THE BIG BOOK

OF LIBRARY GRANT MONEY
1996–97

Profiles of Private and Corporate
Foundations and Direct Corporate Givers
Receptive to Library Grant Proposals

Prepared by
The Taft Group
for the **American Library Association**

American Library Association
Chicago and London 1996

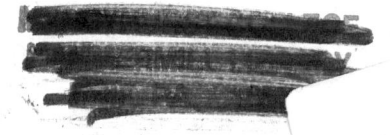

Prepared by The Taft Group for
the American Library Association

The Big Book of Library Grant Money, 1996-97

The Taft Group makes every effort to accurately report information supplied to it by designated program representatives and public sources but is not responsible for and disclaims any liability for information inaccurate at its source or for changes that result from the passage of time. While sharing in efforts to ensure the reliability of information appearing in this book, the American Library Association makes no warranty, express or implied, on the accuracy or reliability of the information, and does not assume and hereby disclaims any liability to any person from any loss or damage caused by errors or omissions in this publication.

∞™ This book is printed on acid-free paper that meets the minimum requirements of American National Standard for Information Sciences—Permanence of Paper for Printed Materials, ANSI Z39.48-1992.

♻ This book is printed on recycled paper that meets Environmental Protection Agency standards.

Printed in the United States of America

ISBN: 0-8389-0683-4

ISSN 1086-0568

The Taft Group is the nation's leading publisher of reference, how-to, and professional information for nonprofit organizations and institutions. For further information or a catalog contact:

The Taft Group, 12300 Twinbrook Parkway, Suite 520, Rockville, MD 20852

(800) 877-TAFT (Customer Service)

I(T)P™ Gale Research, an ITP Information/Reference Group Company.
ITP logo is a trademark under license.

Contents

Indexes

About This Book

The Big Book of Library Grant Money 1996-97 provides detailed descriptive profiles of 1,695 philanthropic programs in the United States—programs associated with private foundations, corporate foundations, and corporate direct givers. All of the funders in this directory have either made grants to libraries in the last reporting period or have listed libraries as a typical recipient category on their questionnaires returned to the Taft Group. The Big Book of Library Grant Money provides fund raisers and researchers with quick and convenient access to important information on the major U.S. funding organizations supporting libraries.

The Big Book of Library Grant Money includes current data on more than 1,130 of the top private foundations, those with assets of at least $1.8 million or grant distributions of at least $250,000. Interfiled with these major private foundations are approximately 400 corporate foundations, and nearly 160 hard-to-find corporate direct givers.

New to This Edition

This second edition of The Big Book of Library Grant Money contains approximately 450 new funders that have been identified as current funding sources for libraries. The directory now excludes funders that do not accept unsolicited requests for funds and those funders that give to only preselected recipients. All of the funders included will consider unsolicited proposals.

The profiles are arranged alphabetically by state. The Recent Grants section of the profile highlights up to five recent library grants and the five highest general grants awarded by the funder during their most recent disclosure period. Publications available from the funder are listed under a new Publications heading located after the Application Information section.

The indexes have also been enhanced in this edition. The **Index to Corporations and Foundations by Headquarters** now lists the funders by their headquarter city and state location, rather than by their state only, as in the previous edition. A new **Index to Corporations and Foundations by Recipient Type** has also been added. This index lists funders by the typical recipient categories they support—in addition to libraries.

Three new practical articles on grantseeking are included in this edition. The articles, Sources on Grantseeking: A Bibliography, Library Fundraising on the Web: Tips and Sites, and Checking Out Cyberspace: Grants from High-Tech Companies, provide additional information to library fundraisers seeking support from private foundations and corporate philanthropic programs.

Content and Arrangement

The funders are arranged alphabetically by state. Foundations named after family members are listed alphabetically by family name, with the last name listed first. For instance, the "Gladys and Roland Harriman Foundation" appears alphabetically in the H's, listed as the "Harriman Foundation, Gladys and Roland." Corporation names and corporate foundation names follow the same convention.

Entries are as detailed as permitted by the information available. Contents of a profile include:

- the foundation name or sponsoring company name and corporate foundation name, if applicable
- corporate financial and major products data
- contact information
- giving histories and additional financial information
- a contributions section that contains donors to the foundation; typical recipients; grant types; nonmonetary support types; geographic distributions; and operating locations
- corporate and philanthropic program officers and directors
- application procedures and restrictions
- publications
- grants analysis
- recent grants listings (library and general)

Method of Compilation

The Big Book of Library Grant Money consists of entries, compiled for the Taft Group's *Directory of Corporate and Foundation Givers,* the *Corporate Giving Directory,* and the *Foundation Reporter*, that support libraries and library services. The profiles are updated annually. Foundation profiles are based on the most recent Form 990-PF available from the IRS, as well as foundations' annual reports, grants lists, guidelines, questionnaire responses, and telephone interviews. Profiles of corporate direct giving programs are based on information provided directly by the companies, press releases, telephone interviews, standard business publications, and data uncovered in extensive surveys of publications in the field. All foundation and corporate contacts were verified by phone within the past year.

Indexes

Seven indexes allow users to quickly locate information presented in the profiles. The first six specialized indexes should be used in conjunction with the **Master Index to Corporations and Foundations** to speed research. Indexes include the following:

Index to Corporations and Foundations by Headquarters. The headquarters index lists foundations and corporations alphabetically by the state and city of their primary location. For foundations, this information is taken from the contact address. For corporations, this information is taken from the headquarters city and state section of the profile. Foundations and corporations primarily support organizations with geographic proximity.

Index to Corporations by Operating Location. The operating location index provides a comprehensive listing of corporations headquartered or operating in your state. The data is taken from the headquarters city and state section of the profile and from the list of operating locations located under the contributions summary section. A company is far more likely to distribute grants in cities and states where it operates than in places where it does not have a direct presence. This pattern reflects the general corporate preference to support causes that benefit employees, stockholders, and other corporate constituencies.

Index to Officers and Directors. Foundation and corporate officers, trustees, directors, and managers are arranged in alphabetical order followed by the name of the foundation.

Index to Corporations and Foundations by Recipient Type. This index, new to the second edition, lists funders by 215 different recipient classifications under nine main categories of giving, including Arts and Humanities, Civic and Public Affairs, Education, Environment, Health, International, Religion, Science, and Social Services. Funders listed under specific program areas typically support organizations and activities in those categories.

Index to Grant Recipients by State. This unique index lists the thousands of grant recipients in *The Big Book of Library Grant Money* by state location when that information was provided by the foundation or corporate giver. If the source of the grant did not supply the recipient's location, the recipient name is matched to our database of more than 200,000 nonprofit organizations, including city and state locations. Each listing includes, as available, the recipient's name and location, size of grant, and donor.

Index to Library Recipients by State. A convenient index to libraries and library-related projects that have received funding. Organizations are listed by state location when that information was provided by the foundation or corporate giver. If the location of the grant recipient was not supplied by the funder, the recipient's name is matched to our database of nonprofit organizations to determine a correct city and state location. Listings include, as available, the recipient's name and location, size of grant, and donor.

Master Index to Corporations and Foundations. An alphabetical arrangement of all corporations, foundations, and corporate foundations profiled in the directory, followed by the page number on which their profiles appear.

Elements of a Profile

Profile Name

Entries within each state are arranged in alphabetical order by the sponsoring company name or the foundation name. (Index citations refer to company name only.) Company-sponsored foundation names follow company names when applicable. Please note that a company may give directly, through a foundation, or both. If no foundation exists, the company is a direct giver.

Sponsoring Company Information

As reported in 1995 issues of *Fortune* magazine (Time, Inc., New York, NY), *Standard & Poor's Register of Corporations, Directors, and Executives 1995* (Standard & Poor's, New York, NY), and *Ward's Business Directory of U.S. Private and Public Companies 1995* (Gale Research Inc., Detroit, MI).

If the sponsoring company is a subsidiary of, or affiliated with another company, this information is listed under Parent Company. Sales, profits, employees, headquarters city and state, and SIC classification give a capsule look at the financial health, primary operating location, and business interests of the profiled company. Corporate giving levels are closely tied to a company's sales and profits: the more profitable a company, the greater its philanthropic potential. Many companies base their giving on a percentage of pretax profits, typically 0.5% to 2.5%, but occasionally as high as 5%. The number of employees also provides a quick measure of a company's size, and corporate programs are always interested in seeing charitable contributions affect the largest number of corporate employees. Company sales, profits, and number of employees are given for 1994, where available.

Company business revolves around corporate headquarters, and charitable giving reflects this orientation. Headquarters information is indexed in the **Index to Corporations and Foundations by Headquarters**. Lastly, a company's field of business or marketing orientation often influences its charitable objectives. The SIC classifications help identify corporations with a special interest in a particular activity due to the nature of their business.

Contact

The name of the person responsible for answering inquiries and receiving grant applications, as well as the individual's title, organization name, mailing address, city, state, zip code, and telephone number. If there is more than one contact, they appear in a note field immediately after the telephone number.

Financial Summary

This section offers a brief picture of a giving program's financial status and giving potential based on the most current reporting periods. When specific figures for contributions were not available, annual giving ranges were often provided by corporate and foundation officers. Financial information includes recent giving, assets, and gifts received (donations received by the foundation). This section ends with a foundation's Employer Identification Number (EIN), the unique nine-digit number assigned to philanthropic institutions by the Internal Revenue Service. The EIN can be used to locate foundation Forms 990-PF, keep track of name changes, and locate foundations registered in states different from current mailing addresses.

Contributions Summary

This section contains current and background information on corporate and foundation giving programs. Original donors to private foundations are listed first, followed by a list of typical nonprofit recipients (see page xxviii for a complete list of nonprofit recipient types). The recipients are based on analysis of the most recent Form 990-PF available, annual reports, and information provided by the organizations.

The grant types section lists types of financial support generally offered by the profiled organization, using the following standard categories: award, capital, challenge, conference/seminar, department, emergency, employee matching gifts, endowment, fellowship, general support, loan, matching gifts, multiyear/continuing support, operating expenses, professor-ship, project, research, scholarship, and seed money.

Information on nonmonetary support types also is provided, using the following categories: cause-related marketing and promotion, donated equipment, donated products, in-kind services, loaned employees, loaned executives, and workplace solicitation.

 The geographic preference for contributions is included in the geographic distribution section. Geographic preferences for funding described here are obtained from the foundations and corporations or by tracking patterns of contributions made over a period of several years. Some programs are national in scope, while others adhere to strict rules limiting support to specific states, counties, or cities. Corporations generally limit contributions to their headquarters and operating communities.

Data on operating locations is included for corporations. This information can help you locate potential donors within your community affiliated with organized giving programs headquartered elsewhere. Operating locations are indexed by state in the **Index to Corporations by Operating Location**.

Corporate Officers/Giving Officers

Provides the names, titles, and biographical information on the principal corporate officers and foundation/giving program officers, directors, and trustees. Biographical information includes date and place of birth, education, current employment, corporate affiliations, nonprofit affiliations, club affiliations, and philanthropic affiliations, when available. A comprehensive list of corporate and contributions program officers is provided in the **Index to Officers and Directors.**

Application Information

Describes application requirements, including initial request procedures, proposal requirements, and deadlines. The restrictions on giving section includes activities, programs, or organizations not supported or ineligible for support by the program profiled.

Other Things to Know

Reports on any recent or significant changes in a giving program's status, affiliated philanthropies, or policies that could affect solicitation efforts.

Publications

Contains a list of publications available from the contributions program.

Grants Analysis

Lists several giving-related statistics based on the most recent year for which figures are available: number of grants, highest grant, typical grant range, and disclosure period. Larger profiles also include the average grant figure. The note contains information on large grants that may skew the average, the year of the recent grants listings, and any other relevant information pertaining to the grants analysis.

Recent Grants

When reported, provides up to five grants awarded to libraries or library-related programs. The top five grants given in the most recent reporting year are also listed. Grants are listed in descending order by amount. When the information is available, the dollar amount, recipient name, recipient location, and a brief description are provided. All grants listed with an identified state are cross-referenced in the **Index to Grant Recipients by State**. All library and library-related grants with an identified state are cross-referenced in the **Index to Library Grants by State**.

Library Grantseeking: Some Practical Advice

by the Staff of The Fund for America's Libraries
American Library Association

The Big Book of Library Grant Money 1996-97, a collaborative effort of the American Library Association and The Taft Group, opens the door wider than ever to sources of alternative funding for libraries. Drawing on the authoritative Taft databases of almost 9,000 top foundation, corporate foundation, and direct corporate givers, it profiles only those givers who have either funded library programs or have expressed willingness to consider proposals from libraries. The total is still large: almost 1,700 potential givers to libraries, some four times more than are identified, profiled, and gathered in any other guide.

The premiere edition of *The Big Book* appeared in 1994. Thanks to an enthusiastic reception and suggestions from users, the directory will now appear every two years, with many new and improved features. In addition to the practical articles in the front section, these features include: organization by state, with a master index to givers; elimination of givers who do not accept unsolicited proposals; indexes to type of program receiving grants, to library recipients, and to corporate headquarters by state and city; and listing of up to five recent library grants (if any) among the ten sample grants for each giver.

Getting Your Share

If you have opened this book you don't need to be sold on the idea of alternative funding. But you will be something of a pioneer when you pursue foundation and corporate support of library projects. Compared to other cultural agencies, libraries have shied from such grant money. Some administrators fear that base operating support might be reduced when grant funding is received. However, such apprehensions have not stopped other grant-seekers from reaching into a pool of some seven billion dollars in annual giving.

Why have libraries garnered so small a share—less than two percent, according to Foundation Center estimates? The abundance of opportunities presented in this guide suggests that funder resistance is not the answer. It is more likely the reluctance to tap private funding and the limited amount of information previously available on receptive givers. Libraries, however, appear ready to overcome their earlier reluctance as they face diminished funding and increased demand for innovative services. As for better access to

information on funders—*The Big Book of Library Grant Money 1996-97* is in your hands.

There are indeed foundation and corporate funds available to libraries. The index of library grants at the back of this book gives a quick snapshot of identifiable recent funding. There will be many more when libraries get the hang of foundation grantseeking. We offer some practical advice in this brief introduction. We think you will be successful. We believe that grants to libraries will snowball when enough successful funded projects are on the books. Your pioneering efforts will benefit not only your own programs, but grant-giving to libraries in general.

Types of Projects Funded

Grant funds are ideal for capital projects such as buildings and equipment or for program development. Many foundations and corporations focus on special areas such as education, the arts, youth, the environment, public health, or community development (see index by type of recipient program); seed money can launch initiatives that will be funded from other sources in the future. Grants are seldom made for operating expenses, and most foundation guidelines make it clear that funds are not provided for business as usual. It is also rare to find foundations contributing to endowments, though sometimes challenge grants are given to leverage other contributions.

Grantmakers are not passive dispensers of cash. Grantmakers want to work with you to solve a problem or meet a need. Your challenge is to convince them that your library is an expertly run organization, indispensable to the people you serve and worthy of their investment. Foundations do not fund the helpless or hopeless. A program officer's job is to recommend winning organizations, projects and people.

Communicating

It helps to have some basic communication tools before you begin grant seeking. You can start with a simple fact sheet that describes your library, including your mission statement, and includes impressive facts and statistics—all organized on one page that is clear and easy to read. A single page of word-processed copy on your letterhead will do the job and can be easily kept up-to-date. Foundations may also ask to see your annual report or a copy of your latest audited financial statement. Most foundations and corporations will award grants only to organizations that have a 501(c)(3) tax exempt status with the Internal Revenue Service. If you don't now have a letter certifying your tax status, you will need to submit IRS forms 1023 and 872-C.

You also need a good idea—a solid project—that matches the grantmaker's interest and your library's mission and goals. It is best to develop your idea from the point of view of the people you serve. For example, all the foundation focus areas mentioned above—from the arts to public health to education—are relevant to libraries, if we consider the needs of people rather than the needs of libraries. If you need to refurbish the children's room, make a case for the children not the furniture.

In addition to the information in this guide, a quick tour through library news journals will give you an idea of the type of projects that receive grant funding. The weekly *Library Hotline* and monthly *College & Research Libraries News* are among the sources of funding news. Another is the *Funding File* column sponsored by Gale Research in the *Library Journal.* You will also find requests from funders seeking grant proposals, particularly for the grants provided through projects of the American Library Association. A prime example is the DeWitt Wallace Reader's Digest grant to ALA for a Library Power program to revitalize school libraries. Here are a few examples of recent library project grants in the news:

The Reader's Digest Foundation planted its first "Tall Tree" grant in Westchester County, N.Y. Westchester Library System Director Maurice Freedman accepted $500,000 from the Foundation in April 1995 on behalf of public school and public library systems county-wide to develop a model program for children. (*American Libraries*, June 1995).

Cornell University and the University of Michigan have received a $750,000 grant from the Andrew W. Mellon Foundation for the pilot phase of the "Making of America" project, which will convert 5,000 historical documents from the 19th century to digital form. The project is designed to preserve the documents and make them widely available to scholars and students via the Internet. (*College and Research Libraries News*, July/August 1995).

Clark University in Massachusetts received a $106,000 grant from the Charles E. Culpeper Foundation to establish a book preservation facility and model training program for the Worcester Area Cooperating Libraries. (*College and Research Libraries News*, May 1995).

At a September 1995 news conference, Bell Atlantic CEO Ray Smith presented Librarian of Congress James Bill-ington a check for $1.5 million for the library's National Digital Library (NDL) Program. (*Library Hotline*, October 2, 1995).

Moving from Prospect to Contact

People give to people. As you begin the prospecting phase, sift through the information in this book and select a few grantmakers with whom you will establish a professional rapport based on thoughtful communication and mutual interest in achieving an end. It is important for any grant-seeker, especially one who performs several other staff functions, to consider Terman's Law. That is, if you want to win the high jump, seek out one person who can jump seven feet, not seven people who can jump one foot. You simply don't have time to research, track giving patterns, and maintain quality communications with seven-score foundations or corporations for each program that needs funding. Better to take a quality approach that begins with identifying the grantmakers whose guidelines and giving practices best fit your project.

Grants are denied most often because the request is outside the scope of a foundation's giving criteria. Newcomers sometimes assume that grantmakers who have already given extensively in one area probably have exhausted their assets or attention. On the contrary, all trends in giving point toward consistency and commitment to specific areas of need.

Use this directory and create a starter list of some twenty companies or foundations that give to programs like yours and can fund at the dollar level you need. Request guidelines from all twenty prospects on your list. Read the guidelines closely to select those that have funded projects similar to those you propose. File the rest for future reference.

To further qualify your prospects, be aware of the various foundation types (examples are given here simply as representative of a type):

- General purpose. These tend to be large and make grants in many categories of interest. They prefer to create funding relationships with organizations like themselves that are large and high-profile. The Ford Foundation, The Pew Charitable Trusts, and The John D. and Catherine MacArthur Foundation are just a few examples. Library partnerships with local agencies such as the YMCA or Headstart that help facilitate broader-based programs may be viewed favorably by a large, general purpose foundation. If the funder is in your geographic region, your chances of being considered also improve.

- Special purpose. Whether large or small in assets, these sources are highly restrictive and give to a narrow set of interests. If your project falls within their scope, they are worth pursuing, especially because they tend to address an issue by giving to a wide variety of organizations, large and small. Both the J. Roderick MacArthur and The Spencer foundations are two such examples.

- Corporate foundation. Corporate giving by companies with well established programs has not increased since 1992. But an upswing may result from an improved economy and other factors. The 1993 Cone/Roper survey on cause-related marketing concluded that social responsibility is more persuasive than advertising; this data may encourage new giving programs. Corporate giving serves to enhance company image and make the community more liveable for its employees. Some companies have set up a formal foundation to disperse a percentage of its profits through grants. Corporations with non-foundation giving programs are also listed in this book.

- Family foundation. These are truly "family affairs" controlled by the philanthropist and his or her relatives. This type of foundation rarely employs full-time staff and can be eclectic in its giving habits; it may be difficult to track patterns in their donations. Using the information in this book, make copies of the "Officer and Director" section of selected entries for your trustees or friends group. Do they know anyone? Most often grants are obtained through insider contact. Enlist your volunteer to initiate contact by letter or phone to request a meeting. Cultivate a person with a family foundation to join your board; many make gifts through their foundations as a function of their leadership.

- Community foundation. These community chests or trusts give to geographic areas. In the past few years many have built impressive assets pooled from smaller foundations that prefer not to staff or administer their own funds. Program officers are typically drawn from the ranks of non-profit leadership and have working knowledge of the program area to which they make grants. Although geographically limited, the giving is typically broad ranging, making this type of foundation an excellent prospect for libraries.

Keeping Up

Information in this book is drawn from the latest updating (before press closing) of the dynamic Taft databases. Current sources such as the *New York Times* business section, *Chronicle of Higher Education* and *Chronicle of Philanthropy* should supplement your prospect research.

Be alert to notices of management changes at the funding source. It is common for a new senior program officer to join a foundation and refocus giving priorities. Or, if you read that a foundation has retained a consultant to evaluate the effectiveness of its giving practices, expect some change in emphasis. Also be aware of the type of assets that fuel the foundation's or corporation's giving. Although a foundation may be an entirely separate creature from the commercial institution that spawned it, the philanthropic entity may still hold the parent company's stock as a primary asset. The amount available to give away each year may depend on the performance of that stock.

With choice prospects in hand, review again your idea. Write it down. Figure the expenses. Be prepared to give a concise background statement on the library, the community and groups it serves, and how your idea can help serve them better. Call ahead to a prospect and check the contact name; sometimes staff changes at giving programs are slow to make it into directories. When you are ready, place a friendly call to the appropriate program officer to ascertain mutual interest in your program or idea. Be polite. Be organized. And above all, be respectful of the donor's time. Grantmakers are justifiably frustrated by well-meaning grantseekers who phone at inopportune times to rattle on about the merits of their organizations. Identify yourself, your organization, your idea (in two sentences or less) and ask if it is a good time to explore the idea. If it's not, schedule another call and keep the appointment. Remember, you are seeking the receptivity that leads to a request for a proposal.

If you establish interest, be prepared to write a proposal if you have not done so already. A prompt and well-written presentation that marries the priorities of the giver to your institution is critical.

Writing your Proposal

Before you begin to write a proposal, try to discuss your idea with a program officer. Be sure to have the grantmaker's guidelines.

There is a wealth of resource material available on how to write proposals. Even older sources, such as *Program Planning and Proposal Writing* by Norton J. Kiritz (Grantsmanship Center, 1980), contain useful advice—such as the following quick outline of proposal elements based on Kiritz suggestions:

1. **Summary.** The cover page should have a concise abstract, summarizing your request. Include as the last item the amount you are asking for.

2. **Introduction.** Briefly establish your library's credibility and the appropriateness of the project to your experience.

3. **Statement of the problem**. Tell a compelling story about the problem you will solve. Focus on the needs of the people you serve or plan to serve.

4. **Goals and objectives**. Define a broad visionary goal for your project, and measurable objectives.

5. **Methods.** Provide more details about how you will go about meeting the goal and objectives. Follow the narrative with a timetable for your work plan.

6. **Evaluation.** Describe how you will determine whether your project meets its goals and objectives.

7. **Future funding.** Discuss your plans for continuing the project after the grant period.

8. **Budget**. Provide the detailed, comprehensive, and realistic budget information with notes—including in-kind contributions or support from other sources.

9. **Addenda.** You may want to append more background information, letters of support, or resumes of personnel who will be involved.

A proposal doesn't have to be long. It does have to be clear, convincing, logical, and concisely written. It must match the interests of the funder. If you follow the above outline, you'll find that writing a proposal helps you think through the elements of your project.

It is always helpful to have your draft read by someone who knows nothing about the idea you are proposing, and very little about your library. The proposal is basically your sales pitch. If you can sell your idea to an impartial outsider, it will have a better chance of inspiring a funder.

The LFRC: A Key Resource

As you progress, you will find many books, workshops and consultants offering detailed advice on how to get grants. (See the all-new bibliography in this book.) You may also contact the Fund for America's Libraries, ALA's new Foundation. Located within the Fund is the Library Fundraising Resource Center (LFRC); 312-280-5050. The central mission of the LFRC is to provide fundraising training through the Library Leadership Fundraising Training project, funded by W.K. Kellogg Foundation and the Carnegie Corporation of New York. This highly visible project helps small and medium sized public libraries meet the challenge for funding by providing training in essential technical skills that will lead to success in fundraising. The LFRC is also developing additional training modules for mid-to-senior level library development professionals and library man-

agement and governing boards. The LFRC will establish training partnerships with state library associations and graduate library schools to make these courses available through a vast network of state association conventions and graduate school programs, as well as at ALA Annual and Midwinter Conferences.

The LFRC also offers professional fundraising counsel to libraries of all types. Staff at the LFRC have over 60 years of combined experience in management and resource development and can provide counsel in all areas of planning implementation of campaigns and stewardship programs.

The Fund for America's Libraries houses a clearinghouse and database of library fundraising literature (available upon request) on topics that include case statements, capital campaigns, foundation/corporate proposals, annual fund, special events, planned/deferred giving, strategic planning, donor recognition, and organizing a foundation. Developed in cooperation with the Fundraising and Financial Development Section of the Library Administration and Management Association of ALA, the clearinghouse gathers literature in more than 50 subject areas about fundraising and fundraising management issues for and concerning libraries.

Ten Quick Pointers

It will take some time and patience to learn all the ropes. Meanwhile, for overburdened development staff, we offer the following "top ten" pointers:

1. Develop a project that enhances the mission and goals of the library.

2. Involve the staff in every step—idea development, funding strategy, the proposal, and its implementation. And don't forget to keep your board or other governance people informed and involved.

3. Be sure the library has the basic resources to support the management of the project.

4. Thoroughly research potential funders (see comments above).

5. Confirm the interest of a potential funder *before* writing your proposal (see comments below).

6. Consider the funder a partner in the project, not a silent source of money.

7. Write a proposal that is clear and concise, demonstrating vision and technical competence.

8. Prepare a budget that is detailed, comprehensive, and realistic.

9. Be prepared to publicize the project when funded, during implementation, and when completed.

10. Build and maintain a relationship with the funding organization.

Leveraging the Proposal

There is some question about when to submit the written presentation. Many seasoned grantseekers believe it is better to ask for a site visit or meeting and then follow with a proposal. A face-to-face meeting always seems a good idea; unfortunately, it does not always suit a grantmaker's style or schedule, and pressing for it before the donor feels ready can create resistance to your project. Many funders prefer to be convinced on paper first before expending their most precious commodity—time. Either way, do strive for a meeting at some point in the cycle if you expect to get the grant.

Follow-through is another critical point for grantseekers. One foundation staff newcomer said recently that nothing in her education or previous careers prepared her for the flood of requests she faced every day. When asked how she made choices, she explained that to a great extent she relied on the tenacity of the grantseeker. If you have done the work and believe in your idea, then make the total investment by following up. Funders expect serious grantseekers to phone within two weeks after you've sent materials to check in and answer any questions. Find out how their process works and what you can expect next. Follow that call with a note of thanks. Have your trustees and community partners write to endorse the project and gently encourage consideration of the proposal.

As you can see, the demands on your time to develop an idea into a funded program will be significant. That is why you must ultimately pursue those few prospects who can help you jump seven feet.

If the Answer Is "No"

If you don't get a grant, don't give up. Although only about one in ten proposals is funded, persistence will pay off. You have created a solid project and made some valuable contacts. Ask the program officer who said "no" for constructive criticism and advice. Ask if the proposal should be reworked and submitted again, or if another funder can be recommended. If you have generated staff and community enthusiasm for the project, re-group and look for other ways to get it going.

Sources on Grantseeking

Dwight F. Burlingame and Janet S. McIntyre

The environment in which nonprofits and governmental agencies, including libraries, operate today has changed in many different ways—not the least of which is the increased pressure to seek additional grant funds. Traditional public funding sources are surely going to be cut back or not grow at the required level for organizations to meet service demands. Libraries are no exception in facing tough financial times, thus the need to be creative in seeking funds. In the publishing world, The Foundation Center, a nonprofit publisher, and The Taft Group, a for-profit publisher, tend to dominate publishing of grant source guides. In the electronic environment, the variety of tools that provide ideas and opportunities for grantseekers continues to grow. [See "Library Fundraising on the Web," following this article. —Ed.]

This annotated bibliography provides a selected overview of the most recent tools available. We have attempted to include works that can be found in most libraries and that go from the general to the specific. In addition, a brief section is presented on periodicals that help to keep one up-to-date in the field. This article updates in part an earlier work by Helen M. Gothberg and Edith H. Ferrell that appeared in the *Reference Services Review*, Summer 1993. Prices given are those available to the authors at press time and are subject to change.

Much of the success of proposal writing and grantseeking can be attributed to research, research, and more research. Of particular importance is finding the right potential funder, and following the guidelines. Many organizations choose to get outside assistance in writing grant proposals. One helpful guide in identifying consultants nationwide is Michele Thrasher's *The Grantseeker's Assistance Network: A Directory of Grants Consultants and Resources* (Alexandria, Va.: Capitol Publications, 1993). It provides the address, phone number, services provided, specialization, geographic area, and other helpful information on more than forty consultants.

One of the primary and most important resources for information and publishing about foundations and the grants they make is the Foundation Center (79 Fifth Ave., New York, NY 10003-3076; 1-800-424-9836). Like its published sources, many of which are included here, the Center's

network of national and regional collections is a must for any grantseeker. Over 200 cooperating libraries in all 50 states and abroad offer free access to major Center publications, free orientations, and microform and photocopying facilities. The Grantsmanship Center (P.O. Box 17220, Los Angeles, Calif. 90017; 1-800-421-9512) is also an important resource. It offers workshops on grantwriting and also provides a free quarterly magazine.

For more in-depth research two publications can be helpful. *Philanthropic Studies Index* (Bloomington, Indiana: Indiana University Press. $75/yr) indexes relevant books, periodical articles, dissertations and other sources that cover the broad field of philanthropy, including volunteerism, nonprofit management, fundraising, and related topics. *The Literature of the Nonprofit Sector: A Bibliography with Abstracts* (New York: The Foundation Center. $45 for vol. 7. ISBN 0-87954-649-2 v. 7) covers the "best" references—translated to mean those that are held by the Foundation Center—in the nonprofit field.

Bibliography

I. Periodicals

The Chronicle of Philanthropy. Biweekly. Washington, D.C.: The Chronicle of Philanthropy. $67.50/yr. ISSN 1040-676x.

This newspaper covers the latest issues in philanthropic activity from case histories and people in the profession to statistical data on major contributions. Sections on recent grants and annual reports of foundations are particularly relevant to the grantseeker.

Corporate Philanthropy Report. Monthly, except Jan. Alexandria, Va: Capitol Publications. $205/yr. ISSN 0885-8365.

Updates on what is happening in the corporate giving world can be found in this newsletter. The spotlight column in each issue focuses on giving profiles of companies and provides contact information.

Grantsmanship Center News. Bimonthly. Los Angeles, Calif.: Grantsmanship Center. $28/yr. ISSN 0364-3115.

Advice on writing grant proposals, articles related to foundation giving, sources for assistance, and helpful advertising.

Dwight F. Burlingame is Director for Academic Programs & Research and Janet S. McIntyre is a Graduate Assistant at the Indiana University Center on Philanthropy.

Grassroots Fundraising Journal. Bimonthly. Berkeley, Calif.: Grassroots Fundraising Journal. $25/yr. ISSN 0740-4832.

Articles on alternative sources of funding, book reviews, and bibliographies are geared to the low-budget organization.

The Nonprofit Times. Monthly. Cedar Knolls, N.J.: Davis Information Group. $59/yr. ISSN 0896-5048.

Focus of this publication is on nonprofit management and fundraising techniques. Helpful advertising particularly on computer software and other technology, as well as printed sources for seeking grants.

II. General Guides to Seeking and Writing Grants

Bauer, David G. *The "How To" Grants Manual: Successful Grantseeking Techniques for Obtaining Public and Private Grants.* 3rd ed. Phoenix, Ariz.: Oryx Press, 1995. 232 p., $29.95. ISBN 0-89774-851-4.

Bauer has written a book that is logical and easy to follow, as well as comprehensive in scope. Part 1 lays out in detail the process of preparing to seek grant support. Part 2 discusses government funding sources and how to meet the requirements. Private funding sources, including helpful details on how to access these resources, are addressed in Part 3. Many worksheets and sample letters, as well information on the use of computer databases and electronic retrieval and searching systems are provided.

Brewer, Ernest W., Charles M. Achilles and Jay R. Fuhriman. *Finding Funding: Grantwriting and Project Management From Start to Finish.* 2nd ed. Thousand Oaks, Calif.: Corwin Press, 1995. 273p., $39.95. ISBN 0-8039-6202-9.

This newly completed second edition of *Finding Funding* contains phone numbers and addresses for new information sources, as well as new data on previously cited works. Section I aids the reader in exploration of grant possibilities and includes a chapter on using the *Catalog of Federal Domestic Assistance* (CFDA). Section II describes the procedure for actually writing and submitting a proposal. Implementation and operation of a funded project are discussed in Section III. Useful "Grant Tips" appear in the margins of many pages of the book.

Gilpatrick, Eleanor G. *Grants for Nonprofit Organizations: A Guide to Funding and Grant Writing.* New York: Praeger, 1989. 213p., $49.95. ISBN 0-275-93274-5.

Designed for those who have the responsibility for preparing grant proposals, this "how-to" comprehensive guide gives attention to program planning and the evaluation portion of the proposal. The first of three main sections covers the preparation stage, including looking for sources of funding

and getting ready to write a proposal. The next six chapters explain and elaborate upon the grant application itself. The last chapters help in budget preparation and other details. Includes helpful examples of real-life situations throughout.

Gooch, Judith. *Writing Winning Proposals.* Washington, D.C: Council for Advancement and Support of Education, 1987. 87p., $32. ISBN 0-89964-249-7.

Beginning with "Research" and ending with "What to Do After the Proposal is in the Mail," this basic guide leads the reader through the grant writing process. It stresses the need for "fit" between the grantseeker's need and the potential funder, whether foundation or corporation. Gooch cautions against seeking money just because it may be available, without being certain the proposed project fits the organization's mission.

Judith B. Margolin, ed. *Foundation Center's User-Friendly Guide: Grantseeker's Guide to Resources.* New York: Foundation Center, 1994. 39p., $14.95. ISBN 0-87954-541-0.

Beginning with the premise that there are ten questions most commonly asked by grantseekers, this booklet answers them and gives a blueprint of where to go next. It offers sources of information on corporate giving, individual donors, and government funding, as well as helpful periodicals and a glossary of terms. Though brief, this book is a good place to start for most grantseekers.

Miner, Lynn E. and Jerry Griffith. *Proposal Planning & Writing.* Phoenix, Ariz.: Oryx Press, 1993. 160p., $29.50. ISBN 0-89774-726-7.

Designed for the use of those seeking grants in many different disciplines including education, social sciences, health care, religion, philanthropy and government, this work presents specific tips used in successful grant proposals which were funded in many of these areas. The book underscores the importance of defining the uniqueness of the grantseeking organization and of the match between funder and grantseeker, so that both parties gain if the proposal is funded. Bibliography, and appendix of publishers and vendors.

111 Secrets to Smarter Grantsmanship. Arlington, Va.: Government Information Services, 1993. 55p. ISBN 0-933544-51-0.

This no-nonsense booklet offers a fresh perspective on the nuances of proposal writing. It stresses the importance of selling the grantseeking organization's capabilities in a truthful and realistic way. Here are found pithy tips on how to search for grant sources, pitfalls to avoid, and what elements are essential to the successful grant. Asserting that, "like it or not, proposal writing skills are often more important in winning grants than is the capability to fulfill the contract," this little book attempts to give the reader a leg-up.

III. Guides to Seeking and Writing Grants in Subject Areas: A Sampling

Barber, Peggy and Linda D. Crowe. *Getting Your Grant: A How-To-Do-It Manual for Librarians*. New York: Neal-Schuman, 1993. 175p., $39.95. ISBN 1-55570-038-1.

Directed at staff of small and medium-sized libraries, this book makes a very convincing case for seeking grants to supplement local tax support. From the importance of being able to state the library's case to the value of making friends and allies for the library through outreach activities, the authors present a step-by-step approach designed just for libraries. The guide covers getting ready and developing the grant idea; most funding sources, including government, foundations, and corporations; and the proposal writing process. Six appendices contain sample grant applications for projects that have been funded.

Bauer, David G. *Grantseeking Primer for Classroom Leaders*. New York: Scholastic, 1994. 131p., $19.95. ISBN 0-590-49216-0.

After presenting the caveat that increased funding for education does not guarantee improved educational outcomes, Bauer suggests that elementary and middle school teachers develop a community advisory committee in order to seek grants. With many sample documents that "classroom leaders" can use in the proposal-writing process, this manual covers the complete process in fifteen easy-to-use chapters. A very helpful bibliography includes government, foundation, and corporate resources as well as computer research services.

Dewey, Barbara I., ed. *Raising Money for Academic and Research Libraries: A How-To-Do-It Manual for Librarians*. New York: Neal-Schuman, 1991. 160p., $39.95. ISBN 1-55570-082-9.

With contributions from eleven experienced fundraisers (founders of DORAL, the Development Officers of Research Academic Libraries, North America), this manual identifies grantwriting as just one of many ways libraries can raise needed funds. Two chapters cover grants from public, private, and corporate entities; the remainder of the work stresses the need for a well integrated development plan which solicits financial support from many constituencies. Most of the ideas presented are applicable to all types of libraries.

Ogden, Thomas E. *Research Proposals: A Guide to Success*. 2nd ed. New York: Raven Press, 1995. 464p., $49. ISBN 0-7817-0313-1.

Essentially a guide for those seeking research grants from the National Institutes of Health, the National Science Foundation, or the Alcohol, Drug Abuse and Mental Health Administration. Not designed to replace the detailed instructions from the funding organization, it offers guidance in the highly competitive grant process, including clear advice on pitfalls.

Ratzlaff, Leslie A., ed. *Education Grant winners: Models of Effective Proposal Structure and Style*. Alexandria, Va.: Capitol Publications, 1995. $73. ISBN 0-937925-75-6.

By reading proposals for actual grants that were awarded by government agencies, grantseekers can see the elements of success firsthand. This book contains nine applications from a cross-section of educational institutions, from public school districts to universities. Designed to spark creativity and new ideas in the grantseeker, it demonstrates the importance of communicating good ideas to the potential funder in a unique and memorable way.

IV. Guides to Grant Sources

A. General

Catalog of Federal Domestic Assistance, 1995. 29th ed. Washington, D.C.: U.S. General Services Administration, sold by Government Printing Office. Annual, with supplements. Looseleaf. 1403p., $57. ISBN 0-614-06319-1.

The 29th edition of this essential guide (CFDA) contains information about 1,390 assistance programs administered by 53 federal agencies. Organized by administering agency, it includes program descriptions under 18 different categories, from "Community Learning Center" to "Transportation." Each entry lists objectives, type of assistance available, eligibility, and application process. Entries are cross-referenced by functional classification, subject, applicant, deadline for application submission, and authorizing legislation.

Corporate 500: The Directory of Corporate Philanthropy. 12th ed. San Francisco: Public Management Institute, 1994. 1491p., $355. ISBN 0-916664-57-0.

Similar in nature to the *Corporate Giving Directory*, this resource has at least one feature which sets it apart. Each corporations's report is accompanied by a graphic summary called *Grants-at-a-Glance*. This box displays: a U.S. map with states shaded where money is given; a pie chart which shows how corporations spend their money; the size of an average grant; the ratio of grants to applications, how giving will change this year (up, down or the same); and a Generosity Index, which is a standardized scale of how generous companies are in relation to each other. The remainder of each company report includes the address, phone and fax numbers, contact person, a business profile, eligibility requirements, a company analysis including quotes from company reports, a contribution profile that includes aggregate giving and sizes of the largest and smallest grants, application procedures, and sample grants. The directory includes over 300 pages of indexes including: Activities Eligible, Funding Areas, Geographic Areas of Giving, and Who's Who in corporate philanthropy. Beginning this year a subscription includes (free) access to Corporate

Philanthropy OnLine. It is accessible one hour a day on working days for one year and includes the full text of the Corporate 500 Directory.

Dame, Kathleen, ed. *Corporate Giving Directory*. 17th ed. Rockville, Md.: Taft Group, 1996. 1875p., $395. ISBN 1-56995-003-2.

This comprehensive directory catalogs 1,001 companies which have given a minimum of $200,000 annually to nonprofit organizations. With $3.5 billion given by corporations last year, this source will be valuable to many grantseekers. Each entry provides contact person, contribution summary, grant types, "other support" given (such as cause- related marketing or donations), giving priorities, typical recipients, where the company (or company foundation) operates, who runs the company and who directs the giving program, the philanthropic philosophy, how to approach the organization, restrictions on giving, and details of recent grants.

DeAngelis, James. *Foundation Reporter, 1996*. 27th ed. Rockville, Md.: The Taft Group, 1995. 1965p., $375. ISBN 1-56995-055-5.

Very similar to the Foundation Center's *The Foundation 1000*, this reference also profiles the 1,000 top-giving private foundations in the U.S. This volume contains additional indexes (officers and directors by alma mater and place of birth, for example), has graphic representations for the top 100 foundations, and a more detailed subcategorization of recipient types.

Directory of New and Emerging Foundations. 3rd ed. New York: Foundation Center, 1994. 375p., $95. ISBN 0-87954-553-4.

Indexed by both geographic location and subject area, this directory lists over 2,900 newer foundations. Each entry contains grantmaking interests and limitations, names of trustees and officers, application procedures, addresses, contact names, and financial data.

Dumouchel, Robert. *Government Assistance Almanac 1995-96*. 9th ed. Detroit, Mich.: Omnigraphics, 1995. 868p., $135. 0-7808-0061-3.

As stated by the author, the purposes of the *Almanac* are to identify all federal domestic assistance programs available (1,370 as of Jan. 1, 1995) and to give users enough information to apply. For each program this almanac gives official and popular titles, types of assistance available, a brief description of objectives and examples of funded projects, eligibility requirements, range and average amounts awarded, summary of recent activity, and addresses and phone numbers of headquarters. This information, which covers financial as well as non-financial assistance, was obtained from the *CFDA* (see above); however the *Almanac* contains entries not in that catalog. It gives funding levels for all programs for the last four fiscal years.

The Foundation Directory. 17th ed. New York: Foundation Center, 1995. 1945p., $195. ISBN 0-87954-597-6.

The Foundation Directory Part 2. 4th ed. New York: Foundation Center, 1995. 987p., $175. ISBN 0-87954-599-2.

The Foundation 1000. New York: Foundation Center, 1995. 2826p., $285. ISBN 0-87954-645-X.

These three directories, all published by the *Foundation Center*, offer information about foundations, both broad and deep. *The Foundation Directory* includes data on over 7,000 larger foundations which have assets of at least $2 million and distribute a minimum of $200,000 in grants/yr. *Part 2* profiles approximately 4,200 mid-sized foundations which give $50,000 to $200,000 annually. Both directories are indexed by subject field, geographic region, donors, officers, and trustees, types of support, new grantmakers, and foundation name. Each entry includes financial information about the foundation, program interests and limitations, application details, and a list of sample grants made by the organization. *The Foundation 1000* offers comprehensive information on the 1,000 wealthiest foundations in the United States; together they award over 210,000 grants worth $7 billion to nonprofits each year. *The Foundation 1000* includes more in-depth information than the others, including extensive lists of sample grants, detailed analyses of grant programs, and required forms, due dates and initial approach information when seeking a grant.

Foundation Grants to Individuals. 9th ed. New York: Foundation Center, 1995. 536p., $65. ISBN 0-87954-604-2.

Since many of America's foundations will not accept grant proposals from individuals, this guide to over 2,600 which do accept such proposals is a real time saver. The foundations listed make grants for educational support, general welfare, arts and culture, awards and prizes, company employees, and students and graduates of specific schools. Each entry includes application procedures and should be especially helpful for financial aid officers, librarians, and guidance counselors. An annotated bibliography of further resources is also included.

Guide to Federal Funding for Governments and Nonprofits. 2 vols. Ed. by Charles J. Edwards, et al. Arlington, Va.: Education Funding Research Council, 1995. 1561p., $294.95. ISBN 0-93354-71-5.

Focusing on federal programs for state and local governments and nonprofit groups of all kinds, this large resource draws information from the CFDA. The chapters are organized by function, such as the environment, jobs, and senior citizens. The lengthy subject index may contain information for grantseekers which is not readily discernible from the chapter headings.

Janowski, Katherine E., ed. *Directory of International Corporate Giving in America and Abroad*. Washington, D.C.: The Taft Group, 1995. 825p. ISBN 1-56995-035-0.

In two separate sections, this directory profiles 1) funding activities in the United States of 465 foreign-owned companies, and 2) international funding endeavors of 160 U.S.-headquartered companies. Nine indexes help the researcher find connections between companies, countries and interests in philanthropy.

Martin, Cheryl L., comp. *Matching Gift Details: Guidebook to Corporate Programs*. Washington, D.C.: Council for Advancement and Support of Education, 1994. 208p., $98. 0-84964-306-X.

This guide gives thirty types of data on 1,020 companies with matching gift programs. Since this is relatively "easy money" for nonprofits, it is a source of revenue that should not be overlooked. Data available in the 1994 update include alphabetical listings of the 1000+ companies followed by detailed information about them, such as number of employees, industry type, date the matching gift program was established, and who administers the programs. The types of organizations eligible for matching gifts are detailed.

National Directory of Corporate Giving. 4th ed. New York: Foundation Center, 1995. 956p., $195. ISBN 0-87954-646-8.

This directory features specific information on 1,900 corporate foundations and over 650 direct giving programs. Application procedures, names of key personnel, types of support usually given, limitations, financial data, and purpose statements are included. The book gives background material on the corporations and recent grants awarded. There are six indexes to help target funding searches.

Who Gets Grants/Who Gives Grants: Nonprofit Organizations and the Foundations Grants They Received. 3rd ed. New York: Foundation Center, 1995. 1469p., $95. ISBN 0-87954-596-8.

Listing 19,000 nonprofit organizations and more than 58,000 grants awarded to them, this book may be helpful to those seeking funds for similar purposes. Entries are arranged by subject area of the recipient organization or program; an examination of recent grant recipients among the nineteen subject fields listed will help grantseekers find successful peers. Within each subject, grants are arranged by geographic area.

B. Arts and Culture

Directory of Grants in the Humanities 1995-96. 9th ed. Phoenix, Ariz.: Oryx Press, 1995. 729p., $84.50. ISBN 0-89774-911-1.

This comprehensive directory covers more than 3,700 organizations and programs that support a broad array of activities in the humanities. It includes such diverse fields as anthropology, religion, folklore, and theater. Funding sources include money for travel, fellowships, conferences, performances, and support for doctoral students. The entries include the purpose of the program, amount of money available, and requirements for applicants.

National Guide to Funding in Arts and Culture. 3rd ed. New York: Foundation Center, 1994. 1055p., $135. ISBN 0-87954-548-8.

Over 4,000 foundations and corporate direct giving programs known for funding theaters, museums, orchestras, dance groups, and other arts and culture activities are profiled in this guide. The book includes 9,000 sample grants funded in the past and indexes to help the grantseeker target possible funding.

C. Education

Guide to Federal Funding for Education 1995. 2 vols. Ed. by Heather C. Bodell, et al. Arlington, Va.: Education Funding Research Council in cooperation with Government Information Services, 1995. $292.95. 1321p. ISBN 0-933538-48-0.

Containing over 1,300 pages of information on 330 federal programs offering financial aid to an array of education organizations, this guide is bound in two looseleaf volumes. Subscribers to the guide receive twice-monthly Federal Grant Deadline Calendars and periodic updates that include new programs. Organized by types of activities (such as Bilingual Education, Substance Abuse) the work incorporates an index cross referencing programs with similar entries in the Catalog of Federal Domestic Assistance.

D. Health & Environment

National Guide to Funding for the Environment and Animal Welfare. 2nd ed. New York: Foundation Center, 1994. 411p., $85. ISBN 0-87954-551-8.

More than 1,300 foundations and corporate direct giving programs are targeted in this guide. It describes 4,000 grants recently awarded to groups involved in ecological research, waste reduction, animal welfare, and litigation and advocacy. The book includes grantmakers' giving parameters, contact names and addresses, financial data, and several indexes to help the grantseeker search for funding.

National Guide to Funding in Health. 4th ed. New York: Foundation Center, 1995. 1142p., $145. ISBN 0-87954-600-X.

Similar in scope to other Foundation Center "National Guides," this work profiles grantmakers in health-related programs. Organizations such as hospitals, universities, and health care associations should locate resources among the 3,400 foundations and corporate givers listed. Over 13,000 recent grants are described in order to help the grantseeker understand funders' priorities.

E. Minorities/Diversity

Directory of Financial Aids for Minorities 1993-95. Prepared by Gail A. Schlachter and R. David Weber. San Carlos, Calif.: Reference Service Press, 1993. 660p., $47.50. ISBN 0-918276-21-7.

For purposes of this directory, minorities are defined as Asian, Black, Hispanic and Native American. Over 2,300 scholarships, fellowships, grants, awards, and internships are available from a broad cross section of 550 organizations: education associations, military and veterans groups, government agencies, professional organizations, corporations, fraternities and sororities. Each entry gives eligibility requirements, financial data, and duration of grant.

Grants for Minorities. New York: Foundation Center, 1995. 359p., $75.

The Foundation Center Grant Guides describe recent grants funded in thirty different subject areas. The grantmakers are listed by specific project (key words) and geographical areas. Minorities include African Americans, Hispanics, Asian Americans, Native Americans, gays and lesbians, and immigrants and refugees.

Grants for Women and Girls. New York: Foundation Center, 1995. 254p., $75.

Grants for education, career guidance, vocational training, equal rights, rape prevention, shelters for victims of domestic abuse, health programs, abortion rights, pregnancy programs, athletics and recreation, arts programs, and social research are all included in this guide.

Meiners, Phyllis A., and Greg A. Sanford, eds. *National Directory of Philanthropy for Native Americans.* Kansas City, Mo.: CRC Publishing, 1992. 139p., $69.95. ISBN 0-9633694-0-7.

This directory contains profiles of 24 foundations, 12 corporations and 3 major religious institutions with a history of providing support for Native American programs. Following the usual format for such directories, the thirty-nine entries include name and address of organization, officers and directors, application deadlines, sample grants descriptions, restrictions and application procedures. The directory is indexed by geography and grantmaker subject area.

F. Religion

Jankowski, Bernard, ed. *Fund Raisers Guide to Religious Philanthropy, 1996.* Rockville, Md.: The Taft Group, 1995. $150. ISBN 1-56995-021-0.

Written to aid a variety of religious organizations such as churches, synagogues, foreign missions, sectarian colleges, hospitals, and health and human service programs, this guide highlights the giving of 550 private grantmakers who have together donated more than $420 million to religious causes. All donors cited give at least $50,000 annually. Each entry provides details on ten recent grants as well as the foundation's regional and denominational preferences.

G. Social Service

National Guide to Funding for Children, Youth and Families. 3rd ed. New York: Foundation Center, 1995. 1095p., $145. ISBN 0-87954-603-4.

As with other Foundation Center National Guides, this volume focuses on a special population. It features 3,400 foundations and corporate giving programs which fund programs for children, youth, and families. As well as all contact information and financial data about the grantmaker, it lists over 13,000 sample grants that have been funded.

National Guide to Funding in Aging. 4th ed. New York: Foundation Center, 1994. 454p., $80. ISBN 0-87954-559-3.

Grantmakers in this guide fund a wide array of programs involved with senior citizens, from hospitals and community centers to legal rights and housing. The book gives detailed information about 220 foundations and descriptions of 1,600 recent grants made by them to seniors' activities. This guide also covers state and federal government programs and voluntary organizations which fund these programs. In all, 1,000 grantmakers are listed.

Library Fundraising on the Web: Tips and Sites

Adam Corson-Finnerty

Director, Library Development, and External Affairs

University of Pennsylvania Library

Our advice is based on the experience of a small team* at Penn that designed a Friends and Benefactors home page for a fifteen-library system. With minor adjustments, the tips that worked for us will serve other libraries and non-profit institutions as they move into fundraising on the Web.

Strategic Storefront

Major university libraries are recording over five million electronic searches a year through their online public access catalogs. Therefore, if your college or university library mounts a Web home page for its main "gateway" to electronic services, you will have one of the best storefront locations on the information superhighway. Here is how you might use that advantage for friend-raising and fundraising:

Create a Library "Friends and Benefactors" home page that links directly from the main library home page. Gather some graphics, write some text, and begin building an interesting, interactive resource for electronic visitors. All you need is access to a color scanner, space on the library server, and the time to teach yourself how to "mark up" a document so that it reads well on the Web. Or hire a student to do it—many have already taught themselves.

Keep in mind that at this stage, your primary audience will be right on campus. Your second audience will be "visitors" from other campuses who have Web-browsing software. Your third will be alumni and anyone else in cyberspace who has the software and wants to see what the library offers electronically. (With the major online services now offering Web-browsing facilities, this third audience is increasing dramatically.)

The team includes Laura Blanchard, who did most of the designing and HTML (Web) mark-up, Richard King, and writers Selden Smith, Brit Ray, and Brett Bonfield. Konrad Hernblad, Miranda Nickles, and Mikaelian Design provided technical and research assistance.

Initial Goals

Here are the key things that you can accomplish at this stage in Web development. I have put them in priority order, and suggest that you spend more time on the first items as you develop your home page.

1. Donor Recognition

The Web allows you to recognize your donors in spectacular ways. Let's take a book fund donor as an example. In the old days about all you could do would be to put a plate in the books and perhaps a plaque on a wall somewhere. With the Web you can create a home page with the donor's picture. If she is memorializing her father, you can put her father's picture up, along with a short comment on what this gift means. You can describe the purpose of the fund, and create "hot links" to other related library resources.

We have been calling this recognition "electronic plaquing." It bestows a little bit of cyberspace upon a donor. It can be a very powerful motivator for new donors, as well as a reenforcement for current donors (and descendants of past donors). However, make sure to get the donor's permission before you launch her into cyberspace. Some people who might be comfortable with a plaque may feel queasy about appearing on the small screen. (And some people will love it!)

Keep in mind the requirements of using copyrighted materials, especially with photos and graphics. Even a photo supplied by the donor might be copyrighted by the photographer; a scanned photo from a magazine article on the donor will probably require permission from the copyright holder.

2. Major Gift Fundraising

So now you have some electronic plaques to show off. Bring a major prospect to your library and show how donors have been recognized on the Web. Or load these pages on your laptop as local files and show them to prospects in his or her own home. Or use a modem and their phone line to take the donor "live" to the library for an interactive tour.

Although you could send your home page address to "wired" donors and let them cruise on their own, I don't recommend this approach; you won't be present to talk about gift opportunities. To alter a familiar fundraising phrase: People don't "give" to the Web, people give to people.

3. Corporate Fundraising

Here's a new idea. Let's say a corporation has donated equipment for your electronic look-up center. With corporations rushing to establish their own Web home pages, you could recognize this gift by providing a hot link to the donor's page. Is this advertising? I don't believe so. Stay away from slogans, mottos, and summary plugs of the kind that our public radio stations are using. Stick to the corporation's name, perhaps its logo, and let browsers decide whether they want to click to the corporate site.

At the Penn Library we are experimenting with a disclaimer page. When you click on the benefactor's name, you first go to a disclaimer that says, "You are leaving Penn Cyberspace," and makes you aware that you will be traveling to another computer server. Since you will be jumping from nonprofit space to commercial space, a border marker will be helpful. A reverse link can also be constructed on the home page of the corporation, should it want to show off the projects it supports.

4. Build Your Friends Group

Put your Friends of the Library group on the Web. For starters, put up your Friends' calendar and a description of what the Friends is all about. Then add an electronic form that allows visitors to join the Friends on the spot. The completed form will be automatically E-mailed to you, or your designee. (You needn't get involved with credit cards; just sign new members up and send a bill through the mail.)

The Friends calendar can be as elaborate and attractive as you wish. Use pictures and graphics as well as descriptive language for your events. You can allow people to RSVP online. And after your event has occurred, you can put up pictures and give a little recognition to Friends leaders and VIPs. Just scan the pictures in and add some captions. It can be done overnight.

Put your Friends Newsletter online. Put up the catalog from your most recent exhibition, or your current one—or the one coming up. Publicize Friends' gifts and recent acquisitions.

Allow the site visitor to send comments and suggestions to the president, the library director, and to you.

But don't get carried away with all this, unless you have an enthusiastic and net-savvy volunteer. As in the real world, development directors could end up spending endless amounts of time on The Friends—without any major gifts to show for it. Don't let your "virtual" Friends eat up your valuable fundraising time.

5. Education About Library Goals and Gift Opportunities

Start putting up the "picture" of where your library is headed. I don't recommend that you start with your forty-page Five Year Plan, but you could easily put it on for anyone who cares to read it. Think short-attention-span. Think pictures. Think lively language. Think playfulness. In a real sense what you will be creating is a huge advertisement for the library.

On the Web, advertisers have to draw people in. They have to create attractive pages and clever inducements to keep site visitors clicking.

Cruise a few Web advertisements and corporate home pages to see what I mean. Check out the playful ads on "Philadelphia Online" (http://www.phillynews.com), a site sponsored by the *Philadelphia Inquirer* and the *Daily News*. Want to see some really inventive uses of the Web? Subscribe online to "Hot Wired" magazine. Last time I looked, it was free (http://www.hotwired.com/login/).

How about a virtual tour of the library? One where you show off recent accomplishments and describe what you hope to do next? If you have an artist's view of what a new facility will look like, scan it and put it up for everyone to admire. Set up clickable floor plans, allowing visitors to check out each new room.

If you are pushing endowed positions in your library, put up a picture of the person who currently holds the position, along with a biography. The possibilities are only limited by the number of fundraising projects you care to manage.

6. Broad-Based Fundraising

Most people think of "fundraising on the Internet" as somehow gathering online gifts and pledges. While this is technically possible, I would not suggest that a library put any great emphasis here. First of all, it is not clear that people will line up in any significant numbers to make pledges based upon your electronic pitch. Record companies may sell CDs over the net, but it seems unlikely that you'll sell a $250,000 renovation to someone cruising your site. Your Web home page will be an aid to your efforts—much as a well-written brochure might be—but it won't do your work for you.

There is no reason not to experiment, however. Public television station KUSM in Montana takes online pledges at its home page. And a number of nonprofit organizations have signed on to a site called "reliefnet," where they can make their case and take gifts via credit card. (Note that using a credit card over the Internet is not yet "secure," and the risk of theft is present.)

Security will get better on the Internet, and more important, people will get used to the idea of making transactions in cyberspace. When that happens, you can be sure that your college or university will develop a method for online giving. Should you and your library be the pioneers in this area? Only if you have a lot of time for endless meetings with campus administrators while the wrinkles are being ironed out.

7. A Surprise Bonus

One of the surprises of developing your Web home page is that you will also be preparing everything you need for your next brochures and publications. After all, you will have written text, gathered pictures, employed graphics—all the things you need to do to prepare a written piece. So here is your first gift from the Web: *Taking the time to develop your Web site does not detract from your publications program; it complements and enhances that program.*

Some Electronic Addresses

Now that you are fired up and ready to develop your own Library Home page, take a few hours and cruise the current sites for ideas. Take a serendipitous approach: Go where your playful instincts lead you and see what draws you in. Most Web cruising software has a "what's cool" and "what's new" facility that quickly take you to interesting sites. Check them out.

For a sampler of sites that relate directly to library fundraising, try:

1. Extensive library fundraising pages:

Penn—http://www.library.upenn.edu/~friends/
Waterloo—http://www.lib.uwaterloo.ca/Gifts.html

2. Library Friends home pages:

Tulane:
http://www.tulane.edu/~lmiller/LibraryFriends.htm
Vermont: http://www.lib.vt.edu/friends/

3. Donor recognition:

Mitchell Multimedia Center:
http://www.library.nwu.edu/media/
Southern Illinois University Library:
http://www.lib.siu.edu/

4. Special Collections:

Georgia: http://www.libs.uga.edu
Tulane:
http://www.tulane.edu/~lmiller/SpecCollHomepage.html
Duke: http://odyssey.lib.duke.edu
Wm. & Mary: http://swem.wm.edu/spcolhp.html

5. Library Special Event/Special Project sites:

Univ. of Va.:
http://www.lib.virginia.edu/etext/fourmill.html
Emory: http://www.cc.emory.edu/ITD/campaign.itd.html
Illinois Urbana-Champaign (Digital Library Proposal):
http://www.grainger.uiuc.edu/dli/

6. University Alumni and Development home pages:

Pitt Alum:
http://info.pitt.edu/~alumni/alumni/relations/alumni.html
Ga. Tech Alum:
http://www.gatech.edu/alumni/alumni.html

7. Sites that promote a university or library capital campaign:

University of Illinois Foundation:
http://www.uiuc.edu/providers/uif/
University of Virginia (click on "Arise and Build"):
http://www.lib.virginia.edu/
Princeton Outdoor Action:
http://www.princeton.edu/~rcurtis/capbroch.html

8. Online Pledging sites:

ReliefNet Home page: http://www.reliefnet.org/
KUSM: http://www.kusm.montana.edu:80/Friends.html

Another Internet resource (not on Web) is a listserv moderated by the ALA Library Administration and Management Association (LAMA). The list, FRFDS-L is an idea exchange focusing on fundraising and resource development for libraries. For information, contact Charles Kratz, FRFDS chair, at 717-941-4008, or the LAMA Office at 800-545-2433, ext. 5031.

An online version of this article (with hotlinks) is mounted on the author's personal home page:
http://pobox.upenn.edu/~adamcf/

Checking Out Cyberspace:
Grants from High-Tech Companies*

Nita L. Martin

As the information superhighway spreads across the world, libraries provide fertile fields for high-tech companies wishing to develop and test-market products, train consumers and professionals, promote economic development, and blunt regulatory restrictions. Whether the new technologies will be extended to low-income communities and to public institutions, or whether many will be left out after demonstration projects end, rests largely with the corporate sector.

The Clinton-Gore administration has made universal access to the information superhighway a priority, and Congress has become a blazing battleground as stakeholders seek to influence legislation that will govern high-tech communications. Nonprofits want discounts for using video and data communication lines, and they want the "fair use" of copyrighted material extended to digitized information available on electronic networks. Telephone and cable companies want deregulation (at least for their competition) and have opposed legislated discount rates for nonprofits. Software and computer companies generally oppose regulation, and look to promote First Amendment freedoms and copyright protection of intellectual property.

In this context, corporate support for upgrading library information technology and making it accessible to the public may come from the business development or the marketing side of a company. Where foundation support is forthcoming, it seems to play a strategic role in positioning the company to benefit from the coming technological proliferation.

But library advocates say there have been only limited links with the corporate world. If the information superhighway is the new frontier for communication, corporate/library partnerships may be considered cutting edge philanthropy. Big opportunities may be waiting for corporations that step down this path.

*Reprinted from *Corporate Philanthropy Report*, August 1995. Reprinted with the permission of the publisher, Capitol Publications, Inc. For more information about *CPR*, call (800) 655-5597.

Telecommunications

Some of the most ambitious initiatives come from the Baby Bells. Bell Atlantic, NYNEX, US West, Pacific West, and other Bell operating companies that emerged from the breakup of AT&T lobbied the Federal Communications Commission to divert $2 billion in access fees to wire schools and school libraries to the information superhighway. The money would come from access fees the long-distance companies pay the Baby Bells. The FCC ignored this proposal, opting instead to lower rates, but commissioners could soon revisit this idea.

Many of the Baby Bells have committed publicly to wiring schools and libraries to the information superhighway. California-based Pacific Bell, for example, wanted to stimulate consumer demand for the new communication technologies. It determined that libraries and librarians had a strong interest in the future of telecommunications and should participate in the national policy debate, learn about and showcase information-age technologies, and network and integrate telecommunications technology into libraries and library systems. To that end, Pac Bell has committed $125 million to two programs.

Pac Bell gave $25 million to the California Research and Education Network (CalREN). CalREN in 1993-94 used the funds for collaborative projects in the San Francisco and Los Angeles Areas. The funded projects were those "whose high-speed applications revolutionize the way organizations communicate and share information." For example, in the heart of Silicon Valley, it funded two projects: an online long-distance master's degree program available statewide through San Jose State University School of Library and Information Studies; and a linked electronic catalog for the Peninsula Public and Community College Library System.

In addition, Pac Bell's Education First program (telephone: 800-901-2210) allocated $100 million for applications based on high-speed telecommunications lines to connect the nearly 8,600 schools, libraries, and community colleges in the company's territory with the communications superhighway in the next few years. Projects include database access for telecomputing, such as Internet access and interactive video conferencing. The company facilitates vendor discounts for hardware, software, and Internet service and a multimedia collaborative development of electronic learning applications.

Twelve demonstration projects at public schools, community colleges, and libraries in Sacramento and Pasadena brought Pac Bell together with AT&T, IBM and Apple to provide the equipment. The Pacific Telesis Foundation provided staff development and training on integrating the new technology, according to foundation chief Jere Jacobs (415-394-3666). The projects are funded for a year, but recipients may apply through 1996 for reduced rates. Pac Bell also advocates a statewide coalition with government and the private sector to ensure that every California classroom and library is wired for full electronic access by 2000.

"We'd like to be able to allow most Americans to have electronic access to libraries," says Michele Daly, media relations manager for Bell Atlantic (202-392-1021). The company is committed to wiring schools in its area (including school libraries) once a full service video dial tone network has been built. The schools will then have to find the funds for the equipment to connect to it. Right now, Bell Atlantic is helping the Library of Congress digitize information to make it available on the Internet.

BellCore, the research and development arm of the Baby Bells, provided Internet links to thirty-two libraries in Morris County, N.J. The company is mainly working with schools and university libraries.

The GTE Foundation has given thirty-eight library-related grants totaling $1.2 million over the last five years, according to Maureen Gorman, vice president of the foundation (203-965-3620). Grantees included the Dallas Museum of Art for the GTE Information Services Center, an education center for teachers and students, classrooms, a visual resource library, and a computerized database of the museum's collection for public reference. In addition, a grant to the University of Illinois/Urbana-Champaign will help fund acquisition of technical equipment for its Information Retrieval Center. The center will house forty computer terminals to access local and remote databases.

GTE California is offering free consulting and $5.5 million in $2,000 credit chunks to libraries and schools for high-tech applications. "As a technology company, we are very interested in building the capacity of the communities where we operate to use products GTE offers" and to improve universities' ability to educate about technology, Gorman says. "I think we would be favorable to other proposals in this area."

US West Foundation (303-793-6686) gave $50,000 to the Siouxland Automated Library Initiative in 1994 to link automated library catalogs of three colleges and the Sioux City Public Library in a tri-state area. The foundation also gave grants to the Colorado State Library in 1992 and 1993 to develop and link public and school libraries to an information network.

But US West recently turned down another, similar request from the state library. The foundation also turned down the Denver Public Library which, like many public libraries, seems to have had little success with corporate donors.

Another much-publicized grant program is the MCI Foundation's three-year, $500,000 LibraryLINK project (202-887-2106). Through the American Library Association's Reference and Adult Services Division (312-280-4397), public libraries receive $20,000 grants to develop technology-based demonstration projects to enhance reference and information services. Most of the first eight grants involve providing public access to the Internet. ALA also received some MCI funds to manage the program.

"Because [MCI's] whole corporate profile is warm and fuzzy, they were interested in a real grassroots, positive feeling in the community," says ALA's Patricia Martin, vice president for development and sponsorship, Fund for America's Libraries (312-280-5045). MCI did not require grant recipients to be MCI customers, but did seek positive media exposure through the program, Martin says.

The MCI Foundation assists "organizations that demonstrate how state-of-the-art technologies enhance the process of learning." Andrea Sarkisian, executive director, noting that second-round recipients would be announced later in 1995, hopes the grants will spark matching funds so libraries can continue the services.

Thus far, AT&T (although it funneled money to selected libraries as part of its giving to the United Negro College Fund) and Sprint have not shown much interest in high-tech library projects, but don't be surprised if that changes.

Computer Companies

Stanly Litow, corporate contributions manager for IBM (914-765-1900), says Big Blue is very interested in creating digital libraries and "in the degree to which school libraries will or will not get access to digitized information." An IBM lab designed a system to digitize the Vatican Library's collection and make it available worldwide, and donated the necessary equipment. IBM also provided a grant to digitize the WPA Federal Theater collection of the Library of Congress. It developed and provided the kiosk technology for the New York Public Library that explains the facility's resources to users. Litow says the next step will be to spread this emerging technology to school libraries. IBM also has a $25 million program, "Reinventing Education," and school libraries in ten states will benefit from the program's grants.

Litow says IBM is concerned with three issues: technical problems in creating digital libraries, providing technical assistance or training to familiarize as many people as possible with the technology and its uses, and addressing with other funders the cost of providing this technology. "We think we have a role trying to get people to cope with this dramatic change," he adds.

Digital Equipment Corp. concentrates on in-kind equipment grants, says spokesperson Mary Ann Hersey (508-493-6369). Recently, it donated $1.5 million in hardware to the British Library for an online public access system; $95,000 in equipment to the Springfield, Mass., Library and Museums Association to network major education and cultural organizations in the city to schools, hospitals, businesses and government offices; and $59,472 for 38 personal computers to the new Grainger Engineering Library Information Center at the University of Illinois.

Impressive as all this is, many libraries believe that computer companies could be doing much more. *Business Week* recently reported a big interest on the part of Silicon Valley firms to give to libraries, but there is little evidence to back up the claim. The San Francisco Public Library has found scant assistance among area high-tech firms for its $30 million capital campaign for a new, state-of-the-art facility. The little it raised from business came mostly from the Bank of America and Pacific Gas & Electric. The only technology-related grant came from the Michigan-based Kresge Foundation (810-643-0533), a private foundation started by Kmart's founders but not affiliated with the corporation. The San Francisco Library's new foundation says it has not given up hope on interesting Silicon Valley firms in its plans for a high-tech showcase.

Apple Computer has been supporting demonstration projects in libraries and museums with equipment and software grants since 1990. The Apple Library of Tomorrow program has helped the Colorado State Library, the San Diego Public Library and the Flint, Mich., Library connect to the Internet. It helped libraries in Telluride, Colo., Cambridge, Mass., and rural New York state build community networks, and has participated in other projects.

The Hewlett-Packard Foundation (415-857-5197), like many other corporate foundations, focused on education, but is open to grant requests from public libraries in its civic grants category. Its one major project with libraries two years ago linked about twelve libraries to the Internet at the University of Colorado, Colorado State University, the Air Force Academy, and other Colorado colleges with public libraries. HP donated equipment and some cash for software.

Cable Television Companies

Cable television, long involved in library projects through cable access requirements, has shown only limited interest in new library projects, but one cooperative venture stands out.

The U.S. Commerce Department last year funded $24.3 million in high-tech projects, seven of ninety-two involving libraries. Although matching funds were required, little corporate money was involved. But in the $1.24 million Charlotte's Web project, the public libraries of Charlotte and Mecklenburg County, N.C., enlisted Time-Warner Cable (203-328-0600) and Vision Cable, as well as Southern Bell, and area schools, universities, public television, and government to create a free-net. It will be an interactive electronic community with free and easy access to education and information. The Commerce Department (202-482-2048) will fund projects in 1995 and 1996, but at reduced levels.

Outlook

The library-corporate giving link has not been fully exploited. Indeed, some of the corporate givers interviewed for this article said they had never even been approached by libraries seeking grants. So, while some libraries have been rebuffed in their efforts to gain funding, the possibilities for corporate funding have not been exhausted for this crucial area.

Nonprofit Recipient Categories

Categories

Recipient Organization Types

Arts & Humanities

Art History, Arts Appreciation, Arts Associations & Councils, Arts Centers, Arts Festivals, Arts Funds, Arts Institutes, Arts Outreach, Ballet, Community Arts, Dance, Ethnic & Folk Art, Film & Video, History & Archeology, Historic Preservation, Libraries, Literary Arts, Museums/Galleries, Music, Opera, Performing Arts, Public Broadcasting, Theater, Visual Arts

Civic & Public Affairs

African American Affairs, Asian American Affairs, Botanical Gardens/Parks, Business/Free Enterprise, Chambers of Commerce, Civil Rights, Clubs, Community Foundations, Economic Development, Economic Policy, Employment/Job Training, Ethnic Organizations, First Amendment Issues, Gay/Lesbian Issues, Hispanic Affairs, Housing, Inner-City Development, Law & Justice, Legal Aid, Minority Business, Municipalities/Towns, Native American Affairs, Nonprofit Management, Parades/Festivals, Philanthropic Organizations, Professional/Trade Associations, Public Policy, Rural Affairs, Safety, Urban/Community Affairs, Women's Affairs, Zoos/Aquariums

Education

Afterschool Enrichment Programs, Agricultural Education, Arts/Humanities Education, Business Education, Business-School Partnerships, Colleges & Universities, Community/Junior Colleges, Continuing Education, Economic Education, Education Associations, Education Funds, Education Reform, Elementary Education (private), Elementary Education (public), Engineering Education, Environmental Education, Faculty Development, Gifted & Talented Programs, Health & Physical Education, International Exchange, International Studies, Journalism/Media Education, Leadership Training, Legal Education, Literacy, Medical Education, Minority Education, Preschool Education, Private Education (precollege), Public Education (precollege), Religious Education, School Volunteerism, Science/Mathematics Education, Secondary Education (private), Secondary Education (public), Social Sciences Education, Special Education, Student Aid, Vocational/Technical Education

Environment

Air/Water Quality, Energy, Forestry, Protection, Research, Resource Conservation, Sanitary Systems, Watershed, Wildlife Protection

Health

Adolescent Health Issues, AIDS/HIV, Alzheimer's Disease, Arthritis, Cancer, Children's Health/Hospitals, Clinics/Medical Centers, Diabetes, Emergency/Ambulance Services, Eyes/Blindness, Geriatric Health, Health Funds, Health Organizations, Health Policy/Cost Containment, Heart, Home-Care Services, Hospices, Hospitals, Hospitals (university affiliated), Kidney, Long-Term Care, Medical Rehabilitation, Medical Research, Medical Training, Mental Health, Multiple Sclerosis, Nursing Services, Nutrition, Outpatient Health Care, Prenatal Health Issues, Preventive Medicine/Wellness Organizations, Public Health, Research/Studies Institutes, Respiratory, Single-Disease Health Associations, Speech & Hearing, Transplant Networks/Donor Banks, Trauma Treatment

International

Foreign Arts Organizations, Foreign Education Institutions, Health Care/Hospitals, Human Rights, International Affairs, International Development, International Environmental Issues, International Law, International Organizations, International

Peace & Security Issues, International Relations, International Relief Efforts, Missionary/Religious Activities, Trade

Religion

Bible Study/Translation, Churches, Dioceses, Jewish Causes, Ministries, Missionary Activities (domestic), Religious Organizations, Religious Welfare, Seminaries, Social/Policy Issues, Synagogues/Temples

Science

Observatories/Planetariums, Science Exhibits/Fairs, Science Museums, Scientific Centers/Institutes, Scientific Labs, Scientific Organizations, Scientific Research

Social Services

Animal Protection, At-Risk Youth, Big Brother/Big Sister, Camps, Child Abuse, Child Welfare, Community Centers, Community Service Organizations, Counseling, Crime Prevention, Day Care, Delinquency/Criminal Rehabilitation, Domestic Violence, Emergency Relief, Family Planning, Family Services, Food & Clothing Distribution, Homes, People With Disabilities, Recreation & Athletics, Refugee Assistance, Scouts, Senior Services, Sexual Abuse, Shelters/Homeless, Special Olympics, Substance Abuse, United Funds/United Way, Veterans, Volunteer Services, YMCA/YMHA/YWCA/YWHA, Youth Organizations

List of Abbreviations

&	And	**Commun**	Communication(s), Community	**Fwy**	Freeway
AA	Associate of Arts	**comptr**	comptroller	**GC**	Golf Club
AB	Arts, Bachelor of	**Conf**	Conference	**gen**	general
Acad	Academy	**Confed**	Confederation	**gov**	governing, governor
acct	accountant	**Cong**	Congress	**govt**	government
admin	administration, administrative, administrator	**Consult**	Consultant, Consulting	**grad**	graduate
adv	advisor, advisory	**contr**	controller		
AFB	Air Force Base	**coo**	chief operating officer	**hon**	honorable, honorary
Aff	Affairs	**Coop**	Cooperating, Cooperative, Cooperation	**Hosp**	Hospital
affil	affiliation			**Hwy**	Highway
AG	Aktiengesellschaft	**Corp**	Corporate, Corporation		
Am	America, American	**Counc**	Council	**Inc**	Incorporated
AM	Arts, Master of	**couns**	counsel, counseling, counselor	**Indus**	Industrial, Industries, Industry
Apt	Apartment	**CPA**	Certified Public Accountant	**Info**	Information, Informational
APO	Army Post Office	**Ct**	Court	**Ins**	Insurance
archt	architect, architecture, architectural	**Ctr**	Center, Centre	**Inst**	Institute, Institution
Assn	Association	**CUNY**	City University of New York	**Intl**	International
Assoc(s)	Associate(s), Associated	**curr**	current		
asst	assistant	**cust**	customer	**JD**	Juris Doctor
atty	attorney			**Jr**	Junior
Ave	Avenue	**DB**	Divinity, Bachelor of		
		DD	Doctor of Divinity	**Legis**	Legislation, Legislative, Legislator
b	born	**del**	delegate		
BA	Bachelor of Arts	**Dem**	Democrat	**Lib(s)**	Library, Libraries
BArch	Bachelor of Architecture	**dep**	deputy	**LLB**	Laws, Bachelor of
BBA	Bachelor of Business Administration	**Dept**	Department	**LLM**	Master of Law
		Devel	Development	**Ln**	Lane
bd	board	**dir**	director	**LP**	Limited Partnership
BE	Bachelor of Engineering	**Distr**	Distributor, Distribution, Distributing	**Ltd**	Limited
BFA	Bachelor of Fine Arts	**Div**	Division	**MA**	Master of Arts
Bldg	Building	**don**	donor	**MArch**	Master of Architecture
Blvd	Boulevard	**Dr**	Doctor	**MBA**	Master of Business Administration
Bros	Brothers	**Dr**	Drive		
BS	Bachelor of Science	**DSW**	Doctor of Social Work	**MD**	Doctor of Medicine
BSChE	Bachelor of Science in Chemical Engineering			**MDiv**	Master of Divinity
		E	East	**Med**	Medical, Medicine
BSME	Bachelor of Science in Mechanical Engineering	**Econ**	Economic, Economics	**mem**	member
		Ed	Education, Educational, Educated	**Meml**	Memorial
Bur	Bureau			**Metro**	Metropolitan
Bus	Business	**EIN**	Employer Identification Number	**MFA**	Master of Fine Arts
				Mfg	Manufacturing
c/o	care of	**empl**	employment	**Mfr**	Manufacturer
CC	Country Club	**Engg**	Engineering	**Mgmt**	Management
ceo	chief executive officer	**engr**	engineer	**mgr**	manager
cfo	chief financial officer	**exec**	executive	**misc**	miscellaneous
Chap	Chapter	**Expy**	Expressway	**Mktg**	Marketing
Chem	Chemical, Chemist, Chemistry			**Mng**	Managing
		f/b/o	for the benefit of	**MS**	Master of Science
chmn	chairman	**Fdn**	Foundation	**MSW**	Master of Social Work
chp	chairperson	**fdr**	founder	**Mt**	Mount
chwm	chairwoman	**Fed**	Federal, Federation, Federated	**Mus**	Museum
Co	Company				
Coll	College	**Fin**	Finance, Financial	**N**	North
comm	committee	**Fl**	Floor	**NAACP**	National Association for the Advancement of Colored People
commn	commission	**FPO**	Fleet Post Office		
commnr	commissioner	**Ft**	Fort		

N. Ap.	Not Applicable	**RD**	Rural Delivery	**SW**	Southwest
N. Av.	Not Available	**rehab**	rehabilitation	**Sys**	System(s)
Natl	National	**rel**	religious, religion		
NE	Northeast	**rels**	relations	**Tech**	Technological, Technical, Technology
No	Number	**rep**	representative		
nonpr	nonprofit	**Repbl**	Republican	**Terr**	Terrace
NW	Northwest	**Res**	Research, Researcher	**ThD**	Doctor of Theology
		ret	retired	**Tpke**	Turnpike
off	office, officer	**RFD**	Rural Free Delivery	**treas**	treasurer
oper	operating, operations	**Rm**	Room	**trust**	trustee
Org	Organization	**RR**	railroad		
		RR	Rural Route	**Un**	United
pers	personnel	**Rte**	Route	**UN**	United Nations
PhB	Philosophy, Bachelor of	**RY**	Railway	**Univ**	University
PhD	Philosophy, Doctor of			**US**	United States
phil	philanthropic	**S**	South	**USA**	United States of America
Pk	Park	**SB**	Science, Bachelor of	**u/w/o**	under the will of
Pke	Pike	**Sch**	School		
Pkwy	Parkway	**Sci**	Science(s), Scientific	**vchmn**	vice chairman
Pl	Place	**SE**	Southeast	**visit**	visiting, visitors
Plz	Plaza	**secy**	secretary	**vp**	vice president
PO	Post Office	**sen**	senator		
Polytech	Polytechnic, Polytechnical	**SM**	Science, Master of	**W**	West
pres	president	**Soc**	Society		
prin	principal	**Sq**	Square	**YC**	Yacht Club
prof	professor	**Sr**	Senior	**YMCA**	Young Men's Christian Association
Prov	Province, Provincial	**SR**	Star/State Route		
Ptnr	Partner	**St**	Saint, State, Street	**YMHA**	Young Men's Hebrew Association
pub(s)	publication(s)	**Sta**	Station		
pub	public	**Ste**	Sainte, Suite	**YWCA**	Young Women's Christian Association
publ(s)	published, publisher, publishing	**Sub(s)**	Subsidiary(ies)		
		SUNY	State University of New York	**YWHA**	Young Women's Hebrew Association
Pvt	Private	**supt**	superintendent		
		supvr	supervisor		
Rd	Road	**Svc(s)**	Service(s)		

Profiles

ALABAMA

Alabama Gas Corp.

Employees: 1,100
Parent Company: Energen Co.
Headquarters: Birmingham, AL
SIC Major Group: Electric, Gas & Sanitary Services

CONTACT
Bill Barber
Director, Corporate Contributions and New Business Admin.
Alabama Gas Corp.
2101 6th Ave. N.
Birmingham, AL 35203-2784
(205) 326-8211

FINANCIAL SUMMARY
Recent Giving: $523,000 (1994)

CONTRIBUTIONS SUMMARY

The company supports nonprofit organizations in its headquarters community, with an emphasis on health and human services and education. Also supports civic organizations and the arts.

Volunteerism: Company encourages volunteerism through a Volunteer Investment Program. The company donates money to approved organizations in which employees volunteer a specified number of hours per year.

Typical Recipients: • *Arts & Humanities:* Arts Associations & Councils, Arts Festivals, Ballet, Community Arts, Dance, General, Historic Preservation, Libraries, Museums/Galleries, Music, Opera, Performing Arts, Public Broadcasting, Theater • *Civic & Public Affairs:* Chambers of Commerce, Civil Rights, Community Foundations, General, Inner-City Development, Law & Justice, Philanthropic Organizations, Public Policy, Urban & Community Affairs, Zoos/Aquariums • *Education:* Colleges & Universities, Elementary Education (Public), Faculty Development, General, Literacy, Science/Mathematics Education, Secondary Education (Public) • *Environment:* General • *Health:* AIDS/HIV, Arthritis, Cancer, Children's Health/Hospitals, Clinics/Medical Centers, Diabetes, Eyes/Blindness, General, Heart, Hospices, Hospitals, Kidney, Medical Rehabilitation, Mental Health, Multiple Sclerosis, Respiratory, Single-Disease Health Associations • *International:* General • *Religion:* General, Religious Welfare • *Science:* General • *Social Services:* At-Risk Youth, Child Welfare, Community Service Organizations, Family Services, General, People with Disabilities, Scouts, Senior Services, Shelters/Homelessness, United Funds/United Ways, Volunteer Services, YMCA/YWCA/YMHA/YWHA

Grant Types: award, capital, emergency, employee matching gifts, general support, multiyear/continuing support, operating expenses, professorship, and scholarship

Nonmonetary Support Types: donated equipment, in-kind services, loaned employees, loaned executives, and workplace solicitation

Geographic Distribution: primarily headquarters area

Operating Locations: AL (Birmingham)

CORP. OFFICERS

Rex Jackson Lysinger: *B* Pittsburgh PA 1937 *ED* Univ Pittsburgh BS 1959 *CURR EMPL* chmn, ceo, dir: Alabama Gas Corp/Energen Corp *CORP AFFIL* chmn, ceo: Taurus Exploration Co; dir: Kirschner Med Corp, South Trust Bank AL *NONPR AFFIL* dir: AL Safety Counc, All Am Bowl, Am Heart Assn, Boy Scouts Am Leadership Birmingham, Salvation Army, Un Way Birmingham; mem: Am Gas Assn, Birmingham Area Chamber Commerce, Southern Gas Assn; mem pres counc: Univ AL Birmingham; trust: Baptist Hosp Fdn, Southern Res Inst *CLUB AFFIL* mem: Newcomen Soc

William Michael Warren, Jr.: *B* Bryan TX 1947 *ED* Auburn Univ BA 1968; Duke Univ JD 1971 *CURR EMPL* pres, coo, dir: Alabama Gas Corp/Energen Corp *CORP AFFIL* dir: AmSouth Bank NA *NONPR AFFIL* dir: Gas Res Inst, Southern Gas Assn; mem: Am Bar Assn, Birmingham Area Chamber Commerce, Relay House; trust: AL Inst Deaf & Blind, Childrens Hosp Birmingham

APPLICATION INFORMATION

Initial Approach: Send a brief letter of inquiry and a full proposal. Include a description of organization, amount requested, purpose of funds sought, recently audited financial statement, and proof of tax-exempt status. Also include a listing of salaries and benefits paid to staff members of the organizations requesting a contribution.

Restrictions on Giving: Does not support individuals, religious organizations for sectarian purposes, political or lobbying groups, organizations outside operating areas, or fraternal organizations.

PUBLICATIONS
Guidelines

GRANTS ANALYSIS
Note: The average contribution size varies. Recent grants are derived from a grants list provided by company in 1995.

RECENT GRANTS

General
Boy Scouts and Girl Scouts, Birmingham, AL
Civil Rights Institute
Kings Ranch, Birmingham, AL
Salvation Army, Birmingham, AL
Talladega College, Talladega, AL

Alabama Power Co. / Alabama Power Foundation

Sales: $2.85 billion
Employees: 7,850
Parent Company: Southern Company
Headquarters: Birmingham, AL
SIC Major Group: Electric Services

CONTACT
Clyde H. Wood
President
Alabama Power Foundation
PO Box 2641, 600 N 18th St.
Birmingham, AL 35291
(205) 250-2508

FINANCIAL SUMMARY
Recent Giving: $4,000,000 (1995 est.); $3,200,000 (1994 approx.); $3,200,000 (1993 approx.)

Assets: $61,912,187 (1992); $43,413,240 (1990); $25,005,939 (1989)

Gifts Received: $12,500,000 (1990); $15,000,000 (1989)

Fiscal Note: Figures include direct corporate and foundation giving. In 1992, direct giving was $1,920,225, and foundation giving was $3,016,590. Above figures exclude nonmonetary support. In 1990, the foundation received funds from Alabama Power Company.

EIN: 57-0901832

CONTRIBUTIONS SUMMARY
Typical Recipients: • *Arts & Humanities:* Arts Associations & Councils, Arts Centers, Arts Festivals, Community Arts, Dance, Libraries, Music, Performing Arts, Theater, Visual Arts • *Civic & Public Affairs:* Business/Free Enterprise, Urban & Community Affairs, Zoos/Aquariums • *Education:* Colleges & Universities, Community & Junior Colleges, Elementary Education (Private), Engineering/Technological Education, Literacy, Minority Education, Public Education (Precollege), Science/Mathematics Education • *Environment:* General • *Health:* Health Organizations, Mental Health, Single-Disease Health Associations • *Science:* Science Exhibits & Fairs • *Social Services:* Child Welfare, Community Centers, Community Service Organizations, Delinquency & Criminal Rehabilitation, Family Services, Food/Clothing Distribution, People with Disabilities, Senior Services, Shelters/Homelessness, Substance Abuse, United Funds/United Ways, Youth Organizations

Grant Types: capital, challenge, employee matching gifts, endowment, general support, matching, multiyear/continuing support, project, scholarship, and seed money

Nonmonetary Support Types: in-kind services, loaned employees, and workplace solicitation

Note: The company reports that nonmonetary support is limited. Total value of nonmonetary support was not available.

Geographic Distribution: primarily in headquarters and operating locations

Operating Locations: AL (Birmingham)

1

CORP. OFFICERS

Art P. Beattie: *B* 1954 *ED* Univ TN BS 1975; Univ AL MBA 1979 *CURR EMPL* vp, secy, treas: AL Power Co *CORP AFFIL* secy: Southern Electric Generating Co

Elmer Beseler Harris: *B* Chilton County AL 1939 *ED* Auburn Univ BS 1962; Auburn Univ MS 1968; Auburn Univ MBA 1970 *CURR EMPL* pres, ceo, dir: AL Power Co *CORP AFFIL* dir: AL Property Co, AmSouth Bank NA; exec vp, dir: Southern Co Inc; pres, dir: Southern Electric Generating Co *NONPR AFFIL* dir: AL Counc Econ Ed, Boy Scouts Am Birmingham Area Counc, Pub Aff Res Counc AL, Un Way Am; mem: Edison Electric Inst, Soc Am Military, Southeastern Electric Exchange; mem adv bd: St Vincent Hosp; trust: Samford Univ, Southern Res Inst *CLUB AFFIL* Cherokee Town & CC, Downtown, Montgomery, Rotary, Summit

Charles D. McCrary: *B* 1952 *ED* Auburn Univ BSME 1973; Birmingham Sch Law JD 1978 *CURR EMPL* sr vp: AL Power Co

GIVING OFFICERS

Art P. Beattie: treas *CURR EMPL* vp, secy, treas: AL Power Co (see above)

W. Roy Crow: dir

Kenneth A. Deal: dir

Banks A. Farris: chmn *B* 1935 *ED* Auburn Univ BCE 1958; Jones Law Sch LLB 1968 *CURR EMPL* vp cust svc & satisfaction: AL Power Co

Charles D. McCrary: exec vp *CURR EMPL* sr vp: AL Power Co (see above)

Jera G. Stribling: exec vp

Anthony J. Topazi: dir *B* Birmingham AL 1950 *ED* Auburn Univ 1972 *CURR EMPL* vp: AL Power Co *CORP AFFIL* dir: AmSouth Bank NA *NONPR AFFIL* mem: Natl Mgmt Assn

Jack Walker, Jr.: dir

Christopher C. Womack: dir

Clyde H. Wood: pres

APPLICATION INFORMATION

Initial Approach: *Initial Contact:* brief letter of inquiry *Include Information On:* description of the organization and its mission, list of officers and board members, amount requested, description of use, sources of other support and amounts of assured or anticipated support for the proposed project, evidence of need, recently audited financial statements, and proof of tax-exempt status *Deadlines:* none

Restrictions on Giving: Does not support individuals, religious organizations for sectarian purposes, political or lobbying groups, or organizations which lack 501(c)(3) status.

Also does not fund organizations which discriminate on the basis of race, color, creed, gender, or national origin or operating expenses which duplicate United Way funding (capital or special project funding will be considered).

PUBLICATIONS

Charitable giving pamphlet, foundation annual report

GRANTS ANALYSIS

Total Grants: $3,016,590*

Number of Grants: 163

Highest Grant: $150,000

Average Grant: $17,000*

Typical Range: $10,000 to $20,000

Disclosure Period: 1992

Note: The total grants figure is for the foundation only. The figure for average grant was provided by the foundation. Recent grants are derived from a 1993 annual report.

RECENT GRANTS

Library
Tuscaloosa Public Library, Tuscaloosa, AL

General
Birmingham-Southern College, Birmingham, AL
Boys and Girls Club of Greater Mobile, Mobile, AL
Family Guidance Center of Montgomery, Montgomery, AL
Montgomery Humane Society, Montgomery, AL
Salvation Army

BE&K Inc. / BE&K Foundation

Employees: 2,900
Headquarters: Birmingham, AL
SIC Major Group: Engineering & Management Services and General Building Contractors

CONTACT

Donna Sanborne
Manager, Corporate Relations
BE&K Inc.
2000 International Park Dr.
Birmingham, AL 35243
(205) 969-3600

FINANCIAL SUMMARY

Recent Giving: $423,726 (fiscal 1994); $243,650 (fiscal 1993)

Assets: $11,333 (fiscal 1994); $179,446 (fiscal 1993)

Gifts Received: $250,750 (fiscal 1994); $54,881 (fiscal 1993)

Fiscal Note: Company gives through the foundation. In fiscal 1994, contributions were received from BE&K Inc.

EIN: 63-0979638

CONTRIBUTIONS SUMMARY

Typical Recipients: • *Arts & Humanities:* Arts Associations & Councils, Arts Festivals, Arts Funds, History & Archaeology, Libraries, Museums/Galleries, Opera, Public Broadcasting • *Civic & Public Affairs:* Business/Free Enterprise, Chambers of Commerce, Civil Rights, Clubs, General, Municipalities/Towns, Professional & Trade Associations, Public Policy, Urban & Community Affairs • *Education:* Arts/Humanities Education, Business Education, Colleges & Universities, Economic Educa-

tion, Education Reform, Engineering/Technological Education, General, Gifted & Talented Programs, Literacy, Minority Education, Private Education (Precollege), Science/Mathematics Education, Special Education • *Health:* AIDS/HIV, Children's Health/Hospitals, Emergency/Ambulance Services, Medical Research, Mental Health, Multiple Sclerosis • *Religion:* Religious Welfare, Social/Policy Issues • *Science:* Science Museums • *Social Services:* Community Service Organizations, Delinquency & Criminal Rehabilitation, Family Services, People with Disabilities, Scouts, United Funds/United Ways, Volunteer Services, Youth Organizations

Grant Types: general support

Geographic Distribution: limited to Birmingham, AL

Operating Locations: AL (Birmingham)

CORP. OFFICERS

T. Michael Goodrich: *CURR EMPL* pres, ceo, dir: BE&K Inc

Theodore C. Kennedy: *CURR EMPL* chmn, dir: BE&K Inc

Donna Sanborne: *CURR EMPL* mgr corp rels: BE&K Inc

Clyde M. Smith: *CURR EMPL* cfo: BE&K Inc

GIVING OFFICERS

T. Michael Goodrich: trust *CURR EMPL* pres, ceo, dir: BE&K Inc (see above)

Theodore C. Kennedy: trust *CURR EMPL* chmn, dir: BE&K Inc (see above)

Clyde M. Smith: trust *CURR EMPL* cfo: BE&K Inc (see above)

APPLICATION INFORMATION

Initial Approach: *Initial Contact:* call requesting application form *Deadlines:* none

GRANTS ANALYSIS

Total Grants: $423,726

Number of Grants: 28

Highest Grant: $93,000

Average Grant: $12,249*

Typical Range: $1,000 to $10,000

Disclosure Period: fiscal year ending March 31, 1994

Note: Average grant figure excludes the highest grant. Recent grants are derived from a partial listing of contributions from a 1994 Form 990.

RECENT GRANTS

General

93,000	United Way of Central Alabama, Birmingham, AL
50,000	Birmingham Area Chamber of Commerce Foundation, Birmingham, AL
20,000	A+ Research Foundation, Birmingham, AL
18,300	Inroads/Birmingham, Birmingham, AL — donation and five sponsorship fees
14,000	Birmingham AIDS Outreach, Birmingham, AL

Bedsole Foundation, J. L.

CONTACT
Mabel B. Ward
Executive Director
J. L. Bedsole Foundation
PO Box 1137
Mobile, AL 36633
(205) 432-3369
Note: Another contact is Ken Niemeyer, vice
president and trust officer of AmSouth Bank,
N.A., at P.O. Drawer 1628, Mobile, AL,
36629, (205) 438-8331.

FINANCIAL SUMMARY
Recent Giving: $1,740,000 (1995 est.);
$1,740,000 (1994 approx.); $1,328,013
(1993)
Assets: $40,578,896 (1993); $33,580,431
(1992); $32,369,258 (1991)
EIN: 23-7225708

CONTRIBUTIONS SUMMARY
Donor(s): The foundation was established
in 1949, with a small donation from J. L.
Bedsole, solely for the purpose of helping
young people achieve a college education.
The foundation was fully funded in 1988 after Mr. Bedsole's death in 1975.

Joseph Linyer Bedsole was born August 7,
1881 in Clarke County, AL. In 1919, he
moved to Mobile where he organized the
Bedsole-Colvin Drug Company. He was a director of the First National Bank of Mobile
for over fifty years and also served as a director of the Alabama Power Company for
twenty years.

Mr. Bedsole was active in many charitable
enterprises. In 1947, as chairman of the Mobile Infirmary Campaign, he organized the
fundraising campaign to build the new hospital, which was dedicated in 1952. In 1951,
he was named "Mobilian of the Year" and
was selected "Man of the Year" by Howard
College (now Samford University), where
he served on the board of trustees from 1939-
62. Mr. Bedsole also received the first honorary degree awarded by the University of
Mobile, where he served as chairman of the
board of trustees from 1962-67.

He was married in 1910 to Phala Bradford.
Their only child, Lt. Joseph Linyer Bedsole,
Jr., a B-17 Bomber pilot with the U.S. Army
Air Corps and holder of the Distinguished
Flying Cross, was killed in a bomber raid
over Germany in April 1944.

Typical Recipients: • *Arts & Humanities:*
Arts Associations & Councils, Arts Centers,
Arts Festivals, Ballet, Historic Preservation,
History & Archaeology, Libraries, Muse-
ums/Galleries, Opera, Performing Arts, Pub-
lic Broadcasting, Theater, Visual Arts •
Civic & Public Affairs: Botanical Gar-
dens/Parks, Clubs, Economic Development,
General, Municipalities/Towns, Rural Af-
fairs, Urban & Community Affairs • *Educa-
tion:* Colleges & Universities, Community
& Junior Colleges, Economic Education,
Education Associations, Education Funds,
Medical Education, Private Education (Prec-

ollege), Public Education (Precollege), Sci-
ence/Mathematics Education, Secondary
Education (Public) • *Environment:* General
• *Health:* Clinics/Medical Centers,
Eyes/Blindness, Health Organizations, Hos-
pitals, Public Health, Single-Disease Health
Associations • *Religion:* Religious Organiza-
tions • *Science:* Observatories & Planetari-
ums, Science Museums, Scientific Centers
& Institutes, Scientific Research • *Social
Services:* Animal Protection, Camps, Child
Welfare, Community Service Organizations,
Day Care, Family Services, Scouts, United
Funds/United Ways, Volunteer Services,
Youth Organizations

Grant Types: capital, operating expenses,
and scholarship

Geographic Distribution: Alabama, with
primary emphasis in Mobile and the southwest part of the state

GIVING OFFICERS
Palmer Bedsole: mem distr comm *B* 1928
CURR EMPL pres, ceo, dir: Bedsole Medi-
cal Companies Inc

T. Massey Bedsole: chmn distr comm, trust
CURR EMPL vp: Mobile Fixture & Equipment Co *CORP AFFIL* sr ptnr: Hand Aren-
dall Bedsole Greaves & Johnston,LLC

Travis M. Bedsole, Jr.: mem distribution
comm

Ken Niemeyer: admin

Mabel B. Ward: exec dir

T. Bestor Ward III: mem distribution comm

Robert Williams: mem distribution comm
PHIL AFFIL pres: MacMillan Bloedel Foundation

APPLICATION INFORMATION
Initial Approach:

Applicants should submit a preliminary letter to the foundation. Application forms and
descriptive brochures for the Bedsole Scholarship Program are sent to high school counselors in southwest Alabama, and to many
four-year Alabama colleges. Application
forms are also sent to individuals upon request.

The preliminary letter should be short and include a brief description of the project and
the name, address, and telephone number of
the contact person for the project.

Applications are accepted continuously. Application forms for the Bedsole Scholars Program are due April 1.

The board meets every other month. If the
foundation has an interest in the proposal
then the applicant will be requested to furnish additional information about the project
and the organization.

Restrictions on Giving: Grants are limited
to Alabama. Bedsole Scholarships are
awarded only to graduates of southwest Alabama high schools who achieve a minimum
high school GPA of 2.50. Preference is
given to high school seniors attending public or private schools in Mobile, Baldwin,
Clarke, Monroe, or Washington Counties
and Sweet Water High School in Marengo
County.

OTHER THINGS TO KNOW
AmSouth Bank, NA, is listed as a corporate
trustee of the foundation.

GRANTS ANALYSIS
Total Grants: $1,328,013
Number of Grants: 37*
Highest Grant: $400,000
Average Grant: $32,514
Typical Range: $2,000 to $50,000
Disclosure Period: 1993

Note: Average grant and number of grants
figures exclude 36 grants totaling $125,000
paid to individuals for the scholars program.
Recent grants are derived from a 1993 Form
990.

RECENT GRANTS
Library
10,000	Clark County Public Library, Little Rock, AR
10,000	Monroe County Public Library, Monroe, MI
10,000	White Smith Memorial Library, Mobile, AL

General
400,000	Exploreum Museum of Discovery, Mobile, AL
153,000	Marine Environmental Science Consortium, New York, NY
100,000	Infirmary Health System, Mobile, AL
75,000	Martin Luther King Avenue Redevelopment Corporation, Chattanooga, TN
63,000	Alabama High School of Mathematics and Science, Birmingham, AL

Blount, Inc. / Blount Foundation

Sales: $691.41 million
Employees: 4,800
Headquarters: Montgomery, AL
SIC Major Group: Nonresidential Construction
Nec, Industrial Buildings & Warehouses,
Water, Sewer & Utility Lines, and Heavy
Construction Nec

CONTACT
D. Joseph McInnes
President
Blount Foundation
4520 Executive Park Dr.
Montgomery, AL 36116-1602
(334) 244-4348

FINANCIAL SUMMARY
Recent Giving: $441,604 (fiscal 1994);
$441,534 (fiscal 1993); $554,439 (fiscal
1992)
Assets: $95,001 (fiscal 1993); $162,272 (fiscal 1992)
Gifts Received: $380,000 (fiscal 1993)
Fiscal Note: Company gives primarily
through the foundation. Direct giving is limited and is not included in above figures. In

fiscal 1993, contributions were received from Blount, Inc.

EIN: 63-6050260

CONTRIBUTIONS SUMMARY

Typical Recipients: • *Arts & Humanities:* Arts Associations & Councils, Arts Centers, Arts Festivals, Arts Institutes, Ballet, Dance, Film & Video, Historic Preservation, Libraries, Literary Arts, Museums/Galleries, Music, Opera, Performing Arts, Public Broadcasting, Theater, Visual Arts • *Civic & Public Affairs:* Community Foundations, Economic Development, Municipalities/Towns, Parades/Festivals, Philanthropic Organizations, Public Policy, Safety, Urban & Community Affairs, Women's Affairs • *Education:* Arts/Humanities Education, Business Education, Colleges & Universities, Economic Education, Education Associations, Education Funds, Education Reform, Engineering/Technological Education, Literacy, Medical Education, Minority Education, Private Education (Precollege), Public Education (Precollege), Religious Education, Science/Mathematics Education, Student Aid • *Environment:* General, Wildlife Protection • *Health:* Arthritis, Health Organizations, Hospitals, Mental Health, Single-Disease Health Associations • *Religion:* Religious Organizations, Religious Welfare • *Social Services:* Child Welfare, Community Service Organizations, Family Services, Food/Clothing Distribution, Homes, Recreation & Athletics, Senior Services, United Funds/United Ways, Youth Organizations

Grant Types: capital, department, employee matching gifts, endowment, fellowship, general support, project, research, and scholarship

Geographic Distribution: emphasis on the state of Alabama, especially the Montgomery area; and operating locations

Operating Locations: AL (Montgomery), CA (Commerce, Compton, Los Angeles, Oakland, Oroville, San Francisco), DE (Wilmington), IA (Webster City), ID (Lewiston), IL (Chicago), IN (Bluffton, Crawfordsville), KS (Coffeyvill), MA (Boston), MI (Detroit, Saginaw, Ypsilanti), MN (Owatonna), NC (Zebulon), NE (Grand Island, York), OK (Oklahoma City, Tulsa), OR (Portland), PA (Washington), SC (Laurens), TX (Amarillo, Dallas, Houston), WI (Onalaska, Prentice, Spencer)

CORP. OFFICERS

Winton Malcolm Blount, Jr.: *B* Union Springs AL 1921 *ED* Univ AL 1939-1941; Judson Coll LHD 1967; Birmingham-Southern Coll LLD 1969; Huntingdon Coll PhD 1969; Univ AL DCL 1969; Seattle Pacific Univ PhD 1971; Univ AL DSci 1971 *CURR EMPL* chmn, dir: Blount Inc *CORP AFFIL* dir: Union Camp Corp; pres: HBC; pres, chmn: B I Indus, Blount Bros Corp *NONPR AFFIL* dir: Un Appeal Montgomery, YMCA Montgomery; life mem: Southern Res Inst; mem: AL Chamber Commerce, Am Enterprise Inst, Am Mgmt Assn, Bus Counc, Conf Bd, Newcomen Soc, US Chamber Commerce; mem adv counc: US Army Aviation Mus; trust: Univ AL; trust, chmn: Rhodes Coll *CLUB AFFIL* Rotary

Duncan Joseph McInnes: *ED* Univ AL BS 1973; Jones Law Sch LLB *CURR EMPL* sr vp admin, corp secy: Blount Inc *NONPR AFFIL* mem: Am Soc Corp Secys

John Michael Panettiere: *B* Kansas City MO 1937 *ED* Westminster Coll 1959; Rockhurst Coll; Univ KS *CURR EMPL* pres, ceo: Blount Inc *CORP AFFIL* chmn: Dixon Indus Inc, Ger Products Inc *NONPR AFFIL* mem: Phi Delta Theta, Westminster Coll Alumni Assn *CLUB AFFIL* Fountain Head CC

GIVING OFFICERS

Winton Malcolm Blount, Jr.: dir *CURR EMPL* chmn, dir: Blount Inc (see above)

Duncan Joseph McInnes: pres, dir *CURR EMPL* sr vp admin, corp secy: Blount Inc (see above)

Katherine Blount Miles: treas, dir

John Michael Panettiere: dir *CURR EMPL* pres, ceo: Blount Inc (see above)

APPLICATION INFORMATION

Initial Approach: *Initial Contact:* brief letter, no longer than two or three pages *Include Information On:* name of organization and contact person; purpose, history, activities, and programs of organization; evidence of need for activity or project, benefits expected, plans for evaluation, and evidence of ability to carry project to completion; projected budget, projected sources and amount of funding needed, and copy of latest financial statement; proof of tax-exempt status *Deadlines:* none

Restrictions on Giving: Foundation declines requests for in-kind grants or courtesy advertising. Member agencies of united funds are not eligible for support unless permission has been granted to conduct a capital fund drive or special benefit. Contributions are not made to individuals; political organizations or candidates; or municipal, state, federal or quasi-governmental agencies.

Foundation usually does not make grants for continuing support.

GRANTS ANALYSIS

Total Grants: $441,604

Typical Range: $1,000 to $10,000

Disclosure Period: fiscal year ending February 28, 1994

Note: Recent grants are derived from a fiscal 1993 Form 990.

RECENT GRANTS

General

25,000	American Enterprise Institute for Public Policy Research, Washington, DC	
25,000	YMCA Capital Fund Drive, Montgomery, AL	
20,000	Birmingham Southern College, Birmingham, AL	
16,668	Brantwood Children's Home, Montgomery, AL	
13,000	RX for Reading, Los Angeles, CA — Riordan Foundation	

Blount Educational and Charitable Foundation, Mildred Weedon

CONTACT
Arnold B. Dopson
Chairman
Mildred Weedon Blount Educational and Charitable Fdn.
PO Box 607
Tallassee, AL 36078
(205) 283-6581

FINANCIAL SUMMARY
Recent Giving: $135,633 (fiscal 1994); $150,800 (fiscal 1991); $147,000 (fiscal 1990)

Assets: $3,263,894 (fiscal 1994); $3,211,466 (fiscal 1991); $2,904,511 (fiscal 1990)

EIN: 63-0817472

CONTRIBUTIONS SUMMARY
Donor(s): the late Mildred W. Blount

Typical Recipients: • *Arts & Humanities:* Arts Associations & Councils, Community Arts, Libraries, Museums/Galleries • *Civic & Public Affairs:* General, Municipalities/Towns, Urban & Community Affairs • *Education:* Business Education, Colleges & Universities, Medical Education, Public Education (Precollege), Secondary Education (Public) • *Health:* Emergency/Ambulance Services, Hospitals • *Religion:* Churches • *Social Services:* Community Service Organizations, Scouts, Substance Abuse, United Funds/United Ways, Youth Organizations

Grant Types: general support and scholarship

Geographic Distribution: focus on AL

GIVING OFFICERS
J. Herbert Boddie: trust
John I. Cottle III: secy
Arnold B. Dopson: chmn
Lloyd F. Emfinger, Jr.: trust
Carl W. Fuller: trust
Charles B. Funderburk: trust
John C. Granger: trust
O. C. Harden, Jr.: trust
Virgil F. Redden: trust
Teddy O. Taylor: trust
Daniel P. Wilbanks: vchmn

APPLICATION INFORMATION
Initial Approach: Request application procedures. Deadline is early May.

OTHER THINGS TO KNOW
Provides scholarships for higher education to students from Elmore County, AL.

GRANTS ANALYSIS
Total Grants: $135,633
Number of Grants: 18
Highest Grant: $15,000
Typical Range: $500 to $10,000

Disclosure Period: fiscal year ending June 30, 1994

Note: Recent grants are derived from a fiscal 1994 Form 990. Number of grants and typical range do not include individual scholarships.

RECENT GRANTS

General

15,000	St. Michael's Church, Kirtland, OH — chimes
10,800	STRATE, Tallassee, AL
10,000	Community Hospital
10,000	Elmore County High School
10,000	Reeltown High School, Reeltown, AL

Comer Foundation

CONTACT
R. Larry Edmunds
Secretary-Treasurer
Comer Fdn.
PO Box 302
Sylacauga, AL 35150
(205) 249-2962

FINANCIAL SUMMARY
Recent Giving: $597,059 (1993); $561,690 (1992); $552,370 (1991)

Assets: $10,830,183 (1993); $10,565,635 (1992); $10,606,841 (1991)

EIN: 63-6004424

CONTRIBUTIONS SUMMARY
Donor(s): Avondale Mills, Comer-Avondale Mills, Inc., Cowikee Mills

Typical Recipients: • *Arts & Humanities:* Arts Associations & Councils, Ballet, Libraries, Museums/Galleries, Music • *Civic & Public Affairs:* General, Housing, Municipalities/Towns, Urban & Community Affairs • *Education:* Colleges & Universities, Economic Education, Education Funds, Education Reform, Engineering/Technological Education, General, Literacy, Medical Education, Public Education (Precollege), Special Education, Student Aid, Vocational & Technical Education • *Environment:* General • *Health:* Children's Health/Hospitals, Clinics/Medical Centers, Hospices, Medical Rehabilitation, Medical Research, Medical Training, Nursing Services • *Religion:* Religious Welfare • *Science:* Science Exhibits & Fairs, Science Museums • *Social Services:* Animal Protection, Camps, Child Welfare, Community Service Organizations, Family Services, Recreation & Athletics, Scouts, Substance Abuse, United Funds/United Ways, Youth Organizations

Grant Types: capital, general support, operating expenses, and research

Geographic Distribution: focus on Birmingham and Sylacauga, AL

GIVING OFFICERS
Richard J. Comer: trust

Francis H. Crockard: trust

Marie M. Edmunds: asst secy, asst treas

R. Larry Edmunds: secy, treas

Gillian C. Goodrich: trust

Dr. Hugh C. Nabers, Jr.: trust

Jane B. Selfe: trust

William Bew White, Jr.: chmn, trust *PHIL AFFIL* trust: Barbara Ingalls Shook Foundation, Susan Mott Webb Charitable Trust

APPLICATION INFORMATION
Initial Approach: Send brief letter of inquiry describing program or project. There are no deadlines.

GRANTS ANALYSIS
Total Grants: $597,059

Number of Grants: 48

Highest Grant: $100,000

Typical Range: $250 to $56,666

Disclosure Period: 1993

Note: Recent grants are derived from a 1993 Form 990.

RECENT GRANTS

Library

19,500	B.B. Comer Memorial Library, Sylacauga, AL — library

General

100,000	Auburn University, Auburn, AL — textile scholarships
53,000	University of Montevallo, Montevallo, AL — supplement for renovation of Comer Hall on campus
30,000	Sylacauga Park and Recreation Board, Sylacauga, AL — support of operations and programs
25,000	Cahaba Girl Scout Council, Birmingham, AL — assistance for programs and operations
25,000	International Science and Engineering Fair, Birmingham, AL — support for programs

Daniel Foundation of Alabama

CONTACT
S. Garry Smith
Foundation Manager
Daniel Foundation of Alabama
820 Shades Creek Pkwy.
Ste. 1200
Birmingham, AL 35209
(205) 879-0902

FINANCIAL SUMMARY
Recent Giving: $1,515,500 (1992); $1,515,500 (1991); $1,535,500 (1990)

Assets: $35,613,728 (1992); $20,940,566 (1990); $21,387,000 (1988)

EIN: 63-0736444

CONTRIBUTIONS SUMMARY
Donor(s): The Daniel Foundation of Alabama was founded in 1977, with assets transferred from the Daniel Foundation of South Carolina. The latter was established posthumously in 1947 by Charles E. Daniel and R. Hugh Daniel. Charles E. Daniel (1895-1964) organized, and was chairman of, Daniel Construction Company. He also was a trustee of Clemson University.

Typical Recipients: • *Arts & Humanities:* Arts Associations & Councils, Arts Festivals, Libraries, Museums/Galleries, Music, Opera • *Civic & Public Affairs:* Economic Policy, Urban & Community Affairs • *Education:* Arts/Humanities Education, Business Education, Colleges & Universities, Education Funds, Engineering/Technological Education, Legal Education, Private Education (Precollege), Public Education (Precollege), Religious Education, Science/Mathematics Education, Secondary Education (Private), Special Education • *Environment:* General, Wildlife Protection • *Health:* Cancer, Clinics/Medical Centers, Eyes/Blindness, Health Organizations, Hospices, Medical Research, Mental Health, Research/Studies Institutes, Single-Disease Health Associations • *Religion:* Churches, Jewish Causes, Religious Welfare • *Science:* Science Museums, Scientific Centers & Institutes • *Social Services:* At-Risk Youth, Camps, Community Service Organizations, Recreation & Athletics, Substance Abuse, United Funds/United Ways, Youth Organizations

Grant Types: general support

Geographic Distribution: primarily Alabama and other southeastern states

GIVING OFFICERS
Frances Daniel Branum: dir

Harry Blackwell Brock, Jr.: pres, dir *B* Fort Payne AL 1926 *ED* Univ AL BS 1949; Northwestern Univ 1957 *CORP AFFIL* chmn, fdr: Compass Bancshares; dir: Marathon Corp *NONPR AFFIL* chmn, dir: Jr Achievement Jefferson County; mem: AL Academy Honor, Chief Execs Forum, Young Pres Org; mem exec bd Birmingham area counc: Boy Scouts Am; mem exec comm: Southern Res Inst; mem pres counc: Univ AL *CLUB AFFIL* Birmingham CC, Shoal Creek CC

Charles W. Daniel: vp

M. C. Daniel: chmn

S. Garry Smith: secy, treas, fdn mgr

APPLICATION INFORMATION
Initial Approach:

Preliminary contact should be made in written form.

The letter should include a description of the proposed program, its purpose, and a breakdown of how the grant will be used.

There is no official deadline for funding requests; however, applications should be received in time for board meetings in April and October.

GRANTS ANALYSIS
Total Grants: $1,515,500

Number of Grants: 67

Highest Grant: $150,000

Average Grant: $22,619

Typical Range: $5,000 to $50,000

Disclosure Period: 1992

Note: Recent grants are derived from a 1992 Form 990.

RECENT GRANTS

Library
25,000	Greenville Butler County Library, Greenville, SC

General
100,000	Alabama Institute for the Deaf and Blind, Talladega, AL
100,000	Birmingham-Southern College, Birmingham, AL
100,000	Citadel, Charleston, SC
100,000	Mayo Foundation, Rochester, MN
100,000	University of Alabama Law School Chair, Tuscaloosa, AL

Ebsco Industries, Inc.

Sales: $400.0 million
Employees: 2,800
Headquarters: Birmingham, AL
SIC Major Group: Periodicals, Partitions & Fixtures Except Wood, Commercial Printing—Lithographic, and Commercial Printing Nec

CONTACT
Elton Bryson Stephens
Chairman
Ebsco Industries, Inc.
PO Box 1943
Birmingham, AL 35201
(205) 991-1197

FINANCIAL SUMMARY
Fiscal Note: Company gives directly. Annual Giving Range: $500,000 to $1 million or 5% of pre-tax earnings

CONTRIBUTIONS SUMMARY
Typical Recipients: • *Arts & Humanities:* General, Libraries • *Civic & Public Affairs:* General • *Education:* General • *Health:* General • *Social Services:* General

Grant Types: general support

Nonmonetary Support Types: donated products and workplace solicitation

Geographic Distribution: worldwide

Operating Locations: AL (Birmingham)

CORP. OFFICERS
Elton Bryson Stephens: *B* Clio AL 1911 *ED* Birmingham-Southern Coll BA 1932; Univ AL Law Sch LLB 1936 *CURR EMPL* fdr, chmn, pres: Ebsco Indus Inc *CORP AFFIL* chmn: AL Bancorp, Bennett-Ebsco Subscription Svcs, RA Brown Agency Ltd, CANEBSCO Subscription Svcs Ltd, Highland Bank; chmn, secy: Ebsco Investment Svcs; chmn, vp: Franklin Sq Agency Overseas; fdr, dir, chmn: Bank SE; trust: Ebsco Employee Savings & Profit Sharing Trust *NONPR AFFIL* chmn: Birmingham-Southern Coll Exec Comm, TN-Tombigbee Waterway Authority Econ Pension Comm; dir: Birmingham Chamber Commerce; fdr,

chmn: Am Counc Arts; mem: AL Election Law Comm, Alpha Tau Omega, Birmingham-Southern Coll Fin & Investment Comm, Future Farmers Am AL Exec Comm, Omicron Delta Kappa, Phi Alpha Delta; mem, don: Un Arts Fund/Metro Arts Counc; trust: Southern Res Inst *CLUB AFFIL* Birmingham Press, The Club, Downtown, Mountain Brook CC, Shades Valley Rotary, Summit

James T. Stephens: *B* 1939 *ED* Yale Univ BA 1961; Harvard Univ MBA 1964 *CURR EMPL* chmn exec comm, pres, ceo, dir: Ebsco Indus Inc

GIVING OFFICERS
Elton Bryson Stephens: *CURR EMPL* fdr, chmn, pres: Ebsco Indus Inc (see above)

APPLICATION INFORMATION
Initial Approach: *Initial Contact:* letter* *Deadlines:* none *Note:* In 1993, the company committed all of its funding for the next four years and is not accepting proposals at this time.

OTHER THINGS TO KNOW
The company reports that two substantial long-term commitments have put the giving program over budget for the next four years.

The directors of the giving program report that the office is overwhelmed with requests that they do not have the time to read or the funds to support. Funding to new programs or organizations has ceased.

Linn-Henley Charitable Trust

CONTACT
Mitzie Hall
Trust Officer
Linn-Henley Charitable Trust
c/o Central Bank of the South, Trust Dept.
PO Box 10566
Birmingham, AL 35296
(205) 558-6717

FINANCIAL SUMMARY
Recent Giving: $266,500 (fiscal 1992); $275,285 (fiscal 1991); $287,315 (fiscal 1990)

Assets: $6,181,563 (fiscal 1992); $5,813,740 (fiscal 1991); $6,780,555 (fiscal 1990)

EIN: 63-6051833

CONTRIBUTIONS SUMMARY
Donor(s): the late Walter E. Henley

Typical Recipients: • *Arts & Humanities:* Community Arts, Historic Preservation, Libraries, Museums/Galleries, Public Broadcasting • *Civic & Public Affairs:* Business/Free Enterprise, Zoos/Aquariums • *Education:* Colleges & Universities, Legal Education, Public Education (Precollege), Special Education • *Environment:* General • *Health:* Hospitals, Medical Research • *Social Services:* Youth Organizations

Grant Types: general support

Geographic Distribution: limited to Jefferson County, AL

GIVING OFFICERS
Central Bank of the South: trust
John C. Henley III: trust

APPLICATION INFORMATION
Initial Approach: Send brief letter of inquiry stating amount and purpose. There are no deadlines.

GRANTS ANALYSIS
Total Grants: $266,500
Number of Grants: 62
Highest Grant: $50,000
Typical Range: $1,000 to $5,000
Disclosure Period: fiscal year ending March 31, 1992

Note: Recent grants are derived from a fiscal 1992 Form 990.

RECENT GRANTS

Library
50,000	Henley Research Library, Birmingham, AL
50,000	Henley Research Library, Birmingham, AL
5,000	Reynolds Historical Library, Birmingham, AL

General
10,000	Baptist Montclair and Princeton Hospitals, Birmingham, AL
10,000	St. Vincent's Hospital, Birmingham, AL
5,000	Birmingham Area Chamber of Commerce, Birmingham, AL
5,000	Cumberland School of Law, Homewood, AL
5,000	Samford University, Birmingham, AL

McMillan Foundation, D. W.

CONTACT
Ed Leigh McMillan II
Trustee
D. W. McMillan Fdn.
329 Belleville Ave.
Brewton, AL 36426
(205) 867-4881

FINANCIAL SUMMARY
Recent Giving: $769,100 (1992); $591,000 (1990); $384,300 (1989)

Assets: $13,338,302 (1992); $10,905,415 (1990); $10,718,472 (1989)

EIN: 63-6044830

CONTRIBUTIONS SUMMARY
Donor(s): D.W. McMillan Trust

Typical Recipients: • *Arts & Humanities:* Libraries • *Civic & Public Affairs:* Clubs, Economic Development, General, Housing, Municipalities/Towns, Urban & Community Affairs • *Education:* General, Special Education, Student Aid • *Health:* Cancer, Children's Health/Hospitals,

Emergency/Ambulance Services, Health Organizations, Heart, Hospices, Hospitals, Medical Rehabilitation, Mental Health, Single-Disease Health Associations • *Religion:* Religious Welfare • *Social Services:* Child Welfare, Community Service Organizations, Family Services, Food/Clothing Distribution, People with Disabilities, United Funds/United Ways, Volunteer Services, Youth Organizations

Grant Types: emergency and general support

Geographic Distribution: limited to Escambia County, AL, and Escambia County, FL

GIVING OFFICERS
John David Finlay, Jr.: trust

Michael N. Hoke, Jr.: trust

Ed L. McMillan II: trust

Allison R. Sinrod: trust

APPLICATION INFORMATION
Initial Approach: Send letter containing proof of need and establishing that they meet qualifications as poor and needy. There are no deadlines.

Restrictions on Giving: Limited to Escambia County, Alabama and Escambia County, Florida.

OTHER THINGS TO KNOW
Provides aid to poor and needy residents of Escambia County, AL.

GRANTS ANALYSIS
Total Grants: $769,100

Number of Grants: 41

Highest Grant: $141,000

Typical Range: $1,000 to $25,000

Disclosure Period: 1992

Note: Recent grants are derived from a 1992 Form 990.

RECENT GRANTS
Library

1,000	Escambia County Co-operative Library System, Brewton, AL
1,000	Escambia County Co-operative Library System, Brewton, AL
1,000	Escambia County Co-operative Library System, Brewton, AL

General

141,000	Escambia County Hospital Board, Brewton, AL
141,000	Escambia County Hospital Board, Brewton, AL
141,000	Escambia County Hospital Board, Brewton, AL
91,500	Bapist Hospital, Pensacola, FL
91,500	Bapist Hospital, Pensacola, FL

Smith, Jr. Foundation, M. W.

CONTACT
Kenneth E. Niemeyer
M. W. Smith, Jr. Fdn.
c/o AmS. Bank, N.A.
PO Drawer 1628
Mobile, AL 36629
(205) 438-8260

FINANCIAL SUMMARY
Recent Giving: $78,300 (fiscal 1994); $68,500 (fiscal 1992); $141,000 (fiscal 1990)

Assets: $2,024,499 (fiscal 1994); $1,918,570 (fiscal 1992); $1,877,717 (fiscal 1990)

EIN: 63-6018078

CONTRIBUTIONS SUMMARY
Donor(s): the late M. W. Smith, Jr.

Typical Recipients: • *Arts & Humanities:* Community Arts, Dance, Historic Preservation, History & Archaeology, Libraries, Museums/Galleries • *Civic & Public Affairs:* Municipalities/Towns, Urban & Community Affairs, Zoos/Aquariums • *Education:* Science/Mathematics Education • *Religion:* Religious Welfare • *Social Services:* Child Welfare, Community Service Organizations, People with Disabilities, United Funds/United Ways, Youth Organizations

Grant Types: capital, emergency, endowment, general support, multiyear/continuing support, operating expenses, project, research, scholarship, and seed money

Geographic Distribution: focus on southwest AL

GIVING OFFICERS
Louis M. Finley, Jr.: comm mem

John Martin: comm mem

Maida S. Pearson: chmn

Mary M. Riser: secy

APPLICATION INFORMATION
Initial Approach: Send brief letter describing program. There are no deadlines.

Restrictions on Giving: Does not support individuals.

GRANTS ANALYSIS
Total Grants: $78,300

Number of Grants: 12

Highest Grant: $25,000

Typical Range: $300 to $25,000

Disclosure Period: fiscal year ending June 30, 1994

Note: Recent grants are derived from a fiscal 1994 Form 990.

RECENT GRANTS
Library

6,500	White Smith Library — education

General

25,000	Alabama School of Math and Science, Mobile, AL — education

25,000	Debakey Fund — community welfare
3,000	ACEE — community welfare
3,000	Forman Chapter Missionary Baptist — community welfare
2,000	Mobile Community Organization, Mobile, AL — community welfare

Sonat Inc. / Sonat Foundation

Sales: $1.74 billion
Employees: 2,230
Headquarters: Birmingham, AL
SIC Major Group: Holding Companies Nec, Crude Petroleum & Natural Gas, Natural Gas Liquids, and Natural Gas Transmission

CONTACT
Darlene O'Donnell
Secretary
Sonat Foundation
PO Box 2563
Birmingham, AL 35202
(205) 325-7460

FINANCIAL SUMMARY
Recent Giving: $1,300,000 (1995 est.); $1,500,000 (1994 approx.); $1,226,378 (1993)

Assets: $6,795,517 (1993); $5,042,487 (1991); $5,089,984 (1990)

Gifts Received: $3,000,000 (1993); $1,000,000 (1991)

Fiscal Note: Above figures reflect foundation giving. Above figures exclude nonmonetary support. In 1993, foundation received contributions from Sonat, Inc.

EIN: 63-0830299

CONTRIBUTIONS SUMMARY
Typical Recipients: • *Arts & Humanities:* Arts Associations & Councils, Arts Centers, Arts Festivals, Historic Preservation, Libraries, Museums/Galleries, Music, Opera, Performing Arts, Public Broadcasting, Theater • *Civic & Public Affairs:* Business/Free Enterprise, Civil Rights, Clubs, Economic Development, Economic Policy, Employment/Job Training, General, Philanthropic Organizations, Professional & Trade Associations, Urban & Community Affairs, Women's Affairs, Zoos/Aquariums • *Education:* Arts/Humanities Education, Business Education, Colleges & Universities, Continuing Education, Economic Education, Education Associations, Education Funds, Engineering/Technological Education, Legal Education, Literacy, Medical Education, Minority Education, Private Education (Precollege), Religious Education, Science/Mathematics Education, Secondary Education (Private) • *Environment:* Resource Conservation • *Health:* Children's Health/Hospitals, Clinics/Medical Centers, Eyes/Blindness, Health Policy/Cost Containment, Health Funds, Health Organizations, Hospitals, Single-Disease Health Associations • *Religion:* Religious Organizations,

Religious Welfare, Seminaries • *Science:* Scientific Centers & Institutes • *Social Services:* Animal Protection, Child Welfare, Community Centers, Community Service Organizations, Family Services, Food/Clothing Distribution, Homes, People with Disabilities, Recreation & Athletics, Scouts, Senior Services, Shelters/Homelessness, Substance Abuse, United Funds/United Ways, Volunteer Services, Youth Organizations

Grant Types: employee matching gifts, general support, project, and seed money

Nonmonetary Support: $96,000 (1993); $320,145 (1989); $134,920 (1988)

Nonmonetary Support Types: donated equipment, in-kind services, and loaned executives

Note: Nonmonetary support is provided by the foundation and the company. Estimated value of nonmonetary support for 1991 is not available. 1993 figure represents in-kind donations only.

Geographic Distribution: communities where company operates, with emphasis on Birmingham, AL

Operating Locations: AL (Birmingham), GA, LA, TX (Houston)

CORP. OFFICERS
Beverly Turner Krannich: *B* Mobile AL 1951 *ED* Rhodes Coll 1973; Samford Univ Sch Law 1976 *CURR EMPL* vp, secy: Sonat Inc

Ronald L. Kuehn, Jr.: *B* Brooklyn NY 1935 *ED* Fordham Univ BS 1957; Fordham Univ LLB 1964 *CURR EMPL* chmn, pres, ceo, dir: Sonat Inc *CORP AFFIL* dir: Am South Bancorp, Protective Life Corp, Sonat Exploration Co, Sonat Offshore Drilling, Southern Natural Gas Co, Teleco Oilfield Svcs, Union Carbide Corp *NONPR AFFIL* dir: Gas Res Inst, Interstate Natural Gas Assn Am, Natl Petroleum Counc; mem: Am Bar Assn, Am Gas Assn, Assn Bar City New York, Bretton Woods Comm, Fed Energy Bar Assn, Newcomen Soc, NY Bar Assn; mem pres counc: Univ AL Birmingham; trust: Birmingham-Southern Coll, Boys Club Am

James Emmett Moylan, Jr.: *B* Savannah GA 1951 *ED* GA Inst Tech BE 1972; Harvard Univ MBA 1976 *CURR EMPL* pres: Sonat Inc *NONPR AFFIL* dir: Birmingham Childrens Theater, Jr Achievement; mem: Am Inst CPAs, Fin Execs Inst; mem acct adv counc: Univ AL

Darlene O'Donnell: *CURR EMPL* exec vp: Sonat Inc

GIVING OFFICERS
Edie James: treas

Leria L. Jordan: vp

Beverly Turner Krannich: pres *CURR EMPL* vp, secy: Sonat Inc (see above)

L. David Mathews: vp

James Emmett Moylan, Jr.: vp *CURR EMPL* pres: Sonat Inc (see above)

Darlene O'Donnell: secy *CURR EMPL* exec vp: Sonat Inc (see above)

William A. Smith: vp

APPLICATION INFORMATION
Initial Approach: *Initial Contact:* brief letter or proposal *Include Information On:* description of the organization, amount requested, list of corporate and foundation support, purpose for which funds are sought, recently audited financial statement, proof of tax-exempt status *Deadlines:* none

Restrictions on Giving: Foundation does not make grants to individuals; organizations already receiving United Way support; or political, religious, fraternal, or veterans organizations.

OTHER THINGS TO KNOW
Scholarships are awarded only to children of active, retired, disabled or deceased employees of Sonat, Inc. and its subsidiaries and affiliates.

GRANTS ANALYSIS
Total Grants: $1,226,378

Number of Grants: 161

Highest Grant: $301,356

Average Grant: $7,617

Typical Range: $1000 to $10,000

Disclosure Period: 1993

Note: Recent grants are derived from a 1993 Form 990.

RECENT GRANTS
General

301,356	Charities Fund, Alexandria, VA
100,500	Tuskegee University, Tuskegee, AL
66,100	Birmingham Southern College, Birmingham, AL
50,000	Civil Rights Museum, Birmingham, AL
25,500	Boy Scouts of America, Birmingham, AL

Tennessee Valley Printing Co. / Decatur Daily Charitable Trust

Sales: $5.5 million
Employees: 110
Headquarters: Decatur, AL

CONTACT
Joe Perrin
Controller
Tennessee Valley Printing Co.
PO Box 2213
Decatur, AL 35609
(205) 353-4612

FINANCIAL SUMMARY
Recent Giving: $21,659 (1993); $16,147 (1991)

Assets: $469,824 (1993); $428,462 (1991)

EIN: 63-6131336

CONTRIBUTIONS SUMMARY
Typical Recipients: • *Arts & Humanities:* Libraries, Theater • *Civic & Public Affairs:* Public Policy • *Education:* Colleges & Universities, Community & Junior Colleges • *Health:* Hospitals • *Religion:* Churches

Grant Types: general support

Geographic Distribution: focus on AL

CORP. OFFICERS
Barrett C. Shelton, Jr.: *CURR EMPL* chmn, pres, ceo: TN Valley Printing Co

GIVING OFFICERS
Am South Bank, N.A.: trust

Barrett C. Shelton, Jr.: mem adv comm *CURR EMPL* chmn, pres, ceo: TN Valley Printing Co (see above)

Tolly G. Shelton: mem

APPLICATION INFORMATION
Initial Approach: Send a brief letter of inquiry. There are no deadlines.

GRANTS ANALYSIS
Total Grants: $21,659

Number of Grants: 7

Highest Grant: $7,250

Typical Range: $1,000 to $5,000

Disclosure Period: 1993

Note: Recent grants are derived from a 1993 Form 990.

RECENT GRANTS
Library

2,909	Wheeler Basin Regional Library, Decatur, AL — for educational purposes

General

7,250	University of Alabama, Tuscaloosa, AL — for educational purposes
3,500	First Presbyterian Church — for religious purposes
1,000	Calhoun Community College Foundation — for educational purposes
1,000	Decatur General Hospital Foundation, Decatur, IL — for charitable purposes
1,000	Public Affairs Research Council of Alabama, Birmingham, AL — for charitable purposes

---

Vulcan Materials Co. / Vulcan Materials Company Foundation

Sales: $1.13 billion
Employees: 6,697
Headquarters: Birmingham, AL
SIC Major Group: Crushed & Broken Limestone, Crushed & Broken Granite, Alkalies & Chlorine, and Cyclic Crudes & Intermediates

---

CONTACT
Mary S. Russom
Administrator, Community Affairs
Vulcan Materials Co.
PO Box 530187
Birmingham, AL 35253-0187
(205) 877-3229

FINANCIAL SUMMARY

Recent Giving: $2,624,000 (fiscal 1995 est.); $2,409,369 (fiscal 1994 approx.); $2,407,941 (fiscal 1993)

Assets: $1,744,811 (fiscal 1993); $1,529,158 (fiscal 1992); $2,665,690 (fiscal 1989)

Fiscal Note: Figures include foundation and direct contributions. In 1993, foundation giving totaled $1,870,874, and direct giving totaled $537,064. Above figures exclude nonmonetary support.

EIN: 63-0971859

CONTRIBUTIONS SUMMARY

Typical Recipients: • *Arts & Humanities:* Arts Associations & Councils, Arts Centers, Arts Festivals, Arts Funds, Arts Institutes, Community Arts, Dance, Ethnic & Folk Arts, Historic Preservation, Libraries, Literary Arts, Museums/Galleries, Music, Opera, Performing Arts, Public Broadcasting, Theater, Visual Arts • *Civic & Public Affairs:* Business/Free Enterprise, Economic Development, Economic Policy, Municipalities/Towns, Zoos/Aquariums • *Education:* Colleges & Universities, Economic Education, Education Funds, Elementary Education (Private), Engineering/Technological Education, Literacy, Minority Education, Public Education (Precollege), Science/Mathematics Education, Special Education • *Environment:* General • *Health:* Health Organizations, Mental Health • *Science:* Science Exhibits & Fairs • *Social Services:* Animal Protection, Child Welfare, Community Centers, Community Service Organizations, Counseling, Delinquency & Criminal Rehabilitation, Emergency Relief, Food/Clothing Distribution, People with Disabilities, Recreation & Athletics, Senior Services, Shelters/Homelessness, Substance Abuse, United Funds/United Ways, Youth Organizations

Grant Types: capital, department, emergency, employee matching gifts, endowment, fellowship, general support, multiyear/continuing support, project, scholarship, and seed money

Note: Employee matching gift ratio: 1 to 1 for donations to hospitals and cultural organizations; 2 to 1 for donations to educational institutions. Annual limit of $10,000 per employee.

Nonmonetary Support Types: donated equipment, donated products, in-kind services, loaned employees, loaned executives, and workplace solicitation

Note: The estimated value of the nonmonetary support provided by the company is not available.

Geographic Distribution: in states where company has operations

Operating Locations: AL (Birmingham, Calera, Childersburg, Gadsder, Glencoe, Helena, Huntsville, Lacon, Madison, Ohatchee, Russelville, Scottsboro, Trinity, Tuscumbia), GA (Adairsville, Columbus, Dalton, Fairmount, Grayson, Kennesaw, LaGrange, Lithia Springs, Lithonia, Newman, Norcross, Rabun, Red Oak, Stockbridge, Villa Rica), IA (Camanche, Cedar Rapids, Garrison, Mentour, Robbins), IL (Casey, Crystal Lake, Decatur, Fairbury, Joliet, Kankakee, Lemont, McCook-Hodgkins, Momence, Pontiac, Weston), IN (Francesville, Lafayette, Monon, South Bend), KS (Wichita), KY (Brandenburg, Elizabethtown, Fort Knox, Lexington, Stephensburg), LA (Geismar), MI (Iuka), NC (Boone, Charlotte, Concord, East Forsyth, Elkin, Enka, Gold Hill, Henderson, Hendersonville, Morgantown, North Wilkesboro, Rockingham, Smith Grove, Winston-Salem), SC (Blacksburg, Gray Court, Greeneville, Liberty, Lyman, Pacolet), TN (Athens, Bristol, Chattanooga, Clarksville, Cleveland, Dayton, Franklin, Greeneville, Holladay, Kingsport, Knox County, Knoxville, Lebanon, Maryville, Morristown, Nashville, Parsons, Rogersville, Savannah, Sevierville, South Pittsburg, Tazewell, Waverly), TX (Abilene, Boyd, Bridgeport, Brownwood, Denison, Knippa, San Antonio, Uvalde), VA (Danville, Edgerton, Manassas, Occoquan, Richmond, South Boston, Stafford, Warrenton), WI (Milwaukee, Oconomowec, Oshkosh, Port Edwards, Racine, Sussex)

CORP. OFFICERS

Herbert Anthony Sklenar: *B* Omaha NE 1931 *ED* Univ Omaha BSBA 1952; Harvard Univ MBA 1954 *CURR EMPL* chmn, ceo: Vulcan Materials Co *CORP AFFIL* dir: AmSouth Bancorp, Protective Life Corp, Temple-Inland Inc *NONPR AFFIL* mem: Am Inst CPAs, Delta Sigma Pi, Omicron Delta Kappa, Phi Eta Sigma, Phi Kappa Phi, US Chamber Commerce; trust: AL Symphony Assn, Birmingham-Southern Coll, Southern Res Inst; vp bd dirs: YMCA Birmingham *CLUB AFFIL* Birmingham CC, Chicago, The Club, Shoal Creek, Univ

GIVING OFFICERS

John A. Heilala: trust

Guy K. Mitchell, Jr.: trust *B* 1948 *CURR EMPL* sr vp: Vulcan Materials Co

Terry W. Reese: asst treas *B* Huntsville AL 1942 *ED* Univ TN 1970 *CURR EMPL* asst treas & dir taxes: Vulcan Materials Co *NONPR AFFIL* mem: Inst Mgmt Accts, Natl Assn Accts, Tax Execs Inst

Mary S. Russom: secy, treas *CURR EMPL* admin comm aff: Vulcan Materials Co

Herbert Anthony Sklenar: chmn, trust *CURR EMPL* chmn, ceo: Vulcan Materials Co (see above)

APPLICATION INFORMATION

Initial Approach: *Initial Contact:* letter or proposal to Mary S. Russom *Include Information On:* description of the organization, amount requested, purpose for which funds are sought, recently audited financial statement, proof of tax-exempt status *Deadlines:* none; applications acted upon throughout the year *Note:* Company does not respond to telephone solicitations.

Restrictions on Giving: Does not give grants to individuals, fraternal organizations, member agencies of united funds, political or lobbying groups, or religious organizations for sectarian purposes; does not support goodwill advertising or dinners or special events.

GRANTS ANALYSIS

Total Grants: $1,870,874

Number of Grants: 567

Average Grant: $3,300

Typical Range: $1,000 to $10,000

Disclosure Period: fiscal year ending November 30, 1993

Note: Financial information is for foundation only. $537,067 was given directly and is not included in the above figures. Recent grants are derived from a 1993 Form 990.

RECENT GRANTS

General

66,666	Birmingham-Southern College, Birmingham, AL
50,000	Birmingham Civil Rights Institute, Birmingham, AL
50,000	University of Alabama Birmingham, Birmingham, AL
45,000	Auburn University Foundation, Auburn, AL
42,840	United Way of Central Alabama, Birmingham, AL

ARIZONA

Morris Foundation, Margaret T.

CONTACT

Eugene P. Polk
Trustee
Margaret T. Morris Foundation
PO Box 592
Prescott, AZ 86302
(602) 445-4010

FINANCIAL SUMMARY

Recent Giving: $1,048,000 (1993); $1,263,350 (1992); $545,850 (1991)

Assets: $25,834,445 (1993); $23,741,661 (1992); $23,884,968 (1991)

EIN: 86-6057798

CONTRIBUTIONS SUMMARY

Donor(s): The foundation was established in 1967 by the late Margaret T. Morris .

Typical Recipients: • *Arts & Humanities:* Art History, Arts Associations & Councils, Arts Centers, Arts Festivals, Arts Funds, Arts Institutes, Arts Outreach, Ballet, Dance, Historic Preservation, History & Archaeology, Libraries, Museums/Galleries, Opera, Theater • *Civic & Public Affairs:* Economic Development, Housing, Law & Justice, Legal Aid, Municipalities/Towns, Urban & Community Affairs, Zoos/Aquariums • *Education:* Arts/Humanities Education, Colleges & Universities, Education Associations, General, Health & Physical

Education, Medical Education, Public Education (Precollege), Science/Mathematics Education, Student Aid • *Environment:* General, Resource Conservation • *Health:* AIDS/HIV, Cancer, Clinics/Medical Centers, Emergency/Ambulance Services, Health Policy/Cost Containment, Health Organizations, Hospices, Hospitals, Medical Research, Single-Disease Health Associations • *International:* Foreign Arts Organizations, Health Care/Hospitals, International Development • *Religion:* Jewish Causes, Religious Organizations • *Science:* Science Museums, Scientific Centers & Institutes, Scientific Organizations • *Social Services:* At-Risk Youth, Child Welfare, Community Service Organizations, Day Care, Family Planning, Family Services, Food/Clothing Distribution, Homes, People with Disabilities, Recreation & Athletics, Scouts, Senior Services, Shelters/Homelessness, Volunteer Services, Youth Organizations

Grant Types: capital, general support, operating expenses, project, and scholarship

Geographic Distribution: focus on New York and Arizona

GIVING OFFICERS
Richard Lee Menschel: trust *B* New York NY 1934 *ED* Syracuse Univ BS 1955; Harvard Univ MBA 1959 *CURR EMPL* ptnr: Goldman Sachs & Co *CORP AFFIL* dir: Kieckhefer Assocs *PHIL AFFIL* près, treas, dir: Charina Foundation; dir: Horace W. Goldsmith Foundation

Eugene P. Polk: trust *PHIL AFFIL* admin off, trust: J. W. Kieckhefer Foundation; dir: Charina Foundation

APPLICATION INFORMATION
Initial Approach:

The foundation requests applications be made in writing.

The written proposal should provide a description of the problem addressed, the nature of the project, the objectives of the program, and a copy of the IRS tax-exempt ruling.

The foundation reports receipt of applications is preferred from May through November.

Restrictions on Giving: The foundation does not make grants to individuals or sectarian religious organizations.

GRANTS ANALYSIS
Total Grants: $1,048,000

Number of Grants: 77

Highest Grant: $100,000

Average Grant: $13,610

Typical Range: $2,500 to $20,000

Disclosure Period: 1993

Note: Recent grants are derived from a 1993 Form 990.

RECENT GRANTS

Library
50,000	Pierpont Morgan Library, New York, NY — capital campaign

General
100,000	Harvard University, Cambridge, MA — capital campaign
70,000	Children's Action Alliance, Phoenix, AZ — in support of Child Welfare Project: 1994
50,000	Harvard School of Public Health, Cambridge, MA — Dean's Discretionary Fund
50,000	Phoenix Zoo, Phoenix, AZ — in support of the Great Deserts of the World exhibit
50,000	Prescott Senior Day Care Center, Prescott, AZ — toward reduction of debt

Mulcahy Foundation

CONTACT
Ashby I. Lohse
Treasurer and Secretary
Mulcahy Fdn.
70 W Franklin St.
Tucson, AZ 85701
(602) 623-6414

FINANCIAL SUMMARY
Recent Giving: $114,050 (fiscal 1994); $117,240 (fiscal 1992); $120,093 (fiscal 1991)

Assets: $1,939,441 (fiscal 1994); $2,104,818 (fiscal 1992); $1,896,721 (fiscal 1991)

Gifts Received: $25,000 (fiscal 1992)

EIN: 86-6053461

CONTRIBUTIONS SUMMARY
Donor(s): the late John A. Mulcahy, Mulcahy Lumber Co.

Typical Recipients: • *Arts & Humanities:* Community Arts, Libraries, Museums/Galleries, Opera • *Civic & Public Affairs:* Hispanic Affairs • *Education:* Arts/Humanities Education, Colleges & Universities, Community & Junior Colleges, Environmental Education, General, Medical Education, Public Education (Precollege), Religious Education, Student Aid • *Religion:* Churches • *Social Services:* Community Service Organizations, Food/Clothing Distribution, United Funds/United Ways, YMCA/YWCA/YMHA/YWHA, Youth Organizations

Grant Types: capital, emergency, endowment, general support, multiyear/continuing support, operating expenses, project, and research

Geographic Distribution: focus on AZ, with emphasis on the Tucson area

GIVING OFFICERS
Cliffton E. Bloom: trust

Ashby I. Lohse: secy, treas

APPLICATION INFORMATION
Initial Approach: Send brief letter describing program. Include a description of organization, amount requested, purpose of funds sought, recently audited financial statement,

and proof of tax-exempt status. There are no deadlines.

Restrictions on Giving: Does not support individuals.

GRANTS ANALYSIS
Total Grants: $114,050

Number of Grants: 16

Highest Grant: $44,164

Typical Range: $300 to $28,700

Disclosure Period: fiscal year ending June 30, 1994

Note: Recent grants are derived from a fiscal 1994 Form 990.

RECENT GRANTS

General
44,164	University of Arizona, Tucson, AZ
28,700	Wilderness Expeditions, Tucson, AZ — scholarship
8,469	Northern Arizona University, Flagstaff, AZ — education
5,000	United Way of Greater Tucson, Tucson, AZ — community charities
4,900	First United Methodist Church, Tucson, AZ — education

Phelps Dodge Corporation / Phelps Dodge Foundation

Revenue: $3.28 billion
Headquarters: Phoenix, AZ
SIC Major Group: Chemicals & Allied Products, Fabricated Metal Products, Metal Mining, and Primary Metal Industries

CONTACT
William C. Tubman
President
Phelps Dodge Foundation
2600 N Central Ave.
Phoenix, AZ 85004
(602) 234-8100

FINANCIAL SUMMARY
Recent Giving: $1,400,000 (1995 est.); $1,243,826 (1994 approx.); $1,231,154 (1993)

Assets: $13,152,516 (1993); $12,847,910 (1992); $11,844,695 (1991)

Fiscal Note: Above figures are for the foundation only. Company also offers direct gifts. Contact for this support is Nicholas S. Balich, vice president. Estimated value of this support was $1,317,000 in 1993. Above figures exclude nonmonetary support.

EIN: 13-6077350

CONTRIBUTIONS SUMMARY
Typical Recipients: • *Arts & Humanities:* Arts Funds, Community Arts, Libraries, Museums/Galleries, Music, Opera, Public Broadcasting, Theater • *Civic & Public Affairs:* Business/Free Enterprise, Civil Rights, Economic Development, Economic Policy, Law & Justice, Public Policy,

Safety, Urban & Community Affairs • *Education:* Colleges & Universities, Community & Junior Colleges, Economic Education, Education Associations, Education Funds, Health & Physical Education, International Exchange, Medical Education, Minority Education, Science/Mathematics Education, Student Aid • *Environment:* General • *Health:* Health Funds, Health Organizations, Hospitals, Medical Training • *International:* Health Care/Hospitals, International Peace & Security Issues, International Relations • *Social Services:* Community Service Organizations, Family Planning, Recreation & Athletics, United Funds/United Ways, Youth Organizations

Grant Types: employee matching gifts, general support, multiyear/continuing support, and scholarship

Note: The foundation reports that it provides multiyear/continuing support only in limited situations.

Nonmonetary Support Types: donated products and in-kind services

Note: Nonmonetary support is provided by the company; estimated value of support is not available.

Geographic Distribution: where company maintains major operating facilities

Operating Locations: AR (El Dorado), AZ (Morenci, Phoenix), CA (Irvine), CT (Norwich), FL (Coral Gables), GA (Atlanta, Trenton), IN (Fort Wayne), KS (Ulysses), KY (Edmonton, Henderson, Hopkinsville), LA (Franklin), MO (St. Louis), NC (Laurinburg), NJ (Bayway, Elizabeth), NM (Hurley, McKinley County, Santa Rita, Tyrone), NY (Ossining), OH (Springfield), SC (Inman), TX (El Paso), WV (Moundsville)

CORP. OFFICERS

Nicholas S. Balich: *B* Bisbee AZ 1936 *ED* Univ AZ 1960 *CURR EMPL* vp: Phelps Dodge Corp *CORP AFFIL* dir: Textrade Inc; pres: Phelps Dodge Mercantile Co

Douglas Cain Yearley: *B* Oak Park IL 1936 *ED* Cornell Univ BE 1958; Harvard Univ 1968-1969 *CURR EMPL* chmn, pres, ceo: Phelps Dodge Corp *CORP AFFIL* dir: Inroads Inc, JP Morgan & Co, Lockheed Corp, Morgan Guaranty Trust Co, Southern Peru Copper Corp, USX Corp, Valley Natl Bank, Valley Natl Corp *NONPR AFFIL* chmn: Copper Devel Assn, Intl Copper Assn; dir: Natl Assn Mfrs, Phoenix Symphony; mem: Alexis de Toqueville Soc, AZ Econ Counc, Bus Roundtable, Natl Electronic Mfrs Assn; vchmn: Am Mining Congress *CLUB AFFIL* AZ, Blind Brook CC, Echo Lake CC, The Links, Paradise Valley CC, Sky

GIVING OFFICERS

Frank J. Longto: vp, treas *B* Kingston NY 1940 *ED* Manhattan Coll BBA 1965; CUNY MBA 1977 *CURR EMPL* vp, treas: Phelps Dodge Corp *CORP AFFIL* secy, treas, dir: Phelphs Dodge Indus Inc; vp, treas, dir: Phelps Dodge Refining Corp

Mark R. Mollison: asst treas

Mary K. Sterling: secy *CURR EMPL* shareholder rel off: Phelps Dodge Corp

William Charles Tubman: pres *B* New York NY 1932 *ED* Fordham Univ BS 1953; Fordham Univ JD 1960 *CURR EMPL* vp, secy: Phelps Dodge Corp *CORP AFFIL* vp, secy, dir: Phelphs Dodge Indus Inc, Phelphs Dodge Refining Corp *NONPR AFFIL* dir: Phoenix Symphony, St Joseph Hosp Fdn; mem: Am Bar Assn, Maricopa County Bar Assn, NY Bar Assn; mem scholarship adv counc: Univ AZ; trust: Phoenix Art Mus

Douglas Cain Yearley: dir *CURR EMPL* chmn, pres, ceo: Phelps Dodge Corp (see above)

APPLICATION INFORMATION

Initial Approach: *Initial Contact:* brief letter *Include Information On:* description of the organization, amount requested, purpose for which funds are sought, recently audited financial statement, and proof of tax-exempt status *Deadlines:* July through September

Restrictions on Giving: Does not support individuals, political or lobbying groups, dinners or special events, or goodwill advertising.

OTHER THINGS TO KNOW

Company matches employee contributions to accredited colleges and universities, including junior colleges; privately financed, nonprofit accredited secondary schools; voluntary hospitals; museums; performing arts organizations; botanical gardens; public broadcasting services; or zoological societies.

PUBLICATIONS

A Tradition of Giving

GRANTS ANALYSIS

Total Grants: $1,231,154

Number of Grants: 113

Highest Grant: $45,000

Average Grant: $10,895

Typical Range: $1,000 to $15,000

Disclosure Period: 1993

Note: Financial information is for the foundation only. Recent grants are derived from a 1993 Form 990.

RECENT GRANTS

General

45,000	Phoenix Zoo, Phoenix, AZ — zoomobile operating account
40,000	Mt. Graham Community Hospital Foundation, Safford, AZ
40,000	Phelps Dodge Scholarships, Phoenix, AZ
38,000	Arizona State University, Tempe, AZ
35,000	Montana Tech Foundation, Butte, MT

Spalding Foundation, Eliot

CONTACT

Peter T. Gianas
Secretary and Trustee
Eliot Spalding Fdn.
4400 E Broadway, Ste. 800
Tucson, AZ 85711
(602) 796-6630

FINANCIAL SUMMARY

Recent Giving: $106,864 (1993)

Assets: $2,424,106 (1993)

EIN: 86-6050507

CONTRIBUTIONS SUMMARY

Typical Recipients: • *Arts & Humanities:* Libraries • *Civic & Public Affairs:* Botanical Gardens/Parks, General • *Education:* Colleges & Universities, Community & Junior Colleges, Student Aid • *Religion:* Religious Welfare • *Social Services:* Food/Clothing Distribution, United Funds/United Ways

Grant Types: general support

Geographic Distribution: focus on Tucson, AZ

GIVING OFFICERS

Peter T. Gianas: dir, secy, trust

Samuel P. Goddard, Jr.: dir, vp, trust

D. M. Lovitt: dir, pres

Clayton E. Niles: dir, treas

J. M. Sakrison: dir

APPLICATION INFORMATION

Initial Approach: Send a brief letter of inquiry. Include a description of organization, amount requested, purpose of funds sought, recently audited financial statement, and proof of tax-exempt status.

GRANTS ANALYSIS

Total Grants: $106,864

Number of Grants: 9

Highest Grant: $82,864

Typical Range: $1,000 to $10,000

Disclosure Period: 1993

Note: Recent grants are derived from a 1993 Form 990.

RECENT GRANTS

Library

2,000	Libraries Limited, Phoenix, AZ

General

82,864	Tucson United Way, Tucson, AZ
10,000	Salvation Army, Tucson, AZ
5,000	Community Food Bank, Tucson, AZ
2,000	Dollars for Scholars, Tucson, AZ
1,500	Amity Foundation, Tucson, AZ

ARKANSAS

Arkansas Power & Light Co.

Sales: $1.52 billion
Employees: 2,916
Parent Company: Entergy Corp.
Headquarters: Little Rock, AR
SIC Major Group: Electric Services

CONTACT
Sandy Alstadt
Manager, Corporate Communications
Arkansas Power & Light Co.
PO Box 551
Little Rock, AR 72203
(501) 377-3547

FINANCIAL SUMMARY
Recent Giving: $1,400,000 (1995 est.);
$1,400,000 (1994 approx.); $1,300,000
(1993 approx.)
Fiscal Note: All giving is direct.

CONTRIBUTIONS SUMMARY
Typical Recipients: • *Arts & Humanities:*
Arts Associations & Councils, Arts Centers,
Community Arts, Dance, Historic Preserva-
tion, Libraries, Museums/Galleries, Music,
Opera, Performing Arts • *Civic & Public Af-
fairs:* Business/Free Enterprise, Civil
Rights, Economic Development, Economic
Policy, Professional & Trade Associations,
Safety, Urban & Community Affairs,
Women's Affairs • *Education:* Colleges &
Universities, Economic Education, Educa-
tion Associations, Education Funds, Engi-
neering/Technological Education, Minority
Education, Public Education (Precollege),
Religious Education, Science/Mathematics
Education, Student Aid • *Environment:* Gen-
eral • *Health:* Health Organizations, Hospi-
tals, Single-Disease Health Associations
• *Religion:* Religious Welfare • *Social Serv-
ices:* Child Welfare, Community Centers,
Community Service Organizations, Domestic Violence, Food/Clothing Distribution,
Homes, Recreation & Athletics, Senior Services, Shelters/Homelessness, Substance
Abuse, United Funds/United Ways, Volunteer Services, Youth Organizations

Grant Types: capital, employee matching
gifts, general support, matching, multi-
year/continuing support, project, and scholarship

Geographic Distribution: primarily Arkansas and southeastern Missouri, with emphasis on operating locations

Operating Locations: AR (Blytheville, El
Dorado, Hot Springs, Little Rock, Pine
Bluff), MO

CORP. OFFICERS
Robert Drake Keith: *B* Breckenridge TX
1935 *ED* TX A&M Univ BS 1961 *CURR
EMPL* pres, dir: AR Power & Light Co

Jerry L. Maulden: *B* North Little Rock AR
1936 *ED* Univ AR BS 1963 *CURR EMPL*
chmn, ceo: MS Power & Light Co *CORP AF-
FIL* chmn, ceo: AR Power & Light Co, LA

Power & Light Co, New Orleans Pub Svc
Inc; dir: Assoc Natl Gas Co, Middle S En-
ergy, Middle S Svcs, Middle S Utilities, Sys
Fuels; group pres: Entergy Svcs Inc; pres,
coo: Entergy Corp; vchmn, coo: Gulf Sts
Utilities Co

GIVING OFFICERS
Sandra R. Alstadt: *CURR EMPL* mgr corp
commun: AR Power & Light Co

APPLICATION INFORMATION
Initial Approach: *Initial Contact:* letter or
proposal *Include Information On:* description of the organization, amount requested,
purpose for which funds are sought, recently
audited financial statement, and proof of tax-
exempt status *Deadlines:* none

GRANTS ANALYSIS
Total Grants: $1,400,000
Typical Range: $1,000 to $5,000
Disclosure Period: 1994

De Queen General Hospital Foundation

CONTACT
C. E. Hendrix, Jr.
President
De Queen General Hospital Fdn.
Cossatot Technical College
De Queen, AR 71832
(501) 584-4471

FINANCIAL SUMMARY
Recent Giving: $151,875 (1993)
Assets: $3,484,623 (1993)
EIN: 71-0405256

CONTRIBUTIONS SUMMARY
Typical Recipients: • *Arts & Humanities:*
Libraries • *Civic & Public Affairs:* Urban &
Community Affairs • *Education:* Student
Aid • *Social Services:* People with Disabili-
ties, Youth Organizations

Grant Types: general support and scholarship

GIVING OFFICERS
Donn Allison: dir
Frank Daniel, M.D.: dir
Dave Elkin: dir
C. E. Hendrix, Jr.: pres
Martha Johnston: secy, treas
Charles Jones, M.D.: dir
Ray Kimball: dir

APPLICATION INFORMATION
Initial Approach: Applications available at
Cossatot Technical College.

OTHER THINGS TO KNOW
Provides scholarships to individuals studying for a medical profession.

GRANTS ANALYSIS
Total Grants: $151,875
Number of Grants: 6
Highest Grant: $50,000

Typical Range: $175 to $34,850
Disclosure Period: 1993

Note: Recent grants are derived from a 1993
Form 990. Number of grants and typical
range do not include matching grants.

RECENT GRANTS

Library
50,000	County of Sevier, Arkansas, AR — library building fund

General
34,850	County of Sevier, Arkansas, AR — county ambulance
3,500	Young Expressions — assist young people
3,000	Sevier County Adult Activities Center, Dequeen, AR — grant to assist developmentally disabled persons
350	University of Arkansas Fayetteville, Fayetteville, AR — student scholarship
175	Quachita Baptist University, Arkadelphia, AR — student scholarship

---

Jones Foundation, Harvey and Bernice

CONTACT
Nan Schoonover
Director
Harvey and Bernice Jones Fdn.
PO Box 233
Springdale, AR 72765
(501) 756-0611

FINANCIAL SUMMARY
Recent Giving: $1,075,304 (fiscal 1993);
$1,075,304 (fiscal 1992); $5,672,472 (fiscal
1991)

Assets: $7,373,736 (fiscal 1993);
$7,378,736 (fiscal 1992); $7,805,155 (fiscal
1991)

Gifts Received: $1,950,000 (fiscal 1989);
$2,500,000 (fiscal 1988)

EIN: 71-6057141

CONTRIBUTIONS SUMMARY
Donor(s): Harvey Jones, Mrs. Harvey Jones,
and their related companies

Typical Recipients: • *Arts & Humanities:*
Arts Centers, Libraries • *Civic & Public Af-
fairs:* Employment/Job Training • *Educa-
tion:* Colleges & Universities, Private
Education (Precollege), Religious Education
• *Religion:* Churches, Religious Organiza-
tions • *Social Services:* Child Welfare, Com-
munity Service Organizations, Counseling,
Day Care, Family Services, Homes, United
Funds/United Ways, Youth Organizations

Grant Types: general support and scholarship

Geographic Distribution: focus on Springdale, AR

GIVING OFFICERS

Herbert G. Frost, Jr.: dir *B* Little Rock AR 1931 *ED* Univ AR 1952 *CURR EMPL* vp: Am Fuel Cell & Coated Fabrics Co *CORP AFFIL* pres, dir: Jack Frost Mgmt Consult *PHIL AFFIL* dir, mgr: Harvey and Bernice Jones Charitable Trust; dir: Harvey and Bernice Jones Charitable Trust 2, MBM Charitable Foundation

Bernice Jones: chmn *PHIL AFFIL* dir: Harvey and Bernice Jones Charitable Trust, Harvey and Bernice Jones Charitable Trust 2, MBM Charitable Foundation

Hugh Means: trust

Nan Schoonover: dir

Gene Thompson: trust

William Walker: trust

APPLICATION INFORMATION

Initial Approach: Send letter requesting application form. There are no deadlines. Board meets November 30.

GRANTS ANALYSIS

Total Grants: $1,075,304

Typical Range: $1,000 to $10,000

Disclosure Period: fiscal year ending November 30, 1992

Note: Recent grants are derived from a fiscal 1991 Form 990. No grants list was provided for fiscal 1992.

RECENT GRANTS

Library
10,000	Springdale Public Library

General
100,000	Arkansas Baptist Children's Home, Little Rock, AR
75,000	Northwest Arkansas Adult Day Care Center, AR
71,000	Single Parent Fund — EOA
50,087	Springdale Schools
40,000	New Life Ranch

Murphy Foundation

CONTACT

Perry Silliman
Secretary and Treasurer
Murphy Foundation
200 N Jefferson St
Ste. 400
Union Building
El Dorado, AR 71730
(501) 862-2884

FINANCIAL SUMMARY

Recent Giving: $410,000 (fiscal 1995 est.); $415,507 (fiscal 1994); $400,000 (fiscal 1993 approx.)

Assets: $8,100,000 (fiscal 1995 est.); $9,336,075 (fiscal 1994); $8,000,000 (fiscal 1993 approx.)

EIN: 71-6049826

CONTRIBUTIONS SUMMARY

Donor(s): The foundation was established in Arkansas in 1958 by Charles Haywood Murphy, Jr., and other members of the Murphy family. Mr. Murphy is chairman of Murphy Oil Corporation.

Typical Recipients: • *Arts & Humanities:* Arts Centers, Historic Preservation, History & Archaeology, Libraries, Museums/Galleries, Music, Performing Arts, Public Broadcasting • *Civic & Public Affairs:* Economic Development, Public Policy • *Education:* Arts/Humanities Education, Colleges & Universities, Elementary Education (Private), Literacy, Medical Education, Secondary Education (Public), Student Aid • *Religion:* Churches, Religious Welfare • *Social Services:* Animal Protection, Crime Prevention, Scouts, United Funds/United Ways, YMCA/YWCA/YMHA/YWHA, Youth Organizations

Grant Types: capital, endowment, and scholarship

Geographic Distribution: primarily southern Arkansas

GIVING OFFICERS

Johnnie W. Murphy: pres, dir *PHIL AFFIL* pres: Murphy Foundation of Louisiana

Lucy A. Ring: dir *PHIL AFFIL* secy, treas, dir: Murphy Foundation of Louisiana

Perry Silliman: secy-treas

APPLICATION INFORMATION

Initial Contact: Requests should be in the form of a letter describing all pertinent details of the proposed project. Educational grant requests for individual student aid should be submitted on a copy of the foundation's standard application form and should include a copy of the applicant's scholastic record. Applicants requesting grants for the general giving program should write a letter to the foundation explaining the program in need of funding.

Deadlines: Applications should be submitted by August 1.

Note: Educational grants are restricted to students from the southern Arkansas area.

Restrictions on Giving: Educational grants are restricted to students from the southern Arkansas area.

GRANTS ANALYSIS

Total Grants: $415,507

Number of Grants: 56

Highest Grant: $61,594

Average Grant: $7,420

Typical Range: $1,000 to $15,000

Disclosure Period: fiscal year ending April 30, 1994

Note: Total grant figure includes $215,574 in gifts of Murphy's Oil Company stock. Recent grants are derived from a fiscal 1994 Form 990.

RECENT GRANTS

Library
20,531	Barton Library, El Dorado, AR — endowment fund in the form of stocks

General
61,594	United Way of Union County, El Dorado, AR —
	endowment fund in the form of stocks
30,797	Boy Scouts of America DeSota Area Council, Desota, AR — in the form of stocks
30,797	Boys and Girls Clubs of El Dorado, El Dorado, AR — in the form of stocks
25,000	University of Arkansas Medical Sciences Foundation Fund, Little Rock, AR
15,000	YWCA of El Dorado, El Dorado, AR — capital campaign

Ottenheimer Brothers Foundation

CONTACT

Steve Bauman
Secretary
Ottenheimer Brothers Fdn.
1400 Union National Bank Bldg.
Little Rock, AR 72201
(501) 376-4531

FINANCIAL SUMMARY

Recent Giving: $206,178 (fiscal 1994)

Assets: $5,008,698 (fiscal 1994)

EIN: 71-6059988

CONTRIBUTIONS SUMMARY

Typical Recipients: • *Arts & Humanities:* History & Archaeology, Libraries • *Civic & Public Affairs:* General • *Education:* Business Education, Literacy • *Religion:* Jewish Causes, Religious Welfare, Social/Policy Issues • *Social Services:* Family Services, Food/Clothing Distribution, People with Disabilities

Grant Types: general support

Geographic Distribution: focus on AR

GIVING OFFICERS

Steve Bauman: secy

Noland Blass, Jr.: bd dir

E. C. Eichenbaum: chmn

Judy Grundfest: bd dir

Edward M. Penick: bd dir

Louis Rosen: bd dir

Fred Selz: bd dir

Sam B. Strauss, Jr.: bd dir

E. Grainger Williams: bd dir

APPLICATION INFORMATION

Initial Approach: Send a brief letter of inquiry. Include a description of organization, amount requested, purpose of funds sought, recently audited financial statement, and proof of tax-exempt status.

GRANTS ANALYSIS

Total Grants: $206,178

Number of Grants: 12

Highest Grant: $150,000

Typical Range: $25 to $25,000

Disclosure Period: fiscal year ending April 30, 1994

Note: Recent grants are derived from a fiscal 1994 Form 990.

RECENT GRANTS

Library

150,000	University of Arkansas Little Rock Ottenheimer Library Expansion, Little Rock, AR
5,000	University of Arkansas Little Rock Law Library, Little Rock, AR

General

20,000	Philander Smith College Ottenheimer Business Center, Little Rock, AR
1,000	Garth Foundation
1,000	Literacy Skills Partners Grant, Little Rock, AR
1,000	National Conference of Christians and Jews, New York, NY
1,000	Potluck, Inc., Little Rock, AR

Riggs Benevolent Fund

CONTACT
Anne Roark
Trust Department
Riggs Benevolent Fund
c/o Worthen Bank and Trust Co., N.A., Trust Dept.
PO Box 1681
Little Rock, AR 72203-1681
(501) 378-1231

FINANCIAL SUMMARY
Recent Giving: $228,850 (1992); $269,550 (1991); $202,200 (1989)

Assets: $4,468,560 (1992); $4,345,756 (1991); $3,558,672 (1989)

Gifts Received: $176,413 (1992); $215,500 (1991); $309,261 (1989)

Fiscal Note: In 1992, contributions were received from Robert Cress ($5,413), Martha Riggs ($60,000), Lamar Riggs ($7,500), Riggs Tractor Co. ($100,000), and Jack Riggs ($3,500).

EIN: 71-6050130

CONTRIBUTIONS SUMMARY
Donor(s): members of the Riggs family, Robert G. Cress, J. A. Riggs Tractor Co.

Typical Recipients: • *Arts & Humanities:* Arts Centers, Libraries, Museums/Galleries, Music, Theater • *Civic & Public Affairs:* Employment/Job Training, General, Municipalities/Towns, Urban & Community Affairs • *Education:* Agricultural Education, Colleges & Universities, Education Funds, Engineering/Technological Education, Literacy, Private Education (Precollege), Science/Mathematics Education, Student Aid • *Health:* Children's Health/Hospitals, Hospitals, Nursing Services • *Religion:* Churches, Religious Welfare • *Social Services:* Child Welfare, Community Service Organizations, Family Services, Homes,

United Funds/United Ways, Youth Organizations

Grant Types: general support and scholarship

Geographic Distribution: focus on AR

GIVING OFFICERS
Worthen Trust Co.: trust

Robert G. Cress: trust *CURR EMPL* pres: JA Riggs Tractor Co

John A. Riggs III: trust *B* Little Rock AR 1934 *ED* Univ AR 1957 *CURR EMPL* chmn: JA Riggs Tractor Co *CORP AFFIL* dir: Worthen Natl Bank AR

APPLICATION INFORMATION
Initial Approach: Foundation requests that application be typed. Include a description of organization, amount requested, purpose of funds sought, recently audited financial statement, and proof of tax-exempt status. There are no deadlines.

GRANTS ANALYSIS
Total Grants: $228,850

Number of Grants: 65

Highest Grant: $12,500

Typical Range: $1,000 to $5,000

Disclosure Period: 1992

Note: Recent grants are derived from a 1992 Form 990.

RECENT GRANTS

Library

12,500	Hendrix College Library Fund, Conway, AR

General

12,500	Arkansas Children's Hospital, Little Rock, AR
12,500	Little Rock Boys Club, Little Rock, AR — capital campaign
9,000	First United Methodist Church, Little Rock, AR
9,000	First United Methodist Church, Little Rock, AR
8,000	First United Methodist Church, Little Rock, AR

Sturgis Charitable and Educational Trust, Roy and Christine

CONTACT
Katie Speer
Trustee
Roy and Christine Sturgis Charitable and Educational Trust
PO Box 92
Malvern, AR 72104
(501) 664-8525

FINANCIAL SUMMARY
Recent Giving: $492,613 (1993)

Assets: $13,786,385 (1993)

EIN: 71-0495345

CONTRIBUTIONS SUMMARY
Typical Recipients: • *Arts & Humanities:* Arts Centers, Libraries, Theater • *Education:* Colleges & Universities, Public Education (Precollege), Secondary Education (Private), Secondary Education (Public), Vocational & Technical Education • *Health:* Arthritis, Children's Health/Hospitals, Hospices, Hospitals • *International:* Missionary/Religious Activities • *Religion:* Churches, Religious Organizations, Religious Welfare • *Social Services:* Community Service Organizations, Recreation & Athletics

Grant Types: general support

Geographic Distribution: focus on AR

GIVING OFFICERS
Barry B. Findley: trust

Katie Speer: trust

APPLICATION INFORMATION
Initial Approach: Send a brief letter of inquiry. Include a description of organization, amount requested, purpose of funds sought, recently audited financial statement, and proof of tax-exempt status.

GRANTS ANALYSIS
Total Grants: $492,613

Number of Grants: 37

Highest Grant: $100,000

Typical Range: $1,000 to $50,000

Disclosure Period: 1993

Note: Recent grants are derived from a 1993 Form 990.

RECENT GRANTS

Library

5,000	Hot Spring County Library, Hot Spring, AR
1,500	Hot Spring County Library, Hot Spring, AR

General

100,000	Ouachita Baptist University, Arkadelphia, AR
50,000	Ouachita Baptist University, Arkadelphia, AR
25,000	Ouachita Technical College Malvern, Ouachita, AR
25,000	University of Arkansas Little Rock, Little Rock, AR
25,000	University of Arkansas Little Rock, Little Rock, AR

Wal-Mart Stores, Inc. / Wal-Mart Foundation

Revenue: $83.41 billion
Employees: 525,000
Headquarters: Bentonville, AR
SIC Major Group: Department Stores

CONTACT
Ginger Sanders
Director of Foundation
Wal-Mart Foundation
702 SW Eighth St.
Bentonville, AR 72716-8071
(501) 273-4000

Note: The company's World Wide Web address is http://www.walldata.com

FINANCIAL SUMMARY

Recent Giving: $10,312,301 (fiscal 1992); $10,000,000 (fiscal 1991 approx.); $11,266,033 (fiscal 1990)

Assets: $15,681,286 (fiscal 1991); $9,332,875 (fiscal 1990); $7,464,586 (fiscal 1989)

Fiscal Note: Company gives through foundation only. Above figures exclude nonmonetary support.

EIN: 71-6107283

CONTRIBUTIONS SUMMARY

Typical Recipients: • *Arts & Humanities:* Arts Festivals, Community Arts, Dance, Historic Preservation, Libraries, Museums/Galleries, Music, Public Broadcasting, Theater • *Civic & Public Affairs:* Business/Free Enterprise, Economic Development, Economic Policy, Law & Justice, Municipalities/Towns, Professional & Trade Associations, Public Policy, Safety, Urban & Community Affairs, Women's Affairs, Zoos/Aquariums • *Education:* Agricultural Education, Business Education, Colleges & Universities, Continuing Education, Economic Education, Education Associations, Education Funds, Elementary Education (Private), Literacy, Medical Education, Minority Education, Preschool Education, Public Education (Precollege), Religious Education, Science/Mathematics Education, Special Education, Student Aid • *Environment:* General • *Health:* Emergency/Ambulance Services, Geriatric Health, Health Funds, Health Organizations, Hospices, Hospitals, Medical Rehabilitation, Medical Research, Mental Health, Nutrition, Public Health, Single-Disease Health Associations • *Religion:* Religious Welfare • *Social Services:* Animal Protection, Child Welfare, Community Centers, Community Service Organizations, Counseling, Domestic Violence, Emergency Relief, Food/Clothing Distribution, Homes, People with Disabilities, Recreation & Athletics, Senior Services, Shelters/Homelessness, Substance Abuse, United Funds/United Ways, Volunteer Services, Youth Organizations

Grant Types: capital, general support, research, and scholarship

Geographic Distribution: in communities where stores are located

Operating Locations: AL, AR (Bentonville, Fayetteville, Ft. Smith, Rogers), AZ, CA, CO, CT, DE, FL, GA, HI, IA, ID, IL, IN, KS, KY, LA, MA, MD, ME, MI, MN, MO, MS, MT, NC, ND, NE, NH, NJ, NM, NV, NY, OH, OK, OR, PA, PR, RI, SC, SD, TN, TX, VA, WA, WI, WV, WY

Note: Operates more than 1,400 stores in 29 states.

CORP. OFFICERS

Paul R. Carter: *B* Monticello AR 1940 *ED* Univ AR BA 1964 *CURR EMPL* exec vp fin, cfo, dir: Wal-Mart Stores Inc *CORP AFFIL* dir: McLane Co Inc; exec vp, cfo, dir: N AR Wholesale Co; exec vp, dir: Nadco Inc *NONPR AFFIL* mem: Am Inst CPAs

David Dayne Glass: *B* Liberty MO 1935 *ED* Southwest MO St Univ BS 1959 *CURR EMPL* pres, ceo, dir: Wal-Mart Stores Inc *CORP AFFIL* dir: Bank of Bentonville, McLane Co Inc, Phillips Food Ctrs

Donald G. Soderquist: *B* Chicago IL 1934 *ED* Wheaton Coll BA 1955 *CURR EMPL* vchmn, coo, dir: Wal-Mart Stores Inc *CORP AFFIL* dir: First Natl Bank Rogers AR, McLane Co Inc, Servicemaster-Consumer Svcs *NONPR AFFIL* dir: Intl Mass Retail Assn

S. Robson Walton: *B* 1945 *ED* Columbia Univ LLB 1969 *CURR EMPL* chmn, dir: Wal-Mart Stores Inc *CORP AFFIL* dir: Acxiom Corp, Cooper Commun; vchmn: N AR Wholesale Co *PHIL AFFIL* trust: Walton Foundation, Sam M. and Helen R. Walton Foundation; dir: Walton Family Foundation

GIVING OFFICERS

Paul R. Carter: dir *CURR EMPL* exec vp fin, cfo, dir: Wal-Mart Stores Inc (see above)

Thomas Martin Coughlin: mem *B* Cleveland OH 1949 *ED* CA St Univ BS 1972 *CURR EMPL* sr vp opers: Wal-Mart Stores Sams Wholesale Div *NONPR AFFIL* dir: Students Free Enterprise; mem: Natl Mass Retail Inst

Bill Fields: mem *B* 1949 *ED* Univ AR BSBA 1971 *CURR EMPL* exec vp: Wal-Mart Stores Inc

David Dayne Glass: trust *CURR EMPL* pres, ceo, dir: Wal-Mart Stores Inc (see above)

Joseph S. Hardin, Jr.: mem *B* Nashville TN 1945 *ED* US Military Acad 1967; N TX St Univ 1972 *CURR EMPL* pres, ceo, dir: Wal-Mart Stores McLane Div *CORP AFFIL* exec vp: Wal-Mart Stores Inc; pres, ceo, dir: McLane/America Inc, McLane Eastern Inc, McLane Foods Inc, McLane/Foodservice-Temple, McLane/High Plains Inc, McLane/Mid Atlantic Inc, McLane/Midwest Inc, McLane/Pacific Inc, McLane/Southern Inc, McLane/Suneast Inc, McLane/Sunwest Inc, McLane/Western Inc, Merit Distr Svcs Inc, Professional Data Solution; pres,ceo, dir: McLane/Southern CA

Bobby L. Martin: mem *B* Giddeon MO 1948 *ED* S TX Univ 1969 *CURR EMPL* sr vp: Wal-Mart Stores Inc *CORP AFFIL* dir: Western Mechandising; mem exec bd: I/S Adv Group Intl Bus Machines *NONPR AFFIL* exec dir: Gen Merchandise Adv Counc

Dean L. Sanders: mem *B* 1950 *ED* Univ AR BA 1972 *CURR EMPL* pres, ceo: Wal-Mart Stores Sams Club Div *CORP AFFIL* ceo, dir: Wholesale Club Inc

Ginger Sanders: dir

Thomas Patrick Seay: mem *B* Little Rock AR 1941 *ED* Univ AR BS 1963; Univ AR MBA 1975 *CURR EMPL* exec vp real estate & construction: Wal-Mart Stores Inc

NONPR AFFIL mem adv counc: Univ AR Mktg Dept; trust: Intl Counc Shopping Ctrs

Donald Shinkel: mem

Donald G. Soderquist: trust *CURR EMPL* vchmn, coo, dir: Wal-Mart Stores Inc (see above)

S. Robson Walton: mem *CURR EMPL* chmn, dir: Wal-Mart Stores Inc *PHIL AFFIL* trust: Walton Foundation, Sam M. and Helen R. Walton Foundation; dir: Walton Family Foundation (see above)

Wesley Wright: mem *CURR EMPL* sr vp special divs: Wal-Mart Stores Inc

APPLICATION INFORMATION

Initial Approach: *Initial Contact:* brief letter or proposal to foundation; or contact local store for application *Include Information On:* description of the organization, amount requested, purpose for which funds are sought, recently audited financial statement, and proof of tax-exempt status *Deadlines:* none *Note:* Company does not accept requests for direct grants. Address grant requests to the foundation only.

Restrictions on Giving: Wal-Mart Foundation only supports organizations that in some way benefit the communities in which their stores are located.

The foundation does not give grants to individuals, except student scholarships.

OTHER THINGS TO KNOW

Wal-Mart Foundation awards one scholarship per year to a graduating high school senior in each of its store communities.

The Wal-Mart Community Involvement Program (CIP) allows each store to hold local fund-raisers on store premises for qualifying charities and organizations. Qualifying projects are matched up to $2,000.

GRANTS ANALYSIS

Total Grants: $10,312,301

Number of Grants: 1,304

Highest Grant: $1,470,433

Average Grant: $7,948

Typical Range: $100 to $2,000 and $10,000 to $20,000

Disclosure Period: fiscal year ending January 31, 1992

Note: Recent grants are derived from a fiscal 1992 Form 990.

RECENT GRANTS

General

1,470,433	Children's Miracle Network, St. Paul, MN
120,000	Students in Free Enterprise, Springfield, MO
106,354	Children's Miracle Network, St. Paul, MN
55,260	Children's Miracle Network, St. Paul, MN
54,000	Texas A&M University, College Station, TX

CALIFORNIA

Ahmanson Foundation

CONTACT
Lee E. Walcott, Jr.
Vice President and Managing Director
Ahmanson Foundation
9215 Wilshire Blvd.
Beverly Hills, CA 90210
(310) 278-0770

FINANCIAL SUMMARY
Recent Giving: $19,530,770 (fiscal 1993);
$21,050,925 (fiscal 1992); $19,441,614 (fiscal 1991)

Assets: $549,776,000 (fiscal 1993);
$465,538,000 (fiscal 1992); $427,155,336 (fiscal 1991)

Gifts Received: $16,421 (fiscal 1991);
$3,553 (fiscal 1990); $270,000 (fiscal 1989)

Fiscal Note: In fiscal 1991, contributions were received from the estate of Rita Wright.

EIN: 95-6089998

CONTRIBUTIONS SUMMARY

Donor(s): The Ahmanson Foundation was incorporated in 1952 as an independent foundation in California with funds donated by the late Howard F. Ahmanson and his wife, Dorothy G. Sullivan, also deceased. Other donors include William H. Ahmanson and Robert H. Ahmanson, both nephews.

A graduate of the University of Southern California, Howard Ahmanson built an extensive financial empire consisting primarily of savings and loan associations and insurance companies. A noted philanthropist, yachtsman, and art collector, Howard Ahmanson served on the boards of the Los Angeles County Museum of Art, University of Southern California, Kennedy Center for the Performing Arts, and California Museum of Science and Industry.

Typical Recipients: • *Arts & Humanities:* Arts Appreciation, Arts Centers, Arts Funds, Arts Institutes, Arts Outreach, Ethnic & Folk Arts, General, Historic Preservation, Libraries, Literary Arts, Museums/Galleries, Music, Performing Arts, Public Broadcasting, Theater, Visual Arts • *Civic & Public Affairs:* Botanical Gardens/Parks, Civil Rights, Economic Policy, Employment/Job Training, General, Hispanic Affairs, Housing, Law & Justice, Legal Aid, Nonprofit Management, Parades/Festivals, Philanthropic Organizations, Public Policy, Safety, Urban & Community Affairs, Zoos/Aquariums • *Education:* Arts/Humanities Education, Business Education, Colleges & Universities, Education Associations, Education Funds, Education Reform, Elementary Education (Private), Elementary Education (Public), Engineering/Technological Education, General, Journalism/Media Education, Legal Education, Literacy, Medical Educa-

tion, Minority Education, Preschool Education, Private Education (Precollege), Public Education (Precollege), Science/Mathematics Education, Secondary Education (Private), Social Sciences Education, Student Aid, Vocational & Technical Education • *Environment:* Air/Water Quality, General, Resource Conservation, Wildlife Protection • *Health:* Adolescent Health Issues, AIDS/HIV, Alzheimers Disease, Cancer, Children's Health/Hospitals, Clinics/Medical Centers, Emergency/Ambulance Services, Eyes/Blindness, Health Organizations, Heart, Hospitals, Long-Term Care, Medical Research, Mental Health, Nursing Services, Prenatal Health Issues, Research/Studies Institutes, Single-Disease Health Associations, Speech & Hearing • *International:* Foreign Arts Organizations, Foreign Educational Institutions, Health Care/Hospitals, International Environmental Issues, International Peace & Security Issues, Missionary/Religious Activities • *Religion:* Churches, Dioceses, Jewish Causes, Religious Welfare, Social/Policy Issues, Synagogues/Temples • *Science:* Scientific Centers & Institutes • *Social Services:* Animal Protection, At-Risk Youth, Child Welfare, Community Service Organizations, Counseling, Crime Prevention, Day Care, Delinquency & Criminal Rehabilitation, Domestic Violence, Emergency Relief, Family Planning, Family Services, Food/Clothing Distribution, Homes, People with Disabilities, Recreation & Athletics, Senior Services, Shelters/Homelessness, Substance Abuse, Youth Organizations

Grant Types: capital, challenge, endowment, general support, matching, project, scholarship, and seed money

Geographic Distribution: primarily in Southern California, with emphasis on Los Angeles County

GIVING OFFICERS

Howard Fieldstead Ahmanson, Jr.: chmn

Robert H. Ahmanson: pres, trust *B* 1927 *CURR EMPL* vp, dir: H F Ahmanson & Co

William H. Ahmanson: vp, trust *B* Omaha NE 1925 *ED* Univ CA Los Angeles BS 1950 *CURR EMPL* chmn bd: H F Ahmanson & Co *CORP AFFIL* chmn: Natl Am Ins Co, Stuyvesant Ins Group; pres: Natl Am Ins Co *NONPR AFFIL* mem: Fdrs Music Ctr; mem bd dirs: Hosp Good Samaritan; trust: CA Inst Arts, Greater Los Angeles Zoo Assn, Los Angeles County Mus Art

Daniel N. Belin: trust *PHIL AFFIL* vchmn, trust: Samuel H. Kress Foundation

Lloyd Edward Cotsen: trust *B* Boston MA 1929 *ED* Princeton Univ BA 1950; Harvard Univ MBA 1957 *CURR EMPL* chmn, ceo, dir: Neutrogena Corp *CORP AFFIL* chmn: Music Ctr Oper Co *NONPR AFFIL* trust: Archaeological Inst Am Southern CA Chap *PHIL AFFIL* dir: Cotsen Family Foundation

Robert M. DeKruif: trust *B* 1919 *CURR EMPL* vchmn, dir: H F Ahmanson & Co

Robert F. Erburu: trust *B* Ventura CA 1930 *ED* Univ Southern CA BA 1952; Harvard Univ JD 1955 *CURR EMPL* chmn, dir: Times Mirror Co *CORP AFFIL* dir: Tejon Ranch Co; dir, chmn: Fed Reserve Bank San Francisco *NONPR AFFIL* chmn: Am Newspaper Publs Assn, Brookings Inst; dir: Independent Colls Southern CA, Los Angeles Festival, Tomas Rivera Ctr; fellow: Am Acad Arts & Sci; mem: Am Bar Assn, Bus Counc, Bus Roundtable, CA Bus Roundtable; mem bd dirs: Counc Foreign Rels; mem trust counc: Natl Gallery Art *PHIL AFFIL* chmn bd trust: J. Paul Getty Trust; dir: Ralph M. Parsons Foundation, Carrie Estelle Doheny Foundation, William and Flora Hewlett Foundation; vp: Fletcher Jones Foundation; dir: Pfaffinger Foundation; chmn, dir: Times Mirror Foundation

Karen A. Hoffman: secy

Donald B. Stark: treas

Lee E. Walcott, Jr.: vp, mng dir

APPLICATION INFORMATION
Initial Approach:
Applicants should review a copy of the foundation's annual report and guidelines before sending in a proposal. After determining that a proposal matches the foundation's interests a brief proposal or letter of inquiry should be sent to the Managing Director.

Applicants should describe the purpose of the organization, project, and overall funding plan. Also include current annual budget, project budget, list of other available sources of support, audited financial statement, a copy of 501(c)(3) tax-exempt status letter, and a list of the organization's governing board and officers.

Applications may be submitted anytime.

After review of proposals, the foundation may request additional information or an interview. Notification generally occurs within 30 to 60 days.

Restrictions on Giving: Generally, no grants are made to individuals, or for endowed chairs, annual campaigns, fellowships or exchange programs, film productions, continuing support, deficit financing, professorships, internships, individual scholarships, conferences, exhibits, films or video production, or loans.

The foundation generally does not fund organizations which make grants to others, religious organizations for sectarian or propagation of faith purposes, traveling exhibits, performance underwriting, seminars, workshops, studies, surveys, general research and development, or operational support of regional and national charities.

PUBLICATIONS
Annual report and guidelines

GRANTS ANALYSIS
Total Grants: $19,530,770
Number of Grants: 128
Highest Grant: $1,000,000
Average Grant: $152,584

Typical Range: $10,000 to $50,000 and $100,000 to $500,000

Disclosure Period: fiscal year ending October 31, 1993

Note: Recent grants are derived from a 1993 Form 990.

RECENT GRANTS

Library

500,000	University of California Los Angeles Foundation University Research Library, Los Angeles, CA — additional support toward library acquisitions for the Ahmanson-Murphy Aldine and First Century of Italian Printing collections
323,500	California Institute of Technology, Pasadena, CA — toward restoration of the Gates and Morgan Libraries
250,000	Claremont University Center, Claremont, CA — toward acquisition of endowment for the Honnold Library
250,000	Library Foundation of Los Angeles, Los Angeles, CA — toward the Public Library Collection's Endowment Fund
250,000	University of California Los Angeles Foundation William Andrews Clark Memorial Library, Los Angeles, CA — toward the Library Acquisition Endowment Fund

General

1,000,000	University of California Los Angeles Foundation/Neuropsychiatric Institute, Los Angeles, CA — toward establishment of the University of California Los Angeles Brain Mapping Center
1,000,000	University of Southern California Norris Cancer Center, Los Angeles, CA — toward the Cancer Pharmacology Laboratory Suite in the new Research Tower of the Kenneth Norris, Jr. Comprehensive Cancer Center
500,000	Foundation for the Junior Blind, Los Angeles, CA — toward the capital campaign for renovation and new facility construction
500,000	Hebrew Union College Jewish Institute of Religion, Los Angeles, CA — toward furnishing and equipping the Ahmanson Resource Center at the Cultural Center for American Jewish Life
500,000	Nature Conservancy, San Francisco, CA — toward the Santa Margarita River/Santa Ana Mountains Project

Amado Foundation, Maurice

CONTACT
Stella Amado Lavis
President
Maurice Amado Foundation
3600 Wilshire Blvd., Ste. 1228
Los Angeles, CA 90010
(213) 381-3632

FINANCIAL SUMMARY
Recent Giving: $898,800 (fiscal 1993); $823,077 (fiscal 1992); $717,049 (fiscal 1991)

Assets: $21,289,629 (fiscal 1993); $20,216,814 (fiscal 1992); $18,500,624 (fiscal 1991)

EIN: 95-6041700

CONTRIBUTIONS SUMMARY
Donor(s): The foundation was incorporated in 1961 by the late Maurice Amado .

Typical Recipients: • *Arts & Humanities:* Arts Outreach, Ethnic & Folk Arts, Libraries, Museums/Galleries, Music • *Civic & Public Affairs:* General, Philanthropic Organizations, Safety • *Education:* Colleges & Universities, Education Funds, Medical Education, Private Education (Precollege), Religious Education, Science/Mathematics Education • *Health:* Clinics/Medical Centers, Health Organizations, Hospitals, Medical Research • *International:* Foreign Arts Organizations, Foreign Educational Institutions, Missionary/Religious Activities • *Religion:* Jewish Causes, Religious Organizations, Synagogues/Temples • *Social Services:* Community Centers, Crime Prevention, People with Disabilities, Recreation & Athletics, Senior Services, United Funds/United Ways, Youth Organizations

Grant Types: capital, conference/seminar, endowment, general support, multiyear/continuing support, operating expenses, project, and research

Geographic Distribution: emphasis on Los Angeles, CA, New York, NY, and Israel

GIVING OFFICERS
Bernice Amado: vp, secy, dir

Ralph D. Amado: dir

Theodore M. Amado: dir

Renee Kaplan: dir

Stella Amado Lavis: pres, dir

Victor R. Lavis: dir

Regina A. Tarica: treas, dir

Samuel R. Tarica: asst secy

APPLICATION INFORMATION
Initial Approach:

There is no formal application procedure. The foundation requests application be made in writing.

Include a description of the program or project and other essential information needed for approval.

Deadlines are March 1 and October 1.

Restrictions on Giving: The foundation does not make grants to individuals.

GRANTS ANALYSIS
Total Grants: $898,800

Number of Grants: 45

Highest Grant: $115,000

Average Grant: $19,973

Typical Range: $2,000 to $50,000

Disclosure Period: fiscal year ending November 30, 1993

Note: Recent grants are derived from a fiscal 1993 grants list.

RECENT GRANTS

Library

7,000	Bala Cynwyd Library, Bala Cynwyd, CA

General

115,000	Jewish Museum, New York, NY
105,000	Los Angeles Sephardic Homes for the Aged, Los Angeles, CA
100,000	Jewish Homes for the Aging of Greater Los Angeles, Los Angeles, CA
100,000	Sephardic Temple Tifereth Israel, Los Angeles, CA — Maurice Amado Perpetual building endowment fund
100,000	University of California Los Angeles Maurice Amado Chair in Sephardic Studies, Los Angeles, CA

American President Companies, Ltd. / American President Companies Foundation

Revenue: $2.79 billion
Employees: 5,000
Headquarters: Oakland, CA
SIC Major Group: Holding Companies Nec, Deep Sea Foreign Transportation of Freight, and Freight Transportation Arrangement

CONTACT
Lora Breed
Corporate Contributions Administrator
American President Companies Foundation
1111 Broadway
Oakland, CA 94607
(510) 272-8177

FINANCIAL SUMMARY
Recent Giving: $540,000 (1995 est.); $550,000 (1994); $442,777 (1993)

Assets: $351,203 (1993); $480,070 (1992); $350,249 (1990)

Gifts Received: $400,000 (1993)

Fiscal Note: Company gives directly and through the foundation. Giving figure for 1993 is foundation giving only. Above figures exclude nonmonetary support. Foundation receives contributions from American President Companies Ltd.

EIN: 94-2955262

CONTRIBUTIONS SUMMARY

Typical Recipients: • *Arts & Humanities:* Arts Associations & Councils, Ballet, Dance, Libraries, Museums/Galleries, Music, Performing Arts, Theater • *Civic & Public Affairs:* African American Affairs, Clubs, Community Foundations, Municipalities/Towns, Parades/Festivals, Professional & Trade Associations, Urban & Community Affairs • *Education:* Colleges & Universities, Continuing Education, Education Associations, Education Funds, International Exchange, International Studies, Legal Education, Minority Education, Private Education (Precollege), Public Education (Precollege) • *Environment:* General • *Health:* AIDS/HIV, Children's Health/Hospitals, Hospitals, Multiple Sclerosis, Single-Disease Health Associations • *Science:* Science Museums • *Social Services:* Community Centers, Community Service Organizations, Domestic Violence, People with Disabilities, Recreation & Athletics, Refugee Assistance, United Funds/United Ways, Youth Organizations

Grant Types: employee matching gifts and matching

Note: The company awards corporate volunteer service grants to nonprofits where employees volunteer their time.

Nonmonetary Support Types: donated equipment, loaned employees, and loaned executives

Note: Estimate of nonmonetary support is unavailable.

Geographic Distribution: employee donations are matched nationally

Operating Locations: CA (Oakland)

CORP. OFFICERS

Maryellen B. Cattani: *B* Bakersfield CA 1943 *ED* Vassar Coll AB 1965; Univ CA Berkeley JD 1968 *CURR EMPL* sr vp, gen couns, secy: Am Pres Cos Ltd *CORP AFFIL* dir: ABM Indus Inc, Bank West *NONPR AFFIL* mem: Am Bar Assn, Am Corp Couns Assn, Bar Assn San Francisco, CA Bar Assn, CA Women Lawyers, Ctr Pub Resources San Francisco, San Francisco Chamber Commerce, Womens Forum W; pres, regent, trust: St Marys Coll CA; trust: Head-Royce Sch

Joji Hayashi: *B* 1939 *ED* Armstrong Coll BBA 1963 *CURR EMPL* pres, ceo, dir: Am Pres Lines Ltd *CORP AFFIL* pres, dir: Eagle Marine Svcs Ltd

John Mitchell Lillie: *B* Chicago IL 1937 *ED* Stanford Univ MS 1959; Stanford Univ MBA 1962-1964 *CURR EMPL* chmn, pres, ceo: Am Pres Cos Ltd *CORP AFFIL* chmn: Am Pres Lines Ltd; dir: The Gap Inc, Vons Cos Inc *NONPR AFFIL* mem: Beta Theta Pi, Tau Beta Pi; trust: Stanford Univ

Timothy J. Rhein: *B* San Francisco CA 1941 *ED* Univ Santa Clara 1962 *CURR EMPL* pres, dir: APL Land Transport Svcs *CORP AFFIL* pres, dir: Am Pres Tracking Ltd

Will Miller Storey: *B* Vancouver WA 1931 *ED* OR St Univ BA 1953; Univ WA *CURR EMPL* exec vp, cfo, treas, dir: Am Pres Cos Ltd *CORP AFFIL* exec vp, cfo, dir: Am Pres Lines Ltd *PHIL AFFIL* trust: Schuller Fund

GIVING OFFICERS

Maryellen B. Cattani: sr vp, gen couns, secy *CURR EMPL* sr vp, gen couns, secy: Am Pres Cos Ltd (see above)

Joji Hayashi: sr vp *CURR EMPL* pres, ceo, dir: Am Pres Lines Ltd (see above)

John Mitchell Lillie: chmn, pres *CURR EMPL* chmn, pres, ceo: Am Pres Cos Ltd (see above)

Timothy J. Rhein: sr vp, dir *CURR EMPL* pres, dir: APL Land Transport Svcs (see above)

Will Miller Storey: exec vp, cfo *CURR EMPL* exec vp, cfo, treas, dir: Am Pres Cos Ltd *PHIL AFFIL* trust: Schuller Fund (see above)

William J. Stuebgen: treas *B* Denver CO 1947 *ED* CO St Univ BS 1969 *CURR EMPL* vp, contr, chief acct off: Am Pres Cos Ltd

Timothy J. Windle: asst secy

APPLICATION INFORMATION

Initial Approach: *Initial Contact:* in writing, using forms provided for this purpose or by means of other documentation acceptable to the foundation *Deadlines:* none *Note:* Gives primarily through employee matching gifts and employee volunteer service awards.

Restrictions on Giving: The following organizations are not eligible: religious, veteran, labor or fraternal organizations (except for programs which benefit the community-at-large), political parties, organizations, candidates or issues.

GRANTS ANALYSIS

Total Grants: $442,777

Number of Grants: 201

Highest Grant: $240,000

Average Grant: $2,203

Typical Range: $500 to $10,000

Disclosure Period: 1993

Note: Analysis is based on foundation giving only. Recent grants are derived from a 1993 Form 990.

RECENT GRANTS

Library

1,000	American Merchant Marine Library Association

General

240,000	United Way
20,000	Oakland Sharing the Vision, Oakland, CA
10,150	Stanford University, Stanford, CA
7,500	Transportation Center
5,701	Project Open Hand, San Francisco, CA

Apple Computer, Inc.

Revenue: $9.18 billion
Employees: 11,963
Headquarters: Cupertino, CA
SIC Major Group: Electronic Computers and Computers, Peripherals & Software

CONTACT

Fred Silverman
Manager, Community Affairs
Apple Computer Inc.
1 Infinite Loop
Cupertino, CA 95014
(408) 974-2974
Note: The company's World Wide Web address is http://www.apple.com

FINANCIAL SUMMARY

Recent Giving: $7,500,000 (fiscal 1993 approx.); $7,500,000 (fiscal 1992 approx.); $8,637,000 (fiscal 1991 approx.)

Fiscal Note: All contributions are made directly by the company, primarily in the form of computer equipment (see below). Above figures include nonmonetary support. Cash grants are made to community-based nonprofit agencies in the San Francisco Bay area.

CONTRIBUTIONS SUMMARY

Typical Recipients: • *Arts & Humanities:* Community Arts, Museums/Galleries, Music, Performing Arts, Theater • *Education:* Elementary Education (Private), Minority Education, Public Education (Precollege) • *Environment:* General • *Health:* Single-Disease Health Associations

Grant Types: employee matching gifts, general support, and project

Note: Company primarily makes equipment grants. Employee matching gift ratio: 1 to 1. Company matches emplyee grants up to $1,000.

Nonmonetary Support: $7,000,000 (fiscal 1993); $8,000,000 (fiscal 1991); $8,620,000 (fiscal 1990)

Nonmonetary Support Types: donated equipment

Note: Donated computer equipment constitutes the bulk of the company's giving. The remaining gifts are usually in the form of cash donations.

Geographic Distribution: nationally

Operating Locations: CA (Cupertino, Napa, Sacramento), CO (Fountain), TX (Austin)

CORP. OFFICERS

Armas Clifford Markkula, Jr.: *B* 1942 *ED* Univ Southern CA MS *CURR EMPL* chmn: Apple Computer Inc *CORP AFFIL* chmn: ACM Aviation; dir: San Jose Jet Ctr; fdr: Echelon Corp

Michael H. Spindler: *B* 1942 *ED* Rheinische Fachochschule MBA *CURR EMPL* pres, ceo, dir: Apple Computer Inc *CORP AFFIL* chmn, dir: Claris Corp

GIVING OFFICERS

Andrea Gooden: *CURR EMPL* program mgr ed grants: Apple Computer Inc

Anne McMullin: *CURR EMPL* program mgr regional & intl programs: Apple Computer Inc

Fred Silverman: *CURR EMPL* mgr commun aff: Apple Computer Inc

APPLICATION INFORMATION

Initial Approach: *Initial Contact:* call or write the Community Affairs department for latest guidelines which outline proposal requirements *Deadlines:* refer to guidelines *Note:* Application procedures should be requested prior to submission of full proposal, as only requests that adhere to Apple's format will be accepted.

Restrictions on Giving: Individuals, government agencies (except those serving as a vital link in a network of private nonprofit groups), and religious or political organizations are ineligible for corporate grants.

Does not make grants for endowment funds, building construction or acquisition, publications, salaries, sponsorship of athletic events, fund-raising events, raffles, auctions, door prizes, or traditionally parent-supported activities, such as P.T.A., Scouts, Little League, etc.

Recipients must adhere to Apple's internal nondiscrimination policies.

GRANTS ANALYSIS

Total Grants: $7,500,000

Number of Grants: 400*

Highest Grant: $150,000*

Average Grant: $6,000*

Typical Range: $5,000 to $10,000

Disclosure Period: fiscal year ending September 30, 1993

Note: The figures for number of grants, average grant, and highest grant were supplied by the company.

Argyros Foundation

CONTACT

Charles E. Packard
Trustee
Argyros Fdn.
950 S Coast Dr., Ste. 200
Costa Mesa, CA 92626
(714) 434-5000

FINANCIAL SUMMARY

Recent Giving: $672,611 (fiscal 1993); $1,228,951 (fiscal 1992); $822,796 (fiscal 1991)

Assets: $16,947,742 (fiscal 1993); $14,451,183 (fiscal 1992); $13,171,869 (fiscal 1991)

Gifts Received: $369,885 (fiscal 1993); $390,000 (fiscal 1992); $402,726 (fiscal 1991)

Fiscal Note: In fiscal 1993, contributions were received from the Argyros Charitable Trust No. 4.

EIN: 95-3421867

CONTRIBUTIONS SUMMARY

Donor(s): the Argyros Charitable Trusts

Typical Recipients: • *Arts & Humanities:* Arts Associations & Councils, Arts Centers, Ballet, Historic Preservation, History & Archaeology, Libraries, Museums/Galleries, Music, Opera, Performing Arts • *Civic & Public Affairs:* Clubs, General, Hispanic Affairs, Philanthropic Organizations, Public Policy, Safety, Women's Affairs • *Education:* Business Education, Colleges & Universities, Education Funds, Student Aid • *Environment:* Resource Conservation • *Health:* AIDS/HIV, Cancer, Clinics/Medical Centers, Hospitals, Medical Research, Preventive Medicine/Wellness Organizations, Single-Disease Health Associations • *International:* International Affairs • *Religion:* Churches, Dioceses, Jewish Causes, Religious Organizations, Religious Welfare, Social/Policy Issues • *Science:* Science Museums, Scientific Centers & Institutes, Scientific Organizations • *Social Services:* Big Brother/Big Sister, Child Abuse, Child Welfare, Community Service Organizations, Domestic Violence, Food/Clothing Distribution, Homes, People with Disabilities, Recreation & Athletics, Scouts, Substance Abuse, United Funds/United Ways, Youth Organizations

Grant Types: capital and project

Geographic Distribution: focus on CA

GIVING OFFICERS

George L. Argyros: secy, dir, trust *B* Detroit MI 1937 *ED* Chapman Coll BS 1959; MI St Univ *CURR EMPL* pres: Arnel Devel Co *CORP AFFIL* chmn: Arnel Homes, Arnel Mgmt; chmn, dir: Air Cal; dir: ACI Holdings, First Am Fin Corp; mem: Baseballs Revenue Sharing Comm; owner, dir: HAL Inc *NONPR AFFIL* chmn: Western WA Un Cerebral Palsy Telethon; chmn bd trust: Chapman Coll; chmn fundraising: Natl Multiple Sclerosis Soc; dir: Am League; mem: Restructuring Comm, World Aff Counc, Young Pres Org *PHIL AFFIL* vchmn, cfo, dir: Arnold and Mabel Beckman Foundation

Julie A. Argyros: pres, dir, trust

Carol Campbell: exec dir

Warren Finley: trust

Charles Packard: trust

APPLICATION INFORMATION

Initial Approach: Include a description of organization, amount requested, purpose of funds sought, recently audited financial statement, and proof of tax-exempt status. Deadline is June 1.

GRANTS ANALYSIS

Total Grants: $672,611

Number of Grants: 59

Highest Grant: $134,666

Typical Range: $500 to $112,500

Disclosure Period: fiscal year ending July 31, 1993

Note: Recent grants are derived from a fiscal 1993 Form 990.

RECENT GRANTS

Library

1,600	Richard Nixon Library and Birthplace, Yorba Linda, CA

General

134,666	Boy Scouts of America, Santa Ana, CA
112,500	Doheny Eye Institute, Los Angeles, CA
55,000	Horatio Alger Association, Washington, DC
50,000	Center for Strategic and International Studies, Washington, DC
48,000	Chapman University, Orange, CA

Arkelian Foundation, Ben H. and Gladys

CONTACT

Frank I. Ford, Jr.
Secretary, Treasurer, Chief Financial Officer
Ben H. and Gladys Arkelian Fdn.
PO Box 1825
Bakersfield, CA 93303
(805) 324-9801

FINANCIAL SUMMARY

Recent Giving: $99,400 (1993); $108,316 (1992); $114,098 (1989)

Assets: $2,041,215 (1993); $2,771,548 (1992); $2,635,045 (1989)

EIN: 95-6103223

CONTRIBUTIONS SUMMARY

Typical Recipients: • *Arts & Humanities:* Historic Preservation, History & Archaeology, Libraries, Museums/Galleries, Music, Opera, Public Broadcasting • *Civic & Public Affairs:* Legal Aid • *Education:* Colleges & Universities, General, Preschool Education, Private Education (Precollege), Public Education (Precollege) • *Health:* Arthritis, Cancer, Emergency/Ambulance Services, Health Funds, Hospitals, Multiple Sclerosis, Single-Disease Health Associations • *International:* Health Care/Hospitals • *Religion:* Churches, Religious Organizations, Religious Welfare • *Social Services:* Child Welfare, Community Service Organizations, Family Services, Homes, People with Disabilities, Recreation & Athletics, Substance Abuse, United Funds/United Ways, Youth Organizations

Grant Types: general support

Geographic Distribution: limited to Kern County, CA

GIVING OFFICERS

D. Bianco: vp, asst secy, dir, trust

Frank I. Ford, Jr.: cfo, secy, treas

Harvey H. Means: pres, dir *PHIL AFFIL* vp, secy: Harry and Ethel West Foundation

APPLICATION INFORMATION
Initial Approach: Send brief letter of inquiry describing program. There are no deadlines.

Restrictions on Giving: Limited to Kern County, CA.

GRANTS ANALYSIS
Total Grants: $99,400
Number of Grants: 30
Highest Grant: $35,840
Typical Range: $200 to $10,000
Disclosure Period: 1993

Note: Recent grants are derived from a 1993 Form 990.

RECENT GRANTS

Library
35,840	Kern County Library Fund, Kern, CA

General
10,000	Cal State University, CA — building fund
7,500	Kern Valley Medical Fund, Kern, CA
5,000	Good Shepherd Foundation, Bakersfield, CA
5,000	Salvation Army, Bakersfield, CA
3,600	Bakersfield Rescue Mission, Bakersfield, CA

BankAmerica Corp. / BankAmerica Foundation

Revenue: $16.53 billion
Employees: 83,200
Headquarters: San Francisco, CA
SIC Major Group: Bank Holding Companies and National Commercial Banks

CONTACT
Caroline O. Boitano
President & Executive Director
BankAmerica Foundation
PO Box 37000
Dept. 3246
San Francisco, CA 94137
(415) 953-3175
Note: The company's World Wide Web address is http://www.bankamerica.com

FINANCIAL SUMMARY
Recent Giving: $26,700,000 (1995 est.); $24,037,289 (1994); $14,854,325 (1993)

Assets: $97,546 (1993); $3,225,929 (1992); $731,211 (1991)

Gifts Received: $12,739,253 (1993)

Fiscal Note: Figures for 1995 and 1994 contain foundation and direct corporate giving. In 1994, foundation giving totaled $14,748,289 and direct contributions totaled $9,289,000. Figure for 1993 represents foundation giving only. Above figures exclude nonmonetary support. In 1993, gifts were received from BankAmerica Corp. and Seafirst Bank Matching Gifts Program.
EIN: 94-1670382

CONTRIBUTIONS SUMMARY

Typical Recipients: • *Arts & Humanities:* Arts Appreciation, Arts Associations & Councils, Arts Centers, Arts Festivals, Arts Funds, Arts Institutes, Ballet, Community Arts, Ethnic & Folk Arts, Historic Preservation, Libraries, Museums/Galleries, Music, Opera, Performing Arts, Public Broadcasting, Theater • *Civic & Public Affairs:* Asian American Affairs, Botanical Gardens/Parks, Business/Free Enterprise, Civil Rights, Community Foundations, Economic Development, Employment/Job Training, Hispanic Affairs, Housing, Native American Affairs, Nonprofit Management, Professional & Trade Associations, Public Policy, Rural Affairs, Urban & Community Affairs, Women's Affairs • *Education:* Afterschool/Enrichment Programs, Agricultural Education, Business Education, Colleges & Universities, Community & Junior Colleges, Economic Education, Education Funds, Education Reform, Elementary Education (Private), Engineering/Technological Education, Environmental Education, General, International Exchange, International Studies, Medical Education, Minority Education, Science/Mathematics Education, Student Aid • *Health:* Children's Health/Hospitals, Clinics/Medical Centers, Emergency/Ambulance Services, Health Organizations, Hospitals, Prenatal Health Issues • *International:* International Relations • *Science:* Science Museums, Scientific Centers & Institutes • *Social Services:* Child Abuse, Child Welfare, Community Service Organizations, Family Services, Food/Clothing Distribution, People with Disabilities, Substance Abuse, United Funds/United Ways, YMCA/YWCA/YMHA/YWHA, Youth Organizations

Grant Types: capital, general support, project, and seed money

Nonmonetary Support: $2,000,000 (1989); $2,000,000 (1988); $3,000,000 (1987)

Nonmonetary Support Types: cause-related marketing & promotion, donated equipment, and loaned employees

Note: Estimated value of nonmonetary support is $2.0 million annually.

Geographic Distribution: nationally, with emphasis on California; some international giving where corporation operates

Operating Locations: CA (Los Angeles, San Francisco, Walnut Creek), FL, IL (Chicago), NY (New York, Woodside), PA (Philadelphia), TX (Dallas, Houston), WA (Seattle)

CORP. OFFICERS
Kathleen J. Burke: *B* 1952 *CURR EMPL* exec vp personnel rels off: BankAm Corp

Lewis Waldo Coleman: *B* San Francisco CA 1942 *ED* Stanford Univ BA 1965 *CURR EMPL* vchmn: BankAm Corp *CORP AFFIL* dir: Chiron Corp; vchmn, cfo, treas, dir: Bank of Am Natl Trust & Savings Assn

Donald A. Mullane: *B* Los Angeles CA 1938 *ED* Univ Southern CA *CURR EMPL* exec vp: BankAm Corp *CORP AFFIL* dir: Maryvale Inc; exec vp: BankAm Natl Trust & Savings Assn *NONPR AFFIL* bd couns: Sch Urban Planning; chmn: CA Commun Reinvestment Corp, Los Angeles Commun Reinvestment Comm, Univ WA Pacific Coast Sch Banking; co-chmn: Commun Reinvestment Inst; dir: AP Giannini Fdn, Las Familias, Los Angeles Sports Counc, St Vincent Hosp; mem: CA Bankers Assn, Los Angeles Chamber Commerce, Retail Bankers Am *CLUB AFFIL* Bankers San Francisco, City Bunker Hill, Hacienda GC *PHIL AFFIL* dir, mem investment comm: Bank of America - Giannini Foundation

Thomas E. Peterson: *B* 1936 *CURR EMPL* vchmn: BankAm Corp

Richard Morris Rosenberg: *B* Fall River MA 1930 *ED* Suffolk Univ BS 1952; Golden St Coll MBA 1963; Golden St Coll LLB 1966 *CURR EMPL* chmn, pres, ceo: BankAm Corp *CORP AFFIL* chmn: Mastercard Intl; dir: Airborne Express Co, Am Magnetics Corp, Northrop Grumman Corp, Potlatch Corp, Seafirst Corp, Seattle-First Natl Bank, Visa USA *NONPR AFFIL* mem: Am Bankers Assn, Bank Mktg Assn, CA Bar Assn; mem bd regents: Univ CO Sch Bank Mktg; trust: CA Inst Tech, Claremont Coll, Golden Gate Univ, Golden St Coll *CLUB AFFIL* Hillcrest CC, Rainier

GIVING OFFICERS
Caroline O. Boitano: pres, exec dir *PHIL AFFIL* asst secy, dir, secy nominating comm: Bank of America - Giannini Foundation

Kathleen J. Burke: trust *CURR EMPL* exec vp personnel rels off: BankAm Corp (see above)

Sandra Cohen: secy

Lewis Waldo Coleman: trust *CURR EMPL* vchmn: BankAm Corp (see above)

Raymond M. McKee: trust

Donald A. Mullane: chmn *CURR EMPL* exec vp: BankAm Corp *PHIL AFFIL* dir, mem investment comm: Bank of America - Giannini Foundation (see above)

Thomas E. Peterson: trust *CURR EMPL* vchmn: BankAm Corp (see above)

Richard Morris Rosenberg: trust *CURR EMPL* chmn, pres, ceo: BankAm Corp (see above)

Judy Tufo: fin off

James Wagele: vp

Kristine Yee: treas

APPLICATION INFORMATION
Initial Approach: *Initial Contact:* brief letter *Include Information On:* name and address of organization and contact; organization's mission; copy of IRS letter of designation with tax ID number; list of board members; population and geographic area served; purpose for which grant is requested; total cost of accomplishing purpose; amount of request; list of funding

sources with amounts of other funding obtained, pledged, or requested *Deadlines:* none; decisions made quarterly

Restrictions on Giving: Generally not receptive to individuals, organizations without 501(c)(3) public charity status, memorial campaigns, fund-raising events, political activities, religious organizations for sectarian purposes, research, athletic events and programs, endowment campaigns, advertising, member agencies of united funds, book or film or video projects, or organizations that discriminate on the basis of age, race, creed, or sex.

OTHER THINGS TO KNOW

In 1992, BankAmerica Corp. and BankAmerica Foundation acquired, respectively, Security Pacific Corp. and Security Pacific Foundation and related entities, Security Pacific Foundation Northwest and Security Pacific Bank Arizona Foundation. The foundations associated with Security Pacific completely dissolved; the giving program for BankAmerica Corp. and its subsidiaries continues to be contained completely within BankAmerica Foundation.

GRANTS ANALYSIS

Total Grants: $14,854,325

Number of Grants: 924

Highest Grant: $450,000

Average Grant: $16,076

Typical Range: $2,500 to $25,000

Disclosure Period: 1993

Note: Recent grants are derived from a 1993 Form 990.

RECENT GRANTS

Library

50,000	Library Foundation of San Francisco, San Francisco, CA — capital support $250,000 over five years
50,000	Ronald Reagan Presidential Foundation, Simi Valley, CA — capital support for library
25,000	Library Foundation of Los Angeles, Los Angeles, CA — $100,000 grant payable over four years for repair and renovation of the historic library building and collection, restoration, and catalogue

General

450,000	United Way of Bay Area, San Francisco, CA — annual gift
450,000	United Way of Bay Area, San Francisco, CA — annual gift
425,000	United Way of Bay Area, San Francisco, CA — annual gift
278,500	Citizens Scholastic Foundation of America, St. Peter, MN — achievement awards program
240,000	United Way of Orange County, Orange, CA — annual payment

Baskin-Robbins USA Co.

Sales: $79.6 million
Employees: 800
Headquarters: Glendale, CA
SIC Major Group: Eating & Drinking Places, Food & Kindred Products, and Holding & Other Investment Offices

CONTACT

Kathie Bellamy
Manager, Consumer Relations
Baskin-Robbins
31 Baskin-Robbins Pl.
Glendale, CA 91201
(818) 956-0031

FINANCIAL SUMMARY

Fiscal Note: Company does not disclose contributions figures.

CONTRIBUTIONS SUMMARY

Baskin-Robbins sponsors children's charities, a trust fund set up to benefit Muscular Dystrophy Association, and St. Jude's Research Hospital. Also is involved in local "Adopt-A-School" program.

Volunteerism: In-house volunteer commitee raises $10,000 to $12,000 each year by hosting fund raising events. Money raised goes to company's Children's Charities Trust Fund. Employees also support Angel Tree, a holiday program benefiting needy children.

Typical Recipients: • *Arts & Humanities:* Libraries • *Education:* General • *Health:* Adolescent Health Issues, Alzheimers Disease, Children's Health/Hospitals, Diabetes, Heart • *Social Services:* At-Risk Youth, Child Welfare, Shelters/Homelessness, Substance Abuse, Volunteer Services

Grant Types: general support

Nonmonetary Support Types: donated equipment, donated products, and in-kind services

Operating Locations: CA (Glendale), CT, MO, NJ, NY

CORP. OFFICERS

Glenn Bacheller: *CURR EMPL* pres: Baskin-Robbins USA Co

GIVING OFFICERS

Kathie Bellamy: *CURR EMPL* mgr, consumer rels: Baskin-Robbins USA Co

APPLICATION INFORMATION

Initial Approach: Applicants should send a brief letter including a description of organization and amount requested.

Restrictions on Giving: Does not support individuals, religious organizations for sectarian purposes, or political or lobbying groups.

Bay Area Foods

Sales: $600.0 million
Employees: 2,300
Headquarters: San Rafael, CA
SIC Major Group: Holding & Other Investment Offices and Wholesale Trade—Nondurable Goods

CONTACT

Kathy Graf
Director, Personnel
Bay Area Foods
33 San Pablo Ave.
San Rafael, CA 94903
(415) 472-5860

FINANCIAL SUMMARY

Fiscal Note: Annual Giving Range: less than $100,000

CONTRIBUTIONS SUMMARY

Social services are the highest priority, with united funds receiving the most support. Youth organizations and community centers also are supported. Civic and public affairs, education, and health receive frequent contributions. Civic contributions go to better government, business and free enterprise, urban and community affairs, safety organizations, and municipalities. Education contributions support colleges and universities and public education (precollege); health contributions support hospitals and substance abuse programs. Libraries also are of interest.

Typical Recipients: • *Arts & Humanities:* Libraries • *Civic & Public Affairs:* Business/Free Enterprise, Municipalities/Towns, Safety, Urban & Community Affairs • *Education:* Colleges & Universities, Public Education (Precollege) • *Health:* Hospitals • *Social Services:* Community Centers, Substance Abuse, United Funds/United Ways, Youth Organizations

Grant Types: capital and general support

Nonmonetary Support Types: donated products

Geographic Distribution: near headquarters and operating locations only

Operating Locations: CA, VA

CORP. OFFICERS

Ron Glass: *CURR EMPL* pres: Bay Area Foods

APPLICATION INFORMATION

Initial Approach: Initial contact may be by phone call or letter. Letter should include a description of the organization, amount requested, and purpose for which funds are sought. Applications are accepted at any time.

Restrictions on Giving: Company does not contribute to fraternal organizations, individuals, political or lobbying groups, or religious organizations for sectarian purposes.

Bechtel, Jr. Foundation, S. D.

CONTACT
Stephen D. Bechtel, Jr.
President
S. D. Bechtel, Jr. Foundation
PO Box 193809
San Francisco, CA 94119-3809
(415) 768-1234

FINANCIAL SUMMARY
Recent Giving: $1,395,767 (1992);
$1,243,008 (1991); $1,122,365 (1990)

Assets: $23,606,301 (1992); $22,918,125
(1991); $19,483,136 (1990)

Gifts Received: $792,152 (1992); $675,099
(1991); $616,639 (1990)

Fiscal Note: In 1992, contributions were received from the S.D. Bechtel Charitable Uni-Trust II and the L.P. Bechtel Charitable Uni-Trust II. In 1991, contributions were received from Mr. and Mrs. S.D. Bechtel, Jr.

EIN: 94-6066138

CONTRIBUTIONS SUMMARY
Donor(s): The foundation was established in 1957 by Mr. and Mrs. S. D. Bechtel, Jr.

Typical Recipients: • *Arts & Humanities:* Historic Preservation, History & Archaeology, Libraries, Museums/Galleries, Music, Opera • *Civic & Public Affairs:* Botanical Gardens/Parks, Clubs, Legal Aid, Philanthropic Organizations, Professional & Trade Associations, Women's Affairs, Zoos/Aquariums • *Education:* Colleges & Universities, Economic Education, Engineering/Technological Education, International Studies, Legal Education, Private Education (Precollege), Science/Mathematics Education, Student Aid • *Environment:* Air/Water Quality, General, Resource Conservation • *Health:* Cancer, Medical Research, Prenatal Health Issues, Single-Disease Health Associations • *Religion:* Churches • *Science:* Science Museums, Scientific Centers & Institutes • *Social Services:* Animal Protection, Homes, People with Disabilities, Recreation & Athletics, United Funds/United Ways, Volunteer Services, Youth Organizations

Grant Types: capital, challenge, general support, operating expenses, and scholarship

Geographic Distribution: focus on the San Francisco Bay area

GIVING OFFICERS
Elizabeth Hogan Bechtel: vp, dir *PHIL AFFIL* dir, vp: Shenandoah Foundation

Riley P. Bechtel: dir *B* 1952 *ED* Univ CA Davis BS 1975; Stanford Univ JD 1980; Stanford Univ MBA 1980 *CURR EMPL* pres, dir: Bechtel Group Inc *CORP AFFIL* chmn, dir: Am Bechtel Inc, Bechtel Energy Corp, Bechtel Intl, Bechtel N Am Power Corp, Bechtel Oper Svcs Corp, Bechtel Overseas Corp, Bechtel Power Corp, Overseas Bechtel Inc; pres, dir: Bechtel Corp *PHIL AFFIL* chmn, dir: Bechtel Foundation; pres, dir: Royal Barney Hogan Foundation

Stephen Davison Bechtel, Jr.: don, pres, dir *B* Oakland CA 1925 *ED* Univ CO 1944; Purdue Univ BS 1946; Stanford Univ MBA 1948 *CURR EMPL* chmn emeritus, dir: Bechtel Group *CORP AFFIL* chmn: Bechtel Investments, Fremont Group, Sequoia Ventures; dir: IBM Corp; vp: Pure Water Corp *NONPR AFFIL* dir: Am Soc French Legion Honor; fellow: Am Acad Arts & Sci, Am Soc Chem Engg; foreign mem: Fellowship Engg UK; hon fellow: Inst Chem Engrs UK; life couns: Conf Bd; mem: Am Inst Mining Metallurgical Petroleum Engrs, Am Soc Engg Ed, Beta Theta Pi, CA Acad Sci, Chi Epsilon, Fellowship Engg, Labor Mgmt Group, Natl Acad Engg, Natl Action Counc Minorities Engg, Natl Soc Professional Engrs, Purdue Univ Pres Counc, Tau Beta Pi; mem adv counc: Stanford Univ Grad Sch Bus; mem policy comm: Bus Roundtable; trust, mem: CA PolyTech Inst *CLUB AFFIL* Augusta Natl GC, Bohemian, Claremont CC, Cypress Point, Links, Metro, Mount Royal, Natl GC, Pacific-Union, Ramada, San Francisco GC, Thunderbird CC, Vancouver, York *PHIL AFFIL* vp, dir: Royal Barney Hogan Foundation; dir: ABC Foundation, Bechtel Foundation

Thomas G. Flynn: vp *PHIL AFFIL* sr vp: Bechtel Foundation

Theodore J. Van Bebber: vp, treas

APPLICATION INFORMATION
Restrictions on Giving: The foundation does not make grants to individuals.

GRANTS ANALYSIS
Total Grants: $1,395,767

Number of Grants: 120

Highest Grant: $400,000

Average Grant: $11,631

Typical Range: $1,000 to $25,000

Disclosure Period: 1992

Note: Recent grants are derived from a 1992 Form 990.

RECENT GRANTS

Library
5,000	University of California, Berkeley, CA — Bancroft Library

General
400,000	California Institute of Technology, Pasadena, CA — fellowships
100,000	California Institute of Technology, Pasadena, CA — campus improvement
100,000	Massachusetts Institute of Technology, Cambridge, MA — Bechtel Lecture Hall
100,000	Purdue University, West Lafayette, IN — Geotech Engineering Lab
100,000	University of Colorado at Boulder, Boulder, CO — Computer Graphics Lap Fund

Berger Foundation, H. N. and Frances C.

CONTACT
Ronald M. Auen
President
H. N. and Frances C. Berger Foundation
PO Box 661178
Arcadia, CA 91006-1178
(818) 447-3551

FINANCIAL SUMMARY
Recent Giving: $13,282,907 (1992);
$10,909,472 (1991); $7,708,560 (1990)

Assets: $232,796,145 (1992); $251,585,168
(1991); $229,500,573 (1990)

Gifts Received: $10,237,342 (1992);
$62,862,521 (1990); $157,799,313 (1989)

Fiscal Note: In 1990, the foundation received $62,862,521 from the H.N. and Frances C. Berger Trust No. 2. In 1992, the foundation received $9,772,884 from H.N and F.C. Berger Trust No. 1, $256,543 from the Berger Family Trust A, and $207,915 from H.N. Berger Estate.

EIN: 95-6048939

CONTRIBUTIONS SUMMARY
Donor(s): The foundation was established in 1961 by H. N. Berger and Francis C. Berger.

Typical Recipients: • *Arts & Humanities:* Arts Associations & Councils, Arts Festivals, Arts Outreach, Libraries, Museums/Galleries, Music • *Civic & Public Affairs:* Botanical Gardens/Parks, Housing, Municipalities/Towns, Professional & Trade Associations, Public Policy, Safety, Zoos/Aquariums • *Education:* Arts/Humanities Education, Colleges & Universities, Education Funds, Engineering/Technological Education, Public Education (Precollege), Science/Mathematics Education, Special Education, Student Aid • *Environment:* General • *Health:* AIDS/HIV, Alzheimers Disease, Cancer, Children's Health/Hospitals, Clinics/Medical Centers, Emergency/Ambulance Services, Heart, Hospices, Hospitals, Medical Research, Nursing Services, Single-Disease Health Associations • *Religion:* Bible Study/Translation, Churches, Religious Organizations • *Social Services:* Child Welfare, Community Centers, Community Service Organizations, Delinquency & Criminal Rehabilitation, Domestic Violence, Food/Clothing Distribution, Substance Abuse, Youth Organizations

Grant Types: capital, endowment, fellowship, general support, project, and scholarship

Geographic Distribution: emphasis on California

GIVING OFFICERS
Shirley Allen: vp, treas *B* 1930 *CORP AFFIL* vp: Utility Boring Inc

Joan Auen: secy, dir

Ronald M. Auen: pres, dir *B* 1932

Robert M. Barton: dir

John N. Berger: vp, dir

Jim Kuhn: dir

Christopher McGuire: vp, dir

Douglas Vance: dir

Lewis Webb, Jr.: vp, dir

APPLICATION INFORMATION
Initial Approach:

Applicants should send a brief letter of inquiry of one to three pages.

The letter should include a description of the project, the amount of the grant request, proof of tax-exempt status, and a short history and purpose of the organization.

There are no deadlines.

The board meets semi-annually.

GRANTS ANALYSIS
Total Grants: $13,282,907

Number of Grants: 72

Highest Grant: $2,751,625

Average Grant: $73,942*

Typical Range: $20,000 to $100,000

Disclosure Period: 1992

Note: Average grant figure excludes four grants totaling $8,254,875. Recent grants are derived from a 1992 Form 990.

RECENT GRANTS

Library

100,000	Henry E. Huntington Library and Art Gallery, San Marino, CA — restoration of the Tempietto and complete relandscaping of the Rose Garden

General

2,751,625	Claremont McKenna College, Claremont, CA — endowment fund
2,751,625	Methodist Hospital Foundation, Arcadia, CA — endowment fund
2,751,625	University of Arizona Foundation, Tucson, AZ — endowment fund
1,375,813	Caney Creek Community Center, Pippa Passes, KY — endowment fund
1,375,813	Cumberland College, Williamsburg, KY — endowment fund

Bettingen Corporation, Burton G.

CONTACT
Patricia A. Brown
Executive Director
Burton G. Bettingen Corporation
9777 Wilshire Blvd., Ste. 611
Beverly Hills, CA 90212
(310) 276-4115

FINANCIAL SUMMARY
Recent Giving: $4,450,000 (fiscal 1993); $3,650,445 (fiscal 1992); $4,917,500 (fiscal 1991)

Assets: $24,491,737 (fiscal 1993); $26,000,000 (fiscal 1992 approx.); $26,198,434 (fiscal 1991)

Gifts Received: $1,482,145 (fiscal 1993); $1,482,145 (fiscal 1992); $1,592,788 (fiscal 1991)

Fiscal Note: In fiscal 1993, the corporation received funds from the Burton G. Bettingen Charitable Lead Annuity Trust.

EIN: 95-3942826

CONTRIBUTIONS SUMMARY
Donor(s): The corporation was established in 1984 by the late Burton G. Bettingen .

Typical Recipients: • *Arts & Humanities:* Libraries, Music, Public Broadcasting • *Civic & Public Affairs:* Business/Free Enterprise, Law & Justice, Legal Aid, Native American Affairs, Philanthropic Organizations, Public Policy • *Education:* Colleges & Universities, Faculty Development, Medical Education, Minority Education, Private Education (Precollege), Religious Education • *Environment:* Resource Conservation • *Health:* Children's Health/Hospitals, Emergency/Ambulance Services, Health Organizations, Hospitals, Medical Research, Preventive Medicine/Wellness Organizations, Research/Studies Institutes, Single-Disease Health Associations • *Religion:* Dioceses, Religious Welfare • *Social Services:* Child Welfare, Community Service Organizations, Family Planning, Homes, People with Disabilities, Shelters/Homelessness, Youth Organizations

Grant Types: capital, endowment, general support, project, and research

Geographic Distribution: focus on, but not limited to, Los Angeles, CA

GIVING OFFICERS
Patricia A. Brown: secy, treas, exec dir, dir *CURR EMPL* admin dir, dir: Burton G Bettingen Corp

Regina Covitt: asst treas

Sandra G. Nowicki: pres, dir *CURR EMPL* pres, dir: Burton G Bettingen Corp

Stuart P. Tobisman: vp, dir, couns *PHIL AFFIL* secy, trust: Norman Lear Foundation

Gyte Van Zyl: vp, dir

Jane Van Zyl: dir

APPLICATION INFORMATION
Initial Approach:

The corporation welcomes letters of inquiry or full proposals from applicants.

Letter of inquiry should state the applicant's background, goals and objectives, and its specific need for funding.

Full proposals should include the following: a concise statement of the project; a statement of the applicant's background, purpose, objectives, or the most recent annual report containing this information; brief budgetary information in relation to the request, and other commitments received for support; a copy of the applicant's most recent financial statements and a copy of the most recent Form 990; a copy of the IRS 501(c)(3) tax-determination letter; and a list of the members of applicant's governing

board showing their business, professional, or community affiliations.

Also, if the applicant is located or conducts operations in California, proposals should include documentation that the applicant is exempt from state franchise or income tax under Section 23701(d), California revenue and taxation code.

Proposals are received year round.

Restrictions on Giving: The corporation does not award grants to individuals, for conferences or seminars, or to organizations that are themsevles grantmaking bodies. In addition, the corporation does not support general fundraising events, dinners, or mass mailings.

PUBLICATIONS
Application guidelines

GRANTS ANALYSIS
Total Grants: $4,450,000

Number of Grants: 41

Highest Grant: $1,000,000

Average Grant: $86,250*

Typical Range: $10,000 to $100,000

Disclosure Period: fiscal year ending September 30, 1993

Note: Average grant figure excludes the largest grant of $1,000,000. Recent grants are derived from a fiscal 1993 grants list.

RECENT GRANTS

Library

10,000	Foundation Center, New York, NY — charitable

General

1,000,000	Father Flanagan's Boys Home, Boys Town, NE — charitable
375,000	Catholic Charities of Los Angeles, Los Angeles, CA — charitable
250,000	Phoenix House of California, Los Angeles, CA — charitable
250,000	San Fernando Valley Child Guidance Clinic, Northridge, CA — charitable
200,000	Catholic Charities of Los Angeles, Los Angeles, CA — charitable

Boswell Foundation, James G.

CONTACT
Greer J. Fearon
Executive Secretary
James G. Boswell Foundation
4600 Security Pacific Plz.
333 South Hope St.
Los Angeles, CA 90071
(213) 485-1717

FINANCIAL SUMMARY
Recent Giving: $1,170,587 (1993); $4,373,291 (1992); $3,290,117 (1991)

Assets: $59,397,436 (1993); $58,812,293 (1992); $59,057,509 (1991)

EIN: 95-6047326

CONTRIBUTIONS SUMMARY

Donor(s): The James G. Boswell Foundation was established in 1947. The donor was the late James G. Boswell , founder of the J. G. Boswell Company, a successful farm and agricultural supplies enterprise. Today, stock from the company constitutes a significant percentage of foundation assets.

Typical Recipients: • *Arts & Humanities:* Arts Centers, History & Archaeology, Libraries, Music, Public Broadcasting • *Civic & Public Affairs:* Business/Free Enterprise, Community Foundations, Law & Justice, Legal Aid, Municipalities/Towns, Philanthropic Organizations, Urban & Community Affairs • *Education:* Agricultural Education, Colleges & Universities, Engineering/Technological Education, Medical Education, Private Education (Precollege), Public Education (Precollege), Science/Mathematics Education, Student Aid • *Environment:* General • *Health:* Health Organizations, Hospitals, Medical Research • *International:* Foreign Arts Organizations, Foreign Educational Institutions • *Social Services:* Child Welfare, People with Disabilities, Recreation & Athletics, Scouts, Special Olympics, United Funds/United Ways, YMCA/YWCA/YMHA/YWHA, Youth Organizations

Grant Types: capital, fellowship, general support, project, and scholarship

Geographic Distribution: primarily California

GIVING OFFICERS

James G. Boswell II: pres, trust *B* 1922 *ED* Stanford Univ BA *CURR EMPL* chmn: JG Boswell Co *CORP AFFIL* dir: Security Pacific Corp

Rosalind M. Boswell: secy-treas, trust

Susan W. Dulin: vp

Greer J. Fearon: exec secy

APPLICATION INFORMATION
Initial Approach:

The foundation does not have a formal application form. A letter of inquiry should be mailed to the foundation.

The letter should include the reason for seeking the grant and sufficient background information to establish the need for funding.

Inquiries may be submitted at any time. The board of directors meets periodically, as the need arises, to consider grant requests.

Restrictions on Giving: Educational grants are limited to high school graduates from the Corcoran, CA, School District.

GRANTS ANALYSIS
Total Grants: $1,170,587

Number of Grants: 29

Highest Grant: $400,000

Average Grant: $40,365

Typical Range: $500 to $5,000 and $10,000 to $100,000

Disclosure Period: 1993

Note: Recent grants are derived from a 1993 Form 990.

RECENT GRANTS
Library

50,000	Polytechnic School, Pasadena, CA — remodeling of James G Boswell library

General

400,000	Agricultural Education Foundation, Templeton, CA — "5x95" campaign
169,447	Corcoran Scholarship Committee, Corcoran, CA — individual scholarship at Corcoran High School
150,000	California Institute of Technology, Pasadena, CA — support James G. Boswell Professor of Neuroscience, emeritus
120,000	Agricultural Education Foundation, Templeton, CA — agricultural leadership training seminars
105,140	New South Wales Scholarship Program, Sydney, Australia — undergraduate scholarship

---

Bothin Foundation

CONTACT
Lyman H. Casey
Executive Director and Treasurer
Bothin Foundation
873 Sutter St., Ste. B
San Francisco, CA 94109
(415) 771-4300

FINANCIAL SUMMARY
Recent Giving: $748,619 (1993); $800,000 (1992 approx.); $462,992 (1991)

Assets: $19,090,635 (1993); $17,000,000 (1992 approx.); $19,757,680 (1991)

EIN: 94-1196182

CONTRIBUTIONS SUMMARY
Donor(s): "The Bothin Foundation, formerly the Bothin Helping Fund, was established by Henry E. Bothin, his wife, Ellen Chabot Bothin, and his daughter, Genevieve Bothin de Limur, and incorporated as a private foundation in the State of California on September 28, 1917." The foundation is administered by a board of directors, several of whom are members of the Bothin family.

Typical Recipients: • *Arts & Humanities:* Arts Associations & Councils, Libraries, Museums/Galleries, Music, Public Broadcasting, Theater • *Civic & Public Affairs:* Asian American Affairs, Employment/Job Training, Hispanic Affairs, Housing, Urban & Community Affairs • *Education:* Leadership Training, Science/Mathematics Education, Secondary Education (Private), Secondary Education (Public), Special Education • *Environment:* Resource Conservation, Wildlife Protection • *Health:* Health Organizations, Hospitals, Kidney, Medical

Rehabilitation, Mental Health • *International:* Human Rights • *Religion:* Ministries, Religious Welfare • *Science:* Scientific Research • *Social Services:* Animal Protection, Camps, Child Welfare, Community Centers, Community Service Organizations, Counseling, Day Care, Family Services, People with Disabilities, Recreation & Athletics, Senior Services, Sexual Abuse, Substance Abuse, Volunteer Services, Youth Organizations

Grant Types: capital

Geographic Distribution: focus on metropolitan San Francisco area (San Francisco, Marin, San Mateo, Sonoma, and Santa Barbara counties)

GIVING OFFICERS
William W. Budge: dir

A. Michael Casey: vp, secy, dir

Lyman H. Casey: exec dir, treas

Genevieve Bothin Lyman Di San Faustino: pres, dir, don granddaughter

Stephanie MacColl: dir

Edmona Lyman Mansell: vp, dir

Robert R. Miller: dir

Rhoda Schultz: dir

APPLICATION INFORMATION
Initial Approach:

Applicants should submit a brief preliminary letter of intention.

Requests for support should include a description of the goals and objectives of the proposed project, purpose, and history of the applying organization, names and qualifications of the project's staff, total operating budget, estimated or proposed budget for the project, amount requested, other sources of income, and proof of tax exemption. If additional information is needed, the foundation will contact the applicant.

The board of directors meets in February, June, and October. Applications should be submitted eight weeks prior to board meetings.

Applicants should expect a waiting period of up to three months before funding decisions are made. All requests are answered with a written response within a reasonable period of time.

Restrictions on Giving: Grants are not made to individuals, for endowment drives, general operating expenses, films or other media presentations, religious groups for sectarian purposes, medical research, conferences, program support, or educational institutions other than thoses directly serving the developmentally disabled.

PUBLICATIONS
Biennial report, grant-making guidelines

GRANTS ANALYSIS
Total Grants: $748,619

Number of Grants: 83

Highest Grant: $25,000

Average Grant: $9,020

Typical Range: $5,000 to $15,000

Disclosure Period: 1993

Note: Recent grants are derived from a 1993 grants list.

RECENT GRANTS

Library
| 7,715 | Friends of San Francisco Public Library, San Francisco, CA |

General
25,000	Central City Hospitality House, San Francisco, CA
25,000	On Lok Senior Health Services, San Francisco, CA
25,000	St. Francis Hospital Foundation, San Francisco, CA
20,000	Mission High School, San Francisco, CA
15,000	Boys and Girls Club of the Peninsula, Menlo Park, CA

Brenner Foundation, Mervyn

CONTACT
John R. Gentry
President
Mervyn Brenner Fdn.
Three Embarcadero Ctr., Ste. 2100
San Francisco, CA 94111
(415) 951-0100

FINANCIAL SUMMARY
Recent Giving: $139,650 (fiscal 1992); $129,270 (fiscal 1991); $156,500 (fiscal 1990)

Assets: $3,819,841 (fiscal 1992); $3,546,673 (fiscal 1991); $3,015,059 (fiscal 1990)

EIN: 94-6088679

CONTRIBUTIONS SUMMARY
Donor(s): the late Mervyn I. Brenner

Typical Recipients: • *Arts & Humanities:* Libraries, Music, Performing Arts, Public Broadcasting, Theater • *Education:* Colleges & Universities, Private Education (Precollege), Public Education (Precollege) • *Health:* Hospitals • *Social Services:* Child Welfare, Community Service Organizations, Family Planning, Family Services, United Funds/United Ways, Youth Organizations

Grant Types: operating expenses

Geographic Distribution: focus on CA

GIVING OFFICERS
William D. Crawford: vp *PHIL AFFIL* cfo, dir: Herbst Foundation

John R. Gentry: pres

Marc H. Monheimer: secy *PHIL AFFIL* trust: Wollenberg Foundation

John T. Seigle: treas *B* 1930 *CORP AFFIL* secy, treas, dir: Little World Travel *PHIL AFFIL* pres: Herbst Foundation

Marvin T. Tepperman: vp

APPLICATION INFORMATION
Initial Approach: Send brief letter of inquiry describing program. There are no deadlines.

Restrictions on Giving: Does not support individuals.

GRANTS ANALYSIS
Total Grants: $139,650

Number of Grants: 66

Highest Grant: $11,000

Typical Range: $1,000 to $5,000

Disclosure Period: fiscal year ending August 31, 1992

Note: Recent grants are derived from a fiscal 1992 Form 990.

RECENT GRANTS

Library
| 5,000 | San Francisco Performing Arts Library and Museum, San Francisco, CA |
| 4,000 | San Mateo Public Library, San Mateo, CA |

General
11,000	University of California Regents, Los Angeles, CA
9,500	University of California San Francisco Foundation, San Francisco, CA
8,000	H.C.S.F. Foundation, San Francisco, CA
6,000	Beaverton United School District, Beaverton, OR
5,000	All Saints Episcopal Day School

Bright Family Foundation

CONTACT
Calvin E. Bright
President
Bright Family Fdn.
1620 N Carpenter Rd., Bldg. B
Modesto, CA 95351
(209) 526-8242

FINANCIAL SUMMARY
Recent Giving: $162,318 (1993); $122,215 (1992); $109,907 (1991)

Assets: $4,367,272 (1993); $3,593,103 (1992); $3,100,437 (1991)

Gifts Received: $400,000 (1993); $400,000 (1992); $400,000 (1991)

Fiscal Note: In fiscal 1993, contributions were received from Calvin and Marjorie Bright.

EIN: 77-0126942

CONTRIBUTIONS SUMMARY
Donor(s): Calvin Bright, Marjorie Bright

Typical Recipients: • *Arts & Humanities:* Libraries, Museums/Galleries, Public Broadcasting • *Civic & Public Affairs:* Clubs, General, Women's Affairs • *Education:* Colleges & Universities, Medical Education, Private Education (Precollege), Secondary Education (Public) • *Health:* Clinics/Medical Centers, Health Organizations, Single-Disease Health Associations • *International:* International Environmental Issues • *Religion:* Churches, Religious Welfare • *Social*

Services: Child Welfare, Community Service Organizations, Domestic Violence, Scouts, Shelters/Homelessness, United Funds/United Ways, Youth Organizations

Grant Types: operating expenses

Geographic Distribution: focus on CA

GIVING OFFICERS
Calvin E. Bright: pres

Lyn Bright: secy, treas

Marjorie Bright: vp

APPLICATION INFORMATION
Initial Approach: Application form required. Deadline is December 1.

GRANTS ANALYSIS
Total Grants: $162,318

Number of Grants: 17

Highest Grant: $30,418

Typical Range: $500 to $10,000

Disclosure Period: 1993

Note: Recent grants are derived from a 1993 Form 990.

RECENT GRANTS

Library
| 2,000 | Friends of Turlock Public Library, Turlock, CA |

General
30,418	California State University, Turlock, CA — Stanislaus Foundation
26,500	Boy Scouts of America, Modesto, CA
20,000	San Francisco School of Medicine, San Francisco, CA — department of Neurology
15,000	Beggs Methodist Church, Beggs, OK
10,000	Modesto Gospel Mission, Modesto, CA

Campini Foundation, Frank A.

CONTACT
Paul J. Ruby
Director
Frank A. Campini Fdn.
220 Montgomery St., 100
San Francisco, CA 94104
(415) 421-4171

FINANCIAL SUMMARY
Recent Giving: $560,042 (1993)

Assets: $12,491,652 (1993)

EIN: 94-6107956

CONTRIBUTIONS SUMMARY
Typical Recipients: • *Arts & Humanities:* Libraries, Museums/Galleries, Music, Opera, Public Broadcasting, Theater • *Civic & Public Affairs:* General, Urban & Community Affairs, Zoos/Aquariums • *Education:* Colleges & Universities, International Studies, Private Education (Precollege), Student

Aid • *Environment:* General • *Health:* AIDS/HIV, Cancer, Clinics/Medical Centers, Hospices, Medical Research, Preventive Medicine/Wellness Organizations, Single-Disease Health Associations • *International:* Missionary/Religious Activities • *Religion:* Jewish Causes, Religious Welfare • *Science:* Scientific Centers & Institutes • *Social Services:* Child Welfare, Community Service Organizations, Crime Prevention, Domestic Violence, Family Services, Food/Clothing Distribution, Youth Organizations

Grant Types: general support

Geographic Distribution: focus on CA

GIVING OFFICERS
Alan Neys: dir

Patricia Neys: secy, treas

Paul J. Ruby: dir

APPLICATION INFORMATION
Initial Approach: Send a brief letter of inquiry. Include a description of organization, amount requested, purpose of funds sought, recently audited financial statement, and proof of tax-exempt status.

GRANTS ANALYSIS
Total Grants: $560,042

Number of Grants: 78

Highest Grant: $70,000

Typical Range: $1,000 to $20,000

Disclosure Period: 1993

Note: Recent grants are derived from a 1993 Form 990.

RECENT GRANTS
Library

5,000	Library Foundation of San Francisco, San Francisco, CA

General

70,000	Audubon Canyon Ranch, Stinson Beach, CA
53,300	Columbia Park Boys Club, San Francisco, CA
20,000	University of California San Francisco Pediatric Oncology Clinical Research, San Francisco, CA
20,000	University of California San Francisco Pediatric Oncology Research, San Francisco, CA
15,000	AIDS Homecare Program, San Francisco, CA

Chartwell Foundation

CONTACT
Andrew J. Perenchio
President
Chartwell Fdn.
1901 Ave. of the Stars, Ste. 680
Los Angeles, CA 90067
(213) 556-7600

FINANCIAL SUMMARY
Recent Giving: $850,325 (fiscal 1993); $822,317 (fiscal 1992); $948,094 (fiscal 1991)

Assets: $147,166 (fiscal 1993); $771,945 (fiscal 1992); $703,957 (fiscal 1991)

Gifts Received: $216,563 (fiscal 1993); $859,782 (fiscal 1992)

Fiscal Note: In fiscal 1993, contributons were received from A. Jerrold Perenchio.

EIN: 95-4080111

CONTRIBUTIONS SUMMARY
Donor(s): A. Jerrold Perenchio

Typical Recipients: • *Arts & Humanities:* Arts Funds, Arts Institutes, Film & Video, Libraries, Museums/Galleries, Music, Opera • *Civic & Public Affairs:* African American Affairs, General, Hispanic Affairs, Public Policy, Women's Affairs • *Education:* Colleges & Universities, Literacy, Medical Education, Private Education (Precollege), Public Education (Precollege), Religious Education • *Environment:* General • *Health:* AIDS/HIV, Alzheimers Disease, Cancer, Children's Health/Hospitals, Diabetes, Eyes/Blindness, Hospitals, Medical Research, Multiple Sclerosis, Prenatal Health Issues, Research/Studies Institutes, Single-Disease Health Associations • *International:* Foreign Arts Organizations, Foreign Educational Institutions, International Relief Efforts, Missionary/Religious Activities • *Religion:* Jewish Causes, Missionary Activities (Domestic), Religious Welfare • *Social Services:* Child Welfare, Community Centers, Community Service Organizations, Domestic Violence, Family Planning, Family Services, Food/Clothing Distribution, People with Disabilities, Recreation & Athletics, Senior Services, Shelters/Homelessness, Substance Abuse, Youth Organizations

Grant Types: general support

Geographic Distribution: focus on CA

GIVING OFFICERS
Robert V. Cahill: vp

Andrew Jerrold Perenchio: pres *B* Fresno CA 1930 *ED* Univ CA Los Angeles BS 1954 *CURR EMPL* pres: Chartwell Partnerships Group *CORP AFFIL* dir: Cablevision Sys Corp, City Natl Corp *CLUB AFFIL* Bel-Air CC, Friars, Westchester CC

John Perenchio: vp

APPLICATION INFORMATION
Initial Approach: Send brief letter of inquiry describing program or project. There are no deadlines.

Restrictions on Giving: Does not support individuals.

GRANTS ANALYSIS
Total Grants: $850,325

Number of Grants: 338

Highest Grant: $34,515

Typical Range: $1,000 to $25,000

Disclosure Period: fiscal year ending November 30, 1993

Note: Recent grants are derived from a fiscal 1993 Form 990.

RECENT GRANTS
Library

5,000	Tom Bradley Library Foundation, Los Angeles, CA

General

34,515	Our Lady of Malibu School, Malibu, CA
25,000	Children's Action Network, Los Angeles, CA
25,000	Children's Diabetes Foundation, Los Angeles, CA
25,000	City of Hope, Los Angeles, CA
25,000	US Committee for UNICEF, Los Angeles, CA

Chevron Corporation

Revenue: $31.06 billion
Employees: 55,123
Headquarters: San Francisco, CA
SIC Major Group: Petroleum Refining, Crude Petroleum & Natural Gas, Oil & Gas Exploration Services, and Lubricating Oils & Greases

CONTACT
J. W. (Skip) Rhodes, Jr.
Manager, Corporate Contributions
Chevron Corporation
PO Box 7753
San Francisco, CA 94120-7753
(415) 894-7700
Note: Mr. Rhodes handles applications for national and international organizations. Regional organizations should direct grant applications to local Chevron public affairs representative. To obtain these names and addresses, contact Chevron Corporation at (415) 894-4193.

FINANCIAL SUMMARY
Recent Giving: $19,019,623 (1993); $25,135,155 (1992); $27,700,000 (1991)

Fiscal Note: All contributions are made directly by the company. International giving is included in the above figures. Above figures include nonmonetary support.

CONTRIBUTIONS SUMMARY
Typical Recipients: • *Arts & Humanities:* Arts Associations & Councils, Arts Centers, Arts Festivals, Arts Funds, Ballet, Community Arts, Dance, Film & Video, Historic Preservation, Libraries, Museums/Galleries, Music, Opera, Performing Arts, Public Broadcasting, Theater • *Civic & Public Affairs:* African American Affairs, Business/Free Enterprise, Economic Development, Economic Policy, Employment/Job Training, Hispanic Affairs, Housing, Law & Justice, Legal Aid, Nonprofit Management, Professional & Trade Associations, Public Policy, Rural Affairs, Safety, Urban & Community Affairs, Women's Affairs, Zoos/Aquariums • *Education:* Agricultural Education, Arts/Humanities Education, Business Education, Colleges & Universities, Economic Education, Education Associations, Education Funds, Education Reform, Elementary Education (Private), En-

gineering/Technological Education, Faculty Development, General, International Studies, Journalism/Media Education, Literacy, Minority Education, Public Education (Precollege), Science/Mathematics Education, Student Aid • *Environment:* General • *Health:* AIDS/HIV, Emergency/Ambulance Services, Health Policy/Cost Containment, Health Funds, Health Organizations, Hospices, Hospitals, Medical Rehabilitation, Mental Health, Public Health, Single-Disease Health Associations • *International:* Foreign Educational Institutions, Health Care/Hospitals, International Affairs, International Peace & Security Issues, International Relations, International Relief Efforts • *Science:* Observatories & Planetariums, Science Exhibits & Fairs, Scientific Centers & Institutes, Scientific Organizations • *Social Services:* Child Welfare, Community Centers, Community Service Organizations, Day Care, Delinquency & Criminal Rehabilitation, Domestic Violence, Emergency Relief, Family Services, Food/Clothing Distribution, Homes, People with Disabilities, Refugee Assistance, Senior Services, Shelters/Homelessness, Substance Abuse, United Funds/United Ways, Volunteer Services, Youth Organizations

Grant Types: conference/seminar, department, employee matching gifts, fellowship, general support, professorship, project, research, scholarship, and seed money

Note: Employee/director/retiree matching programs are available for educational institutions and arts and cultural organizations. Educational gifts will be matched up to $5,000 and cultural gifts up to $1,000, per individual per calendar year.

Nonmonetary Support: $395,341 (1992); $886,000 (1991); $267,000 (1990)

Nonmonetary Support Types: donated equipment

Geographic Distribution: to corporate operating locations nationally and internationally; international operating locations include Canada, England, Spain, Mexico, Columbia, Brazil, and Puerto Rico

Operating Locations: AK (Anchorage, Nikiski), AL, AZ, CA (Bakersfield, El Segundo, La Habra, Los Angeles, Richmond, San Francisco, Santa Barbara, Ventura), CO (Denver), DC, FL, GA (Atlanta), HI (Honolulu), KY, LA (New Orleans), MD (Baltimore), MS (Pascagoula), NM (Albuquerque), NV, OH (Cincinnati), OK (Tulsa), OR (Portland, St. Helens), PA, TX (Cedar Bayou, El Paso, Houston, Orange, Port Arthur), UT (Salt Lake City), WA (Seattle), WY

CORP. OFFICERS
John Dennis Bonney: *B* Blackpool England 1930 *ED* Oxford Univ Hertford Coll BA 1954; Univ CA Berkeley Law Sch LLB 1956; Oxford Univ Hertford Coll MA 1959 *CURR EMPL* vchmn, dir: Chevron Corp *NONPR AFFIL* dir: Am Petroleum Inst *CLUB AFFIL* Commonwealth, Oxford & Cambridge, Univ, World Trade

Kenneth Tindall Derr: *B* Wilkes-Barre PA 1936 *ED* Cornell Univ BS 1959; Cornell Univ MBA 1960 *CURR EMPL* chmn, ceo:

Chevron Corp *CORP AFFIL* dir: Citicorp *NONPR AFFIL* dir: Am Petroleum Inst, Am Productivity & Quality Control Ctr, Bay Area Counc, Invest-In-Am; mem: Bus Counc, Bus Roundtable, CA Bus Roundtable, Stanford Univ Inst Intl Studies; trust: Conf Bd, Cornell Univ; vchmn: Natl Petroleum Counc *CLUB AFFIL* Orinda CC, Pacific-Union, San Francisco GC

James Norman Sullivan: *B* San Francisco CA 1937 *ED* Univ Notre Dame BS 1959 *CURR EMPL* vchmn, dir: Chevron Corp *NONPR AFFIL* dir: San Francisco Chamber Commerce; mem bd regents: St Marys Coll

GIVING OFFICERS
Ken Johnson: *CURR EMPL* program off: Chevron Corp

David McMurry: *CURR EMPL* program off: Chevron Corp

J.W. Skip Rhodes, Jr.: *CURR EMPL* mgr corp contributions: Chevron Corp

APPLICATION INFORMATION
Initial Approach: *Initial Contact:* one- or two-page letter to J. W. (Skip) Rhodes, Jr., Contributions Manager of Chevron Corp., for national and international organizations; community organizations should direct grant applications to a local Chevron public affairs representative *Include Information On:* name, address, contact person, and telephone number; brief description of purpose, objectives, program, and accomplishments of organization; geographic area and number of people served; number of volunteer workers; board members' names and affiliations and brief background of executive director and key staff; financial statement or current operating budget that lists sources of financial support, membership in a united fund or other funding association, and percentage of income devoted to (1) program, (2) administration, and (3) fund raising; and copy of most recent Form 990 *Deadlines:* none *Note:* Before submitting a proposal, organizations should request a copy of Chevron's grant application guidelines.

Restrictions on Giving: Chevron generally does not support individuals; religious, veterans, labor, fraternal, athletic, or political organizations; capital funds for buildings or equipment; endowment funds; operating expenses for organizations receiving support through the United Way; school-related bands and sports events; national health, medical, and human service organizations; travel funds; fund-raising events or benefit tickets; or courtesy advertising.

OTHER THINGS TO KNOW
At more than 30 locations, the Chevron Employee Involvement Fund supports organizations in which company employees provide volunteer services.

PUBLICATIONS
Values in Action, guidelines

GRANTS ANALYSIS
Total Grants: $19,019,623
Number of Grants: 6,187
Highest Grant: $650,000
Average Grant: $3,074

Typical Range: $2,500 to $10,000
Disclosure Period: 1993
Note: Recent grants are derived from a 1993 contributions report.

RECENT GRANTS
Library
50,000	Library Foundation of San Francisco, San Francisco, CA

General
650,000	Oakland Housing Authority, Oakland, CA
309,729	REACH — scholarships for employees children
295,546	University of California Berkeley, Berkeley, CA
189,000	Stanford University, Stanford, CA
160,225	Stanford University, Stanford, CA

Clorox Co. / Clorox Company Foundation

Sales: $1.63 billion
Employees: 5,800
Headquarters: Oakland, CA
SIC Major Group: Polishes & Sanitation Goods, Canned Fruits & Vegetables, Dehydrated Fruits, Vegetables & Soups, and Pickles, Sauces & Salad Dressings

CONTACT
Carmella J. Johnson
Contributions Manager
Clorox Company Foundation
1221 Broadway
PO Box 24305
Oakland, CA 94623
(510) 271-7751

FINANCIAL SUMMARY
Recent Giving: $2,500,000 (fiscal 1995 est.); $2,467,717 (fiscal 1994 approx.); $1,800,000 (fiscal 1993)

Assets: $2,506,094 (fiscal 1993); $2,675,475 (fiscal 1992); $2,878,185 (fiscal 1991)

Gifts Received: $690,000 (fiscal 1993)

Fiscal Note: Totals include contributions by the foundation and direct gifts by the company and its subsidiaries. Above figures exclude nonmonetary support.

EIN: 94-2674980

CONTRIBUTIONS SUMMARY
Typical Recipients: • *Arts & Humanities:* Arts Appreciation, Arts Associations & Councils, Arts Centers, Arts Festivals, Arts Outreach, Ballet, Community Arts, Dance, Ethnic & Folk Arts, Film & Video, Historic Preservation, Libraries, Literary Arts, Museums/Galleries, Music, Opera, Performing Arts, Public Broadcasting, Theater, Visual Arts • *Civic & Public Affairs:* African American Affairs, Asian American Affairs, Civil Rights, Community Foundations, Economic Development, Employment/Job Training, General, Hispanic Affairs, Law &

Justice, Legal Aid, Municipalities/Towns, Nonprofit Management, Safety, Urban & Community Affairs, Women's Affairs, Zoos/Aquariums • *Education:* Arts/Humanities Education, Business Education, Colleges & Universities, Community & Junior Colleges, Continuing Education, Economic Education, Education Associations, Education Funds, Elementary Education (Private), General, Journalism/Media Education, Literacy, Minority Education, Preschool Education, Private Education (Precollege), Public Education (Precollege), School Volunteerism, Science/Mathematics Education, Secondary Education (Public), Special Education, Student Aid • *Environment:* General, Resource Conservation, Wildlife Protection • *Health:* Children's Health/Hospitals, Clinics/Medical Centers, Emergency/Ambulance Services, Geriatric Health, Health Funds, Health Organizations, Hospices, Hospitals, Mental Health, Prenatal Health Issues, Single-Disease Health Associations • *International:* International Affairs, International Development • *Religion:* Religious Organizations, Religious Welfare • *Science:* Science Exhibits & Fairs • *Social Services:* Child Welfare, Community Centers, Community Service Organizations, Counseling, Day Care, Delinquency & Criminal Rehabilitation, Domestic Violence, Family Planning, Family Services, Food/Clothing Distribution, People with Disabilities, Recreation & Athletics, Scouts, Senior Services, Shelters/Homelessness, Substance Abuse, United Funds/United Ways, Volunteer Services, YMCA/YWCA/YMHA/YWHA, Youth Organizations

Grant Types: capital, employee matching gifts, endowment, general support, operating expenses, project, and scholarship

Note: Employee matching gift ratio: 1 to 1 for educational institutions.

Nonmonetary Support: $1,700,000 (fiscal 1993); $1,700,000 (fiscal 1992); $1,200,000 (fiscal 1989)

Nonmonetary Support Types: donated equipment, donated products, in-kind services, and workplace solicitation

Note: Estimated value of nonmonetary support for 1993 was $1.7 million, including product donations to Second Harvest ($1.3 million) and disaster relief product donations ($40,000).

Geographic Distribution: primarily to organizations located in Oakland; the San Francisco East Bay area; communities where Clorox has operating facilities; a few major national causes

Operating Locations: CA (Fairfield, Los Angeles, Oakland, Pleasanton), FL (Tampa), GA (Atlanta, Forest Park), IL (Chicago, Wheeling), KS (Rosedale), KY (Burnside, Louisville), MD (Aberdeen, Frederick), MO (Belle, Kansas City), MS (Jackson), NC (Charlotte), NJ (Carlstadt, Jersey City, Lodi), NV (Reno, Sparks), OH (Cleveland), OR (Springfield), PR, TN (Dyersburg), TX (Houston), WV (Beryl, Parsons)

Note: Clorox operates more than 30 plants in the United States, Canada, Mexico, Puerto Rico, and abroad.

CORP. OFFICERS
William Friend Ausfahl: *B* San Francisco CA 1940 *ED* Univ CA Berkeley BA 1961; Stanford Univ Grad Sch Bus Admin MBA 1963 *CURR EMPL* group vp, cfo, dir: Clorox Co *CORP AFFIL* vp, dir: Clorox Intl Co Inc, Food Svc Products Co, Kingsford Products Co, Prince Castle Inc

G. Craig Sullivan: *B* 1940 *ED* Boston Coll BS 1964 *CURR EMPL* chmn, pres, ceo: Clorox Co

GIVING OFFICERS
William Friend Ausfahl: vp, treas, trust *CURR EMPL* group vp, cfo, dir: Clorox Co (see above)

James O. Cole: pres, trust *B* Florence AL 1941 *ED* Talladega Coll 1962; Harvard Univ Law Sch 1971 *CURR EMPL* vp corp aff: Clorox Co

Edward A. Cutter: vp, secy, trust *B* Berkeley CA 1939 *ED* Stanford Univ BS 1961; Harvard Univ Law Sch JD 1964 *CURR EMPL* sr vp, secy, gen couns: Clorox Co *CORP AFFIL* secy, dir: Clorox Intl Co Inc, Food Svc Products Co, Prince Castle Inc; vp, secy, dir: Kingsford Products Co

Neil P. DeFeo: trust *CURR EMPL* group vp: Clorox Co

Ramon A. Llerado: trust *CURR EMPL* group vp tech: Clorox Co

Peter N. Louras: vp, trust *CURR EMPL* group vp: Clorox Co

G. Craig Sullivan: trust *CURR EMPL* chmn, pres, ceo: Clorox Co (see above)

APPLICATION INFORMATION
Initial Approach: *Initial Contact:* a brief letter or phone call to request application guidelines and application form *Include Information On:* completed standard form; description of the organization; project summary; list of board of directors; organizational and project budgetary information; constituency served; plans for project evaluation; other sources of support; recently audited financial statement; proof of tax-exempt status *Deadlines:* applications for foundation grants are accepted August 1 to June 1 of each fiscal year ending June 30; deadlines are August 1, November 1, March 1, and June 1; requests for special events sponsorship should be submitted in writing at least sixty days prior to the event *Note:* Endowment/capital campaign requests include building funds, purchase of major equipment, or general operating reserve funds. However, the foundation discourages contributions to endowments. The company's operating facilities each have their own particular funding priorities and independent review processes. A complete list of contributions programs at Clorox locations is contained within the guidelines.

Restrictions on Giving: The foundation will not provide grants to political parties, organizations, candidates, or issues; veterans organizations, except for programs benefiting the public at large; religious causes, except nonsectarian activities available to the community at large; field trips, tours, or travel; individuals; benefit costs; raffle tickets; media production; athletic leagues or events; national conventions/meetings; benefit advertising; association or membership dues; or dinners outside the Bay Area.

Only one grant request per organization will be considered within a fiscal year time period (July 1 through June 30).

OTHER THINGS TO KNOW
First-time grants generally range from $1,000 to $5,000 for general operating support and special projects. The foundation considers itself a supplemental funding source, seeking points of intervention where modest grants can be leveraged for greater change.

In addition to cash contributions by the company and foundation, Clorox has invested more than $60 million in low-income housing projects nationwide. Such investments are expected to increase to approximately $100 million.

PUBLICATIONS
Guidelines, application form, foundation annual report

GRANTS ANALYSIS
Total Grants: $2,467,717

Number of Grants: 1,000

Highest Grant: $80,000

Average Grant: $2,468

Typical Range: $1,000 to $10,000

Disclosure Period: fiscal year ending June 30, 1994

Note: Recent grants are derived from a fiscal 1994 annual report.

RECENT GRANTS

General

85,000 East Oakland Youth Development Center/Foundation, Oakland, CA —for the interim executive director position, general operating support, grant writing, and the Summer Youth Program

50,000 East Bay Funders, Oakland, CA —to help East Oakland neighborhood residents develop their capacity to solve problems in their communities

30,000 Castlemont High School, Oakland, CA —for Commencement 2000 Project

30,000 Oakland Community Fund, Oakland, CA —for recreation and academic programs at sites located throughout the city's recreation centers and to publish a comprehensive directory of current programs available for youth

25,000 Allen Temple Foundation, Oakland, CA —for the Family Life Center

Columbia Foundation

CONTACT
Susan Clark Silk
Executive Director
Columbia Foundation
One Lombard St., Ste. 305
San Francisco, CA 94111
(415) 986-5179

FINANCIAL SUMMARY
Recent Giving: $2,841,311 (fiscal 1994);
$2,198,528 (fiscal 1993); $2,190,000 (fiscal 1992)

Assets: $43,600,381 (fiscal 1994);
$44,669,117 (fiscal 1993); $40,084,950 (fiscal 1992)

Gifts Received: $80,000 (fiscal 1993);
$80,000 (fiscal 1992); $80,000 (fiscal 1991)

Fiscal Note: In fiscal 1991, 1992, and 1993, the foundation received $80,000 from a trust established by a member of the board of directors.

EIN: 94-1196186

CONTRIBUTIONS SUMMARY
Donor(s): The Columbia Foundation was established in 1940 by Madeline Haas Russell, donor and president of the foundation. Mrs. Russell is a member of the Haas family, which owns Levi-Strauss and Company, the nation's largest manufacturer of apparel.

Mrs. Russell has been active in Democratic politics, and served on the boards at the San Francisco Museum of Art, and the Asia Foundation, which is located in San Francisco. She has also been active in public broadcasting, health care, and education.

Christine H. Russell, the foundation's treasurer, is also a donor to the foundation.

Typical Recipients: • *Arts & Humanities:* Arts Associations & Councils, Arts Centers, Arts Funds, Arts Institutes, Ballet, Community Arts, Dance, Ethnic & Folk Arts, Film & Video, Historic Preservation, Libraries, Museums/Galleries, Music, Opera, Public Broadcasting, Theater, Visual Arts • *Civic & Public Affairs:* Asian American Affairs, Civil Rights, Economic Development, Employment/Job Training, First Amendment Issues, Gay/Lesbian Issues, Hispanic Affairs, Law & Justice, Legal Aid, Municipalities/Towns, Native American Affairs, Philanthropic Organizations, Professional & Trade Associations, Public Policy, Rural Affairs, Urban & Community Affairs, Women's Affairs • *Education:* Afterschool/Enrichment Programs, Business Education, Colleges & Universities, International Studies, Private Education (Precollege) • *Environment:* Air/Water Quality, Forestry, General, Protection, Research, Resource Conservation • *Health:* AIDS/HIV, Health Funds, Hospices, Medical Research, Preventive Medicine/Wellness Organizations • *International:* Foreign Educational Institutions, International Development, International Environmental Issues, International Peace & Security Issues, International Relations, Missionary/Religious Activities • *Religion:* Jewish Causes, Religious Organizations, Religious Welfare, Synagogues/Temples • *Social Services:* Community Centers, Community Service Organizations, Domestic Violence, Food/Clothing Distribution, Homes, Refugee Assistance, Shelters/Homelessness, Volunteer Services, Youth Organizations

Grant Types: capital, project, and seed money

Geographic Distribution: primarily the San Francisco Bay Area

GIVING OFFICERS
Charles Phillips Russell: vp, don
Christine Haas Russell: treas, don, dir
PHIL AFFIL dir: Levi Strauss Foundation
Madeline Haas Russell: pres, don, dir *B* San Francisco CA 1915 *ED* Smith Coll BA 1937 *NONPR AFFIL* trust: Brandeis Univ, San Francisco Mus Modern Art
Alice Cornelia Russell-Shapiro: secy, dir
Susan Clark Silk: exec dir

APPLICATION INFORMATION
Initial Approach:

Contact the foundation for an application form.

Complete application form with an authorizing signature of the chair of the board of directors. Include a two-page summary describing the need for the project, how the project seeks to meet the need, and what is requested from the Columbia Foundation. The foundation stresses that the proposal summary should be typed and prepared with particular care. The proposal itself should be no more than five pages stating the following: need for the project and strategies for achieving the project's objectives; estimated time required to complete the project; method for measuring accomplishments; relationship to similar projects in the same field; qualifications of the staff; and a description of the applicant's organization. Provide a separate one-page, line-item budget identifying the projected income and expenses of the organization and the program. Funding sources and expenditures from the last two years should be listed by source and amount. Also, applications should include a list of members of the board of directors with identification of their organizational affiliation or occupation, a statement of affirmative action, an IRS tax-exempt determination letter, and any other optional materials, such as newspaper articles or informational brochures. All grantees must provide a report detailing the results of the project funded by the foundation, including an accounting of how all grant funds were spent.

There are two deadlines for applications each year, August 1 and February 1. All materials should be postmarked by the application deadline or the following business day if the deadline falls on a weekend or holiday.

The board meets twice a year for decisions on grant applications. The executive director will notify those applicants whose requests will receive further consideration. The director may arrange a site visit or a meeting with staff or board members to discuss the proposal. The foundation reports that it only grants funds to about thirty new applicants each year.

Restrictions on Giving: The foundation does not customarily provide support for operating budgets of established agencies, for recurring expenses for direct services or ongoing administrative costs, for individual fellowships or scholarships, or for agencies wholly supported by federated campaigns or heavily subsidized by government funds.

PUBLICATIONS
Application guidelines, program policy statement, annual report, grants list, and five-year report

GRANTS ANALYSIS
Total Grants: $2,841,311

Number of Grants: 94

Highest Grant: $200,000

Average Grant: $30,227

Typical Range: $1,000 to $50,000

Disclosure Period: fiscal year ending May 31, 1994

Note: Recent grants are derived from a fiscal 1994 annual report.

RECENT GRANTS

Library
150,000   Library Foundation of San Francisco, San Francisco, CA — for the capital campaign for a new public library for San Francisco; $250,000 over five years

General
100,000   Congregation Emanu-El, San Francisco, CA — a second grant of $250,000 over five years
100,000   Natural Resources Defense Council, New York, NY — for the Campaign for NRDC, $250,000 over five years
80,000   Jewish Home for the Aged, San Francisco, CA — for the construction of the Howard A. Friedman Pavilion, a 120-bed facility for the frail elderly; $200,000 over five years
50,000   Centro del Pueblo, San Francisco, CA — for the capital campaign to complete building renovation of Centro del Pueblo, a Mission District community-based development project that serves a multicultural, low-income population
50,000   Congregation Emanu-El, San Francisco, CA — for the renovation of Temple Emanu-El and for community service programs sponsored by Congregation Emanu-El; $250,000 over five years

Copley Press, Inc. / Copley Foundation, James S.

Sales: $411.0 million
Employees: 3,000
Headquarters: La Jolla, CA
SIC Major Group: Newspapers

CONTACT
Anita A. Baumgardner
Secretary, Trustee
James S. Copley Foundation
7776 Ivanhoe Ave.
PO Box 1530
La Jolla, CA 92038-1530
(619) 454-0411

FINANCIAL SUMMARY
Recent Giving: $1,500,000 (1995 est.);
$1,499,647 (1994); $1,384,677 (1993)
Assets: $22,400,000 (1995 est.);
$22,361,479 (1994); $22,493,674 (1993)
Gifts Received: $30,213 (1992)
Fiscal Note: Totals include foundation contributions only. The company also gives directly through its headquarters and subsidiaries. The amount of this support is unavailable. In 1992, the foundation received a contribution from the San Diego Union Shoe Fund.
EIN: 95-6051770

CONTRIBUTIONS SUMMARY
Typical Recipients: • *Arts & Humanities:* Arts Centers, Dance, General, Libraries, Museums/Galleries, Music, Opera, Performing Arts, Public Broadcasting, Theater • *Civic & Public Affairs:* General, Public Policy, Urban & Community Affairs, Zoos/Aquariums • *Education:* Colleges & Universities, Education Funds, Literacy, Private Education (Precollege), Student Aid • *Health:* AIDS/HIV, Hospices, Hospitals, Mental Health • *International:* International Organizations • *Religion:* Religious Welfare • *Social Services:* Animal Protection, Child Welfare, Community Service Organizations, Homes, People with Disabilities, Recreation & Athletics, Senior Services, Substance Abuse, United Funds/United Ways, Youth Organizations

Grant Types: capital, employee matching gifts, multiyear/continuing support, project, and scholarship

Note: Employee matching gifts apply only to educational institutions; scholarships are given to certain colleges and universities with authorization for them to select recipients. Employee matching gift ratio: 1 to 1.

Geographic Distribution: near headquarters and operating locations only

Operating Locations: CA (La Jolla, San Diego, San Pedro, Santa Monica, Torrance), IL (Aurora, Elgin, Joliet, Lincoln, Naperville, Plainfield, Springfield, Waukegan, Wheaton)

CORP. OFFICERS
David C. Copley: *ED* Menlo Coll BSBA *CURR EMPL* pres, dir: Copley Press Inc *CORP AFFIL* cfo, secy: Copley News Svc, Copley Press Electronics Co; chmn, ceo,

chmn sr mgmt bd: Fox Valley Press Inc; mem editorial Bd: San Diego Union - Tribune; pres: Copley NW Inc, Puller Paper Co, Rio Zorro Publs Inc; publ: Borrego Sun; vchmn: Copley/Colony *NONPR AFFIL* dir: CA Ctr Arts, San Diego Mus Art, St Vincent de Paul Soc; mem: FOCAS, Natl Newspaper Assn, San Diego Aerospace Mus, San Diego Hall Sci, San Diego Historical Soc, US Humane Soc; mem adv bd: San Diego Automotive Mus; mem pres assocs: Zoological Soc San Diego; mem pres club: Univ San Diego; mem pres counc: San Diego Kind Corp, Scripps Clinic & Res Fdn; trust: Am Craft Counc, Canterbury Sch, San Diego Crew Classic Fdn; trust emeritus: La Jolla Playhouse *CLUB AFFIL* Bachelor San Diego

Helen K. Copley: *B* Cedar Rapids IA 1922 *ED* Hunter Coll 1945 *CURR EMPL* chmn, ceo, dir: Copley Press Inc *CORP AFFIL* chmn: Copley News Svc; chmn, editorial bd: Union Tribune Publ Co; publ: San Diego Union-Tribune *NONPR AFFIL* chmn: San Diego Counc Literacy; dir: Washington Crossing Fdn; life mem: Friends Intl Ctr; life patroness: Makua Auxiliary; mem: Am Newspaper Publs Assn, Am Press Inst, CA Newspaper Publs Assn, Inter-Am Press Assn, La Jolla Town Counc, San Diego Hall Sci, San Diego Mus Art, San Diego Soc Natural History, San Diego Symphony Assn, San Diego Zoological Soc, Scripps Meml Hosp Auxiliary, Soc Professional Journalists, Star India Auxiliary, YWCA *CLUB AFFIL* Army & Navy, Aurora CC, Kona Kai, La Jolla Beach Tennis, La Jolla CC, San Diego Univ, San Diego YC *PHIL AFFIL* trust: Howard Hughes Medical Institute

Robert F. Crouch: *CURR EMPL* sr vp, dir: Copley Press Inc

Charles F. Patrick: *CURR EMPL* secy, vp fin: Copley Press Inc

GIVING OFFICERS
Anita A. Baumgardner: secy, trust

David C. Copley: pres, trust *CURR EMPL* pres, dir: Copley Press Inc (see above)

Helen K. Copley: chmn, trust *CURR EMPL* chmn, ceo, dir: Copley Press Inc *PHIL AFFIL* trust: Howard Hughes Medical Institute (see above)

Robert F. Crouch: vp, trust *CURR EMPL* sr vp, dir: Copley Press Inc (see above)

Alex De Bakcsy: vp, trust *CORP AFFIL* dir: Copley Press Inc

Edmund Ludlow Keeney, MD: med adv *B* Shelbyville IN 1908 *ED* IN Univ AB 1930; Johns Hopkins Univ MD 1934 *NONPR AFFIL* dir: Allergy Fdn Am, Univ San Diego; mem: Alpha Omega Alpha, Am Acad Allergy, Am Med Assn, Am Soc Clinical Investigation, Beta Theta Pi, CA Med Assn, Phi Beta Kappa, Western Assn Physicians, Western Soc Clinical Res; pres emeritus: Scripps Clinic Res Fdn *CLUB AFFIL* El Dorado CC, Fox Acres CC, La Jolla CC, Rotary

Charles F. Patrick: treas, trust *CURR EMPL* secy, vp fin: Copley Press Inc (see above)

Richard R. Reilly: cultural & the arts adv

Karl ZoBell: vp, trust *B* La Jolla CA 1932 *ED* UT St Univ 1949-1951; Columbia Univ 1951-1952; Columbia Univ AB 1953; Stanford Univ JD 1958 *CURR EMPL* ptnr: Gray Cary Ames & Frye *CORP AFFIL* dir, fdr: La Jolla Bank & Trust Co; vp, dir: Geisel-Seuss Enterprises Inc *NONPR AFFIL* fellow: Am Coll Trust & Estate Couns; mem: Am Bar Assn, CA Bar Assn, Lambda Alpha; trust: Dr Seuss Fdn *CLUB AFFIL* La Jolla Beach & Tennis, La Jolla Beach & Volleyball *PHIL AFFIL* secy: Dr. Seuss Foundation

APPLICATION INFORMATION
Initial Approach: *Initial Contact:* letter *Include Information On:* name of organization, address, telephone number, and name of contact person; statement of purpose and objectives, succinct summary of project, anticipated cost of project, amount of request, and how funds will be spent; list of board of directors and staff, project budget; current financial report; and proof of tax-exempt status *Deadlines:* board meets in February and thereafter as resources are available; requests to be considered at the February meeting must be submitted in writing no later than January 1

Restrictions on Giving: Foundation does not make grants to individuals, dinners or special events, goodwill advertising, or political or lobbying groups. Grants generally are not made for unrestricted purposes, budgetary support, or operating expenses.

Grants generally are not made to organizations receiving support from United Way; local chapters of national organizations; public elementary and secondary schools; organizations whose activities are mainly international; research projects; courtesy advertising or underwriting for fund-raising events; government agencies; religious, fraternal, political, or athletic organizations; or conferences or seminars.

OTHER THINGS TO KNOW
Foundation does not grant interviews.

Contributions are made for one year and imply no commitment to repeat donations.

GRANTS ANALYSIS
Total Grants: $1,499,647
Number of Grants: 300*
Highest Grant: $100,000
Average Grant: $5,000*
Typical Range: $100 to $10,000
Disclosure Period: 1994

Note: Number of grants and average grant figures exclude 22 scholarships totaling $28,250 and 165 matching gifts totaling $40,320 and were supplied by the foundation. Recent grants are derived from a 1992 Form 990.

RECENT GRANTS

Library
5,000	Athenaeum, Philadelphia, PA	

General
360,274	United Way	
300,000	San Diego National Sports Training Foundation, San Diego, CA	

106,000	YMCA of San Diego County, San Diego, CA
50,000	Scripps Memorial Hospital Foundation, La Jolla, CA
50,000	Sharp Hospital Foundation, San Diego, CA

Cowell Foundation, S. H.

CONTACT
Thomas G. David
Director of Grants Programs
S. H. Cowell Foundation
120 Montgomery St., No. 2570
San Francisco, CA 94111
(415) 397-0285

FINANCIAL SUMMARY
Recent Giving: $8,500,000 (1995 est.);
$7,900,000 (1994 approx.); $7,034,998
(1993)

Assets: $149,640,058 (1993); $85,173,249
(1992); $140,000,000 (1991 approx.)

EIN: 94-1392803

CONTRIBUTIONS SUMMARY
Donor(s): The S. H. Cowell Foundation was
established in 1955 through the will of Sa-
muel Henry Cowell . S. H. Cowell's father,
Henry, was a noted businessman who made
his fortune during the famous California
Gold Rush of the 1850s. By 1888, Henry
Cowell owned the thriving Henry Cowell
Lime and Cement Company, various warehouses and storage companies, prime San
Francisco financial district properties, and
82,491 acres of land stretching from Texas
Island, Canada, to San Louis Obispo, CA.
Henry Cowell's net worth was estimated at
$3,000,000. S. H. Cowell, although one of
four surviving heirs, eventually inherited
this estate in its totality. When S. H. Cowell
died in 1955, his will provided for the creation of a foundation that would continue his
family's philanthropy. The original assets
bequeathed to the foundation exceeded
$12,560,363.

Typical Recipients: • *Arts & Humanities:*
Ballet, Ethnic & Folk Arts, Libraries, Muse-
ums/Galleries, Performing Arts, Theater
• *Civic & Public Affairs:* Asian American
Affairs, Community Foundations, Economic
Development, Employment/Job Training,
General, Housing, Public Policy, Urban &
Community Affairs, Women's Affairs • *Edu-
cation:* Colleges & Universities, Education
Associations, Elementary Education (Pri-
vate), Elementary Education (Public), Gen-
eral, Literacy, Preschool Education, Public
Education (Precollege), Secondary Educa-
tion (Public) • *Environment:* General, Re-
source Conservation • *Health:* AIDS/HIV,
Clinics/Medical Centers, Public Health • *In-
ternational:* Health Care/Hospitals, International Environmental Issues, International
Organizations, International Relief Efforts
• *Religion:* Jewish Causes, Religious Wel-

fare • *Science:* Scientific Centers & Insti-
tutes • *Social Services:* Child Welfare, Com-
munity Service Organizations, Day Care,
Domestic Violence, Family Planning, Fam-
ily Services, Food/Clothing Distribution,
Homes, People with Disabilities, Substance
Abuse, United Funds/United Ways, Youth
Organizations

Grant Types: capital, challenge, and project

Geographic Distribution: mainly Northern
California

GIVING OFFICERS
Thomas G. David: dir (grant program)

J. D. Erickson: pres

George A. Hopiak: secy-treas

Lise Einfeld Maisano: program off

Mary Seawell Metz: dir *B* Rockhill SC
1937 *ED* Furman Univ BA 1958; Inst
Phonetique 1962-1963; Sorbonne 1962-
1963; LA St Univ PhD 1966 *CORP AFFIL*
dir: Longs Drug Stores, Lucky Stores, Pacific Gas & Electric Co, Pacific Telesis
Group, Union Bank *NONPR AFFIL* adv
counc: Stanford Grad Sch Bus, Stanford
Univ Grad Sch Bus; assoc: Freedom Forum
Media Studies Ctr; dean extension: Univ CA
Berkeley; dir, mem: World Aff Counc Northern CA; exec comm: Womens Coll Coalition; mem: Assn Independent CA Colls
Univs, Bus-Higher Ed Forum, Natl Assn Independent Colls Univs, Phi Beta Kappa, Phi
Kappa Phi, Southern Conf Language Teaching, Western Coll Assn, Womens Forum;
mem ed bd: Liberal Ed; mem editorial bd:
Liberal Ed; trust: Am Conservatory Theater
PHIL AFFIL dir: Rosenberg Foundation

Fredric C. Nelson: dir

Max Thelen, Jr.: vp *B* Berkeley CA 1919
ED Univ CA Berkeley AB 1940; Harvard
Univ JD 1946 *NONPR AFFIL* mem: Am
Coll Trial Lawyers, CA Bar Assn, Counc
Foreign Rels; pres, dir: Oramax Fund; trust:
World Aff Counc *CLUB AFFIL* Common-
wealth, Marines Meml, World Trade

Beverly N. White: program off

Stephanie R. Wolf: exec dir

APPLICATION INFORMATION
Initial Approach:

Applicants are asked to submit a preliminary
letter to the foundation's executive director,
outlining the project or need for which support is requested and providing basic facts
relating to the applicant.

The letter should be two or three pages in
length and should include a summary of history, purpose, and goals of the applying
agency; budget and timetable for the project; specific amount requested from the
foundation and an explanation of the particular uses to which these funds would be applied; list of other funding sources and
amount solicited or received; and a copy of
the most recent IRS determination letter of
tax-exempt status.

Letters of inquiry are accepted throughout
the year.

The foundation board generally meets
monthly to consider requests.

Restrictions on Giving: The foundation normally does not make grants outside northern
California or to support individuals. It generally does not fund start-ups of new organizations not included within its affirmative
interests; academic or other research unless
significantly related to policies or activities
of an organization within its affirmative interest fields; general support, routine program administration, and operating
expenses; endowments and repayment of indebtedness, except in unusual cases; annual
fund-raising and development campaigns;
government or governmental agencies;
churches or sectarian religious programs;
hospitals or programs and projects under
hospital sponsorship; medical research or
treatment; conferences, seminars, workshops, symposia, or related activities; or media programs, including publications and
communications projects.

OTHER THINGS TO KNOW
The foundation "prefers to make grants for
unusual capital needs or specific projects,
rather than for general support, operating expenses, or repayment of indebtedness." Priority is given to applicants who have not
received previous grants from the foundation. The foundation is continually increasing its number of matching and challenge
grants to provide agencies with leverage in
fund raising and to amplify the effect of its
support.

PUBLICATIONS
Annual report

GRANTS ANALYSIS
Total Grants: $7,034,998

Number of Grants: 214

Highest Grant: $400,000

Average Grant: $32,874

Typical Range: $30,000 to $70,000

Disclosure Period: 1993

Note: Recent grants are derived from a 1993
Form 990.

RECENT GRANTS
Library
| 200,000 | Library Foundation of San Francisco, San Francisco, CA |

General
400,000	Brentwood Union School District, Brentwood, CA
400,000	Redwood City School District, San Francisco, CA
300,000	Marin Community Foundation, San Rafael, CA
265,000	Chinese Community Housing Corporation, San Francisco, CA
250,000	Mission Housing Development Corporation, San Francisco, CA

Crocker Trust, Mary A.

CONTACT
Charles Crocker
Trustee
Mary A. Crocker Trust
233 Post St., 2nd Fl.
San Francisco, CA 94108
(415) 982-0138

FINANCIAL SUMMARY
Recent Giving: $531,020 (1993); $501,000 (1992); $547,000 (1991)

Assets: $13,750,643 (1993); $12,396,088 (1992); $12,107,117 (1991)

EIN: 94-6051917

CONTRIBUTIONS SUMMARY
Donor(s): the late Mary A. Crocker

Typical Recipients: • *Arts & Humanities:* Community Arts, Film & Video, Libraries, Public Broadcasting • *Civic & Public Affairs:* Botanical Gardens/Parks, Employment/Job Training, Ethnic Organizations, Municipalities/Towns, Nonprofit Management, Philanthropic Organizations, Rural Affairs, Urban & Community Affairs • *Education:* Colleges & Universities, Education Funds, Education Reform, General, Literacy, Minority Education, Private Education (Precollege), Public Education (Precollege), Science/Mathematics Education, Secondary Education (Private), Secondary Education (Public), Special Education • *Environment:* Air/Water Quality, Forestry, General, Resource Conservation, Wildlife Protection • *Health:* Research/Studies Institutes • *International:* Health Care/Hospitals • *Religion:* Religious Welfare • *Science:* Science Museums, Scientific Centers & Institutes, Scientific Organizations • *Social Services:* Child Welfare, Community Centers, Community Service Organizations, Emergency Relief, Family Planning, Family Services, People with Disabilities, Youth Organizations

Grant Types: capital, emergency, general support, project, and seed money

Geographic Distribution: focus on the San Francisco Bay area, CA

GIVING OFFICERS
Elizabeth Atcheson: trust

Lucy Blake: trust

Charles Crocker: trust

Tania W. Stepanian: chmn

Frederick W. Whitridge: trust

APPLICATION INFORMATION
Initial Approach: Send letter requesting application form. There are no deadlines.

Restrictions on Giving: Does not support individuals or provide loans.

PUBLICATIONS
Application Guidelines

GRANTS ANALYSIS
Total Grants: $531,020

Number of Grants: 36

Highest Grant: $50,000

Typical Range: $1,000 to $25,000

Disclosure Period: 1993

Note: Recent grants are derived from a 1993 Form 990.

RECENT GRANTS
Library
50,000	San Francisco Library Foundation, San Francisco, CA	

General
25,000	Mentoring Center, San Francisco, CA	
25,000	Petaluma Wildlife and National Science Museum, San Francisco, CA	
25,000	San Francisco Day School, San Francisco, CA	
20,000	Beacon High School, San Francisco, CA	
20,000	Berkeley High School Development Group, Berkeley, CA	

Darling Foundation, Hugh and Hazel

CONTACT
Richard L. Stack
Trustee
Hugh and Hazel Darling Foundation
777 S Figueroa St., 37th Fl.
Los Angeles, CA 90017
(213) 683-5281

FINANCIAL SUMMARY
Recent Giving: $1,100,000 (1995 est.); $1,050,000 (1994); $1,092,500 (1993)

Assets: $23,000,000 (1995 est.); $22,000,000 (1994 approx.); $22,000,000 (1993 approx.)

EIN: 95-6874901

CONTRIBUTIONS SUMMARY
Donor(s): The foundation was established in 1988 from the estate of Hugh Darling and Hazel Darling after Mr. Darling passed away in 1986 and Mrs. Darling passed away in 1987.

Mr. Darling was a prominent lawyer in Southern California for more than 50 years. As an undergraduate, he attended the University of California at Berkeley, and he received his LL.B degree from the University of Southern California School of Law in 1927. He opened a law office with a partner in 1928 that today is known as the law firm of Darling, Hall & Rae in Los Angeles, CA. Mr. Darling developed an expertise in aviation law and served on the board of directors for Western Airlines.

He also belonged to many civic associations, and served as the mayor of Beverly Hills in 1960-61. A former president of the Los Angeles County Bar Association, he visited law schools as a speaker and used his influence to further the support of legal education in California.

Typical Recipients: • *Arts & Humanities:* History & Archaeology, Libraries • *Education:* Business Education, Colleges & Universities, Education Funds, Legal Education, Science/Mathematics Education, Special Education, Student Aid • *Science:* Science Museums • *Social Services:* Crime Prevention, People with Disabilities

Grant Types: capital, endowment, and scholarship

Geographic Distribution: limited to California

GIVING OFFICERS
Richard L. Stack: trust *B* Los Angeles CA 1947 *ED* Univ CA Los Angeles BA 1969; Loyola Univ JD 1973 *CURR EMPL* atty: Darling Hall & Rae *NONPR AFFIL* mem: St Thomas More Soc

APPLICATION INFORMATION
Initial Approach:

Applicants should submit a detailed one- or two-page letter of proposal.

Letters should include appropriate contact and mailing information, a description of the project, and the amount requested.

There are no deadlines for requesting funds.

Restrictions on Giving: Grants are limited to California educational institutions with a primary emphasis on legal education.

GRANTS ANALYSIS
Total Grants: $1,092,500

Number of Grants: 14

Highest Grant: $500,000

Average Grant: $78,036

Typical Range: $1,000 to $200,000

Disclosure Period: 1993

Note: Recent grants are derived from a 1993 grants list.

RECENT GRANTS
Library
500,000	University of California Los Angeles, Los Angeles, CA — law library	

General
250,000	Pepperdine University, Malibu, CA — endowment fund	
125,000	University of Southern California, Los Angeles, CA — endowment fund	
75,000	University of California, Berkeley, CA — renovation to Law School	
65,000	Azusa Pacific University, Azusa, CA — Business School Building	
25,000	Loyola School of Law, Los Angeles, CA — scholarship fund	

Dr. Seuss Foundation

CONTACT
Audrey S. Geisel
President
Dr. Seuss Fdn.
7301 Encelia Dr.
La Jolla, CA 92037
(619) 454-7384

FINANCIAL SUMMARY
Recent Giving: $433,615 (1993)
Assets: $2,600,102 (1993)
EIN: 95-6029752

CONTRIBUTIONS SUMMARY
Typical Recipients: • *Arts & Humanities:*
Arts Funds, Arts Outreach, Ethnic & Folk
Arts, Libraries, Museums/Galleries, Music,
Opera, Performing Arts, Public Broadcast-
ing, Theater • *Civic & Public Affairs:* Civil
Rights, Community Foundations, General,
Public Policy, Zoos/Aquariums • *Education:*
Colleges & Universities, Education Funds,
Education Reform, Literacy, Secondary Edu-
cation (Private) • *Health:* Cancer, Children's
Health/Hospitals, Clinics/Medical Centers,
Hospices, Prenatal Health Issues, Re-
search/Studies Institutes • *International:* For-
eign Arts Organizations, Human Rights,
International Organizations, International
Relief Efforts • *Religion:* Religious Welfare
• *Social Services:* Child Welfare, Family
Planning, Food/Clothing Distribution, Peo-
ple with Disabilities, Scouts, Senior Serv-
ices, YMCA/YWCA/YMHA/YWHA

Grant Types: general support

Geographic Distribution: focus on CA

GIVING OFFICERS
R. L. Bernstein: vp

Audrey Geisel: pres, asst secy

Edward Lathem: dir

Karl ZoBell: secy *B* La Jolla CA 1932 *ED*
UT St Univ 1949-1951; Columbia Univ
1951-1952; Columbia Univ AB 1953; Stan-
ford Univ JD 1958 *CURR EMPL* ptnr: Gray
Cary Ames & Frye *CORP AFFIL* dir, fdr: La
Jolla Bank & Trust Co; vp, dir: Geisel-Seuss
Enterprises Inc *NONPR AFFIL* fellow: Am
Coll Trust & Estate Couns; mem: Am Bar
Assn, CA Bar Assn, Lambda Alpha; trust:
Dr Seuss Fdn *CLUB AFFIL* La Jolla Beach
& Tennis, La Jolla Beach & Volleyball
PHIL AFFIL vp, trust: James S. Copley
Foundation

APPLICATION INFORMATION
Initial Approach: The foundation has no
formal grant application procedure or application form. There are no deadlines.

GRANTS ANALYSIS
Total Grants: $433,615
Number of Grants: 144
Highest Grant: $215,000
Typical Range: $50 to $22,250
Disclosure Period: 1993
Note: Recent grants are derived from a 1993
Form 990.

RECENT GRANTS
Library
1,000	Lorraine Williams-Oregon Children's Library Center, OR	
1,000	Springfield Library and Museums, Springfield, MA	

General
215,000	San Diego Community Foundation, San Diego, CA
22,250	Green Cancer Center Scripps Clinic
19,650	Zoological Society of San Diego, San Diego, CA
15,600	Scripps Clinic and Research Foundation, La Jolla, CA
10,000	Fund for Free Expression, New York, NY

Durfee Foundation

CONTACT
Robert S. MacFarlane, Jr.
Managing Director
Durfee Fdn.
11444 W Olympic Blvd., Ste. 1017
Los Angeles, CA 90064
(310) 312-9543

FINANCIAL SUMMARY
Recent Giving: $588,734 (1992); $545,849
(1991); $536,670 (1990)

Assets: $14,529,882 (1992); $13,451,929
(1991); $11,797,461 (1990)

EIN: 95-2223738

CONTRIBUTIONS SUMMARY
Donor(s): Ray Stanton Avery, the late
Dorothy Durfee Avery

Typical Recipients: • *Arts & Humanities:*
Community Arts, History & Archaeology,
Libraries, Museums/Galleries, Public Broadcasting • *Civic & Public Affairs:* Hispanic
Affairs, Nonprofit Management, Philanthropic Organizations, Urban & Community
Affairs, Women's Affairs • *Education:* Colleges & Universities, Community & Junior
Colleges, Gifted & Talented Programs, International Studies, Minority Education, Sci-
ence/Mathematics Education • *Environment:*
General • *Health:* Health Organizations • *International:* Foreign Educational Institutions • *Social Services:* Community Service
Organizations, Youth Organizations

Grant Types: project

Geographic Distribution: focus on CA

GIVING OFFICERS
Caroline Avery: secy

Ray Stanton Avery: don, chmn *PHIL AF-
FIL* trust emeritus: John Randolph and Dora
Haynes Foundation

Russell D. Avery: pres

Robert S. MacFarlane, Jr.: mng dir, trust

Judith A. Newkirk: vp, asst treas

Michael A. Newkirk: treas

APPLICATION INFORMATION
Initial Approach: Submit grant application
at request of foundation only.

Restrictions on Giving: Does not fund endowments or operating budgets.

GRANTS ANALYSIS
Total Grants: $588,734
Number of Grants: 20
Highest Grant: $159,524
Typical Range: $2,175 to $100,000
Disclosure Period: 1992
Note: Recent grants are derived from a 1992
Form 990.

RECENT GRANTS
Library
100,000	Huntington Library, San Marino, CA — endow the R. Stanton Avery Chair
12,000	California Historical Society, San Francisco, CA — develop visual imaging system for library automation program
5,000	Huntington Library, San Marino, CA — support the American/Chinese program

General
159,524	Earthwatch, Watertown, MA — support and Expedition Awards program, which provides educational fieldwork for high school students
95,380	Johns Hopkins Center for Talented Youth, Baltimore, MD — support an Expedition Awards program, which provides educational fieldwork for high school students
51,316	Claremont Graduate School, Claremont, CA — support the American/Chinese program
33,658	Boys and Girls Club, Santa Ana, CA — develop full-time computer instructional program
25,792	California Institute of Technology, Pasadena, CA — support the American/Chinese program

Essick Foundation

CONTACT
Bryant Essick
President
Essick Fdn.
PO Box 61030
Pasadena, CA 91116
(213) 626-6658

FINANCIAL SUMMARY
Recent Giving: $158,279 (1993); $159,532
(1992); $154,995 (1991)

Assets: $3,257,092 (1993); $3,296,547 (1992); $3,282,074 (1991)

EIN: 95-6048985

CONTRIBUTIONS SUMMARY
Donor(s): the late Jeanette Marie Essick, Bryant Essick, Essick Investment Co.

Typical Recipients: • *Arts & Humanities:* Arts Institutes, Ethnic & Folk Arts, Libraries, Museums/Galleries, Public Broadcasting • *Civic & Public Affairs:* Clubs, Philanthropic Organizations, Zoos/Aquariums • *Education:* Colleges & Universities, Education Funds, Engineering/Technological Education, Science/Mathematics Education • *Health:* Children's Health/Hospitals, Clinics/Medical Centers, Emergency/Ambulance Services, Eyes/Blindness, Health Organizations, Hospitals, Medical Research, Prenatal Health Issues, Research/Studies Institutes, Single-Disease Health Associations • *Religion:* Churches, Religious Welfare • *Social Services:* Child Welfare, Community Service Organizations, People with Disabilities, Recreation & Athletics, Scouts, Special Olympics, United Funds/United Ways, Volunteer Services, Youth Organizations

Grant Types: general support

Geographic Distribution: primarily in southern CA

GIVING OFFICERS
Bryant Essick: pres

James H. Essick: vp

Robert N. Essick: vp *B* Los Angeles CA 1942 *NONPR AFFIL* mem: Modern Language Assn; mem bd overseers: Huntington Library

APPLICATION INFORMATION
Initial Approach: Send brief letter of inquiry describing program or project and proof of tax-exempt status. There are no deadlines.

GRANTS ANALYSIS
Total Grants: $158,279

Number of Grants: 35

Highest Grant: $50,000

Typical Range: $200 to $25,000

Disclosure Period: 1993

Note: Recent grants are derived from a 1993 Form 990.

RECENT GRANTS

Library
25,000	Huntington Library and Art Gallery, San Marino, CA	

General
50,000	Hospital of the Good Samaritan, Los Angeles, CA	
10,000	United Way, Pasadena, CA	
8,532	American Red Cross, New York, NY	
6,547	University of Rochester, Rochester, NY	
5,000	California Special Olympics, Santa Monica, CA	

Femino Foundation

CONTACT
James J. Femino
President
Femino Fdn.
PO Box 567
West Covina, CA 91793
(818) 915-1641

FINANCIAL SUMMARY
Recent Giving: $116,250 (fiscal 1993); $133,000 (fiscal 1992); $99,000 (fiscal 1991)

Assets: $3,784,395 (fiscal 1993); $3,192,586 (fiscal 1992); $2,862,648 (fiscal 1991)

Gifts Received: $295,500 (fiscal 1993); $265,000 (fiscal 1992); $290,500 (fiscal 1991)

Fiscal Note: In fiscal 1993, contributions were received from James J. and Sue Femino.

EIN: 23-7423792

CONTRIBUTIONS SUMMARY
Donor(s): James J. Femino, Sue Femino, Dominic Femino

Typical Recipients: • *Arts & Humanities:* Arts Centers, Historic Preservation, History & Archaeology, Libraries, Music, Performing Arts • *Civic & Public Affairs:* Botanical Gardens/Parks, General, Hispanic Affairs, Women's Affairs • *Education:* Colleges & Universities, Medical Education, Private Education (Precollege), Student Aid • *Health:* AIDS/HIV, Alzheimers Disease, Cancer, Clinics/Medical Centers, Health Organizations, Hospitals, Hospitals (University Affiliated), Medical Research, Mental Health, Public Health, Research/Studies Institutes, Speech & Hearing • *Social Services:* Child Welfare, Community Service Organizations, Domestic Violence, United Funds/United Ways, Youth Organizations

Grant Types: research and scholarship

Geographic Distribution: focus on Los Angeles, CA

GIVING OFFICERS
Robert L. Bacon: secy

James J. Femino: pres

Sue Femino: vp

APPLICATION INFORMATION
Initial Approach: Send brief letter of inquiry describing program. There are no deadlines.

GRANTS ANALYSIS
Total Grants: $116,250

Number of Grants: 34

Highest Grant: $27,500

Typical Range: $250 to $20,000

Disclosure Period: fiscal year ending September 30, 1993

Note: Recent grants are derived from a fiscal 1993 Form 990.

RECENT GRANTS

Library
20,000	University of Southern California Library, Los Angeles, CA — scripter	
2,000	Huntington Library, Huntington, CA	

General
27,500	University of Southern California, Los Angeles, CA	
10,000	University of Southern California School of Dentists, Los Angeles, CA	
5,000	French Foundation, Los Angeles, CA	
5,000	Northwestern University, Evanston, IL	
5,000	Ortho and Education Foundation, Los Angeles, CA	

Fireman's Fund Insurance Co. / Fireman's Fund Foundation

Employees: 8,900
Parent Company: Allianz of America, Inc.
Headquarters: Novato, CA
SIC Major Group: Fire, Marine & Casualty Insurance and Surety Insurance

CONTACT
Barbara B. Friede
Secretary and Director
Fireman's Fund Fdn.
777 San Marin Dr.
Novato, CA 94998-1406
(415) 899-2757

FINANCIAL SUMMARY
Recent Giving: $1,000,000 (1995 est.); $998,636 (1994); $986,004 (1993)

Assets: $100,000 (1995 est.); $106,335 (1994); $65,253 (1993)

Gifts Received: $993,768 (1993); $1,039,333 (1992)

Fiscal Note: Above figures reflect foundation giving only and do not include subsidiary contributions. Above figures exclude nonmonetary support.

EIN: 94-6078025

CONTRIBUTIONS SUMMARY
Typical Recipients: • *Arts & Humanities:* Arts Centers, Arts Institutes, Arts Outreach, Ballet, Community Arts, Dance, Ethnic & Folk Arts, Historic Preservation, Libraries, Museums/Galleries, Music, Opera, Performing Arts, Public Broadcasting, Theater, Visual Arts • *Civic & Public Affairs:* Economic Development, Employment/Job Training, General, Housing, Nonprofit Management, Parades/Festivals, Philanthropic Organizations, Women's Affairs, Zoos/Aquariums • *Education:* Business Education, Colleges & Universities, Community & Junior Colleges, Continuing Education, Private Education (Precollege), Public Education (Precollege), Religious Education, Secondary Education (Public) • *Environment:* General • *Health:*

Heart, Hospitals, Preventive Medicine/Wellness Organizations • *Religion:* Religious Welfare • *Science:* Observatories & Planetariums, Science Exhibits & Fairs, Science Museums • *Social Services:* Child Welfare, Community Centers, Community Service Organizations, Counseling, Day Care, Domestic Violence, Emergency Relief, Family Services, Food/Clothing Distribution, People with Disabilities, Senior Services, Shelters/Homelessness, Substance Abuse, United Funds/United Ways, Youth Organizations

Grant Types: employee matching gifts and project

Note: Employee matching gift ratio: 1 to 1.

Nonmonetary Support: $100,000 (1993); $100,000 (1992); $100,000 (1991)

Nonmonetary Support Types: donated equipment and in-kind services

Note: Furniture requests should be sent to Judy Anatasia. Requests for use of facilities should be sent to Terri McMahan.

Geographic Distribution: primarily in San Francisco, Sonoma and Marin counties, CA

Operating Locations: CA (Novato, San Francisco), GA (Atlanta), HI (Honolulu), IA (Bettendorf), IL (Chicago), LA (Metairie), MO (St. Louis), NJ (Parsippany), OH (Cincinnati), TX (Dallas), WI (Wauwatosa)

CORP. OFFICERS

Gary E. Black: *CURR EMPL* exec vp, dir: Firemans Fund Ins Co

Herbert E. Hansmeyer: *CURR EMPL* chmn, dir: Firemans Fund Ins Co

Timothy T. Koo: *CURR EMPL* exec vp, dir: Firemans Fund Ins Co

John F. Meyer: *CURR EMPL* exec vp, cfo, dir: FFI Co

David R. Pollard: *CURR EMPL* exec vp: Firemans Fund Ins Co

Joe L. Stinnette, Jr.: *CURR EMPL* pres, ceo, dir: Firemans Fund Ins Co

Thomas A. Swanson: *CURR EMPL* sr vp, gen couns, secy: Firemans Fund Ins Co

GIVING OFFICERS

Gary E. Black: pres, dir *CURR EMPL* exec vp, dir: Firemans Fund Ins Co (see above)

Barbara Friede: secy, operating dir

Timothy T. Koo: dir *CURR EMPL* exec vp, dir: Firemans Fund Ins Co (see above)

Harold Marsh: treas

John F. Meyer: chmn *CURR EMPL* exec vp, cfo, dir: FFI Co (see above)

Kathryn A. Murrell: dir *CURR EMPL* sr vp: Firemans Fund Ins Co

David R. Pollard: dir *CURR EMPL* exec vp: Firemans Fund Ins Co (see above)

Thomas E. Rowe: dir *B* 1950 *ED* Towson St Univ BA 1972 *CURR EMPL* exec vp, dir: Am Ins Co Inc *CORP AFFIL* exec vp, dir: Am Automobile Ins Co, Assoc Indemnity Corp, Natl Surety Corp

Joe L. Stinnette, Jr.: dir *CURR EMPL* pres, ceo, dir: Firemans Fund Ins Co (see above)

Thomas A. Swanson: dir *CURR EMPL* sr vp, gen couns, secy: Firemans Fund Ins Co (see above)

APPLICATION INFORMATION

Initial Approach: *Initial Contact:* brief letter of not more than two pages, plus attachments *Include Information On:* description of the organization; constituency served; statement of mission, objectives and goals; amount requested, and an explanation of how funds will be used to support a specific program or project; also include a program budget showing expenses and income sources, list of current contributors and amounts, recently audited financial statement, proof of tax-exempt status, and list of board members, executive director and other key staff members *Deadlines:* none

Restrictions on Giving: Grants are not made to individuals; religious, veterans, labor, or fraternal organizations; capital campaigns, endowment funds or operating expenses; fund-raising or sporting events; subscription fees or admission tickets; insurance premiums; medical research and health organizations; political candidates; political or lobbying groups; dinners or special events; trips or tours; advertisements; or videos, films, or television productions.

PUBLICATIONS
Guidelines

GRANTS ANALYSIS
Total Grants: $998,636
Number of Grants: 128*
Highest Grant: $30,000
Average Grant: $5,000*
Typical Range: $5,000 to $10,000
Disclosure Period: 1994

Note: Number of grants and average grant figures were provided by the foundation and exclude united fund contributions and matching gifts. Recent grants are derived from a 1993 Form 990.

RECENT GRANTS

General

50,580	United Way of the Bay Area, San Francisco, CA	
10,000	Marin Housing Center, San Rafael, CA	
10,000	San Francisco Zoological Society, San Francisco, CA	
7,880	United Way Crusade of Mercy, Chicago, IL	
7,500	St. Vincent DePaul Society, Marin County, CA	

Fleishhacker Foundation

CONTACT
Christine Elbel
Executive Director
Fleishhacker Fdn.
One Maritime Plaza, Ste. 830
San Francisco, CA 94111
(415) 788-2909

FINANCIAL SUMMARY

Recent Giving: $518,350 (1993); $531,339 (1992); $707,200 (1991)

Assets: $7,907,421 (1993); $7,486,161 (1992); $7,216,408 (1991)

Gifts Received: $55,000 (1992); $190,000 (1991); $245,000 (1990)

Fiscal Note: In fiscal 1992, contributions were received from the Walter & Elise Haas Fund ($50,000) and Grants for the Arts ($5,000).

EIN: 94-6051048

CONTRIBUTIONS SUMMARY

Donor(s): the late Mortimer Fleishhacker, Sr., and Janet Fleishhacker Bates

Typical Recipients: • *Arts & Humanities:* Arts Appreciation, Arts Associations & Councils, Arts Centers, Arts Festivals, Arts Outreach, Ballet, Community Arts, Dance, Ethnic & Folk Arts, Film & Video, Historic Preservation, Libraries, Literary Arts, Museums/Galleries, Music, Performing Arts, Public Broadcasting, Theater • *Civic & Public Affairs:* General, Municipalities/Towns, Parades/Festivals, Urban & Community Affairs • *Education:* Arts/Humanities Education, Colleges & Universities, Education Reform, Minority Education, Private Education (Precollege), Public Education (Precollege), School Volunteerism, Science/Mathematics Education, Secondary Education (Public), Social Sciences Education, Special Education, Student Aid • *Environment:* General • *International:* International Organizations • *Religion:* Jewish Causes, Missionary Activities (Domestic), Religious Organizations • *Social Services:* Child Welfare, Family Services, Youth Organizations

Grant Types: capital, conference/seminar, endowment, fellowship, general support, operating expenses, project, and seed money

Geographic Distribution: limited to northern CA

GIVING OFFICERS
Delia F. Ehrlich: dir
Jodi Ehrlich: dir
John Stephen Ehrlich, Jr.: dir
Christine Elbel: exec dir
David Fleishhacker: pres, dir
Mortimer Fleishhacker III: treas, dir
Lois Gordon: dir
Sandra Fleishhacker Randall: dir
Deborah Sloss: secy
Laurie Sloss: dir
Leon Sloss: vp, dir

APPLICATION INFORMATION

Initial Approach: Fellowship seekers should contact the foundation for detailed application form required for certain grant programs. Send brief letter of inquiry describing program or project. Board meets quarterly. Decisions are made within two to five months.

Restrictions on Giving: Does not provide funds for annual campaigns, deficit financing, or matching gifts.

PUBLICATIONS
Application Guidelines

GRANTS ANALYSIS
Total Grants: $518,350

Highest Grant: $100,000

Typical Range: $500 to $20,000

Disclosure Period: 1993

Note: Recent grants are derived from a 1993 Form 990.

RECENT GRANTS

Library

20,000	Main Library of San Francisco, San Francisco, CA — first payment on a five-year, $100,000 grant to support the furnishing and equipment of the New Main Library building
20,000	New Main Campaign, San Francisco, San Francisco, CA — first of five payments on a $100,000 grant to support the completion of the new Main Library of San Francisco

General

20,000	Fine Arts Museums Foundation, San Francisco, CA — third and final year of a $45,000 grant to support the permanent installation of portions of the Teotihuacan murals from Mexico
10,000	College Preparatory School, Oakland, CA — fifth and final payment on a $50,000 grant to support capital improvements
10,000	Congregation Emanu-El, San Francisco, San Francisco, CA — fifth and final payment of a $90,000 grant to support capital renovations
10,000	Foundation Consortium for School-Linked Services, Sacramento, CA — to help the regional component of this three-year pilot project to undertake systemic reform of school-based support services within the state educational system
10,000	Foundation Consortium for School-Linked Services, Sacramento, CA — to help the regional component of this three-year pilot project to undertake systemic reform of school-based support services within the state educational system

Friedman Family Foundation

CONTACT
Phyllis K. Friedman
President
Friedman Family Fdn.
204 E 2nd Ave., Ste. 719
San Mateo, CA 94401
(415) 342-8750

FINANCIAL SUMMARY
Recent Giving: $232,140 (fiscal 1994); $203,935 (fiscal 1993); $201,950 (fiscal 1992)

Assets: $4,940,680 (fiscal 1994); $4,111,251 (fiscal 1993); $4,058,497 (fiscal 1992)

Gifts Received: $750,929 (fiscal 1994); $427,298 (fiscal 1992)

Fiscal Note: In fiscal 1994, contributions were received from Phyllis K. Friedman.

EIN: 94-6109692

CONTRIBUTIONS SUMMARY
Donor(s): Phyllis K. Friedman, Howard Friedman

Typical Recipients: • *Arts & Humanities:* Arts Festivals, Community Arts, Libraries, Museums/Galleries, Music, Public Broadcasting, Theater • *Civic & Public Affairs:* African American Affairs, Asian American Affairs, Economic Development, Employment/Job Training, Ethnic Organizations, General, Hispanic Affairs, Housing, Law & Justice, Legal Aid, Native American Affairs, Nonprofit Management, Parades/Festivals, Professional & Trade Associations, Public Policy, Urban & Community Affairs, Women's Affairs • *Education:* Colleges & Universities, International Exchange, Private Education (Precollege), Public Education (Precollege) • *Environment:* General • *Health:* AIDS/HIV, Clinics/Medical Centers, Health Policy/Cost Containment, Health Organizations, Hospitals, Medical Research, Public Health, Single-Disease Health Associations • *International:* Human Rights, International Development, International Organizations, International Relations, International Relief Efforts • *Religion:* Jewish Causes, Religious Organizations, Religious Welfare • *Science:* Observatories & Planetariums • *Social Services:* Animal Protection, Child Abuse, Child Welfare, Community Service Organizations, Domestic Violence, Emergency Relief, Family Services, Food/Clothing Distribution, People with Disabilities, Senior Services, Shelters/Homelessness, United Funds/United Ways, YMCA/YWCA/YMHA/YWHA, Youth Organizations

Grant Types: general support

Geographic Distribution: national, with focus on CA

GIVING OFFICERS
Bob Friedman: treas

David Friedman: secy *CURR EMPL* sr vp: Heller Fin *PHIL AFFIL* treas: Friedman Family Foundation

Ellie Friedman: vp

Phyllis K. Friedman: pres

APPLICATION INFORMATION
Initial Approach: Request application form. There are no deadlines.

Restrictions on Giving: The foundation does not make grants to individuals. Limited to the San Francisco Bay Area.

GRANTS ANALYSIS
Total Grants: $232,140

Number of Grants: 87

Highest Grant: $10,000

Typical Range: $50 to $10,000

Disclosure Period: fiscal year ending February 28, 1994

Note: Recent grants are derived from a fiscal 1994 Form 990.

RECENT GRANTS

General

10,000	Bar Association of San Francisco, San Francisco, CA
10,000	Bay Area Women's Resource Center, San Francisco, CA
10,000	Coalition on Homelessness, San Francisco, CA
10,000	Coleman Advocates for Children and Youth, San Francisco, CA
10,000	Community Development Institute, East Palo Alto, CA

Fujitsu America, Inc.

Sales: $1.5 billion
Employees: 4,000
Headquarters: San Jose, CA
SIC Major Group: Industrial Machinery & Equipment

CONTACT
Colleen O'Hare
Contact
Fujitsu America, Inc.
3055 Orchard Dr.
San Jose, CA 95134
(408) 432-1300

CONTRIBUTIONS SUMMARY
Fujitsu America's giving priorities include the arts (libraries, museums), education, health (hospitals, single-disease health associations), and social services (community service organizations, united funds). About 50% goes to education with emphasis on minority-related issues.

Typical Recipients: • *Arts & Humanities:* Libraries, Museums/Galleries • *Education:* Colleges & Universities, Minority Education • *Health:* Hospitals, Single-Disease Health Associations • *Social Services:* Community Service Organizations, United Funds/United Ways

Grant Types: general support

Geographic Distribution: headquarters and operating locations
Operating Locations: CA (San Jose)

CORP. OFFICERS
Yoshio Honda: *CURR EMPL* pres: Fujitsu Am

K. Nogawa: *CURR EMPL* cfo: Fujitsu Am

GIVING OFFICERS
Colleen O'Hare: *CURR EMPL* contact: Fujitsu Am

APPLICATION INFORMATION
Initial Approach: Submit a letter at any time, including a description of the organization, amount and purpose of request, goals and objectives of the organization, and a list of the board of directors.

Restrictions on Giving: Value of monetary and nonmonetary support is not available. Nonmonetary support generally is in the form of donated computers and telecommunications equipment.

GRANTS ANALYSIS
Typical Range: $1,000 to $2,500

Gamble Foundation

CONTACT
Launce E. Gamble
President
Gamble Fdn.
PO Box 2655
San Francisco, CA 94126
(415) 957-9999

FINANCIAL SUMMARY
Recent Giving: $117,500 (1992)
Assets: $2,738,276 (1992)
Gifts Received: $45,000 (1992)
Fiscal Note: In 1992, contributions were received from Mary S. Gamble ($15,000), George F. Gamble ($15,000), and Launce E. Gamble ($15,000).
EIN: 94-1680503

CONTRIBUTIONS SUMMARY
Typical Recipients: • *Arts & Humanities:* Ballet, Libraries, Museums/Galleries, Opera • *Civic & Public Affairs:* Economic Development, General, Legal Aid, Urban & Community Affairs • *Education:* Agricultural Education, Arts/Humanities Education, General, Private Education (Precollege), Science/Mathematics Education, Secondary Education (Private), Secondary Education (Public), Student Aid • *Environment:* Wildlife Protection • *Health:* Arthritis, Clinics/Medical Centers, Emergency/Ambulance Services • *International:* Foreign Educational Institutions • *Religion:* Ministries • *Social Services:* Child Welfare, Community Service Organizations, People with Disabilities, Recreation & Athletics, Scouts, Shelters/Homelessness, United Funds/United Ways, Youth Organizations
Grant Types: general support
Geographic Distribution: focus on CA

GIVING OFFICERS
George F. Gamble: vp, secy,treas
Launce E. Gamble: pres
Mary S. Gamble: vp

APPLICATION INFORMATION
Initial Approach: Send a brief letter of inquiry. There are no deadlines.

GRANTS ANALYSIS
Total Grants: $117,500
Number of Grants: 40
Highest Grant: $15,000
Typical Range: $250 to $10,000
Disclosure Period: 1992

Note: Recent grants are derived from a 1992 Form 990.

RECENT GRANTS
Library

2,500	Friends of Bancroft Library, Berkeley, CA — for support of the arts	
2,500	Friends of Bancroft Library, Berkeley, CA — for support of the arts	
500	Woodside Elementary School Library, Woodside, CA — for support of the arts	

General

15,000	Larkin Street Youth Center, San Francisco, CA — for social rehabilitation	
10,000	Napa Valley Shelter Project Napa County Council for Economic Development, Napa, CA — for social rehabilitation	
10,000	Oak Street House Golden Gate Compassionate Ministries, San Francisco, CA — for social rehabilitation	
10,000	Shelter Network of San Mateo County, San Mateo, CA — for social rehabilitation	
6,250	Thacher School, Ojai, CA — for educational purposes	

Gap, Inc., The / Gap Foundation

Revenue: $3.72 billion
Employees: 39,000
Headquarters: San Francisco, CA
SIC Major Group: Family Clothing Stores

CONTACT
Kim Castner
Foundation Administrator
Gap Foundation
One Harrison St.
San Francisco, CA 94105
(415) 291-2757
Note: Telephone inquiries are discouraged.

FINANCIAL SUMMARY
Recent Giving: $5,300,000 (fiscal 1995 est.); $4,270,000 (fiscal 1994); $4,190,000 (fiscal 1993)

Assets: $5,290,000 (fiscal 1995 est.); $4,800,000 (fiscal 1994); $3,400,000 (fiscal 1993)

Gifts Received: $2,975,000 (fiscal 1994); $615,000 (fiscal 1990); $623,500 (fiscal 1989)

Fiscal Note: Company gives directly and through the foundation. In 1994, foundation giving totaled $2,108,536. Above figures include nonmonetary support. In fiscal 1994, contributions were received from The Gap, Inc.

EIN: 94-2474426

CONTRIBUTIONS SUMMARY
Typical Recipients: • *Arts & Humanities:* Libraries, Music • *Education:* Minority Education, Public Education (Precollege) • *Environment:* General • *Health:* Medical Research, Single-Disease Health Associations • *Social Services:* Child Welfare, Community Service Organizations, Food/Clothing Distribution, Shelters/Homelessness, United Funds/United Ways, Volunteer Services, Youth Organizations

Grant Types: employee matching gifts and general support

Note: In fiscal 1994, matching gifts amounted to $267,395, about 6% of total foundation contributions.

Nonmonetary Support: $1,170,000 (fiscal 1994); $1,693,000 (fiscal 1993); $1,422,000 (fiscal 1992)

Nonmonetary Support Types: donated equipment and donated products

Note: The Gap awards merchandise, office equipment (computers), and gift certificates. Contact Molly White, senior director, for information. The company also offers employee paid leave for volunteer activities.

Geographic Distribution: headquarter counties of San Francisco and San Mateo, CA; with limited giving in New York, NY, Erlanger, KY, Baltimore, MD, and Ventura, CA

Operating Locations: CA (San Bruno, San Francisco)

Note: The Gap and its divisions operate 1,300 stores in the United States, the United Kingdom, France, and Canada.

CORP. OFFICERS
Millard S. Drexler: *B* New York NY 1944 *ED* Boston Univ MBA 1967; SUNY Buffalo MA *CURR EMPL* pres, dir: The Gap Inc *CORP AFFIL* ceo: Banana Republic; pres, ceo, dir: AnnTaylor Stores

Donald George Fisher: *B* 1928 *ED* Univ CA BS 1950 *CURR EMPL* fdr, chmn, ceo: The Gap Inc *CORP AFFIL* dir: Charles Schwab & Co Inc *PHIL AFFIL* trust: D and DF Foundation

Robert J. Fisher: *B* 1955 *CURR EMPL* exec vp, coo: The Gap Inc

Richard M. Lyons: *CURR EMPL* exec vp: The Gap Inc

GIVING OFFICERS
John P. Carver: trust

Kim Castner: admin

Jack Chin: program off

Millard S. Drexler: trust *CURR EMPL* pres, dir: The Gap Inc (see above)

Donald George Fisher: pres *CURR EMPL* fdr, chmn, ceo: The Gap Inc *PHIL AFFIL* trust: D and DF Foundation (see above)

Doris F. Fisher: treas *B* 1931 *PHIL AFFIL* trust: D and DF Foundation

Robert J. Fisher: vp *CURR EMPL* exec vp, coo: The Gap Inc (see above)

Anne Lawrence: dir

Molly White: secy, vp admin

Dianne Yamashiro-Omi: program off

APPLICATION INFORMATION

Initial Approach: *Initial Contact:* a concise one- or two-page letter *Include Information On:* description of the organization and project; services provided, including target population; amount requested; short budget with list of major donors; proof of tax-exempt status; and percentage of overhead cost related to total organizational budget *Deadlines:* if requested, proposals are due quarterly, at the beginning of the month before the month of the next board meeting

Restrictions on Giving: Does not donate to individuals, political candidates, religious organizations for sectarian purposes, promotional/tie-ins or sponsorship, or to fundraising benefits.

OTHER THINGS TO KNOW

The Gap's divisions include Banana Republic, Gap Stores, GapKids, BabyGap, Gap Shoes, and Gap Warehouses.

The Gap Foundation reports that it donates cash, gift certificates, and limited contributions of merchandise.

A full proposal, if requested, should include brief statement of organization's history and goals; exact purpose of project and grant request; target population(s); amount requested total project budget, organization budget, other sources of funds, anticipated or committed; copy of most recent 990, with attached schedule A; most recent, audited financial statement; copy of 501(c)3 designation letter; description of how project will be evaluated; list of board members with affiliations.

Organizations outside of headquarters area should contact regional manager for information on contributions. The regional manager's name and address can be obtained from any Gap, Gapkids, or Banana Republic store.

The company reports that it donates 1% of its pre-tax earnings to the foundation. It also reports that all charitable giving for the its divisions are carried out by the foundation.

PUBLICATIONS

Annual report, funding guidelines

GRANTS ANALYSIS

Total Grants: $3,100,000*

Number of Grants: 830*

Highest Grant: $70,000

Average Grant: $10,000*

Typical Range: $1,000 to $15,000

Disclosure Period: fiscal year ending June 30, 1994

Note: Total grants, number of grants, and average grant include $267,000 in matching gifts. Typical grant range does not include matching gifts.Total grants figure includes $375,000 to the United Way, but not non-monetary support. Recent grants are derived from a fiscal 1994 Form 990.

RECENT GRANTS

General

50,000	Red Cross, San Francisco, CA
25,000	Gay Men's Health Crisis, San Francisco, CA
25,000	Good Samaritan Family Resource Center, San Francisco, CA
25,000	San Francisco Neighborhood Legal Assistance, San Francisco, CA
20,000	California Academy of Sciences, San Francisco, CA

Garland Foundation, John Jewett and H. Chandler

CONTACT

G. E. Morrow
Manager
John Jewett and H. Chandler Garland Fdn.
PO Box 550
Pasadena, CA 91102-0550

FINANCIAL SUMMARY

Recent Giving: $1,473,650 (1992); $1,395,658 (1990); $1,237,301 (1989)

Assets: $392,247 (1992); $142,190 (1991); $165,168 (1989)

Gifts Received: $1,652,727 (1992); $1,419,071 (1991)

Fiscal Note: In 1992, contributions were received from Chandler Trust ($1,511,440) and trust under the will of J.J. Garland ($141,287).

EIN: 95-6023587

CONTRIBUTIONS SUMMARY

Donor(s): members of the Garland family

Typical Recipients: • *Arts & Humanities:* Historic Preservation, Libraries, Public Broadcasting • *Education:* Colleges & Universities, Private Education (Precollege), Public Education (Precollege) • *Environment:* General • *Health:* Hospitals, Single-Disease Health Associations • *Social Services:* Child Welfare, Community Service Organizations, United Funds/United Ways, Youth Organizations

Grant Types: general support

Geographic Distribution: focus on southern CA

GIVING OFFICERS

Ann K. Babcock: trust

Gwendolyn G. Babcock: trust *B* 1936 *ED* Bryn Mawr Coll *CURR EMPL* investor:

Chandis Securities Co *CORP AFFIL* dir: Times Mirror Co; trust: Chandler Trusts

John C. Babcock: trust

Sarah G. Babcock: trust

Susan H. Babcock: trust

G. E. Morrow: mgr, trust

APPLICATION INFORMATION

Initial Approach: Send full description of purpose, program, and amount of grant being sought with a copy of federal and state tax-exempt letter. There are no deadlines.

Restrictions on Giving: The foundation does not make grants to individuals. Limited to Southern California.

GRANTS ANALYSIS

Total Grants: $1,473,650

Disclosure Period: 1992

Note: Grants list for 1992 was not provided.

Gellert Foundation, Carl

CONTACT

Peter J. Brusati
Secretary
Carl Gellert Fdn.
2222 19th Ave.
San Francisco, CA 94116
(415) 566-4420

FINANCIAL SUMMARY

Recent Giving: $498,800 (fiscal 1993); $576,600 (fiscal 1992); $628,800 (fiscal 1991)

Assets: $7,997,738 (fiscal 1993); $8,109,597 (fiscal 1992); $7,936,168 (fiscal 1991)

EIN: 94-6062858

CONTRIBUTIONS SUMMARY

Donor(s): the late Carl Gellert, Atlas Realty Co., Pacific Coast Construction Co., the late Gertrude E. Gellert

Typical Recipients: • *Arts & Humanities:* Community Arts, Libraries, Music • *Civic & Public Affairs:* Legal Aid, Municipalities/Towns • *Education:* Arts/Humanities Education, Colleges & Universities, Private Education (Precollege), Religious Education, Science/Mathematics Education, Secondary Education (Private), Secondary Education (Public), Special Education, Student Aid • *Health:* Alzheimers Disease, Arthritis, Clinics/Medical Centers, Health Organizations, Hospitals, Long-Term Care, Medical Rehabilitation, Medical Research, Mental Health • *Religion:* Churches, Dioceses, Ministries, Religious Organizations, Religious Welfare, Seminaries • *Social Services:* Animal Protection, Big Brother/Big Sister, Child Welfare, Community Centers, Community Service Organizations, Family Planning, Family Services, Food/Clothing Distribution, Homes, People with Disabilities, Recreation & Athletics, Senior Services, Substance Abuse, Youth Organizations

Grant Types: capital, endowment, general support, multiyear/continuing support, operating expenses, project, research, and scholarship

Geographic Distribution: focus on the San Francisco Bay area, CA

GIVING OFFICERS
Fred R. Bahrt: pres, dir *PHIL AFFIL* dir, vchmn: Celia Berta Gellert Foundation

Peter J. Brusati: secy, dir *PHIL AFFIL* secy, mgr, dir: Celia Berta Gellert Foundation

Andrew A. Cresci: dir *PHIL AFFIL* treas, dir: Celia Berta Gellert Foundation

Celia B. Gellert: dir *PHIL AFFIL* dir: Celia Berta Gellert Foundation

Robert J. Grassilli: treas, dir *PHIL AFFIL* dir: Celia Berta Gellert Foundation

Robert L. Pauly: vp, dir

APPLICATION INFORMATION
Initial Approach: Applicants must send five copies of their proof of tax-exempt status, the letter classifying applicant as "not a private foundation" under Section 509(a), and a signed statement that applicant's status under sections 501(c)(3) and 509(a) has not been revoked or modified, Applicants should also include brief outline of information regarding the organization, a brief outline project for which funds are sought and outline of specific funding requirements. All requests received prior to October 1 will be presented to the board for consideration at the directors meeting in November. Requests received after October 1 will be considered in the following fiscal year.

Restrictions on Giving: Does not support individuals or provide loans.

PUBLICATIONS
Application Guidelines

GRANTS ANALYSIS
Total Grants: $498,800

Number of Grants: 83

Highest Grant: $100,000

Typical Range: $1,000 to $10,000

Disclosure Period: fiscal year ending November 30, 1993

Note: Recent grants are derived from a fiscal 1993 Form 990.

RECENT GRANTS
General
100,000	Little Sisters of the Poor, San Francisco, CA — toward operations and reduction of debt of St. Anne's Home for the Aged
25,000	Seton Medical Center, Daly City, CA — for emergency room charity care
25,000	Seton Medical Center, Daly City, CA — towards purchase and installation of wireless patient monitors at the Carl Gellert Emergency Center
15,000	Recreation Center for the Handicapped, San Francisco,

CA — for children's afterschool program
| 15,000 | University of San Francisco, San Francisco, CA — for unrestricted use |

Gellert Foundation, Celia Berta

CONTACT
Peter Brusati
Secretary and Manager
Celia Berta Gellert Fdn.
2222 19th Ave.
San Francisco, CA 94116
(415) 566-4420

FINANCIAL SUMMARY
Recent Giving: $211,500 (fiscal 1993); $211,500 (fiscal 1992); $200,000 (fiscal 1991)

Assets: $3,201,887 (fiscal 1993); $2,836,858 (fiscal 1992); $2,449,238 (fiscal 1991)

Gifts Received: $435,000 (fiscal 1993); $377,000 (fiscal 1992); $350,000 (fiscal 1991)

Fiscal Note: In fiscal 1993, contributions were received from Celia A. Gellert.

EIN: 23-7083733

CONTRIBUTIONS SUMMARY
Donor(s): Celia Berta Gellert

Typical Recipients: • *Arts & Humanities:* Arts Outreach, General, Historic Preservation, History & Archaeology, Libraries, Museums/Galleries • *Civic & Public Affairs:* Ethnic Organizations, Nonprofit Management, Women's Affairs • *Education:* Colleges & Universities, Continuing Education, General, Private Education (Precollege), Public Education (Precollege), Religious Education, Science/Mathematics Education, Secondary Education (Private), Secondary Education (Public), Student Aid • *Health:* AIDS/HIV, Children's Health/Hospitals, Clinics/Medical Centers, Health Policy/Cost Containment, Health Organizations, Heart, Hospitals, Medical Research, Mental Health, Nutrition, Respiratory, Speech & Hearing • *Religion:* Churches, Religious Organizations, Religious Welfare, Seminaries • *Social Services:* Animal Protection, Child Welfare, Community Service Organizations, Day Care, Food/Clothing Distribution, Homes, People with Disabilities, Recreation & Athletics, Senior Services, Shelters/Homelessness, Youth Organizations

Grant Types: capital, endowment, general support, multiyear/continuing support, operating expenses, project, research, and scholarship

Geographic Distribution: focus on the San Francisco, CA, area.

GIVING OFFICERS
Fred R. Bahrt: dir, vchmn *PHIL AFFIL* pres, dir: Carl Gellert Foundation

Peter J. Brusati: secy, mgr, dir *PHIL AFFIL* secy, dir: Carl Gellert Foundation

Andrew A. Cresci: treas, dir *PHIL AFFIL* dir: Carl Gellert Foundation

Celia B. Gellert: dir *PHIL AFFIL* dir: Carl Gellert Foundation

Robert J. Grassilli: dir *PHIL AFFIL* treas, dir: Carl Gellert Foundation

Robert L. Pauley: dir, chmn

APPLICATION INFORMATION
Initial Approach: Send brief letter describing program. Include a description of organization, amount requested, purpose of funds sought, recently audited financial statement, and proof of tax-exempt status. There are no deadlines.

Restrictions on Giving: Does not support individuals.

PUBLICATIONS
Application Guidelines

GRANTS ANALYSIS
Total Grants: $211,500

Number of Grants: 48

Highest Grant: $16,500

Typical Range: $1,000 to $10,000

Disclosure Period: fiscal year ending November 30, 1993

Note: Recent grants are derived from a fiscal 1993 Form 990.

RECENT GRANTS
General
16,500	Seton Medical Center, Daly City, CA — towards the Cost of Marquette pulse oxymeters for intensive care unit and transitional care unit
12,500	College of Notre Dame, Belmont, CA — for financial aid for deserving students
10,500	Together in the Mission of Education, San Francisco, CA — for extended care program
10,000	Immaculate Conception Academy, San Francisco, CA — for endowment fund
10,000	Little Sisters of the Poor, San Francisco, CA — for St. Anne's Home for the Aged

Getty Trust, J. Paul

CONTACT
Getty Grant Program J. Paul Getty Trust
401 Wilshire Blvd., Ste. 1000
Santa Monica, CA 90401-1455
(310) 393-4244
Note: Correspondence should be addressed to the Getty Grant Program. The trust does not list a specific contact person. Initial application inquiries are accepted by fax, but final applications must be mailed.

FINANCIAL SUMMARY

Recent Giving: $6,237,499 (fiscal 1994); $7,539,754 (fiscal 1993); $10,463,661 (fiscal 1992)

Assets: $6,016,488,752 (fiscal 1994); $6,184,252,528 (fiscal 1992); $5,251,845,004 (fiscal 1991)

Gifts Received: $98,700 (fiscal 1994); $147,800 (fiscal 1992); $100,000 (fiscal 1991)

Fiscal Note: The J. Paul Getty Trust occasionally receives works of art and reference materials from individuals, libraries, and other museums. These gifts are listed in terms of their fair market value.

EIN: 95-1790021

CONTRIBUTIONS SUMMARY

Donor(s): "The Getty Grant Program is part of the J. Paul Getty Trust, a private operation foundation dedicated to the visual arts and the humanities. In addition to the Grant Program, the Trust has seven operating programs. The Trust's origins date to 1953 and the founding of the J. Paul Getty Museum as a California charitable trust. When most of Mr. Getty's personal estate passed to the Trust in 1992, the trustees decided that — given the size of the endowment and Mr. Getty's purpose, stated in the trust indenture as 'the diffusion of artistic and general knowledge' — the Trust should make a greater contribution to the visual arts than the museum could alone." Billionaire J. Paul Getty was the son of Oklahoma oilman George Franklin Getty, who founded the Getty Oil Company.

Typical Recipients: • *Arts & Humanities:* Arts Associations & Councils, Arts Funds, Arts Institutes, Ethnic & Folk Arts, Historic Preservation, History & Archaeology, Libraries, Museums/Galleries, Visual Arts • *Civic & Public Affairs:* Municipalities/Towns • *Education:* Arts/Humanities Education, Colleges & Universities, International Exchange, Minority Education • *Environment:* General • *International:* Foreign Arts Organizations, Foreign Educational Institutions, International Environmental Issues, International Peace & Security Issues

Grant Types: fellowship, matching, multi-year/continuing support, project, and research

Geographic Distribution: no geographic restrictions

GIVING OFFICERS

Philippa Calnan: dir pub affairs

Miguel Angel Corzo: dir (Getty Conservation Inst)

Kenneth Nelson Dayton: trust emeritus *B* Minneapolis MN 1922 *ED* Yale Univ BA 1944 *PHIL AFFIL* don, pres, treas, dir: Oakleaf Foundation; vp, trust: Granelda Foundation

Lani Lattin Duke: dir (Getty Ctr Ed Arts)

Robert F. Erburu: chmn bd trust *B* Ventura CA 1930 *ED* Univ Southern CA BA 1952; Harvard Univ JD 1955 *CURR EMPL* chmn, dir: Times Mirror Co *CORP AFFIL* dir: Tejon Ranch Co; dir, chmn: Fed Reserve Bank San Francisco *NONPR AFFIL* chmn: Am

Newspaper Publs Assn, Brookings Inst; dir: Independent Colls Southern CA, Los Angeles Festival, Tomas Rivera Ctr; fellow: Am Acad Arts & Sci; mem: Am Bar Assn, Bus Counc, Bus Roundtable, CA Bus Roundtable; mem bd dirs: Counc Foreign Rels; mem trust counc: Natl Gallery Art *PHIL AFFIL* trust: Ahmanson Foundation; dir: Ralph M. Parsons Foundation, Carrie Estelle Doheny Foundation, William and Flora Hewlett Foundation; vp: Fletcher Jones Foundation; dir: Pfaffinger Foundation; chmn, dir: Times Mirror Foundation

Eleanor Fink: dir art history info program

David Pierpont Gardner: trust *B* Berkeley CA 1933 *ED* Brigham Young Univ BS 1955; Univ CA Berkeley MA 1959; Univ CA Berkeley PhD 1966 *CORP AFFIL* dir: First Security Corp, Fluor Corp *NONPR AFFIL* assoc: Cambridge Univ Clare Hall; dir: CA Econ Devel Corp; mem: Am Academy Arts & Sciences, Am Philosophical Soc, Assn Am Univs, CA Chamber Commerce, Higher Ed Forum, Natl Academy Ed, Natl Academy Pub Admin, Phi Beta Kappa, Phi Kappa Phi; pres, prof higher ed: Univ CA Santa Barbara; trust: Tanner Lectures Human Values *PHIL AFFIL* chmn, dir: George S. and Dolores Dore Eccles Foundation; pres: William and Flora Hewlett Foundation

Gordon Peter Getty: trust *B* Los Angeles CA 1933 *ED* Univ San Francisco BS 1956 *NONPR AFFIL* adv dir: Metro Opera Assn; dir: Marin Opera Co, San Francisco Symphony; trust: Mannes Coll Music *PHIL AFFIL* chmn, trust: L. S. B. Leakey Foundation; chmn, pres, dir: Ann and Gordon Getty Foundation

Vartan Gregorian: trust *B* Tabriz Iran 1934 *ED* Coll Armenien 1955; Stanford Univ BA 1958; Stanford Univ PhD 1964 *NONPR AFFIL* chmn bd visitors: City Univ NY Grad Sch Univ Ctr, NY Pub Library; dir: Boston Univ Inst Advanced Study, Trinity Sch; mem: Am Acad Medicine, Am Assn Advancement Slavic Studies, Am Historical Assn, Am Library Assn, Am Philosophical Soc, Counc Foreign Rels, Intl Fed Library Assn, Intl League Human Rights, Mid-East Studies Assn, Natl Humanities Faculty; pres: Brown Univ; prof: New Sch Social Res; prof history: NY Univ *CLUB AFFIL* Grolier, Round Table *PHIL AFFIL* dir: Aaron Diamond Foundation

Valerie Gross: exec asst to pres

Helene Lois Kaplan: trust *B* New York NY 1933 *ED* Barnard Coll AB 1953; NY Univ JD 1967 *CURR EMPL* of couns: Skadden Arps Slate Meagher & Flom *CORP AFFIL* dir: Chem Bank, Chem Banking Corp, May Dept Stores, Met Life Ins Co, Mobil Corp, NYNEX Corp, Verde Exploration Ltd; ptnr: New York City Partnership; trust: Mitre Corp *NONPR AFFIL* chmn: Barnard Coll; dir: Catskill Ctr Conservation & Devel; mem: Am Academy Arts Sciences, Am Bar Assn, Am Philosophical Soc, Assn Bar City New York, Bretton Woods Comm, Carnegie Commn Science Tech & Govt, Carnegie Counc Adolescent Devel, Century Assn, Counc Foreign Rels, NY St Bar Assn, NY St Govs Task Force Life Law, Womens Forum;

mem counc: Rockefeller Univ; trust: Am Mus Natural History, Inst Advanced Studies, Mt Sinai Hosp Med Ctr, Mt Sinai Med Sch, Olive Free Library *CLUB AFFIL* Coffee House, Cosmopolitan *PHIL AFFIL* trust: John Simon Guggenheim Memorial Foundation; secy, dir: Golden Family Foundation; dir: Commonwealth Fund; dir, mem fin & admin comm: Carnegie Corporation of New York

Joseph James Kearns: vp, treas *B* Sacramento CA 1942 *ED* CA St Univ BA 1964; Stanford Univ MS 1965 *CORP AFFIL* dir: Commerical Ctr Bank, Electro Rent Corp *NONPR AFFIL* mem: Los Angeles Treas Club, Natl Assn Corp Dirs; mem investment comm: Archdiocese Los Angeles

Jon B. Lovelace, Jr.: trust *B* 1927 *CURR EMPL* chmn, dir: Capital Res & Mgmt Co *CORP AFFIL* chmn: Am Mutual Fund *PHIL AFFIL* dir: Capital Group Foundation

Herbert L. Lucas, Jr.: trust

Deborah Marrow: dir (Getty Grant Program)

Stuart Thorne Peeler: trust *B* Los Angeles CA 1929 *ED* Stanford Univ BA 1950; Stanford Univ JD 1953 *CURR EMPL* chmn, pres, ceo: Putumayo Production Co *CORP AFFIL* dir: Calmat Co, Chieftain Intl, Homestake Gold Australia Ltd, Homestake Mining Co *NONPR AFFIL* mem: Am Inst Mining Metallurgical Petroleum Engrs, Am Judicature Soc, CA Bar Assn, Phi Delta Phi, Theta Chi *CLUB AFFIL* Tuscon CC

Stephen D. Roundtree: dir (oper & planning)

Salvatore Settis: dir ctr history of art & humanities

Rocco Carmine Siciliano: trust *B* Salt Lake City UT 1922 *ED* Univ UT BA 1944; Georgetown Univ LLB 1948 *CORP AFFIL* dir: Pacific Enterprises, Un Television *NONPR AFFIL* bd gov: Cedars-Sinai Med Ctr; chmn: Ctr Govermental Studies; co-chmn: CA Commn Campaign Financing; commnr: CA Citizens Budget Commn; mem: Natl Academy Pub Admin; pres: Dwight D Eisenhower World Aff Inst; trust: CA Channel, Comm Econ Devel, Los Angeles Philharmonic Assn *CLUB AFFIL* California, Met

John Walsh, Jr.: dir (J Paul Getty Museum) *ED* Yale Univ BA 1961; Columbia Univ MA 1965; Columbia Univ PhD 1971 *NONPR AFFIL* bd fellows: Claremont Grad Sch Univ Ctr; mem: Am Antiquarian Soc, Am Assn Museums, Archaeological Inst Am, Coll Art Assn; mem gov bd: Smithsonian Counc, Yale Univ Art Gallery; mem, trust: Assn Art Mus Dirs *CLUB AFFIL* Century

J. Patrick Whaley: trust

John Cunningham Whitehead: trust *B* Evanston IL 1922 *ED* Haverford Coll BA 1943; Harvard Univ MBA 1947 *CURR EMPL* chmn: AEA Investors *NONPR AFFIL* chmn: Asia Soc, Intl House, Intl Rescue Comm, UN Nations Assn US Am, Youth Understanding; chmn emeritus: Brookings Inst; mem: Counc Foreign Rels; pres: Boy Scouts America NY Counc; trust: Haverford Coll, Lincoln Ctr Theater, Outward Bound, Rockefeller Univ; trust counc: Natl Gallery Art *CLUB AFFIL* F St DC, Links, Met, Univ

Harold Marvin Williams: pres, ceo *B* Philadelphia PA 1928 *ED* Univ CA Los Angeles AB 1946; Harvard Univ JD 1949; Univ Southern CA Grad Sch Law 1955-1956 *CORP AFFIL* dir: Am Med Intl, Times-Mirror Co *NONPR AFFIL* co-chmn: Pub Commn Los Angeles Govt; mem: CA Bar Assn, Comm Econ Devel, Counc Foreign Rels; mem higher ed review commn: State CA; regent: Univ CA; trust: Natl Humanities Ctr *PHIL AFFIL* trust: Robert Ellis Simon Foundation

Blenda Jacqueline Wilson: trust *B* Woodbridge NJ 1941 *ED* Cedar Crest Coll AB 1962; Seton Hall Univ AM 1965; Boston Coll PhD 1979 *CORP AFFIL* adv bd: MI Consolidated Gas; dir: Alpha Capital Mgmt *NONPR AFFIL* adv bd: Stanford Inst Higher Ed Res, Univ Southern CA District 60 Natl Alliance; Am delegate: US/UK Dialogue About Quality Judgements Higher Ed; dir: Arab Commun Ctr Econ Social Svcs, Henry Ford Health Sys, Henry Ford Hosp-Fairlance Ctr, Intl Fdn Ed & Self-Help, Metro Ctr High Tech, Nothridge Hosp Med Ctr, Race Rels Counc Metro Detroit, Un Way Southeastern MI, Univ Detroit Jesuit High Sch; dir, trust emeritus: Fdn Ctr; dir, vchmn: Metro Aff; mem: Am Assn Higher Ed, Am Assn St Colls & Univs, Am Assn Univ Women, Assn Black Professionals & Admins, Assn Gov Bds, Econ Club, Ed Commn Sts, Intl Womens Forum, MI Womens Forum, Natl Coalition 100 Black Women, Women Execs St Govt, Women & Fdns, Womens Econ Club Detroit; mem exec bd: Boy Scouts Am Detroit Area Counc; mem higher ed colloquium: Am Counc Ed; pres: CA St Univ Northridge; trust: Boston Coll, Childrens TV Workshop, Sammy Davis Jr Natl Liver Inst, Henry Ford Mus; trust assoc: Boston Coll; trust emeritus: Cambridge Coll; visiting comm: Harvard Coll Div Continuing Ed Faculty Arts Sciences, PEW Forum K-12 Ed Reform US *CLUB AFFIL* Rotary *PHIL AFFIL* dir: Commonwealth Fund

APPLICATION INFORMATION
Initial Approach:

Potential applicants should request the Getty Grant program's guidelines brochure. After determining whether their project falls within the scope of these guidelines, they should request the detailed guidelines for the category of support for which they are seeking assistance. The next step, in most cases, is to submit a preliminary letter.

All applications materials must be received in the grant program office before the review process can begin. Applications are reviewed by specialists in relevant fields. For most grants, recommendations are made by committees of experts. The grant program bases its final decisions on the recommendations of outside reviewers and committee members. Final notification is usually within six months of receipt of the complete application.

Restrictions on Giving: The trust generally will not support operating expenses, indirect

costs, endowment funds, building maintenance or construction, and production or acquisition of works of art. Grants to individuals are limited to postdoctoral fellowships and senior research grants.

OTHER THINGS TO KNOW
The trust reports that most grants range between $2,000 and $250,000. The majority of grants are under $50,000. Grants also range from one to four years, and are not renewable.

PUBLICATIONS
Guidelines, grant program description, lists of grants awarded, and biennial report

GRANTS ANALYSIS
Total Grants: $6,237,499

Number of Grants: 220

Highest Grant: $250,000

Average Grant: $28,352

Typical Range: $2,000 to $50,000

Disclosure Period: fiscal year ending June 30, 1994

Note: Recent grants are derived from a fiscal 1993 partial grants list.

RECENT GRANTS

Library

146,500	University of Illinois at Urbana-Champaign, Champaign, IL — for a two-moth research visit by a librarian from Romania
50,000	Slovak National Gallery, Bratislava, Slovakia — for library acquisitions
40,000	Museum of Decorative Arts, Prague, — for library acquisitions
40,000	University of Poznan, Poznan, Poland — for library acquisitions
30,000	Art Libraries Society of North America, Tuscon, AZ — for representatives from Central and Eastern Europe to attend the 1993 Art Libraries Society of North American conference

General

268,000	Hebrew University of Jerusalem, Jerusalem, Israel — for the survey, documentation, and research of Jewish art in Poland
250,000	American Academy in Rome, New York, NY — for the development of a joint bibliographic database for the Unione Internazionale degli Istituti di Archaeologia, Storia e Storia dell'Arte in Rome
250,000	Save Venice, New York, NY — for the Chiesa diSanta Maria dei Miracoli, Venice
160,000	Corporation for Jefferson's Poplar Forest, Forest, VA — for Thomas Jefferson's Poplar Forest

152,204	Loyola University, State University of New York at Binghamton, University of California Davis — senior research grant for three researchers about "Aesthetics of Validation: Rethinking Yoruba Art and Religion"

Ghidotti Foundation

Former Foundation Name: William and Marian Ghidotti Foundation

CONTACT
William Toms
Trustee
Ghidotti Fdn.
3961 De Sablo Rd.
Cameron Park, CA 95682
(916) 677-3994

FINANCIAL SUMMARY
Recent Giving: $402,395 (1993); $380,167 (1992); $435,925 (1991)

Assets: $9,126,818 (1993); $8,593,022 (1992); $8,265,975 (1991)

EIN: 94-6181833

CONTRIBUTIONS SUMMARY
Donor(s): William Ghidotti, the late Marian Ghidotti

Typical Recipients: • *Arts & Humanities:* Historic Preservation, Libraries, Music, Theater • *Education:* Agricultural Education, Elementary Education (Private), Literacy, Private Education (Precollege), Public Education (Precollege) • *Health:* Home-Care Services, Hospices, Hospitals • *Social Services:* Child Welfare, Community Service Organizations, United Funds/United Ways, Volunteer Services, Youth Organizations

Grant Types: general support and scholarship

Geographic Distribution: limited to Nevada County, CA

GIVING OFFICERS
Wells Fargo Bank: trust

Mary Bouma: trust

Erica Erickson: trust

Frank Francis: trust

William Toms: trust

Ruth Halls Ungler: trust

APPLICATION INFORMATION
Initial Approach: Send application form by February for new scholarships, August for renewals. Also send transcript of grades, student and family income, and personal resume.

GRANTS ANALYSIS
Total Grants: $402,395

Number of Grants: 13

Highest Grant: $22,500

Typical Range: $1,000 to $22,000

Disclosure Period: 1993

Note: Recent grants are derived from a 1993 Form 990. Number of grants and typical range do not include scholarships to individuals.

RECENT GRANTS

General

22,500	Forest Lake Christian School
17,020	FFA and 4-H Fair Auction
12,500	Grass Valley School District, Grass Valley, CA
12,000	Hospice, Incline Valley, NV
3,500	Volunteer Action Center of Nevada County, Grass Valley, CA

Gilmore Foundation, William G.

CONTACT
Faye Wilson
Secretary
William G. Gilmore Fdn.
120 Montgomery St., Ste. 1880
San Francisco, CA 94104
(415) 546-1400

FINANCIAL SUMMARY
Recent Giving: $991,700 (1993); $1,030,200 (1992); $989,100 (1991)

Assets: $14,251,773 (1993); $13,553,322 (1992); $13,426,281 (1991)

EIN: 94-6079493

CONTRIBUTIONS SUMMARY
Donor(s): the late William G. Gilmore and Mrs. William G. Gilmore

Typical Recipients: • *Arts & Humanities:* Arts Associations & Councils, Arts Centers, General, Libraries, Museums/Galleries, Music, Opera, Public Broadcasting • *Civic & Public Affairs:* General, Hispanic Affairs, Legal Aid, Zoos/Aquariums • *Education:* Afterschool/Enrichment Programs, Colleges & Universities, Continuing Education, Education Funds, General, Private Education (Precollege), Public Education (Precollege), Religious Education, Science/Mathematics Education, Secondary Education (Private) • *Environment:* Resource Conservation, Wildlife Protection • *Health:* Cancer, Children's Health/Hospitals, Clinics/Medical Centers, Emergency/Ambulance Services, Hospices, Hospitals, Medical Research, Single-Disease Health Associations, Speech & Hearing • *Religion:* Churches, Dioceses, Religious Organizations, Religious Welfare • *Science:* Science Museums, Scientific Centers & Institutes • *Social Services:* Animal Protection, Community Service Organizations, Family Services, Food/Clothing Distribution, People with Disabilities, Scouts, Shelters/Homelessness, United Funds/United Ways, Youth Organizations

Grant Types: general support

Geographic Distribution: mainly in northern CA

GIVING OFFICERS
Thomas B. Boklund: trust

C. Lee Emerson: vp, treas, trust

V. Neil Fulton: asst secy

Robert C. Harris: pres, trust *B* San Francisco CA 1916 *ED* Stanford Univ 1937; Harvard Univ 1940 *CURR EMPL* coun: Heller Ehrman White & McAuliffe

William R. Mackey: trust

Faye Wilson: secy

APPLICATION INFORMATION
Initial Approach: Send brief letter of inquiry describing program or project. Deadline is December 1. Decisions are made within two months.

GRANTS ANALYSIS
Total Grants: $991,700

Number of Grants: 166

Highest Grant: $40,000

Typical Range: $500 to $30,000

Disclosure Period: 1993

Note: Recent grants are derived from a 1993 Form 990.

RECENT GRANTS

Library

25,000	Library Foundation of San Francisco, San Francisco, CA
7,500	Napa City/Country Public Library Foundation, Napa, CA

General

40,000	Summit Medical Center Foundation, Oakland, CA
30,000	Oregon Graduate Institute, Beaverton, OR
30,000	Project Open Hand, San Francisco, CA
30,000	Queen of the Valley Hospital Foundation, San Francisco, CA
28,000	Boy Scouts of America Columbia Pacific Council, WA

Golden West Foundation

CONTACT
Frank S. Whiting
President
Golden West Foundation
1365 Hillcrest AVe.
Pasadena, CA 91106
(818) 286-4465

FINANCIAL SUMMARY
Recent Giving: $133,995 (1992); $54,310 (1990)

Assets: $2,935,447 (1992); $2,447,749 (1990)

EIN: 68-0222103

CONTRIBUTIONS SUMMARY
Typical Recipients: • *Arts & Humanities:* Libraries, Museums/Galleries, Music • *Education:* Colleges & Universities, Science/Mathematics Education • *Health:* Hospitals

Grant Types: general support

GIVING OFFICERS
Lorne J. Brown: vp

Elizabeth L. Whiting: secy, treas

Frank S. Whiting: pres

APPLICATION INFORMATION
Initial Approach: Send a brief letter of inquiry.

GRANTS ANALYSIS
Total Grants: $133,995

Number of Grants: 30

Highest Grant: $29,519

Typical Range: $100 to $6,500

Disclosure Period: 1992

Note: Recent grants are derived from a 1992 Form 990.

RECENT GRANTS

Library

4,100	Fellows of the Huntington Library, San Marino, CA

General

29,519	Huntington Memorial Hospital, Pasadena, CA
23,875	ARCS Foundation, Los Angeles, CA
10,500	Polytechnic School, Pasadena, CA
10,000	Claremont McKenna College, Claremont, CA
10,000	Descanso Gardens Guild, Canada, CA

Goldwyn Foundation, Samuel

CONTACT
Meyer Gottlieb
Treasurer
Samuel Goldwyn Foundation
10203 Santa Monica Blvd., Ste. 500
Los Angeles, CA 90067
(310) 552-2255

FINANCIAL SUMMARY
Recent Giving: $3,910,807 (1991); $990,209 (1990); $950,458 (1989)

Assets: $20,036,942 (1991); $19,968,981 (1990); $20,068,132 (1989)

EIN: 95-6006859

CONTRIBUTIONS SUMMARY
Donor(s): The foundation was established in 1987 by the late Samuel Goldwyn and the late Frances H. Goldwyn .

Typical Recipients: • *Arts & Humanities:* Arts Associations & Councils, Dance, General, Libraries, Museums/Galleries, Public Broadcasting, Theater, Visual Arts • *Civic & Public Affairs:* Civil Rights, Clubs, General, Law & Justice, Professional & Trade Associations, Safety, Urban & Community Affairs • *Education:* Arts/Humanities Education, Colleges & Universities, Education Funds, General, Private Education (Precollege), Special Education, Student Aid • *Environment:* General, Resource Conservation • *Health:* AIDS/HIV, Cancer, Children's Health/Hospitals, Clinics/Medical Centers, Health Funds, Hospitals, Research/Studies Institutes • *Religion:* Jewish Causes, Religious Welfare • *Social Services:* Child Welfare, Community Centers, Community Service Organizations, Emergency Relief, Family Planning, People with Disabilities, Senior Services, United Funds/United Ways

Grant Types: project, research, scholarship, and seed money

Geographic Distribution: some national; focus on Los Angeles, CA, metropolitan area

GIVING OFFICERS
Anthony Goldwyn: trust

Francis Goldwyn: trust

John Goldwyn: trust

Peggy E. Goldwyn: vp, trust

Samuel John Goldwyn, Jr.: pres *B* Los Angeles CA 1926 *ED* Univ VA *CURR EMPL* chmn, ceo: Samuel Goldwyn Co

Meyer Gottlieb: treas, dir *B* 1939 *ED* Univ CA Los Angeles MBA 1965 *CURR EMPL* pres: Samuel Goldwyn Co

GRANTS ANALYSIS
Total Grants: $3,910,807

Number of Grants: 88

Highest Grant: $3,672,872

Average Grant: $2,735*

Typical Range: $100 to $5,000

Disclosure Period: 1991

Note: Average grant figure does not include the highest grant of $3,672,872. Recent grants are derived from a 1991 Form 990.

RECENT GRANTS

Library
10,000	Academy Foundation, Beverly Hills, CA — Herrick Library

General
3,672,872	Motion Picture and Television Relief Fund, Woodland Hills, CA
25,000	Motion Picture Scholarship
15,000	Venice Family Clinic, Venice, CA
12,174	University of California Los Angeles Writing Awards, Los Angeles, CA
12,000	Frostig Education Center

Haas, Jr. Fund, Evelyn and Walter

CONTACT
Ira S. Hirschfield
President
Evelyn and Walter Haas, Jr. Fund
One Lombard St.
San Francisco, CA 94111
(415) 398-3744

FINANCIAL SUMMARY
Recent Giving: $10,000,000 (1995 est.); $9,000,000 (1994); $5,489,658 (1993)

Assets: $230,000,000 (1995 est.); $240,000,000 (1994); $220,040,871 (1993)

Gifts Received: $110,000,000 (1992); $10,000,000 (1991)

Fiscal Note: In 1991, the fund received $10,000,000 from Walter A. Haas, Jr. and Evelyn D. Haas, both donors, officers, and trustees of the foundation. In 1992, the fund received $110,000,000 from the estate of Elise S. Haas.

EIN: 94-6068932

CONTRIBUTIONS SUMMARY
Donor(s): The Evelyn and Walter Haas, Jr. Fund was established in 1953 by Mr. and Mrs. Walter A. Haas, Jr. Walter A. Haas, Jr., is the son of Walter A. Haas, the head of Levi Strauss & Company from 1928 to 1955. His mother, Elise Haas, was the daughter of Sigmund Stern, a nephew of Levi Strauss. Walter Haas, Jr., is honorary chairman and director of Levi Strauss Associates and former chairman of Levi Strauss & Company. He is a former trustee of the Ford Foundation and was an early president of the Guardsmen, a group of young men involved in social welfare. He has been a leader in San Francisco Urban League inner-city activities, and he helped establish a Boys Club at Hunter's Point. His wife, Evelyn Haas, serves on the board of the San Francisco Museum of Art and Children's Hospital of San Francisco.

Typical Recipients: • *Arts & Humanities:* Ballet, Libraries, Museums/Galleries, Music, Opera, Performing Arts • *Civic & Public Affairs:* Asian American Affairs, Clubs, Community Foundations, Employment/Job Training, General, Hispanic Affairs, Housing, Law & Justice, Legal Aid, Nonprofit Management, Philanthropic Organizations, Public Policy, Urban & Community Affairs, Women's Affairs • *Education:* After-school/Enrichment Programs, Business Education, Colleges & Universities, Education Funds, Legal Education, Private Education (Precollege), School Volunteerism • *Environment:* Resource Conservation • *Health:* Alzheimers Disease, Clinics/Medical Centers, Health Organizations, Hospices, Hospitals, Long-Term Care, Nursing Services • *International:* International Affairs • *Religion:* Churches, Jewish Causes, Religious Organizations, Religious Welfare • *Social Services:* Community Centers, Community Service Organizations, Domestic Violence,

Family Services, Food/Clothing Distribution, Homes, People with Disabilities, Refugee Assistance, Senior Services, Shelters/Homelessness, United Funds/United Ways, Volunteer Services, Youth Organizations

Grant Types: challenge, general support, multiyear/continuing support, operating expenses, and project

Geographic Distribution: primarily San Francisco and Alameda Counties, CA

GIVING OFFICERS
Elizabeth Haas Eisenhardt: don daughter, trust *CURR EMPL* ptnr: Oakland Athletics

Evelyn Danzig Haas: don, vchmn, trust

Robert D. Haas: trust, don son *B* San Francisco CA 1942 *ED* Univ CA Berkeley BA 1964; Harvard Univ MBA 1968 *CURR EMPL* chmn, ceo, dir: Levi Strauss Assocs Inc *CORP AFFIL* chmn, ceo: Levi Strauss & Co *PHIL AFFIL* pres, dir: Levi Strauss Foundation; trust: Ford Foundation

Walter Jerome Haas: treas, secy, don son, trust *B* 1949 *CURR EMPL* pres, ceo: Oakland Athletics *PHIL AFFIL* trust: Walter and Elise Haas Fund

Ira S. Hirschfield: pres, trust

APPLICATION INFORMATION
Initial Approach:

Applicants should submit a letter of inquiry briefly stating the purpose of and need for the project, background of the sponsoring organization, project budget, and amount requested before making a formal application. Application forms are not required. The fund will answer letters of inquiry within three weeks.

Applications should include a detailed description of the proposal, including need, objectives, scope, and method of evaluation; proposed budget; organization's total budget; audited financial statement reflecting the most recent fiscal year; list of potential and actual sources of funding; copy of IRS form 501(c)(3); and a list of directors.

There are no deadlines for submitting requests.

The board meets three times a year. Final notification will be made in ninety days.

Restrictions on Giving: No grants are made to other private foundations, individuals, fund-raising campaigns, deficit budgets, or for religious purposes, conferences, publications, media, or research projects. Grants are generally not made outside of San Francisco and Alameda Counties.

PUBLICATIONS
Annual report

GRANTS ANALYSIS
Total Grants: $5,489,658

Number of Grants: 227

Highest Grant: $1,000,000

Average Grant: $40,000*

Typical Range: $5,000 to $50,000

Disclosure Period: 1993

Note: Average grant figure was supplied by the fund. Recent grants are derived from a 1993 Form 990.

RECENT GRANTS

Library
250,000 Library Foundation of San Francisco, San Francisco, CA — capital campaign

General
1,000,000 Wheaton College Board of Trustees, Norton, MA — athletic facility
200,000 Jewish Community Federation of San Francisco, the Peninsula, Marin, and Sonoma Counties, San Francisco, CA
200,000 University of California Berkeley Foundation Haas School of Business, Berkeley, CA
100,000 Congregation Emanu-El, San Francisco, CA
62,500 Jewish Home for the Aged, San Francisco, CA

Hafif Family Foundation

CONTACT
Herbert Hafif
Director
Hafif Family Fdn.
269 W Bonita Ave.
Claremont, CA 91711
(714) 625-7971

FINANCIAL SUMMARY
Recent Giving: $231,825 (1993); $396,992 (1991); $517,080 (1990)

Assets: $4,356,573 (1993); $4,225,764 (1991); $4,234,180 (1990)

Gifts Received: $862,819 (1993); $2,379,199 (1990); $609,770 (1989)

EIN: 95-4081964

CONTRIBUTIONS SUMMARY
Donor(s): the donor is Herbert Hafif, the foundation's director

Typical Recipients: • *Arts & Humanities:* Libraries, Museums/Galleries, Music, Performing Arts • *Civic & Public Affairs:* Clubs, Community Foundations, General, Hispanic Affairs, Law & Justice, Parades/Festivals, Professional & Trade Associations, Public Policy, Urban & Community Affairs • *Education:* Afterschool/Enrichment Programs, Colleges & Universities, General, Private Education (Precollege), Religious Education, Secondary Education (Private) • *Health:* Clinics/Medical Centers, Emergency/Ambulance Services, Health Organizations, Medical Rehabilitation, Nutrition, Prenatal Health Issues, Preventive Medicine/Wellness Organizations, Single-Disease Health Associations • *International:* International Organizations, International Peace & Security Issues, Missionary/Religious Activities • *Re-*

ligion: Churches, Religious Organizations, Religious Welfare, Social/Policy Issues, Synagogues/Temples • *Science:* Scientific Organizations • *Social Services:* Community Centers, Community Service Organizations, Counseling, Crime Prevention, Emergency Relief, Family Services, People with Disabilities, Recreation & Athletics, Senior Services, Sexual Abuse, Shelters/Homelessness, Substance Abuse, United Funds/United Ways, Volunteer Services, YMCA/YWCA/YMHA/YWHA, Youth Organizations

Grant Types: general support

Geographic Distribution: primarily CA, with emphasis on Los Angeles

GIVING OFFICERS
Herbert Hafif: dir *B* Philadelphia PA 1930 *ED* Pomona Coll BA; Univ Southern CA JD

APPLICATION INFORMATION
Initial Approach: The foundation requests applications be made in writing. There are no deadlines.

GRANTS ANALYSIS
Total Grants: $231,825
Number of Grants: 38
Highest Grant: $47,000
Typical Range: $50 to $39,625
Disclosure Period: 1993
Note: Recent grants are derived from a 1993 Form 990.

RECENT GRANTS

Library
10,000 Friends of Claremont Public Library, Claremont, CA

General
47,000 Lestonnac Free Medical Clinic
39,625 American Red Cross, New York, NY
25,000 Los Angeles Mission Foundation, Los Angeles, CA
10,000 Chino Valley YMCA, CA
10,000 LaVerne Rotary Club, LaVerne, CA

Haigh-Scatena Foundation

CONTACT
Ronald W. Clement
Executive Director
Haigh-Scatena Fdn.
PO Box 4399
Davis, CA 95617-4399
(916) 758-5327

FINANCIAL SUMMARY
Recent Giving: $219,620 (fiscal 1992); $266,795 (fiscal 1991); $160,704 (fiscal 1990)

Assets: $3,265,552 (fiscal 1992); $3,160,706 (fiscal 1991); $2,848,381 (fiscal 1990)

EIN: 94-1753746

CONTRIBUTIONS SUMMARY
Donor(s): the late Isabelle Simi Haigh and Vivien Haigh

Typical Recipients: • *Arts & Humanities:* Libraries • *Civic & Public Affairs:* Community Foundations, Employment/Job Training, General, Legal Aid, Nonprofit Management, Philanthropic Organizations, Urban & Community Affairs • *Education:* Colleges & Universities, Continuing Education, General, Public Education (Precollege), Student Aid • *Religion:* Religious Organizations • *Social Services:* Child Welfare, Community Service Organizations, Counseling, Domestic Violence, Family Planning, Family Services, Shelters/Homelessness, Youth Organizations

Grant Types: conference/seminar, loan, project, research, and seed money

Geographic Distribution: limited to northern CA

GIVING OFFICERS
Jean Bacigalupi: pres, dir
Ronald W. Clement: exec dir
Jeanette M. Dunckel: secy, dir *PHIL AFFIL* dir: Zellerbach Family Fund
Andrew Eber: vp, dir
Bruce Goldstein: dir
Gloria Hom: dir
Francis J. Lunger: treas
Arnold Perkins: dir
Gary Templin: dir
Caroline Tower: dir
Joanna Uribe de Mena: dir

APPLICATION INFORMATION
Initial Approach: Application materials issued upon receipt of acceptable concept letter (three pages). There are no deadlines. Board meets bimonthly. Decisions are made within six months.

PUBLICATIONS
Informational Brochure (including application guidelines)

GRANTS ANALYSIS
Total Grants: $219,620
Number of Grants: 26
Highest Grant: $18,750
Typical Range: $1,000 to $10,000
Disclosure Period: fiscal year ending August 31, 1992
Note: Recent grants are derived from a fiscal 1992 Form 990.

RECENT GRANTS

Library
500 Foundation Center

General
18,750 California Consortium for the Prevention of Child Abuse, CA
18,750 Interface Institute
17,250 Youth Law Center
16,250 La Familia Counseling Center
15,000 Legal Services for Children

Hancock Foundation, Luke B.

CONTACT
Ruth Ramel
Administrator
Luke B. Hancock Foundation
360 Bryant St.
Palo Alto, CA 94301
(415) 321-5536

FINANCIAL SUMMARY
Recent Giving: $1,000,000 (fiscal 1995 est.); $974,286 (fiscal 1994); $1,219,320 (fiscal 1993)

Assets: $24,000,000 (fiscal 1995 est.); $24,037,815 (fiscal 1994); $25,076,651 (fiscal 1993)

EIN: 88-6002013

CONTRIBUTIONS SUMMARY
Donor(s): The Luke B. Hancock Foundation, established in 1948, was initiated by a donation from Luke B. Hancock . Mr. Hancock, born in Grand Haven, MI, in 1874, was a businessman involved in oil exploration and production. His first endeavor was marketing petroleum products in Minneapolis and the northwestern states. Later, he worked with petroleum as a refined product and in oil exploration and production in Montana, Wyoming, and the Dakotas. He initiated the Hancock Foundation to promote the well-being of young children. In 1963, with principal assets from Mr. Hancock's estate, the Hancock Foundation's name was changed to the Luke B. Hancock Foundation in order to honor its founder and first president more prominently.

Typical Recipients: • *Arts & Humanities:* Libraries, Museums/Galleries, Music • *Civic & Public Affairs:* Civil Rights, Employment/Job Training, Housing, Municipalities/Towns, Urban & Community Affairs • *Education:* Afterschool/Enrichment Programs, Arts/Humanities Education, Colleges & Universities, Education Associations, Education Funds, Elementary Education (Public), General, Leadership Training, Literacy, Minority Education, Preschool Education, Private Education (Precollege), Public Education (Precollege), Secondary Education (Public), Special Education, Student Aid • *Environment:* Resource Conservation • *Health:* Children's Health/Hospitals, Emergency/Ambulance Services, Health Organizations, Transplant Networks/Donor Banks • *International:* International Relations, International Relief Efforts • *Religion:* Religious Organizations, Religious Welfare • *Science:* Scientific Organizations • *Social Services:* At-Risk Youth, Child Welfare, Community Service Organizations, Counseling, Delinquency & Criminal Rehabilitation, Emergency Relief, Family Services, Food/Clothing Distribution, Homes, People with Disabilities, Recreation & Athletics, Senior Services, Shelters/Homelessness, Volunteer Services, Youth Organizations

Grant Types: emergency, matching, and project

Geographic Distribution: primarily the San Francisco Bay area

GIVING OFFICERS
Linda Catron: secy, dir

Carol E. Hancock: dir

Jane Hancock: pres, dir

Kimberly Hancock: vp, dir

Lorraine Hancock: chwm, dir

Noble Hancock: treas, dir *CURR EMPL* treas, dir: Un States

Ruth Ramel: admin

APPLICATION INFORMATION
Initial Approach:

The foundation requests that applicants submit a preliminary letter prior to sending a proposal.

Preliminary letters should assume the form of a brief summary detailing the amount requested, method of operation, goals, and anticipated results for the particular project. Proposals, if subsequently requested by the foundation, should be accompanied by a recent audited financial report and a copy of the IRS rulings which should show tax-exempt status and not private foundation status. Proposals also should include a statement of the need for the activity, brief history of major funding attempts, methods used by others to support this need, proposed operational method for the program, expected results, qualifications of staff responsible for directing the program, a detailed budget with total costs and all proposed sources of funding, proposed future operational report, and an authorized signature from the board of directors.

The foundation has no application or proposal forms. Preliminary letters will be used to determine if a project falls within the foundation's areas of interest. The foundation strongly emphasizes its desire to receive such preliminary letters before a proposal is prepared or submitted.

Restrictions on Giving: The foundation does not consider grants for personal research or scholarship, publications or films, endowment funds, or building construction or acquisition.

PUBLICATIONS
Annual report

GRANTS ANALYSIS
Total Grants: $974,286

Number of Grants: 60

Highest Grant: $30,000

Average Grant: $21,000*

Typical Range: $5,000 to $35,000

Disclosure Period: fiscal year ending April 30, 1994

Note: The average grant figure was supplied by the foundation. Recent grants are derived from a fiscal 1994 Form 990.

RECENT GRANTS

Library
4,500	Foundation Center, New York, NY

General
30,000	Points of Light/Volunteer Centers, Palo Alto, CA
25,000	American Red Cross, Northridge, CA
25,000	Children Now, Palo Alto, CA
25,000	Commonweal, Bolinas, CA
25,000	Ft. Mason Center, Palo Alto, CA

Hanover Foundation

CONTACT
Ralph J. Shapiro
Chairman
Hanover Fdn.
433 N Camden Dr., Ste. 1200
Beverly Hills, CA 90210
(310) 550-0960

FINANCIAL SUMMARY
Recent Giving: $211,876 (fiscal 1994)

Assets: $2,015,389 (fiscal 1994)

Gifts Received: $140,300 (fiscal 1994)

Fiscal Note: In fiscal 1994, contributions were received from the Fischer Revocable Trust ($5,000) and Ralph J. and Shirley Shapiro ($132,800); others made contributions under $5,000.

EIN: 95-3887151

CONTRIBUTIONS SUMMARY
Typical Recipients: • *Arts & Humanities:* Libraries, Museums/Galleries, Music, Public Broadcasting • *Civic & Public Affairs:* Housing, Law & Justice, Legal Aid, Public Policy, Urban & Community Affairs • *Education:* Colleges & Universities, Education Funds, Education Reform, Legal Education, Minority Education, Student Aid • *Environment:* General, Resource Conservation • *Health:* Cancer, Children's Health/Hospitals, Heart, Hospitals (University Affiliated), Mental Health, Trauma Treatment • *International:* Foreign Arts Organizations, Missionary/Religious Activities • *Religion:* Jewish Causes • *Social Services:* Child Welfare, Community Service Organizations, Family Planning, Recreation & Athletics, Special Olympics, Volunteer Services, YMCA/YWCA/YMHA/YWHA, Youth Organizations

Grant Types: general support

Geographic Distribution: focus on CA

GIVING OFFICERS
Alison D. Shapiro: vp, secy

Peter W. Shapiro: vp, treas

Ralph J. Shapiro: chmn

Shirley Shapiro: pres

APPLICATION INFORMATION
Initial Approach: The foundation has no formal grant application procedure or application form.

GRANTS ANALYSIS
Total Grants: $211,876

Number of Grants: 89

Highest Grant: $100,000

Typical Range: $100 to $15,450

Disclosure Period: fiscal year ending January 31, 1994

Note: Recent grants are derived from a fiscal 1994 Form 990.

RECENT GRANTS

Library

2,000	Library Foundation of Los Angeles, Los Angeles, CA
1,000	Halley Library Friends, Halley, ID

General

100,000	Jewish Community Foundation of Jewish Federation, Council of Greater Los Angeles, Los Angeles, CA
15,450	United Cerebral Palsy/Spastic Children's Foundation, Mothers Auxiliary, Van Nuys, CA
5,000	American Friends of Israel Museum, New York, NY
5,000	Los Angeles County Bar Foundation, Mental Health Advocacy Services, Los Angeles, CA
5,000	Tides Foundation Sustainable Conservation, San Francisco, CA

Haynes Foundation, John Randolph and Dora

CONTACT
Diane Cornwell
Administrative Director
John Randolph and Dora Haynes Foundation
888 W Sixth St., Ste. 1150
Los Angeles, CA 90017-2737
(213) 623-9151

FINANCIAL SUMMARY
Recent Giving: $2,300,000 (fiscal 1995 est.); $2,274,933 (fiscal 1994); $2,092,670 (fiscal 1993)

Assets: $40,300,000 (fiscal 1995 est.); $40,366,564 (fiscal 1994); $42,369,147 (fiscal 1993)

Gifts Received: $10,000 (fiscal 1990); $10,000 (fiscal 1987)

Fiscal Note: In fiscal 1990, the foundation received a gift from Edward Levonlan.

EIN: 95-1644020

CONTRIBUTIONS SUMMARY
Donor(s): The Haynes Foundation was established in 1926 by Dr. John Randolph Haynes, "a distinguished physician, and his wife Dora Haynes, who were active and progressive citizens of Los Angeles during one of the city's most important developmental periods (1887-1937)."

Typical Recipients: • *Arts & Humanities:* Historic Preservation, History & Archaeology, Libraries, Museums/Galleries • *Civic & Public Affairs:* Economic Development, Hispanic Affairs, Housing, Law & Justice, Native American Affairs, Professional & Trade Associations, Public Policy, Urban & Community Affairs, Women's Affairs • *Education:* Business Education, Colleges & Universities, Faculty Development, General, International Studies, Science/Mathematics Education, Social Sciences Education, Student Aid • *Environment:* General • *Health:* Health Policy/Cost Containment • *Religion:* Social/Policy Issues • *Social Services:* Senior Services, Shelters/Homelessness, Substance Abuse

Grant Types: fellowship, research, and scholarship

Geographic Distribution: near headquarters only

GIVING OFFICERS
Ray Stanton Avery: trust emeritus *PHIL AFFIL* don, chmn: Durfee Foundation

Diane Cornwell: admin dir

Robert Ray Dockson: first vp, trust *B* Quincy IL 1917 *ED* Springfield Jr Coll AB 1937; Univ IL BS 1939; Univ Southern CA MS 1940; Univ Southern CA PhD 1946 *CURR EMPL* chmn emeritus: CalFed Inc *CORP AFFIL* chmn emeritus: CA Fed Bank; dir: Computer Sciences Corp, IT Corp, McKesson Corp, TransAmerica Income Shares *NONPR AFFIL* bd regents, chmn univ bd: Pepperdine Univ; chmn housing task force: CA Roundtable; mem: Am Arbitration Assn, Am Econ Assn, Am Fin Assn, Beta Gamma Sigma, CA Chamber Commerce, Los Angeles Chamber Commerce, Newcomen Soc, Hugh O'Brian Youth Fdn, Phi Kappa Phi; mem bd councs: Univ Southern CA Sch Bus Admin; mem hon bd govs: Town Hall; pres, trust: Orthopedic Hosp; trust: CA Counc Econ Ed, Comm Econ Devel *CLUB AFFIL* Birnam Wood GC, Bohemian, California, Los Angeles CC, One Hundred, Silver Dollar, Thunderbird CC

Philip Metschan Hawley: trust *B* Portland OR 1925 *ED* Univ CA Berkeley BS 1946; Harvard Univ Advanced Mgmt Program 1967 *CORP AFFIL* dir: AT&T, Atlantic Richfield Co, Bank Am Corp, Bank Am Natl Trust & Savings Assn, Johnson & Johnson, Weyerhaeuser Co *NONPR AFFIL* chmn, mem: CA Retailers Assn; mem: Beta Alpha Psi, Beta Gamma Sigma, Bus Counc, Bus Roundtable, Conf Bd, Phi Beta Kappa; mem visiting comm: Univ CA Los Angeles Grad Sch Mgmt; trust: CA Inst Tech *CLUB AFFIL* Bohemian, California, Links, Los Angeles, Multnomah, Newport Harbor

Jack King Horton: second vp, trust *B* Stanton NE 1916 *ED* Stanford Univ AB 1936; Oakland Coll Law LLB 1941 *NONPR AFFIL* mem: Bus Counc; pres, bd: Exec Svc Corp Southern CA, Pepperdine Univ; trust: Univ Southern CA *CLUB AFFIL* Bohemian, California, Cypress Point, Los Angeles CC, Pacific Union

F. Haynes Lindley, Jr.: pres, trust

Daniel A. Mazmanian: trust

Chauncey J. Medberry III: trust *B* Los Angeles CA 1917 *ED* Univ CA Los Angeles BA 1938 *CURR EMPL* dir: CP Natl Corp *PHIL AFFIL* vp: Fletcher Jones Foundation; hon dir: Bank of America - Giannini Foundation

Donn Biddle Miller: trust *B* Gallipolis OH 1929 *ED* OH Wesleyan Univ BA 1951; Univ MI JD 1954; Harvard Univ 1974 *CURR EMPL* ptnr: O'Melveny & Myers *CORP AFFIL* dir: Pacific Mutual Life Ins Co, Security Pacific Corp, Security Pacific Natl Bank; gen couns, dir: Carter Hawley Hale Stores; pres, dir: Pearson-Sibert Oil Co TX *NONPR AFFIL* bd dir: Rotary Fdn; chmn bd trusts: Occidental Coll; dir: Automobile Club Southern CA, CA Commun Fdn; mem: Am Bar Assn, CA Bar Assn, Delta Sigma Rho, Los Angeles Chamber Commerce, Los Angeles County Bar Assn, OH Bar Assn, Omicron Delta Kappa, Order Coif, Phi Beta Kappa, Phi Delta Phi, Pi Sigma Alpha, Sigma Chi *CLUB AFFIL* Bel Air Bay, California, Chancery, Los Angeles CC *PHIL AFFIL* dir: James Irvine Foundation

Jane G. Pisano: chmn comm research & grants, trust

Gilbert T. Ray: trust

APPLICATION INFORMATION
Initial Approach:

Applicants should send a cover letter, on the college, university, or research institute's letterhead, signed by an administrative officer, which indicates that the proposal has the endorsement of the institution.

The proposal should include a statement of purpose, problems to be addressed, and a detailed explanation of methodology; names and qualifications of personnel; length of time required for completion of the study; and a detailed budget. Also include copies of the institution's tax exemption letters from the IRS and the California Franchise Tax Board, and twenty copies of the proposal.

Applications should be submitted one month prior to quarterly board meetings.

Requests for grants are considered first by the foundation's committee on research and grants, which then makes its recommendations to the foundation's board of trustees.

Restrictions on Giving: No grants are made to individuals. The foundation does not participate in co-funding projects and does not offer indirect cost support.

PUBLICATIONS
Purposes and program brochure

GRANTS ANALYSIS
Total Grants: $2,274,933

Number of Grants: 32

Highest Grant: $177,320

Average Grant: $71,092

Typical Range: $5,000 to $100,000

Disclosure Period: fiscal year ending August 31, 1994

Note: Recent grants are derived from a partial fiscal 1993 grants list. Recent grants excludes fellowships and grants for publications.

RECENT GRANTS

Library

28,131	Huntington Library, San Marino, CA — cataloging papers of Kenneth Hahn
25,459	University of Southern California, Los Angeles, CA — library cataloging of Historical Society Photography Collection
21,600	Huntington Library, San Marino, CA — history fellowships
12,800	Huntington Library, San Marino, CA — photography, missions, and Native Americans

General

92,289	University of California Santa Barbara, Santa Barbara, CA — religious and public life in Los Angeles
74,847	University of California Los Angeles, Los Angeles, CA — immigrants and the Los Angeles economy
65,494	University of California Los Angeles, Los Angeles, CA — longitudinal study of Los Angeles BEST
42,216	Claremont Graduate School, Claremont, CA — Hispanic gang study
41,909	California State University at Fullerton, Fullerton, CA — 1993 Los Angeles city elections

Hedco Foundation

CONTACT

Mary A. Goriup
Manager
Hedco Fdn.
c/o Fitzgerald, Abbott and Beardsley
1221 Broadway, 21st Fl.
Oakland, CA 94612-1837
(510) 451-3300

FINANCIAL SUMMARY

Recent Giving: $880,744 (fiscal 1992); $531,262 (fiscal 1991); $1,193,673 (fiscal 1990)

Assets: $9,639,541 (fiscal 1992); $8,463,759 (fiscal 1991); $7,640,046 (fiscal 1990)

Gifts Received: $1,400,000 (fiscal 1992); $850,000 (fiscal 1991); $1,500,000 (fiscal 1990)

Fiscal Note: In fiscal 1992, contributions were received from Herrick-Pacific Corporation ($1,000,000), Catalina Associates I ($300,000), and The Herrick Corporation ($100,000).

EIN: 23-7259742

CONTRIBUTIONS SUMMARY

Donor(s): Herrick Corp., Catalina Associates

Typical Recipients: • *Arts & Humanities:* Libraries, Museums/Galleries • *Civic & Public Affairs:* General • *Education:* Colleges & Universities, Private Education (Precollege), Science/Mathematics Education • *Health:* Hospitals, Medical Research, Single-Disease Health Associations • *International:* International Relations, International Relief Efforts • *Religion:* Religious Welfare • *Social Services:* Community Service Organizations, Senior Services, Youth Organizations

Grant Types: capital and scholarship

Geographic Distribution: focus on CA

GIVING OFFICERS

Laine Ainsworth: dir

Dr. James Appleton: trust

David H. Dornsife: vp, dir

Ester M. Dornsife: pres, dir

Harold W. Dornsife: cfo, dir *B* Mishawaka IN 1915 *ED* Univ Southern CA 1939 *CURR EMPL* chmn: Peninsula Steel Products *CORP AFFIL* chmn: Central TX IW, Gillig Corp, Peninsula Steel Products; chmn, ceo: Herrick-Pacific Corp

Mary A. Goriup: mgr

Dorothy Jernstedt: secy, dir

James S. Little: dir

William Picard: dir

J. G. Ross: dir

APPLICATION INFORMATION

Initial Approach: The foundation has no formal grant application procedure or application form. There are no deadlines.

GRANTS ANALYSIS

Total Grants: $880,744

Number of Grants: 12

Highest Grant: $300,000

Typical Range: $30,000 to $50,000

Disclosure Period: fiscal year ending November 30, 1992

Note: Recent grants are derived from a fiscal 1992 Form 990.

RECENT GRANTS

General

300,000	Redlands University
100,000	Bay Area Community Services, Oakland, CA
100,000	Good Shepherd Home, Oakland, CA
50,000	ALS and Neuromuscular Research Center, Norristown, PA
50,000	Dooley Foundation

Heller Charitable Foundation, Clarence E.

CONTACT

Bruce A. Hirsch
Executive Director
Clarence E. Heller Charitable Fdn.
One Lombard St., Ste. 305
San Francisco, CA 94111
(415) 989-9839

FINANCIAL SUMMARY

Recent Giving: $848,524 (1993)

Assets: $28,490,551 (1993)

Gifts Received: $6,596,349 (1993)

Fiscal Note: In 1993, contributions were received from the estate of Clarence F. Heller.

EIN: 94-2814266

CONTRIBUTIONS SUMMARY

Typical Recipients: • *Arts & Humanities:* Arts Outreach, History & Archaeology, Libraries, Music, Theater • *Civic & Public Affairs:* Employment/Job Training, Rural Affairs • *Education:* Arts/Humanities Education, Colleges & Universities, Public Education (Precollege), School Volunteerism, Student Aid • *Environment:* General, Protection, Research, Resource Conservation • *Health:* AIDS/HIV, Medical Research • *International:* International Organizations • *Social Services:* Shelters/Homelessness

Grant Types: general support

Geographic Distribution: focus on CA

GIVING OFFICERS

Anne Heller Anderson: dir

Peter B. Harckham: dir

Alfred Heller: pres

Katherine Heller: dir

Miranda Heller: secy, treas

Bruce A. Hirsch: exec dir

Elizabeth H. Mandell: vp

Peter Mandell: dir

APPLICATION INFORMATION

Initial Approach: Send a brief letter of inquiry. Include a description of organization, amount requested, purpose of funds sought, recently audited financial statement, and proof of tax-exempt status.

GRANTS ANALYSIS

Total Grants: $848,524

Number of Grants: 37

Highest Grant: $200,000

Typical Range: $1,000 to $46,000

Disclosure Period: 1993

Note: Recent grants are derived from a 1993 Form 990.

RECENT GRANTS

Library

20,000	Paine College, Augusta, GA — for an endowment to support the Collins-Callaway Library

1,000	Foundation Center, San Francisco, CA — for general support

General

200,000	University of California Regents, Berkeley, CA — for an initiative to develop sound public policy options designed to prevent the damaging public health effects of pesticide use an air pollution
46,000	San Francisco Unified School District, San Francisco, CA — support teacher participation in curriculum development activities for Project 2061
40,000	Resource Renewal Institute, San Francisco, CA — for research and public education on Green Plans
30,000	Natural Resources Defense Council, San Francisco, CA — develop a plan for sustainable timber management in the eight national forests of the Sierra Nevada
26,890	Community School of Music and Arts, Mountain View, CA — expand chamber music ensemble opportunities and scholarship assistance for music school students

Hewlett Foundation, William and Flora

CONTACT
David P. Gardner
President
William and Flora Hewlett Foundation
525 Middlefield Rd., Ste. 200
Menlo Park, CA 94025-3495
(415) 329-1070

FINANCIAL SUMMARY
Recent Giving: $41,000,000 (1995 est.); $39,332,008 (1994); $45,182,000 (1993)

Assets: $980,000,000 (1995 est.); $974,000,000 (1994 approx.); $875,288,000 (1993)

EIN: 94-1655673

CONTRIBUTIONS SUMMARY
Donor(s): The Hewlett Foundation was established in 1966 by William R. Hewlett; his late wife, Flora Lamson Hewlett ; and their eldest son, Walter B. Hewlett. William Hewlett is a co-founder of the Hewlett-Packard Company, established in 1939 with his partner, David Packard. Mr. Hewlett is retired from the computer and electronics company and is chairman of the foundation. In 1977, the foundation's name changed to the William and Flora Hewlett Foundation, in memory of Mrs. Hewlett who died that

year. She bequeathed $230 million in Hewlett-Packard stock to the foundation.

Typical Recipients: • *Arts & Humanities:* Arts Associations & Councils, Ballet, Dance, Libraries, Music, Opera, Performing Arts, Public Broadcasting, Theater • *Civic & Public Affairs:* Community Foundations, Economic Development, Employment/Job Training, Housing, Native American Affairs, Nonprofit Management, Public Policy, Urban & Community Affairs • *Education:* Colleges & Universities, Education Reform, Environmental Education, Faculty Development, General, International Studies, Literacy, Minority Education, Science/Mathematics Education, Social Sciences Education, Student Aid • *Environment:* General, Resource Conservation • *Health:* Adolescent Health Issues, Health Policy/Cost Containment, Research/Studies Institutes • *International:* Foreign Educational Institutions, Health Care/Hospitals, International Affairs, International Development, International Peace & Security Issues, International Relations • *Social Services:* Child Welfare, Community Service Organizations, Crime Prevention, Family Planning, Shelters/Homelessness, Volunteer Services, Youth Organizations

Grant Types: challenge, endowment, general support, multiyear/continuing support, operating expenses, project, and seed money

Geographic Distribution: national, with emphasis in the San Francisco Bay area; some international giving for population issues

GIVING OFFICERS
Robert F. Erburu: dir *B* Ventura CA 1930 *ED* Univ Southern CA BA 1952; Harvard Univ JD 1955 *CURR EMPL* chmn, dir: Times Mirror Co *CORP AFFIL* dir: Tejon Ranch Co; dir, chmn: Fed Reserve Bank San Francisco *NONPR AFFIL* chmn: Am Newspaper Publs Assn, Brookings Inst; dir: Independent Colls Southern CA, Los Angeles Festival, Tomas Rivera Ctr; fellow: Am Acad Arts & Sci; mem: Am Bar Assn, Bus Counc, Bus Roundtable, CA Bus Roundtable; mem bd dirs: Counc Foreign Rels; mem trust counc: Natl Gallery Art *PHIL AFFIL* trust: Ahmanson Foundation; chmn bd trust: J. Paul Getty Trust; dir: Ralph M. Parsons Foundation, Carrie Estelle Doheny Foundation; vp: Fletcher Jones Foundation; dir: Pfaffinger Foundation; chmn, dir: Times Mirror Foundation

David Pierpont Gardner: pres *B* Berkeley CA 1933 *ED* Brigham Young Univ BS 1955; Univ CA Berkeley MA 1959; Univ CA Berkeley PhD 1966 *CORP AFFIL* dir: First Security Corp, Fluor Corp *NONPR AFFIL* assoc: Cambridge Univ Clare Hall; dir: CA Econ Devel Corp; mem: Am Academy Arts & Sciences, Am Philosophical Soc, Assn Am Univs, CA Chamber Commerce, Higher Ed Forum, Natl Academy Ed, Natl Academy Pub Admin, Phi Beta Kappa, Phi Kappa Phi; pres, prof higher ed: Univ CA Santa Barbara; trust: Tanner Lectures Human Values *PHIL AFFIL* chmn, dir: George S. and Dolores Dore Eccles Foundation; trust: J. Paul Getty Trust

Eleanor H. Gimon: dir

Walter B. Hewlett: chmn *PHIL AFFIL* dir: Packard Humanities Institute; pres: Center for Computer Assisted Research in the Humanities; dir: Stanford Theater Foundation

William Redington Hewlett: chmn emeritus *B* Ann Arbor MI 1913 *ED* Stanford Univ BA 1934; MA Inst Tech MS 1936; Stanford Univ EE 1939 *CURR EMPL* co-fdr, emeritus dir: Hewlett-Packard Co

Roger William Heyns: dir *B* Grand Rapids MI 1918 *ED* Hope Coll 1936-1937; Calvin Coll AB 1940; Univ MI MS 1942; Univ MI PhD 1948 *NONPR AFFIL* fellow: Am Psychological Assn; mem: Counc Foreign Rels, Phi Beta Kappa, Phi Kappa Phi, Sigma Xi *PHIL AFFIL* vchmn, dir: James Irvine Foundation

Mary Hewlett Jaffe: dir

Herant Katchadourian, MD: dir

Walter Massey: dir

Arjay Miller: dir *B* Shelby NE 1916 *ED* Univ CA Los Angeles BS 1937; Univ CA Berkeley 1938-1940 *NONPR AFFIL* counc mem: Conf Bd; dean emeritus: Stanford Univ Grad Sch Bus; fellow: Am Academy Arts & Sciences; hon trust: Brookings Inst; life trust: Urban Inst; mem bd dirs: Stanford Res Inst Intl *CLUB AFFIL* Bohemian, Pacific Union

William Ford Nichols, Jr.: treas *B* Palo Alto CA 1934 *ED* Stanford Univ AB 1956; Stanford Univ MBA 1958 *CURR EMPL* contr: Saga Corp *CORP AFFIL* contr: Saga Corp *NONPR AFFIL* mem: Am Inst CPAs, CA Soc CPAs, Fin Execs Inst, Natl Assn Accts; mem bd trust: Investment Fund Fdns

Marianne Marguerite Pallotti: vp, corp secy *B* Hartford CT 1937 *ED* NY Univ BA 1968; NY Univ MA 1972 *NONPR AFFIL* bd dir: NY Theatre Ballet, Overseas Devel Networks; mem: Northern CA Grantmakers, Peninsula Grantmakers, Women Fdns

Loret Miller Ruppe: dir *B* Milwaukee WI 1936 *NONPR AFFIL* exec: Women Govt; mem: Am Coordinating Counc Norway, Counc Am Ambassadors, Norwegian-Am Historical Assn, Veterans Foreign Wars; trust: Univ Notre Dame

APPLICATION INFORMATION
Initial Approach:

Applicants should submit a letter of inquiry containing a brief statement of need for funds and sufficient factual information to enable the staff to determine whether the proposal falls within the foundation's area of preferred interest. Applicants also should provide reasons and needs for support, taking into account other possible sources of funding.

A formal proposal should include a statement of purpose, budget and financial statement, qualifications of key personnel, list of governing members, evidence of tax-exempt status, and a statement that the proposal has been reviewed and approved by the applicant's governing body.

Applications for music programs should be submitted by January 1, for review in April. Theater program applications should be submitted by April 1, for review in July. Applications from dance programs and film and video service organizations are due by July 1, for review in October. For the Conflict Resolution program, applications from theory organizations and international organizations are due January 1, for review in April; applications from training and promotional organizations and public policy decision making organizations are due July 1, for review in October; and applications from practitioner organizations are due October 1, for review in January. Although the foundation does not expect to be able to adhere rigidly to this schedule, it will make every effort to do so.

Letters of application will be acknowledged briefly upon receipt. Because the foundation prefers to conduct its affairs with a small staff, a more detailed response will be delayed in some cases. Applicants who have not received a substantive reply after a reasonable period of time should make a follow-up inquiry. All inquiries initially are reviewed by the relevant program officer who will request further information, if needed. He or she, in consultation with the president, will either decline those requests which seem unlikely to result in a project the foundation can support, or present the request to the staff for discussion.

Restrictions on Giving: The foundation recognizes that significant programs require time to demonstrate their value, and is therefore willing to consider proposals covering several years of support. While the foundation will fund specific projects in its areas of interest and will occasionally provide general support for organizations of special interest, it expects to work primarily through support of organizations active in its main programs. One exception is the regional grants program, under which the foundation will fund specific projects that meet an immediate community need.

The foundation normally will not consider grants or loans to individuals, or for basic research or capital construction funds. The foundation will not make grants in the areas of medicine or health, criminal justice, juvenile delinquency, drug and alcohol addiction, the elderly, or the handicapped. It will not support general fund-raising drives, films, or videos; or make grants intended directly or indirectly to support candidates for political office or to influence legislation.

OTHER THINGS TO KNOW
The foundation reports that "in its grantmaking decisions as well as in its interests and activities, the Hewlett Foundation is wholly independent of the Hewlett-Packard Company and the Hewlett-Packard Company Foundation."

GRANTS ANALYSIS
Total Grants: $39,332,008

Number of Grants: 275

Highest Grant: $1,207,000

Average Grant: $143,025

Typical Range: $40,000 to $200,000

Disclosure Period: 1994

Note: Recent grants are derived from a 1993 annual report.

RECENT GRANTS

Library

500,000	Research Libraries Group, Mountain View, CA — for general support of research and development for Research Libraries Information Network
200,000	Council on Library Resources, Washington, DC — for general support

General

730,000	Population Council, New York, NY — for general support of the Research Division
670,000	Alan Guttmacher Institute, New York, NY — for policy analysis
550,000	Program for Appropriate Technology in Health, Seattle, WA — for general support of family planning activities
500,000	Development Studies Center, Oakland, CA — to expand the Child Development Study
500,000	Pathfinder International, Watertown, MA — for general support

Hewlett-Packard Co. / Hewlett-Packard Co. Foundation

Revenue: $24.99 billion
Employees: 97,000
Headquarters: Palo Alto, CA
SIC Major Group: Electronic Computers, Computer Peripheral Equipment Nec, Process Control Instruments, and Fluid Meters & Counting Devices

CONTACT
Roy Verley
Director of Corporate Philanthropy
Hewlett-Packard Co.
PO Box 10301
Palo Alto, CA 94303-0890
(415) 857-3053
Note: US universities and colleges should contact US University Grants Manager . US national organizations should contact US National Contributions Manager . Local organizations should contact the nearest major HP facility. International organizations should contact the subsidiary in the country of request. The company's World Wide Web address is http://www.hp.com/home.html"

FINANCIAL SUMMARY
Recent Giving: $65,000,000 (fiscal 1995 est.); $64,400,000 (fiscal 1994 approx.); $67,300,000 (fiscal 1993 approx.)

Asset . $4,890,000 (fiscal 1995); $5 ˙26,233 (fiscal 1994); $3,158,792 (fiscal 1993)

Fiscal Note: Corporation contributes both directly and through the Hewlett-Packard Co. Foundation. Total foundation giving was $534,500 in 1994. Individual departments at major company facilities make grants totaling about $5,400,000 per year, which are included in totals above. Above figures include nonmonetary support.

EIN: 94-2618409

CONTRIBUTIONS SUMMARY
Typical Recipients: • *Arts & Humanities:* Arts Centers, Arts Funds, History & Archaeology, Museums/Galleries, Music • *Civic & Public Affairs:* Law & Justice • *Education:* Business Education, Colleges & Universities, Elementary Education (Private), Elementary Education (Public), Engineering/Technological Education, General, Medical Education, Minority Education, Public Education (Precollege), Science/Mathematics Education • *Environment:* General • *Health:* Emergency/Ambulance Services, Hospitals • *International:* Foreign Arts Organizations, Foreign Educational Institutions, Health Care/Hospitals, International Organizations, International Relations, International Relief Efforts • *Science:* Science Museums, Scientific Organizations • *Social Services:* Community Service Organizations, YMCA/YWCA/YMHA /YWHA, Youth Organizations

Grant Types: employee matching gifts and project

Note: Employee matching gift ratio: 1 to 1, for employee cash gifts to higher education and United Way campaigns only. Company matches product donations 3 to 1, for gifts to higher education and kindergarten through graduate school.

Nonmonetary Support: $53,164,000 (fiscal 1994); $56,420,000 (fiscal 1993); $57,500,000 (fiscal 1992)

Nonmonetary Support Types: donated products

Note: Totals for product donations are computed using list price values. Nonmonetary support is provided by the company. Contacts for nonmonetary support are Tony Napolitan, University Grants and Nancy Thomas, National Grants.

Geographic Distribution: near operating locations and to national organizations

Operating Locations: CA (Cupertino, Mountain View, North Hollywood, Palo Alto, Rocklin, Rohnert Park, Roseville, San Diego, San Jose, Santa Clara, Santa Rosa, Sunnyvale), CO (Colorado Springs, Fort Collins, Greeley, Loveland), DE (Wilmington), GA (Atlanta), ID (Boise), IL (Rolling Meadows), MA (Andover, Chelmsford, Waltham), MD (Rockville), NH (Exeter), NJ (Rockaway), OR (Corvallis, McMinnville), WA (Everett, Spokane, Vancouver)

Note: Also operates in Puerto Rico, Europe, Asia, Australia, Brazil, Canada, and Mexico.

CORP. OFFICERS
Lewis Emmett Platt: *B* Johnson City NY
1941 *ED* Cornell Univ BSME 1963; Univ
PA MBA 1966 *CURR EMPL* chmn, pres,
ceo, dir: Hewlett-Packard Co *CORP AFFIL*
dir: Molex Inc; pres, dir: Calan Inc *NONPR
AFFIL* mem: Inst Electrical & Electronics
Engrs, Sci Apparatus Mfg Assn

GIVING OFFICERS
Roy Verley: exec dir *CURR EMPL* dir corp
philanthropy: Hewlett-Packard Co

APPLICATION INFORMATION
Initial Approach: *Initial Contact:* call for
guidelines and forms; cash or equipment proposals from local education organizations,
community services, and arts agencies to
contributions committee at nearest major facility: national requests to Nancy Thomas,
contributions manager *Include Information
On:* description of the organization, history,
and purpose; amount requested; purpose of
grant; statement of need; sources and status
of other funding; key personnel and qualifications of staff; recently audited financial
statement; and proof of tax-exempt status
Deadlines: general requests, any time; university equipment requests, by August 2 for
consideration for following year *Note:* University requests require an Hewlett-Packard
employee sponsor. Contact Tony Napolitan,
university grants manager

Restrictions on Giving: Equipment is donated only to organizations that have the
staff and budget capacity to manage the new
technology.

Hewlett-Packard does not support fund
drives and annual appeals; fund raising
events and dinners; conferences; memberships; capital campaigns; endowments; faculty chairs; scholarships; grants to
individuals; grants from Hewlett-Packard in
the U.S. to organizations outside the U.S.;
organizations that are not tax-exempt; and
religious or sectarian groups.

OTHER THINGS TO KNOW
Grant seekers should develop a knowledgeable, supportive Hewlett-Packard employee
constituency prior to submitting a formal application. Company places strong emphasis
on programs in which employees volunteer.

PUBLICATIONS
Philanthopic annual report, community report, guidelines

GRANTS ANALYSIS
Total Grants: $64,400,000*

Number of Grants: 2,900*

Highest Grant: $4,573,254

Average Grant: $22,000*

Typical Range: $2,000 to $50,000

Disclosure Period: fiscal year ending October 31, 1994

Note: Total grants includes foundation and
direct giving. Number of grants and average
grants figures were Provided by the company. Recent grants are derived from a 1994
grants list.

RECENT GRANTS
General

4,573,254	University of California, Berkeley, CA —for computer science
1,222,923	Massachusetts Institute of Technology, Cambridge, MA
970,533	Massachusetts Institute of Technology, Cambridge, MA —for electrical and computer engineering
920,064	ESD number 112 School District, Battleground, WA
817,683	University of Southern California, Los Angeles, CA —for electrical and computer engineering

Hoag Family Foundation, George

Former Foundation Name: Hoag Foundation

CONTACT
W. Dickerson Milliken
Secretary and Director
George Hoag Family Foundation
Century Plaza Towers, Ste. 4392
2029 Century Pk., E
Los Angeles, CA 90067
(310) 785-0690

FINANCIAL SUMMARY
Recent Giving: $2,384,100 (1993);
$1,153,000 (1992); $2,212,100 (1990)
Assets: $39,708,201 (1993); $38,983,771
(1992); $32,085,157 (1990)
EIN: 95-6006885

CONTRIBUTIONS SUMMARY
Donor(s): The Hoag Foundation was established in 1940 with funds donated by the
late George Grant Hoag and from bequests
from his estate. His widow, Grace E. Hoag,
and his son, George Grant Hoag II, also
have supported the foundation with donations. George Grant Hoag was a prominent
vice president and director of the J.C. Penney Company. The foundation sponsored the
construction of the Hoag Memorial Hospital
in Newport Beach, CA.

The foundation recently changed its name to
the George Hoag Family Foundation.

Typical Recipients: • *Arts & Humanities:*
Arts Festivals, Libraries, Museums/Galler-
ies, Music, Performing Arts, Theater • *Civic
& Public Affairs:* General, Law & Justice,
Legal Aid • *Education:* Colleges & Universi-
ties, Education Associations, General,
Gifted & Talented Programs, Literacy, Pri-
vate Education (Precollege), Public Educa-
tion (Precollege), Secondary Education
(Private), Secondary Education (Public),
Special Education • *Environment:* Wildlife
Protection • *Health:* Cancer, Children's
Health/Hospitals, Clinics/Medical Centers,
Emergency/Ambulance Services, Heart, Hos-
pitals, Medical Research, Preventive Medi-
cine/Wellness Organizations,
Single-Disease Health Associations • *Relig-*

ion: Churches, Religious Welfare • *Social
Services:* Big Brother/Big Sister, Child
Abuse, Child Welfare, Community Service
Organizations, Domestic Violence,
Food/Clothing Distribution, General,
Homes, People with Disabilities, Recreation
& Athletics, Senior Services, Substance
Abuse, YMCA/YWCA/YMHA/YWHA,
Youth Organizations

Grant Types: general support, project, and
research

Geographic Distribution: California, principally Orange County

GIVING OFFICERS
Albert J. Auer: dir

John L. Curci, Jr.: dir

George Grant Hoag II: pres, dir

Patricia H. Hoag: vp, dir

W. Dickerson Milliken: secy, dir *PHIL AF-
FIL* dir: Del E. Webb Foundation

Gwyn Parry: dir

Melinda Hoag Smith: dir

Del V. Werderman: treas *PHIL AFFIL*
treas: Del E. Webb Foundation

APPLICATION INFORMATION
Initial Approach:

Written requests, not exceeding two pages,
should be sent to the foundation to determine eligibility and to arrange for necessary
forms and any additional information which
may be needed.

Requests should outline aims and specific
needs. Finished applications must be accompanied by IRS determination letter of tax-exempt status, California Franchise Tax Board
letter, Forms 4653 or 2218, and notification
of status under section 509(a). Also include
an audited financial statement; list of officers, directors, and trustees; detailed statement of request; budget; timetable; list of
other funding sources; statement of how the
project would benefit California and/or Orange County residents and the need served;
statement specifying when the organization
will report to the foundation on the disbursement of funds and the results obtained; and a
declaration from the governing body of the
organization authorizing the application.

Deadlines are March 31 and September 30.

The foundation's grant-making criteria include current need for proposed project and
extent to which it duplicates existing services; reasonableness of budget; evidence of
efficient, economical management and experienced, competent personnel; and assurance
of practical results. Final action taken on
each application is communicated to the applicant in writing following the board meetings in April and October at which it is
approved or disapproved.

Restrictions on Giving: The foundation
does not make grants to individuals for any
purpose. It generally does not give to governmental agencies or organizations which receive substantial support from taxation;
sectarian or religious organizations in which
the principal activity benefits the members;
or organizations soliciting funds in support
of projects or programs operated by a party

other than the applicant. The foundation usually does not make grants to any organization two years in succession, and prefers not to grant funds more often than once every three or four years.

GRANTS ANALYSIS
Total Grants: $2,384,100

Number of Grants: 46

Highest Grant: $1,710,000

Average Grant: $14,980*

Typical Range: $2,000 to $20,000

Disclosure Period: 1993

Note: The average grant figure excludes the highest grant of $1,710,000. Recent grants are derived from a 1993 Form 990.

RECENT GRANTS

Library

10,000	Sherman Library and Gardens, Newport Beach, CA

General

1,710,000	Hoag Hospital Foundation, Newport Beach, CA
150,000	Brentwood Presbyterian Church, Los Angeles, CA
50,000	City of Hope, Duarte, CA
45,000	Boys and Girls Club of Huntington Valley, Huntington Beach, CA
38,500	Cuesta College Foundation, San Luis Obispo, CA

Hoover, Jr. Foundation, Margaret W. and Herbert

CONTACT
Sara K. Bond
Vice President
Margaret W. and Herbert Hoover, Jr.
  Foundation
200 S Los Robles Ave., Ste. 520
Pasadena, CA 91101
(818) 796-4014

FINANCIAL SUMMARY
Recent Giving: $1,600,000 (1995 est.); $1,600,000 (1994 approx.); $563,512 (1993)

Assets: $14,000,000 (1995 est.); $13,900,000 (1994 approx.); $13,351,707 (1993)

EIN: 95-2560832

CONTRIBUTIONS SUMMARY
Donor(s): The foundation was incorporated in 1968 by the late Herbert Hoover, Jr. and the late Margaret W. Hoover .

Typical Recipients: • *Arts & Humanities:* Libraries • *Civic & Public Affairs:* General, Nonprofit Management, Philanthropic Organizations, Professional & Trade Associations, Public Policy • *Education:* Colleges & Universities, Education Funds, Medical Education, Science/Mathematics Education • *Environment:* Wildlife Protection • *Health:* Cancer, Diabetes, Emergency/Ambulance Services, Eyes/Blindness, Hospitals, Medical Research, Multiple Sclerosis, Single-Dis-

ease Health Associations, Speech & Hearing, Transplant Networks/Donor Banks • *International:* International Development, International Peace & Security Issues • *Science:* Scientific Centers & Institutes, Scientific Research • *Social Services:* Community Service Organizations, Crime Prevention, Delinquency & Criminal Rehabilitation, Volunteer Services

Grant Types: matching, research, and seed money

Geographic Distribution: national

GIVING OFFICERS
Sara K. Bond: vp, asst secy, trust

Margaret Hoover Brigham: vp, secy, trust

Herbert Hoover III: pres, trust *B* Boston MA 1927 *ED* Univ AZ 1952; Harvard Univ 1955 *CORP AFFIL* chmn, secy: Western Telematics; dir: AMCAP Fund, Bond Fund Am, Cash Mgmt Trust Am

Robert J. Plourde: vp, asst treas, trust *PHIL AFFIL* secy, asst treas, trust: Solomon R. and Rebecca D. Baker Foundation

Joan Hoover Vowles: vp, treas, trust

APPLICATION INFORMATION
Initial Approach:

The foundation requests applications be made in writing and no longer than one page.

The one-page proposal must include a statement explaining why the project is necessary, why the applicant's approach to the problem is unique, how the project will be carried out, the amount of funding required, and a project time table showing well-defined and measurable goals.

The foundation has no deadline for submitting proposals.

Restrictions on Giving: Most of the grants are made to organizations involved in medical and scientific research. The foundation makes grants to tax-exempt organizations only. The foundation does not provide funds for individuals, loans, renovation projects, annual campaigns, deficit financing, land acquisition, scholarships, or fellowships.

PUBLICATIONS
Application guidelines

GRANTS ANALYSIS
Total Grants: $563,512

Number of Grants: 22

Highest Grant: $112,542

Average Grant: $25,614

Typical Range: $2,500 to $75,000

Disclosure Period: 1993

Note: Recent grants are derived from a 1993 Form 990.

RECENT GRANTS

General

112,542	Western Biomedical Research, Eugene, OR — research in multiple sclerosis
75,000	Hoover Institution on War, Revolution, and Peace, Stanford, CA — Russian archives microfilming
51,879	House Ear Institute, Los Angeles, CA — development of binaural hearing aid
49,612	Neuroscience Education and Research Foundation, La Jolla, CA — research in nerve regeneration
48,507	Georgetown University Medical Center, Washington, DC — acoustic emissions as an early indicator of toxicity in cancer patients

Howe and Mitchell B. Howe Foundation, Lucille Horton

CONTACT
Mitchell B. Howe, Jr.
President
Lucille Horton Howe and Mitchell B. Howe
  Fdn.
180 S Lake Ave.
Pasadena, CA 91101
(213) 684-2240

FINANCIAL SUMMARY
Recent Giving: $142,500 (1993); $134,125 (1992); $147,287 (1991)

Assets: $2,054,347 (1993); $2,005,308 (1992); $2,083,806 (1991)

EIN: 95-6081945

CONTRIBUTIONS SUMMARY
Donor(s): the late Mitchell B. Howe

Typical Recipients: • *Arts & Humanities:* Arts Centers, Historic Preservation, Libraries, Music • *Civic & Public Affairs:* General, Law & Justice, Legal Aid, Municipalities/Towns • *Education:* Business Education, Colleges & Universities, Community & Junior Colleges, Private Education (Precollege), Public Education (Precollege), Secondary Education (Private), Student Aid, Vocational & Technical Education • *Health:* Children's Health/Hospitals, Health Organizations, Hospitals, Kidney, Medical Research, Public Health, Research/Studies Institutes, Single-Disease Health Associations • *Religion:* Churches, Religious Organizations, Religious Welfare • *Social Services:* Animal Protection, Child Welfare, Community Service Organizations, Family Services, Homes, People with Disabilities, Recreation & Athletics, United Funds/United Ways, Volunteer Services, YMCA/YWCA/YMHA/YWHA, Youth Organizations

Grant Types: general support

Geographic Distribution: focus on CA

GIVING OFFICERS
John C. Cushman: dir

Mitchell B. Howe, Jr.: pres, treas

Hugh V. Hunter: dir

Lynn H. Myers: chmn

Martha Taylor: secy

APPLICATION INFORMATION
Initial Approach: Send brief letter describing program. Deadline is October 1.

GRANTS ANALYSIS

Total Grants: $142,500

Number of Grants: 32

Highest Grant: $76,000

Typical Range: $500 to $12,000

Disclosure Period: 1993

Note: Recent grants are derived from a 1993 Form 990.

RECENT GRANTS

Library

2,000	Friends of Huntington Library, Los Angeles, CA

General

76,000	Huntington Medical Research Institutes, Huntington, CA
12,000	Children's Hospital, CA — Pasadena guild
8,000	Pasadena City College Foundation, Pasadena, CA
5,000	Azusa Pacific University, Azusa, CA
5,000	Boys and Girls Club of Pasadena, Pasadena, CA

Imperial Bancorp / Imperial Bank Foundation

Gross Operating Earnings: $192.63 million

Employees: 1,500

Headquarters: Los Angeles, CA

SIC Major Group: Holding & Other Investment Offices

CONTACT

Richard Baker
Senior Vice President and Legal Counsel
Imperial Bancorp Foundation
9220 S La Cienega Blvd.
Inglewood, CA 90301
(310) 417-5600

FINANCIAL SUMMARY

Recent Giving: $72,665 (1993); $67,800 (1992); $135,750 (1991)

Assets: $537,398 (1993); $530,565 (1992); $508,573 (1991)

Gifts Received: $60,000 (1993); $60,000 (1992); $60,000 (1991)

Fiscal Note: In 1993, contributions were received from Imperial Bank.

EIN: 95-3655599

CONTRIBUTIONS SUMMARY

Typical Recipients: • *Arts & Humanities:* Libraries, Music • *Education:* After-school/Enrichment Programs, Business Education, Colleges & Universities, Education Associations, Private Education (Precollege) • *Environment:* General, Resource Conservation • *Health:* AIDS/HIV, Alzheimers Disease, Children's Health/Hospitals, Clinics/Medical Centers, Geriatric Health, Health Organizations, Hospitals, Medical Research, Preventive Medicine/Wellness Organizations, Research/Studies Institutes, Single-Disease Health Associations

• *International:* International Relief Efforts • *Religion:* Jewish Causes, Religious Organizations, Religious Welfare • *Social Services:* Child Welfare, Day Care, Food/Clothing Distribution, Scouts, United Funds/United Ways, YMCA/YWCA/YMHA/YWHA, Youth Organizations

Grant Types: capital and general support

Geographic Distribution: giving primarily in CA

Operating Locations: CA (Inglewood)

CORP. OFFICERS

George L. Graziadio, Jr.: *CURR EMPL.* chmn, pres, ceo, dir: Imperial Bancorp

GIVING OFFICERS

Mary Lou Area: dir

Richard M. Baker: secy

George L. Graziadio, Jr.: dir *CURR EMPL* chmn, pres, ceo, dir: Imperial Bancorp (see above)

Bernard G. LeBeau: dir

David A. Sklar: cfo *CURR EMPL* exec vp, cfo: Imperial Bancorp

Sharron A. Walker: pres

APPLICATION INFORMATION

Initial Approach: The foundation requests applications be made in writing. There are no deadlines.

GRANTS ANALYSIS

Total Grants: $72,665

Number of Grants: 22

Highest Grant: $10,000

Typical Range: $500 to $7,500

Disclosure Period: 1993

Note: Recent grants are derived from a 1993 Form 990.

RECENT GRANTS

General

10,000	Torrance Memorial Medical Center Health Care, Torrance, CA — general support
7,500	Boy Scouts of America, Los Angeles, CA — general support
7,000	University of California Los Angeles Foundation, Los Angeles, CA — Anderson School of Management
5,000	AIDS Project Los Angeles, Los Angeles, CA — general support
5,000	Children's Bureau of Southern California, Los Angeles, CA — current support campaign

Irvine Foundation, James

CONTACT

Craig E. McGarvey
Director of Administration
James Irvine Foundation
One Market Plz.
Spear Tower, Ste. 1715
San Francisco, CA 94105
(415) 777-2244

Note: Applications for community services, health, higher education, and special projects should be submitted to the above address. Applications for the cultural arts and youth programs should be submitted to the Los Angeles office at 777 S Figueroa St., Ste. 740, Los Angeles, CA 90017, (213) 236-0552, FAX (213) 236-0537.

FINANCIAL SUMMARY

Recent Giving: $29,000,000 (1994 est.); $27,887,064 (1993); $25,079,693 (1992)

Assets: $670,000,000 (1994 est.); $690,264,425 (1993); $626,228,757 (1992 approx.)

EIN: 94-1236937

CONTRIBUTIONS SUMMARY

Donor(s): The foundation was established by James Irvine in 1937 "to promote the general welfare of the people of California." Mr. Irvine (d. 1947) was president of the Irvine Land and Orchard Company, Napa Valley Railroad, and Moraga Land Company. The original trust property was a significant portion of Irvine Company stock, whose primary asset was approximately 100,000 acres of land in Orange County, CA, known as Irvine Ranch.

Typical Recipients: • *Arts & Humanities:* Arts Institutes, Arts Outreach, Ballet, Film & Video, General, Libraries, Museums/Galleries, Music, Opera, Performing Arts, Public Broadcasting • *Civic & Public Affairs:* Asian American Affairs, Community Foundations, Economic Development, Economic Policy, Hispanic Affairs, Housing, Law & Justice, Nonprofit Management, Philanthropic Organizations, Professional & Trade Associations, Public Policy, Rural Affairs, Urban & Community Affairs, Women's Affairs • *Education:* Colleges & Universities, Education Associations, Engineering/Technological Education, Faculty Development, General, International Studies, Minority Education, Science/Mathematics Education, Student Aid • *Environment:* Air/Water Quality, General, Resource Conservation • *Health:* AIDS/HIV, Children's Health/Hospitals, Clinics/Medical Centers, Health Policy/Cost Containment, Health Organizations, Hospitals, Prenatal Health Issues, Public Health • *Social Services:* Child Welfare, Day Care, Domestic Violence, Family Planning, Family Services, Shelters/Homelessness, United Funds/United Ways, Volunteer Services, Youth Organizations

Grant Types: capital, challenge, loan, project, and seed money

Geographic Distribution: exclusively California

GIVING OFFICERS
Samuel Henry Armacost: dir *B* Newport News VA 1939 *ED* Denison Univ BA 1961; Stanford Univ MBA 1964 *CURR EMPL* gen ptnr: Weiss Peck & Grier *CORP AFFIL* dir: Chevron Corp, Failure Group

Angela Glover Blackwell: dir *ED* Howard Univ; Univ CA Boalt Hall Sch Law *CORP AFFIL* dir: Levi Strauss & Co *NONPR AFFIL* dir: Urban Inst *PHIL AFFIL* dir: Foundation for Child Development; vp: Rockefeller Foundation

Dennis Arthur Collins: pres *B* Yakima WA 1940 *ED* Stanford Univ BA 1962; Stanford Univ MA 1963 *NONPR AFFIL* chmn: Counc Commun Based Devel; dir: Northern CA Grantmakers, Southern CA Assn Philanthropy; mem: Counc Fdns, Independent Sector; trust: Am Farmland Trust, Marin Country Day Sch *CLUB AFFIL* California, University, World Trade

Myron Du Bain: chmn, dir *B* Cleveland OH 1923 *ED* Univ CA Berkeley BA 1946; Stanford Univ 1967 *CORP AFFIL* bd dir: Menlo Park; dir: Carter Hawley Hale Stores, Chronicle Publ Co, First Interstate Bancorp, Pacific Telesis Group, Potlatch Corp, SCIOS Inc, SRI Intl, Transamerica Corp *NONPR AFFIL* dir: San Francisco Opera Assn; sr mem: Conf Bd *CLUB AFFIL* Bohemian, CA Tennis, Lagunitas CC, Pacific Union, Villa Taverna

Larry R. Fies: treas, corp secy

Camilla Chandler Frost: dir *B* 1926 *ED* Wellesley Coll *CURR EMPL* secy/treas, dir: Chandis Securities Co *CORP AFFIL* dir: SCE Corp, Security Pacific Corp, Security Pacific Natl Bank; trust: Chandler Trusts *NONPR AFFIL* trust: CA Inst Tech, Wellesley Coll

James C. Gaither: dir *B* Oakland CA 1937 *ED* Princeton Univ BA 1959; Stanford Univ JD 1964 *CORP AFFIL* dir: Basic Am Foods, Levi Strauss & Co *NONPR AFFIL* mem: Am Bar Assn, CA Bar Assn, Order Coif, Phi Delta Phi, San Francisco Bar Assn; mem exec comm, bd visitors: Stanford Univ Sch Law; mem exec comm, trust: Carnegie Endowment Intl Peace, Rand Corp; pres bd trusts: Stanford Univ; trust: Ctr Biotech Research, St Stephens Parish Day School

Walter Bland Gerken: dir *B* New York NY 1922 *ED* Wesleyan Univ BA 1948; Maxwell Sch Citizenship Pub Aff MPA 1958 *CURR EMPL* chmn exec comm, dir: Pacific Mutual Life Ins Co *CORP AFFIL* dir: Mgmt Compensation Group, Southern CA Edison Co, Whittaker Corp; dir, sr advisor: Boston Consult Group *NONPR AFFIL* chmn: Exec Svc Corps, Nature Conservancy CA; chmn bd overseers: Univ CA Irvine Coll Med; dir: Hoag Meml Presbyterian Hosp; mem bd overseers: RAND/Univ CA Los Angeles Ctr Study Soviet Behavior; trust: Occidental Coll, Wesleyan Univ *CLUB AFFIL* Automobile, Balboa Bay, CA, Dairymens CC, Metro, Pauma Valley CC *PHIL AFFIL* dir: Pacific Mutual Charitable Foundation; vp, dir, mem exec comm, chmn audit comm,

mem dirs grant program comm: W. M. Keck Foundation

Roger William Heyns: vchmn, dir *B* Grand Rapids MI 1918 *ED* Hope Coll 1936-1937; Calvin Coll AB 1940; Univ MI MS 1942; Univ MI PhD 1948 *NONPR AFFIL* fellow: Am Psychological Assn; mem: Counc Foreign Rels, Phi Beta Kappa, Phi Kappa Phi, Sigma Xi *PHIL AFFIL* dir: William and Flora Hewlett Foundation

Joan F. Lane: dir *PHIL AFFIL* trust: George Warren Brown Foundation

Craig E. McGarvey: dir admin

Donn Biddle Miller: dir *B* Gallipolis OH 1929 *ED* OH Wesleyan Univ BA 1951; Univ MI JD 1954; Harvard Univ 1974 *CURR EMPL* ptnr: O'Melveny & Myers *CORP AFFIL* dir: Pacific Mutual Life Ins Co, Security Pacific Corp, Security Pacific Natl Bank; gen couns, dir: Carter Hawley Hale Stores; pres, dir: Pearson-Sibert Oil Co TX *NONPR AFFIL* bd dir: Rotary Fdn; chmn bd trusts: Occidental Coll; dir: Automobile Club Southern CA, CA Commun Fdn; mem: Am Bar Assn, CA Bar Assn, Delta Sigma Rho, Los Angeles Chamber Commerce, Los Angeles County Bar Assn, OH Bar Assn, Omicron Delta Kappa, Order Coif, Phi Beta Kappa, Phi Delta Phi, Pi Sigma Alpha, Sigma Chi *CLUB AFFIL* Bel Air Bay, California, Chancery, Los Angeles CC *PHIL AFFIL* trust: John Randolph and Dora Haynes Foundation

Forrest Nelson Shumway: dir *B* Skowhegan ME 1927 *ED* Stanford Univ BA 1950; Stanford Univ LLB 1952 *CURR EMPL* vchmn: AlliedSignal

Kathryn L. Wheeler: dir *CURR EMPL* employee svcs rep: Cadence Design Sys Inc

Edward Zapanta, MD: dir

APPLICATION INFORMATION
Initial Approach:

Applicants can send a letter of inquiry or a full proposal. The foundation stresses that it is available to assist with questions on guidelines and application requirements.

A full proposal includes a cover letter and the proposal, as well as supporting documents. The cover letter should include a summary of the proposed project, the amount requested from the foundation, general information about the applicant organization and the need to be addressed, the project cost, and the amount requested from the foundation. The proposal should describe the applicant's history, current programs, key leadership, and major funding sources. The proposal should document the need that the project will address, and list the project strategy, staff requirements, timeline, and evaluation criteria. It should also detail the project budget, including current and anticipated revenue sources and amounts.

The full proposal should also include a board endorsement, copies of both 501(c)(3) and 509(a) letters, financial statements for the last three fiscal years, current operating budget, funding sources for the project and the applicant organizations, and a board of directors roster.

The foundation board meets five times annually. Grant recommendations in each field of interest are considered at least twice a year, with the exception of higher education grants which are approved in September. Proposals may be submitted at any time and will be acknowledged promptly. However, higher education proposals must be received by April 1 to be considered for the following September.

When considering requests, the foundation places emphasis on the applicant organization's quality, leadership, and significance in relation to others in the field. It looks for proposals that have the potential for impact beyond the applicant organization. An interview and/or site visit are essential parts of the decision-making process during the final review stage.

Restrictions on Giving: Substantially tax-supported organizations, endowments, general operating expenses, debt reduction, basic research, films, publishing activities, festivals, conferences, religious or sectarian organizations, and private elementary or secondary schools will not be funded. The foundation will usually not make grants to an organization in successive years.

OTHER THINGS TO KNOW
By provision of its trust, the foundation can support only those programs and organizations that provide benefit within the state of California. The trust further restricts the foundation from making grants to organizations that receive substantial support through taxation or that primarily benefit tax-supported entities or agencies of government. The foundation does not fund individuals. Proposals for one-time events are generally not accepted, although conference support will be considered in exceptional cases when the issue being addressed falls within programmatic guidelines and the potential for impact is high. The foundation rarely makes grants for endowment purposes or for the reduction or elimination of deficits.

PUBLICATIONS
Annual report, Grantseeker's Guide

GRANTS ANALYSIS
Total Grants: $27,887,064
Number of Grants: 267
Highest Grant: $1,400,000
Average Grant: $104,446
Typical Range: $50,000 to $150,000
Disclosure Period: 1993

Note: Recent grants are derived from a 1992 annual report.

RECENT GRANTS
Library
120,000   College of Notre Dame, Belmont, CA — to computerize the library catalog system

General
1,200,000   Higher Education Policy Institute, Saratoga, CA — core support

1,000,000	University of Southern California, Los Angeles, CA — for the James Irvine Foundation Center for Scholarly Technology
750,000	University of Redlands, Redlands, CA — toward construction of the University Center
500,000	St. Mary's College, Moraga, CA — toward the cost of a comprehensive program to become a more effective multicultural academic community
400,000	Local Initiatives Support Corporation, Los Angeles, CA — to support the Los Angeles Collaborative for Community Development

Irwin Charity Foundation, William G.

CONTACT
Michael R. Gorman
Executive Director
William G. Irwin Charity Foundation
235 Montgomery St.
711 Russ Bldg.
San Francisco, CA 94104
(415) 362-6954

FINANCIAL SUMMARY
Recent Giving: $3,105,283 (1993); $2,195,000 (1992); $2,360,918 (1991)

Assets: $64,192,833 (1993); $63,689,857 (1992); $63,914,534 (1991)

EIN: 94-6069873

CONTRIBUTIONS SUMMARY
Donor(s): The William G. Irwin Charity Foundation was established by Mrs. Fannie M. Irwin in 1919. The foundation received contributions from Mrs. Fannie M. Irwin and Mrs. Helene Irwin Fagan , both deceased.

Typical Recipients: • *Arts & Humanities:* Ballet, Dance, Libraries, Museums/Galleries, Music, Opera, Performing Arts • *Civic & Public Affairs:* Law & Justice, Urban & Community Affairs • *Education:* Colleges & Universities, Private Education (Precollege), Science/Mathematics Education, Secondary Education (Private) • *Health:* Cancer, Clinics/Medical Centers, Geriatric Health, Health Organizations, Hospitals, Medical Rehabilitation, Medical Research, Research/Studies Institutes, Single-Disease Health Associations • *Religion:* Religious Organizations, Religious Welfare • *Social Services:* Community Service Organizations, Food/Clothing Distribution, People with Disabilities, Shelters/Homelessness, United Funds/United Ways, Youth Organizations

Grant Types: capital, general support, project, and research

Geographic Distribution: only in the states of California and Hawaii

GIVING OFFICERS
George K. Cronin: trust

Michael R. Gorman: exec dir

Frederic R. Grant: trust *PHIL AFFIL* secy, dir: John McIntire Educational Fund

William Lee Olds III: trust

William Lee Olds, Jr.: pres, trust

Jane Olds Ritchie: vp, trust

APPLICATION INFORMATION
Initial Approach:

The foundation has no application forms. Prospective applicants should submit a letter to the foundation.

Grant requests should be accompanied by a summary letter, current financial information (audited, if possible, with a balance sheet and statement of revenue and expenses), budget, list of board members, complete justification for request, history of organization, description of activities, and proof of federal and state tax-exempt status.

Applications should be submitted approximately three weeks prior to a meeting date. Meetings are held approximately every two months.

OTHER THINGS TO KNOW
All subsequent correspondence with the foundation should include reference to the date of original inquiry.

GRANTS ANALYSIS
Total Grants: $2,195,000

Number of Grants: 23

Highest Grant: $300,000

Average Grant: $95,435

Typical Range: $25,000 to $100,000

Disclosure Period: 1992

Note: Recent grants are derived from a 1992 Form 990.

RECENT GRANTS

General

300,000	California Pacific Medical Center, San Francisco, San Francisco, CA — equipment for the Breast Health Center
300,000	Mills College, Oakland, Oakland, CA — renovation of Mills Hall
300,000	St. Ignatius College Preparatory, San Francisco, CA — capital campaign
200,000	Mission Delores Basilica, San Francisco, San Francisco, CA — restoration project
150,000	Dominican College of San Rafael, San Rafael, CA — upgrade three residence halls

Jacobs Family Foundation

CONTACT
Jennifer Vanica
Foundation Manager
Jacobs Family Fdn.
PO Box 261519
San Diego, CA 92196
(619) 578-7256

FINANCIAL SUMMARY
Recent Giving: $1,054,858 (1993)

Assets: $23,772,487 (1993)

Gifts Received: $7,472,500 (1993)

Fiscal Note: In 1993, contributions were received from Joseph J. Jacobs, Cenfed Bank ($5,000), and Ambassador Foundation ($5,000).

EIN: 95-4187111

CONTRIBUTIONS SUMMARY
Typical Recipients: • *Arts & Humanities:* Libraries, Museums/Galleries • *Civic & Public Affairs:* African American Affairs, Business/Free Enterprise, Economic Development, Employment/Job Training, General, Housing, Women's Affairs • *Education:* Arts/Humanities Education, Colleges & Universities, Education Reform, Leadership Training, Private Education (Precollege), School Volunteerism, Student Aid • *Health:* Clinics/Medical Centers, Hospitals, Medical Research, Preventive Medicine/Wellness Organizations • *International:* International Affairs, International Development, International Relations • *Religion:* Religious Welfare • *Science:* Scientific Centers & Institutes • *Social Services:* Child Welfare, Crime Prevention, Family Planning, Family Services, Substance Abuse

Grant Types: general support

Geographic Distribution: focus on CA

GIVING OFFICERS
Norman Hapke: vp

Valerie Hapke: asst secy

Dr. Joseph J. Jacobs: pres, ceo, cfo *B* New York NY 1916 *ED* Polytech Inst BS 1937; Polytech Inst MS 1939; Polytech Inst PhD 1942 *CORP AFFIL* chmn: Bank Audi; vp, gen couns: Graphic Scanning Corp *NONPR AFFIL* dir: CA Econ Devel Corp, CA Round Table, Genetics Inst, Inst Contemporary Studies, Un Way; mem: Assocs CA Inst Tech; trust: Harvey Mudd Coll, Polytech Inst NY *CLUB AFFIL* Annandale GC, Pauma Valley CC *PHIL AFFIL* treas, dir: Jacob Family Foundation; pres, dir: Jacobs Engineering Foundation

Linda K. Jacobs: vp

Margaret E. Jacobs: vp

Violet J. Jacobs: secy

Jennifer Vanica: mgr

APPLICATION INFORMATION
Initial Approach: Send a brief letter of inquiry. Include a description of organization, amount requested, purpose of funds sought,

recently audited financial statement, and proof of tax-exempt status.

GRANTS ANALYSIS
Total Grants: $1,054,858

Number of Grants: 80

Highest Grant: $100,000

Typical Range: $200 to $50,000

Disclosure Period: 1993

Note: Recent grants are derived from a 1993 Form 990.

RECENT GRANTS

Library
10,000	Pasadena Public Library Foundation, Pasadena, CA — for Save the Library campaign

General
100,000	Los Angeles Urban League, Pasadena, CA — for Micro-Small Business Development Collaboration
50,000	Teach for America, Los Angeles, CA — for TEACH! program
50,000	The Door: A Center of Alternatives, New York, NY — for aid and assistance
35,250	Liberty Hill Foundation, Santa Monica, CA — for Los Ninos
35,000	Elementary Institute of Science, San Diego, CA — for capacity building

Jameson Foundation, J. W. and Ida M.

CONTACT
Les M. Huhn
President
J. W. and Ida M. Jameson Fdn.
PO Box 397
Sierra Madre, CA 91024
(818) 355-6973

FINANCIAL SUMMARY
Recent Giving: $1,060,000 (fiscal 1994); $1,000,000 (fiscal 1993); $955,300 (fiscal 1992)

Assets: $889,778 (fiscal 1994); $986,803 (fiscal 1993); $932,382 (fiscal 1992)

Gifts Received: $1,008,851 (fiscal 1994); $953,407 (fiscal 1993); $875,000 (fiscal 1992)

Fiscal Note: In fiscal 1994, contributions were received from the Ida May Jameson Trust.

EIN: 95-6031465

CONTRIBUTIONS SUMMARY
Donor(s): J. W. Jameson Corp., the late Ida M. Jameson

Typical Recipients: • *Arts & Humanities:* Community Arts, Libraries, Museums/Galleries, Music, Public Broadcasting • *Civic & Public Affairs:* Botanical Gardens/Parks, General, Legal Aid, Philanthropic Organizations, Public Policy, Safety, Zoos/Aquariums • *Education:* Colleges & Universities, Community & Junior Colleges, General, Legal Education, Medical Education, Private Education (Precollege), Public Education (Precollege), Religious Education, Secondary Education (Public) • *Health:* Children's Health/Hospitals, Emergency/Ambulance Services, Hospitals, Medical Research, Preventive Medicine/Wellness Organizations, Research/Studies Institutes • *Religion:* Churches, Religious Organizations, Religious Welfare • *Social Services:* Community Service Organizations, Senior Services, Youth Organizations

Grant Types: general support, research, and scholarship

Geographic Distribution: focus on CA

GIVING OFFICERS
Bill B. Betz: dir

William M. Croxton: vp, dir

Les M. Huhn: pres, dir

Frederick Leroy Leydorf: dir *B* Toledo OH 1930 *ED* Univ MI BBA 1953; Univ CA Los Angeles JD 1958 *CURR EMPL* ptnr: Hufstedler Miller Kaus & Beardsley *CORP AFFIL* ptnr: Hufstedler Miller Kaus & Beardsley *NONPR AFFIL* mem: Am Bar Assn, Am Coll Probate Couns, CA Bar Assn, Intl Academy Estate Trust Law, Los Angeles County Bar Assn, Los Angeles World Affs Counc, Univ CA Los Angeles Law Alumni Assn; mem legal comm: Music Ctr Fdn

Pauline Vetrovec: secy, dir

APPLICATION INFORMATION
Initial Approach: Send a brief letter of inquiry. Include a description of organization, amount requested, purpose of funds sought, recently audited financial statement, and proof of tax-exempt status. Deadline is March 1.

GRANTS ANALYSIS
Total Grants: $1,060,000

Number of Grants: 79

Highest Grant: $50,000

Typical Range: $2,000 to $40,000

Disclosure Period: fiscal year ending June 30, 1994

Note: Recent grants are derived from a fiscal 1994 Form 990.

RECENT GRANTS

Library
20,000	Henry E. Huntington Library and Art Gallery, San Marino, CA
20,000	Pasadena City College, Pasadena, CA — Library Fund

General
50,000	Huntington Medical Research Institute, Pasadena, CA
40,000	Amherst College, Amherst, MA
40,000	Southern California School of Theology at Claremont, Claremont, CA
40,000	University of California Los Angeles Foundation, Los Angeles, CA — J. W. and Ida M. Jameson Fund
40,000	University of Michigan, Ann Arbor, MI

Jewett Foundation, George Frederick

CONTACT
Theresa A. Mullen
Executive Director
George Frederick Jewett Foundation
The Russ Bldg.
235 Montgomery St., Ste. 612
San Francisco, CA 94104
(415) 421-1351

FINANCIAL SUMMARY
Recent Giving: $892,297 (1993); $981,330 (1992); $898,598 (1991)

Assets: $29,045,103 (1992); $23,491,058 (1991); $23,556,015 (1989)

Gifts Received: $7,944 (1992); $4,200 (1991); $6,050 (1989)

Fiscal Note: The foundation receives gifts from Berkshire Hathaway.

EIN: 04-6013832

CONTRIBUTIONS SUMMARY
Donor(s): The George Frederick Jewett Foundation was established in 1957 under the will of George Frederick Jewett (1896-1956), whose mother was the former Margaret Weyerhaeuser. Mr. Jewett was chairman of Potlatch Corporation and a trustee of the American University of Cairo.

Typical Recipients: • *Arts & Humanities:* Arts Centers, Arts Festivals, Arts Institutes, Arts Outreach, Dance, Historic Preservation, Libraries, Museums/Galleries, Music, Performing Arts, Public Broadcasting • *Civic & Public Affairs:* Community Foundations, Economic Policy, Nonprofit Management, Philanthropic Organizations, Public Policy • *Education:* Colleges & Universities, Economic Education, Medical Education, Minority Education, Religious Education, Science/Mathematics Education, Special Education • *Environment:* General, Resource Conservation • *Health:* Cancer, Diabetes, Hospitals • *International:* Foreign Educational Institutions, Health Care/Hospitals, International Environmental Issues, International Relations • *Religion:* Churches, Religious Organizations • *Social Services:* Child Welfare, Community Service Organizations, Family Planning, Family Services, People with Disabilities, Senior Services, Substance Abuse, United Funds/United Ways, Youth Organizations

Grant Types: capital, endowment, general support, and project

Geographic Distribution: primarily eastern Washington and the city of San Francisco

GIVING OFFICERS

Mary Jewett Gaiser: don, trust *B* Ogdenburg NY 1901 *ED* Wellesley Coll BA 1923; Whitman Coll LLD 1949 *NONPR AFFIL* mem: Natl Social Welfare Assembly; mem natl bd: Un Svc Org, YWCA; trust: Am Univ Beirut, Wellesley Coll, Whitman Coll

Margaret Weyerhaeuser Jewett Greer: trust *ED* Harvard Univ 1952 *PHIL AFFIL* don: Weyerhaeuser Family Foundation

William Hershey Greer, Jr.: trust *B* Owensboro KY 1928 *ED* Yale Univ BA 1951; Harvard Univ JD 1954 *PHIL AFFIL* don: Weyerhaeuser Family Foundation

George F. Jewett, Jr.: chmn *B* Spokane WA 1927 *ED* Dartmouth Coll BA 1950; Harvard Univ MBA 1952 *CURR EMPL* vchmn, dir: Potlatch Corp *NONPR AFFIL* chmn: Pacific Presbyterian Med Fdn; dir: Carnegie Inst, San Francisco Ballet Assn; trust: Asia Fdn, Natl Gallery Art *CLUB AFFIL* Bohemian, Burlingame CC, Francisco, Ida Lewis YC, Newport Reading Room, NY YC, Pacific-Union, San Diego YC, Spouting Rock Beach, St Francis YC *PHIL AFFIL* vp, trust: Weyerhaeuser Family Foundation; vp: Potlatch Foundation for Higher Education/Potlatch Foundation II

Lucille Winifred McIntyre Jewett: trust *B* St Louis MO 1929 *NONPR AFFIL* collectors comm: Natl Gallery Art; mem: Asian Scholars Selection Comm, Jr League Tacoma, Pi Beta Phi, World Svc Counc; mem natl counc: Sch Am Ballet New York City; trust: San Francisco Ballet Assn, Univ Puget Sound *CLUB AFFIL* Francisco *PHIL AFFIL* don: Weyerhaeuser Family Foundation

Theresa A. Mullen: exec dir

APPLICATION INFORMATION
Initial Approach:

Verbal requests will not be accepted. Before making a formal proposal, however, an applicant is welcome to make written inquiries regarding foundation policies and programs.

Proposals should include the name and address of applicant, names of chief administrative officers, statement of private foundation status, and a letter from an officer endorsing the proposal and agreeing that the applicant will assume full fiscal management and accounting responsibility for any funds received. The statement must be supported either by a copy of an IRS letter regarding private foundation status; a copy of completed form 4653, with a statement from a principal officer providing date filed and IRS response; an opinion of legal status; or a copy of an IRS letter of tax exemption. An applicant should also provide a statement attesting that no portion of a Jewett grant will be used to employ, compensate, or benefit a government official.

The foundation also requires specific information for project proposals. Proposals must contain a brief description of the project, with background information; development plan; evaluation method; expected results; constituency served; and information on key personnel administering the project. Applicants must provide budgetary information on salaries, rent, supplies for technicians,

clerical services, equipment, expendable supplies, and travel. They also must indicate amounts of "in-kind" or cash contributions, sources of income, and amounts received from other philanthropic agencies. The foundation prefers to have a three-year projected budget. Prospective grantees also should indicate start and completion dates, and whether or not the proposal has been submitted to other grant-making organizations, including federal and state agencies.

Applications may be submitted any time.

Proposals are reviewed quarterly, and many are held for final processing at the foundation's annual meeting at the end of the year. The foundation prefers to participate with other donors, and not to assume a major portion of the amount to be raised. A high priority is given to organizations receiving little or no support from public tax funds.

Restrictions on Giving: No grants are made to individuals. Support occasionally may be given to scholarship, fellowship, or research programs of established institutions. Grants generally are not given to other private or operating foundations. While the foundation will not support activities that influence legislation, it may support research on and studies of problems of public concern. Emergency petitions are not favored except when they involve disaster and human suffering.

OTHER THINGS TO KNOW
The administrative officers of each recipient organization must agree in writing to administer the grant in accordance with its stated terms, to submit interim financial and progress reports, to advise the foundation of any changes, to request the termination of a project if the program as approved becomes impossible to carry out, and to refund any unused amounts.

When grants are made to organizations in states that require annual reporting of receipts and expenditures by organizations soliciting general support, the foundation requires evidence that its grant has been reported properly.

No plaques or memorials relating to the foundation can be used without prior approval.

PUBLICATIONS
Annual report, application guidelines

GRANTS ANALYSIS
Total Grants: $892,297

Number of Grants: 122

Highest Grant: $200,000

Average Grant: $5,721*

Typical Range: $1,000 to $15,000

Disclosure Period: 1993

Note: The average grant figure does not a include $200,000 grant to Wellesley College. Recent grants are derived from a 1993 annual report.

RECENT GRANTS

Library
10,000	Friends of the San Francisco Public Library, San

Francisco, CA — in support of the City Guides project, a program of historical and architectural walks in San Francisco's neighborhoods

General
50,000	Roper Hospital, Charleston, SC — general operating support
25,000	Cathedral of St. John the Evangelist, Spokane, WA — third payment on a multiyear commitment for the Endowment Preservation Fund
25,000	Gonzaga University, Spokane, WA — third payment on a five-year commitment in support of the University Center for Information Technology
25,000	Nature Conservancy, Seattle, WA — first payment on a two-year commitment in support of the Willapa Bay Watershed Project
20,000	Cancer Patient Care of Spokane County, Spokane, WA — support of a Home Assessment and Outreach Program for cancer patients in need of financial or emotional assistance

Johnson Charitable Educational Trust, James Hervey

CONTACT
Lawrence Y. True
President
James Hervey Johnson Charitable Educational Trust
5309 Canterbury Dr.
San Diego, CA 92116-0000
(619) 283-8016

FINANCIAL SUMMARY
Recent Giving: $255,400 (fiscal 1993)

Assets: $11,402,161 (fiscal 1993)

EIN: 33-6081439

CONTRIBUTIONS SUMMARY
Typical Recipients: • *Arts & Humanities:* Libraries, Museums/Galleries • *Education:* General • *Health:* Health Organizations • *International:* International Organizations • *Religion:* Religious Organizations, Social/Policy Issues • *Social Services:* Shelters/Homelessness, Substance Abuse

Grant Types: general support

Geographic Distribution: focus on CA

GIVING OFFICERS
Lawrence Y. True: pres, trust

APPLICATION INFORMATION
Initial Approach: Send a brief letter of inquiry. Include a description of organization,

amount requested, purpose of funds sought, recently audited financial statement, and proof of tax-exempt status.

GRANTS ANALYSIS
Total Grants: $255,400

Number of Grants: 17

Highest Grant: $33,000

Typical Range: $2,500 to $25,000

Disclosure Period: fiscal year ending July 31, 1993

Note: Recent grants are derived from a fiscal 1993 Form 990.

RECENT GRANTS
Library
25,000   Council for Democratic and Secular Humanism — for a book acquisition for a freethought library

4,000   James Harvey Johnson Memorial Library — purchase books by Thomas Paine

General
33,000   North American Committee for Humanism, Farmington Hills, MI — publication of Humanism Today magazine and seminar

25,000   Humanist Association of Los Angeles, Los Angeles, CA — publicize humanism on college campuses

21,900   American Natural Hygiene Society, Tampa, FL — produce videotape of convention

20,000   A New Enlightenment — publish the first in a series of books on religion and health

20,000   American Natural Hygiene Society, Tampa, FL — publish a book on natural hygiene

Jones Foundation, Fletcher

CONTACT
John W. Smythe
Executive Director
Fletcher Jones Foundation
One Wilshire Bldg., Ste. 1210
624 S Grand Ave.
Los Angeles, CA 90017
(213) 689-9292

FINANCIAL SUMMARY
Recent Giving: $5,760,000 (1995 est.); $5,800,000 (1994 approx.); $5,805,037 (1993)

Assets: $111,000,000 (1995 est.); $115,000,000 (1994 approx.); $93,995,315 (1993)

EIN: 23-7030155

CONTRIBUTIONS SUMMARY
Donor(s): In 1969, the Jones Foundation was established by the will of Fletcher Jones

with a bequest of approximately $30 million. Mr. Jones was the co-founder, chairman, and chief executive officer of Computer Services Corporation, a computer software services company. He was a collector of fine art, and possessed a large collection of Impressionist paintings. He also assembled one of the West's preeminent stables of thoroughbred racehorses. Mr. Jones died in 1972 at the age of 41. The first distribution of funds from the Jones estate was given to the foundation in 1977; the final distribution of the estate was made in 1981. The foundation donated its first grants in 1974. In March of 1987, the Jones Foundation was renamed the Fletcher Jones Foundation.

Typical Recipients: • *Arts & Humanities:* Arts Institutes, General, History & Archaeology, Libraries, Museums/Galleries, Music, Opera, Performing Arts • *Civic & Public Affairs:* Botanical Gardens/Parks, Community Foundations, General, Law & Justice, Legal Aid • *Education:* Business Education, Colleges & Universities, Continuing Education, Education Funds, Engineering/Technological Education, General, International Studies, Legal Education, Private Education (Precollege), Science/Mathematics Education, Social Sciences Education, Student Aid, Vocational & Technical Education • *Health:* Children's Health/Hospitals, Clinics/Medical Centers, Health Organizations, Hospitals, Nursing Services, Research/Studies Institutes • *International:* International Development, International Peace & Security Issues • *Religion:* Religious Welfare • *Science:* Science Museums • *Social Services:* Child Welfare, Food/Clothing Distribution, People with Disabilities, Recreation & Athletics, Scouts, Volunteer Services, Youth Organizations

Grant Types: professorship and scholarship

Geographic Distribution: primarily California

GIVING OFFICERS
Robert F. Erburu: vp *B* Ventura CA 1930 *ED* Univ Southern CA BA 1952; Harvard Univ JD 1955 *CURR EMPL* chmn, dir: Times Mirror Co *CORP AFFIL* dir: Tejon Ranch Co; dir, chmn: Fed Reserve Bank San Francisco *NONPR AFFIL* chmn: Am Newspaper Publs Assn, Brookings Inst; dir: Independent Colls Southern CA, Los Angeles Festival, Tomas Rivera Ctr; fellow: Am Acad Arts & Sci; mem: Am Bar Assn, Bus Counc, Bus Roundtable, CA Bus Roundtable; mem bd dirs: Counc Foreign Rels; mem trust counc: Natl Gallery Art *PHIL AFFIL* trust: Ahmanson Foundation; chmn bd trust: J. Paul Getty Trust; dir: Ralph M. Parsons Foundation, Carrie Estelle Doheny Foundation, William and Flora Hewlett Foundation, Pfaffinger Foundation; chmn, dir: Times Mirror Foundation

Houston Irvine Flournoy: vp *B* New York NY 1929 *ED* Cornell Univ BA 1950; Princeton Univ MA 1952; Princeton Univ PhD 1956 *CORP AFFIL* dir: Fremont Gen Corp, Lockheed Corp, Lockheed Fin Corp, Tosco Corp *NONPR AFFIL* mem: Natl Acad Pub

Admin, Pi Sigma Alpha *PHIL AFFIL* dir: Lockheed Leadership Fund

Parker S. Kennedy: trust *B* 1948 *ED* Univ Southern CA AB 1970; Hastings Sch Law LLB 1973 *CURR EMPL* pres, dir: First Am Title Ins Co *CORP AFFIL* chmn, dir: First Am Title/TX; pres, dir: First Am Fin Corp *PHIL AFFIL* trust: First American Financial Foundation

Chauncey J. Medberry III: vp *B* Los Angeles CA 1917 *ED* Univ CA Los Angeles BA 1938 *CURR EMPL* dir: CP Natl Corp *PHIL AFFIL* trust: John Randolph and Dora Haynes Foundation; hon dir: Bank of America - Giannini Foundation

Rudolph James Munzer: trust *B* Minneapolis MN 1918 *ED* Stanford Univ BA 1940 *CORP AFFIL* dir: First Am Fin Corp *NONPR AFFIL* mem bd dirs: Long Beach Meml Hosp, Natl Liquefied Petroleum Gas Assn, St Anthony High Sch Fdn

Donald Eugene Nickelson: trust *B* Emporia KS 1932 *ED* Phillips Univ 1960 *CURR EMPL* vchmn bd, dir: Harbour Group Ltd *CORP AFFIL* chmn, dir: Greenfield Indus, Rotan Mosle Fin Corp; dir: Allied Healthcare Products *NONPR AFFIL* dir: Securities Indus Assn

John D. Pettker: secy

John Phleger Pollock: pres *B* Sacramento CA 1920 *ED* Stanford Univ AB 1942; Harvard Univ JD 1948 *CURR EMPL* of couns: Rodi Pollock Pettker Galbraith & Phillips *NONPR AFFIL* active: Boy Scouts Am; fellow: Am Coll Trial Lawyers; mem: Am Bar Assn, Los Angeles County Bar Assn; trust: Good Hope Med Fdn

Dickinson C. Ross: vp

John W. Smythe: exec dir, treas *B* 1925

Jess C. Wilson, Jr.: vp

APPLICATION INFORMATION
Initial Approach:

Organizations should submit a short test letter to the foundation before preparing a formal grant application. There is no special grant application format.

Include a fact sheet summarizing significant statistics and background information about the organization's qualifications, objectives, current programs and services, sources of support, purpose, goals, expense budget, funding, and method of evaluation, and include most recent financial report, proof of nonprofit status, most recent IRS Form 990, list of officers with professional affiliations, and most recent annual report. Also include the name, address, and telephone number of the organization's attorney.

Applications for grants are accepted throughout the year. Grant decisions are made once in each calendar quarter.

Each test letter will be acknowledged with either a denial or an invitation to submit a formal application.

Restrictions on Giving: Grants are not made to individuals, political candidates, projects which are financed by government agencies, or K-12 schools; or for deficit financing, operating funds, contingencies, conferences, seminars, workshops, travel exhibits, surveys, elections, campaigns, voter registration, or propaganda.

PUBLICATIONS
Annual report

GRANTS ANALYSIS
Total Grants: $5,805,037

Number of Grants: 59

Highest Grant: $500,000

Average Grant: $98,390

Typical Range: $5,000 to $25,000 and $50,000 to $150,000

Disclosure Period: 1993

Note: Recent grants are derived from a 1993 annual report.

RECENT GRANTS

Library

500,000	Henry E. Huntington Library and Art Gallery, San Marino, CA — Fletcher Jones Chair, first payment
25,000	Henry E. Huntington Library and Art Gallery, San Marino, CA — operating
10,000	Harvard University Center for Italian Renaissance, Cambridge, MA — Villa I Tatti-Library Catalog

General

500,000	University of San Diego, San Diego, CA — chair in Biology, first payment
500,000	University of San Francisco, San Francisco, CA — chair in Biology, first payment
463,182	University of the Pacific, Stockton, CA — chair in Entrepreneurship, final payment
451,825	University of Redlands, Redlands, CA — chair in American Politics, final payment
434,541	Occidental College, Los Angeles, CA — chair in Chemistry, final payment

Knudsen Foundation, Tom and Valley

CONTACT
Helen B. McGrath
Executive Vice President and Treasurer
Tom and Valley Knudsen Fdn.
900 Wilshire Blvd., Ste. 1434
Los Angeles, CA 90017
(213) 614-1940

FINANCIAL SUMMARY
Recent Giving: $457,000 (1993); $643,750 (1992); $613,000 (1991)

Assets: $3,586,692 (1993); $3,821,745 (1992); $4,152,942 (1991)

Gifts Received: $99,440 (1993); $101,699 (1992); $95,174 (1991)

Fiscal Note: In 1993, contributions were received from the trust fund for M. Christensen.

EIN: 95-6031188

CONTRIBUTIONS SUMMARY
Donor(s): the late T. R. Knudsen, the late Valley M. Knudsen

Typical Recipients: • *Arts & Humanities:* Arts Centers, History & Archaeology, Libraries, Museums/Galleries, Music • *Civic & Public Affairs:* Clubs, Housing, Legal Aid, Municipalities/Towns • *Education:* Colleges & Universities, Engineering/Technological Education, Legal Education, Public Education (Precollege), Science/Mathematics Education, Student Aid • *Environment:* General • *Health:* Clinics/Medical Centers, Emergency/Ambulance Services, Research/Studies Institutes • *Religion:* Churches, Religious Organizations, Religious Welfare • *Science:* Scientific Organizations • *Social Services:* Child Welfare, Community Service Organizations, Day Care, Food/Clothing Distribution, People with Disabilities, Youth Organizations

Grant Types: general support and scholarship

Geographic Distribution: limited to southern CA

GIVING OFFICERS
Christian Castenskiold: dir

William W. Escherich: dir

Doris Holtz: dir

Gene Knudsen-Hoffman: dir

Helen B. McGrath: exec vp, secy, treas, dir

Peter F. O'Malley: dir *B* New York NY 1937 *ED* Univ PA BS 1960 *CURR EMPL* pres: Los Angeles Dodgers *CORP AFFIL* exec vp: Los Angeles Dodgers Baseball Club *NONPR AFFIL* dir: Los Angeles Police Meml Fdn; trust: Little League Fdn; vchmn bd govs: Los Angeles Music Ctr Performing Arts Counc

Robert E. Osborne: dir

Joseph Robert Vaughan: pres, dir *B* Los Angeles CA 1916 *ED* Loyola Univ AB 1937; Loyola Univ JD 1939 *PHIL AFFIL* dir: Fritz B. Burns Foundation

APPLICATION INFORMATION
Initial Approach: Include a description of organization, amount requested, purpose of funds sought, recently audited financial statement, and proof of tax-exempt status. Deadlines are March 1 and September 1.

Restrictions on Giving: Limited to southern California.

PUBLICATIONS
Application Guidelines

GRANTS ANALYSIS
Total Grants: $457,000

Number of Grants: 33

Highest Grant: $100,000

Typical Range: $1,000 to $30,000

Disclosure Period: 1993

Note: Recent grants are derived from a 1993 Form 990.

RECENT GRANTS

Library

15,000	Huntington Library and Art Gallery, San Marino, CA
15,000	Richard Nixon Library and Birthplace, Yorba Linda, CA

General

100,000	Danish Lutheran Church Relocation Committee, Glendale, CA
30,000	Loma Linda University, Loma Linda, CA
30,000	Loyola Marymount University, Los Angeles, CA
30,000	Mt. St. Mary's College, Los Angeles, CA
25,000	Occidental College, Los Angeles, CA

Komes Foundation

CONTACT
Jerome W. Komes
President
Komes Fdn.
1801 Van Ness Ave., Ste. 300
San Francisco, CA 94109
(415) 441-6462

FINANCIAL SUMMARY
Recent Giving: $93,350 (1993); $228,300 (1992); $198,950 (1991)

Assets: $2,922,647 (1993); $2,845,145 (1992); $2,847,523 (1991)

Gifts Received: $6,802 (1993); $75,000 (1992); $100,000 (1991)

Fiscal Note: In 1993, contributions were received from Jerome and Flora Komes.

EIN: 94-1611406

CONTRIBUTIONS SUMMARY
Donor(s): Jerome W. Komes, Flora Komes

Typical Recipients: • *Arts & Humanities:* Community Arts, Ethnic & Folk Arts, Historic Preservation, Libraries, Museums/Galleries, Music, Public Broadcasting • *Civic & Public Affairs:* Economic Policy, General, Law & Justice, Legal Aid, Nonprofit Management, Public Policy, Urban & Community Affairs • *Education:* Arts/Humanities Education, Colleges & Universities, Leadership Training, Literacy, Minority Education, Private Education (Precollege), Religious Education, Secondary Education (Private), Special Education • *Environment:* General • *Health:* Cancer, Clinics/Medical Centers, Emergency/Ambulance Services, Health Organizations, Heart, Hospitals, Medical Research, Mental Health, Single-Disease Health Associations, Speech & Hearing • *International:* International Organizations • *Religion:* Churches, Dioceses, Religious Organizations, Religious Welfare • *Science:* Observatories & Planetariums, Science Exhibits & Fairs, Science Museums, Scientific

Centers & Institutes • *Social Services:* At-Risk Youth, Child Welfare, Community Service Organizations, Day Care, People with Disabilities, Scouts, Senior Services, Shelters/Homelessness, Substance Abuse, United Funds/United Ways, Youth Organizations

Grant Types: capital, endowment, general support, multiyear/continuing support, operating expenses, research, scholarship, and seed money

Geographic Distribution: focus on northern CA

GIVING OFFICERS
Jerome W. Komes: pres, vp

Michael Lawton Mellor: assoc secy *B* Yorkshire England 1922 *ED* Univ CA AB 1943; Univ CA LLB 1950 *CURR EMPL* coun: Thelen Marrin Johnson & Bridges *CORP AFFIL* of coun: Thelen Marrin Johnson & Bridges *NONPR AFFIL* dir: Friends San Francisco Pub Library, Intl Visitors Ctr San Francisco, Robinson Jeffers Tor House Fdn; mem: Am Bar Assn, San Francisco Bar Assn *PHIL AFFIL* secy: Robert and Alice Bridges Foundation

APPLICATION INFORMATION
Initial Approach: Send brief letter describing program. Include a description of organization, amount requested, purpose of funds sought, recently audited financial statement, and proof of tax-exempt status. There are no deadlines.

Restrictions on Giving: Limited to northern California.

PUBLICATIONS
Annual Report (includes application guidelines), Informational Brochure

GRANTS ANALYSIS
Total Grants: $93,350

Number of Grants: 59

Highest Grant: $20,000

Typical Range: $250 to $7,500

Disclosure Period: 1993

Note: Recent grants are derived from a 1993 Form 990.

RECENT GRANTS

Library
1,000	Library Foundation of San Francisco, San Francisco, CA

General
20,000	Maranists, San Francisco, CA
6,600	FADICA, Washington, DC
5,000	Knights of Malta, San Francisco, CA
5,000	Knights of the Holy Seplechre, San Francisco, CA
2,500	AERMIC

Koret Foundation

CONTACT
Michael A. Papo
Chief Executive Officer and Executive Director
Koret Foundation
33 New Montgomery St., Ste. 1090
San Francisco, CA 94105-4509
(415) 882-7740

FINANCIAL SUMMARY
Recent Giving: $11,250,000 (1995 est.); $10,571,530 (1994); $12,311,484 (1993)

Assets: $185,000,000 (1995 est.); $184,000,000 (1994 approx.); $184,314,377 (1993)

Gifts Received: $100,000 (1993); $292,271 (1992); $19,710 (1991)

Fiscal Note: Contributions received are bequests from the Joseph Koret 1980 Irrevocable Trust.

EIN: 94-1624987

CONTRIBUTIONS SUMMARY
Donor(s): The Koret Foundation was established in 1966, with the late Stephanie Koret and the late Joseph Koret as donors.

Typical Recipients: • *Arts & Humanities:* Arts Centers, Ballet, Ethnic & Folk Arts, Libraries, Museums/Galleries, Performing Arts • *Civic & Public Affairs:* Community Foundations, Housing, Zoos/Aquariums • *Education:* Colleges & Universities, Continuing Education, Preschool Education, Public Education (Precollege), Religious Education, Student Aid • *Environment:* Resource Conservation • *Health:* Emergency/Ambulance Services, Geriatric Health, Hospitals (University Affiliated), Long-Term Care • *International:* Foreign Educational Institutions, International Environmental Issues, International Organizations, Missionary/Religious Activities • *Religion:* Jewish Causes • *Social Services:* Camps, Family Services, Food/Clothing Distribution, Shelters/Homelessness, United Funds/United Ways

Grant Types: general support, operating expenses, and project

Geographic Distribution: San Francisco Bay Area (San Francisco, San Mateo, Santa Clara, Alameda, Marin, and Contra Costa); and Israel

GIVING OFFICERS
Richard C. Blum: dir *B* 1935 *ED* Univ CA Berkeley BA; Univ CA Berkeley MBA *CURR EMPL* fdr, chmn, pres: Richard C Blum & Assocs *CORP AFFIL* dir: AGP Indus Corp, Natl Ed Corp, NWA Inc, Shaklee Corp, Sumitomo Bank CA, URS Corp

Michael J. Boskin: dir

William Kraemer Coblentz: dir *B* San Francisco CA 1922 *ED* Univ CA Berkeley BA 1943; Yale Univ LLB 1947 *CURR EMPL* ptnr: Coblentz Cahen McCabe & Breyer *CORP AFFIL* dir: McClatchy Newspapers, Pac Bell, Pacific Telesis Group *NONPR AFFIL* mem: Am Bar Assn, Am Law Inst, Assn Bar City New York, CA Bar

Assn, Counc Foreign Rels, San Francisco Bar Assn

Jack R. Curley: treas, secy *B* San Francisco CA 1928 *ED* Univ CA BS 1949; Minneapolis MN Coll Law 1955-1957; Univ CA Los Angeles Grad Sch Bus Exec Prog 1968 *CORP AFFIL* owner, developer: Pier 31 Warehouse Self- Storage *NONPR AFFIL* mem: CA Newspaper Publs Assn *CLUB AFFIL* mem: Mala Lahaina Boat, Preeminent Albert's Field Intl Tennis

Eugene L. Friend: vchmn, dir *B* 1916 *CURR EMPL* chmn, dir: Kutler Clothiers

Richard L. Greene: dir

Stanley Herzstein: dir

Susan Koret: chmn

Michael A. Papo: exec dir, ceo

Thaddeus N. Taube: pres, dir *B* 1931 *ED* Stanford Univ BS 1954; Stanford Univ MS 1957 *CURR EMPL* chmn, dir: Woodmont Cos *PHIL AFFIL* pres, dir: Taube Family Foundation

APPLICATION INFORMATION
Initial Approach:

Applicants must first submit a one- to three-page preliminary letter to the foundation's executive director or program officer.

The preliminary letter should include a description of the project or need for which support is requested; information about the applicant organization, including experience, programs, or services, and population and geographic area served; summary budget for the proposed project, including amount sought from the foundation and other sources; and copy of the IRS determination letter of tax-exempt status. If the foundation is interested, an application for funding package will be sent; if not, the applicant will be notified in writing within 90 days.

Completed applications for funding are reviewed by a program officer, who may request additional information, an interview, or a visit. The review process may take from three to six months. All grants are subject to the approval of the foundation's board of directors. Once a grant is awarded, a grantee is required to provide narrative and financial reports at specified times detailing accomplishments, problems, and the use of funds.

Restrictions on Giving: The foundation reports that it will only make grants to organizations which have proof of tax-exempt status under Section 501(c)(3) of the IRS Code and which are not private foundations as described in Section 509(a). No grants will be made to fiscal agents soliciting funds in support of programs which are not conducted by the applicant, for propaganda or lobbying activities, or to organizations which have not fulfilled all the terms of a previous grant. Grants generally will not be made for a request in which there are no other sources of funding; for deficit funding, endowments, or emergency funding; for general fund-raising campaigns; for the purchase of equipment or furnishings; or to sectarian, veterans, fraternal, military, religious, or similar groups whose principal activity is for the benefit of their own membership.

GRANTS ANALYSIS
Total Grants: $10,571,530

Number of Grants: 212

Highest Grant: $1,000,000

Average Grant: $49,866

Typical Range: $1,000 to $15,000 and $20,000 to $100,000

Disclosure Period: 1994

Note: Recent grants are derived from a 1993 grants list.

RECENT GRANTS

Library
600,000	Library Foundation of San Francisco, San Francisco, CA — toward furnishings, fixtures, equipment, and endowment of San Francisco's new main library

General
1,220,000	Jewish Home for the Aged, San Francisco, CA — over five years, to help construct a 120-bed skilled nursing facility on the grounds of the Home
714,000	Jewish Community Federation of San Francisco, the Peninsula, Marin and Sonoma Counties, San Francisco, CA
271,500	Jewish Community Federation of San Francisco, the Peninsula, Marin and Sonoma Counties, San Francisco, CA
265,000	Stanford University, Stanford, CA — for graduate fellowships in the School of Humanities and Science
250,000	New Israel Fund, New York, NY — support a portion of Electoral Reform project

Leavey Foundation, Thomas and Dorothy

CONTACT
J. Thomas McCarthy
Chairman and Trustee
Thomas and Dorothy Leavey Foundation
4680 Wilshire Blvd.
Los Angeles, CA 90010
(213) 930-4252

FINANCIAL SUMMARY
Recent Giving: $5,311,237 (1993); $8,678,610 (1992); $8,979,867 (1991)

Assets: $158,245,173 (1993); $150,894,376 (1992); $154,889,628 (1991)

EIN: 95-6060162

CONTRIBUTIONS SUMMARY
Donor(s): The Thomas and Dorothy Leavey Foundation was established in California in 1952 by Thomas E. Leavey and his wife, Dorothy Leavey.

Typical Recipients: • *Arts & Humanities:* Arts Associations & Councils, History & Archaeology, Libraries, Music, Performing Arts, Public Broadcasting • *Civic & Public Affairs:* General, Legal Aid, Philanthropic Organizations, Professional & Trade Associations, Public Policy, Women's Affairs • *Education:* Agricultural Education, Arts/Humanities Education, Colleges & Universities, Education Associations, Education Funds, International Exchange, Medical Education, Minority Education, Private Education (Precollege), Public Education (Precollege), Religious Education, Secondary Education (Private), Special Education, Student Aid • *Health:* Children's Health/Hospitals, Clinics/Medical Centers, Health Funds, Health Organizations, Hospitals, Nursing Services, Prenatal Health Issues • *International:* Foreign Educational Institutions, Health Care/Hospitals, International Peace & Security Issues • *Religion:* Churches, Dioceses, Religious Organizations, Religious Welfare, Social/Policy Issues • *Science:* Science Museums • *Social Services:* Child Welfare, Domestic Violence, Family Planning, Family Services, Food/Clothing Distribution, People with Disabilities, Recreation & Athletics, Senior Services, Special Olympics, Substance Abuse, Volunteer Services, Youth Organizations

Grant Types: capital, endowment, general support, research, and scholarship

Geographic Distribution: primarily California, with special emphasis on the Los Angeles metropolitan area

GIVING OFFICERS
Louis M. Castruccio: trust

Dorothy E. Leavey: don, trust

Joseph James Leavey: trust *B* Oakland CA 1930 *ED* Univ San Francisco AB 1952; Stanford Univ LLB 1955 *CURR EMPL* atty: Early Maslach Leavey & Nutt

J. Thomas McCarthy: chmn, trust *B* Santa Monica CA 1932 *ED* Univ Southern CA BA 1953; Univ Southern CA LLD 1963 *CURR EMPL* sr ptner: Bodkin McCarthy Sargent & Smith

Kathleen Leavey McCarthy: trust *B* Beverly Hills CA 1935 *ED* Univ Southern CA BS 1957

Kenneth Tyler: trust

APPLICATION INFORMATION
Initial Approach:

Applicants should submit a letter to the foundation.

The letter should include descriptions of the organization and the project for which funds are sought, and proof of tax-exempt status.

There are no deadlines for submitting requests.

If the application is accepted, a full proposal will be requested.

Restrictions on Giving: The foundation reports that scholarships are provided only to children of employees of agents of Farmers Insurance Group and its subsidiaries.

GRANTS ANALYSIS
Total Grants: $5,311,237

Number of Grants: 69*

Highest Grant: $1,000,000

Average Grant: $60,239*

Typical Range: $1,000 to $100,000

Disclosure Period: 1993

Note: Number of grants and average grant figures exclude $275,205 in individual grants. The average grant figure also excludes the highest grant of $1,000,000. Recent grants are derived from a 1993 Form 990.

RECENT GRANTS

General
1,000,000	Santa Clara University, Santa Clara, CA
666,666	California Medical Center, Los Angeles, CA
629,340	University of Southern California Department of Nursing, Los Angeles, CA
250,000	Archdiocese of Los Angeles, Los Angeles, CA — Manning House of Prayer
250,000	Daughters of Mary and Joseph, Los Angeles, CA

LEF Foundation

CONTACT
Marina Drummer
Executive Director
LEF Fdn.
1095 Lodi Ln.
St. Helena, CA 94574
(707) 963-9591

FINANCIAL SUMMARY
Recent Giving: $517,000 (fiscal 1994); $297,200 (fiscal 1991); $397,840 (fiscal 1990)

Assets: $8,298,828 (fiscal 1994); $7,686,492 (fiscal 1991); $6,412,660 (fiscal 1990)

Gifts Received: $70,017 (fiscal 1994); $1,028,864 (fiscal 1991)

Fiscal Note: In fiscal 1994, contributions were received from Lyda Kuth ($50,034) and Marion Green ($19,983).

EIN: 68-0070194

CONTRIBUTIONS SUMMARY
Donor(s): Lyda Ebert Trust

Typical Recipients: • *Arts & Humanities:* Arts Associations & Councils, Arts Centers, Arts Funds, Dance, Ethnic & Folk Arts, Film & Video, General, Libraries, Museums/Galleries, Music, Performing Arts, Theater • *Civic & Public Affairs:* African American Affairs, Economic Development, General, Urban & Community Affairs, Women's Affairs • *Environment:* General • *Religion:* Churches • *Social Services:* Camps, Youth Organizations

Grant Types: general support, project, and seed money

Geographic Distribution: focus on northern CA and New England

GIVING OFFICERS
Marina Drummer: exec dir

Laurey Finneran: trust

Marion E. Greene: pres

Dean Kuth: vp

Lyda Ebert Kuth: secy, cfo

APPLICATION INFORMATION
Initial Approach: Send brief letter of inquiry describing program or project (seven copies). Deadlines are March 1 and September 1.

PUBLICATIONS
Application Guidelines

GRANTS ANALYSIS
Total Grants: $517,000

Number of Grants: 86

Highest Grant: $20,000

Typical Range: $500 to $12,000

Disclosure Period: fiscal year ending June 30, 1994

Note: Recent grants are derived from a fiscal 1994 Form 990.

RECENT GRANTS
Library
10,000	Wadsworth Athenaeum, Hartford, CT

General
20,000	Build, Chicago, IL
12,000	Bay Area Women's Resource Center, San Francisco, CA
10,500	Black Panther Party
10,000	Holding Ground Dudley Street Neighborhood Initiative
8,000	Defending Our Lives

Long Foundation, J.M.

CONTACT
Robert M. Long
President
J.M. Long Fdn.
PO Box 5222
Walnut Creek, CA 94596
(510) 944-6701

FINANCIAL SUMMARY
Recent Giving: $1,496,850 (1993); $529,580 (1992); $15,000 (1991)

Assets: $31,890,155 (1993); $32,323,834 (1992); $26,101,785 (1991)

Gifts Received: $1,388,243 (1993); $8,066,684 (1992); $28,806,536 (1991)

EIN: 94-1643626

CONTRIBUTIONS SUMMARY
Donor(s): the late Joseph M. Long and Vera M. Long

Typical Recipients: • *Arts & Humanities:* Libraries, Museums/Galleries • *Civic & Public Affairs:* Botanical Gardens/Parks • *Education:* Business Education, Colleges & Universities, Education Funds, Health & Physical Education, Medical Education, Private Education (Precollege), Public Education (Precollege) • *Environment:* Resource Conservation, Wildlife Protection • *Health:* Health Funds, Hospitals, Preventive Medicine/Wellness Organizations • *Science:* Scientific Research • *Social Services:* Camps, Scouts, Senior Services, Youth Organizations

Grant Types: general support

Geographic Distribution: giving limited to CA

GIVING OFFICERS
W. G. Combs: vp, treas, trust

O. D. Jones: trust

Robert Merril Long: pres, trust *B* Oakland CA 1938 *ED* Brown Univ 1956-1958; Claremont Mens Coll BA 1960 *CURR EMPL* chmn, ceo, dir: Longs Drug Stores Corp *NONPR AFFIL* mem: Natl Assn Chain Drug Stores *PHIL AFFIL* ceo: Vera M. Long Foundation

S. D. Roath: trust *CURR EMPL* pres, dir: Long Drug Stores

M. J. Souyoultzis: trust

C. Tessler: secy

APPLICATION INFORMATION
Initial Approach: Send a brief letter of inquiry. Include a description of organization, amount requested, purpose of funds sought, recently audited financial statement, and proof of tax-exempt status. There are no deadlines.

GRANTS ANALYSIS
Total Grants: $1,496,850

Number of Grants: 121

Highest Grant: $300,000

Typical Range: $1,000 to $10,000

Disclosure Period: 1993

Note: Recent grants are derived from a 1993 Form 990.

RECENT GRANTS
Library
10,000	California State Bakersfield Foundation, Bakersfield, CA — W. Stern Library
10,000	Friends of Vacaville Library, Vacaville, CA

General
300,000	University of Pacific, Stockton, CA
200,000	University of California Santa Cruz, Santa Cruz, CA — J.M. Long marine lab
122,000	Ducks Unlimited, Long Grove, IL — ricelands as wetlands project
110,000	University of California San Francisco, San Francisco, CA
56,000	Oregon State University Foundation, Corvallis, OR

Lund Foundation

CONTACT
Victoria D. Lund
President
Lund Fdn.
PO Box 15159
North Hollywood, CA 91615
(818) 985-2171

FINANCIAL SUMMARY
Recent Giving: $427,950 (1993); $628,865 (1992); $555,640 (1991)

Assets: $72,717,189 (1993); $4,859,924 (1992); $3,798,139 (1991)

Gifts Received: $64,058,678 (1993)

Fiscal Note: In 1993, contributions were received from the Lund Family Trust.

EIN: 23-7306460

CONTRIBUTIONS SUMMARY
Donor(s): Sharon D. Lund

Typical Recipients: • *Arts & Humanities:* Arts Centers, Arts Institutes, Libraries, Music • *Civic & Public Affairs:* Philanthropic Organizations • *Education:* Education Funds, Private Education (Precollege), Special Education • *Health:* Clinics/Medical Centers, Emergency/Ambulance Services, Hospitals • *Social Services:* People with Disabilities, Volunteer Services

Grant Types: general support and operating expenses

Geographic Distribution: focus on CA

GIVING OFFICERS
Lillian B. Disney: pres *B* Lewiston ID *CURR EMPL* owner: Retlaw Enterprises *PHIL AFFIL* pres: Lillian B. Disney Foundation

Ronald E. Gother: asst secy *PHIL AFFIL* dir, vp, cfo: Gibson, Dunn, and Crutcher Foundation

Victoria D. Lund: pres

Robert L. Wilson: vp, secy, treas *PHIL AFFIL* secy, treas: Lillian B. Disney Foundation

APPLICATION INFORMATION
Initial Approach: The foundation has no formal grant application procedure or application form. There are no deadlines.

GRANTS ANALYSIS
Total Grants: $427,950

Number of Grants: 9

Highest Grant: $300,000

Typical Range: $300 to $10,000

Disclosure Period: 1993

Note: Recent grants are derived from a 1993 Form 990.

RECENT GRANTS
Library
5,000	Los Angeles Library Foundation, Los Angeles, CA — general fund

General

65,150	Marianne Frostig Center, Pasadena, CA — general fund
25,000	American Red Cross, Los Angeles, CA — general fund
20,000	Independence Center, Los Angeles, CA — general fund
1,500	Orthopaedic Hospital, Beverly Hills, CA — general fund
1,000	John Tracy Clinic, Los Angeles, CA — general fund

Lurie Foundation, Louis R.

CONTACT
Robert A. Lurie
President
Louis R. Lurie Foundation
555 California St., Ste. 5100
San Francisco, CA 94104
(415) 392-2470

FINANCIAL SUMMARY
Recent Giving: $1,233,000 (1995 est.); $1,233,000 (1994 approx.); $1,233,000 (1993 approx.)

Assets: $15,900,000 (1995 est.); $15,907,000 (1994 approx.); $15,906,624 (1993 approx.)

Gifts Received: $353,534 (1992); $353,534 (1991); $353,534 (1989)

Fiscal Note: The above gifts are contributions from the Charitable Trust under the will of Louis R. Lurie.

EIN: 94-6065488

CONTRIBUTIONS SUMMARY
Donor(s): The Louis R. Lurie Foundation was established in 1948. The donors were the late Louis R. Lurie, the late George S. Lurie, and Robert A. Lurie. Louis R. Lurie made his fortune in real estate and as a producer in the entertainment field. Robert A. Lurie, his son and president of the foundation, owns the San Francisco Giants baseball team.

Typical Recipients: • *Arts & Humanities:* Arts Centers, Ballet, Community Arts, Ethnic & Folk Arts, Libraries, Literary Arts, Museums/Galleries, Music, Opera, Public Broadcasting, Theater • *Civic & Public Affairs:* Botanical Gardens/Parks, Employment/Job Training, Hispanic Affairs, Housing, Law & Justice, Professional & Trade Associations, Urban & Community Affairs, Zoos/Aquariums • *Education:* Colleges & Universities, Education Associations, Education Funds, Education Reform, Health & Physical Education, Minority Education, Private Education (Precollege), Public Education (Precollege), Student Aid • *Environment:* General • *Health:* Clinics/Medical Centers, Emergency/Ambulance Services, Geriatric Health, Health Funds, Health Organizations, Hospitals, Medical Research, Mental Health, Single-Disease Health Associations • *Religion:* Churches, Jewish Causes, Religious Organizations, Religious Welfare • *Sci-*

ence: Science Museums • *Social Services:* Child Welfare, Community Centers, Community Service Organizations, Domestic Violence, Family Services, Food/Clothing Distribution, People with Disabilities, Recreation & Athletics, Senior Services, Substance Abuse, United Funds/United Ways, Youth Organizations

Grant Types: general support and project

Geographic Distribution: primarily metropolitan San Francisco, CA; and Chicago, IL

GIVING OFFICERS
Ms. Patricia R. Fay: dir

James L. Hunt: dir

H. Michael Kurzman: vp, dir *B* 1939 *CORP AFFIL* exec vp, treas, dir: Lurie Co Inc

Robert Alfred Lurie: pres, don, dir *B* 1929 *CURR EMPL* pres: Lurie Co Inc *CORP AFFIL* owner: San Francisco Giants

Eugene L. Valla: cfo, dir *CORP AFFIL* vp, dir: Lurie Co Inc

APPLICATION INFORMATION
Initial Approach:

Initial contact should be a brief letter. The foundation issues guidelines for submitting applications, but it does not have a formal application form.

The letter should include the history and activities of the organization, the specific project for which funding is sought, the names and qualifications of key personnel, the budget, the specific funds requested and how they will be used, and the sources of other funding committed or expected. Applicants should attach copies of the following documents to the letter: names of officers/directors, the latest twelve month financial statement, the current operating budget, and the most recent tax-exempt statement from the IRS.

The foundation's screening committee reviews applications on a continuing basis, and advises whether the requests will be recommended to the board of directors. The board currently meets in November or December each year.

Restrictions on Giving: No grants are made to individuals.

GRANTS ANALYSIS
Total Grants: $1,233,000

Number of Grants: 96

Highest Grant: $275,000

Average Grant: $12,844

Typical Range: $5,000 to $30,000

Disclosure Period: 1992

Note: Recent grants are derived from a 1992 Form 990.

RECENT GRANTS
Library

50,000	Library Foundation of San Francisco, San Francisco, CA

General

275,000	Jewish Community Federation
50,000	Congregation Emanu-El, New York, NY
50,000	Jewish Community Federation, San Francisco, CA — Operation Exodus
30,000	San Francisco Day School, San Francisco, CA
30,000	University of California San Francisco, San Francisco, CA

Lux Foundation, Miranda

CONTACT
Lawrence I. Kramer, Jr.
Executive Director
Miranda Lux Fdn.
57 Post St., Ste. 510
San Francisco, CA 94104
(415) 981-2966

FINANCIAL SUMMARY
Recent Giving: $320,434 (fiscal 1994); $246,600 (fiscal 1993); $241,970 (fiscal 1992)

Assets: $4,593,482 (fiscal 1994); $4,882,322 (fiscal 1993); $4,829,129 (fiscal 1992)

EIN: 94-1170404

CONTRIBUTIONS SUMMARY
Donor(s): the late Miranda W. Lux

Typical Recipients: • *Arts & Humanities:* Libraries, Music, Performing Arts, Public Broadcasting, Theater • *Civic & Public Affairs:* Asian American Affairs, Business/Free Enterprise, Employment/Job Training, Hispanic Affairs, Nonprofit Management • *Education:* Afterschool/Enrichment Programs, Business Education, Business-School Partnerships, Colleges & Universities, Education Funds, Literacy, Private Education (Precollege), Public Education (Precollege), Science/Mathematics Education, Secondary Education (Private), Secondary Education (Public), Student Aid • *Environment:* Resource Conservation • *Health:* Children's Health/Hospitals, Clinics/Medical Centers • *Religion:* Religious Welfare • *Science:* Science Museums • *Social Services:* At-Risk Youth, Child Welfare, Community Centers, Community Service Organizations, Family Services, People with Disabilities, Recreation & Athletics, Youth Organizations

Grant Types: fellowship, multiyear/continuing support, operating expenses, project, scholarship, and seed money

Geographic Distribution: limited to San Francisco, CA

GIVING OFFICERS
Beatrice Bowles: secy, treas

Lawrence I. Kramer, Jr.: exec dir

Benson Bertheau Roe, MD: pres *B* Los Angeles CA 1918 *ED* Univ CA Berkeley AB 1939; Harvard Univ MD 1943 *CORP AFFIL* dir: Control Laser Corp *NONPR AFFIL* fellow: Am Coll Cardiology, Am Coll Surgeons; mem: Am Assn Thoracic Surgery, Am Med Assn, Am Surgical Assn, CA Med Assn; premeritus: Univ CA

Philip F. Spalding: vp

David Wisnom, Jr.: pres

Diana Potter Wolfensperger: trust

APPLICATION INFORMATION
Initial Approach: Send brief letter of inquiry describing program or project. Include a description of organization, amount requested, purpose of funds sought, recently audited financial statement, and proof of tax-exempt status. There are no deadlines.

Restrictions on Giving: Does not support individuals or provide funds for annual campaigns, defcit financing, land acquisition, loans, renovations, publications, or conferences.

PUBLICATIONS
Annual Report, Application Guidelines

GRANTS ANALYSIS
Total Grants: $320,434

Number of Grants: 28

Highest Grant: $25,000

Typical Range: $1,000 to $20,000

Disclosure Period: fiscal year ending June 30, 1994

Note: Recent grants are derived from a fiscal 1994 Form 990.

RECENT GRANTS
General

25,000	NFTE, San Francisco, CA — to support small business entrepreneurship programs	
20,000	Arribe Juntos, San Francisco, CA — to support the Youth at Work program	
18,249	Enterprise for High School Students, San Francisco, CA — to support their collaborative apprenticeship program	
17,500	Healing Kidz, San Francisco, CA — to support various vocational programs	
17,500	Renaissance Technical Training Institute, San Francisco, CA — for Student Opportunity and Resource program	

Magowan Family Foundation

CONTACT
Mary Ann Chapin
Assistant Treasurer
Magowan Family Fdn.
2100 Washington St.
San Francisco, CA 94109
(415) 563-5581

FINANCIAL SUMMARY
Recent Giving: $382,400 (fiscal 1992); $427,880 (fiscal 1991); $419,275 (fiscal 1990)

Assets: $5,570,020 (fiscal 1992); $5,395,006 (fiscal 1991); $4,915,300 (fiscal 1990)

Gifts Received: $14,834 (fiscal 1992); $57,417 (fiscal 1991)

Fiscal Note: In 1992, contributions were received from Merchants National Properties.

EIN: 13-6085999

CONTRIBUTIONS SUMMARY
Donor(s): the late Charles E. Merrill, the late Robert A. Magowan, Doris M. Magowan, Merrill L. Magowan, Robert A. Magowan, Jr.

Typical Recipients: • *Arts & Humanities:* Arts Associations & Councils, Ballet, Community Arts, Dance, Historic Preservation, History & Archaeology, Libraries, Literary Arts, Museums/Galleries, Music, Opera, Performing Arts, Public Broadcasting, Theater • *Civic & Public Affairs:* Botanical Gardens/Parks, Clubs, General, Hispanic Affairs, Philanthropic Organizations, Zoos/Aquariums • *Education:* Colleges & Universities, Private Education (Precollege) • *Environment:* Air/Water Quality, General, Wildlife Protection • *Health:* Emergency/Ambulance Services, Health Organizations, Heart, Hospices, Hospitals, Medical Research, Mental Health, Single-Disease Health Associations • *Religion:* Churches, Religious Organizations • *Social Services:* Child Welfare, Family Planning, Family Services, Recreation & Athletics, United Funds/United Ways, Youth Organizations

Grant Types: general support

Geographic Distribution: focus on NY, CA, and FL

GIVING OFFICERS
Mary Ann Chapin: asst treas

Rolando E. Fernandez: asst treas

Thomas J. Lombardi: treas *PHIL AFFIL* treas, trust: Merrill Lynch & Co. Foundation Inc.

Charles M. Magowan: asst vp

Doris M. Magowan: vp

James Magowan: asst vp

Kimberly Magowan: asst vp

Mark E. Magowan: vp

Merrill L. Magowan: vp

Peter Alden Magowan: off *B* New York NY 1942 *ED* Stanford Univ BA 1964; Oxford Univ MA 1966 *CURR EMPL* chmn: Safeway Inc *CORP AFFIL* dir: Opportunity Funding Corp, Pacific Gas & Electric Co, Vons Cos Inc *NONPR AFFIL* mem: Food Mktg Inst

Robert A. Magowan, Jr.: asst vp

Stephen C. Magowan: vp

Thomas C. Magowan: asst vp

Bernat Rosner: secy *CURR EMPL* sr vp, secy, gen coun: Safeway Stores

APPLICATION INFORMATION
Initial Approach: Send brief letter of inquiry describing program or project. There are no deadlines.

Restrictions on Giving: Does not support individuals.

GRANTS ANALYSIS
Total Grants: $382,400

Number of Grants: 130

Highest Grant: $25,000

Typical Range: $500 to $6,000

Disclosure Period: fiscal year ending October 31, 1992

Note: Recent grants are derived from a fiscal 1992 Form 990.

RECENT GRANTS
Library

5,500	Scouville Memorial Library, Salisbury, CT	
1,500	Rogers Memorial Library, Southampton, NY	

General

25,000	Ozone Society, Marshall, VA	
20,000	Rogosin Institute, New York, NY	
19,650	Grace Cathedral, San Francisco, CA	
13,400	Episcopal School of New York, New York, NY	
13,000	San Francisco Zoological Society, San Francisco, CA	

Margoes Foundation

CONTACT
John S. Blum
Principal Manager
Margoes Fdn.
57 Post St.
San Francisco, CA 94104
(415) 981-2966

FINANCIAL SUMMARY
Recent Giving: $215,040 (fiscal 1994); $214,490 (fiscal 1993); $206,429 (fiscal 1992)

Assets: $3,953,922 (fiscal 1994); $3,919,956 (fiscal 1993); $3,700,056 (fiscal 1992)

Gifts Received: $9,911 (fiscal 1993); $980,559 (fiscal 1992); $502,401 (fiscal 1990)

Fiscal Note: In fiscal 1993, major contributions were received from Margoes Insurance Trust ($8,963).

EIN: 94-2955164

CONTRIBUTIONS SUMMARY
Donor(s): the late John A. Margoes

Typical Recipients: • *Arts & Humanities:* Libraries • *Civic & Public Affairs:* Employment/Job Training, General, Hispanic Affairs, Housing, Nonprofit Management, Philanthropic Organizations • *Education:* Afterschool/Enrichment Programs, Business Education, Colleges & Universities, General, Medical Education, Minority Education, Private Education (Precollege), Public Education (Precollege), Science/Mathematics Education, Student Aid • *Health:* Heart, Hospitals, Medical Research, Mental Health, Research/Studies Institutes • *International:* International Organizations • *Social Serv-*

ices: At-Risk Youth, Community Service Organizations, Counseling, People with Disabilities, Youth Organizations

Grant Types: endowment, multiyear/continuing support, operating expenses, project, research, and scholarship

Geographic Distribution: focus on CA

GIVING OFFICERS
Robert H. Erwin III: cfo, dir

Patrick L. McClung: dir

Neal L. Peterson: secy, dir

Alfred R. Zipf: chmn, dir *B* Buffalo NY 1917 *NONPR AFFIL* adv bd regents: Natl Library Medicine; mem: Natl Academy Sciences

APPLICATION INFORMATION
Initial Approach: Send brief letter describing program. Include a description of organization, amount requested, purpose of funds sought, recently audited financial statement, and proof of tax-exempt status. There are no deadlines.

Restrictions on Giving: Does not support individuals.

PUBLICATIONS
Annual Report

GRANTS ANALYSIS
Total Grants: $215,040

Number of Grants: 22

Highest Grant: $24,376

Typical Range: $600 to $20,000

Disclosure Period: fiscal year ending February 28, 1994

Note: Recent grants are derived from a fiscal 1994 Form 990.

RECENT GRANTS
General

24,376	University of Michigan School of Medicine, Ann Arbor, MI — continuing support of Margoes Scholarships to minority students from Michigan during first year of medical school
20,440	University of Arizona, Tucson, AZ — scholarship support for African nationals to pursue doctoral programs in plant pathology and plant sciences
20,000	Aim High, San Francisco, CA — support of academic and cultural enrichment program for middle school students from low-income families
20,000	Goodwill Industries, San Francisco, CA — partial support of the acquisition of 1500 Mission Street building to expand vocational training and rehabilitation services for people with physical and mental disabilities
20,000	Santa Clara University, Santa Clara, CA — scholarship support Institute of Agribusiness for first-year

MBA students and agribusiness managers from sub-Saharan African countries

---

Mattel, Inc. / Mattel Foundation

Revenue: $3.2 billion
Employees: 20,000
Headquarters: El Segundo, CA
SIC Major Group: Games, Toys & Children's Vehicles and Dolls & Stuffed Toys

CONTACT
Gloria De Necochea
Foundation Manager
Mattel Fdn.
333 Continental Blvd.
El Segundo, CA 90245
(310) 524-3530

FINANCIAL SUMMARY
Recent Giving: $4,200,000 (1995); $3,200,000 (1994); $1,400,000 (1993)

Assets: $1,122,418 (1993); $886,096 (1992); $849,617 (1991)

Gifts Received: $1,566,646 (1993)

Fiscal Note: Other company departments also make limited contributions and product donations. Contact for such support is Glenn Bozarth, VP Corporate Communications. Above figures exclude nonmonetary support. In 1993, Foundation received contributions from Mattel, Inc.

EIN: 95-3263647

CONTRIBUTIONS SUMMARY
Typical Recipients: • *Arts & Humanities:* Arts Institutes, Ballet, Libraries, Music, Performing Arts • *Civic & Public Affairs:* African American Affairs, Business/Free Enterprise, Civil Rights, Community Foundations, Economic Development, Economic Policy, General, Housing, Philanthropic Organizations, Women's Affairs • *Education:* Business Education, Colleges & Universities, Economic Education, Education Funds, Elementary Education (Private), Elementary Education (Public), Engineering/Technological Education, General, Leadership Training, Literacy, Medical Education, Private Education (Precollege), Science/Mathematics Education, Secondary Education (Public), Special Education, Student Aid • *Environment:* General • *Health:* AIDS/HIV, Cancer, Children's Health/Hospitals, Clinics/Medical Centers, Diabetes, Multiple Sclerosis, Single-Disease Health Associations • *International:* International Development, International Relief Efforts • *Religion:* Churches, Jewish Causes, Religious Welfare • *Science:* Scientific Centers & Institutes, Scientific Organizations • *Social Services:* Big Brother/Big Sister, Child Welfare, Community Service Organizations, Delinquency & Criminal Rehabilitation, Family Services, Recreation & Athletics, Substance Abuse, United Funds/United Ways, YMCA/YWCA/YMHA/YWHA, Youth Organizations

Grant Types: award, capital, conference/seminar, employee matching gifts, general support, matching, and scholarship

Note: Employee matching gift ratio: 1 to 1.

Nonmonetary Support: $300,000 (1995); $250,000 (1994); $500,000 (1993)

Nonmonetary Support Types: donated equipment, donated products, and workplace solicitation

Note: A considerable donation of equipment for computer labs was made to special education groups. For information on nonmonetary support, contact the Glenn Bozarth, VP, Corporate Communications at the above address.

Geographic Distribution: nationally

Operating Locations: AZ (Phoenix), CA (City of Industry, El Segundo), IL (Des Plaines), KY, NY (East Aurora, New York), TN, TX (Dallas, Ft. Worth)

CORP. OFFICERS
John W. Amerman: *B* Newark NJ 1932 *ED* Dartmouth Coll BA 1953; Dartmouth Coll Amos Tuck Sch Bus Admin MBA 1954 *CURR EMPL* chmn, ceo: Mattel Inc *CORP AFFIL* dir: Unocal Corp

Jill EliKann Barad: *B* New York NY 1951 *ED* Queens Coll BA 1973 *CURR EMPL* pres, coo, dir: Mattel Inc *CORP AFFIL* dir: Arco Toys, Bandai & Mattel Res Group Co *NONPR AFFIL* charter mem: Rainbow Guild/Amie Karen Cancer Fund; dir: Town Hall Big Sisters; mem: Am Film Inst; trust: Queens Coll

James Arthur Eskridge: *B* San Diego CA 1942 *ED* Univ CA Riverside BS 1968; Harvard Univ MBA 1975 *CURR EMPL* pres: Mattel Inc Fisher Price Div *NONPR AFFIL* mem: NW AR Symphony Guild *CLUB AFFIL* Harvard, Palos Verdes GC

N. Ned Mansour: *ED* Univ Southern CA BS 1970; Univ San Diego Law Sch JD 1973 *CURR EMPL* sr vp, secy, gen couns: Mattel Inc *CORP AFFIL* sr vp, secy, dir: Mattel Sales Corp

GIVING OFFICERS
Jill EliKann Barad: dir *CURR EMPL* pres, coo, dir: Mattel Inc (see above)

Harold Brown, PhD: chmn *B* New York NY 1927 *ED* Columbia Univ AB 1945; Columbia Univ AM 1946; Columbia Univ PhD 1949 *CORP AFFIL* dir: Alumax Inc, AMAX Inc, CBS Inc, Cummins Engine Co Inc, Mattel Inc, Philip Morris Cos Inc; ptnr: Warburg Pincus & Co *NONPR AFFIL* mem: Am Acad Arts & Sci, Am Physical Soc, Counc Foreign Rels, Natl Acad Engg, Natl Acad Sci, Phi Beta Kappa, Polaris Steering Comm, Sigma Xi; trust: CA Inst Tech, Trilateral Commn *CLUB AFFIL* Athenaeum, Bohemian, CA, Metro, River *PHIL AFFIL* chmn, dir: Arnold and Mabel Beckman Foundation

Gloria De Necochea: fdn mgr *PHIL AFFIL* program off: Weingart Foundation

Joseph C. Gandolfo: dir *B* 1942 *CURR EMPL* pres oper: Mattel Inc

Edward N. Ney: dir *B* St. Paul MN 1925 *ED* Amherst Coll BA 1947 *CURR EMPL* chmn bd adv: Burson-Marsteller *CORP AFFIL* dir: Am Barrick Corp, Ctr Commun, Fortune Bank, Horshum Corp, LA Power Fin Corp, Mattel Inc *NONPR AFFIL* bd gov: Foreign Policy Assn; mem adv bd: Counc Foreign Rels, Ctr Strategic Intl Studies; trust: Amherst Coll, Mus Broadcasting

APPLICATION INFORMATION
Initial Approach: *Initial Contact:* brief letter of application *Include Information On:* description of the organization, including legal name, history, activities, and board composition; description of program for which funds are sought; program budget and amount requested; list of other sources of support with amounts indicated; copy of most recently audited annual report and 990; and IRS determination letter *Deadlines:* none *Note:* Grant applications must be received by January 1 in order to be considered for March meeting, April 1 for June meeting, July 1 for September meeting, and October 1 for December meeting.

Restrictions on Giving: Foundation generally does not support capital facilities; research activities; endowments; individuals; religious, fraternal, political, athletic, social, or veterans organizations; labor groups; programs receiving substantial financial support; federal, state, or local government agencies; or courtesy advertising.

OTHER THINGS TO KNOW
Fisher-Price is now part of Mattel, Inc.

In 1992, the foundation committed $1 million to a foundation-administered initiative for educational development. Over three years, Mattel will fund five learning centers that provide educational programs in areas most affected by the Los Angeles riots. The centers will provide educational programs from preschool to adult education. Foundation is not accepting applications for this initiative.

In 1994, the foundation established a program called "Helping Kids Grow." This initial $900,000 fund will provide assistance to underprivileged children's health clinics in several U.S. cities.

PUBLICATIONS
Funding guidelines, newsletter

GRANTS ANALYSIS
Total Grants: $3,019,000

Number of Grants: 387

Highest Grant: $107,000

Average Grant: $8,000

Typical Range: $5,000 to $50,000

Disclosure Period: 1994

Note: Above figures provided by the foundation. Recent grants are derived from a 1993 Form 990.

RECENT GRANTS

Library
5,000	Library Foundation of Los Angeles, Los Angeles, CA — for general operating budget

General
79,000	Foundation for Technology Access, San Rafael, CA — for general operating support
50,000	Puente Learning Center, Los Angeles, CA — for general operating support
36,000	Housing Options for People to Excel, Los Angeles, CA — for general operating support
25,000	Big Sisters of Los Angeles, Los Angeles, CA — for general operating support
25,000	Hamline University, St. Paul, MN — for Antarctic Educational Expedition

---

MCA Inc. / MCA Foundation, Ltd.

Sales: $3.38 billion
Employees: 16,500
Parent Company: Matsushita Electric Industrial Co. Ltd.
Headquarters: Universal City, CA
SIC Major Group: Motion Picture & Video Production, Automotive & Apparel Trimmings, Book Publishing, and Miscellaneous Publishing

CONTACT
Helen D. Yatsko
Administrator
MCA Fdn., Ltd.
100 Universal City Plz.
Ste. 500/3
Universal City, CA 91608
(818) 777-1208

FINANCIAL SUMMARY
Recent Giving: $821,000 (1994 approx.); $749,000 (1993); $920,500 (1992)

Assets: $14,497,828 (1993); $14,237,493 (1992); $14,067,319 (1991)

Gifts Received: $26,000 (1993)

Fiscal Note: Figures are for foundation only. Direct giving usually totals between $200,000 and $500,000 annually. In 1994, direct giving totaled $246,344. In 1993, the foundation received gifts from MCA Inc. and its subsidiaries.

EIN: 13-6096061

CONTRIBUTIONS SUMMARY
Typical Recipients: • *Arts & Humanities:* Arts Associations & Councils, Arts Centers, Arts Funds, Arts Institutes, Dance, Film & Video, Historic Preservation, Libraries, Literary Arts, Museums/Galleries, Music, Performing Arts, Public Broadcasting, Theater • *Civic & Public Affairs:* African American Affairs, Business/Free Enterprise, Civil Rights, Economic Development, Employment/Job Training, General, Law & Justice, Philanthropic Organizations, Professional & Trade Associations, Public Policy, Urban & Community Affairs, Women's Affairs • *Education:* Arts/Humanities Education, Business Education, Colleges & Universities, Community & Junior Colleges, Education Associations, Education Funds, Education Reform, Legal Education, Literacy, Medical Education, Minority Education, Student Aid • *Environment:* General • *Health:* Cancer, Clinics/Medical Centers, Emergency/Ambulance Services, Hospitals, Medical Research, Mental Health, Multiple Sclerosis, Single-Disease Health Associations • *Science:* Scientific Centers & Institutes • *Social Services:* Child Welfare, Community Centers, Community Service Organizations, Counseling, Delinquency & Criminal Rehabilitation, Emergency Relief, Family Planning, Food/Clothing Distribution, People with Disabilities, Recreation & Athletics, Senior Services, United Funds/United Ways, Volunteer Services, Youth Organizations

Grant Types: employee matching gifts, general support, and project

Geographic Distribution: principally near operating locations and to national organizations

Operating Locations: CA (Glendale, Universal City, Yosemite National Park), IL (Pinckneyville), NJ (Pleasantville), NY (Gloversville, New York)

CORP. OFFICERS
Richard Eugene Baker: *B* Sioux City IA 1939 *ED* CA St Univ Long Beach BBA 1961 *CURR EMPL* vp, cfo, dir: MCA Inc *CORP AFFIL* cfo, dir: Hilltop Svcs Inc; treas, dir: UNI Distr Corp *NONPR AFFIL* dir: Motion Picture Indus Pension Plan, Res Prevent Blindness Fdn; mem: Acad Motion Picture Arts Sci, Am Inst CPAs, CA Soc CPAs, Fin Execs Inst; trust: Fin Ed Res Fdn

Ronald Meyer: *B* 1945 *CURR EMPL* pres, dir: MCA Inc

Thomas Pollock: *CURR EMPL* vchmn: MCA Inc

Sidney Jay Sheinberg: *B* Corpus Christi TX 1935 *ED* Columbia Univ AB 1955; Columbia Univ LLB 1958 *CURR EMPL* pres, coo, dir: MCA Inc *CORP AFFIL* dir: Spencer Gifts *NONPR AFFIL* chmn: Assn Motion Picture Television Producers *PHIL AFFIL* trust: Eric P. Sheinberg Foundation

Lew Robert Wasserman: *B* Cleveland OH 1913 *CURR EMPL* chmn emeritus, mem exec comm: MCA Inc *CORP AFFIL* chmn: Universal City Studios; dir: Am Airlines Inc *NONPR AFFIL* bd govs: Ronald Reagan Pres Fdn; chmn: Res Prevent Blindness Fdn; chmn emeritus: Assn Motion Picture Television Producers; dir: Los Angeles Music Ctr Fdn; hon chmn: Los Angeles Music Ctr Theatre Group; pres: Hollywood Canteen Fdn; trust: CA Inst Tech, Carter Ctr, Lyndon Baines Johnson Fdn, John F Kennedy Ctr Performing Arts, John F Kennedy Lib, Jules Stein Eye Inst *PHIL AFFIL* chmn fin comm, dir: Amateur Athletic Foundation of Los Angeles; pres: Wasserman Foundation; chmn, trust: Hollywood Canteen Foundation; chmn: Jules and Doris Stein Foundation

GIVING OFFICERS
Richard Eugene Baker: vp, treas, cfo *CURR EMPL* vp, cfo, dir: MCA Inc (see above)

Pamela F. Cherney: asst treas

Michael Samuel: secy *B* 1936 *CURR EMPL* secy, dir: Geffen Records Inc *CORP AFFIL* secy: Universal Fil Exchange Inc; secy, dir: UNI Distr Corp

Sidney Jay Sheinberg: pres, dir *CURR EMPL* pres, coo, dir: MCA Inc *PHIL AFFIL* trust: Eric P. Sheinberg Foundation (see above)

George A. Smith: vp *CURR EMPL* vp, dir: Geffen Records Inc *CORP AFFIL* vp, dir: Hilltop Svcs Inc, UNI Distr Corp

Thomas Wertheimer: vp, dir *B* New York NY 1938 *ED* Princeton Univ BA 1960; Columbia Univ JD 1963 *CURR EMPL* exec vp, dir: MCA Inc

Helen D. Yatsko: admin

APPLICATION INFORMATION
Initial Approach: *Initial Contact:* full proposal; if foundation is interested in organization it will request further information *Include Information On:* statement of objectives, activities, accomplishments, and geographic scope; detailed description of specific program for which support is sought, grant's expected accomplishment, how program will be carried out, and evaluative criteria; names and business and professional affiliations of officers and board, number of meetings held in previous year, and whether or not board members compensated; number of paid employees and volunteer workers and total compensation paid; current, itemized budget listing major funding sources; purpose for which funds are sought; amount requested; and proof of tax-exempt status *Deadlines:* none *Note:* Foundation also requires a signed statement that the organization will furnish periodic reports indicating the use of funds provided by MCA.

Restrictions on Giving: Does not support individuals, political or lobbying groups, or religious organizations for sectarian purposes.

PUBLICATIONS
Application guidelines

GRANTS ANALYSIS
Total Grants: $749,000

Number of Grants: 68

Highest Grant: $100,000

Average Grant: $11,015

Typical Range: $5,000 to $30,000

Disclosure Period: 1993

Note: Recent grants are derived from a 1993 Form 990.

RECENT GRANTS
Library
30,000	New York Public Library, New York, NY — general

General
100,000	Motion Picture and Television Relief Fund, Woodland Hills, CA — event
50,000	American Red Cross, Los Angeles, CA — general
50,000	Columbia University, New York, NY — event
25,000	Landmark West School, Encino, CA — general
25,000	Los Angeles Educational Alliance for Restructuring Now, Los Angeles, CA — general

McBean Charitable Trust, Alletta Morris

CONTACT
Peter McBean
Trustee
Alletta Morris McBean Charitable Trust
100 California St., Rm. 744
San Francisco, CA 94111
(415) 781-3443

FINANCIAL SUMMARY
Recent Giving: $819,495 (1994); $1,187,750 (1993); $767,400 (1992)

Assets: $28,000,000 (1994 est.); $27,707,735 (1993); $27,367,085 (1992)

EIN: 94-3019660

CONTRIBUTIONS SUMMARY
Donor(s): The trust was established in 1986 by the late Alletta Morris McBean .

Typical Recipients: • *Arts & Humanities:* Arts Associations & Councils, Historic Preservation, Libraries, Museums/Galleries • *Civic & Public Affairs:* General • *Education:* Private Education (Precollege) • *Environment:* General • *Health:* Hospices, Nursing Services • *Religion:* Churches, Religious Organizations • *Social Services:* Animal Protection, Family Services

Grant Types: general support

Geographic Distribution: focus on Newport, RI

GIVING OFFICERS
Donald Christ: trust

Noreen Drexel: trust

Peter McBean: trust *PHIL AFFIL* pres: McBean Family Foundation

John A. Van Beuren: trust *PHIL AFFIL* vp, dir: Van Beuren Charitable Foundation

APPLICATION INFORMATION
Initial Approach:

The trust requests applications be made in writing.

Written proposals should thoroughly explain the program and the project for which the organization is seeking funding.

There are no deadlines.

Restrictions on Giving: The trust does not make grants to individuals.

GRANTS ANALYSIS
Total Grants: $819,495

Number of Grants: 16

Highest Grant: $200,000

Average Grant: $51,218

Typical Range: $10,000 to $100,000

Disclosure Period: 1994

Note: Recent grants are derived from a 1992 grants list.

RECENT GRANTS
Library
17,500	Redwood Library Athenaeum, Newport, RI

General
175,000	Brick Market Foundation, Newport, RI
100,000	Animal Medical Center, New York, NY
100,000	St. George's School, Newport, RI
50,000	Trinity Church, Newport, RI
27,500	St. John the Evangelist, Newport, RI

McConnell Foundation

Former Foundation Name: Carl R. and Leah F. McConnell Foundation

CONTACT
Lee W. Salter
Executive Director
McConnell Foundation
PO Box 991870
Redding, CA 96099-1870
(916) 222-0696
Note: The foundation can also be contacted directly at 292 Hemsted Dr., Ste 100, Redding, CA, 96099.

FINANCIAL SUMMARY
Recent Giving: $4,431,441 (1993); $2,391,276 (1992); $2,062,688 (1991)

Assets: $60,414,742 (1993); $53,716,395 (1992); $51,221,885 (1991)

Gifts Received: $3,708,417 (1993)

Fiscal Note: 1993 contributions were received from Leah F. McConnell.

EIN: 94-6102700

CONTRIBUTIONS SUMMARY
Donor(s): The McConnell Foundation was established in 1964 by Carl R. McConnell and Leah F. McConnell. Mrs. McConnell continues to serve on the foundation's board of directors.

Typical Recipients: • *Arts & Humanities:* Historic Preservation, History & Archaeology, Libraries, Museums/Galleries, Music, Public Broadcasting, Theater • *Civic & Public Affairs:* Botanical Gardens/Parks, Law & Justice, Municipalities/Towns, Parades/Festivals, Philanthropic Organizations, Safety, Urban & Community Affairs, Women's Affairs • *Education:* Colleges & Universities, Education Funds, Literacy, Minority Education, Public Education (Precollege), Science/Mathematics Education, Secondary Education (Private), Student Aid • *Environment:* Forestry, General, Wildlife Protection • *Health:* Clinics/Medical Centers • *Social Services:* Community Centers, Day Care, Family Services, Recreation & Athletics, Senior Services, Substance Abuse, Volunteer Services

Grant Types: project and scholarship

Geographic Distribution: focus on Shasta and Siskiyou counties in California

GIVING OFFICERS
Doreta Domke: dir

John A. Mancasola: dir

Leah F. McConnell: fdr, don, dir

Leonard B. Nelson: dir

William B. Nystrom: dir

Lee W. Salter: dir, exec dir

APPLICATION INFORMATION
Initial Approach:

Applicants should send a letter of intent of one to three pages. Applicants can contact the foundation to obtain a cover sheet that must accompany the letter of intent.

The letter of intent should include the following: opening paragraph including the name of applying organization, the amount requested, and purpose of the grant; a brief history and description of the applying organization; the purpose for which the grant is being requested, identifying why the project is important to the community, why the project would make a difference, and documentation of need; description of the volunteer component; project budget, highlighting areas and amount of proposed McConnell Foundation support; a brief explanation of proposed expenditures, and any anticipated funds and/or in-kind services from other sources expected for the project; experience and expertise of key personnel; plan for continuing the project beyond the one year of McConnell Foundation funding, if necessary; a copy of the organization's profit and loss statement, and balance sheet, including the disclosure of pension plans, deferred compensation plans, and the liability assumed; for non-governmental agencies, a listing of the organization's current board of directors; and for non-governmental agencies, a copy of the IRS tax-exempt determination letters verifying the organization's status as a 501(c)(3). Note, a letter from the state authority in California will not satisfy the tax-exempt determination requirement, and all items listed must be included in the application in order for letter of intent to be considered.

Foundation must receive the letter of intent by February 15. Full proposals must be received by May 31.

Letters of intent will be reviewed and all applicants will be notified by mail on or before March 31. Successful applicants will be invited to submit a full proposal. Full proposals will be reviewed and the applicants notified by July 31.

Restrictions on Giving: The foundation does not make grants to individuals, endowment funds, annual fund drives, sectarian religious purposes, construction or purchase of buildings, and budget deficits. Also, the foundation stresses that applicants should use standard English and avoid "grantsmanship" double talk and jargon. If the services of an independent paid grantwriter are used to compose the letter of intent or proposal, it must be disclosed on the cover sheet, including the amount paid.

PUBLICATIONS
Annual report, grant policies and procedures

GRANTS ANALYSIS
Total Grants: $4,431,441

Number of Grants: 120

Highest Grant: $1,395,579

Average Grant: $36,928

Typical Range: $10,000 to $50,000

Disclosure Period: 1993

Note: Recent grants are derived from a 1993 Form 990.

RECENT GRANTS

Library

250,000	Siskiyou County Public Library, Yreka, CA — expansion and remodeling

General

1,395,579	Shasta Natural Science Association, Shasta, CA — arboretum
250,000	Shasta Natural Science Association, Shasta, CA — Arboretum by the River
100,000	City of Anderson, Parks and Recreation Department, Anderson, CA — instructional and wading pools
75,000	Shasta County Family YMCA, Shasta, CA — equipment for child care program
48,000	College of the Siskiyou, Weed, CA — membership

McDonnell Douglas Corp.-West / McDonnell Douglas Employee's Community Fund-West

Employees: 42,000
Parent Sales: $17.51 billion
Headquarters: Long Beach, CA
SIC Major Group: Aircraft and Aircraft Parts & Equipment Nec

CONTACT
Beverly A. Hoskinson
Executive Director
McDonnell Douglas Employee's Community Fund-West
3855 Lakewood Blvd. (802-11)
Long Beach, CA 90846
(310) 593-2612

FINANCIAL SUMMARY
Recent Giving: $2,000,000 (1995 est.); $2,274,503 (1994); $3,018,599 (1993)

Assets: $4,305,830 (1994); $4,800,000 (1991 approx.); $4,732,923 (1988)

Fiscal Note: Contributions are made primarily through the employee fund, which is a direct-giving program operated from within the company.

CONTRIBUTIONS SUMMARY
Typical Recipients: • *Arts & Humanities:* Arts Associations & Councils, Arts Festivals, Community Arts, Dance, Historic Preservation, Libraries, Museums/Galleries, Music, Opera, Performing Arts, Public Broadcasting, Theater • *Civic & Public Affairs:* Business/Free Enterprise, Housing, Zoos/Aquariums • *Education:* Student Aid • *Environment:* General • *Health:* Health Organizations, Hospices, Hospitals, Medical Rehabilitation, Medical Research, Mental Health, Single-Disease Health Associations • *International:* International Peace & Security Issues • *Religion:* Religious Welfare • *Science:* Scientific Centers & Institutes • *Social Services:* Child Welfare, Community Centers, Community Service Organizations, Counseling, Emergency Relief, Family Services, Food/Clothing Distribution, Homes, People with Disabilities, Recreation & Athletics, Senior Services, Shelters/Homelessness, Substance Abuse, United Funds/United Ways, Volunteer Services, Youth Organizations

Grant Types: capital, challenge, general support, research, and seed money

Geographic Distribution: nationally, primarily in those communities where McDonnell Douglas maintains corporate operations

Operating Locations: AL (Huntsville), AZ (Mesa), CA (Huntington Beach, Long Beach, Los Angeles, Orange), CO, DC, FL, GA (Macon), MD, MO (St. Louis), OK (Tulsa), PA, TX, UT (Salt Lake City)

Note: In 1994, foundation reached 36 states plus Washington, DC.. More than 86% of ECF-W members live in Southern California.

CORP. OFFICERS
David Brown: *CURR EMPL* mgr external rels: McDonnell Douglas Corp

Carol James Dorrenbacher: *B* Mishawaka IN 1928 *ED* Purdue Univ BSEE 1949; Univ IL MSEE 1950; Purdue Univ PhD 1989 *CURR EMPL* sr vp: McDonnell Douglas Corp *NONPR AFFIL* campaign chmn: Discovery Sci Ctr Space & Flight Pavilion; fellow: Am Inst Aeronautics Astronautics; restructuring chmn: LA Ed Partnership *CLUB AFFIL* Natl Space *PHIL AFFIL* dir: McDonnell Douglas Foundation

John Finney McDonnell: *B* Baltimore MD 1938 *ED* Princeton Univ BS 1960; Princeton Univ MS 1962; Washington Univ 1962-1966 *CURR EMPL* chmn: McDonnell Douglas Corp *CORP AFFIL* chmn: McDonnell Douglas Computer Sys Co; dir: McDonnell Douglas Fin Corp, Ralston Purina Co *NONPR AFFIL* bd commnrs: St Louis Sci Ctr; chmn: Natl Counc Faculty Arts & Sci; trust: KETC, Washington Univ *PHIL AFFIL* don, treas: James S. McDonnell Foundation; dir: McDonnell Douglas Foundation

Harrison C. Stonecipher: *B* Scott County TN 1936 *ED* TN Polytech Inst BS 1960 *CURR EMPL* chmn, ceo, pres, dir: McDonnell Douglas Corp West *CORP AFFIL* chmn: Precision Castparts Corp *NONPR AFFIL* chmn: Pre-Paid Legal Agency

GIVING OFFICERS

Kenneth Burdeno: *CURR EMPL* dir, commun fund: McDonnell Douglas Corp-W

Mary W. DeLong: *CURR EMPL* dir, commun fund: McDonnell Douglas Corp-W

Betty Evans: *CURR EMPL* dir, commun fund: McDonnell Douglas Corp-W

Kenneth A. Francis: *B* 1934 *CURR EMPL* exec vp, chmn giving program: McDonnell Douglas Corp

Beverly A. Hoskinson: *CURR EMPL* exec dir, commun fund: McDonnell Douglas Corp-West

Markele Machado: *CURR EMPL* dir, commun fund: McDonnell Douglas Corp-W

James T. McMillan: *B* Alhambra CA 1925 *ED* Univ Southern CA 1951; Univ CA Los Angeles 1954 *CURR EMPL* dir, commun fund: McDonnell Douglas Corp-W *CORP AFFIL* dir: MDC Realty Co; pres: McDonnell Douglas Fin Corp *NONPR AFFIL* fellow: Am Inst Aeronautics & Astronautics; mem: Am Bar Assn, Natl Acad Engg, Natl Space Club Assn; mem engg adv counc: Univ CA Berkeley

Mary Ann Scanlon: *CURR EMPL* dir, commun fund: McDonnell Douglas Corp-W

Betty Smith: *CURR EMPL* dir, commun fund: McDonnell Douglas Corp-W

APPLICATION INFORMATION

Initial Approach: *Initial Contact:* one- to two-page letter or proposal *Include Information On:* description of the organization, amount requested, purpose for which funds are sought, recently audited financial statement, proof of tax-exempt status, area served by organization *Deadlines:* none; requests are considered quarterly; repeat requests are not considered in the same year

Restrictions on Giving: Foundation does not fund political organizations or programs; fraternal, social, religious, or similar groups; educational institutions, except those dedicated solely to the handicapped; tax-supported endeavors, except joint government and private enterprise projects; private foundations; trips or tours; courtesy advertising; conference or dinner tickets; service club activities, scholarships, other than those offered under McDonnell Douglas Scholarship Fund for employee children; endowments; or member organizations of united funds.

Foundation will not consider repeat requests in the same year. A grant does not necessarily indicate that continued support will be available.

OTHER THINGS TO KNOW

Fund is an employee owned and operated nonprofit organization. Fund combines the assets of the former Douglas Aircraft Welfare Foundation and the contributions of McDonnell Douglas-West employees made through payroll deductions to support charitable organziations in areas where contributors live and work. Funds are distributed by an employee board of directors, with allocations based in large part on the amount of ECF-W members' contributions in each community and the comparative need. In areas

where few employees live, contributions are directed toward local United Ways.

GRANTS ANALYSIS

Total Grants: $2,274,503

Number of Grants: 465

Highest Grant: $147,160

Average Grant: $4,891

Typical Range: $1,000 to $5,000

Disclosure Period: 1994

Note: Recent grants are derived from a 1994 grants list.

RECENT GRANTS

General

147,160	McDonnell Douglas Scholarship Foundation, Long Beach, CA
60,000	California Educational Initiatives Fund, San Francisco, CA
50,000	American Red Cross, Disaster Relief Fund, S California, CA
50,000	Lawrence Hall of Science (GEMS), Berkeley, CA
37,500	Executive Service Corps of Southern California, Los Angeles, CA

McMahan Foundation, Catherine L. and Robert O.

CONTACT
Neal W. McMahan
Executive Director
Catherine L. and Robert O. McMahan Fdn.
PO Box 221580
Carmel, CA 93922
(408) 625-6444

FINANCIAL SUMMARY
Recent Giving: $163,200 (1993)
Assets: $4,829,389 (1993)
EIN: 94-6061273

CONTRIBUTIONS SUMMARY
Typical Recipients: • *Arts & Humanities:* Arts Centers, History & Archaeology, Libraries, Music, Theater • *Civic & Public Affairs:* Clubs, Community Foundations, Parades/Festivals, Public Policy, Rural Affairs, Zoos/Aquariums • *Education:* Colleges & Universities, General, Private Education (Precollege) • *Environment:* Forestry • *Health:* Alzheimers Disease, Clinics/Medical Centers, Heart • *Social Services:* Child Welfare, Community Service Organizations, Family Planning, Family Services, Food/Clothing Distribution, People with Disabilities, Recreation & Athletics, Sexual Abuse, YMCA/YWCA/YMHA/YWHA

Grant Types: general support

Geographic Distribution: focus on CA

GIVING OFFICERS
Michael L. McMahan: cfo

Neal W. McMahan: exec dir

Marsha Zelus: secy

APPLICATION INFORMATION
Initial Approach: Send a brief letter of inquiry. Include a description of organization, amount requested, purpose of funds sought, recently audited financial statement, and proof of tax-exempt status.

GRANTS ANALYSIS
Total Grants: $163,200

Number of Grants: 26

Highest Grant: $25,000

Typical Range: $1,000 to $25,000

Disclosure Period: 1993

Note: Recent grants are derived from a 1993 Form 990.

RECENT GRANTS

Library

25,000	Stanford University, Stanford, CA — Alan Baldridge Library Fund
12,500	Carmel Public Library Foundation, Carmel, CA — for first installment of pledge
3,000	Foundation for Monterey County Free Libraries, Monterey, CA — help fund the Hopework Center program

General

25,000	Robert Louis Stevenson School, Pebble Beach, CA
10,000	YWCA, Monterey, CA
7,500	National Coalition Building Institute, Washington, DC — for operating expenses
6,000	Monterey Bay Aquarium, Monterey, CA — help underwrite the 1994 Global Issues Symposium
5,000	American Heart Association, Tulsa, MI

Meyer Fund, Milton and Sophie

CONTACT
Joseph E. Fanucci
Trust Officer
Milton and Sophie Meyer Fund
c/o Wells Fargo Bank
420 Montgomery St.
San Francisco, CA 94163
(415) 396-3895

FINANCIAL SUMMARY
Recent Giving: $197,474 (1993); $185,600 (1992); $210,557 (1991)

Assets: $3,108,032 (1993); $2,993,642 (1992); $2,683,456 (1991)

EIN: 94-6480997

CONTRIBUTIONS SUMMARY
Donor(s): the late Milton Meyer

Typical Recipients: • *Arts & Humanities:* Libraries, Museums/Galleries • *Civic & Public Affairs:* General • *Education:* Colleges & Universities, Continuing Education, Private Education (Precollege) • *Health:* Cancer, Clinics/Medical Centers, Medical Research • *International:* Foreign Educational Institutions, Health Care/Hospitals, International Relations, Missionary/Religious Activities • *Religion:* Jewish Causes, Religious Organizations, Synagogues/Temples • *Social Services:* Community Centers, Community Service Organizations, Senior Services

Grant Types: general support

Geographic Distribution: focus on the San Francisco Bay Area, CA

GIVING OFFICERS

Wells Fargo Bank, N.A.: trust

Harold S. Dobbs: trust

APPLICATION INFORMATION

Initial Approach: Send brief letter of inquiry describing program or project. Include a description of organization, amount requested, purpose of funds sought, recently audited financial statement, and proof of tax-exempt status. There are no deadlines.

Restrictions on Giving: Limited to charitable Jewish organizations.

GRANTS ANALYSIS

Total Grants: $197,474

Number of Grants: 25

Highest Grant: $45,974

Typical Range: $1,000 to $25,000

Disclosure Period: 1993

Note: Recent grants are derived from a 1993 Form 990.

RECENT GRANTS

General

45,974	Jewish Community Federation, San Francisco, CA
25,000	Northern California Hillel, San Francisco, CA
10,000	Berkeley Hillel Foundation, Berkeley, CA
10,000	Congregation Emanu-El, New York, NY
10,000	Ernest Rosenbaum Cancer Research

Mitsubishi Motor Sales of America, Inc.

Sales: $4.0 billion
Employees: 1,900
Headquarters: Cypress, CA
SIC Major Group: Wholesale Trade—Durable Goods

CONTACT

Lisa Dunn
Corporate Relations Manager
Mitsubishi Motor Sales of America
6400 Katella Ave.
Cypress, CA 90630
(714) 372-6000

FINANCIAL SUMMARY

Fiscal Note: Company does not disclose contributions figures.

CONTRIBUTIONS SUMMARY

Company focuses support on organizations that advocate safe driving. Interest areas include projects that promote safe driving in general or target safe driving practices toward such special groups as teenagers or senior citizens; endeavor to widen seatbelt safety awareness; advance automotive safety research; and carry on the war against drunk drivers.

Volunteerism: In 1994, company instituted a formal volunteer program. Volunteer efforts are focused on the communities in which its offices are located. Program suppport varies from project to project.

Typical Recipients: • *Arts & Humanities:* Community Arts, Dance, Ethnic & Folk Arts, General, Libraries, Music, Performing Arts • *Civic & Public Affairs:* African American Affairs, Asian American Affairs, Chambers of Commerce, Ethnic Organizations, General, Hispanic Affairs, Parades/Festivals, Philanthropic Organizations, Professional & Trade Associations, Safety • *Education:* Afterschool/Enrichment Programs, Business Education, Business-School Partnerships, Colleges & Universities, Community & Junior Colleges, Elementary Education (Public), General, International Exchange, Minority Education, Public Education (Precollege), Science/Mathematics Education, Secondary Education (Public), Special Education, Vocational & Technical Education • *Environment:* General • *Health:* General • *International:* General, International Relations • *Science:* General, Science Museums • *Social Services:* At-Risk Youth, Child Welfare, Community Service Organizations, Emergency Relief, Food/Clothing Distribution, General, People with Disabilities, Recreation & Athletics, United Funds/United Ways, Volunteer Services, Youth Organizations

Grant Types: emergency, general support, multiyear/continuing support, operating expenses, project, and seed money

Nonmonetary Support Types: cause-related marketing & promotion, donated equipment, donated products, and in-kind services

Note: Cause-related marketing and promotion is handled by the marketing services department. Company also sponsors an employee volunteer program.

Geographic Distribution: focus is within communities where company has a major presence

Operating Locations: CA (Cypress, Orange County), FL (Orlando), IL (Itasca), NJ (Bridgeport), TX (Irving)

CORP. OFFICERS

Richard D. Recchia: *CURR EMPL* coo, exec vp: Mitsubishi Motor Sales Am

Tohei Takeuchi: *CURR EMPL* pres, ceo: Mitsubishi Motor Sales Am

GIVING OFFICERS

Lisa Dunn: *CURR EMPL* corp rels mgr: Mitsubishi Motor Sales Am

APPLICATION INFORMATION

Initial Approach: All requests must be in writing and directly relate to company's focus. Proposals must include a brief overview of the organization, including the specific project for which funding is requested; the exact amount requested; a short background of the organization, including the number of paid and volunteer employees; specific project information, including the purpose for desired funds, time period of proposed program, goals and how they will be attained, projected results and how they will be assessed, how the organization will report and evaluate results, and geographical area served and number of people who will benefit; and financial disclosure including full budget for current year, current sources of funding, ratio of administrative costs to total budget, and proportion of funding to be derived from contributions. Additional information required is a copy of IRS tax-exempt document per Section 501(c)(3); copy of current Form 990; audited financial statements from the previous two years; list of present board of directors; and support documents such as an annual report, catalogs, brochures, news clippings, and any other pertinent information you may wish to include.

Restrictions on Giving: Does not support political parties, candidates, or lobbying organizations; organizations that are not tax-exempt; individuals; or organizations whose major area of influence is outside the United States.

Company has formulated a series of guidelines by which it reviews all requests. To be considered, applicant organizations must promote safe driving or fall within other areas of support; be focused within communities where company has a major presence; allow company to review its list of contributors; show a specific use for contributions of $10,000 or less; and be able to exist independently of company's contribution. Additionally, the organization should enjoy the support of its local constituency, including community leaders.

Financial support is granted on a one-time basis, and further support or renewal is not implied. However, additional or future funding may be available pending submission of a new request.

PUBLICATIONS

Guidelines for corporate giving

GRANTS ANALYSIS

Typical Range: $2,500 to $5,000

Note: Recent grants are derived from a grants list provided by company in 1995.

RECENT GRANTS

General
Automotive Technology Competitions
Chief Operator Teen Safe Driving Program,
Albany, CA
King Elementary School, Cypress, CA
Minnesota Seat Belt Challenge, MN
Mothers Against Drunk Driving, Orange
County, CA

Muller Foundation

Former Foundation Name: Frank Muller,
Sr., Foundation

CONTACT
R. A. Vilmure
President
Muller Fdn.
11357 Pala Loma Dr.
Valley Center, CA 92082
(619) 742-3378

FINANCIAL SUMMARY
Recent Giving: $328,470 (fiscal 1992);
$364,422 (fiscal 1991); $278,073 (fiscal
1990)

Assets: $6,714,609 (fiscal 1992);
$6,233,082 (fiscal 1991); $6,897,049 (fiscal
1990)

EIN: 95-6121774

CONTRIBUTIONS SUMMARY
Donor(s): Frank Muller

Typical Recipients: • *Arts & Humanities:*
Arts Centers, Libraries, Music, Performing
Arts • *Education:* Colleges & Universities,
Private Education (Precollege) • *Health:*
Hospitals, Medical Research, Single-Disease
Health Associations • *Religion:* Churches,
Religious Organizations • *Social Services:*
Child Welfare, Community Service Organizations, Homes, Recreation & Athletics,
Youth Organizations

Grant Types: general support and operating
expenses

Geographic Distribution: focus on CA

GIVING OFFICERS
James Muller: dir
John Muller: treas, dir
Sheila Muller: vp
Tim Muller: dir
Mary M. Thompson: vp, dir
Richard A. Vilmure: pres, dir

APPLICATION INFORMATION
Initial Approach: Send brief letter of inquiry describing program or project. There
are no deadlines.

Restrictions on Giving: Does not support
individuals.

GRANTS ANALYSIS
Total Grants: $328,470
Number of Grants: 290
Highest Grant: $8,000
Typical Range: $100 to $5,000

Disclosure Period: fiscal year ending July
31, 1992

Note: Grants list for 1992 was incomplete.
Recent grants are derived from a fiscal 1992
Form 990.

RECENT GRANTS

General
8,000	Bellarmine College Preparatory, San Jose, CA

Munger Foundation, Alfred C.

CONTACT
Charles T. Munger
President
Alfred C. Munger Fdn.
355 S Grand Ave., 35th Fl.
Los Angeles, CA 90071-1560
(213) 624-7715

FINANCIAL SUMMARY
Recent Giving: $940,126 (fiscal 1993);
$857,937 (fiscal 1992); $754,769 (fiscal
1991)

Assets: $10,510,488 (fiscal 1993);
$10,300,702 (fiscal 1992); $9,071,071 (fiscal 1991)

Gifts Received: $64,119 (fiscal 1993);
$85,642 (fiscal 1992); $22,900 (fiscal 1991)

Fiscal Note: In fiscal 1993, contributons
were received from Berkshire Hathaway,
Inc.

EIN: 95-2462103

CONTRIBUTIONS SUMMARY
Donor(s): Charles T. Munger and Nancy B.
Munger

Typical Recipients: • *Arts & Humanities:*
Libraries, Museums/Galleries, Music, Public Broadcasting • *Civic & Public Affairs:*
Botanical Gardens/Parks, General, Law &
Justice, Legal Aid • *Education:* Colleges &
Universities, Engineering/Technological
Education, Legal Education, Medical Education, Private Education (Precollege), Science/Mathematics Education • *Environment:*
General • *Health:* Children's Health/Hospitals, Eyes/Blindness, Hospices, Hospitals,
Hospitals (University Affiliated), Medical
Research, Single-Disease Health Associations • *International:* Health Care/Hospitals
• *Religion:* Churches, Missionary Activities
(Domestic), Religious Organizations • *Social Services:* Child Welfare, Family Planning, People with Disabilities, Youth
Organizations

Grant Types: general support

Geographic Distribution: focus on CA

GIVING OFFICERS
Richard D. Esbenshade: secy, treas, trust
PHIL AFFIL secy, trust: Otis Booth Foundation

Charles T. Munger: don, pres, trust *B*
Omaha NE 1924 *ED* CA Inst Tech 1944;
Harvard Univ JD 1948 *CURR EMPL* vchmn,

dir: Berkshire Hathaway *CORP AFFIL*
chmn: Mutual Savings & Loan Assn; chmn,
dir: Daily Journal Corp, Wesco Fin Corp;
dir: Salomon, US Air *NONPR AFFIL* chmn
bd trust: Hosp Good Samaritan; dir: Natl
Corp Housing Partnership; trust: Harvard
Sch Los Angeles CA, Planned Parenthood
Los Angeles *PHIL AFFIL* trust: Caryll M.
and Norman F. Sprague, Jr. Foundation; vp,
treas, trust: Otis Booth Foundation

Nancy B. Munger: treas, asst secy, trust

APPLICATION INFORMATION
Initial Approach: The foundation reports it
only makes contributions to preselected
charitable organizations.

GRANTS ANALYSIS
Total Grants: $940,126
Number of Grants: 15
Highest Grant: $250,075
Typical Range: $200 to $250,000
Disclosure Period: fiscal year ending November 30, 1993

Note: Recent grants are derived from a fiscal
1993 Form 990.

RECENT GRANTS

Library
250,000	Huntington Library, Huntington, CA — Henry E. Endowment

General
250,075	Hospital of the Good Samaritan, Los Angeles, CA
75,000	Planned Parenthood of Los Angeles, Los Angeles, CA — world population
9,600	Lundeen, Los Angeles, CA
5,500	Doheny Eye Institute, Los Angeles, CA
3,000	Las Madrinas, Los Angeles, CA — children's hospital

Murphey Foundation, Lluella Morey

CONTACT
Alfred B. Hastings, Jr.
Trustee
Lluella Morey Murphey Fdn.
PO Box 1419
La Quinta, CA 92253
(619) 564-3488

FINANCIAL SUMMARY
Recent Giving: $83,569 (fiscal 1993);
$119,650 (fiscal 1992); $150,785 (fiscal
1990)

Assets: $4,210,397 (fiscal 1993);
$3,990,156 (fiscal 1992); $3,345,475 (fiscal
1990)

EIN: 95-6152669

CONTRIBUTIONS SUMMARY
Donor(s): the late Lluella Morey Murphey

Typical Recipients: • *Arts & Humanities:*
Historic Preservation, History & Archaeol-

ogy, Libraries, Music • *Civic & Public Affairs:* Community Foundations, Employment/Job Training, General • *Education:* Colleges & Universities, Education Reform, Engineering/Technological Education, General, Preschool Education, Private Education (Precollege), Public Education (Precollege), Special Education, Student Aid • *Health:* Cancer, Clinics/Medical Centers, Emergency/Ambulance Services, Health Organizations, Hospitals, Kidney, Medical Research, Mental Health, Preventive Medicine/Wellness Organizations • *Religion:* Churches, Religious Organizations, Religious Welfare • *Social Services:* Animal Protection, Child Welfare, Community Service Organizations, Crime Prevention, Domestic Violence, Emergency Relief, Family Planning, Family Services, People with Disabilities, Recreation & Athletics, Senior Services, Special Olympics, Substance Abuse, United Funds/United Ways, YMCA/YWCA/YMHA/YWHA, Youth Organizations

Grant Types: capital, general support, research, and scholarship

Geographic Distribution: focus on CA

GIVING OFFICERS
Alfred B. Hastings, Jr.: trust

Leonard M. Marangi: trust

James A. Schlinger: trust

APPLICATION INFORMATION
Initial Approach: The foundation requests applications be made in writing. Include a description of organization, amount requested, purpose of funds sought, recently audited financial statement, and proof of tax-exempt status. There are no deadlines.

GRANTS ANALYSIS
Total Grants: $83,569

Number of Grants: 32

Highest Grant: $5,000

Typical Range: $1,000 to $3,000

Disclosure Period: fiscal year ending November 30, 1993

Note: Recent grants are derived from a fiscal 1993 Form 990.

RECENT GRANTS

Library

3,000	Pasadena Public Library Foundation, Pasadena, CA	

General

5,000	Church Divinity School, Pasadena, CA
3,062	Boys and Girls Club of Poachella Valley, CA
3,000	Abe Recovery Center, Pasadena, CA
3,000	American Cancer Society, Pasadena, CA
3,000	City of Hope, Los Angeles, CA

Nestle USA Inc. / Nestle USA Foundation

Former Foundation Name: Carnation Company Foundation
Sales: $7.5 billion
Employees: 22,000
Parent Company: Nestle S.A.
Headquarters: Glendale, CA
SIC Major Group: Management Consulting Services

CONTACT
Betty A. Dumas
Philanthropy & Gov't Relations Coordinator
Nestle USA Foundation
800 N Brand Blvd.
Glendale, CA 91203
(818) 549-6000

FINANCIAL SUMMARY
Recent Giving: $717,667 (1993); $1,080,950 (1992); $609,500 (1991)

Assets: $13,910,325 (1993); $13,536,102 (1992); $13,587,170 (1991)

Fiscal Note: Above figures are for the foundation only. Figures for direct corporate contributions and nonmonetary support were unavailable.

EIN: 95-6027479

CONTRIBUTIONS SUMMARY
Typical Recipients: • *Arts & Humanities:* Arts Centers, Arts Outreach, History & Archaeology, Libraries, Museums/Galleries, Music, Performing Arts, Theater • *Civic & Public Affairs:* Asian American Affairs, Botanical Gardens/Parks, Business/Free Enterprise, Economic Development, Employment/Job Training, Housing, Urban & Community Affairs, Zoos/Aquariums • *Education:* Agricultural Education, Colleges & Universities, Community & Junior Colleges, General, Literacy, Minority Education, Public Education (Precollege), Science/Mathematics Education, Secondary Education (Private), Student Aid • *Environment:* Resource Conservation • *Health:* Clinics/Medical Centers, Emergency/Ambulance Services, Hospitals, Preventive Medicine/Wellness Organizations • *Science:* Scientific Organizations • *Social Services:* Child Welfare, Community Centers, Community Service Organizations, Food/Clothing Distribution, Homes, United Funds/United Ways, Youth Organizations

Grant Types: general support

Nonmonetary Support: $500,000 (1992)

Nonmonetary Support Types: donated products

Geographic Distribution: near company's manufacturing facilities

Operating Locations: CA (Glendale)

CORP. OFFICERS
Peter Dominic Argentine: *B* Pittsburgh PA 1948 *ED* Univ Pittsburgh 1970; Duquesne Univ 1972 *CURR EMPL* sr vp planning & devel: Nestle USA Inc

James Herington Ball: *B* Kansas City MO 1942 *ED* Univ MO AB 1964; St Louis Univ JD 1973 *CURR EMPL* sr vp, asst secy, gen couns: Nestle USA Inc *CORP AFFIL* secy: Nestles Frozen Food Co; sr vp, gen couns, secy: Nestle Holdings Inc; vp, secy: Stouffer Corp *NONPR AFFIL* dir: Alliance Childrens Rights; mem: MO Bar Assn

Mario A. Corti: *CURR EMPL* sr vp, chief admin off: Nestle USA Inc

Timm F. Crull: *B* 1931 *ED* MI St Univ BA 1955 *CURR EMPL* chmn: Nestle USA Inc *CORP AFFIL* chmn: Nestle Food Co; chmn, pres: T S C Holdings Inc; chmn, pres, ceo: Stouffer Corp; pres, ceo, dir: Nestle Holdings Inc

Cam Starrett: *CURR EMPL* exec vp human resources & corp rels: Nestle USA Inc

Joseph M. Weller: *CURR EMPL* pres, coo, dir: Nestle USA Inc

GIVING OFFICERS
Peter Dominic Argentine: treas *CURR EMPL* sr vp planning & devel: Nestle USA Inc (see above)

James Herington Ball: dir *CURR EMPL* sr vp, asst secy, gen couns: Nestle USA Inc (see above)

Mario A. Corti: vp, dir *CURR EMPL* sr vp, chief admin off: Nestle USA Inc (see above)

N. Paul Devereux: vp, dir *CURR EMPL* vp retirement design: Nestle USA Inc

Betty A. Dumas: philanthropy & govt rels coordinator

M. C. Ewing: secy

Robert H. Sanders: vp

Robert W. Schult: dir *B* 1949 *ED* Univ NC BA 1971 *CURR EMPL* pres, ceo, dir: Nestle Food Co

Cam Starrett: dir *CURR EMPL* exec vp human resources & corp rels: Nestle USA Inc (see above)

Joseph M. Weller: pres, dir *CURR EMPL* pres, coo, dir: Nestle USA Inc (see above)

APPLICATION INFORMATION
Initial Approach: *Initial Contact:* brief letter requesting application guidelines *Include Information On:* copy of IRS exemption certificate and audited financial statement *Deadlines:* none

Restrictions on Giving: Does not support international organizations, fraternal organizations, goodwill advertising, individuals, member agencies of united funds, political or lobbying groups, or religious organizations for sectarian purposes.

PUBLICATIONS
Application guidelines

GRANTS ANALYSIS
Total Grants: $717,667

Number of Grants: 36

Highest Grant: $100,000

Average Grant: $19,935

Typical Range: $5,000 to $25,000

Disclosure Period: 1993

Note: Recent grants are derived from a 1993 Form 990.

RECENT GRANTS

General

100,000	United Negro College Fund Ladders of Hope, New York, NY — general support	
75,000	Cleveland Clinic Research Foundation, Cleveland, OH — general support	
50,000	Mt. St. Mary's College, Los Angeles, CA — general support	
40,000	American Red Cross, Cleveland, OH — general support	
40,000	Wartburg College, Waverly, IA — general support	

Norton Family Foundation, Peter

CONTACT
Peter Norton
Trustee
Peter Norton Family Fdn.
225 Arizona
Santa Monica, CA 90401
(310) 575-7700

FINANCIAL SUMMARY
Recent Giving: $1,292,689 (1993)

Assets: $23,077,435 (1993)

EIN: 95-4195347

CONTRIBUTIONS SUMMARY
Typical Recipients: • *Arts & Humanities:* Arts Associations & Councils, Arts Institutes, Dance, Ethnic & Folk Arts, General, Libraries, Museums/Galleries, Public Broadcasting • *Civic & Public Affairs:* Community Foundations, General, Parades/Festivals, Women's Affairs • *Education:* Arts/Humanities Education, Colleges & Universities, Medical Education, Preschool Education, Science/Mathematics Education • *Environment:* Air/Water Quality • *Health:* Clinics/Medical Centers, Emergency/Ambulance Services, Mental Health • *International:* Foreign Arts Organizations • *Social Services:* Big Brother/Big Sister, Child Welfare, Community Service Organizations

Grant Types: general support

Geographic Distribution: focus on CA

GIVING OFFICERS
Anne Etheridge: secy, treas

Eileen Norton: vp

Peter Norton: don *B* 1943 *CORP AFFIL* dir: Symantec Corp

APPLICATION INFORMATION
Initial Approach: Send a brief letter of inquiry. There are no deadlines.

GRANTS ANALYSIS
Total Grants: $1,292,689

Number of Grants: 114

Highest Grant: $200,000

Typical Range: $250 to $75,000

Disclosure Period: 1993

Note: Recent grants are derived from a 1993 Form 990.

RECENT GRANTS

Library

25,000	New York Public Library of Contemporary Art, New York, NY	

General

51,000	CDF	
50,000	Shakespeare Globe Centre, Brooklyn, NY	
34,500	Minneapolis Fund, Minneapolis, MN	
30,000	School for Arts and Science — for annual giving	
27,183	Five Acres, Altadena, CA	

Odell Fund, Robert Stewart Odell and Helen Pfeiffer

CONTACT
Thomas N. Neville
Trustee
Robert Stewart Odell and Helen Pfeiffer Odell Fund
c/o Wells Fargo Bank Trustee
PO Box 63002
San Francisco, CA 94163
(415) 396-3226

FINANCIAL SUMMARY
Recent Giving: $1,235,846 (1993); $1,175,150 (1992); $1,053,950 (1990)

Assets: $28,926,848 (1993); $29,544,654 (1992); $23,400,077 (1990)

EIN: 94-6132116

CONTRIBUTIONS SUMMARY
Donor(s): The foundation was established in 1967 by the late Robert Stewart Odell and the late Helen Pfeiffer Odell .

Typical Recipients: • *Arts & Humanities:* Arts Festivals, History & Archaeology, Libraries, Museums/Galleries, Music, Performing Arts • *Civic & Public Affairs:* Law & Justice, Parades/Festivals, Public Policy, Safety, Urban & Community Affairs, Zoos/Aquariums • *Education:* Afterschool/Enrichment Programs, Colleges & Universities, Education Funds, Preschool Education, Private Education (Precollege), Secondary Education (Private), Secondary Education (Public), Student Aid • *Environment:* General • *Health:* Children's Health/Hospitals, Clinics/Medical Centers, Eyes/Blindness, Health Organizations, Hospitals, Medical Research • *International:* Human Rights, International Organizations, Missionary/Religious Activities • *Religion:* Churches, Religious Organizations, Religious Welfare • *Science:* Science Museums, Scientific Centers & Institutes • *Social Services:* At-Risk Youth, Child Welfare, Community Service Organizations, Day Care, Family Services, Homes, People with Disabilities, Recreation & Athletics, Shel-

ters/Homelessness, United Funds/United Ways, Youth Organizations

Grant Types: general support

Geographic Distribution: focus on northern California, with emphasis on San Francisco

GIVING OFFICERS
James P. Conn: trust *CURR EMPL* pres, dir: Bay Meadows Catering

Paul B. Fay, Jr.: trust

Thomas N. Neville: trust

APPLICATION INFORMATION
Initial Approach:

The fund requests applications be made in writing.

Written applications should include the purpose for which the funds will be used and a copy of the Federal tax exemption letter showing that the applicant is a public charity.

The foundation requests that applications be sent early in the calendar year to assure consideration.

The trustees intend to make payments between October 15 and December 31 of each year and not earlier.

Restrictions on Giving: The fund only makes grants to public charities. The foundation does not make grants to individuals.

GRANTS ANALYSIS
Total Grants: $1,235,846

Number of Grants: 78

Highest Grant: $100,000

Average Grant: $15,844

Typical Range: $5,000 to $25,000

Disclosure Period: 1993

Note: Recent grants are derived from a 1993 Form 990.

RECENT GRANTS

General

100,000	St. Anthony Foundation, San Francisco, CA	
25,000	Archbishop Alemany Scholarship Fund, San Francisco, CA	
25,000	Blind Babies Foundation, San Francisco, CA	
25,000	Boys and Girls Club of Peninsula, San Francisco, CA	
25,000	Catholic Charities of San Mateo, San Mateo, CA	

Osher Foundation, Bernard

CONTACT
Patricia Tracy-Nagle
Executive Administrator and Secretary
Bernard Osher Foundation
220 San Bruno Ave.
San Francisco, CA 94103
(415) 861-5587

FINANCIAL SUMMARY
Recent Giving: $2,969,759 (1993); $2,183,850 (1992); $3,516,912 (1991)

Assets: $38,487,784 (1993); $35,622,549 (1992); $34,138,227 (1991)

EIN: 94-2506257

CONTRIBUTIONS SUMMARY

Donor(s): The foundation was established in 1977 by Bernard Osher. Mr. Osher is a prominent businessman and community leader in the San Francisco Bay Area.

Typical Recipients: • *Arts & Humanities:* Arts Festivals, Arts Institutes, Ballet, Dance, Ethnic & Folk Arts, Film & Video, General, History & Archaeology, Libraries, Museums/Galleries, Music, Opera, Performing Arts, Public Broadcasting, Theater • *Civic & Public Affairs:* Legal Aid, Parades/Festivals, Public Policy, Urban & Community Affairs • *Education:* Arts/Humanities Education, Colleges & Universities, Continuing Education, International Studies, Journalism/Media Education, Medical Education, Private Education (Precollege) • *Environment:* General, Resource Conservation • *Health:* AIDS/HIV, Diabetes, Health Organizations, Mental Health • *International:* International Organizations, International Peace & Security Issues • *Religion:* Churches, Religious Organizations, Religious Welfare • *Science:* Science Museums, Scientific Centers & Institutes • *Social Services:* Community Centers, Community Service Organizations, Family Planning, Family Services, Food/Clothing Distribution, People with Disabilities, Shelters/Homelessness, Substance Abuse, Youth Organizations

Grant Types: project and scholarship

Geographic Distribution: restricted to San Francisco, Alameda, Contra Costa, Marin or San Mateo counties

GIVING OFFICERS

David Agger: dir

Dr. Frederick E. Balderston: dir

Reeder Butterfield: vp

Judith Ciani: dir

Robert Friend: dir

Ron Kaufman: dir

Barbro Osher: pres

Bernard A. Osher: treas *B* 1928 *CURR EMPL* fdr, pres: Butterfield & Butterfield *CORP AFFIL* dir: Golden W Fin Corp, World Saving & Loan Assn *PHIL AFFIL* dir: Koret Foundation

Patricia Tracy-Nagle: exec admin, secy

Alfred S. Wilsey, Sr.: dir *PHIL AFFIL* pres: Wilsey Foundation

APPLICATION INFORMATION

Initial Approach:

Applicants should submit a letter of inquiry. Initial letters should include a brief background of the organization, including qualifications of people involved; a description of the nature and scope of proposed project or program and anticipated results; a preliminary timetable and budget outline; financial statement for most recent completed year of operation; evidence of tax-exempt status; names of appropriate governing authority; and evidence of request approval.

Applications are accepted at any time.

If the letter of inquiry falls within the foundation's objective, the board will request a more detailed proposal. All applications will receive a prompt response from the foundation.

Restrictions on Giving: Generally, the foundation does not fund requests for capital improvements, normal operating expenses, deficits, or fundraising campaigns. The foundation may not make direct grants to individuals.

PUBLICATIONS

Application guidelines

GRANTS ANALYSIS

Total Grants: $2,969,759

Number of Grants: 123

Highest Grant: $1,000,000

Average Grant: $16,146*

Typical Range: $1,000 to $25,000

Disclosure Period: 1993

Note: The average grant figure excludes the highest grant of $1,000,000. Recent grants are derived from a 1993 grants list.

RECENT GRANTS

Library

360,167	San Francisco Library Foundation, San Francisco, CA
7,500	San Francisco Performing Arts Library, San Francisco, CA

General

72,000	California Academy of Sciences, San Francisco, CA
55,000	University of California San Francisco Neurology Fellowship, San Francisco, CA
50,000	Omega Boys Club, San Francisco, CA
40,000	Planned Parenthood of San Francisco, San Francisco, CA
30,000	Diamond Youth Shelter, San Francisco, CA

Pacific Mutual Life Insurance Co. / Pacific Mutual Charitable Foundation

Revenue: $3.21 billion
Employees: 2,395
Headquarters: Newport Beach, CA
SIC Major Group: Life Insurance, Accident & Health Insurance, Pension, Health & Welfare Funds, and Investors Nec

CONTACT

Robert G. Haskell
President
Pacific Mutual Charitable Foundation
700 Newport Center Dr.
Newport Beach, CA 92660
(714) 640-3787

FINANCIAL SUMMARY

Recent Giving: $1,115,000 (1994 approx.); $851,249 (1993); $816,547 (1992)

Assets: $14,629,063 (1993); $8,561,930 (1991); $7,776,513 (1990)

Gifts Received: $5,729,782 (1993)

Fiscal Note: Company gives directly and through the foundation. In 1994, direct giving totaled approximately $120,000, while foundation giving totaled about $995,000. In 1992, direct giving was $115,347, and foundation contributions were $701,200. Figure for 1993 represents only foundation giving. Contributions were received from Pacific Mutual Life Insurance Company.

EIN: 95-3433806

CONTRIBUTIONS SUMMARY

Typical Recipients: • *Arts & Humanities:* Arts Centers, Arts Festivals, Arts Funds, Dance, Ethnic & Folk Arts, Libraries, Museums/Galleries, Music, Opera, Performing Arts, Public Broadcasting, Theater • *Civic & Public Affairs:* Botanical Gardens/Parks, Civil Rights, Economic Development, Economic Policy, Employment/Job Training, Hispanic Affairs, Housing, Law & Justice, Legal Aid, Municipalities/Towns, Nonprofit Management, Public Policy, Safety, Urban & Community Affairs, Women's Affairs, Zoos/Aquariums • *Education:* Business Education, Colleges & Universities, Economic Education, Education Funds, General, Health & Physical Education, Medical Education, Minority Education, Public Education (Precollege), Student Aid • *Environment:* General • *Health:* AIDS/HIV, Children's Health/Hospitals, Emergency/Ambulance Services, Geriatric Health, Health Policy/Cost Containment, Health Organizations, Hospices, Hospitals, Medical Research, Medical Training, Mental Health, Nutrition, Public Health, Single-Disease Health Associations • *Religion:* Religious Welfare • *Social Services:* Child Welfare, Community Service Organizations, Counseling, Day Care, Delinquency & Criminal Rehabilitation, Emergency Relief, Family Planning, Family Services, Food/Clothing Distribution, Homes, People with Disabilities, Senior Services, Shelters/Homelessness, Substance Abuse, United Funds/United Ways, Volunteer Services, Youth Organizations

Grant Types: capital, employee matching gifts, fellowship, general support, project, research, and scholarship

Nonmonetary Support: $158,958 (1992); $87,000 (1988); $31,000 (1987)

Nonmonetary Support Types: donated equipment and in-kind services

Note: Nonmonetary support is provided by the company.

Geographic Distribution: primarily to local organizations in areas with large concentrations of company employees; some state and national funding

Operating Locations: CA (Fountain Valley, Newport Beach)

CORP. OFFICERS

Harry Geiple Bubb: *B* Trinidad CO 1924 *ED* Stanford Univ BA 1946; Stanford Univ MBA 1949; Harvard Univ Advanced Mgmt Program 1973 *CURR EMPL* chmn emeritus, dir: Pacific Mutual Life Ins Co *CORP AFFIL* dir: Pacific Consulting Corp, Pacific Investment Mgmt Co *NONPR AFFIL* dir: CA Chamber Commerce, CA Econ Devel Corp, Los Angeles Chamber Commerce, Orange County Bus Comm Arts, Un Way Orange County; mem: CA Med Assn; mem adv bd: Town Hall Orange County; mem adv counc: CA St Parks Fdn; trust: Newport Harbor Art Mus, US Acad Decathlon *CLUB AFFIL* Balboa YC, CA, Ctr, Lincoln

William D. Cvengros: *B* 1948 *ED* Univ Notre Dame BA 1970; Northwestern Univ MBA 1972 *CURR EMPL* vchmn, chief invest off: Pacific Mutual Life Ins Co *CORP AFFIL* pres, ceo: Pacific Fin Asset Mgmt Corp

Walter Bland Gerken: *B* New York NY 1922 *ED* Wesleyan Univ BA 1948; Maxwell Sch Citizenship Pub Aff MPA 1958 *CURR EMPL* chmn exec comm, dir: Pacific Mutual Life Ins Co *CORP AFFIL* dir: Mgmt Compensation Group, Southern CA Edison Co, Whittaker Corp; dir, sr advisor: Boston Consult Group *NONPR AFFIL* chmn: Exec Svc Corps, Nature Conservancy CA; chmn bd overseers: Univ CA Irvine Coll Med; dir: Hoag Meml Presbyterian Hosp; mem bd overseers: RAND/Univ CA Los Angeles Ctr Study Soviet Behavior; trust: Occidental Coll, Wesleyan Univ *CLUB AFFIL* Automobile, Balboa Bay, CA, Dairymens CC, Metro, Pauma Valley CC *PHIL AFFIL* dir: James Irvine Foundation; vp, dir, mem exec comm, chmn audit comm, mem dirs grant program comm: W. M. Keck Foundation

Thomas C. Sutton: *B* Atlanta GA 1942 *ED* Univ Toronto BS 1965; Harvard Univ 1982 *CURR EMPL* chmn, ceo, dir: Pacific Mutual Life Ins Co *CORP AFFIL* dir: Pacific Equities Network, Pacific Fin Asset Mgmt Corp; pres, ceo, dir: Group Holding Co, Pacific Fin Holding Co *NONPR AFFIL* fellow: Soc Actuaries; mem: Am Acad Actuaries, Pacific Sts Actuarial Club; mem affiliates adv bd: Univ CA Irvine Sch Mgmt; trust: S Coast Repertory

GIVING OFFICERS

Harry Geiple Bubb: dir *CURR EMPL* chmn emeritus, dir: Pacific Mutual Life Ins Co (see above)

Edward R. Byrd: cfo

William D. Cvengros: dir *CURR EMPL* vchmn, chief invest off: Pacific Mutual Life Ins Co (see above)

Walter Bland Gerken: dir *CURR EMPL* chmn exec comm, dir: Pacific Mutual Life Ins Co *PHIL AFFIL* dir: James Irvine Foundation; vp, dir, mem exec comm, chmn audit comm, mem dirs grant program comm: W. M. Keck Foundation (see above)

Brenda K. Hardwig: asst secy

Robert G. Haskell: pres, dir *B* Orange CA 1952 *ED* Univ Southern CA 1974; Univ Southern CA 1979 *CURR EMPL* vp pub aff: Pacific Mutual Life Ins Co

Patricia A. Kosky: vp *CURR EMPL* commun rels mgr: Pacific Mutual Life Ins Co

Michael T. McLaughlin: gen coun

Audrey L. Milfs: secy *B* 1945 *CURR EMPL* asst vp, secy: Pacific Mutual Life Ins Co *CORP AFFIL* dir: Pacific Fin Asset Mgmt Corp; secy, dir: Group Holding Co, Pacific Equities Network, Pacific Mutual Holding Co, PM Group Life Ins Co

Thomas C. Sutton: chmn *CURR EMPL* chmn, ceo, dir: Pacific Mutual Life Ins Co (see above)

APPLICATION INFORMATION

Initial Approach: *Initial Contact:* letter or proposal *Include Information On:* proof of tax-exempt status; description of the organization and project, including needs, objectives, and evaluative criteria; budget for project, including personnel and operating costs; list of other contributors and levels of funding, and amount requested; current budget for organization, including specific sources of revenue and any contingency funds; description of volunteer support; and list of board of directors and advisory board members *Deadlines:* by September 15

Restrictions on Giving: Foundation does not support individuals; political parties, candidates, or partisan political organizations; professional associations; veterans and labor organizations, fraternal organizations, athletic clubs, or social clubs; religious organizations for sectarian or denominational purposes; or operating expenses for member agencies of United Way, except under special circumstances.

OTHER THINGS TO KNOW

Generally prefers to make annual grants. Organizations may reapply annually, but grants typically are made to one organization for no more than three consecutive years.

Grants for annual operating expenses typically range from $500 to $2,000. Most capital grants range from $10,000 to $25,000 over a two- to five-year period.

The foundation reports that each year it selects two or more areas of special focus (e.g. AIDS, homelessness, Hispanic needs) and makes major grants in that focus area. These grants are usually made later in the calendar year after the foundation has done considerable research.

PUBLICATIONS

Community involvement report

GRANTS ANALYSIS

Total Grants: $851,249

Number of Grants: 90

Highest Grant: $172,379

Average Grant: $9,458

Typical Range: $500 to $10,000

Disclosure Period: 1993

Note: Figures represent foundation giving only. Recent grants are derived from a 1993 Form 990.

RECENT GRANTS

Library

10,000	Newport Beach Public Library Foundation, Newport Beach, CA — capital campaign

General

172,379	United Way of Orange County, Garden Grove, CA
75,000	Southern California Association for Philanthropy, Los Angeles, CA
52,000	Newport-Mesa Schools Foundation, Newport, CA
50,000	Children's Advocacy Institute
50,000	Orange County Trauma Society, Orange, CA

Pacific Telesis Group / Telesis Foundation

Former Foundation Name: Pacific Telesis Foundation
Revenue: $9.49 billion
Employees: 313
Headquarters: San Francisco, CA
SIC Major Group: Holding Companies Nec, Radiotelephone Communications, and Telephone Communications Except Radiotelephone

CONTACT

Jere A. Jacobs
President
Pacific Telesis Foundation
130 Kearny St.
Rm. 3309
San Francisco, CA 94108
(415) 394-3693
Note: Alternate contacts are Mary Leslie, Susan Diekman, and Lee Davis, Executive Directors. The company's World Wide Web address is http://www.pactel.com

FINANCIAL SUMMARY

Recent Giving: $8,157,311 (1993); $7,987,570 (1992); $7,522,528 (1991)

Assets: $68,750,973 (1992); $68,600,272 (1991); $62,460,587 (1990)

Fiscal Note: Above represents foundation contributions only. Company also has a direct giving program administered by Molly Hopp, Director of Community Affairs, Pacific Telesis Group. Operating companies, Pacific Bell, and Nevada Bell, also make direct contributions, not included above. Above figures exclude nonmonetary support.

EIN: 94-2905832

CONTRIBUTIONS SUMMARY

Typical Recipients: • *Arts & Humanities:* Arts Appreciation, Community Arts, Dance, Ethnic & Folk Arts, Libraries, Museums/Galleries, Music, Opera, Performing Arts, Theater, Visual Arts • *Civic & Public Affairs:* Housing, Law & Justice, Nonprofit Management, Urban & Community Affairs, Women's Affairs • *Education:* Arts/Humanities Education, Business Education, Colleges & Universities, Community & Junior Colleges, Economic Education, Elementary

Education (Private), Engineering/Technological Education, Faculty Development, Literacy, Minority Education, Preschool Education, Public Education (Precollege), Science/Mathematics Education, Student Aid • *Social Services:* Child Welfare, Day Care, Homes, People with Disabilities, Senior Services, Shelters/Homelessness, Substance Abuse, United Funds/United Ways, Volunteer Services, Youth Organizations

Grant Types: employee matching gifts, project, and scholarship

Note: Employee matching gift ratio: 1 to 1. Foundation will match gifts from active employees and members of board of directors up to a maximum of $3,000 in a calendar year.

Geographic Distribution: only to regional and local organizations operating within service areas or communities in which significant numbers of employees live; generally does not contribute funds outside the state of California

Operating Locations: CA (Bakersfield, Fresno, Los Angeles, Oakland, Orange, Riverside, Sacramento, Salinas, San Diego, San Francisco, San Jose, San Ramon, Santa Rosa), NV (Reno)

CORP. OFFICERS
James R. Moberg: *B* 1935 *ED* Harvard Univ Grad Sch Bus Admin 1972; Univ Southern CA BS *CURR EMPL* exec vp human resources: Pacific Telesis Group *CORP AFFIL* exec vp: Pacific Bell

Richard William Odgers: *B* Detroit MI 1936 *ED* Univ MI AB 1959; Univ MI JD 1961 *CURR EMPL* exec vp, gen couns, secy: Pacific Telesis Group *CORP AFFIL* exec vp: Pacific Bell Group; exec vp, secy: Pacific Bell *NONPR AFFIL* dir: Legal Aid Soc San Francisco; fellow: Am Bar Fdn, Am Coll Trial Lawyers, Am Judicature Soc; mem: Am Bar Assn, Am Law Inst, San Francisco Bar Assn *CLUB AFFIL* City, Olympic, Pacific-Union *PHIL AFFIL* secy, treas: van Loben Sels Foundation

Philip J. Quigley: *B* 1943 *CURR EMPL* chmn, ceo, pres: Pacific Telesis Group *CORP AFFIL* dir: Vasian Assocs Inc, Wells Fargo Bank, Wells Fargo & Co; pres, ceo: Pacific Bell Group

GIVING OFFICERS
Lee Davis: exec dir

Susan Diekman: exec dir *ED* Stanford Univ BA 1966; Stanford Univ ME 1967

Nancy Ishirashi: mem bd

Jere A. Jacobs: pres, dir

Mary Leslie: exec dir *ED* San Francisco St Univ BA 1969; Golden Gate Univ

James R. Moberg: dir *CURR EMPL* exec vp human resources: Pacific Telesis Group (see above)

Richard William Odgers: secy, dir *CURR EMPL* exec vp, gen couns, secy: Pacific Telesis Group *PHIL AFFIL* secy, treas: van Loben Sels Foundation (see above)

Philip J. Quigley: chmn *CURR EMPL* chmn, ceo, pres: Pacific Telesis Group (see above)

Mike Rodriguez: mem bd
Richard R. Roll: vp, dir

APPLICATION INFORMATION
Initial Approach: *Initial Contact:* organizations that serve California and are statewide or national in scope, send proposal outline to foundation; Bay area, central area, northern area, and southern area of California and Nevada organizations, send outline to appropriate area manager of Pacific Bell or Nevada Bell *Include Information On:* description of the organization's purpose and scope, including short-term and long-range objectives; evidence of how request fits foundation guidelines; standards to evaluate success of program; current total budget for organization; budget for specific project; brief statement explaining why company should provide support and how support would be recognized; proof of 501(c)(3) tax-exempt status; list of corporate and foundation funders and funding levels; evidence of strategies to develop earned income and avoid over-dependence on any single source of contributed income *Deadlines:* none *Note:* Addresses of appropriate regional contacts are available from company.

Restrictions on Giving: Foundation does not make grants to the following organizations and/or causes: organizations without 501(c)(3) status; organizations that discriminate by race, creed, color, sex, sexual preference, age, or national origin; private foundations; "flow-through" organizations; organizations supported by the United Way; individual primary and secondary schools or school districts; capital projects; endowment funds; religious organizations for sectarian purposes; veterans groups or labor organizations when serving only their own members; individuals; general operating purposes; medical clinics or medical research; emergency funds or guarantees; special occassion or goodwill advertising; sports programs or events; political or lobbying activities; or in the form of products or services or cause-related marketing.

OTHER THINGS TO KNOW
Grants are determined on a zero-based budgeting process, which requires annual evaluation of both previously funded projects and new grant requests.

Foundation grants should not be construed as establishing a precedent for further support.

Foundation prefers to make one-time grants, although in special circumstances grants may span up to three years.

Foundation may request post-grant reports from organizations receiving contributions.

Foundation gives preference to organizations with active, diverse boards, effective leadership, and continuity of efficient administration.

GRANTS ANALYSIS
Total Grants: $8,157,311

Typical Range: $15,000 to $25,000

Disclosure Period: 1993

Note: Recent grants are derived from a 1992 grants list.

RECENT GRANTS
Library

50,000	Library Foundation of San Francisco, San Francisco, CA

General

1,150,843	United Way of the Bay Area, San Francisco, CA
873,030	United Way, Los Angeles, CA
231,525	United Way of Orange County, Irvine, CA
211,961	United Way of San Diego County, San Diego, CA
200,000	United Way of the Bay Area, San Francisco, CA

Packard Foundation, David and Lucile

CONTACT
Colburn S. Wilbur
Executive Director
David and Lucile Packard Foundation
300 2nd St., Ste. 200
Los Altos, CA 94022
(415) 948-7658

FINANCIAL SUMMARY
Recent Giving: $55,510,356 (1993); $45,000,000 (1992 approx.); $32,834,909 (1991)

Assets: $1,279,828,472 (1993); $1,100,000,000 (1992 approx.); $681,317,000 (1991)

Gifts Received: $322,375,719 (1993); $285,000,000 (1992 approx.); $407,232,000 (1991)

Fiscal Note: The foundation is to received annual contributions from Hewlett-Packard common stock through 2003. In 1993, the foundation received gifts from David Packard, the David and Lucile S. Packard Trust I, and the David and Lucile S. Packard Trust II.

EIN: 94-2278431

CONTRIBUTIONS SUMMARY
Donor(s): The David and Lucile Packard Foundation was established in 1964. The foundation's donors are David Packard, the foundation's president, and his late wife, Lucile Salter Packard . The couple's four children, David Woodley Packard, Nancy Ann Packard Burnett, Susan Packard Orr, and Julie Elizabeth Packard, all serve on their parents' foundation.

David Packard and William Hewlett founded Hewlett-Packard Company in 1938. The company became a major manufacturer of test and measurement instruments and microcomputers. Mr. Packard also served as U.S. Secretary of Defense between 1969 and 1971.

Typical Recipients: • *Arts & Humanities:* Arts Associations & Councils, Arts Funds, Ballet, Community Arts, Dance, Historic

Preservation, History & Archaeology, Libraries, Literary Arts, Museums/Galleries, Music, Opera, Performing Arts, Theater • *Civic & Public Affairs:* Botanical Gardens/Parks, Community Foundations, Employment/Job Training, Housing, Municipalities/Towns, Nonprofit Management, Philanthropic Organizations, Professional & Trade Associations, Public Policy, Women's Affairs, Zoos/Aquariums • *Education:* Afterschool/Enrichment Programs, Arts/Humanities Education, Business Education, Colleges & Universities, Education Associations, Elementary Education (Private), Engineering/Technological Education, General, International Studies, Medical Education, Public Education (Precollege), School Volunteerism, Science/Mathematics Education, Secondary Education (Public), Student Aid • *Environment:* Air/Water Quality, General, Wildlife Protection • *Health:* Children's Health/Hospitals, Clinics/Medical Centers, Health Policy/Cost Containment, Health Organizations, Hospitals, Long-Term Care, Nursing Services, Nutrition, Prenatal Health Issues, Public Health • *International:* Foreign Educational Institutions, Health Care/Hospitals, International Environmental Issues, International Peace & Security Issues • *Science:* Scientific Centers & Institutes, Scientific Organizations • *Social Services:* Child Welfare, Community Service Organizations, Counseling, Day Care, Family Planning, Family Services, Food/Clothing Distribution, Homes, People with Disabilities, Shelters/Homelessness, Youth Organizations

Grant Types: capital, department, general support, project, research, and seed money

Geographic Distribution: national, with an emphasis on San Mateo, Santa Clara, Santa Cruz, and Monterey counties, CA; Pueblo, CO; also Mexico and Columbia

GIVING OFFICERS
Nancy Packard Burnett: trust

Robin Chandler Duke: trust *PHIL AFFIL* trust: United States-Japan Foundation

Robert Joy Glaser, MD: trust *B* St Louis MO 1918 *ED* Harvard Univ SB 1940; Harvard Univ MD 1943 *CORP AFFIL* dir: Affymax, Alza Corp, CA Water Svc Co, Nellcor *NONPR AFFIL* dir: Kaiser Fdn Hosps, Packard Humanities; editor: Pharos; fellow: Am Academy Arts Sciences, Am Assn Advancement Science; mem: Alpha Omega Alpha, Am Clinical Climatological Assn, Am Fed Clinical Res, Am Soc Clinical Investigation, Am Soc Experimental Pathology, Assn Am Med Colls, Assn Am Physicians, Central Soc Clinical Res, Natl Academy Sciences Inst Medicine, Natl Inst Allergy Infectious Disease, Sigma Xi, Western Assn Physicians; trust: Washington Univ *CLUB AFFIL* Century, Harvard *PHIL AFFIL* dir med science, trust: Lucille P. Markey Charitable Trust; dir: Packard Humanities Institute

Dean O. Morton: trust *B* 1932 *ED* KS St Univ BE 1954; Harvard Univ MBA 1960 *CURR EMPL* ret exec vp, coo, dir: Hewlett-Packard Co

Susan Packard Orr: vp, trust

David Packard: pres, chmn *B* Pueblo CO 1912 *ED* Stanford Univ BA 1934; Stanford Univ MEE 1939 *CORP AFFIL* dir: Boeing Co, Genentech *NONPR AFFIL* dir emeritus: Wolf Trap Fdn; fellow: Inst Electrical Electronics Engrs; hon lifetime mem: Instrument Soc Am; mem: Alpha Delta Phi, Am Enterprise Inst, Am Ordnance Assn, Bus Counc, Bus Roundtable, CA Chamber Commerce, Natl Academy Engg, Phi Beta Kappa, Pres Counc Advs Science Tech, Sigma Xi, Tau Beta Pi, Wilson Counc; mem bd overseers: Hoover Inst; trust: Herbert Hoover Fdn, Ronald Reagan Presidential Fdn; vchmn, trust: CA Nature Conservancy

David Woodley Packard: vp, trust *CURR EMPL* pres, chmn: Ibycus Corp *PHIL AFFIL* pres, chmn: Packard Humanities Institute; chmn, pres: Stanford Theater Foundation

Julie Elizabeth Packard: trust *NONPR AFFIL* secy, dir: Monterey Bay Aquarium Res Inst *PHIL AFFIL* vp, exec dir: Monterey Bay Aquarium Foundation

Frank H. Roberts: trust *PHIL AFFIL* asst secy, trust: Dean Witter Foundation

Edwin E. Van Bronkhurst: treas, trust

Colburn S. Wilbur: exec dir *B* 1935 *PHIL AFFIL* treas, dir: Stanford Theater Foundation

Barbara Wright: secy, trust *PHIL AFFIL* secy: Packard Humanities Institute

APPLICATION INFORMATION
Initial Approach:

Written proposals should be sent to the foundation's executive director.

Proposals should include a cover letter from the executive director or board chair indicating that the proposal has the support of the agency's board. General information should include the name, address, and telephone number of the organization; its background and purpose; list of people and constituent groups served; names and affiliations of directors and trustees; and a copy of the IRS determination letter of tax-exempt status. Financial information should include the prior year's financial statements (preferably audited), sources of the organization's funds (both public and private), budget for the years in which the program will take place, detailed project budget, other sources of support, and the amount requested from the foundation. Program information should include objective and description, evidence of need and value, geographic area served, an outline of program's phases, evaluative methods, and personnel involved and their qualifications.

Proposals are considered at the foundation's quarterly board meetings. The application deadlines for consideration at these meetings are December 15, March 15, June 15, and September 15.

The foundation's board meets in March, June, September, and December.

Restrictions on Giving: The foundation does not support religious programs.

OTHER THINGS TO KNOW
The foundation is affiliated with the Monterey Bay Aquarium Research Institute, the Stanford Theater Foundation, and the Packard Humanities Institute. The foundation provides other services such as managment assistance and loans for land purchase and low-income housing.

The foundation distributes grants primarily in San Mateo, Santa Clara, Santa Cruz, and Monterey Counties, CA; it also awards some grants in Pueblo, CO. National funding is given for child health, science and engineering fellowships, and support for science instruction in African American colleges. In addition, funding is available for conservation and population studies in the US, Mexico, and Columbia.

PUBLICATIONS
Annual report and quarterly journal, *The Future of Children*

GRANTS ANALYSIS
Total Grants: $55,510,356

Number of Grants: 726

Highest Grant: $10,000,000

Average Grant: $76,461

Typical Range: $5,000 to $100,000

Disclosure Period: 1993

Note: Recent grants are derived from a 1993 Form 990.

RECENT GRANTS

Library
125	New York Public Library, New York, NY — for the new Science Industry and Business Library

General
10,000,000	Lucile Salter Packard Children's Hospital at Stanford (LSPCH), Palo Alto, CA — to support LSPCH's use of various facilities and services at Stanford University Hospital
6,659,175	Monterey Bay Aquarium Research Institute, Pacific Grove, CA — for operating expenses, capital equipment and projects, and to apply to the construction of a SWATH vessel
4,840,825	Monterey Bay Aquarium Research Institute, Pacific Grove, CA — for operating and research expenses, capital equipment, and construction contingency funds
1,000,000	Beckman Laser Institute and Medical Clinic, Irvine, CA — for laser treatment and research of disfiguring birthmarks
1,000,000	ETI Institute, Mountain View, CA — support for the Search for Extraterrestrial Intelligence Program

Parsons Foundation, Ralph M.

CONTACT
Christine Sisley
Executive Director and Secretary
Ralph M. Parsons Foundation
1055 Wilshire Blvd., Ste. 1701
Los Angeles, CA 90017
(213) 482-3185

FINANCIAL SUMMARY
Recent Giving: $11,335,392 (1993);
$9,303,793 (1992); $5,773,922 (1991)
Assets: $190,621,148 (1993); $183,232,141
(1992); $178,028,340 (1991)
EIN: 95-6085895

CONTRIBUTIONS SUMMARY
Donor(s): The foundation was established
in 1961 by Ralph M. Parsons (1896-1974).
Despite his modest beginnings as the son of
a Long Island fisherman, Mr. Parsons established and led one of the world's largest engineering and construction firms, Parsons
Corporation. He was a pioneer in missile
and space launch facilities and nuclear
plants.

In 1961, Mr. Parsons established a modest
foundation. Upon his death in 1974, the
grant-making organization received a bequest from his estate valued at approximately $154 million. This foundation is
managed independently of the Parsons Corporation.

Typical Recipients: • *Arts & Humanities:*
Arts Centers, Arts Institutes, Arts Outreach,
Ethnic & Folk Arts, Historic Preservation,
History & Archaeology, Libraries, Muse-
ums/Galleries, Music, Public Broadcasting,
Theater • *Civic & Public Affairs:* Botanical
Gardens/Parks, Civil Rights, Employ-
ment/Job Training, Hispanic Affairs, Hous-
ing, Law & Justice, Nonprofit Management,
Philanthropic Organizations, Professional &
Trade Associations, Public Policy, Safety,
Urban & Community Affairs • *Education:*
Arts/Humanities Education, Colleges & Uni-
versities, Economic Education, Education
Associations, Education Funds, Education
Reform, Elementary Education (Private), En-
gineering/Technological Education, Liter-
acy, Minority Education, Preschool
Education, Public Education (Precollege),
Science/Mathematics Education, Special
Education, Student Aid • *Environment:* Gen-
eral • *Health:* AIDS/HIV, Alzheimers Dis-
ease, Cancer, Children's Health/Hospitals,
Clinics/Medical Centers, Health Organiza-
tions, Hospitals, Long-Term Care, Medical
Research, Mental Health, Prenatal Health Is-
sues, Trauma Treatment • *International:*
Health Care/Hospitals • *Religion:* Jewish
Causes • *Science:* Scientific Centers & Insti-
tutes, Scientific Research • *Social Services:*
At-Risk Youth, Child Abuse, Child Welfare,
Community Centers, Day Care, Delinquency
& Criminal Rehabilitation, Domestic Vio-
lence, Emergency Relief, Family Planning,
Family Services, Food/Clothing Distribu-
tion, People with Disabilities, Recreation &
Athletics, Refugee Assistance, Scouts, Sen-
ior Services, Shelters/Homelessness, Volun-
teer Services, YMCA/YWCA/YMHA
/YWHA, Youth Organizations

Grant Types: capital, challenge, fellowship, general support, project, scholarship,
and seed money

Geographic Distribution: primarily Los
Angeles County, CA, with the exception of
higher education grants distributed to a few
select national institutions in engineering
education

GIVING OFFICERS
Albert A. Dorskind: vp, cfo, dir *B* New
York NY 1922 *ED* Cornell Univ 1943; Cor-
nell Univ LLB 1948 *CURR EMPL* chmn:
MCA Devel Co

Robert F. Erburu: dir *B* Ventura CA 1930
ED Univ Southern CA BA 1952; Harvard
Univ JD 1955 *CURR EMPL* chmn, dir:
Times Mirror Co *CORP AFFIL* dir: Tejon
Ranch Co; dir, chmn: Fed Reserve Bank San
Francisco *NONPR AFFIL* chmn: Am News-
paper Publs Assn, Brookings Inst; dir: Inde-
pendent Colls Southern CA, Los Angeles
Festival, Tomas Rivera Ctr; fellow: Am
Acad Arts & Sci; mem: Am Bar Assn, Bus
Counc, Bus Roundtable, CA Bus Round-
table; mem bd dirs: Counc Foreign Rels;
mem trust counc: Natl Gallery Art *PHIL AF-
FIL* trust: Ahmanson Foundation; chmn bd
trust: J. Paul Getty Trust; dir: Carrie Estelle
Doheny Foundation, William and Flora
Hewlett Foundation; vp: Fletcher Jones
Foundation; dir: Pfaffinger Foundation;
chmn, dir: Times Mirror Foundation

Leroy B. Houghton: vp

Joseph G. Hurley: pres, dir *CURR EMPL*
pres: Hurley Grassini & Wrinkle

Edgar R. Jackson: vp, dir

Everett Broadstone Laybourne: vp, dir *B*
Springfield OH 1911 *ED* OH St Univ BA
1932; Harvard Univ JD 1935 *CURR EMPL*
of couns: Baker & McKenzie *CORP AFFIL*
dir: Brouse-Whited Packaging Co, CA Energy Co, Coldwater Investment Co, McBain
Instruments, Pacific Energy Corp, Viking Indus; trust: Brite-Lite Corp *NONPR AFFIL*
chmn: WAIF Inc; mem: Big Ten Univs Club
Southern CA, Los Angeles County Bar
Assn, Roscomare Valley Assn, Selden Soc,
World Aff Counc; trust: Beta Theta Pi Scholastic Fdn Southern CA *CLUB AFFIL* Bel-
Air CC, California, Town Hall

Christine Sisley: secy, exec dir *PHIL AF-
FIL* treas: Patron Saints Foundation

APPLICATION INFORMATION
Initial Approach:

Applicants should submit a preliminary letter outlining the nature of the project for
which funding is sought, the amount requested, and justification for such a request.
The applicant may also phone and speak to
the foundation staff to discuss proposal
ideas.

The preliminary letter should include brief
information on the applying organization
and proof of tax-exempt status.

The staff submits applications to the board
of directors six times each year, in alternate
months beginning in January. For the sake
of fairness, applications are considered in
chronological order. Due to the large
number of proposals which the foundation
receives, applicants should be prepared for a
period of delay leading up to a final decision.

The foundation's staff makes an initial
screening of the application and a decision
is made within two months on whether the
applicant is qualified. The foundation does
not encourage communications with its directors. If the decision is affirmative, more
detailed information may be requested and a
date set for a meeting or on-site visit.

OTHER THINGS TO KNOW
The foundation considers providing challenge funds to launch new programs which
could become self-sustaining, or to secure
equipment and material which will substantially extend and improve existing services.
When applicable, the foundation prefers to
support programs that are innovative, or in-
troduce new ideas, encourage inventiveness,
and develop more productive methods.

PUBLICATIONS
Annual report

GRANTS ANALYSIS
Total Grants: $11,335,392

Number of Grants: 160

Highest Grant: $1,000,000

Average Grant: $70,846

Typical Range: $10,000 to $50,000 and
$100,000 to $250,000

Disclosure Period: 1993

Note: Recent grants are derived from a 1993
annual report.

RECENT GRANTS

Library

1,000,000	Huntington Library, Gardens and Art Gallery, San Marino, CA — for an integrated security and fire protection system
100,000	Library Foundation of Los Angeles, Los Angeles, CA — for Sunday public service hours at the Central Library of Los Angeles

General

1,000,000	City of Hope, Los Angeles, CA — over five years for a new doctors' wing, part of a $200-million capital improvement program
250,000	AIDS Healthcare Foundation, Los Angeles, CA — for construction of the Carl Bean AIDS Care Center in South Central Los Angeles
250,000	Colorado School of Mines Foundation, Golden, CO — for computer equipment to be used in the EPICS program

250,000	Orbis International, New York, NY — to equip an Engineering Technical Training Center on a DC-10 hospital aircraft which provides sight-saving medical services worldwide
250,000	Puente Learning Center, Los Angeles, CA — over two years to construct a state-of-the-art learning center in East Los Angeles

Parvin Foundation, Albert

CONTACT
Phyllis Parvin
President
Albert Parvin Fdn.
c/o Lewis, Joffee and Co.
10880 Wilshire Blvd., Ste. 520
Los Angeles, CA 90024
(310) 475-5676

FINANCIAL SUMMARY
Recent Giving: $160,062 (1993); $214,850 (1992); $397,800 (1991)

Assets: $6,548,368 (1993); $6,214,041 (1992); $6,039,642 (1991)

EIN: 95-2158989

CONTRIBUTIONS SUMMARY
Donor(s): Albert O. Parvin

Typical Recipients: • *Arts & Humanities:* Film & Video, Libraries, Music • *Civic & Public Affairs:* General, Legal Aid, Parades/Festivals, Public Policy • *Education:* Colleges & Universities, Education Funds, Minority Education • *Health:* Alzheimers Disease, Cancer, Emergency/Ambulance Services, Eyes/Blindness, Geriatric Health, Health Organizations, Heart, Hospitals, Medical Research, Prenatal Health Issues • *International:* Foreign Arts Organizations, Foreign Educational Institutions, International Relief Efforts • *Religion:* Jewish Causes, Religious Organizations • *Social Services:* Community Service Organizations, Family Planning, People with Disabilities

Grant Types: endowment and general support

Geographic Distribution: focus on CA

GIVING OFFICERS
Harvey G. Joffe: cfo, dir

Phyllis Parvin: pres, dir

Stanley Parvin: dir

Bernard Silbert: dir

Steven Silbert: dir

APPLICATION INFORMATION
Initial Approach: Send brief letter of inquiry describing program. Include a description of organization, amount requested, purpose of funds sought, recently audited financial statement, and proof of tax-exempt status. There are no deadlines.

GRANTS ANALYSIS
Total Grants: $160,062

Number of Grants: 25

Highest Grant: $60,000

Typical Range: $100 to $60,000

Disclosure Period: 1993

Note: Recent grants are derived from a 1993 Form 990.

RECENT GRANTS
Library

500	Community Library, Los Angeles, CA

General

60,000	University of California Los Angeles, Los Angeles, CA — Rex Kennamer Teaching Fund
60,000	University of Hawaii, Honolulu, HI
25,000	City of Hope, Los Angeles, CA
2,000	ABC's, Los Angeles, CA
2,000	University of California Los Angeles Center on Aging, Los Angeles, CA

Peppers Foundation, Ann

CONTACT
Jack H. Alexander
Secretary
Ann Peppers Fdn.
PO Box 50146
Pasadena, CA 91115
(818) 449-0793

FINANCIAL SUMMARY
Recent Giving: $362,500 (1993); $373,200 (1992); $372,700 (1991)

Assets: $8,087,572 (1993); $7,449,592 (1992); $6,836,817 (1991)

EIN: 95-2114455

CONTRIBUTIONS SUMMARY
Donor(s): the late Ann Peppers

Typical Recipients: • *Arts & Humanities:* Arts Centers, History & Archaeology, Libraries, Museums/Galleries, Music, Public Broadcasting • *Civic & Public Affairs:* Housing, Law & Justice, Public Policy, Women's Affairs • *Education:* Colleges & Universities, Education Funds, Education Reform, Engineering/Technological Education, General, Leadership Training, Literacy, Minority Education, Private Education (Precollege), Public Education (Precollege), Science/Mathematics Education, Special Education, Student Aid, Vocational & Technical Education • *Environment:* General • *Health:* Cancer, Clinics/Medical Centers, Emergency/Ambulance Services, Health Organizations, Kidney, Medical Research, Mental Health, Speech & Hearing • *International:* Health Care/Hospitals, International Affairs • *Religion:* Churches, Religious Organizations, Religious Welfare, Seminaries • *Social Services:* Child Welfare, Domestic Violence, Family Services, Food/Clothing Distribution, Homes, People with Disabilities, Recreation & Athletics, Scouts, Senior Services, Shelters/Homelessness, Volunteer Services, Youth Organizations

Grant Types: conference/seminar, project, and scholarship

Geographic Distribution: limited to the Los Angeles, CA, metropolitan area

GIVING OFFICERS
Jack H. Alexander: secy *PHIL AFFIL* trust: Stark Brothers Nurseries and Orchards Co. Charitable Trust

A. L. Burford, Jr.: vp, dir

W. Paul Colwell: pres, dir

Howard O. Wilson: treas, dir *PHIL AFFIL* dir, treas: Elizabeth M. Falk Foundation; mem bd advs: Sidney Stern Memorial Trust

APPLICATION INFORMATION
Initial Approach: Send brief letter of inquiry describing program or project. There are no deadlines.

Restrictions on Giving: Does not support individuals.

GRANTS ANALYSIS
Total Grants: $362,500

Number of Grants: 65

Highest Grant: $25,000

Typical Range: $1,000 to $17,500

Disclosure Period: 1993

Note: Recent grants are derived from a 1993 Form 990.

RECENT GRANTS
Library

25,000	Pasadena Library, Pasadena, CA

General

22,600	University of Redlands, Redlands, CA — for equipment and professor for Ann Peppers Art Center
20,000	Braille Institute, Santa Barbara, CA
17,500	Pepperdine University, Malibu, CA — for Ann Peppers Scholarship Fund
15,000	California Institute of Technology, Pasadena, CA — for scholarship program
10,000	Walden School, Baltimore, MD — for heating and cooling equipment

Philibosian Foundation, Stephen

CONTACT
Joyce P. Stein
Trustee
Stephen Philibosian Fdn.
46-930 W El Dorado Dr.
Indian Wells, CA 92210-8649
(619) 568-3920

FINANCIAL SUMMARY
Recent Giving: $741,480 (1993); $528,460 (1991); $445,542 (1990)

Assets: $7,741,830 (1993); $7,588,217 (1991); $6,825,212 (1990)

EIN: 23-7029751

CONTRIBUTIONS SUMMARY
Donor(s): Armenian Missionary Association of America

Typical Recipients: • *Arts & Humanities:* Arts Funds, Arts Institutes, Ballet, Libraries, Museums/Galleries, Music, Opera, Theater • *Civic & Public Affairs:* Ethnic Organizations, General, Hispanic Affairs • *Education:* Arts/Humanities Education, Colleges & Universities, Private Education (Precollege) • *Environment:* General • *Health:* Alzheimers Disease, Cancer, Diabetes, Health Organizations, Hospitals • *International:* Foreign Educational Institutions, Missionary/Religious Activities • *Religion:* Churches, Missionary Activities (Domestic), Religious Organizations, Religious Welfare, Seminaries • *Social Services:* Big Brother/Big Sister, Child Welfare, Community Service Organizations, Homes, Youth Organizations

Grant Types: capital, endowment, multi-year/continuing support, and scholarship

Geographic Distribution: focus on CA

GIVING OFFICERS
Nazar Daghlian: trust

Mrs. Richard Danelian: trust

Stephanie Landes: trust

Albert Momjian: trust

Joyce P. Stein: trust

APPLICATION INFORMATION
Initial Approach: The foundation reports it only makes contributions to preselected charitable organizations.

Restrictions on Giving: Does not support individuals or provide loans.

GRANTS ANALYSIS
Total Grants: $741,480

Number of Grants: 117

Highest Grant: $188,500

Typical Range: $500 to $5,000

Disclosure Period: 1993

Note: Recent grants are derived from a 1993 Form 990.

RECENT GRANTS
Library
3,000	Ronald Reagan Presidential Foundation, Los Angeles, CA

General
188,500	Armenian Missionary Association, Paramus, NJ
145,000	Children, Richmond, VA
50,000	All American Fund, Washington, DC
44,000	Armenian Assembly, Washington, DC
35,200	San Miguel Church, Los Angeles, CA

Pickford Foundation, Mary

CONTACT
Edward C. Stotsenberg
President
Mary Pickford Fdn.
9171 Wilshire Blvd., Ste. 512
Beverly Hills, CA 90210
(310) 273-2770

FINANCIAL SUMMARY
Recent Giving: $634,900 (fiscal 1992); $592,780 (fiscal 1990); $608,220 (fiscal 1989)

Assets: $9,447,724 (fiscal 1992); $8,984,047 (fiscal 1990); $9,151,627 (fiscal 1989)

EIN: 95-6093487

CONTRIBUTIONS SUMMARY
Donor(s): the late Mary Pickford Rogers

Typical Recipients: • *Arts & Humanities:* Historic Preservation, Libraries, Museums/Galleries, Music, Public Broadcasting, Theater • *Education:* Colleges & Universities • *Health:* Hospitals, Medical Research, Single-Disease Health Associations • *Social Services:* Homes, People with Disabilities, Senior Services, Shelters/Homelessness, Youth Organizations

Grant Types: endowment, general support, and scholarship

Geographic Distribution: focus on CA

GIVING OFFICERS
Sull Lawrence: secy, dir

Charles B. Rogers: treas, dir

Edward G. Stotsenberg: pres, ceo, dir

APPLICATION INFORMATION
Initial Approach: Send brief letter of inquiry describing program or project. There are no deadlines.

Restrictions on Giving: Does not support individuals.

GRANTS ANALYSIS
Total Grants: $634,900

Highest Grant: $55,000

Typical Range: $10,000 to $55,000

Disclosure Period: fiscal year ending May 31, 1992

Note: No grants list was provided for fiscal 1992. Recent grants are derived from a fiscal 1991 Form 990.

RECENT GRANTS
Library
50,000	Library of Congress, Washington, DC

General
55,000	University of Southern California School of Gerontology, Los Angeles, CA
50,000	Motion Picture Country Home, Woodland Hills, CA
35,000	Jewish Home for the Aging, Reseda, CA

25,000	Claremont McKenna College, Claremont, CA
10,000	University of California Los Angeles Film and Television Archives, Los Angeles, CA

Rosenberg Foundation

CONTACT
Kirke P. Wilson
Executive Director and Secretary
Rosenberg Foundation
47 Kearny St., Ste. 804
San Francisco, CA 94108
(415) 421-6105

FINANCIAL SUMMARY
Recent Giving: $2,000,000 (1995 est.); $1,706,000 (1994); $2,602,000 (1993)

Assets: $35,000,000 (1995 est.); $35,000,000 (1994 approx.); $37,817,118 (1993)

EIN: 94-1186182

CONTRIBUTIONS SUMMARY
Donor(s): The Rosenberg Foundation was established in 1935 with a bequest from Max L. Rosenberg , a native Californian and head of Rosenberg Brothers and Co., a San Francisco dried fruit firm. In 1969, the foundation received an additional bequest from the estate of Mrs. Charlotte S. Mack , one of the foundation's early directors.

Typical Recipients: • *Arts & Humanities:* Libraries • *Civic & Public Affairs:* Asian American Affairs, Business/Free Enterprise, Civil Rights, Economic Development, Economic Policy, Hispanic Affairs, Housing, Law & Justice, Legal Aid, Philanthropic Organizations, Professional & Trade Associations, Public Policy, Rural Affairs, Urban & Community Affairs, Women's Affairs • *Education:* Minority Education • *International:* Human Rights • *Social Services:* Community Service Organizations, Emergency Relief

Grant Types: project

Geographic Distribution: primarily California

GIVING OFFICERS
Phyllis Cook: dir

Benton W. Dial: pres, dir

Robert F. Friedman: vp, dir

Honorable Thelton Eugene Henderson: dir *B* Shreveport LA 1933 *ED* Univ CA Berkeley BA 1956; Univ CA Berkeley JD 1962 *NONPR AFFIL* judge: US Dist Ct Northern Dist CA; mem: Am Bar Assn, Charles Houston Law Assn, Natl Bar Assn

Bill Ong Hing: dir

Herma Hill Kay: dir *B* Orangeburg SC 1934 *ED* Southern Methodist Univ BA 1956; Univ Chicago JD 1959 *NONPR AFFIL* dean, prof: Univ CA Berkeley; mem: Am Academy Arts & Sciences, Am Law Inst, Assn Am Law Schs, Bar US Supreme Court, CA Bar Assn, CA Women Lawyers,

Order Coif; trust, dir: Equal Rights Advocates CA

Leslie L. Luttgens: dir

Mary Seawell Metz: dir *B* Rockhill SC 1937 *ED* Furman Univ BA 1958; Inst Phonetique 1962-1963; Sorbonne 1962-1963; LA St Univ PhD 1966 *CORP AFFIL* dir: Longs Drug Stores, Lucky Stores, Pacific Gas & Electric Co, Pacific Telesis Group, Union Bank *NONPR AFFIL* adv counc: Stanford Grad Sch Bus, Stanford Univ Grad Sch Bus; assoc: Freedom Forum Media Studies Ctr; dean extension: Univ CA Berkeley; dir, mem: World Aff Counc Northern CA; exec comm: Womens Coll Coalition; mem: Assn Independent CA Colls Univs, Bus-Higher Ed Forum, Natl Assn Independent Colls Univs, Phi Beta Kappa, Phi Kappa Phi, Southern Conf Language Teaching, Western Coll Assn, Womens Forum; mem ed bd: Liberal Ed; mem editorial bd: Liberal Ed; trust: Am Conservatory Theater *PHIL AFFIL* dir: S. H. Cowell Foundation

S. Donley Ritchey: treas, dir *B* Derry Township PA 1933 *ED* San Diego St Univ BS 1955; San Diego St Univ MS 1963

Norvel Smith: dir

Kirke P. Wilson: exec dir, secy

APPLICATION INFORMATION
Initial Approach:

Letters of inquiry describing the proposed project, the applying organization, and anticipated budget should be sent to the foundation. If the proposed project falls within the foundation's program priorities, a formal application will be requested.

A formal application should include a written proposal indicating the problem to be addressed; the plan of the project and its activities and goals; names and qualifications of the staff; the lasting significance of the project; anticipated goals and proposed evaluation of the project; future plans for the project; an itemized budget indicating project cost; grant amount requested; other sources of support; length of time for which support is requested and estimated future budgets; and materials describing the organization such as history, experience, a copy of IRS form indicating tax-exempt status, list of board members, and indication of the organization's status on affirmative action in reference to gender and minority groups.

Applications may be submitted any time.

After a formal application has been received by the foundation, a visit and interview will be arranged. There is generally a two- to three-month waiting period before the foundation reviews an application.

Restrictions on Giving: No grants are given for scholarships, endowments, capital purposes, operating purposes, or matching gifts. Grants are also not paid to individuals or for fundraising events.

OTHER THINGS TO KNOW
Approved grants are paid in installments. Organizations receiving support are required to provide the foundation with periodic progress reports and itemized expenditure lists.

The foundation expects unexpended funds to be returned.

PUBLICATIONS
Policies and procedures brochure, and anniversary report

GRANTS ANALYSIS
Total Grants: $2,602,000*

Number of Grants: 56

Highest Grant: $112,500

Average Grant: $46,464

Typical Range: $5,000 to $55,000

Disclosure Period: 1993

Note: Figures are based on grants authorized for 1993. Recent grants are derived from a 1993 annual report.

RECENT GRANTS

Library
16,000	Foundation Center, New York, NY — national program

General
112,500	Mexican American Legal Defense and Educational Fund (MALDEF), Los Angeles, CA — California Language Rights Program
109,250	Rural Community Assistance Corporation, Sacramento, CA — San Diego Farmworker Housing project
106,000	Immigrant Legal Resource Center, San Francisco, CA — immigrant children's projects
100,000	Legal Services of Northern California, Sacramento, CA — Child Support Enforcement project
98,000	Asian Pacific American Legal Center of Southern California, Los Angeles, CA — language rights project

Rosenberg, Jr. Family Foundation, Louise and Claude

CONTACT
Claude Rosenberg, Jr.
Secretary
Louise and Claude Rosenberg, Jr. Family Fdn.
2465 Pacific Ave.
San Francisco, CA 94115
(415) 921-2465

FINANCIAL SUMMARY
Recent Giving: $823,563 (fiscal 1993); $804,900 (fiscal 1992); $680,895 (fiscal 1991)

Assets: $14,111,377 (fiscal 1993); $13,429,794 (fiscal 1992); $12,362,138 (fiscal 1991)

Gifts Received: $1,200,050 (fiscal 1993); $1,702,096 (fiscal 1992); $2,665,169 (fiscal 1991)

Fiscal Note: In fiscal 1993, contributions were received from Claude and Louise Rosenberg, Jr.
EIN: 94-3031132

CONTRIBUTIONS SUMMARY
Typical Recipients: • *Arts & Humanities:* Arts Appreciation, Arts Centers, Arts Outreach, Ballet, Dance, Ethnic & Folk Arts, Libraries, Literary Arts, Museums/Galleries, Music, Opera, Performing Arts, Public Broadcasting, Theater • *Civic & Public Affairs:* Community Foundations, Economic Development, General, Municipalities/Towns, Philanthropic Organizations, Public Policy, Urban & Community Affairs, Women's Affairs, Zoos/Aquariums • *Education:* Afterschool/Enrichment Programs, Arts/Humanities Education, Business Education, Colleges & Universities, Continuing Education, Education Funds, Elementary Education (Public), General, Private Education (Precollege), Public Education (Precollege), School Volunteerism, Secondary Education (Private), Secondary Education (Public), Student Aid • *Environment:* General, Wildlife Protection • *Health:* Cancer, Clinics/Medical Centers, Diabetes, Eyes/Blindness, Health Organizations, Hospitals, Medical Research, Multiple Sclerosis, Research/Studies Institutes, Single-Disease Health Associations • *International:* Foreign Educational Institutions, Human Rights, International Environmental Issues, International Peace & Security Issues, Missionary/Religious Activities • *Religion:* Jewish Causes, Synagogues/Temples • *Social Services:* Camps, Child Welfare, Community Centers, Family Services, Food/Clothing Distribution, People with Disabilities, Recreation & Athletics, United Funds/United Ways, Volunteer Services

Grant Types: general support and research
Geographic Distribution: focus on San Francisco, CA

GIVING OFFICERS
John P. Levin, Jr.: dir

Claude N. Rosenberg, Jr.: secy, dir *CURR EMPL* ptnr: RCM Capital Mgmt *PHIL AFFIL* chmn, dir: Rosenberg Capital Management Charitable Fund and Welfare Trust

Louise J. Rosenberg: pres, dir

APPLICATION INFORMATION
Initial Approach: The foundation reports no specific application guidelines. There are no deadlines.

GRANTS ANALYSIS
Total Grants: $823,563

Number of Grants: 68

Highest Grant: $100,000

Typical Range: $500 to $10,000

Disclosure Period: fiscal year ending October 31, 1993

Note: Recent grants are derived from a fiscal 1993 Form 990.

RECENT GRANTS

Library
100,000	New Main Library, San Francisco, CA

General

85,436	Developmental Studies Center, San Ramon, CA
75,000	Jewish Family and Children's Services, San Francisco, CA — for Rosenberg School Emigre Resettlement 1993/94
50,000	Jewish Family and Children's Services, San Francisco, CA — for shelter
50,000	Jewish Home for the Aged, San Francisco, CA
50,000	Stanford University, Stanford, CA

Ryan Foundation, David Claude

CONTACT
Jerome D. Ryan
President
David Claude Ryan Fdn.
PO Box 6409
San Diego, CA 92166
(619) 291-7311

FINANCIAL SUMMARY
Recent Giving: $569,277 (1992); $205,278 (1989); $160,942 (1988)

Assets: $2,291,018 (1992); $2,680,257 (1989); $2,525,638 (1988)

Gifts Received: $120,000 (1992); $70,000 (1989); $80,000 (1988)

Fiscal Note: In 1992, contributions were received from Gladys B. Ryan ($85,000) and Jerome D. and Anne M. Ryan ($35,000).

EIN: 95-6051140

CONTRIBUTIONS SUMMARY
Donor(s): Jerome D. Ryan, Gladys B. Ryan

Typical Recipients: • *Arts & Humanities:* Libraries, Museums/Galleries, Public Broadcasting • *Civic & Public Affairs:* General, Legal Aid, Zoos/Aquariums • *Education:* Colleges & Universities, General, Medical Education, Minority Education, Private Education (Precollege) • *Health:* Emergency/Ambulance Services • *International:* Health Care/Hospitals, International Organizations, International Relief Efforts • *Religion:* Bible Study/Translation, Churches, Ministries, Missionary Activities (Domestic), Religious Organizations, Religious Welfare • *Social Services:* Camps, Child Welfare, Community Service Organizations, Food/Clothing Distribution, People with Disabilities, Recreation & Athletics, United Funds/United Ways, Youth Organizations

Grant Types: multiyear/continuing support

Geographic Distribution: focus on CA, with emphasis on San Diego

GIVING OFFICERS
Gladys B. Ryan: vp, secy, treas

Jerome D. Ryan: pres

Stephen M. Ryan: vp, asst secy

APPLICATION INFORMATION
Initial Approach: Include a description of organization, amount requested, purpose of funds sought, recently audited financial statement, and proof of tax-exempt status. There are no deadlines.

Restrictions on Giving: Does not support individuals.

GRANTS ANALYSIS
Total Grants: $569,277

Number of Grants: 45

Highest Grant: $120,000

Typical Range: $500 to $6,000

Disclosure Period: 1992

Note: Recent grants are derived from a 1992 Form 990.

RECENT GRANTS
Library

500	Ryan Aeronautical Library, San Diego, CA

General

120,000	Christian Unified Schools of San Diego, San Diego, CA
99,114	Mission Aviation Fellowship, Redlands, CA
80,272	EAA Aviation Center
69,667	San Diego Rescue Mission, San Diego, CA
33,334	University of Southern California School of Medicine, Los Angeles, CA

Salvatori Foundation, Henry

CONTACT
Henry Salvatori
President
Henry Salvatori Fdn.
1901 Ave. of the Stars, Ste. 230
Los Angeles, CA 90067
(310) 277-3444

FINANCIAL SUMMARY
Recent Giving: $1,950,750 (fiscal 1994); $2,118,843 (fiscal 1992); $606,275 (fiscal 1991)

Assets: $4,415,530 (fiscal 1994); $7,199,181 (fiscal 1992); $8,406,891 (fiscal 1991)

Gifts Received: $8,711,273 (fiscal 1991)

Fiscal Note: In fiscal 1991, contributions were received from Henry Salvatori.

EIN: 95-4287740

CONTRIBUTIONS SUMMARY
Donor(s): Henry Salvatori the late Gail Sarver and Sarver, Inc.

Typical Recipients: • *Arts & Humanities:* Historic Preservation, History & Archaeology, Libraries, Public Broadcasting • *Civic & Public Affairs:* Economic Policy, General, Law & Justice, Legal Aid, Parades/Festivals, Philanthropic Organizations, Professional & Trade Associations, Public Policy • *Education:* Colleges & Universities, Education Funds, Elementary Education (Public), Faculty Development, General, Religious Education, Social Sciences Education, Student Aid • *International:* International Affairs, International Relations

Grant Types: conference/seminar and general support

Geographic Distribution: giving limited to Osborne County, KS

GIVING OFFICERS
Charles Kesler: dir

Edwin Meese III: dir

Henry Salvatori: pres *B* Rome Italy 1901 *ED* Columbia Univ MS; Univ PA BS *NONPR AFFIL* mem: Am Assn Petroleum Geologists, Am Geophysical Union, Am Petroleum Inst, Seismological Soc Am, Soc Exploration Geophysicists; trust: Univ Southern CA

Frederick E. Vandenberg: secy, treas

APPLICATION INFORMATION
Initial Approach: Application form not required for scholarships. Submit one proposal. Deadline is April 1 for scholarships and December 31 for grants. Board meeting dates vary.

Restrictions on Giving: Does not provide grants to individuals.

PUBLICATIONS
Informational brochure

GRANTS ANALYSIS
Total Grants: $1,950,750

Number of Grants: 18

Highest Grant: $300,000

Typical Range: $25,000 to $275,000

Disclosure Period: fiscal year ending June 30, 1994

Note: Recent grants are derived from a fiscal 1994 Form 990.

RECENT GRANTS
Library

250,000	Ronald Reagan Presidential Library, Simi Valley, CA — interactive computer

General

300,000	Hillsdale College, Hillsdale, MI — endow chair on American values
275,000	Intercollegiate Studies Institute, Bryn Mawr, PA — teacher training
200,000	Heritage Foundation, Washington, DC — fellowship and awards for exhibiting American values
200,000	James Madison Foundation, Washington, DC — fellowship
175,000	Claremont Institute, Claremont, CA — teacher seminars

San Diego Gas & Electric

Revenue: $1.98 billion
Employees: 4,166
Headquarters: San Diego, CA
SIC Major Group: Electric & Other Services
Combined

CONTACT
Molly Cartmill
Corporate Contribution Manager
San Diego Gas & Electric
PO Box 1831
San Diego, CA 92112
(619) 696-4299

FINANCIAL SUMMARY
Recent Giving: $1,600,000 (1995 est.);
$1,600,000 (1994 approx.); $1,600,000
(1993 approx.)

Fiscal Note: Company gives directly. Figure for 1993 does not include $18,650 distributed separately. Above figures exclude nonmonetary support.

CONTRIBUTIONS SUMMARY
Typical Recipients: • *Arts & Humanities:*
Arts Centers, Arts Festivals, Arts Funds,
Arts Institutes, Community Arts, Dance, Ethnic & Folk Arts, Historic Preservation, Libraries, Museums/Galleries, Music, Opera,
Performing Arts, Theater, Visual Arts
• *Civic & Public Affairs:* Economic Development, Employment/Job Training, Legal Aid,
Professional & Trade Associations, Safety,
Zoos/Aquariums • *Education:* Arts/Humanities Education, Business Education, Colleges & Universities, Economic Education,
Education Funds, Elementary Education (Private), Engineering/Technological Education,
Health & Physical Education, Literacy,
Medical Education, Minority Education, Preschool Education, Science/Mathematics Education • *Environment:* General • *Health:*
Geriatric Health, Health Organizations, Hospices, Hospitals, Medical Research, Mental
Health, Single-Disease Health Associations
• *Science:* Observatories & Planetariums,
Science Exhibits & Fairs, Scientific Organizations • *Social Services:* Child Welfare,
Community Centers, Community Service Organizations, Counseling, Day Care, Delinquency & Criminal Rehabilitation,
Emergency Relief, Family Services,
Food/Clothing Distribution, People with Disabilities, Recreation & Athletics, Senior
Services, Shelters/Homelessness, Substance
Abuse, United Funds/United Ways, Volunteer Services, Youth Organizations

Grant Types: capital, conference/seminar,
employee matching gifts, matching, and project

Nonmonetary Support: $820,000 (1994);
$35,000 (1992)

Nonmonetary Support Types: donated
equipment, loaned employees, and workplace solicitation

Note: Nonmonetary support is provided by
the company. Company-sponsored volunteer
programs include the Employees Contribution Club and Ambassadors Program, which
raise over $750,000 through the efforts of
more than 150 employees serving in leadership roles on the boards of non-profits.

Geographic Distribution: primarily at headquarters and operating locations

Operating Locations: CA (Carlsbad, Chula
Vista, Coronado, Encina, Escondido, Irvine,
San Diego, San Onofre, Santa Ana, South
Bay)

CORP. OFFICERS
Thomas Alexander Page: *B* Niagara Falls
NY 1933 *ED* Purdue Univ BS 1955; Purdue
Univ MS 1963 *CURR EMPL* chmn, pres,
ceo: San Diego Gas & Electric *CORP AFFIL* chmn: Pacific Diversified Capital Co,
Wahlco Environmental Sys

GIVING OFFICERS
Molly Cartmill: *CURR EMPL* corp contributions mgr: San Diego Gas & Electric

APPLICATION INFORMATION
Initial Approach: *Initial Contact:* brief letter of inquiry and request for application *Include Information On:* brief description of
proposed program and goal; amount and purpose of funds requested; name, address,
phone number, and contact person; current
operating budget; description of target population; evaluative criteria; certification of
tax-exempt status; list of officers and board
of directors; description of volunteer involvement, including SD&G employees
Deadlines: none *Note:* All requests must be
made in writing.

Restrictions on Giving: The company does
not provide funds for general operating expenses; travel expenses; loans or loan guarantees; debt reduction or past operating
deficits; liquidating an organization; reducing or donating the cost of any gas or electric service that other customers must pay
(except for customers who are helped
through our winter assistance program);
multi-year pledges; advertising (the company does, however, appreciate complimentary advertising that results from their
sponsorship of a specific program or project).

OTHER THINGS TO KNOW
The company provides for corporate and regional contributions. Corporate contributions dollars exist to support
communitywide organizations and activities
that benefit citizens throughout the markets
where they do business. Regional contributions dollars exist to support organizations
and activities that benefit citizens living
within certain geographic areas of the community.

There is no deadline for requests. The company makes decisions on a monthly basis all
year long.

GRANTS ANALYSIS
Typical Range: $1,000 to $50,000

Saroyan Foundation, William

CONTACT
Robert Setrakian
Trustee
William Saroyan Fdn.
1905 Baker St.
San Francisco, CA 94115
(415) 563-4444

FINANCIAL SUMMARY
Recent Giving: $1,005 (fiscal 1992); $5,017
(fiscal 1988)

Assets: $2,393,697 (fiscal 1992);
$2,323,188 (fiscal 1991); $2,323,138 (fiscal
1990)

EIN: 94-1657684

CONTRIBUTIONS SUMMARY
Donor(s): William Saroyan

Typical Recipients: • *Arts & Humanities:*
Libraries • *Civic & Public Affairs:* Ethnic Organizations, General

Grant Types: general support

GIVING OFFICERS
William Abrahams: trust *PHIL AFFIL* executor, trust: Lillian Hellman Fund

Dan Dibert: trust

Anthony Melchior Frank: trust *B* Berlin
Germany 1931 *ED* Dartmouth Coll BA
1953; Dartmouth Coll MBA 1954 *CORP AFFIL* chmn, dir: CA Housing Fin Agency; dir:
Allianz Ins Co, Am Fed Home Loan Bank
San Francisco; trust, treas: Blue Shield CA
NONPR AFFIL bd overseers: Tuck Sch;
chmn bd Visitors: Univ CA Los Angeles Sch
Architecture & Planning; mem: Chief Execs
Org, World Bus Forum; trust: Am Conservatory Theater

Jennifer Larson: trust

Haig G. Mardikian: trust

Robert Setrakian: trust

APPLICATION INFORMATION
Initial Approach: The foundation requests
applications be made in writing. There are
no deadlines.

GRANTS ANALYSIS
Total Grants: $1,005

Number of Grants: 2

Highest Grant: $1,000

Disclosure Period: fiscal year ending September 30, 1992

Note: Recent grants are derived from a Fiscal 1992 Form 990.

RECENT GRANTS

General
1,000   Kalfayan Center for Armenians
Armenian Research Center,
Arcadia, CA

Schwab & Co., Inc., Charles / Schwab Corp. Foundation, Charles

Parent Company: The Charles Schwab Corp.
Revenue: $965.01 million
Parent Employees: 6,320
Headquarters: San Francisco, CA
SIC Major Group: Security Brokers & Dealers

CONTACT
Karen Ens
Manager, Community Relations
Charles Schwab & Co., Inc.
101 Montgomery St.
San Francisco, CA 94104
(415) 627-8415

FINANCIAL SUMMARY
Recent Giving: $2,500,000 (1995 est.);
$2,000,000 (1994 approx.); $1,500,000
(1993 approx.)

Fiscal Note: The company gives directly
and through its foundation. Above figures
exclude nonmonetary support.

CONTRIBUTIONS SUMMARY
Typical Recipients: • *Arts & Humanities:*
Arts Associations & Councils, Community
Arts, Libraries, Museums/Galleries, Music,
Opera, Performing Arts, Public Broadcasting • *Civic & Public Affairs:* Employ-
ment/Job Training, Nonprofit Management,
Philanthropic Organizations, Urban & Community Affairs, Zoos/Aquariums • *Education:* Business Education, Economic
Education, Public Education (Precollege) •
Environment: General • *Health:* Single-Disease Health Associations • *Social Services:*
Animal Protection, Community Service Organizations, Emergency Relief, Family Services, Food/Clothing Distribution, People
with Disabilities, Shelters/Homelessness,
United Funds/United Ways, Volunteer Services, Youth Organizations

Grant Types: capital, employee matching
gifts, general support, operating expenses,
and project

Note: Employee matching gift ratio: 2 to 1

Nonmonetary Support: $50,000 (1993)

Nonmonetary Support Types: in-kind services

Note: In-kind services consist of printing.

Geographic Distribution: primarily headquarters and in geographic areas where there
are Schwab branch offices (approximately
200 locations nationwide)

Operating Locations: AZ (Phoenix), CA
(San Francisco), CO (Denver), FL (Orlando), IN (Indianapolis)

CORP. OFFICERS
David S. Pottruck: *B* 1948 *ED* Univ PA BA
1970; Univ PA MBA 1972 *CURR EMPL*
pres, ceo, dir: Charles Schwab & Co Inc
CORP AFFIL pres, coo, dir: Schwab Holdings Inc

Charles R. Schwab: *B* Woodland CA 1937
ED Stanford Univ MBA 1961 *CURR EMPL*
chmn, dir: Charles Schwab & Co Inc *CORP*
AFFIL chmn, ceo, dir: Charles Schwab &
Co Inc; dir: The Gap Inc, Charles Schwab
Family of Funds, Schwab Investments *PHIL*
AFFIL dir: Charles and Helen Schwab Foun-
dation

Lawrence J. Stupski: *B* 1945 *ED* Yale
Univ JD 1970 *CURR EMPL* vchmn: Charles
Schwab & Co Inc *CORP AFFIL* vchmn:
Schwab Holdings Inc

GIVING OFFICERS
Charles R. Schwab: chmn *CURR EMPL*
chmn, dir: Charles Schwab & Co Inc *PHIL*
AFFIL dir: Charles and Helen Schwab Foundation (see above)

APPLICATION INFORMATION
Initial Approach: *Initial Contact:* write to
company for guidelines, then send brief letter and full proposal *Include Information
On:* description of the organization, purpose
of funds sought, recently audited financial
statements, list of board members, list of current funding sources, and proof of tax-exempt status *Deadlines:* none

Restrictions on Giving: Does not provide
capital, challenge, or seed grants; purchase
tickets to fundraisers, banquets, awards dinners, etc.; or purchase advertising in print or
radio.

OTHER THINGS TO KNOW
The Charles Schwab Corporation Foundation was created in December 1993.

PUBLICATIONS
Program guidelines

GRANTS ANALYSIS
Typical Range: $1,000 to $5,000

Scott Foundation, Virginia Steele

CONTACT
Charles Newton
President
Virginia Steele Scott Fdn.
1151 Oxford Rd.
San Marino, CA 91108
(818) 405-2226

FINANCIAL SUMMARY
Recent Giving: $2,300,000 (fiscal 1993);
$375,666 (fiscal 1992); $246,267 (fiscal
1991)

Assets: $9,200,817 (fiscal 1993);
$9,242,422 (fiscal 1992); $8,873,773 (fiscal
1991)

Gifts Received: $5,687,554 (fiscal 1991);
$147,180 (fiscal 1990); $135,141 (fiscal
1989)

Fiscal Note: 1991 contributions were received from Grace C. Scott Trust.

EIN: 23-7365076

CONTRIBUTIONS SUMMARY
Donor(s): the late Virginia Steele Scott and
Grace C. Scott

Typical Recipients: • *Arts & Humanities:*
Arts Associations & Councils, Arts Centers,
Arts Institutes, Community Arts, Libraries,
Museums/Galleries, Music, Performing Arts
• *Civic & Public Affairs:* Botanical Gar-
dens/Parks • *Education:* Arts/Humanities
Education

Grant Types: general support

Geographic Distribution: focus on
Pasadena, CA

GIVING OFFICERS
Blake Reynolds Nevius: dir *B* Winona MN
1916 *ED* Antioch Coll BA 1938; Univ Chi-
cago MA 1941; Univ Chicago PhD 1947
NONPR AFFIL mem: Modern Language
Assn; premeritus: Univ CA Los Angeles

Charles Newton: pres, dir

Henry J. Tanner: fin adv

Robert R. Wark: dir *B* Edmonton Canada
1924 *ED* Univ Alberta BA 1944; Univ Alberta MA 1946; Harvard Univ AM 1949;
Harvard Univ PhD 1952 *NONPR AFFIL*
mem: Coll Art Assn Am

APPLICATION INFORMATION
Initial Approach: The foundation has no
formal grant application procedure or application form. Deadline is September 30.

Restrictions on Giving: Limited to visual
and performing arts in Pasadena and Los Angeles.

GRANTS ANALYSIS
Total Grants: $2,300,000

Number of Grants: 9

Highest Grant: $2,247,500

Typical Range: $2,500 to $10,000

Disclosure Period: fiscal year ending June
30, 1993

Note: Recent grants are derived from a fiscal 1993 Form 990.

RECENT GRANTS

Library
2,247,500   Henry E. Huntington Library
            and Art Gallery, San Marino,
            CA

General
10,000   Art Center College of Design,
            Pasadena, CA
2,500   Descanso Gardens Guild, La
            Canada, CA

Seaver Charitable Trust, Richard C.

CONTACT
Myron E. Harpole
Trustee
Richard C. Seaver Charitable Trust
350 S Figueroa St., Ste. 270
Los Angeles, CA 90071
(213) 624-1311

FINANCIAL SUMMARY
Recent Giving: $451,500 (1993); $231,000
(1992); $189,000 (1991)

Assets: $2,733,761 (1993); $2,533,224 (1992); $3,372,773 (1991)

EIN: 95-3311102

CONTRIBUTIONS SUMMARY

Typical Recipients: • *Arts & Humanities:* Arts Centers, Arts Institutes, Dance, General, Historic Preservation, Libraries, Museums/Galleries, Music, Opera, Performing Arts, Theater • *Civic & Public Affairs:* Botanical Gardens/Parks, Clubs, General, Hispanic Affairs, Municipalities/Towns, Public Policy, Safety • *Education:* Arts/Humanities Education, Colleges & Universities, Education Reform, Elementary Education (Private), General, Legal Education, Private Education (Precollege), Religious Education, Science/Mathematics Education, Secondary Education (Private) • *Health:* Cancer, Eyes/Blindness, Hospices, Hospitals, Medical Research, Research/Studies Institutes • *International:* International Peace & Security Issues, International Relief Efforts, Missionary/Religious Activities • *Religion:* Churches, Religious Organizations • *Social Services:* Child Welfare, Community Service Organizations, Family Services, People with Disabilities, Recreation & Athletics

Grant Types: general support

Geographic Distribution: focus on CA

GIVING OFFICERS

Myron E. Harpole: trust *B* 1927 *ED* Univ CA Berkeley BA 1947; Harvard Univ JD 1949 *CURR EMPL* secy, dir: W & F Mfg *CORP AFFIL* vp, dir: Bristol Indus, H C Merchandisers Inc *PHIL AFFIL* asst secy, dir: Seaver Institute

APPLICATION INFORMATION

Initial Approach: The foundation requests applications be made in writing. There are no deadlines.

GRANTS ANALYSIS

Total Grants: $451,500

Number of Grants: 47

Highest Grant: $25,000

Typical Range: $1,000 to $20,000

Disclosure Period: 1993

Note: Recent grants are derived from a 1993 Form 990.

RECENT GRANTS

Library

4,000	Huntington Library and Art Gallery, San Marino, CA
2,500	Library Foundation of Los Angeles, Los Angeles, CA

General

20,000	Curtis School, Los Angeles, CA
15,000	Al Wooten Jr. Youth Adult Cultural Education Center, Los Angeles, CA
10,000	Doheny Eye Institute, Los Angeles, CA
10,000	Harvard Westlake School, Los Angeles, CA
10,000	Teach for America, Los Angeles, CA

Seaver Institute

CONTACT

Richard W. Call
President and CEO
Seaver Institute
800 W 6th St., Ste. 1410
Los Angeles, CA 90017
(213) 688-7550

FINANCIAL SUMMARY

Recent Giving: $1,600,000 (fiscal 1995 est.); $1,567,316 (fiscal 1994 approx.); $1,378,415 (fiscal 1993)

Assets: $37,000,000 (fiscal 1995 est.); $36,944,259 (fiscal 1994); $36,600,196 (fiscal 1993)

Gifts Received: $66,320 (fiscal 1993); $117,700 (fiscal 1992); $47,256 (fiscal 1991)

Fiscal Note: The foundation receives annual funding from trusts established by Mr. Seaver.

EIN: 95-6054764

CONTRIBUTIONS SUMMARY

Donor(s): The Seaver Institute was created in 1955 by the late Frank R. Seaver . It is the recipient of annual funds under other trusts established by Mr. Seaver.

Typical Recipients: • *Arts & Humanities:* Arts Associations & Councils, Arts Funds, Arts Institutes, General, Libraries, Museums/Galleries, Music • *Civic & Public Affairs:* Ethnic Organizations, General, Public Policy, Zoos/Aquariums • *Education:* Arts/Humanities Education, Business Education, Colleges & Universities, Education Reform, Engineering/Technological Education, International Studies, Private Education (Precollege), Public Education (Precollege), Science/Mathematics Education, Secondary Education (Private) • *Environment:* Resource Conservation, Wildlife Protection • *Health:* Children's Health/Hospitals, Eyes/Blindness, Hospitals, Medical Research, Single-Disease Health Associations • *Religion:* Churches • *Science:* Science Museums, Scientific Organizations, Scientific Research • *Social Services:* Child Welfare, Recreation & Athletics, Substance Abuse, United Funds/United Ways, Volunteer Services, Youth Organizations

Grant Types: project and research

Geographic Distribution: national

GIVING OFFICERS

Dr. David Alexander: dir

Richard Allen Archer: dir *B* Los Angeles CA 1927 *ED* Univ Southern CA BS 1949 *CURR EMPL* chmn: Jardine Emett & Chandler *CORP AFFIL* vchmn bd, dir: Jardine Ins Brokers

Richard W. Call, MD: pres, ceo, dir *B* Los Angeles CA 1924 *ED* Stanford Univ AB 1945; Stanford Univ MD 1947; Harvard Univ 1953 *CORP AFFIL* dir: Execs Svc Corp, TCW Galileo Emerging, TCW Investment Funds *NONPR AFFIL* bd govs, trust: Mus Natural History; dir: Santa Anita Fdn;

fellow: Am Coll Physicians; trust, chmn, emeritus: Childrens Hosp

Cameron Cooper: dir

Victoria Seaver Dean: dir

John F. Hall: vp, treas, dir *PHIL AFFIL* secy, trust: Bloedel Foundation

Myron E. Harpole: asst secy, dir *B* 1927 *ED* Univ CA Berkeley BA 1947; Harvard Univ JD 1949 *CURR EMPL* secy, dir: W & F Mfg *CORP AFFIL* vp, dir: Bristol Indus, H C Merchandisers Inc *PHIL AFFIL* trust: Richard C. Seaver Charitable Trust

Leroy Edward Hood: dir *B* Missoula MT 1938 *ED* CA Inst Tech BS 1960; Johns Hopkins Univ MD 1964; CA Inst Tech Phd 1968 *NONPR AFFIL* dir: Natl Science Fdn Science & Tech Ctr; mem: Am Academy Arts & Sciences, Am Assn Advancement Science, Am Assn Immunologists, Natl Academy Sciences, Sigma Xi

Raymond Jallow: dir *B* Baghdad Iraq 1933 *ED* Univ Baghdad BA 1953; Univ Southern CA MA 1956; Univ CA Los Angeles PhD 1966 *CURR EMPL* chmn: Jallow Intl Ltd

Christopher Seaver: secy, dir

Martha Seaver: dir

Richard Carlton Seaver: chmn, dir *B* Los Angeles CA 1922 *ED* Pomona Coll BA 1946; Univ CA Berkeley JD 1949 *CURR EMPL* chmn: Hydril Co *CORP AFFIL* dir: DeAnza Land & Leisure Corp *NONPR AFFIL* dir: Episcopal Church Fdn, Hosp Good Samaritan; mem: Am Bar Assn, CA Bar Assn, Los Angeles County Bar Assn; trust: Doheny Eye Inst, Episcopal Diocesan Investment Trust, Harvard Westlake Sch, Los Angeles County Mus Natural History, Pomona Coll; vp, dir: Los Angeles Music Ctr Opera Assn *CLUB AFFIL* Los Angeles, Los Angeles YC, Newport Harbor YC, St Franis YC *PHIL AFFIL* trust: Roy E. Thomas Medical Foundation

APPLICATION INFORMATION

Initial Approach:

Proposals should be addressed to the president of the trust.

Applicants seeking support from the trust should submit a letter of inquiry and one copy of a brief proposal. This should include a description of the project, time period needed for completion and funding, amount needed, budget, and any other pertinent information.

There are no deadlines for submitting proposals.

Preliminary reviews are conducted by the president, who then sends favorable proposals to the benefactions committee for final review.

Restrictions on Giving: No grants are made to individuals.

GRANTS ANALYSIS

Total Grants: $1,378,415

Number of Grants: 79

Highest Grant: $159,360

Average Grant: $17,448

Typical Range: $1,000 to $100,000

Disclosure Period: fiscal year ending June 30, 1993

Note: Recent grants are derived from a fiscal 1993 grants list.

RECENT GRANTS

Library

5,000	Huntington Library, Pasadena, CA

General

159,360	Johns Hopkins University, Baltimore, MD
150,000	Massachusetts Institute of Technology, Cambridge, MA — silicon retinal implant
121,275	Woods Hole Oceanographic Institute, Woodshore, MA
119,658	University of Colorado, Denver, CO
100,000	National Geographic Society, Washington, DC

Sierra Pacific Industries / Sierra Pacific Foundation

Sales: $700.0 million
Employees: 2,700
Headquarters: Redding, CA
SIC Major Group: Lumber & Wood Products

CONTACT
Becky Riley
Trustee
Sierra Pacific Foundation
PO Box 496028
Redding, CA 96049
(916) 378-8000

FINANCIAL SUMMARY
Recent Giving: $115,124 (fiscal 1993); $139,018 (fiscal 1992); $126,940 (fiscal 1991)

Assets: $1,626,486 (fiscal 1993); $1,622,207 (fiscal 1992); $1,633,300 (fiscal 1990)

EIN: 94-2574178

CONTRIBUTIONS SUMMARY
Typical Recipients: • *Arts & Humanities:* Arts Associations & Councils, Libraries, Museums/Galleries, Music, Public Broadcasting • *Civic & Public Affairs:* Business/Free Enterprise, Clubs, General, Parades/Festivals, Rural Affairs, Safety, Urban & Community Affairs, Women's Affairs • *Education:* Colleges & Universities, General, Private Education (Precollege), Secondary Education (Public), Student Aid • *Environment:* General, Wildlife Protection • *Health:* Cancer, Health Organizations, Hospices, Medical Research, Nutrition, Single-Disease Health Associations • *Social Services:* Child Welfare, Recreation & Athletics, Senior Services, Shelters/Homelessness, United Funds/United Ways, Youth Organizations

Grant Types: employee matching gifts, general support, and scholarship

CORP. OFFICERS
A. A. Emmerson: *CURR EMPL* pres, ceo, dir: Sierra Pacific Indus

GIVING OFFICERS
Carolyn Emmerson Dietz: treas
Ida Emmerson: pres
Becky Riley: trust
Richard L. Smith: vp

APPLICATION INFORMATION
Initial Approach: Applications should be submitted upon request. Application deadline is March 30.

GRANTS ANALYSIS
Total Grants: $115,124
Number of Grants: 113
Highest Grant: $5,450
Typical Range: $100 to $1,000
Disclosure Period: fiscal year ending June 30, 1993
Note: Recent grants are derived from a fiscal 1993 Form 990.

RECENT GRANTS

Library

1,000	Shingletown Library, Shingletown, CA

General

5,000	Hayfork Volunteer Fire Department, Hayfork, CA
2,664	Trinity County Junior Livestock Committee
2,204	Crater High School, Medford, OR
2,164	Humboldt Buggy Association
2,000	Tehama County Senior Citizens

Skaggs Foundation, L. J. and Mary C.

CONTACT
Philip M. Jelley
Secretary and Foundation Manager
L. J. and Mary C. Skaggs Foundation
1221 Broadway, 21st Fl.
Oakland, CA 94612
(510) 451-3300
Note: The foundation reports that it is still in operation, but grant making is suspended.

FINANCIAL SUMMARY
Recent Giving: $1,299,710 (1994); $1,298,745 (1993); $1,558,245 (1992)

Assets: $2,100,000 (1994 est.); $3,200,000 (1993 approx.); $4,428,028 (1992)

Gifts Received: $480,000 (1994 est.); $480,000 (1993); $480,000 (1992)

Fiscal Note: The foundation has received contributions from the L. J. Skaggs Foundation Trust.

EIN: 94-6174113

CONTRIBUTIONS SUMMARY
Donor(s): The foundation was established in 1967 by L. J. Skaggs and Mary C. Skaggs to provide a funding source for small innovative projects. Grants initially were made in the area of medical research and projects related to diabetes. Following Mr. Skaggs' death in 1970 and an increase in assets due to bequests from his estate, the foundation broadened the scope of its interests.

Typical Recipients: • *Arts & Humanities:* Arts Associations & Councils, Arts Centers, Arts Festivals, Historic Preservation, History & Archaeology, Libraries, Museums/Galleries, Music, Opera, Performing Arts, Theater • *Civic & Public Affairs:* Botanical Gardens/Parks • *Education:* Colleges & Universities • *Environment:* General, Resource Conservation, Wildlife Protection • *Health:* Diabetes • *International:* Foreign Arts Organizations, Foreign Educational Institutions, Health Care/Hospitals

Grant Types: project and research

Geographic Distribution: principally to national organizations; theater grants limited to Northern California

GIVING OFFICERS
Donald D. Crawford, Jr.: treas, mem bd dirs B Long Beach CA 1936
Jayne C. Davis: vp, mem bd dirs
Philip M. Jelley: secy, fdn mgr, mem bd dirs
David Knight: program dir, asst secy
Catherine L. O'Brien: vp, mem bd dirs
Mary C. Skaggs: pres, mem bd dirs

APPLICATION INFORMATION
Initial Contact: Applicants should submit a brief letter of intent describing the organization, and listing the amount requested, purpose for which funds are sought, income and expense information, and key personnel. The foundation staff will then determine whether or not a full proposal is appropriate. Mass-mailed, photocopied, or printed funding requests are not given serious consideration.

Include Information On: A full proposal should include a history and background of the organization, purpose for grant, method for achieving goals and tasks, amount requested, total budget, and an explanation of how funds will be used. Applicants also must include a listing of other committed and anticipated funding, statement illustrating the experience of personnel involved with the program, listing of the organization's board of trustees with professional affiliations, and a copy of the IRS tax-exempt status letter.

Deadlines: Letters of intent are accepted between January 15 and June 1 from applicants interested in being considered for the following year's funding. Full invited proposals must be received by September 1 for consideration at the November board meeting.

Review Process: The foundation evaluates proposals according to various criteria. Full proposals are analyzed with regard to foundation priorities and objectives; stability and integrity of the applicant organization; experience of key personnel; financial position of the applicant; whether the proposal duplicates or works in conjunction with similar projects; whether the project meets a demonstrated need; whether the project will receive continued community support; and, in the case of cultural programs, the level of demonstrated artistic achievement of key personnel. The directors generally favor requests putting forth creative responses to broad social problems. Applications for grants to support opera are by foundation invitation only. Proposals in areas of social concerns not directly related to the foundation's primary interests will not be given strong consideration.

Note: The foundation will not fund individuals, capital or annual fund drives, residence home programs, halfway houses, sectarian religious organizations, or budget deficits.

Restrictions on Giving: The foundation will not fund individuals, capital or annual fund drives, residence home programs, halfway houses, sectarian religious organizations, or budget deficits.

OTHER THINGS TO KNOW
The foundation reports that grant making is suspended.

PUBLICATIONS
Annual report

GRANTS ANALYSIS
Total Grants: $1,299,710
Number of Grants: 80
Highest Grant: $250,000
Average Grant: $16,246
Typical Range: $5,000 to $25,000
Disclosure Period: 1994

Note: Recent grants are derived from a 1994 grants list.

RECENT GRANTS
General
150,000	Westminster Abbey Trust, London, England
50,000	Bath Abbey Trust, Bath, England
50,000	Grace Cathedral, San Francisco, CA
25,000	National Trust, London, England
20,000	Centre for Advanced Welsh and Celtic Studies, Aberystwyth, Wales

Smith Trust, May and Stanley

CONTACT
N. D. Matheny
Trustee
May and Stanley Smith Trust
49 Geary St., Ste. 244
San Francisco, CA 94108
(415) 391-0292

FINANCIAL SUMMARY
Recent Giving: $220,800 (1993); $209,200 (1992); $176,800 (1990)

Assets: $4,780,021 (1993); $4,467,501 (1992); $3,616,538 (1990)
Gifts Received: $134,616,738 (1989)
EIN: 94-6435244

CONTRIBUTIONS SUMMARY
Donor(s): May Smith

Typical Recipients: • *Arts & Humanities:* Arts Outreach, Dance, Ethnic & Folk Arts, Libraries, Music, Visual Arts • *Civic & Public Affairs:* Housing, Parades/Festivals, Urban & Community Affairs • *Education:* Literacy, Science/Mathematics Education, Special Education, Student Aid • *Health:* AIDS/HIV, Arthritis, Children's Health/Hospitals, Eyes/Blindness, Health Organizations, Home-Care Services, Medical Research, Mental Health, Single-Disease Health Associations • *International:* Foreign Educational Institutions, International Organizations, Missionary/Religious Activities • *Religion:* Religious Organizations, Religious Welfare • *Social Services:* Big Brother/Big Sister, Child Welfare, Community Centers, Community Service Organizations, Domestic Violence, Family Services, Food/Clothing Distribution, Homes, People with Disabilities, Recreation & Athletics, Senior Services, YMCA/YWCA/YMHA/YWHA, Youth Organizations

Grant Types: general support

Geographic Distribution: focus on CA

GIVING OFFICERS
John P. Collins, Jr.: trust *PHIL AFFIL* trust: Stanley Smith Horticultural Trust

J. Ronald Gibbs: trust

N. D. Matheny: trust *PHIL AFFIL* trust: Stanley Smith Horticultural Trust

APPLICATION INFORMATION
Initial Approach: Send brief letter of inquiry describing program or project. Include a description of organization, amount requested, purpose of funds sought, recently audited financial statement, and proof of tax-exempt status.

GRANTS ANALYSIS
Total Grants: $220,800
Number of Grants: 43
Highest Grant: $6,000
Typical Range: $2,500 to $6,000
Disclosure Period: 1993

Note: Recent grants are derived from a 1993 Form 990.

RECENT GRANTS
Library
5,000	Trinity Parish School, Menlo Park, CA — library expansion and updating

General
6,000	Catholic Charities, Oakland, CA — department of aging programs
6,000	Catholic Charities, San Mateo, CA — peninsula family resrouce center homeless prvention program
6,000	Columbia Christian Counseling Group Society, Clearbrook, Canada — subsidizing fees for low-income clients
6,000	Community Justice Initiatives Association, Langley, Canada — victim/offender reconciliation program
6,000	Fund for Pediatric Care and Research, Oakland, CA — general budget

Southern California Edison Co.

Sales: $7.4 billion
Employees: 16,487
Parent Company: SCE Corp
Headquarters: Rosemead, CA
SIC Major Group: Electric Services

CONTACT
Rebecca S. Jones
Director, Charitable Contributions
Southern California Edison Co.
2244 Walnut Grove Ave.
PO Box 800
Rosemead, CA 91770
(818) 302-3841

FINANCIAL SUMMARY
Recent Giving: $10,000,000 (1995 est.); $9,800,000 (1994 approx.); $4,500,000 (1993 approx.)

Fiscal Note: Company gives directly. Above figures exclude nonmonetary support.

CONTRIBUTIONS SUMMARY
Typical Recipients: • *Arts & Humanities:* Arts Associations & Councils, Arts Centers, Arts Institutes, Community Arts, Dance, Ethnic & Folk Arts, Historic Preservation, Libraries, Museums/Galleries, Music, Opera, Performing Arts, Public Broadcasting, Theater • *Civic & Public Affairs:* Business/Free Enterprise, Civil Rights, Economic Development, Economic Policy, Housing, Law & Justice, Professional & Trade Associations, Public Policy, Safety, Urban & Community Affairs, Women's Affairs, Zoos/Aquariums • *Education:* Business Education, Colleges & Universities, Economic Education, Engineering/Technological Education, Faculty Development, General, Literacy, Minority Education, Private Education (Precollege), Science/Mathematics Education, Special Education • *Environment:* General • *Health:* Geriatric Health, Health Organizations, Hospices, Hospitals, Nursing Services • *Science:* Science Exhibits & Fairs, Scientific Centers & Institutes, Scientific Organizations • *Social Services:* Child Welfare, Community Centers, Community Service Organizations, Counseling, Emergency Relief, Family Services, People with Disabilities, Recreation & Athletics, Senior Services, Substance Abuse, United Funds/United Ways, Volunteer Services, Youth Organizations

Grant Types: department, employee matching gifts, endowment, general support, and matching

Nonmonetary Support: $200,000 (1994); $80,000 (1989); $80,000 (1988)

Nonmonetary Support Types: donated equipment, in-kind services, and loaned executives

Note: The company provides nonmonetary support. In 1994, nonmonetary support was estimated at $200,000. For more information on nonmonetary support, contact Rebecca S. Jones.

Geographic Distribution: primarily in Southern California service area; limited giving elsewhere

Operating Locations: AZ (Phoenix), CA (Allhambra, Apple Valley, Arcadia, Baldwin Park, Barstow, Bell, Bell Gardens, Bellflower, Beverly Hills, Brea, Buena Park, Burbank, Camarillo, Carson, Cathedral City, Cerritos, Chino, Claremont, Compton, Corona, Costa Mesa, Covina, Cudahy, Culver City, Cypress, Delano, Downey, Duarte, El Monte, Fontana, Fountain Valley, Fullerton, Garden Grove, Gardena, Glendora, Hanford, Hawthorne, Hemet, Hesperia, Highland, Huntington Beach, Huntington Park, Inglewood, Irvine, La Canada-Flintridge, La Habra, La Mirada, La Puente, La Verne, Laguna Beach, Lakewood, Lancaster, Lawndale, Lomita, Long Beach, Los Angeles, Lynwood, Manhattan Beach, Maywood, Mission Viejo, Monclair, Monrovia, Montebello, Monterey Park, Moorpark, Moreno Valley, Newport Beach, Norco, Norwalk, Ontario, Orange, Oxnard, Palm Springs, Palmdale, Palo Verde, Paramount, Pico Rivera, Placentia, Pomona, Port Hueneme, Porterville, Rancho Cucamonga, Rancho Palos Verdes, Redlands, Redondo Beach, Rialto, Ridgecrest, Rosemead, San Bernadino, San Bueno, San Dimas, San Fernando, San Gabriel, Santa Ana, Santa Barbara, Santa Clarita, Santa Monica, Santa Paula, Seal Beach, Seal Beach, Simi Valley, South Gate, South Pasadena, Stanton, Temple City, Thousand Oaks, Torrance, Tulare, Tustin, Upland, Victorville, Visalia, Walnut, West Covina, West Hollywood, Westminster, Whittier, Yorba Linda)

Note: Also operates in 800 cities and communities in Southern California.

CORP. OFFICERS
John E. Bryson: *B* New York NY 1943 *ED* Freie Univ Berlin 1965-1966; Stanford Univ BA 1965; Yale Univ JD 1969 *CURR EMPL* chmn, ceo: Southern CA Edison Co *CORP AFFIL* chmn, ceo: SCE Corp; dir: Pacific Am Income Shares Inc, Times Mirror Co; trust: First Interstate Bancorp *NONPR AFFIL* mem: CA Bar Assn, DC Bar Assn, Natl Assn Regulatory Utility Commnrs, OR Bar Assn, Phi Beta Kappa, Stanford Univ Alumni Assn; mem bd editors, assoc editor: Yale Univ Law Journal; trust: CA Environmental Trust, Claremont Univ Ctr, Stanford Univ Grad Sch Alumni Assn, World Resources Inst

Stephen E. Frank: *CURR EMPL* pres, coo: Southern CA Edison Co

GIVING OFFICERS
Rebecca S. Jones: *CURR EMPL* dir charitable contributions: Southern CA Edison Co

APPLICATION INFORMATION
Initial Approach: *Initial Contact:* brief letter or proposal *Include Information On:* description of the organization, amount requested, purpose for which funds are sought, recently audited financial statement, and proof of tax-exempt status *Deadlines:* none

Restrictions on Giving: Company does not support fraternal, political, veterans, or religious organizations, or public agencies.

GRANTS ANALYSIS
Total Grants: $9,800,000*

Typical Range: $500 to $10,000

Disclosure Period: 1994

Note: Total grants figure is approximate. Recent grants are derived from a partial 1994 grants list.

RECENT GRANTS

General
100,000	East Los Angeles Community Union Education Foundation, Los Angeles, CA	

Specialty Manufacturing Co. / Boss Foundation, William

Sales: $3.5 million
Employees: 26
Headquarters: San Leandro, CA

CONTACT
Bruce Lawin
Specialty Manufacturing Co.
2035 Edison Avenue
San Leandro, CA 94577
(510) 562-6049

FINANCIAL SUMMARY
Recent Giving: $58,800 (fiscal 1993); $4,865 (fiscal 1992)

Assets: $675,601 (fiscal 1993); $626,438 (fiscal 1992)

Gifts Received: $25,000 (fiscal 1993); $25,500 (fiscal 1992)

Fiscal Note: In fiscal 1993, contributions were received from Specialty Manufacturing Co.

EIN: 41-6038452

CONTRIBUTIONS SUMMARY
Typical Recipients: • *Arts & Humanities:* Arts Centers, Arts Funds, Arts Institutes, History & Archaeology, Libraries, Museums/Galleries, Music, Opera, Public Broadcasting, Theater • *Civic & Public Affairs:* Clubs, Native American Affairs • *Education:* Arts/Humanities Education • *Health:* Emergency/Ambulance Services • *Religion:* Churches • *Science:* Science Museums • *Social Services:* Substance Abuse

Grant Types: general support

Geographic Distribution: focus on MN

CORP. OFFICERS
Bruce A. Lawin: *CURR EMPL* pres: Specialty Mfg Co

Mark Nosbush: *CURR EMPL* vp: Specialty Mfg Co

Bobbie Perata: *CURR EMPL* cfo, dir: Specialty Mfr Co

Richard Stallmen: *CURR EMPL* pres, dir: Speciality Mfr Co

GIVING OFFICERS
W. Andrew Boss: pres, dir
Bruce A. Lawin: treas
Heidi McKeown: vp, secy, dir
Nancy B. Sandberg: chmn, dir

APPLICATION INFORMATION
Initial Approach: Send a brief letter of inquiry. Include a description of organization, amount requested, purpose of funds sought, recently audited financial statement, and proof of tax-exempt status.

GRANTS ANALYSIS
Total Grants: $58,800
Number of Grants: 22
Highest Grant: $9,000
Typical Range: $200 to $5,000
Disclosure Period: fiscal year ending June 30, 1993

Note: Recent grants are derived from a fiscal 1993 Form 990.

RECENT GRANTS

Library
200	Friends of St. Paul Public Library, St. Paul, MN	

General
6,000	House of Hope Presbyterian Church, St. Paul, MN	
1,000	College of Associated Arts, St. Paul, MN	
1,000	Science Museum of St. Paul, St. Paul, MN	
500	American Red Cross, St. Paul, MN	
400	Schubert Club, St. Paul, MN	

Stans Foundation

CONTACT
Maurice H. Stans
Chairman, Treasurer
Stans Fdn.
211 S Orange Grove Blvd. No. 12
Pasadena, CA 91105
(818) 795-5947

FINANCIAL SUMMARY
Recent Giving: $146,392 (1992); $175,640 (1990); $179,437 (1989)

Assets: $5,231,139 (1992); $4,694,494 (1990); $4,470,232 (1989)

EIN: 36-6008663

CONTRIBUTIONS SUMMARY
Donor(s): Maurice H. Stans, the late Kathleen C. Stans

Typical Recipients: • *Arts & Humanities:* Historic Preservation, History & Archaeology, Libraries, Museums/Galleries, Music • *Civic & Public Affairs:* Civil Rights, General, Housing, Legal Aid, Parades/Festivals, Public Policy • *Education:* Colleges & Universities, Engineering/Technological Education, General, Journalism/Media Education, Private Education (Precollege) • *Health:* Eyes/Blindness, Hospices, Hospitals, Medical Research, Mental Health, Research/Studies Institutes, Single-Disease Health Associations • *International:* International Affairs, International Environmental Issues, International Peace & Security Issues • *Religion:* Jewish Causes, Ministries, Religious Organizations, Religious Welfare • *Science:* Science Museums • *Social Services:* Animal Protection, Child Welfare, Community Service Organizations, United Funds/United Ways, Youth Organizations

Grant Types: capital, conference/seminar, general support, multiyear/continuing support, and research

Geographic Distribution: focus on CA

GIVING OFFICERS
Mary C. Elia: secy

Marie Gath: asst secy

Maureen Stans Helmick: vp, dir

Terrell S. Manley: asst treas, dir

William Manley: vp, dir

Maurice H. Stans: chmn, treas, dir *B* Shakopee MN 1908 *ED* Northwestern Univ 1925-28; Columbia Univ 1929-30; IL Wesleyan Univ LLD 1954; DePaul Univ 1960; Northwestern Univ 1960; Parsons Coll 1960; Grove City Coll LLD 1969; St Anselms Coll 1969; Gustavus Adolphus Coll 1970; Univ San Diego 1970; Maryville Coll 1971; Pomona Coll 1971; Rio Grande Coll 1972; Natl Univ 1979; Pepperdine Univ 1984 *CORP AFFIL* chmn, dir: Weatherby Inc; dir: Uniglobe Travel Intl *NONPR AFFIL* dir: Chinese Am Med Assistance Fdn, Eisenhower World Affs Inst, Huntington Meml Library, Huntington Meml Res Inst; fin chmn, dir: Nixon Presidential Library; founding dir: African Wildlife Fdn; hon mem: DC Soc CPAs, HI Soc CPAs, Iron Molders & Foundry Workers Union, Natl Assn Postmasters; mem: Am Accounting Assn, Am Inst CPAs, Fed Govt Accts Assn, IL Soc CPAs, Natl Assn Mfrs *PHIL AFFIL* fdr, pres, dir: Stans Foundation *CLUB AFFIL* Adventurers, Adventurers, African Safari, African Safari, Athenaeum, Athenaeum, California, California, Club Intl, E African Professional Hunters, Explorers, Explorers, Jamhuri Garissa, Jamhuri Garissa, Safari Intl, Shikar-Safari, Shikar Safari Intl, Union League, Union League, Valley Hunt, Valley Hunt

Steven H. Stans: pres, dir

Theodore M. Stans: vp, dir

APPLICATION INFORMATION
Initial Approach: Send a brief letter of inquiry. There are no deadlines.

GRANTS ANALYSIS
Total Grants: $146,392

Number of Grants: 125

Highest Grant: $26,520

Typical Range: $100 to $2,000

Disclosure Period: 1992

Note: Recent grants are derived from a 1992 Form 990.

RECENT GRANTS
Library
2,000	Huntington Library, Huntington, CA	
1,800	Nixon Library	

General
16,000	Eisenhower World Affairs Institute
10,000	Pollock Animals Myco
3,500	School Sisters of Notre Dame
3,150	African Wildlife Foundation, Washington, DC
2,500	Murphys Landing

Stauffer Charitable Trust, John

CONTACT
H. Jess Senecal
Trustee
John Stauffer Charitable Trust
301 N Lake Ave., 10th Fl.
Pasadena, CA 91101
(818) 793-9400

FINANCIAL SUMMARY
Recent Giving: $1,500,000 (fiscal 1995 est.); $1,500,000 (fiscal 1994); $1,455,000 (fiscal 1993)

Assets: $38,044,949 (fiscal 1994); $37,000,000 (fiscal 1993); $37,304,448 (fiscal 1992)

EIN: 23-7434707

CONTRIBUTIONS SUMMARY
Donor(s): The terms of the late John Stauffer's will established the John Stauffer Charitable Trust in 1974. John Stauffer was an officer and director of the Stauffer Chemical Company. He was particularly interested in educational concerns and hospitals.

Typical Recipients: • *Arts & Humanities:* Libraries • *Education:* Colleges & Universities, Legal Education, Science/Mathematics Education, Student Aid • *Health:* Cancer, Children's Health/Hospitals, Clinics/Medical Centers, Health Organizations, Hospitals, Medical Rehabilitation, Outpatient Health Care • *International:* Health Care/Hospitals • *Religion:* Churches, Religious Welfare • *Social Services:* Child Welfare, Community Service Organizations, Delinquency & Criminal Rehabilitation, Family Planning, Family Services, Food/Clothing Distribution, People with Disabilities, Scouts, Senior Services, Substance Abuse, YMCA/YWCA/YMHA/YWHA, Youth Organizations

Grant Types: endowment, fellowship, and scholarship

Geographic Distribution: primarily California

GIVING OFFICERS
Carl M. Franklin: co-trust *PHIL AFFIL* trust: Torrey H. and Dorothy K. Webb Educational and Charitable Trust, Rita H. Small Educational and Charitable Trust, Morris S Smith Foundation

H. Jess Senecal: co-trust *PHIL AFFIL* trust: Glen and Dorothy Stillwell Charitable Trust

Michael S. Whalen: co-trust

APPLICATION INFORMATION
Initial Approach:

Three copies of a full proposal must be submitted to the trust in writing. Personal interviews are discouraged. Guidelines are available upon request.

Proposals should include the amount requested; an explanation of the need for the subject of the grant; the goals; the manner in which John Stauffer's name will be memorialized; full financial information, including a detailed budget for the project to be assisted by the grant; and a statement of whether other sources of funding are being sought, and if so, which other sources are providing funding.

All applications must be executed by an officer of the grantee institution. Applications signed by a division or department head must be approved and countersigned by the head of the organization or institution, or by an officer thereof. Applicants should submit the latest IRS tax-exempt determination letter, stating that the grantee is not a private foundation, as well as the latest audited balance sheet and statement of income and expenditures. In addition, the trust would like to see a tax-exempt letter from the State of California. Letters of support from authorities and/or organizations in the applicant's field are encouraged.

All proposals and letters should be submitted in three copies, one for each of the trustees. An applicant desiring the material to be returned in the event of a rejection should state so.

The board meets quarterly and accepts applications any time.

If the proposal needs amplification or clarification, the trust will request the needed information in writing. Applicants are notified in writing whether or not the grant is being given. Decisions are made within six to nine months.

Restrictions on Giving: Those receiving grants are required to send a report on the use of the funds to the trust, including a certification that the funds have been used for the purpose for which the grant was made. The trust reserves the right to call for a reasonable audit of the use of grant funds conducted by its representatives at its own expense. If grants were used for purposes other than that for which the grant was made, the total amount of the grant must be returned.

Grants are usually for one calendar year however, there may be exceptions in unusual situations.

Restrictions on Giving: Grants are not made to organizations which, in turn, distribute them to others at their own discretion. Recipients may be required to provide matching funds. Also, large grants may be distributed over a period of two or more years.

OTHER THINGS TO KNOW
Those denied a grant may submit a new application in the future, but should not request reinstatement of a prior request which has been denied. The trust prefers to participate with other donors when making grants.

PUBLICATIONS
Policy guidelines

GRANTS ANALYSIS
Total Grants: $1,455,000

Number of Grants: 13

Highest Grant: $500,000

Average Grant: $100,000*

Typical Range: $50,000 to $200,000

Disclosure Period: fiscal year ending May 31, 1993

Note: Average grant figure was supplied by the foundation. Recent grants are derived from a fiscal 1993 Form 990.

RECENT GRANTS
Library
300,000   University of California Los Angeles Law School, Los Angeles, CA — remainder of grant made to expand and renovate the University of California Los Angeles law library

General
500,000   University of Southern California, Los Angeles, CA — remainder of grant made as an endowment, income of which underwrites the international symposia held by the Loker Hydrocarbon Research Institute

100,000   Children's Hospital, Los Angeles, CA — assist in equipping an ambulatory care clinic for underprivileged children in the community

100,000   Stanford University, Stanford, CA — remainder of grant toward rehabilitation of the John Stauffer chemistry building

100,000   University of California Boalt Hall School of Law, Berkeley, CA — fund in memory of A Richard Kimbrough for law students going into public service

50,000   Harvey Mudd College, Claremont, CA — renovation of chemistry lab in Jacobs science center

Stauffer Foundation, John and Beverly

CONTACT
Lawrence K. Gould, Jr.
Director
John and Beverly Stauffer Fdn.
333 S Hope St., 48th Fl.
Los Angeles, CA 90071
(213) 620-1780

FINANCIAL SUMMARY
Recent Giving: $164,685 (1993); $161,075 (1992); $169,130 (1991)

Assets: $3,501,344 (1993); $3,514,458 (1992); $3,596,838 (1991)

EIN: 95-2241406

CONTRIBUTIONS SUMMARY
Donor(s): the late John Stauffer and Beverly Stauffer

Typical Recipients: • *Arts & Humanities:* Arts Associations & Councils, Dance, Historic Preservation, History & Archaeology, Libraries, Literary Arts, Museums/Galleries, Music, Opera, Performing Arts, Theater • *Civic & Public Affairs:* Clubs, Economic Policy, General, Hispanic Affairs, Legal Aid, Nonprofit Management, Philanthropic Organizations, Public Policy, Zoos/Aquariums • *Education:* Colleges & Universities, Private Education (Precollege) • *Health:* Cancer, Children's Health/Hospitals, Health Organizations, Hospitals, Medical Research, Single-Disease Health Associations • *International:* International Organizations • *Religion:* Churches, Missionary Activities (Domestic), Religious Organizations, Religious Welfare • *Science:* Science Museums • *Social Services:* Animal Protection, Child Welfare, Community Service Organizations, Crime Prevention, Food/Clothing Distribution, People with Disabilities, Scouts, Shelters/Homelessness, Substance Abuse, Veterans, Youth Organizations

Grant Types: capital, general support, multiyear/continuing support, and scholarship

Geographic Distribution: focus on the southern CA area

GIVING OFFICERS
Leslie E. S. Bartleson: dir

Craig H. Flanagan: dir

Mary Ann Frankenhoff: dir

Laurence K. Gould, Jr.: dir *PHIL AFFIL* trust: Della Martin Foundation

Harriette Hughes: dir

Felix W. Robertson: dir

Brook Sheridan: dir

Jack R. Sheridan: dir

Katherine Stauffer Sheridan: dir

APPLICATION INFORMATION
Initial Approach: The foundation requests applications be made in writing. There are no deadlines.

GRANTS ANALYSIS
Total Grants: $164,685

Number of Grants: 44

Highest Grant: $10,000

Typical Range: $110 to $8,740

Disclosure Period: 1993

Note: Recent grants are derived from a 1993 Form 990.

RECENT GRANTS
Library
5,000   Richard Nixon Library and Birthplace Foundation, Yorba Linda, CA

5,000   Santa Barbara Mission Archive Library, Santa Barbara, CA

General
10,000   Helen Woodward Animal Center, Rancho Santa Fe, CA

8,740   Childhelp USA, Woodland Hills, CA

8,000   Foundation Endowment, Alexandria, VA

7,500   Zoological Society, San Diego, CA

6,000   Boys and Girls Club of Hollywood, Hollywood, CA

Steele Foundation, Harry and Grace

CONTACT
Marie F. Kowert
Assistant Secretary
Harry and Grace Steele Foundation
441 Old Newport Blvd., Ste. 301
Newport Beach, CA 92663
(714) 631-9158

FINANCIAL SUMMARY
Recent Giving: $8,567,936 (fiscal 1993); $7,950,933 (fiscal 1992); $5,925,555 (fiscal 1991)

Assets: $40,818,480 (fiscal 1993); $45,405,458 (fiscal 1992); $50,100,764 (fiscal 1991)

EIN: 95-6035879

CONTRIBUTIONS SUMMARY
Donor(s): The Harry and Grace Steele Foundation, formerly the Harry G. Steele Foundation, was established in California in 1953 by the late Grace C. Steele in memory of her husband, Harry G. Steele. The trustees of the foundation seek to perpetuate Mr. Steele's legacy of social consciousness and philanthropy. The trustees elected to change the name of the foundation to the Harry and Grace Steele Foundation. Mrs. Steele bequeathed the major portion of her estate to the foundation upon her death in 1974.

Typical Recipients: • *Arts & Humanities:* Arts Centers, Arts Institutes, Libraries, Museums/Galleries, Music, Opera, Performing Arts, Public Broadcasting, Theater • *Civic & Public Affairs:* Community Foundations, Nonprofit Management, Public Policy, Urban & Community Affairs, Women's Affairs, Zoos/Aquariums • *Education:*

Colleges & Universities, Faculty Development, Gifted & Talented Programs, Minority Education, Private Education (Precollege), Special Education, Student Aid • *Environment:* General • *Health:* Cancer, Children's Health/Hospitals, Hospitals, Outpatient Health Care • *International:* Health Care/Hospitals, International Peace & Security Issues • *Religion:* Churches, Religious Organizations, Religious Welfare • *Social Services:* Child Welfare, Community Service Organizations, Domestic Violence, Family Planning, Food/Clothing Distribution, People with Disabilities, Recreation & Athletics, Senior Services, Youth Organizations

Grant Types: capital, challenge, endowment, general support, multiyear/continuing support, professorship, project, and scholarship

Geographic Distribution: primarily Orange County, CA

GIVING OFFICERS
Alphonse A. Burnand III: secy *PHIL AFFIL* pres: Alphonse A. Burnand Medical and Educational Foundation

Audrey Steele Burnand: pres

Marie F. Kowert: asst secy

Elizabeth R. Steele: trust

Richard Steele: treas

Barbara Steele Williams: asst secy

APPLICATION INFORMATION
Initial Approach:

The foundation has no formal application forms. Send a single copy of a concise letter with supporting documentation that is signed by an officer of the organization.

Letters of application should be signed by an officer of the organization and include a copy of IRS letter showing section 501(c)(3) status and classification of the organization as "not a private foundation"; current list of officers, directors, or trustees; evidence of need for services or facilities to be funded; list of other outstanding potential sources of support; time schedule for reporting the manner of expenditure and results obtained from foundation funding; analysis of expenditures disbursed for fund raising and administrative costs against amount expended for the purposes intended; and the amount requested from the foundation.

There are no specific deadlines for receipt of proposals. The trustees meet several times a year to consider grant requests.

Grantees will not be considered for grants more often than once every three or four years. Proposals are initially reviewed by staff to see if they conform to legal requirements and foundation guidelines, and contain all essential information. Based on the information in the application, the trustees may request a visit with the applicant and will on occasion request a personal interview. Applicants should allow approximately six months for decisions on proposals.

Restrictions on Giving: The foundation does not make donations to tax-supported organizations or private foundations. No grants are given to individuals or for loans.

The foundation requires progress and financial reports from recipients.

PUBLICATIONS
Annual report, program policy statement

GRANTS ANALYSIS
Total Grants: $8,567,936

Number of Grants: 71

Highest Grant: $1,815,000

Average Grant: $120,675

Typical Range: $5,000 to $25,000 and $100,000 to $500,000

Disclosure Period: fiscal year ending October 31, 1993

Note: Recent grants are derived from a fiscal 1993 Form 990.

RECENT GRANTS
General

1,815,000	Planned Parenthood Federation of America, New York, NY — Emerson Electric stock; general support
500,950	Mills College, Oakland, CA — Emerson Electric stock; improvements and scholarships
500,950	Scripps College, Claremont, CA — Emerson Electric stock; capital improvements
496,800	Children's Hospital Foundation of Orange County, Orange, CA — Emerson Electric stock
486,069	Planned Parenthood Federation of America, New York, NY — Emerson Electric stock; general support

Stein Foundation, Jules and Doris

CONTACT
Linda L. Valliant
Program Officer
Jules and Doris Stein Foundation
PO Box 30
Beverly Hills, CA 90213
(310) 276-2101

FINANCIAL SUMMARY
Recent Giving: $3,799,400 (1994); $724,600 (1992); $3,154,500 (1991)

Assets: $55,000,000 (1993 approx.); $54,372,701 (1992); $46,617,284 (1991)

Gifts Received: $3,921,112 (1993 est.); $3,926,217 (1992); $4,409,266 (1990)

Fiscal Note: The foundation receives contributions from the Doris Jones Stein Charitable Lead Trusts.

EIN: 95-3708961

CONTRIBUTIONS SUMMARY
Donor(s): The foundation was established in 1981 in California, and was formerly named the Doris Jones Stein Foundation.

Typical Recipients: • *Arts & Humanities:* Arts Funds, Arts Institutes, Ballet, Dance, Libraries, Literary Arts, Museums/Galleries, Music, Opera, Performing Arts, Public Broadcasting, Theater • *Civic & Public Affairs:* Civil Rights, Employment/Job Training, Gay/Lesbian Issues, Law & Justice, Legal Aid, Philanthropic Organizations, Professional & Trade Associations, Public Policy, Urban & Community Affairs, Women's Affairs, Zoos/Aquariums • *Education:* Colleges & Universities, Education Funds, Engineering/Technological Education, Legal Education, Private Education (Precollege), Secondary Education (Private), Student Aid • *Environment:* General, Resource Conservation • *Health:* Cancer, Diabetes, Health Organizations, Medical Rehabilitation, Medical Research • *International:* Human Rights, International Relations, Missionary/Religious Activities • *Religion:* Churches, Religious Welfare • *Social Services:* Child Welfare, Community Service Organizations, Delinquency & Criminal Rehabilitation, Family Planning, Family Services, Recreation & Athletics, Shelters/Homelessness, Youth Organizations

Grant Types: project and research

Geographic Distribution: primarily in Los Angeles, CA; Kansas City, MO; and New York, NY

GIVING OFFICERS
Gerald H. Oppenheimer: pres, dir *PHIL AFFIL* trust: Hollywood Canteen Foundation

Reed Oppenheimer: dir

Andrew Shiva: vp, dir

Jean Stein: vp, dir

Linda L. Valliant: program off, secy

Lew Robert Wasserman: chmn *B* Cleveland OH 1913 *CURR EMPL* chmn emeritus, mem exec comm: MCA Inc *CORP AFFIL* chmn: Universal City Studios; dir: Am Airlines Inc *NONPR AFFIL* bd govs: Ronald Reagan Pres Fdn; chmn: Res Prevent Blindness Fdn; chmn emeritus: Assn Motion Picture Television Producers; dir: Los Angeles Music Ctr Fdn; hon chmn: Los Angeles Music Ctr Theatre Group; pres: Hollywood Canteen Fdn; trust: CA Inst Tech, Carter Ctr, Lyndon Baines Johnson Fdn, John F Kennedy Ctr Performing Arts, John F Kennedy Lib, Jules Stein Eye Inst *PHIL AFFIL* chmn fin comm, dir: Amateur Athletic Foundation of Los Angeles; pres: Wasserman Foundation; chmn, trust: Hollywood Canteen Foundation

APPLICATION INFORMATION
Initial Approach:

Prospective applicants must complete the foundation's Grant Application Summary form and submit it with a copy of the IRS determination letter verifying tax-exempt status.

Applicants should provide a description of the purpose for which funds are sought. Funding requests for a special program or project receive more consideration than proposals for the general operating budget. Supporting information may be provided at the applicant's discretion. Also enclose pertinent financial data, including a statement of current assets and liabilities, as well as the source and application of funds. Applicants also should provide information on qualifications of the professional and volunteer staff, organizational history, performance record, and future goals.

Applications may be sent any time.

The grant review committee meets periodically to review new grant applications and make recommendations to the board of directors. Applicants are notified of funding decisions as soon as possible.

Restrictions on Giving: The foundation is fulfilling a pledge to build the Doris Stein Eye Research Center and is not soliciting any new grant applications through the 1995 calendar year.

Grant applications are not held over for consideration at a subsequent time; however, applicants may re-apply and receive consideration.

Restrictions on Giving: The foundation does not provide grants for individuals or political campaigns.

OTHER THINGS TO KNOW
Grant recipients are responsible for reporting on the progress of their programs and verifying the use of grant funds. Reports are due at six-month intervals during grant fund utilization, and a final report of fund application must be submitted.

PUBLICATIONS
Guidelines

GRANTS ANALYSIS
Total Grants: $3,799,400
Number of Grants: 230
Average Grant: $16,519
Typical Range: $1,000 to $10,000
Disclosure Period: 1994

Note: The highest grant for 1994 was unavailable. Recent grants are derived from a 1992 Form 990.

RECENT GRANTS
Library
4,500	Ronald Reagan Presidential Foundation, Los Angeles, CA — general support for program, development of Library and Public Affairs Center
2,500	Lambda Legal Defense and Education Fund, New York, NY — family relationships project and a social science research library

General
56,200	Costume Council of LACMA, Los Angeles, CA — Doris Stein Research and Design Center for Costumes and Textiles
53,125	PEF Israel Endowment Funds, New York, NY — support of several projects including purchase of heart catheterization machine,

	research in Israeli AIDS task Force
20,000	Institute for Policy Studies, Washington, DC — general support for programs on public policy analysis and research
20,000	Trinity School, New York, NY
11,000	Ms. Foundation for Women, New York, NY — general funds

---

Strauss Foundation, Leon

CONTACT
Robert P. Vossler
Trustee
Leon Strauss Fdn.
5332 Harbor St.
Commerce, CA 90040
(213) 728-5440

FINANCIAL SUMMARY
Recent Giving: $240,000 (1992); $400,000 (1990)
Assets: $7,037,279 (1992); $6,546,156 (1989)
Gifts Received: $6,476,359 (1990)
Fiscal Note: In fiscal 1990, contributions were received from the late Leon Strauss.
EIN: 51-0205308

CONTRIBUTIONS SUMMARY
Donor(s): the late Leon Strauss

Typical Recipients: • *Arts & Humanities:* Arts Associations & Councils, Arts Centers, Libraries, Music, Public Broadcasting • *Civic & Public Affairs:* General, Safety • *Education:* Colleges & Universities, Community & Junior Colleges, Secondary Education (Public), Student Aid • *Environment:* General • *Health:* Cancer, Clinics/Medical Centers, Health Organizations, Hospitals, Medical Research, Mental Health, Research/Studies Institutes, Single-Disease Health Associations, Speech & Hearing • *Religion:* Churches, Jewish Causes, Ministries, Religious Welfare • *Social Services:* At-Risk Youth, People with Disabilities, Youth Organizations
Grant Types: endowment and general support

GIVING OFFICERS
Charles Curley: trust
Paul Simon: trust
Ralph Simon: trust
William Simon: trust *CURR EMPL* vchmn: North Face
Robert P. Vossler: trust

APPLICATION INFORMATION
Initial Approach: Send brief letter of inquiry including purpose and I.R.S. identification number. There are no deadlines.

GRANTS ANALYSIS
Total Grants: $240,000
Number of Grants: 46

Highest Grant: $25,000
Typical Range: $1,000 to $15,000
Disclosure Period: 1992

Note: Recent grants are derived from a 1992 Form 990.

RECENT GRANTS
Library
2,500	San Francisco Main Library, San Francisco, CA

General
25,000	City of Hope, Los Angeles, CA
15,000	National Jewish Research
10,000	Airport Marina Mental Health Association
10,000	Claremont McKenna College, Claremont, CA
10,000	Crippled Children Guild of Orthopedic Hospital

Sumitomo Bank of California

Income: $357.06 million
Employees: 1,584
Parent Company: The Sumitomo Bank, Limited
Headquarters: San Francisco, CA
SIC Major Group: State Commercial Banks

CONTACT
Steve Nelson
Public Affairs Officer
Sumitomo Bank of California
320 California St., 8th Fl.
San Francisco, CA 94104
(415) 445-8000

FINANCIAL SUMMARY
Recent Giving: $300,000 (1995 est.); $280,000 (1994 approx.); $325,000 (1993 approx.)
Fiscal Note: Company gives directly.

CONTRIBUTIONS SUMMARY
Typical Recipients: • *Arts & Humanities:* Community Arts, Libraries, Museums/Galleries, Music • *Civic & Public Affairs:* Economic Development, Employment/Job Training, Housing, Urban & Community Affairs • *Education:* Colleges & Universities, Public Education (Precollege) • *Health:* Health Organizations • *Social Services:* Community Service Organizations, Family Services, People with Disabilities, United Funds/United Ways, Youth Organizations
Grant Types: department, employee matching gifts, general support, and project
Note: Employee matching gift ratio: 1 to 1.
Nonmonetary Support Types: in-kind services
Note: Estimate of nonmonetary support is unavailable. For more information, contact Steve Nelson.
Geographic Distribution: contributions restricted to headquarters area
Operating Locations: CA (Albany, Alhambra, Anaheim, Arcadia, Brea, Claremont, Costa Mesa, Cupertino, Fremont, Fresno,

Gardena, Hacienda Heights, Hayward Millbrae, Huntington Beach, La Palma, Long Beach, Los Angeles, Monterey, Mountain View, Oakland, Oxnard, Pleasant Hill, Pomona, Sacramento, San Diego, San Francisco, San Jose, San Mateo, Santa Monica, Sherman Oaks, Stockton, Torrance, Watsonville, West Hollywood)

CORP. OFFICERS
Tadaichi Ikagawa: *B* Kyoto Japan 1939 *ED* Kyoto Univ 1961 *CURR EMPL* pres, ceo, dir: Sumitomo Bank CA *NONPR AFFIL* mem: Japan Chamber Commerce

GIVING OFFICERS
Yukio Kitagawa: *CURR EMPL* sr asst to pres: Sumitomo Bank CA

Steve Nelson: *CURR EMPL* pub aff off: Sumitomo Bank CA

APPLICATION INFORMATION
Initial Approach: *Initial Contact:* brief letter of inquiry *Include Information On:* description of the organization and name of contact person, a statement of purpose, a request for a specific amount of funding, an explanation of why funds are needed and how they will be used, a list of contributors, and a recently audited financial statement *Deadlines:* none *Note:* Individual branches administer small budgets; large grants are referred to the Public Affairs Office.

Restrictions on Giving: Does not support individuals, religious organizations for sectarian purposes, political or lobbying groups, or organizations outside operating areas.

PUBLICATIONS
Guidelines sheet

GRANTS ANALYSIS
Total Grants: $325,000

Typical Range: $1,000 to $25,000

Disclosure Period: 1993

Note: Recent grants are derived from a 1993 grants list.

RECENT GRANTS

General
Big Brothers/Big Sisters of East Bay, CA
La Familia Counseling Center, Sacramento, CA
Low Income Housing Fund, San Francisco, CA
Neighborhood Housing Service, CA
Nonprofit Housing Assistance, San Francisco, CA

Taper Foundation, Mark

CONTACT
Raymond F. Reisler
Executive Director
Mark Taper Fdn.
12011 San Vicente Blvd., Ste. 400
Los Angeles, CA 90049
(310) 476-5413

FINANCIAL SUMMARY
Recent Giving: $800,000 (fiscal 1994); $1,945,000 (fiscal 1993); $1,856,500 (fiscal 1992)

Assets: $5,740,632 (fiscal 1994); $6,578,365 (fiscal 1993); $8,259,157 (fiscal 1992)

EIN: 95-6027846

CONTRIBUTIONS SUMMARY
Donor(s): S. Mark Taper

Typical Recipients: • *Arts & Humanities:* Arts Outreach, Community Arts, Libraries • *Civic & Public Affairs:* Philanthropic Organizations • *Education:* Colleges & Universities, Legal Education • *Health:* Children's Health/Hospitals, Clinics/Medical Centers, Emergency/Ambulance Services, Geriatric Health, Health Organizations, Medical Research, Single-Disease Health Associations • *Social Services:* Child Welfare, Community Service Organizations, Counseling, Homes, Senior Services

Grant Types: capital, general support, and project

Geographic Distribution: focus on CA

GIVING OFFICERS
Janice Anne Lazarof: vp, treas, dir

Dayle McEwen: secy

Raymond F. Reisler: exec dir

Ruth Stegall: asst secy *PHIL AFFIL* asst secy: S. Mark Taper Foundation

Barry H. Taper: vp, secy, dir *PHIL AFFIL* vp, secy, dir: S. Mark Taper Foundation

APPLICATION INFORMATION
Initial Approach: Send a brief letter of inquiry. Include a description of organization, amount requested, purpose of funds sought, recently audited financial statement, and proof of tax-exempt status. There are no deadlines.

Restrictions on Giving: Does not support individuals. Limited to California.

PUBLICATIONS
Application Guidelines

GRANTS ANALYSIS
Total Grants: $800,000

Number of Grants: 3

Highest Grant: $500,000

Typical Range: $100,000 to $200,000

Disclosure Period: fiscal year ending June 30, 1994

Note: Recent grants are derived from a fiscal 1994 Form 990.

RECENT GRANTS

Library
500,000   Los Angeles Public Library, Los Angeles, CA

General
200,000   Los Angeles Free Clinic, Los Angeles, CA

Taube Family Foundation

CONTACT
John Glennon
Treasurer
Taube Family Fdn.
1050 Ralston Ave.
Belmont, CA 94002
(415) 592-3960

FINANCIAL SUMMARY
Recent Giving: $642,235 (fiscal 1993); $310,416 (fiscal 1992); $421,245 (fiscal 1991)

Assets: $5,862,131 (fiscal 1993); $6,100,798 (fiscal 1992); $4,459,572 (fiscal 1991)

Gifts Received: $504,627 (fiscal 1993); $1,714,562 (fiscal 1992); $188,240 (fiscal 1991)

Fiscal Note: In fiscal 1993, contributions were received from the Taube Family Trust.

EIN: 94-2702180

CONTRIBUTIONS SUMMARY
Donor(s): members of the Taube family

Typical Recipients: • *Arts & Humanities:* Ballet, Libraries, Museums/Galleries, Music, Public Broadcasting • *Civic & Public Affairs:* Business/Free Enterprise, Community Foundations, Economic Development, General, Legal Aid, Urban & Community Affairs, Zoos/Aquariums • *Education:* Colleges & Universities, Education Associations, Private Education (Precollege), Religious Education, School Volunteerism, Secondary Education (Private), Social Sciences Education • *Health:* Arthritis, Cancer, Children's Health/Hospitals, Hospices, Hospitals, Medical Research, Multiple Sclerosis, Single-Disease Health Associations • *International:* Foreign Educational Institutions, International Organizations, Missionary/Religious Activities • *Religion:* Jewish Causes, Religious Organizations, Religious Welfare • *Social Services:* Community Centers, Community Service Organizations, Family Services, People with Disabilities, Recreation & Athletics, Scouts, United Funds/United Ways, Volunteer Services, Youth Organizations

Grant Types: general support

Geographic Distribution: national

GIVING OFFICERS
Kerry Dowhan: secy

John Glennon: treas

Kenneth A. Moline: secy, treas

Thaddeus N. Taube: pres, dir *B* 1931 *ED* Stanford Univ BS 1954; Stanford Univ MS 1957 *CURR EMPL* chmn, dir: Woodmont Cos *PHIL AFFIL* pres, dir: Koret Foundation

APPLICATION INFORMATION
Initial Approach: The foundation reports it only makes contributions to preselected charitable organizations.

GRANTS ANALYSIS
Total Grants: $642,235

Number of Grants: 54

Highest Grant: $260,000

Typical Range: $100 to $250,000

Disclosure Period: fiscal year ending November 30, 1993

Note: Recent grants are derived from a fiscal 1993 Form 990.

RECENT GRANTS

Library

500	Library Foundation of San Francisco, San Francisco, CA

General

260,000	United Way, San Francisco, CA
250,000	Stanford University, Stanford, CA
110,250	Jewish Community Federation, San Francisco, CA
2,500	American Friends of Hebrew University, Beverly Hills, CA
2,500	Washington Legal Foundation, Washington, DC

Teichert & Son, A. / Teichert Foundation

Sales: $199.8 million
Employees: 900
Headquarters: Sacramento, CA
SIC Major Group: Stone, Clay & Glass Products

CONTACT
Frederick Teichert
Executive Director
Teichert Foundation
3500 American River Dr.
Sacramento, CA 95864
(916) 484-3011

FINANCIAL SUMMARY
Recent Giving: $101,747 (fiscal 1993); $139,994 (fiscal 1992); $0 (fiscal 1990)

Assets: $447,295 (fiscal 1993); $535,371 (fiscal 1992); $500,000 (fiscal 1990)

Gifts Received: $100,000 (fiscal 1992); $500,000 (fiscal 1990)

Fiscal Note: In fiscal 1992, contributions were received from A. Teichert & Sons Inc.

EIN: 68-0212355

CONTRIBUTIONS SUMMARY
Typical Recipients: • *Arts & Humanities:* Libraries, Museums/Galleries, Music, Opera, Public Broadcasting, Theater • *Civic & Public Affairs:* Economic Development, General, Housing, Nonprofit Management, Public Policy, Safety, Zoos/Aquariums • *Education:* Business Education, Colleges & Universities, Elementary Education (Public), General, Private Education (Precollege) • *Environment:* Air/Water Quality, General, Resource Conservation • *Health:* Children's Health/Hospitals, Heart • *Religion:* Religious Welfare • *Science:* Scientific Centers & Institutes • *Social Services:* Child Welfare, Community Service Organizations, Delinquency & Criminal Rehabilitation, Family

Planning, Family Services, People with Disabilities, Youth Organizations

Grant Types: general support

Operating Locations: CA (Sacramento)

CORP. OFFICERS
Norman E. Eilert: *CURR EMPL* sr vp, cfo: Teichert & Son

Louis V. Riggs: *CURR EMPL* pres, ceo: Teichert & Son

John B. Sandman: *CURR EMPL* exec vp, coo: Teichert & Son

GIVING OFFICERS
Thomas J. Hammer: dir

Anne S. Haslam: secy

Judson T. Riggs: dir

Bruce Stimson: cfo

Frederick A. Teichert: exec dir

Melita M. Teichert: dir

APPLICATION INFORMATION
Initial Approach: Application form required. Deadlines are March 20, June 19, and September 18.

GRANTS ANALYSIS
Total Grants: $101,747

Number of Grants: 73

Highest Grant: $10,000

Typical Range: $500 to $5,000

Disclosure Period: fiscal year ending March 31, 1993

Note: Recent grants are derived from a Fiscal 1993 Form 990.

RECENT GRANTS

Library

10,000	Sacramento Public Library, Sacramento, CA

General

3,500	Families First, Davis, GA
3,000	Davis Science Center, Davis, CA — Explorit
3,000	People Reaching Out, Carmichael, CA
2,500	Diffa, Sacramento, CA — Heart Strings
2,500	Nonprofit Resource Center, Sacramento, CA

Thornton Foundation

CONTACT
Charles B. Thornton, Jr.
President
Thornton Fdn.
523 W Sixth St., Ste. 636
Los Angeles, CA 90016
(213) 629-3867

FINANCIAL SUMMARY
Recent Giving: $359,850 (1992); $330,600 (1991); $347,500 (1990)

Assets: $8,461,691 (1992); $7,799,116 (1991); $6,304,248 (1990)

EIN: 95-6037178

CONTRIBUTIONS SUMMARY
Donor(s): the late Charles B. Thornton and Flora I.Thornton

Typical Recipients: • *Arts & Humanities:* Arts Centers, Libraries, Museums/Galleries, Music, Public Broadcasting • *Civic & Public Affairs:* Economic Development, General, Urban & Community Affairs • *Education:* Business Education, Colleges & Universities, Education Reform, General, Legal Education, Private Education (Precollege), Public Education (Precollege), Science/Mathematics Education, Secondary Education (Private) • *Environment:* Wildlife Protection • *Health:* Cancer, Children's Health/Hospitals, Clinics/Medical Centers, Emergency/Ambulance Services, Hospitals, Research/Studies Institutes • *International:* International Affairs • *Religion:* Churches, Religious Organizations, Religious Welfare • *Social Services:* Day Care, Youth Organizations

Grant Types: operating expenses

Geographic Distribution: focus on CA

GIVING OFFICERS

Robert E. Novell: secy

Charles B. Thornton, Jr.: pres, trust

William Laney Thornton: vp, trust *PHIL AFFIL* trust: Flora L. Thornton Foundation

APPLICATION INFORMATION
Initial Approach: Send brief letter of inquiry describing program or project. There are no deadlines.

GRANTS ANALYSIS
Total Grants: $359,850

Number of Grants: 41

Highest Grant: $93,200

Typical Range: $1,000 to $15,000

Disclosure Period: 1992

Note: Recent grants are derived from a 1992 Form 990.

RECENT GRANTS

Library

2,300	Huntington Library, San Marino, CA

General

93,200	San Francisco Day School, San Francisco, CA
52,500	San Francisco University High School, San Francisco, CA
50,000	Harvard-Westlake School, Los Angeles, CA
27,000	Harvard College, Cambridge, MA
15,000	Harvard Business School, Cambridge, MA

Thornton Foundation, Flora L.

CONTACT
Flora L. Thornton
Trustee
Flora L. Thornton Fdn.
c/o Edward A. Landry Co.
4444 Lakeside Dr., Ste. 300
Burbank, CA 91505
(818) 842-1645

FINANCIAL SUMMARY
Recent Giving: $1,201,650 (fiscal 1992); $805,500 (fiscal 1991); $1,580,550 (fiscal 1990)

Assets: $3,837,738 (fiscal 1992); $4,652,471 (fiscal 1991); $3,823,625 (fiscal 1990)

Gifts Received: $874,428 (fiscal 1991); $1,014,000 (fiscal 1990)

EIN: 95-3855595

CONTRIBUTIONS SUMMARY
Donor(s): Flora L. Thornton

Typical Recipients: • *Arts & Humanities:* Ethnic & Folk Arts, History & Archaeology, Libraries, Museums/Galleries, Music, Opera, Public Broadcasting, Theater • *Civic & Public Affairs:* General, Municipalities/Towns • *Education:* Arts/Humanities Education, Colleges & Universities, Education Funds, Literacy, Private Education (Precollege), Public Education (Precollege), Secondary Education (Private), Student Aid • *Health:* Arthritis, Cancer, Children's Health/Hospitals, Hospitals, Kidney, Medical Research, Multiple Sclerosis, Prenatal Health Issues • *International:* International Affairs • *Religion:* Churches, Jewish Causes • *Science:* Science Museums • *Social Services:* Community Service Organizations, Food/Clothing Distribution, Shelters/Homelessness, United Funds/United Ways, Volunteer Services

Grant Types: general support

GIVING OFFICERS
Edward A. Landry: trust *B* New Orleans LA 1939 *ED* LA St Univ BA 1961; Univ CA Los Angeles JD 1964 *CURR EMPL* atty: Musick Peeler & Garrett *PHIL AFFIL* trust: Dan Murphy Foundation; asst secy, asst treas: Jaquelin Hume Foundation; trust: Walter Lantz Foundation

Glen P. McDaniel: trust

Flora L. Thornton: trust

William Laney Thornton: trust *PHIL AFFIL* vp, trust: Thornton Foundation

APPLICATION INFORMATION
Initial Approach: Send brief letter of inquiry describing program or project. There are no deadlines.

GRANTS ANALYSIS
Total Grants: $1,201,650
Number of Grants: 32
Highest Grant: $250,000
Typical Range: $1,000 to $10,000

Disclosure Period: fiscal year ending November 30, 1992

Note: Recent grants are derived from a Fiscal 1992 Form 990.

RECENT GRANTS
Library
10,000 — Library of Congress James Madison Council, Washington, DC

General
250,000 — Pepperdine University, Malibu, CA
200,000 — University of Southern California Kenneth Norris, Jr., Cancer Center, Los Angeles, CA
125,000 — San Francisco University High School, San Francisco, CA
100,000 — St. John's Hospital and Health Center Foundation
25,000 — Rabbi Louis J. Sigel Endowment Fund, New York, NY

Times Mirror Company, The / Times Mirror Foundation

Revenue: $3.85 billion
Employees: 27,700
Headquarters: Los Angeles, CA
SIC Major Group: Newspapers, Periodicals, Book Publishing, and Cable & Other Pay Television Services

CONTACT
Stephen Meier
Secretary
The Times Mirror Foundation
Times Mirror Sq.
Los Angeles, CA 90053
(213) 237-3993
Note: Ms. Malry is contact for general information and for organizations in Southern California. Organizations outside of Southern California should first apply for support from the Times Mirror Company operating unit in their area.

FINANCIAL SUMMARY
Recent Giving: $6,723,000 (1994 approx.); $6,562,243 (1993); $8,351,463 (1992)

Assets: $5,600,000 (1995 est.); $9,523,694 (1990); $18,183,490 (1989)

Fiscal Note: Giving figures include foundation giving and direct contributions by the corporation and its operating units. In 1993, the foundation gave $2,685,250; the company and its subsidiaries gave $3,876,993. In 1994, the foundation gave $1,045,000; the company and its subsidiaries gave $5,678,000. Above figures include nonmonetary support.

EIN: 95-6079651

CONTRIBUTIONS SUMMARY
Typical Recipients: • *Arts & Humanities:* Arts Associations & Councils, Arts Centers, Dance, Ethnic & Folk Arts, General, Historic Preservation, Libraries, Museums/Galleries, Music, Performing Arts, Public Broadcasting, Theater • *Civic & Public Affairs:* African American Affairs, Asian American Affairs, Chambers of Commerce, Civil Rights, Economic Development, Economic Policy, Employment/Job Training, First Amendment Issues, General, Hispanic Affairs, Housing, Legal Aid, Minority Business, Municipalities/Towns, Native American Affairs, Nonprofit Management, Parades/Festivals, Professional & Trade Associations, Public Policy, Urban & Community Affairs, Women's Affairs, Zoos/Aquariums • *Education:* Arts/Humanities Education, Business Education, Business-School Partnerships, Colleges & Universities, Education Funds, Education Reform, Engineering/Technological Education, General, International Studies, Journalism/Media Education, Literacy, Minority Education, Student Aid • *Environment:* General • *Health:* Cancer, Diabetes, Emergency/Ambulance Services, Eyes/Blindness, General, Respiratory • *International:* Foreign Arts Organizations, International Affairs, International Organizations, International Relations • *Religion:* Religious Welfare • *Science:* Science Museums • *Social Services:* Camps, Child Welfare, Community Centers, Community Service Organizations, Domestic Violence, Family Services, Food/Clothing Distribution, Homes, People with Disabilities, Recreation & Athletics, Scouts, Senior Services, United Funds/United Ways, Volunteer Services, YMCA/YWCA/YMHA/YWHA, Youth Organizations

Grant Types: capital, employee matching gifts, general support, multiyear/continuing support, project, and scholarship

Note: Employee matching gift ratio: 1 to 1. Company will match gifts made by employees and retirees with a minimum contribution of $25 and a maximum of $10,000 per calendar year. The company grants scholarships to children of Times Mirror employees; the foundation has contributed towards limited scholarships to local schools.

Nonmonetary Support: $27,352 (1988); $5,710 (1987)

Nonmonetary Support Types: donated equipment, donated products, and in-kind services

Note: The company provides a small, unspecified amount of nonmonetary support.

Geographic Distribution: primarily nonprofits located in southern California, and in communities where there is a significant employee presence

Operating Locations: AZ, CA (Costa Mesa, Irvine, Laguna Niguel, Long Beach, Los Angeles, San Jose, Santa Ana), CO (Englewood), CT (Greenwich, Hartford, Stamford), DC, IL (Chicago, Homewood), MA (Cambridge), MD (Baltimore, Baltimore), MO (St. Louis), NY (Long Island, Melville, New York), PA (Allentown, Harrisburg), TX (Austin, Dallas)

CORP. OFFICERS
Robert F. Erburu: *B* Ventura CA 1930 *ED* Univ Southern CA BA 1952; Harvard Univ JD 1955 *CURR EMPL* chmn, dir: Times Mir-

ror Co *CORP AFFIL* dir: Tejon Ranch Co; dir, chmn: Fed Reserve Bank San Francisco *NONPR AFFIL* chmn: Am Newspaper Publs Assn, Brookings Inst; dir: Independent Colls Southern CA, Los Angeles Festival, Tomas Rivera Ctr; fellow: Am Acad Arts & Sci; mem: Am Bar Assn, Bus Counc, Bus Roundtable, CA Bus Roundtable; mem bd dirs: Counc Foreign Rels; mem trust counc: Natl Gallery Art *PHIL AFFIL* trust: Ahmanson Foundation; chmn bd trust: J. Paul Getty Trust; dir: Ralph M. Parsons Foundation, Carrie Estelle Doheny Foundation, William and Flora Hewlett Foundation; vp: Fletcher Jones Foundation; dir: Pfaffinger Foundation

Curtis Alan Hessler: *B* Berwyn IL 1943 *ED* Harvard Univ BA 1966; Oxford Univ 1966-1969; Yale Univ JD 1973; Univ CA Berkeley MA 1976 *CURR EMPL* exec vp: Times Mirror Co

Edward Eric Johnson: *B* Park Ridge NJ 1944 *ED* Rensselaer Polytech Inst 1966; Stanford Univ 1968 *CURR EMPL* sr vp: Times Mirror Co

Richard T. Schlosberg III: *B* 1943 *ED* US Air Force Acad BS 1965; Harvard Univ MBA 1972 *CURR EMPL* exec vp: Times Mirror Co *CORP AFFIL* chmn: Times Mirror Magazines Inc *PHIL AFFIL* dir: Pfaffinger Foundation; trust: Hartford Courant Foundation

Mark Hinckley Willes: *B* Salt Lake City UT 1941 *ED* Columbia Univ AB 1963; Columbia Univ PhD 1967 *CURR EMPL* pres, ceo: Times Mirror Co *CORP AFFIL* dir: Black & Decker Corp, Ryder Sys Inc *PHIL AFFIL* trust: General Mills Foundation

Donald Franklin Wright: *B* St Paul MN 1934 *ED* Univ MN BME 1957; Univ MN MBA 1958 *CURR EMPL* sr vp: Times Mirror Co *NONPR AFFIL* dir: Assocs CA Inst Tech, Univ MN Fdn; mem exec comm, bd fellows: Claremont Univ Grad Sch; vchmn, regional pres: Boy Scouts Am *CLUB AFFIL* City Bunker Hill, Univ MN Alumni

GIVING OFFICERS

Shelby Coffey III: dir *CURR EMPL* editor, exec vp: Los Angeles Times

Robert F. Erburu: chmn, dir *CURR EMPL* chmn, dir: Times Mirror Co *PHIL AFFIL* trust: Ahmanson Foundation; chmn bd trust: J. Paul Getty Trust; dir: Ralph M. Parsons Foundation, Carrie Estelle Doheny Foundation, William and Flora Hewlett Foundation; vp: Fletcher Jones Foundation; dir: Pfaffinger Foundation (see above)

Curtis Alan Hessler: dir *CURR EMPL* exec vp: Times Mirror Co (see above)

Edward Eric Johnson: dir *CURR EMPL* sr vp: Times Mirror Co (see above)

Cassandra Malry: treas *CURR EMPL* mgr corp contributions: Times Mirror Co

Stephen Charles Meier: secy, dir *B* Los Angeles CA 1950 *ED* Occidental Coll 1972; Harvard Univ MBA 1977 *CURR EMPL* vp admin & commun aff: Times Mirror Co

Lisa Cleri Reale: asst secy

Charles Robert Redmond: pres, ceo, dir *B* New Brunswick NJ 1926 *ED* Rutgers Univ 1950; Univ Southern CA MBA 1960 *CURR*

EMPL exec vp: Times Mirror Co *PHIL AFFIL* chmn, dir: Pfaffinger Foundation

Richard T. Schlosberg III: dir *CURR EMPL* exec vp: Times Mirror Co *PHIL AFFIL* dir: Pfaffinger Foundation; trust: Hartford Courant Foundation (see above)

Donald Franklin Wright: dir *CURR EMPL* sr vp: Times Mirror Co (see above)

APPLICATION INFORMATION

Initial Approach: *Initial Contact:* two- to three-page letter to foundation *Include Information On:* description of the organization, its purpose, programs, and project to be considered; proof of tax-exempt status; list of current supporting organizations and amount of support; organizational budget for current and upcoming fiscal years *Deadlines:* by May 1 or October 1; board meets in June and November *Note:* Organizations in areas served by Times Mirror subsidiaries with significant employee presence should submit requests to subsidiary directly.

Restrictions on Giving: Company and foundation do not provide grants for religious or fraternal purposes, publications, conferences, television programs, or films, or to individuals. Foundation does not support fund-raising events.

Repeat grant requests will not be considered within a one-year time period.

OTHER THINGS TO KNOW

In 1995, the company reported that the foundation has not made any new grants since June 1994. As a result of the impact the economy has had on the company's operating revenue, the resources available for direct charitable giving purposes have been significantly reduced; at the moment, the company is only making very small direct gifts primarily to organizations located in southern California. On the foundation side, the company is in the process of reviewing the grantmaking program and does not anticipate taking any new proposals under consideration until the end of 1995.

Grants requests to the Times Mirror Co. are considered as received. Company's grants are generally smaller than the foundation and may include support for fund-raising events. Application criteria and eligibility are similar to those for the foundation. Contact Ms. Malry for further information.

Times Mirror also gives through 26 operating units, including the Los Angeles Times, CA; Newsday, Long Island, NY; The Baltimore Sun Newspaper, MD.

PUBLICATIONS

Contributions Annual Report

GRANTS ANALYSIS

Total Grants: $6,723,000

Number of Grants: 226*

Highest Grant: $375,000

Average Grant: $29,748*

Typical Range: $1,000 to $12,000 and $25,000 to $50,000

Disclosure Period: 1994

Note: Number of grants and average grants figures exclude matching gifts, subsidiary

giving, and National Merit Scholarships. Recent grants are derived from a 1994 grants list.

RECENT GRANTS

Library

75,000	Library Foundation of Los Angeles, Los Angeles, CA — for two-year, $150,000 grant toward the capital campaign of the Central Library to establish the Los Angeles Times Literacy Center
50,000	Henry E. Huntington Library and Art Gallery, San Marino, CA — toward seventy-fifth anniversary observances
50,000	University of Southern California University Library System, Los Angeles, CA — for four-year, $200,000 capital grant toward construction of Teaching Library
12,500	Henry E. Huntington Library and Art Gallery, San Marino, CA — for unrestricted annual support
10,000	Wadsworth Atheneum, Hartford, CT — for five-year, $50,000 grant to underwrite "free days" at the Museum every Thursday for five years

General

375,000	Broadcast Capital Fund, Washington, DC — for balance of funds committed to increase minority broadcast ownership under Newhouse agreements
76,104	National Merit Scholarship Corporation, Evanston, IL — for scholarships for 1994-95
75,000	Loyola Marymount University, Los Angeles, CA — for two-year, $150,000 capital grant for Conrad N. Hilton Center for Business
60,000	United Way of Orange County, Garden Grove, CA — for unrestricted annual support
50,000	Learn — for two-year, $100,000 unrestricted support

TransAmerica Corporation / TransAmerica Foundation

Revenue: $5.35 billion
Employees: 10,700
Headquarters: San Francisco, CA
SIC Major Group: Investment Advice

CONTACT

Mary Sawai
Assistant Secretary
TransAmerica Foundation
600 Montgomery St.
San Francisco, CA 94111
(415) 983-4333

FINANCIAL SUMMARY
Recent Giving: $3,439,000 (1993 approx.); $2,902,000 (1992); $3,180,000 (1991)

Assets: $31,947,105 (1993); $29,620,000 (1992); $28,774,177 (1991)

Fiscal Note: Figures represent giving for foundation, corporation, and affiliates. Above figures exclude nonmonetary support.

EIN: 94-3034825

CONTRIBUTIONS SUMMARY
Typical Recipients: • *Arts & Humanities:* Historic Preservation, Libraries, Literary Arts, Museums/Galleries, Music, Opera, Performing Arts, Public Broadcasting • *Civic & Public Affairs:* General, Legal Aid, Nonprofit Management, Philanthropic Organizations, Urban & Community Affairs, Zoos/Aquariums • *Education:* Colleges & Universities, Economic Education, Education Associations, Education Funds, Elementary Education (Private), Private Education (Precollege), Science/Mathematics Education, Secondary Education (Private), Special Education • *Environment:* General • *Health:* Cancer, Clinics/Medical Centers, Health Funds, Hospices, Hospitals, Mental Health, Single-Disease Health Associations • *Religion:* Jewish Causes • *Science:* Observatories & Planetariums • *Social Services:* Child Welfare, Community Centers, Community Service Organizations, Family Services, Food/Clothing Distribution, People with Disabilities, Shelters/Homelessness, Youth Organizations

Grant Types: employee matching gifts, general support, professorship, project, research, and scholarship

Nonmonetary Support: $154,000 (1989); $160,000 (1988)

Nonmonetary Support Types: in-kind services

Geographic Distribution: primarily in operating areas

Operating Locations: CA (Los Angeles, San Francisco), IL (Chicago), NY (Purchase), TX (Houston)

CORP. OFFICERS
Burton Edward Broome: *B* New York NY 1935 *ED* Fordham Univ BS 1963; Univ CA MBA 1964 *CURR EMPL* vp, contr: TransAm Corp *NONPR AFFIL* chmn adv counc: Univ Southern CA Securities Exchange Comm & Fin Reporting Inst; mem: Am Accounting Assn, Am Inst CPAs, CA Soc CPAs, Fin Execs Inst; mem professional accounting program: Univ CA Berkeley *CLUB AFFIL* Commonwealth

Richard Henry Finn: *B* Luanshya Zambia 1934 *ED* Oxford Univ 1956; Oxford Univ 1958 *CURR EMPL* pres, ceo, dir: TransAm Fin Corp *CORP AFFIL* dir: TransAm Assurance Co, TransAm Leasing Inc, TransAm Life Cos, TransAm Life Ins Annuity Co, TransAm Occidental Life Ins Co; exec vp: TransAm Corp; pres, ceo, dir: TransAm Commercial Fin Corp; pres, dir: TA Leasing Holding Co Inc

Edgar Hardd Grubb: *B* Harrisburg PA 1939 *ED* PA St Univ BA 1961; CA St Univ Fullerton MBA 1967 *CURR EMPL* exec vp,

cfo: TransAm Corp *CORP AFFIL* dir: TransAm Fin Corp, TransAm Occidental Life Ins Co; pres, dir: TransAm Telecom Corp *NONPR AFFIL* bd dirs: Goodwill Indus; mem: Am Inst CPAs, CA Soc CPAs, Fin Execs Inst; trust: Mills Coll

James Ross Harvey: *B* Los Angeles CA 1934 *ED* Princeton Univ BS 1956; Univ CA Berkeley Grad Sch Bus Admin MBA 1963 *CURR EMPL* chmn: TransAm Corp *CORP AFFIL* dir: Airtouch Commun Inc, McKesson Corp, Pacific Telesis Group, Charles Schwab & Co Inc, Sedgwick Group, SRI Intl, TransAm Fin Corp, TransAm Ins Corp, TransAm Ins Corp CA, TransAm Interway, TransAm Leasing Inc, TransAm Life Ins Annuity Co, TransAm Occidental Life Ins Co, TransAm Title Ins; vchmn: Pentzer Devel Corp *NONPR AFFIL* dir: Bay Area Counc, CA St Parks Fdn; mem: Mt Land Reliance, Natl Pk Fdn, Nature Conservancy; pres, dir: San Francisco Chamber Commerce; trust: St Marys Coll, Univ CA Bus Sch; vchmn: Presidio Counc *CLUB AFFIL* Bohemian, Fly Fishers, Pacific-Union

Frank Casper Herringer: *B* New York NY 1942 *ED* Dartmouth Coll AB 1964; Dartmouth Coll MBA 1965 *CURR EMPL* pres, ceo, dir: TransAm Corp *CORP AFFIL* dir: Fred S James Corp, Pacific Telesis Group, Sedgwick Group PLC, TransAm Assurance Co, TransAm Equipment Leasing Co, TransAm Fin Corp, TransAm Ins Corp, TransAm Interway, TransAm Leasing Inc, TransAm Life Ins Annuity Co, TransAm Occidental Life Ins Co, Union Oil Co CA, Unocal Corp, Unocal Exploration Corp; pres: TransAm Intl Holdings *NONPR AFFIL* mem: Phi Beta Kappa; trust: CA Pacific Med Ctr, Dartmouth Coll Amos Tuck Sch Bus Admin, Mills Coll, Pacific Presbyterian Med Ctr *CLUB AFFIL* Olympic, Pacific Union, San Francisco GC, Villa Taverna

James Blakeley Lockhart: *B* New York NY 1936 *ED* Boston Univ BS 1956; Boston Univ JD 1959 *CURR EMPL* vp pub aff: TransAm Corp *CORP AFFIL* dir: Budget Rent-a-Car Intl Inc *NONPR AFFIL* chmn: Bay Area Urban League, KQED-FM, KQED-TV; chmn bus counc: Fine Arts Mus San Francisco; chmn pub affairs comm: San Francisco Chamber Commerce; dep: CA Bus Roundtable; dir: Downtown Assn San Francisco, Pub Aff Counc, Pub Broadcasting Svc Enterprises, Pvt Indus Counc San Francisco; mem: Am Bar Assn, Bay Area Counc, Car Truck Rental Leasing Assn Am, IL Bar Assn, Intl Franchise Assn, SC Bar Assn, Sigma Pi Phi, World Aff Counc; vp, dir: Lawrence Hall Sch Boys; vp, dir, mem exec comm: Bd Episcopal Charities *CLUB AFFIL* Bohemian, Boule, City, Lakeview

GIVING OFFICERS
Burton Edward Broome: vp, treas *CURR EMPL* vp, contr: TransAm Corp (see above)

David Roland Carpenter: exec vp, dir *B* Fort Wayne IN 1939 *ED* Univ MI BBA 1961; Univ MI MS 1962 *CORP AFFIL* chmn: TransAm Assurance Co, TransAm Life & Annuity Co; dir: First TransAm Life Ins Co, TransAm Fin Corp, TransAm Ins Corp, TransAm Ins Group, TransAm Intl Ins

Svcs, TransAm Investment Svcs Inc, TransAm Life Ins Co Canada, TransAm Realty Svcs Inc; exec vp: TransAm Corp; group vp: TransAm Corp; pres: TransAm Ins Corp CA *NONPR AFFIL* bd: Am Womens Econ Devel Corp, Century City Assn, Independent Colls Southern CA; bd visit: Univ CA Los Angeles Anderson Grad Sch Bus Mgmt; chmn bd dirs: CA Med Ctr Fdn; dir: Womens Econ Devel Corp; fellow: Soc Actuaries; gov bd: Fords Theatre; mem: Am Acad Actuaries, Assn CA Life Ins Cos, Intl Ins Soc, Los Angeles Chamber Commerce; trust, founding mem: Alliance Aging Res; vchmn: UniHealth Am

Richard Henry Finn: dir *CURR EMPL* pres, ceo, dir: TransAm Fin Corp (see above)

Edgar Hardd Grubb: dir *CURR EMPL* exec vp, cfo: TransAm Corp (see above)

James Ross Harvey: chmn, dir *CURR EMPL* chmn: TransAm Corp (see above)

Frank Casper Herringer: vchmn, dir *CURR EMPL* pres, ceo, dir: TransAm Corp (see above)

Richard Neal Latzer: vp, dir *B* New York NY 1937 *ED* Univ PA BA 1959; Univ PA MA 1961 *CURR EMPL* sr vp, chief investment off: TransAm Corp *CORP AFFIL* chief investment off: ARC Reinsurance Corp; chief investment off, mem investment comm: TransAm Ins Group; chmn, chief investment off, dir: TransAm Life Ins & Annuity Co, TransAm Occidental Life Ins Co; dir: TransAm Assurance Co, TransAm Cash Reserve Inc, TransAm Income Shares, TransAm Realty Investment Corp; dir, mem exec comm: TransAm Realty Svcs Inc; pres: TransAm Investment Svcs Inc *NONPR AFFIL* mem: Chartered Fin Analysts, Security Analysts San Francisco

James Blakeley Lockhart: pres, dir *CURR EMPL* vp pub aff: TransAm Corp (see above)

Christopher M. McLain: vp, secy, dir *B* San Luis Obispo CA 1943 *ED* Univ CA Berkeley BS 1965; Univ CA Berkeley JD 1968 *CURR EMPL* sr vp, gen couns, secy: TransAm Corp *NONPR AFFIL* mem: Alameda County Bar Assn, Am Bar Assn, Am Soc Corp Secys, CA Bar Assn

Richard James Olsen: dir *B* San Francisco CA 1938 *ED* Stanford Univ 1964 *CURR EMPL* vp corp rels: TransAm Corp

Mary Sawai: asst secy

APPLICATION INFORMATION
Initial Approach: *Initial Contact:* brief letter or proposal *Include Information On:* description of the organization, amount requested, purpose for which funds are sought, recently audited financial statement, proof of tax-exempt status, and a list of board of directors *Deadlines:* none

Restrictions on Giving: Does not support individuals; political, religious, or fraternal organizations; advertisements in charitable publications; or loans.

OTHER THINGS TO KNOW
Company reports that certain aspects of the giving program are undergoing changes and that giving may be somewhat curtailed in the future.

GRANTS ANALYSIS
Total Grants: $1,419,403

Number of Grants: 2,932

Highest Grant: $50,000

Average Grant: $484

Typical Range: $100 to $5,000

Disclosure Period: 1993

Note: Figures above reflect foundation contributions only and include matching gifts. Recent grants are derived from a 1993 Form 990.

RECENT GRANTS

Library

12,500	San Francisco Library, San Francisco, CA

General

50,000	Glide Memorial Foundation, San Francisco, CA — food program
25,000	Glide Memorial Foundation, San Francisco, CA — 30th anniversary celebration
25,000	National Parks Foundation, Washington, DC
25,000	Salvation Army of the Bay Area, San Francisco, CA
20,000	San Francisco Food Bank, San Francisco, CA

Trust Funds

CONTACT
Albert J. Steiss
President
Trust Funds
100 Broadway, 3rd Fl.
San Francisco, CA 94111
(415) 434-3323

FINANCIAL SUMMARY
Recent Giving: $204,074 (1993); $237,080 (1992); $290,225 (1991)

Assets: $4,134,005 (1993); $4,008,003 (1992); $4,048,050 (1991)

Gifts Received: $1,000 (1993); $500 (1992)

EIN: 94-6062952

CONTRIBUTIONS SUMMARY
Donor(s): Bartley P. Oliver

Typical Recipients: • *Arts & Humanities:* Libraries, Museums/Galleries, Music, Opera • *Civic & Public Affairs:* Employment/Job Training, Housing, Nonprofit Management, Public Policy, Rural Affairs, Women's Affairs • *Education:* Colleges & Universities, Elementary Education (Public), Faculty Development, General, Minority Education, Private Education (Precollege), Religious Education, Science/Mathematics Education, Secondary Education (Private), Student Aid • *Health:* Emergency/Ambulance Services, Geriatric Health, Hospitals, Mental Health • *International:* International Peace & Security Issues, Missionary/Religious Activities • *Religion:* Churches, Dioceses, Religious Organizations, Religious Welfare, Social/Policy Issues • *Social Services:* Community Service Organizations, Family Planning, Family Services, Food/Clothing Distribution, Senior Services, Youth Organizations

Grant Types: conference/seminar, emergency, general support, research, scholarship, and seed money

Geographic Distribution: focus on the San Francisco Bay area, CA

GIVING OFFICERS
James T. Healy: cfo, vp, dir

David Ramsey: dir

Albert J. Steiss: pres, dir

Rev. James J. Ward: vp, secy, dir

APPLICATION INFORMATION
Initial Approach: Send a brief letter of inquiry. Include a description of organization, amount requested, purpose of funds sought, recently audited financial statement, and proof of tax-exempt status. There are no deadlines.

Restrictions on Giving: Limited to Catholic charities in the San Francisco Bay Area.

PUBLICATIONS
Application Guidelines

GRANTS ANALYSIS
Total Grants: $204,074

Number of Grants: 27

Highest Grant: $20,000

Typical Range: $450 to $15,528

Disclosure Period: 1993

Note: Recent grants are derived from a 1993 Form 990.

RECENT GRANTS

Library

1,000	Foundation Center, San Francisco, CA — for support of library research publication for foundations

General

20,000	Archdiocese of San Francisco, San Francisco, CA — for planning commission
18,000	Human Life Center, University of Steubenville, Steubenville, OH — for salary of research assistant
15,528	Sacramento Life Center, Sacramento, CA — for anti-abortion counseling
15,000	Americans United for Life, Chicago, IL — for anti-abortion initiative through courts
10,000	Archdiocese of San Francisco, San Francisco, CA — for Respect for Life Commission

Union Bank / Union Bank Foundation

Assets: $16.39 billion
Employees: 8,000
Parent Company: Bank of Tokyo, Ltd., Tokyo, Japan
Headquarters: San Francisco, CA
SIC Major Group: State Commercial Banks

CONTACT
Christopher I. M. Houser
President
Union Bank Foundation
Terminal Annex
PO Box 3100
Los Angeles, CA 90051
(213) 236-5826
Note: Call (415)705-7396 for the Public Relations department.

FINANCIAL SUMMARY
Recent Giving: $1,446,787 (1993); $1,144,563 (1992); $2,340,000 (1991 approx.)

Assets: $638,635 (1993); $874,199 (1992); $862,144 (1991)

Gifts Received: $1,200,000 (1993); $1,137,421 (1992)

Fiscal Note: Above figures include both foundation contributions and direct giving by the bank. Above figures exclude nonmonetary support. In 1993, contributions were received from Union Bank.

EIN: 95-6023551

CONTRIBUTIONS SUMMARY
Typical Recipients: • *Arts & Humanities:* Arts Centers, Arts Funds, Arts Institutes, Dance, Ethnic & Folk Arts, Historic Preservation, Libraries, Museums/Galleries, Music, Opera, Performing Arts, Public Broadcasting, Theater • *Civic & Public Affairs:* African American Affairs, Asian American Affairs, Botanical Gardens/Parks, Chambers of Commerce, Community Foundations, Economic Development, General, Housing, Nonprofit Management, Urban & Community Affairs, Women's Affairs • *Education:* Arts/Humanities Education, Business Education, Colleges & Universities, Economic Education, Education Funds, Education Reform, Engineering/Technological Education, Minority Education • *Environment:* General • *Health:* Emergency/Ambulance Services, Hospitals, Medical Rehabilitation, Medical Research, Single-Disease Health Associations • *International:* International Affairs, International Relations • *Science:* Scientific Organizations • *Social Services:* Community Service Organizations, Domestic Violence, Family Services, People with Disabilities, United Funds/United Ways, Youth Organizations

Grant Types: capital, general support, and project

Nonmonetary Support Types: donated equipment

Note: No estimate is available for value of nonmonetary support.

Geographic Distribution: primarily in California

Operating Locations: CA (Los Angeles)

CORP. OFFICERS
Tamotsu Yamaguchi: *B* Hokkaido Japan 1930 *ED* Univ Tokyo BS 1953 *CURR EMPL* chmn: Union Bank *CORP AFFIL* chmn: Bank Tokyo Trust Co *NONPR AFFIL* dir: Asia Soc, CA Bus Roundtable, Japan Am Soc, KCET, Los Angeles Sports Counc, Los Angeles World Aff Counc; mem bd overseers: Huntington Lib; mem ceo bd adv: Univ Southern CA

Kanetaka Yoshida: *CURR EMPL* pres, ceo, dir: Union Bank

GIVING OFFICERS
Christopher I. M. Houser: pres *B* Los Angeles CA 1936 *ED* Stanford Univ 1958

APPLICATION INFORMATION
Initial Approach: *Initial Contact:* brief letter or proposal *Include Information On:* description of the organization, amount requested, purpose for which funds are sought, recently audited financial statement, and proof of tax-exempt status *Deadlines:* none; board meets quarterly

Restrictions on Giving: Foundation does not support individuals, primary or secondary education, or religious or political organizations.

OTHER THINGS TO KNOW
The foundation lists Union Bank as a corporate trustee.

GRANTS ANALYSIS
Total Grants: $1,146,787

Number of Grants: 324

Highest Grant: $125,000

Average Grant: $3,539

Typical Range: $500 to $5,000

Disclosure Period: 1993

Note: Financial information is for the foundation only. Recent grants are derived from a 1993 Form 990.

RECENT GRANTS
Library

50,000	San Francisco Library Foundation, San Francisco, CA — first payment of three-year pledge
12,500	University of California San Francisco, San Francisco, CA — Health Services Library, final payment of two-year pledge
10,000	Los Angeles Public Library, Los Angeles, CA

General

125,000	United Way of Los Angeles, Los Angeles, CA
99,750	United Way of Los Angeles, Los Angeles, CA
99,750	United Way of Los Angeles, Los Angeles, CA
50,000	United Way of San Diego, San Diego, CA
50,000	United Way of San Diego, San Diego, CA

Unocal Corp. / Unocal Foundation

Revenue: $7.07 billion
Employees: 14,687
Headquarters: Los Angeles, CA
SIC Major Group: Chemicals & Allied Products, Oil & Gas Extraction, Petroleum & Coal Products, and Wholesale Trade—Nondurable Goods

CONTACT
Judith Barker
President and Director
Unocal Foundation
1201 W 5th St.
Los Angeles, CA 90017
(213) 977-6171

FINANCIAL SUMMARY
Recent Giving: $4,000,000 (fiscal 1995 est.); $3,700,000 (fiscal 1994 approx.); $3,089,818 (fiscal 1993)

Assets: $3,859,519 (fiscal 1994); $1,050,000 (fiscal 1993); $4,646,623 (fiscal 1991)

Gifts Received: $6,336,000 (fiscal 1994)

Fiscal Note: In fiscal 1994, the foundation gave $2,485,025 and the company gave approximately $1,214,975. Above figures exclude nonmonetary support. In 1994, Foundation received contributions from Union Oil Company of California ($6,336,000).
EIN: 95-6071812

CONTRIBUTIONS SUMMARY
Typical Recipients: • *Arts & Humanities:* Arts Centers, Arts Institutes, Community Arts, Dance, Historic Preservation, Libraries, Museums/Galleries, Music, Opera, Performing Arts, Theater • *Civic & Public Affairs:* African American Affairs, Business/Free Enterprise, Civil Rights, Economic Development, Economic Policy, Employment/Job Training, Hispanic Affairs, Housing, Law & Justice, Legal Aid, Minority Business, Nonprofit Management, Professional & Trade Associations, Public Policy, Safety, Urban & Community Affairs, Women's Affairs • *Education:* Agricultural Education, Arts/Humanities Education, Business Education, Colleges & Universities, Continuing Education, Economic Education, Education Associations, Education Funds, Education Reform, Engineering/Technological Education, Faculty Development, International Exchange, International Studies, Leadership Training, Legal Education, Medical Education, Minority Education, Public Education (Precollege), Science/Mathematics Education, Secondary Education (Public), Social Sciences Education, Student Aid • *Environment:* General, Resource Conservation • *Health:* Arthritis, Clinics/Medical Centers, Emergency/Ambulance Services, Health Organizations, Hospitals, Medical Rehabilitation, Medical Research, Medical Training, Mental Health, Single-Disease

Health Associations • *International:* International Affairs, International Organizations, International Relations • *Religion:* Religious Welfare • *Science:* Science Exhibits & Fairs, Scientific Centers & Institutes, Scientific Organizations • *Social Services:* Big Brother/Big Sister, Community Service Organizations, General, Homes, People with Disabilities, Recreation & Athletics, Scouts, Special Olympics, Substance Abuse, United Funds/United Ways, YMCA/YWCA/YMHA/YWHA, Youth Organizations

Grant Types: challenge, department, employee matching gifts, fellowship, general support, professorship, project, research, and scholarship

Geographic Distribution: nationally, with preference given to areas where Unocal maintains corporate facilities

Operating Locations: AK, CA, LA, TX

CORP. OFFICERS
Claude Stout Brinegar: *B* Rockport CA 1926 *ED* Stanford Univ BA 1950; Stanford Univ MS 1951; Stanford Univ PhD 1954 *CURR EMPL* vchmn, exec vp, dir: Unocal Corp *CORP AFFIL* bd dirs: Maxicare Health Plans Inc; exec vp, chief fin off: Union Oil Co CA; founding dir: Consolidated Rail Corp; pres, dir: Unocal Intl Corp *NONPR AFFIL* bd adv: Farnsworth Art Mus; chmn: CA Citizens Compensation Commn; mem: Am Petroleum Inst, Phi Beta Kappa, Sigma Xi *CLUB AFFIL* Boothbay Harbor YC, CA, Georgetown, Intl, Southport YC

Richard Joseph Stegemeier: *B* Alton IL 1928 *ED* Univ MO BS 1950; TX A&M Univ MS 1951 *CURR EMPL* chmn, ceo: Unocal Corp *CORP AFFIL* dir: First Interstate Bancorp, Northrop Grumman Corp, Outboard Marine Corp *NONPR AFFIL* adv counc: CA St Univ Long Beach; bd govs: Los Angeles County Music Ctr, Town Hall CA; bd overseers: Exec Counc Foreign Diplomats, Huntington Lib; bd visit: Univ CA Los Angeles Anderson Grad Sch Bus Mgmt, Univ MO Rolla; chmn: Boy Scouts Am Los Angeles Area Counc, Los Angeles World Aff Counc; dir: Am Petroleum Inst, CA Econ Devel Corp, French Fdn Alzheimer Res, Los Angeles Philharmonic Assn, Natl Counc Bus Advs, Orange County Performing Arts Ctr, John Tracy Clinic, YMCA Metro Los Angeles; dir, mem: Natl Assn Mfrs; mem: Am Inst Chem Engrs, CA Bus Roundtable, CA Counc Sci & Tech, Conf Bd, Counc Foreign Rels, Natl Acad Engg, Natl Petroleum Counc, Soc Petroleum Engrs; mem adv bd: CA St Univ Fullerton, Northwestern Univ JL Kellogg Grad Sch Bus Mgmt; trust: Comm Econ Devel, Harvey Mudd Coll, Los Angeles Archdiocese Fdn, Loyola Marymount Univ, Hugh OBrian Youth Fdn, Univ Southern CA *CLUB AFFIL* CA CC

GIVING OFFICERS
Judith Barker: pres, dir

MacDonald G. Becket: dir

Claude Stout Brinegar: dir *CURR EMPL* vchmn, exec vp, dir: Unocal Corp (see above)

D. D. Chessum: treas *CURR EMPL* treas, dir: Unocal Intl Corp *CORP AFFIL* treas: Poco Graphite Inc; vp, dir: Southcap Pipe Line Co

Jon S. Gibby: vp

Karen Ann Sikkema: dir *B* Kalamazoo MI 1946 *ED* Kalamazoo Coll 1968; Univ MI 1970 *CURR EMPL* vp corp commun: Unocal Corp *NONPR AFFIL* dir: Alliance Bus Childcare Devel

Richard Joseph Stegemeier: dir *CURR EMPL* chmn, ceo: Unocal Corp (see above)

APPLICATION INFORMATION

Initial Approach: *Initial Contact:* brief letter *Include Information On:* background of organization, including its goals and objectives; necessity/purpose of grant; amount budgeted for project; most recent audited financial statement and annual report; current year's budget; evaluative criteria; other organizations solicited and amounts received, pledged, or anticipated; copy of IRS determination letter; copy of most recent IRS Form 990 *Deadlines:* none

Restrictions on Giving: Foundation does not support grants to individuals; elementary or secondary education; political or lobbying groups; veterans, fraternal, sectarian, social, religious, athletic, choral, band, or similar groups; courtesy advertising; conferences, films, or contests; supplemental operating support for organizations eligible for united funds; governmental agencies or departments; or trade, business, or professional associations; most capital campaigns or endowments.

Grants are not renewed automatically; a request for support must be submitted each year.

GRANTS ANALYSIS

Total Grants: $2,485,025

Number of Grants: 199

Highest Grant: $740,561

Average Grant: $12,488

Typical Range: $1,000 to $20,000

Disclosure Period: fiscal year ending January 31, 1994

Note: Above information for foundation only. Excludes $1,214,975 in direct giving. Recent grants are derived from a fiscal 1994 Form 990.

RECENT GRANTS

General

740,561	United Way Campaign, Los Angeles, CA — for welfare
100,000	California Institute of Technology, Pasadena, CA — for Center for Air Quality Analysis
94,000	Citizens Scholarship Foundation of America, St. Peter, MN — for scholarships and fellowships
50,000	Archdiocese of Los Angeles Education Foundation, Los Angeles, CA — for education
50,000	Carter Center, Atlanta, GA — for welfare

USL Capital Corporation

Revenue: $564.5 million
Employees: 719
Parent Company: Ford Motor Co.
Headquarters: San Francisco, CA
SIC Major Group: Miscellaneous Business Credit Institutions and Equipment Rental & Leasing Nec

CONTACT

Tom Donahoe
Manager, Corporate Contributions
USL Capital
733 Front St.
San Francisco, CA 94111
(415) 627-9710

FINANCIAL SUMMARY

Recent Giving: $600,000 (1995 est.); $597,500 (1994); $500,000 (1993)

Fiscal Note: Company gives directly. Above figures include nonmonetary support.

CONTRIBUTIONS SUMMARY

Typical Recipients: • *Arts & Humanities:* Arts Associations & Councils, Arts Festivals, Arts Outreach, Ballet, Dance, Ethnic & Folk Arts, Libraries, Museums/Galleries, Music, Opera, Performing Arts, Public Broadcasting, Theater • *Civic & Public Affairs:* Asian American Affairs, Business/Free Enterprise, Employment/Job Training, Housing, Legal Aid, Municipalities/Towns, Parades/Festivals, Public Policy, Women's Affairs, Zoos/Aquariums • *Education:* Arts/Humanities Education, Colleges & Universities, Education Funds, Minority Education, Public Education (Precollege) • *Health:* AIDS/HIV, Clinics/Medical Centers, Hospices, Prenatal Health Issues, Preventive Medicine/Wellness Organizations • *Religion:* Religious Welfare • *Science:* Science Museums, Scientific Centers & Institutes • *Social Services:* At-Risk Youth, Child Welfare, Community Centers, Community Service Organizations, Domestic Violence, Family Services, Food/Clothing Distribution, People with Disabilities, Recreation & Athletics, Scouts, Shelters/Homelessness, United Funds/United Ways, Volunteer Services, Youth Organizations

Grant Types: employee matching gifts, general support, and project

Note: Employee matching gift ratio: 2 to 1 for first $500, and 1 to 1 for gifts greater than $500. The maximum total matched is $2,000.

Nonmonetary Support: $47,500 (1994)

Nonmonetary Support Types: donated equipment

Geographic Distribution: primarily to San Francisco or Bay Area organizations

Operating Locations: CA (San Francisco, San Mateo)

CORP. OFFICERS

James George Duff: *B* Pittsburg KS 1938 *ED* Univ KS BA 1960; Univ KS MBA 1961 *CURR EMPL* chmn, ceo, dir: USL Capital

Corp *CORP AFFIL* dir: Airlease Mgmt Svcs, US Fleet Leasing Inc, US Rail Svcs *NONPR AFFIL* dir: Bay Area Counc; mem: Conf Bd, San Francisco Chamber Commerce; mem adv bd: Univ KS Sch Bus; trust: San Francisco Mus Modern Art

William Selover: *CURR EMPL* vp corp communs: USL Capital Corp

GIVING OFFICERS

Tom Donahoe: *CURR EMPL* mgr corp contributions: USL Capital Corp

APPLICATION INFORMATION

Initial Approach: *Initial Contact:* brief letter *Include Information On:* description of the organization, proposed use of funds, other sources of funds applicable to the proposal, and a description of how USL Capital support would be recognized. *Deadlines:* none

Restrictions on Giving: Does not support religious organizations for sectarian purposes; organizations that do not have current 501(c)(3) tax exempt status; individual primary and secondary schools (except as an employee matching gift); political or lobbying activities; sports programs without other charitable purpose; or endowment funds.

OTHER THINGS TO KNOW

Gives priority to organizations in which company's employees are active in a regular volunteer capacity.

Company was formerly known as US Leasing International.

PUBLICATIONS

Guidelines

GRANTS ANALYSIS

Total Grants: $550,000

Number of Grants: 89

Highest Grant: $47,500

Average Grant: $5,098

Typical Range: $3,000 to $5,000

Disclosure Period: 1994

Note: Total grants, Number of grants and average grant figures exclude matching gifts. Recent grants are derived from a 1994 contributions report.

RECENT GRANTS

General

14,000	Children's Garden of California, San Rafael, CA
10,000	CORO Foundation, Los Angeles, CA
10,000	San Francisco School Volunteers, San Francisco, CA
7,500	San Francisco AIDS Foundation, San Francisco, CA
7,500	San Francisco Education Fund, San Francisco, CA

Van Nuys Foundation, I. N. and Susanna H.

CONTACT
George A. Bender
Co-Trustee
I. N. and Susanna H. Van Nuys Fdn.
444 S Flower St., Ste. 2340
Los Angeles, CA 90071
(213) 362-0900

FINANCIAL SUMMARY
Recent Giving: $650,098 (fiscal 1994); $712,462 (fiscal 1993); $679,435 (fiscal 1992)

Assets: $10,894,217 (fiscal 1994); $11,501,488 (fiscal 1993); $11,716,305 (fiscal 1992)

EIN: 95-6006019

CONTRIBUTIONS SUMMARY
Typical Recipients: • *Arts & Humanities:* Historic Preservation, Libraries, Museums/Galleries • *Civic & Public Affairs:* Urban & Community Affairs • *Education:* Colleges & Universities, Engineering/Technological Education, Private Education (Precollege), Public Education (Precollege), Student Aid • *Health:* Children's Health/Hospitals, Hospitals, Long-Term Care • *Religion:* Churches, Religious Welfare • *Science:* Science Museums • *Social Services:* Animal Protection, Child Welfare, Community Service Organizations, Homes, People with Disabilities, Substance Abuse, Youth Organizations

Grant Types: general support

Geographic Distribution: focus on CA

GIVING OFFICERS
Bank of America: trust

George A. Bender: co-trust

Arthur L. Crowe, Jr.: dir

George H. Whitney: trust

APPLICATION INFORMATION
Initial Approach: The foundation requests applications be made in writing. Include a description of organization, amount requested, purpose of funds sought, recently audited financial statement, and proof of tax-exempt status. There are no deadlines.

Restrictions on Giving: Limited to scientific and educational purposes.

GRANTS ANALYSIS
Total Grants: $650,098

Number of Grants: 20

Highest Grant: $339,593

Typical Range: $500 to $67,918

Disclosure Period: fiscal year ending May 31, 1994

Note: Recent grants are derived from a fiscal 1994 Form 990.

RECENT GRANTS

Library
25,000	Library Foundation of Los Angeles, Los Angeles, CA
13,584	Henry E. Huntington Library and Art Gallery, San Marino, CA

General
339,593	Hospital of the Good Samaritan, Los Angeles, CA
67,918	Wellesley College, Wellesley, MA
63,958	California Institute of Technology, Pasadena, CA
40,751	Children's Hospital, Los Angeles, CA
10,000	Foothill Country Day School, Claremont, CA

Weingart Foundation

CONTACT
John G. Ouellet
President and Chief Administrative Officer
Weingart Foundation
PO Box 17982
Los Angeles, CA 90017-0982
(213) 688-7799

FINANCIAL SUMMARY
Recent Giving: $25,000,000 (fiscal 1995 est.); $25,254,704 (fiscal 1994); $25,147,402 (fiscal 1993)

Assets: $500,000,000 (fiscal 1995 est.); $485,559,047 (fiscal 1994); $494,859,808 (fiscal 1993)

Gifts Received: $50,000 (fiscal 1992 est.); $12,142 (fiscal 1991); $12,906,340 (fiscal 1990)

Fiscal Note: The foundation received $10,428,992 from the distribution of the Ben Weingart Charitable Testamentary Trust and $1,876,981 from a revocable trust, which terminated during the 1990 fiscal year.

EIN: 95-6054814

CONTRIBUTIONS SUMMARY
Donor(s): Ben Weingart (1888-1980) was a real estate developer in Southern California who helped create a new town, the City of Lakewood, during the 1950s. It was the first planned city in Southern California. Mr. Weingart was born in Atlanta, GA. He attended school through the eighth grade and arrived in Los Angeles when he was 18 years old.

The Weingart Foundation was established in California in 1951 as the B. W. Foundation. The name of the foundation was changed in April 1978. Funds for the foundation's incorporation were donated by the late Ben Weingart and Stella Weingart, who bequeathed their estates to the foundation.

Typical Recipients: • *Arts & Humanities:* Arts Centers, Arts Institutes, Arts Outreach, Libraries, Museums/Galleries, Public Broadcasting • *Civic & Public Affairs:* Community Foundations, Law & Justice, Public Policy • *Education:* Arts/Humanities Education, Business Education, Colleges & Universities, Education Reform, Elementary Education (Private), Engineering/Technological Education, Faculty Development, Literacy, Medical Education, Minority Education, Preschool Education, Private Education (Precollege), Public Education (Precollege), Science/Mathematics Education, Special Education, Student Aid, Vocational & Technical Education • *Health:* Cancer, Children's Health/Hospitals, Clinics/Medical Centers, Emergency/Ambulance Services, Health Organizations, Hospices, Hospitals, Medical Research, Nursing Services, Outpatient Health Care, Prenatal Health Issues • *International:* Missionary/Religious Activities • *Religion:* Jewish Causes, Religious Welfare • *Science:* Science Museums, Scientific Centers & Institutes • *Social Services:* At-Risk Youth, Camps, Child Abuse, Child Welfare, Community Centers, Community Service Organizations, Counseling, Crime Prevention, Day Care, Delinquency & Criminal Rehabilitation, Emergency Relief, Family Services, Food/Clothing Distribution, People with Disabilities, Recreation & Athletics, Scouts, Shelters/Homelessness, Substance Abuse, Volunteer Services, YMCA/YWCA/YMHA/YWHA, Youth Organizations

Grant Types: capital, challenge, project, and seed money

Geographic Distribution: nine counties in Southern California

GIVING OFFICERS
Roy Arnold Anderson: chmn, ceo *B* Ripon CA 1920 *ED* Stanford Univ AB 1947; Stanford Univ Grad Sch Bus 1949 *CURR EMPL* chmn emeritus: Lockheed Corp *CORP AFFIL* dir: Atlantic Richfield Co, First Interstate Bancorp, First Interstate Bank CA, Southern CA Edison Co

Steven D. Broidy: dir *B* 1938 *CURR EMPL* vchmn bd: City Natl Bank *CORP AFFIL* vchmn bd, dir: City Natl Corp

Gloria De Necochea: program off *PHIL AFFIL* fdn mgr: Mattel Foundation

Susan H. Grimes: corp secy, program off

John Thomas Gurash: dir, mem audit comm *B* Oakland CA 1910 *ED* Loyola Univ Sch Law 1938-1939 *CURR EMPL* chmn: Horace Mann Educators Corp *CORP AFFIL* dir: St Gobain Corp *NONPR AFFIL* mem: Am Soc French Legion Honor, Newcomen Soc, PA Soc; trust: Orthopedic Hosp; trust emeritus: Occidental Coll *CLUB AFFIL* Annandale GC, California, Los Angeles CC, Pine Valley GC, Senior Golf Assn Southern CA, Valley Hunt

Barbara Kaze: program off

William J. McGill: dir *PHIL AFFIL* dir: Richard Lounsbery Foundation

John G. Ouellet: pres, chief admin off

Sol Price: dir *B* Chicago IL 1932 *ED* Northwestern Univ 1954 *CURR EMPL* chmn emeritus, dir: Price Co *CORP AFFIL* chmn, dir: Price Reit; treas: IL Glove Co *PHIL AFFIL* pres, dir, don: Sol and Helen Price Foundation

Dennis Carothers Stanfill: dir *B* Centerville TN 1927 *ED* US Naval Academy BS 1949; Oxford Univ MA 1953 *CURR EMPL* pres: Stanfill Bowen & Co *CORP AFFIL* co-chmn, ceo: Metro-Goldwyn Mayer; co-chmn, co-ceo, dir: Pathe Commun Corp; dir:

Broadway Stores Inc, Carter Hawley Hale Stores, Dial Corp *NONPR AFFIL* trust: CA Inst Tech, John F Kennedy Ctr Performing Arts

Ann L. Van Dormolen: vp, treas *B* 1947 *ED* DePaul Univ Coll 1968-1973

Harry J. Volk: chmn, ceo, dir *B* Trenton NJ 1905 *ED* Rutgers Univ AB 1927; Rutgers Univ LLB 1930 *NONPR AFFIL* mem: CA Inst Tech Assocs, Los Angeles Chamber Commerce, Los Angeles County Mus Art, Univ Southern CA Assocs *CLUB AFFIL* Bohemian, California, Founders, Los Angeles CC

Laurence A. Wolfe: vp (admin)

APPLICATION INFORMATION
Initial Approach:

A qualified organization that believes it meets the foundation's criteria for a grant should first submit a brief, to-the-point "test letter."

The letter, not to exceed two pages, should contain a concise statement of the need for funds, amount sought, and enough factual information to enable the foundation to determine an initial response. Supporting data may be included. Fifteen copies are required. If the project meets the foundation's priorities, a formal application will be sent to the organization.

Applications are accepted throughout the year.

Final notification arrives three to four months after receiving the proposal.

Restrictions on Giving: The foundation does not make grants for propagandizing, influencing legislation and/or elections, promoting voter registration, for political candidates, political campaigns or organizations engaged in political activities. The foundation does not make grants to federated appeals or to organizations that collect funds for redistribution to other nonprofit groups. It does not make grants for support of national charities, for operating budgets of agencies served by the United Way or other federated sources (except for approved special projects), for operating expenses of performing arts organizations, or for the benefit of individuals or small groups. The foundation does not consider requests for support of projects that normally would be financed from government funds. It ordinarily does not make grants for endowment funds, contingencies, or deficits. As a general rule, it does not make grants for conferences, seminars, workshops, exhibits, travel, surveys, publishing activities, or films. Nor does the foundation encourage applications for funding the projects of environmental, consumer, refugee, and religious groups; international organizations; or governmental or quasi-governmental agencies. Applicant organizations must be tax-exempt under section 501(c)(3) of the IRS code.

OTHER THINGS TO KNOW
The foundation expects applicant organizations to show project support from internal sources as well as outside sources. Grants may cover a multiyear period in some cases, but the foundation generally does not make

a grant to any organization on an annual basis.

PUBLICATIONS
Annual report, guidelines, and application procedures

GRANTS ANALYSIS
Total Grants: $25,254,704

Number of Grants: 745

Highest Grant: $2,500,000

Average Grant: $33,899

Typical Range: $25,000 to $100,000

Disclosure Period: fiscal year ending June 30, 1994

Note: Recent grants are derived from a fiscal 1994 annual report.

RECENT GRANTS
Library

250,000	George Bush Presidential Library Foundation, Houston, TX — toward Library Center at Texas A&M University
100,000	University of La Verne, La Verne, CA — toward expansion and renovation of Wilson Library and related facilities

General

2,500,000	American Red Cross Los Angeles Chapter, Los Angeles, CA — Northridge Earthquake Relief
1,150,000	Los Angeles Mission, Los Angeles, CA — toward renovation of hotel for multipurpose use and support of transient housing program
1,000,000	California Institute of Technology, Pasadena, CA — to support Dr. Lee A. DuBridge Postdoctoral Prize Fellows Award Fund
600,000	American Red Cross Los Angeles Chapter, Los Angeles, CA — to support new Central East District headquarters facility and toward the Missouri/Mississippi River disaster relief fund
510,000	City of Hope, Los Angeles, CA — to support medical services for children without insurance

West Foundation, Harry and Ethel

CONTACT
Harvey H. Means
Vice President and Secretary
Harry and Ethel West Fdn.
PO Box 1825
Bakersfield, CA 93303
(805) 324-9801

FINANCIAL SUMMARY
Recent Giving: $151,185 (1993)

Assets: $5,736,800 (1993)

EIN: 23-7168492

CONTRIBUTIONS SUMMARY
Typical Recipients: • *Arts & Humanities:* History & Archaeology, Libraries, Museums/Galleries, Music, Public Broadcasting • *Civic & Public Affairs:* Business/Free Enterprise, Clubs, General, Hispanic Affairs, Law & Justice, Public Policy, Rural Affairs, Safety, Urban & Community Affairs • *Education:* Colleges & Universities, General, Public Education (Precollege), Secondary Education (Public) • *Environment:* General • *Health:* Arthritis, Hospitals, Medical Research, Single-Disease Health Associations • *Religion:* Religious Welfare • *Social Services:* Animal Protection, At-Risk Youth, Child Welfare, Senior Services, YMCA/YWCA/YMHA/YWHA, Youth Organizations

Grant Types: general support

Geographic Distribution: focus on Kern County, CA

GIVING OFFICERS
A. O. Knapp: pres

Richard G. McBurnie: dir

Harvey H. Means: vp, secy *PHIL AFFIL* pres, dir: Ben H. and Gladys Arkelian Foundation

APPLICATION INFORMATION
Initial Approach: Send a brief letter of inquiry. There are no deadlines.

GRANTS ANALYSIS
Total Grants: $151,185

Number of Grants: 37

Highest Grant: $35,000

Typical Range: $60 to $13,000

Disclosure Period: 1993

Note: Recent grants are derived from a 1993 Form 990.

RECENT GRANTS

Library

13,000	Kern County Library Foundation, Bakersfield, CA

General

35,000	Kern Agricultural Foundation, Bakersfield, CA
12,500	California State University Bakersfield, Bakersfield, CA
7,000	Garces Memorial High School, Bakersfield, CA
6,000	Fisheries Foundation of California, Richmond, CA
5,088	YMCA of Kern County, Bakersfield, CA

Whitecap Foundation

CONTACT
Elizabeth Duker
President
Whitecap Fdn.
800 Wilshire Blvd., Ste. 1010
Los Angeles, CA 90017
(213) 624-5401

FINANCIAL SUMMARY
Recent Giving: $831,766 (fiscal 1994)

Assets: $8,138,937 (fiscal 1994)

Gifts Received: $500,000 (fiscal 1994)

Fiscal Note: In fiscal 1994, contributions were received from Mr. and Mrs. Brack Duker.

EIN: 95-4111120

CONTRIBUTIONS SUMMARY
Typical Recipients: • *Arts & Humanities:* Dance, Libraries • *Civic & Public Affairs:* Asian American Affairs, General, Hispanic Affairs, Nonprofit Management, Professional & Trade Associations, Urban & Community Affairs • *Education:* Colleges & Universities, Elementary Education (Public), General, Literacy, Private Education (Precollege), Public Education (Precollege) • *Environment:* General, Wildlife Protection • *Health:* Mental Health • *International:* International Relief Efforts • *Religion:* Religious Organizations, Religious Welfare • *Social Services:* Community Centers, Emergency Relief, Family Services, Scouts, Youth Organizations

Grant Types: general support

Geographic Distribution: focus on CA

GIVING OFFICERS
Brack Duker: cfo, secy

Elizabeth Duker: pres

APPLICATION INFORMATION
Initial Approach: Send a brief letter of inquiry. Include a description of organization, amount requested, purpose of funds sought, recently audited financial statement, and proof of tax-exempt status. There are no deadlines.

GRANTS ANALYSIS
Total Grants: $831,766

Number of Grants: 38

Highest Grant: $136,029

Typical Range: $900 to $95,200

Disclosure Period: fiscal year ending November 30, 1994

Note: Recent grants are derived from a fiscal 1994 Form 990.

RECENT GRANTS

Library
25,000	Library Foundation of Los Angeles, Los Angeles, CA

General
136,029	Our Savior Center
95,200	Ducks Unlimited, Jackson, WY
42,100	Mt. St. Mary's College

33,817	Valle Lindo School District
33,517	Rx for Reading, Milwaukee, WI

Witter Foundation, Dean

CONTACT
Dean Witter III
President
Dean Witter Fdn.
601 Montgomery, No. 900
San Francisco, CA 94111
(415) 788-8855

FINANCIAL SUMMARY
Recent Giving: $519,137 (fiscal 1993); $358,260 (fiscal 1992); $328,300 (fiscal 1991)

Assets: $12,308,666 (fiscal 1993); $10,489,535 (fiscal 1992); $9,938,935 (fiscal 1991)

Gifts Received: $36,925 (fiscal 1989); $9,500 (fiscal 1988)

EIN: 94-6065150

CONTRIBUTIONS SUMMARY
Donor(s): the late Dean Witter, Mrs. Dean Witter, Dean Witter and Co.

Typical Recipients: • *Arts & Humanities:* Historic Preservation, History & Archaeology, Libraries, Museums/Galleries • *Civic & Public Affairs:* Botanical Gardens/Parks, Economic Policy, General, Nonprofit Management, Philanthropic Organizations, Public Policy, Zoos/Aquariums • *Education:* Business Education, Colleges & Universities, Public Education (Precollege) • *Environment:* Air/Water Quality, General, Resource Conservation, Wildlife Protection • *International:* International Peace & Security Issues • *Science:* Scientific Centers & Institutes, Scientific Labs • *Social Services:* Animal Protection, Community Service Organizations

Grant Types: capital and project

Geographic Distribution: limited to northern CA

GIVING OFFICERS
James Ramsey Bancroft: vp *B* Ponca City OK *ED* Univ CA Berkeley AB 1940; Univ CA Berkeley MBA 1941; Hastings Coll JD 1949 *CURR EMPL* chmn: Adams Capital Mgmt Co *CORP AFFIL* mem: CA Consumers Inc, Canadian Ins Co CA; of coun: Bancroft Avery & McAlister, owner, mgr: Bancroft Vineyard; pres: Madison Properties Inc *NONPR AFFIL* dir: CA Urology Fdn, Fdn Res Ed Orthopedic Surgery, Pacific Vascular Res Fdn; mem: Am Bar Assn

Salvador O. Gutierrez: trust

Stephen Nessier: trust

Frank H. Roberts: asst secy, trust *PHIL AFFIL* trust: David and Lucile Packard Foundation

Roland E. Tognazzini, Jr.: trust

Dean Witter III: pres, dir

Malcolm G. Witter: trust

William D. Witter: secy, treas

APPLICATION INFORMATION
Initial Approach: Send brief letter of inquiry describing program or project. Include a description of organization, amount requested, purpose of funds sought, recently audited financial statement, and proof of tax-exempt status.

Restrictions on Giving: Does not support individuals or provide endowment funds.

PUBLICATIONS
Annual Report (including application guidelines)

GRANTS ANALYSIS
Total Grants: $519,137

Highest Grant: $105,000

Typical Range: $5,000 to $25,000

Disclosure Period: fiscal year ending November 30, 1993

Note: Recent grants are derived from a fiscal 1993 Form 990.

RECENT GRANTS

General
105,000	Walter A. Hass School of Business, San Francisco, CA
105,000	Walter A. Hass School of Business, San Francisco, CA
75,000	Stanford Graduate School of Business, Stanford, CA
50,000	National Bureau of Economic Research, Cambridge, MA
25,000	Center for Economic Policy Research, Chicago, IL

Y and H Soda Foundation

CONTACT
Judith Murphy
Chief Executive Officer and Vice President
Y and H Soda Fdn.
2 Theatre Square, Ste. 211
Orinda, CA 94563
(510) 253-2630

FINANCIAL SUMMARY
Recent Giving: $2,000,000 (fiscal 1993)

Assets: $69,647,987 (fiscal 1993)

Gifts Received: $5,943,446 (fiscal 1993)

Fiscal Note: In fiscal 1993, contributions were received from the Y. Charles Soda Trust.

EIN: 94-1611668

CONTRIBUTIONS SUMMARY
Typical Recipients: • *Arts & Humanities:* Libraries, Museums/Galleries, Music • *Civic & Public Affairs:* Clubs, General • *Education:* Arts/Humanities Education, Colleges & Universities, Private Education (Precollege), Secondary Education (Private) • *Environment:* General, Wildlife Protection • *Health:* AIDS/HIV, Cancer, Health Organizations • *Religion:* Churches, Dioceses, Jewish Causes, Religious Organizations,

Religious Welfare, Seminaries • *Social Services:* Animal Protection, Community Service Organizations, Day Care, Domestic Violence, Family Services, Food/Clothing Distribution, Senior Services, Youth Organizations

Grant Types: general support

Geographic Distribution: focus on CA

GIVING OFFICERS
Alfred Dossa: pres

James Dye: secy

Alan Holloway: treas, cfo

Judith Murphy: vp, ceo

Rosemary Soda: vp

APPLICATION INFORMATION
Initial Approach: Send a brief letter of inquiry. Include a description of organization, amount requested, purpose of funds sought, recently audited financial statement, and proof of tax-exempt status.

GRANTS ANALYSIS
Total Grants: $2,000,000

Number of Grants: 56

Highest Grant: $12,500

Typical Range: $1,000 to $2,000

Disclosure Period: fiscal year ending November 30, 1993

Note: Recent grants are derived from a fiscal 1993 Form 990.

RECENT GRANTS
Library

1,500	Foundation Center, New York, NY

General

12,500	St. Mary's College, CA
5,000	Beresford Northern Light School
5,000	Heart to Heart, Kansas City, MO
5,000	Salesian Boys and Girls Club, Los Angeles, CA
5,000	Seminary Avenue Development Corp, Oakland, CA

COLORADO

Bacon Foundation, E. L. and Oma

Former Foundation Name: E. L. Bacon Foundation

CONTACT
Herbert L. Bacon
President
E. L. and Oma Bacon Fdn.
855 25 Rd.
Grand Junction, CO 81505
(303) 242-1174

FINANCIAL SUMMARY
Recent Giving: $124,250 (fiscal 1992); $112,292 (fiscal 1991); $102,627 (fiscal 1990)

Assets: $3,235,287 (fiscal 1992); $2,996,834 (fiscal 1991); $2,298,010 (fiscal 1990)

EIN: 84-0772667

CONTRIBUTIONS SUMMARY
Donor(s): the late E. L. Bacon, the late Oma Bacon

Typical Recipients: • *Arts & Humanities:* Libraries, Public Broadcasting • *Civic & Public Affairs:* Civil Rights, Economic Development, Housing, Municipalities/Towns, Urban & Community Affairs, Zoos/Aquariums • *Education:* Colleges & Universities, Religious Education • *Health:* Clinics/Medical Centers, Hospitals, Mental Health • *Religion:* Religious Organizations, Religious Welfare • *Social Services:* Community Service Organizations, Domestic Violence, People with Disabilities, Substance Abuse, United Funds/United Ways, Youth Organizations

Grant Types: general support

Geographic Distribution: focus on CO

GIVING OFFICERS
Herbert L. Bacon: pres

Laura M. Bacon: treas

Patrick A. Gormley: vp

APPLICATION INFORMATION
Initial Approach: Send brief letter of inquiry describing program. There are no deadlines.

Restrictions on Giving: Does not support individuals.

PUBLICATIONS
Application Guidelines

GRANTS ANALYSIS
Total Grants: $124,250

Number of Grants: 17

Highest Grant: $50,000

Typical Range: $5,000 to $10,000

Disclosure Period: fiscal year ending August 31, 1992

Note: Recent grants are derived from a fiscal 1992 Form 990.

RECENT GRANTS
General

50,000	Iliff School of Theology, Denver, CO
10,000	Marillac Clinic, Grand Junction, CO — indigent care
10,000	Resource Center, Grand Junction, CO — domestic violence
10,000	United Way of Mesa County, Grand Junction, CO
7,500	City of Grant Junction, Grand Junction, CO — economic development

Boettcher Foundation

CONTACT
William A. Douglas
President and Executive Director
Boettcher Foundation
600 Seventeenth St., Ste. 2210 S
Denver, CO 80202
(303) 534-1937

FINANCIAL SUMMARY
Recent Giving: $7,000,000 (1994 approx.); $7,109,606 (1993); $7,080,826 (1992)

Assets: $150,000,000 (1994 approx.); $153,965,000 (1993); $142,490,130 (1992)

EIN: 84-0404274

CONTRIBUTIONS SUMMARY
Donor(s): The Boettcher family established the foundation in 1937, with substantial gifts from Charles and Fanny Augusta Boettcher, their son Claude K. Boettcher, his wife Edna Boettcher, and other family members, for general charitable purposes within the state of Colorado. Charles Boettcher (1852-1948), a German immigrant, helped organize the Great Western Sugar Company and the Ideal Cement Company.

Typical Recipients: • *Arts & Humanities:* Arts Centers, Historic Preservation, History & Archaeology, Libraries, Museums/Galleries, Music, Opera, Performing Arts, Public Broadcasting • *Civic & Public Affairs:* African American Affairs, Botanical Gardens/Parks, Economic Development, Housing, Parades/Festivals, Rural Affairs, Zoos/Aquariums • *Education:* Business Education, Colleges & Universities, Economic Education, Elementary Education (Private), Engineering/Technological Education, Literacy, Private Education (Precollege), Science/Mathematics Education, Student Aid • *Environment:* General, Resource Conservation • *Health:* AIDS/HIV, Children's Health/Hospitals, Clinics/Medical Centers, Emergency/Ambulance Services, Hospices, Long-Term Care, Mental Health • *Science:* Science Museums • *Social Services:* At-Risk Youth, Community Centers, Community Service Organizations, Day Care, Domestic Violence, Family Planning, Family Services, Food/Clothing Distribution, People with Disabilities, Recreation & Athletics, Scouts, Senior Services, United Funds/United Ways, Volunteer Services, YMCA/YWCA/YMHA/YWHA, Youth Organizations

Grant Types: capital, challenge, general support, and scholarship

Geographic Distribution: Colorado only

GIVING OFFICERS
Mrs. Charles Boettcher II: trust

William Allan Douglas: pres, exec dir *B* St Louis MO 1929 *CLUB AFFIL* Boulder CC, Denver Athletic, Rotary Denver

E. Atwill Gilman: trust

A. Barry Hirschfeld: trust *B* 1942 *ED* Univ Denver MBA 1967; CA State Polytechnic

Univ *CURR EMPL* dir: AB Hirschfeld Press Inc

Edward Lehman: trust *B* Denver CO 1925 *ED* Univ Denver 1947; Univ Denver Law Sch 1951 *CURR EMPL* chrm, ceo: Lehman Communs Corp *CORP AFFIL* pres, publ: Canon City Daily Record, Longmont Daily Times-Call, Loveland Daily Reporter-Herald

Hover T. Lentz: vchmn, trust *B* Denver CO 1923 *ED* Princeton Univ BS 1946; Univ Denver LLB 1948

Harry T. Lewis, Jr.: trust *B* Cincinnati OH 1933 *CURR EMPL* sr vp Rocky Mountain oper: Dain Bosworth

Edith R. Mattson: asst treas

Claudia Boettcher Merthan: chmn, trust

John Clark Mitchell II: secy, trust *B* Denver CO 1917 *ED* Yale Univ BA 1938; Rutgers Univ 1952 *CORP AFFIL* dir: Un Bank Denver, Un Banks CO *NONPR AFFIL* dir: Boy Scouts Am Denver Area Counc, Denver Symphony Assn, Downtown Denver, Inst Intl Ed, Western Stock Show Assn; mem: Assn CO Fdns, Chevaliers du Tastevin, Denver Orchid Soc, Rocky Mountain Wine Food Soc; trust: Denver Botanical Gardens

Frederick A. Trask III: asst secy

George Merritt Wilfley: treas, trust *B* Denver CO 1924 *ED* Univ CO BA 1950; Univ Denver *CURR EMPL* chmn, dir: AR Wilfley & Sons *CORP AFFIL* chmn bd: Boy Club of Denver Inc; dir: First Interstate Bank NA; pres, dir: Western Foundries *NONPR AFFIL* chmn bd: Boys Club Denver; dir, mem: Natl Assn Mfrs; mem: Am Inst Mining Metallurgical Petroleum Engrs, Coal Mining Assn, Natl Assn Corrosion Engrs *CLUB AFFIL* Alto Lake, Castle Pines, Denver CC, Univ

APPLICATION INFORMATION
Initial Approach:

The foundation has no standard application form. A succinct letter describing the project and its intended purpose will suffice.

If the foundation is interested in a project, it requests a formal application which includes the organization's name and address, IRS statement of tax-exempt status, title of application signer, list of officers and directors, brief history of the organization and its principal programs and accomplishments, latest annual report and current budget, and plan for evaluation of the proposed project.

The applicant must describe the intended project, its need and proposed solution, its social significance, and benefit to Colorado citizens. Applicants must also provide a detailed budget, qualifications of the involved personnel, the endorsements of the relevant authorities, and a plan for evaluation of the program.

Applicants should allow two or three months for the application to be processed.

OTHER THINGS TO KNOW
Grantees are required to submit reports on the use of grants and project results.

PUBLICATIONS
Annual report; biennial scholarship report

GRANTS ANALYSIS
Total Grants: $7,109,606
Number of Grants: 140*
Highest Grant: $500,000
Average Grant: $41,490*
Typical Range: $1,000 to $10,000 and $25,000 to $100,000
Disclosure Period: 1993

Note: The number of grants and average grant figures exclude scholarships. Recent grants are derived from a 1993 Form 990.

RECENT GRANTS
Library
342,000   Denver Public Library, Denver, CO — toward equipment for Western History Department's photo automation project
210,000   Eleanor Roosevelt Institute, Denver, CO — toward library renovation
75,000   Northeastern Junior College, Sterling, CO — toward construction of new library

General
455,390   Colorado College, Colorado Springs, CO — scholarships
400,000   Graland Country Day School, Denver, CO — toward campus capital campaign
390,053   University of Colorado, Boulder, CO — scholarships
350,000   Denver Museum of Natural History, Denver, CO — toward prehistoric journey exhibits
350,000   University of Denver, Denver, CO — toward Walter K. Koch Chair in entrepreneurship in the College of Business Administration

Comprecare Foundation

CONTACT
Comprecare Fdn.
1390 Logan
Denver, CO 80203
(303) 695-6685

FINANCIAL SUMMARY
Recent Giving: $161,135 (1993); $153,617 (1992); $476,783 (1991)
Assets: $4,848,150 (1993); $4,551,246 (1992); $4,539,643 (1991)
Gifts Received: $400 (1993); $3,425 (1992); $500 (1991)
EIN: 84-0641406

CONTRIBUTIONS SUMMARY
Typical Recipients: • *Arts & Humanities:* Libraries • *Civic & Public Affairs:* General, Hispanic Affairs, Law & Justice, Urban & Community Affairs • *Health:* Geriatric Health, Health Organizations, Mental Health, Nursing Services, Single-Disease Health Associations • *Religion:* Churches, Ministries, Religious Organizations • *Science:* Science Museums • *Social Services:* Community Service Organizations, Domestic Violence, Family Services, People with Disabilities, Senior Services, Substance Abuse, Youth Organizations
Grant Types: general support
Geographic Distribution: focus on CO

GIVING OFFICERS
Marcus B. Bond, MD: vchmn
Bradford L. Darling: dir
Raymond C. Delisle: dir
Ellen J. Mangione: dir
Joseph P. Natele: chmn, dir
Richard F. Negri: secy, treas, dir
M. Eugene Sherman, MD: dir

APPLICATION INFORMATION
Initial Approach: The foundation has no formal grant application procedure or application form. Deadline is December 1.
Restrictions on Giving: Limited to wellness, maintenance, and to improve the mental health in Colorado's elderly population.

PUBLICATIONS
Annual Report

GRANTS ANALYSIS
Total Grants: $161,135
Number of Grants: 14
Highest Grant: $53,000
Typical Range: $4,000 to $10,000
Disclosure Period: 1993

Note: Recent grants are derived from a 1993 Form 990.

RECENT GRANTS
General
53,000   Colorado Action for Healthy People, Denver, CO
12,000   Kids in Need of Dentistry, Denver, CO
10,800   Bent County Nursing Service, Las Animas, CO
10,600   Grand Valley Senior Daybreak, Grand Junction, CO
10,600   Southern Ute Community Action Programs, Ignacio, CO

Coors Foundation, Adolph

CONTACT
Linda S. Tafoya
Executive Director
Adolph Coors Foundation
3773 Cherry Creek N Dr., Ste. 955
Denver, CO 80209-3829
(303) 388-1636

FINANCIAL SUMMARY
Recent Giving: $5,293,750 (fiscal 1993); $5,374,975 (fiscal 1992); $4,819,995 (fiscal 1991)

Assets: $146,924,928 (fiscal 1993); $125,344,399 (fiscal 1992); $113,933,773 (fiscal 1991)

Gifts Received: $2,390,787 (fiscal 1988)

Fiscal Note: In fiscal 1988, the foundation received gifts totaling $2,000,000 from Janet H. Coors and contributions totaling $390,787 from the J. H. Coors Irrevocable Trust.

EIN: 51-0172279

CONTRIBUTIONS SUMMARY

Donor(s): Adolph Coors, Sr., a native German, came to the United States to escape his country's political and economic oppression. In 1873, he founded the Coors brewery in Golden, CO.

In 1912, Adolph Coors, Jr., became brewery superintendent and continued the profitable operation of the family's brewery and porcelain company. Later, during the prohibition years, he established what has become one of the largest malted milk operations in the country. Adolph Coors, Jr., died in 1970. In October 1975, the Adolph Coors Foundation was established with funds from his trust.

Typical Recipients: • *Arts & Humanities:* Arts Associations & Councils, Arts Centers, Historic Preservation, Libraries, Museums/Galleries, Music, Performing Arts, Public Broadcasting, Theater • *Civic & Public Affairs:* Business/Free Enterprise, Economic Development, Economic Policy, Employment/Job Training, First Amendment Issues, Housing, Law & Justice, Legal Aid, Native American Affairs, Nonprofit Management, Parades/Festivals, Public Policy, Women's Affairs, Zoos/Aquariums • *Education:* Arts/Humanities Education, Business Education, Colleges & Universities, Economic Education, Education Associations, Education Funds, Education Reform, Engineering/Technological Education, General, Health & Physical Education, Journalism/Media Education, Leadership Training, Literacy, Minority Education, Private Education (Precollege), Religious Education, Science/Mathematics Education • *Environment:* General • *Health:* Clinics/Medical Centers, Health Organizations, Hospitals, Medical Rehabilitation, Medical Research • *International:* International Development, International Peace & Security Issues • *Religion:* Jewish Causes, Ministries, Religious Organizations, Religious Welfare • *Social Services:* Child Welfare, Community Centers, Community Service Organizations, Delinquency & Criminal Rehabilitation, Domestic Violence, Family Services, Food/Clothing Distribution, Homes, People with Disabilities, Recreation & Athletics, Scouts, Senior Services, Shelters/Homelessness, Substance Abuse, United Funds/United Ways, YMCA/YWCA/YMHA/YWHA, Youth Organizations

Grant Types: capital, endowment, general support, operating expenses, project, and scholarship

Geographic Distribution: Colorado only

GIVING OFFICERS

Ambassador Holland Coors: dir

Jeffrey H. Coors: treas *B* Denver CO 1945 *ED* Cornell Univ BSChE 1967; Cornell Univ MSChE 1968 *CURR EMPL* chmn, pres, ceo, dir: Adolph Coors Co *CORP AFFIL* chmn, ceo: Coors Techs; pres: ACX Techs; prin: Golden Aluminum Co *PHIL AFFIL* treas, trust: Castle Rock Foundation

Peter Hanson Coors: vp, trust *B* Denver CO 1946 *ED* Cornell Univ BS 1969; Univ Denver MBA 1970 *CURR EMPL* ceo: Adolph Coors Co *CORP AFFIL* chmn: Coors Brewing Co; chmn, dir: Coors Distr Co *NONPR AFFIL* dir: Wildlife Legis Fund; hon dir: Special Olympics CO; mem: Natl Individuals Advancement Counc, Opportunities Ctrs Am, Young Pres Org; mem exec comm: Ducks Unlimited; trust: CO Univ, Outward Bound CO, Pres Leadership Comm; trust, chmn devel comm: Regis Coll Natl Comm Future *CLUB AFFIL* Metro Denver Execs *PHIL AFFIL* vp, trust: Castle Rock Foundation

William K. Coors: pres *B* Golden CO 1916 *ED* Princeton Univ BSChE 1938; Princeton Univ MSChE 1939 *CURR EMPL* chmn: Adolph Coors Co *CORP AFFIL* dir: Coors Porcelain Co *PHIL AFFIL* vp: A. V. Hunter Trust; pres, treas: Castle Rock Foundation

Linda S. Tafoya: exec dir, secy *PHIL AFFIL* secy: Castle Rock Foundation

Rev. Robert G. Windsor: dir *PHIL AFFIL* trust: Castle Rock Foundation

APPLICATION INFORMATION
Initial Approach:

A preliminary letter with a general description of the proposed project is suggested and should be sent to the executive director.

After the initial letter is sent, the applying organization should send one copy of a complete proposal, including the organization's legal name and address; contact person and phone number; proof of tax exemption; history, description, and goals of the organization; factors which set the proposed project apart from similar programs; amount needed and how it will be spent; project budget; proof of need, and expected goals of project; other sources of funding; list of board members (indicate occupations); financial statement of most recent year (foundation prefers a copy of audit); and current and/or proposed income and expense budget.

The board of directors generally meets in January, April, July, and October to select grant recipients. Applications must be received at least eight weeks prior to the meeting at which consideration is desired.

Restrictions on Giving: The foundation does not make grants to individuals, or for endowment funds, research, film production or other media projects, churches, preschools, day-care centers, nursing homes, extended care centers, conduit funding, deficit financing or retirement of debt, special benefit programs, purchase of membership, or purchase of blocks of tickets.

OTHER THINGS TO KNOW

Presentations by applicants are to be made to staff rather than to board members. If possible, an on-site visit will be conducted as a part of the application review process. If a proposal is approved, a grant agreement is required.

PUBLICATIONS
Annual report

GRANTS ANALYSIS
Total Grants: $5,293,750

Number of Grants: 117

Highest Grant: $700,000

Average Grant: $45,246

Typical Range: $10,000 to $100,000

Disclosure Period: fiscal year ending November 30, 1993

Note: Recent grants are derived from a fiscal 1993 Form 990.

RECENT GRANTS

Library

100,000	Colorado College, Colorado Springs, CO — upgrade computer system in the library

General

700,000	Colorado State Fair Authority, Pueblo, CO — construction of new indoor arena
500,000	University of Colorado Foundation, Denver, CO — renovation of Dal Ward Center
300,000	Boys and Girls Clubs of Metro Denver, Denver, CO — remodeling, expansion, and modernization of facilities
300,000	Up With People, Tucson, AZ — relocate its headquarters to Denver
250,000	Graland Country Day School, Denver, CO — rebuild the Graland Campus to enhance delivery of quality education

Duncan Trust, John G.

CONTACT
Yvonne Baca
Trust Officer
John G. Duncan Trust
c/o First Interstate Bank of Denver, N.A.
PO Box 5825
Denver, CO 80217
(303) 293-2211

FINANCIAL SUMMARY
Recent Giving: $167,700 (1993); $184,000 (1992); $154,500 (1991)

Assets: $3,752,249 (1993); $3,581,068 (1992); $3,527,713 (1991)

EIN: 84-6016555

CONTRIBUTIONS SUMMARY
Donor(s): the late John G. Duncan

Typical Recipients: • *Arts & Humanities:* Arts Centers, Arts Outreach, History & Archaeology, Libraries, Music, Performing Arts, Theater • *Civic & Public Affairs:* Employment/Job Training, General, Housing, Legal Aid, Urban & Community Affairs, Women's Affairs • *Education:* Colleges & Universities, Continuing Education, Elementary Education (Private), Minority Education, Private Education (Precollege), Science/Mathematics Education • *Health:* Cancer, Children's Health/Hospitals, Health Organizations, Hospices, Hospitals, Medical Rehabilitation, Medical Research, Single-Disease Health Associations • *International:* International Organizations • *Religion:* Jewish Causes, Religious Welfare, Synagogues/Temples • *Social Services:* At-Risk Youth, Child Welfare, Community Service Organizations, Family Services, Homes, People with Disabilities, Senior Services, Shelters/Homelessness, Substance Abuse, Volunteer Services, Youth Organizations

Grant Types: capital, emergency, operating expenses, project, research, and seed money

Geographic Distribution: limited to CO

GIVING OFFICERS
First Interstate Bank of Denver: trust

APPLICATION INFORMATION
Initial Approach: The foundation requests applications be made in writing. Include a description of organization, amount requested, purpose of funds sought, recently audited financial statement, and proof of tax-exempt status. There are no deadlines.

Restrictions on Giving: Limited to charities in CO.

PUBLICATIONS
Application Guidelines

GRANTS ANALYSIS
Total Grants: $167,700

Number of Grants: 34

Highest Grant: $10,000

Typical Range: $2,500 to $5,000

Disclosure Period: 1993

Note: Recent grants are derived from a 1993 Form 990.

RECENT GRANTS

General

10,000	Community Technical Skill Center, Denver, CO
10,000	Denver Academy, Denver, CO
10,000	Epilepsy Foundation of Colorado, Englewood, CO
10,000	Stanley British Primary School, Denver, CO
10,000	Temple Center, Denver, CO

El Pomar Foundation

CONTACT
William J. Hybl
Chairman and Chief Executive Officer
El Pomar Foundation
10 Lake Circle
Colorado Springs, CO 80906
(719) 633-7733
Note: The foundation also has a toll-free number of 1-800-534-7711.

FINANCIAL SUMMARY
Recent Giving: $13,500,000 (1995 est.); $13,000,000 (1994 approx.); $12,805,487 (1993)

Assets: $300,000,000 (1995 est.); $300,000,000 (1994 approx.); $300,000,000 (1993 approx.)

EIN: 84-6002373

CONTRIBUTIONS SUMMARY
Donor(s): The El Pomar Foundation was established in 1937 by the late Spencer Penrose. Upon his death in 1939, the foundation received a portion of his estate. Mrs. Spencer Penrose, who died in 1956, also made gifts to the foundation. Mr. Penrose and his associate, Charles L. Tutt, were involved in the gold and copper mining and real estate businesses. He was founder of the Utah Copper Company, and built the Broadmoor Hotel in Colorado Springs. His private zoo became the Cheyenne Mountain Zoo, which the foundation still supports.

Typical Recipients: • *Arts & Humanities:* Arts Associations & Councils, Arts Centers, Community Arts, Historic Preservation, History & Archaeology, Libraries, Museums/Galleries, Music, Opera, Public Broadcasting, Theater • *Civic & Public Affairs:* Economic Development, Hispanic Affairs, Housing, Municipalities/Towns, Nonprofit Management, Urban & Community Affairs, Zoos/Aquariums • *Education:* Business Education, Colleges & Universities, Economic Education, Minority Education, Private Education (Precollege), Public Education (Precollege), Student Aid • *Environment:* General • *Health:* Alzheimers Disease, Arthritis, Cancer, Clinics/Medical Centers, Emergency/Ambulance Services, Health Organizations, Hospitals, Medical Rehabilitation, Medical Research, Mental Health, Nursing Services • *Religion:* Religious Welfare • *Science:* Science Museums, Scientific Centers & Institutes • *Social Services:* Child Welfare, Community Centers, Community Service Organizations, Day Care, Domestic Violence, Emergency Relief, Family Services, Food/Clothing Distribution, Homes, People with Disabilities, Recreation & Athletics, Senior Services, Shelters/Homelessness, Substance Abuse, United Funds/United Ways, Youth Organizations

Grant Types: award, capital, general support, and project

Geographic Distribution: Colorado only

GIVING OFFICERS
Karl E. Eitel: chmn exec comm, trust *B* Chicago IL 1928 *ED* MI St Univ BS 1951 *CORP AFFIL* dir: Affiliated Bankshares CO, El Pomar Investment Co, First Natl Bank CO Springs, Garden City Co, Manitou & Pikes Railway Co; vchmn, exec commr: Broadmoor Mgmt Co *NONPR AFFIL* dir: Goodwill Indus; mem: Am Hotel Motel Assn, Assn US Army, CO Springs Chamber Commerce, CO-WY Hotel Motel Assn, Hotel Greeters Am, Hotel Sales Mgmt Assn, Inter-Am Hotel Assn, Natl Assn Travel Orgs *CLUB AFFIL* Broadmoor GC, CC CO, Chey-

enne Mountain CC, Navy League US, Rio Verde CC, US Tennis Lawn Assn

Dolores C. Fowler: dir (El Pomar Center)

Robert Hilbert: secy, treas, vp (admin), trust *CURR EMPL* secy, treas, dir: Garden City Co

William J. Hybl: chmn, ceo, trust *B* Des Moines IA 1942 *ED* CO Coll BA 1964; Univ CO JD 1967 *CURR EMPL* vchmn: Broadmoor Hotel Inc *CORP AFFIL* dir: Bank One CO, Bank One Colorado Springs, KN Energy, Manitou & Pikes Peak RY Co; exec vp, dir: Garden City Co

Kent Oliver Olin: trust *B* Chicago IL 1930 *ED* Ripon Coll BS 1955 *CURR EMPL* vchmn, dir: Affiliated Bankshares CO *NONPR AFFIL* secy, treas: Air Force Academy Fdn *CLUB AFFIL* Broadmoor GC, Cherry Hills CC

David J. Palenchar: vp (programs)

Russell Thayer Tutt, Jr.: pres, trust

APPLICATION INFORMATION
Initial Approach:

There are no set application forms. A detailed and complete application should be sent to the foundation.

Applications should include name, address, and title of person signing the application; list of officers and directors; statement of amount requested and explanation of need; names of foundations from which aid has been requested in the last three years; tax-exempt letter and classification; latest audited balance sheet and income statement; history, purpose, and accomplishments of the organization; description of project's purpose; budget for project; the endorsement of the principal officer; and a copy of the most recent IRS Form 990.

Applications may be submitted at any time.

Applications are studied by the trustees, voted on, and acted upon as soon as possible.

Restrictions on Giving: The foundation does not make grants to individuals, other distributing organizations, tax-supported institutions (except for specific purposes), or camps or seasonal facilities; for deficits, endowments, films or other media projects, travel, or conferences. Grantees are precluded from applying for a grant for three years following notification of a grant. Applicants whose proposals are not funded must wait one year before they are eligible to submit another proposal. Applicants must be residents of the state of Colorado.

OTHER THINGS TO KNOW
The foundation reports that it also sponsors a limited number of seminars, workshops, and conferences.

PUBLICATIONS
Annual report

GRANTS ANALYSIS
Total Grants: $12,346,303*

Number of Grants: 164

Highest Grant: $5,573,899

Average Grant: $41,295*

Typical Range: $5,000 to $25,000 and $50,000 to $125,000

Disclosure Period: 1992

Note: Total grants include the foundation's program-related investments. Average grant figure excludes the foundation's highest expenditure, a program-related investment to the El Pomar Center for $5,573,899. Recent grants are derived from a 1992 Form 990.

RECENT GRANTS

Library

235,000	University of Denver, Denver, CO — for upgrading the Penrose Library
100,000	Denver Public Library, Denver, CO — for children's books at Children's Pavilion
15,000	Penrose Community Library, Penrose, CO — for the renovation of the new library building

General

800,000	Junior Achievement, Colorado Springs, CO — for headquarters expansion and annex building
500,000	Foundation Valley School of Colorado, Colorado Springs, CO — for the renovation of the Froelicher academic building
335,000	Penrose-St. Francis Healthcare System, Colorado Springs, CO — for new kitchen facilities at Namaste
260,000	Colorado College, Colorado College, CO — 1992 scholarships
250,000	Cheyenne Mountain Zoo, Colorado Springs, CO — for general operating support

Fishback Foundation Trust, Harmes C.

CONTACT
Katharine H. Stapleton
Trustee
Harmes C. Fishback Fdn Trust
8 Village Rd.
Englewood, CO 80110
(303) 623-2700

FINANCIAL SUMMARY
Recent Giving: $90,605 (1993); $75,767 (1991); $74,310 (1990)

Assets: $2,228,961 (1993); $1,923,510 (1991); $1,724,191 (1990)

EIN: 84-6094542

CONTRIBUTIONS SUMMARY
Donor(s): the late Harmes C. Fishback

Typical Recipients: • *Arts & Humanities:* Arts Centers, Community Arts, Historic Preservation, History & Archaeology, Libraries, Museums/Galleries, Music, Opera, Performing Arts • *Civic & Public Affairs:* Botanical Gardens/Parks, Economic Development, General, Legal Aid, Zoos/Aquariums • *Education:* Colleges & Universities,

Continuing Education, International Studies, Leadership Training, Private Education (Precollege) • *Environment:* General • *Health:* AIDS/HIV, Cancer, Diabetes, Hospices, Medical Rehabilitation, Medical Research, Respiratory, Transplant Networks/Donor Banks • *Religion:* Religious Welfare • *Science:* Science Museums • *Social Services:* Child Welfare, Community Service Organizations, Day Care, Family Planning, Family Services, Food/Clothing Distribution, People with Disabilities, Senior Services, United Funds/United Ways, YMCA/YWCA/YMHA/YWHA, Youth Organizations

Grant Types: endowment, multiyear/continuing support, and scholarship

Geographic Distribution: limited to the metropolitan Denver, CO, area

GIVING OFFICERS
Katharine H. Stapleton: trust

APPLICATION INFORMATION
Initial Approach: Send brief letter describing program. There are no deadlines.

Restrictions on Giving: Does not support individuals.

GRANTS ANALYSIS
Total Grants: $90,605

Number of Grants: 35

Highest Grant: $10,000

Typical Range: $500 to $5,000

Disclosure Period: 1993

Note: Recent grants are derived from a 1993 Form 990.

RECENT GRANTS

General

10,000	American Diabetes Association, Denver, CO
5,000	Denver Museum of Natural History, Denver, CO
5,000	Porter Hospice, Denver, CO
5,000	Spalding Rehabilitation Hospital, Denver, CO
4,500	Colorado University Foundation for AIDS Research, Denver, CO

Gates Foundation

CONTACT
Thomas C. Stokes
Executive Director and Secretary
Gates Foundation
3200 Cherry Creek South Dr., Ste. 630
Denver, CO 80209
(303) 722-1881

FINANCIAL SUMMARY
Recent Giving: $5,340,000 (1995 est.); $4,725,248 (1994); $5,416,034 (1993)

Assets: $122,641,452 (1993); $116,013,207 (1992); $110,215,250 (1991)

EIN: 84-0474837

CONTRIBUTIONS SUMMARY
Donor(s): The Gates Foundation was established in Colorado in 1946 by the late Charles C. Gates, Sr. , and members of the Gates family. Gates Corporation, an aircraft parts, instruments, and mechanical rubber goods company, was founded in 1911 by Mr. Gates. In 1961, he transferred the presidency of the company to his son, Charles C. Gates, Jr. The company is one of the largest privately-owned companies in the country, and Charles Gates, Jr., remains the chairman, president, and chief executive officer.

Typical Recipients: • *Arts & Humanities:* Arts Centers, Arts Funds, Dance, Historic Preservation, History & Archaeology, Libraries, Museums/Galleries, Music, Opera, Performing Arts, Public Broadcasting, Theater, Visual Arts • *Civic & Public Affairs:* Botanical Gardens/Parks, Business/Free Enterprise, Economic Development, Employment/Job Training, Housing, Municipalities/Towns, Parades/Festivals, Public Policy, Urban & Community Affairs, Women's Affairs, Zoos/Aquariums • *Education:* Arts/Humanities Education, Business Education, Colleges & Universities, Continuing Education, Economic Education, Education Associations, Engineering/Technological Education, General, Leadership Training, Literacy, Private Education (Precollege), Public Education (Precollege), Science/Mathematics Education, Secondary Education (Private), Student Aid • *Environment:* General, Resource Conservation • *Health:* Health Policy/Cost Containment • *Religion:* Religious Welfare • *Science:* Science Museums, Scientific Organizations • *Social Services:* Child Welfare, Community Centers, Domestic Violence, Family Planning, Family Services, Food/Clothing Distribution, People with Disabilities, Recreation & Athletics, Senior Services, Shelters/Homelessness, Substance Abuse, United Funds/United Ways, YMCA/YWCA/YMHA/YWHA, Youth Organizations

Grant Types: capital, challenge, and general support

Geographic Distribution: primarily Colorado, with emphasis on the Denver area

GIVING OFFICERS
George B. Beardsley: trust

Charles G. Cannon: trust

Ellen Kingman Fisher: program off

F. Charles Froelicher: trust

Charles Cassius Gates, Jr.: pres, trust, don son *B* Morrison CO 1921 *ED* MA Inst Tech 1939-1941; Stanford Univ BS 1943 *CURR EMPL* chmn, pres, ceo, dir: Gates Corp *CORP AFFIL* chmn: Gates Energy Products; chmn, ceo: Gates Rubber Co; chmn, dir: Cody Co; dir: BHP Petroleum, Hamilton Oil Corp, TX Gas Corp *NONPR AFFIL* dir: CO Wildlife Heritage Fdn; trust: CA Inst Tech, Denver Mus Natural History, Nature Conservancy CO Chapter *CLUB AFFIL* Augusta Natl GC, Boone & Crockett, Castle Pines GC, CC CO, Cherry Hills CC, Club Ltd, Denver CC, Old Baldy, Outrigger Canoe,

Roundup Riders Rockies, Shikar Safari, Waialae CC

Thomas Joseph Gibson: treas *B* Washington DC 1935 *ED* Rensselaer Polytech Inst BEE 1956; George Washington Univ JD 1962 *CURR EMPL* exec vp, cfo, secy, dir: Gates Corp *CORP AFFIL* dir: Conexiones Hidraulicas, Gates Hydraulics Ltd, Gates Hydraulique, Gates Ltd (UK), Protection Mutual Ins Co; exec vp, secy, dir: Cody Resources; pres, dir: Cody Co; secy, dir: Fiber Extrusion; sr vp, secy, cfo, dir: Gates Rubber Co; vp, dir: Gates Canada, Natl Products; vp, secy, dir: A Bar A Ranch, Gates Formed-Fibre Products, Gates Power Drive Products, Uniroyal Power Transmission Co; vp, secy, treas, dir: Gates Energy Products, Gates Export Corp; vp, treas, secy, dir: Gates Land Co *NONPR AFFIL* dir: Denver Counc Pub Television; mem: CO Assn Commerce Indus, Denver Chamber Commerce *CLUB AFFIL* Econ Denver, Rotary

William West Grant III: trust *B* New York NY 1932 *ED* Yale Univ BA 1954; NY Univ 1958 *CURR EMPL* chmn, dir: CO Natl Bank *CORP AFFIL* chmn: CO Capital Adv; dir: CO Natl Bankshares, Plains Petroleum Co *NONPR AFFIL* dir: Inst Intl Ed, KRMA-TV, Mountain St Employers Counc, New World Airport Commn, Samaritan Inst; mem: CO Bankers Assn, Denver Chamber Commerce; trust: Denver Mus Natural History, Midwest Res Inst; vchmn CO chap: Nature Conservancy *CLUB AFFIL* Denver CC

Peter G. Huidekoper: program off

Karen W. Mather: grants mgr

Thomas C. Stokes: exec dir, secy

Christina H. Turissini: comptr

Diane Gates Wallach: vp, trust *CURR EMPL* systems project mgr: Gates Rubber Co

Mike Wilfley: trust *CURR EMPL* pres, dir: A R Wilfley & Sons

APPLICATION INFORMATION
Initial Approach:

Prospective applicants should telephone or write to a program officer in order to review the substance of a project before sending a formal proposal. Applicants should also request a new copy of the application guidelines pamphlet which is updated annually.

The application should include name, address, description, and history of organization; copy of most recent tax-exempt IRS ruling and IRS Form 990; copy of most recent annual audit and accompanying management letter; current year's budget of income and expenses and year-to-date record of income and expenses; description of proposed project, its importance, and potential effect; amount needed; detailed budget and timetable; review of other private and public sources of support, with special attention to trustee support, foundation support by name and amount, corporate support, and community support; full descriptions of all participating personnel, including names, occupations, titles, addresses, and phone numbers; an endorsement from administrative head stating priority of project; access to pertinent files and records; and a list of board of directors with addresses, phone

numbers, and primary business or professional affiliations.

In general, final proposals should be submitted at least eight weeks prior to a meeting of the board of trustees. Deadlines for the coming year are January 15 for the April 1 meeting, April 1 for the June 15 meeting, July 15 for the October 1 meeting, and October 1 for the December 15 meeting. Highly specialized requests and proposals requiring on-site study or outside consultation may require even more time for review.

The foundation's staff acknowledges and reviews all applications, and notifies each applicant in writing regarding funding decisions within two weeks following each quarterly meeting.

Restrictions on Giving: Generally the foundation does not make grants outside Colorado; make loans or grants to individuals or loans to organizations; support projects involving court actions; provide operating funds to organizations funded by dwindling grants; consider previously denied proposals; make grants to other grant-making foundations; give funds to retire debts; support annual operating expenses; give funds to United Way agencies except through its annual grant to the United Way; grant individual awards or scholarships; give grants for the purchase of vehicles; or make grants directly to individual public schools or public school districts; or makes grants for the construction of medical facilities or medical research. The foundation does not make grants for projects, conferences, or meetings which will be held or completed prior to the next trustees' meeting. It also does not purchase tickets for fund-raising dinners, parties, balls, or other social fund-raising events.

PUBLICATIONS
Annual report including information for grant applications

GRANTS ANALYSIS
Total Grants: $5,416,034

Number of Grants: 115

Highest Grant: $800,000

Average Grant: $47,096

Typical Range: $5,000 to $30,000 and $50,000 to $100,000

Disclosure Period: 1993

Note: Recent grants are derived from a 1993 Form 990.

RECENT GRANTS

Library
250,000	Denver Public Library Foundation, Denver, CO

General
800,000	Denver Botanical Gardens, Denver, CO
650,000	Graland Country Day School, Denver, CO
200,000	Boys and Girls Clubs of Metro Denver, Denver, CO
200,000	Boys and Girls Clubs of Metro Denver, Denver, CO
155,000	Education Commission of States, Denver, CO

Great-West Life Assurance Co.

Assets: $1.5 billion
Employees: 2,500
Headquarters: Englewood, CO
SIC Major Group: Insurance Carriers

CONTACT
John Clayton
Vice President, Corporate Services
Great-West Life Assurance Co.
8515 E Orchard Rd.
Englewood, CO 80111
(303) 889-3000

FINANCIAL SUMMARY
Fiscal Note: Annual Giving Range: $100,000 to $250,000

CONTRIBUTIONS SUMMARY
Supports all categories of giving, with emphasis on social services and United Way.

Typical Recipients: • *Arts & Humanities:* Arts Associations & Councils, Arts Centers, Community Arts, Dance, Libraries, Museums/Galleries, Music, Performing Arts • *Civic & Public Affairs:* Women's Affairs • *Education:* Business Education, Colleges & Universities, Economic Education, Minority Education, Student Aid • *Health:* Health Policy/Cost Containment, Hospitals, Medical Research, Mental Health • *Social Services:* Community Service Organizations, Domestic Violence, Family Services, People with Disabilities, Substance Abuse, United Funds/United Ways, Youth Organizations

Grant Types: general support, research, and scholarship

Nonmonetary Support Types: donated equipment, in-kind services, loaned employees, and loaned executives

Geographic Distribution: primarily at the Englewood, CO, headquarters, but also in 48 states (NY and RI excepted) where there are company offices; mainly through United Way

Operating Locations: CO (Englewood)

CORP. OFFICERS
W. T. McCallum: *CURR EMPL* pres, ceo: Great-West Life Assurance Co

APPLICATION INFORMATION
Initial Approach: Send letter any time, including a description of the organization, amount and purpose of funds sought, and proof of tax-exempt status.

Restrictions on Giving: Program does not support goodwill advertising, individuals, or fraternal, political, or religious organizations.

OTHER THINGS TO KNOW
Program gives approximately $125,000 in nonmonetary support each year. This amount is not included in the contributions budget or figures above.

GRANTS ANALYSIS
Typical Range: $500 to $1,000

Heginbotham Trust, Will E.

CONTACT
Dave O. Colver
Trustee
Will E. Heginbotham Trust
PO Box 245
Holyoke, CO 80734
(303) 854-2497

FINANCIAL SUMMARY
Recent Giving: $197,044 (1993); $333,751 (1992); $419,287 (1991)

Assets: $4,185,252 (1993); $4,123,103 (1992); $4,206,855 (1991)

Gifts Received: $9,000 (1992)

EIN: 84-6053496

CONTRIBUTIONS SUMMARY
Donor(s): the late Will E. Heginbotham

Typical Recipients: • *Arts & Humanities:* Arts Associations & Councils, Historic Preservation, Libraries, Museums/Galleries • *Civic & Public Affairs:* Clubs, Housing, Law & Justice, Municipalities/Towns, Safety, Urban & Community Affairs • *Education:* Preschool Education, Public Education (Precollege), Secondary Education (Public) • *Health:* Emergency/Ambulance Services, Hospitals, Prenatal Health Issues • *Religion:* Churches • *Social Services:* Child Welfare, Community Service Organizations, Homes, Recreation & Athletics, Youth Organizations

Grant Types: capital, general support, and operating expenses

Geographic Distribution: focus on Phillips County, CO

GIVING OFFICERS
Ted Clark: trust

Dave O. Colver: trust

Josephine McWilliams: trust

APPLICATION INFORMATION
Initial Approach: Send brief letter of inquiry describing program or project. There are no deadlines.

GRANTS ANALYSIS
Total Grants: $197,044

Number of Grants: 15

Highest Grant: $50,000

Typical Range: $68 to $40,000

Disclosure Period: 1993

Note: Recent grants are derived from a 1993 Form 990.

RECENT GRANTS
General

50,000	Haxtun RE-2J School District, Haxtun, CO — for balance of new school building grant
40,000	Holyoke Housing Authority, Holyoke, CO — for 1993 installment payment per November 1991 grant
25,000	Town of Haxtun, Haxtun, CO — for final grant for fire truck
19,000	Melissa Memorial Hospital, Holyoke, CO — for balance of capital improvement grant
15,000	City of Holyoke, Holyoke, CO — for swimming pool roof

Hewit Family Foundation

CONTACT
William D. Hewit
President, Treasurer
Hewit Family Fdn.
621 17th St., Ste. 2555
Denver, CO 80293
(303) 292-0697

FINANCIAL SUMMARY
Recent Giving: $105,000 (fiscal 1993); $100,000 (fiscal 1992); $90,000 (fiscal 1991)

Assets: $2,733,114 (fiscal 1993); $2,217,755 (fiscal 1992); $2,160,874 (fiscal 1991)

Gifts Received: $400,000 (fiscal 1993); $75,000 (fiscal 1991); $600,000 (fiscal 1989)

Fiscal Note: In fiscal 1993, contributions were received from William D. Hewit ($200,000) and Betty Ruth Hewit ($200,000).

EIN: 74-2397040

CONTRIBUTIONS SUMMARY
Donor(s): members of the Hewit family

Typical Recipients: • *Arts & Humanities:* Historic Preservation, Libraries, Museums/Galleries, Public Broadcasting • *Civic & Public Affairs:* Zoos/Aquariums • *Education:* Education Funds, General, Science/Mathematics Education • *Health:* Children's Health/Hospitals, Health Organizations, Hospitals • *Science:* Science Museums • *Social Services:* Child Welfare, Community Service Organizations, United Funds/United Ways, Youth Organizations

Grant Types: general support

Geographic Distribution: focus on Denver, CO

GIVING OFFICERS
Christie F. Andrews: vp, dir

Richard J. Andrews: dir

Robert S. Brown: dir

Betty R. Hewit: vp, dir

William D. Hewit: pres, treas, dir

William E. Hewit: vp, dir

Jack E. Kennedy: dir

APPLICATION INFORMATION
Initial Approach: Send brief letter describing program. Include a description of organization, amount requested, purpose of funds sought, recently audited financial statement, and proof of tax-exempt status. There are no deadlines.

Restrictions on Giving: Limited to organizations that qualify under Section 501(c)(3) of the Internal Revenue Code.

GRANTS ANALYSIS
Total Grants: $105,000

Typical Range: $2,000 to $10,000

Disclosure Period: fiscal year ending November 30, 1993

Note: Recent grants are derived from a fiscal 1992 Form 990. Grants list was not provided in fiscal 1993 Form 990.

RECENT GRANTS
Library

5,000	Denver Public Library, Denver, CO

General

10,000	Boy Scouts of America Denver Area Council, Denver, CO
10,000	Children's Hospital, Red Wagon Club, Denver, CO
10,000	Denver Museum of Natural History, Denver, CO
10,000	Denver Zoological Foundation, Denver, CO
10,000	Girl Scouts of America Mile Hi Council, Denver, CO

JFM Foundation

CONTACT
JFM Fdn.
PO Box 5083
Denver, CO 80217
(303) 832-3131

FINANCIAL SUMMARY
Recent Giving: $632,144 (fiscal 1993); $604,961 (fiscal 1992); $639,318 (fiscal 1990)

Assets: $38,375 (fiscal 1993); $16,433 (fiscal 1992); $68,779 (fiscal 1991)

Gifts Received: $657,900 (fiscal 1993); $567,800 (fiscal 1992); $809,491 (fiscal 1991)

Fiscal Note: In fiscal 1993, contributions were received from Frederick R. Mayer ($349,900), Charitable Lead Trust II ($192,000), Charitable Lead Trust I ($96,000), and State of Colorado Family Grant Center ($20,000).

EIN: 84-0833163

CONTRIBUTIONS SUMMARY
Donor(s): Frederick R. Mayer

Typical Recipients: • *Arts & Humanities:* Arts Centers, Arts Funds, Arts Outreach, Community Arts, Dance, History & Archaeology, Libraries, Museums/Galleries, Music, Opera, Public Broadcasting • *Civic & Public Affairs:* Community Foundations, Economic Development, General, Hispanic Affairs, Legal Aid, Nonprofit Management, Parades/Festivals, Philanthropic Organizations, Urban & Community Affairs, Women's Affairs • *Education:* Arts/Humanities Education, Colleges & Universities,

Continuing Education, Education Associations, Education Reform, Elementary Education (Private), General, International Studies, Private Education (Precollege), Public Education (Precollege), Secondary Education (Public), Social Sciences Education • *Health:* Hospices • *Religion:* Religious Welfare • *Social Services:* Child Welfare, Community Service Organizations, Food/Clothing Distribution, Scouts, Shelters/Homelessness, United Funds/United Ways, Youth Organizations

Grant Types: endowment, general support, and project

Geographic Distribution: limited to CO

GIVING OFFICERS
Gloria J. Higgins: dir

Anthony R. Mayer: dir

Frederick Miller Mayer: dir *B* Youngstown OH 1898 *ED* Heidelberg Coll BA 1920; Harvard Univ JD 1924; Heidelberg Coll LLD 1948 *NONPR AFFIL* hon trust: Dallas Mus Fine Arts; mem: Acacia, Am Petroleum Inst, IN Petroleum Assn, Mid-Continent Oil Gas Assn, Petroleum Equipment Suppliers Assn; trust: Dallas Fdn Arts, Heidelberg Coll *CLUB AFFIL* mem: Huguenot Soc OH, Phi Kappa Delta, SAR

Frederick R. Mayer: pres *B* Youngstown OH 1928 *ED* Yale Univ BA 1950 *CURR EMPL* pres, owner: Captiva Corp *NONPR AFFIL* chmn: Denver Art Mus; mem: Independent Petroleum Assn Am, Natl Petroleum Counc; mem, dir: Am Petroleum Inst

Jan Perry Mayer: vp, secy, treas

APPLICATION INFORMATION
Initial Approach: Send brief concept paper describing program or project. Include a description of organization, amount requested, purpose of funds sought, recently audited financial statement, and proof of tax-exempt status.

PUBLICATIONS
Application Guidelines

GRANTS ANALYSIS
Total Grants: $632,144

Number of Grants: 50

Highest Grant: $200,000

Typical Range: $425 to $50,000

Disclosure Period: fiscal year ending November 30, 1993

Note: Recent grants are derived from a fiscal 1993 Form 990.

RECENT GRANTS

Library

10,000	Denver Public Library, Denver, CO

General

41,113	University of Denver, Denver, CO
38,000	Charter Fund, Denver, CO
20,000	Adult Learning Source, Denver, CO
15,000	School District No. 1, Denver, CO
15,000	St. Stephen's Episcopal School, Austin, TX

Johnson Foundation, Helen K. and Arthur E.

CONTACT
Stan Kamprath
Vice President and Executive Director
Helen K. and Arthur E. Johnson Foundation
1700 Broadway, Ste. 2302
Denver, CO 80290
(303) 861-4127

FINANCIAL SUMMARY
Recent Giving: $3,900,000 (1995 est.); $4,166,000 (1994); $3,256,731 (1993)

Assets: $92,000,000 (1995 est.); $88,000,000 (1994 approx.); $93,201,572 (1993)

Gifts Received: $228 (1988); $119,522 (1986)

EIN: 84-6020702

CONTRIBUTIONS SUMMARY
Donor(s): Incorporated in 1948 as the Arthur E. Johnson Foundation, the foundation became the Helen K. and Arthur E. Johnson Foundation in 1975.

Typical Recipients: • *Arts & Humanities:* History & Archaeology, Libraries, Museums/Galleries, Music, Opera, Public Broadcasting • *Civic & Public Affairs:* Employment/Job Training, General, Hispanic Affairs, Housing, Native American Affairs, Urban & Community Affairs, Zoos/Aquariums • *Education:* Colleges & Universities, Economic Education, Elementary Education (Private), General, Leadership Training, Minority Education, Private Education (Precollege), Public Education (Precollege), Secondary Education (Private), Student Aid • *Environment:* Air/Water Quality, General, Resource Conservation • *Health:* AIDS/HIV, Alzheimers Disease, Cancer, Clinics/Medical Centers, Health Organizations, Hospitals, Medical Research, Nursing Services, Single-Disease Health Associations, Speech & Hearing • *International:* International Environmental Issues • *Religion:* Churches, Religious Welfare, Seminaries • *Social Services:* Animal Protection, Child Welfare, Community Centers, Community Service Organizations, Emergency Relief, Family Planning, Family Services, Food/Clothing Distribution, Homes, People with Disabilities, Recreation & Athletics, Senior Services, Shelters/Homelessness, Substance Abuse, United Funds/United Ways, Volunteer Services, YMCA/YWCA/YMHA/YWHA, Youth Organizations

Grant Types: capital, general support, project, and scholarship

Geographic Distribution: Colorado only

GIVING OFFICERS
Lynn H. Campion: vp, treas, trust

Thomas B. Campion, Jr.: trust *PHIL AFFIL* trust: Chubb Foundation

Mrs. James R. Hartley: pres, trust

Charles R. Hazelrigg: trust

Gerald R. Hillyard, Jr.: secy, trust

Stanley Kamprath: vp, exec dir

Roger D. Knight, Jr.: trust

Ronald L. Lehr: trust

Stanley D. Neeleman: trust

Betty J. Penner: asst secy

APPLICATION INFORMATION
Initial Approach:

Applicants should send a brief preliminary letter outlining the project. If interested, the foundation will request a full proposal.

Include in a full proposal the amount requested and objective of the project (including methods to be used), relevance of project to others, timetable for accomplishing goals, history of organization and current board members, documentation of financial support and list of other funding agencies, operating and project budget, recent financial statements, proposed evaluation plan, plans for possible long-term funding, and IRS tax exemption letter.

Proposals for spring, summer, fall, and winter board meetings should be sent by January 1, April 1, July 1, and October 1, respectively.

If interested, the foundation will review requested proposals at board meetings.

Restrictions on Giving: The foundation does not support organizations whose purpose is to influence the legislative or judicial process in any manner or for any cause. It is not foundation policy to make multiple-year grant commitments. Regional and national programs rarely receive support. Requests for operational or capital support are more likely to be approved than requests for loans, endowment support, purchase of blocks of tickets, individual scholarships, or support for conferences. The foundation requires reports from grantees as to the specific use of the funds and the results achieved by the program.

PUBLICATIONS
Annual report

GRANTS ANALYSIS
Total Grants: $4,166,000

Number of Grants: 165

Highest Grant: $380,000

Average Grant: $15,000*

Typical Range: $5,000 to $30,000

Disclosure Period: 1994

Note: Average grant was supplied by the foundation. Recent grants are derived from a 1993 Form 990.

RECENT GRANTS

Library

50,000	Western State College, Gunnison, CO — Savage library

General

250,000	Christian Living Campus, Littleton, CO — expansion project
150,000	Colorado Uplift, Denver, CO — new programs

130,634	Arapaho House, Sheridan, CO — advocacy case management
125,000	University of Colorado Foundation, Boulder, CO — AIDS research
100,000	Cenikor Foundation, Lakewood, CO

Joslin-Needham Family Foundation

CONTACT
Judy Gunnon
Joslin-Needham Family Fdn.
c/o Farmers State Bank
200 Clayton St.
Brush, CO 80723
(303) 842-5101

FINANCIAL SUMMARY
Recent Giving: $166,821 (1993); $161,190 (1992); $161,560 (1991)

Assets: $3,584,889 (1993); $3,526,126 (1992); $3,603,519 (1991)

EIN: 84-6038670

CONTRIBUTIONS SUMMARY
Donor(s): the late Gladys Joslin

Typical Recipients: • *Arts & Humanities:* Libraries • *Civic & Public Affairs:* Municipalities/Towns, Safety, Urban & Community Affairs • *Education:* Agricultural Education, Public Education (Precollege), Secondary Education (Public) • *Health:* Emergency/Ambulance Services, Health Organizations, Hospitals, Long-Term Care • *Religion:* Churches, Ministries, Religious Organizations, Religious Welfare • *Social Services:* Community Service Organizations, Food/Clothing Distribution, Scouts, United Funds/United Ways, Youth Organizations

Grant Types: general support

Geographic Distribution: focus on the Brush, CO, area

GIVING OFFICERS
Farmers State Bank: trust

Robert V. Hansen: trust

Robert Petteys: trust

Helen Watrous: off

APPLICATION INFORMATION
Initial Approach: Send brief letter of inquiry describing program. Include a description of organization, amount requested, purpose of funds sought, recently audited financial statement, and proof of tax-exempt status. There are no deadlines.

GRANTS ANALYSIS
Total Grants: $166,821

Number of Grants: 16

Highest Grant: $55,000

Typical Range: $300 to $54,757

Disclosure Period: 1993

Note: Recent grants are derived from a 1993 Form 990.

RECENT GRANTS
Library
27,000	East Morgan County Library District, Brush, CO

General
55,000	East Morgan County Hospital Foundation, Brush, CO
54,757	Ebenezer Lutheran Care Center Foundation, Brush, CO
13,564	City of Brush, Brush, CO
3,000	East Morgan County Hospital Foundation, Brush, CO
2,700	Rankin Presyterian Church, Rankin, CO

Kitzmiller/Bales Trust

CONTACT
Robert U. Hansen
Trustee
Kitzmiller/Bales Trust
PO Box 96
Wray, CO 80758
(303) 332-4824

FINANCIAL SUMMARY
Recent Giving: $334,582 (1993); $341,249 (1991); $294,330 (1990)

Assets: $5,635,944 (1993); $5,863,434 (1991); $5,089,005 (1990)

EIN: 84-6178085

CONTRIBUTIONS SUMMARY
Donor(s): the late Edna B. Kitzmiller

Typical Recipients: • *Arts & Humanities:* History & Archaeology, Libraries, Museums/Galleries • *Civic & Public Affairs:* Municipalities/Towns, Safety, Urban & Community Affairs • *Education:* General, Public Education (Precollege), Secondary Education (Public) • *Health:* Emergency/Ambulance Services, Hospitals, Medical Rehabilitation • *Social Services:* Community Centers, Family Services, Recreation & Athletics, Scouts

Grant Types: capital and operating expenses

Geographic Distribution: limited to projects within the area of East Yuma County School District, CO

GIVING OFFICERS
Duard Fix: trust

Robert U. Hansen: trust

APPLICATION INFORMATION
Initial Approach: Send brief letter of inquiry describing program or project. There are no deadlines.

GRANTS ANALYSIS
Total Grants: $334,582

Number of Grants: 17

Highest Grant: $117,000

Typical Range: $2,000 to $10,000

Disclosure Period: 1993

Note: Recent grants are derived from a 1993 Form 990.

RECENT GRANTS
Library
3,500	Wray Public Library, Wray, CO — copier and encyclopedia set

General
117,000	Wray Rehabilitation and Activities Center, Wray, CO — building project
95,000	Wray Rehabilitation and Activities Center, Wray, CO — building project
50,500	East Yuma County School District RJ-2, Wray, CO — capital expenditures
30,000	Wray Rehabilitation and Activities Center, Wray, CO — rehabilitation pool
12,000	Wray Rehabilitation and Activities Center, Wray, CO — operating funds

KN Energy, Inc. / KN Energy Foundation

Revenue: $493.35 million
Employees: 1,735
Headquarters: Hastings, NE
SIC Major Group: Coal Mining, Electric, Gas & Sanitary Services, and Oil & Gas Extraction

CONTACT
Stuart Wheeler
Director, Public Affairs
KN Energy, Inc.
PO Box 281304
Lakewood, CO 80228-8304
(303) 989-1740
Note: Company headquarters is located at PO Box 608, Hastings, NE 68902, (303) 989-1740.

FINANCIAL SUMMARY
Recent Giving: $125,366 (1992)

Assets: $3,099,558 (1992)

EIN: 84-1148161

CONTRIBUTIONS SUMMARY
Typical Recipients: • *Arts & Humanities:* Arts Associations & Councils, Arts Centers, General, Historic Preservation, History & Archaeology, Libraries, Museums/Galleries, Music, Performing Arts • *Civic & Public Affairs:* Chambers of Commerce, Clubs, Community Foundations, Economic Development, General, Municipalities/Towns, Rural Affairs, Urban & Community Affairs • *Education:* Colleges & Universities, Engineering/Technological Education, General • *Environment:* General • *Health:* General, Hospitals • *Social Services:* Community Centers, Delinquency & Criminal Rehabilitation, Family Planning, General, People with Disabilities, Recreation & Athletics, Senior Services, Youth Organizations

Grant Types: employee matching gifts and general support

Geographic Distribution: headquarters and operating locations in CO, KS, NE, and WY.

Operating Locations: CO (Lakewood), NE (Hastings), WY (Casper)

CORP. OFFICERS

Charles W. Battey: *B* 1932 *ED* Univ NE BBA 1954 *CURR EMPL* chmn, dir: KN Energy *CORP AFFIL* dir: Boatmens Natl Bank Kansas City *NONPR AFFIL* dir: Counc Ed, Heart Am Un Way, Kansas City Crime Commn, Kansas City Pub TV, Midwest REs Inst

Larry D. Hall: *CURR EMPL* pres, ceo, dir: KN Energy

Stuart L. Wheeler: *CURR EMPL* dir pub aff: KN Energy

GIVING OFFICERS

Judy A. Aden: treas

Charles W. Battey: pres, dir *CURR EMPL* chmn, dir: KN Energy (see above)

Robert L. Boumann: asst secy

William S. Garner, Jr.: secy, dir

Larry D. Hall: vp, dir *CURR EMPL* pres, ceo, dir: KN Energy (see above)

Stuart L. Wheeler: asst secy, dir *CURR EMPL* dir pub aff: KN Energy (see above)

James F. Williams: asst treas

APPLICATION INFORMATION

Initial Approach: Send a brief letter of inquiry. Not more than three pages. Include a description of organization, amount requested, purpose of funds sought, recently audited financial statement, and proof of tax-exempt status. There are no deadlines.

GRANTS ANALYSIS

Total Grants: $125,366

Number of Grants: 111

Highest Grant: $24,078

Typical Range: $100 to $5,000

Disclosure Period: 1992

Note: Recent grants are derived from a 1992 Form 990.

RECENT GRANTS

Library
2,000	City of Kearney Library and Information Center Bookmobile, Kearney, NE
2,000	O'Neill Friends of the Library, O'Neill, NE
1,750	Holdrege Public Library, Holdrege, CO

General
24,078	Huck Boyd Foundation
5,000	Cheyenne County Community Center Foundation, Sydney, NE
2,605	Hastings College Foundation, Hastings, NE
2,500	Chadron State College, Chadron, NE
2,500	Wyoming Community Foundation, Wyoming, MI

Monfort Family Foundation

Former Foundation Name: Monfort Charitable Foundation

CONTACT

Dave Evans
Administrator
Monfort Family Foundation
PO Box 890
Greeley, CO 80632
(303) 356-3611

FINANCIAL SUMMARY

Recent Giving: $1,594,971 (1993); $1,821,635 (1992); $979,602 (1991)

Assets: $33,407,538 (1993); $34,000,396 (1992); $35,088,683 (1991)

Gifts Received: $54,963 (1992); $1,691,360 (1991); $1,973,752 (1990)

Fiscal Note: In 1991, contributions were received from estate of Margery Monfort Wilson ($1,680,000) and Richard L. Monfort ($11,360). In 1992, contributions were from the estate of Margery Monfort Wilson.

EIN: 23-7068253

CONTRIBUTIONS SUMMARY

Donor(s): The foundation was established in 1970.

Typical Recipients: • *Arts & Humanities:* Libraries, Music, Performing Arts, Public Broadcasting, Theater • *Civic & Public Affairs:* Community Foundations, General, Hispanic Affairs, Housing, Municipalities/Towns, Parades/Festivals, Professional & Trade Associations, Women's Affairs • *Education:* Agricultural Education, Colleges & Universities, Community & Junior Colleges, Economic Education, Elementary Education (Public), Literacy, Private Education (Precollege), Public Education (Precollege), Student Aid • *Health:* AIDS/HIV, Arthritis, Cancer, Children's Health/Hospitals, Clinics/Medical Centers, Medical Rehabilitation, Multiple Sclerosis, Prenatal Health Issues, Single-Disease Health Associations, Speech & Hearing • *Religion:* Churches • *Social Services:* Animal Protection, Community Centers, Community Service Organizations, Crime Prevention, Food/Clothing Distribution, Recreation & Athletics, Scouts, Senior Services, Shelters/Homelessness, Substance Abuse, United Funds/United Ways, Veterans, Youth Organizations

Grant Types: general support

Geographic Distribution: focus on Greeley, CO

GIVING OFFICERS

Dave Evans: admin

Kyle Futo: vp

Myra Monfort: secy

Kaye C. Montera: pres

APPLICATION INFORMATION

Initial Approach:

Contact the foundation for application guidelines.

Applications should include organization's name, total budget of organization, total project budget, amount requested, summary of proposal, other sources of funding, future funding, and list of board members.

Deadlines for applications are May 1 and October 1.

GRANTS ANALYSIS

Total Grants: $1,594,971

Number of Grants: 48

Highest Grant: $510,000

Average Grant: $33,229

Typical Range: $1,000 to $35,000

Disclosure Period: 1993

Note: Recent grants are derived from a 1993 Form 990.

RECENT GRANTS

Library
4,000	Friends of Lincoln Park Library, Greeley, CO — purchase books

General
510,000	University of Northern Colorado, Greeley, CO — toward building of new stadium
304,159	University of Colorado Foundation, Boulder, CO — cancer research
101,884	Humane Society of Weld County, Greeley, CO — toward building of animal shelter
100,000	United Way, Greeley, CO
100,000	Weld County Veterans Memorial, Greeley, CO — toward building of memorial

Morrison Charitable Trust, Pauline A. and George R.

CONTACT

L. D. Hoyt
Trustee
Pauline A. and George R. Morrison Charitable Trust
1801 York St.
Denver, CO 80206
(303) 320-1066

FINANCIAL SUMMARY

Recent Giving: $95,580 (fiscal 1993); $48,853 (fiscal 1992); $454,000 (fiscal 1991)

Assets: $7,982,522 (fiscal 1993); $7,338,366 (fiscal 1992); $6,828,060 (fiscal 1991)

EIN: 84-6166335

CONTRIBUTIONS SUMMARY

Donor(s): George R. Morrison

Typical Recipients: • *Arts & Humanities:* Historic Preservation, Libraries, Museums/Galleries, Visual Arts • *Civic & Public Affairs:* Botanical Gardens/Parks, Zoos/Aquariums • *Environment:* General, Wildlife Protection • *Religion:* Religious Organizations • *Science:* Science Museums • *Social Services:* People with Disabilities, Recreation & Athletics

Grant Types: capital and general support

Geographic Distribution: focus on CO

GIVING OFFICERS
Robert W. Findlay: trust

L. Douglas Hoyt: trust

Robert D. Ibbotson: trust

Jerry I. Maine: trust

APPLICATION INFORMATION
Initial Approach: Include a description of organization, amount requested, purpose of funds sought, recently audited financial statement, and proof of tax-exempt status. There are no deadlines.

Restrictions on Giving: Limited to tax exempt organizations in Colorado. Requests for grants to defray general operating costs will not be considered.

GRANTS ANALYSIS
Total Grants: $95,580

Number of Grants: 5

Highest Grant: $34,696

Typical Range: $5,000 to $30,884

Disclosure Period: fiscal year ending November 30, 1993

Note: Recent grants are derived from a fiscal 1993 Form 990.

RECENT GRANTS
General
34,696	Ute Mountain Tribal Cultural Park Recreation and Education Center, Towaoc, CO — restabilization of Bone Awl or Sandal House
30,884	Rocky Mountain National Park Association, Estes Park, CO — Colorado River Handicapped Access Trail
15,000	Denver Museum of Natural History, Denver, CO — operations
5,000	Colorado Wildlife Heritage Foundation, Denver, CO — Barrier-Free Wildlife Facility

Muchnic Foundation

CONTACT
David Mize
Secretary and Treasurer
Muchnic Fdn.
104 S. Cascade Ave., Ste. 202
Colorado Springs, CO 80903-5102
(913) 367-4164

FINANCIAL SUMMARY
Recent Giving: $507,454 (fiscal 1993)

Assets: $8,670,116 (fiscal 1993)

EIN: 48-6102818

CONTRIBUTIONS SUMMARY
Typical Recipients: • *Arts & Humanities:* Arts Associations & Councils, Arts Funds,

History & Archaeology, Libraries, Museums/Galleries, Performing Arts • *Civic & Public Affairs:* Municipalities/Towns • *Education:* Colleges & Universities, Engineering/Technological Education, International Studies, Private Education (Precollege), Student Aid • *Environment:* General, Resource Conservation • *Health:* Arthritis, Cancer, Children's Health/Hospitals, Prenatal Health Issues, Research/Studies Institutes, Single-Disease Health Associations • *International:* Health Care/Hospitals, International Relief Efforts • *Religion:* Churches, Ministries • *Science:* Science Museums • *Social Services:* Animal Protection, Scouts, Substance Abuse, United Funds/United Ways, YMCA/YWCA/YMHA/YWHA, Youth Organizations

Grant Types: general support

Geographic Distribution: focus on CO

GIVING OFFICERS
Elizabeth M. Elicker: pres, trust

Ann Mize Kovats: dir

David C. Mize: secy, treas

APPLICATION INFORMATION
Initial Approach: The foundation has no formal grant application procedure or application form. Deadline is October 31.

GRANTS ANALYSIS
Total Grants: $507,454

Number of Grants: 67

Highest Grant: $131,477

Typical Range: $500 to $48,000

Disclosure Period: fiscal year ending November 30, 1993

Note: Recent grants are derived from a fiscal 1993 Form 990.

RECENT GRANTS
Library
8,000	Atchison Library, Atchison, KS
2,000	Atchison Library, Atchison, KS — funds for special big print books

General
48,000	Drexel University, Philadelphia, PA
30,000	St. Francis Boys Home
25,000	Duke University, Durham, NC
25,000	Kansas University Endowment Association, Topeka, KS
17,000	Benedictine College, Atchison, KS

Mullen Foundation, J. K.

Former Foundation Name: The John K. and Catherine S. Mullen Benevolent Corporation

CONTACT
John F. Malo
Secretary
J. K. Mullen Fdn.
1640 Logan St.
Denver, CO 80203
(303) 830-1148

FINANCIAL SUMMARY
Recent Giving: $293,590 (fiscal 1992); $299,000 (fiscal 1991); $324,100 (fiscal 1990)

Assets: $4,529,353 (fiscal 1992); $4,433,136 (fiscal 1991); $4,273,738 (fiscal 1990)

EIN: 84-6002475

CONTRIBUTIONS SUMMARY
Donor(s): the late John K. Mullen and Catherine S. Mullen, the J. K. Mullen Co.

Typical Recipients: • *Arts & Humanities:* Libraries, Museums/Galleries, Music • *Civic & Public Affairs:* Zoos/Aquariums • *Education:* Colleges & Universities, Private Education (Precollege), Religious Education • *Health:* Hospices, Hospitals, Mental Health, Single-Disease Health Associations • *Religion:* Religious Organizations • *Social Services:* Community Service Organizations, Food/Clothing Distribution, People with Disabilities, Youth Organizations

Grant Types: general support

Geographic Distribution: focus on Denver, CO

GIVING OFFICERS
John F. Malo: secy, dir

Timothy M. O'Connor: dir

Edith M. Roberts: dir

Sheila Sevier: dir

Anne H. Weckbaugh: dir

J. Kernan Weckbaugh: pres, dir

John K. Weckbaugh: vp, dir

Walter S. Weckbaugh: treas, dir

APPLICATION INFORMATION
Initial Approach: Send cover letter and full proposal. Deadline is September 1.

Restrictions on Giving: Does not support individuals.

GRANTS ANALYSIS
Total Grants: $293,590

Number of Grants: 45

Highest Grant: $35,000

Typical Range: $1,000 to $5,000

Disclosure Period: fiscal year ending July 31, 1992

Note: Recent grants are derived from a fiscal 1992 Form 990.

RECENT GRANTS
Library
20,090	Denver Public Library, Denver, CO
20,000	Denver Public Library, Denver, CO

General
35,000	Catholic University, Washington, DC
25,000	Regis High School, Denver, CO
25,000	Regis/Loretto Heights College, Denver, CO
20,000	Children's Hospital, Denver, CO
12,500	St. Thomas Seminary, Denver, CO

Norgren Foundation, Carl A.

CONTACT
Leigh H. Norgren
President
Carl A. Norgren Fdn.
2696 S Colorado Blvd., No. 585
Denver, CO 80222
(303) 758-8392

FINANCIAL SUMMARY
Recent Giving: $142,948 (1993); $145,600 (1991); $170,370 (1990)

Assets: $2,972,039 (1993); $2,643,096 (1991); $2,386,289 (1990)

EIN: 84-6034195

CONTRIBUTIONS SUMMARY
Donor(s): the late Carl A. Norgren and Juliet E. Norgren, C.A. Norgren Co.

Typical Recipients: • *Arts & Humanities:* Historic Preservation, Libraries, Museums/Galleries, Music, Opera • *Civic & Public Affairs:* General, Philanthropic Organizations, Zoos/Aquariums • *Education:* Agricultural Education, Colleges & Universities, Environmental Education, Private Education (Precollege) • *Health:* Cancer, Children's Health/Hospitals, Clinics/Medical Centers, Hospitals, Medical Rehabilitation, Medical Research, Single-Disease Health Associations • *Religion:* Churches, Ministries, Missionary Activities (Domestic) • *Science:* Science Museums • *Social Services:* Child Welfare, Community Service Organizations, Family Planning, Family Services, Food/Clothing Distribution, People with Disabilities, Recreation & Athletics, Scouts, Shelters/Homelessness, United Funds/United Ways, Youth Organizations

Grant Types: capital and general support

Geographic Distribution: focus on Denver, CO

GIVING OFFICERS
Gene N. Koelbel: vp, trust

Donald K. Norgren: trust

Leigh H. Norgren: pres, treas, trust

Vanda N. Werner: secy

APPLICATION INFORMATION
Initial Approach: Send a brief letter of inquiry. Include a description of organization, amount requested, purpose of funds sought, recently audited financial statement, and proof of tax-exempt status. There are no deadlines.

PUBLICATIONS
Annual Report (including application guidelines)

GRANTS ANALYSIS
Total Grants: $142,948

Number of Grants: 62

Highest Grant: $10,000

Typical Range: $500 to $5,000

Disclosure Period: 1993

Note: Recent grants are derived from a 1993 Form 990.

RECENT GRANTS
Library
8,000	Arapahoe Library Foundation, Littleton, CO
1,500	Bud Werner Library, Steamboat Springs, CO

General
10,000	Yours for Life Ministries, Santa Ana, CA
6,000	Children's Hospital Foundation, Denver, CO
5,500	Colorado State University Foundation, Ft. Collins, CO
5,000	Colorado Outdoor Education Center, Breckenridge, CO
5,000	National Sports Center for the Disabled, Winter Park, CO

O'Fallon Trust, Martin J. and Mary Anne

CONTACT
Alfred O'Meara, Jr.
Chairman
Martin J. and Mary Anne O'Fallon Trust
2800 S University Blvd 61
Denver, CO 80210
(303) 753-1727

FINANCIAL SUMMARY
Recent Giving: $216,250 (1992); $157,750 (1991); $145,450 (1990)

Assets: $2,726,386 (1992); $2,629,743 (1991); $2,409,509 (1990)

EIN: 84-0415830

CONTRIBUTIONS SUMMARY
Donor(s): the late Martin J. O'Fallon

Typical Recipients: • *Arts & Humanities:* Community Arts, Historic Preservation, Libraries, Museums/Galleries, Music, Theater • *Civic & Public Affairs:* Botanical Gardens/Parks, Economic Development, General, Women's Affairs, Zoos/Aquariums • *Education:* Legal Education, Minority Education, Private Education (Precollege), Student Aid • *Environment:* General • *Health:* Hospices, Mental Health • *Religion:* Churches, Religious Organizations, Religious Welfare • *Science:* Science Museums • *Social Services:* Community Service Organizations, Day Care, Family Planning, Family Services, Food/Clothing Distribution, Homes, United Funds/United Ways, Youth Organizations

Grant Types: capital and project

Geographic Distribution: limited to CO; priority always given to Denver.

GIVING OFFICERS
Margaret H. Carey: secy, trust

Alfred O'Meara, Jr.: chmn, trust

Brian O'Meara: trust

Patrick E. Purcell: treas, trust

APPLICATION INFORMATION
Initial Approach: Grant applications from agencies outside CO not accepted. Send letter requesting application form. Submit proposal preferably between May and August

Restrictions on Giving: Does not support individuals.

PUBLICATIONS
Annual Report (including application guidelines)

GRANTS ANALYSIS
Total Grants: $216,250

Number of Grants: 25

Highest Grant: $100,000

Typical Range: $1,000 to $10,000

Disclosure Period: 1992

Note: Recent grants are derived from a 1992 Form 990.

RECENT GRANTS
Library
10,000	St. Anne's Episcopal School, Denver, CO — capital costs of library

General
100,000	Denver Museum of Natural History, Denver, CO — in support of Prehistoric Journey
25,000	Rocky Mountain National Park Associates, Estes Park, CO — for the Colorado River Accessibility Trail project
10,000	Boys and Girls Club of Metro Denver, Denver, CO — special campaign
10,000	University of Denver Law School, Denver, CO — Martin J. Harrington Scholarship Fund
5,000	Dominican Sisters Home Health Agency of Denver, Denver, CO — general support

Petteys Memorial Foundation, Jack

CONTACT
Jack Petteys Memorial Fdn.
PO Box 324
Brush, CO 80723
(303) 842-5101

FINANCIAL SUMMARY
Recent Giving: $218,890 (1993); $176,950 (1992); $158,522 (1991)

Assets: $4,298,501 (1993); $4,121,445 (1992); $3,661,364 (1991)

EIN: 84-6036239

CONTRIBUTIONS SUMMARY
Typical Recipients: • *Arts & Humanities:* Arts Associations & Councils, Libraries, Museums/Galleries, Public Broadcasting • *Civic & Public Affairs:* General, Municipali-

ties/Towns, Safety, Urban & Community Affairs • *Education:* Colleges & Universities, Community & Junior Colleges, Public Education (Precollege), Student Aid • *Health:* Children's Health/Hospitals, Clinics/Medical Centers, Emergency/Ambulance Services, Geriatric Health, Health Organizations, Hospitals, Medical Rehabilitation • *Social Services:* Community Service Organizations, People with Disabilities, Senior Services, United Funds/United Ways

Grant Types: general support and scholarship

Geographic Distribution: limited to northeastern CO

GIVING OFFICERS
Farmers State Bank: trust

Robert Hansen: trust

Robert A. Petteys: trust

Helen C. Watrous: dir

APPLICATION INFORMATION
Initial Approach: Send brief letter describing program. Deadline is December 1.

GRANTS ANALYSIS
Total Grants: $218,890

Number of Grants: 29

Highest Grant: $115,000

Typical Range: $435 to $18,000

Disclosure Period: 1993

Note: Recent grants are derived from a 1993 Form 990.

RECENT GRANTS
General

115,000	East Morgan County Hospital Foundation, Brush, CO
10,000	City of Brush, Brush, CO
10,000	RE-1 Valley School District, Sterling, CO
3,005	Peetz Plateau School District RE-5, Peetz, CO
3,000	Eastern Colorado Services for the Developmentally Disabled, Sterling, CO

Pittsburg Midway Coal Mining Co.

Sales: $462.37 million
Employees: 1,500
Parent Company: Chevron Corp.
Headquarters: Englewood, CO
SIC Major Group: Coal Mining

CONTACT
Fred Meurer
Manager Public Affairs
Pittsburg Midway Coal Mining Co.
PO Box 6518
Englewood, CO 80155-6518
(303) 930-4065

FINANCIAL SUMMARY
Fiscal Note: Annual Giving Range: less than $100,000

CONTRIBUTIONS SUMMARY
Company reports that 40% of contributions are allocated to health and human services; 30% to civic and public affairs; 20% to education; and 10% to arts and humanities.

Typical Recipients: • *Arts & Humanities:* Arts Appreciation, Arts Associations & Councils, Arts Centers, Arts Festivals, Community Arts, General, Libraries, Museums/Galleries, Music, Public Broadcasting • *Civic & Public Affairs:* Botanical Gardens/Parks, Chambers of Commerce, Clubs, General, Native American Affairs, Parades/Festivals, Professional & Trade Associations, Urban & Community Affairs • *Education:* Colleges & Universities, Community & Junior Colleges, Education Funds, Education Reform, Elementary Education (Public), Engineering/Technological Education, General, Public Education (Precollege), Science/Mathematics Education • *Environment:* Air/Water Quality, Energy, General, Resource Conservation, Wildlife Protection • *Health:* Children's Health/Hospitals, Clinics/Medical Centers, Emergency/Ambulance Services, Eyes/Blindness, General, Hospitals, Medical Rehabilitation, Prenatal Health Issues • *Science:* General, Science Exhibits & Fairs, Scientific Organizations • *Social Services:* Child Welfare, Community Centers, Community Service Organizations, Crime Prevention, Day Care, Delinquency & Criminal Rehabilitation, Domestic Violence, Emergency Relief, Family Services, General, Recreation & Athletics, Senior Services, United Funds/United Ways, Volunteer Services, Youth Organizations

Grant Types: award, emergency, general support, multiyear/continuing support, and scholarship

Geographic Distribution: principally near operating locations and to national organizations

Operating Locations: AL (Tuscaloosa), NM (Gallup, Raton), WY (Kemmerer)

CORP. OFFICERS
Barry G. McGrath: *CURR EMPL* chmn, pres: Pittsburg Midway Coal Mining Co

APPLICATION INFORMATION
Initial Approach: Send a brief letter of inquiry. Include a description of organization, amount requested, purpose of funds sought, and proof of tax-exempt status. Must coincide with company business interests.

Restrictions on Giving: Does not support group or individual travel expenses.

OTHER THINGS TO KNOW
Generally charitable contributions are made upon requests/recommendations by mine managers. The company are not soliciting additional requests for contributions.

GRANTS ANALYSIS
Typical Range: $10 to $1,000

Note: Typical grant size is less than $1,000. Recent grants are derived from a grants list provided by company in 1995.

RECENT GRANTS

General
Chief Manuelito Awards Banquet
Council of Energy Resource Tribes
Ducks Unlimited, Jackson, WY
Lions Club, Englewood, CO
March of Dimes, Englewood, CO

Rabb Foundation, Harry W.

CONTACT
Richard A. Zarlengo
Secretary-Treasurer
Harry W. Rabb Fdn.
6242 S Elmira Circle
Englewood, CO 80111
(303) 721-0048

FINANCIAL SUMMARY
Recent Giving: $112,566 (fiscal 1993); $131,410 (fiscal 1991); $112,770 (fiscal 1990)

Assets: $1,918,906 (fiscal 1993); $2,014,162 (fiscal 1991); $1,980,827 (fiscal 1990)

EIN: 23-7236149

CONTRIBUTIONS SUMMARY
Typical Recipients: • *Arts & Humanities:* Community Arts, Libraries, Museums/Galleries, Music, Opera, Performing Arts, Public Broadcasting • *Civic & Public Affairs:* Employment/Job Training, General, Public Policy • *Education:* Colleges & Universities, Education Reform • *Health:* AIDS/HIV, Arthritis, Cancer, Diabetes, Hospices, Multiple Sclerosis, Single-Disease Health Associations • *International:* International Organizations, International Relations • *Religion:* Churches, Jewish Causes, Religious Organizations, Religious Welfare • *Social Services:* Child Welfare, Community Service Organizations, Homes, People with Disabilities, Senior Services, United Funds/United Ways, Youth Organizations

Grant Types: general support

Geographic Distribution: focus on Denver, CO

GIVING OFFICERS
Myles Dolan: trust, vp

Jacob B. Kaufman: trust, pres

Richard A. Zarlengo: trust, secy, treas

APPLICATION INFORMATION
Initial Approach: Send brief letter describing program. There are no deadlines.

GRANTS ANALYSIS
Total Grants: $112,566

Number of Grants: 52

Highest Grant: $25,000

Typical Range: $500 to $5,000

Disclosure Period: fiscal year ending June 30, 1993

Note: Recent grants are derived from a fiscal 1993 Form 990.

RECENT GRANTS

Library

500	Denver Public Library Friends, Denver, CO

General

25,000	Allied Jewish Federation, Denver, CO
12,500	Mile High United Way, Denver, CO
6,000	Mt. St. Vincent Home, Denver, CO
5,500	Hospice of Peace, Denver, CO
5,000	Hospice of Metro Denver, Denver, CO

Schuller International / Schuller Fund

Former Foundation Name: Manville Fund
Revenue: $1.2 billion
Employees: 7,500
Headquarters: Denver, CO
SIC Major Group: Holding & Other
Investment Offices, Paper & Allied Products, and Stone, Clay & Glass Products

CONTACT
Joni Baird
Vice President
Schuller Fund
PO Box 5108
Denver, CO 80217-0008
(303) 978-2000

FINANCIAL SUMMARY
Recent Giving: $190,011 (1994); $255,254 (1993); $289,752 (1992 approx.)

Assets: $191,865 (1993); $181,585 (1992); $508,174 (1990)

Gifts Received: $275,000 (1993); $200,000 (1992)

Fiscal Note: Figures represent fund contributions only. Company does not reveal direct giving information. In 1993, contributions were received from Schuller International.

EIN: 13-6034039

CONTRIBUTIONS SUMMARY
Typical Recipients: • *Arts & Humanities:* Arts Associations & Councils, Arts Centers, Arts Outreach, Ballet, Community Arts, General, Historic Preservation, Libraries, Literary Arts, Museums/Galleries, Performing Arts, Theater, Visual Arts • *Civic & Public Affairs:* Botanical Gardens/Parks, Clubs, Economic Development, General, Housing, Inner-City Development, Urban & Community Affairs, Zoos/Aquariums • *Education:* Agricultural Education, Colleges & Universities, Community & Junior Colleges • *Health:* AIDS/HIV, Cancer, Emergency/Ambulance Services, Health Organizations, Respiratory, Single-Disease Health Associations • *International:* Human Rights • *Religion:* Ministries, Religious Organizations • *Social Services:* At-Risk Youth, Community Centers, Community Service Organizations, Counseling, Domestic Violence, Emergency Relief, Family Services, Food/Clothing Distribution, Homes, People with Disabilities, Recreation & Athletics, Scouts, Senior Services, Sexual Abuse, Shelters/Homelessness, Substance Abuse, United Funds/United Ways, Volunteer Services, Youth Organizations

Grant Types: award, challenge, emergency, employee matching gifts, general support, scholarship, and seed money

Nonmonetary Support Types: donated equipment, donated products, in-kind services, loaned executives, and workplace solicitation

Geographic Distribution: primarily in company operating locations

Operating Locations: AZ (Tucson), CA (Pittsburg, Santa Ana, Willows), GA (Winder), IL (Rockdale, Waukegan), IN (Elkhart, Richmond), KS (McPherson), ME (Lewiston), MS (Natchez), NC (Laurinburg), NJ (Edison, Penbryn), OH (Defiance, Waterville), TN (Etowah), TX (Cleburne, Ennis, Ft. Worth), VA (Richmond, Shenandoah Valley), WV (Parkersburg)

CORP. OFFICERS
William Thomas Stephens: *ED* Univ AR BS 1965; Univ AR MS 1966 *CURR EMPL* chmn, pres, ceo, dir: Schuller Intl.

GIVING OFFICERS
Joni Baird: vp, fund admin

Cecil Vanoy Draper: pres *B* El Paso TX 1940 *ED* North TX St Univ 1967

Robert E. Fowler, Jr.: trust

Dave Pullen: vp

M. K. Rhinehart: vp, treas *CURR EMPL* dir fin & admin: Schuller Intl

William Spink: asst secy

William Thomas Stephens: trust *CURR EMPL* chmn, pres, ceo, dir: Schuller Intl. (see above)

Will Miller Storey: trust *B* Vancouver WA 1931 *ED* OR St Univ BA 1953; Univ WA *CURR EMPL* exec vp, cfo, treas, dir: Am Pres Cos Ltd *CORP AFFIL* exec vp, cfo, dir: Am Pres Lines Ltd *PHIL AFFIL* exec vp, cfo: American President Companies Foundation

Raymond S. Troubh: trust

APPLICATION INFORMATION
Initial Approach: Send a full proposal.

Include Information On: names, addresses, and professional affiliation of members of the board of directors of the organization; copy of the organization's determination letter from the IRS; most recent audited financial statements; interim statement of income and expenses for the current fiscal year; complete budget including all sources of income and projected expenses of the project; timetable and action plan for the project; any printed materials describing the organization and its activities, such as brochures, newspaper articles, and annual reports; any additional information relevant to the proposal

When to Submit: by quarterly deadlines: May 15, August 15, and December 15

Restrictions on Giving: The fund does not give to hospitals, organizations involved in private education, religious activities, organizations without 501(c)(3) tax-exempt status, special events, or organizations that receive more than 20% of their annual income from the United Way or similar community fund drives.

Organizations that have previously been awarded a grant from the fund may not reapply until two years after the application date of the funded request.

OTHER THINGS TO KNOW
Religious institutions may receive funding for programs that are secular and not religious or ceremonial in nature.

In 1994, the Manville Fund reorganized as the Schuller Fund. Its program description includes the following areas. (1) Community Grants: Supports a range of organizations involved with the arts, culture, and social service activities. Recent recipients include child recreation groups, training for the handicapped, and health organizations. (2) Education Grants: Grants are available to high school seniors with a parent or guardian who has been a company employee for at least one year. (3) Matching Grants: The fund matches dollar-for-dollar personal donations of $50 to $249 by company employees or their families to colleges and universities.

Program details, including budgets, deadlines, procedures, and forms can be obtained from representatives at company sites or from headquarters in Denver, CO.

Fund officers give preference to proposals that reflect Schuller employee's volunteerism at all levels and all locations.

Priority will be given to applicants for matching funds, challenge grants, and proposals that yield some significant multiple.

GRANTS ANALYSIS
Total Grants: $255,254

Number of Grants: 339*

Highest Grant: $10,000

Typical Range: $500 to $6,000

Disclosure Period: 1993

Note: Recent grants are derived from a 1993 Form 990. Number of grants is approximate.

RECENT GRANTS

Library

6,000	Manville Public Library, Manville, NJ

General

10,000	Volunteer Federal Bank, Madisonville, TN
6,000	Denver Inner-City Parish, Denver, CO
5,000	American Lung Association, Denver, CO
5,000	Cancer Care of Defiance County, Defiance, OH
5,000	Cenikor Foundation, Lakewood, CO

Security Life of Denver Insurance Co.

Revenue: $626.98 million
Employees: 656
Parent Company: Internationale Nederlanden U.S. Insurance Holdings, Inc.
Headquarters: Denver, CO
SIC Major Group: Insurance Carriers

CONTACT
Ellen Sturmer
Marketing Systems Coordinator
Security Life of Denver Insurance Co.
Security Life Ctr.
1290 Broadway
Denver, CO 80203
(303) 860-1290

FINANCIAL SUMMARY
Recent Giving: $75,000 (1992); $100,000 (1991); $100,000 (1990)

CONTRIBUTIONS SUMMARY
Program supports the range of typical contributions categories: arts and humanities, civic and public affairs, education, health, and social services.

Typical Recipients: • *Arts & Humanities:* Arts Appreciation, Arts Associations & Councils, Arts Centers, Arts Festivals, Community Arts, Dance, Ethnic & Folk Arts, General, Historic Preservation, Libraries, Literary Arts, Museums/Galleries, Music, Opera, Performing Arts, Public Broadcasting, Theater, Visual Arts • *Civic & Public Affairs:* Economic Development, General, Philanthropic Organizations, Public Policy, Urban & Community Affairs, Women's Affairs, Zoos/Aquariums • *Education:* Arts/Humanities Education, Business Education, Colleges & Universities, Economic Education, Education Funds, Elementary Education (Private), General, Health & Physical Education, Literacy, Minority Education, Private Education (Precollege), Public Education (Precollege) • *Environment:* General • *Health:* General, Health Policy/Cost Containment, Health Organizations, Medical Research, Public Health • *Science:* Scientific Centers & Institutes • *Social Services:* Child Welfare, Community Service Organizations, Domestic Violence, Emergency Relief, Family Services, Food/Clothing Distribution, General, Recreation & Athletics, Shelters/Homelessness, Substance Abuse, United Funds/United Ways, Volunteer Services, Youth Organizations

Grant Types: award, capital, employee matching gifts, general support, multi-year/continuing support, and project

Nonmonetary Support Types: donated equipment, in-kind services, and workplace solicitation

Geographic Distribution: in CO, with emphasis on Denver, and in states where there is an agent

Operating Locations: CO (Denver), DC, GA, IN, NH

CORP. OFFICERS
Steven Christopher: *CURR EMPL* pres: Security Life Denver Ins Co
Frederick Arthur Deering: *CURR EMPL* chmn, dir: Security Life Denver Ins Co
Robert Glen Hillard: *CURR EMPL* ceo, dir: Security Life Denver Ins Co

GIVING OFFICERS
Ellen Sturmer: *CURR EMPL* commun cordinator: Security Life Denver

APPLICATION INFORMATION
Initial Approach: Send brief letter of inquiry including a description of the organization, amount requested, purpose of funds sought, and time frame within which contribution is needed.

Restrictions on Giving: Does not support political or lobbying groups or religious organizations for sectarian purposes.

GRANTS ANALYSIS
Typical Range: $100 to $1,000

Stone Trust, H. Chase

CONTACT
Sanara J. Koster
Trust Officer
H. Chase Stone Trust
c/o Bank One, Colorado Springs, NA
PO Box 1699
Colorado Springs, CO 80942
(719) 471-5000

FINANCIAL SUMMARY
Recent Giving: $136,825 (1993); $124,975 (1992); $99,608 (1991)

Assets: $2,667,829 (1993); $2,694,011 (1992); $2,558,360 (1991)

EIN: 84-6066113

CONTRIBUTIONS SUMMARY
Typical Recipients: • *Arts & Humanities:* Arts Centers, Arts Outreach, Libraries, Museums/Galleries, Music, Opera, Performing Arts • *Civic & Public Affairs:* Municipalities/Towns, Safety, Urban & Community Affairs • *Education:* Colleges & Universities, Literacy, Private Education (Precollege), Public Education (Precollege), Science/Mathematics Education • *Health:* Cancer, Health Organizations, Medical Research, Single-Disease Health Associations • *Social Services:* Community Service Organizations, Substance Abuse, United Funds/United Ways, Youth Organizations

Grant Types: general support

Geographic Distribution: limited to El Paso County, CO

GIVING OFFICERS
Affiliated National Bank Trust Department: trust

APPLICATION INFORMATION
Initial Approach: Send brief letter describing program. Include a description of organization, amount requested, purpose of funds sought, recently audited financial statement, and proof of tax-exempt status. Deadlines are April 30 and October 31.

Restrictions on Giving: Does not support individuals.

GRANTS ANALYSIS
Total Grants: $136,825

Typical Range: $1,000 to $10,000

Disclosure Period: 1993

Note: Recent grants are derived from a 1992 Form 990. No grants list was provided for 1993.

RECENT GRANTS
Library
6,000	Pikes Peak Library District for Imagination Celebration, Colorado Springs, CO — for 1993 functions

General
40,000	Penrose-St. Francis Healthcare Foundation, Colorado Springs, CO — toward development of Penrose Cancer Center
12,500	City of Colorado Springs Drug Abuse Awareness Program, Colorado Springs, CO — for drug prevention program presented to local fifth and sixth grade students
10,000	Webb-Waring Institute for Biomedical Research, Denver, CO — toward renovation and special equipment for infectious-bacterial disease research facility
7,500	Assistance League of Colorado Springs, Colorado Springs, CO — Operation School bell program
5,000	Colorado Springs Mounted Patrol, Colorado Springs, CO — funding for start-up costs

---

Taylor Foundation, Ruth and Vernon

CONTACT
Friday A. Green
Trustee
Ruth and Vernon Taylor Foundation
1670 Denver Club Bldg.
Denver, CO 80202
(303) 893-5284

FINANCIAL SUMMARY
Recent Giving: $1,269,000 (fiscal 1993); $1,254,930 (fiscal 1992); $1,317,382 (fiscal 1991)

Assets: $29,511,752 (fiscal 1993); $25,915,006 (fiscal 1992); $26,252,629 (fiscal 1991)

Gifts Received: $958,125 (fiscal 1985)

EIN: 84-6021788

CONTRIBUTIONS SUMMARY

Donor(s): The Colorado-based foundation was established in 1950 by Ruth Taylor and Vernon Taylor . Vernon F. Taylor (1888-1972) was president of Peerless Oil and Gas Company (San Antonio) and chairman of Wytana Cattle Company. He was a director of Trinity University and Tulane University. Three of the four members of the current board of trustees are members of the Taylor family, the children of the foundation's donors.

Typical Recipients: • *Arts & Humanities:* Arts Associations & Councils, Arts Centers, Arts Festivals, Arts Institutes, Ballet, Community Arts, Dance, Historic Preservation, Libraries, Museums/Galleries, Opera, Performing Arts, Public Broadcasting • *Civic & Public Affairs:* Economic Policy, General, Legal Aid, Municipalities/Towns, Philanthropic Organizations, Public Policy, Zoos/Aquariums • *Education:* Arts/Humanities Education, Colleges & Universities, Education Funds, International Studies, Literacy, Preschool Education, Private Education (Precollege), Religious Education, Science/Mathematics Education, Student Aid • *Environment:* General, Resource Conservation, Wildlife Protection • *Health:* Cancer, Emergency/Ambulance Services, Health Funds, Health Organizations, Hospitals, Medical Rehabilitation, Medical Research, Research/Studies Institutes, Single-Disease Health Associations • *International:* Foreign Educational Institutions, International Organizations, International Relations • *Religion:* Religious Welfare • *Science:* Science Museums • *Social Services:* Child Welfare, Emergency Relief, Family Planning, Homes, People with Disabilities, Recreation & Athletics, Senior Services, Shelters/Homelessness, Substance Abuse, Youth Organizations

Geographic Distribution: national, with some preference for Texas, Colorado, Wyoming, Montana, Illinois, and the Mid-Atlantic states

GIVING OFFICERS

Ruth Taylor Campbell: trust, don daughter

Friday Ann Green: trust *B* Chicago IL 1940 *ED* Wichita St Univ BA 1968 *NONPR AFFIL* bd dir, treas, co-fdr: Art Students League Denver

Sara Taylor Swift: trust, don daughter

Vernon F. Taylor, Jr.: trust, don *B* 1916 *ED* Dartmouth Coll *CURR EMPL* pres, dir: Westhoma Oil Co *CORP AFFIL* dir: AMAX Gold, CO Natl Bankshares, Cyprus Minerals Co; pres, dir: Peerless Oil Co

APPLICATION INFORMATION

Initial Approach:

The foundation suggests that initial contact be made in writing. There are no official application guidelines. Only one proposal copy should be sent.

Applications are accepted anytime.

GRANTS ANALYSIS

Total Grants: $1,269,000

Number of Grants: 160

Highest Grant: $75,750

Average Grant: $7,931

Typical Range: $1,000 to $25,000

Disclosure Period: fiscal year ending June 30, 1993

Note: Recent grants are derived from a fiscal 1993 Form 990.

RECENT GRANTS
General
42,000	Proctor Academy, Andover, NH	
39,000	St. Mary's Hall, San Antonio, TX	
32,000	San Antonio Academy, San Antonio, TX	
31,250	Mountain States Legal Foundation, Denver, CO	
30,000	Denver's Ocean Journey, Denver, CO	

US WEST, Inc. / US WEST Foundation

Sales: $2.58 billion
Employees: 60,778
Headquarters: Englewood, CO
SIC Major Group: Holding Companies Nec and Telephone Communications Except Radiotelephone

CONTACT
Janet Rash
Grants Manager
US WEST Foundation
7800 E Orchard Rd., Ste. 300
Englewood, CO 80111
(303) 793-6648
Note: Proposals should be sent to the nearest of 13 foundation offices throughout the western United States; a list can be obtained by contacting Ms. Rash at the above address. The company's World Wide Web address is http://www.uswest.com

FINANCIAL SUMMARY
Recent Giving: $25,000,000 (1995 est.); $25,830,000 (1994); $23,277,000 (1993)

Assets: $18,500,000 (1995 est.); $16,029,000 (1994); $13,989,000 (1993)

Gifts Received: $24,438,101 (1992)

Fiscal Note: All contributions are made through the foundation. The foundation received contributions in 1992 from US West and its subsidiaries.

EIN: 84-0978668

CONTRIBUTIONS SUMMARY
Typical Recipients: • *Arts & Humanities:* Arts Associations & Councils, Historic Preservation, Museums/Galleries, Music, Opera, Public Broadcasting, Theater • *Civic & Public Affairs:* Business/Free Enterprise, Economic Development, Employment/Job Training, Law & Justice, Nonprofit Management, Urban & Community Affairs, Women's Affairs • *Education:* Business Education, Colleges & Universities, Economic Education, Education Funds, Engineering/Technological Education, Minority Education, Science/Mathematics Education • *Environment:* General • *Social Services:* Child Welfare, Family Services, United Funds/United Ways, Youth Organizations

Grant Types: employee matching gifts, general support, matching, and multiyear/continuing support

Note: Employee matching gift ratio: 1 to 1.

Geographic Distribution: 14 Western states served by company

Operating Locations: AZ, CO, IA, ID, MN, MT, ND, NE, NM, OR, SD, UT, WA, WY

GIVING OFFICERS
Leon Marks: secy

Richard David McCormick: pres *B* Ft Dodge IA 1940 *ED* IA St Univ BS 1961 *CURR EMPL* chmn, pres, ceo, dir: US W Inc *CORP AFFIL* dir: Majers Corp, Norwest Bank MN NA, Norwest Corp, Prin Fin Group, SuperValu Inc *NONPR AFFIL* dir: Regis Coll; fdr: Osage Initiatives; mem: Phi Gamma Delta

James Marvin Osterhoff: treas *B* Lafayette IN 1936 *ED* Purdue Univ BSME 1958; Stanford Univ MBA 1963 *CURR EMPL* exec vp, cfo: US W Inc *CORP AFFIL* dir: GenCorp Inc *NONPR AFFIL* dir, cfo: Pvt Sector Counc; mem: Fin Execs Inst; mem fin counc: Conf Bd

Jane Prancan: exec dir *CURR EMPL* dir corp commun aff: US W Inc

Janet Rash: grants mgr

APPLICATION INFORMATION
Initial Approach: *Initial Contact:* proposal, not to exceed ten pages, sent to one of thirteen local operatings offices (Colorado office only accepts proposals on a referral basis—unsolicited proposals sent to Colorado office will not be considered) *Include Information On:* name of organization, mailing address, telephone number, contact person, list of organization's board of directors, copy of IRS form 501(c)(3) *Deadlines:* deadlines vary according to giving category; Arts and Culture, February 15; Education, May 15; Human Services, August 15; Civic and Community Improvement, October 15 *Note:* Foundation only accepts proposals for the general grants category of giving.

Restrictions on Giving: Foundation does not fund political campaigns; telephone service or communications equipment; computer hardware or software; individuals; fraternal organizations, clubs, school organizations, and school athletic funds; general operating budgets of organizations that receive more than 40% of their budget from the United Way; religious organizations for sectarian purposes; international organizations; national health agencies or their local affiliates; general operating budgets of tax-supported educational institutions; debt retirement or operational deficits; foundations that are themselves grantmaking bodies; or trips and tours.

OTHER THINGS TO KNOW
The US WEST Foundation was formed in July 1988 and began making grants in 1989. The foundation serves to combine US WEST's giving program with those of its subsidiaries, Mountain Bell, Pacific Northwest Bell, and Northwestern Bell, which

have now been combined into one company, US WEST Communications. The foundation also gives on behalf of the holding company's other subsidiaries, which include companies involved in cellular communications, and advanced technologies.

PUBLICATIONS
US West Foundation Review

GRANTS ANALYSIS
Total Grants: $25,830,000
Number of Grants: 1,976
Highest Grant: $600,000
Average Grant: $13,072
Typical Range: $1,000 to $25,000
Disclosure Period: 1994
Note: Figures supplied by the company

Weckbaugh Foundation, Eleanore Mullen

CONTACT
Edward J. Limes
President
Eleanore Mullen Weckbaugh Fdn.
PO Box 31678
Aurora, CO 80041
(303) 367-1545

FINANCIAL SUMMARY
Recent Giving: $368,200 (fiscal 1994); $385,220 (fiscal 1993); $418,280 (fiscal 1992)
Assets: $6,771,735 (fiscal 1994); $7,405,527 (fiscal 1993); $6,525,102 (fiscal 1992)
EIN: 23-7437761

CONTRIBUTIONS SUMMARY
Donor(s): the late Eleanore Mullen Weckbaugh

Typical Recipients: • *Arts & Humanities:* Libraries, Music, Opera, Performing Arts, Public Broadcasting • *Civic & Public Affairs:* Employment/Job Training, Ethnic Organizations, General, Housing, Professional & Trade Associations, Safety, Urban & Community Affairs • *Education:* Afterschool/Enrichment Programs, Colleges & Universities, Continuing Education, Education Funds, Private Education (Precollege), Public Education (Precollege), Secondary Education (Private), Secondary Education (Public) • *Health:* Eyes/Blindness, Heart, Hospitals • *Religion:* Churches, Ministries, Missionary Activities (Domestic), Religious Organizations, Religious Welfare • *Science:* Science Museums • *Social Services:* Child Welfare, Community Centers, Community Service Organizations, Domestic Violence, Family Planning, Food/Clothing Distribution, Homes, People with Disabilities, Scouts, Senior Services, Sexual Abuse, Substance Abuse, Youth Organizations

Grant Types: general support
Geographic Distribution: focus on CO

GIVING OFFICERS
Jean Guyton: trust

Samuel Percy Guyton: trust *B* Jackson MS 1937 *ED* MS St Univ BA 1959; Univ VA LLB 1965 *CURR EMPL* ptnr: Holland & Hart *NONPR AFFIL* dir: Genesis Jobs; fellow: Am Coll Tax Counc, Am Tax Policy Inst, CO Bar Fdn; mem: CO Bar Assn, Denver Bar Assn; trust: CO Historical Fdn

Edward J. Limes: pres, treas, trust

Michael Polakovic: trust

Teresa Polakovic: secy, trust

APPLICATION INFORMATION
Initial Approach: Send brief letter of inquiry describing program or project. There are no deadlines.

Restrictions on Giving: Does not support individuals.

GRANTS ANALYSIS
Total Grants: $368,200
Number of Grants: 45
Highest Grant: $25,000
Typical Range: $5,000 to $10,000
Disclosure Period: fiscal year ending March 31, 1994
Note: Recent grants are derived from a fiscal 1994 Form 990.

RECENT GRANTS
Library

15,000	Denver Public Library, Denver, CO	

General

25,000	Sacred Heart House, Denver, CO	
20,000	Regis University Weckbaugh, Denver, CO — Lascor endowment	
15,000	Genesis Jobs, Denver, CO	
12,500	Jefferson County Adult ESL Program, Lakewood, CO	
10,000	Adult Learning Source, Denver, CO	

CONNECTICUT

Aetna Life & Casualty Co. / Aetna Foundation

Revenue: $17.52 billion
Employees: 42,631
Headquarters: Hartford, CT
SIC Major Group: Life Insurance, Accident & Health Insurance, Fire, Marine & Casualty Insurance, and Insurance Agents, Brokers & Service

CONTACT
Michael C. Alexander
Vice President & Executive Director
Aetna Foundation
151 Farmington Ave., RE1B
Hartford, CT 06156-3180
(203) 273-1932

Note: Contact person for international and direct corporate contributions is Diana Kinosh, management information supervisor, phone (203) 273-7580, address is the same as above.

FINANCIAL SUMMARY
Recent Giving: $8,800,000 (1995 est.); $9,425,322 (1994); $11,568,324 (1993)
Assets: $28,078,077 (1994); $29,978,352 (1993); $29,764,302 (1992)
Fiscal Note: Company makes contributions both directly and through the Foundation. Foundation grants totaled $8,393,006 in 1993. International giving figures are included in above figures. Above figures exclude nonmonetary support. Other departments make contributions. See "Other Things To Know" for more details.
EIN: 23-7241940

CONTRIBUTIONS SUMMARY
Typical Recipients: • *Arts & Humanities:* Arts Associations & Councils, General, History & Archaeology, Libraries • *Civic & Public Affairs:* African American Affairs, Chambers of Commerce, Economic Development, Employment/Job Training, Hispanic Affairs, Law & Justice • *Education:* Afterschool/Enrichment Programs, Business Education, Business-School Partnerships, Colleges & Universities, Education Associations, Education Funds, Education Reform, General, Leadership Training, Minority Education, Public Education (Precollege), Science/Mathematics Education, Secondary Education (Private), Secondary Education (Public), Student Aid • *Health:* Children's Health/Hospitals, Clinics/Medical Centers, Emergency/Ambulance Services, Health Organizations, Hospitals, Nursing Services, Prenatal Health Issues • *International:* Foreign Educational Institutions, Health Care/Hospitals, International Development, International Organizations • *Religion:* Churches • *Science:* Scientific Centers & Institutes • *Social Services:* Child Welfare, People with Disabilities, Scouts, United Funds/United Ways, Volunteer Services

Grant Types: employee matching gifts, general support, multiyear/continuing support, and project

Note: Employee matching gift ratio: 1 to 1 for colleges and universities only ($10 to $2500), up to the program budget cap designated by the Aetna Foundation, Inc. each year. Matching grants will be pro-rated when the maximum is exceeded.

Nonmonetary Support: $134,239 (1994); $157,083 (1993); $188,409 (1992)

Nonmonetary Support Types: donated equipment, donated products, and in-kind services

Note: Company offers the use of its facilities. Contact person for nonmonetary support is Susan Shaw, program assistant, phone (203) 273-2645.

Geographic Distribution: 1) headquarters programs: emphasizing the greater Hartford, CT, metropolitan area and cities selected under the FOCUS program; 2) field programs: nationally, where company has a significant

        The Big Book of Library Grant Money

local presence through its field office operations; 3)national initiatives: national organizations that can influence local, state, or federal policies and programs; and 4)international organizations

Operating Locations: CT (Hartford), IL (Downers Grove), NJ (Princeton)

Note: Aetna operates in more than 100 cities nationwide.

CORP. OFFICERS

Ronald E. Compton: *B* 1933 *ED* Northwestern Univ BS 1954 *CURR EMPL* chmn, pres, ceo: Aetna Life & Casualty Co *CORP AFFIL* chmn, pres: Aetna Casualty & Surety Co Inc, Aetna Life Ins Co, Automobile Ins Co, Standard Fire Ins Co

Timothy Arthur Holt: *B* Hartford CT 1953 *ED* Univ CT BA 1975; Dartmouth Coll Amos Tuck Sch Bus Admin MBA 1977 *CURR EMPL* vp portfolio mgmt: Aetna Life & Casualty Co *CORP AFFIL* treas, dir: Farmington Casualty Co *NONPR AFFIL* corp adv bd: Natl Head Start Assn; mem: Phi Beta Kappa; mem investment comm: Hartford Univ

Amin I. Khalifa: *CURR EMPL* cfo: Aetna Life & Casualty Co

Lucille M. Nickerson: *B* Canaan CT 1947 *ED* CT Coll BA 1968; Univ CT MS 1980; Univ CT JD 1980 *CURR EMPL* couns, corp secy: Aetna Casualty & Surety Co Inc *CORP AFFIL* couns, corp secy: Standard Fire Ins Co *NONPR AFFIL* mem: Am Bar Assn, Assn Life Ins Counc

GIVING OFFICERS

Michael C. Alexander: vp, exec dir

Wallace W. Barnes: chmn *B* Bristol CT 1926 *ED* Williams Coll BA 1949; Yale Univ LLB 1952 *CURR EMPL* chmn, dir: Barnes Group Inc *CORP AFFIL* chmn: NHKA Assoc Spring Suspension Components; chmn, dir: Rohr Inc; dir: Autoliasons France SA, Loctite Corp, Motalink Ltd, Rogers Corp, Wiltshire; dir exec comm: Aetna Life & Casualty Co; pres: Assoc Spring Asia Ltd, Assoc Spring Corp, Wallace Barnes Ltd, Bowman Products Ltd, Resortes Barnes; pres, dir: Resortes Indus N SA, Resortes Mecanicos SA *NONPR AFFIL* chmn bd regents: Univ Hartford; corporator: Inst Living; dir: Bus-Indus Political Action Comm, CT Bus & Indus Assn, CT Econ Devel Corp, Natl Assn Mfrs; mem: Am Arbitration Assn, Am Bar Assn, Am Judicature Soc, Bristol Historical Soc, CT Bar Assn, Jr Achievement N Central CT, Newcomen Soc; trust: Am Clock & Watch Mus, Bristol Regional Environment Ctr, Girls Club Assn Bristol, New England Air Mus *CLUB AFFIL* Am Legion, Econ, Elks, 100 CT, Williams, Yale *PHIL AFFIL* dir: Barnes Group Foundation Inc., New England Legal Foundation

Ronald E. Compton: pres, dir *CURR EMPL* chmn, pres, ceo: Aetna Life & Casualty Co (see above)

Marian Wright Edelman: dir *B* Bennettsville SC 1939 *ED* Univ Paris 1958-1959; Spelman Coll BA 1960; Yale Univ LLB 1963 *NONPR AFFIL* dir: Citizens Constitutional Concerns, City Lights, Ctr Law Social Policy, Leadership Conf Civil Rights, NAACP Legal Defense Ed Fund, Natl Alliance Bus, Parents As Teachers Natl Ctr; mem: Natl Commn Children; mem adv bd: Hampshire Coll; mem adv counc: Martin Luther King Jr Meml Ctr; pres, fdr: Childrens Defense Fund; trust: Joint Ctr Political Studies, Martin Luther King Jr Meml Ctr, March Dimes, Spelman Coll; US comm: UN Children's Fund *PHIL AFFIL* dir: Aaron Diamond Foundation; trust: Skadden, Arps, Slate, Meagher & Flom Fellowship Foundation

Earl Gilbert Graves: dir *B* Brooklyn NY 1935 *ED* Morgan St Univ BA 1958 *CURR EMPL* chmn, ceo: Pepsi-Cola Washington DC *CORP AFFIL* chmn, editor, publ: Black Enterprise Magazine; dir: Aetna Life & Casualty Co, Chrysler Corp, Federated Dept Stores Inc, New Am Schs Devel Corp, Rohm & Haas Co, St Urban Devel Corp; editor, publ: Black Enterprise Magazine; pres, dir: Earl G Graves Ltd Inc, Earl G Graves Publ Co Inc *NONPR AFFIL* dir: Advertising Counc, Bus Mktg Corp, Coalition NY, Glass Ceiling Commn, Magazine Publs Assn, Natl Supplier Devel Counc, NY St Urban Devel Corp, TransAfrica Forum, US Intl Counc, Young Pres Org; gov: John F Kennedy Ctr Performing Arts Corp Fund; mem: Interracial Counc Bus Opportunity, NAACP, Omega Psi Phi, Pres Comm Small & Minority Bus, Sigma Pi Phi, Southern Christian Leadership Conf; mem pres counc bus admin: Univ VT; mem visit comm: Harvard Univ John F Kennedy Sch Govt; natl commnr scouting: Boy Scouts Am; trust: Am Mus Natural History & Planetarium Authority, Howard Univ *CLUB AFFIL* Econ

Edward K. Hamilton: dir *CURR EMPL* pres: Hamilton Rabinovitz & Szanton

Timothy Arthur Holt: treas, investment mgr *CURR EMPL* vp portfolio mgmt: Aetna Life & Casualty Co (see above)

Judith H. Jones: asst secy

Robert A. Morse: contr

Lucille M. Nickerson: secy *CURR EMPL* couns, corp secy: Aetna Casualty & Surety Co Inc (see above)

APPLICATION INFORMATION

Initial Approach: *Initial Contact:* preliminary proposal to the foundation; if interested, foundation will request full proposal *Include Information On:* organization's history and purpose, project description and budget, level of support requested, and proof of tax-exempt status *Deadlines:* none *Note:* When appropriate, staff refers inquiries to field officers.

Restrictions on Giving: Foundation does not support individuals, capital or endowment campaigns, medical research, private secondary schools, political activities, relig-

ious organizations, fund-raising dinners or other similar special events, sporting events and conferences, or organizations that do not have tax-exempt status.

OTHER THINGS TO KNOW

Individual departments at Aetna also make contributions. There is no established budget for this support. The contact for these funds is Diana Kinosh, Management Information Supervisor.

The contact for international contributions is also Diana Kinosh, Management Information Supervisor.

GRANTS ANALYSIS

Total Grants: $9,559,561

Number of Grants: 600*

Highest Grant: $300,000

Average Grant: $13,054*

Typical Range: $5,000 to $25,000

Disclosure Period: 1994

Note: Number of grants figure and average grant are approximate, represent foundation and direct giving, include nonmonetary support, Health Appeal, colleges and universities, and various other gifts totaling $1,727,180. Recent grants are derived from a 1994 grants list.

RECENT GRANTS

General

300,000	Hartford Childhood Immunization Project (HCIP), Hartford, CT — final payment of a 1992-94, $850,000 commitment to a broad-based community coalition, led by the City of Hartford Health Department, to develop a computerized registry to track the immunization status of all Hartford children
297,550	Saturday Academy — in celebration of the 10-year anniversary of this academic enrichment program that serves minority and disadvantaged middle school students
200,000	Children's Fund, Hartford, CT — 1992-95, $1,000,000 commitment toward a $25 million fund to support community-based primary and preventive pediatric care for Hartford children
200,000	State of Texas Department of Health, Austin, TX — three-year, $500,000 grant for the funding of statewide community-based immunization grants program
200,000	University of Pittsburgh Allegheny County Health Department, Pittsburgh, PA — grant to provide mobile van to work with three neighborhood health clinics to improve on-time

immunization rates and primary care for at-risk children

American Brands, Inc.

Revenue: $8.44 billion
Employees: 45,000
Headquarters: Old Greenwich, CT
SIC Major Group: Holding Companies Nec, Distilled & Blended Liquors, Cigarettes, and Cigars

CONTACT
Roger W. W. Baker
Secretary, Corporate Responsibility & Public Affairs Committee
American Brands, Inc.
1700 E Putnam Ave.
PO Box 811
Old Greenwich, CT 06870
(203) 698-5148

FINANCIAL SUMMARY
Recent Giving: $13,058,853 (1994); $12,320,241 (1993); $15,847,668 (1992)

Fiscal Note: Figures exclude contributions by U.S. and foreign subsidiaries. The corporation gives directly. Above figures include nonmonetary support.

CONTRIBUTIONS SUMMARY
Typical Recipients: • *Arts & Humanities:* Arts Centers, Community Arts, Historic Preservation, Libraries, Museums/Galleries, Music, Opera, Performing Arts, Public Broadcasting, Theater • *Civic & Public Affairs:* Civil Rights, Economic Development, Employment/Job Training, Legal Aid, Urban & Community Affairs, Women's Affairs, Zoos/Aquariums • *Education:* Arts/Humanities Education, Business Education, Colleges & Universities, Community & Junior Colleges, Continuing Education, Economic Education, Education Associations, Elementary Education (Private), Literacy, Minority Education, Private Education (Precollege), Public Education (Precollege), Special Education • *Environment:* General • *Health:* Emergency/Ambulance Services, Health Organizations, Hospitals, Medical Research, Public Health, Single-Disease Health Associations • *International:* Health Care/Hospitals, International Peace & Security Issues, International Relations • *Social Services:* Child Welfare, Community Centers, Community Service Organizations, Day Care, Food/Clothing Distribution, People with Disabilities, Recreation & Athletics, Shelters/Homelessness, Substance Abuse, United Funds/United Ways, Volunteer Services, Youth Organizations

Grant Types: capital, emergency, employee matching gifts, general support, multi-year/continuing support, and operating expenses

Note: Employee matching gift ratio: 2 to 1

Nonmonetary Support: $434,614 (1993); $497,731 (1992); $523,099 (1991)

Nonmonetary Support Types: in-kind services

Geographic Distribution: near headquarters and in operating locations only

Operating Locations: AL (Auburn), CT (Old Greenwich, Stamford), IA (Waterloo), IL (Deerfield, Elmhurst, Niles, Springfield, Wheeling), IN (Jasper), KY (Clermont), MA (Brockton, Fairhaven, New Bedford), NC (Durham, Reidsville), NY (Long Island City), OH (Elyria, North Olmsted), PA (East Texas), TX (Duncanville), VA (Chester, Richmond), WI (Milwaukee)

Note: Also has major operations in Weybridge, Surrey, England.

CORP. OFFICERS
Thomas Chandler Hays: *B* Chicago IL 1935 *ED* CA Inst Tech BS 1957; CA Inst Tech MS 1958; Harvard Univ Grad Sch Bus Admin MBA 1963 *CURR EMPL* chmn, ceo, dir: Am Brands Inc *CORP AFFIL* dir: ACCO World Corp, Acushnet Co, Am Tobacco Co, Am Tobacco Intl Corp, Callaher Ltd, Franklin Life Ins Co, Jim Beam Brands Co, Master Lock Co, MasterBrand Indus, MCM Products; vp, dir: Am Franklin Co *NONPR AFFIL* dir: Commun Fdns Fairfield County; trust: Five Town Commun Fund *CLUB AFFIL* BelAir Bay, Cincinnati CC, Darien CC, Tokeneke *PHIL AFFIL* trust: Andrew Jergens Foundation

John T. Ludes: *B* 1936 *ED* Northern IL Univ BS; Northern IL Univ MS; Northern IL Univ BS; Northern IL Univ MS *CURR EMPL* group vp: Am Brands Inc *CORP AFFIL* pres, ceo, dir: Acushnet Co

GIVING OFFICERS
Roger William Weatherburn Baker: *B* 1944 *ED* St Edmunds Coll 1961 *CURR EMPL* secy corp responsibility & pub aff comm: Am Brands Inc *NONPR AFFIL* dir: Stamford Symphony Orchestra; mem: Intl Assn Bus Commun; trust: Silvermine Guild & Arts Ctr

Robert J. Rukeyser: *B* New Rochelle NY 1942 *ED* Cornell Univ BA 1964; NY Univ MBA 1969 *CURR EMPL* vchmn corp responsibility & pub aff comm: Am Brands Inc *CORP AFFIL* dir: Acushnet Co, Am Brands Intl Corp, Am Franklin Co, Am Tobacco Co, Golden Belt Mfg Co, Jim Beam Brands Co, Masterbrand Indus, Swingline, Wilson Jones Co; vp opers: ACCO World Corp *NONPR AFFIL* dir: Hole in Wall Gang Camp, Stamford Ctr Arts; mem: Natl Off Products Assn, Wholesale Stationers Assn

APPLICATION INFORMATION
Initial Approach: *Initial Contact:* brief letter *Include Information On:* organization's purpose, list of other corporate contributors, and proof of tax-exempt status *Deadlines:* none

Restrictions on Giving: Generally does not support individuals, fraternal organizations, organizations funded by the United Way, or religious organizations for sectarian purposes.

GRANTS ANALYSIS
Total Grants: $13,058,853

Typical Range: $500 to $5,000

Disclosure Period: 1994

Note: Recent grants are derived from a 1992 grants list.

RECENT GRANTS
General
25,000   Long Island Sound Taskforce — an unrestricted grant to be paid over a three year period

Auerbach Foundation, Beatrice Fox

CONTACT
Dorothy A. Schiro
Vice President and Treasurer
Beatrice Fox Auerbach Foundation
25 Brookside Blvd.
West Hartford, CT 06107
(203) 232-5854

FINANCIAL SUMMARY
Recent Giving: $1,842,973 (1993); $1,629,550 (1992); $1,464,232 (1991)

Assets: $36,043,384 (1993); $34,952,484 (1992); $33,829,777 (1991)

EIN: 06-6033334

CONTRIBUTIONS SUMMARY
Donor(s): The foundation was established in 1941 by the late Beatrice Fox Auerbach .

Typical Recipients: • *Arts & Humanities:* Arts Associations & Councils, Arts Centers, History & Archaeology, Libraries, Museums/Galleries, Music, Performing Arts, Public Broadcasting, Theater • *Civic & Public Affairs:* Botanical Gardens/Parks, Civil Rights, Economic Development, Employment/Job Training, General, Hispanic Affairs, Municipalities/Towns, Nonprofit Management, Philanthropic Organizations, Professional & Trade Associations, Public Policy, Urban & Community Affairs, Women's Affairs • *Education:* Agricultural Education, Colleges & Universities, Community & Junior Colleges, Education Funds, Literacy, Private Education (Precollege), Special Education, Student Aid • *Environment:* Forestry, General, Resource Conservation • *Health:* AIDS/HIV, Children's Health/Hospitals, Emergency/Ambulance Services, Health Funds, Heart, Hospices, Hospitals, Nursing Services, Prenatal Health Issues, Public Health, Research/Studies Institutes, Single-Disease Health Associations • *International:* International Affairs, International Relations • *Religion:* Churches, Jewish Causes, Religious Organizations, Religious Welfare, Synagogues/Temples • *Social Services:* At-Risk Youth, Camps, Child Welfare, Community Centers, Community Service Organizations, Family Planning, Family Services, Food/Clothing Distribution, People with Disabilities, Recreation & Athletics, Scouts, Senior Services, Shelters/Homelessness, Substance Abuse, United Funds/United Ways, Youth Organizations

Grant Types: capital, department, general support, and project

Geographic Distribution: focus on the Hartford, CT area

GIVING OFFICERS

Georgette A. Koopman: pres, trust *PHIL AFFIL* pres, trust: Koopman Fund; trust: Schiro Fund

Rena Koopman: trust *PHIL AFFIL* secy, trust: Koopman Fund

Bernard W. Schiro: chmn, trust *PHIL AFFIL* pres, trust: Schiro Fund

Dorothy A. Schiro: vp, treas, trust *PHIL AFFIL* asst secy, trust: Koopman Fund; secy, treas, trust: Schiro Fund

Elizabeth A. Schiro: secy *PHIL AFFIL* trust: Schiro Fund

APPLICATION INFORMATION
Initial Approach:

Applicants should send a brief letter of inquiry.

The proposal should include the purpose of the grant, verfication of the tax-exempt status, as well as a financial statement.

There are generally no deadlines for submitting proposals. Although the foundation does request that proposals submitted near the end of the year should be submitted by November 15.

GRANTS ANALYSIS
Total Grants: $1,842,973

Number of Grants: 50

Highest Grant: $1,000,000

Average Grant: $16,959*

Typical Range: $2,500 to $50,000

Disclosure Period: 1993

Note: The highest grant of $1,000,000 was not included in the average grant figure. Recent grants are derived from a 1993 Form 990.

RECENT GRANTS

Library
25,000	Hartford Public Library, Hartford, CT
7,000	Bancroft Library, Friends University of California, Berkeley, CA

General
1,000,000	Jewish Federation of Greater Hartford, W. Hartford, CT — annual fund
150,000	Jewish Federation of Greater Hartford, W. Hartford, CT — annual fund
105,000	HFPG, Hartford, CT — advise fund
100,000	McLean Association, Simsbury, CT — hospice program
80,000	Hartford Foundation for Public Giving, Hartford, CT — Temple Beth Israel

Bissell Foundation, J. Walton

CONTACT
J. Danford Anthony, Jr.
Trustee
J. Walton Bissell Fdn.
City Pl., 25th Fl.
Hartford, CT 06103
(203) 275-0136

FINANCIAL SUMMARY
Recent Giving: $651,000 (1992 approx.); $293,500 (1989); $534,000 (1988)

Assets: $15,000,000 (1992 est.); $12,579,763 (1989); $10,696,374 (1988)

EIN: 06-6035614

CONTRIBUTIONS SUMMARY
Donor(s): the late J. Walton Bissell

Typical Recipients: • *Arts & Humanities:* Dance, Libraries, Music, Performing Arts • *Education:* Colleges & Universities, Public Education (Precollege) • *Health:* Health Organizations • *Social Services:* Family Planning, People with Disabilities, Senior Services

Grant Types: general support

Geographic Distribution: focus on CT, MA, VT, and NH

GIVING OFFICERS
J. Danford Anthony, Jr.: trust *B* Boston MA 1935 *ED* Wesleyan Univ AB 1957; Harvard Univ LLB 1960 *CURR EMPL* ptnr: Day Berry & Howard *NONPR AFFIL* mem: Am Bar Assn, CT Bar Assn, Natl Assn Bond Lawyers; mem exec comm: Fed Tax Inst New England

P. R. Reynolds: trust

D. M. Rockwell: secy, trust

L. Steiner: trust

APPLICATION INFORMATION
Initial Approach: Send brief letter of inquiry describing program or project. There are no deadlines.

Restrictions on Giving: Does not support individuals.

GRANTS ANALYSIS
Total Grants: $293,500

Number of Grants: 36

Highest Grant: $41,000

Typical Range: $1,000 to $7,500

Disclosure Period: 1989

Note: Recent grants are derived from a 1989 Form 990.

RECENT GRANTS

General
41,000	New England Kurn Hattin Homes, Boston, MA
20,000	Miss Porter's School, Farmington, CT
17,500	Cumberland College, Williamsburg, KY
15,000	American School for the Deaf, Hartford, CT

15,000	Hartford College for Women, Hartford, CT

Chadwick Fund, Dorothy Jordan

CONTACT
Berkley D. Johnson, Jr.
Trustee
Dorothy Jordan Chadwick Fund
c/o Davison Dawson & Clark
PO Box 298
New Canann, CT 06840

FINANCIAL SUMMARY
Recent Giving: $405,500 (fiscal 1993); $387,500 (fiscal 1992); $351,000 (fiscal 1991)

Assets: $11,310,163 (fiscal 1993); $11,188,535 (fiscal 1992); $10,363,572 (fiscal 1991)

EIN: 13-6069950

CONTRIBUTIONS SUMMARY
Donor(s): the late Donothy J. Chadwick, Dorothy R. Kidder

Typical Recipients: • *Arts & Humanities:* Arts Associations & Councils, Arts Centers, Arts Outreach, General, Libraries, Literary Arts, Museums/Galleries, Music, Performing Arts, Public Broadcasting, Theater • *Civic & Public Affairs:* Botanical Gardens/Parks, General, Urban & Community Affairs, Zoos/Aquariums • *Education:* Arts/Humanities Education, Colleges & Universities, Education Reform, Private Education (Precollege) • *Environment:* General • *Health:* Alzheimers Disease, Clinics/Medical Centers • *International:* International Environmental Issues, International Peace & Security Issues • *Religion:* Churches • *Social Services:* Child Welfare, Senior Services, Youth Organizations

Grant Types: general support

Geographic Distribution: focus on New York, NY, and Washington, DC

GIVING OFFICERS
US Trust Company of NY: trust

Berkley D. Johnson: trust

APPLICATION INFORMATION
Initial Approach: Send brief letter of inquiry describing program or project. There are no deadlines.

GRANTS ANALYSIS
Total Grants: $405,500

Number of Grants: 38

Highest Grant: $50,000

Typical Range: $1,000 to $15,000

Disclosure Period: fiscal year ending May 31, 1993

Note: Recent grants are derived from a fiscal 1993 Form 990.

RECENT GRANTS

Library

5,000	Library of Congress, Washington, DC

General

36,000	African Wildlife Foundation, Washington, DC
20,000	Friends of the National Arboretum, Washington, DC
15,000	Alzheimers Disease and Related Disorders Association, Washington, DC
15,000	Council for Basic Education, Washington, DC
15,000	President and Fellows of Harvard University, Cambridge, MA

Champion International Corporation / Champion International Foundation

Revenue: $5.31 billion
Employees: 25,300
Headquarters: Stamford, CT
SIC Major Group: Wood Products Nec and Paper Mills

CONTACT

Gael Doar
Director, Contributions and Community Support Program
Champion International Corp.
One Champion Plz.
Stamford, CT 06921
(203) 358-7000
Note: Ms. Doar is the contact for the giving program and the foundation.

FINANCIAL SUMMARY

Recent Giving: $7,426,000 (1995 est.); $7,426,000 (1994); $7,712,000 (1993)

Assets: $372,722 (1993); $344,910 (1992)

Fiscal Note: Contributions are made directly by the company. The foundation awards a small grant every year. In 1993, the foundation gave $15,000. Foundation giving is included in the above figures. Above figures include nonmonetary support.

EIN: 31-6022258

CONTRIBUTIONS SUMMARY

Typical Recipients: • *Arts & Humanities:* Libraries, Museums/Galleries, Visual Arts • *Civic & Public Affairs:* Community Foundations, Urban & Community Affairs • *Education:* Colleges & Universities, Engineering/Technological Education, Literacy, Minority Education, Public Education (Precollege) • *Environment:* General • *Health:* Hospitals • *Social Services:* Community Service Organizations, Substance Abuse

Grant Types: employee matching gifts, general support, multiyear/continuing support, and project

Note: Employee matching gift ratio: 1 to 1.

Nonmonetary Support: $105,000 (1993); $167,000 (1992); $125,000 (1990)

Nonmonetary Support Types: donated products

Geographic Distribution: near headquarters and operating locations only

Operating Locations: AL (Abbeville, Citronelle, Courtland), FL (Cantonment, Pensacola, Whitehouse), GA (Waycross), ME (Bucksport, Costigan), MI (Norway, Quinnesec), MN (Sartell), NC (Canton, Roanoke Rapids), NY (Deferiet), OH (Hamilton), TX (Camden, Lufkin, Sheldon), WA (Klickitat)

CORP. OFFICERS

Lewis Clark Heist: *B* Bridgeport CT 1931 *ED* Yale Univ BA 1953; Yale Univ MF 1957 *CURR EMPL* pres, coo, dir: Champion Intl Corp *CORP AFFIL* dir: Lyman Farm, Ryland Group, Stamford Hosp Health Corp; pres, ceo: Gateway Homes *NONPR AFFIL* chmn bd govs: Natl Counc Pulp & Paper Indus Air & Stream Improvement; dir: Forest Indus Counc Taxation, Greenwich Fdn Commun Gifts, Natl Forest Products Assn, Stamford Hosp Fdn; founding dir: Drugs Dont Work; mem: Am Forestry Assn, Soc Am Foresters, Southwestern Area Commerce & Indus Assn CT; mem adv bd: Yale Univ Forestry Sch; trust: Inst Paper Sci & Tech

Kenwood C. Nichols: *B* 1940 *ED* Auburn Univ BA; Duke Univ MA *CURR EMPL* vchmn, dir: Champion Intl Corp *CORP AFFIL* dir: Weldwood Canada Ltd *NONPR AFFIL* dir: Stamford Mus Nature Ctr; mem bd visit: Duke Univ Sch Forestry Environmental Sci; trust: King & Low-Heywood Thomas Sch

Andrew Clark Sigler: *B* Brooklyn NY 1931 *ED* Dartmouth Coll AB 1953; Dartmouth Coll Amos Tuck Grad Sch Bus Admin MBA 1956 *CURR EMPL* chmn, ceo, dir: Champion Intl Corp *CORP AFFIL* dir: Bristol-Myers Squibb Co, Chem Bank, Chem Banking Corp, Gen Electric Co *NONPR AFFIL* mem: Bus Counc, Bus Roundtable; trust: Dartmouth Coll

Robert W. Tume: *CURR EMPL* vp pub aff: Champion Intl Corp

GIVING OFFICERS

Gael Doar: *CURR EMPL* dir contributions & commun support program: Champion Intl Corp

Cheryl Esquivel: *CURR EMPL* mgr contributions programs: Champion Intl Corp

APPLICATION INFORMATION

Initial Approach: *Initial Contact:* preliminary letter *Include Information On:* name, address, and telephone number of organization; contact person and title; names of executive director, directors, and their affiliations; copy of IRS exemption letter; description of how proposed project relates to company giving guidelines; description of how project's success will be determined; description of experience and qualifications organization has for implementing project; copy of most recent audited financial statement; sources of income; and budget for organization and proposed project *Deadlines:* none *Note:* Grant requests may be submitted to headquarters or to the contributions coor-

dinator at the nearest Champion facility. A complete list of operating facility addresses is available from the company.

Restrictions on Giving: Grants are not made to individuals; organizations without 501(c)(3) status; political candidates or organizations; religious, fraternal, or veterans organizations, unless they furnish services to benefit the general public; dinners, benefits, exhibits, conferences, sports events, and other one-time, short-term activities; journal advertisements and the purchase of tickets; supplementary operating funds for agencies in a United Way already supported by company; and community organizations not located within a company location.

OTHER THINGS TO KNOW

The Champion International Foundation is an inactive foundation. It awards a small grant of $15,000 to $25,000 a year. In 1995, the foundation plans to pay out all of its assets. These contributions will be made to organizations that would normally receive grants from the corporate giving program.

PUBLICATIONS

Giving guidelines, volunteer pamphlet, annual report

GRANTS ANALYSIS

Total Grants: $7,712,000*

Highest Grant: $125,000*

Typical Range: $2,500 to $10,000

Disclosure Period: 1993

Note: Figures were supplied by the company. Recent grants are derived from a 1993 Form 990.

Chesebrough-Pond's USA Co. / Chesebrough Foundation

Sales: $920.2 million
Employees: 4,045
Parent Company: Unilever N.V.
Headquarters: Greenwich, CT
SIC Major Group: Toilet Preparations, Pharmaceutical Preparations, and Surgical Appliances & Supplies

CONTACT

Elizabeth Cummiskey
Manager, Corporate Contributions
Chesebrough-Pond's USA Co.
33 Benedict Pl.
Box 6000
Greenwich, CT 06836-6000
(203) 625-1757

FINANCIAL SUMMARY

Recent Giving: $725,000 (1995 est.); $1,290,000 (1994 approx.); $646,080 (1993)

Assets: $352,466 (1993); $488,392 (1992); $394,992 (1991)

Gifts Received: $501,738 (1993); $843,750 (1992)

Fiscal Note: 1994 figures include foundation and direct giving. All other figures are for foundation giving only. Above figures exclude nonmonetary support. In 1993, the foundation received 18,000 shares of Colgate-Palmolive stock.

EIN: 22-3043105

CONTRIBUTIONS SUMMARY

Typical Recipients: • *Arts & Humanities:* Arts Centers, Arts Institutes, History & Archaeology, Libraries, Museums/Galleries, Music, Opera, Performing Arts, Public Broadcasting, Theater • *Civic & Public Affairs:* African American Affairs, Business/Free Enterprise, Civil Rights, Economic Development, Employment/Job Training, General, Housing, Minority Business, Municipalities/Towns, Urban & Community Affairs • *Education:* Arts/Humanities Education, Business-School Partnerships, Colleges & Universities, Economic Education, Education Associations, Education Funds, Engineering/Technological Education, General, Medical Education, Minority Education, Private Education (Precollege), Student Aid • *Environment:* General • *Health:* Cancer, Clinics/Medical Centers, Emergency/Ambulance Services, Health Organizations • *Religion:* Religious Organizations • *Social Services:* Big Brother/Big Sister, Community Service Organizations, Counseling, Emergency Relief, Food/Clothing Distribution, Recreation & Athletics, Scouts, Senior Services, Substance Abuse, United Funds/United Ways, Volunteer Services, Youth Organizations

Grant Types: award, capital, employee matching gifts, and general support

Note: Employee matching gift ratio: 1 to 1.

Nonmonetary Support: $500,000 (1994)

Nonmonetary Support Types: donated products

Geographic Distribution: neighborhoods and communities near corporate headquarters and operating locations

Operating Locations: CA, CT (Clinton), IL (Chicago), MO (Jefferson City), NC (Raeford), PR (Las Piedras)

CORP. OFFICERS

Patrick J. Choel: *CURR EMPL* pres, ceo: Chesebrough-Pond's USA Co

Leo P. Kroes: *CURR EMPL* cfo: Chesebrough-Pond's USA Co

Melvin H. Kurtz: *B* New York NY 1936 *ED* CUNY BSCHE 1959; Fordham Univ JD 1963 *CURR EMPL* vp, dir, secy, gen couns: Chesebrough-Pond's USA Co *NONPR AFFIL* dir: Stamford Symphony Orchestra; mem: Am Bar Assn, Intl Patent & Trademark Assn, NY Bar Assn, NY Patent Law Assn; mem trademark aff pub adv comm: Patent & Trademark Off

GIVING OFFICERS

Anthony Chiafari: dir

Elizabeth Cummiskey: fdn contact *CURR EMPL* mgr corp contributions: Chesebrough-Pond's USA Co

Melvin H. Kurtz: secy, dir *CURR EMPL* vp, dir, secy, gen couns: Chesebrough-Pond's USA Co (see above)

James W. McCall: pres, dir *CURR EMPL* vp pers & pub rels: Chesebrough-Pond's USA Co

Robert Orlando: asst treas

Barbara Tarasovich: treas

APPLICATION INFORMATION

Initial Approach: *Initial Contact:* call to request *Programs for People,* brochure, which contains corporate giving guidelines, application procedures, and nonprofit questionnaire *Include Information On:* questionnaire requests: description of goals and activities, amount requested, special programs and/or other pertinent information relating to need, and proof of tax-exempt status *Deadlines:* August 31 of year before funding is requested

Restrictions on Giving: Company does not provide grants for endowments.

Company only considers requests from not-for-profit, nonpolitical, nonsectarian organizations that possess IRS 501(c)(3) status.

OTHER THINGS TO KNOW

The company does not release direct giving figures, as giving program is under periodic review.

GRANTS ANALYSIS

Total Grants: $646,080

Number of Grants: 126

Highest Grant: $60,000

Average Grant: $5,128

Typical Range: $1,000 to $10,000

Disclosure Period: 1993

Note: Above figures are for the foundation only and do not reflect direct gifts. Recent grants are derived from a 1993 Form 990.

RECENT GRANTS

Library

5,000	Greenwich Library Cole Auditorium, Greenwich, CT — $10,000 pledge for1992-93

General

60,000	JRF Scholarships
23,525	JRF King and Low Heywood Thomas Prep School
20,000	Boys and Girls Club of Stamford, Stamford, CT — five-year pledge 1989-93
20,000	United Way of Greenwich, Greenwich, CT
13,000	Opportunities Industrialization Council, Philadelphia, PA — additional payment

Connecticut Mutual Life Insurance Company / Connecticut Mutual Life Foundation

Assets: $11.52 billion
Employees: 1,935
Headquarters: Hartford, CT
SIC Major Group: Life Insurance and Security & Commodity Services Nec

CONTACT

Bertina Williams
Corporate Responsibility Officer
Connecticut Mutual Life Fdn.
140 Garden St.
Hartford, CT 06154
(203) 727-6500

FINANCIAL SUMMARY

Recent Giving: $1,100,000 (1995 est.); $1,054,000 (1994 approx.); $1,044,311 (1993)

Assets: $14,533,817 (1993); $14,512,476 (1992); $14,374,122 (1991)

Fiscal Note: Company also makes direct contributions. Grants of up to $1 million are made to nonprofit organizations which focus on education, housing, and health issues in the Hartford, CT area. Above figures exclude nonmonetary support.

EIN: 51-0192500

CONTRIBUTIONS SUMMARY

Typical Recipients: • *Arts & Humanities:* Arts Associations & Councils, Arts Funds, Community Arts, Historic Preservation, History & Archaeology, Libraries, Museums/Galleries, Performing Arts, Public Broadcasting • *Civic & Public Affairs:* African American Affairs, Business/Free Enterprise, Chambers of Commerce, Civil Rights, Economic Development, Economic Policy, Employment/Job Training, Housing, Law & Justice, Legal Aid, Nonprofit Management, Professional & Trade Associations, Public Policy, Urban & Community Affairs, Women's Affairs • *Education:* Arts/Humanities Education, Business Education, Colleges & Universities, Community & Junior Colleges, Economic Education, Education Associations, Education Reform, Elementary Education (Private), Literacy, Medical Education, Minority Education, Private Education (Precollege), Public Education (Precollege), Religious Education, Secondary Education (Public), Special Education, Student Aid • *Environment:* General • *Health:* AIDS/HIV, Children's Health/Hospitals, Clinics/Medical Centers, Health Policy/Cost Containment, Health Funds, Health Organizations, Hospitals, Prenatal Health Issues, Public Health, Single-Disease Health Associations • *Religion:* Jewish Causes • *Social Services:* At-Risk Youth, Child Welfare, Community Service Organizations, Day Care, Delinquency & Criminal Rehabilitation, Family Services, Food/Clothing Distribution, Homes, Senior Services, Shelters/Homelessness, Substance Abuse,

United Funds/United Ways, Volunteer Services, Youth Organizations

Grant Types: capital, employee matching gifts, general support, and project

Note: Employee gifts of up to $750 per year to an accredited educational institution are matched.

Nonmonetary Support: $23,000 (1987)

Nonmonetary Support Types: loaned executives

Note: Nonmonetary support is estimated at $200,000 annually.

Geographic Distribution: Primarily giving is reserved for the greater Hartford area and to Connecticut.

Operating Locations: CT (Hartford)

CORP. OFFICERS

Walter Joseph Gorski: *B* New Britain CT 1943 *ED* Univ CT BS 1964; Univ CT JD 1967 *CURR EMPL* sr vp, gen couns, asst secy: CT Mutual Life Ins Co *CORP AFFIL* asst secy: Group Am Ins Co; pres, dir: CT Mutual Fin Svcs Fund Inc, CT Mutual Investment Accounts; ptnr: Schatz Schatz Ribicoff & Kotkin *NONPR AFFIL* mem: Am Counc Life Ins, Assn Life Ins Counc, CT Bar Assn

Denis Francis Mullane: *B* Astoria NY 1930 *ED* US Military Acad BS 1952 *CURR EMPL* chmn: CT Mutual Life Ins Co *CORP AFFIL* dir: CT Natural Gas Co; pres, dir: DHC Inc *NONPR AFFIL* chmn: Am Coll; dir: Am Counc Life Ins, St Francis Hosp; mem: Am Soc Corp Execs, Natl Assn Life Underwriters; pres: Assn Grads US Military Acad; trust: US Military Acad

GIVING OFFICERS

Constance E. Clayton: dir *CORP AFFIL* dir: CT Mutual Life Ins Co *NONPR AFFIL* superintendent: Philadelphia Pub Sch Sys

Myron P. Curzan: dir *CURR EMPL* ptnr: Arnold & Porter *CORP AFFIL* dir: CT Mutual Life Ins Co

William Ben Ellis: pres, dir *B* Vicksburg MS 1940 *ED* Carnegie-Mellon Univ BS 1962; LA St Univ 1966; Univ MD PhD 1966; Am Univ 1968 *CURR EMPL* chmn: NW Utilities Co *CORP AFFIL* chmn: N Atlantic Energy Svc Corp, Northeast Utilities Svc Co, Pub Svc Co NH, Western MA Electric Co; chmn, ceo: CT Light & Power Co Inc, Holyoke Water Power Co, Northeast Nuclear Energy Co, Rocky River Realty Co; dir: CT Mutual Life Ins Co, Nuclear Electric Ins Ltd *NONPR AFFIL* bd regents: Univ Hartford; corporator: Inst Living, St Francis Hosp; critic, commentator: Sci-Fi Channel; elector: Wadsworth Atheneum; mem: Atomic Indus Forum, CT Bus & Indus Assn, Greater Hartford Chamber Commerce, Sci Fiction Writers Am, Writers Guild Am

Robert M. Furek: dir *B* Jersey City NJ 1942 *ED* Colby Coll BS 1964; Columbia Univ MS 1966 *CURR EMPL* pres, ceo, dir: Heublein Inc *CORP AFFIL* dir: CT Mutual Life Ins Co, Dexter Corp; ceo, pres, dir: Heublein Holdings Corp *NONPR AFFIL* vchmn: Am Red Cross Hartford Chap *PHIL AFFIL* chmn: Heublein Foundation, Inc.

Walter Joseph Gorski: vp, dir *CURR EMPL* sr vp, gen couns, asst secy: CT Mutual Life Ins Co (see above)

Katherine K. Miller: secy

Denis Francis Mullane: dir *CURR EMPL* chmn: CT Mutual Life Ins Co (see above)

Astrida R. Olds: asst vp, exec dir

William J. Sullivan: treas *CURR EMPL* vp: CT Mutual Life Ins Co

Bertina Williams: corp responsibility off

APPLICATION INFORMATION

Initial Approach: *Initial Contact:* a brief letter *Include Information On:* brief description of the organization and programs, an income and expense statement for the organization, goals and objectives, budget, copy of IRS 501(c)(3), 509(a)(1) determination letter, and a list of board members *Deadlines:* none

Restrictions on Giving: Grants are generally not made to religious organizations for sectarian purposes; partisan political organizations; United Way or other federated drives outside the Hartford area; or goodwill advertising.

Capital grants must meet certain requirements; policy regarding capital grants may be obtained by writing the foundation. Endowments rarely are considered, and only when endowment is reserved for a particular project or program.

OTHER THINGS TO KNOW

CM Alliance also contributes to company-sponsored programs.

GRANTS ANALYSIS

Total Grants: $1,044,311

Number of Grants: 620

Highest Grant: $262,000

Average Grant: $1,684

Typical Range: $500 to $10,000

Disclosure Period: 1993

Note: Above figures include $209,149 in scholarship grants to educational organizations. Recent grants are derived from a 1993 Form 990.

RECENT GRANTS

General

59,250	United Way/Combined Health Appeal, Hartford, CT — operating grant	
59,250	United Way/Combined Health Appeal, Hartford, CT — operating grant	
59,250	United Way/Combined Health Appeal, Hartford, CT — operating grant	
59,250	United Way/Combined Health Appeal, Hartford, CT — operating grant	
47,500	Hartford Action Plan on Infant Health, Hartford, CT — operating grant	

Crabtree & Evelyn / Crabtree & Evelyn Foundation

Sales: $82.5 million
Employees: 284
Headquarters: Woodstock, CT
SIC Major Group: Wholesale Trade—Nondurable Goods

CONTACT
Irving J. Schoppe
Treasurer and Director
Crabtree & Evelyn
PO Box 167
Peake Brook RD.
Woodstock, CT 06281
(203) 928-2761

FINANCIAL SUMMARY
Recent Giving: $100,400 (fiscal 1994); $98,605 (fiscal 1993); $54,040 (fiscal 1992)

Assets: $7,805 (fiscal 1994); $15,710 (fiscal 1993); $24,065 (fiscal 1992)

Gifts Received: $90,250 (fiscal 1993); $85,750 (fiscal 1992)

Fiscal Note: In fiscal 1993, contributions were received from Crabtree & Evelyn ($47,250), Crabtree & Evelyn Retail Stores ($3,000), Windham Toiletries ($9,000), and Scarborough & Co. ($31,000).

EIN: 06-1303762

CONTRIBUTIONS SUMMARY
Typical Recipients: • *Arts & Humanities:* Libraries • *Civic & Public Affairs:* General, Municipalities/Towns • *Education:* Special Education • *Health:* Cancer, Home-Care Services, Hospices, Hospitals • *International:* International Environmental Issues • *Social Services:* Child Abuse, Child Welfare, Community Service Organizations, Day Care, Domestic Violence, People with Disabilities, Recreation & Athletics

Grant Types: general support and scholarship

Geographic Distribution: principally near operating locations and to national organizations

Operating Locations: CT (Woodstock), NH (Milford)

CORP. OFFICERS
Cyrus I. Harvey, Jr.: *CURR EMPL* chmn, dir: Crabtree & Evelyn Ltd

GIVING OFFICERS
William C. Brewer: dir

Alan G. Cummings: secy, dir

Cyrus I. Harvey, Jr.: ceo, dir *CURR EMPL* chmn, dir: Crabtree & Evelyn Ltd (see above)

Rebecca M. Harvey: vp, dir

Paula M. Kroll: pres, dir *CURR EMPL* pres, dir: Crabtree & Evelyn

Irving J. Schoppe: treas, dir

APPLICATION INFORMATION
Initial Approach: Send a brief letter of inquiry. Include a description of organization.

There are no deadlines. For scholarships, request application form.

Restrictions on Giving: Does not support individuals, religious organizations for sectarian purposes, or political or lobbying groups.

OTHER THINGS TO KNOW
Company reported in August 1995 that contributions had been temporarily suspended.

GRANTS ANALYSIS
Total Grants: $100,400

Number of Grants: 15

Highest Grant: $34,100

Typical Range: $100 to $15,000

Disclosure Period: fiscal year ending May 31, 1994

Note: Recent grants are derived from a fiscal 1994 Form 990. Number of grants and typical range do not include individual scholarships.

RECENT GRANTS
Library
1,000	Helaine Dauphinais Library Restoration, Thompson, CT

General
34,000	Day Kimball Hospital, Putnam, CT
15,000	Town of Thompson, North Grosvenordale, CT
6,250	Project Reach, Dorchester, MA
5,000	Monadnock Hospice, Peterborough, NH
2,500	Conservation International Seed Ventures, Washington, DC

Crane Co. / Crane Foundation

Sales: $1.65 billion
Employees: 8,400
Headquarters: Stamford, CT
SIC Major Group: Fabricated Metal Products, Industrial Machinery & Equipment, Lumber & Wood Products, and Rubber & Miscellaneous Plastics Products

CONTACT
Barry Manasse
Manager
Crane Co.
100 1st. Stamford Pl.
Stamford, CT 06902
(203) 363-7268

FINANCIAL SUMMARY
Recent Giving: $170,939 (1993); $178,267 (1992); $160,000 (1991)

Assets: $4,027,455 (1993); $3,484,412 (1992); $3,611,834 (1991)

EIN: 43-6051752

CONTRIBUTIONS SUMMARY
Typical Recipients: • *Arts & Humanities:* Arts Associations & Councils, Arts Centers, Ballet, Historic Preservation, Libraries, Mu-

seums/Galleries, Music, Performing Arts, Public Broadcasting, Theater • *Civic & Public Affairs:* Botanical Gardens/Parks, Business/Free Enterprise, Economic Development, Economic Policy, Hispanic Affairs, Housing, Law & Justice, Legal Aid, Minority Business, Parades/Festivals, Public Policy, Safety, Urban & Community Affairs, Women's Affairs • *Education:* Arts/Humanities Education, Business Education, Colleges & Universities, Community & Junior Colleges, Economic Education, Education Funds, Education Reform, General, Literacy, Private Education (Precollege), Public Education (Precollege), Secondary Education (Private), Secondary Education (Public), Student Aid • *Environment:* General • *Health:* Cancer, Emergency/Ambulance Services, Health Organizations, Hospitals, Medical Research, Mental Health, Transplant Networks/Donor Banks • *International:* Health Care/Hospitals, International Peace & Security Issues, International Relief Efforts • *Religion:* Bible Study/Translation, Religious Welfare • *Social Services:* Child Abuse, Child Welfare, Community Service Organizations, Domestic Violence, Food/Clothing Distribution, Homes, People with Disabilities, Special Olympics, Substance Abuse, United Funds/United Ways, Volunteer Services, Youth Organizations

Grant Types: emergency, employee matching gifts, and general support

Geographic Distribution: focus on NY and PA

Operating Locations: AZ (Goodyear), CA (Burbank), FL (Jacksonville), IL (Joilet), MI (Sterling Heights), MO (Chesterfield, St. Louis), NC (Marion), NY (New Rochelle, New York), OH (Salem, Washington Court House), PA (King of Prussia, Warrington)

CORP. OFFICERS
L. Hill Clark: *CURR EMPL* exec vp: Crane Co

Gil Dickoff: *CURR EMPL* treas: Crane Co

Robert Sheldon Evans: *B* Pittsburgh PA 1944 *ED* Univ PA BA 1966; Columbia Univ MBA 1968 *CURR EMPL* chmn, pres, ceo, coo: Crane Co *CORP AFFIL* chmn: Medusa Corp; dir: HBD Indus *NONPR AFFIL* mem deans adv counc: Columbia Univ Grad Sch Bus; trust: Allen Stevenson Sch, Eaglebrook Sch *PHIL AFFIL* trust: Edward P. Evans Foundation

Robert J. Muller, Jr.: *CURR EMPL* exec vp: Crane Co

GIVING OFFICERS
Gil Dickoff: treas *CURR EMPL* treas: Crane Co (see above)

Robert Sheldon Evans: chmn, pres, dir *CURR EMPL* chmn, pres, ceo, coo: Crane Co *PHIL AFFIL* trust: Edward P. Evans Foundation (see above)

Paul R. Hundt: secy, dir *B* New York NY 1939 *ED* Univ Notre Dame 1960; Columbia Univ 1963 *CURR EMPL* vp, secy, gen coun: Crane Co *PHIL AFFIL* trust: Crane Fund for Widows and Children

Richard B. Phillips: vp *CURR EMPL* vp: Crane Co *PHIL AFFIL* trust: Crane Fund for Widows and Children

David S. Smith: exec vp, dir

APPLICATION INFORMATION
Initial Approach: Send brief letter on organization letterhead describing program. There are no deadlines.

Restrictions on Giving: The foundation does not make grants to individuals.

GRANTS ANALYSIS
Total Grants: $170,939

Number of Grants: 166

Highest Grant: $10,000

Typical Range: $50 to $10,000

Disclosure Period: 1993

Note: Recent grants are derived from a 1993 Form 990.

RECENT GRANTS
Library
2,500	Pierpont Morgan Library, New York, NY
1,500	New York Public Library, New York, NY

General
10,000	Manhattan College, New York, NY
10,000	Stamford Hospital Foundation, Stamford, CT — "Pneumonia Pnockout" Campaign
5,500	LEAD Program in Business, New York, NY
5,000	AmeriCares Foundation, New Canaan, CT
5,000	Morning Star Mission

Culpeper Foundation, Charles E.

CONTACT
Linda E. Jacobs
Vice President for Programs
Charles E. Culpeper Foundation
Financial Centre
695 E Main St., Ste. 404
Stamford, CT 06901-2138
(203) 975-1240

FINANCIAL SUMMARY
Recent Giving: $6,750,000 (1995 est.); $6,706,196 (1994); $5,838,080 (1993)

Assets: $157,000,000 (1995); $150,000,000 (1994); $157,392,846 (1993)

Gifts Received: $1,300 (1995); $1,265 (1994); $1,368 (1993)

EIN: 13-1956297

CONTRIBUTIONS SUMMARY
Donor(s): The Culpeper Foundation was established under the will of Charles E. Culpeper, a pioneer in the bottling and marketing of Coca-Cola. He was born in Rome, GA, in 1874, and served as president and chairman of the Coca-Cola Bottling

Company of New York. His will gave most of his fortune to establish the foundation. He requested that a portion of the principal be conserved for the benefit of future generations. The foundation was established when he died in 1940.

Typical Recipients: • *Arts & Humanities:* Arts Centers, Arts Outreach, Ballet, Dance, Historic Preservation, Libraries, Museums/Galleries, Music, Opera, Performing Arts, Public Broadcasting, Theater • *Civic & Public Affairs:* Botanical Gardens/Parks, Law & Justice, Zoos/Aquariums • *Education:* Colleges & Universities, Environmental Education, General, International Exchange, International Studies, Medical Education, Religious Education, Student Aid • *Health:* Cancer, Clinics/Medical Centers, Emergency/Ambulance Services, Health Policy/Cost Containment, Hospitals, Medical Research • *International:* International Affairs • *Religion:* Seminaries • *Science:* Scientific Labs • *Social Services:* Crime Prevention

Grant Types: multiyear/continuing support, project, and research

Geographic Distribution: wide range of distribution within the United States

GIVING OFFICERS

Mary Ellen Bucci: program off

Colin Goetze Campbell: dir *B* New York NY 1935 *ED* Cornell Univ AB 1957; Columbia Univ JD 1960 *CORP AFFIL* dir: Hartford Steam Boiler Inspection & Ins Co, Middlesex Mutual Assurance Co, Pitney Bowes, Sysco Corp, Winrock Intl Inst Agriculture Devel *NONPR AFFIL* dir: Inst Future; mem: Counc Foreign Rels, Phi Delta Phi, Psi Upsilon; pres emeritus: Wesleyan Univ; trust: Colonial Williamsburg Fdn, Goodspeed Opera House Fdn *CLUB AFFIL* mem: Century *PHIL AFFIL* pres, trust: Rockefeller Brothers Fund

Philip M. Drake: vp, secy, treas, dir *B* Flushing NY 1925 *CURR EMPL* ptnr: Cummings & Lockwood

Joseph Francis Fahey, Jr.: dir *B* Stamford CT 1925 *ED* Univ Notre Dame BA 1949; Univ CT 1951; Bridgeport Univ 1952; Stanford Univ 1958; Northwestern Univ 1960; Columbia Univ 1965 *CURR EMPL* pres, dir: Stamford Devel Corp *CORP AFFIL* dir: Norco Inc, Samford Devel Corp *NONPR AFFIL* dir: Congregate Care Ctrs Am, Stamford Hosp; mem: Am Bankers Assn, CT Bankers Assn, Southwestern Area Commerce Indus Assn *PHIL AFFIL* pres: Rich Foundation, Inc. *CLUB AFFIL* Club Pelican Bay, Landmark, Roasters, Stamford YC, Woodway CC

John A. Huston: dir

Linda E. Jacobs: vp for programs

Nancy J. Kelly: comptr

Ronald P. Lynch: dir *B* New York NY 1935 *ED* Cornell Univ BS 1958 *CURR EMPL* mng ptnr: Lord Abbett & Co *CORP AFFIL* chmn: Affiliated Fund Inc, Lord Abbett Bond-Debenture Fund Inc, Lord Abbett Cash Reserve Fund Inc, Lord Abbett Developing Growth Fund Inc, Lord Abbett Equity Fund Inc, Lord Abbett Fundamental Value Fund, Lord Abbett Global Fund Inc, Lord Abbett Income Fund Inc, Lord Abbett Tax-Free Income Fund Inc, Lord Abbett US Govt Securities Fund, Lord Abbett Value Appreciation Fund Inc

Francis Joseph McNamara, Jr.: pres, dir *B* Boston MA 1927 *ED* Georgetown Univ AB 1949; Georgetown Univ LLB 1951 *NONPR AFFIL* fellow: Am Bar Fdn, Am Coll Trial Lawyers; mem: Am Bar Assn, Am Law Inst, CT Bar Assn, Fed Bar Assn, Knight Holy Sepulchre, Knight St Gregory Great, Navy League US; trust: US Supreme Ct Historical Soc; trust emeritus: Fairfield Univ *CLUB AFFIL* Belleair CC, Turf & Field, WeeBurn

John Morning: dir *B* Cleveland OH 1932 *CURR EMPL* pres: John Morning Design *CORP AFFIL* dir: Dime Savings Bank *NONPR AFFIL* chmn bd trusts: Pratt Inst; co-chmn: Ctr African Art; dir: Assn Gov Bds Colls & Univs; mem: Am Inst Graphic Arts, Century Assn; mem bd dir: NY Landmarks Conservancy; mem ed comm: Mus Modern Art; trust: Am Academy Dramatic Arts, Wilberforce Univ

John Charles Rose: dir *B* New York NY 1924 *ED* Fordham Univ BS 1946; Georgetown Univ MD 1950 *NONPR AFFIL* assoc editor: Academy Medicine; diplomatic: Am Bd Family Practice, Am Bd Internal Medicine; fellow: Am Coll Physicians; mem: Am Heart Assn, Am Physiological Soc, Biophysics Soc, Royal Soc Medicine, Soc Experimental Biology & Medicine; prof emeritus: Georgetown Univ Sch Medicine *CLUB AFFIL* Cosmos

Michael G. Ulasky: comptr

APPLICATION INFORMATION
Initial Approach:

Applicants should send a brief letter of inquiry.

Letters should provide a description of the project and its purpose, a detailed budget, a short statement of the applicant's history and background, information on other sources of funding (current and anticipated), and a copy of the IRS tax-exempt determination letter.

There are no deadlines for submitting proposals.

The foundation's board meets quarterly to consider and take final action on grant requests. Every applicant receives written notification of the action taken by the foundation. If the project falls within the scope of the foundation's interests and if there is a possibility that the project will be funded, the applicant will be asked to furnish a full proposal. Interviews and on-site visits are made at the foundation's discretion only after receiving pertinent materials.

Restrictions on Giving: The foundation rarely approves grants for endowments, building programs, conferences or seminars.

Although the foundation is not inclined to make scholarship grants, consideration will be given to requests from higher education organizations or consortia seeking to develop new approaches to providing financial assistance to undergraduates. It does not make grants to individuals, or to conduit organizations. There are no specific dollar limitations. The foundation only supports projects located in the United States.

GRANTS ANALYSIS
Total Grants: $6,706,196

Number of Grants: 138

Highest Grant: $250,000

Average Grant: $48,105*

Typical Range: $25,000 to $250,000

Disclosure Period: 1994

Note: Average grant figure provided by the foundation. Recent grants are derived from a 1993 Form 990.

RECENT GRANTS
Library

150,000	Mountain College Library Network, Swannanoa, NC — toward the establishment of a single automated library system for the consortium
108,000	Cornell University, Ithaca, NY — toward development of a multidiscipline digital library preservation and access project on America's infrastructure, "The Making of America"
100,000	New York Botanical Garden, Bronx, NY — toward library computerization and the expansion of information and reference services
87,500	Commission on Preservation and Access, Washington, DC — toward seminars for library school deans, meetings of the College Libraries Committee, and communications and publications program
73,333	Northeast Document Conservation Center, Andover, MA — toward advanced internship program for library conservators

General

150,000	Choate Rosemary Hall, Wallingford, CT — for Charles E. Culpeper Scholarship Fund in memory of Dr. Hermann Karl Scheyning
127,400	Critical Languages and Area Studies Consortium, Peacham, VT — toward Japanese language and culture studies for high school students
122,478	Macalester College, St. Paul, MN — toward equipment to expand and upgrade the language laboratory and

120,438	curriculum development stipends
	Drew University, Madison, NJ — toward the creation of a multimedia classroom and for faculty training across the curriculum
108,000	Johns Hopkins University, Baltimore, MD — 1993 Medical Science Scholar

Culpeper Memorial Foundation, Daphne Seybolt

CONTACT
Nicholas Nardi
Secretary and Treasurer
Daphne Seybolt Culpeper Memorial Fdn.
PO Box 206
Norwalk, CT 06852-0206
(203) 762-3984

FINANCIAL SUMMARY
Recent Giving: $617,990 (1993); $312,250 (1990); $444,748 (1989)

Assets: $12,391,158 (1993); $10,624,895 (1990); $10,071,717 (1989)

EIN: 22-2478755

CONTRIBUTIONS SUMMARY
Donor(s): the late Daphne Seybolt Culpeper

Typical Recipients: • *Arts & Humanities:* Arts Centers, Historic Preservation, History & Archaeology, Libraries, Museums/Galleries, Music • *Education:* Arts/Humanities Education, Colleges & Universities, Community & Junior Colleges, Legal Education, Private Education (Precollege), Student Aid • *Health:* Cancer, Clinics/Medical Centers, Health Organizations, Heart, Hospices, Hospitals, Medical Research, Prenatal Health Issues, Single-Disease Health Associations • *Religion:* Churches, Religious Organizations, Religious Welfare • *Science:* Scientific Centers & Institutes • *Social Services:* Child Welfare, Community Service Organizations, Day Care, Family Services, Senior Services, United Funds/United Ways, YMCA/YWCA/YMHA/YWHA, Youth Organizations

Grant Types: general support and multi-year/continuing support

Geographic Distribution: focus on CT

GIVING OFFICERS
Rodney S. Eielson: pres

Nicholas J. Nardi: secy, treas

APPLICATION INFORMATION
Initial Approach: Send brief letter of inquiry describing program or project. There are no deadlines.

Restrictions on Giving: Does not support individuals.

PUBLICATIONS
Application Guidelines

GRANTS ANALYSIS

Total Grants: $617,990

Number of Grants: 140

Highest Grant: $50,000

Typical Range: $1,000 to $5,000

Disclosure Period: 1993

Note: Recent grants are derived from a 1993 Form 990.

RECENT GRANTS

Library

30,000	Norwalk Public Library, Norwalk, CT — acquisition of local area network

General

50,000	Bethesda Hospital Association, Boynton Beach, FL — magnetic resonance imaging system
40,000	Don Shula Foundation, Miami, FL — youth investigator awards program
40,000	Norwalk Hospital Foundation, Norwalk, CT — pulmonary, cardiology, and geriatrics sections
25,000	Norton Gallery and School of Art, West Palm Beach, FL — education programs both within and outside of the museum
20,000	First Presbyterian Church, Delray Beach, FL

Day Foundation, Nancy Sayles

CONTACT
John R. Disbrow
Vice President
Nancy Sayles Day Fdn.
c/o Union Trust Co.
300 Main St.
Stamford, CT 06904
(203) 348-6211

FINANCIAL SUMMARY
Recent Giving: $401,030 (fiscal 1993); $389,000 (fiscal 1992); $368,012 (fiscal 1991)

Assets: $9,295,016 (fiscal 1993); $9,114,398 (fiscal 1992); $8,420,233 (fiscal 1991)

Gifts Received: $104,057 (fiscal 1993); $64,850 (fiscal 1990); $50,313 (fiscal 1989)

EIN: 06-6071254

CONTRIBUTIONS SUMMARY
Donor(s): the late Nancy Sayles Day, Mrs. Lee Day Gillespie

Typical Recipients: • *Arts & Humanities:* Arts Centers, Community Arts, Dance, Historic Preservation, History & Archaeology, Libraries, Museums/Galleries, Music, Opera, Performing Arts, Public Broadcasting, Theater • *Civic & Public Affairs:* General • *Education:* Colleges & Universities, Education Reform, General, International Exchange, Leadership Training, Private Education (Precollege), Religious Education • *Environment:* General, Resource Conservation • *Health:* Health Organizations, Hospices, Hospitals • *International:* International Development, International Environmental Issues, International Peace & Security Issues • *Religion:* Churches • *Social Services:* Child Welfare, Community Service Organizations, Delinquency & Criminal Rehabilitation, Family Planning, People with Disabilities, Recreation & Athletics, Youth Organizations

Grant Types: general support and multi-year/continuing support

Geographic Distribution: focus on MA

GIVING OFFICERS
Union Trust Co.: trust

APPLICATION INFORMATION
Initial Approach: The foundation has no formal grant application procedure or application form. There are no deadlines.

GRANTS ANALYSIS
Total Grants: $401,030

Number of Grants: 36

Highest Grant: $50,015

Typical Range: $1,000 to $5,000

Disclosure Period: fiscal year ending September 30, 1993

Note: Recent grants are derived from a fiscal 1993 Form 990.

RECENT GRANTS

Library

25,000	Nantucket Athaeneum, Nantucket, MA

General

20,000	Nantucket Cottage Hospital, Nantucket, MA
15,000	St. Paul's Church, Nantucket, MA
10,000	Bowdoin College, Brunswick, ME — for Beckwith Chair
10,000	Health Resource Network, Boston, MA
10,000	Hospice of Cambridge, Boston, MA

Dell Foundation, Hazel

CONTACT
June M. Powers
President
Hazel Dell Fdn.
c/o Law Offices Carroll & Lane
PO Box 771
Norwalk, CT 06852
(203) 853-6565

FINANCIAL SUMMARY
Recent Giving: $128,000 (1992); $123,750 (1991); $160,000 (1990)

Assets: $2,751,972 (1992); $2,735,859 (1991); $2,505,857 (1990)

EIN: 13-6161744

CONTRIBUTIONS SUMMARY
Donor(s): the late Harry C. McClarity

Typical Recipients: • *Arts & Humanities:* Arts Festivals, Libraries, Theater • *Civic & Public Affairs:* Housing, Municipalities/Towns, Parades/Festivals, Safety • *Education:* Colleges & Universities, Private Education (Precollege), Secondary Education (Public) • *Health:* Children's Health/Hospitals, Clinics/Medical Centers, Emergency/Ambulance Services, Health Organizations, Hospitals, Medical Rehabilitation • *Religion:* Churches, Religious Welfare • *Social Services:* Animal Protection, Child Welfare, Community Service Organizations, Counseling, Recreation & Athletics, United Funds/United Ways, Youth Organizations

Grant Types: general support

Geographic Distribution: focus on CT, MA, and NJ

GIVING OFFICERS
Joy S. Dunlop: secy, dir

Gail A. Fallon: dir

June M. Powers: pres, dir

Thomas F. Ryan: treas

Diane Schroeder: dir

William J. Sullivan: trust *CURR EMPL* dir adv: Rolex Watch USA Inc

APPLICATION INFORMATION
Initial Approach: The foundation has no formal grant application procedure or application form. There are no deadlines.

Restrictions on Giving: No support for individuals.

GRANTS ANALYSIS
Total Grants: $128,000
Number of Grants: 47
Highest Grant: $14,000
Typical Range: $500 to $2,500
Disclosure Period: 1992

Note: Recent grants are derived from a 1992 Form 990.

RECENT GRANTS
Library
2,000	Pequot Library, Southport, CT

General
14,000	Centrastate Medical Center, Freehold, NJ
10,000	Norwalk Hospital, Norwalk, CT
7,500	Bangs Avenue School, Asbury, NJ
7,350	Medical Center of Ocean County Foundation, Point Pleasant, NJ — pediatric building fund
5,000	St. Labre Indian School, Ashland, MT

Dexter Corporation / Dexter Corp. Foundation

Sales: $887.11 million
Employees: 4,800
Headquarters: Windsor Locks, CT
SIC Major Group: Chemical Preparations Nec, Industrial Inorganic Chemicals Nec, Medicinals & Botanicals, and Biological Products Except Diagnostic

CONTACT
K. Grahame Walker
President and CEO
Dexter Corp. Fdn.
One Elm St.
Windsor Locks, CT 06096
(203) 627-9051

FINANCIAL SUMMARY
Recent Giving: $433,200 (1993); $474,665 (1992); $491,270 (1991)

Assets: $125,557 (1991); $198,318 (1990); $715,481 (1989)

Gifts Received: $400,000 (1993); $400,000 (1991)

Fiscal Note: Company gives through foundation only. Gifts include employee matching funds for education and for United Ways.

EIN: 06-1013754

CONTRIBUTIONS SUMMARY
Typical Recipients: • *Arts & Humanities:* Arts Associations & Councils, Dance, Historic Preservation, Libraries, Museums/Galleries, Music, Opera, Public Broadcasting, Theater • *Civic & Public Affairs:* Economic Development, Urban & Community Affairs, Women's Affairs • *Education:* Colleges & Universities, Community & Junior Colleges, Minority Education, Public Education (Precollege), Religious Education • *Environment:* General • *Health:* Health Funds, Health Organizations, Hospitals, Mental Health, Nursing Services, Single-Disease Health Associations • *Social Services:* Community Service Organizations, Delinquency & Criminal Rehabilitation, Domestic Violence, Food/Clothing Distribution, People with Disabilities, Shelters/Homelessness, Substance Abuse, United Funds/United Ways, Youth Organizations

Grant Types: employee matching gifts, general support, project, and research

Nonmonetary Support: $100,000 (1989); $100,000 (1988)

Nonmonetary Support Types: loaned employees and loaned executives

Note: Estimated nonmonetary support is not available and is not included in the above figures. Loaned employees and loaned executives are provided for local United Way drives.

Geographic Distribution: one-half of grants go to the greater Hartford area; most of the remaining funds go to areas near operating locations, especially where Dexter employees will benefit

Operating Locations: AL (Birmingham), CA (City of Industry, Fremont, Pittsburg, Sunnyvale), CT (Hartford, Windsor Locks), DE (Wilmington), IL (Elk Grove Village, Waukegan), IN (Indianapolis), MA (Canton, Lowell), MD (Frederick, Gaithersburg), MI (Auburn Hills), MO (Kansas City), NC (Pineville), NH (Londonderry, Seabrook), NJ (Newark), NY (Grand Island, Olean), OH (Aurora, Chagrin Falls), SC (Greenville), TX (Brownsville, Grand Prairie, Richardson)

CORP. OFFICERS
Robert Ernest McGill III: *B* San Francisco CA 1931 *ED* Williams Coll BA 1954; Harvard Univ Grad Sch Bus Admin MBA 1956 *CURR EMPL* exec vp fin & admin, dir: Dexter Corp *CORP AFFIL* bd mgrs: Travelers Funds Variable Annuities; dir: Analytical Tech Inc, Inroads Inc, Travelers Equity Funds, Travelers Funds Variable Commodities; pres: Kettlebrook Ins Co Ltd; trust: Colt Bequest Inc; vchmn: Life Techs Inc *NONPR AFFIL* bd dirs: Hartford Symphony Orchestra; bd overseers sch bus: Univ CT; dir: CT Pub Expenditures Counc; mem: Fin Execs Inst, NY Soc Security Analysts; mem exec comm: Greater Hartford Arts Counc; trust: Pub Expenditure Counc

Keith Grahame Walker: *B* West Bridgford England 1937 *ED* Britannia Royal Naval Coll 1957; Royal Naval Engg Coll 1962 *CURR EMPL* pres, ceo, chmn: Dexter Corp *CORP AFFIL* dir: Barnes Group Inc, Life Techs Inc *NONPR AFFIL* bd dirs: Greater Hartford Arts Counc; dir: New England Air Mus; mem: CT Bus & Indus Assn; trust: Hartford Grad Ctr *CLUB AFFIL* Hartford GC *PHIL AFFIL* vchmn exec comm: CBIA Education Foundation

GIVING OFFICERS
Bruce H. Beatt: secy

Lanie Kretschmar: coordinator

Robert Ernest McGill III: vp *CURR EMPL* exec vp fin & admin, dir: Dexter Corp (see above)

John D. Thompson: treas

Glen L. Urban: dir *CORP AFFIL* dir: Dexter Corp

Keith Grahame Walker: pres *CURR EMPL* pres, ceo, chmn: Dexter Corp *PHIL AFFIL* vchmn exec comm: CBIA Education Foundation (see above)

Arthur E. Wegner: dir

APPLICATION INFORMATION

Initial Approach: *Initial Contact:* brief letter requesting guidelines *Include Information On:* proposal on organization's letterhead stationery describing organization and its goals, where funds will be directed, amount requested, recently audited financial statement, proof of tax-exempt status (501(c)(3) mandatory) *Deadlines:* none

Restrictions on Giving: Does not support individuals.

Organization must have 501(c)(3) status.

GRANTS ANALYSIS

Total Grants: $433,200

Number of Grants: 316

Highest Grant: $15,000

Average Grant: $1,371

Typical Range: $1,000 to $5,000

Disclosure Period: 1993

Note: Recent grants are derived from a 1992 grants list.

RECENT GRANTS

General

15,000	United Way
14,070	Youth for Understanding, Washington, DC — international exchange
10,000	St. Bonaventure University, St. Bonaventure, NY
10,000	Trinity College, Deerfield, IL
8,000	United Way/Combined Health Appeal

Ensign-Bickford Industries / Ensign-Bickford Foundation

Sales: $173.6 million
Employees: 1,500
Headquarters: Simsbury, CT
SIC Major Group: Chemicals & Allied Products, Stone, Clay & Glass Products, and Textile Mill Products

CONTACT

Linda Angelastro
Executive Director, Corporate Communications
Ensign-Bickford Industries
Ten Mill Pond Lane
Simsbury, CT 06070
(203) 658-4411

FINANCIAL SUMMARY

Recent Giving: $261,600 (1993); $215,538 (1992); $274,433 (1991)

Assets: $15,496 (1993); $37,519 (1992); $10,422 (1991)

Gifts Received: $240,500 (1993); $240,000 (1992); $268,000 (1991)

Fiscal Note: In 1993, contributions were received from Ensign-Bickford Industries, Inc.

EIN: 06-6041097

CONTRIBUTIONS SUMMARY

Typical Recipients: • *Arts & Humanities:* Arts Associations & Councils, Historic Preservation, History & Archaeology, Libraries, Museums/Galleries, Music, Performing Arts, Theater • *Civic & Public Affairs:* Economic Development, Employment/Job Training, General, Municipalities/Towns, Parades/Festivals, Professional & Trade Associations, Public Policy, Safety, Urban & Community Affairs • *Education:* Colleges & Universities, Medical Education, Private Education (Precollege), Secondary Education (Public), Student Aid • *Environment:* General • *Health:* Cancer, Children's Health/Hospitals, Health Organizations, Hospitals • *Religion:* Churches, Religious Organizations • *Social Services:* Child Welfare, Community Centers, People with Disabilities, Recreation & Athletics, Senior Services, United Funds/United Ways, Volunteer Services, Youth Organizations

Grant Types: capital, conference/seminar, employee matching gifts, general support, multiyear/continuing support, project, research, scholarship, and seed money

Geographic Distribution: primarily in areas of company operations, particularly in the Simsbury and Avon, CT, area

CORP. OFFICERS

Herman J. Fonteyne: *CURR EMPL* pres, ceo, dir: Ensign-Bickford Indus

Joseph E. Lovejoy: *CURR EMPL* chmn, dir: Ensign-Bickford Indus

GIVING OFFICERS

Linda W. Angelastro: exec dir

David R. Bailey: dir

Austin D. Barney: dir

Pamela Bartlett: dir

Robert E. Darling, Jr.: chmn *B* Oakland CA 1937 *ED* San Francisco St Univ BA 1959; Yale Univ Sch Drama MFA 1963 *CURR EMPL* artistic producer: Acorn Theatre *NONPR AFFIL* mem: Actors Equity - Canada, Am Guild Musical Artists, Logan Circle Assn, OPERA Am, Un Scenic Artists

Jeanne M. Delehanty: dir

John E. Ellsworth: dir *B* Simsbury CT 1904 *ED* Yale Univ 1926 *CORP AFFIL* dir: Ensign-Bickford Realty Corp

Beatrice Murdock France: dir

Sandra Ginnis: dir

Jeffrey J. Nelb: treas, dir

Frank S. Wilson: dir

APPLICATION INFORMATION

Initial Approach: Send a letter stating purpose of request, annual budget, other funding, and geographic area in which proceeds will be distributed. There are no deadlines.

Restrictions on Giving: Generally limited to organizations within the geographic area of its corporate offices.

OTHER THINGS TO KNOW

Foundation also donates equipment.

GRANTS ANALYSIS

Total Grants: $261,600

Number of Grants: 81

Highest Grant: $40,000

Typical Range: $50 to $1,000

Disclosure Period: 1993

Note: Recent grants are derived from a 1993 Form 990.

RECENT GRANTS

General

40,000	United Way
25,000	FRWA — endowment
25,000	Simsbury Soccer, Simsbury, CT
25,000	St. Francis Hospital, Los Angeles, CA
12,000	Connecticut Forum, Hartford, CT

Fairchild Foundation, Sherman

CONTACT

Patricia A. Lydon
Vice President
Sherman Fairchild Foundation
71 Arch St.
Greenwich, CT 06830
(203) 661-9360

FINANCIAL SUMMARY

Recent Giving: $9,737,600 (1993); $11,122,542 (1992); $10,244,320 (1991)

Assets: $247,816,427 (1993); $225,259,036 (1992); $223,901,433 (1991)

Gifts Received: $3,477 (1993); $3,477 (1992); $3,477 (1991)

Fiscal Note: The foundation receives contributions from the Sherman M. Fairchild Annuity Trust.

EIN: 13-1951698

CONTRIBUTIONS SUMMARY

Donor(s): The Sherman Fairchild Foundation was incorporated in 1955 by Sherman M. Fairchild, inventor of the Fairchild aerial camera, chairman of Fairchild Camera Instrument Co. and of Fairchild Hiller Corp., owner of Fairchild Recording Equipment Co., and a director, and one of the largest single stockholders of IBM. When Mr. Fairchild died in 1971, he left most of his estate to the foundation.

Typical Recipients: • *Arts & Humanities:* Arts Centers, Arts Institutes, Historic Preservation, Libraries, Museums/Galleries, Performing Arts • *Education:* Arts/Humanities Education, Colleges & Universities, Engineering/Technological Education, Faculty Development, General, Legal Education, Medical Education, Private Education (Precollege), Religious Education, Science/Mathematics Education, Secondary Education (Private), Student Aid • *Health:* Cancer, Hospitals, Medical Research • *International:* International Peace & Security Issues • *Religion:* Jewish Causes, Religious Welfare, Seminaries • *Science:* Science Museums, Scientific Research • *Social Services:* Child Welfare, Community Service Organizations, Recreation & Athletics, Youth Organizations

Grant Types: capital, endowment, fellowship, general support, project, research, and scholarship

Geographic Distribution: no geographic restrictions; emphasis on New York City metropolitan area

GIVING OFFICERS

Laura Bachman: asst secy

Walter Burke: pres, treas, dir

Walter F. Burke III: dir

William Elfers: dir *B* New York NY 1918 *ED* Princeton Univ BA 1941; Harvard Univ MBA 1943 *CURR EMPL* dir: Greylock Mgmt Corp *CORP AFFIL* dir: B & B Intl Holdings Inc, Hartford Fire Ins Co, Westvaco Corp; ptnr: Greylock Capital Ltd, Greylock Ventures Ltd Partnership *NONPR AFFIL* chmn bd overseers: Northwestern Univ; trust: Mus Fine Arts; trust emeritus: Hotchkiss Sch, Northeastern Univ *CLUB AFFIL* Algonquin, Commercial, Longwood Cricket, Princeton, River, Wellesley CC

Robert P. Henderson: dir

Bonnie Himmelman: exec vp, dir

Patricia A. Lydon: vp, asst treas

Michele Tolela Myers: dir *B* Rabat Morocco 1941 *ED* Univ Paris 1962; Univ Denver MA 1966; Univ Denver PhD 1967; Trinity Univ MA 1977 *CORP AFFIL* dir: Bank One OH *NONPR AFFIL* dir: Am Counc Ed; dir, mem: Am Counc Ed; mem: Intl Commun Assn, Speech Commun Assn; mem pres commn: Natl Collegiate Atletic Assn; pres: Denison Univ *CLUB AFFIL* San Antonio 100

Paul Donnelly Paganucci: dir *B* Waterville ME 1931 *ED* Dartmouth Coll AB 1953; Dartmouth Coll MBA 1954; Harvard Univ JD 1957 *CURR EMPL* chmn: Ledyard Natl Bank *CORP AFFIL* dir: Allmerica Securities Trust Inc, Filenes Basement Inc, HRE Properties, Hypertherm Inc, Meriden-Stinehour Inc, Occupational Health & Rehab Inc, St Mutual Securities *NONPR AFFIL* mem: Inst Chartered Fin Analysts, NY Soc Security Analysts, Pres Pvt Sector Survey Cost Control; overseer: Dartmouth Catholic Student Ctr; trust: Casque & Gauntlet, Colby Coll, Coll Mt St Vincent *PHIL AFFIL* dir: Grace Foundation, Inc. *CLUB AFFIL* Dartmouth NY

Agnar Pytte: dir *B* Kongsberg Norway 1932 *ED* Princeton Univ AB 1953; Harvard Univ AM 1954; Harvard Univ PhD 1958 *CORP AFFIL* dir: AO Smith Corp,

Goodyear Tire & Rubber Co *NONPR AFFIL* dir: Greater Cleveland Growth Assn, Un Way Am; mem: Am Physical Soc, Cleveland Roundtable, Cleveland Tech Leadership Counc, OH Counc Res & Econ Devel, Phi Beta Kappa, Sigma Xi; pres: Case Western Reserve Univ; trust: Cleveland Inst Music, Cleveland Orchestra, OH Aerospace Inst, Univs Res Assn *PHIL AFFIL* trust: Goodyear Tire & Rubber Company Fund

James Wright: dir

APPLICATION INFORMATION
Initial Approach:

Applicants should send a letter to the foundation.

The letter should include a description of the proposed project and proof of the organization's tax-exempt status.

There are no deadlines for funding requests.

Restrictions on Giving: No grants are made to individuals.

GRANTS ANALYSIS
Total Grants: $9,737,600

Number of Grants: 60

Highest Grant: $1,000,000

Average Grant: $162,293

Typical Range: $50,000 to $350,000

Disclosure Period: 1993

Note: Recent grants are derived from a 1993 Form 990.

RECENT GRANTS

Library
1,000,000	Pierpont Morgan Library, New York, NY — endowment

General
750,000	Case Western Reserve University, Cleveland, OH — construction of science building
500,000	Union Theological Seminary, New York, NY — renovation of Hastings Hall
500,000	University of Chicago, Chicago, IL — virtual learning center
450,000	University of California San Francisco, San Francisco, CA — degenerative diseases research
350,000	Boys Club of New York, New York, NY — general

Harcourt Foundation, Ellen Knowles

CONTACT
Paul Altermatt
President
Ellen Knowles Harcourt Fdn.
51 Main St.
New Milford, CT 06776
(203) 355-2631

FINANCIAL SUMMARY

Recent Giving: $92,225 (1993); $92,735 (1992); $86,049 (1990)

Assets: $2,104,675 (1993); $2,218,889 (1992); $1,787,423 (1990)

EIN: 06-1068025

CONTRIBUTIONS SUMMARY

Donor(s): the late Ellen Knowles Harcourt

Typical Recipients: • *Arts & Humanities:* Historic Preservation, History & Archaeology, Libraries, Literary Arts, Music, Performing Arts, Public Broadcasting • *Civic & Public Affairs:* Botanical Gardens/Parks, Employment/Job Training, General, Housing, Parades/Festivals • *Education:* Agricultural Education, Arts/Humanities Education, Colleges & Universities, General, Minority Education, Private Education (Precollege), Science/Mathematics Education, Secondary Education (Public), Student Aid • *Environment:* General, Resource Conservation • *Health:* Hospitals, Nursing Services • *Social Services:* Animal Protection, Child Welfare, Community Centers, Community Service Organizations, Recreation & Athletics, Shelters/Homelessness, United Funds/United Ways, Volunteer Services, YMCA/YWCA/YMHA/YWHA, Youth Organizations

Grant Types: general support

Geographic Distribution: focus on New Milford, CT

GIVING OFFICERS

Paul B. Altermatt: pres, dir *B* New Haven CT 1930 *ED* Wesleyan Univ BA 1951; Georgetown Univ LLB 1956 *CURR EMPL* ptnr: Cramer & Anderson *CORP AFFIL* dir: Cologne Life Reinsurance Co, Cologne Reinsurance Am *NONPR AFFIL* fellow: Am Bar Assn, Am Bar Fdn, Am Law Inst, CT Bar Assn; fellow, dir: New England Bar Assn; pres, dir: New Milford

Roger Chace: asst treas

Barbara Chappuis: secy, dir

Adele F. Ghisalbert: dir

Alice McCallister: dir

Leandro Pasqual: dir

George Verenes: treas, dir

APPLICATION INFORMATION

Initial Approach: Include a description of organization, amount requested, purpose of funds sought, recently audited financial statement, and proof of tax-exempt status. There are no deadlines.

Restrictions on Giving: Limited to New Milford, CT, and surrounding areas.

GRANTS ANALYSIS
Total Grants: $92,225

Number of Grants: 23

Highest Grant: $25,000

Typical Range: $500 to $7,500

Disclosure Period: 1993

Note: Recent grants are derived from a 1993 Form 990.

RECENT GRANTS

General

25,000	New Milford Hospital Foundation, New Milford, CT — Operating Room Equipment
12,000	J.P. Memorial Scholarship, New Milford, CT — scholarship program
7,500	Housatonic Valley Association, Cornwall, CT — Greenway program
5,000	Elliot Pratt Center, New Milford, CT — land program
5,000	Habitat for Humanity, Kent, CT — program support

Heublein Inc. / Heublein Foundation, Inc.

Sales: $1.9 billion
Employees: 3,500
Parent Company: Grand Metropolitan PLC
Headquarters: Farmington, CT
SIC Major Group: Wines, Brandy & Brandy Spirits, Distilled & Blended Liquors, and Wines & Distilled Beverages

CONTACT

Moira E. Burke
Treasurer
Heublein Foundation, Inc.
PO Box 388
Farmington, CT 06034-0388
(203) 231-5000
Note: Contact for direct gifts is John Shea, director, community affairs.

FINANCIAL SUMMARY

Recent Giving: $1,000,000 (1995 est.); $995,000 (1994 approx.); $989,488 (1993)

Assets: $155,335 (1993); $91,280 (1991)

Gifts Received: $999,445 (1993); $1,004,646 (1991)

Fiscal Note: Company gives though the foundation and directly. Company departments also make contributions. Budget for this support is unknown and is not included in above figures. Above figures exclude non-monetary support. In 1993, contributions were received from Heublein, Inc.

EIN: 06-6051280

CONTRIBUTIONS SUMMARY

Typical Recipients: • *Arts & Humanities:* Arts Associations & Councils, Libraries, Museums/Galleries, Public Broadcasting, Visual Arts • *Civic & Public Affairs:* Economic Development, Housing, Urban & Commu-

nity Affairs • *Education:* Colleges & Universities, Literacy, Minority Education • *Health:* Health Funds, Health Organizations, Hospitals • *Social Services:* Child Welfare, Community Service Organizations, Emergency Relief, Family Services, People with Disabilities, Shelters/Homelessness, United Funds/United Ways, Youth Organizations

Grant Types: employee matching gifts, general support, and scholarship

Note: Employee matching gift ratio: 1 to 1. Scholarships are available to Heublein employees only.

Geographic Distribution: only in areas where company has operating locations

Operating Locations: CA (Madera, Menlo Park, Napa Valley), CT (Farmington, Hartford), MI (Allen Park)

CORP. OFFICERS

Robert M. Furek: *B* Jersey City NJ 1942 *ED* Colby Coll BS 1964; Columbia Univ MS 1966 *CURR EMPL* pres, ceo, dir: Heublein Inc *CORP AFFIL* dir: CT Mutual Life Ins Co, Dexter Corp; pres, dir: Heublein Holdings Corp *NONPR AFFIL* vchmn: Am Red Cross Hartford Chap *PHIL AFFIL* dir: Connecticut Mutual Life Foundation

John A. Powers: *B* New York NY 1926 *ED* St Peters Coll BA 1950 *CURR EMPL* chmn, dir: Heublein Inc *CORP AFFIL* dir: CT Natl Bank, Hartford Natl Corp, Hartford Steam Boiler Inspection & Ins Co *NONPR AFFIL* dep chmn: Intl Distillers Vinters Ltd; mem: CT Bus & Indus Assn; mem bus adv counc: Skidmore Coll; regent: Harvard Univ; trust: Hartford Grad Ctr

GIVING OFFICERS

Moira E. Burke: contr, secy

Robert M. Furek: chmn, dir *CURR EMPL* pres, ceo, dir: Heublein Inc *PHIL AFFIL* dir: Connecticut Mutual Life Foundation (see above)

Peter M. Seremet: pres

Douglas M. Waddell: dir *CURR EMPL* sr vp fin, treas, dir: Heublein Inc

Richard E. Walton: secy, dir *CURR EMPL* sr vp, secy, gen couns, dir: Heublein Inc

APPLICATION INFORMATION

Initial Approach: *Initial Contact:* brief letter and one copy of full proposal *Include Information On:* description of the organization, amount requested, purpose for which funds are sought, recently audited financial statement, and proof of tax-exempt status *Deadlines:* none; board meets as required

Restrictions on Giving: Does not support dinners or special events, fraternal organizations, goodwill advertising, individuals, member agencies of united funds, political or lobbying groups, or religious organizations for sectarian purposes.

Company stresses that they do not give outside of the local areas where the company has operations.

GRANTS ANALYSIS

Total Grants: $989,488

Number of Grants: 456

Highest Grant: $230,500

Average Grant: $2,117

Typical Range: $1,000 to $5,000

Disclosure Period: 1993

Note: Recent grants are derived from a 1993 Form 990.

RECENT GRANTS

General

230,500	United Way — federated drives
87,200	Education Testing Service, Princeton, NJ — scholarship program
75,000	Hartford Public Schools, Hartford, CT — "Building Blocks" Montessori school
50,000	Horace Bushnell Memorial Hall Corporation, Hartford, CT — Arts-in-Education program
36,500	University of Connecticut Health Center, Farmington, CT — bimolecular structure analysis center

Hoffman Foundation, Maximilian E. and Marion O.

CONTACT

Doris C. Chaho
President
Maximillian E. and Marion O. Hoffman Foundation
970 Farmington Ave., Ste. 203
West Hartford, CT 06117
(203) 521-2949

FINANCIAL SUMMARY

Recent Giving: $1,691,552 (fiscal 1993); $1,601,550 (fiscal 1992); $1,409,720 (fiscal 1991)

Assets: $36,415,999 (fiscal 1993); $35,226,137 (fiscal 1992); $33,710,985 (fiscal 1991)

EIN: 22-2648036

CONTRIBUTIONS SUMMARY

Donor(s): The foundation was established in 1986 in Connecticut as a successor foundation of the Maximilian E. and Marion O. Hoffman Foundation, which was established in New York in 1984 by Marion O. Hoffman.

Typical Recipients: • *Arts & Humanities:* Arts Associations & Councils, Arts Centers, Libraries, Music, Public Broadcasting

• *Civic & Public Affairs:* Economic Policy, Employment/Job Training, Housing, Law & Justice, Public Policy, Safety, Urban & Community Affairs, Women's Affairs • *Education:* Colleges & Universities, Education Funds, International Exchange, Literacy, Medical Education, Private Education (Precollege), Science/Mathematics Education, Secondary Education (Private), Social Sciences Education, Special Education, Student Aid • *Environment:* Air/Water Quality, Energy, General, Resource Conservation • *Health:* Adolescent Health Issues, Children's Health/Hospitals, Emergency/Ambulance Services, Geriatric Health, Health Organizations, Heart, Hospitals, Hospitals (University Affiliated), Medical Rehabilitation, Nursing Services, Nutrition • *International:* International Development, International Organizations, International Relief Efforts, Missionary/Religious Activities • *Religion:* Jewish Causes, Religious Welfare • *Science:* Scientific Centers & Institutes, Scientific Organizations • *Social Services:* Camps, Child Welfare, Food/Clothing Distribution, Homes, People with Disabilities, United Funds/United Ways, Volunteer Services, Youth Organizations

Grant Types: capital, endowment, general support, project, and scholarship

Geographic Distribution: no geographic restrictions, with an emphasis on the Northeast

GIVING OFFICERS
Bahij Chaho: treas
Doris C. Chaho: pres

APPLICATION INFORMATION
Initial Approach:
Applicants should send written grant proposals.

Proposals should include a copy of the IRS tax-exempt determination letter.

Proposals should be received by the foundation 2 to 3 weeks before board meetings.

The board meets three times a year.

GRANTS ANALYSIS
Total Grants: $1,691,552
Number of Grants: 58
Highest Grant: $300,000
Average Grant: $29,165
Typical Range: $15,000 to $50,000
Disclosure Period: fiscal year ending June 30, 1993

Note: Recent grants are derived from a fiscal 1993 Form 990.

RECENT GRANTS
General
300,000	St. Francis Hospital and Medical Center, Hartford, CT — cardiac catheterization laboratory
200,000	Avon Old Farms School, Avon, CT — University of Connecticut health center project
100,000	Bates College, Lewiston, ME — fund for student research
100,000	University of Hartford, West Hartford, CT — occupational therapy program expansion
86,000	Syrian Orthodox Church, Beirut, Lebanon — land for high school

Huisking Foundation

CONTACT
Frank R. Huisking
Treasurer
Huisking Fdn.
PO Box 353
Botsford, CT 06404
(203) 426-8618

FINANCIAL SUMMARY
Recent Giving: $330,750 (1993); $332,612 (1992); $361,850 (1991)

Assets: $6,749,498 (1993); $7,105,093 (1992); $7,579,313 (1991)

Gifts Received: $8,216 (1991); $7,796 (1990); $6,941 (1989)

Fiscal Note: In 1991, contributions were received from Charles L. Huisking in form of stock.

EIN: 13-6117501

CONTRIBUTIONS SUMMARY
Donor(s): members of the Huisking family and family-related corporations

Typical Recipients: • *Arts & Humanities:* Libraries • *Civic & Public Affairs:* Botanical Gardens/Parks • *Education:* Colleges & Universities, Education Funds, Engineering/Technological Education, General, Private Education (Precollege), Secondary Education (Private), Student Aid • *Environment:* Resource Conservation • *Health:* Emergency/Ambulance Services, Hospitals, Long-Term Care, Medical Research, Multiple Sclerosis, Single-Disease Health Associations • *Religion:* Churches, Dioceses, Religious Organizations, Religious Welfare, Seminaries • *Social Services:* At-Risk Youth, Community Centers, Community Service Organizations, Day Care, Family Services, Homes, United Funds/United Ways, Youth Organizations

Grant Types: operating expenses, project, and research

Geographic Distribution: national

GIVING OFFICERS
Helen Crawford: dir
Evelyn F. Daly: dir
Robert P. Daly: dir
John E. Haigney: dir, pres
Claire F. Hanavan: dir
Taylor W. Hanavan: dir
Frank R. Huisking: treas, dir
Richard V. Huisking, Jr.: secy, dir
Richard V. Huisking, Sr.: dir
William Huisking, Jr.: vp, dir
Jean M. Steinschneider: dir

APPLICATION INFORMATION
Initial Approach: Send brief letter describing program. There are no deadlines.

Restrictions on Giving: Does not support individuals.

GRANTS ANALYSIS
Total Grants: $330,750
Number of Grants: 153
Highest Grant: $25,000
Typical Range: $100 to $5,000
Disclosure Period: 1993

Note: Recent grants are derived from a 1993 Form 990.

RECENT GRANTS
Library
24,000	Spring Hill College, Mobile, AL — library upgrade
3,000	Byram Shubert Library, Greenwich, CT — operating needs

General
25,000	Georgetown University, Washington, DC — alumni fund
25,000	Georgetown University, Washington, DC — alumni fund
25,000	University of Notre Dame, Notre Dame, IN
17,500	St. Marys College, Notre Dame, IN
16,000	Regional Y of Western Connecticut, Brookfield, CT — child care

ITT Hartford Insurance Group, Inc. / ITT Hartford Insurance Group Foundation

Parent Company: ITT Corp.
Parent Sales: $10.06 billion
Parent Employees: 19,700
Headquarters: Hartford, CT
SIC Major Group: Fire, Marine & Casualty Insurance

CONTACT
Richard Madden
Director, Corporate Communications
ITT Hartford Insurance Group
Hartford Plz.
690 Asylum Ave.
Hartford, CT 06115
(203) 547-5818

FINANCIAL SUMMARY

Recent Giving: $2,800,000 (1995 est.); $2,600,000 (1994 approx.); $2,215,540 (1993)

Assets: $76,033 (1993); $176,805 (1992); $125,862 (1991)

Gifts Received: $2,100,000 (1993); $2,421,855 (1992)

Fiscal Note: Figures include foundation and direct contributions. Above figures exclude nonmonetary support. In 1993, contributions were received from Hartford Fire Insurance Co.

EIN: 06-6079761

CONTRIBUTIONS SUMMARY

Typical Recipients: • *Arts & Humanities:* Arts Associations & Councils, Arts Centers, Arts Funds, Community Arts, Dance, Libraries, Literary Arts, Museums/Galleries, Music, Opera, Performing Arts, Public Broadcasting, Theater • *Civic & Public Affairs:* African American Affairs, Business/Free Enterprise, Civil Rights, Economic Development, Employment/Job Training, General, Hispanic Affairs, Housing, Law & Justice, Nonprofit Management, Professional & Trade Associations, Public Policy, Safety, Urban & Community Affairs, Women's Affairs • *Education:* Agricultural Education, Business Education, Colleges & Universities, Community & Junior Colleges, Education Funds, Health & Physical Education, International Studies, Journalism/Media Education, Legal Education, Literacy, Medical Education, Minority Education, Private Education (Precollege), Public Education (Precollege), Religious Education, Science/Mathematics Education, Special Education, Student Aid • *Environment:* General • *Health:* Children's Health/Hospitals, Clinics/Medical Centers, Geriatric Health, Health Policy/Cost Containment, Health Organizations, Hospices, Hospitals, Medical Rehabilitation, Medical Research, Prenatal Health Issues, Public Health • *Religion:* Religious Welfare • *Social Services:* Camps, Child Welfare, Community Service Organizations, Day Care, Delinquency & Criminal Rehabilitation, Domestic Violence, Emergency Relief, Food/Clothing Distribution, General, Homes, People with Disabilities, Recreation & Athletics, Senior Services, Shelters/Homelessness, Substance Abuse, United Funds/United Ways, Youth Organizations

Grant Types: capital, challenge, employee matching gifts, endowment, general support, project, research, and scholarship

Nonmonetary Support: $400,000 (1990); $600,000 (1989); $3,000,000 (1987)

Nonmonetary Support Types: donated equipment, in-kind services, and loaned executives

Geographic Distribution: mainly in Hartford, CT; company also considers requests from organizations in the 42 office communities in which it operates

Operating Locations: AZ (Phoenix), CA (Brea, Diamond Bar, Sacramento, San Francisco), CO (Denver), CT (Bridgeport, East Hartford, Hartford, Southington), DC, FL (Maitland), GA (Atlanta), IL (Bolingbrook, Chicago), IN (Indianapolis), KS (Overland Park), LA (Metairie), MA (Cambridge), MD (Hunt Valley), MI (Grand Rapids, Troy), MN (Bloomington, Minneapolis), MO (St. Louis), NC (Charlotte), NE (Omaha), NH (Manchester), NJ (Rockaway Township, Secaucus, Vogrhes), NV (Reno), NY (Albany, Hauptaute, New Hartford, New York, Syracuse, West Amherst), OH (Cincinnati, Independence), OK (Oklahoma City), PA (Lancaster, Pittsburgh), TX (Dallas, Houston, San Antonio), VA (Richmond), WA (Seattle)

Note: Also operates in Canada and Western Europe.

CORP. OFFICERS

Ramani Ayer: *B* India 1947 *CURR EMPL* pres, coo: ITT Hartford Ins Group

Donald Robert Frahm: *CURR EMPL* chmn, ceo, dir: ITT Hartford Ins Group

GIVING OFFICERS

Christine L. Charter: asst treas

Donald Robert Frahm: pres, dir *CURR EMPL* chmn, ceo, dir: ITT Hartford Ins Group (see above)

Joseph H. Gareau: dir *CORP AFFIL* exec vp, dir: Hartford Casualty Ins Co; sr vp: Hartford Accident Indemnity Co; sr vp, chief investment off, dir: Hartford Ins Midwest

J. Richard Garrett: treas *CURR EMPL* treas: ITT Hartford Ins Group

Edward L. Morgan: sr vp, dir *CURR EMPL* vp, dir corp rels: ITT Hartford Ins Group

Michael S. O'Halloran: secy

Michel S. Wilder: vp, dir *CURR EMPL* mem contributions comm: ITT Hartford Ins Group

APPLICATION INFORMATION

Initial Approach: *Initial Contact:* organizations in Hartford should send a brief two-page letter requesting application form to headquarters; organizations near the company's regional offices should send requests to the local general manager for consideration, who may forward it to Hartford depending on the size of the grant requested *Include Information On:* brief description of the organization and project, including legal name, history, activities, and constituency served; summary of project for which funds are sought, including verification of need; goals and means for accomplishing them, including how many people will be affected; other organizations providing similar programs (if any) and how they differ; budget for organization and project; amount re-

quested; actual and potential sources and amounts of funding; proof of tax-exempt and non-private foundation status; list of officers, directors, executive director, and other key people *Deadlines:* none

Restrictions on Giving: Excluded from consideration are political parties or candidates, political or lobbying groups, endowments, single disease health associations, public and state-supported educational institutions, individuals, trips and parades, sectarian programs, fraternal organizations, conferences and seminars, courtesy advertising, memberships in professional or trade associations, or fund-raising dinners.

Capital support generally limited to agencies in Greater Hartford. Organizations accepted for a capital grant may not also receive operating support in the same year.

Funding is generally not provided to agencies that receive United Way funding. Special programs can be an exception, but the agency must have the permission of the United Way before it solicits funding.

OTHER THINGS TO KNOW

Directors have a limited role in administering the foundation program.

Generally seeks to support organizations that enable individuals to help themselves and that are supported by creative and ultimately self-supporting funding initiatives.

Where possible, the Hartford will try to leverage its funds through matching and challenge grants and consider awarding multiple-year grants if appropriate and where desirable.

GRANTS ANALYSIS

Total Grants: $1,934,495*

Number of Grants: 441*

Highest Grant: $520,000

Average Grant: $4,387*

Typical Range: $500 to $20,000

Disclosure Period: 1993

Note: Above figures exclude $281,045 in matching gifts. Recent grants are derived from a 1993 Form 990.

RECENT GRANTS

Library

25,000	Wadsworth Atheneum, Hartford, CT

General

520,000	United Way/Combined Health Appeal, Hartford, CT
219,637	United Way of the Regional Offices, Hartford, CT
96,000	Urban League of Greater Hartford, Hartford, CT
65,000	Newington Children's Hospital, Hartford, CT
65,000	St. Francis Hospital, New York, NY

Kohn-Joseloff Foundation

Former Foundation Name: Morris Joseloff
Foundation

CONTACT
Bernhard L. Kohn, Sr.
President
Kohn-Joseloff Fdn.
125 La Salle Rd., Rm. 200
West Hartford, CT 06107
(203) 521-7010

FINANCIAL SUMMARY

Recent Giving: $410,755 (1993); $489,150
(1992); $673,850 (1991)

Assets: $10,104,743 (1993); $9,909,508
(1992); $10,147,199 (1991)

EIN: 13-6062846

CONTRIBUTIONS SUMMARY

Donor(s): the late Lillian L. Joseloff, Morris Joseloff Foundation Trust

Typical Recipients: • *Arts & Humanities:*
Arts Associations & Councils, History & Archaeology, Libraries, Literary Arts, Museums/Galleries, Music, Opera, Performing
Arts, Public Broadcasting, Theater • *Civic &
Public Affairs:* Botanical Gardens/Parks,
Clubs, General, Native American Affairs,
Women's Affairs • *Education:* Colleges &
Universities, Minority Education, Private
Education (Precollege), Public Education
(Precollege), Special Education • *Environment:* General • *Health:* Cancer, Children's
Health/Hospitals, Emergency/Ambulance
Services, Hospitals, Medical Research, Nursing Services, Single-Disease Health Associations • *Religion:* Jewish Causes, Religious
Organizations, Religious Welfare • *Social
Services:* Camps, Community Service Organizations, Family Services, People with
Disabilities, Scouts, Senior Services, United
Funds/United Ways, Youth Organizations

Grant Types: general support

Geographic Distribution: focus on CT

GIVING OFFICERS
Bernhard L. Kohn, Jr.: vp, dir
Bernhard L. Kohn, Sr.: pres, dir
Joan J. Kohn: secy, treas, dir
Kathryn K. Rieger: vp, dir

APPLICATION INFORMATION

Initial Approach: The foundation has no
formal grant application procedure or application form. There are no deadlines.

Restrictions on Giving: Does not support
individuals.

GRANTS ANALYSIS
Total Grants: $410,755
Number of Grants: 65
Highest Grant: $135,000

Typical Range: $100 to $1,000
Disclosure Period: 1993
Note: Recent grants are derived from a 1993
Form 990.

RECENT GRANTS

Library

52,250	Wadsworth Athaeneum, Hartford, CT

General

135,000	Jewish Federation of Greater Hartford, Hartford, CT
63,000	University of Hartford Art School, Hartford, CT
20,200	Greater Hartford Easter Seal Rehabilitation Center, Hartford, CT
15,000	Women's League, Hartford, CT
11,250	Loomis Chaffee School, Hartford, CT

Koopman Fund

CONTACT
Georgette Koopman
President
Koopman Fund
17 Brookside Blvd.
West Hartford, CT 06107
(203) 232-6406

FINANCIAL SUMMARY

Recent Giving: $465,152 (1993); $392,766
(1992); $351,113 (1991)

Assets: $8,767,281 (1993); $8,103,323
(1992); $7,790,153 (1991)

EIN: 06-6050431

CONTRIBUTIONS SUMMARY

Donor(s): the late Richard Koopman, Georgette Koopman

Typical Recipients: • *Arts & Humanities:*
Community Arts, Dance, Historic Preservation, History & Archaeology, Libraries, Museums/Galleries, Music, Public
Broadcasting, Theater • *Civic & Public Affairs:* Civil Rights, Economic Development,
General, Hispanic Affairs, Housing, Nonprofit Management, Philanthropic Organizations, Safety, Urban & Community Affairs,
Women's Affairs, Zoos/Aquariums • *Education:* Agricultural Education, Colleges &
Universities, Engineering/Technological
Education, Private Education (Precollege),
Special Education, Student Aid • *Health:*
AIDS/HIV, Clinics/Medical Centers, Emergency/Ambulance Services, Health Organizations, Hospices, Hospitals, Medical
Rehabilitation, Medical Research, Nursing
Services, Single-Disease Health Associations • *International:* International Affairs,
International Peace & Security Issues, International Relations • *Religion:* Jewish
Causes, Religious Organizations, Religious
Welfare, Synagogues/Temples • *Science:*

Scientific Centers & Institutes, Scientific Organizations • *Social Services:* Child Welfare, Community Service Organizations,
Crime Prevention, Emergency Relief, Family Planning, Family Services, Food/Clothing Distribution, Homes, People with
Disabilities, United Funds/United Ways,
YMCA/YWCA/YMHA/YWHA, Youth Organizations

Grant Types: capital, emergency, endowment, general support, multiyear/continuing
support, and scholarship

Geographic Distribution: focus on CT

GIVING OFFICERS

Beatrice Koopman: trust

Dorothy B. Koopman: trust

Georgette A. Koopman: pres, trust *PHIL
AFFIL* pres, trust: Beatrice Fox Auerbach
Foundation; trust: Schiro Fund

Rena Koopman: secy, trust *PHIL AFFIL*
trust: Beatrice Fox Auerbach Foundation

Richard Koopman, Jr.: trust

Dorothy A. Schiro: asst secy, trust *PHIL
AFFIL* vp, treas, trust: Beatrice Fox Auerbach Foundation; secy, treas, trust: Schiro
Fund

APPLICATION INFORMATION

Initial Approach: The foundation has no
formal grant application procedure or application form. There are no deadlines.

GRANTS ANALYSIS
Total Grants: $465,152
Number of Grants: 180
Highest Grant: $100,000
Typical Range: $100 to $75,000
Disclosure Period: 1993
Note: Recent grants are derived from a 1993
Form 990.

RECENT GRANTS

Library

5,000	Hartford Public Library, Hartford, CT
5,000	Wadsworth Athaeneum, Hartford, CT
1,470	Wadsworth Athaeneum, Hartford, CT

General

100,000	Hartford Foundation for Public Giving, Hartford, CT — advise fund
75,100	Jewish Federation of Hartford, West Hartford, CT — endowment fund
52,500	Hartford College for Women, Hartford, CT — capital campaign
50,000	Temple Beth Israel, West Hartford, CT
25,000	Jewish Federation of Hartford, West Hartford, CT

Kreitler Foundation

CONTACT
Hobart C. Kreitler
President
Kreitler Foundation
2960 Post Rd.
Southport, CT 06490-1242
(203) 259-8585

FINANCIAL SUMMARY

Recent Giving: $121,925 (1993); $120,525 (1992); $50,160 (1991)

Assets: $3,472,013 (1993); $3,125,400 (1992); $3,048,889 (1991)

Gifts Received: $3,138,293 (1991)

Fiscal Note: In 1991, contributions were received from Hobart C. and Sally S. Kreitler.

EIN: 06-1311676

CONTRIBUTIONS SUMMARY

Typical Recipients: • *Arts & Humanities:* General, History & Archaeology, Libraries, Museums/Galleries, Performing Arts • *Civic & Public Affairs:* Community Foundations, General, Public Policy, Rural Affairs, Urban & Community Affairs, Women's Affairs • *Education:* Afterschool/Enrichment Programs, Arts/Humanities Education, Business Education, Colleges & Universities, Community & Junior Colleges, Education Funds, General, Student Aid • *Environment:* General • *Health:* Diabetes, Home-Care Services, Hospitals, Medical Rehabilitation, Prenatal Health Issues • *International:* Health Care/Hospitals, International Relief Efforts • *Religion:* Churches, Ministries, Religious Organizations, Religious Welfare • *Science:* Science Museums • *Social Services:* Child Welfare, Community Centers, Community Service Organizations, Crime Prevention, Family Services, Food/Clothing Distribution, People with Disabilities, Recreation & Athletics, Senior Services, Shelters/Homelessness, United Funds/United Ways, YMCA/YWCA/YMHA/YWHA, Youth Organizations

Grant Types: general support

Geographic Distribution: focus on CT

GIVING OFFICERS
Katherine K. Hodge: treas
Hobart C. Kreitler: pres
James S. Kreitler: dir
John M. Kreitler: dir
Karen R. Kreitler: dir
Sally S. Kreitler: secy
Thomas Kreitler: vp

APPLICATION INFORMATION

Initial Approach: Send a brief letter of inquiry. Include a description of organization, amount requested, purpose of funds sought, recently audited financial statement, and proof of tax-exempt status. There are no deadlines.

GRANTS ANALYSIS
Total Grants: $121,925
Number of Grants: 57
Highest Grant: $12,442
Typical Range: $25 to $12,000
Disclosure Period: 1993

Note: Recent grants are derived from a 1993 Form 990.

RECENT GRANTS
General

12,442	First Church Congregational
12,442	First Church Congregational
12,000	Connecticut Scholars Program, Hartford, CT
12,000	Connecticut Scholars Program, CT
10,000	Family and Children's Aid, Bridgeport, CT

Larsen Fund

CONTACT
Patricia S. Palmer
Grants Administrator
Larsen Fund
2960 Post Rd.
Southport, CT 06490
(201) 255-5318

FINANCIAL SUMMARY

Recent Giving: $456,347 (1993); $384,884 (1990); $378,334 (1989)

Assets: $8,692,578 (1993); $7,092,524 (1990); $7,578,928 (1989)

EIN: 13-6104430

CONTRIBUTIONS SUMMARY

Donor(s): the late Roy E. Larsen

Typical Recipients: • *Arts & Humanities:* Arts Institutes, History & Archaeology, Libraries, Museums/Galleries, Music, Performing Arts, Theater • *Civic & Public Affairs:* General, Professional & Trade Associations • *Education:* Colleges & Universities, General, Journalism/Media Education, Minority Education, Private Education (Precollege), Science/Mathematics Education, Secondary Education (Public) • *Environment:* Air/Water Quality, General, Resource Conservation, Wildlife Protection • *Health:* Health Organizations, Hospitals, Outpatient Health Care, Single-Disease Health Associations • *International:* International Affairs • *Religion:* Churches • *Science:* Science Museums, Scientific Centers & Institutes • *Social Services:* Child Welfare, Community Service Organizations, Family Planning, Youth Organizations

Grant Types: capital, conference/seminar, endowment, fellowship, general support, project, research, and scholarship

Geographic Distribution: focus on the New York, NY, area; Minneapolis, MN, area; and CT

GIVING OFFICERS

David L. Johnson: treas

Christopher Larsen: vp, dir

Jonathan Zerbe Larsen: secy, dir B New York NY 1940 *ED* Harvard Univ BA 1961; Harvard Univ MAT 1963 *CURR EMPL* editor in chief: Village Voice *NONPR AFFIL* trust: Cambridge Coll, Natural Resources Defense Counc

Robert R. Larsen: pres, dir

Patricia S. Palmer: grants admin

Anne Larsen Simonson: vp, dir

APPLICATION INFORMATION

Initial Approach: Send brief letter of inquiry describing program or project. There are no deadlines.

Restrictions on Giving: Does not support individuals.

PUBLICATIONS
Annual Report (including application guidelines)

GRANTS ANALYSIS
Total Grants: $456,347
Number of Grants: 61
Highest Grant: $55,000
Typical Range: $500 to $26,000
Disclosure Period: 1993

Note: Recent grants are derived from a 1993 Form 990.

RECENT GRANTS
Library

7,000	New York Public Library, New York, NY — for charitable purposes
6,000	Wadsworth Atheneum, Hartford, CT — for charitable purposes

General

55,000	Sarah Lawrence School — for educational purposes
41,000	Cambridge Trust Company, Cambridge, MA — for educational purposes
26,000	Nantucket Cottage Hospital, Nantucket, MA — for medical purposes
25,000	Natural Resources Defense Council, New York, NY — for charitable purposes
25,000	Sisconset Union Chapel, Sisconset, CT — for religious purposes

Lydall, Inc.

Revenue: $157.4 million
Employees: 944
Headquarters: Manchester, CT
SIC Major Group: Chemicals & Allied
 Products, Paper & Allied Products, Textile
 Mill Products, and Transportation Equipment

CONTACT
Margaret R. Murphy
Assistant Manager, Operations
Lydall, Inc.
PO Box 151
Manchester, CT 06045-0151
(203) 646-1233

FINANCIAL SUMMARY
Recent Giving: $135,000 (1993)

Fiscal Note: Annual Giving Range: less
than $100,000

CONTRIBUTIONS SUMMARY
Typical Recipients: • *Arts & Humanities:*
Arts Associations & Councils, Arts Centers,
Arts Funds, Arts Institutes, Ballet, Commu-
nity Arts, General, Historic Preservation, Li-
braries, Literary Arts, Museums/Galleries,
Music, Opera, Performing Arts, Public
Broadcasting, Theater • *Civic & Public Af-
fairs:* Chambers of Commerce, Economic
Development, General, Housing, Nonprofit
Management, Philanthropic Organizations,
Urban & Community Affairs • *Education:*
Business Education, Business-School Part-
nerships, Colleges & Universities, Commu-
nity & Junior Colleges, Continuing
Education, Economic Education, General,
Literacy • *Environment:* Air/Water Quality,
Resource Conservation • *Health:* Alzhe-
imers Disease, Arthritis, Cancer, Children's
Health/Hospitals, Eyes/Blindness, General,
Health Policy/Cost Containment, Health Or-
ganizations, Heart, Hospices, Hospitals,
Medical Rehabilitation, Medical Research,
Mental Health, Multiple Sclerosis, Nursing
Services, Nutrition, Public Health, Single-
Disease Health Associations • *Social Serv-
ices:* Child Welfare, Community Centers,
Community Service Organizations, Counsel-
ing, Domestic Violence, Emergency Relief,
Family Services, Food/Clothing Distribu-
tion, General, Homes, People with Disabili-
ties, Shelters/Homelessness, Substance
Abuse, United Funds/United Ways, Youth
Organizations

Grant Types: capital, emergency, employee
matching gifts, general support, multi-
year/continuing support, operating expenses,
project, research, and scholarship

Nonmonetary Support Types: donated
equipment, loaned employees, and loaned executives

Geographic Distribution: headquarters and
operating locations

Operating Locations: CT (Manchester),
NC (Hamptonville), NH (Rochester), NY
(Green Island, Hoosick Falls), VA (Rich-
mond)

CORP. OFFICERS
Leonard R. Jaskol: *B* New Rochelle NY
1937 *ED* Am Univ 1958; City Univ NY
1969 *CURR EMPL* chmn, pres, ceo, dir: Lydall

APPLICATION INFORMATION
Initial Approach: Send a brief letter of request. Include a description of organization,
amount requested, purpose of funds sought,
recently audited financial statement, and
proof of tax-exempt status. Deadline is Sep-
tember/October for the following year.

Restrictions on Giving: Does not support
individuals, religious organizations for sectarian purposes, or political or lobbying
groups.

GRANTS ANALYSIS
Typical Range: $500 to $1,000

MacCurdy Salisbury Educational Foundation

CONTACT
Ward Bing
Secretary and Treasurer
MacCurdy Salisbury Educational Fdn.
Nine Mansewood Rd.
Old Lyme, CT 06371
(203) 434-2647

FINANCIAL SUMMARY
Recent Giving: $122,735 (fiscal 1993);
$117,172 (fiscal 1992); $133,467 (fiscal
1990)

Assets: $3,355,435 (fiscal 1993);
$3,179,386 (fiscal 1991); $3,001,909 (fiscal
1990)

EIN: 06-6044250

CONTRIBUTIONS SUMMARY
Typical Recipients: • *Arts & Humanities:*
Community Arts, Libraries, Museums/Gal-
leries, Music • *Civic & Public Affairs:* Mu-
nicipalities/Towns • *Education:* Private
Education (Precollege) • *Social Services:*
Child Welfare, Community Service Organi-
zations, Youth Organizations

Grant Types: general support and scholarship

Operating Locations: CT (Old Lyme)

GIVING OFFICERS
Ward Bing: secy, treas

APPLICATION INFORMATION
Initial Approach: Application form available. Deadlines are April 30 and November
15.

Restrictions on Giving: Restricted to residents of Lyme and Old Lyme, CT.

GRANTS ANALYSIS
Total Grants: $122,735

Typical Range: $2,500 to $5,000

Disclosure Period: fiscal year ending May
31, 1993

Note: Recent grants are derived from a fiscal 1992 Form 990.

RECENT GRANTS
General
5,000	Lyme Academy, Lyme, CT
2,500	Lyme/Old Lyme School, Lyme, CT

Matthies Foundation, Katharine

CONTACT
Art Stone
Trustee
Katharine Matthies Fdn.
PO Box 0046
Waterbury, CT 06721
(203) 597-6631

FINANCIAL SUMMARY
Recent Giving: $583,065 (1993)

Assets: $11,543,158 (1993)

EIN: 06-6261860

CONTRIBUTIONS SUMMARY
Typical Recipients: • *Arts & Humanities:*
History & Archaeology, Libraries, Music •
Civic & Public Affairs: General, Urban &
Community Affairs • *Education:* Faculty De-
velopment, General, Literacy • *Environ-
ment:* Resource Conservation, Wildlife
Protection • *Health:* Emergency/Ambulance
Services, Health Organizations, Hospitals
• *International:* Missionary/Religious Activi-
ties • *Religion:* Religious Organizations, Re-
ligious Welfare • *Social Services:* Child
Welfare, Crime Prevention, People with Dis-
abilities, Recreation & Athletics, Substance
Abuse, United Funds/United Ways,
YMCA/YWCA/YMHA/YWHA, Youth Organizations

Grant Types: general support

Geographic Distribution: focus on CT

GIVING OFFICERS
Shawmut Bank: trust

APPLICATION INFORMATION
Initial Approach: The foundation has no
formal grant application procedure or application form.

GRANTS ANALYSIS
Total Grants: $583,065

Number of Grants: 44

Highest Grant: $70,000

Typical Range: $1,000 to $31,430

Disclosure Period: 1993

Note: Recent grants are derived from a 1993
Form 1990.

RECENT GRANTS
Library
70,000	Seymour Public Library
25,000	Derby Public Library, Derby, CT
18,200	Friends of Ansonia Library — building

General

31,430	Valley YMCA — locker room renovation	
25,000	Castles in Seymour	
25,000	Valley Instructor Network	
20,000	Area Co-Operative Education	
20,000	Valley Emergency Medical Service	

Moore Charitable Foundation, Marjorie

CONTACT
Maria Delsesto
Marjorie Moore Charitable Fdn.
c/o Connecticut National Bank
1 Exchange Pl.
Waterbury, CT 06751
(203) 597-6631

FINANCIAL SUMMARY
Recent Giving: $133,222 (fiscal 1993); $94,596 (fiscal 1992); $40,962 (fiscal 1991)

Assets: $2,364,725 (fiscal 1993); $2,365,676 (fiscal 1992); $2,192,650 (fiscal 1991)

EIN: 06-6050196

CONTRIBUTIONS SUMMARY
Donor(s): the late Marjorie Moore

Typical Recipients: • *Arts & Humanities:* Arts Associations & Councils, History & Archaeology, Libraries, Museums/Galleries • *Civic & Public Affairs:* Chambers of Commerce, General, Law & Justice, Municipalities/Towns, Safety • *Education:* Literacy, Private Education (Precollege) • *Health:* AIDS/HIV, Emergency/Ambulance Services, Health Organizations, Hospices, Hospitals, Medical Research, Mental Health, Nursing Services, Single-Disease Health Associations • *Religion:* Churches • *Social Services:* Child Welfare, Community Centers, Community Service Organizations, Delinquency & Criminal Rehabilitation, People with Disabilities, Recreation & Athletics, Senior Services, United Funds/United Ways, Youth Organizations

Grant Types: capital, endowment, multi-year/continuing support, operating expenses, project, and seed money

Geographic Distribution: limited to Kensington, CT

GIVING OFFICERS
Connecticut National Bank: trust

APPLICATION INFORMATION
Initial Approach: The foundation has no formal grant application procedure or application form. There are no deadlines.

Restrictions on Giving: Limited to charities that will benefit Kensington, CT, residents.

GRANTS ANALYSIS
Total Grants: $133,222

Number of Grants: 11

Highest Grant: $46,222

Typical Range: $1,500 to $20,000

Disclosure Period: fiscal year ending July 31, 1993

Note: Recent grants are derived from a fiscal 1993 Form 990.

RECENT GRANTS

Library

14,500	Berlin Peck Memorial Library, Berlin, CT	

General

46,222	South Kensington Fire Department, South Kensington, CT	
25,500	Kensington United Methodist Church, Kensington, CT	
6,000	Griswold School Playground, Griswold, CT	
5,000	Connecticut Community Care, Hartford, CT	
4,000	Berlin Children's Fund, Berlin, CT	

Moore Foundation, Edward S.

CONTACT
John W. Cross III
President
Edward S. Moore Foundation
47 Arch St.
Greenwich, CT 06830
(203) 629-4591
Note: Another contact for the foundation is Donald Vail, secretary, who is an attorney at Walter, Conston, Alexander and Green, 90 Park Avenue, New York, NY, 10016 at (212) 210-9400.

FINANCIAL SUMMARY
Recent Giving: $1,465,556 (1992); $1,388,270 (1991); $1,213,170 (1990)

Assets: $28,524,001 (1992); $30,939,656 (1991); $26,331,420 (1990)

EIN: 13-6127365

CONTRIBUTIONS SUMMARY
Donor(s): The foundation was established in 1957, and donors include Edward S. Moore, Jr. and Evelyn N. Moore, both deceased, and Carolyn N. Moore.

Typical Recipients: • *Arts & Humanities:* Historic Preservation, History & Archaeology, Libraries, Museums/Galleries, Music, Opera, Public Broadcasting • *Civic & Public Affairs:* Philanthropic Organizations • *Education:* Business Education, Colleges & Universities, Economic Education, Elementary Education (Private), Elementary Education (Public), Medical Education, Private Education (Precollege), Religious Education • *Environment:* Air/Water Quality, General • *Health:* Health Organizations, Hospitals, Medical Research, Mental Health • *Religion:* Churches, Religious Welfare • *Science:* Scientific Centers & Institutes • *Social Services:* Camps, Child Welfare, Community Centers, Community Service Organizations, Family Services, General, People with Disabilities, Recreation & Athletics, Shelters/Homelessness, Youth Organizations

Grant Types: general support

Geographic Distribution: focus on New York and Connecticut

GIVING OFFICERS
John W. Cross III: pres, dir

Louisa Gilbert: dir

Marion Moore Gilbert: vp, dir

Alexander Jackson: treas, asst secy, dir

Donald Vail: secy, dir *B* Yonkers NY 1921 *ED* Princeton Univ AB 1942; Harvard Univ Law Sch JD 1948 *CURR EMPL* atty: Walter Conston Alexander & Green PC

Lois Cross Willis: dir

APPLICATION INFORMATION
Initial Approach:

Applicants should send a preliminary letter.

Grant proposals should include a description of the project, the approximate budget, a list of other funding sources, a copy of the organization's balance sheet, an income statement, and a copy of the IRS tax-exempt certification letter.

There are no deadlines for submitting proposals.

The board meets quarterly in January, April, July, and October. Final notification usually takes three to six months.

Restrictions on Giving: No grants are made to individuals.

PUBLICATIONS
Annual report

GRANTS ANALYSIS
Total Grants: $1,465,556

Number of Grants: 92

Highest Grant: $200,000

Average Grant: $15,930*

Typical Range: $10,000 to $25,000

Disclosure Period: 1992

Note: Recent grants are derived from a 1992 Form 990.

RECENT GRANTS

Library

10,000	Darien Library, Darien, CT	
10,000	Greenwich Library, Greenwich, CT	
10,000	New York Public Library, New York, NY	

General

40,000	Children's Aid Society, New York, NY	
30,000	Belle Baruch Institute for Marine Biology, Columbia, SC	
30,000	Clear Pool Camp, Carmel, NY	
30,000	Fresh Air Fund, New York, NY	
30,000	Greenwich Hospital Association, Greenwich, CT	

Mosbacher, Jr. Foundation, Emil

CONTACT
Emil Mosbacher, Jr.
President
Emil Mosbacher, Jr. Fdn.
The Meridian Bldg.
170 Mason St.
Greenwich, CT 06830
(203) 869-4100

FINANCIAL SUMMARY
Recent Giving: $78,900 (fiscal 1993); $55,883 (fiscal 1992); $95,957 (fiscal 1991)

Assets: $3,537,876 (fiscal 1993); $3,358,200 (fiscal 1992); $3,028,750 (fiscal 1991)

EIN: 23-7454106

CONTRIBUTIONS SUMMARY
Donor(s): Emil Mosbacher, Jr., Emil Mosbacher III, John D. Mosbacher, R. Bruce Mosbacher

Typical Recipients: • *Arts & Humanities:* History & Archaeology, Libraries, Museums/Galleries, Public Broadcasting • *Civic & Public Affairs:* Botanical Gardens/Parks, Civil Rights, General, Hispanic Affairs • *Education:* Colleges & Universities, Legal Education, Medical Education, Private Education (Precollege) • *Health:* Cancer, Children's Health/Hospitals, Clinics/Medical Centers, Health Organizations, Hospices, Hospitals, Medical Rehabilitation, Medical Research, Single-Disease Health Associations • *International:* Foreign Educational Institutions, Health Care/Hospitals, International Organizations, International Peace & Security Issues • *Religion:* Churches, Religious Welfare • *Social Services:* Animal Protection, Community Service Organizations, Family Services, People with Disabilities, Scouts, Substance Abuse, United Funds/United Ways, YMCA/YWCA/YMHA/YWHA, Youth Organizations

Grant Types: general support

Geographic Distribution: focus on NY and CT

GIVING OFFICERS
Emil Mosbacher, Jr.: pres, dir *B* White Plains NY 1922 *ED* Dartmouth Coll BA 1943 *CORP AFFIL* dir: Amax Gold, Avon Products, Chemical Bank, Chubb Corp, Fed Ins Co, Vigilant Ins Co *NONPR AFFIL* mem: Independent Petroleum Assn Am, Pilgrims US, US Seniors Golf Assn, US Yacht Racing Assn; mem bd overseers: Hoover Inst; trust: Lenox Hill Hosp *PHIL AFFIL* trust: Arnold D. Frese Foundation

Patricia Mosbacher: vp

R. Bruce Mosbacher: vp, secy, treas, trust

APPLICATION INFORMATION
Initial Approach: Send brief letter describing program. Include a description of organization, amount requested, purpose of funds sought, recently audited financial statement, and proof of tax-exempt status. There are no deadlines.

Restrictions on Giving: Does not support individuals.

GRANTS ANALYSIS
Total Grants: $78,900

Number of Grants: 35

Highest Grant: $5,000

Typical Range: $100 to $1,000

Disclosure Period: fiscal year ending November 30, 1993

Note: Recent grants are derived from a fiscal 1993 Form 990.

RECENT GRANTS

General

5,000	Barry University, Miami Shores, FL
5,000	Dartmouth College, Hanover, NH
5,000	New York Medical College, Valhalla, NY
3,500	Hospital for Special Surgery, New York, NY
3,000	United Way, New York, NY

Newman's Own, Inc. / Newman's Own Foundation

Sales: $28.0 million
Employees: 11
Headquarters: Westport, CT
SIC Major Group: Groceries & Related Products Nec

CONTACT
Aaron E. Hotchner
Vice President
Newman's Own Foundation
246 Post Rd. E
Westport, CT 06880-3615
(203) 222-0136

FINANCIAL SUMMARY
Recent Giving: $361,600 (fiscal 1994); $324,500 (fiscal 1993); $461,900 (fiscal 1992)

Assets: $24,108 (fiscal 1994); $46,857 (fiscal 1993); $27,670 (fiscal 1992)

Gifts Received: $334,865 (fiscal 1994); $331,886 (fiscal 1993); $487,799 (fiscal 1992)

Fiscal Note: Contributes through foundation only. In 1992, contributions were received from Mauri Foods ($302,799), Paul L. Newman ($164,000), and from Wyandot Popcorn Museum ($21,000).

EIN: 06-1247230

CONTRIBUTIONS SUMMARY
Typical Recipients: • *Arts & Humanities:* Community Arts, Libraries, Museums/Galleries, Public Broadcasting, Theater • *Civic & Public Affairs:* Housing, Public Policy • *Education:* Literacy, Public Education (Precollege) • *Environment:* General • *Health:* Health Funds, Hospitals, Single-Disease Health Associations • *International:* Foreign Educational Institutions, Health Care/Hospitals, International Organizations, International Peace & Security Issues, International Relations, International Relief Efforts, Missionary/Religious Activities • *Religion:* Religious Welfare • *Social Services:* Child Welfare, Community Centers, Community Service Organizations, Delinquency & Criminal Rehabilitation, Domestic Violence, Family Services, Food/Clothing Distribution, Homes, People with Disabilities, Shelters/Homelessness, Youth Organizations

Grant Types: general support

Operating Locations: CT (Westport)

CORP. OFFICERS
Aaron Edward Hotchner: *B* St Louis MO 1920 *ED* WA Univ AB 1941; WA Univ LLB *CURR EMPL* vp, treas: Newmans Own Inc *NONPR AFFIL* mem: Dramatists Guild, MO Bar Assn, Writers Guild Am; vp: Hole Wall Gang Camp *CLUB AFFIL* Century

Paul L. Newman: *B* Cleveland OH 1925 *ED* Kenyon Coll BA 1949; Yale Univ Sch Drama 1951; Yale Univ LHD 1988 *CURR EMPL* pres: Newmans Own Inc *NONPR AFFIL* pres, dir: Hole Wall Gang Fund

GIVING OFFICERS
Jamie K. Gerard: secy

Aaron Edward Hotchner: vp, dir *CURR EMPL* vp, treas: Newmans Own Inc (see above)

Paul L. Newman: pres, dir, don *CURR EMPL* pres: Newmans Own Inc (see above)

Joanne Gignilliat Woodward: dir *B* Thomasville GA 1930 *ED* LA St Univ 1947-1949; Neighborhood Playhouse Dramatic Sch

APPLICATION INFORMATION
Initial Approach: *Initial Contact:* detailed written proposal *Include Information On:* commitment to charitable or educational purposes; detailed description of the activities normally carried on and conducted; a description of typical activities; detailed proposal setting forth the specific amount requested and the specific purpose; details on how grant will be administered and under whose supervision; publications, brochures, or soliciting materials concerning the activities of organization; proof of charitable and tax-exempt status; most recent audited financial statements; list and description of board of directors; and any annual reports issued during last three years *Deadlines:* none

Restrictions on Giving: Funds may not be used for propaganda purposes or to attempt to influence legislation.

OTHER THINGS TO KNOW
Foundation requires regular reports of the progress of the project for which funds are granted.

PUBLICATIONS
Guidelines sheet

GRANTS ANALYSIS
Total Grants: $361,600

Number of Grants: 31

Highest Grant: $74,000

Average Grant: $11,665

Typical Range: $5,000 to $25,000

Disclosure Period: fiscal year ending August 31, 1994

Note: Recent grants are derived from a fiscal 1994 Form 990.

RECENT GRANTS

General

74,000	Women's and Children's Hospital
40,000	Child Abuse Prevention Service, New South Wales, Australia
21,800	National Aunties and Uncles, Queensland, Australia
20,000	Royal Blind Society, New South Wales, Australia
16,800	Shepherd Centre for Deaf Children, South Wales, Australia

NewMil Bancorp / New Milford Savings Bank Foundation

Sales: $5.09 million
Employees: 122
Headquarters: New Milford, CT
SIC Major Group: Holding & Other Investment Offices

CONTACT
Anthony J. Nania
President
NewMil Bancorp
PO Box 600
New Milford, CT 06776-0600
(203) 354-4411

FINANCIAL SUMMARY
Recent Giving: $27,021 (1994); $19,929 (1993); $9,697 (1992)

Assets: $775,478 (1993); $753,437 (1992); $663,050 (1991)

Gifts Received: $145,000 (1989)

EIN: 06-1140115

CONTRIBUTIONS SUMMARY
Typical Recipients: • *Arts & Humanities:* Arts Associations & Councils, Historic Preservation, History & Archaeology, Libraries, Music, Performing Arts • *Civic & Public Affairs:* Chambers of Commerce, Clubs, Economic Development, General, Housing, Parades/Festivals, Safety, Urban & Community Affairs, Women's Affairs • *Education:* Arts/Humanities Education, Private Education (Precollege), Public Education (Precollege), Secondary Education (Public), Student Aid • *Environment:* General • *Health:* Emergency/Ambulance Services, Health Funds, Home-Care Services, Hospices, Hospitals, Mental Health • *Religion:* Churches, Jewish Causes, Religious Welfare • *Social Services:* Child Welfare, Community Centers, Community Service Organizations, Day Care, Food/Clothing Distribution, Recreation & Athletics, Senior Services,

Shelters/Homelessness, United Funds/United Ways, Youth Organizations

Grant Types: general support

Geographic Distribution: giving limited to northwest CT

Operating Locations: CT (New Milford)

CORP. OFFICERS
Ian McMahon: *CURR EMPL* cfo, treas: NewMil Bancorp

Anthony J. Nania: *CURR EMPL* chmn, ceo: NewMil Bancorp

Francis J. Wiatr: *CURR EMPL* pres: NewMil Bancorp

GIVING OFFICERS
Willis H. Barton, Jr.: vp

Herbert E. Bullock: dir

Laurie G. Gonthier: dir

John V. Haxo, MD: dir

Ian McMahon: cfo, treas *CURR EMPL* cfo, treas: NewMil Bancorp (see above)

Anthony J. Nania: pres, dir *CURR EMPL* chmn, ceo: NewMil Bancorp (see above)

Betty F. Pacocha: secy

Suzanne L. Powers: dir

Mary C. Williams: dir

APPLICATION INFORMATION
Initial Approach: The foundation has no formal grant application procedure or application form. There are no deadlines.

GRANTS ANALYSIS
Total Grants: $19,929

Number of Grants: 96

Highest Grant: $1,500

Typical Range: $30 to $1,500

Disclosure Period: 1993

Note: Recent grants are derived from a 1993 Form 990.

RECENT GRANTS

Library

1,000	Kent Library Association, Kent, CT
125	Friends of Burnham Library
100	Hotchkiss Library of Sharon, Sharon, CT
100	Morris Public Library, Morris, CT

General

1,500	Canaan Fire Company, Canaan, NJ
1,500	North Canaan Elementary School Music Department, Canaan, CT
1,000	Children's Center of New Mexico, NM
1,000	Sharon Fire Department, Sharon, PA
663	A New England New Year, New Milford, CT

Oaklawn Foundation

CONTACT
Ann K. Arnold
President
Oaklawn Fdn.
280 Railroad Ave.
Greenwich, CT 06830
(203) 629-1911

FINANCIAL SUMMARY
Recent Giving: $460,260 (1993); $507,260 (1992); $345,660 (1991)

Assets: $11,374,759 (1993); $11,109,126 (1992); $11,427,917 (1991)

Gifts Received: $6,000 (1993); $21,500 (1992); $16,005 (1990)

Fiscal Note: In 1993, contributions were received from William S. Kies, III.

EIN: 13-6127896

CONTRIBUTIONS SUMMARY
Donor(s): the late Mabel B. Kies, the late W.S. Kies, Margaret K. Gibb

Typical Recipients: • *Arts & Humanities:* Community Arts, Libraries, Music, Opera, Public Broadcasting • *Civic & Public Affairs:* Public Policy, Zoos/Aquariums • *Education:* Colleges & Universities, Education Funds, Education Reform, Medical Education, Minority Education, Private Education (Precollege), Secondary Education (Private), Special Education • *Environment:* General • *Health:* Hospitals, Nursing Services • *Religion:* Churches • *Science:* Scientific Centers & Institutes • *Social Services:* Community Service Organizations, Family Services, People with Disabilities, Youth Organizations

Grant Types: endowment and scholarship

Geographic Distribution: focus on the Northeast

GIVING OFFICERS
Ann K. Arnold: pres, dir

Walter B. Levering: chmn, dir

John L. Montgomery: vp, dir

Audrey S. Paight: treas, asst secy, dir

APPLICATION INFORMATION
Initial Approach: Send a brief letter of inquiry. Include a description of organization, amount requested, purpose of funds sought, recently audited financial statement, and proof of tax-exempt status. There are no deadlines.

GRANTS ANALYSIS
Total Grants: $460,260

Number of Grants: 57

Highest Grant: $90,260

Typical Range: $1,000 to $10,000

Disclosure Period: 1993

Note: Recent grants are derived from a 1993 Form 990.

RECENT GRANTS

General

90,260	Hill School, Pottstown, PA

35,000	Brunswich Secondary School, Brunswich, CT
25,000	Greenwich Hospital, Greenwich, CT
20,000	Choate Rosemary Hall Secondary School, Wallingford, CT
20,000	Cumberland College, Williamsburg, KY

Olin Corp. / Olin Corporation Charitable Trust

Revenue: $2.65 billion
Employees: 12,400
Headquarters: Stamford, CT
SIC Major Group: Alkalies & Chlorine, Industrial Inorganic Chemicals Nec, Plastics Materials & Resins, and Cyclic Crudes & Intermediates

CONTACT
Carmella V. Piacentini
Administrator
Olin Corp. Charitable Trust
120 Long Ridge Rd.
Stamford, CT 06904
(203) 356-3301

FINANCIAL SUMMARY
Recent Giving: $2,000,000 (1995 est.); $2,000,000 (1994 approx.); $2,036,820 (1993)

Assets: $8,000,000 (1995); $10,000,000 (1994); $10,454,499 (1993)

Fiscal Note: Company gives primarily through the foundation. Direct giving, not included above, is generally around $10,000 to $25,000 annually. Above figures exclude nonmonetary support.

EIN: 43-6022750

CONTRIBUTIONS SUMMARY
Typical Recipients: • *Arts & Humanities:* Arts Associations & Councils, Arts Centers, Arts Institutes, Community Arts, Dance, Historic Preservation, Libraries, Museums/Galleries, Music, Opera, Performing Arts, Public Broadcasting, Theater, Visual Arts • *Civic & Public Affairs:* Business/Free Enterprise, Civil Rights, Public Policy • *Education:* Business Education, Colleges & Universities, Community & Junior Colleges, Engineering/Technological Education, Literacy, Minority Education, Private Education (Precollege), Public Education (Precollege), Science/Mathematics Education • *Environment:* General • *Health:* Emergency/Ambulance Services, Health Organizations, Hospices, Hospitals, Medical Rehabilitation, Mental Health, Single-Disease Health Associations • *International:* Foreign Educational Institutions • *Science:* Scientific Centers & Institutes • *Social Services:* Community Centers, Family Services, Food/Clothing Distribution, Shelters/Homelessness, Substance Abuse, United Funds/United Ways, Volunteer Services, Youth Organizations

Grant Types: capital, challenge, department, employee matching gifts, fellowship, general support, multiyear/continuing support, project, scholarship, and seed money

Note: Employee matching gift ratio: 1 to 1 for active employees, and 0.5 to 1 for retirees.

Nonmonetary Support Types: donated equipment, donated products, in-kind services, loaned employees, and loaned executives

Note: Estimated value of nonmonetary support is unavailable. Annual competitive award program for long-term significant employee, retiree or family member volunteer affiliation. Contact Carmella Piacentini, manager corporate contributions at the above address.

Geographic Distribution: principally near operating locations and to national organizations

Operating Locations: AL (McIntosh), AZ (Chandler), CA (San Leandro, Santa Clara), CT (Cheshire, New Haven, Stamford, Stratford, Waterbury), DC, FL (St. Marks, St. Petersburg), GA (Augusta), IA, IL (East Alton, Marion), KS, KY, LA (Lake Charles, Shreveport), MA, MO (Independence), NJ (West Paterson), NY (Niagara Falls, Rochester), PA, SC, TN (Charleston), TX, VT, WA (Redmond), WI (Baraboo), WV (South Charleston)

CORP. OFFICERS
Donald Wayne Griffin: *B* Evansville IN 1937 *ED* Syracuse Univ; Univ Evansville BA *CURR EMPL* pres, coo, dir: Olin Corp *CORP AFFIL* chmn: Ravenna Arsenal Inc; chmn, ceo: Gen Defense Corp, Pacific Electro Dynamics Corp, Physics Intl Corp, Rocket Res Corp; dir: IL St Bank E Alton, Indy Electronics Inc, Rayonier Inc, Rayonier Timberlands LP, Riverbend Bancshares *NONPR AFFIL* dir: Leadership Counc SW IL; life mem: Navy League US; mem: Am Defense Preparedness Assn, Am Soc Metals, Assn US Army, IL Chamber Commerce, Natl Shooting Sports Fdn, Small Arms Ammunition Mfrs, SW IL Indus Assn, Wildlife Mgmt Inst

John William Johnstone, Jr.: *B* Brooklyn NY 1932 *ED* Hartwick Coll BA 1954; Harvard Univ Advanced Mgmt Program 1970 *CURR EMPL* chmn, ceo: Olin Corp *CORP AFFIL* chmn: Olin-Asahi Interconnect Tech, Phoenix Home Life Ins Co; dir: Am Brands Inc, HL Fin Group, Res Corp *NONPR AFFIL* dir: Am Productivity & Quality Control Ctr, Chem Mfrs Assn, Soap Detergent Assn; mem: Am Mgmt Assn, Soc Chem Indus; policy comm: Bus Roundtable; vchmn: Conf Bd *CLUB AFFIL* Blind Brook, Landmark, Links, Woodway CC *PHIL AFFIL* dir: Research Corporation

GIVING OFFICERS
Donald Wayne Griffin: trust *CURR EMPL* pres, coo, dir: Olin Corp (see above)

John William Johnstone, Jr.: trust *CURR EMPL* chmn, ceo: Olin Corp *PHIL AFFIL* dir: Research Corporation (see above)

Carmella V. Piacentini: admin

APPLICATION INFORMATION
Initial Approach: *Initial Contact:* one- or two-page letter *Include Information On:* description of the organization, amount requested, purpose for which funds are sought, recently audited financial statement, and proof of tax-exempt status *Deadlines:* none

Restrictions on Giving: Foundation does not support endowments or loans, dinners or special events, fraternal organizations, goodwill advertising, individuals, political or lobbying groups or religious organizations for sectarian purposes.

Does not provide general support to member agencies of united funds. May consider capital campaign support.

GRANTS ANALYSIS
Total Grants: $2,000,000

Number of Grants: 3,000

Highest Grant: $775,000

Average Grant: $667

Typical Range: $100 to $5,000

Disclosure Period: 1994

Note: Figures are approximate. Recent grants are derived from a 1993 Form 990.

RECENT GRANTS
General

90,000	River Bend United Way, Alton, IL — charitable contribution
50,000	American Red Cross Alton-Wood — charitable contribution
42,000	Inroads, St. Louis, MO — charitable contribution
30,000	Alabama School of Mathematics and Science Foundation, Mobile, AL — charitable contribution
30,000	Conference Board, New York, NY — charitable contribution

Palmer Fund, Frank Loomis

CONTACT
Mildred E. Devine
Vice President and Administrator
Frank Loomis Palmer Fund
c/o Shawmut Bank
250 State St.
New London, CT 06320
(203) 447-6133

FINANCIAL SUMMARY
Recent Giving: $760,000 (fiscal 1995 est.); $756,841 (fiscal 1994 approx.); $999,168 (fiscal 1993)

Assets: $17,500,000 (fiscal 1995 est.); $17,419,481 (fiscal 1994 approx.); $17,397,946 (fiscal 1993)

EIN: 06-6026043

CONTRIBUTIONS SUMMARY
Donor(s): The foundation was established in 1936 by the late Virginia Palmer in memory of her father, Frank Loomis Palmer.

Typical Recipients: • *Arts & Humanities:* Arts Centers, Arts Festivals, Arts Outreach, Historic Preservation, History & Archaeology, Libraries, Museums/Galleries, Music, Opera, Theater • *Civic & Public Affairs:* Economic Development, General, Hispanic Affairs, Housing, Municipalities/Towns, Professional & Trade Associations, Safety, Urban & Community Affairs, Women's Affairs, Zoos/Aquariums • *Education:* Afterschool/Enrichment Programs, Arts/Humanities Education, Colleges & Universities, Education Reform, Engineering/Technological Education, Literacy, Private Education (Precollege), Public Education (Precollege), Secondary Education (Private), Social Sciences Education, Student Aid • *Environment:* General • *Health:* AIDS/HIV, Children's Health/Hospitals, Emergency/Ambulance Services, Health Organizations, Hospices, Hospitals, Mental Health, Nursing Services, Single-Disease Health Associations • *Religion:* Churches, Religious Welfare • *Science:* Scientific Centers & Institutes, Scientific Organizations • *Social Services:* Big Brother/Big Sister, Child Welfare, Community Centers, Community Service Organizations, Counseling, Emergency Relief, Family Planning, Family Services, Food/Clothing Distribution, People with Disabilities, Recreation & Athletics, Scouts, Shelters/Homelessness, Substance Abuse, United Funds/United Ways, YMCA/YWCA/YMHA/YWHA, Youth Organizations

Grant Types: capital, conference/seminar, matching, project, research, scholarship, and seed money

Geographic Distribution: primarily limited to New London, CT

GIVING OFFICERS
Mildred E. Devine: vp, admin

APPLICATION INFORMATION
Initial Approach:

Initial contact should be by telephone to request an application and guidelines.

Proposal should include a completed application form, an audited financial statement for the most recent year or a treasurer's report, and a project budget (for organizations in the formative stages), an IRS tax-exempt letter dated after 1969, and a proposed operating budget for the period of time in which the desired grant will be used. For organizations that are new or unfamiliar to the foundation, a brief organizational background is required. Please see guidelines for additional requirements for churches and municipalities.

Completed applications including all required supporting data for grants must be submitted by May 15 and November 15 of each year. If these dates fall on a Saturday or Sunday, the deadline is not extended. Applications postmarked on the day of the deadline are accepted.

Restrictions on Giving: Grants will be limited to activities conducted or organizations located in New London. Special consideration may be given to grantees whose programs offer the possibility of matching

grants. Grants are not made to individuals, for endowments, for deficit financing, or for reimbursement for items purchased prior to grant request.

OTHER THINGS TO KNOW
The foundation lists the Shawmut Bank as a corporate trustee.

PUBLICATIONS
Informational brochure including application guidelines

GRANTS ANALYSIS
Total Grants: $999,168

Number of Grants: 50

Highest Grant: $174,000

Average Grant: $16,840*

Typical Range: $1,000 to $35,000

Disclosure Period: fiscal year ending July 31, 1993

Note: Average grant figure excludes the highest grant of $174,000. Recent grants are derived from a fiscal 1993 Form 990.

RECENT GRANTS
General

174,000	Connecticut College for New London Community Center, New London, CT
50,000	Easter Seal Rehabilitation Center, New London, CT
50,000	Mitchell College, Statesville, NC — implement phase one technology enhancement of the campus
41,500	Child and Family Agency, New London, CT
37,700	Thames Science Center, New London, CT

Perkin-Elmer Corp.

Sales: $1.02 billion
Employees: 5,954
Headquarters: Norwalk, CT
SIC Major Group: Industrial Machinery & Equipment and Instruments & Related Products

CONTACT
Zelda Jacobs
Senior Corporate Relations Specialist
Perkin-Elmer Corp.
761 Main Ave.
Norwalk, CT 06859-0246
(203) 762-1000

CONTRIBUTIONS SUMMARY
Typical Recipients: • *Arts & Humanities:* Community Arts, Libraries, Museums/Galleries, Performing Arts, Public Broadcasting • *Civic & Public Affairs:* Economic Development, Economic Policy, Employment/Job Training, Housing, Law & Justice, Legal Aid, Urban & Community Affairs, Women's Affairs, Zoos/Aquariums • *Education:* Business Education, Colleges & Universities, Community & Junior Colleges, Continuing Education, Economic Education, Education Associations, Education Funds, Faculty De-

velopment, Literacy, Minority Education, Private Education (Precollege), Public Education (Precollege), Science/Mathematics Education • *Environment:* General • *Health:* Health Organizations, Hospices, Hospitals, Medical Rehabilitation, Medical Research, Mental Health, Nursing Services, Nutrition, Public Health • *Science:* Scientific Centers & Institutes, Scientific Organizations • *Social Services:* Child Welfare, Community Centers, Community Service Organizations, Counseling, Day Care, Delinquency & Criminal Rehabilitation, Domestic Violence, Emergency Relief, Family Services, Food/Clothing Distribution, Homes, People with Disabilities, Recreation & Athletics, Senior Services, Shelters/Homelessness, Substance Abuse, United Funds/United Ways, Volunteer Services, Youth Organizations

Grant Types: capital, challenge, conference/seminar, emergency, employee matching gifts, fellowship, general support, loan, multiyear/continuing support, operating expenses, professorship, project, research, scholarship, and seed money

Nonmonetary Support Types: donated equipment and donated products

Operating Locations: CA (Pomona), CT (Norwalk), MN (Eden Prairie), NY (Westbury)

CORP. OFFICERS
Gaynor N. Kelley: *B* New Canaan CT 1931 *ED* Delehanty Institute 1952 *CURR EMPL* chmn, ceo, dir: Perkin-Elmer Corp *CORP AFFIL* dir: Clark Equipment Co, Gateway Bank-Norwalk, Hercules *PHIL AFFIL* vchmn exec comm: CBIA Education Foundation

APPLICATION INFORMATION
Initial Approach: Send brief letter of inquiry, and a full proposal including a description of the organization, amount requested, purpose of funds sought, recently audited financial statements, and proof of tax-exempt status. There are no dealines.

Restrictions on Giving: Does not support individuals, religious organizations for sectarian purposes, or political or lobbying groups.

GRANTS ANALYSIS
Typical Range: $250 to $1,000

Price Foundation, Lucien B. and Katherine E.

CONTACT
Rev. Francis V. Krukowski
President
Lucien B. and Katherine E. Price Fdn.
896 Main St.
Manchester, CT 06040
(203) 643-1129

FINANCIAL SUMMARY
Recent Giving: $87,800 (1993); $122,500 (1992); $124,300 (1991)

Assets: $3,637,487 (1993); $3,241,199 (1992); $3,243,082 (1991)

EIN: 06-6068868

CONTRIBUTIONS SUMMARY
Typical Recipients: • *Arts & Humanities:* Libraries • *Civic & Public Affairs:* General • *Education:* Colleges & Universities, Legal Education, Preschool Education, Private Education (Precollege), Religious Education, Secondary Education (Private), Secondary Education (Public), Student Aid • *Health:* Hospitals, Medical Rehabilitation • *International:* Health Care/Hospitals, International Relief Efforts • *Religion:* Churches, Dioceses, Religious Organizations, Religious Welfare, Seminaries • *Social Services:* Camps, Community Service Organizations, Youth Organizations

Grant Types: general support

Geographic Distribution: focus on CT and VT

GIVING OFFICERS
Morgan P. Ames: treas
Rev. Joseph L. Federal: dir
Rev. J. T. Fitzgerald: vp
Dr. Edward P. Flanagan: secy
Rev. Francis V. Krukowski: pres

APPLICATION INFORMATION
Initial Approach: The foundation requests applications be made in writing. There are no deadlines.

GRANTS ANALYSIS
Total Grants: $87,800
Number of Grants: 22
Highest Grant: $19,000
Typical Range: $1,000 to $12,500
Disclosure Period: 1993

Note: Recent grants are derived from a 1993 Form 990.

RECENT GRANTS
Library
8,000   St. James School Library Fund, Manchester, CT

General
19,000   St. James School, Manchester, CT
12,500   Judge Memorial High School, Salt Lake City, UT
10,000   Diocese of Salt Lake City, Salt Lake City, UT
10,000   Notre Dame School, Price, UT
4,000   St. James School Equipment Fund, Manchester, CT

Schiro Fund

CONTACT
Bernard Schiro
President
Schiro Fund
25 Brookside Blvd.
West Hartford, CT 06107
(203) 232-5854

FINANCIAL SUMMARY
Recent Giving: $362,114 (1993); $375,166 (1992); $328,105 (1991)
Assets: $5,071,529 (1993); $6,741,223 (1992); $6,665,625 (1991)
EIN: 06-6056977

CONTRIBUTIONS SUMMARY
Donor(s): Bernard W. Schiro, the late Beatrice Fox Auerbach

Typical Recipients: • *Arts & Humanities:* Ballet, Dance, Libraries, Music, Opera, Public Broadcasting • *Civic & Public Affairs:* Civil Rights, General, Philanthropic Organizations, Urban & Community Affairs, Women's Affairs • *Education:* Colleges & Universities, Faculty Development, Private Education (Precollege), Public Education (Precollege), Student Aid • *Environment:* General, Resource Conservation, Wildlife Protection • *Health:* AIDS/HIV, Cancer, Emergency/Ambulance Services, Hospitals, Medical Research, Preventive Medicine/Wellness Organizations, Single-Disease Health Associations • *International:* Foreign Educational Institutions, Health Care/Hospitals, Human Rights • *Religion:* Churches, Jewish Causes, Religious Organizations, Religious Welfare, Synagogues/Temples • *Social Services:* Camps, Community Service Organizations, Family Planning, Family Services, People with Disabilities, United Funds/United Ways, Youth Organizations

Grant Types: general support

Geographic Distribution: focus on CT

GIVING OFFICERS
Linda S. Glickstein: trust
Georgette A. Koopman: trust *PHIL AFFIL* pres, trust: Beatrice Fox Auerbach Foundation, Koopman Fund
Bernard W. Schiro: pres, trust *PHIL AFFIL* chmn, trust: Beatrice Fox Auerbach Foundation
Dorothy A. Schiro: secy, treas, trust *PHIL AFFIL* vp, treas, trust: Beatrice Fox Auerbach Foundation; asst secy, trust: Koopman Fund
Elizabeth A. Schiro: trust *PHIL AFFIL* secy: Beatrice Fox Auerbach Foundation
Robert G. Schiro: trust
Susan F. Schiro: trust
Helen B. Schiro Kaplan: trust
Jean L. Schiro-Zarela: trust

APPLICATION INFORMATION
Initial Approach: Send a brief letter of inquiry. Include a description of organization, amount requested, purpose of funds sought, recently audited financial statement, and proof of tax-exempt status. There are no deadlines.

GRANTS ANALYSIS
Total Grants: $362,114
Number of Grants: 185*
Highest Grant: $214,000
Typical Range: $25 to $25,000
Disclosure Period: 1993

Note: Recent grants are derived from a 1993 Form 990. Number of grants is approximate.

RECENT GRANTS
Library
1,450   Wadsworth Athenaeum, Hartford, CT

General
214,000   Hartford Foundation for Public Giving, Hartford, CT
16,000   United Way of Southeastern Pennsylvania, Philadelphia, PA
13,000   Jewish Federation of Greater Hartford, West Hartford, CT
7,000   Farmington Valley Jewish Congregation, Simsbury, CT
5,200   Planned Parenthood Association, New Haven, CT

Shawmut National Corp. / Shawmut Charitable Foundation

Revenue: $2.31 billion
Employees: 11,588
Headquarters: Boston, MA
SIC Major Group: Bank Holding Companies

CONTACT
Maxine Dean
Assistant Vice President, Community Relations
Shawmut National Corp.
777 Main St.
MSN 355
Hartford, CT 06115
(203) 728-2274

FINANCIAL SUMMARY
Recent Giving: $3,000,000 (1995 est.); $3,100,000 (1994 approx.); $3,000,000 (1992 approx.)
Assets: $35,621 (1992); $45,995 (1991)
Gifts Received: $1,753,521 (1992)
Fiscal Note: Company gives directly and through the foundation. In 1992, the foundation gave $1,777,509. In 1992, the foundation received a contribution from Shawmut Bank, N.A.
EIN: 04-6023794

CONTRIBUTIONS SUMMARY
Typical Recipients: • *Arts & Humanities:* Arts Associations & Councils, Arts Centers, Arts Funds, Arts Institutes, Community Arts, Dance, Ethnic & Folk Arts, Historic Preservation, History & Archaeology, Libraries, Museums/Galleries, Music, Opera, Performing Arts, Public Broadcasting, Theater, Visual Arts • *Civic & Public Affairs:* African American Affairs, Business/Free Enterprise, Civil Rights, Economic Development, Economic Policy, Employment/Job Training, Housing, Law & Justice, Nonprofit Management, Urban & Community Affairs, Women's Affairs, Zoos/Aquariums • *Education:* Arts/Humanities Education, Business Education, Colleges & Universities, Community & Junior Colleges, Continuing Education, Economic Education, Education Associations, Education Reform, Engineering/Technological Education, Health &

Physical Education, Literacy, Minority Education, Private Education (Precollege), Public Education (Precollege), Social Sciences Education, Student Aid • *Environment:* General • *Health:* AIDS/HIV, Clinics/Medical Centers, Emergency/Ambulance Services, Health Funds, Health Organizations, Hospices, Hospitals, Medical Rehabilitation, Medical Training, Mental Health, Nutrition, Public Health • *Religion:* Synagogues/Temples • *Science:* Scientific Centers & Institutes • *Social Services:* Child Welfare, Community Centers, Community Service Organizations, Counseling, Day Care, Delinquency & Criminal Rehabilitation, Domestic Violence, Family Planning, Family Services, Food/Clothing Distribution, Homes, People with Disabilities, Recreation & Athletics, Refugee Assistance, Senior Services, Shelters/Homelessness, Substance Abuse, United Funds/United Ways, Volunteer Services, Youth Organizations

Grant Types: capital, employee matching gifts, general support, and operating expenses

Geographic Distribution: throughout Massachusetts, Connecticut, and Rhode Island

Operating Locations: CT, FL (Stuart), MA, NY (New York), RI

Note: Maintains dual headquarters in Connecticut and Massachusetts and operates 350 branches throughout Connecticut, Massachusetts, and Rhode Island.

CORP. OFFICERS
Joel Barnes Alvord: *B* Manchester CT 1938 *ED* Dartmouth Coll AB 1960; Dartmouth Coll Amos Tuck Grad Sch Bus Admin MBA 1961 *CURR EMPL* chmn, ceo, dir: Shawmut Natl Corp *CORP AFFIL* chmn, ceo: Shawmut Bank NA, Shawmut Corp; chmn, pres, dir: Hartford Natl Corp; dir: Hartford Steam Boiler Inspection & Ins Co *NONPR AFFIL* dir: Inst Living, Jobs MA, Mus Fine Arts, Wang Ctr Performing Arts; mem: Assn Reserve City Bankers, MA Bus Roundtable

David L. Eyles: *CURR EMPL* vchmn, chief credit policy off, dir: Shawmut Natl Corp

Gunnar S. Overstrom, Jr.: *B* Buffalo NY 1942 *ED* Babson Coll BS 1965; Suffolk Univ Sch Law LLB 1968 *CURR EMPL* pres, coo: Shawmut Natl Corp *CORP AFFIL* chmn, ceo: Shawmut Bank CT NA; pres, ceo: Hartford Natl Corp; pres, coo: Shawmut Corp *NONPR AFFIL* mem: Am Bankers Assn, Am Bar Assn, Assn Reserve City Bankers

GIVING OFFICERS
Maxine Dean: *CURR EMPL* asst vp commun rels: Shawmut Natl Corp

APPLICATION INFORMATION
Initial Approach: *Initial Contact:* proposal or telephone call to a SNC affiliate bank *Include Information On:* description of the organization, amount requested, purpose for which funds are sought, budget, recently audited financial statement, annual report, proof of tax-exempt status, list of board members, list of other supporters *Deadlines:*

application deadlines vary by state (contact local SNC affiliate bank)

Restrictions on Giving: Does not support individuals, national medical foundations, or political, religious, or fraternal organizations.

OTHER THINGS TO KNOW
Matching gifts program is for cultural, private secondary, public and private postsecondary educational institutions only.

Connecticut organizations may contact Maxine Dean, Assistant Vice President, Community Relations, at above address. Massachusetts organizations may contact Dinah Waldsmith, Shawmut Bank Boston, One Federal Street, Boston, MA 02211, (617) 292-3748. Rhode Island organizations may contact Harold Greene, Assistant Vice President, Administration, People's Bank, 333 Central Avenue, Johnstown, RI 02919, (401) 275-1000.

GRANTS ANALYSIS
Total Grants: $1,766,509

Number of Grants: 609

Highest Grant: $382,259

Average Grant: $2,901

Typical Range: $1,000 to $10,000

Disclosure Period: 1992

Note: Figures represent foundation giving only. Recent grants are derived from a 1992 Form 990.

RECENT GRANTS
Library
50,000	Boston Public Library Foundation, Boston, MA	
12,000	Springfield Library/Museums Association, Springfield, MA	

General
382,259	United Way of Eastern New England	
72,000	United Way of Central Massachusetts, Worcester, MA	
50,000	Metropolitan Boston Housing Partnership, Boston, MA	
50,000	Northeastern University, Boston, MA	
50,000	Northeastern University, Boston, MA	

Smart Family Foundation

CONTACT
Raymond Smart
President
Smart Family Foundation
15 Benders Dr.
Greenwich, CT 06831
(203) 531-1474

FINANCIAL SUMMARY
Recent Giving: $3,000,000 (1994 est.); $2,033,254 (1993); $2,400,000 (1992)

Assets: $65,689,849 (1993); $63,000,000 (1992 approx.); $60,400,000 (1991)

EIN: 06-1232323

CONTRIBUTIONS SUMMARY
Donor(s): The Smart Family Foundation was established in 1951. Donors are members of the Smart family.

Typical Recipients: • *Arts & Humanities:* Arts Festivals, Ballet, History & Archaeology, Libraries, Museums/Galleries, Music, Opera, Performing Arts, Theater • *Civic & Public Affairs:* Professional & Trade Associations • *Education:* Arts/Humanities Education, Colleges & Universities, Elementary Education (Private), General, Private Education (Precollege), Public Education (Precollege) • *Environment:* General, Resource Conservation • *Health:* Eyes/Blindness, Health Organizations, Hospitals, Medical Research, Research/Studies Institutes • *International:* Human Rights • *Religion:* Jewish Causes • *Science:* Scientific Centers & Institutes • *Social Services:* Animal Protection, Child Welfare, Community Service Organizations, Crime Prevention, People with Disabilities

Grant Types: project and research

Geographic Distribution: broad geographic distribution

GIVING OFFICERS
Joan Feitler: dir, mem

Robert Feitler: chmn *B* Chicago IL 1930 *ED* Univ PA BS 1951; Harvard Univ JD 1954 *CURR EMPL* pres: Weyco Group *CORP AFFIL* chmn: Hynite Corp; dir: Assoc Banc-Corp, Assoc Commerce Bank, Champion Parts, Mfrs Box Co, TC Mfg Co; vchmn bd, dir: Nunn-Bush Shoe Co *NONPR AFFIL* pres: Milwaukee Art Mus; trust: Univ Chicago Newberry Library *CLUB AFFIL* Harvard, Milwaukee, Milwaukee Athletic, Univ

Ellen Oswald: dir, mem

William Oswald: treas

Mary Smart: secy

Raymond Smart: pres

David Kendal Stone: dir *B* Natick MA 1942 *ED* Franklin & Marshall Coll AB 1964 *CURR EMPL* exec vp, dir oper: Fiduciary Trust Co Intl *NONPR AFFIL* mem: Am Inst CPAs, Comm Banking Inst Taxation, NY St Bankers Assn, NY St Soc CPAs

Sue Smart Stone: mem

Barbara Wald: dir *B* Council Bluffs IA 1935 *NONPR AFFIL* mem: Home Based Bus Professionals, Independent Computer Consults, Main Line Womens Bus Network, Natl Better Bus Bureau

APPLICATION INFORMATION
Initial Approach:

A one page summary of the project should submitted to the Foundation. It should be sent by regular first-class mail.

Applicant should include a brief description of the project, including cost, and copy of the IRS letter indicating them as a 501 (c)(3) organization.

Deadlines for proposals are January 1 and June 1 each year.

Restrictions on Giving: The Foundation does not give grants to individuals or for-profit businesses.

GRANTS ANALYSIS
Total Grants: $2,033,254

Number of Grants: 45

Highest Grant: $500,000

Average Grant: $45,183

Typical Range: $5,000 to $25,000 and $45,000 to $100,000

Disclosure Period: 1993

Note: Recent grants are derived from a 1993 Form 990.

RECENT GRANTS

Library
25,000	Newberry Library, Chicago, IL

General
500,000	Hyde Foundation, Bath, ME
221,734	University of Chicago, Chicago, IL — HALP
138,610	Harvard Medical School, Cambridge, MA — Retinitis Pigmentosa Program
130,000	Stanford University Accelerated Schools Program, Stanford, CA
90,000	State University of New York, NY

Southern New England Telephone Company

Sales: $1.65 billion
Employees: 9,600
Parent Company: Southern New England Telecommunications Corporation
Headquarters: New Haven, CT
SIC Major Group: Telephone Communications Except Radiotelephone and Communications Services Nec

CONTACT
Daphne Ross
Manager, Contributions
SNET
227 Church St.
New Haven, CT 06506
(203) 771-2546

FINANCIAL SUMMARY
Recent Giving: $1,500,000 (1994 est.); $1,500,000 (1993); $1,500,000 (1992)

Fiscal Note: Company gives directly. Above figures exclude nonmonetary support.

CONTRIBUTIONS SUMMARY
Typical Recipients: • *Arts & Humanities:* Arts Associations & Councils, Dance, Libraries, Music, Performing Arts, Theater • *Civic & Public Affairs:* Economic Development, Public Policy • *Education:* Colleges & Universities, Community & Junior Colleges, Education Associations, Engineering/Technological Education, Literacy, Minority Education, Private Education (Precollege), Science/Mathematics Education • *Health:* Hospitals • *Social Services:* Child Welfare,

Community Service Organizations, People with Disabilities, Senior Services, Substance Abuse, United Funds/United Ways, Youth Organizations

Grant Types: capital and employee matching gifts

Note: Employee matching gift ratio: 1 to 1.

Nonmonetary Support: $200,000 (1993); $200,000 (1992); $200,000 (1990)

Nonmonetary Support Types: donated equipment, in-kind services, and loaned executives

Geographic Distribution: Connecticut

Operating Locations: CT

CORP. OFFICERS
Daniel Joseph Miglio: *B* Philadelphia PA 1940 *ED* Univ PA Wharton Sch BS 1962 *CURR EMPL* chmn, pres: Southern New England Telephone Co *CORP AFFIL* dir: Aristotle Corp, First Constitution Bank *NONPR AFFIL* chmn: Southern New England Telephone Co Political Action Comm; fin chmn: CT Joint Counc Econ Ed; mem: Kappa Alpha; mem exec comm, dir: US Telephone Assn

GIVING OFFICERS
Toni Boulay: *CURR EMPL* staff assoc matching gifts: Southern New England Telephone Co

Linda D. Hershman: *B* Pittsburgh PA 1947 *ED* Univ Pittsburgh 1967; Univ CT Law Sch 1970 *CURR EMPL* vp external aff: Southern New England Telephone Co *CORP AFFIL* mem bd dir: Colony Savings Bank *NONPR AFFIL* dir: Hartford Advocates Arts; mem: Am Bar Assn, CT Bar Assn, Greater Hartford Chamber Commerce, Hartford Womens Network, Natl Policies Panel, St Govt Rels Comm, St Legislation Comm, Temple Beth David, US Tennis Assn; mem bd trust: Univ CT Law Sch Fdn

Daphne Ross: *CURR EMPL* mgr contributions: Southern New England Telephone Co

APPLICATION INFORMATION
Initial Approach: *Initial Contact:* letter or proposal *Include Information On:* description of the organization, amount requested, purpose for which funds are sought, recently audited financial statement, proof of tax-exempt status, and other corporate funding sources *Deadlines:* none

Restrictions on Giving: Company does not support endowments; fraternal, political, or religious organizations; member agencies of united funds; goodwill advertising; or individuals.

GRANTS ANALYSIS
Total Grants: $1,500,000

Typical Range: $500 to $1,000

Disclosure Period: 1993

Stanley Charitable Foundation, A.W.

CONTACT
Maria Delsesto
Treasurer
A.W. Stanley Charitable Fdn.
1 Exchange Pl.
Waterbury, CT 06721
(203) 597-6633

FINANCIAL SUMMARY
Recent Giving: $487,890 (1993); $527,900 (1992); $446,250 (1991)

Assets: $12,928,873 (1993); $12,719,701 (1992); $12,663,001 (1991)

Gifts Received: $515 (1993); $41,439 (1992)

Fiscal Note: In 1992, contributions were received from Mildred Derby Trust.

EIN: 06-0724195

CONTRIBUTIONS SUMMARY
Donor(s): the late Alix W. Stanley

Typical Recipients: • *Arts & Humanities:* Community Arts, Historic Preservation, Libraries, Museums/Galleries, Music, Opera, Performing Arts, Public Broadcasting • *Civic & Public Affairs:* Chambers of Commerce, Employment/Job Training, General, Housing, Safety, Women's Affairs • *Education:* Colleges & Universities, General, Private Education (Precollege), Special Education • *Health:* Hospices, Hospitals, Medical Research, Mental Health • *Religion:* Churches, Religious Welfare • *Social Services:* Child Welfare, Community Service Organizations, Family Planning, Family Services, United Funds/United Ways, Youth Organizations

Grant Types: capital, emergency, and multi-year/continuing support

Geographic Distribution: focus on New Britain, CT, and surrounding areas

GIVING OFFICERS
William E. Attwood: pres

Donald W. Davis: dir, trust *B* Springfield MA 1921 *ED* Harvard Univ MBA; PA St Univ AB *CORP AFFIL* chmn exec comm, dir: Stanley Works; dir: Allied-Signal, Northeast Utilities, Pitney Bowes *NONPR AFFIL* dir: CT Pub TV, Natl Captioning Inst, Natl Inst Dispute Resolution, New Britain Gen Hosp; mem: Natl Assn Mfrs; vchmn bd regents: Univ Hartford

Maria Delsesto: treas

Marie S. Gustin: dir, trust

Susan Rathgeber: dir, trust

Catherine Rogers: dir, trust

John W. Shumaker: dir, trust

Rev. James A. Simpson: dir, trust

Talcott Stanley: vp, trust

APPLICATION INFORMATION
Initial Approach: The foundation has no formal grant application procedure or application form. There are no deadlines.

Restrictions on Giving: Limited to the residents of New Britain, CT.

GRANTS ANALYSIS
Total Grants: $487,890

Number of Grants: 27

Highest Grant: $100,000

Typical Range: $1,000 to $75,000

Disclosure Period: 1993

Note: Recent grants are derived from a 1993 Form 990.

RECENT GRANTS

Library

11,000	New Britain Public Library, New Britain, CT
5,000	Wadsworth Athaeneum, Hartford, CT

General

100,000	United Way
75,000	New Britain Memorial Hospital, New Britain, CT
67,000	Boys and Girls Club of New Britain, New Britain, CT
50,000	Constructive Workshops, New Britain, CT — educational
15,000	Mooreland Hill School, Kensington, CT — building

Stanley Works / Stanley Works Foundation

Revenue: $2.51 billion
Employees: 19,000
Headquarters: New Britain, CT
SIC Major Group: Hand & Edge Tools Nec, Partitions & Fixtures Except Wood, Steel Wire & Related Products, and Hardware Nec

CONTACT
Cheryl Farmer
Contributions and Public Affairs
Stanley Works
1000 Stanley Dr.
New Britain, CT 06053
(203) 225-5111

FINANCIAL SUMMARY
Recent Giving: $1,300,000 (1995); $1,100,675 (1994); $1,310,166 (1993)

Assets: $4,523 (1993); $1,246,241 (1992); $1,468,588 (1991)

Gifts Received: $1,000,050 (1992)

Fiscal Note: As of 1994, company will give directly and not through the foundation. Above figures exclude nonmonetary support.

EIN: 06-6088099

CONTRIBUTIONS SUMMARY
Typical Recipients: • *Arts & Humanities:* Arts Associations & Councils, Community Arts, Dance, General, Libraries, Museums/Galleries, Music, Opera, Performing Arts, Public Broadcasting, Theater • *Civic & Public Affairs:* African American Affairs, Business/Free Enterprise, Community Foundations, Economic Policy, Employment/Job Training, General, Housing, Urban & Community Affairs • *Education:* Business Education, Colleges & Universities, Economic Education, Elementary Education (Private), Elementary Education (Public), Engineering/Technological Education, Literacy, Minority Education, Public Education (Precollege), Science/Mathematics Education • *Environment:* General, Resource Conservation • *Health:* Cancer, Children's Health/Hospitals, Emergency/Ambulance Services, Hospitals, Medical Research • *International:* International Development • *Religion:* Churches, Religious Welfare • *Science:* Science Exhibits & Fairs • *Social Services:* Community Service Organizations, Family Services, Homes, People with Disabilities, Shelters/Homelessness, Substance Abuse, United Funds/United Ways, Youth Organizations

Grant Types: capital, challenge, employee matching gifts, general support, and seed money

Nonmonetary Support: $150,000 (1992); $150,000 (1991); $150,000 (1990)

Nonmonetary Support Types: donated equipment and in-kind services

Note: Nonmonetary support is valued at $150,000 annually.

Geographic Distribution: primarily in communities in which company has operating locations

Operating Locations: AZ (Phoenix), CA (Chatsworth, Costa Mesa, Monrovia, Rancho Cucamonga, San Dimas, Visalia), CT (Clinton, Farmington, New Britain), FL (Orlando), GA (Atlanta, Covington), IN (Shelbyville), KS (Kansas City, Lenexa), MA (Worcester), MI (Birmingham, Novi, Troy), MN (Two Harbors), MO (St. Louis), MS (Tupelo), NC (Charlotte, Hamlet, Sanford), NH (Claremont), OH (Cleveland, Columbus, Covington, Georgetown, Sabina, Washington Court House), OR (Milwaukie), PA (Allentown, Royersford, York), RI (East Greenwich), SC (Cheraw), TN (Pulaski, Shelbyville), TX (Carrollton, Dallas, Wichita Falls), VA (Richmond, Winchester), VT (Pittsfield, Shaftsbury)

CORP. OFFICERS
Richard H. Ayers: *B* Newton MA 1942 *ED* MA Inst Tech BS 1965; MA Inst Tech MS 1965 *CURR EMPL* chmn, ceo: Stanley Works *CORP AFFIL* assoc dir: Perkin Elmer Corp; chmn: Stanley Atlantic Inc; dir: CT Mutual Funds, CT Mutual Investment Accounts Inc, Southern New England Telecommun Corp; vp: Jensen Tools Inc; vp, dir: Stanley Access Tech *NONPR AFFIL* dir: New Britain Gen Hosp; mem: Hand Tools Inst, Hartford Bus Econ Advs, Natl Assn Mfrs; trust: Hartford Grad Ctr *CLUB AFFIL* Econ NY, Farmington CC

GIVING OFFICERS
Cheryl Farmer: *CURR EMPL* contributions & pub aff: Stanley Works

APPLICATION INFORMATION
Initial Approach: *Initial Contact:* brief letter or proposal *Include Information On:* description of the organization and how it will affect Stanley employees, amount requested, purpose for which funds are sought, recently audited financial statement, proof of 501(c)(3) tax-exempt status, identification of company employees involved with organization *Deadlines:* none

Restrictions on Giving: No funds will be given outside of where Stanley has operations. Foundation does not fund endowments and generally does not support United Way-supported organizations, individuals, political organizations, dinners, special events, fraternal organizations, goodwill advertising, athletic events, or religious organizations for sectarian purposes.

OTHER THINGS TO KNOW
Foundation particularly supports capital projects and funding for building, equipment, or seed money projects in Stanley communities.

GRANTS ANALYSIS
Total Grants: $1,310,166

Number of Grants: 1,056*

Highest Grant: $100,000

Average Grant: $1,240

Typical Range: $1,000 to $5,000

Disclosure Period: 1993

Note: Fiscal information is for foundation only. Figures include matching gifts and scholarships. Number of grants is approximate. Recent grants are derived from a 1993 Form 990.

RECENT GRANTS

Library

40,000	New Britain Institute, New Britain, CT — library
10,000	New Britain Institute, New Britain, CT — library

General

100,000	City of Hope, Duarte, CA
50,000	Boys and Girls Club of New Britain, New Britain, CT
50,000	Constructive Workshops, New Britain, CT
40,000	New Britain Memorial Hospital, New Britain, CT
25,000	Central Connecticut State University Foundation, New Britain, CT

Tetley, Inc.

Sales: $300.0 million
Employees: 1,000
Headquarters: Shelton, CT
SIC Major Group: Food & Kindred Products

CONTACT
Dorothy Young
Contributions Coordinator
Tetley, Inc.
100 Commerce Dr.
Shelton, CT 06484
(203) 929-9200

FINANCIAL SUMMARY
Recent Giving: $100,000 (1990); $60,000 (1989); $50,000 (1988)

CONTRIBUTIONS SUMMARY

Emphasis of support goes to health; also funds the arts, social services, and civic affairs. Colleges and universities are supported via an educational matching grant program. Limited support to local chapters of national organizations. Company's charitable contributions policy states, "It is the policy of the Company to participate in the betterment of the society in which the Company conducts its business affairs. The Company acknowledges its responsibility to assist in the preservation of values which form the basis of the free enterprise system. The Company also acknowledges its commitment to help the citizens of our society fulfill their human needs. A means by which the Company can fulfill its social responsibility and act upon its commitment is to make cash contributions to charitable, not-for-profit organizations which engage in activities consistent with the Company's stated policy."

Typical Recipients: • *Arts & Humanities:* Arts Centers, Community Arts, Dance, Historic Preservation, Libraries, Museums/Galleries, Music, Performing Arts, Public Broadcasting • *Civic & Public Affairs:* Economic Development, Safety • *Education:* Colleges & Universities • *Health:* Hospitals, Medical Research, Mental Health, Single-Disease Health Associations • *Social Services:* Community Centers, Community Service Organizations, Domestic Violence, Senior Services, Substance Abuse, United Funds/United Ways, Youth Organizations

Grant Types: employee matching gifts, general support, and multiyear/continuing support

Nonmonetary Support Types: loaned employees

Geographic Distribution: primarily near headquarters and operating locations; limited support to national organizations

Operating Locations: CT (Shelton), FL, GA, MO, NJ, NY, PA

CORP. OFFICERS
Henry F. McInerney: *CURR EMPL* ceo, pres: Tetley

GIVING OFFICERS
Dorothy Young: *CURR EMPL* contributions comm: Tetley

APPLICATION INFORMATION
Initial Approach: Send letter in spring or fall including a description of the organization, amount and purpose of funds sought, and proof of tax-exempt status.

Restrictions on Giving: Program does not support political or religious groups; groups which receive contributions from United Way offices to which the company has made a contribution; or groups that do not qualify as exempt under section 501 (c)(3) of the Internal Revenue Code, unless there is an overriding community interest involved.

GRANTS ANALYSIS
Typical Range: $100 to $5,000

Thomson Information Publishing Group

Parent Company: Thomson Holdings
Parent Sales: $103.9 million
Headquarters: Stamford, CT
SIC Major Group: Printing & Publishing and Security & Commodity Brokers

CONTACT
Gerald Tenser
Vice President
Thomson Information Publishing Group
One Sta. Pl.
Stamford, CT 06902
(203) 969-8700

FINANCIAL SUMMARY
Fiscal Note: Annual Giving Range: $50,000 to $100,000

CONTRIBUTIONS SUMMARY
Typical Recipients: • *Arts & Humanities:* Libraries • *Education:* Colleges & Universities • *Social Services:* General

Grant Types: general support and scholarship

Nonmonetary Support Types: donated products

Geographic Distribution: primarily in headquarters area

Operating Locations: CT (Stamford)

CORP. OFFICERS
Michael Brown: *CURR EMPL* ceo, pres: Thomson Info Publ Group

Robert C. Hall: *CURR EMPL* vp: Thomson Info Publ Group

Nigel Harrison: *CURR EMPL* cfo: Thomson Info Publ Group

APPLICATION INFORMATION
Initial Approach: Send brief letter or proposal, including information on the organization, the amount requested, purpose of the grant, and proof of tax-exempt status. Company accepts applications at any time, but the best time to apply is mid-year for funding the following year.

GRANTS ANALYSIS
Typical Range: $500 to $1,500

Valentine Foundation, Lawson

CONTACT
Alice P. Doyle
Trustee
Lawson Valentine Fdn.
998 Farmington Ave., Ste. 123
West Hartford, CT 06107
(203) 521-3108

FINANCIAL SUMMARY
Recent Giving: $663,122 (fiscal 1994); $372,947 (fiscal 1993); $266,278 (fiscal 1992)

Assets: $8,201,257 (fiscal 1994); $8,737,224 (fiscal 1993); $8,656,884 (fiscal 1992)

EIN: 13-6920044

CONTRIBUTIONS SUMMARY
Donor(s): Alice P. Doyle

Typical Recipients: • *Arts & Humanities:* Arts Associations & Councils, Dance, History & Archaeology, Libraries, Opera, Performing Arts, Public Broadcasting, Theater • *Civic & Public Affairs:* Botanical Gardens/Parks, Civil Rights, General, Municipalities/Towns, Public Policy, Rural Affairs, Urban & Community Affairs, Women's Affairs • *Education:* Arts/Humanities Education, Colleges & Universities, Literacy, Private Education (Precollege), Secondary Education (Public) • *Environment:* Air/Water Quality, Forestry, General, Resource Conservation • *Health:* Cancer, Medical Research • *International:* Human Rights, International Development, International Environmental Issues, International Organizations, International Peace & Security Issues, International Relations • *Religion:* Churches, Seminaries • *Social Services:* Child Welfare, Delinquency & Criminal Rehabilitation, Domestic Violence, Family Services, Food/Clothing Distribution, Volunteer Services

Grant Types: general support

Geographic Distribution: focus on AK, NJ, and NY

GIVING OFFICERS
Alice P. Doyle: trust

Allen Doyle: trust

Valentine Doyle: trust

Lucy Miller: trust

Paul E. Vawter: trust

William D. Zabel: trust *B* Omaha NE 1936 *ED* Princeton Univ AB 1958; Harvard Univ LLB 1961 *CURR EMPL* ptnr: Schulte Roth & Zabel *NONPR AFFIL* mem: Am Bar Assn, Am Coll Trust Estate Counc, Am Law Inst, FL Bar Assn, Lawyers Comm Human Rights, New York City Bar Assn, NY Bar Assn *PHIL AFFIL* vchmn, dir: Soros Foundation-Hungary; trust: Harold and Mimi Steinberg Charitable Trust; dir: Fund for Reform and Opening of China; secy: Soros Foundation-Soviet Union; dir: Open Society Fund; trust: Central European University Foundation Trust, Soros Charitable Foundation Tr, Soros Humanitarian Foundation Tr

APPLICATION INFORMATION
Initial Approach: Send brief letter of inquiry. Include a description of organization, amount requested, purpose of funds sought, recently audited financial statement, and proof of tax-exempt status. There are no deadlines.

GRANTS ANALYSIS
Total Grants: $663,122

Number of Grants: 102

Highest Grant: $62,000

Typical Range: $50 to $55,000

Disclosure Period: fiscal year ending February 28, 1994

Note: Recent grants are derived from a fiscal 1994 Form 990.

RECENT GRANTS

General

62,000	Bennington College Corporation, Bennington, VT
55,000	Warren Wilson College, Swann, NC
53,000	International Alliance for Sustainable Agriculture, Minneapolis, MN
29,000	University of Michigan, Ann Arbor, MI
27,000	American Friends Service Committee, Philadelphia, PA

Vance Charitable Foundation, Robert C.

CONTACT
Herbert E. Carlson, Jr.
President and Trustee
Robert C. Vance Charitable Fdn.
21 Winesap Rd.
Kensington, CT 06037
(203) 828-6037

FINANCIAL SUMMARY
Recent Giving: $269,003 (fiscal 1994); $254,546 (fiscal 1993); $246,694 (fiscal 1992)

Assets: $6,471,420 (fiscal 1994); $6,568,821 (fiscal 1993); $6,622,587 (fiscal 1992)

EIN: 06-6050188

CONTRIBUTIONS SUMMARY
Donor(s): the late Robert C. Vance

Typical Recipients: • *Arts & Humanities:* Community Arts, Libraries, Museums/Galleries, Music • *Civic & Public Affairs:* General • *Education:* Colleges & Universities, General, Literacy, Private Education (Precollege), Special Education • *Health:* Hospices, Hospitals, Medical Research, Mental Health • *Religion:* Religious Organizations, Religious Welfare • *Social Services:* Child Welfare, Community Centers, Community Service Organizations, Family Planning, Family Services, People with Disabilities, United Funds/United Ways, Youth Organizations

Grant Types: general support

Geographic Distribution: limited to the Berlin, CT, area

GIVING OFFICERS
Shawmut Bank: mgr
Rita H. Beaulieu: secy, trust
Cheryl Carlson: trust
Elizabeth M. Carlson: asst secy, trust
Herbert Carlson, Sr.: treas, trust
Herbert E. Carlson, Jr.: pres, trust

APPLICATION INFORMATION
Initial Approach: Send brief letter describing program. There are no deadlines.

Restrictions on Giving: Does not support individuals.

PUBLICATIONS
Application Guidelines

GRANTS ANALYSIS
Total Grants: $269,003
Number of Grants: 23
Highest Grant: $62,000
Typical Range: $500 to $25,000
Disclosure Period: fiscal year ending January 31, 1994

Note: Recent grants are derived from a fiscal 1994 Form 990.

RECENT GRANTS

Library

5,000	Capitol Region Library Council, Windsor, CT — educational
500	Peck Memorial Library of Berlin, Berlin, CT — educational

General

62,000	United Community Services, Orwell, OH — operational
25,000	Boys and Girls Club of New Britain, New Britain, CT — building
25,000	Friendship Center, New Britain, CT — building
25,000	Hospital for Special Care, Hartford, CT — building
25,000	Klingberg Family Centers, New Britain, CT — building

Vanderbilt Trust, R. T.

CONTACT
Hugh B. Vanderbilt
Chairman
R. T. Vanderbilt Trust
30 Winfield St.
Norwalk, CT 06855
(203) 853-1400

FINANCIAL SUMMARY
Recent Giving: $361,500 (1993); $344,195 (1992); $310,065 (1991)

Assets: $8,652,806 (1993); $7,917,554 (1992); $7,849,861 (1991)

EIN: 06-6040981

CONTRIBUTIONS SUMMARY
Typical Recipients: • *Arts & Humanities:* Historic Preservation, History & Archaeology, Libraries, Museums/Galleries, Performing Arts • *Civic & Public Affairs:* General, Zoos/Aquariums • *Education:* Colleges & Universities, Private Education (Precollege) • *Environment:* Air/Water Quality, General, Resource Conservation, Wildlife Protection • *Health:* AIDS/HIV, Cancer, Children's Health/Hospitals, Emergency/Ambulance Services, Heart, Hospitals, Kidney, Medical Research, Single-Disease Health Associations • *International:* Health Care/Hospitals • *Religion:* Churches, Ministries, Religious Organizations • *Social Services:* Animal Protection, Child Welfare, Community Service Organizations, Family Planning, Substance Abuse, United Funds/United Ways, Youth Organizations

Grant Types: capital, endowment, and operating expenses

Geographic Distribution: focus on CT and NY

GIVING OFFICERS
Hugh Bedford Vanderbilt, Sr.: chmn, trust *B* New York NY 1921 *ED* Trinity Coll 1942 *CURR EMPL* chmn, ceo: Vanderbilt (RT) Co *NONPR AFFIL* hon trust: Greenwich Historical Soc; mem: Chem Mfrs Assn; trust: Historic Deerfield *CLUB AFFIL* Blind Brook, Everglades, Greenwich CC, Lyford CC, Round Hill

Robert T. Vanderbilt, Jr.: trust

APPLICATION INFORMATION
Initial Approach: Send brief letter describing program. There are no deadlines.

Restrictions on Giving: Does not support individuals.

GRANTS ANALYSIS
Total Grants: $361,500
Number of Grants: 92
Highest Grant: $100,000
Typical Range: $100 to $85,000
Disclosure Period: 1993

Note: Recent grants are derived from a 1993 Form 990.

RECENT GRANTS

General

85,000	Planned Parenthood International Assistance, New York, NY
15,000	New York Zoological Society, Bronx, NY
10,000	Greenwich Hospital Association, Greenwich, CT
10,000	Massachusetts General Hospital, Boston, MA
6,000	Berkshire School, Sheffield, MA

Wheeler Foundation, Wilmot

CONTACT
Wilmot F. Wheeler, Jr.
President
Wilmot Wheeler Fdn.
PO Box 429
Southport, CT 06490

FINANCIAL SUMMARY
Recent Giving: $76,350 (fiscal 1993); $70,925 (fiscal 1991); $62,100 (fiscal 1990)

Assets: $2,691,568 (fiscal 1993); $2,013,327 (fiscal 1991); $2,024,506 (fiscal 1990)

EIN: 06-6039119

CONTRIBUTIONS SUMMARY

Donor(s): the late Wilmot F. Wheeler, Hulda C. Wheeler

Typical Recipients: • *Arts & Humanities:* Community Arts, Dance, History & Archaeology, Libraries, Museums/Galleries, Music, Opera, Public Broadcasting • *Civic & Public Affairs:* Clubs, General, Municipalities/Towns • *Education:* Colleges & Universities, Economic Education, Preschool Education, Private Education (Precollege), Student Aid • *Environment:* General • *Health:* Emergency/Ambulance Services • *International:* International Development • *Religion:* Churches, Religious Organizations, Religious Welfare • *Science:* Scientific Centers & Institutes • *Social Services:* Community Service Organizations, Emergency Relief, United Funds/United Ways, Youth Organizations

Grant Types: general support

Geographic Distribution: focus on CT

GIVING OFFICERS

Halsted W. Wheeler: secy

Wilmont F. Wheeler III: vp, treas

Wilmot Fitch Wheeler, Jr.: pres *B* Southport CT 1923 *ED* Yale Univ BA 1945; NY Univ postgrad 1947-1948 *CURR EMPL* chmn, dir: Jelliff Corp *CORP AFFIL* dir: Peoples Bank CT, Sormir Petroleum; trust: Peoples Mutual Holdings *NONPR AFFIL* bd dir: Wilmot Wheeler Fdn; trust: Am Farm Sch, Bridgeport Hosp *PHIL AFFIL* vp, dir: William T. Morris Foundation *CLUB AFFIL* Fairfield CC, Sky, Yale

APPLICATION INFORMATION

Initial Approach: Send brief letter describing program. There are no deadlines.

GRANTS ANALYSIS

Total Grants: $76,350

Number of Grants: 52

Highest Grant: $22,500

Typical Range: $50 to $7,000

Disclosure Period: fiscal year ending June 30, 1993

Note: Recent grants are derived from a fiscal 1993 Form 990.

RECENT GRANTS

Library
1,250	Pequot Library
250	Darien Library, Darien, CT

General
22,500	St. Luke's Parish
9,500	St. Paul's Church
7,000	Proctor Academy
3,500	Brown University, Providence, RI
3,000	Sun Sentinel — Hurricane Andrew

Wiremold Co. / Wiremold Foundation

Sales: $126.34 million
Employees: 1,300
Headquarters: West Hartford, CT
SIC Major Group: Electronic & Other Electrical Equipment

CONTACT

John Davis Murphy
President
Wiremold Foundation
60 Woodlawn St.
West Hartford, CT 06110
(203) 233-6251

FINANCIAL SUMMARY

Recent Giving: $184,501 (1993); $192,690 (1992); $190,660 (1989)

Assets: $221,379 (1993); $200,124 (1992); $640,620 (1989)

Gifts Received: $204,000 (1993); $49,000 (1992)

EIN: 06-6089445

CONTRIBUTIONS SUMMARY

Typical Recipients: • *Arts & Humanities:* Arts Associations & Councils, Ballet, General, Historic Preservation, Libraries, Museums/Galleries, Music, Performing Arts, Public Broadcasting • *Civic & Public Affairs:* African American Affairs, Employment/Job Training, General, Housing, Public Policy, Urban & Community Affairs • *Education:* Business Education, Colleges & Universities, Education Funds, General, Literacy, Minority Education, Student Aid • *Environment:* General • *Health:* AIDS/HIV, Children's Health/Hospitals, General, Hospitals • *Religion:* Religious Welfare • *Social Services:* Camps, Child Welfare, Community Service Organizations, Family Services, Food/Clothing Distribution, General, People with Disabilities, Recreation & Athletics, United Funds/United Ways, Youth Organizations

Grant Types: employee matching gifts and general support

Geographic Distribution: primarily headquarters area

Operating Locations: CT (West Hartford)

CORP. OFFICERS

Arthur P. Byrne: *CURR EMPL* chmn, pres, dir: Wiremold Co

John Davis Murphy: *CURR EMPL* chmn emeritus, dir: Wiremold Co

Robert H. Murphy: *CURR EMPL* vchmn emeritus, dir: Wiremold Co

GIVING OFFICERS

Arthur P. Byrne: treas *CURR EMPL* chmn, pres, dir: Wiremold Co (see above)

Joan L. Johnson: secy

John Davis Murphy: pres *CURR EMPL* chmn emeritus, dir: Wiremold Co (see above)

Robert H. Murphy: vp *CURR EMPL* vchmn emeritus, dir: Wiremold Co (see above)

APPLICATION INFORMATION

Initial Approach: The foundation has no formal grant application procedure or application form. There are no deadlines.

GRANTS ANALYSIS

Total Grants: $184,501

Number of Grants: 73

Highest Grant: $65,000

Typical Range: $500 to $15,000

Disclosure Period: 1993

Note: Recent grants are derived from a 1993 Form 990. Number of grants and typical range do not include matching gifts.

RECENT GRANTS

Library
5,000	Wadsworth Athenaeum, Hartford, CT

General
65,000	United Way/Combined Health Appeal of Hartford, Hartford, CT
7,000	YMCA of Hartford, Hartford, CT — capital fund drive
5,000	Greater Hartford Easter Seals Rehabilitation Center, Hartford, CT
5,000	Hartford Hospital, Hartford, CT
5,000	NAED Education Foundation, Wilton, CT

Young Foundation, Robert R.

CONTACT

David W. Wallace
President
Robert R. Young Foundation
PO Box 1423
Greenwich, CT 06836
Note: The foundation does not publish its telephone number.

FINANCIAL SUMMARY

Recent Giving: $1,900,000 (1995 est.); $1,941,627 (1994 approx.); $2,012,958 (1993)

Assets: $30,500,000 (1995 est.); $30,862,106 (1994 approx.); $36,666,361 (1993)

Gifts Received: $265,607 (1992); $6,863,706 (1989)

Fiscal Note: The foundation received gifts of $6,863,706 and $265,607 from the estate of Anita O'Keeffe Young.

EIN: 13-6131394

CONTRIBUTIONS SUMMARY

Donor(s): The foundation was established by the late Anita O'Keefe Young .

Typical Recipients: • *Arts & Humanities:* Ballet, History & Archaeology, Libraries,

Museums/Galleries, Music, Performing Arts • *Civic & Public Affairs:* Clubs, Safety • *Education:* Colleges & Universities, Minority Education, Private Education (Precollege), Secondary Education (Private), Secondary Education (Public), Student Aid • *Environment:* General, Resource Conservation, Wildlife Protection • *Health:* Arthritis, Cancer, Children's Health/Hospitals, Clinics/Medical Centers, Diabetes, Emergency/Ambulance Services, Heart, Hospices, Hospitals, Medical Research, Mental Health, Multiple Sclerosis, Single-Disease Health Associations • *International:* International Relations • *Religion:* Churches, Jewish Causes, Religious Organizations, Religious Welfare • *Social Services:* Animal Protection, Community Service Organizations, Counseling, Crime Prevention, Emergency Relief, Family Planning, Family Services, Food/Clothing Distribution, People with Disabilities, Recreation & Athletics, Scouts, Senior Services, Substance Abuse, United Funds/United Ways, YMCA/YWCA/YMHA/YWHA, Youth Organizations

Grant Types: general support, project, and research

Geographic Distribution: New York and New England

GIVING OFFICERS
David William Wallace: pres, trust *B* New York NY 1924 *ED* Yale Univ BS 1948; Harvard Univ JD 1951 *CURR EMPL* chmn: Todd Shipyards Corp *CORP AFFIL* ceo, chmn, dir, mem exec comm: Lone Star Indus; chmn: FECO Engrg Sys, Natl Securities & Res Corp, Piper Acceptance Corp, Piper Aircraft Corp; dir: Eastern Air Lines, Holme Protection Corp, Producers Cotton Oil Co, Putnam Trust Co, SCM Corp, Zurn Indus; mem: Lloyds London *CLUB AFFIL* Brook, Econ, Greenwich CC, Sky, St Andrews Soc NY, Yale

Jean M. Wallace: dir, secy

APPLICATION INFORMATION
Initial Approach:

Applications should be in letter form.

Letters should include a description of the organization requesting funds, qualifications of individuals responsible for program or project, and an outline of proposed use of funds.

Applications are accepted at any time.

Applicants may expect a reply, usually within three months.

GRANTS ANALYSIS
Total Grants: $2,012,958

Number of Grants: 45

Highest Grant: $937,000

Average Grant: $24,454*

Typical Range: $100 to $30,000

Disclosure Period: 1993

Note: Average grant figure excludes the highest grant of $937,000. Recent grants are derived from a 1993 Form 990.

RECENT GRANTS
Library
5,500	Eagle Hill Library, Southport, CT	
4,500	Greenwich Library Development, Greenwich, CT	
100	Friends of Greenwich Library, Greenwich, CT	

General
937,000	New York Hospital, New York, NY	
501,000	Greenwich Hospital, Greenwich, CT	
315,003	Greenwich Academy, Greenwich, CT	
30,000	Boys and Girls Club, Greenwich, CT	
30,000	Boys and Girls Club, Newport, RI	

DELAWARE

Borkee Hagley Foundation

CONTACT
Henry H. Silliman, Jr.
President
Borkee Hagley Fdn.
PO Box 4590
Greenville, DE 19807
(302) 652-8616

FINANCIAL SUMMARY
Recent Giving: $209,000 (1993); $125,400 (1990); $100,600 (1989)

Assets: $5,158,236 (1993); $2,584,729 (1990); $2,814,736 (1989)

EIN: 51-6011644

CONTRIBUTIONS SUMMARY
Typical Recipients: • *Arts & Humanities:* History & Archaeology, Libraries • *Civic & Public Affairs:* Clubs, Employment/Job Training, General, Housing, Professional & Trade Associations, Urban & Community Affairs • *Education:* Environmental Education, Private Education (Precollege) • *Environment:* General • *Health:* Emergency/Ambulance Services, Geriatric Health, Hospices, Hospitals, Long-Term Care • *Religion:* Jewish Causes, Religious Organizations, Religious Welfare • *Social Services:* Big Brother/Big Sister, Child Welfare, Community Service Organizations, Day Care, Food/Clothing Distribution, Homes, Special Olympics, YMCA/YWCA/YMHA/YWHA, Youth Organizations

Grant Types: capital and general support

Geographic Distribution: focus on DE

GIVING OFFICERS
Thomas F. Husbands: trust

Eleanor Silliman Maroney: secy *PHIL AFFIL* trust: Crystal Trust

Mariana Silliman Richards: trust

George A. Sandbach: trust

Henry Harper Silliman: trust *CORP AFFIL* dir: Sigma Investment Shares

Henry Harper Silliman, Jr.: pres *PHIL AFFIL* treas, trust: Longwood Foundation

John E. Silliman: vp *B* Scarsdale NY 1934 *ED* Yale Univ BA 1956; Columbia Univ LLB 1959 *CURR EMPL* ptnr: Murtha Cullina Richter Pinney

Robert M. Silliman: vp, treas *ED* Yale Univ

Doris Silliman Stockly: trust

APPLICATION INFORMATION
Initial Approach: Send a brief letter of inquiry. Include a description of organization, amount requested, purpose of funds sought, recently audited financial statement, and proof of tax-exempt status. There are no deadlines.

GRANTS ANALYSIS
Total Grants: $209,000

Number of Grants: 39

Highest Grant: $20,000

Typical Range: $1,000 to $10,000

Disclosure Period: 1993

Note: Recent grants are derived from a 1993 Form 990.

RECENT GRANTS
Library
10,000	Hagley Museum and Library, Wilmington, DE	

General
20,000	Emily Tybout duPont Memorial Endowment	
15,000	Delaware Nature Education Society, Wilmington, DE	
10,000	American Red Cross	
10,000	Big Brothers and Big Sisters	
10,000	Delaware Special Olympics, Wilmington, DE	

Caspersen Foundation for Aid to Health and Education, O. W.

CONTACT
Lois E. Hansen
Secretary, Assistant Treasurer
O. W. Caspersen Fdn for Aid to Health and Education
PO Box 911
Wilmington, DE 19899
(201) 786-5354

FINANCIAL SUMMARY
Recent Giving: $221,000 (1993); $543,500 (1992); $163,000 (1991)

Assets: $5,011,121 (1993); $3,790,398 (1992); $3,756,282 (1991)

Gifts Received: $696,030 (1992)

Fiscal Note: In 1993, contributions were received from Freda R. Caspersen Charitable

Lead Unitrust ($323,530) and Finn M.W. Caspersen ($372,500).
EIN: 51-0101350

CONTRIBUTIONS SUMMARY
Donor(s): the late O. W. Caspersen

Typical Recipients: • *Arts & Humanities:* Arts Associations & Councils, Libraries • *Education:* Colleges & Universities, General, Legal Education, Private Education (Precollege) • *Environment:* Resource Conservation • *Health:* Emergency/Ambulance Services, Health Organizations, Hospitals, Single-Disease Health Associations • *Social Services:* Recreation & Athletics

Grant Types: capital, emergency, multi-year/continuing support, operating expenses, and research

Geographic Distribution: focus on the Eastern coastal states

GIVING OFFICERS
Barbara M. Caspersen: vp, treas, dir

Erik Michael Westby Caspersen: dir, vp

Finn M. W. Caspersen, Jr.: vp, dir *B* New York NY 1941 *ED* Brown Univ BA 1963; Harvard Univ LLB 1966; Hood Coll LLD; Washington Univ HHD *CURR EMPL* chmn, ceo, dir: Beneficial Corp *CORP AFFIL* chmn: Beneficial Bank PLC; dir: Clark Hill; mem exec comm, dir: Beneficial Natl Bank; pres, dir: Tri Farms, Westby Corp, Westby Mgmt Corp *NONPR AFFIL* adv bd: Inst Law & Econ; chmn: Gladstone Equestrian Assn, Harbour Island; dir: Shelter Harbor Fire District; emeritus trust: Brown Univ, Camp Nejeda Fdn Diabetic Children; mem: Am Bar Assn, Am Fin Svcs Assn, Cardigan Mountain Sch, Conf Bd, FL Bar Assn, Harvard Univ Resources Comm, NY Bar Assn, Partnership NJ; mem adv comm: Boy Scouts Am Morris-Sussex Area; mem bd advs: Univ PA Inst Law Econ; mem driving comm: Am Horse Shows Assn; pres: Coalition Svc Indus; pres, chmn: US Equestrian Team; speaker: Univ PA; trust: Peddie Sch *PHIL AFFIL* vp, dir: Beneficial Foundation, Inc.; chmn: Waterloo Foundation Arts, Waterloo Foundation Arts *CLUB AFFIL* Harvard, Knickerbocker, Univ, Wilmington CC

Samuel Michael Westby Caspersen: dir, vp

Lois E. Hansen: secy, asst treas

John O. Williams: asst secy, asst treas *PHIL AFFIL* dir: Beneficial Foundation, Inc.

APPLICATION INFORMATION
Initial Approach: The foundation has no formal grant application procedure or application form. There are no deadlines.

Restrictions on Giving: Health and education grants only.

GRANTS ANALYSIS
Total Grants: $221,000

Number of Grants: 4

Highest Grant: $125,000

Typical Range: $1,000 to $5,000

Disclosure Period: 1993

Note: Recent grants are derived from a 1993 Form 990.

RECENT GRANTS
General

125,000	Wellesley College, Wellesley, MA
90,000	Gladstone Equestrian Association, Gladstone, NJ
5,000	Shipley School, Bryn Mawr, PA
1,000	Groton School, Groton, MA

Crestlea Foundation

CONTACT
Stephen A. Martinenza
Treasurer
Crestlea Foundation
1004 Wilmington Trust Center
Wilmington, DE 19801
(302) 654-2477

FINANCIAL SUMMARY
Recent Giving: $800,000 (1994); $1,133,410 (1993); $809,208 (1992)

Assets: $17,500,000 (1994 est.); $17,320,170 (1993); $16,821,361 (1992)

Gifts Received: $200 (1994); $329,881 (1993); $10,762 (1992)

Fiscal Note: In 1993, the foundation received contributions from the Wilmington Trust Co.

EIN: 51-6015638

CONTRIBUTIONS SUMMARY
Donor(s): The foundation was incorporated in 1955 by the late Henry B. duPont .

Typical Recipients: • *Arts & Humanities:* Arts Centers, Arts Funds, Historic Preservation, History & Archaeology, Libraries, Museums/Galleries, Music, Theater • *Civic & Public Affairs:* Business/Free Enterprise, Clubs, Economic Development, General, Law & Justice, Nonprofit Management, Professional & Trade Associations, Public Policy, Urban & Community Affairs, Zoos/Aquariums • *Education:* Arts/Humanities Education, Colleges & Universities, Health & Physical Education, Medical Education, Private Education (Precollege), Secondary Education (Private), Secondary Education (Public), Student Aid, Vocational & Technical Education • *Environment:* Air/Water Quality, General, Resource Conservation • *Health:* Cancer, Clinics/Medical Centers, Geriatric Health, Health Organizations, Hospices, Hospitals, Long-Term Care, Single-Disease Health Associations • *Religion:* Churches, Ministries, Religious Welfare • *Social Services:* Animal Protection, Camps, Child Welfare, Community Centers, Community Service Organizations, Day Care, Family Planning, Family Services, Food/Clothing Distribution, Homes, People with Disabilities, Recreation & Athletics, Senior Services, Special Olympics, United Funds/United Ways, Veterans, YMCA/YWCA/YMHA/YWHA, Youth Organizations

Grant Types: capital and operating expenses

Geographic Distribution: majority of grants given to organizations within 50 miles of Wilmington, DE

GIVING OFFICERS
Robert C. Barlow: pres *B* 1931 *CURR EMPL* treas, dir: DE Savings Bank *NONPR AFFIL* asst treas, dir: Red Clay Reservation *PHIL AFFIL* asst secy: Welfare Foundation, Longwood Foundation

Otto C. Fad: vp

Stephen A. Martinenza: treas *PHIL AFFIL* asst treas: Welfare Foundation, Longwood Foundation

APPLICATION INFORMATION
Initial Approach:

The foundation requests applications be made in writing.

Applicants should include the reason for the grant, any pertinent financial statements, and a copy of the IRS exemption approval letter.

Applications must be received by November 1.

Restrictions on Giving: Grants are given to organizations within 50 miles of Wilmington, DE. The foundation does not make grants to individuals.

GRANTS ANALYSIS
Total Grants: $1,133,410

Number of Grants: 61

Highest Grant: $400,000

Average Grant: $18,580

Typical Range: $1,000 to $20,000

Disclosure Period: 1993

Note: Recent grants are derived from a 1993 grants list.

RECENT GRANTS

Library

400,000	Hagley Museum and Library, Wilmington, DE — endowment campaign
50,000	Wilmington Institute Free Library, Wilmington, DE — building fund
5,000	Hagley Museum and Library, Wilmington, DE
5,000	Hagley Museum and Library, Wilmington, DE — Eleutherian Mills Endowment Fund

General

145,410	Pomfret School, Pomfret, CT — scholarship aid
50,000	Yale University, New Haven, CT — capital campaign
35,000	YMCA of Delaware, Dover, DE — capital campaign
25,000	Nature Conservancy, Dover, DE — land purchase
25,000	Pilot School, Wilmington, DE — building repairs

Crystal Trust

CONTACT
Stephen C. Doberstein
Executive Director
Crystal Trust
1088 du Pont Bldg.
Wilmington, DE 19898
(302) 774-8421

FINANCIAL SUMMARY
Recent Giving: $2,974,015 (1994 approx.);
$5,011,781 (1993); $3,745,525 (1992)

Assets: $65,996,014 (1993); $66,113,196
(1991); $56,993,596 (1990)

EIN: 51-6015063

CONTRIBUTIONS SUMMARY
Donor(s): The donor of the trust, the late
Irenee du Pont , established the trust in
1947. Under the terms of Mr. du Pont's will,
the trust received an additional endowment
in 1964, and has since operated under its present name. Mr. du Pont served as president
of E. I. du Pont de Nemours & Co., a Wil-
mington-based manufacturing and chemical
firm. Currently, the board of advisory trustees includes three descendants of the donor.

Typical Recipients: • *Arts & Humanities:*
Historic Preservation, History & Archaeol-
ogy, Libraries, Museums/Galleries, Music,
Opera, Theater • *Civic & Public Affairs:*
Clubs, Employment/Job Training, General,
Housing, Nonprofit Management, Urban &
Community Affairs • *Education:* Colleges &
Universities, Private Education (Precollege),
Secondary Education (Private) • *Environ-
ment:* General, Resource Conservation
• *Health:* Cancer, Health Organizations, Hos-
pices, Hospitals, Single-Disease Health As-
sociations • *Religion:* Ministries, Religious
Welfare • *Science:* Scientific Centers & In-
stitutes, Scientific Organizations • *Social
Services:* Child Welfare, Community Centers, Community Service Organizations, Domestic Violence, Family Planning, Family
Services, Food/Clothing Distribution, People with Disabilities, Recreation & Athletics, Senior Services, Special Olympics,
YMCA/YWCA/YMHA/YWHA, Youth Organizations

Grant Types: capital

Geographic Distribution: the state of Delaware

GIVING OFFICERS
Robert W. Crump: fin off

Stephen C. Doberstein: exec dir

Irenee du Pont, Jr.: trust *B* 1920 *ED* Dartmouth Coll; MA Inst Tech *CORP AFFIL*
dir: MIT Corp, Wilmington Trust Co
NONPR AFFIL chmn, dir: Wilmington Coll
PHIL AFFIL vp, trust: Longwood Gardens;
dir: Unidel Foundation; vp: Bredin Foundation *CLUB AFFIL* Wilmington CC

David Greenewalt: adv trust, don grandson

Eleanor Silliman Maroney: trust *PHIL AF-
FIL* secy: Borkee Hagley Foundation

APPLICATION INFORMATION
Initial Approach:

The trust does not use standard application
forms. Detailed letters of request should be
submitted.

Letters should include a history of the applicant organization, organizational purposes
and activities, information about the proposal and its priority within the applicant organization, certification of tax-exempt
status, and information on the governing
group and finances of the organization.

Requests may be submitted any time prior to
October 1. Early application is recommended.

Grant decisions are formulated by the end of
the year.

Restrictions on Giving: The trust does not
support individuals, endowment funds, research, scholarships, fellowships, matching
programs, loans, or continuing expenses of
operations or deficits.

OTHER THINGS TO KNOW
In unique cases, requests can be considered
at times other than those specified by the
trust. One-time support is preferred, usually
for capital or for the needs of a program in
its early stages.

Requests should be submitted by an appropriate volunteer officer or board member of
the organization, or by a member of its executive staff to whom the responsibility is
specifically delegated by its governing body.

GRANTS ANALYSIS
Total Grants: $5,011,781

Number of Grants: 53

Highest Grant: $2,500,000

Average Grant: $48,303*

Typical Range: $10,000 to $100,000

Disclosure Period: 1993

Note: Average grant figure excludes highest
grant of $2,500,000. Recent grants are de-
rived from a 1993 Form 990.

RECENT GRANTS
Library

250,000	Eleutherian Mills-Hagley Museum and Library, Wilmington, DE — research library
100,000	Hockessin Library, Hockessin, DE — payment of challenge grant
50,000	Delaware Technical and Community College, Georgetown, DE — electronic system for library

General

2,500,000	Wilmington College, New Castle, DE — capital campaign
250,000	Independence School, Newark, DE — capital needs
182,645	Delaware Nature Society, Hockessin, DE — landowner contact program
100,000	Food Bank of Delaware, Newark, DE — expansion
100,000	Ingleside Homes, Wilmington, DE — capital campaign

du Pont de Nemours & Co., E. I.

Revenue: $34.96 billion
Employees: 114,000
Headquarters: Wilmington, DE
SIC Major Group: Crude Petroleum & Natural
Gas, Bituminous Coal—Underground,
Natural Gas Liquids, and Nonwoven Fabrics

CONTACT
Peter C. Morrow
Manager, Corporate Contributions
E. I. du Pont de Nemours & Co.
Nemours Bldg.
Rm. 9541
1007 Market St.
Wilmington, DE 19898
(302) 774-2036
Note: Dr. Claibourne D. Smith, Vice President,
Technology and Professional Development,
is the contact for DuPont's educational
program. His number is (302)774-5025. Mr
Morrow is the contact for national
organizations and the headquarters area.
Organizations with regional scope should
contact their nearest DuPont site for more
information.

FINANCIAL SUMMARY
Recent Giving: $28,000,000 (1995 est.);
$28,000,000 (1994 approx.); $28,000,000
(1993 approx.)

Fiscal Note: Company gives directly. Above
figures include nonmonetary support. Figures also include international giving.

CONTRIBUTIONS SUMMARY
Typical Recipients: • *Arts & Humanities:*
Arts Appreciation, Arts Associations &
Councils, Arts Centers, Arts Festivals, Arts
Funds, Arts Institutes, Community Arts,
Dance, Ethnic & Folk Arts, Historic Preser-
vation, Libraries, Literary Arts, Muse-
ums/Galleries, Music, Opera, Performing
Arts, Public Broadcasting, Theater, Visual
Arts • *Civic & Public Affairs:* Business/Free
Enterprise, Civil Rights, Economic Develop-
ment, Economic Policy, Employment/Job
Training, Housing, Law & Justice, Legal
Aid, Municipalities/Towns, Nonprofit Man-
agement, Philanthropic Organizations, Pro-
fessional & Trade Associations, Public
Policy, Safety, Urban & Community Affairs,
Women's Affairs, Zoos/Aquariums • *Educa-
tion:* Agricultural Education, Business Edu-
cation, Colleges & Universities, Community
& Junior Colleges, Economic Education,
Education Associations, Education Funds,
Engineering/Technological Education, Fac-
ulty Development, International Exchange,

International Studies, Journalism/Media Education, Legal Education, Literacy, Minority Education, Preschool Education, Private Education (Precollege), Public Education (Precollege), Science/Mathematics Education, Social Sciences Education, Student Aid • *Environment:* General • *Health:* Emergency/Ambulance Services, Geriatric Health, Health Policy/Cost Containment, Health Organizations, Hospices, Hospitals, Medical Rehabilitation, Medical Research, Medical Training, Mental Health, Single-Disease Health Associations • *International:* Foreign Educational Institutions, Health Care/Hospitals, International Peace & Security Issues, International Relations • *Science:* Science Exhibits & Fairs, Scientific Centers & Institutes, Scientific Organizations • *Social Services:* Animal Protection, Child Welfare, Community Centers, Community Service Organizations, Counseling, Day Care, Delinquency & Criminal Rehabilitation, Domestic Violence, Emergency Relief, Family Services, Food/Clothing Distribution, Homes, People with Disabilities, Recreation & Athletics, Senior Services, Shelters/Homelessness, Substance Abuse, United Funds/United Ways, Volunteer Services, Youth Organizations

Grant Types: capital, conference/seminar, emergency, fellowship, general support, and multiyear/continuing support

Nonmonetary Support: $1,400,000 (1994); $860,000 (1993); $741,000 (1992)

Nonmonetary Support Types: donated equipment

Note: Company also donates property. Contact the nearest DuPont site or Peter C. Morrow at above address for more information on nonmonetary support.

Geographic Distribution: near headquarters and operating locations and to some national and international organizations

Operating Locations: AL (Axis), AR (Hazen, Lonoke), CA (Antioch, Huntington Beach, Santa Clara), CO (Commerce City, Rangley), CT (Danbury, Newtown), DE (Edge Moor, Glasgow, Newark, Newport, Seaford, Wilmington), FL (Starke), GA (Athens), IA (Clinton, Fort Madison), IL (El Paso), IN (East Chicago, Kokomo), KS (Kansas City), KY (Louisville, Wurtland), LA (Darrow, Egan, Grand Chenier, La Place, Lake Charles, Westlake), MA (Boston), MI (Flint, Mason, Montague, Mt. Clemens, Troy), MS (Pass Christian), MT (Billings), NC (Brevard, Denton, Fayetteville, Kinston, Research Triangle Park, Wilmington), NJ (Deepwater, Gibbstown, Linden, Parlic, Pompton Lakes), NM (Bloomfield, Maljamar), NY (Buffalo, Ilion, Niagara Falls, Rochester), OH (Circleville, Findley, North Bend, Stow, Toledo), OK (Ada, Hennessy, Laverne, Medford, Ponca City, Tuttle), PA (Boothwyn, Dunbar, Philadelphia, Pittsburgh, Towanda), SC (Camden, Charleston, Florence), TN (Chattanooga, Memphis, New Johnsonville, Old Hickory), TX (Beaumont, El Dorado, Hamlin, Houston, Ingelside, La Porte, McKinney, Mertzon, Mont Belvieu, Orange, Orla, Pasadena, Round Rock, San Angelo, Sterling City, Victoria), VA (Front Royal, Martinsville, Mavisdale, Richmond, Waynesboro), WV (Belle, Martinsburg, Moundsville, Parkersburg)

Note: Also operates in Canada, Mexico, Puerto Rico, Japan, China, Europe, Asia, and Africa.

CORP. OFFICERS

Edgar Smith Woolard, Jr.: *B* Washington NC 1934 *ED* NC St Univ BS 1956 *CURR EMPL* chmn, ceo, dir: EI du Pont de Nemours & Co *CORP AFFIL* dir: Citicorp, Intl Bus Machines Corp, Seagram Co *NONPR AFFIL* dir: NC Textile Fdn; trust: Natl Counc Econ Ed, NC St Univ, Protestant Episcopal Theological Seminary, Winterthur Mus Gardens

GIVING OFFICERS

Peter C. Morrow: *CURR EMPL* mgr corp contributions, exec secy contributions comm: EI du Pont de Nemours & Co

Dr. Claibourne D. Smith: *CURR EMPL* vp tech & professional devel: EI du Pont de Nemours & Co

APPLICATION INFORMATION

Initial Approach: *Initial Contact:* corporation prefers to initiate contact for education grants; requests for support of national organizations or programs in corporate headquarters community should be addressed to Peter C. Morrow; requests for support of projects in operating communities should be addressed to the manager of the nearest company site *Include Information On:* brief description of the organization and program to be funded, how it relates to corporate and community interests, and extent of utilization of facilities or services by DuPont employees and community members

Restrictions on Giving: Du Pont does not make contributions to individuals other than through certain scholarship and fellowship programs; member agencies of united funds, except for capital needs; charitable organizations not eligible for support under the Internal Revenue Code; sectarian organizations whose programs are limited to members of one religious group; fraternal and veterans groups; or organizations that discriminate by sex, race, color, creed, or national origin.

OTHER THINGS TO KNOW

The company awards between 5,000 and 6,000 grants annually.

DuPont plans to expand its international giving program to better reflect the company's global business interests.

PUBLICATIONS

Brochure

GRANTS ANALYSIS

Total Grants: $28,000,000*

Typical Range: $5,000 to $10,000

Disclosure Period: 1994

Note: Recent grants are derived from a partial 1993 grants list. Total Grants figure is approximate.

RECENT GRANTS

General

2,000,000	Business/Public Education Council, Wilmington, DE
2,000,000	University of Delaware
105,000	Drexel University, Philadelphia, PA — undergraduate engineering
32,000	Manhattan College, Riverdale, NY — environmental science program
15,000	Spelman College, Atlanta, GA

Fair Play Foundation

CONTACT

Blaine T. Phillips
President
Fair Play Fdn.
350 Delaware Trust Bldg.
Wilmington, DE 19801
(302) 658-6771

FINANCIAL SUMMARY

Recent Giving: $480,998 (1993); $492,722 (1992); $650,000 (1991)

Assets: $7,595,263 (1993); $8,073,349 (1992); $11,455,888 (1991)

EIN: 51-6017779

CONTRIBUTIONS SUMMARY

Typical Recipients: • *Arts & Humanities:* Arts Centers, Arts Festivals, Arts Institutes, General, Historic Preservation, History & Archaeology, Libraries, Museums/Galleries, Music, Theater • *Civic & Public Affairs:* Botanical Gardens/Parks, General, Philanthropic Organizations, Zoos/Aquariums • *Education:* Agricultural Education, Colleges & Universities, Education Funds, Legal Education, Private Education (Precollege) • *Environment:* Air/Water Quality, General, Resource Conservation, Wildlife Protection • *Health:* Arthritis, Hospices, Medical Research, Single-Disease Health Associations • *International:* International Environmental Issues • *Religion:* Churches • *Social Services:* Child Welfare, Community Service Organizations, Day Care, Family Services, Recreation & Athletics

Grant Types: capital and general support

Geographic Distribution: focus on DE

GIVING OFFICERS

James F. Burnett: vp, trust

George P. Edmonds: trust

L. E. Grimes: treas, trust

Blaine T. Phillips: pres, trust

D. P. Ross, Jr.: trust

APPLICATION INFORMATION

Initial Approach: Send brief letter of inquiry describing program or project. There are no deadlines or restrictions.

GRANTS ANALYSIS

Total Grants: $480,998

Number of Grants: 32

Highest Grant: $100,000

Typical Range: $5,000 to $30,000

Disclosure Period: 1993

Note: Recent grants are derived from a 1993 Form 990.

RECENT GRANTS

Library
148	Hagley Museum, Wilmington, DE — library

General
100,000	Chesapeake Bay Foundation, Annapolis, MD — Nanticoke project
65,000	University of Virginia, Charlottesville, VA — chair
25,000	University of Virginia, Charlottesville, VA — Carr's Hill Stonework
15,000	African Wildlife Foundation, Washington, DC — gorilla project in Uganda
15,000	Chesapeake Wildlife Heritage, Easton, MD — Woodducks/Bluebirds Project

Glencoe Foundation

CONTACT
Ellice McDonald, Jr.
President
Glencoe Fdn.
Greenville Ctr.
3801 Kennett Pke.
Bldg. C, Ste. 300
Greenville, DE 19807
(302) 654-9933

FINANCIAL SUMMARY
Recent Giving: $342,294 (1993); $322,013 (1992); $443,647 (1991)

Assets: $4,147,102 (1993); $4,207,076 (1992); $4,595,865 (1991)

Gifts Received: $146,318 (1993); $101,076 (1992); $71,670 (1991)

Fiscal Note: In 1993, contributions were received from Mr. and Mrs. Ellice McDonald, Jr. ($144,218).

EIN: 51-0164761

CONTRIBUTIONS SUMMARY
Donor(s): Ellice McDonald, Jr., Rosa H. McDonald

Typical Recipients: • *Arts & Humanities:* Libraries, Museums/Galleries, Music • *Education:* Private Education (Precollege) • *Health:* Hospitals, Mental Health • *International:* Foreign Arts Organizations, Foreign Educational Institutions, International Environmental Issues, International Organizations, International Peace & Security Issues

Grant Types: capital, emergency, general support, multiyear/continuing support, and operating expenses

Geographic Distribution: Gives to the city of Glencoe, Scotland.

GIVING OFFICERS
Gregory A. Inskip: dir

Walter J. Laird, Jr.: dir

Ellice McDonald, Jr.: pres, dir

Rosa H. McDonald: vp, dir

John C. Milner: secy, treas

John P. Sinclair: dir

APPLICATION INFORMATION
Initial Approach: Send brief letter requesting application form. There are no deadlines.

Restrictions on Giving: Limited to the Highland and Island Region of Scotland.

PUBLICATIONS
Application Guidelines

GRANTS ANALYSIS
Total Grants: $342,294

Number of Grants: 8

Highest Grant: $154,836

Typical Range: $8,877 to $63,040

Disclosure Period: 1993

Note: Recent grants are derived from a 1993 Form 990.

RECENT GRANTS
General
154,836	Clan Donald Lands Trust, Isle of Skye, Scotland — operating grant
63,040	Clan Donald Lands Trust, Isle of Skye, Scotland — small project grants
38,776	Royal Caledonian Schools, Herfordshire, England — operating grant
29,338	Royal Caledonian Schools, Herfordshire, England — facilities grant
16,576	National Trust for Scotland, Edinburgh, Scotland — project funds

Good Samaritan

CONTACT
E. N. Carpenter II
Secretary and Treasurer
Good Samaritan
600 Ctr. Mill Rd.
Wilmington, DE 19807
(302) 654-7558

FINANCIAL SUMMARY
Recent Giving: $556,260 (1993); $779,298 (1992); $685,900 (1991)

Assets: $3,266,170 (1993); $3,698,123 (1992); $1,694,805 (1991)

EIN: 51-6000401

CONTRIBUTIONS SUMMARY
Donor(s): the late Elias Ahuja

Typical Recipients: • *Arts & Humanities:* Libraries • *Civic & Public Affairs:* Community Foundations, Law & Justice, Public Policy, Urban & Community Affairs • *Education:* Colleges & Universities, Community & Junior Colleges, Education Funds, Engineering/Technological Education, Faculty Development, Minority Education, Private Education (Precollege), Public Education (Precollege), Science/Mathematics Education, Special Education, Student Aid • *Environment:* General, Resource Conservation • *Health:* Hospitals • *International:* Foreign Educational Institutions • *Religion:* Ministries • *Social Services:* At-Risk Youth, Child Welfare, Day Care, Delinquency & Criminal Rehabilitation, Family Planning, Recreation & Athletics, YMCA/YWCA/YMHA/YWHA, Youth Organizations

Grant Types: general support

Geographic Distribution: focus on East Coast

GIVING OFFICERS
Edmund N. Carpenter II: secy, treas, dir

Elizabeth Lee DuPont: vp

Rev. Henry W. Sherrill: pres, dir

APPLICATION INFORMATION
Initial Approach: The foundation requests applications be made in writing. There are no deadlines.

PUBLICATIONS
Application Guidelines

GRANTS ANALYSIS
Total Grants: $556,260

Number of Grants: 23

Highest Grant: $50,000

Typical Range: $4,000 to $50,000

Disclosure Period: 1993

Note: Recent grants are derived from a 1993 Form 990.

RECENT GRANTS
Library
15,000	Library of the Boston Athenaeum, Boston, MA — for an endowment fund for interns

General
50,000	Princeton-Blairstown Center, Blairstown, NJ — provide funds for the center's programs
50,000	Roxbury Community College, Boston, MA — support college's endowment
50,000	YWCA, Wilmington, DE
48,600	University of Delaware, Newark, DE — to support Improving School Board Effectiveness program
35,000	Benedictine Homes of Delaware, Wilmington, DE — provide scholarship funds

ICI Americas Inc.

Sales: $1.2 billion
Employees: 6,500
Parent Company: Imperial Chemical Industries PLC
Headquarters: Wilmington, DE
SIC Major Group: Plastics Materials & Resins, Industrial Inorganic Chemicals Nec, Medicinals & Botanicals, and Biological Products Except Diagnostic

CONTACT
Barbara Sanson Curran
Corporate Secretary
ICI Americas Inc.
Concord Plz.
3411 Silverside Rd.
PO Box 15391
Wilmington, DE 19850
(302) 887-3073

FINANCIAL SUMMARY
Recent Giving: $400,000 (1995 est.); $400,000 (1994 approx.); $400,000 (1993 approx.)

Fiscal Note: Above figures exclude nonmonetary support. Above figures also exclude subsidiary contributions. Company gives about $1 million annually. About $400,000 represents new grants to organizations. About $600,000 represents prior commitments and multiyear/continuing support.

CONTRIBUTIONS SUMMARY
Typical Recipients: • *Arts & Humanities:* Arts Associations & Councils, Community Arts, Libraries, Museums/Galleries, Music, Opera, Performing Arts, Public Broadcasting, Theater • *Civic & Public Affairs:* Business/Free Enterprise, Civil Rights, Employment/Job Training, Public Policy • *Education:* Colleges & Universities, Community & Junior Colleges, Literacy, Minority Education, Science/Mathematics Education • *Environment:* General • *Health:* Geriatric Health, Hospices, Hospitals, Medical Research, Mental Health, Nursing Services, Single-Disease Health Associations • *Science:* Scientific Organizations • *Social Services:* Child Welfare, Community Centers, Community Service Organizations, Day Care, People with Disabilities, Senior Services, Shelters/Homelessness, Substance Abuse, United Funds/United Ways

Grant Types: employee matching gifts, general support, multiyear/continuing support, and operating expenses

Nonmonetary Support Types: donated equipment, in-kind services, and loaned executives

Note: Nonmonetary support is provided by individual businesses.

Geographic Distribution: primarily in Delaware Valley

Operating Locations: AZ, DE (Wilmington), FL, IL, MA, MN, NJ, PA

CORP. OFFICERS
John R. Danzeisen: *B* 1948 *ED* Ursinus Coll BS; Widener Univ MBA *CURR EMPL* chmn, dir: ICI Ams Inc *CORP AFFIL* chmn, ceo, dir: ICI Am Holdings Inc; pres, dir: Glidden Co

Bruce Peters: *CURR EMPL* vp fin: ICI Ams Inc

GIVING OFFICERS
Barbara Sanson Curran: *B* Wiesbaden Germany 1955 *ED* Bryn Mawr Coll AB 1977; Dickinson Coll Law Sch JD 1980 *CURR EMPL* corp secy: ICI Ams Inc *CORP AFFIL* secy: ICI Am Holdings Inc *NONPR AFFIL* mem: Am Bar Assn, PA Bar Assn, Philadelphia Bar Assn *PHIL AFFIL* trust: Chubb Foundation

APPLICATION INFORMATION
Initial Approach: *Initial Contact:* brief letter or proposal *Include Information On:* outline the scope of the program or project, the impact it is expected to have, its associated costs, plans for achievement, listing of the board of directors, tax determination letter, and budget *Deadlines:* none *Note:* Grant applications should be sent to Ms. Barbara Curran at the above contact address. Proposals are forwarded to Delaware Community Foundation for screening.

Restrictions on Giving: Fund donates only to qualified nonprofit organizations defined by section 501(c)(3) of IRS code.

Does not support individuals; sectarian organizations for sectarian purposes; private, elementary, or secondary schools; political campaigns; payment of existing debts or obligations; natural disaster or emergency funds or expeditions; fraternal or veterans groups; advocacy groups; purchase of advertising space in a program or other medium; organizations under the umbrella of a larger organization to which ICI already contributes (such as United Way); special events or activities more suitably funded by other sources; or sports organizations.

Fund only gives in Daleware.

OTHER THINGS TO KNOW
The ICI Americas Fund is administered by the Delaware Community Foundation. Its grant-making activities are overseen by a contribution committee comprised of ICI representatives.

Minimum grant made is $1,000.

On June 1, 1993, ICI split into two separate organizations—ICI and ZENECA PLC. ICI is now a $2.7 billion company with 10,000 employees and fifty-seven manufacturing sites in North America. ICI is composed of the following international business: Materials (Acrylics, Composites, Films, and Polyurethanes), Paints, Explosives, Industrial Chemicals, Tioxide, as well as regional businesses. Company representative reports that the demerger should not affect giving of ICI Americas Inc. Fund.

ZENECA also has a giving program. The contact for the program is Ms. Patricia Preston.

GRANTS ANALYSIS
Total Grants: $400,000*

Typical Range: $5,000 to $10,000

Disclosure Period: 1994

Note: Annual giving is approximately $1 million. Total grants figure does not include company's prior commitments. Recent grants are derived from a 1991 grants list.

RECENT GRANTS
General
A.C.E.S., Wilmington, DE
Boys Club of Delaware, Wilmington, DE
Delaware Council on Economic Education, Newark, DE
Delaware Hospice, Wilmington, DE
Delaware Nature Society, Hockessin, DE

Kent-Lucas Foundation

CONTACT
Elizabeth K. Van Alen
President
Kent-Lucas Fdn.
101 Springer Bldg.
3411 Silverside Rd.
Wilmington, DE 19810
(302) 478-4383

FINANCIAL SUMMARY
Recent Giving: $174,300 (1993); $180,650 (1992); $155,400 (1991)

Assets: $2,527,360 (1993); $2,626,431 (1992); $2,853,022 (1991)

EIN: 23-7010084

CONTRIBUTIONS SUMMARY
Donor(s): Atwater Kent Foundation

Typical Recipients: • *Arts & Humanities:* Arts Associations & Councils, Historic Preservation, History & Archaeology, Libraries, Museums/Galleries, Public Broadcasting, Theater • *Civic & Public Affairs:* Clubs, Employment/Job Training, General, Municipalities/Towns, Philanthropic Organizations, Public Policy, Safety • *Education:* Arts/Humanities Education, Colleges & Universities, International Exchange, International Studies, Medical Education, Religious Education, Special Education, Student Aid • *Environment:* General, Resource Conservation • *Health:* Children's Health/Hospitals, Clinics/Medical Centers, Emergency/Ambulance Services, Hospitals, Medical Research, Nursing Services • *Religion:* Churches, Religious Organizations, Religious Welfare • *Social Services:* Animal Protection, Child Welfare, Community Service Organizations, Crime Prevention, Family Services, Food/Clothing Distribution, Recreation & Athletics, Shelters/Homelessness, United Funds/United Ways, Youth Organizations

Grant Types: capital, general support, multiyear/continuing support, and operating expenses

Geographic Distribution: focus on the Philadelphia, PA, metropolitan area, ME, and FL

GIVING OFFICERS
Cassandra Ludington: trust

Elizabeth K. Van Alen: pres, treas, trust

James L. Van Alen II: trust

William L. Van Alen: vp, trust

William L. Van Alen, Jr.: trust

James R. Weaver: secy

Stella R. Williams: asst secy

APPLICATION INFORMATION

Initial Approach: Send a brief letter of inquiry. Include a description of organization, amount requested, purpose of funds sought, recently audited financial statement, and proof of tax-exempt status. There are no deadlines.

Restrictions on Giving: Does not support individuals.

PUBLICATIONS
Application Guidelines

GRANTS ANALYSIS
Total Grants: $174,300

Number of Grants: 72

Highest Grant: $40,000

Typical Range: $50 to $25,000

Disclosure Period: 1993

Note: Recent grants are derived from a 1993 Form 990.

RECENT GRANTS

Library

1,000	Northeast Harbor Library, Northeast Harbor, ME

General

25,000	Children's Hospital of Philadelphia, Philadelphia, PA — The Campaign for CHOP
14,200	University of Pennsylvania, Philadelphia, PA — graduate school of fine arts
10,000	Jupiter Hospital, Jupiter, FL
5,000	American Red Cross, West Palm Beach, FL — disaster relief fund
5,000	Fellowship Christians University and Schools, Greenwich, CT

Kutz Foundation, Milton and Hattie

CONTACT
Toni Young
President, Bd. of Dirs.
Milton and Hattie Kutz Fdn.
c/o Jewish Federation of Delaware
101 Garden of Eden Rd.
Wilmington, DE 19803
(302) 478-6200

FINANCIAL SUMMARY
Recent Giving: $137,851 (fiscal 1993); $120,725 (fiscal 1992); $143,575 (fiscal 1991)

Assets: $2,615,145 (fiscal 1993); $2,474,407 (fiscal 1992); $2,334,581 (fiscal 1991)

EIN: 51-0187055

CONTRIBUTIONS SUMMARY
Donor(s): Milton Kutz, Hattie Kutz

Typical Recipients: • *Arts & Humanities:* Libraries • *Civic & Public Affairs:* Community Foundations, Housing • *Education:* Colleges & Universities, Private Education (Precollege), Secondary Education (Private), Student Aid • *International:* Missionary/Religious Activities • *Religion:* Jewish Causes, Missionary Activities (Domestic), Religious Organizations, Synagogues/Temples • *Social Services:* Community Service Organizations, Day Care, Homes, Youth Organizations

Grant Types: capital, emergency, general support, operating expenses, project, scholarship, and seed money

Geographic Distribution: focus on DE

GIVING OFFICERS
Dr. Cas Anolick: trust

Dr. Bennett N. Epstein: secy

Rolf F. Erikson: treas

Martin G. Mand: trust *B* Norfolk VA 1936 *ED* State Univ NY *CURR EMPL* chmn, ceo, dir: Paramount Pictures Corp *CORP AFFIL* dir: Burke Rehabilitation Ctr, Museum Broadcasting, NY-Cornell Med Ctr, Will Rogers Memorial Fund; mem: Academy Motion Pictures Arts Sciences, Am Film Inst, Motion Pictures Assn, Motion Pictures Pioneers, Variety Clubs Intl *NONPR AFFIL* dir: Univ CA Los Angeles Med Ctr

David Margules, Esq.: trust

Irving Morris, Esq.: trust

Barbara Schoenberg: trust

Jeremiah Patrick Shea: trust *B* Philadelphia PA 1926 *ED* Yale Univ BA 1946; Catholic Univ Am MA 1950 *CURR EMPL* chmn, ceo, dir: Bank DE Wilmington *CORP AFFIL* asst secy, treas: Santa Fe Natural Resources; chmn: Bank DE Corp Wilmington; pres: Wilmington Fin Co; treas; dir: Santa Fe Indus *NONPR AFFIL* dir: St Marks High Sch; mem: Am Bankers Assn, Natl Alliance Businessmen, Robert Morris Assocs; vp: Un Way

Bernard L. Siegel: trust

Judy Wortman: trust

Toni Young: pres

Dr. Leo Zeftel: trust

APPLICATION INFORMATION
Initial Approach: Send a brief letter describing financial position of student's family and requesting application form. The deadline is March 15.

Restrictions on Giving: Limited to freshmen who are residents of Delaware.

GRANTS ANALYSIS
Total Grants: $137,851

Number of Grants: 7

Highest Grant: $33,156

Typical Range: $3,000 to $14,915

Disclosure Period: fiscal year ending June 30, 1993

Note: Recent grants are derived from a fiscal 1993 Form 990. Number of grants and

typical range do not include scholarships to individuals.

RECENT GRANTS

General

33,156	Jewish Federation of Delaware, Wilmington, DE
20,009	Jewish Family Services, Wilmington, DE
18,511	Albert Einstein Academy, Wilmington, DE
14,915	Jewish Community Center, Wilmington, DE
5,790	Gratz Hebrew High School, Wilmington, DE

Laffey-McHugh Foundation

CONTACT
Thomas S. Lodge
Secretary
Laffey-McHugh Foundation
PO Box 2207
Wilmington, DE 19899-2207
(302) 658-9141

FINANCIAL SUMMARY
Recent Giving: $1,933,730 (1993); $1,908,630 (1992); $1,773,640 (1991)

Assets: $53,966,073 (1993); $47,666,526 (1992); $44,877,591 (1991)

EIN: 51-6015095

CONTRIBUTIONS SUMMARY
Donor(s): The principal donor of the Laffey-McHugh Foundation was Frank A. McHugh, who died in 1949. Mr. McHugh was secretary to Pierre S. duPont at the E. I. duPont de Nemours Company. Other donors to the foundation included the late Alice L. McHugh and the late Marie Louise McHugh.

Typical Recipients: • *Arts & Humanities:* Arts Funds, Libraries, Museums/Galleries, Public Broadcasting • *Civic & Public Affairs:* Botanical Gardens/Parks, Clubs, Employment/Job Training, General, Housing, Urban & Community Affairs, Zoos/Aquariums • *Education:* Colleges & Universities, Education Associations, Education Funds, Minority Education, Private Education (Precollege), Public Education (Precollege), Secondary Education (Private), Student Aid • *Environment:* Resource Conservation • *Health:* Cancer, Geriatric Health, Hospices, Hospitals, Single-Disease Health Associations • *Religion:* Churches, Dioceses, Ministries, Religious Organizations, Religious Welfare • *Social Services:* Animal Protection, At-Risk Youth, Child Abuse, Child Welfare, Community Centers, Community Service Organizations, Counseling, Day Care, Emergency Relief, Family Planning, Family Services, Food/Clothing Distribution, Homes, People with Disabilities, Recreation & Athletics, Senior Services, Shelters/Homelessness, Special Olympics, Substance Abuse, United Funds/United Ways, Youth Organizations

Grant Types: capital, general support, project, and scholarship

Geographic Distribution: primarily Delaware

GIVING OFFICERS

Arthur Gould Connolly, Jr.: treas, dir *B* Wilmington DE *ED* Georgetown Univ BSS 1959; Georgetown Univ LLB 1962 *CURR EMPL* atty: Connolly Bove Lodge & Hutz

Arthur Gould Connolly, Sr.: pres *B* Boston MA 1905 *ED* MA Inst Tech BS 1927; Harvard Univ LLB 1930 *CURR EMPL* sr ptnr: Connolly Bove Lodge & Hutz *NONPR AFFIL* fellow: Am Coll Trial Lawyers; mem: Am Bar Assn, DE Bar Assn, New Castle County Bar Assn; pres, dir: Arguild Fdn *CLUB AFFIL* Harvard DE, Lago Mar, Wilmington CC

Edward G. Goett: dir

Thomas S. Lodge: secy *B* Lewes DE 1917 *ED* Univ VA BA 1949; Univ VA LLB 1951 *CURR EMPL* ptnr: Connolly Bove Lodge & Hutz *NONPR AFFIL* mem: Am Bar Assn, DE Bar Assn

Marie L. McHugh: vp, dir

Collins Jacques Seitz: vp, dir *B* Wilmington DE 1914 *ED* Univ DE AB 1937; Univ VA LLB 1940 *NONPR AFFIL* judge: US Ct Appeals 3rd Circuit; mem: Am Bar Assn, DE Bar Assn *CLUB AFFIL* Wilmington CC

APPLICATION INFORMATION
Initial Approach:

There are no application forms. Applicants should send a succinct, two-page letter.

Application letters should include background information on the organization and project, goals of the project, amount requested, listing of other funding sources, and indication of IRS tax-exempt status. The foundation will request any additional information.

Applications should be submitted by April 15 or October 15, as the directors normally meet in May and November.

Restrictions on Giving: Grants are not made to individuals.

OTHER THINGS TO KNOW
Trustees prefer capital investments/improvements rather than studies or projects.

GRANTS ANALYSIS
Total Grants: $1,933,730

Number of Grants: 80

Highest Grant: $165,000

Average Grant: $24,172

Typical Range: $5,000 to $50,000

Disclosure Period: 1993

Note: Recent grants are derived from a 1993 Form 990.

RECENT GRANTS

Library
35,000 Hockessin Library, Hockessin, DE — building fund

General
165,000 United Way of Delaware, Wilmington, DC — annual campaign

75,000 Catholic Diocese of Wilmington, Wilmington, DE — educational trust
75,000 Salesianum School, Wilmington, DC — capital campaign
75,000 Visitation Sisters of St. Joseph Convent, Pittsfield, MA — construction of new monastery
65,000 Ministry of Caring, Wilmington, DE — capital improvements and work with the homeless

Longwood Foundation

CONTACT
David Wakefield
Executive Secretary
Longwood Foundation
1004 Wilmington Trust Ctr.
Wilmington, DE 19801
(302) 654-2477

FINANCIAL SUMMARY
Recent Giving: $20,000,000 (fiscal 1994 approx.); $15,749,988 (fiscal 1993); $20,000,000 (fiscal 1992 approx.)

Assets: $425,000,000 (fiscal 1994 approx.); $458,381,428 (fiscal 1993); $400,000,000 (fiscal 1992 approx.)

EIN: 51-0066734

CONTRIBUTIONS SUMMARY
Donor(s): The Longwood Foundation was created in 1937 by Pierre Samuel du Pont and became the principal beneficiary of his estate upon his death in 1954.

Typical Recipients: • *Arts & Humanities:* Arts Centers, Arts Funds, Historic Preservation, Libraries, Museums/Galleries, Music • *Civic & Public Affairs:* Botanical Gardens/Parks, Clubs, Economic Development, Employment/Job Training, Housing, Nonprofit Management, Parades/Festivals, Urban & Community Affairs, Women's Affairs, Zoos/Aquariums • *Education:* Colleges & Universities, Environmental Education, General, Literacy, Preschool Education, Private Education (Precollege), Public Education (Precollege), Secondary Education (Private), Special Education, Student Aid • *Environment:* General • *Health:* Children's Health/Hospitals, Clinics/Medical Centers, Emergency/Ambulance Services, Health Organizations, Hospices, Hospitals, Long-Term Care • *Religion:* Ministries, Religious Welfare • *Science:* Science Museums • *Social Services:* Child Welfare, Community Centers, Community Service Organizations, Counseling, Day Care, Family Planning, Family Services, Food/Clothing Distribution, Homes, People with Disabilities, Recreation & Athletics, Senior Services, Shelters/Homelessness, Substance Abuse, United Funds/United Ways, Veterans, Youth Organizations

Grant Types: capital and challenge

Geographic Distribution: limited to Delaware, primarily the greater Wilmington area

GIVING OFFICERS
Robert C. Barlow: asst secy *B* 1931 *CURR EMPL* treas, dir: DE Savings Bank *NONPR AFFIL* asst treas, dir: Red Clay Reservation *PHIL AFFIL* asst secy: Welfare Foundation; pres: Crestlea Foundation

Gerret van Sweringen Copeland: trust *CLUB AFFIL* Knickerbocker, Leash, Piping Rock

David Laird Craven: trust *B* Winston-Salem NC 1953 *ED* Davidson Coll 1975; Wake Forest Univ 1978 *CURR EMPL* sr vp, secy, couns: Southern Natl Corp *CORP AFFIL* sr vp, secy: Southern Natl Bank NC

Edward Bradford du Pont: vp, trust *B* Wilmington DE 1934 *ED* Yale Univ ED 1956; Harvard Univ MBA 1959 *CURR EMPL* chmn, dir: Atlantic Aviation Corp *CORP AFFIL* dir: EI du Pont de Nemours & Co; vp: Wilmington Trust Co *NONPR AFFIL* treas: Red Clay Reservation; trust: Easter Corp, Eleutherian Mills-Hagley Fdn, Hagley Mus & Library *CLUB AFFIL* New York YC, Wilmington CC

Pierre Samuel du Pont IV: trust *B* Wilmington DE 1935 *ED* Princeton Univ BS 1956; Harvard Univ LLB 1963 *CURR EMPL* ptnr: Richards Layton & Finger *CORP AFFIL* dir: Pet Inc, Whitman Corp; trust: Northwestern Mutual Life Ins Co *PHIL AFFIL* secy, trust: Longwood Gardens *CLUB AFFIL* Acorn, Colony, Country, New York YC, Wilmington CC

Stephen A. Martinenza: asst treas *PHIL AFFIL* asst treas: Welfare Foundation; treas: Crestlea Foundation

Irenee du Pont May: secy, trust

Hugh Rodney Sharp III: pres, trust *CURR EMPL* EI du Pont de Nemours & Co

Henry Harper Silliman, Jr.: treas, trust *PHIL AFFIL* pres: Borkee Hagley Foundation

David Wakefield: exec secy *PHIL AFFIL* exec secy: Welfare Foundation

APPLICATION INFORMATION
Initial Approach:

The foundation has no standard application form. Prospective applicants should send a two-page letter to the foundation.

The letter of inquiry should include a general description of the project, financial position of the organization, and a copy of the IRS 501(c)(3) tax-exempt status letter.

Proposals should be submitted by April 15 or October 1.

Restrictions on Giving: Grants are generally not made to fraternal organizations or to political or lobbying groups, or for special projects and/or dinners.

OTHER THINGS TO KNOW
About 10% of the grantees in any given year are first-time recipients of foundation aid.

GRANTS ANALYSIS
Total Grants: $15,749,988

Number of Grants: 68

Highest Grant: $6,350,000

Average Grant: $140,298*

Typical Range: $10,000 to $25,000 and $50,000 to $200,000

Disclosure Period: fiscal year ending September 30, 1993

Note: Average grant figure excludes highest grant of $6,350,000. Recent grants are derived from a fiscal 1993 Form 990.

RECENT GRANTS

Library

200,000	Hagley Museum and Library, Wilmington, DE — replace heating and air conditioning
60,000	Bayard Taylor Memorial Library, Kennett Square, PA — computerize card file

General

6,350,000	Longwood Gardens, Kennett Square, PA — project expenses
580,000	University of Delaware, Newark, DE — capital campaign
500,000	Beebe Hospital, Lewes, DE — building campaign
500,000	Newark Senior Center, Newark, DE — capital campaign
500,000	Planned Parenthood of Delaware, Wilmington, DE — endowment campaign

Lovett Foundation

CONTACT
Michael J. Robinson III
Vice President
Lovett Fdn.
82 Governor Printz Blvd.
Claymont, DE 19703
(302) 798-6604

FINANCIAL SUMMARY
Recent Giving: $234,380 (fiscal 1993); $199,462 (fiscal 1992); $168,810 (fiscal 1991)

Assets: $3,030,454 (fiscal 1993); $2,967,130 (fiscal 1992); $2,772,024 (fiscal 1991)

Gifts Received: $100,005 (fiscal 1993); $201,300 (fiscal 1992)

Fiscal Note: In fiscal 1993, contributions were received from Walter L. Morgan.

EIN: 23-6253918

CONTRIBUTIONS SUMMARY
Donor(s): Walter I. Morgan

Typical Recipients: • *Arts & Humanities:* Historic Preservation, History & Archaeology, Libraries, Museums/Galleries, Music, Public Broadcasting • *Civic & Public Affairs:* General, Philanthropic Organizations, Urban & Community Affairs, Zoos/Aquariums • *Education:* Arts/Humanities Education, Colleges & Universities, Medical Education, Private Education (Precollege), Secondary Education (Private), Special Edu-

cation • *Health:* Alzheimers Disease, Cancer, Children's Health/Hospitals, Emergency/Ambulance Services, Heart, Hospitals, Hospitals (University Affiliated), Medical Research, Nursing Services, Respiratory, Single-Disease Health Associations • *Religion:* Churches, Religious Welfare, Seminaries • *Science:* Scientific Centers & Institutes • *Social Services:* Community Service Organizations, Delinquency & Criminal Rehabilitation, People with Disabilities, Recreation & Athletics, United Funds/United Ways, Youth Organizations

Grant Types: general support

Geographic Distribution: focus on the Wilmington, DE, and Philadelphia, PA, areas

GIVING OFFICERS
Walter L. Morgan: trust, pres

Michael J. Robinson III: vp, trust

Leanor H. Silver: trust, secy

Andrew Brodbeck Young, Esq.: trust *B* Philadelphia PA 1907 *ED* Princeton Univ AB 1928; Harvard Univ LLB 1931 *CURR EMPL* ptnr: Stradley Ronon Stevens & Young *CORP AFFIL* dir: MA Bruder & Sons, Holmes Investment Co, Welding Engineers; dir, vp: WW Interests; trust, dir: Philadelphia Belt LineRy Co *NONPR AFFIL* chmn bd trust: Mary Jocobs Memorial Library Fdn; fellow: Am Bar Fdn; mem: Am Arbitration Assn, Am Bar Assn, Am Coll Tax Counc, Am Law Inst, PA Bar Assn, Phi Beta Kappa, Philadelphia Chamber Commerce; trust: Frank Michaels Scholarship Fdn, Lovett Fdn, Michael Bruder Fdn, Penjerdel Fdn *PHIL AFFIL* trust: Brosman Family Scholarship Trust, Michael Bruder Foundation, Lovett Foundation, Penjerdel Foundation *CLUB AFFIL* Anglers, Commanderie de Bordeaux, Penn Wilderness, Philadelphia Sunday Breakfast, Sunnybrook GC, Tunkhannock Creek Assn; mem: Phi Beta Kappa

APPLICATION INFORMATION
Initial Approach: Send brief letter of inquiry describing program. There are no formal deadlines, but foundation prefers requests prior to March 15.

Restrictions on Giving: Does not support individuals. Limited to Philadelphia, PA, and Wilmington, DE, metropolitan area.

GRANTS ANALYSIS
Total Grants: $234,380

Number of Grants: 77

Highest Grant: $50,000

Typical Range: $100 to $25,000

Disclosure Period: fiscal year ending November 30, 1993

Note: Recent grants are derived from a fiscal 1993 Form 990.

RECENT GRANTS

Library

10,000	Ludington Library, Bryn Mawr, PA
500	Library Company of Philadelphia, Philadelphia, PA

General

50,000	Wills Eye Hospital, Philadelphia, PA
25,000	BRSI Beaumont, Bryn Mawr, PA
15,000	Our Mother of Good Counsel Church, Bryn Mawr, PA
10,000	Bryn Mawr Hospital Foundation, Bryn Mawr, PA
10,000	St. Luke United Methodist Church, Bryn Mawr, PA

Marmot Foundation

CONTACT
Endsley P. Fairman
Secretary
Marmot Foundation
1004 Wilmington Trust Ctr.
Wilmington, DE 19801
(302) 654-2477

FINANCIAL SUMMARY
Recent Giving: $1,100,000 (1993); $1,000,000 (1992); $805,000 (1990)

Assets: $25,227,446 (1993); $22,999,895 (1992); $17,781,046 (1990)

EIN: 51-6022487

CONTRIBUTIONS SUMMARY
Donor(s): The foundation was established in 1968 by the Margaret F. duPont Trust.

Typical Recipients: • *Arts & Humanities:* Arts Associations & Councils, Arts Centers, Arts Funds, General, Historic Preservation, Libraries, Museums/Galleries • *Civic & Public Affairs:* Community Foundations, Employment/Job Training, General, Philanthropic Organizations, Professional & Trade Associations, Urban & Community Affairs, Zoos/Aquariums • *Education:* Colleges & Universities, General, Medical Education, Preschool Education, Private Education (Precollege), Public Education (Precollege), Secondary Education (Private), Social Sciences Education, Special Education • *Environment:* General, Resource Conservation • *Health:* Children's Health/Hospitals, Clinics/Medical Centers, Diabetes, Emergency/Ambulance Services, Eyes/Blindness, Heart, Hospitals, Research/Studies Institutes, Trauma Treatment • *Religion:* Dioceses, Religious Organizations, Religious Welfare • *Science:* Science Museums, Scientific Centers & Institutes • *Social Services:* Community Centers, Community Service Organizations, Family Planning, Family Services, Food/Clothing Distribution, People with Disabilities, Recreation & Athletics, Scouts, Senior Services, Special Olympics, United Funds/United Ways, YMCA/YWCA/YMHA/YWHA, Youth Organizations

Grant Types: capital, matching, and research

Geographic Distribution: focus on Delaware and Florida

GIVING OFFICERS
Lammot Joseph du Pont: trust

Miren de Amezola du Pont: trust

Willis Harrington du Pont: pres, trust *B* Wilmington DE 1936 *ED* Wesleyan Univ 1958; Cornell Univ 1960 *NONPR AFFIL* trust: Miami Science Mus

Endsley P. Fairman: secy, trust

George S. Harrington: trust

APPLICATION INFORMATION
Initial Approach:

The foundation has no formal grant application procedure or application form.

The foundation has no deadline for submitting proposals.

The board meets in May and November. Decisions are made two weeks after the board meeting.

Restrictions on Giving: The foundation does not support religious organizations, individuals, operating budgets, or scholarships, and does not make loans.

GRANTS ANALYSIS
Total Grants: $1,100,000

Number of Grants: 89

Highest Grant: $65,000

Average Grant: $12,360

Typical Range: $10,000 to $25,000

Disclosure Period: 1993

Note: Recent grants are derived from a 1993 Form 990.

RECENT GRANTS

Library
10,000	Hagley Museum and Library, Wilmington, DE

General
65,000	Rollins College, Winter Park, FL
50,000	United Way of Delaware, Wilmington, DE
35,000	Bascom Palmer Eye Institute, Miami, FL
25,000	Columbia University Department of Psychiatry, New York, NY
25,000	Food Bank of Delaware, Newark, DE

Mohasco Corp. / Mohasco Foundation

Revenue: $300.0 million
Employees: 3,800
Parent Company: MHS Holdings Corp.
Headquarters: Wilmington, DE
SIC Major Group: Furniture & Fixtures

CONTACT
Mohasco Corp.
1201 N Orange St., Ste. 1
Wilmington, DE 19801
(302) 573-2500

FINANCIAL SUMMARY
Recent Giving: $84,565 (1992); $110,679 (1991); $120,373 (1990)

Assets: $826,696 (1992); $868,998 (1991); $1,299,072 (1990)

Gifts Received: $30,000 (1992)

Fiscal Note: In 1992, contributions were received from Mohasco Corp.

EIN: 14-6019132

CONTRIBUTIONS SUMMARY
Typical Recipients: • *Arts & Humanities:* Arts Associations & Councils, Libraries • *Civic & Public Affairs:* Economic Policy, General, Municipalities/Towns, Philanthropic Organizations, Urban & Community Affairs • *Education:* Colleges & Universities, Community & Junior Colleges, Education Reform, Private Education (Precollege), Student Aid • *Health:* Emergency/Ambulance Services, Hospitals • *Social Services:* Child Welfare, Community Service Organizations, People with Disabilities, Recreation & Athletics, United Funds/United Ways, Youth Organizations

Grant Types: employee matching gifts and general support

Geographic Distribution: focus on VA

Operating Locations: GA (Atlanta, Dublin), MS (Eupora, Greenville, New Albany, Okolona, Senatobia, Tupelo), NC (Clinton), SC (Bennettsville, Dillon, Liberty), VA (Fairfax)

Note: List includes plant locations.

GIVING OFFICERS
Joseph P. Lamb: secy

John B. Sganga: treas *B* Bronx NY 1931 *ED* Brooklyn Coll BS 1961 *CURR EMPL* exec vp, cfo, dir: Mahasco Corp *NONPR AF-FIL* mem: Fin Execs Inst, Inst Certified Mgmt Consult, Inst Mgmt Accts *CLUB AF-FIL* Apple Ridge CC, Brookside Racquet & Swim, Treasurers

APPLICATION INFORMATION
Initial Approach: Send a brief letter of inquiry. Deadline is May 1 for scholarships; there is no deadline for general charities.

GRANTS ANALYSIS
Total Grants: $84,565

Number of Grants: 8

Highest Grant: $75,750

Typical Range: $500 to $2,000

Disclosure Period: 1992

Note: Recent grants are derived from a 1992 Form 990.

RECENT GRANTS

General
75,750	Citizens Scholarship Foundation, St. Peter, MN
1,000	Association for Excellence in Education, Tupelo, MA
1,000	Boy Scouts of America, Tupelo, MS
1,000	Financial Executives Research Foundation, Morristown, NJ
500	American Red Cross, Union County Chapter, New Albany, MS

Vale Foundation, Ruby R.

CONTACT
Richard E. Menkiewicz
Sr. Trust Administrator
Ruby R. Vale Fdn.
c/o Bank of Delaware
222 Delaware Ave.
Wilmington, DE 19899
(302) 429-1278

FINANCIAL SUMMARY
Recent Giving: $266,500 (1993); $173,000 (1992); $179,000 (1990)

Assets: $2,921,810 (1993); $3,004,105 (1992); $2,772,385 (1990)

EIN: 51-6018883

CONTRIBUTIONS SUMMARY
Donor(s): the late Ruby R. Vale

Typical Recipients: • *Arts & Humanities:* Libraries, Visual Arts • *Education:* Colleges & Universities, Legal Education, Private Education (Precollege) • *Health:* Children's Health/Hospitals • *Social Services:* Child Welfare, Community Service Organizations, Day Care, Family Services

Grant Types: general support

Geographic Distribution: focus on East Coast

GIVING OFFICERS
Bank DE: trust

APPLICATION INFORMATION
Initial Approach: The foundation has no formal grant application procedure or application form. Deadline is September 1.

GRANTS ANALYSIS
Total Grants: $266,500

Number of Grants: 15

Highest Grant: $50,000

Typical Range: $5,000 to $35,000

Disclosure Period: 1993

Note: Recent grants are derived from a 1993 Form 990.

RECENT GRANTS

Library
25,000	Milford District Free Public Library, Milford, DE

General
50,000	Dartmouth College, Hanover, NH
35,000	Dickinson School of Law, Carlisle, PA
25,000	Easter Seal Society of Del-Mar, New Castle, DE
20,000	Family and Children's Services of Delaware, Wilmington, DE
15,000	Hotchkiss School, Lakeville, CT

Welfare Foundation

CONTACT
David Wakefield
Executive Secretary
Welfare Foundation
1004 Wilmington Trust Center
Wilmington, DE 19801
(302) 654-2477

FINANCIAL SUMMARY
Recent Giving: $3,000,000 (1994 est.); $2,251,280 (1993); $2,472,100 (1992)

Assets: $55,000,000 (1994 est.); $64,499,094 (1993); $56,600,000 (1992)

EIN: 51-6015916

CONTRIBUTIONS SUMMARY

Donor(s): The foundation was established in 1930 by the late Pierre Samuel du Pont (d. 1954) to support initial plans for a public secondary school system. When that project was completed, the foundation turned its support to the community at large.

Du Pont family members are the descendants of Pierre Samuel du Pont de Nemours (1739-1817), a Frenchman who emigrated to America in 1800. His son, Eleuthere Irenee, founded a gunpowder factory in 1801 which was the precursor to E. I. du Pont de Nemours & Company, a manufacturer of chemicals, plastics, fibers, and specialty products. Edward B. du Pont, a treasurer of the foundation, is a director of the company.

Typical Recipients: • *Arts & Humanities:* Arts Centers, Arts Funds, History & Archaeology, Libraries, Museums/Galleries, Public Broadcasting • *Civic & Public Affairs:* Economic Development, Employment/Job Training, General, Nonprofit Management, Zoos/Aquariums • *Education:* Colleges & Universities, General, Minority Education, Private Education (Precollege), Science/Mathematics Education, Secondary Education (Private), Special Education, Student Aid • *Environment:* General, Resource Conservation, Watershed • *Health:* Health Organizations, Hospices, Prenatal Health Issues • *Religion:* Religious Welfare • *Science:* Scientific Centers & Institutes • *Social Services:* At-Risk Youth, Camps, Child Welfare, Community Centers, Community Service Organizations, Counseling, Day Care, Family Services, Food/Clothing Distribution, Homes, People with Disabilities, Senior Services, Special Olympics, Substance Abuse, United Funds/United Ways, YMCA/YWCA/YMHA/YWHA, Youth Organizations

Grant Types: capital

Geographic Distribution: Delaware, with emphasis on the greater Wilmington area

GIVING OFFICERS

Robert C. Barlow: asst secy *B* 1931 *CURR EMPL* treas, dir: DE Savings Bank *NONPR*

AFFIL asst treas, dir: Red Clay Reservation *PHIL AFFIL* asst secy: Longwood Foundation; pres: Crestlea Foundation

Robert H. Bolling, Jr.: pres, trust *ED* Princeton Univ 1948 *CORP AFFIL* dir: Wilmington Trust Co

J. Simpson Dean, Jr.: vp, trust

Edward Bradford du Pont: treas, trust *B* Wilmington DE 1934 *ED* Yale Univ ED 1956; Harvard Univ MBA 1959 *CURR EMPL* chmn, dir: Atlantic Aviation Corp *CORP AFFIL* dir: EI du Pont de Nemours & Co; vp: Wilmington Trust Co *NONPR AFFIL* treas: Red Clay Reservation; trust: Easter Corp, Eleutherian Mills-Hagley Fdn, Hagley Mus & Library *PHIL AFFIL* vp, trust: Longwood Foundation *CLUB AFFIL* New York YC, Wilmington CC

Stephen A. Martinenza: asst treas *PHIL AFFIL* asst treas: Longwood Foundation; treas: Crestlea Foundation

Mrs. W. Laird Stabler, Jr.: secy, trust

David Wakefield: exec secy *PHIL AFFIL* exec secy: Longwood Foundation

APPLICATION INFORMATION
Initial Approach:

Applicants should send a preliminary letter to the foundation.

Letters should state the reason for the grant request, and include pertinent financial statements and a copy of an IRS tax-exempt status letter.

The deadlines for submitting proposals are April 15 and November 1.

GRANTS ANALYSIS
Total Grants: $2,251,280

Number of Grants: 60

Highest Grant: $200,000

Average Grant: $37,521

Typical Range: $10,000 to $50,000

Disclosure Period: 1993

Note: Recent grants are derived from a 1993 Form 990.

RECENT GRANTS

General
200,000	Brandywine Conservancy, Chadds Ford, PA — conservation easement program
100,000	Delaware Special Olympics, Newark, DE — capital campaign
100,000	Food Bank of Delaware, Newark, DE
100,000	Layton Homes for Aged, Wilmington, DE — building renovations
100,000	South Chester County Medical Society, West Grove, PA — capital campaign

Wilmington Trust Co. / Wilmington Trust Co. Foundation

Gross Operating Earnings: $404.64 million
Employees: 2,188
Headquarters: Wilmington, DE
SIC Major Group: Depository Institutions

CONTACT
Beryl A. Barmore
Assistant Vice President
Wilmington Trust Co.
1100 N Market St.
Wilmington, DE 19890
(302) 651-1462

FINANCIAL SUMMARY
Recent Giving: $87,000 (1992); $213,780 (1991); $327,500 (1990)

Assets: $3,548 (1992); $635 (1991); $2,496 (1990)

Gifts Received: $90,392 (1992); $211,739 (1991); $308,287 (1990)

Fiscal Note: In 1992, contributions were received from Wilmington Trust Co.

EIN: 51-6021540

CONTRIBUTIONS SUMMARY
Typical Recipients: • *Arts & Humanities:* Arts Institutes, Community Arts, Libraries, Museums/Galleries, Music, Opera, Performing Arts, Public Broadcasting, Theater • *Civic & Public Affairs:* Economic Development, Employment/Job Training, Housing, Municipalities/Towns, Professional & Trade Associations, Public Policy, Zoos/Aquariums • *Education:* Colleges & Universities • *Environment:* General • *Health:* Clinics/Medical Centers, Health Funds, Health Organizations, Hospitals • *Religion:* Ministries • *Social Services:* At-Risk Youth, Community Centers, Community Service Organizations, Day Care, Recreation & Athletics, Senior Services, United Funds/United Ways, Youth Organizations

Grant Types: general support

Geographic Distribution: focus on DE

Operating Locations: DE (Wilmington)

CORP. OFFICERS
Beryl A. Barmore: *CURR EMPL* asst vp: Wilmington Trust Co

Ted T. Cecala: *CURR EMPL* exec vp, cfo: Wilmington Trust Co

Leonard W. Quill: *CURR EMPL* chmn, pres, ceo, dir: Wilmington Trust Co

GIVING OFFICERS
Wilmington Trust Co.: trust

Beryl A. Barmore: trust *CURR EMPL* asst vp: Wilmington Trust Co (see above)

Bernard J. Taylor II: trust *ED* Univ PA BS 1949 *CORP AFFIL* chmn, ceo, dir: Wilmington Trust Co *NONPR AFFIL* treas, dir: PA Opera Theatre *CLUB AFFIL* Orpheus, Wilmington CC

APPLICATION INFORMATION
Initial Approach: Include a description of organization, amount requested, purpose of funds sought, recently audited financial statement, and proof of tax-exempt status. There are no deadlines.

Restrictions on Giving: Limited to the State of Delaware.

GRANTS ANALYSIS
Total Grants: $87,000

Number of Grants: 24

Highest Grant: $9,000

Typical Range: $500 to $3,000

Disclosure Period: 1992

Note: Recent grants are derived from a 1992 Form 990.

RECENT GRANTS

Library
7,000	Wilmington Library, Wilmington, DE

General
9,000	Police Athletic League of Delaware, Wilmington, DE
8,500	University of Delaware, Newark, DE
7,000	Chesapeake Bay Girl Scout Council, Annapolis, MD
6,000	Beebe Medical Foundation, Lewes, DE
5,000	Delaware Adolescent Program, Wilmington, DE

DISTRICT OF COLUMBIA

Appleby Trust, Scott B. and Annie P.

CONTACT
Virginia M. Herrin
Trust Officer
Scott B. and Annie P. Appleby Trust
c/o Crestar Bank, N.A.
15th St. & New York Ave.
Washington, DC 20005
(804) 782-5204

FINANCIAL SUMMARY
Recent Giving: $129,500 (1993); $160,500 (1992); $114,000 (1990)

Assets: $3,709,322 (1993); $3,613,184 (1992); $3,126,453 (1990)

EIN: 52-6334302

CONTRIBUTIONS SUMMARY
Typical Recipients: • *Arts & Humanities:* Community Arts, Libraries, Museums/Galleries, Music, Theater • *Civic & Public Affairs:* General, Municipalities/Towns, Safety, Women's Affairs • *Education:* Colleges & Universities, Minority Education,

Private Education (Precollege), Special Education • *Environment:* Resource Conservation • *Health:* Cancer, Children's Health/Hospitals, Emergency/Ambulance Services, Health Organizations, Hospices, Hospitals • *Religion:* Churches • *Social Services:* Child Welfare, Community Service Organizations, People with Disabilities, YMCA/YWCA/YMHA/YWHA, Youth Organizations

Grant Types: general support

Geographic Distribution: focus on GA, FL, and Washington, DC

GIVING OFFICERS
F. Jordan Colby: trust

Sarah P. Williams: trust

APPLICATION INFORMATION
Initial Approach: Send a brief letter of inquiry. There are no deadlines.

GRANTS ANALYSIS
Total Grants: $129,500

Number of Grants: 23

Highest Grant: $50,000

Typical Range: $500 to $10,000

Disclosure Period: 1993

Note: Recent grants are derived from a 1993 Form 990.

RECENT GRANTS

Library
5,000	Augusta Public Library, Augusta, GA

General
50,000	Georgia Department of Human Services, Atlanta, GA
10,000	Gallaudet University, Washington, DC
7,000	Arah's Circle, Washington, DC
5,000	Black Student Fund, Washington, DC
5,000	Easter Seal Society, Washington, DC

Bloedorn Foundation, Walter A.

CONTACT
F. Elwood Davis
President
Walter A. Bloedorn Fdn.
888 17th St., NW, Ste. 1075
Washington, DC 20006
(202) 452-8553

FINANCIAL SUMMARY
Recent Giving: $220,000 (1993); $211,500 (1992); $359,350 (1989)

Assets: $6,276,212 (1993); $5,834,831 (1992); $5,652,170 (1989)

EIN: 52-0846147

CONTRIBUTIONS SUMMARY
Donor(s): the late Walter A. Bloedorn

Typical Recipients: • *Arts & Humanities:* Historic Preservation, History & Archaeol-

ogy, Libraries, Music, Public Broadcasting • *Civic & Public Affairs:* Municipalities/Towns, Philanthropic Organizations, Urban & Community Affairs • *Education:* Colleges & Universities, Legal Education, Private Education (Precollege), Religious Education • *Health:* Children's Health/Hospitals, Emergency/Ambulance Services, Hospices, Hospitals, Hospitals (University Affiliated), Long-Term Care • *Religion:* Religious Welfare • *Science:* Scientific Centers & Institutes • *Social Services:* Child Welfare, Community Service Organizations, Food/Clothing Distribution, Homes, People with Disabilities, Senior Services, United Funds/United Ways, Youth Organizations

Grant Types: capital, general support, and professorship

Geographic Distribution: focus on the Washington, DC, metropolitan area

GIVING OFFICERS
John H. Bloedorn, Jr.: dir

John E. Boice, Jr.: secy, treas, dir

F. Elwood Davis: pres, dir

Robert E. Davis: dir *B* Madison IL 1931 *ED* Univ MO 1953; Washington Univ *CORP AFFIL* dir: H&R Block, Erbamont NV, HIMONT, Rheometrics, USF&G Corp *NONPR AFFIL* mem: Am Mgmt Assn

Lloyd H. Elliot: dir *PHIL AFFIL* chmn, trust: Walter G. Ross Foundation

J. Hillman Zahn: dir *PHIL AFFIL* trust: Walter G. Ross Foundation

APPLICATION INFORMATION
Initial Approach: Send cover letter, full proposal, and proof of tax-exempt status. Deadline is March 31. Board meets in April.

GRANTS ANALYSIS
Total Grants: $220,000

Number of Grants: 28

Highest Grant: $125,000

Typical Range: $500 to $14,500

Disclosure Period: 1993

Note: Recent grants are derived from a 1993 Form 990.

RECENT GRANTS

General
125,000	George Washington University, Washington, DC — hospital construction
14,500	Boys and Girls Club of Washington, Washington, DC
10,000	Boys Club of America, Atlanta, GA
10,000	George Washington University Law School, Washington, DC
10,000	National Geographic Society Education Foundation, Washington, DC

Cafritz Foundation, Morris and Gwendolyn

CONTACT
Calvin Cafritz
Chairman, President, Chief Executive Officer, Treasurer
Morris and Gwendolyn Cafritz Foundation
1825 K St., NW
Washington, DC 20006
(202) 223-3100

FINANCIAL SUMMARY
Recent Giving: $8,600,000 (fiscal 1995 est.); $8,620,000 (fiscal 1994 approx.); $8,010,285 (fiscal 1993)

Assets: $185,500,000 (fiscal 1995 est.); $185,600,000 (fiscal 1994 approx.); $185,000,000 (fiscal 1993)

Gifts Received: $20,000 (fiscal 1988); $25,000 (fiscal 1987); $13,633,300 (fiscal 1985)

Fiscal Note: In fiscal 1988, the GDC Corporation of Washington, DC, contributed $20,000 to the foundation.

EIN: 52-6036989

CONTRIBUTIONS SUMMARY
Donor(s): The foundation was established in 1948 by Morris Cafritz and Gwendolyn Cafritz . Morris Cafritz (d.1964) was a major real estate developer and prominent philanthropist in the Washington, DC, area. Gwendolyn Cafritz died in 1988.

Typical Recipients: • *Arts & Humanities:* Arts Associations & Councils, Arts Centers, Arts Institutes, Arts Outreach, Ballet, Community Arts, Dance, Historic Preservation, History & Archaeology, Libraries, Literary Arts, Museums/Galleries, Music, Opera, Performing Arts, Public Broadcasting, Theater • *Civic & Public Affairs:* Employment/Job Training, Housing, Nonprofit Management, Professional & Trade Associations, Urban & Community Affairs • *Education:* Arts/Humanities Education, Colleges & Universities, Education Associations, Education Funds, International Studies, Medical Education, Preschool Education, Private Education (Precollege), Public Education (Precollege), Science/Mathematics Education, Special Education, Student Aid • *Environment:* Air/Water Quality, General • *Health:* Adolescent Health Issues, AIDS/HIV, Children's Health/Hospitals, Emergency/Ambulance Services, Geriatric Health, Health Organizations, Hospices, Hospitals, Medical Rehabilitation, Mental Health, Nursing Services, Single-Disease Health Associations • *Social Services:* Child Welfare, Community Centers, Community Service Organizations, Counseling, Domestic Violence, Emergency Relief, Family Planning, People with Disabilities, Recreation & Athletics, Refugee Assistance, Senior Services, Shelters/Homelessness, Substance Abuse, United Funds/United Ways, Volunteer Services, Youth Organizations

Grant Types: challenge, general support, project, scholarship, and seed money

Geographic Distribution: Washington, DC, metropolitan area only

GIVING OFFICERS
Martin Atlas: dir *CURR EMPL* pres, ceo, treas: Cafritz Cos

Daniel J. Boorstin: dir *B* Atlanta GA 1914 *ED* Harvard Univ AB; Oxford Univ BCL; Oxford Univ Balliol Coll BA; Yale Univ JSD *CORP AFFIL* mem bd editors: Encyclopaedia Britannica *NONPR AFFIL* hon fellow: Am Geographical Soc; librarian emeritus: Library Congress; mem: Am Academy Arts Sciences, Am Antiquarian Soc, Am Philosophical Soc, Am Studies Assn, Colonial Soc MA, Commn Critical Choices Ams, Intl House Japan, MA Historical Soc, Org Am Historians, Phi Beta Kappa, Royal Historical Soc; trust: Colonial Williamsburg Fdn, John F Kennedy Ctr Performing Arts, Thomas Gilcrease Mus, Woodrow Wilson Ctr Intl Scholars *CLUB AFFIL* mem: Cosmos, Elizabethan, Jewish, Natl Press

Warren Earl Burger: dir *B* St. Paul MN 1907 *ED* Univ MN 1925-1927; St Paul Coll Law (Mitchell Coll Law) LLB *NONPR AFFIL* chancellor emeritus: Smithsonian Inst; chmn: Commn Bicentennial US Constitution, Fed Judicial Ctr, Judicial Conf US; hon chmn: Inst Judicial Admin, Natl Ctr St Courts, Natl Judicial Coll, US Supreme Ct Historical Soc; trust: Natl Geographic Soc; trust emeritus: Macalester Coll, Mayo Fdn, Mitchell Coll Law *CLUB AFFIL* pres emeritus: Bentham

Calvin Cafritz: chmn, pres, ceo, treas *B* Washington DC 1931 *CURR EMPL* fdr: Calvin Cafritz Enterprises

Roger Arthur Clark: secy *B* Chicago IL 1932 *ED* Univ IL BS 1954; Univ IL LLB 1958 *CURR EMPL* sr ptnr: Rogers & Wells *CORP AFFIL* dir: Cafritz Cos *NONPR AFFIL* mem: Am Bar Assn, DC Bar Assn, Order of Coif *CLUB AFFIL* Chevy Chase, Metro

William P. Rogers: dir *B* Norfolk NY 1913 *CURR EMPL* sr ptnr: Rogers & Wells

APPLICATION INFORMATION
Initial Approach:

There is no official application form. Applications should be in writing, with the proposal narrative limited to ten, double-spaced typewritten pages, if possible.

In addition to the narrative, include with grant requests a separate fact sheet of not more than two pages in 2 skeleton form. Information should be under the following headings in this order: organization name; address; telephone and FAX numbers including area code; description of the organization; annual budget of entire organization; budget for project; previous Cafritz Foundation support; purpose of request; support from public and private sources (names and amounts); balance needed to complete project; amount requested; and period that grant will cover. Proposals must be signed by the head of the applying organization

Submit proposals by March 1, July 1, and November 1.

Applicants are notified as soon as possible after proposals are reviewed by the foundation's advisory board or board of directors. It takes six to nine months from the deadline date to process a proposal before submitting it to the board of directors.

Restrictions on Giving: Grants generally are made on a project basis. Support is not given to private foundations or individuals, or for capital purposes or endowments. It is not a general policy to commit funds for a project for more than one year at a time.

PUBLICATIONS
Annual report, application procedures

GRANTS ANALYSIS
Total Grants: $8,010,285

Number of Grants: 166

Highest Grant: $400,000

Average Grant: $48,255

Typical Range: $10,000 to $100,000

Disclosure Period: fiscal year ending April 30, 1993

Note: Recent grants are derived from a fiscal 1993 grants list.

RECENT GRANTS

Library

200,000	Library of Congress, Washington, DC — to purchase the Watterston House, to be used as a temporary residence for visiting scholars
100,000	Folger Shakespeare Library, Washington, DC — one-to-one general support
100,000	Shakespeare Theatre at the Folger Library, Washington, DC — general support
75,000	Library of Congress — to support Washingtoniana II, A Guide to the Architecture, Design, and Engineering Collections of the Washington, DC, Metropolitan Area, in the Prints and Photographs Division

General

400,000	Planned Parenthood of Metropolitan Washington, Washington, DC — general support
250,000	Local Initiatives Support Corporation, Washington, DC — to develop 450 units of affordable housing and for commercial development
200,000	District of Columbia Committee on Public Education, Washington, DC — general support for 1991-92 school year
200,000	Georgetown University Medical Center, Washington, DC — for the HIV/AIDS Women's Program, to provide comprehensive health care services to women and children

150,000   Washington Regional Association of Grantmakers, Washington, DC — for the Community Development Support Collaborative

Covington and Burling / Covington and Burling Foundation

Revenue: $124.78 million
Employees: 896
Headquarters: Washington, DC
SIC Major Group: Legal Services

CONTACT
Newman T. Halvorson, Jr.
Secretary
Covington and Burling Foundation
PO Box 7566
Washington, DC 20044
(202) 662-5432

FINANCIAL SUMMARY
Recent Giving: $222,731 (1993); $213,295 (1992); $112,051 (1991)

Assets: $219,822 (1993); $286,764 (1992); $388,933 (1991)

Gifts Received: $150,000 (1993); $100,300 (1992); $100,000 (1991)

Fiscal Note: In 1993, contributions were received from Covington & Burling.

EIN: 23-7150671

CONTRIBUTIONS SUMMARY
Typical Recipients: • *Arts & Humanities:* Historic Preservation, Libraries • *Civic & Public Affairs:* Civil Rights, General, Housing, Law & Justice, Legal Aid, Professional & Trade Associations, Public Policy, Women's Affairs • *Education:* Colleges & Universities, General, Legal Education • *Environment:* General • *Health:* Clinics/Medical Centers • *International:* Foreign Educational Institutions, Human Rights, International Development • *Science:* Scientific Centers & Institutes • *Social Services:* Delinquency & Criminal Rehabilitation, Senior Services, Youth Organizations

Grant Types: employee matching gifts and general support

Geographic Distribution: focus on DC

Operating Locations: DC (Washington)

CORP. OFFICERS
Newman Thorbus Halvorson, Jr.: *B* Detroit MI 1936 *ED* Princeton Univ AB 1958; Harvard Univ LLB 1961 *CURR EMPL* ptnr: Covington & Burling *NONPR AFFIL* mem: Am Bar Assn, Comm 100 Fed City, DC Bar Assn *CLUB AFFIL* Chevy Chase, Chevy Chase CC, Metropolitan, Metropolitan *PHIL AFFIL* asst secy/treas, chmn emeritus: Eugene and Agnes E. Meyer Foundation

Charles A. Miller: *CURR EMPL* ptnr: Covington and Burling

Charles F. C. Ruff: *CURR EMPL* ptnr: Covington and Burling

GIVING OFFICERS
David N. Brown: dir

Newman Thorbus Halvorson, Jr.: secy, dir *CURR EMPL* ptnr: Covington & Burling *PHIL AFFIL* asst secy/treas, chmn emeritus: Eugene and Agnes E. Meyer Foundation (see above)

Michael S. Horne: dir

Charles A. Miller: pres, dir *CURR EMPL* ptnr: Covington and Burling (see above)

Charles F. C. Ruff: dir *CURR EMPL* ptnr: Covington and Burling (see above)

John P. Rupp: dir

APPLICATION INFORMATION
Initial Approach: Send a brief letter of inquiry. Include a a description of organization, amount requested, and a description of the project under consideration. There are no deadlines.

Restrictions on Giving: Foundation generally supports legal education and law-related activities of an educational or charitable nature.

GRANTS ANALYSIS
Total Grants: $222,731

Typical Range: $500 to $5,000

Disclosure Period: 1993

Note: Recent grants are derived from a 1992 Form 990.

RECENT GRANTS

Library
5,000   Friends of the Law Library of Congress, Washington, DC

General
50,000   University District of Columbia Foundation, Washington, DC
32,845   Harvard Law School, Cambridge, MA
25,000   Council for Court Excellence, Washington, DC
25,000   Legal Aid Society of the District of Columbia, Washington, DC
7,250   George Washington University National Law Center, Washington, DC

Folger Fund

CONTACT
Kathrine Dulin Folger
President
Folger Fund
2800 Woodley Rd., NW
Washington, DC 20008
(202) 667-2991

FINANCIAL SUMMARY
Recent Giving: $1,016,995 (fiscal 1993); $453,715 (fiscal 1991); $688,698 (fiscal 1990)

Assets: $15,409,463 (fiscal 1993); $12,780,825 (fiscal 1991); $14,998,725 (fiscal 1990)

Gifts Received: $72,160 (fiscal 1991); $187,015 (fiscal 1990); $220,813 (fiscal 1988)

Fiscal Note: In fiscal 1991, contributions were received from Katherine Dulin Folger Charitable Trust.

EIN: 52-0794388

CONTRIBUTIONS SUMMARY
Donor(s): the late Eugenia O. Dulin, Kathrine Dulin Folger

Typical Recipients: • *Arts & Humanities:* Arts Associations & Councils, Arts Centers, Historic Preservation, Libraries, Museums/Galleries, Music, Opera, Performing Arts, Public Broadcasting • *Civic & Public Affairs:* Botanical Gardens/Parks, Chambers of Commerce, Clubs, Native American Affairs, Public Policy • *Education:* Arts/Humanities Education, Education Reform, Minority Education, Private Education (Precollege), Social Sciences Education, Student Aid • *Health:* Cancer, Emergency/Ambulance Services, Health Organizations, Hospitals, Medical Rehabilitation, Single-Disease Health Associations • *International:* International Relief Efforts • *Religion:* Churches, Religious Organizations • *Science:* Scientific Centers & Institutes • *Social Services:* Child Welfare, Community Service Organizations, Family Services, People with Disabilities, Recreation & Athletics, Scouts, United Funds/United Ways, Youth Organizations

Grant Types: general support and operating expenses

Geographic Distribution: Donations only to IRS approved charities in Palm Beach County, FL; Knox County, TN; and Washington, DC

GIVING OFFICERS
John Dulin Folger: trust

Kathrine Dulin Folger: pres, treas *B* Springfield TN *ED* Finch Jr Coll 1923 *NONPR AFFIL* chmn womens comm: Corcoran Gallery Art; fdr: Am Cancer Soc DC, Dulin Meml Gallery Art; mem womens comm: Smithsonian Assocs; pres: Jr League Knoxville; trust: Commun Chest Palm Beach FL, John F Kennedy Ctr Performing Arts, Soc Four Arts *CLUB AFFIL* Bath & Tennis, Everglades

Lee Merritt Folger: vp, secy

APPLICATION INFORMATION
Initial Approach: Send cover letter and full proposal. Include a description of organization, amount requested, purpose of funds sought, recently audited financial statement, and proof of tax-exempt status. Decisions are made within three months.

Restrictions on Giving: Does not support individuals.

PUBLICATIONS
Annual Report

GRANTS ANALYSIS
Total Grants: $1,016,995

Number of Grants: 63

Highest Grant: $217,500

Typical Range: $250 to $188,850

Disclosure Period: fiscal year ending August 31, 1993

Note: Recent grants are derived from a fiscal 1993 Form 990.

RECENT GRANTS

Library

120,000	Folger Shakespeare Library, Washington, DC — endowment fund, Cabot Memorial fund, and general operations
10,000	Smithsonian Institution, Washington, DC — Ripley Endowment fund to benefit Smithsonian libraries

General

217,500	Protestant Episcopal Cathedral Foundation, Mt. St. Albans, Washington, DC
188,850	St. Albans School, Washington, DC — capital fund, capital improvements, general operations
60,950	Harvard University, Cambridge, MA — JFK School of Government Public Studies, Memorial Church, Fairbanks Center, and general operations
32,500	Washington Cathedral, Mt. St. Alban, Washington, DC — capital improvements and general operations
27,000	Trustees of Reservations, Beverly, MA — Coolidge Point Reservation and Essex River Estuary

Freed Foundation

CONTACT
Lorraine Barnhart
Executive Director
Freed Foundation
3050 K St., NW, Ste. 335
Washington, DC 20007
(202) 337-5487

FINANCIAL SUMMARY
Recent Giving: $812,700 (fiscal 1994); $397,900 (fiscal 1993); $621,500 (fiscal 1992)

Assets: $17,450,022 (fiscal 1994); $18,100,068 (fiscal 1993); $17,465,821 (fiscal 1992)

Gifts Received: $96,842 (fiscal 1994); $268,000 (fiscal 1993); $101,218 (fiscal 1992)

Fiscal Note: In fiscal 1993, $268,000 was received from the estate of Gerald Freed. In fiscal 1994, $96,842 was received from the estate of Gerald Freed.

EIN: 52-6047591

CONTRIBUTIONS SUMMARY
Donor(s): The foundation was incorporated in 1954 by the late Frances W. Freed and the late Gerald A. Freed .

Typical Recipients: • *Arts & Humanities:* Arts Outreach, Libraries, Museums/Galleries • *Civic & Public Affairs:* Employment/Job Training, General, Housing, Professional & Trade Associations, Women's Affairs, Zoos/Aquariums • *Education:* Continuing Education, Education Funds, Literacy, Medical Education • *Environment:* Air/Water Quality, General, Resource Conservation, Wildlife Protection • *Health:* AIDS/HIV, Clinics/Medical Centers, Emergency/Ambulance Services, Hospitals, Mental Health, Nutrition • *Religion:* Religious Welfare • *Science:* Scientific Centers & Institutes • *Social Services:* Animal Protection, Child Abuse, Child Welfare, Community Service Organizations, Crime Prevention, Day Care, Domestic Violence, Family Planning, Family Services, People with Disabilities, Sexual Abuse, Substance Abuse

Grant Types: general support, multi-year/continuing support, operating expenses, and project

Geographic Distribution: focus on the Mid-Atlantic States

GIVING OFFICERS
Lorraine Barnhart: exec dir *PHIL AFFIL* asst secy, exec dir, trust: Huber Foundation

Lloyd J. Derrickson: secy, trust

Elizabeth Ann Freed: pres, trust

Joan F. Kahn: trust

Sherwood Monahan: trust

APPLICATION INFORMATION
Initial Approach:

Applicants should write to the foundation for an application form.

A formal application should be accompanied by a program plan for which the grant is requested.

The foundation has no deadline for submitting proposals. The foundation does not support foreign organizations, international projects, individuals, scholarships, endowment funds, research, conferences, or meetings.

Restrictions on Giving: Only tax-exempt organizations located in or benefitting Metropolitan Washington, DC, New Jersey, or New York City will be considered for funding.

PUBLICATIONS
Annual report including application guidelines

GRANTS ANALYSIS
Total Grants: $812,700

Number of Grants: 42

Highest Grant: $75,000

Average Grant: $19,350

Typical Range: $1,000 to $25,000

Disclosure Period: fiscal year ending May 31, 1994

Note: Recent grants are derived from a fiscal 1994 Form 990.

RECENT GRANTS

Library

59,000	City of Long Branch, Long Branch, NJ — computerize elementary school libraries
40,000	Anxiety Disorders Association of America, Rockville, MD — for establishment of library
1,500	Foundation Center, New York, NY — for general support

General

75,000	New York Zoological Society, Bronx, NY — for Species Survival Fund
50,000	American Red Cross, Washington, DC — for Disaster Relief Fund
45,000	Center for Mental Health, Washington, DC — for outpatient treatment for substance abuse
25,000	Boys and Girls Club of Monmouth County, Asbury Park, NJ — for mental health project
25,000	Martin Luther King Day Care Center, Camden, NJ — Sikora Center for Child Development

Giant Food Inc. / Giant Food Foundation

Revenue: $3.56 billion
Employees: 24,500
Headquarters: Landover, MD
SIC Major Group: Grocery Stores and Drug Stores & Proprietary Stores

CONTACT
David W. Rutstein
Secretary
Giant Food Foundation
PO Box 1804, D-593
Washington, DC 20013
(301) 341-4301

FINANCIAL SUMMARY
Recent Giving: $500,000 (fiscal 1995 est.); $527,024 (fiscal 1994); $553,040 (fiscal 1993)

Assets: $750,000 (fiscal 1995 est.); $743,000 (fiscal 1994 approx.); $528,714 (fiscal 1993)

Gifts Received: $700,000 (fiscal 1993)

Fiscal Note: Above figures represent foundation giving only. Company also sponsors a direct giving program. For information about direct giving, contact Barry F. Scher, Vice President of Public Affairs. Above figures exclude nonmonetary support.

EIN: 52-6045041

CONTRIBUTIONS SUMMARY
Typical Recipients: • *Arts & Humanities:* Arts Centers, Ballet, Community Arts, Dance, Libraries, Museums/Galleries, Music, Opera, Performing Arts, Public Broad-

casting, Theater • *Civic & Public Affairs:* African American Affairs, Chambers of Commerce, Employment/Job Training, Law & Justice, Urban & Community Affairs, Women's Affairs, Zoos/Aquariums • *Education:* Arts/Humanities Education, Colleges & Universities, Community & Junior Colleges, Education Funds, Medical Education, Minority Education, Special Education, Student Aid • *Health:* Cancer, Heart, Hospitals, Mental Health, Single-Disease Health Associations • *Religion:* Jewish Causes, Religious Organizations, Religious Welfare, Social/Policy Issues • *Social Services:* Child Welfare, Community Centers, Community Service Organizations, Family Services, Food/Clothing Distribution, People with Disabilities, Recreation & Athletics, Senior Services, Shelters/Homelessness, United Funds/United Ways, Youth Organizations

Grant Types: general support

Nonmonetary Support: $400,000 (fiscal 1994); $75,000 (fiscal 1993); $75,000 (fiscal 1992)

Nonmonetary Support Types: cause-related marketing & promotion, donated equipment, donated products, and in-kind services

Note: Contact for nonmonetary support is Barry F. Scher, Vice President of Public Affiars.

Geographic Distribution: Maryland, District of Columbia, and Virginia

Operating Locations: CA (Fresno), DC (Washington), MD (Baltimore, Burtonsville, Frederick, Gaithersburg, Jessup, Joppa Heights, Landover, Lanham, Lutherville, Pikesville, Prince Frederick, Rockville, Salisbury, Silver Spring, Upper Marlboro, Westminster), VA (Annandale, Charlottesville, Fredericksburg, Herndon, Lakeridge, McLean, Springfield, Warrenton)

CORP. OFFICERS

Israel Cohen: *B* Jerusalem Palestine 1912 *CURR EMPL* chmn, ceo, dir: Giant Food Inc *CORP AFFIL* chmn, ceo, dir: Giant Automatic Money Sys; chmn, dir: Giant MD; pres, dir: Bayside Traffic Svc Inc *PHIL AFFIL* secy, treas: Naomi and Nehemiah Cohen Foundation

GIVING OFFICERS

Israel Cohen: pres, dir *CURR EMPL* chmn, ceo, dir: Giant Food Inc *PHIL AFFIL* secy, treas: Naomi and Nehemiah Cohen Foundation (see above)

David W. Rutstein: secy *B* New York NY 1944 *ED* Univ PA BA 1966; George Washington Univ JD 1969 *CURR EMPL* sr vp, gen couns: Giant Food Inc *NONPR AFFIL* dir, asst treas, trust: Washington DC Metro Bd Trade; dir, mem exec comm: Fed City Counc; mem: Am Bar Assn, DC Bar Assn, Washington Metro Area Corp Couns Assn; trust: Greater Washington Res Ctr *PHIL AFFIL* chmn, chmn investment comm: Eugene and Agnes E. Meyer Foundation

Millard Farrar West, Jr.: trust *B* Washington DC 1910 *ED* Princeton Univ AB 1932; Natl Univ LLB 1935 *CURR EMPL* vp: Prudential Securities Inc *CORP AFFIL* dir: Dewey Electronics Corp; dir emeritus: Giant Food Inc *NONPR AFFIL* dir: Active Un Giv-

ers Fund; dir, treas, chmn fin comm: VA Theological Seminary; mem fin comm, chmn: Washington Cathedral Chap; mem fin comm, treas: Episcopal Diocese WA

APPLICATION INFORMATION

Initial Approach: *Initial Contact:* brief letter or proposal *Include Information On:* description of the organization, amount requested, purpose for which funds are sought, recently audited financial statement, and proof of Internal Revenue Service Section 170(c) status *Deadlines:* none

GRANTS ANALYSIS

Total Grants: $527,024

Number of Grants: 150

Highest Grant: $200,000

Average Grant: $500

Typical Range: $100 to $5,000

Disclosure Period: fiscal year ending January 31, 1994

Note: Above figures provided by the company. Recent grants are derived from a Fiscal 1993 Form 990.

RECENT GRANTS

General

175,000	United Way of National Capital Area, Washington, DC
100,000	United Jewish Appeal Federation of Greater Washington, New York, NY
100,000	United Jewish Appeal Federation of Greater Washington, New York, NY
42,000	United Way of Central Maryland, Baltimore, MD — 1991-92 pledge
8,333	Howard County General Hospital, Columbia, MD

Graham Fund, Philip L.

CONTACT
Mary Bellor
President and Secretary
Philip L. Graham Fund
1150 15th St., NW
Washington, DC 20071
(202) 334-6640

FINANCIAL SUMMARY
Recent Giving: $2,750,000 (1995 est.); $2,825,000 (1994 approx.); $2,772,798 (1993)

Assets: $60,550,830 (1993); $56,527,000 (1992); $49,932,333 (1991)

EIN: 52-6051781

CONTRIBUTIONS SUMMARY
Donor(s): The fund, established in 1963, is named after the former publisher and president of *The Washington Post*, Philip L. Graham. His widow, Katharine Meyer Graham, friends, and the Washington Post Company provided the initial gifts for the fund.

Typical Recipients: • *Arts & Humanities:* Arts Outreach, Ballet, Dance, Ethnic & Folk Arts, Libraries, Museums/Galleries, Music, Opera, Performing Arts, Theater, Visual Arts • *Civic & Public Affairs:* Economic Development, Employment/Job Training, First Amendment Issues, Hispanic Affairs, Housing, Municipalities/Towns, Public Policy, Urban & Community Affairs • *Education:* Arts/Humanities Education, Business Education, Colleges & Universities, Journalism/Media Education, Minority Education, Preschool Education, Public Education (Precollege), Science/Mathematics Education, Secondary Education (Private) • *Environment:* Watershed • *Health:* AIDS/HIV, Children's Health/Hospitals, Clinics/Medical Centers, Health Organizations, Home-Care Services, Hospices, Mental Health • *International:* International Organizations, International Relations • *Religion:* Churches, Jewish Causes, Religious Organizations, Religious Welfare • *Social Services:* At-Risk Youth, Child Welfare, Community Centers, Community Service Organizations, Delinquency & Criminal Rehabilitation, Domestic Violence, Family Services, Food/Clothing Distribution, People with Disabilities, Recreation & Athletics, Scouts, Senior Services, Shelters/Homelessness, Substance Abuse, Volunteer Services, YMCA/YWCA/YMHA/YWHA, Youth Organizations

Grant Types: capital, endowment, and project

Geographic Distribution: emphasis on metropolitan Washington, DC

GIVING OFFICERS
Mary Bellor: pres, secy

Martin Cohen: trust, treas *B* New York NY 1932 *ED* Brown Univ AB 1953; Univ PA Wharton Sch MBA 1957 *CURR EMPL* vp, dir: Washington Post Co *CORP AFFIL* dir: Bowater Mersey Paper Co, Intl Herald Tribune *NONPR AFFIL* dir, treas: Natl Mus Health & Medicine; mem: Am Inst CPAs, Fin Execs Inst; mem bd govs: Childrens Hosp Natl Med Ctr

Donald Edward Graham: trust *B* Baltimore MD 1945 *ED* Harvard Univ BA 1966 *CURR EMPL* chmn, ceo, pres: Washington Post Co *CORP AFFIL* dir: Bowater Mersey Paper Co *NONPR AFFIL* mem: Am Antiquarian Soc, Phi Beta Kappa; trust: Fed City Counc *PHIL AFFIL* dir: Washington Post Company Educational Foundation

Katharine Meyer Graham: trust, don *B* New York NY 1917 *ED* Univ Chicago AB 1938 *CURR EMPL* chmn exec comm, dir: Washington Post Co *CORP AFFIL* co-chmn: Intl Herald Tribune; dir: Bowater Mersey Paper Co, Reuters Founders Share Co Ltd *NONPR AFFIL* dir: Counc Aid Ed, Fed City Counc, Urban Inst; fellow: Am Acad Arts & Sci; hon trust: George Washington Univ; life trust: Univ Chicago; mem: Am Soc Newspaper Editors, Counc Foreign Rels, Overseas Devel Counc; mem sr adv bd: Joan Shorenstein Barone Ctr Press Politics Pub Policy, Harvard Univ *CLUB AFFIL* Cosmopolitan, Metro, Natl Press, 1925 F St

Leonade Diane Jones: asst treas *B* Bethesda MD 1947 *ED* Simmons Coll BA 1969; Stanford Univ JD 1973; Stanford Univ MBA 1973 *CURR EMPL* treas: Washington Post Co *NONPR AFFIL* dir: Washington Performing Arts Soc; mem: Am Bar Assn, CA Bar Assn, DC Bar Assn, Natl Assn Corp Treas, Stanford Univ Bus Sch Alumni Assn; mem adv counc: Stanford Univ Sch Bus; mem corp: Simmons Coll; trust: Am Inst Mng Diversity

Vincent Emory Reed: trust *B* St Louis MO 1928 *ED* WV St Coll BS 1952; Howard Univ MA 1965 *CORP AFFIL* dir: Home Fed Savings & Loan Assn *NONPR AFFIL* dir: DC Goodwill Indus, 12 Neediest Kids, Washington YMCA; mem: Am Assn Sch Pers Admins, Am Soc Bus Officals, DC Parent Teacher Assn, Kappa Alpha Psi, NAACP, Natl Assn Sch Security Offs, Natl Assn Secondary Sch Prins, Natl Ed Assn, Phi Delta Kappa; staff mem: DC Pub Schs; volunteer: SE Boys Club, SE Youth Football Assn *CLUB AFFIL* Kiwanis, Pigskin *PHIL AFFIL* dir: Hattie M. Strong Foundation

John W. Sweeterman: trust *PHIL AFFIL* dir: George Preston Marshall Foundation

APPLICATION INFORMATION
Initial Approach:

A telephone call should be made to the fund before submitting a proposal. If the fund is interested, it will request a formal proposal.

A proposal of no more than ten pages should describe the organization, its purpose, and the people it benefits. Applicants should also include a description of the project, benefits, costs, amount requested from the fund, other funding sources, the organization's qualifications to accomplish its goals, and potential future support (if relevant). Applicants also should submit a recent financial statement, current budget, project budget, list of the organization's governing board, and a copy of the organization's IRS letter of tax-exempt status.

The fund's trustees meet four times a year to make funding decisions. Proposals may be submitted any time; however, to be considered at these meetings, proposals must be received by March 1, June 1, September 1, and November 1. Proposals from theaters are considered only at the summer and fall meetings. Proposals from other cultural organizations are reviewed during the fall and winter meetings.

Restrictions on Giving: Funds generally are not disbursed outside the Washington, DC, metropolitan area, and are not used to support national or international organizations. To a limited degree and on the initiative of the fund only, grants occasionally are made in communities where the Washington Post Company has significant business interests. Grants are not made to individuals, organizations without IRS 501(c)(3) status, membership groups, or for religious purposes. In addition, grants are not given for research, meetings, conferences, seminars, workshops, medical services, annual giving campaigns, travel expenses, tickets for benefits, support of fundraising events, produc-

tion of films, publications, or courtesy advertising.

PUBLICATIONS
History and proposal guidelines, and summary of grants

GRANTS ANALYSIS
Total Grants: $2,772,798

Number of Grants: 128

Highest Grant: $250,000

Average Grant: $21,662

Typical Range: $5,000 to $25,000

Disclosure Period: 1993

Note: Recent grants are derived from a 1993 annual report.

RECENT GRANTS

Library
15,000   Folger Shakespeare Library, Washington, DC — full pledge of $60,000, to support 1994 Student Shakespeare Festival

General
250,000   Federal City Council, Washington, DC — to support expansion of the Anacostia Early Childhood Education Project to a second facility

180,000   DC Jewish Community Center, Washington, DC — first payment on a pledge of $300,000, to support the capital campaign for acquisition and renovation of the organization's former facility

100,000   Enterprise Foundation, Columbia, MD — fulfills three-year pledge of $300,000, to support large-scale development of affordable housing in Washington, DC

100,000   Gallaudet University, Washington, DC — to support capital campaign for the Hall Memorial Building

80,000   Salvation Army, Washington, DC — second payment on pledge of $250,000, to support a capital campaign for expansion and upgrading of facilities throughout the metro area

Higginson Trust, Corina

CONTACT
Charles Abeles
Trustee
Corina Higginson Trust
1717 Massachusetts Ave., NW, Ste. 101
Washington, DC 20036
(202) 265-1313

FINANCIAL SUMMARY
Recent Giving: $116,000 (1993); $122,200 (1992); $109,592 (1991)

Assets: $3,392,542 (1993); $3,455,376 (1992); $3,460,476 (1991)

Gifts Received: $10,171 (1992)

EIN: 52-6055743

CONTRIBUTIONS SUMMARY
Donor(s): the late Corina Higginson

Typical Recipients: • *Arts & Humanities:* Arts Associations & Councils, Arts Centers, Ballet, Community Arts, Dance, Ethnic & Folk Arts, History & Archaeology, Libraries, Museums/Galleries, Music, Performing Arts, Theater • *Civic & Public Affairs:* Community Foundations, Economic Development, Employment/Job Training, General, Law & Justice, Nonprofit Management, Philanthropic Organizations, Professional & Trade Associations, Public Policy, Women's Affairs • *Education:* Arts/Humanities Education, Gifted & Talented Programs, Literacy, Minority Education, Private Education (Precollege), Science/Mathematics Education, Secondary Education (Public) • *Environment:* General, Resource Conservation • *Health:* Clinics/Medical Centers, Geriatric Health, Prenatal Health Issues • *International:* Health Care/Hospitals, International Environmental Issues • *Religion:* Jewish Causes, Religious Organizations • *Social Services:* Community Service Organizations, Food/Clothing Distribution, Refugee Assistance, Senior Services, Sexual Abuse, Shelters/Homelessness, United Funds/United Ways, Volunteer Services, Youth Organizations

Grant Types: emergency, general support, multiyear/continuing support, operating expenses, project, research, and seed money

Geographic Distribution: focus on the Washington, DC, area

GIVING OFFICERS
Charles C. Abeles: trust *B* Norfolk VA 1929 *ED* Harvard Univ AB 1952; Univ VA JD 1958 *CURR EMPL* ptnr: Piper & Marbury *CORP AFFIL* dir: D & D Ventures Corp *NONPR AFFIL* mem: Bar Assn VA, DC Bar Assn; mem adv bd: Bur Natl Aff Corp

Milton C. Corken: trust

John Perkins: trust

Jean Head Sisco: trust

APPLICATION INFORMATION
Initial Approach: Application form required. Deadlines are March 1 and September 1.

Restrictions on Giving: Does not support individuals or provide funds for endowments. Limited to the Washington metropolitan area.

PUBLICATIONS
Application Guidelines

GRANTS ANALYSIS
Total Grants: $116,000

Number of Grants: 22

Highest Grant: $7,500

Typical Range: $2,000 to $5,000

Disclosure Period: 1993

Note: Recent grants are derived from a 1993 Form 990.

RECENT GRANTS

Library

7,500   Library Theater, Bethesda, MD — summer books alive

General

7,500   Ayuda, Washington, DC — representation of immigrant women

7,500   Levin School of Music, Washington, DC — LINC program

7,500   Washington Lawyer's Committee, Washington, DC — public education project

5,000   CARE, Washington, DC — Shaw flexible response elder care program

5,000   Chesapeake Bay Foundation, Annapolis, MD — for its public school program

Kiplinger Foundation

CONTACT

Andrea Wilkes
Secretary
Kiplinger Foundation
1729 H St., NW
Washington, DC 20006
(202) 887-6559

FINANCIAL SUMMARY

Recent Giving: $1,249,935 (1993); $550,143 (1991); $836,060 (1990)

Assets: $20,270,400 (1993); $20,647,805 (1991); $20,515,983 (1990)

Gifts Received: $250,000 (1993); $1,000,000 (1990); $125,000 (1989)

Fiscal Note: In 1993, contributions were received from the Kiplinger Washington Editors, Inc.

EIN: 52-0792570

CONTRIBUTIONS SUMMARY

Donor(s): The foundation was incorporated in 1948 by the late Willard M. Kiplinger .

Typical Recipients: • *Arts & Humanities:* Arts Associations & Councils, Arts Centers, Arts Institutes, Ballet, Historic Preservation, History & Archaeology, Libraries, Museums/Galleries, Music, Performing Arts, Public Broadcasting, Theater • *Civic & Public Affairs:* Economic Development, Employment/Job Training, General, Housing, Legal Aid, Philanthropic Organizations, Professional & Trade Associations, Public Policy, Safety, Urban & Community Affairs, Women's Affairs • *Education:* Arts/Humanities Education, Colleges & Universities, Community & Junior Colleges, Education Funds, Engineering/Technological Education, International Exchange, Journalism/Media Education, Literacy, Minority Education, Private Education (Precollege), Public Education (Precollege), Sci-

ence/Mathematics Education • *Environment:* General • *Health:* Children's Health/Hospitals, Emergency/Ambulance Services, Health Organizations, Hospices, Hospitals, Mental Health, Nursing Services, Public Health • *Religion:* Religious Welfare • *Science:* Science Exhibits & Fairs • *Social Services:* Child Welfare, Community Centers, Community Service Organizations, Family Planning, Family Services, Food/Clothing Distribution, Homes, People with Disabilities, Senior Services, Shelters/Homelessness, United Funds/United Ways, Volunteer Services, Youth Organizations

Grant Types: capital, endowment, general support, matching, multiyear/continuing support, and operating expenses

Geographic Distribution: focus on the greater Washington, DC, metropolitan area

GIVING OFFICERS

David M. Daugherty: treas

Austin Huntington Kiplinger: pres, trust *B* Washington DC 1918 *ED* Cornell Univ AB 1939; Harvard Univ *CURR EMPL* chmn: Kiplinger Washington Editors *CORP AFFIL* chmn: Editors Press, Fairview Properties, KCMS, Kiplinger Washington Editors, May Properties, Outlook *NONPR AFFIL* chmn: Washington Intl Horse Show; mem: Assn Radio & Television News Analysts, Delta Upsilon, Phi Beta Kappa, Soc Professional Journalists, Telluride Assn; pres: Fed City Counc; trust: Washington Journalism Ctr; trust emeritus: Cornell Univ *CLUB AFFIL* Alfalfa, Alibi, Chevy Chase CC, Commonwealth, Cornell, Metropolitan, Natl Press, Overseas Writers, Potomac Hunt

Knight A. Kiplinger: trust *B* Washington DC 1948 *ED* Cornell Univ BA 1969; Princeton Univ *CURR EMPL* pres: Kiplinger Washington Editors *CORP AFFIL* chmn: Editors Press; exec vp: KCMS *NONPR AFFIL* chmn: Oratorio Soc; mem: Soc Am Bus Editors & Writers, Soc Professional Journalists; mem adv bd: Levine Sch Music, Mt Vernon Ladies Assn; mem natl adv bd: Natl Mus Women Arts; trust: Greater Washington Res Ctr *CLUB AFFIL* Natl Press

Todd L. Kiplinger: trust *CURR EMPL* vp & vchmn investments, dir: Kiplinger Washington Editors

Frances Turgeon: trust

Andrea Wilkes: secy, trust

APPLICATION INFORMATION

Initial Approach:

The foundation requests applications be made in writing.

Written proposals must state the purpose and the background of the organization.

The foundation has no deadline for submitting proposals.

The board meets four times a year. Decisions are made within three to six months.

Restrictions on Giving: Grants are limited to education, health, welfare, civic, and cultural organizations. No grants or scholarships are made to individuals.

PUBLICATIONS

Application guidelines

GRANTS ANALYSIS

Total Grants: $1,249,935

Number of Grants: 142

Highest Grant: $506,500

Average Grant: $8,802

Typical Range: $200 to $25,000

Disclosure Period: 1993

Note: Recent grants are derived from a 1993 Form 990.

RECENT GRANTS

Library

5,000   Library Foundation of Martin County, Stuart, FL

1,500   Foundation Center, Washington, DC

General

506,500   Cornell University, Ithaca, NY

90,000   Washington Journalism Center, Washington, DC

52,500   United Way Campaign, Washington, DC

50,500   McDonogh School, McDonogh, MD

30,000   Ohio State University Kiplinger Fellows, Columbus, OH

Koch Charitable Foundation, Charles G.

CONTACT

Lynn Taylor
Managing Director
Charles G. Koch Charitable Foundation
1401 I St., NW
Ste. 300
Washington, DC 20005
(202) 842-4616

FINANCIAL SUMMARY

Recent Giving: $1,507,221 (1992); $663,300 (1991); $1,150,620 (1990)

Assets: $12,370,126 (1992); $11,881,872 (1991); $11,791,198 (1990)

EIN: 48-0918408

CONTRIBUTIONS SUMMARY

Donor(s): The foundation was established in 1981 by Charles G. Koch, chairman and chief executive officer of Koch Industries, which has interests in chemical technology, oil field services, oil exploration and production, crude oil trading and distribution, hydrocarbon and natural gas liquids, and real estate (including cattle ranches and industrial and residential properties). Charles Koch's father, the late Fred C. Koch (1900-1967), founded Rock Island Oil and Refining Company, the forerunner to Koch Industries, now run by two Koch brothers.

Charles Koch has been a strong supporter of classical liberal causes. He helped found Citizens for a Sound Economy and serves on the board of the Institute of Humane Studies at George Mason University.

Typical Recipients: • *Arts & Humanities:* Arts Associations & Councils, Libraries • *Civic & Public Affairs:* Business/Free Enterprise, Economic Policy, General, Legal Aid, Public Policy • *Education:* Colleges & Universities, Private Education (Precollege) • *International:* International Organizations • *Social Services:* Animal Protection

Grant Types: general support and project

Geographic Distribution: no geographic restrictions

GIVING OFFICERS
Richard M. Fink: vp, dir *PHIL AFFIL* pres: Claude R. Lambe Charitable Foundation; vp, dir: Fred C. and Mary R. Koch Foundation, Inc.

Mary Ann Fox: secy *PHIL AFFIL* secy: Claude R. Lambe Charitable Foundation

Vonda Holliman: treas *PHIL AFFIL* treas: Fred C. and Mary R. Koch Foundation, Inc., David H. Koch Charitable Trust, Claude R. Lambe Charitable Foundation

Charles de Ganahl Koch: dir *B* Wichita KS 1935 *ED* MA Inst Tech BSE 1957; MA Inst Tech MSME 1958; MA Inst Tech MSChE 1959 *CURR EMPL* chmn, ceo, dir: Koch Indus Inc *CORP AFFIL* dir: First Natl Bank Wichita *NONPR AFFIL* chmn, dir: George Mason Univ Inst Humane Studies; dir: Wichita Collegiate Sch; mem: Mont Pelerin Soc, Natl Petroleum Counc *CLUB AFFIL* NY Athletic, Wichita CC

Elizabeth B. Koch: vp, dir *PHIL AFFIL* vp, dir: Claude R. Lambe Charitable Foundation, Fred C. and Mary R. Koch Foundation, Inc.

Lynn Taylor: mng dir *PHIL AFFIL* vp, mng dir: Claude R. Lambe Charitable Foundation

APPLICATION INFORMATION
Initial Approach:

Applicants should submit a short letter of proposal.

The letter should describe the organization and project for which funding is sought. Applicants also should include a project budget.

There are no deadlines.

Restrictions on Giving: No grants are given to individuals.

OTHER THINGS TO KNOW
Besides making grants, the foundation also offers conferences and seminars/workshops.

GRANTS ANALYSIS
Total Grants: $1,507,221
Number of Grants: 29
Highest Grant: $500,000
Average Grant: $51,973
Typical Range: $2,000 to $55,000
Disclosure Period: 1992
Note: Recent grants are derived from a 1992 Form 990.

RECENT GRANTS
Library
10,000   Center for the Study of Public Choice, Fairfax, VA — Buchanan Library project

General
500,000   Wichita Collegiate School, Wichita, KS — building fund
160,000   Center for the Study of Market Process, Fairfax, VA — new faculty and student assistance
141,950   National Foundation for Teaching Entrepreneurship, New York, NY — Wichita Program
128,900   National Foundation for Teaching Entrepreneurship, New York, NY — Wichita Program
96,000   Center for the Study of Market Process, Fairfax, VA — summer faculty and student fund

Lea Foundation, Helen Sperry

CONTACT
Sperry Lea
President
Helen Sperry Lea Fdn.
3534 Fulton St., NW
Washington, DC 20007
(202) 337-7339

FINANCIAL SUMMARY
Recent Giving: $150,450 (1993); $17,241 (1992); $103,800 (1990)

Assets: $3,496,430 (1993); $2,889,027 (1992); $2,096,306 (1990)

EIN: 13-6161749

CONTRIBUTIONS SUMMARY
Donor(s): the late Helen Sperry Lea

Typical Recipients: • *Arts & Humanities:* Ballet, Dance, Historic Preservation, Libraries, Museums/Galleries, Music, Performing Arts, Public Broadcasting, Theater • *Civic & Public Affairs:* Ethnic Organizations, General, Philanthropic Organizations, Public Policy • *Education:* Colleges & Universities, Legal Education, Private Education (Precollege), School Volunteerism, Secondary Education (Private) • *Environment:* General • *International:* International Affairs, International Organizations, International Peace & Security Issues, International Relations • *Social Services:* Community Service Organizations, Shelters/Homelessness

Grant Types: general support

Geographic Distribution: Giving generally limited to the Washington, DC, area

GIVING OFFICERS
Anna Lea: dir, vp
Helena Lea: dir, vp
R. Brooke Lea II: dir, vp
Sperry Lea: dir, pres, treas
Carol A. Rhees: secy

APPLICATION INFORMATION
Initial Approach: The foundation has no formal grant application procedure or application form. There are no deadlines.

GRANTS ANALYSIS
Total Grants: $150,450
Number of Grants: 28
Highest Grant: $28,000
Typical Range: $500 to $18,000
Disclosure Period: 1993
Note: Recent grants are derived from a 1993 Form 990.

RECENT GRANTS
General
28,000   Sidwell Friends School, Chinese Student Exchange, Washington, DC
18,000   Friends of Meridian Hill, Washington, DC
13,500   Society for the Preservation of the Greek Heritage, Reston, VA
10,000   Growing Together, Washington, DC
7,500   Center for Teaching Peace, Washington, DC

Marpat Foundation

CONTACT
Marpat Fdn.
c/o John M. Bixler, Miller and Chevalier
655 15th St., NW
Washington, DC 20005
(202) 626-5830
Note: Foundation does not list a contact person.

FINANCIAL SUMMARY
Recent Giving: $915,823 (1993); $754,000 (1992); $689,923 (1991)

Assets: $13,476,672 (1993); $12,956,245 (1992); $12,848,662 (1991)

EIN: 52-1358159

CONTRIBUTIONS SUMMARY
Donor(s): Marvin Breckinridge Patterson

Typical Recipients: • *Arts & Humanities:* Arts Associations & Councils, Arts Outreach, Ethnic & Folk Arts, Historic Preservation, History & Archaeology, Libraries, Literary Arts, Museums/Galleries, Music, Public Broadcasting, Theater • *Civic & Public Affairs:* Botanical Gardens/Parks, Employment/Job Training, Law & Justice, Professional & Trade Associations, Safety, Women's Affairs • *Education:* Arts/Humanities Education, Colleges & Universities, Environmental Education, International Exchange, International Studies, Private Education (Precollege), Science/Mathematics Education, Special Education • *Environment:* Air/Water Quality, General, Protection, Resource Conservation, Watershed • *Health:* Children's Health/Hospitals, Health Organizations, Home-Care Services, Hospitals, Nursing Services • *International:* Foreign Arts Organizations, Foreign Educational Institutions, General, Health Care/Hospitals, International Affairs, International Organizations, International Peace & Security Issues • *Religion:* Churches, Jewish Causes, Ministries, Religious Welfare • *Science:* Science Museums, Scientific Centers & Institutes, Scientific Organizations • *Social Services:* At-Risk Youth, Child Abuse, Community Service Organizations, Family Planning, Food/Clothing Distribution, Scouts, Senior Services, Shelters/Homelessness, Volunteer Services, YMCA/YWCA/YMHA/YWHA

Grant Types: capital, fellowship, general support, operating expenses, and research

Geographic Distribution: focus on the Washington, DC, metropolitan area

GIVING OFFICERS
Charles Thomas Akre: vp, dir *B* Washington DC 1942 *ED* Am Univ 1968 *CURR EMPL* sr vp, dir: Johnston Lemon & Co

Isabella B. Dubow: dir

Joan F. Koven: secy, treas, dir

Marvin Breckinridge Patterson: pres, dir

Mrs. John Farr Simons: dir

Samuel N. Stokes: dir

APPLICATION INFORMATION
Initial Approach: Send full proposal describing program or project, amount requested, and proof of tax-exempt status under IRS code section 501(c)(3). Submit five copies. Deadline is October 1.

Restrictions on Giving: Does not support individuals.

PUBLICATIONS
Informational Brochure (including application guidelines)

GRANTS ANALYSIS
Total Grants: $915,823
Number of Grants: 67
Highest Grant: $28,000
Typical Range: $5,000 to $28,000
Disclosure Period: 1993

Note: Recent grants are derived from a 1993 Form 990.

RECENT GRANTS

Library
15,000   Kentucky Historical Society, Frankfort, KY — toward construction and equipment of a museum and library to house and exhibit Kentucky's history for all Kentuckians

General
28,000   Friends of Jefferson Patterson Park, St. Leonard, MD — six-month funding for three staff people to present school programs, manage a visitor center, and conduct special activities for visitors

25,000   Accokeek Foundation, Accokeek, MD — preserve natural, historical, cultural resources of Potomac River

basin, foster public education programs to make people aware of its diverse heritage and encourage land stewardship

25,000   International Council on Monuments and Sites, Washington, DC — summer intern program

20,000   Academy of Natural Sciences of Philadelphia, Philadelphia, PA — toward building and equipping new Estuarine Research center

20,000   Columbia Road Health Services, Washington, DC — make primary health care available to a greater number of poor inner-city residents through the services of an additional family physician and registered nurse

Marriott Foundation, J. Willard

CONTACT
Kay Bodeen
Administrator
J. Willard Marriott Foundation
One Marriott Dr.
Washington, DC 20058
(301) 380-7523

FINANCIAL SUMMARY
Recent Giving: $7,505,330 (1992); $1,358,620 (1991); $8,741,200 (1990)

Assets: $69,322,896 (1992); $55,846,384 (1991); $38,080,134 (1990)

Gifts Received: $10,365,675 (1992); $10,365,671 (1991); $10,365,694 (1990)

Fiscal Note: The foundation receives substantial contributions from the J. Williard Marriott Charitable Annuity Trust.

EIN: 52-6068678

CONTRIBUTIONS SUMMARY
Donor(s): The foundation was established in Washington, DC, in 1966 by J. Willard Marriott and his wife, Alice S. Marriott. In 1927, J. Willard and his wife opened their first coffee shop, an enterprise that eventually grew into several hotels and an airline catering service. J. Willard, who died in 1985, was founder and chairman of the Marriott Corporation. J. Willard Marriott, Jr., the eldest son of the founder, succeeded his father as president in 1964, and developed the corporation into one of the nation's largest hotel chains.

Typical Recipients: • *Arts & Humanities:* Arts Associations & Councils, Historic Preservation, Libraries, Museums/Galleries, Music, Performing Arts, Theater • *Civic & Public Affairs:* Economic Development, Professional & Trade Associations, Public Policy • *Education:* Business Education, Colleges & Universities, Education Associations, Education Reform, Student Aid

• *Health:* Eyes/Blindness, Health Organizations, Hospitals, Hospitals (University Affiliated), Prenatal Health Issues • *International:* International Development, International Relations • *Religion:* Churches, Missionary Activities (Domestic), Religious Organizations, Religious Welfare • *Social Services:* People with Disabilities, Senior Services, Youth Organizations

Grant Types: capital, general support, and scholarship

Geographic Distribution: national, with emphasis on Utah and the Washington, DC, area

GIVING OFFICERS
Kay Bodeen: admin

Sterling Don Colton: mgr *ED* Univ Utah BS 1951; Stanford Univ JD 1954 *CURR EMPL* gen couns, vp, dir: Marriott Intl *CORP AFFIL* dir, vp: Colton Ranch Corp *NONPR AFFIL* chmn: Natl Chamber Litigation Ctr; dir: Polynesian Cultural Ctr; mem: Am Bar Assn, CA Bar Assn, DC Bar Assn, Sigma Chi, UT St Bar Assn, Washington Metro Area Corp Couns Assn

Alice Marriott: don, off *B* Salt Lake City UT 1907 *ED* Univ UT AB 1927 *CURR EMPL* co-fdr, vp, dir: Marriott Corp *NONPR AFFIL* dir: Arthritis Rheumatism Fdn Metro Washington, Washington Ballet Guild, Washington Home Rule Comm; hon trust: Natl Arthritis Fdn; mem: Am Newspaper Womens Club, Capitol Speakers Club, Chi Omega, League Repbl Women, Natl Symphony Orchestra Assn, Phi Kappa Phi; mem adv comm: Natl Comm Child Abuse; mem adv counc: Natl Insts Health Natl Inst Arthritis & Musculoskeletal Skin Diseases; treas, dir: Welcome to Washington Intl Clubs; trust: John F Kennedy Ctr Performing Arts *PHIL AFFIL* trust: Alice S. Marriott Foundation *CLUB AFFIL* Capitol Hill, Washington

John Willard Marriott, Jr.: don, off *B* Washington DC 1932 *ED* Univ UT BS 1954 *CURR EMPL* chmn, ceo, pres, dir: Marriott Intl Inc *CORP AFFIL* dir: Gen Motors Corp, Outboard Marine Corp *NONPR AFFIL* Sigma Chi; mem: Bus Roundtable, Latter Day Sts Church; mem conf bd: Bus Counc, US Chamber Commerce; mem natl adv bd: Boy Scouts Am; trust: Eisenhower Med Ctr, Exec Counc Foreign Diplomats, Mayo Fdn, Natl Geographic Soc *PHIL AFFIL* trust: Alice S. Marriott Foundation *CLUB AFFIL* Burning Tree, Metro

Richard Edwin Marriott: off *B* Washington DC 1939 *ED* Univ UT BS 1963; Harvard Univ MBA 1965 *CORP AFFIL* chmn: Media Corp; dir: Marriott Intl, Potomac Electric Power Co, Riggs Natl Bank WA; pres, dir: Farrells Ice Cream Parlour Restaurants, Marriott Family Restaurants, MDS Distr Svcs, Willmar Distr Inc; prin: Marriott Condominium Devel Corp *NONPR AFFIL* mem: Natl Commn Against Drunk Driving, Natl Restaurant Assn, Sigma Chi; trust: Boy Scouts Am, Boys Clubs Am, Dole Fdn Employment Persons Disabilities

APPLICATION INFORMATION
Restrictions on Giving: The foundation does not have a formal grants program. Con-

tributions are made solely to organizations that are of interest to the manager. The foundation is not inviting applications through 1995. No grants are made to individuals.

GRANTS ANALYSIS
Total Grants: $7,505,330

Number of Grants: 262

Highest Grant: $1,000,000

Average Grant: $28,646

Typical Range: $1,000 to $50,000

Disclosure Period: 1992

Note: Recent grants are derived from a 1992 Form 990.

RECENT GRANTS

Library

200,000	University of Utah Library, Salt Lake City, UT
200,000	University of Utah Library, Salt Lake City, UT
50,000	Ronald Reagan Presidential Foundation, Los Angeles, CA

General

1,000,000	Marriott Foundation for People with Disabilities, Washington, DC
500,000	Marriott Foundation for People with Disabilities, Washington, DC
500,000	Rebuild Los Angeles, Los Angeles, CA
300,000	Massachusetts General Hospital, Boston, MA
250,000	Stanford University, Neonatal Department, Stanford, CA

MCI Communications Corp. / MCI Foundation

Revenue: $13.33 billion
Employees: 34,000
Headquarters: Washington, DC
SIC Major Group: Communications Services Nec and Telephone Communications Except Radiotelephone

CONTACT
Adrea Sarkisian
Executive Director
MCI Foundation
1801 Pennsylvania Ave., NW
Washington, DC 20006
(202) 887-3247
Note: Local organizations requesting funds should contact regional offices. See "Other Things To Know" for more details. The company's World Wide Web address is http://www.mci.com

FINANCIAL SUMMARY
Recent Giving: $2,500,000 (1995 est.); $2,200,000 (1994 approx.); $2,229,665 (1993)

Assets: $5,292,081 (1993); $4,557,714 (1992); $6,973,600 (1991)

Gifts Received: $2,800,000 (1993); $2,001,000 (1990)

Fiscal Note: Above figures are for the foundation only. Above figures exclude nonmonetary support. In 1993, the foundation received $2,800,000 from MCI Communications Corp.

EIN: 51-0294683

CONTRIBUTIONS SUMMARY
Typical Recipients: • _Arts & Humanities:_ Arts Centers, Arts Outreach, Film & Video, Museums/Galleries, Music, Performing Arts, Public Broadcasting • _Civic & Public Affairs:_ African American Affairs, Business/Free Enterprise, Economic Development, Employment/Job Training, General, Housing, Nonprofit Management, Professional & Trade Associations, Public Policy, Urban & Community Affairs • _Education:_ Business Education, Colleges & Universities, Economic Education, Education Associations, Education Funds, International Studies, Legal Education, Medical Education, Private Education (Precollege), Public Education (Precollege), Science/Mathematics Education, Student Aid • _Environment:_ General • _Health:_ Arthritis, Cancer, Emergency/Ambulance Services, Health Organizations, Hospitals, Medical Training, Single-Disease Health Associations • _Religion:_ Religious Welfare • _Science:_ Science Museums, Scientific Centers & Institutes • _Social Services:_ Child Welfare, Emergency Relief, Family Planning, Homes, People with Disabilities, Recreation & Athletics, United Funds/United Ways, Youth Organizations

Grant Types: capital, emergency, general support, multiyear/continuing support, operating expenses, project, research, and scholarship

Nonmonetary Support Types: donated equipment

Note: MCI donates telecom equipment for educational purposes only. Estimated value of nonmonetary support is not available.

Geographic Distribution: headquarters and operating locations

Operating Locations: CA (San Francisco), CO (Colorado Springs), DC, GA (Atlanta), IA (Cedar Rapids), IL (Chicago), NC (Cary), NJ (Piscataway), NY (Rye Brook), TX (Richardson)

Note: MCI Communications Corp. subsidiaries are MCI Telecommunications Corp., MCI International, and Telecom USA.

CORP. OFFICERS
John Rice Worthington: _B_ Chicago IL 1930 _ED_ Univ MI BA 1952; Univ MI MBA 1954; Univ MI JD 1955 _CURR EMPL_ sr vp, gen couns, dir: MCI Commun Corp _CORP AFFIL_ secy: QWest Commun Inc; secy, dir: Teleconnect Co; sr vp, secy, gen counc: MCI Telecommun Corp

John H. Zimmerman: _B_ Akron OH 1932 _ED_ Colgate Univ BA 1954; Kent St Univ MBA 1962 _CURR EMPL_ sr vp: MCI Commun Corp _NONPR AFFIL_ chmn adv bd: Am Mgmt Assn; mem: Phi Beta Kappa; mem adv bd: George Washington Univ Sch Bus Pub Mgmt

GIVING OFFICERS
Adrea Sarkisian: exec dir

John Rice Worthington: dir _CURR EMPL_ sr vp, gen couns, dir: MCI Commun Corp (see above)

John H. Zimmerman: dir _CURR EMPL_ sr vp: MCI Commun Corp (see above)

APPLICATION INFORMATION
Initial Approach: _Initial Contact:_ brief letter of inquiry or proposal _Include Information On:_ name and address of organization, purpose of grant requested, copy of IRS 501 (c)(3) tax letter, and detailed description of how funds will be used _Deadlines:_ none

Restrictions on Giving: The foundation does not support individuals, religious organizations for sectarian purposes, or political or lobbying groups. The foundation also does not buy advertising as a form of contribution.

OTHER THINGS TO KNOW
Regional or local nonprofit organizations should submit written proposals to the public relations directors at the following MCI divisional headquarters offices:

MCI Eastern Division, 5 International Dr., Rye Brook, NY 10573 handles inquiries for Connecticut, Delaware, Maine, Massachusetts, Maryland, New Hampshire, New Jersey, New York, Pennsylvania, Rhode Island, Vermont, Virginia, and West Virginia.

MCI Central Division, 205 N Michigan Ave., Ste. 3200, Chicago, IL 60601 handles inquiries for Illinois, Indiana, Iowa, Michigan, Minnesota, Nebraska, North Dakota, Ohio, South Dakota, and Wisconsin.

MCI West Division, 201 Spear St., 9th Fl., San Francisco, CA 94105 handles inquiries for Alaska, Arizona, California, Colorado, Hawaii, Idaho, Montana, Nevada, New Mexico, Oregon, Utah, Washington, and Wyoming.

MCI Southern Division, 400 Perimeter Ctr., Ste. 400, Atlanta, GA 30346 handles inquiries for Alabama, Arkansas, Florida, Georgia, Kansas, Kentucky, Louisiana, Mississippi, Missouri, North Carolina, South Carolina, Oklahoma, Tennessee, and Texas.

GRANTS ANALYSIS
Total Grants: $2,229,665

Number of Grants: 312

Highest Grant: $100,000

Average Grant: $7,146

Typical Range: $5,000 to $10,000

Disclosure Period: 1993

Note: Recent grants are derived from a 1993 Form 990.

RECENT GRANTS

General

100,000	Marine Toys for Tots Foundation, Snyder, NY — community outreach program
100,000	National Consumers League, Washington, DC — Fraud Information Center

50,000 Ronald McDonald Children's Charity, Oak Brook, IL — general support
38,650 March of Dimes Birth Defects, Eugene, OR — general support
35,000 Education Excellence Partnership, New York, NY — general support

Potomac Electric Power Co.

Revenue: $1.73 billion
Employees: 5,100
Headquarters: Washington, DC
SIC Major Group: Electric Services

CONTACT
William Torgerson
Chairman, Contributions Committee
Potomac Electric Power Co.
1900 Pennsylvania Ave., NW, Rm 841
Washington, DC 20068
(202) 872-2365
Note: Alternative contact is Mark Tool.

FINANCIAL SUMMARY
Recent Giving: $1,700,000 (1992 approx.); $1,773,000 (1991); $1,700,000 (1990)
Fiscal Note: Company gives directly.

CONTRIBUTIONS SUMMARY
Typical Recipients: • *Arts & Humanities:* Arts Associations & Councils, Arts Centers, Dance, Historic Preservation, Libraries, Museums/Galleries, Music, Opera, Performing Arts, Public Broadcasting, Theater • *Civic & Public Affairs:* Business/Free Enterprise, Civil Rights, Employment/Job Training, Municipalities/Towns, Urban & Community Affairs, Women's Affairs • *Education:* Colleges & Universities, Education Associations, Education Funds, Literacy, Minority Education, Public Education (Precollege), Science/Mathematics Education, Student Aid • *Environment:* General • *Health:* Health Organizations, Hospices, Hospitals, Medical Research, Single-Disease Health Associations • *International:* International Peace & Security Issues • *Religion:* Churches, Religious Organizations • *Social Services:* Animal Protection, Child Welfare, Community Service Organizations, Family Services, Food/Clothing Distribution, People with Disabilities, Recreation & Athletics, Senior Services, Shelters/Homelessness, Substance Abuse, United Funds/United Ways, Youth Organizations
Grant Types: capital and project
Note: Does not fund general operating funds.
Geographic Distribution: Washington, DC, area
Operating Locations: DC, MD, PA, TX

CORP. OFFICERS
Edward Franklin Mitchell: *B* Harrisonburg VA 1931 *ED* Univ VA 1956; George Washington Univ 1960 *CURR EMPL* pres, ceo, dir: Potomac Electric Power Co *CORP AFFIL* dir: Acacia Mutual Life Ins Co, Roggs Natl Bank, Suburban Bank *NONPR AFFIL*

bd dirs: Natl Rehab Hosp; bd dirs DC Chapter: ARC; mem adv counc: Univ MD Energy Coll; mem, dir: MD Chamber Commerce

GIVING OFFICERS
William T. Torgerson: *B* Annapolis MD 1944 *ED* Princeton Univ 1966; Univ MD 1973 *CURR EMPL* vp, gen couns: Potomac Electric Power Co

APPLICATION INFORMATION
Initial Approach: *Initial Contact:* letter or proposal *Include Information On:* description of the organization, amount requested, purpose for which funds are sought, recently audited financial statement, proof of tax-exempt status *Deadlines:* none

Restrictions on Giving: Funds only organizations in company's service territory; does not fund organizations outside of the metropolitan Washington, D.C., area.

GRANTS ANALYSIS
Total Grants: $1,700,000*
Disclosure Period: 1992
Note: Total grants figure is approximate.

Public Welfare Foundation

CONTACT
Larry Kressley
Executive Director
Public Welfare Foundation
2600 Virginia Ave., NW, Ste. 505
Washington, DC 20037-1977
(202) 965-1800

FINANCIAL SUMMARY
Recent Giving: $18,500,000 (fiscal 1995 est.); $17,326,713 (fiscal 1994); $17,193,500 (fiscal 1993)
Assets: $287,518,000 (fiscal 1995 est.); $288,167,230 (fiscal 1994); $277,308,139 (fiscal 1993)
EIN: 54-0597601

CONTRIBUTIONS SUMMARY
Donor(s): The Public Welfare Foundation was founded in 1947 by Charles Edward Marsh, an Ohio newspaperman. Mr. Marsh believed that newspapers were semi-public utilities which contributed to the improvement of society. This philosophy, coupled with a strong humanitarian instinct, inspired him to use the income from some of the newspapers he owned to establish a foundation.

Typical Recipients: • *Arts & Humanities:* Libraries • *Civic & Public Affairs:* African American Affairs, Business/Free Enterprise, Civil Rights, Economic Development, Employment/Job Training, Housing, Law & Justice, Legal Aid, Nonprofit Management, Public Policy, Rural Affairs, Safety, Urban & Community Affairs, Women's Affairs • *Education:* Colleges & Universities, Legal Education • *Environment:* Air/Water Quality, General, Resource Conservation • *Health:* Adolescent Health Issues, AIDS/HIV, Children's Health/Hospitals,

Clinics/Medical Centers, Geriatric Health, Health Organizations, Hospitals, Mental Health, Prenatal Health Issues, Public Health • *International:* Health Care/Hospitals, International Development, International Environmental Issues, International Peace & Security Issues, International Relief Efforts • *Religion:* Social/Policy Issues • *Science:* Scientific Organizations • *Social Services:* Child Welfare, Community Service Organizations, Counseling, Delinquency & Criminal Rehabilitation, Domestic Violence, Family Planning, Family Services, Food/Clothing Distribution, Homes, People with Disabilities, Refugee Assistance, Senior Services, Shelters/Homelessness, Youth Organizations

Grant Types: general support, matching, operating expenses, project, and seed money
Geographic Distribution: international and national

GIVING OFFICERS
Linda J. Campbell: secy, asst treas
Peter Edelman: dir *B* Minneapolis MN 1938 *ED* Harvard Univ AB 1958; Harvard Univ LLB 1961 *NONPR AFFIL* chmn: Ctr Commun Change, Fair Employment Counc Greater Washington; co-chmn: Am Peace Now; dir: Ctr Natl Policy, Food Res Action Ctr, Pub Voice; mem exec comm: Washington Lawyers Commn Civil Rights Under Law; mem natl gov bd: Common Cause
Antoinette M. Haskell: dir
Robert H. Haskell: dir
Veronica T. Keating: treas, dir
Larry Kressley: exec dir
Claudia Haines Marsh: dir emeritus
Robert R. Nathan: dir *B* Dayton OH 1908 *ED* Univ PA BS 1931; Univ PA MA 1933; Georgetown Univ LLB 1938 *CURR EMPL* chmn: Robert R Nathan Assocs
Myrtis H. Powell: dir
Thomas J. Scanlon: vchmn, dir
Thomas W. Scoville: dir
Jerome W. D. Stokes: dir
Donald T. Warner: chmn, dir

APPLICATION INFORMATION
Initial Approach:
Applicants should send a letter of inquiry to the foundation, and call for application guidelines.

A two page letter should describe the work to be conducted. The letter should be accompanied by a cover sheet, which includes: the name and address of the organization, contact person, telephone and fax numbers, one paragraph summarizing the organization's purpose and activities, one paragraph summarizing the proposal, the relationship of the proposal to the organization's mission statement, total annual organizational budget and fiscal year, total project budget, dollar amount requested, and time period the grant will cover (with beginning and ending dates).

Requests for grants may be submitted at any time and are reviewed by the screening committee on a daily basis.

The foundation requests that all materials be written in English and that applicants not request preliminary meetings until a letter of inquiry has been submitted. Within one month of receiving the request, the foundation will notify the applicant whether the request has been accepted for consideration. If accepted, a proposal will be requested at that time. It generally takes an additional two to three months for the foundation to notify the applicant if it has approved the proposal. Funds should be sought for the following operating year in most cases. Decisions are made by the board of directors which meets regularly during the year.

Restrictions on Giving: The foundation generally does not fund conferences, endowments, foreign study, graduate work, individuals, publications, research projects, scholarships, seminars, and workshops.

OTHER THINGS TO KNOW
Each year a good portion of the grantees are first-time recipients.

PUBLICATIONS
Annual report; application guidelines (Spanish translation available)

GRANTS ANALYSIS
Total Grants: $17,326,713

Number of Grants: 426

Highest Grant: $250,000

Average Grant: $40,673

Typical Range: $25,000 to $50,000

Disclosure Period: fiscal year ending October 31, 1994

Note: Recent grants are derived from a fiscal 1993 annual report.

RECENT GRANTS

Library
50,000   National Library Support Project, Blue Mountain Lake, NY — general operating support

General
250,000   Friends of the Earth, Washington, DC — general support

250,000   N Street Village, Washington, DC — for a model low-income permanent rental apartment community

250,000   Natural Resources Defense Council, New York, NY — for the atmosphere protection initiative

250,000   Warren Wilson College, Swannanoa, NC — to support the college providing a four-year liberal arts education to students largely from Appalachia

200,000   Environmental Defense Fund, New York, NY — for the global atmosphere and international programs

Strong Foundation, Hattie M.

CONTACT
Judith B. Cyphers
Secretary and Director of Grants
Hattie M. Strong Foundation
1620 Eye St., NW, Ste. 700
Washington, DC 20006
(202) 331-1619

FINANCIAL SUMMARY
Recent Giving: $721,495 (fiscal 1993); $739,190 (fiscal 1992); $761,645 (fiscal 1991)

Assets: $18,649,585 (fiscal 1993); $18,647,095 (fiscal 1992); $17,855,823 (fiscal 1991)

Gifts Received: $1,655 (fiscal 1993); $1,880 (fiscal 1992); $1,820 (fiscal 1990)

EIN: 53-0237223

CONTRIBUTIONS SUMMARY
Donor(s): The foundation was incorporated in 1928 by the late Hattie M. Strong .

Typical Recipients: • *Arts & Humanities:* Arts Outreach, Libraries, Performing Arts, Public Broadcasting, Theater • *Civic & Public Affairs:* Employment/Job Training, Hispanic Affairs, Nonprofit Management, Philanthropic Organizations, Professional & Trade Associations • *Education:* After-school/Enrichment Programs, Colleges & Universities, Community & Junior Colleges, Education Funds, Education Reform, Elementary Education (Public), General, Health & Physical Education, Leadership Training, Literacy, Minority Education, Public Education (Precollege), Special Education • *Health:* Children's Health/Hospitals, Medical Rehabilitation • *Religion:* Churches, Ministries, Religious Organizations, Religious Welfare • *Social Services:* At-Risk Youth, Child Welfare, Community Service Organizations, Crime Prevention, Family Services, People with Disabilities, Recreation & Athletics, Senior Services, Shelters/Homelessness, United Funds/United Ways, Volunteer Services, YMCA/YWCA/YMHA/YWHA, Youth Organizations

Grant Types: loan and project

Geographic Distribution: the Washington, DC, metropolitan area only for community education grant program; no geographic restrictions for student loan program

GIVING OFFICERS
Barbara B. Cantrell: dir

Judith B. Cyphers: secy, dir grants

Thelma L. Eichman: dir

Mary Draper Janney: dir *PHIL AFFIL* dir: Marjorie Merriweather Post Foundation of D.C.

John M. Lynham, Jr.: dir *PHIL AFFIL* trust: Dimick Foundation

Richard S. T. Marsh: dir *PHIL AFFIL* trust: Foundation for Middle East Peace

Patricia Mascari: dir

Vincent Emory Reed: dir *B* St Louis MO 1928 *ED* WV St Coll BS 1952; Howard Univ MA 1965 *CORP AFFIL* dir: Home Fed Savings & Loan Assn *NONPR AFFIL* dir: DC Goodwill Indus, 12 Neediest Kids, Washington YMCA; mem: Am Assn Sch Pers Admins, Am Soc Bus Officals, DC Parent Teacher Assn, Kappa Alpha Psi, NAACP, Natl Assn Sch Security Offs, Natl Assn Secondary Sch Prins, Natl Ed Assn, Phi Delta Kappa; staff mem: DC Pub Schs; volunteer: SE Boys Club, SE Youth Football Assn *CLUB AFFIL* Kiwanis, Pigskin *PHIL AFFIL* trust: Philip L. Graham Fund

Sigrid S. Reynolds: dir

C. Peter Strong: dir

Henry Strong: chmn, pres, off *B* Rochester NY 1923 *ED* Williams Coll AB 1949 *NONPR AFFIL* dir: Mt Vernon Coll, Natl Symphony Orchestra Assn; vchmn bd trusts, hon trust: John F Kennedy Ctr Performing Arts *CLUB AFFIL* Chevy Chase, Gibson Island, Metropolitan

Henry L. Strong: vp, off

Robin C. Tanner: treas, dir loans

APPLICATION INFORMATION
Initial Approach:

For the loan program, students should send an initial letter to the foundation. For the grant program, organizations interested in submitting a proposal should first contact the foundation and request written materials explaining proposal procedures and requirements.

For the loan program, students should send an initial letter providing a brief personal history and identification of the educational institution attended, the subjects studied, the date studies are expected to be completed, and the amount of funds needed. If the student qualifies for consideration, application forms are then sent out to be completed and returned to the foundation. For the grant program, organizations should follow the foundation's proposal procedures and requirements as directed.

Students should apply between January 1 and March 31 for loans covering the academic year beginning the following September. Deadlines for grant proposals are January 15, April 15, July 15, and October 15 to be considered for March, June, September, and December, respectively.

Loan applicants are normally notified of the foundation's decision in early July. After a full review of grant proposals by foundation staff, including personal interviews if necessary, proposals are presented to the board for action. Applicants are notified in writing of the board's decision.

Restrictions on Giving: For the loan program, foreign students temporarily in the

United States do not qualify. For the grant program, the foundation generally does not support building or endowment funds, requests for equipment, research, conferences, projects designed to educate the general public, or programs of national or international scope. The foundation does not make grants to individuals or provide scholarships.

PUBLICATIONS
Annual report and informational brochure including application guidelines

GRANTS ANALYSIS
Total Grants: $222,645*

Number of Grants: 62

Highest Grant: $6,000

Average Grant: $3,591

Typical Range: $1,000 to $5,000

Disclosure Period: fiscal year ending August 31, 1993

Note: Total grants figure is for the community grants program. It excludes $498,850 for the student loan program. Recent grants are derived from a fiscal 1993 grants list.

RECENT GRANTS

Library

5,000	DC Public Schools, Washington, DC — expansion of Home/School Resource and Toy Lending Library's services
5,000	DC Public Schools, Washington, DC — Toy Lending Library
2,500	Library Theater, Washington, DC — Summer Books Alive/Summer Storybuilders program to motivate children to read

General

6,000	Gallaudet University, Washington, DC — implementation of Project Success to help prepare deaf and hard of hearing teachers for certification in DC
6,000	George Mason University, Fairfax, VA — curriculum development of the Community Youth Leadership component for Project LEAD
6,000	Latin American Youth Center, Washington, DC — in support of multifaceted educational program at the Teen Drop-In Center
6,000	YWCA, Harrison Center for Career Education, Washington, DC — support of direct training expenses of the practical nursing and home health aid programs
5,000	Academy of Hope, Washington, DC — support for new staff position and expanded services of community-based literacy and basic education program for 100 adult students

FLORIDA

Adams Foundation, Arthur F. and Alice E.

CONTACT
Tom Dean
Trustee
Arthur F. and Alice E. Adams Foundation
c/o First Union National Bank
214 N Hogan St.
Jacksonville, FL 32231
(904) 361-1399

FINANCIAL SUMMARY
Recent Giving: $811,000 (fiscal 1992); $667,410 (fiscal 1991); $312,500 (fiscal 1990)

Assets: $16,875,443 (fiscal 1992); $15,981,339 (fiscal 1991); $9,088,660 (fiscal 1990)

Gifts Received: $6,063,661 (fiscal 1991); $5,727,634 (fiscal 1990)

Fiscal Note: In 1990, the foundation received $5,658,636 from the Alice E. Adams Trust and $68,997 from the Alice E. Adams Charitable Remainder Trust 1983.

EIN: 65-6003785

CONTRIBUTIONS SUMMARY
Typical Recipients: • *Arts & Humanities:* Dance, Libraries, Museums/Galleries, Music, Opera, Theater • *Civic & Public Affairs:* Philanthropic Organizations, Zoos/Aquariums • *Education:* Colleges & Universities, Education Associations, Private Education (Precollege), Student Aid • *Health:* Hospitals, Medical Rehabilitation, Public Health • *International:* Health Care/Hospitals • *Social Services:* Child Welfare, Community Service Organizations, Emergency Relief, People with Disabilities

Grant Types: general support and scholarship

Geographic Distribution: eastern United States with an emphasis on Miami, FL

GIVING OFFICERS
Dewey Ballantine: trust

Richard H. Chapman: mgr, contact person, vp (Southeast Bank)

GRANTS ANALYSIS
Total Grants: $811,000

Number of Grants: 15

Highest Grant: $405,000

Typical Range: $10,000 to $50,000

Disclosure Period: fiscal year ending September 30, 1992

Note: Recent grants are derived from a fiscal 1992 Form 990.

RECENT GRANTS

Library

80,000	John Carter Brown Library, Providence, RI

General

405,000	Greater Miami Opera, Miami, FL
75,000	Opera Memphis, Memphis, TN
50,000	Coconut Grove Playhouse, Miami, FL
50,000	Miami Heart Institute, Miami Beach, FL
35,000	Metropolitan Museum of Art, New York, NY

Beattie Foundation Trust, Cordelia Lee

CONTACT
Robert E. Perkins
Administrative Agent
Cordelia Lee Beattie Fdn Trust
1800 2nd St., Ste. 905
Sarasota, FL 34236

FINANCIAL SUMMARY
Recent Giving: $94,900 (fiscal 1992); $110,883 (fiscal 1991); $129,102 (fiscal 1990)

Assets: $1,971,179 (fiscal 1992); $1,984,104 (fiscal 1991); $1,728,393 (fiscal 1990)

EIN: 59-6540711

CONTRIBUTIONS SUMMARY
Donor(s): the late Cordelia Lee Beattie

Typical Recipients: • *Arts & Humanities:* Arts Associations & Councils, Arts Festivals, Ballet, Community Arts, Dance, Libraries, Museums/Galleries, Music, Opera, Performing Arts, Theater • *Civic & Public Affairs:* Municipalities/Towns, Zoos/Aquariums • *Education:* Colleges & Universities, Private Education (Precollege), Public Education (Precollege), Student Aid • *Environment:* General • *Health:* Single-Disease Health Associations • *Social Services:* Youth Organizations

Grant Types: capital and scholarship

Geographic Distribution: limited to Sarasota County, FL

GIVING OFFICERS
First Union National Bank: trust

Dr. Robert E. Perkins: admin agent *PHIL AFFIL* exec dir: William G. Selby and Marie Selby Foundation; admin agent: Leslie T. and Frances U. Posey Foundation; trust: Goldsmith Greenfield Foundation

James R. Rodgers: trust *PHIL AFFIL* trust: Cordelia Lunceford Beatty Trust

William W. Rodgers: trust *PHIL AFFIL* trust: Cordelia Lunceford Beatty Trust

APPLICATION INFORMATION
Initial Approach: Application form required. There are no deadlines.

PUBLICATIONS
Application Guidelines

GRANTS ANALYSIS
Total Grants: $94,900

Number of Grants: 13

Highest Grant: $20,000

Typical Range: $3,000 to $10,000

Disclosure Period: fiscal year ending October 31, 1992

Note: Recent grants are derived from a fiscal 1992 Form 990.

RECENT GRANTS

Library

5,000	Friends of Library of Venice Area, Venice, FL — construction/equipment
5,000	Sarasota County Public Library System, Sarasota, FL
5,000	Sarasota County Public Library System, Sarasota, FL — materials/equipment

General

20,000	Florida West Coast Symphony, Sarasota, FL — scholarships
10,000	Sarasota County Area Council, Sarasota, FL — programming/production
6,000	Pines of Sarasota, Sarasota, FL
5,500	School Board of Sarasota Company, Sarasota, FL
5,500	School Board of Sarasota County, Sarasota, FL — band uniforms

Beveridge Foundation, Frank Stanley

CONTACT
Philip Caswell
President and Director
Frank Stanley Beveridge Foundation
301 Yamato Rd., Ste. 1130
Boca Raton, FL 33431-4929
(407) 241-8388

FINANCIAL SUMMARY
Recent Giving: $1,688,963 (1991); $1,921,093 (1990); $1,579,224 (1989)

Assets: $42,161,192 (1991); $37,014,567 (1990); $36,934,996 (1989)

EIN: 04-6032164

CONTRIBUTIONS SUMMARY
Donor(s): The foundation was established in 1947 in Massachusetts by the late Frank Stanley Beveridge (1879-1956). Mr. Beveridge was the founder of Stanhome, Inc. (formerly Stanley Home Products, Inc.) and the Stanley Park of Westfield, Inc.

Typical Recipients: • *Arts & Humanities:* Arts Associations & Councils, Arts Funds, Dance, Historic Preservation, Libraries, Museums/Galleries, Music, Performing Arts, Public Broadcasting • *Civic & Public Affairs:* Housing, Philanthropic Organizations, Urban & Community Affairs, Zoos/Aquariums • *Education:* Colleges & Universities, Education Associations, Education Funds, Preschool Education, Private Education (Precollege), Special Education • *Environment:* General • *Health:* Geriatric Health, Health Organizations, Hospices, Hospitals, Mental Health, Single-Disease Health Associations • *Religion:* Churches • *Social Services:* Child Welfare, Community Centers, Community Service Organizations, Emergency Relief, Family Services, People with Disabilities, Senior Services, Youth Organizations

Grant Types: capital, challenge, conference/seminar, emergency, general support, multiyear/continuing support, project, and seed money

Geographic Distribution: primarily Hampden and Hampshire counties, MA; and the Tampa and Palm Beach, FL, areas

GIVING OFFICERS
Sarah Caswell Bartelt: dir

William R. Cass: dir

John Beveridge Caswell: dir *B* Hartford CT 1938 *ED* Brown Univ BA 1960; Columbia Univ MBA 1961 *CURR EMPL* pres: Omnia Group *CORP AFFIL* dir: Berkshire Life Ins Co

Philip Caswell: pres, dir

John G. Gallup: dir *B* Bridgeport CT 1927 *NONPR AFFIL* dir: Visiting Nurses Assn; hon dir: Assn Indus MA; mem: Am Paper Inst, Boston Paper Trade Assn, Greater Springfield Chamber Commerce; pres: Springfield Orchestra Assn; trust: Commun Fdn Western MA *CLUB AFFIL* Colony, Longmeadow CC

Carole S. Lenhart: treas

Joseph Beveridge Palmer: dir

Homer G. Perkins: dir *B* New Haven CT 1916 *ED* Yale Univ 1938 *CURR EMPL* dir: Stanhome *CORP AFFIL* dir: Daniel OConnells Sons; treas, dir: Stanley Park Westfield; trust, chmn bd: Cooley Dickinson Hosp *NONPR AFFIL* mem: Direct Selling Assn *CLUB AFFIL* Lions

Evelyn Beveridge Russell: dir

Patsy Palmer Stecher: dir

J. Thomas Touchton: dir

David F. Woods: clerk, dir *B* 1936 *ED* Loyola Coll BS 1964 *CORP AFFIL* trust: Baystate Health Sys *NONPR AFFIL* mem: Assn Advanced Life Underwriting, MA Assn Life Underwriters, Natl Assn Life Underwriters

APPLICATION INFORMATION
Initial Approach:

Applicants should request guidelines and an application form by letter.

The letter should describe the organization and project for which funds are sought. Applicants also should include evidence of 509(a) classification. Formal applications should include purpose and history of the organization; proposal objective; time period of project; total project budget and amount requested; list of special fund raising activities; and name of person completing form.

Applicants should also include proof of IRS 501(c)(3) status; IRS Form 990 for the two most recent years; latest balance sheet and detailed income statement; statement that the grant request is executed by a person authorized to submit on the behalf of the requesting organization; list of other sources of funding for the project; names and affiliations of board members; name and qualification of the individual proposed to administer the grant; and a table of organization.

The suggested deadlines for applications are February 1 and August 1. Grant proposals must be completed 60 days before the next scheduled board meeting.

Board meetings generally are held in April and October. Applicants are notified in writing of the action taken by the board relative to grant proposals usually within two weeks of board meetings.

Restrictions on Giving: The foundation usually does not fund endowments; foreign organizations or expenditures; organizations outside the approved geographic area; individuals; private foundations; operating expenses, except for research or start-up programs; budget deficits; travel; fund-raising activities; program-related investment loans; United Ways and their foundations; chiefly tax-supported institutions and their foundations; or organizations that receive more than 50% of their operating revenues from taxes.

Any requests outside Hampden or Hampshire counties require the support of one or more directors. Applicants should not solicit such support. The foundation will contact these applicants if interested, after initial proposals are received.

PUBLICATIONS
Grant proposal guidelines

GRANTS ANALYSIS
Total Grants: $1,688,963

Number of Grants: 79

Highest Grant: $665,000

Average Grant: $13,128*

Typical Range: $1,000 to $50,000

Disclosure Period: 1991

Note: The average grant figure excludes the largest grant of $665,000. Recent grants are derived from a 1991 Form 990.

RECENT GRANTS

Library

5,000	Company of the Redwood Library and Athenaeum, Newport, RI

General

665,000	Stanley Park of Westfield, Westfield, MA
50,400	Community Foundation of Western Massachusetts
50,000	Cooley Dickinson Health Care Corporation, Northampton, MA
50,000	Watkinson School, Hartford, CT
40,500	Community Foundation of Greater Tampa, Tampa, FL

Breyer Foundation

CONTACT
Henry W. Breyer III
President
Breyer Fdn.
354 Chilean Ave.
Palm Beach, FL 33480
(407) 655-2205

FINANCIAL SUMMARY
Recent Giving: $85,550 (1993); $110,250 (1992); $122,215 (1991)

Assets: $2,271,912 (1993); $2,097,335 (1992); $2,146,961 (1991)

Gifts Received: $300 (1993); $300 (1992); $300 (1991)

EIN: 23-6295924

CONTRIBUTIONS SUMMARY
Donor(s): Henry W. Breyer III

Typical Recipients: • *Arts & Humanities:* Arts Associations & Councils, Arts Centers, Historic Preservation, History & Archaeology, Libraries, Museums/Galleries, Music, Opera, Performing Arts, Public Broadcasting, Theater • *Civic & Public Affairs:* Botanical Gardens/Parks, Clubs, Community Foundations, General, Safety, Urban & Community Affairs, Zoos/Aquariums • *Education:* Arts/Humanities Education, Colleges & Universities, Private Education (Precollege), Special Education • *Environment:* General, Resource Conservation, Wildlife Protection • *Health:* Arthritis, Cancer, Children's Health/Hospitals, Diabetes, Emergency/Ambulance Services, Health Organizations, Heart, Hospices, Hospitals, Medical Research, Public Health • *International:* Foreign Educational Institutions, Human Rights, International Affairs • *Religion:* Churches, Religious Welfare • *Social Services:* Community Service Organizations, Day Care, Family Planning, Food/Clothing Distribution, People with Disabilities, Substance Abuse, United Funds/United Ways, Youth Organizations

Grant Types: general support

Geographic Distribution: focus on PA

GIVING OFFICERS
Henry W. Breyer III: dir, pres

Henry W. Breyer IV: treas

Joanne Breyer: secy, trust

APPLICATION INFORMATION
Initial Approach: Send brief letter describing program. There are no deadlines.

GRANTS ANALYSIS
Total Grants: $85,550

Number of Grants: 65

Highest Grant: $15,000

Typical Range: $100 to $11,000

Disclosure Period: 1993

Note: Recent grants are derived from a 1993 Form 990.

RECENT GRANTS

Library

100	Friends of Library, The Pennsylvania Horticultural Society, Philadelphia, PA
100	Gladwyne Free Library, Gladwyne, PA
100	Ludington Public Library, Bryn Mawr, PA

General

15,000	Church of the Redeemer
11,000	Planned Parenthood, Washington, DC
6,200	American Red Cross, New York, NY
5,200	Pennsylvania Horticultural Society, Philadelphia, PA
3,000	Church Farm School, Paoli, PA

Burdines Inc.

Sales: $1.18 billion
Employees: 11,800
Headquarters: Miami, FL
SIC Major Group: Department Stores

CONTACT
Peggy Hurst
Director, Public Affairs
Burdines Inc.
22 E Flagler St.
Miami, FL 33131
(305) 835-5151

FINANCIAL SUMMARY
Recent Giving: $540,000 (1993 approx.); $2,000,000 (1992 approx.); $325,000 (1991 approx.)

Fiscal Note: Company makes direct contributions.

CONTRIBUTIONS SUMMARY
Typical Recipients: • *Arts & Humanities:* Arts Associations & Councils, Arts Centers, Arts Funds, Community Arts, Dance, Historic Preservation, Libraries, Museums/Galleries, Music, Opera, Performing Arts, Public Broadcasting, Theater, Visual Arts • *Civic & Public Affairs:* Civil Rights • *Education:* Arts/Humanities Education, Business Education, Colleges & Universities, Community & Junior Colleges, Education Funds, Private Education (Precollege), Public Education (Precollege) • *Environment:* General • *Science:* Observatories & Planetariums, Science Exhibits & Fairs • *Social Services:* Food/Clothing Distribution, United Funds/United Ways

Grant Types: award, capital, challenge, department, general support, and matching

Nonmonetary Support Types: donated equipment, donated products, in-kind services, loaned employees, and loaned executives

Note: Contact for nonmonetary support is Christian Immodino.

Geographic Distribution: limited to Florida

Operating Locations: FL (Miami)

CORP. OFFICERS
Douglas Flom: *CURR EMPL* cfo: Burdines Inc

James Gray: *CURR EMPL* pres: Burdines Inc

J. David Scheiner: *CURR EMPL* vchmn: Burdines Inc

Howard Socol: *CURR EMPL* chmn, ceo: Burdines Inc

GIVING OFFICERS
Peggy Hurst: *CURR EMPL* dir pub aff: Burdines Inc

APPLICATION INFORMATION
Initial Approach: *Initial Contact:* brief phone call or written proposal *Include Information On:* a description of organization, amount requested, purpose of funds sought, recently audited financial statement, and proof of tax-exempt status *Deadlines:* after February 1

Restrictions on Giving: Program does not support individuals, fraternal organizations, goodwill advertising, health causes (except through the United Way), sports-related events, religious organizations for sectarian purposes, scholarships, advertising, out-of-state organizations, door prizes, gift certificates, or political or lobbying groups.

OTHER THINGS TO KNOW
Burdines Federated Department Stores emerged from bankruptcy in 1992 and resumed corporate contributions in February 1993. The Campeau Foundation was not a company resource as of 1992.

GRANTS ANALYSIS
Total Grants: $540,000*

Typical Range: $1,000 to $25,000

Disclosure Period: 1993

Note: Total grants figure is approximate.

Catlin Charitable Trust, Kathleen K.

CONTACT
Kathleen K. Catlin Charitable Trust
c/o First Florida Bank
PO Box 676
Venice, FL 34284-0676
(813) 488-2261

FINANCIAL SUMMARY
Recent Giving: $307,871 (fiscal 1992); $7,501 (fiscal 1991); $328,210 (fiscal 1990)

Assets: $5,711,861 (fiscal 1992); $5,374,806 (fiscal 1991); $4,924,597 (fiscal 1990)

EIN: 59-6877094

CONTRIBUTIONS SUMMARY
Typical Recipients: • *Arts & Humanities:* Libraries • *Civic & Public Affairs:* Urban & Community Affairs • *Education:* Elementary Education (Public), Public Education (Precollege), Secondary Education (Public) • *Environment:* Wildlife Protection • *Health:* Arthritis, Cancer, Hospices, Hospitals, Mul-

tiple Sclerosis, Single-Disease Health Associations • *Religion:* Religious Welfare • *Social Services:* Big Brother/Big Sister, Child Welfare, Community Centers, Community Service Organizations, Day Care, Food/Clothing Distribution, Recreation & Athletics, Senior Services, Substance Abuse, YMCA/YWCA/YMHA/YWHA, Youth Organizations

Grant Types: capital and general support

Geographic Distribution: primarily Venice and Sarasota, FL

APPLICATION INFORMATION
Initial Approach: Request application form. There are no deadlines.

GRANTS ANALYSIS
Total Grants: $307,871

Number of Grants: 24

Highest Grant: $177,620

Typical Range: $1,000 to $25,000

Disclosure Period: fiscal year ending February 28, 1992

Note: Recent grants are derived from a fiscal 1992 Form 990.

RECENT GRANTS

Library
25,000	Friends of Venice Library, Venice, FL — library expansion

General
177,620	Senior Friendship Center, Sarasota, FL — center building
25,000	Hospice Foundation, Sarasota, FL — building campaign for Venice Hospice House
14,136	Deborah Hospital Foundation, Browns Mills, NJ — workstation purchase
10,000	Children's Haven and Adult Center, Sarasota, FL — various capital improvements
10,000	Venice Elementary School, Venice, FL — math/science lab

Chastain Charitable Foundation, Robert Lee and Thomas M.

CONTACT
Robert Lee and Thomas M. Chastain
Charitable Fdn.
c/o First Union National Bank of Florida
40 Cocoanut Row
Palm Beach, FL 33480
(407) 838-5616

FINANCIAL SUMMARY
Recent Giving: $201,000 (1993); $140,000 (1992); $134,000 (1991)

Assets: $4,134,618 (1993); $3,911,219 (1992); $3,836,369 (1991)

EIN: 59-6171294

CONTRIBUTIONS SUMMARY
Donor(s): the late Robert Lee Chastain

Typical Recipients: • *Arts & Humanities:* Arts Centers, Arts Festivals, Arts Funds, Arts Institutes, Community Arts, Dance, Libraries, Music, Opera, Performing Arts, Public Broadcasting, Theater • *Civic & Public Affairs:* Botanical Gardens/Parks, Urban & Community Affairs, Zoos/Aquariums • *Education:* Colleges & Universities, Community & Junior Colleges • *Environment:* General • *Health:* Cancer, Emergency/Ambulance Services, Mental Health • *International:* International Environmental Issues, International Peace & Security Issues • *Religion:* Religious Welfare • *Science:* Science Museums • *Social Services:* At-Risk Youth, Child Welfare, Community Service Organizations, Counseling, Youth Organizations

Grant Types: general support

Geographic Distribution: focus on the Palm Beach and Martin County, FL, area

GIVING OFFICERS
First Union National Bank of Florida: trust

Thomas M. Chastain: trust

Harry A. Johnston II: trust

APPLICATION INFORMATION
Initial Approach: The foundation has no formal grant application procedure or application form. There are no deadlines.

GRANTS ANALYSIS
Total Grants: $201,000

Number of Grants: 24

Highest Grant: $27,000

Typical Range: $2,500 to $10,000

Disclosure Period: 1993

Note: Recent grants are derived from a 1993 Form 990.

RECENT GRANTS

General
28,000	Ann Norton Sculpture Gardens, Palm Beach, FL
15,000	Caribbean Conservation, Gainsville, FL
12,000	Florida Atlantic University, Boca Raton, FL
10,000	American Red Cross
10,000	Pine Jog Environmental Education

Chatlos Foundation

CONTACT
William J. Chatlos
President
Chatlos Foundation
PO Box 915048
Longwood, FL 32791-5048
(407) 862-5077
Note: The foundation also can be contacted through the office of its accountant, Eugene Miller, 655 Third Avenue, 14th Fl., New York, NY, 10017.

FINANCIAL SUMMARY
Recent Giving: $3,500,000 (1995 est.); $3,464,480 (1994); $3,638,363 (1993)

Assets: $87,153,662 (1993); $84,753,223 (1992); $85,646,041 (1991)

Gifts Received: $50,000 (1989)

Fiscal Note: In 1989, the foundation received $50,000 in the form of interest on a bond due in 2004.

EIN: 13-6161425

CONTRIBUTIONS SUMMARY
Donor(s): William Frederick Chatlos , the foundation's donor, was born in Bridgeport, CT, in 1889. In his youth, he began working for a builder and lumberman while studying the drafting of housing plans in night school at the YMCA. At the age of 17, Mr. Chatlos built his first house. He continued to construct buildings in Connecticut, New York, New Jersey, and Florida until his death in 1977. Mr. Chatlos established the foundation in 1953.

Typical Recipients: • *Arts & Humanities:* Libraries • *Civic & Public Affairs:* Housing, Safety, Women's Affairs • *Education:* Colleges & Universities, Religious Education, Special Education, Student Aid • *Health:* AIDS/HIV, Arthritis, Cancer, Clinics/Medical Centers, Emergency/Ambulance Services, Eyes/Blindness, Health Organizations, Hospitals, Medical Research, Nursing Services, Trauma Treatment • *International:* Health Care/Hospitals, International Development, International Peace & Security Issues, International Relief Efforts, Missionary/Religious Activities • *Religion:* Bible Study/Translation, Churches, Ministries, Missionary Activities (Domestic), Religious Organizations, Religious Welfare, Seminaries, Social/Policy Issues • *Social Services:* Child Welfare, Community Centers, Food/Clothing Distribution, People with Disabilities, Shelters/Homelessness

Grant Types: challenge, general support, project, and scholarship

Geographic Distribution: national; no geographic restrictions

GIVING OFFICERS
Alice E. Chatlos: chmn, sr vp, trust *CORP AFFIL* vp: Sun Ray Homes

William J. Chatlos: pres, treas, trust *CORP AFFIL* pres: Sun Ray Homes Inc

Joy E. D'Arata: vp, trust

Carol W. Leongomez: secy, trust

Charles O. Morgan: trust

Kathryn A. Randle: vchmn bd, trust

Michele C. Roach: asst secy, asst treas, trust

APPLICATION INFORMATION
Initial Approach:

The foundation requests that all inquiries be in writing.

All requests must include a cover letter with amount requested, one- to two-page proposal summary (if not included in the letter), evidence of IRS tax exemption, copies of the organization's last two audited financial statements and form 990, budget for the current year, project budget, list of officers and directors, and an indication of commitments already made to the projected budget.

The full board meets in February, May, August, and November. There are no application deadlines, but proposals may be forwarded for consideration at a subsequent meeting.

A preliminary review committee considers all proposals at its monthly meetings. If significant interest is evidenced, a proposal is considered by the full board. Applicants are notified if their proposal is to be considered by the full board. Meetings with the foundation are by appointment only, and are not granted initially.

Restrictions on Giving: The foundation does not support medical research, individual church congregations, individuals, the arts, state universities, or organizations in existence for less than two years. It also does not provide seed money, loans, deficit financing, or endowment funds.

OTHER THINGS TO KNOW

Organizations are allowed to submit a proposal every six months, however, no more than one project will be funded in a twelve month period.

PUBLICATIONS
Application guidelines

GRANTS ANALYSIS
Total Grants: $3,464,480

Number of Grants: 224

Highest Grant: $300,000

Average Grant: $15,466

Typical Range: $500 to $5,000 and $10,000 to $30,000

Disclosure Period: 1994

Note: Recent grants are derived from a 1993 Form 990.

RECENT GRANTS

Library
50,000	Covenant Theological Seminary, St. Louis, MO — Phase III of renovation/development of J. Oliver Buswell Library
30,000	Columbia Bible College and Seminary, St. Louis, MO — Phase III of renovation/development of J. Oliver Buswell Library
25,000	Clearwater Christian College, Clearwater, FL — retrospective conversion project for Easter Library
25,000	Kennedy Kreiger Institute, Baltimore, MD — establishment of a lending library for assistive technology equipment

General
200,000	Orlando Regional Medical Center Foundation, Orlando, FL — second payment of 1991 commitment
200,000	Orlando Regional Medical Center Foundation, Orlando,

	FL — third payment of commitment
196,800	Retinitis Pigmentosa Foundation Fighting Blindness, Baltimore, MD — final payment on commitment
113,750	Haggai Institute, Atlanta, GA — final payment of 1992 commitment
100,000	Asbury Theological Seminary, Wilmore, KY — increase endowed World Missions scholarship fund

Davis Foundations, Arthur Vining

CONTACT
Max King Morris
Executive Director
Arthur Vining Davis Foundations
111 Riverside Ave., Ste. 130
Jacksonville, FL 32202-4921
(904) 359-0670

FINANCIAL SUMMARY
Recent Giving: $6,650,000 (1994); $7,050,000 (1993 approx.); $6,075,500 (1992)

Assets: $145,000,000 (1994); $146,500,000 (1993 approx.); $134,051,000 (1992)

EIN: 25-6018909

CONTRIBUTIONS SUMMARY
Donor(s): Arthur Vining Davis , the son of a Congregational minister, graduated from Amherst College in 1888. By 1910, he became the president of the Aluminum Company of America (ALCOA). He later served for many years as chairman of the board. During his years at Alcoa, he began developing interests in Florida and the Bahamas. At the age of 82, he moved his numerous activities from Pittsburgh and New York to Florida, investing substantially in land, banks, airlines, shipping companies, nurseries, construction, and hotels. Arthur Vining Davis died in 1962 at the age of 95.

Three foundations function as a single philanthropic organization. Foundation No. 1 was organized by Mr. Davis in 1952. Foundations No. 2 and No. 3 were created by his will from a major share of his estate. Although Mr. Davis did not delegate his giving during his lifetime, he did designate six individual trustees in his will to run his foundations' giving programs.

Typical Recipients: • *Arts & Humanities:* Arts Centers, Film & Video, History & Archaeology, Libraries, Public Broadcasting • *Education:* Arts/Humanities Education, Colleges & Universities, International Studies, Medical Education, Public Education (Precollege), Religious Education, Science/Mathematics Education, Social Sciences Education • *Environment:* Resource Conservation • *Health:* Children's Health/Hospitals, Health Organizations, Hospices, Hospitals, Mental Health, Research/Studies Institutes • *International:*

Missionary/Religious Activities • *Religion:* Religious Organizations, Religious Welfare, Seminaries • *Social Services:* Community Service Organizations, United Funds/United Ways

Grant Types: capital, challenge, endowment, general support, and project

Geographic Distribution: national; no grants outside the United States

GIVING OFFICERS
Carl H. Bruns: trust emeritus

Rev. A. Stanley Bullock, Jr.: dir

Holbrook R. Davis: trust

J. H. Dow Davis: trust

Joel P. Davis: trust

Dr. Jonathan P. Davis: trust

Maynard K. Davis: trust

Nathanael V. Davis: chmn *B* Pittsburgh PA 1915 *ED* Harvard Univ 1938

Atwood Dunwoody: trust *B* 1912 *ED* Univ FL LLB 1933 *CURR EMPL* ptnr: Sawyer Johnston Mershon

Jane M. Estes: comptr

Doreen D. Flippin: exec asst

Rev. Davis Given: trust

Jonathan T. Howe: assoc dir

Mrs. John L. Kee, Jr.: trust

Dr. William G. Kee: trust

Dr. Max King Morris: exec dir *B* Springfield MD 1924 *ED* US Naval Academy BS 1947; Tufts Univ MA 1960; Tufts Univ MA Econ 1961; Tufts Univ Phd 1967 *CURR EMPL* pres: Thalassa Res Co *NONPR AFFIL* mem: Counc Foreign Rels, Inst Intl Strategic Studies, Middle East Inst, US Naval Inst

Mary Sizemore: admin asst

Judson Tharin: program off

William R. Wright: trust

APPLICATION INFORMATION
Initial Approach:

A statement describing the institution and the project should be addressed to the executive director of the foundations. Applicants are advised that no advantage is gained in addressing requests to one of the individual foundations, or to members of the board. A detailed budget should be appended.

Colleges, universities, and seminaries must furnish enrollment information, average SAT/ACT scores of entering students for at least a three-year period, a brief synopsis of the institution's development program, and audited financial statements for three years.

Applications for grants from a hospice or medical program must provide full details of the project, a history of the applicant organization, copies of audited financial statements for the past three years, and an accounting of sources of support.

All proposals must emanate from the president or primary executive of an organization, rather than from department or unit heads. They must contain a statement by the chief officer of the applying organization regarding the priority of the project.

The foundations report no deadlines for funding requests.

A preliminary review of a proposal is made to determine whether or not a request falls within the foundations' areas of interest. If it does, a request for additional materials, or a staff visit to the organization may be indicated. The board meets three times a year.

Restrictions on Giving: The foundations do not support organizations outside of the U.S.; individuals, except participants chosen by the grantee institution in an organized scholarship program; voter registration drives; voter education; efforts to influence elections or legislation; publicly governed colleges and universities, and other entities (except medical institutions) which are supported primarily by government funds; and projects incurring obligations extending over several years.

OTHER THINGS TO KNOW
The three foundations' assets are invested by corporate trustees and administered as separate legal entities. For the purposes of grantmaking, however, the three foundations function as a single philanthropic organization. The foundations also share a single administrative office in Jacksonville, FL.

Grants generally are made out of annual income, with minimal future commitments. Grantees are expected to prepare a brief written progress report one year after receipt of a grant, or sooner if the project is completed. A more detailed final report also will be required.

The foundations state that a decision not to fund a project is more often the result of funding limitations rather than a judgment of the quality of an applicant or its program. A decision not to fund does not preclude the future submission of a new proposal.

Mellon Bank, N.A., of Pittsburgh, PA, serves as corporate trustee for Foundations No. 1 and No. 2. Sun Bank/North Florida, N.A., of Jacksonville, FL, serves as corporate trustee for Foundation No. 3.

PUBLICATIONS
Annual report, and programs, policies, and procedure statement

GRANTS ANALYSIS
Total Grants: $6,650,000

Number of Grants: 72

Highest Grant: $500,000

Average Grant: $92,361

Typical Range: $50,000 to $125,000

Disclosure Period: 1994

Note: Recent grants are derived from a 1994 grants list.

RECENT GRANTS

Library

125,000	Ohio Wesleyan University, Delaware, OH — to help fund the library automation project
125,000	St. John's College, Santa Fe, NM — to help endow a teaching chair and to help fund library renovation
125,000	Washington Theological Union, Washington, DC — to help fund the library renovation project
125,000	Wesley Theological Seminary, Washington, DC — to help fund the library automation project
100,000	Agnes Scott College, Decatur, GA — to help fund the library computerization project

General

250,000	Rockefeller University, New York, NY — to help fund the development of the Program in the Neurobiology of Behavior
200,000	Pilgrim Place, Claremont, CA — to provide additional funding for the Davis Health Endowment
180,000	University of Florida School of Medicine, Gainesville, FL — to help fund the establishment of the Center for Caregiver/Patient Interactions
150,000	Mayo Foundation Graduate School of Medicine, Rochester, MN — to help fund the development of new programs at the Center for Humanities in Medicine
125,000	Drew University, Madison, NJ — to help fund construction of the language resource center

---

duPont Foundation, Alfred I.

CONTACT
Rosemary C. Wills
Assistant Secretary and Assistant Treasurer
Alfred I. du Pont Foundation
PO Box 1380
Jacksonville, FL 32201
(904) 396-6600

FINANCIAL SUMMARY
Recent Giving: $850,000 (1995 est.); $800,000 (1994 approx.); $825,000 (1993 approx.)

Assets: $19,000,000 (1995 est.); $18,000,000 (1994 approx.); $18,500,000 (1993 approx.)

Gifts Received: $168,000 (1988)

EIN: 59-1297267

CONTRIBUTIONS SUMMARY
Donor(s): The foundation was incorporated in 1936 by the late Jessie Dew Ball duPont .

Typical Recipients: • *Arts & Humanities:* Historic Preservation, History & Archaeology, Libraries, Museums/Galleries, Music, Theater • *Civic & Public Affairs:* Public Policy • *Education:* Afterschool/Enrichment Programs, Agricultural Education, Colleges & Universities, Community & Junior Colleges, Continuing Education, Education Funds, Medical Education, Religious Education, Science/Mathematics Education, Student Aid • *Environment:* General • *Health:* Alzheimers Disease, Arthritis, Children's Health/Hospitals, Emergency/Ambulance Services, Health Organizations, Hospices, Nursing Services, Public Health, Single-Disease Health Associations • *International:* Foreign Educational Institutions, Health Care/Hospitals • *Religion:* Churches, Religious Organizations, Religious Welfare • *Social Services:* Child Welfare, Community Service Organizations, Emergency Relief, Food/Clothing Distribution, Homes, Senior Services, Shelters/Homelessness, United Funds/United Ways, Youth Organizations

Grant Types: emergency and general support

Geographic Distribution: southeastern United States, focus on Florida

GIVING OFFICERS
Braden Ball: pres, dir

Jacob Chapman Belin: vp, treas, dir *B* DeFuniak Springs FL 1914 *ED* George Washington Univ 1935-1938 *CURR EMPL* ceo, dir: St Joe Paper Co *CORP AFFIL* chmn: Florola Telephone Co, Gulf Telephone Co; dir: FL E Coast RY Co, St Joseph Land & Devel Co; pres, dir: Apalachicola Northern Railroad Co, St Joseph Tel & Tel Co *NONPR AFFIL* dir: Alfred I duPont Inst, Nemours Fdn; mem: Kappa Alpha; trust: Alfred I duPont Estate *CLUB AFFIL* Elks, Rotary

Edward Carter Brownlie: asst secy, asst treas *B* Birmingham AL 1937 *ED* Samford Univ 1963 *CURR EMPL* vp, admin, dir: St. Joe Paper Co *CORP AFFIL* asst treas, dir: Talisman Sugar Corp; treas, dir: Apalachicola Northern Railroad Co, Gen Die & Mfg Corp, St Joe Commun Inc, St Joe Container Co, St Joe Oil Co, St Joseph Tel & Tel Co; vp, dir: St Joe Forest Products Co, St Joseph Land & Devel Co; vp, treas, dir: St Joe Indus Inc *PHIL AFFIL* treas: St. Joe Foundation

Lillie S. Land: secy, dir

Robert E. Nedley: dir *B* 1938 *CURR EMPL* pres, coo, dir: St Joe Paper Co *CORP AFFIL* pres: St Joe Industries Inc; pres, coo, dir: St Joe Forest Products Co; v pres: St Joe Container Co; vp, dir: Gulf Telephone Co, St Joe Commun Inc, St Joe Land & Devel Co, St Joseph Tel & Tel Co

Rosemary C. Wills: asst secy, asst treas

APPLICATION INFORMATION
Initial Approach:

The foundation reports that requests should be made for a formal application form.

The foundation has no deadline for submitting proposals.

Restrictions on Giving: The foundation reports that individual grants are generally limited to elderly individuals residing in the southeastern United States who are in distressed economic situations.

GRANTS ANALYSIS
Total Grants: $413,439*

Number of Grants: 81*

Highest Grant: $25,000

Average Grant: $5,104*

Typical Range: $500 to $10,000

Disclosure Period: 1992

Note: Figures above exclude regular monthly grants, temporary grants, and special Christmas grants made to individuals in 1992 totaling $412,691. Recent grants are derived from a 1992 Form 990.

RECENT GRANTS

Library

6,900	Gulf County Public Library, Mobile, AL
5,000	Liberty County Public Library

General

25,000	University of Florida College of Medicine, Gainesville, FL — Alzheimers Disease
20,000	Baptist Medical Center Children's Hospital, Birmingham, AL
20,000	Baptist Medical Center Children's Hospital, Birmingham, AL
20,000	James Madison Institute — public policy studies
15,000	US Industrial Council Scholarship Fund

Einstein Fund, Albert E. and Birdie W.

CONTACT

Joyce Boyer
President
Albert E. and Birdie W. Einstein Fund
PO Box 6297
Hollywood, FL 33081
(305) 963-1739

FINANCIAL SUMMARY

Recent Giving: $437,250 (fiscal 1994); $406,433 (fiscal 1992); $358,050 (fiscal 1991)

Assets: $7,744,963 (fiscal 1994); $7,886,309 (fiscal 1992); $7,474,323 (fiscal 1991)

EIN: 59-6127412

CONTRIBUTIONS SUMMARY

Donor(s): the late Albert E. Einstein and Birdie W. Einstein

Typical Recipients: • *Arts & Humanities:* Libraries, Opera, Performing Arts • *Civic & Public Affairs:* Municipalities/Towns, Professional & Trade Associations, Public Policy, Zoos/Aquariums • *Education:* Business Education, Colleges & Universities, Community & Junior Colleges, Education Funds, Medical Education • *Health:* Cancer, Health Organizations, Heart, Hospitals, Hospitals (University Affiliated), Kidney, Medical Rehabilitation, Multiple Sclerosis, Single-Disease Health Associations • *Religion:* Churches, Jewish Causes, Ministries, Religious Organizations, Religious Welfare, Syna-

gogues/Temples • *Science:* Science Museums • *Social Services:* Child Welfare, Community Centers, Community Service Organizations, Crime Prevention, Food/Clothing Distribution, People with Disabilities, Senior Services, Shelters/Homelessness, United Funds/United Ways, YMCA/YWCA/YMHA/YWHA, Youth Organizations

Grant Types: general support

Geographic Distribution: focus on Broward, Dade, and Palm Beach counties, FL

GIVING OFFICERS

Joyce Boyer: pres

R. M. Gardner: vp

Harold Satchell: secy, treas

APPLICATION INFORMATION

Initial Approach: Application form required. There are no deadlines.

Restrictions on Giving: Does not support individuals.

GRANTS ANALYSIS

Total Grants: $437,250

Number of Grants: 32

Highest Grant: $100,000

Typical Range: $250 to $50,000

Disclosure Period: fiscal year ending June 30, 1994

Note: Recent grants are derived from a fiscal 1994 Form 990.

RECENT GRANTS

General

100,000	University of Florida Fund Shands Teaching Hospital, Gainesville, FL
50,000	Museum of Discovery and Science Center, Ft. Lauderdale, FL
25,000	Jewish Federation of South Broward, Hollywood, FL
25,000	Nova University, Davis, FL
25,000	YMCA, Hollywood, CA

Frueauff Foundation, Charles A.

CONTACT

Zoe Cole Golloway
Assistant Executive Director
Charles A. Frueauff Foundation
307 E 7th Ave.
Tallahassee, FL 32303
(904) 561-3508

FINANCIAL SUMMARY

Recent Giving: $3,750,000 (1995 est.); $3,788,000 (1994 approx.); $3,909,500 (1993)

Assets: $75,000,000 (1994 approx.); $77,802,284 (1993); $75,061,481 (1992)

EIN: 13-5605371

CONTRIBUTIONS SUMMARY

Donor(s): The foundation was established in 1950, with the late Charles A. Frueauff as donor.

Typical Recipients: • *Arts & Humanities:* History & Archaeology, Libraries, Public Broadcasting • *Civic & Public Affairs:* Employment/Job Training, Legal Aid • *Education:* Business Education, Colleges & Universities, Education Funds, Engineering/Technological Education, Faculty Development, General, Medical Education, Minority Education, Student Aid • *Health:* Children's Health/Hospitals, Clinics/Medical Centers, Health Organizations, Hospices, Hospitals • *Religion:* Religious Welfare • *Social Services:* At-Risk Youth, Child Welfare, Community Centers, Community Service Organizations, Counseling, Family Services, Food/Clothing Distribution, Homes, People with Disabilities, Recreation & Athletics, Scouts, Senior Services, Shelters/Homelessness, Substance Abuse, United Funds/United Ways, YMCA/YWCA/YMHA/YWHA, Youth Organizations

Grant Types: capital, endowment, general support, operating expenses, project, and scholarship

Geographic Distribution: broad geographic distribution

GIVING OFFICERS

James P. Fallon: trust

Karl P. Fanning: trust

David Frueauff: exec dir, secy

Sue M. Frueauff: trust

Anna Kay Frueauff-Cochran: trust

Zoe Cole Golloway: asst exec dir

Charles T. Klein: vp, trust

Dr. A. C. McCully: pres, trust

APPLICATION INFORMATION
Initial Approach:

Organizations should send a letter of request or make a phone call to the foundation.

Letters of request should include complete financial data and a copy of the organization's IRS determination letter of tax-exempt status.

Submit requests between January 1 and March 15.

The foundation will notify only those organizations that will receive a grant in late May.

Restrictions on Giving: The foundation does not make grants to individuals, to organizations outside of the United States, or for loans, emergency funds, or research.

GRANTS ANALYSIS

Total Grants: $3,909,500

Number of Grants: 145

Highest Grant: $75,000

Average Grant: $26,962

Typical Range: $10,000 to $60,000

Disclosure Period: 1993

Note: Recent grants are derived from a 1993 Form 990.

179

RECENT GRANTS

Library

50,000	Millsaps College, Jackson, MS — library automation project
50,000	Regis University, Denver, CO — library expansion and renovation
35,000	Ogelthorpe University, Atlanta, GA — expansion of library holdings

General

50,000	Arkansas Children's Hospital, Little Rock, AR — ECMO unit support
50,000	Big Bend Hospice, Tallahassee, FL — rural country program expansion
50,000	Boys and Girls Club of the Arkansas River Valley, Russellville, AR — capital campaign
50,000	Boys Club of New York, New York, NY — learning center program support
50,000	Catholic Charities Diocese of Brooklyn, Brooklyn, NY — St. John's community life center and future fund campaign

Gulf Power Co. / Gulf Power Foundation

Sales: $583.0 million
Employees: 1,565
Parent Company: Southern Co.
Headquarters: Pensacola, FL
SIC Major Group: Electric, Gas & Sanitary Services

CONTACT
Candy Klinglesmith
Gulf Power Foundation, Inc.
PO BOX 1151
Pensacola, FL 32520-0783
(904) 444-6380

FINANCIAL SUMMARY
Recent Giving: $176,100 (1993); $151,165 (1992); $128,138 (1990)

Assets: $1,853,608 (1993); $886,059 (1992); $20,130 (1990)

Gifts Received: $1,082,484 (1993); $1,000,000 (1992); $150,000 (1990)

Fiscal Note: In 1993, contributions were received from Gulf Power Company.

EIN: 59-2817740

CONTRIBUTIONS SUMMARY
Typical Recipients: • *Arts & Humanities:* Arts Associations & Councils, Historic Preservation, History & Archaeology, Libraries, Museums/Galleries, Public Broadcasting • *Civic & Public Affairs:* African American Affairs, Business/Free Enterprise, Chambers of Commerce, Clubs, Housing, Professional & Trade Associations, Public Policy, Rural Affairs, Safety, Urban & Community Affairs, Women's Affairs • *Education:* Agricul-

tural Education, Business Education, Colleges & Universities, Community & Junior Colleges, Education Associations, Education Funds, Elementary Education (Private), Elementary Education (Public), Engineering/Technological Education, General, Literacy, Public Education (Precollege), Secondary Education (Public), Student Aid • *Environment:* General, Wildlife Protection • *Health:* Cancer, Clinics/Medical Centers, Emergency/Ambulance Services, Health Funds, Health Organizations, Hospices, Hospitals, Prenatal Health Issues, Single-Disease Health Associations, Transplant Networks/Donor Banks • *Religion:* Ministries, Religious Organizations, Religious Welfare, Social/Policy Issues • *Social Services:* Animal Protection, Child Welfare, Community Service Organizations, Counseling, Food/Clothing Distribution, Homes, People with Disabilities, Recreation & Athletics, Scouts, Senior Services, Shelters/Homelessness, Substance Abuse, United Funds/United Ways, Youth Organizations

Grant Types: capital, conference/seminar, general support, and scholarship

Geographic Distribution: northwest Florida and service territory of Gulf Power

CORP. OFFICERS
Travis J. Bowden: *B* Greenville AL 1938 *ED* Univ AL 1960 *CURR EMPL* pres, ceo, dir: Gulf Power Co *CORP AFFIL* pres, ceo, dir: Gulf Power Co

Francis M. Fisher, Jr.: *CURR EMPL* vp: Gulf Power Co

GIVING OFFICERS
Francis M. Fisher, Jr.: chmn *CURR EMPL* vp: Gulf Power Co (see above)

John E. Hodges, Jr.: trust

G. Edison Holland, Jr.: trust

Ronnie R. Labrato: secy

Earl B. Parsons, Jr.: trust

Arlan E. Scarbrough: trust

Warren E. Tate: treas

APPLICATION INFORMATION
Initial Approach: Send a brief letter of inquiry and a full proposal. Include a description of organization, amount requested, purpose of funds sought, recently audited financial statement, and proof of tax-exempt status. Foundation meets quarterly.

Restrictions on Giving: The foundation does not support individuals or organizations outside service area.

GRANTS ANALYSIS
Total Grants: $176,100

Number of Grants: 73

Highest Grant: $25,000

Typical Range: $210 to $10,000

Disclosure Period: 1993

Note: Recent grants are derived from a 1993 Form 990.

RECENT GRANTS

Library

1,000	Washington County Public Library, Chipley, FL — capital funds

General

25,000	United Way of Escambia County, Pensacola, FL
10,000	University of West Florida, Pensacola, FL — capital funds
8,700	United Way of Northwest Florida, Panama City, FL
5,900	Community Drug and Alcohol Commission, Pensacola, FL
5,000	Association for Retarded Citizens, Chipley, FL — capital funds

Howell Foundation of Florida

CONTACT
Manley H. Thaler
President
Howell Fdn of Florida
700 North Olive
West Palm Beach, FL 33401
(407) 832-3829

FINANCIAL SUMMARY
Recent Giving: $32,842 (1993); $46,787 (1992)

Assets: $3,235,110 (1993); $3,268,621 (1992)

EIN: 65-0301944

CONTRIBUTIONS SUMMARY
Typical Recipients: • *Arts & Humanities:* Arts Centers, Libraries, Music • *Education:* Colleges & Universities • *Health:* Emergency/Ambulance Services, Hospices, Hospitals • *Social Services:* Domestic Violence, Senior Services

Grant Types: general support

GIVING OFFICERS
Manley H. Thaler: pres

APPLICATION INFORMATION
Initial Approach: Include a description of organization, amount requested, purpose of funds sought, recently audited financial statement, and proof of tax-exempt status. There are no deadlines.

GRANTS ANALYSIS
Total Grants: $32,842

Number of Grants: 16

Highest Grant: $15,000

Typical Range: $25 to $4,000

Disclosure Period: 1993

Note: Recent grants are derived from a 1993 Form 990.

RECENT GRANTS

Library

3,000	Public Library

General

10,000	Ithaca College Endowment, Ithaca, NY
6,500	Tompkins County Hospital
3,400	Senior Citizens Council — art classes
3,295	Hospicare
2,600	Palm Beach County Red Cross, Palm Beach, FL

Kelly Tractor Co. / Kelly Foundation

Sales: $1.0 million
Employees: 350
Headquarters: Miami, FL
SIC Major Group: Wholesale Trade—Durable Goods

CONTACT
Patrick Kelly
President
Kelly Tractor Co.
8255 NW 58th St.
Miami, FL 33166
(305) 592-5360

FINANCIAL SUMMARY
Recent Giving: $122,350 (1993); $99,600 (1992); $91,321 (1989)

Assets: $1,714,670 (1993); $1,170,679 (1992); $1,123,304 (1989)

Gifts Received: $556,446 (1993); $22,250 (1992); $26,825 (1989)

Fiscal Note: In 1993, contributions were received from Kelly Tractor Co.

EIN: 59-6153269

CONTRIBUTIONS SUMMARY
Typical Recipients: • *Arts & Humanities:* History & Archaeology, Libraries, Museums/Galleries, Public Broadcasting • *Civic & Public Affairs:* Botanical Gardens/Parks, General, Hispanic Affairs, Housing, Zoos/Aquariums • *Education:* Colleges & Universities, Elementary Education (Public), Private Education (Precollege), Religious Education, Student Aid • *Environment:* General • *Health:* Cancer, Emergency/Ambulance Services, Health Organizations, Hospitals • *Religion:* Churches, Religious Organizations, Religious Welfare • *Social Services:* Animal Protection, Community Service Organizations, People with Disabilities, Scouts, Youth Organizations

Grant Types: general support and scholarship

Geographic Distribution: focus on FL

Operating Locations: FL (Clewiston)

CORP. OFFICERS
L. Patrick Kelly: *CURR EMPL* pres: Kelly Tractor Co

Loyd G. Kelly: *CURR EMPL* chmn, dir: Kelly Tractor Co

GIVING OFFICERS
Eileen I. Kelly: dir

Joy Kelly: dir

L. Patrick Kelly: dir *CURR EMPL* pres: Kelly Tractor Co (see above)

Loyd G. Kelly: vp, dir *CURR EMPL* chmn, dir: Kelly Tractor Co (see above)

Marjorie H. Kelly: dir

Nick Kelly: dir

Robert W. Kelly: pres, dir

Robert W. Kelly, Jr.: dir

Evelyn D. Shelley: dir

Alden M. Wyse: secy, treas, dir

APPLICATION INFORMATION
Initial Approach: Send brief letter describing program. Students applying for educational assistance should request an application form. There are no deadlines.

GRANTS ANALYSIS
Total Grants: $122,350

Number of Grants: 43

Highest Grant: $16,800

Typical Range: $100 to $1,000

Disclosure Period: 1993

Note: Recent grants are derived from a 1993 Form 990. Number of grants, highest grant, and typical grant range do not include educational grants to individuals.

RECENT GRANTS

General

16,800	Habitat for Humanity, Miami, FL
8,000	First Baptist Church, Clewiston, FL
8,000	Palm Beach Atlantic College, Palm Beach, FL
5,000	Church of Little Flower, Coral Gables, FL
5,000	Cuban American National Foundation, Miami, FL

Kirbo Charitable Trust, Thomas M. and Irene B.

CONTACT
R. Murray Jenks
President and Trustee
Thomas M. and Irene B. Kirbo Charitable Trust
112 W Adams St., Ste. 1111
Jacksonville, FL 32202-3865
(904) 354-7212

FINANCIAL SUMMARY
Recent Giving: $1,800,000 (fiscal 1994 approx.); $1,486,000 (fiscal 1993 approx.); $876,000 (fiscal 1990)

Assets: $34,000,000 (fiscal 1994 approx.); $36,000,000 (fiscal 1993 approx.); $25,811,158 (fiscal 1990)

EIN: 59-2151720

CONTRIBUTIONS SUMMARY
Donor(s): The trust was established in 1959 by Irene Kirbo and the late Thomas M. Kirbo.

Typical Recipients: • *Arts & Humanities:* Arts Centers, Libraries, Music, Performing Arts • *Civic & Public Affairs:* Municipalities/Towns • *Education:* Colleges & Universities, Legal Education, Medical Education, Public Education (Precollege) • *Environment:* General • *Health:* Hospitals, Nursing Services • *Religion:* Churches, Religious Organizations, Religious Welfare • *Social Services:* Community Centers, Counseling, Day Care, Food/Clothing Distribution, People with Disabilities, Shelters/Homelessness, Youth Organizations

Grant Types: general support

Geographic Distribution: Georgia and Florida

GIVING OFFICERS
John T. Jenks: trust

R. Murray Jenks: pres, trust

Bruce W. Kirbo: trust *CURR EMPL* secy: Stones Inc

Charles Hughes Kirbo: chmn, trust *B* Bainbridge GA 1917 *ED* Univ GA LLB 1939 *PHIL AFFIL* treas, trust: Global 2000

APPLICATION INFORMATION
Initial Approach:

Applicants should write to the trust to receive a formal application.

The formal application should include the amount of funds requested, a list of grants received by the organization in the last three years, a statement that the organization will furnish reports as to the status of the funds during the project's existence, a list of directors and their affiliations, the names and qualifications of the personnel involved in the project for which the grant is requested, and a statement by the chief officer of the organization as to the validity of the request. The trust also requests the following attachments: a copy of the most recent letter of exemption from the IRS, a copy of the form or letter from the IRS classifying the organization as not a private foundation, a statement from the chief officer that the organization's tax-exempt status has not been revoked, and the organization's latest balance sheet.

The trust has no deadline for submitting proposals.

Restrictions on Giving: The foundation does not make grants to individuals.

GRANTS ANALYSIS
Total Grants: $876,000

Number of Grants: 26

Highest Grant: $125,000

Average Grant: $26,083*

Typical Range: $5,000 to $35,000

Disclosure Period: fiscal year ending September 30, 1990

Note: The average grant figure excludes the two highest grants of $125,000 each. Recent grants are derived from a fiscal 1990 grants list.

RECENT GRANTS

Library

50,000	Carter Presidential Library, Atlanta, GA

General

125,000	Henrietta Egleston Hospital, Atlanta, GA
125,000	Scottish Rite Children's Hospital, Atlanta, GA
100,000	National Benevolent Association of Christ, Jacksonville, FL
50,000	Andrew College, Cuthbert, GA
50,000	Berry College, Rome, GA

Knight Foundation, John S. and James L.

Former Foundation Name: Knight Foundation

CONTACT
Creed Black
President
John S. and James L. Knight Foundation
2 S Biscayne Blvd., Ste. 3800
Miami, FL 33131-1803
(305) 539-0009
Note: Grant proposals should be addressed: Attn: Grant Request. Name change from the former Knight Foundation was effective January 1, 1993.

FINANCIAL SUMMARY
Recent Giving: $39,000,000 (1995 est.); $34,200,000 (1994 approx.); $32,069,323 (1993)

Assets: $800,031,371 (1993); $639,165,141 (1992); $605,039,445 (1991)

Gifts Received: $107,829,417 (1993); $10,780,041 (1992); $6,629,326 (1991)

Fiscal Note: During 1991 and 1992, the foundation received a total of $117,409,367 from the estate of James L. Knight. Further distributions to the foundation from the estate with an estimated worth of more than $200,000,000 are expected, but the timing is unknown.

EIN: 34-6519827

CONTRIBUTIONS SUMMARY
Donor(s): The John S. and James L. Knight Foundation was established in Akron, OH, on December 29, 1950. Its forerunner was the Charles Landon Knight Memorial Education Fund. Upon the death of John S. Knight in 1981, his brother James was elected chairman of the foundation and served in that capacity until his death in February 1991. In March 1991, Lee Hills, a foundation trustee for more than 30 years and vice chairman since 1986, was elected chairman. Foundation funds have been provided by the estates of John S. and James L. Knight and their mother, Clara I. Knight.

Typical Recipients: • *Arts & Humanities:* Arts Associations & Councils, Arts Funds, Arts Institutes, Dance, Ethnic & Folk Arts, Historic Preservation, History & Archaeology, Libraries, Museums/Galleries, Music, Opera, Performing Arts, Public Broadcasting, Theater • *Civic & Public Affairs:* Botanical Gardens/Parks, Community Foundations, Economic Development, Em-

ployment/Job Training, Housing, Municipalities/Towns, Philanthropic Organizations, Professional & Trade Associations, Public Policy, Women's Affairs, Zoos/Aquariums • *Education:* Arts/Humanities Education, Colleges & Universities, Elementary Education (Public), Faculty Development, General, Journalism/Media Education, Legal Education, Literacy, Minority Education, Public Education (Precollege), Science/Mathematics Education, Student Aid • *Environment:* Air/Water Quality • *Health:* Cancer, Children's Health/Hospitals, Emergency/Ambulance Services, Hospices, Hospitals, Prenatal Health Issues • *International:* Human Rights, International Organizations • *Religion:* Religious Welfare, Seminaries • *Social Services:* Child Welfare, Community Service Organizations, Family Services, Recreation & Athletics, Shelters/Homelessness, United Funds/United Ways, Youth Organizations

Grant Types: capital, challenge, endowment, and project

Geographic Distribution: selected areas in California, Colorado, Florida, Georgia, Indiana, Kansas, Kentucky, Michigan, Minnesota, Mississippi, North Carolina, North Dakota, Ohio, Pennsylvania, South Carolina, and South Dakota

GIVING OFFICERS
W. Gerald Austen: vchmn, trust *B* Akron OH 1930 *ED* MA Inst Tech BS 1951; Harvard Univ MD 1955 *CURR EMPL* chief surgeon: MA Gen Hosp

Creed Carter Black: pres, ceo, trust *B* Harlan KY 1925 *ED* Northwestern Univ BS 1949; Univ Chicago MA 1952 *NONPR AFFIL* mem: Am Newspaper Publs Assn, Am Soc Newspaper Editors, Kappa Tau Alpha, Lambda Chi Alpha, Natl Conf Editorial Writers, Sigma Delta Chi; pres, mem: Southern Newspaper Publs Assn *CLUB AFFIL* Bankers, Riviera CC

Alvah Herman Chapman, Jr.: trust *B* Columbus GA 1921 *ED* Citadel BS 1942 *CURR EMPL* chmn exec comm, dir: Knight-Ridder *NONPR AFFIL* chmn: Commun Anti-Drug Coalitions Am, Govs Commn Homelessness, We Will Rebuild; chmn emeritus: FL Intl Univ Fdn; mem: Am Newspaper Publs Assn, Pres Drug Adv Counc, Southern Newspaper Publs Assn; vchmn: Miami Coalition Drug-Free Commun *PHIL AFFIL* pres, trust: Alvah H. and Wyline P. Chapman Foundation

Jill Cathryn Ker Conway: trust *B* New South Wales Australia 1934 *ED* Univ Sydney BA 1958; Harvard Univ PhD 1969 *PHIL AFFIL* dir: Kresge Foundation

Marjorie Knight Crane: trust

Timothy J. Crowe: vp, cfo

Charles Colmery Gibson: trust *B* Edwards MS 1914 *ED* Harvard Univ BA 1937; Harvard Univ Advanced Mgmt Program 1953

Jay Terrence Harris: trust

Gordon Emory Heffern: trust *B* Utica PA 1924 *ED* Stevens Inst Tech 1944; Univ VA 1949 *CORP AFFIL* dir: Biskind Devel Co, Pioneer-Standard Electronics, A Schulman Inc, Scripps Howard Broadcasting Co

NONPR AFFIL fellow: Christian Athletes; pres, ceo: Akron Commun Fdn *CLUB AFFIL* Akron City, Congress Lake, 50, Pepper Pike, Portage CC, Union

Lee Hills: chmn, trust *B* Granville ND 1906 *ED* Univ MO 1929; Oklahoma City Univ LLB 1935 *CURR EMPL* dir: Seattle Times Co

Larry Jinks: chmn journalism adv comm *B* Mt Pleasant TX 1929 *ED* Univ MO BS 1950; Columbia Coll MO MS 1956

Wyatt Thomas Johnson, Jr.: trust *B* Macon GA 1941 *ED* Univ GA AB 1963; Harvard Univ MBA 1965 *CURR EMPL* vchmn, dir: Times Mirror Co *CORP AFFIL* publ, ceo: Los Angeles Times *NONPR AFFIL* dir: Trilateral Commn; mem: Am Newspaper Publs Assn, Counc Foreign Rels, Sigma Delta Chi *PHIL AFFIL* trust: Rockefeller Foundation; secy, treas, trust: Edward Arthur Mellinger Educational Foundation

Beverly Knight Olson: trust

James D. Spaniolo: vp, chief program off *ED* MI St Univ BA 1968; Univ MI Law Sch JD 1975; Univ MI Law Sch MPA

Henry King Stanford: trust *B* Atlanta GA 1916 *ED* Emory Univ AB 1936; Univ Heidelberg 1936-1937; Emory Univ MA 1940; Univ Denver MS 1943; NY Univ PhD 1949 *CORP AFFIL* dir: Avatar Holdings *NONPR AFFIL* chmn adv commn: Jimmy Carter Historical Site; dir: Golden Key Honor Soc; mem: Alpha Kappa Psi, Assn Caribbean Univs & Res Insts, Delta Phi Alpha, Intl Assn Univ Pres, Natl Assn Independent Colls & Univs, Phi Beta Kappa, Phi Kappa Phi, Phi Mu Alpha, Phi Sigma Iota, Southern Assn Colls & Schs; pres emeritus: Univ GA, Univ Miami; trust: Caribbean Resources Devel Fdn *CLUB AFFIL* Rotary

APPLICATION INFORMATION
Initial Approach:

Contact the foundation to receive its "How to Apply for a Grant" publication. An original and one copy of a brief letter on the organization's letterhead should be submitted. The letter should include a description of the organization and scope of its current activities; a statement of need; a statement of the project objectives; a description of project activities and timetable for their accomplishment; a statement concerning the overall cost of the project for which funding is sought, the amount of funding requested from the foundation and the amounts, sources, and status (committed or pending) of additional support for the project.

A full application should include an original and one copy of the entire proposal. The proposal packet should include the Knight Foundation's proposal cover sheet; the application letter (described above); a project budget; the organization's current annual operating budget; a list of the organization's governing board and its officers, including the members' business, professional, and community affiliations; only one copy of the most current IRS determination letter of 501(c)(3) and 509(a) tax-exempt status; and the most recent audited financial statements. Supporting documents may be sent as additional information, not as a substitute for specific application information. The proposal should not be bound, inserted in protective sleeves, or prepared in any type of notebook form, because materials are disassembled during the review process. The foundation encourages an emphasis on substance rather than presentation. Special supplementary materials such as videos cannot be returned to applicants.

The foundation's board of trustees meets four times a year to review proposals. Grant requests must be received by 5:00 p.m. on January 1, April 1, July 1, and October 1, for the June, September, December, and March agendas, respectively. Grant requests will be considered at the board meeting six months after deadlines. If any of the above dates fall on a weekend or holiday, the deadline will be the first working day following the published deadline.

Applicants are usually notified of the foundation's decisions in writing within two weeks after the trustees' meeting.

Restrictions on Giving: The foundation does not fund individuals. It prefers not to make grants to the following: international programs, except in support of a free press around the world; agencies that are supported by the United Way, except for pilot programs or capital expenditures; annual fund-raising campaigns; fund-raising dinners; ongoing requests for general operating support; operating deficits; production costs of films, videos, or television programs; organizations which in turn make grants to others (except for community foundations); activities to propagate a religious faith; support of political candidates; purchase of band uniforms or trips for bands; purchase of commercial television or radio time; honoraria; charities operated by service clubs; scholarly research leading to a book; group travel; memorials; medical research; organizations whose mission is to prevent, eradicate, and/or alleviate the effects of a disease; and requests from hospitals, unless they are for community-wide capital campaigns with a stated goal and beginning and ending dates. The foundation also will not fund activities that are normally the responsibility of government, or projects or services for which tax support has been cut, though in selective cases it will join with units of government in supporting special projects of interest to the foundation. The foundation prefers not to consider applications more frequently than once a year, whether the result of the previous proposal was positive or negative. The trustees also prefer not to consider applications from any institutions receiving a multi-year grant until all payments of that grant have been made. Also trustees prefer not to fund a second request for a capital project for which the foundation previously approved a grant. Applicants for Community Initiatives must be located where the foundation's founders were involved in publishing newspapers. The eligible twenty-six cities are listed under the geographic distribution section of the "Contributions Summary" portion of this profile. Applicants from anywhere in the

U.S. are eligible for the Journalism and national Arts and Culture Programs. Applicants for the Excellence in Education Program are by invitation only. Progress, financial, and other reports are requested by the foundation as needed. The foundation no longer makes Presidential Discretionary Grants.

OTHER THINGS TO KNOW
The foundation reports that a major portion of the proposals are rejected because they fail to meet published criteria.

The foundation has specific geographic restrictions for its programs. Grants for the Communities Initiatives program are awarded in: Long Beach and San Jose, CA; Boulder, CO; Boca Raton, Bradenton, Miami, and Tallahassee, FL; Columbus, Macon, and Milledgeville, GA; Fort Wayne and Gary, IN; Wichita, KS; Lexington, KY; Detroit MI; Duluth and St. Paul, MN; Biloxi, MS; Charlotte, NC; Grand Forks, ND; Akron, OH; Philadelphia and State College, PA; Columbia and Myrtle Beach, SC; and Aberdeen, SD.

Education and Arts and Culture programs award grants nationally and locally (twenty-six communities). Although the journalism program is national in focus, U.S. organizations funded by the foundation may support international journalism organizations.

PUBLICATIONS
Annual report, grant application brochure, quarterly newsletter, Knight Commission on Intercollegiate Athletics reports

GRANTS ANALYSIS
Total Grants: $34,200,000*

Number of Grants: 456*

Highest Grant: $2,000,000*

Average Grant: $75,000*

Typical Range: $5,000 to $50,000 and $100,000 to $250,000

Disclosure Period: 1994

Note: Total grants, number of grants, average grant, and highest grant are approximate and were supplied by the foundation. The number of grants figure includes one program-related investment. Recent grants are derived from a 1993 grants list.

RECENT GRANTS

Library
1,112,000   University of Maryland Foundation, Washington, DC — to create a national resource library on freedom of information issues relating to schools and colleges

General
5,000,000   National Community Development Initiative, New York, NY — for the second three-year round of this consortium organized to support community development corporations in 23 US cities

3,000,000   Center for Foreign Journalists, Reston, VA — for the Knight International Press Fellowship Program

2,000,000   Community Partnership for Homeless, Coral Gables, FL — to implement the Dade County Community Homeless Plan

1,000,000   Dade County Public Schools, Miami, FL — for the development of two prototype full-service elementary schools as part of Project Phoenix, the district's rebuilding plan following Hurricane Andrew

1,000,000   Local Initiatives Support Corporation, New York, NY — for support of Campaign for Communities, a national effort to expand community development corporation programs

Landegger Charitable Foundation

CONTACT
John F. Bolt
Secretary
Landegger Charitable Fdn.
219 Live Oak St.
New Smyrna Beach, FL 32170
(904) 426-1755

FINANCIAL SUMMARY
Recent Giving: $557,950 (fiscal 1994); $644,000 (fiscal 1991); $549,700 (fiscal 1990)

Assets: $11,187,241 (fiscal 1994); $10,438,456 (fiscal 1991); $9,357,484 (fiscal 1990)

EIN: 51-0180544

CONTRIBUTIONS SUMMARY
Typical Recipients: • *Arts & Humanities:* Arts Centers, Historic Preservation, Libraries • *Civic & Public Affairs:* General, Urban & Community Affairs • *Education:* Colleges & Universities, Community & Junior Colleges, Private Education (Precollege), Religious Education, Student Aid • *Health:* Clinics/Medical Centers, Hospitals • *International:* International Affairs, Missionary/Religious Activities • *Religion:* Churches, Jewish Causes • *Social Services:* Community Service Organizations, Family Services, Recreation & Athletics

Grant Types: general support and multi-year/continuing support

Geographic Distribution: focus on DC

GIVING OFFICERS
John F. Bolt: secy

Carl Clement Landegger: treas, dir *B* Vienna Austria 1930 *ED* Georgetown Univ BS 1951 *CURR EMPL* chmn, dir: Black Clawson Co *CORP AFFIL* chmn: AL River Pulp Co, St Anne Nackawic Pulp & Paper

Co; dir: Downingtown Mfg Co; vchmn: Parsons & Whittemore *NONPR AFFIL* dir: Georgetown Univ; trust: NY Historical Soc *CLUB AFFIL* Explorers, Road Runners

George Francis Landegger: pres, dir *B* 1938 *CURR EMPL* chmn, pres, dir: Parsons & Whittemore

Arthur L. Schwartz: vp *CURR EMPL* pres, dir: Parsons & Whittemore

APPLICATION INFORMATION
Initial Approach: Send brief letter of inquiry describing program or project. There are no deadlines.

GRANTS ANALYSIS
Total Grants: $557,950

Number of Grants: 64

Highest Grant: $100,000

Typical Range: $200 to $100,000

Disclosure Period: fiscal year ending October 31, 1994

Note: Recent grants are derived from a fiscal 1994 Form 990.

RECENT GRANTS
General

100,000	Georgetown University, Washington, DC — Distinguished Professorship
100,000	International Business Diplomacy Program
75,000	Georgetown University, Washington, DC — Distinguished Professorship of Theology
50,000	Georgetown University, Washington, DC — Landegger program Continuing Grant
30,000	Lenox Hill Neighborhood Association, New York, NY

Lattner Foundation, Forrest C.

CONTACT
Susan L. Lloyd
President and Secretary
Forrest C. Lattner Foundation
777 E Atlantic Ave., Ste. 317
Delray Beach, FL 33483
(407) 278-3781
Note: Another contact is Martha L. Connelly, chairman, at the above address.

FINANCIAL SUMMARY
Recent Giving: $3,669,400 (1992); $3,041,135 (1990); $225,000 (1988)

Assets: $64,237,153 (1992); $58,247,654 (1990); $5,504,542 (1988)

Gifts Received: $51,591,212 (1990); $159,550 (1988)

Fiscal Note: In 1990, contributions were received from Francis H. Lattner.

EIN: 59-2147657

CONTRIBUTIONS SUMMARY
Donor(s): The foundation was incorporated in 1981 by Mrs. Forrest C. Lattner, Mrs. Frances H. Lattner, and the late Forrest C. Lattner .

Typical Recipients: • *Arts & Humanities:* Libraries, Museums/Galleries, Performing Arts, Public Broadcasting • *Civic & Public Affairs:* Employment/Job Training, Philanthropic Organizations, Women's Affairs, Zoos/Aquariums • *Education:* Community & Junior Colleges, Literacy, Medical Education, Private Education (Precollege), Science/Mathematics Education, Special Education • *Environment:* Air/Water Quality, General • *Health:* AIDS/HIV, Alzheimers Disease, Cancer, Children's Health/Hospitals, Clinics/Medical Centers, Eyes/Blindness, Health Funds, Hospices, Hospitals, Medical Research, Mental Health, Research/Studies Institutes, Single-Disease Health Associations • *Religion:* Religious Organizations, Religious Welfare • *Social Services:* Child Welfare, Community Service Organizations, Day Care, Domestic Violence, Family Planning, Family Services, Food/Clothing Distribution, General, Homes, People with Disabilities, Youth Organizations

Grant Types: general support

Geographic Distribution: focus on midwestern United States and Florida

GIVING OFFICERS
Forrest C. Brown, MD: trust

Martha L. Connelly: chmn, trust

Susan L. Lloyd: pres, secy, trust *PHIL AFFIL* trust: Susan L. Hollenbeck Charitable Trust

APPLICATION INFORMATION
Initial Approach:

Applicants should send an initial letter of request to the foundation.

Initial proposal should include the applicant's name, address, and phone number; the name of person to be contacted, with title; a brief statement of the history of the applicant and the purpose of the grant request; supplemental information about the applicant, including a list of officers and directors, an audited financial statement (receipts and disbursements and a balance sheet) for the most recent fiscal year, a budget for the current fiscal year, and an IRS tax-exempt letter.

Grant proposals are accepted in May and October. If the request falls within the foundation's guidelines, it will be acknowledged. If necessary, supplemental information will be requested.

The foundation's grant review committee meets to consider final proposals. If the request is approved and a grant is awarded, the applicant will be notified in June or December following the grant review committee's meeting.

GRANTS ANALYSIS
Total Grants: $3,669,400

Number of Grants: 124

Highest Grant: $440,000

Average Grant: $29,592

Typical Range: $5,000 to $35,000

Disclosure Period: 1992

Note: Recent grants are derived from a 1992 Form 990.

RECENT GRANTS
Library

110,000	Delray Beach Library, Delray Beach, FL

General

440,000	Alzheimers Association, Boca Raton, FL — funds to be used as needed
150,000	Girl Scouts of the Wichita Area, Wichita, KS
150,000	Unity School, Delray Beach, FL
100,000	Alton Ochsner Clinic, New Orleans, LA
100,000	Boy Scouts of America Quivera Council, Wichita, KS

MacLeod Stewardship Foundation

CONTACT
John A. MacLeod
President
MacLeod Stewardship Fdn.
1929 Princess Ct.
Naples, FL 33942
(813) 566-1806

FINANCIAL SUMMARY
Recent Giving: $108,121 (1993); $72,625 (1990); $75,694 (1989)

Assets: $2,414,850 (1993); $2,115,176 (1990); $1,926,323 (1989)

Gifts Received: $201,875 (1989); $150,000 (1988)

Fiscal Note: In 1989, contributions were received from John A. MacLeod.

EIN: 59-2492096

CONTRIBUTIONS SUMMARY
Donor(s): John A. MacLeod

Typical Recipients: • *Arts & Humanities:* Libraries • *Civic & Public Affairs:* Community Foundations, General, Housing, Philanthropic Organizations, Public Policy • *Education:* Business Education, Private Education (Precollege), Public Education (Precollege) • *Health:* Health Organizations, Hospices • *International:* Foreign Educational Institutions, International Relief Efforts • *Religion:* Churches, Religious Organizations, Religious Welfare • *Social Services:* Community Centers, Community Service Organizations, Crime Prevention, Family Services, Food/Clothing Distribution, People with Disabilities, Recreation & Athletics, United Funds/United Ways, Youth Organizations

Grant Types: general support

Geographic Distribution: focus on Southeast

GIVING OFFICERS
Cynthia MacLeod: trust

John A. MacLeod II: dir

John Amend MacLeod: pres, secy, dir *B* Manila 1942 *ED* Univ Notre Dame BBA 1963; Univ Notre Dame JD 1969 *CURR EMPL* ptnr: Crowell & Moring *NONPR AFFIL* dir: St Francis Ctr; mem: Am Bar Assn, DC Bar Assn, Notre Dame Law Assn; trust, mem exec comm: Eastern Mineral Law Fdn

Muriel D. MacLeod: trust

Roderick A. MacLeod: trust

APPLICATION INFORMATION
Initial Approach: Send brief letter describing program. There are no deadlines.

GRANTS ANALYSIS
Total Grants: $108,121

Number of Grants: 17

Highest Grant: $34,078

Typical Range: $1,000 to $2,000

Disclosure Period: 1993

Note: Recent grants are derived from a 1993 Form 990.

RECENT GRANTS

General
34,078	Community Foundation of Collier County, Naples, FL
20,000	Youth For Christ
10,000	Dunnegan Foundation
10,000	Junior Achievement
5,000	English Language Institute of China, San Dimas, CA

Morgan Foundation, Louie R. and Gertrude

CONTACT
Robert Summerall, Jr.
Director
Louie R. and Gertrude Morgan Fdn.
PO Box 550
Arcadia, FL 33821
(813) 494-1551

FINANCIAL SUMMARY
Recent Giving: $129,500 (1992); $125,200 (1991); $131,000 (1990)

Assets: $2,408,669 (1992); $2,458,735 (1991); $2,462,259 (1990)

EIN: 59-6142359

CONTRIBUTIONS SUMMARY
Donor(s): the late Louie R. Morgan, the late Mildred Morgan, Gertrude Morgan, Eleanor Morgan

Typical Recipients: • *Arts & Humanities:* Libraries • *Civic & Public Affairs:* Hispanic Affairs, Municipalities/Towns • *Education:* Secondary Education (Public) • *Health:* Hospitals • *Religion:* Churches, Religious Organizations, Religious Welfare

Grant Types: general support

Geographic Distribution: focus on FL

GIVING OFFICERS
Lewis W. Smith: trust

Robert Summerall, Jr.: dir

Jane Weller: secy

APPLICATION INFORMATION
Initial Approach: The foundation requests applications be made in writing. There are no deadlines.

GRANTS ANALYSIS
Total Grants: $129,500

Number of Grants: 25

Highest Grant: $10,000

Typical Range: $2,000 to $5,000

Disclosure Period: 1992

Note: Recent grants are derived from a 1992 Form 990.

RECENT GRANTS

Library
2,000	Arcadia Library

General
10,000	Arcadia Church of God, Arcadia, FL
10,000	Nocatee Church of God, Nocatee, FL
5,000	Brethren Church
5,000	Brownville Baptist Church, Brownville, FL
5,000	Brownville Church of God, Brownville, FL

Peterson Charitable Foundation, Folke H.

CONTACT
Howard Usher
Trustee
Folke H. Peterson Charitable Foundation
c/o SunBank S Florida
PO Box 14728
Ft. Lauderdale, FL 33302
(305) 765-7477

FINANCIAL SUMMARY
Recent Giving: $503,000 (fiscal 1992)

Assets: $12,829,768 (fiscal 1992)

Gifts Received: $1,126,200 (fiscal 1992)

Fiscal Note: In fiscal 1992, contributions were received from the estate of Folke H. Peterson.

EIN: 65-6040055

CONTRIBUTIONS SUMMARY
Typical Recipients: • *Arts & Humanities:* Libraries • *Education:* Colleges & Universities • *Environment:* General • *Social Services:* Animal Protection

Grant Types: general support

GIVING OFFICERS
SunBank South Florida: trust

Don E. Champion: trust

Richard K. Kornmeier: trust

Emily Van Vliet: trust

Frank Van Vliet: trust

APPLICATION INFORMATION
Initial Approach: Send a brief letter of inquiry. There are no deadlines.

GRANTS ANALYSIS
Total Grants: $503,000

Number of Grants: 20

Highest Grant: $125,000

Typical Range: $5,000 to $13,000

Disclosure Period: fiscal year ending November 30, 1992

Note: Recent grants are derived from a fiscal 1992 Form 990.

RECENT GRANTS

Library
10,000	Broward Public Library, Broward, FL

General
125,000	Society for the Prevention of Cruelty to Animals of Broward County, Fort Lauderdale, FL
125,000	University of Florida Foundation, Gainesville, FL
125,000	University of Miami, Miami, FL
13,000	Miami Museum of Science, Miami, FL
13,000	Ocean Impact, Fort Lauderdale, FL

Royal Foundation, May Mitchell

CONTACT
Richard O. Hartley
Chairman, Grant Committee
May Mitchell Royal Fdn.
2266 Kings Lake Blvd.
Naples, FL 33962
(813) 774-0420

FINANCIAL SUMMARY
Recent Giving: $91,000 (fiscal 1993); $111,465 (fiscal 1992); $114,790 (fiscal 1991)

Assets: $2,305,362 (fiscal 1993); $2,195,610 (fiscal 1992); $2,065,351 (fiscal 1991)

EIN: 38-2387140

CONTRIBUTIONS SUMMARY
Donor(s): May Mitchell Royal Trust Foundation

Typical Recipients: • *Arts & Humanities:* Libraries • *Education:* Colleges & Universities, Medical Education, Student Aid • *Health:* Children's Health/Hospitals, Clinics/Medical Centers, Diabetes, Emergency/Ambulance Services, Eyes/Blindness, Health Organizations, Hospices, Hospitals, Medical Research, Public Health, Single-Disease Health Associations, Transplant Networks/Donor Banks • *Religion:* Churches • *Social Services:* Child Welfare, Community Service Organizations, Domestic Violence, Family Services, People with

Disabilities, Substance Abuse, Youth Organizations

Grant Types: research and scholarship

Geographic Distribution: focus on MT, FL, and HI

GIVING OFFICERS

Comerica Bank Midland: trust

Tyrone W. Gillespie: grant comm

Richard O. Hartley: chmn, grant comm

Ruth C. Lishman: grant comm

APPLICATION INFORMATION

Initial Approach: Application form required. Deadline is May 31.

GRANTS ANALYSIS

Total Grants: $91,000

Number of Grants: 10

Highest Grant: $20,000

Typical Range: $1,000 to $20,000

Disclosure Period: fiscal year ending September 30, 1993

Note: Recent grants are derived from a fiscal 1993 Form 990.

RECENT GRANTS

General

20,000	Shriners Hospital for Crippled Children, Honolulu, HI — equipment for playground and Radiology Department
20,000	St. Joseph Mercy Hospital, Pontiac, MI — purchase accu-care telemetry monitoring system
10,000	American Red Cross, West Palm Beach, FL — flood relief disaster fund
10,000	Hawaii Lions Foundation Eye Bank, Holualoa, HI — corneal transplant program
10,000	Kresge Eye Institute, Detroit, MI — support research associate for visual lab

Selby and Marie Selby Foundation, William G.

CONTACT

Robert E. Perkins
Executive Director
William G. Selby and Marie Selby Foundation
1800 Second St., Ste. 905
Sarasota, FL 34236
(813) 957-0442

FINANCIAL SUMMARY

Recent Giving: $2,720,230 (fiscal 1995 est.); $2,663,192 (fiscal 1994); $2,603,042 (fiscal 1993)

Assets: $56,379,000 (fiscal 1995 est.); $55,393,179 (fiscal 1994); $57,475,734 (fiscal 1993)

Gifts Received: $2,245,267 (fiscal 1993); $1,500 (fiscal 1991)

EIN: 59-6121242

CONTRIBUTIONS SUMMARY

Donor(s): The William G. Selby and Marie Selby Foundation was endowed by William G. Selby and his wife in 1955. Mr. Selby, who died in 1956, was a co-founder of the Selby Oil Company in Ohio. In addition, he was a large stockholder in Texaco, and owned extensive mineral interests in the Colorado Rocky Mountain region. The foundation is affiliated with the Beattie, Sarasota County, Paddock, and Posey Foundations, all of First Union Bank.

Typical Recipients: • *Arts & Humanities:* Arts Associations & Councils, Film & Video, Libraries, Museums/Galleries, Performing Arts, Theater • *Civic & Public Affairs:* Community Foundations, Economic Policy, Hispanic Affairs, Housing, Women's Affairs • *Education:* Agricultural Education, Arts/Humanities Education, Business Education, Colleges & Universities, Community & Junior Colleges, Economic Education, Minority Education, Preschool Education, Public Education (Precollege), Science/Mathematics Education, Secondary Education (Private), Secondary Education (Public), Student Aid • *Environment:* Air/Water Quality • *Health:* Children's Health/Hospitals, Emergency/Ambulance Services, Hospices, Medical Research, Mental Health, Single-Disease Health Associations • *Religion:* Ministries, Religious Welfare • *Science:* Scientific Labs • *Social Services:* Animal Protection, At-Risk Youth, Day Care, Domestic Violence, Family Planning, Family Services, Food/Clothing Distribution, People with Disabilities, Recreation & Athletics, Senior Services, Youth Organizations

Grant Types: capital, general support, and scholarship

Geographic Distribution: Sarasota, FL, and adjoining counties

GIVING OFFICERS

C. William Curtis: mem admin comm

John Davidson: mem admin comm

Wendel Kent: mem admin comm

Dr. Robert E. Perkins: exec dir *PHIL AFFIL* admin agent: Cordelia Lee Beattie Foundation Trust, Leslie T. and Frances U. Posey Foundation; trust: Goldsmith Greenfield Foundation

Sid Schwalbe: mem admin comm

Charles E. Stottlemyer: chmn, mem admin comm

APPLICATION INFORMATION

Initial Approach:

Applicants should contact the administrative agent for a copy of their application procedures and application form.

Applications must include a proposal abstract, using a form available from the foundation, that provides a brief description of the proposal; its objective, time period, and total budget; amount requested; and name, telephone number, and address of person completing the application. Required documentation includes proof of IRS tax-exempt and nonprivate foundation status, balance sheet and income statement, project budget,

names and affiliations of directors or trustees, name and qualifications of person proposed to administer the grant, and a statement that the request is executed by an authorized person. Supporting information may be submitted to describe the organization and the project. Three copies of the proposal abstract must be submitted, with one copy accompanying required documentation.

Application deadlines are February 1 and August 1.

The grants committee reviews proposals and notifies applicants of their decisions within five months of the deadline. The trustees evaluate applications on the basis of the proposed project's value to society, soundness of sponsoring organization, sources of other financial support, and assurance of future maintenance of the project without an undesirable financial burden to the sponsoring organization or taxpayer.

Restrictions on Giving: No grants are given to individuals, or for endowment funds, operating budgets, continuing support, annual campaigns, deficit financing, seed money, or emergency funds. It also does not support special projects, research, graduate study, publications, travel, surveys, seminars, workshops, conferences, loans, fund raising, or program advertising. The foundation generally does not give to organizations outside of Sarasota and adjoining counties, to other foundations, or to the United Way. It prefers not to support projects that are normally financed by public tax funds. The foundation usually does not make grants payable in installments in future years.

OTHER THINGS TO KNOW

A representative of First Union Bank serves as a corporate trustee for the foundation.

In order to be eligible for a Selby scholarship, a student must be a bona fide resident of Sarasota or Manatee counties before attending college, and must attend a participating Florida college or university. A minimum grade point average of 3.0 is required. Students seeking a scholarship should write to the Florida college or university in which he or she has an interest. The foundation reports that scholarships are also available for Sarasota County residents who choose to attend college outside the State of Florida. These students should apply directly to the Foundation office.

PUBLICATIONS

Application guidelines

GRANTS ANALYSIS

Total Grants: $2,663,192

Number of Grants: 72

Highest Grant: $200,000

Average Grant: $36,989

Typical Range: $5,000 to $50,000

Disclosure Period: fiscal year ending May 31, 1994

Note: Grants analysis includes 20 scholarship programs totaling $469,150. Recent grants are derived from a fiscal 1993 grants list.

RECENT GRANTS

Library
50,000   Friends of the Gulf Gate Library, Sarasota, FL

General
200,000   Cardinal Mooney High School, Sarasota, FL
164,000   Sarasota County Public Schools Foundation, Sarasota, FL
162,000   Mote Marine Laboratory, Orlando, FL
150,000   Goodwill Industries Manasota, Manasota, FL
150,000   Sarasota Day Nursery, Sarasota, FL

Speer Foundation, Roy M.

CONTACT
Richard W. Baker
Trustee
Roy M. Speer Foundation
1803 U.S. Hwy. 19
Holiday, FL 34691
(813) 938-8521

FINANCIAL SUMMARY
Recent Giving: $310,000 (fiscal 1993); $40,000 (fiscal 1991); $35,000 (fiscal 1990)

Assets: $3,674,356 (fiscal 1993); $2,006,083 (fiscal 1991); $1,988,671 (fiscal 1990)

EIN: 59-2785945

CONTRIBUTIONS SUMMARY
Typical Recipients: • *Arts & Humanities:* Libraries • *Education:* Colleges & Universities, Religious Education • *Health:* Hospitals, Single-Disease Health Associations • *Religion:* Churches, Jewish Causes, Religious Organizations, Religious Welfare • *Social Services:* Senior Services

Grant Types: endowment, general support, and research

GIVING OFFICERS
Richard W. Baker: trust

APPLICATION INFORMATION
Initial Approach: Foundation requests a written narrative. There are no deadlines.

GRANTS ANALYSIS
Total Grants: $310,000

Number of Grants: 5

Highest Grant: $250,000

Typical Range: $5,000 to $25,000

Disclosure Period: fiscal year ending June 30, 1993

Note: Recent grants are derived from a Fiscal 1993 Form 990.

RECENT GRANTS

General
250,000   Hilltop Baptist Temple, Cedar Park, TX

25,000   Stetson University, St. Petersburg, FL
20,000   Christian Resources Center, Tampa, FL
10,000   Neighborly Senior Services Foundation, Clearwater, FL
5,000   Morton F. Plant Hospital, Clearwater, FL

Wahlstrom Foundation

CONTACT
Eleonora W. McCabe
President
Wahlstrom Fdn.
2855 Ocean Dr. No. D-4
Vero Beach, FL 32963
(407) 231-0373

FINANCIAL SUMMARY
Recent Giving: $266,870 (1993); $247,076 (1992); $218,792 (1990)

Assets: $5,984,331 (1993); $5,849,629 (1992); $5,310,291 (1990)

EIN: 06-6053378

CONTRIBUTIONS SUMMARY
Donor(s): the late Magnus Wahlstrom

Typical Recipients: • *Arts & Humanities:* Arts Centers, Ballet, Community Arts, Dance, History & Archaeology, Libraries, Museums/Galleries, Music, Performing Arts, Theater • *Civic & Public Affairs:* Housing, Municipalities/Towns, Professional & Trade Associations, Urban & Community Affairs • *Education:* Business Education, Colleges & Universities, Engineering/Technological Education, General, Literacy, Private Education (Precollege), Student Aid • *Environment:* General • *Health:* AIDS/HIV, Cancer, Emergency/Ambulance Services, Health Organizations, Hospices, Hospitals, Nursing Services • *Religion:* Churches, Religious Organizations, Religious Welfare • *Social Services:* Animal Protection, Camps, Child Welfare, Domestic Violence, Food/Clothing Distribution, People with Disabilities, Recreation & Athletics, Senior Services, Shelters/Homelessness, Substance Abuse, United Funds/United Ways, Volunteer Services, YMCA/YWCA/YMHA/YWHA, Youth Organizations

Grant Types: capital, endowment, multi-year/continuing support, project, research, scholarship, and seed money

Geographic Distribution: focus on Indian River County, FL, and CT

GIVING OFFICERS
Lois J. Hughes: vp, dir

Bruce R. Johnson: vp, dir

Charles B. Kaufman: secy

Jim D. Machen: treas

Eleonora W. McCabe: pres, dir

Agnes S. Wahlstrom: chmn emeritus

APPLICATION INFORMATION
Initial Approach: Send letter requesting application form. Deadlines are May 1 and November 1.

Restrictions on Giving: Limited to Bridgeport, CT, and Vero Beach, FL.

PUBLICATIONS
Application Guidelines

GRANTS ANALYSIS
Total Grants: $266,870

Number of Grants: 63

Highest Grant: $100,000

Typical Range: $100 to $5,000

Disclosure Period: 1993

Note: Recent grants are derived from a 1993 Form 990.

RECENT GRANTS

General
100,000   Bridgeport Area Foundation, Bridgeport, CT — scholarship support
20,000   Indian River County Council on Aging, Vero Beach, FL — to underwrite community coach bus service
11,000   Bridgeport Area Foundation, Bridgeport, CT — operational support
10,000   Association for Retarded Children, Vero Beach, FL — repairs to group homes
7,500   Treasure Coast Food Bank, Ft. Pierce, FL — to provide freezer

Wertheim Foundation, Dr. Herbert A.

CONTACT
Herbert A. Wertheim
President
Dr. Herbert A. Wertheim Fdn.
4470 S.W. 74th Ave.
Miami, FL 33155
(305) 264-4465

FINANCIAL SUMMARY
Recent Giving: $189,170 (fiscal 1993); $208,042 (fiscal 1992); $204,793 (fiscal 1989)

Assets: $5,056,692 (fiscal 1993); $4,515,947 (fiscal 1992); $4,160,469 (fiscal 1989)

EIN: 59-1778605

CONTRIBUTIONS SUMMARY
Donor(s): Herbert A. Wertheim

Typical Recipients: • *Arts & Humanities:* Arts Appreciation, Arts Associations & Councils, Ballet, Community Arts, Dance, Libraries, Public Broadcasting, Theater • *Civic & Public Affairs:* Botanical Gardens/Parks, Clubs, General, Urban & Community Affairs, Zoos/Aquariums • *Education:* Arts/Humanities Education, Colleges & Universities, General, Medical

Education, Private Education (Precollege), Student Aid • *Health:* Eyes/Blindness, Hospitals, Medical Research • *Religion:* Religious Welfare • *Social Services:* Community Service Organizations, Youth Organizations

Grant Types: research

Geographic Distribution: focus on FL and CO

GIVING OFFICERS
Dr. Herbert A. Wertheim: pres, dir

Nicole J. Wertheim: secy, dir

APPLICATION INFORMATION
Initial Approach: Send a brief letter of inquiry. Include a description of organization, amount requested, purpose of funds sought, recently audited financial statement, and proof of tax-exempt status. There are no deadlines.

GRANTS ANALYSIS
Total Grants: $189,170

Number of Grants: 8

Highest Grant: $101,000

Typical Range: $500 to $56,000

Disclosure Period: fiscal year ending September 30, 1993

Note: Recent grants are derived from a fiscal 1993 Form 990. Number of grants and typical range do not include miscellaneous small grants.

RECENT GRANTS

General

101,000	Florida International University, Miami, FL
56,000	Vail Mountain School, Vail, CO
16,900	Crystal Ball Foundation, Vail, CO
3,000	Jerry Ford Foundation, Vail, CO
3,000	University of Miami, Miami, FL

Whitehead Charitable Foundation

CONTACT
Thomas Victory, Jr.
Principal Manager
Whitehead Charitable Fdn.
1001 N. US Highway 1
Jupiter, FL 33477
(407) 746-8444

FINANCIAL SUMMARY
Recent Giving: $2,935,150 (fiscal 1993); $1,367,000 (fiscal 1992); $5,000 (fiscal 1991)

Assets: $6,230,349 (fiscal 1993); $8,941,394 (fiscal 1992); $8,970,235 (fiscal 1991)

Gifts Received: $753,849 (fiscal 1993); $3,000,000 (fiscal 1989); $1,000,000 (fiscal 1988)

Fiscal Note: In fiscal 1993, contributions were received from Article Ten Trust under the will of Edwin C. Whitehead.

EIN: 06-0956618

CONTRIBUTIONS SUMMARY
Donor(s): Edwin C. Whitehead

Typical Recipients: • *Arts & Humanities:* Libraries, Museums/Galleries • *Civic & Public Affairs:* Business/Free Enterprise, Civil Rights, General, Urban & Community Affairs • *Education:* Colleges & Universities, Medical Education • *Health:* Geriatric Health, Health Organizations, Medical Research, Prenatal Health Issues, Single-Disease Health Associations • *Science:* Science Museums, Scientific Centers & Institutes, Scientific Organizations

Grant Types: endowment and research

Geographic Distribution: national, with giving in DC, NC, NY, and VA

GIVING OFFICERS
Arthur W. Brill: secy, dir

Elaine Unschuld: asst secy

John J. Whitehead: pres, dir

Peter J. Whitehead: vp, dir

Susan Whitehead: dir

APPLICATION INFORMATION
Initial Approach: The foundation has no formal grant application procedure or application form. There are no deadlines.

GRANTS ANALYSIS
Total Grants: $2,935,150

Number of Grants: 9

Highest Grant: $2,000,000

Typical Range: $1,000 to $750,000

Disclosure Period: fiscal year ending November 30, 1993

Note: Recent grants are derived from a fiscal 1993 Form 990.

RECENT GRANTS

Library

28,400	National Library of Medicine

General

2,000,000	Duke University, Durham, NC
750,000	Whitehead Institute of Biomedical Research
117,498	Husic Capital Management
50,000	Horizons Initiative, Cambridge, MA
40,000	American Civil Liberties Union Foundation, New York, NY

Wiggins Memorial Trust, J. J.

CONTACT
John H. Holbrook
Trustee
J. J. Wiggins Memorial Trust
PO Drawer 1111
Moore Haven, FL 33471
(813) 946-3400

FINANCIAL SUMMARY
Recent Giving: $92,760 (fiscal 1994); $105,863 (fiscal 1992); $170,048 (fiscal 1991)

Assets: $5,558,748 (fiscal 1994); $5,715,337 (fiscal 1992); $5,407,647 (fiscal 1991)

Gifts Received: $1,482,367 (fiscal 1990); $2,060,993 (fiscal 1989)

EIN: 59-2675273

CONTRIBUTIONS SUMMARY
Donor(s): the late J. J. Wiggins

Typical Recipients: • *Arts & Humanities:* Libraries • *Civic & Public Affairs:* Law & Justice, Municipalities/Towns, Professional & Trade Associations, Safety • *Education:* Colleges & Universities, Community & Junior Colleges, Elementary Education (Private), Public Education (Precollege), Student Aid • *Religion:* Religious Organizations • *Social Services:* Crime Prevention, Homes, Scouts, Youth Organizations

Grant Types: capital, operating expenses, and scholarship

Geographic Distribution: focus on Glades County, FL

GIVING OFFICERS
Joseph P. Branch: trust

John H. Holbrook: trust

L. E. Strope: trust

A. E. Wells: trust

APPLICATION INFORMATION
Initial Approach: Scholarship applicants must be nominated by high school or college level educators. Application form required. Deadline is May 1.

GRANTS ANALYSIS
Total Grants: $92,760

Number of Grants: 33

Highest Grant: $16,800

Typical Range: $100 to $10,800

Disclosure Period: fiscal year ending April 30, 1994

Note: Recent grants are derived from a fiscal 1994 Form 990.

RECENT GRANTS

Library

250	Friends of the Library, Tyler, TX — for operating expenses

General

16,800	Edison Community College, Ft. Myers, FL — for scholarship
10,800	Southern Florida Community College, FL — for scholarship
5,475	Glades County Youth Livestock, Moore Haven, FL — for operating expenses
4,800	Harding College — for scholarship
4,800	University of Florida, Gainesville, FL — for scholarship

GEORGIA

Alumax Inc.

Revenue: $2.75 billion
Employees: 14,000
Parent Company: Amax, Inc.
Headquarters: Norcross, GA
SIC Major Group: Holding Companies Nec, Primary Aluminum, Secondary Nonferrous Metals, and Aluminum Sheet, Plate & Foil

CONTACT
Thomas Hagley
Director, Public & Investor Relations
Alumax Inc.
5655 Peachtree Pkwy.
Norcross, GA 30092-2812
(404) 246-6600

FINANCIAL SUMMARY
Recent Giving: $500,000 (1993 approx.); $500,000 (1992 approx.); $700,000 (1991 approx.)
Fiscal Note: All contributions are made directly by the company.

CONTRIBUTIONS SUMMARY
Typical Recipients: • *Arts & Humanities:* Arts Associations & Councils, Arts Centers, Arts Festivals, Arts Funds, Community Arts, Dance, Ethnic & Folk Arts, Historic Preservation, Libraries, Museums/Galleries, Music, Opera, Performing Arts, Public Broadcasting, Theater • *Civic & Public Affairs:* Business/Free Enterprise, Economic Development, Employment/Job Training, Public Policy, Women's Affairs, Zoos/Aquariums • *Education:* Business Education, Colleges & Universities, Community & Junior Colleges, Economic Education, Engineering/Technological Education, International Studies, Literacy, Minority Education • *Health:* Health Organizations, Hospices, Hospitals, Medical Research, Single-Disease Health Associations • *Science:* Science Exhibits & Fairs, Scientific Organizations • *Social Services:* Community Centers, Community Service Organizations, Day Care, Delinquency & Criminal Rehabilitation, Emergency Relief, Food/Clothing Distribution, People with Disabilities, Senior

Services, Substance Abuse, United Funds/United Ways, Youth Organizations
Grant Types: emergency and general support
Geographic Distribution: near headquarters and operating locations only
Operating Locations: AL (Moulton), AR (Springdale), AZ (Mesa), CA (Cerritos, Hayward, Norwalk, Perris Valley, Riverside, Visalia, Woodland), CO (Loveland), FL (Ocala, Orlando, Plant City), GA (Jonesboro, Norcross), ID (Boise), IL (Des Plaines, Hinsdale, Morris, Rosemont, St. Charles, Westmont), IN (Bristol, Franklin, Lebanon), KS (McPherson), KY (Carrollton), MA (Billerica), MD (Columbia, Frederick), MI (Eau Claire, Grand Rapids, Southfield), MO (North Kansas City, St. Louis), MS (Hernando), NC (Reidsville), NJ (Carlstadt), NY (Dunkirk, New York), OH (Cleveland, Mentor, Rocky River), OR (Stayton), PA (Bloomsburg, Lancaster, Leola), SC (Goose Creek), SD (Yankton), TX (Dallas, Denison, Houston, Irving, Mansfield, Mesquite, Rockwall, Texarkana), VA (Harrisonburg), WA (Ferndale, Kent), WI (Marshfield)

CORP. OFFICERS
Allen Born: *B* Durango CO 1933 *ED* Univ TX El Paso BS 1958 *CURR EMPL* chmn, ceo: Amax Inc *CORP AFFIL* chmn: Alumax Inc, Amax Gold Inc; co-chmn: Cyprus Amax Minerals Co; dir: Aztec Mining Co Ltd, Aztec Resources, Canadian Tungsten Mining Corp *NONPR AFFIL* chmn, chmn fin comm: Am Mining Congress; dir: Mineral Info Inst; mem: Am Inst Mining Metallurgical Petroleum Engrs *CLUB AFFIL* Indian Harbor YC, Sky, Vancouver

GIVING OFFICERS
Thomas Hagley: *CURR EMPL* dir pub & investor rels: Alumax Inc

APPLICATION INFORMATION
Initial Approach: *Initial Contact:* brief letter or proposal *Include Information On:* description of the organization, statement of goals, proposed budget for project, anticipated time frame for the project, membership and community support, other sources of support, copy of IRS 501(c)(3) determination letter, list of organization's board of directors and corporate officers, copy of organization's budget, and audited financial statement *Deadlines:* none
Restrictions on Giving: Company does not support individuals, fraternal or religious organizations, political or lobbying groups, or goodwill advertising.

OTHER THINGS TO KNOW
Amax, Inc., the parent company of Alumax, Inc., also sponsors a contributions program (see separate entry).

GRANTS ANALYSIS
Total Grants: $500,000*
Number of Grants: 500*
Highest Grant: $20,000
Average Grant: $1,000
Typical Range: $1,000 to $5,000

Disclosure Period: 1992
Note: Figures are approximate.

Arnold Fund

CONTACT
John C. Sawyer
Executive Director
Arnold Fund
1201 W Peachtree St., Ste. 4200
Atlanta, GA 30309
(404) 881-7000

FINANCIAL SUMMARY
Recent Giving: $503,800 (1993); $273,900 (1992); $164,500 (1989)
Assets: $13,952,052 (1993); $13,094,853 (1992); $3,560,702 (1989)
Gifts Received: $5,029,894 (1992)
EIN: 58-6032079

CONTRIBUTIONS SUMMARY
Donor(s): Florence Arnold

Typical Recipients: • *Arts & Humanities:* Community Arts, Libraries, Music • *Civic & Public Affairs:* Community Foundations, Municipalities/Towns, Urban & Community Affairs • *Education:* Colleges & Universities, Engineering/Technological Education, Private Education (Precollege), Public Education (Precollege), Secondary Education (Public), Special Education, Student Aid • *Environment:* Wildlife Protection • *Health:* Hospitals • *Religion:* Churches • *Social Services:* Community Service Organizations, Scouts, United Funds/United Ways, YMCA/YWCA/YMHA/YWHA, Youth Organizations
Grant Types: general support
Geographic Distribution: focus on GA

GIVING OFFICERS
Robert F. Fowler III: trust
David Newman: trust
John C. Sawyer: exec dir
Frank B. Turner: trust

APPLICATION INFORMATION
Initial Approach: Send brief letter of inquiry describing program or project. Include a description of organization, amount requested, purpose of funds sought, recently audited financial statement, and proof of tax-exempt status. There are no deadlines.
Restrictions on Giving: Limited to Georgia.

GRANTS ANALYSIS
Total Grants: $503,800
Number of Grants: 30
Highest Grant: $123,500
Typical Range: $1,000 to $100,000
Disclosure Period: 1993
Note: Recent grants are derived from a 1993 Form 990.

RECENT GRANTS
Library

20,000	Porter Library, Atlanta, GA

General

123,500	Fish and Wildlife Foundation, Atlanta, GA — Alcovy River
100,000	Newton County Board of Education, Newton, GA — auditorium
48,800	Oxford College of Emory University, Atlanta, GA — scholarship
30,000	Newton General Hospital, Newton, GA
27,500	Kiwanis Scholarship Fund, Newton, GA — scholarship

Callaway Foundation

CONTACT
J. T. Gresham
President
Callaway Foundation
PO Box 790
209 Broome St.
La Grange, GA 30241
(706) 884-7348

FINANCIAL SUMMARY
Recent Giving: $7,242,541 (fiscal 1994); $6,178,043 (fiscal 1993); $13,508,562 (fiscal 1992)

Assets: $154,895,018 (fiscal 1994); $160,392,159 (fiscal 1993); $152,487,158 (fiscal 1992)

EIN: 58-0566147

CONTRIBUTIONS SUMMARY
Donor(s): The Callaway Foundation's origins date back to 1907 when the late Fuller E. Callaway, Sr. , and his companies backed the establishment of a new hospital in La-Grange, GA, and to 1919, when he founded a charitable, religious, and educational corporation called the Textile Benefit Association. Mr. Callaway was chairman of Callaway Mills and numerous other businesses. After his death in 1928, Mr. Callaway's charitable organizations were managed by boards of trustees. In 1932, the organizations combined their assets under the name of the Textile Benefit Association. In 1943, Fuller E. Callaway, Jr., organized the Callaway Community Foundation which received the assets of the Textile Benefit Association in 1944. In 1962, the Callaway Community Foundation changed its name to the Callaway Foundation.

Typical Recipients: • *Arts & Humanities:* Arts Associations & Councils, Community Arts, Historic Preservation, History & Archaeology, Libraries, Museums/Galleries, Music, Performing Arts • *Civic & Public Affairs:* Botanical Gardens/Parks, Business/Free Enterprise, Clubs, Economic Development, Employment/Job Training, Municipalities/Towns, Urban & Community Affairs • *Education:* Arts/Humanities Education, Colleges & Universities, Economic Education, Education Associations, Education Funds, Education Reform, International Exchange, Literacy, Medical Education, Preschool Education, Vocational & Technical

Education • *Environment:* General • *Health:* Alzheimers Disease, Cancer, Clinics/Medical Centers, Emergency/Ambulance Services, Health Organizations, Heart, Hospitals, Medical Rehabilitation, Single-Disease Health Associations, Transplant Networks/Donor Banks • *Religion:* Churches, Religious Organizations, Religious Welfare, Synagogues/Temples • *Social Services:* Animal Protection, Camps, Community Service Organizations, People with Disabilities, Recreation & Athletics, Substance Abuse, United Funds/United Ways, Youth Organizations

Grant Types: capital, challenge, general support, matching, and operating expenses

Geographic Distribution: Georgia, primarily in the city of LaGrange and Troup County

GIVING OFFICERS
Mark Clayton Callaway: trust *PHIL AFFIL* trust: Fuller E. Callaway Foundation

J. T. Gresham: pres, gen mgr, treas *B* 1937 *CURR EMPL* dir: Atlantic Realty Co *PHIL AFFIL* pres, gen mgr, treas: Fuller E. Callaway Foundation

Charles D. Hudson, Jr.: trust *PHIL AFFIL* trust: Fuller E. Callaway Foundation

Charles Daugherty Hudson: vp, trust *B* La Grange GA 1927 *ED* Auburn Univ 1945-1948 *CURR EMPL* pres: Hammond Hudson & Holder *CORP AFFIL* chmn: Hosp Equip Fin Authority; chmn, dir: First Annuity Corp; dir: C & S GA Corp, C & S Investment Advs, Citizens & Southern GA Corp; ptnr: PCH Properties; vp, bd dir: Hudson Maddox Enterprises, La Grange Industries Inc *NONPR AFFIL* area dir, mem: GA Sch Bd Assn; bd dir: Auburn Univ Fund; chmn bd trusts: La Grange Coll; dir, mem: La Grange Chamber Commerce; mem: Beta Gamma Sigma, Downtown La Grange Devel Authority, GA Assn Independent Agents, Newcomen Soc, Sigma Alpha Epsilon, Sons Am Revolution, Univ GA Gridiron Secret Soc; mem exec comm, chmn bd trusts: Camp Viola; mem pres, adv bd: Med Coll GA; mem pres adv counc: GA St Univ; mem 21st century commn: Auburn Univ; trust: GA Baptist Fdn, GA Hosp Assn, GA Trust Historic Preservation, GA Youth Council, Scottish Rite Childrens Hosp, Troup County Historical Soc; trust, chmn: Florence Hand Home Charitable Trust *CLUB AFFIL* Aetna Life and Casualty Pres, Commerce, Elks, Highland CC, Lafayette, Masons, Rotary, Shriners *PHIL AFFIL* vp, trust: Fuller E. Callaway Foundation

James R. Lewis: trust *PHIL AFFIL* trust: Fuller E. Callaway Foundation

C. L. Pitts: secy *PHIL AFFIL* secy: Fuller E. Callaway Foundation

Fred Lamar Turner: trust *B* La Grange GA 1949 *ED* Troup Tech School AA 1969; Columbus Coll BA 1973; GA St Univ MS 1979; GA St Univ JD 1986 *CURR EMPL* prin, owner, pres, dir: J K Boatwright Co *NONPR AFFIL* bd dir: Troup County Certified Devel Corp, Troup County Planning Comm; chmn: La Grange Indus Devel Authority; mem: Am Inst CPAs, GA Soc

CPAs, La Grange Chamber Commerce; pres: Troup County Chamber Commerce; trust: Clark Holder Clinic Ed Fdn, La Grange Coll; trust, bd dir: Chattahoochee Valley Art Assn *CLUB AFFIL* Rotary, Troup CC *PHIL AFFIL* trust: Fuller E. Callaway Foundation

APPLICATION INFORMATION
Initial Approach:

Applicants should send a letter containing pertinent information about the organization to the foundation office.

Initial letters should contain an outline of the purpose of the request, a proposed budget, the needs of the applicant, and proof of tax-exempt status.

The board of trustees meets in January, April, July, and October. Applications may be submitted any time; however, optimum times for application are four to six weeks before the quarterly meetings.

Restrictions on Giving: Grants are not made for endowment, debt retirement, or loans. No grants are made to individuals.

OTHER THINGS TO KNOW
The foundation prefers to support organizations on a one-time basis rather than on a long-term basis.

PUBLICATIONS
Annual report

GRANTS ANALYSIS
Total Grants: $7,242,541

Number of Grants: 83

Highest Grant: $1,412,762

Average Grant: $87,260

Typical Range: $1,000 to $10,000 and $25,000 to $100,000

Disclosure Period: fiscal year ending September 30, 1994

Note: Recent grants are derived from a fiscal 1994 grants list.

RECENT GRANTS

Library

658,622	LaGrange Memorial Library, LaGrange, GA — for expansion project
138,048	LaGrange Memorial Library, LaGrange, GA — for operating support

General

1,412,762	LaGrange College, LaGrange, GA — for renovation project
500,000	Medical College of Georgia, Augusta, GA — for research facility project
349,480	LaGrange College, LaGrange, GA — for natatorium complex
320,000	LaGrange College, LaGrange, GA — for operating and maintaining property
257,272	LaGrange College, LaGrange, GA — for operating and maintaining property

English Memorial Fund, Florence C. and H. L.

CONTACT
Victor A. Gregory
Secretary
Florence C. and H. L. English Memorial Fund
PO Box 4655
Atlanta, GA 30302

FINANCIAL SUMMARY
Recent Giving: $438,497 (1993); $351,247 (1992); $472,254 (1991)

Assets: $11,493,183 (1993); $10,568,893 (1992); $9,930,244 (1991)

EIN: 58-6045781

CONTRIBUTIONS SUMMARY
Donor(s): the late Florence Cruft English

Typical Recipients: • *Arts & Humanities:* Arts Centers, Arts Festivals, Ballet, Dance, Historic Preservation, History & Archaeology, Libraries, Museums/Galleries, Theater • *Civic & Public Affairs:* Business/Free Enterprise, Economic Development, Employment/Job Training, General, Housing, Municipalities/Towns, Public Policy, Zoos/Aquariums • *Education:* Colleges & Universities, Economic Education, Education Reform, Engineering/Technological Education, Legal Education, Private Education (Precollege), Science/Mathematics Education • *Environment:* General, Resource Conservation • *Health:* Cancer, Emergency/Ambulance Services, Health Organizations, Hospices, Hospitals, Medical Rehabilitation, Medical Research, Single-Disease Health Associations • *International:* International Peace & Security Issues • *Religion:* Jewish Causes, Ministries, Religious Organizations, Religious Welfare, Seminaries • *Science:* Science Museums • *Social Services:* Camps, Child Welfare, Community Service Organizations, Counseling, Family Services, Food/Clothing Distribution, People with Disabilities, Recreation & Athletics, Scouts, Special Olympics, United Funds/United Ways, Volunteer Services, Youth Organizations

Grant Types: multiyear/continuing support

Geographic Distribution: limited to the metropolitan Atlanta, GA, area

GIVING OFFICERS
Trust Company Bank: trust

Edward P. Gould: chmn *B* Chattanooga TN 1931 *ED* Emory Univ 1953 *CURR EMPL* chmn: Trust Co Bank Atlanta *CORP AFFIL* chmn: Trust Co GA; chmn, mem exec comm: Munich Am Reassurance Co *NONPR AFFIL* mem: Assn Reserve City Bankers *PHIL AFFIL* chmn: Trust Co. of Georgia Foundation

Victor A. Gregory: secy

L. Phillip Humann: trust *CURR EMPL* chmn, dir: Trust Co Bank *PHIL AFFIL* mem: Trust Co. of Georgia Foundation; trust: Camp Younts Foundation, Mattie H. Marshall Foundation

Robert Strickland: trust *B* Atlanta GA 1927 *ED* Davidson Coll BS 1948; Atlanta Law Sch LLB 1953 *CURR EMPL* chmn, ceo, dir: SunTrust Banks

APPLICATION INFORMATION
Initial Approach: Request application form from foundation.

Restrictions on Giving: Does not support individuals; no loans.

PUBLICATIONS
Application Guidelines

GRANTS ANALYSIS
Total Grants: $438,497

Number of Grants: 118

Highest Grant: $25,000

Typical Range: $2,000 to $10,000

Disclosure Period: 1993

Note: Recent grants are derived from a 1993 Form 990.

RECENT GRANTS
Library
5,000	Atlanta-Fulton Public Library Foundation, Atlanta, GA

General
25,000	Emory University, Atlanta, GA
16,667	Atlanta Neighborhood Development Partnership, Atlanta, GA
15,000	Georgia Tech Foundation, Atlanta, GA
14,000	Fernbank Museum of Natural History, Atlanta, GA
12,500	University of Georgia Dean Rusk Law Center, Athens, GA — operating grant

Evans Foundation, Lettie Pate

CONTACT
Charles H. McTier
President
Lettie Pate Evans Foundation
50 Hurt Plz., Ste. 1200
Atlanta, GA 30303
(404) 522-6755

FINANCIAL SUMMARY
Recent Giving: $7,614,000 (1995 est.); $7,610,000 (1994 approx.); $7,195,000 (1993)

Assets: $166,014,286 (1994); $156,970,024 (1993); $151,974,007 (1992)

Fiscal Note: Asset increase from rise in value of foundation's holdings of Coca Cola stock, which doubled after a two-for-one split.

EIN: 58-6004644

CONTRIBUTIONS SUMMARY
Donor(s): Mrs. Lettie Pate Evans established this foundation in Georgia in 1945. It is one of three related foundations. The other two, the Lettie Pate Whitehead Foundation and the Joseph B. Whitehead Foundation, were set up by Mrs. Evans' children by her first marriage. All three foundations share the same office and staff. The foundation also shares a common administrative arrangement with the Robert W. Woodruff Foundation.

Typical Recipients: • *Arts & Humanities:* Arts Centers, Arts Funds, Film & Video, Historic Preservation, Libraries, Museums/Galleries, Performing Arts, Theater • *Civic & Public Affairs:* African American Affairs, Community Foundations, Zoos/Aquariums • *Education:* Business Education, Colleges & Universities, Education Reform, General, Literacy, Minority Education, Private Education (Precollege), Public Education (Precollege), Science/Mathematics Education, Student Aid • *Health:* Nursing Services • *Religion:* Religious Welfare • *Science:* Science Museums • *Social Services:* Community Centers, Homes

Grant Types: capital and project

Geographic Distribution: primarily Georgia

GIVING OFFICERS
Roberto Crispulo Goizueta: trust *B* Havana Cuba 1931 *ED* Yale Univ BS 1953; Yale Univ BSChE 1953 *CURR EMPL* chmn, ceo, chmn exec bd, dir: Coca-Cola Co *CORP AFFIL* chmn, dir: Coca-Cola Export Corp; dir: Eastman Kodak Co, Ford Motor Co, Sonat Inc, Suntrust Banks, Trust Co GA *NONPR AFFIL* mem: Bus Counc, Roundtable Policy Comm; mem, founding dir: Points Light Fdn; trust: Am Assembly, Boys Club Am, Emory Univ, Robert W Woodruff Arts Ctr *PHIL AFFIL* trust: Joseph B. Whitehead Foundation, Goizueta Foundation

P. Russell Hardin: secy, treas *CURR EMPL* secy, treas: Ichauway Inc *PHIL AFFIL* vp, secy: Joseph B. Whitehead Foundation, Robert W. Woodruff Foundation, Lettie Pate Whitehead Foundation

Joseph Wayne Jones: chmn, trust *B* Wilmington DE 1936 *ED* Univ FL BS 1958 *CURR EMPL* chmn, pres: Moms Best Cookies *CORP AFFIL* chmn bd: Ichauway Inc *NONPR AFFIL* mem: Assn Natl Advertisers, Sigma Nu; mem nuisance abatement bd: City Winter Pk; trust: Winter Pk Meml Hosp; vchmn: YMCA Winter Pk *PHIL AFFIL* chmn, trust: Joseph B. Whitehead Foundation; mem: Goizueta Foundation *CLUB AFFIL* Groose Pointe, Interlachen FL

Charles H. McTier: pres *CURR EMPL* pres: Ichauway Inc *PHIL AFFIL* pres: Joseph B. Whitehead Foundation, Robert W. Woodruff Foundation, Lettie Pate Whitehead Foundation

James Malcolm Sibley: trust *B* Atlanta GA 1919 *ED* Princeton Univ AB 1941; Woodrow Wilson Sch Law 1942; Harvard Univ Law Sch 1945-1946 *CURR EMPL* ptnr: King & Spalding *CORP AFFIL* chmn exec comm, dir: Trust Co GA; dir: Rock-Tenn Co, Summit Indus, SunTrust Banks, Trust Co Bank; dir emeritus: Life Ins Co GA *NONPR AFFIL* mem: Am Bar Assn, Am Bar Fdn, Am Coll Probate Couns, Am Law Inst, Atlanta Bar Assn, GA Bar Assn; mem bd dirs: Callaway Gardens *CLUB AFFIL* Commerce, Piedmont Driving *PHIL AFFIL* vchmn, trust: Joseph B. Whitehead Foundation; trust: John and Wilhelmina D. Harland Charitable Foundation; vchmn, trust: Robert W. Woodruff Foundation; trust: Lettie Pate Whitehead Foundation

Hughes Spalding, Jr.: vchmn, trust *ED* Georgetown Univ; Univ GA *PHIL AFFIL* chmn: Lettie Pate Whitehead Foundation

J. Lee Tribble: treas *CURR EMPL* bus mgr: Ichauway Inc *PHIL AFFIL* treas: Robert W. Woodruff Foundation, Lettie Pate Whitehead Foundation

James Bryan Williams: trust *B* Sewanee TN 1933 *ED* Emory Univ AB 1955 *CURR EMPL* chmn, ceo, dir: SunTrust Banks *CORP AFFIL* dir: Boral Indus, Coca-Cola Co, Fed Reserve Bank Atlanta, GA-Pacific Corp, Genuine Parts Co, Rollins, RPC Energy Svcs, Sonat Inc *NONPR AFFIL* chmn bd trusts: Robert R Woodruff Health Sci Ctr; trust: Emory Univ *CLUB AFFIL* Augusta Natl GC, Capital City, Commerce, Piedmont Driving *PHIL AFFIL* trust: Robert W. Woodruff Foundation; mem distr comm: Trust Co. of Georgia Foundation

APPLICATION INFORMATION
Initial Approach:

There is no standard application form. Proposals should be made in letter form.

Proposal letters should include a brief description of the organization, its purposes, programs, staffing and governing board; the organization's latest financial statements, including the most recent audit report; a description of the proposed project and full justification for its funding; an itemized project budget, including other sources of support in hand or anticipated; and evidence from the IRS of the organization's tax-exempt status and that the applicant organization is not a private foundation.

The board meets in April and November; proposals should be submitted by February 1 and September 1.

Requests are reviewed upon receipt. If a proposal clearly is not within the giving interests of the foundation, the applicant will be notified immediately. The foundation grants an interview at the request of an applicant, but only after the proposal is determined to be of interest. Applicants are given final notification of grant decisions within thirty days of board meetings.

Restrictions on Giving: Grants generally are limited to tax-exempt public charities located and operating in Georgia. The foundation does not make loans or give grants to individuals.

OTHER THINGS TO KNOW
Occasionally, the foundation provides support to institutions in Virginia favored by Mrs. Evans. The foundation prefers to make grants for one-time capital projects; awards for basic operating expenses are usually avoided.

The foundation shares offices and administrative staff with the Robert W. Woodruff Foundation, Joseph B. Whitehead Foundation, and Ichauway, Inc. Grant and proposals submitted to the Lettie Pate Evans

Foundation may also be considered by one or more of the associated foundations. It is not necessary to communicate separately with more than one of these foundations in seeking information or requesting grant support.

GRANTS ANALYSIS
Total Grants: $7,195,000

Number of Grants: 32

Highest Grant: $1,500,000

Average Grant: $224,844

Typical Range: $50,000 to $250,000

Disclosure Period: 1993

Note: Recent grants are derived from a 1993 partial grants list.

RECENT GRANTS

Library
25,000	Effingham County Library Board, Springfield, GA — for construction of a new county public library

General
1,500,000	Friends of Zoo Atlanta, Atlanta, GA — toward $8.5 million capital campaign for improvements
700,000	Berry College, Rome, GA — for support for the Bonner Scholarship Program, computer system enhancements, and installation of elevator in Evans Hall
500,000	Georgia Partnership for Excellence in Education, Atlanta, GA — for support for reform efforts of state and local school systems
500,000	Mercer University, Macon, GA — for establishment of the Ferrol A. Sams Endowed Chair of English
500,000	Wesleyan College, Macon, GA — for campus modernization and renovations

Fuqua Foundation, J. B.

CONTACT
J. B. Fuqua
President
J. B. Fuqua Fdn.
One Atlantic Ctr., Ste. 5000
1201 W Peachtree St., N.E.
Atlanta, GA 30309

FINANCIAL SUMMARY
Recent Giving: $311,368 (fiscal 1992); $878,367 (fiscal 1990); $1,841,851 (fiscal 1989)

Assets: $16,242,391 (fiscal 1992); $10,714,494 (fiscal 1990); $18,379,505 (fiscal 1989)

Gifts Received: $1,650,000 (fiscal 1992); $8,156,250 (fiscal 1989); $7,500 (fiscal 1988)

EIN: 23-7122039

CONTRIBUTIONS SUMMARY
Donor(s): J. B. Fuqua

Typical Recipients: • *Arts & Humanities:* Arts Centers, Historic Preservation, Libraries, Museums/Galleries, Music, Public Broadcasting • *Civic & Public Affairs:* Botanical Gardens/Parks, General, Philanthropic Organizations, Public Policy, Urban & Community Affairs, Zoos/Aquariums • *Education:* Business Education, Colleges & Universities, Education Associations, International Studies, Private Education (Precollege), Special Education • *Environment:* General, Resource Conservation • *Health:* Arthritis, Children's Health/Hospitals, Clinics/Medical Centers, Eyes/Blindness, Hospitals, Medical Research, Nursing Services, Single-Disease Health Associations • *International:* International Affairs, International Relations • *Religion:* Churches, Religious Organizations, Religious Welfare • *Science:* Science Museums • *Social Services:* Child Welfare, Community Service Organizations, Family Services, Homes, People with Disabilities, United Funds/United Ways, Youth Organizations

Grant Types: general support and operating expenses

Geographic Distribution: focus on GA

GIVING OFFICERS
K. Robert Draughon: vp

Dorothy C. Fuqua: secy

J. Rex Fuqua: treas

John Brooks Fuqua: pres *B* Prince Edward County VA 1918 *ED* Hampden-Sydney Coll LLD (hon) 1972; Duke Univ LLD (hon) 1973; FL Meml Coll LHD (hon) 1982; Oglethorpe Univ LLD (hon) 1986; Queens Coll LHD (hon) 1987; Longwood Coll LHD (hon) 1990 *CORP AFFIL* fdr, former chmn: Fuqua Indus; mem adv bd: Fin World, Norfolk Southern Corp *NONPR AFFIL* dir: Horatio Alger Assn Distinguished Ams, Lyndon B Johnson Fdn; mem: Bus Higher Ed Forum, Chief Execs Org, Conf Bd, World Bus Counc; mem bd visitors: Duke Univ Fuqua Sch Bus; overseer: Exec Counc Foreign Diplomats; trust: Hampden-Sydney Coll

APPLICATION INFORMATION
Initial Approach: Send brief letter of inquiry describing program or project. There are no deadlines.

Restrictions on Giving: Does not support individuals.

PUBLICATIONS
Annual Report

GRANTS ANALYSIS
Total Grants: $311,368

Number of Grants: 51

Highest Grant: $77,848

Typical Range: $1,000 to $12,000

Disclosure Period: fiscal year ending September 30, 1992

Note: Recent grants are derived from a fiscal 1992 Form 990.

RECENT GRANTS

General

77,848	Prince Edward Academy, Farmville, VA
30,000	American Enterprise Institute for Public Policy Research, Washington, DC
27,000	Prince Edward Academy Foundation, Farmville, VA
25,000	Executive Council on Foreign Diplomats, Armonk, NY
25,000	Fuqua School of Business, Atlanta, GA

Georgia-Pacific Corporation / Georgia-Pacific Foundation

Revenue: $12.33 billion
Employees: 50,000
Headquarters: Atlanta, GA
SIC Major Group: Lumber, Plywood & Millwork, Logging, Sawmills & Planing Mills—General, and Millwork

CONTACT

Joan E. Leininger
Director, Community Programs
Georgia-Pacific Fdn.
133 Peachtree St. NE
Atlanta, GA 30303
(404) 652-5229

Note: Company also gives on behalf of the Great Northern Nekoosa Corp. Send requests for information to Sharon Davidson, PO Box 105605, Atlanta, GA 30348. See "Other Things To Know" for more details.

FINANCIAL SUMMARY

Recent Giving: $2,548,953 (1992); $2,277,572 (1991); $2,463,857 (1990)

Assets: $701,341 (1992); $2,445,982 (1991); -$87,361 (1990)

Gifts Received: $759,081 (1992)

Fiscal Note: Direct giving by local plants is not included in the figures above.

EIN: 93-6023726

CONTRIBUTIONS SUMMARY

Typical Recipients: • *Arts & Humanities:* Arts Associations & Councils, Arts Centers, Arts Festivals, Dance, Historic Preservation, Libraries, Museums/Galleries, Music, Opera, Public Broadcasting, Theater • *Civic & Public Affairs:* Business/Free Enterprise, Civil Rights, Economic Development, Law & Justice, Municipalities/Towns, Urban & Community Affairs, Zoos/Aquariums • *Education:* Business Education, Colleges & Universities, Economic Education, Education Associations, Education Funds, General, Literacy, Minority Education, Private Education (Precollege), Science/Mathematics Education, Special Education, Student Aid • *Environment:* Air/Water Quality, General • *Health:* Children's Health/Hospitals, Emergency/Ambulance Services, Health Funds, Health Organizations, Hospitals, Medical Rehabilitation, Medical Research, Single-Disease Health Associations • *Religion:* Jewish Causes, Religious Welfare • *Science:* Science Museums • *Social Services:* Child Welfare, Community Service Organizations, Family Services, Food/Clothing Distribution, People with Disabilities, Recreation & Athletics, Substance Abuse, United Funds/United Ways, Youth Organizations

Grant Types: capital, employee matching gifts, endowment, general support, and scholarship

Note: Employee matching gift ratio: 2 to 1.

Nonmonetary Support Types: donated equipment and donated products

Note: Value of nonmonetary support is unavailable.

Geographic Distribution: areas where corporation maintains facilities

Operating Locations: AL (Belk, Fayette, Monroeville, Talladega, Thomasville), AR (Crossett, El Dorado, Fordyce, Little Rock, Pine Bluff), AZ (Phoenix), CA (Buena Park, Cottonwood, Elk Grove, Ft. Bragg, Madera, Marysville, Modesto, Montebello, Porterville, San Francisco, Tracy, Ukiah, Vernon, Yreka), CO, CT (Wilton), DE (Wilmington), FL (Cross City, Hawthorne, Highland City, Jacksonville, Lake Placid, Palatka), GA (Albany, Atlanta, Brunswick, Claxton, Doraville, Durand, Ellabell, Hampton, Marietta, McRae, Monticello, Peachtree City, Port Wentworth, Savannah, Vienna, Warrenton), IA (Burlington, Dubuque, Ft. Dodge, Monticello), IL (Taylorville), IN (Gary), KS (Blue Rapids), LA (West Monroe, Zachary), ME (Woodland), MI (Gaylord, Grand Rapids, Grayling, Kalamazoo, Owosso), MN (Bemidji, Duluth, Minneapolis), MO (Cuba, Maryville), MS (Bay Springs, Columbia, Duckhill, Gloster, Louisville, Monticello, Oxford, Roxie, Taylorsville), NC (Ahoskie, Asheboro, Bridgeton, Conway, Creedmoor, Dudley, Enfield, Hamlet, Marion, Murfreesboro, Whiteville), NJ (Delair), NY (Akron, Buchanan, Buffalo, Lyons Falls, Oneonta, Plattsburg, Schenectady, Warwick), OH (Canton, Cincinnati, Cleveland, Columbus, Franklin, Newark), OK (Ardmore, Pryor), OR (Albany, Canby, Coquille, Eugene, Lebanon, Portland, Springfield, Sutherlin, Tigard, Toledo), PA (Mount Wolf, Pittsburgh, Quakertown, Reading), SC (Aiken, Alcolu, Bowdens, Catawba, Conway, Holly Hill, Orangeburg, Prosperity, Russellville, Spartanburg, Varnville, Walterboro, Whiteville), TX (Carrollton, Daingerfield, Ft. Worth, Garland, Houston, Lufkin, Plano, Quanah), UT (Sigurd), VA (Emporia, Jarrett, McKenny, Milford, Richmond, Skippers, South Boston, Wakefield), VT (Gilman), WA (Auburn, Bellingham, Olympia), WI (Milwaukee, Oshkosh, Phillips, Sheboygan, Superior), WV (Grafton, Iaeger, Rainelle, Richwood), WY (Lovell)

Note: Also operates in Canada, Europe, and South and Central America.

CORP. OFFICERS

Alston Dayton "Pete" Correll, Jr.: *B* Brunswick GA 1941 *ED* Univ GA BS 1963; Univ ME MS 1966; Univ ME MSCHE 1967 *CURR EMPL* chmn, pres, ceo: GA-Pacific Corp *CORP AFFIL* chmn: Great Northern Nekoosa Corp, Nekoosa Papers Inc; dir: British Columbia Forest Products Ltd, Brunswick Pulp & Paper Co, Engraph Inc, Kraft Co GA, Northwood Pulp & Timber Ltd; pres: GA-Pacific Resins Inc, Mead Timber Co; pres, dir: Mill Svcs & Mfg *PHIL AFFIL* dir: Housing People Economically

GIVING OFFICERS

Cornelia B. Brewer: asst secy

Alston Dayton "Pete" Correll, Jr.: trust *CURR EMPL* chmn, pres, ceo: GA-Pacific Corp *PHIL AFFIL* dir: Housing People Economically (see above)

Rebecca M. Crockford: pres, treas

Diane Durgin: asst secy *B* Albany NY 1946 *ED* Wellesley Coll BA 1970; Boston Coll Law Sch JD 1974 *CURR EMPL* sr vp law, gen couns: GA-Pacific Corp *CORP AFFIL* secy, dir: Mill Svcs & Mfg *NONPR AFFIL* dir: Am Arbitration Assn, Am Red Cross Metro Atlanta Chap, Atlanta Symphony Orchestra, Nature Conservancy; dir, mem exec comm: Alliance Theatre Co Atlanta; mem: Am Bar Assn, Am Corp Couns Assn, Am Law Inst, Am Soc Corp Secys, GA Exec Womens Network, NY Bar Assn, Order Coif *CLUB AFFIL* Commerce Atlanta

Thomas Marshall Hahn, Jr.: dir *B* Lexington KY 1926 *ED* Univ KY BS 1945; MA Inst Tech PhD 1950 *CURR EMPL* dir: GA-Pacific Corp *CORP AFFIL* dir: Cincinnati Inc, Coca-Cola Enterprises Inc, Norfolk Southern Corp, SunTrust Banks, Trust Co GA *NONPR AFFIL* dir: Am Forest & Paper Assn, Am Paper Inst, Atlanta Arts Alliance, Bus Counc GA, Central Atlanta Progress, Ferrum Jr Coll, Keep Am Beautiful; fellow: Am Physics Soc; mem: Atlanta Action Forum, Boy Scouts Am Atlanta Chap Adv Bd, Carter Ctr, Conf Bd, Emory Univ Bd Councilors, Omicron Delta Kappa, Phi Beta Kappa, Pres Export Counc, Salvation Army Greater Atlanta Natl Adv Bd, Sigma Xi; mem (bd visitors): Callaway Gardens; mem (exec comm): Natl Counc Pulp & Paper Indus Air & Stream Improvement; trust: Clark Atlanta Univ, Emory Univ, Inst Paper Chem, Robert W Woodruff Arts Ctr *CLUB AFFIL* Atlanta CC, Capital City, Commerce, The Links, Ocean Reef, Piedmont Driving, Shenandoah *PHIL AFFIL* dir: Housing People Economically

Kenneth F. Khoury: secy

Joan E. Leininger: dir commun programs

James Combs Van Meter: chmn *B* Lexington KY 1938 *ED* Univ KS MS 1963 *CURR EMPL* exec vp fin, cfo: GA-Pacific Corp *CORP AFFIL* exec vp, cfo, dir: GA-Pacific Resins Inc; exec vp fin, dir: GA-Pacific Intl Corp; vp, dir: Nekoosa Papers Inc *NONPR AFFIL* bd visit: Berry Coll; mem: Fin Execs Inst; trust: Centre Coll

Beth C. Zoffmann: trust

APPLICATION INFORMATION

Initial Approach: *Initial Contact:* brief letter or proposal *Include Information On:* description of the organization, amount requested, purpose for which funds are sought, recently audited financial statement, and proof of tax-exempt status *Deadlines:* none

OTHER THINGS TO KNOW

Georgia Pacific has merged with Great Northern Nekoosa Corporation. All giving is done through Georgia Pacific.

Requests for basic information and detailed application procedures should be addressed to Sharon Davidson at PO Box 105605, Atlanta, GA 30348. Joan E. Leininger will be the contact for any subsequent relations.

GRANTS ANALYSIS

Total Grants: $2,548,953

Highest Grant: $448,845

Typical Range: $1,000 to $10,000

Disclosure Period: 1992

Note: Average grant and number of grants figures are unavailable. Recent grants are derived from a 1992 Form 990.

RECENT GRANTS

General

448,845	National Merit Scholarship Corporation, Evanston, IL
186,000	United Way of Metropolitan Atlanta, Atlanta, GA
50,000	Oregon Conservancy, OR
48,297	United Way of South Wood County, Wisconsin Rapids, WI
32,573	United Givers Fund of Forrest County, Hattiesburg, MS

Georgia Power Co. / Georgia Power Foundation

Sales: $4.45 billion
Employees: 12,600
Parent Company: Southern Co.
Headquarters: Atlanta, GA
SIC Major Group: Electric Services

CONTACT

Judy M. Anderson
Executive Director
Georgia Power Foundation
333 Piedmont Ave.
20th Fl.
Atlanta, GA 30308
(404) 526-6784

FINANCIAL SUMMARY

Recent Giving: $6,000,000 (1995 est.); $6,261,000 (1994 approx.); $5,967,000 (1993 approx.)

Assets: $60,000,000 (1995); $59,000,000 (1994); $64,328,765 (1993)

Gifts Received: $2,566,083 (1993)

Fiscal Note: Above figures include both corporate contributions and foundation giving. Above figures exclude nonmonetary support. In 1993, foundation received contributions from Georgia Power Co.

EIN: 58-1709417

CONTRIBUTIONS SUMMARY

Typical Recipients: • *Arts & Humanities:* Arts Associations & Councils, Arts Centers, Arts Festivals, Arts Funds, Arts Institutes, Community Arts, Dance, Ethnic & Folk Arts, Historic Preservation, Libraries, Museums/Galleries, Music, Performing Arts, Theater • *Civic & Public Affairs:* Civil Rights, Economic Development, Economic Policy, Employment/Job Training, Housing, Philanthropic Organizations, Professional & Trade Associations, Rural Affairs, Women's Affairs, Zoos/Aquariums • *Education:* Agricultural Education, Arts/Humanities Education, Business Education, Colleges & Universities, Community & Junior Colleges, Economic Education, Education Associations, Education Funds, Elementary Education (Private), Engineering/Technological Education, Faculty Development, Health & Physical Education, Journalism/Media Education, Literacy, Minority Education, Private Education (Precollege), Public Education (Precollege), Science/Mathematics Education • *Health:* Geriatric Health, Health Organizations, Hospices, Hospitals, Medical Rehabilitation, Medical Research, Mental Health, Single-Disease Health Associations • *Science:* Scientific Centers & Institutes • *Social Services:* Child Welfare, Community Centers, Community Service Organizations, Delinquency & Criminal Rehabilitation, Family Planning, Family Services, Food/Clothing Distribution, Homes, People with Disabilities, Recreation & Athletics, Senior Services, Shelters/Homelessness, Substance Abuse, United Funds/United Ways, Youth Organizations

Grant Types: award, capital, challenge, conference/seminar, emergency, employee matching gifts, endowment, fellowship, general support, multiyear/continuing support, operating expenses, professorship, project, research, and scholarship

Note: Also provides funds for sports.

Nonmonetary Support: $138,000 (1991); $34,062 (1990)

Nonmonetary Support Types: cause-related marketing & promotion, donated equipment, donated products, in-kind services, loaned employees, and loaned executives

Geographic Distribution: service territory, inside the state of Georgia

Operating Locations: GA

CORP. OFFICERS

Judy M. Anderson: *B* Jay FL 1948 *ED* Troy St Univ 1971; Atlanta Law Sch 1979 *CURR EMPL* vp, corp secy: GA Power Co *CORP AFFIL* dir: GA Housing & Fin Authority; secy: Piedmont-Forrest Corp *NONPR AFFIL* mem: Am Bar Assn

James K. Davis: *CURR EMPL* sr vp, corp rels: GA Power Co

H. Allen Franklin: *B* 1945 *ED* Univ AL BEE 1966 *CURR EMPL* pres: GA Power Co *CORP AFFIL* exec vp: Southern Co Inc

Warren Yancey Jobe: *B* Burlington NC 1940 *ED* Univ NC BS 1963 *CURR EMPL* exec vp, cfo, treas, dir: GA Power Co *CORP AFFIL* vp, dir: Piedmont-Forrest Corp *NONPR AFFIL* mem: Am Inst CPAs, At-

lanta Chamber Commerce, Fin Execs Inst, GA Soc CPAs, NC Assn CPAs, Soc Intl Bus Fellows; mem adv bd: GA Southern Univ Sch Bus, N Arts Ctr; mem funding bd: Success By Six; trust: Dekalb Counc Econ Ed *CLUB AFFIL* Capital City, Peachtree World Tennis, Rotary *PHIL AFFIL* dir: Pittulloch Foundation

Gale Klappa: *CURR EMPL* sr vp, mktg: GA Power Co

GIVING OFFICERS

Judy M. Anderson: exec dir, secy, treas *CURR EMPL* vp, corp secy: GA Power Co (see above)

Robert L. Boyer: dir *CURR EMPL* vp various plants: GA Power Co

Wayne Theodore Dahlke: dir *B* Birmingham AL 1941 *ED* Univ AL BSCE 1965; Harvard Univ Advanced Mgmt Program 1985; Emory Univ *CURR EMPL* sr vp power delivery: GA Power Co *CORP AFFIL* dir: GA Affiliate Inc *NONPR AFFIL* dir: Am Diabetes Assn, Am Red Cross Metro Chap, Natl Families Action; mem: Am Soc Civil Engrs, NSPE

James K. Davis: dir

Robert H. Haubein, Jr.: dir *B* 1940 *ED* Univ MO BSEE 1963; Harvard Univ Advanced Mgmt Program 1987; Stanford Univ Exec Program 1989 *CURR EMPL* sr vp admin svcs: GA Power Co

Gene R. Hodges: dir *B* 1938 *ED* GA St Univ BBA 1963 *CURR EMPL* exec vp customer opers: GA Power Co

Warren Yancey Jobe: pres, dir *CURR EMPL* exec vp, cfo, treas, dir: GA Power Co *PHIL AFFIL* dir: Pittulloch Foundation (see above)

Charles O. Rawlins: treas, asst secy

APPLICATION INFORMATION

Initial Approach: *Initial Contact:* brief letter or proposal *Include Information On:* brief description of the organization, list of officers and board members, amount requested, purpose for which funds are sought, sources of other support and the amounts assured or anticipated for the project proposed, and proof of tax-exempt status *Deadlines:* none

Restrictions on Giving: Does not give to individuals or political or lobbying groups.

OTHER THINGS TO KNOW

The Georgia Power Foundation was established in December 1986 with a $10.5 million grant from Georgia Power Co., although the company also continues to give directly.

Southern Co., Georgia Power's parent company, does not administer a contributions program. However, several other subsidiares administer direct giving programs: Alabama Power Co. (see separate entry for details); Gulf Power Company/Gulf Power Foundation, 500 Bayfront Parkway, PO Box 1151, Pensacola, FL 32520, 904-444-6325; and Mississippi Power Company/Mississippi Power Foundation (see separate entry for details).

PUBLICATIONS

Brochure

GRANTS ANALYSIS
Total Grants: $6,261,000*

Number of Grants: 1,500

Highest Grant: $1,250,000

Average Grant: $2,000

Typical Range: $1,000 to $5,000

Disclosure Period: 1994

Note: Fiscal information includes both direct and foundation giving. Total grants figure is approximate. Above figures are provided by the company. Recent grants are derived from a 1993 Form 990.

RECENT GRANTS

General

250,000	Georgia Partnership for Excellence in Education, Atlanta, GA — operating expenses
100,000	Carter Center, Atlanta, GA — capital
100,000	United Negro College Fund, New York, NY — operating expenses
100,000	United Negro College Fund, Morris Brown College, New York, NY — operating expenses
76,000	Georgia Fund for Education, Atlanta, GA — operating expenses

Haley Foundation, W. B.

CONTACT
Eloise Haley
President
W. B. Haley Fdn.
1612 Orchard Dr.
Albany, GA 31707
(912) 435-3686

FINANCIAL SUMMARY
Recent Giving: $183,000 (fiscal 1994); $137,307 (fiscal 1993); $94,917 (fiscal 1991)

Assets: $2,198,074 (fiscal 1994); $2,379,412 (fiscal 1993); $2,343,338 (fiscal 1991)

EIN: 58-6113405

CONTRIBUTIONS SUMMARY
Donor(s): the late W. B. Haley, Jr.

Typical Recipients: • *Arts & Humanities:* Community Arts, Historic Preservation, History & Archaeology, Libraries, Museums/Galleries, Music, Opera, Theater • *Civic & Public Affairs:* Women's Affairs • *Education:* Colleges & Universities • *Health:* Cancer, Heart, Hospitals, Medical Research, Single-Disease Health Associations • *International:* International Affairs, International Relations • *Religion:* Religious Welfare • *Social Services:* Community Centers, Community Service Organizations, Family Services, Scouts, United Funds/United Ways, Youth Organizations

Grant Types: general support

Geographic Distribution: focus on Albany, GA

GIVING OFFICERS
Eloise Haley: pres

Virginia Holman: trust

Emily Jean H. McAfee: trust

Joseph B. Powell, Jr.: trust *PHIL AFFIL* dir: Lockhart Vaughan Foundation

Stuart Watson: secy

Harry Wilson: trust

APPLICATION INFORMATION
Initial Approach: Send brief letter of inquiry describing program. There are no deadlines.

GRANTS ANALYSIS
Total Grants: $183,000

Number of Grants: 20

Highest Grant: $145,000

Typical Range: $500 to $1,000

Disclosure Period: fiscal year ending February 28, 1994

Note: Recent grants are derived from a fiscal 1994 Form 990.

RECENT GRANTS

General

2,500	United Way of Southern Georgia, Albany, GA
2,000	Boys Club of Albany, Albany, GA
2,000	Girls Incorporated, Albany, GA
1,000	Carter Center, Atlanta, GA
1,000	Phoebe Putney Hospital Foundation, Albany, NY

Harland Charitable Foundation, John and Wilhelmina D.

CONTACT
John A. Conant
Secretary
John and Wilhelmina D. Harland Charitable
  Foundation
Two Piedmont Center, Ste. 106
Atlanta, GA 30305
(404) 264-9912

FINANCIAL SUMMARY
Recent Giving: $1,342,009 (1993); $1,088,625 (1992); $1,038,000 (1991)

Assets: $21,398,132 (1993); $24,784,806 (1992); $19,538,306 (1990)

Gifts Received: $28,000 (1993); $96,000 (1990); $235,000 (1988)

Fiscal Note: In 1993, the foundation received contributions of $14,000 each from Miriam H. Conant and John A. Conant.

EIN: 23-7225012

CONTRIBUTIONS SUMMARY
Donor(s): The foundation was established by Mr. John Harland and his wife, Wilhelmina D. Harland in May 1972 through a gift of 125,000 shares of John H. Harland Company common stock. Mr. Harland, originally from Northern Ireland, came to Atlanta in 1906. In 1923, he founded the John H. Harland Company which now operates 44 plants in the United States and Puerto Rico. Mrs. Harland was born in Atlanta, and studied at the New England Conservatory of Music in Boston. She also offered voluntary service in France and Serbia during and immediately following World War I.

Typical Recipients: • *Arts & Humanities:* Arts Outreach, Ballet, Film & Video, Historic Preservation, Libraries, Museums/Galleries, Performing Arts, Theater • *Civic & Public Affairs:* Botanical Gardens/Parks, Community Foundations, Economic Development, Employment/Job Training, Ethnic Organizations, General, Housing, Law & Justice, Legal Aid, Philanthropic Organizations, Urban & Community Affairs • *Education:* Colleges & Universities, Education Funds, General, International Studies, Literacy, Private Education (Precollege), Public Education (Precollege), Religious Education, Special Education • *Environment:* Resource Conservation • *Health:* Children's Health/Hospitals, Clinics/Medical Centers, Emergency/Ambulance Services, Health Organizations, Hospitals, Long-Term Care, Mental Health, Single-Disease Health Associations • *Religion:* Religious Organizations, Religious Welfare • *Social Services:* At-Risk Youth, Camps, Child Welfare, Community Service Organizations, Counseling, Delinquency & Criminal Rehabilitation, Domestic Violence, Family Services, Homes, People with Disabilities, Recreation & Athletics, Scouts, Shelters/Homelessness, United Funds/United Ways, YMCA/YWCA/YMHA/YWHA, Youth Organizations

Grant Types: capital, endowment, general support, and project

Geographic Distribution: focus on metropolitan Atlanta, GA

GIVING OFFICERS
John A. Conant: secy *B* 1923 *NONPR AFFIL* chmn: Columbia Theological Seminary

Miriam Harland Conant: pres

Margaret C. Dickson: vp, treas

James Malcolm Sibley: trust *B* Atlanta GA 1919 *ED* Princeton Univ AB 1941; Woodrow Wilson Sch Law 1942; Harvard Univ Law Sch 1945-1946 *CURR EMPL* ptnr: King & Spalding *CORP AFFIL* chmn exec comm, dir: Trust Co GA; dir: Rock-Tenn Co, Summit Indus, SunTrust Banks, Trust Co Bank; dir emeritus: Life Ins Co GA *NONPR AFFIL* mem: Am Bar Assn, Am Bar Fdn, Am Coll Probate Couns, Am Law Inst, Atlanta Bar Assn, GA Bar Assn; mem bd dirs: Callaway Gardens *CLUB AFFIL* Commerce, Piedmont Driving *PHIL AFFIL* vchmn, trust: Joseph B. Whitehead Foundation; trust: Lettie Pate Evans Foundation; vchmn, trust: Robert W. Woodruff Foundation; trust: Lettie Pate Whitehead Foundation

Allison F. Williams: trust

APPLICATION INFORMATION
Initial Approach:

Requests should be in the form of a letter to the foundation.

Proposals should include a brief description of the organization; description of the proposed program, including need, method of operation, expected outcome, staffing and financial requirements; amount requested from the foundation and potential support from other sources; and a copy of the IRS determination letter of tax-exempt status.

Proposals may be submitted anytime, but consideration generally is given to new proposals during the spring and fall board meetings; such proposals should be received no later than March 1 and September 1.

Restrictions on Giving: The foundation does not make grants to private primary or secondary schools except for those serving the disabled.

OTHER THINGS TO KNOW
The foundation requires a written report on the use of the grant at the end of the grant period. The foundation has put more of a focus on the social needs of the community.

PUBLICATIONS
Annual report

GRANTS ANALYSIS
Total Grants: $1,342,009
Number of Grants: 63
Highest Grant: $244,375
Average Grant: $21,302
Typical Range: $5,000 to $25,000
Disclosure Period: 1993

Note: Recent grants are derived from a 1993 Form 990.

RECENT GRANTS
General

244,375	Egleston Hospital for Children at Emory, Atlanta, GA
89,750	Roosevelt Warm Springs, Atlanta, GA
54,375	Atlanta Union Mission, Atlanta, GA
54,375	Howard Schools, Atlanta, GA
54,375	Northwest Georgia Girl Scout Council, Atlanta, GA

Jewell Memorial Foundation, Daniel Ashley and Irene Houston

CONTACT
William H. Jewell
Chairman
Daniel Ashley and Irene Houston Jewell Memorial Fdn.
40 28th St., N.W.
Atlanta, GA 30309
(615) 757-3203

FINANCIAL SUMMARY
Recent Giving: $92,025 (fiscal 1994);
$101,579 (fiscal 1992); $88,745 (fiscal 1991)

Assets: $3,186,942 (fiscal 1994); $3,115,772 (fiscal 1992); $2,902,287 (fiscal 1991)
EIN: 58-6034213

CONTRIBUTIONS SUMMARY
Donor(s): Crystal Springs Textiles Corp.

Typical Recipients: • *Arts & Humanities:* Libraries • *Education:* Colleges & Universities, Engineering/Technological Education, Literacy, Private Education (Precollege), Public Education (Precollege), Secondary Education (Private), Secondary Education (Public), Student Aid • *Environment:* General • *Health:* Emergency/Ambulance Services, Hospitals • *Religion:* Bible Study/Translation • *Social Services:* Recreation & Athletics, United Funds/United Ways

Grant Types: capital, multiyear/continuing support, operating expenses, and scholarship

Geographic Distribution: limited to Chickamauga, GA

GIVING OFFICERS
Elizabeth J. Barry: trust
C. Ann Barton: treas
Carol J. Browder: trust
Juanita C. Crowder: trust
D. Ashley Jewell V: secy, trust
E. Dunbar Jewell: trust
William H. Jewell: trust, chmn
Frank W. McDonald: trust
George M. McMillan: trust, vchmn
Ellen J. Siegfried: trust

APPLICATION INFORMATION
Initial Approach: Send brief letter of inquiry describing program. There are no deadlines.

Restrictions on Giving: Scholarships available only to high school seniors who are residents of Walker, Dade, and Catoosa counties, GA.

GRANTS ANALYSIS
Total Grants: $92,025
Number of Grants: 21
Highest Grant: $16,700
Typical Range: $325 to $15,000
Disclosure Period: fiscal year ending June 30, 1994

Note: Recent grants are derived from a fiscal 1994 Form 990.

RECENT GRANTS
Library

15,000	Chickamauga Public Library, Chickamauga, GA — general operation fund

General

16,700	Chickamauga City Schools, Chickamauga, GA — general operation fund
10,000	Clemson University Foundation, Clemson, SC — general operation fund
10,000	McCallie School, Chattanooga, TN — general operation fund

6,000	Gordon Lee High School, Chickamauga, GA — Chickamauga athletic field renovation
5,500	United Way, Chattanooga, TN — general operation fund

Life Insurance Co. of Georgia

Employees: 3,034
Parent Company: ING America Life Corp.
Headquarters: Atlanta, GA
SIC Major Group: Insurance Carriers

CONTACT
Nonni Stowe
Vice President, Corporate Affairs
Life Insurance Co. of Georgia
5780 Powers Ferry Rd. NW
Atlanta, GA 30327
(404) 980-5100

CONTRIBUTIONS SUMMARY
Half of the contributions budget goes to the Atlanta United Way. The other half supports company's primary areas of interest: education and health. Limited contributions support the arts and civic and public affairs. Contributions are made to community service organizations directly, but the donation to the United Way covers most of the welfare interest.

Typical Recipients: • *Arts & Humanities:* Arts Associations & Councils, Arts Centers, Dance, Ethnic & Folk Arts, Historic Preservation, Libraries, Museums/Galleries, Music, Theater • *Civic & Public Affairs:* Business/Free Enterprise, Employment/Job Training, Professional & Trade Associations, Safety, Zoos/Aquariums • *Education:* Business Education, Colleges & Universities, Economic Education, Education Associations, Literacy, Minority Education, Science/Mathematics Education • *Health:* Health Policy/Cost Containment, Health Organizations, Medical Research, Mental Health, Single-Disease Health Associations • *Religion:* Religious Welfare • *Social Services:* Child Welfare, Community Service Organizations, Domestic Violence, Family Services, Senior Services, Substance Abuse, United Funds/United Ways, Youth Organizations

Grant Types: general support, operating expenses, and project

Nonmonetary Support Types: in-kind services and loaned executives

Geographic Distribution: primarily in the state of GA, but occasionally in other southern states

Operating Locations: GA (Atlanta)

CORP. OFFICERS
Jim Brooks: *CURR EMPL* pres: Life Ins Co GA

Robert H. St. Jacques: *B* Pawtucket RI 1924 *ED* Cornell Univ 1948 *CURR EMPL* chmn, pres, ceo, dir: Life Ins Co GA *CORP AFFIL* clerk, dir: Little Harbor Co; dir: Plymouth Saving Bank; pres: Hayden Mfg Co; pres, dir: Porter Bog

GIVING OFFICERS
Nonni Stowe: *CURR EMPL* vp corp aff: Life Ins Co GA

APPLICATION INFORMATION
Initial Approach: Send proposal any time, including a description and history of organization, amount and purpose of funds sought, a recently audited financial statement, proof of tax-exempt status, a list of directors and officers, and a budget breakdown including administrative expenses. The National Charities Information Bureau's review of organization will be heavily considered in determining soundness of contribution.

OTHER THINGS TO KNOW
Company reports contributions level and value of nonmonetary support are confidential.

GRANTS ANALYSIS
Typical Range: $1,000 to $2,500

Marshall Foundation, Mattie H.

CONTACT
Thomas O. Marshall
Chairman, Secretary
Mattie H. Marshall Fdn.
c/o Trust Co. Bank
PO Box 4655
Atlanta, GA 30302

FINANCIAL SUMMARY
Recent Giving: $120,000 (1993); $100,000 (1992); $93,000 (1990)
Assets: $4,017,148 (1993); $3,806,471 (1992); $2,586,910 (1990)
EIN: 58-6042019

CONTRIBUTIONS SUMMARY
Typical Recipients: • *Arts & Humanities:* Historic Preservation, History & Archaeology, Libraries • *Civic & Public Affairs:* Women's Affairs • *Education:* Colleges & Universities, Legal Education, Private Education (Precollege), Religious Education • *Health:* Children's Health/Hospitals, Clinics/Medical Centers, Hospitals, Medical Research • *Religion:* Churches, Religious Organizations, Religious Welfare, Seminaries • *Social Services:* Animal Protection, Community Service Organizations, Scouts, Youth Organizations

Grant Types: operating expenses
Geographic Distribution: focus on GA

GIVING OFFICERS
Trust Company Bank: trust
Martha M. Dykes: dir
Jesse Seaborn Hall: trust *B* Atlanta GA 1929 *ED* Emory Univ AB 1950; Emory Univ LLB 1955 *CURR EMPL* exec vp: Sun-Trust Banks *CORP AFFIL* dir: Crawford & Co; exec vp: Trust Co Bank *NONPR AFFIL* mem: Am Bankers Assn, Trust Mgmt Assn;

trust: Henrietta Egleston Hosp Children, Oglethorpe Univ *CLUB AFFIL* Capital City, Commerce

L. Phillip Humann: trust *CURR EMPL* chmn, dir: Trust Co Bank *PHIL AFFIL* mem: Trust Co. of Georgia Foundation; trust: Camp Younts Foundation, Florence C. and H. L. English Memorial Fund

Thomas Oliver Marshall, Jr.: chmn, secy *B* Americus GA 1920 *ED* US Naval Academy BS 1941; Univ GA JD 1948 *NONPR AFFIL* mem: Am Bar Assn, Am Judicature Soc, Am Legion, Atlanta Bar Assn, GA Bar Assn, Judicial Coll GA, Natl Judicial Coll, St Bar GA, Veterans Foreign Wars; trust: Andrew Coll, Southern GA Methodist Home Aged *CLUB AFFIL* Kiwanis, Masons, Shriners *PHIL AFFIL* bd mem: William H. and Lula E. Pitts Foundation

APPLICATION INFORMATION
Initial Approach: Send brief letter describing program. There are no deadlines.

GRANTS ANALYSIS
Total Grants: $120,000
Number of Grants: 20
Highest Grant: $42,000
Typical Range: $1,000 to $5,000
Disclosure Period: 1993
Note: Recent grants are derived from a 1993 Form 990.

RECENT GRANTS
Library
5,000	Lake Blackshear Regional Library, Americus, GA

General
42,000	South Georgia Methodist Home for the Aging, Americus, GA
15,000	Sumter Humane Society, Americus, GA
10,000	League of the Good Samaritans, Americus, GA
5,000	Agnes Scott College, Decatur, GA
5,000	Andrew College, Cuthbert, GA

Marshall Trust in Memory of Sanders McDaniel, Harriet McDaniel

CONTACT
Victor E. Gregory
Trust Officer
Harriet McDaniel Marshall Trust in Memory of Sanders McDaniel
c/o Trust Co. Bank
PO Box 4655
Atlanta, GA 30302
(404) 588-7442

FINANCIAL SUMMARY
Recent Giving: $301,831 (fiscal 1993); $88,133 (fiscal 1992); $248,636 (fiscal 1990)

Assets: $5,626,996 (fiscal 1993); $5,305,262 (fiscal 1992); $3,938,148 (fiscal 1990)
EIN: 58-6089937

CONTRIBUTIONS SUMMARY
Donor(s): Harriet McDaniel Marshall

Typical Recipients: • *Arts & Humanities:* Arts Associations & Councils, Arts Centers, Ballet, Dance, Historic Preservation, History & Archaeology, Libraries, Museums/Galleries, Theater • *Civic & Public Affairs:* Botanical Gardens/Parks, Business/Free Enterprise, Economic Development, Housing, Urban & Community Affairs, Zoos/Aquariums • *Education:* Colleges & Universities, Economic Education, Education Reform, Engineering/Technological Education, General, Legal Education, Literacy, Private Education (Precollege), Religious Education • *Environment:* General • *Health:* Geriatric Health, Hospices, Hospitals, Single-Disease Health Associations • *International:* Missionary/Religious Activities • *Religion:* Religious Organizations, Religious Welfare • *Social Services:* At-Risk Youth, Camps, Community Service Organizations, Family Planning, People with Disabilities, Recreation & Athletics, Scouts, Senior Services, United Funds/United Ways, Youth Organizations

Grant Types: capital and project
Geographic Distribution: focus on the Atlanta, GA, metropolitan area

GIVING OFFICERS
Trust Co Bank: trust

APPLICATION INFORMATION
Initial Approach: Send letter requesting policy statement. Deadline is first of month preceding month in which board meeting is held. Board meets in January, April, July, and October.

Restrictions on Giving: The foundation generally does not fund operating needs such as maintenance and debt service, requests by political organizations, churches, or individuals.

OTHER THINGS TO KNOW
The foundation requests periodic program reports from grant recipients.

PUBLICATIONS
Policy statement, including guidelines

GRANTS ANALYSIS
Total Grants: $301,831
Number of Grants: 59
Highest Grant: $15,000
Typical Range: $1,000 to $5,000
Disclosure Period: fiscal year ending November 30, 1993
Note: Recent grants are derived from a fiscal 1993 Form 990.

RECENT GRANTS
Library
5,000	Atlanta-Fulton Public Library Foundation, Atlanta, GA — operating grant

General

15,000	Emory University, Atlanta, GA — operating grant
12,500	University of Georgia Dean Rusk Law Center, Athens, GA
12,500	University of Georgia Dean Rusk Law Center, Athens, GA — operating grant
10,000	Vanderbilt University, Nashville, TN — operating grant
10,000	Vanderbilt University, Nashville, TN — operating grant

McCarty Foundation, John and Margaret

CONTACT
William H. Cheney, Sr.
President
John and Margaret McCarty Fdn.
944 Nawench Dr., NW
Atlanta, GA 30327

FINANCIAL SUMMARY
Recent Giving: $1,136,525 (1993); $1,175,298 (1992); $743,500 (1990)

Assets: $12,364,181 (1993); $12,389,234 (1992); $12,102,301 (1990)

Gifts Received: $6,050,000 (1990)

EIN: 58-1867301

CONTRIBUTIONS SUMMARY
Typical Recipients: • *Arts & Humanities:* Film & Video, Historic Preservation, Libraries • *Civic & Public Affairs:* Civil Rights, Housing, Law & Justice, Municipalities/Towns, Public Policy • *Education:* Colleges & Universities, General, Private Education (Precollege), Religious Education, Secondary Education (Private), Student Aid • *Health:* Alzheimers Disease, Children's Health/Hospitals, Health Organizations, Hospitals, Mental Health, Nursing Services, Single-Disease Health Associations • *International:* International Organizations, Missionary/Religious Activities • *Religion:* Churches, Ministries, Religious Organizations, Religious Welfare • *Social Services:* Community Service Organizations, Family Services, United Funds/United Ways, YMCA/YWCA/YMHA/YWHA

Grant Types: general support

GIVING OFFICERS
Eleanor M. Cheney: secy

William H. Cheney, Sr.: pres

APPLICATION INFORMATION
Initial Approach: Send a brief letter of inquiry. Include a description of organization, amount requested, purpose of funds sought, recently audited financial statement, and proof of tax-exempt status. There are no deadlines.

GRANTS ANALYSIS
Total Grants: $1,136,525

Number of Grants: 31

Highest Grant: $500,000

Typical Range: $1,000 to $10,000

Disclosure Period: 1993

Note: Recent grants are derived from a 1993 Form 990.

RECENT GRANTS
Library

10,000	Park City Municipal Court, Park City, UT — children's library

General

500,000	Visiting Nurse Association, Atlanta, GA — Alzheimers care
130,000	Episcopal Renewal Ministries, Marietta, GA
98,500	Younglife, Colorado Springs, CO
50,000	Psychological Studies Institute, Atlanta, GA — building fund
30,000	Marion Military Institute, Marion, AL

Porter Testamentary Trust, James Hyde

CONTACT
James Hyde Porter Testamentary Trust
c/o Trust Co. Bank of Middle Georgia, N.A.
PO Box 4248
Macon, GA 31208
(912) 741-2265

FINANCIAL SUMMARY
Recent Giving: $146,955 (1993); $219,056 (1992); $192,020 (1990)

Assets: $5,031,954 (1993); $4,777,209 (1992); $3,900,792 (1990)

EIN: 58-6034882

CONTRIBUTIONS SUMMARY
Donor(s): the late James Hyde Porter

Typical Recipients: • *Arts & Humanities:* Arts Associations & Councils, Arts Festivals, Arts Institutes, Arts Outreach, Ethnic & Folk Arts, Historic Preservation, History & Archaeology, Libraries, Museums/Galleries, Music, Opera, Theater • *Civic & Public Affairs:* Clubs, General, Housing • *Education:* Arts/Humanities Education, Colleges & Universities, Medical Education, Private Education (Precollege), Public Education (Precollege) • *Health:* Children's Health/Hospitals, Emergency/Ambulance Services, Hospices, Speech & Hearing • *Religion:* Ministries, Religious Welfare • *Science:* Science Museums • *Social Services:* Child Welfare, Community Centers, Community Service Organizations, Food/Clothing Distribution, People with Disabilities, Recreation & Athletics, Shelters/Homelessness, United Funds/United Ways, YMCA/YWCA/YMHA/YWHA, Youth Organizations

Grant Types: capital and general support

Geographic Distribution: limited to Bibb and Newton counties, GA

GIVING OFFICERS
Trust Co. Bank of Middle GA, NA: trust

Dr. Rodney M. Browne: dir

Dr. W. L. Dobbs: dir

Rabbi Vri Goren: dir

Rev. Ben F. Hendricks: mgr, dir

Larry Justice: dir

Katherine M. Kalish: dir

Davis Morgan: dir

Tommy Olmstead: dir

Dr. Henry Patton: dir

Ed S. Sell, Jr.: dir *B* Athens GA 1917 *ED* Univ GA BA 1937; Univ GA JD 1939 *CURR EMPL* ptnr: Sell & Melton *NONPR AFFIL* mem: Am Bar Fdn, City Lions, GA Bar Assn, Macon Bar Assn, Macon Circuit Bar Assn, Phi Beta Kappa, Phi Delta Phi, Phi Kappa Phi, Shriners; trust: Wesleyan Coll *CLUB AFFIL* Masons, 191, River North *PHIL AFFIL* trust: Peyton Anderson Foundation

Rev. Jack Wilson: dir

APPLICATION INFORMATION
Initial Approach: Application form required. Deadline is April 20.

PUBLICATIONS
Application Guidelines

GRANTS ANALYSIS
Total Grants: $146,955

Number of Grants: 20

Highest Grant: $38,000

Typical Range: $2,500 to $10,000

Disclosure Period: 1993

Note: Recent grants are derived from a 1993 Form 990.

RECENT GRANTS
Library

25,000	Newton County Library Board, Newton, TX — purchase of books and other materials
7,000	James Hyde Porter Memorial Library, Macon, GA — purchase of books, microfilm, periodicals, and genealogical aids

General

38,000	Mercer Medical School, Atlanta, GA — purchase equipment for visual learning system
25,000	YMCA of Metropolitan Atlanta Covington Branch, Atlanta, GA — funding local building program
23,000	Association of Retarded Citizens, Macon, GA — building renovation and repairs
20,000	St. Peter Claver School, Macon, GA — construction of building
18,000	Museum of Arts and Sciences — capital expansion

Schwob Foundation, Simon

CONTACT
Henry Schwob
President
Simon Schwob Fdn.
c/o Schwob Realty
PO Box 1014
Columbus, GA 31902
(706) 327-4582

FINANCIAL SUMMARY
Recent Giving: $180,000 (1993); $185,000
(1992); $150,815 (1991)
Assets: $4,374,761 (1993); $4,277,936
(1992); $4,219,238 (1991)
EIN: 58-6038932

CONTRIBUTIONS SUMMARY
Donor(s): Schwob Manufacturing Co.,
Schwob Realty Co., Schwob Co. of Florida

Typical Recipients: • *Arts & Humanities:*
Community Arts, Libraries, Museums/Galleries, Music, Opera, Public Broadcasting
• *Civic & Public Affairs:* Civil Rights, Urban & Community Affairs • *Education:*
Arts/Humanities Education, Colleges & Universities, Private Education (Precollege),
Science/Mathematics Education, Social Sciences Education, Vocational & Technical
Education • *Health:* Arthritis, Cancer, Children's Health/Hospitals, Clinics/Medical
Centers, Emergency/Ambulance Services,
Geriatric Health, Heart, Hospices, Hospitals,
Medical Research, Outpatient Health Care,
Respiratory • *International:* International Relief Efforts, Missionary/Religious Activities
• *Religion:* Churches, Jewish Causes, Religious Organizations, Synagogues/Temples
• *Social Services:* Community Service Organizations, Homes, Youth Organizations

Grant Types: general support

Geographic Distribution: focus on GA

GIVING OFFICERS
Jan Heiman: trust

Simone Nehman: secy, treas

Henry C. Schwob: pres, trust

Joyce Schwob: vp

APPLICATION INFORMATION
Initial Approach: The foundation has no
formal grant application procedure or application form. There are no deadlines.

GRANTS ANALYSIS
Total Grants: $180,000
Number of Grants: 43
Highest Grant: $50,000
Typical Range: $100 to $36,000
Disclosure Period: 1993

Note: Recent grants are derived from a 1993
Form 990.

RECENT GRANTS
Library
2,500   Medical Center, Columbus,
GA — library fund

General
50,000   Jewish Welfare Federation,
Columbus, GA
36,000   Columbus College Foundation,
Columbus, GA
10,000   Anti-Defamation League,
Atlanta, GA
10,000   Schwob Department of Music,
Columbus, GA
5,000   Emory Geriatric Hospital,
Atlanta, GA

Trust Company Bank / Trust Co. of Georgia Foundation

Assets: $10.37 billion
Employees: 2,853
Parent Company: Sun Trust Banks, Inc.
Headquarters: Atlanta, GA
SIC Major Group: State Commercial Banks

CONTACT
William R. Bowdoin, Jr.
Secretary
Trust Co. of Georgia Foundation
Mail Code 041
PO BOX 4418
Atlanta, GA 30302
(404) 588-8246

FINANCIAL SUMMARY
Recent Giving: $2,226,426 (1995);
$2,035,762 (1994); $1,714,963 (1993)
Assets: $17,000,000 (1995); $16,812,382
(1994); $15,415,764 (1993)

Fiscal Note: Company gives primarily
through the foundation. Above figures exclude nonmonetary support.
EIN: 58-6026063

CONTRIBUTIONS SUMMARY
Typical Recipients: • *Arts & Humanities:*
Arts Appreciation, Arts Associations &
Councils, Arts Centers, Arts Festivals, Arts
Funds, Community Arts, Dance, Ethnic &
Folk Arts, Historic Preservation, Libraries,
Museums/Galleries, Music, Opera, Performing Arts, Public Broadcasting, Theater
• *Civic & Public Affairs:* Business/Free Enterprise, Civil Rights, Economic Development, Economic Policy, Employment/Job
Training, Housing, Law & Justice, Legal
Aid, Municipalities/Towns, Nonprofit Management, Public Policy, Safety, Urban &
Community Affairs, Women's Affairs,
Zoos/Aquariums • *Education:* Arts/Humanities Education, Business Education, Colleges & Universities, Economic Education,
Education Funds, International Exchange, International Studies, Legal Education, Medical Education, Minority Education, Private
Education (Precollege), Public Education
(Precollege), Religious Education, Sci-

ence/Mathematics Education, Special Education • *Environment:* General • *Health:* Geriatric Health, Health Organizations,
Hospitals, Medical Rehabilitation, Medical
Training, Mental Health, Nursing Services,
Single-Disease Health Associations • *Science:* Scientific Centers & Institutes • *Social
Services:* Child Welfare, Community Centers, Community Service Organizations,
Counseling, Delinquency & Criminal Rehabilitation, Domestic Violence, Emergency
Relief, Family Services, Food/Clothing Distribution, Homes, People with Disabilities,
Recreation & Athletics, Senior Services,
Shelters/Homelessness, Substance Abuse,
United Funds/United Ways, Youth Organizations

Grant Types: capital, employee matching
gifts, general support, multiyear/continuing
support, project, and seed money

Geographic Distribution: metropolitan Atlanta area

Operating Locations: GA (Atlanta)

Note: Operates numerous branches in Fulton
and Dekalb counties.

CORP. OFFICERS
William R. Bowdoin, Jr.: *CURR EMPL*
group vp: Trust Co Bank

Edward P. Gould: *B* Chattanooga TN 1931
ED Emory Univ 1953 *CURR EMPL* chmn:
Trust Co Bank Atlanta *CORP AFFIL* chmn:
Trust Co GA; chmn, mem exec comm: Munich Am Reassurance Co *NONPR AFFIL*
mem: Assn Reserve City Bankers *PHIL AFFIL* chmn: Florence C. and H. L. English
Memorial Fund

GIVING OFFICERS
William R. Bowdoin, Jr.: secy *CURR
EMPL* group vp: Trust Co Bank (see above)

Edward P. Gould: chmn *CURR EMPL*
chmn: Trust Co Bank Atlanta *PHIL AFFIL*
chmn: Florence C. and H. L. English Memorial Fund (see above)

L. Phillip Humann: mem *CURR EMPL*
chmn, dir: Trust Co Bank *PHIL AFFIL* trust:
Camp Younts Foundation, Florence C. and
H. L. English Memorial Fund, Mattie H.
Marshall Foundation

John W. Spiegel: mem *B* Indianapolis IN
1941 *ED* Wabash Coll 1963; Emory Univ
1965 *CURR EMPL* exec vp, cfo: Sun Trust
Banks Inc *CORP AFFIL* dir: Rock Tenn Co;
exec vp: Trust Co GA *NONPR AFFIL* dir:
Atlanta Opera, High Mus Art; dir, mem exec
comm: Morehouse Coll Sch Med; mem: Atlanta Chamber Commerce, Bank Admin
Inst, Emory Univ Bus Sch Alumni Assn, Fin
Execs Inst; mem adv bd: Young Audiences
Atlanta; mem exec comm: Robert W Woodruff Arts Ctr; mem exec comm, dir: Alliance Theatre Atlanta; trust: Leadership
Atlanta; vp exec bd: Boy Scouts Am Atlanta
Area Counc *CLUB AFFIL* Cherokee Town
& CC

James Bryan Williams: mem distr comm *B*
Sewanee TN 1933 *ED* Emory Univ AB 1955

199

CURR EMPL chmn, ceo, dir: SunTrust Banks *CORP AFFIL* dir: Boral Indus, Coca-Cola Co, Fed Reserve Bank Atlanta, GA-Pacific Corp, Genuine Parts Co, Rollins, RPC Energy Svcs, Sonat Inc *NONPR AFFIL* chmn bd trusts: Robert R Woodruff Health Sci Ctr; trust: Emory Univ *CLUB AFFIL* Augusta Natl GC, Capital City, Commerce, Piedmont Driving *PHIL AFFIL* trust: Robert W. Woodruff Foundation, Lettie Pate Evans Foundation

Edward Jenner Wood: mem *B* Danville VA 1951 *ED* Univ NC 1974; GA St Univ 1984 *CURR EMPL* exec vp: Sun Trust Banks Inc *CORP AFFIL* dir: Cotton States Life Ins Co

APPLICATION INFORMATION

Initial Approach: *Initial Contact:* call or write *Include Information On:* organization, objectives, amount requested, total amount needed, purpose for grant, proposed objective and community benefit, other contributors, financial data, annual report, list of board of directors and their affiliations, proof of tax-exempt status *Deadlines:* December 1, March 1, June 1, or September 1; board meets in January, April, July, and October

Restrictions on Giving: Foundation does not make loans or grants for maintenance or debt service. Does not support political organizations, churches, individuals, dinners or special events, or conferences.

OTHER THINGS TO KNOW

Nonmatching grants may be made to national organizations but must benefit the metropolitan Atlanta area.

The committee expects periodic program reports from recipients.

PUBLICATIONS

Application guidelines

GRANTS ANALYSIS

Total Grants: $2,035,762

Highest Grant: $500,000

Typical Range: $3,000 to $5,000

Disclosure Period: 1994

Note: Total grants figure includes matching gifts. Recent grants are derived from a 1993 Form 990.

RECENT GRANTS

General

160,606	United Way of Metropolitan Atlanta, Atlanta, GA	
160,606	United Way of Metropolitan Atlanta, Atlanta, GA	
160,606	United Way of Metropolitan Atlanta, Atlanta, GA	
160,599	United Way of Metropolitan Atlanta, Atlanta, GA	
100,000	Atlanta Project, Atlanta, GA	

Winter Construction Co.

Sales: $37.68 million
Employees: 140
Headquarters: Atlanta, GA
SIC Major Group: General Building
   Contractors

CONTACT
Patty Nally
Marketing Director
Winter Construction Co.
530 Means St. NW, Ste. 200
Atlanta, GA 30318-5730
(404) 588-3300

FINANCIAL SUMMARY
Recent Giving: $25,000 (1993); $30,000 (1992 approx.); $30,000 (1991)

CONTRIBUTIONS SUMMARY
Typical Recipients: • *Arts & Humanities:* Arts Appreciation, Arts Associations & Councils, Arts Centers, Arts Festivals, Arts Funds, Community Arts, Dance, Ethnic & Folk Arts, Historic Preservation, Libraries, Literary Arts, Museums/Galleries, Music, Opera, Performing Arts, Theater, Visual Arts • *Civic & Public Affairs:* Philanthropic Organizations, Safety, Urban & Community Affairs, Zoos/Aquariums • *Education:* Arts/Humanities Education, Business Education, Continuing Education • *Environment:* General • *Social Services:* Community Centers, Volunteer Services

Grant Types: award and general support

Nonmonetary Support Types: donated equipment, in-kind services, loaned employees, and loaned executives

Geographic Distribution: in headquarters and operating communities

Operating Locations: GA (Atlanta)

CORP. OFFICERS
Sean Durkin: *CURR EMPL* cfo: Winter Construction Co

Jack Jones: *CURR EMPL* vp: Winter Construction Co

Arnold P. Silverman: *CURR EMPL* pres, coo: Winter Construction Co

Robert L. Silverman: *CURR EMPL* chmn, ceo: Winter Construction Co

APPLICATION INFORMATION
Initial Approach: Send brief letter of inquiry. There are no deadlines. Include a description of organization, amount requested, and purpose of funds sought.

Restrictions on Giving: Does not support individuals.

GRANTS ANALYSIS
Typical Range: $1,000 to $2,500

Woolley Foundation, Vasser

CONTACT
Benjamin T. White
Secretary, Treasurer
Vasser Woolley Fdn.
c/o Alston and Bird
One Atlantic Ctr., 1201 W Peachtree St.
Atlanta, GA 30309-3424
(404) 881-7000

FINANCIAL SUMMARY
Recent Giving: $332,233 (1993); $265,000 (1992); $236,000 (1990)

Assets: $7,022,282 (1993); $6,463,472 (1992); $5,648,883 (1990)

EIN: 58-6034197

CONTRIBUTIONS SUMMARY
Donor(s): the late Vasser Woolley

Typical Recipients: • *Arts & Humanities:* Arts Centers, Arts Outreach, Community Arts, Historic Preservation, History & Archaeology, Libraries, Museums/Galleries, Music, Theater • *Civic & Public Affairs:* Employment/Job Training, Housing, Law & Justice • *Education:* Arts/Humanities Education, Colleges & Universities, Legal Education, Literacy, Private Education (Precollege) • *Environment:* Resource Conservation • *Health:* Children's Health/Hospitals, Hospitals • *Religion:* Religious Organizations, Religious Welfare • *Social Services:* Child Welfare, Community Service Organizations, People with Disabilities, United Funds/United Ways, YMCA/YWCA/YMHA/YWHA, Youth Organizations

Grant Types: department, general support, and multiyear/continuing support

Geographic Distribution: focus on the Atlanta, GA, area

GIVING OFFICERS
R. Neal Batson: trust *B* Nashville TN 1941 *ED* Vanderbilt Univ BA 1963; Vanderbilt Univ JD 1966 *CURR EMPL* ptnr: Alston & Bird *NONPR AFFIL* fellow: Am Coll Bankruptcy, Am Coll Trial Lawyers; mem,: Am Bankruptcy Inst; mem: Am Law Inst, Atlanta Bar Assn, Southeastern Bankruptcy Law Inst

Alexander P. Gaines: trust *B* Atlanta GA 1910 *ED* Univ GA AB 1932; Emory Univ LLB 1935 *CURR EMPL* mem: Alston & Bird *NONPR AFFIL* fellow: Am Coll Probate Couns; mem: Am Bar Assn, Atlanta Bar Assn, DC Bar Assn, GA Bar Assn; trust: Piedmont Hosp Fdn; trust emeritus: Agnes Scott Coll, Berry Schs, Univ GA Fdn

Oscar N. Persons: trust

John R. Seydel: trust

Paul V. Seydel: trust

Tom Smith: pres

Benjamin T. White: secy, treas, trust *PHIL AFFIL* secy, treas, trust: Charles Loridans Foundation; asst secy: Lenora and Alfred Glancy Foundation

L. Neil Williams, Jr.: chmn, trust *B* Charlotte NC 1936 *ED* Duke Univ AB 1958; Duke Univ JD 1961 *CURR EMPL* mng ptnr: Alston & Bird *CORP AFFIL* dir: Natl Data Corp *NONPR AFFIL* dir: Atlanta Symphony Orchestra, Woodruff Arts Ctr; mem: Am Bar Assn, Am Law Inst; mem bd couns: Central Atlanta Progress Assn *PHIL AFFIL* dir: Gay and Erskine Love Foundation

APPLICATION INFORMATION

Initial Approach: Send brief letter of inquiry describing program or project. There are no deadlines.

PUBLICATIONS

Informational Brochure, Application Guidelines

GRANTS ANALYSIS

Total Grants: $332,233

Number of Grants: 13

Highest Grant: $100,000

Typical Range: $5,000 to $30,000

Disclosure Period: 1993

Note: Recent grants are derived from a 1993 Form 990.

RECENT GRANTS

Library
3,000	APPLE Corps, Atlanta, GA — to support efforts to obtain a Readers Digest/DeWitt-Wallace Library Power Grant for the Atlanta public schools

General
50,000	Emory University, Atlanta, GA — for Phillip H. Alston endowment for use at the Carter Center
30,000	Atlanta Neighborhood Development Partnership, Atlanta, GA — to support campaign for housing and neighborhood revitalization in Atlanta
25,000	Atlanta Union Mission, Atlanta, GA — to support current expansion and renovation campaign
25,000	Exodus, Atlanta, GA — to support renovation of Exodus' St. Lukes and West End Burger King Academies
15,000	7 Stages, Atlanta, GA — to support capital improvement campaign

HAWAII

Amfac/JMB Hawaii Inc.

Sales: $116.1 million
Employees: 1,545
Parent Company: JMB Realty Corp. (Chicago, IL)
Headquarters: Honolulu, HI
SIC Major Group: Subdividers & Developers Nec and Sugarcane & Sugar Beets

CONTACT
Phyllis O. Kacher
Director of Marketing
Amfac/JMB Hawaii, Inc.
700 Bishop St.
PO Box 3230
Honolulu, HI 96801
(808) 543-8922

FINANCIAL SUMMARY
Recent Giving: $566,000 (1989); $580,000 (1988); $800,414 (1987)

Fiscal Note: Company gives directly; figures include contributions by subsidiaries. In 1989, company went private and has not since released giving figures.

EIN: 23-7418207

CONTRIBUTIONS SUMMARY
Typical Recipients: • *Arts & Humanities:* Arts Appreciation, Arts Associations & Councils, Arts Centers, Arts Funds, Arts Institutes, Community Arts, Dance, Historic Preservation, Libraries, Museums/Galleries, Music, Opera, Performing Arts, Public Broadcasting, Theater • *Civic & Public Affairs:* Business/Free Enterprise, Civil Rights, Economic Development, Housing, Professional & Trade Associations, Safety, Urban & Community Affairs, Women's Affairs • *Education:* Agricultural Education, Business Education, Colleges & Universities, Economic Education, Education Funds, Journalism/Media Education, Medical Education, Private Education (Precollege), Public Education (Precollege), Science/Mathematics Education, Special Education, Student Aid • *Environment:* General • *Health:* Emergency/Ambulance Services, Hospices, Hospitals, Medical Rehabilitation, Single-Disease Health Associations • *International:* International Relations • *Religion:* Churches, Religious Organizations, Religious Welfare, Synagogues/Temples • *Social Services:* Child Welfare, Community Centers, Community Service Organizations, Counseling, Delinquency & Criminal Rehabilitation, Domestic Violence, Emergency Relief, Family Services, Food/Clothing Distribution, Homes, People with Disabilities, Recreation & Athletics, Senior Services, Shelters/Homelessness, Substance Abuse, United Funds/United Ways, Volunteer Services, Youth Organizations

Grant Types: capital, employee matching gifts, general support, and multiyear/continuing support

Nonmonetary Support Types: donated equipment, donated products, in-kind services, loaned employees, and loaned executives

Note: Value of nonmonetary support is unavailable and is not included in above figures.

Geographic Distribution: exclusively in Hawaii

Operating Locations: HI (Honolulu, Keaau, Kekaha, Lahaina, Lihue, Waipahu)

CORP. OFFICERS
Phyllis Okada Kacher: *CURR EMPL* dir mktg: Amfac/JMB HI Inc

Roderick T. Wilson: *B* 1944 *ED* Univ KS BS 1970; Univ KS JD 1970 *CURR EMPL* pres, ceo: Amfac/JMB HI Inc *CORP AFFIL* exec vp: Amfac; pres: Kekaha Sugar Co, Oahu Sugar Co, Pioneer Mill Co, Wilson Miller Capital Corp

GIVING OFFICERS
Donald DeCastro: *CURR EMPL* exec vp, cfo: Amfac/JMB HI Inc

Phyllis Okada Kacher: *CURR EMPL* dir mktg: Amfac/JMB HI Inc (see above)

APPLICATION INFORMATION
Initial Approach: *Initial Contact:* brief letter of inquiry *Include Information On:* description of the organization and project, amount requested, total project cost, other sources of funding, recently audited financial statement, proof of tax-exempt status *Deadlines:* none; council members review grants quarterly

Restrictions on Giving: Grants generally will not be made to veterans, labor, sectarian, political, fraternal, or athletic groups (except in special cases in which such groups provide needed services to the community at large); individuals; activities primarily supported by a united fund; or activities supported solely by tax funds. Program advertisements and trip and travel expenses are not supported.

OTHER THINGS TO KNOW
Grant making is restricted to Hawaii. No more information was available at the time of publication.

GRANTS ANALYSIS
Typical Range: $250 to $5,000

Atherton Family Foundation

CONTACT
Chris Sunada
Grants Manager
Atherton Family Foundation
c/o Hawaii Community Foundation
222 Merchant St.
Honolulu, HI 96813
(808) 537-6333

FINANCIAL SUMMARY
Recent Giving: $3,500,000 (1995 est.); $2,500,000 (1994 approx.); $3,092,435 (1993)

Assets: $56,750,000 (1995 est.); $56,500,500 (1994); $56,425,518 (1993)

EIN: 51-0175971

CONTRIBUTIONS SUMMARY

Donor(s): The Atherton Family Foundation was established in 1975 to continue the charitable work of the original donor and trustees of the Juliette M. Atherton Trust (established in 1915).

Juliette M. Atherton was the daughter of pioneer American missionaries in Hawaii. Her husband, Joseph Ballard Atherton, was the son-in-law of Samuel Northrup Castle, the president of Castle and Cooke. Mrs. Atherton entrusted her estate to three of her children, Charles H. Atherton, Mary A. Richards, and Frank C. Atherton, to continue the charitable work in which she was interested. In 1976, the assets of her trust, as well as the assets of the Frank C. Atherton Trust (which had provided support for charitable organizations since 1935) were transferred to the Atherton Family Foundation. The charitable giving patterns of both original trusts were similar through the years.

Consolidation of the two trusts was carried out to provide more efficient administration, greater flexibility in foundation policies, and greater protection and growth of the investment assets. It also permitted an increase in the number of members and directors for a broader representation of charitable interests.

Typical Recipients: • *Arts & Humanities:* Arts Centers, Arts Funds, Community Arts, Dance, History & Archaeology, Libraries, Museums/Galleries, Music, Opera, Performing Arts, Public Broadcasting, Theater • *Civic & Public Affairs:* Botanical Gardens/Parks, Community Foundations, General, Housing, Legal Aid, Public Policy, Safety, Urban & Community Affairs • *Education:* Afterschool/Enrichment Programs, Arts/Humanities Education, Colleges & Universities, Education Associations, Education Funds, Elementary Education (Private), Faculty Development, Medical Education, Preschool Education, Private Education (Precollege), Religious Education, Special Education, Student Aid • *Environment:* General, Resource Conservation • *Health:* Clinics/Medical Centers, Geriatric Health, Health Funds, Health Organizations, Hospices, Hospitals, Medical Rehabilitation, Medical Research, Medical Training, Mental Health, Nursing Services • *International:* International Affairs • *Religion:* Churches, Religious Organizations, Religious Welfare • *Science:* Scientific Centers & Institutes, Scientific Organizations • *Social Services:* At-Risk Youth, Child Welfare, Community Centers, Community Service Organizations, Counseling, Delinquency & Criminal Rehabilitation, Domestic Violence, Emergency Relief, Family Services, Food/Clothing Distribution, Homes, People with Disabilities, Recreation & Athletics, Senior Services, Shelters/Homelessness, Substance Abuse, United Funds/United Ways, Volunteer Services, Youth Organizations

Grant Types: capital, endowment, general support, project, and scholarship

Geographic Distribution: only Hawaii

GIVING OFFICERS

Frank C. Atherton: vp, dir

Judith Dawson: vp, secy, dir

Robert Richards Midkiff: pres, dir *B* Honolulu HI 1920 *ED* Yale Univ BA 1942; Harvard Univ AMP 1962 *CURR EMPL* chmn, dir: Am Trust Co HI *CORP AFFIL* chmn bd: Bishop Trust Co Ltd; dir: Persis Corp; pres, ceo: Am Fin Svcs HI; pres, ceo, dir: Am Trust Co *NONPR AFFIL* dir: Downtown Improvement Assn, HI Visitors Bur; mem: Counc Fdns, Phi Beta Kappa, Profit Sharing Res Fdn; mem bd dirs: Lahaina Restoration Fdn; mem, dir: Employee Stock Ownership Plan Assn Am, Profit Sharing Counc Am; treas, dir: HI Community Fdn *PHIL AFFIL* treas, trust: Samuel N. and Mary Castle Foundation *CLUB AFFIL* Oahu CC, Pacific, Waialea GC

James F. Morgan, Jr.: vp, dir

Joan H. Rohlfing: vp, dir

Chris Sunada: grants mgr

APPLICATION INFORMATION
Initial Approach:

Applicants should send two copies of a written proposal to the foundation or deliver them to the charitable trust department of the Hawaiian Trust Company.

The proposal should include a two- or three-page letter describing the proposed program, a list of the governing board members of the organization, the income and expenditures budget for the project, and the organization's financial statement for its most recently completed accounting period. Optional materials may include one or two letters of endorsement and printed material describing the organization's purpose. Both the signature of the presiding officer of the board of directors and the chief administrator must be on the proposal. The address of the applicant and the telephone number of the appropriate contact person are also required. Organizations that have never applied to the foundation in the past, or who have not received foundation funding during the previous three years, must include proof of tax-exempt status, organization charter and by-laws, and descriptive literature about the organization.

Written requests may be submitted to the foundation anytime. However, if an organization wishes to have its request considered at a particular meeting, its proposal must be received by the first of the month two months prior to the month in which there is a meeting. Meetings are scheduled on the third Wednesday of February, April, June, August, October, and December.

Restrictions on Giving: The directors give grants to tax-exempt, charitable organizations only. Grants are rarely made to organizations outside Hawaii.

OTHER THINGS TO KNOW
Any organization receiving a grant from the foundation will be required to submit a brief report summarizing the outcome of the project and a fiscal accounting of the grant expenditures as soon as the operating period for which the funds were used is completed.

Hawaiian Trust Company is listed as the treasurer of the foundation.

PUBLICATIONS
Annual report, grant guidelines, scholarship guidelines

GRANTS ANALYSIS
Total Grants: $2,080,425

Number of Grants: 113

Highest Grant: $200,000

Average Grant: $18,411

Typical Range: $1,000 to $15,000 and $20,000 to $50,000

Disclosure Period: 1992

Note: Recent grants are derived from a 1992 Form 990.

RECENT GRANTS

Library

15,000	Hawaii Preparatory Academy, Honolulu, HI — for upgrade and renovation of Dyer library

General

200,000	United Way Aloha, Honolulu, HI — for 1992 campaign
100,000	Academy of the Pacific, Honolulu, HI — for capital campaign
100,000	Punahou School, Honolulu, HI —- for sesquicentennial campaign
100,000	YMCA Metropolitan, Honolulu, HI — for comprehensive capital expansion program
50,000	Kawaiahao Church Endowment Trust, Kawaiahao, HI — for church preservation

Baldwin Memorial Foundation, Fred

CONTACT
Janis Reischmann
Trust Officer
Fred Baldwin Memorial Fdn.
c/o Hawaii Community Foundation
212 Merchant St.
Honolulu, HI 96813
(808) 537-6333

FINANCIAL SUMMARY
Recent Giving: $154,400 (1993); $142,100 (1992); $135,750 (1991)

Assets: $4,361,438 (1993); $4,047,906 (1992); $4,049,676 (1991)

Gifts Received: $4,374 (1988)

EIN: 99-0075264

CONTRIBUTIONS SUMMARY

Typical Recipients: • *Arts & Humanities:* Arts Centers, Community Arts, Dance, General, History & Archaeology, Libraries, Museums/Galleries, Music, Performing Arts, Public Broadcasting, Theater, Visual Arts • *Civic & Public Affairs:* Economic Development, General, Professional & Trade Associations, Urban & Community Affairs, Women's Affairs • *Education:* Arts/Humanities Education, Private Education (Precollege), Secondary Education (Public), Special Education • *Environment:* General, Resource Conservation • *Health:* AIDS/HIV, Diabetes, Hospices, Hospitals, Medical Rehabilitation, Nutrition • *International:* International Relations • *Religion:* Churches, Religious Organizations, Religious Welfare • *Social Services:* Animal Protection, Child Welfare, Community Service Organizations, Emergency Relief, Family Services, Food/Clothing Distribution, People with Disabilities, Scouts, United Funds/United Ways, Youth Organizations

Grant Types: general support

Geographic Distribution: limited to HI, with emphasis on Maui County

GIVING OFFICERS

Bennet M. Baldwin: trust

John C. Baldwin: trust

Joseph P. Cooke, Jr.: secy, treas, trust *B* Baltimore MD 1947 *ED* Communtiy Coll Baltimore AA 1972; Univ Baltimore BS 1975 *CURR EMPL* pres, ceo: Thomas P Harkins *NONPR AFFIL* chmn: Govs Construction Indus Employers Adv Counc; dir: Archdiocese Baltimore, Harbor Bank of MD, Prince Georges Chamber Commerce, St Louis Church; mem: Assoc Builders & Contractors, Natl Housing & Rehab Assn; trust: Howard County Hosp *CLUB AFFIL* dir: Cattail Creek CC

Michael H. Lyons II: pres, trust

Shaun L. McKay: vp, trust

Frances C. Ort: trust

Henry F. Rice: trust

Claire C. Sanford: trust

Mary Cameron Sanford: trust *B* 1930 *CURR EMPL* chmn: Maui Land & Pineapple Co *CORP AFFIL* chmn: Maui Publ Co Ltd; dir: Haleakala Ranch Co, Kapalua Land Co Ltd; pub: Maui News

Emily Young: trust

APPLICATION INFORMATION

Initial Approach: Send cover letter and full proposal. Include a description of organization, amount requested, purpose of funds sought, recently audited financial statement, and proof of tax-exempt status. There are no deadlines or restrictions.

GRANTS ANALYSIS

Total Grants: $154,400

Number of Grants: 37

Highest Grant: $12,000

Typical Range: $500 to $10,000

Disclosure Period: 1993

Note: Recent grants are derived from a 1993 Form 990.

RECENT GRANTS

Library
10,000	Haleakala School Library, Kula, HI
3,000	Imua Rehab, Honolulu, HI

General
12,000	Makawao Union Church, Makawao, HI
10,000	Aloha House, Paia, HI
7,500	Maui Hi Maloma, Maui, HI
7,000	Catholic Charities, Honolulu, HI
6,000	Lokan Pacific, Honolulu, HI

Castle Foundation, Harold K. L.

CONTACT

Katherine F. Braden
Vice President and Treasurer
Harold K. L. Castle Foundation
146 Hekili St., Ste. 203A
Kailua, HI 96734
(808) 262-9413

FINANCIAL SUMMARY

Recent Giving: $4,500,000 (1995 est.); $4,700,000 (1994); $4,260,000 (1993)

Assets: $95,000,000 (1995 est.); $94,000,000 (1994 approx.); $96,240,000 (1993)

EIN: 99-6005445

CONTRIBUTIONS SUMMARY

Donor(s): The foundation was established in 1962, with the late Harold K. L. Castle and his wife, the late Alice Hedemann Castle, as donors. Mr. Castle, a prominent landowner and community leader, owned the Kaneohe Ranch. The ranch company was dissolved upon Mr. Castle's death; some of the land and commercial properties from the original ranch provide the base for the foundation's assets.

Typical Recipients: • *Arts & Humanities:* Arts Centers, Community Arts, Historic Preservation, History & Archaeology, Libraries, Museums/Galleries, Music, Public Broadcasting, Theater • *Civic & Public Affairs:* Botanical Gardens/Parks, Employment/Job Training, Legal Aid, Public Policy • *Education:* Arts/Humanities Education, Colleges & Universities, Economic Education, Elementary Education (Private), Environmental Education, General, Literacy, Private Education (Precollege) • *Environment:* Air/Water Quality, General • *Health:* Clinics/Medical Centers, Health Organizations, Hospitals, Medical Rehabilitation, Single-Disease Health Associations • *International:* International Environmental Issues • *Religion:* Ministries, Religious Organizations • *Science:* Scientific Centers & Institutes • *Social Services:* Animal Protection, At-Risk Youth, Domestic Violence, Food/Clothing Distribution, People with Disabilities, Scouts, Substance Abuse, United Funds/United Ways,

YMCA/YWCA/YMHA/YWHA, Youth Organizations

Grant Types: capital, general support, multiyear/continuing support, project, and seed money

Geographic Distribution: primarily Hawaii, particularly Windward Oahu

GIVING OFFICERS

William C. Aull: dir *CURR EMPL* treas, dir: Mid Pacific Inst *PHIL AFFIL* vp, trust: Samuel N. and Mary Castle Foundation

John C. Baldwin: dir *B* 1937 *CURR EMPL* secy, treas, dir: H N J 2 Inc

Katherine F. Braden: vp, treas

James C. Castle, Jr.: vp

Carol Conrad: secy

Henry Mitchell D'Olier: dir *B* Chicago IL 1946 *ED* Univ IA BA 1968; Univ IA JD 1972 *CURR EMPL* ptnr tax & health mgmt comm: Goodsil Anderson Quinn & Stifel *CORP AFFIL* dir: Reyns Mens Wear *NONPR AFFIL* dir: Central Union Church; dir, chmn: Boys & Girls Club Honolulu; mem: Am Bar Assn, Am Coll Hosp Attys, HI St Bar Assn, Natl Health Lawyers Assn, Omicron Delta Kappa, Order of Coif *CLUB AFFIL* Plaza, Rotary

Elaine L. Hogue: assoc admin

James C. McIntosh: pres, dir *PHIL AFFIL* trust: Samuel N. and Mary Castle Foundation

Randolph Graves Moore: exec vp *B* Honolulu HI 1939 *ED* Swarthmore Coll 1961; Stanford Univ 1963 *CURR EMPL* ceo: Kaneohe Ranch *CORP AFFIL* dir: Grove Farm Co, Ltd, Hawaii Stevedores

Peter E. Russell: dir

APPLICATION INFORMATION
Initial Approach:

Applicants should send a preliminary letter to the foundation requesting guidelines.

One original and six copies of a written proposal with a cover letter or executive summary signed by the organization's board chairman and president as well as a contact person's name and daytime telephone number. The proposal should include the purpose of the requested grant, the budget for the organization and the specifc project for which funds are being requested, together with an indication of other funding sources. A list of the organization's current officers and directors should also be included as well as a description of what will be done to determine the effectiveness of the project. The organization's most recent annual report and a copy of the IRS Section 501(c)(3) determination letter should also be included.

The deadline for proposals is the first of the month prior to the month of the meeting date (i.e., January 1, March 1, May 1, etc.). The board generally meets every other month.

The foundation directors will generally notify recipients within one week of the meeting. Larger grants (more than $100,000) are usually paid in December.

Restrictions on Giving: The foundation does not give grants to individuals.

OTHER THINGS TO KNOW

All funded organizations are required to sign a written grant agreement detailing the use of the grant funds, reporting requirements, and other specifics of the grant.

The foundation approves about 25% of all proposals it receives.

Organizations should not resubmit a proposal until the next fiscal year.

PUBLICATIONS

Annual report, guidelines

GRANTS ANALYSIS

Total Grants: $4,260,000

Number of Grants: 55

Highest Grant: $530,000

Average Grant: $77,000*

Typical Range: $5,000 to $25,000 and $50,000 to $100,000

Disclosure Period: 1993

Note: Average grant figure was supplied by the foundation. Recent grants are derived from a 1993 partial grants list.

RECENT GRANTS

Library

100,000	Seabury Hall, Honolulu, HI — capital fund drive for new gymnasium and library

General

500,000	Hawaii Pacific University, Honolulu, HI — toward the cost of the merger with Hawaii Loa College
250,000	Center for a Sustainable Future, Honolulu, HI — toward development of a center for study of the optimum uses of resources of the globe to permit a sustainable means of production and consumption in an environmentally acceptable manner
200,000	St. Andrews Priory, Honolulu, HI — capital fund drive toward new gymnasium
175,000	Sacred Hearts Academy, Honolulu, HI — capital improvement drive
150,000	Punahou School, Honolulu, HI — capital renovations of Castle Hall

Cooke Foundation

CONTACT

Susan Jones
Grants Administrator
Cooke Foundation
222 Merchant St.
Honolulu, HI 96813
(808) 537-6333

FINANCIAL SUMMARY

Recent Giving: $665,518 (fiscal 1993); $859,000 (fiscal 1992); $1,269,600 (fiscal 1991)

Assets: $18,740,601 (fiscal 1993); $17,975,779 (fiscal 1992); $16,152,450 (fiscal 1991 est.)

EIN: 23-7120804

CONTRIBUTIONS SUMMARY

Donor(s): The Cooke Foundation was established in 1920 as the Charles M. Cooke and Anna C. Cooke Trust, with funds bequeathed by their estates. The Cooke family was one of the early pioneers in the development of Hawaii. The family was instrumental in the growth of the Honolulu Academy of Arts, and, to this day, in honor of Anna C. Cooke, the first grant authorized by the foundation's trustees each fiscal year goes to the academy. Through the Cooke Foundation, the Cooke family continues to support the interests and needs of Hawaii.

Typical Recipients: • _Arts & Humanities:_ Arts Associations & Councils, Arts Centers, Film & Video, General, Historic Preservation, History & Archaeology, Libraries, Museums/Galleries, Music, Opera, Performing Arts, Public Broadcasting, Theater • _Civic & Public Affairs:_ Asian American Affairs, Botanical Gardens/Parks, Business/Free Enterprise, Clubs, Employment/Job Training, General, Housing, Legal Aid, Parades/Festivals, Public Policy, Urban & Community Affairs, Zoos/Aquariums • _Education:_ Arts/Humanities Education, Colleges & Universities, Education Funds, Preschool Education, Private Education (Precollege), Public Education (Precollege), Special Education • _Environment:_ Air/Water Quality, General, Resource Conservation, Wildlife Protection • _Health:_ AIDS/HIV, Health Organizations, Heart, Hospices, Hospitals, Mental Health, Single-Disease Health Associations • _Religion:_ Churches, Religious Organizations, Religious Welfare • _Science:_ Scientific Research • _Social Services:_ At-Risk Youth, Child Welfare, Community Centers, Community Service Organizations, Crime Prevention, Domestic Violence, Emergency Relief, Family Planning, Family Services, Food/Clothing Distribution, People with Disabilities, Recreation & Athletics, Scouts, Senior Services, Shelters/Homelessness, Substance Abuse, United Funds/United Ways, Volunteer Services, Youth Organizations

Grant Types: capital, general support, matching, multiyear/continuing support, operating expenses, and project

Geographic Distribution: only in Hawaii, with emphasis on Oahu

GIVING OFFICERS

Dale Bachman: trust

Anna Delby Blackwell: trust _B_ Honolulu HI 1932 _ED_ Vassar Coll 1950-1952; Univ HI 1952-1953; Univ Canterbury New Zealand 1985; HI Pacific Univ BA 1991 _CURR EMPL_ consult: ANNAgram _NONPR AFFIL_ asst mgr: Cathedral Assocs St Marks; fdr: Womens Fund HI

Richard A. Cooke, Jr.: vp, trust

Samuel A. Cooke: pres, trust _CURR EMPL_ vp, dir: Honolulu Academy Arts

Betty P. Dunford: vp, trust

Susan Jones: grants admin _PHIL AFFIL_ grants admin: Samuel N. and Mary Castle Foundation

Charles C. Spalding: vp, trust

Anita Watanabe: secy

APPLICATION INFORMATION

Initial Approach:

Two copies of an one- to two-page executive summary of the proposal should be sent to the foundation.

The following materials should be included a cover page stating the name of organization, its address and phone number, amount requested, and a contact person; a copy of a proposal in narrative form, signed by the organization's office of the board and executive officer; two copies of a list of organization's governing board including their occupations and affiliations; two copies of the agency's current operating budget including a budget for specific project, if separate from the operating budget; a copy of most recently audited financial statement; a copy of the IRS determination letter for the organization; and copy of the charter and bylaws for the organization, if a proposal has never been submitted to the foundation.

The full proposal should include the following—the organization's mission statement; a description of program or project including a timetable, program objectives, action plan, and methods of evaluation; a statement of need for the service including a description of population served; and any documentation or citations from independent sources addressing the issues.

Funding requests may be submitted at any time. Deadlines for board meetings are: May 1st for the July meeting; August 1st for the October meeting; December 1st for the February meeting; and April 1st for June meeting.

Restrictions on Giving: Grants are not given to individuals; to churches or for religious programs, except for a few churches which Cooke family forebears were instrumental in founding; or for scholarships; regranting or discretionary funds; or loans to individuals or institutions. Only one grant will be awarded to an organization in any one year.

OTHER THINGS TO KNOW

Organizations receiving grants must submit a brief report summarizing the outcome of the project and an expenditure report at the completion of the project or accounting period.

The Hawaii Community Foundation is the grants administrator for the Cooke Foundation, Ltd.

PUBLICATIONS

Annual report and application procedures

GRANTS ANALYSIS

Total Grants: $665,518

Number of Grants: 76

Highest Grant: $50,000

Average Grant: $8,757

Typical Range: $1,000 to $15,000

Disclosure Period: fiscal year ending June 30, 1993

Note: Recent grants are derived from a fiscal 1993 Form 990.

RECENT GRANTS

General

50,000	Honolulu Academy of Arts, Honolulu, HI
50,000	Punahou School, Honolulu, HI — support for Cooke Hall
25,000	Bishop Museum, Honolulu, HI — capital improvements to Amy B.1 Greenwell Ethnobotanical Garden
25,000	Boy Scouts of America, Honolulu, HI — support to upgrade Camp Pupukea
25,000	Na Pua O Kauai Island School, Honolulu, HI — support for capital campaign

First Hawaiian, Inc. / First Hawaiian Foundation

Income: $511.61 million
Employees: 3,369
Headquarters: Honolulu, HI
SIC Major Group: Holding Companies Nec, State Commercial Banks, and Miscellaneous Business Credit Institutions

CONTACT

Herbert E. Wolff
Director/Secretary
First Hawaiian Foundation
165 S King St.
Honolulu, HI 96813
(808) 525-8144

FINANCIAL SUMMARY

Recent Giving: $1,325,452 (1993); $1,475,774 (1992); $900,000 (1991 approx.)

Assets: $8,927,979 (1993); $9,372,976 (1992); $9,978,513 (1991)

Gifts Received: $177,276 (1993); $667 (1992)

Fiscal Note: Company gives mainly through foundation. Individual branches also may make grants at the discretion of the branch manager. Total direct giving figures for the branches are not available. Gifts were received from First Hawaiian Credit Corp., First Hawaiian Bank, and First Hawaiian Leasing.

EIN: 23-7437822

CONTRIBUTIONS SUMMARY

Typical Recipients: • *Arts & Humanities:* Arts Centers, Historic Preservation, History & Archaeology, Libraries, Museums/Galleries, Music, Public Broadcasting • *Civic & Public Affairs:* Asian American Affairs, Housing, Law & Justice, Urban & Community Affairs • *Education:* Arts/Humanities Education, Business Education, Colleges & Universities, Economic Education, Education Funds, International Studies, Literacy, Private Education (Precollege), Public Education (Precollege), Religious Education, Science/Mathematics Education, Special Education, Student Aid • *Environment:* General, Resource Conservation • *Health:* Clinics/Medical Centers, Emergency/Ambulance Services, Hospitals • *International:* Foreign Educational Institutions, Missionary/Religious Activities • *Religion:* Churches, Religious Welfare • *Science:* Scientific Research • *Social Services:* Child Welfare, Community Centers, Day Care, Family Services, Food/Clothing Distribution, Recreation & Athletics, Senior Services, Shelters/Homelessness, Substance Abuse, United Funds/United Ways, Youth Organizations

Grant Types: capital and project

Geographic Distribution: primarily in Hawaii, with emphasis on Honolulu, but sometimes makes gifts in Guam and the continental United States

Operating Locations: HI (Honolulu)

CORP. OFFICERS

Walter Arthur Dods, Jr.: *B* Honolulu HI 1941 *ED* Univ HI BBA 1968 *CURR EMPL* chmn, ceo: First Hawaiian Inc *CORP AFFIL* chmn, ceo: First Hawaiian Leasing Inc; chmn, ceo, dir: First Hawaiian Creditcorp Inc; dir: A&B HI, Alexander & Baldwin Inc, First Ins Co HI, Grace Pacific Corp, GTE CA, GTE HI, GTE Northwest, Matson Navigation Co, Oceanic Cablevision, Pacific Guardian Life Ins Co, Restaurant Suntory US, RHP Inc, Suntory Resorts; mem adv bd: Duty Free; pres, dir: FHB Properties, First Hawaiian Overseas Corp *NONPR AFFIL* bd govs: HI Employers Counc; chmn: Japan-HI Econ Counc; chmn, dir: Pacific Intl Ctr High-Tech Res; dir: Coalition Drug-Free HI, E-W Ctr Fdn, HI Visit Bur, World Cup Honolulu; exec comm: HI Open; mem: Am Bankers Assn, Bank Mktg Assn, HI Bankers Assn, HI Bus Roundtable, HI Chamber Commerce, Honolulu Chamber Commerce, Honolulu Press Club, Japanese Cultural Ctr HI; mem bd govs: Pacific Peace Fdn; mem exec bd: Aloha Counc, Boy Scouts Am; mem govs adv bd: Geothermal-Interisland Cable Project; treas: Rehab Hosp Pacific; trust: Blood Bank HI, Contemporary Mus, HI Maritime Ctr, Japan-Am Soc, Nature Conservancy HI, Punahou Sch *CLUB AFFIL* 200

GIVING OFFICERS

Harriet Aoki: dir

Kenneth J. Bentley: dir

Philip H. Ching: vp, dir *B* Honolulu HI 1931 *ED* Colgate Univ BA 1952; Univ CA LLB 1955 *CURR EMPL* exec vp: First Hawaiian Inc *CORP AFFIL* dir: AIG HI Ins Consulting Inc, Bacon-Universal, First Hawaiian Creditcorp Inc, First Hawaiian Leasing Inc, Nordic Construction; vchmn: First Hawaiian Bank *NONPR AFFIL* dir, trust: Castle Med Ctr; mem: Am Bar Assn, Chinese Chamber Commerce, HI Bar Assn; secy, treas: Bobby Benson Fdn; treas, bd govs: HI Commun Fdn; trust: Chaminade Univ *CLUB AFFIL* Pacific, Waialae CC

Walter Arthur Dods, Jr.: pres, dir *CURR EMPL* chmn, ceo: First Hawaiian Inc (see above)

Anthony R. Guerrero, Jr.: dir *B* Honolulu HI 1945 *ED* Univ Portland 1967 *CURR EMPL* exec vp branch oper group: First Hawaiian Bank

John Arthur Hoag: vp, dir *B* Freeport NY 1932 *ED* Univ MO BS 1955; Pacific Coast Banking Sch 1970; Univ HI MBA 1977 *CURR EMPL* pres, dir: First Hawaiian Inc *CORP AFFIL* chmn, pres: HI Reserves Inc; dir: First Hawaiian Leasing Inc; pres, dir: First Hawaiian Bank, First Hawaiian Creditcorp Inc; vchmn: First Hawaiian Interstate Bank, Pioneer Fed Savings Bank *NONPR AFFIL* dir: HI Med Svc Assn, Honolulu Polynesian Cultural Ctr, Kapiolani Med Ctr Women & Children; mem: HI Bankers Assn, HI Chamber Commerce, Univ HI Pres Club

Donald G. Horner: vp, dir *B* Fayetteville NC 1950 *ED* Univ NC 1972; Univ Southern CA 1977 *CURR EMPL* exec vp: First Hawaiian Inc *CORP AFFIL* chmn: First Hawaiian Creditcorp Inc; pres, dir: First Hawaiian Leasing Inc; sr vp (bus devel & planning group): First Hawaiian Bank

Gary K. Kai: dir *CURR EMPL* sr vp retail loan group: First Hawaiian Bank

Howard Henry Karr: treas, dir *B* Honolulu HI 1943 *ED* Univ HI 1966 *CURR EMPL* exec vp, treas: First Hawaiian Inc *CORP AFFIL* treas, dir: Am Security Properties Inc, FIH Intl Inc, Real Estate Delivery Inc; vchmn, cfo: First Hawaiian Bank; vp, treas, dir: FHB Properties Inc, FHI Intl Inc, First Hawaiian Creditcorp Inc, First Hawaiian Ctr Inc, First Hawaiian Leasing Inc, First Hawaiian Overseas Corp, First Interstate HI Bank *NONPR AFFIL* mem: Am Inst CPAs, Fin Execs Inst, Natl Assn Accts

Gerald M. Pang: dir *B* Honolulu HI 1948 *ED* Univ HI 1970 *CURR EMPL* exec vp wholesale loan group: First Hawaiian Bank

Norwood W. Pope: dir

Herbert E. Wolff: secy, dir *B* Cologne Germany 1925 *ED* Rutgers Univ BA 1953; Univ MD BS 1957; George Washington Univ MA 1962 *CURR EMPL* sr vp, secy: First Hawaiian Inc *CORP AFFIL* secy: First Hawaiian Creditcorp Inc; sr vp, secy: First Hawaiian Bank *NONPR AFFIL* bd dirs: Un Svc Orgs; dir: Girl Scouts US; mem: Am Bankers Assn, Am Soc Corp Secys, Assn US Army, First Cavalry Div Assn, First Infantry Div Assn, HI Comm Foreign Rels, Phi Kappa Phi, Silver Jubilee Comm St HI, US Army Mus Soc; mem exec bd: Boy Scouts Am Aloha Counc; pres: HI Army Mus Soc, Pacific Asian Aff Counc *CLUB AFFIL* Plz, Rotary, Waialae CC

APPLICATION INFORMATION

Initial Approach: *Initial Contact:* letter of request with specific details *Include Information On:* description of the organization, amount requested, project budget, purpose for which funds are sought, recently audited financial statement, proof of tax-exempt status *Deadlines:* none

Restrictions on Giving: Company will only fund organizations with tax-exempt status.

GRANTS ANALYSIS

Total Grants: $1,325,452

Number of Grants: 93

Highest Grant: $225,000

Average Grant: $14,252

Typical Range: $1,000 to $35,000

Disclosure Period: 1993

Note: Recent grants are derived from a 1993 Form 990.

RECENT GRANTS

General

225,000	Aloha United Way Oahu, Honolulu, HI — social welfare
49,166	ASSETS School for Gifted/Dyslexic Children, Honolulu, HI — capital fund campaign
43,334	Hawaii Pacific University, Honolulu, HI — renovation of Hawaii Loa campus
33,333	North Hawaii Community Hospital, Kamuela, HI — capital campaign
30,000	University of Hawaii Foundation, Honolulu, HI — support of athletic programs

Frear Eleemosynary Trust, Mary D. and Walter F.

CONTACT

Mary D. and Walter F. Frear Eleemosynary Trust
c/o Bishop Trust Co., Ltd.
PO Box 3170
Honolulu, HI 96802
(808) 538-4540

FINANCIAL SUMMARY

Recent Giving: $512,413 (1993); $581,890 (1992); $621,552 (1991)

Assets: $13,078,414 (1993); $12,746,645 (1992); $12,651,006 (1991)

Gifts Received: $78,809 (1991); $18,248 (1988)

Fiscal Note: In 1991, contributions were received from Mary D. and Walter F. Frear Special Trust "A".

EIN: 99-6002270

CONTRIBUTIONS SUMMARY

Donor(s): the late Mary D. Frear and Walter F. Frear

Typical Recipients: • *Arts & Humanities:* Arts Festivals, Arts Funds, Community Arts, Dance, Libraries, Museums/Galleries, Music, Opera, Public Broadcasting, Theater • *Civic & Public Affairs:* Botanical Gardens/Parks, General, Law & Justice • *Education:* Arts/Humanities Education, Business Education, Colleges & Universities, Eco-

nomic Education, Faculty Development, Literacy, Preschool Education, Private Education (Precollege), Secondary Education (Private), Student Aid • *Environment:* General • *Health:* Hospitals, Medical Rehabilitation, Medical Research • *Religion:* Churches, Religious Organizations, Religious Welfare • *Science:* Scientific Centers & Institutes • *Social Services:* Child Welfare, Community Centers, Community Service Organizations, Day Care, Food/Clothing Distribution, Recreation & Athletics, United Funds/United Ways, Youth Organizations

Grant Types: capital, general support, multiyear/continuing support, and operating expenses

Geographic Distribution: focus on HI

GIVING OFFICERS

Bishop Trust Co.: trust

APPLICATION INFORMATION

Initial Approach: Send cover letter and full proposal (four copies). Deadlines are January 15, April 15, July 15, and October 15.

Restrictions on Giving: Does not support individuals.

PUBLICATIONS

Annual Report (including application guidelines)

GRANTS ANALYSIS

Total Grants: $512,413

Number of Grants: 48

Highest Grant: $12,000

Typical Range: $1,000 to $11,000

Disclosure Period: 1993

Note: Recent grants are derived from a 1993 Form 990.

RECENT GRANTS

Library

1,500	Koloa Early School, Kauai, HI — replace books and equipment in the library corner following Hurricane Iniki

General

12,000	Assets School, Honolulu, HI — pledge payment for the capital fund drive
11,000	Hawaii Pacific University, Honolulu, HI — scholarship program
10,000	Island School, Lihue, HI — rebuild the school following Hurricane Iniki
9,000	Assets School, Honolulu, HI — tuition aid program
7,500	Chaminade University of Honolulu, Honolulu, HI — Master of Science in Teaching program

McInerny Foundation

CONTACT

Lois C. Loomis
Contact Person
McInerny Foundation
Hawaiian Trust Company, Ltd.
PO Box 3170
Honolulu, HI 96802
(808) 528-4944

FINANCIAL SUMMARY

Recent Giving: $1,950,000 (fiscal 1995 est.); $1,876,380 (fiscal 1994); $1,785,834 (fiscal 1993)

Assets: $47,000,000 (fiscal 1995 est.); $46,672,037 (fiscal 1994); $39,755,434 (fiscal 1993)

EIN: 99-6002356

CONTRIBUTIONS SUMMARY

Donor(s): The McInerny Foundation was established in 1937, by William H. McInerny and James D. McInerny and their sister, Ella McInerny. They were descendants of Patrick Michael McInerny who arrived in the Hawaiian Islands from Ireland during the mid-nineteenth century whaling period. The first distribution committee of the McInerny Foundation consisted of James and William McInerny. After the death of James in 1945, William constituted the distribution committee until his death in 1947. Since then, as provided in the trust indenture, the distribution committee has consisted of three members appointed by the board of directors of Hawaiian Trust Company, Ltd., corporate trustee of the foundation.

Typical Recipients: • *Arts & Humanities:* Community Arts, Dance, Historic Preservation, History & Archaeology, Libraries, Museums/Galleries, Music, Opera, Performing Arts, Public Broadcasting, Theater • *Civic & Public Affairs:* Botanical Gardens/Parks, Community Foundations, Employment/Job Training, General, Housing, Parades/Festivals • *Education:* Arts/Humanities Education, Colleges & Universities, Economic Education, Education Reform, Elementary Education (Private), Faculty Development, Gifted & Talented Programs, Literacy, Preschool Education, Private Education (Precollege), Public Education (Precollege), Science/Mathematics Education, Special Education, Student Aid • *Environment:* General • *Health:* AIDS/HIV, Cancer, Children's Health/Hospitals, Clinics/Medical Centers, Emergency/Ambulance Services, Health Organizations, Hospices, Hospitals, Medical Rehabilitation, Mental Health, Prenatal Health Issues, Single-Disease Health Associations • *Religion:* Religious Welfare • *Social Services:* Child Welfare, Community Centers, Community Service Organizations, Day Care, Family Planning, Family Services, Food/Clothing Distribution, People with Disabilities, Scouts, Senior Services, United Funds/United Ways, Volunteer Services, YMCA/YWCA/YMHA/YWHA, Youth Organizations

Grant Types: capital, challenge, general support, project, scholarship, and seed money

Geographic Distribution: exclusively Hawaii

GIVING OFFICERS

Haunani Apoliona: alternate mem distribution comm

Gerry Ching: mem distr comm

Henry Benjamin Clark, Jr.: vchmn distribution comm *B* Chevy Chase MD 1915 *ED* Northwestern Univ BCS 1937; Harvard Univ MBA 1940 *NONPR AFFIL* chmn: Honolulu Academy Arts; dir: Goodwill Indus, Hanahauoli Sch, Honolulu YMCA, Palolo Chinese Home Rehab Hosp; mem: Academy Pacific, HI Bus Roundtable, HI Chamber Commerce *CLUB AFFIL* Outrigger, Pacific, Pacific-Union

Mark H. Fukunaga: alternate mem distr comm *CURR EMPL* chmn, ceo, dir: Servco Pacific

Lois C. Loomis: contact person *CURR EMPL* vp, secy charitable fdns off: Hawaiian Trust Co Ltd

Thomas J. MacDonald: chmn *B* Providence RI 1940 *ED* Univ RI BA 1962; Stanford Univ MA 1965 *CURR EMPL* pres: Hawaiian Trust Co Ltd *CORP AFFIL* coo, exec vp: Client Svcs Group; dir: Bancorp Investments Group Ltd, Black Devel Corp; pres: Am Fin Svcs HI, Am Trust Co, Bishop Trust Co Ltd *NONPR AFFIL* dir: YMCA Honolulu; pres, dir: Intl Wine & Food Soc; treas, dir: Bank Securities Assn, Un Way Aloha

Thurston Twigg-Smith: alternate mem *B* Honolulu HI 1921 *ED* Yale Univ BA 1942 *CURR EMPL* chmn, pres, ceo, dir: Persis Corp *CORP AFFIL* chmn: Honolulu Advertiser; chmn, ceo: Maryville Alcoa Daily Times, NW Media; dir: Am Fin Svcs HI, Am Savings Bank, Am Trust Co HI, HI Electric Co Inc *NONPR AFFIL* mem: Honolulu Chamber Commerce; trust: Contemporary Mus, Honolulu Acad Arts, Punahou Sch, Yale Univ Art Gallery *CLUB AFFIL* Oahu CC, Outrigger Canoe, Pacific, Waialae CC *PHIL AFFIL* pres: Persis Hawaii Foundation; dir: Twigg-Smith Art Foundation

APPLICATION INFORMATION
Initial Approach:

Applicants seeking capital grants, tuition aid (schools only), or scholarships (schools only) should contact the foundation to obtain required questionnaires. Organizations requesting general support should first contact the foundation office to ascertain whether a project falls within the foundation's stated goals and focus. If it does, the organization will be asked to submit a proposal.

The proposal should include a letter of not more than three pages, signed by the presiding officer of the board of directors of the organization, containing a summary of the proposed activity, amount needed from the foundation, list of other funding sources, description of how the proposed project is to be carried out, indication of the population to be benefited, and a plan for evaluating the project's effectiveness. Financial information should include project and organization budgets, income and expenditure statements, and plans for continued support of the project. The foundation also requires a statement of relevant qualifications of the person(s) responsible for carrying out the project, a statement of active participation of the board members, and the name and telephone number of the contact person. A list of the governing board members and their professional or business affiliations, as well as three or four letters endorsing the activity should accompany the proposal. The above information should include a statement of not more than one page, double-spaced, clearly explaining how the proposed activity will benefit the lives of Hawaii's people and how the people of Hawaii will be adversely affected if the activity is not carried out. Seven copies of the proposal should be included, as well as a single copy of each of the organization's certifications of tax-exempt and non-private foundation status, its charters and by-laws, and its most recently audited financial statement.

There are no deadlines for applications for general support. The distribution committee meets frequently to consider grant proposals. Requests for capital fund drives are considered only at the committee's September meetings. Requests from schools for tuition aid and scholarships are considered only at the committee's March meetings. Complete questionnaires and accompanying proposals should be submitted by January 15 or July 15 for consideration in March or September, as appropriate.

Sixty days are required to process a proposal, allowing for a possible visit to the site and for studying the proposal in relation to other foundation activities. An exception to this schedule is the review of proposals for capital fund drives and school tuition aid and scholarship programs.

Restrictions on Giving: Under the deed of trust, the foundation does not give grants or scholarships to individuals, nor does it provide grants for deficit funding or endowments, or to religious organizations.

OTHER THINGS TO KNOW
Hawaiian Trust Company, Ltd. is the foundation's corporate trustee.

PUBLICATIONS
Annual report

GRANTS ANALYSIS
Total Grants: $1,876,380

Number of Grants: 133

Highest Grant: $67,500

Average Grant: $14,108

Typical Range: $5,000 to $25,000

Disclosure Period: fiscal year ending September 30, 1994

Note: Recent grants are derived from a fiscal 1993 annual report.

RECENT GRANTS
General

67,500	Child and Family Service, Honolulu, HI — capital campaign
50,000	Punahou School, Honolulu, HI — capital fund drive
50,000	Punahou School, Honolulu, HI — financial aid program
45,500	Hawaii Pacific University, Honolulu, HI — scholarship program
40,000	Chaminade University Educational Foundation, Honolulu, HI — scholarship program

IDAHO

Albertson's Inc.

Revenue: $11.89 billion
Employees: 75,000
Headquarters: Boise, ID
SIC Major Group: Grocery Stores

CONTACT
David I. Connolly
Vice President & Treasurer
Albertson's Inc.
250 Park Ctr. Blvd.
PO Box 20
Boise, ID 83726
(208) 385-6334

FINANCIAL SUMMARY
Recent Giving: $2,650,000 (1995 est.); $2,500,000 (1994 approx.); $2,100,000 (1993 approx.)

Fiscal Note: Company gives directly. Above figures include nonmonetary support.

CONTRIBUTIONS SUMMARY
Typical Recipients: • *Arts & Humanities:* Arts Appreciation, Arts Centers, Community Arts, Historic Preservation, Libraries, Music, Opera, Performing Arts, Public Broadcasting • *Education:* Business Education, Colleges & Universities, Community & Junior Colleges, Economic Education, Elementary Education (Private), Minority Education • *Health:* Emergency/Ambulance Services, Geriatric Health, Hospitals, Medical Rehabilitation, Mental Health, Public Health • *Social Services:* Child Welfare, Community Centers, Community Service Organizations, Emergency Relief, Food/Clothing Distribution, Senior Services, Shelters/Homelessness, Substance Abuse, United Funds/United Ways, Youth Organizations

Grant Types: capital, conference/seminar, emergency, employee matching gifts, and general support

Note: Employee matching gift ratio: 1 to 1, up to $1000 (for higher education only).

Nonmonetary Support: $1,300,000 (1994)

Nonmonetary Support Types: donated equipment and donated products

Note: Nonmonetary support is provided by the company. Mr. Connolly is the contact person for such support.

Geographic Distribution: headquarters and operating locations

Operating Locations: AR, AZ (Chandler, Phoenix), CA (Brea, Long Beach, Sacramento), CO (Aurora, Denver), FL (Orlando, Plant City), ID (Boise), KS, LA, MT, NE (Omaha), NM, NV, OK (Ponca City), OR (Portland), SD, TX (Ft. Worth, San Antonio), UT (Salt Lake City), WA (Bellevue, Spokane), WY

Note: Company operates fifteen divisions in locations listed above.

CORP. OFFICERS
John Blythe Carley: *B* Spokane WA 1934 *ED* Boise Jr Coll AA 1955; Univ WA 1956-1957; Stanford Univ Exec Program 1973 *CURR EMPL* pres, coo, dir: Albertsons Inc *CLUB AFFIL* Arid, Hillcrest CC

A. Craig Olson: *B* 1951 *ED* Univ ID BS 1974 *CURR EMPL* cfo, sr vp fin: Albertsons Inc

Michael Read: *CURR EMPL* dir pub aff: Albertsons Inc

GIVING OFFICERS
David I. Connolly: *B* Juntura OR 1934 *ED* Univ OR BS 1957; Harvard Univ 1977 *CURR EMPL* vp, treas: Albertsons Inc *NONPR AFFIL* mem: Admin Mgmt Soc, Boise Area Econ Devel Counc, Fin Execs Inst, Natl Assn Accts, Natl Assn Corp Treas

APPLICATION INFORMATION
Initial Approach: *Initial Contact:* brief letter of inquiry *Include Information On:* description of the organization, amount requested, purpose of funds sought, recently audited financial statement, and proof of tax-exempt status *Deadlines:* none

Restrictions on Giving: Does not support religious organizations for sectarian purposes, or political or lobbying groups.

PUBLICATIONS
Contributions Policy and Procedures

Boise Cascade Corporation

Revenue: $4.14 billion
Employees: 17,362
Headquarters: Boise, ID
SIC Major Group: Sawmills & Planing Mills—General, Softwood Veneer & Plywood, Structural Wood Members Nec, and Reconstituted Wood Products

CONTACT
Connie E. Weaver
Contributions Administrator
Boise Cascade Corp.
PO Box 50
Boise, ID 83728-0001
(208) 384-7673

FINANCIAL SUMMARY
Recent Giving: $500,000 (1993 approx.); $1,000,000 (1992); $1,017,000 (1991)

Fiscal Note: Totals include cash contributions (about 90%) and nonmonetary support (about 10%). Company reported in early 1992 that giving had been temporarily curtailed. See "Other Things To Know" for more details.

CONTRIBUTIONS SUMMARY
Typical Recipients: • *Arts & Humanities:* Community Arts, Dance, Libraries, Museums/Galleries, Music, Opera, Performing Arts, Theater • *Civic & Public Affairs:* Business/Free Enterprise, Civil Rights, Economic Development, Economic Policy, Public Policy, Women's Affairs, Zoos/Aquariums • *Education:* Business Education, Colleges & Universities, Community & Junior Colleges, Economic Education, Engineering/Technological Education, Literacy, Minority Education, Special Education • *Environment:* General • *Health:* Emergency/Ambulance Services, Hospitals • *Social Services:* Community Centers, Homes, Recreation & Athletics, Senior Services, Substance Abuse, United Funds/United Ways, Youth Organizations

Grant Types: capital, employee matching gifts, and project

Nonmonetary Support: $50,000 (1992); $300,000 (1989); $115,000 (1988)

Nonmonetary Support Types: donated equipment and donated products

Geographic Distribution: principally near operating locations

Operating Locations: AL, AR, AZ, CA, CO, CT, FL, GA, HI, ID, IL, IN, KS, KY, LA, MA, MD, ME, MI, MN, MO, MT, NC, NJ, NV, NY, OH, OR, PA, SC, TN, TX, UT, WA, WI

CORP. OFFICERS
John Bruce Fery: *B* Bellingham WA 1930 *ED* Univ WA BA 1953; Stanford Univ MBA 1955 *CURR EMPL* chmn, ceo, dir, coo: Boise Cascade Corp *CORP AFFIL* dir: Albertsons Inc, Boeing Co, Hewlett-Packard Co, W One Bancorp *NONPR AFFIL* bd govs, mem exec comm: Natl Counc Air & Stream Improvement; chmn: ID Commun Fdn; dir mem exec comm: Am Forest & Paper Assn; dir, mem exec comm: Am Paper Inst; mem: Bus Counc *CLUB AFFIL* Arid, Arlington, Hillcrest CC, Links

John Henry Wasserlein: *B* Evergreen Park IL 1941 *ED* MA Inst Tech BSME 1963 *CURR EMPL* pres, dir: Boise Cascade Canada Ltd *CORP AFFIL* dir: Noranda Forest USA; pres, dir: Fraser Paper Ltd; sr vp, gen mgr publs: Boise Cascade Corp *NONPR AFFIL* dir: Canada Pulp & Paper Assn; mem: Am Mgmt Assn, Am Paper Inst, ASME, Chi Phi, Fourdinier Kraft Bd Group, Intl Bicycle Touring Soc, Mensa, Natl Rifle Assn, Paper Indus Mgmt Assn, Pi Tau Sigma, TAPPI

GIVING OFFICERS
Connie Weaver: *CURR EMPL* contributions admin: Boise Cascade Corp

APPLICATION INFORMATION
Initial Approach: *Initial Contact:* local community organizations: write to nearest Boise Cascade facility; colleges and universities where company recruits potential employees: write to Connie Weaver, contributions administrator, Boise Cascade Corp; application forms available from most Boise Cascade offices *Include Information On:* description of the organization and its purpose; proof of tax-exempt status; list of officers and directors; current operating budget and sources of funding; recently audited financial statement or most recent Form 990; purpose of grant; project budget and estimated fund-raising costs; and sources of funding, both committed and proposed *Deadlines:* none

Restrictions on Giving: Company does not support organizations located in areas where the company has few or no operations; individuals; private foundations; international organizations; fraternal, social, labor, or veterans organizations; requests of a political nature and organizations or programs that are sensitive, controversial, harmful, or which pose a potential conflict of interest for the company; operating expenses of United Way member agencies; school trips or tours; courtesy advertising; testimonial dinners; loans or investments; or churches or religious organizations.

Company generally will not support memorials, grants to cover operating deficits, or projects that are primarily fund-raising events; organizations that channel funds to donee agencies, except for United Way; or endowments at educational institutions or funds or associations whose sole purpose is to raise funds for educational institutions or other organizations.

OTHER THINGS TO KNOW
Company reported in early 1992 that giving has been temporarily suspended. Funds have been limited to previously-committed long-terms pledges and to the United Way.

Priority is given to organizations and programs in communities where the company operates and to those in which company employees are involved.

PUBLICATIONS
Guidelines

GRANTS ANALYSIS
Total Grants: $500,000*

Typical Range: $1,000 to $10,000

Disclosure Period: 1993

Note: Total grants figure is an approximation. Recent grants are derived from a 1990 grants list.

RECENT GRANTS
Library
250,000   Gonzaga University — to establish a regional library

General
500,000   University of Washington College of Forestry Resources, Seattle, WA — Pulp and Paper Program

150,000	Lake of the Woods Hospital, Kenora, ON, Canada
30,000	Boys and Girls Club, Salem, OR
25,000	Community Hospital, Council, ID
25,000	Primary Children's Medical Center, Salt Lake City, UT — to help build a new hospital serving the Intermountain West

CHC Foundation

CONTACT
Joan C. Hahn-Struhs
President
CHC Fdn.
PO Box 1644
Idaho Falls, ID 83403
(208) 522-2368

FINANCIAL SUMMARY
Recent Giving: $417,988 (1993); $399,420 (1992); $343,139 (1991)

Assets: $11,484,318 (1993); $11,102,722 (1992); $10,850,615 (1991)

EIN: 82-0211282

CONTRIBUTIONS SUMMARY
Typical Recipients: • *Arts & Humanities:* Arts Associations & Councils, History & Archaeology, Libraries, Theater • *Civic & Public Affairs:* Clubs, Economic Development, Employment/Job Training, General, Municipalities/Towns, Professional & Trade Associations, Safety, Zoos/Aquariums • *Education:* Education Funds, Public Education (Precollege) • *Environment:* General, Wildlife Protection • *Health:* Emergency/Ambulance Services, Health Organizations, Hospitals • *Religion:* Religious Organizations • *Science:* Scientific Centers & Institutes • *Social Services:* At-Risk Youth, Child Welfare, Community Service Organizations, Counseling, Crime Prevention, Domestic Violence, Family Planning, Family Services, General, Homes, Recreation & Athletics, Scouts, Senior Services, Substance Abuse

Grant Types: general support

Geographic Distribution: limited to ID; majority of grants in greater eastern ID region

GIVING OFFICERS
Milton F. Adam: secy

Donald R. Bjornson, MD: mem

Joan Chesbro: mem

Ernest C. Craner: mem

Joan C. Hahn-Struhs: pres

Ralph Isom: mem

Janice C. Matthews: treas

Maureen McFadden: mem

Charles M. Rice: vp

Gerald H. Scheid: mem

Anne S. Voilleque: mem

APPLICATION INFORMATION
Initial Approach: Send brief letter or proposal; proposal cover sheet (form from foundation) required. Proposal must include the following: name and address of organization; name, title, address, and telephone number of submitter or of project director; description of the organization, including background, purpose, objectives, and experience; financial status; proof of tax-exempt status. Must also include detailed information about the project and the project's finances. Applications must be received by February 1st and August 1st. Board meets in February and August. Grant cycles are publicly announced.

Restrictions on Giving: Foundation supports only tax-exempt nonprofit organizations. Foundation does not support individuals; religious groups or churches; political or legislative action groups; athletic teams, bands, trips or tours, or contests and competitions; scholarships; general operating expenses of organizations; annual fund drives; advertising for benefit purposes; general activities not clearly linked to specifici charitable objectives; general planning or work in which achievements cannot be measured; projects that involve the basic delivery of educational services, except for unique or innovatve special programs that serve students or enhance teaching skills or otherwise add a desireable educational dimension not provided by or appropriately printed by regular school operating budgets; national or regional organizations except as may be a specific project or activity within the foundation's region. Foundation prefers short-term projects; will consider longer term projects which demonstrate a potential for ongoing matching funds or operating funding independent of foundation funds.

OTHER THINGS TO KNOW
The CHC Foundation, an independent philanthropic foundation, was created in 1985. Its immediate antecedent was Community Hospital of Idaho Falls, which owned the hospital until 1984.

GRANTS ANALYSIS
Total Grants: $417,988

Number of Grants: 70

Highest Grant: $80,000

Typical Range: $52 to $30,000

Disclosure Period: 1993

Note: Recent grants are derived from a 1993 Form 990.

RECENT GRANTS
Library

4,135	Jefferson Free Library District, Jefferson, ID — Henan-Annis
3,500	Hackay Free Library District, Hackay, ID
1,625	Ririe City Library, Ririe, ID

General

80,000	FAITH, Idaho Falls, ID
40,000	School District 91, Idaho Falls, ID — Skyline teen parenting

26,438	City of Idaho Falls, Idaho Falls, ID — Tautphaus Zoo
20,845	School District 60, Idaho Falls, ID — Hobbs Middle School
20,000	Rigby Area Senior Citizens, Rigby, ID

Daugherty Foundation

CONTACT
Hal Peterson
Trust Manager
Daugherty Fdn.
PO Box 51448
Idaho Falls, ID 83405

FINANCIAL SUMMARY
Recent Giving: $608,130 (1993); $634,799 (1992); $727,081 (1991)

Assets: $4,239,069 (1993); $4,544,969 (1992); $5,082,006 (1991)

EIN: 82-6010665

CONTRIBUTIONS SUMMARY
Donor(s): West One Bank, Idaho, N.A.

Typical Recipients: • *Arts & Humanities:* Arts Associations & Councils, Libraries • *Civic & Public Affairs:* Clubs, Community Foundations, Employment/Job Training • *Education:* Colleges & Universities, Medical Education, Public Education (Precollege) • *Environment:* General • *Health:* Children's Health/Hospitals, Clinics/Medical Centers, Hospitals, Medical Rehabilitation • *Religion:* Churches, Religious Welfare • *Social Services:* Child Welfare, Community Service Organizations, Food/Clothing Distribution, Homes, People with Disabilities, Recreation & Athletics, Special Olympics, United Funds/United Ways, Youth Organizations

Grant Types: general support

Geographic Distribution: focus on eastern ID

GIVING OFFICERS
West One Bank Idaho, N.A.: trust

APPLICATION INFORMATION
Initial Approach: Send brief letter of inquiry describing program or project. Include a description of organization, amount requested, purpose of funds sought, recently audited financial statement, and proof of tax-exempt status. Deadline is July 31.

PUBLICATIONS
Informational Brochure (including application guidelines)

GRANTS ANALYSIS
Total Grants: $608,130

Number of Grants: 23

Highest Grant: $116,626

Typical Range: $1,000 to $9,000

Disclosure Period: 1993

Note: Recent grants are derived from a 1993 Form 990.

RECENT GRANTS

Library
9,000   Idaho Falls Public Library, Idaho Falls, ID — eastern Idaho science and technology MTRL

General
116,626   Elks Rehabilitation Hospital, Idaho Falls, ID — eastern Idaho youth organization
116,626   Epworth Village, Idaho Falls, ID — eastern Idaho youth organization
116,626   Shriners Hospital, Idaho Falls, ID — eastern Idaho youth organization
25,000   Idaho Community Foundation, Boise, ID — eastern Idaho youth organization
25,000   Idaho Falls ISU/IU Center for Higher Education, Idaho Falls, ID — eastern Idaho youth organization

Helms Foundation

CONTACT
John T. Hastings, Jr.
Assistant Secretary and Treasurer
Helms Fdn.
PO Box 10130
Ketchum, ID 83340
(208) 726-5603

FINANCIAL SUMMARY
Recent Giving: $443,599 (fiscal 1994); $356,329 (fiscal 1993); $547,502 (fiscal 1992)

Assets: $3,994,136 (fiscal 1994); $4,482,087 (fiscal 1993); $4,325,833 (fiscal 1992)

EIN: 95-6091335

CONTRIBUTIONS SUMMARY
Donor(s): Helms family, Helms Bakeries

Typical Recipients: • *Arts & Humanities:* Libraries, Museums/Galleries, Music • *Civic & Public Affairs:* General, Philanthropic Organizations • *Education:* Colleges & Universities, General, Private Education (Precollege), Religious Education • *Environment:* Air/Water Quality, General • *Health:* Children's Health/Hospitals, Clinics/Medical Centers, Health Organizations, Hospitals, Research/Studies Institutes • *Religion:* Churches, Ministries, Religious Organizations, Religious Welfare • *Social Services:* Family Planning, Family Services, People with Disabilities, Youth Organizations

Grant Types: general support

Geographic Distribution: focus on CA

GIVING OFFICERS
Elizabeth Helms Adams: vp, secy, treas, trust

Stephen Helms Bell: asst secy, asst treas

John T. Hastings, Jr.: trust, asst secy, asst treas

Peggy Helms Hurtig: pres, trust
Frank J. Kanne, Jr.: trust

APPLICATION INFORMATION
Initial Approach: The foundation reports it only makes contributions to preselected charitable organizations.

GRANTS ANALYSIS
Total Grants: $443,599
Number of Grants: 86
Highest Grant: $126,262
Typical Range: $250 to $28,000
Disclosure Period: fiscal year ending June 30, 1994
Note: Recent grants are derived from a fiscal 1994 Form 990.

RECENT GRANTS
Library
5,000   Ronald Reagan Presidential Foundation, Simi Valley, CA

General
126,262   Thacher School, Ojai, CA
28,000   Bard College, Annandale-on-Hudson, NY
20,500   Calvary Bible Church
11,552   James Madison University, Harrisonburg, VA
11,231   Regent University, Virginia Beach, VA

Morrison Knudsen Corporation / Morrison Knudsen Corporation Foundation

Revenue: $2.5 billion
Employees: 12,850
Headquarters: Boise, ID
SIC Major Group: Holding Companies Nec, Metal Mining Services, Coal Mining Services, and Industrial Buildings & Warehouses

CONTACT
Marlene Puckett
Chairman
Morrison Knudsen Corporation Foundation
One Morrison Knudsen Plz.
Boise, ID 83729
(208) 386-5000

FINANCIAL SUMMARY
Recent Giving: $692,906 (1993); $713,535 (1991)

Assets: $7,489,455 (1993); $8,244,299 (1991)

Gifts Received: $100 (1991)

Fiscal Note: Now contributes through foundation only. In 1991, direct contributions totalled $280,048.

EIN: 82-6005410

CONTRIBUTIONS SUMMARY
Typical Recipients: • *Arts & Humanities:* Arts Centers, Arts Festivals, Community Arts, Libraries, Museums/Galleries, Music,

Performing Arts, Public Broadcasting • *Civic & Public Affairs:* Business/Free Enterprise, Civil Rights, Economic Development, Philanthropic Organizations, Professional & Trade Associations, Public Policy, Safety, Urban & Community Affairs, Zoos/Aquariums • *Education:* Arts/Humanities Education, Colleges & Universities, Education Funds, Private Education (Precollege), Public Education (Precollege), Student Aid • *Environment:* General • *Health:* Emergency/Ambulance Services, Health Organizations, Medical Rehabilitation, Single-Disease Health Associations • *International:* International Relations • *Religion:* Religious Organizations • *Social Services:* Child Welfare, Community Centers, Community Service Organizations, Day Care, Recreation & Athletics, Youth Organizations

Grant Types: employee matching gifts

Note: Foundation makes matching gifts to educational institutions, and matches employees' and spouses' gifts on a one-to-one basis up to $2,000 per person.

Nonmonetary Support Types: donated equipment, in-kind services, loaned employees, and loaned executives

Geographic Distribution: nationally, with a focus on Idaho and operating locations

Operating Locations: AZ (Phoenix), CA (Costa Mesa, Sacramento, San Francisco, Walnut Creek), FL (Fort Lauderdale, Jacksonville), HI (Honolulu), ID (Boise), IL (Chicago), MA (Boston), MD (Columbia), MI (Troy), MT (Billings), NY (Forest Hills, Hormell, New York, Rochester), OH (Cleveland), PA (Mountaintop), TX (Dallas, San Antonio)

Note: Company maintains offices and properties in the United States, Canada, Australia, New Zealand, Micronesia, Melanesia, and Indonesia.

CORP. OFFICERS
Stephen G. Hanks: *B* 1951 *ED* Brigham Young Univ 1970-1975; Univ ID 1975-1978 *CURR EMPL* exec vp fin admin, secy: Morrison Knudsen Corp *CORP AFFIL* secy: MK Pacific Inc; secy, dir: Atascosa Mining Co, Natl Projects Inc, Natl Structures Inc, Western Aircraft Inc

Robert A. Tinsman: *B* 1946 *ED* WI St Univ 1968 *CURR EMPL* chmn: Morrison Knudsen Corp *CORP AFFIL* pres, dir: Atascosa Mining Co, Navasota Mining Co

GIVING OFFICERS
James F. Cleary: treas

Jack Granger: dir *B* 1940 *ED* WA St Univ BS 1963 *CURR EMPL* pres: Natl Projects Inc *CORP AFFIL* dir: MK Pacific Inc; pres, dir: Natl Structures Inc

Stephen G. Hanks: secy *CURR EMPL* exec vp fin admin, secy: Morrison Knudsen Corp (see above)

Daniel J. Kunz: dir *B* 1952

Marlene Puckett: chmn

Marie Sarsten: dir

APPLICATION INFORMATION
Initial Approach: *Initial Contact:* written request no longer than four pages *Include Information On:* activities of the applying organization, specific amount requested, outline of how grant would be used, proof of 501(c)(3) status, and prescribed financial statement *Deadlines:* none

GRANTS ANALYSIS
Total Grants: $692,906

Number of Grants: 594*

Highest Grant: $50,000

Average Grant: $1,167*

Typical Range: $1,000 to $2,500

Disclosure Period: 1993

Note: Number of grants and average grant figures include 240 grants totaling $324,265 awarded to individuals. Recent grants are derived from a 1993 grants list.

RECENT GRANTS

Library

3,000	Smithsonian Institution Library, Washington, DC — Tunnels Exhibition

General

27,433	United Way of Ada County, Ada, OK
25,000	Catholic Schools Foundation Inner-City Scholarship, Boston, MA
12,000	Discovery Center of Idaho, Boise, ID
10,000	Americares, New Canaan, CT
10,000	Catholic University of America, Washington, DC

Ore-Ida Foods, Inc. / Heinz Foundation

Sales: $500.0 million
Employees: 5,300
Parent Company: H. J. Heinz Co.
Headquarters: Boise, ID
SIC Major Group: Food & Kindred Products

CONTACT
Grant Jones
Manager, Public Relations
Ore-Ida Foods, Inc.
220 W Park Center Blvd.
Boise, ID 83706
(208) 383-6100

CONTRIBUTIONS SUMMARY
Typical Recipients: • *Arts & Humanities:* Arts Funds, Dance, General, Libraries, Museums/Galleries, Music, Performing Arts, Public Broadcasting • *Civic & Public Affairs:* General, Philanthropic Organizations, Professional & Trade Associations, Zoos/Aquariums • *Education:* Agricultural Education, Colleges & Universities, Elementary Education (Private), General, Literacy, Preschool Education, Private Education (Precollege), Public Education (Precollege) • *Health:* Hospitals, Nutrition • *Social Services:* Day Care, Family Services,

Food/Clothing Distribution, Shelters/Homelessness, Volunteer Services, Youth Organizations

Grant Types: employee matching gifts and scholarship

Nonmonetary Support Types: donated equipment and in-kind services

Geographic Distribution: in headquarters and operating communities

Operating Locations: ID (Boise), OR, WI

CORP. OFFICERS
Richard M. Wamhoff: *CURR EMPL* pres: Ore-Ida Foods

APPLICATION INFORMATION
Initial Approach: Send a brief letter of inquiry. Include a description of organization, amount requested, purpose of funds sought, recently audited financial statement, and proof of tax-exempt status.

Restrictions on Giving: Does not support individuals, religious organizations for sectarian purposes, or political or lobbying groups.

OTHER THINGS TO KNOW
Company gives through its parent company's foundation, the Heinz Foundation. Profile reflects Ore-Ida's priorities.

GRANTS ANALYSIS
Typical Range: $2,500 to $5,000

RECENT GRANTS

General

100,000	College of Idaho, Caldwell, ID — scholarship funds

West One Bancorp

Revenue: $599.83 million
Employees: 4,000
Headquarters: Boise, ID
SIC Major Group: Bank Holding Companies and State Commercial Banks

CONTACT
MelloDee Thornton
Assistant Vice President Community Affairs
West One Bancorp
PO Box 8247
Boise, ID 83733
(208) 383-7275
Note: An alternate address is 101 S Capital Blvd., Boise, ID 83733

FINANCIAL SUMMARY
Recent Giving: $1,000,000 (1995 est.); $1,000,000 (1994 approx.); $850,000 (1993 approx.)

Fiscal Note: Company gives directly.

CONTRIBUTIONS SUMMARY
Typical Recipients: • *Arts & Humanities:* Community Arts, Dance, General, Libraries, Museums/Galleries, Music, Opera, Performing Arts, Public Broadcasting, Theater, Visual Arts • *Civic & Public Affairs:* Economic Policy, General, Housing, Law & Justice, Women's Affairs, Zoos/Aquariums • *Educa-*

tion: Agricultural Education, Arts/Humanities Education, Business Education, Elementary Education (Private), General, Literacy • *Health:* Emergency/Ambulance Services, General, Health Policy/Cost Containment, Hospitals • *Social Services:* Community Centers, Community Service Organizations, Domestic Violence, General, Homes, People with Disabilities, Shelters/Homelessness, United Funds/United Ways, Youth Organizations

Grant Types: capital, challenge, employee matching gifts, general support, multi-year/continuing support, and project

Nonmonetary Support Types: donated equipment, in-kind services, loaned employees, and loaned executives

Note: Value of nonmonetary support is unavailable.

Geographic Distribution: primarily at headquarters and operating locations

Operating Locations: ID (Boise), OR (Hillsboro, Portland), UT (Salt Lake City), WA (Bellevue)

CORP. OFFICERS
D. Michael Jones: *CURR EMPL* pres: W One Bancorp

Daniel Raymond Nelson: *B* Spokane WA 1938 *ED* WA St Univ 1962 *CURR EMPL* chmn, ceo, dir: W One Bancorp *CORP AFFIL* chmn, dir: W One Bank ID

GIVING OFFICERS
MelloDee Thornton: *CURR EMPL* asst vp commun aff: W One Bancorp

APPLICATION INFORMATION
Initial Approach: *Initial Contact:* brief letter requesting copy of contributions request form *Include Information On:* description of the organization; amount requested; purpose of funds sought; recently audited financial statements; list of board of directors; list of other corporate and major donors, including contribution amounts; and proof of tax-exempt status *Deadlines:* none *Note:* Completed form is to be returned with other requested information.

Restrictions on Giving: Does not support individuals, private foundations, international or fraternal organizations, service or veteran's organizations, beauty or talent contests, general operating expenses of United Way organizations, national disease-related organizations, athletic team events, direct support of religious groups, organizations outside of operating areas, or political or lobbying groups.

PUBLICATIONS
Contributions guidelines

GRANTS ANALYSIS
Total Grants: $1,000,000*

Typical Range: $1,000 to $2,500

Disclosure Period: 1994

Note: Total grants figure is approximate.

Whiting Foundation, Macauley and Helen Dow

CONTACT
Macauley Whiting
President
Macauley and Helen Dow Whiting Fdn.
PO Box 1980
Sun Valley, ID 83353
(208) 622-9331

FINANCIAL SUMMARY
Recent Giving: $172,500 (1993); $151,500 (1992); $233,462 (1991)

Assets: $4,316,928 (1993); $3,467,638 (1992); $4,122,871 (1991)

EIN: 23-7418814

CONTRIBUTIONS SUMMARY
Typical Recipients: • *Arts & Humanities:* Ballet, Dance, Libraries, Music, Public Broadcasting • *Civic & Public Affairs:* Municipalities/Towns, Zoos/Aquariums • *Education:* Colleges & Universities, Economic Education, Education Funds, Private Education (Precollege) • *Environment:* General, Resource Conservation • *Health:* Clinics/Medical Centers, Hospitals

Grant Types: general support

Geographic Distribution: gives throughout the United States

GIVING OFFICERS
Helen Dow Whiting: treas, trust

Macauley Whiting: pres, trust

Mary Macauley Whiting: secy, trust

Sara Whiting: trust

APPLICATION INFORMATION
Initial Approach: Send brief letter of inquiry describing program or project. Include a description of organization, amount requested, purpose of funds sought, recently audited financial statement, and proof of tax-exempt status. There are no deadlines.

Restrictions on Giving: Does not support individuals.

GRANTS ANALYSIS
Total Grants: $172,500

Number of Grants: 12

Highest Grant: $46,000

Typical Range: $5,000 to $25,000

Disclosure Period: 1993

Note: Recent grants are derived from a 1993 Form 990.

RECENT GRANTS

Library
12,500	Winter Park Public Library
8,000	Community Library Association, Ketchum, ID

General
46,000	Hotchkiss School, Lakesville, CT
25,000	Trinity Preparatory School, Winter Park, FL
20,000	Northwood University, Midland, MI
10,000	Blaine County School District Education Fund, Hailey, IN
10,000	Methodist Hospital, Los Angeles, CA

Whittenberger Foundation, Claude R. and Ethel B.

CONTACT
William J. Rankin
Chairman
Claude R. and Ethel B. Whittenberger Fdn.
PO Box 1073
Caldwell, ID 83605
(208) 459-4649

FINANCIAL SUMMARY
Recent Giving: $207,043 (1993); $228,785 (1992); $205,189 (1990)

Assets: $4,135,266 (1993); $3,787,896 (1992); $2,884,376 (1990)

EIN: 23-7092604

CONTRIBUTIONS SUMMARY
Donor(s): the late Ethel B. Whittenberger

Typical Recipients: • *Arts & Humanities:* Arts Associations & Councils, Arts Outreach, Ballet, Community Arts, Dance, History & Archaeology, Libraries, Literary Arts, Museums/Galleries, Music, Public Broadcasting, Theater • *Civic & Public Affairs:* Botanical Gardens/Parks, Community Foundations, Economic Development, Hispanic Affairs, Housing, Law & Justice, Municipalities/Towns, Nonprofit Management • *Education:* Arts/Humanities Education, Business Education, Colleges & Universities, Economic Education, Education Funds, Education Reform, Elementary Education (Public), Faculty Development, Gifted & Talented Programs, Minority Education, Public Education (Precollege), Secondary Education (Public), Student Aid • *Environment:* Resource Conservation, Wildlife Protection • *Social Services:* At-Risk Youth, Child Abuse, Child Welfare, Community Service Organizations, Day Care, Family Services, Scouts, Substance Abuse, United Funds/United Ways, Youth Organizations

Grant Types: general support and scholarship

Geographic Distribution: limited to ID

GIVING OFFICERS
Margaret Gigray: treas

D. Whitman Jones: dir

Joe Miller: secy

Donald Price: dir

William J. Rankin: chmn

APPLICATION INFORMATION
Initial Approach: Send outline and budget of project. There are no deadlines.

Restrictions on Giving: Limited to qualified Idaho organizations.

PUBLICATIONS
Application Guidelines, Informational Brochure

GRANTS ANALYSIS
Total Grants: $207,043

Number of Grants: 40

Highest Grant: $41,410

Typical Range: $1,000 to $8,000

Disclosure Period: 1993

Note: Recent grants are derived from a 1993 Form 990.

RECENT GRANTS

Library
2,500	Caldwell Public Library, Caldwell, ID — foundation center

General
41,410	Albertson College, Caldwell, OH — scholars program
30,000	City of Caldwell, Caldwell, OH — city improvement projects
9,189	Caldwell Fine Arts, Caldwell, ID — student enrichment
8,500	Hispanic Issues Committee, Caldwell, ID — ending discrimination program
8,193	School District 139, Caldwell, ID — drug prevention

ILLINOIS

Abbott Laboratories / Abbott Laboratories Fund

Revenue: $9.15 billion
Employees: 49,700
Headquarters: Abbott Park, IL
SIC Major Group: Pharmaceutical Preparations, Medicinals & Botanicals, X-Ray Apparatus & Tubes, and Laboratory Apparatus & Furniture

CONTACT
Cindy Schwab
Vice President
Abbott Laboratories Fund
One Abbott Park Rd.
D379/AP6C
Abbott Park, IL 60064-3500
(708) 937-8686

FINANCIAL SUMMARY
Recent Giving: $7,574,243 (1993); $6,000,000 (1992); $4,500,000 (1991)

Assets: $48,448,427 (1993); $55,252,084 (1992); $33,325,399 (1990)

Fiscal Note: Figure for 1993 represents fund giving and $1,070,408 in matching gifts. Figures for 1992 and 1991 include fund contributions, direct giving and matching gifts.

Figures exclude donations to international relief efforts and nonmonetary support.
EIN: 36-6069793

CONTRIBUTIONS SUMMARY

Typical Recipients: • *Arts & Humanities:* Arts Institutes, Community Arts, Dance, General, Historic Preservation, Libraries, Museums/Galleries, Music, Opera, Performing Arts, Public Broadcasting, Theater • *Civic & Public Affairs:* Clubs, Community Foundations, Economic Development, Economic Policy, General, Hispanic Affairs, Housing, Law & Justice, Professional & Trade Associations, Public Policy, Safety, Urban & Community Affairs, Women's Affairs, Zoos/Aquariums • *Education:* Business Education, Colleges & Universities, Community & Junior Colleges, Continuing Education, Education Associations, Engineering/Technological Education, Health & Physical Education, Legal Education, Medical Education, Minority Education, Science/Mathematics Education, Student Aid • *Environment:* General • *Health:* Children's Health/Hospitals, Clinics/Medical Centers, Emergency/Ambulance Services, Geriatric Health, Health Organizations, Heart, Hospices, Hospitals, Kidney, Medical Rehabilitation, Medical Research, Medical Training, Nursing Services, Nutrition, Public Health, Single-Disease Health Associations • *International:* Health Care/Hospitals • *Religion:* Religious Welfare • *Science:* Observatories & Planetariums, Science Museums, Scientific Centers & Institutes, Scientific Research • *Social Services:* Child Welfare, Community Centers, Community Service Organizations, Delinquency & Criminal Rehabilitation, Emergency Relief, Family Services, People with Disabilities, Sexual Abuse, Shelters/Homelessness, Substance Abuse, United Funds/United Ways, Volunteer Services, Youth Organizations

Grant Types: employee matching gifts, general support, and research

Nonmonetary Support: $9,000,000 (1992); $19,200,000 (1991); $5,000,000 (1989)

Nonmonetary Support Types: donated products

Note: Product donations are directed primarily to organizations that support overseas medical missions and hospitals.

Geographic Distribution: in communities where company has significant operations or number of employees

Operating Locations: AZ (Casa Grande), CA (Madera, Mountain View, Santa Clara), IL (Abbott Park, Long Grove, North Chicago), MA (Andover), MI (Sturgis), NC (Laurinburg, Rocky Mount), OH (Ashland, Columbus), PR (Barceloneta), TX (Austin, Dallas, Irving), UT (Salt Lake City), VA (Altavista)

CORP. OFFICERS

Duane Lee Burnham: *B* Excelsior MN 1942 *ED* Univ MN BS 1963; Univ MN MBA 1972 *CURR EMPL* chmn, ceo, dir: Abbott Laboratories *CORP AFFIL* chmn: Abbott Health Products; chmn, dir: Sequoia Turner Corp; dir: Bell Howell Co, Fed Reserve Bank Chicago, RTE Corp, Sara Lee

Corp *NONPR AFFIL* chmn: Emergency Comm Am Trade; dir: Evanston Hosp, Healthcare Leadership Counc, Lyric Opera Chicago; mem: Bus Roundtable; mem adv bd: Northwestern Univ Kellogg Grad Sch Bus Mgmt; trust: Mus Sci Indus, Northwestern Univ *PHIL AFFIL* pres,dir: D.L. & S.E. Burnham Foundation

Gary Patrick Coughlan: *B* Fresno CA 1944 *ED* St Marys Coll BA 1966; Univ CA Los Angeles MA 1967; Wayne St Univ MBA 1971 *CURR EMPL* cfo, sr vp fin: Abbott Laboratories *CORP AFFIL* dir: Blvd Bank Chicago, Pet Inc; sr vp, cfo: Kraft Foodservice Inc *NONPR AFFIL* mem: Conf Bd, Counc Fin Execs, Fin Execs Inst, Pharmaceutical Mfrs Assn; mem bus adv counc: Counc Foreign Rels, De Paul Univ Coll Commerce, Univ IL Chicago *CLUB AFFIL* Econ Chicago

Thomas Richard Hodgson: *B* Lakewood OH 1941 *ED* Purdue Univ BSChE 1963; Univ MI MSE 1964; Harvard Univ MBA 1969 *CURR EMPL* pres, coo, dir: Abbott Laboratories *CORP AFFIL* dir: MacLean Fogg Co; pres, coo: Abbott Health Products *NONPR AFFIL* mem: Chicago Counc Foreign Rels, Univ MI Natl Adv Comm Engg; trust: Rush-Presbyterian-St Lukes Med Ctr *CLUB AFFIL* Chicago, Econ, Harvard Bus Sch Chicago, Knollwood

GIVING OFFICERS

Duane Lee Burnham: dir *CURR EMPL* chmn, ceo, dir: Abbott Laboratories *PHIL AFFIL* pres,dir: D.L. & S.E. Burnham Foundation (see above)

Gary Patrick Coughlan: dir *CURR EMPL* cfo, sr vp fin: Abbott Laboratories (see above)

Kenneth W. Farmer: pres, dir *CURR EMPL* vp admin: Abbott Laboratories

Lael Frederic Johnson: dir *B* Yakima WA 1938 *ED* Wheaton Coll AB 1960; Northwestern Univ Law Sch JD 1963 *CURR EMPL* sr vp, secy, gen couns: Abbott Laboratories *NONPR AFFIL* mem: Am Bar Assn, Assn Gen Couns, Chicago Bar Assn, IL Bar Assn; mem adv comm: IL Secy St Corp Accts; mem corp couns inst: Northwestern Univ Law Sch; mem planning comm: Corp Couns Inst

Paul E. Roge: secy

Cindy A. Schwab: vp

Barry Wojtak: treas *CURR EMPL* treas: Abbott Laboratories

APPLICATION INFORMATION

Initial Approach: *Initial Contact:* brief letter *Include Information On:* description of project, outlining needs and goals; current financial status of project and organization; copy of 501(c)(3) tax-exempt letter; and list of current supporters and donors *Deadlines:* none; contributions committee meets continuously throughout the year

Restrictions on Giving: Does not award grants to individuals, political or lobbying groups, or religious organizations for sectarian purposes; does not support dinners, special events, or goodwill advertising.

OTHER THINGS TO KNOW

Abbott Laboratories Fund is supported by contributions from Abbott Laboratories employees, retirees, and the corporation.

PUBLICATIONS

Abbott Laboratories Fund Contributions Policy

GRANTS ANALYSIS

Total Grants: $7,574,243
Number of Grants: 990*
Highest Grant: $676,561
Average Grant: $6,570*
Typical Range: $1,000 to $10,000
Disclosure Period: 1993

Note: Figures represent foundation giving only. Number of grants figure is approximate. Number of grants and average grant figures exclude $1,070,408 in matching gifts. Recent grants are derived from a 1993 Form 990.

RECENT GRANTS

Library

25,000	Community Library Endowment, Barceloneta, PR

General

676,561	United Way Lake County, Green Oaks, IL
242,442	United Way Franklin County, Columbus, OH
202,500	Museum of Science and Industry, Chicago, IL
125,000	American Red Cross National Disaster Relief Fund, Chicago, IL
100,000	Commercial Club Foundation, Chicago, IL

Akzo America / Akzo America Foundation

Sales: $2.3 billion
Employees: 10,650
Parent Company: Akzo N.V.
Headquarters: Chicago, IL
SIC Major Group: Chemicals & Allied Products, Leather & Leather Products, Petroleum & Coal Products, and Rubber & Miscellaneous Plastics Products

CONTACT

Donna Rogan
Secretary to President
Akzo America
300 S Riverside Plza.
Chicago, IL 60606
(312) 906-7647

FINANCIAL SUMMARY

Recent Giving: $208,386 (1992); $132,575 (1991); $290,669 (1990)

Assets: $193,278 (1992); $165,189 (1991); $84,301 (1990)

Gifts Received: $231,102 (1992); $209,750 (1990); $50,000 (1989)

Fiscal Note: In 1990, contributions were received from Organon Teknika Corporation

($50,000) and Akzo Chemicals, Inc. ($159,750).

EIN: 56-6061194

CONTRIBUTIONS SUMMARY
Typical Recipients: • *Arts & Humanities:* Community Arts, General, Libraries, Music, Opera, Public Broadcasting • *Civic & Public Affairs:* Economic Development, Law & Justice, Philanthropic Organizations, Public Policy, Safety • *Education:* Colleges & Universities, Community & Junior Colleges, Economic Education, Education Associations, General, International Exchange, Minority Education, Science/Mathematics Education, Special Education • *Environment:* General • *Health:* AIDS/HIV, Clinics/Medical Centers, Emergency/Ambulance Services, Health Organizations, Heart, Hospitals, Single-Disease Health Associations • *Social Services:* Community Service Organizations, United Funds/United Ways, Youth Organizations

Grant Types: capital, employee matching gifts, fellowship, matching, and scholarship

Geographic Distribution: in company operating locations

Operating Locations: AL (Birmingham), CA (Los Angeles), CO (Colorado Springs, Denver), DE (Millsboro), GA (Baxley, Norcross), IL (Addison, Chicago, East St. Louis, Morton Grove), KY (Louisville), MI (Manistee), NC (Asheville, Durham, High Point), NJ (Neshanic Station, New Brunswick, West Orange), NY (Burt, New York), OH (Akron, Columbus), OK (Oklahoma City), PA (Clarks Summit), TN (Rockwood), TX (Pasadena), WI (Janesville)

CORP. OFFICERS
Eugene Wilcauskas: *CURR EMPL* pres, dir: Akzo Am

GIVING OFFICERS
Peter Stephen Gold: trust *B* Shelby NC 1941 *ED* Duke Univ 1963; Duke Univ law 1966 *CURR EMPL* vp, gen coun: Akzo Am

Alan B. Graf: trust *CURR EMPL* pres, dir: Akzo Salt Co

Eugene Wilcauskas: trust *CURR EMPL* pres, dir: Akzo Am (see above)

APPLICATION INFORMATION
Initial Approach: At time of publication, contributions policy was under review. No new information was expected until late 1994.

GRANTS ANALYSIS
Total Grants: $208,386
Number of Grants: 29
Highest Grant: $25,000
Typical Range: $500 to $5,000
Disclosure Period: 1992
Note: Recent grants are derived from a 1992 Form 990.

RECENT GRANTS
General

25,000	American Chemical Society, Detroit, MI
19,143	American Red Cross
11,000	Duke University Medical Center, Durham, NC
10,000	United Way of Greater Durham, Durham, NC
5,000	Foreign Student Service Council, Washington, DC

Akzo Chemicals Inc.

Sales: $513.0 million
Employees: 2,100
Headquarters: Chicago, IL
SIC Major Group: Chemicals & Allied Products

CONTACT
Sharon Augustyn
Secretary
Akzo Chemicals Inc.
300 S Riverside Plz.
Chicago, IL 60606
(312) 906-7500

CONTRIBUTIONS SUMMARY
Contributions are made in all major categories of support: arts and humanities, civic and public affairs, education, health, and social services. Also matches grants to cultural and educational institutions.

Typical Recipients: • *Arts & Humanities:* Historic Preservation, Libraries, Museums/Galleries, Music, Public Broadcasting • *Civic & Public Affairs:* Economic Development, Safety • *Education:* Colleges & Universities, Economic Education, Minority Education, Public Education (Precollege), Student Aid • *Health:* Health Organizations, Hospitals, Medical Research, Mental Health, Single-Disease Health Associations • *Religion:* Religious Welfare • *Social Services:* Child Welfare, Community Service Organizations, People with Disabilities, United Funds/United Ways, Youth Organizations

Grant Types: general support and matching

Nonmonetary Support Types: donated equipment, donated products, and workplace solicitation

Geographic Distribution: primarily near headquarters and operating locations

Operating Locations: DE, IL (Chicago), MI, NC, NJ, PA, TN

CORP. OFFICERS
J. S. Kimmel: *CURR EMPL* vp: Akzo Chems

GIVING OFFICERS
Sharon Augustyn: *CURR EMPL* secy: Azko Chem

APPLICATION INFORMATION
Initial Approach: Send a letter prior to August for funding the following year. Include a description of the organization, amount and purpose of funds sought, and proof of tax-exempt status.

Restrictions on Giving: Program does not support fraternal, political, or religious organizations. Goodwill advertising is handled by the Advertising Department.

AMCORE Bank, N.A. Rockford / AMCORE Foundation, Inc.

Assets: $2.1 billion
Employees: 1,100
Parent Company: Amcore Financial, Inc.
Headquarters: Rockford, IL
SIC Major Group: Depository Institutions

CONTACT
Charles E. Gagnier
President
Amcore Foundation
501 7th St., PO Box 1537
Rockford, IL 61110
(815) 961-7500

FINANCIAL SUMMARY
Recent Giving: $157,725 (fiscal 1993); $138,588 (fiscal 1992); $186,395 (fiscal 1991)

Assets: $56 (fiscal 1993); $1,014 (fiscal 1992); $35,531 (fiscal 1990)

Gifts Received: $156,700 (fiscal 1993); $130,400 (fiscal 1992); $150,000 (fiscal 1989)

EIN: 36-6042947

CONTRIBUTIONS SUMMARY
Typical Recipients: • *Arts & Humanities:* Arts Associations & Councils, Dance, General, Historic Preservation, Libraries, Literary Arts, Museums/Galleries, Music, Performing Arts, Theater • *Civic & Public Affairs:* Botanical Gardens/Parks, Business/Free Enterprise, Chambers of Commerce, Clubs, Economic Development, Employment/Job Training, General, Minority Business, Parades/Festivals, Philanthropic Organizations, Public Policy, Safety, Urban & Community Affairs, Women's Affairs • *Education:* Business Education, Colleges & Universities, Community & Junior Colleges, Economic Education, General, Health & Physical Education, Literacy, Minority Education, Preschool Education, Private Education (Precollege), Public Education (Precollege), Secondary Education (Public), Special Education • *Health:* Cancer, Emergency/Ambulance Services, General, Health Organizations, Hospices, Hospitals, Long-Term Care, Mental Health, Nursing Services, Nutrition, Public Health, Single-Disease Health Associations • *Science:* Science Museums • *Social Services:* Child Welfare, Community Centers, Community Service Organizations, Counseling, Crime Prevention, Day Care, Delinquency & Criminal Rehabilitation, Domestic Violence, Emergency Relief, Family Services, Food/Clothing Distribution, General, Homes, People with Disabilities, Scouts, Senior Services, Shelters/Homelessness, Substance Abuse, United Funds/United Ways, Volunteer Services, YMCA/YWCA/YMHA/YWHA, Youth Organizations

Grant Types: capital and general support

Geographic Distribution: focus on Rockford, IL and surrounding communities

Operating Locations: IL (Rockford)

CORP. OFFICERS

Carl J. Dargene: *B* Rockford IL 1930 *ED* Univ SC 1951; Univ IL *CURR EMPL* pres, ceo (until Dec. 1995): Amcore Fin

Charles E. Gagnier: *CURR EMPL* pres, ceo, dir: AMCORE Bank

GIVING OFFICERS

F. Taylor Carlin: dir

Carl J. Dargene: dir *CURR EMPL* pres, ceo (until Dec. 1995): Amcore Fin (see above)

Robert A. Doyle: dir

Charles E. Gagnier: dir *CURR EMPL* pres, ceo, dir: AMCORE Bank (see above)

Robert H. Henry, MD: dir

Robert J. Meuleman: dir *B* South Bend IL 1937 *ED* Univ Notre Dame 1961; MI St Univ 1962 *CURR EMPL* pres, ceo (as of Dec. 1995): AMCORE Fin

William D. Nelson: dir

Richard Nordlof: dir

Michael Tulley: dir

James S. Waddell: adv

APPLICATION INFORMATION

Initial Approach: a brief letter of inquiry. Include a description of organization, amount requested, purpose of funds sought, recently audited financial statement, proof of tax-exempt status, a list of officers and board members, most recent annual report, operating budget for last two years, and a list of other donors. There are no deadlines.

Restrictions on Giving: Does not support individuals, religious organizations for sectarian purposes, political or lobbying groups, organizations outside operating areas, or loans of any kind. It does support organizations located in the company's immediate market area.

GRANTS ANALYSIS

Total Grants: $157,725

Number of Grants: 42

Highest Grant: $55,000

Typical Range: $200 to $30,000

Disclosure Period: fiscal year ending November 30, 1993

Note: Recent grants are derived from a fiscal 1993 Form 990.

RECENT GRANTS

General

55,000	United Way Services, Rockford, IL
17,000	Rockford Public Schools Foundation, Rockford, IL
10,000	Davis Memorial Park Board, Rockford, IL
7,000	Rockford College, Rockford, IL
5,000	Milestone, Rockford, IL

American National Bank & Trust Co. of Chicago / American National Bank & Trust Co. of Chicago Foundation

Employees: 2,015
Parent Company: First Chicago Corp.
Headquarters: Chicago, IL
SIC Major Group: National Commercial Banks

CONTACT

Joan M. Klaus
Foundation Director, Trustee
American National Bank & Trust Co. of
　Chicago Foundation
33 N LaSalle St.
Chicago, IL 60690
(312) 661-6115

FINANCIAL SUMMARY

Recent Giving: $1,200,000 (1995 est.); $1,075,000 (1994 approx.); $15,500 (1993)

Assets: $828,595 (1993); $18,164 (1992); $220,196 (1991)

Gifts Received: $825,000 (1993); $782,250 (1992)

Fiscal Note: All contributions are made through the foundation. Above figures exclude nonmonetary support. In 1993, the foundation received gifts from American National Bank & Trust Company of Chicago and the Beatrice Delaney Trust.

EIN: 36-6052269

CONTRIBUTIONS SUMMARY

Typical Recipients: • *Arts & Humanities:* Arts Associations & Councils, Arts Centers, Arts Funds, Arts Institutes, Community Arts, Dance, History & Archaeology, Libraries, Museums/Galleries, Music, Opera, Public Broadcasting, Theater, Visual Arts • *Civic & Public Affairs:* African American Affairs, Chambers of Commerce, Economic Development, General, Housing, Law & Justice, Nonprofit Management, Parades/Festivals, Philanthropic Organizations, Urban & Community Affairs, Women's Affairs, Zoos/Aquariums • *Education:* Colleges & Universities, Education Funds, Engineering/Technological Education, Health & Physical Education, Minority Education, Private Education (Precollege), Science/Mathematics Education, Social Sciences Education, Special Education • *Health:* Alzheimers Disease, Cancer, Clinics/Medical Centers, Diabetes, Eyes/Blindness, Health Funds, Hospices, Hospitals, Medical Rehabilitation, Medical Research, Single-Disease Health Associations • *International:* International Relations • *Religion:* Jewish Causes, Ministries • *Science:* Science Museums • *Social Services:* Child Welfare, Community Centers, Community Service Organizations, Domestic Violence, Family Services, Food/Clothing Distribution, Homes, People with Disabilities, Recreation & Athletics, Shelters/Homelessness, United Funds/United Ways, Youth Organizations

Grant Types: capital, employee matching gifts, and general support

Geographic Distribution: within the six-county Chicago metropolitan area

Operating Locations: IL (Chicago)

CORP. OFFICERS

Alan F. Delp: *B* 1934 *CURR EMPL* pres, ceo, dir: Am Natl Bank & Trust Co Chicago *CORP AFFIL* pres, ceo: Am Natl Corp

Leo Francis Mullin: *B* Concord MA 1943 *ED* Harvard Univ AB 1964; Harvard Univ MS 1965; Harvard Univ Grad Sch Bus Admin MBA 1967 *CURR EMPL* chmn: Am Natl Bank & Trust Co Chicago *CORP AFFIL* chmn: Am Natl Corp; pres, coo, dir: First Chicago Corp, First Natl Bank Chicago *NONPR AFFIL* dir: Childrens Meml Hosp, Juvenile Diabetes Assn, Metro Planning Counc; mem: Assn Reserve City Bankers, Bankers Roundtable, Harvard Univ Alumni Assn, IL Bankers Assn; treas: Chicago Econ Devel Commn; trust: Field Mus Natural History, Northwestern Univ; vchmn: Urban League Chicago *CLUB AFFIL* Chicago, Econ, Harvard

GIVING OFFICERS

Alan S. Adams: sr vp

Thomas H. Adams: exec vp

David Bender: bond *PHIL AFFIL* vp: Bender Foundation

Samuel Crayton, Jr.: CRA

Joan Klaus: trust

Timothy P. Moen: chmn *B* San Antonio TX *ED* Southern Methodist Univ BBA 1974; Southern Methodist Univ MBA 1975 *CURR EMPL* exec vp human: Am Natl Bank & Trust Co Chicago

Leo Francis Mullin: trust *CURR EMPL* chmn: Am Natl Bank & Trust Co Chicago (see above)

John F. Reuss: trust *CURR EMPL* exec vp treas dept: Am Natl Bank & Trust Co Chicago

APPLICATION INFORMATION

Initial Approach: *Initial Contact:* send annual report and letter requesting application form *Include Information On:* statement of purpose; amount requested; description of current program activities, accomplishments, and future plans; statement of revenues and expenditures; current annual budget; proof of tax-exempt status; list of board members; list of corporate donors in previous calendar year and the amounts of their contributions *Deadlines:* none; proposals are reviewed continuously throughout the year

Restrictions on Giving: Foundation does not support organizations outside the six-county Chicago metropolitan area; individuals; propaganda influencing legislation or election of candidates to public office; sectarian religious organizations; the purchase of advertising in program books; contributions to eliminate operating deficits; or start-up ventures.

Except in circumstances of special need, the foundation does not support primary, elementary, or secondary education.

OTHER THINGS TO KNOW

Upon expiration of any pledge, the contributions committee conducts an in-depth review of recipients's program before additional funding is approved.

Foundation trustees have determined that the foundation's contributions should be measured by earnings of the sponsoring corporation rather than by the foundation's earnings. The corporation will make contributions to the foundation as necessary to maintain it at a minimum of about $1.0 million.

GRANTS ANALYSIS

Total Grants: $1,075,000

Number of Grants: 450

Highest Grant: $260,000

Average Grant: $1,500

Typical Range: $250 to $10,000

Disclosure Period: 1994

Note: Above figures provided by the company. Recent grants are derived from a 1993 Form 990.

RECENT GRANTS

General

3,080	Lutheran Outdoor Ministries, Chicago, IL
2,400	Sabin School, Chicago, IL
2,108	Lutheran Outdoor Ministries, Chicago, IL
1,500	City Year, Chicago, IL
1,069	Sabin School, Chicago, IL

Amoco Corporation / Amoco Foundation

Revenue: $26.95 billion
Employees: 47,000
Headquarters: Chicago, IL
SIC Major Group: Holding Companies Nec, Crude Petroleum & Natural Gas, Natural Gas Liquids, and Broadwoven Fabric Mills—Manmade

CONTACT

Patricia D. Wright
Executive Director and Secretary
Amoco Foundation
200 E Randolph Dr.
Chicago, IL 60601
(312) 856-6305
Note: For general inquiries contact Ms. Wright. For information on specific programs and where grant proposals should be mailed to, see "Other Things You Should Know."

FINANCIAL SUMMARY

Recent Giving: $20,000,000 (1994 approx.); $19,875,117 (1993); $23,702,088 (1992)

Assets: $73,886,279 (1993); $68,816,244 (1992); $63,800,216 (1991)

Gifts Received: $24,606,250 (1993); $27,047,546 (1992)

Fiscal Note: Most contributions are made through the foundation. Company also administers a direct giving program. Figures include both foundation and direct corporate giving, with direct giving totaling $5.8 million in 1993. Above figures exclude nonmonetary support. Foundation receives contributions from the Amoco Production Company. Figure for 1993 represents donated shares. Figure for 1992 reflects donated shares and $8,091,296 in donated working interest from company shallow rights.

EIN: 36-6046879

CONTRIBUTIONS SUMMARY

Typical Recipients: • *Arts & Humanities:* Arts Centers, Arts Institutes, Ethnic & Folk Arts, Libraries, Museums/Galleries, Performing Arts • *Civic & Public Affairs:* African American Affairs, Business/Free Enterprise, Community Foundations, Economic Policy, Employment/Job Training, Hispanic Affairs, Housing, Law & Justice, Professional & Trade Associations, Public Policy, Urban & Community Affairs, Women's Affairs, Zoos/Aquariums • *Education:* Business Education, Colleges & Universities, Community & Junior Colleges, Engineering/Technological Education, Minority Education, Public Education (Precollege), Science/Mathematics Education, Student Aid • *Environment:* Air/Water Quality, General, Resource Conservation • *Health:* Children's Health/Hospitals, Clinics/Medical Centers, Emergency/Ambulance Services, Hospitals, Single-Disease Health Associations • *International:* Foreign Educational Institutions, Health Care/Hospitals, International Affairs, International Organizations, Missionary/Religious Activities • *Science:* Scientific Organizations • *Social Services:* Child Welfare, Community Service Organizations, Delinquency & Criminal Rehabilitation, General, Homes, People with Disabilities, Recreation & Athletics, United Funds/United Ways, Youth Organizations

Grant Types: capital, employee matching gifts, fellowship, general support, loan, and scholarship

Note: Employee matching gift ratio: 1 to 1.

Nonmonetary Support: $588,230 (1989); $148,900 (1988); $494,000 (1987)

Nonmonetary Support Types: donated equipment and donated products

Note: Nonmonetary gifts are distributed through local corporate divisions.

Geographic Distribution: near operating locations, nationally, and internationally

Operating Locations: AL (Decatur), CO (Denver), GA (Atlanta, Norcross), IL (Chicago, Joliet, Oakbrook), IN (Whiting), LA (New Orleans), SC (Cooper River), TX (Houston, Texas City), VA (Yorktown)

CORP. OFFICERS

R. Wayne Anderson: *CURR EMPL* sr vp human resources: Amoco Corp

John L. Carl: *B* Huntingdon IN 1948 *ED* Purdue Univ BS 1970; Purdue Univ MBA 1972 *CURR EMPL* exec vp, cfo: Amoco Corp *NONPR AFFIL* mem: Am Petroleum Inst, Fin Execs Inst, IN Univ Sch Bus Deans Adv Counc

Patrick Joseph Early: *B* Lincoln NE 1933 *ED* CO Sch Mines BS 1955; Univ W Ontario 1971; Harvard Univ 1980 *CURR EMPL* vchmn, dir: Amoco Corp *NONPR AFFIL* dir: Am Petroleum Inst, Childrens Meml Hosp, Soc Petroleum Engrs; trust: Chicago Mus Sci Indus, Natl Urban League *CLUB AFFIL* Chicago, Econ, Execs, Mid-Am, Naperville CC

Harry Laurance Fuller: *B* Moline IL 1938 *ED* Cornell Univ BSChE 1961; DePaul Univ JD 1965 *CURR EMPL* chmn, pres, ceo, dir: Amoco Corp *CORP AFFIL* dir: Abbott Laboratories Am, Chase Manhattan Bank, Chase Manhattan Corp *NONPR AFFIL* dir: Chicago Rehab Inst, Chicago Un; mem: Am Petroleum Inst, IL Bar Assn; trust: Northwestern Univ Orchestral Assn *CLUB AFFIL* Chicago, Chicago GC, Mid-Am

James M. Griffith: *CURR EMPL* vp pub and govt aff: Amoco Corp

George S. Spindler: *B* Omaha NE 1938 *ED* GA Inst Tech BCE 1961; DePaul Univ JD 1966 *CURR EMPL* sr vp, gen coun exec off: Amoco Corp

Lawrason D. Thomas: *B* 1934 *ED* Univ MI BSCLE 1957; Univ MI MBA 1957 *CURR EMPL* vchmn, dir: Amoco Corp

GIVING OFFICERS

R. Wayne Anderson: chmn, dir *CURR EMPL* sr vp human resources: Amoco Corp (see above)

Jerry M. Brown: dir *B* 1937 *ED* TX A&M Univ BS 1959 *CURR EMPL* vp, exec: Amoco Production Co

John L. Carl: dir *CURR EMPL* exec vp, cfo: Amoco Corp (see above)

Richard E. Evans: dir *CURR EMPL* vp refining: Amoco Oil Co

James M. Griffith: dir *CURR EMPL* vp pub and govt aff: Amoco Corp (see above)

John R. Laubenstein: asst secy

Kevin P. Lynch: dir *CURR EMPL* former pres: Amoco Chem Indonesia Ltd

John S. Ruey: treas

George S. Spindler: pres, dir *CURR EMPL* sr vp, gen coun exec off: Amoco Corp (see above)

Mark E. Thompson: asst treas

Patricia Donovan Wright: exec dir, secy *B* 1952 *ED* Univ WI 1974 *CURR EMPL* mgr corp commun rels: Amoco Corp *NONPR AFFIL* mem: Women Commun *CLUB AFFIL* Publicity Chicago

APPLICATION INFORMATION

Initial Approach: *Initial Contact:* one- or two-page letter *Include Information On:* brief description of the organization (including legal name, primary purpose, and history); specific purpose of grant request and expected benefits; amount requested and evaluative criteria; budget information including annual report or financial statement listing sources of support; most recent IRS Form 990; copy of IRS determination letter; list of board members *Deadlines:* none; foundation prefers to receive applications before September 1 *Note:* In 1991, foundation formed 14 local area contributions committees that evaluate and recommend proposals to the foundation. If organization is located near one, contact its local representative. If request is from another country, contact nearest Amoco facility. A list of area contacts can be found in the foundation annual report.

Restrictions on Giving: Foundation does not provide grants for endowments or loans. Foundation does not support individuals, private foundations, or religious, fraternal, social, or athletic organizations. Ordinarily does not make grants to member agencies of the United Way, except for occasional capital funding.

OTHER THINGS TO KNOW

Contacts for specific programs include the following: John R. Laubenstein, 312-856-2049, for public policy, international, environmental, and higher education programs; Marcene Broadwater, 312-856-5063, for precollege education and other youth programs; Irene Brown, 312-856-6355, for community programs; Iris Cross, 312-856-6651, for Employee Volunteer Programs; and Brian K. Dinges, 312-856-2051, for Retiree Volunteer Programs and matching gifts program.

In 1991, the foundation board directed the formation of contributions committees at 14 Amoco locations in the U.S. to better gauge the local needs and make grant recommendations to the foundation. The foundation recommends that applicants submit their proposal for a preliminary review to the committee located in the same geographic area. A list of the 14 geographic areas is included in the foundation's annual report.

PUBLICATIONS
Amoco Foundation Annual Report

GRANTS ANALYSIS
Total Grants: $19,875,117

Number of Grants: 1,280

Average Grant: $15,527

Typical Range: $1,000 to $25,000

Disclosure Period: 1993

Note: Recent grants are derived from a 1993 grants list.

RECENT GRANTS

Library
Chicago Public Library Foundation, Chicago, IL

General
Academy for Mathematics and Science Teachers, Chicago, IL
Alliance for the Chespeake Bay, Baltimore, MD
Alvin Community College, League City, TX
American Association of Engineering Societies, Washington, DC
American Enterprise Institute for Public Policy Research, Washington, DC

Andreas Foundation

CONTACT
Michael D. Andreas
Vice President
Andreas Fdn.
c/o Doris Carlson Adm. Co.
PO Box 1470
Decatur, IL 62525
800-637-5843

FINANCIAL SUMMARY

Recent Giving: $3,163,235 (fiscal 1992); $3,537,608 (fiscal 1991); $950,525 (fiscal 1989)

Assets: $8,833,868 (fiscal 1992); $2,627,342 (fiscal 1991); $3,140,519 (fiscal 1990)

Gifts Received: $4,837,429 (fiscal 1992); $3,000,000 (fiscal 1991); $4,500 (fiscal 1990)

Fiscal Note: In fiscal 1992, contributions were received from Archer Daniels Midland Company ($4,827,429) and Lowell W. Andreas ($10,000).

EIN: 41-6017057

CONTRIBUTIONS SUMMARY

Donor(s): Dwayne O. Andreas, Lowell W. Andreas, Glenn A. Andreas

Typical Recipients: • *Arts & Humanities:* Arts Festivals, Historic Preservation, Libraries, Music, Theater • *Civic & Public Affairs:* Business/Free Enterprise, Civil Rights, General, Hispanic Affairs, Legal Aid, Public Policy • *Education:* Arts/Humanities Education, Colleges & Universities, Elementary Education (Private), General, Private Education (Precollege), Religious Education, Secondary Education (Public), Student Aid • *Environment:* General • *Health:* Cancer, Clinics/Medical Centers, Emergency/Ambulance Services, Heart, Hospitals, Medical Research, Single-Disease Health Associations • *International:* Missionary/Religious Activities • *Religion:* Churches, Dioceses, Jewish Causes, Missionary Activities (Domestic), Religious Organizations, Religious Welfare • *Social Services:* Emergency Relief, Family Planning, People with Disabilities, Recreation & Athletics, Senior Services, Shelters/Homelessness, Youth Organizations

Grant Types: general support and multi-year/continuing support

GIVING OFFICERS

Dorothy Inez Andreas: trust *CORP AFFIL* dir: Natl City Bancorp

Dwayne Orville Andreas: pres *B* Worthington MN 1918 *ED* Wheaton Coll 1936 *CURR EMPL* chmn, ceo: Archer-Daniels-Midland Co *CORP AFFIL* dir: Columbia Pictures Entertainment, Lone Star

Indus, Salomon Inc; pres: Seaview Hotel Corp *NONPR AFFIL* chmn: Pres Task Force Intl Pvt Enterprise, US-USSR Trade Econ Counc; dir: Boys Club Am; mem: Foreign Policy Assn, Trilateral Commn; trust: Freedom From Hunger Fdn, Hoover Inst, US Naval Acad Fdn, Woodrow Wilson Ctr Intl Scholars *CLUB AFFIL* Blind Brook CC, Friars, Indian Creek CC, Knickerbocker, Links, Minikahda, Union League

Lowell Willard Andreas: exec vp, treas, dir *B* Lisbon IA 1922 *ED* Wheaton Coll 1941; Univ IA *CURR EMPL* chmn fin comm, mem exec comm, dir: Archer-Daniels-Midland Co *CORP AFFIL* dir: Hickory Tech Corp, Natl City Bancorp, Natl City Bank Minneapolis *NONPR AFFIL* mem: Phi Delta Theta *PHIL AFFIL* pres: Archer-Daniels-Midland Foundation

Michael Dwayne Andreas: vp, secy, trust *B* Coral Gables FL 1948 *ED* Northwestern Univ BA 1970 *CURR EMPL* exec vp, dir: Archer-Daniels-Midland *CORP AFFIL* chmn: Golden Peanut Co; dir: Toepfer Intl *NONPR AFFIL* dir: Chicago Bd Trade, Decatur Chamber Commerce *CLUB AFFIL* Decatur CC, Indian Creek CC, Southside CC

Terry Herbert-Burns: trust

Sandra Andreas McMurtrie: trust

APPLICATION INFORMATION

Initial Approach: The foundation reports it only makes contributions to preselected charitable organizations.

Restrictions on Giving: Does not support individuals.

GRANTS ANALYSIS
Total Grants: $3,163,235

Number of Grants: 113

Highest Grant: $1,000,000

Typical Range: $1,000 to $10,000

Disclosure Period: fiscal year ending November 30, 1992

Note: Recent grants are derived from a fiscal 1992 Form 990.

RECENT GRANTS

Library
10,000	Roman Antheneum, New Rochelle, NY

General
1,000,000	We Will Rebuild, Coral Gables, FL
500,000	American Red Cross, Washington, DC
220,000	School for Field Studies, Beverly, MA
205,000	Cell Therapy Research Foundation, Memphis, TN
200,000	Barry University, Miami Shores, FL

AON Corporation / AON Foundation

Revenue: $4.15 billion
Employees: 22,000
Headquarters: Chicago, IL
SIC Major Group: Holding Companies Nec and Insurance Agents, Brokers & Service

CONTACT

Carolyn E. Labutka
Director, AON Foundation
AON Corporation
123 N Wacker Dr.
Chicago, IL 60606
(312) 701-3035

FINANCIAL SUMMARY

Recent Giving: $4,000,000 (1995 est.); $3,200,000 (1994 approx.); $5,090,472 (1993)

Assets: $288,198 (1993); $1,575,703 (1992); $1,345,985 (1991)

Gifts Received: $3,000,000 (1992)

Fiscal Note: Company gives through foundation only. Above figures exclude nonmonetary support. In 1992, contributions were received from AON Corporation and its subsidiaries.

EIN: 36-3337340

CONTRIBUTIONS SUMMARY

Typical Recipients: • _Arts & Humanities:_ Arts Associations & Councils, Arts Festivals, Arts Institutes, Dance, Historic Preservation, Libraries, Museums/Galleries, Music, Opera, Performing Arts, Public Broadcasting, Theater • _Civic & Public Affairs:_ Business/Free Enterprise, Civil Rights, Economic Development, Economic Policy, Employment/Job Training, Law & Justice, Philanthropic Organizations, Public Policy, Safety, Urban & Community Affairs, Zoos/Aquariums • _Education:_ Arts/Humanities Education, Business-School Partnerships, Colleges & Universities, Education Funds, Elementary Education (Private), Faculty Development, Health & Physical Education, Legal Education, Public Education (Precollege), Religious Education, Science/Mathematics Education, Student Aid • _Environment:_ General • _Health:_ AIDS/HIV, Alzheimers Disease, Children's Health/Hospitals, Clinics/Medical Centers, Emergency/Ambulance Services, Health Funds, Hospitals, Medical Rehabilitation, Medical Research, Single-Disease Health Associations • _International:_ International Affairs, International Relations • _Religion:_ Churches, Jewish Causes, Religious Organizations, Religious Welfare • _Science:_ Scientific Centers & Institutes • _Social Services:_ At-Risk Youth, Child Welfare, Community Centers, Community Service Organizations, Counseling, Food/Clothing Distribution, Homes, People with Disabilities, Recreation & Athletics, Refugee Assistance, Senior Services, United Funds/United Ways, Volunteer Services, Youth Organizations

Grant Types: award, capital, challenge, department, employee matching gifts, endow-

ment, general support, operating expenses, and research

Note: Employee matching gift ratio: 1 to 1.

Nonmonetary Support Types: donated equipment

Note: Nonmonetary support is provided by the company and the foundation. The company reports that it donates computer and office equipment.

Geographic Distribution: primarily in operating locations; also internationally

Operating Locations: AK (Anchorage), CA (Los Angeles, Palo Alto, Pasadena), HI (Honolulu), IL (Chicago), IN (Indianapolis), MA (Boston), MN (Minneapolis), MT (Billings), NJ (Old Bridge), NY (Albany, New York), OH (Cleveland), OK (Oklahoma City), OR (Portland), PA (Trevose), TX (Houston), VA (Richmond), WI (Milwaukee)

CORP. OFFICERS

Daniel T. Cox: _B_ 1946 _ED_ Univ NC 1968; Vanderbilt Univ MA 1971 _CURR EMPL_ exec vp: AON Corp _CORP AFFIL_ chmn, dir: Life Ins Co VA; vp, dir: Rollins Hudig Hall Group

Harvey Norman Medvin: _B_ Chicago IL 1936 _ED_ Univ IL BS 1958 _CURR EMPL_ exec vp, treas, cfo: AON Corp _CORP AFFIL_ dir: LaSalle Natl Bank Chicago, LaSalle Natl Corp, Schwarz Paper Co; exec, vp, cfo, dir: Combined Ins Co Am; pres, treas, dir: Ryan Warranty Svcs; sr vp, dir: Globe Life Ins Co; treas, vp: Ryan Ins Group; vp, treas, dir: Rollins Hudig Hall Group _NONPR AFFIL_ bd govs: Chicago Lighthouse Blind; dir: Highland Pk Hosp, Northbrook IL Symphony Orchestra; trust: Ravina Festival Highland Pk

Patrick G. Ryan: _B_ Milwaukee WI 1937 _ED_ Northwestern Univ BS 1959 _CURR EMPL_ chmn, ceo, pres, dir: AON Corp _CORP AFFIL_ chmn: Globe Life Ins Co, James S Kemper & Co, Pat Ryan & Assocs, Ryan Ins Group DE, Union Fidelity Life Ins Co, VA Surety Co; chmn, ceo: Combined Ins Co Am, Rollins Burdick Hunter Co; chmn, pres, ceo: Rollins Hudig Hall Group; dir: Commonwealth Edison Co, First Chicago Corp, First Natl Bank, Gould Inc, Penske Corp; pres: Dearborn Life Ins Co, Riverside Acceptance Corp, Ryan Properties; pres, dir: Abacus Life Ins, Geneva Surety Ins Co, Lincoln-Standard Life Ins Co; vp: Ryan Construction Co MN; vp, dir: AMRA Svcs, Self-Insurers Svc Inc _NONPR AFFIL_ trust: Field Mus Natural History, Northwestern Univ, Rush-Presbyterian-St Lukes Med Ctr _PHIL AFFIL_ vp, dir: Patrick G. and Shirley W. Ryan Foundation

Raymond Inwood Skilling: _B_ Enniskillen England 1939 _ED_ Queens Univ LLB 1961; Univ Chicago JD 1962 _CURR EMPL_ exec vp, chief couns, dir: AON Corp _CORP AFFIL_ exec vp, chief couns; dir: Combined Ins Co Am _NONPR AFFIL_ mem: Am Bar Assn, Chicago Bar Assn, IL Bar Assn; underwriting mem: Lloyds London _CLUB AFFIL_ Casino, Chicago, Econ, Racquet Chicago, Saddle & Cycle

GIVING OFFICERS

Franklin Alan Cole: dir _B_ Park Falls WI 1926 _ED_ Univ IL BA 1947; Northwestern Univ JD 1950 _CURR EMPL_ chmn: Croesus Corp _CORP AFFIL_ dir: Am Natl Bank & Trust Co Chicago, Am Natl Corp, AON Corp, CNA Income Shares, Duff & Phelps Utilitites Income, GATX Corp, Local Initiative Support Corp, Peoples Energy Corp _NONPR AFFIL_ chmn: Chicago Human Rels Fdn; vchmn, trust: Northwestern Univ

Carolyn E. Labutka: dir

Andrew James McKenna: chmn, dir _B_ Chicago IL 1929 _ED_ Univ Notre Dame BS 1951; DePaul Univ JD 1954 _CURR EMPL_ chmn, pres, ceo: Schwarz Paper Co _CORP AFFIL_ bd govs: Chicago Stock Exchange; dir: AON Corp, Dean Foods Co, First Chicago Corp, First Natl Bank Chicago, Lake Shore Bancorp, McDonalds Corp, Skyline Corp, Tribune Co _NONPR AFFIL_ chmn: Univ Notre Dame; dir: Assn Gov Bds Colls & Univs, Catholic Charities Chicago, Childrens Meml Med Ctr, Mus Sci & Indus; trust: La Lumiere Sch _CLUB AFFIL_ Casino, Chicago, Chicago Athletic, Chicago Bears Football, Chicago Natl League Ball, Commercial, Econ, Glen View GC, Island _PHIL AFFIL_ trust: Arthur J. Decio Foundation

Harvey Norman Medvin: treas _CURR EMPL_ exec vp, treas, cfo: AON Corp (see above)

Donald S. Perkins: dir _B_ St Louis MI 1927 _ED_ Yale Univ 1949; Harvard Univ 1951 _CORP AFFIL_ dir: AON Corp, AT&T, Cummins Engine Co Inc, Firestone Tire & Rubber Co, Freeport-McMoran Inc, Inland Steel Indus Inc, Kmart Corp, LaSalle St Fund, GD Searle & Co, Springs Indus Inc, TBG Inc, Time Warner; mem intl counc: Morgan Guaranty Trust Co; trust: Putnam Investors Fund

Arthur Foster Quern: corp secy _B_ Jamaica NY 1942 _ED_ St Johns Univ 1965; SUNY _CURR EMPL_ chmn, ceo: Rollins Burdick Hunter Co _CORP AFFIL_ chmn, dir: RHH/Albert G. Ruben Ins Svcs; chmn, pres, dir: Rollins Hudig Hall Co; dir: Combined Ins Co Am, Life Ins Co VA, Self-Insurers Svc Inc, Union Fidelity Life Ins Co; vp, dir: Rollins Hudig Hall Group _NONPR AFFIL_ chmn, dir: Univ Chicago Hosp _PHIL AFFIL_ dir: Field Foundation of Illinois

Paul I. Rabin: asst treas _B_ Chicago IL 1938 _ED_ Roosevelt Univ 1961 _CORP AFFIL_ asst treas: Am Combined Life Ins Co, AON Auto Capital, AON Capital Corp, AON Corp, Cananwill Inc, Fed Investors Life Ins; treas: AON Speciality Group, CICA Realty Corp, Combined Credit Corp, Combined Premium Fin, Credit Life Ins Co, Godwins Inc, Rollins Burdick Hunter Co, Miller Mason & Dickenson, Rollins Hudig Hall Co, Ryan Ins Group; treas, dir: Dearborn Life Ins Co, Globe Life Ins Co, Rollins Hudig Hall Fl, Ryan Svcs Corp, Union Fidelity Life Ins Co, VA Surety Co; vp, treas: AON Risk Svcs, Combined Life Ins Co, Godwins Intl Holdings _NONPR AFFIL_ mem: Natl Corp Cash Mgmt Assn

Patrick G. Ryan: pres, dir _CURR EMPL_ chmn, ceo, pres, dir: AON Corp _PHIL AF-_

FIL vp, dir: Patrick G. and Shirley W. Ryan Foundation (see above)

Raymond Inwood Skilling: dir *CURR EMPL* exec vp, chief couns, dir: AON Corp (see above)

APPLICATION INFORMATION

Initial Approach: *Initial Contact:* letter or proposal *Include Information On:* name, address, phone number of organization, and name of executive director; one paragraph description of the organization; description of project, including specific objectives, evidence of need, proof that program would not duplicate existing services, and history of organization with such projects; amount requested and purpose of request; list of other potential funding sources and amounts; description of the greatest challenges facing organization in the next two or three years, and evaluation of organization's strengths and weaknesses; list of current contributors and amounts; proof of 501(c)3 status, and annual report *Deadlines:* quarterly: March 31, June 30, September 30, December 31

Restrictions on Giving: Grants are not made to individuals or political organizations.

OTHER THINGS TO KNOW

AON Corporation was formerly Combined International Corporation. The AON Foundation was formerly the Combined International Foundation.

GRANTS ANALYSIS

Total Grants: $5,090,472

Number of Grants: 1,572

Highest Grant: $275,000

Average Grant: $9,815*

Typical Range: $1,000 to $10,000

Disclosure Period: 1993

Note: Average grant figure was supplied by the company and excludes employee matching gifts. The average employee gift is $167. Recent grants are derived from a 1992 Form 990.

RECENT GRANTS

Library
20,000   Newberry Library, Chicago, IL — pledge payment

General
200,000   Boys and Girls Club, Chicago, IL — pledge payment
100,000   Archdiocese of Chicago Big Brothers Shoulders Fund, Chicago, IL — pledge payment
100,000   Boy Scouts of America, Chicago, IL — pledge payment
100,000   Corporate/Community Schools of America, Chicago, IL — support school program
100,000   Northwestern Memorial Foundation, Chicago, IL — pledge payment

Archer-Daniels-Midland Co. / Archer-Daniels-Midland Foundation

Revenue: $11.37 billion
Employees: 14,000
Headquarters: Decatur, IL
SIC Major Group: Prepared Flour Mixes & Doughs, Flour & Other Grain Mill Products, Wet Corn Milling, and Cottonseed Oil Mills

CONTACT

Miranda Rothrock
Grants Coordinator
Archer-Daniels-Midland Foundation
4666 Faries Pkwy.
PO Box 1470
Decatur, IL 62526
(217) 424-2570
Note: Telephone inquiries are strongly discouraged.

FINANCIAL SUMMARY

Recent Giving: $4,287,227 (fiscal 1993); $3,000,000 (fiscal 1992 approx.); $2,728,589 (fiscal 1991)

Assets: $7,424,107 (fiscal 1993); $5,670,685 (fiscal 1991); $3,831,151 (fiscal 1990)

Gifts Received: $9,002,438 (fiscal 1993)

Fiscal Note: Company gives through foundation only. Above figures exclude nonmonetary support. In fiscal 1993, the foundation received 252,700 shares of Saloman, Inc., stock from Archer-Daniels-Midland Co.

EIN: 41-6023126

CONTRIBUTIONS SUMMARY

Typical Recipients: • *Arts & Humanities:* Arts Associations & Councils, Arts Centers, Arts Festivals, Arts Funds, Arts Institutes, Ethnic & Folk Arts, Historic Preservation, Libraries, Museums/Galleries, Music, Opera, Performing Arts, Public Broadcasting, Theater • *Civic & Public Affairs:* Business/Free Enterprise, Civil Rights, Economic Development, Economic Policy, Law & Justice, Public Policy, Rural Affairs, Safety, Urban & Community Affairs, Women's Affairs, Zoos/Aquariums • *Education:* Agricultural Education, Business Education, Colleges & Universities, Community & Junior Colleges, Economic Education, Education Associations, Education Funds, Faculty Development, General, Health & Physical Education, International Studies, Legal Education, Medical Education, Minority Education, Private Education (Precollege), Religious Education, Science/Mathematics Education, Secondary Education (Private), Student Aid • *Environment:* General • *Health:* Cancer, Health Organizations, Hospitals • *International:* Health Care/Hospitals, International Affairs, International Development, International Peace & Security Issues, International Relations, International Relief Efforts • *Religion:* Churches, Jewish Causes, Religious Organizations, Religious Welfare • *Social Services:* Child Welfare, Community Service Organizations, Day Care, Emergency Re-

lief, Family Planning, Food/Clothing Distribution, People with Disabilities, Recreation & Athletics, Senior Services, Substance Abuse, United Funds/United Ways, Volunteer Services, Youth Organizations

Grant Types: employee matching gifts and general support

Note: Employee matching gift ratio: 1 to 1.

Nonmonetary Support Types: donated equipment and loaned employees

Note: Company also loans workspace. Value of nonmonetary support is not available.

Geographic Distribution: emphasis on corporate operating locations, particularly Illinois; also gives nationally

Operating Locations: AL, AR, CA, CO (Arriba, Hugo), FL, GA, IA (Cedar Rapids), IL (Decatur, Farmer City, Oakland), IN, KS (Asherville, Brownell, Canton, Goodland, Kanorado, Longford, Lyons, Minneapolis, Oakley, Palco, Park, Salina, Shawnee Mission), KY, LA (New Orleans), MI (Detroit), MN (Minneapolis), MO, MS, MT, NC, ND, NE (Lincoln), NY, OH, OK (Enid, Texahoma), OR (Portland), PA, SC, TN, TX (Plainview), VA, WA, WI, WY (Albin, Chugwater)

CORP. OFFICERS

Dwayne Orville Andreas: *B* Worthington MN 1918 *ED* Wheaton Coll 1936 *CURR EMPL* chmn, ceo: Archer-Daniels-Midland Co *CORP AFFIL* dir: Columbia Pictures Entertainment, Lone Star Indus, Salomon Inc; pres: Seaview Hotel Corp *NONPR AFFIL* chmn: Pres Task Force Intl Pvt Enterprise, US-USSR Trade Econ Counc; dir: Boys Club Am; mem: Foreign Policy Assn, Trilateral Commn; trust: Freedom From Hunger Fdn, Hoover Inst, US Naval Acad Fdn, Woodrow Wilson Ctr Intl Scholars *CLUB AFFIL* Blind Brook CC, Friars, Indian Creek CC, Knickerbocker, Links, Minikahda, Union League *PHIL AFFIL* pres: Andreas Foundation

Lowell Willard Andreas: *B* Lisbon IA 1922 *ED* Wheaton Coll 1941; Univ IA *CURR EMPL* chmn fin comm, mem exec comm, dir: Archer-Daniels-Midland Co *CORP AFFIL* dir: Hickory Tech Corp, Natl City Bancorp, Natl City Bank Minneapolis *NONPR AFFIL* mem: Phi Delta Theta *PHIL AFFIL* exec vp, treas, dir: Andreas Foundation

John Hancock Daniels: *B* St Paul MN 1921 *ED* Yale Univ BA 1943; Harvard Univ Advanced Mgmt Program 1957 *CURR EMPL* pres: Mulberry Resources *NONPR AFFIL* dir: Bus Counc; mem: Masters Foxhounds Assn Am; trust: Comm Econ Devel *CLUB AFFIL* Grolier, Links, Minneapolis, Sprindale Hall, Woodhill

James R. Randall: *B* 1924 *ED* Univ WI BSCE 1948 *CURR EMPL* pres, dir: Archer-Daniels-Midland Co

Richard P. Reising: *B* 1944 *ED* Univ MO 1969; Stanford Univ BA *CURR EMPL* secy, vp, gen. couns: Archer-Daniels-Midland Co *CORP AFFIL* secy: Tabor Grain Co; vp, dir: Chokee Creek Elevator Co *CLUB AFFIL* CC Decatur

GIVING OFFICERS

Lowell Willard Andreas: pres *CURR EMPL* chmn fin comm, mem exec comm, dir: Archer-Daniels-Midland Co *PHIL AFFIL* exec vp, treas, dir: Andreas Foundation (see above)

Howard G. Buffett: vp, asst to pres

John Hancock Daniels: chmn *CURR EMPL* pres: Mulberry Resources (see above)

Richard P. Reising: secy *CURR EMPL* secy, vp, gen, couns: Archer-Daniels-Midland Co (see above)

Miranda Rothrock: grants coordinator

APPLICATION INFORMATION

Initial Approach: *Initial Contact:* brief letter or proposal—no telephone calls *Include Information On:* description of the organization, amount requested, purpose for which funds are sought, recently audited financial statement, and proof of tax-exempt status *Deadlines:* none

Restrictions on Giving: Does not support individuals.

Generally does not give to united funds except in the form of matching gifts.

GRANTS ANALYSIS

Total Grants: $3,771,629

Number of Grants: 230

Highest Grant: $1,000,000

Average Grant: $16,398

Typical Range: $500 to $50,000

Disclosure Period: fiscal year ending June 30, 1993

Note: Figures exclude 1,544 matching gifts totaling $515,598. Recent grants are derived from a fiscal 1993 Form 990.

RECENT GRANTS

General

1,000,000	Financial Services Volunteer Corps, New York, NY
100,000	American Farmland Trust, Washington, DC
100,000	Anti-Defamation League of B'nai B'rith, Washington, DC
100,000	Anti-Defamation League of B'nai B'rith, Washington, DC
100,000	Business Council of United Nations, New York, NY

Beloit Foundation

CONTACT

Gary G. Grabowski
Executive Director
Beloit Fdn.
11722 Main St.
Roscoe, IL 61073
(815) 623-6600

FINANCIAL SUMMARY

Recent Giving: $1,456,660 (1992); $674,125 (1990); $566,427 (1989)

Assets: $15,489,080 (1992); $13,165,554 (1990); $13,611,890 (1989)

Gifts Received: $10,648 (1989); $17,010 (1988)

EIN: 39-6068763

CONTRIBUTIONS SUMMARY

Donor(s): the late Elbert H. Neese

Typical Recipients: • *Arts & Humanities:* Historic Preservation, Libraries, Museums/Galleries, Music, Theater • *Civic & Public Affairs:* Community Foundations, Economic Development, Employment/Job Training, Housing • *Education:* Agricultural Education, Colleges & Universities, Gifted & Talented Programs, Private Education (Precollege), Science/Mathematics Education, Secondary Education (Public), Student Aid • *Health:* Prenatal Health Issues • *Religion:* Religious Welfare • *Social Services:* Camps, Community Service Organizations, Domestic Violence, Family Planning, Family Services, Recreation & Athletics, Substance Abuse, United Funds/United Ways, Youth Organizations

Grant Types: capital and general support

Geographic Distribution: focus on Beloit, WI

GIVING OFFICERS

Gary G. Grabowski: exec dir, treas, dir *PHIL AFFIL* exec dir, treas: Neese Family Foundation; trust: Warner Electric Foundation

Kim M. Kotthaus: secy

Harry C. Moore, Sr.: dir

Alonzo A. Neese, Jr.: dir

Elbert Haven Neese: pres, dir *B* Chicago IL 1923 *ED* Purdue Univ BS 1944 *CORP AFFIL* dir: First Natl Bank & Trust Co Beloit, Regal-Beloit Corp *NONPR AFFIL* mem: Beloit City Counc; trust: Beloit Coll *PHIL AFFIL* vp, secy: Neese Family Foundation

Laura Neese-Malik: dir

Jane Petit-Moore: dir

APPLICATION INFORMATION

Initial Approach: Send letter requesting application form. There is no deadline.

Restrictions on Giving: Limited to Beloit, WI, stateline area.

GRANTS ANALYSIS

Total Grants: $1,456,660

Number of Grants: 39

Highest Grant: $342,480

Typical Range: $1,000 to $45,000

Disclosure Period: 1992

Note: Recent grants are derived from a 1992 Form 990.

RECENT GRANTS

Library

100,000	Beloit College, Beloit, WI — library

General

342,480	Beloit 2000 Development Corporation, Beloit, WI — property acquisitions
271,035	Beloit YMCA, Beloit, WI — renovation fund raiser
150,000	Beloit College, Beloit, WI — help yourself program
71,124	City of Beloit, Beloit, WI — alternative human services delivery
53,036	Robinson School, Beloit, WI — start-up funding for excel-tech program

Blair and Co., William / Blair and Co. Foundation, William

Employees: 542
Headquarters: Chicago, IL
SIC Major Group: Security & Commodity Brokers

CONTACT

E. David Coolidge III
Managing Partner
William Blair and Co.
222 W Adams St.
Chicago, IL 60606
(312) 236-1600

FINANCIAL SUMMARY

Recent Giving: $377,550 (fiscal 1993); $275,000 (fiscal 1992 approx.); $284,150 (fiscal 1991)

Assets: $1,275,841 (fiscal 1991); $1,096,904 (fiscal 1990); $1,170,521 (fiscal 1989)

Gifts Received: $150,000 (fiscal 1991); $150,000 (fiscal 1990); $125,000 (fiscal 1989)

Fiscal Note: In 1991, contributions were received from William Blair & Company.

EIN: 36-3092291

CONTRIBUTIONS SUMMARY

Typical Recipients: • *Arts & Humanities:* Arts Appreciation, Arts Centers, Arts Institutes, Dance, General, Libraries, Opera, Performing Arts, Theater • *Civic & Public Affairs:* Economic Development, General, Law & Justice, Philanthropic Organizations, Safety, Zoos/Aquariums • *Education:* Economic Education, Elementary Education (Private), General, Literacy • *Health:* General, Hospitals, Medical Research, Single-Disease Health Associations • *Science:* Observatories & Planetariums, Scientific Organizations • *Social Services:* Child Welfare, Community Centers, Community Service Organizations, Counseling, Day Care, Delinquency & Criminal Rehabilitation, Family Services, General, People with Disabilities, Senior Services, Substance Abuse, Youth Organizations

Grant Types: endowment, general support, multiyear/continuing support, and operating expenses

Geographic Distribution: primarily in the metropolitan Chicago, IL, area

Operating Locations: IL (Chicago)

CORP. OFFICERS

E. David Coolidge III: *CURR EMPL* mng ptnr, ceo: William Blair & Co *CORP AFFIL* dir: Pittway Corp *PHIL AFFIL* vp: Pittway Corp. Charitable Foundation

GIVING OFFICERS
Stephen Campbell: treas

E. David Coolidge III: vp *CURR EMPL* mng ptnr, ceo: William Blair & Co *PHIL AFFIL* vp: Pittway Corp. Charitable Foundation (see above)

Edgar D. Jannotta: pres *B* Evanston IL 1931 *ED* Princeton Univ 1953; Harvard Univ MBA 1959 *CORP AFFIL* dir: AAR Corp, Bandag, Molex Inc, Oil-Dri Corp Am, Safety-Kleen Corp, Sloan Valve Co

James M. McMullan: vp

Gregory N. Thomas: secy

APPLICATION INFORMATION
Initial Approach: Send a brief letter of inquiry and a full proposal. Include a description of organization, amount requested, purpose of funds sought, recently audited financial statement and proof of tax-exempt status. There are no deadlines.

OTHER THINGS TO KNOW
The general activities of the organization or the specific purpose should have significant impact on the Chicago area.

GRANTS ANALYSIS
Total Grants: $284,150

Number of Grants: 138

Highest Grant: $10,000

Typical Range: $500 to $5,000

Disclosure Period: fiscal year ending August 31, 1991

Note: Recent grants are derived from a fiscal 1991 Form 990.

RECENT GRANTS

General

10,000	Lake Forest Academy, Lake Forest, IL
9,500	Maryville City of Youth, Chicago, IL
7,000	Better Government Association, Chicago, IL
6,000	Hull House, Chicago, IL
5,000	Hoover Outdoor Education Center, Chicago, IL

Blowitz-Ridgeway Foundation

CONTACT
Robert N. Di Leonardi
Administrator
Blowitz-Ridgeway Foundation
2700 River Rd., Ste. 211
Des Plaines, IL 60018
(708) 298-2378

FINANCIAL SUMMARY
Recent Giving: $700,000 (fiscal 1994 est.); $656,010 (fiscal 1993); $629,916 (fiscal 1992)

Assets: $17,453,264 (fiscal 1993); $16,773,915 (fiscal 1992); $17,293,652 (fiscal 1991)

EIN: 36-2488355

CONTRIBUTIONS SUMMARY
Donor(s): The Blowitz-Ridgeway Foundation was founded in 1984 using the proceeds of the sale of Chicago's Ridgeway Hospital, a non-profit, psychiatric facility focusing on low-income adolescents.

Typical Recipients: • *Arts & Humanities:* Libraries • *Health:* AIDS/HIV, Cancer, Children's Health/Hospitals, Clinics/Medical Centers, Health Organizations, Home-Care Services, Hospices, Hospitals, Long-Term Care, Medical Rehabilitation, Medical Research, Mental Health, Single-Disease Health Associations • *Social Services:* Child Welfare, Community Centers, Community Service Organizations, Counseling, Emergency Relief, Family Planning, Family Services, Homes, People with Disabilities, Senior Services, Shelters/Homelessness, Youth Organizations

Grant Types: capital, multiyear/continuing support, project, and research

Geographic Distribution: focus on Illinois

GIVING OFFICERS
Arthur Collision: trust

Tony Dean: treas, trust

Robert N. DiLeonardi: admin

J. W. Jackson: trust

Daniel Kline: vp, trust

Joanne Lanigan: trust

Patricia A. MacAlister: trust

Max Pastin: pres, trust

Marvin Pitluk: trust

Samuel Winston: trust

APPLICATION INFORMATION
Initial Approach:

The foundation requests applicants write the foundation for a formal application form.

The foundation has no deadline for submitting proposals.

The board meets monthly.

Restrictions on Giving: The foundation does not support government agencies or organizations which subsist on third party funding. The foundation does not make grants to individuals. Grants will not be made for religious or political purposes, nor generally for the production or writing of audio-visual materials.

PUBLICATIONS
Information brochure, including application guidelines and an annual report

GRANTS ANALYSIS
Total Grants: $656,010

Number of Grants: 55

Highest Grant: $31,750

Average Grant: $11,927

Typical Range: $5,000 to $25,000

Disclosure Period: fiscal year ending September 30, 1993

Note: Recent grants are derived from a fiscal 1993 annual report.

RECENT GRANTS

Library

1,500	Foundation Center, New York, NY — library and resource center on US grantmakers

General

31,750	University of Chicago Medical Center, Chicago, IL — research on drug-resistant infections
30,000	Gastro-Intestinal Research Foundation, Chicago, IL — towards new IBD research center at the University of Chicago
28,090	Austin Special, Austin, TX — capital needs, sheltered workshop for mentally disabled
26,000	University of Illinois, Chicago, IL — research on chemical reactions in cancer causing agents
25,000	Children's Memorial Hospital, Chicago, IL — towards new pediatric research facility

Blum Foundation, Harry and Maribel G.

CONTACT
H. Jonathan Kovler
President
Harry and Maribel G. Blum Foundation
919 N Michigan Ave., Ste. 2800
Chicago, IL 60611
(312) 664-5050

FINANCIAL SUMMARY
Recent Giving: $1,000,000 (1995 est.); $1,000,073 (1994 approx.); $1,900,500 (1993 approx.)

Assets: $12,000,000 (1995 est.); $11,548,000 (1994 approx.); $12,337,000 (1993 approx.)

EIN: 36-6152744

CONTRIBUTIONS SUMMARY
Donor(s): The foundation was established in 1967 by the late Harry Blum .

Typical Recipients: • *Arts & Humanities:* Arts Centers, Arts Funds, Historic Preservation, Libraries, Museums/Galleries • *Civic & Public Affairs:* Employment/Job Training, Zoos/Aquariums • *Education:* Business-School Partnerships, Colleges & Universities • *Health:* Clinics/Medical Centers, Diabetes, Hospitals, Medical Research, Single-Disease Health Associations, Transplant Networks/Donor Banks • *Religion:* Jewish Causes, Religious Organizations, Synagogues/Temples • *Social Services:* Child Welfare, Community Service Organizations, Food/Clothing Distribution, Recreation & Athletics, United Funds/United Ways

Grant Types: general support

Geographic Distribution: national, with emphasis on Illinois

GIVING OFFICERS
H. H. Bregar: secy, dir *PHIL AFFIL* secy: Blum-Kovler Foundation

H. Jonathan Kovler: pres, dir *PHIL AFFIL* treas: Blum-Kovler Foundation

Peter Kovler: dir *PHIL AFFIL* asst secy: Blum-Kovler Foundation

APPLICATION INFORMATION
Initial Approach:

The foundation reports that no specific application form is required.

The foundation has no deadline for submitting proposals.

Restrictions on Giving: The foundation does not make grants to individuals.

GRANTS ANALYSIS
Total Grants: $902,750

Number of Grants: 16

Highest Grant: $200,000

Average Grant: $56,422

Typical Range: $100 to $3,500 and $100,000 to $200,000

Disclosure Period: 1992

Note: Recent grants are derived from a 1992 Form 990.

RECENT GRANTS
Library
200,000	Chicago Public Library Foundation, Chicago, IL — education

General
200,000	Jewish United Fund, Chicago, IL — general welfare
200,000	Northwestern Memorial Hospital-Kovler Organ Transplant, Chicago, IL — medical
150,000	US Holocaust Memorial Museum, Washington, DC — cultural and civic
100,000	University of Chicago Diabetes Research, Chicago, IL — medical
30,000	Corporate/Community Schools of America, Chicago, IL — education

Blum-Kovler Foundation

CONTACT
H. Jonathan Kovler
Treasurer
Blum-Kovler Foundation
919 N Michigan Ave., Ste. 2800
Chicago, IL 60611
(312) 664-5050

FINANCIAL SUMMARY
Recent Giving: $3,000,000 (1995 est.); $3,250,000 (1994 approx.); $2,926,000 (1993 approx.)

Assets: $35,300,000 (1995 est.); $36,600,000 (1994); $36,200,000 (1993)

EIN: 36-2476143

CONTRIBUTIONS SUMMARY
Donor(s): The foundation was established in 1953, with the late Harry Blum and Everette Kovler as donors. Both men served as chairman of the James B. Distilling Company, a subsidiary of American Brands, Inc. The Blum-Kovler Foundation is administered primarily by family members. Maribel Blum, widow of Harry Blum, served as the foundation's chairperson until her death in 1985.

Typical Recipients: • *Arts & Humanities:* Arts Centers, Arts Festivals, Arts Funds, Arts Institutes, Dance, Historic Preservation, Libraries, Museums/Galleries, Music, Opera, Performing Arts, Public Broadcasting, Theater • *Civic & Public Affairs:* African American Affairs, Business/Free Enterprise, Civil Rights, Legal Aid, Philanthropic Organizations, Public Policy, Urban & Community Affairs, Zoos/Aquariums • *Education:* Arts/Humanities Education, Business Education, Business-School Partnerships, Colleges & Universities, Economic Education, Education Associations, Education Funds, International Studies, Medical Education, Minority Education, Private Education (Precollege), Science/Mathematics Education, Student Aid • *Environment:* General • *Health:* Children's Health/Hospitals, Clinics/Medical Centers, Diabetes, Health Funds, Hospices, Hospitals, Medical Rehabilitation, Medical Research, Mental Health, Single-Disease Health Associations • *International:* Foreign Educational Institutions, Health Care/Hospitals, International Affairs, International Peace & Security Issues, International Relations, International Relief Efforts, Missionary/Religious Activities • *Religion:* Jewish Causes, Religious Organizations, Synagogues/Temples • *Science:* Science Museums • *Social Services:* Animal Protection, Child Welfare, Community Centers, Community Service Organizations, Food/Clothing Distribution, Homes, People with Disabilities, Recreation & Athletics, Refugee Assistance, Shelters/Homelessness, Substance Abuse, Youth Organizations

Grant Types: general support

Geographic Distribution: primarily in the Chicago, IL, metropolitan area; also Washington, DC, and New York, NY

GIVING OFFICERS
H. H. Bregar: secy *PHIL AFFIL* secy, dir: Harry and Maribel G. Blum Foundation

Everett Kovler: pres

H. Jonathan Kovler: treas *PHIL AFFIL* pres, dir: Harry and Maribel G. Blum Foundation

Peter Kovler: asst secy *PHIL AFFIL* dir: Harry and Maribel G. Blum Foundation

APPLICATION INFORMATION
Initial Approach:

Interested parties may submit proposals to the foundation office.

The foundation does not issue application guidelines.

Applications may be submitted at any time.

GRANTS ANALYSIS
Total Grants: $1,698,832

Number of Grants: 215

Highest Grant: $202,000

Average Grant: $7,902

Typical Range: $200 to $20,000

Disclosure Period: 1992

Note: Recent grants are derived from a 1992 Form 990.

RECENT GRANTS
General
107,000	Citizens Vote, Washington, DC
100,000	American University, Washington, DC — Kovler Family Scholarship
100,000	University of Chicago Diabetes Research, Chicago, IL — Kovler Diabetes Center
75,000	Travelers and Immigrants Aid, Chicago, IL
70,000	Corporate/Community Schools of America, Chicago, IL

Boothroyd Foundation, Charles H. and Bertha L.

CONTACT
Bruce E. Brown
President
Charles H. and Bertha L. Boothroyd Fdn.
120 W Madison St., Ste. 14-L
Chicago, IL 60602
(312) 346-8333

FINANCIAL SUMMARY
Recent Giving: $178,000 (fiscal 1992); $164,500 (fiscal 1991); $167,500 (fiscal 1990)

Assets: $3,663,015 (fiscal 1992); $3,498,904 (fiscal 1991); $3,370,174 (fiscal 1990)

Gifts Received: $3 (fiscal 1992); $360 (fiscal 1991)

Fiscal Note: In 1992, contributions were received from Miss Agness K. McAvoy.

EIN: 36-6047045

CONTRIBUTIONS SUMMARY
Donor(s): the late Mary T. Palzkill, Agnes K. McAvoy Trust

Typical Recipients: • *Arts & Humanities:* Arts Institutes, Libraries, Opera • *Civic & Public Affairs:* General, Legal Aid, Municipalities/Towns, Women's Affairs • *Education:* Colleges & Universities, Medical Education • *Environment:* Resource Conservation • *Health:* Alzheimers Disease, Health Funds, Health Organizations, Hospitals, Medical Research, Mental Health, Nursing Services, Single-Disease Health Associations • *Religion:* Religious Welfare • *Social Services:* Community Service Organizations, Senior Services

Grant Types: research and scholarship

Geographic Distribution: focus on IL

GIVING OFFICERS
Bruce E. Brown: pres

Donald C. Gancer: vp *B* Chicago IL 1933 *ED* Marquette Univ LLB 1957 *CURR EMPL* prin: Querrey & Harrow Ltd *CORP AFFIL* dir: Bank Commerce & Indus, Heritage/Pullman Bank, Suburban Trust & Savings Bank *NONPR AFFIL* mem: Am Bar Assn, Chicago Bar Assn, Chicago Counc Lawyers, IL Bar Assn, WI Bar Assn

Lorraine Marcus: secy

APPLICATION INFORMATION
Initial Approach: Send brief letter describing program. There are no deadlines.

GRANTS ANALYSIS
Total Grants: $178,000

Number of Grants: 24

Highest Grant: $15,000

Typical Range: $1,000 to $10,000

Disclosure Period: fiscal year ending June 30, 1992

Note: Recent grants are derived from a fiscal 1992 Form 990.

RECENT GRANTS

Library
1,000	Newberry Library, Chicago, IL

General
15,000	Clarence Darrow Convention Center, Chicago, IL
15,000	University of Chicago, Chicago, IL — Chicago Brown Book
10,000	Alzheimers Foundation, Chicago, IL
10,000	Bethel New Life, Chicago, IL
10,000	Chicago Volunteer Legal Services Foundation, Chicago, IL

Brach Foundation, Helen

CONTACT
Raymond F. Simon
President and Director
Helen Brach Foundation
55 W Wacker Dr., Ste. 701
Chicago, IL 60601
(312) 372-4417

FINANCIAL SUMMARY
Recent Giving: $2,676,799 (fiscal 1993); $2,598,159 (fiscal 1992); $2,226,460 (fiscal 1991)

Assets: $68,788,181 (fiscal 1993); $63,496,233 (fiscal 1992); $56,040,936 (fiscal 1991)

Gifts Received: $2,831,333 (fiscal 1991); $13,042,899 (fiscal 1989); $13,000,000 (fiscal 1988)

Fiscal Note: In fiscal year 1992 the foundation received a gift of $8,915 from the Frank Brach Marital Trust. In fiscal 1991, the foundation received $2,793,094 from the estate of Helen V. Brach and $38,239 from the Frank Brach Marital Trust. A contribution of $42,899 was received from the Frank Brach Marital Trust in 1989. The foundation received a bequest of $13,000,000 from the estate of Helen V. Brach in the fiscal years of 1988 and 1989.

EIN: 23-7376427

CONTRIBUTIONS SUMMARY
Donor(s): The Helen Brach Foundation was incorporated in 1974 in Chicago, IL. Helen V. Brach was the wife of Frank Brach, owner of the E.J. Brach and Sons Candy Company in Chicago. Frank Brach's father founded the company, which in 1966 was sold upon Frank Brach's retirement. After his death in 1970, Helen Brach became heir to the family fortune.

In February 1977, Helen Brach disappeared without a trace. Seven years later, she was declared legally dead, with her death presumed to have occurred in 1977. As the foundation was the primary beneficiary under her will, it received a significant bequest from her estate when she was declared deceased. Charles M. Vorhees (Helen Brach's brother) was an original member and director of the foundation, and remains on the board of directors.

Typical Recipients: • *Arts & Humanities:* Arts Centers, Arts Institutes, Community Arts, Dance, Historic Preservation, Libraries, Museums/Galleries, Music • *Civic & Public Affairs:* Employment/Job Training, Hispanic Affairs, Housing, Inner-City Development, Philanthropic Organizations, Public Policy, Urban & Community Affairs, Women's Affairs, Zoos/Aquariums • *Education:* Afterschool/Enrichment Programs, Arts/Humanities Education, Colleges & Universities, Community & Junior Colleges, Education Associations, Education Funds, Minority Education, Preschool Education, Private Education (Precollege), Public Education (Precollege), Religious Education, Secondary Education (Private), Special Education, Student Aid • *Environment:* General • *Health:* AIDS/HIV, Children's Health/Hospitals, Clinics/Medical Centers, Geriatric Health, Health Funds, Health Organizations, Hospices, Hospitals, Nursing Services, Nutrition, Public Health • *International:* Missionary/Religious Activities • *Religion:* Churches, Dioceses, Ministries, Missionary Activities (Domestic), Religious Organizations, Religious Welfare • *Science:* Science Museums • *Social Services:* Animal Protection, Child Welfare, Community Centers, Counseling, Family Services, Food/Clothing Distribution, People with Disabilities, Senior Services, Shelters/Homelessness, Volunteer Services, Youth Organizations

Grant Types: capital, department, endowment, general support, operating expenses, project, and scholarship

Geographic Distribution: national, with emphasis on Illinois

GIVING OFFICERS
James John O'Connor: vp, dir *B* Chicago IL 1937 *ED* Holy Cross Coll BS 1958; Harvard Univ MBA 1960; Georgetown Univ JD 1963 *CURR EMPL* chmn, ceo, dir: Commonwealth Edison Co *CORP AFFIL* UN Airlines Lines Corp; chmn: Advanced Reactor Corp; dir: Am Natl Canada, Chicago Stock Exchange, Corning Inc, First Chicago Corp, First Natl Bank Chicago, Scotsman Indus Inc, Tribune Co *NONPR AFFIL* bd advs: Mercy Hosp Med Ctr; chmn: Cardinal Bernardins Big Shoulders Fund; chmn, dir: Chicago Assn Commerce Indus; dir: Am Nuclear Energy Counc, Catholic Charities, Chicago Urban League, Edison Electric Inst, Harvard Univ Grad Sch Bus Admin Assocs, Leadership Counc Metro Open Commun, Lyric Opera Chicago, Mus Sci & Indus, Reading Is Fundamental, St Xavier Coll, US Counc Energy Awareness; mem: Am Bar Assn, Bus Counc, Chicago Bar Assn, IL Bar Assn, IL Bus Roundtable; mem exec bd: Boy Scouts Am Chicago Area Counc; trust: Northwestern Univ *CLUB AFFIL* Hundred Cook County *PHIL AFFIL* chmn corp responsibility comm

John J. Sheridan: secy, treas, dir

R. Matthew Simon: dir

Raymond F. Simon: pres, dir *PHIL AFFIL* dir: Polk Brothers Foundation

Charles A. Vorhees: dir

Charles M. Vorhees: chmn, dir

APPLICATION INFORMATION
Initial Approach:

Applicants should contact the foundation by letter for application form and a report on the foundation.

Include one copy of each of the following items: a grant proposal; description of qualified personnel assigned to the project, if special talents or skills are required; financial statement for latest fiscal year; list of principal officers and/or directors; name, title, and salary of three highest paid persons affiliated with the organization; copy of IRS determination that applicant is tax exempt under 501(c)(3) of the Internal Revenue Code; and a signature and date on the application form.

The deadline for proposals is December 31 for consideration by March 31. To receive optimum consideration, proposals should be received by the foundation in completed form several months before the end of the year and precede a board meeting.

The board follows a schedule of regular quarterly meetings to consider grant applications and review the progress of currently funded projects. Final consideration is given to all applications received in any year at the board's first meeting the following year, which is usually in March. At the foundation's discretion, a site visit or interview may be scheduled as part of the review process. All eligible requests will be acknowledged.

Restrictions on Giving: Except for well-established organizations which the foundation has supported in the past, the board prefers to consider relatively smaller grants and to distribute them among a number of applicants. The foundation usually does not make multiyear grants or commitments, although it will consider such requests where exceptional circumstances support the need or value of such an approach. Except where the foundation has made an express commitment for successive years' funding, a grant made in one year in no way implies the recipient will receive priority for funding in future years.

PUBLICATIONS
Annual report, program guidelines, application form.

GRANTS ANALYSIS
Total Grants: $2,676,799

Number of Grants: 151

Highest Grant: $100,000

Average Grant: $10,000*

Typical Range: $5,000 to $25,000

Disclosure Period: fiscal year ending March 31, 1993

Note: Average grant figure supplied by the foundation. Recent grants are derived from a fiscal 1992 grants list.

RECENT GRANTS

Library

50,000	De Paul University, Chicago, IL — toward construction costs of new library on Lincoln Park Campus
33,000	Earth Action Network Magazine, Norwalk, CT — to subsidize subscription for Illinois high school and college libraries

General

100,000	Big Shoulders Fund, Chicago, IL — to help support long-range planning process and support for teaching corps serving 130 inner-city schools
100,000	Miscericordia Home, Chicago, IL — to help subsidize young adults being transferred to Independent Living Complex who need additional time to become self-supporting
100,000	United Animal Nations, Chicago, IL — to increase donor base and to continue new-member acquisition program
75,000	Housing Opportunities and Maintenance for the Elderly H.O.M.E., Chicago, IL — for development of 55-unit intergenerational, shared living community for low-income elderly
75,000	Loyola University of Chicago, Chicago, IL — to support crisis intervention and family counseling program of Charles Doyle Center

Brunswick Corp. / Brunswick Foundation

Revenue: $2.83 billion
Employees: 18,000
Headquarters: Skokie, IL
SIC Major Group: Boat Building & Repairing, Internal Combustion Engines Nec, and Sporting & Athletic Goods Nec

CONTACT
Wendy L. Smith
President
Brunswick Foundation
One N Field Ct.
Lake Forest, IL 60045
(708) 735-4700
Note: Foundation does not accept telephone solicitations.

FINANCIAL SUMMARY
Recent Giving: $1,500,000 (1995 est.); $1,097,000 (1994 approx.); $690,838 (1993)

Assets: $7,600,000 (1995 est.); $7,600,000 (1994 approx.); $8,691,492 (1993)

Gifts Received: $650,000 (1993)

Fiscal Note: All contributions are made through the foundation. Figures include matching gifts. Above figures exclude nonmonetary support. Contributions are received from Brunswick Corp.

EIN: 36-6033576

CONTRIBUTIONS SUMMARY
Typical Recipients: • *Arts & Humanities:* Arts Funds, Arts Institutes, Community Arts, Dance, Historic Preservation, Libraries, Museums/Galleries, Music, Performing Arts • *Civic & Public Affairs:* Civil Rights, Clubs, Community Foundations, Economic Development, Legal Aid, Rural Affairs, Urban & Community Affairs, Women's Affairs • *Education:* Business Education, Colleges & Universities, Community & Junior Colleges, Education Associations, Engineering/Technological Education, Leadership Training, Literacy, Minority Education, Science/Mathematics Education, Student Aid • *Environment:* General • *Health:* Children's Health/Hospitals, Emergency/Ambulance Services, Health Organizations, Hospices, Hospitals, Mental Health, Nursing Services, Prenatal Health Issues, Single-Disease Health Associations • *Religion:* Religious Organizations, Religious Welfare • *Social Services:* Big Brother/Big Sister, Child Welfare, Community Centers, Community Service Organizations, Delinquency & Criminal Rehabilitation, Family Planning, Family Services, Food/Clothing Distribution, People with Disabilities, Recreation & Athletics, Scouts, Senior Services, Shelters/Homelessness, Substance Abuse, United Funds/United Ways, YMCA/YWCA/YMHA/YWHA, Youth Organizations

Grant Types: capital, challenge, employee matching gifts, general support, project, and research

Nonmonetary Support: $2,000,000 (1994); $3,000,000 (1987); $2,196,418 (1986)

Nonmonetary Support Types: donated equipment, donated products, and in-kind services

Note: Local managers are the contacts for nonmonetary support. Each division and each location independently handle over 150 separate units.

Geographic Distribution: emphasis on areas where company has major facilities

Operating Locations: AL, AR (Camden), AZ, CA (Anaheim, Costa Mesa, Los Angeles, San Diego, Santa Ana), CT (Torrington), FL (De Land, St. Cloud), GA, IL (Chicago, Morton Grove, Niles, Skokie), IN, KY (Eminence), LA, MD (Timonium), MI (Muskegon), MN, MS, NC, NE (Lincoln), OH (Willard), OK (Red Fork, Stillwater, Tulsa), SC, TN (Knoxville), TX (Houston), VA (Marion), WA (Arlington, Seattle, Spokane), WI (Brookfield, Fond du Lac, Oshkosh)

CORP. OFFICERS
Dianne Mary Yaconetti: *B* Chicago IL 1946 *ED* Mallinckrodt Coll 1984-1985 *CURR EMPL* vp admin, corp secy: Brunswick Corp *NONPR AFFIL* dir: Lambs; mem: Am Soc Corp Secys

GIVING OFFICERS
Paul Kilius: treas

Robert N. Rasmus: dir

Michael Schmitz: secy

Wendy L. Smith: pres, dir *B* Chicago IL 1950 *ED* Oakton Commun Coll 1986; Mundelein Coll 1990 *NONPR AFFIL* asst secy: Brunswick Public Charitable Fdn; dir: Assn Colls IL; mem: Chicago Women Philanthropy, Counc Fdns, Independent Sector, Suburban Contributions Network, Women Philanthropy Corp Fdns; mem adv counc: Fdn Independent Higher Ed; treas, mem: Don Forum Chicago

Dianne Mary Yaconetti: vp, dir *CURR EMPL* vp admin, corp secy: Brunswick Corp (see above)

APPLICATION INFORMATION
Initial Approach: *Initial Contact:* brief letter *Include Information On:* objectives and purpose for which grant is sought; plans for implementation and evaluation of project; benefits expected; evidence of need for project; budget; proof of tax-exempt status; and most recently audited financial statement *Deadlines:* none *Note:* Foundation does not accept telephone solicitation.

Restrictions on Giving: Foundation does not make grants to individuals or provide loans; usually support religious or political organizations, veterans groups, fraternal orders; labor groups; preschool, primary or secondary schools; contribute toward trips, tours, tickets, dinnerss, special events or advertising; donate company equipment or products; or make capital or endowment grants.

PUBLICATIONS
Annual report

GRANTS ANALYSIS
Total Grants: $1,097,000

Highest Grant: $100,000
Average Grant: $10,000
Typical Range: $1,000 to $10,000
Disclosure Period: 1994

Note: Above figures were provided by the foundation. Total grantsfigure is approximate. Recent grants are derived from a 1993 grants list.

RECENT GRANTS
General
27,100	Lambs, Libertyville, IL — unrestricted
25,000	Muscular Dystrophy Association, Tucson, AZ — unrestricted
20,000	Every Women's Place, Muskegon, MI — capital campaign
20,000	Muskegon Community College, Muskegon, MI — expansion fund
12,000	Boy Scouts of America Great Smoky Mountain Council, Knoxville, TN — capital campaign

Butz Foundation

CONTACT
Tom Boyden
Administrator
Butz Fdn.
c/o The Northern Trust Co.
50 S La Salle St.
Chicago, IL 60675
(312) 630-6000

FINANCIAL SUMMARY
Recent Giving: $128,450 (1993); $137,600 (1990); $133,000 (1989)
Assets: $3,059,761 (1993); $2,546,757 (1990); $2,502,799 (1989)
EIN: 36-6008818

CONTRIBUTIONS SUMMARY
Donor(s): the late Theodore C. Butz, Jean Butz James

Typical Recipients: • *Arts & Humanities:* Arts Associations & Councils, Arts Festivals, Community Arts, Libraries, Music, Performing Arts • *Civic & Public Affairs:* Botanical Gardens/Parks, Zoos/Aquariums • *Education:* Colleges & Universities, General, Private Education (Precollege), Special Education • *Health:* AIDS/HIV, Hospitals, Medical Research, Multiple Sclerosis, Prenatal Health Issues • *Science:* Science Museums • *Social Services:* People with Disabilities, Shelters/Homelessness

Grant Types: multiyear/continuing support, operating expenses, and research
Geographic Distribution: focus on IL

GIVING OFFICERS
Barbara T. Butz: dir
Elvira M. Butz: vp, trust
Theodore H. Butz: pres, dir

Thompson H. Butz: treas, trust
Vera M. Dover: secy
Jean Butz James: dir
Ronald E. James: dir

APPLICATION INFORMATION
Initial Approach: Send brief letter describing program. There are no deadlines.
Restrictions on Giving: Does not support individuals.

GRANTS ANALYSIS
Total Grants: $128,450
Number of Grants: 24
Highest Grant: $10,000
Typical Range: $250 to $10,000
Disclosure Period: 1993
Note: Recent grants are derived from a 1993 Form 990.

RECENT GRANTS
Library
5,000	Blue Ridge School, Dyke, VA — for library

General
10,000	Evanston Hospital, Evanston, IL — arrhythmia research
10,000	Multiple Sclerosis Society, Chicago/Northern Illinois Chapter, Chicago, IL — for research
10,000	Northwestern Memorial Foundation, Chicago, IL
7,500	Boarder Baby Project, Washington, DC
7,000	Barnesville School, Barnesville, IL — for handicapped facilities

Caestecker Foundation, Charles and Marie

CONTACT
Frank Karaba
Trustee
Charles and Marie Caestecker Fdn.
20 S Clark, Ste. 2310
Chicago, IL 60603-1802
(312) 726-2468
Note: Scholarship application address: c/o Guidance Counselor, Green Lake Public High School, Green Lake, WI 54941

FINANCIAL SUMMARY
Recent Giving: $1,338,453 (fiscal 1994); $364,745 (fiscal 1991); $261,968 (fiscal 1990)
Assets: $4,704,070 (fiscal 1994); $6,211,684 (fiscal 1991); $6,211,454 (fiscal 1990)
EIN: 36-3154453

CONTRIBUTIONS SUMMARY
Donor(s): the late Charles E. Caestecker
Typical Recipients: • *Arts & Humanities:* Historic Preservation, History & Archaeology, Libraries • *Education:* Colleges & Universities, Engineering/Technological

Education, Religious Education, Science/Mathematics Education, Student Aid
• *Health:* Clinics/Medical Centers, Hospitals
• *Religion:* Churches, Religious Welfare
• *Social Services:* Community Service Organizations
Grant Types: operating expenses and scholarship
Geographic Distribution: focus on WI

GIVING OFFICERS
Thomas E. Caestecker: trust
Frank Andrew Karaba: trust *B* Chicago IL 1927 *ED* Northwestern Univ BS 1949; Northwestern Univ JD 1951 *CURR EMPL* mng ptnr: Crowley Barrett & Karaba *NONPR AFFIL* mem: Am Bar Assn, IL Bar Assn

APPLICATION INFORMATION
Initial Approach: Request application form for scholarships. Deadline is February 1 of graduation year.

GRANTS ANALYSIS
Total Grants: $1,338,453
Number of Grants: 11
Highest Grant: $1,268,604
Typical Range: $1,000 to $15,000
Disclosure Period: fiscal year ending April 30, 1994
Note: Recent grants are derived from a fiscal 1994 Form 990.

RECENT GRANTS
Library
1,268,604	Caestecker Public Library Foundation, Green Lake, WI — library building

General
15,000	Ripon College, Ripon, WI
10,000	Carleton College, Northfield, MN — scholarship
10,000	Luther College, Decorah, IA — scholarship
9,915	Coastal Carolina College, Conway, SC — scholarship
7,934	Michigan Technological University, Houghton, MI — scholarship

CBI Industries, Inc. / CBI Foundation

Sales: $1.67 billion
Employees: 14,000
Headquarters: Oak Brook, IL
SIC Major Group: Holding Companies Nec, Drilling Oil & Gas Wells, Heavy Construction Nec, and Industrial Gases

CONTACT
Susan E. Marks
Secretary
CBI Foundation
800 Jorie Blvd.
Oak Brook, IL 60521-2268
(708) 572-7000

FINANCIAL SUMMARY

Recent Giving: $432,331 (1993); $425,000 (1992 approx.); $275,000 (1991)

Assets: $930 (1993); -$2,168 (1990); $42,980 (1989)

Gifts Received: $365,000 (1993); $256,000 (1990); $266,344 (1989)

Fiscal Note: Foundation receives funding through CBI Industries, Inc.

EIN: 36-6050115

CONTRIBUTIONS SUMMARY

Typical Recipients: • *Arts & Humanities:* Arts Associations & Councils, Arts Centers, Arts Institutes, Dance, Historic Preservation, Libraries, Museums/Galleries, Music, Opera, Performing Arts, Theater • *Education:* Arts/Humanities Education, Business Education, Colleges & Universities, Education Associations, Engineering/Technological Education • *Health:* Health Organizations, Hospices, Hospitals, Medical Rehabilitation, Medical Research, Single-Disease Health Associations • *Science:* Scientific Centers & Institutes • *Social Services:* Child Welfare, Community Centers, Community Service Organizations, People with Disabilities, Volunteer Services, Youth Organizations

Grant Types: award, emergency, employee matching gifts, general support, operating expenses, and research

Geographic Distribution: primarily in the Chicago, IL, area

Operating Locations: AL (Birmingham, Cordova, Florence), CA (Fontana), DE (New Castle), GA (Norcross), IL (Aurora, Bourbonnais, Chicago, Kankakee, Plainfield), LA (Belle Chasse), MN (Minneapolis), OK (Tulsa), SC (Columbia), TX (Brownsville, Houston)

CORP. OFFICERS

John Cahill: *CURR EMPL* sr vp, cfo: KY Fried Chicken Corp

John Earl Jones: *B* Kansas City MO 1934 *ED* Carleton Coll BA 1956; Univ Chicago 1958-1960; Northwestern Univ 1960-1961 *CURR EMPL* chmn, ceo, pres: CBI Indus Inc *CORP AFFIL* dir: Allied Products Corp, INDREX, Interlake Corp, Liquid Carbonic Corp, NICOR Inc, Sea Con Svcs, TNDREX, Valmont Indus Inc, Walker Process Corp *NONPR AFFIL* mem bus adv counc: Univ IL; trust: Glenwood Sch Boys

George Louis Schueppert: *B* Merrill WI 1938 *ED* Univ WI BBA 1961; Univ Chicago MBA 1969 *CURR EMPL* exec vp, cfo, dir: CBI Indus Inc *CORP AFFIL* dir: Wells Mfg Co *NONPR AFFIL* bd adv: CPAs Pub Interest, Govt Asst Project *CLUB AFFIL* Econ

GIVING OFFICERS

Buel Thomas Adams: mem mgmt comm *B* Mansfield OH 1933 *ED* St Josephs Coll BS 1954; Univ PA MBA 1960 *CURR EMPL* vp, treas: CBI Indus Inc *NONPR AFFIL* mem: Fin Execs Inst, Machinery & Allied Products Inst

Stephen M. Duffy: pres *CURR EMPL* vp human resources: CBI Indus Inc

Susan E. Marks: secy

J. J. McDevitt: mem mgmt comm

W.R. Robinson: mem mgmt comm

C. O. Ziemer: vp, dir, trust

APPLICATION INFORMATION

Initial Approach: *Initial Contact:* brief letter and full proposal *Include Information On:* description of the organization, amount requested, purpose of funds sought, a list of officers and directors, audited financial statement, and proof of tax-exempt status *Deadlines:* no deadlines

Restrictions on Giving: The foundation does not make loans.

The foundation does not support individuals, religious organizations for sectarian purposes, building or endowment funds, political or lobbying groups, foreign organizations, or individual organizations that receive United Way funds.

GRANTS ANALYSIS

Total Grants: $432,331

Number of Grants: 100

Highest Grant: $78,926

Average Grant: $4,323

Typical Range: $500 to $1,000

Disclosure Period: 1993

Note: Recent grants are derived from a 1993 Form 990.

RECENT GRANTS

General

78,926	United Way Crusade of Mercy, Chicago, IL
42,585	United Way Crusade of Mercy, Chicago, IL
28,612	United Way Houston Area, Houston, TX
25,000	Rush Presbyterian-St. Luke's Medical Center, Chicago, IL
24,355	United Way Kankakee County, Kankakee, IL

Centralia Foundation

CONTACT

Wendell D. Lamblin
Chairman
Centralia Foundation
PO Box 709
Centralia, IL 62801-0709

FINANCIAL SUMMARY

Recent Giving: $47,287 (1993); $78,656 (1992); $422,890 (1990)

Assets: $11,557,865 (1993); $6,756,781 (1992); $8,913,244 (1990)

Gifts Received: $4,263,880 (1993); $236,388 (1992); $4,790,000 (1990)

Fiscal Note: In 1993, contributions were received from Ken Bauer ($20,000), Dee C. and Sue Boswell ($25,000), A. L. Boyll ($88,460), D. G. Geary ($237,146), Carillon Bell Charitable Fdn. (48,672), the John J. Parish Charitable Remainder Trust ($2,664,534), and Virginia Speith

($60,000); there were many miscellaneous contributions of $20,000 or less.

EIN: 37-6029269

CONTRIBUTIONS SUMMARY

Typical Recipients: • *Arts & Humanities:* Arts Associations & Councils, Libraries • *Civic & Public Affairs:* Clubs, Community Foundations, General, Municipalities/Towns • *Health:* Children's Health/Hospitals, Emergency/Ambulance Services, Hospitals • *Religion:* Religious Welfare • *Social Services:* Child Welfare, Community Service Organizations, Day Care, Food/Clothing Distribution, Homes, Scouts, YMCA/YWCA/YMHA/YWHA, Youth Organizations

Grant Types: general support and scholarship

Geographic Distribution: focus on IL

GIVING OFFICERS

Lloyd Allen: trust *PHIL AFFIL* vchmn: CENEX Foundation

Verle Besant: vchmn

Joel L. Fleishman: dir

Bruce Geary: trust

John Lackey: trust

Wendell Lamblin: chmn

Dan Nichols: trust

William Sprehe: trust

APPLICATION INFORMATION

Initial Approach: Send request for scholarship procedures.

OTHER THINGS TO KNOW

Provides scholarships to individuals for higher education.

GRANTS ANALYSIS

Total Grants: $47,287

Number of Grants: 20

Highest Grant: $6,893

Typical Range: $225 to $5,000

Disclosure Period: 1993

Note: Recent grants are derived from a 1993 Form 990. Number of grants and typical range do not include scholarships to individuals.

RECENT GRANTS

Library

2,557	Centralia Public Library, Centralia, IL

General

6,893	City of Centralia, Centralia, IL
5,000	Youth Sports Program, Centralia, IL — Marion County Housing Authority
2,657	Shriners Children's Hospital, St. Louis, MO
2,557	Masonic Lodge Number 201, Centralia, IL
2,557	St. Mary's Hospital, Centralia, IL

Chicago Sun-Times, Inc. / Chicago Sun-Times Charity Trust

Sales: $99.6 million
Employees: 1,700
Headquarters: Chicago, IL
SIC Major Group: Printing & Publishing

CONTACT
Patricia L. Dudek
Manager Community and Client Services
Chicago Sun-Times, Inc.
401 N Wabash Ave., Rm. 356
Chicago, IL 60611
(312) 321-3121

FINANCIAL SUMMARY
Recent Giving: $100,000 (fiscal 1993);
$203,211 (fiscal 1992); $100,000 (fiscal
1991)

Assets: $397,510 (fiscal 1992); $437,230
(fiscal 1990); $277,935 (fiscal 1988)

Gifts Received: $209,003 (fiscal 1992)

Fiscal Note: In 1992, contributions were received from Beat the Champs Bowling Contest ($14,734), Kup's Purple Heart Cruise ($30,893), Poplar Creek ($50,216), Chicago Sun-Time Sports Show ($20,640), Zazz Mixer ($19,300), Great America (15,000), Barnum P. Bailey Circus ($15,000), Sports Luncheon ($14,569), Ice Capades ($8,889), Zaslow Party ($4,994), Sesame Street ($3,911), WWBZ Blazefest ($2,000), and miscellaneous contributors ($8,727).

EIN: 36-6059459

CONTRIBUTIONS SUMMARY
Typical Recipients: • *Arts & Humanities:* Art History, Arts Appreciation, Arts Associations & Councils, Arts Centers, Arts Festivals, Arts Institutes, Arts Outreach, Ballet, Community Arts, Dance, Ethnic & Folk Arts, General, Historic Preservation, Libraries, Literary Arts, Museums/Galleries, Music, Opera, Performing Arts, Public Broadcasting, Theater, Visual Arts • *Civic & Public Affairs:* African American Affairs, Community Foundations, Economic Development, Employment/Job Training, Ethnic Organizations, General, Hispanic Affairs, Housing, Inner-City Development, Public Policy, Urban & Community Affairs, Women's Affairs • *Education:* Afterschool/Enrichment Programs, Arts/Humanities Education, General, Journalism/Media Education, Literacy, Minority Education • *Health:* AIDS/HIV, Alzheimers Disease • *Religion:* Religious Organizations • *Social Services:* Child Welfare, Community Centers, Community Service Organizations, Counseling, Day Care, Delinquency & Criminal Rehabilitation, Domestic Violence, Emergency Relief, Family Planning, Family Services, Food/Clothing Distribution, General, Homes, People with Disabilities, Recreation & Athletics, Senior Services, Shelters/Homelessness, Substance Abuse, United Funds/United Ways, Volunteer Services, Youth Organizations

Grant Types: general support, multiyear/continuing support, operating expenses, project, and seed money

Geographic Distribution: primarily Chicago, IL

Operating Locations: IL (Chicago)

CORP. OFFICERS
Sam S. McKeel: *CURR EMPL* pres, ceo: Chicago Sun-Times

GIVING OFFICERS
Dennis A. Britton: trust

Chuck Champion: trust

Tom Foster: trust *CURR EMPL* ceo: Foster Farms

Tom Neri: trust

Charles Price: pres, trust

APPLICATION INFORMATION
Initial Approach: Send a brief letter of inquiry and a full proposal. Include a description of organization, amount requested, purpose of funds sought, recently audited financial statement, and proof of tax-exempt status.

PUBLICATIONS
Policies and Procedures Fact Sheet

GRANTS ANALYSIS
Total Grants: $203,211

Number of Grants: 18

Highest Grant: $50,216

Typical Range: $1,215 to $15,000

Disclosure Period: fiscal year ending September 30, 1992

Note: Recent grants are derived from a fiscal 1992 Form 990.

RECENT GRANTS

General
50,216	Poplar Creek, Chicago, IL
30,893	Kup's Purple Heart Cruise, Chicago, IL
20,640	Chicago Sun-Time Sports Show, Chicago, IL
19,430	Zazz Mixer, Chicago, IL
15,000	Great America, Chicago, IL

CLARCOR Inc. / CLARCOR Foundation

Sales: $225.0 million
Employees: 2,200
Headquarters: Rockford, IL
SIC Major Group: Metal Cans, Paper Mills, Fiber Cans, Drums & Similar Products, and Unsupported Plastics Profile Shapes

CONTACT
William Knese
Chairman
CLARCOR Foundation
PO Box 7007
Rockford, IL 61125
(815) 962-8867

FINANCIAL SUMMARY
Recent Giving: $550,000 (1995 est.);
$798,000 (1994 approx.); $555,558 (1993)

Assets: $6,400,000 (1995); $6,365,000 (1994); $7,700,966 (1993)

Fiscal Note: Grants are made only through the foundation. Individual company departments also make direct contributions (contact David Lindsay, vice president of group services). The budget for department grants is $20,000 and is included in the figures above. Above figures include nonmonetary support.

EIN: 36-6032573

CONTRIBUTIONS SUMMARY
Typical Recipients: • *Arts & Humanities:* Arts Associations & Councils, Dance, History & Archaeology, Libraries, Museums/Galleries, Music, Theater • *Civic & Public Affairs:* Botanical Gardens/Parks, General, Hispanic Affairs, Women's Affairs • *Education:* Business Education, Colleges & Universities, Economic Education, Legal Education, Private Education (Precollege) • *Health:* Health Organizations, Hospitals, Mental Health, Nursing Services • *Religion:* General, Religious Welfare • *Science:* Science Museums • *Social Services:* At-Risk Youth, Big Brother/Big Sister, Child Welfare, Community Centers, Community Service Organizations, Day Care, Emergency Relief, Food/Clothing Distribution, Homes, People with Disabilities, Recreation & Athletics, Scouts, United Funds/United Ways, YMCA/YWCA/YMHA/YWHA, Youth Organizations

Grant Types: capital, employee matching gifts, general support, matching, and project

Note: Employee matching gift ratio: 1 to 1. Only gifts to educational institutions are matched.

Nonmonetary Support: $20,000 (1992); $20,000 (1991); $20,000 (1990)

Nonmonetary Support Types: loaned employees, loaned executives, and workplace solicitation

Note: For more information on nonmonetary support, contact David Lindsay.

Geographic Distribution: operating locations only

Operating Locations: AL (Birmingham), CA (Corona), GA (Atlanta), IL (Downers Grove, Rockford), IN (New Albany), KY (Louisville), NE (Kearney), OH (Cincinnati), PA (Lancaster), TN (Nashville), TX (Dallas, Garland)

CORP. OFFICERS
Lawrence Eugene Gloyd: *B* Milan IN 1932 *ED* Hanover Coll BA 1954 *CURR EMPL* chmn, pres, ceo, dir: CLARCOR Inc *CORP AFFIL* dir: AMcore Fin Inc, GUD Holdings Ltd, Thomas Indus Inc; mem adv bd: Liberty Mutual Ins Co; trust: Swedish Am Corp *NONPR AFFIL* chmn bd trusts: Rockford Coll; dir: IL Counc Econ Ed; dir, trust: Counc 100; mem: Am Hardware Mfrs Assn, Pres Assn; natl dir: Big Bros/Big Sisters *CLUB AFFIL* Masons

William F. Knese: *CURR EMPL* vp, treas, contr: CLARCOR Inc

Ronald A. Moreau: *B* Penetanguishene Ontario Canada 1947 *ED* Rensselaer Polytech Inst 1970 *CURR EMPL* vp consumer products group: CLARCOR Inc *NONPR AFFIL* mem: Canadian Mfrs Inst, Natl Metal Decorators

GIVING OFFICERS

Marshall C. Arne: trust *B* Forest City IA 1930 *ED* Univ IA 1952 *CURR EMPL* vp, secy: CLARCOR Inc *CORP AFFIL* sec: JL Clark Inc; secy: JA Baldwin Filters Mfg Co, MI Spring Co

Lawrence Eugene Gloyd: trust *CURR EMPL* chmn, pres, ceo, dir: CLARCOR Inc (see above)

Norman E. Johnson: trust *B* Lake Mills IA 1948 *ED* Univ IA 1970; Drake Univ 1972 *CURR EMPL* vp, gen mgr: Baldwin Filters Inc

William F. Knese: chmn, trust *CURR EMPL* vp, treas, contr: CLARCOR Inc (see above)

Ronald A. Moreau: trust *CURR EMPL* vp consumer products group: CLARCOR Inc (see above)

APPLICATION INFORMATION

Initial Approach: *Initial Contact:* brief letter; grant application *Include Information On:* amount requested, purpose for which funds are sought, description of the organization, recently audited financial statement, and proof of tax-exempt status *Deadlines:* none

OTHER THINGS TO KNOW

In 1988, J.L. Clark Manufacturing Co. was reincorporated as CLARCOR Inc. The foundation name was changed from the Clark Foundation to the CLARCOR Foundation.

GRANTS ANALYSIS

Total Grants: $555,558

Number of Grants: 84

Highest Grant: $85,153

Average Grant: $6,614

Typical Range: $1,000 to $10,000

Disclosure Period: 1993

Note: Recent grants are derived from a 1993 Form 990.

RECENT GRANTS

Library
1,500	Kearney Public Library, Kearney, NE	

General
85,153	United Way, Rockford, IL
50,000	Davis Memorial Park
50,000	Swedish American Medical Foundation, Rockford, IL
30,000	Northern Illinois Botanical Society, Rockford, IL
30,000	St. Elizabeth Community Center

CNA Financial Corporation/CNA Insurance Companies / CNA Foundation

Sales: $11.01 billion
Employees: 16,800
Parent Company: Loews Corporation
Headquarters: Chicago, IL
SIC Major Group: Accident & Health Insurance, Life Insurance, and Fire, Marine & Casualty Insurance

CONTACT
Sarada- Amani
Manager, Community Relations
CNA Insurance Cos.
CNA Plz.
Chicago, IL 60685
(312) 822-5318
Note: The company's World Wide Web address is http://www.cna.com

FINANCIAL SUMMARY

Recent Giving: $3,500,000 (1995 est.); $2,000,000 (1994 approx.); $1,689,413 (1993)

Assets: $0 (1992); $38,190 (1989)

Gifts Received: $60,000 (1989); $14,000 (1988)

Fiscal Note: Above figures include foundation and direct corporate gifts. Above figures exclude nonmonetary support. Contribution for 1989 was received from CNA.

EIN: 36-6214412

CONTRIBUTIONS SUMMARY

Typical Recipients: • *Arts & Humanities:* Arts Institutes, Dance, Historic Preservation, Libraries, Literary Arts, Museums/Galleries, Music, Opera, Performing Arts, Theater • *Civic & Public Affairs:* Business/Free Enterprise, Employment/Job Training, General, Housing, Law & Justice, Public Policy, Safety, Urban & Community Affairs, Women's Affairs, Zoos/Aquariums • *Education:* Arts/Humanities Education, Business Education, Economic Education, General, Literacy, Minority Education, Preschool Education, Private Education (Precollege), Public Education (Precollege) • *Health:* General, Health Organizations, Hospitals • *Social Services:* Child Welfare, Community Service Organizations, Counseling, Delinquency & Criminal Rehabilitation, Family Services, Food/Clothing Distribution, General, People with Disabilities, Shelters/Homelessness, United Funds/United Ways, Youth Organizations

Grant Types: employee matching gifts, general support, multiyear/continuing support, operating expenses, and scholarship

Note: Employee matching gift ratio: 1 to 1.

Nonmonetary Support Types: donated equipment and in-kind services

Note: Nonmonetary support is provided by the company; the contact for this support is Sarada-Amani (see above). The estimated value of nonmonetary support is not available.

Geographic Distribution: focus on Illinois

Operating Locations: FL (Orlando), IL (Chicago), PA (Reading), TN (Nashville)

CORP. OFFICERS

Dennis Haig Chookaszian: *B* Chicago IL 1943 *ED* Northwestern Univ BSCHE 1965; Univ Chicago MBA 1967; London Sch Econ MS 1968 *CURR EMPL* chmn, ceo: CNA Fin Corp *CORP AFFIL* chmn: Agency Mgmt Svcs; dir: Mercury Fin *NONPR AFFIL* chmn: Fdn Health Enhancement; exec vp, dir: Boy Scouts Am Chicago Area Counc; mem: Am Inst CPAs, Beta Gamma Sigma, IL Soc CPAs; trust: Commun Church Wilmette *CLUB AFFIL* mem: Bank, Westmoreland CC

GIVING OFFICERS

William H. Sharkey, Jr.: dir

APPLICATION INFORMATION

Initial Approach: *Initial Contact:* brief letter *Include Information On:* description of the organization, amount requested, purpose of funds sought, audited financial statement, proof of tax-exempt status, and names and amounts of other contributers *Deadlines:* none

Restrictions on Giving: Does not support individuals, religious organizations for sectarian purposes, capital campaigns, political or lobbying groups, or veterans' organizations.

OTHER THINGS TO KNOW

All giving through foundation is in the form of matching gifts. Information above is for corporate grant program.

Matching gifts are available only to company employees.

Company publishes a corporate contribution guidelines sheet.

CNA Insurance Companies is affiliated with CNA Financial Corporation, Continental Casualty Company, and Continental Assurance Company.

GRANTS ANALYSIS
Total Grants: $2,000,000

Typical Range: $2,500 to $5,000

Disclosure Period: 1994

Commerce Clearing House, Incorporated / Thorne Foundation, Oakleigh L.

Revenue: $577.99 million
Employees: 5,800
Headquarters: Riverwoods, IL
SIC Major Group: Book Publishing, Periodicals, Miscellaneous Publishing, and Computer Programming Services

CONTACT
Terry Milone
Vice President and Assistant Secretary
Commerce Clearing House, Incorporated
2700 Lake Cook Rd.
Riverwoods, IL 60015
(708) 940-4600

FINANCIAL SUMMARY
Recent Giving: $300,000 (1995 est.); $300,000 (1994 approx.); $196,000 (1993)

Assets: $286,667 (1993); $180,255 (1992); $158,345 (1991)

Gifts Received: $300,000 (1993); $300,000 (1992); $300,000 (1991)

Fiscal Note: Contributes through foundation only. The foundation receives gifts from Commerce Clearing House, Incorporated.

EIN: 51-0243758

CONTRIBUTIONS SUMMARY
Typical Recipients: • *Arts & Humanities:* Arts Associations & Councils, Arts Centers, Arts Festivals, Arts Institutes, Community Arts, General, Historic Preservation, History & Archaeology, Libraries, Museums/Galleries, Music, Opera, Performing Arts, Public Broadcasting, Theater • *Civic & Public Affairs:* Employment/Job Training, General, Law & Justice, Legal Aid, Professional & Trade Associations, Public Policy, Urban & Community Affairs, Women's Affairs, Zoos/Aquariums • *Education:* Arts/Humanities Education, Colleges & Universities, Education Associations, Education Funds, Elementary Education (Private), Literacy, Minority Education, Private Education (Precollege), Secondary Education (Public), Special Education • *Environment:* Air/Water Quality, General, Resource Conservation, Wildlife Protection • *Health:* Arthritis, Cancer, Health Funds, Hospitals, Nursing Services, Single-Disease Health Associations • *International:* International Organizations • *Religion:* Churches, Religious Welfare • *Science:* Observatories & Planetariums, Science Museums • *Social Services:* Animal Protection, Child Welfare, Community Centers, Community Service Organizations, Delinquency & Criminal Rehabilitation, Domestic Violence, Family Services, Recreation & Athletics, Shelters/Homelessness, Substance Abuse, United Funds/United Ways, Volunteer Services, Youth Organizations

Grant Types: capital and general support

Nonmonetary Support Types: donated equipment

Geographic Distribution: emphasis on Chicago and New York City

Operating Locations: CA (San Francisco, San Rafael, Torrance), DC, IL (Riverwoods, Springfield), NJ (Jersey City), NY (New York)

CORP. OFFICERS
Oakleigh Blakeman Thorne: *B* Santa Barbara CA 1932 *ED* Harvard Univ BA 1954 *CURR EMPL* chmn, dir: Commerce Clearing House *CORP AFFIL* chmn: CCH Computax; dir: Bank Millbrook; pres: CT Corp Sys, Legal Information Svcs *PHIL AFFIL* pres, trust: Millbrook Tribute Garden; pres: Oakleigh L. Thorne Foundation; chmn, pres, dir *CLUB AFFIL* Brook, Racquet & Tennis

GIVING OFFICERS
Joseph Finora: asst treas

Theresa A. Milone: vp, asst secy *CURR EMPL* asst secy, dir: CCH Legal Info Svcs

Oakleigh Thorne: vp, secy *PHIL AFFIL* vp, secy: Millbrook Tribute Garden

Oakleigh Blakeman Thorne: chmn, pres, treas, dir *CURR EMPL* chmn, dir: Commerce Clearing House *PHIL AFFIL* pres, trust: Millbrook Tribute Garden; pres: Oakleigh L. Thorne Foundation (see above)

Mary Walters: head of pub rels

APPLICATION INFORMATION
Initial Approach: *Initial Contact:* brief letter of inquiry and full proposal *Include Information On:* a description of organization, amount requested, and purpose of funds sought *Deadlines:* none

Restrictions on Giving: Does not support individuals, scholarships, fellowships, or matching gifts. Does not make loans.

GRANTS ANALYSIS
Total Grants: $196,000
Number of Grants: 59
Highest Grant: $33,000
Average Grant: $3,322
Typical Range: $1,000 to $5,000
Disclosure Period: 1993

Note: Recent grants are derived from a 1993 grants list.

RECENT GRANTS
General

33,000	United Way New York City, New York, NY
10,000	Chicago Horticultural Society, Chicago, IL
10,000	Project Rush
6,000	United Way Marin County, CA
6,000	Young Adult Institute, New York, NY

Commonwealth Edison Co.

Revenue: $5.26 billion
Employees: 19,000
Parent Company: Unicom Corp.
Headquarters: Chicago, IL
SIC Major Group: Electric Services

CONTACT
Edward M. Peterson
Corporate Responsibility Manager
Commonwealth Edison Co.
PO Box 767
Chicago, IL 60690
(312) 394-3062

FINANCIAL SUMMARY
Recent Giving: $3,400,000 (1995 est.); $2,891,000 (1994); $3,317,000 (1993)

Fiscal Note: All contributions are made directly by the company. Above figures exclude nonmonetary support.

CONTRIBUTIONS SUMMARY
Typical Recipients: • *Arts & Humanities:* Arts Institutes, Community Arts, Dance, Ethnic & Folk Arts, Libraries, Museums/Galleries, Opera, Performing Arts, Public Broadcasting, Theater • *Civic & Public Affairs:* Civil Rights, Economic Development, Housing, Urban & Community Affairs, Zoos/Aquariums • *Education:* Colleges & Universities • *Health:* Health Organizations, Hospitals, Single-Disease Health Associations • *Social Services:* Community Service Organizations, Substance Abuse, United Funds/United Ways, Youth Organizations

Grant Types: capital, employee matching gifts, and general support

Note: The company also reports benefits as a typical grant type. Employee matching gift ratio: 1 to 1 for education only.

Nonmonetary Support: $400,000 (1994)

Nonmonetary Support Types: in-kind services and loaned executives

Geographic Distribution: limited to company service area (Chicago and northern Illinois)

Operating Locations: IL (Chicago)

CORP. OFFICERS
John J. Costello: *CURR EMPL* dir pub aff: Commonwealth Edison Co

James John O'Connor: *B* Chicago IL 1937 *ED* Holy Cross Coll BS 1958; Harvard Univ MBA 1960; Georgetown Univ JD 1963 *CURR EMPL* chmn, ceo, dir: Commonwealth Edison Co *CORP AFFIL* UN Airlines Lines Corp; chmn: Advanced Reactor Corp; dir: Am Natl Canada, Chicago Stock Exchange, Corning Inc, First Chicago Corp, First Natl Bank Chicago, Scotsman Indus Inc, Tribune Co *NONPR AFFIL* bd advs: Mercy Hosp Med Ctr; chmn: Cardinal Bernardins Big Shoulders Fund; chmn, dir: Chicago Assn Commerce Indus; dir: Am Nuclear Energy Counc, Catholic Charities, Chicago Urban League, Edison Electric Inst, Harvard Univ Grad Sch Bus Admin Assocs, Leadership Counc Metro Open Commun, Lyric Opera Chicago, Mus Sci & Indus,

Reading Is Fundamental, St Xavier Coll, US Counc Energy Awareness; mem: Am Bar Assn, Bus Counc, Chicago Bar Assn, IL Bar Assn, IL Bus Roundtable; mem exec bd: Boy Scouts Am Chicago Area Counc; trust: Northwestern Univ *CLUB AFFIL* Hundred Cook County *PHIL AFFIL* vp, dir: Helen Brach Foundation

Donald Allen Petkus: *B* Chicago IL 1941 *ED* Marquette Univ MSME 1962; Northwestern Univ MBA 1968 *CURR EMPL* sr vp: Commonwealth Edison Co *NONPR AFFIL* adv: Mercy Hosp Med Ctr; bd govs: Orchestral Assn; chmn: Am Cancer Soc; dir: Boy Scouts Am, WFMT; trust: Mus Contemporary Art, WTTW-TV

Cordell Reed: *B* Chicago IL 1938 *ED* Univ IL BSME 1960 *CURR EMPL* sr vp: Commonwealth Edison Co *CORP AFFIL* dir: LaSalle Natl Bank, LaSalle Natl Corp, Walgreen Co *NONPR AFFIL* mem: Am Nuclear Soc, Natl Tech Assn; trust: Chicago Commun Trust, Abraham Lincoln Ctr, John G Shedd Aquarium

Samuel Knox Skinner: *B* Chicago IL 1938 *ED* Univ IL BS 1960; DePaul Univ JD 1966 *CURR EMPL* pres, dir: Commonwealth Edison Co *NONPR AFFIL* mem: Am Bar Assn, Chicago Bar Assn, IL Bar Assn *CLUB AFFIL* Chicago, Shoreacres

Pamela Strobel: *B* Chicago IL 1952 *ED* Univ IL BS 1974; Univ IL JD 1977 *CURR EMPL* vp, gen couns: Commonwealth Edison Co

GIVING OFFICERS

James John O'Connor: chmn corp responsibility comm *CURR EMPL* chmn, ceo, dir: Commonwealth Edison Co *PHIL AFFIL* vp, dir: Helen Brach Foundation (see above)

Edward M. Peterson: *CURR EMPL* mgr corp responsibility: Commonwealth Edison Co

Donald Allen Petkus: mem corp responsibility comm *CURR EMPL* sr vp: Commonwealth Edison Co (see above)

Cordell Reed: mem (corp responsibility comm) *CURR EMPL* sr vp: Commonwealth Edison Co (see above)

Pamela Strobel: mem corp responsibility comm *CURR EMPL* vp, gen couns: Commonwealth Edison Co (see above)

APPLICATION INFORMATION

Initial Approach: *Initial Contact:* brief letter *Include Information On:* outline of proposal, description of the organization, amount requested, and proof of tax-exempt status *Deadlines:* none

Restrictions on Giving: The company does not purchase ads for benefit programs or make grants to religious or political organizations, individuals, or fraternal organizations. Capital support typically is limited to one-half of 1% of total drive.

GRANTS ANALYSIS
Total Grants: $2,891,000
Number of Grants: 400
Typical Range: $1,000 to $5,000
Disclosure Period: 1994

CR Industries

Sales: $153.0 million
Employees: 1,800
Parent Company: SKF USA, Inc.
Headquarters: Elgin, IL
SIC Major Group: Industrial Machinery & Equipment and Transportation Equipment

CONTACT
Jane Graves
Personnel
CR Industries
900 N State
Elgin, IL 60123
(708) 742-7840

FINANCIAL SUMMARY
Fiscal Note: Annual Giving Range: $100,000 to $250,000

CONTRIBUTIONS SUMMARY
Highest priorities are social services and higher education. Social service support goes to united funds, drug and alcohol programs, and community service organizations. In education, concentration is on colleges and universities, with an interest in business and economic education. Arts centers, museums, business and free enterprise, and professional and trade associations also receive support. Health funding goes to local hospitals.

Typical Recipients: • *Arts & Humanities:* Arts Associations & Councils, Arts Centers, Historic Preservation, Libraries, Museums/Galleries, Music, Performing Arts • *Civic & Public Affairs:* Business/Free Enterprise, Economic Development, Law & Justice, Professional & Trade Associations, Public Policy, Urban & Community Affairs, Zoos/Aquariums • *Education:* Business Education, Colleges & Universities, Economic Education, Engineering/Technological Education • *Health:* Hospitals • *Social Services:* Community Service Organizations, People with Disabilities, Substance Abuse, United Funds/United Ways

Grant Types: capital, challenge, endowment, general support, project, research, and seed money

Nonmonetary Support Types: donated equipment and loaned executives

Geographic Distribution: near headquarters and operating locations only

Operating Locations: IL (Elgin), IN, KS, MO, NC, OK, SD

CORP. OFFICERS
Dennis Clark: *CURR EMPL* pres: CR Indus
James Meyer: *CURR EMPL* vp, cfo: CR Indus

APPLICATION INFORMATION
Initial Approach: Submit a brief letter or proposal, including proof of tax-exempt status, a description of the organization, and the purpose for which funds are sought. Applications are accepted any time.

Restrictions on Giving: The following are not considered for charitable contributions: fraternal organizations, goodwill advertis-

ing, or religious organizations for fraternal purposes.

GRANTS ANALYSIS
Typical Range: $1,000 to $2,500

Crown Memorial, Arie and Ida

CONTACT
Rebecca Stimson
Executive Director
Arie and Ida Crown Memorial
222 N LaSalle St., Ste. 2000
Chicago, IL 60601
(312) 236-6300

FINANCIAL SUMMARY
Recent Giving: $4,545,209 (1992); $5,141,555 (1990); $4,061,485 (1989)
Assets: $91,153,637 (1992); $77,900,185 (1990); $110,305,020 (1989)
Gifts Received: $125,463 (1987)
Fiscal Note: Listed donors in 1987 were Lester Crown, John J. Crown, and Joanne Crown.
EIN: 36-6076088

CONTRIBUTIONS SUMMARY
Donor(s): The foundation was established in honor of Arie and Ida Crown by their children in 1947. The Crown family was headed by noted industrialist Henry Crown. Henry and his brother Sol started a building supply company that became the largest in the Chicago area, and the basis for the Crown family fortune.

John J. Crown, Lester Crown and Joanne Crown have all donated more than 2% of the total contributions received by the foundation.

Typical Recipients: • *Arts & Humanities:* Community Arts, Libraries, Museums/Galleries, Music, Opera, Performing Arts, Theater • *Civic & Public Affairs:* Civil Rights, Employment/Job Training, Municipalities/Towns, Public Policy, Women's Affairs, Zoos/Aquariums • *Education:* Colleges & Universities, General, Literacy, Private Education (Precollege), Religious Education • *Environment:* Air/Water Quality • *Health:* Alzheimers Disease, Children's Health/Hospitals, Clinics/Medical Centers, Diabetes, Hospitals, Mental Health, Single-Disease Health Associations • *International:* Foreign Educational Institutions, International Affairs, Missionary/Religious Activities • *Religion:* Jewish Causes • *Science:* Science Museums • *Social Services:* Child Welfare, Community Service Organizations, Domestic Violence, Emergency Relief, Family Services, Food/Clothing Distribution, Homes, People with Disabilities, Refugee Assistance, Senior Services, United Funds/United Ways, Youth Organizations

Grant Types: capital, endowment, and general support

Geographic Distribution: metropolitan Chicago, IL

GIVING OFFICERS

Arie Steven Crown: vp, dir *B* Chicago IL
1952 *ED* Claremont McKenna Coll 1974;
Univ CA Los Angeles 1977 *CURR EMPL*
gen ptnr: Henry Crown & Co *CORP AFFIL*
dir: Aspen Ski Co, Farmers Investment Co,
Hilton Hotels Corp, Parks Devel Co, Sierra
Tucson Companies Inc; pres: Ojai Valley
Inn Co

James Schine Crown: vp, dir *B* 1953 *ED*
Hampshire Coll BA 1976; Stanford Univ JD
1980 *CURR EMPL* gen ptnr: Henry Crown
& Co *CORP AFFIL* vp: Am Envelope Co;
vp, dir: CC Indus Inc, Exchange Bldg Corp

Lester Crown: don, vp, treas, dir *B* Chicago
IL 1925 *ED* Northwestern Univ BSCE 1947;
Harvard Univ MBA 1949 *CURR EMPL*
chmn, dir: Material Svc Corp *CORP AFFIL*
chmn, dir: CC Indus Inc, Exchange Bldg
Corp, Material Svc Resource Corp; dir:
Maytag Corp; exec vp, chmn exec comm,
dir: Gen Dynamics Corp; pres, dir: Henry
Crown & Co; ptnr: NY Yankees Partnership
NONPR AFFIL chmn: Jewish Theological
Seminary; dir: Childrens Meml Hosp, Lyric
Opera; mem: Harvard Univ Grad Sch Bus
Admin Alumni Assn, Phi Eta Sigma, Pi Mu
Epsilon, Tau Beta Pi; mem bd advs: Chicago
Zoological Soc; trust: Northwestern Univ
Aspen Inst Humanistic Studies, Michael
Reese Fdn *CLUB AFFIL* Chicago, Commer-
cial, Econ, Lake Shore CC, Marco Polo,
Mid-Am, Mid-Am, Northmoor CC, North-
western Univ John Evans, Standard

Susan Crown: pres

Charles B. Goodman: vp, dir *PHIL AFFIL*
dir: Edward and Marion Goodman Foundation; trust: Edward A. Crown Charitable
Fund

Barbara Goodman Manilow: vp, dir

Byron S. Miller: vp, dir

Rebecca Stimson: exec dir

APPLICATION INFORMATION
Initial Approach:
Prospective applicants should submit a letter
of inquiry before submitting a proposal.
January 31 and July 31

GRANTS ANALYSIS
Total Grants: $4,545,209
Number of Grants: 649
Highest Grant: $200,000
Average Grant: $7,003
Typical Range: $100 to $10,000
Disclosure Period: 1992
Note: Recent grants are derived from a 1992
Form 990.

RECENT GRANTS
Library
50,000   Chicago Public Library
          Foundation, Chicago, IL

General
250,000   American Committee for the
          Weizmann Institute of
          Science, New York, NY
200,000   Brown University, Providence,
          RI

200,000   Yale University, New Haven,
          CT
180,000   Jewish United Fund of
          Metropolitan Chicago,
          Chicago, IL
170,000   Covenant Foundation,
          Chicago, IL

CT Corp. System / Thorne Foundation, Oakleigh L.

Employees: 1,115
Parent Company: Commerce Clearing House
Headquarters: New York, NY
SIC Major Group: Engineering & Management Services

CONTACT
Terry Milone
Assistant Secretary
CT Corp. System
c/o CCH Inc.
2700 Lake Crook Rd.
Riverwoods, IL 60015
(708) 940-4600

FINANCIAL SUMMARY
Fiscal Note: Company does not disclose contributions figures.

CONTRIBUTIONS SUMMARY
Typical Recipients: • *Arts & Humanities:*
Art History, Arts Associations & Councils,
Arts Institutes, Film & Video, General, Li-
braries, Museums/Galleries, Performing
Arts, Public Broadcasting, Theater • *Civic &
Public Affairs:* Botanical Gardens/Parks,
Clubs, Housing, Women's Affairs,
Zoos/Aquariums • *Education:* Colleges &
Universities, General • *Environment:* Re-
source Conservation, Wildlife Protection
• *Health:* Hospices, Hospitals • *Social Serv-
ices:* Child Welfare, Community Service Or-
ganizations, Family Services,
Shelters/Homelessness, Substance Abuse,
United Funds/United Ways, Youth Organiza-
tions

Grant Types: capital, general support,
matching, and multiyear/continuing support

Geographic Distribution: only in headquarters area

Operating Locations: NY (New York)

CORP. OFFICERS
Robyn Staaterman: *CURR EMPL* pres: CT
Corp

GIVING OFFICERS
Oakleigh Blakeman Thorne: pres *B* Santa
Barbara CA 1932 *ED* Harvard Univ BA
1954 *CURR EMPL* chmn, dir: Commerce
Clearing House *CORP AFFIL* chmn: CCH
Computax; dir: Bank Millbrook; pres: CT
Corp Sys, Legal Information Svcs *PHIL AF-
FIL* chmn, pres, treas, dir: Oakleigh L.
Thorne Foundation; pres, trust: Millbrook

Tribute Garden; chmn, pres, dir *CLUB AF-
FIL* Brook, Racquet & Tennis

APPLICATION INFORMATION
Initial Approach: Send a full proposal. Include a description of organization, amount
requested, and purpose of funds sought.
Restrictions on Giving: Does not support
individuals.

OTHER THINGS TO KNOW
Company gives through the Oakleigh B.
Thorne Foundation. See Commerce Clearing
House entry for more information on the
Oakleigh B. Thorne Foundation.

GRANTS ANALYSIS
Typical Range: $1,000 to $2,500

Cuneo Foundation

CONTACT
John F. Cuneo, Jr.
President
Cuneo Foundation
9101 N Greenwood, Ste. 210
Niles, IL 60714
(708) 296-3351

FINANCIAL SUMMARY
Recent Giving: $732,729 (1994); $783,337
(1991); $797,496 (1990)
Assets: $25,528,082 (1991); $22,378,610
(1990); $17,313,589 (1989)
EIN: 36-2261606

CONTRIBUTIONS SUMMARY
Donor(s): The foundation was incorporated
in 1945 by John F. Cuneo and the Milwaukee Golf Development Corp.

Typical Recipients: • *Arts & Humanities:*
Libraries, Music • *Civic & Public Affairs:*
Law & Justice • *Education:* Colleges & Uni-
versities, Medical Education, Private Educa-
tion (Precollege), Public Education
(Precollege), Religious Education, Secon-
dary Education (Public) • *Health:* Alzhe-
imers Disease, Cancer, Children's
Health/Hospitals, Heart, Hospices, Hospi-
tals, Medical Research, Single-Disease
Health Associations • *Religion:* Bible
Study/Translation, Churches, Religious Or-
ganizations, Religious Welfare, Seminaries
• *Social Services:* Child Welfare, Commu-
nity Service Organizations, Food/Clothing
Distribution, General, Homes, People with
Disabilities, Recreation & Athletics, Shel-
ters/Homelessness, United Funds/United
Ways, Youth Organizations

Grant Types: capital, general support, and
matching

Geographic Distribution: focus on the Chicago, IL, metropolitan area

GIVING OFFICERS

Herta Cuneo: dir

John F. Cuneo, Jr.: pres, dir *B* Chicago IL 1931 *ED* Georgetown Univ *CURR EMPL* ptnr, pres: Milwaukee Golf Develo[D Co *CORP AFFIL* pres: Grasmere Corp, Hawthorn Corp

Rev. Msgr. Harry C. Koenig: dir

Consuela Cuneo McAlister: dir

Tim McAlister: dir

Charles Lucien McEvoy: vp, asst secy, dir *B* Bradford PA 1917 *ED* Georgetown Univ AB 1938-1941; Chicago Kent Coll Law JD 1950 *CLUB AFFIL* Chicago Athletic, Chicago GC

Rosemary McEvoy: dir

Father George Rassas: dir

Robert F. Routh: secy, treas

John Tomisek: secy, treas, dir

APPLICATION INFORMATION
Initial Approach:

The foundation requests applications be made in writing.

The foundation requests that the application include any supporting materials that might be necessary before a decision can be made.

The foundation has no deadline for submitting proposals.

The board of directors meets in May and October of each year. Decisions are usually made within two months.

Restrictions on Giving: The foundation reports that at least 60% of the annual contributions are for religious, charitable, educational, or scientific purposes directly or indirectly associated with the Roman Catholic Church.

Restrictions on Giving: The foundation has set no fixed limit on the amount of the grants, but its policy has been to confine the amounts to no more than $75,000 in any one year. At present, grants are not being made to individuals, or for scholarships, fellowships, research projects, or loans.

GRANTS ANALYSIS
Total Grants: $732,729

Highest Grant: $50,000

Typical Range: $1,000 to $15,000

Disclosure Period: 1994

Note: Recent grants are derived from a 1991 Form 990.

RECENT GRANTS

Library
7,000	Library of International Relations, Chicago, IL

General
45,000	St. Joseph Church, Chicago, IL
32,500	Children's Home and Aid Society, Chicago, IL
29,000	Stritch School of Medicine, Chicago, IL
25,000	Franciscan Friars of Maryville, Maryville, IL
25,000	St. Mary's Parish, Chicago, IL

Deere & Co. / Deere Foundation, John

Sales: $7.75 billion
Employees: 34,500
Headquarters: Moline, IL
SIC Major Group: Farm Machinery & Equipment, Internal Combustion Engines Nec, Lawn & Garden Equipment, and Construction Machinery

---

CONTACT
Donald R. Margenthaler
President
John Deere Foundation
John Deere Rd.
Moline, IL 61265
(309) 765-5030

FINANCIAL SUMMARY
Recent Giving: $7,500,000 (fiscal 1995); $5,800,000 (fiscal 1994); $3,781,387 (fiscal 1993)

Assets: $21,000,000 (fiscal 1995); $19,400,000 (fiscal 1994); $17,600,000 (fiscal 1993)

Gifts Received: $2,809,000 (fiscal 1993); $6,525,000 (fiscal 1990)

Fiscal Note: Above figures include foundation giving and direct contributions by the company and its operating units. In fiscal 1994, foundation giving was $4,200,000 and direct giving was $1,600,000. International giving is included in the above figures. Above figures exclude nonmonetary support. In fiscal 1993, foundation received contributions from: Deere & Co. ($2,000,000), John Deere Credit Company ($500,000), John Deere Insurance Company ($26,210), Tahoe Insurance Company ($169,290), Sierra General Life Insurance Company ($13,500), Heritage National Healthplan Services, Inc. ($100,000).

EIN: 36-6051024

CONTRIBUTIONS SUMMARY
Typical Recipients: • *Arts & Humanities:* Arts Centers, Community Arts, Libraries, Museums/Galleries, Music, Opera • *Civic & Public Affairs:* Community Foundations, Economic Development, Municipalities/Towns, Parades/Festivals, Rural Affairs, Urban & Community Affairs • *Education:* Agricultural Education, Business Education, Colleges & Universities, Community & Junior Colleges, Economic Education, Engineering/Technological Education, General, Minority Education, Private Education (Precollege), Public Education (Precollege), Science/Mathematics Education, Secondary Education (Private) • *Environment:* General • *Health:* Emergency/Ambulance Services, Health Organizations • *Religion:* Religious Welfare • *Social Services:* Community Centers, Community Service Organizations, Day Care, Family Services, Homes, People with Disabilities, Senior Services, Substance Abuse, United Funds/United Ways, Youth Organizations

Grant Types: capital, department, general support, and project

Nonmonetary Support: $375,000 (fiscal 1994); $433,000 (fiscal 1993); $306,000 (fiscal 1992)

Nonmonetary Support Types: in-kind services and loaned executives

Note: Nonmonetary support is provided by the company.

Geographic Distribution: in areas where company has facilities and to some national organizations

Operating Locations: GA (Augusta), IA (Davenport, Des Moines, Dubuque, Ottumwa, Waterloo), IL (East Moline, Jacksonville, Milan, Moline), KS (Coffeyville), MN (Minneapolis), NV (Reno), TN (Greeneville), WI (Horicon, Madison)

CORP. OFFICERS
Hans Walter Becherer: *B* Detroit MI 1935 *ED* Trinity Coll BA 1957; Munich Univ 1958; Harvard Univ MBA 1962 *CURR EMPL* chmn, ceo: John Deere & Co *CORP AFFIL* chmn: John Deere Capital Corp, John Deere Credit Co; dir: AlliedSignal Inc, Schering-Plough Corp; mem adv comm: Chase Manhattan Bank Intl; pres: John Deere Indus Equipment Co, Deere Mktg Svcs Inc *NONPR AFFIL* dir: US/Yugoslavia Trade Econ Counc; mem: Bus Counc, Bus Roundtable, Conf Bd, Counc Foreign Rels, Equipment Mfrs Inst; mem (industry sector adv comm): US Dept Commerce; trust: Comm Econ Devel; vp, trust: St Katherines-St Marks Sch *CLUB AFFIL* Arsenal GC, Chicago, Rock Island

Wade Clark: *CURR EMPL* dir govt aff: John Deere & Co

David H. Stowe, Jr.: *B* Winston-Salem NC 1936 *ED* Amherst Coll BA Econ 1958; MA Inst Tech 1961 *CURR EMPL* pres, coo, dir: John Deere & Co *CORP AFFIL* dir: John Deere Capital Corp, John Deere Catalog Co, John Deere Co, John Deere Credit Co, John Deere Fin Ltd, John Deere Health Care, John Deere Indus Equipment Co, John Deere Ins Group, John Deere Leasing Co, John Deere Ltd, Deere Mktg Svcs Inc, John Deere SA, Heritage Natl Healthplan Svcs Inc

GIVING OFFICERS
Hans Walter Becherer: dir *CURR EMPL* chmn, ceo: John Deere & Co (see above)

Darlene S. Ellis: asst secy

Joseph Walker England: chmn, dir *B* Moline IL 1940 *ED* Univ IL BS 1962 *CURR EMPL* sr vp worldwide parts & corp admin: John Deere & Co *CORP AFFIL* dir: John Deere Indus Equipment Co, First Midwest Bank Corp; vp, dir: John Deere Capital Corp *NONPR AFFIL* chmn: Moline Fdn; dir: Arrowhead Ranch, Natl Assn Mfrs, Un Way Am; mem: Am Inst CPAs, Fin Execs Inst, IL Soc CPAs, Natl Assn Accts, Univ IL Alumni Assn *CLUB AFFIL* Short Hills CC

Donald R. Margenthaler: pres, dir

Michael Stewart Plunkett: treas, dir *B* Moline IL 1937 *ED* Augustana Coll BA 1968 *CURR EMPL* sr vp engg, tech & human resources: John Deere & Co *CORP AF-FIL* dir: John Deere Ins Group, First Natl Bank Moline, Heritage Natl Healthplan Svcs Inc, HON Indus Inc *NONPR AFFIL* dir: Jr Achievement Quad Cities Area, Quad City Devel Group, YMCA Upper Rock Island County; mem: Machinery Allied Products Inst, Mfrs Alliance Productivity & Innovation; trust: St Ambrose Coll

Sonja J. Sterling: secy

David H. Stowe, Jr.: dir *CURR EMPL* pres, coo, dir: John Deere & Co (see above)

APPLICATION INFORMATION
Initial Approach: *Initial Contact:* one-page letter to Donald R. Margenthaler, President of the John Deere Foundation, if organization is located in Moline, IL, or is national in scope; organizations serving communities where John Deere units are located should direct letters to the unit's general manager *Include Information On:* description of the organization and statement of objectives; explanation of purpose or goals for which support is requested; description of benefits and geographic area to be served; budget information, sources of revenue and other contributions; plans for reporting results; amount requested and rationale for the request; and verification of tax-exempt status *Deadlines:* none

Restrictions on Giving: John Deere Foundation will not provide support for individuals; dinners or special events; fraternal organizations; goodwill advertising; or political or lobbying groups.

OTHER THINGS TO KNOW
In 1992 and 1993, Deere & Co. and its employees, through payroll deductions, provided more than $7 million (each year) to support various nonprofit organizations, including major support for the United Way.

GRANTS ANALYSIS
Total Grants: $4,276,815*

Number of Grants: 278

Highest Grant: $500,000

Average Grant: $5,000*

Typical Range: $1,000 to $5,000

Disclosure Period: fiscal year ending October 31, 1994

Note: Total grants figure represents foundation giving only. Foundation supplied average grant figure. Recent grants are derived from a fiscal 1993 Form 990.

RECENT GRANTS

General
500,000	Iowa State Fair Board, Des Moines, IA
310,000	Cedar Valley United Way, Waterloo, IA
250,000	St. Ambrose University, Davenport, IA
221,000	Urban Foundation, New York, NY
200,000	Renew Moline, Moline, IL

Demos Foundation, N.

CONTACT
William C. Diebel
Secretary and Director
N. Demos Fdn.
c/o The Northern Trust Co.
50 S LaSalle St.
Chicago, IL 60675
(312) 630-6000

FINANCIAL SUMMARY
Recent Giving: $194,000 (fiscal 1992); $157,200 (fiscal 1990); $150,000 (fiscal 1989)

Assets: $3,533,065 (fiscal 1992); $3,212,149 (fiscal 1990); $3,004,501 (fiscal 1989)

EIN: 36-6165689

CONTRIBUTIONS SUMMARY
Donor(s): the late Nicholas Demos

Typical Recipients: • *Arts & Humanities:* Libraries • *Civic & Public Affairs:* General • *Education:* Agricultural Education, Colleges & Universities • *Health:* Children's Health/Hospitals • *International:* Foreign Educational Institutions, International Organizations, International Peace & Security Issues • *Social Services:* Child Welfare, Community Service Organizations, Family Services, People with Disabilities, Youth Organizations

Grant Types: scholarship

Geographic Distribution: limited to Greece

GIVING OFFICERS
William C. Diebel: secy, dir

Elizabeth R. Gebhard: dir

Charles M. Gray: dir

Bishop Iakvos: dir

J. Terrance Murray: treas, dir *PHIL AF-FIL* asst secy, treas, dir: Bert William Martin Foundation

Robert F. Reusche: dir *B* New Rochelle NY 1927 *ED* OH St Univ BS 1949; Univ Chicago MBA 1955 *CURR EMPL* vchmn, dir: Northern Trust Co *CORP AFFIL* chmn, dir: Northern Trust FL Corp; dir: Banque Scandinave Suisse, Griffin Group *NONPR AFFIL* dir: JR Bowman Health Ctr; mem: Am Bankers Assn, Corp Fiduciary Assn, Fin Analysts Federation; mem adv bd: Catholic Charities; trust: Chicago Home Incurables, Ravinia Festival Assn

Mrs. Irving Seaman, Jr.: pres, dir

Gordon H. Smith: chmn, dir *PHIL AFFIL* dir: Gordon and Norma Smith Family Foundation

Mrs. Theodore D. Tieken: dir

APPLICATION INFORMATION
Initial Approach: Send a brief letter of inquiry. There are no deadlines.

Restrictions on Giving: Limited to charities in Greece.

PUBLICATIONS
Application Guidelines

GRANTS ANALYSIS
Total Grants: $194,000

Number of Grants: 12

Highest Grant: $50,000

Typical Range: $5,000 to $25,000

Disclosure Period: fiscal year ending June 30, 1992

Note: Recent grants are derived from a fiscal 1992 Form 990.

RECENT GRANTS

Library
12,000	Gennadius Library, American School of Classical Studies

General
50,000	Spastics Society
25,000	Anatolia College
20,000	American Farm School, New York, NY
20,000	Society for Thalassemic Children
19,000	Social Work Foundation

Dillon Foundation

CONTACT
Peter W. Dillon
President and Director
Dillon Foundation
PO Box 537
Sterling, IL 61081
(815) 626-9000

FINANCIAL SUMMARY
Recent Giving: $1,765,706 (fiscal 1993); $1,367,634 (fiscal 1991); $1,203,088 (fiscal 1990)

Assets: $29,581,911 (fiscal 1991); $23,835,337 (fiscal 1990); $23,179,465 (fiscal 1989)

EIN: 36-6059349

CONTRIBUTIONS SUMMARY
Donor(s): The foundation was incorporated in 1953 by members of the Dillon family.

Typical Recipients: • *Arts & Humanities:* History & Archaeology, Libraries, Music, Opera • *Civic & Public Affairs:* Botanical Gardens/Parks, Community Foundations, Economic Development, Municipalities/Towns, Safety, Urban & Community Affairs, Zoos/Aquariums • *Education:* Colleges & Universities, Community & Junior Colleges, Economic Education, Education Associations, Education Funds, Private Education (Precollege), Public Education (Precollege), Science/Mathematics Education, Secondary Education (Public) • *Environment:* General • *Health:* Cancer, Children's Health/Hospitals, Clinics/Medical Centers, Emergency/Ambulance Services, Health Organizations, Hospitals, Medical Research, Research/Studies Institutes, Single-Disease Health Associations • *International:* International Organizations • *Religion:* Churches, Religious Organizations, Religious Welfare • *Social Services:* Community Service Organizations, Family

Planning, People with Disabilities, Recreation & Athletics, Senior Services, United Funds/United Ways, Youth Organizations

Grant Types: capital, emergency, general support, matching, multiyear/continuing support, research, scholarship, and seed money

Geographic Distribution: focus on the Sterling, IL, area

GIVING OFFICERS
James M. Boesen: treas, dir

John P. Conway: vp, secy, dir

Margo Dillon: asst secy, dir

Peter W. Dillon: pres, dir

Gale Inglee: asst treas, dir

APPLICATION INFORMATION
Initial Approach:

The foundation requests applications be made in writing.

Written proposals should describe the details of the program or project for which the applicant is requesting assistance.

There are no deadlines.

Restrictions on Giving: No grants are made to individuals. The foundation does not make loans.

GRANTS ANALYSIS
Total Grants: $1,765,706

Number of Grants: 78

Highest Grant: $976,458

Average Grant: $10,250*

Typical Range: $500 to $12,000

Disclosure Period: fiscal year ending October 31, 1993

Note: Average grant figure excludes the highest grant of $976,458. Recent grants are derived from a fiscal 1993 grants list.

RECENT GRANTS
Library
36,000	Sterling Park Library, Sterling, IL

General
976,458	City of Sterling, Sterling, IL
183,484	Sterling Schools Foundation, Sterling, IL
121,373	Sterling Park District, Sterling, IL
60,000	United Way, Sterling, IL
38,475	Sterling High School Activity Fund, Sterling, IL

Donnelley Foundation, Gaylord and Dorothy

CONTACT
Jane Rishel
President
Gaylord and Dorothy Donnelley Fdn.
350 E 22nd St.
Chicago, IL 60616-1428
(312) 326-7255

FINANCIAL SUMMARY
Recent Giving: $1,742,573 (1993); $749,445 (1992); $696,050 (1991)

Assets: $12,000,553 (1993); $12,209,591 (1992); $9,555,226 (1991)

Gifts Received: $292,969 (1993); $188,029 (1992); $545,000 (1991)

Fiscal Note: In 1993, contributions were received from Gaylord Donnelley Estate.

EIN: 36-6108460

CONTRIBUTIONS SUMMARY
Donor(s): Gaylord Donnelley, Dorothy Ranney Donnelley

Typical Recipients: • *Arts & Humanities:* Arts Associations & Councils, Arts Centers, Arts Festivals, Historic Preservation, History & Archaeology, Libraries, Literary Arts, Museums/Galleries, Theater • *Civic & Public Affairs:* Botanical Gardens/Parks, Civil Rights, Clubs, Community Foundations, Economic Development, First Amendment Issues, General, Professional & Trade Associations, Public Policy, Rural Affairs, Urban & Community Affairs • *Education:* Colleges & Universities, General, Private Education (Precollege), Social Sciences Education • *Environment:* General, Resource Conservation, Wildlife Protection • *Health:* Medical Rehabilitation, Medical Research, Respiratory, Single-Disease Health Associations • *International:* Foreign Educational Institutions, International Environmental Issues • *Religion:* Churches, Religious Organizations • *Social Services:* Animal Protection, Child Welfare, Community Service Organizations, Senior Services, Shelters/Homelessness, Youth Organizations

Grant Types: general support, operating expenses, and project

Geographic Distribution: focus on the Chicago, IL, area

GIVING OFFICERS
Gerald W. Adelmann: dir

Larry D. Berning: secy, dir *B* Kendallville IN 1940 *ED* IN Univ AB 1963; IN Univ JD 1968 *CURR EMPL* Sidley & Austin: ptnr *NONPR AFFIL* mem: Am Bar Assn, Am Coll Trust & Estate Counc, Chicago Bar Assn, Chicago Estate Planning Counc, Il Bar Assn, IN Bar Assn; pres: Alice T Miner Colonial Collection, William H. Miner Fdn; trust: Old Peoples Home Chicago *CLUB AFFIL* Law, Legal, Mid-Day

Robert T. Carter: dir

Robert W. Carton, MD: dir

Dorothy R. Donnelley: vp *CLUB AFFIL* Womens Athletic

Elliott R. Donnelley: vp, dir

Strachan Donnelley: chmn, dir

Laura Donnelley-Morton: vp, dir

James Burrows Edwards: dir *B* Hawthorne FL 1927 *ED* Coll Charleston BS 1950; Univ Louisville DMD 1955; Coll Charleston LiHD 1975; Univ Louisville DSS 1982 *CORP AFFIL* dir: Brendles, Chemical Waste Mgmt, Com Satellite Corp, Encyclopedia Britannica, IMD Industries, Natl Data Corp, Phillips Petroleum, Wachovia Bank SC; mem adv bd: Norfolk-Southern Corp *NONPR AFFIL* dir: William Benton Fdn, Harry Frank Guggenheim Fdn, Pi Kappa Phi Fdn; fellow: Am Coll Dentists, Intl Coll Dentists; mem: AHEPA, Am Dental Assn, Am Hellenic Ed Progressive Assn, Am Soc Oral & Maxillofacial Surgeons, British Assn Oral & Maxillofacial Surgeons, Chalmers J Lyons Academy Oral Surgery, Coastal District Dental Soc, Delta Sigma Delta, Fed Dentaire Intl, Intl Soc Oral & Maxillofacial Surgeons, Masons, Navy League US, Omicron Delta Kappa, Oral Surgery Political Action Comm, Pi Kappa Phi, Rotary, SC Dental Soc, SC Soc Oral & Maxillofacial Surgeons, Southeastern Soc Oral & Maxillofacial Surgeons; pres: Med Univ SC

C. Bouton McDougal: dir

Kathleen A. McShane: asst secy

Jane Rishel: pres, treas, dir

APPLICATION INFORMATION
Initial Approach: Send a brief letter of inquiry. Not more than one page. Include a description of organization, amount requested, purpose of funds sought, recently audited financial statement, and proof of tax-exempt status. There are no deadlines.

PUBLICATIONS
Application Guidelines

GRANTS ANALYSIS
Total Grants: $1,742,573

Number of Grants: 197

Highest Grant: $210,000

Typical Range: $500 to $181,000

Disclosure Period: 1993

Note: Recent grants are derived from a 1993 Form 990.

RECENT GRANTS
Library
75,000	Newberry Library, Chicago, IL
60,000	Chicago Public Library Foundation, Chicago, IL

General
210,000	Chicago Horticultural Society, Glencoe, IL
181,000	American Friends of Cambridge University, Washington, DC
113,578	University of Chicago, Chicago, IL
100,000	Ducks Unlimited Foundation, Memphis, TN
50,000	University of Illinois Foundation, Urbana, IL

Donnelley & Sons Co., R.R.

Revenue: $4.88 billion
Employees: 30,000
Headquarters: Chicago, IL
SIC Major Group: Commercial Printing Nec,
Book Printing, Commercial
Printing—Lithographic, and Commercial
Printing—Gravure

CONTACT

Susan M. Levy
Community Relations Manager
R.R. Donnelley & Sons Co.
77 W Wacker Dr.
Chicago, IL 60601
(312) 326-8102

FINANCIAL SUMMARY

Recent Giving: $3,600,000 (1995 est.);
$2,977,258 (1994); $2,687,000 (1993)

Fiscal Note: All contributions are made directly by the company and its operating divisions. Above figures include nonmonetary support.

CONTRIBUTIONS SUMMARY

Typical Recipients: • *Arts & Humanities:* Arts Institutes, Historic Preservation, Libraries, Literary Arts, Museums/Galleries, Performing Arts, Theater • *Civic & Public Affairs:* Employment/Job Training, Public Policy, Urban & Community Affairs, Zoos/Aquariums • *Education:* Colleges & Universities, Education Associations, Literacy • *Health:* Hospitals, Mental Health • *Social Services:* Domestic Violence, Family Services, People with Disabilities, Shelters/Homelessness, United Funds/United Ways, Youth Organizations

Grant Types: capital, emergency, employee matching gifts, general support, multi-year/continuing support, and seed money

Nonmonetary Support Types: donated equipment and loaned executives

Note: Value of nonmonetary support is unavailable. Company donates only used equipment. Company loans executives to the United Way only. Contact Susan M. Levy for more information.

Geographic Distribution: in communities where there are manufacturing facilities and where employees live; and limited number of national organizations

Operating Locations: AZ (Casa Grande), CA (Fremont, Los Angeles, Newark), CO (Greeley), CT (Old Saybrook), FL (Daytona), IA (Des Moines, Mt. Pleasant), IL (Chicago, Dwight, Elgin, Lombard, Mattoon, Mendota, Pontiac, Wheeling, Willowbrook), IN (Crawfordsville, Warsaw), KY (Danville, Glasgow), MA (Hudson), MS (Senatobia), NC (Greensboro, Newton, Raleigh), NE (Lincoln), NV (Reno), NY (New York), OH (Willard), OR (Beaverton, Portland, Tigard), PA (Allentown, Bloomsburg, Lancaster, Pittsburgh, Scranton), SC (Spartanburg), TN (Gallatin, Newburn), TX (Houston, McAllen), UT (Orem, Provo), VA (Harrisonburg, Lynchburg), VT (Rutland), WA (Preston, Seattle)

Note: Also operates in England; Ireland; the Far East; Spain; Mexico City and Reynosa, Mexico; France; Germany; Korea; the Netherlands; Scotland; and Barbados.

CORP. OFFICERS

Rory J. Cowan: *B* 1953 *ED* Harvard Univ ABA; Harvard Univ MBA *CURR EMPL* exec vp, info tech: RR Donnelley & Sons Co

Dan Davis: *CURR EMPL* vp magazine sales: RR Donnelley & Sons Co

James R. Donnelley: *B* Chicago IL 1935 *ED* Dartmouth Coll BA 1957; Univ Chicago MBA 1962 *CURR EMPL* vchmn, chmn contributions comm: RR Donnelley & Sons Co *PHIL AFFIL* dir: Elliott and Ann Donnelley Foundation; mgr: Barker Welfare Foundation; vp, treas, trust: John C. Griswold Foundation; don, pres, treas: Nina H. and James R. Donnelley Foundation; dir: Thomas E. II Donnelley Foundation

Frank Robert Jarc: *B* Waukegan IL 1942 *ED* Univ MI BS 1964; Harvard Univ MBA 1967 *CURR EMPL* exec vp fin: RR Donnelley & Sons Co *CORP AFFIL* dir: Urban Gateways *NONPR AFFIL* bd mgrs: YMCA; mem: Evans Scholarship Alumni Assn *CLUB AFFIL* Chicago, Commonwealth, Econ, Execs

Cheryl Malmloff: *CURR EMPL* commun rels admin: RR Donnelley & Sons Co

W. Ed Taylor: *CURR EMPL* pres network svc: RR Donnelley & Sons Co

Ed Tyler: *CURR EMPL* group pres: RR Donnelley & Sons Co

John Robert Walter: *B* Pittsburgh PA 1947 *ED* Miami Univ BS 1969 *CURR EMPL* chmn, ceo: RR Donnelley & Sons Co *CORP AFFIL* dir: Abbott Laboratories, Dayton Hudson Corp, John Deere & Co *NONPR AFFIL* chmn: Un Way/Crusade Mercy Metro Chicago; dir: Evanston Hosp; mem: IL Mfrs Assn; trust: Chicago Historical Soc, Northwestern Univ, Orchestral Assn *CLUB AFFIL* Commercial, Commonwealth, Execs, Links, River

Jon Ward: *CURR EMPL* group pres: RR Donnelley & Sons Co

GIVING OFFICERS

James R. Donnelley: *CURR EMPL* vchmn, chmn contributions comm: RR Donnelley & Sons Co *PHIL AFFIL* dir: Elliott and Ann Donnelley Foundation; mgr: Barker Welfare Foundation; vp, treas, trust: John C. Griswold Foundation; don, pres, treas: Nina H. and James R. Donnelley Foundation; dir: Thomas E. II Donnelley Foundation (see above)

Susan M. Levy: secy, contributions comm *CURR EMPL* secy contributions comm, commun rels mgr: RR Donnelley & Sons Co

APPLICATION INFORMATION

Initial Approach: *Initial Contact:* proposal *Include Information On:* description of the organization, amount requested, purpose for which funds are sought, recently audited financial statement, proof of tax-exempt status, and list of board of directors *Deadlines:* before November 1 to be considered for that year *Note:* Nonprofits may also include a limited amount of supporting materials, such as annual reports, brochures, or newsletters.

Restrictions on Giving: The company does not support individuals, religious or fraternal organizations, political or lobbying groups, dinners or special events, or goodwill advertising, and seldom supports taxsupported organizations.

OTHER THINGS TO KNOW

Part of Donnelley's annual giving is administered by manufacturing divisions, although division grants tend to be smaller than those awarded by the corporate office. In general, manufacturing divisions award grants ranging from $25 to $15,000 each, while the corporate office awards grants ranging from $1,000 to $125,000 each.

In general, company does not contribute its printing services. Consideration will be given only to unusual, one-time items which meet company's normal funding priorities and which will have a significant impact on its communities. Specifically excluded are ongoing publications such as annual reports, newsletters, or any items connected with fund raising.

GRANTS ANALYSIS

Total Grants: $2,977,258*
Number of Grants: 300*
Highest Grant: $50,000*
Average Grant: $9,924
Typical Range: $1,000 to $10,000
Disclosure Period: 1994

Note: Total grants, number of grants, and highest grant figures were supplied by the company.

Duchossois Industries Inc. / Duchossois Foundation

Sales: $481.0 million
Employees: 6,000
Headquarters: Elmhurst, IL
SIC Major Group: Electrical Equipment & Supplies Nec, Racing Including Track Operations, Ammunition Except for Small Arms, and Small Arms

CONTACT

Kimberly D. Lenczuk
President
Duchossois Foundation
845 N Larch Ave.
Elmhurst, IL 60126
(708) 381-6278

FINANCIAL SUMMARY

Recent Giving: $351,841 (1993); $385,094 (1992); $247,460 (1991)

Assets: $845,396 (1993); $208,081 (1992); $107,341 (1991)

Gifts Received: $1,000,000 (1993); $500,000 (1992)

Fiscal Note: Company gives primarily through foundation. Above figures exclude nonmonetary support. In 1993, contributions were received from Duchossois Industries.

EIN: 36-3327987

CONTRIBUTIONS SUMMARY

Typical Recipients: • *Arts & Humanities:* Arts Associations & Councils, Arts Institutes, Arts Outreach, Ballet, Community Arts, Dance, Ethnic & Folk Arts, General, Libraries, Literary Arts, Museums/Galleries, Music, Opera, Performing Arts, Public Broadcasting, Theater, Visual Arts • *Civic & Public Affairs:* Chambers of Commerce, Clubs, Economic Development, Philanthropic Organizations, Public Policy, Safety, Urban & Community Affairs, Women's Affairs, Zoos/Aquariums • *Education:* Arts/Humanities Education, Business Education, Colleges & Universities, Education Funds, Education Reform, Elementary Education (Private), Engineering/Technological Education, Faculty Development, Minority Education, Private Education (Precollege), Public Education (Precollege), Special Education, Student Aid • *Environment:* General • *Health:* AIDS/HIV, Cancer, Children's Health/Hospitals, Clinics/Medical Centers, Health Funds, Hospices, Hospitals, Medical Research, Mental Health, Research/Studies Institutes, Single-Disease Health Associations, Speech & Hearing • *International:* Missionary/Religious Activities • *Religion:* Churches, Jewish Causes, Religious Welfare • *Science:* Scientific Organizations • *Social Services:* At-Risk Youth, Child Welfare, Community Service Organizations, Family Services, Homes, People with Disabilities, Recreation & Athletics, Substance Abuse, United Funds/United Ways, Volunteer Services, Youth Organizations

Grant Types: capital, endowment, general support, project, and seed money

Geographic Distribution: primarily in Chicago, IL

Operating Locations: IL (Chicago Heights, Elmhurst)

CORP. OFFICERS

Richard Louis Duchossois: *B* Chicago IL 1921 *ED* Washington & Lee Univ *CURR EMPL* chmn, ceo, dir: Duchossois Indus Inc *CORP AFFIL* chmn: Arlington Intl Racecourse Ltd, Chamberlain Consumer Products, Chamberlain Tech Co, Duchossois Commun Co, Thrall Car Mfg Co, Transportation Corp Am; dir: Hill n Dale Farm, LaSalle Natl Bank; pres, ceo: Chamberlain Mfg Corp *NONPR AFFIL* dir: Thoroughbred Racing Assn; mem: Chief Execs Org, Econ Comm *CLUB AFFIL* Execs, Jockey

GIVING OFFICERS

Dayle Paige Duchossois: dir

R. Bruce Duchossois: dir

Richard Louis Duchossois: secy *CURR EMPL* chmn, ceo, dir: Duchossois Indus Inc (see above)

Kimberly Duchossois Lenczuk: pres

Richard J. Rogers: asst secy

APPLICATION INFORMATION

Initial Approach: *Initial Contact:* one-page letter *Include Information On:* description of the organization, budget for current year, list of board of directors, copy of IRS determination letter, copy of most recent audit, specific recommendations as to how foundation can support organization's efforts *Deadlines:* end of November (for following year)

Restrictions on Giving: The foundation does not support individuals, including scholarships or fellowships; tickets, benefits, or program advertisements; political or lobbying groups; religious organizations for sectarian purposes; fraternal organizations; goodwill advertising; or organizations that are not tax-exempt.

OTHER THINGS TO KNOW

Most contributions in the area of medical research are pledged to cancer research through the University of Chicago. Other requests are considered as funding allows.

PUBLICATIONS

Guidelines

GRANTS ANALYSIS

Total Grants: $351,841

Number of Grants: 66

Highest Grant: $66,200

Average Grant: $5,331

Typical Range: $1,000 to $10,000

Disclosure Period: 1993

Note: Recent grants are derived from a 1993 Form 990.

RECENT GRANTS

Library

10,000	J.W. Barriger III National RR Library, St. Louis, MO — Library Endowment Campaign

General

28,000	Boys and Girls Clubs of America, Streamwood, IL — legends and fans; general support
26,000	Grayson-Jockey Club Research Foundation, New York, NY — pledge first installment
20,000	Campaign to Save Hitchcock Woods, Aiken, SC — capital campaign pledge; second installment
18,500	Mental Health Association in Illinois, Chicago, IL — general support
10,750	Ingalls Development Foundation, Harvey, IL —

membership and benefit support

Encyclopaedia Britannica, Inc.

Revenue: $586.0 million
Headquarters: Chicago, IL
SIC Major Group: Printing & Publishing

CONTACT

Tom Panelas
Director
Encyclopaedia Britannica, Inc.
310 S Michigan Ave.
Chicago, IL 60604
(312) 347-7000

FINANCIAL SUMMARY

Fiscal Note: Company does not disclose contributions figures.

CONTRIBUTIONS SUMMARY

Typical Recipients: • *Arts & Humanities:* Dance, General, Libraries, Museums/Galleries, Music, Opera, Performing Arts, Public Broadcasting, Theater, Visual Arts • *Civic & Public Affairs:* First Amendment Issues, General, Professional & Trade Associations, Women's Affairs • *Education:* Business Education, Elementary Education (Private), General, Literacy • *Health:* General, Health Organizations, Hospitals • *Social Services:* General, United Funds/United Ways, Youth Organizations

Grant Types: award

Operating Locations: IL (Chicago)

CORP. OFFICERS

Peter B. Norton: *B* London England 1929 *CURR EMPL* pres, ceo, dir: Encyclopaedia Britannica *CORP AFFIL* chmn: Am Learning Corp, Encyclopaedia Brittanica Educational Corp *NONPR AFFIL* fellow: Chartered Inst Administrators, Chartered Inst Secys, UK Chartered Inst Dirs; mem: Intl Ed, Japan Am Soc Chicago *PHIL AFFIL* dir: William Benton Foundation *CLUB AFFIL* mem: Chicago Club

APPLICATION INFORMATION

Initial Approach: Send a full proposal. Include a description of organization, amount requested, purpose of funds sought, recently audited financial statement, and proof of tax-exempt status.

Restrictions on Giving: Does not support individuals, religious organizations for sectarian purposes, or political or lobbying groups.

First Chicago Corp. / First National Bank of Chicago Foundation

Revenue: $5.09 billion
Employees: 17,355
Headquarters: Chicago, IL
SIC Major Group: Bank Holding Companies and National Commercial Banks

CONTACT
Diane M. Smith
Vice President
First National Bank of Chicago Foundation
1 First Natl Plz.
Ste. 356
Chicago, IL 60670
(312) 732-6948

FINANCIAL SUMMARY

Recent Giving: $3,500,000 (1992 approx.); $3,792,000 (1991 approx.); $4,148,621 (1990)

Fiscal Note: Figures above represent both direct and foundation giving. Above figures exclude nonmonetary support.

EIN: 36-6033828

CONTRIBUTIONS SUMMARY

Typical Recipients: • *Arts & Humanities:* Community Arts, Dance, Ethnic & Folk Arts, Libraries, Museums/Galleries, Music, Opera, Performing Arts, Public Broadcasting, Theater • *Civic & Public Affairs:* Civil Rights, Economic Development, Housing, Law & Justice, Urban & Community Affairs, Zoos/Aquariums • *Education:* Business Education, Colleges & Universities, Economic Education, Education Associations, Education Funds, Minority Education • *Environment:* General

Grant Types: capital, employee matching gifts, endowment, fellowship, general support, operating expenses, and project

Nonmonetary Support: $1,300,000 (1990); $800,000 (1988); $1,400,000 (1987)

Nonmonetary Support Types: donated equipment, in-kind services, and loaned executives

Geographic Distribution: Chicago, IL

Operating Locations: IL (Chicago), NY (New York)

CORP. OFFICERS

Richard Lee Thomas: *B* Marion OH 1931 *ED* Kenyon Coll BA 1953; Harvard Univ MBA 1958 *CURR EMPL* chmn, ceo: First Chicago Corp *CORP AFFIL* chmn, pres, ceo: First Natl Bank Chicago; dir: Am Natl Corp, CNA Fin Corp, Sara Lee Corp *NONPR AFFIL* adv: Chicago Christian Indus League; life trust: Orchestral Assn; mem: Beta Theta Phi, Chicago Counc Foreign Rels, Phi Beta Kappa; trust: Kenyon Coll, Northwestern Univ, Rush-Presbyterian-

St Lukes Med Ctr *CLUB AFFIL* Casino, Chicago, Commercial, Indian Hills CC, Mid-Am, Sunningdale GC

David J. Vitale: *B* Beverly MA 1946 *ED* Harvard Univ 1968; Univ Chicago 1976 *CURR EMPL* vchmn: First Chicago Corp *CORP AFFIL* pres, dir: First Chicago Intl Fin Corp; vchmn: First Natl Bank Chicago *NONPR AFFIL* vchmn: Glenwood Sch Boys

GIVING OFFICERS

Ilona M. Berry: secy *ED* Bradley Univ 1977; Univ IL 1980 *CURR EMPL* secy, dir: First Chicago Fin Corp *CORP AFFIL* secy, dir: First Capital Corp Chicago, First Chicago Natl Processing

Clark D. Burrus: vp, dir *B* Chicago IL 1928 *ED* Roosevelt Univ BS 1954; Roosevelt Univ MPA 1972 *CURR EMPL* sr vp: First Natl Bank Chicago *CORP AFFIL* chmn: Chicago Transit Authority; dir: Cosmopolitan Chamber Commerce, Natl Urban Aff

Marion Foote: vp, dir

Lawrence E. Fox: vp, dir

Diane M. Smith: vp, dir

Richard Lee Thomas: vp *CURR EMPL* chmn, ceo: First Chicago Corp (see above)

David J. Vitale: vp, dir *CURR EMPL* vchmn: First Chicago Corp (see above)

APPLICATION INFORMATION

Initial Approach: *Initial Contact:* letter or proposal *Include Information On:* goals and objectives of requesting organization, list of board members and key personnel, background information on organization and specific project, purpose for which funds are sought, current budget and principal funding sources, recently audited financial statement or annual report, proof of tax-exempt status *Deadlines:* none

Restrictions on Giving: In general, the foundation does not support individuals; religious or fraternal organizations; preschool, elementary, or secondary schools; agencies receiving United Way/Crusade of Mercy funds; public agencies; multiyear operating pledges; or consecutive multiyear capital pledges.

OTHER THINGS TO KNOW
The company refused to give updated contributions figures.

GRANTS ANALYSIS
Total Grants: $3,500,000

Typical Range: $1,000 to $10,000

Disclosure Period: 1992

Note: Fiscal information represents combined giving. Recent grants are derived from a 1990 grants list.

RECENT GRANTS

General

32,853	University of Chicago, Chicago, IL
27,955	Harvard University, Cambridge, MA
23,615	Northwestern University, Evanston, IL
15,350	Kenyon College, Gambier, OH
12,365	DePaul University, Chicago, IL

Fry Foundation, Lloyd A.

CONTACT
Lloyd A. Fry Foundation
135 S LaSalle St., Ste. 1910
Chicago, IL 60603
(312) 580-0310
Note: The foundation does not list a specific contact person.

FINANCIAL SUMMARY
Recent Giving: $4,665,870 (fiscal 1994); $4,381,550 (fiscal 1993); $3,626,820 (fiscal 1992)

Assets: $95,354,538 (fiscal 1994); $97,088,220 (fiscal 1993); $87,091,730 (fiscal 1992)

Gifts Received: $1,715,049 (fiscal 1994); $5,463,278 (fiscal 1993); $1,123,018 (fiscal 1991)

Fiscal Note: The foundation is a residual beneficiary of several trusts established by the estate of the founder.

EIN: 36-6108775

CONTRIBUTIONS SUMMARY

Donor(s): Born in San Antonio, TX, in 1895, Lloyd A. Fry established a roofing business in Chicago in 1931. The Lloyd A. Fry Roofing Company grew into the world's largest producer of asphalt roofing products until its sale to Owens-Corning Fiberglass Corporation in 1977. The foundation was established in 1959 by Mr. Fry. Upon his death in 1981, the foundation received a significant testamentary bequest which led to an increase in its philanthropic activity.

Typical Recipients: • *Arts & Humanities:* Arts Appreciation, Arts Centers, Arts Institutes, Dance, Ethnic & Folk Arts, Historic Preservation, Libraries, Museums/Galleries, Music, Opera, Performing Arts, Public Broadcasting, Theater • *Civic & Public Affairs:* Economic Development, Employment/Job Training, Housing, Law & Justice, Legal Aid, Nonprofit Management, Public Policy, Urban & Community Affairs, Zoos/Aquariums • *Education:* Arts/Humanities Education, Colleges & Universities, Education Associations, Education Funds, Education Reform, Elementary Education (Private), Faculty Development, General, International Exchange, Literacy, Minority Education, Preschool Education, Private Education (Precollege), Public Education (Precollege), Science/Mathematics Educa-

237

tion, Secondary Education (Public), Special Education, Student Aid • *Environment:* General • *Health:* AIDS/HIV, Clinics/Medical Centers, Geriatric Health, Health Policy/Cost Containment, Health Organizations, Hospitals, Mental Health, Nursing Services, Prenatal Health Issues, Public Health, Single-Disease Health Associations • *International:* Health Care/Hospitals, International Relations, International Relief Efforts • *Religion:* Churches, Religious Welfare • *Social Services:* Child Welfare, Community Centers, Community Service Organizations, Counseling, Delinquency & Criminal Rehabilitation, Domestic Violence, Food/Clothing Distribution, People with Disabilities, Refugee Assistance, Senior Services, Shelters/Homelessness, Substance Abuse, United Funds/United Ways, Volunteer Services, Youth Organizations

Grant Types: project

Geographic Distribution: metropolitan Chicago, IL

GIVING OFFICERS

Roger E. Anderson: vchmn, dir *B* Chicago IL 1921 *ED* Northwestern Univ BA 1942 *CORP AFFIL* dir: Amstead Indus, Eastman Kodak Co

Jill C. Darrow: exec dir

Lloyd A. Fry III: dir

Howard McDowell McCue III: vp, secy, dir *B* Sumter SC 1946 *ED* Princeton Univ AB 1968; Harvard Univ JD 1971 *CURR EMPL* ptnr: Mayer Brown & Platt *NONPR AFFIL* adjunct prof law: IL Inst Tech Chicago-Kent Coll Law; dir: Lawrence Hall Sch Boys, Harvard Law Soc IL, Intl Academy Estate & Trust Law, Ravinia Festival Assn; dir, mem: Chicago Bar Fdn; mem: Am Bar Assn, Am Coll Tax Couns, Chicago Bar Assn, IL Bar Assn, Phi Beta Kappa; mem editorial adv bd: Trusts & Estates Mag *CLUB AFFIL* Chicago, Kenilworth, Westmoreland CC *PHIL AFFIL* asst secy: Washington Square Health Foundation; asst secy, asst treas: Lannan Foundation; secy, dir: Elizabeth F. Cheney Foundation; asst secy, asst treas, dir: Andrew Greeley Foundation; asst secy, asst treas: Elliott and Ann Donnelley Foundation

Edmund Anton Stephan: chmn, dir *B* Chicago IL 1911 *ED* Univ Notre Dame AB 1933; Harvard Univ LLB 1939 *CURR EMPL* sr ptnr: Mayer Brown & Platt *CORP AFFIL* dir: Marsh & McLennan Cos; hon dir: Brunswick Corp *NONPR AFFIL* emeritus chmn bd trusts: Univ Notre Dame; mem: Am Bar Assn, Chicago Bar Assn, IL Bar Assn *CLUB AFFIL* Bob-O-Link GC, Chicago, Harvard, Law, Legal, MI Shores, Mid-Day, Westmoreland CC *PHIL AFFIL* secy: Arthur J. Schmitt Foundation

M. James Termondt: pres, treas, dir *PHIL AFFIL* treas, dir: A. C. Buehler Foundation; dir: Walter E. Heller Foundation; secy, dir: Todd Wehr Foundation

APPLICATION INFORMATION
Initial Approach:

Applicants may submit an inquiry before a full proposal. Inquiries should include a brief statement of the project and a project budget.

Full proposals should include a brief history of the organization with functions and goals; brief proposal summary, including need to be addressed, budget, and an evaluation plan; most recent audited financial report and approved operating budget; other sources of support; list of board members and key personnel; and copy of IRS tax-exempt status letter.

Applications may be submitted at any time.

The board of directors meets in February, May, August, and November. Although the foundation considers requests for operating support and capital campaigns, it prefers to fund projects directed at the solution of specific problems. Priority is given to proposals for new programs rather than for support of ongoing direct service programs.

Restrictions on Giving: Grants rarely are made to organizations outside metropolitan Chicago. No grants are made to individuals, government agencies, fund-raising benefits, or tax-supported educational institutions for services that fall within their normal responsibilities.

PUBLICATIONS
Annual report

GRANTS ANALYSIS
Total Grants: $4,381,550

Number of Grants: 319

Highest Grant: $113,200

Average Grant: $13,735

Typical Range: $5,000 to $50,000

Disclosure Period: fiscal year ending June 30, 1993

Note: Recent grants are derived from a fiscal 1993 annual report.

RECENT GRANTS

General

113,200	University of Chicago, Chicago, IL — for the 1993 summer seminars for high school teachers
100,000	Big Shoulders Fund, Chicago, IL — first payment of five-year $500,000 grant for teacher training and staff development in inner-city schools of the Archdiocese of Chicago
100,000	Rush-Presbyterian-St. Luke's Medical center, Chicago, IL — for the Pilsen senior health advocates program
75,000	Rosary College, River Forest, IL — for the master of arts in educational leadership program for prospective school principals
75,000	Travelers and Immigrants Aid of Chicago, Chicago, IL — first payment of a three-year $225,000 grant for the Families Building Community project

GATX Corp.

Income: $1.02 billion
Employees: 3,500
Headquarters: Chicago, IL
SIC Major Group: Rental of Railroad Cars, Freight Transportation on the Great Lakes, Refined Petroleum Pipelines, and Miscellaneous Business Credit Institutions

CONTACT
Christiane S. Wilczura
Manager, Community Affairs
GATX Corp.
500 W Monroe St.
Chicago, IL 60661
(312) 621-6221

FINANCIAL SUMMARY
Recent Giving: $1,200,000 (1995 est.); $1,400,000 (1994 approx.); $1,230,800 (1993)

Fiscal Note: All contributions are made directly by the company and its subsidiaries, American Steamship Company of Buffalo, NY., GATX Leasing Corporation of San Francisco, CA., and Unit Associated Companies of Jacksonville, FL. Above figures include nonmonetary support.

CONTRIBUTIONS SUMMARY
Typical Recipients: • *Arts & Humanities:* Arts Associations & Councils, Arts Institutes, Arts Outreach, Community Arts, Dance, Ethnic & Folk Arts, Historic Preservation, Libraries, Museums/Galleries, Music, Opera, Performing Arts, Public Broadcasting, Theater, Visual Arts • *Civic & Public Affairs:* Economic Development, Employment/Job Training, Housing, Public Policy, Urban & Community Affairs, Zoos/Aquariums • *Education:* After-school/Enrichment Programs, Arts/Humanities Education, Colleges & Universities, Education Reform, Faculty Development, Literacy, Minority Education, Preschool Education, Private Education (Precollege), Student Aid • *Health:* AIDS/HIV, Cancer, Clinics/Medical Centers, Geriatric Health, Health Organizations, Hospices, Hospitals, Medical Rehabilitation, Mental Health, Nutrition, Single-Disease Health Associations • *Social Services:* At-Risk Youth, Child Welfare, Community Centers, Community Service Organizations, Counseling, Delinquency & Criminal Rehabilitation, Domestic Violence, Family Services, Food/Clothing Distribution, People with Disabilities, Senior Services, Shelters/Homelessness, Substance Abuse, United Funds/United Ways, Youth Organizations

Grant Types: challenge, employee matching gifts, general support, operating expenses, project, and seed money

Nonmonetary Support: $60,000 (1994); $12,000 (1993); $44,018 (1992)

Nonmonetary Support Types: donated equipment, in-kind services, loaned employees, and workplace solicitation

Geographic Distribution: principally in Chicago, IL, and other company locations

Operating Locations: CA (Carson, Compton, Richmond, San Francisco, San Pedro, Wilmington), FL (Jacksonville, Taft, Tampa), GA, IL (Argo, Chicago), IN (East Chicago), LA (Good Hope), NJ (Carteret), NY (Buffalo), OH (Youngstown), OR (Portland), PA, TX (Galena Park, Houston, Norco, Pasadena), UT, WA (Seattle, Vancouver)

CORP. OFFICERS
James Jay Glasser: *B* Chicago IL 1934 *ED* Yale Univ BA 1955; Harvard Univ JD 1958 *CURR EMPL* chmn, pres, ceo: GATX Corp *CORP AFFIL* dir: BF Goodrich Co, Harris Bankcorp Inc, Harris Trust & Savings Bank, Mutual Trust Life Ins Co, Stone Container Corp *NONPR AFFIL* dir: Chicago Assn Commerce Indus, Chicago Central Area Comm, D&R Fund, Lake Forest Hosp, Natl Merit Scholarship Corp, Northwestern Meml Fdn, Voices IL Children; mem: Chi Psi; trust: Better Govt Assn, Chicago Zoological Soc, Univ Chicago *CLUB AFFIL* Casino, Chicago, Commercial, Econ Chicago, Lake Shore CC, Onwentsia, Racquet, Shoreacres, Tavern, Winter

GIVING OFFICERS
Jim Herbert: *CURR EMPL* mem contributions comm: GATX Corp

Steve Kuhrtz: *CURR EMPL* mem contributions comm: GATX Corp

Jean Luber: *CURR EMPL* mem contributions comm: GATX Corp

Bob Moran: *CURR EMPL* mem contributions comm: GATX Corp

Bronna Wasserman: *CURR EMPL* mem contributions: GATX Corp

Christiane S. Wilczura: mgr commun aff *CURR EMPL* mgr: GATX Corp

Dick Wood: *CURR EMPL* mem contributions comm: GATX Corp

APPLICATION INFORMATION
Initial Approach: *Initial Contact:* letter *Include Information On:* name, address, and phone number of organization; contact person and title; name of executive director; list of members of board of directors; proof of tax-exempt status; audited financial statement; annual report; budget; list of other sources of support; statement of purpose and history of organization; current program activities and goals; specifics regarding project to be funded and program budget, as applicable; IRS 990 if audit is not available *Deadlines:* by the 15th day of January, April, July, or October

Restrictions on Giving: Corporation does not support individuals, political or fraternal organizations, religious organizations for sectarian purposes, trips or tours, courtesy advertising, tickets or tables for benefit purposes, private foundations, capital cam-

paigns, endowment funds, local chapters of national organizations, land acquisition, deficit financing, member organizations of united funds for general operating support, national health organizations, individual primary, secondary, or preschools, or health research.

OTHER THINGS TO KNOW
Recipients must submit progress reports as a condition of funding.

Grant renewals are not automatic.

GRANTS ANALYSIS
Total Grants: $1,230,800

Number of Grants: 150

Highest Grant: $30,000

Average Grant: $8,205

Typical Range: $3,000 to $10,000

Disclosure Period: 1993

Note: Recent grants are derived from a 1993 grants list.

RECENT GRANTS
General
30,000	University of Chicago, Chicago, IL — scholarship endowment fund
20,000	Chicago Zoological Society, Chicago, IL — capital campaign
20,000	Corporate Community Schools of America — operations of school only
20,000	Travelers and Immigrants Aid, Chicago, IL — GATX New Beginning II
15,000	Bonaventure House, Chicago, IL — unrestricted

Geifman Family Foundation

CONTACT
Morris M. Geifman
President
Geifman Family Fdn.
2239 29th St.
Rock Island, IL 61201
(309) 788-9531

FINANCIAL SUMMARY
Recent Giving: $158,360 (1993); $161,810 (1992); $125,665 (1991)

Assets: $2,834,970 (1993); $3,430,706 (1992); $3,294,743 (1991)

EIN: 36-6123096

CONTRIBUTIONS SUMMARY
Typical Recipients: • *Arts & Humanities:* Community Arts, Libraries, Museums/Galleries • *Civic & Public Affairs:* General, Urban & Community Affairs • *Education:* Colleges & Universities, Student Aid • *Health:* Alzheimers Disease, Cancer, Emergency/Ambulance Services, Heart, Prenatal Health Issues, Research/Studies Institutes, Single-Disease Health Associations • *International:* Health Care/Hospitals, Missionary/Religious Activities • *Religion:* Jewish

Causes, Religious Organizations, Religious Welfare, Synagogues/Temples • *Social Services:* Community Centers, Community Service Organizations, Homes, People with Disabilities, Substance Abuse, United Funds/United Ways, Youth Organizations

Grant Types: endowment and general support

Geographic Distribution: focus on IL

GIVING OFFICERS
Geraldine Geifman: secy, dir

Morris M. Geifman: pres, dir

Stephen Geifman: vp, treas, dir

Terri Geifman: asst treas, dir

Cherie Handler: asst secy, dir

APPLICATION INFORMATION
Initial Approach: Application must be typewritten. The foundation has no formal grant application procedure or application form. There are no deadlines.

GRANTS ANALYSIS
Total Grants: $158,360

Number of Grants: 96

Highest Grant: $50,000

Typical Range: $50 to $20,000

Disclosure Period: 1993

Note: Recent grants are derived from a 1993 Form 990.

RECENT GRANTS
Library
20,000	Rock Island Library Foundation, Rock Island, IL — endowment fund

General
50,000	Tri City Jewish Center Building Fund, Rock Island, IL
17,000	Jewish Federation of Quad Cities, Rock Island, IL
7,500	Cabbages and Kings, Dallas, TX
6,000	Tri City Jewish Center, Rock Island, IL — endowment
5,500	Congregation B'nai Tikvah, Deerfield, IL

Geneseo Foundation

CONTACT
Gary W. Joyner
Trust Officer
Geneseo Fdn.
c/o Central Trust and Savings Bank
101 N. State St.
Geneseo, IL 61254
(309) 944-5601

FINANCIAL SUMMARY
Recent Giving: $158,323 (fiscal 1992); $53,010 (fiscal 1991); $113,354 (fiscal 1990)

Assets: $3,119,534 (fiscal 1992); $3,051,702 (fiscal 1991); $2,556,251 (fiscal 1990)

Gifts Received: $546 (fiscal 1992); $255,520 (fiscal 1991)

Fiscal Note: In 1991, contributions were received from the estate of Catherine Cambell.

EIN: 36-6079604

CONTRIBUTIONS SUMMARY

Donor(s): George B. Dedrick

Typical Recipients: • *Arts & Humanities:* Arts Associations & Councils, Community Arts, Libraries • *Civic & Public Affairs:* Botanical Gardens/Parks, Community Foundations, Economic Development, Municipalities/Towns, Urban & Community Affairs, Zoos/Aquariums • *Education:* Education Reform, Public Education (Precollege) • *Health:* Cancer, Hospitals, Single-Disease Health Associations • *Religion:* Churches, Religious Welfare • *Social Services:* Child Welfare, Community Service Organizations, Recreation & Athletics, Scouts, Senior Services, United Funds/United Ways, Youth Organizations

Grant Types: general support and scholarship

GIVING OFFICERS

A. Dean Decker: mgr *PHIL AFFIL* adv comm mem, trust: Kenneth S. Moore and Arletta E. Moore Foundation

Bruce Fehlman: mgr

John L. Greenwood: mgr

Raymond Johnson: mgr

Darwin Knudtsen: mgr

Eugene Lohman: chmn

Robert Schaefer: mgr

Todd W. Sieben: mgr

Dean D. Urick: mgr

APPLICATION INFORMATION

Initial Approach: Applications available upon request.

OTHER THINGS TO KNOW

Awards scholarships for higher education to graduates of Geneseo High School.

GRANTS ANALYSIS

Total Grants: $158,323

Number of Grants: 26

Highest Grant: $50,000

Typical Range: $132 to $25,000

Disclosure Period: fiscal year ending March 31, 1992

Note: Recent grants are derived from a fiscal 1992 Form 990. Number of grants and typical range do not include college scholarships totaling $11,250.

RECENT GRANTS

Library

10,000	Geneseo Public Library, Geneseo, NY	

General

50,000	Arrowhead Ranch, Coal Valley, IL	
25,000	Geneseo Community Park District, Geneseo, NY	
18,500	Geneseo Youth Baseball, Geneseo, NY	
12,550	Geneseo Downtown Development, Geneseo, NY	
10,000	Geneseo Endowment for Excellence in Education, Geneseo, NY	

Graham Foundation for Advanced Studies in the Fine Arts

CONTACT

Richard Solomon
Director
Graham Foundation for Advanced Studies in the Fine Arts
4 W Burton Pl.
Chicago, IL 60610
(312) 787-4071

FINANCIAL SUMMARY

Recent Giving: $1,156,772 (1993); $1,069,694 (1992); $716,275 (1991)

Assets: $22,848,501 (1993); $22,245,874 (1992); $20,761,153 (1991)

Gifts Received: $15,000 (1992)

Fiscal Note: In 1992, the foundation received paintings valued at $15,000 from Charles F. Murphy, Jr.

EIN: 36-2356089

CONTRIBUTIONS SUMMARY

Donor(s): The foundation was established in 1956 by a bequest from Ernest R. Graham (1866-1936), a Chicago architect. Under the guidance of Daniel Burnham, Mr. Graham was the principal assistant in overseeing construction of the 1893 World's Columbian Exhibition and later was associated with the D. H. Burnham & Co. architectural firm. After Mr. Burnham's death in 1912, Graham built the company into one of the nation's largest designers of railroad stations, banks, office buildings, museums, department stores, theaters, and post offices. Ernest Graham's died during the Depression, leaving his estate severely undervalued. It took 20 years for his associate and executor, the late Charles F. Murphy, to rebuild the estate and begin the foundation.

Typical Recipients: • *Arts & Humanities:* Arts Associations & Councils, Arts Centers, Arts Institutes, Ethnic & Folk Arts, Film & Video, General, Historic Preservation, History & Archaeology, Libraries, Literary Arts, Museums/Galleries, Performing Arts, Visual Arts • *Civic & Public Affairs:* Housing, Municipalities/Towns, Urban & Community Affairs • *Education:* Arts/Humanities Education, Colleges & Universities, Engineering/Technological Education • *Environment:* General • *International:* Foreign Arts Organizations, Foreign Educational Institutions

Grant Types: challenge, conference/seminar, department, fellowship, project, and research

Geographic Distribution: no geographic restrictions

GIVING OFFICERS

Irwin J. Askow: trust *CURR EMPL* secy, dir: Allied World Travel

Thomas H. Beeby: trust *CURR EMPL* ptnr: Hammond Beeby & Babka *NONPR AFFIL* fellow: Am Inst Arch; mem exec comm: Chicago Inst Architecture & Urbanism

Miles Lee Berger: secy, treas, trust *B* Chicago IL 1930 *ED* Brown Univ 1952 *CURR EMPL* chmn: Berger Fin Svcs Corp *CORP AFFIL* chmn, dir: Midtown Bancorp, Midtown Bank Chicago; vchmn: Columbia Natl Bank Chicago, Heitman Fin Svcs Co Ltd; vchmn, dir: CNBC Bancorp *NONPR AFFIL* mem: Am Inst Real Estate Appraisers, Soc Real Estate Appraisers, Soc Real Estate Counsellors *PHIL AFFIL* pres: Albert E. Berger Foundation

Sally Kitt Chappell: trust

Roberta Felman: trust

Henry Kuehn: trust

James Nagle: trust

James Otis, Jr.: trust *B* Chicago IL 1931 *ED* Princeton Univ BA 1953; Univ Chicago 1955-1957 *CURR EMPL* pres: Otis Co *CORP AFFIL* dir: Pioneer Bank, Southern Mineral Corp *NONPR AFFIL* bd govs: Chicago Zoological Soc; chmn bd trusts: N Suburban YMCA; gov bd: Shedd Aquarium; mem: Am Inst Archts, Natl Counc Architectural Registration Bds, Northwestern Univ Assocs, Urban Land Inst; mem adv bd: Cook County Forest Preserve District; mem, assoc: Chicago Counc Foreign Rels; mem fdrs counc: Field Mus Natural History; trust: Better Govt Assn, Evanston Hosp *CLUB AFFIL* Anglers, Chicago, Coleman Lake, Commercial, Commonwealth, Econ, Glenview, Princeton

John James Schornack: trust *B* Chicago IL 1930 *ED* Loyola Univ BS 1951; Northwestern Univ MBA 1956; Harvard Bus Sch 1969 *CURR EMPL* vchmn, mng ptnr: Ernst & Young Midwest Region *CORP AFFIL* chmn, ceo, dir: Kraftseal Corp *NONPR AFFIL* chmn counc: Barat Coll; chmn, dir: Ernst & Young Fdn; chmn, mem: Midwest-Japan Assn; dir: Met Planning Counc, Un Way Chicago; mem: Am Accounting Assn, Am Inst CPAs, IL Soc CPAs, Japan Am Soc, Loyola Univ Citizens Bd; trust: Chicago Symphony Orchestra; vchmn trust: St Francis Hosp *CLUB AFFIL* Chicago Glen View Ocean, Commercial Economic, Traven

Charles H. Shaw: trust *B* 1931 *ED* Williams Coll 1951 *CURR EMPL* ptnr: Charles H Shaw Co

Richard Solomon: dir

Benjamin Horace Weese: pres, trust *B* Evanston IL 1929 *ED* Harvard Univ BArch 1951; Ecole des Beaux Arts 1956; Harvard Univ MArch 1957 *CURR EMPL* prin: Weese Langley Weese *NONPR AFFIL* co-fdr, pres: Chicago Archts Fdn, Glessner House; fellow: Am Inst Archts; mem: Natl Counc Architectural Registration Bds

APPLICATION INFORMATION

Initial Approach:

A proposal should be sent to the foundation. There is no formal application form.

The proposal should include a succinct description of the project and its objectives, a list of persons involved, timetable, budget, amount requested, and IRS determination letter. Applications also should describe how participants intend to proceed, and why they believe they have unique capabilities to bring the project to a successful conclusion. Applicants are requested to send three letters of reference from individuals knowledgeable in the area and familiar with their ability.

Applications should be postmarked no later than July 15 and January 15.

Notification of the decision on the proposal is usually made within 90 days.

Restrictions on Giving: Grants are not made for endowment, general support, operating expenses, construction or other capital expenditures, architectural fees for construction, or direct scholarship aid to students or projects in pursuit of a degree. Grants to institutions will not fund fringe benefits or overhead.

OTHER THINGS TO KNOW

Grants to individuals do not exceed $10,000. If a large sum of money is requested, other sources of funding should be included. Although grants are typically reserved for the early stages of a project, in a few compelling cases, grants may be made to help match a previous challenge grant by another institution.

In addition to making grants, the foundation conducts lectures and exhibits. The foundation also reports that it makes its Madlener House available to other organizations, at a nominal fee, for activities that relate to the foundation's purposes and do not conflict with its schedule. Applicants seeking permission to use the house should apply in writing well in advance of the date desired and must comply with strict rules governing use of the building.

PUBLICATIONS

Annual report

GRANTS ANALYSIS

Total Grants: $1,156,772

Number of Grants: 134

Highest Grant: $100,000

Average Grant: $8,633

Typical Range: $5,000 to $10,000

Disclosure Period: 1993

Note: Recent grants are derived from a 1993 annual report.

RECENT GRANTS

Library
20,000	Library of Congress, Washington, DC — in support of the Center for American Architecture
10,000	Finnish Foundation for the Visual Arts, New York, NY — exhibition of Aalto's Viipuri Library
6,000	Library of American Landscape History, Amherst,

MA — book about landscape artist
5,000	Athenaeum of Philadelphia, Philadelphia, PA — exhibition, catalog and symposium about American perspective drawings prior to Latrobe
5,000	Chicago Athenaeum, Chicago, IL — exhibition: "20th Century Industrial Design in Chicago"

General
16,000	Business and Professional People for the Public Interest, Chicago, IL — exhibition and symposium about Chicago's scattered-site housing program
10,000	Catholic University of America, Washington, DC — design and build Starter House of 300 square feet
10,000	Mission Housing Development Corporation, San Francisco, CA — workshop for training developers of low-income housing
10,000	Roosevelt University, Chicago, IL — video about Adler and Sullivan's auditorium building
10,000	University of Cincinnati, Cincinnati, OH — three round table discussions at the Center for the Study of the Practice of Architecture

Harrison Foundation, Fred G.

CONTACT

Ed Goodwin
President and Trust Officer
Fred G. Harrison Fdn.
c/o The Bank of Herrin
PO Box B
Herrin, IL 62948
(618) 942-6666

FINANCIAL SUMMARY

Recent Giving: $69,711 (1993); $56,325 (1991); $40,574 (1989)

Assets: $2,018,014 (1993); $1,971,891 (1991); $1,825,628 (1989)

EIN: 37-6085205

CONTRIBUTIONS SUMMARY

Donor(s): Julia Harrison Bruce, Fred G. Harrison

Typical Recipients: • *Arts & Humanities:* Arts Centers, Libraries • *Civic & Public Affairs:* Business/Free Enterprise, Chambers of Commerce, Clubs, General, Municipalities/Towns, Zoos/Aquariums • *Education:* General, Public Education (Precollege) • *Environment:* General • *Religion:* Churches • *Social Services:* Community Service Or-

ganizations, Counseling, Recreation & Athletics, Shelters/Homelessness, United Funds/United Ways, Youth Organizations

Grant Types: general support and scholarship

Geographic Distribution: focus on Herrin, IL

GIVING OFFICERS

Bank of Herrin: trust

Carl Bruce: adv

Julia Harrison Bruce: adv

APPLICATION INFORMATION

Initial Approach: Send brief letter describing program. There are no deadlines.

GRANTS ANALYSIS

Total Grants: $69,711

Number of Grants: 20

Highest Grant: $12,500

Typical Range: $200 to $10,255

Disclosure Period: 1993

Note: Recent grants are derived from a 1993 Form 990.

RECENT GRANTS

Library
5,000	Herrin City Library, Herrin, IL

General
12,500	Herrin Sports Complex, Herrin, IL
10,000	Herrin School District, Herrin, IL
6,750	Herrin Junior Ball League, Herrin, IL
5,000	Herrin Doughboy Foundation, Herrin, IL
5,000	Herrin Memorial Baptist Church, Herrin, IL

Hartmarx Corporation / Hartmarx Charitable Foundation

Sales: $732.0 million
Employees: 11,200
Headquarters: Chicago, IL
SIC Major Group: Holding Companies Nec, Men's/Boys' Suits & Coats, Men's/Boys' Trousers & Slacks, and Men's/Boys' Clothing Nec

CONTACT

Kay C. Nalbach
President
Hartmarx Charitable Foundation
101 N Wacker Dr.
Chicago, IL 60606
(312) 357-5331
Note: Foundation reports that it is not accepting unsolicited requests for funds in 1995.

FINANCIAL SUMMARY

Recent Giving: $350,000 (fiscal 1995 est.); $311,000 (fiscal 1994 approx.); $296,283 (fiscal 1993)

Assets: $75,849 (fiscal 1993); $54,769 (fiscal 1992); $45,876 (fiscal 1990)

Fiscal Note: All corporate and subsidiary contributions are made through the foundation. Figure for 1993 includes $16,155 in employee matching gifts.

EIN: 36-6152745

CONTRIBUTIONS SUMMARY

Typical Recipients: • *Arts & Humanities:* Arts Festivals, Arts Institutes, General, Historic Preservation, History & Archaeology, Libraries, Museums/Galleries, Music, Opera, Performing Arts, Public Broadcasting, Theater • *Civic & Public Affairs:* African American Affairs, Business/Free Enterprise, Economic Development, Housing, Law & Justice, Legal Aid, Professional & Trade Associations, Public Policy, Safety, Urban & Community Affairs, Women's Affairs, Zoos/Aquariums • *Education:* Business Education, Colleges & Universities, Community & Junior Colleges, Economic Education, Education Funds, Engineering/Technological Education, Minority Education, Private Education (Precollege), Public Education (Precollege), Science/Mathematics Education, Student Aid • *Health:* Cancer, Clinics/Medical Centers, Health Organizations, Hospitals, Respiratory, Single-Disease Health Associations • *Religion:* Jewish Causes, Religious Organizations, Religious Welfare • *Social Services:* At-Risk Youth, Child Welfare, Community Centers, Community Service Organizations, Family Planning, Family Services, People with Disabilities, Recreation & Athletics, Senior Services, United Funds/United Ways, Volunteer Services, YMCA/YWCA/YMHA/YWHA, Youth Organizations

Grant Types: capital, employee matching gifts, general support, research, and scholarship

Note: Matching gifts are matched on a 1 to 1 basis up to $1,500 for each individual in any calendar year. Foundation will not match bequests, dues, tuition fees, subscription fees, loan payments, or contributions not made as direct donations.

Geographic Distribution: near headquarters and operating locations only

Operating Locations: AL (Anniston), AR (Rector), GA (Loganville, Norcross), IL (Chicago, Des Plaines), IN (Michigan City), KY (Elizabethtown, Winchester), MD (Baltimore), MO (Cape Girardeau, Chaffee, Farmington, St. Louis), NC (Whiteville), NY (Buffalo, New York, Rochester), PA (Easton)

CORP. OFFICERS

Elbert O. Hand: *B* 1939 *ED* Hamilton Coll BS 1961 *CURR EMPL* chmn, ceo: Hartmarx Corp *CORP AFFIL* chmn: Am Apparel Brands Inc, Hart Schaffner & Marx

Homi Burjor Patel: *B* Bombay India 1949 *ED* Univ Bombay BS 1973; Columbia Univ

MBA 1975 *CURR EMPL* pres, coo, dir: Hartmarx Corp *CORP AFFIL* pres, ceo: Johnny Carson Apparel, Intercontinental Apparel, M Wile & Co; treas, dir: Textile Clothing Tech Corp *NONPR AFFIL* exec vp, mem, dir: Clothing Mfrs Assn Am *CLUB AFFIL* Chicago, Univ

GIVING OFFICERS

James Edward Condon: treas *B* Chicago IL 1950 *ED* IL Inst Tech BS 1972; IL Inst Tech MS 1973; Univ Chicago MBA 1976 *CURR EMPL* vp long term planning: Hartmarx Corp *CORP AFFIL* treas: Am Apparel Brands Inc; treas, dir: Hart Schaffner & Marx *NONPR AFFIL* mem: Assn Investment Mgmt & Res, Natl Assn Corp Treas; mem bd overseers: IL Inst Tech

Glenn R. Morgan: comm mem *B* Chicago IL 1947 *ED* Northwestern Univ 1968; Northwestern Univ 1970 *CURR EMPL* sr vp fin & admin: Hartmarx Corp *NONPR AFFIL* mem: Fin Execs Inst

Kay C. Nalbach: pres

APPLICATION INFORMATION

Initial Approach: *Initial Contact:* brief letter or proposal *Include Information On:* description of the organization, amount requested, purpose for which funds are sought, recently audited financial statement, proof of tax-exempt status *Deadlines:* none

Restrictions on Giving: Does not support goodwill advertising, political or lobbying groups, individuals, or religious organizations for sectarian purposes.

OTHER THINGS TO KNOW

The foundation reports that it is not accepting unsolicited requests for grants in 1995.

GRANTS ANALYSIS

Total Grants: $280,128

Number of Grants: 117

Highest Grant: $55,000

Average Grant: $2,394

Typical Range: $500 to $5,500

Disclosure Period: fiscal year ending November 30, 1993

Note: Figures represent foundation giving only and include subsidiary giving. Figures exclude $16,155 in employee matching gifts. Recent grants are derived from a 1993 Form 990.

RECENT GRANTS

General

55,000	United Way Crusade of Mercy, Chicago, IL
25,000	Northwestern University Kellogg Graduate School of Management, Evanston, IL
20,000	United Way of Michigan City/Michiana, Michigan City, IN
14,000	United Way, Greater Buffalo Chapter, Buffalo, NY
13,000	United Way of Greater Rochester, Rochester, NY

Hastings Charitable Foundation, Oris B.

CONTACT
John G. Holland
Trustee
Oris B. Hastings Charitable Foundation
230 Eighth St.
Cairo, IL 62914-2135
(618) 734-2800

FINANCIAL SUMMARY
Recent Giving: $132,528 (1993); $98,396 (1991)

Assets: $2,767,901 (1993); $2,697,152 (1991)

EIN: 37-1105036

CONTRIBUTIONS SUMMARY
Typical Recipients: • *Arts & Humanities:* Historic Preservation, History & Archaeology, Libraries • *Civic & Public Affairs:* Clubs, Municipalities/Towns, Urban & Community Affairs • *Education:* Private Education (Precollege), Secondary Education (Private) • *Health:* Emergency/Ambulance Services, Health Organizations • *Social Services:* Domestic Violence, Senior Services

Grant Types: general support

Geographic Distribution: focus on Cairo, IL

GIVING OFFICERS
John G. Holland: trust *PHIL AFFIL* trust: Hastings Trust

APPLICATION INFORMATION
Initial Approach: Send a brief letter of inquiry. There are no deadlines.

GRANTS ANALYSIS
Total Grants: $132,528

Number of Grants: 16

Highest Grant: $15,000

Typical Range: $3,000 to $14,956

Disclosure Period: 1993

Note: Recent grants are derived from a 1993 Form 990.

RECENT GRANTS

Library

11,500	Cairo Public Library, Cairo, IL

General

15,000	City of Cairo, Cairo, IL
14,957	Community Health and Emergency Services, Cairo, IL
13,770	Daystar Community Program, Cairo, IL
13,000	St. Joseph School, Cairo, IL
10,500	Daystar Care Center, Cairo, IL

Heller Financial, Inc.

Employees: 1,400
Parent Company: Fuji Bank, Ltd.
Headquarters: Chicago, IL
SIC Major Group: Short-Term Business Credit and Personal Credit Institutions

CONTACT
Judy Korba
Executive Assistant
Heller Financial Inc.
500 W Monroe St.
Chicago, IL 60661
(312) 441-6748

FINANCIAL SUMMARY
Recent Giving: $600,000 (1995 est.); $600,000 (1994 approx.); $600,000 (1992 approx.)

Fiscal Note: Company gives directly. Above figures exclude nonmonetary support.

CONTRIBUTIONS SUMMARY
Typical Recipients: • *Arts & Humanities:* Libraries, Music, Public Broadcasting • *Civic & Public Affairs:* Business/Free Enterprise, Professional & Trade Associations, Public Policy • *Education:* Colleges & Universities, Elementary Education (Private), Literacy, Minority Education, Private Education (Precollege), Public Education (Precollege) • *Health:* Mental Health • *Social Services:* United Funds/United Ways, Youth Organizations

Grant Types: employee matching gifts, project, scholarship, and seed money

Note: Matching gifts are for academic purposes only.

Nonmonetary Support Types: cause-related marketing & promotion, donated equipment, and donated products

Geographic Distribution: near headquarters and operating locations only

Operating Locations: CA, GA, IL (Chicago), NY, TX

CORP. OFFICERS
Michael S. Blum: *B* New York NY 1939 *ED* City Coll NY BCE 1960; Rutgers Univ MBA 1965 *CURR EMPL* chmn, pres, ceo: Heller Fin Inc *CORP AFFIL* chmn, ceo: Heller Intl Corp, Heller Intl Group; dir: Fuji Bank & Trust Co, Fuji Securities; pres, ceo: Abacus Real Estate Fin Group *NONPR AFFIL* dir: Cities Schs, Jewish Comm Chicago; mem: Urban Land Inst

GIVING OFFICERS
John Brooklier: *CURR EMPL* vp mktg: Heller Fin Inc

APPLICATION INFORMATION
Initial Approach: *Initial Contact:* brief letter of inquiry and a full proposal *Include Information On:* a description of the organization, amount requested, purpose for which funds are sought, list of board of trustees or directors, percentage of budget used for administration and overhead, evidence of 501(c)(3) status, outcomes expected, measurement tools, and list of funding from other organizations or government agencies *Deadlines:* none

Restrictions on Giving: Heller Financial, Inc. does not support individuals, organizations outside its operating areas, political or lobbying groups, United Way-supported organizations, or religious organizations for sectarian purposes.

OTHER THINGS TO KNOW
The majority of Heller Financial, Inc.'s charitable contributions are distributed by the corporate headquarters office in Chicago, IL, but a small percentage of funding is distributed through its various regional offices.

GRANTS ANALYSIS
Total Grants: $600,000*

Typical Range: $1,000 to $25,000

Disclosure Period: 1994

Note: Total grants figure is approximate. Recent grants are derived from a 1992 grants lists.

RECENT GRANTS

General
Cabrini-Green Youth Program, Chicago, IL
Chicago Cities in Schools, Chicago, IL
Day School, Chicago, IL
Good News Partners, Chicago, IL
Look to the Future Foundation, Chicago, IL

Hermann Foundation, Grover

CONTACT
Paul K. Rhoads
President and Director
Grover Hermann Foundation
7200 Sears Tower
233 South Wacker Dr.
Chicago, IL 60606
(312) 876-1000
Note: Monterey County, CA, organizations should contact the foundation at PO Box 596, Pebble Beach, CA 93953.

FINANCIAL SUMMARY
Recent Giving: $3,370,201 (1993); $3,370,201 (1992); $3,565,112 (1991)

Assets: $6,101,416 (1992); $14,126,669 (1990); $18,635,048 (1989)

EIN: 36-6064489

CONTRIBUTIONS SUMMARY
Donor(s): The Grover Hermann Foundation was established in 1955. Its donors are Grover Hermann and Sarah T. Hermann.

Typical Recipients: • *Arts & Humanities:* Historic Preservation, Libraries, Music • *Civic & Public Affairs:* Legal Aid, Professional & Trade Associations, Public Policy • *Education:* Colleges & Universities, Education Funds, Engineering/Technological Education, Faculty Development, General, Health & Physical Education, Journalism/Media Education, Legal Education, Literacy, Minority Education, Private Education (Precollege), Special Education, Student Aid • *Environment:* General • *Health:* Health Organizations, Hospices, Hospitals, Medical Rehabilitation, Mental Health, Nursing Services, Single-Disease Health Associations, Speech & Hearing • *International:* Health Care/Hospitals, International Organizations, International Relations • *Religion:* Religious Welfare • *Social Services:* Animal Protection, Child Welfare, Community Service Organizations, Domestic Violence, Emergency Relief, Family Services, Food/Clothing Distribution, General, People with Disabilities, Senior Services, Youth Organizations

Grant Types: capital, challenge, endowment, fellowship, general support, project, research, and scholarship

Geographic Distribution: broad geographic distribution, with grants for community-related activities favoring Chicago, IL, and Monterey County, CA

GIVING OFFICERS
Katheryn V. Rhoads: dir

Paul Kelly Rhoads: pres, dir *B* La Grange IL 1940 *ED* Washington & Lee Univ BA 1962; Loyola Univ JD 1967 *CURR EMPL* ptnr: Schiff Hardin & Waite *CORP AFFIL* dir: Hamler Indus, Haymarsh Corp *NONPR AFFIL* adv comm: Heritage Fdn Thomas A Roe Inst Econ Policy Studies; bd overseers: IL Inst Tech Chicago-Kent Coll Law; dir: Cyrus Tang Scholarship Fdn; mem: Chicago Bar Assn, IL Bar Assn, Union League; mem adv comm: Loyola Univ; trust: Western Springs Historical Soc; trust, mem exec comm: IL Inst Tech *CLUB AFFIL* Manistee GC & CC, Metro, Portage Lake YC, Salt Creek

APPLICATION INFORMATION
Initial Approach:

Organizations should submit a brief letter to the foundation. Telephone inquiries are not considered. The foundation has no formal application form.

Requests for funds should provide a concise description of the proposed project or other use for requested funds; specific objectives to be accomplished; background and qualifications of the organization and the individuals involved; the methods by which the organization will evaluate the results of the proposed project; a budget, including amount requested; latest audited financial statement; and a copy of the organization's most recent evidence of its federal tax-exempt status, accompanied by a separate representation that no change in that status has occurred since it was issued or is currently anticipated.

There are no deadlines for submitting requests.

The foundation's board meets four times a year. Responses normally will be received from several weeks to two or three months following application.

Restrictions on Giving: The foudnation will not provide funds for individuals, nonexempt organizations, general operating expenses, fraternal organizations, foreign organizations, athletic organizations, other private foundations, or political entities.

GRANTS ANALYSIS

Total Grants: $3,370,201

Number of Grants: 133

Highest Grant: $375,000

Average Grant: $25,340

Typical Range: $1,000 to $50,000

Disclosure Period: 1993

Note: Recent grants are derived from a 1993 Form 990.

RECENT GRANTS

General

375,000	Pacific Legal Foundation, Sacramento, CA
250,000	MAP International, Brunswick, GA — payment due on endowment fund
200,000	Boys and Girls Club of the Monterey Peninsula, Seaside, CA — final payment on challenge grant for new building
200,000	CARE Foundation, Western Region, San Francisco, CA — help establish permanent endowment fund
200,000	Heritage Foundation, Washington, DC — support Grover Hermann Fellow and general operations

Illinois Consolidated Telephone Co. / Lumpkin Foundation

Sales: $53.0 million
Employees: 664
Parent Company: Consolidated Communications
Headquarters: Mattoon, IL
SIC Major Group: Communications

CONTACT

Richard Anthony Lumpkin
President
Illinois Consolidated Telephone Co.
121 S 17th St.
Mattoon, IL 61938
(217) 235-3361

FINANCIAL SUMMARY

Recent Giving: $16,000 (1992); $130,500 (1991); $159,350 (1990)

Assets: $7,308,583 (1992); $6,519,933 (1991); $4,853,657 (1990)

Gifts Received: $309,500 (1992); $913,050 (1991); $180,000 (1990)

Fiscal Note: In 1992, contributions were received from the Illinois Consolidated Telephone Co.

EIN: 23-7423640

CONTRIBUTIONS SUMMARY

Typical Recipients: • *Arts & Humanities:* Arts Institutes, Libraries, Music • *Civic & Public Affairs:* General • *Education:* Colleges & Universities, Private Education (Precollege) • *Health:* Clinics/Medical Centers, Emergency/Ambulance Services, Health Organizations, Hospitals, Medical Rehabilitation, Nursing Services • *Religion:* Religious Welfare • *Social Services:* Child Welfare, Community Service Organizations, Family Services, Youth Organizations

Grant Types: general support

Geographic Distribution: focus on central IL

CORP. OFFICERS

R. J. Currey: *CURR EMPL* pres, coo, dir: IL Consolidated Telephone Co

Richard Anthony Lumpkin: *CURR EMPL* chmn, ceo, dir: IL Consolidated Tel Co

GIVING OFFICERS

S. L. Grissom: vp, secy, treas

Richard Anthony Lumpkin: pres, dir *CURR EMPL* chmn, ceo, dir: IL Consolidated Tel Co (see above)

Margaret Lumpkin Keon: dir

Mary Lumpkin Sparks: dir

L. M. Wilson: asst secy

APPLICATION INFORMATION

Initial Approach: Send cover letter and full proposal. Include a description of organization, amount requested, purpose of funds sought, recently audited financial statement, and proof of tax-exempt status. Deadline is November 30. Board meets in June and December.

Restrictions on Giving: Does not support individuals.

GRANTS ANALYSIS

Total Grants: $16,000

Number of Grants: 4

Highest Grant: $5,000

Typical Range: $1,000 to $5,000

Disclosure Period: 1992

Note: Recent grants are derived from a 1992 Form 990.

RECENT GRANTS

General

5,000	American National Red Cross, Mattoon, IL
5,000	International Red Cross, Mattoon, IL
1,000	Rehabilitation Institute of Chicago, Chicago, IL

Illinois Tool Works, Inc. / Illinois Tool Works Foundation

Revenue: $3.46 billion
Employees: 19,000
Headquarters: Glenview, IL
SIC Major Group: Plastics Products Nec, Chemical Preparations Nec, Unsupported Plastics Profile Shapes, and Hardware Nec

CONTACT

Stephen B. Smith
Director
Illinois Tool Works Foundation
3600 W Lake Ave.
Glenview, IL 60025
(708) 724-7500

FINANCIAL SUMMARY

Recent Giving: $2,540,236 (1993); $1,896,768 (1992); $1,800,000 (1989)

Assets: $12,535,258 (1992); $12,984,517 (1989)

Fiscal Note: Above figures include foundation and direct contributions. Direct giving amounts to approximately $300,000 annually.

EIN: 36-6087160

CONTRIBUTIONS SUMMARY

Typical Recipients: • *Arts & Humanities:* Arts Associations & Councils, Arts Institutes, Dance, Historic Preservation, Libraries, Museums/Galleries, Music, Opera, Performing Arts, Public Broadcasting, Theater • *Civic & Public Affairs:* Business/Free Enterprise, Civil Rights, Economic Development, Employment/Job Training, Housing, Law & Justice, Legal Aid, Nonprofit Management, Professional & Trade Associations, Public Policy, Urban & Community Affairs, Women's Affairs, Zoos/Aquariums • *Education:* Business Education, Colleges & Universities, Community & Junior Colleges, Economic Education, Education Funds, Engineering/Technological Education, Literacy, Minority Education, Science/Mathematics Education, Student Aid • *Health:* Hospitals, Medical Rehabilitation, Medical Research, Mental Health, Nursing Services • *Science:* Observatories & Planetariums, Science Exhibits & Fairs • *Social Services:* Family Planning, Family Services, Homes, People with Disabilities, Senior Services, Substance Abuse, United Funds/United Ways, Volunteer Services, Youth Organizations

Grant Types: capital, employee matching gifts, general support, and scholarship

Note: Employee matching gift ratio: 3 to 1 for donations to not-for-profit charitable organizations not already sponsored by company.

Geographic Distribution: mainly in Illinois, and where company maintains operating facilities

Operating Locations: AR (Pine Bluff), CA (Hawthorne), CO (Colorado Springs), CT (Waterbury), IL (Chicago, Des Plaines, Downers Grove, Elk Grove Village, Elmhurst, Frankfort, Glenview, Itasca, Lincolnshire, Lincolnwood, Schaumburg, Wood Dale), MA (Danvers), MI (Detroit, Ferndale), MN (Alexandria), NJ (Piscataway), NY (Orangeburg), OH (Loveland), PA (Montgomeryville, Philadelphia), TN (Erin), TX (Arlington, Irving), VA (Lynchburg), WI (Plymouth)

CORP. OFFICERS

W. James Farrell: *B* 1942 *ED* Univ Detroit BA 1968 *CURR EMPL* exec vp: IL Tool Works Inc *CORP AFFIL* pres, dir: Balance Engg Corp, Ransburg Corp

Stewart Skinner Hudnut: *B* Cincinnati OH 1939 *ED* Princeton Univ AB 1961; Oxford Univ JD 1962; Harvard Univ 1965 *CURR EMPL* vp, gen couns, secy: IL Tool Works Inc *CORP AFFIL* contributing editor: Modern Banking Forms; secy, dir: Balance Engg Corp *NONPR AFFIL* dir: Am Red Cross, Greater Waterbury Chamber Commerce, Litchfield Land Trust CT; dir, mem exec comm: Un Way Naugatuck Valley; mem: Am Bar Assn, CT Bar Assn, IL Bar Assn, Phi Beta Kappa; secy, trust: Assn Protection Adirondacks

John Karpen: *CURR EMPL* vp human resources: IL Tool Works Inc

Micheal Lynch: *CURR EMPL* mgr govt aff: IL Tool Works Inc

John Doane Nichols: *B* Shanghai People's Republic of China 1930 *ED* Harvard Univ BA 1953; Harvard Univ MBA 1955 *CURR EMPL* chmn, ceo: IL Tool Works Inc *CORP AFFIL* dir: Household Intl Inc, NICOR Inc, Northern IL Gas Co, Philip Morris Cos Inc, Ransburg Corp, Rockwell Intl Corp, Stone Container Corp; trust: Argonne Natl Laboratory *NONPR AFFIL* trust: Art Inst Chicago, Bus Roundtable, Chicago Commerce Civic Commn, Chicago Symphony Orchestra, Jr Achievement Chicago, Lyric Opera Chicago, Mus Sci & Indus, Univ Chicago *CLUB AFFIL* Chicago Commercial, Harvard, Indian Hills CC, Olympic

Harold Byron Smith, Jr.: *B* Chicago IL 1933 *ED* Princeton Univ BS 1955; Northwestern Univ MBA 1957 *CURR EMPL* chmn exec comm, dir: IL Tool Works Inc *CORP AFFIL* dir: WW Grainger Inc, Northern Trust Co, Northwestern Mutual Life Ins Co *NONPR AFFIL* dir: Adler Planetarium, Boys & Girls Clubs Am, Mfrs Alliance Productivity & Innovation, Newberry Lib, Northwestern Univ, Rush-Presbyterian-St Lukes Med Ctr; mem: Repbl Natl Comm IL *CLUB AFFIL* Chicago, Commercial, Commonwealth, Econ, Northwestern, Princeton *PHIL AFFIL* secy, dir: Bellebyron Foundation

GIVING OFFICERS

W. James Farrell: dir *CURR EMPL* exec vp: IL Tool Works Inc (see above)

Stewart Skinner Hudnut: secy, dir *CURR EMPL* vp, gen couns, secy: IL Tool Works Inc (see above)

John Karpen: dir *CURR EMPL* vp human resources: IL Tool Works Inc (see above)

John Doane Nichols: trust *CURR EMPL* chmn, ceo: IL Tool Works Inc (see above)

Michael J. Robinson: treas, dir *CURR EMPL* treas, dir: Balance Engg Corp

Harold Byron Smith, Jr.: chmn, pres, dir *CURR EMPL* chmn exec comm, dir: IL Tool Works Inc *PHIL AFFIL* secy, dir: Bellebyron Foundation (see above)

Stephen Byron Smith: dir *NONPR AFFIL* mem: Soc Colonial Wars *PHIL AFFIL* pres, dir: Bellebyron Foundation, Bellebyron Foundation *CLUB AFFIL* Chicago

APPLICATION INFORMATION

Initial Approach: *Initial Contact:* brief letter or proposal *Include Information On:* description of the organization; amount requested and purpose for which funds are sought; recently audited financial statement; and proof of tax-exempt status *Deadlines:* none

GRANTS ANALYSIS

Total Grants: $2,540,236

Typical Range: $1,000 to $10,000

Disclosure Period: 1993

Note: Recent grants are derived from a 1992 Form 990.

RECENT GRANTS

Library
10,000	Newberry Library, Chicago, IL
3,500	Newberry Library, Chicago, IL

General
225,000	United Way/Crusade of Mercy, Chicago, IL
57,500	Citizens Scholarship Foundation of America, St. Peter, MN
50,000	Civic Committee Foundation, Chicago, IL
25,305	National Merit Scholarship Corporation, Evanston, IL
25,000	Academy for Mathematics and Science Teachers, Chicago, IL

Kelly Foundation, T. Lloyd

CONTACT
M. C. Ryan
Treasurer
T. Lloyd Kelly Fdn.
c/o Continental Bank
30 N LaSalle St.
Chicago, IL 60697
(312) 828-1785

FINANCIAL SUMMARY
Recent Giving: $149,050 (1992); $128,400 (1990); $122,360 (1989)

Assets: $2,650,642 (1992); $2,142,037 (1990); $2,160,326 (1989)

Gifts Received: $303,523 (1992)

EIN: 36-6050341

CONTRIBUTIONS SUMMARY
Donor(s): Mildred Wetten Kelly McDermott

Typical Recipients: • *Arts & Humanities:* Arts Institutes, Historic Preservation, History & Archaeology, Libraries, Opera, Public Broadcasting, Theater • *Civic & Public Affairs:* Women's Affairs • *Education:* Colleges & Universities, Private Education (Precollege), Special Education • *Health:* Children's Health/Hospitals, Hospices, Hospitals, Medical Research, Prenatal Health Issues • *Religion:* Religious Welfare • *Social Services:* Child Welfare, Community Service Organizations, Counseling, Family Planning, Youth Organizations

Grant Types: general support

GIVING OFFICERS
Barbara K. Hull: dir

Arthur L. Kelly: dir

Robert A. Malstrom: dir, pres

Mildred Wetten Kelly McDermott: dir, vp

Sally Morris: dir

M. C. Ryan: treas, dir

H. Blair White: secy, dir *B* Burlington IA 1927 *ED* Univ IA BA 1950; Univ IA BA 1950; Univ IA JD 1951; Univ IA JD 1951 *CURR EMPL* ptnr: Sidley & Austin *CORP AFFIL* dir: Bankmont Fin Corp, DeKalb Energy Co, DeKalb Energy Corp, DeKalb Genetics Co, DeKalb Genetics Corp, RR Donnelley & Sons Co, RR Donnelley & Sons Co, Kimberly-Clark Corp *NONPR AFFIL* dir: Auxiliary Cook County Hosp, Childrens Meml Hosp Chicago, Childrens Memorial Hosp, Rush-Presbyterian-St Lukes Med Ctr; mem: Am Bar Assn, Am Coll Trial Lawyers, Chicago Bar Assn, IL Bar Assn, 7th Fed Circuit Bar Assn

APPLICATION INFORMATION
Initial Approach: Send brief letter describing program. There are no deadlines.

GRANTS ANALYSIS
Total Grants: $149,050

Number of Grants: 26

Highest Grant: $51,000

Typical Range: $100 to $2,000

Disclosure Period: 1992

Note: Recent grants are derived from a 1992 Form 990.

RECENT GRANTS

Library
200	University of Chicago Library Society, Chicago, IL

General
51,000	Planned Parenthood, St. Louis, MO
18,000	Planned Parenthood, Ashville, NC
15,000	Planned Parenthood, Chicago, IL
12,000	St. Paul's School, Concord, NH
10,000	Rush-Presbyterian St. Luke's Medical Center, Chicago, IL

Kemper National Insurance Cos. / Kemper Foundation, James S.

Revenue: $2.3 billion
Employees: 6,335
Headquarters: Long Grove, IL
SIC Major Group: Holding & Other Investment Offices, Insurance Agents, Brokers & Service, and Insurance Carriers

CONTACT
James R. Connor
Executive Director
James S. Kemper Foundation
One Kemper Dr.
Long Grove, IL 60049
(708) 320-2847
Note: Contact Howard L. Knight, chairman, or Charles W. Meinhardt, secretary, of the corporate contributions committee for information about the direct giving program.

FINANCIAL SUMMARY
Recent Giving: $970,000 (fiscal 1995 est.); $971,636 (fiscal 1994); $834,073 (fiscal 1993)

Assets: $29,000,000 (fiscal 1995 est.); $29,573,800 (fiscal 1994); $17,960,265 (fiscal 1993)

Fiscal Note: In addition to foundation figures above, corporation provides direct grants totaling approximately $100,000 annually. Direct giving supports youth, health, and cultural activities. Above figures exclude nonmonetary support.

EIN: 36-6007812

CONTRIBUTIONS SUMMARY
Typical Recipients: • *Arts & Humanities:* Arts Festivals, Libraries, Museums/Galleries, Music, Opera, Public Broadcasting, Theater • *Education:* Arts/Humanities Education, Business Education, Colleges & Universities, Community & Junior Colleges, Economic Education, Engineering/Technological Education, Faculty Development, General, International Studies, Legal Education, Medical Education, Minority Education, Student Aid • *Health:* Medical Rehabilitation, Single-Disease Health Associations • *Science:* Science Museums • *Social Services:* Substance Abuse

Grant Types: award, department, endowment, and multiyear/continuing support

Nonmonetary Support: $50,000 (fiscal 1991)

Nonmonetary Support Types: in-kind services

Note: Company contributes printing and creative support in the way of writing and design. Contact Mr. Meinhardt for information.

Geographic Distribution: primarily to organizations in the Chicago metropolitan area, and nationally

Operating Locations: CA (Los Angeles, Menlo Park, Pasadena), CO (Denver), IA (Mason City), IL (Chicago, Long Grove), OH (Cleveland), WI (Milwaukee)

CORP. OFFICERS
Alfred K. Kenyon: *ED* St Matthews Univ *CURR EMPL* pres, coo: Lumbermens Mutual Casualty Co *CORP AFFIL* pres, coo: Kemper Natl Ins Cos

Gerald Leonard Maatman: *B* Chicago IL 1930 *ED* IL Inst Tech BS 1951 *CURR EMPL* chmn, ceo: Kemper Natl Ins Cos *CORP AFFIL* chmn: Underwriters Laboratories; chmn, ceo: Am Mfgs Mutual Ins Co, Am Motorists Ins Co, Lumbermens Mutual Casualty Co; dir: Am Protection Ins Co, Kemper Intl Corp *NONPR AFFIL* dir: Advocates Hwy & Auto Safety, Am Ins Assn, Ins Inst Hwy Safety, Jr Achievement Chicago, Natl Commn Against Drunk Driving, Natl Down Syndrome Soc, Natl Fire Protection Assn, Soc Fire Protection Engrs; mem: Tau Beta Pi; trust: Am Inst Chartered Property & Casualty Underwriters *CLUB AFFIL* Wynstone GC

GIVING OFFICERS
J. Reed Coleman: trust *PHIL AFFIL* pres, trust: Norman Bassett Foundation

James Richard Connor: exec dir *B* Indianapolis IN 1928 *ED* Univ IA BA 1951; Univ WI MS 1954; Univ WI PhD 1961 *NONPR AFFIL* mem: Am Assn Univ Profs, Beta Gamma Sigma, Blue Key, Delta Sigma Pi, Golden Key, Order Omega, Org Am Historians, Phi Alpha Theta, Phi Beta Kappa, Phi Delta Kappa, Phi Eta Sigma, Phi Kappa Phi; mem natl adv comm: Woodrow Wilson Natl Fellowship Fdn

James Scott Kemper, Jr.: hon chmn *B* Chicago IL 1914 *ED* Harvard Univ LLB 1938; Yale Univ AB 1955 *CURR EMPL* chmn: Kemper Sports Mgmt *CORP AFFIL* chmn: Kemper Corp; pres: Lumbermens Mutual Casualty Co *NONPR AFFIL* dir: Am Mutual Ins Alliance, Arthritis Fdn, Boys Club Am, Chicago Boys Club, Lyric Opera Chicago, Natl Counc Alcoholism; mem: Alpha Sigma Phi; mem adv bd: Chicago Metro Counc Alcoholism; mem adv comm: Drug Abuse & Alcoholism Program; trust: Conf Bd, IL Inst Tech, Mus Sci & Indus, Northwestern Meml Hosp *CLUB AFFIL* Bohemian, Chicago, Glen View GC, Ironwood CC, Pauma Valley CC

George D. Kennedy: trust *B* Pittsburgh PA 1926 *ED* Williams Coll BA 1948 *CURR EMPL* chmn exec comm: Mallinckrodt Group Inc *CORP AFFIL* chmn: Mallinckrodt Veterinary Inc; chmn, dir, comm mem: Brunswick Corp; dir: Am Natl Can Co, IL Tool Works Inc, Kemper Natl Ins Cos, Medcare Am Inc, Scotsman Indus Inc, Stone Container Corp; dir, mem exec comm: Kemper Corp *NONPR AFFIL* dir: Childrens Meml Hosp & Med Ctr, Critical Care Am, Lyric Opera Chicago, McGaw Med Ctr, Northwestern Univ; gov mem: Chicago Orchestra Assn; mem: Mid Am Chicago Comm; mem bus adv counc: Carnegie-Mellon Univ Grad Sch Indus Admin; mem, dir: Chicago Assn Commerce Indus, Chicago Counc Foreign Rels; natl bd trust: Boy Scouts Am; regional trust: Boys & Girls Clubs Am; trust: Chicago Symphony Orchestra, Comm Econ Devel, Ctr Workforce Preparation & Quality Ed, Natl Commn

Against Drunk Driving; vchmn, mem: Am Mining Congress *CLUB AFFIL* Bd Rm, Commercial, Larchmont YC, NY Athletic, Skokie CC; mem: Sleepy Hallow CC

Dalton L. Knauss: trust *B* Imboden AK 1928 *ED* DeVry Inst Tech 1951; IL Inst Tech

George Ralph Lewis: trust *B* Burgess VA 1941 *ED* Hampton Univ BS 1963; Iona Coll MBA 1968 *CURR EMPL* vp, treas: Philip Morris Cos Inc *CORP AFFIL* dir: Central Fidelity Banks Inc, Kemper Natl Ins Cos *NONPR AFFIL* corp adv bd: Natl Bankers Assn; dir: Natl Urban League; mem: Natl Corp Treas Assn, Omega Psi Phi, Sigma Pi Phi; Natl adv comm: Professional Golfers Assn Am; trust: Hampton Univ *PHIL AFFIL* trust: Charles Sanders Trust

Katharine Culbert Lyall: trust *B* Lancaster PA 1941 *ED* Cornell Univ BA 1963; NY Univ MBA 1965; Cornell Univ PhD 1969 *CORP AFFIL* dir: Kemper Ins Co, WI Power & Light Co *NONPR AFFIL* mem: Am Econ Assn, Phi Beta Kappa; mem exec comm: Assn Am Univs; prof: Univ WI Madison

Gerald Leonard Maatman: chmn, pres, trust *CURR EMPL* chmn, ceo: Kemper Natl Ins Cos (see above)

Shirley Neil Pettis: trust *B* Mountain View CA *ED* Andrews Univ 1942; Univ CA 1944; Andrews Univ 1945 *NONPR AFFIL* mem: Am Historical Assn, Commn Presidential Scholars, Natl Womens Econ Alliance Fdn, Political Sci Assn; trust: Loma Linda Univ *CLUB AFFIL* Capitol Hill, Congressional, Morningside CC

Bernard William Rogers: trust *B* Fairview KS 1921 *ED* US Military Acad BS 1943; Oxford Univ BA 1950; Oxford Univ MA 1954 *CORP AFFIL* dir: Gen Dynamics Corp, Kemper Group, Thomas Indus Inc; sr consult: Coca Cola Co *NONPR AFFIL* chmn: Un Svs Org World Bd Govs; dir: Assn US Army, Atlantic Counc US, Inst Defense Analysts, Logistics Mgmt Inst, George C Marshall Fdn; hon fellow: Oxford Univ; mem: Am Soc French Legion Honor, Assn Am Rhodes Scholars, Counc Foreign Rels, Military Order World Wars, Phi Delta Theta, Retired Offs Assn, Veterans Foreign Wars, Washington World Aff Counc; trust: WA Inst Foreign Aff *CLUB AFFIL* Alfalfa, Army & Navy, Army-Navy CC, Pilgrims

Richard Nathaniel Rosett: trust *B* Baltimore MD 1928 *ED* Columbia Univ BA 1953; Yale Univ MA 1954; Yale Univ PhD 1957 *CORP AFFIL* dir: Hutchinson Techs, Lumbermans Mutual Ins Co *NONPR AFFIL* dean: Rochester Inst Tech Coll Bus, Univ Chicago Sch Bus; dir: Ctr Governmental Res; mem: Am Econ Assn, Phi Beta Kappa; pres: US Bus Sch Prague; trust: Keuka Coll; vchmn, dir: Mont Pelerin Soc *CLUB AFFIL* Chicago, Cosmos, Genesee Valley, Valley, Yale

Daniel Roger Toll: trust *B* Denver CO 1927 *ED* Princeton Univ AB 1949; Harvard Univ MBA 1955 *CURR EMPL* chmn: Corona Corp *CORP AFFIL* dir: AP Green Indus Inc, Brown Group Inc, AP Green Indus, Kemper Corp, Kemper Natl Ins Cos, Lincoln Natl Convertible Securities Fund, Lincoln Natl Direct Placement Fund, Lincoln Natl Income

Fund, Mallinckrodt Group Inc, NICOR Inc *NONPR AFFIL* chief crusader: Chicago Crusade Mercy; dir: Boy Scouts Am; dir, exec comm, chmn fin comm & hosp aff comm: Evanston Hosp; mem: Chicago Assn Commerce & Indus, Phi Beta Kappa; natl vchmn: INROADS; pres: Chicago Metro Planning Commn *CLUB AFFIL* Chicago, Commercial, Econ, Harvard Bus Sch, Indian Hill, Princeton, Union League *PHIL AFFIL* trust: George Warren Brown Foundation

Walter Lucas White: secy, treas, trust *B* Des Moines IA 1940 *ED* Coe Coll 1962; IN Univ MBA 1964 *CURR EMPL* cfo: Lumbermans Mutual Casualty Co *CORP AFFIL* cfo, dir: Am Motorists Ins Co; sr vp, dir: Am Mfgs Mutual Ins Co

APPLICATION INFORMATION
Initial Approach: *Initial Contact:* brief letter *Include Information On:* description of project, time frame, amount needed to complete project, and amount requested *Deadlines:* applications must be received by November 1

Restrictions on Giving: Does not support dinners or special events, fraternal organizations, good-will advertising, member agencies of united funds, political or lobbying groups, religious organizations for sectarian purposes, or individuals.

GRANTS ANALYSIS
Total Grants: $971,636

Number of Grants: 140

Highest Grant: $83,000

Average Grant: $6,940

Typical Range: $1,000 to $20,000

Disclosure Period: fiscal year ending July 31, 1994

Note: Recent grants are scholar, nursing student, and project grants. Direct grants from Kemper National Insurance Companies are not included in these figures. Recent grants are derived from a fiscal 1994 annual report.

RECENT GRANTS

Library
15,000	College of St. Francis, Joliet, IL — for faculty and curriculum development and library enhancement
5,000	Brumback Library, Van Wert, OH — to support automation of the library

General
83,000	Museum of Science and Industry, Chicago, IL — to support the "Kemper Back Seat Drive In" driver safety exhibit
30,930	La Salle University, Philadelphia, PA — for Kemper Scholar Grants
30,300	Loyola University, Chicago, IL — for Kemper Scholar Grants
30,000	University of the Pacific School of Business and Public Administration, Stockton, CA — for funding
29,200	to upgrade and enhance computer resources Brigham Young University, Provo, UT — for Kemper Scholar Grants

---

Kern Foundation Trust

CONTACT
David W. Holman
Corporate Trustee Representative
Kern Foundation Trust
c/o The Northern Trust Co.
50 S LaSalle St.
Chicago, IL 60675
(312) 557-2703

FINANCIAL SUMMARY
Recent Giving: $750,000 (1993 est.); $681,950 (1992); $746,700 (1991)

Assets: $18,000,000 (1993 est.); $17,239,610 (1992); $17,162,301 (1991)

EIN: 36-6107250

CONTRIBUTIONS SUMMARY
Donor(s): The foundation was established in 1959 by the late Herbert A. Kern , who felt that the basic theosophical concepts such as the essential unity of all in manifestation was a critical starting point for changing peoples' attitudes about race, culture, responsibility towards one another and the environment. It became operational in 1966 and is not affiliated with or related to any other charitable trust or foundation.

Typical Recipients: • *Arts & Humanities:* Libraries, Museums/Galleries • *Education:* Arts/Humanities Education, Colleges & Universities, Private Education (Precollege), Public Education (Precollege) • *Religion:* Religious Organizations • *Social Services:* People with Disabilities

Grant Types: fellowship, general support, project, and scholarship

Geographic Distribution: primarily in Illinois and California

GIVING OFFICERS
David W. Holman: corp trust rep

Herbert A. Kern, Jr.: trust

John C. Kern: trust

APPLICATION INFORMATION
Initial Approach:

The foundation has no formal grant application procedure or application form.

The foundation has no deadline for submitting proposals.

Upon receipt of a proposal which includes sufficient detail to make a case for support, the proposal is routed to a qualified professional to evaluate it.

Restrictions on Giving: The foundation reports that it limits grant making to religious foundations chartered to advance the cause of theosophy. Grants are not made to individuals or private building funds.

OTHER THINGS TO KNOW
The Northern Trust Company of Chicago operates as a corporate trustee.

The foundation reports that it provides all types of services to its principal theosophical organizations receiving grants. It gives only financial support to universities and colleges to which a grant has been made to assist a graduate student or faculty member.

PUBLICATIONS
Program policy statement

GRANTS ANALYSIS
Total Grants: $750,000

Number of Grants: 5

Highest Grant: $500,000

Average Grant: $150,000*

Typical Range: $1,000 to $60,000*

Disclosure Period: 1993

Note: Average grant figure and typical grant range was provided by the foundation. Recent grants are derived from a 1991 Form 990.

RECENT GRANTS

Library
13,200	University of Chicago Library, Chicago, IL

General
533,000	Theosophical Society in America, Wheaton, IL
159,300	Krotona Institute of Theosophy, Ojai, CA
31,200	Happy Valley School, Ojai, CA
10,000	California Institute of Integral Studies, San Francisco, CA

Lederer Foundation, Francis L.

CONTACT
Robert I. Ury
Secretary, Director
Francis L. Lederer Fdn.
120 S Riverside Plz. No. 1200
Chicago, IL 60606
(312) 876-7100

FINANCIAL SUMMARY
Recent Giving: $213,000 (1993); $236,000 (1991); $236,500 (1990)

Assets: $5,028,824 (1993); $5,022,583 (1991); $4,285,472 (1990)

EIN: 36-2594937

CONTRIBUTIONS SUMMARY
Typical Recipients: • *Arts & Humanities:* Arts Institutes, Historic Preservation, History & Archaeology, Libraries, Museums/Galleries, Music, Opera, Public Broadcasting, Theater • *Civic & Public Affairs:* Housing, Public Policy, Urban & Community Affairs • *Education:* Colleges & Universities, Education Funds, Private Education (Precollege), Science/Mathematics Education • *Health:* AIDS/HIV, Alzheimers Disease, Clinics/Medical Centers, Health Or-

ganizations, Medical Research, Multiple Sclerosis, Prenatal Health Issues, Single-Disease Health Associations • *Religion:* Jewish Causes, Religious Organizations, Synagogues/Temples • *Science:* Science Museums • *Social Services:* Child Abuse, Community Service Organizations, Domestic Violence, People with Disabilities, Scouts, Youth Organizations

Grant Types: general support

Geographic Distribution: focus on Chicago, IL

GIVING OFFICERS
Adrienne Lederer: vp, dir

Francis L. Lederer II: pres, treas, dir

Robert I. Ury: secy, dir

APPLICATION INFORMATION
Initial Approach: Send a brief letter of inquiry. Include a description of organization, amount requested, purpose of funds sought, recently audited financial statement, and proof of tax-exempt status. There are no deadlines.

GRANTS ANALYSIS
Total Grants: $213,000

Number of Grants: 21

Highest Grant: $35,000

Typical Range: $500 to $25,000

Disclosure Period: 1993

Note: Recent grants are derived from a 1993 Form 990.

RECENT GRANTS
Library

10,000	Chicago Historical Society, Chicago, IL — library
2,000	Anshe Emet Library Fund, Chicago, IL

General

35,000	National Committee for the Prevention of Child Abuse, Chicago, IL — toll-free telephone number
25,000	Jewish United Fund, Chicago, IL
20,000	University of Chicago, Chicago, IL — support student/biological science/Pritzker
10,000	Alzheimers Disease and Related Disorders Association, Chicago, IL
10,000	Child Abuse Prevention Services, Chicago, IL — children's group programs

Lehmann Foundation, Otto W.

CONTACT
Richard J. Peterson
Trustee
Otto W. Lehmann Fdn.
PO Box 11194
Chicago, IL 60611
(708) 895-0175

FINANCIAL SUMMARY
Recent Giving: $175,000 (fiscal 1994); $175,000 (fiscal 1993); $160,000 (fiscal 1991)

Assets: $2,293,300 (fiscal 1994); $2,484,667 (fiscal 1993); $2,288,555 (fiscal 1991)

EIN: 36-6160836

CONTRIBUTIONS SUMMARY
Donor(s): the late Otto W. Lehmann

Typical Recipients: • *Arts & Humanities:* Arts Institutes, History & Archaeology, Libraries, Music, Opera • *Civic & Public Affairs:* Employment/Job Training, Zoos/Aquariums • *Education:* Colleges & Universities, Engineering/Technological Education, Private Education (Precollege), Special Education, Student Aid • *Health:* Alzheimers Disease, Cancer, Children's Health/Hospitals, Emergency/Ambulance Services, Eyes/Blindness, Health Organizations, Hospitals, Medical Rehabilitation, Medical Research, Nursing Services, Single-Disease Health Associations • *Religion:* Religious Organizations, Religious Welfare • *Science:* Science Museums • *Social Services:* Child Welfare, Community Service Organizations, Domestic Violence, Food/Clothing Distribution, People with Disabilities, Shelters/Homelessness, United Funds/United Ways, Youth Organizations

Grant Types: general support

Geographic Distribution: limited to the Chicago, IL, area

GIVING OFFICERS
David W. Peterson: trust

Lucille S. Peterson: trust

Richard J. Peterson: trust

Orris Seng: trust *PHIL AFFIL* trust: Harry L. and John L. Smysor Memorial Fund

APPLICATION INFORMATION
Initial Approach: Send brief letter describing program. Include a description of organization, amount requested, purpose of funds sought, recently audited financial statement, and proof of tax-exempt status. Deadline is July 31.

GRANTS ANALYSIS
Total Grants: $175,000

Number of Grants: 65

Highest Grant: $12,000

Typical Range: $1,000 to $12,000

Disclosure Period: fiscal year ending July 31, 1994

Note: Recent grants are derived from a fiscal 1994 Form 990.

RECENT GRANTS
General

12,000	Loyola University, Chicago, IL — scholarships
12,000	Northwestern University, Evanston, IL — scholarships
6,500	DePaul University, Chicago, IL — scholarships
5,000	Boys and Girls Clubs of America, Chicago, IL — scholarships
5,000	Children's Memorial Medical Center, Chicago, IL — health facility

MacArthur Foundation, John D. and Catherine T.

CONTACT
John D. and Catherine T. MacArthur Foundation
c/o Office of Grant Management, Research, and Information
140 S Dearborn St., Ste 1100
Chicago, IL 60603
(312) 726-8000
Note: Inquiries about the foundation's programs should be sent directly to the grant's management office. Details concerning the interests of the programs can be obtained by writing. In a few cases, such as fellowships done jointly with the Social Science Research Council, applications should be sent to the partner organization, but details about these programs can be obtained from the foundation. See "Other Things To Know" for more details.

FINANCIAL SUMMARY
Recent Giving: $151,000,000 (1994 approx.); $151,164,925 (1993); $156,000,000 (1992 approx.)

Assets: $3,000,000,000 (1994 approx.); $3,098,244,000 (1993); $2,948,361,000 (1992)

EIN: 23-7093598

CONTRIBUTIONS SUMMARY
Donor(s): The foundation was incorporated in 1970 in Illinois, with funds donated by John D. MacArthur . Mr. MacArthur, who died in 1978, built his fortune through the Bankers Life and Casualty Company of Chicago, of which he was the sole owner. He also owned an array of related companies and over 100,000 acres of land, primarily in the Palm Beach, FL, area. He left the assets of his insurance fortune and real estate holdings, ultimately valued at more than $3 billion, to the foundation. His wife, Catherine T. MacArthur, was a board member of both Bankers Life and Casualty and the foundation prior to her death in 1981. Mr. MacArthur left the selection of areas of interest, programs, and guidelines for the foundation entirely up to its board of trustees.

Typical Recipients: • *Arts & Humanities:* Arts Associations & Councils, Arts Centers, Arts Festivals, Arts Institutes, Community Arts, Dance, Ethnic & Folk Arts, Historic Preservation, History & Archaeology, Libraries, Museums/Galleries, Music, Opera, Performing Arts, Public Broadcasting, Theater, Visual Arts • *Civic & Public Affairs:* African American Affairs, Business/Free Enterprise, Civil Rights, Economic Development, Economic Policy, Hispanic Affairs, Housing, Law & Justice, Legal Aid, Minority Business, Philanthropic Organizations, Professional & Trade Associations, Public Policy, Urban & Community Affairs, Women's Affairs, Zoos/Aquariums • *Education:* Business Education, Colleges & Universities, Education Reform, Health & Physical Education, International Exchange, International Studies, Journalism/Media Education, Literacy, Medical Education, Minority Education, Science/Mathematics Education • *Environment:* Air/Water Quality, Energy, General, Resource Conservation, Wildlife Protection • *Health:* Geriatric Health, Health Organizations, Medical Research, Mental Health, Preventive Medicine/Wellness Organizations • *International:* Foreign Educational Institutions, Health Care/Hospitals, Human Rights, International Affairs, International Development, International Environmental Issues, International Organizations, International Peace & Security Issues, International Relations, Missionary/Religious Activities • *Religion:* Religious Welfare, Seminaries, Social/Policy Issues • *Science:* Observatories & Planetariums, Scientific Centers & Institutes, Scientific Research • *Social Services:* Child Welfare, Community Service Organizations, Crime Prevention, Family Planning, Family Services, Senior Services, United Funds/United Ways, Volunteer Services

Grant Types: fellowship, general support, matching, multiyear/continuing support, project, and research

Geographic Distribution: international and national: education reform grants primarily in Chicago, IL, and cultural grants primarily in Chicago, IL, and Palm Beach County, FL

GIVING OFFICERS
Carmen Barroso: dir (population program)

Kennette Benedict: dir (peace & intl coop)

Ray Boyer: dir (communs)

David S. Chernoff: asst secy, assoc gen coun

John Edward Corbally: dir *B* South Bend WA 1924 *ED* Univ WA BS 1947; Univ WA MA 1950; Univ CA Berkeley PhD 1955 *NONPR AFFIL* mem: Alpha Phi Omega, Beta Gamma Sigma, Chi Gamma Iota, Omicron Delta Kappa, Phi Beta Kappa, Phi Kappa Phi, Phi Kappa Sigma; pres emeritus: Univ IL *CLUB AFFIL* Tavern, Useless Bay CC, Wayfarers *PHIL AFFIL* dir: Univ WA Foundation

Nancy Best Ewing: secy, assoc gen coun

Robert P. Ewing: dir *B* Kirksville MO 1925 *ED* NE MO St Univ BS 1948 *PHIL AFFIL* trust, secy: Retirement Research Foundation

William H. Foege, M.D.: dir *PHIL AFFIL* secy, exec dir: Global 2000

James Merle Furman: dir *B* Kansas City MO 1932 *ED* OH St Univ BA 1954 *NONPR AFFIL* chmn: IL Comm Higher Ed Scope Structure & Productivity, Natl Task Force Higher Ed & Pub Interest, State Higher Ed Exec Offs; mem: Ed Commn Sts, Natl Ctr Higher Ed Mgmt Systems, Student Fin Assistance Study Group, Western Interstate Commn Higher Ed; mem bd: Donors Forum; mem bd advs: Fund Improvement Postsecondary Ed; mem corp adv bd: Univ MD; mem exec comm: State Higher Ed Planning Comm US Off Ed; mem mgmt adv comm:

Northwestern Univ; mem panel politics & st univs: Carnegie Fdn; trust: Bradley Univ, Loyola Univ

Murray Gell-Mann: dir *B* New York NY 1929 *ED* Yale Univ BS 1948; MA Inst Tech PhD 1951; Yale Univ ScD 1959 *NONPR AFFIL* adv: IN Univ Sch Bus

Peter H. Gerber: dir (ed program)

Philip M. Grace: treas

Alan Montgomery Hallene: dir *B* Moline IL 1929 *ED* Oak Ridge Sch Reactor Tech 1951-1952; Univ IL BS 1951 *CURR EMPL* pres: Montgomery Elevator Intl *CORP AFFIL* dir: Butler Mfg Co, First Midwest Bank Moline, Montgomery Elevator Co, Rolscreen Co *NONPR AFFIL* dir: Inst IL, Univ IL Fdn; mem: IL Gov Adv Counc, Univ IL Alumni Assn; trust: Butterworth Meml Trust, Lincoln Academy IL *PHIL AFFIL* trust: Montgomery Elevator Co. Charitable Trust; mem: Alice Butler Foundation *CLUB AFFIL* mem: Rotary

Ralph E. Hamilton: dir (FL philanthropy)

Paul Harvey: dir *B* Tulsa OK 1918 *CURR EMPL* commentator: ABC News *CORP AFFIL* sundicated columnist: Los Angeles Times Syndicate *NONPR AFFIL* mem: Aircraft Owners & Pilots Assn, Washington Radio & TV Correspondents Assn; mem, bd govs: Chicago Symphony Orchestral Assn *CLUB AFFIL* Chicago Press; mem: Chicago Press

John Paul Holdren: dir *B* Sewickley PA 1944 *ED* MA Inst Tech SB 1965; MA Inst Tech SM 1966; Stanford Univ PhD 1970 *CORP AFFIL* consult: Lawrence Livermore Labs; sr investigator: Rocky Mountain Biological Labs *NONPR AFFIL* bd sponsors: Am Physical Soc; chmn: US Pugwash Comm; chmn, mem exec comm: Pugwash Conf Science & World Aff; fellow: Am Academy Arts & Sciences, Am Assn Advancement Science, CA Academy Sciences; mem: Fed Am Scientists, Natl Academy Sciences

Shirley Mount Hufstedler: dir *B* Denver CO 1925 *ED* Univ NM BBA 1945; Stanford Univ LLB 1949 *CURR EMPL* ptnr: Hufstedler Kaus & Ettinger *CORP AFFIL* dir: Harman Indus Intl, Hewlett-Packard Co, US West *NONPR AFFIL* mem: Am Bar Assn, Am Bar Fdn, Am Judicature Soc, Am Law Inst, Assn Bar City New York, Counc Foreign Rels, Los Angeles County Bar Assn, Order Coif, Town Hall, Women Lawyers Assn; trust: Aspen Inst Humanistic Studies, CA Inst Tech, Carnegie Endowment Intl Peace, Colonial Williamsburg Fdn

John Hurkey: assoc vp

Richard J. Kaplan: dir grants mgmt, res and information

Lawrence L. Landry: vp, cfo

Sara Lawrence Lightfoot: dir

Paul E. Lingenfelter: assoc vp planning evaluation, dir program investments

William F. Lowry: dir (human resources)

Margaret Ellerbe Mahoney: dir *B* Nashville TN 1924 *ED* Vanderbilt Univ BA 1946 *NONPR AFFIL* dir: Alliance Aging Res, Overseas Devel Counc; mem: Alpha Omega

Alpha, Am Academy Arts & Sciences, Am Assn Advancement Science, Counc Foreign Rels, Fin Womens Assn, Natl Academy Sciences Inst Medicine, NY Academy Sciences; mem adv bd: Barnard Coll Inst Medicine Res, Office Chief Med Examiner New York City; trust: Columbia Univ, Smith Coll; vchmn: New York City Mayors Comm Pub/Pvt Partnership; vchmn bd govs: NY Academy Medicine *PHIL AFFIL* pres, dir: Commonwealth Fund *CLUB AFFIL* mem: Alpha Omega Alpha

Dan M. Martin: dir world environment & resources program, population program

Elizabeth J. McCormack: chmn, dir *CURR EMPL* assoc: Rockefeller Family & Assocs *PHIL AFFIL* trust: Trust for Mutual Understanding

Joshua J. Mintz: gen couns

Victor Rabinowitch: sr vp

George A. Ranney, Jr.: dir *B* Chicago IL 1940 *ED* Harvard Univ BA 1962; Univ Chicago JD 1966 *CURR EMPL* ptnr: Mayer Brown & Platt *PHIL AFFIL* dir: Field Foundation of Illinois, Spencer Foundation, George M. Pullman Educational Foundation

Rebecca Riley: dir (community initiatives program), vp (Chicago aff)

Robert M. Rose: dir health program

Camille E. Seamans: dir (human resources)

Adele Smith Simmons: pres *B* Lake Forest IL 1941 *ED* Radcliffe Coll BA 1963; Oxford Univ PhD 1969 *CORP AFFIL* dir: Affiliated Pubs, Boston Globe, First Chicago Corp, Marsh & McLennan New York City *NONPR AFFIL* dir: Synergos Inst; mem: Counc Foreign Rels, Phi Beta Kappa; trust: Union Concerned Scientists *CLUB AFFIL* Cosmopolitan *PHIL AFFIL* trust: Norwottock Charitable Trust

Dale E. Smith: dir (FL real estate)

Thomas Charles Theobald: dir *B* Cincinnati OH 1937 *ED* Coll Holy Cross AB 1958; Harvard Univ MBA 1960 *CURR EMPL* ptner, investor: William Blair Capital Mgmt Co *CORP AFFIL* chmn: Chicago Clearing House Assn; chmn, dir: Continental Bank NA; dir: Xerox Corp; pres: Moorpark Holding Inc *NONPR AFFIL* bd dir assocs: Harvard Univ Grad Sch Bus Admin; dir: Boy Scouts Am Chicago Area Counc, Chicago Counc Foreign Rels; mem: Chicago Inst Archt Urbanism, Chicago Un, IL Bus Roundtable; mem commn architecture: Art Inst Chicago; trust: Natl Lekotek Ctr, Northwestern Univ *CLUB AFFIL* Commercial, Econ Chicago

Woodward A. Wickham: vp (pub affairs), dir (gen program)

APPLICATION INFORMATION
Initial Approach:
The application and proposal process varies from program to program. Prospective applicants should contact the foundation for information and specific program guidelines before submitting an application.

For programs in which applications are accepted, a letter of inquiry may be submitted. It should include a brief summary of the problem to be addressed, and proposed solution. Financial details and a description of the applicant orgnization should also be included. If the proposed project is of interest to the foundation, it may request a ful proposal.

Most proposals are considered by the board of directors or by a board committee. The foundation notifies applicants in wiring of final action taken on their proposals.

Restrictions on Giving: The foundation will not fund programs or activities which are routinely the responsibility of government, political activities or campaigns, capital campaigns, annual fund-raising drives, regular development campaigns, institutional benefits, honorary functions, publications, tuition and scholarships, conferences, religious programs, or awards to individuals, except by way of the MacArthur Fellows Program and research grants of the Program on Peace and International Cooperation.

OTHER THINGS TO KNOW
The foundation's e-mail address is: 4answers%macfdntsmcimail.com

PUBLICATIONS
Annual report, programs and policies, individual booklets concerning each program as well as program-related investments

GRANTS ANALYSIS
Total Grants: $151,164,925

Number of Grants: 810

Highest Grant: $13,500,000*

Average Grant: $186,623

Typical Range: $15,000 to $50,000 and $100,000 to $500,000

Disclosure Period: 1993

Note: The foundation reports that the highest grant will be paid over a three year period. Recent grants are derived from a 1993 annual report.

RECENT GRANTS

General

13,500,000	Energy Foundation, San Francisco, CA — in support of general operations over three years
6,000,000	National Community Development Initiative, Washington, DC — to increase the scale of community development activities nationwide (over three years; program-related investment)
3,825,000	University of Virginia, Charlottesville, VA — for the research and communications activities of the collaborative research Network on Mental Health and the Law, over three years
1,950,000	University of Pittsburgh, Pittsburgh, PA — to develop a new Network on Psychopathology and Development, over two years
1,500,000	Human Rights Watch, New York, NY — in support of operations over three years

McCormick Foundation, Chauncey and Marion Deering

CONTACT
Charles E. Schroeder
Secretary and Treasurer
Chauncey and Marion Deering McCormick Foundation
410 North Michigan Ave., Rm. 590
Chicago, IL 60611
(312) 644-6720

FINANCIAL SUMMARY
Recent Giving: $804,000 (fiscal 1991); $695,600 (fiscal 1990); $492,700 (fiscal 1989 approx.)

Assets: $24,949,821 (fiscal 1991); $15,251,387 (fiscal 1990); $13,871,559 (fiscal 1988)

Gifts Received: $23,500 (fiscal 1991); $4,250 (fiscal 1990); $5,000 (fiscal 1985)

EIN: 36-6054815

CONTRIBUTIONS SUMMARY
Donor(s): The Chauncey and Marion Deering McCormick Foundation was established in 1957 by Brooks McCormick (b. 1917), and named after his parents. Mr. McCormick was the last member of his family to run International Harvester; he stepped down in 1977. International Harvester was formed through the merger of the McCormick and Deering Harvester Companies. The McCormick Company was founded in 1831 by Cyrus McCormick, inventor of the reaper.

Typical Recipients: • *Arts & Humanities:* Arts Institutes, Libraries, Music, Public Broadcasting • *Civic & Public Affairs:* Philanthropic Organizations, Rural Affairs, Zoos/Aquariums • *Education:* Colleges & Universities, Education Funds • *Environment:* General • *Health:* Health Organizations, Medical Research, Single-Disease Health Associations • *Social Services:* Homes

Grant Types: capital, endowment, general support, project, and scholarship

Geographic Distribution: primarily metropolitan Chicago area

GIVING OFFICERS
Brooks McCormick: vp *B* Chicago IL 1917 *ED* Yale Univ BA 1940 *NONPR AFFIL* adv, gov mem: Chicago Zoological Soc; hon dir: Open Lands Project; life trust: Art Inst Chicago, St Lukes Med Ctr

Charles Deering McCormick: pres *B* Chicago IL 1915 *ED* Yale Univ BA 1938 *NONPR AFFIL* life trust: Northwestern Univ

Charlotte Deering McCormick: vp

Charles Edgar Schroeder: secy, treas, dir *B* Chicago IL 1935 *ED* Dartmouth Coll BA 1957; Dartmouth Coll Amos Tuck Grad Sch Bus MBA 1958 *CURR EMPL* chmn, dir: Blvd Bancorp *CORP AFFIL* dir: Blvd Bank N Am, Natl Blvd Bank Chicago, Natl Standard Co; pres, dir: Cutler Oil & Gas Corp, Mi-

ami Corp *NONPR AFFIL* mem: Fin Analysts Soc Chicago; trust: Northwestern Meml Hosp, Northwestern Univ *CLUB AFFIL* Chicago, Commercial, Glen View GC, MI Shores, Mid-Am *PHIL AFFIL* secy, treas, dir: Danielson Foundation; vp, treas: James Deering Danielson Foundation; secy, treas: Gibbett Hill Foundation; secy, treas, dir: Deering Foundation

APPLICATION INFORMATION
Initial Approach:

The foundation has no formal application procedure; it reports, "Grants, scholarships, fellowships, loans, etc. generally are not made based upon an application."

Restrictions on Giving: Recipients are limited to organizations described in Section 170(c) IRS Code and are determined by the foundation's board of directors.

OTHER THINGS TO KNOW
In addition to giving grants, the foundation owns a 500-acre plot of land which is made available to various charitable organizations for conferences and meetings.

GRANTS ANALYSIS
Total Grants: $804,000

Number of Grants: 38

Highest Grant: $110,000

Average Grant: $21,158

Typical Range: $1,000 to $25,000

Disclosure Period: fiscal year ending July 31, 1991

Note: Recent grants are derived from a fiscal 1991 Form 990.

RECENT GRANTS

Library

25,000	Northwestern University, Evanston, IL — Deering Library fund

General

75,000	Children's Home and Aid Society of Illinois, Chicago, IL
65,000	Chicago Community Foundation, Chicago, IL — the McCormick Family Fund
55,000	Lincoln Park Zoological Society, Chicago, IL
50,000	Brooks and Hope B. McCormick Foundation, Chicago, IL
50,000	Roger McCormick Foundation, Chicago, IL

Mellinger Educational Foundation, Edward Arthur

CONTACT
Edward Arthur Mellinger Educational Fdn.
1025 E Broadway
Monmouth, IL 61462
(309) 734-2419

FINANCIAL SUMMARY
Recent Giving: $655,279 (1992); $960,407 (1989); $429,912 (1988)

Assets: $16,624,686 (1992); $13,372,567 (1989); $12,325,307 (1988)

EIN: 36-2428421

CONTRIBUTIONS SUMMARY
Donor(s): the late Mrs. Inez M. Hensleigh

Typical Recipients: • *Arts & Humanities:* Libraries

Grant Types: loan and scholarship

Geographic Distribution: limited to students residing or attending college in the Midwest

GIVING OFFICERS
David D. Fleming: pres, trust

Wyatt Thomas Johnson, Jr.: secy, treas, trust *B* Macon GA 1941 *ED* Univ GA AB 1963; Harvard Univ MBA 1965 *CURR EMPL* vchmn, dir: Times Mirror Co *CORP AFFIL* publ, ceo: Los Angeles Times *NONPR AFFIL* dir: Trilateral Commn; mem: Am Newspaper Publs Assn, Counc Foreign Rels, Sigma Delta Chi *PHIL AFFIL* trust: John S. and James L. Knight Foundation, Rockefeller Foundation

Merle R. Yontz: vp, trust

APPLICATION INFORMATION
Initial Approach: Request application form. Deadline is May 1.

PUBLICATIONS
Application Guidelines, program policy statement. Provides scholarships for higher education.

Monticello College Foundation

CONTACT
Winifred G. Delano
Executive Director
Monticello College Fdn.
The Evergreens
Godfrey, IL 62035
(618) 466-7911

FINANCIAL SUMMARY
Recent Giving: $220,600 (fiscal 1993); $1,306,600 (fiscal 1992); $282,000 (fiscal 1990)

Assets: $6,141,872 (fiscal 1993); $5,733,560 (fiscal 1992); $6,202,661 (fiscal 1990)

Gifts Received: $14,093 (fiscal 1993)

EIN: 37-0681538

CONTRIBUTIONS SUMMARY
Typical Recipients: • *Arts & Humanities:* Arts Centers, Ballet, Dance, Libraries, Museums/Galleries, Music • *Civic & Public Affairs:* Women's Affairs • *Education:* Colleges & Universities, Community & Junior Colleges, Engineering/Technological Education, Medical Education, Private Education (Precollege), Student Aid

Grant Types: fellowship, project, and scholarship

Geographic Distribution: focus on IL and MO

GIVING OFFICERS
Winifred G. Delano: exec dir

APPLICATION INFORMATION
Initial Approach: Include a description of organization, amount requested, purpose of funds sought, recently audited financial statement, and proof of tax-exempt status. Deadline is September 1 and April 1.

PUBLICATIONS
Annual Report (including application guidelines)

GRANTS ANALYSIS
Total Grants: $220,600

Number of Grants: 21

Highest Grant: $110,000

Typical Range: $1,500 to $10,000

Disclosure Period: fiscal year ending June 30, 1993

Note: Recent grants are derived from a fiscal 1993 Form 990.

RECENT GRANTS
Library
12,500   Newbury Library, Chicago, IL — post-doctoral scholarship for women

General
110,000   Washington University, St. Louis, MO — Olin Fellowship program

18,000   Illinois College, Jacksonville, IL — scholarships for women

11,250   Lewis and Clark College, Godfrey, IL — Monticello College Foundation scholarship for women

10,000   Blackburn College, Carlinville, IL — scholarships for women

10,000   Westminster College, Fulton, MO — scholarships for women

Nalco Chemical Co. / Nalco Foundation

Sales: $1.39 billion
Employees: 6,800
Headquarters: Naperville, IL
SIC Major Group: Chemical Preparations Nec, Industrial Inorganic Chemicals Nec, Surface Active Agents, and Industrial Organic Chemicals Nec

CONTACT
Joanne C. Ford
President
Nalco Foundation
One Nalco Center
Naperville, IL 60563-1198
(708) 305-1556

FINANCIAL SUMMARY
Recent Giving: $1,700,000 (1995 est.); $1,839,011 (1994 approx.); $1,592,645 (1993)

Assets: $3,497,926 (1993); $1,212,154 (1992); $1,618,572 (1991)

Fiscal Note: Figures do not include direct giving. In 1994, direct corporate giving totaled $1,401,920. Above figures exclude nonmonetary support.

EIN: 36-6065864

CONTRIBUTIONS SUMMARY
Typical Recipients: • *Arts & Humanities:* Arts Funds, Arts Institutes, Community Arts, Dance, Historic Preservation, Libraries, Museums/Galleries, Music, Opera, Performing Arts, Public Broadcasting • *Civic & Public Affairs:* Business/Free Enterprise, Employment/Job Training, Law & Justice, Legal Aid, Nonprofit Management, Urban & Community Affairs, Women's Affairs, Zoos/Aquariums • *Education:* Business Education, Colleges & Universities, Economic Education, Education Associations, Engineering/Technological Education, Literacy, Medical Education, Minority Education, Science/Mathematics Education, Social Sciences Education, Special Education • *Environment:* General • *Health:* Emergency/Ambulance Services, Health Policy/Cost Containment, Health Organizations, Hospices, Hospitals, Medical Rehabilitation, Mental Health, Single-Disease Health Associations • *Social Services:* Child Welfare, Community Centers, Community Service Organizations, Counseling, Delinquency & Criminal Rehabilitation, Domestic Violence, Family Services, Food/Clothing Distribution, People with Disabilities, Substance Abuse, Youth Organizations

Grant Types: capital, challenge, employee matching gifts, general support, operating expenses, project, and scholarship

Note: Company sponsors employee matching gifts to colleges and universities and not-for-profit hospitals and cultural organizations.

Nonmonetary Support Types: donated equipment and loaned executives

Note: Value of nonmonetary support is unavailable. Support is provided by the company. Loaned executives are granted to United Way.

Geographic Distribution: towns where Nalco has major manufacturing facilities or subsidiaries; emphasis on Chicago metropolitan area, including DuPage County; few to U.S.-based nonprofit organizations with an international focus

Operating Locations: CA (Carson), GA (Jonesboro), IL (Chicago, Naperville), LA (Garyville), NJ (Paulsboro), TX (Freeport, Sugar Land)

CORP. OFFICERS
David R. Bertran: *CURR EMPL* vp info services: Nalco Chem Co

Graham Jackson: *CURR EMPL* vp pub rels: Nalco Chem Co

James F. Lambe: *B* 1945 *ED* Univ IL
BSCE 1968; DePaul Univ JD 1972 *CURR
EMPL* sr vp human resources: Nalco Chem
Co

Edward J. Mooney, Jr.: *B* Omar WV 1941
ED Univ TX BS 1964; Univ TX JD 1967
CURR EMPL pres, ceo, dir: Nalco Chem Co
NONPR AFFIL mem: Am Patent Law Assn,
IL Bar Assn, St Bar TX

GIVING OFFICERS
David R. Bertran: dir *CURR EMPL* vp info
services: Nalco Chem Co (see above)

Mary F. Carhart: secy

Joanne C. Ford: pres, dir

Craig J. Holderness: asst treas

James F. Lambe: dir *CURR EMPL* sr vp human resources: Nalco Chem Co (see above)

Terrence J. Taylor: treas

APPLICATION INFORMATION
Initial Approach: *Initial Contact:* request
guidelines *Include Information On:* legal
name and history of organization, summary
of specified project or need, intended use of
funds, latest financial statement or budget,
list of board of directors and their affiliations and addresses, list of corporate and
foundation contributions, proof of tax-exempt status, and IRS Form 990 *Deadlines:*
none

Restrictions on Giving: The foundation generally does not support individuals, political
activities or lobbying groups, churches or religious education, secondary or elementary
schools, state-supported colleges or universities, endowment funds, advertising in charitable publications, or purchase of tickets for
fund-raising activities.

OTHER THINGS TO KNOW
The company sponsors a "Community Involvement" program, which is defined as the
"giving of time and effort by individuals to
special causes, with the company participating as originator or organizer." In addition,
the program also includes the establishment
of Community Advisory Groups at facilities
around the country, facility tours for students, teachers and neighbors, and the hiring
of college students in the Cooperative Education program. In 1993, employees also contributed $8,500 to a relief fund for Midwest
flood victims.

GRANTS ANALYSIS
Total Grants: $1,839,011

Typical Range: $2,000 to $10,000

Disclosure Period: 1994

Note: Above figures reflect foundation giving only. Recent grants are derived from a
1992 grants list.

RECENT GRANTS

General
Adler Planetarium, Chicago, IL — general
support
Alivio Medical Center, Chicago, IL — general
support
American Council on Science and Health,
New York, NY — general support

American Indian Science and Engineering
Society, Boulder, CO — chemical
engineering scholarship
American Lung Association of DuPage and
McHenry Counties, Glen Ellyn, IL — Camp
Gottago for asthmatic children

Norton Memorial
Corporation, Geraldi

CONTACT
Roger P. Eklund
President and Treasurer
Geraldi Norton Memorial Corporation
One First National Plaza, Ste. 3148
Chicago, IL 60603
(312) 726-0212

FINANCIAL SUMMARY
Recent Giving: $237,450 (1993); $211,700
(1990); $228,082 (1989)

Assets: $2,552,079 (1993); $2,329,172
(1990); $3,017,145 (1989)

EIN: 36-6069997

CONTRIBUTIONS SUMMARY
Donor(s): the late Grace Geraldi Norton

Typical Recipients: • *Arts & Humanities:*
Arts Centers, Arts Festivals, Arts Institutes,
Historic Preservation, History & Archaeol-
ogy, Libraries, Museums/Galleries, Music,
Opera, Public Broadcasting, Theater • *Civic
& Public Affairs:* Clubs, Zoos/Aquariums
• *Education:* Colleges & Universities, Educa-
tion Funds, Legal Education, Minority Edu-
cation, Private Education (Precollege),
Secondary Education (Private), Student Aid
• *Health:* Cancer, Children's Health/Hospi-
tals, Diabetes, Health Organizations, Hos-
pices, Hospitals, Medical Rehabilitation,
Medical Research, Mental Health, Prenatal
Health Issues, Research/Studies Institutes,
Single-Disease Health Associations, Speech
& Hearing • *Social Services:* Child Welfare,
Community Service Organizations, Recrea-
tion & Athletics, Shelters/Homelessness,
United Funds/United Ways, Youth Organiza-
tions

Grant Types: general support

Geographic Distribution: focus on the Chicago, IL, area

GIVING OFFICERS
Dariel Ann Eklund: vp

Roger P. Eklund: pres, treas

Sally S. Eklund: secy

APPLICATION INFORMATION
Initial Approach: Send brief letter of inquiry describing program. Include a description of organization, amount requested,
purpose of funds sought, recently audited financial statement, and proof of tax-exempt
status. There are no deadlines.

Restrictions on Giving: Does not support
individuals.

GRANTS ANALYSIS
Total Grants: $237,450

Number of Grants: 74

Highest Grant: $30,000

Typical Range: $250 to $20,000

Disclosure Period: 1993

Note: Recent grants are derived from a 1993
Form 990.

RECENT GRANTS

Library
1,000 Newberry Library, Chicago, IL

General
30,000 Juvenile Diabetes Foundation,
    New York, NY
25,000 University of Chicago,
    Chicago, IL — Department
    of Radiation and Cellular
    Oncology; Gene Therapy,
    Prostate Cancer
20,000 University of Chicago,
    Chicago, IL — molecular
    genetics lab
15,000 Harvard College Fund,
    Cambridge, MA —
    scholarships
15,000 Northwestern Memorial
    Hospital, Chicago, IL —
    Campaign for Institute of
    Psychiatry

Offield Family Foundation

CONTACT
Marie Larson
Secretary
Offield Family Foundation
400 N Michigan Ave., Rm. 470
Chicago, IL 60611
(312) 467-5480

FINANCIAL SUMMARY
Recent Giving: $3,395,000 (fiscal 1993);
$2,139,250 (fiscal 1992); $1,768,661 (fiscal
1991)

Assets: $59,039,328 (fiscal 1993);
$51,130,485 (fiscal 1992); $40,932,081 (fiscal 1991)

Gifts Received: $71,417 (fiscal 1993);
$17,998 (fiscal 1992)

Fiscal Note: In 1993, the foundation received funds from James S. Offield
($55,000) and from Split Income Trusts
($16,417).

EIN: 36-6066240

CONTRIBUTIONS SUMMARY
Donor(s): The foundation was incorporated
in 1940 by Dorothy Wrigley Offield.

Typical Recipients: • *Arts & Humanities:*
Arts Associations & Councils, Arts Centers,
Film & Video, History & Archaeology, Libraries, Museums/Galleries, Music, Public
Broadcasting • *Civic & Public Affairs:* Botanical Gardens/Parks, Community Foundations, General, Public Policy, Women's
Affairs • *Education:* Colleges & Universities, Education Funds, General, Medical Education, Private Education (Precollege),
Public Education (Precollege), Student Aid

• *Environment:* Air/Water Quality, General, Resource Conservation, Watershed, Wildlife Protection • *Health:* Children's Health/Hospitals, Clinics/Medical Centers, Emergency/Ambulance Services, Health Funds, Health Organizations, Hospitals, Medical Research, Transplant Networks/Donor Banks, Trauma Treatment • *Religion:* Churches, Religious Welfare • *Science:* Science Museums • *Social Services:* Child Welfare, Community Service Organizations, Day Care, Family Planning, Food/Clothing Distribution, People with Disabilities, Scouts, Substance Abuse, United Funds/United Ways, Youth Organizations

Grant Types: general support

Geographic Distribution: nationally

GIVING OFFICERS

Raymond Hibner Drymalski: treas *B* Chicago IL 1936 *ED* Georgetown Univ BA 1958; Univ MI JD 1961 *CURR EMPL* ptnr: Bell Boyd & Lloyd *NONPR AFFIL* counc govs: Northwestern Healthcare Network; dir: Lincoln Park Zoological Soc, Northwestern Meml Hosp; mem: Am Bar Assn, Chicago Bar Assn *CLUB AFFIL* Econ

Marie Larson: secy, dir

Edna Jean Offield: pres

James S. Offield: vp

Paxson H. Offield: vp

APPLICATION INFORMATION

Initial Approach:

Applicants should mail a letter of inquiry describing the proposed project, information about the organization, and its future goals.

There are no deadlines. The board makes final decisions on grants at its meeting in June.

OTHER THINGS TO KNOW

Although the Santa Catalina Island Conservancy is a private foundation, the Offield Family Foundation maintains expenditures responsibility.

GRANTS ANALYSIS

Total Grants: $3,395,000

Number of Grants: 62

Highest Grant: $750,000

Average Grant: $54,758

Typical Range: $10,000 to $100,000

Disclosure Period: fiscal year ending June 30, 1993

Note: Recent grants are derived from a fiscal 1993 Form 990.

RECENT GRANTS

Library
50,000	Sedona Public Library, Sedona, AZ

General
750,000	Catalina Conservancy, Avalon, CA
250,000	Catalina Conservancy, Avalon, CA
100,000	Billfish Foundation, Ft. Lauderdale, FL
100,000	Laguna Beach Unified School District, Laguna Beach, CA

100,000	Little Traverse Conservancy, Harbor Springs, MI

Outboard Marine Corp. / OMC Foundation

Sales: $1.03 billion
Employees: 8,449
Headquarters: Waukegan, IL
SIC Major Group: Industrial Machinery & Equipment and Transportation Equipment

CONTACT

Laurin M. Baker
Secretary and Director
OMC Fdn.
100 Sea Horse Dr.
Waukegan, IL 60085
(708) 689-6200

FINANCIAL SUMMARY

Recent Giving: $264,500 (1993); $280,000 (1992 approx.); $277,670 (1991)

Assets: $3,942,387 (1990); $1,646,666 (1989)

Gifts Received: $2,500,000 (1990); $1,087,500 (1989)

Fiscal Note: In 1990, contributions were received from Outboard Marine Corp.

EIN: 39-6037139

CONTRIBUTIONS SUMMARY

Typical Recipients: • *Arts & Humanities:* Arts Institutes, Libraries, Museums/Galleries, Performing Arts, Public Broadcasting • *Civic & Public Affairs:* Business/Free Enterprise, Public Policy, Zoos/Aquariums • *Education:* Colleges & Universities, Community & Junior Colleges, Engineering/Technological Education • *Health:* Hospitals • *Social Services:* United Funds/United Ways

Grant Types: employee matching gifts, project, and scholarship

Geographic Distribution: in headquarters and operating communities

Operating Locations: FL (Sarasota, Stuart), GA (Calhoun), IL (Waukegan), IN (Syracuse), MI (Cadillac), MO (Lebanon), NC (Andrews, Burnsville, Spruce Pine), SC (Columbia), TN (Murfreesboro, Old Hickory), WI (Milwaukee)

Note: List includes plant and division locations.

CORP. OFFICERS

Laurin M. Baker: *CURR EMPL* dir pub aff: Outboard Marine Corp

Harold Bowman: *CURR EMPL* chmn, pres, ceo, dir: Outboard Marine Corp

GIVING OFFICERS

Laurin M. Baker: secy, dir *CURR EMPL* dir pub aff: Outboard Marine Corp (see above)

James C. Chapman: pres, dir *B* Detroit MI 1931 *ED* Univ Detroit BME 1965 *CORP AFFIL* dir: Advance Machine Co *NONPR AFFIL* mem: Soc Automotive Engrs, Soc Mfg Engrs, Wankegan-Lake County Chamber

Commerce; pres: Boy Scouts Am NE IL Counc; trust: Univ Detroit Mercy

Richard Medland: vp, dir

APPLICATION INFORMATION

Initial Approach: Send a brief letter of inquiry including a description of organization, amount requested, purpose of funds sought, and proof of tax-exempt status. Deadline is September.

Restrictions on Giving: Does not support individuals, religious organizations for sectarian purposes, political or lobbying groups, or organizations outside operating areas.

GRANTS ANALYSIS

Total Grants: $402,200

Number of Grants: 5

Highest Grant: $22,445

Typical Range: $1,000 to $5,000

Disclosure Period: 1990

Note: Recent grants are derived from a 1990 Form 990.

RECENT GRANTS

Library
10,369	City Libraries, Milwaukee, WI

General
22,445	United Way, Libertyville, IL
21,002	United Way, Milwaukee, WI
9,313	United Way, Brunsville, NC
7,919	United Way, Rutherfordton, NC

Packaging Corporation of America

Sales: $2.0 billion
Employees: 14,000
Parent Company: Tenneco Inc.
Headquarters: Evanston, IL
SIC Major Group: Corrugated & Solid Fiber Boxes, Sawmills & Planing Mills—General, Pulp Mills, and Paperboard Mills

CONTACT

Warren Hazelton
Director, Corporate Relations
Packaging Corporation of America
1603 Orrington Ave.
Evanston, IL 60201
(708) 492-6968

FINANCIAL SUMMARY

Fiscal Note: Company gives directly. Annual Giving Range: $250,00 to $500,000. Above figures exclude nonmonetary support.

CONTRIBUTIONS SUMMARY

Typical Recipients: • *Arts & Humanities:* Community Arts, General, Libraries, Museums/Galleries, Public Broadcasting • *Civic & Public Affairs:* General, Municipalities/Towns • *Education:* Arts/Humanities Education, Business Education, Colleges & Universities, Economic Education, Elementary Education (Private), Engineering/Technological Education, General, Minority Education, Public Education (Precollege), Science/Mathematics Education, Special

Education • *Health:* Emergency/Ambulance Services, General, Hospices, Hospitals, Nursing Services, Single-Disease Health Associations • *Social Services:* Community Service Organizations, Emergency Relief, Food/Clothing Distribution, General, Recreation & Athletics, Shelters/Homelessness, United Funds/United Ways, Youth Organizations

Grant Types: award, emergency, employee matching gifts, general support, and scholarship

Nonmonetary Support Types: cause-related marketing & promotion and donated products

Geographic Distribution: in headquarters and operating communities

Operating Locations: IL (Evanston)

Note: Packaging Corporation of America operates in 100 field locations.

CORP. OFFICERS
Robert A. Page: *B* 1951 *ED* Lamar Univ BS 1974 *CURR EMPL* vp, cfo: Packaging Corp Am

Paul T. Stecko: *B* 1944 *ED* PA St Univ BS; Univ Pittsburgh MS; Univ Pittsburgh MBA *CURR EMPL* ceo, pres: Packaging Corp Am

GIVING OFFICERS
Warren Hazelton: *CURR EMPL* dir corp rels: Packaging Corp Am

APPLICATION INFORMATION
Initial Approach: *Initial Contact:* brief letter of inquiry *Include Information On:* a description of organization, amount requested, purpose of funds sought, recently audited financial statement, and proof of tax-exempt status *Deadlines:* none; annual budget developed in July *Note:* No phone calls will be accepted, and local requests must be made through local operating facilities.

Restrictions on Giving: The company does not support individuals, religious organizations for sectarian purposes, or political or lobbying groups.

GRANTS ANALYSIS
Typical Range: $500 to $2,500

RECENT GRANTS
General
Adopt-a-School, Omaha, NE
Clarke School for the Deaf, Northampton, MA
Golden Apple Foundation, Chicago, IL
Holy Cross Hospital, Salt Lake City, UT
Junior Achievement, Chicago, IL

Payne Foundation, Frank E. and Seba B.

CONTACT
M. Catherine Ryan
Second Vice President
Frank E. and Seba B. Payne Foundation
c/o Bank of America
231 S LaSalle St.
Chicago, IL 60697
(312) 987-0806

FINANCIAL SUMMARY
Recent Giving: $3,619,460 (fiscal 1993); $3,284,980 (fiscal 1992); $3,182,840 (fiscal 1991)

Assets: $82,840,954 (fiscal 1993); $77,619,347 (fiscal 1992); $72,330,527 (fiscal 1991)

EIN: 23-7435471

CONTRIBUTIONS SUMMARY
Donor(s): The Frank E. and Seba B. Payne Foundation was established in 1962 by Seba B. Payne, the widow of Frank E. Payne.

Typical Recipients: • *Arts & Humanities:* Historic Preservation, History & Archaeology, Libraries, Literary Arts, Museums/Galleries, Public Broadcasting, Theater • *Civic & Public Affairs:* Economic Development, General, Law & Justice, Municipalities/Towns • *Education:* Arts/Humanities Education, Colleges & Universities, Education Associations, Education Funds, Literacy, Minority Education, Private Education (Precollege), Religious Education, Science/Mathematics Education, Student Aid • *Health:* AIDS/HIV, Clinics/Medical Centers, Emergency/Ambulance Services, Hospitals, Nursing Services, Speech & Hearing, Transplant Networks/Donor Banks • *Religion:* Churches, Dioceses, Ministries, Religious Organizations, Religious Welfare • *Social Services:* Child Welfare, Community Service Organizations, Crime Prevention, Domestic Violence, Food/Clothing Distribution, Homes, People with Disabilities, Senior Services, Shelters/Homelessness, Substance Abuse, United Funds/United Ways, YMCA/YWCA/YMHA/YWHA, Youth Organizations

Grant Types: capital, general support, operating expenses, and project

Geographic Distribution: principally Chicago, IL, and Bethlehem, PA, areas

GIVING OFFICERS
Susan Hurd Cummings: trust

Doug Hurd: trust

Priscilla Payne Hurd: trust

Charles M. Nisen: trust *B* Milwaukee WI 1913 *ED* Univ MI AB 1934; Univ MI LLB 1935 *CURR EMPL* atty, ptnr: Nisen & Elliott

M. Catherine Ryan: bank rep, contact person *CURR EMPL* second vp: Continental IL Natl Bank & Trust Co

APPLICATION INFORMATION
Initial Approach:

Requests should be submitted in writing.

Requests should include the name, address, and a brief history of the organization; a list of its officers and directors; purpose for which funds are requested; evidence of need for the proposed project; most recent financial statements, including sources of funds and information on fund-raising activities and costs; estimate of time and funds required to complete project; and proof of tax-exempt status.

There are no set deadlines for submitting requests.

The foundation board generally meets in the Spring and Fall.

Restrictions on Giving: Grants are not made to individuals.

OTHER THINGS TO KNOW
Bank of America serves as a corporate trustee for the foundation.

PUBLICATIONS
Instructions to applicants

GRANTS ANALYSIS
Total Grants: $3,619,460

Number of Grants: 44

Highest Grant: $1,300,000

Average Grant: $53,491*

Typical Range: $5,000 to $60,000

Disclosure Period: fiscal year ending June 30, 1993

Note: The average grant figure excludes the highest grant of $1,300,000. Recent grants are derived from a fiscal 1993 Form 990.

RECENT GRANTS

Library

26,000	Bethlehem Public Library, Bethlehem, PA
5,000	Hellertown Area Library, Hellertown, PA

General

1,300,000	St. Lukes Hospital, Bethlehem, PA — construction
814,000	Lehigh University, Bethlehem, PA
250,000	Madiera School, McLean, VA — new facility
100,000	Cathedral Church of the Nativity, Bethlehem, PA — capital improvements
100,000	Church of the Assumption, B.V.M., Bethlehem, PA — construction

Peoples Energy Corp.

Revenue: $1.26 billion
Employees: 3,441
Headquarters: Chicago, IL
SIC Major Group: Holding Companies Nec and Natural Gas Distribution

CONTACT
Kenneth L. Gogins
Manager, Corporate Contributions
Peoples Energy Corp.
130 E Randolph Dr.
Chicago, IL 60601
(312) 240-4393

FINANCIAL SUMMARY
Recent Giving: $950,000 (1995 est.); $950,000 (1994 approx.); $950,000 (1993 approx.)

Fiscal Note: Company gives directly.

CONTRIBUTIONS SUMMARY
Typical Recipients: • *Arts & Humanities:* Arts Associations & Councils, Arts Institutes, Dance, Ethnic & Folk Arts, Historic Preservation, Libraries, Museums/Galleries, Opera, Performing Arts, Public Broadcast-

ing, Theater • *Civic & Public Affairs:* Civil Rights, Economic Development, Economic Policy, Employment/Job Training, Housing, Law & Justice, Professional & Trade Associations, Urban & Community Affairs, Women's Affairs, Zoos/Aquariums • *Education:* Colleges & Universities, Community & Junior Colleges, Elementary Education (Private), Literacy, Private Education (Precollege), Public Education (Precollege) • *Health:* Health Organizations, Hospitals • *Science:* Observatories & Planetariums • *Social Services:* Child Welfare, Community Centers, Community Service Organizations, Family Services, Homes, Senior Services, Shelters/Homelessness, United Funds/United Ways, Volunteer Services, Youth Organizations

Grant Types: capital, employee matching gifts, endowment, fellowship, general support, and multiyear/continuing support

Note: Employee matching gift ratio: 2 to 1 for primary and secondary schools and to hospitals. Employee matching gift ratio: 1 to 1 for other eligible institutions.

Nonmonetary Support Types: donated equipment, in-kind services, loaned employees, and loaned executives

Geographic Distribution: company service area

Operating Locations: IL (Chicago, Waukegan)

CORP. OFFICERS
J. Bruce Hasch: *CURR EMPL* pres, coo: Peoples Energy Corp

James D. Pitts: *CURR EMPL* vp urban aff: Peoples Energy Corp

Richard Edward Terry: *B* Green Bay WI 1937 *ED* St Norbert Coll BA 1959; Univ WI LLB 1964 *CURR EMPL* chmn, ceo, dir: Peoples Energy Corp *CORP AFFIL* dir: Amsted Indus Inc, Harris Bankcorp Inc, Harris Trust & Savings Bank, N Shore Gas Co, Peoples Gas Light & Coke Co *NONPR AFFIL* dir: Big Shoulders Fund, Chicago Chamber Commerce, Chicago Mus Sci & Indus, IL Counc Econ Ed, Inst Gas Tech, Mus Sci & Indus; mem: Am Gas Assn, Chicago Area Central Comm, Midwest Gas Assn, Natl Petroleum Counc; mem bus adv counc: Chicago Urban League; trust: St Norbert Coll, Xavier Univ *CLUB AFFIL* Chicago, Commercial, Econ, Mid-Am, Univ

GIVING OFFICERS
Kenneth L. Gogins: *CURR EMPL* mgr corp commun: Peoples Energy Corp

APPLICATION INFORMATION
Initial Approach: *Initial Contact:* brief letter and proposal *Include Information On:* name, full mailing address, and telephone number of organization; background and purpose of the organization; type of request (operating or capital); geographical area served; sources of income; most recent financial statement (preferably audited); current budget and list of programs; proof of tax-exempt status; names of officers and directors; and number of professional, clerical, and volunteer staff members *Deadlines:* none

Restrictions on Giving: Contributions will not be made to individuals; organizations not eligible for tax-deductible support; organizations that discriminate by race, color, creed, or national origin; political organizations or campaigns; organizations whose prime purpose is to influence legislation; religious organizations for purely sectarian purposes; agencies or institutions owned and operated by local, state, or federal governments; trips or tours; or special occasion or goodwill advertising.

PUBLICATIONS
Contribution guidelines

GRANTS ANALYSIS
Total Grants: $950,000*
Disclosure Period: 1994
Note: Figure is approximate.

Pick, Jr. Fund, Albert

CONTACT
Nadine Van Sant
Executive Director and Secretary
Albert Pick, Jr. Fund
30 N Michigan Ave.
Chicago, IL 60602
(312) 236-1192

FINANCIAL SUMMARY
Recent Giving: $990,000 (1993 est.); $800,067 (1992); $821,767 (1991)

Assets: $17,299,469 (1992); $15,506,335 (1991); $14,336,635 (1990)

Gifts Received: $11,521 (1992); $10,850 (1991); $1,445,216 (1990)

Fiscal Note: In 1991 and 1992, the foundation received gifts from Harris Associates.

EIN: 36-6071402

CONTRIBUTIONS SUMMARY
Donor(s): The foundation was incorporated in 1947 by the late Albert Pick, Jr.

Typical Recipients: • *Arts & Humanities:* Arts Associations & Councils, Arts Festivals, Arts Institutes, Dance, Libraries, Museums/Galleries, Music, Opera, Public Broadcasting, Theater • *Civic & Public Affairs:* Asian American Affairs, Economic Development, Employment/Job Training, General, Hispanic Affairs, Philanthropic Organizations, Urban & Community Affairs • *Education:* Agricultural Education, Arts/Humanities Education, Colleges & Universities, Education Associations, International Studies, Literacy, Minority Education, Public Education (Precollege), Science/Mathematics Education, Special Education • *Environment:* Air/Water Quality, Resource Conservation • *Health:* AIDS/HIV, Children's Health/Hospitals, Clinics/Medical Centers, Emergency/Ambulance Services, Health Organizations, Hospitals, Long-Term Care, Preventive Medicine/Wellness Organizations, Public Health, Single-Disease Health Associations • *Religion:* Jewish Causes, Religious Organizations, Religious Welfare • *Science:* Obser-

vatories & Planetariums, Science Museums, Scientific Organizations • *Social Services:* Child Welfare, Community Service Organizations, Day Care, Domestic Violence, Family Planning, Family Services, Homes, People with Disabilities, Scouts, Sexual Abuse, Shelters/Homelessness, Substance Abuse, United Funds/United Ways, YMCA/YWCA/YMHA/YWHA, Youth Organizations

Grant Types: capital, general support, multiyear/continuing support, and project

Geographic Distribution: focus on Chicago, IL

GIVING OFFICERS
Arthur W. Brown, Jr.: vp, dir

Burton B. Kaplan: dir *PHIL AFFIL* treas: Mayer and Morris Kaplan Foundation

Ralph I. Lewy: treas, dir *B* Leiwen Germany 1931 *ED* Roosevelt Univ BS 1953 *CURR EMPL* pres: Ralph Lewy Ltd *NONPR AFFIL* mem: Am Inst CPAs

Edward Neisser: dir

Albert Pick III: vp, dir

Nadine Van Sant: exec dir, secy

APPLICATION INFORMATION
Initial Approach:

Call or write the fund for application form.

Proposals should be as brief as possible and include the following: a history of the organization, a description of current programs, a description of the proposed project, and the intended use of the funds requested; proof of tax-exempt status from the IRS and a ruling that the organization is publicly supported under section 509(a) of the IRS code; the names, affiliations, and addresses of governing board members, officers, and staff; a current financial statement, preferably audited; the projected annual budgets for the organization and the project; a list of principal sources of income; and a description of the geographic area served.

The deadlines for submitting proposals are February 1, April 1, July 1, and October 1. Proposals from cultural organizations should be submitted by the July 1 deadline.

The board meets in March or April, June, September, and December.

Restrictions on Giving: The fund will not consider proposals from organizations whose fiscal year ends on the same month as the board meeting's review of that request. Grants are not made to religious organizations or for political purposes. The fund does not support individuals, hospitals, local chapters of single-disease associations, umbrella organizations, building or endowment funds, deficit financing, long-term projects, advertising, scholarships, fundraising, or fraternal, veterans, labor, or athletic groups. Additionally, the fund does not support student aid, scholarship programs, or campaigns for reduction of debts.

PUBLICATIONS
Program policy statement and application guidelines

GRANTS ANALYSIS
Total Grants: $800,067
Number of Grants: 129
Highest Grant: $47,917
Average Grant: $6,202
Typical Range: $1,500 to $10,000
Disclosure Period: 1992

Note: Recent grants are derived from a 1992 Form 990.

RECENT GRANTS

General

47,917	LaRabida Children's Hospital and Research Center, Chicago, IL — Lakeside Gardens playground
33,800	United Charities of Chicago, Chicago, IL — life management skills
20,000	Adler Planetarium, Chicago, IL — moon shadows exhibit
17,500	University of Chicago, Chicago, IL — Albert Pick, Jr. Lecturer on International Relations
12,000	Jewish United Fund, Chicago, IL

Playboy Enterprises, Inc. / Playboy Foundation

Revenue: $218.99 million
Employees: 619
Headquarters: Chicago, IL
SIC Major Group: Periodicals, Cable & Other Pay Television Services, Catalog & Mail-Order Houses, and Patent Owners & Lessors

CONTACT
Cleo F. Wilson
Executive Director
Playboy Foundation
680 N Lakeshore Dr.
Chicago, IL 60611
(312) 751-8000
Note: The company's World Wide Web address is http://www.playboy.com

FINANCIAL SUMMARY
Recent Giving: $350,000 (1995 est.); $360,602 (1994); $290,000 (1993)

Fiscal Note: Contributes through foundation only. Above figures exclude nonmonetary support.

CONTRIBUTIONS SUMMARY
Typical Recipients: • *Arts & Humanities:* Community Arts, Ethnic & Folk Arts, Libraries, Public Broadcasting • *Civic & Public Affairs:* Civil Rights, First Amendment Issues, Law & Justice, Legal Aid, Philanthropic Organizations, Public Policy, Women's Affairs • *Education:* Journalism/Media Education • *Health:* Medical Research, Single-Disease Health Associations • *Social Services:* Community Service Organizations, Delinquency & Criminal Rehabilitation, Domestic Violence, Family Planning, People with Dis-

abilities, Refugee Assistance, Senior Services, Shelters/Homelessness, Youth Organizations

Grant Types: matching

Note: Employee matching gift ratio: 1 to 1

Nonmonetary Support: $60,000 (1995); $200,000 (1993)

Nonmonetary Support Types: donated equipment, donated products, and in-kind services

Geographic Distribution: nationally

Operating Locations: CA (Beverly Hills, Holmby Hills, Los Angeles, San Francisco), GA (Atlanta), IL (Chicago, Itasca), MI (Detroit), NY (New York)

CORP. OFFICERS
Christie A. Hefner: *B* Chicago IL 1952 *ED* Brandeis Univ BA 1974 *CURR EMPL* ceo: Playboy Enterprises Inc *CORP AFFIL* dir: Sealy Corp *NONPR AFFIL* dir: Am Civil Liberties Union IL Chap, Brandeis Univ, Magazine Publs Assn, Natl Coalition Crime Delinquency, Phi Beta Kappa, Rush-Presbyterian-St Lukes Med Ctr; mem: Brandeis Natl Womens Comm, Chicago Network, Comm 200, Goodman Theatre, Voters Choice, Young Pres Org

Hugh Marston Hefner: *B* Chicago IL 1926 *ED* Univ IL BS 1949 *CURR EMPL* chmn emeritus, fdr: Playboy Enterprises Inc *CORP AFFIL* dir: Playboy Clubs Intl; publ, editor-in-chief: Playboy Magazine

GIVING OFFICERS
Christie A. Hefner: dir *CURR EMPL* chmn, ceo: Playboy Enterprises Inc (see above)

Burton Joseph: chmn, dir *ED* CUNY

Cleo F. Wilson: exec dir

APPLICATION INFORMATION
Initial Approach: *Initial Contact:* brief letter of inquiry *Include Information On:* description of the organization, amount requested, purpose of funds sought, audited financial statement, and proof of tax-exempt status *Deadlines:* none

Restrictions on Giving: Does not support individuals, religious organizations for sectarian purposes, scholarships, or political groups.

OTHER THINGS TO KNOW
Also provides printing and design services, and public service advertising space in *Playboy* magazine.

PUBLICATIONS
Foundation annual report, newsletter

GRANTS ANALYSIS
Total Grants: $360,602
Typical Range: $5,000 to $10,000
Disclosure Period: 1994

Prince Trust, Abbie Norman

CONTACT
Abbie Norman Prince Trust
Ten S Wacker Dr., Ste. 2575
Chicago, IL 60606
(312) 454-9130

FINANCIAL SUMMARY
Recent Giving: $608,000 (1992); $601,500 (1990); $776,500 (1989)

Assets: $12,265,516 (1992); $10,404,955 (1990); $11,238,698 (1989)

EIN: 36-2411865

CONTRIBUTIONS SUMMARY
Typical Recipients: • *Arts & Humanities:* Arts Funds, Ballet, Dance, General, Historic Preservation, Libraries, Literary Arts, Museums/Galleries, Music, Opera, Performing Arts, Theater • *Civic & Public Affairs:* Economic Development, General, Housing, Urban & Community Affairs • *Education:* Colleges & Universities, Elementary Education (Public), Faculty Development, Preschool Education, Private Education (Precollege) • *Environment:* General • *Health:* AIDS/HIV, Alzheimers Disease, Clinics/Medical Centers, Health Policy/Cost Containment, Health Organizations, Hospitals, Medical Rehabilitation • *Religion:* Churches, Ministries, Religious Welfare • *Social Services:* Child Welfare, Community Service Organizations, Family Services, Recreation & Athletics, Senior Services, Shelters/Homelessness, United Funds/United Ways, Youth Organizations

Grant Types: capital, general support, multi-year/continuing support, project, research, and seed money

Geographic Distribution: limited to Chicago, IL, and RI

GIVING OFFICERS
Frederick Henry Prince: trust *PHIL AFFIL* trust, mgr: Frederick and Diana Prince Foundation

William Wood Prince: trust *B* St. Louis MO 1914 *ED* Princeton Univ AB 1936 *CURR EMPL* vchmn: FH Prince & Co *CORP AFFIL* dir: WR Grace & Co *NONPR AFFIL* trust: Art Inst Chicago *PHIL AFFIL* pres, trust: Prince Foundation; trust: Prince Charitable Trusts

APPLICATION INFORMATION
Initial Approach: Send a brief letter of inquiry. Include a description of organization, amount requested, purpose of funds sought, recently audited financial statement, and proof of tax-exempt status. There are no deadlines.

Restrictions on Giving: Does not support individuals.

GRANTS ANALYSIS
Total Grants: $608,000
Number of Grants: 42
Highest Grant: $100,000
Typical Range: $5,000 to $20,000

Disclosure Period: 1992

Note: Recent grants are derived from a 1992 Form 990.

RECENT GRANTS

Library

10,000	Library of Congress, Washington, DC — patron support

General

100,000	Madeira School, Greenway, VA — capital campaign
50,000	Rehabilitation Institute, Chicago, IL — for the Henry Betts Award
30,000	North Country School, Lake Placid, NY — for Prince Faculty Fund endowment
30,000	Trustees of Amherst College, Folger Shakespeare College, Washington, DC — operating support
25,000	Eugene and Agnes E. Meyer Foundation, Washington, DC — funding pool

R. F. Foundation

CONTACT
R. F. Fdn.
One First National Plaza, Rm. 4700
Chicago, IL 60603
(815) 758-3461

FINANCIAL SUMMARY
Recent Giving: $172,000 (1993); $270,000 (1990); $220,000 (1989)

Assets: $3,428,229 (1993); $6,113,384 (1990); $6,340,347 (1989)

EIN: 36-6069098

CONTRIBUTIONS SUMMARY
Donor(s): Thomas H. Roberts, Thomas H. Roberts, Jr., Eleanor T. Roberts, Mary R. Roberts

Typical Recipients: • *Arts & Humanities:* Libraries • *Civic & Public Affairs:* Community Foundations, General • *Education:* Colleges & Universities, Minority Education • *Health:* Children's Health/Hospitals, Clinics/Medical Centers, Health Organizations, Hospitals, Public Health • *International:* International Development, Missionary/Religious Activities • *Religion:* Religious Organizations • *Social Services:* Child Welfare, Community Service Organizations, Food/Clothing Distribution, People with Disabilities, Senior Services, Shelters/Homelessness, United Funds/United Ways

Grant Types: emergency, multiyear/continuing support, and operating expenses

Geographic Distribution: limited to the Chicago and DeKalb County, IL, area

GIVING OFFICERS
Thomas H. Roberts III: vp, dir

Thomas Humphrey Roberts, Jr.: treas, dir *B* DeKalb IL 1924 *ED* IA St Univ BS 1949; Harvard Univ MBA 1955 *CURR EMPL* dir:

DeKalb Genetics Corp *CORP AFFIL* dir: Continental IL Natl Bank & Trust Co, IMC Fertilizer Group, Pride Petroleum Svcs; vchmn exec comm, dir: DeKalb Energy Co *NONPR AFFIL* bd visitors: Harvard Univ Bus Sch; trust: Rush-Presbyterian-St Lukes Med Ctr

Thomas E. Swaney: secy, dir

APPLICATION INFORMATION
Initial Approach: Send cover letter and full proposal. Include a description of organization, amount requested, purpose of funds sought, recently audited financial statement, and proof of tax-exempt status. There are no deadlines.

Restrictions on Giving: Does not support individuals or provide scholarships or loans.

GRANTS ANALYSIS
Total Grants: $172,000

Number of Grants: 15

Highest Grant: $87,000

Typical Range: $500 to $22,500

Disclosure Period: 1993

Note: Recent grants are derived from a 1993 Form 990.

RECENT GRANTS

Library

500	Sycamore Public Library, Sycamore, NY

General

87,000	Rush-Presbyterian-St. Lukes Medical Center, Chicago, IL
22,500	Hiawatha Children's Home
18,000	VAC
12,000	Sycamore United Way, Sycamore, NY
6,000	Meals on Wheels, New York, NY

Rand McNally & Co. / Rand McNally Foundation

Employees: 4,000
Headquarters: Skokie, IL
SIC Major Group: Printing & Publishing

CONTACT
Edward C. McNally
Secretary
Rand McNally Foundation
PO Box 7600
Chicago, IL 60680
(708) 329-8100

FINANCIAL SUMMARY
Recent Giving: $193,758 (1993); $192,836 (1991); $191,795 (1989)

Assets: $1,591,663 (1993); $1,380,145 (1991); $968,190 (1989)

Gifts Received: $250,000 (1993); $250,000 (1991); $250,000 (1989)

Fiscal Note: In 1993, contributions were received from Rand McNally & Company.

EIN: 36-3514596

CONTRIBUTIONS SUMMARY
Typical Recipients: • *Arts & Humanities:* Arts Institutes, History & Archaeology, Libraries, Music • *Civic & Public Affairs:* Community Foundations, Economic Development, General, Urban & Community Affairs, Zoos/Aquariums • *Education:* Business Education, Colleges & Universities, Economic Education, Education Associations • *Health:* Children's Health/Hospitals • *Social Services:* Community Service Organizations, Scouts, United Funds/United Ways, Volunteer Services, YMCA/YWCA/YMHA/YWHA, Youth Organizations

Grant Types: employee matching gifts and general support

Geographic Distribution: focus on IL

GIVING OFFICERS
James J. Habschmidt: vp, treas

Joseph L. Landers, Jr.: asst secy

Andrew McNally IV: chmn, dir *B* Chicago IL 1939 *ED* Univ NC BA 1963; Univ Chicago MBA 1969 *CURR EMPL* pres, ceo, dir: Rand McNally & Co *CORP AFFIL* dir: Allendale Ins, First IL Corp, Walter Foster Publs, Hubbell Inc, Mercury Fin, Probus Publ, Val Pak, Zenith Electronics Corp *NONPR AFFIL* active visitor comm library: Univ Chicago; dir: Childrens Meml Hosp, Graphic Arts Tech Fdn; mem: Chicago Map Soc, Young Pres Org; mem visitor comm: Univ NC Bus Sch; trust: Newberry Library *CLUB AFFIL* Chicago, Commercial, Commonwealth, Glen View GC, Links, Saddle & Cycle

Edward C. McNally: vp, secy

APPLICATION INFORMATION
Initial Approach: The foundation does not report any specific application guidelines. Send a brief letter of inquiry.

GRANTS ANALYSIS
Total Grants: $193,758

Number of Grants: 80

Highest Grant: $35,090

Typical Range: $200 to $12,500

Disclosure Period: 1993

Note: Recent grants are derived from a 1993 Form 990.

RECENT GRANTS

Library

35,090	Newberry Library, Chicago, IL
2,500	Northwestern University Library, Evanston, IL

General

12,500	United Way/Crusade of Mercy, Chicago, IL
12,500	United Way/Crusade of Mercy, Chicago, IL
10,000	Chicago Lighthouse for the Blind, Chicago, IL
5,000	Rochester Institute of Technology, Rochester, NY
3,500	Artis Trees/Children Celebrate Children, Children's Memorial Hospital, Chicago, IL

Regenstein Foundation

CONTACT
Joseph Regenstein, Jr.
President
Regenstein Foundation
8600 W Bryn Mawr Ave., Ste. 705N
Chicago, IL 60631
(312) 693-6464

FINANCIAL SUMMARY
Recent Giving: $9,206,094 (1993); $3,145,026 (1992); $2,432,244 (1990)

Assets: $96,418,668 (1993); $99,830,232 (1992); $85,667,771 (1990)

EIN: 36-3152531

CONTRIBUTIONS SUMMARY
Donor(s): The foundation was established in 1950, with the late Joseph Regenstein and Helen Regenstein as donors.

Typical Recipients: • *Arts & Humanities:* Arts Institutes, Historic Preservation, History & Archaeology, Libraries, Museums/Galleries, Music, Opera, Public Broadcasting • *Civic & Public Affairs:* Clubs, Nonprofit Management, Philanthropic Organizations, Professional & Trade Associations, Public Policy, Zoos/Aquariums • *Education:* Colleges & Universities, General, Medical Education, Preschool Education, Private Education (Precollege) • *Health:* Hospitals, Medical Rehabilitation, Nursing Services, Prenatal Health Issues • *Religion:* Jewish Causes, Religious Welfare • *Science:* Science Museums • *Social Services:* Child Welfare, Community Service Organizations, Delinquency & Criminal Rehabilitation, Family Planning, Food/Clothing Distribution, Homes, People with Disabilities, Scouts, Sexual Abuse, United Funds/United Ways, Volunteer Services, Youth Organizations

Grant Types: capital, endowment, general support, loan, multiyear/continuing support, and project

Geographic Distribution: Illinois, primarily the metropolitan Chicago area

GIVING OFFICERS
Ramona D. Baiocchi: asst secy

Anita Bury: asst secy

John Eggum: secy, treas, dir *B* Chicago IL 1913 *ED* Walton Sch Commerce *CORP AFFIL* dir: Arvey Corp

Betty Regenstein Hartman: vp, dir

Robert A. Mecca: vp, dir *B* 1951

Joseph Regenstein, Jr.: pres, dir *B* Chicago IL 1923 *ED* Brown Univ 1945 *CURR EMPL* chmn: Arvey Corp

Randall A. Watkins: contr, asst treas

APPLICATION INFORMATION
Initial Approach:

Brief requests in letter form should be addressed to the foundation's president.

Requests should include a cover letter, signed or approved by the organization's chief executive, summarizing the request, and describing the organization, proposed use of funds, desired results, and other sources of funds; one copy of the proposal; copy of the IRS determination letter of tax-exempt status; recently audited financial statement; budget statement for the current and subsequent year; and the amount requested. Additional information often is requested by the foundation.

There are no deadlines for submitting proposals.

Restrictions on Giving: The foundation reports that most grants are made on the initiative of the foundation's trustees; only a very small percentage of applicants can expect to obtain funds. Because long-range pledges often make income unavailable for substantial periods of time, it is suggested that applicants needing immediate help apply to individuals or businesses in a position to make immediate grants. The foundation does not make grants to individuals. The foundation does not conduct personal interviews with an applicant except upon the foundation's initiative.

PUBLICATIONS
General information letter

GRANTS ANALYSIS
Total Grants: $9,206,094

Number of Grants: 41

Highest Grant: $5,500,000

Average Grant: $69,387*

Typical Range: $1,000 to $10,000 and $25,000 to $75,000

Disclosure Period: 1993

Note: The average grant figure excludes the two highest grants totally $6,500,000. Recent grants are derived from a 1993 Form 990.

RECENT GRANTS

Library

1,000,000	University of Chicago, Chicago, IL — library renovation	
250,000	Newberry Library, Chicago, IL — endowment reading room	
2,000	Foundation Center, New York, NY	
2,000	Newberry Library, Chicago, IL	

General

5,500,000	Lincoln Park Zoo, Chicago, IL — construct mammal house	
700,000	Rush Presbyterian, Chicago, IL — diagnostic center	
400,000	Northwestern Memorial Foundation, Chicago, IL — four fellowships	
250,000	Chicago Horticultural Society, Glencoe, IL — fund exhibit	
114,000	Summit School, Dundee, IL — Elgin campus	

Retirement Research Foundation

CONTACT
Marilyn Hennessy
President
Retirement Research Foundation
8765 W Higgins Rd., No. 401
Chicago, IL 60631
(312) 714-8080

FINANCIAL SUMMARY
Recent Giving: $8,202,790 (1994); $6,436,216 (1993); $5,626,564 (1992)

Assets: $145,000,000 (1995 est.); $143,000,000 (1994 approx.); $140,000,000 (1993)

EIN: 36-2429540

CONTRIBUTIONS SUMMARY
Donor(s): "The Retirement Research Foundation was established by John D. MacArthur, a Chicago resident and businessman, in 1950. Upon Mr. MacArthur's death in 1978, the foundation was the recipient of major assets and began active grant making in 1979. MacArthur also established the John D. and Catherine T. MacArthur Foundation. However, each foundation is separate and totally independent of the other."

Typical Recipients: • *Arts & Humanities:* Film & Video, Libraries • *Civic & Public Affairs:* Asian American Affairs, Economic Development, Employment/Job Training, General, Housing, Legal Aid, Nonprofit Management, Professional & Trade Associations, Public Policy, Urban & Community Affairs • *Education:* Colleges & Universities, Community & Junior Colleges, Continuing Education, Literacy • *Health:* Clinics/Medical Centers, Diabetes, Emergency/Ambulance Services, Geriatric Health, Health Policy/Cost Containment, Health Organizations, Home-Care Services, Hospices, Hospitals, Long-Term Care, Medical Research, Mental Health, Nursing Services, Single-Disease Health Associations • *Religion:* Religious Organizations, Religious Welfare, Seminaries • *Social Services:* Community Centers, Community Service Organizations, Counseling, Family Services, Food/Clothing Distribution, Homes, People with Disabilities, Senior Services, Shelters/Homelessness, Volunteer Services

Grant Types: challenge, multiyear/continuing support, project, research, and seed money

Geographic Distribution: U.S. only

GIVING OFFICERS
Duane Chapman: trust

Robert P. Ewing: trust, secy *B* Kirksville MO 1925 *ED* NE MO St Univ BS 1948 *PHIL AFFIL* dir: John D. and Catherine T. MacArthur Foundation

Marilyn Hennessy: pres, exec dir *B* 1936

Brian F. Hofland, PhD: vp, program off

Webster H. Hurley: trust

Edward J. Kelly: chmn bd, trust *B* Des Moines IA 1911 *ED* IA St Univ BA 1934; IA St Univ JD 1936 *CURR EMPL* atty, ptnr: Whitfield Musgrave Selvy Kelly & Eddy

Marilyn Stein Le Feber: assoc vp

Sister Stella Louise: trust *B* 1920 *NONPR AFFIL* pres, dir: St Mary Nazareth Hosp

Sharon F. Markham: assoc vp

Nathaniel P. McParland, MD: trust

Marvin Meyerson: trust

John F. Santos: trust

Harry D. Sutphen: treas

Ruth Ann Watkins: trust

APPLICATION INFORMATION
Initial Approach:

The foundation does not have a standard application form. Applications must be submitted in writing.

Applications should include a two- to three-page summary of the project, its significance, and its cost. In addition, proposals should address specific project objectives, and give a detailed description of methods. A timetable and line item budget, including other sources of funds and a budget justification, should be included. If relevant, plans for continued support should be described. Curricula vitae, not to exceed five pages, should be included for project directors and key staff. Information on the applicant organization should include its history, accomplishments, financial reports, annual reports, and specific qualifications for the proposed project. A copy of the applicant's tax-exempt status under Section 501(c)(3), and of classification as "not a private foundation" under Section 509(a) of the Internal Revenue Code, must be included. All applications must be signed by the chief executive officer of the applicant organization and submitted in triplicate.

Research proposals should describe the experimental design, procedures to be used to accomplish the objectives, sequence of the investigation, kinds of data to be obtained, and the means by which data will be analyzed and interpreted.

Model projects and service proposals should describe the project design, target group, change to be effected, resources and method of delivery, sequence of activities planned to meet project objectives, and methods and criteria to be used to evaluate the outcome of the project.

Education and training proposals should describe the target group; educational needs to be met; content, methods, sequence, and location of educational experiences; and the methods and criteria which will be used to evaluate the educational program.

Deadlines for receipt of applications are February 1, May 1, and August 1.

Decisions are usually made four months after the deadline dates. The foundation is particularly interested in innovative projects which develop and demonstrate new approaches to the problems of the aged and which have the potential for regional or national impact. Funding of service development projects is limited to the seven Midwestern states (Illinois, Indiana, Iowa, Kentucky, Michigan, Missouri, Wisconsin) and Florida. When projects of equal significance are being considered, priority will be given to organizations serving the Chicago metropolitan area.

Restrictions on Giving: The foundation does not provide support for construction of facilities; general operating expenses of established organizations; endowment or developmental campaigns; scholarships; loans; grants to individuals; projects outside the United States; dissertation research; production of films or videos; or conferences, publications, and travel, unless they are components of foundation-funded projects. Generally, support of projects beyond a three-year period will not be provided.

PUBLICATIONS
Program guidelines and application procedures, two-year report, 10-year retrospective report

GRANTS ANALYSIS
Total Grants: $8,202,790

Number of Grants: 132

Highest Grant: $390,676

Average Grant: $62,142

Typical Range: $20,000 to $125,000

Disclosure Period: 1994

Note: Recent grants are derived from a 1994 grants list.

RECENT GRANTS
General

390,676 Lutheran General Medical Center Foundation, Park Ridge, IL — two-year grant to expand and evaluate the use of critical care pathways across senior settings

389,663 Rush-Presbyterian-St. Luke's Medical Center, Chicago, IL — three-year grant for research to vigorously evaluate whether an integrated, multimodality program of health promotion practices can slow or possibly reverse aging processes in the elderly

309,391 Yale University, New Haven, CT — three-year grant to identify effective strategies to prevent delirium among hospitalized elderly patients

265,066 Vanderbilt University, Nashville, TN — three-year grant for research to assess the benefits elderly individuals with hearing loss receive from personal amplification

239,352 Florida A&M University, Tallahassee, FL — two-year grant to establish a Health Promotion Center and Consortium for low-income African American older adults at risk for diabetes and hypertension

Rice Foundation

CONTACT
Arthur A. Nolan, Jr.
President and Director
Rice Foundation
8600 Gross Point Rd.
Skokie, IL 60077-2151
(708) 581-9999

FINANCIAL SUMMARY
Recent Giving: $5,875,000 (1995 est.); $5,861,102 (1994); $5,784,124 (1993)

Assets: $80,107,653 (1995 est.); $80,000,670 (1994); $80,100,040 (1993)

Gifts Received: $300 (1992); $1,000 (1990); $3,581,415 (1988)

Fiscal Note: In 1988, the foundation received two contributions totaling $3,579,915 from the estate of Ada Rice, and $1,500 from James Daugherty III.

EIN: 36-6043160

CONTRIBUTIONS SUMMARY
Donor(s): The Rice Foundation was established in 1947 by the late Daniel F. Rice .

Typical Recipients: • *Arts & Humanities:* Arts Associations & Councils, Arts Funds, Arts Institutes, Historic Preservation, History & Archaeology, Libraries, Museums/Galleries, Performing Arts, Public Broadcasting • *Civic & Public Affairs:* Botanical Gardens/Parks, Law & Justice, Safety, Zoos/Aquariums • *Education:* Arts/Humanities Education, Colleges & Universities, Education Funds, Medical Education, Private Education (Precollege), Science/Mathematics Education • *Environment:* General, Resource Conservation • *Health:* Arthritis, Cancer, Clinics/Medical Centers, Geriatric Health, Health Organizations, Hospitals, Medical Rehabilitation, Mental Health, Single-Disease Health Associations • *Religion:* Religious Organizations, Religious Welfare • *Science:* Science Museums • *Social Services:* Child Welfare, Community Centers, Family Services, People with Disabilities, Recreation & Athletics, Senior Services, Shelters/Homelessness, Volunteer Services, Youth Organizations

Grant Types: general support

Geographic Distribution: focus on Illinois, primarily Chicago

GIVING OFFICERS
Marilynn Bruder Alsdorf: dir *ED* Northwestern Univ 1946 *NONPR AFFIL* dir: Chicago Horticultural Soc; treas: Mus Contemporary Art Chicago; vp: Art Inst Chicago *CLUB AFFIL* Casino, Contemporary, Friday, Womens Athletic *PHIL AFFIL* pres, treas, dir: Alsdorf Foundation

John Grey: dir

Arthur A. Nolan, Jr.: pres, dir

Patricia Nolan: vp, treas, dir

Peter Nolan: vp, dir, secy

Edward Reilly: grants coordinator

David P. Winchester: dir

Barbara M. J. Wood: dir

APPLICATION INFORMATION
Initial Approach:

Applications should be submitted in writing.

Applications should include a statement describing the applicant organization and its activities, the amount and purpose of the grant requested, and proof of IRS tax-exempt status.

The foundation reports no application deadlines.

Restrictions on Giving: No grants are made to individuals.

GRANTS ANALYSIS
Total Grants: $5,796,264

Number of Grants: 53

Highest Grant: $1,750,000

Average Grant: $11,381*

Typical Range: $1,000 to $25,000

Disclosure Period: 1992

Note: The average grant figure excludes five grants totaling $5,250,000. Recent grants are derived from a 1992 Form 990.

RECENT GRANTS

Library
10,000	Library of International Relations, Chicago, IL

General
1,500,000	Field Museum of Natural History, Chicago, IL
1,000,000	Rehabilitation Institute of Chicago Foundation, Chicago, IL
500,000	John G. Shedd Aquarium, Chicago, IL
500,000	Maryville Academy, Des Plaines, IL
50,000	Evanston Hospital, Evanston, IL

Ringier-America

Sales: $600.0 million
Employees: 4,000
Headquarters: Itasca, IL
SIC Major Group: Printing & Publishing

CONTACT
Francine Overton
Corporate Manager, Human Resources
Ringier-America
One Pierce Pl., Ste. 800
Itasca, IL 60143-1272
(708) 285-6000

FINANCIAL SUMMARY
Fiscal Note: Annual Giving Range: $100,000 to $150,000

CONTRIBUTIONS SUMMARY
Typical Recipients: • *Arts & Humanities:* Libraries, Museums/Galleries • *Education:* Colleges & Universities, Education Associations, Private Education (Precollege), Public Education (Precollege) • *Health:* Hospitals, Single-Disease Health Associations • *Social Services:* Child Welfare, United Funds/United Ways, Youth Organizations

Grant Types: general support

Geographic Distribution: no geographic restrictions

Operating Locations: AR, AZ, CA, IL (Itasca), KS, MS, NC, TN, WI

CORP. OFFICERS
Edward C. Nytko: *CURR EMPL* pres, ceo, dir: Ringier-Am

LaVerne F. Schmidt: *CURR EMPL* sr vp, cfo: Ringier-Am

APPLICATION INFORMATION
Initial Approach: Submit a letter before September in order to receive funding for the following year. Include a description of the organization, purpose for which funds are sought, the benefits of the organization/project, and a recent annual report.

Restrictions on Giving: Does not provide nonmonetary support.

OTHER THINGS TO KNOW
Company reports that corporate giving has ceased.

Russell Charitable Foundation, Tom

CONTACT
Leslie R. Bishop
Secretary
Tom Russell Charitable Fdn.
1315 W 22nd St., Ste. 300
Oak Brook, IL 60521
(708) 571-4600

FINANCIAL SUMMARY
Recent Giving: $450,000 (fiscal 1992); $455,000 (fiscal 1991); $440,000 (fiscal 1990)

Assets: $10,290,119 (fiscal 1992); $10,068,656 (fiscal 1991); $9,522,514 (fiscal 1990)

EIN: 36-6082517

CONTRIBUTIONS SUMMARY
Donor(s): the late Thomas C. Russell, Wrap-On Co., Inc., Huron and Orleans Building Corp.

Typical Recipients: • *Arts & Humanities:* Historic Preservation, Libraries • *Education:* Colleges & Universities • *Health:* Medical Research, Single-Disease Health Associations • *Religion:* Churches • *Science:* Scientific Organizations • *Social Services:* Child Welfare, Community Service Organizations, Senior Services, Shelters/Homelessness, Youth Organizations

Grant Types: general support

Geographic Distribution: focus on the metropolitan Chicago, IL, area

GIVING OFFICERS
Leslie R. Bishop: secy, dir

Thomas A. Hearn: vp, dir

John Lindquist: asst secy, dir

J. Tod Meserow: pres, dir

APPLICATION INFORMATION
Initial Approach: The foundation has no formal grant application procedure or application form. There are no deadlines.

PUBLICATIONS
Application Guidelines

GRANTS ANALYSIS
Total Grants: $450,000

Number of Grants: 67

Highest Grant: $20,000

Typical Range: $2,000 to $10,000

Disclosure Period: fiscal year ending August 31, 1992

Note: Recent grants are derived from a Fiscal 1991 Form 990. No grants list was provided for fiscal 1992.

RECENT GRANTS

General
20,000	Boys and Girls Club, Chicago, IL
20,000	Cumberland College, Williamsburg, KY
20,000	Duke Comprehensive Cancer Center, Durham, NC
20,000	LaGrange Memorial Treatment Pavilion, Hinsdale, IL
20,000	Senior Friends, Hartford, CT

Santa Fe Pacific Corporation / Santa Fe Pacific Foundation

Revenue: $2.95 billion
Employees: 15,431
Headquarters: Schaumburg, IL
SIC Major Group: Holding Companies Nec, Railroads—Line-Haul Operating, and Refined Petroleum Pipelines

CONTACT
Catherine A. Westphal
President
Santa Fe Pacific Foundation
1700 E Golf Rd.
Schaumburg, IL 60173-5860
(708) 995-6000

FINANCIAL SUMMARY
Recent Giving: $1,200,000 (1995 est.); $1,200,000 (1994 approx.); $1,260,809 (1993)

Assets: $139,847 (1993); $1,225,299 (1992); $2,113,556 (1991)

Gifts Received: $143,000 (1993)

Fiscal Note: Almost all contributions are made through the foundation, but individual departments occasionally make direct grants. Direct gifts are not included in total giving figures. Above figures exclude nonmonetary support. In 1993, foundation received contributions from Santa Fe Pacific Gold Corporation and Santa Fe Pacific Pipelines, Inc.

EIN: 36-6051896

CONTRIBUTIONS SUMMARY

Typical Recipients: • *Arts & Humanities:* Arts Associations & Councils, Arts Centers, Arts Funds, Arts Institutes, Community Arts, Dance, Historic Preservation, Libraries, Museums/Galleries, Music, Opera, Performing Arts, Theater • *Civic & Public Affairs:* Economic Policy, Employment/Job Training, Law & Justice, Legal Aid, Public Policy, Urban & Community Affairs, Women's Affairs • *Education:* Agricultural Education, Business Education, Colleges & Universities, Continuing Education, Economic Education, Education Associations, Engineering/Technological Education, Health & Physical Education, Medical Education, Minority Education, Public Education (Precollege), Science/Mathematics Education, Social Sciences Education, Special Education, Student Aid • *Environment:* General • *Health:* Medical Rehabilitation, Medical Training, Mental Health • *Social Services:* Child Welfare, Community Service Organizations, Counseling, Domestic Violence, Emergency Relief, Food/Clothing Distribution, Homes, People with Disabilities, Senior Services, Shelters/Homelessness, Substance Abuse, Volunteer Services, Youth Organizations

Grant Types: capital, employee matching gifts, general support, operating expenses, and scholarship

Nonmonetary Support Types: donated equipment and in-kind services

Note: The foundation does not specify value of nonmonetary support.

Geographic Distribution: company service areas, principally the midwestern, southwestern, and western United States

Operating Locations: AZ, CA (Los Angeles, San Diego, San Francisco), CO, IL (Chicago), KS, MO (Kansas City), NM (Albuquerque), OK, TX (Dallas, Houston)

CORP. OFFICERS

Robert Duncan Krebs: *B* Sacramento CA 1942 *ED* Stanford Univ BA 1964; Harvard Univ MBA 1966 *CURR EMPL* chmn, pres, ceo: Santa Fe Southern Pacific Corp *CORP AFFIL* chmn: Streeterville Corp; chmn, pres, ceo: Atchison Topeka & Santa Fe Railway Co; dir: Catellus Devel Corp, Northern Trust Co, Phelps Dodge Corp, Santa Fe Energy Resources Inc, Santa Fe Indus, Santa Fe Pacific Pipelines Inc, Santa Fe Pacific Realty Corp; pres, dir: SFELP Inc *NONPR AFFIL* chmn: Northwestern Meml Hosp Chicago; mem: Assn Am RRs, Kappa Sigma, Northwestern Univ Assocs, Phi Beta Kappa, Stanford Univ Alumni Assn; trust: Glenwood Sch Boys, Lake Forest Coll, John G Shedd Aquarium *CLUB AFFIL* Bohemian, Chicago, Onwentsia, Pacific Union, World Trade

Jeff Williams: *CURR EMPL* dir pub aff: Santa Fe Pacific Corp

GIVING OFFICERS

Russell E. Hagberg: dir *B* 1950 *ED* Northern IL Univ BS 1971; Univ Chicago MBA 1978 *CURR EMPL* vp transportation, dir: Atchison Topeka & Santa Fe Railway Co

Carl R. Ice: dir

Dennis R. Johnson: asst treas *PHIL AFFIL* treas: Rivendell Stewards Trust

Max W. Prosser: vp, secy, treas

Erben J. Schulot: asst treas

Irvin Toole, Jr.: dir *B* 1941 *CURR EMPL* chmn, ceo, pres: Santa Fe Pacific Pipeline Ptnrs LP *CORP AFFIL* chmn, pres, ceo: SFP Pipeline Holdings Inc

Catherine A. Westphal: pres, dir

Sharon Williams: asst secy, asst treas

APPLICATION INFORMATION

Initial Approach: *Initial Contact:* proposal with a brief cover letter *Include Information On:* description of the organization, amount requested, copy of IRS tax-exempt ruling, list of organization's officers and directors, narrative detailing organization's purpose and concerns, program objectives and methods by which they will be accomplished, outline of future funding of ongoing projects, other sources of support, recently audited financial statement, budget data *Deadlines:* none *Note:* Major requests in excess of $20,000 are reviewed annually in the fall if received prior to September 1; proposals received later are considered in the following year.

Restrictions on Giving: In general, the foundation does not support individuals; political, religious, fraternal, or veterans organizations; hospitals; national health organizations or their local chapters; preschool, primary, or secondary schools; goodwill advertising; tax-supported schools or agencies; operating funds of organizations funded by United Way; tours, conferences, dinners, seminars, workshops, testimonials, or endowment funds; grant-making foundations; or programs beyond stated geographic areas of interest.

OTHER THINGS TO KNOW

Organizations wishing to be considered for future funding should submit a progress report for evaluation and a proposal containing current information.

The foundation matches employee gifts to eligible educational and cultural organizations. Private hospitals are also eligible for funds. Gifts are matched on a dollar-for-dollar basis from $25 to $5,000. Foundation limits funds matched to $5,000 per employee per calendar year.

GRANTS ANALYSIS

Total Grants: $1,260,809

Number of Grants: 291

Highest Grant: $187,000

Average Grant: $4,333

Typical Range: $500 to $10,000

Disclosure Period: 1993

Note: Recent grants are derived from a 1993 grants list.

RECENT GRANTS

Library

10,000	St. Louis Mercantile Library/Barriger National Railroad Library, St. Louis, MO	

General

187,000	United Way Crusade of Mercy, Chicago, IL	
100,000	United Way of Greater Topeka, Topeka, KS	
83,484	National Merit Scholarship Corporation, Evanston, IL	
60,000	National 4-H Educational Awards Program, Chevy Chase, MD	
40,125	American Indian Science and Engineering Society, Boulder, CO	

Sara Lee Corp. / Sara Lee Foundation

Revenue: $15.53 billion
Employees: 146,000
Headquarters: Chicago, IL
SIC Major Group: Frozen Specialties Nec, Meat Packing Plants, Sausages & Other Prepared Meats, and Canned Specialties

CONTACT

Robin Tryloff
Executive Director
Sara Lee Foundation
Three First Natl. Plz.
Chicago, IL 60602-4260
(312) 558-8448
Note: Ms. Tryloff is also Senior Manager, Community Relations of the Sara Lee Corporation. The foundation gives only in the Chicago area. Requests for support from organizations in operating communities should be addressed directly to local divisions.

FINANCIAL SUMMARY

Recent Giving: $12,800,000 (fiscal 1995 est.); $14,400,000 (fiscal 1994); $14,900,000 (fiscal 1993)

Assets: $2,800,000 (fiscal 1990); $4,700,000 (fiscal 1989)

Fiscal Note: Above figures include worldwide cash contributions by the company and foundation. Foundation giving totaled about $5.4 million in 1994 and $6.4 million in 1993. 1994 contributions by other company departments totaled $177,000; in 1993, $231,000; and in 1992, about $150,000. Contact Elynor Williams, Vice President, Sara Lee Corp. Above figures exclude nonmonetary support.

EIN: 36-3150460

CONTRIBUTIONS SUMMARY

Typical Recipients: • *Arts & Humanities:* Arts Associations & Councils, Arts Centers, Arts Festivals, Arts Institutes, Community Arts, Dance, Ethnic & Folk Arts, Historic Preservation, Libraries, Museums/Galleries, Music, Opera, Performing Arts, Theater, Visual Arts • *Civic & Public Affairs:* Civil Rights, Economic Development, Employment/Job Training, Housing, Law & Justice, Legal Aid, Philanthropic Organizations, Urban & Community Affairs, Women's Affairs, Zoos/Aquariums • *Education:* Arts/Humanities Education, Business Education, Colleges & Universities, International Exchange, Literacy, Minority Education • *Health:* Health Organizations • *International:* International Peace & Security Issues • *Science:* Observatories & Planetariums • *Social Services:* Child Welfare, Community Centers, Community Service Organizations, Counseling, Day Care, Domestic Violence, Family Planning, Family Services, Food/Clothing Distribution, Homes, People with Disabilities, Refugee Assistance, Senior Services, Shelters/Homelessness, Substance Abuse, United Funds/United Ways, Volunteer Services, Youth Organizations

Grant Types: award, employee matching gifts, general support, multiyear/continuing support, operating expenses, project, and seed money

Note: Employee matching gift ratio: 2 to 1, up to $1,000 per gift. Employee matching gift ratio: 1 to 1, up to $10,000.

Nonmonetary Support: $8,100,000 (fiscal 1994); $3,000,000 (fiscal 1993); $7,000,000 (fiscal 1992)

Nonmonetary Support Types: donated products, in-kind services, loaned executives, and workplace solicitation

Note: See "Other Things To Know" for more details.

Geographic Distribution: Chicago metropolitan area and where divisions operate; limited support for national organizations

Operating Locations: AL (Athens, Florence, Montgomery, Scottsboro, Slocomb), AR (Clarksville, Little Rock), AZ (Glendale), CA (Hayward, LaMirada, Los Angeles, Modesto, San Diego, San Francisco, San Lorenzo), CT (Stamford), DE (Dover), FL (Miami, Pinellas Park, Tampa), GA (Atlanta, Calhoun, Cartersville, Eastman, Eatonton, Fitzgerald, Midway, Milledgeville, Newnan, Raburn Gap, Wrightsville), IA (Des Moines, New Hampton, Storm Lake), IL (Batavia, Bensenville, Champaign, Chicago, Elk Grove Village, Schaumburg), IN (Dubois, Indianapolis), KS (Lenexa), KY (Alexandria), LA (New Orleans), MI (Detroit, Grand Rapids, Livonia, Traverse City, Zeeland), MN (Minneapolis), MO (Kansas City, St. Joseph, St. Louis), MS (Forest, Jackson, Olive Branch, West Point), NC (Advance, Asheboro, Asheville, Carey, Charlotte, Clayton, Dunn, Eden, Forest City, High Point, Jefferson, Kernersville, Laurel Hill, Lumberton, Maxton, Mocksville, Morganton, Mt. Airy, Rockingham, Rural Hill, Sanford, Sparta, Tarboro, Weaverville, Winston-Salem, Yadkinville), ND (Fargo), NJ (Secaucus), NM (Las Cruces), NV (Henderson), NY (New York, Perry, Rochester), OH (Cincinnati, Columbus, Valley View), OR (Portland), PA (Douglassville, Philadelphia, Pittsburgh), SC (Barnwell, Bennettsville, Charleston, Columbia, Conway, Florence, Gaffrey, Greenville, Harsville, Marion), TN (Cordova, Lavergne, Martin, Memphis, Mountain City, Nasville, Newbern), TX (Dallas), VA (Galax, Gretna, Hillsville, Martinsville, Rocky Mount, Salem), WA (Algona, Tacoma), WI (Greenbay, Milwaukee, New London)

CORP. OFFICERS

John H. Bryan: *B* West Point MS 1936 *ED* Rhodes Coll BA 1958; SUNY Grad Sch Bus Admin MS 1960 *CURR EMPL* chmn, ceo, dir: Sara Lee Corp *CORP AFFIL* dir: Amoco Corp, First Chicago Corp, First Natl Bank Chicago, Gen Motors Corp *NONPR AFFIL* chmn bus adv counc: Chicago Urban League; dir: Bus Comm Arts, Grocery Mfrs Am, Natl Womens Econ Alliance, Un Way Crusade Mercy Metro Chicago; mem: Bus Counc, Bus Roundtable; mem natl corps comm: Un Negro Coll Fund; mem trust counc: Natl Gallery Art; trust: Comm Econ Devel, Rush Presbyterian St Lukes Med Ctr, Univ Chicago; vp, treas, trust: Art Inst Chicago

Maureen Murray Culhane: *B* Milwaukee WI 1948 *ED* NY Univ 1970; Univ Chicago 1983 *CURR EMPL* vp fin, treas: Sara Lee Corp *CORP AFFIL* dir: Consolidated Foodservice Cos, JP Foodservice; treas: PLA Monarch Inc

Robert L. Lauer: *B* Crook CO 1933 *ED* Bowling Green St Univ BS 1956 *CURR EMPL* sr vp: Sara Lee Corp *NONPR AFFIL* dir: Advertising Counc, Intl Theatre Festival Chicago, Arthur W Page Soc, Pub Aff Counc, Second Harvest Natl Food Bank Network; mem: Bus Comm Arts New York City, Pub Rels Soc Am *CLUB AFFIL* Chicago, Commonwealth, Econ Chicago, Execs, Univ

Michael Emmett Murphy: *B* Winchester MA 1936 *ED* Boston Coll BS 1958; Harvard Univ Sch Bus Admin MBA 1962 *CURR EMPL* vchmn, cfo, chief admin off: Sara Lee Corp *CORP AFFIL* corp controller, vp admin: Hanes Corp; dir: GATX Corp *NONPR AFFIL* dir: Lyric Opera Chicago, Northwestern Meml Hosp; mem: Beta Gamma Sigma, Fin Execs Inst, Hoboken Chamber Commerce, Intl Platform Assn, Miami Chamber Commerce, Ouiment Scholar Alumni Group, UN Assn, Winston-Salem Chamber Commerce; mem, dir: Natl Assn Mfrs; trust: Boston Coll

Gordon Harold Newman: *B* Sioux City IA 1933 *ED* Univ IA BS 1955; Univ IA JD 1961 *CURR EMPL* sr vp, secy, gen couns: Sara Lee Corp *CORP AFFIL* pres, dir: PYA Gen Ptnr Corp; secy, dir: Bali Co, Playtex Apparel Inc; vp, secy, dir: Rice Hosiery Corp *NONPR AFFIL* mem: Am Bar Assn, Am Soc Corp Secys, Chicago Bar Assn, IL Bar Assn, Northwestern Univ Assocs; vchmn: Counc Auditorium Theatre *CLUB AFFIL* Standard

Elynor Alberta Williams: *B* Baton Rouge LA 1946 *ED* Spelman Coll BS 1966; Cornell Univ Grad Sch Bus Admin MS 1973 *CURR EMPL* vp pub responsibility: Sara Lee Corp *NONPR AFFIL* deacon: Chicago Un Church; mem: Alpha Kappa Alpha, Cosmopolitan Chamber Commerce, Exec Leadership Counc, Intl Assn Bus Commun, Intl Network Women Enterprise & Trade, League Women Voters, NAACP, Natl Assn Female Execs, Natl Org Women, Pub Rels Soc Am; mem exec comm: Natl Womens Econ Alliance; mem natl tech adv comm: OICs Am Inc

GIVING OFFICERS

John H. Bryan: dir *CURR EMPL* chmn, ceo, dir: Sara Lee Corp (see above)

Maureen Murray Culhane: treas *CURR EMPL* vp fin, treas: Sara Lee Corp (see above)

David B. Ellis: asst treas

Robert L. Lauer: pres, dir *CURR EMPL* sr vp: Sara Lee Corp (see above)

William Lipsman: asst secy

Gina Mullen: asst dir

Michael Emmett Murphy: dir *CURR EMPL* vchmn, cfo, chief admin off: Sara Lee Corp (see above)

Gordon Harold Newman: vp, secy *CURR EMPL* sr vp, secy, gen couns: Sara Lee Corp (see above)

Robin Tryloff: exec dir

Elynor Alberta Williams: dir *CURR EMPL* vp pub responsibility: Sara Lee Corp (see above)

APPLICATION INFORMATION

Initial Approach: *Initial Contact:* brief letter or telephone call requesting annual contributions report and application; to apply to divisions, call local division for information *Include Information On:* along with application, submit most recently audited financial statement, current operating budget, annual report (or other materials summarizing programs), list of directors and their affiliations, proof of tax-exempt status, list of public and private support of $500 or more received during the most recently completed fiscal year *Deadlines:* no later than first working day of March, September, or December for consideration at quarterly meetings held after those months *Note:* Proposals must be submitted on the foundation's application form.

Restrictions on Giving: The following are not eligible for grants: capital and endowment campaigns; individuals; organizations with a limited constituency, such as fraternal or veterans groups; organizations that limit services to members of one religious group or seek to propagate a particular belief or creed; political organizations or groups promoting one ideological view; elementary or secondary schools, either public or private; single-disease health organizations; tickets to dinners and other events; goodwill advertising in yearbooks or dinner programs; or national or international organizations with limited relationship to local Sara Lee operations.

OTHER THINGS TO KNOW

Sara Lee's contributions program is decentralized. About two-fifths of total contributions are made by the foundation, which is the main philanthropic vehicle for the Chicago corporate office. The remainder is distributed by divisions, which administer their own programs, including nonmonetary giving and volunteer services.

Organizations should not submit a contribution application more than once in any 12-month period. Grants are not automatically renewed, and recipients desiring renewed support should submit a request approximately two months prior to the anniversary of their grant(s). A renewal request should include the organization's most recent audited financial statement, current year's operating budget, updated board of directors list, and summary of how the previous year's grant was used. An application form is not necessary for grant renewal requests.

Sara Lee maintains a policy that annual cash and product contributions shall represent at least 2% of domestic pretax income.

At the corporate and division levels, company forms active partnerships with particularly effective local organizations and encourages employee involvement.

GRANTS ANALYSIS

Total Grants: $5,438,000*

Typical Range: $1,000 to $10,500

Disclosure Period: fiscal year ending July 2, 1994

Note: Recent grants are derived from a fiscal 1993 grants list. Figures represent foundation giving only.

RECENT GRANTS

Library
10,000   Chicago Public Library Foundation, Chicago, IL

General
381,925   United Way Crusade of Mercy, Chicago, IL
166,000   J.L. Kellogg Graduate School of Management, Evanston, IL
125,000   Field Museum of Natural History, Chicago, IL
100,000   Second Harvest National Food Bank Network, Chicago, IL
61,000   Youth Guidance, Chicago, IL

Scholl Foundation, Dr.

CONTACT

Pamela Scholl Mahaffee
President
Dr. Scholl Foundation
11 S La Salle St., Ste. 2100
Chicago, IL 60603
(312) 782-5210

FINANCIAL SUMMARY

Recent Giving: $8,611,800 (1994); $8,437,075 (1992); $7,363,250 (1991)

Assets: $138,700,000 (1995 est.); $142,400,000 (1994); $136,877,781 (1992)

EIN: 36-6068724

CONTRIBUTIONS SUMMARY

Donor(s): The Dr. Scholl Foundation (formerly William M. Scholl Foundation) was created in 1947 by Dr. William M. Scholl . "At 18, he enrolled in Illinois Medical College, now Loyola University, and was awarded his M.D. degree in 1904. That same year, he established Scholl, Inc., a manufacturer of orthopedic devices and footwear. He died in 1968 leaving Scholl, Inc., and the foundation in the hands of his nephews. The foundation received the bulk of his estate, and Scholl, Inc., was sold in 1979."

Typical Recipients: • *Arts & Humanities:* History & Archaeology, Libraries, Museums/Galleries, Music, Opera, Public Broadcasting • *Civic & Public Affairs:* Employment/Job Training, Law & Justice, Professional & Trade Associations, Public Policy, Zoos/Aquariums • *Education:* Arts/Humanities Education, Colleges & Universities, Education Associations, Elementary Education (Private), Engineering/Technological Education, Faculty Development, Legal Education, Medical Education, Minority Education, Private Education (Precollege), Science/Mathematics Education, Special Education, Student Aid • *Health:* Cancer, Eyes/Blindness, Health Organizations, Heart, Hospitals, Medical Research, Research/Studies Institutes, Single-Disease Health Associations • *International:* Foreign Arts Organizations, Foreign Educational Institutions, Health Care/Hospitals, International Affairs, International Organizations, International Peace & Security Issues • *Religion:* Churches, Religious Organizations, Religious Welfare • *Science:* Science Museums, Scientific Organizations • *Social Services:* Child Welfare, Community Centers, Family Services, Food/Clothing Distribution, Homes, People with Disabilities, Recreation & Athletics, Senior Services, Shelters/Homelessness, Volunteer Services, Youth Organizations

Grant Types: project

Geographic Distribution: no geographic restrictions; an emphasis on Illinois

GIVING OFFICERS

George W. Alexander: asst secy-treas, dir
Neil Flanagin: dir *B* Chicago IL 1930 *ED* Yale Univ BA 1953; Univ MI JD 1956 *CURR EMPL* ptnr: Sidley & Austin (Chicago)
William B. Jordan III: dir
Leonard J. Knirko: treas
Pamela Scholl Mahaffee: pres, dir
Jack E. Scholl: secy, exec dir, dir
Michael L. Scholl: dir

William H. Scholl: chmn, dir
Douglas C. Witherspoon: dir

APPLICATION INFORMATION
Initial Approach:

Applicants should obtain a copy of the foundation's standard application form and guidelines. The form is required along with one copy of a full proposal.

Applications must be received by May 15 to be considered for current year program.

Applications are acknowledged. The foundation notifies applicants of its decisions in November, and distribution of grants occurs in December.

Restrictions on Giving: "In general, the Foundation does not consider the following for funding: organizations not eligible for tax-deductible support; political organizations or campaigns, or groups whose prime purpose is to influence legislation; foundations that are themselves grant-making bodies; public education; grants to individuals; general endowment grants; unrestricted purpose grants; general support grants; grants for the reduction of an operating deficit or to liquidate a debt; testimonial dinners and similar benefit programs involving purchases of tables, tickets, or advertisements; or installment grants, but the Foundation gives consideration to subsequent applications pertaining to the same project."

OTHER THINGS TO KNOW

Applicants must present their request in the form of a special project or program designed to achieve a desirable result. All grantees are asked to sign an agreement which requires a full report to be filed at the conclusion of the project, including a statement of the results achieved by the grant. Only one application per organization will be considered annually.

PUBLICATIONS

Program guidelines and application procedures

GRANTS ANALYSIS

Total Grants: $8,611,800

Number of Grants: 356

Highest Grant: $500,000

Average Grant: $24,190

Typical Range: $10,000 to $50,000

Disclosure Period: 1994

Note: Recent grants are derived from a 1992 grants list.

RECENT GRANTS

General
500,000   Center for Strategic and International Studies, Washington, DC — funding

425,000	for Scholl Chair and expenses as requested Dr. William M. Scholl College, Chicago, IL — funding for museum and scholarship programs as requested
400,000	Loyola University of Chicago, Chicago, IL — partial funding for endowed chair
150,000	Georgetown University Medical Center, Washington, DC — funding for Lombardi endowed professorship and cardiology project
125,000	Clearbrook Center, Rolling Meadows, IL — funding for expansion for vocational rehabilitation center

Square D Co. / Square D Foundation

Revenue: $1.65 billion
Employees: 19,300
Parent Company: Schneider S.A.
Headquarters: Palatine, IL
SIC Major Group: Switchgear & Switchboard Apparatus, Metal Foil & Leaf, Fabricated Metal Products Nec, and Transformers Except Electronic

CONTACT
Becky Murdock
Secretary
Square D Foundation
1415 S Roselle
Palatine, IL 60067
(708) 397-2610 ext. 3480

FINANCIAL SUMMARY

Recent Giving: $1,400,000 (1994 est.); $2,119,695 (1993); $1,294,947 (1992)

Assets: $580,500 (1993); $2,084,433 (1992); $1,502,806 (1990)

Fiscal Note: Total giving figures above are for foundation only. Contributions are primarily made through the foundation; company occasionally makes direct contributions. Above figures exclude nonmonetary support.

EIN: 36-6054195

CONTRIBUTIONS SUMMARY

Typical Recipients: • *Arts & Humanities:* Arts Associations & Councils, Arts Centers, Arts Festivals, Arts Funds, Arts Institutes, Dance, Libraries, Museums/Galleries, Music, Opera, Public Broadcasting, Theater • *Civic & Public Affairs:* Business/Free Enterprise, Rural Affairs, Safety • *Education:* Arts/Humanities Education, Business Education, Colleges & Universities, Community & Junior Colleges, Economic Education, Education Funds, Engineering/Technological Education, Minority Education, Student Aid • *Health:* Emergency/Ambulance Services,

Health Funds, Hospitals, Medical Research, Mental Health, Single-Disease Health Associations • *Social Services:* Child Welfare, Community Centers, Community Service Organizations, Emergency Relief, Food/Clothing Distribution, Homes, People with Disabilities, Senior Services, United Funds/United Ways, Youth Organizations

Grant Types: capital, conference/seminar, department, employee matching gifts, fellowship, general support, research, and scholarship

Nonmonetary Support Types: donated equipment

Note: The foundation does not specify the value of nonmonetary support. Individual plants and plant managers should be contacted for nonmonetary support.

Geographic Distribution: areas where Square D Co. maintains manufacturing facilities

Operating Locations: AL (Clanton, Leeds), CA (Costa Mesa), FL (Clearwater, Pinellas Park), IA (Cedar Rapids), IL (Niles, Palatine, Schiller Park), IN (Huntington, Peru), KY (Florence, Lexington), MO (Columbia), NC (Asheville, Knightdale, Monroe, Raleigh), NE (Lincoln), OH (Dublin, Middletown, Oxford), SC (Columbia, Seneca), TN (Elkton, Memphis, Nashville, Smyrna), TX (Dallas, Ft. Worth, Mesquite), WI (Milwaukee, Oshkosh)

CORP. OFFICERS

William P. Brink: *CURR EMPL* exec vp fin, contr, cfo: Square D Co

Charles W. Denny: *CURR EMPL* coo, pres, dir: Square D Co *CORP AFFIL* coo: Schneider NA

Walter W. Kurczewski: *CURR EMPL* vp, secy, gen couns: Square D Co

GIVING OFFICERS

William P. Brink: treas, dir *CURR EMPL* exec vp fin, contr, cfo: Square D Co (see above)

R. P. Fiorani: vp, dir

Philip H. Francis: vp, dir *B* San Diego CA 1938 *ED* CA Polytech St Univ 1959; St Marys Univ 1972 *CURR EMPL* vp tech: Schneider NA *NONPR AFFIL* dir assessment: Natl Inst Standards & Tech

Walter W. Kurczewski: pres, dir *CURR EMPL* vp, secy, gen couns: Square D Co (see above)

Becky Murdock: secy

APPLICATION INFORMATION

Initial Approach: *Initial Contact:* brief letter or proposal *Include Information On:* description of the organization, amount requested, evaluative plans, purpose for which funds are sought, recently audited financial statement, proof of tax-exempt status, operating budget for the current year showing breakdown of expenses and sources

of income, members of the agency's governing board, and corporate and foundation contributors and amount each has contributed in the last calendar year *Deadlines:* to local Square D facilities/plants between June and August for funding the next calendar year

Restrictions on Giving: Does not make contributions to religious organizations (except where is support used for nondenominational social service); political groups and organizations; labor unions and organizations; organizations making requests by telephone; organizations listed by the U.S. Attorney General as subversive or front organizations; or individuals.

Since foundation supports United Way in corporate communities, donations normally are not made to organizations receiving support through United Way.

GRANTS ANALYSIS
Total Grants: $2,119,695
Number of Grants: 242
Highest Grant: $1,000,000
Average Grant: $4,646*
Typical Range: $1,000 to $5,000
Disclosure Period: 1993

Note: Average grant excludes the highest grant of $1,000,000. Recent grants are derived from a 1991 Form 990.

RECENT GRANTS

General

150,000	Community Youth Creative Learning Experience, Palatine, IL
125,000	North Carolina A&T State University, Greensboro, NC
100,000	American-Ireland Fund
100,000	University of Iowa Foundation, Iowa City, IA
75,000	Northern Illinois University, DeKalb, IL

United Airlines, Inc. / United Airlines Foundation

Parent Company: UAL Corporation
Revenue: $11.0 billion
Parent Employees: 76,000
Headquarters: Elk Grove, IL
SIC Major Group: Air Transportation—Scheduled

CONTACT
Eileen Younglove
Secretary & Contributions Manager
United Airlines Foundation
PO Box 66100
Chicago, IL 60666
(708) 952-5714

FINANCIAL SUMMARY

Recent Giving: $2,537,259 (1993); $2,713,684 (1992); $2,830,135 (1991)

Assets: $2,618,120 (1993); $2,757,727 (1992); $2,856,000 (1990)

Fiscal Note: Figures are for foundation only. Company also maintains an annual direct giving program of about $500,000, and in-kind transportation donations of about $2 million.

EIN: 36-6109873

CONTRIBUTIONS SUMMARY

Typical Recipients: • *Arts & Humanities:* Arts Associations & Councils, Arts Institutes, Ballet, Dance, Ethnic & Folk Arts, Libraries, Museums/Galleries, Music, Opera • *Civic & Public Affairs:* African American Affairs, Business/Free Enterprise, Civil Rights, Economic Development, Employment/Job Training, Safety, Urban & Community Affairs, Women's Affairs, Zoos/Aquariums • *Education:* Arts/Humanities Education, Business Education, Business-School Partnerships, Colleges & Universities, Literacy, Minority Education, Public Education (Precollege), Science/Mathematics Education, Student Aid • *Environment:* Resource Conservation • *Health:* Alzheimers Disease, Cancer, Children's Health/Hospitals, Heart, Hospitals, Single-Disease Health Associations • *Religion:* Dioceses, Religious Welfare • *Science:* Observatories & Planetariums, Science Museums • *Social Services:* Community Centers, Emergency Relief, Senior Services, United Funds/United Ways, Youth Organizations

Grant Types: general support and project

Nonmonetary Support: $2,000,000 (1991); $1,000,000 (1989)

Nonmonetary Support Types: in-kind services

Geographic Distribution: primarily in Washington, DC; Los Angeles and San Francisco, CA; Denver, CO; Honolulu, HI; Chicago, IL; and Seattle, WA

Operating Locations: CA (Los Angeles, San Francisco), DC, HI (Honolulu), IL (Chicago), WA (Seattle)

Note: Also operates in London, England and Tokyo, Japan.

CORP. OFFICERS

John Charles Pope: *B* Newark NJ 1949 *ED* Yale Univ BA 1971; Harvard Univ MBA 1973 *CURR EMPL* pres, coo, dir: Un Airlines Inc *CORP AFFIL* chmn: Air WI Inc, Air WI Svcs Inc; dir: Fed Mogul Corp; pres, coo, dir: UAL Corp; trust: WTTW *NONPR AFFIL* mem: Air Transport Assn Am

Stephen M. Wolf: *B* Oakland CA 1941 *ED* San Francisco St Univ BA 1965 *CURR EMPL* chmn, ceo, pres: UAL Corp *CORP AFFIL* chmn, ceo, pres: Un Airlines Inc; dir: ConAgra Inc; pres: Un Airlines Credit Corp *NONPR AFFIL* dir: Alzheimers Disease & Related Disorders Assn, Chicago Symphony Orchestra, Conf Bd, Mus Flight, Northwest-

ern Univ Kellogg Grad Sch Bus Mgmt, Rush Presbyterian-St Lukes Med Ctr

GIVING OFFICERS

Paul George: vp, dir *CURR EMPL* sr vp human resources: Un Airlines Inc

James M. Guyette: dir *B* Fresno CA 1945 *ED* St Marys Coll BS 1967 *CURR EMPL* exec vp opers: Un Airlines Inc *CORP AFFIL* chmn: Un Airlines Employees Credit Union; dir: Private Bancorp; exec vp: UAL Corp *NONPR AFFIL* bd regents: St Marys Coll; bd regents, mem adv counc: Univ IL; devel counc: Alexian Bros Med Ctr; dir: Un Way Am

Lawrence M. Nagin: dir *B* San Francisco CA 1941 *ED* Univ Southern CA BA 1962; Univ CA JD 1965 *CURR EMPL* sr vp corp & external aff, gen couns: Un Airlines Inc *CORP AFFIL* sr vp, gen couns: Air WI Inc, Air WI Svcs Inc *NONPR AFFIL* mem: Am Bar Assn

Joseph R. O'Gorman, Jr.: dir *B* 1943 *ED* GA Inst Tech BS 1966; IL Inst Tech MBA 1973 *CURR EMPL* exec vp: UAL Corp *CORP AFFIL* exec vp: Un Airlines Inc; pres: Air WI Inc, Air WI Svcs Inc

John Charles Pope: dir *CURR EMPL* pres, coo, dir: Un Airlines Inc (see above)

Stephen M. Wolf: pres, dir *CURR EMPL* chmn, ceo, pres: UAL Corp (see above)

Eileen M. Younglove: secy *CURR EMPL* contributions mgr: Un Airlines Inc

APPLICATION INFORMATION

Initial Approach: *Initial Contact:* submit the proposal in writing on the organization's letterhead (there are no application forms for requests). The proposal should explain the organization and the project or event that the grant will benefit.*Include Information On:* all supporting documentation. For example, if a ticket is requested, attach promotional literature advertising the event; for dinners, attach the invitation and response cards; for grants, attach the list of board of directors, other contributers, an audited financial statement, a previous and current year's budget and a copy of the organization's IRS tax exempt letter. *Deadlines:* 60 days prior to quarterly meetings; meetings are held in March, June, September, and December. *Note:* Do not send video tapes to the foundation. Supporting documentation will not be returned.

Restrictions on Giving: The United Airlines Foundation does not provide in-kind gifts or funding in the following areas: capital or building grants, development campaigns, endowments, individuals, political organizations, United Way-funded agencies, individual public or private schools, churches, the purchase of tickets to dinners or other fund-raising events, or goodwill advertising.

GRANTS ANALYSIS

Total Grants: $2,537,259

Number of Grants: 202

Highest Grant: $308,250

Average Grant: $12,561

Typical Range: $1,000 to $25,000

Disclosure Period: 1993

Note: Recent grants are derived from a 1993 Form 990.

RECENT GRANTS

Library
25,000 — Chicago Public Library Foundation, Chicago, IL — four-year pledge totaling $100,000

General
308,250 — United Way of the Bay Area, San Francisco, CA
286,975 — United Way Crusade of Mercy, Chicago, IL
200,000 — Museum of Science and Industry, Chicago, IL — aviation exhibit, two-year pledge totaling $400,000
93,200 — Mile High United Way, Denver, CO
87,450 — United Way, Los Angeles, CA

USG Corporation / USG Foundation

Revenue: $2.29 billion
Employees: 11,500
Headquarters: Chicago, IL
SIC Major Group: Gypsum Products, Paper Mills, Adhesives & Sealants, and Mineral Wool

CONTACT

Harold E. Pendexter, Jr.
President
USG Fdn.
125 S Franklin
Chicago, IL 60606
(312) 606-4594

FINANCIAL SUMMARY

Recent Giving: $300,000 (1995 est.); $290,959 (1994); $176,093 (1993)

Assets: $106,985 (1993); $477,156 (1991); $1,011,359 (1989)

Fiscal Note: Company gives through foundation only.

EIN: 36-2984045

CONTRIBUTIONS SUMMARY
Typical Recipients: • *Arts & Humanities:* Arts Institutes, Historic Preservation, Libraries, Museums/Galleries, Opera, Public Broadcasting, Theater • *Civic & Public Affairs:* Economic Development, Law & Justice, Public Policy, Urban & Community Affairs, Zoos/Aquariums • *Education:* Colleges & Universities • *Health:* Health Or-

ganizations, Hospices, Hospitals, Medical Research, Mental Health • *Social Services:* Community Service Organizations, Emergency Relief, Food/Clothing Distribution, People with Disabilities, United Funds/United Ways, Youth Organizations

Grant Types: capital, employee matching gifts, general support, and scholarship

Geographic Distribution: nationally, with emphasis on Illinois and corporate operating locations

Operating Locations: AL (Birmingham), CA (Fremont, La Miranda, Plaster City, Santa Fe Springs, South Gate, Torrance), FL (Jacksonville), GA (Atlanta, Chamblee), IA (Fort Dodge, Sperry), IL (Chicago), IN (East Chicago, Shoals, Shoals, Wabash), LA (New Orleans, New Orleans), MA (Boston), MD (Baltimore), MI (Detroit), MN (Cloquet, Red Wing), MO (North Kansas City), MS (Greenville), NC (Spruce Pine), NJ (Clark, Port Reading), NV (Empire, Empire), NY (Oakfield, Oakfield, Oakfield, Stony Point), OH (Gypsum, Tipp City, Westlake), OK (Southard), TX (Dallas, Galena Park, Sweetwater), UT (Sigurd), VA (Norfolk, Plasterco), WA (Tacoma, Tacoma), WI (Walworth)

Note: Above is only a partial list of major plant and subsidiary locations.

CORP. OFFICERS

Eugene B. Connolly: *B* New York NY 1932 *ED* Hofstra Univ BS 1954; Hofstra Univ MBA 1964 *CURR EMPL* chmn, ceo: USG Corp *CORP AFFIL* dir: BPB Indus, CGC Inc, US Can Corp *NONPR AFFIL* adv: JL Kellogg Grad Sch Mgmt; dir: Natl Assn Mfrs, Un Way Chicago; mem: Mid-Am Comm *CLUB AFFIL* Biltmore CC, Chicago, Metro

Richard Harrison Fleming: *B* Milwaukee WI 1947 *ED* Univ Pacific 1969; Dartmouth Coll 1971 *CURR EMPL* cfo, vp: USG Corp *CORP AFFIL* pres, treas, dir: USG Foreign Investments Ltd; vp, treas, dir: USG Interiors Inc

Harold E. Pendexter, Jr.: *B* Portland ME 1934 *ED* Bowdoin Coll 1957 *CURR EMPL* sr vp admin, chief admin off: USG Corp

GIVING OFFICERS

Richard Harrison Fleming: treas, trust *CURR EMPL* cfo, vp: USG Corp (see above)

Matthew P. Gonring: vp, trust *CURR EMPL* vp: USG Corp *NONPR AFFIL* vp: Youth Guidance

Peter K. Maitland: dir

Harold E. Pendexter, Jr.: pres, dir *CURR EMPL* sr vp admin, chief admin off: USG Corp (see above)

Donald E. Roller: vp *CURR EMPL* vp: USG Corp

Susan K. Torrey: secy *CURR EMPL* vp, asst secy, dir: USG Interiors Inc *CORP AFFIL* secy, dir: USG Interiors Intl Inc

APPLICATION INFORMATION

Initial Approach: *Initial Contact:* full proposal *Include Information On:* statement of need or problem and summary of background; amount requested and how it will be used; copy of IRS determination letter and most recent financial statements; list of board members; detailed description of proposed project, its purpose, and qualifications of organization to obtain objectives; goals and plan to achieve goals; supporting literature *Deadlines:* none (board meets quarterly); foundation attempts to respond to all proposals within 2 months

Restrictions on Giving: The foundation does not contribute to sectarian organizations having an exclusively religious nature; individuals; political parties, offices, or candidates; fraternal or veterans organizations; primary or secondary schools; organizations that cannot provide adequate accounting records or procedures; or courtesy advertising. In general, organizations already receiving funds through united campaigns will not be considered for additional support.

GRANTS ANALYSIS

Total Grants: $127,153*

Number of Grants: 53

Highest Grant: $25,000

Average Grant: $2,399

Typical Range: $500 to $5,000

Disclosure Period: 1993

Note: Total grants figure excludes $48,940 worth of matching gifts. Recent grants are derived from a 1993 Form 990.

RECENT GRANTS

General

25,000	United Way Crusade of Mercy, Chicago, IL
24,290	National Merit Scholarship Corporation, Evanston, IL
8,000	City of Hope, Duarte, CA
6,500	City of Hope, Duarte, CA
3,600	Chicago Council of Urban Affairs, Chicago, IL

INDIANA

American General Finance Corp. / American General Finance Foundation

Former Foundation Name: Credithrift Financial

Assets: $6.46 billion

Employees: 4,507

Parent Company: American General Finance Inc.

Headquarters: Evansville, IN

SIC Major Group: Personal Credit Institutions

CONTACT

Michelle Dixon
Community Relations Coordinator
American General Finance Corp.
601 NW Second St.
Evansville, IN 47708
(812) 468-5413

Note: Inquiries regarding scholarships should be directed toward the University of Evansville, Director of Financial Aid.

FINANCIAL SUMMARY

Recent Giving: $435,000 (1994 approx.); $386,272 (1993); $388,102 (1992)

Assets: $552,882 (1993); $922,111 (1992); $1,270,565 (1991)

Gifts Received: $1,000 (1992); $202,093 (1988)

Fiscal Note: Company gives through the foundation.

EIN: 35-6042566

CONTRIBUTIONS SUMMARY

Typical Recipients: • *Arts & Humanities:* Arts Associations & Councils, Dance, Libraries, Museums/Galleries, Music, Public Broadcasting, Theater • *Civic & Public Affairs:* Botanical Gardens/Parks, Clubs, Economic Development, General, Housing, Municipalities/Towns, Parades/Festivals, Urban & Community Affairs • *Education:* Agricultural Education, Business Education, Colleges & Universities, Education Funds, Literacy, Private Education (Precollege), Public Education (Precollege), Secondary Education (Public), Student Aid • *Health:* Alzheimers Disease, Arthritis, Cancer, Children's Health/Hospitals, Diabetes, Emergency/Ambulance Services, Heart, Hospices, Hospitals, Medical Rehabilitation, Mental Health, Prenatal Health Issues, Single-Disease Health Associations • *Religion:* Religious Organizations, Religious Welfare • *Science:* Science Museums • *Social Services:* Community Service Organizations, Day Care, Emergency Relief, Family Services, People with Disabilities, Scouts, Senior Services, Shelters/Homelessness, Substance Abuse, United Funds/United Ways, Volunteer Services, YMCA/YWCA/YMHA/YWHA, Youth Organizations

Grant Types: capital, general support, matching, multiyear/continuing support, operating expenses, and scholarship

Geographic Distribution: primarily in IN; emphasis on Evansville, IN

Operating Locations: IN (Evansville), PR, VI

Note: The company has 1,301 offices in 40 states, Puerto Rico, and the Virgin Islands.

CORP. OFFICERS

Michelle Dixon: *CURR EMPL* commun rels coordinator: Am Gen Fin Corp

Daniel Leitch III: *B* Bryn Mawr PA 1933 *ED* Univ PA Wharton Sch 1978 *CURR EMPL* pres, ceo, dir: Am Gen Fin Corp *NONPR AFFIL* dir: Am Fin Svcs Assn, IN Dept Fin Inst

James R. Tuerff: *B* Gary IN 1941 *ED* St Josephs Coll BA 1963 *CURR EMPL* chmn, dir: Am Gen Fin Corp *CORP AFFIL* pres:

Am Gen Corp, Am Gen Life & Accident Ins Co *NONPR AFFIL* fellow: Life Mgmt Inst Soc Houston; mem adv comm: St Josephs Coll

GIVING OFFICERS

Bryan A. Binyon: treas *CURR EMPL* treas: Am Gen Fin Corp

James L. Gleaves: asst treas

Roy L. Hardison: asst secy

Harold Swanson Hook, Sr.: mem *B* Kansas City MO 1931 *ED* Univ MO BS 1953; Univ MO MA 1954 *CURR EMPL* chmn, ceo: Am Gen Corp *CORP AFFIL* chmn: Am Gen Life & Accident Ins Co; dir: Chem Banking Corp, Cooper Indus Inc, Panhandle Eastern Corp, Sprint Corp, TX Commerce Bancshares Inc, TX Commerce Bank NA; fdr, pres: Main Event Mgmt Corp *NONPR AFFIL* dir: Greater Houston Partnership, Houston Assn Life Underwriters, Soc Performing Arts Houston, TX Med Ctr, TX Res League, TX Taxpayers Assn; mem: Beta Gamma Sigma, Exec Mgmt Soc, Natl Assn Life Underwriters, Philosophy Soc TX; mem adv bd: Boy Scouts Am Sam Houston Area Counc; mem natl exec bd: Boy Scouts Am *CLUB AFFIL* Heritage, Petroleum, Ramada, River Oaks CC, Univ

James R. Jerwers: dir *CURR EMPL* sr vp, dir: Am Gen Fin Corp

Daniel Leitch III: chmn, ceo, pres, dir *CURR EMPL* pres, ceo, dir: Am Gen Fin Corp (see above)

David M. McManigal: asst treas

Joseph M. Moore: asst treas

George W. Schmidt: contr, asst secy *CURR EMPL* contr, asst secy: Am Gen Fin Corp

David C. Seeley: mem *CURR EMPL* sr vp, dir: Am Gen Fin Corp

Gary M. Smith: vp, secy, gen coun, dir *CURR EMPL* vp, secy, gen coun: Am Gen Fin Corp

Leonard J. Winiger: asst treas, asst contr

APPLICATION INFORMATION

Initial Approach: *Initial Contact:* application form required for employee-related scholarships; for general support, send brief letter of inquiry and one copy of proposal *Include Information On:* a description of organization, amount requested, proof of tax-exempt status, description of project and population that benefits from project *Deadlines:* June 1 for scholarships; no set deadline for contributions

GRANTS ANALYSIS

Total Grants: $386,272

Number of Grants: 54*

Highest Grant: $82,034

Average Grant: $7,153*

Typical Range: $500 to $25,000

Disclosure Period: 1993

Note: Number of grants and average grant figures do not include scholarships or matching grants to education. Recent grants are derived from a 1993 Form 990.

RECENT GRANTS

Library
500   Willard Library, Evansville, IN

General
82,034	United Way and Related Agencies, Evansville, IN
54,190	University of Evansville, Evansville, IN
54,190	University of Evansville, Evansville, IN
19,920	Field Community Involvement Program
15,000	American Red Cross, Evansville, IN

American United Life Insurance Co. / AUL Foundation Inc.

Income: $608.9 billion
Employees: 880
Headquarters: Indianapolis, IN
SIC Major Group: Life Insurance

CONTACT
Judy Boyle
Corporate Contributions Committee
American United Life Insurance Co.
PO Box 368
Indianapolis, IN 46206-0368
(317) 263-1517

FINANCIAL SUMMARY

Recent Giving: $1,543,000 (1995 est.); $1,462,000 (1994); $1,980,853 (1993)

Assets: $4,000,000 (1995 est.); $3,098,000 (1994); $3,276,101 (1993)

Gifts Received: $973,741 (1993); $115,903 (1988)

Fiscal Note: Figures above include both foundation giving and direct corporate contributions. Foundation giving totaled $539,500 in 1994 and $317,500 in 1993. Above figures include nonmonetary support. The foundation receives contributions from American United Life Insurance Company.

EIN: 31-1146437

CONTRIBUTIONS SUMMARY

Typical Recipients: • *Arts & Humanities:* Arts Associations & Councils, Arts Centers, Libraries, Museums/Galleries, Music, Opera, Performing Arts, Public Broadcasting, Theater, Visual Arts • *Civic & Public Affairs:* Business/Free Enterprise, Economic Development, Employment/Job Training, Legal Aid, Professional & Trade Associations, Urban & Community Affairs, Zoos/Aquariums • *Education:* Colleges & Universities, Economic Education, Legal Education, Medical Education, Minority Education

• *Health:* Health Organizations, Hospitals, Medical Research, Medical Training, Mental Health, Nursing Services, Single-Disease Health Associations • *Social Services:* Animal Protection, Child Welfare, Community Centers, Community Service Organizations, Counseling, Day Care, Delinquency & Criminal Rehabilitation, Domestic Violence, Emergency Relief, Family Services, Food/Clothing Distribution, People with Disabilities, Recreation & Athletics, Senior Services, Shelters/Homelessness, Substance Abuse, United Funds/United Ways, Volunteer Services, Youth Organizations

Grant Types: capital, endowment, and general support

Nonmonetary Support: $100,000 (1994); $20,000 (1993); $15,647 (1992)

Nonmonetary Support Types: in-kind services, loaned employees, loaned executives, and workplace solicitation

Note: The company also provides nonprofits with in-house printing services. Contact person for nonmonetary support is Ron Fritz (see "contact" for further information).

Geographic Distribution: near operating location, with emphasis on Indiana

Operating Locations: IN (Indianapolis)

CORP. OFFICERS

Jim Freeman: *CURR EMPL* vp, corp commun: Am Un Life Ins Co

James W. Murphy: *B* 1936 *CURR EMPL* sr vp corp fin: Am Un Life Ins Co

R. Stephen Radcliffe: *B* 1945 *CURR EMPL* sr vp, chief actuary: Am Un Life Ins Co

Jerry D. Semler: *B* Indianapolis IN 1937 *ED* Purdue Univ BS 1958 *CURR EMPL* chmn, pres, ceo: Am Un Life Ins Co *NONPR AFFIL* bd adv: IN Univ Sch Med; bd assocs: Rose-Hulman Inst Tech; chmn: Ctr Leadership Devel, Noble Fdn; dir: Boy Scouts Am Crossroads Counc, IN Repertory Theatre, IN Sports Corp, Indianapolis Convention & Visit Bur, Jr Achievement Central IN, Life Off Mgmt Assn, Marion County Assn Retarded Citizens, MDRT Fdn, Un Way Central IN; dir, mem exec comm: Commn Downtown; hon dir: 500 Festival Assoc; mem: Alpha Tau Omega, Am Coll Life Underwriters, Health Ins Assn Am, IN Chamber Commerce, Million Dollar Round Table, Natl Assn Life Underwriters, Purdue Univ Pres Counc; mem deans adv counc: Purdue Univ Krannert Sch Mgmt; mem exec comm: Assn IN Life Ins Cos; trust: Eiteljorg Mus

GIVING OFFICERS

Judy Boyle: corp contributions comm

James E. Dora: dir *B* 1936 *ED* Purdue Univ 1958 *CURR EMPL* pres: James E Dora Inc *CORP AFFIL* dir: Am Un Life Ins Co; ptnr: Airport Inn Developers, B&D Assoc, Holiday Inn North, I-70 East Inn Devel

Ron Fritz: chmn, corp contributions comm

James Thomas Morris: dir *B* Terre Haute IN 1943 *ED* IN Univ AB 1965; Butler Univ MBA 1970 *CURR EMPL* chmn, ceo, dir: Indianapolis Water Co *CORP AFFIL* chmn: Utility Data Corp; dir: Am UN Life Ins Co *NONPR AFFIL* dir: Boy Scouts Am, Goodwill Indus IN, Greater Indianapolis Progress Comm, Un Way Greater Indianapolis, YMCA Greater Indianapolis; mem: Indianapolis Chamber Commerce *CLUB AFFIL* Meridian

James W. Murphy: treas *CURR EMPL* sr vp corp fin: Am Un Life Ins Co (see above)

Jerry D. Semler: chmn, dir *CURR EMPL* chmn, pres, ceo: Am Un Life Ins Co (see above)

APPLICATION INFORMATION

Initial Approach: *Initial Contact:* brief letter *Include Information On:* description of the organization, amount requested, purpose for which funds are sought, recently audited financial statement, and proof of tax-exempt status *Deadlines:* by the first of each month

Restrictions on Giving: Does not support individuals, religious organizations for sectarian purposes, or political or lobbying groups.

OTHER THINGS TO KNOW

Foundation only makes contributions to pre-selected organizations.

Corporate direct giving program is open to applicants.

In 1992, company broadened its employee matching gift program to not only colleges and universities but also secondary schools in central Indiana. The company also increased the maximum amount matched from $2,500 for one individual per calendar year to $5,000 per one individual per calendar year.

Company donates at least 2% of its pre-tax income to support charitable organizations.

GRANTS ANALYSIS
Total Grants: $1,462,000
Number of Grants: 229*
Highest Grant: $150,000
Typical Range: $1,000 to $15,000
Disclosure Period: 1994

Note: Above figures include both corporate and foundation giving. In 1994, foundation giving totaled $539,500. Number of grants excludes college matching grants. Recent grants are derived from a 1993 Form 990.

RECENT GRANTS

General
100,000	Life and Leadership Development, Indianapolis, IN — capital fund
34,500	Independent Colleges of Indiana Foundation, Indianapolis, IN — operating and capital funds
25,000	Indiana State University Foundation, Terre Haute, IN — insurance program
25,000	Life and Health Insurance Medical Research Fund, Washington, DC — Otis Bowen research center
15,000	Life and Health Insurance Medical Research Fund, Washington, DC — scholarship fund

Anderson Foundation, John W.

CONTACT
Paul G. Wallace
Secretary and Trustee
John W. Anderson Foundation
402 Wall St.
Valparaiso, IN 46383
(219) 462-4611

FINANCIAL SUMMARY

Recent Giving: $4,951,801 (1992); $4,396,911 (1991); $4,400,000 (1990)

Assets: $127,201,216 (1992); $126,530,817 (1991); $99,731,172 (1989)

EIN: 35-6070695

CONTRIBUTIONS SUMMARY

Donor(s): The John W. Anderson Foundation was established in Indiana in 1967, with funds donated by the late John W. Anderson . Mr. Anderson was both an inventor and president of Anderson Company, a manufacturer of automobile accessories.

Typical Recipients: • *Arts & Humanities:* Libraries, Public Broadcasting • *Civic & Public Affairs:* Law & Justice, Legal Aid, Philanthropic Organizations • *Education:* Colleges & Universities, Continuing Education, Education Associations, Education Funds, Medical Education, Minority Education, Private Education (Precollege), Religious Education, Special Education, Student Aid • *Health:* Cancer, Children's Health/Hospitals, Clinics/Medical Centers, Emergency/Ambulance Services, Health Organizations, Hospices, Mental Health, Nursing Services, Research/Studies Institutes, Single-Disease Health Associations • *Religion:* Churches, Religious Welfare • *Social Services:* At-Risk Youth, Community Service Organizations, Counseling, Delinquency & Criminal Rehabilitation, Family Planning, Family Services, Food/Clothing Distribution, People with Disabilities, United Funds/United Ways, Youth Organizations

Grant Types: general support, project, and research

Geographic Distribution: mainly Lake and Porter counties area of Northwestern Indiana

GIVING OFFICERS

Richard S. Melvin: chmn, trust

William Vinovich: trust

Paul G. Wallace: trust, secy *B* Gary IN 1923 *CURR EMPL* secy, gen couns: Anderson Co

Bruce W. Wargo: trust *B* East Chicago IN 1938 *CURR EMPL* cfo: Nyloncraft

Wilfred G. Wilkins: vchmn, trust

APPLICATION INFORMATION
Initial Approach:

Applicants should submit five copies of a proposal.

Proposals should include the organization's purpose, planned use for the grant, list of officers, financial and budget statements, and proof of tax exemption.

The foundation reports no application deadlines.

Restrictions on Giving: No grants are made to individuals.

OTHER THINGS TO KNOW
Funds for scholarships are provided through universities only.

GRANTS ANALYSIS

Total Grants: $4,951,801

Number of Grants: 186*

Highest Grant: $952,800

Average Grant: $19,142*

Typical Range: $1,500 to $50,000

Disclosure Period: 1992

Note: The average grant figure excludes two grants totaling $1,429,600. Number of grants includes 17 scholarships. Recent grants are derived from a 1992 Form 990.

RECENT GRANTS

General
952,800	Boys and Girls Club of Northwest Indiana, Gary, IN
476,041	Boys and Girls Club of Porter County, Valparaiso, IN
404,000	Indiana University Foundation, Bloomington, IN
322,500	Independent Colleges of Indiana Foundation, Indianapolis, IN
300,000	Purdue University, West Lafayette, IN

Ayres Foundation, Inc.

CONTACT
John E. D. Peacock
President
Ayres Fdn, Inc.
6355 Morenci Trail
Indianapolis, IN 46258
(317) 299-2200

FINANCIAL SUMMARY

Recent Giving: $97,150 (1993); $85,450 (1992); $80,275 (1991)

Assets: $2,167,638 (1993); $2,132,626 (1992); $2,060,704 (1991)

EIN: 35-6018437

CONTRIBUTIONS SUMMARY

Donor(s): L.S. Ayres & Co., the late Theodore B. Griffith and Mrs. Theodore B. Griffith

Typical Recipients: • *Arts & Humanities:* Arts Institutes, Historic Preservation, Libraries, Museums/Galleries, Music, Theater • *Civic & Public Affairs:* Botanical Gardens/Parks, Community Foundations, General, Municipalities/Towns, Zoos/Aquariums • *Education:* Colleges & Universities, Education Funds, Engineering/Technological Education, General, Medical Education, Private Education (Precollege) • *Environment:* Resource Conservation • *Health:* Cancer, Health Organizations, Home-Care Services, Hospitals, Long-Term Care, Nursing Services, Single-Disease Health Associations • *Religion:* Churches, Religious Welfare • *Social Services:* Big Brother/Big Sister, Community Service Organizations, Day Care, Family Planning, Family Services, Food/Clothing Distribution, People with Disabilities, Scouts, Senior Services, Shelters/Homelessness, Volunteer Services, Youth Organizations

Grant Types: capital, general support, and operating expenses

Geographic Distribution: primarily in IN, with emphasis on Indianapolis

Operating Locations: IN (Indianapolis)

GIVING OFFICERS

Lyman S. Ayres: dir *B* Indianapolis IN 1908 *ED* Yale Univ 1930

Daniel F. Evans: vp, treas, dir *B* Crawfordsville IN 1922 *ED* Wabash Coll AB 1943; Harvard Univ MBA 1948; Univ Indianapolis LLD 1969; Wabash Coll LLD 1976 *NONPR AFFIL* chmn: Govs Comm Utility Future; mem: IN Academy, IN Retail Counc, Natl Assn Advancement Colored People, Phi Beta Kappa, Soc IN Pioneers; trust: Oak Hill Cemetery Co, Wabash Coll

Alvin C. Fernandes, Jr.: vp, secy, dir

John E. D. Peacock: pres, dir

William J. Stout: dir *B* Bloomington IN 1914 *ED* IN Univ AB 1937 *CORP AFFIL* pres, dir: Citizens Gas & Coke Utility *NONPR AFFIL* dir: St Richards Day Sch, St Vincent Hosp; mem: Indianapolis Chamber Commerce, Indianapolis Merchants Assn, Indianapolis Personnel Assn, Natl Retail Merchants Assn; pres, dir: Flanner House

David P. Williams III: dir

APPLICATION INFORMATION

Initial Approach: Send brief proposal including name, address, telephone number, proof of IRS tax-exempt status, financial data, nature of request, information on current sources of funding, amount requested, and recently audited financial statement. There are no deadlines.

GRANTS ANALYSIS
Total Grants: $97,150
Number of Grants: 41
Highest Grant: $25,000
Typical Range: $200 to $3,000
Disclosure Period: 1993

Note: Recent grants are derived from a 1993 Form 990.

RECENT GRANTS

Library
1,500	Indianapolis Library Foundation, Indianapolis, IN — operating fund

General
25,000	Indiana University Medical School, Bloomington, IN — capital fund
20,000	Goodwill Industries of Central Indiana, Indianapolis, IN — capital fund
5,000	Indianapolis Foundation, Indianapolis, IN — operating fund
4,500	Associated Colleges of Indiana, Indianapolis, IN — operating fund
3,000	Planned Parenthood, Indianapolis, IN — operating fund

Ball Brothers Foundation

CONTACT
Douglas A. Bakken
Executive Director
Ball Brothers Foundation
PO Box 1408
Muncie, IN 47308
(317) 741-5500

FINANCIAL SUMMARY

Recent Giving: $3,100,000 (1995 est.); $2,500,000 (1994 approx.); $2,983,166 (1993)

Assets: $81,000,000 (1995 est.); $83,000,000 (1994 approx.); $84,456,404 (1993)

Gifts Received: $5,000 (1992); $1,000 (1990); $1,520 (1987)

EIN: 35-0882856

CONTRIBUTIONS SUMMARY

Donor(s): The Ball Brothers Foundation was established in 1926 by Edmund B. Ball, Frank C. Ball, George A. Ball, Lucius L. Ball, and William A. Ball, all of whom are deceased. The estate of Edmund B. Ball provided the foundation's initial endowment, with securities valued at about $3.5 million. His brothers subsequently donated additional money and securities to augment the foundation's assets. The foundation is affiliated with the George and Frances Ball Foundation.

Edmund Burke Ball was one of the founders of the Ball Brothers Company, which grew over the years to become the Ball Corporation, a large and diversified manufacturer whose best-known product is the Ball glass preserving jar.

Typical Recipients: • *Arts & Humanities:* Arts Associations & Councils, Arts Funds, Arts Outreach, Historic Preservation, History & Archaeology, Libraries, Museums/Galleries, Public Broadcasting, Theater • *Civic & Public Affairs:* Botanical Gardens/Parks, Clubs, Community Foundations, Economic Development, Housing, Municipalities/Towns, Philanthropic Organizations, Public Policy, Urban & Community Affairs • *Education:* Business Education, Colleges & Universities, Economic Education, Education Funds, International Exchange, Journalism/Media Education, Literacy, Private Education (Precollege), Public Education (Precollege), Science/Mathematics Education • *Environment:* General, Resource Conservation • *Health:* AIDS/HIV, Heart, Hospitals, Preventive Medicine/Wellness Organizations • *Religion:* Religious Organizations, Religious Welfare • *Social Services:* Community Service Organizations, Family Services, People with Disabilities, Recreation & Athletics, Special Olympics, United Funds/United Ways, YMCA/YWCA/YMHA/YWHA, Youth Organizations

Grant Types: challenge, general support, operating expenses, and project

Geographic Distribution: Indiana

GIVING OFFICERS

Douglas Adair Bakken: exec dir *B* 1939

Edmund Ferdinand Ball: chmn, dir *B* Muncie IN 1905 *CORP AFFIL* dir: Minnetrista Corp

Frank E. Ball: vp, dir *B* 1938 *CURR EMPL* pres: Minnetrista Corp *CORP AFFIL* pres: B B & S Properties Inc

William M. Bracken: dir

John Wesley Fisher: pres, dir *B* Walland TN 1915 *ED* Univ TN BS 1938; Harvard Univ MBA 1942 *CURR EMPL* chmn emeritus: Ball Corp *CORP AFFIL* chmn bd: Am Natl Trust & Investment Co, Corp Innovation Devel; dir: Devon Energy Corp, Kindel Furniture Co, Minnetrista Corp; ptnr: Blackwood & Nichols Corp *NONPR AFFIL* chmn bd dirs: Ball Meml Hosp; mem: Conf Bd, Glass Packaging Inst, Grocery Mfrs Am, IN Academy, IN Chamber Commerce, Muncie Chamber Commerce, Natl Assn Mfrs, Repbl St Fin Comm *CLUB AFFIL* Columbia, Delaware CC, Indianapolis CC, Muncie, Naples YC, Quail CC, Rotary, Royal Provincia CC

Douglas J. Foy: treas, asst secy, dir *CURR EMPL* secy, dir: Pri Pak *CORP AFFIL* secytreas, dir: B B & S Properties Inc, Minnetrista Corp *PHIL AFFIL* treas, asst secy: George and Frances Ball Foundation

Lucina B. Moxley: dir

John J. Pruis: dir *B* Borculo MI 1923 *ED* Western MI Univ BS 1947; Northwestern Univ MA 1949; Northwestern Univ PhD 1951 *NONPR AFFIL* chmn, dir: Ball Meml Hosp; dir: Big Brothers/Big Sisters, IN Legal Fdn, Muncie Symphony Assn, N Central Assn, Un Way Delaware County; mem: Am Assn Higher Ed, Beta Gamma Sigma, Muncie Chamber Commerce, Omicron Delta Kappa, Phi Delta Kappa, Speech Commun Assn *PHIL AFFIL* exec vp, dir: George and Frances Ball Foundation *CLUB AFFIL* Blue Key, Rotary

APPLICATION INFORMATION

Initial Approach:

Applicants should send a detailed letter of inquiry to the foundation.

Letters should include a description of the project; list of staff members; budget; IRS certification of nonprofit status; and a statement indicating the objectives, anticipated results, and method of evaluation of the proposed project.

Letters of application are preferred prior to October.

Restrictions on Giving: The foundation does not fund individual or student grant requests.

OTHER THINGS TO KNOW

The foundation reports that, in addition to grant making, it also offers proposal writing assistance and conducts seminars and workshops.

PUBLICATIONS
Grants list

GRANTS ANALYSIS
Total Grants: $2,983,166
Number of Grants: 62
Highest Grant: $1,400,044
Average Grant: $25,953*
Typical Range: $5,000 to $35,000
Disclosure Period: 1993

Note: The average grant figure excludes the highest grant of $1,400,044. Recent grants are derived from a 1993 Form 990.

RECENT GRANTS

Library
15,000	Indiana University Lilly Library, Bloomington, IN — Ball/Fisher fellowships for visiting scholars

General
600,000	Ball State University Foundation, Muncie, IN — '93 Wings payment
110,000	Community Foundation of Muncie and Delaware County, Muncie, IN — Cardinal Greenways
100,900	Ball State University Foundation, Teachers College, Muncie, IN — PEP Sesame Street
100,000	Ball Memorial Hospital Foundation, Muncie, IN — challenge grant
65,000	United Way, Muncie, IN

Ball Foundation, George and Frances

CONTACT
Joyce M. Beck
Administrative Secretary
George and Frances Ball Foundation
PO Box 1408
Muncie, IN 47308
(317) 741-5500

FINANCIAL SUMMARY

Recent Giving: $3,200,000 (1995 est.); $2,800,000 (1994 approx.); $3,050,000 (1993)

Assets: $68,000,000 (1995 est.); $68,000,000 (1994 approx.); $68,516,260 (1993)

EIN: 35-6033917

CONTRIBUTIONS SUMMARY

Donor(s): The foundation was established in 1937, with the late George A. Ball as donor.

Typical Recipients: • *Arts & Humanities:* Arts Associations & Councils, Arts Festivals, Arts Funds, Historic Preservation, History & Archaeology, Libraries, Museums/Galleries, Music, Public Broadcasting • *Civic & Public Affairs:* Botanical Gardens/Parks, Community Foundations, Economic Development, General, Housing, Philanthropic Organizations, Safety • *Education:* Business Education, Colleges & Universities, Economic Education, Education Funds, Faculty Development, Minority Education, Public Education (Precollege), Secondary Education (Public), Vocational &

Technical Education • *Environment:* General, Resource Conservation • *Health:* Children's Health/Hospitals, Health Organizations, Hospitals, Medical Rehabilitation, Medical Research • *Religion:* Religious Welfare • *Social Services:* Community Service Organizations, Day Care, Family Planning, Family Services, People with Disabilities, Recreation & Athletics, Scouts, Special Olympics, Substance Abuse, United Funds/United Ways, YMCA/YWCA/YMHA/YWHA, Youth Organizations

Grant Types: project

Geographic Distribution: mainly Indiana and immediate surrounding area

GIVING OFFICERS

Stefan Stolen Anderson: dir *B* Madison WI 1934 *ED* Harvard Univ AB 1956; Univ Chicago MBA 1960 *CURR EMPL* chmn, pres, dir: Merchants Natl Bank Muncie *CORP AFFIL* dir: BMH Health Svcs, Fed Reserve Bank Chicago, Maxon Corp; pres: Delaware Advancement Corp, First Merchants Corp *NONPR AFFIL* dir: Commun Fdn Muncie & Delaware County, Delaware County Chamber Commerce, IN Chamber Commerce, Muncie Symphony Assn, Un Way Delaware County; mem: IN Bankers Assn, Independent Bankers Assn IN; trust: Nature Conservancy, YMCA Muncie Family *CLUB AFFIL* Delaware CC, Rotary, Skyline *PHIL AFFIL* trust: Ziegler Foundation, BMH Foundation

Joyce M. Beck: admin secy

Frank A. Bracken: pres, dir *B* 1934

Rosemary B. Bracken: dir emeritus

Douglas J. Foy: treas, asst secy *CURR EMPL* secy, dir: Pri Pak *CORP AFFIL* secytreas, dir: B B & S Properties Inc, Minnetrista Corp *PHIL AFFIL* treas, asst secy, dir: Ball Brothers Foundation

John J. Pruis: exec vp, dir *B* Borculo MI 1923 *ED* Western MI Univ BS 1947; Northwestern Univ MA 1949; Northwestern Univ PhD 1951 *NONPR AFFIL* chmn, dir: Ball Meml Hosp; dir: Big Brothers/Big Sisters, IN Legal Fdn, Muncie Symphony Assn, N Central Assn, Un Way Delaware County; mem: Am Assn Higher Ed, Beta Gamma Sigma, Muncie Chamber Commerce, Omicron Delta Kappa, Phi Delta Kappa, Speech Commun Assn *PHIL AFFIL* dir: Ball Brothers Foundation *CLUB AFFIL* Blue Key, Rotary

Samuel L. Reed: dir

Mary R. Sissel: dir

Robert M. Smitson: dir *B* 1936

APPLICATION INFORMATION

Initial Approach:

Applications should be addressed to the administrative secretary of the foundation.

Applications should include a complete description of the project, budget, and a copy of the organization's IRS tax exemption letter.

Applications are accepted any time.

GRANTS ANALYSIS

Total Grants: $2,800,000

Number of Grants: 40

Highest Grant: $1,000,000

Average Grant: $46,154*

Typical Range: $1,000 to $10,000 and $15,000 to $60,000

Disclosure Period: 1994

Note: The average grant figure excludes the largest grant of $1,000,000. Recent grants are derived from a 1993 Form 990.

RECENT GRANTS

General

896,000	Minnetrista Cultural Foundation, Muncie, IN — Oakhurst Gardens	
500,000	Ball State University Foundation, Muncie, IN — academic excellence	
300,000	BMH Foundation, Muncie, IN — facilities	
250,000	Cardinal Greenway, Muncie, IN — Rails to Trails	
200,000	Berea College, Berea, KY — capital campaign	

CINergy / CINergy Foundation

Former Foundation Name: PSI Energy Foundation
Revenue: $1.12 billion
Employees: 4,154
Headquarters: Plainfield, IN
SIC Major Group: Electric Services

CONTACT

Connie E. Carter
Foundation Assistant
CINergy
251 N Illinois St., Ste. 1400
Indianapolis, IN 46204
(317) 488-3516
Note: The toll free number for the foundation is 800-428-4337. The foundation may be contacted for general information and an application form. However, applicants are requested to submit their proposals to the district office closest to them for review and endorsement. A complete list of district offices is available in the foundation's grant application packet.

FINANCIAL SUMMARY

Recent Giving: $4,000,000 (1995 est.); $1,900,000 (1994 approx.); $1,954,053 (1993)

Fiscal Note: Contributes through foundation only. Above figures include nonmonetary support.

EIN: 03-1755088

CONTRIBUTIONS SUMMARY

Typical Recipients: • *Arts & Humanities:* Ballet, Community Arts, General, History & Archaeology, Libraries, Museums/Galleries, Music, Opera, Performing Arts, Public Broadcasting, Theater • *Civic & Public Affairs:* Botanical Gardens/Parks, Chambers of Commerce, Community Foundations, Economic Development, General, Urban & Community Affairs, Zoos/Aquariums • *Education:* Business-School Partnerships, Colleges & Universities, Education Reform, Elementary Education (Private), Faculty Development, General, Leadership Training, Literacy, Public Education (Precollege), Student Aid • *Environment:* General, Resource Conservation • *Health:* Children's Health/Hospitals, General, Mental Health, Prenatal Health Issues • *Religion:* Religious Welfare • *Social Services:* General, People with Disabilities, Recreation & Athletics, Scouts, Special Olympics, Substance Abuse, United Funds/United Ways, Youth Organizations

Grant Types: conference/seminar, project, scholarship, and seed money

Nonmonetary Support: $100,000 (1993)

Nonmonetary Support Types: donated equipment, in-kind services, and workplace solicitation

Note: The value of nonmonetary support for 1993 is an approximate figure for donated equipment only.

Geographic Distribution: company service area, comprised of 69 counties in Indiana

Operating Locations: IN (Attica, Aurora, Bedford, Bloomington, Brazil, Brookville, Carmel, Cedar Grove, Clarksville, Clinton, Columbus, Connersville, Corydon, Danville, Franklin, Greencastle, Greendale, Greensburg, Greenwood, Huntington, Indianapolis, Kokomo, Lafayette, Lawrenceburg, Madison, Martinsville, New Castle, Noblesville, North Manchester, Princeton, Rising Sun, Rochester, Seymour, Shelbyville, Sullivan, Terre Haute, Vincennes, Wabash, West Harrison), KY (Covington, Newport), OH (Cincinnati, Middletown, Monroe)

CORP. OFFICERS

Renae Conley: *CURR EMPL* gen mgr corp commun: CINergy

Cheryl M. Foley: *B* Warren OH 1947 *ED* Mt Holyoke Coll 1969; Capital Univ Sch Law 1978 *CURR EMPL* vp, secy, gen couns: CINergy

M. Steven Harkness: *B* Princeton IN 1948 *ED* Univ Evansville BS 1970; IN Univ MBA 1985 *CURR EMPL* treas: CINergy *CORP AFFIL* treas: PSI Resources Inc

J. Wayne Leonard: *CURR EMPL* group vp, cfo: CINergy

Jackson H. Randolph: *B* Cincinnati OH 1930 *ED* Univ Cincinnati 1958; Univ Cincinnati 1968 *CURR EMPL* chmn, ceo: CINergy *CORP AFFIL* dir: Cincinnati Fin Corp, Jackson Trust Co NA, PNC Fin Corp; pres, ceo, dir: Lawrenceburg Gas Co, Miami Power Corp, Tri-St Improvement Co, Union Light Heat & Power Co, W Harrison Gas & Electric Co, YGK

James E. Rogers, Jr.: *B* Birmingham AL 1947 *ED* Univ KY 1970 *CURR EMPL* vp: CINergy *CORP AFFIL* chmn, ceo: PSI Resources Inc; dir: Bankers Life Holding Co Inc, NBD IN Inc

GIVING OFFICERS

Constance E. Carter: asst

Cheryl M. Foley: secy *CURR EMPL* vp, secy, gen couns: CINergy (see above)

J. Joseph Hale, Jr.: pres, dir

M. Steven Harkness: treas *CURR EMPL* treas: CINergy (see above)

J. Wayne Leonard: dir *CURR EMPL* group vp, cfo: CINergy (see above)

James E. Rogers, Jr.: chmn *CURR EMPL* vp: CINergy (see above)

Rhonda R. Whitaker: fdn coordinator

APPLICATION INFORMATION

Initial Approach: *Initial Contact:* phone call to request application guidelines and grant application form *Include Information On:* grant application form requests the following information: organization name, address, phone number, and federal tax identification number; name and title of contact person; a brief description of the organization's mission, goals, and objectives; and project information, including name, date of project, total project cost, dollar amount requested, number of people project benefits, county within which project is located, additional counties benefiting from project, project description, and a list of CINergy employees involved in the project and a description of their roles; attachments requested include a copy of 501(c)(3) tax exemption letter; a copy of organization's current budget and the project budget, showing all project revenues and expenses; the names and addresses of the organization's board of directors; and other supplementary material that describe the organization *Deadlines:* January 1, April 1, July 1, and October 1 *Note:* Applicants are encouraged to call the foundation to discuss their proposals prior to submission. Applicants are requested to submit their grant application to the district office closest to them for review and endorsement by the district manager. Managers and employees are involved in the decision-making process, and the foundation reports it is important for the CINergy district manager in applicant's service area to be well informed about project.

Restrictions on Giving: The foundation does not fund advertising; post-event funding; organizations benefiting an individual or a few persons; or veterans, labor, religious, politcal, or fraternal groups.

Generally, gifts for athletic programs and facilities are beyond the scope of foundation's program.

OTHER THINGS TO KNOW

Company is looking for partnerships between the company and organizations that enhance the future of Indiana communities. Grants are for specific projects or designated programs.

Grants are made on a one-year basis. Re-application is necessary for consideration of a grant renewal.

Special consideration is given to programs with a statewide scope that benefit citizens in company's service area.

Some organizations receiving grants from the Cinergy Foundation will be offered the added benefit of an energy audit of their facilities at CINergy's expense. The audit provides the organization with recommendations to save on energy costs.

GRANTS ANALYSIS
Total Grants: $1,954,053

Number of Grants: 734

Highest Grant: $50,000

Average Grant: $2,662

Typical Range: $200 to $5,000

Disclosure Period: 1993

Note: Recent grants are derived from a 1993 grants list.

RECENT GRANTS

Library
Indiana Libraries, IN — for Summer Family Reading Program

General
Bloomington Community Foundation, Bloomington, IN — for endowment building for the community
Boy Scouts of America — for professional position for development of rural scouting
Boy Scouts of America — for statewide programs and services for youth
Brownsburg Community School Corporation, Brownsburg, IN — for Challenger Learning Center
Butler University, Indianapolis, IN — for Partnership for Excellence

Clowes Fund

CONTACT
Allen W. Clowes
President and Treasurer
Clowes Fund
250 E 38th St.
Indianapolis, IN 46205
(317) 923-3264

FINANCIAL SUMMARY
Recent Giving: $1,915,807 (1993); $2,183,512 (1992); $1,686,934 (1991)

Assets: $42,556,679 (1993); $41,240,258 (1992); $48,623,141 (1991)

EIN: 35-1079679

CONTRIBUTIONS SUMMARY
Donor(s): The Clowes Fund was established in 1952 by the late Edith W. Clowes , George H.A. Clowes, and Allen W. Clowes.

Typical Recipients: • *Arts & Humanities:* Arts Associations & Councils, Arts Outreach, Ballet, Dance, Historic Preservation, History & Archaeology, Libraries, Museums/Galleries, Music, Opera, Performing Arts, Public Broadcasting, Theater • *Civic & Public Affairs:* Employment/Job Training, Law & Justice, Philanthropic Organizations, Public Policy, Urban & Community Affairs, Zoos/Aquariums • *Education:* Arts/Humanities Education, Business-School Partnerships, Colleges & Universities, Education Associations, Elementary Education (Public), Literacy, Medical Education, Minority Education, Preschool Education, Private Education (Precollege), Science/Mathematics Education • *Environment:* Wildlife Protection • *Health:* Diabetes, Health Funds, Health Organizations, Hospitals, Hospitals (University Affiliated), Medical Research • *Religion:* Churches, Ministries, Religious Organizations, Religious Welfare • *Science:* Scientific Centers & Institutes, Scientific Labs, Scientific Organizations • *Social Services:* Big Brother/Big Sister, Camps, Child Welfare, Community Service Organizations, Family Planning, Family Services, Food/Clothing Distribution, Homes, People with Disabilities, Recreation & Athletics, Scouts, Shelters/Homelessness, Substance Abuse, United Funds/United Ways, Youth Organizations

Grant Types: capital, endowment, general support, operating expenses, and research

Geographic Distribution: primarily Indiana and Massachusetts

GIVING OFFICERS
Margaret C. Bowles: secy

Alexander W. Clowes: dir

Allen W. Clowes: pres, treas *ED* Harvard Univ 1939

Jonathan J. Clowes: dir

Margaret J. Clowes: vp *ED* Bryn Mawr Coll 1937

Thomas J. Clowes: dir

Byron P. Hollett: dir *PHIL AFFIL* dir: Lilly Endowment

Thomas M. Lofton: dir *B* Indianapolis IN 1929 *CURR EMPL* ptnr: Baker & Daniels *NONPR AFFIL* dir: IN Univ Fdn; mem: Beta Gamma Sigma, Order Coif; mem bd visitors: IN Univ Law Sch *CLUB AFFIL* Masons, Skyline *PHIL AFFIL* chmn: Lilly Endowment

William H. Marshall: dir

APPLICATION INFORMATION
Initial Approach:
Applicants should submit a letter or proposal to the fund.

Proposals should include a description of the organization, purpose for which the grant is sought, specific amount requested, budget for the proposal, financial statement, and copy of the IRS ruling of tax-exempt status. Two copies of this information is required. If any of the listed criteria is not included in the proposal, it will be considered unacceptable with no written notice given.

The deadline for applications is January 31.

The fund's board meets once a year between February 1 and June 1 to consider proposals.

Restrictions on Giving: The fund does not make grants to individuals, or for publications, conferences, or seminars.

OTHER THINGS TO KNOW

The fund does not acknowledge receipt of grant proposals. The Clowes Fund does not make available any kind of printed material for distribution and does not have a printed application.

GRANTS ANALYSIS
Total Grants: $1,915,807

Number of Grants: 62

Highest Grant: $280,000

Average Grant: $26,817*

Typical Range: $3,000 to $25,000 and $50,000 to $100,000

Disclosure Period: 1993

Note: The average grant figure excludes the highest grant of $280,000. Recent grants are derived from a 1993 Form 990.

RECENT GRANTS
Library

50,000	Athenaeum Foundation, Indianapolis, IN — roof restoration

General

280,000	Bryn Mawr College, Bryn Mawr, PA — professorship in science and public policy
150,000	Putney School, Putney, VT — renovation of physical plant
100,000	Marine Biological Laboratory, Woods Hole, MA — for the Young Investigators Endowment at Ecosystems Center
75,000	Boy Scouts of America Crossroads of American Council, Indianapolis, IN — swimming pool
75,000	Rockport Apprenticeship, Rockport, ME — renovation of facilities

Cole Foundation, Olive B.

CONTACT
John E. Hogan
Executive Vice President
Olive B. Cole Foundation
6207 Constitution Dr.
Ft. Wayne, IN 46804
(219) 436-2182

FINANCIAL SUMMARY
Recent Giving: $964,025 (fiscal 1994);
$1,470,575 (fiscal 1993); $857,833 (fiscal
1992)

Assets: $21,056,637 (fiscal 1994);
$21,614,181 (fiscal 1993); $20,841,829 (fiscal 1992)

EIN: 35-6040491

CONTRIBUTIONS SUMMARY
Donor(s): The Olive B. Cole Foundation
was established in Indiana in 1954 with
funds donated by the late Richard R. Cole
and Olive B. Cole . Mr. Cole set up the foundation in honor of his mother. The money
for the foundation came from stock in Flint
and Walling, a water pump and conditioner
manufacturer.

Typical Recipients: • *Arts & Humanities:*
Arts Appreciation, Arts Outreach, Dance,
Historic Preservation, Libraries, Museums/Galleries, Music, Opera • *Civic & Public Affairs:* Botanical Gardens/Parks,
Chambers of Commerce, Community Foundations, Economic Development, Employment/Job Training, General,
Municipalities/Towns, Parades/Festivals,
Philanthropic Organizations, Safety, Urban
& Community Affairs, Zoos/Aquariums
• *Education:* Business Education, Colleges
& Universities, Education Associations, Education Funds, Engineering/Technological
Education, General, International Studies,
Literacy, Private Education (Precollege),
Public Education (Precollege), Science/Mathematics Education, Secondary
Education (Public), Special Education, Student Aid • *Environment:* General, Resource
Conservation • *Health:* AIDS/HIV, Cancer,
Emergency/Ambulance Services, Health Organizations, Home-Care Services • *Science:*
Science Exhibits & Fairs • *Social Services:*
Child Welfare, Community Centers, Community Service Organizations, Day Care, Emergency Relief, Food/Clothing Distribution,
People with Disabilities, Recreation & Athletics, Scouts, Senior Services, United
Funds/United Ways, Youth Organizations

Grant Types: capital, general support, loan,
operating expenses, project, and scholarship

Geographic Distribution: primarily Kendallville, Noble County, and northeastern Indiana

GIVING OFFICERS
Donald Fischer: dir

John E. Hogan: exec vp *PHIL AFFIL* pres:
M. E. Raker Foundation; pres, dir: Eloc
Foundation

Maclyn T. Parker: secy, dir *PHIL AFFIL*
vp, dir: Eloc Foundation; dir: Howard P. Arnold Foundation

John N. Pichon: pres *PHIL AFFIL* dir: M.
E. Raker Foundation

Victor B. Porter: dir *B* 1913 *CURR EMPL*
chmn bd: Porter Inc

Paul Schirmeyer: dir

Gwendlyn I. Tipton: scholarship admin, dir

APPLICATION INFORMATION
Initial Approach:
A letter of inquiry is the preferred method
of initial contact.

Applicants must complete an application
form that is supplied upon request. The foundation publishes a statement of its program
policy and application guidelines.

Applications may be submitted any time.
The board meets in February, May, August,
and November.

Applicants will be notified of the board's decision after four months.

Restrictions on Giving: Scholarship eligibility is limited to residents of Noble
County or graduates of Noble County, IN,
secondary schools. Grants are not given to
individuals, religious organizations, or funds
for redistribution.

OTHER THINGS TO KNOW
Scholarship applications also are available
at high school offices throughout Noble
County, IN.

PUBLICATIONS
Application form

GRANTS ANALYSIS
Total Grants: $964,025*

Number of Grants: 48*

Highest Grant: $200,000

Average Grant: $20,084*

Typical Range: $5,000 to $30,000

Disclosure Period: fiscal year ending
March 31, 1994

Note: Above figures exclude $154,841 in
scholarships designated for individuals. Recent grants are derived from a fiscal 1994
Form 990.

RECENT GRANTS

Library

5,000	Joyce Public Library, Orlando, IN — for upgrading and expansion	

General

200,000	Noble County Community Foundation, Albion, IN — for establishment	
100,000	LaGrange County Community Foundation, LaGrange, IN — for operating budget	
100,000	Steuben County Community Foundation, Angola, IN — for operating funds	
40,000	Community Harvest Food Bank, Ft. Wayne, IN	
34,000	Nature Conservancy, Indianapolis, IN — for	

Hoosier Landscapes: Saving
Our Last Great Places

Cummins Engine Co. / Cummins Engine Foundation

Revenue: $4.73 billion
Employees: 23,400
Headquarters: Columbus, IN
SIC Major Group: Automotive Services Nec
and Internal Combustion Engines Nec

CONTACT
Adele J. Vincent
Executive Director
Cummins Engine Fdn.
Box 3005, Mail Code 60814
Columbus, IN 47202
(812) 377-3114

FINANCIAL SUMMARY
Recent Giving: $3,000,000 (fiscal 1995
est.); $2,644,264 (fiscal 1994); $1,992,336
(fiscal 1992)

Assets: $4,614,350 (fiscal 1994); $600,000
(fiscal 1992); $3,293,202 (fiscal 1991)

Gifts Received: $4,000,000 (fiscal 1994)

Fiscal Note: Above figures are for foundation only. Foundation awards 90% to 95% of
all corporate support; balance is direct corporate, subsidiary, and nonmonetary contributions. The company operates on a fiscal
calendar from March through February.
Above figures exclude nonmonetary support. In fiscal 1994, the foundation received
contributions from Fleetguard, Inc.

EIN: 35-6042373

CONTRIBUTIONS SUMMARY
Typical Recipients: • *Arts & Humanities:*
Arts Appreciation, Arts Associations &
Councils, Arts Festivals, Arts Funds, Community Arts, Dance, Historic Preservation,
Libraries, Museums/Galleries, Music, Performing Arts, Public Broadcasting • *Civic &
Public Affairs:* Botanical Gardens/Parks,
Civil Rights, Economic Development, Employment/Job Training, Housing, Legal Aid,
Municipalities/Towns, Public Policy, Rural
Affairs, Urban & Community Affairs,
Women's Affairs • *Education:* Arts/Humanities Education, Business Education, Colleges & Universities, Community & Junior
Colleges, Education Funds, Elementary Education (Private), Engineering/Technological
Education, International Exchange, Minority
Education, Private Education (Precollege),
Public Education (Precollege), Science/Mathematics Education • *Environment:*
General • *Health:* Hospices, Mental Health,
Public Health • *International:* Foreign Educational Institutions, International Peace &
Security Issues, International Relations • *Social Services:* Child Welfare, Community
Centers, Community Service Organizations,
Counseling, Domestic Violence, Emergency
Relief, Family Planning, Family Services,
Food/Clothing Distribution, Senior Services,
Shelters/Homelessness, Substance Abuse,

United Funds/United Ways, Volunteer Services, Youth Organizations

Grant Types: capital, challenge, conference/seminar, employee matching gifts, endowment, general support, project, and seed money

Nonmonetary Support: $95,000 (fiscal 1990); $200,000 (fiscal 1989); $25,000 (fiscal 1988)

Nonmonetary Support Types: donated equipment and loaned executives

Note: The company committed to a program in Indiana to donate unwanted computers to schools. Value of the gifts is unavailable.

Geographic Distribution: funds local projects only in locations where company has manufacturing operations; gives limited support to selected national and international organizations

Operating Locations: IA (Lake Mills), IN (Columbus, Madison, Seymour), NC (Rocky Mount), NY (Jamestown), OH (Findlay, Fostoria), SC (Charleston), SD (Sioux Falls), TN (Cookeville, Memphis)

CORP. OFFICERS

James Alan Henderson: *B* South Bend IN 1934 *ED* Princeton Univ AB 1956; Harvard Univ 1961-1963 *CURR EMPL* pres, coo, dir: Cummins Engine Co Inc *CORP AFFIL* dir: Ameritech Corp, Inland Steel Indus Inc, Landmark Communs Inc, Rohm & Haas Co *NONPR AFFIL* trust: Culver Ed Fdn; trust, chmn exec comm: Princeton Univ *PHIL AFFIL* dir: Ameritech Foundation

Henry Brewer Schacht: *B* Erie PA 1934 *ED* Yale Univ BS 1956; Harvard Univ MBA 1962 *CURR EMPL* chmn, ceo: Cummins Engine Co Inc *CORP AFFIL* dir: Aluminum Co Am, AT&T, CBS Inc, Chase Manhattan Bank NA Inc, Chase Manhattan Corp *NONPR AFFIL* dir: Bus Enterprise Trust, Bus Roundtable; mem: Bus Counc, Counc Foreign Rels, Harvard Univ Grad Sch Bus Admin Assocs, Mgmt Execs Soc, Tau Beta Pi; sr mem: Conf Bd; trust: Brookings Inst, Comm Econ Devel, Yale Corp *PHIL AFFIL* chmn bd: Ford Foundation

GIVING OFFICERS

Mark E. Chesnut: dir *CURR EMPL* vp plan & org effectiveness: Cummins Engine Co Inc

George Fauerbach, Jr.: dir *B* New York NY 1946 *ED* GA Inst Tech BSME 1968; Univ VA MBA 1973 *CURR EMPL* vp power systems group: Cummins Engine Co Inc *CORP AFFIL* chmn: Cummins Power Generation Inc, Onan Corp

Hanna Holborn Gray, PhD: dir *B* Heidelberg Germany 1930 *ED* Bryn Mawr Coll AB 1950; Harvard Univ PhD 1957; Yale Univ MA 1971 *CORP AFFIL* dir: Ameritech Corp, Atlantic Richfield Co, Cummins Engine Co Inc, JP Morgan & Co, Morgan Guaranty Trust Co *NONPR AFFIL* bd overseers: Marlboro Sch Music; bd regents: Smithsonian Inst; dir: Chicago Counc Foreign Rels; fellow: Am Acad Arts & Sci; hon fellow: Oxford Univ, St Anns Coll; mem: Am Philosophical Soc, Natl Acad Ed, Phi Beta Kappa, Renaissance Soc Am; mem bd overseers: Harvard Univ; prof: Univ Chicago;

trust: Bryn Mawr Coll *PHIL AFFIL* trust: Howard Hughes Medical Institute

Peter Bannerman Hamilton: dir *B* Philadelphia PA 1946 *ED* Princeton Univ AB 1968; Yale Univ JD 1971 *CURR EMPL* vp, cfo: Cummins Engine Co Inc *CORP AFFIL* dir: Kemper Corp; treas, dir: Cadec Sys Inc

James Alan Henderson: vchmn, dir *CURR EMPL* pres, coo, dir: Cummins Engine Co Inc *PHIL AFFIL* dir: Ameritech Foundation (see above)

Joseph C. High: dir

F. Joseph Loughrey: dir *CORP AFFIL* dir: Onan Corp

Ted Leroy Marston: dir *CURR EMPL* consult: Cummins Engine Co Inc

Joseph Irwin Miller: dir *B* Columbus IN 1909 *ED* Yale Univ AB 1931; Oxford Univ MA 1933 *CURR EMPL* chmn exec comm, chmn fin comm, dir: Cummins Engine Co Inc *CORP AFFIL* chmn exec comm, dir: Irwin-Union Corp; dir: Irwin Fin Corp *NONPR AFFIL* fellow: Am Acad Arts & Sci, Branford Coll, Royal Inst; hon fellow: Balliol Coll, British Archts, Royal Inst British Archts; mem: Am Philosophical Soc, Beta Gamma Sigma, Bus Counc, Conf Bd, Phi Beta Kappa; trust: Natl Humanities Ctr *PHIL AFFIL* dir: Irwin-Sweeney-Miller Foundation

William Irwin Miller: dir *B* Indianapolis IN 1956 *ED* Yale Univ BA 1978; Stanford Univ MBA 1981 *CURR EMPL* chmn: Irwin Fin Corp *CORP AFFIL* chmn: Tipton Lakes Co; dir: Cummins Engine Co Inc, Irwin Union Corp *NONPR AFFIL* dir: Am Pub Radio St Paul; trust: Christian Theological Seminary, Taft Sch *PHIL AFFIL* dir: Irwin-Sweeney-Miller Foundation; trust: Xenia S. and Irwin Miller Trust, Clementine M. Tangeman Trust

Brenda S. Pitte: dir

Henry Brewer Schacht: vchmn, dir *CURR EMPL* chmn, ceo: Cummins Engine Co Inc *PHIL AFFIL* chmn bd: Ford Foundation (see above)

Theodore Mathew Solso: dir *B* Spokane WA 1947 *ED* DePauw Univ 1969; Harvard Univ MBA 1971 *CURR EMPL* exec vp oper: Cummins Engine Co Inc *CORP AFFIL* chmn: Holset Engring Co Ltd, Onan Corp; dir: AMAX Inc, Dampers Iberica SA, Kirloska Cummins Ltd

Richard B. Stoner, Jr.: vchmn *B* Indianapolis IN 1946 *CURR EMPL* pres: Holset Engring Co Ltd (England) *CORP AFFIL* chmn: Dampers Iberica SA, Dampers SA; pres: Holset Engg Co USA, Onan Corp; vp: Cummins Power Generation Inc

Adele J. Vincent: exec dir

Bernard Joseph White: dir *NONPR AFFIL* assoc dean, prof: Univ MI Sch Bus Admin

APPLICATION INFORMATION
Initial Approach: *Initial Contact:* written inquiry or proposal; local projects outside Indiana should be sent to local plant manager *Include Information On:* brief description of problem being addressed, what program hopes to achieve, operating plan and cost, description of key leadership, criteria for

evaluating success of program, and documentation of tax-exempt status *Deadlines:* none

Restrictions on Giving: Does not support political causes or candidates, sectarian religious activities, fraternal organizations, goodwill advertising, or individuals. Scholarships only go to employees' children.

OTHER THINGS TO KNOW
Cummins contributes 5% of its domestic pretax profits and 1% of its international profits for charitable activities.

GRANTS ANALYSIS
Total Grants: $2,644,264

Number of Grants: 200*

Highest Grant: $530,000

Average Grant: $23,492*

Typical Range: $1,000 to $10,000 and $10,000 to $25,000

Disclosure Period: fiscal year ending February 28, 1994

Note: Number of grants and average grant figures are approximations. Recent grants are derived from a fiscal 1994 Form 990.

RECENT GRANTS

General

530,000	City of Columbus, Columbus, IN — donation of land to Mill Race Park
100,000	Bartholomew Consolidated School Corporation, Columbus, IN — architect fees for expansion of Northside and Schmitt schools
50,000	Otter Creek, Columbus, IN — architect fees for expansion of golf course
50,000	South Africa Free Elections Fund, New York, NY — support for non-partisan voter education and registration in preparation for the April 1994 elections
40,000	North Carolina Wesleyan College, Rocky Mt., NC — support for capital campaign

Dekko Foundation

CONTACT
Myrna Zymslony
Program Officer
Dekko Foundation
PO Box 548
Kendallville, IN 46755-0548
(219) 347-1278
Note: The foundation can be contacted directly at 1208 Lakeside Dr., Kendallville, IN 46775.

FINANCIAL SUMMARY
Recent Giving: $3,589,168 (fiscal 1993); $1,385,603 (fiscal 1992); $1,131,872 (fiscal 1991)

Assets: $73,649,524 (fiscal 1993); $46,207,967 (fiscal 1992); $28,578,525 (fiscal 1991)

Gifts Received: $25,433,987 (fiscal 1993); $15,464,000 (fiscal 1992); $9,576,000 (fiscal 1991)

Fiscal Note: In fiscal 1993, the foundation received $25,430,462 from the estate of Chester E. Dekko. In fiscal 1992, the foundation received $15,400,000 from the late Chester E. Dekko. In fiscal 1991, the foundation received $9,550,000 from the late Chester E. Dekko, former president and donor of the Dekko Foundation.

EIN: 35-1528135

CONTRIBUTIONS SUMMARY

Donor(s): The foundation was established in 1981 by its founder and donor, the late Chester E. Dekko . Dekko also formerly served as the chairman, president, and chief executive officer of Group Dekko International in Kendallville, IN. The company manufactured electric current-carrying wiring equipment and was formerly known as Lyall Electric.

Typical Recipients: • *Arts & Humanities:* Arts Outreach, Historic Preservation, History & Archaeology, Libraries, Museums/Galleries • *Civic & Public Affairs:* Botanical Gardens/Parks, Community Foundations, Economic Development, Law & Justice, Municipalities/Towns, Philanthropic Organizations, Public Policy, Safety, Urban & Community Affairs, Women's Affairs • *Education:* Arts/Humanities Education, Colleges & Universities, Elementary Education (Public), Engineering/Technological Education, Faculty Development, International Studies, Literacy, Minority Education, Private Education (Precollege), Public Education (Precollege), Religious Education, Science/Mathematics Education, Secondary Education (Public), Student Aid, Vocational & Technical Education • *Social Services:* Big Brother/Big Sister, Child Welfare, Day Care, Domestic Violence, Food/Clothing Distribution, People with Disabilities, Recreation & Athletics, Senior Services, YMCA/YWCA/YMHA/YWHA

Grant Types: general support

Geographic Distribution: focus on communities in which Group Dekko International has plants, including Noble, Steuben, Whitley, DeKalb, LaGrange, and Kosciusko, IN; Union, Clarke, Lucas, Ringgold, and Decatur, IA; Limestone, AL; Collier, FL; and El Paso, TX

GIVING OFFICERS

Chester E. Dekko, Jr.: pres *B* 1954

Erica Dekko: vp

Lorene Dekko Salsbery: vp *B* 1961

Linda Speakman: secy-treas

Myrna Zymslony: program off

APPLICATION INFORMATION

Initial Approach:

Applicants should send a written grant request.

The grant request should include the following: name and address of the organization requesting funds; copy of the IRS 501(c)(3) letter of exemption; statement of purpose and principal service of organization; organization affiliations; name, title, and address of person making application; detailed project description; complete project budget; timeline for completion of project; list of all sources and other requests for funds for this particular project; and a statement of how this program will affect the local community in which Group Dekko International has a plant. Applicants should allow approximately three months for a decision on the proposal.

There are no deadlines for submitting proposals.

PUBLICATIONS

Application guidelines

GRANTS ANALYSIS

Total Grants: $3,589,168

Number of Grants: 193

Highest Grant: $510,000

Average Grant: $18,597

Typical Range: $1,000 to $75,000

Disclosure Period: fiscal year ending August 31, 1993

Note: Recent grants are derived from a fiscal 1993 Form 990.

RECENT GRANTS

Library

22,483	LaGrange County Library, LaGrange, IN
10,000	Noble County Community Fair, Albion, IN — to establish library flag fund

General

510,000	Limestone Area Community Foundation, Athens, AL
510,000	South Central Iowa Community Foundation, IA
500,000	Noble County Community Foundation, Albion, IN — for Central Noble auditorium
250,000	University of Minnesota Foundation, Minneapolis, MN
250,000	Whitley County YMCA, Columbia City, IN

First Source Corp. / First Source Corp. Foundation

Income: $16.72 million
Employees: 732
Headquarters: South Bend, IN
SIC Major Group: Depository Institutions, Holding & Other Investment Offices, Insurance Agents, Brokers & Service, and Transportation Services

CONTACT

Mary Sonneborn Hugus
Trust Officer
First Source Corp.
c/o First Source Bank
PO Box 1602
South Bend, IN 46601
(219) 236-2790

FINANCIAL SUMMARY

Recent Giving: $241,150 (1993); $156,600 (1992); $127,898 (1991)

Assets: $2,780,184 (1993); $2,466,984 (1992); $2,225,390 (1991)

Gifts Received: $258,445 (1993); $195,000 (1992); $59,151 (1989)

Fiscal Note: In 1993, contributions were received from 1st Source Corp.

EIN: 35-6034211

CONTRIBUTIONS SUMMARY

Typical Recipients: • *Arts & Humanities:* Arts Centers, History & Archaeology, Libraries, Museums/Galleries, Music, Public Broadcasting • *Civic & Public Affairs:* Business/Free Enterprise, Community Foundations, Economic Development, Economic Policy, General, Housing, Minority Business, Municipalities/Towns, Parades/Festivals, Urban & Community Affairs • *Education:* Arts/Humanities Education, Business Education, Colleges & Universities, Economic Education, Education Associations, Engineering/Technological Education, General, Private Education (Precollege), Student Aid • *Health:* Health Funds, Health Organizations, Hospitals • *Religion:* Religious Organizations, Religious Welfare • *Social Services:* Crime Prevention, Delinquency & Criminal Rehabilitation, People with Disabilities, Recreation & Athletics, Shelters/Homelessness, United Funds/United Ways, YMCA/YWCA/YMHA/YWHA, Youth Organizations

Grant Types: general support

Geographic Distribution: focus on IN

Operating Locations: IN (Hamlet)

CORP. OFFICERS

Christopher J. Murphy III: *B* Washington DC 1946 *ED* Univ Notre Dame BA 1968; Univ VA JD 1971; Harvard Univ Sch Bus Admin MBA 1973 *CURR EMPL* pres, dir: 1st Source Corp *CORP AFFIL* chmn: Discover Re Ins, 1st Source Ins Inc, Memorial Health Sys, Quality Dining, Trust Corp Mortgage; dir: Comair Inc, 1st Source Bank *NONPR AFFIL* adv counc: Arts & Letters, Notre Dame Coll; dir: Natl Assn OTC Cos., South Bend Chamber Commerce; dir, chmn: Natl Assn Publically Traded Cos; intl bd dir, mem: Young Pres Org; mem: Am Bankers Assn, Am Bar Assn, Indiana Bar Assn, Natl Assn Bus Economists, Natl Assn Security Dealers, Robert Morris Assocs, St Joseph County Bar Assn, VA Bar Assn; pres: N Central IN Med Ed Fdn

Ernestine Morris Raclin: *B* South Bend IN 1927 *ED* St Marys Coll 1947; Univ Notre Dame (hon) LLD 1978 *CURR EMPL* chmn, dir: 1st Source Corp *CORP AFFIL* chmn: 1st Natl Bank Chicago, 1st Source Bank; dir: N IN Public Svc Co *NONPR AFFIL* adv bd: IN Univ South Bend; dir: MI Public Broadcasting, Project Future, United Way IN; mem: IN State Chamber Commerce, St Joseph County Chamber Commerce; trust: Univ Notre Dame *CLUB AFFIL* Audubon, Ocean, Signal Point, Summit

GIVING OFFICERS

First Source Bank: trust

Van E. Gates: chmn *PHIL AFFIL* pres: Gates Foundation

Terry Gerber: dir

Joann Meehan: dir

Christopher J. Murphy III: dir *CURR EMPL* pres, dir: 1st Source Corp (see above)

Ernestine Raclin: dir

Ernestine Morris Raclin: dir *CURR EMPL* chmn, dir: 1st Source Corp (see above)

APPLICATION INFORMATION
Initial Approach: Send statement of purpose concerning grant request. There are no deadlines.

GRANTS ANALYSIS
Total Grants: $241,150

Number of Grants: 34

Highest Grant: $100,000

Typical Range: $500 to $46,000

Disclosure Period: 1993

Note: Recent grants are derived from a 1993 Form 990.

RECENT GRANTS

General

100,000	Community Foundation, South Bend, IN
46,000	United Way of St. Joseph County, South Bend, IN
30,000	Community Foundation, South Bend, IN
20,000	Community Foundation of St. Joseph County, South Bend, IN
7,500	Homeless Center, Notre Dame, IN

Fort Wayne National Bank / Fort Wayne National Bank Foundation

Sales: $84.68 million
Employees: 682
Parent Company: Fort Wayne National Corp
Headquarters: Fort Wayne, IN
SIC Major Group: Depository Institutions

CONTACT
Fort Wayne National Bank
110 W Berry St.
PO Box 110
Fort Wayne, IN 46802
(219) 426-0555

FINANCIAL SUMMARY
Recent Giving: $223,273 (fiscal 1993); $197,916 (fiscal 1992)

Assets: $596,218 (fiscal 1993); $414,713 (fiscal 1992)

Gifts Received: $400,000 (fiscal 1993); $400,000 (fiscal 1992)

Fiscal Note: In fiscal 1993, contributions were received from Fort Wayne National Bank.

EIN: 35-6020622

CONTRIBUTIONS SUMMARY
Typical Recipients: • *Arts & Humanities:* Arts Associations & Councils, Libraries, Public Broadcasting • *Civic & Public Affairs:* Botanical Gardens/Parks, Parades/Festivals, Zoos/Aquariums • *Education:* Business Education, Education Funds, Engineering/Technological Education, Minority Education • *Health:* Hospitals • *Religion:* Religious Welfare • *Social Services:* Big Brother/Big Sister, Community Service Organizations, People with Disabilities, Recreation & Athletics, United Funds/United Ways, YMCA/YWCA/YMHA/YWHA

Grant Types: general support

Geographic Distribution: focus on IN

CORP. OFFICERS
M. James Johnston: *CURR EMPL* pres. dir: Fort Wayne National Bank

Jackson R. Lehman: *CURR EMPL* chmn, ceo, dir: Fort Wayne National Bank

Paul E. Shaffer: *CURR EMPL* vchmn: Fort Wayne National Bank

GIVING OFFICERS
Fort Wayne National Bank: trust

APPLICATION INFORMATION
Initial Approach: Send a brief letter of inquiry. Include a description of organization, amount requested, purpose of funds sought, recently audited financial statement, and proof of tax-exempt status. There are no deadlines.

GRANTS ANALYSIS
Total Grants: $223,273

Number of Grants: 22

Highest Grant: $57,875

Typical Range: $1,500 to $10,000

Disclosure Period: fiscal year ending February 28, 1993

Note: Recent grants are derived from a fiscal 1993 Form 990.

RECENT GRANTS

Library

4,000	Allen County Public Library Foundation, Ft. Wayne, IN — for charitable purposes

General

57,875	United Way of Allen County, Ft. Wayne, IN — for charitable purposes
15,000	YMCA, Ft. Wayne, IN — for charitable purposes
15,000	YWCA, Ft. Wayne, IN — for charitable purposes
12,500	Ft. Wayne Bicentennial Council, Ft. Wayne, IN — for charitable purposes
10,000	Ft. Wayne Zoological Society, Ft. Wayne, IN — for charitable purposes

Glick Foundation, Eugene and Marilyn

CONTACT
Barbara Gunn
Director
Eugene and Marilyn Glick Fdn.
PO Box 40177
Indianapolis, IN 46240
(317) 469-5836

FINANCIAL SUMMARY
Recent Giving: $290,157 (fiscal 1993); $193,824 (fiscal 1992); $199,553 (fiscal 1990)

Assets: $10,804,976 (fiscal 1993); $9,213,668 (fiscal 1992); $5,217,699 (fiscal 1990)

Gifts Received: $1,140,750 (fiscal 1993); $1,282,000 (fiscal 1992); $1,000,000 (fiscal 1990)

Fiscal Note: In fiscal 1993, contributions were received from Eugene and Marilyn Glick.

EIN: 35-1549707

CONTRIBUTIONS SUMMARY
Donor(s): Eugene B. Glick, Marilyn K. Glick

Typical Recipients: • *Arts & Humanities:* Arts Associations & Councils, Community Arts, General, Libraries, Museums/Galleries, Music, Opera, Public Broadcasting, Theater • *Civic & Public Affairs:* African American Affairs, Employment/Job Training, General, Nonprofit Management, Public Policy, Women's Affairs, Zoos/Aquariums • *Education:* Colleges & Universities, Education Funds, Public Education (Precollege) • *Health:* Cancer, Diabetes, Emergency/Ambulance Services, Health Organizations, Hospitals, Medical Research, Mental Health, Single-Disease Health Associations • *International:* Foreign Arts Organizations • *Religion:* Jewish Causes, Missionary Activities (Domestic), Religious Organizations, Synagogues/Temples • *Social Services:* Child Welfare, Community Service Organizations, Family Planning, Recreation & Athletics, Scouts, Senior Services, United Funds/United Ways, Youth Organizations

Grant Types: capital, general support, operating expenses, and project

Geographic Distribution: focus on Indianapolis, IN

GIVING OFFICERS
Eugene B. Glick: pres

Marilyn K. Glick: secy, treas

Barbara Gunn: dir

APPLICATION INFORMATION
Initial Approach: Send a brief letter of inquiry. Include a description of organization, amount requested, purpose of funds sought, recently audited financial statement, and proof of tax-exempt status.

GRANTS ANALYSIS
Total Grants: $290,157

Number of Grants: 145

Highest Grant: $48,281

Typical Range: $100 to $45,351

Disclosure Period: fiscal year ending November 30, 1993

Note: Recent grants are derived from a fiscal 1993 Form 990.

RECENT GRANTS

Library
1,000   Indianapolis Marion County Public Library Foundation, Indianapolis, IN — support of summer reading program

General
48,281   Indianapolis Network for Employment and Training, Indianapolis, IN — support of Pro-100 Program

45,351   Indianapolis Network for Employment and Training, Indianapolis, IN — Pro-100 reimbursement

34,000   Indianapolis Jewish Home, Indianapolis, IN — building fund

25,000   Jewish Federation of Greater Indianapolis, Indianapolis, IN — Gene B. Glick Family Rent Loan fund

18,189   Jewish Family and Children's Services, Indianapolis, IN

Griffith Foundation, W. C.

CONTACT
Michael Miner
Senior Vice President-Trust Officer
W. C. Griffith Fdn.
c/o National City Bank
PO Box 5031
Indianapolis, IN 46255
(317) 267-7290

FINANCIAL SUMMARY
Recent Giving: $400,000 (fiscal 1993); $367,500 (fiscal 1992); $349,500 (fiscal 1991)

Assets: $8,485,786 (fiscal 1993); $8,610,580 (fiscal 1992); $7,773,663 (fiscal 1991)

EIN: 35-6007742

CONTRIBUTIONS SUMMARY
Donor(s): the late William C. and Ruth Perry Griffith

Typical Recipients: • *Arts & Humanities:* Arts Associations & Councils, Community Arts, Ethnic & Folk Arts, Historic Preservation, History & Archaeology, Libraries, Museums/Galleries, Music, Opera, Performing Arts, Public Broadcasting, Theater • *Civic & Public Affairs:* Botanical Gardens/Parks, Economic Development, General, Housing, Municipalities/Towns, Parades/Festivals, Public Policy, Safety, Urban & Community Affairs, Zoos/Aquariums • *Education:* Business Education, Colleges & Universities,

Education Funds, Education Reform, Faculty Development, International Studies, Private Education (Precollege), Student Aid • *Environment:* General, Resource Conservation • *Health:* AIDS/HIV, Cancer, Emergency/Ambulance Services, Health Organizations, Hospitals, Medical Rehabilitation, Medical Research, Mental Health, Single-Disease Health Associations • *Religion:* Religious Organizations, Religious Welfare • *Social Services:* Animal Protection, At-Risk Youth, Big Brother/Big Sister, Child Welfare, Community Service Organizations, Counseling, Family Planning, Food/Clothing Distribution, People with Disabilities, Recreation & Athletics, Substance Abuse, United Funds/United Ways, YMCA/YWCA/YMHA/YWHA, Youth Organizations

Grant Types: capital and multiyear/continuing support

Geographic Distribution: focus on Indianapolis, IN

GIVING OFFICERS
Ruthelen Griffith Burns: adv

Charles P. Griffith, Jr.: adv

Walter S. Griffith: adv

William C. Griffith III: adv

Wendy G. Kortepeter: adv

APPLICATION INFORMATION
Initial Approach: Send brief letter of inquiry describing program or project. Include a description of organization, amount requested, purpose of funds sought, recently audited financial statement, and proof of tax-exempt status. There are no deadlines. Board meets in June and November.

Restrictions on Giving: Does not support individuals.

GRANTS ANALYSIS
Total Grants: $400,000

Number of Grants: 83

Highest Grant: $25,000

Typical Range: $1,000 to $25,000

Disclosure Period: fiscal year ending November 30, 1993

Note: Recent grants are derived from a fiscal 1993 Form 990.

RECENT GRANTS

General
25,000   Boys and Girls Clubs of Indianapolis, Indianapolis, IN

25,000   Indianapolis Zoological Society, Indianapolis, IN

25,000   Memorial Sloan-Kettering Cancer Center, New York, NY

20,000   Methodist Hospital Foundation, Indianapolis, IN

15,000   Crossroads Rehabilitation Center, Indianapolis, IN

Habig Foundation, Arnold F.

CONTACT
Arnold F. Habig
President
Arnold F. Habig Fdn.
1500 Main St.
Jasper, IN 47546
(812) 634-1010

FINANCIAL SUMMARY
Recent Giving: $226,706 (1993); $311,109 (1992); $237,711 (1991)

Assets: $3,429,766 (1993); $3,226,742 (1992); $3,052,622 (1991)

Gifts Received: $550 (1992); $50,000 (1991); $73,975 (1990)

Fiscal Note: In 1992, contributions were received from Arnold F. Habig.

EIN: 35-6074146

CONTRIBUTIONS SUMMARY
Donor(s): Arnold F. Habig

Typical Recipients: • *Arts & Humanities:* Arts Associations & Councils, Historic Preservation, History & Archaeology, Libraries, Museums/Galleries, Music • *Civic & Public Affairs:* Clubs, General, Philanthropic Organizations, Safety, Urban & Community Affairs • *Education:* Agricultural Education, Arts/Humanities Education, Colleges & Universities, Engineering/Technological Education, Private Education (Precollege), Religious Education, Secondary Education (Public), Student Aid, Vocational & Technical Education • *Environment:* Resource Conservation • *Health:* Emergency/Ambulance Services, Geriatric Health, Hospitals, Long-Term Care, Research/Studies Institutes • *Religion:* Churches, Dioceses, Religious Organizations, Religious Welfare • *Social Services:* Big Brother/Big Sister, Community Service Organizations, Counseling, Crime Prevention, Delinquency & Criminal Rehabilitation, Homes, Scouts, Senior Services, United Funds/United Ways, Youth Organizations

Grant Types: general support

Geographic Distribution: focus on IN

GIVING OFFICERS
Arnold F. Habig: off, pres

Douglas A. Habig: dir *B* Louisville KY 1946 *ED* St Louis Univ BS 1968; IN Univ MBA 1972 *CURR EMPL* pres, ceo, dir: Kimball Intl Inc *CORP AFFIL* chmn, ceo: Kimball Electronics Inc; pres, ceo, dir: Kimball Inc, Kimball Intl Mfg Inc; pres, dir: Harpers Inc, Kimball Intl Mktg, Kimball Intl Transit Inc, W Jefferson Wood Products Inc *PHIL AFFIL* pres, dir: Habig Foundation

John Basil Habig: secy *B* Jasper IN 1933 *ED* Bellarmine Coll BA 1957 *CURR EMPL* sr exec vp, coo, dir: Kimball Intl Inc *CORP AFFIL* dir: Hen/Hills Cabinets, Hospitality Furniture, Springs Valley Bank & Trust Co; sr exec vp: Artec, Kimball Furniture Reproductions Inc, Kimball Piano & Organ Co, Kimball Upholstered Products, Kimco SA, McAllen-Am Corp; sr exec vp, dir: Kimball

Electronics Inc, Kimball Inc, Kimball Intl Mktg, W Jefferson Wood Products Inc; vp, dir: Kimball Intl Transit Inc *PHIL AFFIL* vp, dir: Habig Foundation

Thomas Louis Habig: treas *B* Jasper IN 1928 *ED* Tulane Univ BBA 1950 *CURR EMPL* chmn: Kimball Intl Inc *CORP AFFIL* chmn: Artec, Batesville Am Mfg Co, Chandler Veneers, Dale-Wood Mfg Co, Evansville Veneer & Lumber Co, Greensburg Mfg Co, Heritage Hills, IN Hardwoods, IN Hardwoods Cloverport Mill, Jasper Corp, Jasper Laminates, Jasper Plastics, Kimball Electronics Inc, Kimball Exports Inc, Kimball Furniture Reproductions Inc, Kimball Hospitality Furniture, Kimball Inc, Kimball Intl Mfg Inc, Kimball Intl Mktg, Kimball Intl Transit Inc, Kimball Off Furniture Co, Kimball Piano & Organ Co, Kimball Upholstered Products, Kimball World Inc, Lafayette Mfg Co, McAllen-Am Mfg Co, Natl Off Furniture Co, Tool Pro, W Jefferson Wood Products Inc; dir: Springs Valley Bank & Trust Co; secy, dir: SVB&T *NONPR AFFIL* mem: Am Legion, Sigma Chi *CLUB AFFIL* KC *PHIL AFFIL* chmn, dir: Habig Foundation

APPLICATION INFORMATION
Initial Approach: The foundation has no formal grant application procedure or application form. There are no deadlines.

GRANTS ANALYSIS
Total Grants: $226,706

Number of Grants: 86

Highest Grant: $60,000

Typical Range: $25 to $40,628

Disclosure Period: 1993

Note: Recent grants are derived from a 1993 Form 990.

RECENT GRANTS
Library
90	Jasper Public Library, Jasper, IN	

General
60,000	Sisters of St. Benedict, Ferdinand, IN
40,628	St. Joseph's Church, Jasper, IN
25,000	St. Meinrad Archabbey, St. Meinrad, IN
25,000	University of Evansville, Evansville, IN
21,125	Holy Family School, Tulsa, OK

Hook Drugs / Hook Drug Foundation

Employees: 4,900
Headquarters: Indianapolis, IN
SIC Major Group: Miscellaneous Retail

CONTACT
Hook Drug Fdn.
PO Box 199054
Indianapolis, IN 46219
(216) 487-1000

FINANCIAL SUMMARY
Recent Giving: $171,212 (1993); $122,898 (1992); $134,682 (1991)

Assets: $2,394,909 (1993); $2,334,434 (1992); $2,297,741 (1991)

Gifts Received: $50 (1993); $2,024 (1992); $175 (1991)

EIN: 23-7046664

CONTRIBUTIONS SUMMARY
Typical Recipients: • *Arts & Humanities:* Arts Associations & Councils, Ballet, Dance, Libraries, Museums/Galleries, Music • *Civic & Public Affairs:* Business/Free Enterprise, Economic Development, General, Professional & Trade Associations, Public Policy, Safety, Zoos/Aquariums • *Education:* Agricultural Education, Business Education, Colleges & Universities, Continuing Education, Education Funds, Medical Education, Minority Education, Science/Mathematics Education, Student Aid, Vocational & Technical Education • *Health:* Alzheimers Disease, Clinics/Medical Centers, Diabetes, Emergency/Ambulance Services, Eyes/Blindness, Health Organizations, Hospitals, Medical Rehabilitation, Nursing Services, Single-Disease Health Associations, Transplant Networks/Donor Banks • *Religion:* Ministries, Religious Welfare • *Social Services:* Camps, Child Abuse, Community Service Organizations, Crime Prevention, Day Care, Domestic Violence, Emergency Relief, Family Services, Food/Clothing Distribution, Homes, People with Disabilities, Recreation & Athletics, Scouts, Senior Services, Shelters/Homelessness, Substance Abuse, United Funds/United Ways, Volunteer Services, Youth Organizations

Grant Types: general support and scholarship

Geographic Distribution: Grants are awarded in headquarters and operating communities.

Operating Locations: IL, IN, KY, MI, OH

CORP. OFFICERS
Russell D. Mesalam: *CURR EMPL* pres: Hook Drugs

GIVING OFFICERS
Thomas Dingledy: secy, dir

John J. Kelly: treas, dir

Russell D. Mesalam: pres *CURR EMPL* pres: Hook Drugs (see above)

James Richter: vp, dir *B* Indianapolis IN 1942 *ED* Hanover Coll 1965 *CURR EMPL* vp human resources: Hook-Superx

John R. Roesch: dir

Mark A. Varnau: dir *B* Kokomo IN 1934 *ED* Purdue Univ 1956 *CURR EMPL* vp mktg: Hook Drugs *CORP AFFIL* dir: Marquette Monor

APPLICATION INFORMATION
Initial Approach: Send a brief letter of inquiry and a full proposal. Include a description of organization, amount requested, purpose of funds sought, recently audited financial statement, and proof of tax-exempt status.

Restrictions on Giving: Does not support individuals, religious organizations for sectarian purposes, political or lobbying groups, or organizations outside operating areas.

GRANTS ANALYSIS
Total Grants: $171,212

Number of Grants: 82

Highest Grant: $20,000

Typical Range: $100 to $10,000

Disclosure Period: 1993

Note: Recent grants are derived from a 1993 Form 990.

RECENT GRANTS
General
20,000	Indianapolis Zoological Society, Indianapolis, IN	
20,000	Purdue University Family Pharmacy Project, West Lafayette, IN	
10,000	Boys and Girls Clubs of Indianapolis, Indianapolis, IN	
10,000	Respond Now, Chicago Heights, IL	
6,000	Butler University, Indianapolis, IN	

Inland Container Corp. / Inland Container Corp. Foundation

Revenue: $1.25 billion
Employees: 7,500
Parent Company: Temple-Inland Inc.
Headquarters: Indianapolis, IN
SIC Major Group: Corrugated & Solid Fiber Boxes

CONTACT
Frank F. Hirschman
President
Inland Container Corp. Foundation
4030 Vincennes Rd.
Indianapolis, IN 46268-0937
(317) 879-4308

FINANCIAL SUMMARY
Recent Giving: $1,600,000 (1995 est.); $1,490,000 (1994 approx.); $1,306,726 (1993)

Assets: $13,647,733 (1993); $12,727,592 (1992); $12,895,058 (1991)

Fiscal Note: Company gives through foundation only. Parent company, Temple-Inland Inc., sponsors the Temple-Inland Foundation, an independent giving program (see separate entry). Above figures exclude nonmonetary support.

EIN: 35-6014640

CONTRIBUTIONS SUMMARY
Typical Recipients: • *Arts & Humanities:* Arts Associations & Councils, Arts Centers, Arts Festivals, Arts Funds, Historic Preservation, Libraries, Museums/Galleries, Music, Performing Arts, Public Broadcasting, Theater • *Civic & Public Affairs:* Business/Free Enterprise, Civil Rights, Economic Develop-

ment, Urban & Community Affairs, Zoos/Aquariums • *Education:* Colleges & Universities, Education Associations, Minority Education, Public Education (Precollege), Science/Mathematics Education • *Environment:* General • *Health:* Health Organizations, Hospitals, Single-Disease Health Associations • *Social Services:* Child Welfare, Community Centers, Emergency Relief, People with Disabilities, Senior Services, Shelters/Homelessness, Substance Abuse, United Funds/United Ways, Youth Organizations

Grant Types: capital, general support, operating expenses, and scholarship

Geographic Distribution: near company operating locations

Operating Locations: AL, AR (Fort Smith), CA (Bell, Newark, Ontario, Santa Fe Springs, Tracy), CO (Wheat Ridge), FL (Orlando), GA (Macon, Rome), IL (Chicago), IN (Crawfordsville, Evansville, Indianapolis, Newport), KS (Garden City, Kansas City), KY (Louisville), LA, MN (Shakopee), MO (St. Louis), MS (Hattiesburg), NE (Omaha), NJ (Spotswood), OH (Middletown), PA (Biglerville, Erie, Hazleton), SC (Lexington, Rock Hill), TN (Elizabethtown, New Johnsonville), TX (Dallas, Edinburg, Orange), VA (Richmond, Winchester), WI (Milwaukee)

CORP. OFFICERS
Patricia Foley: *B* Buffalo NY 1942 *ED* IN Univ 1971; IN Univ MBA 1977 *CURR EMPL* asst secy: Inland Container Corp *NONPR AFFIL* asst treas, dir: Campfire Girls

James C. Foxworthy: *CURR EMPL* vp human resources: Inland Container Corp

Frank Frederick Hirschman: *B* Indianapolis IN 1936 *ED* DePauw Univ 1958; Northwestern Univ 1960 *CURR EMPL* asst vp fin, asst secy: Inland Container Corp

William B. Howes: *B* Washington DC 1937 *ED* Furman Univ 1959; Harvard Univ 1976 *CURR EMPL* chmn, ceo: Inland Container Corp

Joseph Ernest Tomlinson: *B* Sycamore IL 1939 *ED* Univ IL BS 1962 *CURR EMPL* vp, treas, contr: Inland Container Corp *CLUB AFFIL* Crooked Stick GC

GIVING OFFICERS
Patricia Foley: secy, treas, dir *CURR EMPL* asst secy: Inland Container Corp (see above)

James C. Foxworthy: vp, dir *CURR EMPL* vp human resources: Inland Container Corp (see above)

Frank Frederick Hirschman: pres, dir *CURR EMPL* asst vp fin, asst secy: Inland Container Corp (see above)

Steven L. Householder: vp, dir

William B. Howes: vp, dir *CURR EMPL* chmn, ceo: Inland Container Corp (see above)

Joseph Ernest Tomlinson: vp, treas, contr: Inland Container Corp (see above)

APPLICATION INFORMATION
Initial Approach: *Initial Contact:* brief letter *Include Information On:* description of project and sponsoring organization, project's importance and relevance to foundation, geographic area served, total funds needed, amount requested, other sources of income, and, if appropriate, other organizations being approached for funding *Deadlines:* prior to October 30 *Note:* Requests from operating communities outside of Indianapolis should be sent to nearest site manager for initial review.

Restrictions on Giving: The foundation does not support individuals, religious organizations for sectarian purposes, individual professors or departments within universities, organizations or projects outside operating locations or headquarter areas, dinners or special events, fraternal organizations, goodwill advertising, or political or lobbying groups.

GRANTS ANALYSIS
Total Grants: $1,490,000*

Average Grant: $1,000*

Typical Range: $100 to $2,500

Disclosure Period: 1994

Note: Total Grants figure provided by the company. Average Grant figure is an approximation. Recent grants are derived from a 1993 Form 990.

RECENT GRANTS

General

163,331	Inland Scholarships, Indianapolis, IN
65,519	United Way of Central Indiana, Indianapolis, IN
51,596	United Givers Fund of Rome and Floyd County, Rome, GA
50,477	United Fund of Orange, Orange, TX
18,275	Youth for Understanding, Washington, DC — Foreign Exchange Scholarships

Journal-Gazette Co. / Journal-Gazette Foundation, Inc.

Headquarters: Ft. Wayne, IN
SIC Major Group: Communications

CONTACT
Richard G. Inskeep
President
Journal-Gazette Foundation, Inc.
701 S Clinton St.
Ft. Wayne, IN 46802
(219) 461-8202

FINANCIAL SUMMARY
Recent Giving: $450,000 (1995 est.); $432,640 (1994); $461,085 (1993)

Assets: $3,757,627 (1993); $3,386,692 (1992); $2,962,275 (1991)

Gifts Received: $705,625 (1993); $729,000 (1992); $712,000 (1991)

Fiscal Note: Contributes through foundation only. In 1992, contributions were received from Richard G. Inskeep and Harriett J. Inskeep. Above figures exclude nonmonetary support.

EIN: 31-1134237

CONTRIBUTIONS SUMMARY
Typical Recipients: • *Arts & Humanities:* Arts Appreciation, Arts Associations & Councils, Arts Funds, History & Archaeology, Libraries, Museums/Galleries, Music, Performing Arts, Public Broadcasting, Theater • *Civic & Public Affairs:* Botanical Gardens/Parks, Employment/Job Training, Hispanic Affairs, Municipalities/Towns, Parades/Festivals, Public Policy, Rural Affairs, Urban & Community Affairs, Women's Affairs, Zoos/Aquariums • *Education:* Business Education, Colleges & Universities, Continuing Education, Education Associations, Education Funds, Journalism/Media Education, Literacy, Private Education (Precollege), Public Education (Precollege), Student Aid • *Environment:* Resource Conservation • *Health:* AIDS/HIV, Children's Health/Hospitals, Emergency/Ambulance Services, Health Organizations, Hospitals, Mental Health, Research/Studies Institutes, Single-Disease Health Associations • *Religion:* Churches, Religious Organizations, Religious Welfare • *Science:* Scientific Centers & Institutes • *Social Services:* Camps, Child Welfare, Community Service Organizations, Family Planning, Food/Clothing Distribution, People with Disabilities, Recreation & Athletics, Senior Services, Substance Abuse, United Funds/United Ways, Volunteer Services, Youth Organizations

Grant Types: capital and operating expenses

Geographic Distribution: primarily in northeastern IN

Operating Locations: IN (Ft. Wayne)

CORP. OFFICERS
Richard G. Inskeep: *CURR EMPL* publ: Journal Gazette Co

Craig Klugman: *CURR EMPL* editor: Journal Gazette Co

GIVING OFFICERS
Jerry D. Fox: secy, treas, dir

Harriet J. Inskeep: dir

Richard G. Inskeep: pres, dir *CURR EMPL* publ: Journal Gazette Co (see above)

Julia Inskeep Walda: dir

APPLICATION INFORMATION
Initial Approach: *Initial Contact:* brief letter *Include Information On:* need for financial assistance, period of time assistance is required *Deadlines:* none

Restrictions on Giving: Recipient organization must be in the general geographic area of northeast Indiana.

GRANTS ANALYSIS
Total Grants: $461,085

Number of Grants: 90

Highest Grant: $74,250

Average Grant: $5,123

Typical Range: $500 to $10,000

Disclosure Period: 1993

Note: Recent grants are derived from a 1993 Form 990.

RECENT GRANTS

General

74,250	United Way Allen County, Ft. Wayne, IN — operating
61,600	Indiana University Foundation, Bloomington, IN — operating
28,000	Allen County Stadium Fund, Ft. Wayne, IN — capital
25,605	Ft. Wayne Bicentennial Celebration Council, Ft. Wayne, IN — capital
25,000	Headwaters State Park — capital

Kuehn Foundation

CONTACT
Mary C. Powell
Chairman
Kuehn Fdn.
PO Box 207
Evansville, IN 47702
(812) 476-1709

FINANCIAL SUMMARY
Recent Giving: $302,590 (1993); $168,000 (1992); $116,000 (1991)

Assets: $5,564,720 (1993); $6,142,368 (1992); $5,943,380 (1991)

Gifts Received: $3,330,050 (1991); $98,400 (1990); $3,285,000 (1989)

Fiscal Note: In 1991, contributions were received from Nicholas E. Kuehn Trust.

EIN: 23-7021199

CONTRIBUTIONS SUMMARY
Typical Recipients: • *Arts & Humanities:* Arts Outreach, Ballet, Community Arts, Libraries, Museums/Galleries, Music, Performing Arts, Theater • *Civic & Public Affairs:* Botanical Gardens/Parks, General, Municipalities/Towns, Parades/Festivals, Professional & Trade Associations, Urban & Community Affairs, Women's Affairs, Zoos/Aquariums • *Education:* Business Education, Colleges & Universities, Community & Junior Colleges, General, Private Education (Precollege) • *Environment:* General • *Health:* Emergency/Ambulance Services, Hospices, Hospitals, Medical Rehabilitation, Nursing Services • *International:* Foreign Arts Organizations, International Affairs, International Organizations • *Religion:* Churches, Religious Welfare, Seminaries • *Science:* Science Museums • *Social Services:* Animal Protection, Camps, Child Welfare, Community Centers, Community Service Organizations, Crime Prevention, Delinquency & Criminal Rehabilitation, People with Disabilities, Scouts, United Funds/United Ways, Youth Organizations

Grant Types: general support

Geographic Distribution: focus on IN

GIVING OFFICERS
George Everett Powell, Jr.: vchmn *B* Kansas City MO 1926 *ED* Northwestern Univ 1946 *CURR EMPL* chmn, dir: Yellow Corp *CORP AFFIL* dir: Butler Mfg Co, First Natl Charter Corp *NONPR AFFIL* assoc trust: Nelson-Atkins Mus Art; bd govs: Kansas City Art Inst; dir: Kansas City Symphony; mem: Kansas City Chamber Commerce, Northwestern Univ Bus Adv Comm; trust, mem exec comm: MidWest Res Inst *PHIL AFFIL* pres, dir: Powell Family Foundation; trust: Yellow Corporate Foundation

Mary C. Powell: chmn

Nicholas K. Powell: secy *PHIL AFFIL* dir: Powell Family Foundation

Peter E. Powell: trust

Richard K. Powell: trust

APPLICATION INFORMATION
Initial Approach: The foundation has no formal grant application procedure or application form. There are no deadlines.

GRANTS ANALYSIS
Total Grants: $302,590

Number of Grants: 54

Highest Grant: $150,000

Typical Range: $250 to $25,000

Disclosure Period: 1993

Note: Recent grants are derived from a 1993 Form 990.

RECENT GRANTS

Library

500	Willard Library, Evansville, IN
250	Winston Churchill Memorial and Library, London, England

General

20,000	Powell Gardens, Kingsville, MO
6,000	Powell Gardens, Kingsville, MO
5,340	Rollins College, Winter Park, FL — Roy E. Crummer Graduate School
5,000	Ad Hoc Group Against Crime, Kansas City, MO
5,000	Wildwood Outdoor Education Center, Lacygne, KS

Leighton-Oare Foundation

CONTACT
Judd C. Leighton
Secretary-Treasurer
Leighton-Oare Foundation
112 W Jefferson Blvd., Ste. 603
South Bend, IN 46601
(219) 232-5977

FINANCIAL SUMMARY
Recent Giving: $1,865,312 (1993); $1,189,922 (1992); $1,233,830 (1991)

Assets: $20,262,436 (1993); $15,089,915 (1992); $14,201,394 (1991)

Gifts Received: $531,443 (1993); $512,180 (1991); $360,000 (1990)

Fiscal Note: In 1993, contributions were received from Judd C. and Mary Morris Leighton.

EIN: 35-6034243

CONTRIBUTIONS SUMMARY
Donor(s): The foundation was incorporated in 1955 by Mary Morris Leighton and Judd C. Leighton.

Typical Recipients: • *Arts & Humanities:* Arts Associations & Councils, Arts Festivals, Dance, History & Archaeology, Libraries, Museums/Galleries, Music, Opera, Public Broadcasting • *Civic & Public Affairs:* Clubs, Community Foundations, Philanthropic Organizations, Safety • *Education:* Arts/Humanities Education, Colleges & Universities, Legal Education, Minority Education, Private Education (Precollege), Science/Mathematics Education • *Health:* Children's Health/Hospitals, Geriatric Health, Health Funds, Multiple Sclerosis, Research/Studies Institutes • *Religion:* Churches • *Social Services:* Community Service Organizations, United Funds/United Ways, YMCA/YWCA/YMHA/YWHA

Grant Types: endowment, general support, and professorship

Geographic Distribution: national, with a focus on Indiana

GIVING OFFICERS
John E. Fink: dir

Nancy L. Ickler: dir

Judd C. Leighton: secy, treas, dir

Mary Morris Leighton: pres, dir

James F. Thornburg: vp, dir

APPLICATION INFORMATION
Initial Approach:

The foundation requests applications be made in writing.

Written applications should include information which supports that the requesting organization is of an educational, scientific, literary, religious, or charitable nature.

The foundation reports that applications should be submitted so as to allow reasonable time to act on an application.

Restrictions on Giving: The foundation does not make grants to individuals, or for capital, endowment, or emergency funds, operating budgets, annual campaigns, seed money, deficit financing, matching gifts, scholarships, fellowships, or loans.

GRANTS ANALYSIS
Total Grants: $1,865,312

Number of Grants: 34

Highest Grant: $498,512

Average Grant: $54,862*

Typical Range: $300 to $1,000 and $10,000 to $200,000

Disclosure Period: 1993

Note: Recent grants are derived from a 1993 Form 990.

RECENT GRANTS
Library

| 200,000 | Hillsdale College, Hillsdale, MI — library addition |

General

250,000	Northwestern University, Chicago, IL — endowed Law School chair and research fund
200,000	Memorial Health Foundation, South Bend, IN — senior center building fund
100,000	Corporation of St. Marys College, Notre Dame, IN — science hall renovation
100,000	Mayo Foundation, Rochester, MN
99,600	Community Foundation of St. Joseph County, South Bend, IN — endowment fund

National Steel Corp.

Sales: $2.42 billion
Employees: 10,000
Parent Company: NKK U.S.A. Corp. and NII Capital Corp.
Headquarters: Mishawaka, IN
SIC Major Group: Primary Metal Industries

CONTACT
Bob Toothman
Controller
National Steel Corp.
4100 Addison Lakes Pkwy.
Mishawaka, IN 46545
(219) 273-7000

FINANCIAL SUMMARY
Fiscal Note: Giving Range: about $450,000 annually

CONTRIBUTIONS SUMMARY
Makes contributions in all traditional categories. Arts interests include museums, libraries, and music. Health funding exclusively supports hospitals. Social services are primarily supported through the United Way. Education support is limited, except through matching gift program. Civic and public affairs also is a low priority.

Typical Recipients: • *Arts & Humanities:* Dance, Historic Preservation, Libraries, Museums/Galleries, Music, Theater • *Civic & Public Affairs:* Business/Free Enterprise, Civil Rights, Economic Development, Employment/Job Training, Public Policy, Safety, Zoos/Aquariums • *Education:* Colleges & Universities • *Health:* Health Organizations • *Religion:* Religious Welfare • *Social Services:* Community Service Organizations, Family Services, People with Disabilities, Senior Services, Substance Abuse, United Funds/United Ways, Youth Organizations

Grant Types: employee matching gifts and general support

Nonmonetary Support Types: donated equipment, loaned employees, and loaned executives

Geographic Distribution: primarily near headquarter and operating locations

Operating Locations: IN (Mishawaka)

CORP. OFFICERS
V. John Goodwin: *CURR EMPL* pres, ceo: Natl Steel

Kokichi Hagiwara: *CURR EMPL* chmn: Natl Steel

APPLICATION INFORMATION
Initial Approach: Send a brief letter including a description of the organization, amount and purpose of funds sought, and proof of tax-exempt status.

Restrictions on Giving: Does not support individuals.

GRANTS ANALYSIS
Typical Range: $1,000 to $3,000

NBD Indiana, Inc.

Parent Company: NBD Bancorp, Inc.
Assets: $45.23 billion
Parent Employees: 18,512
Headquarters: Indianapolis, IN
SIC Major Group: State Commercial Banks

CONTACT
Jean M. Smith
First Vice President, Public Relations & Community Affairs
NBD Indiana, Inc.
One Indiana Sq., Ste. 540
Indianapolis, IN 46266
(317) 266-5271

FINANCIAL SUMMARY
Recent Giving: $1,500,000 (1995 est.); $1,300,000 (1994 approx.); $1,523,000 (1993)

Fiscal Note: All contributions are made directly by the company. The budget for giving from other departments is $70,000 and is included in the above figures. Above figures exclude nonmonetary support.

CONTRIBUTIONS SUMMARY
Typical Recipients: • *Arts & Humanities:* Arts Associations & Councils, Dance, Historic Preservation, Libraries, Museums/Galleries, Music, Opera, Performing Arts, Public Broadcasting, Theater • *Civic & Public Affairs:* Economic Development, Economic Policy, Housing, Zoos/Aquariums • *Education:* Colleges & Universities, Economic Education, Minority Education • *Health:* Hospitals • *Social Services:* Family Services, United Funds/United Ways, Youth Organizations

Grant Types: capital, employee matching gifts, endowment, general support, and operating expenses

Note: Employee matching gift ratio: 1 to 1. Employee matching gift ratio: 2 to 1 for the first $250 given during each calendar year. Above figures exclude nonmonetary support.

Nonmonetary Support Types: loaned employees, loaned executives, and workplace solicitation

Note: Estimated value of nonmonetary support is not available. Please contact Jean M. Smith, vice president, for nonmonetary gifts.

Geographic Distribution: Indiana, with emphasis on central Indiana

Operating Locations: IN (Bloomington, Carmel, Chesterton, Corydon, Delphi, Elkhart, Evansville, Frankfort, Ft. Wayne, Indianapolis, Jeffersonville, Lafayette, Lowell, Marion, Merrillville, Muncie)

CORP. OFFICERS
David T. Fronek: *B* 1943 *CURR EMPL* exec vp, dir commun rels: NBD IN Inc *CORP AFFIL* chmn: NBD Leasing Inc

Andrew J. Paine, Jr.: *B* Chicago IL 1937 *ED* DePauw Univ BA 1959; IN Univ MBA 1967; Rutgers Univ Stonier Grad Sch Banking 1969 *CURR EMPL* vchmn: NBD Bancorp Inc *CORP AFFIL* dir: Hammond Co, Indianapolis Life Ins Co; pres, dir: NBD Bank NA, NBD IN Inc; vchmn: IN Natl Corp; vchmn, dir: INB Fin Corp *NONPR AFFIL* bd govs, mem exec comm: IN Univ Sch Bus Devel Cabinet Assn; chmn ed counc, dir: Indianapolis Chamber Commerce; chmn govt rels counc: Am Bankers Assn; dir: Commun Svc Counc, Un Way Greater Indianapolis; mem: IN Univ Sch Bus Alumni Assn, Indianapolis Mus Art, Young Pres Org; natl bd dirs: Jr Achievement; trust: Childrens Mus, DePauw Univ *CLUB AFFIL* Columbia, Meridian Hills CC *PHIL AFFIL* chmn, trust: Arthur Jordan Foundation

GIVING OFFICERS
Thomas W. Binford: mem commun concerns comm *CURR EMPL* chmn, dir: Binford Assocs *CORP AFFIL* dir: Heritage Mgmt Group, INB Natl Bank *NONPR AFFIL* chmn: Methodist Occupational Health Ctr

Daniel R. Efroymson: mem commun concerns comm *B* Indianapolis IN 1941 *ED* Harvard Univ 1963; George Washington Univ Sch Law 1972 *CURR EMPL* pres, dir: Real Silk Investments Inc *CORP AFFIL* dir: Lincoln Natl Corp *NONPR AFFIL* chmn: Un Way Allocations Subcomm; comm chmn: Off Equal Opportunity; dir: Training Inc; treas: Un Negro Coll Fund IN Campaign

David T. Fronek: *CURR EMPL* exec vp, dir commun rels: NBD IN Inc (see above)

Thomas Milton Miller: mem commun concerns comm *B* Corydon IN 1930 *ED* IN Univ BS 1952; Univ WI Sch Bank Admin 1961 *CURR EMPL* chmn, ceo: INB Fin Corp *CORP AFFIL* chmn: NBD IN Inc; chmn, pres: NBD Bank NA; dir: NBD Bancorp Inc *NONPR AFFIL* chmn, mem exec comm: Indianapolis Convention & Visit Bur; dir, mem exec comm: IN Univ Fdn; mem: Am Bankers Assn, City Bankers Assn, IN Soc Chicago, IN Univ Alumni Assn, Indianapolis Chamber Commerce, Sigma Chi; mem bd advs: IN Univ, Purdue Univ; mem, dir: Assn Bank Holding Cos; mem exec comm, dir: IN Chamber Commerce; trust, mem exec comm: Methodist Hosp *CLUB AFFIL* Econ, IN Univ Varsity, Masons, Meridian Hills CC

Andrew J. Paine, Jr.: pres, ceo *CURR EMPL* vchmn: NBD Bancorp Inc *PHIL AF-*

281

FIL chmn, trust: Arthur Jordan Foundation (see above)

Michael Rodman: mem commun concerns comm *CURR EMPL* vp: NBD IN Inc

Sallie W. Rowland: *CURR EMPL* mem commun concerns comm: NBD IN Inc

Jean M. Smith: vchmn commun concerns comm *CURR EMPL* first vp pub rels & commun aff: NBD IN Inc *NONPR AFFIL* chmn communications comm, mem exec comm: Natl League Cities Congress; mem: Circle City Classic Organizing Comm, Un Way Campaign Cabinet; trust: Winona Health Fdn; trust, mem exec comm: Butler Univ

Edward E. Whitehead: mem commun concerns comm *CURR EMPL* vp: NBD IN Inc

APPLICATION INFORMATION

Initial Approach: *Initial Contact:* letter or proposal *Include Information On:* clear definition of program and its merits; evidence of past success of program and its leaders; proof that bank community will benefit; financial stability; future financing information; other support for program; tax-exempt status; plans to report results; names of entire board, officers, and staff; statement of aims with respect to ethical promotion and fund-raising techniques; most recent balance sheet; income and expense statement for the year; current budget; and unique nature of program *Deadlines:* forty five days in advance of committee meetings, which occur on the second Friday of March, September, and December

Restrictions on Giving: The following categories are not considered for grants: national organizations (health, social services, veterans, business, etc.), political parties and candidates, religious or fraternal organizations, primary or secondary educational institutions (public or private), or individuals.

OTHER THINGS TO KNOW

In 1993, INB National Bank merged with NBD Bancorp. The company reports that its giving program will remain independent and that funding will remain focused on organizations in the Indianapolis area.

GRANTS ANALYSIS

Total Grants: $1,300,000
Disclosure Period: 1994

Note: Recent grants are derived from a partial 1992 grants list.

RECENT GRANTS
General
400,000   United Way

Old National Bank in Evansville / Old National Bank Charitable Trust

Assets: $1.1 billion
Employees: 500
Parent Company: Old National Bancorp.
Headquarters: Evansville, IN
SIC Major Group: National Commercial Banks

CONTACT
Jonathan Weinzapfel
Manager, Public Relations
Old National Bank in Evansville
PO Box 207
Evansville, IN 47702
(812) 464-1507

FINANCIAL SUMMARY
Recent Giving: $313,800 (1994); $234,825 (1993); $259,119 (1992)

Assets: $966,612 (1993); $1,088,588 (1992); $1,076,022 (1991)

Gifts Received: $36,955 (1993); $207,228 (1992); $136,251 (1991)

Fiscal Note: Company primarily gives through its trust; however, a small discretionary budget exists for contributions that fall outside the trust's guidelines.

EIN: 35-6015583

CONTRIBUTIONS SUMMARY
Typical Recipients: • *Arts & Humanities:* Arts Associations & Councils, Community Arts, Dance, General, Historic Preservation, History & Archaeology, Libraries, Museums/Galleries, Music, Performing Arts, Theater • *Civic & Public Affairs:* African American Affairs, Business/Free Enterprise, Clubs, Community Foundations, Economic Development, General, Hispanic Affairs, Housing, Inner-City Development, Minority Business, Municipalities/Towns, Parades/Festivals, Philanthropic Organizations, Professional & Trade Associations, Safety, Urban & Community Affairs, Zoos/Aquariums • *Education:* After-school/Enrichment Programs, Business Education, Colleges & Universities, Education Funds, Elementary Education (Private), General, Private Education (Precollege), Public Education (Precollege), Religious Education, Special Education, Student Aid • *Environment:* General, Resource Conservation • *Health:* Adolescent Health Issues, Children's Health/Hospitals, Clinics/Medical Centers, Emergency/Ambulance Services, General, Health Organizations, Home-Care Services, Hospitals, Medical Rehabilitation, Respiratory • *Religion:* General, Ministries, Religious Organizations, Religious Welfare • *Social Services:* At-Risk Youth, Community Service Organizations, Delinquency & Criminal Rehabilitation, Family Planning, Family Services, Food/Clothing Distribution, General, Recreation & Athletics, Scouts, Shelters/Homelessness, Substance Abuse, United Funds/United Ways, YMCA/YWCA/YMHA/YWHA, Youth Organizations

Grant Types: capital, challenge, conference/seminar, general support, operating expenses, and project

Geographic Distribution: Warrick, Vanderberg, and Posey counties, IN, and Henderson County, KY

Operating Locations: IN (Evansville)

CORP. OFFICERS
Michael R. Hinton: *B* Evansville IN 1954 *ED* Univ Evansville 1975; Univ Evansville 1982 *CURR EMPL* pres, coo, dir: Old Natl Bank Evansville *CORP AFFIL* dir: Old Natl

Svc Corp *NONPR AFFIL* dir: St Marys Med Ctr

James A. Risinger: *B* Logansport IN 1948 *ED* NC St Univ 1971; Rutgers Univ Stonier Grad Sch Banking 1989 *CURR EMPL* chmn, ceo: Old Natl Bank Evansville

Jonathan Weinzapfel: *CURR EMPL* mgr pub rels: Old Natl Bank Evansville

APPLICATION INFORMATION
Initial Approach: *Initial Contact:* one-page letter *Include Information On:* a description of organization, amount requested, who will benefit from the program or project, and proof of tax-exempt status *Deadlines:* none

Restrictions on Giving: Does not support individuals, political or lobbying groups, or organizations outside operating areas.

OTHER THINGS TO KNOW
Profile reflects contributions by the Evansville-headquartered subsidiary of Old National Bancorp. Separate banks administer independent programs.

GRANTS ANALYSIS
Total Grants: $313,800

Typical Range: $500 to $2,000

Disclosure Period: 1994

Note: Recent grants are derived from a 1993 Form 990.

RECENT GRANTS

General
84,717	United Way of Southwestern Indiana, Evansville, IN
22,700	University of Evansville, Evansville, IN
20,166	YMCA
11,300	Rehabilitation Center, Evansville, IN
10,250	University of Southern Indiana, Evansville, IN

Oliver Memorial Trust Foundation

CONTACT
Robijo M. Burzynski
Principal Manager
Oliver Memorial Trust Fdn.
c/o Norwest Bank Indiana, N.A.
112 W Jefferson Blvd.
South Bend, IN 46601
(219) 237-3340

FINANCIAL SUMMARY
Recent Giving: $313,874 (1993); $291,877 (1992); $342,400 (1990)

Assets: $7,564,571 (1993); $7,532,199 (1992); $5,972,829 (1990)

Gifts Received: $50,000 (1993); $450,518 (1992); $40,000 (1990)

Fiscal Note: In 1993, contributions were received from Jane C. Warriner ($25,000) and J. Oliver Cunningham ($25,000).

EIN: 35-6013076

CONTRIBUTIONS SUMMARY

Donor(s): the late C. Frederick Cunningham, Gertrude Oliver Cunningham, the late Walter C. Steenburg, Jane Cunningham Wanner, J. Oliver Cunningham.

Typical Recipients: • *Arts & Humanities:* Arts Associations & Councils, Community Arts, Historic Preservation, History & Archaeology, Libraries, Museums/Galleries, Music • *Civic & Public Affairs:* Botanical Gardens/Parks, General, Parades/Festivals, Zoos/Aquariums • *Education:* Business Education, Colleges & Universities, Education Associations, Education Funds, Journalism/Media Education, Minority Education, Religious Education, Student Aid • *Health:* Hospitals • *Religion:* Churches, Religious Organizations • *Social Services:* At-Risk Youth, Child Welfare, Community Service Organizations, People with Disabilities, United Funds/United Ways, Youth Organizations

Grant Types: capital, endowment, multi-year/continuing support, and seed money

Geographic Distribution: focus on IN

GIVING OFFICERS
Norwest Bank Indiana, NA: trust

APPLICATION INFORMATION
Initial Approach: Include a description of organization, amount requested, purpose of funds sought, recently audited financial statement, and proof of tax-exempt status. There are no deadlines.

GRANTS ANALYSIS
Total Grants: $313,874

Number of Grants: 25

Highest Grant: $134,930

Typical Range: $300 to $50,000

Disclosure Period: 1993

Note: Recent grants are derived from a 1993 Form 990.

RECENT GRANTS

General

50,000	University of Notre Dame, Notre Dame, IN
25,000	Bethel College, Mishawaka, IN
25,000	Smith College, Northampton, MA
10,500	United Way of St. Joseph County, South Bend, IN
10,000	St. Mary's College, Notre Dame, IN

Plumsock Fund

CONTACT
John G. Rauch, Jr.
Secretary-Treasurer
Plumsock Fund
9292 N Meridian St., Ste. 312
Indianapolis, IN 46260
(317) 846-8115

FINANCIAL SUMMARY
Recent Giving: $1,461,665 (1993); $1,438,799 (1992); $1,300,154 (1991)

Assets: $4,353,563 (1993); $4,560,958 (1992); $6,072,206 (1991)

Gifts Received: $1,466,000 (1993); $1,663,910 (1992); $1,330,000 (1991)

Fiscal Note: In 1993, contributions were received from Sarah L. Lutz ($1,425,000) and Christopher H. Lutz ($41,000).

EIN: 35-6014719

CONTRIBUTIONS SUMMARY

Donor(s): the late Evelyn L. Lutz, Herbert B. Lutz, Sarah L. Lutz

Typical Recipients: • *Arts & Humanities:* Arts Associations & Councils, Arts Centers, Dance, Ethnic & Folk Arts, Historic Preservation, History & Archaeology, Libraries, Literary Arts, Museums/Galleries, Theater • *Civic & Public Affairs:* General, Hispanic Affairs, Native American Affairs, Rural Affairs, Urban & Community Affairs, Women's Affairs • *Education:* Arts/Humanities Education, Colleges & Universities, Engineering/Technological Education, General, Journalism/Media Education, Private Education (Precollege), Social Sciences Education • *Environment:* General, Resource Conservation • *Health:* Hospitals • *International:* Foreign Educational Institutions, Health Care/Hospitals, International Organizations, International Peace & Security Issues • *Religion:* Churches • *Social Services:* Community Service Organizations, Family Planning, United Funds/United Ways, Veterans, Youth Organizations

Grant Types: endowment, general support, and scholarship

Geographic Distribution: national

GIVING OFFICERS
Edwin Fancher: pres

Marianne H. Hughes: asst secy

Dr. Christopher H. Lutz: mng dir

Sarah L. Lutz: dir

John G. Rauch, Jr.: secy, treas

William T. Rauch: asst treas

Daniel A. Wolf: vp

APPLICATION INFORMATION
Initial Approach: Send brief letter of inquiry describing program or project. Include a description of organization, amount requested, purpose of funds sought, recently audited financial statement, and proof of tax-exempt status. There are no deadlines.

Restrictions on Giving: Does not support individuals or provide scholarships or fellowships.

GRANTS ANALYSIS
Total Grants: $1,461,665

Number of Grants: 147*

Highest Grant: $148,500

Typical Range: $100 to $106,000

Disclosure Period: 1993

Note: Recent grants are derived from a 1993 Form 990. Number of grants is approximate.

RECENT GRANTS

Library

8,000	Friends of Manchester Library, Manchester, MA

General

148,500	Center for Regional Mesoamerican Investigations, Antiqua, Guatemala
106,000	Bonnet House, Ft. Lauderdale, FL
61,000	USS Indianapolis Survivors Memorial Organization, Indianapolis, IN
60,000	Gesundheit Institute, Arlington, VA
59,500	CIRMA, South Woodstock, VT

Rieke Corp. / Rieke Corp. Foundation

Employees: 350
Parent Company: TriMas Corp.
Headquarters: Auburn, IN
SIC Major Group: Fabricated Metal Products, Industrial Machinery & Equipment, and Rubber & Miscellaneous Plastics Products

CONTACT
Ricke Corp. Foundation
500 W Seventh St.
Auburn, IN 46706
(219) 925-3700

FINANCIAL SUMMARY
Recent Giving: $28,500 (fiscal 1992); $26,000 (fiscal 1991); $26,000 (fiscal 1990)

Assets: $656,526 (fiscal 1992); $618,346 (fiscal 1991); $517,367 (fiscal 1990)

Gifts Received: $10,000 (fiscal 1992); $10,000 (fiscal 1991); $10,000 (fiscal 1990)

Fiscal Note: In 1992, contributions were received from Rieke Corporation.

EIN: 51-0158651

CONTRIBUTIONS SUMMARY
Typical Recipients: • *Arts & Humanities:* Historic Preservation, History & Archaeology, Libraries, Museums/Galleries • *Civic & Public Affairs:* Chambers of Commerce, Municipalities/Towns, Urban & Community Affairs • *Education:* Special Education • *Health:* Geriatric Health, Health Organizations, Hospitals • *Social Services:* Animal Protection, Child Welfare, Community Service Organizations, People with Disabilities, Senior Services, Substance Abuse, United Funds/United Ways, Youth Organizations

Grant Types: general support

Geographic Distribution: focus on IN

Operating Locations: IN (Auburn)

CORP. OFFICERS
Phil Keedy: *CURR EMPL* pres: Rieke Corp

GIVING OFFICERS
Lincoln National Bank & Trust Co.: trust

Donald E. Kelley: trust

Glenn T. Rieke: trust

Mahlon E. Rieke: trust

APPLICATION INFORMATION
Initial Approach: Submit either a written or personal request. Deadline is August 31.

GRANTS ANALYSIS
Total Grants: $28,500

Number of Grants: 10

Highest Grant: $7,500

Typical Range: $1,000 to $3,000

Disclosure Period: fiscal year ending September 30, 1992

Note: Recent grants are derived from a fiscal 1992 Form 990.

RECENT GRANTS

Library

3,000	Eckhart Public Library, Eckhart, IN

General

7,500	United Way of DeKalb, DeKalb, IN — annual funding
6,000	DeKalb County Council on Aging, DeKalb, IN — William A. Heimach Center
2,000	City of Auburn, Auburn, IN — drug and alcohol resistance education
2,000	DeKalb County Parent Group for Handicapped Children, DeKalb, IN — preschool for handicapped
2,000	DeKalb Humane Society, DeKalb, IN

South Bend Tribune / Schurz Communications Foundation

Employees: 270
Parent Company: Schurz Communications
Headquarters: South Bend, IN
SIC Major Group: Printing & Publishing

CONTACT
James M. Schurz
President
Schurz Communications Foundation
225 W Colfax Ave.
South Bend, IN 46626
(219) 287-1001

FINANCIAL SUMMARY
Recent Giving: $170,788 (1993); $179,505 (1992); $136,883 (1991)

Assets: $957,750 (1993); $1,010,269 (1992); $1,126,714 (1991)

Gifts Received: $85,445 (1993); $40,987 (1992); $50,321 (1991)

Fiscal Note: In 1993, contributions were received from South Bend Tribune ($73,320) and WSBT ($12,125).

EIN: 35-6024357

CONTRIBUTIONS SUMMARY
Typical Recipients: • *Arts & Humanities:* Arts Centers, Arts Festivals, Historic Preservation, History & Archaeology, Libraries, Museums/Galleries, Music, Performing Arts, Public Broadcasting • *Civic & Public Affairs:* Botanical Gardens/Parks, Community Foundations, Municipalities/Towns, Parades/Festivals, Urban & Community Affairs • *Education:* Business Education, Colleges & Universities, Education Funds, Private Education (Precollege) • *Health:* Hospices • *Social Services:* United Funds/United Ways, YMCA/YWCA/YMHA/YWHA, Youth Organizations

Grant Types: general support

Geographic Distribution: limited to South Bend, IN

Operating Locations: IN (South Bend)

CORP. OFFICERS
Todd Schurz: *CURR EMPL* pres, publ, editor, dir: South Bend Tribune

GIVING OFFICERS
John J. McGann: vp

James Montgomery Schurz: pres, dir *B* South Bend IN 1933 *ED* Stanford Univ 1956 *CURR EMPL* vp, dir: Schurz Communs

E. Berry Smith: secy, treas

APPLICATION INFORMATION
Initial Approach: The foundation has no formal grant application procedure or application form. There are no deadlines.

Restrictions on Giving: Limited to the South Bend, IN, area.

GRANTS ANALYSIS
Total Grants: $170,788

Number of Grants: 21

Highest Grant: $50,000

Typical Range: $500 to $40,000

Disclosure Period: 1993

Note: Recent grants are derived from a 1993 Form 990.

RECENT GRANTS

General

50,000	Community Foundation of St. Joseph County, Indianapolis, IN
28,188	United Way of St. Joseph County, South Bend, IN
15,000	University of Notre Dame, Notre Dame, IN — outreach program
12,000	United Way of St. Joseph County, South Bend, IN
5,000	YMCA, Elkhart, IN

Vevay-Switzerland County Foundation

CONTACT
Ralph Tilley
President
Vevay-Switzerland County Fdn.
102 W Main St.
Vevay, IN 47043
(812) 427-2323

FINANCIAL SUMMARY
Recent Giving: $172,500 (1993); $928,471 (1991); $254,844 (1990)

Assets: $4,829,781 (1993); $5,398,056 (1991); $5,723,040 (1990)

Gifts Received: $546,948 (1993); $1,000,000 (1991)

Fiscal Note: In 1993, contributions were received from Paul Ogle Foundation ($500,000).

EIN: 35-1472069

CONTRIBUTIONS SUMMARY
Donor(s): Paul W. Ogle

Typical Recipients: • *Arts & Humanities:* Arts Appreciation, History & Archaeology, Libraries, Music, Theater • *Civic & Public Affairs:* Clubs, Municipalities/Towns, Safety, Urban & Community Affairs • *Education:* Community & Junior Colleges, General • *Health:* Emergency/Ambulance Services • *Religion:* Churches • *Social Services:* Senior Services

Grant Types: multiyear/continuing support and project

Geographic Distribution: limited to the town of Vevay and Switzerland County, IN

GIVING OFFICERS
Evelina Brown: treas

Martha Cole: secy

Woodie Reeves: vp

Ralph W. Tilley: pres

APPLICATION INFORMATION
Initial Approach: Application form required. There are no deadlines.

GRANTS ANALYSIS
Total Grants: $172,500

Number of Grants: 14

Highest Grant: $50,000

Typical Range: $250 to $41,481

Disclosure Period: 1993

Note: Recent grants are derived from a 1993 Form 990.

RECENT GRANTS

General

50,000	Town of Vevay, Vevay, IN — East Enterprise sewer project
41,481	Town of Vevay, Vevay, IN — water/sewer extension project
27,647	Town of Vevay, Vevay, IN — tourism/marketing project
15,000	East Enterprise Fire Department, Vevay, IN
15,000	Switzerland County Church, Switzerland County, IN — various programs

Winchester Foundation

CONTACT
Chris L. Talley
Chairman
Winchester Fdn.
100 S Meridian St.
Winchester, IN 47394
(317) 584-3501

FINANCIAL SUMMARY
Recent Giving: $121,752 (1993); $142,665 (1992); $103,447 (1991)

Assets: $3,346,067 (1993); $3,012,160 (1992); $2,813,946 (1991)

Gifts Received: $2,447 (1993); $932 (1992); $51,210 (1991)

Fiscal Note: In 1993, contributions were received from Kevin D. Gulley Scholarship Fund ($1,741), Robert G. Jones Scholarship Fund ($666), and Winchester Athena Club ($40).

EIN: 23-7422941

CONTRIBUTIONS SUMMARY
Typical Recipients: • *Arts & Humanities:* Arts Associations & Councils, Community Arts, Libraries, Music, Visual Arts • *Civic & Public Affairs:* Philanthropic Organizations, Professional & Trade Associations, Public Policy, Urban & Community Affairs • *Education:* Business Education, Colleges & Universities, Economic Education, Education Funds, Education Reform, International Studies, Secondary Education (Public), Social Sciences Education, Student Aid, Vocational & Technical Education • *Social Services:* Animal Protection, Community Service Organizations

Grant Types: general support and scholarship

Geographic Distribution: focus on IN

GIVING OFFICERS
Ruth Connally: trust

Helen Garlotte: trust

Enid Goodrich: vchmn *PHIL AFFIL* vchmn, dir: Thirty-Five Twenty, Inc.

Terri E. Matchett: secy

Linda Pugh: asst secy

Chris L. Talley: chmn

Don E. Welch: trust *PHIL AFFIL* dir: Thirty-Five Twenty, Inc.

APPLICATION INFORMATION
Initial Approach: The foundation has no formal grant application procedure or application form. Application form required for scholarships. There are no deadlines for grants. Scholarship deadlines are in the spring on a date designated by the Board of Trustees.

OTHER THINGS TO KNOW
Provides scholarships to graduating students of Winchester Community High School.

GRANTS ANALYSIS
Total Grants: $121,752

Number of Grants: 29

Highest Grant: $15,422

Typical Range: $150 to $15,000

Disclosure Period: 1993

Note: Recent grants are derived from a 1993 Form 990.

RECENT GRANTS
Library
5,000	Winchester Community Library, Winchester, IN

General
15,422	DePauw University, Greencastle, IN — Pierre Goodrich Scholarship Fund
15,000	DePauw University, Greencastle, IN — Pierre Goodrich Scholarship Fund
14,000	Butler University, Butler, IN — Pierre Goodrich Scholarship Fund
10,000	Grace College — Pierre Goodrich Scholarship Fund
10,000	Hanover College, Hanover, IN — Pierre Goodrich Scholarship Fund

Zollner Foundation

CONTACT
Alice Kopfer
Administrator
Zollner Fdn.
c/o Norwest Bank
PO Box 960
Ft. Wayne, IN 46801
(219) 461-6000

FINANCIAL SUMMARY
Recent Giving: $405,376 (1993); $245,505 (1992); $230,415 (1990)

Assets: $7,431,010 (1993); $8,656,008 (1992); $6,711,394 (1990)

EIN: 35-6381471

CONTRIBUTIONS SUMMARY
Typical Recipients: • *Arts & Humanities:* History & Archaeology, Libraries, Museums/Galleries, Public Broadcasting • *Civic & Public Affairs:* Clubs, Community Foundations, Economic Development, General, Philanthropic Organizations, Professional & Trade Associations, Urban & Community Affairs, Zoos/Aquariums • *Education:* Business Education, Colleges & Universities, Engineering/Technological Education, Vocational & Technical Education • *Health:* Health Organizations, Hospitals • *Social Services:* Scouts, United Funds/United Ways, YMCA/YWCA/YMHA/YWHA, Youth Organizations

Grant Types: general support

Geographic Distribution: focus on IN

GIVING OFFICERS
Norwest Bank: trust

APPLICATION INFORMATION
Initial Approach: Send a brief letter of inquiry. There are no deadlines.

GRANTS ANALYSIS
Total Grants: $405,376

Number of Grants: 24

Highest Grant: $65,000

Typical Range: $2,000 to $55,000

Disclosure Period: 1993

Note: Recent grants are derived from a 1993 Form 990.

RECENT GRANTS
General
65,000	United Way, Ft. Wayne, IN
55,000	Tri-State University, Angola, IN
37,000	Indiana Institute of Technology, Ft. Wayne, IN
35,000	Ft. Wayne Community Foundation, Ft. Wayne, IN
23,000	IPFW, Ft. Wayne, IN

IOWA

Adler Foundation Trust, Philip D. and Henrietta B.

CONTACT
Philip D. and Henrietta B. Adler Fdn Trust
c/o Norwest Bank Iowa, N.A.
203 W Third St.
Davenport, IA 52801
(319) 583-3226

FINANCIAL SUMMARY
Recent Giving: $313,936 (1993); $283,760 (1991); $339,500 (1990)

Assets: $7,394,940 (1993); $5,103,511 (1991); $5,536,735 (1990)

EIN: 42-6262655

CONTRIBUTIONS SUMMARY
Typical Recipients: • *Arts & Humanities:* Arts Centers, Community Arts, Historic Preservation, Libraries, Museums/Galleries, Music, Theater • *Civic & Public Affairs:* General • *Education:* Colleges & Universities, Public Education (Precollege) • *Health:* Emergency/Ambulance Services • *Social Services:* Child Welfare, Community Service Organizations, Food/Clothing Distribution, Shelters/Homelessness, YMCA/YWCA/YMHA/YWHA, Youth Organizations

Grant Types: general support

Geographic Distribution: focus on Davenport, IA

GIVING OFFICERS
Northwest Bank of Iowa, N.A.: trust

Betty Schlermer: trust

APPLICATION INFORMATION
Initial Approach: The foundation has no formal grant application procedure or application form.

GRANTS ANALYSIS
Total Grants: $313,936

Number of Grants: 9

Highest Grant: $100,000

Typical Range: $5,000 to $100,000

Disclosure Period: 1993

Note: Recent grants are derived from a 1993 Form 990.

RECENT GRANTS

Library

25,000	Maureen and Mike Mansfield Foundation, Missoula, MT — Mansfield Library	

General

100,000	Davenport Schools Foundation, Davenport, IA
25,000	Scott County YMCA, Davenport, IA
25,000	University of Iowa Foundation, Iowa City, IA — School of Religion
15,000	John Lewis Coffee Shop, Davenport, IA
12,500	Friendly House, Portland, OR

Audubon State Bank / Audubon State Bank Charitable Foundation

Headquarters: Audubon, IA

CONTACT

Richard Harms
Audubon State Bank
Audubon, IA 50025
(712) 563-2644

FINANCIAL SUMMARY

Recent Giving: $42,511 (1993); $28,256 (1991)

Assets: $55,383 (1993); $46,038 (1991)

Gifts Received: $48,000 (1993); $50,000 (1991)

Fiscal Note: In 1993, contributions were received from Audubon State Bank.

EIN: 42-1366431

CONTRIBUTIONS SUMMARY

Typical Recipients: • *Arts & Humanities:* Libraries, Museums/Galleries, Music, Public Broadcasting • *Civic & Public Affairs:* Botanical Gardens/Parks, Business/Free Enterprise, Economic Development, General, Municipalities/Towns, Urban & Community Affairs, Women's Affairs • *Education:* Agricultural Education, Colleges & Universities, International Exchange, Secondary Education (Private), Student Aid • *Health:* Emergency/Ambulance Services, Heart • *Religion:* Churches, Religious Organizations, Religious Welfare • *Social Services:* Emergency Relief, Family Planning, Homes, People with Disabilities, Recreation & Athletics, Scouts, Senior Services

Grant Types: general support

Geographic Distribution: focus on IA

GIVING OFFICERS

M.P. Barron: dir

F.J. Boyd: pres, dir

John Chrystal: dir

Mary Garst: dir

Stephen Garst: dir *PHIL AFFIL* dir: Iowa Savings Bank Charitable Trust Foundation; treas, dir: Home State Bank Charitable Foundation

Stephen Garst: dir

Richard Harms: secy, treas, dir

William C. Hess: vp, dir *CURR EMPL* pres: Iowa Savings Bank *PHIL AFFIL* secy, treas, dir: Iowa Savings Bank Charitable Trust Foundation; secy, dir: Home State Bank Charitable Foundation

John C. Parrott, Jr.: dir

APPLICATION INFORMATION

Initial Approach: Send a brief letter of inquiry. Include a description of organization, amount requested, purpose of funds sought, recently audited financial statement, and proof of tax-exempt status. There are no deadlines.

GRANTS ANALYSIS

Total Grants: $42,511

Number of Grants: 48

Highest Grant: $10,000

Typical Range: $200 to $1,000

Disclosure Period: 1993

Note: Recent grants are derived from a 1993 Form 990.

RECENT GRANTS

Library

250	Audubon Library, Audubon, IA	
25	Audubon Library, Audubon, IA	

General

10,000	Carroll County Auditor, Carroll, IA — Four Corners Park
10,000	Friendship Home, Audubon, IA
2,000	New Hope Village Corporation, Carroll, IA
2,000	St. Patrick's Cemetery Association, Audubon, IA
1,550	Iowa College Foundation, Des Moines, IA

Bechtel Charitable Remainder Uni-Trust, Marie H.

CONTACT

Lucy Boedeker
Office Manager
Marie H. Bechtel Charitable Remainder Uni-Trust
201 W Second St.
1000 Firstar Ctr.
Davenport, IA 52801
(319) 328-3333

FINANCIAL SUMMARY

Recent Giving: $1,000,000 (1995 est.); $1,000,000 (1994 approx.); $1,001,000 (1993 approx.)

Assets: $18,500,000 (1995 est.); $18,500,000 (1994 approx.); $18,500,000 (1993 approx.)

EIN: 42-6288500

CONTRIBUTIONS SUMMARY

Donor(s): The Marie H. Bechtel Charitable Remainder Uni-Trust is the largest of four trusts and a corporate foundation which were created either by Harold R. Bechtel or by Marie H. Bechtel during their lifetimes. The other charitable organizations are the following: the Bechtel Foundation, the H. Reimers Bechtel Uni-Trust, the H. R. Bechtel Testamentary Charitable Trust, and the Harold R. Bechtel Charitable Remainder Uni-Trust.

Harold R. Bechtel was one of Iowa's foremost bankers until his death in 1987. Marie H. Bechtel was highly regarded for her cultural activities and interests in Scott County, IA, as well as her devotion to the health care needs of the community.

Both Harold and Marie were born in Davenport, IA. Harold served in both World War I and World War II, rising to the rank of lieutenant colonel. He became engaged in the banking industry in 1935 when the Bechtel Trust Company received its state banking charter.

Typical Recipients: • *Arts & Humanities:* Libraries • *Civic & Public Affairs:* Employment/Job Training, Municipalities/Towns, Philanthropic Organizations • *Education:* Colleges & Universities, Medical Education, Private Education (Precollege) • *Environment:* General • *Social Services:* Community Centers, Community Service Organizations

Grant Types: general support and scholarship

Geographic Distribution: limited to Scott County, IA

GIVING OFFICERS

R. Richard Bittner: trust, dir *PHIL AFFIL* trust: Harold R. Bechtel Charitable Remainder Uni-Trust, H. Reimers Bechtel Charitable Remainder Uni-Trust, H. R. Bechtel Testamentary Charitable Trust

Lucy Boedeker: off mgr

APPLICATION INFORMATION

Initial Approach:

Contact the trust to request a copy of the grant application.

Grant applications will require the following: a brief description of the organization, including its legal name, history, activities, purpose, and governing body; a clear description of the purpose for which the grant is requested and the goals to be achieved; the amount requested and a list of other current and potential sources of financial support; a copy of the organization's most recent audited financial statement; a copy of the IRS tax-exempt determination letter; and a copy of the organization's last 990-income tax return.

There are no deadlines for grant applications.

The trust will send a written notice to applicants within a reasonable time, whether the request for a grant has been approved or declined.

Restrictions on Giving: The foundation generally does not support endowment funds; past operating deficits or debt retirement; general and continuing operating support; or basic scholarly research within established academic disciplines.

Grants are currently confined to nonprofit, public tax-exempt organizations to be used for their charitable purposes. Grants may be made to individuals in the future, but are not currently available.

Grants are made to Scott County, IA only.

PUBLICATIONS
Information for grant applications

GRANTS ANALYSIS
Total Grants: $1,003,953

Number of Grants: 21

Highest Grant: $200,000

Average Grant: $22,847*

Typical Range: $10,000 to $50,000

Disclosure Period: 1992

Note: The average grant figure excludes two grants totaling $250,000. Recent grants are derived from a 1992 partial.

RECENT GRANTS

General
200,000	St. Ambrose University, Davenport, IA
50,000	Palmer College of Chiropractic
50,000	Scott County Family YMCA, Davenport, IA — capital campaign challenge matching grant
46,000	Family Resources, Davenport, IA
35,000	Salvation Army, Davenport, IA

Bechtel Testamentary Charitable Trust, H. R.

CONTACT
R. Richard Bittner
Trustee
H. R. Bechtel Testamentary Charitable Trust
201 W Second St.
Davenport, IA 52801
(319) 328-3333

FINANCIAL SUMMARY
Recent Giving: $249,000 (fiscal 1991); $0 (fiscal 1989)

Assets: $5,085,002 (fiscal 1991); $4,371,324 (fiscal 1989)

Gifts Received: $100,028 (fiscal 1991)

Fiscal Note: In fiscal 1991, contributions were received from the estate of Harold Bechtel.

EIN: 42-6428369

CONTRIBUTIONS SUMMARY
Typical Recipients: • *Arts & Humanities:* Libraries, Museums/Galleries, Public Broadcasting • *Education:* Colleges & Universities

Grant Types: general support

GIVING OFFICERS
R. Richard Bittner: trust *PHIL AFFIL* trust, dir: Marie H. Bechtel Charitable Remainder Uni-Trust; trust: Harold R. Bechtel Charitable Remainder Uni-Trust, H. Reimers Bechtel Charitable Remainder Uni-Trust

APPLICATION INFORMATION
Initial Approach: The foundation reports that applicants should request a grant application form from the trustee.

GRANTS ANALYSIS
Total Grants: $249,000

Number of Grants: 11

Highest Grant: $35,000

Typical Range: $8,000 to $35,000

Disclosure Period: fiscal year ending October 30, 1991

Note: Recent grants are derived from a Fiscal 1991 Form 990.

RECENT GRANTS

Library
35,000	Herbert Hoover Presidential Library, West Branch, IA

General
35,000	Augustan College, Rock Island, IL
35,000	Iowa Public TV, Johnston, IA
30,000	Iowa College Foundation, Ames, IA
30,000	Iowa State University Foundation, Ames, IA
30,000	University of Iowa Foundation, Iowa City, IA

Carver Charitable Trust, Roy J.

CONTACT
Roger A. Hughes
Executive Administrator
Roy J. Carver Charitable Trust
PO Box 76
Muscatine, IA 52761
(319) 263-4010

FINANCIAL SUMMARY
Recent Giving: $8,500,000 (fiscal 1995 est.); $8,403,128 (fiscal 1994); $7,099,267 (fiscal 1993)

Assets: $180,000,000 (fiscal 1995 est.); $174,338,641 (fiscal 1994); $168,000,000 (fiscal 1993 est.)

Gifts Received: $8,947,445 (fiscal 1987); $26,290,921 (fiscal 1986)

Fiscal Note: In fiscal 1987, the foundation received $5,021,586 from the estate of Roy J. Carver and $3,925,859 from converted stock shares and interest on real estate.

EIN: 42-1186589

CONTRIBUTIONS SUMMARY
Donor(s): The trust was established in 1982 under the will of Roy J. Carver, an Iowa industrialist and philanthropist whose interests and activities were worldwide. Mr. Carver founded Bandag, Inc., the Carver Pump Company, and Carver Foundry Products, and remained active in the management of each firm until his death in 1981.

Typical Recipients: • *Arts & Humanities:* Arts Outreach, History & Archaeology, Libraries, Museums/Galleries • *Civic & Public Affairs:* Asian American Affairs, General, Hispanic Affairs, Urban & Community Affairs • *Education:* Arts/Humanities Education, Colleges & Universities, Community & Junior Colleges, Education Funds, Elementary Education (Private), General, Medical Education, Public Education (Precollege), Science/Mathematics Education, Student Aid • *Environment:* General • *Science:* Science Museums, Scientific Centers & Institutes, Scientific Research • *Social Services:* Community Service Organizations, Family Services, People with Disabilities, Recreation & Athletics, Youth Organizations

Grant Types: capital, project, research, scholarship, and seed money

Geographic Distribution: primarily in the state of Iowa, and organizations outside Iowa with which the founder had a significant association

GIVING OFFICERS
Willard Lee Boyd: trust *B* St. Paul MN 1927 *ED* Univ MN BS 1949; Univ MI LLB 1951; Univ MI LLM 1952; Univ MI SJD 1962 *NONPR AFFIL* adv bd: Cabrina-Green Legal Aid Clinic; dir: Am Counc Arts, Childrens Meml Hosp, IL Arts Counc, Natl Mus Svcs; mem: Am Bar Assn, IA Bar Assn; mem adv bd: Chicago Dept Cultural Aff, Chicago Meml Hosp, Elderhostel; pres: Field Mus Natural History; pres emeritus: Univ IA Law Sch

Lucille Avis Carver: trust *B* 1919 *CURR EMPL* treas, dir: Bandag Inc *CORP AFFIL* treas, dir: Carver Pump Co

Roy James Carver, Jr.: trust *B* Davenport IA 1943 *ED* Univ IA MA 1968; Univ CA Berkeley 1970 *CURR EMPL* chmn, dir: Carver Pump Co *CORP AFFIL* dir: Bandag Inc; pres, dir: Carver Hardware

William F. Cory: trust

Arthur Ernest Dahl: trust *B* Alexis IL 1916 *ED* Augustana Coll 1935-1939 *CURR EMPL* consult, dir: Bank Alexis

J. Larry Griffith: trust

Roger A. Hughes: exec adm

Clay Le Grand: trust *B* St Louis MO 1911 *ED* St Ambrose Coll 1931; Catholic Univ Am LLB 1934 *CURR EMPL* of couns: Stanley Rehling Lande & Van Der Kamp *NONPR AFFIL* mem: Am Bar Assn, Am Judicature Soc, IA Bar Assn, Inst Judicial Admin, Scott County Bar Assn

APPLICATION INFORMATION
Initial Approach:

Applicants should forward a letter of proposal to the trust.

The proposal letter should contain a description of the organization, including its purpose, activities, and governing board; clear description of the desired purpose and goals; amount of the request and potential sources of funding; and statement of why support from the trust is vital to the success of the project. Applicants should also include a copy of the IRS determination letter indicating 501(c)(3) tax-exempt status, copy of the organization's most recent audited financial statement, name of the contact person, and telephone number.

Deadlines for submitting proposals are December 1, March 1, June 1, and September 1. The board of trustees meets in January, April, July, and October.

Staff will consider meeting with applicants after reading their proposals. All grants are acted upon by the board of trustees after thorough screening and evaluation by the staff. The trust will send written notices to applicants within a reasonable time period.

Restrictions on Giving: The trust does not direct grants to individuals or fund religious activities; annual campaigns or continuing support; political parties, offices, or candidates; fundraising benefits; or program advertising.

OTHER THINGS TO KNOW

Once a grant is approved, the grantee must accept the terms and conditions of an Agreement of Donee, which includes financial reporting and summary results. This practice enables the trust to review and evaluate grant performance periodically.

GRANTS ANALYSIS

Total Grants: $8,403,128

Number of Grants: 55

Highest Grant: $1,117,166

Average Grant: $152,784

Typical Range: $20,000 to $200,000

Disclosure Period: fiscal year ending April 30, 1994

Note: Recent grants are derived from a fiscal 1993 Form 990.

RECENT GRANTS

Library

40,000	University of Iowa Library, Iowa City, IA — library linking research
20,000	Dike Public Library — construction of new library

General

1,446,881	Muscatine County, Muscatine, IA — construction of soccer complex
978,864	Mississippi Bend Area Education Agency, Mississippi Bend, MS —

	juvenile court project and playground planning
669,100	Carver Statewide Scholarship Program, New York, NY — college and university scholarships
645,799	Iowa State University Institute for Physical Research, Ames, IA — center for emerging manufacturing
635,440	University of Iowa College of Medicine, Iowa City, IA — medical research grants and therapy

Century Companies of America

Assets: $2.3 billion
Employees: 1,225
Headquarters: Waverly, IA
SIC Major Group: Insurance Carriers

CONTACT

Justin Tolan
Manager, Advertising & Corporate
  Communications
Century Companies of America
2000 Heritage Way
Waverly, IA 50677
(319) 352-4090

FINANCIAL SUMMARY

Recent Giving: $177,000 (1993)

CONTRIBUTIONS SUMMARY

development, disaster relief, and environmental programs. Limited support to local and statewide arts organizations. About 60% of contributions go to education; 15% to health/safety/welfare; 12% to urban/civic services; 5% to culture/arts; 5% to the United Way; and 3% to other organizations.

Volunteerism: Company has been involved in county walk-a-thons.

Typical Recipients: • *Arts & Humanities:* Arts Appreciation, Community Arts, Historic Preservation, Libraries, Museums/Galleries, Public Broadcasting, Theater • *Civic & Public Affairs:* Philanthropic Organizations, Safety, Urban & Community Affairs • *Education:* Colleges & Universities, Community & Junior Colleges • *Health:* Emergency/Ambulance Services, Health Organizations, Hospices, Medical Rehabilitation • *Social Services:* Child Welfare, Recreation & Athletics, United Funds/United Ways

Grant Types: challenge, employee matching gifts, general support, and multiyear/continuing support

Nonmonetary Support Types: donated equipment and in-kind services

Geographic Distribution: company service areas, in descending order by priority: Waverly, Cedar Falls/Waterloo, and Des Moines, IA

Note: Century Companies of America has operating locations in all states except New Hampshire.

CORP. OFFICERS

Richard M. Heins: *CURR EMPL* ceo: Century Cos Am

Kevin Lentz: *CURR EMPL* coo: Century Cos Am

Daniel E. Meylink, Sr.: *CURR EMPL* pres: Century Cos Am

APPLICATION INFORMATION

Initial Approach: Send letter requesting application guidelines. Guidelines state that an an officer of the requesting organization write and sign a letter requesting the grant. The letter may be sent at any time and should include the following information: organization's legal name and brief statement of overall objectives; address; name and address of principal administrative officer; name and title of organization's contact person; copy of letter documenting tax-exempt status under section 501(c)(3); amount of funding requested; description of service or program that the grant will fund; how the request fits with company's priorities as outlined in the guidelines brochure; and any supporting background information. For funding requests of $500 or more, the request must be accompanied by the contributions committee form CC-21 plus letter of tax-exemption. The form can be obtained by writing to the contribution's committee chairperson.

Restrictions on Giving: The contributions committee will not consider grants for individual use; political parties, candidates, and partisan political campaigns; professional associations; operating expenses for organizations that receive United Way funding, unless of an emergency nature; or religious groups for religious purposes. The company does not make multiple-year pledges to organizations that fall in a category that is at or above company's stated goals. The Century Cos. may provide multiple-year (up to five years) grants to organizations that are below stated goals.

OTHER THINGS TO KNOW

Preference is given to programs in which company associates and their families are involved. Preference also is given to projects involving more than just monetary funding. Training, management assistance, and involvement by Century Companies associates can be more important than dollars. The committee also gives preference to projects that are leveraged through challenge grants, matching grants, or cooperative funding from other sources.

PUBLICATIONS

Century Companies of America Corporate Contributions brochure

GRANTS ANALYSIS

Typical Range: $1,000 to $2,500

Cowles Foundation, Gardner and Florence Call

CONTACT
David Krudenier
President and Trustee
Gardner and Florence Call Cowles Foundation
715 Locust St.
Des Moines, IA 50304
(515) 284-8116

FINANCIAL SUMMARY
Recent Giving: $1,576,680 (1993); $1,500,000 (1992); $1,482,000 (1991)

Assets: $13,440,221 (1993); $16,000,000 (1992 est.); $15,521,398 (1991)

Gifts Received: $5,000 (1993); $1,225 (1990); $1,200 (1989)

Fiscal Note: In 1993, the foundation received a contribution from Thomas R. Hutchison—the foundation's treasurer and trustee.

EIN: 42-6054609

CONTRIBUTIONS SUMMARY
Donor(s): The Gardner and Florence Call Cowles Foundation (originally the Gardner Cowles Foundation) was established in Iowa in 1934 by Gardner Cowles and Florence Cowles. Gardner Cowles was born in Oskaloosa, IA, in 1861. He spent twenty years in the investment and banking businesses, and in 1903, purchased the *Des Moines Register*. He continued to buy newspaper concerns in Iowa, including the *Des Moines Tribune*, now the *Des Moines Register and Tribune*. He served as director of several corporations and banks, and was a trustee of colleges and hospitals. In 1931, Mr. Cowles served as the director of the Reconstruction Finance Corporation at the request of President Herbert Hoover. He died in 1946. His son, Gardner Cowles, Jr., established the Cowles Charitable Trust in 1948, and founded Cowles Communications. Gardner Cowles's grandson, Gardner Cowles III, is a trustee of the Cowles Charitable Trust.

Typical Recipients: • *Arts & Humanities:* Arts Centers, Libraries, Museums/Galleries, Music, Opera, Performing Arts, Theater • *Civic & Public Affairs:* Urban & Community Affairs • *Education:* Colleges & Universities, Private Education (Precollege) • *Social Services:* Community Centers, Family Planning, Senior Services, Youth Organizations

Grant Types: capital, challenge, endowment, general support, and operating expenses

Geographic Distribution: Iowa

GIVING OFFICERS
Elizabeth Ballantine: trust

Morley Cowles Ballantine: don granddaughter, trust *B* Des Moines IA 1925 *ED* Ft Lewis Coll AB 1975 *CURR EMPL* chmn, publ, editor: Durango Herald *CORP AFFIL* dir: First Natl Bank Durango *NONPR AFFIL* mem: CO Assoc Press Assn, CO Forum, Fed Women, Ft Lewis Coll Fdn, Natl Soc Colo-

nial Dames; trust: Simpson Coll, Univ Denver *CLUB AFFIL* Mill Reef

Charles C. Edwards, Jr.: trust *B* Denver CO 1947 *ED* Univ CO BA 1970; Drake Univ 1973 *CURR EMPL* pres, publ: Des Moines Register *CORP AFFIL* dir: Norwest Bank *NONPR AFFIL* bd dir: IA Coll Fdn; mem bd gov: Drake Univ; pres: IA Group Econ Devel

Luther Lyons Hill, Jr.: secy, trust *B* Des Moines IA 1922 *ED* Williams Coll BA 1947; Harvard Univ LLB 1950 *CURR EMPL* of couns: Nymaster Goode McLaughlin Voigts West Hansell & O'Brien *CORP AFFIL* couns admin: IA Life Health Guaranty Assn; dir: Equitable IA, FM Hubbell Son Cos *NONPR AFFIL* dir: Science Ctr IA, Un Commun Svcs Greater Des Moines; mem: Am Bar Assn, Assn Life Ins Couns, IA Bar Assn, Polk County Bar Assn; trust: Des Moines Metro Opera, Simpson Coll, Thompson Trust *CLUB AFFIL* Des Moines, Wakonda

Thomas R. Hutchinson: treas, trust

Elizabeth Stuart Kruidenier: trust

Kenneth MacDonald: vp, trust *B* Jefferson IA 1905 *ED* Univ IA AB 1926 *NONPR AFFIL* mem: Am Soc Newspaper Editors, Sigma Delta Chi *CLUB AFFIL* Des Moines

Terry Tinson Saario: trust *PHIL AFFIL* pres, secy, asst treas: Northwest Area Foundation

APPLICATION INFORMATION
Initial Approach:

Initial contact should consist of a cover letter and proposal describing the organization and the program for which funding is sought. There are no formal guidelines or application forms.

The eight-member board of trustees, composed of members of the Cowles family and the Cowles Media Company, meets as required to review grant proposals. Applications may be submitted at any time.

Restrictions on Giving: No grants are made to individuals or to institutions outside of Iowa.

GRANTS ANALYSIS
Total Grants: $1,576,680

Number of Grants: 10

Highest Grant: $700,000

Average Grant: $157,668

Typical Range: $100,000 to $500,000

Disclosure Period: 1993

Note: Recent grants are derived from a 1993 Form 990.

RECENT GRANTS
General

700,000	Drake University, Des Moines, IA — endowment fund
500,000	Simpson College, Indianola, IA — building expansion
100,000	Grand View College, Des Moines, IA — building expansion
100,000	Planned Parenthood, Des Moines, IA — equipment purchase

75,000	Wartburg College, Waverly, IA — building expansion

Forster Charitable Trust, James W. and Ella B.

CONTACT
James W. and Ella B. Forster Charitable Trust
c/o First Bank and Trust
Rock Rapids, IA 51246
(712) 472-2537

FINANCIAL SUMMARY
Recent Giving: $93,857 (fiscal 1993); $117,942 (fiscal 1990)

Assets: $2,173,167 (fiscal 1993); $1,870,337 (fiscal 1990)

EIN: 42-1305882

CONTRIBUTIONS SUMMARY
Typical Recipients: • *Arts & Humanities:* Historic Preservation, History & Archaeology, Libraries • *Civic & Public Affairs:* Economic Development, Parades/Festivals, Safety • *Education:* Student Aid • *Health:* Hospitals • *Social Services:* Community Centers, Youth Organizations

Grant Types: department and general support

GIVING OFFICERS
John Appel: trust

Edward Ladd: trust

APPLICATION INFORMATION
Initial Approach: The foundation reports no specific application guidelines. Send a brief letter of inquiry, including statement of purpose, amount requested, and proof of tax-exempt status.

GRANTS ANALYSIS
Total Grants: $93,857

Number of Grants: 6

Highest Grant: $50,969

Typical Range: $5,000 to $14,500

Disclosure Period: fiscal year ending June 30, 1993

Note: Recent grants are derived from a Fiscal 1993 Form 990.

RECENT GRANTS
Library

5,000	Rock Rapids Public Library, Rock Rapids, IA — purchase of art prints

General

50,969	City of Rock Rapids, Rock Rapids, IA — multi-use community center
14,500	Lyon County Fair Association, Rock Rapids, IA — restoration of round barn
10,000	Merrill Pioneer Hospital, Rock Rapids, IA — purchase of anesthesia machine

2,350   Central Lyon FCA, Rock
         Rapids, IA — leadership
         camp scholarships

Gazette Co. / Gazette Foundation

Sales: $39.0 million
Employees: 673
Headquarters: Cedar Rapids, IA
SIC Major Group: Printing & Publishing

CONTACT
Joseph F. Hladky III
President & Director
Gazette Co.
500 Third Ave. SE
Cedar Rapids, IA 52401
(319) 398-8202

FINANCIAL SUMMARY
Recent Giving: $173,270 (1993); $117,188
(1992); $97,550 (1991)

Assets: $368,007 (1993); $340,966 (1992);
$311,855 (1991)

Gifts Received: $177,500 (1993); $137,500
(1992); $112,500 (1991)

Fiscal Note: In 1993, contributions were received from the Cedar Rapids Television
Co. ($27,500), the Cedar Rapids Gazette
($75,000), and the Gazette Co. ($75,000).

EIN: 42-6075177

CONTRIBUTIONS SUMMARY
Typical Recipients: • *Arts & Humanities:*
Arts Associations & Councils, Ethnic &
Folk Arts, History & Archaeology, Libraries, Museums/Galleries, Music, Performing
Arts, Theater • *Civic & Public Affairs:*
Chambers of Commerce, Clubs, General,
Housing, Philanthropic Organizations, Professional & Trade Associations, Public Policy, Safety, Women's Affairs • *Education:*
Agricultural Education, Business Education,
Colleges & Universities, Community & Junior Colleges, Leadership Training, Private
Education (Precollege), Student Aid • *Environment:* General • *Health:* Cancer, Children's Health/Hospitals, Health
Organizations, Kidney, Outpatient Health
Care • *Religion:* Religious Welfare • *Social
Services:* Community Service Organizations, Counseling, Domestic Violence, Family Services, Food/Clothing Distribution,
Scouts, Substance Abuse, United
Funds/United Ways,
YMCA/YWCA/YMHA/YWHA, Youth Organizations

Grant Types: capital and general support

Geographic Distribution: focus on Cedar
Rapids, IA

Operating Locations: IA (Cedar Rapids)

CORP. OFFICERS
Joseph F. Hladky III: *CURR EMPL* ed,
publ: Gazette Co

Ken Slaughter: *CURR EMPL* cfo: Gazette
Co

GIVING OFFICERS
Elizabeth T. Barry: dir

John L. Donnelly: treas, dir

J. F. Hladky, Jr.: dir

Joseph F. Hladky III: pres, dir *CURR
EMPL* ed, publ: Gazette Co (see above)

Ken Slaughter: dir, vp *CURR EMPL* cfo:
Gazette Co (see above)

APPLICATION INFORMATION
Initial Approach: Application form required. There are no deadlines. Review process takes three months.

Restrictions on Giving: Does not support
individuals. Limited to Cedar Rapids, IA.

PUBLICATIONS
Guidelines Sheet

GRANTS ANALYSIS
Total Grants: $173,270

Number of Grants: 56

Highest Grant: $32,500

Typical Range: $200 to $29,700

Disclosure Period: 1993

Note: Recent grants are derived from a 1993
Form 990.

RECENT GRANTS
Library
   500   Friends of Public Library,
          Cedar Rapids, IA

General
 32,500   Greater Cedar Rapids
          Foundation, Cedar Rapids,
          IA
 29,700   United Way, Cedar Rapids, IA
 22,050   University of Iowa
          Foundation, Iowa City, IA
 10,000   Make-A-Wish Foundation,
          Cedar Rapids, IA
  7,000   Kirkwood Community College
          Foundation, Cedar Rapids,
          IA

Guaranty Bank & Trust Co. / Guaranty Bank and Trust Co. Charitable Trust

Employees: 56
Headquarters: Cedar Rapids, IA
SIC Major Group: Depository Institutions

CONTACT
Larry Johnson
President
Guaranty Bank & Trust Co.
PO Box 1807
Cedar Rapids, IA 52406-1807
(319) 362-2111

FINANCIAL SUMMARY
Recent Giving: $13,230 (1993); $13,075
(1991); $12,550 (1989)

Assets: $61,194 (1993); $39,001 (1991);
$29,719 (1989)

Gifts Received: $20,000 (1993); $17,000
(1991); $12,000 (1989)

Fiscal Note: In 1993, contributions were received from Guaranty Bank and Trust Company.

EIN: 51-0182485

CONTRIBUTIONS SUMMARY
Typical Recipients: • *Arts & Humanities:*
Community Arts, Ethnic & Folk Arts, Historic Preservation, Libraries, Music • *Civic
& Public Affairs:* Clubs, General, Housing,
Urban & Community Affairs • *Education:*
Business Education, Colleges & Universities, Education Funds, Public Education
(Precollege) • *Environment:* General
• *Health:* Alzheimers Disease, Emergency/Ambulance Services, Health Organizations, Single-Disease Health Associations
• *Religion:* Jewish Causes • *Science:* Scientific Centers & Institutes • *Social Services:*
Animal Protection, Camps, Community Centers, Community Service Organizations, Domestic Violence, Food/Clothing
Distribution, People with Disabilities, Senior Services, Substance Abuse, United
Funds/United Ways,
YMCA/YWCA/YMHA/YWHA

Grant Types: general support

Geographic Distribution: focus on IA

Operating Locations: IA (Cedar Rapids)

CORP. OFFICERS
Harold M. Becker: *CURR EMPL* chmn, dir:
Guaranty Bank & Trust Co

Larry Johnson: *CURR EMPL* pres: Guaranty Bank & Trust Co

GIVING OFFICERS
Harold M. Becker: dir *CURR EMPL* chmn,
dir: Guaranty Bank & Trust Co (see above)

Dennis J. Evans: dir

D. Bruce Gibson: dir

Thomas F. Nugent: dir

APPLICATION INFORMATION
Initial Approach: Send brief letter describing program. There are no deadlines.

GRANTS ANALYSIS
Total Grants: $13,230

Number of Grants: 29

Highest Grant: $2,000

Typical Range: $100 to $2,000

Disclosure Period: 1993

Note: Recent grants are derived from a 1993
Form 990.

RECENT GRANTS
Library
   25   Marion Public Library,
         Marion, IA

General
 2,000   United Way of East Central
         Iowa, Cedar Rapids, IA
 1,500   Jane Boyd Community House,
         Cedar Rapids, IA
 1,000   Mt. Mercy College Project
         Access, Cedar Rapids, IA
 1,000   YMCA The Promise of
         Tomorrow, Cedar Rapids, IA
   750   Iowa College Foundation, Des
         Moines, IA

IES Industries, Inc. / IES Industries Charitable Foundation

Sales: $801.27 million
Employees: 2,462
Headquarters: Cedar Rapids, IA
SIC Major Group: Holding Companies Nec, Railroads—Line-Haul Operating, Electric Services, and Natural Gas Distribution

CONTACT

Robert J. Kucharski
Treasurer
IES Industries Charitable Foundation
PO Box 351
Cedar Rapids, IA 52406
(319) 398-4572

FINANCIAL SUMMARY

Recent Giving: $700,000 (1995 est.); $722,000 (1994 approx.); $732,875 (1993)

Assets: $3,878,180 (1993); $4,300,000 (1992); $1,880,889 (1990)

Gifts Received: $1,500,000 (1989)

Fiscal Note: Above figures are for the foundation only. Company does not offer direct gifts. Above figures exclude nonmonetary support.

EIN: 42-1305874

CONTRIBUTIONS SUMMARY

Typical Recipients: • *Arts & Humanities:* Arts Associations & Councils, Historic Preservation, Libraries, Music, Public Broadcasting, Theater • *Education:* Agricultural Education, Colleges & Universities, Community & Junior Colleges, Education Funds, Public Education (Precollege) • *Environment:* General • *Health:* Hospitals, Single-Disease Health Associations • *Social Services:* Child Welfare, Community Centers, Community Service Organizations, Food/Clothing Distribution, People with Disabilities, Recreation & Athletics, Senior Services, Shelters/Homelessness, United Funds/United Ways, Youth Organizations

Grant Types: capital, employee matching gifts, and general support

Note: Employee matching gift ratio: 1 to 1 for in state schools, .50 to 1 for out of state schools.

Geographic Distribution: headquarters and service territory

Operating Locations: IA (Cedar Rapids)

CORP. OFFICERS

Blake O. Fisher, Jr.: *B* 1943 *ED* Univ MI BS 1965; Univ MI MS 1967 *CURR EMPL* exec vp, cfo, dir: IES Indus Inc *CORP AFFIL* cfo, exec vp: IA Southern Utilities Co; chmn, pres: IA Land & Bldg Co; exec vp, cfo, dir: IA Electric Light & Power Co, IES Utilities Inc; exec vp, dir: IES Diversified Inc, IES Energy Inc; pres, dir: IES Investments Inc, SIDCO Inc, Village Resorts Inc; vp, dir: Plateau Resources Ltd

Robert Joseph Kucharski: *B* Milwaukee WI 1932 *ED* Univ WI BBA 1959 *CURR EMPL* vp, secy: IES Indus Inc *CORP AFFIL*

chmn, treas: EnDyna Power Corp; dir: Aegon USA Capital Appreciation Portfolio, Aegon USA Growth Portfolio, Aegon USA High Yield Portfolio, Aegon USA Money Mkt Portfolio, Aegon USA Tax Exempt Portfolio; ptnr: Juneau Village I; secy: IES Container Svcs Corp, IES Diversified Inc, IES Energy Inc, IES Investments Inc, IES Leasing Inc, IES Railcar Svc Ctr, Metro Devel Corp, SIDCO Inc, SIRCO, Southern IA Mfg Co, Terra Comfort; secy, dir: Cedar Rapids & IA City RY Co, IES Transportation Inc; secy, treas: Indus Energy Applications Inc; secy, treas, dir: IES Barge Svcs Inc; treas: IA Southern Utilities Co, Micro Fuel Corp, Southern IA Mfg Co; vp: IA Land & Bldg Co; vp admin, secy: IES Utilities Inc; vp, treas: IA Electric Light & Power Co *NONPR AFFIL* chmn: Jr Achievement Cedar Rapids; chmn fin comm: All Sts Parish; dir: Big Bros/Big Sisters, Cedar Rapids Symphony Assn, IA Bus Devel Credit Corp, Un Way E Central IA; mem: Am Inst CPAs, Edison Electric Inst, IA Soc CPAs, Midwest Gas Assn, MO Valley Electronic Assn, Natl Assn Accts

Lee Liu: *B* Hunan People's Republic of China 1933 *ED* IA St Univ 1957 *CURR EMPL* chmn, ceo, pres, dir: IES Indus Inc *CORP AFFIL* chmn, ceo: IA Southern Utilities Co; chmn, pres, ceo: IA Electric Light & Power Co; dir: Firstar Bank Cedar Rapids NA, HON Indus Inc, Muscatine, Prin Fin Group Des Moines; pres, dir: Cedar Rapids & IA City RY Co, IA Land & Bldg Co, IES Container Svcs Corp, Indus Energy Applications Inc *NONPR AFFIL* bd trust: Univ Northern IA; bd visit: Univ IA Coll Bus Admin; dir: Electric Power Res Inst; mem: IA Bus Counc, IA St Univ Pres Counc, IA Utility Assn; trust: Fine Fdn, Hoover Presidential Lib Assn, IA Natl Heritage Fdn, Mercy Med Ctr *CLUB AFFIL* Cedar Rapids CC

GIVING OFFICERS

Robert Joseph Kucharski: secy, treas *CURR EMPL* vp, secy: IES Indus Inc (see above)

Lee Liu: pres *CURR EMPL* chmn, ceo, pres, dir: IES Indus Inc (see above)

APPLICATION INFORMATION

Initial Approach: *Initial Contact:* brief letter describing program *Include Information On:* description of the organization, amount requested, purpose of donation, tax-exempt status *Deadlines:* company begins taking requests in September; executive committee then reviews requests and makes final decisions on them in November or December

Restrictions on Giving: Gives only to IRS 501(c)(3) organizations which are based within the United States. Does not make international contributions.

GRANTS ANALYSIS

Total Grants: $732,875

Number of Grants: 195

Highest Grant: $105,000

Average Grant: $3,758

Typical Range: $2,500 to $10,000

Disclosure Period: 1993

Note: Recent grants are derived from a 1993 grants list.

RECENT GRANTS

Library

31,100	Mt. Mercy College, Cedar Rapids, IA — construction of new library and support academic programs
12,375	Coe College, Cedar Rapids, IA — capital growth annual fund, expansion of library, general operations, endowment for faculty salaries, endowment for student financial aid, faculty and program development, instructional equipment, and sponsor cultural events
5,000	Manchester Public Library, Manchester, IA — construction project
4,000	West Branch Public Library, West Branch, IA — construction project
3,500	Fairfield Public Library, Fairfield, IA — construction project

General

105,000	United Way East Central Iowa, Cedar Rapids, IA — community assistance
33,077	Iowa State University Foundation, Ames, IA — scholarship funding support academic programs
29,130	University of Northern Iowa Foundation, Cedar Falls, IA — support academic programs
26,370	University of Iowa Foundation, Iowa City, IA — support academic and scholarship programs
24,500	Kirkwood Community College Foundation, Cedar Rapids, IA — scholarship program support academic program

Iowa-Illinois Gas & Electric Co.

Sales: $545.41 million
Employees: 1,350
Headquarters: Davenport, IA
SIC Major Group: Electric Services, Crude Petroleum & Natural Gas, and Natural Gas Transmission

CONTACT

Lance E. Cooper
Vice President Finance, Chief Financial Officer
Iowa-Illinois Gas & Electric Co.
206 E 2nd St.
Davenport, IA 52801
(319) 326-7313
Note: For contributions under $250, contact Sam Wilson, director, corporate communications, at 319-326-7278.

FINANCIAL SUMMARY

Recent Giving: $500,000 (1995 est.); $500,000 (1994 approx.); $540,000 (1993 approx.)

Fiscal Note: Company gives directly. Gifts of less than $250 are available from other company departments; they have a budget of $40,000, which is included in the above figures. Please contact Sam Wilson, director, corporate communications.

CONTRIBUTIONS SUMMARY

Typical Recipients: • *Arts & Humanities:* Community Arts, Libraries, Music • *Civic & Public Affairs:* Economic Development, Urban & Community Affairs • *Education:* General • *Social Services:* Family Services, People with Disabilities, United Funds/United Ways

Grant Types: capital and employee matching gifts

Note: Employee matching gift ratio: 1 to 1, with a limit of $1,000.

Geographic Distribution: headquarters and operating locations

Operating Locations: IA (Bettendorf, Bluff, Cedar Rapids, Chillicothe, Coralville, Council Bluffs, Davenport, Fruitland, Ft. Dodge, Iowa City, Ottumwa), IL (Cordova, Moline, Rock Island)

CORP. OFFICERS

Stanley J. Bright: *B* Rochester NY 1940 *ED* George Washington Univ BBA 1963 *CURR EMPL* chmn, pres, ceo: IA-IL Gas & Electric Co *CORP AFFIL* chmn, ceo: Intercoast Energy Co *NONPR AFFIL* mem: Am Inst CPAs *CLUB AFFIL* Arsenal GC, Outing, Union League

Lance E. Cooper: *CURR EMPL* cfo, vp fin: IA-IL Gas & Electric Co

Sam Wilson: *CURR EMPL* dir corp commun: IA-IL Gas & Electric Co

APPLICATION INFORMATION

Initial Approach: *Initial Contact:* brief letter of inquiry and concise proposal *Include Information On:* description of the project and organization; amount requested; list of board of directors, trustees, officers, and other key people and their affiliations; list of additional sources approached for funding as well as other donors, with amount of support; audited financial statement; proof of tax-exempt status; who benefits from program; number of people served; and percentage of donation going to administrative or fund raising costs *Deadlines:* none

Restrictions on Giving: The company does not support individuals, churches, national health organizations, or organizations already funded by the United Way.

GRANTS ANALYSIS

Total Grants: $500,000

Disclosure Period: 1994

Note: Total grants figure is approximate.

Kinney-Lindstrom Foundation

CONTACT
Lowell K. Hall
Secretary
Kinney-Lindstrom Foundation
PO Box 520
Mason City, IA 50401
(515) 896-3888

FINANCIAL SUMMARY
Recent Giving: $188,445 (1993); $355,510 (1991); $374,425 (1990)

Assets: $6,528,067 (1993); $6,553,790 (1991); $6,421,596 (1990)

EIN: 42-6037351

CONTRIBUTIONS SUMMARY
Donor(s): The Kinney-Lindstrom Foundation was incorporated in Iowa in 1957. The donor was the late Ida Lindstrom Kinney, a native of Iowa and a nurse. Her husband, William D. Kinney, was a practicing doctor in several Iowa towns. Oil discovered on land in Texas owned by the Kinneys was the basis of the endowment. Currently, the foundation receives half of its income from farming in Iowa, in addition to the income from oil.

Typical Recipients: • *Arts & Humanities:* Arts Associations & Councils, Arts Festivals, Historic Preservation, History & Archaeology, Libraries, Museums/Galleries, Music, Performing Arts, Public Broadcasting, Theater • *Civic & Public Affairs:* Employment/Job Training, Municipalities/Towns, Parades/Festivals • *Education:* Colleges & Universities, Special Education, Student Aid • *Environment:* General, Resource Conservation • *Health:* Cancer, Emergency/Ambulance Services • *International:* International Environmental Issues • *Religion:* Churches • *Social Services:* Day Care, Recreation & Athletics, Scouts, United Funds/United Ways, YMCA/YWCA/YMHA/YWHA

Grant Types: capital and general support

Geographic Distribution: exclusively IA

GIVING OFFICERS
Lowell K. Hall: secy, treas, trust

E. J. Hermanson: trust

Thor Jenson: chmn, trust

APPLICATION INFORMATION
Initial Approach: Applicants should send a brief letter to the foundation.

Include Information On: The foundation has no specific requirements regarding the form in which applications should be submitted.

Deadlines: The deadline for submitting applications is March 1.

Review Process: The board meets ten times a year. Applicants are notified of the foundation's decision two weeks after a board meeting.

GRANTS ANALYSIS
Total Grants: $188,445

Number of Grants: 33

Highest Grant: $35,000

Typical Range: $250 to $25,000

Disclosure Period: 1993

Note: Recent grants are derived from a 1993 Form 990.

RECENT GRANTS

General
35,000	United Way of Northern Central Iowa, IA
25,000	American Red Cross, IA — Iowa flood disaster
20,000	City of Mason, Mason, IA — park and recreation ball diamonds
15,000	Iowa College Foundation, Des Moines, IA — educational
8,343	YMCA Mason City, Mason City, IA — repairs building and sidewalks

Kuyper Foundation, Peter H. and E. Lucille

CONTACT
Joan Kuyper Farver
President
Peter H. and E. Lucille Kuyper Fdn.
c/o Pella Corp.
102 Main St.
Pella, IA 50219
(515) 628-1000

FINANCIAL SUMMARY
Recent Giving: $679,000 (fiscal 1994); $658,089 (fiscal 1993); $844,310 (fiscal 1991)

Assets: $12,027,391 (fiscal 1994); $12,631,396 (fiscal 1993); $12,242,290 (fiscal 1991)

Gifts Received: $100,000 (fiscal 1991)

EIN: 23-7068402

CONTRIBUTIONS SUMMARY
Donor(s): Peter H. Kuyper, E. Lucille Gaass Kuyper

Typical Recipients: • *Arts & Humanities:* Arts Associations & Councils, Arts Centers, Historic Preservation, Libraries, Museums/Galleries, Opera, Public Broadcasting • *Civic & Public Affairs:* Community Foundations, General • *Education:* Colleges & Universities, Private Education (Precollege), Public Education (Precollege), Religious Education • *Environment:* Resource Conservation • *Health:* Health Organizations, Hospitals, Single-Disease Health Associations • *Religion:* Churches, Religious Organizations, Religious Welfare • *Social Services:* Child Welfare, Community Service Organizations, Day Care, People with Disabilities, Recreation & Athletics, United Funds/United Ways, Youth Organizations

Grant Types: general support

Geographic Distribution: focus on the Pella, IA, area

GIVING OFFICERS
William J. Anderson: treas *B* Fort Dodge IA 1946 *CURR EMPL* asst secy: Pella Corp *PHIL AFFIL* treas, asst secy admin: Pella Rolscreen Foundation

William J. Anderson: treas *CURR EMPL* asst secy: Pella Corp *PHIL AFFIL* treas, asst secy admin: Pella Rolscreen Foundation (see above)

Thomas W. Carpenter: secy

Joan Kuyper Farver: pres, dir *B* 1919 *ED* Grinnell Coll BA 1941 *CURR EMPL* chmn emeritus, dir: Pella Rolscreen Corp *NONPR AFFIL* mem bd: IA Coll Fdn; mem exec comm, dir: Central Coll *CLUB AFFIL* Pella Garden, PEO Sisterhood *PHIL AFFIL* pres, trust: Pella Rolscreen Foundation

Suzanne Farver: vp, dir

Ann F. Lennartz: vp, dir

APPLICATION INFORMATION
Initial Approach: The foundation has no formal grant application procedure or application form. There are no deadlines.

Restrictions on Giving: Focus on the Pella, IA area.

GRANTS ANALYSIS
Total Grants: $679,000

Number of Grants: 46

Highest Grant: $201,400

Typical Range: $500 to $25,000

Disclosure Period: fiscal year ending April 30, 1994

Note: Recent grants are derived from a fiscal 1994 Form 990. Number of grants and typical range do not include matching gifts.

RECENT GRANTS
General

201,400	Central College, Pella, IA
25,000	Dorott College, Sioux Center, IA
20,000	Community Foundation, Pella, IA
20,000	Community Hospital, Pella, IA
20,000	Nature Conservancy, Seattle, WA

Lee Endowment Foundation

CONTACT
Lee Endowment Fdn.
c/o Boatmen's Bank
PO Box 1407
Mason City, IA 50402
(515) 421-0507
Note: Applications for the affiliated Elizabeth Muse Norris Charitable Fund and Lorraine and Ray Rorick Fund should be sen to the Globe-Gazette, Mason City, IA 50401.

FINANCIAL SUMMARY
Recent Giving: $676,410 (1993); $615,892 (1992); $754,832 (1990)

Assets: $16,187,972 (1993); $14,483,211 (1992); $12,191,303 (1990)

EIN: 42-1074052

CONTRIBUTIONS SUMMARY
Donor(s): the late Elizabeth Norris

Typical Recipients: • *Arts & Humanities:* Community Arts, Libraries, Museums/Galleries, Music, Performing Arts, Theater • *Civic & Public Affairs:* Economic Development, General, Municipalities/Towns, Parades/Festivals • *Education:* Colleges & Universities, Community & Junior Colleges, Minority Education, Preschool Education, Private Education (Precollege), Public Education (Precollege) • *Environment:* General • *Health:* Emergency/Ambulance Services, Health Organizations, Hospices, Hospitals, Public Health • *Religion:* Churches, Religious Organizations • *Social Services:* Camps, Child Welfare, Community Service Organizations, Counseling, Delinquency & Criminal Rehabilitation, Family Services, People with Disabilities, Recreation & Athletics, Scouts, Senior Services, United Funds/United Ways, Youth Organizations

Grant Types: general support and scholarship

Geographic Distribution: focus on Mason City and Cerro Gordo County, IA, for scholarships; north central IA for other grants

GIVING OFFICERS
Donald G. Harrer: pres

Douglas F. Sherwin: vp

J. Martin Wolman: vp, treas

APPLICATION INFORMATION
Initial Approach: Application form required for scholarships. Deadline is March 1 for scholarships; no deadline for charitable fund applications.

GRANTS ANALYSIS
Total Grants: $676,410

Number of Grants: 30

Highest Grant: $225,021

Typical Range: $1,500 to $84,000

Disclosure Period: 1993

Note: Recent grants are derived from a 1993 Form 990. Number of grants and typical range do not include awards to individuals.

RECENT GRANTS
Library

13,000	Mason City Public Library, Mason City, IA

General

225,021	Globe-Gazette Christmas Cheer Fund, Mason City, IA
84,000	Hospice, Mason City, IA
31,250	City of Mason City, Mason City, IA
20,000	Handicap Village, Clear Lake, IA
17,200	Mason City Parks and Recreation, Mason City, IA

Lee Enterprises / Lee Foundation

Sales: $372.91 million
Employees: 4,900
Headquarters: Davenport, IA
SIC Major Group: Communications and Printing & Publishing

CONTACT
Russell Kennel
Secretary
Lee Enterprises
215 N Main
Davenport, IA 52801
(319) 383-2100

FINANCIAL SUMMARY
Recent Giving: $374,983 (fiscal 1993); $232,618 (fiscal 1991); $273,220 (fiscal 1990)

Assets: $6,034,114 (fiscal 1993); $4,509,018 (fiscal 1991); $4,312,703 (fiscal 1990)

Gifts Received: $500,000 (fiscal 1989); $1,000,000 (fiscal 1988)

Fiscal Note: In 1989, contributions were received from Lee Enterprises, Inc.

EIN: 42-6057173

CONTRIBUTIONS SUMMARY
Typical Recipients: • *Arts & Humanities:* General, Historic Preservation, History & Archaeology, Libraries, Museums/Galleries, Public Broadcasting, Theater • *Civic & Public Affairs:* Community Foundations, Employment/Job Training, Professional & Trade Associations, Zoos/Aquariums • *Education:* Colleges & Universities, Education Funds, International Studies, Private Education (Precollege) • *Environment:* Resource Conservation • *Health:* Clinics/Medical Centers, Emergency/Ambulance Services, Geriatric Health, Hospitals, Single-Disease Health Associations • *Religion:* Jewish Causes, Religious Welfare • *Social Services:* Community Centers, Community Service Organizations, Day Care, Emergency Relief, Family Services, Food/Clothing Distribution, Homes, Scouts, Senior Services, United Funds/United Ways, YMCA/YWCA/YMHA/YWHA, Youth Organizations

Grant Types: capital, endowment, and general support

Geographic Distribution: primarily in areas of company operations in IA, IL, WI, MT, ND, and OR

Operating Locations: AZ (Tucson), CA (San Marcos), HI (Honolulu), IA (Mason City, Muscatine, Ottumwa, Rapid City), IL (Carbondale, Decatur, Kewanee), MN (Winona), MT (Billings, Butte, Helena, Missoula), ND (Bismarck), NE (Lincoln, Omaha), NM (Albuquerque), OR (Corvallis, Portland), WI (La Crosse, Racine), WV (Huntington)

CORP. OFFICERS
Richard Gottlieb: *CURR EMPL* ceo, pres: Lee Enterprises

Lloyd G. Schermer: *B* St. Louis MO 1927 *ED* Amherst Coll 1950; Harvard Univ Sch Bus Admin MBA 1952 *CURR EMPL* chmn, dir: Lee Enterprises *CORP AFFIL* dir: Davenport Bank & Trust Co, NAPP Sys *NONPR AFFIL* chmn: Am Newspaper Publ Assn; dir: Conservation Fdn, Newspaper Advertising Bur, Smithsonian Inst, Univ MT Fdn, World Wildlife Fund; mem: Am Soc Newspaper Editors; mem bd visitors: Northwestern Univ Medill Sch Journalism

GIVING OFFICERS

Richard B. Belkin: vp, dir *CURR EMPL* vp, dir: Lee Enterprises

Richard P. Galligan: secy, dir *CURR EMPL* dir fin svcs: Lee Enterprises

Ronald L. Rickman: vp, dir *CURR EMPL* vp, dir: Lee Enterprises

Michael J. Riley: treas, dir *CURR EMPL* treas, cfo: Lee Enterprises *CORP AFFIL* treas, cfo: Lee Enterprises

Lloyd G. Schermer: chmn *CURR EMPL* chmn, dir: Lee Enterprises (see above)

APPLICATION INFORMATION

Initial Approach: The foundation has no formal grant application procedure or application form.

Restrictions on Giving: Does not support individuals.

GRANTS ANALYSIS

Total Grants: $374,983

Number of Grants: 56

Highest Grant: $50,000

Typical Range: $1,000 to $25,300

Disclosure Period: fiscal year ending September 30, 1993

Note: Recent grants are derived from a fiscal 1993 Form 990.

RECENT GRANTS

Library

3,000	Bettendorf Public Library, Bettendorf, IA — endowment fund	
2,500	Kohrs Memorial Library, Deer Lodge, MT	

General

50,000	Mansfield Foundation, Missoula, MT — endowment	
26,300	American Red Cross Quad-Cities Chapter, Rock Island, IL	
16,667	Montana Community Foundation, Billings, MT — endowment fund	
10,000	St. Ambrose University, Davenport, IA — endowment fund	
10,000	St. Louis Jewish Center for the Aged, St. Louis, MO — endowment fund	

Maytag Family Foundation, Fred

CONTACT

Francis C. Miller
Foundation Manager
Fred Maytag Family Foundation
200 First St. S
PO Box 426
Newton, IA 50208
(515) 792-1800

FINANCIAL SUMMARY

Recent Giving: $1,028,392 (1993); $1,267,241 (1990); $1,236,277 (1989)

Assets: $31,324,481 (1993); $21,259,955 (1990); $28,543,362 (1989)

EIN: 42-6055654

CONTRIBUTIONS SUMMARY

Donor(s): The Fred Maytag Family Foundation was established in 1945 by the late Fred Maytag II .

Typical Recipients: • *Arts & Humanities:* Arts Centers, Ballet, Dance, Historic Preservation, History & Archaeology, Libraries, Museums/Galleries, Music, Opera, Performing Arts, Public Broadcasting, Theater • *Civic & Public Affairs:* General, Law & Justice, Nonprofit Management • *Education:* Colleges & Universities, General, Medical Education, Minority Education, Private Education (Precollege), Public Education (Precollege), Science/Mathematics Education, Student Aid • *Environment:* General, Resource Conservation • *Health:* Cancer, Clinics/Medical Centers, Health Organizations, Hospices, Hospitals, Medical Rehabilitation, Mental Health, Single-Disease Health Associations • *International:* Health Care/Hospitals, International Peace & Security Issues, International Relations • *Religion:* Religious Organizations, Religious Welfare • *Social Services:* Child Welfare, Community Centers, Community Service Organizations, Family Planning, Family Services, People with Disabilities, Recreation & Athletics, Scouts, Senior Services, Shelters/Homelessness, Substance Abuse, United Funds/United Ways, Volunteer Services, YMCA/YWCA/YMHA/YWHA, Youth Organizations

Grant Types: capital, general support, multiyear/continuing support, operating expenses, research, and scholarship

Geographic Distribution: exclusively the Des Moines and Newton, IA, area

GIVING OFFICERS

Frederick L. Maytag III: trust

Kenneth P. Maytag: trust *CURR EMPL* vp: Maytag Dairy Farms

Francis C. Miller: mgr *CURR EMPL* secy: Maytag Dairy Farms

APPLICATION INFORMATION
Initial Approach:

Applicants should submit a written request to the foundation.

There is no specific application format.

Applications are accepted any time, preferably April-May.

Restrictions on Giving: Preference is given to Newton and central Iowa organizations.

GRANTS ANALYSIS

Total Grants: $1,028,392

Number of Grants: 69

Highest Grant: $250,000

Average Grant: $14,904

Typical Range: $1,000 to $25,000

Disclosure Period: 1993

Note: Recent grants are derived from a 1993 Form 990.

RECENT GRANTS

Library

50,000	City of Newton Library, Newton, IA	

General

250,000	Wesley Retirement Services, Des Moines, IA	
51,200	Iowa Methodist Medical Center, Des Moines, IA	
50,000	Iowa College Foundation, Des Moines, IA	
50,000	Nature Conservancy, Des Moines, IA	
40,000	Scattergood Friends School Foundation, W. Branch, IA	

McElroy Trust, R. J.

CONTACT

Linda L. Klinger
Executive Director
R. J. McElroy Trust
KWWL Building, Ste. 318
Waterloo, IA 50703
(319) 291-1299

FINANCIAL SUMMARY

Recent Giving: $1,805,658 (1994); $1,770,530 (1993); $1,620,917 (1992)

Assets: $33,556,383 (1994); $35,589,041 (1993); $33,532,136 (1991)

EIN: 42-6173496

CONTRIBUTIONS SUMMARY

Donor(s): The trust was founded in 1965 with funds from the estate of Ralph J. McElroy , the owner of Black Hawk Broadcasting. McElroy's company included television and radio stations throughout Iowa and southern Minnesota.

McElroy started his career at the age of thirteen, when he left home, took off on a freight train, and worked the wheat fields. In 1935, McElroy became a salesman and air personality for WMT in Waterloo, IA. Twelve years later, he founded the Black Hawk Broadcasting Company.

McElroy died in 1965 and his will established a trust fund, the proceeds of which are to be used for the educational benefit of deserving youth. "It is ironic that McElroy's own accomplishments were achieved without the benefit of higher education, and he had no natural children of his own. Yet his strong commitment to youth and education has extended far beyond his lifetime to the enoumous benefit of many, many young people."

Typical Recipients: • *Arts & Humanities:* Arts Centers, Arts Outreach, Historic Preservation, Libraries, Museums/Galleries, Music, Performing Arts, Public Broadcasting, Theater • *Civic & Public Affairs:* Employment/Job Training, Municipalities/Towns, Philanthropic Organizations, Rural Affairs, Urban & Community Affairs, Women's Affairs • *Education:* Arts/Humanities Education, Colleges & Universities, Community & Junior Colleges, Economic Education, Education Funds, Elementary Education (Private), Faculty Development, General, Gifted & Talented Programs, International Exchange, Journalism/Media Education, Minority Education, Preschool Education, Private Education (Precollege), Public Education (Precollege), Science/Mathematics Education, Student Aid • *Environment:* General, Resource Conservation, Wildlife Protection • *Health:* Children's Health/Hospitals, Medical Training • *Religion:* Religious Welfare • *Social Services:* Child Welfare, Day Care, Domestic Violence, Family Planning, Family Services, Food/Clothing Distribution, People with Disabilities, Recreation & Athletics, Substance Abuse, Volunteer Services, Youth Organizations

Grant Types: capital, endowment, fellowship, general support, project, and scholarship

Geographic Distribution: primarily Iowa, with emphasis on the Waterloo area

GIVING OFFICERS
Raleigh D. Buckmaster: chmn, dir

Ross D. Christensen: trust *B* 1940 *ED* Univ IA *CURR EMPL* vp, dir: Heartland Midwest Mgmt *CORP AFFIL* ptnr: Jo Ro Gen Partnership

Linda L. Klinger: exec dir

James B. Waterbury: trust

Richard C. Young: trust

APPLICATION INFORMATION
Initial Approach:

Applicants should send a proposal to the trust.

Proposals should contain general information including the following: name of organization, address, names and qualifications of persons who will administer the grant, contact person including title and phone number, a copy of 501(c)(3) determination letter, and the articles of confederation. Background information should include a statement of purpose and a description of the organization and its activities. A project description should explain community need and benefits to be derived by the community, long-term goals of the project, specific short-term measurable objectives, specific activities planned, number of young people to be served and from what age group, and timetable for the project. Financial information should include a copy of organization's most recently audited financial statement, a

copy of project budget including: payroll (hourly rate), payroll taxes and fringes, materials and supplies, taxes, rent transportation, utilities, and miscellaneous; amount requested from McElroy Trust and desired timing of grant payment; amount requested from all other funding sources; and plans for ongoing funding.

Submission deadlines are March 1, June 1, September 1, and December 1.

Requests for funds are voted upon by the board; the trust will send written notice of the trustees' decision. Decisions are made by May 1, August 1, November 1, and February 1.

Restrictions on Giving: The trust does not grants to individuals. The trust also gives gives preference to organization in Black Hawk County and rural counties in the KWWL viewing area.

OTHER THINGS TO KNOW
The trust prefers to fund programs rather than capital projects. It also perfers to fund a project over a period of time (one to three years).

PUBLICATIONS
Application guidelines

GRANTS ANALYSIS
Total Grants: $1,620,917

Number of Grants: 88

Highest Grant: $250,000

Average Grant: $18,420

Typical Range: $1,000 to $10,000 and $25,000 to $75,000

Disclosure Period: 1992

Note: Recent grants are derived from a 1992 annual report.

RECENT GRANTS
Library
25,000	Hoover Presidential Library Association, West Branch, IA — to provide educational programming
5,000	Mechanicsville Public Library, Mechanicsville, IA — to purchase reference materials for students

General
250,000	Student Loan Fund — to provide a revolving student loan fund at each of the private colleges located in the KWWL viewing area and the KTIV viewing area
183,000	Northeast Iowa High School Scholarships, IA — to provide scholarships of $1,000 each for high school graduates to be used to further their education
100,000	University of Northern Iowa, Cedar Falls, IA — to help fund the Youth Leadership Studies program
95,000	Hawkeye Community College — to provide student loans, Black Student Scholarships,

	and to help fund Second Chance
70,000	Warburg College — to help fund a Communications Center

---

Mid-Iowa Health Foundation

CONTACT
Rex Burns
Secretary
Mid-Iowa Health Fdn.
550 39th St., Ste. 104
Des Moines, IA 50312
(515) 277-6411

FINANCIAL SUMMARY
Recent Giving: $603,920 (1993); $517,050 (1991); $502,079 (1990)

Assets: $14,509,744 (1993); $13,588,991 (1991); $12,578,873 (1990)

EIN: 42-1235348

CONTRIBUTIONS SUMMARY
Typical Recipients: • *Arts & Humanities:* Libraries, Public Broadcasting • *Civic & Public Affairs:* Employment/Job Training, General, Housing, Women's Affairs • *Education:* Afterschool/Enrichment Programs, Agricultural Education, Colleges & Universities, Community & Junior Colleges, Health & Physical Education, Medical Education • *Health:* AIDS/HIV, Arthritis, Cancer, Children's Health/Hospitals, Clinics/Medical Centers, Diabetes, Emergency/Ambulance Services, Geriatric Health, Health Organizations, Home-Care Services, Hospices, Hospitals, Mental Health, Nursing Services, Public Health, Respiratory, Trauma Treatment • *Religion:* Churches, Religious Welfare • *Social Services:* Big Brother/Big Sister, Child Welfare, Community Service Organizations, Counseling, Day Care, Family Planning, Family Services, Food/Clothing Distribution, People with Disabilities, Recreation & Athletics, Scouts, Senior Services, Shelters/Homelessness, Special Olympics, Substance Abuse, United Funds/United Ways, YMCA/YWCA/YMHA/YWHA, Youth Organizations

Grant Types: capital, general support, operating expenses, and scholarship

Geographic Distribution: limited to Polk County, IA, and seven surrounding counties

GIVING OFFICERS
Rex Burns: secy, treas

Simon Casady: dir

Donna Drees: dir

Don C. Green: dir

Dale Grunewald: dir

Thomas Jeschke: dir

Ivan Johnson: chmn, dir

Bernard Mercer: vchmn, dir *CURR EMPL* chmn, dir: Preferred Risk Mutual Ins Co

T. Ward Phillips: dir

F. F. Satterlee: dir

APPLICATION INFORMATION

Initial Approach: Application form required. Approach foundation with brief letter of inquiry or telephone. There are no deadlines.

PUBLICATIONS

Application Guidelines

GRANTS ANALYSIS

Total Grants: $603,920

Number of Grants: 50

Highest Grant: $50,000

Typical Range: $3,000 to $25,000

Disclosure Period: 1993

Note: Recent grants are derived from a 1993 Form 990.

RECENT GRANTS

General

50,000	Broadlawns Hospital, Des Moines, IA
25,000	American Red Cross, Des Moines, IA — flood relief
25,000	Convalescent Home for Children, Johnston, IA — renovation/remodeling
25,000	Family Planning Council of Iowa, Des Moines, IA — nurse practitioner program
25,000	Food Bank of Central Iowa, Des Moines, IA — operations/flood response

Owen Industries, Inc. / Owen Foundation

Sales: $110.0 million
Employees: 460
Headquarters: Center Lake, IA
SIC Major Group: Fabricated Metal Products and Holding & Other Investment Offices

CONTACT

Carl Harrison
Chief Financial Officer
Owen Industries, Inc.
5th Ave N,5
Center Lake, IA
(712) 347-5500

FINANCIAL SUMMARY

Recent Giving: $109,035 (fiscal 1993); $125,520 (fiscal 1992); $89,500 (fiscal 1991)

Assets: $522,193 (fiscal 1993); $463,352 (fiscal 1992); $369,852 (fiscal 1991)

Gifts Received: $150,000 (fiscal 1993); $200,000 (fiscal 1992); $200,000 (fiscal 1991)

Fiscal Note: In fiscal year 1992, contributions were received from Owen Industries, Inc.

EIN: 47-6025298

CONTRIBUTIONS SUMMARY

Typical Recipients: • *Arts & Humanities:* Arts Appreciation, Arts Associations & Councils, Community Arts, Libraries, Museums/Galleries, Music, Performing Arts, Theater • *Civic & Public Affairs:* Botanical Gardens/Parks, General, Women's Affairs, Zoos/Aquariums • *Education:* Colleges & Universities, Private Education (Precollege) • *Health:* Health Organizations, Hospitals • *Religion:* Religious Welfare • *Social Services:* Community Service Organizations, People with Disabilities, Recreation & Athletics, United Funds/United Ways, Youth Organizations

Grant Types: general support

Geographic Distribution: primarily in NE

Operating Locations: IA (Carter Lake)

CORP. OFFICERS

Carl Harrison: *CURR EMPL* cfo: Owens Indus

Robert F. Owen: *B* Omaha NE 1943 *ED* IA St Univ 1966 *CURR EMPL* chmn, pres: Owen Indus *CORP AFFIL* pres: Paxton & Veiling Steel Co; pres, dir: Central Plains Steel Co, Lincoln Steel Co, MO Valley Steel Co; vp, dir: Northern Plains Steel Co

GIVING OFFICERS

Sam R. Brower: secy, treas

Dolores C. Owen: trust

Richard F. Owen: vp, trust

Robert F. Owen: pres, trust *CURR EMPL* chmn, pres: Owen Indus (see above)

APPLICATION INFORMATION

Initial Approach: The foundation has no formal grant application procedure or application form. There are no deadlines.

GRANTS ANALYSIS

Total Grants: $109,035

Number of Grants: 24

Highest Grant: $15,000

Typical Range: $1,000 to $10,000

Disclosure Period: fiscal year ending November 30, 1993

Note: Recent grants are derived from a fiscal 1993 Form 990.

RECENT GRANTS

General

15,000	Pembroke Hills — charitable
12,500	Goodwill Industries, Omaha, NE
12,500	Goodwill Industries, Omaha, NE — charitable
12,500	Hastings College — charitable
10,500	Omaha Zoo Foundation, Omaha, NE — charitable

Pella Corporation / Pella Rolscreen Foundation

Sales: $400.0 million
Employees: 2,500
Headquarters: Pella, IA
SIC Major Group: Millwork and Products of Purchased Glass

CONTACT

William J. Anderson
Assistant Secretary, Administration
Pella Rolscreen Foundation
102 Main St.
Pella, IA 50219
(515) 628-1000

FINANCIAL SUMMARY

Recent Giving: $1,400,000 (1995 est.); $820,494 (1994); $846,081 (1993)

Assets: $11,800,000 (1995 est.); $11,726,958 (1994); $11,322,598 (1993)

Fiscal Note: All contributions are made through the foundation.

EIN: 23-7043881

CONTRIBUTIONS SUMMARY

Typical Recipients: • *Arts & Humanities:* Historic Preservation, History & Archaeology, Libraries, Museums/Galleries, Music, Opera, Performing Arts, Public Broadcasting, Theater • *Civic & Public Affairs:* Botanical Gardens/Parks, Chambers of Commerce, Clubs, Housing, Municipalities/Towns, Urban & Community Affairs • *Education:* Colleges & Universities, Community & Junior Colleges, Education Funds, Preschool Education, Private Education (Precollege), Public Education (Precollege), Science/Mathematics Education, Secondary Education (Private), Secondary Education (Public), Student Aid • *Environment:* General • *Health:* AIDS/HIV, Emergency/Ambulance Services, Hospitals, Transplant Networks/Donor Banks • *Religion:* Churches, Ministries, Religious Organizations, Religious Welfare • *Science:* Scientific Centers & Institutes • *Social Services:* Camps, Child Abuse, Child Welfare, Community Centers, Community Service Organizations, Day Care, Family Services, Food/Clothing Distribution, People with Disabilities, Recreation & Athletics, Senior Services, United Funds/United Ways, Volunteer Services, Youth Organizations

Grant Types: capital and employee matching gifts

Note: Employee matching gift ratio: 1 to 1.

Geographic Distribution: almost exclusively in Iowa, with emphasis on Marion, Mahaska, and Carroll Counties

Operating Locations: IA (Pella)

CORP. OFFICERS

William J. Anderson: *B* Fort Dodge IA 1946 *CURR EMPL* asst secy: Pella Corp

PHIL AFFIL treas: Peter H. and E. Lucille Kuyper Foundation

James Wayne Bevis: *B* Quincy FL 1934 *ED* Univ FL BS 1959 *CURR EMPL* vchmn, ceo, dir: Pella Corp *CORP AFFIL* dir: IA Electric Indus Inc, IES Indus Inc, IES Utilities Inc *NONPR AFFIL* dir: Natl Assn Mfrs

Gary M. Christensen: *B* 1943 *CURR EMPL* sr vp mktg & sales, dir: Pella Corp

Joan Kuyper Farver: *B* 1919 *ED* Grinnell Coll BA 1941 *CURR EMPL* chmn emeritus, dir: Pella Rolscreen Corp *NONPR AFFIL* mem bd: IA Coll Fdn; mem exec comm, dir: Central Coll *CLUB AFFIL* Pella Garden, PEO Sisterhood *PHIL AFFIL* pres, dir: Peter H. and E. Lucille Kuyper Foundation

Beth Wilson: *CURR EMPL* dir pub aff: Pella Corp

GIVING OFFICERS
William J. Anderson: treas, asst secy admin *CURR EMPL* asst secy: Pella Corp *PHIL AFFIL* treas: Peter H. and E. Lucille Kuyper Foundation (see above)

James Wayne Bevis: secy, trust *CURR EMPL* vchmn, ceo, dir: Pella Corp (see above)

Joan Kuyper Farver: pres, trust *CURR EMPL* chmn emeritus, dir: Pella Rolscreen Corp *PHIL AFFIL* pres, dir: Peter H. and E. Lucille Kuyper Foundation (see above)

APPLICATION INFORMATION
Initial Approach: *Initial Contact:* full proposal (two copies) *Include Information On:* description of the organization, statement of need, amount requested, purpose for which funds are sought, project budget, recently audited financial statement, and proof of tax-exempt status *Deadlines:* none; board meets quarterly

Restrictions on Giving: Grants are not made to individuals, except under scholarship programs. Product donations are not made.

GRANTS ANALYSIS
Total Grants: $820,494*
Number of Grants: 125*
Highest Grant: $150,500
Average Grant: $6,564*
Typical Range: $500 to $10,000
Disclosure Period: 1994

Note: Figures provided by the foundation. Number of grants and average grant figures exclude $236,798 in matching gifts. Recent grants are derived from a 1993 partial grants list.

RECENT GRANTS
Library
5,000	Eddyville Public Library, Eddyville, IA — for new library building
5,000	Hoover Presidential Library Association, West Branch, IA — for five year commitment

General
150,500	Central College, Pella, IA — for first year commitment

70,000	Pella Corporation Employees Scholarships, Pella, IA — for scholarship program
20,770	Pella Community Hospital, Pella, IA — for matching gift
20,000	Pella Christian Grade School, Pella, IA — for building expansion
20,000	Pella Community Hospital, Pella, IA — for third installment

Ruan Foundation Trust, John

CONTACT
John Ruan III
Trustee
John Ruan Fdn Trust
3200 Ruan Ctr.
Des Moines, IA 50309
(515) 245-2552

FINANCIAL SUMMARY
Recent Giving: $72,740 (fiscal 1992); $1,157,458 (fiscal 1991); $191,717 (fiscal 1990)

Assets: $4,173,713 (fiscal 1992); $3,833,031 (fiscal 1991); $5,076,067 (fiscal 1990)

Gifts Received: $120,000 (fiscal 1992); $240,000 (fiscal 1990); $20,000 (fiscal 1989)

Fiscal Note: In 1992, contributions were received from Ruan Transport.

EIN: 42-6059463

CONTRIBUTIONS SUMMARY
Donor(s): John Ruan

Typical Recipients: • *Arts & Humanities:* Community Arts, Historic Preservation, Libraries, Music • *Civic & Public Affairs:* African American Affairs, Botanical Gardens/Parks, Chambers of Commerce, Clubs, General, Public Policy, Urban & Community Affairs • *Education:* Agricultural Education, Business Education, Business-School Partnerships, Colleges & Universities, Secondary Education (Private) • *Environment:* Wildlife Protection • *Health:* Emergency/Ambulance Services, Health Organizations, Kidney, Prenatal Health Issues • *International:* Human Rights • *Religion:* Religious Welfare • *Science:* Scientific Centers & Institutes • *Social Services:* Animal Protection, Child Welfare, Community Centers, Community Service Organizations, Counseling, Family Planning, Homes, People with Disabilities, Recreation & Athletics, United Funds/United Ways, Youth Organizations

Grant Types: general support

Geographic Distribution: focus on Des Moines, IA

GIVING OFFICERS
Elizabeth J. Ruan: trust *PHIL AFFIL* dir: World Food Prize Foundation

John Ruan III: trust *B* Des Moines IA 1943 *ED* Northwestern Univ 1966 *CURR EMPL*

pres: Ruan Ctr Corp *PHIL AFFIL* secy, dir: World Food Prize Foundation

APPLICATION INFORMATION
Initial Approach: The foundation has no formal grant application procedure or application form. There are no deadlines.

GRANTS ANALYSIS
Total Grants: $72,740
Number of Grants: 110
Highest Grant: $26,000
Typical Range: $50 to $5,000
Disclosure Period: fiscal year ending June 30, 1992

Note: Recent grants are derived from a Fiscal 1992 Form 990.

RECENT GRANTS
Library
1,000	Hoover Presidential Library Association

General
26,000	Variety Club, Des Moines, IA
25,000	YMCA of Greater Des Moines, Des Moines, IA
15,000	Capital Research, Des Moines, IA
15,000	Orchard Place, Des Moines, IA
12,500	Iowa State University Foundation, Ames, IA

Sheaffer Inc.

Sales: $75.0 million
Employees: 750
Headquarters: Ft. Madison, IA
SIC Major Group: Miscellaneous Manufacturing Industries and Paper & Allied Products

CONTACT
Walter Pensak
Vice President, Treasurer, Human Resources Manager
Sheaffer Inc.
301 Ave. H
Ft. Madison, IA 52627
(319) 372-3300

CONTRIBUTIONS SUMMARY
Program makes at least one large capital grant a year and then gives multiple smaller gifts to health, the arts, and social services.

Typical Recipients: • *Arts & Humanities:* Arts Associations & Councils, Arts Centers, Community Arts, Dance, Historic Preservation, Libraries, Museums/Galleries, Music, Performing Arts, Theater • *Civic & Public Affairs:* Employment/Job Training • *Education:* Colleges & Universities • *Health:* Health Policy/Cost Containment, Health Organizations, Hospitals, Mental Health, Single-Disease Health Associations • *Social Services:* Child Welfare, Community Centers, Community Service Organizations, Family Services, People with Disabilities, Substance Abuse, United Funds/United Ways, Youth Organizations

Grant Types: capital and general support

Nonmonetary Support Types: donated products and workplace solicitation

Operating Locations: IA (Fort Madison)

CORP. OFFICERS
David Connars: *CURR EMPL* ceo, dir: Sheaffer Inc

Shane Dolohanty: *CURR EMPL* cfo: Sheaffer Inc

Owen James: *CURR EMPL* coo, dir: Sheaffer Inc

GIVING OFFICERS
Walter Waltz: *CURR EMPL* contr: Sheaffer

APPLICATION INFORMATION
Initial Approach: For large grants, write letter one year in advance. Include a description of the organization, amount and purpose of funds sought, a recently audited financial statement, and proof of tax-exempt status. For smaller contributions, send a letter any time including the same information.

Van Buren Foundation

CONTACT
John A. Manning
Treasurer
Van Buren Fdn.
c/o Farmers State Bank
Keosauqua, IA 52565
(319) 293-3794

FINANCIAL SUMMARY
Recent Giving: $64,744 (1993); $85,292 (1991); $181,411 (1990)

Assets: $3,112,035 (1993); $2,743,084 (1991); $2,435,085 (1990)

Gifts Received: $961 (1993); $1,283 (1989); $1,206 (1988)

EIN: 42-6062589

CONTRIBUTIONS SUMMARY
Donor(s): the late Ralph S. Roberts

Typical Recipients: • *Arts & Humanities:* History & Archaeology, Libraries, Music • *Civic & Public Affairs:* Economic Development, Municipalities/Towns, Safety, Urban & Community Affairs • *Education:* Agricultural Education, Arts/Humanities Education, Elementary Education (Private), Preschool Education, Private Education (Precollege), Public Education (Precollege), Secondary Education (Private), Secondary Education (Public) • *Environment:* Resource Conservation • *Health:* Emergency/Ambulance Services, Health Organizations, Hospitals • *Religion:* Churches • *Social Services:* Crime Prevention, Recreation & Athletics, Senior Services, Shelters/Homelessness

Grant Types: capital, general support, project, and scholarship

Geographic Distribution: limited to Van Buren County, IA

GIVING OFFICERS
Connie Davenport: dir

James A. Dorothy: dir

Jon Finney: vchmn

Mike Gunn: dir

Richard A. Lytle: secy

John O. Manning: treas

Sandy McLain: 2nd vp

Arthur P. Ovrom: chmn

Davis E. Pollock: pres

Rex Strait: first vp

APPLICATION INFORMATION
Initial Approach: Application forms for scholarships available from foundation or high school counselors in Van Buren County.

OTHER THINGS TO KNOW
Provides scholarships for higher education to healthcare and medical students from Van Buren county, IA.

GRANTS ANALYSIS
Total Grants: $64,744

Number of Grants: 28

Highest Grant: $17,000

Typical Range: $200 to $10,000

Disclosure Period: 1993

Note: Recent grants are derived from a 1993 Form 990. Number of grants and typical range do not include scholarships to individuals.

RECENT GRANTS

Library
732	Keosauqua Public Library, Keosauqua, IA — copier	
640	Birmingham Public Library, Birmingham, IA — Ralph Schott Memorial	

General
17,000	City of Keosauqua, Keosauqua, IA	
10,000	Van Buren Schools, Keosauqua, IA — elementary playground equipment	
7,000	City of Farmington, Farmington, IA — community shelter house	
3,000	Harmony Community School, Bonaparte, IA — elementary playground equipment	
2,400	Harmony Schools, Bonaparte, IA — work experience program	

Winnebago Industries, Inc. / Winnebago Industries Foundation

Sales: $452.11 million
Employees: 3,052
Headquarters: Forest City, IA
SIC Major Group: Transportation Equipment

CONTACT
Elsie Felland
Corporate Cashier
Winnebago Industries
PO Box 152
Forest City, IA 50436-0152

(515) 582-3535

FINANCIAL SUMMARY
Recent Giving: $52,750 (fiscal 1994); $49,425 (fiscal 1993); $54,100 (fiscal 1992 approx.)

Assets: $1,195,893 (fiscal 1994); $1,127,446 (fiscal 1993); $1,040,610 (fiscal 1991)

EIN: 23-7174206

CONTRIBUTIONS SUMMARY
Typical Recipients: • *Arts & Humanities:* Arts Associations & Councils, Arts Centers, Arts Festivals, Community Arts, History & Archaeology, Libraries, Museums/Galleries, Public Broadcasting • *Civic & Public Affairs:* Clubs, Economic Development, General, Municipalities/Towns, Parades/Festivals, Rural Affairs, Safety, Urban & Community Affairs • *Education:* Colleges & Universities, General, International Exchange, Private Education (Precollege), Public Education (Precollege), Secondary Education (Public), Student Aid • *Environment:* General, Resource Conservation • *Health:* Cancer, Emergency/Ambulance Services, Eyes/Blindness, Health Organizations, Heart, Hospices, Hospitals, Nursing Services • *Religion:* Jewish Causes, Religious Welfare • *Social Services:* Community Centers, Community Service Organizations, Crime Prevention, Emergency Relief, Family Planning, Food/Clothing Distribution, Recreation & Athletics, Scouts, Special Olympics, Substance Abuse, United Funds/United Ways, Youth Organizations

Grant Types: general support

Geographic Distribution: focus on IA

Operating Locations: IA (Forest City)

CORP. OFFICERS
Edwin F. Barker: *CURR EMPL* vp, cfo: Winnebago Indus

Fred G. Dohrmann: *CURR EMPL* pres, ceo, dir: Winnebago Indus

John K. Hanson: *B* Thor IA 1913 *ED* Waldorf Coll AA 1932; Univ MN BS 1934 *CURR EMPL* chmn, dir: Winnebago Indus *PHIL AFFIL* trust: Hanson Foundation

GIVING OFFICERS
Gerald E. Boman: pres

Keith Elwick: trust

Luise V. Hanson: trust *PHIL AFFIL* trust: Hanson Foundation

Paul D. Hanson: trust

APPLICATION INFORMATION
Initial Approach: Send a full proposal. There are no deadlines.

Restrictions on Giving: Does not support individuals, religious organizations for sectarian purposes, political or lobbying groups, or organizations outside operating areas.

GRANTS ANALYSIS
Total Grants: $52,750

Number of Grants: 92

Highest Grant: $2,000

Typical Range: $125 to $2,000

Disclosure Period: fiscal year ending February 28, 1994

Note: Recent grants are derived from a fiscal 1994 Form 990.

RECENT GRANTS

Library

1,000	Rockwell Public Library, Rockwell, IA
500	Fertile Public Library, Fertile, IA
500	Forest City Public Library, Forest City, IA

General

2,000	Puckerbrush, Forest City, IA
2,000	Sister Robertelle Center of North Iowa, Forest City, IA
1,670	Waldorf College, Forest City, IA
1,500	American Field Service, Forest City, IA
1,500	Forest City Rotary Club, Forest City, IA

KANSAS

Baehr Foundation, Louis W. and Dolpha

CONTACT
Carl F. Gump
Chairman
Louis W. and Dolpha Baehr Fdn.
Miami County National Bank and Trust
PO Box 369
Paola, KS 66071
(913) 294-4311

FINANCIAL SUMMARY
Recent Giving: $136,104 (fiscal 1994); $142,081 (fiscal 1993); $148,441 (fiscal 1992)

Assets: $2,950,510 (fiscal 1994); $3,074,651 (fiscal 1993); $3,098,974 (fiscal 1992)

EIN: 48-6129741

CONTRIBUTIONS SUMMARY
Donor(s): the late L. W. Baehr, the late Dolpha Baehr

Typical Recipients: • *Arts & Humanities:* Arts Centers, Historic Preservation, Libraries • *Civic & Public Affairs:* Urban & Community Affairs • *Education:* Colleges & Universities, Community & Junior Colleges, General, Minority Education, Private Education (Precollege), Public Education (Precollege), Secondary Education (Public) • *Health:* Health Organizations, Hospitals, Mental Health • *International:* International Relations • *Social Services:* Child Welfare, Community Service Organizations, People with Disabilities, Recreation & Athletics, Scouts, United Funds/United Ways, Youth Organizations

Grant Types: capital, endowment, project, research, and seed money

Geographic Distribution: limited to the greater Kansas City area

GIVING OFFICERS
Miami County National Bank & Trust: trust

APPLICATION INFORMATION
Initial Approach: Send a brief letter of inquiry. Include a description of organization, amount requested, purpose of funds sought, recently audited financial statement, and proof of tax-exempt status. Meetings are scheduled for January, April, August, and October. Proposals must be received at least four weeks prior to the month in which the request is to be reviewed.

Restrictions on Giving: Does not support individuals or provide funds for advertising. Limited to the Kansas City Area.

PUBLICATIONS
Application Guidelines

GRANTS ANALYSIS
Total Grants: $136,104

Number of Grants: 15

Highest Grant: $70,000

Typical Range: $300 to $17,225

Disclosure Period: fiscal year ending April 30, 1994

Note: Recent grants are derived from a fiscal 1994 Form 990.

RECENT GRANTS

Library

5,000	Oswatomic Library, Oswatomic, KS

General

70,000	Unified School District 368, Paola, KS — Together Project
17,225	Kansas University Endowment Association, Lawrence, KS
10,000	Lakemary Endowment, Paola, KS
7,000	Children's center for Visually Handicapped, Overland Park, KS
6,278	Miami County Hospital, Paola, KS

Baughman Foundation

CONTACT
Eugene W. Slaymaker
President
Baughman Foundation
PO Box 1356
Liberal, KS 67905-1356
(316) 624-1371

FINANCIAL SUMMARY
Recent Giving: $700,000 (1995 est.); $700,000 (1994 approx.); $701,676 (1993)

Assets: $15,000,000 (1995 est.); $15,829,191 (1994); $16,644,972 (1993)

EIN: 48-6108797

CONTRIBUTIONS SUMMARY
Donor(s): The foundation was incorporated in 1958 by the late Robert W. Baughman and John W. Baughman Farms Co.

Typical Recipients: • *Arts & Humanities:* Arts Associations & Councils, Arts Funds, Ethnic & Folk Arts, Historic Preservation, History & Archaeology, Libraries, Museums/Galleries, Public Broadcasting • *Civic & Public Affairs:* Chambers of Commerce, Economic Development, Employment/Job Training, General, Law & Justice, Municipalities/Towns, Philanthropic Organizations, Safety, Urban & Community Affairs • *Education:* Agricultural Education, Colleges & Universities, Community & Junior Colleges, Economic Education, Education Funds, Private Education (Precollege), Public Education (Precollege), Religious Education, Science/Mathematics Education, Student Aid • *Health:* Diabetes, Emergency/Ambulance Services, Health Organizations, Hospitals, Single-Disease Health Associations • *Religion:* Missionary Activities (Domestic), Religious Organizations, Religious Welfare • *Science:* Science Museums • *Social Services:* Community Service Organizations, Day Care, Domestic Violence, Family Services, People with Disabilities, Recreation & Athletics, Scouts, Senior Services, Sexual Abuse, Youth Organizations

Grant Types: capital, endowment, operating expenses, project, and scholarship

Geographic Distribution: emphasis on Liberal, KS

GIVING OFFICERS
Carol Feather Francis: vp, trust

Eugene W. Slaymaker: pres, trust

James R. Yoxall: secy, treas, trust

APPLICATION INFORMATION
Initial Approach:

The foundation requests applications be made in writing.

Applicants should submit proposal stating need, availability of other funding, and amount requested.

Applicants must submit proposals prior to 10 a.m. central time on the second Wednesday of each month.

The foundation reviews proposals on a monthly basis.

Restrictions on Giving: Grants are made only to organizations with tax-exempt status under IRS section 501(c)(3) and which are not private foundations. No grants are given to individuals.

GRANTS ANALYSIS
Total Grants: $701,676

Number of Grants: 60

Highest Grant: $104,500

Average Grant: $11,695

Typical Range: $2,000 to $12,000

Disclosure Period: 1993

Note: Recent grants are derived from a 1993 Form 990.

RECENT GRANTS

Library

5,000	Town of Flaglen, Flaglen, CO — reservation assistance, town hall/library
2,700	City of Kismet, Kismet, KS — library software
2,500	Ashland City Library, Ashland, KS — computer equipment
2,000	Liberal Memorial Library, Liberal, KS — book purchases

General

104,500	Seward County Community College Development Foundation, Liberal, KS — scholarships, public relations, liability insurance
100,000	Southwest Kansas Medical Foundation, Liberal, KS — capital fund drive
34,204	USD 480, Liberal, KS — tri-agency
32,875	Liberal Good Samaritan Center, Liberal, KS — part 1992 and all 1993 capital drive
25,000	LAVTS Foundation, Liberal, KS — instructional equipment, scholarships

Beech Aircraft Corp. / Beech Aircraft Foundation

Sales: $1.25 billion
Employees: 9,500
Parent Company: Raytheon Co.
Headquarters: Wichita, KS
SIC Major Group: Aircraft, Fabricated Plate Work—Boiler Shops, Aircraft Parts & Equipment Nec, and Space Vehicle Equipment Nec

CONTACT

Robert B. Welton
Secretary-Treasurer
Beech Aircraft Foundation
9709 E Central
Wichita, KS 67206
(316) 676-8785

FINANCIAL SUMMARY

Recent Giving: $450,000 (1995 est.); $450,000 (1994 approx.); $482,028 (1993)

Assets: $6,103,577 (1993); $6,006,332 (1992); $6,034,825 (1991)

Gifts Received: $200,850 (1993); $150,000 (1992); $145,000 (1991)

Fiscal Note: Contributes through foundation only. Above figures exclude nonmonetary support. In 1993, contributions were received from the Beech Aircraft Corp.

EIN: 48-6125881

CONTRIBUTIONS SUMMARY

Typical Recipients: • *Arts & Humanities:* Arts Associations & Councils, Ballet, Historic Preservation, Libraries, Museums/Galleries, Music, Public Broadcasting, Theater • *Civic & Public Affairs:* Botanical Gardens/Parks, Clubs, General, Law & Justice, Philanthropic Organizations, Professional & Trade Associations, Public Policy, Safety, Zoos/Aquariums • *Education:* Agricultural Education, Business Education, Colleges & Universities, Community & Junior Colleges, Economic Education, Education Funds, General, Literacy, Medical Education, Science/Mathematics Education, Secondary Education (Public), Special Education, Student Aid • *Environment:* General, Resource Conservation • *Health:* Cancer, Clinics/Medical Centers, Hospices, Hospitals, Medical Rehabilitation, Multiple Sclerosis, Preventive Medicine/Wellness Organizations, Single-Disease Health Associations • *Science:* Observatories & Planetariums, Scientific Organizations • *Social Services:* Child Welfare, Community Service Organizations, Crime Prevention, Emergency Relief, Food/Clothing Distribution, Homes, People with Disabilities, Scouts, Senior Services, United Funds/United Ways, Volunteer Services, Youth Organizations

Grant Types: capital, challenge, employee matching gifts, general support, multi-year/continuing support, project, scholarship, and seed money

Geographic Distribution: primarily in communities with company facilities, with an emphasis on Kansas

Operating Locations: KS (Wichita)

CORP. OFFICERS

Wayne W. Wallace: *CURR EMPL* gen couns, corp secy: Beech Aircraft Corp *CORP AFFIL* secy, dir: Beech Aerospace Svcs Inc; vp, secy, dir: Beech Holdings Inc

Arthur E. Wegner: *CURR EMPL* chmn: Beech Aircraft Corp *CORP AFFIL* chmn: Beech Aerospace Svcs Inc; chmn, pres: Beech Holdings Inc

Robert Breen Welton: *B* Waterbury CT 1938 *ED* Quinnipiac Coll BS 1961 *CURR EMPL* vp, asst contr: Beech Aircraft Corp *CORP AFFIL* cfo,vp (bus devel): Beech Holdings Inc *NONPR AFFIL* dir: Boys & Girls Clubs Witchita, Wichita St Univ Endowment Fund; mem: Natl Assn Accts *CLUB AFFIL* Rotary

GIVING OFFICERS

Max Emil Bleck: dir *B* Buffalo NY 1927 *ED* Rensselaer Polytech Inst BS 1949; Univ Buffalo MS 1950-1951 *CURR EMPL* pres, dir: Raytheon Co *CORP AFFIL* chmn, ceo: Beech Aircraft Corp

J. A. Elliot: dir

Richard Griffiths: vp, dir

Wayne W. Wallace: dir *CURR EMPL* gen couns, corp secy: Beech Aircraft Corp (see above)

Arthur E. Wegner: pres *CURR EMPL* chmn: Beech Aircraft Corp (see above)

Robert Breen Welton: secy-treas *CURR EMPL* vp, asst contr: Beech Aircraft Corp (see above)

APPLICATION INFORMATION

Initial Approach: *Initial Contact:* brief letter of inquiry, contact foundation for pre-printed standard form for scholarships *Include Information On:* state whether organization is affiliated with the United Way *Deadlines:* none for grants, by March 15 for scholarships

Restrictions on Giving: The foundation does not support individuals (except for employee-related scholarships), athletics, endowments, or loans. Educational scholarships must be to accredited schools.

GRANTS ANALYSIS

Total Grants: $482,028

Number of Grants: 110

Highest Grant: $103,000

Average Grant: $4,382

Typical Range: $500 to $4,500

Disclosure Period: 1993

Note: Recent grants are derived from a 1993 grants list.

RECENT GRANTS

Library

5,000	Dwight D. Eisenhower Library, Abilene, KS — for culture and the arts

General

103,000	United Way of the Plains, Wichita, KS — for community service
50,000	Kansas Independent College Fund, Topeka, KS — for universities and schools
32,126	Scholarship Program Beech Aircraft Foundation, Wichita, KS — for universities and schools
27,500	Cerebral Palsy Research Foundation of Kansas — for hospitals and research
25,000	Sedgwick County Zoological Association, Wichita, KS — for community service

Central National Bank / Central Charities Foundation

Sales: $6.0 million
Employees: 150
Headquarters: Junction City, KS
SIC Major Group: Depository Institutions

CONTACT

Central National Bank
802 N Washington St.
Junction City, KS 66441
(913) 238-4114

FINANCIAL SUMMARY

Recent Giving: $43,960 (1993); $21,753 (1991)

Assets: $671,533 (1993); $608,036 (1991)

Gifts Received: $34,608 (1993); $28,000 (1991)

EIN: 48-6143983

CONTRIBUTIONS SUMMARY
Typical Recipients: • *Arts & Humanities:* Libraries, Literary Arts, Opera, Theater • *Civic & Public Affairs:* Safety • *Education:* Agricultural Education, Colleges & Universities, Economic Education, Private Education (Precollege), Secondary Education (Public) • *Health:* Hospices, Hospitals • *Religion:* Churches, Religious Welfare • *Social Services:* At-Risk Youth, Community Service Organizations, Recreation & Athletics, Scouts, United Funds/United Ways, YMCA/YWCA/YMHA/YWHA

Grant Types: general support

Geographic Distribution: focus on KS

CORP. OFFICERS
E. J. Rolfs: *CURR EMPL* chmn, dir: Central National Bank

Ed C. Rolfs: *CURR EMPL* pres, dir: Central National Bank

GIVING OFFICERS
DeCourcy E. McIntosh: mem *PHIL AFFIL* exec dir, secy: Helen Clay Frick Foundation

E. J. Rolfs: mem *CURR EMPL* chmn, dir: Central National Bank (see above)

Ed C. Rolfs: mem *CURR EMPL* pres, dir: Central National Bank (see above)

Evelina Rolfs: mem

Galen K. Unruh: mem

James R. Waters: mem

Robert K. Weary: mem *PHIL AFFIL* pres: Jellison Benevolent Society

Bruce J. Woner: mem

APPLICATION INFORMATION
Initial Approach: Request application form. There are no deadlines.

GRANTS ANALYSIS
Total Grants: $43,960

Number of Grants: 32

Highest Grant: $16,707

Typical Range: $100 to $1,000

Disclosure Period: 1993

Note: Recent grants are derived from a 1993 Form 990.

RECENT GRANTS
Library
1,164	Frank Carlson Library, Concordia, KS

General
16,707	Presbyterian Church, Junction City, KS
6,116	United Way of Geary County, Junction City, KS
2,500	Sunflower State Games, Topeka, KS
2,500	YMCA, Junction City, KS
1,350	Boy Scouts of America, Junction City, KS

Davis Foundation, James A. and Juliet L.

CONTACT
William Y. Chalfant
Secretary
James A. and Juliet L. Davis Fdn.
PO Box 2027
Hutchinson, KS 67504-2027
(316) 663-5021

FINANCIAL SUMMARY
Recent Giving: $130,153 (1993); $113,480 (1991); $120,682 (1990)

Assets: $3,005,098 (1993); $3,000,463 (1991); $2,671,682 (1990)

EIN: 48-6105748

CONTRIBUTIONS SUMMARY
Typical Recipients: • *Arts & Humanities:* Arts Associations & Councils, Community Arts, History & Archaeology, Libraries, Museums/Galleries, Music, Public Broadcasting • *Civic & Public Affairs:* Employment/Job Training, General, Zoos/Aquariums • *Education:* Afterschool/Enrichment Programs, Colleges & Universities, Community & Junior Colleges, Education Funds, Preschool Education, Student Aid • *Environment:* General • *Health:* Emergency/Ambulance Services, Hospices, Mental Health, Single-Disease Health Associations • *Religion:* Churches, Ministries • *Social Services:* Big Brother/Big Sister, Child Welfare, Community Service Organizations, Day Care, Emergency Relief, Family Planning, Food/Clothing Distribution, Scouts, Shelters/Homelessness, United Funds/United Ways, Youth Organizations

Grant Types: general support and scholarship

Geographic Distribution: limited to the Hutchinson, KS, area

GIVING OFFICERS
William Y. Chalfant: secy

Kent Longenecker: trust

Peter M. McDonald: pres

Merl F. Sellers: trust

V. Carol Shaft: trust

APPLICATION INFORMATION
Initial Approach: Scholarships limited to students graduating from Hutchinson High School who will attend college in KS or MO. Deadline is March 15.

GRANTS ANALYSIS
Total Grants: $130,153

Number of Grants: 41

Highest Grant: $30,000

Typical Range: $100 to $1,000

Disclosure Period: 1993

Note: Recent grants are derived from a 1993 Form 990. Number, high, and typical grant figures do not include scholarship grants and awards.

RECENT GRANTS
Library
30,000	Living Land Foundation, Hutchinson, KS — new library

General
6,000	Hutchinson Community College Endowment Association, Hutchinson, KS — general scholarships
3,000	Hospice of Reno County, Hutchinson, KS — new office
3,000	Living Land Foundation, Hutchinson, KS
3,000	Training and Evaluation Center of Hutchinson (TECH), Hutchinson, KS
2,000	Kids After School, Hutchinson, KS

DeVore Foundation

CONTACT
Richard A. DeVore
President
DeVore Fdn.
1199 E Central
Wichita, KS 67201
(316) 267-3211

FINANCIAL SUMMARY
Recent Giving: $134,285 (fiscal 1993); $124,133 (fiscal 1992); $45,856 (fiscal 1990)

Assets: $3,136,977 (fiscal 1993); $3,032,961 (fiscal 1992); $2,311,591 (fiscal 1990)

Gifts Received: $8,000 (fiscal 1993); $43,275 (fiscal 1992); $35,000 (fiscal 1990)

EIN: 48-6109754

CONTRIBUTIONS SUMMARY
Donor(s): the late Floyd DeVore, Richard A. DeVore, William O. DeVore

Typical Recipients: • *Arts & Humanities:* Arts Associations & Councils, Arts Centers, Libraries, Music • *Civic & Public Affairs:* Municipalities/Towns, Native American Affairs, Zoos/Aquariums • *Education:* Colleges & Universities, Private Education (Precollege) • *Environment:* Air/Water Quality • *Health:* Cancer, Hospitals, Medical Research, Single-Disease Health Associations • *Religion:* Churches, Religious Welfare • *Social Services:* At-Risk Youth, Big Brother/Big Sister, Child Welfare, Community Service Organizations, Homes, People with Disabilities, Special Olympics, Substance Abuse, United Funds/United Ways, YMCA/YWCA/YMHA/YWHA, Youth Organizations

Grant Types: capital, endowment, general support, multiyear/continuing support, operating expenses, and project

Geographic Distribution: focus on Wichita, KS

GIVING OFFICERS
Richard A. DeVore: pres, secy

William O. DeVore: vp, treas

APPLICATION INFORMATION
Initial Approach: Send a brief letter of inquiry. Include a description of organization, amount requested, purpose of funds sought, recently audited financial statement, and proof of tax-exempt status. There are no deadlines.

PUBLICATIONS
Application Guidelines, Annual Report

GRANTS ANALYSIS
Total Grants: $134,285

Number of Grants: 71

Highest Grant: $50,000

Typical Range: $100 to $5,000

Disclosure Period: fiscal year ending November 30, 1993

Note: Recent grants are derived from a fiscal 1993 Form 990.

RECENT GRANTS

Library
1,000	Wichita Public Library Foundation, Wichita, KS

General
50,000	YMCA, Wichita, KS
10,000	Harvard College Fund, Cambridge, MA
6,250	First Presbyterian Church, Wichita, KS
6,250	First Presbyterian Church, Wichita, KS
5,000	Arkansas River Foundation, Wichita, KS

Exchange National Bank / Adair-Exchange Bank Foundation

Headquarters: Atchison, KS

CONTACT
Paul H. Adair
Treasurer & Director
Exchange National Bank
600 Commercial St.
Atchison, KS 66002

FINANCIAL SUMMARY
Recent Giving: $27,850 (1993); $21,750 (1991)

Assets: $169,536 (1993); $166,024 (1991)

Gifts Received: $29,000 (1993); $23,000 (1991)

Fiscal Note: In 1993, contributions were received from Exchange National Bank ($26,000) and Fort National Bank ($3,000).

EIN: 23-7389214

CONTRIBUTIONS SUMMARY
Typical Recipients: • *Arts & Humanities:* Arts Associations & Councils, Libraries, Museums/Galleries, Theater • *Civic & Public Affairs:* Business/Free Enterprise, General, Municipalities/Towns, Urban & Community Affairs • *Education:* Agricultural Education, Business Education, Colleges & Universities, Community & Junior Colleges, Education Funds, Preschool Education, Private Education (Precollege) • *Health:* Cancer, Mental Health • *Religion:* Churches, Religious Welfare • *Social Services:* Community Centers, Community Service Organizations, Domestic Violence, Scouts, YMCA/YWCA/YMHA/YWHA

Grant Types: general support

Geographic Distribution: focus on KS

GIVING OFFICERS
Grace Adair: pres

Paul H. Adair: treas

Richard J. Bruggen: dir

Richard R. Dickason: vp, dir

Sharon Rains: secy

APPLICATION INFORMATION
Initial Approach: The foundation has no formal grant application procedure or application form. There are no deadlines.

GRANTS ANALYSIS
Total Grants: $27,850

Number of Grants: 32

Highest Grant: $5,000

Typical Range: $100 to $1,000

Disclosure Period: 1993

Note: Recent grants are derived from a 1993 Form 990.

RECENT GRANTS

Library
250	Atchison Public Library Multi-Media, Atchison, KS

General
5,000	Kansas Independent College Fund, Topeka, KS
4,000	Santa Fe Depot Enhancement Project, Atchison, KS
2,000	Trinity Episcopal Church, Atchison, KS
1,000	Atchison YMCA Foundation, Atchison, KS
1,000	Benedictine College Capital Campaign, Atchison, KS

First National Bank / First National Bank Charitable Trust

Sales: $4.7 million
Employees: 49
Headquarters: Goodland, KS
SIC Major Group: Depository Institutions

CONTACT
Mona K. McGinley
First National Bank
202 E 11th St.
Goodland, KS 67735
(913) 899-5611

FINANCIAL SUMMARY
Recent Giving: $12,416 (1993); $22,837 (1991)

Assets: $134,627 (1993); $137,993 (1991)

Gifts Received: $32,907 (1993)

EIN: 48-6133921

CONTRIBUTIONS SUMMARY
Typical Recipients: • *Arts & Humanities:* Libraries • *Civic & Public Affairs:* Economic Development • *Education:* Colleges & Universities, General • *Health:* Children's Health/Hospitals, Health Organizations • *Religion:* Churches

Grant Types: general support

Geographic Distribution: focus on KS

CORP. OFFICERS
Lawrence L. McCants: *CURR EMPL* pres, dir: First National Bank

GIVING OFFICERS
Mona K. McGinley: trust *PHIL AFFIL* trust off: Ordie T. Billenwillms Charitable Trust

APPLICATION INFORMATION
Initial Approach: Send a brief letter of inquiry. Include a description of organization, amount requested, purpose of funds sought, recently audited financial statement, and proof of tax-exempt status. There are no deadlines.

GRANTS ANALYSIS
Total Grants: $12,416

Number of Grants: 9

Highest Grant: $6,767

Typical Range: $150 to $1,000

Disclosure Period: 1993

Note: Recent grants are derived from a 1993 Form 990.

RECENT GRANTS

Library
150	Goodland Public Library, Goodland, KS — for educational purposes

General
6,767	Our Lady of Perpetual Help Church, Goodland, KS — for religious purposes
1,900	Greater Goodland Development, Goodland, KS — for governmental purposes
1,005	Goodland Activities Center, Goodland, KS — for educational purposes
1,000	Kansas Action for Children, Topeka, KS — for health purposes
894	Sherman County, Goodland, KS — for health purposes

Mingenback Foundation, Julia J.

CONTACT
Don Steffes
President
Julia J. Mingenback Fdn.
1008 Turkey Creek Drive
McPherson, KS 67460
(316) 241-0700

FINANCIAL SUMMARY
Recent Giving: $185,167 (1993); $183,667 (1992); $188,666 (1991)

Assets: $3,728,635 (1993); $3,715,786 (1992); $3,708,341 (1991)

EIN: 48-6109567

CONTRIBUTIONS SUMMARY
Donor(s): the late E.C. Mingenback

Typical Recipients: • *Arts & Humanities:* Arts Associations & Councils, Community Arts, Libraries, Museums/Galleries • *Education:* Colleges & Universities, Private Education (Precollege) • *Health:* Hospitals • *Social Services:* Community Centers, Homes, Senior Services, YMCA/YWCA/YMHA/YWHA, Youth Organizations

Grant Types: capital and operating expenses

Geographic Distribution: focus on McPherson County, KS

GIVING OFFICERS
Bank IV Kansas NA: trust

James Lee Ketcherside: dir *B* Topeka KS 1935 *CURR EMPL* chmn, pres: Farmers Alliance Mutual Ins Co

Ruth Lancaster: treas

Edwin T. Pyle: dir

Don C. Steffes: pres

APPLICATION INFORMATION
Initial Approach: Send brief letter of inquiry describing program or project. There are no deadlines.

GRANTS ANALYSIS
Total Grants: $185,167

Number of Grants: 6

Highest Grant: $60,000

Typical Range: $6,000 to $50,000

Disclosure Period: 1993

Note: Recent grants are derived from a 1993 Form 990.

RECENT GRANTS
Library
1,500	McPherson Public Library, McPherson, KS — programs and operations

General
60,000	McPherson Memorial Hospital, McPherson, KS — capital improvements
50,000	St. Josephs Catholic School, McPherson, KS — capital improvements
27,000	Elyria Christian School, McPherson, KS — to purchase building and addition of classrooms
25,000	Lindsborg Hospital, Lindsborg, KS — new construction
15,000	YMCA, McPherson, KS — programs and operations

Schowalter Foundation

CONTACT
Willis Harder
President
Schowalter Fdn.
726 Main St.
Newton, KS 67114
(316) 283-3720

FINANCIAL SUMMARY
Recent Giving: $123,950 (1993); $191,150 (1992); $209,400 (1991)

Assets: $5,564,403 (1993); $4,201,007 (1992); $4,103,616 (1991)

EIN: 48-0623544

CONTRIBUTIONS SUMMARY
Donor(s): the late J. A. Schowalter

Typical Recipients: • *Arts & Humanities:* History & Archaeology, Libraries, Literary Arts, Music • *Civic & Public Affairs:* Economic Development, Housing • *Education:* Colleges & Universities, Minority Education, Private Education (Precollege), Religious Education, Student Aid • *Health:* Emergency/Ambulance Services • *International:* Health Care/Hospitals, International Peace & Security Issues, Missionary/Religious Activities • *Religion:* Bible Study/Translation, Churches, Ministries, Missionary Activities (Domestic), Religious Organizations, Religious Welfare, Seminaries, Social/Policy Issues • *Social Services:* At-Risk Youth, Community Service Organizations, Day Care, United Funds/United Ways

Grant Types: capital, project, and scholarship

Geographic Distribution: limited to the Midwest

GIVING OFFICERS
Howard E. Baumgartner: trust

Allen Becker: trust

Willis Harder: pres, trust

Howard Hershberger: trust

Sue Ann Jantz: trust

Eugene Unruh: trust

Elvin D. Yoder: trust

APPLICATION INFORMATION
Initial Approach: Send cover letter and full proposal. Include a description of organization, amount requested, purpose of funds sought, recently audited financial statement, and proof of tax-exempt status. Deadlines are March 1 and September 1.

Restrictions on Giving: The foundation does not make grants to individuals.

PUBLICATIONS
Application Guidelines

GRANTS ANALYSIS
Total Grants: $123,950

Number of Grants: 33

Highest Grant: $10,000

Typical Range: $1,000 to $10,000

Disclosure Period: 1993

Note: Recent grants are derived from a 1993 Form 990.

RECENT GRANTS
General
10,000	Bethel College, North Newton, KS — strengthen church ties
10,000	Bluffton College, Bluffton, OH — minority scholarships
10,000	Goshen College, Goshen, IN — scholarships
8,000	Hesston College, Hesston, KS — peace studies program
5,200	Anabaptist Curriculum Publishers Council, Newton, KS — jubilee curriculum development

Williams Charitable Trust, Mary Jo

CONTACT
Michael E. Collins
Trustee
Mary Jo Williams Charitable Trust
607 N 7th
Garden City, KS 67846
(316) 276-3203

FINANCIAL SUMMARY
Recent Giving: $325,403 (1993); $269,420 (1991); $116,150 (1990)

Assets: $2,565,814 (1993); $2,521,590 (1991); $2,223,721 (1990)

EIN: 48-6276428

CONTRIBUTIONS SUMMARY
Typical Recipients: • *Arts & Humanities:* Libraries, Music • *Civic & Public Affairs:* Housing, Professional & Trade Associations • *Education:* Arts/Humanities Education, Community & Junior Colleges, Education Funds, Preschool Education, Public Education (Precollege), Science/Mathematics Education • *Environment:* General, Resource Conservation • *Religion:* Ministries, Religious Welfare • *Social Services:* At-Risk Youth, Community Service Organizations, Emergency Relief, Senior Services, United Funds/United Ways, Youth Organizations

Grant Types: emergency, endowment, general support, and scholarship

Geographic Distribution: Garden City, KS

GIVING OFFICERS
Michael E. Collins: trust

Leonard Rich: trust

Jack Williamson: trust

APPLICATION INFORMATION
Initial Approach: The foundation reports that only written proposals are considered for religious, charitable, scientific, literary, or educational purposes or for the prevention of cruelty to children or animals. The foundation does not support athletics or athletic competitions.

GRANTS ANALYSIS
Total Grants: $325,403

Number of Grants: 11

Highest Grant: $200,000

Typical Range: $1,000 to $63,903

Disclosure Period: 1993

Note: Recent grants are derived from a 1993 Form 990.

RECENT GRANTS

General

200,000	Montessori Learning Center, Garden City, KS — preschool child care
63,903	Garden City Community College Endowment Association, Garden City, KS — PC computers and software for science lecture hall; software and firearms for police science; FATS training for musicians in residence
15,000	Emmaus House, Garden City, KS — aid to needy
11,000	Nature Conservancy, Topeka, KS — nature conservation
10,000	Finney County United Way, Garden City, KS — various

KENTUCKY

Brown & Williamson Tobacco Corp.

Sales: $1.4 billion
Employees: 5,200
Parent Company: B.A.T. Industries p.l.c.
Headquarters: Louisville, KY
SIC Major Group: Cigarettes and Chewing & Smoking Tobacco

CONTACT
Joseph Helewicz
Vice President, Corporate Communications & Administration
Brown & Williamson Tobacco Corp.
1500 Brown & Williamson Tower
Louisville, KY 40202
(502) 568-7000
Note: Mr. Helewicz is also Chairman of the Contributions Committee.

FINANCIAL SUMMARY
Recent Giving: $1,600,000 (1995 est.); $1,600,000 (1994 approx.); $2,100,000 (1992 approx.)

Fiscal Note: Company gives directly. Above figures exclude nonmonetary support.

CONTRIBUTIONS SUMMARY
Typical Recipients: • *Arts & Humanities:* Arts Associations & Councils, Dance, Ethnic & Folk Arts, Historic Preservation, Libraries, Museums/Galleries, Public Broadcasting • *Civic & Public Affairs:* Business/Free Enterprise, Economic Development, Employment/Job Training, Law & Justice, Public Policy, Urban & Community Affairs, Women's Affairs, Zoos/Aquariums • *Education:* Colleges & Universities, Education Associations, Minority Education, Science/Mathematics Education • *Environment:* General • *Science:* Scientific Organizations • *Social Services:* Child Welfare, Community Centers, Community Service Organizations, Family Services, Senior Services, Substance Abuse, United Funds/United Ways

Grant Types: award, capital, employee matching gifts, general support, operating expenses, research, and scholarship

Nonmonetary Support Types: donated equipment and workplace solicitation

Geographic Distribution: near headquarters and operating locations only

Operating Locations: GA, KY (Louisville), NC, PA, SC

CORP. OFFICERS
Nick Brookes: *CURR EMPL* chmn, ceo: Brown & Williamson Tobacco Corp

Joseph S. Helewicz: *CURR EMPL* vp corp commun: Brown & Williamson Tobacco Corp

Earl Eugene Kohnhorst: *B* Louisville KY 1947 *ED* Univ Louisville 1970; Univ Louisville 1971 *CURR EMPL* exec vp, coo, dir: Brown & Williamson Tobacco Corp

Patricia A. Lafollette: *CURR EMPL* pub aff asst: Brown & Williamson Tobacco Corp

Michael J. McGraw: *CURR EMPL* sr vp law & human resources: Brown & Williamson Tobacco Corp

Carl L. Schoenbachler, Jr.: *CURR EMPL* sr vp, cfo, dir: Brown & Williamson Tobacco Corp

T. E. Whitehair, Jr.: *CURR EMPL* exec vp, mktg and sales: Brown & Williamson Tobacco Corp

GIVING OFFICERS
Joseph S. Helewicz: chmn contributions comm *CURR EMPL* vp corp commun: Brown & Williamson Tobacco Corp (see above)

APPLICATION INFORMATION
Initial Approach: *Initial Contact:* letter requesting formal application form *Include Information On:* description of the organization, amount requested, purpose of funds sought, recently audited financial statement, and proof of tax-exempt status *Deadlines:* August

Restrictions on Giving: The company does not support individuals, dinners or special events, fraternal organizations, goodwill advertising, member agencies of united funds, political or lobbying groups, or religious organizations for sectarian purposes.

GRANTS ANALYSIS
Total Grants: $1,600,000

Typical Range: $2,500 to $5,000

Disclosure Period: 1994

Note: Recent grants are derived from a 1994 partial grants list.

RECENT GRANTS

General

5,000	American Indian College Fund, Louisville, KY — to ensure the survival and growth of their institutions, all of which are located on or near reservations in 12 western and midwestern states

Commercial Bank / Commercial Bank Foundation

Sales: $11.5 million
Employees: 70
Parent Company: Commercial Bancorp.
Headquarters: Grayson, KY
SIC Major Group: Depository Institutions

CONTACT
Jack W. Strother
President and Chief Executive Officer
Commercial Bank
208 E Main St.
Grayson, KY 41143
(606) 474-7811
Note: Corporate address is 1918 Cumberland Ave., Drawer 520, Middlesboro, KY 40965; Tel: (606) 248-1450.

FINANCIAL SUMMARY
Recent Giving: $8,667 (1993); $7,000 (1992); $9,125 (1991)

Assets: $220,496 (1993); $199,739 (1992); $175,720 (1991)

Gifts Received: $25,000 (1993); $25,000 (1992); $25,000 (1991)

Fiscal Note: In 1993, contributions were received from the Commercial Bank of Grayson.

EIN: 61-1087988

CONTRIBUTIONS SUMMARY
Typical Recipients: • *Arts & Humanities:* Libraries • *Education:* Colleges & Universities, Public Education (Precollege), Student Aid

Grant Types: scholarship

Geographic Distribution: limited to Carter County, KY

Operating Locations: KY (Grayson)

CORP. OFFICERS
Jack W. Strother, Sr.: *CURR EMPL* chmn: Commercial Bank

Jack W. Strother, Sr.: *CURR EMPL* pres, ceo, dir: Commercial Bank

GIVING OFFICERS
Jack W. Strother, Sr.: trust *CURR EMPL* chmn: Commercial Bank (see above)

Jack W. Strother, Sr.: trust *CURR EMPL* pres, ceo, dir: Commercial Bank (see above)

APPLICATION INFORMATION
Initial Approach: Application form required for scholarships. Other applications in writing. Deadline for graduating seniors is April 15.

Restrictions on Giving: Scholarships restricted to Carter County seniors.

OTHER THINGS TO KNOW
Provides higher education scholarships to graduates of Carter County, KY, high schools.

GRANTS ANALYSIS
Total Grants: $8,667

Number of Grants: 17

Highest Grant: $667

Disclosure Period: 1993

Note: Recent grants are derived from a 1993 Form 990.

RECENT GRANTS
Library
500	Olive Hill Public Library, KY

General
667	Northern Kentucky University, Highland Heights, KY — scholarship
500	Georgetown College, Georgetown, KY — scholarship
500	Georgetown College, Georgetown, KY — scholarship
500	Georgetown College, Georgetown, KY — scholarship
500	McDavid/Hicks Memorial Scholarship Fund, KY

Gheens Foundation

CONTACT
James N. Davis
Executive Director and Treasurer
Gheens Foundation
One Riverfront Plz., Ste. 705
Louisville, KY 40202
(502) 584-4650

FINANCIAL SUMMARY
Recent Giving: $2,087,313 (fiscal 1993); $2,117,210 (fiscal 1992); $1,551,556 (fiscal 1990)

Assets: $53,119,248 (fiscal 1993); $52,539,533 (fiscal 1992); $44,629,378 (fiscal 1990)

Gifts Received: $28,061,635 (fiscal 1986)

EIN: 61-6031406

CONTRIBUTIONS SUMMARY
Donor(s): The foundation was established in 1957, with the late C. Edwin Gheens and the late Mary Jo Gheens Hill as donors.

Typical Recipients: • *Arts & Humanities:* Arts Centers, Historic Preservation, History & Archaeology, Libraries, Museums/Galleries, Opera, Public Broadcasting, Theater • *Civic & Public Affairs:* African American Affairs, Clubs, Economic Development, General, Legal Aid, Philanthropic Organizations • *Education:* Agricultural Education, Business Education, Colleges & Universities, Economic Education, Education Associations, Education Reform, Elementary Education (Private), General, Literacy, Medical Education, Private Education (Precollege), Public Education (Precollege), Religious Education, Secondary Education (Private), Special Education • *Environment:* Air/Water Quality, Resource Conservation, Wildlife Protection • *Health:* Cancer, Children's Health/Hospitals, Diabetes, Eyes/Blindness, Geriatric Health, Medical Rehabilitation, Mental Health, Single-Disease Health Associations • *Religion:* Churches, Jewish Causes, Ministries, Religious Organizations, Religious Welfare • *Science:* Science Museums • *Social Services:* At-Risk Youth, Child Welfare, Family Planning, Family Services, Food/Clothing Distribution, People with Disabilities, Scouts, Senior Services, Substance Abuse, United Funds/United Ways, Youth Organizations

Grant Types: capital, challenge, department, endowment, project, and research

Geographic Distribution: emphasis on Louisville, KY, and Louisiana

GIVING OFFICERS
Oscar Sims Bryant, Jr.: secy, trust *B* Jakin GA 1920 *ED* Draughn Sch Commerce 1946 *CURR EMPL* exec vp, mem exec comm, dir: Liberty Natl Bank & Trust Co KY *NONPR AFFIL* dir: Filson Club, Louisville Soc Prevention Blindness, Recordings Blind; mem exec comm: Boy Scouts Am Old KY Home Counc; pres: Fairmont Fund *CLUB AFFIL* Masons, Owl Creek CC, Pendennis, Shriners

Walter S. Coe: trust

James N. Davis: treas, exec dir

Donald W. Doyle: trust

John M. Smith: trust

Joseph E. Stopher: pres, trust *B* 1914 *ED* Univ Louisville LLB 1938 *CURR EMPL* ptnr: Boehl Stopher & Graves

APPLICATION INFORMATION
Initial Approach:

The foundation provides an application form; ten copies of the completed application should be sent to the foundation.

The application form requests the following information: name of organization, contact person and title, address, program summary, describing the activities of the organization and the particular activity that the grant would fund; and a financial summary detailing the amount of the request, total annual budget of the organization, and the budget for the project which the grant would support.

There are no deadlines for submitting applications.

GRANTS ANALYSIS
Total Grants: $1,916,500*

Number of Grants: 62

Highest Grant: $250,000

Average Grant: $30,911

Typical Range: $5,000 to $60,000

Disclosure Period: fiscal year ending October 31, 1993

Note: Total grants figure excludes $170,813 in grant-related expenses. Recent grants are derived from a fiscal 1993 Form 990.

RECENT GRANTS
Library
250,000	Bellarmine College, Louisville, KY — new library

General
200,000	Jefferson County Board of Education, Louisville, KY — education
175,000	Boy Scouts of America Old Kentucky Home Council, Louisville, KY — operating costs
100,000	David School, David, KY — capital costs
100,000	University of Kentucky, Sanders-Brown Center of Aging, Lexington, KY — capital costs
70,000	Metro United Way, Louisville, KY — operating costs

Houchens Foundation, Ervin G.

Former Foundation Name: Houchens Foundation

CONTACT
George S. Houchens
Director
Ervin G. Houchens Fdn.
PO Box 90009
Bowling Green, KY 42102
(502) 843-3252

FINANCIAL SUMMARY
Recent Giving: $75,047 (1992); $34,259 (1991); $69,435 (1990)

Assets: $3,862,973 (1992); $3,872,847 (1991); $3,872,180 (1990)

Gifts Received: $17,486 (1992); $15,528 (1991)

Fiscal Note: In 1992, major contributions were received from Ervin G. Houchens Foundation, Inc. ($17,436).

EIN: 61-0623087

CONTRIBUTIONS SUMMARY

Donor(s): Houchens Markets, Inc., B.G. Wholesale

Typical Recipients: • *Arts & Humanities:* Arts Associations & Councils, Arts Funds, Historic Preservation, History & Archaeology, Libraries, Theater • *Civic & Public Affairs:* Safety • *Education:* Business Education, Colleges & Universities, Education Funds, Literacy, Student Aid • *Environment:* General • *Health:* Single-Disease Health Associations • *Religion:* Churches, Missionary Activities (Domestic), Religious Welfare • *Social Services:* Child Welfare, Community Service Organizations, Recreation & Athletics, United Funds/United Ways, Youth Organizations

Grant Types: general support

Geographic Distribution: limited to southwest KY

GIVING OFFICERS

Covella H. Biggers: treas, dir

Erin Biggers: dir

Gil E. Biggers: dir

Gil M. Biggers: dir

Ervin G. Houchens: pres, dir

George Suel Houchens: dir

C. Cecil Martin: dir

Lois Lynne Martin: secy, dir

APPLICATION INFORMATION

Initial Approach: Send a brief letter of inquiry. Include a description of organization, amount requested, purpose of funds sought, recently audited financial statement, and proof of tax-exempt status. There are no deadlines.

OTHER THINGS TO KNOW

Provides loans to local higher education institutions, churches, and youth clubs in southwest Kentucky.

GRANTS ANALYSIS

Total Grants: $75,047

Number of Grants: 28

Highest Grant: $10,000

Typical Range: $1,000 to $5,000

Disclosure Period: 1992

Note: Recent grants are derived from a 1992 Form 990.

RECENT GRANTS

Library

5,000	Bowling Green Public Library, Bowling Green, IN	

General

10,000	Child Protection, Bowling Green, IN	
9,500	Clear Creek Bible College, Pineville, KY	
5,000	Kentucky Wesleyan College, Owensboro, KY	
5,000	Oakland City College, Oakland City, IN	
4,000	Audubon Council, Owensboro, KY	

Humana, Inc. / Humana Foundation

Revenue: $3.65 billion
Employees: 11,431
Headquarters: Louisville, KY
SIC Major Group: General Medical & Surgical Hospitals, Accident & Health Insurance, Hospital & Medical Service Plans, and Insurance Agents, Brokers & Service

CONTACT

Virginia Lewman
Foundation Manager
Humana Fdn.
500 W Main St.
PO Box 1438
Louisville, KY 40201
(502) 580-3041

FINANCIAL SUMMARY

Recent Giving: $5,300,000 (fiscal 1995 est.); $5,000,000 (fiscal 1994 approx.); $4,440,137 (fiscal 1993)

Assets: $31,284,989 (fiscal 1993); $36,511,433 (fiscal 1991); $21,581,174 (fiscal 1990)

Gifts Received: $1,804,184 (fiscal 1993); $6,599,870 (fiscal 1991)

Fiscal Note: All contributions are made through the foundation. Above figures exclude nonmonetary support. In fiscal 1993, the foundation received $1,804,184 in stock from Humana.

EIN: 61-1004763

CONTRIBUTIONS SUMMARY

Typical Recipients: • *Arts & Humanities:* Arts Associations & Councils, Arts Centers, Arts Festivals, Arts Funds, Community Arts, Dance, Historic Preservation, History & Archaeology, Libraries, Museums/Galleries, Music, Performing Arts, Public Broadcasting, Theater • *Civic & Public Affairs:* Asian American Affairs, Business/Free Enterprise, Civil Rights, Community Foundations, Economic Development, General, Hispanic Affairs, Legal Aid, Nonprofit Management, Philanthropic Organizations, Professional & Trade Associations, Urban & Community Affairs, Women's Affairs, Zoos/Aquariums • *Education:* Business Education, Colleges & Universities, Continuing Education, Education Associations, Education Funds, Education Reform, Elementary Education (Private), Medical Education, Minority Education, Preschool Education, Private Education (Precollege), Public Education (Precollege), Secondary Education (Private), Special Education, Student Aid • *Environment:* General • *Health:* Children's Health/Hospitals, Clinics/Medical Centers, Emergency/Ambulance Services, Heart, Hospitals, Medical Research, Mental Health, Nursing Services, Single-Disease Health Associations • *International:* Foreign Educational Institutions • *Religion:* Dioceses, Religious Welfare • *Science:* Science Museums, Scientific Organizations • *Social Services:* Child Welfare, Community Centers, Community Service Organizations, Family

Planning, Family Services, Food/Clothing Distribution, Homes, People with Disabilities, Senior Services, United Funds/United Ways, Youth Organizations

Grant Types: capital, conference/seminar, department, endowment, general support, research, and scholarship

Geographic Distribution: emphasis on Louisville, KY

Operating Locations: AL, AZ, DC, FL (Jacksonville), IL, KS, KY (Lexington, Louisville), MO, NV, OH, TX (San Antonio)

CORP. OFFICERS

David Allen Jones: *B* Louisville KY 1931 *ED* Univ Louisville BS 1954; Yale Univ JD 1960 *CURR EMPL* co-fdr, chmn, ceo, dir: Humana Inc *CORP AFFIL* dir: Abbott Laboratories, Royal Crown Cos; mem exec comm, dir: First KY Natl Corp, First KY Trust Co, First Natl Bank Louisville *NONPR AFFIL* mem: Louisville Area Chamber Commerce

Wayne Thomas Smith: *B* Painesville OH 1943 *ED* Auburn Univ BS 1968; Auburn Univ MS 1969; Trinity Univ 1971-1973 *CURR EMPL* pres, coo, dir: Humana Ins Co *CORP AFFIL* chmn: Managed Care Indemnity Inc; dir, exec vp: Humana Inc; pres: Humana Health Ins Co FL, Humana Health Ins Co NV; pres, coo, dir: Health Value Mgmt Inc, HMPK Inc, HPLAN Inc, Humana Broadway Corp, Humana Enterprises Inc, Humana Health Plan AK Inc, Humana Health Plan AL Inc, Humana Health Plan AR Inc, Humana Health Plan FL Inc, Humana Health Plan GA Inc, Humana Health Plan Inc, Humana Health Plan LA Inc, Humana Health Plan MD Inc, Humana Health Plan MI Inc, Humana Health Plan NC Inc, Humana Health Plan OH Inc, Humana Health Plan PA Inc, Humana Health Plan TX Inc, Humana Health Plan UT Inc, Humana Health Plan WA Inc, Humana HealthChicago Ins Co, Humana Ins Agency Inc, Humana Kansas City Inc, Humana Med Plan CA Inc, Humana Med Plan Inc, Humana Military Healthcare Svcs Inc, Humco Inc, Humrealty Inc, Managed Prescription Svcs Inc, MedBenefixx Inc, Prescription Benefits Inc, Prime Benefits Sys Inc, Prime Health KS Inc, Prime Health Mgmt Svcs Inc, Randmark Inc

GIVING OFFICERS

George G. Bauernfeind: vp (taxes) *CURR EMPL* vp taxes: Humana Inc

Martha E. Clark: assoc secy *CURR EMPL* assoc secy: Humana Health Plan Inc

Darlene A. Curlee: asst secy *CURR EMPL* asst secy, dir: Humana Health Plan Inc

James Willard Doucette: vp, treas *B* Louisville KY 1951 *ED* Univ Louisville 1972; Univ PA Wharton Sch 1976 *CURR EMPL* vp investment mgmt, treas: Humana Inc *CORP AFFIL* treas, dir: Humana Health Ins NV Inc, Humana HealthChicago Ins Co; vp investments, treas, dir: Humana Health Plan Inc *NONPR AFFIL* mem: Am Philatelic Soc, Assn Investment Mgmt & Res, Natl Assn HMO Regulators

W. Roger Drury: sr vp *CURR EMPL* cfo: Humana Inc *CORP AFFIL* treas, dir: Hurstbourne CC Inc

David Allen Jones: chmn, ceo, dir *CURR EMPL* co-fdr, chmn, ceo, dir: Humana Inc (see above)

Virginia Lewman: fdn mgr

James E. Murray: vp *CURR EMPL* vp, contr, dir: Humana Health Plan Inc

Walter Emerson Neely: vp *CURR EMPL* secy, dir: Humana Med Plan Inc *CORP AFFIL* secy, dir: Humana Health Ins NV Inc, Humana Health Plan OH Inc, Humana HealthChicago Ins Co; vp, gen couns, secy: Humana Health Plan Inc

Wayne Thomas Smith: pres, dir *CURR EMPL* pres, coo, dir: Humana Ins Co (see above)

APPLICATION INFORMATION
Initial Approach: *Initial Contact:* request application *Include Information On:* description of the organization, amount requested, purpose for which funds are sought, recently audited financial statement, and proof of tax-exempt status *Deadlines:* none

Restrictions on Giving: Company does not give to fraternal organizations, political or lobbying groups, religious organizations for sectarian purposes, or individuals.

OTHER THINGS TO KNOW
The company reports that it is presently restructuring its giving program.

On August 31, 1993, the foundation made a distribution of assets with a fair market value of $17,676,453 to the Galen Foundation. The Galen Foundation is the philanthropic arm of Galen Corp., which recently merged with Columbia Healthcare Systems. Columbia Healthcare merged in 1994 with Hospital Corp. of America to form Columbia/HCA Healthcare Systems (see separate entry for details).

GRANTS ANALYSIS
Total Grants: $4,440,137

Number of Grants: 77

Highest Grant: $673,700

Average Grant: $57,664

Typical Range: $1,000 to $25,000 and $100,000 to $325,000

Disclosure Period: fiscal year ending August 31, 1993

Note: Recent grants are derived from a fiscal 1993 Form 990.

RECENT GRANTS

General
673,700	Humana Foundation Scholarship Program, Educational Testing Service, Princeton, NJ
325,000	University of Kentucky, Lexington, KY
275,000	American Red Cross, Louisville Chapter, Louisville, KY
250,000	Claremont Graduate School, Claremont, CA
247,500	Kentucky School Reform Corporation, Lexington, KY

Norton Foundation Inc.

Former Foundation Name: George Norton Foundation

CONTACT
Lucy Crawford
Executive Director
Norton Fdn Inc.
4350 Brownsboro Rd., Ste. 133
Louisville, KY 40207
(502) 893-9549

FINANCIAL SUMMARY
Recent Giving: $592,172 (1992); $497,844 (1991); $468,420 (1990)

Assets: $12,675,377 (1992); $12,703,998 (1991); $10,939,559 (1990)

Gifts Received: $4,000,040 (1989)

EIN: 61-6024040

CONTRIBUTIONS SUMMARY
Donor(s): Mrs. George W. Norton

Typical Recipients: • *Arts & Humanities:* Arts Centers, Arts Festivals, Arts Funds, Community Arts, Ethnic & Folk Arts, Libraries, Museums/Galleries, Public Broadcasting, Theater, Visual Arts • *Civic & Public Affairs:* African American Affairs, Community Foundations, General, Urban & Community Affairs, Women's Affairs • *Education:* Colleges & Universities, Economic Education, Education Funds, General, Public Education (Precollege), Special Education • *Environment:* General, Resource Conservation • *International:* International Peace & Security Issues • *Religion:* Ministries, Religious Organizations • *Social Services:* Child Welfare, Community Centers, Community Service Organizations, Family Planning, Family Services, Food/Clothing Distribution, Homes, People with Disabilities, Shelters/Homelessness, United Funds/United Ways, Volunteer Services, Youth Organizations

Grant Types: operating expenses

Geographic Distribution: focus on KY

GIVING OFFICERS
Richard Clay: dir

Lucy Crawford: exec dir

Jane Norton Dulaney: pres, dir

Robert W. Dulaney: vp, dir

APPLICATION INFORMATION
Initial Approach: Send cover letter and full proposal. There are no deadlines. Board meets quarterly. Decisions are made within 90 days.

Restrictions on Giving: Does not support individuals or provide endowment funds.

GRANTS ANALYSIS
Total Grants: $592,172

Number of Grants: 40

Highest Grant: $66,002

Typical Range: $2,500 to $15,000

Disclosure Period: 1992

Note: Recent grants are derived from a 1992 Form 990.

RECENT GRANTS

General
66,002	University of Louisville Foundation, Louisville, KY
35,000	Family Place
30,000	Governor's Scholars, Effective Learning Project
30,000	Kentucky Youth Advocates, Louisville, KY
30,000	Morton Center

Providian Corporation

Revenue: $2.95 billion
Employees: 9,300
Headquarters: Louisville, KY
SIC Major Group: Holding Companies Nec, Life Insurance, and Accident & Health Insurance

CONTACT
Diane Everse
Manager, Corporate Relations
Providian Corp.
PO Box 32830
Louisville, KY 40232
(502) 560-2190

FINANCIAL SUMMARY
Recent Giving: $1,944,900 (1995 est.); $1,635,678 (1994); $1,622,240 (1993)

Fiscal Note: Above figures reflect both foundation and direct corporate giving. Above figures exclude nonmonetary support.

CONTRIBUTIONS SUMMARY
Typical Recipients: • *Arts & Humanities:* Arts Associations & Councils, Arts Centers, Arts Funds, Arts Institutes, Community Arts, Film & Video, Historic Preservation, Libraries, Museums/Galleries, Music, Opera, Performing Arts, Public Broadcasting, Theater • *Civic & Public Affairs:* Economic Development, General, Housing, Legal Aid, Nonprofit Management, Philanthropic Organizations, Safety, Urban & Community Affairs, Women's Affairs, Zoos/Aquariums • *Education:* Business Education, Colleges & Universities, Community & Junior Colleges, Continuing Education, Economic Education, Education Associations, Education Funds, Elementary Education (Private), General, Literacy, Minority Education, Preschool Education, Private Education (Precollege), Public Education (Precollege), Special Education • *Health:* General, Geriatric Health, Medical Research, Single-Disease Health Associations • *Social Services:* Child Welfare, Community Centers, Community Service Organizations, Family Services, Food/Clothing Distribution, General, Homes, People with Disabilities, Senior Services, Shelters/Homelessness, United Funds/United Ways, Volunteer Services, Youth Organizations

Grant Types: capital, emergency, employee matching gifts, general support, and multi-year/continuing support

Note: Employee matching gift ratio: 1 to 1.

Nonmonetary Support: $65,000 (1993)

Nonmonetary Support Types: donated equipment, in-kind services, loaned employees, and loaned executives

Geographic Distribution: primarily Louisville and operating locations

Operating Locations: CA (Pleasanton, Redding, San Francisco), KY (Louisville), MO (St. Louis), NC (Durham), PA (Frazer, Valley Forge)

CORP. OFFICERS
Irving Widmer Bailey II: *B* Cambridge MA 1941 *ED* Univ CO 1963; NY Univ 1968 *CURR EMPL* chmn: Commonwealth Life Ins Co *CORP AFFIL* chmn, pres, ceo, dir: Providian Corp; dir: BellSouth Telecommun Inc, Capital Holding Corp *NONPR AFFIL* dir: Fed Reserve Bank St Louis Louisville Branch

Shailesh J. Mehta: *B* Bombay India 1949 *ED* Indian Inst Tech 1971; Case Western Reserve Univ 1975 *CURR EMPL* pres, ceo: Providian Corp *CORP AFFIL* pres, ceo: First Deposit Corp

Robert L. Walker: *CURR EMPL* sr vp planning & fin, cfo: Providian Corp

GIVING OFFICERS
Diane Everse: *CURR EMPL* mgr, corp rels: Providian Corp

APPLICATION INFORMATION
Initial Approach: *Initial Contact:* brief letter of inquiry *Include Information On:* description of the organization, including fiscal year and geographic area served; description of program for which funds are sought, including program budget; list of training needs that can be met by Providian associate volunteers (if program is for education); identity of other corporate or foundation sources approached for funding, including commitments to date; number of people served by program, including available demographic data; current listing of officers and directors and their professional affiliations; copy of most recent audited financial statements and annual report; positive promotional opportunities available to Providian as a result of request; proof of tax-exempt status *Deadlines:* none

Restrictions on Giving: Does not support individuals or political campaigns.

OTHER THINGS TO KNOW
In 1993 the company changed its name from Capital Holding Corporation to Providian Corporation.

GRANTS ANALYSIS
Total Grants: $2,300,000

Typical Range: $1,000 to $2,500

Disclosure Period: 1994

Note: Total grants figure provided by company. Figures for number of grants and average grants not available.

RECENT GRANTS
Library
Louisville Library, Louisville, KY

General
American Red Cross, Washington, DC
Campaign for Greater Louisville, Louisville, KY
Insurance Industry AIDS Initiative, Washington, DC
Metro United Way, Louisville, KY
Salvation Army, Washington, DC

Thomas Foundation, Joan and Lee

CONTACT
Lee B. Thomas
Director
Joan and Lee Thomas Fdn.
2602 Grassland Dr.
Louisville, KY 40299-2524
(502) 495-1958

FINANCIAL SUMMARY
Recent Giving: $557,140 (fiscal 1994); $557,687 (fiscal 1993); $210,000 (fiscal 1991)

Assets: $13,156,794 (fiscal 1994); $13,174,515 (fiscal 1993); $10,793,746 (fiscal 1991)

Gifts Received: $420,000 (fiscal 1994); $700,000 (fiscal 1993); $250,000 (fiscal 1991)

Fiscal Note: In fiscal 1994, contributions were received from Lee B. and Joan E. Thomas.

EIN: 61-1166955

CONTRIBUTIONS SUMMARY
Donor(s): the donor is Lee B. Thomas, Jr., a director of the foundation

Typical Recipients: • *Arts & Humanities:* Arts Centers, Libraries, Music • *Civic & Public Affairs:* Economic Policy, First Amendment Issues, General, Housing, Law & Justice, Legal Aid, Philanthropic Organizations, Public Policy, Urban & Community Affairs, Women's Affairs • *Education:* Colleges & Universities, General, Literacy, Preschool Education, Private Education (Precollege), Student Aid • *Health:* Nursing Services • *International:* International Environmental Issues, International Peace & Security Issues, International Relations • *Religion:* Religious Organizations, Religious Welfare, Social/Policy Issues • *Social Services:* At-Risk Youth, Child Welfare, Community Centers, Community Service Organizations, Family Services, Homes, Senior Services, United Funds/United Ways, Youth Organizations

Grant Types: general support

Geographic Distribution: primarily KY

GIVING OFFICERS
Glenn E. Thomas: dir

Dr. Joan E. Thomas: dir

Lee B. Thomas: dir

APPLICATION INFORMATION
Initial Approach: The foundation has no formal grant application procedure or application form. There are no deadlines.

GRANTS ANALYSIS
Total Grants: $557,140

Number of Grants: 20

Highest Grant: $200,140

Typical Range: $1,000 to $65,000

Disclosure Period: fiscal year ending June 30, 1994

Note: Recent grants are derived from a fiscal 1994 Form 990.

RECENT GRANTS
General

200,140	Center for Women and Families, Louisville, KY
65,000	Home of the Innocents, Louisville, KY
62,000	Lincoln Foundation, Louisville, KY
50,000	Council on Economic Priorities, New York, NY
50,000	National Center for Family Literacy, Louisville, KY

Thomas Industries / Thomas Foundation

Revenue: $450.15 million
Employees: 3,500
Headquarters: Louisville, KY
SIC Major Group: Industrial Machinery & Equipment

CONTACT
Phil J. Stuecker
Vice President and Chief Financial Officer
Thomas Industries
4360 Brownsboro Rd.
Ste. 300
Louisville, KY 40207
(502) 893-4600

FINANCIAL SUMMARY
Recent Giving: $43,500 (1993); $66,750 (1992); $25,100 (1991)

Assets: $4,515 (1993); $3,015 (1992); $8,765 (1991)

Gifts Received: $45,000 (1993); $61,000 (1992); $29,500 (1991)

Fiscal Note: In 1993, contributions were received from Thomas Industries, Inc.

EIN: 39-6075230

CONTRIBUTIONS SUMMARY
Typical Recipients: • *Arts & Humanities:* Arts Associations & Councils, History & Archaeology, Libraries, Museums/Galleries, Music • *Civic & Public Affairs:* Botanical Gardens/Parks, Clubs, Economic Development, General, Housing, Urban & Community Affairs • *Education:* Business Education, Colleges & Universities, Community & Junior Colleges, Economic Education, Education Funds, Public Education (Precollege) • *Health:* Arthritis, Emer-

gency/Ambulance Services, Health Funds, Hospices, Hospitals, Medical Rehabilitation • *Social Services:* Camps, Child Welfare, Family Services, Homes, People with Disabilities, Scouts, Senior Services, Shelters/Homelessness, United Funds/United Ways, Volunteer Services, Youth Organizations

Grant Types: capital and general support

Geographic Distribution: focus on Louisville, KY

Operating Locations: KY (Louisville)

CORP. OFFICERS

Timothy Charles Brown: *B* Louisville KY 1950 *ED* Eastern KY Univ BBA 1972; Univ Louisville MBA *CURR EMPL* pres, ceo, dir: Thomas Indus *NONPR AFFIL* mem: AICPA, Kentucky Soc CPAs

Phillip J. Stuecker: *CURR EMPL* vp, cfo: Thomas Indus

GIVING OFFICERS

Timothy Charles Brown: pres *CURR EMPL* pres, ceo, dir: Thomas Indus (see above)

C. Barr Schuler: vp

Phillip J. Stuecker: cfo, vp, secy *CURR EMPL* vp, cfo: Thomas Indus (see above)

David J. Stumler: asst secy

Ronald D. Wiseman: treas

APPLICATION INFORMATION

Initial Approach: Submit a brief letter of inquiry. Deadline is October 1.

GRANTS ANALYSIS

Total Grants: $43,500

Number of Grants: 12

Highest Grant: $25,000

Typical Range: $300 to $5,000

Disclosure Period: 1993

Note: Recent grants are derived from a 1993 Form 990.

RECENT GRANTS

Library
4,000	Henderson County Public Library, Henderson, KY

General
25,000	Friends of Audubon State Park
20,000	Electrical Contracting Foundation
5,295	Chaney House Group Home, Henderson, KY
5,000	Brescia College, Owensboro, KY
5,000	Cliff Hagan Boys Club, Owensboro, KY

Yeager Charitable Trust, Lester E.

CONTACT
Donald W. Haas
Trustee
Lester E. Yeager Charitable Trust
PO Box 964
Owensboro, KY 42302-0964
(502) 686-8254

FINANCIAL SUMMARY
Recent Giving: $141,195 (1993); $143,225 (1992); $222,527 (1990)

Assets: $4,114,568 (1993); $4,040,293 (1992); $3,824,457 (1990)

Gifts Received: $148,947 (1990); $531,595 (1989)

Fiscal Note: In 1990, contributions were received from the estate of Lester E. Yeager.

EIN: 61-1159548

CONTRIBUTIONS SUMMARY
Donor(s): the donor is the estate of Lester E. Yeager

Typical Recipients: • *Arts & Humanities:* Arts Associations & Councils, Libraries, Museums/Galleries, Music • *Civic & Public Affairs:* Botanical Gardens/Parks, Clubs, Housing, Municipalities/Towns, Urban & Community Affairs, Zoos/Aquariums • *Education:* Business Education, Colleges & Universities, Community & Junior Colleges, Education Associations, Education Funds, Private Education (Precollege) • *Environment:* General • *Health:* Emergency/Ambulance Services, Hospices, Hospitals, Single-Disease Health Associations • *Religion:* Churches • *Social Services:* Child Welfare, Community Centers, Homes, People with Disabilities, Recreation & Athletics, Senior Services, Shelters/Homelessness, United Funds/United Ways, Volunteer Services, Youth Organizations

Grant Types: general support

Geographic Distribution: primarily in Daviess County, KY

GIVING OFFICERS
Ruth F. Adkins: trust

Donald W. Haas: trust

Nancy C. Kennedy: trust

William L. Wilson: trust

APPLICATION INFORMATION
Initial Approach: Request application form. Deadline is December 15.

Restrictions on Giving: The foundation does not make grants to individuals.

GRANTS ANALYSIS
Total Grants: $141,195

Number of Grants: 35

Highest Grant: $25,000

Typical Range: $1,000 to $20,000

Disclosure Period: 1993

Note: Recent grants are derived from a 1993 Form 990.

RECENT GRANTS

Library
5,000	Henderson County Public Library, Henderson, KY

General
25,000	RiverPark Center, Owensboro, KY
15,000	Brescia College, Owensboro, KY
15,000	Kentucky Wesleyan College, Owensboro, KY
7,500	College Foundation
7,500	Owensboro Community College, Owensboro, KY

LOUISIANA

Babcock & Wilcox Co.

Revenue: $1.59 billion
Employees: 19,000
Parent Company: Babcock & Wilcox Investment Company
Headquarters: New Orleans, LA
SIC Major Group: Electronic & Other Electrical Equipment, Fabricated Metal Products, Industrial Machinery & Equipment, and Primary Metal Industries

CONTACT
Don Washington
Manager, Communications & Investor Relations
Babcock & Wilcox Co.
PO Box 60035
New Orleans, LA 70160
(504) 587-4080
Note: Company is located at 1450 Poydras Street, New Orleans, LA.

FINANCIAL SUMMARY
Fiscal Note: Annual Giving Range: $500,000 to $1 million

CONTRIBUTIONS SUMMARY
Education: 40% of total contributions. Interests include business, elementary, and engineering education, as well as colleges and universities.

Civic & Public Affairs: Approximately 30%. Supports economic development, environmental affairs, national security, and professional and trade associations. 1 **Health & Human Services:** About 20%. Primarily supports community service organizations and united funds.

Arts & Humanities: 10%. Includes performing arts, museums, and various arts organizations in the New Orleans area.

Typical Recipients: • *Arts & Humanities:* Arts Centers, Historic Preservation, Libraries, Museums/Galleries, Music • *Civic & Public Affairs:* Business/Free Enterprise, Economic Development, Philanthropic Organizations, Professional & Trade Associations • *Education:* Business Education,

Colleges & Universities, Elementary Education (Private), Engineering/Technological Education, Public Education (Precollege) • *Environment:* General • *Health:* Hospitals, Medical Research • *Science:* Scientific Organizations • *Social Services:* Community Centers, Community Service Organizations, Food/Clothing Distribution, United Funds/United Ways

Grant Types: capital, general support, multiyear/continuing support, and scholarship

Nonmonetary Support Types: in-kind services, loaned employees, and workplace solicitation

Geographic Distribution: principally near operating locations and to national organizations

Operating Locations: LA (New Orleans)

CORP. OFFICERS
Brock A. Hattox: *CURR EMPL* sr vp, cfo: Babcock & Wilcox Co

GIVING OFFICERS
Don Washington: *CURR EMPL* mgr commun & investor rels: Babcock & Wilcox Co *PHIL AFFIL* mem contributions comm

APPLICATION INFORMATION
Initial Contact: written proposal

Include Information On: name, address, and nature of program or description of the organization; pertinent financial material; names of other supporters; and the amount requested

Deadlines: none

Restrictions on Giving: The company does not support individuals or religious organizations for sectarian purposes.

OTHER THINGS TO KNOW
Babcock & Wilcox is a subsidiary of McDermott, Inc. (see separate entry). Both contributions programs are administered through the headquarters office in New Orleans. The company gives under the name from where the proposal originates. Babcock & Wilcox and McDermott have operating facilities throughout the United States.

During the past several years, funds for the contributions program have been limited as a result of a decline in business. The company's first priority is to continue support to organizations with whom the company has traditional, established relationships. However, the company continues to review proposals from new organizations.

The company reviews all requests for support of charitable, civic, and cultural causes in light of their benefit to the communities in which the company's operations or offices are located. Aid-to-education grants and scholarships are closely aligned with the college recruiting program.

GRANTS ANALYSIS
Typical Range: $1,000 to $2,500

Coughlin-Saunders Foundation

CONTACT
Coughlin-Saunders Fdn.
1412 Centre Ct., Ste. 202
Alexandria, LA 71301
(318) 445-9342

FINANCIAL SUMMARY
Recent Giving: $498,990 (fiscal 1992); $457,650 (fiscal 1990); $328,125 (fiscal 1989)

Assets: $10,330,626 (fiscal 1992); $9,095,124 (fiscal 1990); $9,064,379 (fiscal 1989)

Gifts Received: $1,547,820 (fiscal 1989); $3,660 (fiscal 1988)

EIN: 72-6027641

CONTRIBUTIONS SUMMARY
Donor(s): the late Anne S. Coughlin, R. R. Saunders, the late F. H. Coughlin, J. A. Adams

Typical Recipients: • *Arts & Humanities:* Arts Associations & Councils, Ballet, General, Libraries, Museums/Galleries, Music, Performing Arts, Theater • *Civic & Public Affairs:* Botanical Gardens/Parks, General • *Education:* Colleges & Universities, General, Literacy, Medical Education, Private Education (Precollege), Science/Mathematics Education, Secondary Education (Private), Student Aid • *Health:* Emergency/Ambulance Services, Health Organizations, Hospitals • *Religion:* Churches, Jewish Causes, Religious Welfare • *Social Services:* Child Welfare, Community Service Organizations, Food/Clothing Distribution, United Funds/United Ways, Youth Organizations

Grant Types: capital, fellowship, loan, professorship, and scholarship

Geographic Distribution: focus on central LA

GIVING OFFICERS
John Adams: vp

Nellie Adams: dir

Homer Adler: dir

Scott O. Brame: dir *B* Alexandria LA 1928 *ED* LA St Univ BS 1949 *CURR EMPL* pres, ceo, dir: Central LA Electric Co *CORP AFFIL* dir: Security First Natl Bank *NONPR AFFIL* chmn: St Francis Cabrini Hosp; regional vp: Counc Better LA

Ed Crump: secy, treas

Carolyn Saunders: dir

R. R. Saunders: pres

APPLICATION INFORMATION
Initial Approach: Send brief letter of inquiry describing program or project. Deadline is March 15. Board meets in March and September. Decisions are made between March 31 and October 31.

Restrictions on Giving: Does not support individuals or provide matching gifts.

PUBLICATIONS
Application Guidelines

GRANTS ANALYSIS
Total Grants: $498,990

Number of Grants: 111

Highest Grant: $50,000

Typical Range: $1,000 to $10,000

Disclosure Period: fiscal year ending November 30, 1992

Note: Recent grants are derived from a fiscal 1992 Form 990.

RECENT GRANTS
Library
10,000   Rapides Parish Library, Alexandria, LA — books and equipment

General
50,000   Louisiana College, Pineville, LA — nursing program
50,000   Louisiana State University at Alexandria, Alexandria, LA — endowment challenge
44,000   YMCA, Alexandria, LA — building program
20,000   Mason Preparatory School, Charleston, SC — Rife Alexander Kadry Memorial scholarship
14,000   YWCA, Alexandria, LA — air conditioning and heating repairs

Freeport-McMoRan Inc.

Sales: $1.61 billion
Employees: 7,300
Headquarters: New Orleans, LA
SIC Major Group: Crude Petroleum & Natural Gas, Copper Ores, Gold Ores, and Silver Ores

CONTACT
Everett J. Williams, PhD
Manager of Community Relations
Freeport-McMoRan Inc.
1615 Poydras St.
PO Box 61119
New Orleans, LA 70112
(504) 582-1952

FINANCIAL SUMMARY
Recent Giving: $10,200,000 (1995 est.); $10,200,000 (1994); $11,100,000 (1993)

Fiscal Note: All contributions are made directly through the company and its subsidiaries. The giving figures for 1992 and 1993 include grants made through the matching gifts program.

CONTRIBUTIONS SUMMARY
Typical Recipients: • *Arts & Humanities:* Arts Appreciation, Arts Associations & Councils, Arts Centers, Arts Festivals, Arts Funds, Arts Institutes, Ballet, Community Arts, Dance, Ethnic & Folk Arts, Historic Preservation, History & Archaeology, Libraries, Museums/Galleries, Music, Opera, Performing Arts, Public Broadcasting, Theater • *Civic & Public Affairs:* African American

Affairs, Botanical Gardens/Parks, Business/Free Enterprise, Economic Development, Employment/Job Training, Housing, Legal Aid, Minority Business, Municipalities/Towns, Public Policy, Rural Affairs, Safety, Urban & Community Affairs, Women's Affairs, Zoos/Aquariums • *Education:* Agricultural Education, Business Education, Colleges & Universities, Community & Junior Colleges, Economic Education, Education Associations, Education Reform, Elementary Education (Private), Elementary Education (Public), Engineering/Technological Education, General, Leadership Training, Legal Education, Literacy, Minority Education, Preschool Education, Private Education (Precollege), Public Education (Precollege), Science/Mathematics Education, Special Education, Student Aid • *Environment:* General, Resource Conservation, Wildlife Protection • *Health:* Cancer, Children's Health/Hospitals, Clinics/Medical Centers, Emergency/Ambulance Services, Health Organizations, Hospitals, Medical Research, Mental Health, Prenatal Health Issues • *International:* International Affairs • *Religion:* Churches, Dioceses, Jewish Causes, Ministries, Religious Organizations • *Science:* Science Exhibits & Fairs, Science Museums, Scientific Centers & Institutes, Scientific Organizations • *Social Services:* Big Brother/Big Sister, Child Welfare, Community Service Organizations, Counseling, Crime Prevention, Delinquency & Criminal Rehabilitation, Domestic Violence, Emergency Relief, Family Services, Food/Clothing Distribution, People with Disabilities, Recreation & Athletics, Senior Services, Substance Abuse, United Funds/United Ways, Volunteer Services, YMCA/YWCA/YMHA/YWHA, Youth Organizations

Grant Types: capital, challenge, employee matching gifts, endowment, general support, multiyear/continuing support, operating expenses, project, and research

Nonmonetary Support Types: donated equipment, loaned employees, loaned executives, and workplace solicitation

Note: Value of nonmonetary support is unavailable. Above figures exclude nonmonetary support.

Geographic Distribution: principally near operating locations and to national organizations

Operating Locations: LA (New Orleans)

CORP. OFFICERS
James Robert Moffett: *B* Houma LA 1938 *ED* Univ TX BS 1961; Tulane Univ MS 1963 *CURR EMPL* chmn, ceo, dir: Freeport-McMoRan Inc *CORP AFFIL* chmn: Freeport-McMoRan Copper & Gold; dir: Daniel Indus, Hibernia Natl Bank; fdr, dir: McMoRan Oil & Gas *NONPR AFFIL* bd govs: Tulane Univ Med Ctr; chmn: Bus Counc New Orleans; dir: Am Cancer Soc Greater New Orleans; mem: All-Am Wildcatters Assn, Natl Petroleum Counc, New Orleans Geological Soc, Univ TX Devel Bd, Univ TX Geology Fdn; vp: Southern LA Mid-Continent Oil Gas Assn *CLUB AFFIL* Green Wave, Petroleum Club New Orleans

GIVING OFFICERS
Daniel D. Dreiling, Jr.: *CURR EMPL* vp: Freeport-McMoRan Inc

Rene Louis Latiolais: *B* New Orleans 1942 *ED* LA St Univ BSChE 1965; Harvard Univ Grad Sch Bus Admin 1978 *CURR EMPL* pres, coo, dir: Freeport-McMoRan Inc *CORP AFFIL* pres, ceo: Freeport-McMoRan Resource Partners *NONPR AFFIL* mem: Am Soc Petroleum Engrs

Everett J. Williams, PhD: *CURR EMPL* mgr commun rels: Freeport-McMoRan Inc

APPLICATION INFORMATION
Initial Approach: *Initial Contact:* telephone call or letter, followed by full proposal; interview or site visit arranged thereafter *Include Information On:* description of project and organization, list of other sources of support, financial statements, proof of tax-exempt status *Deadlines:* none

Restrictions on Giving: Does not support individuals; distributing foundations; national disease agencies; or religious, political, fraternal, veterans, national, or tax-supported organizations.

OTHER THINGS TO KNOW
Giving is based on earnings; therefore the contributions budget varies from year to year.

PUBLICATIONS
Freeport-McMoRan Corporate Giving Program

GRANTS ANALYSIS
Total Grants: $7,000,000*

Number of Grants: 450*

Highest Grant: $1,000,000

Average Grant: $13,333*

Typical Range: $2,500 to $15,000

Disclosure Period: 1992

Note: Total grant figure excludes $1.7 million in matching gifts, bringing total 1992 giving to $8.7 million. Number of grants figure excludes matching gifts. Average grant figure excludes a $1 million grant. Recent grants are derived from a 1994 grants list.

RECENT GRANTS

Library
Friends of New Orleans Public Library, New Orleans, LA
Westbank Community Library, TX — endowment

General
Academy of the Sacred Heart, LA
AGAPE Ministries, LA
American Cancer Society, TX — Camp Discovery
American Jewish Committee, Chicago, IL
American Red Cross, TX

German Protestant Orphan Asylum Association

CONTACT
Everett T. Aultman
Executive Director
German Protestant Orphan Asylum Association
5342 St. Charles Ave.
New Orleans, LA 70115
(504) 895-2361

FINANCIAL SUMMARY
Recent Giving: $322,606 (fiscal 1993); $261,952 (fiscal 1992); $278,049 (fiscal 1991)

Assets: $7,170,391 (fiscal 1993); $7,159,242 (fiscal 1992); $6,734,718 (fiscal 1991)

Gifts Received: $90 (fiscal 1993)

EIN: 72-0423621

CONTRIBUTIONS SUMMARY
Typical Recipients: • *Arts & Humanities:* Libraries, Museums/Galleries, Public Broadcasting • *Civic & Public Affairs:* African American Affairs, Employment/Job Training, General, Housing, Women's Affairs • *Education:* Arts/Humanities Education, Colleges & Universities, Private Education (Precollege), Public Education (Precollege) • *Health:* Children's Health/Hospitals, Health Organizations, Hospitals, Medical Rehabilitation, Single-Disease Health Associations • *Religion:* Churches, Jewish Causes, Religious Organizations, Religious Welfare • *Science:* Scientific Centers & Institutes • *Social Services:* At-Risk Youth, Child Welfare, Community Centers, Counseling, Day Care, Domestic Violence, Family Planning, Family Services, Homes, People with Disabilities, Volunteer Services, YMCA/YWCA/YMHA/YWHA, Youth Organizations

Grant Types: general support and operating expenses

Geographic Distribution: limited to LA

GIVING OFFICERS
Everett T. Aultman: exec dir

Charles Bennett: dir

P. W. Bohne: vp, dir

Albert J. Flettrich: dir

Walter C. Flower III: dir

J. Gary Haller: secy, dir

Robert L. Hattier: treas, dir

Charles B. Mayer: dir

George J. Mayer: pres, dir

APPLICATION INFORMATION
Initial Approach: Send brief letter of inquiry describing program or project. Deadlines are December, March, June, and September. Board meets in January, April, July, and September.

PUBLICATIONS
Annual report (including Application Guidelines)

GRANTS ANALYSIS

Total Grants: $322,606

Number of Grants: 31

Highest Grant: $23,030

Typical Range: $4,000 to $19,700

Disclosure Period: fiscal year ending November 30, 1993

Note: Recent grants are derived from a fiscal 1993 Form 990.

RECENT GRANTS

General

23,030	Youth Service Bureau of St. Tammany, Covington, LA — Power of Choice Program
19,875	Associated Catholic Charities of New Orleans, New Orleans, LA
19,700	Family Services of Greater New Orleans, New Orleans, LA — second year of new start program
17,875	Children's Hospital, New Orleans, LA — Project LD
17,312	Boys and Girls Villages, Lake Charles, LA — second year of family development program

Southwestern Electric Power Co.

Revenue: $837.2 million
Employees: 1,997
Parent Company: Central & South West Corp.
Headquarters: Shreveport, LA
SIC Major Group: Electric, Gas & Sanitary Services

CONTACT

Johnie Wise
Division Manager
Southwestern Electric Power Co.
6300 Line Ave.
Shreveport, LA 71106
(318) 222-2141

FINANCIAL SUMMARY

Recent Giving: $719,739 (1993)

CONTRIBUTIONS SUMMARY

Typical Recipients: • *Arts & Humanities:* Arts Associations & Councils, Arts Festivals, Community Arts, Historic Preservation, Libraries, Public Broadcasting, Theater • *Civic & Public Affairs:* Chambers of Commerce, Clubs, Community Foundations, Economic Development, Parades/Festivals, Urban & Community Affairs • *Education:* Colleges & Universities, Community & Junior Colleges, General, Health & Physical Education, Science/Mathematics Education • *Health:* Cancer, Children's Health/Hospitals, Clinics/Medical Centers, General, Heart, Hospitals, Medical Research • *Social Services:* Community Centers, Community Service Organizations, Emergency Relief, Family Services, General, Recreation & Athletics, United Funds/United Ways, Youth Organizations

Grant Types: capital, general support, and seed money

Nonmonetary Support Types: donated equipment and loaned employees

Geographic Distribution: in headquarters and operating communities

Operating Locations: AR (Fayetteville, Texarkana), LA (Shreveport), TX (Longview)

CORP. OFFICERS

Richard H. Bremer: *CURR EMPL* chmn exec comm, ceo, pres, dir: Southwestern Electric Power Co

W.J. Googe III: *CURR EMPL* vp: Southwestern Electric Power Co

Marvin McGregor: *CURR EMPL* vp: Southwestern Electric Power Co

APPLICATION INFORMATION

Initial Approach: Send a brief letter of inquiry. Include a description of organization, amount requested, and purpose of funds sought.

Restrictions on Giving: Does not support individuals, religious organizations for sectarian purposes, or political or lobbying groups.

GRANTS ANALYSIS

Total Grants: $719,739

Disclosure Period: 1993

Note: Typical grant size is less than $1,000. Recent grants are derived from a grants list provided by company in 1994.

RECENT GRANTS

General

Fayetteville Chamber of Commerce, Fayetteville, AR
Henderson Civic Center, Henderson, TX
Junior Achievement of East Texas, Longview, TX
Louisiana Tech University, Ruston, LA
Texarkana Opportunities, Texarkana, TX

MAINE

Central Maine Power Co.

Revenue: $893.58 million
Employees: 2,400
Headquarters: Augusta, ME
SIC Major Group: Electric & Other Services Combined

CONTACT

David F. Allen
Director, Governmental & Regulatory Affairs
Central Maine Power Co.
Edison Dr.
Augusta, ME 04336
(207) 623-3521

FINANCIAL SUMMARY

Recent Giving: $200,000 (1995 est.); $200,000 (1994 approx.); $300,000 (1993)

Fiscal Note: Company gives directly. Above figures exclude nonmonetary support.

CONTRIBUTIONS SUMMARY

Typical Recipients: • *Arts & Humanities:* Arts Associations & Councils, Arts Festivals, Arts Institutes, Community Arts, Dance, Ethnic & Folk Arts, General, Historic Preservation, Libraries, Literary Arts, Museums/Galleries, Music, Performing Arts, Public Broadcasting, Theater, Visual Arts • *Civic & Public Affairs:* Civil Rights, Economic Development, Economic Policy, Employment/Job Training, Housing, Professional & Trade Associations, Public Policy, Rural Affairs, Safety, Urban & Community Affairs, Women's Affairs • *Education:* Arts/Humanities Education, Business Education, Colleges & Universities, Community & Junior Colleges, Continuing Education, Economic Education, Education Associations, Education Funds, Elementary Education (Private), Engineering/Technological Education, Faculty Development, Literacy, Minority Education, Preschool Education, Public Education (Precollege), Science/Mathematics Education, Social Sciences Education, Student Aid • *Environment:* General • *Health:* Emergency/Ambulance Services, General, Geriatric Health, Health Organizations, Hospices, Hospitals, Medical Rehabilitation, Mental Health, Nutrition, Public Health, Single-Disease Health Associations • *Science:* Science Exhibits & Fairs, Scientific Centers & Institutes • *Social Services:* Child Welfare, Community Centers, Community Service Organizations, Counseling, Day Care, Delinquency & Criminal Rehabilitation, Domestic Violence, Emergency Relief, Family Planning, Family Services, Food/Clothing Distribution, General, People with Disabilities, Recreation & Athletics, Senior Services, Shelters/Homelessness, Substance Abuse, United Funds/United Ways, Volunteer Services, Youth Organizations

Grant Types: award, capital, challenge, conference/seminar, emergency, employee matching gifts, general support, matching, multiyear/continuing support, project, research, scholarship, and seed money

Note: Employee matching gift ratio: 1 to 1.

Nonmonetary Support: $30,000 (1994); $50,000 (1993)

Nonmonetary Support Types: cause-related marketing & promotion, donated equipment, donated products, in-kind services, loaned employees, and loaned executives

Note: Mentoring-engineering help with science 'design and build' program. In school help-Portland employees donate time in elementary school. Contact Tim Vrabek, Community Relations.

Geographic Distribution: primarily central and southern Maine

Operating Locations: ME (Augusta, Lewiston, Portland)

Note: Company also has fourteen district offices throughout the state of Maine.

CORP. OFFICERS

David T. Flanagan: *B* Bangor MA 1947 *ED* Harvard Univ BA 1969; Univ London Kings Coll MA 1970; Boston Coll Law Sch JD 1973 *CURR EMPL* pres, ceo, dir: Central ME Power Co *CORP AFFIL* chmn: ME Yankee Atomic Power Co

Mark Ishkenian: *CURR EMPL* pub aff: Central ME Power Co

David E. Marsh: *ED* NH Coll 1971 *CURR EMPL* vp fin, cfo: Central ME Power Co *CORP AFFIL* treas, dir: ME Electric Power Co

GIVING OFFICERS

David F. Allen: *CURR EMPL* dir governmental & regulatory aff: Central ME Power Co

APPLICATION INFORMATION

Initial Approach: *Initial Contact:* a brief letter of inquiry *Include Information On:* a description of organization, amount requested, purpose of funds sought, recently audited financial statement, and proof of tax-exempt status *Deadlines:* none

Restrictions on Giving: Company does not support individuals, religious organizations for sectarian purposes, political or lobbying groups, or organizations outside operating areas.

GRANTS ANALYSIS

Total Grants: $300,000

Typical Range: $50 to $1,000

Disclosure Period: 1993

Davenport Trust Fund

Former Foundation Name: George P. Davenport Trust Fund

CONTACT

John W. Coombs
Trustee
Davenport Trust Fund
55 Front St.
Bath, ME 04530
(207) 443-3431

FINANCIAL SUMMARY

Recent Giving: $256,160 (1993); $316,944 (1992); $335,075 (1991)

Assets: $5,368,967 (1993); $5,258,818 (1992); $5,267,315 (1991)

Gifts Received: $3,060 (1993); $5,050 (1992); $28,087 (1991)

Fiscal Note: In 1993, contributions were received from the Maine Woman's Christian Temperance Union ($3,000).

EIN: 01-6009246

CONTRIBUTIONS SUMMARY

Donor(s): the late George P. Davenport

Typical Recipients: • *Arts & Humanities:* Libraries, Public Broadcasting • *Civic & Public Affairs:* General, Municipalities/Towns, Urban & Community Affairs • *Education:* Arts/Humanities Education, Colleges & Universities, Engineering/Technological Education, General, Medical Education, Public Education (Precollege), Student Aid • *Health:* Clinics/Medical Centers, Health Organizations • *Religion:* Churches, Religious Organizations, Religious Welfare • *Social Services:* Food/Clothing Distribution, People with Disabilities, YMCA/YWCA/YMHA/YWHA, Youth Organizations

Grant Types: general support, loan, and scholarship

Geographic Distribution: focus on ME

GIVING OFFICERS

John W. Coombs: trust *B* Salt Lake City UT 1905 *ED* Univ UT AB 1926; George Washington Univ LLB 1934 *CURR EMPL* chmn: Transintl Hotel Co *CORP AFFIL* consult: Transam Corp, Transam Mtg Adv

J. Franklin Howe: trust

Barry M. Sturgeon: trust

APPLICATION INFORMATION

Initial Approach: Application form required for scholarships. Include a description of organization, amount requested, purpose of funds sought, recently audited financial statement, and proof of tax-exempt status. There are no deadlines.

Restrictions on Giving: Limited to the Bath, ME, area.

OTHER THINGS TO KNOW

Provides undergraduate scholarships to local students.

GRANTS ANALYSIS

Total Grants: $256,160

Number of Grants: 62

Highest Grant: $25,000

Typical Range: $500 to $20,000

Disclosure Period: 1993

Note: Recent grants are derived from a 1993 Form 990.

RECENT GRANTS

Library

3,400	Patten Free Library, Bath, ME

General

25,000	Maine Medical Center, Portland, ME
20,000	Elmhurst Association for Retarded Citizens, Bath, ME
15,000	Salvation Army, Bath, ME
14,000	University of Maine Orono, Orono, ME — scholarships
10,000	University of Southern Maine, Portland, ME — scholarships

Gannett Publishing Co., Guy / Gannett Foundation, Guy P.

Sales: $100.0 million
Employees: 2,000
Headquarters: Portland, ME
SIC Major Group: Printing & Publishing

CONTACT

James E. Baker
Chief Financial Officer
Guy Gannett Publishing Co.
One City Ctr.
PO Box 15277
Portland, ME 04101
(207) 828-8100

FINANCIAL SUMMARY

Recent Giving: $142,235 (1993); $115,303 (1992); $126,835 (1991)

Assets: $2,029,987 (1993); $2,071,666 (1992); $2,079,864 (1991)

Gifts Received: $133,351 (1991); $132,225 (1989); $105,946 (1988)

Fiscal Note: In 1991, contributions were received from Guy Gannet Publishing Company.

EIN: 01-6003797

CONTRIBUTIONS SUMMARY

Typical Recipients: • *Arts & Humanities:* Arts Associations & Councils, History & Archaeology, Libraries, Museums/Galleries, Music, Opera, Performing Arts, Public Broadcasting, Theater • *Civic & Public Affairs:* General, Municipalities/Towns, Philanthropic Organizations, Urban & Community Affairs • *Education:* Colleges & Universities, Community & Junior Colleges, Leadership Training, Public Education (Precollege), Science/Mathematics Education, Student Aid • *Environment:* Resource Conservation • *Health:* Clinics/Medical Centers, Emergency/Ambulance Services, Health Organizations, Hospitals, Medical Research • *Religion:* Ministries, Religious Welfare • *Social Services:* Child Welfare, Community Centers, Community Service Organizations, Family Services, Homes, People with Disabilities, Scouts, Senior Services, United Funds/United Ways, YMCA/YWCA/YMHA/YWHA, Youth Organizations

Grant Types: project

Geographic Distribution: primarily in ME

Operating Locations: ME (Portland)

CORP. OFFICERS

James Shaffer: *B* Boston MA 1945 *ED* Purdue Univ BS 1967; Indiana Univ MBA 1969 *CURR EMPL* pres, ceo, dir: Guy P. Gannett Publishing Co *NONPR AFFIL* trust: Portland Symphony *PHIL AFFIL* vp: Briggs Family Foundation

GIVING OFFICERS

James E. Baker: treas

Madeline G. Corson: dir

John H. Gannett: dir

Jean Gannett Hawley: pres, dir

APPLICATION INFORMATION

Initial Approach: Send brief letter of inquiry. Applications are reviewed only once a year. Deadline is March 1st.

Restrictions on Giving: Does not support individuals. Organizations must be tax-exempt under 501(c)(3). Encourages requests for specific projects rather than for normal operating expenses or continuing support.

GRANTS ANALYSIS

Total Grants: $142,235

Number of Grants: 26

Highest Grant: $85,360

Typical Range: $100 to $35,000

Disclosure Period: 1993

Note: Recent grants are derived from a 1993 Form 990.

RECENT GRANTS

Library

1,000	Portland Public Library, Portland, ME	

General

85,360	United Way, Portland, ME
35,000	Greater Portland Cares, Portland, ME
8,000	Portland YMCA, Portland, ME
1,000	Preble Street Resource Center, Portland, ME
1,000	Prop, Portland, ME

Mulford Trust, Clarence E.

CONTACT

David R. Hastings II
Trustee
Clarence E. Mulford Trust
PO Box 290
Fryeburg, ME 04037
(207) 935-2061

FINANCIAL SUMMARY

Recent Giving: $266,983 (1993); $269,397 (1992); $270,239 (1991)

Assets: $5,951,831 (1993); $5,898,704 (1992); $5,959,817 (1991)

EIN: 01-0247548

CONTRIBUTIONS SUMMARY

Donor(s): the late Clarence E. Mulford

Typical Recipients: • *Arts & Humanities:* Historic Preservation, History & Archaeol-

ogy, Libraries, Music • *Civic & Public Affairs:* Municipalities/Towns, Urban & Community Affairs, Women's Affairs • *Education:* Colleges & Universities, Literacy, Private Education (Precollege), Public Education (Precollege) • *Health:* Health Organizations, Hospices, Hospitals • *Religion:* Churches, Religious Organizations • *Social Services:* Animal Protection, Community Service Organizations, Senior Services, United Funds/United Ways, Youth Organizations

Grant Types: general support

Geographic Distribution: focus on Fryeburg, ME, and neighboring towns

GIVING OFFICERS

David R. Hastings II: trust

Peter G. Hastings: trust

APPLICATION INFORMATION

Initial Approach: Include a description of organization, amount requested, purpose of funds sought, recently audited financial statement, and proof of tax-exempt status. Deadlines are January 10 and July 10.

Restrictions on Giving: Does not support individuals or provide loans, matching gifts, or scholarships. Limited to Fryeburg, ME, and surrounding area.

GRANTS ANALYSIS

Total Grants: $266,983

Number of Grants: 26

Highest Grant: $48,500

Typical Range: $500 to $8,000

Disclosure Period: 1993

Note: Recent grants are derived from a 1993 Form 990.

RECENT GRANTS

Library

8,000	Fryeburg Library Club, Fryeburg, ME
5,000	Bridgton Public Library, Bridgton, ME
1,000	Woman's Library Club of Lovell, Lovell, ME
500	Brownfield Public Library, Brownfield, ME
250	Denmark Public Library, Denmark, ME

General

159,237	Fryeburg Academy, Fryeburg, ME
55,709	Town of Fryeburg, Fryeburg, ME
7,000	Church of the New Jerusalem, Fryeburg, ME
7,000	Fryeburg Congregational Church, Fryeburg, ME
5,000	School Administrative District 72, Fryeburg, ME

Webber Oil Co. / Webber Oil Foundation

Sales: $200.0 million
Employees: 850
Headquarters: Bangor, ME
SIC Major Group: Miscellaneous Retail and Wholesale Trade—Nondurable Goods

CONTACT

Larry K. Mahoney
Trustee
Webber Oil Co.
PO Box 929
Bangor, ME 02929
(207) 942-5501

FINANCIAL SUMMARY

Recent Giving: $33,670 (fiscal 1993); $57,400 (fiscal 1992); $65,850 (fiscal 1991)

Assets: $238,886 (fiscal 1993); $197,393 (fiscal 1992); $239,730 (fiscal 1990)

Gifts Received: $25,000 (fiscal 1993); $50,000 (fiscal 1992)

Fiscal Note: In fiscal 1993, contributions were received from Parish Land Co, ($10,000) and Tyler and West Sargent ($6,000). Three other donors made contributions of $3,000 each.

EIN: 23-7046575

CONTRIBUTIONS SUMMARY

Typical Recipients: • *Arts & Humanities:* General, Libraries, Museums/Galleries, Music, Opera, Theater • *Civic & Public Affairs:* Economic Development, General, Municipalities/Towns • *Education:* Colleges & Universities, General, Private Education (Precollege), Secondary Education (Private), Vocational & Technical Education • *Health:* General, Hospitals, Public Health • *Religion:* Churches • *Social Services:* Child Welfare, Community Service Organizations, Counseling, General, People with Disabilities, Recreation & Athletics, YMCA/YWCA/YMHA/YWHA, Youth Organizations

Grant Types: capital and scholarship

Geographic Distribution: focus on Bangor, ME

Operating Locations: ME (Bangor)

CORP. OFFICERS

Larry K. Mahaney: *CURR EMPL* chmn, pres, dir: Webber Oil Co

GIVING OFFICERS

Linda F. Harnum: trust

Larry K. Mahaney: trust *CURR EMPL* chmn, pres, dir: Webber Oil Co (see above)

Louise F. Witham: trust

APPLICATION INFORMATION

Initial Approach: Send a brief letter of inquiry. Include a description of organization, amount requested, and purpose of funds sought.

Restrictions on Giving: Limited to Bangor, ME, area high schools.

OTHER THINGS TO KNOW
Provides scholarships to high school students.

GRANTS ANALYSIS
Total Grants: $33,670

Number of Grants: 17

Highest Grant: $5,000

Typical Range: $370 to $4,000

Disclosure Period: fiscal year ending August 31, 1993

Note: Recent grants are derived from a fiscal 1993 Form 990. Number of grants and typical range do not include individual scholarships.

RECENT GRANTS

Library
500	William Farnsworth Library and Museum, Rockland, ME

General
5,000	Eastern Maine Charities Children's Campaign, Bangor, ME
4,000	Husson College, Bangor, ME
4,000	Mission College, Bangor, ME
3,000	East Orrington Congregational Church, Orrington, ME
2,500	Community Health and Counsel, Bangor, ME

MARYLAND

AEGON USA Inc.

Employees: 5,474
Parent Company: Aegon N.V.
Headquarters: Baltimore, MD
SIC Major Group: Holding Companies Nec and Life Insurance

CONTACT
Rosmary Kostmayer
Director of Communications
AEGON USA, Inc.
1111 N Charles St.
Baltimore, MD 21201
(410) 576-4583

FINANCIAL SUMMARY
Recent Giving: $900,000 (1995 est.); $900,000 (1994 approx.); $700,000 (1993 approx.)

Fiscal Note: Company gives directly.

CONTRIBUTIONS SUMMARY
Typical Recipients: • *Arts & Humanities:* Community Arts, Dance, Historic Preservation, Libraries, Museums/Galleries, Music, Public Broadcasting • *Education:* Colleges & Universities, Private Education (Precollege), Public Education (Precollege) • *Health:* Hospitals, Single-Disease Health Associations • *Social Services:* United Funds/United Ways

Grant Types: capital, employee matching gifts, general support, project, and scholarship

Nonmonetary Support Types: in-kind services and loaned executives

Note: Contact Rosemary Kostmayer for information on nonmonetary support.

Geographic Distribution: principally near operating locations in central Maryland and eastern Iowa

Operating Locations: AR, CA, FL, GA, IA, IL, MD, NJ, PA, TX

CORP. OFFICERS
Patrick S. Baird: *B* 1954 *ED* Univ IA BS 1976 *CURR EMPL* cfo, sr vp: AEGON USA Inc *CORP AFFIL* vp, cfo: Bankers Un Life Assurance Co, Life Investors Ins Co Am; vp, cfo, dir: Ausa Holding Co, First Ausa Life Ins Co

Larry G. Brown: *B* Halstad MN 1942 *ED* Univ MN 1963; Univ MN 1966 *CURR EMPL* sr vp, secy, gen couns: AEGON USA Inc *CORP AFFIL* chmn: Intl Life Investors Ins Co; chmn, pres, dir: First Ausa Life Ins Co; pres: Cadet Holding Co, Transunion Casualty Co; pres, dir: Ausa Holding Co; secy, dir: Bankers Un Life Assurance Co, Gen Svcs Life Ins Co, Life Holding Reins Co; sr vp, secy, dir: Life Investors Ins Co Am, PFL Life Ins Co; vp, dir: Monumental Life Ins Co

Patrick E. Falconio: *B* Pittsburgh PA 1941 *ED* Duquesne Univ 1963; Univ GA MBA 1971 *CURR EMPL* chief investment off, exec vp: AEGON USA Inc *CORP AFFIL* chmn: Aegon USA Securities Inc, Cedar Income Fund Ltd, Landauer Assoc Inc, Landauer Real Estate Couns, USP Real Estate Investment; chmn, pres: Aegon USA Investment Mgmt, Cedas Income Fund, USP REIT; dir: Firstar Bank NA, Teleres; exec vp: Monumental Gen Casualty Co; sr vp: Life Holding Reins Co; sr vp, chief investment off: Bankers Un Life Assurance Co, First Ausa Life Ins Co, Gen Svcs Life Ins Co, Life Investors Ins Co Am, PFL Life Ins Co; sr vp, dir: Ausa Holding Co, Transunion Casualty Co

Donald James Shepard: *B* Cedar Rapids IA 1946 *ED* Univ Chicago MBA 1981 *CURR EMPL* chmn, pres, ceo: AEGON USA Inc *CORP AFFIL* chmn, pres: Life Investors Ins Co Am, NN Investors Life Ins Co, Pacific Fidelity Life Ins Co, Transunion Casualty Co; chmn, pres, ceo: AUSA Life Ins Co; dir: COPA, Creditor Resources, Creditor Resources CA, Ennia Reinsurance Co Am, Investors Warranty Am, Lease Am Corp, Lease Am Investment Co, Natl Old Line Life Ins Co, S Central Underwriting Co; exec vp, dir: Intl Life Investors Ins Co; pres: Investors Life Ins Co, Un Standard Asset Growth Corp, Un Standard Asset Growth Corp; pres, ceo: Bankers Un Life Assurance Co; pres, dir: IA Fidelity Life Ins Co; sr exec vp: Gen Svcs Life Ins Co, GSL Holding Corp; sr vp, dir: Cadet Holding Co, Hawkeye Holding, Money Svcs; vp: Zahorik Co

GIVING OFFICERS
Rosmary Kostmayer: *CURR EMPL* dir commun: AEGON USA Inc

APPLICATION INFORMATION
Initial Approach: *Initial Contact:* brief letter *Include Information On:* a description of the organization, amount requested, and the purpose for which funds are sought; a recently audited financial statement and proof of tax-exempt status are helpful but not necessary *Deadlines:* none

GRANTS ANALYSIS
Typical Range: $500 to $2,500

Note: Recent grants are derived from a 1993 grants list.

RECENT GRANTS

General
Kinkwood Community College
Loyola College, Baltimore, MD
United Way of Central Maryland, Baltimore, MD
United Way of Eastern Iowa, IA
University of Iowa Business School, Iowa City, IA

Blaustein Foundation, Louis and Henrietta

CONTACT
David Hirschhorn
Vice President
Louis and Henrietta Blaustein Fdn.
Blaustein Bldg.
PO Box 238
Baltimore, MD 21203
(410) 347-7112

FINANCIAL SUMMARY
Recent Giving: $1,089,418 (1993); $1,112,334 (1992); $1,153,354 (1991)

Assets: $14,175,717 (1993); $12,879,349 (1992); $12,347,942 (1991)

Gifts Received: $616,700 (1993); $666,500 (1992); $666,500 (1991)

Fiscal Note: In fiscal 1993, contributions were received from American Trading and Production Corp.

EIN: 52-6038381

CONTRIBUTIONS SUMMARY
Donor(s): the late Louis Blaustein, the late Henrietta Blaustein, American Trading and Production Corp., and members of the Blaustein family

Typical Recipients: • *Arts & Humanities:* Arts Funds, Community Arts, Libraries, Museums/Galleries, Music • *Civic & Public Affairs:* Community Foundations, Housing, Safety, Urban & Community Affairs • *Education:* Colleges & Universities, Literacy, Private Education (Precollege), Religious Education, Special Education, Student Aid, Vocational & Technical Education • *Environment:* Air/Water Quality, General, Resource Conservation, Wildlife Protection • *Health:* Cancer, Clinics/Medical Centers,

Emergency/Ambulance Services, Health Organizations, Hospitals, Medical Research, Multiple Sclerosis • *International:* International Development • *Religion:* Jewish Causes, Religious Organizations, Religious Welfare • *Social Services:* Child Welfare, Community Service Organizations, Domestic Violence, Family Planning, Family Services, Food/Clothing Distribution, People with Disabilities, Youth Organizations

Grant Types: general support

Geographic Distribution: focus on the greater Baltimore, MD, metropolitan area

GIVING OFFICERS
David Hirschhorn: vp, trust *CURR EMPL* vchmn, dir: Am Trading & Production Corp *PHIL AFFIL* don, vp, trust: Jacob and Hilda Blaustein Foundation; pres, trust: David and Barbara B. Hirschhorn Foundation

Dale E. Maxson: asst secy *PHIL AFFIL* asst secy: Alvin and Fanny Blaustein Thalheimer Foundation

Henry A. Rosenberg, Jr.: vp, trust *B* Pittsburgh PA 1929 *ED* Hobart Coll BA 1952 *CURR EMPL* chmn, chmn exec comm, ceo, dir: Crown Central Petroleum Corp *CORP AFFIL* chmn, dir: Crown Central Holding Corp, F Z Corp, Pride Baltimore; dir: Am Trading & Production Corp, Signet Banking Corp, US Fidelity & Guaranty Co; pres, dir: Locot Inc *NONPR AFFIL* chmn, dir, mem exec comm: Natl Petroleum Refiners Assn; dir: Crohns & Colitis Fdn, Goucher Coll, Johns Hopkins Hosp, McDonogh Sch, Natl Aquarium Baltimore, Natl Flag Day Fdn, Un Way Central MD, YMCA Greater Baltimore; mem: Am Petroleum Inst, Natl Petroleum Counc; mem adv bd: William Donald Schaefer Ctr Pub Policy; mem natl exec bd: Boy Scouts Am *CLUB AFFIL* 25 Year Petroleum Indus *PHIL AFFIL* pres, trust: Henry and Ruth Blaustein Rosenberg Foundation; vp, trust: Alvin and Fanny Blaustein Thalheimer Foundation

Frank A. Strzelczyk: secy, treas

Louis B. Thalheimer: vp, trust *B* 1944 *ED* Amherst Coll 1966; NY Univ 1969 *CURR EMPL* chmn, ceo, dir: Am Trading & Production Corp *PHIL AFFIL* trust: Henry and Ruth Blaustein Rosenberg Foundation

APPLICATION INFORMATION
Initial Approach: Send brief letter of inquiry describing program or project. There are no deadlines.

GRANTS ANALYSIS
Total Grants: $1,089,418

Number of Grants: 26

Highest Grant: $625,668

Typical Range: $750 to $80,000

Disclosure Period: 1993

Note: Recent grants are derived from a 1993 Form 990.

RECENT GRANTS
General

625,668	Associated Jewish Charities and Welfare Fund, Baltimore, MD
80,000	Johns Hopkins University, Baltimore, MD
50,000	US Holocaust Memorial Museum, Washington, DC
20,000	Kennedy Kreiger Institute, Baltimore, MD
20,000	Maryland Food Bank, Baltimore, MD

Campbell Foundation

CONTACT
Bruce S. Campbell III
Secretary
Campbell Fdn.
100 W Pennsylvania Ave.
Baltimore, MD 21204
(410) 825-0545

FINANCIAL SUMMARY
Recent Giving: $122,500 (1993); $95,900 (1992); $104,900 (1990)

Assets: $2,321,094 (1993); $2,239,978 (1992); $1,867,421 (1990)

EIN: 52-0794348

CONTRIBUTIONS SUMMARY
Donor(s): R. McLean Campbell

Typical Recipients: • *Arts & Humanities:* Arts Centers, Arts Outreach, Community Arts, General, History & Archaeology, Libraries, Museums/Galleries, Music, Opera, Performing Arts, Theater • *Civic & Public Affairs:* Clubs, Economic Development, General, Parades/Festivals, Urban & Community Affairs, Zoos/Aquariums • *Education:* Arts/Humanities Education, Colleges & Universities, Education Funds, Minority Education, Private Education (Precollege), Special Education, Student Aid • *Environment:* General • *Health:* AIDS/HIV, Children's Health/Hospitals, Clinics/Medical Centers, Eyes/Blindness, Hospitals • *Religion:* Churches, Religious Organizations, Religious Welfare • *Social Services:* Animal Protection, Camps, Child Welfare, Community Service Organizations, Counseling, Family Planning, People with Disabilities, Shelters/Homelessness, Special Olympics, United Funds/United Ways, YMCA/YWCA/YMHA/YWHA, Youth Organizations

Grant Types: capital and endowment

Geographic Distribution: focus on the greater Baltimore, MD area

GIVING OFFICERS
Carolyn C. Beall: asst treas

Bruce S. Campbell III: trust, secy

Bruce S. Campbell, Jr.: trust, vp

Mary Jo Campbell: asst treas

R. McLean Campbell: trust, vp

William B. Campbell: pres

Margaret C. W. Davis: treas

APPLICATION INFORMATION
Initial Approach: Include a description of organization, amount requested, purpose of funds sought, recently audited financial

statement, and proof of tax-exempt status. There are no deadlines.

Restrictions on Giving: Does not support individuals. Limited to the greater Baltimore, MD, area.

GRANTS ANALYSIS
Total Grants: $122,500

Number of Grants: 51

Highest Grant: $12,500

Typical Range: $500 to $10,500

Disclosure Period: 1993

Note: Recent grants are derived from a 1993 Form 990.

RECENT GRANTS
Library

1,000	Museum and Library of Maryland History, Baltimore, MD

General

12,500	McDonogh School, Owings Mills, MD
10,500	Gilman School Scholarship Fund, Baltimore, MD — provide funds for financial support
10,000	Trinity Church, Baltimore, MD
6,000	Bryn Mawr School, Baltimore, MD
6,000	Maryland Society for the Prevention of Blindness, Baltimore, MD

Crown Books / Crown Books Foundation

Sales: $240.68 million
Employees: 2,300
Parent Company: Dart Group Corp.
Headquarters: Landover, MD
SIC Major Group: Miscellaneous Retail

CONTACT
Carol Thompson
Secretary
Crown Books
3300 75th Ave.
Landover, MD 20785
(301) 731-1200

FINANCIAL SUMMARY
Recent Giving: $75,500 (1993); $284,433 (1992); $77,855 (1991)

Assets: $3,490,235 (1993); $3,455,694 (1992); $3,630,116 (1991)

EIN: 52-1590726

CONTRIBUTIONS SUMMARY
Typical Recipients: • *Arts & Humanities:* Arts Associations & Councils, Arts Funds, Ballet, History & Archaeology, Libraries, Literary Arts, Music, Opera, Public Broadcasting, Theater • *Civic & Public Affairs:* General, Philanthropic Organizations, Women's Affairs • *Education:* Arts/Humanities Education, Colleges & Universities, Legal Education, Literacy, Minority Education, Private Education (Precollege), Secondary

Education (Public) • *Health:* AIDS/HIV, Cancer, Children's Health/Hospitals, Diabetes, Emergency/Ambulance Services, Heart, Hospitals, Kidney, Multiple Sclerosis, Research/Studies Institutes • *International:* Foreign Arts Organizations, Foreign Educational Institutions, Missionary/Religious Activities • *Religion:* Churches, Jewish Causes, Religious Welfare • *Social Services:* Community Service Organizations, Family Services, Youth Organizations

Grant Types: general support

Geographic Distribution: national, with giving in CA, CT, DC, MD, and VA

CORP. OFFICERS

Herbert H. Haft: *B* 1920 *CURR EMPL* chmn, ceo, dir: Dart Group Corp *CORP AFFIL* chmn, ceo, dir: Trak Auto Corp; chmn, dir: Crown Books *PHIL AFFIL* chmn: Dart Group Foundation; trust: Crown Book Foundation

GIVING OFFICERS

Ron Marshall: treas, asst secy *PHIL AFFIL* asst secy: Dart Group Foundation

APPLICATION INFORMATION

Initial Approach: Send a brief letter of inquiry. Include a description of organization, amount requested, purpose of funds sought, recently audited financial statement, and proof of tax-exempt status. There are no deadlines.

GRANTS ANALYSIS

Total Grants: $75,500

Number of Grants: 23

Highest Grant: $50,000

Typical Range: $150 to $5,000

Disclosure Period: 1993

Note: Recent grants are derived from a 1993 Form 990.

RECENT GRANTS

Library
50,000	Library Foundation of Los Angeles, Los Angeles, CA

General
5,000	Georgetown Day School, Washington, DC
5,000	Reading is Fundamental, Washington, DC
4,000	Sidwell Friends School, Washington, DC
1,500	American Academy in Rome, New York, NY
1,250	Jewish Social Service Agency, Rockville, MD

Dart Group Corp. / Dart Group Foundation

Sales: $1.38 billion
Employees: 9,800
Headquarters: Landover, MD
SIC Major Group: Automotive Dealers & Service Stations and Miscellaneous Retail

CONTACT
Laverne Murphy
Executive Committee
Dart Group Corp.
3300 75th Ave.
Landover, MD 20785
(301) 731-1200

FINANCIAL SUMMARY
Recent Giving: $36,351 (1993); $93,148 (1992); $99,045 (1990)

Assets: $2,287,823 (1993); $2,249,366 (1992); $1,997,540 (1989)

Gifts Received: $850,000 (1989); $600,000 (1988)

Fiscal Note: In 1989, contributions were from the Dart Group Corp.

EIN: 52-1497671

CONTRIBUTIONS SUMMARY
Typical Recipients: • *Arts & Humanities:* Arts Centers, Libraries, Literary Arts, Museums/Galleries, Opera, Performing Arts, Theater • *Civic & Public Affairs:* Economic Development, Employment/Job Training, Zoos/Aquariums • *Education:* Arts/Humanities Education, Colleges & Universities, Education Reform, General, Legal Education, Medical Education, Preschool Education, Private Education (Precollege), Secondary Education (Public), Student Aid • *Health:* AIDS/HIV, Cancer, Children's Health/Hospitals, Geriatric Health, Medical Research, Prenatal Health Issues, Single-Disease Health Associations • *International:* Missionary/Religious Activities • *Religion:* Jewish Causes, Religious Organizations • *Social Services:* Child Welfare, Community Service Organizations, People with Disabilities, Substance Abuse, United Funds/United Ways

Grant Types: capital, general support, and scholarship

Geographic Distribution: DC metropolitan area, including surrounding MD

CORP. OFFICERS
Herbert H. Haft: *B* 1920 *CURR EMPL* chmn, ceo, dir: Dart Group Corp *CORP AFFIL* chmn, ceo, dir: Trak Auto Corp; chmn, dir: Crown Books *PHIL AFFIL* trust: Crown Book Foundation

GIVING OFFICERS
Herbert H. Haft: chmn *CURR EMPL* chmn, ceo, dir: Dart Group Corp (see above)

Ron Marshall: asst secy *PHIL AFFIL* treas, asst secy: Crown Books Foundation

APPLICATION INFORMATION
Initial Approach: Send a brief letter of inquiry. Include a description of organization, amount requested, purpose of funds sought,

recently audited financial statement, and proof of tax-exempt status. There are no deadlines.

Restrictions on Giving: Does not support individuals.

GRANTS ANALYSIS
Total Grants: $36,351

Number of Grants: 30

Highest Grant: $10,000

Typical Range: $100 to $10,000

Disclosure Period: 1993

Note: Recent grants are derived from a 1993 Form 990.

RECENT GRANTS

General
10,000	Leukemia Society of America, Washington, DC
3,000	American Athletic Association of the Deaf, Washington, DC
1,333	Neediest Kids, Washington, DC
1,310	American Cancer Society, Washington, DC
1,000	American University, Washington, DC — president's circle

France Foundation, Jacob and Annita

CONTACT
Fredrick W. Lafferty
Executive Director
Jacob and Annita France Foundation
1122 Kenilworth Dr., Ste. 118
Baltimore, MD 21204
(410) 832-5700

FINANCIAL SUMMARY
Recent Giving: $3,160,474 (fiscal 1993); $2,925,365 (fiscal 1992); $2,298,620 (fiscal 1991)

Assets: $69,105,325 (fiscal 1993); $63,841,371 (fiscal 1992); $59,483,217 (fiscal 1991)

Gifts Received: $375,824 (fiscal 1993); $536,868 (fiscal 1990 est.)

Fiscal Note: In fiscal 1990, donations were from the termination of a pension plan created by Jacob France.

EIN: 52-0794585

CONTRIBUTIONS SUMMARY
Donor(s): The foundation was established in 1959 by Jacob France and his wife, Annita France. The late Mr. France, a prominent Baltimore lawyer and banker, founded the Equitable Trust Company, now known as Equitable Bancorp.

Typical Recipients: • *Arts & Humanities:* Arts Institutes, Historic Preservation, History & Archaeology, Libraries, Museums/Galleries, Music, Opera, Theater • *Civic & Public Affairs:* Chambers of Commerce, Community Foundations, Philanthropic Organizations, Zoos/Aquariums • *Education:* Arts/Humanities Education,

Colleges & Universities, Economic Education, Education Funds, Education Reform, General, Health & Physical Education, Legal Education, Literacy, Medical Education, Private Education (Precollege), Science/Mathematics Education, Student Aid • *Environment:* Air/Water Quality, General • *Health:* Hospices, Hospitals, Trauma Treatment • *International:* International Affairs • *Religion:* Churches, Dioceses, Religious Welfare • *Science:* Scientific Centers & Institutes • *Social Services:* Community Service Organizations, Family Services, People with Disabilities, United Funds/United Ways, Youth Organizations

Grant Types: capital, general support, and project

Geographic Distribution: Maryland, primarily the metropolitan Baltimore area

GIVING OFFICERS
Redmond C. S. Finney: dir

Frederick W. Lafferty: exec dir *PHIL AFFIL* exec dir: Robert G. and Anne M. Merrick Foundation

Robert G. Merrick III: dir *PHIL AFFIL* dir: Robert G. and Anne M. Merrick Foundation

Anne M. Pinkard: pres *PHIL AFFIL* pres: Robert G. and Anne M. Merrick Foundation

Robert M. Pinkard: secy/treas, dir *PHIL AFFIL* vp: Robert G. and Anne M. Merrick Foundation

Walter D. Pinkard, Jr.: vp, dir *B* 1949 *ED* Yale Univ 1971; Harvard Univ MBA 1975 *CURR EMPL* pres, dir: Colliers Pinkard *PHIL AFFIL* secy, treas: Robert G. and Anne M. Merrick Foundation

Vernon T. Pittinger: dir *PHIL AFFIL* dir: Robert G. and Anne M. Merrick Foundation

Donna C. Silbersack: asst secy, treas *PHIL AFFIL* asst secy, treas: Robert G. and Anne M. Merrick Foundation

APPLICATION INFORMATION
Initial Approach:

Grant requests should be submitted in letter form.

Letters of application should describe the purpose of the grant, operational procedures, time schedule, key staff members, approximate budget, and references to other sources of funding. In addition, a copy of the most recent financial report and IRS tax-exempt 501(c)(3) ruling letter should be enclosed.

Applications may be submitted at any time.

An interview may follow if requests are within the guidelines and interests of the foundation.

Restrictions on Giving: Applications are limited to organizations that are tax-exempt under section 501(c)(3) of the Internal Revenue Code and that are based in Maryland. Grantees must have the financial potential to sustain the project on a continuing basis after funding ceases. The foundation requests that an organization wait one year after final payment before submitting a subsequent proposal.

OTHER THINGS TO KNOW
The recipient of a grant is expected to make periodic progress reports. The foundation shares its officers and directors with the Robert G. and Anne M. Merrick Foundation, located at the same address.

GRANTS ANALYSIS
Total Grants: $3,160,474

Number of Grants: 89

Highest Grant: $385,664

Average Grant: $35,511

Typical Range: $5,000 to $50,000

Disclosure Period: fiscal year ending May 31, 1993

Note: Recent grants are derived from a fiscal 1993 Form 990.

RECENT GRANTS

General

385,664	Echo Hill Outdoor School, Worton, MD — Billy B. Bay Project
243,760	Johns Hopkins University, Baltimore, MD — success for all programs
192,500	Johns Hopkins University, Baltimore, MD — Zanvyl Kreiger Mind/Brain Institute
144,667	Gilman School, Baltimore, MD
137,500	Johns Hopkins University, Baltimore, MD — athletic facility

Goldseker Foundation of Maryland, Morris

CONTACT
Timothy D. Armbruster
President
Morris Goldseker Foundation of Maryland
Latrobe Bldg.
2 E Read St., 9th Fl.
Baltimore, MD 21202
(410) 837-5100

FINANCIAL SUMMARY
Recent Giving: $2,025,029 (1993); $1,736,272 (1992); $1,462,649 (1991)

Assets: $54,664,368 (1993); $52,000,000 (1992); $49,462,944 (1991)

EIN: 52-0983502

CONTRIBUTIONS SUMMARY
Donor(s): The Morris Goldseker Foundation of Maryland was established in 1973 by the will of Morris Goldseker expressly to support programs directly benefiting the people of the Baltimore metropolitan area.

Typical Recipients: • *Arts & Humanities:* Libraries • *Civic & Public Affairs:* African American Affairs, Civil Rights, Community Foundations, Economic Development, Employment/Job Training, Housing, Law & Justice, Parades/Festivals, Philanthropic Organizations, Professional & Trade Associations, Urban & Community Affairs, Women's Affairs • *Education:* Colleges & Universities, Education Funds, General, Literacy, Medical Education, Preschool Education, Special Education, Student Aid • *Health:* Mental Health • *Religion:* Jewish Causes, Religious Organizations • *Social Services:* At-Risk Youth, Child Welfare, Community Service Organizations, Counseling, Crime Prevention, Domestic Violence, Family Planning, Family Services, Food/Clothing Distribution, Shelters/Homelessness, Youth Organizations

Grant Types: multiyear/continuing support, project, and seed money

Geographic Distribution: Baltimore, MD

GIVING OFFICERS
Timothy Armbruster: pres

Frank P. Borzymowski: secy

Sheila Dodson: treas

Sheldon Goldseker: chmn, trust

Simon Goldseker: vchmn, trust

APPLICATION INFORMATION
Initial Approach:

Applicants should submit a preliminary letter to the foundation.

Applicants should include evidence of IRS tax-exempt status under sections 501(c)(3) and 509 of the Internal Revenue Code, background information, statement of need and objectives of the proposed project, methods for accomplishing objectives, projected program budget, and amount sought.

The deadlines for requests are April 1, August 1, and December 1.

The foundation's board meets three times a year in March, June, and October to consider proposals. Applicants are notified in writing of the outcome of their requests immediately after each meeting.

Restrictions on Giving: In order to be considered for funding, an organization must carry on its work and activities principally in the Baltimore metropolitan area.

The foundation does not make grants in support of religious programs or purposes, endowments, individuals, building campaigns, deficit financing, annual giving, publications, or operating budgets. Also the foundation reports it does not support arts and culture, ongoing operating budgets, political action groups, specific diseases or disabilities groups, or projects normally financed with public funds.

OTHER THINGS TO KNOW
The foundation lists Security Trust Company of Baltimore as a corporate trustee. The foundation is affiliated with the Baltimore Community Foundation.

PUBLICATIONS
Annual report, program guidelines

GRANTS ANALYSIS
Total Grants: $2,025,029

Number of Grants: 58

Highest Grant: $119,660

Average Grant: $34,914

Typical Range: $5,000 to $70,000

Disclosure Period: 1993

Note: Recent grants are derived from a 1993 Form 990.

RECENT GRANTS

Library

50,000	Enoch Pratt Free Library, Baltimore, MD

General

119,660	Associated Jewish Community, Baltimore, MD
119,660	Johns Hopkins University, Baltimore, MD
119,660	Morgan State University Foundation, Baltimore, MD
119,600	Baltimore Community Foundation, Baltimore, MD
119,000	Advocates for Children and Youth, Baltimore, MD

Hechinger Co. / Hechinger Foundation, Sidney L.

Revenue: $2.45 billion
Employees: 15,000
Headquarters: Landover, MD
SIC Major Group: Hardware Stores, Lumber & Other Building Materials, Paint, Glass & Wallpaper Stores, and Retail Nurseries & Garden Stores

CONTACT
John W. Hechinger, Sr.
Trustee
Sidney L. Hechinger Fdn. c/o Ms. Gwen Morris
3500 Pennsy Dr.
Landover, MD 20785-1691
(301) 341-0999

FINANCIAL SUMMARY
Recent Giving: $850,000 (fiscal 1995 est.); $692,575 (fiscal 1994); $831,090 (fiscal 1993)

Assets: $745,615 (fiscal 1994); $378,126 (fiscal 1993); $1,247,104 (fiscal 1992)

Gifts Received: $600,000 (fiscal 1994); $500,000 (fiscal 1993)

Fiscal Note: Company gives primarily through the foundation. The foundation receives gifts from Hechinger Co.

EIN: 52-6054428

CONTRIBUTIONS SUMMARY
Typical Recipients: • *Arts & Humanities:* Arts Appreciation, Arts Associations & Councils, Arts Centers, Arts Festivals, Arts Outreach, Ballet, Dance, Historic Preservation, Libraries, Literary Arts, Museums/Galleries, Music, Opera, Performing Arts, Public Broadcasting, Theater, Visual Arts • *Civic & Public Affairs:* African American Affairs, Business/Free Enterprise, Civil Rights, Economic Development, Employment/Job Training, Housing, Law & Justice, Legal Aid, Municipalities/Towns, Professional & Trade Associations, Public Policy, Safety, Urban & Community Affairs, Women's Affairs, Zoos/Aquariums • *Education:* Arts/Humanities Education, Business Education, Colleges & Universities, Community & Junior Colleges, Economic Educa-

tion, Education Associations, Engineering/Technological Education, Medical Education, Minority Education, Private Education (Precollege), Public Education (Precollege), Religious Education, Student Aid • *Environment:* General • *Health:* Cancer, Children's Health/Hospitals, Emergency/Ambulance Services, Geriatric Health, Health Funds, Health Organizations, Hospices, Hospitals, Medical Rehabilitation, Mental Health, Nursing Services, Nutrition, Public Health, Single-Disease Health Associations • *International:* International Relations • *Religion:* Churches, Jewish Causes, Religious Organizations, Religious Welfare, Synagogues/Temples • *Science:* Scientific Centers & Institutes • *Social Services:* Animal Protection, At-Risk Youth, Child Welfare, Community Centers, Community Service Organizations, Counseling, Day Care, Delinquency & Criminal Rehabilitation, Domestic Violence, Family Planning, Family Services, Food/Clothing Distribution, Homes, People with Disabilities, Recreation & Athletics, Senior Services, Sexual Abuse, Shelters/Homelessness, Substance Abuse, United Funds/United Ways, Volunteer Services, Youth Organizations

Grant Types: award, capital, endowment, general support, multiyear/continuing support, operating expenses, and scholarship

Geographic Distribution: only near headquarters and operating locations

Operating Locations: DC, DE, MD (Landover), NJ, NY, OH, PA, VA

CORP. OFFICERS
Richard England: *B* Pittsfield MA 1920 *ED* Harvard Univ 1942 *CURR EMPL* chmn emeritus, dir: Hechinger Co *PHIL AFFIL* mgr: Sydney L. Hechinger Foundation, Sidney L Hechinger Foundation

John Walter Hechinger, Jr.: *B* 1950 *ED* Boston Univ BBA 1972 *CURR EMPL* ceo, pres, dir: Hechinger Co *CORP AFFIL* chmn, dir: Home Quarters Warehouse *PHIL AFFIL* treas, dir: Community Foundation Greater Washington, Community Foundation Greater Washington

John Walter Hechinger, Sr.: *B* Washington DC 1920 *ED* Yale Univ BS 1941 *CURR EMPL* chmn, dir: Hechinger Co *NONPR AFFIL* dir: Handgun Control, Natl Urban Coalition *PHIL AFFIL* mgr: Sydney L. Hechinger Foundation, Sidney L Hechinger Foundation

S. Ross Hechinger: *B* 1952 *ED* Syracuse Univ *CURR EMPL* sr vp admin: Hechinger Co

GIVING OFFICERS
John Walter Hechinger, Jr.: trust *CURR EMPL* ceo, pres, dir: Hechinger Co *PHIL AFFIL* treas, dir: Community Foundation Greater Washington (see above)

John Walter Hechinger, Sr.: trust *CURR EMPL* chmn, dir: Hechinger Co *PHIL AFFIL* mgr: Sydney L. Hechinger Foundation (see above)

S. Ross Hechinger: pres *CURR EMPL* sr vp admin: Hechinger Co (see above)

APPLICATION INFORMATION
Initial Approach: *Initial Contact:* brief letter or proposal *Include Information On:* description of the organization, amount requested, purpose for which funds are sought, recently audited financial statement, proof of tax-exempt status, and list of board of directors *Deadlines:* none *Note:* Trustees do not meet with organizations to discuss proposals; applicants should not call the foundation to inquire on the status of a proposal; foundation only awards one grant per year to an organization.

Restrictions on Giving: Grants are not made to individuals.

OTHER THINGS TO KNOW
The foundation is considered a separate legal entity from the company.

The foundation requests that organizations not call to inquire on the status of proposals.

PUBLICATIONS
Proposal guidelines

GRANTS ANALYSIS
Total Grants: $692,575

Number of Grants: 159

Highest Grant: $159,000

Average Grant: $4,356

Typical Range: $500 to $5,000

Disclosure Period: fiscal year ending June 30, 1994

Note: Recent grants are derived from a fiscal 1994 Form 990.

RECENT GRANTS

General

159,000	United Jewish Appeal Federation of Jewish Philanthropies, Rockville, MD
145,000	United Way, Washington, DC — National Capital Area
40,000	Sidwell Friends School, Washington, DC
25,000	Local Initiatives Support Corporation, Washington, DC
21,900	Citizens Scholarship Foundation of America, St. Peter, MN

Hecht-Levi Foundation

CONTACT
Florence Grant
Hecht-Levi Fdn.
c/o Mercantile-Safe Deposit and Trust Co.
2 Hopkins Plz.
Baltimore, MD 21202
(410) 237-5322

FINANCIAL SUMMARY
Recent Giving: $314,150 (1993); $399,150 (1992); $380,569 (1991)

Assets: $8,543,949 (1993); $8,102,376 (1992); $7,915,008 (1991)

EIN: 52-6035023

CONTRIBUTIONS SUMMARY

Donor(s): the late Alexander Hecht, the late Selma H. Hecht, Robert H. Levi, Ryda H. Levi

Typical Recipients: • *Arts & Humanities:* Arts Funds, Arts Institutes, Arts Outreach, Ballet, Dance, Historic Preservation, Libraries, Museums/Galleries, Music, Opera, Performing Arts, Theater • *Civic & Public Affairs:* Community Foundations, General, Housing, Legal Aid, Philanthropic Organizations, Urban & Community Affairs, Zoos/Aquariums • *Education:* Arts/Humanities Education, Business Education, Colleges & Universities, Education Funds, Leadership Training, Private Education (Precollege), Religious Education • *Environment:* Resource Conservation • *Health:* Health Organizations, Mental Health • *Religion:* Churches, Jewish Causes, Religious Organizations, Synagogues/Temples • *Science:* Scientific Centers & Institutes • *Social Services:* Child Welfare, Community Service Organizations, Family Planning, United Funds/United Ways

Grant Types: general support

Geographic Distribution: focus on Baltimore, MD, metropolitan area

GIVING OFFICERS

Sandra L. Gerstung: pres

Frank Albert Kaufman: dir *B* Baltimore MD 1916 *ED* Dartmouth Coll AB 1937; Harvard Univ LLB 1940 *CURR EMPL* judge: US District Court MD *NONPR AFFIL* mem: Am Bar Assn, Am Judicature Soc, Am Law Inst, Baltimore Bar Assn, Fed Bar Assn, Fed Judges Assn, MD Bar Assn; trust emeritus: Goucher Coll, MD Inst Coll Art

Alexander H. Levi: vp, dir

Richard H. Levi: vp, treas, dir

Robert Henry Levi: vp, dir *B* Baltimore MD 1915 *ED* Johns Hopkins Univ AB 1936 *CURR EMPL* chmn: Catalyst Recovery Intl *CORP AFFIL* dir: Am Gen Ins Co, Fidelity & Deposit Co, Hittman Assocs *NONPR AFFIL* dir: Associated Jewish Charities Baltimore, Johns Hopkins Univ; dir (metro Baltimore): Jr Achievement; mem: Am Retail Federation, Natl Retail Merchants Assn; trust: Goucher Coll, Johns Hopkins Hosp

Ryda H. Levi: vp, dir

Wilbert H. Sirota: secy, dir *PHIL AFFIL* secy: Nathan and Suzanne Cohen Foundation, Merrill Foundation

APPLICATION INFORMATION

Initial Approach: The foundation requests applications be made in writing. There are no deadlines.

GRANTS ANALYSIS

Total Grants: $314,150

Number of Grants: 62

Highest Grant: $100,000

Typical Range: $500 to $5,000

Disclosure Period: 1993

Note: Recent grants are derived from a 1993 Form 990.

RECENT GRANTS

General

50,000	Associated Jewish Charities, Baltimore, MD
12,000	Johns Hopkins Medical Fund, Baltimore, MD
7,000	Park School, Baltimore, MD
5,250	Johns Hopkins University, Baltimore, MD
5,000	Baltimore Community Foundation, Baltimore, MD

Knapp Foundation

CONTACT

Robert B. Vojvoda
Vice President
Knapp Foundation
PO Box O
St. Michaels, MD 21663
(301) 745-5660

FINANCIAL SUMMARY

Recent Giving: $722,564 (1993); $837,759 (1992); $419,625 (1991)

Assets: $20,694,332 (1993); $20,917,548 (1992); $20,793,386 (1991)

EIN: 13-6001167

CONTRIBUTIONS SUMMARY

Donor(s): The foundation was incorporated in 1929 by the late Joseph Palmer Knapp .

Typical Recipients: • *Arts & Humanities:* Historic Preservation, History & Archaeology, Libraries, Museums/Galleries • *Civic & Public Affairs:* General, Municipalities/Towns, Public Policy, Safety, Urban & Community Affairs, Zoos/Aquariums • *Education:* Colleges & Universities, Engineering/Technological Education, Medical Education, Private Education (Precollege), Public Education (Precollege), Religious Education, Science/Mathematics Education, Secondary Education (Public), Special Education • *Environment:* General, Resource Conservation, Wildlife Protection • *Health:* Cancer, Emergency/Ambulance Services, Hospitals, Single-Disease Health Associations • *Religion:* Religious Welfare • *Science:* Science Museums, Scientific Labs • *Social Services:* Community Service Organizations, People with Disabilities, United Funds/United Ways, Youth Organizations

Grant Types: project

Geographic Distribution: focus on Mid-Atlantic United States

GIVING OFFICERS

Ruth Capranica: secy

Margaret P. Newcombe: trust

George L. Penny: trust

Sylvia V. Penny: trust *CURR EMPL* secy: George L Penny Inc *PHIL AFFIL* trust: Knapp Educational Fund

Antoinette P. Vojvoda: pres *PHIL AFFIL* pres: Knapp Educational Fund

Robert B. Vojvoda: vp *PHIL AFFIL* vp: Knapp Educational Fund

APPLICATION INFORMATION

Initial Approach:

The foundation requests detailed letters of application.

The foundation has no deadline for submitting proposals.

Restrictions on Giving: The foundation does not support individuals or provide funds for loans, scholarships, fellowships, research, endowment or building funds, or operating budgets.

PUBLICATIONS

Application guidelines

GRANTS ANALYSIS

Total Grants: $722,564

Number of Grants: 40

Highest Grant: $298,364

Average Grant: $18,064

Typical Range: $1,000 to $20,000

Disclosure Period: 1993

Note: Recent grants are derived from a 1993 Form 990.

RECENT GRANTS

Library

50,000	University of North Carolina, Chapel Hill, NC — National Endowment for the Humanities Challenge Grant to libraries
10,000	Berea College, Berea, KY— grant for Hutchins Library Acquisition Fund
10,000	Canandaigua City School District, Canandaigua, NY — grant for new multi-media creation station in library
10,000	Columbia University in the City of New York, New York, NY — purchase of microfilm reader/printer
10,000	Emmanuel College Library, Boston, MA — purchase of equipment for library automation system

General

298,364	Wildfowl Trust of North America, Grasonville, MD — maintenance of habitat for waterfowl and wildlife for educational purposes
133,000	Nature Conservancy, Carrboro, NC — to purchase additional land at Nags Head Woods Preserve
30,000	Tufts University School of Veterinary Medicine, N. Grafton, MA — purchase of equipment to modernize the surgical facilities at Wildlife Clinic
11,250	Delaware Nature Society, Hockessin, DE — purchase of audio-visual equipment
10,000	Capitol College, Laurel, MD — equipment for the CD-ROM reference collection

Leidy Foundation, John J.

CONTACT
Sharon Shaefer
Secretary
John J. Leidy Fdn.
217 E Redwood St., Rm. 1600
Baltimore, MD 21202
(410) 727-4136

FINANCIAL SUMMARY
Recent Giving: $298,920 (1993); $226,874 (1991); $286,450 (1990)

Assets: $7,090,635 (1993); $6,649,382 (1991); $5,863,774 (1990)

EIN: 52-6034785

CONTRIBUTIONS SUMMARY
Donor(s): the late John J. Leidy

Typical Recipients: • *Arts & Humanities:* Arts Institutes, Community Arts, Libraries, Music, Opera • *Civic & Public Affairs:* Clubs, Economic Development, Legal Aid, Philanthropic Organizations, Urban & Community Affairs • *Education:* Colleges & Universities, Education Reform, Elementary Education (Private), Legal Education, Literacy, Private Education (Precollege), Special Education, Student Aid • *Health:* Emergency/Ambulance Services, Health Organizations, Hospitals, Medical Research, Public Health, Single-Disease Health Associations • *Religion:* Jewish Causes, Religious Organizations • *Social Services:* Big Brother/Big Sister, Child Welfare, Community Service Organizations, Family Services, Food/Clothing Distribution, People with Disabilities, United Funds/United Ways, Youth Organizations

Grant Types: scholarship

Geographic Distribution: focus on MD

GIVING OFFICERS
Allan Herbert Fisher, Jr.: secy, trust *B* Baltimore MD 1922 *ED* Johns Hopkins Univ AB 1942; Univ MD LLB 1949 *NONPR AFFIL* fellow: Am Coll Probate Counc; mem: Am Bar Assn, Baltimore Bar Assn, DC Bar Assn, MD Bar Assn

Henry E. Pear: treas, trust

Robert Pierson: vp

W. Michel Pierson: vp, trust

Sharon Shaefer: secy

APPLICATION INFORMATION
Initial Approach: Send cover letter and full proposal. There are no deadlines.

Restrictions on Giving: Does not support individuals.

GRANTS ANALYSIS
Total Grants: $298,920
Number of Grants: 107
Highest Grant: $19,000
Typical Range: $300 to $18,000
Disclosure Period: 1993

Note: Recent grants are derived from a 1993 Form 990.

RECENT GRANTS
Library
10,000	Enoch Pratt Free Library, Baltimore, MD
3,500	Board of Library Trustees, Baltimore, MD

General
19,000	Associated Jewish Charities, Baltimore, MD
18,000	Maryland Food Committee, Baltimore, MD
15,000	Boys and Girls Club of Maryland, Baltimore, MD
10,000	Big Brothers and Big Sisters of Baltimore, Baltimore, MD
10,000	Boys and Girls Club of Maryland, Baltimore, MD

Lockhart Vaughan Foundation

CONTACT
Joseph B. Powell, Jr.
Director
Lockhart Vaughan Fdn.
250 W. Pratt St., No. 13
Baltimore, MD 21201
(410) 539-5541

FINANCIAL SUMMARY
Recent Giving: $471,390 (1993)
Assets: $16,581,712 (1993)
EIN: 52-1693184

CONTRIBUTIONS SUMMARY
Typical Recipients: • *Arts & Humanities:* Libraries • *Civic & Public Affairs:* Botanical Gardens/Parks, Community Foundations, Employment/Job Training, Housing, Urban & Community Affairs, Women's Affairs • *Education:* Colleges & Universities, Elementary Education (Public), General, Leadership Training, Science/Mathematics Education, Social Sciences Education • *Environment:* General, Resource Conservation • *Health:* Cancer, Children's Health/Hospitals, Emergency/Ambulance Services, Health Organizations, Mental Health • *Religion:* Churches, Ministries, Religious Welfare • *Science:* Scientific Centers & Institutes • *Social Services:* Big Brother/Big Sister, Child Abuse, Family Planning, Family Services, Food/Clothing Distribution, Shelters/Homelessness, Substance Abuse, YMCA/YWCA/YMHA/YWHA, Youth Organizations

Grant Types: general support

Geographic Distribution: focus on MD

GIVING OFFICERS
Benjamin M. Baker III: dir

Julia Baker Menzies: dir

Joseph B. Powell, Jr.: dir *PHIL AFFIL* trust: W. B. Haley Foundation

Susan Baker Powell: dir *PHIL AFFIL* trust: Susan Vaughan Foundation

APPLICATION INFORMATION
Initial Approach: Send a brief letter of inquiry. Include a description of organization, amount requested, purpose of funds sought, recently audited financial statement, and proof of tax-exempt status.

GRANTS ANALYSIS
Total Grants: $471,390
Number of Grants: 45
Highest Grant: $25,000
Typical Range: $1,000 to $25,000
Disclosure Period: 1993

Note: Recent grants are derived from a 1993 Form 990.

RECENT GRANTS
Library
10,000	Enoch Pratt Free Library, Baltimore, MD — for educational purposes

General
25,000	Baltimore Community Foundation, Baltimore, MD — for collaborative children and families initiative
25,000	Health Care for the Homeless, Baltimore, MD — for medical purposes
20,000	Big Brothers and Big Sisters of Central Maryland, Baltimore, MD — for general support
20,000	Chesapeake Bay Foundation, Annapolis, MD — for educational purposes
20,000	Irvine Natural Science Center, Stevenson, MD — urban environmental education project

M.E. Foundation

CONTACT
F. Carroll Brown
Vice President
M.E. Fdn.
PO Box 448
Linthicum, MD 21090
(410) 636-0094

FINANCIAL SUMMARY
Recent Giving: $624,601 (1993); $777,744 (1992); $650,272 (1991)

Assets: $10,451,783 (1993); $9,945,220 (1992); $12,373,125 (1991)

Gifts Received: $440 (1993); $1,069,601 (1991)

EIN: 13-6205356

CONTRIBUTIONS SUMMARY

Donor(s): Margaret Brown Trimble and Frances Carroll Brown

Typical Recipients: • *Arts & Humanities:* Libraries, Music • *Civic & Public Affairs:* Economic Development, General • *Education:* Colleges & Universities, International Exchange, Private Education (Precollege), Religious Education, Special Education • *International:* International Development, International Organizations, International Peace & Security Issues, International Relations, Missionary/Religious Activities • *Religion:* Churches, Ministries, Missionary Activities (Domestic), Religious Organizations, Religious Welfare, Seminaries, Social/Policy Issues • *Social Services:* At-Risk Youth, Community Service Organizations, Family Services, Homes, People with Disabilities, Substance Abuse, Youth Organizations

Grant Types: general support

Geographic Distribution: national

GIVING OFFICERS

Frances Carroll Brown: vp, treas, dir

Charles Wendell Colson: vp, dir *B* Boston MA 1931 *ED* Brown Univ AB 1953; George Washington Univ JD 1959 *NONPR AFFIL* assoc: Prison Fellowship

Margaret Brown Trimble: pres, secy, dir

APPLICATION INFORMATION

Initial Approach: Send brief letter of inquiry describing program or project. Include a description of organization, amount requested, purpose of funds sought, recently audited financial statement, and proof of tax-exempt status. There are no deadlines.

GRANTS ANALYSIS

Total Grants: $624,601

Number of Grants: 93

Highest Grant: $45,000

Typical Range: $1,000 to $25,000

Disclosure Period: 1993

Note: Recent grants are derived from a 1993 Form 990.

RECENT GRANTS

General

45,000	Prison Fellowship Ministries, Washington, DC
42,500	Mini Bible College, Hampton, VA
35,000	Joni and Friends, Agoura Hills, CA
27,000	The Door, Louisville, KY
25,000	Association of Christian Schools International, Northport, AL

Martin Marietta Corp. / Martin Marietta Corp. Foundation

Revenue: $9.87 billion
Employees: 92,786
Headquarters: Bethesda, MD
SIC Major Group: Guided Missiles & Space Vehicles, Construction Sand & Gravel, Clay Refractories, and Ammunition Except for Small Arms

CONTACT

Donna S. Price
Coordinator, Gifts and Grants
Martin Marietta Corp. Foundation
6801 Rockledge Dr.
Bethesda, MD 20817
(301) 897-6284

FINANCIAL SUMMARY

Recent Giving: $7,181,000 (1994 approx.); $5,974,430 (1993); $6,456,315 (1992)

Assets: $676,024 (1993); $818,520 (1992); $785,838 (1990)

Gifts Received: $6,044,000 (1993); $6,364,000 (1992)

Fiscal Note: Total for 1992 includes $1,668,360 in matching gifts, $557,235 in scholarships and $4,955,405 in cash giving. Company departments also make contributions directly from corporate funds. Above figures exclude nonmonetary support. In 1993, the foundation received contributions from Martin Marietta Corp.

EIN: 13-6161566

CONTRIBUTIONS SUMMARY

Typical Recipients: • *Arts & Humanities:* Arts Associations & Councils, Arts Centers, Arts Festivals, Arts Funds, Ballet, Dance, Historic Preservation, Libraries, Museums/Galleries, Music, Opera, Performing Arts, Public Broadcasting, Theater • *Civic & Public Affairs:* African American Affairs, Business/Free Enterprise, General, Housing, Municipalities/Towns, Parades/Festivals, Professional & Trade Associations, Public Policy, Safety, Urban & Community Affairs, Women's Affairs, Zoos/Aquariums • *Education:* Business Education, Colleges & Universities, Community & Junior Colleges, Economic Education, Education Funds, Education Reform, Engineering/Technological Education, General, Legal Education, Medical Education, Private Education (Precollege), Public Education (Precollege), Science/Mathematics Education, Secondary Education (Public), Social Sciences Education, Special Education • *Environment:* General • *Health:* Cancer, Emergency/Ambulance Services, Hospices, Hospitals, Medical Research, Single-Disease Health Associations • *Religion:* Jewish Causes, Religious Welfare • *Science:* Science Museums, Scientific Organizations, Scientific Research • *Social Services:* Community Centers, Community Service Organizations, Family Planning, Food/Clothing Distribution, Homes, People with Disabilities, Recreation & Athletics, Shelters/Home-lessness, United Funds/United Ways, Youth Organizations

Grant Types: employee matching gifts, general support, and scholarship

Note: Employee gifts are only matched to colleges and universities. Employee matching gift ratio: 1 to 1.

Geographic Distribution: near headquarters and operating locations only

Operating Locations: CO (Denver, Littleton), FL (Orlando), LA (New Orleans), MA (Western), MD (Baltimore, Bethesda), NJ (Moorestown, Trenton), NY (Central, South Central), PA (Philadephia), TN (Oak Ridge), VT

CORP. OFFICERS

Norman Ralph Augustine: *B* Denver CO 1935 *ED* Princeton Univ BS 1957; Princeton Univ MSE 1959 *CURR EMPL* chmn, ceo, dir: Martin Marietta Corp *CORP AFFIL* chmn: Martin Marietta Overseas Corp; dir: Phillips Petroleum Co, Procter & Gamble Co, Riggs Natl Bank *NONPR AFFIL* chmn: Am Red Cross, Assn US Army, Defense Sci Bd, Space Sys Tech Adv Bd; chmn adv counc: MA Inst Tech Lincoln Lab; chmn natl prog evaluation comm: Boy Scouts Am; consult: US Dept Air Force, US Dept Army, US Dept Energy, US Dept Navy, US Dept Transportation, US Fed Aviation Admin; consult off: Off US Secy Defense; dir: New Am Schs Devel Corp; fellow: Am Astronautical Soc, Am Inst Aeronautics Astronautics, Inst Electrical Electronics Engrs; mem: Am Acad Arts & Sci, Am Assn Advancement Sci, Am Helicopter Soc, Armed Forces Communs Electronics Assn, Bus Counc, Indus Coll Armed Forces, Intl Acad Astronautics, Natl Acad Engg, Natl Security Indus Assn, Phi Beta Kappa, Sigma Xi, Tau Beta Pi, US Air Force Sci Adv Bd; mem bd advs: Ctr Adv Procurement, Journal Defense Res; mem policy counc: Bus Roundtable; trust: Johns Hopkins Univ, Princeton Univ *CLUB AFFIL* Natl Space, Rotary

Buzz Bartlett: *CURR EMPL* dir pub & commun rels: Martin Marietta Corp

Marcus C. Bennett: *B* Atlanta GA 1936 *ED* GA Inst Tech BS 1958 *CURR EMPL* vp, cfo, dir: Martin Marietta Corp *CORP AFFIL* chmn: Chesapeake Pk Inc, Martin Marietta Materials Inc, Orlando Pk Inc; sr vp, cfo, dir: Martin Marietta Techs

A. Thomas Young: *B* Wachapreague VA 1938 *ED* Univ VA BS 1961; MA Inst Tech MS 1972 *CURR EMPL* pres, coo, dir: Martin Marietta Corp *CORP AFFIL* chmn, pres, coo: Martin Marietta Techs; dir: Cooper Indus Inc, Dial Corp *NONPR AFFIL* dir: Univ VA Sch Engg & Applied Sci VA Engg Fdn; fellow: Aerospace Indus Assn Am, Am Astronautical Soc, Am Inst Aeronautics Astronautics; mem: Natl Acad Engg, Natl Assn Engrs

GIVING OFFICERS

Phillip S. Giaramita: chmn gifts & grants comm *CURR EMPL* vp pub & commun aff: Martin Marietta Corp

Donna S. Price: coordinator gifts and grants

Wayne F. Shaner: trust

Peter F. Warren, Jr.: trust

APPLICATION INFORMATION
Initial Approach: *Initial Contact:* letter or full proposal *Include Information On:* description of the organization, amount requested, purpose for which funds are sought, recently audited financial statements, and proof of tax-exempt status *Deadlines:* none

Restrictions on Giving: Does not give to political or religious organizations, or individuals except through scholarship program. Grants are seldom made for athletic events.

GRANTS ANALYSIS
Total Grants: $5,974,430
Number of Grants: 375*
Highest Grant: $600,000
Average Grant: $15,932*
Typical Range: $1,000 to $10,000
Disclosure Period: 1993

Note: Financial information is for the foundation only. The figures for average grant and number of grants are approximations and exclude matching grants and scholarships. Recent grants are derived from a 1993 Form 990.

RECENT GRANTS
General

600,000	New American Schools Development Corporation, Arlington, VA
250,000	University of Central Florida Foundation, Orlando, FL
235,000	University of Tennessee Academy for Teachers of Math/Science, Knoxville, TN
204,000	University of Maryland Foundation, College Park, MD
200,000	University of Colorado Boulder Foundation, Boulder, CO

McCormick & Co. Inc.

Sales: $1.56 billion
Employees: 7,501
Headquarters: Sparks, MD
SIC Major Group: Potato Chips & Similar Snacks, Frozen Specialties Nec, Edible Fats & Oils Nec, and Flavoring Extracts & Syrups Nec

CONTACT
Allen M. Barrett, Jr.
Vice President, Corporate Communications
McCormick & Co. Inc.
18 Loveton Circle
Sparks, MD 21152-6000
(410) 771-7310

FINANCIAL SUMMARY
Recent Giving: $1,500,000 (1994 approx.); $1,200,000 (1993 approx.); $1,225,000 (1992 approx.)

Fiscal Note: Company gives directly. Above figures exclude nonmonetary support.

CONTRIBUTIONS SUMMARY
Typical Recipients: • *Arts & Humanities:* Historic Preservation, Libraries, Museums/Galleries, Music, Public Broadcasting, Theater • *Civic & Public Affairs:* Business/Free Enterprise, Economic Development, Law & Justice, Professional & Trade Associations, Urban & Community Affairs • *Education:* Business Education, Colleges & Universities, Economic Education, Minority Education, Science/Mathematics Education, Student Aid • *Environment:* General • *Health:* Health Organizations, Medical Research, Nutrition • *Science:* Scientific Organizations • *Social Services:* Community Service Organizations, Family Planning, Family Services, Food/Clothing Distribution, United Funds/United Ways, Volunteer Services, Youth Organizations

Grant Types: capital, employee matching gifts, and scholarship

Note: Employee matching gift ratio: 1 to 1.

Nonmonetary Support Types: donated products

Note: Value of nonmonetary support is not available.

Geographic Distribution: near headquarters and operating locations

Operating Locations: CA (Anaheim, Carlsbad, Fremont, Gilroy, Hayward, Salinas), GA (Atlanta, Doraville), IL (Chicago), IN (South Bend), MA (East Hampton), MD (Baltimore, Hunt Valley), NJ (Freehold), NY, TX (Dallas, Irving), VA (Bedford)

CORP. OFFICERS
H. Eugene Blattman: *B* Kansas City MO 1936 *ED* Whitman Coll BA 1958 *CURR EMPL* pres, ceo, coo: McCormick & Co Inc

Richard Wayne Single, Sr.: *B* Baltimore MD 1938 *ED* Univ MD AB 1959; Univ MD JD 1961 *CURR EMPL* vp, secy, gen couns, dir: McCormick & Co Inc *CORP AFFIL* dir: Club House Foods, McCormick Can, McCormick de Mex *NONPR AFFIL* mem: Am Bar Assn, MD Bar Assn; trust: Franklin Sq Hosp

GIVING OFFICERS
Allen M. Barrett, Jr.: *CURR EMPL* vp, corp commun: McCormick & Co

Richard Wayne Single, Sr.: *CURR EMPL* vp, secy, gen couns, dir: McCormick & Co Inc (see above)

APPLICATION INFORMATION
Initial Approach: *Initial Contact:* letter and proposal *Include Information On:* description of the organization, amount requested, purpose for which funds are sought, and proof of tax-exempt status *Deadlines:* late fall

Restrictions on Giving: Company does not support individuals; religious, fraternal, political, or lobbying groups; or goodwill advertising or benefit events.

OTHER THINGS TO KNOW
The McCormick Fund is the vehicle through which the company makes direct contributions.

GRANTS ANALYSIS
Total Grants: $1,500,000*

Typical Range: $5,000 to $10,000
Disclosure Period: 1994
Note: Figure is approximate.

Merck Family Fund

CONTACT
Betsy Taylor
Executive Director
Merck Family Fund
6930 Carroll Ave.
Ste. 500
Takoma Park, MD 20912
(301) 270-2970
Note: The fund has recently moved. See "Other Things To Know" for more details.

FINANCIAL SUMMARY
Recent Giving: $1,160,000 (1994 est.); $1,255,500 (1993); $1,200,000 (1992)

Assets: $26,665,379 (1993); $28,508,384 (1992); $32,314,670 (1991)

Gifts Received: $120 (1993)

EIN: 22-6063382

CONTRIBUTIONS SUMMARY
Donor(s): The fund was incorporated in 1954 by members of the Merck family.

Typical Recipients: • *Arts & Humanities:* Arts Funds, History & Archaeology, Libraries, Museums/Galleries, Music, Theater • *Civic & Public Affairs:* Economic Development, Municipalities/Towns, Philanthropic Organizations, Public Policy, Urban & Community Affairs, Women's Affairs • *Education:* Environmental Education, General, Literacy, Public Education (Precollege), Secondary Education (Public) • *Environment:* Air/Water Quality, Forestry, General, Resource Conservation • *Health:* Home-Care Services, Hospitals, Long-Term Care, Preventive Medicine/Wellness Organizations • *International:* International Environmental Issues • *Science:* Scientific Centers & Institutes, Scientific Organizations • *Social Services:* Child Welfare, Day Care, Family Planning, Food/Clothing Distribution, Shelters/Homelessness, Youth Organizations

Grant Types: project

Geographic Distribution: national

GIVING OFFICERS
Sharman B. Altshuler: mem

Katherine A. Arthaud: mem

Patience Chamberlin: pres, trust

Olivia H. Farr: mem

Francis W. Hatch III: vp, trust

George W. M. Hatch: mem

Serena Merck Hatch: mem *B* 1928 *PHIL AFFIL* trust: John Merck Fund

Albert W. Merck, Jr.: trust

Antony M. Merck: trust

George F. Merck: mem

Josephine A. Merck: trust

Wilhelm M. Merck: treas, trust

Anne Merck-Abeles: secy, trust

Betsy Taylor: exec dir *PHIL AFFIL* trust: Town Creek Foundation

Dinah B. Vischer: mem

Serena H. Whitridge: trust

APPLICATION INFORMATION
Initial Approach:

The fund requests initial contact be made through a brief letter of inquiry or written proposal.

Applications should describe the activities of the organization and specific details of the proposal, including the amount requested.

Applications are due in March and August.

Restrictions on Giving: The fund awards grants only to tax-exempt organizations in the United States. It does not make grants to individuals or for-profit organizations. It does not support debt reduction, annual fundraising campaigns, capital construction, purchase of equipment, acquisition of land, or film or video projects. The fund does not generally support academic research or books.

OTHER THINGS TO KNOW
The fund's administrative office has moved from Charleston, SC, to the above Maryland address.

PUBLICATIONS
Annual report

GRANTS ANALYSIS
Total Grants: $1,255,500

Number of Grants: 39

Highest Grant: $100,000

Average Grant: $32,192

Typical Range: $25,000 to $45,000

Disclosure Period: 1993

Note: Recent grants are derived from a 1993 grants list.

RECENT GRANTS
Library
1,000	Foundation Center, New York, NY — general support

General
100,000	Institute for Educational Inquiry, Seattle, WA
55,000	New York University, New York, NY — the development of a curriculum on environmentally sustainable business practices for business schools and executives
50,000	Appalachian Center for Economic Networks, Athens, OH — specialty foods initiative, a flexible manufacturing network of low-income women in Ohio
50,000	Appalachian Mountain Club, Montpelier, VT — an outreach and communications coordinator for the Northern Forest Alliance
50,000	Enterprise Foundation, Columbia, MD — "Greenstreets," the gardening/open space component of the Sandtown-Winchester community revitalization project in Baltimore

Meyerhoff Fund, Joseph

CONTACT
Louis L. Kaplan
Executive Vice President
Joseph Meyerhoff Fund
25 S Charles St.
Baltimore, MD 21201
(410) 727-3200

FINANCIAL SUMMARY
Recent Giving: $1,300,000 (1995 est.); $1,300,000 (1994 approx.); $1,197,335 (1993)

Assets: $27,000,000 (1995 est.); $27,000,000 (1994 approx.); $27,997,212 (1993)

EIN: 52-6035997

CONTRIBUTIONS SUMMARY
Donor(s): The fund was incorporated in 1953 by Mrs. Joseph Meyerhoff and the late Joseph Meyerhoff .

Typical Recipients: • *Arts & Humanities:* Libraries, Music • *Civic & Public Affairs:* General, Native American Affairs, Philanthropic Organizations, Public Policy, Urban & Community Affairs • *Education:* Colleges & Universities, Education Funds, Education Reform, Literacy, Private Education (Precollege), Religious Education, Student Aid • *Health:* Hospitals, Speech & Hearing • *International:* Foreign Arts Organizations, Foreign Educational Institutions, International Peace & Security Issues, Missionary/Religious Activities • *Religion:* Jewish Causes, Religious Organizations, Synagogues/Temples • *Social Services:* Child Welfare, Community Service Organizations, Scouts, Senior Services, United Funds/United Ways, Volunteer Services, YMCA/YWCA/YMHA/YWHA

Grant Types: capital, emergency, endowment, matching, multiyear/continuing support, professorship, scholarship, and seed money

Geographic Distribution: focus on Baltimore, MD; New York, NY; and the United Kingdom

GIVING OFFICERS
George B. Hess: vp, exec dir

Louis L. Kaplan: exec vp

Harvey M. Meyerhoff: pres *ED* Univ WI BBA 1948 *CURR EMPL* pres: Joseph Meyerhoff Fund

Joseph Meyerhoff II: treas *NONPR AFFIL* vp: Jewish Commun Ctr Baltimore

Marvin S. Williams: secy

APPLICATION INFORMATION
Initial Approach:

The fund requests applications be made in writing.

Written applications should include a list of the organization's directors, amount of the contribution sought, and a copy of a current budget.

The fund has no deadline for submitting proposals.

Restrictions on Giving: The fund does not make grants to individuals.

GRANTS ANALYSIS
Total Grants: $1,197,335

Number of Grants: 216

Highest Grant: $175,000

Average Grant: $5,543

Typical Range: $250 to $10,000

Disclosure Period: 1993

Note: Recent grants are derived from a 1993 Form 990.

RECENT GRANTS
Library
6,000	New York Public Library, New York, NY

General
175,000	Israel Endowment Fund, New York, NY
75,000	Associated H and LPM Fund, Baltimore, MD
50,000	Fund for Educational Excellence, Baltimore, MD
40,000	New Israel Fund, Washington, DC
33,000	American Society for Technion, New York, NY

Middendorf Foundation

CONTACT
E. Phillips Hathaway
President and Trustee
Middendorf Foundation
5 E Read St.
Baltimore, MD 21202
(410) 752-7088

FINANCIAL SUMMARY
Recent Giving: $739,987 (fiscal 1994); $707,373 (fiscal 1993); $607,800 (fiscal 1992)

Assets: $19,000,159 (fiscal 1994); $19,484,215 (fiscal 1993); $17,040,916 (fiscal 1992)

EIN: 52-6048944

CONTRIBUTIONS SUMMARY
Donor(s): The foundation was incorporated in 1953 by the late J. William Middendorf, Jr. , and the late Alice C. Middendorf .

Typical Recipients: • *Arts & Humanities:* Arts Centers, Arts Institutes, Dance, Historic Preservation, Libraries, Museums/Galleries, Music, Opera, Public Broadcasting • *Civic & Public Affairs:* Botanical Gardens/Parks,

Community Foundations, Economic Development, Employment/Job Training, Philanthropic Organizations, Professional & Trade Associations, Zoos/Aquariums • *Education:* Arts/Humanities Education, Colleges & Universities, Education Funds, Medical Education, Private Education (Precollege) • *Environment:* Wildlife Protection • *Health:* Cancer, Clinics/Medical Centers, Eyes/Blindness, Geriatric Health, Health Organizations, Hospitals, Mental Health, Prenatal Health Issues, Preventive Medicine/Wellness Organizations, Single-Disease Health Associations • *International:* International Organizations • *Religion:* Churches, Religious Organizations, Religious Welfare • *Science:* Scientific Centers & Institutes • *Social Services:* Child Welfare, Community Service Organizations, Emergency Relief, Family Planning, Family Services, Food/Clothing Distribution, People with Disabilities, Recreation & Athletics, Shelters/Homelessness, United Funds/United Ways, YMCA/YWCA/YMHA/YWHA, Youth Organizations

Grant Types: endowment, general support, matching, and professorship

Geographic Distribution: focus on Maryland

GIVING OFFICERS
Forrest F. Bramble, Jr.: vp, trust *CURR EMPL* ptnr: Barton & Wilmer Niles

E. Phillips Hathaway: pres, trust

Philips Hathaway: trust

Sealy H. Hopkinson: trust

Craig Lewis: treas, trust *B* 1930 *CURR EMPL* prin, dir: Investment Couns MD

Robert B. Russell II: trust *CURR EMPL* prin-treas, dir: Investment Couns MD

APPLICATION INFORMATION
Initial Approach:

The foundation requests applications be made in writing.

The foundation requests applicants include all supporting documentation in the initial proposal.

The foundation has no deadline for submitting proposals.

Restrictions on Giving: The foundation does not make grants to individuals.

GRANTS ANALYSIS
Total Grants: $739,987

Number of Grants: 36

Highest Grant: $87,500

Average Grant: $20,555

Typical Range: $5,000 to $25,000

Disclosure Period: fiscal year ending March 31, 1994

Note: Recent grants are derived from a fiscal 1994 grants list.

RECENT GRANTS
General

87,500	Johns Hopkins University School of Medicine — medical research
50,000	Boys Latin School of Maryland, Baltimore, MD — acquisition of books and information system
50,000	Hammond Harwood House Association, Annapolis, MD — for an endowment
50,000	Salvation Army, St. Louis, MO — flood relief
50,000	Salvation Army, Los Angeles, CA — Los Angels earthquake relief

---

Mulford Foundation, Vincent

CONTACT
Paul Klender
Vice President
Vincent Mulford Fdn.
c/o Mercantile Safe Deposit and Trust Co.
2 Hopkins Plz.
Baltimore, MD 21201
(410) 237-5518

FINANCIAL SUMMARY
Recent Giving: $401,000 (1993); $325,000 (1992); $207,000 (1990)

Assets: $7,780,563 (1993); $6,986,856 (1992); $5,044,737 (1990)

Gifts Received: $307,947 (1993); $665,893 (1992)

Fiscal Note: In 1993, contributions were received from Vincent Mulford, Jr.

EIN: 22-6043594

CONTRIBUTIONS SUMMARY
Donor(s): the late Vincent S. Mulford, the late Edith Mulford

Typical Recipients: • *Arts & Humanities:* Ballet, Community Arts, History & Archaeology, Libraries, Museums/Galleries, Music, Opera, Performing Arts • *Civic & Public Affairs:* Economic Development, Urban & Community Affairs • *Education:* Colleges & Universities, Education Funds, Engineering/Technological Education, Private Education (Precollege), Religious Education • *Health:* Emergency/Ambulance Services, Hospitals, Medical Rehabilitation • *International:* International Relations • *Religion:* Churches, Dioceses, Ministries, Religious Organizations, Religious Welfare, Seminaries • *Social Services:* Community Service Organizations, Family Planning, United Funds/United Ways, Volunteer Services, Youth Organizations

Grant Types: general support

Geographic Distribution: focus on MA, NJ, and NY

GIVING OFFICERS
Madeline H. Grant: trust

Christian R. Sonne: trust

APPLICATION INFORMATION
Initial Approach: The foundation requests applications be made in writing. There are no deadlines.

GRANTS ANALYSIS
Total Grants: $401,000

Number of Grants: 74

Highest Grant: $50,000

Typical Range: $250 to $2,000

Disclosure Period: 1993

Note: Recent grants are derived from a 1993 Form 990.

RECENT GRANTS
Library

1,250	Pierpont Morgan Library, New York, NY

General

25,000	Massachusetts Institute of Technology, Cambridge, MA
25,000	Montclair Volunteer Ambulance Corps, Montclair, NJ
10,000	American Red Cross Disaster, Montclair, NJ
10,000	Berkeley Divinity School, New Haven, CT
10,000	Trinity Episcopal Church, Tulsa, OK

PHH Corporation / PHH Foundation, Inc.

Former Foundation Name: PHH Group Foundation
Revenue: $2.02 billion
Employees: 4,834
Headquarters: Hunt Valley, MD
SIC Major Group: Management Services, Local Passenger Transportation Nec, Local Trucking Without Storage, and Transportation Services Nec

CONTACT
Pilar M. Page
Vice President
PHH Foundation, Inc.
11333 McCormick Rd.
Hunt Valley, MD 21031
(410) 771-2733

Note: The foundation is funding only current projects and is not accepting new grant applications until April 30, 1995.

FINANCIAL SUMMARY
Recent Giving: $500,000 (fiscal 1995 est.); $469,415 (fiscal 1994); $468,777 (fiscal 1993)

Assets: $97,622 (fiscal 1994); $78,432 (fiscal 1993); $52,502 (fiscal 1992)

Gifts Received: $486,847 (fiscal 1994); $482,799 (fiscal 1993); $162,900 (fiscal 1992)

Fiscal Note: Contributes through foundation only.

EIN: 52-6040911

CONTRIBUTIONS SUMMARY
Typical Recipients: • *Arts & Humanities:* Community Arts, General, History & Archaeology, Libraries, Museums/Galleries, Music, Opera, Performing Arts, Theater

• *Civic & Public Affairs:* African American Affairs, Economic Policy, General, Municipalities/Towns, Philanthropic Organizations, Professional & Trade Associations, Safety, Urban & Community Affairs, Zoos/Aquariums • *Education:* Business Education, Colleges & Universities, Economic Education, Education Funds, General, Literacy, Minority Education, Preschool Education, Private Education (Precollege), Public Education (Precollege), Religious Education, Secondary Education (Public), Student Aid • *Health:* Children's Health/Hospitals, Clinics/Medical Centers, Emergency/Ambulance Services, General, Health Organizations, Hospitals, Medical Research, Multiple Sclerosis, Respiratory, Single-Disease Health Associations • *Religion:* Religious Organizations • *Science:* Scientific Centers & Institutes • *Social Services:* Child Welfare, Community Service Organizations, Domestic Violence, Emergency Relief, Family Services, Food/Clothing Distribution, General, People with Disabilities, Shelters/Homelessness, Substance Abuse, United Funds/United Ways, Youth Organizations

Grant Types: award, capital, employee matching gifts, general support, and project

Note: Employee matching gift ratio: 1 to 1 up to $2,000 per employee per year.

Nonmonetary Support Types: cause-related marketing & promotion

Geographic Distribution: limited to community where corporation headquarters is located; Baltimore, MD, area

Operating Locations: CA (Huntington), CO (Englewood), CT (Danbury, Wilton), IL (Chicago), MD (Hunt Valley), NC (Edenton), NJ (Mt. Laurel), TX (Ft. Worth), VA (Williamsburg)

CORP. OFFICERS
Peter Brinch: *CURR EMPL* dir pub rels: PHH Corp

Robert Dietrich Kunisch: *B* Norwalk CT 1941 *ED* NY Univ BS 1963 *CURR EMPL* chmn, pres, ceo: PHH Corp *CORP AFFIL* chmn, ceo: PHH Holdings Inc; dir: Alex Brown & Sons Inc, CSX Corp, GenCorp Inc, Greater Baltimore Co, Mercantile Bankshares Corp, Mercantile Safe Deposit & Trust, Preston Corp; trust: Johns Hopkins Health Sys, Johns Hopkins Hospital *NONPR AFFIL* mem: Un Way Central MD; trust: Johns Hopkins Univ

Roy A. Meierhenry: *B* Norfolk NE 1938 *ED* Univ NE BS 1960; Creighton Univ MBA 1966 *CURR EMPL* sr vp, cfo: PHH Corp *CORP AFFIL* cfo, treas, dir: Dealers Holdings Inc; dir: Dome Corp *NONPR AFFIL* dir: Greater Baltimore Med Ctr; mem: Fin Execs Inst

GIVING OFFICERS
Eugene A. Arbaugh: pres, dir *B* Manchester MD 1938 *ED* Western MD Coll 1960; Univ MD 1966 *CURR EMPL* sr vp, secy, chief mktg off: PHH Corp

Robert Dietrich Kunisch: chmn, dir *CURR EMPL* chmn, pres, ceo: PHH Corp (see above)

R. W. Mitchell: treas

Pilar M. Page: vp
Samuel H. Wright: secy *B* Baltimore MD 1946 *ED* Un Coll 1968; Univ MD 1972 *CURR EMPL* vp, gen couns: PHH Corp *NONPR AFFIL* mem: Am Bar Assn

APPLICATION INFORMATION
Initial Approach: *Initial Contact:* write for application form and guidelines *Include Information On:* name, affiliation, address, and phone number of organization; how long organization has existed and geographic area served; list of principal staff and board members; list of board members employed by organization and whether the board has authorized request; list of current sources of other income, including percentages for the last three years; indication of amounts and percentages of total income spent on program services, fund-raising, administrative, and general; and copy of IRS tax exemption ruling or determination letter, current financial statement, and recent audit by a certified public accountant *Deadlines:* none *Note:* Requests for less than $1,000 may be submitted on the foundation's short application form. Proposals for funds in excess of $1,000 should be submitted on a PHH Foundation Form or on the applicant's organization letterhead. Responses on application form for requests for more than $1,000 must be in numeric sequence as listed above.

Restrictions on Giving: The foundation does not support organizations with major support from government funding; individuals; political activities and organizations; goodwill; journal advertisements; products; or dinners or related social activities. Grants are made only to organizations having tax-exempt status under Section 501(c)(3) of the IRS code.

OTHER THINGS TO KNOW
The foundation is currently funding only previous commitments. New grant applications will not be accepted until after April 30, 1995.

PUBLICATIONS
Policy statement

GRANTS ANALYSIS
Total Grants: $469,415

Number of Grants: 44*

Highest Grant: $130,000

Average Grant: $9,403*

Typical Range: $1,000 to $10,000

Disclosure Period: fiscal year ending April 30, 1994

Note: Number of grants and average grant figures do not include matching gifts totaling $55,665. Recent grants are derived from a fiscal 1994 grants list. .

RECENT GRANTS
General

130,000	United Way Central Maryland, Baltimore, MD
40,000	College Bound Foundation, Baltimore, MD
25,000	Johns Hopkins University, Baltimore, MD
20,000	Loyola College, Baltimore, MD
10,000	GBMC Foundation, Baltimore, MD

Price Associates, T. Rowe / Price Associates Foundation, T. Rowe

Sales: $310.04 million
Employees: 1,665
Headquarters: Baltimore, MD
SIC Major Group: Investment Advice

CONTACT
Brenda K. Ashworth
Program Officer
T. Rowe Price Associates Foundation
100 E Pratt St., 9th Fl.
Baltimore, MD 21202
(410) 547-2100

FINANCIAL SUMMARY
Recent Giving: $800,000 (1995 est.); $763,000 (1994); $680,726 (1993)

Assets: $5,776,265 (1993); $4,026,247 (1992); $1,733,442 (1991)

Gifts Received: $2,300,640 (1993); $400,700 (1992); $50,000 (1990)

Fiscal Note: Above figures are for the foundation only. Company reports that it gives primarily through the foundation. Above figures exclude nonmonetary support. In 1993, contributions were received from T. Rowe Price Associates.

EIN: 52-1231953

CONTRIBUTIONS SUMMARY
Typical Recipients: • *Arts & Humanities:* Arts Festivals, Arts Funds, Arts Institutes, Community Arts, Historic Preservation, History & Archaeology, Libraries, Museums/Galleries, Music, Opera, Public Broadcasting, Theater • *Civic & Public Affairs:* Professional & Trade Associations, Public Policy, Urban & Community Affairs, Zoos/Aquariums • *Education:* Arts/Humanities Education, Business Education, Colleges & Universities, Education Funds, Elementary Education (Private), Literacy, Minority Education, Private Education (Precollege), Public Education (Precollege), Secondary Education (Private), Student Aid • *Environment:* General, Resource Conservation • *Health:* Health Organizations, Hospitals, Single-Disease Health Associations • *Social Services:* Child Welfare, Community Service Organizations, Family Services, Food/Clothing Distribution, People with Disabilities, Recreation & Athletics, Shelters/Homelessness, United Funds/United Ways, Youth Organizations

Grant Types: capital, employee matching gifts, and general support

Nonmonetary Support Types: donated equipment and workplace solicitation

Note: T. Rowe Price Associates only offers nonmonetary support to the United Way. Estimated value of nonmonetary support is not available.

Geographic Distribution: focus on headquarters and operating locations

Operating Locations: MD (Baltimore)

CORP. OFFICERS

George A. Roche: *B* Rochester NY 1941 *ED* Georgetown Univ 1963; Harvard Univ Sch Bus Admin 1966 *CURR EMPL* mng dir, cfo, vp: T Rowe Price Assoc *CORP AFFIL* dir: BRP Inc; pres, dir: T Rowe Price New Era Fund Inc *NONPR AFFIL* dir: Enoch Pratt Free Lib *CLUB AFFIL* Ctr, Harvard, L'Hirondelle, MD

GIVING OFFICERS

Brenda K. Ashworth: program off

Stephen W. Boesel: vp *B* Niles OH 1944 *ED* Baldwin-Wallace Coll 1968; Univ Denver 1969 *CURR EMPL* vp: T Rowe Price Assoc *CORP AFFIL* vp: T Rowe Price New Era Fund Inc

Thomas H. Broadus, Jr.: vp *CURR EMPL* mng dir: T Rowe Price Assoc *CORP AFFIL* mng dir: T Rowe Price Assoc

Patricia O. Goodyear: secy

Carter O. Hoffman: vp, treas *CURR EMPL* mng dir: T Rowe Price Assoc

Albert C. Hubbard, Jr.: chmn, pres

APPLICATION INFORMATION

Initial Approach: *Initial Contact:* brief letter or proposal *Include Information On:* description of program, list of organization's board members, annual report, statement of need *Deadlines:* none

Restrictions on Giving: Company does not support individuals, religious organizations for sectarian purposes, or political or lobbying groups.

GRANTS ANALYSIS

Total Grants: $680,726

Number of Grants: 371

Highest Grant: $75,000

Average Grant: $1,835

Typical Range: $500 to $3,000

Disclosure Period: 1993

Note: Recent grants are derived from a 1993 Form 990.

RECENT GRANTS

General

75,000	United Way, Baltimore, MD
21,225	Roland Park Country School, Baltimore, MD — for secondary education
20,000	Baltimore Educational Scholarship Trust, Baltimore, MD — for secondary education
19,700	St. Paul School, Brooklandville, MD — for secondary education
15,000	Collegebound Foundation, Baltimore, MD — for secondary education

Rouse Co. / Rouse Co. Foundation

Revenue: $5.6 million
Employees: 94
Headquarters: Columbia, MD
SIC Major Group: General Building Contractors, Holding & Other Investment Offices, and Real Estate

CONTACT

Margaret P. Mauro
Executive Director
The Rouse Co. Fdn.
10275 Little Patuxent Pkwy.
Columbia, MD 21044
(410) 992-6375
Note: Another telephone number is (410) 994-3436.

FINANCIAL SUMMARY

Recent Giving: $161,170 (1993); $148,000 (1992); $120,168 (1991)

Assets: $3,057,996 (1993); $2,910,651 (1992); $2,667,304 (1991)

Gifts Received: $174,176 (1993); $108,161 (1992); $80,825 (1991)

Fiscal Note: In 1993, contributions were received from the Rouse Company.

EIN: 52-6056273

CONTRIBUTIONS SUMMARY

Typical Recipients: • *Arts & Humanities:* Arts Associations & Councils, Arts Centers, Arts Funds, Community Arts, Dance, Ethnic & Folk Arts, Libraries, Literary Arts, Museums/Galleries, Music, Opera, Performing Arts, Public Broadcasting, Theater, Visual Arts • *Civic & Public Affairs:* Economic Development, Employment/Job Training, General, Housing, Zoos/Aquariums • *Education:* Arts/Humanities Education, Business Education, Colleges & Universities, Community & Junior Colleges, Legal Education, Student Aid • *Health:* Clinics/Medical Centers, Hospices, Hospitals, Prenatal Health Issues • *International:* International Relations • *Science:* Scientific Centers & Institutes • *Social Services:* Child Welfare, Community Service Organizations, Domestic Violence, Food/Clothing Distribution, Homes, Senior Services, Sexual Abuse, Shelters/Homelessness, Substance Abuse, United Funds/United Ways, Volunteer Services, Youth Organizations

Grant Types: capital, challenge, department, endowment, general support, multi-year/continuing support, operating expenses, project, scholarship, and seed money

Nonmonetary Support Types: donated equipment and in-kind services

Geographic Distribution: primarily in the central MD area

Operating Locations: AR (Fayetteville), CA (Santa Monica), CO (Colorado Springs, Denver), CT (New Haven), DC (Washington), FL (Jacksonville, Miami, Tallahassee, Tampa), GA (Atlanta, Augusta, Decatur), IA (Ames, Cedar Falls, Keokuk, Marshalltown, Muscatine, W. Burlington), IL (Mt. Pros-

pect), KY (Louisville), LA (Gretna, New Orleans, Shreveport), MA (Boston, Springfield), MD (Baltimore, Easton, Glen Burnie, Owings Mills, Parkville), MI (Taylor), MN (Minnetonka), MO (St. Louis), NC (Charlotte), NJ (Burlington, Cherry HIll, Paramus, Voorhees, Wayne, Woodbridge), NY (New York, Staten Island), OH (Dayton, Toledo), PA (Exton, Greensburg, Philadelphia, Plymouth Meeting), TX (Austin, Ft. Worth, Galveston, Houston, San Antonio), VA (Norfolk), WA (Seattle), WI (Milwaukee)

CORP. OFFICERS

R. Harwood Beville: *B* Philadelphia PA 1940 *ED* Univ MD BS 1962; Harvard Univ MBA 1964 *CURR EMPL* exec vp: Rouse Co *NONPR AFFIL* dir: Traditional Acupuncture Inst; mem bus adv counc: Anne Arundel County, Univ MD; trust: Intl Counc Shopping Ctrs

Anthony W. Deering: *CURR EMPL* pres, coo, dir: Rouse Co

Mathias Joseph DeVito: *B* Trenton NJ 1930 *ED* Univ MD BA 1954; Univ MD LLB 1956 *CURR EMPL* chmn, ceo: Rouse Co *CORP AFFIL* dir: First MD Bancorp, Nova Pharmaceutical Corp, Trizec Corp, USAir Group *NONPR AFFIL* chmn: Greater Baltimore Commn; mem: Order Coif *CLUB AFFIL* Adirondack League, Elkridge, Union League

Jeffrey H. Donahue: *CURR EMPL* sr vp, cfo: Rouse Co

GIVING OFFICERS

Edwin A. Daniels, Jr.: exec dir, trust

Anthony W. Deering: treas, trust *CURR EMPL* pres, coo, dir: Rouse Co (see above)

Richard G. McCauley: secy-treas, trust

APPLICATION INFORMATION

Initial Approach: Send brief letter of inquiry. If initial review suggests that a request for funding is appropriate, such requests should include request for a specific amount of money and an explanation of its intended use; a brief description of the organization, its history and activity; the names and qualifications of the persons who will administer the grant; and a copy of most recent tax exemption statement. For a specific project or program, include goals and objectives, population to be served, schedule for implementation, and method of evaluating its effectiveness. There are no deadlines.

Restrictions on Giving: Does not support religious programs, individuals, or political advocacy. Organizations must be tax-exempt under 501(c)(3).

PUBLICATIONS

Informational Brochure (including Application Guidelines)

GRANTS ANALYSIS

Total Grants: $161,170

Number of Grants: 12

Highest Grant: $100,000

Typical Range: $2,000 to $10,000

Disclosure Period: 1993

Note: Recent grants are derived from a 1993 Form 990.

RECENT GRANTS

General

100,000	United Way of Central Maryland, Baltimore, MD	
20,000	Greater Baltimore Medical Center, Baltimore, MD — redevelopment campaign fund	
10,000	Build, Baltimore, MD	
10,000	Chase-Brexton Clinic, Baltimore, MD — capital fund	
10,000	Joseph Richey House, Baltimore, MD	

Smith Foundation, Gordon V. and Helen C.

CONTACT
Gordon V. Smith
Director
Gordon V. and Helen C. Smith Fdn.
8716 Crider Brook Way
Potomac, MD 20854
(301) 469-8597

FINANCIAL SUMMARY
Recent Giving: $97,540 (1993); $241,992 (1992); $446,949 (1991)

Assets: $5,683,508 (1993); $5,243,374 (1992); $5,064,001 (1991)

Gifts Received: $4,000 (1992); $579,848 (1991); $10,280 (1990)

EIN: 52-1440846

CONTRIBUTIONS SUMMARY
Donor(s): Gordon V. Smith, Helen C. Smith, Miller and Smith, Inc.

Typical Recipients: • *Arts & Humanities:* Arts Centers, Libraries, Music, Performing Arts, Public Broadcasting • *Civic & Public Affairs:* Clubs, Public Policy, Safety, Women's Affairs • *Education:* Business Education, Colleges & Universities, Legal Education, Private Education (Precollege), Religious Education • *Health:* Cancer, Diabetes, Emergency/Ambulance Services, Health Organizations, Heart, Hospitals, Multiple Sclerosis, Prenatal Health Issues, Respiratory • *International:* International Organizations, International Relief Efforts, Missionary/Religious Activities • *Religion:* Churches, Religious Organizations, Religious Welfare, Seminaries • *Social Services:* Big Brother/Big Sister, Recreation & Athletics, Youth Organizations

Grant Types: general support

Geographic Distribution: national

GIVING OFFICERS
Cynthia Skarbek: dir

Bruce G. Smith: dir

Douglas I. Smith: dir

Gordon Victor Smith: dir *B* 1932 *ED* Harvard Univ MBA 1959 *CURR EMPL* fdr, chmn: Miller & Smith Cos

Helen C. Smith: dir

APPLICATION INFORMATION
Initial Approach: Send brief letter of inquiry describing program or project. There are no deadlines.

GRANTS ANALYSIS
Total Grants: $97,540

Number of Grants: 37

Highest Grant: $28,000

Typical Range: $20 to $24,000

Disclosure Period: 1993

Note: Recent grants are derived from a 1993 Form 990.

RECENT GRANTS

Library

25	Ohio Wesleyan University, Delaware, OH — Friends of the Library	

General

28,000	Wesley Theological Seminary, Washington, DC — President's Discretionary Fund	
24,000	Wesley Theological Seminary, Washington, DC — endowment campaign	
20,000	Ohio Wesleyan University, Delaware, OH	
6,600	Wesley Theological Seminary, Washington, DC	
6,560	Bethesda United Methodist Church, Bethesda, MD	

Unger Foundation, Aber D.

CONTACT
Eugene M. Feinblatt
President
Aber D. Unger Fdn.
223 E Redwood St.
Baltimore, MD 21202
(410) 576-4211

FINANCIAL SUMMARY
Recent Giving: $95,050 (fiscal 1994); $93,550 (fiscal 1993); $120,010 (fiscal 1992)

Assets: $2,314,371 (fiscal 1994); $2,238,515 (fiscal 1993); $2,043,340 (fiscal 1992)

EIN: 52-6034758

CONTRIBUTIONS SUMMARY
Typical Recipients: • *Arts & Humanities:* Arts Centers, Arts Institutes, Community Arts, Libraries, Music, Theater • *Civic & Public Affairs:* Employment/Job Training, General, Housing, Municipalities/Towns, Philanthropic Organizations, Urban & Community Affairs • *Education:* Arts/Humanities Education, Colleges & Universities, Education Reform, General, Health & Physical Education, Literacy, Student Aid

• *Health:* AIDS/HIV, Arthritis, Health Organizations, Hospitals, Mental Health • *International:* Health Care/Hospitals, Human Rights, International Development • *Religion:* Churches, Religious Organizations, Religious Welfare • *Social Services:* Community Service Organizations, Domestic Violence, Family Planning, Family Services, Food/Clothing Distribution, People with Disabilities, Sexual Abuse, Shelters/Homelessness, United Funds/United Ways

Grant Types: general support

Geographic Distribution: focus on MD

GIVING OFFICERS
Eugene M. Feinblatt: pres, treas

John Feinblatt: dir

Marjorie W. Feinblatt: dir

Paul C. Wolman III: dir

APPLICATION INFORMATION
Initial Approach: Send brief letter describing program. There are no deadlines.

GRANTS ANALYSIS
Total Grants: $95,050

Number of Grants: 25

Highest Grant: $13,000

Typical Range: $300 to $12,500

Disclosure Period: fiscal year ending February 28, 1994

Note: Recent grants are derived from a fiscal 1994 Form 990.

RECENT GRANTS

General

12,500	Union Memorial Hospital Foundation, Baltimore, MD	
10,000	Family Life Foundation, Baltimore, MD	
10,000	Interns for Peace, Baltimore, MD — Center of Jewish-Arab Economic Development	
8,000	Villa Julie College, Baltimore, MD	
5,000	Fund for Educational Excellence, Baltimore, MD	

Warfield Memorial Fund, Anna Emory

CONTACT
Charles B. Reeves, Jr.
President
Anna Emory Warfield Memorial Fund
1210 Merc. Bldg.
Baltimore, MD 21201
(301) 547-0612

FINANCIAL SUMMARY
Recent Giving: $158,910 (1993); $159,540 (1992); $164,450 (1991)

Assets: $4,011,232 (1993); $3,928,522 (1992); $3,774,685 (1991)

Gifts Received: $1,500 (1992); $22,130 (1989)

EIN: 52-0785672

CONTRIBUTIONS SUMMARY

Donor(s): the late S. Davies Warfield

Typical Recipients: • *Arts & Humanities:* Libraries • *Civic & Public Affairs:* Philanthropic Organizations • *Health:* Hospitals • *Religion:* Religious Welfare • *Social Services:* Child Welfare, Family Services, Homes

Grant Types: general support

Geographic Distribution: focus on the Baltimore, MD, metropolitan area

GIVING OFFICERS

Mrs. W. Page Dame, Jr.: trust

Edward K. Dunn, Jr.: treas, trust *B* Baltimore MD 1935 *ED* Princeton Univ AB 1958; Harvard Univ MBA 1960 *CURR EMPL* pres, chmn exec comm, dir: Mercantile-Safe Deposit & Trust Co *CORP AFFIL* pres, dir: Mercantile Bankshares Corp *NONPR AFFIL* dir: Green Mt Cemetery; mem corp adv bd: Natl Assn Securities Dealers; mem fin adv bd: Archdiocese Baltimore; trust: Assoc Catholic Charities, Johns Hopkins Health System, Johns Hopkins Hosp, Wilson (Thomas) Sanitarium *PHIL AFFIL* trust: Thomas Wilson Sanitarium for Children of Baltimore City

Mrs. William E. Grose: trust

Louis W. Hargrave: trust

Mrs. Thomas H. Maddux: trust

Braxton D. Mitchell: vp, trust

Charles B. Reeves, Jr.: pres, trust *B* Baltimore MD 1923 *ED* Princeton Univ BA 1947; Univ VA LLB 1951 *CURR EMPL* ptnr: Venable Baetjer & Howard *NONPR AFFIL* mem: Am Bar Assn, Am Judicature Soc, MD Bar Assn; pres: Kernan (James Lawrence) Hosp

Mrs. William F. Schmick, Jr.: trust

Mrs. John R. Sherwood: trust

Mrs. Lewis C. Strudwick: trust

APPLICATION INFORMATION

Initial Approach: Send brief letter including purpose and personal and financial data. There are no deadlines.

OTHER THINGS TO KNOW

Provides grants to individuals to alleviate poverty and human distress.

PUBLICATIONS

Application Guidelines

GRANTS ANALYSIS

Total Grants: $158,910

Typical Range: $200 to $750

Disclosure Period: 1993

Note: Recent grants are derived from a 1992 Form 990. All grants in 1993 were scholarships to individuals.

RECENT GRANTS

Library

750	Foundation Center, New York, NY

General

500	Associated Catholic Charities, Baltimore, MD
200	Union Memorial Hospital, Baltimore, MD
200	Wesley Home, Baltimore, MD

Widgeon Foundation

CONTACT

Elizabeth H. Robinson
President
Widgeon Fdn.
PO Box 1084
Easton, MD 21601
(301) 822-7707

FINANCIAL SUMMARY

Recent Giving: $58,955 (1993); $82,290 (1992); $91,465 (1990)

Assets: $2,443,365 (1993); $2,315,766 (1992); $2,008,790 (1990)

EIN: 13-6113927

CONTRIBUTIONS SUMMARY

Donor(s): Elizabeth H. Robinson

Typical Recipients: • *Arts & Humanities:* Arts Centers, History & Archaeology, Libraries, Museums/Galleries • *Civic & Public Affairs:* General, Public Policy, Safety, Urban & Community Affairs, Zoos/Aquariums • *Education:* Colleges & Universities, Faculty Development, Medical Education, Private Education (Precollege), Public Education (Precollege) • *Environment:* Wildlife Protection • *Health:* Alzheimers Disease, Cancer, Children's Health/Hospitals, Diabetes, Emergency/Ambulance Services, Heart, Hospices • *International:* Foreign Educational Institutions • *Religion:* Churches, Religious Organizations, Religious Welfare • *Social Services:* Animal Protection, Community Service Organizations, Homes, People with Disabilities, Recreation & Athletics, Scouts, United Funds/United Ways, YMCA/YWCA/YMHA/YWHA, Youth Organizations

Grant Types: general support

Geographic Distribution: focus on MD, PA, and VA

GIVING OFFICERS

Elizabeth H. Robinson: dir, pres, treas

Richard Robinson: dir, vp *B* 1937 *ED* Harvard Univ 1959 *CURR EMPL* pres, ceo, chmn, dir: Scholastic

George V. Strong, Jr.: dir, secy

APPLICATION INFORMATION

Initial Approach: The foundation requests applications be made in writing. There are no deadlines.

GRANTS ANALYSIS

Total Grants: $58,955

Number of Grants: 34

Highest Grant: $10,350

Typical Range: $100 to $6,900

Disclosure Period: 1993

Note: Recent grants are derived from a 1993 Form 990.

RECENT GRANTS

Library

3,000	Dorchester County Public Library, Cambridge, MD

General

10,350	University of Maryland Foundation, College Park, MD
6,900	Steward School, Richmond, VA
5,000	Busick Tennis Foundation
5,000	Morehead College, Atlanta, GA
5,000	University of Virginia Experimental Farm, Charlottesville, VA

MASSACHUSETTS

Acushnet Co. / Acushnet Foundation

Sales: $416.0 million
Employees: 3,400
Headquarters: Fairhaven, MA
SIC Major Group: Sporting & Athletic Goods Nec, Fabricated Rubber Products Nec, Synthetic Rubber, and Footwear Except Rubber Nec

CONTACT

Edward Powers
Foundation Manager
Acushnet Fdn.
21 Francis St.
Fairhaven, MA 02719
(508) 992-0820
Note: The Acushnet Co. is no longer involved in administering the Acushnet Foundation.

FINANCIAL SUMMARY

Recent Giving: $300,000 (fiscal 1995 est.); $275,430 (fiscal 1994); $300,000 (fiscal 1993 approx.)

Assets: $6,236,319 (fiscal 1993); $7,019,217 (fiscal 1992); $6,609,772 (fiscal 1991)

Fiscal Note: Contributes through foundation only.

EIN: 04-6032197

CONTRIBUTIONS SUMMARY

Typical Recipients: • *Arts & Humanities:* Arts Associations & Councils, Community Arts, Historic Preservation, History & Archaeology, Libraries, Museums/Galleries, Music, Public Broadcasting, Theater • *Civic & Public Affairs:* Civil Rights, Law & Justice, Legal Aid, Philanthropic Organizations, Public Policy, Urban & Community Affairs • *Education:* Business Education, Colleges & Universities, Economic Education, Education Funds, Engineering/Technological Education, General, International Exchange, Minority Education, Public Education (Precollege), Science/Mathematics Education, Secondary Education (Public), Special Education, Student Aid • *Environment:* General • *Health:* Children's Health/Hospitals, Health Funds, Health Organizations, Hospitals, Medical Rehabilitation • *Religion:* Churches, Religious Organizations, Religious Welfare • *Science:* Science Exhibits & Fairs • *Social Services:* Child Welfare, Community Centers, Community Service Organizations, Day Care, Family Services, Scouts, Substance Abuse, United Funds/United Ways, YMCA/YWCA/YMHA/YWHA, Youth Organizations

Grant Types: capital, emergency, general support, multiyear/continuing support, scholarship, and seed money

Geographic Distribution: generally limited to the greater New Bedford, MA, area

Operating Locations: MA (Acushnet, Brockton, Fairhaven)

CORP. OFFICERS
John T. Ludes: *CURR EMPL* pres, ceo, dir: Acushnet Co

Walter R. Uihlein: *ED* Univ MA BA *CURR EMPL* vp, dir: Acushnet Co *CORP AFFIL* pres, ceo, dir: Titleist & Foot-Joy Worldwide Co

GIVING OFFICERS
William Russell Bommer: trust *B* Akron OH 1942 *CURR EMPL* secy: Teachers Protective Mutual Life Ins Co

Robert Dubiel: trust

Grame L. Flanders: trust

Glenn Johnson: trust

Edward Powers: fdn mng, trust

Thomas C. Weaver: trust

Richard B. Young: trust

APPLICATION INFORMATION
Initial Approach: *Initial Contact:* letter *Include Information On:* amount desired, purpose, and other pertinent information *Deadlines:* none

Restrictions on Giving: Does not support endowments, operating expenses, or matching gifts.

Grants are made in the New Bedford area unless a project receives specific board approval.

OTHER THINGS TO KNOW
The foundation favors organizations with no other means of support. Grant seekers currently receiving government aid are not encouraged to apply.

The Acushnet Co. was the original donor to the Acushnet Foundation. It is currently not involved with administering the foundation.

GRANTS ANALYSIS
Total Grants: $275,430
Number of Grants: 51
Highest Grant: $70,000
Average Grant: $5,401
Typical Range: $1,000 to $6,500
Disclosure Period: fiscal year ending June 30, 1994

Note: Recent grants are derived from a fiscal 1994 grants list.

RECENT GRANTS
General
70,000	United Way of New Bedford, New Bedford, MA — general support
50,000	St. Luke's Hospital, New Bedford, MA — general support
27,180	National Merit Scholarship Corporation, Evanston, IL — general support
15,000	St. Luke's Hospital, New Bedford, MA — general support
10,000	YMCA Camp Massasoit, New Bedford, MA — general support

---

American Optical Corp. / American Optical Foundation

Sales: $200.0 million
Employees: 250
Headquarters: Southbridge, MA
SIC Major Group: Instruments & Related Products, Rubber & Miscellaneous Plastics Products, Stone, Clay & Glass Products, and Wholesale Trade—Durable Goods

CONTACT
Ernest Duquette
Director, Employee Benefits
American Optical Corp.
14 Mechanic St.
Southbridge, MA 01550
(508) 765-2060

FINANCIAL SUMMARY
Recent Giving: $36,695 (1994); $36,954 (1993); $39,614 (1992)

Assets: $1,158,644 (1993); $1,096,220 (1992); $1,020,350 (1991)

Gifts Received: $26,895 (1993); $29,070 (1992); $41,600 (1991)

EIN: 04-6028058

CONTRIBUTIONS SUMMARY
Typical Recipients: • *Arts & Humanities:* Libraries • *Civic & Public Affairs:* General, Municipalities/Towns • *Education:* Colleges & Universities, Education Funds, Engineering/Technological Education, International Exchange, Private Education (Precollege), Public Education (Precollege), Science/Mathematics Education, Student Aid • *Health:* Children's Health/Hospitals, Health Organizations • *Social Services:* Youth Organizations

Grant Types: employee matching gifts and scholarship

Geographic Distribution: focus on MA

Operating Locations: MA (Southbridge)

CORP. OFFICERS
Maurice J. Cunniffe: *CURR EMPL* chmn, ceo: Am Optical Corp

Neil M. Henderson: *CURR EMPL* pres, dir: Am Optical Corp

John W. Van Dyke: *CURR EMPL* cfo: Am Optical Corp

GIVING OFFICERS
American Optical Corp.: trust

Steven J. Beckett: trust *CURR EMPL* treas: Am Optical Corp

Ernest A. Duquette: trust

APPLICATION INFORMATION
Initial Approach: Submit two letters of recommendation, transcripts, formal application, SAT scores, and essay on career objectives. Deadline is April 25.

Restrictions on Giving: Limited to children of company employees.

OTHER THINGS TO KNOW
Provides individual scholarships for education at accredited colleges and universities.

GRANTS ANALYSIS
Total Grants: $36,954
Number of Grants: 9
Highest Grant: $8,360
Typical Range: $1,000 to $2,000
Disclosure Period: 1993

Note: Information listed does not include scholarships. Recent grants are derived from a 1993 Form 990.

RECENT GRANTS
Library
1,000	Notre Dame Library, Notre Dame, IN

General
8,360	Youth for Understanding, New York, NY
3,464	West Street School, Vassalboro, ME
3,000	Wheaton College, Norton, MA — scholarship
2,300	Rochester Polytechnical Institute, Rochester, NY — scholarship
2,200	Washington University, St. Louis, MO — scholarship

Ansin Private Foundation, Ronald M.

CONTACT
Ronald M. Ansin
Trustee
Ronald M. Ansin Private Fdn.
One Main St.
Leominster, MA 01453

FINANCIAL SUMMARY
Recent Giving: $752,660 (fiscal 1993); $30,260 (fiscal 1992); $135,547 (fiscal 1991)

Assets: $9,797,909 (fiscal 1993); $8,634,023 (fiscal 1992); $3,123,575 (fiscal 1991)

Gifts Received: $1,400,000 (fiscal 1993); $3,941,484 (fiscal 1992); $220,000 (fiscal 1991)

Fiscal Note: In fiscal 1993, contributions were received from Ronald M. Ansin.

EIN: 04-2786469

CONTRIBUTIONS SUMMARY
Donor(s): Ronald M. Ansin

Typical Recipients: • *Arts & Humanities:* Community Arts, General, History & Archaeology, Libraries, Museums/Galleries, Music, Performing Arts, Theater • *Civic & Public Affairs:* Civil Rights, Clubs, Community Foundations, General, Legal Aid, Municipalities/Towns, Public Policy, Urban & Community Affairs • *Education:* Colleges & Universities, Community & Junior Colleges, Private Education (Precollege), Vocational & Technical Education • *Environment:* Air/Water Quality, General, Resource Conservation, Watershed • *Health:* AIDS/HIV, Children's Health/Hospitals, Clinics/Medical Centers, Hospitals, Single-Disease Health Associations • *International:* International Environmental Issues, International Organizations, International Peace & Security Issues, International Relations • *Religion:* Churches, Jewish Causes, Religious Organizations, Religious Welfare, Synagogues/Temples • *Social Services:* Community Service Organizations, Family Planning, Family Services, Scouts, United Funds/United Ways, Youth Organizations

Grant Types: general support

Geographic Distribution: focus on MA

GIVING OFFICERS
Ronald M. Ansin: trust *B* Worcester MA 1934 *ED* Harvard Univ BA 1955; Yale Univ JD 1958 *CURR EMPL* chmn, treas, dir: LB Evans & Son Co *CORP AFFIL* chmn: Am Footwear Corp, Ansewn Shoe Corp, Anwelt Corp, Merchants Natl Bank; dir: Cole-Haan; dir, pres: Cleghorn Shoe Corp *NONPR AFFIL* treas: Lawrence Academy; trust: Applewild Sch, Fitchburg Art Mus, Fitchburg St Coll, Leominster Hosp

Ronald M. Ansin: trust *CURR EMPL* chmn, treas, dir: LB Evans & Son Co (see above)

APPLICATION INFORMATION
Initial Approach: Send brief letter describing program. Include a description of organization, amount requested, purpose of funds sought, recently audited financial statement, and proof of tax-exempt status. There are no deadlines.

GRANTS ANALYSIS
Total Grants: $752,660

Number of Grants: 60

Highest Grant: $308,552

Typical Range: $100 to $10,000

Disclosure Period: fiscal year ending November 30, 1993

Note: Recent grants are derived from a fiscal 1993 Form 990.

RECENT GRANTS
Library

2,000	John F. Kennedy Library Foundation, Boston, MA

General

308,552	Lawrence Academy, Groton, MA
144,858	New England Deaconess Hospital, Boston, MA
30,000	Nashua River Watershed Association, Groton, MA
25,000	Campaign for Military Service Education Fund, Washington, DC
25,000	Worcester County Horticultural Society, Boylston, MA

Arakelian Foundation, Mary Alice

CONTACT
John H. Pramberg, Jr.
President
Mary Alice Arakelian Fdn.
PO Box 510
Newburyport, MA 01950

FINANCIAL SUMMARY
Recent Giving: $130,000 (1992); $158,000 (1990); $211,600 (1989)

Assets: $5,082,498 (1992); $4,270,947 (1990); $4,327,039 (1989)

EIN: 04-6155695

CONTRIBUTIONS SUMMARY
Typical Recipients: • *Arts & Humanities:* Arts Funds, Community Arts, Historic Preservation, Libraries, Museums/Galleries, Public Broadcasting • *Civic & Public Affairs:* Municipalities/Towns • *Education:* Special Education • *Health:* Hospitals, Prenatal Health Issues • *Religion:* Churches, Religious Organizations, Synagogues/Temples • *Social Services:* Community Service Organizations, United Funds/United Ways

Grant Types: general support

GIVING OFFICERS
Fleet Trust Company: trust

Rose M. Marshall: trust

Donald D. Mitchell: trust

John H. Pramberg, Jr.: pres, dir *PHIL AFFIL* trust: Wheelwright Scientific School, Swasey Fund for Relief of Public School Teachers of Newburyport

Charles P. Richmond: trust

APPLICATION INFORMATION
Initial Approach: The foundation has no formal grant application procedure or application form. Deadline is September 15.

GRANTS ANALYSIS
Total Grants: $130,000

Number of Grants: 7

Highest Grant: $30,000

Typical Range: $10,000 to $15,000

Disclosure Period: 1992

Note: Recent grants are derived from a 1992 Form 990.

RECENT GRANTS
Library

15,000	Friends of the Newburyport Public Library, Newburyport, MA

General

25,000	Anna Jacques Hospital, Newburyport, MA — special care nursery
20,000	First Religious Society of Newburyport, Newburyport, MA
15,000	Link House, Boston, MA — renovations
15,000	United Way of Merrimack Valley, Lawrence, MA
10,000	Haverhill/Newburyport Human Services, Newburyport, MA

Babson Foundation, Paul and Edith

CONTACT
Elizabeth D. Nichols
Trustee
Paul and Edith Babson Fdn.
c/o Nichols and Pratt
50 Congress St.
Boston, MA 02109
(617) 523-6800

FINANCIAL SUMMARY
Recent Giving: $328,697 (1993); $259,500 (1992); $285,660 (1991)

Assets: $6,922,884 (1993); $6,793,208 (1992); $6,682,589 (1991)

EIN: 04-6037891

CONTRIBUTIONS SUMMARY
Donor(s): the late Paul T. Babson

Typical Recipients: • *Arts & Humanities:* History & Archaeology, Libraries, Museums/Galleries, Music, Opera, Performing Arts, Public Broadcasting, Theater • *Civic & Public Affairs:* Economic Development, Employment/Job Training, General, Hispanic Affairs, Municipalities/Towns, Public Policy, Urban & Community Affairs • *Education:* Colleges & Universities, General, Leadership Training, Medical Education, Minority Education, Private Education (Precollege), Public Education (Precollege), Student Aid • *Environment:* General • *Health:* Hospitals, Public Health • *International:* Foreign Arts Organizations, International Relief Efforts • *Religion:* Religious Organizations • *Science:* Science Museums • *Social Services:* Child Welfare, Community Centers, Community Service Organizations, Crime Prevention, Family Planning, Family Services, Food/Clothing Distribution, Homes, Shelters/Homelessness, United Funds/United Ways, YMCA/YWCA/YMHA/YWHA, Youth Organizations

Grant Types: general support

Geographic Distribution: focus on MA

GIVING OFFICERS

Donald Paul Babson: trust *B* Newton MA 1924 *ED* Cornell Univ 1948; Harvard Univ Sch Bus Admin 1950 *CURR EMPL* chmn: Babson-United Investment Advs *CORP AFFIL* chmn, pres: Un Bus Svc; dir: Multibank Fin Corp, South Shore Bank

Susan Averill Babson: trust *B* Birmingham MI 1924 *ED* MI St Univ 1946 *CURR EMPL* secy, clerk, dir: Un Bus Svc *CORP AFFIL* dir: Babson-United Investment Advs

James R. Nichols: trust *PHIL AFFIL* trust: Harold Whitworth Pierce Charitable Trust, Elisha V. Ashton Trust

APPLICATION INFORMATION

Initial Approach: Send a brief letter of inquiry. Include a description of organization, amount requested, purpose of funds sought, recently audited financial statement, and proof of tax-exempt status. There are no deadlines.

Restrictions on Giving: Limited to Massachusetts.

GRANTS ANALYSIS

Total Grants: $328,697

Number of Grants: 38

Highest Grant: $50,000

Typical Range: $2,000 to $30,000

Disclosure Period: 1993

Note: Recent grants are derived from a 1993 Form 990.

RECENT GRANTS

General

50,000	Wellesley Community Center, Wellesley, MA
30,000	Museum of Science, Boston, MA
23,500	United Way, Boston, MA
15,000	Thresholds Foundation, Chicago, IL
15,000	Tides Foundation, San Francisco, CA

Balfour Foundation, L. G.

CONTACT

Kerry H. Sullivan
Director of Grant Making
L.G. Balfour Foundation
c/o Fleet Investment Services
75 State St., 7th Fl.
Mail Code: MABOFO7B
Boston, MA 02109
(617) 346-2484

FINANCIAL SUMMARY

Recent Giving: $3,275,000 (fiscal 1995 est.); $3,275,000 (fiscal 1994 approx.); $5,286,952 (fiscal 1993)

Assets: $56,000,000 (fiscal 1995 est.); $56,581,475 (fiscal 1994); $58,460,023 (fiscal 1993)

Gifts Received: $26,400 (fiscal 1988)

Fiscal Note: In fiscal 1988, the foundation received funds totaling $26,400 from Manning, Fulton and Skinner Attorneys; McNamara, Pipkin and Knott; and Winmark Sports.

EIN: 04-6397138

CONTRIBUTIONS SUMMARY

Donor(s): Lloyd G. Balfour (d.1978) founded and was the sole owner of the L. G. Balfour Company, producer of class rings and fraternity pins. After Mr. Balfour's death in 1973, the company was managed for a number of years by the Bank of New England, first as executor of L. G. Balfour's estate, and then as trustee of the L. G. Balfour Foundation, which was established in 1973. The company was sold in 1983, but the foundation retains a significant financial interest.

Typical Recipients: • *Arts & Humanities:* Libraries • *Education:* Colleges & Universities, Education Associations, Education Funds, Minority Education, Public Education (Precollege), Student Aid • *Health:* Hospitals • *Social Services:* Day Care

Grant Types: capital, general support, and scholarship

Geographic Distribution: primarily Massachusetts and the New England area

GIVING OFFICERS

Kerry H. Sullivan: trust off, dir grant making *CURR EMPL* vp: Fleet Investment Svcs

APPLICATION INFORMATION
Initial Approach:

Applicants should submit a letter of intent to the trustee for review and response before a formal grant proposal is prepared.

The letter should describe the nature and objective of the program to be funded and include a list of the organization's board members or trustees along with the names and qualifications of officers and staff; evidence of tax-exempt status; detailed budget for the projects; Form 990 and audited financial statement for the most recent fiscal year; statement of other sources of funding, both private and public; and a statement of agreement to report on the results of the project and on the expenditure of grant funds.

Proposals should be submitted by January 31 for consideration in the spring, or by July 31 for consideration in the fall.

The foundation's distribution committee usually meets twice each year, in the spring and fall.

Restrictions on Giving: No grants are made to individuals or private foundations. Grant proposals for capital projects such as construction, renovation, or equipment purchase will be considered, but will be given less priority.

OTHER THINGS TO KNOW

Fleet Bank of Massachusetts is listed as corporate trustee for the foundation.

PUBLICATIONS

Grant application procedures

GRANTS ANALYSIS

Total Grants: $3,100,525

Number of Grants: 22

Highest Grant: $650,000

Average Grant: $116,692*

Typical Range: $25,000 to $250,000

Disclosure Period: fiscal year ending March 31, 1990

Note: The average grant figure excludes a single grant totaling $650,000. Recent grants are derived from a fiscal 1990 Form 990.

RECENT GRANTS

Library

150,000	Norton Public Library — grant

General

650,000	Wheaton College, Wheaton, IL -- grant/renovation
250,000	Bowdoin College, Brunswick, ME — grants
200,000	Massachusetts Institute of Technology, Cambridge, MA — scholarships
200,000	National Association of Secondary School Principals, Reston, VA — scholarships
200,000	Rhode Island School of Design, Providence, RI — scholarships

Bank of Boston / Mechanics Bank Foundation

Sales: $42.0 million
Employees: 188
Parent Company: Multibank Financial Corp.
Headquarters: Worcester, MA
SIC Major Group: Depository Institutions

CONTACT

Richard Collins
President
Bank of Boston
100 Front St.
Worcester, MA 01608
(508) 798-6400

FINANCIAL SUMMARY

Recent Giving: $60,072 (1993); $70,225 (1989)

Assets: $45,089 (1993); $139,572 (1989); $90,230 (1988)

Gifts Received: $90,000 (1993); $112,000 (1989); $80,000 (1988)

Fiscal Note: In 1993, contributions were received from the Mechanics Bank.

EIN: 04-6144189

CONTRIBUTIONS SUMMARY

Typical Recipients: • *Arts & Humanities:* Community Arts, Historic Preservation, Libraries • *Civic & Public Affairs:* Botanical Gardens/Parks • *Education:* Business Education, Colleges & Universities, Engineering/Technological Education • *Environment:* Air/Water Quality • *Health:* Children's Health/Hospitals, Clinics/Medical Centers, Health Organizations, Medical Research • *International:* Foreign Arts Organizations • *Religion:* Religious Organizations • *Science:* Scientific Centers & Institutes • *Social Serv-*

ices: Child Welfare, Community Service Organizations, Family Services, United Funds/United Ways, YMCA/YWCA/YMHA/YWHA, Youth Organizations

Grant Types: employee matching gifts and general support

Geographic Distribution: focus on MA

Operating Locations: MA (Worcester)

CORP. OFFICERS
Richard B. Collins: *B* Newport News VA 1942 *ED* Princeton Univ 1964; Harvard Univ Sch Bus Admin 1969 *CURR EMPL* ceo, pres, dir: Mechanics Bank

GIVING OFFICERS
Richard B. Collins: trust *CURR EMPL* ceo, pres, dir: Mechanics Bank (see above)

Fairman C. Cowan: trust

Francis H. Dewey III: trust *PHIL AFFIL* chmn, trust: George I. Alden Trust

APPLICATION INFORMATION
Initial Approach: Send brief letter describing program. There are no deadlines.

GRANTS ANALYSIS
Total Grants: $60,072

Number of Grants: 18

Highest Grant: $3,000

Typical Range: $500 to $2,500

Disclosure Period: 1993

Note: Recent grants are derived from a 1993 Form 990. Number of grants and typical range do not include matching gifts.

RECENT GRANTS
Library
2,000	Notre Dame Academy Library

General
3,000	Tower Hill Botanical Garden, Worcester, MA
2,500	DYNAMY, Worcester, MA
2,500	Worcester Children's Friend Society, Worcester, MA
2,000	Family Services of Central Massachusetts, Worcester, MA
2,000	International Artists Series, Worcester, MA

Bank of Boston Corp. / Bank of Boston Corp. Charitable Foundation

Income: $7.4 billion
Employees: 16,800
Headquarters: Boston, MA
SIC Major Group: Bank Holding Companies and National Commercial Banks

---

CONTACT
Michele Courton Brown
Director, Corporate Contributions
Bank of Boston Corporation Charitable Foundation
Government & Community Affairs Department
PO Box B2016

01-17-04
Boston, MA 02106-2016
(617) 434-2171
Note: Regional contributions officers are located in Springfield, New Bedford, and Yarmouth Port, MA, and in home office of out-of-state subsidiaries. Names and addresses for these officers are available from foundation. The company's World Wide Web address is http://www.llnl.gov/fstc/bank_of_boston.html"

FINANCIAL SUMMARY
Recent Giving: $7,000,000 (1995 est.); $5,800,000 (1994 approx.); $4,697,714 (1993)

Assets: $5,145,213 (1993); $12,607,252 (1991); $14,531,164 (1990)

Fiscal Note: Company gives directly and through its foundation. Above figures exclude nonmonetary support.

EIN: 04-2748070

CONTRIBUTIONS SUMMARY
Typical Recipients: • *Arts & Humanities:* Arts Associations & Councils, Arts Institutes, Community Arts, Ethnic & Folk Arts, General, Historic Preservation, Libraries, Museums/Galleries, Music, Performing Arts, Public Broadcasting, Theater, Visual Arts • *Civic & Public Affairs:* Business/Free Enterprise, Economic Development, Housing, Municipalities/Towns, Public Policy, Urban & Community Affairs • *Education:* Business Education, Colleges & Universities, Engineering/Technological Education, Literacy, Preschool Education, Public Education (Precollege) • *Health:* AIDS/HIV, Clinics/Medical Centers, Health Organizations, Hospitals • *Science:* Science Museums • *Social Services:* Child Welfare, Community Centers, Community Service Organizations, Family Services, Food/Clothing Distribution, People with Disabilities, Recreation & Athletics, Shelters/Homelessness, United Funds/United Ways, Youth Organizations

Grant Types: challenge, employee matching gifts, project, and seed money

Nonmonetary Support: $100,000 (1993); $1,500,000 (1990); $715,000 (1988)

Nonmonetary Support Types: donated equipment, in-kind services, and loaned employees

Note: Contact for nonmonetary support is Michele C. Brown, director of Corporate Contributions.

Geographic Distribution: only in New England; branches located outside of New England may make small grants locally

Operating Locations: AL (Birmingham), AZ (Phoenix), CA (Los Angeles), CT (Greenwich, Hartford, Waterbury), DE (Wimington), FL (Boca Raton, Deerfield Beach, Jacksonville, Palm Beach, Sarasota), LA (Metairie), MA (Boston, Burlington, Cambridge, Cape Cod, Haverhill, Holyoke, New Bedford, Wellesley, Worcester), ME (Portland), NC (Charlotte), RI (Providence), SC (Hilton Head Island), TX (Dallas), VT (Burlington)

Note: Bank operates 251 branches throughout New England.

CORP. OFFICERS
Michele Courton Brown: *CURR EMPL* dir corp contributions: Bank Boston Corp

Charles Kilvert Gifford: *B* Providence RI 1942 *ED* Princeton Univ BA 1964 *CURR EMPL* pres, dir: Bank Boston Corp *CORP AFFIL* chmn: MA Minority Enterprise Investment Corp; dir: Boston Edison Co, MA Mutual Life Ins Co; pres, dir: First Natl Bank Boston *NONPR AFFIL* dir: Assn Reserve City Bankers, Boston Private Independent Counc, Un Way Am; mem: Boston Chamber Commerce; trust: New England Aquarium

William J. Shea: *B* 1948 *CURR EMPL* exec vp, treas, cfo, vchmn: Bank Boston Corp

Ira Stepanian: *B* Cambridge MA 1936 *ED* Tufts Univ BA 1958; Boston Coll MBA 1971 *CURR EMPL* chmn, ceo: Bank Boston Corp *CORP AFFIL* dir: Liberty Mutual Fire Ins Co, Liberty Mutual Ins Co, NYNEX New England *NONPR AFFIL* dir: MA Bus Roundtable; mem: Assn Bank Holding Cos, Assn Reserve City Bankers; overseer: Boston Mus Fine Arts; trust: Boston Mus Sci, Boston Symphony Orchestra, Gen Hosp, Tufts Univ

GIVING OFFICERS
Michele Courton Brown: dir *CURR EMPL* dir corp contributions: Bank Boston Corp (see above)

Charles Kilvert Gifford: trust *CURR EMPL* pres, dir: Bank Boston Corp (see above)

Ira A. Jackson: trust

William J. Shea: trust *CURR EMPL* exec vp, treas, cfo, vchmn: Bank Boston Corp (see above)

Ira Stepanian: trust *CURR EMPL* chmn, ceo: Bank Boston Corp (see above)

Eliot N. Vestner: trust *B* Bronxville NY 1935 *ED* Amherst Coll BA 1957; Univ MI MA 1958; Columbia Univ LLB 1962

APPLICATION INFORMATION
Initial Approach: *Initial Contact:* brief letter requesting guidelines or proposal on organization letterhead *Include Information On:* history and description of the organization; name, address, and telephone number of applicant; purpose and amount of grant request; budget for current and previous years (or current and proposed budgets); sources and amounts of support for most recently completed year; total project budget (if request is for a project); recently audited financial statement; most recent Form 990; proof of tax-exempt status; names and affiliations of directors and/or trustees; report on last grant received from Bank of Boston *Deadlines:* before board meetings, which are held in February, April, June, August, and October. *Note:* Requests for in-kind contributions should be sent to Greater Boston Region.

Restrictions on Giving: Does not support individuals, religious programs, fraternal organizations, political or lobbying groups, national health organizations, research projects, conferences, forums, benefits, goodwill advertising, or travel expenses.

Repeat requests are not considered within the calendar year. Multiyear grants generally are limited to capital and/or endowment campaigns and usually for no more than three years. Two years must elapse between multiyear campaign requests.

GRANTS ANALYSIS
Total Grants: $5,800,000*

Number of Grants: 500*

Average Grant: $11,600*

Typical Range: $1,000 to $5,000 and $25,000 to $50,000

Disclosure Period: 1994

Note: Grants figures are approximations and are provided by the Company. Recent grants are derived from a 1993 Form 990.

RECENT GRANTS
Library
50,000	Boston Public Library Foundation, Boston, MA

General
675,000	United Way of Eastern New England, Boston, MA
150,000	United Way of Southeastern Maine, ME
104,425	United Way of Connecticut, Hartford, CT
100,000	Metropolitan Boston Housing Partnership, Boston, MA
60,320	United Way of Portland, Portland, ME

Beaucourt Foundation

CONTACT
Beaucourt Fdn.
Testa, Hurwitz & Thibeault
53 State St.
Boston, MA 02109-2809
(617) 248-7426

FINANCIAL SUMMARY
Recent Giving: $110,000 (1993); $140,000 (1992); $100,000 (1991)

Assets: $2,593,400 (1993); $2,437,629 (1992); $2,552,928 (1991)

EIN: 04-2979426

CONTRIBUTIONS SUMMARY
Typical Recipients: • *Arts & Humanities:* Libraries • *Education:* Business Education, Colleges & Universities, International Studies

Grant Types: general support

Geographic Distribution: Boston, MA

GIVING OFFICERS
Henry W. Comstock: dir

Arnaud De Vitry: dir

Richard J. Testa: pres, treas, dir *PHIL AFFIL* trust: Keel Foundation

APPLICATION INFORMATION
Initial Approach: The foundation has no formal grant application procedure or application form. There are no deadlines.

GRANTS ANALYSIS
Total Grants: $110,000

Number of Grants: 2

Highest Grant: $100,000

Disclosure Period: 1993

Note: Recent grants are derived from a 1993 Form 990.

RECENT GRANTS
Library
100,000	French Library in Boston, Boston, MA

General
10,000	Emerson College, Boston, MA

Bird Corp. / Bird Corp. Charitable Foundation

Revenue: $212.43 million
Employees: 800
Headquarters: Norwood, MA
SIC Major Group: Industrial Machinery & Equipment, Transportation Equipment, and Wholesale Trade—Durable Goods

CONTACT
Lyz Acieri
Trustee
Bird Corp. Charitable Fdn.
1077 Pleasant St.
Norwood, MA 02062
(617) 551-0656

FINANCIAL SUMMARY
Recent Giving: $25,486 (1992); $29,320 (1991); $24,868 (1990)

Assets: $29,785 (1992); $15,790 (1991); $13,829 (1990)

Gifts Received: $39,774 (1992); $31,980 (1991); $28,245 (1990)

Fiscal Note: In 1992, contributions were received from Bird Inc.

EIN: 23-7067725

CONTRIBUTIONS SUMMARY
Typical Recipients: • *Arts & Humanities:* Libraries, Museums/Galleries, Public Broadcasting • *Civic & Public Affairs:* Business/Free Enterprise, General, Housing, Public Policy, Safety, Zoos/Aquariums • *Education:* Business Education, Colleges & Universities, Education Associations, Education Funds, Private Education (Precollege), Public Education (Precollege), Student Aid • *Environment:* Air/Water Quality, General • *Health:* Emergency/Ambulance Services, Health Organizations, Single-Disease Health Associations • *Religion:* Religious Welfare • *Science:* Science Museums, Scientific Organizations • *Social Services:* Animal Protection, Child Welfare, Community Service Organizations, Food/Clothing Distribution, People with Disabilities, Recreation & Athletics, Senior Services, Substance Abuse, Youth Organizations

Grant Types: general support

Nonmonetary Support Types: in-kind services, loaned employees, and loaned executives

Geographic Distribution: focus on MA

Operating Locations: CA (Martinez, San Mateo, Wilmington), KY (Bardstown), LA (Shreveport), MA (Dedham, Norwood), OR (Portland), SC (Charleston)

Note: List includes plant locations

CORP. OFFICERS
Richard Maloof: *CURR EMPL* pres, coo: Bird Corp

Joseph D. Vecchiolla: *CURR EMPL* chmn: Bird Corp

GIVING OFFICERS
Lyz Acieri: trust

Frank S. Antony: secy, dir

Robert P. Bass, Jr.: dir

Charles S. Bird, Jr.: dir

David Bird: dir

Robert Cooper: dir

Francis J. Dunleavy: dir

John T. Dunlop: trust

Guy W. Fiske: dir *B* Upton MA 1924 *ED* Brown Univ BA 1946 *CURR EMPL* chmn: Fiske Assocs *CORP AFFIL* dir: Bird Corp, CA Ed Publ Corp, Graphic Controls Corp, SEV Corp *NONPR AFFIL* dir: Voice Fdn

George J. Haufler: pres, dir *B* Philadelphia PA 1932 *ED* Drexel Univ 1958

William A. Krivsky: dir *B* Stafford Springs CT 1929

APPLICATION INFORMATION
Initial Approach: Send brief letter describing program. There are no deadlines.

PUBLICATIONS
Guidelines

GRANTS ANALYSIS
Total Grants: $25,486

Number of Grants: 61

Highest Grant: $2,550

Typical Range: $25 to $1,000

Disclosure Period: 1992

Note: Recent grants are derived from a 1992 Form 990.

RECENT GRANTS
Library
25	Richards Memorial Library

General
2,550	Northeastern University, Boston, MA
2,500	SNARC
2,250	University of Kentucky, Lexington, KY
2,000	Chi Chi Rodriguez Youth Foundation, Clearwater, FL
1,700	Norwood Scholarship Foundation, Norwood, MA

Blake Foundation, S. P.

CONTACT
Stewart P. Blake
Trustee
S. P. Blake Fdn.
666 Bliss Rd.
Longmeadow, MA 01106
(413) 567-9483

FINANCIAL SUMMARY
Recent Giving: $218,368 (1993); $395,118 (1992); $414,490 (1991)

Assets: $3,693,594 (1993); $3,458,133 (1992); $3,778,148 (1991)

EIN: 23-7185871

CONTRIBUTIONS SUMMARY
Donor(s): S. Prestley Blake

Typical Recipients: • *Arts & Humanities:* Arts Centers, Historic Preservation, Libraries, Museums/Galleries, Music, Performing Arts, Public Broadcasting • *Civic & Public Affairs:* General, Philanthropic Organizations, Public Policy • *Education:* Business Education, Colleges & Universities, Education Funds, Private Education (Precollege), Student Aid • *Health:* Children's Health/Hospitals • *International:* Foreign Educational Institutions • *Religion:* Churches • *Social Services:* Community Service Organizations, People with Disabilities, United Funds/United Ways

Grant Types: general support

Geographic Distribution: focus on the western MA area

GIVING OFFICERS
Bensen P. Blake: trust

Stewart P. Blake: trust *B* Jersey City NJ 1914 *ED* Trinity Coll LLD 1976 *CORP AFFIL* co-founder: Friendly Ice Cream Corp *NONPR AFFIL* trust: Bay Path Jr Coll *CLUB AFFIL* Colony, Longmeadow CC

APPLICATION INFORMATION
Initial Approach: The foundation has no formal grant application procedure or application form. There are no deadlines.

GRANTS ANALYSIS
Total Grants: $218,368

Number of Grants: 17

Highest Grant: $167,648

Typical Range: $1000 to $25,000

Disclosure Period: 1993

Note: Recent grants are derived from a 1993 Form 990.

RECENT GRANTS
Library
2,500	Springfield Library and Museums, Springfield, MA

General
167,648	Wilbraham Monson Academy, Wilbraham, MA
10,000	Community United Way of Pioneer, Springfield, MA
1,000	Bates College, Lewiston, MA
1,000	Junior Achievement, Springfield, MA
500	Marina Sands Chapel, Stuart, FL

Boston Edison Co. / Boston Edison Foundation

Revenue: $1.48 billion
Employees: 4,654
Headquarters: Boston, MA
SIC Major Group: Electric Services

CONTACT
John J. Connolly
Director
Boston Edison Fdn.
800 Boylston St. P1071
Boston, MA 02199-2599
(617) 424-2235

FINANCIAL SUMMARY
Recent Giving: $877,000 (1995 est.); $877,000 (1994 approx.); $834,959 (1993)

Assets: $590,524 (1993); $326,765 (1992); $335,064 (1991)

Gifts Received: $1,100,000 (1993); $700,000 (1992)

Fiscal Note: Company gives exclusively through the foundation. Contributions are received from the Boston Edison Co.

EIN: 04-2754285

CONTRIBUTIONS SUMMARY
Typical Recipients: • *Arts & Humanities:* Arts Institutes, Arts Outreach, Ballet, Dance, Libraries, Museums/Galleries, Music, Performing Arts • *Civic & Public Affairs:* Economic Development, Employment/Job Training, Housing, Municipalities/Towns, Philanthropic Organizations, Professional & Trade Associations, Safety, Urban & Community Affairs, Zoos/Aquariums • *Education:* Afterschool/Enrichment Programs, Business-School Partnerships, Colleges & Universities, Engineering/Technological Education, Minority Education, Private Education (Precollege), Religious Education, Science/Mathematics Education, Student Aid • *Health:* AIDS/HIV, Alzheimers Disease, Cancer, Clinics/Medical Centers, Emergency/Ambulance Services, Health Organizations, Hospices, Hospitals, Nursing Services, Single-Disease Health Associations • *Science:* Science Museums • *Social Services:* Community Service Organizations, Counseling, Family Services, Food/Clothing Distribution, Recreation & Athletics, Senior Services, Shelters/Homelessness, United Funds/United Ways, Youth Organizations

Grant Types: employee matching gifts, project, and scholarship

Note: Employee matching gift ratio: 1 to 1.

Nonmonetary Support Types: donated equipment and in-kind services

Note: The company donates used furniture. Estimated value of nonmonetary support is unavailable.

Geographic Distribution: in greater Boston and eastern Massachusetts areas

Operating Locations: MA (Boston)

CORP. OFFICERS
John J. Connolly: *CURR EMPL* dir corp rels: Boston Edison Co

George Wilmont Davis: *B* Columbia SC 1933 *ED* US Naval Acad BS 1955; US Naval Acad MS 1963 *CURR EMPL* pres, coo, dir: Boston Edison Co *NONPR AFFIL* bd av: US Navy Postgrad Sch; mem: Natl Nuclear Accreditation Bd; mem sci adv bd: Univ MA

Ronald A. Ledgett: *B* 1938 *ED* Stanford Univ *CURR EMPL* sr vp power delivery: Boston Edison Co

Thomas J. May: *B* Hartford CT 1947 *ED* Stonehill Coll BS 1969; Bentley Coll MS 1980 *CURR EMPL* chmn, ceo: Boston Edison Co *CORP AFFIL* dir: Connection Yankee Electric, Dana Farber Inc, Yankee Atomic Electric Co; exec vp, treas, dir: Harbor Electric Energy Co *NONPR AFFIL* mem: Am Inst CPAs

GIVING OFFICERS
E. Thomas Boulette: trust *B* 1942 *ED* Colby Coll BA; IA St Univ MS; IA St Univ PhD *CURR EMPL* sr vp nuclear: Boston Edison Co

Ann L. Cardello: admin

John J. Connolly: dir *CURR EMPL* dir corp rels: Boston Edison Co (see above)

Theodora S. Convisser: trust *B* New York NY 1947 *ED* Brandeis Univ BA 1969; Northeastern Univ JD 1975; Boston Univ LLM 1979 *CURR EMPL* corp clerk, asst gen couns: Boston Edison Co *CORP AFFIL* clerk, dir: Harbor Electric Energy Co *NONPR AFFIL* mem: Am Bar Assn, Am Soc Corp Secys

Cameron H. Daley: trust *ED* Northeastern Univ BSEE 1968; Rensselaer Polytech Inst MS 1969 *CURR EMPL* sr vp power supply: Boston Edison Co

George Wilmont Davis: trust *CURR EMPL* pres, coo, dir: Boston Edison Co (see above)

Lester Carl Gustin: trust *B* 1942 *ED* Boston Univ BS 1967 *CURR EMPL* sr vp mktg & customer svc: Boston Edison Co

John Joseph Higgins: trust *B* 1932 *ED* Northeastern Univ BBA 1966 *CURR EMPL* sr vp human resources: Boston Edison Co *CORP AFFIL* contr: Continental Bank Corp *NONPR AFFIL* mem: Bank Admin Inst, Fin Execs Inst

C. S. Daisy Jao: tax adv

Catherine J. Keuthen: legal adv

Ronald A. Ledgett: trust *CURR EMPL* sr vp power delivery: Boston Edison Co (see above)

Thomas J. May: chmn *CURR EMPL* chmn, ceo: Boston Edison Co (see above)

Emilie F. O'Neill: treas

Charles E. Peters, Jr: trust *B* 1951 *ED* Univ MA BSBA 1973; Bentley Coll MSF 1984 *CURR EMPL* sr vp fin: Boston Edison Co *CORP AFFIL* vp, dir: Harbor Electric Energy Co

Walter E. Salvi: mgr

APPLICATION INFORMATION

Initial Approach: *Initial Contact:* written proposals to the foundation in advance of any personal or telephone contact *Include Information On:* recent annual report, budget for organization and specific project requiring funding, specific amount of funding requested, other funding sources either at hand or anticipated, provision for accountability to project sponsors, proof of tax-exempt status *Deadlines:* March 1, June 1, September 1, and December 1

Restrictions on Giving: Proposals for same project will not be considered more than once within a one-year period.

GRANTS ANALYSIS
Total Grants: $834,959

Number of Grants: 69

Highest Grant: $332,846

Average Grant: $5,000*

Typical Range: $500 to $10,000

Disclosure Period: 1993

Note: Number of grants and average grant figures exclude matched gifts to cultural organizations totaling $11,856 and matched gifts to education totaling $57,152. Average grant figure is an approximation provided by the company. Recent grants are derived from a 1993 Form 990.

RECENT GRANTS

Library

10,000	John F. Kennedy Library Foundation Dinner, Boston, MA	

General

332,846	United Way Massachusetts Bay, Boston, MA	
50,000	Northeastern University, Boston, MA	
38,247	Fund for Boston Parks and Recreation, Boston, MA	
25,000	South Boston Health Center, South Boston, MA	
25,000	Thompson Island Outward Bound Education Center, Boston, MA	

Cabot Corp. / Cabot Corp. Foundation

Sales: $1.61 billion
Employees: 5,400
Headquarters: Boston, MA
SIC Major Group: Carbon Black, Industrial Inorganic Chemicals Nec, Plastics Materials & Resins, and Mechanical Rubber Goods

CONTACT
Dorothy L. Forbes
Executive Director & Vice President
Cabot Corp. Foundation
75 State St.
Boston, MA 02109
(617) 345-0100

Note: Organizations also may contact the appropriate individual at a Cabot facility. Ms. Forbes is also the contact person for international contributions.

FINANCIAL SUMMARY
Recent Giving: $717,916 (fiscal 1994); $701,318 (fiscal 1993); $774,436 (fiscal 1992)

Assets: $1,200,000 (fiscal 1995 est.); $900,000 (fiscal 1994 approx.); $850,000 (fiscal 1991)

Fiscal Note: Contributions of $5,000 to $25,000 are made locally by Cabot's various operations, an estimated $500,000 globally, For local contributions, contact local managing director at area office. Cabot's Reasearch and Development department makes contributions of approximately $175,000 annually. Above figures exclude nonmonetary support.

EIN: 04-6035227

CONTRIBUTIONS SUMMARY
Typical Recipients: • *Arts & Humanities:* Arts Appreciation, Arts Associations & Councils, Arts Centers, Arts Funds, Arts Institutes, Arts Outreach, Community Arts, Dance, Ethnic & Folk Arts, Historic Preservation, Libraries, Literary Arts, Museums/Galleries, Music, Opera, Performing Arts, Theater • *Civic & Public Affairs:* African American Affairs, Business/Free Enterprise, Economic Development, Economic Policy, Employment/Job Training, Law & Justice, Legal Aid, Municipalities/Towns, Public Policy, Safety, Women's Affairs, Zoos/Aquariums • *Education:* Business Education, Colleges & Universities, Community & Junior Colleges, Economic Education, Education Funds, Elementary Education (Private), Engineering/Technological Education, Faculty Development, General, Health & Physical Education, International Exchange, International Studies, Minority Education, Preschool Education, Private Education (Precollege), Public Education (Precollege), Science/Mathematics Education, Special Education, Student Aid • *Environment:* General • *Health:* Cancer, Health Organizations, Heart, Hospitals • *International:* General, Health Care/Hospitals, International Development, International Relations • *Science:* Science Exhibits & Fairs, Science Museums, Scientific Organizations • *Social Services:* At-Risk Youth, Child Welfare, Community Centers, Community Service Organizations, Counseling, Day Care, Emergency Relief, Food/Clothing Distribution, Homes, People with Disabilities, Recreation & Athletics, Senior Services, Substance Abuse, United Funds/United Ways, Volunteer Services, Youth Organizations

Grant Types: capital, challenge, employee matching gifts, fellowship, general support, professorship, project, research, scholarship, and seed money

Note: Employee matching gift ratio: 1 to 1. Gifts go to schools and united funds.

Nonmonetary Support: $200,000 (fiscal 1994); $300,000 (fiscal 1993); $200,000 (fiscal 1992)

Nonmonetary Support Types: donated equipment, donated products, in-kind services, loaned employees, and loaned executives

Note: Nonmonetary support was supplied by both the c company and the foundation in 1994. For information on nonmonetary support, contact local Cabot facilities manager. Dorothy Forbes also handles some requests (see above - Contact)

Geographic Distribution: areas where Cabot employees live and work

Operating Locations: DE (Newark), GA (Atlanta, Newnan, Norcross), IL (Tuscola), IN (Indianapolis, Plymouth), LA (Franklin, Villeplatte), MA (Billarica, Boston, Everett, Southbridge), OK (Chickasha), PA (Boyertown, Reading), TX (Amarillo, Pampa), WV (Waverly)

Note: Also operates in Argentina, Canada, Brazil, Columbia, Germany, Spain, Mexico, India, Indonesia, the Netherlands, Belgium, Australia, Venezuela, and Malaysia.

CORP. OFFICERS
Samuel Wright Bodman III: *B* Chicago IL 1938 *ED* Cornell Univ BS 1961; MA Inst Tech PhD 1964 *CURR EMPL* chmn, pres, ceo, dir: Cabot Corp *CORP AFFIL* dir: Am Oil & Gas Corp, Bank Boston Corp, Cabot Oil & Gas Corp, Continental Cablevision, Distrigas MA Corp, First Natl Bank Boston, John Hancock Mutual Life Ins Co, Index Tech Corp, Mitre Corp, Westvaco Corp *NONPR AFFIL* mem: Am Acad Arts & Sci; trust: Babson Coll, Isabella Stewart Gardner Mus, New England Aquarium; trust, mem exec comm: MA Inst Tech

Charles Agustus Gray: *B* Washington DC 1938 *ED* Cornell Univ BSCHE 1961; MA Inst Tech PhD 1965 *CURR EMPL* vp tech: Cabot Corp

GIVING OFFICERS
Samuel Wright Bodman III: pres, dir *CURR EMPL* chmn, pres, ceo, dir: Cabot Corp (see above)

Carroll Cabot: dir

Maryellen Cabot: dir

John Dorian Curtin, Jr.: vp, treas *B* Tulsa OK 1932 *ED* Yale Univ BA 1954; Harvard Univ MBA 1956 *CURR EMPL* exec vp, dir: Cabot Corp *CORP AFFIL* dir: Am Oil & Gas Corp, Cabot Oil & Gas Corp, Midco Acquisition Corp, Modar; vp, dir: Cabot Safety Corp *CLUB AFFIL* Ramada, Somerset

Dorothy L. Forbes: vp, exec dir

Charles D. Gerlinger: clerk *B* Sioux Falls SD 1933 *ED* Princeton Univ AB 1955; Univ MI Law Sch LLB 1958; Boston Univ MBA 1972 *CURR EMPL* secy, sr couns: Cabot Corp *CORP AFFIL* secy, dir: Cabot Safety Corp *NONPR AFFIL* mem: Am Bar Assn, Am Soc Corp Secys

Charles Agustus Gray: dir *CURR EMPL* vp tech: Cabot Corp (see above)

Karen M. Morressey: dir

APPLICATION INFORMATION
Initial Approach: *Initial Contact:* brief telephone inquiry; if within guidelines, a proposal will be requested *Include Information*

On: statement of proposed project (no more than two pages), including its purpose, uniqueness, long-term goals, specific short-term objectives, estimated time required for completion, and manner by which results are measured; brief background information on organization, board of directors, and those leading proposed effort; proof of tax-exempt status; total project cost, present and potential funding sources, and amount requested of Cabot; include latest audited financial statement if organization's budget exceeds $100,000 *Deadlines:* at least one month before board meetings held in March, June, September, and December *Note:* Organizations receiving grants are expected to provide periodic progress reports.

Restrictions on Giving: Cabot Corporation Foundation does not make contributions to individuals, political or fraternal organizations, religious institutions for sectarian purposes, advertising, or dinner-table sponsorship.

OTHER THINGS TO KNOW

Cabot strongly encourages requests from projects under way in plant locations. The contributions program has expanded its involvement in plant communities, tying contributions more closely to the nature of business, encouraging greater employee participation in community volunteer activities, and addressing significant societal concerns. Foundation particularly considers recommendations from teams formed by local employees, which initiate community projects and consider local requests for support.

Company prefers to support specific projects or programs rather than general operating expenses.

Strong consideration is given to projects that combine financial support with company manpower, technical assistance, or in-kind support to achieve objectives.

Company often conducts "needs assessments" surveys to determine if projects will have a long-term effect on the community they serve.

Cabot is especially interested in projects involved with science and technology.

GRANTS ANALYSIS
Total Grants: $717,916

Number of Grants: 57

Highest Grant: $45,000

Average Grant: $12,595

Typical Range: $1,000 to $10,000

Disclosure Period: fiscal year ending September 30, 1994

Note: Recent grants are derived from a 1993 grants list.

RECENT GRANTS

Library
27,000	Parkersburg and Wood County Public Library, Parkersburg, WV — to construct a new library at the Waverly School
25,000	Boston Public Library Foundation, Boston, MA — capital campaign to restore historic library

General
150,310	United Way Funds
50,000	Massachusetts Institute of Technology, Cambridge, MA — support for the Hoyt Hotel Career Development professorship
50,000	Museum of Science, Boston, MA — final payment of three-year pledge to build a chemistry laboratory classroom
25,000	Massachusetts General Hospital, Boston, MA — restricted support for Clinic Research project
25,000	New England Aquarium, Boston, MA — commemorative gift

Cabot Family Charitable Trust

CONTACT
Ruth C. Scheer
Executive Director
Cabot Family Charitable Trust
75 State St.
Boston, MA 02109
(617) 342-6007

FINANCIAL SUMMARY
Recent Giving: $623,930 (1993); $691,080 (1992); $581,779 (1991)

Assets: $16,579,524 (1993); $13,558,932 (1992); $10,720,412 (1991)

EIN: 04-6036446

CONTRIBUTIONS SUMMARY
Donor(s): the late Godfrey L. Cabot

Typical Recipients: • *Arts & Humanities:* Arts Funds, Film & Video, Historic Preservation, History & Archaeology, Libraries, Music, Public Broadcasting, Theater • *Civic & Public Affairs:* Civil Rights, Clubs, Native American Affairs, Philanthropic Organizations, Public Policy • *Education:* Colleges & Universities, Health & Physical Education, International Studies, Journalism/Media Education, Leadership Training, Legal Education, Private Education (Precollege), Science/Mathematics Education • *Environment:* General • *Health:* Clinics/Medical Centers, Health Organizations, Hospitals, Mental Health • *International:* Foreign Educational Institutions, Health Care/Hospitals, Human Rights, International Peace & Security Issues • *Science:* Scientific Organizations • *Social Services:* Family Planning, Youth Organizations

Grant Types: capital, endowment, general support, multiyear/continuing support, and project

Geographic Distribution: focus on CA and MA

GIVING OFFICERS
Jane C. Bradley: trust

John Godfrey Lowell Cabot: trust *B* Rio de Janeiro Brazil 1934 *ED* Harvard Univ AB 1956; Harvard Univ MBA 1960 *CURR EMPL* vchmn, dir: Cabot Corp *CORP AFFIL* dir: Am Oil & Gas Corp, Cabot Oil & Gas Corp, Distrigas MA Corp, Eaton Vance Corp, Hollingsworth & Vose Co *NONPR AFFIL* chmn, dir: New England Legal Fdn; mem corp: MA Gen Hosp; overseer: WGBH Ed Fdn; overseer, gov: New England Med Ctr; trust: Tufts Univ

Louis Wellington Cabot: trust *B* Boston MA 1921 *ED* Harvard Univ AB 1943; Harvard Univ MBA 1948 *CORP AFFIL* dir: Kendall Sq Res *NONPR AFFIL* fellow: Am Academy Arts Sciences; mem: Bus Counc, Conf Bd, Counc Foreign Rels, MA Bus Roundtable, Natl Counc US-China Trade, Phi Beta Kappa, Sigma Xi, US Chamber Commerce; mem corp: MA Inst Tech; trsut: Brookings Inst; trust: Mus Science Boston, Natl Humanities Ctr, Northeastern Univ *CLUB AFFIL* Commercial, Harvard, Metropolitan, New York YC, River, Somerset, Wianno

Ruth C. Scheer: exec dir

APPLICATION INFORMATION
Initial Approach: Send a brief letter of inquiry. Include a description of organization, amount requested, purpose of funds sought, recently audited financial statement, and proof of tax-exempt status. Deadlines are April 1 and October 1.

Restrictions on Giving: Limited to organizations that deal with population control, environmental quality, and educational awards.

PUBLICATIONS
Annual Report

GRANTS ANALYSIS
Total Grants: $623,930

Number of Grants: 40

Highest Grant: $50,079

Typical Range: $5,000 to $25,000

Disclosure Period: 1993

Note: Recent grants are derived from a 1993 Form 990.

RECENT GRANTS

Library
25,044	Boston Public Library Foundation, Boston, MA

General
25,044	Global Fund for Women, Menlo Park, CA
25,044	Pathfinder International, Oakland, CA
25,044	Population Action International, Washington, DC
25,041	Meridian International Center, Meridian, ID
25,040	Appalachian Mountain Club, Boston, MA

Childs Charitable Foundation, Roberta M.

CONTACT
John R. D. McClintock
Trustee
Roberta M. Childs Charitable Fdn.
PO Box 639
North Andover, MA 01845
(508) 685-4113

FINANCIAL SUMMARY
Recent Giving: $187,500 (fiscal 1994); $165,000 (fiscal 1993); $122,500 (fiscal 1992)

Assets: $3,498,654 (fiscal 1994); $3,763,625 (fiscal 1993); $3,677,024 (fiscal 1992)

EIN: 04-2660275

CONTRIBUTIONS SUMMARY
Donor(s): the late Roberta M. Childs

Typical Recipients: • *Arts & Humanities:* Ethnic & Folk Arts, Historic Preservation, Libraries, Public Broadcasting • *Civic & Public Affairs:* General, Housing, Law & Justice, Philanthropic Organizations, Urban & Community Affairs • *Education:* Colleges & Universities, Legal Education, Medical Education, Minority Education, Private Education (Precollege), Special Education • *Environment:* General, Resource Conservation • *Health:* Children's Health/Hospitals, Clinics/Medical Centers, Home-Care Services, Hospitals, Medical Rehabilitation, Medical Research, Single-Disease Health Associations, Trauma Treatment • *Religion:* Ministries, Religious Organizations, Religious Welfare • *Social Services:* Animal Protection, Child Welfare, Community Service Organizations, Emergency Relief, Family Services, Homes, People with Disabilities, Senior Services, Shelters/Homelessness, Substance Abuse, United Funds/United Ways, Youth Organizations

Grant Types: general support and operating expenses

Geographic Distribution: focus on MA

GIVING OFFICERS
John R. D. McClintock: trust

APPLICATION INFORMATION
Initial Approach: The foundation has no formal grant application procedure or application form. There are no deadlines.

GRANTS ANALYSIS
Total Grants: $187,500

Number of Grants: 67

Highest Grant: $5,000

Typical Range: $1,000 to $5,000

Disclosure Period: fiscal year ending March 31, 1994

Note: Recent grants are derived from a fiscal 1994 Form 990.

RECENT GRANTS
Library
5,000	Stevens Memorial Library, North Andover, MA

General
5,000	Brighten Your Future, Logan, OH
5,000	FCD Foundation, Needham, MA
5,000	Helping Hands Simian Aides, Boston, MA
5,000	Institute of Charity, Peoria, IL
5,000	Sankaty Head Foundation, Siasconset, MA

Davis Foundation, Irene E. and George A.

CONTACT
Ann T. Keiser
Manager, Financial Administration
Irene E. and George A. Davis Foundation
301 Chestnut St.
PO Box 504
East Longmeadow, MA 01028-0504
(413) 525-3961

FINANCIAL SUMMARY
Recent Giving: $1,532,521 (1993); $1,442,069 (1992); $1,456,835 (1991)

Assets: $31,031,754 (1993); $26,520,093 (1992); $26,193,981 (1991)

Gifts Received: $3,621,356 (1993); $2,000,000 (1991); $2,325,000 (1990)

Fiscal Note: In 1990, contributions were from the American Saw & Manufacturing Co. In 1993, contributions were from Amercian Saw & Manufacturing Co.

EIN: 23-7102734

CONTRIBUTIONS SUMMARY
Donor(s): The foundation was established in 1970 by the late Irene E. Davis and George A. Davis, and was incorporated under the laws of the Commonwealth of Massachusetts in 1972.

Typical Recipients: • *Arts & Humanities:* Arts Associations & Councils, Arts Funds, Historic Preservation, History & Archaeology, Libraries, Museums/Galleries • *Civic & Public Affairs:* Clubs, Community Foundations, Public Policy, Zoos/Aquariums • *Education:* Business Education, Colleges & Universities, Education Associations, General, International Studies, Minority Education, Private Education (Precollege), Public Education (Precollege), School Volunteerism, Special Education • *Health:* Children's Health/Hospitals, Clinics/Medical Centers, Emergency/Ambulance Services, Hospitals, Nursing Services, Single-Disease Health Associations • *International:* Health Care/Hospitals, International Affairs • *Religion:* Churches, Dioceses, Jewish Causes, Religious Welfare • *Social Services:* At-Risk Youth, Big Brother/Big Sister, Child Welfare, Community Service Organizations, Food/Clothing Distribution, General, People with Disabilities, Recreation & Athletics, United Funds/United Ways, YMCA/YWCA/YMHA/YWHA, Youth Organizations

Grant Types: general support and multi-year/continuing support

Geographic Distribution: limited to western Massachusetts

GIVING OFFICERS
John H. Davis: trust *B* 1949 *ED* Nichols Coll 1972 *CURR EMPL* pres-treas, dir: Am Saw Mfg Co

Mary Davis: trust

Stephen A. Davis: trust *B* 1957 *CURR EMPL* pres-purchasing-clerk, dir: Am Saw Mfg Co

Ann T. Keiser: mgr fin admin

Robert R. Lepak: trust

APPLICATION INFORMATION
Initial Approach:
Applicants should send a letter of intent to request an application.

The letter of intent should outline the purpose, scope, estimated cost and method of evaluation of specific goals. The organization will be notified if the foundation would like to review a full proposal.

Requests may be submitted at any time. Complete proposals must be received no later than the first day of the month, two months prior to the regularly scheduled meeting.

The trustees meet quarterly to review proposals.

Restrictions on Giving: The foundation's guidelines usually preclude support for individuals, scholarships, internships, continuing support of current programs, debt reduction, multiple proposals per year from the same organizations, other private foundations, and program-related loans.

GRANTS ANALYSIS
Total Grants: $1,532,521

Number of Grants: 95*

Highest Grant: $205,000

Average Grant: $16,027*

Typical Range: $1,000 to $20,000

Disclosure Period: 1993

Note: The figures for average grant and number of grants excludes 10 scholarships totaling $10,000. Recent grants are derived from a 1993 Form 990.

RECENT GRANTS
Library
10,000	Nantucket Athaeneum, Nantucket, MA
7,500	Springfield Library and Museums, Springfield, MA
5,000	East Longmeadow Public Library, East Longmeadow, MA

General
205,000	Nichols College, Dudley, MA
176,266	Community United Way of Pioneer Valley, Springfield, MA

150,000	YMCA, Springfield, MA
125,000	MacDuffie School, Springfield, MA
110,000	Baystate Medical Center, Springfield, MA

Demoulas Supermarkets Inc. / Demoulas Foundation

Sales: $885.0 million
Employees: 7,000
Headquarters: Tewksbury, MA
SIC Major Group: Grocery Stores

CONTACT
Elizabeth Miliotis
Demoulas Foundation
875 East St.
Tewksbury, MA 01876
(508) 851-8000

FINANCIAL SUMMARY
Recent Giving: $1,223,465 (1994); $747,680 (1993); $1,220,838 (1992)
Assets: $32,021,351 (1993); $30,981,894 (1992); $30,039,223 (1991)
Gifts Received: $600,000 (1989)
Fiscal Note: Above figures are for the foundation only.
EIN: 04-2723441

CONTRIBUTIONS SUMMARY
Typical Recipients: • *Arts & Humanities:* Arts Associations & Councils, Arts Centers, Ballet, Dance, General, Historic Preservation, History & Archaeology, Libraries, Museums/Galleries, Music, Opera • *Civic & Public Affairs:* Clubs, Municipalities/Towns, Parades/Festivals, Philanthropic Organizations, Safety, Urban & Community Affairs • *Education:* Business Education, Colleges & Universities, Education Funds, General, Medical Education, Private Education (Precollege), Religious Education, Secondary Education (Private), Student Aid • *Environment:* General • *Health:* Cancer, Children's Health/Hospitals, Diabetes, Health Organizations, Hospitals, Long-Term Care, Medical Rehabilitation, Medical Research, Respiratory, Single-Disease Health Associations • *Religion:* Churches, Religious Organizations, Religious Welfare • *Science:* Science Museums • *Social Services:* Camps, Community Centers, Community Service Organizations, Food/Clothing Distribution, Homes, People with Disabilities, Recreation & Athletics, Scouts, Senior Services, Substance Abuse, Veterans, Youth Organizations

Grant Types: endowment and general support
Geographic Distribution: primarily New England
Operating Locations: MA (Tewksbury)

CORP. OFFICERS
Telemachus A. Demoulas: *B* 1923 *CURR EMPL* pres, ceo, dir: Demoulas Supermarkets Inc *CORP AFFIL* pres, ceo: Market Share Inc

GIVING OFFICERS
Arthur T. Demoulas: trust *CURR EMPL* vp, dir: Demoulas Supermarkets Inc

Telemachus A. Demoulas: trust *CURR EMPL* pres, ceo, dir: Demoulas Supermarkets Inc (see above)

Elizabeth Miliotis: contact

D. Harold Sullivan: trust *CURR EMPL* vp fin, treas, dir: Demoulas Supermarkets Inc

APPLICATION INFORMATION
Initial Approach: *Initial Contact:* brief letter of inquiry *Include Information On:* brief history of organization and description of need *Deadlines:* none

OTHER THINGS TO KNOW
Foundation donors are Demoulas Supermarkets Inc and the Demoulas Family.

GRANTS ANALYSIS
Total Grants: $747,680
Number of Grants: 164
Highest Grant: $52,500
Average Grant: $4,559
Typical Range: $5,000 to $10,000
Disclosure Period: 1993
Note: Recent grants are derived from a 1993 Form 990.

RECENT GRANTS
General

52,500	Bentley College, Waltham, MA
36,500	Boys Club, Lowell, MA
30,000	Boston College, Boston, MA
25,000	Holy Trinity Greek Orthodox Church, Lowell, MA
25,000	Immaculate Conception Church, Lowell, MA

Dewing Foundation, Frances R.

CONTACT
Margaret Corley
Manager
Frances R. Dewing Fdn.
10 Kearney Rd., Ste. 301
Needham, MA 02194
(617) 449-2110

FINANCIAL SUMMARY
Recent Giving: $152,957 (1993); $165,427 (1992); $134,577 (1991)
Assets: $2,742,864 (1993); $2,547,513 (1992); $2,424,193 (1991)
EIN: 04-6114839

CONTRIBUTIONS SUMMARY
Donor(s): Frances R. Dewing

Typical Recipients: • *Arts & Humanities:* Arts Associations & Councils, Arts Centers, Arts Institutes, Arts Outreach, Community Arts, Dance, General, Historic Preservation, Libraries, Literary Arts, Museums/Galleries, Music, Opera, Performing Arts, Theater • *Civic & Public Affairs:* General, Hispanic Affairs, Housing, Urban & Community Af-

fairs • *Education:* Afterschool/Enrichment Programs, Colleges & Universities, Education Reform, General, Literacy, Private Education (Precollege), Public Education (Precollege), Special Education • *Environment:* General, Resource Conservation, Watershed, Wildlife Protection • *Health:* Health Organizations • *International:* International Relations • *Science:* Science Museums, Scientific Centers & Institutes, Scientific Organizations • *Social Services:* At-Risk Youth, Child Welfare, Community Service Organizations, Counseling, Day Care, Family Services, Food/Clothing Distribution, Homes, People with Disabilities, Recreation & Athletics, Refugee Assistance, Youth Organizations

Grant Types: project and seed money

Geographic Distribution: focus on New England, NY, and CA

GIVING OFFICERS
Abigail D. Avery: trust

Roger C. Avery: trust

Margaret Corley: mgr

Ruth D. Ewing: trust

APPLICATION INFORMATION
Initial Approach: Send a brief letter of inquiry. Include a description of organization, amount requested, purpose of funds sought, recently audited financial statement, and proof of tax-exempt status. There are no deadlines.

PUBLICATIONS
Application Guidelines

GRANTS ANALYSIS
Total Grants: $152,957
Number of Grants: 44
Highest Grant: $5,000
Typical Range: 1,000 to $5,000
Disclosure Period: 1993
Note: Recent grants are derived from a 1993 Form 990.

RECENT GRANTS
Library

5,000	Crandall Public Library, Crandall, MA

General

5,000	Associated Day Care Services, Boston, MA
5,000	Phillips Brooke House, Boston, MA
5,000	Unh Image Making, Boston, MA
4,800	Science for All Seasons, Boston, MA
4,660	Westport River Watershed, Boston, MA

339

Dexter Charitable Fund, Eugene A.

CONTACT
Jane Corwin
Trust Officer
Eugene A. Dexter Charitable Fund
c/o BayBank
PO Box 3422
Burlington, MA 01803
(617) 273-1700

FINANCIAL SUMMARY
Recent Giving: $381,113 (1993); $390,519 (1992); $419,915 (1991)

Assets: $10,408,555 (1993); $10,138,269 (1992); $9,911,646 (1991)

EIN: 04-6018698

CONTRIBUTIONS SUMMARY
Donor(s): the late Henrietta F. Dexter

Typical Recipients: • *Arts & Humanities:* Arts Associations & Councils, Community Arts, History & Archaeology, Libraries, Literary Arts, Music, Performing Arts, Theater • *Civic & Public Affairs:* African American Affairs, Business/Free Enterprise, Community Foundations, Employment/Job Training, Ethnic Organizations, General, Hispanic Affairs, Housing, Municipalities/Towns, Philanthropic Organizations, Professional & Trade Associations, Urban & Community Affairs, Zoos/Aquariums • *Education:* Arts/Humanities Education, Colleges & Universities, General, Minority Education, Public Education (Precollege), School Volunteerism, Special Education • *Environment:* General • *Health:* AIDS/HIV, Clinics/Medical Centers, Health Organizations, Hospitals, Mental Health, Research/Studies Institutes • *International:* International Affairs • *Religion:* Churches, Religious Organizations, Religious Welfare • *Social Services:* At-Risk Youth, Child Welfare, Community Centers, Community Service Organizations, Day Care, Family Planning, Food/Clothing Distribution, Senior Services, United Funds/United Ways, YMCA/YWCA/YMHA/YWHA, Youth Organizations

Grant Types: capital, conference/seminar, and seed money

Geographic Distribution: limited to Hampden County, MA, with emphasis on the greater Springfield area

GIVING OFFICERS
Baybank: trust

APPLICATION INFORMATION
Initial Approach: Send a brief letter of inquiry. There are no deadlines.

Restrictions on Giving: Limited to charitable organizations in Springfield, MA.

PUBLICATIONS
Informational Brochure (including application guidelines)

GRANTS ANALYSIS
Total Grants: $381,113

Number of Grants: 45
Highest Grant: $50,000
Disclosure Period: 1993
Note: Recent grants are derived from a 1993 Form 990.

RECENT GRANTS
Library

5,000	Library and Museums Association

General

50,000	Community Foundation of Western Massachusetts, Springfield, MA
30,000	Community Foundation of Western Massachusetts, Springfield, MA
25,000	Bayside Health Systems, Springfield, MA
25,000	Community Foundation of Western Massachusetts, Springfield, MA
25,000	Urban League of Springfield, Springfield, MA

Digital Equipment Corp.

Revenue: $13.45 billion
Employees: 92,000
Headquarters: Maynard, MA
SIC Major Group: Electronic Computers, Computer Peripheral Equipment Nec, Electronic Components Nec, and Magnetic & Optical Recording Media

CONTACT
Jane M. Hamel
Manager, Corporate Contributions Program
Digital Equipment Corp.
111 Powder Mill Rd., MSO1-1/L14
Maynard, MA 01754
(508) 493-9210
Note: The company's World Wide Web address is
http://www.digital.com/info/home.html"

FINANCIAL SUMMARY
Recent Giving: $12,600,000 (fiscal 1994 approx.); $28,000,000 (fiscal 1993 approx.); $25,000,000 (fiscal 1992 approx.)

Fiscal Note: All contributions are made directly by the company; international giving is included. Above figures include nonmonetary support. Company's business group also provides substantial support to education through various programs, including a multimillion dollar grant program devoted to external research. See "Other Things To Know" for more details.

CONTRIBUTIONS SUMMARY
Typical Recipients: • *Arts & Humanities:* Community Arts, Dance, Libraries, Museums/Galleries, Performing Arts, Public Broadcasting • *Civic & Public Affairs:* Employment/Job Training, Housing, Nonprofit Management, Urban & Community Affairs • *Education:* Colleges & Universities, Elementary Education (Private), Engineering/Technological Education, Literacy, Minority Education, Science/Mathematics Education • *Environment:* General • *Health:* Health Organizations, Medical Rehabilitation, Medical Research, Mental Health • *International:* Foreign Educational Institutions, International Organizations • *Science:* Science Exhibits & Fairs • *Social Services:* Child Welfare, Community Service Organizations, Domestic Violence, Emergency Relief, Food/Clothing Distribution, People with Disabilities, Senior Services, Shelters/Homelessness, Substance Abuse, Youth Organizations

Grant Types: challenge, general support, and project

Note: Company also provides equipment grants on computer systems.

Nonmonetary Support: $22,000,000 (fiscal 1993); $17,000,000 (fiscal 1992); $22,000,000 (fiscal 1991)

Nonmonetary Support Types: donated equipment

Note: Company focuses its equipment support in the areas of education, healthcare and community programs. In 1995, the company reported that the employee matching gift program has been suspended.

Geographic Distribution: mainly in Digital communities; also to regional, national, and international organizations

Operating Locations: CA (Los Angeles, San Francisco), CO (Colorado Springs), DC, GA (Atlanta), IL (Chicago), MA (Acton, Hudson, Marlboro, Maynard, Northboro, Shrewsbury, Westfield, Westminster), NH (Southern New Hampshire), NM (Albuquerque)

Note: Also operates in 100 countries worldwide.

CORP. OFFICERS
Robert B. Palmer: *B* 1941 *ED* TX Tech Univ BS; TX Tech Univ MS *CURR EMPL* pres, ceo, dir, chmn: Digital Equipment Corp

GIVING OFFICERS
Jane M. Hamel: *CURR EMPL* mgr corp contributions program: Digital Equipment Corp

APPLICATION INFORMATION
Initial Approach: *Initial Contact:* telephone call or brief letter requesting guidelines *Include Information On:* two to three page summary of proposed program, detailed description of how company funds will be used, audience served, summary of grant impact on overall program, impact on community/region/nation, statement of organization's history and objectives, budget and organizational structure, most recent audited financial statement, other sources of support, list of directors, and proof of tax-exempt status *Deadlines:* none *Note:* Additional information may be requested during the review process. Equipment proposals must also include a listing of the Digital equipment being requested along with the part numbers and prices.

Restrictions on Giving: Contributions are typically not considered for capital campaigns; individuals; political activities; religious organizations for sectarian or denominational purposes; veterans organizations; organizations having illegal or discriminatory practices; multiyear grants; endowment funds; foundations that are grantmaking institutions; trips, tours, or transportation; tickets, tables, or advertising for benefit purposes; or organizations that violate any company principles.

OTHER THINGS TO KNOW
For information concerning the external research program, contact Jean Bonney, (508) 493-3503.

GRANTS ANALYSIS
Total Grants: $12,600,000

Disclosure Period: fiscal year ending June 30, 1994

Note: Recent grants are derived from a 1993 grants list.

RECENT GRANTS

General
1,400,000	Iowa State University, Ames, IA—computer equipment
456,000	Children International, Kansas City, MO
100,000	YWCA of the USA, New York, NY

Fletcher Foundation

CONTACT
Warner S. Fletcher
Treasurer
Fletcher Fdn.
370 Main St., 12th Fl.
Worcester, MA 01608
(508) 798-8621

FINANCIAL SUMMARY
Recent Giving: $735,100 (1993); $170,000 (1992); $99,500 (1991)

Assets: $17,369,216 (1993); $2,890,152 (1992); $2,832,319 (1991)

Gifts Received: $14,395,402 (1993); $323,856 (1991); $778,340 (1990)

Fiscal Note: In 1993, contributions were received from the estate of Marion S. Fletcher.

EIN: 04-6470890

CONTRIBUTIONS SUMMARY
Typical Recipients: • *Arts & Humanities:* Community Arts, Historic Preservation, History & Archaeology, Libraries, Museums/Galleries, Music, Public Broadcasting, Theater • *Civic & Public Affairs:* Clubs, General, Hispanic Affairs, Housing, Law & Justice, Legal Aid, Municipalities/Towns, Urban & Community Affairs, Women's Affairs • *Education:* Colleges & Universities, Education Funds, Private Education (Precollege) • *Environment:* General, Resource Conservation • *Health:* Cancer, Children's Health/Hospitals, Clinics/Medical Centers • *International:* Foreign Arts Organizations • *Social Services:* At-Risk Youth, Community Centers, Community Service Organizations, Crime Prevention, Family Planning, Homes, Shelters/Homelessness, Substance

Abuse, United Funds/United Ways, Youth Organizations

Grant Types: general support

Geographic Distribution: focus on Worcester County, MA

GIVING OFFICERS
Allen W. Fletcher: chmn, trust *PHIL AFFIL* trust: Stoddard Charitable Trust

Mary F. Fletcher: trust

Nina M. Fletcher: trust

Patricia A. Fletcher: trust

Warner S. Fletcher: treas, trust *B* Worcester MA 1945 *ED* Williams Coll BA 1967; Boston Univ JD 1973 *CURR EMPL* treas: Fletcher Tilton & Whipple *NONPR AFFIL* mem: Am Bar Assn, MA Bar Assn, Worcester County Bar Assn; treas, dir: Worcester Art Mus *PHIL AFFIL* chmn, trust: Stoddard Charitable Trust; secy, trust: George I. Alden Trust

APPLICATION INFORMATION
Initial Approach: Send brief letter describing program. There are no deadlines.

GRANTS ANALYSIS
Total Grants: $735,100

Number of Grants: 52

Highest Grant: $390,000

Typical Range: $1,000 to $30,000

Disclosure Period: 1993

Note: Recent grants are derived from a 1993 Form 990.

RECENT GRANTS

Library
5,000	Frick Art Reference Library, New York, NY

General
390,000	Bancroft School, Worcester, MA
30,000	Spectrum House, Worcester, MA
25,000	Greater Worcester Land Trust, Worcester, MA
17,500	MCCM Foundation, Worcester, MA
15,000	Massachusetts Audubon Society, Lincoln, MA

Friendship Fund

CONTACT
Judy Casey
Trust Officer
Friendship Fund
c/o Boston Safe Deposit and Trust Co.
One Boston Pl.
Boston, MA 02108
(617) 722-6818

FINANCIAL SUMMARY
Recent Giving: $145,720 (fiscal 1992); $147,000 (fiscal 1991); $139,579 (fiscal 1990)

Assets: $3,320,820 (fiscal 1992); $3,113,445 (fiscal 1991); $3,008,210 (fiscal 1990)

EIN: 13-6089220

CONTRIBUTIONS SUMMARY
Donor(s): the late Charles R. Crane

Typical Recipients: • *Arts & Humanities:* Film & Video, Libraries, Museums/Galleries, Music, Opera, Performing Arts, Public Broadcasting • *Civic & Public Affairs:* Civil Rights, Community Foundations, General, Housing, Public Policy, Safety, Urban & Community Affairs, Women's Affairs • *Education:* Colleges & Universities, General, Legal Education, Private Education (Precollege), Public Education (Precollege), Science/Mathematics Education, Student Aid • *Environment:* General • *Health:* Clinics/Medical Centers, Health Organizations, Hospitals, Prenatal Health Issues • *International:* International Affairs, International Organizations, International Peace & Security Issues • *Religion:* Churches, Religious Organizations • *Science:* Scientific Labs, Scientific Organizations • *Social Services:* Community Service Organizations, Family Planning, Sexual Abuse, Substance Abuse

Grant Types: capital, project, and scholarship

GIVING OFFICERS
Darby Bradley: secy, trust

Charles M. Crane: trust

Richard T. Crane: trust

Sylvia E. Crane: vp, trust

Josephine DeGive: pres, trust

Mrs. Bruce C. Fisher: trust

Nancy F. Fitzpatrick: dir

Elizabeth McLane-Bradley: trust

APPLICATION INFORMATION
Initial Approach: Send a brief letter of inquiry. Include a description of organization, amount requested, purpose of funds sought, recently audited financial statement, and proof of tax-exempt status. Applications are accepted during the month of May only.

GRANTS ANALYSIS
Total Grants: $145,720

Number of Grants: 91

Highest Grant: $10,000

Typical Range: $500 to $3,000

Disclosure Period: fiscal year ending June 30, 1992

Note: Recent grants are derived from a fiscal 1992 Form 990. Information listed does not include 1 grant for scholarship assistance to an individual.

RECENT GRANTS

Library
3,000	Woods Hole, Woods Hole, MA — library renovations
1,000	New York Public Library, New York, NY — extend library's hours

General
10,000	Flight Safety Foundation, Arlington, VA — internship

5,000	Coolidge Center for Environmental, Cambridge, MA
5,000	University of Rochester, Rochester, NY — scholarship fund
4,740	Harvard Law School, Cambridge, MA — student loan repayment
4,600	Citizen's Fund, Washington, DC — support for study "Dying Before Their Time"

GenRad / GenRad Foundation

Revenue: $158.7 million
Employees: 2,800
Headquarters: Concord, MA
SIC Major Group: Business Services and Instruments & Related Products

CONTACT
Linda B. Schuler
Trustee
Genrad Foundation
300 Baker Ave.
Concord, MA 01742
(508) 287-7743

FINANCIAL SUMMARY
Recent Giving: $56,500 (1994); $36,175 (1993); $39,585 (1992)

Assets: $1,448,546 (1993); $1,421,608 (1992); $714,020 (1990)

EIN: 04-6043570

CONTRIBUTIONS SUMMARY
Typical Recipients: • *Arts & Humanities:* Arts Associations & Councils, Community Arts, General, Historic Preservation, Libraries, Music, Performing Arts, Public Broadcasting, Theater • *Civic & Public Affairs:* General, Zoos/Aquariums • *Education:* Colleges & Universities, Engineering/Technological Education, General, Public Education (Precollege), Science/Mathematics Education, Secondary Education (Public), Special Education • *Health:* General, Geriatric Health, Health Organizations, Home-Care Services, Hospitals, Mental Health, Single-Disease Health Associations • *Science:* General, Observatories & Planetariums, Science Exhibits & Fairs, Science Museums, Scientific Centers & Institutes, Scientific Organizations • *Social Services:* Animal Protection, At-Risk Youth, Child Welfare, Community Service Organizations, Counseling, Delinquency & Criminal Rehabilitation, Domestic Violence, Family Services, General, People with Disabilities, Senior Services, Shelters/Homelessness, Substance Abuse, Volunteer Services, Youth Organizations

Grant Types: capital, challenge, endowment, general support, multiyear/continuing support, operating expenses, and seed money

Geographic Distribution: primarily in MA

Operating Locations: MA (Concord)

CORP. OFFICERS
James F. Lyons: *CURR EMPL* pres, ceo, dir: GenRad

GIVING OFFICERS
Raymond F. McNulty: trust *B* Salem MA 1946 *ED* Bowdoin Coll 1968 *CURR EMPL* corp rels dir: GenRad *NONPR AFFIL* mem: Natl Investor Rels Inst, Pub Rels Soc Am

Jane Pflugradt: secy

Linda B. Schuler: trust

Barbara J. Wahler: trust

APPLICATION INFORMATION
Initial Approach: Send a brief letter of inquiry. Include a description of organization, amount requested, purpose of funds sought, recently audited financial statement, and proof of tax-exempt status. There are no deadlines. Call to request guidelines.

Restrictions on Giving: Docs not support individuals, religious organizations for sectarian purposes, political or lobbying groups, or organizations outside operating areas.

PUBLICATIONS
Application Guidelines

GRANTS ANALYSIS
Total Grants: $36,175

Number of Grants: 18

Highest Grant: $10,000

Typical Range: $300 to $5,000

Disclosure Period: 1993

Note: Recent grants are derived from a 1993 Form 990.

RECENT GRANTS

General

10,000	Science Discovery Museum, Boston, MA
5,000	Emerson Health Systems, Emerson, MA
4,333	Concord-Assabet Adolescent Services, Concord, MA
3,750	Concord Family Service, Concord, MA
2,500	Minuteman Home Care Corporation, Boston, MA

Germeshausen Foundation, Kenneth J.

CONTACT
Martin S. Kaplan
Trustee
Kenneth J. Germeshausen Fdn.
c/o Hale and Dorr
60 State St.
Boston, MA 02109
(616) 526-6000

FINANCIAL SUMMARY
Recent Giving: $635,000 (1993)

Assets: $17,225,396 (1993)

EIN: 04-6179459

CONTRIBUTIONS SUMMARY
Typical Recipients: • *Arts & Humanities:* Historic Preservation, Libraries, Museums/Galleries, Music, Public Broadcasting • *Education:* Engineering/Technological Education • *Science:* Science Museums • *Social Services:* Food/Clothing Distribution

Grant Types: general support

Geographic Distribution: focus on MA

GIVING OFFICERS
Paline S. Germeshausen: trust

Martin S. Kaplan: trust *PHIL AFFIL* trust: Harold E. Edgerton Foundation

Nancy G. Klavans: trust

APPLICATION INFORMATION
Send a brief letter of inquiry. Include a description of organization, amount requested, purpose of funds sought, recently audited financial statement, and proof of tax-exempt status.

GRANTS ANALYSIS
Total Grants: $635,000

Number of Grants: 9

Highest Grant: $200,000

Typical Range: $10,000 to $100,000

Disclosure Period: 1993

Note: Recent grants are derived from a 1993 Form 990.

RECENT GRANTS

Library

25,000	Weston Library, Weston, MA — for general purpose

General

100,000	Massachusetts Institute of Technology, Cambridge, MA — for general purpose
75,000	Museum of Science, Boston, MA — for new exhibits plan
50,000	Greater Boston Food Bank, Boston, MA — for general purpose

Gillette Co. / Gillette Charitable & Educational Foundation

Revenue: $6.07 billion
Employees: 33,400
Headquarters: Boston, MA
SIC Major Group: Cutlery, Toilet Preparations, Electric Housewares & Fans, and Pens & Mechanical Pencils

CONTACT
James P. Furlong
Director, Civic Affairs
Gillette Charitable and Educational Fdn.
Prudential Tower Bldg.
48th Fl.
Boston, MA 02199
(617) 421-7722

FINANCIAL SUMMARY
Recent Giving: $2,750,000 (1992 approx.); $2,400,000 (1991); $224,000 (1990)

Assets: $2,283,905 (1992); $2,634,220 (1991); $2,021,993 (1990)

Fiscal Note: Majority of contributions are given directly by the Gillette Co. Figures for 1992 include matching gifts, program support, and $50,000 in foundation giving. Above figures exclude nonmonetary support.

EIN: 13-6047626

CONTRIBUTIONS SUMMARY

Typical Recipients: • *Arts & Humanities:* Arts Centers, Dance, Libraries, Museums/Galleries, Music, Public Broadcasting • *Civic & Public Affairs:* Economic Policy, Employment/Job Training, Law & Justice, Urban & Community Affairs, Zoos/Aquariums • *Education:* Business Education, Colleges & Universities, Education Funds, Private Education (Precollege), Religious Education • *Health:* Health Organizations, Hospitals, Medical Rehabilitation, Medical Research, Mental Health, Nursing Services, Single-Disease Health Associations • *International:* Foreign Educational Institutions • *Religion:* Religious Organizations • *Social Services:* Community Centers, Food/Clothing Distribution, Recreation & Athletics, Shelters/Homelessness, United Funds/United Ways, Volunteer Services, Youth Organizations

Grant Types: award, capital, challenge, conference/seminar, department, employee matching gifts, endowment, general support, multiyear/continuing support, operating expenses, professorship, research, and scholarship

Note: Scholarships provided only through the National Merit Scholarship Program and similar programs. Matching gifts awarded to higher education up to $10,000 and to hospitals and cultural groups up to $500.

Nonmonetary Support: $6,740,000 (1992)

Nonmonetary Support Types: cause-related marketing & promotion, donated equipment, donated products, in-kind services, loaned employees, loaned executives, and workplace solicitation

Geographic Distribution: primarily in Boston and other operating locations

Operating Locations: CA (Redwood City, Santa Monica, Westlake Village), IA (Iowa City), IL (North Chicago), MA (Andover, Boston, Lynnfield), MN (St. Paul), WI (Janesville)

CORP. OFFICERS

Gaston Raymond Levy: *B* Alexandria Egypt 1928 *ED* Victoria Coll 1945 *CURR EMPL* exec vp: Gillette Intl

Derwyn Fraser Phillips: *B* St Catherines Ontario Canada 1930 *ED* Univ W Ontario BA 1954 *CURR EMPL* vchmn N Atlantic: Gillette Co *CORP AFFIL* dir: MFS Sun Life Series Funds *NONPR AFFIL* mem: Cosmetic Toiletry Fragrance Assn; mem, dir: Greater Boston Chamber Commerce

Lorne R. Waxlax: *B* Two Harbors MN 1933 *ED* Univ MN BBA 1955; Northwestern Univ MBA 1967 *CURR EMPL* exec vp diversified oper: Gillette Co *CORP AFFIL* chmn, ceo: Braun AG; mem admin bd: BHF Bank; mem adv bd: Deutsche Bank *NONPR AFFIL* dir: Natl Assn Mfrs; mem: Beta Gamma Sigma *CLUB AFFIL* Algonquin Boston, Brae Burn CC, Hawks Nest CC, Kronberg Golf & Land

Alfred Michael Zeien: *B* New York NY 1930 *ED* Webb Inst Architecture BS 1952; Harvard Univ MBA 1955 *CURR EMPL* chmn, ceo: Gillette Co *CORP AFFIL* dir: Bank Boston Corp, First Natl Bank Boston, MA Mutual Life Ins Co, Polaroid Corp, Raytheon Co, Repligen Corp *NONPR AFFIL* trust: Univ Hosp Boston

GIVING OFFICERS

James P. Furlong: dir civic aff

John McGowan: dir

William J. McMorrow: off *B* Boston MA 1931 *ED* Boston Coll AB 1953; Boston Coll MBA 1971 *CURR EMPL* sr vp admin: Gillette Co *CORP AFFIL* vp, dir: Compania Giva SA

Thomas Francis Skelly: off *B* Boston MA 1934 *ED* Northeastern Univ BS 1956; Babson Coll MBA 1966 *CURR EMPL* sr vp fin, cfo: Gillette Co *CORP AFFIL* dir: Newworld Bank; pres, dir: Compania Giva SA *NONPR AFFIL* dir: Natl Foreign Trade Counc; dir natl counc: Northeastern Univ; mem: Am Inst CPAs, Fin Execs Inst

APPLICATION INFORMATION

Initial Approach: *Initial Contact:* brief letter *Include Information On:* description of the organization or project; information on goals or objectives; who it serves; list of directors or trustees; budget information; and information on other sources of funding *Deadlines:* none

Restrictions on Giving: Contributions are made largely, but not exclusively, to the Boston area and other major plant locations.

GRANTS ANALYSIS
Total Grants: $2,400,000

Typical Range: $5,000 to $10,000

Disclosure Period: 1993

Note: Figures include $50,000 in foundation giving and $1,900,000 in direct giving. Recent grants are derived from a partial grants list.

RECENT GRANTS

General
50,000   Northeastern University, Boston, MA

Globe Newspaper Co. / Boston Globe Foundation

Sales: $416.0 million
Employees: 2,101
Parent Company: Affiliated Publications, Inc.
Headquarters: Boston, MA
SIC Major Group: Newspapers

CONTACT
Suzanne W. Maas
Executive Director
The Boston Globe Foundation
135 Morrissey Blvd.
Boston, MA 02107-2378
(617) 929-2895

FINANCIAL SUMMARY
Recent Giving: $1,928,513 (fiscal 1994); $1,814,767 (fiscal 1993); $1,663,676 (fiscal 1992)

Assets: $109,048 (fiscal 1993); $18,069 (fiscal 1991); $58,022 (fiscal 1990)

Gifts Received: $2,082,783 (fiscal 1993)

Fiscal Note: Above figures reflect foundation giving only. Contact for direct support is Skip Griffin, Director, Community Relations and Public Affairs. Above figures exclude nonmonetary support. Contributions received from Globe Newspaper Company.

EIN: 22-2821421

CONTRIBUTIONS SUMMARY
Typical Recipients: • *Arts & Humanities:* Arts Associations & Councils, Arts Festivals, Arts Funds, Ballet, Dance, Ethnic & Folk Arts, Libraries, Museums/Galleries, Music, Performing Arts, Public Broadcasting, Theater, Visual Arts • *Civic & Public Affairs:* Economic Development, Employment/Job Training, Hispanic Affairs, Housing, Nonprofit Management, Philanthropic Organizations, Urban & Community Affairs, Women's Affairs • *Education:* After-school/Enrichment Programs, Colleges & Universities, Education Reform, Elementary Education (Private), General, Journalism/Media Education, Literacy, Medical Education, Preschool Education, Private Education (Precollege), Public Education (Precollege), Science/Mathematics Education, Special Education, Student Aid • *Health:* AIDS/HIV, Children's Health/Hospitals, Clinics/Medical Centers, Health Organizations, Hospitals, Medical Research, Mental Health, Nutrition • *International:* Human Rights • *Science:* Science Museums • *Social Services:* Camps, Child Welfare, Community Centers, Community Service Organizations, Counseling, Day Care, Domestic Violence, Family Services, Food/Clothing Distribution, Homes, People with Disabilities, Recreation & Athletics, Shelters/Homelessness, Substance Abuse, United Funds/United Ways, Youth Organizations

Grant Types: challenge, employee matching gifts, general support, multiyear/continuing support, operating expenses, project, and seed money

Nonmonetary Support Types: cause-related marketing & promotion

Note: Nonmonetary support is provided by the company. Contact for support is Skip Griffin, Director, Community Relations and Public Affairs.

Geographic Distribution: Boston, Cambridge, Somerville, Chelsea, and Billerica, MA

Operating Locations: MA (Billerica, Boston, Waltham)

CORP. OFFICERS
John Peter Giuggio: *B* Boston MA 1930 *ED* Boston Coll BSBA 1951 *CURR EMPL* vchmn, dir: Globe Newspaper Co *CORP AFFIL* dir: Affiliated Broadcasting, McCaw Cellular Communs, Million Market Newspaper; pres, coo, dir: Affiliated Pubs Inc *NONPR AFFIL* assoc chmn: Better Bus Bur Boston; dir: Commun Newsdealers, Greater Boston Chamber Commerce, N Conway Inst, Newspaper Advertising Bur; mem: Boston Coll Alumni Assn; trust: Emmanuel Coll; trust, dir: Boston Coll High Sch, Carney Hosp *CLUB AFFIL* Univ

Richard C. Ockerbloom: *B* Medford MA 1929 *ED* Northwestern Univ BSBA 1952 *CURR EMPL* pres, coo, dir: Globe Newspaper Co *CORP AFFIL* chmn: Commun News Inc, Metro Sunday Newspapers *NONPR AFFIL* dir: Greater Boston Convention Visit Bur, Newspapers First, Un Way MA Bay, Winchester Hosp; mem adv bd: Univ MA; mem, trust: Natl Assn Coop Ed; trust: Northeastern Univ *CLUB AFFIL* Advertising Boston, Algonquin, Winchester CC

William Osgood Taylor: *B* Boston MA 1932 *ED* Harvard Univ BA 1954 *CURR EMPL* chmn, ceo, dir: Affiliated Pubs Inc *CORP AFFIL* chmn: Globe Newspaper Co, GNC; dir: McCaw Cellular Communs; publ: Boston Globe Pubs *NONPR AFFIL* chmn: Am Press Inst; mem adv counc: Trust Reservations; mem corp: MA Gen Hosp; trust: Cotting Sch Handicapped Children, John F Kennedy Lib Fdn, New England Aquarium, Wellesley Coll *CLUB AFFIL* Chilton, Country, Somerset, Tavern

GIVING OFFICERS
Leslie Griffin: dir

Alexander Boyd Hawes, Jr.: treas *B* Washington DC 1947 *ED* Univ Denver 1965-1969 *CURR EMPL* asst to pres: Globe Newspaper Co *NONPR AFFIL* dir: Friends Sakonnet Lighthouse, Literacy Volunteers MA

Catherine Emily Campbell Henn: pres *B* St. Louis MO 1942 *ED* Wellesley Coll 1964; Harvard Univ 1969 *CURR EMPL* vp, clerk: Affiliated Pubs Inc

Suzanne W. Maas: exec dir

Mary Marty: treas asst *B* 1942 *ED* Marycrest Coll 1964 *CURR EMPL* treas: Affiliated Pubs Inc

Loretta McLoughton: dir

Sylvia Payton: secy

Claire Shaw: asst dir

Benjamin B. Taylor: dir *B* 1947 *ED* Harvard Univ *NONPR AFFIL* trust: Pk Sch, Radcliffe Coll

William Osgood Taylor: pres, dir *CURR EMPL* chmn, ceo, dir: Affiliated Pubs Inc (see above)

APPLICATION INFORMATION
Initial Approach: *Initial Contact:* brief letter requesting foundation guidelines and application *Include Information On:* amount requested; purpose of request; total cost, amount raised, total to be raised, priorities and objectives, description of services, other sources of funding and amounts, agency's operating experience, and coordination with other agencies; public relations efforts; projected duration of program(s); evidence of need and nonduplication and population served (number, age, income levels, ethnic groups, geographic distribution, special needs); site (location, occupancy status, accessibility to target population, feasibility of space for program); staff (number, composition, experience, training, orientation, ratio to clients, and applicable use of volunteers and turnover); board (function, composition, decision-making process); evaluative criteria, financial statement, proof of tax-exempt status; budget; description of in-kind goods or services; and potential of organization to be self-supporting *Deadlines:* none *Note:* The foundation strongly suggests that proposals be submitted on a Boston Globe Proposal form. The foundation also asks all grant recipients to complete three questionnaires regarding accessibility for the disabled to programs and program spaces and diversity of staff and board.

Restrictions on Giving: The foundation does not make grants to individuals or for the purchase of tables, tickets, or advertising. The foundation does not make more than one grant per fiscal year to any one organization.

OTHER THINGS TO KNOW
The Globe Santa Fund solicits through advertising and publicity contributions to purchase Christmas gifts for needy children. The company also administers several scholarship programs, including the L.L. Winship Scholarship Fund (for children of full-time company employees), the I. Arthur Seigel Scholarship Fund (athletic), the Marjorie L. Adams Scholarship Fund (for children of employees), and the Louis Shriber Scholarship Fund (for Globe newsboys). The company also sponsors scholastic art awards and the Globe Interscholastic Festival.

The New York Times Company acquired the Globe newspaper Co.'s parent corporation, Affiliated Publications, in 1993.

GRANTS ANALYSIS
Total Grants: $1,928,513

Number of Grants: 227

Highest Grant: $263,500

Average Grant: $8,496

Typical Range: $5,000 to $10,000

Disclosure Period: fiscal year ending June 30, 1994

Note: Recent grants are derived from a fiscal 1993 Form 990.

RECENT GRANTS
Library
100,000 Boston Public Library, Boston, MA — a 1991 donation to the "Endowment for Literacy" campaign, partial payment on a multiyear $1,000,000 pledge

15,000 Hampshire College, Amherst, MA — to be used toward the Library Foreign Periodical Fund

General
125,000 University of Massachusetts, Amherst, MA — Taylor Scholarship — support the Taylor Scholars Program

50,000 University of Massachusetts Boston, Amherst, MA — in support of the 1993 Taylor Scholars Program

40,000 Metropolitan Boston Housing Partnership, Boston, MA

37,000 Project Bread/The Walk for Hunger, Boston, MA — support the Emergency Feeding Network

30,000 United Way of Massachusetts Bay/Child Care Initiative, Boston, MA — pledge toward the Child Care Initiative Funding Collaboratives to strengthen nonprofit child care providers by focusing resources on physical facilities and staff retention

Goldberg Family Foundation
Former Foundation Name: Avram and Carol Goldberg Charitable Foundation

CONTACT
Avram J. Goldberg
Trustee
Goldberg Family Fdn.
225 Franklin St., Ste. 2700
Boston, MA 02108
(617) 695-1300

FINANCIAL SUMMARY
Recent Giving: $290,268 (fiscal 1993); $130,731 (fiscal 1991); $250,050 (fiscal 1990)

Assets: $7,226,584 (fiscal 1993); $6,882,067 (fiscal 1991); $6,031,655 (fiscal 1990)

Gifts Received: $24,000 (fiscal 1993); $15,719 (fiscal 1991); $529,546 (fiscal 1990)

Fiscal Note: In 1993, contributions were received from Carol R. Goldberg.

EIN: 04-6039556

CONTRIBUTIONS SUMMARY
Typical Recipients: • *Arts & Humanities:* Arts Centers, Community Arts, Libraries, Museums/Galleries, Music, Performing Arts, Public Broadcasting, Theater • *Civic & Public Affairs:* Economic Development, Philan-

thropic Organizations • *Education:* Business Education, Colleges & Universities, Education Funds, Minority Education, Private Education (Precollege), Social Sciences Education • *Environment:* General • *Health:* Children's Health/Hospitals, Geriatric Health, Hospitals, Medical Rehabilitation, Medical Research, Single-Disease Health Associations • *International:* International Organizations, Missionary/Religious Activities • *Religion:* Jewish Causes, Religious Organizations, Synagogues/Temples • *Science:* Science Museums, Scientific Centers & Institutes • *Social Services:* Community Service Organizations, People with Disabilities, United Funds/United Ways

Grant Types: general support

Geographic Distribution: focus on MA

GIVING OFFICERS

Avram Jacob Goldberg: trust *B* Brookline MA 1930 *ED* Harvard Univ AB 1951; Harvard Univ JD 1954 *CURR EMPL* chmn: AVCAR Group *CORP AFFIL* dir: Boston Co, Boston Safe Deposit & Trust Co *NONPR AFFIL* fellow: Am Academy Arts & Sciences, Brandeis Univ; hon life trust: Beth Israel Hosp; hon trust, vp: Combined Jewish Philanthropies Greater Boston; mem exec comm, dir: Food Mktg Inst; trust: Boston Plan Excellence Pub Schs, MA Eye Ear Infirmary; vp, dir: Natl Retail Merchants Assn *PHIL AFFIL* trust: Joseph F. and Clara Ford Foundation

Carol Rabb Goldberg: trust *B* Newton MA 1931 *ED* Tufts Univ BA 1955; Harvard Univ Sch Bus Admin 1969 *CURR EMPL* pres: AVCAR Group *CORP AFFIL* dir: Aicorp, Gillette Co, Lotus Devel Corp; trust: Putnam Fund Group *NONPR AFFIL* bd overseers: WGBH Ed Fdn; bd regents: Higher Ed Comm; bd visitors: Boston Univ Med Sch; dir: Greater Boston Arts Fund, Harvard Univ Bus Sch Alumni Assn, John F Kennedy Library Fdn; mem: Babson Coll Fdn; mem bus adv counc: Carnegie-Mellon Univ; mem natl counc adv comm: Tufts Univ Ctr Pub Svc *CLUB AFFIL* Commercial Merchants Boston *PHIL AFFIL* trust: Sidney and Esther Rabb Charitable Foundation, Sidney R. Rabb Charitable Trust

APPLICATION INFORMATION

Initial Approach: Send brief letter describing program. There are no deadlines.

GRANTS ANALYSIS

Total Grants: $290,268

Number of Grants: 110

Highest Grant: $36,550

Typical Range: $25 to $30,000

Disclosure Period: fiscal year ending June 30, 1993

Note: Recent grants are derived from a fiscal 1993 Form 990.

RECENT GRANTS

Library
4,500	JFK Library Foundation, Boston, MA	

General
36,550	Beth Israel Hospital, Boston, MA	
34,036	United Way, Boston, MA	
30,000	Tufts University Lincoln Filene Center, Medford, MA — New England Institute for Non-Profit Organizations	
18,500	Putney School, Putney, VT	
2,590	Congregation Kehillath Israel, Brookline, MA	

Harcourt General, Inc. / Harcourt General Charitable Foundation

Former Foundation Name: General Cinema Foundation
Revenue: $3.64 billion
Employees: 27,714
Headquarters: Chestnut Hill, MA
SIC Major Group: Motion Picture Theaters Except Drive-In, Miscellaneous Publishing, Miscellaneous Retail Stores Nec, and Insurance Carriers Nec

CONTACT
Kay M. Kilpatrick
Contributions Administrator
Harcourt General, Inc.
27 Boylston St.
Chestnut Hill, MA 02167
(617) 232-8200

FINANCIAL SUMMARY
Recent Giving: $1,474,305 (fiscal 1993); $1,022,615 (fiscal 1992); $272,000 (fiscal 1990)

Assets: $28,771,877 (fiscal 1993); $23,509,222 (fiscal 1992); $21,672,297 (fiscal 1990)

Fiscal Note: Above figures are for the foundation only. The company gives directly and through the foundation. Annual giving range is $3,000,000 to $3,500,000.

EIN: 22-3026002

CONTRIBUTIONS SUMMARY
Typical Recipients: • *Arts & Humanities:* Arts Associations & Councils, Ballet, General, Historic Preservation, History & Archaeology, Libraries, Museums/Galleries, Music, Performing Arts, Theater • *Civic & Public Affairs:* African American Affairs, Economic Development, Hispanic Affairs, Legal Aid, Philanthropic Organizations, Public Policy, Urban & Community Affairs, Zoos/Aquariums • *Education:* Business Education, Colleges & Universities, Continuing Education, Education Associations, Education Funds, Education Reform, Engineering/Technological Education, General, Health & Physical Education, Legal Education, Medical Education, Public Education (Precollege) • *Health:* Children's Health/Hospitals, Clinics/Medical Centers, Diabetes, Health Funds, Hospices, Hospitals, Medical Research, Prenatal Health Issues • *Religion:* Jewish Causes, Religious Organizations, Religious Welfare • *Science:*

Science Museums • *Social Services:* At-Risk Youth, Big Brother/Big Sister, Child Welfare, Community Service Organizations, Counseling, Domestic Violence, Family Services, General, People with Disabilities, Shelters/Homelessness, Volunteer Services, Youth Organizations

Grant Types: capital, employee matching gifts, general support, and project

Nonmonetary Support Types: donated products

Note: Company provides movie passes for raffles and auctions.

Geographic Distribution: only in Greater Boston area

Operating Locations: CA (Los Angeles), DC, FL (Orlando), IL (Lake Forest), MA (Chestnut Hill), NY (New York), PR, TX (Dallas, Las Colinas)

CORP. OFFICERS
Richard Alan Smith: *B* Boston MA 1924 *ED* Harvard Univ BS 1946 *CURR EMPL* chmn, dir: Harcourt Gen Inc *CORP AFFIL* chmn, ceo: Neiman Marcus Group Inc; dir: First Natl Bank Boston, Liberty Life Assurance Co, Liberty Mutual Fire Ins Co, Liberty Mutual Life Ins Co, Wang Laboratories *NONPR AFFIL* vchmn: Dana Farber Cancer Inst *CLUB AFFIL* Belmont CC, Harvard, Hazel Hotchkiss Wightman Tennis, Suburban Indoor Tennis Ctr, Variety *PHIL AFFIL* vp, treas, asst secy, dir: Margaret T. Biddle Foundation; treas, dir: Arvin Foundation; don: Richard and Susan Smith Foundation

GIVING OFFICERS
Kay M. Kilpatrick: trust *CURR EMPL* contributions adm: Hartcort Gen Inc

Brian J. Knez: trust *CURR EMPL* pres: Harcourt Brace & Co *CORP AFFIL* pres, ceo: Harcourt Brace Jovanovich *PHIL AFFIL* trust: Richard and Susan Smith Foundation

Robert A. Smith: trust *B* 1959 *ED* Harvard Univ MBA 1985 *CURR EMPL* group vp, dir: Harcourt Gen Inc *CORP AFFIL* group vp: Neiman Marcus Group Inc

APPLICATION INFORMATION
Initial Approach: *Initial Contact:* brief letter, no more than three pages in length *Include Information On:* organizational history; project's goals and objectives, its impact, and its relation to Harcourt General's and applicant's priorities; amount requested; plans for evaluating project and for maintaining it after grant period; detailed operating budget, including list of other sources of funds; names and qualifications of project's personnel; audited financial statements for the most recent two years; breakdown of current financial support (i.e. corporate, foundation, government, etc.); list of major donors and board members; most recent tax return; proof of tax-exempt status *Deadlines:* January 1, April 1, July 1, and October 1; board meets in January, May, August, and November

Restrictions on Giving: Does not support sectarian religious activities, political or lobbying activities, projects usually supported by the general public, recent grantees, organizations whose applications have been denied in the past year, individuals, operating budgets, deficits, or organizations where Harcourt General may become the predominant source of support.

OTHER THINGS TO KNOW
Please note name of General Cinema Corporation changed in March 1993 to Harcourt General, Inc., as well as the name of the foundation from General Cinema Corporate Charitable Foundation to Harcourt General Charitable Foundation.

GRANTS ANALYSIS
Total Grants: $1,474,305

Number of Grants: 105

Highest Grant: $150,000

Average Grant: $14,041

Typical Range: $1,000 to $20,000

Disclosure Period: fiscal year ending October 31, 1993

Note: Financial information is for the foundation only. Recent grants are derived from a fiscal 1993 Form 990.

RECENT GRANTS

Library
50,000	Boston Public Library Foundation, Boston, MA

General
90,000	Combined Jewish Philanthropies, Boston, MA
50,000	Beth Israel Hospital, Boston, MA
50,000	Boston Educational Development Foundation, Boston, MA
50,000	Children's Hospital, Boston, MA
50,000	Harvard Medical School, Cambridge, MA

Harrington Foundation, Francis A. and Jacquelyn H.

CONTACT
Sumner B. Tilton, Jr.
Trustee
Francis A. and Jacquelyn H. Harrington Fdn.
370 Main St., 12th Fl.
Worcester, MA 01608
(508) 798-8621

FINANCIAL SUMMARY
Recent Giving: $532,333 (1993); $643,083 (1992); $405,500 (1991)

Assets: $9,289,560 (1993); $9,091,318 (1992); $9,648,295 (1991)

EIN: 04-6125088

CONTRIBUTIONS SUMMARY
Donor(s): Francis A. Harrington, Charles A. Harrington Foundation

Typical Recipients: • *Arts & Humanities:* Arts Centers, History & Archaeology, Libraries, Museums/Galleries, Music, Performing Arts, Public Broadcasting, Theater

• *Civic & Public Affairs:* Botanical Gardens/Parks, Community Foundations, Housing, Municipalities/Towns, Native American Affairs, Rural Affairs, Urban & Community Affairs • *Education:* Colleges & Universities, Community & Junior Colleges, Private Education (Precollege), Science/Mathematics Education, Student Aid • *Environment:* General, Resource Conservation, Wildlife Protection • *Health:* Cancer • *International:* Foreign Arts Organizations • *Religion:* Churches • *Science:* Science Museums, Scientific Centers & Institutes, Scientific Organizations • *Social Services:* Big Brother/Big Sister, Child Welfare, Community Centers, Community Service Organizations, Crime Prevention, Family Planning, Family Services, United Funds/United Ways, YMCA/YWCA/YMHA/YWHA, Youth Organizations

Grant Types: capital, general support, and project

Geographic Distribution: focus on Worcester, MA

GIVING OFFICERS
Francis A. Harrington, Jr.: trust

James H. Harrington: trust

Sumner B. Tilton, Jr.: trust *CURR EMPL* jr, clerk: New England Newspaper Supply Co *CORP AFFIL* clerk: R H White Co, R H White Construction Co, Whiteater Inc, Whitinsville Water Co *NONPR AFFIL* pres: Greater Worcester Commmun Fdn *PHIL AFFIL* trust: Ruth H. and Warren A. Ellsworth Foundation, Mildred H. McEvoy Foundation

APPLICATION INFORMATION
Initial Approach: Send a brief letter of inquiry. Include a description of organization, amount requested, purpose of funds sought, recently audited financial statement, and proof of tax-exempt status. There are no deadlines.

GRANTS ANALYSIS
Total Grants: $532,333

Number of Grants: 49

Highest Grant: $100,000

Typical Range: $2,000 to $33,000

Disclosure Period: 1993

Note: Recent grants are derived from a 1993 Form 990.

RECENT GRANTS

Library
30,000	American Antiquarian Society, Worcester, MA — to establish endowment to fund the Marcus A. McCorison Librarianship

General
100,000	Greater Worcester Community Foundation, Worcester, MA — to fund a human services fund
43,000	Greater Worcester Community Foundation, Worcester, MA — annual "pass-through" funds to provide distributable income for social service grants from

	Harrington Human Services Fund
33,333	New England Science Center, Worcester, MA — support of Jason Video Teleconferencing project
20,000	Big Brothers and Big Sisters of Worcester County, Worcester, MA — capital campaign to create the center
20,000	Greater Worcester Community Foundation, Worcester, MA — contribution to the United Way Endowment Fund

Henderson Foundation, George B.

CONTACT
Henry R. Guild, Jr.
Trustee
George B. Henderson Fdn.
50 Congress St., Ste. 1020
Boston, MA 02109
(617) 523-1320

FINANCIAL SUMMARY
Recent Giving: $134,270 (1993); $244,097 (1992); $186,334 (1991)

Assets: $6,495,656 (1993); $6,513,972 (1992); $6,849,958 (1991)

EIN: 04-6089310

CONTRIBUTIONS SUMMARY
Donor(s): the late George B. Henderson

Typical Recipients: • *Arts & Humanities:* Arts Associations & Councils, Arts Centers, Historic Preservation, History & Archaeology, Libraries, Theater • *Civic & Public Affairs:* Botanical Gardens/Parks, Clubs, Economic Development, Municipalities/Towns, Urban & Community Affairs, Zoos/Aquariums • *Education:* Colleges & Universities, Education Funds • *Environment:* General, Resource Conservation • *Health:* Clinics/Medical Centers, Health Organizations • *Religion:* Churches • *Social Services:* Community Centers, Community Service Organizations, Recreation & Athletics, Veterans

Grant Types: capital and general support

Geographic Distribution: limited to Boston, MA

GIVING OFFICERS
Thomas B. Adams: bd mem

Valerie Burns: secy

Pauline Chase-Harrell: bd mem

Nancy Coolidge: bd mem

John deMonchaux: bd mem

Jonathan Fairbank: bd mem

Henry Rice Guild, Jr.: trust *B* Boston MA 1928 *ED* Harvard Univ 1950-1953 *CURR EMPL* pres: Guild Monrad & Oates *CORP AFFIL* dir: Tampa Electric Co, TECO Energy Inc

Ernest Henderson III: trust *B* Boston MA 1924 *ED* Harvard Univ SB 1944; Harvard

Univ MBA 1949 *CURR EMPL* pres, ceo: Fidelity Products Corp *CORP AFFIL* dir: Boston Biotechnology Corp; pres: Henderson Houses Am *NONPR AFFIL* dir: Wellesley Commun Ctr; mem: Chief Execs Org; pres: Sudbury Nursing Home; treas, dir: Boston Biomedical Res Inst *PHIL AFFIL* trust: Henderson Foundation

Gerard C. Henderson: trust

Carol R. Johnson: chmn

Alan Shestack: bd mem

APPLICATION INFORMATION
Initial Approach: Send letter requesting application form. There are no deadlines. Applicants usually notified within three months.

Restrictions on Giving: Does not support individuals for endowment funds or operating expenses. Grants solely for enhancement of physical appearance of Boston city.

GRANTS ANALYSIS
Total Grants: $134,270

Number of Grants: 8

Highest Grant: $30,000

Typical Range: $3,800 to $25,000

Disclosure Period: 1993

Note: Recent grants are derived from a 1993 Form 990.

RECENT GRANTS

Library
30,000 Boston Public Library, Boston, MA — casting a copy of MacMonnies' Bacchante

General
20,000 Dimock Community Health Center, Roxbury, MA — restoration of cupoola and stork weathervane on Sewell Building
10,170 South End-Lower Roxbury Open Space Land Trust, Boston, MA — ornamental picket fencing around two highly visible gardens in the South End
10,000 Parish of Christ Church, Hyde Park, MA — restoration of roofing elements
3,800 Forest Hills Educational Trust, Jamaica Plain, MA — reconditioning of the City of Roxbury Union Soldiers Monument

Hershey Foundation, Barry J.

CONTACT
Barry J. Hershey
Trustee
Barry J. Hershey Foundation
900 Tanglewood Dr.
Concord, MA 01742-4947
(508) 369-8933

FINANCIAL SUMMARY
Recent Giving: $153,000 (1992); $30,000 (1991); $21,500 (1990)

Assets: $8,699,853 (1992); $868,295 (1991); $971,529 (1990)

Gifts Received: $3,056,500 (1992); $12,500 (1991); $360,000 (1990)

Fiscal Note: In 1992, contributions were received from Barry J. Hershey.

EIN: 34-1574366

CONTRIBUTIONS SUMMARY
Typical Recipients: • *Arts & Humanities:* Ballet, Libraries, Music • *Education:* Education Funds, Private Education (Precollege) • *Health:* Health Organizations • *International:* International Organizations, International Peace & Security Issues • *Religion:* Religious Organizations • *Social Services:* Child Welfare

Grant Types: general support

GIVING OFFICERS
Barry J. Hershey: trust

Connie Hershey: trust

APPLICATION INFORMATION
Initial Approach: The foundation reports no specific application guidelines. Send a brief letter of inquiry, including statement of purpose, amount requested, and proof of tax-exempt status.

GRANTS ANALYSIS
Total Grants: $153,000

Number of Grants: 8

Highest Grant: $100,000

Typical Range: $2,500 to $19,000

Disclosure Period: 1992

Note: Recent grants are derived from a 1992 Form 990.

RECENT GRANTS

Library
4,000 Ganden Shartse Library

General
100,000 Tibetan Children's Village
19,000 Mind and Life Institute
10,000 Mind and Life Institute
10,000 Penn School
5,000 Wisdom Publications

Heydt Fund, Nan and Matilda

CONTACT
Jane Corvin
Trust Officer
Nan and Matilda Heydt Fund
c/o BayBank
PO Box 3422
Burlington, MA 01803
(617) 273-1700

FINANCIAL SUMMARY
Recent Giving: $123,802 (1993); $190,024 (1992); $176,827 (1991)

Assets: $4,547,736 (1993); $4,386,850 (1992); $4,305,738 (1991)

EIN: 04-6136421

CONTRIBUTIONS SUMMARY
Donor(s): the late Matilda L. Heydt

Typical Recipients: • *Arts & Humanities:* Historic Preservation, Libraries, Opera • *Civic & Public Affairs:* Botanical Gardens/Parks, General, Hispanic Affairs, Housing, Legal Aid, Public Policy, Safety, Urban & Community Affairs • *Education:* Colleges & Universities, Elementary Education (Public), General, Special Education • *Environment:* General, Resource Conservation • *Health:* Children's Health/Hospitals, Health Funds, Hospitals, Mental Health, Nursing Services • *Religion:* Churches • *Social Services:* At-Risk Youth, Child Welfare, Community Service Organizations, Counseling, Family Planning, Food/Clothing Distribution, United Funds/United Ways, Youth Organizations

Grant Types: capital, project, and seed money

Geographic Distribution: limited to Hampden County, MA

GIVING OFFICERS
Baybank: trust

APPLICATION INFORMATION
Initial Approach: Contact foundation for more information. There are no deadlines.

PUBLICATIONS
Informational Brochure (including application guidelines)

GRANTS ANALYSIS
Total Grants: $123,802

Number of Grants: 24

Highest Grant: $20,000

Typical Range: $500 to $10,000

Disclosure Period: 1993

Note: Recent grants are derived from a 1993 Form 990.

RECENT GRANTS

Library
3,500 Friends of West Springfield Public Library, West Springfield, MA

General
20,000 Western Massachusetts Food Bank, Springfield, MA
10,000 Frank Newhall Look Memorial Park, Northampton, MA
10,000 Holyoke Visiting Nurse Association, Holyoke, MA
7,500 Douglas A. Thom Clinic for Children, Boston, MA
5,945 Casa of Springfield, Springfield, MA

Hopedale Foundation

CONTACT
H. Raymond Grant
Treasurer
Hopedale Fdn.
PO Box 123, 43 Hope St.
Hopedale, MA 01747
(508) 473-2871

FINANCIAL SUMMARY
Recent Giving: $165,682 (fiscal 1993); $197,718 (fiscal 1992); $179,000 (fiscal 1991)

Assets: $5,330,558 (fiscal 1993); $4,985,163 (fiscal 1992); $4,594,470 (fiscal 1991)

EIN: 04-6044779

CONTRIBUTIONS SUMMARY
Donor(s): Draper Corp., the late Thomas H. West, the late John D. Gannett

Typical Recipients: • *Arts & Humanities:* Arts Associations & Councils, Historic Preservation, Libraries, Museums/Galleries, Music, Public Broadcasting • *Civic & Public Affairs:* Botanical Gardens/Parks, Economic Development, Municipalities/Towns, Zoos/Aquariums • *Education:* Colleges & Universities, Education Funds, Elementary Education (Private), Elementary Education (Public), Medical Education, Science/Mathematics Education • *Health:* Children's Health/Hospitals, Clinics/Medical Centers, Hospitals, Hospitals (University Affiliated), Nursing Services • *Religion:* Religious Welfare • *Science:* Science Museums • *Social Services:* Community Service Organizations, Crime Prevention, Food/Clothing Distribution, Recreation & Athletics, Senior Services, United Funds/United Ways, YMCA/YWCA/YMHA/YWHA

Grant Types: capital, general support, and loan

Geographic Distribution: focus on Hopedale, MA, area

GIVING OFFICERS
Vincent J. Arone: trust
W. Gregory Burrill: trust
Peter S. Ellis: trust
William B. Gannett: trust
H. Raymond Grant: treas
Alfred H. Sparling, Jr.: trust
Thomas H. West, Jr.: trust

APPLICATION INFORMATION
Initial Approach: Send brief letter of inquiry describing program or project. Deadline is June 1 for student loans; no set deadline for grants. Board meets in February, June, and October.

Restrictions on Giving: Student loans restricted to Hopedale High School graduates.

GRANTS ANALYSIS
Total Grants: $165,682
Number of Grants: 21
Highest Grant: $75,000

Typical Range: $500 to $20,000
Disclosure Period: fiscal year ending October 31, 1993

Note: Recent grants are derived from a fiscal 1993 Form 990.

RECENT GRANTS
Library
1,500	Friends of Hopedale Library, Hopedale, MA

General
75,000	Milford-Whitinsville Regional Hospital, Milford, MA
20,000	Hopedale School Department Computer Lab, Hopedale, MA
11,782	Town of Hopedale Master Plan, Hopedale, MA
10,000	New England Colleges Fund, Boston, MA
6,000	Visiting Nurse Association, Milford, MA

Housatonic Curtain Co. / High Meadow Foundation

Sales: $5.2 million
Employees: 90
Headquarters: Stockbridge, MA

CONTACT
Tammy Stevens
Foundation Coordinator
High Meadow Fdn.
c/o Country Curtains, Inc.
PO Box 955
Stockbridge, MA 01262
(413) 298-5565

FINANCIAL SUMMARY
Recent Giving: $934,696 (1992)
Assets: $932,903 (1992)
Gifts Received: $882,813 (1992)

Fiscal Note: In fiscal 1992, major contributions were received from John H. & Jane P. Fitzpatrick ($345,331), Country Curtains, Inc. ($230,667), and Housatonic Curtain Co. ($184,267).

EIN: 22-2527419

CONTRIBUTIONS SUMMARY
Typical Recipients: • *Arts & Humanities:* General, Historic Preservation, History & Archaeology, Libraries, Museums/Galleries, Music, Opera, Performing Arts, Theater • *Civic & Public Affairs:* Employment/Job Training, Ethnic Organizations, General, Parades/Festivals, Public Policy • *Education:* Arts/Humanities Education, Private Education (Precollege) • *Environment:* General, Resource Conservation • *Health:* Hospitals, Prenatal Health Issues • *Religion:* Churches • *Social Services:* Child Welfare, Community Service Organizations, People with Disabilities, United Funds/United Ways, Youth Organizations

Grant Types: scholarship

Operating Locations: MA (Stockbridge)

CORP. OFFICERS
Jo Ann Fitzpatrick Brown: *CURR EMPL* vp: Country Curtains Inc *CORP AFFIL* vp: Housatonic Curtain Co *PHIL AFFIL* dir: High Meadow Foundation

John H. Fitzpatrick: *CURR EMPL* vchmn, chmn plan and fin comm: Country Curtains Inc *CORP AFFIL* pres: Housatonic Curtain Co *PHIL AFFIL* pres: High Meadow Foundation

GIVING OFFICERS
Jo Ann Fitzpatrick Brown: dir *CURR EMPL* vp: Country Curtains Inc *PHIL AFFIL* dir: High Meadow Foundation (see above)

Jane P. Fitzpatrick: chmn, treas *CURR EMPL* chmn, ceo, treas: Country Curtains Inc *PHIL AFFIL* chmn: High Meadow Foundation

John H. Fitzpatrick: pres *CURR EMPL* vchmn, chmn plan and fin comm: Country Curtains Inc *PHIL AFFIL* pres: High Meadow Foundation (see above)

Mary Ann Snyder: dir *PHIL AFFIL* dir: High Meadow Foundation, Chicago Resource Center

APPLICATION INFORMATION
Initial Approach: Send a brief letter of inquiry. There are no deadlines.

OTHER THINGS TO KNOW
For more information about the High Meadow Foundation, see Country Curtains.

GRANTS ANALYSIS
Total Grants: $934,696
Number of Grants: 321
Highest Grant: $150,000
Typical Range: $200 to $10,000
Disclosure Period: 1992

Note: Information listed does not include grants to individuals or scholarships. Recent grants are derived from a 1992 Form 990.

RECENT GRANTS
Library
11,150	Lenox Library Association, Lenox, MA
3,100	Stockbridge Library Association

General
60,000	Berkshire Medical Center, Stockbridge, MA
55,000	Berkshire Country Day School, Stockbridge, MA
53,000	Berkshire United Way, Stockbridge, MA
25,000	Berkshire 21 Campaign, Stockbridge, MA
25,000	Berkshire Natural Resource Council, Stockbridge, MA — pledge

John Hancock Mutual Life Insurance Co.

Revenue: $5.66 billion
Employees: 19,000
Headquarters: Boston, MA
SIC Major Group: Life Insurance

CONTACT
James H. Young
General Director & Assistant Secretary
John Hancock Mutual Life Insurance Co.
Box 111
Boston, MA 02117
(617) 572-6607

FINANCIAL SUMMARY
Recent Giving: $3,600,000 (1995 est.);
$3,400,000 (1994 approx.); $3,300,000
(1993 approx.)
Fiscal Note: All contributions are made directly by the company.

CONTRIBUTIONS SUMMARY
Typical Recipients: • *Arts & Humanities:*
Arts Appreciation, Arts Associations &
Councils, Arts Centers, Arts Institutes, Community Arts, Dance, Ethnic & Folk Arts,
Historic Preservation, Libraries, Museums/Galleries, Music, Opera, Performing
Arts, Public Broadcasting, Theater • *Civic & Public Affairs:* Business/Free Enterprise,
Civil Rights, Economic Development, Economic Policy, Employment/Job Training,
Law & Justice, Professional & Trade Associations, Public Policy, Urban & Community Affairs, Women's Affairs • *Education:*
Business Education, Continuing Education,
Economic Education, Education Funds,
Medical Education, Minority Education, Science/Mathematics Education, Special Education • *Environment:* General • *Health:*
Health Policy/Cost Containment, Hospitals,
Medical Research, Nutrition, Public Health,
Single-Disease Health Associations • *Social Services:* Child Welfare, Community Centers, Community Service Organizations,
Counseling, Delinquency & Criminal Rehabilitation, Family Services, Food/Clothing
Distribution, Homes, People with Disabilities, Recreation & Athletics, Senior Services, Shelters/Homelessness, Substance
Abuse, United Funds/United Ways, Volunteer Services, Youth Organizations
Grant Types: capital, employee matching
gifts, general support, and multiyear/continuing support
Note: Employee matching gift ratio: .5 to 1.
Nonmonetary Support Types: in-kind services, loaned employees, and loaned executives
Note: Company sponsors nonmonetary support program that provides space for meetings, printing and graphic services, public
relations assistance, photography, special
events planning, and loaned executives and
employees. Estimated value of this support
is not available.
Geographic Distribution: giving is restricted to Boston-based organizations
Operating Locations: MA (Boston)

Note: Operates in all 50 states and the District of Columbia.

CORP. OFFICERS
William L. Boyan: *B* Medford MA 1937
ED Harvard Univ 1958 *CURR EMPL* pres,
coo, dir: John Hancock Mutual Life Ins Co
CORP AFFIL dir: El Paso Electric Co,
Shawmut Bank

Stephen Lee Brown: *B* Providence RI 1937
ED Middlebury Coll BA 1958 *CURR EMPL*
chmn, ceo, dir: John Hancock Mutual Life
Ins Co *CORP AFFIL* dir: Boston Housing
Partnership, John Hancock Subsidiaries,
Towle Mfg Co *NONPR AFFIL* dir: Million
Dollar Round Table Fdn, Un Way MA Bay;
fellow: Soc Actuaries; mem: Am Acad Actuaries; trust: Mus Sci Boston, Wang Ctr Performing Arts *CLUB AFFIL* Algonquin,
Commercial *PHIL AFFIL* trust, mem: Alfred
P. Sloan Foundation

Kathy Dristal: *CURR EMPL* vp: John Hancock Mutual Life Ins Co

GIVING OFFICERS
James H. Young: *CURR EMPL* gen dir,
asst secy: John Hancock Mutual Life Ins Co

APPLICATION INFORMATION
Initial Approach: *Initial Contact:* brief letter or proposal *Include Information On:* objectives, services, program activities, and
accomplishments of organization; purpose
for which funds are sought; proof of tax-exempt status; names and affiliations of officers, trustees, and members of the board of
directors; population served and their socioeconomic composition; and annual budget
for the project or program to be assisted
Deadlines: none *Note:* All organizations receiving company grants are requested to submit periodic reports on how funds are used.
All continuing grants are reviewed at least
once in three years.

Restrictions on Giving: Does not support
dinners or special events, fraternal or political organizations, religious organizations for
sectarian purposes, individuals, or goodwill
advertising.

GRANTS ANALYSIS
Total Grants: $3,400,000

Disclosure Period: 1994

Note: Total grants figure is an approximation.

Johnson Fund, Edward C.

CONTACT
Anne-Marie Soulliere
Foundation Director
Edward C. Johnson Fund
82 Devonshire St., S3
Boston, MA 02109
(617) 563-6806

FINANCIAL SUMMARY
Recent Giving: $3,156,278 (1993);
$2,434,067 (1992); $2,320,806 (1991)

Assets: $66,390,800 (1993); $43,963,383
(1992); $32,425,211 (1991)

Gifts Received: $19,776,372 (1993);
$10,776,509 (1992); $2,420,720 (1991)

Fiscal Note: In 1991, contributions were received from Edward C. Johnson III. In 1993,
contributions were received from Sun Dune
Investments, Swallows Cave Investments,
FMR Corp., Edward C. Johnson III, and the
Edward C. Johnson II Charitable Lead Trust.

EIN: 04-6108344

CONTRIBUTIONS SUMMARY
Donor(s): The fund was established in 1964
by Edward C. Johnson, III and the late Edward C. Johnson II .

Typical Recipients: • *Arts & Humanities:*
Arts Associations & Councils, Ethnic &
Folk Arts, Film & Video, General, Historic
Preservation, History & Archaeology, Libraries, Museums/Galleries, Music • *Civic & Public Affairs:* Botanical Gardens/Parks,
Clubs, General, Native American Affairs,
Philanthropic Organizations, Public Policy •
Education: Colleges & Universities, Private
Education (Precollege) • *Environment:* Resource Conservation • *Health:* Alzheimers
Disease, Cancer, Emergency/Ambulance
Services, Eyes/Blindness, Hospitals, Medical Research, Preventive Medicine/Wellness
Organizations • *International:* Health
Care/Hospitals, International Organizations
• *Religion:* Churches • *Science:* Scientific
Centers & Institutes • *Social Services:* Animal Protection, Child Welfare, Recreation &
Athletics

Grant Types: capital, endowment, and project

Geographic Distribution: focus on New
England

GIVING OFFICERS
Abigail P. Johnson: trust

Edward Crosby Johnson III: trust *B* Boston MA 1930 *ED* Harvard Univ AB 1954
CURR EMPL chmn, pres, ceo, dir: FMR
Corp *CORP AFFIL* chmn, pres: Magellan
Fund; dir: Fidelity Distributors Corp; mgr,
gen ptnr: Fidelity Govt Securities Fund;
pres: Fidelity Cash Reserve Fund, Fidelity
Daily Income Trust, Fidelity Fund, Fidelity
Group Mutual Funds; pres, trust: Fidelity Equity-Income Fund, Fidelity Intermediate
Bond Fund, Fidelity Municipal Bond Portfolio *NONPR AFFIL* dir: Boston Biomed Res
Inst, Boston Mus Fine Arts, Childrens Hosp,
MA Gen Hosp, New England Deaconess
Hosp, Northeastern Univ; mem: Am Acad
Arts Sci, Am Antiquarian Soc, Boston Econ
Club, Boston Soc Security Analysts, City
Club Corp, Fin Analysts Fed *CLUB AFFIL*
Badminton & Tennis, Chilton, Mayflower
Descendents, Union *PHIL AFFIL* trust: Fidelity Foundation; pres: Charles River
Square Antique Foundation Inc

Edward Crosby Johnson IV: trust

Elizabeth L. Johnson: trust

Caleb Loring, Jr.: trust *B* Boston MA 1921
ED Harvard Univ AB 1943; Harvard Univ
LLB 1948 *CURR EMPL* mng dir: FMR Corp
CORP AFFIL dir: Fidelity Investments;
pres, treas, dir: Fidelity Properties Inc

NONPR AFFIL mem: Am Bar Assn, Boston Bar Assn, MA Bar Assn *PHIL AFFIL* trust: Fidelity Foundation

Anne-Marie Soulliere: dir *PHIL AFFIL* dir: Fidelity Foundation

APPLICATION INFORMATION
Initial Approach:

Applicant should contact the fund for a summary of request form.

A full application is made in a letter of request with supporting materials including the following: an organizational history and the organization's objectives; current audited financial statements; a project budget; a list of officers and directors; an IRS 501(c)(3) determination letter; reports on previous Edward C. Johnson Fund grants; and a brief development summary, including a list of other foundations and corporations receiving proposals.

Applications should be received by March 30 or September 30 for consideration in June or December, respectively.

Restrictions on Giving: The fund does not make multiyear pledges and does not normally award grants to any organization in successive years. No grants are made to individuals or for scholarships.

PUBLICATIONS
Application guidelines and summary form

GRANTS ANALYSIS

Total Grants: $3,156,278

Number of Grants: 44

Highest Grant: $1,224,550

Average Grant: $44,924*

Typical Range: $5,000 to $70,000

Disclosure Period: 1993

Note: Average grant figure excludes the highest grant. Recent grants are derived from a 1993 Form 990.

RECENT GRANTS

Library
600	Library of the Boston Athenaeum, Boston, MA

General
575,000	Foundation for Neurological Diseases, New York, NY
380,000	Proctor Academy, Andover, NH
250,000	Bradford College, Bradford, MA
201,000	Garrison Forest School, Owings Mills, MD
173,828	Fidelity Investments Charitable Gift Fund

Kelley and Elza Kelley Foundation, Edward Bangs

CONTACT
Henry L. Murphy, Jr.
Administrator Manager
Edward Bangs Kelley and Elza Kelley Fdn.
PO Drawer M
Hyannis, MA 02601
(508) 775-3116

FINANCIAL SUMMARY
Recent Giving: $181,550 (1993); $169,200 (1992); $181,789 (1991)

Assets: $3,553,352 (1993); $3,483,519 (1992); $3,506,682 (1991)

Gifts Received: $1,065 (1993); $1,150 (1992); $3,575 (1991)

EIN: 04-6039660

CONTRIBUTIONS SUMMARY
Donor(s): the late Edward Bangs Kelley, the late Elza deHorvath Kelley

Typical Recipients: • *Arts & Humanities:* Arts Centers, Community Arts, Historic Preservation, History & Archaeology, Libraries, Literary Arts, Museums/Galleries, Music, Performing Arts, Theater • *Civic & Public Affairs:* Housing, Philanthropic Organizations, Urban & Community Affairs • *Education:* Arts/Humanities Education, Colleges & Universities, Community & Junior Colleges, Private Education (Precollege), Secondary Education (Private), Student Aid • *Environment:* Air/Water Quality, General, Resource Conservation, Wildlife Protection • *Health:* Alzheimers Disease, Eyes/Blindness, Hospitals, Medical Rehabilitation, Medical Research, Preventive Medicine/Wellness Organizations, Research/Studies Institutes, Single-Disease Health Associations • *International:* International Organizations • *Religion:* Religious Welfare • *Science:* Science Museums • *Social Services:* Animal Protection, Big Brother/Big Sister, Child Welfare, Community Service Organizations, Day Care, Senior Services, Substance Abuse, United Funds/United Ways, Youth Organizations

Grant Types: capital, emergency, operating expenses, project, research, and scholarship

Geographic Distribution: limited to Barnstable County, MA

GIVING OFFICERS
John F. Aylmer: dir

Jocelyn Bowman: dir

Palmer Davenport: dir

Townsend Hornor: dir

John M. Kayajan: dir

Ruth B. Kelley: dir

Kenneth S. MacAffer, Jr.: dir

Stephen W. Malaquias, M.D.: dir

Mary L. Montgomery: clerk, dir

Henry L. Murphy, Jr.: vp,admin, mgr, dir

E. Carlton Nickerson: dir

Frank L. Nickerson: dir

Joshua A. Nickerson, Jr.: dir

Thomas S. Olsen: treas, dir

Milton L. Penn: pres, dir

Walter G. Robinson: dir

Barbara H. Sheaffer: dir

APPLICATION INFORMATION
Initial Approach: Send letter requesting application form. Deadline is April 30 for scholarships; no deadline for grants.

PUBLICATIONS
Annual Report (includes Application Guidelines).

GRANTS ANALYSIS
Total Grants: $181,550

Number of Grants: 29

Highest Grant: $15,000

Typical Range: $1,000 to $10,000

Disclosure Period: 1993

Note: Recent grants are derived from a 1993 Form 990. Number of grants and typical range do not include scholarships to individuals.

RECENT GRANTS

General
15,000	Cape and Island Partnership to Reduce Substance Abuse, Hyannis, MA — helping communities help themselves
10,000	Cape Cod Hospital Foundation, Hyannis, MA — new emergency center
10,000	Friends of Cape Cod National Seashore, MA — establishment of the Joshua A. Nickerson, Sr. Conservation Fund
10,000	Housing Assistance Corporation — NOAH Facilities expansion/renovation
6,000	Big Brothers and Big Sisters of Cape Cod and the Islands, Orleans, MA — continuation and expansion of the position of Research Development Coordinator

Ladd Charitable Corporation, Helen and George

CONTACT
Charles A. Rosebrock
Director
Helen and George Ladd Charitable Corporation
One International Pl.
Boston, MA 02210-2699
(617) 439-2000

FINANCIAL SUMMARY
Recent Giving: $184,310 (fiscal 1993); $201,255 (fiscal 1992); $182,210 (fiscal 1991)

Assets: $4,747,567 (fiscal 1993); $3,569,274 (fiscal 1992); $2,865,368 (fiscal 1991)

Gifts Received: $520,168 (fiscal 1993); $520,188 (fiscal 1992); $516,188 (fiscal 1991)

Fiscal Note: In 1993, contributions were received from George and Helen Ladd.

EIN: 04-2767890

CONTRIBUTIONS SUMMARY

Donor(s): George E. Ladd, Jr. Charitable Trust

Typical Recipients: • *Arts & Humanities:* Community Arts, History & Archaeology, Libraries, Music, Performing Arts, Public Broadcasting, Theater • *Civic & Public Affairs:* African American Affairs, Economic Development, Employment/Job Training, General, Municipalities/Towns, Public Policy, Urban & Community Affairs, Women's Affairs, Zoos/Aquariums • *Education:* Colleges & Universities, Minority Education, Private Education (Precollege) • *Environment:* General, Resource Conservation • *Health:* Arthritis, Hospices, Hospitals, Single-Disease Health Associations • *International:* International Affairs • *Religion:* Churches, Ministries, Religious Welfare • *Social Services:* Big Brother/Big Sister, Child Welfare, Community Centers, Community Service Organizations, Counseling, Domestic Violence, People with Disabilities, United Funds/United Ways, YMCA/YWCA/YMHA/YWHA, Youth Organizations

Grant Types: general support

Geographic Distribution: focus on ME

GIVING OFFICERS

George E. Ladd III: dir *PHIL AFFIL* dir: Lincoln and Therese Filene Foundation

Lincoln F. Ladd: dir *PHIL AFFIL* dir: Lincoln and Therese Filene Foundation

Robert M. Ladd: dir *PHIL AFFIL* dir: Lincoln and Therese Filene Foundation

Charles A. Rosebrock: dir *PHIL AFFIL* treas, secy: Lincoln and Therese Filene Foundation

APPLICATION INFORMATION

Initial Approach: Send brief letter describing program. Include a description of organization, amount requested, purpose of funds sought, recently audited financial statement, and proof of tax-exempt status. There are no deadlines.

GRANTS ANALYSIS

Total Grants: $184,310

Number of Grants: 33

Highest Grant: $45,000

Typical Range: $50 to $41,000

Disclosure Period: fiscal year ending February 1, 1993

Note: Recent grants are derived from a fiscal 1993 Form 990.

RECENT GRANTS

Library

360	Cary Memorial Library, Cary, NC

General

45,000	Skidmore College, Saratoga Springs, NY
41,000	Bates College, Lewiston, ME
37,600	Town of Wayne, Wayne, ME
5,100	YWCA, Auburn, ME
5,000	Rural Community Action Ministry, North Leeds, ME

Levy Foundation, June Rockwell

CONTACT

James W. Noonan
Secretary
June Rockwell Levy Foundation
136 Ridgeway Rd.
Weston, MA 02193
(617) 237-4037

FINANCIAL SUMMARY

Recent Giving: $695,000 (1993); $712,500 (1992); $736,646 (1991)

Assets: $17,789,802 (1993); $17,782,025 (1992); $17,873,158 (1991)

EIN: 04-6074284

CONTRIBUTIONS SUMMARY

Donor(s): The foundation was incorporated in 1947 by the late Austin T. Levy .

Typical Recipients: • *Arts & Humanities:* Libraries, Museums/Galleries, Music, Public Broadcasting, Theater • *Civic & Public Affairs:* African American Affairs, General, Hispanic Affairs, Housing, Municipalities/Towns, Nonprofit Management, Philanthropic Organizations, Urban & Community Affairs, Zoos/Aquariums • *Education:* Arts/Humanities Education, Colleges & Universities, Engineering/Technological Education, Medical Education, Private Education (Precollege), Secondary Education (Private), Secondary Education (Public), Special Education • *Environment:* Air/Water Quality, Resource Conservation • *Health:* Cancer, Children's Health/Hospitals, Emergency/Ambulance Services, Geriatric Health, Health Funds, Health Organizations, Hospices, Hospitals, Medical Research, Nursing Services, Single-Disease Health Associations • *International:* International Affairs, International Organizations, International Relations • *Religion:* Ministries, Religious Organizations • *Science:* Science Museums • *Social Services:* Child Welfare, Community Centers, Community Service Organizations, Family Planning, Family Services, Food/Clothing Distribution, Homes, People with Disabilities, Scouts, Substance Abuse, United Funds/United Ways, Volunteer Services, Youth Organizations

Grant Types: capital, general support, research, scholarship, and seed money

Geographic Distribution: focus on Rhode Island and Massachusetts

GIVING OFFICERS

James K. Edwards: trust

George T. Helm: trust

Jonathan B. Loring: chmn, pres, trust

Raymond N. Menard: trust

James W. Noonan: secy, trust

Edward H. Osgood: trust *B* Wenham MA 1916 *ED* Harvard Univ 1938 *CORP AFFIL* dir: Fiduciary Trust Co

Nancy Smith: treas *B* Meridian MS 1951 *ED* Tulane Univ BFA 1973; Harvard Univ MA 1989 *NONPR AFFIL* chmn adv bd: Boston Writers Rm; dir: Artists Fdn; mem: Counc Advancement & Support Ed, Natl Writers Un Svcs Org, Natl Writers Union, Women Commun

James M. White, Jr.: trust *NONPR AFFIL* asst clerk, dir: NE Health Svs

APPLICATION INFORMATION

Initial Approach:

The foundation requests applications be made in writing.

The application should include any materials the organization feels is necessary.

The foundation has no deadline for submitting proposals.

Restrictions on Giving: The foundation does not make grants for religious purposes or to individuals.

GRANTS ANALYSIS

Total Grants: $695,000

Number of Grants: 94

Highest Grant: $50,000

Average Grant: $7,394

Typical Range: $2,000 to $15,000

Disclosure Period: 1993

Note: Recent grants are derived from a 1993 Form 990.

RECENT GRANTS

Library

15,000	Glocester-Manton Free Public Library, Chepacket, RI
10,000	Cumberland Public Library, Cumberland, RI
6,000	Providence Public Library, Providence, RI

General

50,000	Massachusetts General Hospital, Boston, MA
50,000	Medical Foundation, Boston, MA
40,000	United Way of Southeastern New England, Providence, RI
28,000	Lincoln School, Providence, RI
28,000	Northwest Community Nursing and Health Services, Harmony, RI

Linnell Foundation

CONTACT
Arthur G. Carlson, Jr.
Executive Director
Linnell Fdn.
PO Box 79220
Waverley, MA 02179
(617) 484-1051

FINANCIAL SUMMARY
Recent Giving: $243,700 (1993); $503,730 (1990); $213,770 (1988)

Assets: $1,574,624 (1993); $7,322,838 (1990); $7,386,045 (1988)

EIN: 04-2625173

CONTRIBUTIONS SUMMARY
Typical Recipients: • *Arts & Humanities:* Libraries, Museums/Galleries, Music • *Civic & Public Affairs:* Clubs, Law & Justice, Professional & Trade Associations • *Education:* Colleges & Universities, Private Education (Precollege), Student Aid • *Environment:* General, Wildlife Protection • *Health:* Hospitals, Medical Research, Single-Disease Health Associations • *Social Services:* Animal Protection, People with Disabilities, Substance Abuse, United Funds/United Ways

Grant Types: general support

Geographic Distribution: national, with focus on FL

GIVING OFFICERS
Arthur G. Carlson, Jr.: exec dir

Russell N. Cox: trust

Robert J. Richards: trust

Robert C. Silver: trust

APPLICATION INFORMATION
Initial Approach: Send brief letter of inquiry describing program or project.

GRANTS ANALYSIS
Total Grants: $243,700

Number of Grants: 15

Highest Grant: $205,000

Typical Range: $100 to $25,000

Disclosure Period: 1993

Note: Recent grants are derived from a 1993 Form 990.

RECENT GRANTS

Library
1,000	Boston University Friends of Libraries, Boston, MA
1,000	Friends of Libraries, Boston University, Boston, MA

General
205,000	Criminal Justice Policy Foundation, Waverley, MA
25,000	Drug Policy Foundation, Washington, DC
2,500	Boston University Medical Center Hospital Hematology Fund, Boston, MA
2,500	Dr. Bernard Tolnick Scholarship Fund
1,000	Boca Raton Animal Shelter, Boca Raton, FL

Little, Inc., Arthur D. / Little Foundation, Arthur D.

Revenue: $341.0 million
Employees: 2,400
Headquarters: Cambridge, MA
SIC Major Group: Management Consulting Services and Commercial Physical Research

CONTACT
Ann Farrington
Secretary for the Trustees
Arthur D. Little Fdn.
25 Acorn Pk.
Cambridge, MA 02140
(617) 498-5524

FINANCIAL SUMMARY
Recent Giving: $350,000 (1995 est.); $419,072 (1994 approx.); $368,553 (1993)

Assets: $350,000 (1995 est.); $350,000 (1994 approx.); $110,000 (1993)

Gifts Received: $306,147 (1990); $230,000 (1989); $337,341 (1988)

Fiscal Note: Contributes through foundation only. Above figures exclude nonmonetary support. In 1989 and 1990, contributions were from Arthur D. Little, Inc.

EIN: 04-6079132

CONTRIBUTIONS SUMMARY
Typical Recipients: • *Arts & Humanities:* Arts Associations & Councils, Arts Outreach, Libraries, Museums/Galleries, Music, Performing Arts, Theater • *Civic & Public Affairs:* Economic Development, Employment/Job Training, Housing, Legal Aid, Nonprofit Management, Philanthropic Organizations, Professional & Trade Associations, Urban & Community Affairs, Women's Affairs, Zoos/Aquariums • *Education:* Business Education, Colleges & Universities, Continuing Education, Education Funds, Engineering/Technological Education, Minority Education, Public Education (Precollege), Science/Mathematics Education, Special Education, Student Aid • *Environment:* General • *Health:* Adolescent Health Issues, AIDS/HIV, Hospices, Hospitals, Medical Research, Mental Health • *Science:* Science Exhibits & Fairs, Science Museums, Scientific Centers & Institutes • *Social Services:* Child Welfare, Community Centers, Community Service Organizations, Counseling, Emergency Relief, Family Services, Homes, People with Disabilities, Sexual Abuse, Shelters/Homelessness, United Funds/United Ways, Volunteer Services, Youth Organizations

Grant Types: award, fellowship, general support, multiyear/continuing support, and project

Nonmonetary Support Types: in-kind services

Note: In-kind services are in the form of printing.

Geographic Distribution: primarily in areas of company operations, particularly in home-office community, Cambridge, MA

Operating Locations: CA (Los Angeles, San Francisco, Santa Barbara), DC, MA (Cambridge), NY (New York), PA (Philadelphia), TX (Houston)

CORP. OFFICERS
Judith C. Harris: *CURR EMPL* vp: Arthur D Little Inc

Charles Robert LaMantia: *B* New York NY 1939 *ED* Columbia Univ 1960; Columbia Univ 1965 *CURR EMPL* pres, ceo, dir: Arthur D Little Inc *NONPR AFFIL* mem: Am Inst Chem Engrs, Soc Chem Indus; mem bd govs: New England Med Ctr; mem bd overseers: Mus Sci; mem engg counc: Columbia Univ; overseer: WGBH; trust: Meml Dr Trust

John Francis Magee: *B* Bangor ME 1926 *ED* Bowdoin Coll 1946; Harvard Univ Sch Bus Admin 1948 *CURR EMPL* chmn, dir: Arthur D Little Inc *CORP AFFIL* dir: John Hancock Mutual Life Ins Co, Houghton Mifflin Co

P. Ranganath Nayak: *B* New Delhi India 1942 *ED* Victoria Jubilee Tech Inst Bombay BE 1963; MA Inst Tech PhD 1968 *CURR EMPL* sr vp: Arthur D Little Inc

David C. Shanks: *B* Indianapolis, IN 1939 *ED* Cornell Univ 1962; Univ DE 1968 *CURR EMPL* vp, mng dir: Arthur D Little Inc *CORP AFFIL* dir: Corion Corp; mng: E Air Lines *NONPR AFFIL* dir: Assn Indus MA

GIVING OFFICERS
Ann Farrington: secy

Ann Gillespie: trust

Judith C. Harris: trust *CURR EMPL* vp: Arthur D Little Inc (see above)

Theodore Paul Heuchling: trust *B* Chicago IL 1925 *ED* MA Inst Tech 1946-1948 *CURR EMPL* sr vp: Arthur D Little Inc *CORP AFFIL* sr vp: Arthur D Little Enterprises

P. Ranganath Nayak: trust *CURR EMPL* sr vp: Arthur D Little Inc (see above)

David C. Shanks: trust *CURR EMPL* vp, mng dir: Arthur D Little Inc (see above)

APPLICATION INFORMATION
Initial Approach: *Initial Contact:* written proposal, preliminary inquiry *Include Information On:* operations of organization and a recent balance sheet *Deadlines:* none

Restrictions on Giving: Does not support individuals, religious or political organizations, national health organizations, or events such as dinners, lunches, galas, or marches, or individual scholarships and individual research. Geographic restriction to areas where the company has an office.

PUBLICATIONS
Application guidelines

GRANTS ANALYSIS
Total Grants: $368,553

Number of Grants: 85

Highest Grant: $40,000

Average Grant: $4,336

Typical Range: $1,000 to $5,000

Disclosure Period: 1993

Note: Recent grants are derived from a 1993 grants list.

RECENT GRANTS

General

40,000	United Way of New England, Boston, MA — corporate contribution
30,000	Harvard University Graduate School of Business Administration, Boston, MA
19,650	John F. Kennedy School of Government, Cambridge, MA — full tuition scholarship for Cambridge city employees to attend Mid-Career Master in Public Education program
10,000	Massachusetts Corporation for Educational Telecommunications, Cambridge, MA — support for pilot program, FirstMath
10,000	Mount Auburn Foundation, Cambridge, MA — Campaign 2000

M/A-COM, Inc. / M/A-COM Foundation

Sales: $250.0 million
Employees: 3,500
Headquarters: Wakefield, MA
SIC Major Group: Electrical Equipment & Supplies Nec and Electronic Components Nec

CONTACT
Victoria Dillon
Corporate Communications
M/A-COM, Inc.
100 Chelmsford St.
Lowell, MA 01851
(508) 442-5000

FINANCIAL SUMMARY
Recent Giving: $208,540 (fiscal 1993); $216,994 (fiscal 1992); $323,785 (fiscal 1991)

Assets: $21,642 (fiscal 1993); $57 (fiscal 1992); $65,457 (fiscal 1991)

Gifts Received: $230,000 (fiscal 1993); $152,290 (fiscal 1992); $100,000 (fiscal 1991)

Fiscal Note: Contributes through foundation only. In fiscal 1993, contributions were received from M/A-COM, Inc.

EIN: 04-6169568

CONTRIBUTIONS SUMMARY
Typical Recipients: • *Arts & Humanities:* Ballet, Libraries, Museums/Galleries, Music, Performing Arts, Public Broadcasting, Theater • *Civic & Public Affairs:* African American Affairs, Economic Development, General, Safety, Urban & Community Affairs • *Education:* Colleges & Universities, Education Funds, Engineering/Technological Education, Legal Education, Minority Education, Private Education (Precollege), Religious Education, Secondary Education (Public), Student Aid • *Health:* AIDS/HIV, Arthritis, Cancer, Health Organizations, Hospitals, Single-Disease Health Associations • *Religion:* Seminaries • *Science:* Science Museums • *Social Services:* Camps, Child Welfare, Community Service Organizations, Family Services, United Funds/United Ways, Youth Organizations

Grant Types: employee matching gifts, general support, and scholarship

Note: Scholarships are awarded to children of employees only. Employee matching gift ratio: 1 to 1.

Geographic Distribution: primarily in Massachusetts

Operating Locations: CA (San Diego, Torrance), MA (Amesbury, Burlington, Wakefield, Waltham), MD (Hunt Valley)

Note: Twelve different company names are listed as a division of either M/A-COM Inc. or Adams-Russell Inc.

CORP. OFFICERS
Allan Laverne Rayfield: *B* Mobile AL 1935 *ED* PA St Univ BSCE 1959; Rensselaer Polytech Inst MBA 1965; Harvard Univ Adv Mgmt Program 1976 *CURR EMPL* pres, ceo, dir: M/A-COM Inc *CORP AFFIL* pres, dir: M/A-COM Omni Spectra Inc *NONPR AFFIL* mem: Chi Epsilon, Tau Beta Pi *CLUB AFFIL* Peugot YC

Thomas Aquinas Vanderslice: *B* Philadelphia PA 1932 *ED* Boston Coll BS 1953; Catholic Univ Am PhD 1956 *CURR EMPL* chmn: M/A-COM Inc *CORP AFFIL* dir: Bank Boston Corp, Computer Consoles, Texaco Inc *NONPR AFFIL* mem: Alpha Sigma Nu, Am Chem Soc, Am Inst Physics, Am Soc Testing & Materials, Am Vacuum Soc, Natl Acad Engg, Sigma Pi Sigma, Sigma Xi, Tau Beta Pi; trust: Boston Coll, Comm Econ Devel *CLUB AFFIL* Oyster Harbors, Patterson, Royal Poinciana GC, St Andrews GC

GIVING OFFICERS
Ralph V. G. Bakkensen: asst secy

John Kermit Birchfield, Jr.: secy, trust *B* Roanoke VA 1940 *ED* Roanoke Coll BS 1968; Univ VA JD 1971 *CURR EMPL* mng dir: Century Ptnrs *CORP AFFIL* clerk, dir: M/A-COM Omni Spectra Inc; dir: HPSC Inc, Intermountain Gas Indus, WSHCB Properties; sr vp, gen couns, corp secy: M/A-COM Inc *NONPR AFFIL* chmn collections comm: Cape Ann Historic Assn; dir: Atlanta Music Festival Assn, Emory Univ Mus Art Archaeology; mem: Am Arbitration Assn, Am Bar Assn, Am Law Inst, Assn Bar City New York, Atlanta Bar Assn, NY Bar Assn; trust: Chatham Hall Sch, Roanoke Coll *CLUB AFFIL* Annisquaim YC, Carlton London, Farmington CC, India House, Piedmont Driving, Racquet & Tennis, Roanoke CC, Union Boat

Victoria Dillon: trust

Robert H. Glaudel: trust

Philip A. Orlando: asst vp taxation

Stephen P. Zezima: vp taxation

APPLICATION INFORMATION
Initial Approach: *Initial Contact:* a brief letter of inquiry *Include Information On:* a description of organization, amount requested, and purpose of funds sought *Deadlines:* none

Restrictions on Giving: Does not support individuals, religious organizations for sectarian purposes, or political or lobbying groups.

GRANTS ANALYSIS
Total Grants: $208,540

Number of Grants: 75*

Highest Grant: $11,500

Average Grant: $2,341*

Typical Range: $500 to $3,500

Disclosure Period: fiscal year ending October 2, 1993

Note: Number of grants and average grant figures exclude scholarships to individuals totaling $33,000. Recent grants are derived from a fiscal 1993 Form 990.

RECENT GRANTS

Library

10,000	Boston Public Library Foundation, Boston, MA

General

11,350	Rensselaer Polytechnic Institute, Troy, NY
10,000	Boston College, Boston, MA
10,000	Concord Coalition, Washington, DC
10,000	Greater Boston One to One, Boston, MA
10,000	Immaculate Conception Seminary

Massachusetts Mutual Life Insurance Co.

Revenue: $5.33 billion
Employees: 3,959
Headquarters: Springfield, MA
SIC Major Group: Life Insurance and Accident & Health Insurance

CONTACT
Ronald A. Copes
Second Vice President
Massachusetts Mutual Life Insurance Co.
1295 State St.
Springfield, MA 01111
(413) 788-8411

FINANCIAL SUMMARY
Recent Giving: $1,466,496 (1994); $1,371,033 (1993); $1,306,846 (1992)

Fiscal Note: Above figures exclude non-monetary support.

CONTRIBUTIONS SUMMARY
Typical Recipients: • *Arts & Humanities:* General, Libraries, Museums/Galleries, Music, Public Broadcasting, Theater • *Civic & Public Affairs:* General • *Education:* Colleges & Universities, Community & Junior Colleges, Education Funds, Public Educa-

tion (Precollege) • *Health:* Medical Research • *Social Services:* At-Risk Youth

Grant Types: capital, challenge, emergency, employee matching gifts, general support, multiyear/continuing support, operating expenses, and project

Note: Employee matching gift ratio: 1 to 1, up to $750 (1993) and up to $1,500 (1993, for director's only).

Nonmonetary Support: $25,532 (1993)

Nonmonetary Support Types: donated equipment, in-kind services, and loaned employees

Note: In 1993, the company provided $17,323 in donated equipment and $8,209 in in-kind printing. The contact for nonmonetary support is Annette Holmes, Community Affairs Specialist.

Geographic Distribution: only in headquarters area

Operating Locations: MA (Springfield)

Note: In support of business objectives, company will sometimes, though rarely, provide contributions outside of its immediate operating area.

CORP. OFFICERS

William J. Clark: *B* Kansas City MO 1923 *ED* Univ MO BS 1947 *CURR EMPL* chmn: MA Mutual Life Ins Co *NONPR AFFIL* dir: Springfield Coll; mem: Am Soc Chartered Life Underwriters, Life Ins Assn MA, Life Ins Mktg & Res Assn *CLUB AFFIL* Audubon CC, Colony, Long Meadow CC *PHIL AFFIL* dir: I Have A Dream Foundation - Springfield, MA

Gary Edward Wendlandt: *B* Milwaukee WI 1950 *ED* WA Univ BS 1972 *CURR EMPL* exec vp, chief investment off: MA Mutual Life Ins Co *CORP AFFIL* dir: Concert Capital Mgmt, Merrill Lynch Derivatives Products Inc, Oppenheimer Mgmt Corp; pres, dir: MassMutual Holding Co; pres, trust: MassMutual Corp Investors Inc, MassMutual Participation Investors

Thomas B. Wheeler: *B* Buffalo NY 1936 *ED* Yale Univ BA 1958 *CURR EMPL* pres, ceo, dir: MA Mutual Life Ins Co *CORP AFFIL* chmn: Concert Capital Mgmt, Oppenheimer Acquisition Corp; dir: Bank Boston Corp, Textron Inc *NONPR AFFIL* chmn: MA Bus Roundtable; mem: Am Soc CLUs, Boston Underwriters Assn, Health Ins Assn Am, MA Assn Life Underwriters, Million Dollar Round Table, Springfield Life Underwriters Assn, Yale Univ Devel Bd; st chmn: US Olympic Comm; trust: Basketball Hall Fame, Springfield Coll, Springfield Orchestral Assn *CLUB AFFIL* Boca Grande, Chapoquoit Yacht, Colony, Links, Long Meadow CC, Yale

GIVING OFFICERS

Ronald A. Copes: *CURR EMPL* second vp: MA Mutual Life Ins Co

APPLICATION INFORMATION

Initial Approach: *Initial Contact:* written request for copy of application and contribution guidelines *Include Information On:* pertinent organizational data, including name, address, phone number, date of incorpora-

tion, fiscal year, geographic area served, and number of staff and volunteers (identifying MassMutual employees by name); concise description of the organization's mission; description of the program for which funding is requested, including the program budget; specific criteria to be used for measuring success of the program; list of other corporate and foundation sources approached for funding, noting commitments to date; current listing of officers and board of directors, with their professional affiliations; copy of the organization's most recent audited financial statement and annual report; and copy of IRS 501(c)(3) tax-exemption letter *Deadlines:* all properly documented requests within program guidelines must be received by the last day of the month to be given consideration for the next scheduled meeting *Note:* All requests for contributions must be submitted on a MassMutual application form.

Restrictions on Giving: Does not support individuals, religious organizations for sectarian purposes, political or lobbying groups, or organizations outside operating areas. Also does not support fund-raising activities for operating costs and ancillary expenses or deficit reduction campaigns.

OTHER THINGS TO KNOW

Those organizations which receive support are required to provide a status report of the program funded at the end of the grant period, usually within six months of funding. A MassMutual report form will be provided for this purpose when the grant is awarded. Any future support will be contingent on MassMutual's receipt of this information in a timely manner.

PUBLICATIONS

Social Report

GRANTS ANALYSIS

Total Grants: $1,466,496

Typical Range: $1,000 to $2,500

Disclosure Period: 1994

RECENT GRANTS

General
5A Sports Program, Springfield, MA
Baystate Health Systems, Springfield, MA
College of Our Lady of the Elms, Chicopee, MA
Community Foundation of Western Massachusetts, Springfield, MA
Junior Achievement, Springfield, MA

McEvoy Foundation, Mildred H.

CONTACT
Sumner B. Tilton, Jr.
Trustee
Mildred H. McEvoy Foundation
370 Main St., 11th Fl.
Worcester, MA 01608
(508) 798-8621

FINANCIAL SUMMARY

Recent Giving: $1,177,250 (1993); $1,031,250 (1992); $1,110,680 (1991)

Assets: $23,112,121 (1993); $23,412,740 (1992); $24,269,865 (1991)

EIN: 04-6069958

CONTRIBUTIONS SUMMARY

Donor(s): The foundation was established in 1963 by the late Mildred H. McEvoy .

Typical Recipients: • *Arts & Humanities:* Arts Appreciation, Arts Associations & Councils, Ethnic & Folk Arts, Historic Preservation, History & Archaeology, Libraries, Museums/Galleries, Music, Performing Arts, Public Broadcasting • *Civic & Public Affairs:* Botanical Gardens/Parks, Clubs, Community Foundations, Economic Development, General • *Education:* Colleges & Universities, Community & Junior Colleges, Engineering/Technological Education, Private Education (Precollege), Public Education (Precollege), Science/Mathematics Education, Student Aid • *Environment:* General • *Health:* Cancer, Children's Health/Hospitals, Clinics/Medical Centers, Emergency/Ambulance Services, Hospitals, Medical Research, Single-Disease Health Associations • *International:* Foreign Arts Organizations • *Religion:* Churches, Religious Organizations, Religious Welfare • *Science:* Science Museums, Scientific Centers & Institutes, Scientific Research • *Social Services:* Big Brother/Big Sister, Child Welfare, Community Centers, Community Service Organizations, Family Planning, Family Services, Senior Services, Substance Abuse, United Funds/United Ways, YMCA/YWCA/YMHA/YWHA, Youth Organizations

Grant Types: general support

Geographic Distribution: focus on Worcester, MA, and Boothbay Harbor, ME

GIVING OFFICERS

George H. McEvoy: trust

Paul Robert Rossley: trust *B* Worcester MA 1938 *ED* Clark Univ BSBA 1960 *CURR EMPL* State Mutual Life Assurance Co Am *CORP AFFIL* trust: Leicester Savings Bank

Sumner B. Tilton, Jr.: trust *CURR EMPL* jr, clerk: New England Newspaper Supply Co *CORP AFFIL* clerk: R H White Co, R H White Construction Co, Whiteater Inc, Whitinsville Water Co *NONPR AFFIL* pres: Greater Worcester Commmun Fdn *PHIL AFFIL* trust: Ruth H. and Warren A. Ellsworth Foundation, Francis A. and Jacquelyn H. Harrington Foundation

APPLICATION INFORMATION
Initial Approach:

The foundation requests applications be made in writing.

Written applications should include a copy of the organization's federal determination letter.

The foundation reports requests received by July 1 are acted on for December payments.

Restrictions on Giving: The foundation reports applicants must qualify for the federal cumulative list. The foundation does not make grants to individuals or for endowment funds.

GRANTS ANALYSIS
Total Grants: $1,177,250
Number of Grants: 58
Highest Grant: $300,000
Average Grant: $20,297
Typical Range: $5,000 to $37,500
Disclosure Period: 1993

Note: Recent grants are derived from a 1993 Form 990.

RECENT GRANTS

Library
5,000	Clark University, Worcester, MA — library cataloging project

General
50,000	Assumption College, Worcester, MA — pledge over four years toward the construction of a student recreation facility
50,000	Clark University, Worcester, MA — pledge over four years to Robert H. Wetzel Memorial Scholarship Fund
50,000	Worcester Foundation for Experimental Biology, Shrewsbury, MA — to assist with the recruitment of new scientists
50,000	YMCA of Boothbay Region, Boothbay Harbor, ME — capital fund
30,000	Congregational Church of Boothbay Harbor, Boothbay Harbor, ME — four-year pledge for renovations

Memorial Foundation for the Blind

Former Foundation Name: Memorial Homes for the Blind

CONTACT
Alice Taylor
President
Memorial Fdn for the Blind
51 Harvard St.
Worcester, MA 01609
(508) 791-8237

FINANCIAL SUMMARY
Recent Giving: $176,909 (fiscal 1992); $181,760 (fiscal 1991); $209,268 (fiscal 1990)
Assets: $2,888,358 (fiscal 1992); $2,836,637 (fiscal 1991); $2,814,826 (fiscal 1990)
Gifts Received: $20 (fiscal 1992); $2,030 (fiscal 1991)
EIN: 04-1611615

CONTRIBUTIONS SUMMARY
Typical Recipients: • *Arts & Humanities:* Libraries, Public Broadcasting • *Education:*

Colleges & Universities, Special Education • *Health:* Health Organizations, Hospitals, Single-Disease Health Associations • *Social Services:* People with Disabilities

Grant Types: general support
Geographic Distribution: focus on the Worcester, MA, area

GIVING OFFICERS
Stephanie Burnett: dir, treas
Elizabeth C. Congdon: trust
Gilbert S. Davis: dir, vp
Sharon Davis: vp
Carolyn Dik: trust
Alice Taylor: dir, pres

APPLICATION INFORMATION
Initial Approach: Send brief letter of inquiry describing program. There are no deadlines.

GRANTS ANALYSIS
Total Grants: $176,909
Number of Grants: 8
Highest Grant: $79,583
Typical Range: $3,000 to $20,000
Disclosure Period: fiscal year ending March 31, 1992

Note: Recent grants are derived from a fiscal 1992 Form 990.

RECENT GRANTS

Library
28,000	Talking Book Library, Worcester, MA

General
79,583	Massachusetts Association for the Blind, Worcester, MA
16,500	University of Massachusetts Medical Center, Worcester, MA
9,950	Deaf Blind Contract Center, Worcester, MA
3,750	Paski's Out on the Town, Worcester, MA
761	Memorial Hospital, Worcester, MA — Kidney Dialysis Unit

Morgan Construction Co. / Morgan-Worcester, Inc.

Sales: $75.0 million
Employees: 500
Headquarters: Worcester, MA
SIC Major Group: Industrial Machinery & Equipment

CONTACT
Gail M. Wilcox
Secretary, Treasurer
Morgan-Worcester, Inc.
15 Belmont St.
Worcester, MA 01605
(508) 849-6259

FINANCIAL SUMMARY
Recent Giving: $180,527 (fiscal 1993); $156,650 (fiscal 1992); $134,542 (fiscal 1991)

Assets: $861,108 (fiscal 1993); $785,794 (fiscal 1992); $728,310 (fiscal 1991)
Gifts Received: $200,000 (fiscal 1993); $150,000 (fiscal 1992); $160,000 (fiscal 1991)
Fiscal Note: In fiscal 1993, contributions were received from Morgan Construction Co.
EIN: 04-6111693

CONTRIBUTIONS SUMMARY
Typical Recipients: • *Arts & Humanities:* Arts Centers, Arts Institutes, Community Arts, Historic Preservation, History & Archaeology, Libraries, Museums/Galleries, Music, Performing Arts, Public Broadcasting, Theater • *Civic & Public Affairs:* Clubs, General, Urban & Community Affairs, Zoos/Aquariums • *Education:* Colleges & Universities, Education Funds, Engineering/Technological Education, Private Education (Precollege), Student Aid • *Environment:* Resource Conservation, Watershed • *Health:* Clinics/Medical Centers, Emergency/Ambulance Services, Medical Research • *International:* Foreign Arts Organizations • *Religion:* Religious Welfare • *Science:* Scientific Centers & Institutes • *Social Services:* Community Service Organizations, Family Planning, Substance Abuse, United Funds/United Ways, YMCA/YWCA/YMHA/YWHA, Youth Organizations

Grant Types: employee matching gifts and general support
Geographic Distribution: focus on Worcester, MA
Operating Locations: MA (Worcester)

CORP. OFFICERS
Paul S. Morgan: *CURR EMPL* chmn, dir: Morgan Construction Co
Philip R. Morgan: *CURR EMPL* pres, dir: Morgan Construction

GIVING OFFICERS
Daniel M. Morgan: dir
Paul B. Morgan, Jr.: dir
Paul S. Morgan: pres *CURR EMPL* chmn, dir: Morgan Construction Co (see above)
Peter S. Morgan: dir
Philip R. Morgan: dir *CURR EMPL* pres, dir: Morgan Construction (see above)
Gail M. Wilcox: secy, treas *CURR EMPL* secy: Morgan Construction Co

APPLICATION INFORMATION
Initial Approach: Send brief letter describing program. There are no deadlines.
Restrictions on Giving: Limited to Worcester County, MA.

GRANTS ANALYSIS
Total Grants: $180,527
Number of Grants: 135
Highest Grant: $70,000
Typical Range: $2,100 to $12,538
Disclosure Period: fiscal year ending September 30, 1993

Note: Provides employee matching gifts. Recent grants are derived from a fiscal 1993 Form 990.

RECENT GRANTS

Library
1,000	Notre Dame Library, Notre Dame, IN

General
70,000	United Way, Worcester, MA
5,100	Friendly House, Worcester, MA
5,000	Letters of Intent Higgins Armory, Worcester, MA
5,000	Planned Parenthood, Worcester, MA
5,000	Worcester County Horticultural Society, Boylston, MA

New England Business Service / NEBS Foundation

Sales: $237.14 million
Employees: 2,045
Headquarters: Groton, MA
SIC Major Group: Printing & Publishing

CONTACT

John Fairbanks
Treasurer, Secretary
New England Business Service
500 Main St.
Groton, MA 01450
(508) 448-6111

FINANCIAL SUMMARY

Recent Giving: $84,000 (fiscal 1993); $123,600 (fiscal 1992)

Assets: $18,001 (fiscal 1993); $79,616 (fiscal 1992)

Gifts Received: $25,000 (fiscal 1993)

Fiscal Note: Company gives directly and through a foundation. Figures above represent foundation giving only. Direct giving is between $450,000 and $550,000 annually. In fiscal 1993, contributions were received from New England Business Service.

EIN: 04-2772172

CONTRIBUTIONS SUMMARY

Typical Recipients: • *Arts & Humanities:* Community Arts, Libraries, Music, Performing Arts • *Civic & Public Affairs:* Employment/Job Training, Zoos/Aquariums • *Education:* Colleges & Universities, Community & Junior Colleges, Education Funds, Private Education (Precollege), Public Education (Precollege) • *Environment:* Air/Water Quality, Watershed • *Health:* Hospitals • *Science:* Observatories & Planetariums • *Social Services:* Community Centers, Community Service Organizations, United Funds/United Ways

Grant Types: capital, employee matching gifts, general support, and operating expenses

Geographic Distribution: in headquarters and operating communities only

Operating Locations: AZ (Flagstaff), MA (Groton), MO (Maryville), NH (Peterborough), WI (Madison)

CORP. OFFICERS

William C. Lowe: *CURR EMPL* pres, ceo, dir: New England Bus Svc

Richard H. Rhoads: *CURR EMPL* chmn, dir: New England Bus Svc

GIVING OFFICERS

Peter A. Brook: dir

Benjamin H. Lacy: treas, dir *PHIL AFFIL* pres, dir: Clipper Ship Foundation

Jay R. Rhoads, Jr.: pres, dir *PHIL AFFIL* pres: Birch Cove Foundation

APPLICATION INFORMATION

Initial Approach: Send a brief letter of inquiry and a full proposal. Include a description of organization, amount requested, purpose of funds sought, recently audited financial statement, and proof of tax-exempt status. Foundation's board mets in April and October. Deadlines for applying are March 31 and September 30.

Restrictions on Giving: Does not support individuals, religious organizations for sectarian purposes, political or lobbying groups, or organizations outside operating areas.

GRANTS ANALYSIS

Total Grants: $84,000

Number of Grants: 12

Highest Grant: $17,500

Typical Range: $2,500 to $12,500

Disclosure Period: fiscal year ending August 31, 1993

Note: Recent grants are derived from a fiscal 1993 Form 990.

RECENT GRANTS

General
17,500	United Fund of North Central, MA
17,500	United Fund of North Central Massachusetts, MA
12,500	Nashoba Community Hospital, Nashoba, MA
12,500	Nashoba Community Hospital, MA
10,000	Jobs for Youth, Boston, MA

Norton Co. / Norton Co. Foundation

Revenue: $1.53 billion
Employees: 16,800
Parent Company: Compagnie de Saint-Gobain
Headquarters: Worcester, MA
SIC Major Group: Abrasive Products, Oil & Gas Field Services Nec, Industrial Inorganic Chemicals Nec, and Plastics Products Nec

CONTACT

Judi Cutts
Contributions Coordinator
Norton Co. Fdn.
1 New Bond St.
PO Box 15008
Worcester, MA 01615-0008
(508) 795-2605

FINANCIAL SUMMARY

Recent Giving: $1,091,201 (1994); $1,200,000 (1993 approx.); $1,167,867 (1992)

Assets: $0 (1993); $0 (1992); $120 (1991)

Gifts Received: $1,091,201 (1993); $1,180,193 (1992)

Fiscal Note: Company gives primarily through its foundation. Above figures exclude nonmonetary support.

EIN: 23-7423043

CONTRIBUTIONS SUMMARY

Typical Recipients: • *Arts & Humanities:* Arts Appreciation, Arts Associations & Councils, Arts Centers, Arts Funds, Community Arts, Dance, Ethnic & Folk Arts, Historic Preservation, Libraries, Literary Arts, Museums/Galleries, Music, Opera, Performing Arts, Public Broadcasting, Theater, Visual Arts • *Civic & Public Affairs:* Business/Free Enterprise, Civil Rights, Clubs, Community Foundations, Economic Development, Economic Policy, Employment/Job Training, Hispanic Affairs, Minority Business, Municipalities/Towns, Nonprofit Management, Parades/Festivals, Professional & Trade Associations, Public Policy, Rural Affairs, Safety, Urban & Community Affairs, Women's Affairs, Zoos/Aquariums • *Education:* Arts/Humanities Education, Business Education, Colleges & Universities, Community & Junior Colleges, Economic Education, Education Associations, Education Funds, Education Reform, Engineering/Technological Education, Faculty Development, Health & Physical Education, Literacy, Preschool Education, Private Education (Precollege), Public Education (Precollege), Science/Mathematics Education, Secondary Education (Public); Student Aid • *Environment:* General • *Health:* AIDS/HIV, Cancer, Children's Health/Hospitals, Clinics/Medical Centers, Emergency/Ambulance Services, Geriatric Health, Health Policy/Cost Containment, Health Organizations, Hospices, Hospitals, Medical Rehabilitation, Medical Research, Mental Health, Nursing Services, Nutrition, Public Health • *International:* International Organizations • *Religion:* Churches, Religious Welfare • *Science:* Observatories & Planetariums, Science Exhibits & Fairs, Scientific Centers & Institutes, Scientific Organizations • *Social Services:* Camps, Child Welfare, Community Centers, Community Service Organizations, Counseling, Delinquency & Criminal Rehabilitation, Domestic Violence, Emergency Relief, Family Planning, Family Services, General, Homes, People with Disabilities, Recreation & Athletics, Scouts, Senior Services, Sexual Abuse, Shelters/Homelessness, Substance Abuse, United Funds/United Ways, Volunteer Services, YMCA/YWCA/YMHA/YWHA, Youth Organizations

Grant Types: employee matching gifts, general support, and project

Nonmonetary Support: $10,500 (1988)

Nonmonetary Support Types: donated equipment, donated products, and in-kind services

Note: Nonmonetary support is supplied primarily through the foundation. Contact for this support is listed above.

Geographic Distribution: communities where Norton Co. maintains facilities

Operating Locations: AK (Hot Springs), AL (Huntsville), CA (Fullerton), CT (Bloomfield, East Granby), GA (Gainesville), IL (Elk Grove), MA (Northampton, Northboro, Worcester), MI (Warren), NC (Arden, Greensboro), NH (Hillsboro, Littleton, Milford), NJ (Wayne), NY (Granville, Niagara Falls, Troy), OH (Akron, Ravenna, Stow, Tallmadge), PA (Latrobe), TN (Daisy), TX (Brownsville, Bryan, Dallas, Stephenville)

CORP. OFFICERS

Robert C. Ayotte: *B* 1939 *ED* Univ RI BS 1959; Harvard Univ Sch Bus Admin PhD *CURR EMPL* chmn, dir: Corhart Refractories Corp *CORP AFFIL* chmn: Norton Chem Process Products Corp; pres, dir: St-Gobain Advanced Metals Corp, St-Gobain/Norton Indus

Michel Louis Besson: *B* Nancy France 1934 *ED* Ecole Centrale des Arts et Manufactures 1959; MA Inst Tech MS 1960 *CURR EMPL* vchmn, pres, ceo, dir: CertainTeed Corp *CORP AFFIL* chmn, pres, ceo: Norton Co; dir: St-Gobain Corp, World Aff Couns *NONPR AFFIL* bus ptnr: Am Acad Fine Arts, PA Acad Fine Arts; corp ptnr: Philadelphia Mus Art; dir: Greater Philadelphia Intl Network, St Josephs Univ, Urban Aff Partnership; French Foreign trade adv: Comite Natl des Conseillers du Commerce Exterieur; mem: French-Am Chamber Commerce US, Greater Philadelphia Chamber Commerce, Philadelphia Comm Foreign Rels, World Aff Counc; trust: Acad Natural Sci, Inst Intl Ed *CLUB AFFIL* Links, Sunday Breakfast, Union League, Worcester *PHIL AFFIL* pres, dir: CertainTeed Corp. Foundation

Thomas Andrew Decker: *B* Philadelphia PA 1946 *ED* Univ PA BA 1968; Univ VA JD 1971 *CURR EMPL* exec vp, secy, gen couns: CertainTeed Corp *CORP AFFIL* exec vp, secy, gen couns: Norton Co, St-Gobain Corp *NONPR AFFIL* dir: Am Bar Assn; mem: Am Corp Couns Assn *PHIL AFFIL* vp: CertainTeed Corp. Foundation

Michael J. Walsh: *B* Portland OR 1932 *ED* Georgetown Univ JD; Univ Portland BA *CURR EMPL* treas: Norton Co *CORP AFFIL* treas: Norton Co *NONPR AFFIL* chmn: Employees Compensation Appeals Bd; mem: Am Arbitration Assn, Am Bar Assn, Am Judicature Soc, Am Trial Lawyers Assn, DC Bar Assn, Multnomah County Bar Assn, Natl Assn Coll & Univ Attys, OR Bar Assn, Portland Chamber Commerce *PHIL AFFIL* treas: CertainTeed Corp. Foundation

GIVING OFFICERS

Robert C. Ayotte: vp, dir *CURR EMPL* chmn, dir: Corhart Refractories Corp (see above)

Dennis J. Baker: vp, dir

Michel Louis Besson: pres, ceo, dir *CURR EMPL* vchmn, pres, ceo, dir: CertainTeed Corp *PHIL AFFIL* pres, dir: CertainTeed Corp. Foundation (see above)

Peter Richard Dachowski: vp, dir *B* Hillingdon, Middlesex England *ED* Queens Coll MA 1969; Univ Chicago MBA 1971 *CURR EMPL* exec vp: CertainTeed Corp *CORP AFFIL* chmn: Air Vent Inc, Ludowici - Celadon; dir: Mexalit SA *NONPR AFFIL* mem: Beta Gamma Sigma, British-Am Chamber Commerce, Univ Grad Sch Bus Alumni Assn, Young Pres Org *CLUB AFFIL* Univ

Thomas Andrew Decker: vp, dir *CURR EMPL* exec vp, secy, gen couns: CertainTeed Corp *PHIL AFFIL* vp: CertainTeed Corp. Foundation (see above)

Lee Faust: vp

James F. Harkins, Jr.: asst treas *PHIL AFFIL* asst treas: CertainTeed Corp. Foundation

Donald Scott Huml: vp fin, dir *B* Lake Geneva WI 1946 *ED* Marquette Univ BBA 1969; Temple Univ MBA 1980 *CURR EMPL* vp, cfo: CertainTeed Corp *CORP AFFIL* dir: Air Vent Inc, Cameron Ashley Inc; treasury mgr: Allis-Chalmers Corp *NONPR AFFIL* mem: Am Mgmt Assn, Beta Gamma Sigma, Conf Bd, Fin Execs Inst *PHIL AFFIL* vp, dir: CertainTeed Corp. Foundation

Thomas Milton Landin: vp *B* Bradford PA 1937 *ED* Grove City Coll BS 1959; Univ Denver JD 1967 *NONPR AFFIL* dir: Am Music Theatre Festival, Citizens Crime Commn, Mfrs Assn DE Valley, Pub Aff Counc, YMCA Greater Philadelphia; mem: Am Bar Assn, DC Bar Assn; trust: Caribbean/Latin Am Action *CLUB AFFIL* Army & Navy, Capitol Hill, Georgetown, Union League Philadelphia, Vesper

John R. Mesher: asst secy *PHIL AFFIL* asst secy: CertainTeed Corp. Foundation

Curtis M. Pontz: asst secy *PHIL AFFIL* asst secy: CertainTeed Corp. Foundation

Dorothy C. Wackerman: secy, clerk, dir *PHIL AFFIL* vp, dir: CertainTeed Corp. Foundation

Michael J. Walsh: treas, dir *CURR EMPL* treas: Norton Co *PHIL AFFIL* treas: CertainTeed Corp. Foundation (see above)

APPLICATION INFORMATION

Initial Approach: *Initial Contact:* submit brief description of organization and a description of the request, including evidence of the need to be met; the implementation plan; and the appropriateness of your request to the Norton Company Foundation. *Include Information On:* the specific amount requested, the timeline of the project, and a list of other sources of support. Also submit a copy of the IRS letter indicating 501(c)(3) tax exemption, a brief description of current operating budget for the requested project, a copy of IRS form 990, and a list of current corporate and foundation grants. And, send a list of the organization's board of directors and their affiliations. *Deadlines:* none; applications are accepted throughout the year

Restrictions on Giving: Support is ordinarily restricted to communities where Norton has plant facilities and to programs that demonstrate ability to have a significant impact on the need being addressed over a significant period of time.

Foundation does not make contributions to individuals; political candidates; national organizations (including health agencies); a single sectarian or denominational religious, veteran, or fraternal organization (unless for a specific project that benefits the community); fund-raising dinners and events, or courtesy or journal advertising for nonprofit groups (unless there is a direct community relations benefit to Norton Company); large hospitals; capital/endowment drive unless an institution makes extraordinary contributions to Norton communities or to Norton Company; to any project for which Norton is the only donor; or programs receiving United Way support in locations where Norton makes an annual contribution to the United Way.

OTHER THINGS TO KNOW

Each Norton location has a contributions budget and annually identifies one or two priorities in that community for special emphasis. You may approach local operations for contributions. Their priorities vary and may not be reflected in information listed above.

GRANTS ANALYSIS

Total Grants: $576,175

Number of Grants: 318*

Highest Grant: $240,000

Average Grant: $989*

Typical Range: $100 to $5,000

Disclosure Period: 1993

Note: The figures for number of grants and average grant exclude $261,705 in matching gifts. Recent grants are derived from a 1993 Form 990.

RECENT GRANTS

Library
5,000	Brownsville Public Library Foundation, Brownsville, TX
2,450	Ohio Library Foundation, Columbus, OH

General
240,000	United Way of Central Massachusetts, Worcester, MA
30,000	Clark University, Worcester, MA
25,000	City of Worcester, Worcester, MA — South High School
20,000	United Way of Northeastern New York, Albany, NY
10,000	American Ceramic Society, Westerville, OH

Peabody Charitable Fund, Amelia

CONTACT
JoAnne Borek
Executive Director
Amelia Peabody Charitable Fund
201 Devonshire St.
Boston, MA 02110
(617) 451-6178

FINANCIAL SUMMARY
Recent Giving: $4,650,000 (1994 approx.);
$4,686,264 (1992); $4,281,273 (1991)

Assets: $105,000,000 (1995 est.);
$102,000,000 (1993 approx.); $103,558,771
(1992)

Gifts Received: $4,960,188 (1991);
$10,846,654 (1988)

Fiscal Note: In 1988, the fund received a
contribution of $10,846,654 from the estate
of Amelia Peabody. In 1991, the fund received $2,503,885 from the estate of Amelia
Peabody and $2,456,303 from the Frank E.
Peabody Trust.

EIN: 23-7364949

CONTRIBUTIONS SUMMARY
Donor(s): The Amelia Peabody Charitable
Fund was established in 1974 in Massachusetts. In 1985, the fund absorbed a share of
the assets of the Eaton Foundation, also
based in Massachusetts.

Typical Recipients: • *Arts & Humanities:*
Ballet, Historic Preservation, Libraries, Mu-
seums/Galleries, Music, Theater • *Civic &
Public Affairs:* Botanical Gardens/Parks,
General, Housing, Women's Affairs,
Zoos/Aquariums • *Education:* Colleges &
Universities, Education Associations, Engi-
neering/Technological Education, Minority
Education, Private Education (Precollege),
Science/Mathematics Education, Special
Education • *Environment:* General, Re-
source Conservation • *Health:* Children's
Health/Hospitals, Clinics/Medical Centers,
Heart, Hospitals, Nursing Services, Single-
Disease Health Associations • *Religion:*
Churches • *Social Services:* At-Risk Youth,
Child Welfare, Community Service Organi-
zations, Family Planning, People with Dis-
abilities, Shelters/Homelessness, Youth
Organizations

Grant Types: capital and endowment

Geographic Distribution: usually New England and largely greater Boston area

GIVING OFFICERS
JoAnne Borek: exec dir

Richard Leahy: trust

J. Elisabeth Rice: trust

Patricia E. Rice: trust

APPLICATION INFORMATION
Initial Approach:

Applicants should request guidelines from
the foundation.

Proposals should be made by letter. The letter should explain the nature of the nonprofit operation, and must include a copy of
the IRS exemption letter. Include figures indicating the amount of the budget spent on
overhead and the amount for programs, financial statements for the last fiscal year,
and a list of directors/trustees. Also, proposals should identify applications pending
with other foundations and any commitments resulting.

February 1, June 1, and October 1 are proposal deadlines. Proposals for summer program funding must be submitted by the
February deadline.

The officers meet as necessary to review proposals. In general, the final decision meetings take place in early April, early August,
and early December. Requests for funding
are considered only once, but applicants
may reapply after two years. The trustees do
not grant interviews or make site visits except when they consider it necessary.

Restrictions on Giving: No grants are
given to individuals. Multi-year grants are
not made. Also, the foundation does not
make loans, nor does it make grants to support fund-raising efforts or for the purpose
of producing any type of film. "Grants are
not made to religious organizations, organizations that are supported by or have access
to public funds, nonprofits that carry out
their programs outside the United States, or
political action groups." Proposals of nonprofits under the exemption of another umbrella organization will not be considered.

GRANTS ANALYSIS
Total Grants: $4,686,264

Number of Grants: 107

Highest Grant: $1,000,000

Average Grant: $25,583*

Typical Range: $1,000 to $5,000 and
$10,000 to $50,000

Disclosure Period: 1992

Note: Average grant figure excludes the two
largest grants of $1,000,000 each. Recent
grants are derived from a 1992 Form 990.

RECENT GRANTS

Library

1,000,000	Boston Public Library Foundation, Boston, MA
35,000	Southwest Harbor Public Library, Saw Harbor, ME

General

1,000,000	Massachusetts Institute of Technology, Cambridge, MA
500,000	Winsor School, Boston, MA
100,000	Franciscan Children's Hospital and Rehabilitation
75,000	Cotting School, Lexington, MA
50,000	Children's Medical Center Corporation, Boston, MA

Phillips Foundation, Ellis L.

CONTACT
Ellis L. Phillips, Jr.
Vice President, and Director
Ellis L. Phillips Fdn.
29 Commonwealth Ave.
Boston, MA 02116
(617) 424-7607

FINANCIAL SUMMARY
Recent Giving: $142,750 (fiscal 1994);
$269,210 (fiscal 1992); $253,825 (fiscal
1991)

Assets: $5,126,260 (fiscal 1994);
$5,206,624 (fiscal 1992); $5,248,241 (fiscal
1991)

EIN: 13-5677691

CONTRIBUTIONS SUMMARY
Donor(s): the late Ellis L. Phillips

Typical Recipients: • *Arts & Humanities:*
Arts Associations & Councils, Arts Festi-
vals, Arts Funds, Community Arts, Film &
Video, Historic Preservation, History & Ar-
chaeology, Libraries, Museums/Galleries,
Music, Opera, Public Broadcasting, Theater
• *Civic & Public Affairs:* Employment/Job
Training, Housing, Public Policy, Urban &
Community Affairs • *Education:* Arts/Hu-
manities Education, Colleges & Universi-
ties, Engineering/Technological Education,
Environmental Education, Private Education
(Precollege), Religious Education, Sci-
ence/Mathematics Education, Secondary
Education (Private), Social Sciences Educa-
tion • *Environment:* General, Wildlife Protec-
tion • *Health:* Clinics/Medical Centers,
Health Funds, Prenatal Health Issues • *Religion:* Churches, Ministries • *Science:* Science
Museums, Scientific Centers & Institutes
• *Social Services:* Child Welfare, Community Service Organizations, Family Planning, Family Services

Grant Types: conference/seminar, endowment, general support, multiyear/continuing
support, and seed money

Geographic Distribution: focus on northern New England

GIVING OFFICERS
David Lloyd Brown: dir

Cornelia Grumman: dir

David L. Grumman: dir, mem

Dr. George E. McCully: dir

Walter C. Paine: dir

Ellis L. Phillips III: pres, dir, mem

Ellis L. Phillips, Jr.: vp, dir, mem *B* New
York NY 1921 *ED* Princeton Univ AB 1942;
Columbia Univ LLB 1948; Keuka Coll LLD
1956 *CORP AFFIL* dir: Grumman Corp

George C. Thompson: treas, dir

Elise Phillips Watts: dir

K. Noel P. Zimmermann: secy, dir

APPLICATION INFORMATION
Initial Approach: The foundation has no
formal grant application procedure or application form. There are no deadlines.

Restrictions on Giving: Does not support individuals or provide funds for scholarships.

PUBLICATIONS
Annual Report (including application guidelines)

GRANTS ANALYSIS
Total Grants: $142,750

Number of Grants: 24

Highest Grant: $25,000

Typical Range: $200 to $10,000

Disclosure Period: fiscal year ending June 30, 1994

Note: Recent grants are derived from a fiscal 1994 Form 990.

RECENT GRANTS

Library
10,000	Concord Free Public Library, Concord, MA — in support of the Concord Collections project, to survey and document historic book and document collections
10,000	Longy School of Music, Cambridge, MA — assist in making Bakalar Library collection accessible through computerization of its holdings
2,500	Richards Free Library, Newport, NH — challenge grant to provide continued support to the Mill Tapestry Project

General
25,000	Concord Program, Concord, NH — initiate project aimed at forming a collaborative of Concord, MA, area organizations concerned with history, the environment, the arts, education, and values
8,000	Audubon Society of New Hampshire, Concord, NY — complete and publish publication, which will document avian biodiversity of New Hampshire
6,800	Emerson College, Boston, MA — conserve six murals, painted in 1902 and 1903 by William deLeftwich Dodge
6,000	Engineering and Scientific Resources for Advancement, Woburn, MA — support year-round community leadership and economic training in math, science, and leadership program for middle-school youth
5,000	Long Trail School, Dorset, VT — sponsor the artist-in-residence music education program

Pierce Charitable Trust, Harold Whitworth

CONTACT
Elizabeth D. Nichols
Harold Whitworth Pierce Charitable Trust
c/o Nichols and Pratt
50 Congress St.
Boston, MA 02109
(617) 523-6800

FINANCIAL SUMMARY
Recent Giving: $532,540 (1993); $593,771 (1992); $37,000 (1991)

Assets: $13,398,099 (1993); $13,333,962 (1992); $13,210,564 (1991)

EIN: 04-6019896

CONTRIBUTIONS SUMMARY
Donor(s): the late Harold Whitworth Pierce

Typical Recipients: • *Arts & Humanities:* Libraries, Museums/Galleries, Music, Public Broadcasting • *Civic & Public Affairs:* Botanical Gardens/Parks, Economic Development, Employment/Job Training, General, Hispanic Affairs, Municipalities/Towns, Zoos/Aquariums • *Education:* Colleges & Universities, Education Associations, Education Funds, General, Minority Education, Science/Mathematics Education, Student Aid, Vocational & Technical Education • *Environment:* General, Wildlife Protection • *Health:* Health Organizations, Hospitals, Medical Research • *International:* Human Rights • *Religion:* Churches • *Science:* Science Museums, Scientific Centers & Institutes • *Social Services:* At-Risk Youth, Community Service Organizations, Family Planning, Family Services, Food/Clothing Distribution, Recreation & Athletics, Youth Organizations

Grant Types: general support

Geographic Distribution: focus on MA

GIVING OFFICERS
James R. Nichols: trust *PHIL AFFIL* trust: Paul and Edith Babson Foundation, Elisha V. Ashton Trust

Harold I. Pratt: trust

APPLICATION INFORMATION
Initial Approach: Include a description of organization, amount requested, purpose of funds sought, recently audited financial statement, and proof of tax-exempt status. There are no deadlines.

GRANTS ANALYSIS
Total Grants: $532,540

Number of Grants: 27

Highest Grant: $141,740

Typical Range: $1,000 to $100,000

Disclosure Period: 1993

Note: Recent grants are derived from a 1993 Form 990.

RECENT GRANTS

Library
5,000	Nativity Preparatory School, Roxbury, MA — library project
3,800	Center for Coastal Studies, Provincetown, MA — purchase of a computerized reference filing system and inter-library communications system for the library

General
141,740	Milton Hospital, Milton, MA
100,000	Museum of Science, Boston, MA — Discovery Campaign
60,000	New England Aquarium, Boston, MA — support for a new energy management system
28,500	Medical Foundation, Boston, MA — funding for one biomedical research fellowship
25,000	Appalachian Mountain Club, Boston, MA — help pay for data collection and Landsat work involved in the Northern Forest Lands project

Polaroid Corp. / Polaroid Foundation

Revenue: $2.31 billion
Employees: 12,359
Headquarters: Cambridge, MA
SIC Major Group: Photographic Equipment & Supplies

CONTACT
Marcia Schiff
Executive Director
Polaroid Foundation
750 Main St., 2nd Fl.
Cambridge, MA 02139
(617) 386-8289
Note: Contact person listed above also handles nonmonetary requests.

FINANCIAL SUMMARY
Recent Giving: $2,349,000 (1995 est.); $2,351,686 (1994 approx.); $2,552,986 (1993)

Assets: $1,049,027 (1994); $1,103,306 (1993); $1,059,727 (1992)

Gifts Received: $2,492,384 (1993); $2,383,691 (1992)

Fiscal Note: Total giving figures above are for foundation only. Company also makes divisional grants to various nonprofits. Above figures include nonmonetary support.

EIN: 23-7152261

CONTRIBUTIONS SUMMARY
Typical Recipients: • *Arts & Humanities:* Arts Associations & Councils, Arts Centers, Arts Funds, Arts Outreach, Ballet, Community Arts, Dance, Libraries, Museums/Galleries, Music, Opera, Performing Arts, Theater,

Visual Arts • *Civic & Public Affairs:* Civil Rights, Community Foundations, Ethnic Organizations, Housing, Law & Justice, Nonprofit Management, Philanthropic Organizations, Safety, Urban & Community Affairs, Women's Affairs • *Education:* Arts/Humanities Education, Business Education, Colleges & Universities, Community & Junior Colleges, Continuing Education, Elementary Education (Private), Engineering/Technological Education, Literacy, Medical Education, Minority Education, Preschool Education, Private Education (Precollege), Public Education (Precollege), Science/Mathematics Education, Secondary Education (Public), Special Education, Student Aid • *Environment:* General • *Health:* AIDS/HIV, Diabetes, Hospices, Hospitals, Mental Health, Nursing Services, Public Health • *International:* Human Rights • *Religion:* Religious Welfare, Social/Policy Issues • *Science:* Scientific Labs • *Social Services:* Child Welfare, Community Service Organizations, Family Services, Food/Clothing Distribution, Recreation & Athletics, Shelters/Homelessness, United Funds/United Ways

Grant Types: capital, employee matching gifts, general support, operating expenses, project, and seed money

Nonmonetary Support: $50,000 (1992); $98,000 (1990)

Nonmonetary Support Types: donated products

Note: Nonmonetary support is donated through the foundation.

Geographic Distribution: primarily low-income areas of greater Boston and New Bedford, MA area; small number of grants awarded in areas where distribution centers are located; considers funding outside of Massachusetts in areas of minority higher education and photographic acquisition and exhibition; donates products nationwide

Operating Locations: CA (Santa Ana), GA (Atlanta), IL (Chicago), MA (Bedford, Boston, Cambridge, Freetown, Needham, New Bedford, Newton, Norwood, Waltham), NJ (Paramus), PR

CORP. OFFICERS
Joseph G. Parham, Jr.: *CURR EMPL* vp human resources: Polaroid Corp

GIVING OFFICERS
Graham M. Brown, Jr.: treas

Sheldon A. Buckler: trust *B* New York NY 1931 *ED* NY Univ BA 1951; Columbia Univ PhD 1954 *CURR EMPL* chmn bd trusts: Commonwealth Energy Sys *CORP AFFIL* dir: Lord Corp *NONPR AFFIL* bd mgrs: MA Eye Ear Infirmary; mem: Am Chem Soc, Phi Beta Kappa; mem adv bd: Am Repertory Theatre

Richard Ford DeLima: trust *B* New York NY 1930 *ED* Amherst Coll 1951; Harvard Univ Law Sch 1955 *CURR EMPL* vp, secy, gen couns: Polaroid Corp

Peter Otto Kliem: trust *B* Berlin Germany 1938 *ED* Bates Coll BS 1960; Northeastern Univ MS 1965 *CURR EMPL* sr vp bus devel: Polaroid Corp *CORP AFFIL* chmn:

NOVIRx Inc *NONPR AFFIL* assoc: Woods Hole Oceanographic Inst; mem: Am Chem Soc; trust: Boston Biomed Res Inst

Michael LeBlanc: trust

William J. O'Neill, Jr.: pres *CURR EMPL* exec vp, cfo: Polaroid Corp

Joseph Oldfield: trust *CURR EMPL* vp worldwide mfg opers, dir: Polaroid Corp *NONPR AFFIL* dir: Natl Assn Mfrs

Joseph G. Parham, Jr.: trust *CURR EMPL* vp human resources: Polaroid Corp (see above)

Joseph Paulam, Jr.: trust

Marcia Schiff: exec dir, secy, mem oper comm

Carole J. Uhrich: trust *B* Providence RI 1943 *ED* Northeastern Univ 1966; Northeastern Univ 1972 *NONPR AFFIL* mem: Product Devel Mgmt Assn, Soc Photographic Sci & Engrs; trust: Northeastern Univ

APPLICATION INFORMATION
Initial Approach: *Initial Contact:* grant application, letter, or proposal on organization letterhead *Include Information On:* completed grant application together with brief history of program, population served, outline of project for which support is requested, annual budget for project or for overall program if general support requested, proof of tax-exempt status, and most recently audited financial statement *Deadlines:* none

Restrictions on Giving: The foundation does not make more than one grant to a recipient in any calendar year, or make contributions commitments beyond the current funding year; does not make contributions in the form of purchasing advertisements; and does not make grants to individuals. Also does not support political or lobbying groups, religious organizations for sectarian purposes, or dinners or special events, and does not fund research.

OTHER THINGS TO KNOW
The foundation occasionally provides short-term, no-interest loans.

The foundation also makes limited donations of photographic materials. Requests for such support must be on organization letterhead, provide a statement justifying the organization's ability to qualify under Polaroid Foundation guidelines, along with an overview of how photography will be integrated into the program. No budget or statement from the accounting department is required. The organization must work with a low-income or poverty-level population, with the mentally or physically handicapped, or with the retarded. Requests should be directed to Jill Healy, Product Donation Program, Polaroid Foundation, 750 Main St., 2nd Fl., Cambridge, MA, 02139.

A list of committee members may be obtained from the foundation.

Skills Bank is a company-sponsored employee volunteer program. It is run through the community relations office. For information, contact Verna Brookins.

PUBLICATIONS
Annual report

GRANTS ANALYSIS
Total Grants: $2,351,686
Number of Grants: 350
Highest Grant: $358,904
Average Grant: $6,719
Typical Range: $100 to $10,000
Disclosure Period: 1994

Note: Figures were supplied by the foundation. Fiscal information for foundation only. Recent grants are derived from a 1993 Form 990.

RECENT GRANTS
Library

10,000	Public Library of the City of Boston Trustees, Boston, MA — for Boston Public Library

General

358,904	United Way Eastern New England, Boston, MA
47,096	Community Works
45,000	Associated Grantmakers of Massachusetts, Boston, MA
34,577	National Merit Scholarship Corporation, Evanston, IL
28,688	American College Testing, Iowa City, IA

Prouty Foundation, Olive Higgins

CONTACT
George Robbins
Sr. Vice President
Olive Higgins Prouty Fdn.
c/o State St. Bank & Trust Co.
PO Box 351 M-3
Boston, MA 02010
(508) 752-0092

FINANCIAL SUMMARY
Recent Giving: $121,000 (1993); $116,000 (1992); $111,000 (1990)

Assets: $2,286,580 (1993); $2,288,228 (1992); $1,890,479 (1990)

EIN: 04-6046475

CONTRIBUTIONS SUMMARY
Donor(s): Olive Higgins Prouty

Typical Recipients: • *Arts & Humanities:* Arts Centers, History & Archaeology, Libraries, Museums/Galleries, Music, Performing Arts, Public Broadcasting • *Civic & Public Affairs:* Community Foundations, General, Legal Aid, Philanthropic Organizations, Public Policy, Urban & Community Affairs, Women's Affairs • *Education:* Agricultural Education, Colleges & Universities, Continuing Education, Education Associations, Engineering/Technological Education, Private Education (Precollege) • *Environment:* General, Resource Conservation • *Health:* Alzheimers Disease, Children's Health/Hospitals, Clinics/Medical Centers, Diabetes, Health Organizations, Hospices, Hospitals, Medical

Research, Single-Disease Health Associations • *International:* International Relief Efforts • *Religion:* Churches • *Social Services:* Domestic Violence, Family Services, Youth Organizations

Grant Types: capital, general support, and operating expenses

Geographic Distribution: focus on the Greater Worcester, MA, area

GIVING OFFICERS

State Street Bank & Trust Co.: trust

Thomas P. Jalkut: trust *PHIL AFFIL* clerk: MWC Foundation

Lewis J. Prouty: treas

Richard Prouty: trust, pres

William M. Smith III: trust

APPLICATION INFORMATION

Initial Approach: Send brief letter describing program. Include a description of organization, amount requested, purpose of funds sought, recently audited financial statement, and proof of tax-exempt status. Deadline is September 30.

PUBLICATIONS
Application Guidelines

GRANTS ANALYSIS

Total Grants: $121,000

Number of Grants: 42

Highest Grant: $23,000

Typical Range: $1,000 to $5,000

Disclosure Period: 1993

Note: Recent grants are derived from a 1993 Form 990.

RECENT GRANTS

Library
2,000   Friends of Goddard Library

General
23,000   Children's Hospital, Boston, MA
5,000   Austen Riggs Center, Stockbridge, MA
5,000   Cambridge Center for Adult Education, Cambridge, MA
4,000   American Health Assistance Foundation, Boston, MA — for Alzheimers disease research
4,000   Massachusetts Coalition for Battered Women Service Corps, Boston, MA — Jane Doe Safety Fund

Rabb Charitable Foundation, Sidney and Esther

CONTACT
Carol R. Goldberg
Trustee
Sidney and Esther Rabb Charitable Fdn.
c/o Boston Safe Deposit & Trust Co.
One Boston Pl.
Boston, MA 02108
(617) 722-3533

FINANCIAL SUMMARY
Recent Giving: $170,067 (1993); $249,697 (1991); $102,652 (1990)
Assets: $3,895,655 (1993); $3,779,503 (1991); $3,501,254 (1990)
EIN: 04-6039595

CONTRIBUTIONS SUMMARY
Donor(s): the late Sidney R. Rabb

Typical Recipients: • *Arts & Humanities:* History & Archaeology, Libraries, Museums/Galleries, Music, Public Broadcasting • *Civic & Public Affairs:* Parades/Festivals • *Education:* Arts/Humanities Education, Colleges & Universities • *Health:* Children's Health/Hospitals, Hospitals, Medical Rehabilitation • *Religion:* Jewish Causes, Synagogues/Temples • *Science:* Science Museums • *Social Services:* Day Care, Family Planning

Grant Types: general support

Geographic Distribution: focus on MA, with emphasis on Boston

GIVING OFFICERS
Helene R. Cahners-Kaplan: trust *PHIL AFFIL* trust: Sidney R. Rabb Charitable Trust

Carol Rabb Goldberg: trust *B* Newton MA 1931 *ED* Tufts Univ BA 1955; Harvard Univ Sch Bus Admin 1969 *CURR EMPL* pres: AVCAR Group *CORP AFFIL* dir: Aicorp, Gillette Co, Lotus Devel Corp; trust: Putnam Fund Group *NONPR AFFIL* bd overseers: WGBH Ed Fdn; bd regents: Higher Ed Comm; bd visitors: Boston Univ Med Sch; dir: Greater Boston Arts Fund, Harvard Univ Bus Sch Alumni Assn, John F Kennedy Library Fdn; mem: Babson Coll Fdn; mem bus adv counc: Carnegie-Mellon Univ; mem natl counc adv comm: Tufts Univ Ctr Pub Svc *CLUB AFFIL* Commercial Merchants Boston *PHIL AFFIL* trust: Sidney R. Rabb Charitable Trust, Goldberg Family Foundation

APPLICATION INFORMATION
Initial Approach: Send brief letter of inquiry describing program or project. There are no deadlines.

GRANTS ANALYSIS
Total Grants: $170,067
Number of Grants: 16
Highest Grant: $54,000
Typical Range: $500 to $25,000
Disclosure Period: 1993

Note: Recent grants are derived from a 1993 Form 990.

RECENT GRANTS
Library
4,000   Boston Public Library, Boston, MA — capital campaign

General
54,000   Combined Jewish Philanthropies, Boston, MA — annual campaign
25,000   Northeastern University, Boston, MA — century campaign
19,000   Beth Israel Hospital, Boston, MA — playroom at the child care center
13,000   McLean Hospital, Belmont, MA — Shervert H. Frazier Institute campaign
13,000   Tufts University/Lincoln Filene, Medford, MA — New England Institute for nonprofit organization

Reisman Charitable Trust, George C. and Evelyn R.

CONTACT
David Andelman
Trustee
George C. and Evelyn R. Reisman Charitable Trust
c/o Lourie and Cutler, P. C.
60 State St.
Boston, MA 02109
(617) 742-6720

FINANCIAL SUMMARY
Recent Giving: $543,365 (1993); $506,760 (1992); $439,545 (1990)
Assets: $9,474,271 (1993); $9,594,170 (1992); $9,410,936 (1990)
EIN: 04-2743096

CONTRIBUTIONS SUMMARY
Donor(s): George C. Reisman and Apparel Retail Corp.

Typical Recipients: • *Arts & Humanities:* Libraries, Museums/Galleries, Music, Public Broadcasting • *Civic & Public Affairs:* General, Housing, Law & Justice, Philanthropic Organizations, Women's Affairs • *Education:* Colleges & Universities, Private Education (Precollege) • *Health:* Alzheimers Disease, Arthritis, Cancer, Children's Health/Hospitals, Emergency/Ambulance Services, Health Organizations, Heart, Home-Care Services, Hospitals, Medical Rehabilitation, Medical Research, Nursing Services, Single-Disease Health Associations • *International:* Health Care/Hospitals • *Religion:* Jewish Causes, Religious Organizations, Religious Welfare, Seminaries, Synagogues/Temples • *Social Services:* Child Welfare, Community Service Organizations, Emergency Relief, Food/Clothing Distribution, People with Disabilities, Special Olympics, United Funds/United Ways

Grant Types: general support

Geographic Distribution: focus on CO, MA, and RI

GIVING OFFICERS
David Andelman: trust

Evelyn R. Reisman: trust

Howard Reisman: trust

Robert Reisman: trust

David Rothstein: trust

APPLICATION INFORMATION
Initial Approach: Send brief letter of inquiry describing program or project. There are no deadlines.

GRANTS ANALYSIS
Total Grants: $543,365

Number of Grants: 39

Highest Grant: $250,000

Typical Range: $100 to $100,000

Disclosure Period: 1993

Note: Recent grants are derived from a 1993 Form 990.

RECENT GRANTS
General

250,000	Combined Jewish Philanthropies, Boston, MA
100,000	Beth Israel Hospital, Boston, MA
100,000	Brown University, Providence, RI
50,000	Spalding Rehabilitation Hospital, Denver, CO
24,100	Hebrew Rehabilitation Center, Roslindale, MA

Rice Charitable Foundation, Albert W.

CONTACT
Stephen Fritch
Vice President
Albert W. Rice Charitable Fdn.
c/o Shawmut Bank
446 Main St.
Worcester, MA 01810
(508) 793-4205

FINANCIAL SUMMARY
Recent Giving: $163,813 (1993); $205,534 (1992); $219,333 (1991)

Assets: $4,199,372 (1993); $4,074,463 (1992); $4,036,642 (1991)

EIN: 04-6028085

CONTRIBUTIONS SUMMARY
Donor(s): the late Albert W. Rice

Typical Recipients: • *Arts & Humanities:* Arts Associations & Councils, Arts Centers, Community Arts, Historic Preservation, History & Archaeology, Libraries, Museums/Galleries, Music, Performing Arts, Public Broadcasting, Theater • *Civic & Public Affairs:* Clubs, Rural Affairs • *Education:* Community & Junior Colleges, Engineering/Technological Education, Private Education (Precollege) • *Environment:* General, Resource Conservation • *Health:* Clinics/Medical Centers, Hospices • *Religion:* Churches • *Science:* Scientific Centers & Institutes, Scientific Research • *Social Services:* Community Service Organizations, Substance Abuse, United Funds/United Ways, Youth Organizations

Grant Types: general support

Geographic Distribution: focus on Worcester, MA

GIVING OFFICERS
Shawmut Bank, N.A.: trust

APPLICATION INFORMATION
Initial Approach: Send brief letter of inquiry describing program or project. Deadlines are April 1 and October 1.

Restrictions on Giving: Limited to charitable organizations in Worcester, MA.

GRANTS ANALYSIS
Total Grants: $163,813

Number of Grants: 12

Highest Grant: $33,333

Typical Range: $2,500 to $10,000

Disclosure Period: 1993

Note: Recent grants are derived from a 1993 Form 990.

RECENT GRANTS
General

33,333	Medical Center of Central Massachusetts, Worcester, MA — operational
25,000	United Way of Central Massachusetts, Worcester, MA
20,000	All Saints Church, Worcester, MA — operational
10,000	New England Science Center, Worcester, MA — operational
10,000	Spectrum Addiction Services, Worcester, MA — operational

Rogers Family Foundation

CONTACT
Irving E. Rogers, Jr.
Trustee
Rogers Family Fdn.
PO Box 100
Lawrence, MA 01842
(508) 685-1000

FINANCIAL SUMMARY
Recent Giving: $441,100 (1993); $436,025 (1992); $399,200 (1991)

Assets: $10,789,334 (1993); $10,377,246 (1992); $9,970,909 (1991)

Gifts Received: $185,510 (1993); $189,170 (1992); $139,301 (1991)

Fiscal Note: In 1993, contributions were received from Eagle-Tribune Publishing Co. ($150,790) and Eagle-Tribune Realty Trust ($13,000); four other donors made contributions of $9,000 or less.

EIN: 04-6063152

CONTRIBUTIONS SUMMARY
Donor(s): Irving E. Rogers, Eagle-Tribune Publishing Co., Martha B. Rogers

Typical Recipients: • *Arts & Humanities:* Arts Festivals, Community Arts, Ethnic & Folk Arts, Historic Preservation, History & Archaeology, Libraries, Museums/Galleries, Music, Theater • *Civic & Public Affairs:* Community Foundations, General, Housing, Urban & Community Affairs • *Education:* Business Education, Colleges & Universities, General, Minority Education, Private Education (Precollege), Student Aid • *Environment:* Watershed • *Health:* Clinics/Medical Centers, Emergency/Ambulance Services, Home-Care Services, Hospitals, Medical Rehabilitation, Medical Research • *Religion:* Churches, Religious Welfare • *Social Services:* Big Brother/Big Sister, Community Centers, Community Service Organizations, Day Care, Homes, People with Disabilities, Recreation & Athletics, Shelters/Homelessness, United Funds/United Ways, Youth Organizations

Grant Types: general support

Geographic Distribution: limited to the greater Lawrence, MA, area

GIVING OFFICERS
Irving E. Rogers, Jr.: trust *CURR EMPL* pres, publisher, treas, gen mgr: Eagle-Tribune Publishing Co

Irving E. Rogers III: trust

Stephen H. Rogers: trust

APPLICATION INFORMATION
Initial Approach: The foundation has no formal grant application procedure or application form. There are no deadlines.

Restrictions on Giving: Does not support individuals. Limited to Lawrence, MA, and the surrounding communities.

GRANTS ANALYSIS
Total Grants: $441,100

Number of Grants: 58

Highest Grant: $50,000

Typical Range: $1,000 to $50,000

Disclosure Period: 1993

Note: Recent grants are derived from a 1993 Form 990.

RECENT GRANTS
Library

12,500	Town of North Andover/Stevens Memorial Library, North Andover, MA — READCOM
2,000	Lawrence Public Library, Lawrence, MA
1,500	Haverhill Public Library, Haverhill, MA

General

50,000	Brooks School, North Andover, MA — capital campaign

50,000	Home Health Foundation, Andover, MA
34,000	United Fund of Merrimack Valley, Lawrence, MA
25,000	Holy Family Hospital and Medical Center, Methuen, MA
25,000	Lahey Clinic Foundation, Burlington, MA

Rowland Foundation

CONTACT
Philip DuBois
Vice President
Rowland Foundation
PO Box 13
Cambridge, MA 02238
(617) 497-4634

FINANCIAL SUMMARY
Recent Giving: $2,434,761 (fiscal 1993); $1,618,145 (fiscal 1991); $1,959,536 (fiscal 1990)

Assets: $46,165,538 (fiscal 1993); $43,502,411 (fiscal 1991); $36,484,938 (fiscal 1990)

Gifts Received: $49,860 (fiscal 1993); $5,335,036 (fiscal 1991)

Fiscal Note: In 1991 and 1992, the foundation received gifts from the Estate of Edwin H. Land.

EIN: 04-6046756

CONTRIBUTIONS SUMMARY
Donor(s): The Rowland Foundation was established by Edwin H. Land and Helen M. Land in 1960 as Edwin H. Land-Helen M. Land, Inc. The foundation has been operating under its present name since 1972. Edwin Land, inventor of the light polarizer and the Land camera (which introduced the one-step, self-developing film process), founded Polaroid Corporation in 1937, and has served as its chairman, president, and director of research. A major philanthropist, he founded the Rowland Institute for Science and created a $100 million charitable trust for the Land Education Development Fund at the Massachusetts Institute of Technology.

Typical Recipients: • *Arts & Humanities:* Arts Associations & Councils, Arts Centers, Historic Preservation, History & Archaeology, Libraries, Museums/Galleries, Music, Public Broadcasting • *Civic & Public Affairs:* African American Affairs, Employment/Job Training, General • *Education:* Arts/Humanities Education, Colleges & Universities, Medical Education, Minority Education, Private Education (Precollege), Special Education, Student Aid • *Environment:* General, Resource Conservation • *Health:* Cancer, Children's Health/Hospitals, Eyes/Blindness, Health Organizations, Heart, Hospitals, Medical Rehabilitation, Medical Research, Single-Disease Health Associations • *Religion:* Jewish Causes, Religious Welfare • *Science:* Science Museums, Scientific Centers & Institutes, Scientific Organizations • *Social Services:*

Family Planning, People with Disabilities, United Funds/United Ways

Grant Types: general support, project, research, and scholarship

Geographic Distribution: primarily New England

GIVING OFFICERS
Jennifer Land DuBois: trust, don daughter

Philip DuBois: vp, trust *NONPR AFFIL* pres, dir: Rowland Inst Science

Edwin Herbert Land: don, pres, trust *B* Bridgeport CT 1909 *ED* Harvard Univ; Norwich Univ

Helen Maislen Land: vp, treas, trust *B* 1911 *NONPR AFFIL* treas, dir: Rowland Inst Science

Julius Silver: secy *B* Philadelphia PA 1900 *ED* NY Univ BA 1922; Columbia Univ JD 1924 *CURR EMPL* sr ptnr: Silver & Solomon *PHIL AFFIL* pres, treas, trust: Jurodin Fund

APPLICATION INFORMATION
Initial Approach:

Applicants should send a brief letter.

The letter should outline the nature of the request, amount needed, and background information on the history and objectives of the organization. Also include proof of IRS tax exemption.

Applications may be submitted throughout the year; the board meets as necessary.

Restrictions on Giving: No grants are made to individuals or for buildings or endowment funds.

OTHER THINGS TO KNOW
The foundation is now a separate entity from the Rowland Institute.

GRANTS ANALYSIS
Total Grants: $2,434,761

Number of Grants: 41

Highest Grant: $1,000,000

Average Grant: $35,869*

Typical Range: $10,000 to $35,000 and $50,000 to $150,000

Disclosure Period: fiscal year ending November 30, 1993

Note: The average grant figure excludes the highest grant. Recent grants are derived from a fiscal 1993 partial grants list.

RECENT GRANTS

Library

25,000	Boston Athenaeum, Boston, MA
25,000	New York Public Library, New York, NY

General

1,000,000	Rowland Institute for Science, Cambridge, MA
155,195	Harvard University and Colleges, Cambridge, MA — research
120,701	Massachusetts General Hospital, Boston, MA
100,000	Mt. Auburn Hospital Foundation, Cambridge, MA

100,000	Tufts College Veterinary School, N. Grafton, MA

Rubin Family Fund, Cele H. and William B.

CONTACT
Ellen R. Gordon
President
Cele H. and William B. Rubin Family Fund
32 Monadnock Rd.
Wellesley Hills, MA 02181
(617) 235-1075

FINANCIAL SUMMARY
Recent Giving: $1,000,000 (1995 est.); $990,990 (1994 approx.); $1,130,650 (1993)

Assets: $25,000,000 (1995 est.); $25,000,000 (1994 est.); $24,938,631 (1993)

Gifts Received: $700,000 (1993); $650,000 (1992); $575,000 (1991)

Fiscal Note: In 1993, contributions were received from Tootsie Roll Industries, Inc.

EIN: 11-6026235

CONTRIBUTIONS SUMMARY
Donor(s): The foundation was incorporated in 1943 by members of the Joseph Rubin family, the Sweets Co. of America, Inc., Joseph Rubin and Sons, Inc., Tootsie Roll Industries, Inc., and others.

Typical Recipients: • *Arts & Humanities:* Arts Funds, Ballet, Historic Preservation, Libraries, Music • *Civic & Public Affairs:* Economic Development, General, Hispanic Affairs, Law & Justice, Philanthropic Organizations, Public Policy, Urban & Community Affairs, Women's Affairs • *Education:* Business Education, Colleges & Universities, Continuing Education, Education Funds, Engineering/Technological Education, General, Legal Education, Medical Education, Preschool Education, Private Education (Precollege), Secondary Education (Private) • *Environment:* General, Resource Conservation, Wildlife Protection • *Health:* Cancer, Diabetes, Health Organizations, Heart, Hospitals, Kidney, Medical Rehabilitation, Prenatal Health Issues, Public Health, Single-Disease Health Associations • *Religion:* Jewish Causes, Religious Organizations • *Science:* Observatories & Planetariums, Science Museums, Scientific Centers & Institutes • *Social Services:* Child Welfare, Community Service Organizations, Family Services, Food/Clothing Distribution, People with Disabilities, Shelters/Homelessness, United Funds/United Ways, Youth Organizations

Grant Types: general support

Geographic Distribution: focus on Massachusetts and New York

GIVING OFFICERS
Ellen R. Gordon: pres, dir *B* New York NY 1931 *ED* Brandeis Univ BA 1965; Harvard Univ; Vassar Coll *CURR EMPL* pres, coo, dir: Tootsie Roll Indus *CORP AFFIL* dir: CPC Intl; vp, dir: HDI Investment Corp

NONPR AFFIL chp, pres: Comm 200; mem: Natl Confectioners Assn; mem adv counc: Stanford Univ Grad Sch Bus; mem bd fellows: Harvard Univ Med Sch

Melvin Jay Gordon: vp, dir *B* Boston MA 1919 *ED* Harvard Univ BA 1941; Harvard Univ MBA 1943 *CURR EMPL* chmn, ceo: Tootsie Roll Indus *CORP AFFIL* pres: Lisa Gordon Inc, Wendy Gordon Inc, HDI Investment Corp, MJG *NONPR AFFIL* dir: Inst Man Science; visiting comm: Russian Res Ctr *CLUB AFFIL* Harvard, Varsity

APPLICATION INFORMATION
Initial Approach:

The foundation has no formal grant application procedure or application form.

The foundation has no deadline for submitting proposals.

GRANTS ANALYSIS
Total Grants: $1,130,650

Number of Grants: 55

Highest Grant: $594,000

Average Grant: $5,880*

Typical Range: $100 to $5,000

Disclosure Period: 1993

Note: Average grant figure excludes two grants of $594,000 and $225,000. Recent grants are derived from a 1993 Form 990.

RECENT GRANTS

Library

1,000	Wellesley Free Library, Wellesley, MA

General

594,000	Old Colony Charitable Fund, Boston, MA
225,000	Harvard University, Cambridge, MA
125,000	University of Chicago, Chicago, IL
70,000	Harvard Business School, Cambridge, MA
33,000	Combined Jewish Philanthropies of Greater Boston, Boston, MA

Russell Trust, Josephine G.

CONTACT
Clifford E. Elias
Trustee
Josephine G. Russell Trust
70 East St.
Methuen, MA 01844
(617) 687-0501

FINANCIAL SUMMARY
Recent Giving: $353,747 (1993); $330,360 (1992); $284,550 (1991)

Assets: $6,309,553 (1993); $5,959,615 (1992); $5,918,340 (1991)

EIN: 04-2136910

CONTRIBUTIONS SUMMARY
Typical Recipients: • *Arts & Humanities:* History & Archaeology, Libraries, Museums/Galleries • *Civic & Public Affairs:* Asian American Affairs, Chambers of Commerce, Community Foundations, General, Hispanic Affairs, Housing, Municipalities/Towns, Urban & Community Affairs • *Education:* Business Education, Colleges & Universities, General, Private Education (Precollege), Public Education (Precollege), Secondary Education (Private) • *Health:* Children's Health/Hospitals, Hospitals, Medical Research, Nursing Services • *International:* International Organizations • *Religion:* Churches, Jewish Causes, Religious Welfare • *Social Services:* Big Brother/Big Sister, Child Welfare, Community Service Organizations, Family Services, Food/Clothing Distribution, People with Disabilities, Recreation & Athletics, Scouts, United Funds/United Ways, YMCA/YWCA/YMHA/YWHA, Youth Organizations

Grant Types: capital, emergency, general support, project, and scholarship

Geographic Distribution: limited to the greater Lawrence, MA, area

GIVING OFFICERS
Clifford E. Elias: trust *PHIL AFFIL* trust: Artemas W. Stearns Trust

Marsha E. Rich: trust *PHIL AFFIL* trust: Artemas W. Stearns Trust

APPLICATION INFORMATION
Initial Approach: Send brief letter of inquiry describing program or project. Include a description of organization, amount requested, purpose of funds sought, recently audited financial statement, and proof of tax-exempt status. Deadline is January 31.

Restrictions on Giving: Does not support individuals.

PUBLICATIONS
Application Guidelines

GRANTS ANALYSIS
Total Grants: $353,747

Number of Grants: 30

Highest Grant: $70,000

Typical Range: $1,200 to $40,000

Disclosure Period: 1993

Note: Recent grants are derived from a 1993 Form 990.

RECENT GRANTS

Library

12,000	Lawrence Public Library, Lawrence, MA
100	Weare Public Library Trustees, Weare, MA

General

70,000	Lawrence General Hospital, Lawrence, MA
40,000	Holy Family Hospital, Lawrence, MA
25,000	Lawrence Boys and Girls Club, Lawrence, MA
23,000	Big Brothers and Big Sisters, Lawrence, MA
22,000	Brooks School, Andover, MA

Safety Fund National Bank / Safety Fund Foundation

Sales: $257.77 million
Employees: 192
Parent Company: Safety Fund Corporation
Headquarters: Fitchburg, MA
SIC Major Group: Depository Institutions

CONTACT
Martin F. Connors
Treasurer, Director
Safety Fund Foundation
470 Main St.
Fitchburg, MA 01420
(508) 343-6406

FINANCIAL SUMMARY
Recent Giving: $81,308 (1993); $50,533 (1992)

Assets: $19,432 (1993); $1,029 (1992)

Gifts Received: $99,746 (1993); $49,937 (1992)

Fiscal Note: In 1993, contributions were received from Safety Fund National Bank ($49,937).

EIN: 04-2618572

CONTRIBUTIONS SUMMARY
Typical Recipients: • *Arts & Humanities:* Libraries, Museums/Galleries, Music • *Civic & Public Affairs:* Chambers of Commerce, Economic Development, General, Housing, Legal Aid, Public Policy, Urban & Community Affairs • *Education:* Business Education, Colleges & Universities • *Environment:* Resource Conservation • *Health:* Hospitals • *Religion:* Religious Welfare • *Social Services:* Community Service Organizations, Recreation & Athletics, United Funds/United Ways, Youth Organizations

Grant Types: general support

Geographic Distribution: focus on MA

CORP. OFFICERS
Christopher W. Bramley: *CURR EMPL* chmn, ceo: Safety Fund National Bank

GIVING OFFICERS
Christopher W. Bramley: pres, dir *CURR EMPL* chmn, ceo: Safety Fund National Bank (see above)

Martin F. Connors: treas, dir

Joseph A. Giavono: dir

APPLICATION INFORMATION
Initial Approach: Send a brief letter of inquiry. There are no deadlines.

GRANTS ANALYSIS
Total Grants: $81,308

Number of Grants: 19

Highest Grant: $26,250

Typical Range: $250 to $20,000

Disclosure Period: 1993

Note: Recent grants are derived from a 1993 Form 990.

RECENT GRANTS

Library
1,000	Worcester Public Library, Worcester, MA

General
26,250	United Way of North Central Massachusetts, Fitchburg, MA
20,000	Chamber of Commerce, Fitchburg, MA — Cornerstone Program
8,333	Fitchburg State College, Fitchburg, MA
5,000	Henry Heywood Memorial Hospital — capital campaign
5,000	Worcester Chamber of Commerce, Worcester, MA — convention center

Saltonstall Charitable Foundation, Richard

CONTACT
Dudley H. Willis
Trustee
Richard Saltonstall Charitable Fdn.
50 Congress St., Rm. 800
Boston, MA 02109
(617) 227-8660

FINANCIAL SUMMARY
Recent Giving: $550,000 (1993); $525,000 (1992); $475,000 (1991)

Assets: $10,859,879 (1993); $10,883,679 (1992); $13,504,872 (1991)

EIN: 04-6078934

CONTRIBUTIONS SUMMARY
Typical Recipients: • *Arts & Humanities:* Dance, Libraries, Museums/Galleries, Music, Public Broadcasting • *Civic & Public Affairs:* Botanical Gardens/Parks, Clubs, General, Native American Affairs, Rural Affairs, Women's Affairs, Zoos/Aquariums • *Education:* Agricultural Education, Medical Education • *Environment:* Air/Water Quality, General, Resource Conservation, Watershed • *Health:* Alzheimers Disease, Children's Health/Hospitals, Clinics/Medical Centers, Hospitals • *Science:* Science Museums • *Social Services:* Counseling, Family Services, People with Disabilities, Substance Abuse, United Funds/United Ways, Youth Organizations

Grant Types: general support and research

Geographic Distribution: focus on MA

GIVING OFFICERS
Robert Ashton Lawrence: trust *B* Brookline MA 1926 *ED* Yale Univ 1947 *CURR EMPL* exec vp, dir: State Street Res & Mgmt Co *CORP AFFIL* mem exec comm, dir: Affiliated Publs; vp, dir: State St Growth Fund Inc, State St Investment Corp

Emily S. Lewis: trust

Dudley H. Willis: trust

Sally S. Willis: trust

APPLICATION INFORMATION
Initial Approach: Send brief letter of inquiry describing program or project. There are no deadlines.

GRANTS ANALYSIS
Total Grants: $550,000

Number of Grants: 26

Highest Grant: $70,000

Typical Range: $1,000 to $64,000

Disclosure Period: 1993

Note: Recent grants are derived from a 1993 Form 990.

RECENT GRANTS

Library
50,000	Sherborn Public Library, Sherborn, MA

General
70,000	Trustees of Reservations, Beverly, MA
64,000	United Way of Massachusetts Bay, Boston, MA
60,000	Sherborn Rural Land Foundation, Sherborn, MA
50,000	Brigham and Women's Hospital, Boston, MA — Alzheimers research
40,000	New England Medical Center, Boston, MA

Sawyer Charitable Foundation

CONTACT
Carol S. Parks
Executive Director
Sawyer Charitable Fdn.
142 Berkeley St.
Boston, MA 02116
(617) 267-2414

FINANCIAL SUMMARY
Recent Giving: $278,388 (1993); $275,497 (1992); $232,950 (1991)

Assets: $4,914,992 (1993); $5,075,304 (1992); $5,156,492 (1991)

Gifts Received: $55,200 (1992); $5,200 (1991); $38,400 (1990)

Fiscal Note: In 1992, contributions were received from First Federal Parking Corporation ($52,000), General Land Corporation ($2,000), and Brattle Co. ($1,200).

EIN: 04-6088774

CONTRIBUTIONS SUMMARY
Donor(s): Frank Sawyer, William Sawyer, The Brattle Co. Corp., St. Botolph Holding Co., First Franklin Parking Corp.

Typical Recipients: • *Arts & Humanities:* Arts Centers, Historic Preservation, Libraries, Museums/Galleries, Performing Arts • *Civic & Public Affairs:* African American Affairs, Employment/Job Training, General, Public Policy, Urban & Community Affairs, Women's Affairs • *Education:* Community & Junior Colleges, Legal Education, Private Education (Precollege), Secondary Education (Public), Special Education • *Environment:* Air/Water Quality • *Health:* AIDS/HIV, Cancer, Children's Health/Hospitals, Emergency/Ambulance Services, Health Organizations, Hospices, Hospitals, Medical Research, Respiratory, Single-Disease Health Associations, Transplant Networks/Donor Banks, Trauma Treatment • *International:* Health Care/Hospitals, International Relief Efforts • *Religion:* Churches, Jewish Causes, Religious Organizations, Religious Welfare, Synagogues/Temples • *Science:* Science Museums • *Social Services:* Animal Protection, Camps, Child Welfare, Community Service Organizations, Family Services, Homes, People with Disabilities, Scouts, Shelters/Homelessness, Substance Abuse, United Funds/United Ways, Youth Organizations

Grant Types: endowment and general support

Geographic Distribution: focus on the greater New England area

GIVING OFFICERS
Carol S. Parks: exec dir, trust

Mary S. Quinn: mgr

John R. Sawyer: mgr

Mildred F. Sawyer: trust

APPLICATION INFORMATION
Initial Approach: Send cover letter and full proposal. Include a description of organization, amount requested, purpose of funds sought, recently audited financial statement, and proof of tax-exempt status. Deadline is October 15.

Restrictions on Giving: Does not support individuals or provide funds for operating budgets or building projects.

GRANTS ANALYSIS
Total Grants: $278,388

Number of Grants: 86

Highest Grant: $60,000

Typical Range: $100 to $21,263

Disclosure Period: 1993

Note: Recent grants are derived from a 1993 Form 990.

RECENT GRANTS

Library
21,263	Suffolk University, Boston, MA — MFS Library

General
60,000	Newton Country Day School of Sacred Heart, Newton, MA
18,125	Carroll Center for the Blind, Newton, MA
18,000	Rosie's Place, Boston, MA
11,000	Shriners Burn Institute Boston Unit, Boston, MA
10,000	Cardinal Bernard Law Fund, Boston, MA

Stearns Trust, Artemas W.

CONTACT
Clifford E. Elias, Esq.
Trustee
Artemas W. Stearns Trust
70 East St.
Methuen, MA 01844
(508) 687-0151

FINANCIAL SUMMARY
Recent Giving: $257,100 (1993); $258,200 (1992); $185,500 (1991)

Assets: $3,397,523 (1993); $3,303,899 (1992); $3,420,256 (1991)

EIN: 04-2137061

CONTRIBUTIONS SUMMARY
Donor(s): the late Artemas W. Stearns

Typical Recipients: • *Arts & Humanities:* History & Archaeology, Libraries • *Civic & Public Affairs:* Chambers of Commerce, Community Foundations, General, Hispanic Affairs, Housing, Municipalities/Towns, Women's Affairs • *Education:* Colleges & Universities, Private Education (Precollege), Religious Education, Secondary Education (Private) • *Health:* Children's Health/Hospitals, Clinics/Medical Centers, Health Organizations, Hospitals • *International:* International Affairs • *Religion:* Churches, Jewish Causes • *Social Services:* Child Welfare, Community Service Organizations, Counseling, Crime Prevention, Family Services, Food/Clothing Distribution, People with Disabilities, Recreation & Athletics, Senior Services, Shelters/Homelessness, United Funds/United Ways, YMCA/YWCA/YMHA/YWHA, Youth Organizations

Grant Types: capital, emergency, general support, project, and scholarship

Geographic Distribution: limited to the greater Lawrence, MA, area

GIVING OFFICERS
Clifford E. Elias: trust *PHIL AFFIL* trust: Josephine G. Russell Trust

Vincent P. Morton, Jr.: trust

Marsha E. Rich: trust *PHIL AFFIL* trust: Josephine G. Russell Trust

APPLICATION INFORMATION
Initial Approach: Send a brief letter of inquiry. Include a description of organization, amount requested, purpose of funds sought, recently audited financial statement, and proof of tax-exempt status. Deadline is January 31.

PUBLICATIONS
Application Guidelines

GRANTS ANALYSIS
Total Grants: $257,100

Number of Grants: 21

Highest Grant: $40,000

Typical Range: $1,500 to $35,000

Disclosure Period: 1993

Note: Recent grants are derived from a 1993 Form 990.

RECENT GRANTS
General
40,000	Lawrence General Hospital, Lawrence, MA
35,000	Holy Family Hospital, Lawrence, MA
25,000	United Way of Merrimack Valley, Lawrence, MA
20,000	Lazarus House, Lawrence, MA
15,000	Lawrence Boys and Girls Club, Lawrence, MA

Stevens Foundation, Abbot and Dorothy H.

CONTACT
Elizabeth A. Beland
Administrator
Abbot and Dorothy H. Stevens Foundation
PO Box 111
N Andover, MA 01845
(508) 688-7211

FINANCIAL SUMMARY
Recent Giving: $748,632 (1993); $758,884 (1992); $614,806 (1991)

Assets: $14,617,179 (1993); $14,179,493 (1992); $14,086,783 (1991)

EIN: 04-6107991

CONTRIBUTIONS SUMMARY
Donor(s): The foundation was established in 1953 by the late Abbot Stevens .

Typical Recipients: • *Arts & Humanities:* Ballet, Dance, Ethnic & Folk Arts, Film & Video, Historic Preservation, History & Archaeology, Libraries, Museums/Galleries, Music, Opera, Performing Arts, Public Broadcasting, Theater • *Civic & Public Affairs:* Housing, Municipalities/Towns, Philanthropic Organizations, Safety, Urban & Community Affairs • *Education:* Arts/Humanities Education, Business Education, Colleges & Universities, Community & Junior Colleges, Education Funds, General, Minority Education, Private Education (Precollege), Secondary Education (Private), Social Sciences Education, Special Education • *Environment:* General, Resource Conservation, Watershed • *Health:* Children's Health/Hospitals, Clinics/Medical Centers, Home-Care Services, Hospitals, Nursing Services • *International:* Missionary/Religious Activities • *Religion:* Churches, Religious Organizations • *Science:* Science Museums • *Social Services:* At-Risk Youth, Community Service Organizations, Delinquency & Criminal Rehabilitation, Family Services, Food/Clothing Distribution, General, Homes, People with Disabilities, Recreation & Athletics, Senior Services, Substance Abuse, United Funds/United Ways, Youth Organizations

Grant Types: capital, endowment, matching, operating expenses, project, and seed money

Geographic Distribution: limited to Massachusetts, with an emphasis on Greater Lawrence area

GIVING OFFICERS
Elizabeth A. Beland: admin

Phebe S. Miner: trust *PHIL AFFIL* trust: Nathaniel and Elizabeth P. Stevens Foundation, Quaker Hill Foundation

Christopher W. Rogers: trust

Samuel S. Rogers: trust *PHIL AFFIL* trust: Nathaniel and Elizabeth P. Stevens Foundation

APPLICATION INFORMATION
Initial Approach:

The foundation requests applications be made in writing and do not exceed 10 pages. Appendices may be attached.

Formal applications should include a copy of an IRS determination letter, proof of incorporation in Massachusetts, the names of the organization's officers and directors, the most recent annual financial statement, institutional income and an expense budget for the current fiscal year, a detailed program budget for which support is requested, the starting and completion dates of the project and the proposed cash flow, and the current status of fundraising program and anticipated sources.

Proposals may be submitted throughout the year.

Restrictions on Giving: No grants will be made to individuals, state or federal agencies, annual campaigns, deficit financing, exchange programs, internships, fellowships, professorships, scholarships, loans, or to organizations for the use of another agency that has not been determined tax-exempt. The trustees will not normally consider more than one application from an agency in the same calendar year.

OTHER THINGS TO KNOW
The foundation reports an affiliation with the Nathaniel and Elizabeth P. Stevens Foundation, also located in Massachusetts.

PUBLICATIONS
Program policy statement and application guidelines

GRANTS ANALYSIS
Total Grants: $748,632

Number of Grants: 89

Highest Grant: $122,557

Average Grant: $8,412

Typical Range: $1,000 to $10,000

Disclosure Period: 1993

Note: Recent grants are derived from a 1993 Form 990.

RECENT GRANTS
Library
8,000	Memorial Hall Library, Boston, MA

General
48,000	Merrimack Valley Community Foundation, Andover, MA
44,000	South Church in Andover, Andover, MA

30,000	Visiting Nurse Association Home Care, Boston, MA
25,000	Greater Lawrence Family Health Center, Lawrence, MA
25,000	Lawrence General Hospital Foundation, Lawrence, MA

Stone Charitable Foundation

CONTACT
Stephen A. Stone
President
Stone Charitable Fdn.
PO Box 728
Wareham, MA 02571
(508) 759-3503

FINANCIAL SUMMARY
Recent Giving: $333,960 (fiscal 1993); $330,064 (fiscal 1992); $352,650 (fiscal 1991)

Assets: $7,307,130 (fiscal 1993); $6,966,363 (fiscal 1992); $6,408,031 (fiscal 1991)

Gifts Received: $15,000 (fiscal 1993); $20,000 (fiscal 1992); $450,000 (fiscal 1991)

Fiscal Note: In fiscal 1993, contributions were received from Stephen A. Stone.

EIN: 04-6114683

CONTRIBUTIONS SUMMARY
Donor(s): the late Dewey D. Stone, Stephen A. Stone, Anne A. Stone, Thelma Finn, Jack Finn, the late Harry K. Stone

Typical Recipients: • *Arts & Humanities:* Arts Funds, Historic Preservation, Libraries, Museums/Galleries, Music, Public Broadcasting • *Civic & Public Affairs:* African American Affairs, General, Nonprofit Management, Philanthropic Organizations, Urban & Community Affairs • *Education:* Colleges & Universities, Education Associations, Minority Education, Private Education (Precollege) • *Health:* Clinics/Medical Centers, Health Funds, Health Organizations, Hospitals, Medical Rehabilitation, Single-Disease Health Associations • *International:* Foreign Educational Institutions, International Peace & Security Issues, Missionary/Religious Activities • *Religion:* Jewish Causes, Religious Organizations, Religious Welfare, Social/Policy Issues • *Social Services:* Child Welfare, Community Service Organizations, Family Planning, Family Services, Senior Services, Youth Organizations

Grant Types: capital, endowment, and general support

Geographic Distribution: focus on MA

GIVING OFFICERS
Deborah A. Stone: treas, trust

Stephen A. Stone: pres, trust *ED* Univ MI 1938; Harvard Univ 1939 *CURR EMPL* pres: Agawam Farms *CORP AFFIL* dir: Malden Trust Co

Theodore Herzl Teplow: secy, trust *ED* US Merchant Marine Academy BS 1950; Har-

vard Univ MBA 1953 *CORP AFFIL* consultant: Crosby Valve & Gage Co *NONPR AFFIL* trust: Am Merchant Marine Mus Fdn; vchmn, trust: Hebrew Coll MA

APPLICATION INFORMATION
Initial Approach: Send brief letter of inquiry describing program or project. There are no deadlines.

Restrictions on Giving: Does not support individuals.

GRANTS ANALYSIS
Total Grants: $333,960

Number of Grants: 43

Highest Grant: $60,000

Typical Range: $200 to $43,000

Disclosure Period: fiscal year ending November 30, 1993

Note: Recent grants are derived from a fiscal 1993 Form 990.

RECENT GRANTS

Library
| 1,000 | Malden Public Library, Malden, MA |

General
60,000	New Israel Fund, New York, NY
43,000	Hebrew College, Boston, MA
40,000	Jewish Family and Children's Services, Boston, MA
35,000	American Committee for Weizmann Institute of Science, New York, NY
35,000	American Committee for Weizmann Institute of Science, New York, NY

Thermo Electron Corp. / Thermo Electron Foundation

Sales: $1.25 billion
Employees: 10,000
Headquarters: Waltham, MA
SIC Major Group: Industrial Machinery & Equipment and Instruments & Related Products

CONTACT
Linda C. Nordberg
Assistant to President
Thermo Electron Corp.
81 Wyman St.
Waltham, MA 02254
(617) 622-1000

FINANCIAL SUMMARY
Recent Giving: $532,750 (1993); $343,000 (1992); $71,500 (1990)

Assets: $91,755 (1993); $121,044 (1992); $371,989 (1990)

Gifts Received: $500,000 (1993); $150,000 (1992); $125,000 (1990)

Fiscal Note: In 1993, contributions were received from Thermo Electron Corporation.

EIN: 22-2778152

CONTRIBUTIONS SUMMARY
Typical Recipients: • *Arts & Humanities:* Arts Centers, Ballet, Dance, Libraries, Museums/Galleries, Music, Performing Arts, Public Broadcasting • *Civic & Public Affairs:* Business/Free Enterprise, Civil Rights, Economic Development, Economic Policy, Employment/Job Training, General, Legal Aid, Municipalities/Towns, Native American Affairs, Philanthropic Organizations, Professional & Trade Associations, Public Policy, Urban & Community Affairs • *Education:* Business Education, Colleges & Universities, Community & Junior Colleges, Economic Education, Engineering/Technological Education, General, Health & Physical Education, Literacy, Private Education (Precollege), Religious Education, Science/Mathematics Education • *Environment:* General, Resource Conservation • *Health:* AIDS/HIV, Emergency/Ambulance Services, Hospices, Hospitals • *International:* International Development, International Organizations • *Religion:* Jewish Causes, Religious Welfare • *Science:* Observatories & Planetariums, Science Exhibits & Fairs, Science Museums • *Social Services:* Child Welfare, Community Service Organizations, Counseling, Emergency Relief, Food/Clothing Distribution, People with Disabilities, Senior Services, Shelters/Homelessness, United Funds/United Ways, Volunteer Services

Grant Types: award, capital, challenge, general support, and scholarship

Geographic Distribution: focus on headquarters area

Operating Locations: MA (Waltham)

CORP. OFFICERS
Dr. George Nicholas Hatsopoulos: *B* Athens Greece 1927 *ED* MA Inst Tech BS 1949; MA Inst Tech MS 1950; MA Inst Tech 1956 *CURR EMPL* fdr, chmn, pres, ceo, dir: Thermo Electron Corp *CORP AFFIL* dir: Bolt Beranek & Newman, Thermedics, Thermo Cardiosystems, Thermo Fibertek, Thermo Instrument Sys, Thermo Power Corp, Thermo Process Sys, ThermoTrex Corp *NONPR AFFIL* dir: Am Counc Capital Fdn, Ctr Policy Res; mem: Pi Tau Sigma, Sigma Xi; mem governing counc: Natl Academy Engg; trust: Boston Mus Science; vchmn: Am Bus Conf *PHIL AFFIL* trust: Costas and Mary Maliotis Charitable Foundation

John Nicholas Hatsopoulos: *B* Athens Greece 1934 *ED* Northwestern Univ 1959 *CURR EMPL* exec vp, cfo: Thermo Electron Corp *CORP AFFIL* cfo, dir: Thermo Voltek Corp; vp, cfo: Thermedics; vp, cfo, dir: Thermo Cardiosystems, Thermo Fibertek, Thermo Instrument Sys, Thermo Power Corp, Thermo Process Sys, ThermoTrex Corp

GIVING OFFICERS
Robert V. Aghababian: trust

Dr. George Nicholas Hatsopoulos: pres, dir *CURR EMPL* fdr, chmn, pres, ceo, dir: Thermo Electron Corp *PHIL AFFIL* trust: Costas and Mary Maliotis Charitable Foundation (see above)

John Nicholas Hatsopoulos: dir *CURR EMPL* exec vp, cfo: Thermo Electron Corp (see above)

Robert C. Howard: vp, dir

Paul F. Kelleher: trust

Sandra L. Lambert: trust

Theo Melas-Kyriazi: treas

Linda C. Nordberg: mgr

APPLICATION INFORMATION

Initial Approach: The foundation has no formal grant application procedure or application form. There are no deadlines.

GRANTS ANALYSIS

Total Grants: $532,750

Number of Grants: 57

Highest Grant: $250,000

Typical Range: $1,000 to $100,000

Disclosure Period: 1993

Note: Recent grants are derived from a 1993 Form 990.

RECENT GRANTS

General

250,000	Columbia University, New York, NY
100,000	Massachusetts Institute of Technology, Cambridge, MA
25,000	National Academy of Engineering, Washington, DC
10,000	Massachusetts General Hospital, Boston, MA
9,250	Association of Jesuit Colleges and Universities, Washington, DC

Thompson Trust, Thomas

CONTACT

Daniel W. Fawcett
Trustee
Thomas Thompson Trust
31 Milk St., Ste. 201
Boston, MA 02109
(617) 338-2798

FINANCIAL SUMMARY

Recent Giving: $378,845 (fiscal 1993); $392,741 (fiscal 1992); $345,340 (fiscal 1990)

Assets: $9,670,010 (fiscal 1993); $9,689,099 (fiscal 1992); $9,426,325 (fiscal 1990)

EIN: 03-0179429

CONTRIBUTIONS SUMMARY

Donor(s): the late Thomas Thompson

Typical Recipients: • *Arts & Humanities:* Arts Centers, Community Arts, Historic Preservation, Libraries, Music • *Civic & Public Affairs:* General, Safety • *Education:* International Exchange, Private Education (Precollege), Secondary Education (Public), Student Aid • *Environment:* General • *Health:* Health Funds, Hospitals, Mental Health • *Religion:* Religious Organizations, Religious Welfare • *Social Services:* At-

Risk Youth, Community Centers, Community Service Organizations, Counseling, Homes, Recreation & Athletics, Senior Services, Shelters/Homelessness, United Funds/United Ways, Youth Organizations

Grant Types: capital, emergency, general support, and project

Geographic Distribution: limited to Brattleboro, VT, and Rhinebeck, NY, and surrounding areas

GIVING OFFICERS

Daniel W. Fawcett: trust

William B. Tyler: trust *PHIL AFFIL* trust: John W. Alden Trust

APPLICATION INFORMATION

Initial Approach: Initial contact by telephone. Grants awarded only to organizations that have been in operation for three consecutive years. Application form required. Approach foundation by telephone. There are no deadlines. Board meets monthly except in August. Decisions are made within six weeks.

GRANTS ANALYSIS

Total Grants: $378,845

Number of Grants: 24

Highest Grant: $92,000

Typical Range: $2,500 to $34,710

Disclosure Period: fiscal year ending May 31, 1993

Note: Recent grants are derived from a fiscal 1993 Form 990.

RECENT GRANTS

Library

15,666	Starr Library, Rhinebeck, NY

General

92,000	Northern Dutchess Hospital, Rhinebeck, NY
34,710	Benefit of Seamstresses, Needlewomen, and Shop Girls
30,500	Brattleboro Mutual Aid Association, Brattleboro, VT
30,000	Rescue, Brattleboro, VT
25,000	Experiment in International Living, Brattleboro, VT

Tupancy-Harris Foundation of 1986

CONTACT

Robert N. Karelitz
Vice President
Fiduciary Trust Co.
c/o Fiduciary Trust Co.
175 Federal St.
Boston, MA 02110
(617) 482-5270

FINANCIAL SUMMARY

Recent Giving: $423,968 (1993); $437,443 (1992); $439,995 (1991)

Assets: $14,938,736 (1993); $14,653,268 (1992); $11,771,416 (1991)

Gifts Received: $27,309 (1993); $372 (1992)

EIN: 04-6547989

CONTRIBUTIONS SUMMARY

Donor(s): the late Oswald A. Tupancy

Typical Recipients: • *Arts & Humanities:* Arts Associations & Councils, Ethnic & Folk Arts, Historic Preservation, History & Archaeology, Libraries, Music, Public Broadcasting, Theater • *Civic & Public Affairs:* General, Urban & Community Affairs • *Education:* Colleges & Universities, Community & Junior Colleges, Public Education (Precollege) • *Environment:* General, Resource Conservation • *Health:* AIDS/HIV, Clinics/Medical Centers, Hospices, Hospitals, Prenatal Health Issues, Single-Disease Health Associations • *Religion:* Religious Organizations • *Social Services:* Child Welfare, Community Service Organizations, Delinquency & Criminal Rehabilitation, General, Recreation & Athletics, Youth Organizations

Grant Types: general support

Geographic Distribution: focus on Nantucket, MA

GIVING OFFICERS

Fiduciary Trust Co: trust

APPLICATION INFORMATION

Initial Approach: Send brief letter of inquiry describing program or project. There are no deadlines.

GRANTS ANALYSIS

Total Grants: $423,968

Number of Grants: 22

Highest Grant: $193,000

Typical Range: $1,000 to $100,000

Disclosure Period: 1993

Note: Recent grants are derived from a 1993 Form 990.

RECENT GRANTS

General

193,000	Nantucket Conservation Foundation, Nantucket, MA
39,000	Nantucket Cottage Hospital, Nantucket, MA
24,000	Nantucket Boys and Girls Club, Nantucket, MA
20,000	Cape Cod Community College Educational Foundation, West Bonnstable, MA
18,000	A Safe Place, Nantucket, MA

Wallace Foundation, George R.

CONTACT

George R. Wallace Fdn.
c/o Boston Safe Deposit & Trust Co.
One Boston Pl.
Boston, MA 02108
(617) 722-6818

FINANCIAL SUMMARY

Recent Giving: $394,500 (1993); $617,500 (1992); $265,000 (1991)

Assets: $6,530,306 (1993); $6,570,672 (1992); $6,938,454 (1991)

Gifts Received: $7,803 (1990)

EIN: 04-6130518

CONTRIBUTIONS SUMMARY

Donor(s): the late George R. Wallace

Typical Recipients: • *Arts & Humanities:* Dance, Historic Preservation, History & Archaeology, Libraries, Museums/Galleries, Music, Public Broadcasting • *Civic & Public Affairs:* Clubs, Community Foundations, General • *Education:* Business Education, Colleges & Universities, Community & Junior Colleges, Engineering/Technological Education, Minority Education, Private Education (Precollege), Public Education (Precollege), Religious Education • *Environment:* General, Resource Conservation • *Health:* Hospices, Hospitals • *Religion:* Churches, Religious Organizations • *Social Services:* Child Welfare, Domestic Violence, Family Planning, United Funds/United Ways, YMCA/YWCA/YMHA/YWHA, Youth Organizations

Grant Types: capital and endowment

Geographic Distribution: focus on MA

GIVING OFFICERS

John Grado, Jr.: trust

Henry B. Shepard, Jr.: trust

George R. Wallace III: trust

APPLICATION INFORMATION

Initial Approach: Send a brief letter of inquiry. Include a description of organization, amount requested, purpose of funds sought, recently audited financial statement, and proof of tax-exempt status. There are no deadlines.

Restrictions on Giving: Does not support individuals.

GRANTS ANALYSIS

Total Grants: $394,500

Number of Grants: 33

Highest Grant: $55,000

Typical Range: $500 to $50,000

Disclosure Period: 1993

Note: Recent grants are derived from a 1993 Form 990.

RECENT GRANTS

General

55,000	Conservancy, Naples, FL
50,000	Applewild School, Fitchburg, MA
50,000	Community Foundation of Collier County, Naples, FL
25,000	Fitchburg State College, Fitchburg, MA
20,000	Stoneleigh Burnham, Greenfield, MA

Weber Charities Corp., Frederick E.

CONTACT

Mary Ann Dailey
President
Frederick E. Weber Charities Corp.
34 1/2 Beacon St.
Boston, MA 02108
(617) 523-1455

FINANCIAL SUMMARY

Recent Giving: $152,998 (fiscal 1994); $185,212 (fiscal 1993); $220,988 (fiscal 1992)

Assets: $4,976,325 (fiscal 1994); $5,192,271 (fiscal 1993); $4,364,982 (fiscal 1992)

EIN: 04-2133244

CONTRIBUTIONS SUMMARY

Donor(s): the late Frederick E. Weber

Typical Recipients: • *Arts & Humanities:* Libraries, Performing Arts • *Civic & Public Affairs:* Employment/Job Training, Ethnic Organizations, General, Hispanic Affairs, Housing, Law & Justice, Municipalities/Towns, Philanthropic Organizations, Urban & Community Affairs, Women's Affairs • *Education:* Arts/Humanities Education, General, Minority Education, Private Education (Precollege), Student Aid • *Environment:* General • *Health:* AIDS/HIV, Children's Health/Hospitals, Geriatric Health, Health Organizations, Hospices, Hospitals, Medical Research, Mental Health • *International:* Health Care/Hospitals, International Affairs • *Religion:* Churches, Religious Organizations, Religious Welfare • *Social Services:* Camps, Child Welfare, Community Service Organizations, Counseling, Crime Prevention, Emergency Relief, Family Planning, Family Services, Food/Clothing Distribution, General, Homes, People with Disabilities, Recreation & Athletics, Shelters/Homelessness, Substance Abuse, United Funds/United Ways, YMCA/YWCA/YMHA/YWHA, Youth Organizations

Grant Types: emergency, endowment, and scholarship

Geographic Distribution: focus on the greater Boston, MA, area

GIVING OFFICERS

Mary Ann Daily: pres, dir

Janet W. Eustis: clerk, dir

Daniel Anthony Phillips: vp, treas, dir *B* Boston MA 1938 *ED* Harvard Univ 1960-1963 *CURR EMPL* pres, ceo, dir: Fiduciary Trust Co *CORP AFFIL* vp, mem exec comm, dir: Fiduciary Trust Co *NONPR AFFIL* dir: Family Fdn North Am, Family Svc Am; mem: Boston Econ Club, Boston Soc Security Analysts, Harvard Univ Alumni Assn; pres, dir: Am Meml Hosp; vp, treas: Frederick E Weber Charities Corp

APPLICATION INFORMATION

Initial Approach: Send a brief letter of inquiry. Include a description of organization, amount requested, purpose of funds sought, recently audited financial statement, and proof of tax-exempt status. There are no deadlines.

Restrictions on Giving: Limited to Massachusetts organizations.

PUBLICATIONS

Annual Report

GRANTS ANALYSIS

Total Grants: $152,998

Number of Grants: 75

Highest Grant: $20,000

Typical Range: $100 to $10,000

Disclosure Period: fiscal year ending March 31, 1994

Note: Recent grants are derived from a fiscal 1994 Form 990.

RECENT GRANTS

Library

10,000	Boston Public Library, Boston, MA

General

20,000	Associated Grantmakers of Massachusetts, Boston, MA — camperships
10,000	United Way of Massachusetts Bay, Boston, MA
7,500	Travelers Aid of Boston, Boston, MA — revolving fund
7,000	Children's Friend and Family Service Society of the N.S., Salem, MA — revolving fund
5,130	Department of Social Services, Boston, MA — emergency client assistance

Winthrop Trust, Clara B.

CONTACT

Denise Barron
Trust Officer
Clara B. Winthrop Trust
c/o Welch & Forbes
45 School St., 5th Flr.
Boston, MA 02108
(617) 523-1635

FINANCIAL SUMMARY

Recent Giving: $87,800 (1993); $86,574 (1992); $86,700 (1991)

Assets: $2,453,521 (1993); $2,395,861 (1992); $2,394,745 (1991)

EIN: 04-6039972

CONTRIBUTIONS SUMMARY

Typical Recipients: • *Arts & Humanities:* Community Arts, Historic Preservation, History & Archaeology, Libraries, Museums/Galleries, Music, Public Broadcasting, Theater • *Civic & Public Affairs:* General, Municipalities/Towns, Native American Affairs, Public Policy, Urban & Community Affairs, Zoos/Aquariums • *Education:* Colleges & Universities, Education Associations, Private Education (Precollege), Secondary Education (Private) • *Environment:* General, Resource Conservation • *Health:* Hospitals, Nursing Services • *International:* International Organizations • *Religion:* Churches • *Science:* Science Museums • *Social Services:* Child Welfare, Community Service Organizations, Youth Organizations

Grant Types: general support

Geographic Distribution: focus on MA

GIVING OFFICERS
Welch & Forbes: trust

APPLICATION INFORMATION
Initial Approach: Send a brief letter of inquiry. Include a description of organization, amount requested, purpose of funds sought, recently audited financial statement, and proof of tax-exempt status. There are no deadlines.

Restrictions on Giving: Does not support individuals.

GRANTS ANALYSIS
Total Grants: $87,800

Number of Grants: 24

Highest Grant: $9,000

Typical Range: $1,000 to $7,500

Disclosure Period: 1993

Note: Recent grants are derived from a 1993 Form 990.

RECENT GRANTS
Library

2,000	Library of Boston Athenaeum, Boston, MA
2,000	Manchester-by-the-Sea Library, Boston, MA

General

7,000	Winsor School, Boston, MA
6,800	Beverly Hospital, Beverly, MA
5,500	Town of Manchester-by-the-Sea, Boston, MA
4,000	English Speaking Union, Boston, MA
4,000	Friends of Manchester-by-the-Sea Trees, Boston, MA

MICHIGAN

Abrams Foundation, Talbert and Leota

CONTACT
Joe C. Foster, Jr.
Secretary
Talbert and Leota Abrams Fdn.
1000 Michigan Natl. Tower
Lansing, MI 48933
(517) 482-5800

FINANCIAL SUMMARY
Recent Giving: $96,967 (1992); $127,700 (1990); $82,200 (1989)

Assets: $5,999,153 (1992); $3,155,586 (1990); $3,037,822 (1989)

Gifts Received: $2,358,812 (1992); $5,000 (1990); $5,000 (1989)

Fiscal Note: In fiscal 1992, contributions were received from Talbert Abram Trust.

EIN: 38-6082194

CONTRIBUTIONS SUMMARY
Donor(s): the late Leota Abrams, Talbert Abrams

Typical Recipients: • *Arts & Humanities:* Libraries • *Civic & Public Affairs:* Clubs • *Education:* Business Education, Colleges & Universities, Community & Junior Colleges, Engineering/Technological Education • *Health:* Medical Research, Single-Disease Health Associations • *Social Services:* United Funds/United Ways, Youth Organizations

Grant Types: endowment

Geographic Distribution: focus on central MI

GIVING OFFICERS
Kyle C. Abbott: dir

Barbara J. Brown: pres, dir

Craig C. Brown: dir

Joe C. Foster, Jr.: secy, dir *B* Lansing MI 1925 *ED* Wabash Coll 1943-1944; Univ MI JD 1949 *CURR EMPL* ptnr: Fraser Trebilcock Davis & Foster *NONPR AFFIL* fellow: Am Bar Fdn, Am Coll Tax Couns, Am Coll Trust & Estate Couns, MI Bar Fdn; mem: Am Bar Assn, Joint Editorial Bd Uniform Probate Code, MI Bar Assn, Phi Beta Kappa, Phi Gamma Delta, Rotary; mem, exec couns: Intl Academy Estate & Trust Law

Thomas M. Schafer: vp

APPLICATION INFORMATION
Initial Approach: Send two-page letter of inquiry describing program or project. Deadline is June 30 for next calendar year.

Restrictions on Giving: Limited to scientific and educational purposes in central Michigan.

PUBLICATIONS
Annual Report

GRANTS ANALYSIS
Total Grants: $96,967

Number of Grants: 11

Highest Grant: $50,000

Typical Range: $1,000 to $15,000

Disclosure Period: 1992

Note: Recent grants are derived from a 1992 Form 990.

RECENT GRANTS
Library

15,000	Library of Michigan Foundation, Lansing, MI

General

50,000	Michigan State University, E. Lansing, MI
15,000	Michigan Dyslexia Institute, Lansing, MI
6,250	Architectural Studies Foundation, Lansing, MI
2,017	YWCA, Lansing, MI
2,000	Capital Area United Way, Lansing, MI

American Natural Resources Company / ANR Foundation, Inc.

Sales: $2.6 billion
Employees: 10,865
Parent Company: Coastal Natural Gas Co.
Headquarters: Detroit, MI
SIC Major Group: Holding Companies Nec, Bituminous Coal & Lignite—Surface, Anthracite Mining, and Crude Petroleum & Natural Gas

CONTACT
Bernard V. Quinlan
Director, Corporate & Community Affairs
ANR Foundation, Inc.
1 Woodward Ave.
Detroit, MI 48226
(313) 496-3781

FINANCIAL SUMMARY
Recent Giving: $973,861 (1993); $1,013,358 (1992); $1,073,944 (1991)

Assets: $1,727,708 (1993); $1,225,795 (1992); $1,002,040 (1991)

Gifts Received: $1,320,000 (1993); $1,300,000 (1992)

Fiscal Note: All contributions are made through the foundation. In 1993, the foundation received $1,275,000 from ANR Pipeline Co. and $45,000 from ANR Storage Co..

EIN: 38-2602116

CONTRIBUTIONS SUMMARY
Typical Recipients: • *Arts & Humanities:* Arts Appreciation, Arts Associations & Councils, Arts Centers, Arts Institutes, Community Arts, Historic Preservation, Libraries, Museums/Galleries, Music, Opera, Performing Arts, Public Broadcasting, Theater, Visual Arts • *Civic & Public Affairs:* Business/Free Enterprise, Economic Development, Employment/Job Training, Parades/Festivals, Public Policy, Urban & Community Affairs, Zoos/Aquariums • *Education:* Agricultural Education, Arts/Humanities Education, Business Education, Colleges & Universities, Education Associations, Education Reform, Engineering/Technological Education, Faculty Development, Legal Education, Minority Education, Public Education (Precollege), Science/Mathematics Education, Student Aid • *Environment:* General • *Health:* Emergency/Ambulance Services, Health Policy/Cost Containment, Health Organizations, Hospices, Hospitals, Medical Rehabilitation, Medical Research, Public Health, Single-Disease Health Associations • *International:* International Relations • *Religion:* Religious Welfare • *Science:* Science Exhibits & Fairs, Scien-

tific Centers & Institutes, Scientific Organizations • *Social Services:* Child Welfare, Community Service Organizations, Emergency Relief, Food/Clothing Distribution, People with Disabilities, Recreation & Athletics, United Funds/United Ways, Volunteer Services, Youth Organizations

Grant Types: capital, challenge, general support, research, and scholarship

Nonmonetary Support Types: donated equipment and in-kind services

Note: Value of nonmonetary support is not available and is not included in the giving figures.

Geographic Distribution: operating locations

Operating Locations: CO (Golden), MA (Revere), MI (Detroit, Grand Rapids), NY (New York), PA (West Mifflin), TX (Fort Worth, Houston), VA (Roanoke), WV (Birch River)

CORP. OFFICERS

Harold Burrow: *B* Navasota TX 1914 *CURR EMPL* chmn: Am Natural Resources Co *CORP AFFIL* chmn: CO Interstate Gas Co, CO Interstate Gas Co; chmn, ceo: Coastal Natural Gas Co; dir: Coastal Oil & Gas Corp

James F. Cordes: *B* St Louis MO 1940 *ED* St Louis Univ BS 1963; Creighton Univ MBA 1968; Univ NE MS 1976 *CURR EMPL* pres, ceo, dir: Am Natural Resources Co *CORP AFFIL* chmn: ANR Pipeline Co, ANR Storage Co; chmn, ceo: ANR Blue Lake Co; dir: Five Flags Holding Co, Great Lakes Gas Transmission Co, Mfrs Bank Detroit, Mfrs Natl Corp; exec vp, dir: Coastal Corp, Coastal Natural Gas Co

Austin Martin O'Toole: *B* New Bedford MA 1935 *ED* Coll Holy Cross BBA 1957; Georgetown Univ JD 1963 *CURR EMPL* secy: Am Natural Resources Co *CORP AFFIL* asst secy: Coastal Belcher Petroleum Ltd, Coastal Bermuda Petroleum Ltd, Coastal Great Lakes Inc, Coastal Offshore Ins Ltd, Eaton Rapids Gas Storage Sys; asst secy, dir: ANR Storage Co, ANR Western Storage Co, Coastal Mgmt Svcs Singapore Ltd, Coastal Petroleum Far East Ltd, Unitex Offshore Transmission Co; assy secy, dir: TX Offshore Pipeline Sys Inc; clerk, dir: Coastal Oil New England Inc; dir: Coastal Fin Antilles NV, Coastal Fin BV, Coastal Gas Mktg Co, Coastal Multi-Fuels Inc, Coastal Netherlands Fin BV, Coastal St Gas Transmission, Coastal St Holdings UK Ltd, TND Beverage Corp; secy: Coastal Chem Sales Co, Coastal Coal Sales Inc, Javelina Co, Javelina Pipeline Co; secy, dir: ANR Venture Eagle Point Co, ANRFS Holdings Inc, CIC-Canyon Compression Co, CIG Gas Supply Co, Coastal Chem Inc, Coastal Devel Co, Coastal Power Revere Co, Empire St Pipeline Co Inc, Enterprise Coal Co, Greenbrier Coal Co, Kingwood Coal Co, Skyline Coal Co, Southern UT Fuel Co, Transport USA Inc, Unique Mining Sys Inc, UT Fuel Co, VA City Coal Co, VA Iron Coal & Coke Co; sr vp, secy: CO Interstate Gas Co, Coastal Aruba Refining Co, Coastal Oil Chelsea Inc, Coastal Tug & Barge Inc,

Coscol Petroleum Corp; sr vp, secy, dir: ANR Venture Fulton Co, ANR Venture Mgmt Co, CIC Indus Inc, CIC Stock Corp, CIG Exploration Inc, CIG Overthrust Inc, CO Solar-Tech Inc, CO Water Supply Co, Coastal Aruba Holding Co NV, Coastal Aruba Maintenance/Oper Co NV, Coastal Capital Corp, Coastal Cat Process Mktg Inc, Coastal Dril Inc, Coastal Eagle Point Oil Co, Coastal Energy Corp, Coastal Fin Corp, Coastal Fuels Mktg Inc, Coastal Holding Corp, Coastal Javelina Inc, Coastal Ltd Ventures Inc, Coastal Mart Inc, Coastal Midland Inc, Coastal Natural Gas Co, Coastal Oil & Gas Corp, Coastal Oil NY Inc, Coastal Pan Am Corp, Coastal Pipeline Co, Coastal Power Production Co, Coastal Refining & Mktg Inc, Coastal St Crude Gathering Co, Coastal St Energy Co, Coastal St Mgmt Corp, Coastal St Trading Co Inc, Coastal Tankships USA Inc, Coastal Unilube Inc, Coastal W Ventures Inc, Cosbel Petroleum Corp, Coscol Marine Corp, TX Tank Ship Agency Inc, WY Gas Supply Inc; sr vp, sr couns, secy: Coastal Corp; vp, secy, dir: Coastal Tech Inc, Golden Carriers Corp *NONPR AFFIL* mem: Am Arbitration Assn, Am Bar Assn, Am Soc Corp Secys, Houston Bar Assn, TX Bar Assn

James Robert Paul: *B* Wichita KS 1934 *ED* Wichita St Univ BS 1956 *CURR EMPL* chmn, ceo: Coastal St Energy Co *CORP AFFIL* chmn: UT Fuel Co; pres, coo, ceo, dir: Coastal Corp *NONPR AFFIL* mem: Am Petroleum Inst, Fin Execs Inst

GIVING OFFICERS

David A. Arledge: treas *B* 1944 *ED* Univ TX BBA 1965; Univ TX LLB 1968 *CURR EMPL* pres, coo, dir: Coastal Corp *CORP AFFIL* exec vp: Am Natural Resources Co, ANR Storage Co; exec vp, dir: ANR Blue Lake Co, Coastal Tug & Barge Inc, Manatee Towing Co Inc; sr exec vp: ABCO Leasing Inc, ANR Pipeline Co, Coastal Tankships USA Inc; sr vp, dir: Coastal St Trading Co Inc

James F. Cordes: pres, dir *CURR EMPL* pres, ceo, dir: Am Natural Resources Co (see above)

Lawrence Paul Doss: dir *B* Cleveland OH 1927 *ED* OH St Univ 1947-1949; Fenn Coll 1949-1951; Am Univ 1954; Nova Univ MPA *NONPR AFFIL* chmn bd trusts: Doctors Hosp; co-chmn: Move Detroit Forward; dir, mem exec comm: Detroit Econ Growth Corp; mem: MI Commn Jobs Econ Devel, Omega Psi Phi; treas: Congressional Black Caucus; trust: Un Fdn; vchmn, mem exec c omm: Martin Luther King Ctr Nonviolent Social Change *PHIL AFFIL* trust: Hudson-Webber Foundation; pres: Coleman Young Foundation

William L. Johnson: vp *CURR EMPL* vp, contr, dir: ANR Blue Lake Co

Austin Martin O'Toole: secy *CURR EMPL* secy: Am Natural Resources Co (see above)

James Robert Paul: chmn, dir *CURR EMPL* chmn, ceo: Coastal St Energy Co (see above)

Bernard V. Quinlan: dir corp & commun aff

APPLICATION INFORMATION

Initial Approach: *Initial Contact:* written request to chairman, ANR Community Investment Program, at nearest operating company, or to Bernard V. Quinlan, director of corporate and community affairs *Include Information On:* most recent annual report, amount requested, purpose of request, financial and budget information, and proof of tax-exempt status *Deadlines:* none

Restrictions on Giving: Contributions do not support individuals; organizations that are not tax-exempt; organizations practicing discrimination; organizations already supported through the United Way; political organizations or campaigns; religious groups for sectarian purposes; or fund-raising events, conventions, or goodwill advertising.

OTHER THINGS TO KNOW

Principal subsidiaries of American Natural Resources Co. contributing to the foundation include ANR Pipeline Co., Detroit, MI; ANR Coal Company, Roanoke, VA; ANR Freight System, Inc., Lakewood, CO; ANR Storage Company, Detroit, MI; and Great Lakes Gas Transmission Company, Detroit, MI.

GRANTS ANALYSIS

Total Grants: $973,861

Number of Grants: 175

Highest Grant: $90,000

Average Grant: $5,565

Typical Range: $3,000 to $25,000

Disclosure Period: 1993

Note: Recent grants are derived from a 1993 Form 990.

RECENT GRANTS

Library

5,000	Friends of the Detroit Public Library, Detroit, MI — sponsor of Junior Great Books Program and Community Programming

General

90,000	United Way for Southeastern Michigan, Detroit, MI — corporate pledge
48,000	Detroit Renaissance Foundation, Detroit, MI — Detroit Strategic Plan Support
36,000	Wayne State University, Detroit, MI — Faculty Research Awards Program
30,000	Forward Wisconsin, Milwaukee, WI — operating support
28,830	United Way of Southeastern Michigan, Detroit, MI — New Detroit Fund operating support

Batts Foundation

CONTACT
John H. Batts
President
Batts Fdn.
200 Franklin St.
Zeeland, MI 49464
(616) 669-1020

FINANCIAL SUMMARY
Recent Giving: $108,110 (1993); $129,750 (1992); $112,280 (1991)

Assets: $2,169,334 (1993); $1,903,741 (1992); $1,658,575 (1991)

Gifts Received: $250,000 (1993); $250,000 (1992); $250,000 (1991)

Fiscal Note: In 1993, contributions were received from the Batts Group, Ltd.

EIN: 38-2782168

CONTRIBUTIONS SUMMARY
Typical Recipients: • *Arts & Humanities:* Arts Centers, Libraries, Museums/Galleries, Music, Opera, Performing Arts • *Civic & Public Affairs:* Chambers of Commerce, Employment/Job Training, General, Housing, Municipalities/Towns, Zoos/Aquariums • *Education:* Business Education, Colleges & Universities, Community & Junior Colleges, Education Funds, Private Education (Precollege), Public Education (Precollege), Science/Mathematics Education • *Environment:* General, Resource Conservation • *Health:* Emergency/Ambulance Services, Health Funds, Health Organizations, Hospitals, Long-Term Care • *Religion:* Churches, Religious Organizations, Religious Welfare • *Social Services:* Family Planning, Food/Clothing Distribution, Homes, Substance Abuse, United Funds/United Ways, Youth Organizations

Grant Types: general support

Geographic Distribution: focus on MI

GIVING OFFICERS
James L. Batts: dir

John H. Batts: pres, dir

John T. Batts: dir

Michael A. Batts: dir

Robert H. Batts: dir

Warren Leighton Batts: pres *B* Norfolk VA 1932 *ED* GA Inst Tech BS 1961; Harvard Univ MBA 1963 *CURR EMPL* chmn: Ralph Wilson Plastics *CORP AFFIL* dir: Cooper Indus, Sears Roebuck & Co, Sprint Corp *NONPR AFFIL* trust: Northwestern Univ; v chmn, trust: Childrens Meml Hosp *CLUB AFFIL* Chicago, Citrus, Econ, Glen View GC, Indian Hills CC, Los Angeles CC, Moraine CC

Maurice R. Wertenberger: vp

APPLICATION INFORMATION
Initial Approach: The foundation has no formal grant application procedure or application form. There are no deadlines.

GRANTS ANALYSIS
Total Grants: $108,110

Number of Grants: 42

Highest Grant: $20,000

Typical Range: $150 to $15,000

Disclosure Period: 1993

Note: Recent grants are derived from a 1993 Form 990.

RECENT GRANTS
Library
20,000	City of Zeeland Library Fund, Zeeland, MI

General
15,000	Grand Valley State University, Allendale, MI
10,000	United Way of Grand Rapids, Grand Rapids, MI
5,000	American Red Cross, Ottawa County, MI
5,000	Hope College Community Campaign, Holland, MI
5,000	John Ball Zoological Society, Grand Rapids, MI

Bauervic Foundation, Charles M.

CONTACT
Theodore Leonard
Director
Charles M. Bauervic Fdn.
PO Box 170, Rte. 2
Suttons Bay, MI 49682
(616) 271-6885

FINANCIAL SUMMARY
Recent Giving: $139,000 (1993); $150,500 (1992); $136,000 (1991)

Assets: $3,404,350 (1993); $3,605,958 (1992); $3,728,970 (1991)

EIN: 38-6146352

CONTRIBUTIONS SUMMARY
Donor(s): the late Charles M. Bauervic

Typical Recipients: • *Arts & Humanities:* Arts Centers, History & Archaeology, Libraries, Museums/Galleries, Music • *Civic & Public Affairs:* Employment/Job Training, Housing, Public Policy, Safety • *Education:* Arts/Humanities Education, Colleges & Universities, Continuing Education, General, Medical Education, Private Education (Precollege), Religious Education, Science/Mathematics Education, Secondary Education (Private) • *Health:* Alzheimers Disease, Health Organizations, Long-Term Care, Medical Research • *Religion:* Religious Organizations, Religious Welfare, Social/Policy Issues • *Science:* Science Exhibits & Fairs • *Social Services:* At-Risk Youth, Camps, People with Disabilities, Special Olympics, Youth Organizations

Grant Types: general support, operating expenses, and project

Geographic Distribution: focus on MI

GIVING OFFICERS
Kathryn Leonard: treas

Patricia A. Leonard: pres, secy

Theodore J. Leonard: dir

Timothy J. Leonard: dir

Rose Bauervic Wright: vp

APPLICATION INFORMATION
Initial Approach: Send letter requesting application form. Deadline is April 30.

Restrictions on Giving: Limited to Michigan.

GRANTS ANALYSIS
Total Grants: $139,000

Number of Grants: 35

Highest Grant: $20,000

Typical Range: $500 to $10,000

Disclosure Period: 1993

Note: Recent grants are derived from a 1993 Form 990.

RECENT GRANTS
Library
20,000	Hillsdale College-Hillsdale Academy, Hillsdale, MI — Venture Capital Awards and library books
10,000	Northwood University, Midland, MI — External Degree program and Master Degree Library additions

General
10,000	Institute in Basic Life Principles, Oak Brook, IL — tools and equipment for wood shop
8,000	Legion of Christ — kitchen renovation and new dormitory windows
7,500	Boysville of Michigan, Clinton, MI — food service equipment
7,000	Walsh College, North Canton, OH — economic books and student writing awards
6,000	Educational Center for Live, Pontiac, MI — computer equipment

Besser Foundation

CONTACT
J. Richard Wilson
President
Besser Fdn.
123 N Second Ave.
Alpena, MI 49707
(517) 354-4722

FINANCIAL SUMMARY
Recent Giving: $840,761 (1993); $1,395,856 (1992); $681,178 (1991)

Assets: $13,681,607 (1993); $13,133,327 (1992); $13,410,921 (1991)

EIN: 38-6071938

CONTRIBUTIONS SUMMARY
Donor(s): the late J. H. Besser, Besser Co.

Typical Recipients: • *Arts & Humanities:* Arts Associations & Councils, Libraries, Museums/Galleries • *Civic & Public Affairs:* Community Foundations, General, Professional & Trade Associations, Safety • *Education:* Colleges & Universities, Community & Junior Colleges, Minority Education, Public Education (Precollege), Science/Mathematics Education, Secondary Education (Public), Student Aid • *Health:* Health Organizations, Hospices, Hospitals, Medical Rehabilitation, Mental Health, Transplant Networks/Donor Banks • *International:* Health Care/Hospitals, International Relief Efforts • *Religion:* Churches, Synagogues/Temples • *Social Services:* Animal Protection, Big Brother/Big Sister, Camps, Child Welfare, Community Service Organizations, Domestic Violence, Family Services, Food/Clothing Distribution, Shelters/Homelessness, United Funds/United Ways, Youth Organizations

Grant Types: general support, multi-year/continuing support, operating expenses, and scholarship

Geographic Distribution: limited to the Alpena, MI, area

GIVING OFFICERS
Rev. Robert M. Barksdale: trust

James C. Park: trust

Carl F. Reitz: secy, trust

Harold A. Ruemenapp: trust

J. Richard Wilson: pres, trust

APPLICATION INFORMATION
Initial Approach: The foundation requests applications be made in writing. Deadline is the end of second month in calendar quarter.

Restrictions on Giving: Does not support individuals or provide funds for endowments or research. Limited to organizations in Alpena, MI.

PUBLICATIONS
Annual report (including application guidelines)

GRANTS ANALYSIS
Total Grants: $840,761

Number of Grants: 58

Highest Grant: $153,280

Typical Range: $300 to $153,180

Disclosure Period: 1993

Note: Recent grants are derived from a 1993 Form 990.

RECENT GRANTS

General

34,000	United Way of Northeast Michigan, Alpena, MI
31,400	Alpena Community College, Alpena, MI — toward construction of new building, to be paid over three-years
30,000	Child and Family Services, Northeast Michigan Branch, Alpena, MI
26,700	Africare, Washington, DC — water project

24,000	Alpena Community College, Alpena, MI — expenses of operating an adult volunteer center

Borman's Inc. / Borman Fund, The

Sales: $922.0 million
Employees: 8,500
Headquarters: Detroit, MI
SIC Major Group: Grocery Stores and Drug Stores & Proprietary Stores

CONTACT
Gilbert Borman
Secretary-Treasurer
The Borman Fund
20500 Civic Center Dr., Ste. 2750
Southfield, MI 48076
(810) 350-0300

FINANCIAL SUMMARY
Recent Giving: $551,748 (1993); $258,809 (1992); $602,168 (1991)

Assets: $609,849 (1993); $1,051,865 (1992); $949,787 (1991)

Gifts Received: $310,840 (1993); $300,000 (1992); $320,000 (1991)

Fiscal Note: Contributions are made through the foundation only. In 1993, contributions were received from Great Atlantic & Pacific Tea Company ($300,000) and MS. GEP Partnership ($10,000).

EIN: 38-6069267

CONTRIBUTIONS SUMMARY
Typical Recipients: • *Arts & Humanities:* Arts Associations & Councils, Arts Centers, Arts Institutes, Community Arts, Dance, Ethnic & Folk Arts, Historic Preservation, Libraries, Literary Arts, Museums/Galleries, Music, Performing Arts, Theater • *Civic & Public Affairs:* Civil Rights, General, Housing, Parades/Festivals, Philanthropic Organizations, Public Policy, Urban & Community Affairs, Zoos/Aquariums • *Education:* Colleges & Universities, Minority Education, Private Education (Precollege), Religious Education, Science/Mathematics Education, Secondary Education (Public) • *Environment:* General • *Health:* AIDS/HIV, Alzheimers Disease, Cancer, Children's Health/Hospitals, Emergency/Ambulance Services, Eyes/Blindness, Geriatric Health, Health Organizations, Hospices, Hospitals, Mental Health, Multiple Sclerosis, Single-Disease Health Associations • *International:* Foreign Educational Institutions, International Affairs, International Organizations, Missionary/Religious Activities • *Religion:* Churches, Jewish Causes, Religious Organizations, Religious Welfare, Synagogues/Temples • *Science:* Scientific Centers & Institutes, Scientific Organizations • *Social Services:* Animal Protection, Child Welfare, Community Centers, Community Service Organizations, Day Care, Delinquency & Criminal Rehabilitation, Domestic Violence, Emergency Relief, Family Planning, Family Services, Food/Clothing Distri-

bution, People with Disabilities, Recreation & Athletics, Senior Services, Shelters/Homelessness, Substance Abuse, United Funds/United Ways, Youth Organizations

Grant Types: award, general support, and project

Geographic Distribution: focus on southeastern Michigan area

Operating Locations: MI (Detroit, Southfield)

Note: Two divisions are located in Detroit, MI.

CORP. OFFICERS
Paul Borman: *B* Detroit MI 1932 *ED* MI St Univ 1954 *CURR EMPL* chmn: Bormans Inc *CORP AFFIL* dir: First Fed MI

GIVING OFFICERS
Gilbert Borman: secy, treas, dir

Marlene Borman: vp, dir *B* Grant County ND 1936 *ED* Air Force Inst Tech; Cleveland Inst Tech *CURR EMPL* vp res engg: Disc Instruments *NONPR AFFIL* mem: Am Mgmt Assn, Natl Soc Professional Engrs

Paul Borman: pres, dir *CURR EMPL* chmn: Bormans Inc (see above)

APPLICATION INFORMATION
Initial Approach: *Initial Contact:* written request *Include Information On:* amount needed, purpose of the grant, and organizational and financial information of applicant *Deadlines:* none

Restrictions on Giving: The company does not support individuals or political or lobbying groups.

GRANTS ANALYSIS
Total Grants: $551,748

Number of Grants: 110

Highest Grant: $81,500

Average Grant: $5,016

Typical Range: $100 to $10,000

Disclosure Period: 1993

Note: Recent grants are derived from a 1993 Form 990.

RECENT GRANTS

Library

1,000	Detroit Public Library, Detroit, MI

General

81,500	University of Michigan, Ann Arbor, MI
75,000	United Jewish Appeal, New York, NY
54,550	Sisterhood of the Congregation, Southfield, MI
41,450	Civil Liberties Action League, New York, NY
36,000	Allied Jewish Campaign, Bloomfield Hills, MI

Boutell Memorial Fund

Former Foundation Name: Arnold and Gertrude Boutell Memorial Fund

CONTACT
Louise Rhode
Trust Administrator
Boutell Memorial Fund
c/o Second National Bank Saginaw
101 N Washington
Saginaw, MI 48607
(517) 776-7582

FINANCIAL SUMMARY
Recent Giving: $408,798 (fiscal 1994); $383,491 (fiscal 1993); $357,547 (fiscal 1992)

Assets: $7,984,328 (fiscal 1994); $7,976,258 (fiscal 1993); $7,834,168 (fiscal 1992)

EIN: 38-6040492

CONTRIBUTIONS SUMMARY
Donor(s): the late Arnold and Gertrude Boutell

Typical Recipients: • *Arts & Humanities:* Community Arts, Libraries, Music • *Civic & Public Affairs:* Community Foundations, Economic Development, Employment/Job Training, Housing, Municipalities/Towns, Parades/Festivals, Safety, Urban & Community Affairs, Zoos/Aquariums • *Education:* Business-School Partnerships, Colleges & Universities, Public Education (Precollege) • *Health:* Hospitals • *Religion:* Religious Welfare • *Social Services:* Child Welfare, Community Service Organizations, Crime Prevention, Recreation & Athletics, Shelters/Homelessness, United Funds/United Ways, Youth Organizations

Grant Types: general support

Geographic Distribution: limited to Saginaw County, MI

GIVING OFFICERS
Second National Bank of Saginaw: trust

APPLICATION INFORMATION
Initial Approach: Send letter requesting application form. There are no deadlines.

Restrictions on Giving: Does not support individuals.

GRANTS ANALYSIS
Total Grants: $408,798

Number of Grants: 17

Highest Grant: $80,000

Typical Range: $500 to $80,000

Disclosure Period: fiscal year ending March 31, 1994

Note: Recent grants are derived from a fiscal 1994 Form 990.

RECENT GRANTS

General
80,000	Opportunities Industrialization Center, Saginaw, MI
80,000	Saginaw Community Foundation, Saginaw, MI
50,000	Saginaw Future, Saginaw, MI
47,500	United Way of Saginaw, Saginaw, MI
30,000	City Rescue Mission, Saginaw, MI

Chrysler Corp. / Chrysler Corporation Fund

Revenue: $52.22 billion
Employees: 123,000
Headquarters: Highland Park, MI
SIC Major Group: Motor Vehicles & Car Bodies, Electronic Components Nec, Motor Vehicle Parts & Accessories, and Personal Credit Institutions

CONTACT
Lynn A. Feldhouse
Manager & Secretary
Chrysler Corporation Fund
CIMS: 416-13-22
12000 Chrysler Dr.
Highland Park, MI 48288-0001
(313) 956-5194
Note: Kim-Lan Trinh, administrator and assistant secretary, is another contact at the above address.

FINANCIAL SUMMARY
Recent Giving: $21,000,000 (1995 est.); $16,900,000 (1994 approx.); $8,129,998 (1993)

Assets: $50,500,000 (1994 approx.); $32,456,611 (1993); $15,300,000 (1992 approx.)

Gifts Received: $19,940,000 (1993)

Fiscal Note: Company gives only through fund. Above figures exclude nonmonetary support. Contributions were received from Chrysler Corp.

EIN: 38-6087371

CONTRIBUTIONS SUMMARY
Typical Recipients: • *Arts & Humanities:* Arts Associations & Councils, Arts Centers, Arts Institutes, Libraries, Museums/Galleries, Music, Opera, Performing Arts, Public Broadcasting • *Civic & Public Affairs:* Economic Development, Public Policy, Safety, Urban & Community Affairs, Women's Affairs, Zoos/Aquariums • *Education:* Business Education, Colleges & Universities, Economic Education, Education Associations, Engineering/Technological Education, Health & Physical Education, Minority Education, Science/Mathematics Education • *Social Services:* Child Welfare, Community Service Organizations, Emergency Relief, Food/Clothing Distribution, Recreation & Athletics, Senior Services, Substance Abuse, United Funds/United Ways, Volunteer Services, Youth Organizations

Grant Types: employee matching gifts and general support

Note: Employee matching gift ratio: 2 to 1 for the first $500. Employee matching gift ratio: 1 to 1 for gifts of more than $500 up to a maximum of $7,000.

Nonmonetary Support: $6,000,000 (1994); $6,000,000 (1993); $4,500,000 (1992)

Nonmonetary Support Types: donated equipment and donated products

Note: Nonmonetary support is principally in the form of vehicles donated to educational institutions for use in training mechanics.

Geographic Distribution: near operating locations and nationally

Operating Locations: AL (Huntsville, Muscle Shoals), CA (Fullerton, Long Beach, Los Angeles, Ontario, San Leandro), CO (Denver), CT (Farmington, Greenwich), DE (Newark), FL (Miami, Orlando), GA (Atlanta, Savannah), IL (Belvedere, Elk Grove Village, Itasca, Normal, Oak Brook), IN (Indianapolis, Kokomo, New Castle), MA (Natick), MI (Brownstown, Center Line, Detroit, Evart, Highland Park, Marysville, Mount Clemens, Sterling Heights, Trenton, Troy, Warren), MN (Minneapolis, Plymouth Village), MO (Fenton, Hazelwood), NJ (Princeton), NY (Armonk, East Syracuse, Tappan), OH (Dayton, Old Fort, Perrysburg, Sandusky, Solon, Twinsburg, Van Wert), OK (Bethany, Oklahoma City), OR (Beaverton), PA (Allentown), SC (Taylors), TN (Memphis), TX (Ballinger, Carrollton, El Paso, Houston, Richardson), VA (Arlington, Richmond), WI (Beaver Dam, Coleman), WY (Green River)

CORP. OFFICERS
Robert James Eaton: *B* Buena Vista CO 1940 *ED* Univ KS 1963 *CURR EMPL* chmn, ceo: Chrysler Corp *CORP AFFIL* chmn: Saab Automobile; dir: Group Lotus *NONPR AFFIL* chmn: Chevaliers du Tastevin; fellow: Engg Soc Detroit, Soc Automotive Engrs; mem: Indus Tech Inst, Natl Acad Engg; mem adv counc: Univ MI Coll Engg; mem indus adv counc: Stanford Univ Coll Engg

A. C. Liebler: *CURR EMPL* vp commun & mktg: Chrysler Corp

Robert Anthony Lutz: *B* Zurich Switzerland 1932 *ED* Univ CA Berkeley BS 1961; Univ CA Berkeley MBA 1962 *CURR EMPL* pres, coo: Chrysler Corp *NONPR AFFIL* dir: Natl Assn Mfrs; mem: Atlantic Inst Intl Aff, Soc Automotive Engrs; mem adv bd: Univ CA Berkeley Grad Sch Bus Admin; mem econ policy counc: UN Assn

William J. O'Brien III: *ED* Coll Holy Cross BS 1965; Univ Grenoble 1967; Yale Univ Law Sch LLB 1969 *CURR EMPL* vp, secy, gen couns: Chrysler Corp

Kathleen M. Oswald: *CURR EMPL* vp corp pers: Chrysler Corp

Dennis K. Pawley: *B* 1941 *ED* Oakland Univ BS 1982 *CURR EMPL* exec vp mfg: Chrysler Corp

Leroy C. Richie: *B* Buffalo NY 1941 *ED* City Coll NY BA 1970; NY Univ JD 1973 *CURR EMPL* vp, gen couns, auto legal aff: Chrysler Corp *CORP AFFIL* chmn: Highland Park Devel Corp *NONPR AFFIL* bd mem: Marygrove Coll, St Joseph Mercy Hosp; chmn: Visit Nurses Assn; mem: Am Corp Couns Assn, Detroit Bar Assn

Gary C. Valade: *B* 1942 *ED* MI St Univ BS 1966; MI St Univ MBA 1968 *CURR EMPL* exec vp, cfo: Chrysler Corp *CORP AFFIL* chmn, dir: Chrysler Pentastar Aviation

GIVING OFFICERS
S. W. Bergeron: treas, trust

F. J. Castaing: trust

Lynn Alexandra Feldhouse: mgr, secy *B* Detroit MI 1951 *ED* Wayne St Univ BS 1981 *NONPR AFFIL* dir: Citizens Scholarship Fdn Am, Leadership Detroit, Un Commun Svcs

M. M. Glusac: trust

J. A. Kozlowski: asst secy *CORP AFFIL* asst secy: Chrysler Realty Corp, Chrysler Transport

A. C. Liebler: pres, trust *CURR EMPL* vp commun & mktg: Chrysler Corp (see above)

William J. O'Brien III: trust *CURR EMPL* vp, secy, gen couns: Chrysler Corp (see above)

T. J. Osborn: asst treas

Kathleen M. Oswald: trust *CURR EMPL* vp corp pers: Chrysler Corp (see above)

E. T. Pappert: trust

Dennis K. Pawley: trust *CURR EMPL* exec vp mfg: Chrysler Corp (see above)

L. J. Piedra: trust

Leroy C. Richie: trust *CURR EMPL* vp, gen couns, auto legal aff: Chrysler Corp (see above)

R. M. Sherwood: asst treas

C. A. Smith: contr

K. L. Trinh: adm, asst secy

Gary C. Valade: trust *CURR EMPL* exec vp, cfo: Chrysler Corp (see above)

APPLICATION INFORMATION
Initial Approach: *Initial Contact:* brief letter *Include Information On:* goals, objectives, and historical description of the organization; amount requested and total budget or project cost; list of current contributors, particularly companies and foundations; explanation of relationship (if any) to a United Way organization or governmental agency; list of officers and board of directors; proof of tax-exempt status; and most recently audited financial statement *Deadlines:* none *Note:* The fund asks that organizations request guidelines prior to submitting formal letter.

Restrictions on Giving: The fund does not support individuals; discriminatory organizations; endowment funds; primary or secondary schools; political organizations or campaigns; religious organizations for religious purposes; fraternal associations or athletic groups; veterans or labor organizations, social clubs, or similar associations; local chapters of national organizations receiving fund support; organizations or projects outside the United States; research projects; debt retirement programs; operating expenses of single-disease health associations or of organizations already supported through United Way; national health organizations, other than through United Way; the purchase of courtesy advertising; or conferences, seminars, or similar events.

GRANTS ANALYSIS
Total Grants: $16,900,000*

Number of Grants: 1,370*

Highest Grant: $1,000,000

Average Grant: $10,000*

Typical Range: $500 to $20,000

Disclosure Period: 1994

Note: Total grants figure is approximate. Number of grants excludes matching gifts. Average grant figure was supplied by the fund. Recent grants are derived from a 1993 Form 990.

RECENT GRANTS
General

254,072	Michigan Colleges Foundation, Southfield, MI
208,000	Reading Is Fundamental, Washington, DC
208,000	Reading is Fundamental, Washington, DC
200,000	Purdue University Center for Manufacturing, West Lafayette, IN
200,000	US Holocaust Memorial Museum, Washington, DC

Comerica Incorporated

Revenue: $2.55 billion
Employees: 12,000
Headquarters: Detroit, MI
SIC Major Group: Bank Holding Companies and State Commercial Banks

CONTACT
Karla Hall
Corporate Contributions Manager
Comerica Incorporated
PO Box 75000
Detroit, MI 48275-3352
(313) 222-7356
Note: An alternative FAX number is (313)222-8720.

FINANCIAL SUMMARY
Recent Giving: $3,394,000 (1995 est.); $3,381,689 (1994); $3,022,500 (1993)

Fiscal Note: All contributions are made directly by the company. Above figures exclude nonmonetary support.

CONTRIBUTIONS SUMMARY
Typical Recipients: • *Arts & Humanities:* Arts Institutes, Libraries, Music, Opera, Public Broadcasting • *Civic & Public Affairs:* Business/Free Enterprise, Economic Development, Urban & Community Affairs • *Education:* Colleges & Universities, Minority Education, Public Education (Precollege) • *Health:* Hospitals, Mental Health, Single-Disease Health Associations • *Social Services:* United Funds/United Ways, Youth Organizations

Grant Types: award, capital, challenge, employee matching gifts, general support, matching, and project

Note: Company sponsors a special one-time Holiday match program.

Nonmonetary Support: $200,000 (1992); $93,000 (1988); $52,000 (1987)

Nonmonetary Support Types: donated equipment and in-kind services

Note: Please contact Kathryn Bryant, vice president civic affairs, for nonmonetary gifts.

Geographic Distribution: top consideration to organizations within company principal market areas (southeastern Michigan)

Operating Locations: CA (San Jose), FL, IL, MI (Auburn Hills, Battle Creek, Detroit), MN (South St. Paul), TX (Dallas)

CORP. OFFICERS
Donna Kellstrom: *CURR EMPL* vp, exec asst to ceo: Comerica Inc

John D. Lewis: *B* 1950 *CURR EMPL* vchmn: Comerica Bank *CORP AFFIL* vchmn, dir: Comerica Inc

Eugene A. Miller: *B* Detroit MI 1937 *ED* Detroit Inst Tech BBA 1964; Univ WI Sch Bank Admin 1968 *CURR EMPL* chmn, ceo: Comerica Inc *CORP AFFIL* chmn, ceo: Comerica Bank *PHIL AFFIL* trust: McGregor Fund

Michael T. Monahan: *B* 1939 *CURR EMPL* pres, coo, dir: Comerica Bank (MI) *CORP AFFIL* pres, coo, dir: Comerica Inc *NONPR AFFIL* vp, dir: Boys & Girls Clubs Southwestern MI

GIVING OFFICERS
Karla Hall: *CURR EMPL* corp contributions mgr: Comerica Inc

APPLICATION INFORMATION
Initial Approach: *Initial Contact:* proposal *Include Information On:* concise statements about project or agency describing programs, need, budget, management, goals, and accomplishments; itemized projection of proposal costs; organizational operating budgets for past two years (preferably audited statements); list of existing funding sources; current board of directors; and proof of tax-exempt status *Deadlines:* none; proposals reviewed quarterly

Restrictions on Giving: The company does not support national associations, individuals, or religious or fraternal organizations and typically does not support organizations supported by united funds.

The company avoids controversial organizations and causes.

OTHER THINGS TO KNOW
The company gives primarily to private and public 501(c)(3) organizations, and prefers innovative organizations, which demonstrate the ability to solve problems and provide direct services relating to economic development.

The company matches employee gifts to accredited colleges and universities to a maximum of $2,000 per employee per year.

The company reports that three permanent funds have been established with the Community Foundation of Southeastern Michigan to address specific needs of the community in the areas of the arts, youth activities, and economic development. Contact the Community Foundation of Southeastern Michigan at (313) 961-6675.

In early 1993, the company announced an agreement to acquire First of Michigan.

PUBLICATIONS
Comerica Contributions Policy

GRANTS ANALYSIS
Total Grants: $3,381,689*

Average Grant: $6,000

Typical Range: $500 to $30,000

Disclosure Period: 1994

Note: Total includes tickets and goodwill advertising.

Consumers Power Co. / Consumers Power Foundation

Revenue: $2.96 billion
Employees: 10,400
Parent Company: CMS Energy Corp.
Headquarters: Jackson, MI
SIC Major Group: Electric & Other Services Combined

CONTACT
Dennis H. Marvin
Secretary/Treasurer
Consumers Power Fdn.
212 W Michigan Ave.
Jackson, MI 49201
(517) 788-0318

FINANCIAL SUMMARY
Recent Giving: $1,200,000 (1994 approx.); $1,183,352 (1993); $1,106,307 (1992)

Assets: $1,063,546 (1993); $819,365 (1992); $1,866,335 (1991)

Gifts Received: $1,400,000 (1993)

Fiscal Note: Above figures are for the foundation only and, in 1993, include $651,950 in grants, $323,400 in United Way payments, $27,774 in regional grants, and $180,228 in employee matching gifts. The Company's Public Affairs division continues to make some direct gifts. See "Other Things To Know" for more details. In 1993, contributions were received from Consumers Power Company.

EIN: 38-2935534

CONTRIBUTIONS SUMMARY
Typical Recipients: • *Arts & Humanities:* Arts Funds, Arts Institutes, General, Historic Preservation, History & Archaeology, Libraries, Museums/Galleries, Music, Opera, Public Broadcasting, Theater • *Civic & Public Affairs:* Community Foundations, Economic Development, General, Housing, Parades/Festivals, Philanthropic Organizations, Public Policy, Urban & Community Affairs, Zoos/Aquariums • *Education:* Agricultural Education, Business Education, Colleges & Universities, Community & Junior Colleges, Economic Education, Engineering/Technological Education, Public Education (Precollege), Science/Mathematics Education, Secondary Education (Public) • *Environment:* General • *Health:* Alzheimers Disease, Children's Health/Hospitals, Hospitals • *International:* International Relations • *Religion:* Religious Welfare • *Science:* Scientific Centers & Institutes • *Social

Services: Community Service Organizations, Family Services, Substance Abuse, United Funds/United Ways, Youth Organizations

Grant Types: capital, employee matching gifts, general support, operating expenses, and project

Note: Company matches employee donations to colleges, universities and public broadcasting stations within Michigan. Contributions are matched dollar for dollar of $2,000 per employee or retiree in any calendar year.

Nonmonetary Support Types: in-kind services

Note: Value of nonmonetary support provided by the company is not available. Requests should be addressed to Mr. Dennis H. Marvin, who will forward them to the appropriate Region General Manager if necessary.

Geographic Distribution: primarily in Michigan, with some support to national organizations

Operating Locations: MI (Battle Creek, Bay City, Charlevoix, Detroit, Erie, Essexville, Flint, Grand Rapids, Jackson, Kalamazoo, Lansing, Muskegon, Pontiac, Royal Oak, Saginaw, South Haven, Traverse City, West Olive)

CORP. OFFICERS
William Thomas McCormick, Jr.: *B* Washington DC 1944 *ED* Cornell Univ BS 1966; MA Inst Tech PhD 1969 *CURR EMPL* chmn: CMS Energy Corp *CORP AFFIL* chmn: Consumers Power Co; chmn, ceo: CMS Enterprises Co; dir: Bancorp, CMS Generation Co, Edison Electric Inst, Natl Bank Detroit, NBD Bancorp Inc, Rockwell Intl Corp, Schumberger *NONPR AFFIL* dir: Am Gas Assn, Detroit Symphony Orchestra, St John Hosp; dir, mem: Econ Alliance MI, Greater Detroit Chamber Commerce *CLUB AFFIL* CC Detroit, Cosmos, Detroit Athletic, Econ Detroit *PHIL AFFIL* trust: McGregor Fund

Michael G. Morris: *B* 1946 *ED* Eastern MI Univ BS 1969; Detroit Coll Law JD 1973 *CURR EMPL* exec vp, coo: Consumers Power Co *CORP AFFIL* pres, dir: CMS Gas Marketing Co, CMS Midland Inc, Midland Group Ltd

Stanton Kinnie Smith, Jr.: *B* Rockford IL 1931 *ED* Yale Univ BA 1953; Univ WI JD 1956 *CURR EMPL* vchmn: Consumers Power Co *CORP AFFIL* dir: CLARCOR Inc, MI Natl Corp, Oxford Energy Co; vchmn: CMS Enterprises Co; vchmn, gen couns: CMS Energy Corp *NONPR AFFIL* bd advs: MI ST Univ, Univ WI Sch Law; trust: Detroit Inst Art Fdrs Soc, MI Opera Theater, Rockford Coll, Yale Univ Devel Bd

GIVING OFFICERS
Carolyn A. Bloodworth: asst secy

John W. Clark: pres *B* 1945 *ED* IN Univ 1968 *CURR EMPL* sr vp communs: CMS Energy Corp *CORP AFFIL* sr vp communs: Consumers Power Co

Victor J. Fryling: dir *B* 1948 *ED* Wayne St Univ *CURR EMPL* vchmn: Consumers Power Co *CORP AFFIL* chmn: CMS Gas

Marketing Co, CMS Generation Co, CMS Generation Oper Co; pres, dir: CMS Energy Corp

Dennis H. Marvin: secy, treas *CURR EMPL* dir commun planning & programs: Consumers Power Co

William Thomas McCormick, Jr.: chmn *CURR EMPL* chmn: CMS Energy Corp *PHIL AFFIL* trust: McGregor Fund (see above)

Michael G. Morris: dir *CURR EMPL* exec vp, coo: Consumers Power Co (see above)

Stanton Kinnie Smith, Jr.: dir *CURR EMPL* vchmn: Consumers Power Co (see above)

APPLICATION INFORMATION
Initial Approach: *Initial Contact:* brief letter or proposal, no longer than two pages *Include Information On:* description of the organization, amount requested, purpose for which funds are sought, recently audited financial statement, and proof of tax-exempt status *Deadlines:* none, request reviewed quarterly *Note:* applications must be directed to one of the four regional community service managers in Royal Oak, Saginaw, Lansing, or Grand Rapids

Restrictions on Giving: Does not support individuals, political or lobbying groups, endowments, member agencies of united funds, religious organizations for sectarian purposes, or labor, veterans, fraternal and social clubs.

Also does not contribute to organizations which discriminate on the basis of race, sex, creed, age or national origin.

OTHER THINGS TO KNOW
In 1993, the foundation contributed $180,228 in employee matching gifts to qualifying colleges and universities, Michigan public broadcasting stations, and Michigan's certified community foundations. Donations are matched dollar-for-dollar up to a combined maximum of $2,000 a year per donor.

In April 1990, Consumer Power Co. created the Consumer Power Foundation to improve the consistency of CPCo's philanthropic support. Formerly a direct giver, the company gives primarily through the foundation. Company's public affairs department makes limited contributions, about $100,000 annually, to organizations. Also regional general managers have budgeted about $55,000 annually to support local fund-raising activities. These figures are not included in total giving figure.

GRANTS ANALYSIS
Total Grants: $1,183,352

Number of Grants: 278*

Highest Grant: $48,000

Average Grant: $3,608*

Typical Range: $1,000 to $5,000

Disclosure Period: 1993

Note: Number of grants and average grants figures do not include employee matching gifts totaling $180,228. Recent grants are derived from a 1993 form 990.

RECENT GRANTS

General

48,000	Detroit Renaissance Foundation, Detroit, MI — program support
30,000	Jackson Community Foundation, Jackson, MI — program support
20,000	Averill Career Opportunities Center Education Initiatives — program support
20,000	Cranbrook Institute of Science, Bloomfield Hills, MI — program support
20,000	University of Michigan, Ann Arbor, MI — capital contribution

Delano Foundation, Mignon Sherwood

CONTACT
John Simpson, Jr.
Vice President and Sr. Trust Officer
Mignon Sherwood Delano Fdn.
c/o First of America Bank
Trust Dept.
Kalamazoo, MI 49007
(616) 376-8046

FINANCIAL SUMMARY
Recent Giving: $143,663 (1993); $131,965 (1992); $126,599 (1991)

Assets: $3,699,578 (1993); $3,357,795 (1992); $3,204,172 (1991)

EIN: 38-2557743

CONTRIBUTIONS SUMMARY
Donor(s): the late Mignon Sherwood Delano

Typical Recipients: • *Arts & Humanities:* Arts Festivals, Arts Funds, Community Arts, Historic Preservation, History & Archaeology, Libraries, Theater • *Civic & Public Affairs:* General, Municipalities/Towns, Urban & Community Affairs, Women's Affairs • *Education:* Agricultural Education, Elementary Education (Public), Public Education (Precollege) • *Health:* Clinics/Medical Centers, Eyes/Blindness, Hospices, Hospitals • *Social Services:* Child Abuse, Child Welfare, Domestic Violence, Family Planning, Family Services, People with Disabilities, Substance Abuse, United Funds/United Ways, Youth Organizations

Grant Types: general support

Geographic Distribution: focus on Allegan, MI

GIVING OFFICERS
First of America Bank: trust

Ellen Altamore: adv

Rebecca Burnett: adv

G. Phillip Dietrich: adv

Bernard Riker: adv

David Ticknor: adv

Helen Tremble: off

APPLICATION INFORMATION
Initial Approach: Application form available. There are no deadlines.

GRANTS ANALYSIS
Total Grants: $143,663

Number of Grants: 24

Highest Grant: $20,000

Typical Range: $500 to $15,000

Disclosure Period: 1993

Note: Recent grants are derived from a 1993 Form 990.

RECENT GRANTS

Library

7,007	Dorr Township Library, Allegan, MI
6,200	Fennville District Library, Fennville, MI
5,495	Charles A. Ransom District Library, Allegan, MI
4,646	Otsego District Library, Otsego, MI
2,800	Salem Township Library, Allegan, MI

General

20,000	Prevention of Child Abuse, Allegan, MI
10,000	Allegan Public Schools, Allegan, MI
10,000	Family Planning Association, Allegan, MI
8,000	Center for Women in Transition, Allegan, MI
8,000	Child and Family Services, Holland, MI

DeRoy Foundation, Helen L.

CONTACT
Leonard Weiner
Vice President and Trustee
Helen L. DeRoy Fdn.
3274 Penobscot Bldg.
Detroit, MI 48226
(313) 961-3814

FINANCIAL SUMMARY
Recent Giving: $318,145 (1993); $295,820 (1992); $262,325 (1991)

Assets: $7,281,649 (1993); $7,068,977 (1992); $7,154,876 (1991)

EIN: 38-6082108

CONTRIBUTIONS SUMMARY
Donor(s): Helen L. DeRoy

Typical Recipients: • *Arts & Humanities:* Arts Associations & Councils, Arts Centers, Arts Funds, Arts Institutes, Arts Outreach, Community Arts, History & Archaeology, Libraries, Museums/Galleries, Music, Performing Arts, Public Broadcasting, Theater • *Civic & Public Affairs:* General, Legal Aid, Municipalities/Towns, Public Policy, Safety, Women's Affairs, Zoos/Aquariums • *Education:* Agricultural Education, Arts/Humanities Education, Colleges & Universities, Community & Junior Colleges, Engineering/Technological Education, Literacy, Private Education (Precollege), Student Aid • *Health:* Emergency/Ambulance Services, Medical Research, Nursing Services, Prenatal Health Issues, Respiratory, Single-Disease Health Associations • *Religion:* Churches, Jewish Causes, Religious Organizations, Synagogues/Temples • *Science:* Scientific Centers & Institutes • *Social Services:* At-Risk Youth, Camps, Child Welfare, Community Service Organizations, Delinquency & Criminal Rehabilitation, Domestic Violence, Family Services, Food/Clothing Distribution, People with Disabilities, Scouts, Shelters/Homelessness, United Funds/United Ways, YMCA/YWCA/YMHA/YWHA, Youth Organizations

Grant Types: capital, emergency, general support, operating expenses, and scholarship

Geographic Distribution: focus on MI

GIVING OFFICERS
Bernice Michel: secy, trust *PHIL AFFIL* secy, trust: DeRoy Testamentary Foundation

Arthur Rudecker: pres, trust *PHIL AFFIL* vp, trust: DeRoy Testamentary Foundation

Leonard H. Weiner: vp, trust *PHIL AFFIL* pres, trust: DeRoy Testamentary Foundation

APPLICATION INFORMATION
Initial Approach: Request an application form. There are no deadlines.

Restrictions on Giving: Limited to Michigan.

GRANTS ANALYSIS
Total Grants: $318,145

Number of Grants: 165

Highest Grant: $30,000

Typical Range: $200 to $25,000

Disclosure Period: 1993

Note: Recent grants are derived from a 1993 Form 990.

RECENT GRANTS

Library

2,500	Friends of the Detroit Public Library, Detroit, MI

General

30,000	Focus HOPE, Detroit, MI — Machinist Training Institute scholarships
25,000	Temple Beth El, Bloomfield Hills, MI — Torah gift-endowment campaign
7,500	MCHS Infant Mortality Project, Southfield, MI — jubilee program
6,250	Allied Jewish Campaign, Bloomfield Hills, MI — annual pledge
6,250	Allied Jewish Campaign, Bloomfield Hills, MI — annual pledge

DeRoy Testamentary Foundation

CONTACT
Leonard H. Weiner
President
Deroy Testamentary Foundation
3274 Penobscot Bldg.
Detroit, MI 48226
(313) 961-3814

FINANCIAL SUMMARY
Recent Giving: $918,457 (1993); $860,463 (1992); $804,228 (1991)

Assets: $21,398,570 (1993); $20,860,513 (1992); $20,223,095 (1991)

EIN: 38-2208833

CONTRIBUTIONS SUMMARY
Donor(s): The foundation was established in 1979 by the late Helen L. DeRoy .

Typical Recipients: • *Arts & Humanities:* Arts Centers, Arts Institutes, Arts Outreach, Libraries, Museums/Galleries, Music, Opera, Performing Arts, Public Broadcasting, Theater • *Civic & Public Affairs:* General, Municipalities/Towns, Parades/Festivals, Urban & Community Affairs, Women's Affairs • *Education:* Agricultural Education, Arts/Humanities Education, Business Education, Colleges & Universities, Community & Junior Colleges, Engineering/Technological Education, Faculty Development, General, International Exchange, Leadership Training, Legal Education, Medical Education, Minority Education, Preschool Education, Private Education (Precollege), Public Education (Precollege), Science/Mathematics Education, Secondary Education (Private), Student Aid • *Environment:* Air/Water Quality, General • *Health:* Cancer, Children's Health/Hospitals, Eyes/Blindness, Health Organizations, Hospices, Hospitals, Medical Rehabilitation, Medical Research, Mental Health, Trauma Treatment • *Religion:* Churches, Jewish Causes, Religious Organizations, Synagogues/Temples • *Science:* Scientific Centers & Institutes • *Social Services:* Animal Protection, Child Welfare, Community Centers, Community Service Organizations, Day Care, Domestic Violence, Family Planning, Family Services, Homes, People with Disabilities, Recreation & Athletics, Senior Services, United Funds/United Ways, Youth Organizations

Grant Types: general support, professorship, project, and scholarship

Geographic Distribution: focus on Michigan

GIVING OFFICERS
Bernice Michel: secy, trust *PHIL AFFIL* secy, trust: Helen L. DeRoy Foundation

Arthur Rudecker: vp, trust *PHIL AFFIL* pres, trust: Helen L. DeRoy Foundation

Joan Sultana: asst secy, asst treas

Leonard H. Weiner: pres, trust *PHIL AFFIL* vp, trust: Helen L. DeRoy Foundation

APPLICATION INFORMATION
Initial Approach:
The foundation reports that applications may vary depending upon the nature of the request.

The foundation has no deadline for submitting proposals.

Restrictions on Giving: The foundation reports that it principally makes grants to institutes of established excellence in Michigan. The foundation does not make grants to individuals.

GRANTS ANALYSIS
Total Grants: $918,457

Number of Grants: 83

Highest Grant: $125,000

Average Grant: $11,066

Typical Range: $1,000 to $25,000

Disclosure Period: 1993

Note: Recent grants are derived from a 1993 Form 990.

RECENT GRANTS

Library

7,200	Friends of the Detroit Public Library, Detroit, MI

General

125,000	Temple Beth El, Bloomfield Hills, MI — Torah Gift Endowment campaign
100,000	Providence Hospital Foundation, Southfield, MI — Ambulatory Surgery Center
50,000	University of Michigan Law School, Ann Arbor, MI — visiting professorship
50,000	Wayne State University, Detroit, MI — Volunteerism Lecture Series
33,136	Michigan Humane Society, Cruelty Investigation Division, Auburn Hills, MI

Detroit Edison Co. / Detroit Edison Foundation

Revenue: $3.51 billion
Employees: 9,357
Headquarters: Detroit, MI
SIC Major Group: Electric Services and Electric & Other Services Combined

CONTACT
Katherine W. Hunt
Secretary
Detroit Edison Fdn.
2000 Second Avenue-1046 WCB
Detroit, MI 48226
(313) 237-9271

FINANCIAL SUMMARY
Recent Giving: $3,800,000 (1995 est.); $3,755,000 (1994 approx.); $3,284,716 (1993)

Assets: $10,689,000 (1994 approx.); $13,494,181 (1993); $16,365,409 (1992)

Gifts Received: $5,000,000 (1992)

Fiscal Note: The above 1994 figure represents $3,335,000 in foundation giving and $434,000 in direct giving. Above figures exclude nonmonetary support. In 1992, gifts were received from the Detroit Edison Co.

EIN: 38-2708636

CONTRIBUTIONS SUMMARY
Typical Recipients: • *Arts & Humanities:* Arts Associations & Councils, Arts Centers, Historic Preservation, Libraries, Museums/Galleries, Music, Opera, Performing Arts, Public Broadcasting, Theater • *Civic & Public Affairs:* Business/Free Enterprise, Civil Rights, Economic Development, Economic Policy, Professional & Trade Associations, Safety, Women's Affairs, Zoos/Aquariums • *Education:* Business Education, Colleges & Universities, Community & Junior Colleges, Economic Education, Education Associations, Education Funds, Engineering/Technological Education, Literacy, Minority Education, Private Education (Precollege), Public Education (Precollege), Science/Mathematics Education, Student Aid • *Health:* Health Funds, Hospitals, Mental Health, Single-Disease Health Associations • *Science:* Scientific Centers & Institutes, Scientific Organizations • *Social Services:* Community Centers, Community Service Organizations, Delinquency & Criminal Rehabilitation, Family Services, Food/Clothing Distribution, Recreation & Athletics, Substance Abuse, United Funds/United Ways, Youth Organizations

Grant Types: capital, challenge, conference/seminar, employee matching gifts, endowment, general support, and project

Note: Foundation matches employee gifts to all educational and Michigan cultural institutions up to a limit of $5,000 per donor per year. Foundation also sponsors "Holiday Season Matching Gifts" program between November 1 and December 31 each year through which it matches employee gifts to agencies that provide emergency food and shelter services.

Nonmonetary Support Types: donated equipment, in-kind services, loaned executives, and workplace solicitation

Note: Value of nonmonetary support is not available.

Geographic Distribution: solely in customer service area of southeastern Michigan

Operating Locations: MI (Detroit)

CORP. OFFICERS
Frank Emanuel Agosti: *B* Dearborn MI 1936 *ED* MI Tech Univ BSME 1958 *CURR EMPL* sr vp: Detroit Edison Co *CORP AFFIL* chmn: UTS Sys Inc

Haven E. Cockerham: *CURR EMPL* vp human resources: Detroit Edison Co

Anthony Francis Earley, Jr.: *B* Jamaica NY 1949 *ED* Univ Notre Dame BS; Univ Notre Dame MS; Univ Notre Dame JD *CURR EMPL* pres, coo, dir: Detroit Edison Co *CORP AFFIL* dir: Mutual Am *NONPR AFFIL* dir, vchmn: Un Way Long Island; mem: Am Bar Assn, Nassau County Bar

Assn; mem adv counc: Univ Notre Dame Coll Engg

Larry Gailbert Garberding: *B* Albert City IA 1938 *CURR EMPL* cfo, exec vp: Detroit Edison Co *NONPR AFFIL* mem: Am Inst CPAs

John E. Lobbia: *B* Chicago IL 1941 *ED* Univ Detroit BSEE 1964 *CURR EMPL* chmn, ceo: Detroit Edison Co *CORP AFFIL* chmn: Midwest Energy Resources Co; dir: Natl Bank Detroit, NBD Bancorp Inc *NONPR AFFIL* chmn, dir: Un Way Southeastern MI *PHIL AFFIL* trust: Hudson-Webber Foundation

Christopher C. Nern: *CURR EMPL* vp, gen couns: Detroit Edison Co

GIVING OFFICERS
Susan M. Beale: dir *B* Richmond IN 1948 *ED* MI St Univ 1970; Univ MI 1976 *CURR EMPL* secy: Detroit Edison Co *CORP AFFIL* dir: Edison Illuminating Co Detroit, St Clair Energy Corp; secy, asst treas: UTS Sys Inc

Robert J. Buckler: dir *B* 1949 *ED* Univ MI BSME 1971; Univ MI MSME 1973 *CURR EMPL* sr vp: Detroit Edison Co

Larry Gailbert Garberding: dir *CURR EMPL* cfo, exec vp: Detroit Edison Co (see above)

Katherine W. Hunt: secy *CURR EMPL* admin corp contributions, commun & govt aff: Detroit Edison Co

Leslie Louis Loomans: treas, dir *B* Greenville MI 1943 *ED* Univ MI BS 1966; Univ MI MBA 1973 *CURR EMPL* vp, treas: Detroit Edison Co *CORP AFFIL* treas, dir: Midwest Energy Resources Co *NONPR AFFIL* mem: NSF Intl

Christopher C. Nern: dir *CURR EMPL* vp, gen couns: Detroit Edison Co (see above)

S. Martin Taylor: pres, dir

APPLICATION INFORMATION
Initial Approach: *Initial Contact:* brief letter or proposal signed by organization's chief executive or senior development officer *Include Information On:* organization's general or historical purpose, current need to be met, geographic area and population served, anticipated timetable, budget for current year or proposed project, brief profile of current staff and volunteers, most recently audited financial statement, list of major contributors for current and past year together with amounts donated or list of local corporations being approached, proof of tax-exempt status, Michigan Charitable Solicitation license number (if applicable), and any volunteer involvement by Detroit Edison employees *Deadlines:* none

Restrictions on Giving: In general, company does not support individuals; political organizations; sectarian or denominational groups; fraternal, veterans, or labor organizations or social clubs; conventions, parties, or conferences; trips, seminars, or related activities; goodwill advertising; or national or international organizations unless services provided directly benefit company's service area.

Generally does not support United Way-supported organizations.

In the education area, does not support campus-based student chapters of professional organizations or individual faculty research projects.

OTHER THINGS TO KNOW
Prefers to fund specific projects rather than annual operating budgets or multi-purpose capital campaigns.

PUBLICATIONS
Guidelines, application form

GRANTS ANALYSIS
Total Grants: $3,284,716

Number of Grants: 509

Highest Grant: $544,000

Average Grant: $6,453

Typical Range: $3,000 to $25,000

Disclosure Period: 1993

Note: Matching gifts included in total grants figure. Recent grants are derived from a 1993 Form 990.

RECENT GRANTS

General

136,000	United Way for Southeastern Michigan, Detroit, MI
136,000	United Way for Southeastern Michigan, Detroit, MI
136,000	United Way for Southeastern Michigan, Detroit, MI
136,000	United Way for Southeastern Michigan, Detroit, MI
100,000	University of Detroit Mercy, Detroit, MI

Douglas & Lomason Company

Sales: $567.0 million
Employees: 6,700
Headquarters: Farmington Hills, MI
SIC Major Group: Fabricated Metal Products, Furniture & Fixtures, Industrial Machinery & Equipment, and Transportation Equipment

CONTACT
Patricia L. Shelton
Assistant Secretary & Assistant Vice President
Douglas & Lomason Company
24600 Hallwood Ct.
Farmington Hills, MI 48335-1671
(810) 442-4203

FINANCIAL SUMMARY
Recent Giving: $143,000 (fiscal 1994); $70,000 (fiscal 1993); $90,000 (fiscal 1992)

Assets: $11,561 (fiscal 1992)

Gifts Received: $100,000 (fiscal 1992)

CONTRIBUTIONS SUMMARY
Support goes to local education, human service, health, arts, and civic organizations.

Typical Recipients: • *Arts & Humanities:* Arts Associations & Councils, Arts Institutes, General, Historic Preservation, Libraries, Museums/Galleries, Music, Opera,

Public Broadcasting, Theater • *Civic & Public Affairs:* Business/Free Enterprise, Economic Development, General, Professional & Trade Associations, Public Policy, Safety, Urban & Community Affairs, Zoos/Aquariums • *Education:* Business Education, Colleges & Universities, Community & Junior Colleges, Education Associations, Engineering/Technological Education, General, Minority Education • *Health:* Eyes/Blindness, General, Hospices, Hospitals, Medical Research, Mental Health, Single-Disease Health Associations • *Religion:* Religious Organizations • *Science:* Science Exhibits & Fairs • *Social Services:* Animal Protection, Child Welfare, Community Centers, Community Service Organizations, Family Services, Recreation & Athletics, United Funds/United Ways, Volunteer Services, Youth Organizations

Grant Types: capital, challenge, conference/seminar, emergency, general support, matching, operating expenses, project, research, and scholarship

Nonmonetary Support Types: donated products and workplace solicitation

Geographic Distribution: primarily MI

Operating Locations: AR (Marianna), GA (Carrollton, Columbus, La Grange), IA (Dakota City, Humboldt, Red Oak), IL (Normal), MI (Farmington Hills), MO (Excelsior Springs, Kansas City, Troy), MS (Amory, Cleveland), NE (Columbus), TN (Milan), TX (Del Rio)

CORP. OFFICERS
James J. Hoey: *CURR EMPL* sr vp, cfo: Douglas & Lomason Co

Harry A. Lomason II: *B* Detroit MI 1934 *ED* GA St Univ 1959 *CURR EMPL* chmn, pres, ceo, dir: Douglas & Lomason Co *CORP AFFIL* chmn: Bloomington-Normal Seating Co; mem exec comm, dir: Amerisure Cos; vp, dir: Douglas Y Lomason de Mexico SA de CV *NONPR AFFIL* chmn: MI Mfrs Assn; mem: Engring Soc Detroit; mem exec comm, dir: Am Supplier Inst; meme: Soc Automotive Engrs

APPLICATION INFORMATION
Initial Approach: Send a brief letter of inquiry and a full proposal. Include a description of the organization, amount requested, purpose of funds sought, recently audited financial statements, and proof of tax-exempt status. There are no deadlines.

Restrictions on Giving: Does not support individuals, religious organizations for sectarian purposes, or political or lobbying groups.

GRANTS ANALYSIS
Total Grants: $143,000

Typical Range: $500 to $1,000

Disclosure Period: fiscal year ending September 30, 1994

Note: Recent grants are derived from a grants list provided by company in 1995.

RECENT GRANTS

General
American Lung Association, Detroit, MI

Boy Scouts of America, Detroit, MI
Boy Scouts of America, Pontiac, MI
Farmington Hills YMCA, Farmington Hills, MI

Dow Corning Corp. / Dow Corning Foundation

Revenue: $2.2 billion
Employees: 8,691
Parent Company: 50/50 joint venture of Dow
Chemical Co. & Corning Incorporated
Headquarters: Midland, MI
SIC Major Group: Plastics Materials & Resins
and Industrial Organic Chemicals Nec

CONTACT
Anne M. DeBoer
Executive Director, Foundation/Manager,
Corporate Contributions
Dow Corning Corp.
Corporate Contributions Department
Midland, MI 48686-0994
(517) 496-6290

FINANCIAL SUMMARY
Recent Giving: $3,600,000 (1995 est.);
$3,300,000 (1994 approx.); $2,800,000
(1993 approx.)

Assets: $9,777,984 (1993); $9,124,406
(1992); $9,066,459 (1991)

Gifts Received: 350 (1993)

Fiscal Note: Above figures consist of direct
giving and foundation contributions. Foundation giving in 1993 was $274,000. Although
other company departments make contributions directly, all requests should be directed to Anne M. DeBoer, Manager of
Corporate Contributions.

EIN: 38-2376485

CONTRIBUTIONS SUMMARY
Typical Recipients: • *Arts & Humanities:*
Arts Associations & Councils, Arts Centers,
Arts Festivals, Arts Institutes, Community
Arts, Dance, Historic Preservation, Libraries, Museums/Galleries, Music, Performing
Arts, Public Broadcasting, Theater, Visual
Arts • *Civic & Public Affairs:* Community
Foundations, Economic Development, Municipalities/Towns, Professional & Trade Associations, Urban & Community Affairs,
Zoos/Aquariums • *Education:* Colleges &
Universities, Community & Junior Colleges,
Engineering/Technological Education, Minority Education, Science/Mathematics Education • *Environment:* General • *Science:*
Science Exhibits & Fairs, Scientific Centers
& Institutes • *Social Services:* Community
Centers, Community Service Organizations,
Scouts, United Funds/United Ways, Youth
Organizations

Grant Types: employee matching gifts, general support, and seed money

Geographic Distribution: near headquarters and operating locations

Operating Locations: CT, IN (Kendallville), KY (Carrollton, Elizabethtown),
MI (Bay, Midland, Saginaw area), NC
(Greensboro), TN (Memphis)

Note: Also operates in the Australia, Belgium, Brazil, France, Japan, Mexico, Republic of Korea, United Kingdom and West
Germany.

CORP. OFFICERS
Richard A. Hazleton: *B* 1941 *CURR EMPL*
pres, ceo, dir: Dow Corning Corp

Keith Robert McKennon: *B* Condon OR
1933 *ED* OR St Univ BS 1955 *CURR EMPL*
chmn: Dow Corning Corp *CORP AFFIL* dir:
Chem Bank & Trust Co, Chem Fin Corp,
Dowell Schlumberger Inc, Marion Merrell
Dow Inc, PacifiCorp Inc, Tektronix Inc;
exec vp: Dow Chem Co; pres: Dow Chem
USA *NONPR AFFIL* mem exec comm: Soc
Chem Indus; trust: Georgetown Univ Inst
Health Policy Analysis, Keystone Ctr, Natl
Legal Ctr Pub Interest; vp: Boy Scouts Am
Lake Huron Counc Midland

GIVING OFFICERS
Anne M. DeBoer: exec dir *CURR EMPL*
mgr corp contributions: Dow Corning Corp

Paul A. Marcella: secy

Kenneth Yerrich: pres

APPLICATION INFORMATION
Initial Approach: *Initial Contact:* application form available from Dow Corning's
Corporate Contributions Office *Include Information On:* complete application *Deadlines:* January 15 and August 15 (K-12
Reform and Higher Education), March 15
and October 15 (New Community Development and Local Arts), and May 15 and November 15 (Environment)

Restrictions on Giving: Does not support
individuals; fraternal organizations; political, religious, or veterans organizations; athletic groups at the college/university level;
or dinners or fund-raising events.

OTHER THINGS TO KNOW
Contributions of Dow Corning products, material, or equipment usually are not provided; promotional items and samples are
distributed when appropriate.

Dow Corning also sponsors a speakers' bureau.

PUBLICATIONS
Guidelines

GRANTS ANALYSIS
Total Grants: $3,300,000

Typical Range: $10,000 to $50,000

Disclosure Period: 1994

Note: Total grants figure includes direct and
foundation contributions. Recent grants are
derived from a 1993 Form 990.

RECENT GRANTS
General
89,000	Michigan State University, East Lansing, MI
60,000	American Chemical Society, Detroit, MI
50,000	Carrollton College, Carrollton, KY
50,000	Michigan Tech Fund, Houghton, MI
15,000	Pere Marquette Rail Trail, MI

Dow Foundation, Herbert H. and Grace A.

CONTACT
Herbert H. Dow
President
Herbert H. and Grace A. Dow Foundation
PO Box 2184
Midland, MI 48641-2184
(517) 631-3699

FINANCIAL SUMMARY
Recent Giving: $10,679,467 (1993);
$8,946,000 (1992); $8,125,409 (1991)

Assets: $277,214,733 (1993); $265,715,921
(1992); $251,213,909 (1991)

Gifts Received: $383,169 (1993); $17,080
(1990); $6,891 (1987)

Fiscal Note: In 1990, the foundation received $17,080 from the Dow Chemical
Company.

EIN: 38-1437485

CONTRIBUTIONS SUMMARY
Donor(s): The foundation was established
by Mrs. Grace A. Dow in 1936 in memory
of her husband, Dr. Herbert H. Dow,
founder of the Dow Chemical Company. Dr.
Dow maintained two strong interests during
his lifetime: horticulture and an obligation
to the workers and families at Dow Chemical Company "to share in the growing physical and cultural benefits which an
industrially healthy community could provide." Mrs. Dow was a school teacher in
Midland, and avidly studied the town's history. The foundation's trustees hope to perpetuate and expand its donors' interests in
these areas.

Typical Recipients: • *Arts & Humanities:*
Arts Centers, Libraries • *Civic & Public Affairs:* Botanical Gardens/Parks, Community
Foundations, Municipalities/Towns, Native
American Affairs, Philanthropic Organizations, Safety, Urban & Community Affairs,
Zoos/Aquariums • *Education:* Colleges &
Universities, Education Associations, Public
Education (Precollege), Science/Mathematics Education • *Health:* Children's
Health/Hospitals, Clinics/Medical Centers,
Emergency/Ambulance Services, Hospitals
• *Religion:* Churches, Religious Organizations, Religious Welfare, Synagogues/Temples • *Science:* Scientific Centers &
Institutes • *Social Services:* Community Centers, Community Service Organizations,
Family Services, Homes, People with Disabilities, Recreation & Athletics, Senior
Services, Special Olympics, Substance
Abuse, United Funds/United Ways, Youth
Organizations

Grant Types: capital, general support,
matching, operating expenses, research, and
seed money

Geographic Distribution: Michigan; with
emphasis on the Midland area

GIVING OFFICERS
Julie Carol Arbury: trust, don great granddaughter

Kriss A. Arbury: assoc *CURR EMPL* vp, dir: MI Police Equipment Co

Ruth Hale Buchanan: trust

Herbert Dow Doan: secy *B* Midland MI 1922 *ED* Cornell Univ 1949 *CURR EMPL* chmn: Doan Resources Group

Herbert H. Dow: pres *B* Midland MI 1927 *ED* MA Inst Tech BS 1952; Central MI Univ LLD 1972 *CURR EMPL* vp: Dow Chem Co *PHIL AFFIL* pres, trust: Herbert H. and Barbara C. Dow Foundation

Michael Lloyd Dow: treas *B* Saginaw MI 1935 *ED* Williams Coll 1953-1956; MI St Univ BS 1961 *CURR EMPL* dir: Dow Chem Co *CORP AFFIL* dir: Chem Bank & Trust Co, Chem Fin Corp; fdr, chmn, ceo: Gen Aviation; owner: Beachhouse Devel, Classic Aircraft Corp, Michael L Dow Assocs; part owner: Harbor Corp, MLD, Pohlcat Inc, Sail N; ptnr: Northern MI Inns; treas: Assoc Newspapers, Kalamazoo Printing Machinery Co, Panax Corp; vp, ptnr: Central MI Inns; vp, treas: Mellus Newspapers *NONPR AF-FIL* dir: Sparrow Hosp; trust: Leelanau Schs Glen Arbor MI *PHIL AFFIL* treas: Alden and Vada Dow Fund

Michael Lloyd Dow: treas *CURR EMPL* dir: Dow Chem Co *PHIL AFFIL* treas: Alden and Vada Dow Fund (see above)

Michael Lorence Dow: assoc

John T. Riecker: assoc

Margaret Ann Riecker: vp, trust, don granddaughter *PHIL AFFIL* pres, trust: Harry A. and Margaret D. Towsley Foundation

APPLICATION INFORMATION
Initial Approach:

The foundation has no formal application form. Proposals should be sent in the form of a letter.

The letter of inquiry should describe the nature and potential results of the proposed program, institutions and personnel responsible for the work, total project cost, amount requested, means of disbursing the funds to the recipient, proof of tax-exempt status, latest audited financial statement, current budget, names of management, names and occupations of the organization's trustees or directors, and provisions and procedures for evaluating the program.

The board meets bi-monthly to make final decisions, and grants are made in December.

Initial evaluation of proposals is followed by full consideration by the appropriate program committee of the board of trustees. Additional information, site visits, or meetings in Midland may be requested.

Restrictions on Giving: The foundation does not fund individuals, organizations outside of Michigan, or those which are not tax-exempt; political or lobbying groups; and religious organizations for sectarian purposes (except churches in the Midland community). The foundation does not accept preset "formulas for giving" prepared by nonprofit agencies.

OTHER THINGS TO KNOW
The foundation reports that in recent years its funding has been almost completely committed for several years in advance.

PUBLICATIONS
Annual report

GRANTS ANALYSIS
Total Grants: $10,679,467

Number of Grants: 134

Highest Grant: $3,350,000

Average Grant: $79,698

Typical Range: $10,000 to $100,000 and $250,000 to $750,000

Disclosure Period: 1993

Note: Recent grants are derived from a 1993 Form 990.

RECENT GRANTS

Library

3,350,000	City of Midland Grace A. Dow Memorial Library, Midland, MI — building expansion
46,000	Frankfort City Library, Frankfort, MI — automation of library
2,000	City of Midland Grace A. Dow Memorial Library, Midland, MI — operating fund

General

1,512,341	Contribution of Property, Midland, MI — transfer of investment property to exempt purposes
1,500,000	Midland Foundation, Midland, MI — Riverside Place building fund
500,000	City of Midland, Midland, MI — Downtown Streetscape project
400,000	Michigan Molecular Institute, Midland, MI — operating and capital
300,000	Alma College, Alma, MI — remodel Dow Science Center

Eddy Family Memorial Fund, C. K.

CONTACT
Louise Rohde
Trust Officer
C. K. Eddy Family Memorial Fund
c/o Second National Bank of Saginaw
101 N Washington
Saginaw, MI 48607
(517) 776-7360
Note: The contact person for educational loans, located at the same address, is Helen James.

FINANCIAL SUMMARY
Recent Giving: $526,538 (fiscal 1994); $487,835 (fiscal 1993); $407,236 (fiscal 1991)

Assets: $10,199,347 (fiscal 1994); $10,582,830 (fiscal 1993); $9,943,292 (fiscal 1991)

EIN: 38-6040506

CONTRIBUTIONS SUMMARY
Donor(s): the late Arthur D. Eddy

Typical Recipients: • *Arts & Humanities:* Dance, Historic Preservation, History & Archaeology, Libraries, Music, Performing Arts, Theater • *Civic & Public Affairs:* African American Affairs, Business/Free Enterprise, Employment/Job Training, Municipalities/Towns, Safety • *Education:* Business Education, Colleges & Universities, Engineering/Technological Education, Public Education (Precollege), Student Aid • *Health:* Children's Health/Hospitals, Clinics/Medical Centers, Hospitals, Nursing Services • *Religion:* Religious Welfare • *Social Services:* Child Welfare, Community Centers, Community Service Organizations, Food/Clothing Distribution, Recreation & Athletics, United Funds/United Ways, Volunteer Services, Youth Organizations

Grant Types: project and scholarship

Geographic Distribution: limited to Saginaw County, MI

GIVING OFFICERS
Second National Bank of Saginaw: trust

APPLICATION INFORMATION
Initial Approach: Send a brief letter of inquiry. There are no deadlines. Application form required for educational loans. Deadline is May 1.

Restrictions on Giving: Limited to organizations and residents of Saginaw County or City, MI.

PUBLICATIONS
Application Guidelines. Provides scholarships to individuals for higher education.

GRANTS ANALYSIS
Total Grants: $526,538

Number of Grants: 118

Highest Grant: $65,000

Typical Range: $500 to $50,000

Disclosure Period: fiscal year ending June 30, 1994

Note: Recent grants are derived from a fiscal 1994 Form 990.

RECENT GRANTS

General

50,000	Opportunities Industrialization Center, Saginaw, MI — building
50,000	Saginaw Business Incubator, Saginaw, MI — building
42,500	United Way of Saginaw, Saginaw, MI
25,000	Delta College, Saginaw, MI
25,000	St. Mary's Medical Center, Saginaw, MI — equipment

Fabri-Kal Corp. / Fabri-Kal Foundation

Sales: $75.0 million
Parent Employees: 480
Headquarters: Kalamazoo, MI
SIC Major Group: Rubber & Miscellaneous Plastics Products

CONTACT
Robert P. Kittredge
Chairman
Fabri-Kal Corp.
Plastics Pl.
Kalamazoo, MI 49001
(616) 385-5050

FINANCIAL SUMMARY
Recent Giving: $93,284 (1993); $47,510 (1992); $58,149 (1991)

Assets: $976 (1993); $42 (1992); $90 (1991)

Gifts Received: $94,264 (1993); $47,510 (1992); $58,017 (1991)

Fiscal Note: In 1993, contributions were received from the Fabri-Kal Corp.

EIN: 23-7003366

CONTRIBUTIONS SUMMARY
Typical Recipients: • *Arts & Humanities:* General, Historic Preservation, Libraries • *Civic & Public Affairs:* General, Housing, Legal Aid, Urban & Community Affairs • *Education:* Business Education, Colleges & Universities, General, Private Education (Precollege) • *Environment:* General • *Health:* General • *International:* International Organizations • *Religion:* Religious Organizations, Religious Welfare • *Social Services:* Big Brother/Big Sister, Child Welfare, Community Centers, Community Service Organizations, Counseling, Day Care, General, Senior Services, United Funds/United Ways, YMCA/YWCA/YMHA/YWHA, Youth Organizations

Grant Types: capital and general support

Nonmonetary Support Types: loaned executives

Geographic Distribution: focus on MI, PA, and SC

Operating Locations: PA, SC

CORP. OFFICERS
Robert P. Kittredge: *B* Bellevue PA 1925 *ED* Univ MI 1948 *CURR EMPL* chmn, dir: Fabri-Kal Corp

John D. Michael: *CURR EMPL* pres, dir: Fabri-Kal Corp

GIVING OFFICERS
John Dobrowolski: treas

Robert P. Kittredge: pres *CURR EMPL* chmn, dir: Fabri-Kal Corp (see above)

R. L. Weyhing III: secy

APPLICATION INFORMATION
Initial Approach: Send a brief letter of inquiry. There are no deadlines.

Restrictions on Giving: Limited to charities located in Kalamazoo, MI, Hazleton, PA, and Greenville, SC.

GRANTS ANALYSIS
Total Grants: $93,284
Number of Grants: 15
Highest Grant: $10,600
Typical Range: $186 to $10,400
Disclosure Period: 1993

Note: Recent grants are derived from a 1993 Form 990. Number of grants and typical range do not include grants to individuals.

RECENT GRANTS

General
10,600	United Way of Greenville County, Greenville, SC
10,400	United Way of Greater Hazleton, Hazleton, PA
7,500	MMU Business College, Kalamazoo, MI
7,500	Western Michigan University Business College, Kalamazoo, MI
5,000	Bronson Health Foundation, Kalamazoo, MI

Federal-Mogul Corporation / Federal-Mogul Corp. Charitable Trust Fund

Sales: $1.58 billion
Employees: 15,500
Headquarters: Southfield, MI
SIC Major Group: Ball & Roller Bearings, Gaskets, Packing & Sealing Devices, Valves & Pipe Fittings Nec, and Commercial Lighting Fixtures

CONTACT
Christine Cusmano
Secretary, Contributions Committee
Federal-Mogul Corp. Charitable Trust Fund
Corporate Communications
PO Box 1966
Detroit, MI 48235
(810) 354-8663

FINANCIAL SUMMARY
Recent Giving: $363,715 (1993); $367,629 (1992); $1,000,000 (1991 approx.)

Assets: $188,901 (1993); $52,069 (1992); $14,182 (1991)

Gifts Received: $500,000 (1993); $405,000 (1992)

Fiscal Note: Figures are for foundation giving only. Foundation receives contributions from Federal-Mogul Corporation.

EIN: 38-6046512

CONTRIBUTIONS SUMMARY
Typical Recipients: • *Arts & Humanities:* Arts Associations & Councils, Arts Centers, Arts Festivals, Arts Funds, Arts Institutes, Community Arts, Historic Preservation, Libraries, Museums/Galleries, Music, Opera, Performing Arts, Public Broadcasting, Theater • *Civic & Public Affairs:* African American Affairs, Business/Free Enterprise, Civil Rights, Economic Development, Economic Policy, Employment/Job Training, Housing, Law & Justice, Professional & Trade Associations, Public Policy, Rural Affairs, Safety, Urban & Community Affairs, Women's Affairs, Zoos/Aquariums • *Education:* Business Education, Business-School Partnerships, Colleges & Universities, Economic Education, Education Associations, Education Funds, Elementary Education (Private), Engineering/Technological Education, Legal Education, Minority Education, Public Education (Precollege), Religious Education, Science/Mathematics Education, Student Aid • *Health:* Cancer, Children's Health/Hospitals, Clinics/Medical Centers, Health Funds, Health Organizations, Hospices, Hospitals, Medical Research, Single-Disease Health Associations • *International:* International Peace & Security Issues • *Religion:* Religious Welfare • *Science:* Science Exhibits & Fairs, Scientific Centers & Institutes • *Social Services:* Animal Protection, Child Welfare, Community Centers, Community Service Organizations, Delinquency & Criminal Rehabilitation, Food/Clothing Distribution, People with Disabilities, Recreation & Athletics, Substance Abuse, United Funds/United Ways, Volunteer Services, Youth Organizations

Grant Types: capital, employee matching gifts, general support, multiyear/continuing support, operating expenses, and research

Geographic Distribution: near corporate operating locations; a relatively small portion of the budget goes to regional and national activities

Operating Locations: IN (Frankfort, Greensburg, Indianapolis, Leiters Ford, Logansport, Mooresville), MI (Ann Arbor, Detroit, Greenville, Milan, Plymouth, Romulus, Southfield, St. Johns), MN, MO (Malden, St. Louis), NJ (Somerset), OH (Gallipolis, Van Wert), PA (Lititz), SC (Summerton), TN (Lafayette), VA (Blacksburg)

Note: Federal-Mogul operates 29 plants in 13 states nationwide. Above is list of principal subsidiary locations.

CORP. OFFICERS
Dennis James Gormley: *B* New York NY 1939 *ED* Rensselaer Polytech Inst 1963 *CURR EMPL* chmn, ceo, dir: Fed Mogul Corp *CORP AFFIL* chmn: Westwind Air Bearings; dir: Cooper Tire & Rubber Co, NBD Bancorp Inc *NONPR AFFIL* dir: Comm Econ Devel, Jr Achievement Southeastern MI, Un Way Southeastern MI; mem: Automotive Original Equipment Mfrs, Automotive Pres Counc, Motor & Equipment Mfrs Assn; mem adv bd: Fin World; trust: Citizens Res Counc MI, MAPI *CLUB AFFIL* Econ

Martin E. Welch III: *B* Detroit MI 1948 *ED* Univ Detroit BS 1970; Univ Detroit MBA 1973 *CURR EMPL* sr vp, cfo: Fed Mogul Corp *CORP AFFIL* cfo, dir: Fed-Mogul World Trade Inc

GIVING OFFICERS
George N. Bashara, Jr.: chmn contributions comm *B* 1934 *ED* Detroit Coll Law JD 1960; Univ MI *CURR EMPL* vp, secy, gen couns: Fed Mogul Corp *CORP AFFIL* secy, dir: Fed-Mogul World Trade Inc

Christine Cusmano: secy contributions comm

Dennis James Gormley: mem contributions comm *CURR EMPL* chmn, ceo, dir: Fed Mogul Corp (see above)

APPLICATION INFORMATION
Initial Approach: *Initial Contact:* brief letter (two pages or less) *Include Information On:* description of the organization, statement of purpose, amount requested, and how funds will be spent; attach a recently audited financial statement showing budget for past two years and for year contribution is sought, proof of tax-exempt status, list of board of directors and their affiliations, and corporate donor list for past 12 months *Deadlines:* none; applicants notified within several weeks of action taken on request

Restrictions on Giving: Does not support individuals; political or lobbying groups; goodwill advertising; fraternal organizations; loans or investments; projects that support specific elementary or secondary educational institutions. Never makes grants to political parties.

OTHER THINGS TO KNOW
Special consideration given to activities in which employees participate.

Contributions generally are made for one year.

PUBLICATIONS
Guidelines

GRANTS ANALYSIS
Total Grants: $363,715

Number of Grants: 141

Highest Grant: $92,169

Average Grant: $2,580

Typical Range: $100 to $5,000

Disclosure Period: 1993

Note: Above figures are for the foundation only. Recent grants are derived from a 1993 Form 990.

RECENT GRANTS

Library
1,500	Friends of the Detroit Public Library, Detroit, MI

General
92,169	United Way for Southeastern Michigan, Detroit, MI
20,000	Cleveland Clinic, Cleveland, OH
16,300	Detroit Renaissance Foundation, Detroit, MI
14,000	Awda University Foundation, Kansas City, MO

12,000	Detroit Renaissance Foundation, Detroit, MI

Ford Fund, William and Martha

CONTACT
Pierre V. Heftler
Secretary
William and Martha Ford Fund
100 Renaissance Ctr., 34th Fl.
Detroit, MI 48243
(313) 259-7777

FINANCIAL SUMMARY
Recent Giving: $753,937 (1993); $821,038 (1992); $818,984 (1991)

Assets: $1,942,712 (1993); $2,520,431 (1992); $3,185,866 (1991)

Gifts Received: $145,491 (1991); $588,015 (1990)

Fiscal Note: In 1991, contributions were received from a trust agreement between William Clay Ford and Manufacturers National Bank of Detroit.

EIN: 38-6066335

CONTRIBUTIONS SUMMARY
Donor(s): William Clay Ford, Martha Firestone Ford

Typical Recipients: • *Arts & Humanities:* Arts Centers, Arts Funds, Arts Institutes, Historic Preservation, History & Archaeology, Libraries, Music, Performing Arts, Public Broadcasting • *Civic & Public Affairs:* Clubs, General, Municipalities/Towns, Parades/Festivals, Urban & Community Affairs, Zoos/Aquariums • *Education:* Colleges & Universities, General, Minority Education, Private Education (Precollege), Science/Mathematics Education, Special Education, Student Aid • *Environment:* General • *Health:* Children's Health/Hospitals, Emergency/Ambulance Services, Health Organizations, Heart, Hospitals, Medical Research, Nursing Services • *International:* Foreign Arts Organizations, Human Rights • *Religion:* Churches • *Science:* Scientific Centers & Institutes, Scientific Labs • *Social Services:* Child Welfare, Community Service Organizations, Delinquency & Criminal Rehabilitation, Family Planning, Homes, Recreation & Athletics, Substance Abuse, United Funds/United Ways, Youth Organizations

Grant Types: general support and scholarship

Geographic Distribution: giving in MI, NY and TX

GIVING OFFICERS
Richard M. Cundiff: treas, trust *PHIL AFFIL* treas: Walter and Josephine Ford Fund, Eleanor and Edsel Ford Fund; treas, trust: Henry Ford II Fund, Benson and Edith Ford Fund; treas: Edsel B. Ford II Fund

Martha F. Ford: trust, mem *PHIL AFFIL* trust: Harvey Firestone, Jr. Foundation

William Clay Ford: pres, trust, mem *B* Detroit MI 1925 *ED* Yale Univ BS 1949 *CURR EMPL* chmn exec comm, chmn fin comm, dir: Ford Motor Co *CORP AFFIL* owner, pres: Detroit Lions *NONPR AFFIL* chmn emeritus: Edison Inst; dir: Boy Scouts Am, Natl Tennis Hall Fame; mem: Automobile Old Timers, Phelps Assn, Psi Upsilon, Soc Automotive Engrs; mem, dir: Econ Club Detroit; trust: Thomas A Edison Fdn, Eisenhower Med Ctr *CLUB AFFIL* Detroit, KT, Masons *PHIL AFFIL* pres, trust, mem: Eleanor and Edsel Ford Fund

Pierre V. Heftler: secy, trust, mem *B* Paris France 1910 *ED* Dartmouth Coll AB 1930; Univ MI BS 1931; Univ MI JD 1934 *CURR EMPL* ptnr: Bodman & Longley *PHIL AFFIL* secy, trust, mem: Eleanor and Edsel Ford Fund; secy, trust: Henry Ford II Fund; secy, trust, mem: Walter and Josephine Ford Fund; pres, trust: Matilda R. Wilson Fund; secy, trust: Benson and Edith Ford Fund

Pierre V. Heftler: secy, trust, mem *CURR EMPL* ptnr: Bodman & Longley *PHIL AFFIL* secy, trust, mem: Eleanor and Edsel Ford Fund; secy, trust: Henry Ford II Fund; secy, trust, mem: Walter and Josephine Ford Fund; pres, trust: Matilda R. Wilson Fund; secy, trust: Benson and Edith Ford Fund (see above)

George A. Straitor: asst treas *PHIL AFFIL* asst treas: Benson and Edith Ford Fund, Eleanor and Edsel Ford Fund, Walter and Josephine Ford Fund

APPLICATION INFORMATION
Initial Approach: Send a brief letter of inquiry. Include a description of organization, amount requested, purpose of funds sought, recently audited financial statement, and proof of tax-exempt status. There are no deadlines.

Restrictions on Giving: Does not support individuals.

GRANTS ANALYSIS
Total Grants: $753,937

Number of Grants: 56

Highest Grant: $200,000

Typical Range: $100 to $100,000

Disclosure Period: 1993

Note: Recent grants are derived from a 1993 Form 990.

RECENT GRANTS

General
200,000	Edison Institute, Dearborn, MI
100,000	Texas Heart Institute, Houston, TX
58,000	Henry Ford Health System, Detroit, MI
50,000	Boys Clubs of America, New York, NY
50,000	Children's Home of Detroit, Grosse Pointe Woods, MI

Ford II Fund, Henry

CONTACT
Pierre V. Heftler
Secretary and Trustee
Henry Ford II Fund
100 Renaissance Center, 34th Fl.
Detroit, MI 48243
(313) 259-7777

FINANCIAL SUMMARY

Recent Giving: $760,500 (1993); $815,000 (1992); $1,001,500 (1991)

Assets: $14,232,144 (1993); $13,761,947 (1992); $13,326,814 (1991)

Gifts Received: $403,396 (1993); $403,319 (1992); $775,078 (1991)

Fiscal Note: In 1992, the fund received gifts from a trust agreement between Henry Ford II and Comerica Bank. In 1991 and 1990, gifts were received from a trust agreement between Henry Ford II and Manufacturers National Bank of Detroit.

EIN: 38-6066332

CONTRIBUTIONS SUMMARY

Donor(s): The fund was established in 1953. The donor was the late Henry Ford II (d. 1987), a grandson of Ford Motor Company founder Henry Ford, and a chairman and chief executive of the automobile company.

Typical Recipients: • *Arts & Humanities:* Arts Institutes, History & Archaeology, Libraries, Performing Arts, Public Broadcasting • *Civic & Public Affairs:* Clubs, Municipalities/Towns, Urban & Community Affairs • *Education:* Colleges & Universities, Community & Junior Colleges, Education Associations, Minority Education, Private Education (Precollege), Secondary Education (Public), Special Education • *Health:* Children's Health/Hospitals, Emergency/Ambulance Services, Eyes/Blindness, Health Organizations, Hospitals, Medical Rehabilitation, Medical Research • *Religion:* Churches, Religious Welfare • *Science:* Scientific Centers & Institutes • *Social Services:* Child Welfare, Community Service Organizations, Food/Clothing Distribution, People with Disabilities, Recreation & Athletics, United Funds/United Ways, Volunteer Services, Youth Organizations

Grant Types: general support, research, and scholarship

Geographic Distribution: emphasis on Detroit, MI

GIVING OFFICERS

Richard M. Cundiff: treas, trust *PHIL AFFIL* treas: Walter and Josephine Ford Fund, Eleanor and Edsel Ford Fund; treas, trust: Benson and Edith Ford Fund, William and

Martha Ford Fund; treas: Edsel B. Ford II Fund

Edsel B. Ford II: pres, trust, mem *B* 1949 *CURR EMPL* exec dir marketing staff: Ford Motor Co *CORP AFFIL* pres, dir: Ford Motor Credit Co; vchmn: Ford Life Ins Co; vchmn, dir: Am Rd Svcs Co *NONPR AFFIL* adv: Detroit Arts Comm; chmn: Edsel & Eleanor Ford House; mem corp: Babson Coll Fdn; trust: Detroit Inst Children, Englebrook Sch, Henry Ford Commun Coll, Henry Ford Mus, Greenfield Village, Gunnery Sch

Pierre V. Heftler: secy, trust *B* Paris France 1910 *ED* Dartmouth Coll AB 1930; Univ MI BS 1931; Univ MI JD 1934 *CURR EMPL* ptnr: Bodman & Longley *PHIL AFFIL* secy, trust, mem: Eleanor and Edsel Ford Fund, Walter and Josephine Ford Fund, pres, trust: Matilda R. Wilson Fund; secy, trust: Benson and Edith Ford Fund; secy, trust, mem: William and Martha Ford Fund

APPLICATION INFORMATION
Initial Approach:

The fund generally limits support to causes already favorably known to the foundation. However, letters of inquiry may be addressed to the fund's secretary.

Applications should be in the form of a brief letter and include the organization's financial statement and a copy of the IRS determination letter of tax-exempt status.

There are no deadlines for submitting letters of request.

Restrictions on Giving: The fund does not make grants to individuals.

GRANTS ANALYSIS
Total Grants: $760,500

Number of Grants: 21

Highest Grant: $150,000

Average Grant: $36,214

Typical Range: $1,000 to $40,000 and $50,000 to $75,000

Disclosure Period: 1993

Note: Recent grants are derived from a 1993 Form 990.

RECENT GRANTS

General

150,000	University Liggett School, Grosse Pointe, MI
125,000	Yale University, New Haven, CT
100,000	Henry Ford Hospital, Detroit, MI
60,000	United Way for Southeastern Michigan, Detroit, MI
50,000	Detroit Institute for Children, Detroit, MI

Ford Motor Co. / Ford Motor Co. Fund

Revenue: $128.43 billion
Employees: 332,700
Headquarters: Dearborn, MI
SIC Major Group: Truck & Bus Bodies and Truck Trailers

CONTACT
Leo J. Brennan, Jr.
Vice President and Executive Director
Ford Motor Co. Fund
The American Rd., Rm. 949
PO Box 1899
Dearborn, MI 48121
(313) 845-8711

FINANCIAL SUMMARY
Recent Giving: $35,300,000 (1995 est.), $30,900,000 (1994 approx.); $29,418,435 (1993)

Assets: $30,700,000 (1995 est.); $34,900,000 (1994 approx.); $8,954,670 (1993)

Fiscal Note: Above figures include both fund contributions and direct giving by the company. The direct giving program reports contributions of $12,900,000 in 1993 and $14,000,000 in 1992, which includes giving by all foreign and domestic subsidiaries. See "Other Things To Know" for more details. Above figures exclude nonmonetary support.

EIN: 38-1459376

CONTRIBUTIONS SUMMARY
Typical Recipients: • *Arts & Humanities:* Arts Associations & Councils, Arts Centers, Arts Festivals, Arts Institutes, Community Arts, Historic Preservation, Libraries, Museums/Galleries, Music, Opera, Performing Arts, Public Broadcasting, Theater • *Civic & Public Affairs:* African American Affairs, Botanical Gardens/Parks, Business/Free Enterprise, Civil Rights, Community Foundations, Economic Development, Economic Policy, Employment/Job Training, Housing, Law & Justice, Professional & Trade Associations, Public Policy, Safety, Urban & Community Affairs • *Education:* Agricultural Education, Business Education, Colleges & Universities, Economic Education, Education Associations, Education Reform, Engineering/Technological Education, General, Health & Physical Education, Journalism/Media Education, Minority Education, Public Education (Precollege), Science/Mathematics Education, Secondary Education (Public) • *Environment:* General • *Health:* Emergency/Ambulance Services, Health Policy/Cost Containment, Health Organizations, Hospitals, Kidney • *International:* International Development, International Relations • *Social Services:* Child Welfare, Community Service Organizations, Delinquency & Criminal Rehabilitation, Recreation & Athletics, Substance Abuse, United Funds/United Ways, Volunteer Services, Youth Organizations

Grant Types: capital, conference/seminar, department, employee matching gifts, gen-

The Big Book of Library Grant Money　　　　　　　　　　Fruehauf Foundation / MICHIGAN

eral support, and multiyear/continuing support

Note: Employee matching gift ratio: 1 to 1.

Nonmonetary Support: $300,000 (1994); $286,100 (1993); $249,400 (1992)

Nonmonetary Support Types: donated equipment

Note: The contact for nonmonetary support is Ray Byers, Manager of Contribution Programs, The American Rd., Dearborn, MI, 48121, (313) 248-4745.

Geographic Distribution: near headquarters and operating locations and to national organizations

Operating Locations: MI (Dearborn)

Note: Company operates in over 70 locations in the United States. Also operates in Europe, Canada, Mexico, South America, and Australia.

CORP. OFFICERS

John William Martin, Jr.: *B* Evergreen Park IL 1936 *ED* DePaul Univ AB 1958; DePaul Univ JD 1961 *CURR EMPL* vp, gen couns: Ford Motor Co *NONPR AFFIL* dir: Natl Assn Pub Interest Law Fellowships, Natl Legal Aid & Defender Assn; mem: Am Bar Assn, Am Law Inst, Assn Gen Couns, MI Bar Assn *CLUB AFFIL* Little Traverse YC

David Noel McCammon: *B* Topeka KS 1934 *ED* Univ NE 1957; Harvard Univ 1962 *CURR EMPL* vp fin, treas: Ford Motor Co *CORP AFFIL* affiliate: Ford Intl Fin Corp (Bermuda); chmn: Ford Intl Capital Corp (Bermuda); trust: Henry Ford Health Care Corp *CLUB AFFIL* Harvard Bus Sch

Peter John Pestillo: *B* Bristol CT 1938 *ED* Fairfield Univ BSS 1960; Georgetown Univ LLB 1963 *CURR EMPL* exec vp corp rels: Ford Motor Co *CORP AFFIL* co-pres, dir: UAW-Ford Natl *NONPR AFFIL* dir: Am Arbitration Assn, Natl Assn Mfrs; mem: Bus Roundtable, DC Bar Assn, Labor Policy Assn, UBA, US Chamber Commerce; mem adv bd: Un Fdn

John M. Rintamaki: *CURR EMPL* secy: Ford Holdings Inc *CORP AFFIL* secy: Predelivery Svc Corp

David William Scott: *B* Shillong India 1940 *CURR EMPL* vp pub aff: Ford Motor Co *NONPR AFFIL* bd visitors: Northwestern Univ Medill Sch Journalism; mem: Fdn Am Communs, Intl Pub Rels Assn, Pub Rels Soc Am

Stanley A. Seneker: *ED* Santa Clara Univ BS 1953; Univ PA MBA 1957 *CURR EMPL* corp exec vp, cfo: Ford Motor Co

Alex James Trotman: *B* 1933 *ED* MI St Univ MBA 1972 *CURR EMPL* chmn, pres, ceo: Ford Motor Co

GIVING OFFICERS

Leo Joseph Brennan, Jr.: vp, exec dir *B* Hancock MI 1930 *ED* Univ Notre Dame BA 1951; Univ Notre Dame MA 1952; Georgetown Univ 1953 *NONPR AFFIL* dir: Arts Fdn MI, Lourdes Nursing Home, MI Bach Festival; mem: Detroit Zoological Soc, MI Historical Soc; mem bus adv comm: Independent Colls Am; mem contributions counc: Conf Bd; mem fdrs soc: Detroit Inst

Art; trust: Counc MI Fdns, MI 4-H Counc *CLUB AFFIL* Otsego Ski

Alfred B. Ford: trust *B* 1934

Sheila F. Hamp: trust

John William Martin, Jr.: trust *CURR EMPL* vp, gen couns: Ford Motor Co (see above)

David Noel McCammon: treas, trust *CURR EMPL* vp fin, treas: Ford Motor Co (see above)

Peter John Pestillo: trust *CURR EMPL* exec vp corp rels: Ford Motor Co (see above)

John M. Rintamaki: secy *CURR EMPL* secy: Ford Holdings Inc (see above)

David William Scott: trust *CURR EMPL* vp pub aff: Ford Motor Co (see above)

Stanley A. Seneker: trust *CURR EMPL* corp exec vp, cfo: Ford Motor Co (see above)

Dennis A. Tosh: asst treas

Alex James Trotman: pres, trust *CURR EMPL* chmn, pres, ceo: Ford Motor Co (see above)

APPLICATION INFORMATION

Initial Approach: *Initial Contact:* national organizations should submit a brief letter; organizations located in communities where Ford operates may submit requests to the fund or to the community relations committee at local plants *Include Information On:* description of the organization/project, proof of tax-exempt status, amount requested, recently audited financial statement *Deadlines:* none

OTHER THINGS TO KNOW

Contributions to international organizations by foreign subsidiaries totaled $5.1 million in 1993.

PUBLICATIONS

Ford Motor Company Fund Annual Report

GRANTS ANALYSIS

Total Grants: $22,267,752*

Number of Grants: 1,600

Average Grant: $13,917

Typical Range: $100 to $25,000

Disclosure Period: 1994

Note: Fiscal information for fund only and includes nonmonetary support. Recent grants are derived from a 1993 Form 990.

RECENT GRANTS

Library

60,000		Shakespeare Theatre of the Folger Library, Washington, DC

General

665,000		United Way for Southeastern Michigan, Detroit, MI
665,000		United Way for Southeastern Michigan, Detroit, MI
312,500		Michigan State University, East Lansing, MI
312,500		Michigan State University, East Lansing, MI
305,000		Ohio State University, Columbus, OH

Fruehauf Foundation

CONTACT
Elizabeth J. Woods
Assistant Secretary
Fruehauf Fdn.
100 Maple Pk. Blvd., Ste. 106
St. Clair Shores, MI 48081
(313) 774-5130

FINANCIAL SUMMARY
Recent Giving: $399,700 (1993); $436,200 (1992); $146,682 (1991)

Assets: $4,594,345 (1993); $3,788,661 (1992); $3,029,876 (1991)

Gifts Received: $518,263 (1993); $375,843 (1992); $112,000 (1990)

Fiscal Note: In 1993, contributions were received from Barbara F. Bristol ($368,263) and Harvey C. Fruehauf, Jr. ($150,000).

EIN: 23-7015744

CONTRIBUTIONS SUMMARY
Donor(s): Angela Fruehauf

Typical Recipients: • *Arts & Humanities:* Arts Funds, Arts Institutes, Historic Preservation, History & Archaeology, Libraries, Music, Public Broadcasting • *Civic & Public Affairs:* General, Law & Justice, Philanthropic Organizations, Public Policy, Safety, Urban & Community Affairs • *Education:* Business Education, Colleges & Universities, Private Education (Precollege), Religious Education • *Environment:* Resource Conservation • *Health:* Cancer, Children's Health/Hospitals, Clinics/Medical Centers, Hospitals, Medical Research, Mental Health, Nursing Services, Single-Disease Health Associations • *International:* Health Care/Hospitals, International Organizations, International Relief Efforts • *Religion:* Churches, Ministries, Missionary Activities (Domestic), Religious Organizations, Religious Welfare, Seminaries, Social/Policy Issues • *Social Services:* Animal Protection, Community Service Organizations, Family Services, Homes, People with Disabilities, Recreation & Athletics, Substance Abuse, United Funds/United Ways, Youth Organizations

Grant Types: general support

Geographic Distribution: focus on MI

GIVING OFFICERS
Barbara F. Bristol: vp

Harvey C. Fruehauf, Jr.: pres, dir *B* Grosse Pointe Park MI 1929 *ED* Univ MI 1952 *CURR EMPL* pres, dir: HCF Enterprises *CORP AFFIL* chmn: Miami Oil Producers; dir: Georgia Pacific Corp; pres, treas, dir: HCF Realty *PHIL AFFIL* trust: E. L. Wiegand Foundation

Robert B. Joslyn: trust

Frederick R. Keydel: trust *PHIL AFFIL* trust: Conrad-Johnston Foundation

Julie Stranahan: trust

Elizabeth J. Woods: asst secy

385

APPLICATION INFORMATION
Initial Approach: Send brief letter describing program. There are no deadlines.

GRANTS ANALYSIS
Total Grants: $399,700

Number of Grants: 18

Highest Grant: $300,000

Typical Range: $200 to $20,000

Disclosure Period: 1993

Note: Recent grants are derived from a 1993 Form 990.

RECENT GRANTS
General

300,000	University of Michigan Business School, Ann Arbor, MI — funding of endowed seniors
20,000	Billy Graham Evangelical Association, Minneapolis, MN
10,000	Brown University, Providence, RI
10,000	Coral Ridge Ministries, Ft. Lauderdale, FL — religious
10,000	Focus on the Family, Colorado Springs, CO — religious

General Motors Corp. / General Motors Foundation

Revenue: $154.95 billion

Employees: 711,000

Headquarters: Detroit, MI

SIC Major Group: Motor Vehicles & Car Bodies, Turbines & Turbine Generator Sets, Internal Combustion Engines Nec, and Radio & T.V. Communications Equipment

CONTACT
Jeffrey M. Krause
General Motors Foundation
3044 W Grand Blvd.
Ste. 11-128
Detroit, MI 48202
(313) 556-2057

Note: Jeffrey Krause is the contact for broad-based national support. Local groups should contact the company's public affairs director in their community. For educational support, contact the GM executive liaison at your university; if none exists, contact the public affairs officer at the nearest GM facility.

FINANCIAL SUMMARY
Recent Giving: $21,383,457 (1993); $21,047,222 (1992); $24,119,122 (1991)

Assets: $113,458,520 (1993); $125,892,022 (1992); $140,254,279 (1991)

Fiscal Note: Figures reflect foundation giving only. Above figures exclude nonmonetary support.

EIN: 38-2132136

CONTRIBUTIONS SUMMARY
Typical Recipients: • *Arts & Humanities:* Arts Associations & Councils, Arts Centers, Arts Festivals, Arts Funds, Arts Institutes, Dance, Historic Preservation, Libraries, Museums/Galleries, Music, Opera, Performing Arts, Public Broadcasting, Theater, Visual Arts • *Civic & Public Affairs:* African American Affairs, Business/Free Enterprise, Civil Rights, Community Foundations, Economic Development, Economic Policy, Employment/Job Training, Ethnic Organizations, First Amendment Issues, General, Hispanic Affairs, Housing, Law & Justice, Municipalities/Towns, Nonprofit Management, Professional & Trade Associations, Public Policy, Rural Affairs, Safety, Urban & Community Affairs, Women's Affairs, Zoos/Aquariums • *Education:* Agricultural Education, Arts/Humanities Education, Business Education, Colleges & Universities, Community & Junior Colleges, Continuing Education, Economic Education, Education Associations, Education Funds, Education Reform, Elementary Education (Private), Engineering/Technological Education, Faculty Development, General, Health & Physical Education, International Exchange, International Studies, Legal Education, Literacy, Minority Education, Public Education (Precollege), Science/Mathematics Education, Student Aid • *Environment:* General • *Health:* Alzheimers Disease, Cancer, Emergency/Ambulance Services, Health Organizations, Hospices, Hospitals, Medical Rehabilitation, Medical Training, Mental Health, Public Health, Single-Disease Health Associations • *International:* International Affairs, International Relations • *Religion:* Religious Welfare • *Science:* Science Exhibits & Fairs, Scientific Centers & Institutes, Scientific Organizations • *Social Services:* Child Welfare, Community Centers, Community Service Organizations, Family Services, Food/Clothing Distribution, Homes, People with Disabilities, Senior Services, Shelters/Homelessness, Substance Abuse, United Funds/United Ways, Volunteer Services, Youth Organizations

Grant Types: capital, challenge, conference/seminar, department, employee matching gifts, fellowship, general support, project, research, and scholarship

Nonmonetary Support Types: donated equipment, donated products, and in-kind services

Note: Will not donate products for on-highway use. Exact value of nonmonetary support is unavailable.

Geographic Distribution: nationally, with local contributions awarded primarily in communities with significant numbers of GM employees

Operating Locations: AL (Eufaula, Foley), AZ (Tucson), CA (Canoga Park, Carlsbad, El Segundo, Fremont, Fullerton, Goleta, Irvine, Los Angeles, Malibu, Newport Beach, Palo Alto, Simi Valley, Sylmar, Torrance), FL (Winter Park), GA (La Grange), IL (Chicago, Danville, Des Plaines, La Grange), IN (Anderson, Indianapolis, Kokomo, Muncie), KY (Elizabethtown), MD (Baltimore, Bethesda), MI (Ann Arbor, Detroit, Grand Rapids, Lansing, Pontiac, Saginaw, Southfield, Three Rivers, Troy, Warren, Ypsilanti), MS (Forest), NY (Hauppauge, Lockport, New York, Rochester, Syracuse), OH (Cleveland, Dayton, Mansfield, Sandusky, Warren), PA (Elkins Park, Pittsburgh), SC (Orangeburg), TX (Dallas, Plano, San Antonio), WI (Milwaukee)

Note: Above list covers GM's domestic facility locations; principal employment centers are in California, Illinois, Indiana, Michigan, New York, and Ohio.

CORP. OFFICERS
Louis R. Hughes: *B* 1949 *ED* Gen Motors Inst BSME 1971; Harvard Univ MBA *CURR EMPL* exec vp intl oper: Gen Motors Corp *CORP AFFIL* pres: GM Europe

Robert Thomas O'Connell: *B* New Haven CT 1938 *ED* Yale Univ BA 1960; Harvard Univ MBA 1965 *CURR EMPL* sr vp: Gen Motors Corp *CORP AFFIL* chmn: C I M Ins Corp, Motors Ins Corp; chmn, ceo: GMAC Detroit *PHIL AFFIL* treas, trust: General Motors Cancer Research Foundation

John Gray Smale: *B* Listowel Ontario Canada 1927 *ED* Miami Univ OH BS 1949 *CURR EMPL* chmn: Gen Motors Corp *CORP AFFIL* dir: Berol Corp, JP Morgan & Co, Morgan Guaranty Trust Co NY, Procter & Gamble Co *NONPR AFFIL* dir: Atlantic Salmon Fed; mem: Bus Counc; mem bd govs: Nature Conservancy; trust emeritus: Kenyon Coll *CLUB AFFIL* Cincinnati CC, Commercial, Commonwealth, Queen City, Zanesfield Rod & Gun *PHIL AFFIL* mem governing bd: Greater Cincinnati Foundation

G. Richard Wagoner: *B* 1953 *ED* Duke Univ BA 1975; Harvard Univ MBA 1977 *CURR EMPL* exec vp, pres N Am oper: Gen Motors Corp

GIVING OFFICERS
Graham D. Briggs: dir

W. W. Creek: secy

Deborah I. Dingell: pres

William Elis Hoglund: trust *B* Stockholm Sweden 1934 *ED* Princeton Univ AB 1956; Univ MI MBA 1958 *CURR EMPL* exec vp, dir: Gen Motors Corp *NONPR AFFIL* mem visit comm: Univ MI Grad Sch Bus; trust: William Beaumont Hosp *CLUB AFFIL* Bloomfield Hills, Bloomfield Hills CC, Detroit Athletic *PHIL AFFIL* chmn bd trusts: Skillman Foundation

Leon J. Krain: treas *CURR EMPL* treas: Gen Motors Corp

Jeffrey M. Krause: contact

Ed Pasternak: asst treas *B* 1943

Nancy E. Polis: mgr

John Francis Smith, Jr.: trust *B* Worcester MA 1938 *ED* Univ MA BBA 1960; Boston Univ MBA 1965 *CURR EMPL* pres, ceo, dir: Gen Motors Corp *CORP AFFIL* dir: GMHE, Saturn Corp *NONPR AFFIL* bd trust, mem fin comm: MI Cancer Ctr; co-chmn: Bd Econ Alliance MI; dir: Bds Global Bus Mgmt Counc, EDS, Natl Foreign Trade Counc, Polish-Am Enterprise Fund; intl campaign comm: Boston Univ; mem: Am Soc Corp Execs, Beta Gamma Sigma, Bus Roundtable Policy Comm; mem chancellors adv comm: Univ MA *CLUB AFFIL* Econ Detroit

APPLICATION INFORMATION

Initial Approach: *Initial Contact:* letter *Include Information On:* history of organization, purpose for which funds are sought, detailed budget and major annual contributors for previous three years, detailed budget proposal, brief description of activities and operations for current year, proof of tax-exempt status *Deadlines:* none; allow five to six weeks for review

Restrictions on Giving: Generally does not support endowments, special interest groups, or individuals, except through established programs. Does not support elementary or secondary schools; medical or nursing schools; or medical, business, or other research not related to marketing. Will not contribute to political or lobbying groups; religious organizations for sectarian purposes; organizations that discriminate on the basis of race or sex; special interest groups or projects; or industrial affiliate programs; or conferences, workshops, or seminars.

OTHER THINGS TO KNOW

For recorded message with giving guidelines, call (313) 556-4260.

General Motors has established a nonprofit organization, the GM Cancer Research Foundation, which awards substantial prizes for outstanding individual achievement in cancer research. As an extension of the foundation's ongoing commitment in the fight against cancer, the foundation established an international science journalism awards program in 1989. This program recognizes excellence in reporting about biomedical research with application to cancer and cancer research. Three awards, one each for newspaper, magazine and book, and broadcast coverage, carry a $10,000 cash award and a limited-edition work of art.

In addition to its philanthropic activities, General Motors provides funding for numerous educational and public interest programs as a corporate sponsor (examples include the nationwide telecast of "The Kennedy Center Honors: A Celebration of the Performing Arts" and a national concerto competition).

Program has no written guidelines. However, the Public Interest Report provides an overview. Write GM's Public Affairs Library, Room 11-235, 3044 W. Grand Boulevard, Detroit, MI 48702 for a copy of this report.

Company actively works to increase educational opportunities for minorities and women inside the corporation and in the business community.

GRANTS ANALYSIS

Total Grants: $21,383,457*

Number of Grants: 1,050

Highest Grant: $1,000,000

Average Grant: $20,365

Typical Range: $5,000 to $100,000

Disclosure Period: 1993

Note: Total grants are for foundation only. Recent grants are derived from a 1993 Form 990.

RECENT GRANTS

General

1,000,000	General Motors Cancer Research Foundation, New York, NY —for annual payment on pledge
689,100	United Way Southeastern Michigan, Detroit, MI
580,000	United Way of Genesee and Lapeer Counties, Flint, MI —for unrestricted operating grant
500,000	Massachusetts Institute of Technology, Cambridge, MA —for annual payment on unrestricted operating grant
500,000	Michigan State University, East Lansing, MI —for annual payment on capital campaign 1988-97

Grand Rapids Label Co. / Grand Rapids Label Foundation

Sales: $17.0 million
Employees: 115
Headquarters: Grand Rapids, MI
SIC Major Group: Printing & Publishing

CONTACT

William W. Muir, Jr.
President
Grand Rapids Label Co.
2351 Oak Industrial Dr. NE
Grand Rapids, MI 49505-6073
(616) 459-8134
Note: Contact's extension number is 208.

FINANCIAL SUMMARY

Recent Giving: $62,000 (fiscal 1994); $50,000 (fiscal 1993 approx.); $45,322 (fiscal 1992)

Assets: $48,016 (fiscal 1992); $24,306 (fiscal 1991); $25,592 (fiscal 1989)

Gifts Received: $66,876 (fiscal 1992); $40,725 (fiscal 1991); $38,696 (fiscal 1989)

Fiscal Note: In fiscal 1992, contributions were received form Grand Rapids Label Co.

EIN: 38-2281916

CONTRIBUTIONS SUMMARY

Typical Recipients: • *Arts & Humanities:* Arts Associations & Councils, Arts Festivals, Ballet, Ethnic & Folk Arts, General, Historic Preservation, Libraries, Museums/Galleries, Opera, Performing Arts, Public Broadcasting, Theater, Visual Arts • *Civic & Public Affairs:* Botanical Gardens/Parks, General, Parades/Festivals, Professional & Trade Associations, Zoos/Aquariums • *Education:* Arts/Humanities Education, Colleges & Universities, Education Associations, Education Funds, Elementary Education (Public), General, Literacy, Minority Education, Special Education • *Environment:* Air/Water Quality, Resource Conservation, Wildlife Protection • *Health:* Alzheimers Disease, Cancer, Children's Health/Hospitals, Eyes/Blindness,

General, Medical Research • *Religion:* Religious Welfare • *Social Services:* At-Risk Youth, Camps, Child Welfare, Community Centers, Community Service Organizations, Counseling, Domestic Violence, Family Planning, Family Services, Food/Clothing Distribution, General, People with Disabilities, Recreation & Athletics, Senior Services, United Funds/United Ways, Youth Organizations

Grant Types: award, capital, general support, multiyear/continuing support, operating expenses, and research

Geographic Distribution: focus on Grand Rapids, MI

Operating Locations: MI (Grand Rapids)

CORP. OFFICERS

William W. Muir, Jr.: *B* Grand Rapids MI 1936 *ED* Bowling Green St Univ 1958 *CURR EMPL* pres: Grand Rapids Label Co

Thomas Topel: *CURR EMPL* coo: Grand Rapids Label Co

GIVING OFFICERS

Kathleen M. Allen: dir

Martin Allen: dir *B* Grand Rapids MI *ED* Univ Notre Dame 1958; MI St Univ 1962 *CURR EMPL* sr vp, secy: Old Kent Fin Corp *CORP AFFIL* dir: Grand Rapids Label Co

Michael P. Allen: dir

Stephen J. Allen: dir

Susan J. Allen: secy, dir

Elizabeth J. Crosby: vp, dir

James S. Crosby: dir

John F. Crosby: dir

David F. Muir: dir

Elizabeth M. Muir: dir

Kathleen Muir: dir

William M. Muir: dir

William W. Muir, Jr.: pres, dir *CURR EMPL* pres: Grand Rapids Label Co (see above)

APPLICATION INFORMATION

Initial Approach: Send a brief letter of inquiry and a full proposal. Include a description of organization, amount requested, purpose of funds sought, and prf.

Restrictions on Giving: Does not support individuals, religious organizations for sectarian purposes, political or lobbying groups, or organizations outside operating areas.

OTHER THINGS TO KNOW

Company emphasizes that grants are not given to organizations outside the the operating areas.

GRANTS ANALYSIS

Total Grants: $45,322

Number of Grants: 38

Highest Grant: $20,000

Typical Range: $100 to $1,000

Disclosure Period: fiscal year ending June 30, 1992

Note: Recent grants are derived from a fiscal 1992 Form 990.

RECENT GRANTS

General

20,000	United Way of Greater Grand Rapids, Grand Rapids, MI
2,000	United Methodist Community, Grand Rapids, MI
1,230	First of America Classic, Grand Rapids, MI
1,000	Gerald R. Ford Foundation, Grand Rapids, MI
1,000	Porter Hills Presbyterian, Grand Rapids, MI

Herrick Foundation

CONTACT

Kenneth G. Herrick
Chairman, President, Treasurer, and Trustee
Herrick Foundation
150 W Jefferson, Ste. 2500
Detroit, MI 48226
(313) 963-6420

FINANCIAL SUMMARY

Recent Giving: $2,797,545 (fiscal 1992); $5,213,628 (fiscal 1991); $10,187,933 (fiscal 1990).

Assets: $165,702,996 (fiscal 1992); $136,907,581 (fiscal 1991); $126,916,179 (fiscal 1990).

Gifts Received: $30,000 (fiscal 1990); $5,000 (fiscal 1986).

Fiscal Note: In 1990, the foundation received a refund of $30,000 of a previous grant to the Muskegon Rotary Foundation.

EIN: 38-6041517

CONTRIBUTIONS SUMMARY

Donor(s): The foundation was established in 1949, with the late Ray Wesley Herrick and his wife, the late Hazel M. Herrick, as donors. In the early days of the automotive industry in Detroit, Mr. Herrick was in charge of production for the Ford Motor Company. In the early 1930s, he moved to Tecumseh, MI, where he founded and became chairman of the board of directors of the predecessor of the Tecumseh Products Company. Through the Herrick Foundation, he helped build Adrian College in Michigan and the Howe (Indiana) Military Academy. He also gave the city of Holland, MI, a public library now bearing his name. A majority of the foundation's assets consist of shares in the Tecumseh Products Company.

Typical Recipients: • *Arts & Humanities:* History & Archaeology, Libraries, Music, Performing Arts, Public Broadcasting • *Civic & Public Affairs:* Community Foundations, Economic Development, Housing, Municipalities/Towns, Native American Affairs, Safety, Zoos/Aquariums • *Education:* Arts/Humanities Education, Business Education, Colleges & Universities, Community & Junior Colleges, Education Associations, Elementary Education (Private), Faculty Development, Health & Physical Education, Medical Education, Private Education (Precollege), Public Education (Precollege), Religious Education, Science/Mathematics Education, Secondary Education (Public), Student Aid • *Health:* Children's Health/Hospitals, Health Funds, Health Organizations, Hospices, Hospitals, Single-Disease Health Associations • *Religion:* Churches, Religious Organizations, Religious Welfare • *Social Services:* Child Welfare, Community Service Organizations, Family Services, Food/Clothing Distribution, Homes, People with Disabilities, Recreation & Athletics, Senior Services, Substance Abuse, United Funds/United Ways, Youth Organizations

Grant Types: capital, endowment, fellowship, general support, project, research, and scholarship

Geographic Distribution: no geographic restrictions; some emphasis in Michigan

GIVING OFFICERS

Catherine R. Cobb: trust *PHIL AFFIL* trust

John William Gelder: vp, secy, trust *B* Buffalo NY 1933 *ED* Univ MI BBA 1956; Univ MI JD 1959 *CURR EMPL* mng ptnr: Miller Canfield Paddock & Stone *CORP AFFIL* dir: Tecumseh Products Co; secy: Harlan Electric Co *NONPR AFFIL* mem: Order Coif *PHIL AFFIL* vp, secy, trust *CLUB AFFIL* Bloomfield Hills CC, Detroit Athletic

Kenneth Gilbert Herrick: chmn, pres, treas, trust *B* Jackson MI 1921 *CORP AFFIL* chmn: Little Giant Pump Co *NONPR AFFIL* mem exec adv bd: St Jude Childrens Hosp *CLUB AFFIL* Elks, Lenawee CC, Masons, Tecumseh CC

Todd Wesley Herrick: vp, trust *B* Tecumseh MI 1942 *ED* Univ Notre Dame BA 1967 *CURR EMPL* pres, ceo, dir: Tecumseh Products Co *CORP AFFIL* chb, dir: MP Pumps; dir: OH Citizens Trust Co, Sociedad Intercontinental Compressores Hermitocos, Tecnamotor, Un Savings Bank; pres, dir: Vitrus; vp, dir: Little Giant Pump Co *NONPR AFFIL* mem: Am Soc Heating Refrigerating Air Conditioning Engrs, Am Soc Metals

APPLICATION INFORMATION

Initial Approach:

The foundation has no formal application requirements and procedures. Prospective grantees should send the foundation a letter of inquiry.

The letter should include the amount requested, the goal to be accomplished, methods to be used, plans for evaluation, copy of the most current IRS 501(c)(3) tax-exempt ruling, name of the person to contact who will be administering the program, and any other information that would aid the board of trustees in making their decision.

Funding requests may be submitted any time.

Restrictions on Giving: There are no restrictions as to geographical area, charitable fields, kind of institution, or other factors. In general, the foundation funds organizations that further charitable, religious, scientific, literary, and educational purposes.

GRANTS ANALYSIS

Total Grants: $2,797,545

Number of Grants: 109

Highest Grant: $200,000

Average Grant: $25,666

Typical Range: $5,000 to $50,000

Disclosure Period: fiscal year ending September 30, 1992

Note: Recent grants are derived from a fiscal 1992 Form 990.

RECENT GRANTS

Library

20,000	Sequatchie County, Tennessee, Dunlap, TN — to pay and defray, in part, the costs of new bookshelves, furniture, and equipment to complete the Sequatchie County Library Renovation project

General

200,000	Siena Heights College, Adrian, MI — final payment of Herrick Foundation's $500,000 gift to further the objects and purposes of Vision 2000 Program of the college
200,000	Siena Heights College, Adrian, MI — second partial payment of the second installment of Herrick Foundation's $500,000 gift or contribution to further the objectives and purposes of its Vision 2000 program
158,000	Charter Township of Madison, Adrian, MI — for exclusively public purposes, namely to pay and defray the costs of a new fire truck to replace its 1972 Mack Snorkel fire truck and for no other purposes
100,000	Adrian College, Adrian, MI — to be used for facility renovations and improvements
100,000	Allegan General Hospital, Allegan, MI — to defray, in part, the costs for the expansion and renovation of the hospital

Holnam

Revenue: $946.18 million
Employees: 2,400
Parent Company: Holderbank Financiere Glaris Ltd.
Headquarters: Dundee, MI
SIC Major Group: Stone, Clay & Glass Products

CONTACT

Linda McCormick
Public Affairs Administrator
Holnam
6211 N Ann Arbor Rd.
PO Box 122
Dundee, MI 48131
(313) 529-2411

FINANCIAL SUMMARY
Fiscal Note: Annual Giving Range: $100,000 to $250,000

CONTRIBUTIONS SUMMARY
Company reports that 60% of contributions go to education; 20% to civic and public affairs; 15% to health and human services; and 5% to the arts.

Typical Recipients: • *Arts & Humanities:* Arts Associations & Councils, Arts Festivals, General, Historic Preservation, Libraries, Music, Performing Arts, Public Broadcasting • *Civic & Public Affairs:* Chambers of Commerce, Community Foundations, Economic Development, General, Parades/Festivals, Professional & Trade Associations, Safety, Urban & Community Affairs • *Education:* Agricultural Education, Business Education, Business-School Partnerships, Colleges & Universities, Community & Junior Colleges, Continuing Education, General • *Environment:* General, Wildlife Protection • *Health:* General • *Science:* General • *Social Services:* General

Grant Types: capital, conference/seminar, emergency, employee matching gifts, general support, multiyear/continuing support, project, and scholarship

Nonmonetary Support Types: cause-related marketing & promotion, donated equipment, donated products, and loaned employees

Geographic Distribution: in headquarters and operating communities

Operating Locations: MI (Dundee)

CORP. OFFICERS
Peter Byland: *CURR EMPL* chmn: Holnam

Paul Yhouse: *CURR EMPL* pres, ceo: Holnam

APPLICATION INFORMATION
Initial Approach: Send a full proposal. Include a description of organization, amount requested, purpose of funds sought, and proof of tax-exempt status.

Restrictions on Giving: Does not support individuals, religious organizations for sectarian purposes, political or lobbying groups, or organizations outside operating areas.

GRANTS ANALYSIS
Typical Range: $10 to $1,000

Note: Typical grant size is less than $1,000. Recent grants are derived from a grants list provided by company in 1994.

RECENT GRANTS

General
American Heart Association
American Red Cross
Association of Retarded Citizens
Humane Society
March of Dimes

Hudson-Webber Foundation

CONTACT
Gilbert Hudson
President and Trustee
Hudson-Webber Foundation
333 W Fort St., Ste. 1310
Detroit, MI 48226
(313) 963-7777

FINANCIAL SUMMARY
Recent Giving: $2,889,823 (1993); $4,025,148 (1992); $3,562,664 (1991)

Assets: $103,671,050 (1993); $96,753,933 (1992); $92,961,349 (1991)

Gifts Received: $2,250 (1993); $40,000 (1988); $5,000 (1987)

Fiscal Note: In 1988, the foundation received gifts totaling $15,000 from Elizabeth Webber Tost and a gift of $25,000 from Mary Webber Parker.

EIN: 38-6052131

CONTRIBUTIONS SUMMARY
Donor(s): The Hudson-Webber Foundation was organized in 1943, with funds donated by the J. L. Hudson Company and by Richard Webber, Joseph Webber, and Oscar Webber. Significant contributions also were provided by company employees and other members of the family. At the close of 1983, the foundation merged with two other foundations: the Eloise and Richard Webber Foundation (established in 1939, with Richard and Eloise Webber; their daughters, Jean Webber Sutphin and Mary Webber Parker; and Richard Webber's sister, Louise Webber O'Brien as donors) and the Richard H. and Eloise Jenks Webber Charitable Fund (established in 1960, with Richard and Eloise Webber; their daughters, Jean and Mary; and Richard Webber's brother, Joseph L. Webber, as donors).

Joseph L. Hudson, Jr., chairman of the foundation, and Gilbert Hudson, its president and chief executive, are grandnephews of Joseph L. Hudson (1846-1912), who founded J. L. Hudson Company (1881), a major Detroit merchandiser. Joseph L. Hudson was a generous benefactor of local charities and a leader of civic boards and committees. The Webber family's relationship to the company derives from the founder's sister, Mary, who married Joseph T. Webber. When Mr. Hudson died, his four nephews inherited the majority of the company's stock, and Richard Hudson Webber became president of J. L. Hudson Company.

Typical Recipients: • *Arts & Humanities:* Arts Associations & Councils, Arts Centers, Arts Institutes, General, Historic Preservation, History & Archaeology, Libraries, Museums/Galleries, Music, Opera, Performing Arts, Theater • *Civic & Public Affairs:* Business/Free Enterprise, Chambers of Commerce, Community Foundations, Economic Development, Employment/Job Training, Hispanic Affairs, Housing, Law & Justice, Municipalities/Towns, Parades/Festivals, Urban & Community Affairs, Women's Af-

fairs, Zoos/Aquariums • *Education:* Arts/Humanities Education, Business Education, Colleges & Universities, Public Education (Precollege), Secondary Education (Public) • *Environment:* General • *Health:* Cancer, Children's Health/Hospitals, Health Organizations, Hospitals, Public Health, Transplant Networks/Donor Banks • *International:* International Peace & Security Issues • *Religion:* Religious Organizations, Religious Welfare • *Science:* Scientific Centers & Institutes • *Social Services:* Community Service Organizations, Counseling, Crime Prevention, Delinquency & Criminal Rehabilitation, Domestic Violence, Food/Clothing Distribution, Substance Abuse, United Funds/United Ways, Youth Organizations

Grant Types: capital, general support, operating expenses, project, and seed money

Geographic Distribution: Southeastern Michigan, primarily Wayne, Oakland, and Macomb counties; emphasis on Detroit

GIVING OFFICERS
Lawrence Paul Doss: trust *B* Cleveland OH 1927 *ED* OH St Univ 1947-1949; Fenn Coll 1949-1951; Am Univ 1954; Nova Univ MPA *NONPR AFFIL* chmn bd trusts: Doctors Hosp; co-chmn; Move Detroit Forward; dir, mem exec comm: Detroit Econ Growth Corp; mem: MI Commn Jobs Econ Devel, Omega Psi Phi; treas: Congressional Black Caucus; trust: Un Fdn; vchmn, mem exec comm: Martin Luther King Ctr Nonviolent Social Change *PHIL AFFIL* dir: ANR Foundation, Inc.; pres: Coleman Young Foundation

Alfred Robinson Glancy III: trust *B* Detroit MI 1938 *ED* Princeton Univ BA 1960; Harvard Univ MA 1962 *CURR EMPL* chmn, pres, ceo: MCN Corp *CORP AFFIL* chmn, ceo: MI Consolidated Gas Co; dir: MLX Corp, NBD Bancorp Inc, NBD Bank NA; vchmn: UNICO Properties *NONPR AFFIL* chmn: Detroit Med Ctr, Detroit Renaissance, Detroit Symphony Orchestra; dir: Am Gas Assn, Citizens Res Counc MI, Commun Fdn Southeastern MI, Detroit Econ Growth Corp, Greater Detroit Chamber Commerce, New Detroit; trust, mem exec comm: Detroit Inst Art Fdrs Soc; vchmn: Un Way Southeastern MI *CLUB AFFIL* CC Detroit, Detroit, Princeton *PHIL AFFIL* vchmn: Lenora and Alfred Glancy Foundation; dir: Coleman Young Foundation; vchmn: MichCon Foundation

Frank Martin Hennessey: treas, trust *B* Lynn MA 1938 *ED* Northeastern Univ BS 1964 *CURR EMPL* pres, ceo: CEO Emco Ltd *CORP AFFIL* dir: MCN Corp, New Detroit *NONPR AFFIL* dir-at-large natl counc: Northeastern Univ; dir, treas: Greater Detroit & Windsor Japan-Am Soc; dir, trust: Citizens Res Counc MI; mem SE MI adv bd: Un Way *CLUB AFFIL* Clum, Detroit, Detroit, London

Hudson Holland, Jr.: secy, trust *B* Springfield MA 1939 *ED* Williams Coll BA 1961 *CURR EMPL* pres: Nantucket House *CLUB AFFIL* Fontinalis, Nantucket YC

Gilbert Hudson: pres, trust, ceo

Joseph L. Hudson IV: trust

Joseph Lowthian Hudson, Jr.: chmn, trust *PHIL AFFIL* dir: Anderson Fund

John E. Lobbia: trust *B* Chicago IL 1941 *ED* Univ Detroit BSEE 1964 *CURR EMPL* chmn, ceo: Detroit Edison Co *CORP AFFIL* chmn: Midwest Energy Resources Co; dir: Natl Bank Detroit, NBD Bancorp Inc *NONPR AFFIL* chmn, dir: Un Way Southeastern MI

Philip J. Meathe: trust *B* Grosse Pointe MI 1926 *ED* Univ MI B 1948 *CURR EMPL* chmn, ceo, dir: Smith Hinchman & Grylls Assocs

Theodore Hart McCalla Mecke, Jr.: trust *B* Philadelphia PA 1923 *ED* La Salle Coll 1941 *CURR EMPL* pres: Hartwood Assocs *CORP AFFIL* dir: Comerica, Comerica Bank-Detroit, Detroit Legal News *NONPR AFFIL* mem: Am Legion, Military Order Loyal Legion *CLUB AFFIL* Am Legion, CC Detroit, Detroit, Yondotega

Marianne Schwartz: trust

APPLICATION INFORMATION
Initial Approach:

Applicants should send a brief letter, signed by a senior officer of the requesting organization.

The letter of request should include a brief description of the organization; description of the proposed program, including an explanation of its importance and a clear statement of its goals; detailed income and expense budget for the program; potential sources of other funding; and amount requested and time period during which the funds will be used. Proof of the organization's tax-exempt status is required.

Grant requests should be submitted by April 15, August 15, or December 15. Requests received after these dates are reviewed during the next period.

Restrictions on Giving: The foundation does not make grants for endowments, fundraising social events, conferences, or exhibits. Also, the foundation does not fund individuals, except under the Hudson-Webber program for Hudsonians. Programs outside the foundation's geographical area of interest are not supported.

PUBLICATIONS
Annual report

GRANTS ANALYSIS
Total Grants: $2,849,265*

Number of Grants: 124

Highest Grant: $170,000

Average Grant: $22,978

Typical Range: $5,000 to $50,000

Disclosure Period: 1993

Note: The total grants figure excludes $40,558 in grants to needy employees or former employees of the J. L. Hudson Company. Recent grants are derived from a 1993 Form 990.

RECENT GRANTS

Library
44,000	Friends of the Detroit Public Library, Detroit, MI —	

	Greater Detroit Job Brokers Association	

General
170,000	United Way for Southeastern Michigan, Detroit, MI — Torch Drive for affiliated agencies	
90,000	National Conference of Christians and Jews, New York, NY — Greater Detroit Interfaith Round Table's Police Community Relations Program	
90,000	United Way for Southeastern Michigan, Detroit, MI — comprehensive strategic planning	
81,000	Wayne State University Center for Peace and Conflict Studies, Detroit, MI — coordination of Community Dispute Resolution Programs	
80,000	Harper Hospital, Detroit, MI — photodynamic cancer therapy program	

Interkal, Inc.

Sales: $30.0 million
Employees: 190
Headquarters: Kalamazoo, MI
SIC Major Group: Furniture & Fixtures

CONTACT
Brian Gould
Controller, Treasurer
Interkal, Inc.
PO Box 2107
Kalamazoo, MI 49003
(616) 349-1521

FINANCIAL SUMMARY
Fiscal Note: Giving Range: less than $25,000

CONTRIBUTIONS SUMMARY
Contributions evaluated on a case-by-case basis.

Typical Recipients: • *Arts & Humanities:* Arts Associations & Councils, Arts Centers, Community Arts, Libraries, Music, Performing Arts • *Civic & Public Affairs:* Economic Development • *Education:* Business Education, Colleges & Universities, International Exchange, International Studies • *Social Services:* Family Services, United Funds/United Ways

Grant Types: general support

Nonmonetary Support Types: donated equipment and donated products

Geographic Distribution: principally near headquarters and operating locations

Operating Locations: MI (Kalamazoo)

CORP. OFFICERS
Minoru Amemiya: *CURR EMPL* chmn, ceo: Interkal

Richard Patterson: *CURR EMPL* pres: Interkal

GIVING OFFICERS
Brian Gould: *CURR EMPL* contr, treas: Interkal

APPLICATION INFORMATION
Initial Approach: Send brief letter of inquiry, including a description of the organization and purpose of funds sought.

GRANTS ANALYSIS
Typical Range: $250 to $500

Kantzler Foundation

CONTACT
Robert D. Sarrow
Secretary
Kantzler Fdn.
900 Center Ave.
Bay City, MI 48708
(517) 892-0591

FINANCIAL SUMMARY
Recent Giving: $251,913 (1993); $211,408 (1992); $199,987 (1990)

Assets: $5,130,180 (1993); $4,952,212 (1992); $4,325,257 (1990)

EIN: 23-7422733

CONTRIBUTIONS SUMMARY
Donor(s): Leopold I. Kantzler

Typical Recipients: • *Arts & Humanities:* Arts Associations & Councils, Community Arts, Historic Preservation, Libraries, Theater • *Civic & Public Affairs:* Botanical Gardens/Parks, Community Foundations, General, Housing, Municipalities/Towns, Urban & Community Affairs • *Education:* Colleges & Universities, Public Education (Precollege) • *Environment:* General • *Health:* Health Organizations, Hospitals • *Religion:* Ministries • *Social Services:* Family Services, People with Disabilities, Recreation & Athletics, Scouts, Senior Services, United Funds/United Ways, YMCA/YWCA/YMHA/YWHA, Youth Organizations

Grant Types: capital, operating expenses, and seed money

Geographic Distribution: limited to the greater Bay City, MI, area

GIVING OFFICERS
Robbie L. Baker: trust

Ruth Jaffe: trust

D. Brian Law: dir

Dominic Monastiere: vp

Robert D. Sarrow: secy

Clifford D. Van Dyke: pres *B* Ft Madison IA 1929 *ED* Knox Coll BA 1951; Harvard Univ MBA 1955 *CURR EMPL* sr vp: First Am Bank-Mid MI NA *NONPR AFFIL* dir: Delta Coll Fdn; mem: Bay Area Chamber Commerce; pres, dir: Bay County Growth Alliance; trust: Kantzler Fdn *CLUB AFFIL* Bay City CC, Elks, Rotary, Saginaw Bay YC, Saginaw Valley Torch

Jerome Yantz: dir

APPLICATION INFORMATION
Initial Approach: Send cover letter and full proposal. Include a description of organization, amount requested, purpose of funds sought, recently audited financial statement, and proof of tax-exempt status. There are no deadlines.

Restrictions on Giving: Limited to the greater Bay City community.

PUBLICATIONS
Application Guidelines

GRANTS ANALYSIS
Total Grants: $251,913

Number of Grants: 16

Highest Grant: $50,000

Typical Range: $2,663 to $35,000

Disclosure Period: 1993

Note: Recent grants are derived from a 1993 Form 990.

RECENT GRANTS
General

50,000	Bay Area Community Foundation, Bay City, MI — pedestrian bridge for riverwalk
35,000	YWCA, Bay City, MI — facility renovation project
25,000	Bay Area Community Foundation, Bay City, MI — housing rehabilitation program
25,000	Hospital Council Foundation, Bay City, MI — operate business healthcare partnership
20,000	Bay Area Community Foundation, Bay City, MI

Kmart Corporation

Revenue: $34.31 billion
Employees: 320,000
Headquarters: Troy, MI
SIC Major Group: Variety Stores

CONTACT
Leslie Kota
Manager, Comunity Affairs
Kmart Corp.
3100 W Big Beaver Rd.
Troy, MI 48084
(810) 643-1776

FINANCIAL SUMMARY
Recent Giving: $10,000,000 (1993 approx.); $11,000,000 (1992 approx.); $10,000,000 (1991 approx.)

Fiscal Note: Company gives directly. Figures represent total contributions by headquarters, subsidiaries, regional offices, distribution offices, and stores. Above figures exclude nonmonetary support.

CONTRIBUTIONS SUMMARY
Typical Recipients: • *Arts & Humanities:* Arts Institutes, Libraries, Museums/Galleries, Music, Opera, Performing Arts, Public Broadcasting, Theater • *Civic & Public Affairs:* Safety, Urban & Community Affairs, Women's Affairs, Zoos/Aquariums • *Education:* Colleges & Universities, Literacy, Minority Education • *Social Services:* Community Service Organizations, Family Services, Food/Clothing Distribution, United Funds/United Ways, Youth Organizations

Grant Types: emergency and employee matching gifts

Note: Employee matching gift ratio: 1 to 1.

Nonmonetary Support: $11,000,000 (1993); $10,000,000 (1991); $1,000,000 (1989)

Nonmonetary Support Types: cause-related marketing & promotion, donated products, and loaned executives

Geographic Distribution: areas in which Kmart maintains facilities, and to selected national organizations

Note: Kmart operates 2,400 stores in all 50 states and Puerto Rico.

CORP. OFFICERS
Floyd Hall: *CURR EMPL* pres, chmn, ceo: Kmart Corp

GIVING OFFICERS
Shann Kahle: *CURR EMPL* vp corp aff: Kmart Corp

Leslie Kota: *CURR EMPL* mgr commun aff: Kmart Corp

APPLICATION INFORMATION
Initial Approach: *Initial Contact:* phone for copy of guidelines and Kmart Funds application; submit in writing a letter of intent, totalling no more than two pages, and a completed application *Include Information On:* IRS letter of determination of 501(c)(3) tax exemption. Also submit a cover letter signed by a senior official, outlining: whether it is a new or ongoing project; the extent of community and volunteer involvement; how Kmart associates may participate as volunteers in the program; and how the activity could take place at a Kmart facility. Other supporting documentation should include your annual report and a roster of your Board of Directors. *Deadlines:* None; allow at least 2 months for processing

Restrictions on Giving: Kmart does not make contributions to organizations devoted exclusively to research projects or to individuals. Kmart also does not support the following: organizations not granted IRS 501(c)(3) status; local chapters of national organizations already supported; alumni associations; veterans, religious or political organizations; group travel expenses; school extra-curricular activities such as sports, band, etc.; or organizations or programs outside the U.S.. The company does not provide individual scholarships.

OTHER THINGS TO KNOW
Contributions usually are made on an annual basis or for a limited, fixed term. Multiyear requests are not encouraged nor does a contribution ensure future aid. The company also makes nonmonetary contributions such as merchandise.

GRANTS ANALYSIS
Total Grants: $10,000,000*

Highest Grant: $500,000

Average Grant: $10,000*

Disclosure Period: 1993

Note: Total grants and average grants figures are approximate. Recent grants are derived from a 1994 partial grants list.

RECENT GRANTS
General

250,000	Share Our Strength, Washington, DC — for hunger relief efforts

Kresge Foundation

CONTACT
John E. Marshall III
President and Secretary
Kresge Foundation
3215 W Big Beaver Rd.
PO Box 3151
Troy, MI 48007-3151
(810) 643-9630

FINANCIAL SUMMARY
Recent Giving: $58,898,400 (1993); $67,233,121 (1992); $62,989,400 (1991)

Assets: $1,543,183,104 (1993); $1,459,852,521 (1992); $1,422,418,786 (1991)

EIN: 38-1359217

CONTRIBUTIONS SUMMARY
Donor(s): The foundation was established in 1924 by Sebastian S. Kresge (1867-1966), the founder of the Kresge chain of retail stores now known as the Kmart Corporation. As owner of S. S. Kresge Company, Mr. Kresge amassed a fortune of $100 million by 1924. He established the foundation with an initial personal contribution of almost $2 million. Family representation is continued on the board of trustees through Dr. Bruce A. Kresge. The foundation has never been affiliated with Kmart Corporation.

Typical Recipients: • *Arts & Humanities:* Arts Centers, Arts Institutes, Ballet, Historic Preservation, History & Archaeology, Libraries, Museums/Galleries, Music, Performing Arts, Public Broadcasting, Theater • *Civic & Public Affairs:* African American Affairs, Botanical Gardens/Parks, Clubs, Community Foundations, Economic Development, Gay/Lesbian Issues, Professional & Trade Associations, Public Policy, Zoos/Aquariums • *Education:* Arts/Humanities Education, Business Education, Colleges & Universities, Engineering/Technological Education, Faculty Development, Journalism/Media Education, Legal Education, Medical Education, Private Education (Precollege), Science/Mathematics Education, Special Education • *Environment:* Air/Water Quality, General, Resource Conservation, Wildlife Protection • *Health:* AIDS/HIV, Cancer, Children's Health/Hospitals, Clinics/Medical Centers, Emergency/Ambulance

Services, Eyes/Blindness, Health Organizations, Hospices, Hospitals, Medical Rehabilitation, Medical Research, Nursing Services, Outpatient Health Care, Preventive Medicine/Wellness Organizations, Research/Studies Institutes • *International:* Foreign Educational Institutions, Health Care/Hospitals, International Environmental Issues, International Relations • *Religion:* Jewish Causes, Religious Welfare, Seminaries • *Science:* Science Museums, Scientific Centers & Institutes • *Social Services:* Animal Protection, Camps, Child Welfare, Community Centers, Community Service Organizations, Domestic Violence, Family Planning, Family Services, Food/Clothing Distribution, People with Disabilities, Recreation & Athletics, Scouts, Senior Services, Sexual Abuse, Shelters/Homelessness, Substance Abuse, YMCA/YWCA/YMHA/YWHA, Youth Organizations

Grant Types: capital and challenge

Geographic Distribution: no geographic restrictions

GIVING OFFICERS

Sandra McAlister Ambrozy: sr program off

Jill Cathryn Ker Conway: dir *B* New South Wales Australia 1934 *ED* Univ Sydney BA 1958; Harvard Univ PhD 1969 *PHIL AFFIL* trust: John S. and James L. Knight Foundation

Barbara J. Getz: sr program off

Ernest B. Gutierrez: sr program off

Edward M. Hunia: sr vp, treas *B* Sharon PA 1946 *ED* Carnegie Mellon Univ BSME 1967; Carnegie Mellon Univ MSME 1968; Univ Pittsburgh MBA 1971

Bruce Anderson Kresge: vp, trust *B* Detroit MI 1931 *ED* Albion Coll BA 1953; Wayne St Univ MD 1956 *CURR EMPL* physician, staff mem: Crittenton Hosp *NONPR AFFIL* mem: Am Med Assn; trust: Albion Coll

George Dorland Langdon, Jr.: dir *B* Putnam CT 1933 *ED* Harvard Univ AB 1954; Amherst Coll MA 1957; Yale Univ PhD 1961 *NONPR AFFIL* pres: Am Museum Natural History; pres emeritus: Colgate Univ; trust: St Lukes-Roosevelt Hosp *PHIL AFFIL* trust: Wenner-Gren Foundation for Anthropological Research

Edward H. Lerchen: dir

John Elbert Marshall III: pres, secy, trust *B* Providence RI 1942 *ED* Brown Univ BA 1964 *NONPR AFFIL* dir: Counc Fdns, MI Campus Compact; mem bd dirs: Counc MI Fdns; vchmn, dir: Family Svcs Detroit Wayne County

Mark E. Neithercut: program off

David A. Page: dir

David Keith Page: dir *B* Detroit MI 1933 *ED* Dartmouth Coll AB 1955; Harvard Univ LLB 1958 *CURR EMPL* sr ptnr: Honigman Miller Schwartz & Cohn *NONPR AFFIL* pres, dir: Jewish Fed Metro Detroit

Miguel A. Satut: vp

Margaret T. Smith: chmn

Elizabeth C. Sullivan: grants coordinator

Alfred Hendricks Taylor, Jr.: chmn, trust *B* Evanston IL 1930 *ED* Williams Coll BA 1952 *CORP AFFIL* dir: Comerica *NONPR AFFIL* dir: Conservation Fund, Independent Sector, Un Way Detroit; mem: Williams Coll Alumni Assn; trust: Am Farmland Trust; trust emeritus: Natl Trust Historic Preservation *CLUB AFFIL* Birmingham Athletic, Econ Detroit

APPLICATION INFORMATION
Initial Approach:

Telephone calls or meetings are encouraged prior to sending an application.

An application should include a cover letter (signed by the senior administrative official) describing the project's purpose, impact, and priority. The proposal narrative should include proof of the applicant's tax-exempt status, copy of IRS ruling letter stating the organization is not a private foundation as described in IRS section 509(a), detailed financial data including the estimated or contract cost of the project and proposed method of financing it, fund-raising details, and the proposed use of a challenge grant.

Applications also should include a listing of all presently available and anticipated sources of funding; expected completion date of fund raising; estimated operating and maintenance cost of the project, with method proposed to finance such cost; schedule of construction or project commencement; and estimated completion, occupancy, or use dates. Applications must include reasonable assurances that the applicant considers its present and projected status sound. In addition, it must include an audited financial report for the most recently completed fiscal year and a complete copy of the most recent accreditation and/or licensure report. Evidence of existing partial financial support for the project is considered essential. Major regulatory approvals or long-term financing must be secured prior to application.

Applications may be submitted at any time, but only once in a twelve-month period. Those postmarked by February 15 are decided upon by the trustees in the latter part of June; by May 15, in the latter part of September; by July 15, in the latter part of November; by August 15, in the latter part of December; by November 15, in the latter part of March; and by January 15, in the latter part of May.

The trustees prefer to fund organizations that, having raised some funds toward a project, are requesting a challenge grant to provide leverage to complete funding.

Restrictions on Giving: The foundation does not give grants to initiate or complete projects, for debt retirement, furnishings, church building projects, or projects which are substantially completed at the time of application. Also, operating or research budget support and grants to individuals are excluded from consideration.

OTHER THINGS TO KNOW

Full accreditation is required of higher education and hospital applicants.

PUBLICATIONS

Annual report and informational pamphlets

GRANTS ANALYSIS

Total Grants: $58,898,400

Number of Grants: 156

Highest Grant: $3,278,400

Average Grant: $377,554

Typical Range: $50,000 to $450,000

Disclosure Period: 1993

Note: Recent grants are derived from a 1994 partial grants list.

RECENT GRANTS

Library

750,000	St. Ambrose University, Davenport, IA — toward the construction of a new library
600,000	Bellarmine College, Louisville, KY — toward the construction of a library

General

1,000,000	Detroit Community Development Funder's Collaborative, Detroit, MI — toward the establishment of a $20,495,000 fund to provide grants for operating support, intensive technical assistance, and project funding for 16 selected community development corporations operating in Detroit
750,000	Rhodes College, Memphis, TN — toward the renovation of recreational facilities as part of the construction and renovation of buildings for a Campus Life Center
750,000	Salvation Army, Harbor Treatment Facility, Washington, DC — toward the construction of the Harbor Light Treatment Facility in Washington
600,000	District of Columbia Jewish Community Center, Washington, DC — toward the purchase and renovation of a facility
600,000	Juniata College, Huntingdon, PA — toward the renovation of a student residence (The Cloister)

La-Z-Boy Chair Co. / La-Z-Boy Foundation

Sales: $684.0 million
Employees: 7,828
Headquarters: Monroe, MI
SIC Major Group: Upholstered Household Furniture

CONTACT
Donald E. Blohm
Administrator
La-Z-Boy Foundation
1284 N Telegraph Rd.
Monroe, MI 48161
(313) 242-1444

FINANCIAL SUMMARY
Recent Giving: $675,000 (1995 est.); $675,950 (1994 approx.); $663,450 (1993)

Assets: $12,700,000 (1995 est.); $12,666,547 (1994 approx.); $13,103,875 (1993)

Fiscal Note: Company gives through foundation only.

EIN: 38-6087673

CONTRIBUTIONS SUMMARY
Typical Recipients: • *Arts & Humanities:* Arts Centers, Community Arts, Historic Preservation, Libraries, Museums/Galleries, Music • *Civic & Public Affairs:* Community Foundations, Economic Development, Municipalities/Towns, Safety, Women's Affairs • *Education:* Colleges & Universities, Community & Junior Colleges, Education Funds, Elementary Education (Public), Public Education (Precollege), Religious Education, Secondary Education (Public) • *Health:* Diabetes, Emergency/Ambulance Services, Hospices, Hospitals, Single-Disease Health Associations • *Religion:* Churches, Ministries, Religious Welfare • *Social Services:* Community Centers, Community Service Organizations, Senior Services, United Funds/United Ways, Youth Organizations

Grant Types: general support

Geographic Distribution: in communities with manufacturing locations and corporate offices in the United States

Operating Locations: AR (Siloam Springs), CA (Redlands), MI (Grand Rapids, Monroe), MO (Neosho), MS (Lelend, Newton), NC (Hudson, Lenior, Lincolnton), SC (Florence), TN (Dayton), UT (Tremonton)

CORP. OFFICERS
John Case: *CURR EMPL* admin, pub rels: La-Z-Boy Chair Co

Charles Thair Knabusch: *B* Detroit MI 1939 *ED* Cleary Coll AB 1962 *CURR EMPL* chmn, pres, ceo: La-Z-Boy Chair Co *CORP AFFIL* dir: Monroe Bank & Trust *NONPR AFFIL* mem: Natl Assn Furniture Mfrs

GIVING OFFICERS
Donald E. Blohm: admin

Warren W. Gruber: dir *CORP AFFIL* dir: La-Z-Boy Chair Co; pres, dir: Grubers Value World Inc

Gene M. Hardy: dir *B* Selma AL 1937 *ED* Univ AL 1959 *CURR EMPL* secy, treas, dir: La-Z-Boy Chair Co *NONPR AFFIL* mem: Fin Execs Inst

David K. Hehl: dir *CORP AFFIL* dir: La-Z-Boy Chair Co

Frederick H. Jackson: dir *B* Cleveland OH 1927 *ED* Bowling Green St Univ 1951; Case Western Reserve Univ 1960 *CURR EMPL* vp fin, dir: La-Z-Boy Chair Co *NONPR AFFIL* mem: Am Inst CPAs, Fin Execs Inst

James W. Johnston: dir *CORP AFFIL* dir: La-Z-Boy Chair Co

Charles Thair Knabusch: chmn *CURR EMPL* chmn, pres, ceo: La-Z-Boy Chair Co (see above)

Patrick H. Norton: dir *B* 1923 *CURR EMPL* sr vp sales & mktg, dir: La-Z-Boy Chair Co

Edwin J. Shoemaker: vchmn *B* 1907 *CURR EMPL* vchmn, exec vp engring: La-Z-Boy Chair Co

Lorne G. Stevens: dir *CORP AFFIL* dir: La-Z-Boy Chair Co

John F. Weaver: dir *CORP AFFIL* dir: La-Z-Boy Chair Co; exec vp, dir: Monroe Bank & Trust

APPLICATION INFORMATION
Initial Approach: *Initial Contact:* brief letter or proposal *Include Information On:* description of the organization, amount requested, purpose for which funds are sought, recently audited financial statement, proof of 501(c)(3) tax-exempt status, how and by whom program is to be carried out, time span, benefits to the community *Deadlines:* February 15, May 15, August 15, November 15; board of trustees meets quarterly in March, June, September, and December *Note:* Personal interviews upon the foundation's initiative only.

Restrictions on Giving: Foundation does not make direct grants to individuals or for travel and conferences.

GRANTS ANALYSIS
Total Grants: $675,950

Number of Grants: 191

Highest Grant: $37,500

Average Grant: $3,539

Typical Range: $250 to $5,000

Disclosure Period: 1994

Note: Recent grants are derived from a 1993 Form 990.

RECENT GRANTS

General

40,000	Rush Hospital/Newton, Newton, MS — health	
36,000	United Way Monroe County, Monroe, MI — human services	
35,000	Salvation Army of Monroe, Monroe, MI — human services	
30,000	Mercy Memorial Hospital Foundation, Monroe, MI — health	
25,000	Michigan United Conservation, MI — other	

Mardigian Foundation

CONTACT
Edward S. Mardigian, Sr.
President
Mardigian Fdn.
1400 N Woodward Ave., Ste. 225
Bloomfield Hills, MI 48304
(313) 222-3687

FINANCIAL SUMMARY
Recent Giving: $379,080 (1993); $387,445 (1992); $402,630 (1991)

Assets: $9,437,779 (1993); $8,240,759 (1992); $7,400,749 (1991)

Gifts Received: $475,000 (1993); $404,572 (1992); $870,800 (1991)

EIN: 38-6048886

CONTRIBUTIONS SUMMARY
Donor(s): Edward S. Mardigian, Helen Mardigian

Typical Recipients: • *Arts & Humanities:* Arts Associations & Councils, Arts Institutes, Dance, Ethnic & Folk Arts, Libraries, Music, Public Broadcasting, Theater • *Civic & Public Affairs:* Community Foundations, Ethnic Organizations, General, Zoos/Aquariums • *Education:* Colleges & Universities, International Studies, Minority Education, Private Education (Precollege) • *Health:* Alzheimers Disease, Children's Health/Hospitals, Heart, Single-Disease Health Associations • *International:* International Affairs, International Peace & Security Issues, International Relief Efforts, Missionary/Religious Activities • *Religion:* Churches, Dioceses, Jewish Causes, Religious Organizations • *Social Services:* Community Service Organizations, Food/Clothing Distribution, United Funds/United Ways, Youth Organizations

Grant Types: general support

Geographic Distribution: national

GIVING OFFICERS
Edward S. Mardigian, Jr.: dir

Helen Mardigian: dir

Robert Mardigian: dir

Marilyn Varbedian: dir

APPLICATION INFORMATION
Initial Approach: Send brief letter of inquiry describing program or project. There are no deadlines.

GRANTS ANALYSIS
Total Grants: $379,080

Number of Grants: 34

Highest Grant: $100,000

Typical Range: $20 to $83,500

Disclosure Period: 1993

Note: Recent grants are derived from a 1993 Form 990.

RECENT GRANTS

General

100,000	Armenia Fund USA

83,500	Diocese of the Armenian Church, New York, NY
34,200	Armenian General Benevolent Union, Los Angeles, CA
31,000	St. Johns Armenian Church
26,000	National Association for Armenian Studies

Merkley Charitable Trust

CONTACT
Ellie Matestic
Manager
Merkley Charitable Trust
c/o Citizens Commercial & Savings Bank
Trust Division
One Citizens Banking Ctr.
Flint, MI 48502-0000
(313) 257-2448

FINANCIAL SUMMARY
Recent Giving: $134,396 (fiscal 1993); $160,568 (fiscal 1992); $376,469 (fiscal 1991)

Assets: $3,477,212 (fiscal 1993); $3,297,601 (fiscal 1992); $3,169,622 (fiscal 1991)

Gifts Received: $230 (fiscal 1992); $1,911 (fiscal 1991)

Fiscal Note: In fiscal 1992, contributions were received from the family of Dorothy Church.

EIN: 38-6528749

CONTRIBUTIONS SUMMARY
Typical Recipients: • *Arts & Humanities:* Arts Institutes, General, Libraries, Theater • *Civic & Public Affairs:* Urban & Community Affairs • *Education:* Public Education (Precollege) • *Environment:* General • *Health:* Geriatric Health, Respiratory • *Religion:* Jewish Causes, Religious Welfare • *Science:* Science Exhibits & Fairs • *Social Services:* Animal Protection, Community Service Organizations, Recreation & Athletics, YMCA/YWCA/YMHA/YWHA, Youth Organizations

Grant Types: general support

Geographic Distribution: focus on MI

GIVING OFFICERS
Citizens Commercial & Savings Bank: trust

APPLICATION INFORMATION
Initial Approach: The foundation reports no specific application guidelines. Send a brief letter of inquiry, including statement of purpose, amount requested, and proof of tax-exempt status.

GRANTS ANALYSIS
Total Grants: $134,396

Number of Grants: 13

Highest Grant: $63,273

Typical Range: $500 to $21,094

Disclosure Period: fiscal year ending November 30, 1993

Note: Recent grants are derived from a fiscal 1993 Form 990.

RECENT GRANTS
General

63,273	Genesee County Parks and Recreation, Flint, MI
21,094	Genesee County Humane Society, Burton, MI
15,600	Jewish Family and Children's Services, Flint, MI
15,000	Center for Gerontology, Flint, MI
7,300	Salvation Army, Flint, MI

Miller Foundation

Former Foundation Name: Albert L. and Louise B. Miller Foundation

CONTACT
Arthur W. Angood
Chief Operating Officer and Executive Vice President
Miller Fdn.
310 WahWahTaySee Way
Battle Creek, MI 49015
(616) 964-2052

FINANCIAL SUMMARY
Recent Giving: $531,100 (fiscal 1993); $551,284 (fiscal 1991)

Assets: $13,197,815 (fiscal 1993); $12,952,731 (fiscal 1991)

Gifts Received: $68,163 (fiscal 1993); $1,056,839 (fiscal 1991)

Fiscal Note: In 1993, contributions were received from an anonymous donor.

EIN: 38-6064925

CONTRIBUTIONS SUMMARY
Donor(s): the late Louise B. Miller, Robert B. Miller

Typical Recipients: • *Arts & Humanities:* Arts Associations & Councils, History & Archaeology, Libraries • *Civic & Public Affairs:* Economic Development, Housing, Municipalities/Towns, Philanthropic Organizations, Urban & Community Affairs, Zoos/Aquariums • *Education:* Business Education, Colleges & Universities, Education Funds, Preschool Education, Public Education (Precollege), Science/Mathematics Education, Student Aid • *Health:* Hospices, Nursing Services • *Religion:* Religious Organizations • *Social Services:* Community Service Organizations, Counseling, Day Care, People with Disabilities, Senior Services, Substance Abuse, United Funds/United Ways, Youth Organizations

Grant Types: capital, emergency, endowment, general support, loan, scholarship, and seed money

Geographic Distribution: focus on the Battle Creek, MI, area

GIVING OFFICERS
Arthur W. Angood: exec vp, coo, trust *PHIL AFFIL* vp, treas, trust: Miller House

Barbara L. Comai: treas, trust

Gary Edward Costley: trust *B* Caldwell ID 1943 *ED* OR State Univ BS 1966; OR State Univ PhD 1970; OR State Univ MS *CURR EMPL* exec vp: Kellogg Co *CORP AFFIL* pres: Kellogg USA *NONPR AFFIL* mem: Am Inst Nutrition; trust: Am Health Fdn, Duke Univ Med Sch- Sarah W. Stedman Ctr, Youth Understanding Intl Exchange

Rebecca A. Engelhardt: secy, trust, contr *PHIL AFFIL* secy, contr, trust: Miller House

W. James McQuiston: pres, ceo, trust *PHIL AFFIL* pres, trust: Miller House

Allen L. Miller: trust

Olive T. Miller: trust emeritus

Robert Branson Miller, Jr.: trust *B* Battle Creek MI 1935 *ED* MI St Univ BA 1959 *CURR EMPL* publ: Battle Creek Enquirer *NONPR AFFIL* dir Battle Creek MI chapter: Am Red Cross

Robert Branson Miller, Sr.: trust emeritus *B* Ottawa KS 1906 *ED* Williams Coll BA 1929

Arnold VanZanten: treas, trust *B* Holland MI 1912 *ED* Hope Coll 1935; Rutgers Univ 1950 *CORP AFFIL* dir: Intl Res & Devel Corp

Fred M. Woodruff, Jr.: trust

APPLICATION INFORMATION
Initial Approach: Send brief letter of inquiry requesting application form. There are no deadlines.

PUBLICATIONS
Annual Report

GRANTS ANALYSIS
Total Grants: $531,100

Number of Grants: 31

Highest Grant: $125,000

Typical Range: $600 to $100,000

Disclosure Period: fiscal year ending February 28, 1993

Note: Recent grants are derived from a fiscal 1993 Form 990.

RECENT GRANTS

Library

5,000	Willard Library, Battle Creek, MI — indexing film

General

125,000	Neighborhoods of Battle Creek, Battle Creek, MI — housing program
100,000	Central City Development Corporation, Battle Creek, MI — building renovation
75,000	Burnham Brook Center, Battle Creek, MI — senior center construction
40,000	Battle Creek Public Schools, Battle Creek, MI — math/science center
33,000	Binder Park Zoo, Battle Creek, MI — children's zoo

Mills Fund, Frances Goll

CONTACT
Louise Rohde
Trustee
Frances Goll Mills Fund
101 N Washington Ave.
Saginaw, MI 48607
(517) 776-7360

FINANCIAL SUMMARY
Recent Giving: $132,853 (fiscal 1992); $218,450 (fiscal 1990); $155,455 (fiscal 1988)

Assets: $3,451,260 (fiscal 1992); $3,363,196 (fiscal 1990); $3,084,295 (fiscal 1988)

EIN: 38-2434002

CONTRIBUTIONS SUMMARY
Donor(s): the late Frances Goll Mills

Typical Recipients: • *Arts & Humanities:* History & Archaeology, Libraries, Museums/Galleries • *Civic & Public Affairs:* African American Affairs, Housing, Legal Aid, Parades/Festivals • *Education:* Colleges & Universities, Engineering/Technological Education, Public Education (Precollege), Science/Mathematics Education, Student Aid • *Health:* Children's Health/Hospitals, Emergency/Ambulance Services • *Religion:* Churches, Religious Organizations, Religious Welfare • *Social Services:* At-Risk Youth, Community Service Organizations, People with Disabilities, United Funds/United Ways, Youth Organizations

Grant Types: capital, multiyear/continuing support, operating expenses, and seed money

Geographic Distribution: focus on Saginaw County, MI

GIVING OFFICERS
Second National Bank: trust

APPLICATION INFORMATION
Initial Approach: Send brief letter of inquiry and full proposal. There are no deadlines.

PUBLICATIONS
Application guidelines

GRANTS ANALYSIS
Total Grants: $132,853

Number of Grants: 20

Highest Grant: $29,200

Typical Range: $1,000 to $5,000

Disclosure Period: fiscal year ending September 30, 1992

Note: Recent grants are derived from a fiscal 1992 Form 990.

RECENT GRANTS
Library
3,100   Zuael Memorial Library, Saginaw, MI — computers

General
29,200   First Congregational Church, Saginaw, MI — equipment and construction

25,000   Boysville of Michigan, Clinton, MI — roof replacement on St. Vincent's Home

19,500   United Way of Saginaw County, Saginaw, MI — operating

11,800   City Rescue Mission of Saginaw, Saginaw, MI — computer software

5,500   Neighborhood House, Saginaw, MI — Christmas baskets

Mott Foundation, Charles Stewart

CONTACT
Charles Stewart Mott Foundation
1200 Mott Foundation Bldg.
Flint, MI 48502-1851
(810) 238-5651
Note: The foundation does not list a specific contact person. Inquiries should be addressed to the Office of Communications. Proposals should be sent to the Office of Proposal Entry.

FINANCIAL SUMMARY
Recent Giving: $55,000,000 (1995 est.); $52,000,000 (1994 approx.); $49,031,475 (1993)

Assets: $1,200,000,000 (1995 est.); $1,200,000,000 (1994 approx.); $1,273,300,000 (1993 approx.)

Gifts Received: $3,852,404 (1988)

Fiscal Note: In 1988, the foundation received cash and stock from the estate of Edith Davis, a member of the Mott Family.

EIN: 38-1211227

CONTRIBUTIONS SUMMARY
Donor(s): Charles Stewart Mott established the foundation in Flint, MI, in 1926. From his earliest years in his adopted community, Mr. Mott was concerned with the city's welfare, and served two years as mayor. He also served as chairman of U.S. Sugar Corporation, president of the Northern Illinois Water Company, director of and one of the largest individual stockholders in General Motors, a principal stockholder in the Continental Water Company, and a trustee of Stevens Institute of Technology. Mr. Mott also started a medical and dental clinic for children and helped establish the YMCA and the Boy Scouts in Flint, as well as the Whaley Children's Center. Mr. Mott died in 1973. His son, Charles Stewart Harding Mott, guided the foundation from its earliest days until his death in 1989.

Typical Recipients: • *Arts & Humanities:* Libraries, Public Broadcasting • *Civic & Public Affairs:* African American Affairs, Business/Free Enterprise, Civil Rights, Community Foundations, Economic Development, Economic Policy, Employment/Job Training, Hispanic Affairs, Housing, Native American Affairs, Nonprofit Management, Philanthropic Organizations, Professional & Trade Associations, Public Policy, Rural Affairs, Urban & Community Affairs, Women's Affairs • *Education:* Colleges & Universities, Education Associations, Education Reform, Engineering/Technological Education, International Exchange, Leadership Training, Minority Education • *Environment:* General, Resource Conservation • *Health:* AIDS/HIV, Home-Care Services, Research/Studies Institutes • *International:* Foreign Educational Institutions, International Development, International Environmental Issues, International Organizations, International Peace & Security Issues, International Relations • *Religion:* Religious Welfare • *Social Services:* At-Risk Youth, Family Planning, Volunteer Services, Youth Organizations

Grant Types: challenge, general support, project, and seed money

Geographic Distribution: national and international; some emphasis on Flint, MI, but no geographic restrictions

GIVING OFFICERS
Alonzo A. Crim: trust *B* Chicago IL 1928 *ED* Roosevelt Coll BA 1950; Chicago Teachers Coll 1953-1954; Univ Chicago Coll MA 1958; Harvard Univ EdD 1969 *NONPR AFFIL* mem: Am Assn Sch Admins, Natl Alliance Black Sch Educators *CLUB AFFIL* Rotary

Charles B. Cumings: trust emeritus

Katherine Woodruff Fanning: trust *B* Chicago IL 1927 *ED* Smith Coll BA 1949 *CORP AFFIL* dir: Affiliated Pubs Inc Boston Globe Newspaper Co *NONPR AFFIL* adj prof journalism: Boston Univ; bd overseers: Boston Symphony Orchestra; bd visitors: Stanford Univ Knight Fellowships Journalists; dir: Boston Pub Library Fdn, Ctr Foreign Journalists, New Directions News; fall fellow: Harvard Univ Inst Politics; mem: Counc Foreign Rels, Inter-Am Dialogue, Soc Professional Journalists; mem, dir: Am Soc Newspaper Editors; sr adv bd: Harvard Univ Joan Shorenstein Barone Ctr; trust: Kettering Fdn *CLUB AFFIL* Badminton & Tennis, St Botolph *PHIL AFFIL* vp, secy: Tiny Tiger Foundation

Rushworth M. Kidder: trust

Jim L. Krause: asst treas

Webb Franklin Martin: trust *B* Flint MI 1944 *ED* MI St Univ 1966; Wayne St Univ JD 1969 *CURR EMPL* fin 1st vp: NBD Bank NA

Charles S. Harding Mott II: trust *PHIL AFFIL* ceo, pres, treas, trust: Charles Stewart Harding Foundation

Maryanne T. Mott: trust *PHIL AFFIL* pres: Warsh-Mott Legacy; pres, trust: Ruth Mott Fund; don, pres: C. S. Fund

Ruth Rawlings Mott: trust emeritus *B* El Paso TX 1901 *NONPR AFFIL* dir: El Paso Mus, Flint Art Inst *CLUB AFFIL* Quota *PHIL AFFIL* fdr, trust: Ruth Mott Fund; don: Stewart R. Mott Charitable Trust

Douglas Xavier Patino: trust *B* Calexico CA 1939 *ED* Imperial Valley Coll AA 1960; CA St Univ BA 1962; CA St Univ MA 1966; US Intl Univ PhD 1972 *NONPR AF-*

FIL dir: Am Pub Welfare Assn, CA Leadership, CA Sch Professional Psychology, Hispanic Commun Fund; mem: Hispanics Philanthropy, Independent Sector, Northern CA Grantmakers *CLUB AFFIL* mem: Rotary

William H. Piper: trust, mem investment comm *B* Flint MI 1933 *ED* Yale Univ BA 1955 *CURR EMPL* sr vp: NBD Bancorp *PHIL AFFIL* dir: YWCA Foundation

Willa B. Player: trust

John Wilson A. Porter: trust, chmn audit comm *B* Fort Wayne IN 1931 *ED* Albion Coll BA 1953; MI St Univ MA 1957; MI St Univ PhD 1962 *CURR EMPL* ceo: Urban Ed Alliance *NONPR AFFIL* chmn: Am Assn St Colls & Univs Task Force Excellence Ed; dir: MI Congress Parents & Teachers, MI Intl Counc; hon life mem: MI Parent Teachers Assn; mem: Am Assn Sch Admins, Greater Detroit Chamber Commerce, Catherine McAuley Health Sys Bd, MI Govs Blue Ribbon Comm Welfare Reform, MI Martin Luther King Jr Holiday Commn, MI St Chamber Commerce, Natl Ed Goals Panel, Natl Measurement Counc, Phi Delta Kappa, Sigma Pi Phi, Tuskegee Airmen; mem ed comm: NAACP; trust: Albion Coll *CLUB AFFIL* Econ

Richard Kent Rappleye: vp, secy, treas *B* Oswego NY 1940 *ED* Boston Univ 1962-1963; Miami Univ AB 1962; Univ PA Wharton Sch MBA 1964; DePaul Univ 1965-1966 *CORP AFFIL* bd dir: MI Natl Bank, Stoneridge Resources Inc *NONPR AFFIL* bd dir: Stoneridge Resources Inc, Treas Counc MI Fdn; lecturer: Univ MI Flint; mem: Am Inst CPAs, Fin Execs Inst, MI Assn CPAs, Rotary *CLUB AFFIL* Masons

Judy Y. Samelson: vp (communications)

Maureen H. Smyth: vp (programs)

Robert E. Swaney, Jr.: vp, chief investment off

William Samuel White: chmn, pres, ceo, trust, chmn several comms *B* Cincinnati OH 1937 *ED* Dartmouth Coll BA 1959; Dartmouth Coll MBA 1960 *CURR EMPL* chmn: US Sugar Corp *CORP AFFIL* chmn: US Sugar Corp; dir: Continental Water Corp *NONPR AFFIL* chmn: Flint Area Focus Counc *PHIL AFFIL* trust: Charles Stewart Harding Foundation

George S. Whyel: trust emeritus

APPLICATION INFORMATION
Initial Approach:

Grant applications may be handled in one of two ways. The prospective grantee may either submit a brief letter outlining the details of the project being considered, or send a full proposal to the Office of Proposal Entry.

Proposals should include a description of the project; anticipated accomplishments and the population to be served; explanation of why the project is needed; line-item budget for the proposed grant period; institutional budget based on applicant's fiscal year; and the starting and ending dates for the project. Information about the organization seeking funds, starting and ending dates for project, and plans for project evaluation and dissemination also are required.

Proposals may be submitted any time. The board of trustees meets quarterly.

Restrictions on Giving: To prevent conflict-of-interest problems, grant applicants should not route proposals through trustees or solicit their assistance. Trustees are prohibited from voting on grant proposals where they have a conflict of interest. Because of the large number of requests, foundation visits, unless by invitation, are discouraged. Requests for meetings with foundation trustees and staff will be initiated only by the foundation.

Restrictions on Giving: The foundation does not make grants or loans to individuals or for religious activities or programs that serve a specific religious group. Outside the Flint, MI, area, the foundation makes capital and endowment grants only when necessary to carry out other foundation objectives. The foundation does not support research except when it is instrumental for other grant-making purposes. It does not provide ongoing support for projects normally supported or which should be supported by taxpayers. The foundation also does not grant scholarships.

OTHER THINGS TO KNOW
The foundation occasionally considers activities of a non-grant nature that help to achieve program objectives. These may include program-related investments, direct technical or fundraising assistance, research, and the dissemination of findings. Most foundation grants are for up to one year, although applicants may submit multi-year proposals.

PUBLICATIONS
Annual report; facts on grants; philosophy, programs, and procedures; and quarterly newsletter

GRANTS ANALYSIS
Total Grants: $49,031,475

Number of Grants: 371

Highest Grant: $9,598,969

Average Grant: $126,600*

Typical Range: $20,000 to $500,000

Disclosure Period: 1993

Note: The average grant figure was supplied by the foundation. Recent grants are derived from a 1993 Form 990.

RECENT GRANTS

Library

200,000	Baker College, Flint, MI — to support a 3,000 square foot expansion of the college's Flint Library

General

9,598,969	Flint Downtown Development Authority, Flint, MI — to defease the AutoWorld Revenue bonds issued by the Flint Downtown Development Authority
2,000,000	United Negro College Fund, New York, NY — to support Campaign 2000, a campaign to raise $250 million for

	general endowments for the 41 UNCF member institutions
997,702	Focus HOPE, Detroit, MI — to assist in completing the renovation of a 50-year-old plant/office structure in its Industry Mall
535,000	Center for Community Change, Washington, DC — to provide the center with resources to retire the mortgage on its headquarters building located in the Georgetown section of Washington
500,000	Fisk University, Nashville, TN — to provide endowment challenge funds to strengthen the long-term financial stability of the institution

Mott Fund, Ruth

CONTACT
Ruth Mott Fund
1726 Genesee Towers
Flint, MI 48502
(313) 232-3180

FINANCIAL SUMMARY
Recent Giving: $1,023,135 (fiscal 1993); $1,688,003 (fiscal 1992); $1,206,346 (fiscal 1991)

Assets: $2,256,850 (fiscal 1993); $2,405,748 (fiscal 1992); $2,530,823 (fiscal 1991)

Gifts Received: $1,800,000 (fiscal 1993); $2,353,115 (fiscal 1992); $2,216,838 (fiscal 1991)

Fiscal Note: In fiscal 1993, contributions were received from Ruth Mott.

EIN: 38-2284264

CONTRIBUTIONS SUMMARY
Donor(s): Ruth R. Mott

Typical Recipients: • *Arts & Humanities:* Arts Associations & Councils, Arts Centers, Arts Festivals, Community Arts, Dance, Ethnic & Folk Arts, General, Historic Preservation, History & Archaeology, Libraries, Museums/Galleries, Music, Performing Arts, Public Broadcasting, Theater, Visual Arts • *Civic & Public Affairs:* African American Affairs, Economic Policy, Hispanic Affairs, Native American Affairs, Public Policy, Rural Affairs, Urban & Community Affairs, Zoos/Aquariums • *Education:* Colleges & Universities, Private Education (Precollege), Public Education (Precollege) • *Environment:* Forestry, General, Protection, Resource Conservation • *Health:* Children's Health/Hospitals, Health Policy/Cost Containment, Health Organizations, Hospitals, Medical Research, Nutrition, Single-Disease Health Associations • *International:* Human Rights, International Affairs, International Development, International Environmental Issues, International Peace & Security Issues, International Relations, Trade • *Science:* Scientific Organizations • *Social*

Services: Child Welfare, Community Service Organizations, Crime Prevention, Family Services, Food/Clothing Distribution, Refugee Assistance, Youth Organizations

Grant Types: conference/seminar, general support, multiyear/continuing support, operating expenses, project, and seed money

Geographic Distribution: focus on MI

GIVING OFFICERS
Brooks Bollman III: trust

Dudley Cocke: vchmn, trust

Leslie W. Dunbar: trust *B* Lewisburg WV 1921 *ED* Cornell Univ MA; Cornell Univ PhD *NONPR AFFIL* dir: NC Counc Churches, Winston Fdn World Peace; dir, vp: Roosevelt (Franklin & Eleanor) Inst

Jean E. Fairfax: trust

Susan Kleinpell: secy, trust

Donna H. Metcalf: trust

Maryanne T. Mott: pres, trust *PHIL AFFIL* trust: Charles Stewart Mott Foundation; pres: Warsh-Mott Legacy; don, pres: C. S. Fund

Ruth Rawlings Mott: fdr, trust *B* El Paso TX 1901 *NONPR AFFIL* dir: El Paso Mus, Flint Art Inst *CLUB AFFIL* Quota *PHIL AFFIL* trust emeritus: Charles Stewart Mott Foundation; don: Stewart R. Mott Charitable Trust

Melissa Patterson: trust

Joseph R. Robinson: chmn, trust

Virginia M. Sullivan: secy, treas, trust

Herman E. Warsh: trust *PHIL AFFIL* secy, cfo: Warsh-Mott Legacy

APPLICATION INFORMATION
Send a brief letter of inquiry.

Initial Approach: Include a description of organization, amount requested, purpose of funds sought, recently audited financial statement, and proof of tax-exempt status. Deadlines are November 7, March 15, and July 15.

PUBLICATIONS
Application Guidelines

GRANTS ANALYSIS
Total Grants: $1,023,135

Number of Grants: 130

Highest Grant: $30,000

Typical Range: 25 to $30,000

Disclosure Period: fiscal year ending November 30, 1993

Note: Recent grants are derived from a fiscal 1993 Form 990.

RECENT GRANTS
Library
25,000	Richards Free Library, Newport, NH — continued support for the Mill Tapestry Project

General
30,000	Center to Prevent Handgun Violence, Washington, DC — support for the Center's "Second Amendment Campaign"
30,000	Government Accountability Project, Washington, DC — support for GAP's national security program
30,000	Pool Research and Action Center, Washington, DC — continued support of the Campaign to End Childhood Hunger
25,000	California Food Policy Advocates, San Francisco, CA — support for continuation of School Breakfast Organizing Campaign
25,000	Center for the Study of Political Graphics, Los Angeles, CA — general operating support

R&B Machine Tool Co. / Redies Foundation, Edward F.

Sales: $37.0 million
Employees: 230
Headquarters: Saline, MI
SIC Major Group: Industrial Machinery & Equipment

CONTACT
Milton Stemen
President
R & B Machine Tool Co.
PO Box 100
Saline, MI 48176
(313) 429-9421

FINANCIAL SUMMARY
Recent Giving: $111,000 (1993); $106,000 (1992); $86,500 (1991)

Assets: $2,961,354 (1993); $2,673,966 (1992); $2,629,958 (1991)

Gifts Received: $150,000 (1993); $200,000 (1991); $250,000 (1990)

Fiscal Note: In 1993, contributions were received from the R&B Machine Tool Co.

EIN: 38-2391326

CONTRIBUTIONS SUMMARY
Typical Recipients: • *Arts & Humanities:* Libraries, Theater • *Civic & Public Affairs:* General, Municipalities/Towns • *Education:* Community & Junior Colleges, Public Education (Precollege), Student Aid • *Health:* Children's Health/Hospitals, Clinics/Medical Centers, Emergency/Ambulance Services, Health Organizations, Hospitals, Long-Term Care, Nursing Services • *Religion:* Religious Organizations, Religious Welfare • *Social Services:* At-Risk Youth, Camps, Community Service Organizations, Homes, Senior Services, United Funds/United Ways, Youth Organizations

Grant Types: general support

Geographic Distribution: focus on MI

Operating Locations: MI (Saline)

CORP. OFFICERS
Robert D. Redies: *CURR EMPL* chmn, dir: R&B Machine Tool Co

Milton E. Stemen: *CURR EMPL* pres, dir: R&B Machine Tool Co

GIVING OFFICERS
James D. Buhr: trust

Wilbur K. Pierpont: trust

Robert D. Redies: trust *CURR EMPL* chmn, dir: R&B Machine Tool Co (see above)

Milton E. Stemen: trust *CURR EMPL* pres, dir: R&B Machine Tool Co (see above)

APPLICATION INFORMATION
Initial Approach: Send a brief letter of inquiry and a full proposal. Include a description of organization, amount requested, purpose of funds sought, recently audited financial statement, and proof of tax-exempt status. Deadline is February 1, 1992.

GRANTS ANALYSIS
Total Grants: $111,000

Number of Grants: 15

Highest Grant: $50,000

Typical Range: $1,000 to $20,000

Disclosure Period: 1993

Note: Recent grants are derived from a 1993 Form 990.

RECENT GRANTS
Library
5,000	Saline Library, Saline, MI

General
50,000	City of Saline, Saline, MI
20,000	Saline Community Hospital, Saline, MI
10,000	Evangelical Home of Saline, Saline, MI
5,000	Ronald McDonald House, Saline, MI
4,000	Glacier Hills Nursing Home

Ratner Foundation, Milton M.

CONTACT
Charles R. McDonald
Vice President, Secretary, and Trustee
Milton M. Ratner Fdn.
17515 W Nine Mile Rd., Ste. 875
Southfield, MI 48075
(313) 424-9373

FINANCIAL SUMMARY
Recent Giving: $393,100 (fiscal 1992); $209,300 (fiscal 1990); $218,300 (fiscal 1989)

Assets: $6,435,359 (fiscal 1992); $5,668,196 (fiscal 1990); $5,548,520 (fiscal 1989)

EIN: 38-6160330

CONTRIBUTIONS SUMMARY
Donor(s): Milton M. Ratner Trust

Typical Recipients: • *Arts & Humanities:* Libraries, Music • *Civic & Public Affairs:*

General, Municipalities/Towns • *Education:* Colleges & Universities, Continuing Education, Education Funds, Legal Education, Medical Education, Private Education (Precollege), Public Education (Precollege), Religious Education • *Health:* Children's Health/Hospitals, Clinics/Medical Centers, Emergency/Ambulance Services, Health Organizations, Heart, Hospices, Hospitals, Medical Research, Single-Disease Health Associations • *Religion:* Churches, Jewish Causes, Ministries, Religious Organizations, Religious Welfare • *Social Services:* Animal Protection, Child Welfare, Community Service Organizations, Delinquency & Criminal Rehabilitation, Family Services, People with Disabilities, Recreation & Athletics, United Funds/United Ways, Volunteer Services, Youth Organizations

Grant Types: capital, endowment, general support, project, research, and scholarship

Geographic Distribution: focus on MI and GA

GIVING OFFICERS
Mary Jo Ratner Corley: pres, trust

J. Beverly Langford: treas, trust

Charles R. McDonald: vp, secy, trust

APPLICATION INFORMATION
Initial Approach: The foundation has no formal grant application procedure or application form. Deadline is October 15.

Restrictions on Giving: Does not support individuals.

GRANTS ANALYSIS
Total Grants: $393,100

Number of Grants: 55

Highest Grant: $50,000

Typical Range: $1,000 to $10,000

Disclosure Period: fiscal year ending August 31, 1992

Note: Recent grants are derived from a fiscal 1992 Form 990.

RECENT GRANTS
General

50,000	Emory University School of Medicine, Atlanta, GA
24,420	Gordon County Board of Education, Calhoun, GA
20,000	American Red Cross, Washington, DC
13,200	United Way, Detroit, MI
11,000	Children's Hospital of Detroit, Detroit, MI

Scherer Foundation, Karla

CONTACT
Karla Scherer
Chairman
Karla Scherer Fdn.
100 Renaissance Ctr., Ste. 1680
Detroit, MI 48243
(313) 396-3300

FINANCIAL SUMMARY
Recent Giving: $120,910 (1993); $115,725 (1992); $163,151 (1990)

Assets: $4,402,590 (1993); $4,322,448 (1992); $4,109,283 (1990)

Gifts Received: $5,000 (1992); $2,008,921 (1989)

Fiscal Note: In fiscal 1992, contributions were received from Leon and Toby Cooperman Foundation.

EIN: 38-2877392

CONTRIBUTIONS SUMMARY
Donor(s): the donor is Karla Scherer, the foundation's chairman

Typical Recipients: • *Arts & Humanities:* Arts Centers, Arts Institutes, History & Archaeology, Libraries, Museums/Galleries, Music, Theater • *Civic & Public Affairs:* Business/Free Enterprise, Civil Rights, General, Urban & Community Affairs, Women's Affairs • *Education:* Arts/Humanities Education, Business Education, Colleges & Universities, Education Associations, Engineering/Technological Education, General, Legal Education, Preschool Education, Private Education (Precollege), Student Aid • *Environment:* General • *Health:* Cancer, Children's Health/Hospitals, Clinics/Medical Centers, Health Organizations, Hospitals, Medical Research, Mental Health, Prenatal Health Issues • *Religion:* Religious Welfare • *Social Services:* Animal Protection, Child Welfare, Family Planning, People with Disabilities, Youth Organizations

Grant Types: general support and scholarship

Geographic Distribution: nationally

GIVING OFFICERS
David Hempstead: asst secy

John S. Scherer: trust

Karla Scherer: chmn, ceo *B* Detroit MI 1937 *ED* Univ MI BA 1957 *NONPR AFFIL* dir: Econ Club of Detroit; mem: Women's Econ Club Detroit, Women's Forum MI; mem visit comm: Fordham Univ Grad Sch Bus Admin; trust: Eton Acad *CLUB AFFIL* Detroit, Detroit Athletic, Detroit CC, Grosse Pointe, Renaissance

Theodore Souris: asst secy, trust

APPLICATION INFORMATION
Initial Approach: The foundation requests applications be made in writing. There are no deadlines.

OTHER THINGS TO KNOW
Scholarships are provided to women for use in pursuit of education in the field of business.

GRANTS ANALYSIS
Total Grants: $120,910

Number of Grants: 45

Highest Grant: $25,000

Typical Range: $100 to $6,000

Disclosure Period: 1993

Note: Recent grants are derived from a 1993 Form 990.

RECENT GRANTS
General

29,000	Eton Academy, Birmingham, MI
25,000	Lahey Clinic, Burlington, MA
6,000	Harvard University, Cambridge, MA — scholarship
6,000	University of Michigan, Ann Arbor, MI — scholarship
4,000	Columbia University, New York, NY — scholarship

Seidman Family Foundation

CONTACT
Augusta Eppinga
Trustee
Seidman Family Fdn.
99 Monroe Ave., NW, Ste. 800
Grand Rapids, MI 49503
(616) 453-7719

FINANCIAL SUMMARY
Recent Giving: $141,250 (1993); $122,850 (1992); $117,000 (1990)

Assets: $3,139,903 (1993); $2,839,790 (1992); $2,583,930 (1990)

Gifts Received: $5,000 (1992)

Fiscal Note: In fiscal 1992, contributions were received from American Institute of Certified Public Accountants.

EIN: 13-6098204

CONTRIBUTIONS SUMMARY
Donor(s): the late Frank E. Seidman, the late Esther I. Seidman

Typical Recipients: • *Arts & Humanities:* Arts Associations & Councils, Arts Outreach, Community Arts, History & Archaeology, Libraries, Museums/Galleries, Performing Arts, Public Broadcasting • *Civic & Public Affairs:* Botanical Gardens/Parks, General, Native American Affairs, Urban & Community Affairs, Women's Affairs • *Education:* Business Education, Colleges & Universities, Literacy, Science/Mathematics Education, Special Education, Student Aid • *Environment:* General • *Health:* Emergency/Ambulance Services, Hospitals • *International:* Health Care/Hospitals, International Relief Efforts • *Religion:* Churches • *Science:* Scientific Centers & Institutes • *Social Services:* Community Service Organizations, Counseling, Domestic Violence, Family Planning, Food/Clothing Distribution, Recreation & Athletics, Substance Abuse, United Funds/United Ways, Youth Organizations

Grant Types: capital, endowment, general support, multiyear/continuing support, and research

Geographic Distribution: focus on MI

GIVING OFFICERS
Augusta Eppinga: trust

B. Thomas Seidman: trust

L. William Seidman: trust

Sarah B. Seidman: trust

APPLICATION INFORMATION
Initial Approach: The foundation has no formal grant application procedure or application form. There are no deadlines.

GRANTS ANALYSIS
Total Grants: $141,250

Number of Grants: 25

Highest Grant: $25,000

Typical Range: $250 to $25,000

Disclosure Period: 1993

Note: Recent grants are derived from a 1993 Form 990.

RECENT GRANTS

Library

5,000   Sierra Vista Elementary School, Albuquerque, NM — books for school library

General

25,000   Dartmouth College, Hanover, NH

25,000   Grand Valley State University, Allendale, MI — Seidman School of Business

25,000   Rhodes College, Memphis, TN — Seidman Awards program

10,000   Arizona State University College of Business, Tempe, AZ — Seidman Research Institute

5,000   Care Foundation, Los Angeles, CA — mother/child community health outreach program in Guatemala

Skillman Foundation

CONTACT
Leonard W. Smith
President
Skillman Foundation
333 W Fort St., Ste. 1350
Detroit, MI 48226
(313) 961-8850

FINANCIAL SUMMARY
Recent Giving: $19,000,000 (1995 est.); $18,761,881 (1994); $17,342,243 (1993)

Assets: $400,000,000 (1994 est.); $405,599,485 (1993); $364,756,091 (1992)

Gifts Received: $7,032,649 (1989); $499,000 (1988); $457,000 (1987)

Fiscal Note: The foundation receives unrestricted, annual cash contributions from the estate of Rose P. Skillman.

EIN: 38-1675780

CONTRIBUTIONS SUMMARY
Donor(s): The Skillman Foundation is a private foundation incorporated in Detroit, MI, in 1960 by Rose P. Skillman , who was the widow of Robert Skillman (d. 1945), an early and longtime officer and director of 3M Corporation. During their lifetimes, the Skillman's philanthropic interests focused on providing assistance and care for children and young people, especially the disadvantaged living in Southeastern Michigan.

The foundation operated as a conduit for Rose Skillman's philanthropic giving until her death in 1983, after which time her assets were distributed to the foundation.

Typical Recipients: • *Arts & Humanities:* Arts Associations & Councils, Arts Centers, Arts Institutes, History & Archaeology, Libraries, Music, Opera, Performing Arts, Public Broadcasting, Theater • *Civic & Public Affairs:* Economic Development, Employment/Job Training, Hispanic Affairs, Housing, Native American Affairs, Parades/Festivals, Professional & Trade Associations • *Education:* Agricultural Education, Colleges & Universities, Education Funds, Education Reform, Literacy, Minority Education, Preschool Education, Private Education (Precollege), Public Education (Precollege), Science/Mathematics Education, Secondary Education (Public), Social Sciences Education, Student Aid, Vocational & Technical Education • *Health:* Children's Health/Hospitals, Health Organizations, Mental Health, Nursing Services, Public Health, Respiratory, Trauma Treatment • *International:* Health Care/Hospitals, International Relief Efforts • *Religion:* Religious Welfare • *Science:* Scientific Centers & Institutes • *Social Services:* At-Risk Youth, Child Abuse, Child Welfare, Community Service Organizations, Counseling, Crime Prevention, Day Care, Delinquency & Criminal Rehabilitation, Domestic Violence, Emergency Relief, Family Planning, Family Services, Food/Clothing Distribution, Homes, People with Disabilities, Recreation & Athletics, Scouts, Senior Services, Shelters/Homelessness, Substance Abuse, Youth Organizations

Grant Types: capital, general support, matching, multiyear/continuing support, operating expenses, project, scholarship, and seed money

Geographic Distribution: Detroit area and Southeastern Michigan metropolitan

GIVING OFFICERS
James A. Aliber: trust *CURR EMPL* chmn, ceo, dir: First Fed MI

Lillian Bauder: trust

William McNulty Brodhead: chmn, trust *B* Cleveland OH 1941 *ED* Wayne St Univ AB 1965; Univ MI JD 1967 *CURR EMPL* ptnr: Plunkett & Cooney

Bernadine N. Denning: trust

Walter E. Douglas: trust *B* 1933 *CURR EMPL* pres: Avis Ford *NONPR AFFIL* chmn bd: Univ Detroit Jesuit Home

Jean E. Gregory: vp, treas *B* 1928

William Elis Hoglund: chmn bd trusts *B* Stockholm Sweden 1934 *ED* Princeton Univ AB 1956; Univ MI MBA 1958 *CURR EMPL* exec vp, dir: Gen Motors Corp *NONPR AFFIL* mem visit comm: Univ MI Grad Sch Bus; trust: William Beaumont Hosp *CLUB AFFIL* Bloomfield Hills, Bloomfield Hills CC, Detroit Athletic *PHIL AFFIL* trust: General Motors Foundation

Kari Schlachtenhaufen: vp programs

Alan Earl Schwartz: trust *B* Detroit MI 1925 *ED* Univ MI BA 1947; Harvard Univ JD 1950 *CURR EMPL* sr ptnr: Honigman Miller Schwartz & Cohn *CORP AFFIL* dir: Comerica, Core Indus, Detroit Edison Co, Hardleman Co, Howell Indus Inc, PHM Corp, Unisys Corp *NONPR AFFIL* dir: Detroit Econ Growth Corp, Detroit Renaissance, Jewish Welfare Fdn Detroit; mem: MI Bar Assn, NY St Bar Assn; trust: Commun Fdn Southeastern MI, Harper-Grace Hosp, Interlochen Ctr Arts; vp, dir: Un Fdn; vp, mem exec comm: Detroit Symphony Orchestra *CLUB AFFIL* Detroit, Econ, Franklin Hills CC *PHIL AFFIL* secy, trust: Nate S. and Ruth B. Shapero Foundation

Leonard W. Smith: pres, secy, trust *B* 1934 *CORP AFFIL* secy, dir: Detroit Mortgage and Realty Co, DMR Properties Inc

Jane R. Thomas: vchmn, trust

APPLICATION INFORMATION
Initial Approach:

Call or write the foundation for guidelines. In general, the foundation does not consider letters of inquiry but responds only to grant applications.

The foundation does not have a standard application form. Grant requests should be clear and concise. They should contain a cover letter, including an authorized statement signed by the organization chair and the individual responsible for the program, title page, containing the name of organization, the name of the department or division administering the grant, the name of the organization's president and/or the individual responsible for the project, the organization's address and phone number, the amount of grant request, the time period for support, name of the project, the program area to which the proposal is directed, and type of support requested, and a two-page summary of the proposal's essential elements.

Full proposals should be no longer than eight pages and should contain the following: one-sentence statement of purpose; need for the project and problems it addresses; goal of the project, including objectives and results to be achieved; project plan describing project history and past accomplishments, target population, number of people to be served, timeline, and a list of specific activities; description of the organization, including a short history, mission statement, and description of services; revenue plan, including list of other sources of funding; evaluation plan, including method of evaluation, any additional questions, information sources and analysis, the individual who will conduct the evaluation; plan for continued support of the project following the conclusion of the foundation's funding; total project budget, including the foundation's portion itemized and budget narrative; an audited financial statment or unaudited Form 990; list of staff or principal persons responsible for implementing, supervising, and evaluating the project, as well as their qualifications; list of the nonprofit's board, including occupations and affiliations; copy of organization's proof of tax-exempt status; letter of support from collaborating organizations; and an organization brochure and most recent annual report.

There are no deadlines for submission of applications except for requests from arts and culture organizations. The deadline for those organizations is April 1 of each year.

The foundation's trustees review grant applications five times each year, generally in February, April, June, September, and November. The review process for applications takes three months and the foundation will notify the organization in writing when a decision has been made. Other than applications which fall outside the foundation's geographic focus or program areas, the foundation does not provide applicants with assessments of their chances for approval.

Restrictions on Giving: The foundation reports that it does not make grants which may jeopardize an organization's public charity status because the amount requested is too large in relation to the past level of public support. It does not make grants to new organizations or to organizations that had revenues of less than $100,000 for the preceding year. It does not make grants for the purpose of purchasing or constructing facilities or buildings owned by units of government; for endowments, annual drives, fund-raising events, research, or deficit funding; for generic fund-raising requests; or for loans. It does not make grants to individuals, including scholarships, or to organizations that discriminate against people because of age, race, sex, or ethnicity. In general, the foundation also does not make grants of less than $10,000.

OTHER THINGS TO KNOW
The foundation asks all prospective applicants to review its Grantmaking Policies and Procedures before submitting a proposal. The foundation discourages contact with any trustee regarding specific applications. Generally, only one grant will be made to an organization within a year.

One month after notification of grant approval, the foundation meets with nonprofits to discuss reporting requirements. The foundation requires organizations to submit period reports and information about the program, including a signed copy of award letter, six-month progress and expenditure report, final evaluation and expenditure reports, etc.

PUBLICATIONS
Annual report, newsletter, grantmaking policies and procedures

GRANTS ANALYSIS
Total Grants: $18,761,881

Number of Grants: 109

Highest Grant: $8,000,000

Average Grant: $172,127

Typical Range: $25,000 to $200,000

Disclosure Period: 1994

Note: Recent grants are derived from a 1994 partial grants list.

RECENT GRANTS
Library
543,000	Detroit Associated Libraries, Detroit, MI — improve information, and referral services

General
700,000	State of Michigan Department of Social Serivces, Lansing, MI — Independent Living Initiative
385,000	City of Detroit Management Information Services Department, Detroit, MI — information technology strategic planning project
300,000	Hunger Action Coalition for Southeastern Michigan, Detroit, MI — minigrants for emergency food providers
300,000	School District of the City of Detroit, Detroit, MI — comprehensive substance abuse prevention program
265,000	Office of the Wayne County Executive, Department of Public Health, Detroit, MI — youth violence prevention project

SPX Corp. / SPX Foundation

Former Foundation Name: Sealed Power Foundation
Sales: $756.5 million
Employees: 8,600
Headquarters: Muskegon, MI
SIC Major Group: Hand & Edge Tools Nec, Hardware Nec, Industrial Valves, and Special Dies, Tools, Jigs & Fixtures

CONTACT
James M. Sheridan
President
SPX Foundation
700 Terrace Point Dr.
Muskegon, MI 49443-3301
(616) 724-5000

FINANCIAL SUMMARY
Recent Giving: $260,000 (1994 approx.); $388,901 (1993); $235,058 (1991)

Assets: $4,935 (1993); $657 (1991); $24,748 (1990)

Gifts Received: $392,641 (1993); $205,948 (1991); $196,269 (1990)

Fiscal Note: Company makes charitable contributions through the foundation only. In 1993, contributions were received from SPX Corp.

EIN: 38-6058308

CONTRIBUTIONS SUMMARY
Typical Recipients: • *Arts & Humanities:* Arts Centers, General, Libraries, Museums/Galleries, Music, Performing Arts, Public Broadcasting, Theater • *Civic & Public Affairs:* Clubs, Economic Development, Economic Policy, General, Housing, Municipalities/Towns, Parades/Festivals, Professional & Trade Associations, Urban & Community Affairs, Women's Affairs • *Education:* Business Education, Colleges & Universities, Community & Junior Colleges, Education Funds, General, Minority Education, Public Education (Precollege), Science/Mathematics Education • *Health:* Emergency/Ambulance Services, General, Health Organizations, Hospitals • *Religion:* Churches, Religious Organizations, Religious Welfare • *Science:* Scientific Centers & Institutes, Scientific Organizations • *Social Services:* Child Abuse, Community Service Organizations, Crime Prevention, Family Planning, Family Services, Food/Clothing Distribution, General, Special Olympics, Substance Abuse, United Funds/United Ways, YMCA/YWCA/YMHA/YWHA, Youth Organizations

Grant Types: capital, employee matching gifts, and general support

Geographic Distribution: primarily in plant communities

Operating Locations: GA, IL (Des Plaines), IN (Auburn, Rochester), KY (Franklin), MI (Alma, Dowagiac, Jackson, Kalamazoo, Muskeogon, Saint Johns, Warren, Whitehall, Zeeland), MN (Owatonna), MS, OH (Montpelier), PA

CORP. OFFICERS
Curtis T. Atkisson, Jr.: *B* Miami FL 1933 *ED* Univ MI 1956; Stanford Univ 1961 *CURR EMPL* pres, coo, dir: SPX Corp *NONPR AFFIL* dir: Muskegon Econ Growth Alliance; trust: Mercy Hosp

Dale A. Johnson: *B* 1937 *ED* Mankato St Univ BS 1959; Univ MN MA 1966; Univ MN PhD 1968 *CURR EMPL* chmn, ceo, dir: SPX Corp *CORP AFFIL* dir: Douglas & Lomason Co, MCN Corp *NONPR AFFIL* mem, chmn, dir: Motor & Equipment Mfrs Assn; mem, dir: MI Mfg Assn

GIVING OFFICERS
Curtis T. Atkisson, Jr.: trust *CURR EMPL* pres, coo, dir: SPX Corp (see above)

Tina L. Betlejewski: secy

Robert C. Huff: treas, trust *CURR EMPL* treas: SPX Corp

Dale A. Johnson: trust *CURR EMPL* chmn, ceo, dir: SPX Corp (see above)

Stephen A. Lison: vp, trust *CURR EMPL* vp human resources: SPX Corp

James M. Sheridan: pres, trust *CURR EMPL* vp, secy, gen coun: SPX Corp

John D. Tyson: pres, trust *CURR EMPL* vp corp rels: SPX Corp

Albert A. Zagotta: trust *CURR EMPL* exec vp: SPX Corp

APPLICATION INFORMATION
Initial Approach: *Initial Contact:* letter of inquiry *Include Information On:* a description of organization, amount requested, purpose of funds sought, proof of tax-exempt status *Deadlines:* none

GRANTS ANALYSIS
Total Grants: $388,901

Number of Grants: 49*
Highest Grant: $52,000
Average Grant: $7,937*
Typical Range: $100 to $10,000
Disclosure Period: 1993

Note: Recent grants are derived from a 1993 Form 990. Number of grants and average grant figures do not include matching gifts.

RECENT GRANTS

Library
2,000	Friends of Hackley Library, Muskegon, MI

General
30,000	Mercy Hospital
30,000	Muskegon Community College, Muskegon, MI
27,416	Steele County United Way, Owatonna, MN
26,000	United Way of Muskegon County, Muskegon, MI
21,000	Y Family Christian Association

Taubman Foundation, A. Alfred

CONTACT
Guy L. Schmidt
Executive Assistant
A. Alfred Taubman Fdn.
PO Box 200
200 E Long Lake Rd.
Bloomfield Hills, MI 48303-0200
(313) 258-6800

FINANCIAL SUMMARY
Recent Giving: $1,598,275 (fiscal 1993); $1,636,325 (fiscal 1992); $1,799,160 (fiscal 1990)

Assets: $8,611 (fiscal 1993); $7,910 (fiscal 1992); $3,931 (fiscal 1990)

Gifts Received: $1,602,285 (fiscal 1993); $1,636,523 (fiscal 1992); $1,800,673 (fiscal 1990)

Fiscal Note: In fiscal 1992, contributions were received from A. Alfred Taubman.

EIN: 38-2219625

CONTRIBUTIONS SUMMARY
Donor(s): A. Alfred Taubman

Typical Recipients: • *Arts & Humanities:* Arts Festivals, Historic Preservation, History & Archaeology, Libraries • *Civic & Public Affairs:* African American Affairs, Employment/Job Training, General, Hispanic Affairs, Legal Aid, Municipalities/Towns, Public Policy, Urban & Community Affairs, Women's Affairs • *Education:* Colleges & Universities, Education Associations, General, Medical Education, Minority Education, Private Education (Precollege) • *Environment:* General, Resource Conservation • *Health:* AIDS/HIV, Arthritis, Cancer, Clinics/Medical Centers, Diabetes, Health Organizations, Hospices, Hospitals, Long-Term Care, Medical Research, Single-Disease Health Associations •

International: International Relations, Missionary/Religious Activities • *Religion:* Bible Study/Translation, Jewish Causes, Religious Organizations, Religious Welfare, Synagogues/Temples • *Science:* Science Exhibits & Fairs, Scientific Centers & Institutes • *Social Services:* Camps, Child Welfare, Community Service Organizations, Delinquency & Criminal Rehabilitation, Domestic Violence, Family Planning, Family Services, People with Disabilities, Recreation & Athletics, Scouts, Senior Services, Substance Abuse, United Funds/United Ways, Volunteer Services, YMCA/YWCA/YMHA/YWHA, Youth Organizations

Grant Types: operating expenses and research

Geographic Distribution: focus on MI, with emphasis on Detroit

GIVING OFFICERS
Max M. Fisher: trust *B* Pittsburgh PA 1908 *ED* OH St Univ BS 1930 *CORP AFFIL* chmn: Chiquita Brands Intl; dir: Mfrs Natl Corp, Taubman Co *NONPR AFFIL* chmn bd: Detroit Renaissance; dir: Sinai Hosp Detroit; hon chmn: Un Fdn Detroit; mem: Petroleum Inst *PHIL AFFIL* vchmn: Community Foundation Southeastern MI *CLUB AFFIL* Chicago, Economic, Franklin Hills CC, Harmonie, Palm Beach CC, Recess, Standard

Gayle T. Kalisman: pres

Jeffrey H. Miro: secy, trust *CURR EMPL* secy: Sothebys Holdings *CORP AFFIL* dir: Taubman Co, Woodward & Lothrop Inc *PHIL AFFIL* secy: Taubman Charitable Foundation

Gerald R. Poissant: asst treas

Dean Eugene Richardson: trust *B* West Branch MI 1927 *CORP AFFIL* dir: Detroit Edison Co, Ford Holdings, Tecumseh Products Co *NONPR AFFIL* chmn: AAA MI; mem: Detroit Bar Assn, MI Bar Assn

A. Alfred Taubman: chmn, treas, trust *B* Pontiac MI 1925 *ED* Lawrence Inst Tech; Univ MI *CURR EMPL* chmn: Taubman Co *CORP AFFIL* chmn: A&W Restaurants Inc, Sothebys Holdings; dir: Chase Manhattan Corp, Detroit Renaissance, RH Macy & Co; owner: Woodward & Lothrop Co *NONPR AFFIL* chmn: Univ PA Wharton Real Estate Ctr; chmn emeritus: Smithsonian Inst Am Art; dir: Detroit Symphony Orchestra, Econ Club Detroit, Friends Art Preservation Embassies, Natl Realty Comm; mem: City Detroit Arts Comm; nat bd: Smithsonian Assocs; prin benefactor: A Alfred Taubman Health Care Ctr, A Alfred Taubman Med Library Univ MI; trust: Ctr Creative Studies, Detroit Inst Art, Harper-Grace Hosp, Urban Land Inst, Whitney Mus Am Art *PHIL AFFIL* chmn, treas, trust: Taubman Charitable Foundation; pres, chmn, treas, trust: Taubman Endowment Arts *CLUB AFFIL* Econ Detroit

Robert S. Taubman: trust *CURR EMPL* pres, ceo, dir: Taubman Co *CORP AFFIL* dir: A&W Restaurants Inc, Mfrs Natl Bank Detroit, Woodward & Lothrop Inc *NONPR*

AFFIL dir: Sinai Hosp; mem: Intl Counc Shopping Ctrs; mem bd govs: Cranbrook Sch

William S. Taubman: trust *CORP AFFIL* dir: A&W Restaurants Inc

APPLICATION INFORMATION
Initial Approach: Send brief letter of inquiry describing program or project. Include a description of organization, amount requested, purpose of funds sought, recently audited financial statement, and proof of tax-exempt status. There are no deadlines.

GRANTS ANALYSIS
Total Grants: $1,598,275
Number of Grants: 65
Highest Grant: $1,520,000
Typical Range: $100 to $20,000
Disclosure Period: fiscal year ending July 31, 1993

Note: Recent grants are derived from a fiscal 1993 Form 990.

RECENT GRANTS

General
1,520,000	Allied Jewish Campaign, Detroit, MI
20,000	American Jewish Committee, New York, NY
12,000	United Way, New York, NY
5,000	Casita Maria Fiesta '92, New York, NY
3,000	Crittenton Hospital, Rochester, MI

Tecumseh Products Co.

Sales: $1.31 billion
Employees: 12,320
Headquarters: Detroit, MI
SIC Major Group: Industrial Machinery & Equipment and Transportation Equipment

CONTACT
Tecumseh Products Co.
150 W Jefferson Ste. 2500
Detroit, MI 48226
(313) 526-9880

CONTRIBUTIONS SUMMARY
Typical Recipients: • *Arts & Humanities:* History & Archaeology, Libraries, Museums/Galleries, Public Broadcasting • *Civic & Public Affairs:* Community Foundations, Housing, Nonprofit Management, Safety • *Education:* Arts/Humanities Education, Colleges & Universities, Legal Education, Minority Education, Preschool Education, Private Education (Precollege), Public Education (Precollege), Secondary Education (Public), Student Aid • *Health:* Children's Health/Hospitals, Hospices, Hospitals, Medical Rehabilitation • *Religion:* Churches, Synagogues/Temples • *Social Services:* Animal Protection, Child Welfare, Delinquency & Criminal Rehabilitation, Family Services, Food/Clothing Distribution, People with Disabilities, Recreation & Athletics, Senior Services, Youth Organizations

Operating Locations: MI (Detroit, Tecumseh)

CORP. OFFICERS

John H. Foss: *CURR EMPL* vp, treas, cfo, dir: Tecumseh Products Co

Todd Wesley Herrick: *B* Tecumseh MI 1942 *ED* Univ Notre Dame BA 1967 *CURR EMPL* pres, ceo, dir: Tecumseh Products Co *CORP AFFIL* chb, dir: MP Pumps; dir: OH Citizens Trust Co, Sociedad Intercontinental Compressores Hermitocos, Tecnamotor, Un Savings Bank; pres, dir: Vitrus; vp, dir: Little Giant Pump Co *NONPR AFFIL* mem: Am Soc Heating Refrigerating Air Conditioning Engrs, Am Soc Metals *PHIL AFFIL* vp, trust: Herrick Foundation

GIVING OFFICERS

Catherine R. Cobb: trust *PHIL AFFIL* trust: Herrick Foundation

John William Gelder: vp, secy, trust *B* Buffalo NY 1933 *ED* Univ MI BBA 1956; Univ MI JD 1959 *CURR EMPL* mng ptnr: Miller Canfield Paddock & Stone *CORP AFFIL* dir: Tecumseh Products Co; secy: Harlan Electric Co *NONPR AFFIL* mem: Order Coif *PHIL AFFIL* vp, secy, trust: Herrick Foundation *CLUB AFFIL* Bloomfield Hills CC, Detroit Athletic

OTHER THINGS TO KNOW

A majority of the Herrick Foundation's assets consist of shares of the Tecumseh Products Co.

GRANTS ANALYSIS

Number of Grants: 97

Highest Grant: $200,000

Typical Range: $5,000 to $10,000

Disclosure Period: fiscal year ending September 30, 1992

Note: Recent grants are derived from a Fiscal 1992 Form 990.

RECENT GRANTS

Library

20,000	Sequatchie County, Dunlap, TN — for the costs of new bookshelves, furniture and equipment to complete the Sequatchie County Library Renovation Project
10,000	Adrian Masonic Historical Association, Adrian, MI — for the restoration of the Adrian Masonic Temple and the establishment of a Masonic Library and Museum

General

200,000	Siena Heights College, Adrian, MI — to further the objects and purposes of the Vision 2000 Program of Siena Heights College
200,000	Sienna Heights College, Adrian, MI — to further the objectives and purposes of its Vision 2000 program
158,000	Charter Township of Madison, Adrian, MI — to pay and defray costs, for a new fire truck to replace its 1972 Mack Snorkel fire truck and for no other purposes
100,000	Adrian College, Adrian, MI — for facility renovations and improvements
100,000	Allegan General Hospital, Allegan, MI — to be used by it to defray, in part, the costs for the expansion and renovation of the hospital

---

Tiscornia Foundation

CONTACT

Laurianne T. Davis
President and Trustee
Tiscornia Fdn.
1010 Main St., Ste. A
St. Joseph, MI 49085
(616) 926-0700

FINANCIAL SUMMARY

Recent Giving: $182,950 (1993); $173,735 (1992); $154,630 (1991)

Assets: $4,234,150 (1993); $4,376,175 (1992); $4,424,735 (1991)

EIN: 38-1777343

CONTRIBUTIONS SUMMARY

Donor(s): late James W. Tiscornia, the late Waldo V. Tiscornia, Auto Specialties Manufacturing Co., Lambert Brake Corp.

Typical Recipients: • *Arts & Humanities:* Arts Associations & Councils, Arts Centers, History & Archaeology, Libraries, Museums/Galleries, Music • *Civic & Public Affairs:* Economic Policy, General • *Education:* Colleges & Universities, Education Funds, Literacy, Minority Education, Student Aid • *Environment:* General • *Health:* Clinics/Medical Centers, Health Funds, Health Organizations, Hospices, Prenatal Health Issues • *Religion:* Churches, Religious Welfare • *Social Services:* Camps, Community Service Organizations, Counseling, Family Planning, Recreation & Athletics, Shelters/Homelessness, United Funds/United Ways, Volunteer Services, YMCA/YWCA/YMHA/YWHA, Youth Organizations

Grant Types: capital, emergency, general support, multiyear/continuing support, scholarship, and seed money

Geographic Distribution: focus on MI

GIVING OFFICERS

Laurianne T. Davis: pres, trust

Albert Dexel: asst secy, asst treas

Henry H. Tippett: secy, treas, trust

Bernice Tiscornia: first vp, trust

James Tiscornia: second vp, trust

Lester C. Tiscornia: pres, trust *ED* Coll Pacific AB 1932; Andrews Univ LLD 1971 *CURR EMPL* chmn, dir: Auto Specialties Mfg Co *CORP AFFIL* dir: Peoples St Bank *NONPR AFFIL* mem: Soc Automotive Engrs; mem adv bd Twin Cities chapter: Salvation Army; pres: St Joseph Commun Chest

APPLICATION INFORMATION

Initial Approach: Send a brief letter of inquiry. Scholarships only for Northern Berrien County high school students and children of Auto Specialties Manufacturing Co. employees. Deadline is April 1 for scholarships; October 1 for general grants.

Restrictions on Giving: Does not support individuals (except for employee-related scholarships).

GRANTS ANALYSIS

Total Grants: $182,950

Number of Grants: 27

Highest Grant: $45,000

Typical Range: $200 to $12,000

Disclosure Period: 1993

Note: Recent grants are derived from a 1993 Form 990. Number of grants and typical range do not include scholarships to individuals.

RECENT GRANTS

General

45,000	Mercy Memorial Health Fund, Benton Harbor, MI
10,000	Gateway, Berrien Springs, MI
10,000	Planned Parenthood Association, Benton Harbor, MI
10,000	YWCA, St. Joseph, MI
8,000	Blossomland United Way, Benton Harbor, MI

Todd Co., A.M. / Todd Co. Foundation, A.M.

Sales: $130.0 million
Employees: 275
Headquarters: Kalamazoo, MI
SIC Major Group: Chemicals & Allied Products and Food & Kindred Products

---

CONTACT

Ian Blair
Vice President, Trading
A.M. Todd Co.
1717 Douglas Ave.
Kalamazoo, MI 49007
(616) 343-2603

FINANCIAL SUMMARY

Recent Giving: $42,900 (1993); $47,700 (1992); $38,300 (1991)

Assets: $297,096 (1993); $248,155 (1992); $234,706 (1991)

Gifts Received: $75,000 (1993); $50,000 (1992); $50,000 (1991)

Fiscal Note: In 1993, contributions were received from A.M. Todd Co.

EIN: 38-6055829

CONTRIBUTIONS SUMMARY

Typical Recipients: • *Arts & Humanities:* Arts Associations & Councils, Arts Institutes, Community Arts, Historic Preservation, History & Archaeology, Libraries, Music, Performing Arts • *Civic & Public Affairs:* Botanical Gardens/Parks, General, Housing, Municipalities/Towns, Parades/Festivals, Urban & Community Affairs, Zoos/Aquariums • *Education:* Agricultural Education, Business Education, Colleges & Universities, Education Associations, Education Reform, Special Education • *Environment:* General • *Health:* Diabetes, Health Organizations, Prenatal Health Issues • *Religion:* Churches, Religious Welfare • *Science:* Scientific Centers & Institutes • *Social Services:* Big Brother/Big Sister, Camps, Child Welfare, Community Service Organizations, Family Planning, People with Disabilities, Scouts, United Funds/United Ways, YMCA/YWCA/YMHA/YWHA, Youth Organizations

Grant Types: general support

Geographic Distribution: focus on Kalamazoo County, MI

Operating Locations: MI (Kalamazoo)

CORP. OFFICERS

Thomas F. Rose: *CURR EMPL* vp, cfo: AM Todd Co

A. J. Todd III: *CURR EMPL* pres: AM Todd Co

GIVING OFFICERS

Old Kent Bank: trust

Ian D. Blair: trust *CURR EMPL* vp trading: AM Todd Co

A. J. Todd III: trust *CURR EMPL* pres: AM Todd Co (see above)

APPLICATION INFORMATION

Initial Approach: Send a brief letter of inquiry. Include a description of organization, amount requested, purpose of funds sought, and proof of tax-exempt status. There are no deadlines.

Restrictions on Giving: Does not support individuals, religious organizations for sectarian purposes, political or lobbying groups, or organizations outside operating areas.

OTHER THINGS TO KNOW

Education support is primarily provided directly by A.M. Todd Co., not the foundation.

GRANTS ANALYSIS

Total Grants: $42,900

Number of Grants: 28

Highest Grant: $9,300

Typical Range: $100 to $5,000

Disclosure Period: 1993

Note: Recent grants are derived from a 1993 Form 990.

RECENT GRANTS

General

9,300	Greater Kalamazoo United Way, Kalamazoo, MI
5,000	Kalamazoo Child Guidance Clinic, Kalamazoo, MI
5,000	Kalamazoo Foundation, Kalamazoo, MI — YMCA — capital campaign
3,500	Michigan State University KCMS, Kalamazoo, MI — building project
3,000	CEO Council, Kalamazoo, MI

Towsley Foundation, Harry A. and Margaret D.

CONTACT

Margaret Ann Riecker
President and Trustee
Harry A. and Margaret D. Towsley Foundation
3055 Plymouth Rd., Ste. 200
Ann Arbor, MI 48105
(313) 662-6777

FINANCIAL SUMMARY

Recent Giving: $1,708,340 (1993); $2,132,035 (1992); $1,577,623 (1990)

Assets: $37,933,074 (1993); $38,114,614 (1992); $32,527,082 (1990)

Gifts Received: $100,000 (1985)

EIN: 38-6091798

CONTRIBUTIONS SUMMARY

Donor(s): Margaret Dow Towsley established the foundation in 1959 in Michigan with a gift of Dow Chemical Company common stock.

Typical Recipients: • *Arts & Humanities:* Arts Associations & Councils, Arts Funds, Arts Institutes, Libraries, Museums/Galleries, Music, Theater • *Civic & Public Affairs:* Economic Development, Housing, Philanthropic Organizations • *Education:* Colleges & Universities, Community & Junior Colleges, Education Reform, Faculty Development, Medical Education, Minority Education, Preschool Education, Private Education (Precollege), Science/Mathematics Education, Student Aid • *Health:* AIDS/HIV, Cancer, Children's Health/Hospitals, Hospitals, Medical Rehabilitation, Medical Research, Nursing Services, Public Health, Single-Disease Health Associations • *Religion:* Churches, Religious Welfare • *Social Services:* Child Welfare, Community Service Organizations, Family Planning, Family Services, Scouts, Substance Abuse, Volunteer Services, Youth Organizations

Grant Types: emergency, general support, multiyear/continuing support, operating expenses, project, and research

Geographic Distribution: Michigan, especially Ann Arbor and Washtenaw County

GIVING OFFICERS

Robert L. Bring: trust

C. Wendell Dunbar: treas, trust

Jennifer Poteat-Flores: trust

Steven Reicker: trust

John E. Riecker: secy

Margaret Ann Riecker: pres, trust *PHIL AFFIL* vp, trust, don granddaughter: Herbert H. and Grace A. Dow Foundation

Judith Dow Rumelhart: vp, trust

Margaret E. Thompson, MD: trust

Lynn T. White: trust

Susan T. Wyland: trust

APPLICATION INFORMATION

Initial Approach:

Prospective applicants should submit a letter and proposal to the foundation. The foundation does not provide application forms for requests. Elaborate presentations are discouraged.

Applicants should submit a copy of the tax-exempt letter from the IRS; letter establishing that the applicant is not a private foundation; amount requested, need, and intended use; and organization's latest financial statements with an operating budget and other funding sources.

Applications should be submitted between January 1 and March 31 of each year. Send two copies of proposals.

Final notification to applicants usually is made within 60 to 90 days.

Restrictions on Giving: The foundation does not make direct grants to individuals, provide loan funds, grants to students for scholarships, or grants for travel and conferences.

OTHER THINGS TO KNOW

The trustees do not conduct personal interviews with applicants except upon the foundation's initiative. Additional information is frequently requested by the foundation after the application is received.

PUBLICATIONS

Annual report, application guidelines

GRANTS ANALYSIS

Total Grants: $1,708,340

Number of Grants: 40

Highest Grant: $250,000

Average Grant: $42,709

Typical Range: $5,000 to $50,000

Disclosure Period: 1993

Note: Recent grants are derived from a 1993 Form 990.

RECENT GRANTS

Library
90,000   Culver Academies, Culver, IN — new library
2,000   Foundation Center, New York, NY

General
250,000   University of Michigan Center for the Education of Women, Ann Arbor, MI — Margaret Dow Towsley Scholarship Fund endowment
250,000   University of Missouri School of Medicine, Columbia, MO
200,000   Children's Play School, Ann Arbor, MI — preschool education
200,000   Michigan State University College of Natural Sciences, E. Lansing, MI — Center for Science and Mathematics Teachers
165,000   McKenley Foundation, Ann Arbor, MI — Huron River - North Main Development Project

Upjohn Foundation, Harold and Grace

CONTACT
Floyd L. Parks
Secretary and Treasurer
Harold and Grace Upjohn Fdn.
Mall Plaza, Ste. 90
157 S Kalamazoo Mall
Kalamazoo, MI 49007
(616) 344-2818

FINANCIAL SUMMARY

Recent Giving: $317,904 (fiscal 1993); $368,324 (fiscal 1992); $604,355 (fiscal 1991)

Assets: $8,084,687 (fiscal 1993); $7,784,735 (fiscal 1992); $7,672,786 (fiscal 1991)

Gifts Received: $237,875 (fiscal 1991)

Fiscal Note: In fiscal 1991, contributions were received from Mary U. Meader.

EIN: 38-6052963

CONTRIBUTIONS SUMMARY

Donor(s): the late Grace G. Upjohn

Typical Recipients: • *Arts & Humanities:* Libraries, Music • *Civic & Public Affairs:* Botanical Gardens/Parks, Housing, Municipalities/Towns, Philanthropic Organizations, Safety, Urban & Community Affairs • *Education:* Colleges & Universities, Community & Junior Colleges, Education Associations, Education Reform, Private Education (Precollege), Public Education (Precollege), Science/Mathematics Education • *Environment:* General • *Health:* Clinics/Medical Centers, Hospitals, Nursing Services, Preventive Medicine/Wellness Organizations • *Religion:* Ministries, Religious Organizations, Religious Welfare • *Social Services:* Child Welfare, Community Service Organizations, People with Disabilities, Recreation & Athletics, Senior Services, Substance Abuse, United Funds/United Ways, YMCA/YWCA/YMHA/YWHA, Youth Organizations

Grant Types: capital, project, and seed money

Geographic Distribution: focus on MI

GIVING OFFICERS

Gene R. Conrad: off

Joseph J. Dunnigan: vp, trust

Edwin E. Meader: pres, trust

Mary U. Meader: trust

C. H. Mullin: trust

Floyd L. Parks: secy, treas *PHIL AFFIL* vp, treas, trust: Irving S. Gilmore Foundation

Elizabeth H. Thompson: trust

APPLICATION INFORMATION

Initial Approach: Application form available upon request.

Restrictions on Giving: Does not support individuals.

PUBLICATIONS

Annual Report, Application Guidelines

GRANTS ANALYSIS

Total Grants: $317,904

Number of Grants: 12

Highest Grant: $100,000

Typical Range: $2,500 to $50,000

Disclosure Period: fiscal year ending October 31, 1993

Note: Recent grants are derived from a fiscal 1993 Form 990.

RECENT GRANTS

General
100,000   University of Michigan, Ann Arbor, MI — operations
50,000   Kalamazoo Valley Habitat for Humanity, Kalamazoo, MI — facilities
43,904   Community Medical Center Foundation, Kalamazoo, MI — equipment
25,000   Visiting Nurse Association of Southwest Michigan, Kalamazoo, MI — facilities
20,000   Kalamazoo Academic Partnership, Kalamazoo, MI — operations

Upton Foundation, Frederick S.

CONTACT
Stephen E. Upton
Chairman of the Board of Trustees
Frederick S. Upton Foundation
100 Ridgeway
St. Joseph, MI 49085
(616) 982-0272

FINANCIAL SUMMARY

Recent Giving: $1,200,000 (1995 est.); $1,200,000 (1994 approx.); $1,050,655 (1993)

Assets: $25,000,000 (1995 est.); $25,000,000 (1994 approx.); $29,401,906 (1993)

Gifts Received: $3,153,634 (1989); $5,000,000 (1988)

EIN: 36-6013317

CONTRIBUTIONS SUMMARY

Donor(s): The foundation was established in 1954, with Frederick S. Upton as donor. In 1911, Mr. Upton was a co-founder of the Upton Machine Company, the predecessor of the Whirlpool appliance company.

Typical Recipients: • *Arts & Humanities:* Arts Centers, Arts Festivals, Arts Funds, Arts Institutes, Dance, General, Historic Preservation, History & Archaeology, Libraries, Museums/Galleries, Music, Visual Arts • *Civic & Public Affairs:* Philanthropic Organizations, Urban & Community Affairs • *Education:* Arts/Humanities Education, Business Education, Colleges & Universities, Education Funds, General, Literacy, Minority Education, Private Education (Precollege), Public Education (Precollege), Religious Education, Student Aid • *Environment:* General • *Health:* Health Organizations, Hospitals • *Religion:* Churches, Ministries, Religious Organizations, Religious Welfare, Synagogues/Temples • *Social Services:* Animal Protection, Child Welfare, Community Centers, Community Service Organizations, Counseling, Family Planning,

Family Services, People with Disabilities, United Funds/United Ways, Volunteer Services, YMCA/YWCA/YMHA/YWHA, Youth Organizations

Grant Types: general support, project, and scholarship

Geographic Distribution: primarily Michigan

GIVING OFFICERS

Priscilla U. Byrns: trust

David F. Upton: trust

Stephen E. Upton: chmn bd trusts *B* Benton Harbor MI 1924 *ED* Univ MI 1949 *CURR EMPL* sr vp: Whirlpool Corp

Sylvia Upton Wood: secy, trust

APPLICATION INFORMATION
Initial Approach:

Applicants should submit a letter of inquiry to the foundation and request an application form.

Applications may be submitted any time. The board of trustees usually meets four to five times annually.

GRANTS ANALYSIS
Total Grants: $1,050,655

Number of Grants: 136

Highest Grant: $75,190

Average Grant: $7,725

Typical Range: $1,000 to $10,000

Disclosure Period: 1993

Note: Recent grants are derived from a 1993 Form 990.

RECENT GRANTS

Library
10,000	Clements Library

General
75,190	YWCA of Southwestern Michigan, MI
60,725	Lake Michigan College, Benton Harbor, MI
51,000	Olivet College, Olivet, MI
29,000	Salvation Army
25,000	Hospital Foundation

Vicksburg Foundation

CONTACT
Barbara Hoekzema
Secretary and Treasurer
Vicksburg Fdn.
c/o First of America Bank-Michigan N.A.
108 E Michigan Ave.
Kalamazoo, MI 49007
(616) 376-8021

FINANCIAL SUMMARY

Recent Giving: $215,864 (1993); $244,510 (1992); $193,113 (1991)

Assets: $4,336,043 (1993); $4,187,992 (1992); $4,220,616 (1991)

Gifts Received: $46,908 (1993); $26,640 (1992); $51,992 (1991)

Fiscal Note: In 1993, contributions were received from the Stanley J. Herman Charitable Unitrust.

EIN: 38-6065237

CONTRIBUTIONS SUMMARY

Typical Recipients: • *Arts & Humanities:* Arts Funds, Libraries • *Civic & Public Affairs:* General, Law & Justice, Municipalities/Towns, Safety, Urban & Community Affairs • *Education:* Business Education, Colleges & Universities, Education Funds, Education Reform, General, Private Education (Precollege), Public Education (Precollege), Student Aid • *Health:* Hospices, Nursing Services • *International:* Foreign Arts Organizations • *Religion:* Jewish Causes, Religious Organizations, Religious Welfare • *Social Services:* Community Centers, Community Service Organizations, Crime Prevention, Delinquency & Criminal Rehabilitation, Family Services, United Funds/United Ways, Youth Organizations

Grant Types: operating expenses and project

Geographic Distribution: focus on MI

GIVING OFFICERS
First Am Bank MI NA: trust

Dennis Boyle: dir

Meredith Clarke: dir

Gordon Daniels: dir

Barbara Hoekzema: secy, treas

Warren Lawrence: dir

William Oswalt: pres, trust

Butch Peeler: trust

APPLICATION INFORMATION

Initial Approach: Send brief letter of inquiry describing program. Include a description of organization, amount requested, purpose of funds sought, recently audited financial statement, and proof of tax-exempt status. There are no deadlines.

GRANTS ANALYSIS

Total Grants: $215,864

Number of Grants: 19

Highest Grant: $73,724

Typical Range: $100 to $35,500

Disclosure Period: 1993

Note: Recent grants are derived from a 1993 Form 990. Number of grants and typical range do not include assistance to individuals.

RECENT GRANTS

Library
1,500	Vicksburg District Library, Vicksburg, MI — equipment

General
73,724	Village of Vicksburg, Vicksburg, MI — improvements
35,500	Vicksburg Community Schools, Vicksburg, MI
8,000	Kalamazoo College, Kalamazoo, MI — scholarships
8,000	Vicksburg United Way, Vicksburg, MI
8,000	Western Michigan University, Kalamazoo, MI — scholarships

Vollbrecht Foundation, Frederick A.

CONTACT
Kenneth J. Klebba
President
Frederick A. Vollbrecht Fdn.
31700 Telegraph Rd., Ste. 220
Birmingham, MI 48025
(313) 646-7440

FINANCIAL SUMMARY

Recent Giving: $165,950 (1993); $140,000 (1992); $141,500 (1991)

Assets: $2,494,549 (1993); $2,512,913 (1992); $2,518,440 (1991)

EIN: 38-6056173

CONTRIBUTIONS SUMMARY
Donor(s): the late Frederick A. Vollbrecht

Typical Recipients: • *Arts & Humanities:* Libraries, Music • *Civic & Public Affairs:* Business/Free Enterprise, Clubs, Economic Development, General, Public Policy, Urban & Community Affairs • *Education:* Business Education, Colleges & Universities, Community & Junior Colleges, Literacy, Student Aid • *Health:* Cancer, Children's Health/Hospitals, Diabetes, Emergency/Ambulance Services, Health Organizations, Heart, Hospitals, Kidney, Medical Research, Respiratory, Single-Disease Health Associations • *Religion:* Religious Welfare • *Social Services:* At-Risk Youth, Camps, Child Welfare, Community Service Organizations, Family Services, Food/Clothing Distribution, People with Disabilities, Scouts, United Funds/United Ways, Youth Organizations

Grant Types: general support and research

Geographic Distribution: focus on MI

GIVING OFFICERS

Kenneth J. Klebba: trust, pres, treas

Richard E. Mida: trust, vp, secy

APPLICATION INFORMATION

Initial Approach: The foundation requests applications to be made in writing. The foundation has no formal grant application procedure or application form. There are no deadlines.

PUBLICATIONS

Annual Report

GRANTS ANALYSIS

Total Grants: $165,950

Number of Grants: 41

Highest Grant: $30,000

Typical Range: $1,000 to $20,000

Disclosure Period: 1993

Note: Recent grants are derived from a 1993 Form 990.

RECENT GRANTS

Library

1,000	St. Thomas Aquinas Catholic School, Detroit, MI — library materials

General

30,000	Walsh College of Accountancy and Business Administration, Troy, MI — capital campaign pledge
20,000	Spaulding for Children, Southfield, MI
10,000	Business Enterprise Development Center, Troy, MI
10,000	Community House Association, Birmingham, MI — capital campaign
10,000	Walsh College of Accountancy and Business Administration, Troy, MI — scholarship fund

Wege Foundation

CONTACT

Peter M. Wege
President
Wege Fdn.
PO Box 6388
Grand Rapids, MI 49516
(616) 957-0480

FINANCIAL SUMMARY

Recent Giving: $436,475 (1993); $220,950 (1992); $350,549 (1991)

Assets: $14,770,349 (1993); $12,970,409 (1992); $6,703,784 (1991)

Gifts Received: $4,579 (1993); $7,200 (1992); $147,040 (1991)

Fiscal Note: In 1993, contributions were received from Peter M. Wege.

EIN: 38-6124363

CONTRIBUTIONS SUMMARY

Donor(s): Peter M. Wege

Typical Recipients: • *Arts & Humanities:* Arts Centers, Community Arts, Libraries, Literary Arts, Museums/Galleries, Music, Public Broadcasting, Theater • *Civic & Public Affairs:* Botanical Gardens/Parks, Economic Development, Employment/Job Training, Hispanic Affairs, Native American Affairs, Public Policy, Urban & Community Affairs, Zoos/Aquariums • *Education:* Arts/Humanities Education, Business Education, Colleges & Universities, Community & Junior Colleges, Education Funds, Environmental Education, General, Literacy, Private Education (Precollege), Public Education (Precollege), Special Education • *Environment:* General, Resource Conservation • *Health:* Emergency/Ambulance Services, Health Organizations, Hospitals • *International:* International Environmental Issues • *Religion:* Religious Organizations, Religious Welfare • *Social Services:* Camps, Child Welfare, Community Service Organizations, Family Planning, Homes, Refugee Assistance, Senior Services, Substance Abuse, Youth Organizations

Grant Types: general support

Geographic Distribution: focus on Greater Kent County, MI, with emphasis on the Grand Rapids area

GIVING OFFICERS

Charles Lundstrom: secy

Peter M. Wege: pres *B* Grand Rapids MI 1920 *ED* Univ MI *CURR EMPL* vchmn, dir: Steelcase Inc *PHIL AFFIL* trust: Steelcase Foundation

Peter M. Wege II: vp

APPLICATION INFORMATION

Initial Approach: Include a description of organization, amount requested, purpose of funds sought, recently audited financial statement, and proof of tax-exempt status. Deadline is February 15.

GRANTS ANALYSIS

Total Grants: $436,475

Number of Grants: 35

Highest Grant: $100,000

Typical Range: $500 to $75,000

Disclosure Period: 1993

Note: Recent grants are derived from a 1993 Form 990.

RECENT GRANTS

Library

1,000	Ryerson Public Library, Ryerson, MI

General

100,000	Blodgett/St. Mary's MRI, Grand Rapids, MI — community development
75,000	City of East Grand Rapids, East Grand Rapids, MI — community development
65,000	Michigan Botanical Gardens, Grand Rapids, MI — community development
53,500	Center for Environmental Study, Grand Rapids, MI — environmental education
39,000	John Ball Zoological Society, Grand Rapids, MI — community development

Westerman Foundation, Samuel L.

CONTACT

Martha Muir
Vice President, Assistant Secretary
Samuel L. Westerman Fdn.
14532 Indian Trails Dr.
Grand Haven, MI 49417
(810) 642-5770

FINANCIAL SUMMARY

Recent Giving: $369,750 (1993); $354,550 (1992); $303,350 (1991)

Assets: $831,835 (1993); $8,366,846 (1992); $7,503,520 (1991)

EIN: 23-7108795

CONTRIBUTIONS SUMMARY

Typical Recipients: • *Arts & Humanities:* Arts Centers, Arts Institutes, History & Archaeology, Libraries, Music, Opera, Performing Arts, Theater • *Civic & Public Affairs:* Botanical Gardens/Parks, Community Foundations, General, Housing, Women's Affairs • *Education:* Colleges & Universities, Gifted & Talented Programs, International Exchange, Private Education (Precollege), Special Education, Student Aid • *Environment:* Air/Water Quality, General • *Health:* Alzheimers Disease, Arthritis, Children's Health/Hospitals, Heart, Hospices, Hospitals, Medical Research, Respiratory, Single-Disease Health Associations, Transplant Networks/Donor Banks • *International:* Foreign Educational Institutions, International Peace & Security Issues, International Relief Efforts, Missionary/Religious Activities • *Religion:* Churches, Jewish Causes, Religious Welfare, Seminaries • *Social Services:* Animal Protection, Camps, Child Welfare, Community Centers, Community Service Organizations, Delinquency & Criminal Rehabilitation, General, People with Disabilities, Special Olympics, United Funds/United Ways, Youth Organizations

Grant Types: general support and project

Geographic Distribution: focus on MI

GIVING OFFICERS

James H. LoPrete: pres *B* Detroit MI 1929 *ED* Univ MI AB 1951; Univ MI JD 1953

CURR EMPL stnr, pres: Monaghan, Lo-Prete, McDonald, Yakima & Grenke PC *CORP AFFIL* dir: Drake's Batter Mix Co, Oraco Inc *NONPR AFFIL* fellow: Am Coll Trust & Estate Couns, Intl Academy Estate & Trust Law; mem: Am Bar Assn, Oakland County Bar Assn, State Bar Michigan; trust: John R & M Margrite Davis Fdn, Presbyterian Village Michigan; trust, pres: Univ Michigan Club of Detroit Scholarhip Fund *CLUB AFFIL* Detroit Athletic, Orchard Lake CC, Univ Michigan Greater Detroit

Kent G. LoPrete: vp, asst treas

Mary M. Lyneis: secy

Keith H. Muir: vp

Martha M. Muir: vp, asst secy

APPLICATION INFORMATION
Initial Approach: Send brief letter of inquiry describing program or project. There are no deadlines.

GRANTS ANALYSIS
Total Grants: $369,750

Number of Grants: 129

Highest Grant: $20,000

Typical Range: $500 to $11,000

Disclosure Period: 1993

Note: Recent grants are derived from a 1993 Form 990.

RECENT GRANTS

Library

5,000	Friends of Detroit Public Library, Detroit, MI
5,000	Friends of the Detroit Public Library, Detroit, MI

General

20,000	Grand Valley State University, Allendale, MI — Westerman Foundation Scholarship for Nursing
13,500	Huron River Watershed Council, Ann Arbor, MI
12,000	First Baptist Church, Spring Lake, MI
11,000	Kirk in the Hills, Bloomfield Hills, MI
11,000	University of Michigan Department of Athletics, Ann Arbor, MI

Whirlpool Corporation / Whirlpool Foundation

Revenue: $8.1 billion
Employees: 39,590
Headquarters: Benton Harbor, MI
SIC Major Group: Household Laundry Equipment, Commercial Laundry Equipment, Refrigeration & Heating Equipment, and Household Cooking Equipment

CONTACT
Colleen D. Keast
Executive Director
Whirlpool Foundation
400 Riverview Dr.
Ste. 410
Benton Harbor, MI 49022
(616) 923-4934
Note: An alternative contact is Christopher Wyse, manager of communications. The company's World Wide Web address is http://www.whirlpool.com

FINANCIAL SUMMARY
Recent Giving: $7,000,000 (1995 est.); $5,178,482 (1994 approx.); $4,128,410 (1993)

Assets: $19,890,678 (1994); $15,572,410 (1993); $14,852,269 (1991)

Fiscal Note: Company gives directly and through the foundation; figures above represent combined giving. Above figures exclude nonmonetary support.

EIN: 38-6077342

CONTRIBUTIONS SUMMARY
Typical Recipients: • *Arts & Humanities:* Arts Associations & Councils, Arts Centers, Arts Funds, Arts Institutes, Ballet, Community Arts, Dance, Ethnic & Folk Arts, Historic Preservation, History & Archaeology, Libraries, Literary Arts, Museums/Galleries, Music, Opera, Performing Arts, Public Broadcasting, Theater, Visual Arts • *Civic & Public Affairs:* Botanical Gardens/Parks, Business/Free Enterprise, Civil Rights, Clubs, Economic Development, Economic Policy, Employment/Job Training, First Amendment Issues, General, Housing, Law & Justice, Municipalities/Towns, Nonprofit Management, Professional & Trade Associations, Public Policy, Safety, Urban & Community Affairs, Women's Affairs • *Education:* Afterschool/Enrichment Programs, Arts/Humanities Education, Business Education, Colleges & Universities, Community & Junior Colleges, Economic Education, Education Associations, Education Funds, Education Reform, Elementary Education (Private), Engineering/Technological Education, General, International Studies, Journalism/Media Education, Literacy, Medical Education, Minority Education, Private Education (Precollege), Public Education (Precollege), Science/Mathematics Education, Secondary Education (Private), Social Sciences Education, Student Aid, Vocational & Technical Education • *Environment:* General • *Health:* Clinics/Medical Centers, Health Organizations, Hospitals • *International:* Foreign Educational Institutions, Health Care/Hospitals, International Organizations, International Relations • *Religion:* Religious Welfare • *Science:* Science Exhibits & Fairs, Scientific Centers & Institutes, Scientific Organizations • *Social Services:* Animal Protection, Big Brother/Big Sister, Child Welfare, Community Centers, Community Service Organizations, Counseling, Day Care, Delinquency & Criminal Rehabilitation, Domestic Violence, Family Planning, Family Services, Food/Clothing Distribution, General, Homes, People with Disabilities, Recreation & Athletics, Senior Services, Shelters/Homelessness, Substance Abuse, United Funds/United Ways, Volunteer Services, Youth Organizations

Grant Types: employee matching gifts, project, and scholarship

Note: Employee matching gift ratio: 1 to 1. Scholarships are for employees' children only.

Geographic Distribution: only areas where Whirlpool maintains manufacturing facilities

Operating Locations: AR (Fort Smith), IN (Evansville, La Porte), MI (Benton Harbor), MS (Oxford), OH (Clyde, Findlay, Marion), SC (Columbia, Greenville), TN (Knoxville, Lavergne)

Note: Also operates in Toronto, Canada.

CORP. OFFICERS
Bradley J. Bell: *B* Chicago IL 1952 *ED* Univ IL 1974; Harvard Univ MBA 1978 *CURR EMPL* vp, treas: Whirlpool Corp

Bruce K. Berger: *CURR EMPL* corp vp corp aff: Whirlpool Corp

William D. Marohn: *B* Toledo OH 1940 *ED* Univ Toledo BSME 1964 *CURR EMPL* pres, coo, dir: Whirlpool Corp *CORP AFFIL* dir: Cooper Tire & Rubber Co, Vitromatic

James Rogers Samartini: *B* Cleveland OH 1935 *ED* Dartmouth Coll BA 1957; Harvard Univ MBA 1961 *CURR EMPL* exec vp, chief admin off: Whirlpool Corp *CORP AFFIL* dir: Peoples St Bank, Whirlpool Fin Corp, Whirlpool Intl BV *NONPR AFFIL* mem: Fin Execs Inst; mem adv bd: Salvation Army; trust: Dayton Opera Assn

David Ray Whitwam: *B* Madison WI 1942 *ED* Univ WI BS 1967 *CURR EMPL* chmn, ceo: Whirlpool Corp *CORP AFFIL* dir: PPG Indus Inc, USX Corp *NONPR AFFIL* fellow: Aspen Inst; mem: Assn Home Appliance Mfrs, Bus Higher Ed Forum, Bus Roundtable, Indus Policy Adv Comm, Natl Counc Housing; pres, dir: Soup Kitchen *CLUB AFFIL* Point O Woods *PHIL AFFIL* dir: David and Barbara Whitwam Foundation

GIVING OFFICERS
J. C. Anderson: trust

Bradley J. Bell: treas *CURR EMPL* vp, treas: Whirlpool Corp (see above)

Bruce K. Berger: pres, trust *CURR EMPL* corp vp corp aff: Whirlpool Corp (see above)

Colleen D. Keast: exec dir *ED* OH St Univ BA

Frank Luongo: treas

Charles D. Miller: trust

David E. Mitchell: trust

James Rogers Samartini: chmn *CURR EMPL* exec vp, chief admin off: Whirlpool Corp (see above)

Nancy T. Snyder: trust

Jay Van Den Berg: trust

J. Christopher Wyse: mgr commun

Gloria Zamora: trust

APPLICATION INFORMATION
Initial Approach: *Initial Contact:* brief letter or telephone call to get guidelines and application form *Deadlines:* by January 31, April 1, July 1, or October 1

Restrictions on Giving: Does not support dinners or special events, fraternal organizations, goodwill advertising, individuals, political or lobbying groups, or religious organizations for sectarian purposes.

GRANTS ANALYSIS

Total Grants: $5,178,482

Number of Grants: 262

Highest Grant: $200,000

Average Grant: $19,765

Typical Range: $5,000 to $25,000

Disclosure Period: 1994

Note: Recent grants are derived from a 1994 grants list.

RECENT GRANTS

General

200,000	Families and Work Institute, New York, NY — for a study to uncover social, work, and family concerns in American family life
200,000	Family Service America, Milwaukee, WI — for one year of a two-year grant to support enhancements to "Celebrate Families," a national, public education media campaign to highlight the value of and diverse experiences of American families today
129,252	Andrews University Center for Intercultural Relations, Berrien Springs, MI — for one year of a three-year contribution to develop the Whirlpool Foundation Program in Cultural Diversity
100,000	University of Michigan School of Business Administration, Ann Arbor, MI — to fund the implementation of a "Whirlpool Community MBA Corps" over the next three years
68,000	Family Violence Prevention Fund, San Francisco, CA — to fund a national prevention and public awareness advertising campaign entitled, "There's No Excuse for Domestic Violence"

Whiting Foundation

CONTACT

Donald E. Johnson, Jr.
President
Whiting Fdn.
901 Citizens Bank Bldg.
Flint, MI 48502
(313) 767-3600

FINANCIAL SUMMARY

Recent Giving: $900,274 (fiscal 1994); $426,350 (fiscal 1992); $545,412 (fiscal 1991)

Assets: $16,611,345 (fiscal 1994); $14,593,768 (fiscal 1992); $12,273,920 (fiscal 1991)

Gifts Received: $100,000 (fiscal 1990); $133,000 (fiscal 1988)

Fiscal Note: In 1990, contributions were received from the estate of Donald E. Johnson.

EIN: 38-6056693

CONTRIBUTIONS SUMMARY

Donor(s): members of the Johnson family

Typical Recipients: • *Arts & Humanities:* Arts Associations & Councils, Arts Centers, Arts Institutes, Libraries, Museums/Galleries, Music, Theater • *Civic & Public Affairs:* Community Foundations, General, Parades/Festivals, Safety • *Education:* Arts/Humanities Education, Business Education, Colleges & Universities, Education Funds, Gifted & Talented Programs, Medical Education, Minority Education, Private Education (Precollege), Public Education (Precollege), Religious Education, Secondary Education (Public), Special Education • *Environment:* General, Resource Conservation • *Health:* AIDS/HIV, Cancer, Children's Health/Hospitals, Clinics/Medical Centers, Emergency/Ambulance Services, Geriatric Health, Hospitals, Medical Research, Multiple Sclerosis, Single-Disease Health Associations, Trauma Treatment • *International:* Health Care/Hospitals, International Relations • *Religion:* Churches, Religious Welfare • *Social Services:* Animal Protection, Big Brother/Big Sister, Child Welfare, Community Service Organizations, Family Services, Food/Clothing Distribution, Homes, People with Disabilities, Scouts, Senior Services, Shelters/Homelessness, Substance Abuse, United Funds/United Ways, Volunteer Services, YMCA/YWCA/YMHA/YWHA, Youth Organizations

Grant Types: general support, project, and research

Geographic Distribution: focus on MI

GIVING OFFICERS

Mary Alice J. Heaton: trust

Donald E. Johnson, Jr.: pres, trust *CORP AFFIL* pres: Advertisers Press

Marsha A. Kump: exec dir

Linda J. LeMieux: trust

John T. Lindholm: secy, treas, trust

APPLICATION INFORMATION

Initial Approach: Send a brief letter of inquiry. Include a description of organization, amount requested, purpose of funds sought, recently audited financial statement, and proof of tax-exempt status. Deadline is April 30.

Restrictions on Giving: Limited to the greater Flint metropolitan area.

GRANTS ANALYSIS

Total Grants: $900,274

Number of Grants: 55

Highest Grant: $321,874

Typical Range: $500 to $110,000

Disclosure Period: fiscal year ending June 30, 1994

Note: Recent grants are derived from a fiscal 1994 Form 990.

RECENT GRANTS

General

35,000	Flint Institute of Music, Flint, MI
25,000	Endicott College, Beverly, MA — Tupper Hall restoration
22,000	St. Paul's Episcopal Church, Flint, MI — capital improvements
15,000	Genesee County Free Medical Clinic, Flint, MI
15,000	Genesee County Humane Society, Flint, MI — capital campaign

Whitney Fund, David M.

CONTACT

Peter P. Thurber
President and Treasurer
David M. Whitney Fund
150 W Jefferson, Ste. 2500
Detroit, MI 48226
(313) 963-6420

FINANCIAL SUMMARY

Recent Giving: $466,200 (1993); $415,020 (1992); $299,200 (1991)

Assets: $26,142,413 (1994); $25,905,500 (1993); $24,593,642 (1992)

Gifts Received: $3,433,351 (1989); $80,532 (1988)

EIN: 38-6040080

CONTRIBUTIONS SUMMARY

Donor(s): The fund was established in 1949.

Typical Recipients: • *Arts & Humanities:* Arts Associations & Councils, Arts Centers, Arts Funds, Arts Institutes, Community Arts, Film & Video, Libraries, Music, Opera, Public Broadcasting • *Civic & Public Affairs:* Clubs, Community Foundations, Municipalities/Towns, Philanthropic Organizations, Zoos/Aquariums • *Education:* Colleges & Universities, Minority Education, Private Education (Precollege), Religious Education, Secondary Education (Private) • *Environment:* General • *Health:* Children's Health/Hospitals, Emergency/Ambulance Services, Hospitals, Single-Disease Health Associations • *International:* Missionary/Religious Activities • *Religion:* Religious Organizations, Religious Welfare • *Science:* Scientific Centers & Institutes, Scientific Organizations • *Social Services:* Child Welfare, Community Centers, Community Service Organizations, Family Planning, Food/Clothing Distribution, Homes, Recreation & Athletics, Scouts, Shelters/Homelessness, United Funds/United Ways, Youth Organizations

Grant Types: general support

Geographic Distribution: focus on southeastern Michigan

GIVING OFFICERS

Richard Bordley Gushee: trust, vp *B* Detroit MI 1926 *ED* Williams Coll BA 1947; Univ MI JD 1951 *CURR EMPL* ptnr: Miller Canfield Paddock & Stone *CORP AFFIL* bd dir: First MI Capital Corp, Motor City Electric Co *NONPR AFFIL* mem: Am Bar Assn, Corp & Securities Bur Securities Adv Comm, Detroit Bar Assn

George Edward Parker III: trust, vp, secy *B* Detroit MI 1934 *ED* Princeton Univ AB 1956; Univ MI JD 1959 *CURR EMPL* ptnr: Miller Canfield Paddock & Stone *NONPR AFFIL* trust: Hannan House

Peter Palms Thurber: pres, treas, trust *B* Detroit MI 1928 *ED* Williams Coll BA 1950; Harvard Univ Sch Law JD 1953 *CURR EMPL* atty: Miller Canfield Paddock & Stone *CORP AFFIL* dir: Detroit Legal News *NONPR AFFIL* dir: Detroit Symphony Orchestra; fellow: Am Bar Fdn; mem: Am Bar Assn, MI Bar Assn; trust: Commun Fdn Southeastern MI, Counc MI Fdns *CLUB AFFIL* mem: CC Detroit

APPLICATION INFORMATION
Initial Approach:

The fund requests applications be made in writing.

Written proposals should briefly state the specific purpose of the request and a complete explanation of the necessity. A copy of the organization's tax exemption and foundation status letter from the IRS should also be included.

The fund has no deadline for submitting proposals.

Restrictions on Giving: The fund makes grants only to tax-exempt organizations. The fund does not make grants to individuals.

GRANTS ANALYSIS
Total Grants: $466,200

Number of Grants: 40

Highest Grant: $60,000

Average Grant: $11,655

Typical Range: $1,000 to $15,000

Disclosure Period: 1993

Note: Recent grants are derived from a 1993 Form 990.

RECENT GRANTS

Library
2,500	Friends of the Detroit Public Library, Detroit, MI

General
50,000	Community Foundation for Southeastern Michigan, Detroit, MI
40,000	University Liggett School, Grosse Pointe Woods, MI
35,000	Crossroads, Detroit, MI
25,000	Cottage Hospital of Grosse Pointe, Grosse Pointe Farms, MI
20,000	Marygrove College, Detroit, MI

Wickes Foundation, Harvey Randall

CONTACT
James V. Finkbeiner
President
Harvey Randall Wickes Foundation
4800 Fashion Sq. Blvd.
Plaza North, Rm. 472
Saginaw, MI 48604
(517) 799-1850

FINANCIAL SUMMARY
Recent Giving: $1,300,000 (1995 est.); $1,283,546 (1994); $1,282,293 (1993)

Assets: $27,000,000 (1995 est.); $27,000,000 (1994); $28,349,158 (1993)

Gifts Received: $600 (1992)

Fiscal Note: In 1992, the foundation received $600 from an anonymous donor.

EIN: 38-6061470

CONTRIBUTIONS SUMMARY
Donor(s): The foundation was established in 1945 in Michigan with donations primarily from Harvey Randall Wickes. Mr. Wickes was president and later chairman of Wickes Corporation, which has diversified interests including the merchandising of building supplies.

Typical Recipients: • *Arts & Humanities:* Historic Preservation, History & Archaeology, Libraries, Museums/Galleries, Music • *Civic & Public Affairs:* Botanical Gardens/Parks, Business/Free Enterprise, Community Foundations, Economic Development, Employment/Job Training, Housing, Safety, Urban & Community Affairs, Zoos/Aquariums • *Education:* Business Education, Colleges & Universities, Education Funds, Minority Education, Public Education (Precollege), Student Aid • *Health:* Clinics/Medical Centers, Health Funds, Health Organizations, Hospitals, Medical Rehabilitation • *Religion:* Religious Welfare • *Social Services:* Child Welfare, Food/Clothing Distribution, Homes, People with Disabilities, Recreation & Athletics, Senior Services, Shelters/Homelessness, Substance Abuse, United Funds/United Ways, Volunteer Services, Youth Organizations

Grant Types: capital and scholarship

Geographic Distribution: Saginaw County, MI

GIVING OFFICERS
Hugo E. Braun, Jr.: vp, secy, trust *B* Saginaw MI 1932 *ED* Yale Univ BA 1954; Univ MI LLB 1957 *CURR EMPL* atty: Braun Kendrick Finkbeiner Schafer & Murphy *CORP AFFIL* dir: Wolohan Lumber Co

James V. Finkbeiner: pres, trust *B* Green Bay WI 1914 *ED* Univ MI BA 1935; Univ MI JD 1937 *CURR EMPL* atty: Braun Kendrick Finkbeiner Schafer Murphy

William A. Hendrick: trust

Richard P. Heuschele, MD: trust

Craig W. Horn: trust

Frank M. Johnson: trust

William W. Kessel: trust

Lee Knutson: trust

William F. Nelson, Jr.: trust

Michele D. Pavlicek: asst secy

David F. Wallace: trust *B* 1923 *ED* MI St Univ BSME 1949; MI St Univ MBA 1960 *CURR EMPL* chmn bd, dir: Wolohan Lumber Co *PHIL AFFIL* trust: Egenton Home

Lloyd J. Yeo: treas, trust *PHIL AFFIL* treas: Charles F. and Adeline L. Barth Charitable Foundation; pres, treas, trust: Wickson-Link Memorial Foundation

Melvin J. Zahnow: chmn, trust

APPLICATION INFORMATION
Initial Approach:

Applications should be in letter form.

Letters should include specific details as to the proposed use of funds. The foundation will request additional information if necessary.

Information should be submitted three weeks prior to the first of January, April, June, and October.

The board of trustees meets in January, April, June, and October.

Restrictions on Giving: The foundation does not make grants to individuals or churches.

GRANTS ANALYSIS
Total Grants: $1,282,293

Number of Grants: 35

Highest Grant: $233,334

Average Grant: $36,637

Typical Range: $5,000 to $100,000

Disclosure Period: 1993

Note: Recent grants are derived from a 1993 Form 990.

RECENT GRANTS

General
233,334	Saginaw Valley State University Foundation, University Center, MI — conference center
125,000	Saginaw Business Incubator, Saginaw, MI — startup funds
102,000	Saginaw Community Foundation, Saginaw, MI
100,000	City Rescue Mission of Saginaw, Saginaw, MI — renovations at Community Village
75,000	Health Council Foundation, Saginaw, MI — operations

Wickson-Link Memorial Foundation

CONTACT
Lloyd J. Yeo
President
Wickson-Link Memorial Fdn.
PO Box 3275
3023 Davenport St.
Saginaw, MI 48605
(517) 793-9830

FINANCIAL SUMMARY
Recent Giving: $158,735 (1993); $177,598 (1992); $160,045 (1991)

Assets: $3,993,121 (1993); $3,096,400 (1992); $3,870,251 (1991)

EIN: 38-6083931

CONTRIBUTIONS SUMMARY
Donor(s): the late James Wickson, the late Meta Wickson

Typical Recipients: • *Arts & Humanities:* Arts Associations & Councils, Historic Preservation, History & Archaeology, Libraries, Museums/Galleries, Music • *Civic & Public Affairs:* Community Foundations, Employment/Job Training, General, Housing, Municipalities/Towns, Urban & Community Affairs, Zoos/Aquariums • *Education:* Business Education, Colleges & Universities, Public Education (Precollege), Secondary Education (Public) • *Health:* Emergency/Ambulance Services, Geriatric Health, Hospitals, Nursing Services • *Religion:* Churches, Religious Welfare • *Social Services:* At-Risk Youth, Big Brother/Big Sister, Child Abuse, Child Welfare, Community Service Organizations, Domestic Violence, Family Services, People with Disabilities, Recreation & Athletics, Shelters/Homelessness, Special Olympics, United Funds/United Ways, Volunteer Services, Youth Organizations

Grant Types: general support

Geographic Distribution: focus on Saginaw County, MI

GIVING OFFICERS
B. J. Humphreys: vp, secy

C. Ward Lauderbach: dir

Lloyd J. Yeo: pres, treas, trust *PHIL AFFIL* treas: Charles F. and Adeline L. Barth Charitable Foundation; treas, trust: Harvey Randall Wickes Foundation

APPLICATION INFORMATION
Initial Approach: Send cover letter and full proposal. Include a description of organization, amount requested, purpose of funds sought, recently audited financial statement, and proof of tax-exempt status. There are no deadlines.

GRANTS ANALYSIS
Total Grants: $158,735

Number of Grants: 40

Highest Grant: $14,000

Typical Range: $300 to $10,000

Disclosure Period: 1993

Note: Recent grants are derived from a 1993 Form 990.

RECENT GRANTS
Library

4,500	Saginaw Public Libraries, Saginaw, MI	
2,500	City of Frankenmuth Wickson Memorial Library, Frankenmuth, MI	

General

14,000	Saginaw Valley State University Foundation, Saginaw, MI	
10,000	Hospital Council Foundation, Saginaw, MI	
10,000	Saginaw Valley Zoological Society, Saginaw, MI	
10,000	Visiting Nurse Association, Saginaw, MI	
8,400	Boys and Girls Club of Saginaw, Saginaw, MI	

Wilson Fund, Matilda R.

CONTACT
Pierre V. Heftler
President
Matilda R. Wilson Foundation
100 Renaissance Ctr., Ste. 3400
Detroit, MI 48243
(313) 259-7777

FINANCIAL SUMMARY
Recent Giving: $2,069,780 (1993); $1,560,901 (1991); $1,345,622 (1990)

Assets: $39,641,872 (1993); $39,076,819 (1991); $32,598,493 (1990)

Gifts Received: $204,127 (1985)

EIN: 38-6087665

CONTRIBUTIONS SUMMARY
Donor(s): The foundation was incorporated in 1944 in Michigan. The donors were the late Matilda R. Wilson and Alfred G. Wilson.

Typical Recipients: • *Arts & Humanities:* Arts Associations & Councils, Arts Centers, Arts Institutes, History & Archaeology, Libraries, Museums/Galleries, Music, Opera, Performing Arts, Public Broadcasting, Theater • *Civic & Public Affairs:* Chambers of Commerce, Economic Policy, General, Law & Justice, Legal Aid, Philanthropic Organizations, Professional & Trade Associations, Public Policy, Urban & Community Affairs, Zoos/Aquariums • *Education:* Arts/Humanities Education, Colleges & Universities, Education Associations, Elementary Education (Private), General, Minority Education, Private Education (Precollege), Science/Mathematics Education • *Environment:* General • *Health:* Children's Health/Hospitals, Emergency/Ambulance Services, Eyes/Blindness, Hospitals • *International:* Foreign Arts Organizations • *Religion:* Churches, Religious Organizations, Religious Welfare • *Science:* Scientific Centers & Institutes • *Social Services:* At-Risk Youth, Child Welfare, Food/Clothing Distribution, People with Disabilities, Scouts, Volunteer Services, Youth Organizations

Grant Types: capital and operating expenses

Geographic Distribution: national, with emphasis on Michigan

GIVING OFFICERS
Pierre V. Heftler: pres, trust *B* Paris France 1910 *ED* Dartmouth Coll AB 1930; Univ MI BS 1931; Univ MI JD 1934 *CURR EMPL* ptnr: Bodman & Longley *PHIL AFFIL* secy, trust, mem: Eleanor and Edsel Ford Fund; secy, trust: Henry Ford II Fund; secy, trust, mem: Walter and Josephine Ford Fund; secy, trust: Benson and Edith Ford Fund; secy, trust, mem: William and Martha Ford Fund

George Miller: trust

Robert McCellan Surdam: treas, trust *B* Albany NY 1917 *ED* Williams Coll BA 1939 *CLUB AFFIL* CC Detroit, Detroit, Grosse Pointe Hunt, Hobe Sound YC, Jupiter Island, Little Harbor, Rolling Rock, Yondotega *PHIL AFFIL* treas, trust: McGregor Fund; trust: Elizabeth, Allan and Warren Shelden Fund

APPLICATION INFORMATION
Initial Approach:

Prospective applicants should submit a letter explaining the need and use of requested funds.

The foundation reports no application deadlines.

The board meets quarterly to consider proposals, usually in January, April, July, and October.

Restrictions on Giving: The foundation does not make loans or grants to individuals.

GRANTS ANALYSIS
Total Grants: $2,069,780

Number of Grants: 60

Highest Grant: $125,000

Average Grant: $34,496

Typical Range: $4,000 to $50,000

Disclosure Period: 1993

Note: Recent grants are derived from a 1993 Form 990.

RECENT GRANTS
General

125,000	Greater Detroit Chambers Foundation, Detroit, MI — capital	
100,000	American Red Cross, Southeastern Michigan Endowment, Detroit, MI — endowment	
100,000	Children's Hospital of Detroit Hematology/Oncology Department, Detroit, MI — capital	
100,000	Walsh College, Troy, MI — capital	
95,700	Oakland University, Rochester, MI — capital	

MINNESOTA

Allianz Life Insurance Co. of North America

Employees: 430
Parent Company: Allianz of America, Inc.
Headquarters: Minneapolis, MN
SIC Major Group: Insurance Carriers

CONTACT
Alan Grove
Vice President, Law & Secretary
Allianz Life Insurance Co. of North America
1750 Hennepin Ave.
Minneapolis, MN 55403
(612) 347-6500

FINANCIAL SUMMARY
Recent Giving: $230,000 (1994)

CONTRIBUTIONS SUMMARY
Company gives mainly in the greater Minneapolis area. Supports arts and humanities (galleries and music) and civic organizations (housing, economic development, and urban affairs). Company supports colleges and universities and sponsors an employee matching gifts program to higher education institutions. Also supports health organizations and the United Way.

Volunteerism: Contributions are made to organizations at which employees volunteer. Applications are submitted and reviewed for approval by a committee consisting of Allianz Life employees.

Typical Recipients: • *Arts & Humanities:* Libraries, Museums/Galleries, Music • *Civic & Public Affairs:* Economic Development, Housing, Urban & Community Affairs • *Education:* Colleges & Universities, Economic Education, Education Funds • *Health:* Health Organizations, Heart, Hospitals • *Religion:* Churches, Religious Organizations • *Social Services:* People with Disabilities, Scouts, United Funds/United Ways, YMCA/YWCA/YMHA/YWHA, Youth Organizations

Grant Types: capital, general support, and matching

Nonmonetary Support Types: loaned employees and workplace solicitation

Geographic Distribution: near headquarters only

Operating Locations: MN (Minneapolis)

CORP. OFFICERS
Lowell C. Anderson: *B* Minneapolis MN 1937 *ED* Macalester Coll 1963 *CURR EMPL* chmn, pres, ceo: Allianz Life Ins Co N Am *CORP AFFIL* ceo, dir: Preferred Life Ins Co NY; dir: NALAC Fin Plans

GIVING OFFICERS
Alan A. Grove: *CURR EMPL* vp, corp legal off & secy: Allianz Life Ins Co N Am

APPLICATION INFORMATION
Initial Approach: Send a brief letter of inquiry and a full proposal. Include a description of the organization, amount requested, and purpose for which funds are sought. It is best to apply by the end of the third quarter, as the review board meets in the fall.

Restrictions on Giving: Company does not support individuals, political or lobbying groups, or religious organizations for sectarian purposes.

OTHER THINGS TO KNOW
According to Allianz of America, Inc., each local office administers independent contributions programs, with Allianz Life's being the largest. Local offices decide on recipients and support levels, with nonmonetary support such as loaned employees included in programs.

GRANTS ANALYSIS
Typical Range: $1,000 to $2,500
Note: Recent grants are derived from a grants list provided by company in 1995.

RECENT GRANTS

Library
Augsburg College Library Fund, Minneapolis, MN

General
Basillilca, Minneapolis, MN
Boy Scouts of America, Minneapolis, MN
Minneapolis Heart Institute, Minneapolis, MN
Minneapolis/St Paul Housing Fund, Minneapolis, MN
Minnesota Private College Fund, Minneapolis, MN

Andersen Corp. / Bayport Foundation

Sales: $963.0 million
Employees: 3,950
Headquarters: Bayport, MN
SIC Major Group: Millwork

CONTACT
Keith D. Olson
Secretary & Treasurer
Bayport Foundation
100 Fourth Ave. N
Bayport, MN 55003-1096
(612) 430-7395

FINANCIAL SUMMARY
Recent Giving: $1,312,057 (fiscal 1992); $813,700 (fiscal 1991); $721,778 (fiscal 1989)
Assets: $28,265,935 (fiscal 1992); $26,080,319 (fiscal 1991); $21,769,887 (fiscal 1989)
Gifts Received: $1,000,000 (fiscal 1992)
Fiscal Note: All contributions are made through the foundation.
EIN: 41-6020912

CONTRIBUTIONS SUMMARY
Typical Recipients: • *Arts & Humanities:* Arts Centers, Arts Institutes, Historic Preservation, Libraries, Museums/Galleries, Music, Public Broadcasting, Theater • *Civic & Public Affairs:* Business/Free Enterprise, Civil Rights, Legal Aid, Municipalities/Towns, Public Policy, Safety, Urban & Community Affairs, Zoos/Aquariums • *Education:* Arts/Humanities Education, Colleges & Universities, Economic Education, Education Associations, Education Funds, Elementary Education (Private), Engineering/Technological Education, General, Minority Education, Preschool Education, Private Education (Precollege), Public Education (Precollege), Religious Education, Science/Mathematics Education, Special Education, Student Aid • *Environment:* General • *Health:* Clinics/Medical Centers, Emergency/Ambulance Services, Health Organizations, Hospitals, Kidney, Medical Research, Single-Disease Health Associations • *Religion:* Churches, Religious Organizations, Religious Welfare • *Science:* Science Museums • *Social Services:* Animal Protection, Camps, Child Welfare, Community Service Organizations, Emergency Relief, Family Planning, Family Services, Food/Clothing Distribution, Homes, People with Disabilities, Recreation & Athletics, Refugee Assistance, Substance Abuse, United Funds/United Ways, Volunteer Services, Youth Organizations

Grant Types: fellowship, general support, and project

Geographic Distribution: predominantly in Minnesota, especially the Twin Cities area; also in St. Croix, WI, area, and to national organizations

Operating Locations: MN (Bayport), WI (St. Croix)

CORP. OFFICERS
Albert Dewayne Hulings: *B* 1913 *ED* Carleton Coll 1936 *CURR EMPL* hon chmn: Andersen Corp *PHIL AFFIL* vp, dir: Mahadh Foundation

Jerold W. Wulf: *B* St Croix Falls WI 1930 *ED* Univ MN 1954 *CURR EMPL* pres, dir: Andersen Corp *CORP AFFIL* dir: Firstar Corp MN

GIVING OFFICERS
Georgia Aleppo: trust *PHIL AFFIL* trust: Aurora Foundation

Katherine B. Andersen: trust

Albert Dewayne Hulings: vp *CURR EMPL* hon chmn: Andersen Corp *PHIL AFFIL* vp, dir: Mahadh Foundation (see above)

Mary A. Hulings: vp *CORP AFFIL* dir: Andersen Corp

Harold C. Meissner: vp *B* 1917

Keith D. Olson: secy, treas

Earl C. Swanson: trust *PHIL AFFIL* dir: Andersen Foundation; trust: Tozer Foundation; dir: Katzenberger Foundation

APPLICATION INFORMATION
Initial Approach: *Initial Contact:* brief letter or proposal *Include Information On:* description of the organization, amount requested, purpose for which funds are sought, recently audited financial statement, and proof of tax-exempt status *Deadlines:* none

GRANTS ANALYSIS
Total Grants: $1,312,057

Number of Grants: 129

Highest Grant: $155,500

Average Grant: $10,171

Typical Range: 1,000 to $15,000

Disclosure Period: fiscal year ending November 30, 1992

Note: Recent grants are derived from a fiscal 1992 Form 990.

RECENT GRANTS

General

155,500	American Red Cross
150,000	Lakeview Memorial Hospital, Stillwater, MN — Kidney Dialysis Program
100,000	Lakeview Memorial Hospital, Stillwater, MN
100,000	National Right to Work Legal Defense Foundation, Springfield, VA
100,000	St. Croix Area United Way, Stillwater, MN

Andersen Foundation

CONTACT

Mary Gillstrom
Assistant Secretary
Andersen Corporation
100 Fourth Ave., N
Bayport, MN 55003
(612) 439-5150

FINANCIAL SUMMARY

Recent Giving: $10,822,450 (1993); $13,739,075 (1991); $11,052,982 (1990)

Assets: $308,682,728 (1993); $242,763,690 (1991); $209,995,194 (1990)

Gifts Received: $550,000 (1985)

EIN: 41-6020920

CONTRIBUTIONS SUMMARY

Donor(s): The Andersen Foundation was incorporated in Minnesota in 1959 by the late Fred C. Andersen . Mr. Andersen served as a director and former president of Andersen Corporation, a producer of wood and vinyl-clad windows and door units. His wife, Katherine B. Andersen, has made several contributions to the foundation.

Typical Recipients: • *Arts & Humanities:* Arts Centers, Arts Funds, Arts Institutes, Historic Preservation, Libraries, Music, Opera, Performing Arts, Public Broadcasting, Theater • *Civic & Public Affairs:* Municipalities/Towns, Public Policy, Urban & Community Affairs, Zoos/Aquariums • *Education:* Colleges & Universities, Community & Junior Colleges, Education Funds, Elementary Education (Private), General, Minority Education, Private Education (Precollege), Public Education (Precollege), Religious Education, Secondary Education (Public), Special Education • *Environment:* Air/Water Quality • *Health:* Cancer, Children's Health/Hospitals, Clinics/Medical Centers, Emergency/Ambulance Services, Health Organizations, Heart, Hospices, Hospitals, Kidney, Medical Research, Mental Health,

Research/Studies Institutes, Single-Disease Health Associations • *Religion:* Churches, Religious Organizations, Religious Welfare, Seminaries • *Science:* Science Museums • *Social Services:* Animal Protection, Child Welfare, Community Centers, Community Service Organizations, Domestic Violence, Family Services, General, Homes, People with Disabilities, Scouts, Senior Services, Substance Abuse, United Funds/United Ways, Volunteer Services, YMCA/YWCA/YMHA/YWHA, Youth Organizations

Grant Types: general support

Geographic Distribution: emphasis on Minnesota, with some national giving

GIVING OFFICERS

Katherine B. Andersen: don

Keith R. Clements: pres, dir

Mary Gillstrom: asst secy

Leonard W. Kedrowski: asst treas, dir *CURR EMPL* asst treas, contr: Andersen Corp

Earl C. Swanson: dir *PHIL AFFIL* trust: Bayport Foundation, Tozer Foundation; dir: Katzenberger Foundation

APPLICATION INFORMATION

Initial Approach:

The foundation has no formal application requirements or procedures. Prospective applicants should send a letter to the foundation.

The letter should describe the organization and the project for which funds are sought.

Restrictions on Giving: Grants are not given to colleges that receive federal aid.

GRANTS ANALYSIS

Total Grants: $13,739,075

Number of Grants: 107

Highest Grant: $2,400,000

Average Grant: $128,403

Typical Range: $5,000 to $200,000

Disclosure Period: 1991

Note: Recent grants are derived from a 1991 Form 990.

RECENT GRANTS

Library

48,000	Bayport Public Library, Bayport, MN

General

2,400,000	Lakeview Memorial Hospital, Stillwater, MN
1,115,000	Boy Scouts of America, St. Paul, MN — Indianhead Council
500,000	Hazelden Foundation, Center City, MN
225,000	Alice Lloyd College, Pippa Passes, KY
225,000	Asbury College, Wilmore, KY

Bell Foundation, James F.

CONTACT

Diane B. Neimann
Executive Director
James F. Bell Fdn.
601 Lakeshore Pkwy., Ste. 350
Minnetonka, MN 55305-5211
(612) 540-4312

FINANCIAL SUMMARY

Recent Giving: $836,098 (1993)

Assets: $15,259,101 (1993)

EIN: 41-6023099

CONTRIBUTIONS SUMMARY

Typical Recipients: • *Arts & Humanities:* Arts Institutes, Dance, History & Archaeology, Libraries, Museums/Galleries, Music, Opera, Performing Arts, Public Broadcasting, Theater • *Civic & Public Affairs:* Botanical Gardens/Parks, Employment/Job Training, General, Housing, Urban & Community Affairs, Women's Affairs • *Education:* Arts/Humanities Education, Colleges & Universities, Legal Education, Private Education (Precollege), Student Aid • *Environment:* General, Resource Conservation, Wildlife Protection • *International:* International Environmental Issues • *Religion:* Churches • *Science:* Scientific Research • *Social Services:* Big Brother/Big Sister, Community Service Organizations, Scouts

Grant Types: general support

Geographic Distribution: focus on MN

GIVING OFFICERS

Ford W. Bell: trust

Samuel H. Bell, Jr.: trust *B* Rochester NY 1925 *ED* Coll Wooster BA 1947; Univ Akron JD 1952 *NONPR AFFIL* fellow, trust: Akron Bar Fdn; mem: Akron Univ Sch Law Alumni Assn, Am Bar Assn, Fed Bar Assn, Fed Judges Assn, OH Bar Assn

David B. Hartwell: trust

Diane B. Neimann: exec dir

APPLICATION INFORMATION

Initial Approach: Send a brief letter of inquiry. Include a description of organization, amount requested, purpose of funds sought, recently audited financial statement, and proof of tax-exempt status.

GRANTS ANALYSIS

Total Grants: $836,098

Number of Grants: 83

Highest Grant: $50,000

Typical Range: $100 to $50,000

Disclosure Period: 1993

Note: Recent grants are derived from a 1993 Form 990.

RECENT GRANTS

Library

5,000	University of Minnesota, Minneapolis, MN — for James Ford Bell Library

General

50,000	Belwin Foundation, Minnetonka, MN — purchase real estate
33,500	University of Minnesota Foundation James Ford Bell Museum of Natural History, Minneapolis, MN — for staffing and scholarships
30,000	Greater Minneapolis Girl Scout Council (Capital Grant), Minneapolis, MN
30,000	Jason Foundation, Weltham, MA
30,000	Minneapolis College of Art and Design, Minneapolis, MN — for general operating expenses

Bemis Company, Inc. / Bemis Company Foundation

Sales: $1.2 billion
Employees: 7,950
Headquarters: Minneapolis, MN
SIC Major Group: Bags—Uncoated Paper & Multiwall, Bags—Plastics, Laminated & Coated, Platemaking Services, and Plastics Materials & Resins

CONTACT
Lawrence E. Schwanke
Trustee
Bemis Company Fdn.
222 S 9th St.
Ste. 2300
Minneapolis, MN 55402-4099
(612) 376-3000

FINANCIAL SUMMARY
Recent Giving: $1,350,000 (1995 est.); $1,317,487 (1994 approx.); $1,328,823 (1993)

Assets: $1,500,000 (1995 est.); $1,484,544 (1994 approx.); $1,457,209 (1993)

Fiscal Note: Company gives almost exclusively through the foundation.

EIN: 41-6038616

CONTRIBUTIONS SUMMARY
Typical Recipients: • *Arts & Humanities:* Arts Appreciation, Arts Associations & Councils, Arts Centers, Libraries, Museums/Galleries, Music, Opera, Performing Arts, Theater, Visual Arts • *Civic & Public Affairs:* Business/Free Enterprise, Economic Development, Employment/Job Training, Public Policy, Safety, Urban & Community Affairs, Women's Affairs, Zoos/Aquariums • *Education:* Colleges & Universities, Education Funds, Health & Physical Education, Legal Education, Medical Education, Minority Education, Private Education (Precollege), Public Education (Precollege), Religious Education, Student Aid • *Environment:* General • *Health:* Emergency/Ambulance Services, Health Policy/Cost Containment, Health Funds, Hospitals, Single-Disease Health Associations • *Social*

Services: Child Welfare, Community Service Organizations, Counseling, Family Planning, Family Services, Food/Clothing Distribution, Homes, People with Disabilities, Recreation & Athletics, Senior Services, Shelters/Homelessness, Substance Abuse, United Funds/United Ways, Youth Organizations

Grant Types: capital, employee matching gifts, general support, and matching

Note: Employee matching gift ratio: 2 to 1 for education and Food Shelves.

Geographic Distribution: in areas where company has facilities, with emphasis on Minneapolis, MN

Operating Locations: AR (Crossett), CA (Union City), IL (Chicago, Murphysboro, Peoria), IN (Terre Haute), KS (Wichita), KY (Florence, Henderson), MA (Pepperell), MN (Hopkins, Mankato, Minneapolis, Minnetonka), MO (St. Louis), NE (Omaha), NJ (Flemington), NV (Nellis), OH (Fremont, Sandusky, Stow), PA (Hazelton, Scranton, West Hazelton), SC (Duncan), SD (Duncan), TN (Memphis), WA (Seattle, Vancouver), WI (Green Bay, Lancaster, Milwaukee, New London, Oshkosh, Sheboygan)

CORP. OFFICERS
John H. Roe: *B* St. Paul MN 1939 *ED* Williams Coll BA 1962; Harvard Univ MBA 1964 *CURR EMPL* pres, ceo, dir: Bemis Co Inc *CORP AFFIL* dir: First Trust Co

GIVING OFFICERS
LeRoy Francis Bazany: trust *B* Chicago IL 1932 *ED* Univ Notre Dame BS 1954 *CURR EMPL* vp, contr: Bemis Co Inc *NONPR AFFIL* fin adv: Project Pride Living; mem: Fin Execs Inst *CLUB AFFIL* KC, Minneapolis

Audrey Kirchner: secy

Lawrence E. Schwanke: trust *CURR EMPL* vp human resources: Bemis Co Inc

APPLICATION INFORMATION
Initial Approach: *Initial Contact:* brief letter or proposal *Include Information On:* description of the organization; amount requested; purpose for which funds are sought; budget including existing and possible sources of income; officers and board members; details on how objectives will be attained; and proof of tax-exempt status *Deadlines:* none

Restrictions on Giving: Grants do not support individuals, organizations for religious or political purposes, or lobbying efforts or campaigns. Company prefers not to give to educational capital funds, endowments, or trips or tours.

Grants will not exceed 5% of total requirements of any organization or campaign.

No grants for more than three years. No more than 10% of foundation budget is committed to multiyear grants. No more than 20% of annual expenditures is for capital projects.

OTHER THINGS TO KNOW
The basis for charitable contributions is 2% of company's domestic pretax profits.

GRANTS ANALYSIS
Total Grants: $1,328,823*
Number of Grants: 220*
Highest Grant: $158,226
Average Grant: $6,040*
Typical Range: $1,000 to $5,000
Disclosure Period: 1993

Note: The total grants, number of grants, and highest grant figures include matching gifts. Recent grants are derived from a 1993 Form 990.

RECENT GRANTS
General

158,226	United Way — social, welfare, and health
66,355	National Merit Scholarship Corporation, Evanston, IL — educational
63,950	Citizen's Scholarship Foundation of America, St. Peter, MN — educational
60,000	Science Museum of Minnesota, St. Paul, MN — educational
50,000	American Red Cross National Headquarters, Washington, DC — social, welfare, and health

Bigelow Foundation, F. R.

CONTACT
Paul A. Verret
Secretary and Treasurer
F. R. Bigelow Foundation
600 Norwest Ctr.
St. Paul, MN 55101
(612) 224-5463

FINANCIAL SUMMARY
Recent Giving: $3,807,194 (1992 approx.); $3,308,724 (1991); $2,809,945 (1990)

Assets: $81,419,643 (1991); $68,973,345 (1990); $67,877,829 (1989)

Gifts Received: $100 (1987); $85,700 (1985)

EIN: 51-0232651

CONTRIBUTIONS SUMMARY
Donor(s): The F. R. Bigelow Foundation was established in 1934. The late Frederic Russell Bigelow , the foundation's donor, served for many years as president and chairman of the board of directors of the St. Paul Fire and Marine Insurance Company, a subsidiary of the St. Paul Companies.

Typical Recipients: • *Arts & Humanities:* Libraries, Museums/Galleries, Music, Performing Arts, Public Broadcasting, Theater • *Civic & Public Affairs:* Employment/Job Training, Housing, Legal Aid, Municipalities/Towns, Nonprofit Management • *Education:* Colleges & Universities, Education Associations, Education Funds, Literacy, Minority Education • *Environment:* General • *Health:* Single-Disease Health Associations • *Social Services:* Child Welfare, Community Service Organizations, Homes, Senior Services, United Funds/United Ways

Grant Types: capital, operating expenses, project, and seed money

Geographic Distribution: primarily metropolitan St. Paul, MN

GIVING OFFICERS

Robert L. Bullard: trust *PHIL AFFIL* trust: Minnesota Foundation, Blandin Foundation; treas: H. William Lurton Foundation

Iris H. Cornelius: trust

Carl Bigelow Drake, Jr.: chmn, trust *B* St Paul MN 1919 *CURR EMPL* dir: St Paul Cos

Eugene U. Frey: trust

John N. Jackson: trust

Malcolm W. McDonald: trust *PHIL AFFIL* treas, dir: Grotto Foundation; secy, treas, trust: McNeely Foundation; trust: Lee and Rose Warner Foundation

Rev. Mary Bigelow McMillan: trust *B* 1919 *ED* Vassar Coll BA 1941; United Theol Sem MDiv 1978 *NONPR AFFIL* bd dir, trust: Inst Ecumenical Cultural Res; mem: St Paul Health Welfare Planning Comm; trust: MN Charitable Fdn, Wilder Fdn *CLUB AFFIL* mem: New Century

Edward G. Pendergast: trust

Kathleen C. Ridder: trust

Wendy H. Rubin: trust

Jon A. Theobald: trust *B* St Paul MN 1945 *ED* St Johns Univ 1967; St Johns Univ 1970 *CURR EMPL* sr vp: First Trust Co *CORP AFFIL* sr vp trust div: Am Natl Bank & Trust Co *PHIL AFFIL* dir: Tozer Foundation

Paul A. Verret: secy, treas *B* 1941 *PHIL AFFIL* exec dir, secy: Mardag Foundation; secy: Minnesota Foundation

APPLICATION INFORMATION
Initial Approach:

The applicant may submit a preliminary proposal to ascertain whether the project falls within foundation guidelines. Full proposals may be submitted without preliminary reports.

Preliminary summary proposals must address the questions in the application concisely in no more than three or four pages.

Full proposals must include the applicant's name and address; description of the organization's general purpose and objectives; indication of the scope of its operations; copy of the IRS determination letter of tax-exempt status; amount requested; statement of project purpose and objectives; significance of project to society; and an estimate of the number of Minnesota citizens that will benefit from the project. Applicants should also include a project evaluation plan; the applicant's relationship to the organization; detailed budget; indication of other sources of support; statement of need; verification that donated funds will be used solely for the purposes requested and that the applicant will submit progress reports to the foundation; proposed length of time for support (including schedule of support commencement and termination); names and affiliations of board members; qualifications of principal

staff members for project implementation; staff availability throughout duration of the project and replaceability should they not be available; recent balance sheet and audited income sheet; acknowledgement that payment of funds will be at the convenience of the foundation and that modifications of original payment agreements may occur; and indication that application has been received and endorsed by the governing body of applicant organization. If possible, a formal board resolution confirming this should be included. Two copies of the proposal must be submitted.

The board of trustees meets three times a year usually in April, August, and November. Proposals may be submitted any time. Applicants must allow time for ample review prior to formal trustee consideration.

The foundation encourages interviews with applicants when possible. Grant decisions are relayed three to six months after applications are received.

Restrictions on Giving: Grants are not made to individuals.

PUBLICATIONS
Annual report, list of application requirements

GRANTS ANALYSIS
Total Grants: $3,308,724

Number of Grants: 124

Highest Grant: $250,000

Average Grant: $26,683*

Typical Range: $5,000 to $50,000

Disclosure Period: 1991

Note: Average grant for new commitments is $28,447. Recent grants are derived from a 1991 annual report.

RECENT GRANTS

Library
25,000 Friends of the St. Paul Public Library, St. Paul, MN — campaign for the library

General
202,700 United Way of the St. Paul Area, St. Paul, MN — 1990 annual campaign
175,000 Mounds Park Academy, Maplewood, MN — capital campaign
160,000 United Way of the St. Paul Area, St. Paul, MN — Challenge Match Program
146,315 F. R. Bigelow Foundation, St. Paul, MN — the Children, Families and Community Initiative
125,000 United Way of the St. Paul Area, St. Paul, MN — 1989 capital campaign

Blandin Foundation

CONTACT
Paul M. Olson
President
Blandin Foundation
100 N Pokegama Ave.
Grand Rapids, MN 55744
(218) 326-0523

FINANCIAL SUMMARY
Recent Giving: $9,095,000 (1994); $11,499,290 (1993); $8,700,000 (1992 approx.)

Assets: $240,000,000 (1993 est.); $250,000,000 (1992 approx.); $220,000,000 (1991)

Gifts Received: $8,252,028 (1988); $6,452,554 (1987)

Fiscal Note: In 1987 and 1988, the foundation received major distributions from the C. K. Blandin Residuary Trust; smaller amounts were also received from the C. K. Blandin Trust, Insurance Trust, and Cemetery Trust. The foundation notes that their two major trusts combined in 1989. Foundation assets for 1989 reflect the combined assets of the two trusts.

EIN: 41-6038619

CONTRIBUTIONS SUMMARY
Donor(s): The foundation was established in 1941 by the late Charles K. Blandin. As owner of a paper mill, Mr. Blandin began his career with the *St. Paul Pioneer Press and Dispatch*, and by the late 1920s, rose to the position of owner and publisher. Eventually he sold the newspaper but retained ownership of the Blandin Paper Company and various other companies. After his death, most of Mr. Blandin's estate was placed in trust for the foundation. Although the trustees sold the trust's stock in Blandin Paper Company in 1977, the foundation remains committed to serving the community where its income was earned. Most of the foundation's income is derived from the Blandin Residuary Trust.

Mr. Blandin set no specific funding restrictions on the foundation's areas of interest.

Typical Recipients: • *Arts & Humanities:* Arts Appreciation, Arts Associations & Councils, Arts Centers, Arts Institutes, Arts Outreach, Historic Preservation, History & Archaeology, Libraries, Literary Arts, Museums/Galleries, Music, Opera, Performing Arts, Public Broadcasting, Theater • *Civic & Public Affairs:* Botanical Gardens/Parks, Community Foundations, Economic Development, Employment/Job Training, Housing, Municipalities/Towns, Native American Affairs, Nonprofit Management, Professional & Trade Associations, Rural Affairs, Safety, Urban & Community Affairs • *Education:* Arts/Humanities Education, Colleges & Universities, Community & Junior Colleges, Education Reform, Elementary Education (Public), Engineering/Technological Education, Faculty Development, General, Medical Education, Minority Education, Public

Education (Precollege), Science/Mathematics Education, Secondary Education (Public), Special Education, Student Aid • *Environment:* Air/Water Quality, Forestry, General, Resource Conservation • *Health:* Emergency/Ambulance Services, Health Organizations, Hospices, Medical Research, Nursing Services, Outpatient Health Care • *Religion:* Religious Welfare • *Social Services:* At-Risk Youth, Camps, Child Welfare, Community Centers, Crime Prevention, Domestic Violence, Family Services, People with Disabilities, Substance Abuse, United Funds/United Ways, Youth Organizations

Grant Types: multiyear/continuing support, project, scholarship, and seed money

Geographic Distribution: Grand Rapids, Itasca County, and rural areas of Minnesota

GIVING OFFICERS
Kenneth Albrecht: trust

Kathleen Annette: trust

Robert L. Bullard: trust *PHIL AFFIL* trust: Minnesota Foundation, F. R. Bigelow Foundation; treas: H. William Lurton Foundation

Robert L. Comstock, Jr.: trust, mem exec comm *B* 1940 *CURR EMPL* asst vp: Blandin Paper

Henry Doerr: trust *PHIL AFFIL* dir: North Star Research Foundation

Vernae Hasbargen: secy, trust

Peter A. Heegaard: trust, mem exec comm

James Hoolihan: trust *B* 1952 *ED* Univ MN 1973-1977; William Mitchell Coll of Law JD 1979 *CURR EMPL* pres, dir: Indus Lubricant

Kathryn L. Jensen: vp

Mary Jo Jess: vchwn, mem exec comm *PHIL AFFIL* dir: Marshall H. and Nellie Alworth Memorial Fund

Sandy Layman: trust

Marcie Mclaughlin: trust

Paul M. Olson: pres *B* 1944

James Richard Oppenheimer: trust *B* St Paul MN 1921 *ED* Dartmouth Coll BA 1942; Yale Univ JD 1948 *CURR EMPL* of couns: Oppenheimer Wolff & Donnelly *NONPR AFFIL* mem: Am Bar Assn, MN Bar Assn, Ramsey County Bar Assn, St Paul Chamber Commerce; trust: Charles K Blandin Residuary Trust *CLUB AFFIL* Rotary, White Bear YC *PHIL AFFIL* dir: Tozer Foundation

Steven M. Shaler: treas, trust

Bruce W. Stender: chmn, mem exec comm *B* 1942 *ED* FL St Univ PhD 1969 *CURR EMPL* pres, coo, dir: Lyric Block Devel

Brian Vergin: trust *B* 1943 *CURR EMPL* sr vp mktg, dir: Blandin Paper

APPLICATION INFORMATION
Initial Approach:

A preliminary letter of inquiry or a call to a staff member is the initial procedure. A grant proposal may be submitted, depending on the outcome of the inquiry.

The grant proposal should include an organization description with mission, goals, objectives, personnel, and operating budget; description of project; and a summary of the

project including how outcomes will be achieved. Also include a budget detailing expenditures, other funding sources, and how project will be sustained in the future; a list of staff and board of directors; recently audited financial statement; copy of IRS determination letter of tax-exempt status; qualifications of key personnel; and an evaluation plan.

The board meets three times a year. Deadlines are January 2, for the April meeting; May 1, for the August meeting; and August 1, for the January meeting.

Receipt of grant proposals will be acknowledged by a postcard. Applications are reviewed by the Trustees Grants Screening Committee. After review by the full board, approval or denial letters will be sent as soon as possible.

Restrictions on Giving: The foundation does not make grants directly to individuals or for religious activities, camping programs, medical research, travel, ordinary government services, capital campaigns beyond Grand Rapids/Itasca County, renovation, equipment purchases, endowments, publications, films, videos, general operating funds, or programs to influence legislation.

OTHER THINGS TO KNOW
In addition to making grants, the foundation provides services for conferences and community leadership training for rural Minnesota.

PUBLICATIONS
Annual report, application guidelines, and program policy statement

GRANTS ANALYSIS
Total Grants: $9,095,000

Number of Grants: 23

Highest Grant: $2,100,000

Average Grant: $395,435

Typical Range: $50,000 to $400,000

Disclosure Period: 1994

Note: Recent grants are derived from a 1994 grants list.

RECENT GRANTS
General

2,100,000 Wolf Ridge Environmental Learning Center, Finland, MN — over five years challenge grant for the Residential Environmental Learning Center Expansion Project

1,650,000 Forest Resource Center, Lanesboro, MN — over five years, challenge grant for the Residential Environmental Learning Center Expansion project

1,470,000 Deep Portage Conservation Foundation, Hackensack, MN — over five years, challenge grant for the Residential Environmental Learning Center Expansion Project

1,200,000 Long Lake Conservation Center, Palisade, MN — over five years, challenge grant for the Residential Environmental Learning Center Expansion Project

1,080,000 Northwoods Audubon Center, Sandstone, MN — over five years, challenge grant for the Residential Environmental Learning Center Expansion Project

Bremer Foundation, Otto

CONTACT
John Kostishack
Executive Director
Otto Bremer Foundation
445 Minnesota St., Ste. 2000
St. Paul, MN 55101-2107
(612) 227-8036

FINANCIAL SUMMARY
Recent Giving: $7,500,000 (1995); $6,752,652 (1994); $5,624,367 (1993)

Assets: $162,000,000 (1995 est.); $162,000,000 (1994); $113,000,000 (1992 approx.)

EIN: 41-6019050

CONTRIBUTIONS SUMMARY
Donor(s): Otto Bremer , a German immigrant of humble origins, has become an established symbol of philanthropy in the Minnesota, North Dakota, and Wisconsin regions. He began his career as a bookkeeper in the National German American Bank in St. Paul, initiating what proved to be an enduring attachment to that area. Mr. Bremer was an active participant in a wide variety of community affairs throughout his lifetime. In 1921, he became chairman of the American National Bank, and in 1939, he assumed the presidency of the Schmidt Brewing Company.

In addition to these corporate activities, Mr. Bremer was treasurer of the City of St. Paul, aided in the formation of the Minnesota Democratic Farmer-Labor Party, counseled Presidents Woodrow Wilson and Franklin D. Roosevelt, and administered the Federal Home Owners' Loan Corporation in Minnesota. Yet, it was his participation in banking that was most important to Otto Bremer. His holdings were vast, yet his association with "countryside banks" proved to be most satisfying. One of his creeds was that "banks should be home banks, independently operated by people of their communities."

In a biography of Otto Bremer, he is described as firmly believing that individuals do not live or grow in isolation; they fulfill themselves only by helping one another. It was his commitment to this belief that led Mr. Bremer to act with concern for the rural communities in his area that were threatened by poverty. During the Depression, Mr. Bremer liquidated personal assets and placed them in banks serving these rural communities. His support sustained these struggling banks and communities. Later, Mr. Bremer became concerned with maintaining support to these communities after his death. In 1943, he established the Bremer Financial Corporation which received assets from the banks of which Mr. Bremer was principal shareholder. The assets from the Bremer Financial Corporation were then transferred to the Otto Bremer Foundation, which was formed in 1944 due to his deep concern for his holdings in Minnesota, North Dakota, and Wisconsin. Through the foundation, he sought to insure the perpetuation of the Bremer banks and the ultimate return of his wealth to the trade territories of the banks and the city of St. Paul. Money placed in Otto Bremer's banks was funneled into the corporation, and finally to the foundation, which dispensed it to needy causes in the community. In this way, Mr. Bremer formulated an enduring system which would continue to use his wealth to "serve the community in which it was invested first, last and always."

Typical Recipients: • *Arts & Humanities:* Libraries, Music, Public Broadcasting • *Civic & Public Affairs:* African American Affairs, Asian American Affairs, Botanical Gardens/Parks, Civil Rights, Community Foundations, Employment/Job Training, Legal Aid, Native American Affairs, Rural Affairs, Women's Affairs • *Education:* Agricultural Education, Colleges & Universities, Community & Junior Colleges, Continuing Education, Literacy, Medical Education, Minority Education, Preschool Education, Private Education (Precollege), Religious Education • *Health:* AIDS/HIV, Clinics/Medical Centers, Emergency/Ambulance Services, Geriatric Health, Health Organizations, Hospices, Hospitals, Mental Health, Nursing Services • *Religion:* Churches, Jewish Causes, Religious Welfare • *Social Services:* Child Welfare, Community Centers, Community Service Organizations, Counseling, Crime Prevention, Domestic Violence, Family Services, Food/Clothing Distribution, Homes, People with Disabilities, Recreation & Athletics, Refugee Assistance, Senior Services, Shelters/Homelessness, Substance Abuse, United Funds/United Ways, Youth Organizations

Grant Types: capital, general support, loan, project, and seed money

Geographic Distribution: specific rural communities in Minnesota, North Dakota, and Wisconsin

GIVING OFFICERS
Charlotte Johnson: trust

John Kostishack: exec dir

William H. Lipschultz: trust *B* St Paul MN 1930 *ED* Univ MN 1956 *CURR EMPL* vp, regional mgr: Stone Container Corp *CORP AFFIL* vp, dir: Otto Bremer Co; vp, treas: Bremer Fin Corp

Lynda Miner: grants mgr

Karen Starr: sr program off

APPLICATION INFORMATION
Initial Approach:

Applicants should write or call the foundation for an application and for assistance in the development of a proposal.

Proposals should include legal name, address, telephone number, and brief description of the organization; documentation of organization's nonprofit and tax-exempt status, including a copy of the ruling from the IRS; evidence that the request is endorsed by the board of directors, with a list of those members; clear description of project for which funds are being sought, what it is designed to achieve, and how it will be accomplished; names and qualifications of individuals responsible for implementing the project; complete budget for the project including an indication of the time period in which funds are to be spent; audited financial statement (if available) for the organization's previous fiscal year; current operational budget; copy of most recent IRS Form 990; other funding support to be used in connection with the project; description of the project's future funding plans; and a description of the procedure for accounting for expenditures of grant funds and the progress of the project.

The board of trustees meets monthly; however, proposals should be submitted for review three months prior to the date the funding decision is required.

All complete proposals will be reviewed first by the staff and then submitted to the trustees, with whom final responsibility for grant approval resides.

Restrictions on Giving: Grants are given only to projects impacting the service areas of Bremer-affiliated organizations in Wisconsin, North Dakota, Minnesota, and within the city of St. Paul. Grants are rarely made to organizations in other communities unless they affect these specified geographic areas. Grants are not made to individuals, or to endowment funds.

OTHER THINGS TO KNOW
Grants are evaluated at the conclusion of the first year of funding. Grants made for more than one year may be reconsidered at the end of each year.

PUBLICATIONS
Annual report and information brochure

GRANTS ANALYSIS
Total Grants: $6,752,652*

Number of Grants: 586*

Highest Grant: $90,000

Average Grant: $11,523

Typical Range: $200 to $20,000

Disclosure Period: 1994

Note: Figures exclude $1,060,500 in program-related investments. Recent grants are derived from a partial 1994 grants list.

RECENT GRANTS
Library

25,000	Deer Park Public Library, Deer Park, WI — to construct a new library
15,000	Cedar Mountain Public Schools, Franklin, MN — to expand the public library

General

90,000	North Dakota Council on Abused Women's Services, Bismarck, ND — to support the Criminal Justice System Monitoring Program, an effort to demonstrate the need for a statewide data collection system on incidents of domestic violence
75,000	Hmong American Community Association, Menomonie, WI — for the development of a mutual assistance organization that will provide cultural, educational, employment, and legal services to refugees
75,000	United Way of Dunn County, Menomonie, WI — to establish and run a community information and referral service
75,000	Whisper, St. Paul, MN — for the operations of the Juvenile Prevention Program which works to keep young people out of prostitution
67,000	Minnesota Consortium of Theological Schools, St. Paul, MN — for the Northland Ministry Partnership, an ecumenical training program that is based in the changing context of regional communities

Bush Foundation

CONTACT
Humphrey Doermann
President
Bush Foundation
E-900 First National Bank Bldg.
332 Minnesota St.
St. Paul, MN 55101
(612) 227-0891

FINANCIAL SUMMARY
Recent Giving: $21,000,000 (fiscal 1995 est.); $21,663,383 (fiscal 1994); $21,448,818 (fiscal 1993)

Assets: $426,783,000 (fiscal 1994); $480,000,000 (fiscal 1993 approx.); $450,145,000 (fiscal 1992)

EIN: 41-6017815

CONTRIBUTIONS SUMMARY
Donor(s): The Bush Foundation was established in 1953 by Archibald Granville Bush and his wife, Edyth Bassler Bush . Mr. Bush (1887-1966) rose to chairman of the executive committee of Minnesota Mining and Manufacturing Co. (3M). He was active in St. Paul civic affairs and was a trustee of

Hamline University. Mrs. Bush, a former actress and dancer, maintained a strong interest in the performing arts, and founded the Edyth Bassler Bush Theatre. She was chairman of the Bush Foundation from 1966 until her death in 1972.

Typical Recipients: • *Arts & Humanities:* Arts Associations & Councils, Arts Centers, Ethnic & Folk Arts, General, Libraries, Music, Opera, Performing Arts, Public Broadcasting, Theater, Visual Arts • *Civic & Public Affairs:* Economic Development, Employment/Job Training, General, Native American Affairs, Urban & Community Affairs • *Education:* Colleges & Universities, Community & Junior Colleges, Engineering/Technological Education, Faculty Development, General, Medical Education, Minority Education, Public Education (Precollege), School Volunteerism, Science/Mathematics Education, Secondary Education (Private), Social Sciences Education • *Environment:* General, Resource Conservation • *Health:* AIDS/HIV, Children's Health/Hospitals, Clinics/Medical Centers, Health Organizations, Medical Rehabilitation, Medical Training, Mental Health • *Religion:* Religious Welfare • *Social Services:* Big Brother/Big Sister, Child Welfare, Community Centers, Community Service Organizations, Day Care, Domestic Violence, Family Planning, Family Services, People with Disabilities, Refugee Assistance, Senior Services, Substance Abuse, United Funds/United Ways, Youth Organizations

Grant Types: capital, challenge, fellowship, and project

Geographic Distribution: primarily Minnesota, North Dakota, and South Dakota; faculty development grants are made to tribally controlled colleges both inside and outside the primary geographic region

GIVING OFFICERS

Sharon Sayles Belton: secy, dir

Shirley Clark: dir

Merlin E. Dewing: dir *B* Portal ND 1934 *ED* Univ ND BS 1956; Univ ND MS 1958 *CURR EMPL* intl ptnr: KPMG Peat Marwick *NONPR AFFIL* dir: Am Symphony Orchestra League; mem: Am Inst CPAs, Downtown Kiwanis, Greater Minneapolis Chamber Commerce, MN Soc CPAs, NY St Soc CPAs

Humphrey Doermann: pres *B* Toledo OH 1930 *ED* Harvard Univ AB 1952; Harvard Univ MBA 1958; Harvard Univ PhD 1967

Phyllis B. France: dir

Ellen Z. Green, MD: first vchmn, dir

Frank Joseph Hammond: gen couns *B* Harvey IL 1919 *ED* Carleton Coll AB 1941; Harvard Univ LLB 1948 *CURR EMPL* atty: Briggs & Morgan *CORP AFFIL* dir: First Trust Co St Paul *NONPR AFFIL* adjunct prof commercial law: Hamline Univ Sch Law; advocate: Am Bd Trial Advocates; fellow: Am Bar Fdn, Am Coll Trial Lawyers; mem: Delta Sigma Rho, Intl Platform Assn, Phi Beta Kappa; mem exec comm: Boy Scouts Am Indianhead Counc; mem planned gifts comm: MN Orchestra Assn; trust: Carleton Coll *PHIL AFFIL* trust: Charles and El-

lora Alliss Educational Foundation; chmn, trust: Minnesota Foundation *CLUB AFFIL* Informal, Minnesota, St Paul Athletic

Thomas Edward Holloran: chmn bd *B* Minneapolis MN 1929 *ED* Univ MN BS 1951; Univ MN JD 1955 *CURR EMPL* dir: Amdura Corp *CORP AFFIL* dir: ADC Telecommunications, Am Hoist & Derrick Co, Donovan Cos, Flexsteel Indus, Malt-O-Meal Co, Medtronic, Midwest Commun, MTS Sys Corp, Natl City Bank Minneapolis *NONPR AFFIL* mem: Am Bar Assn; prof sch bus: Univ St Thomas; trust: Minneapolis Art Inst

Richard D. McFarland: dir *B* Chicago IL 1930 *ED* Dartmouth Coll 1951; Dartmouth Coll MBA 1952 *CURR EMPL* chmn, ceo: Inter-Regional Fin Group *CORP AFFIL* dir: Dain Bosworth Inc, Graco Inc, IFG Info Svcs, Rauscher Pierce Refsnes *NONPR AFFIL* dir: Abbott-Northwestern Hosp, Childrens Heart Fund, Securities Indus Assn, Un Way Minneapolis; mem: MN Bus Partnership

John A. McHugh: dir *PHIL AFFIL* mem adv comm: Minnesota Foundation; chmn, dir: Minnesota Valley Bancshares Foundation

Diana E. Murphy: dir *B* Faribault MN 1934 *ED* Johannes Gutenburg Univ 1954-1955; Univ MN BA 1954; Univ MN JD 1974 *NONPR AFFIL* dir, treas: Un Way Minneapolis; fellow: Am Bar Fdn; instructor (law sch): Univ MN; mem: Am Bar Assn, Am Judicature Soc, Am Law Inst, Hennepin County Bar Assn, MN Bar Assn, MN Women Lawyers, Order Coif, Order of Coif, Phi Beta Kappa; mem, dir: Fed Judges Assn, Fed Judges Ctr, Natl Assn Women Judges; regent: St Johns Univ; trust: Univ MN Fdn, Univ St Thomas; trust, chmn bd: Twin Cities Pub TV; vice chmn, bd dirs: Science Mus MN

Anita M. Pampusch: dir *B* St Paul MN 1938 *ED* Coll St Catherine BA 1962; Univ Notre Dame MA 1970; Univ Notre Dame PhD 1972 *CORP AFFIL* dir: St Paul Cos *NONPR AFFIL* district chmn: Rhodes Scholarship Selection Comm; fellow: Goucher Coll; mem: Am Philosophical Soc, Phi Beta Kappa, St Paul Chamber Commerce, Womens Econ Roundtable; mem adv comm: Columbia Univ Institutional Leadership Project; mem, chr: Counc Independent Colls; mem exec comm: Womens Coll; pres: Coll St Catherine *CLUB AFFIL* Minneapolis, St Pauls Athletic

Kennon V. Rothchild: treas, dir

W. Richard West, Jr.: second vchmn, dir

Frank B. Wilderson, Jr.: dir *B* Lutcher LA

Ann Wynia: dir *PHIL AFFIL* dir: H. B. Fuller Co. Foundation

APPLICATION INFORMATION
Initial Approach:

Contact the foundation to request a detailed list of its application requirements before drafting a final proposal.

Proposals should include a brief description of the organization; names and primary affiliations of the organization's directors and trustees; name(s) and qualifications of the person(s) who would administer the grant;

recently audited balance sheet and income statement; clear description of the project, its importance, and anticipated results; detailed income and expense budget indicating plans for funding, amount requested, and when payment is desired; statement detailing funds received and pledged; plans for future support; and proposed evaluative criteria. Proposals also should include proof of tax-exempt status.

The board meets in February, June, and October. In odd-numbered years, the board has an additional April meeting. Proposals should be submitted no less than four months prior to a board meeting.

Ordinarily, one member of the program staff is assigned to work on a specific proposal. As necessary, this individual will contact the applicant, seek outside opinions, obtain consultant review assistance, and undertake background research. The results will be presented to the grants committee and the board. The grants committee reviews proposals and makes recommendations to the board. All commitments of grant funds are made by the board. Written notice of grant decisions is usually sent within ten days of a board meeting.

Restrictions on Giving: The foundation ordinarily does not contribute to other foundations or individuals (except through three of its fellowship programs), or for project research in the biomedical and health sciences. Capital funds for medicine and public higher education, hospital construction, grants for debt retirement, and general and continuing operating support are considered low priorities.

OTHER THINGS TO KNOW
The foundation requires progress reports from grant recipients. The reports should include a list of expenditures. Uncommitted funds must be returned at the end of the grant period.

Fellowship grants limited to Minnesota, North Dakota, South Dakota, and western Wisconsin. The Bush Public School Superintendents Program has been discontinued.

PUBLICATIONS
Annual report, information for grant applicants, guidelines

GRANTS ANALYSIS
Total Grants: $21,663,383

Number of Grants: 145*

Highest Grant: $1,000,000

Average Grant: $133,462

Typical Range: $10,000 to $50,000 and $75,000 to $200,000

Disclosure Period: fiscal year ending November 30, 1994

Note: Number of grants and average grant figures exclude $2,311,400 in support for the Bush fellowship programs. Recent grants are derived from a fiscal 1993 grants list.

RECENT GRANTS

Library
116,372   Cheyenne River Sioux Tribe, Eagle Butte, SD — purchase

	of a law library collection for the tribal court
113,299	Flandreau Santee Sioux Tribe, Flandreau, SD — purchase of a law library collection for the tribal court
92,690	Lower Brule Sioux Tribe, Lower Brule, SD — purchase of a law library collection for the tribal court

General

875,000	Shaw University, Raleigh, NC
500,000	St. Johns University, Collegeville, MN — capital challenge grants to Minnesota and Dakota private colleges
496,548	Bush Leadership Fellows Programs, St. Paul, MN — 1992 program that provides mid-career study and internship opportunities for selected residents of Minnesota, North Dakota, South Dakota, and western Wisconsin
492,000	College of St. Benedict, St. Joseph, MN — capital challenge grants to Minnesota and Dakota private colleges
385,000	Livingstone College, Salisbury, NC

Cargill Inc. / Cargill Foundation

Sales: $60.0 million
Employees: 70,000
Headquarters: Minneapolis, MN
SIC Major Group: Grain & Field Beans, Deep Sea Domestic Transportation of Freight, Commodity Contracts Brokers & Dealers, and Flour & Other Grain Mill Products

CONTACT
James S. Hield
Secretary, Contributions Committee
Cargill Inc.
PO Box 9300
Minneapolis, MN 55440
(612) 742-6213
Note: James S. Hield, Executive Director, is also the contact for the foundation. Subsidiaries and divisions also operate separate giving programs in local communities; organizations should contact their local Cargill facility for more information.

FINANCIAL SUMMARY
Recent Giving: $7,262,323 (1994); $4,875,553 (1993); $7,309,004 (1992)

Assets: $41,900,000 (1992 approx.); $41,088,000 (1991); $33,843,000 (1990)

Fiscal Note: Figures include both foundation grants and direct corporate giving. Figures do not include direct corporate contributions by foreign subsidiaries to local organizations. In 1993, foundation giving

was $3,774,231, and direct giving was $1,101,322. Above figures exclude nonmonetary support.
EIN: 41-6020221

CONTRIBUTIONS SUMMARY
Typical Recipients: • *Arts & Humanities:* Arts Institutes, Libraries, Museums/Galleries, Music, Opera, Public Broadcasting, Theater • *Civic & Public Affairs:* Employment/Job Training, Housing • *Education:* Colleges & Universities, Economic Education, Student Aid • *Environment:* General • *Health:* Hospitals • *Social Services:* Community Service Organizations, Food/Clothing Distribution, People with Disabilities, United Funds/United Ways, Youth Organizations

Grant Types: capital, general support, operating expenses, project, and scholarship

Nonmonetary Support Types: donated equipment, loaned executives, and workplace solicitation

Note: Nonmonetary support is provided by the company. Figures for nonmonetary support are not available. Workplace solicitation is for United Way only.

Geographic Distribution: primarily in Minneapolis and St. Paul, MN and seven-county metropolitan area; also where company has a significant presence and, on a limited basis, nationally

Operating Locations: MN

CORP. OFFICERS
James S. Hield: *CURR EMPL* secy contributions comm: Cargill Inc

Whitney MacMillan: *B* 1929 *CURR EMPL* chmn, ceo, dir: Cargill Inc *CORP AFFIL* dir: Continental Bank Corp, Deluxe Corp *NONPR AFFIL* co-chmn: E-W Security Studies *PHIL AFFIL* vchmn, dir: Wem Foundation

Gerald M. Mitchell: *CURR EMPL* exec vp: Cargill Inc *CORP AFFIL* chmn: N Star Steel KY Inc *PHIL AFFIL* vp, dir: Ladish Malting Co. Foundation

Ernest S. Mycek: *CURR EMPL* pres, coo, dir: Cargill Inc

Warren R. Staley: *CURR EMPL* vp, dir: Cargill Inc

GIVING OFFICERS
James S. Hield: exec dir *CURR EMPL* secy contributions comm: Cargill Inc (see above)

Cargill MacMillan, Jr.: vp, dir *B* 1927 *CORP AFFIL* dir: Cargill Inc

Thomas O. Moe: secy, treas *B* Des Moines IA 1938 *ED* Univ MN BA 1960 *CURR EMPL* Mng dir: Dorsey & Whitney *CORP AFFIL* secy: EA Sween Co

William R. Pearce: pres

John Edgar Pearson: vp, dir *B* Minneapolis MN 1927 *ED* Gustavus Adolphus Coll 1944-1945; Northwestern Univ 1945-1946; Univ MN BBA 1948 *CURR EMPL* chmn, ceo: Northwestern Natl Life Ins Co *CORP AFFIL* chmn: N Atlantic Life Ins Co, Northern Life Ins Co; dir: Northern Sts Power Co, Norwest Bank MN NA, Norwest Corp *NONPR AFFIL* dir: Minneapolis Commun Bus Empl Alliance, MN Bus Partnership,

Un Way Greater Minneapolis Area; mem: Am Counc Life Ins, Health Ins Assn Am, Ins Fed MN

APPLICATION INFORMATION
Initial Approach: *Initial Contact:* letter of inquiry *Include Information On:* organization's history, mission, programs and services and staffing report; description of specific use of funds requested, including dollar amount, goals and objectives, and timetable; evidence of IRS 501(c)(3) tax-exempt status; itemized annual budget and sources of support; most recent audited financial statements; list of board of directors *Deadlines:* none; grants are reviewed as they are received

Restrictions on Giving: Foundation does not support political organizations or campaigns; organizations designed primarily for lobbying and advocacy; individuals and their projects; religious organizations for direct religious activities; endowment campaigns; fraternal organizations, societies, or orders; veterans organizations; travel, either by groups or by individuals; purchase of program advertising space; or telephone solicitations.

Foundation generally does not support conferences, seminars, workshops, or symposia; national or local campaigns to eliminate or control specific diseases; athletic scholarships; benefits, fundraisers, or testimonial, recognition, or honoring dinners; subsidization of publications, recordings, television, or film production.

Foundation does not provide seed money or start-up funding for new organizations.

OTHER THINGS TO KNOW
Foundation places primary support on operating and program support and secondary emphasis on capital grants.

First-time grants usually fall in the $5,000 to $10,000 range. Fewer grants are made in the upper range and most often are made to organizations with whom the foundation has had a long-term relationship.

Low priority is given to organizations supported by the United Way or similar funds.

GRANTS ANALYSIS
Total Grants: $3,774,231*

Number of Grants: 148

Highest Grant: $425,000

Average Grant: $25,502

Typical Range: $5,000 to $10,000 and $50,000 to $150,000

Disclosure Period: 1993

Note: Total grants for foundation only; figure does not include direct giving. Recent grants are derived from a 1993 partial grants list.

RECENT GRANTS
Library

50,000	American Library Association, MN

General

425,000	United Way of Minneapolis Area, Minneapolis, MN

264,000	FFA Foundation/Cargill Scholarship Program for Rural America, MN
166,666	Minneapolis Children's Medical Center, Minneapolis, MN
83,333	Metropolitan State University, MN
50,000	Farm Safety for Just Kids, MN

Carolyn Foundation

CONTACT
Carol J. Fetzer
Foundation Administrator
Carolyn Foundation
4800 First Bank Pl.
Minneapolis, MN 55402-4320
(612) 339-7101

FINANCIAL SUMMARY
Recent Giving: $1,200,000 (1995 est.); $1,241,087 (1994); $1,287,669 (1993)

Assets: $27,000,000 (1995 est.); $27,000,000 (1994 approx.); $26,320,938 (1993)

EIN: 41-6044416

CONTRIBUTIONS SUMMARY
Donor(s): The Carolyn Foundation was established in Minnesota in 1964 under the terms of the will of Carolyn McKnight Christian , who died that year. She was the daughter of real estate entrepreneur and lumberman, Sumner T. McKnight.

Typical Recipients: • *Arts & Humanities:* Arts Associations & Councils, Arts Funds, Arts Outreach, Community Arts, Dance, Ethnic & Folk Arts, Historic Preservation, Libraries, Museums/Galleries, Music, Public Broadcasting, Theater • *Civic & Public Affairs:* Asian American Affairs, Botanical Gardens/Parks, Economic Development, Employment/Job Training, General, Housing, Native American Affairs, Nonprofit Management, Public Policy, Rural Affairs, Urban & Community Affairs, Women's Affairs, Zoos/Aquariums • *Education:* Afterschool/Enrichment Programs, Colleges & Universities, Education Associations, Education Reform, Elementary Education (Private), General, Literacy, Private Education (Precollege), Public Education (Precollege), Science/Mathematics Education • *Environment:* Air/Water Quality, Forestry, General, Resource Conservation, Watershed, Wildlife Protection • *Health:* Children's Health/Hospitals, Clinics/Medical Centers, Health Organizations, Hospitals, Nursing Services • *International:* Health Care/Hospitals, International Environmental Issues • *Religion:* Churches, Religious Welfare • *Social Services:* At-Risk Youth, Child Welfare, Community Service Organizations, Counseling, Day Care, Domestic Violence, Family Planning, Family Services, Homes, People with Disabilities, Recreation & Athletics, Senior Services, Shelters/Homelessness, Substance Abuse, Youth Organizations

Grant Types: capital, operating expenses, and project

Geographic Distribution: metropolitan New Haven, CT; and Minneapolis and St. Paul, MN

GIVING OFFICERS
Beatrice Crosby Booth: trust

Guido Calabresi: trust *B* Milan Italy 1932 *ED* Yale Univ BS 1953; Oxford Univ BA 1955; Yale Univ LLB 1958; Oxford Univ MA 1959 *CORP AFFIL* pres, dir: Crosby Co *NONPR AFFIL* fellow: Accademia Delle Scienze Di Torino, Am Academy Arts Sciences, Associazione Italiana Di Diritto Comparato, British Academy, Royal Swedish Academy Sciences, Timothy Dwight Coll; hon trust: Hopkins Grammar Sch; mem: Assn Am Law Schs, CT Bar Assn; Sterling prof, dean: Yale Univ Law Sch; trust: Yale Univ St. Thomas More Chapel

Charles W. Case, Jr.: trust

Eugenie T. Copp: trust

Edwin L. Crosby: vchmn, trust

Franklin M. Crosby III: trust

G. Christian Crosby: trust

Sumner McKnight Crosby, Jr.: chmn, trust

Thomas Manville Crosby, Jr.: trust *B* Minneapolis MN 1938 *ED* Yale Univ BA 1960; Yale Univ JD 1965 *CURR EMPL* atty: Faegre & Benson *NONPR AFFIL* mem: Am Bar Assn

Carol J. Fetzer: fdn admin, secy, trust *PHIL AFFIL* asst secy: Southways Foundation

Carolyn C. Graham: treas, trust

Lucy C. Mitchell: chmn, trust *PHIL AFFIL* asst treas, trust: Southways Foundation

APPLICATION INFORMATION
Initial Approach:

There is no application form; written proposals should be sent to the foundation.

Applicants must provide the name and address of the contact person; description of the organization; list of officers, directors, and executive staff; IRS number and copy of determination letter; state registration certificate; amount requested; timetable; and purpose, objective, and goals of project. Applicants also should include a history of the project; operational plan; future plans; licensing requirements; evaluation methods; reason foundation is being approached for funding; detailed budget; income from prior three years; provisions for financial support of project in future; audited financial report; and an annual report.

The deadline for major contribution funding ($10,000 or larger) is July 1. Requests for minor contributions should be submitted by March 1.

Restrictions on Giving: The foundation does not fund individuals, religious organizations for religious purposes, political or veterans organizations, annual fund drives, debts, and legal costs. The foundation generally will not sponsor conferences, seminars, or projects in foreign countries.

PUBLICATIONS
Annual report

GRANTS ANALYSIS
Total Grants: $1,241,087

Number of Grants: 62

Highest Grant: $50,000

Average Grant: $20,018

Typical Range: $5,000 to $25,000

Disclosure Period: 1994

Note: Recent grants are derived from a 1993 annual report.

RECENT GRANTS
General

100,000	LEAP, New Haven, CT
60,000	New Haven Board of Education, New Haven, CT
50,000	American Wildlands, Lakewood, CO
50,000	Baseball Foundation of Connecticut, New Haven, CT
50,000	Connecticut Audubon Society, Hartford, CT

Cowles Media Co. / Cowles Media Foundation

Sales: $358.2 million
Employees: 2,634
Headquarters: Minneapolis, MN
SIC Major Group: Newspapers and Periodicals

CONTACT
Jan Veith
Contributions Coordinator
Cowles Media Co.
329 Portland Ave.
Minneapolis, MN 55415-1112
(612) 673-7051
Note: Ms. Veith is the contact for the foundation and headquarters corporate giving program. Organizations in other operating locations should contact the company in their area.

FINANCIAL SUMMARY
Recent Giving: $1,500,000 (fiscal 1995 est.); $1,450,974 (fiscal 1994); $1,396,754 (fiscal 1993)

Assets: $8,155,864 (fiscal 1993); $7,040,364 (fiscal 1991); $8,000,000 (fiscal 1989)

Fiscal Note: About one-half of total annual giving is disbursed through the foundation; headquarters and operating companies provide the remainder. Above figures include foundation giving only.

EIN: 41-6031373

CONTRIBUTIONS SUMMARY
Typical Recipients: • *Arts & Humanities:* Arts Associations & Councils, Arts Centers, Arts Festivals, Arts Funds, Arts Institutes, Community Arts, Dance, Ethnic & Folk Arts, Historic Preservation, Libraries, Museums/Galleries, Music, Opera, Performing Arts, Public Broadcasting, Theater, Visual Arts • *Civic & Public Affairs:* Civil Rights,

Economic Development, Employment/Job Training, First Amendment Issues, Housing, Professional & Trade Associations, Urban & Community Affairs, Women's Affairs, Zoos/Aquariums • *Education:* Arts/Humanities Education, Business Education, Colleges & Universities, Community & Junior Colleges, Economic Education, Education Associations, Education Funds, Elementary Education (Private), Engineering/Technological Education, Faculty Development, Journalism/Media Education, Literacy, Minority Education, Private Education (Precollege), Public Education (Precollege) • *Science:* Science Exhibits & Fairs • *Social Services:* Child Welfare, Community Centers, Community Service Organizations, Day Care, Delinquency & Criminal Rehabilitation, Domestic Violence, Emergency Relief, Family Planning, Family Services, Food/Clothing Distribution, People with Disabilities, Refugee Assistance, Shelters/Homelessness, Substance Abuse, United Funds/United Ways, Volunteer Services, Youth Organizations

Grant Types: capital, employee matching gifts, endowment, and general support

Note: Endowment and capital grants are made through the foundation.

Geographic Distribution: near headquarters and operating locations only

Operating Locations: AZ (Scottsdale), CT (Stamford), MN (Minneapolis), PA (Harrisburg)

CORP. OFFICERS

James Arthur Alcott: *B* Stillwater OK 1930 *ED* OK St Univ BS 1952; Stanford Univ MBA 1956 *CURR EMPL* vp admin: Cowles Media Co *CORP AFFIL* dir: Cowles Magazines Inc *NONPR AFFIL* dir: Literary Resources, MN Ctr Book Arts; mem: Beta Gamma Sigma, MN Adult Literacy Campaign, Phi Delta Theta, Phi Kappa Phi; trust: Midwest Res Inst, MN Pub Radio

John Cowles III: *CURR EMPL* chmn: Cowles Media Co

David Carson Cox: *B* Orange City NJ 1937 *ED* Stanford Univ AB 1959; Harvard Univ MBA 1961 *CURR EMPL* pres, ceo, dir: Cowles Media Co *CORP AFFIL* chmn: ADX Distr Co, Cowles Magazines Inc; dir: Natl Computer Sys Inc, NWNL Cos Inc, Tennant Co *NONPR AFFIL* chmn: Guthrie Theater; dir: MN Bus Partnership, Spring Hill Ctr, Un Way Minneapolis; mem: Am Newspaper Publs Assn, Counc Foreign Rels Minneapolis, Greater Minneapolis Chamber Commerce, Harvard Univ Grad Sch Bus Admin Alumni Assn, Newspaper Assn Am, Stanford Univ Alumni Assn; trust: Macalester Coll *CLUB AFFIL* Minikahda, Minneapolis

Joel Roy Kramer: *B* Brooklyn NY 1948 *ED* Harvard Univ BA 1969 *CURR EMPL* pres: Media Cowles Co *CORP AFFIL* dir: Harvard Crimson Inc; publ: Star Tribune *NONPR AFFIL* dir: World Press Inst; mem: Am Soc Newspaper Editors, Assn Press Mng Editors Assn

Randy Miller Lebedoff: *B* Washington DC 1949 *ED* Smith Coll BA 1971; IN Univ JD 1975 *CURR EMPL* asst secy: Cowles Media

Co *CORP AFFIL* sr vp, gen couns: Star Tribune *NONPR AFFIL* dir: Abbott-Northwestern Hosp, Fund Legal Aid Soc; mem: Newspaper Assn Am, Order Coif

Georgina Y. Stephens: *B* Seoul Republic of Korea 1955 *ED* Cornell Univ 1977; Univ MI 1979 *CURR EMPL* treas: Cowles Media Co

James Joseph Viera: *B* Erie PA 1940 *ED* Rensselaer Polytech Inst BS 1962; Columbia Univ Sch Bus Admin MBA 1970 *CURR EMPL* vp, cfo: Cowles Media Co *CORP AFFIL* vp: ADX Distr Co, Cowles Magazines Inc; vp, dir: Scottsdale Publ Inc *NONPR AFFIL* mem: Minneapolis Chamber Commerce; trust: Sci Mus MN *CLUB AFFIL* Rotary

GIVING OFFICERS

James Arthur Alcott: chmn, dir *CURR EMPL* vp admin: Cowles Media Co (see above)

John Cowles III: dir *CURR EMPL* chmn: Cowles Media Co (see above)

David Carson Cox: vp, dir *CURR EMPL* pres, ceo, dir: Cowles Media Co (see above)

Joel Roy Kramer: dir *CURR EMPL* pres: Media Cowles Co (see above)

Randy Miller Lebedoff: secy, dir *CURR EMPL* asst secy: Cowles Media Co (see above)

Chris E. Mahai: dir

Georgina Y. Stephens: dir *CURR EMPL* treas: Cowles Media Co (see above)

Jan Veith: contributions coordinator

James Joseph Viera: dir *CURR EMPL* vp, cfo: Cowles Media Co (see above)

APPLICATION INFORMATION

Initial Approach: *Initial Contact:* brief letter or proposal *Include Information On:* purpose of funds being sought; total project budget; description of the organization, its objectives, and how program will be administered; information about organization's officers and directors, current finances, and current contributors; copy of current IRS tax-exempt ruling *Deadlines:* none, but applications received early in the calendar year preferred *Note:* Preliminary applications or inquiries may be useful in determining the extent to which a proposed project relates to guidelines and existing commitments.

Restrictions on Giving: Generally does not support health-related organizations, religious organizations, international programs, dinners or special events, publications or conferences, social action agencies not participating in the United Way, individuals, fund-raising events, or political or lobbying groups.

OTHER THINGS TO KNOW

Individual operating units have contributions programs related to the needs of their communities; the company tends to make smaller grants, often directed toward community-based organizations.

GRANTS ANALYSIS

Total Grants: $1,450,974

Number of Grants: 515

Highest Grant: $205,000

Average Grant: $2,817

Typical Range: $1,000 to $15,000

Disclosure Period: fiscal year ending March 31, 1994

Note: Above figures reflect foundation giving only. Recent grants are derived from a fiscal 1994 Form 990.

RECENT GRANTS

General

205,000	United Way of Minneapolis Area, Minneapolis, MN — funding provided to more than 350 health and human service programs at over 130 United Way participating agencies serving people who live in Anoka, Carver, Dakota, Hennepin, and Scott counties
30,000	St. Paul Foundation, St. Paul, MN — program to enhance the achievement of low-income minority students in the St. Paul Public Schools
25,000	Minnesota Early Learning Design (MELD), Minneapolis, MN — support Twentieth Anniversary Campaign
25,000	Page Education Foundation, Minneapolis, MN — organizational development
25,000	Twin Cities Rise!, Minneapolis, MN — a pilot project aimed to turn low-wage unskilled and semiskilled people into skilled workers earning higher salaries

Davis Foundation, Edwin W. and Catherine M.

CONTACT

Bette D. Moorman
President
Edwin W. and Catherine M. Davis Fdn.
332 Minnesota St., Ste. 2100
St. Paul, MN 55101
(612) 228-0935

FINANCIAL SUMMARY

Recent Giving: $372,500 (1993); $389,357 (1992); $396,600 (1991)

Assets: $11,915,469 (1993); $10,755,225 (1992); $8,165,806 (1991)

Gifts Received: $142 (1993); $908,028 (1992); $1,500 (1991)

Fiscal Note: In 1993, contributions were received from the 1974 Irrevocable Trust of Catherine M. Davis.

EIN: 41-6012064

CONTRIBUTIONS SUMMARY

Donor(s): The Davis Foundation was established in 1956 by Edwin Weyerhaeuser Davis and members of his family. The Davis family is related to the Weyerhaeuser family, who founded the Weyerhaeuser Company.

Typical Recipients: • *Arts & Humanities:* Arts Associations & Councils, Arts Outreach, Historic Preservation, History & Archaeology, Libraries, Museums/Galleries, Music, Opera, Public Broadcasting, Theater • *Civic & Public Affairs:* Asian American Affairs, Botanical Gardens/Parks, Business/Free Enterprise, Civil Rights, Nonprofit Management, Philanthropic Organizations, Public Policy, Safety, Zoos/Aquariums • *Education:* Colleges & Universities, General, Medical Education, Minority Education, Private Education (Precollege), Religious Education, Social Sciences Education, Student Aid • *Environment:* General, Resource Conservation, Wildlife Protection • *Health:* AIDS/HIV, Cancer, Children's Health/Hospitals, Clinics/Medical Centers, Emergency/Ambulance Services, Eyes/Blindness, Health Funds, Health Organizations, Hospitals, Medical Rehabilitation, Medical Research, Mental Health, Nursing Services, Research/Studies Institutes, Single-Disease Health Associations • *International:* Human Rights, International Peace & Security Issues, International Relations, International Relief Efforts • *Religion:* Churches • *Social Services:* Animal Protection, Child Welfare, Community Service Organizations, Day Care, Emergency Relief, Family Services, Recreation & Athletics, Refugee Assistance, United Funds/United Ways, Youth Organizations

Grant Types: fellowship, general support, operating expenses, project, research, and scholarship

Geographic Distribution: national

GIVING OFFICERS

Frederick W. Davis II: secy, dir

Mary E. Davis: vp, dir

Richard T. Holm: asst treas

Joseph S. Micallef: asst secy, dir *B* 1933 *CURR EMPL* pres-ceo-treas, dir: Fiduciary Counselling Inc *CORP AFFIL* secy, treas: Rock Island Co *PHIL AFFIL* secy: Driscoll Foundation; secy, treas, dir: Charles A. Weyerhaeuser Memorial Foundation; treas: Rodman Foundation; dir: Musser Fund; asst secy, asst treas: Weyerhaeuser Family Foundation

Bette D. Moorman: pres, dir *CORP AFFIL* dir: NCR Corp

APPLICATION INFORMATION

Initial Contact: There is no formal application form; applicants should send an inititial letter of inquiry to the foundation.

Include Information On: Letters of inquiry should be no longer than three pages in length and should include the following: a description of the organization's background; the need for service or project, including its goal; an organizational plan to address the need, including a description of benefits provided by the service or project; a method of evaluation of service or program; a project or organization budget; and any other pertinent background information. All applicants must include a copy of their tax-exempt ruling from the IRS. The foundation will request additional information if necessary.

Deadlines: There are no deadlines for submitting proposals.

Review Process: When directors reach their decision on grants, a letter is sent to the applicant in approximately four to six weeks. The foundation generally does not grant personal interviews.

Restrictions on Giving: The foundation does not make grants to individuals, although it may support scholarships, fellowships, and research programs of established organizations. The foundation generally does not make grants for capital purposes, building and equipment, endowment, or loans. The foundation also prefers not to make long-term commitments in order to preserve flexibility for changing social conditions.

PUBLICATIONS

Report on programs, policies, and procedures

GRANTS ANALYSIS

Total Grants: $372,500

Number of Grants: 41

Highest Grant: $45,000

Typical Range: $1,000 to $40,000

Disclosure Period: 1993

Note: Recent grants are derived from a 1993 Form 990.

RECENT GRANTS

Library

5,000	St. Johns University, Collegeville, MN — Hill Monastic Manuscript Library

General

45,000	National Tropical Botanical Garden, Lawai, HI — education building fund and Kahanu Gardens
30,000	International Rescue Committee, New York, NY
30,000	International Rescue Committee, New York, NY — for general operating support
30,000	National Medical Fellowships, New York, NY — scholarships
20,000	Children's Cancer Research Institute, San Francisco, CA

Donaldson Company, Inc. / Donaldson Foundation

Sales: $533.33 million
Employees: 4,250
Headquarters: Minneapolis, MN
SIC Major Group: Internal Combustion Engines Nec

CONTACT

Raymond F. Vodovnik
Trustee & Secretary
Donaldson Foundation
PO Box 1299
Minneapolis, MN 55440
(612) 887-3010

FINANCIAL SUMMARY

Recent Giving: $575,000 (fiscal 1995 est.); $523,000 (fiscal 1994 approx.); $492,000 (fiscal 1993)

Assets: $1,035,534 (fiscal 1994); $782,000 (fiscal 1993); $749,279 (fiscal 1992)

Gifts Received: $550,000 (fiscal 1992); $300,000 (fiscal 1990); $400,000 (fiscal 1989)

Fiscal Note: Contributes through foundation only. In fiscal 1992, contributions were received from Donaldson Co.

EIN: 41-6052950

CONTRIBUTIONS SUMMARY

Typical Recipients: • *Arts & Humanities:* Arts Centers, Arts Funds, Arts Institutes, Community Arts, Dance, Historic Preservation, Libraries, Museums/Galleries, Music, Opera, Performing Arts, Public Broadcasting, Theater • *Civic & Public Affairs:* Economic Development, Employment/Job Training, Housing, Legal Aid, Nonprofit Management, Zoos/Aquariums • *Education:* Agricultural Education, Business Education, Colleges & Universities, Community & Junior Colleges, Economic Education, Education Funds, Engineering/Technological Education, Faculty Development, Legal Education, Literacy, Minority Education, Private Education (Precollege), Public Education (Precollege), Science/Mathematics Education, Special Education, Student Aid • *Environment:* General • *Health:* Health Funds, Hospices, Hospitals, Mental Health • *Religion:* Churches, Religious Organizations • *Science:* Observatories & Planetariums • *Social Services:* Child Welfare, Community Centers, Community Service Organizations, Counseling, Day Care, Delinquency & Criminal Rehabilitation, Domestic Violence, Emergency Relief, Family Planning, Family Services, Food/Clothing Distribution, Homes, People with Disabilities, Shelters/Homelessness, Substance Abuse, United Funds/United Ways, Youth Organizations

Grant Types: capital, employee matching gifts, endowment, general support, multi-year/continuing support, operating expenses, project, and scholarship

Geographic Distribution: focus on Minnesota

Operating Locations: CA (Ontario), IA (Cresco, Grinnell, Oelwein), IL (Champaign, Dixon), IN (Frankfurt, Resselaer), KY (Nicholasville), MN (Minneapolis), MO (Chillicothe), PA (Philadelphia), WI (Baldwin, Stevens Point)

Note: Company operates plants in all locations.

CORP. OFFICERS

William Alan Hodder: *B* Lincoln NE 1931 *ED* Univ NE 1954; Harvard Univ Grad Sch Bus Admin 1961 *CURR EMPL* chmn, pres, ceo: Donaldson Co Inc *CORP AFFIL* dir: Cowles Media Co, Norwest Corp, NWNL Cos Inc, Supervalu Inc, Tennant Co

GIVING OFFICERS

H. Young Chung: trust

F. A. Sandy Donaldson: trust

Tim Grafe: trust

Donna Hedlund: trust

Jim Martin: trust

Pat Patton: trust

Lynne Roe: trust

Susan Rossow: trust

Bonnie Schneider: trust

Randy Thiele: trust

Aileen Torgeson: trust

Raymond F. Vodovnik: secy, trust *B* Chisholm MN 1935 *ED* MN Inst Tech 1961; Univ MN Law Sch 1964 *CURR EMPL* vp law, secy: Donaldson Co Inc

APPLICATION INFORMATION

Initial Approach: *Initial Contact:* brief letter of inquiry or proposal *Include Information On:* describe organization and its purpose, list of officers and directors, decribe program or project needing assistance, discuss current progress toward goal, a budget and list of contributors, IRS tax exemption letter, and IRS letter stating organization is not a private foundation *Deadlines:* one month prior to trustee meetings

Restrictions on Giving: The foundation limits its support to local or regional drives in communities where Donaldson employees live. The foundation does not support individuals, religious purposes, groups that influence legislation, or political campaigns. Applicants must qualify for tax exemption under the IRS Code and can not be a private foundation.

OTHER THINGS TO KNOW

The foundation considers capital grants, but limits them to 30% of the yearly giving.

Applicants receiving grants are furnished with a form of Statement of Donee, which must be returned to the foundation before payments can be made. The statement may be recalled for any future grant payments.

PUBLICATIONS

Application guidelines and annual report

GRANTS ANALYSIS

Total Grants: $523,000

Number of Grants: 166

Highest Grant: $111,000

Average Grant: $3,151

Typical Range: $1,000 to $5,000

Disclosure Period: fiscal year ending July 31, 1994

Note: Recent grants are derived from a 1992 grants list.

RECENT GRANTS

Library

2,500	Cresco Public Library, Cresco, IA

General

111,000	Minneapolis United Way, Minneapolis, MN
12,500	Mercy Hospital, Oelwein, IA
11,000	Minnesota Private College Fund, St. Paul, MN
10,000	United Way, Minneapolis, MN
10,000	University of Minnesota

Federated Mutual Insurance Co. / Federated Insurance Foundation

Former Foundation Name: Federated Mutual Insurance Foundation
Premiums: $800.0 million
Employees: 2,700
Headquarters: Owatonna, MN
SIC Major Group: Insurance Carriers

CONTACT

Rick Kraus
Manager, Corporate Human Resources
Federated Mutual Insurance Co.
121 E Park Sq.
Owatonna, MN 55060
(507) 455-5200

FINANCIAL SUMMARY

Recent Giving: $122,673 (1994); $104,185 (1993); $105,114 (1992)

Assets: $19,551 (1993); $16,074 (1992); $4,367 (1990)

Gifts Received: $4,458 (1993); $3,602 (1992)

Fiscal Note: In 1993, could not locate contributor.

EIN: 23-7173646

CONTRIBUTIONS SUMMARY

Typical Recipients: • *Arts & Humanities:* Art History, Arts Appreciation, Arts Associations & Councils, Arts Centers, Arts Festivals, Arts Funds, Arts Institutes, Arts Outreach, Community Arts, General, Historic Preservation, History & Archaeology, Libraries, Literary Arts, Museums/Galleries, Music, Performing Arts, Public Broadcasting, Theater, Visual Arts • *Civic & Public Affairs:* Botanical Gardens/Parks, Business/Free Enterprise, Chambers of Commerce, Clubs, Community Foundations, Economic Development, Economic Policy, Employment/Job Training, General, Law & Justice, Parades/Festivals, Philanthropic Organizations, Professional & Trade Associations, Safety, Zoos/Aquariums • *Education:* Afterschool/Enrichment Programs, Agricultural Education, Arts/Humanities Education,

Business Education, Business-School Partnerships, Colleges & Universities, Continuing Education, Economic Education, Education Associations, Education Funds, Elementary Education (Public), General, Health & Physical Education, International Exchange, Literacy, Preschool Education, Science/Mathematics Education, Secondary Education (Public), Social Sciences Education, Special Education, Vocational & Technical Education • *Environment:* General • *Health:* Adolescent Health Issues, AIDS/HIV, Cancer, Children's Health/Hospitals, Clinics/Medical Centers, General, Geriatric Health, Health Policy/Cost Containment, Health Organizations, Heart, Home-Care Services, Hospices, Hospitals, Long-Term Care, Medical Rehabilitation, Medical Research, Nutrition, Prenatal Health Issues, Preventive Medicine/Wellness Organizations, Public Health, Single-Disease Health Associations • *Science:* General, Science Museums • *Social Services:* At-Risk Youth, Camps, Community Centers, Community Service Organizations, Counseling, Day Care, Domestic Violence, Emergency Relief, Family Planning, Family Services, Food/Clothing Distribution, Homes, People with Disabilities, Recreation & Athletics, Senior Services, Shelters/Homelessness, Substance Abuse, United Funds/United Ways, Volunteer Services, Youth Organizations

Grant Types: general support and project

Geographic Distribution: Initial Approach: In the home office, division and major operating communities.

Operating Locations: AZ (Phoenix), GA (Atlanta), MN (Minneapolis, Owatonna, St. Paul)

CORP. OFFICERS

Charles I. Buxton II: *B* Owatonna MN 1924 *ED* US Naval Academy BS 1946; Univ PA postgrad *CURR EMPL* chmn, ceo: Federated Ins Co *CORP AFFIL* chmn, ceo: Fed Life Ins Co, Fed Svc Ins Co; pres, dir: Fed Acceptance Corp, Fed Mutual Agency *NONPR AFFIL* bd govs: Am Inst Property Liability Underwriters; dir: Alliance Am Insurers, MN Ins Federation, MN Ins Information Svc; trust: Assoc Churches Owatonna

Kirk N. Nelson: *CURR EMPL* pres, coo: Federated Ins Co

GIVING OFFICERS

Charles I. Buxton II: pres *CURR EMPL* chmn, ceo: Federated Ins Co (see above)

J. E. Meilahn: secy, treas

Kirk N. Nelson: vp *CURR EMPL* pres, coo: Federated Ins Co (see above)

J. L. Sheard: vp, asst treas

APPLICATION INFORMATION

Initial Approach: Send Send a brief letter of inquiry and a full proposal.. Include a a description of organization, amount requested, purpose of funds sought, recently audited financial statement, and proof of tax-exempt status. Also include the name of the contact perosn. There are no deadlines.

Restrictions on Giving: Does not support individuals, religious organizations for sectarian purposesigious organizations, political or lobbying groups, or organizations outside operating areas.

OTHER THINGS TO KNOW
Company supports human services with 46% of contributions; education, 20%; youth, 10%; arts and humanities, 5.5%; unallocated, 10%; health and wellness, 3.5%; civic and community, 4%; and environment, 1%.

GRANTS ANALYSIS
Total Grants: $104,185

Number of Grants: 105*

Highest Grant: $25,652

Typical Range: $100 to $3,000

Disclosure Period: 1993

Note: Recent grants are derived from a 1993 Form 990.

RECENT GRANTS
Library

5,000	Owatonna Public Library, Owatonna, MN

General

20,000	Steele County United Way
7,000	Dartts Park Baseball Renovation — youth development
5,754	United Way of Metropolitan Atlanta, Atlanta, GA
4,700	Minnesota Private College Fund, St. Paul, MN
3,373	United Way of Steele County

General Mills, Inc. / General Mills Foundation

Revenue: $8.51 billion
Employees: 121,300
Headquarters: Minneapolis, MN
SIC Major Group: Cereal Breakfast Foods, Fluid Milk, Dehydrated Fruits, Vegetables & Soups, and Frozen Fruits & Vegetables

CONTACT
Cindy Thelen
Coordinator
General Mills Foundation
PO Box 1113
Minneapolis, MN 55440
(612) 540-7890

Note: General Mills Foundation's express mail address is General Mills Foundation, One General Mills Blvd., Minneapolis, MN 55426. Foundation also has an alternative contact for the Orlando area. See "Other Things To Know" for more details.

FINANCIAL SUMMARY
Recent Giving: $20,000,000 (fiscal 1994 approx.); $17,206,933 (fiscal 1993); $14,209,236 (fiscal 1992)

Assets: $59,466,476 (fiscal 1993); $44,473,040 (fiscal 1992); $41,893,547 (fiscal 1991)

Gifts Received: $16,900,000 (fiscal 1993); $14,700,000 (fiscal 1992)

Fiscal Note: Above figures represent foundation giving only. Company also gives directly through the corporation and its subsidiaries. The foundation receives contributions from General Mills and its subsidiaries. Above figures exclude nonmonetary support.

EIN: 41-6018495

CONTRIBUTIONS SUMMARY
Typical Recipients: • *Arts & Humanities:* Arts Associations & Councils, Arts Centers, Arts Institutes, Dance, Film & Video, General, Historic Preservation, History & Archaeology, Libraries, Literary Arts, Museums/Galleries, Music, Opera, Performing Arts, Public Broadcasting, Theater • *Civic & Public Affairs:* Asian American Affairs, Business/Free Enterprise, Civil Rights, Economic Development, Employment/Job Training, General, Housing, Law & Justice, Municipalities/Towns, Professional & Trade Associations, Public Policy, Urban & Community Affairs, Women's Affairs, Zoos/Aquariums • *Education:* Agricultural Education, Arts/Humanities Education, Business Education, Business-School Partnerships, Colleges & Universities, Community & Junior Colleges, Continuing Education, Economic Education, Education Associations, Education Funds, Education Reform, Elementary Education (Public), Engineering/Technological Education, Faculty Development, General, Gifted & Talented Programs, International Exchange, International Studies, Legal Education, Literacy, Medical Education, Minority Education, Preschool Education, Private Education (Precollege), Public Education (Precollege), Religious Education, Science/Mathematics Education, Special Education, Student Aid • *Environment:* General • *Health:* Cancer, Emergency/Ambulance Services, Geriatric Health, Health Policy/Cost Containment, Health Organizations, Hospitals, Medical Rehabilitation, Medical Research, Mental Health, Nutrition • *Social Services:* At-Risk Youth, Child Welfare, Community Centers, Community Service Organizations, Counseling, Day Care, Delinquency & Criminal Rehabilitation, Domestic Violence, Emergency Relief, Family Planning, Family Services, Food/Clothing Distribution, Homes, People with Disabilities, Recreation & Athletics, Refugee Assistance, Senior Services, Shelters/Homelessness, Substance Abuse, United Funds/United Ways, Volunteer Services, Youth Organizations

Grant Types: capital, conference/seminar, employee matching gifts, general support, operating expenses, and project

Note: Foundation makes a limited number of capital grants and only for spcial purposes that meet specific community needs within the foundation's funding focus.

Nonmonetary Support: $5,300,000 (fiscal 1992); $5,500,000 (fiscal 1990)

Nonmonetary Support Types: donated products, loaned employees, and loaned executives

Note: General Mills donates a substantial amount of food products primarily through Second Harvest food banks. More than 10

million pounds of food were donated to food banks and relief efforts in fiscal 1992. Contact David Nasby, Vice President, at (612) 540-4351 for more information on nonmonetary support.

Geographic Distribution: primarily in communities where the company has a substantial number of employees

Operating Locations: AL, AR, AZ, CA (Lodi, Vallejo, Vernon), CO, CT, DE, FL (Ocala, Orlando), GA (Covington), HI, IA (Avon, Cedar Rapids), ID, IL (Chicago, South Chicago, St. Charles, West Chicago), IN, KS, KY, LA, MA (Gloucester), MD, ME, MI, MN (Golden Valley, Minneapolis), MO (Kansas City), MS, MT (Great Falls), NC, ND, NE, NH, NJ, NM (Albuquerque), NV, NY (Buffalo, New York), OH (Toledo), OK, OR, PA (Carlisle), RI, SC, SD, TN (Johnson City), TX, UT, VA, VT, WA, WI, WV, WY

CORP. OFFICERS
Horace Brewster Atwater, Jr.: *B* Minneapolis MN 1931 *ED* Princeton Univ AB 1952; Stanford Univ MBA 1954 *CURR EMPL* chmn, ceo, dir: Gen Mills Inc *CORP AFFIL* dir: Gen Electric Co, Merck & Co Inc, Natl Broadcasting Co; mem intl counc: JP Morgan & Co *NONPR AFFIL* adv bd mem: Whitney Mus Am Art; dir: Am Pub Radio; mem: Bus Counc; mem adv counc: Stanford Univ Grad Sch Bus; mem bd: MN Bus Partnership, Walker Art Ctr; mem policy comm: Bus Roundtable *PHIL AFFIL* trust: Merck Co. Foundation; chmn mems, chmn bd trusts: General Mills Fdn; trust: Merck Co Fdn *CLUB AFFIL* Woodhill CC

Leslie M. Frecon: *B* 1954 *CURR EMPL* sr vp, corp fin: Gen Mills Inc

Joe R. Lee: *B* Jessup GA 1940 *ED* Univ GA; US Air Force Acad; Valdosta St Coll *CURR EMPL* vchmn, ceo of Darden: Gen Mills Inc *CORP AFFIL* dir: Graco Inc

David Asher Nasby: *B* Chicago IL 1939 *ED* St Olaf Coll BA 1963; Luther Theological Seminary BD 1966 *CURR EMPL* vp, dir commun aff: Gen Mills Inc *NONPR AFFIL* bd mem: Assn Gov Bds; chmn: Luther Northwestern Seminary; mem: Grocery Mfrs Am, Minneapolis Commun Coll Fdn, Pvt Indus Counc *CLUB AFFIL* 5:55, Minneapolis

Thomas P. Nelson: *CURR EMPL* sr vp, contr: Gen Mills Inc

Michael A. Peel: *B* 1950 *CURR EMPL* sr vp: Gen Mills Inc

Stephen W. Sanger: *B* 1945 *CURR EMPL* chmn, ceo: Gen Mills Inc *NONPR AFFIL* treas: Guthrie Theater Fdn

Clifford Lane Whitehill: *B* Houston TX 1931 *ED* Rice Univ BA 1954; Univ TX LLB 1957; Harvard Univ LLM 1958 *CURR EMPL* sr vp, gen couns, secy: Gen Mills Inc *NONPR AFFIL* assoc bd mem: MN Opera; dir: Am Arbitration Assn, Fund Legal Aid Soc, MN Assn Commerce Indus, MN Special Olympics, MN-Uruguay Ptnrs Ams, Natl Hispanic Scholarship Comm, UN Assn, US Assn Gen Couns; mem: Am Bar Assn, Bus Roundtable, MN Bar Assn, MN Minority Corp Couns, Natl Assn Mfrs, TX Bar Assn; mem adv comm: Natl Chamber Litigation

Ctr; mem corp adv bd: Natl Commn Children, Practicing Law Inst; mem dean's counc: Hamline Univ Law Sch; mem exec comm: Ctr Pub Resources; mem legal exec comm: Grocery Mfrs Am; treas, dir: Better Bus Bur MN; trust: Food Drug Law Inst, Meridian House Intl, William Mitchell Coll Law; vchmn: Better Bus Bur *CLUB AFFIL* Harvard, Lafayette

GIVING OFFICERS

Horace Brewster Atwater, Jr.: chmn, trust *CURR EMPL* chmn, ceo, dir: Gen Mills Inc *PHIL AFFIL* trust: Merck Co. Foundation (see above)

Leslie M. Frecon: trust *CURR EMPL* sr vp, corp fin: Gen Mills Inc (see above)

Joe R. Lee: trust *CURR EMPL* vchmn, ceo of Darden: Gen Mills Inc (see above)

David Asher Nasby: vp *CURR EMPL* vp, dir commun aff: Gen Mills Inc (see above)

Thomas P. Nelson: trust *CURR EMPL* sr vp, contr: Gen Mills Inc (see above)

Michael A. Peel: trust *CURR EMPL* sr vp: Gen Mills Inc (see above)

Stephen W. Sanger: trust *CURR EMPL* chmn, ceo: Gen Mills Inc (see above)

Cindy Thelen: coordinator

David Van Benschoten: treas

Clifford Lane Whitehill: secy, trust *CURR EMPL* sr vp, gen couns, secy: Gen Mills Inc (see above)

Mark Hinckley Willes: trust *B* Salt Lake City UT 1941 *ED* Columbia Univ AB 1963; Columbia Univ PhD 1967 *CURR EMPL* pres, ceo: Times Mirror Co *CORP AFFIL* dir: Black & Decker Corp, Ryder Sys Inc

APPLICATION INFORMATION

Initial Approach: *Initial Contact:* brief letter or proposal *Include Information On:* description of the organization, with a list of its officers and board members; description of the purpose for which the grant is sought and the constituency that will benefit from the project; amount requested, plus justification for that amount; specific details on how this purpose will be achieved by the grant; evidence of need for the project and that the persons proposing the project are able to carry it to completion; planned method for evaluating the proposal program; proof of tax-exempt status, a recently audited financial statement, and the most recent 990 tax form; a specific budget for the project, as well as operating budget for current year; and a major donor list giving the amount of assured and anticipated support for the project proposed *Deadlines:* none; board meets periodically throughout the year *Note:* Application form is available from the foundation.

Restrictions on Giving: Does not support individuals; political, or lobbying organizations; recreation or travel; campaigns to eliminate or control specific diseases; basic or applied research programs; athletic

events; testimonial dinners or fundraisers; for-profit organizations; advertising; sponsorship; or local organizations other than those serving General Mills communities.

Generally does not make grants to subsidize publications, films, television shows, or endowment campaigns.

OTHER THINGS TO KNOW

The company sponsors a number of nutrition education services to improve Americans' health through increased knowledge of nutrition.

The company's corporate citizenship thrust is in three major areas: foundation giving, employee volunteerism, and Altcare, a joint venture of General Mills and the Wilder Foundation of St. Paul, MN. Altcare is an established health-care program concerned with long-term care of the elderly, in particular, alternatives to nursing homes.

The contact in the Orlando area is Patty DeYoung, Community Relations Representative, General Mills Restaurants, 5900 Lake Ellenor Dr., Orlando, FL 32809, (407)850-5213, or FAX (407)856-6648.

The foundation conducts both pre- and post-grant evaluations and seeks the participation of the nonprofit in this process. The foundation also keeps a confidential record of all grants requests that have been accepted for nine years. Records of grants requests that are declined are kept for three years.

PUBLICATIONS
Annual report

GRANTS ANALYSIS
Total Grants: $20,000,000*

Typical Range: $5,000 to $30,000

Disclosure Period: fiscal year ending May 31, 1994

Note: Fiscal data for foundation only. Total grants figure is approximate. Recent grants are derived from a fiscal 1993 annual report.

RECENT GRANTS

General

1,472,086	United Way of Minneapolis Area, Minneapolis, MN — operating support
250,000	United Negro College Fund, New York, NY — capital campaign for UNCF member institutions
230,000	Susan G. Komen Foundation, Dallas, TX — regional breast cancer summits
187,500	Messiah Willard Day Care Center, Minneapolis, MN — Northside Family Connection Way to Grow program
150,000	Carleton College, Northfield, MN — excellence in science program

Griggs and Mary Griggs Burke Foundation, Mary Livingston

CONTACT
Marvin J. Pertzik
Secretary and Treasurer
Mary Livingston Griggs and Mary Griggs
  Burke Foundation
55 E Fifth St.
1400 Norwest Center
St. Paul, MN 55101-1792
(612) 227-7683

FINANCIAL SUMMARY
Recent Giving: $900,000 (fiscal 1995 est.); $900,000 (fiscal 1994 approx.); $900,000 (fiscal 1993 approx.)

Assets: $19,000,000 (fiscal 1995 est.); $19,000,000 (fiscal 1994 approx.); $19,300,000 (fiscal 1993 approx.)

EIN: 41-6052355

CONTRIBUTIONS SUMMARY
Donor(s): The Mary Livingston Griggs and Mary Griggs Burke Foundation was established in 1966. The donor was Mary Livingston Griggs.

Typical Recipients: • *Arts & Humanities:* Arts Associations & Councils, Arts Centers, Arts Funds, Arts Outreach, Ballet, Dance, Historic Preservation, Libraries, Museums/Galleries, Music, Opera, Public Broadcasting, Theater, Visual Arts • *Civic & Public Affairs:* Botanical Gardens/Parks, Employment/Job Training, Nonprofit Management, Philanthropic Organizations, Urban & Community Affairs, Zoos/Aquariums • *Education:* Arts/Humanities Education, Colleges & Universities, International Studies, Literacy, Minority Education, Private Education (Precollege), Science/Mathematics Education, Student Aid • *Environment:* General, Resource Conservation • *Health:* Heart, Medical Research • *International:* International Peace & Security Issues, International Relations • *Science:* Science Museums, Scientific Organizations • *Social Services:* Family Planning, Shelters/Homelessness, United Funds/United Ways

Grant Types: capital, challenge, department, endowment, general support, professorship, and project

Geographic Distribution: primarily St. Paul and Minneapolis, MN; and New York, NY

GIVING OFFICERS
Eleanor Briggs: dir

Mary Livingston Griggs Burke: pres, dir *ED* Columbia Univ; Sarah Lawrence Coll *PHIL AFFIL* don, pres: Mary & Jackson Burke Foundation

Gale Lansing Davis: dir

C. E. Bayliss Griggs: vp, dir

Marvin J. Pertzik: secy, treas, dir

APPLICATION INFORMATION
Initial Approach:

Applicants should send a proposal that includes four copies of the cover letter.

Proposals should include a copy of the IRS tax-exempt determination letter. If the letter is more than one-year old, the foundation requests a statement indicating that there has been no change in the applicant's tax-exempt status. The proposal should also describe, clearly and concisely, the purposes of the grant, amount needed, the budget for the project, and whether or not assistance is sought from any other foundation. The proposal should also include the latest audited financial statements.

There is no deadline for submitting proposals.

Restrictions on Giving: The foundation does not make contributions to individuals, for dinners or special events, to fraternal organizations, political or lobbying groups, religious organizations for sectarian purposes, or for goodwill advertising.

GRANTS ANALYSIS

Total Grants: $1,055,847

Number of Grants: 94

Highest Grant: $175,000

Average Grant: $11,232

Typical Range: $1,000 to $25,000

Disclosure Period: fiscal year ending June 30, 1992

Note: Recent grants are derived from a fiscal 1992 Form 990.

RECENT GRANTS

Library
25,000	New York Library, New York, NY — Astor, Lenox and Tilden Foundations, Oriental Division
10,000	International Crane Foundation, Baraboo, WI — Ron Sauey Memorial Library
5,000	Pierpont Morgan Library, New York, NY — capital campaign

General
175,000	Mary and Jackson Burke Foundation, St. Paul, MN — acquisition
67,500	Cable Natural History Museum, Cable, WI — general operating
56,000	Columbia University, New York, NY — graduate assistance
50,000	Asia Society, New York, NY — annual fund
50,000	Mary and Jackson Burke Foundation, St. Paul, MN — administration

Hallett Charitable Trust, E. W.

Former Foundation Name: Hallett Charitable Trust

CONTACT
Margaret Poley
Trust Officer
E. W. Hallett Charitable Trust
c/o First Bank, N.A.
PO Box 64704
St. Paul, MN 55402
(612) 973-0052

FINANCIAL SUMMARY
Recent Giving: $499,109 (fiscal 1994); $605,975 (fiscal 1991); $582,846 (fiscal 1990)

Assets: $10,363,458 (fiscal 1994); $10,119,941 (fiscal 1991); $9,792,186 (fiscal 1990)

EIN: 41-6261160

CONTRIBUTIONS SUMMARY
Typical Recipients: • *Arts & Humanities:* Libraries • *Civic & Public Affairs:* Economic Development, Municipalities/Towns, Urban & Community Affairs • *Education:* Colleges & Universities, Education Funds, Public Education (Precollege), Religious Education, Science/Mathematics Education, Student Aid • *Health:* Clinics/Medical Centers, Hospices, Hospitals, Medical Rehabilitation • *Religion:* Churches • *Social Services:* Camps, Child Welfare, Homes, People with Disabilities, Recreation & Athletics, Scouts, Youth Organizations

Grant Types: general support

Geographic Distribution: focus on MN

GIVING OFFICERS
N. Jean Rude: trust

Paul D. Schliesman: exec dir *PHIL AFFIL dir:* Tom and Frances Leach Foundation

Osmon R. Springsted: trust

APPLICATION INFORMATION
Initial Approach: Send brief letter of inquiry describing program or project. Include a description of organization, amount requested, purpose of funds sought, recently audited financial statement, and proof of tax-exempt status. There are no deadlines.

Restrictions on Giving: Does not support individuals.

GRANTS ANALYSIS
Total Grants: $499,109

Number of Grants: 28

Highest Grant: $57,000

Typical Range: $3,235 to $50,000

Disclosure Period: fiscal year ending November 30, 1994

Note: Recent grants are derived from a fiscal 1994 Form 990.

RECENT GRANTS

General
57,000	Crosby-Ironton Independent School District 182, Crosby, MN — electronics laboratory
50,000	Cuyana Regional Medical Center, Crosby, MN — long-term care program
49,180	Crosby-Ironton Independent School District 182, Crosby, MN — alternative education program
43,040	Cuyana Regional Medical Center, Crosby, MN — helicopter landing site
30,000	Crosby-Ironton Independent School District 182, Crosby, MN — scholarship fund

Hallett Charitable Trust, Jessie F.

CONTACT
Paul D. Schliesman
Fund Administrator
Jessie F. Hallett Charitable Trust
c/o First Bank N.A.
PO Box 64704
Saint Paul, MN 55164
(612) 973-0047
Note: Application address: c/o First Bank, N.A., 120 South Sixth St., Minneapolis, MN 55480

FINANCIAL SUMMARY
Recent Giving: $293,883 (fiscal 1993); $343,711 (fiscal 1992); $322,449 (fiscal 1990)

Assets: $7,523,470 (fiscal 1993); $7,161,989 (fiscal 1992); $6,115,063 (fiscal 1990)

EIN: 41-6211994

CONTRIBUTIONS SUMMARY
Donor(s): the late Jessie F. Hallett the Bat Handiv Foundation and the Bat Hanadiv Foundation No. 2

Typical Recipients: • *Arts & Humanities:* Libraries • *Civic & Public Affairs:* Economic Development, Municipalities/Towns • *Education:* Colleges & Universities, Religious Education • *Health:* Eyes/Blindness, Health Organizations • *Religion:* Bible Study/Translation, Churches, Religious Organizations, Religious Welfare, Seminaries • *Social Services:* Child Welfare, Homes, People with Disabilities, Scouts, Youth Organizations

Grant Types: general support

Geographic Distribution: national

GIVING OFFICERS
A. C. Jensen: trust

Osmond R. Springsted: trust

APPLICATION INFORMATION
Initial Approach: Send a brief letter of inquiry. Include a description of organization, amount requested, purpose of funds sought,

recently audited financial statement, and proof of tax-exempt status. There are no deadlines.

Restrictions on Giving: Does not provide grants to individuals. Trust is set up for religious, charitable, scientific, literary, and educational purposes.

GRANTS ANALYSIS
Total Grants: $293,883

Number of Grants: 17

Highest Grant: $45,514

Typical Range: $250 to $45,514

Disclosure Period: fiscal year ending November 30, 1993

Note: Recent grants are derived from a fiscal 1993 Form 990.

RECENT GRANTS
Library

500	Village of Crosby Public Library, Crosby, MN

General

45,514	Berea College, Beara, KY
45,514	Bethel College and Seminary, St. Paul, MN
45,514	Moody Bible Institute, Chicago, IL
30,343	Concordia College, Moorehead, MN
30,343	Jamestown Presbyterian College, Jamestown, ND

Hartz Foundation

CONTACT
Onealee Hartz
Secretary and Treasurer
Hartz Fdn.
PO Box 642
Thief River Falls, MN 56701
(803) 449-7155

FINANCIAL SUMMARY
Recent Giving: $214,000 (fiscal 1994); $265,050 (fiscal 1992); $260,050 (fiscal 1991)

Assets: $4,703,115 (fiscal 1994); $4,835,235 (fiscal 1992); $4,632,894 (fiscal 1991)

Gifts Received: $395 (fiscal 1992)

EIN: 41-6041638

CONTRIBUTIONS SUMMARY
Typical Recipients: • *Arts & Humanities:* Libraries, Public Broadcasting • *Civic & Public Affairs:* Botanical Gardens/Parks, Employment/Job Training, Law & Justice, Parades/Festivals, Urban & Community Affairs • *Education:* Community & Junior Colleges, Education Funds, Vocational & Technical Education • *Environment:* General, Watershed • *Health:* Emergency/Ambulance Services, Hospices, Medical Research, Research/Studies Institutes • *Religion:* Churches, Missionary Activities (Domestic), Religious Organizations • *Social Services:* Big Brother/Big Sister, Community Centers,

Community Service Organizations, Recreation & Athletics, Scouts, Senior Services

Grant Types: general support

Geographic Distribution: focus on MN

GIVING OFFICERS
Gene Beito: pres

Onealee Hartz: secy, treas

Dwight Tanquist: vp

APPLICATION INFORMATION
Initial Approach: Send cover letter and full proposal. Include a description of organization, amount requested, purpose of funds sought, recently audited financial statement, and proof of tax-exempt status. There are no deadlines.

Restrictions on Giving: Does not support individuals.

GRANTS ANALYSIS
Total Grants: $214,000

Number of Grants: 39

Highest Grant: $25,000

Typical Range: $100 to $25,000

Disclosure Period: fiscal year ending July 31, 1994

Note: Recent grants are derived from a fiscal 1994 Form 990.

RECENT GRANTS
Library

3,300	Warroad Public Library, Warroad, MN — computer equipment

General

25,000	Thief River Falls Golf Course, Thief River Falls, MN — new construction
25,000	Thief River Falls Soo Line Depot, Thief River Falls, MN
20,000	Mayo Foundation, Rochester, MN
15,000	Northland Community College, Thief River Falls, MN — scholarships
15,000	Northwest Technical College — scholarships

Hickory Tech Corp. / Hickory Tech Corp. Foundation

Former Foundation Name: Mankato Citizens Telephone Co. Foundation
Sales: $56.6 million
Employees: 435
Headquarters: Mankato, MN
SIC Major Group: Telephone Communications Except Radiotelephone

CONTACT
Jane L. Rush
President
Hickory Tech Corp. Fdn.
221 E Hickory St.
PO Box 3248
Mankato, MN 56002-3248
(507) 387-1866

FINANCIAL SUMMARY
Recent Giving: $264,542 (fiscal 1994); $290,683 (fiscal 1993); $169,659 (fiscal 1991)

Assets: $3,461,472 (fiscal 1994); $3,416,179 (fiscal 1993); $2,560,227 (fiscal 1991)

Gifts Received: $70,000 (fiscal 1994); $450,000 (fiscal 1993); $425,000 (fiscal 1991)

Fiscal Note: Company gives through its foundation only. In fiscal 1994, contributions were received from Mankato Citizens Telephone Co.

EIN: 41-6034001

CONTRIBUTIONS SUMMARY
Typical Recipients: • *Arts & Humanities:* Arts Outreach, General, Libraries, Music, Performing Arts, Public Broadcasting, Theater • *Civic & Public Affairs:* Botanical Gardens/Parks, Business/Free Enterprise, Chambers of Commerce, Community Foundations, Economic Development, General, Housing, Parades/Festivals, Urban & Community Affairs • *Education:* Business Education, Business-School Partnerships, Colleges & Universities, Community & Junior Colleges, Economic Education, Education Funds, Engineering/Technological Education, Faculty Development, General, International Studies, Leadership Training, Minority Education, Private Education (Precollege), Public Education (Precollege), Religious Education, Science/Mathematics Education, Secondary Education (Private), Secondary Education (Public), Student Aid, Vocational & Technical Education • *Environment:* General • *Health:* Hospitals, Multiple Sclerosis, Trauma Treatment • *Religion:* Religious Organizations, Religious Welfare • *Science:* Science Exhibits & Fairs • *Social Services:* Camps, Food/Clothing Distribution, General, Recreation & Athletics, Scouts, Senior Services, United Funds/United Ways, Volunteer Services, YMCA/YWCA/YMHA/YWHA, Youth Organizations

Grant Types: capital, employee matching gifts, multiyear/continuing support, and scholarship

Geographic Distribution: primarily in the areas of company operations; emphasis on Mankato, MN

Operating Locations: CA (Los Angeles), IA (Homestead), MN (Mankato, St. Paul), TX (Allen)

CORP. OFFICERS
Robert D. Alton, Jr.: *CURR EMPL* chmn, pres, ceo: Hickory Tech Corp *CORP AFFIL* chmn, dir: Mankato Citizens Tel Co

David A. Christensen: *CURR EMPL* vp, secy, cfo: Hickory Tech Corp

GIVING OFFICERS
Robert D. Alton, Jr.: trust *CURR EMPL* chmn, pres, ceo: Hickory Tech Corp (see above)

Lyle T. Bosacker: trust *CORP AFFIL* dir: Hickory Tech Corp, Mankato Citizens Tel Co

David A. Christensen: secy, treas *CURR EMPL* vp, secy, cfo: Hickory Tech Corp (see above)

Robert K. Else: trust *CORP AFFIL* dir: Hickory Tech Corp, Mankato Citizens Tel Co

James H. Holdrege: trust *CORP AFFIL* dir: Hickory Tech Corp, Mankato Citizens Tel Co

Lyle G. Jacobson: trust *CORP AFFIL* dir: Hickory Tech Corp, Mankato Citizens Tel Co

R. Wynn Kearney, Jr.: trust *CORP AFFIL* dir: Hickory Tech Corp, Mankato Citizens Tel Co

Starr J. Kirklin: trust *CORP AFFIL* dir: Hickory Tech Corp, Mankato Citizens Tel Co

Jane L. Rush: pres

APPLICATION INFORMATION

Initial Approach: *Initial Contact:* a brief letter of inquiry *Include Information On:* a description of organization, amount requested, proof of tax-exempt status, audited financial statement, and descriptive brochures or materials *Deadlines:* December 15

Restrictions on Giving: Does not support individuals, religious organizations for sectarian purposes, political or lobbying groups, organizations outside operating areas, or organizations that discriminate.

GRANTS ANALYSIS

Total Grants: $264,542

Number of Grants: 67

Highest Grant: $65,000

Average Grant: $3,948

Typical Range: $500 to $5,000

Disclosure Period: fiscal year ending February 28, 1994

Note: Recent grants are derived from a fiscal 1994 Form 990.

RECENT GRANTS

Library
500	Minnesota Valley Regional Library, Mankato, MN

General
65,000	Mankato Lutheran Home, Mankato, MN — capital funds
40,000	Citizen's Scholarship Foundation of America, Minneapolis, MN
25,000	Bethany Lutheran College, Mankato, MN
24,950	Mankato State University Foundation, Mankato, MN — scholarships
20,031	Greater Mankato Area United Way, Mankato, MN

Jostens, Inc. / Jostens Foundation Inc., The

Sales: $827.0 million
Employees: 8,000
Headquarters: Minneapolis, MN
SIC Major Group: Jewelry & Precious Metal, Apparel & Accessories Nec, Miscellaneous Publishing, and Commercial Printing—Lithographic

CONTACT

Gregory J. Bailey
Manager
The Jostens Foundation Inc.
5501 Norman Center Dr.
Minneapolis, MN 55437
(612) 830-3235
Note: An additional contact is Veronica R. Theobald, Foundation Specialist, at the above address and phone number. The company's World Wide Web address is http://gopher.jostens.com:2071

FINANCIAL SUMMARY

Recent Giving: $487,000 (fiscal 1995 est.); $405,962 (fiscal 1994); $1,109,620 (fiscal 1993)

Assets: $952,183 (fiscal 1989)

Fiscal Note: Figures are for foundation giving only.

EIN: 41-1280587

CONTRIBUTIONS SUMMARY

Typical Recipients: • *Arts & Humanities:* Arts Associations & Councils, Arts Centers, Arts Institutes, Ethnic & Folk Arts, General, Libraries, Museums/Galleries, Music, Opera, Performing Arts, Public Broadcasting, Theater • *Civic & Public Affairs:* Employment/Job Training, Housing, Legal Aid, Nonprofit Management, Public Policy • *Education:* Business Education, Economic Education, Education Associations, Education Funds, Education Reform, General, Gifted & Talented Programs, Literacy, Minority Education, Public Education (Precollege) • *Health:* Arthritis, Cancer, Children's Health/Hospitals, Eyes/Blindness, Prenatal Health Issues, Trauma Treatment • *Science:* Science Museums • *Social Services:* Child Abuse, Community Centers, Community Service Organizations, Family Services, Scouts, Special Olympics, Substance Abuse, United Funds/United Ways, Youth Organizations

Grant Types: emergency, employee matching gifts, general support, and multiyear/continuing support

Nonmonetary Support: $50,000 (fiscal 1992); $228,000 (fiscal 1989)

Nonmonetary Support Types: donated products, in-kind services, loaned employees, and loaned executives

Note: Nonmonetary support is provided by Jostens, Inc. The contact for nonmonetary support is Gregory J. Bailey, Manager of Corporate Communications, Jostens, Inc., at the above address.

Geographic Distribution: near Jostens operating locations, with emphasis on the Minneapolis-St. Paul, MN area

Operating Locations: AZ (Phoenix), CA (Anaheim, Porterville, San Diego, Visalia), GA (Atlanta), IL (Princeton, Springfield), KS (Abilene, Manhattan, Omaha, Overland Park, Topeka, Yates Center), MA (Attleboro), MI (Dimondale, Lansing), MN (Burnsville, Eden Prairie, Lakeville, Minneapolis, Owatanna, Red Wing, St. Paul), MO (Boonville), MS (Jackson), NC (Winston-Salem), NE (Omaha), NY (Webster), PA (Exton, State College), SC (Laurens), TN (Clarksville, Memphis, Shelbyville), TX (Denton, Irving), UT (Orem)

Note: Operates over 30 plants in the United States and Canada, including Winnipeg, Manitoba; Toronto, Ontario; and Montreal and Sherbrooke, Quebec.

CORP. OFFICERS

Robert C. Buhrmaster: *B* Schenectady NY 1947 *ED* Rensselaer Polytech Inst BS 1969; Dartmouth Coll MBA 1974 *CURR EMPL* pres, ceo, dir: Jostens Inc *CORP AFFIL* pres, dir: Jostens Photography Inc

Orville Earl Fisher, Jr.: *B* LaCrosse WI 1944 *ED* Univ MN BA; Univ MN JD *CURR EMPL* sr vp, gen couns, secy: Jostens Inc *NONPR AFFIL* dir: Am Inc, Bus Econ Ed Fdn, Citizens Scholarship Fdn Am, Sch District 227; mem: Am Assn Corp Couns, Am Bar Assn, Am Soc Corp Secys, Direct Selling Assn, Fed Bar Assn, Hennepin County Bar Assn, MN Bar Assn

John L. Jones: *CURR EMPL* sr vp human resources: Jostens Inc

Charles W. Schmid: *CURR EMPL* sr vp, chief mktg off: Jostens Inc

GIVING OFFICERS

Gregory J. Bailey: mgr *CURR EMPL* mgr corp commun: Jostens Inc

Orville Earl Fisher, Jr.: treas, mem contributions comm *CURR EMPL* sr vp, gen couns, secy: Jostens Inc (see above)

Jennifer Olson-Goude: dir

Trudy A. Rautio: dir *CURR EMPL* vp, contr: Jostens Inc

Charles W. Schmid: dir *CURR EMPL* sr vp, chief mktg off: Jostens Inc (see above)

Veronica R. Theobold: fdn specialist

Kevin Whalen: dir

APPLICATION INFORMATION

Initial Approach: *Initial Contact:* letter or phone inquiry to recive application *Include Information On:* most recent annual report or list of directors and staff; recently audited financial report; copy of current year's budget with prior year comparisons; current and pending sources of support; 501(c)(3) tax-exempt certification; most recent IRS Form 990; and a completed Jostens Foundation Grant Application Form *Deadlines:* contact foundation to receive deadline dates

Restrictions on Giving: In general, does not make grants directly to schools, school districts, scholarship funds or educational foundations established on behalf of an individual or institution; fundraising or special event sponsorship, including ticket purchases; churches or religious groups; endowment funds and capital campaigns; organizations providing services located outside of Jostens' operating area.

Foundation gives grants only to 501(c)(3) organizations.

OTHER THINGS TO KNOW
Program grants generally made during the current year and not in installments for future years.

In 1987, Jostens organized employee contributions committees in several operating locations across the country. These committees make charitable grants within employees' local communities from dollars allocated by the foundation.

PUBLICATIONS
Annual Report of The Jostens Foundation Inc.

GRANTS ANALYSIS
Total Grants: $183,750

Number of Grants: 39

Average Grant: $4,712

Typical Range: $1000 to $5,000

Disclosure Period: fiscal year ending June 30, 1994

Note: Figures for total grants, number of grants, and average grant exclude $201,212 in matching gifts and $21,000 in scholarships. Recent grants are derived from a from fiscal 1993 grants list.

RECENT GRANTS

Library
Friends of the Red Wing Library, Red Wing, MN — for the arts, civic, and cultural purposes

General
Alisa Ann Ruch California Burn Foundation, Canoga Park, CA — for health and human services

American Cancer Society: Topeka, KS; Attleboro, MA; Shelbyville, TN — for health and human services

Arthritis Foundation, Atlanta, GA — for health and human services

Association of Governing Boards of Universities and Colleges, Washington, DC — for education

Boys and Girls Club of St. Paul, St. Paul, MN — for health and human services

Mahadh Foundation
Former Foundation Name: Mary Andersen Hulings Foundation

CONTACT
Peggie Scott
Grants Consultant
MAHADH Foundation
287 Central Ave.
Bayport, MN 55003
(612) 439-1557

FINANCIAL SUMMARY
Recent Giving: $1,268,325 (fiscal 1994); $1,624,831 (fiscal 1993); $2,033,125 (fiscal 1991)

Assets: $16,958,378 (fiscal 1994); $16,554,055 (fiscal 1993); $13,839,440 (fiscal 1991)

Gifts Received: $3,125,310 (fiscal 1991); $508,750 (fiscal 1990)

Fiscal Note: In fiscal 1991, contributions were received from the MEAH 1970 Trust.

EIN: 41-6020911

CONTRIBUTIONS SUMMARY
Donor(s): The foundation was established by Mary A. Hulings, Katherine B. Andersen, and the late Fred C. Andersen . The foundation reports that it is affiliated with the Croix Wood Trust and the Pine Wood Trust, both located in Minnesota.

Typical Recipients: • _Arts & Humanities:_ Arts Centers, Historic Preservation, History & Archaeology, Libraries, Music, Opera, Performing Arts, Public Broadcasting • _Civic & Public Affairs:_ Clubs, General, Housing, Professional & Trade Associations, Women's Affairs • _Education:_ Colleges & Universities, Community & Junior Colleges, Education Funds, Minority Education, Private Education (Precollege), Public Education (Precollege), Religious Education • _Environment:_ General, Resource Conservation, Wildlife Protection • _Health:_ Clinics/Medical Centers, Emergency/Ambulance Services, Health Funds, Hospitals, Mental Health, Single-Disease Health Associations, Transplant Networks/Donor Banks • _International:_ Health Care/Hospitals, International Environmental Issues, International Relief Efforts • _Religion:_ Churches, Religious Welfare • _Social Services:_ Child Welfare, Community Service Organizations, Family Services, Homes, People with Disabilities, Scouts, Substance Abuse, United Funds/United Ways, Volunteer Services, Youth Organizations

Grant Types: general support and operating expenses

Geographic Distribution: focus on Minnesota, with emphasis in St. Paul, the Bayport area, and western Wisconsin

GIVING OFFICERS
Kathleen R. Conley: secy, dir

Albert Dewayne Hulings: vp, dir _B_ 1913 _ED_ Carleton Coll 1936 _CURR EMPL_ hon chmn: Andersen Corp _PHIL AFFIL_ vp: Bayport Foundation

Mary Andersen Hulings: pres, dir

Arthur W. Kaemmer, M.D.: vp

Martha H. Kaemmer: vp

Mary H. Rice: vp

Peggie Scott: grants consult

Rodney M. Wilson: treas

APPLICATION INFORMATION
Initial Approach:

The foundation requests applications be made in writing. Applicants should request a printed questionnaire and guidelines.

The foundation requests that applicants include the following: completed questionnaire, copy of IRS 501 (c)(3) tax-exempt status, copy of most recent audited financial statement, list of other sources of funding, brief history of organization, description of expected results, list and qualifications of key management, list of the organization's board with their affiliations, and letters of support for organization or project.

Deadlines are December 15, April 15, and August 15.

Requests are generally reviewed in January, May, and September.

Restrictions on Giving: The foundation does not support individuals, businesses, or provide funds for scholarships.

OTHER THINGS TO KNOW
The foundation changed its name from the Mary Andersen Foundation to the MAHADH Foundation in 1994.

PUBLICATIONS
Annual report including application guidelines

GRANTS ANALYSIS
Total Grants: $1,268,325

Number of Grants: 82

Highest Grant: $200,000*

Average Grant: $15,467

Typical Range: $1,000 to $20,000

Disclosure Period: fiscal year ending February 28, 1994

Note: The highest grant figure is for fiscal 1993. Recent grants are derived from a fiscal 1994 partial grants list.

RECENT GRANTS

Library
5,000	Bayport Public Library, Bayport, MN

General
15,000	Hope House of St. Croix Valley, Stillwater, MN — capital support
10,000	Education Foundation of Hudson, Hudson, WI — endowment and operating
10,000	Human Services, Oakdale, MN — capital support
5,000	Resources for Child Caring, St. Paul, MN
4,500	Girl Scout Council of St. Croix Valley, St. Paul, MN

Marbrook Foundation

CONTACT
Conley Brooks, Jr.
Executive Director
Marbrook Fdn.
400 Baker Bldg.
Minneapolis, MN 55402
(612) 332-2454

FINANCIAL SUMMARY
Recent Giving: $325,000 (1993); $260,000 (1990); $260,000 (1989)

Assets: $8,711,954 (1993); $5,948,415 (1990); $6,400,028 (1989)

Gifts Received: $189,222 (1993)

Fiscal Note: In 1993, contributions were received from Markell Brooks.

EIN: 41-6019899

CONTRIBUTIONS SUMMARY
Donor(s): the late Edward Brooks, the late Markell C. Brooks, Markell C. Brooks Charitable Trust

Typical Recipients: • *Arts & Humanities:* Arts Institutes, Community Arts, History & Archaeology, Libraries, Museums/Galleries, Music, Public Broadcasting, Theater • *Civic & Public Affairs:* Economic Policy, Urban & Community Affairs • *Education:* Colleges & Universities, Economic Education, Private Education (Precollege) • *Environment:* Air/Water Quality, Resource Conservation • *Health:* Cancer, Hospitals • *Social Services:* Child Welfare, Community Service Organizations, Family Planning, Family Services, United Funds/United Ways, Youth Organizations

Grant Types: capital, conference/seminar, emergency, endowment, general support, multiyear/continuing support, operating expenses, professorship, project, research, and seed money

Geographic Distribution: limited to the Minneapolis-St. Paul, MN, area

GIVING OFFICERS
John E. Andrus III: trust *B* Fergus Falls MN 1909 *ED* Wesleyan Univ BA 1933 *PHIL AFFIL* dir, chmn emeritus: Surdna Foundation

Conley Brooks, Jr.: trust

Conley Brooks, Jr.: trust (see above)

Markell Brooks: trust

William R. Humphrey, Jr.: trust

APPLICATION INFORMATION
Initial Approach: Send cover letter and full proposal. Include a description of organization, amount requested, purpose of funds sought, recently audited financial statement, and proof of tax-exempt status. Deadlines are May 15 and October 15.

PUBLICATIONS
Annual Report (including application guidelines)

GRANTS ANALYSIS
Total Grants: $325,000

Number of Grants: 70

Highest Grant: $25,000

Typical Range: $500 to $20,000

Disclosure Period: 1993

Note: Recent grants are derived from a 1993 Form 990.

RECENT GRANTS
General

25,000	University of Minnesota Eastcliff Renovation, MN
15,000	MacAlester College Junior Facilities, St. Paul, MN
12,000	Breck School, Minneapolis, MN
11,000	Minneapolis Children's Foundation, Minneapolis, MN
10,000	Abbott-Northwestern Hospital Piper Cancer Center, Coon Rapids, MN

Mardag Foundation

CONTACT
Paul A. Verret
Executive Director and Secretary
Mardag Foundation
600 Norwest Ctr.
St. Paul, MN 55101
(612) 224-5463

FINANCIAL SUMMARY
Recent Giving: $1,600,000 (1995 est.); $1,555,675 (1994); $1,555,675 (1993)

Assets: $33,500,000 (1995 est.); $33,000,000 (1994 est.); $32,753,472 (1993)

EIN: 23-7022429

CONTRIBUTIONS SUMMARY
Donor(s): The Mardag Foundation was established in 1969. Originally known as the Ober Charitable Foundation, it was created by the estate of Agnes E. Ober . Mrs. Ober, who died at the age of eighty-two in 1969, was interested in the education of youth and in securing the welfare of the elderly. She served on the boards of trustees of several charitable foundations in St. Paul. Much of her estate was left to benefit charitable foundations in Minnesota.

The Mardag Foundation continues to distribute grants that reflect the philanthropic interests of Mrs. Ober.

Typical Recipients: • *Arts & Humanities:* Historic Preservation, Libraries, Museums/Galleries, Theater • *Civic & Public Affairs:* Business/Free Enterprise, Economic Development, Employment/Job Training, Housing, Legal Aid, Nonprofit Management, Philanthropic Organizations, Rural Affairs, Urban & Community Affairs • *Education:* Colleges & Universities, Elementary Education (Private), Literacy, Preschool Education, Private Education (Precollege), Public Education (Precollege), Special Education • *Environment:* General • *Health:* Geriatric Health, Health Organizations, Hospices, Hospitals, Mental Health, Single-Disease Health Associations • *Social Services:* Animal Protection, Child Welfare, Community Centers, Community Service Organizations, Counseling, Day Care, Delinquency & Criminal Rehabilitation, Domestic Violence, Emergency Relief, Family Services, Food/Clothing Distribution, Homes, People with Disabilities, Refugee Assistance, Senior Services, Shelters/Homelessness, Substance Abuse, United Funds/United Ways, Volunteer Services, Youth Organizations

Grant Types: capital, challenge, conference/seminar, department, emergency, endowment, general support, multiyear/continuing support, professorship, project, research, scholarship, and seed money

Geographic Distribution: Minnesota

GIVING OFFICERS
James E. Davidson: dir

Jean E. Hart: asst secy *B* 1933 *NONPR AFFIL* vp: St Paul Fdn

Dolores Henderson: dir

Katherine V. Lilly: dir

Thomas G. Mairs: pres

Gayle M. Ober: vp, dir

Richard B. Ober: treas, dir

Timothy M. Ober: dir

Paul A. Verret: exec dir, secy *B* 1941 *PHIL AFFIL* secy, treas: F. R. Bigelow Foundation; secy: Minnesota Foundation

APPLICATION INFORMATION
Initial Approach:

Applicants should submit a brief summary of their projects to determine whether or not they meet the interests of the foundation.

A full proposal should include the name and address of the applicant, amount requested, project objective, proof of tax-exempt status, and (if applicable) the estimated number of Minnesota citizens who will benefit from the project. Applicants should also include the position of the individual signing the application, detailed budget, other sources of funding, statement that applicant will spend the funds awarded solely for the purpose stated, length of time for which support will be needed, detailed income statement, and a description of each staff member assigned to the project.

There is no deadline for submitting applications.

The board meets quarterly, with more frequent meetings as needed. The board provides start-up costs for new programs with sound management and clear goals relevant to community needs, funds established agencies seeking to expand services or solve temporary financial difficulty, makes grants payable over a number of years, and provides matching funds.

Restrictions on Giving: The foundation generally will not fund sectarian religious programs, individuals, fiscal agents, or projects without other sources of financial support. The foundation will not make ongoing, open-ended grants.

PUBLICATIONS
Annual report

GRANTS ANALYSIS
Total Grants: $1,067,059

Number of Grants: 73

Highest Grant: $100,000

Average Grant: $14,617

Typical Range: $5,000 to $25,000

Disclosure Period: 1991

Note: Recent grants are derived from a 1991 annual report.

RECENT GRANTS

Library

25,000	Friends of the St. Paul Public Library, St. Paul, MN
11,975	Southcentral Minnesota Inter-Library Exchange, Mankato, MN
10,000	Minnesota Library Foundation, St. Paul, MN

General

100,000	Courage Center, Golden Valley, MN
50,000	Boys and Girls Club of St. Paul, St. Paul, MN
50,000	St. Paul Foundation, St. Paul, MN
37,500	Union Gospel Mission Association of St. Paul, St. Paul, MN
25,000	American Indian Opportunities Industrialization Center, Minneapolis, MN

Medtronic, Inc. / Medtronic Foundation

Sales: $1.33 billion
Employees: 6,303
Headquarters: Minneapolis, MN
SIC Major Group: Surgical & Medical Instruments

CONTACT

Penny Hunt
Director, Community Affairs & Foundation
Medtronic Foundation
7000 Central Ave., NE
Minneapolis, MN 55432
(612) 574-3024

FINANCIAL SUMMARY

Recent Giving: $3,800,000 (fiscal 1995 est.); $3,226,000 (fiscal 1994); $2,656,000 (fiscal 1993)

Assets: $453,000 (fiscal 1995 est.); $253,000 (fiscal 1994 approx.); $3,359,000 (fiscal 1993)

Fiscal Note: Above figures include both foundation contributions and direct corporate gifts. Direct giving for fiscal 1994 totalled was $360,000. Direct gifts usually support employee supported groups in their communities. Above figures exclude nonmonetary support. See "Other Things To Know" for more details.

EIN: 41-1306950

CONTRIBUTIONS SUMMARY

Typical Recipients: • *Arts & Humanities:* Arts Centers, Arts Institutes, Libraries, Museums/Galleries, Music, Opera, Performing Arts, Public Broadcasting, Theater, Visual Arts • *Civic & Public Affairs:* African American Affairs, Employment/Job Training, Hispanic Affairs, Housing, Urban & Community Affairs, Zoos/Aquariums • *Education:* Colleges & Universities, Community & Junior Colleges, Elementary Education (Private), Engineering/Technological Educa-

tion, Faculty Development, Health & Physical Education, Medical Education, Minority Education, Private Education (Precollege), Public Education (Precollege), Science/Mathematics Education • *Health:* Adolescent Health Issues, Cancer, Emergency/Ambulance Services, Geriatric Health, Health Policy/Cost Containment, Health Organizations, Nursing Services, Public Health, Trauma Treatment • *International:* Health Care/Hospitals • *Religion:* Religious Welfare • *Science:* Science Museums • *Social Services:* At-Risk Youth, Community Centers, Community Service Organizations, Family Services, Senior Services, United Funds/United Ways, Volunteer Services, YMCA/YWCA/YMHA/YWHA

Grant Types: employee matching gifts, general support, and project

Note: The Medtronic Foundation matching gift to education program matches up to $4,000 per employee per year, for contributions to educational institutions.

Nonmonetary Support: $4,700,000 (fiscal 1994); $3,500,000 (fiscal 1993); $660,000 (fiscal 1992)

Nonmonetary Support Types: donated equipment, donated products, and workplace solicitation

Note: Nonmonetary support is provided by the company. Workplace solicitation is for the United Way only.

Geographic Distribution: in Minneapolis-St. Paul; also in nine Medtronic plant communities

Operating Locations: AZ (Tempe), CA (Anaheim, Irvine, San Diego), CO (Englewood), MA (Danvers), MI, MN (Milaca, Minneapolis), NY (Forest Hills), PR (Humacao, Villalba), TX

Note: Also operates in Canada, Europe, and Asia.

CORP. OFFICERS

Celici K. Barnes: *CURR EMPL* vp: Medtronic Inc

Arthur D. Collins, Jr.: *CURR EMPL* pres, coo: Medtronic Inc

William Wallace George: *B* Muskegon MI 1942 *ED* GA Inst Tech BS 1964; Harvard Univ MBA 1966 *CURR EMPL* pres: Medtronic Inc *CORP AFFIL* dir: Abbott-Northwestern Hosp, Valspar Corp; pres: Space & Aviation Sys; vp: Litton Indus Inc *NONPR AFFIL* trust: Macalester Coll *CLUB AFFIL* Minikahda, Minneapolis

Glen David Nelson, MD: *CURR EMPL* vchmn, dir: Medtronic Inc *CORP AFFIL* dir: Carolson Holdings, Interstudy Minneapolis, Northwestern Natl Life Ins Co, St Paul Cos Inc *NONPR AFFIL* mem: Am Acad Med Dirs, Am Coll Physician Execs, Am Med Assn, Greater Minneapolis Chamber Commerce, Hennepin County Med Assn; prof: Univ MN

GIVING OFFICERS

Arthur D. Collins, Jr.: vchmn *CURR EMPL* pres, coo: Medtronic Inc (see above)

M. Jacqueline Eastwood: chmn health comm *CURR EMPL* vp, gen mgr, dir: Bio-Medicus

Janet S. Fiola: chmn, mem ed comm *CURR EMPL* senior vp human resources: Medtronic Inc

Penny Hunt: contact *CURR EMPL* dir commun aff: Medtronic Inc

Michael John Kallok: dir, chmn (ed comm) *B* Gary IN 1948 *ED* Univ CO BS 1970; Purdue Univ MS 1974; Univ MN PhD 1978 *CURR EMPL* dir res heart valve div, fellow, sr res med Instrumentation & Tech, sci editor: Medtronic Inc *CORP AFFIL* sci editor: Biomed Instrumentation & Tech *NONPR AFFIL* fellow: Am Coll Cardiology, Am Heart Assn; founding fellow: Am Inst Med & Biological Engg; mem: Am Physiological Soc, Am Soc Mechanical Engrs, Am Thoracic Soc, Assn Advancement Med Instrumentation, Biomed Engg Soc, Inst Electrical Electronics Engrs

Bonnie Labosky: dir, mem health comm

Ray LaVoie: dir, mem health comm

John A. Meslow: dir, mem communs comm *B* 1938 *ED* St Olaf Coll BA 1960 *CURR EMPL* pres: Medtronic Inc Neurological Bus

Stan Myrum: chmn communs comm

Tom Rooney: treas

Marcea Bland Staten: mem communs comm *B* 1948 *CURR EMPL* pres, dir: Ran-Mar Inc *CORP AFFIL* sr legal couns: Medtronic Inc

Steve Tranter: mem ed comm *CURR EMPL* vp: Medtronic Inc

APPLICATION INFORMATION

Initial Approach: *Initial Contact:* send written request for a grant application form to a Medtronic plant manager; Twin Cities applicants may submit a written request directly to Community Affairs Department *Include Information On:* brief description of organization; all previous Medtronic Foundation grants received by organization; current requested amount of funds and purpose for their use; project description, including constituents served, geographic area, use of volunteers, major accomplishments; implementation timetable; evaluation criteria; organization's current operating budget, including income (with top five donors and amounts given), and anticipated expenses; budget for proposed project, including income, expenses and grants pending; for requests for renewal of support provide brief, but specific, report on results of grant; copy of IRS 501(c)(3) nonprofit determination letter; list of officers and directors and their affiliations; latest annual report; most recent audited financial statement; any other information that aids in understanding how the organization or program operates *Deadlines:* none for grants of $5,000 or less; for $5,000 or more the deadlines are the 15th of February, June, September, and December *Note:* Organizations must fill out an application form.

Restrictions on Giving: The foundation does not support research; advertising; primarily social organizations or functions; fund-raising events; lobbying, religious, or political activities; individuals; or fraternal organizations; building endowments; general support for educational institutions; United Way funded agencies.

Only in special situations will foundation consider programs outside of operating communities, multiyear commitments, or capital and endowment grants requests.

OTHER THINGS TO KNOW
Company is committed to contributing at least 2% of pretax profits to charitable organizations.

Company sponsors employee volunteer programs and supports minority vendors whenever possible.

Company sponsors a STAR (Science and Technology Are Rewarding) education initiative, whereby 55,000 young people have benefitted from hands on approach to science education. Seventy percent of this funding has provided opportunities for girls, children of color and economically disadvantaged children.

For direct gifts, a committee—comprised of the company's president and ceo, company's vice-chairman, and the foundation's chairman—considers grants request. Most of contributions are for one-time projects or events and to organizations supported by employees in their communities. Some corporate contributions are leveraged with additional support from public relations, employee relations, or customer relations. Medtronic facilities also provide some contributions to projects and programs in their immediate vicinity and are generally less than $250.

PUBLICATIONS
Medtronic Community Affairs Annual Report, Medtronic Foundation Matching Gifts to Education Program and Form, and Medtronic Foundation Community Impact Fund Program and Form.

GRANTS ANALYSIS
Total Grants: $3,266,000
Number of Grants: 226*
Highest Grant: $500,000
Average Grant: $14,451*
Typical Range: $2,000 to $20,000
Disclosure Period: fiscal year ending April 30, 1994
Note: Number of grants and average grants figures exclude matching gifts to education and Community Impact Fund, and direct giving. Recent grants are derived from a fiscal 1994 annual report.

RECENT GRANTS
Library
11,500 Bakken Library of Electricity in Life, Minneapolis, MN — for Rediscovering Science: Hands-on History of Science

General
390,000 United Way of Minneapolis Area, Minneapolis, MN
325,000 University of Minnesota, Minneapolis, MN — for Bakken Chair in Biomedical Engineering and the Biomedical Engineering Center

100,000 Fondation de France, Paris, France — for indigent patient services at Ho Chi Minh Ville Heart Hospital
100,000 Minnesota Medical Foundation, Minneapolis, MN — for University of Minnesota Cancer Center
50,000 Medecins Sans Frontieres US, New York, NY — for health care project in Romania

---

Minnesota Mining & Mfg. Co. / 3M Foundation

Revenue: $14.02 billion
Employees: 87,015
Headquarters: St. Paul, MN
SIC Major Group: Coated & Laminated Paper Nec, Nonwoven Fabrics, Die-Cut Paper & Board, and Converted Paper Products Nec

CONTACT
Cynthia F. Kleven
Assistant Secretary, 3M Foundation
Community Affairs
591-30-02 3M Ctr.
St. Paul, MN 55144-1000
(612) 733-1110
Note: Inquiries from the St. Paul, MN, area should be addressed to the designated staff person at the above address. See "Other Things To Know" for more details. The company's World Wide Web address is http://www.mmm.com

FINANCIAL SUMMARY
Recent Giving: $40,000,000 (1995 est.); $38,200,000 (1994 approx.); $43,400,000 (1993)
Assets: $9,769,998 (1993); $12,951,001 (1992); $18,000,000 (1991)
Fiscal Note: Above figures include both foundation giving and direct contributions by the company. Foundation giving totaled $15,333,000 in 1993, $10,768,742 in 1992, and $10,647,376 in 1991. Figures include international contributions. Above figures exclude nonmonetary support.
EIN: 41-6038262

CONTRIBUTIONS SUMMARY
Typical Recipients: • *Arts & Humanities:* Arts Institutes, Ethnic & Folk Arts, Historic Preservation, Libraries, Museums/Galleries, Music, Opera, Performing Arts, Public Broadcasting • *Civic & Public Affairs:* Economic Development, Employment/Job Training, Nonprofit Management, Safety, Urban & Community Affairs • *Education:* Colleges & Universities, Education Associations, Education Funds, Engineering/Technological Education, Journalism/Media Education, Minority Education, Science/Mathematics Education • *Environment:* General • *Health:* Geriatric Health, Health Policy/Cost Containment, Health Organizations, Hospices, Hospitals, Mental Health • *Social Services:* Child Welfare, Community Centers, Community Service Organizations, Counseling, Day Care, Delinquency & Criminal Rehabilita-

tion, Domestic Violence, Emergency Relief, Family Services, Food/Clothing Distribution, Homes, People with Disabilities, Recreation & Athletics, Senior Services, Shelters/Homelessness, Substance Abuse, United Funds/United Ways, Volunteer Services, Youth Organizations

Grant Types: challenge, employee matching gifts, fellowship, general support, operating expenses, project, and scholarship

Note: Employee matching gift ratio: 1 to 1.

Nonmonetary Support: $28,000,000 (1993); $24,000,000 (1992); $14,000,000 (1991)

Nonmonetary Support Types: donated equipment, donated products, in-kind services, loaned employees, and workplace solicitation

Note: David Ginkel, Manager Special Community Projects, is the contact for nonmonetary support; he can be reached at 612-733-1420.

Geographic Distribution: near headquarters and operating locations only

Operating Locations: AK (Anchorage), AL (Birmingham, Decatur, Guin), AR (Little Rock), AZ (Phoenix, Tucson), CA (Camarillo, Chico, Corona, Costa Mesa, Fresno, Irvine, Los Angeles, Monrovia, Northridge, Ontario, Petaluma, San Francisco, Stockton, Tustin, Unitek/Monrovia), CO (Denver), CT (Wallingford, West Haven), DC, FL (Pompano, Sanford), GA (Atlanta, Dalton), HI (Honolulu), IA (Ames, Forest City, Knoxville), IL (Bedford Park, Chicago, Cordova, Dekalb, Hinsdale), IN (Hartford City, Indianapolis), KY (Cynthiana), MA (Boston, Cambridge, Chelmsford), MD (Westminster), MI (Ann Arbor, Detroit, Midland), MN (Alexandria, Cottage Grove, Eagan, Fairmont, Hutchinson, New Ulm, Park Rapids, Pine City, St. Paul, Staples), MO (Columbia, Nevada, Springfield, St. Louis), NC (Charlotte, High Point), ND (Wahpeton), NE (Valley), NJ (Belle Mead, Eatontown, Freehold, West Caldwell, West Deptford), NY (Honeoye, Lennox Hill, Rochester, Tonawanda), OH (Baltimore, Cincinnati, Cleveland, Columbus, Grove City, Mentor), OK (Weatherford), OR (Eugene, White City), PA (Bristol, Philadelphia), SC (Greenville, North Charleston), SD (Aberdeen, Brookings), TN (Nashville), TX (Austin, Brownwood, Dallas, El Paso, Fort Worth, Houston, Rio Grande), UT (Salt Lake City), VA (Richmond), WA (Seattle), WI (Cumberland, Menomonie, Nekoosa, Prairie du Chien, Wausau, Wisconsin Rapids), WV (Middleway)

CORP. OFFICERS
Livio Diego DeSimone: *B* Montreal Quebec Canada 1936 *ED* McGill Univ BS 1957 *CURR EMPL* chmn, ceo, dir: MN Mining & Mfg Co *CORP AFFIL* dir: Cray Res Inc, Dayton Hudson Corp, Gen Mills Inc, Vulcan Materials Co *NONPR AFFIL* mem: Bus Roundtable, MN Bus Partnership; natl bd chmn: Jr Achievement; trust: Univ MN Fdn

Raymond C. Richelson: *CURR EMPL* group vp Memory Tech: MN Mining & Mfg

Co *CORP AFFIL* pres, dir: MN Mining & Mfg France

GIVING OFFICERS
M. Kay Grenz: dir

Cynthia F. Kleven: asst secy *CURR EMPL* dir commun aff: MN Mining & Mfg Co

William J. McLellan: dir

Raymond C. Richelson: dir *CURR EMPL* group vp Memory Tech: MN Mining & Mfg Co (see above)

APPLICATION INFORMATION
Initial Approach: *Initial Contact:* letter of inquiry; no phone requests are accepted but company will provide direction *Include Information On:* proof of tax-exempt status, brief history of organization, project description (need, objective, target group), and specific contribution request *Deadlines:* January 1: Health/Human Services; June 1: Arts and Civic/Community; October 1: Education

Restrictions on Giving: The company does not support individuals; religious endeavors; propaganda or lobbying efforts; fraternal, social, political, veterans, or military organizations; for-profit organizations; travel; subsidization of books, magazines, or articles in professional journals (except those relating to other 3M-supported projects); commercial advertising; or purchase of equipment not manufactured by 3M.

Generally does not consider organizations and causes that do not impact 3M communities; workshops, symposia, conferences, seminars, and publication of proceedings; fund-raising, testimonial, and athletic events; endowments; or emergency operating support.

Multiple proposals from one organization per calendar year are discouraged.

The company will not normally fund a program or project beyond three years, or support more than 10% of an organization's campaign goal or annual budget.

OTHER THINGS TO KNOW
In countries where 3M has subsidiary operations, requests should be directed to that location.

3M sponsors a volunteer program for a community project called Community Action Retired Employees Services (CARES).

After the initial inquiry, if further consideration is to be given to the funding request, a grant application form will be sent which should be completed and include the following aditional information: program/project timetable; evaluation; sources and amounts of other support; annual report; and listing of directors and officers and their affiliations.

Inquiries from the St. Paul, MN, area should be addressed to the designated staff person at the above address. The contact people include the following: Wendell J. Butler, health & human services at 612-736-3781; David E. Ginkel, civic/community and contribution of product and property at 612-733-1420; and Barbara W. Kaufmann, arts and education at 612-733-1241. For locations

outside of St.Paul where 3M has an operation, contact Cynthia Kleven at 613-733-1721.

PUBLICATIONS
Giving guidelines

GRANTS ANALYSIS
Total Grants: $38,200,000*

Typical Range: $5,000 to $20,000

Disclosure Period: 1994

Note: Recent grants are derived from a 1992 Form 990.

RECENT GRANTS
General

1,088,000	United Way of St. Paul Area, St. Paul, MN
201,794	United Way of St. Paul, St. Paul, MN
200,000	Junior Achievement
148,418	American Red Cross, St. Paul, MN
100,000	American Chemical Society, Washington, DC

Northern States Power Co. (Minnesota)

Revenue: $2.48 billion
Employees: 7,884
Headquarters: Minneapolis, MN
SIC Major Group: Electric & Other Services Combined and Gas & Other Services Combined

---

CONTACT
Malinda A. Marson
Chairman, Contributions Committee
Northern States Power Co. (Minnesota)
414 Nicollet Mall
Minneapolis, MN 55401
(612) 330-6026
Note: Applicants can call (612) 330-6933 for a grant application and guidelines. Depending upon the geographic location within NSP's service area of Minnesota, North Dakota, South Dakota, and Wisconsin, grant requests should be directed to the appropriate contact persons. See "Other Things To Know" for more details.

FINANCIAL SUMMARY
Recent Giving: $4,500,000 (1995 est.); $4,424,514 (1994 approx.); $4,331,451 (1993)

Fiscal Note: Company and divisions give directly. Above figures include contributions by operating divisions. Above figures exclude nonmonetary support.

CONTRIBUTIONS SUMMARY
Typical Recipients: • *Arts & Humanities:* Arts Centers, Arts Funds, Arts Institutes, Community Arts, Ethnic & Folk Arts, History & Archaeology, Libraries, Museums/Galleries, Music, Opera, Performing Arts, Public Broadcasting, Theater • *Civic & Public Affairs:* Botanical Gardens/Parks, Employment/Job Training, Hispanic Affairs, Housing, Legal Aid, Municipalities/Towns,

Native American Affairs, Nonprofit Management, Parades/Festivals, Safety, Urban & Community Affairs, Women's Affairs, Zoos/Aquariums • *Education:* After-school/Enrichment Programs, Business Education, Colleges & Universities, Community & Junior Colleges, Education Reform, Elementary Education (Public), Legal Education, Minority Education, Preschool Education, Student Aid • *Environment:* General, Wildlife Protection • *Health:* AIDS/HIV, Cancer, Clinics/Medical Centers, Health Organizations, Hospitals, Mental Health, Nursing Services, Single-Disease Health Associations • *Religion:* Religious Welfare • *Social Services:* Child Welfare, Community Centers, Community Service Organizations, Counseling, Day Care, Delinquency & Criminal Rehabilitation, Domestic Violence, Emergency Relief, Family Services, Food/Clothing Distribution, Homes, People with Disabilities, Refugee Assistance, Senior Services, Shelters/Homelessness, Substance Abuse, United Funds/United Ways, Volunteer Services, Youth Organizations

Grant Types: capital, employee matching gifts, general support, operating expenses, and project

Nonmonetary Support: $1,320,000 (1993); $485,000 (1991); $250,000 (1990)

Nonmonetary Support Types: donated equipment and loaned executives

Geographic Distribution: near headquarters and operating locations only

Operating Locations: MN (Brooklyn Center, Edina, Excelsior, Mankato, Minneapolis, Newport, St. Cloud, St. Paul, White Bear Lake, Winona), ND (Fargo, Grand Forks, Minot), SD (Sioux Falls)

CORP. OFFICERS
James J. Howard III: *B* Pittsburgh PA 1935 *ED* Univ Pittsburgh BS 1957; MA Inst Tech MS 1970 *CURR EMPL* chmn, ceo, mem exec contributions comm: Northern Sts Power Co *CORP AFFIL* dir: Ecolab Inc, Equitable Life Assurance Soc US, Honeywell Inc, Walgreen Co *NONPR AFFIL* bd overseers: Univ MN, Univ MN Curtis L Carlson Sch Mgmt; bd trusts: Univ St Thomas; mem: Am Nuclear Energy Counc, Conf Bd NY, Greater Minneapolis Chamber Commerce; trust: Am Counc Radwaste Disposal

Tom Micheletti: *CURR EMPL* vp pub aff: Northern Sts Power Co

Edwin Mathew Theisen: *B* Cold Spring MN 1930 *ED* St Johns Univ BA 1952 *CURR EMPL* pres, coo, dir: Northern Sts Power Co MN *CORP AFFIL* dir: Health One Corp; vchmn: Advantage MN Inc

GIVING OFFICERS
Linda J. Granoien: *CURR EMPL* corp contributions consult, mem exec contributions comm: Northern Sts Power Co

James J. Howard III: *CURR EMPL* chmn, ceo, mem exec contributions comm: Northern Sts Power Co (see above)

Malinda Marson: *CURR EMPL* chmn contributions comm: Northern Sts Power Co

Tom Micheletti: *CURR EMPL* vp pub aff: Northern Sts Power Co (see above)

APPLICATION INFORMATION

Initial Approach: *Initial Contact:* brief letter of inquiry *Include Information On:* description of the organization and its purpose, objectives of program to be funded, intended beneficiaries of program, total amount needed, anticipated amount of request, method of evaluation, audited financial information, list of major donors including amounts pledged, proof of tax status *Deadlines:* none *Note:* Requests for application form should be sent to Linda Granoien, consultant, corporate contributions.

Restrictions on Giving: Company does not support national organizations; research programs; endowments; multi-year pledges; religious, political, or fraternal organizations, except for programs for the direct benefit of the community; government agencies; individuals; travel, fund-raising activities, meetings, dinners, special events, conferences, or seminars; advertisements; agencies/programs receiving more than 50% of budget from United Way; disease-specific organizations; or sports and athletic programs.

OTHER THINGS TO KNOW

Within one year of receiving grant payment, recipient must submit report detailing the expenditures and results of project.

Addresses and names of the appropriate contact persons are contained in the company's funding guidelines.

PUBLICATIONS

Funding guidelines, application form

GRANTS ANALYSIS

Total Grants: $4,331,451

Number of Grants: 408*

Typical Range: $2,500 to $5,000

Disclosure Period: 1993

Note: Number of grants figure excludes contributions by NSP operating divisions to local community service, civic/cultural, education, and health programs totaling $287,158. Recent grants are derived from a 1993 grants list.

RECENT GRANTS

Library
Augsburg College, Minneapolis, MN — capital for library

General
Alexandra House, Circle Pines, MN — general operating/capital
Alliance for the Mentally Ill of Minnesota, St. Paul, MN
Alternatives for People with Autism, Brooklyn Park, MN
American Indian Opportunities Industrialization Center, Minneapolis, MN
Anew Dimension Child Enrichment Center, Minneapolis, MN — capital

Norwest Corporation / Norwest Foundation

Revenue: $6.03 billion
Employees: 39,590
Headquarters: Minneapolis, MN
SIC Major Group: Bank Holding Companies, National Commercial Banks, State Commercial Banks, and Nondeposit Trust Facilities

CONTACT

Diane P. Lilly
President
Norwest Foundation
Norwest Ctr.
6th & Marquette
Minneapolis, MN 55479-1055
(612) 667-7860
Note: Grants applicants should contact nearest local Norwest subsidiary directly. For general questions and for proposals relating to the Minneapolis-St. Paul area, contact Norwest Foundation at the above address. The company's World Wide Web address is http://www.norwest.com

FINANCIAL SUMMARY

Recent Giving: $16,000,000 (1995 est.); $14,697,904 (1994); $9,075,049 (1992)

Assets: $70,000,000 (1995 est.); $80,000,000 (1994 approx.); $79,412,425 (1993 approx.)

Gifts Received: $69,838,480 (1993)

Fiscal Note: Figures include direct and foundation giving for parent and subsidiaries, including Norwest Financial Corporation and Norwest Mortgage. Foundation received gifts from Norwest Equity Capital, Inc., Norwest Growth Fund, Inc., and Norwest Limited in 1993.

EIN: 41-1367441

CONTRIBUTIONS SUMMARY

Typical Recipients: • *Arts & Humanities:* Arts Funds, Libraries, Museums/Galleries, Music, Opera, Public Broadcasting, Theater • *Civic & Public Affairs:* Housing, Urban & Community Affairs • *Education:* Colleges & Universities, Community & Junior Colleges, Education Funds • *Social Services:* United Funds/United Ways

Grant Types: capital, employee matching gifts, general support, multiyear/continuing support, operating expenses, and project

Note: Various grant types are determined and awarded by each bank and business location in response to local needs. Check with specific banks for details about local giving priorities and programs.

Geographic Distribution: primarily in AZ, CO, IA, IN, IL, MN, MT, ND, NE, NM, OH, SD, TX, WI, and WY

Operating Locations: AZ (Phoenix, Scottsdale, Sun City), CA (Concord, Fremont, Richmond, Riverside, Roseville, San Diego, San Francisco), CO (Aurora, Colorado Springs, Denver, Englewood, Fort Collins, Grand Junction, Lakewood,

Westminster), FL (Clearwater, Maitland, West Palm Beach), GA (Atlanta), IA (Atlantic, Badger, Bettendorf, Cedar Falls, Cedar Rapids, Clive, Davenport, Denison, Des Moines, Fort Dodge, Keokuk, Marion, Mason City, Ottumwa, Sioux City, Urbandale, Waterloo), IL (Chicago, Glen Ellyn, Lincolnshire, Lombard, Palos Heights, Peoria), IN (Indianapolis), KS (Overland Park, Shawnee Mission), MD (Baltimore, Rossville, Waldorf), MN (Albert Lea, Austin, Bloomington, Brooklyn Park, Burnsville, Coon Rapids, Dawson, Dodge Center, Duluth, Eagan, Eden Prairie, Edina, Ely, Evelyth, Faribault, Fergus Falls, Golden Valley, Hastings, Hill City, Hopkins, Hoyt Lakes, Jordan, Litchfield, Luverne, Mankato, Maple Grove, Maplewood, Marshall, Minneapolis, Montevideo, Moorhead, Northfield, Ortonville, Osseo, Owatonna, Plymouth, Red Wing, Redwood Falls, Rochester, Sartell, Sauk Rapids, Shoreview, Silver Bay, Slayton, St. Cloud, St. Louis Park, St. Paul, Stillwater, Thief River Falls, Tracy, Two Harbors, Virginia, Winona, Woodbury, Worthington), MT (Anaconda, Billings, Butte, Dillon, Great Falls, Helena, Kalispell, Lewistown), ND (Bismarck, Crystal, Fargo, Grafton, Grandin, Hillsboro, Jamestown, Mandan, Minot, Tower City, Valley City, Wahpeton), NE (Grand Island, Hastings, Norfolk, Omaha, York), NJ (Morristown), NY (New York), OH (Columbus, Springfield), OK (Oklahoma City, Tulsa), PA (King of Prussia), SD (Aberdeen, Belle Foruche, Bristol, Britton, Brookings, Chamberlain, Deadwood, Dell Rapids, Gregory, Groton, Hecla, Hot Springs, Huron, Lake Preston, Lead, Madison, Milbank, Mitchell, Newell, Parker, Rapid City, Redfield, Sioux Falls, Spearfish, Springfield, Watertown), TX (Arlington, Austin, Corpus Christi, Dallas, Houston, Hurst, Pasadena, Richardson, San Antonio), UT (Salt Lake City), WI (Brookfield, La Crosse, Madison, Milwaukee), WY (Casper, Cheyenne, Gillette, Lovell, Wheatland)

Note: Also maintains corporate banking offices in Buenos Aires, Argentina; Hong Kong; Mexico City, Mexico; Santiago, Chile; and Sao Paulo, Brazil.

CORP. OFFICERS

Richard M. Kovacevich: *B* Tacoma WA 1943 *ED* Stanford Univ BS 1965; Stanford Univ MS 1967; Stanford Univ MBA 1967 *CURR EMPL* pres, ceo: Norwest Corp *CORP AFFIL* dir: Fingerhut Cos, Northern Sts Power Co, Northwestern Natl Life Ins Co, NWNL Cos Inc, VISA USA *NONPR AFFIL* dir: Greater Minneapolis Housing Corp, Guthrie Theater, Walker Art Ctr; mem: MN Project Corp Responsibility; trust: Twin Cities Pub Television, Voyageur Outward Bound Sch

Stanley Stephenson Stroup: *B* Los Angeles CA 1944 *ED* Univ IL BA 1966; Univ MI JD 1969 *CURR EMPL* gen couns, exec vp: Norwest Corp *CORP AFFIL* vp, dir: GST Co *NONPR AFFIL* mem: Am Bar Assn, CA Bar Assn, IL Bar Assn, MN Bar Assn; mem adjunct faculty: William Mitchell Coll Law *CLUB AFFIL* Wayzata CC

John T. Thornton: *B* New York NY 1937 *ED* St Johns Univ BBA 1959; St Johns Univ JD 1972 *CURR EMPL* cfo, exec vp: Norwest Corp *CORP AFFIL* ceo, dir: Norwest Ltd Inc; dir: Exel Ltd, Norwest Bank MN NA *NONPR AFFIL* mem: NY Bar Assn

GIVING OFFICERS
Pat Donovan: dir

Richard M. Kovacevich: dir *CURR EMPL* pres, ceo: Norwest Corp (see above)

Diane P. Lilly: pres

Bruce Moland: secy

Carolyn H. Roby: asst secy, asst treas, program mgr

John T. Thornton: treas *CURR EMPL* cfo, exec vp: Norwest Corp (see above)

APPLICATION INFORMATION
Initial Approach: *Initial Contact:* organizations serving a specific neighborhood or city should apply directly to the nearest Norwest affiliate in that area; those serving the seven-county Minneapolis-St. Paul area should apply to Norwest Foundation-Metro; and those serving the state of Minnesota, the Upper Midwest region, should apply to Diane P. Lilly, President of the Norwest Foundation *Include Information On:* name of organization, including contact, address, and phone number; description of the organization, including any special population or geographic areas served; amount requested; purpose for which funds are sought; budget and other sources of income for organization and proposed project; proof of tax-exempt status, 501(c)(3) letter from the IRS *Deadlines:* none

Restrictions on Giving: The foundation does not award single grants to organizations of greater than 10% of the contributions budget except to United Way.

The foundation generally does not support tickets or tables for benefit purposes; travel, tours, or conferences; religious organizations for religious purposes; political campaigns; organizations designed primarily for lobbying; fraternal organizations; goodwill advertising; or individuals.

OTHER THINGS TO KNOW
Norwest Corporation and Norwest Foundation operate a highly decentralized giving program, in which the parent company, the foundation, and numerous banking subsidiaries throughout the country provide grants to qualified recipients in the communities in which the Norwest entities are located. Applicants are advised to target their inquiries to the nearest local Norwest bank for fastest turnaround. If you are unsure about which subsidiary to contact, call the foundation for assistance; the foundation will direct you to the appropriate subsidiary in your project's area.

The Norwest Foundation giving committee exercises control primarily over giving in the Twin Cities area of Minnesota. The foundation also acts as the repository of all contributions data for the parent company and its subsidiaries.

United Banks of Colorado merged into Norwest Corporation in April 1991, and, in April 1992, changed their name to Norwest Bank Colorado. The giving program for Norwest Bank Colorado and Norwest Bank Denver (formerly United Bank of Denver) are now contained within that of the parent company, Norwest Corporation and its foundation, Norwest Foundation.

PUBLICATIONS
Guidelines (includes list of branch offices)

GRANTS ANALYSIS
Total Grants: $14,697,904

Typical Range: $1,000 to $10,000

Disclosure Period: 1994

Note: Recent grants are derived from a 1991 Form 990.

RECENT GRANTS
General

353,500	United Way, Minneapolis, MN	
353,500	United Way, Minneapolis, MN	
85,000	University of Minnesota Foundation, Minneapolis, MN	
83,826	Citizens Scholarship Foundation of America, St. Peter, MN	
82,000	United Way of Central Iowa, Des Moines, IA	

Phillips Family Foundation, Jay and Rose

CONTACT
Patricia A. Cummings
Executive Director
Jay and Rose Phillips Family Foundation
2345 Kennedy St., NE
Minneapolis, MN 55413
(612) 331-6230

FINANCIAL SUMMARY
Recent Giving: $3,686,000 (1995 est.); $3,686,522 (1994 approx.); $3,593,524 (1993)

Assets: $95,450,000 (1995 est.); $90,086,926 (1994 approx.); $97,700,000 (1993 approx.)

Gifts Received: $243,025 (1994); $13,208,515 (1993); $1,360,157 (1992)

Fiscal Note: In 1994, the foundation received a gift from Jay and Rose Phillips in the form of charitable remainder trusts. In 1993 and 1994, the foundation received gifts from the estate of Jay Phillips.

EIN: 41-6019578

CONTRIBUTIONS SUMMARY
Donor(s): The Jay and Rose Phillips Family Foundation was incorporated in 1944, with funds donated by Jay Phillips and members of the Phillips family.

Typical Recipients: • *Arts & Humanities:* Arts Associations & Councils, Arts Centers, Historic Preservation, Libraries, Museums/Galleries, Music, Public Broadcasting, Theater • *Civic & Public Affairs:* Civil Rights, Economic Development, Housing, Philanthropic Organizations, Public Policy, Urban & Community Affairs, Women's Affairs • *Education:* Colleges & Universities, Education Associations, Education Funds, General, Legal Education, Medical Education, Minority Education, Religious Education, Social Sciences Education, Student Aid • *Environment:* General • *Health:* Clinics/Medical Centers, Health Organizations, Hospitals, Long-Term Care, Medical Research, Multiple Sclerosis, Research/Studies Institutes, Single-Disease Health Associations • *International:* Health Care/Hospitals • *Religion:* Jewish Causes, Religious Organizations, Religious Welfare, Social/Policy Issues, Synagogues/Temples • *Science:* Science Museums • *Social Services:* Child Welfare, Community Centers, Community Service Organizations, Counseling, Emergency Relief, Homes, People with Disabilities, Recreation & Athletics, Senior Services, Sexual Abuse, Shelters/Homelessness, United Funds/United Ways, Volunteer Services, Youth Organizations

Grant Types: capital and general support

Geographic Distribution: primarily metropolitan Minneapolis/St. Paul, MN

GIVING OFFICERS
Erik Bernstein: trust

Paula P. Bernstein: trust

William Bernstein: trust

Thomas P. Cook: secy, trust

Patricia A. Cummings: exec dir

Jack I. Levin: trust

John Levin: trust

Suzan Levin: trust

Jeanne Phillips: trust

Morton B. Phillips: don, co-chmn

Pauline Phillips: trust

Rose Phillips: don, co-chmn

Neil I. Sell: asst secy *B* Minneapolis MN 1941 *ED* Univ MN 1963; William Mitchell Coll Law 1968 *CURR EMPL* sr ptnr: Maslon Edelman Borman & Brand *CORP AFFIL* secy, dir: Rykoff-Sexton Inc, John Sexton & Co; secy, gen couns: Wilson Learning Corp *NONPR AFFIL* mem: Am Bar Assn, Am Inst CPAs *PHIL AFFIL* asst secy: Max and Helen Winter Family Foundation

APPLICATION INFORMATION
Initial Approach:

Applicants who are unsure about whether they meet the foundation's funding criteria are encouraged to submit a one-page letter of interest to the foundation. The foundation staff reviews all letters of interest, and the applicant will be notified regarding whether the foundation would like the organization to submit a full proposal.

The letter should describe the reasons for seeking support and the geographic area(s) and population(s) to be served. The letter should also include a brief description of the organization, amount requested, an outline of the purpose for which a grant is sought, a definition of the project, and the specific goals the project is designed to meet. Proposals should also include an explanation of how the request addresses the foundation's funding priorities; a description of population served including geographical area(s) served, number of persons served, ages, income level(s), and special needs of individuals served; evidence of need for organization or project; evidence of organization's capacity to manage program or project including staff qualifications and experience; and method of evaluating effectiveness and success of program(s) or project. Other information which should be included is: itemized project budget; donor's list showing corporate and foundation support during the past twelve months; proof of tax-exempt status; copy of IRS Form 990 with schedule A; list of the board of directors, officers, and their affiliations; and a copy of the most recent audited financial statements. If nonprofit is requesting funds for a special or capital project, the following must also be submitted: a board-approved special project or capital project budget; total amount and sources of funds received or committed; and list of proposals pending with other funding sources.

Applications are accepted throughout the year.

The foundation will send confirmation of application receipt. The trustees meet approximately every three months and completed applications are reviewed in the order in which they are received. The foundation reports that the review process usually takes about three to four months.

Restrictions on Giving: The foundation will not make grants to organizations operating for profit, political campaigns or lobbying efforts to influence legislation, endowment campaigns, or individuals. The foundation requests that all initial inquiries from prospective applicants be by mail, not by telephone or by personal visits to the foundation office.

OTHER THINGS TO KNOW
The foundation was formerly called Phillips Foundation.

PUBLICATIONS
Application brochure, annual report

GRANTS ANALYSIS
Total Grants: $3,593,524
Number of Grants: 301
Highest Grant: $200,000
Average Grant: $11,939
Typical Range: $1,000 to $25,000
Disclosure Period: 1993

Note: Recent grants are derived from a 1993 grants list.

RECENT GRANTS

General

200,000	Mayo Clinic, Rochester, MN — Phillips endowment
200,000	Minneapolis Federation for Jewish Service, Minneapolis, MN — Phillips endowment
200,000	University of Minnesota, Minneapolis, MN — Phillips scholarship endowment
125,000	Beth Israel at Shalom Park, Denver, CO — pledge
103,375	Jewish Family Service of Colorado, Denver, CO — older adults services department

---

Piper Jaffray Companies Inc. / Piper Jaffray Companies Foundation

Revenue: $410.0 million
Employees: 1,834
Parent Company: Piper Jaffray
Headquarters: Minneapolis, MN
SIC Major Group: Holding Companies Nec and Security Brokers & Dealers

---

CONTACT
Marina Lyon
Community Affairs Manager
Piper Jaffray Companies Inc.
222 S Ninth St.
Minneapolis, MN 55402
(612) 342-6082
Note: Brenda Cich is also a contact for the contributions program.

FINANCIAL SUMMARY
Recent Giving: $1,250,000 (1995 est.); $2,400,000 (1994 approx.); $3,899,000 (1993)

Fiscal Note: 1994 figure includes foundation giving ($2,197,000), direct contributions ($969,000), grants from the Piper Jaffray Cos. donor-advised fund of the Minneapolis Foundation ($609,000), and employee matching gifts ($124,000). Above figures exclude nonmonetary support.

CONTRIBUTIONS SUMMARY
Typical Recipients: • *Arts & Humanities:* Arts Centers, Arts Festivals, Arts Institutes, Libraries, Museums/Galleries, Music, Opera, Performing Arts, Theater • *Civic & Public Affairs:* Community Foundations, Employment/Job Training, General, Housing, Native American Affairs, Urban & Community Affairs • *Education:* Business Education, Colleges & Universities, Economic Education, Education Reform, Elementary Education (Private), Gifted & Talented Programs, Public Education (Precollege), Student Aid, Vocational & Technical Education • *Environment:* Resource Conservation • *Health:* Cancer, Medical Rehabilitation, Multiple Sclerosis • *Religion:* Dioceses, Jewish Causes, Religious Welfare, Social/Policy Issues • *Science:* Science Museums • *Social Services:* Child Welfare, Community Centers, Community Service Organizations, Domestic Violence, Emergency Relief, Family Services, Food/Clothing Distribution, General, People with Disabilities, Recreation & Athletics, United Funds/United Ways, Volunteer Services, Youth Organizations

Grant Types: employee matching gifts, general support, and operating expenses

Note: Company matches employee contributions to accredited educational institutions and nonprofit organizations, with a minimum of $50 and a maximum of $250 per calendar year.

Nonmonetary Support: $20,000 (1995)

Nonmonetary Support Types: loaned employees

Note: The above figure is an estimate for 1995.

Geographic Distribution: near headquarters and branch locations

Operating Locations: AZ (Phoenix, Tucson), CA (Los Angeles, Sacramento, San Francisco), CO (Boulder, Colorado Springs, Denver, Pueblo), IA (Davenport, Des Moines, Mason City, Oskaloosa, Sioux City, Storm Lake, Ames, Waterloo), ID (Boise, Idaho Falls, Pocatello), KS (Lawrence, Topeka), MN (Alexandria, Austin, Bloomington, Duluth, Mankato, Minneapolis, Rochester, St. Cloud, St. Paul, Stillwater, Two Harbors, Wayzata), MO (Kansas City), MT (Billings, Bozeman, Butte, Great Falls, Missoula), ND (Bismarck, Fargo, Grand Forks), NE (Lincoln, Omaha), OR (Lake Oswego, Portland), SD (Mitchell, Pierre, Rapid City, Sioux Falls), UT (Provo, Salt Lake City), WA (Aberdeen, Bellevue, Everett, Richland, Seattle, Spokane, Tacoma, Wenatchee), WI (Appleton, Eau Claire, Green Bay, La Crossse, Madison, Menomonie, Milwaukee, Wausau), WY (Casper, Sheridan)

Note: Company has 73 branch offices, most of which are in the western U.S.

CORP. OFFICERS
William H. Ellis: *CURR EMPL* pres, coo, dir: Piper Jaffray Cos Inc

Charles N. Hayssen: *CURR EMPL* cfo: Piper Jaffray Cos Inc *CORP AFFIL* treas: Am Municipal Term Trust Inc IL, MN Municipal Income Portfolio Inc

Marina Lyon: *CURR EMPL* commun aff mgr: Piper Jaffray Cos Inc

Addison Lewis Piper: *B* Minneapolis MN 1946 *ED* Williams Coll BA 1968; Stanford Univ MBA 1972 *CURR EMPL* chmn, ceo, dir: Piper Jaffray Cos Inc *NONPR AFFIL* dir: Guthrie Theater, Minneapolis Abbott NW Hosp, MN Bus Partnership, MN Pub Radio, Stanford Univ Bus Sch Assn, Washburn Child Guidance Ctr; dir, mem exec comm: Minneapolis Downtown Counc; mem: Securities Indus Assn *CLUB AFFIL* CC Rockies, Minneapolis, Woodhill CC *PHIL AFFIL* dir: Piper Jaffray Foundation

GIVING OFFICERS
Karen M. Bohn: pres *B* Grand Forks ND 1953 *ED* Univ ND 1975; Univ ND 1976 *CURR EMPL* pres, ceo: Piper Trust Co *CORP AFFIL* dir: Blue Cross Blue Shield MN, Piper Jaffray Cos Inc *PHIL AFFIL* pres: Piper Jaffray Foundation

Brenda Cich: secy *PHIL AFFIL* secy: Piper Jaffray Foundation

Kathy Henderson: treas

APPLICATION INFORMATION

Initial Approach: *Initial Contact:* for Minneapolis-St. Paul organizations, send brief letter of inquiry *Include Information On:* description of the organization, amount requested, purpose of funds sought, recently audited financial statement, and proof of tax-exempt status *Deadlines:* deadlines are February 28, May 31, August 31, and November 30 *Note:* organizations outside the Minneapolis/St. Paul metro area should submit their requests to the branch office nearest to them; organizations in the Minneapolis/St. Paul area may submit requests to a branch office or to The Piper Jaffray Foundation, Karen Bohn, President.

Restrictions on Giving: The company will not consider requests from: newly formed nonprofit organizations, individuals, teams, religious, political, veterans or fraternal organizations or organizations working to treat or eliminate specific diseases. Support is not available for basic and applied research, travel, event sponsorship, benefits or tickets, or to eliminate an organization's operating deficit. The company does not respond to mass mail requests.

OTHER THINGS TO KNOW

Company reports that it donates over 5% of pretax earnings to charitable organizations.

The Piper Jaffray Companies Foundation was established in December 1992, to distribute a large portion of the corporation's charitable funds. In addition to its own foundation, the company also maintains a donor-advised fund at the Minneapolis Foundation.

PUBLICATIONS

Community involvment report

GRANTS ANALYSIS

Total Grants: $2,400,000

Number of Grants: 2,000

Average Grant: 1,200

Typical Range: $1,000 to $5,000

Disclosure Period: 1994

Note: Above figures include employee matching gifts. Recent grants are derived from a 1993 Form 990.

RECENT GRANTS

Library
Library Foundation of Hennepin County, Minnetonka, MN — capital support

General
Alexandra House, Circle Pines, MN — capital support
American Indian Opportunities Industrialization Center, Minneapolis, MN
American Jewish Community, Portland, OR
Archdiocese of Omaha, Omaha, NE
Boys and Girls Club of Minneapolis, Minneapolis, MN

Saint Paul Companies, Inc.

Revenue: $4.7 billion
Employees: 12,200
Headquarters: Saint Paul, MN
SIC Major Group: Fire, Marine & Casualty Insurance

CONTACT
Mary Ojile
Community Affairs Secretary
St. Paul Companies, Inc.
385 Washington St.
St. Paul, MN 55102
(612) 221-7757

FINANCIAL SUMMARY
Recent Giving: $10,000,000 (1995 est.); $9,043,605 (1994); $9,247,566 (1993)

Fiscal Note: Company gives directly. Above figures exclude nonmonetary support.

CONTRIBUTIONS SUMMARY
Typical Recipients: • *Arts & Humanities:* Arts Associations & Councils, Arts Centers, Arts Funds, Arts Institutes, Arts Outreach, Community Arts, Dance, Ethnic & Folk Arts, History & Archaeology, Libraries, Literary Arts, Museums/Galleries, Music, Performing Arts, Public Broadcasting, Theater • *Civic & Public Affairs:* African American Affairs, Asian American Affairs, Business/Free Enterprise, Chambers of Commerce, Clubs, Economic Development, Employment/Job Training, General, Hispanic Affairs, Housing, Native American Affairs, Nonprofit Management, Urban & Community Affairs, Women's Affairs • *Education:* Business Education, Colleges & Universities, Community & Junior Colleges, Education Reform, Faculty Development, International Studies, Leadership Training, Literacy, Minority Education, Private Education (Precollege), Public Education (Precollege), Social Sciences Education, Student Aid • *Health:* Adolescent Health Issues, AIDS/HIV, Cancer, Clinics/Medical Centers • *International:* International Affairs • *Religion:* Religious Welfare • *Science:* Science Museums • *Social Services:* At-Risk Youth, Child Welfare, Community Service Organizations, Day Care, Emergency Relief, Family Services, Recreation & Athletics, United Funds/United Ways, Volunteer Services, Youth Organizations

Grant Types: capital, employee matching gifts, endowment, fellowship, general support, matching, multiyear/continuing support, operating expenses, project, and seed money

Note: Employee matching gift ratio: 1 to 1; Employee matching gift ratio: 2 to 1 with 50 hours volunteer time and financialcontributions.

Nonmonetary Support Types: donated equipment and workplace solicitation

Note: Value of nonmonetary support is not available. The company also provides printing services to nonprofits. Ron McKinley, Community Affairs Program Manager, is the contact for nonmonetary support.

Geographic Distribution: primarily St. Paul and Minneapolis, MN; state of Minnesota; and communities in which company has major operations; national and international organizations have low priority

Operating Locations: CO, CT, DE, FL, HI, ID, IL, IN, KS, LA, MA, MN, MT, ND, NE, NJ, NY, OH, OR, PA, TX, WA, WI

CORP. OFFICERS
Douglas West Leatherdale: *B* Morden Canada 1936 *ED* Un Coll Canada BA 1957 *CURR EMPL* chmn, pres, ceo: St Paul Cos Inc *CORP AFFIL* ceo, dir: Athena Assurance Co; chmn: Ramsey Ins Co; chmn, ceo: St Paul Surplus Lines Ins Co; chmn, pres, ceo: St Paul Fire & Marine Ins Co; dir: Atwater McMillian, Carlyle Capital LP, Graham Resources Inc, Natl Ins Wholesalers, Northern Sts Power Co MN, John Nuveen & Co Inc, 77 Water St Inc, St Paul Fin Group Inc, St Paul Fire & Marine Ins Co (UK) Ltd, St Paul Land Resources Inc, St Paul Oil & Gas Corp, St Paul Plymouth Ctr Inc, St Paul Properties Inc, St Paul Real Estate IL Inc, St Paul Risk Svcs Inc, Un HealthCare Corp; pres, dir: St Paul Guardian Ins Co, St Paul Mercury Ins Co *NONPR AFFIL* chmn: MN Ins Fed; chmn-elect: Am Ins Assn; dir: Twin Cities Pub Television; mem: Fin Execs Inst, Twin Cities Soc Security Analysts; trust: Carleton Coll, KCTA Pub Television *CLUB AFFIL* MN

Greg Lee: *CURR EMPL* sr vp, human resources: St Paul Cos Inc

Ron McKinley: *CURR EMPL* program mgr commun aff: St Paul Cos Inc

Kim Vetter: *CURR EMPL* commun aff admin: St Paul Cos Inc

GIVING OFFICERS
Thomas McKeown: *B* Albert Lea MN 1929 *ED* St Johns Univ 1952 *CURR EMPL* exec vp, chief admin off: St Paul Cos Inc

Polly Nyberg: *CURR EMPL* commun aff mgr: St Paul Cos Inc

Mary Ojile: *CURR EMPL* commun aff secy: St Paul Cos Inc

Mary Pickard: *CURR EMPL* commun aff off: St Paul Cos Inc

APPLICATION INFORMATION
Initial Approach: *Initial Contact:* completed application materials *Include Information On:* name, address, contact person, telephone number, and date of application; history and purpose of organization; three-year budget history and three-year projected budget; list of board members and affiliations; proof of tax-exemption and Minnesota Charities Registration; purpose of request (including organization's involvement in concept, needs assessment, goals, and benefits); amount of request (including duration, additional sources of support, and amounts pledged); program budget; evaluative criteria; plans for ongoing funding; and evidence of cooperation with similar agencies *Deadlines:* none (applicants seeking funds before end of calendar year should submit applications no later than September 15) *Note:* All the information listed in the applications requirements must be included for re-

quest to be considered. Organizations seeking funds for programs that have not previously received funding from The St. Paul Cos. should begin the process by submitting a one-page letter describing the new request.

Restrictions on Giving: Contribution funds will not be used for religious organizations unless seeking funds in the direct interest of the entire community; veterans, fraternal, political, or lobbying organizations; benefits or fund raisers; advertising; individuals; scholarships to individuals unless part of ongoing scholarship program of an educational institution or other nonprofit organization which selects the scholarship recipients; sectarian purposes; and generally not to organizations which are part of a United Way or other federated giving drive to which company is contributing, except to provide funding for management technical assistance, housing or education for communities of color.

OTHER THINGS TO KNOW
Corporate contributions currently average about 2% of pretax operating earnings averaged over a three-year period.

PUBLICATIONS
Community affairs report

Regional offices have separate giving programs.

GRANTS ANALYSIS
Total Grants: $9,043,605

Number of Grants: 302

Highest Grant: $634,000

Average Grant: $29,946

Typical Range: $5,000 to $55,000

Disclosure Period: 1994

Note: Recent grants are derived from a 1994 annual report.

RECENT GRANTS
Library
25,000	Augsburg College, Minneapolis, MN — for support to increase the recruitment and retention of Hispanic student

General
410,000	United Way of the St. Paul Area, St. Paul, MN — for operating support
250,000	Family Tree Clinic/East Metro Community Health Network, St. Paul, MN — for match for a project that will support the growth and development of the St. Paul Community-based clinics
200,000	Family Housing Fund of Minneapolis and St. Paul, Minneapolis, MN — for support for a special project to improve the functioning of the rental housing market and support to stabilize low-income housing projects owned by nonprofit community development corporations
150,000	Boys and Girls club of St. Paul, St. Paul, MN — for capital support for the construction of a new facility on the East Side of St. Paul which will house education and other programs for low-income youth
115,775	United Way Field Office Locations — for corporate donation to cities where the St. Paul has offices

Sundet Foundation

CONTACT
Kim Burns
Trust Officer
Sundet Fdn.
9231 Penn Ave. S.
Minneapolis, MN 55344
(612) 941-0242

FINANCIAL SUMMARY
Recent Giving: $377,061 (1993); $308,705 (1992); $186,591 (1990)

Assets: $6,248,731 (1993); $5,158,780 (1992); $3,360,155 (1990)

Gifts Received: $808,418 (1993); $800,463 (1992); $489,377 (1990)

Fiscal Note: In 1993, contributions were received from Century Manufacturing ($546,705), Goodwill Mfg. Co. ($110,552), MDSC Building Partners ($41,161), and Lee and Louise Sundet ($110,000).

EIN: 41-1378654

CONTRIBUTIONS SUMMARY
Donor(s): Century Manufacturing Co., Fountain Industries Co., Goudall Manufacturing Co.

Typical Recipients: • *Arts & Humanities:* Arts Institutes, Libraries, Museums/Galleries, Music, Public Broadcasting • *Civic & Public Affairs:* Clubs, Economic Development, General, Urban & Community Affairs • *Education:* Colleges & Universities, General, Private Education (Precollege), Student Aid • *Health:* Health Organizations, Heart, Medical Rehabilitation, Single-Disease Health Associations • *International:* International Development, International Organizations, Missionary/Religious Activities • *Religion:* Churches, Ministries, Religious Organizations, Religious Welfare, Seminaries • *Social Services:* Community Service Organizations, Day Care, United Funds/United Ways, Youth Organizations

Grant Types: general support and scholarship

Geographic Distribution: focus on MN

GIVING OFFICERS
Leland N. Sundet: pres, dir

Louise C. Sundet: vp, dir

Scott A. Sundet: secy, treas, dir

APPLICATION INFORMATION
Initial Approach: Application form required for scholarships. Deadline is February 28.

OTHER THINGS TO KNOW
Provides scholarships to children of employees of Central Manufacturing.

GRANTS ANALYSIS
Total Grants: $377,061

Number of Grants: 117

Highest Grant: $55,000

Typical Range: $100 to $50,000

Disclosure Period: 1993

Note: Recent grants are derived from a 1993 Form 990.

RECENT GRANTS
Library
20,000	Augsburg College, Minneapolis, MN

General
55,000	Tentmakers — endowment fund
50,000	Tentmakers
30,000	University of Minnesota Foundation, Minneapolis, MN — men's athletic pledge
21,000	Prison Fellowship, Washington, DC
20,000	International Millarden Group

Tozer Foundation

CONTACT
Robert S. Davis
President
Tozer Foundation
385 Washington St.
St. Paul, MN 55102
(612) 221-7031

FINANCIAL SUMMARY
Recent Giving: $869,015 (fiscal 1994); $799,750 (fiscal 1991); $746,220 (fiscal 1990)

Assets: $22,000,000 (fiscal 1994); $18,659,892 (fiscal 1991); $15,767,854 (fiscal 1990)

EIN: 41-6011518

CONTRIBUTIONS SUMMARY
Donor(s): The foundation was incorporated in 1946 by the late David Tozer .

Typical Recipients: • *Arts & Humanities:* Arts Centers, Arts Funds, History & Archaeology, Libraries, Music, Opera, Public Broadcasting • *Civic & Public Affairs:* Business/Free Enterprise, Municipalities/Towns, Nonprofit Management, Parades/Festivals, Professional & Trade Associations, Public Policy • *Education:* Business Education, Colleges & Universities, Economic Education, General, Minority Education, Public Education (Precollege), Science/Mathematics Education, Secondary Education (Public) • *Health:* Clinics/Medical Centers, Hospitals • *International:* International Relations • *Re-

ligion: Religious Organizations, Religious Welfare • *Science:* Science Museums • *Social Services:* Family Services, Recreation & Athletics, United Funds/United Ways, Volunteer Services, Youth Organizations

Grant Types: general support and scholarship

Geographic Distribution: focus on Minnesota; Washington, Pine, and Kanabec counties for scholarship program

GIVING OFFICERS
Robert S. Davis: pres *B* Stillwater MN 1914 *ED* Univ MN 1934 *CURR EMPL* dir: HM Smyth Co *PHIL AFFIL* treas, trust: Minnesota Foundation; pres, trust: Saint Croix Foundation

James Richard Oppenheimer: dir *B* St Paul MN 1921 *ED* Dartmouth Coll BA 1942; Yale Univ JD 1948 *CURR EMPL* of couns: Oppenheimer Wolff & Donnelly *NONPR AFFIL* mem: Am Bar Assn, MN Bar Assn, Ramsey County Bar Assn, St Paul Chamber Commerce; trust: Charles K Blandin Residuary Trust *CLUB AFFIL* Rotary, White Bear YC *PHIL AFFIL* trust: Blandin Foundation

John Thomas Simonet: dir *B* Stillwater MN 1926 *ED* Univ MN BBA 1948; Univ MN LLB 1951 *CORP AFFIL* bd dir: Mairs & Power Growth Fund, Mairs & Power Income Fund; dir: Carondelet Life Care Corp, Donovan Cos, First Trust Co, Mairs & Power Funds *NONPR AFFIL* trust: St Paul Seminary *CLUB AFFIL* St Paul Athletic

Earl C. Swanson: trust *PHIL AFFIL* dir: Andersen Foundation; trust: Bayport Foundation; dir: Katzenberger Foundation

Jon A. Theobald: dir *B* St Paul MN 1945 *ED* St Johns Univ 1967; St Johns Univ 1970 *CURR EMPL* sr vp: First Trust Co *CORP AFFIL* sr vp trust div: Am Natl Bank & Trust Co *PHIL AFFIL* trust: F. R. Bigelow Foundation

John F. Thoreen: dir
Grant T. Waldref: chmn

APPLICATION INFORMATION
Initial Approach:
The foundation requests applications be made in writing. Applications for scholarships may be received through high school guidance counselors.

Grant applications must outline the nature of the request.

The foundation has no deadline for submitting proposals.

The board meets periodically throughout the year. The board considers scholarship requests at their annual May meeting. Decisions are made immediately after the meeting.

GRANTS ANALYSIS
Total Grants: $283,515*
Number of Grants: 48*
Highest Grant: $50,000
Average Grant: $5,900*
Typical Range: $1,000 to $10,000
Disclosure Period: fiscal year ending October 31, 1994

Note: Total grants and number of grants exclude $585,500 in individual scholarships. Average grant figure was provided by the foundation. Recent grants are derived from a fiscal 1991 grants list.

RECENT GRANTS

Library
5,000   Osceola Public Library, Osceola, WI — capital drive
5,000   Somerset Library, Somerset, WI — capital drive

General
54,500   United Way of St. Paul, St. Paul, MN — capital campaign
15,000   Courage Center, Golden Valley, MN — St. Croix Valley aquatics and therapy facility
15,000   St. Paul Union Gospel Mission, St. Paul, MN — first installment of three-year grant
13,500   Boy Scouts of America Indianhead Council, St. Paul, MN — general
10,000   Lakeview Memorial Hospital, Stillwater, MN — general

---

Weyerhaeuser Memorial Foundation, Charles A.

CONTACT
Lucy R. McCarthy
President
Charles A. Weyerhaeuser Memorial Fdn.
2100 First National Bank Bldg.
St. Paul, MN 55101
(612) 228-0935

FINANCIAL SUMMARY
Recent Giving: $120,976 (fiscal 1991); $289,139 (fiscal 1990); $296,850 (fiscal 1989)

Assets: $3,704,020 (fiscal 1991); $3,452,280 (fiscal 1990); $3,269,740 (fiscal 1989)

Gifts Received: $21,656 (fiscal 1991); $19,453 (fiscal 1990); $43,045 (fiscal 1989)

Fiscal Note: In 1991, contributions were received from Berkshire Hathaway ($1,236), Lucy R. McCarthy ($20,000), and the Carl A. Weyerhaeuser 1972 Trust ($420).

EIN: 41-6012063

CONTRIBUTIONS SUMMARY
Donor(s): Carl A. Weyerhaeuser Trusts

Typical Recipients: • *Arts & Humanities:* Arts Centers, Community Arts, Libraries, Music, Performing Arts, Public Broadcasting • *Civic & Public Affairs:* Nonprofit Management, Zoos/Aquariums • *Education:* Colleges & Universities, Elementary Education (Private) • *Religion:* Churches • *Social Services:* Community Service Organizations, United Funds/United Ways

Grant Types: general support, multi-year/continuing support, and project

Geographic Distribution: focus on MN

GIVING OFFICERS
Elise R. Donohue: dir
Gordon E. Hed: dir
Lucy R. McCarthy: pres, dir
Joseph S. Micallef: secy, treas, dir *B* 1933 *CURR EMPL* pres-ceo-treas, dir: Fiduciary Counselling Inc *CORP AFFIL* secy, treas: Rock Island Co *PHIL AFFIL* secy: Driscoll Foundation; asst secy, dir: Edwin W. and Catherine M. Davis Foundation; treas: Rodman Foundation; dir: Musser Fund; asst secy, asst treas: Weyerhaeuser Family Foundation
Charles W. Rosenberry II: dir
Walter Samuel Rosenberry III: off *ED* Harvard Univ AB 1953 *NONPR AFFIL* chmn: Denver Art Mus *PHIL AFFIL* treas, trust, don: Weyerhaeuser Family Foundation; dir: Musser Fund
Robert J. Sivertsen: vp, dir

APPLICATION INFORMATION
Initial Approach: Send cover letter and full proposal. There are no deadlines.
Restrictions on Giving: Does not support individuals.

MISSISSIPPI

Armstrong Foundation

Former Foundation Name: Texas Educational Association

CONTACT
Thomas K. Armstrong
President
Armstrong Fdn.
PO Drawer 2299
Natchez, MS 39120
(601) 442-0122

FINANCIAL SUMMARY
Recent Giving: $646,834 (1993); $484,216 (1992); $244,583 (1991)
Assets: $14,160,804 (1993); $13,738,411 (1992); $13,544,058 (1991)
EIN: 75-6003209

CONTRIBUTIONS SUMMARY
Donor(s): the late George W. Armstrong, Sr.

Typical Recipients: • *Arts & Humanities:* Arts Associations & Councils, Community Arts, History & Archaeology, Libraries • *Civic & Public Affairs:* Business/Free Enterprise, Economic Policy, Legal Aid, Professional & Trade Associations, Public Policy • *Education:* Business Education, Colleges & Universities, Economic Education, Education Funds, Education Reform, General, Leadership Training, Private Education (Precollege) • *Environment:* General, Resource Conservation • *Health:* Emergency/Ambulance Services • *Religion:* Churches, Religious Organizations, Religious Welfare • *Social Services:* Child Welfare, Community Service Organizations, United Funds/United Ways, Youth Organizations

Grant Types: conference/seminar, general support, and research

Geographic Distribution: focus on TX

GIVING OFFICERS
Allen J. Armstrong: trust

Thomas K. Armstrong: pres

Thomas K. Armstrong, Jr.: vp *B* Ft Polk LA 1955 *ED* GA Inst Tech 1976 *CURR EMPL* pres, dir: TX Steel Co *NONPR AFFIL* mem: Am Cast Metals Assn, Am Foundrymens Assn

Laura J. Harrison: secy

J. Hatcher James III: vp

John H. James: vp, treas

APPLICATION INFORMATION
Initial Approach: The foundation has no formal grant application procedure or application form. Include IRS tax exempt status and private foundation status. There are no deadlines.

Restrictions on Giving: Does not support individuals.

PUBLICATIONS
Application Guidelines

GRANTS ANALYSIS
Total Grants: $646,834

Number of Grants: 120

Highest Grant: $100,000

Typical Range: $250 to $50,000

Disclosure Period: 1993

Note: Recent grants are derived from a 1993 Form 990.

RECENT GRANTS
General
100,000	Free Congress Research and Education Foundation, Washington, DC — preparation and broadcast of PSAs on free enterprise system
30,134	American Enterprise Forum for Economic Understanding, Dallas, TX — teacher training and student programs in economics and American Heritage
25,000	Media Research Center, Alexandria, VA — free enterprise and Media Institute
25,000	National Center for Policy Analysis, Dallas, TX — public policy education
25,000	National Center for Policy Analysis, Dallas, TX — research on US economy and budget

Feild Co-Operative Association

CONTACT
Ann Stephenson
Secretary
Feild Co-Operative Association
PO Box 5054
Jackson, MS 39216
(601) 939-9295

FINANCIAL SUMMARY
Recent Giving: $694,070 (1993); $1,014,017 (1991); $890,450 (1989)

Assets: $10,402,324 (1993); $9,220,472 (1991); $8,048,057 (1989)

EIN: 64-0155700

CONTRIBUTIONS SUMMARY
Donor(s): sons of the late Dr. and Mrs. Monfort Jones

Typical Recipients: • *Arts & Humanities:* Community Arts, Dance, Libraries, Literary Arts, Music, Opera, Public Broadcasting • *Civic & Public Affairs:* Clubs, Municipalities/Towns • *Education:* General, Private Education (Precollege), School Volunteerism, Special Education • *Health:* Medical Research, Public Health, Single-Disease Health Associations • *International:* Foreign Arts Organizations, Missionary/Religious Activities • *Religion:* Ministries, Religious Organizations, Religious Welfare • *Science:* Scientific Centers & Institutes • *Social Services:* Child Welfare, Community Centers, Family Services, Substance Abuse, Youth Organizations

Grant Types: general support and loan

Geographic Distribution: limited to MS residents

GIVING OFFICERS
Bernard B. Jones II: chmn, dir

Bernard Bryan Jones III: 1st vp, dir

William M. Link, Jr.: 2nd vp, dir

Betty May: treas

Hobson C. McGehee III: dir

Hobson C. McGehee, Jr.: pres, dir

Ann Stephenson: secy

Kenneth Wills: dir

APPLICATION INFORMATION
Initial Approach: Send a brief letter of inquiry. Application form and personal interview required for student loans.

Restrictions on Giving: No grants for endowments or operating expenses.

PUBLICATIONS
Informational Brochure, Application Guidelines

GRANTS ANALYSIS
Total Grants: $694,070

Number of Grants: 18

Highest Grant: $22,500

Typical Range: $500 to $5,000

Disclosure Period: 1993

Note: Recent grants are derived from a 1993 Form 990. Number of grants and typical range do not include loans to students.

RECENT GRANTS
General
22,500	Junior League, Jackson, MS
7,500	Mississippi Forum on Children and Families, Jackson, MS
5,000	International Ballet Competition, Jackson, MS
3,000	French Camp Academy, French Camp, MS
2,500	Magnolia Speech School, Jackson, MS

Hardin Foundation, Phil

CONTACT
C. Thompson Wacaster
Vice President
Phil Hardin Foundation
PO Box 187
Meridian, MS 39302-0187
(601) 483-4282

FINANCIAL SUMMARY
Recent Giving: $906,935 (1993); $954,413 (1992); $753,732 (1991)

Assets: $26,754,810 (1993); $22,052,366 (1990); $22,774,836 (1989)

EIN: 64-6024940

CONTRIBUTIONS SUMMARY
Donor(s): The foundation was incorporated in 1964 by the late Philip Bernard Hardin and Hardin's Bakeries Corp.

Typical Recipients: • *Arts & Humanities:* Arts Associations & Councils, Arts Institutes, History & Archaeology, Libraries, Literary Arts, Museums/Galleries, Public Broadcasting, Visual Arts • *Civic & Public Affairs:* Community Foundations, Economic Policy, Nonprofit Management, Professional & Trade Associations, Urban & Community Affairs • *Education:* Arts/Humanities Education, Colleges & Universities, Community & Junior Colleges, Education Associations, Education Funds, Education Reform, Elementary Education (Private), Faculty Development, General, Gifted & Talented Programs, International Studies, Leadership Training, Literacy, Preschool Education, Private Education (Precollege), Public Education (Precollege), Religious Education, Science/Mathematics Education, Special Education, Student Aid • *Environment:* Resource Conservation • *Health:* Health Policy/Cost Containment, Hospitals (University Affiliated), Medical Rehabilitation, Medical Research, Speech & Hearing • *Religion:* Religious Welfare • *Social Services:* Child Welfare, Community Service Organizations, People with Disabilities, Volunteer Services, Youth Organizations

Grant Types: capital, conference/seminar, endowment, fellowship, matching, multi-year/continuing support, professorship, project, research, and scholarship

Geographic Distribution: focus on Mississippi, but some national support for programs benefiting the education of Mississippians

GIVING OFFICERS
Joe S. Covington, MD: dir

R. B. Deen, Jr.: secy, dir

Edwin E. Downer: dir

Archie R. McDonnell, Sr.: treas, dir

Stephen O. Moore: dir

Mark M. Porter: vp, dir

Lynne Taleff: dir

C. Thompson Wacaster: vp *B* 1941 *ED* Yale Univ BS 1963; Univ VA MA 1965; Univ OR PhD 1973

Robert F. Ward: dir *B* Eden NC 1949 *ED* NC St Univ postgrad 1976-1977; NC St Univ BS *CURR EMPL* sr vp: Mantech Environmental Technology

APPLICATION INFORMATION
Initial Approach:

The foundation requests grant applicants submit two copies of a written proposal. Scholarship applications can be obtained by contacting the foundation.

Written proposals should include a brief summary statement describing the project and the amount requested, a statement of need for the project, the project's goals, a calendar of the project's major activities and a description of each, a budget and schedule of expenditures, a description of the organization and a list of officers associated with the project, a description of the staff member's qualifications who will be working with the project, a statement of approval for the project from the organization's chief officer, and a statement of the organization's tax-exempt status and a copy of the tax exemption letter from the IRS.

Deadlines for submitting proposals are three months before the project's preparation period begins.

The trustees meet every two months to consider proposals.

Restrictions on Giving: The foundation reports most grants are given for projects that directly benefit education. No grants are made for land acquisition or deficit financing.

PUBLICATIONS
Application guidelines and program policy statement

GRANTS ANALYSIS
Total Grants: $906,935

Number of Grants: 49

Highest Grant: $82,500

Average Grant: $18,509

Typical Range: $2,500 to $45,000

Disclosure Period: 1993

Note: Recent grants are derived from a 1993 annual report.

RECENT GRANTS

Library

3,200	Meridian Public Library, Meridian, MS — equipment
2,500	Kemper-Newton Regional Library, Union, MS — educational material
2,500	Town of Beaumont, Beaumont, MS — library renovation
2,000	Foundation Center, New York, NY

General

82,500	Mississippi State University Development Foundation, Meridian, MS — Mississippi State University-Meridian building
75,000	Mississippi Community College Economic Development Foundations, Raymond, MS — a project to assess need and develop an agenda for the next generation of state education reform in Mississippi
71,000	Gulf Coast Community Foundation, Gulfport, MS — challenge grant to establish public education endowments and annual funds
46,900	State Department of Education, Jackson, MS — a state "Onward to Excellence" training and networking project
45,000	Public Education Forum, Jackson, MS — Core Knowledge project

MISSOURI

ACF Industries, Inc. / ACF Foundation

Sales: $646.43 million
Employees: 1,987
Parent Company: Icahn Holding Corp.
Headquarters: Hazelwood, MO
SIC Major Group: Holding & Other Investment Offices, Transportation Equipment, and Transportation Services

CONTACT
Janet Kniffen
Assistant Secretary
ACF Industries, Inc.
3301 Rider Trail S.
Hazelwood, MO 63045
(314) 344-4200

FINANCIAL SUMMARY
Recent Giving: $54,559 (fiscal 1994); $33,301 (fiscal 1993); $47,000 (fiscal 1992)

Assets: $753,647 (fiscal 1994); $786,551 (fiscal 1993); $798,012 (fiscal 1992)

EIN: 13-6085065

CONTRIBUTIONS SUMMARY
Typical Recipients: • *Arts & Humanities:* Libraries, Museums/Galleries • *Civic & Public Affairs:* Clubs, Employment/Job Training, Municipalities/Towns • *Education:* Business Education, Colleges & Universities, Community & Junior Colleges, Engineering/Technological Education, Private Education (Precollege), Religious Education, Special Education, Student Aid, Vocational & Technical Education • *Health:* Children's Health/Hospitals, Emergency/Ambulance Services, Health Funds • *Religion:* Jewish Causes, Religious Organizations, Religious Welfare • *Social Services:* At-Risk Youth, Child Welfare, Community Centers, Community Service Organizations, Food/Clothing Distribution, Homes, People with Disabilities, Shelters/Homelessness, United Funds/United Ways, YMCA/YWCA/YMHA/YWHA, Youth Organizations

Grant Types: employee matching gifts and general support

Geographic Distribution: focus on WV and PA

Operating Locations: MO (Earth City)

CORP. OFFICERS
James C. Bates: *CURR EMPL* vp, cfo: ACF Indus

Carl Celian Icahn: *B* Queens NY 1936 *ED* Princeton Univ BA 1957; NY Univ Sch Medicine *CURR EMPL* chmn, ceo, dir: Icahn & Co *CORP AFFIL* chmn, ceo, dir: ACF Indus Inc; chmn, pres: Icahn Holding Corp; chmn, pres, ceo: Trans World Airlines; dir: Fairchild Corp

Robert J. Mitchell: *CURR EMPL* treas: ACF Industries

James J. Unger: *CURR EMPL* pres: ACF Indus

Roger D. Wynkoop: *CURR EMPL* exec vp: ACF Industries

GIVING OFFICERS
Gail Golden: secy, asst treas, dir

Carl Celian Icahn: pres, treas *CURR EMPL* chmn, ceo, dir: Icahn & Co (see above)

Alfred D. Kingsley: vp, asst secy, dir

APPLICATION INFORMATION
Initial Approach: The foundation has no formal grant application procedure or application form. There are no deadlines.

Restrictions on Giving: The foundation does not make grants to individuals.

PUBLICATIONS
Contributions Guidelines Sheet

GRANTS ANALYSIS
Total Grants: $54,559

Number of Grants: 50

Highest Grant: $26,000

Typical Range: $10 to $3,000

Disclosure Period: fiscal year ending April 30, 1994

Note: Recent grants are derived from a fiscal 1994 Form 990.

RECENT GRANTS

General

26,000	American Red Cross, St. Louis, MO
3,000	Ranken Technical Institute, St. Louis, MO — for educational purposes
1,500	Junior Achievement, St. Louis, MO — for educational purposes
1,250	Boys Hope, St. Louis, MO
1,250	St. Louis Association for Retarded Citizens, St. Louis, MO

Anheuser-Busch Companies, Inc. / Anheuser-Busch Foundation/Anheuser-Busch Charitable Trust

Revenue: $12.05 billion
Employees: 43,345
Headquarters: St. Louis, MO
SIC Major Group: Malt Beverages, Bread, Cake & Related Products, Wet Corn Milling, and Holding Companies Nec

CONTACT

Sylvia Morris
Contributions Specialist
Anheuser-Busch Companies, Inc.
One Busch Pl.
St. Louis, MO 63118
(314) 577-2453
Note: An additional contact is JoBeth Goode Brown, vice president and secretary, at the above address.

FINANCIAL SUMMARY

Recent Giving: $8,971,752 (1993); $25,000,000 (1992 approx.); $25,000,000 (1991 approx.)

Assets: $73,330,936 (1993); $76,722,825 (1992); $65,316,788 (1990)

Gifts Received: $7,287 (1993)

Fiscal Note: Company contributes directly, through the foundation, and through the charitable trust. The foundation gave $8,606,827 in 1992. The remainder was contributed by the trust and the company. 1993 figure is for foundation giving only. Above figures exclude nonmonetary support.

EIN: 51-0168084

CONTRIBUTIONS SUMMARY

Typical Recipients: • *Arts & Humanities:* Arts Associations & Councils, Arts Centers, Arts Funds, Community Arts, Historic Preservation, Libraries, Museums/Galleries, Music, Performing Arts • *Civic & Public Affairs:* Civil Rights, Clubs, Employment/Job Training, Hispanic Affairs, Law & Justice, Public Policy, Rural Affairs, Urban & Community Affairs, Zoos/Aquariums • *Education:* Agricultural Education, Arts/Humanities Education, Business Educa-

tion, Colleges & Universities, Continuing Education, Education Funds, Education Reform, Engineering/Technological Education, General, Health & Physical Education, International Exchange, Literacy, Minority Education, Private Education (Precollege), Science/Mathematics Education, Secondary Education (Private), Secondary Education (Public), Special Education • *Environment:* General • *Health:* Children's Health/Hospitals, Health Policy/Cost Containment, Health Organizations, Heart, Hospitals, Medical Research, Public Health, Single-Disease Health Associations • *Religion:* Dioceses, Religious Organizations, Seminaries • *Science:* Scientific Centers & Institutes, Scientific Organizations, Scientific Research • *Social Services:* Child Welfare, Community Service Organizations, Delinquency & Criminal Rehabilitation, Food/Clothing Distribution, People with Disabilities, Recreation & Athletics, Shelters/Homelessness, Substance Abuse, United Funds/United Ways, Volunteer Services, Youth Organizations

Grant Types: capital, employee matching gifts, and general support

Nonmonetary Support Types: donated products

Note: No estimate is available for value of nonmonetary support.

Geographic Distribution: primarily in communities in which company has major production facilities

Operating Locations: AR (Jonesboro), CA (Carson, Fairfield, Los Angeles, Riverside, San Diego, Slymar, Stockton, Visalia, Woodland), CO (Denver, Ft. Collins, Windsor), FL (Gainesville, Jacksonville, Orlando, Tampa, Winter Haven), GA (Cartersville, Rome), ID (Idaho Falls), IL (Chicago), LA (New Orleans), MA (Boston, Hyannis), MN (Clearbrook, Moorhead), MO (Arnold, St. Louis), NC (Robersonville), NH (Merrimack), NJ (Newark), NY (Baldwinsville, Manhattan, Newburgh), OH (Aurora, Columbus), OK (Oklahoma City, Tulsa), PA (Langhorne, York), TN (Fayetteville), TX (Houston, San Antonio), VA (Williamsburg), WI (Ft. Atkinson, Manitowoc)

CORP. OFFICERS

August Adolphus Busch III: *B* St Louis MO 1937 *ED* Univ AZ 1957; Siebel Inst Tech 1960 *CURR EMPL* chmn, pres, dir: Anheuser-Busch Cos, Inc *CORP AFFIL* dir: Civic Center Corp, Emerson Electric Co, Gen Am Life Ins Co, Mfrs Railway Co, Southwestern Bell Corp, St Louis Natl Baseball Club; trust: St Louis Refrigerator Co *NONPR AFFIL* bd overseers: Univ PA Wharton Sch Bus; chmn adv bd: St Johns Mercy Med Ctr; dir: Un Way Greater St Louis; pres exec bd: Boy Scouts Am *PHIL AFFIL* don, trust: August A. III Busch Charitable Trust, August A III Busch Charitable Trust; mem bd control: Anheuser-Busch Charitable Trust; trust: Anheuser-Busch Foundation *CLUB AFFIL* Frontenac Racquet, Log

Cabin, Noonday, Racquet, St Louis, St Louis CC, Stadium

GIVING OFFICERS

JoBeth Goode Brown: trust *B* Oakdale LA 1950 *ED* Tulane Univ Newcomb Coll BA 1972; Washington Univ JD 1979 *CURR EMPL* vp, secy: Anheuser-Busch Cos Inc *CORP AFFIL* dir: Busch Creative Svcs Corp; secy: St Louis Natl Baseball Club *NONPR AFFIL* mem: Am Bar Assn, Am Soc Corp Secys, Bar Assn Metro St Louis, MO Bar Assn, Order Coif; mem adv bd: Greater MO Focus Leadership, MI Fdn Women's Resources; mem devel bd: St Louis Childrens Hosp; secy: Intl Womens Forum *CLUB AFFIL* Algonquin GC

August Adolphus Busch III: trust *CURR EMPL* chmn, pres, dir: Anheuser-Busch Cos, Inc *PHIL AFFIL* don, trust: August A. III Busch Charitable Trust (see above)

Sylvia Morris: *CURR EMPL* contributions specialist: Anheuser-Busch Cos Inc

APPLICATION INFORMATION

Initial Approach: *Initial Contact:* write or call to request grant application form *Include Information On:* information on the organization, amount of request, purpose of request *Deadlines:* none

Restrictions on Giving: Does not support individuals, political organizations, religious organizations, social or fraternal groups, athletic organizations, hospital operating budgets, or organizations that do not have tax-exempt status.

GRANTS ANALYSIS

Total Grants: $8,971,752

Number of Grants: 440*

Highest Grant: $1,102,250

Average Grant: $20,390

Typical Range: $500 to $25,000

Disclosure Period: 1993

Note: Number of grants figure is approximate. Recent grants are derived from a 1993 Form 990.

RECENT GRANTS

Library

25,000	St. Louis Public Library, St. Louis, MO

General

1,102,250	United Way Greater St. Louis, St. Louis, MO
700,000	Hole in the Wall Gang Fund, New Haven, CT
500,000	River Network, Portland, OR
500,000	St. Louis University, St. Louis, MO
400,000	Archdiocese of St. Louis, St. Louis, MO

Block, H&R / Block Foundation, H&R

Sales: $1.53 billion
Employees: 82,000
Headquarters: Kansas City, MO
SIC Major Group: Tax Return Preparation Services

CONTACT

Barbara Allmon
President of Foundation
The H&R Block Foundation
4410 Main St.
Kansas City, MO 64111
(816) 753-6900
Note: Lin Dunlap handles general inquiries and contribution requests for the Kansas City, MO, area. See "Other Things You Should Know" for details on giving in the Columbus, OH, area. Grants are no longer awarded in the Ft. Lauderdale, FL, area.

FINANCIAL SUMMARY

Recent Giving: $1,036,586 (1994); $1,235,000 (1993); $1,033,987 (1992)

Assets: $24,047,704 (1992); $18,520,302 (1991); $17,011,091 (1990)

Gifts Received: $2,516,157 (1992)

Fiscal Note: Company gives through foundation only. Other company departments make contributions from corporate funds. Budget for this is not available. Contact Terrance R. Ward for information.

EIN: 23-7378232

CONTRIBUTIONS SUMMARY

Typical Recipients: • *Arts & Humanities:* Arts Appreciation, Arts Associations & Councils, Arts Centers, Arts Festivals, Arts Funds, Arts Institutes, Arts Outreach, Ballet, Community Arts, Dance, Ethnic & Folk Arts, Libraries, Literary Arts, Museums/Galleries, Music, Opera, Performing Arts, Theater, Visual Arts • *Civic & Public Affairs:* Business/Free Enterprise, Civil Rights, Economic Development, Employment/Job Training, Housing, Law & Justice, Legal Aid, Nonprofit Management, Public Policy, Safety, Urban & Community Affairs, Women's Affairs, Zoos/Aquariums • *Education:* Arts/Humanities Education, Business Education, Colleges & Universities, Community & Junior Colleges, Continuing Education, Economic Education, Education Funds, Education Reform, General, Legal Education, Literacy, Minority Education, Preschool Education, Private Education (Precollege), Public Education (Precollege), Science/Mathematics Education, Social Sciences Education, Special Education • *Health:* Cancer, Children's Health/Hospitals, Clinics/Medical Centers, Geriatric Health, Health Funds, Health Organizations, Hospices, Hospitals, Medical Rehabilitation, Mental Health, Public Health • *International:* International Relations • *Religion:* Jewish Causes, Religious Organizations • *Science:* Science Exhibits & Fairs • *Social Services:* At-Risk Youth, Child Welfare, Community Centers, Community Service Organizations, Counseling, Day Care, Delinquency & Criminal Rehabilitation, Domestic Violence, Emergency Relief, Family Planning, Family Services, Food/Clothing Distribution, Homes, People with Disabilities, Recreation & Athletics, Refugee Assistance, Senior Services, Shelters/Homelessness, Substance Abuse, United Funds/United Ways, Volunteer Services, Youth Organizations

Grant Types: capital, challenge, employee matching gifts, general support, multi-year/continuing support, operating expenses, project, and scholarship

Geographic Distribution: major emphasis on Kansas City, MO, and Columbus, OH

Operating Locations: KS (Kansas City), MO (Kansas City), OH (Columbus)

Note: The list includes headquarters offices for Personnel Pool of America and CompuServe, Inc., H&R Block's operating companies.

CORP. OFFICERS

Henry Wollman Bloch: *B* Kansas City MO 1922 *ED* Univ MI BS 1943 *CURR EMPL* chmn: H&R Block *CORP AFFIL* dir: Commerce Bancshares, CompuServe Inc *NONPR AFFIL* dir: Civic Counc Greater Kansas City, Greater Kansas City Commun Fdn, Intl Pub Rels Counc, Kansas City Symphony, Mid-Am Coalition Health, St Lukes Hosp; dir, trust: Nelson-Atkins Mus Art; gen chmn: Un Negro Coll Fund, Un Way Heart Am; pres trusts: Univ Kansas City; trust: Jr Achievement Mid-Am; vchmn, dir: Midwest Res Inst; vp, dir: Kansas City Area Health Planning Counc *CLUB AFFIL* Carriage, Kansas City Racquet, Oakwood CC, River *PHIL AFFIL* ceo, pres, dir: Henry W. and Marion H. Bloch Foundation

Thomas Morton Bloch: *B* Kansas City MO 1954 *ED* Claremont McKenna Coll BS 1976 *CURR EMPL* ceo, pres, dir: H&R Block *CORP AFFIL* dir: Bus Mens Assurance Co Am, Commerce Bank Kansas City, CompuServe Inc

Thomas Morton Bloch: *B* Kansas City MO 1954 *ED* Claremont Coll BA 1976 *CURR EMPL* pres, ceo, dir: H&R Block *CORP AFFIL* dir: Bus Mens Assurance Co Am, Commerce Bank Kansas City, CompuServe Inc *PHIL AFFIL* dir: Henry W. and Marion H. Bloch Foundation, Henry W. and Marion H. Bloch Foundation

GIVING OFFICERS

Barbara Allmon: pres

Henry Wollman Bloch: chmn *CURR EMPL* chmn: H&R Block *PHIL AFFIL* ceo, pres, dir: Henry W. and Marion H. Bloch Foundation (see above)

Robert L. Bloch: secy, program off

Charles E. Curran: dir

Edward A. Smith: vchmn, dir *B* Worcester MA 1918 *ED* Clark Univ 1939; Harvard Univ JD 1942 *CURR EMPL* pres, dir: Smith Gill Fisher & Butts *CORP AFFIL* dir: Brown & Loe, Koch Supplies, Milbank Mfg, Woolford Enterprises *NONPR AFFIL* mem: Am Bar Assn *PHIL AFFIL* dir: Henry W. and Marion H. Bloch Foundation

Morton Irvin Sosland: dir *B* Kansas City MO 1925 *ED* Harvard Coll 1946 *CURR EMPL* chmn: Sosland Publ Co *CORP AFFIL* dir: Brown Group Inc, Commerce Bancshares, H&R Block, Hallmark Cards Inc, Kansas City Southern Indus *PHIL AFFIL* dir: Hall Family Foundation; pres, dir: Sosland Foundation; trust: George Warren Brown Foundation

APPLICATION INFORMATION

Initial Approach: *Initial Contact:* one- or two-page letter *Include Information On:* description of purpose for grant; program description of the organization; detailed analysis of amount sought and when it is needed; financial statement for most recent year; total program budget; current list of trustees or directors; and copy of IRS determination letter *Deadlines:* none *Note:* Organizations may be asked to submit additional information or to meet with a member of the foundation's board of directors or staff

Restrictions on Giving: Foundation generally does not make grants to institutions or programs outside the greater Kansas City area; endowment funds or research projects; projects for which foundation must exercise expenditure responsibility; single-disease agencies; travel, conferences, or telethons; literary journals; or historic preservation projects.

OTHER THINGS TO KNOW

Foundation favors making proportionately significant grants to relatively few activities, rather than relatively minor grants to a great many activities. Generally, grants of less than $500 are not made.

Foundation usually makes one-year grants but, in appropriate circumstances, will consider requests for up to three years for special project funding.

Foundation publishes an annual report.

For information on contributions in the Columbus, OH, area, contact: Carrie Brown, Assistant to the CEO, CompuServe, 5000 Arlington Centre Blvd., Columbus, OH 43220, (614) 457-8600.

GRANTS ANALYSIS

Total Grants: $1,036,589

Typical Range: $500 to $6,000

Disclosure Period: 1994

Note: Recent grants are derived from a 1992 Form 990.

RECENT GRANTS

Library
25,000   Greater Kansas City Community Foundation, Kansas City, MO — to establish an endowment fund to provide financial stability and adequate library materials for residents in the metropolitan area

General
133,200   University of Missouri Kansas City, Kansas City, MO — to construct the Henry W.

Bloch School of Business and Public Administration

51,000	Heart of America United Way, Kansas City, MO — funding for United Way agencies during 1992
40,000	Children's Mercy Hospital, Kansas City, MO — to support the Centennial Fund, which will expand and renovate the facility
30,000	Palestine Gardens Senior Citizen Center, Kansas City, MO — to construct the senior citizens center
25,000	Friends of the Zoo, Kansas City, MO — to help construct an educational facility at the entrance to the new zoo

Boatmen's Bancshares, Inc. / Boatmen's Bancshares Charitable Trust

Revenue: $2.29 billion
Employees: 14,400
Headquarters: St. Louis, MO
SIC Major Group: Bank Holding Companies and National Commercial Banks

CONTACT
Carol A. Gruen
Administrative Officer
Boatmen's Bancshares Charitable Trust
PO Box 236
St. Louis, MO 63166
(314) 466-7565
Note: Organizations outside of St. Louis should submit proposals to the Boatmen's subsidiary nearest to them.

FINANCIAL SUMMARY
Recent Giving: $2,435,000 (1993 approx.); $2,662,921 (1992); $2,526,000 (1991 approx.)

Assets: $1,882,817 (1992); $1,415,224 (1990); $1,326,271 (1989)

Fiscal Note: The company also gives directly from corporate funds, which is not reflected in the figures above. Larry D. Bayliss, Senior Vice-President, is the contact person for this support. Above figures exclude nonmonetary support.

EIN: 43-1363004

CONTRIBUTIONS SUMMARY
Typical Recipients: • *Arts & Humanities:* Arts Associations & Councils, Arts Funds, Community Arts, Dance, Historic Preservation, Libraries, Museums/Galleries, Music, Performing Arts • *Civic & Public Affairs:* Business/Free Enterprise, Employment/Job Training, Urban & Community Affairs, Women's Affairs, Zoos/Aquariums • *Education:* Business Education, Colleges & Universities, Economic Education • *Health:* Health Organizations, Hospitals • *Social Services:* Child Welfare, Community Service Organizations, Delinquency & Criminal

Rehabilitation, Recreation & Athletics, United Funds/United Ways, Youth Organizations

Nonmonetary Support Types: cause-related marketing & promotion and donated products

Note: Nonmonetary support is provided by the company. Estimated value is unavailable and varies. Contact for this support is Larry D. Bayliss, Senior Vice President for information.

Geographic Distribution: near operating locations

Operating Locations: AR, IA, IL, KS, MO (St. Louis), NM, OK, TN, TX

CORP. OFFICERS
Andrew Billings Craig III: *B* Buffalo NY 1931 *ED* Cornell Univ 1950-1954; Univ Buffalo BA 1955 *CURR EMPL* chmn, ceo: Boatmens Bancshares Inc *CORP AFFIL* dir: Andco Inc, Anheuser-Busch Cos Inc, BancOhio Corp, Boatman Bank DE, Boatmens Natl Bank St Louis, Calspan Corp, 1st Empire Overseas Corp, Firstmark Fin Corp, Kistler Instrument Corp, Loblaw Inc, M & T Capital Corp, Mfrs & Traders Trust Co, Moubot Inc, NY Standard Mirror Co, Petrolite Corp, Transelco Inc *NONPR AFFIL* bd deacons, trust: Westminster Presbyterian Church; dir: Buffalo Fdn, Niagara Frontier Housing Devel Corp, NY St Assn Retarded Children, Univ Buffalo Sch Mgmt, WNY Nuclear Res Ctr; mem: Assn Reserve City Bankers, Erie County Indus Devel Agency, Small Bus Admin Syracuse District Adv Counc; mem adv bd: Jr League Buffalo; mem banking monetary & fiscal affairs comm: US Chamber Commerce; pres, dir: Boy Scouts Am Greater St Louis; trust: Buffalo Gen Hosp, Columbus Fdn, Ctr Sci Indus, Riverside Methodist Hosp; vchmn: Cornell Univ Counc *CLUB AFFIL* Buffalo CC

GIVING OFFICERS
Carol A. Gruen: admin off

APPLICATION INFORMATION
Initial Approach: *Initial Contact:* brief proposal *Include Information On:* description of the organization; amount requested; purpose for which funds are sought; recently audited financial statement; proof of tax-exempt status *Deadlines:* none

Restrictions on Giving: Only gives to organizations with IRS 501(c)(3) status.

Trust does not support individuals; private secondary schools; tickets or advertisements for dinners, benefits, sports events, and other primarily public relations activities; religious, fraternal, political, labor, or veterans groups unless they furnish services to benefit the general public; and organizations deriving major support from government funding or recipients of major funding from United Ways or the Arts and Education Councils (specific capital campaigns will be considered).

GRANTS ANALYSIS
Total Grants: $2,662,921

Number of Grants: 226

Highest Grant: $200,000

Average Grant: $11,783

Typical Range: $1,000 to $5,000

Disclosure Period: 1992

Note: Recent grants are derived from a 1992 Form 990.

RECENT GRANTS
General

200,000	Washington University, St. Louis, MO
200,000	Washington University, St. Louis, MO
144,500	United Way of Greater St. Louis, St. Louis, MO
144,500	United Way of Greater St. Louis, St. Louis, MO
144,500	United Way of Greater St. Louis, St. Louis, MO

Commerce Bancshares, Inc. / Commerce Bancshares Foundation

Former Foundation Name: Commerce Foundation
Gross Operating Earnings: $581.84 million
Employees: 3,728
Headquarters: Kansas City, MO
SIC Major Group: Bank Holding Companies and National Commercial Banks

CONTACT
Michael Fields
Vice President & Treasurer
Commerce Bancshares Foundation
PO Box 13095
Kansas City, MO 64199-3095
(816) 234-2112

FINANCIAL SUMMARY
Recent Giving: $900,000 (1995 est.); $745,153 (1994); $758,477 (1993)

Assets: $4,730,589 (1993); $5,037,004 (1992); $4,631,369 (1989)

Gifts Received: $16,453 (1993); $657,899 (1992); $371,067 (1990)

Fiscal Note: Company primarily gives through its foundation. In addition, it participates in the Missouri Neigborhood Assistance Program and has a small discretionary budget for activities that fall outside the foundation's guidelines. Figures for these activities are not available and are not included above. In 1993, contributions were received from County Tower Trust.

EIN: 44-6012453

CONTRIBUTIONS SUMMARY
Typical Recipients: • *Arts & Humanities:* Arts Associations & Councils, Community Arts, Historic Preservation, History & Archaeology, Libraries, Museums/Galleries, Music, Opera, Public Broadcasting, Theater • *Civic & Public Affairs:* African American Affairs, Botanical Gardens/Parks, Community Foundations, Economic Development, General, Housing, Legal Aid, Municipalities/Towns, Parades/Festivals, Urban & Community Affairs, Zoos/Aquariums • *Edu-*

cation: Agricultural Education, Arts/Humanities Education, Business Education, Business-School Partnerships, Colleges & Universities, Literacy, Private Education (Precollege), Public Education (Precollege), Secondary Education (Private) • *Health:* Cancer, Children's Health/Hospitals, Emergency/Ambulance Services, Health Organizations • *Religion:* Missionary Activities (Domestic), Religious Organizations, Religious Welfare • *Science:* Scientific Centers & Institutes • *Social Services:* Child Welfare, Community Centers, Community Service Organizations, Counseling, Domestic Violence, Family Planning, Family Services, Food/Clothing Distribution, Shelters/Homelessness, Substance Abuse, United Funds/United Ways, Youth Organizations

Grant Types: general support

Geographic Distribution: primarily Missouri

Operating Locations: MO (Clayton, Kansas City, Springfield, St. Joseph, St. Louis)

CORP. OFFICERS

David Woods Kemper II: *B* Kansas City MO 1950 *ED* Harvard Univ AB 1972; Oxford Univ Worcester Coll MA 1974; Stanford Univ Grad Sch Bus MBA 1976 *CURR EMPL* chmn, pres, ceo, dir: Commerce Bancshares *CORP AFFIL* chmn, ceo: Commerce Bank St Louis; dir: BMA Corp, Seafield Capital Corp, Tower Properties Co, Venture Stores *NONPR AFFIL* adv dir: Friends Chamber Music; dir: Arts & Ed Counc Greater St Louis, Civic Progress, Downtown St Louis Inc, Midwest Res Inst, St Louis Symphony Orchestra; mem: Assn Reserve City Bankers, Young Pres Org; mem exec comm: Kansas City Econ Devel; st chair: Task Force Higher Ed MO; trust: MO Botanical Gardens, Washington Univ *CLUB AFFIL* Kansas City CC, Old Warson CC, Racquet, River, St Louis, Univ *PHIL AFFIL* vp: David Woods Kemper Memorial Foundation

Warren W. Weaver: *CURR EMPL* vchmn: Commerce Bancshares *CORP AFFIL* pres: Commerce Bank Kansas City

GIVING OFFICERS

Michael D. Fields: vp, treas

Thomas Alan Peschka: secy, dir *B* Great Bend KS 1931 *CURR EMPL* vp, secy, treas, gen coun: Commerce Bancshares *CORP AFFIL* pres, dir: CBI Ins; secy, dir: Mid-Am Fin Corp *NONPR AFFIL* mem: MO Bar Assn

Charles E. Templer: vp *CURR EMPL* treas, contr: Commerce Bancshares

Warren W. Weaver: pres, dir *CURR EMPL* vchmn: Commerce Bancshares (see above)

APPLICATION INFORMATION

Initial Approach: *Initial Contact:* address letter of inquiry to or visit local branch president *Include Information On:* description of organization and its purpose, amount requested, time frame, and proof of tax-exempt status *Deadlines:* none

GRANTS ANALYSIS

Total Grants: $758,477

Number of Grants: 445*

Highest Grant: $34,712

Average Grant: $1,704*

Typical Range: $500 to $5,000

Disclosure Period: 1993

Note: Number of grants and average grant figures are approximate. Recent grants are derived from a 1993 Form 990.

RECENT GRANTS

General

34,713	United Way, St. Louis, MO — fourth of four payments
34,713	United Way, St. Louis, MO — third of four payments
34,712	United Way, St. Louis, MO — first of four payments
34,712	United Way, St. Louis, MO — second of four payments
30,000	Missouri Department of Social Services, Jefferson City, MO

Gaylord Foundation, Clifford Willard

CONTACT

Karen Munger
Trust Officer
Clifford Willard Gaylord Fdn.
c/o Boatmen's Trust Co.
100 N Broadway
PO Box 14737
St. Louis, MO 63178
(314) 466-6126

FINANCIAL SUMMARY

Recent Giving: $254,500 (1993); $531,600 (1990); $483,500 (1989)

Assets: $7,587,482 (1993); $6,508,236 (1990); $6,556,089 (1989)

EIN: 43-6027517

CONTRIBUTIONS SUMMARY

Donor(s): the late Clifford W. Gaylord

Typical Recipients: • *Arts & Humanities:* Community Arts, History & Archaeology, Libraries, Museums/Galleries, Performing Arts • *Civic & Public Affairs:* Botanical Gardens/Parks, General, Municipalities/Towns, Women's Affairs • *Education:* Colleges & Universities, General, Legal Education, Private Education (Precollege), Secondary Education (Private) • *Health:* Health Organizations, Hospitals, Medical Research • *Religion:* Religious Welfare • *Social Services:* Child Welfare, People with Disabilities, United Funds/United Ways, YMCA/YWCA/YMHA/YWHA, Youth Organizations

Grant Types: general support

Geographic Distribution: focus on St. Louis, MO

GIVING OFFICERS

Frances M. Barnes III: trust

Clair Stephens Cullenbine: trust *B* Beardstown IL 1905 *ED* Washington Univ LLB 1928 *CORP AFFIL* dir: Crown Zellerbach

Corp *NONPR AFFIL* mem: Am Arbitration Assn, CA Mfrs Assn

Robert G. H. Hoester: trust

Barbara P. Lawton: trust

James F. Wolfe: trust

APPLICATION INFORMATION

Initial Approach: Send brief letter of inquiry describing program or project. There are no deadlines.

Restrictions on Giving: Does not support individuals.

GRANTS ANALYSIS

Total Grants: $254,500

Number of Grants: 40

Highest Grant: $100,000

Typical Range: $1,000 to $20,000

Disclosure Period: 1993

Note: Recent grants are derived from a 1993 Form 990.

RECENT GRANTS

Library

10,000	Mercantile Library Association, St. Louis, MO

General

100,000	Washington University School of Law, St. Louis, MO
20,000	St. Louis University, St. Louis, MO
10,000	City of St. Genevieve Charitable Contributions, St. Genevieve, MO
10,000	Matthews-Dickey Boys Club, St. Louis, MO
7,500	Washington University, St. Louis, MO

General American Life Insurance Co. / General American Charitable Foundation

Premiums: $1.18 billion
Employees: 2,869
Headquarters: St. Louis, MO
SIC Major Group: Life Insurance and Accident & Health Insurance

CONTACT

Charles L. Larance
President
General American Charitable Foundation
700 Market St.
PO Box 396
St. Louis, MO 63101
(314) 444-0681

FINANCIAL SUMMARY

Recent Giving: $800,000 (fiscal 1995 est.); $747,000 (fiscal 1994 approx.); $679,000 (fiscal 1993 approx.)

Assets: $4,780,291 (fiscal 1992); $2,500,000 (fiscal 1991); $2,234,552 (fiscal 1990)

Fiscal Note: Above figures include both foundation and direct giving.
EIN: 43-1401687

CONTRIBUTIONS SUMMARY
Typical Recipients: • *Arts & Humanities:* Arts Funds, Arts Outreach, Community Arts, Dance, Libraries, Music, Opera, Performing Arts, Theater • *Civic & Public Affairs:* Employment/Job Training, General, Municipalities/Towns, Parades/Festivals, Philanthropic Organizations, Professional & Trade Associations, Public Policy, Urban & Community Affairs, Women's Affairs, Zoos/Aquariums • *Education:* Business Education, Colleges & Universities, Economic Education, Education Associations, Education Funds, Medical Education, Minority Education, Public Education (Precollege), Secondary Education (Public), Student Aid • *Health:* AIDS/HIV, Alzheimers Disease, Diabetes, Emergency/Ambulance Services, Hospitals, Hospitals (University Affiliated), Medical Rehabilitation, Medical Research, Single-Disease Health Associations • *Religion:* Churches, Jewish Causes, Ministries, Religious Welfare • *Science:* Scientific Centers & Institutes • *Social Services:* At-Risk Youth, Child Welfare, Community Centers, Community Service Organizations, Counseling, Domestic Violence, Emergency Relief, Family Planning, Food/Clothing Distribution, Homes, People with Disabilities, Recreation & Athletics, Senior Services, Substance Abuse, United Funds/United Ways, Volunteer Services, Youth Organizations

Grant Types: capital, general support, professorship, project, research, and scholarship
Geographic Distribution: primarily in the St. Louis, MO, area
Operating Locations: GA (Atlanta), MO (Clayton, St. Louis)

CORP. OFFICERS
Charles L. Larance: *CURR EMPL* vp corp rels: Gen Am Life Ins Co
Richard A. Liddy: *B* 1935 *ED* IA St Univ BS 1957 *CURR EMPL* pres, dir: Gen Am Life Ins Co *CORP AFFIL* chmn: Reins Group Am Inc
Leonard Mark Rubenstein: *B* New London CT 1946 *ED* Washington Univ AB 1968; Univ MO MBA 1972 *CURR EMPL* exec vp, treas: Gen Am Life Ins Co *CORP AFFIL* pres, dir: Gen Am Investment Mgmt Co; treas, dir: St Louis Reins Co Inc; vp, treas: GenCare Health Sys Inc *NONPR AFFIL* mem: St Louis Soc Fin Analysts
H. Edwin Trusheim: *B* Chicago IL 1927 *ED* Concordia Teachers Coll BS 1948; WA Univ 1951-1954; Northwestern Univ MA 1955 *CURR EMPL* chmn, ceo: Gen Am Life Ins Co *CORP AFFIL* bd dirs: Am Counc Life Ins, Angelica Corp; chmn bd: Fed Reserve Bank St Louis *NONPR AFFIL* bd dirs: Un Way Greater St Louis; dir: Civic Progress St Louis

GIVING OFFICERS
Joseph M. Gorman: secy
Charles L. Larance: pres *CURR EMPL* vp corp rels: Gen Am Life Ins Co (see above)

Leonard Mark Rubenstein: vp, dir *CURR EMPL* exec vp, treas: Gen Am Life Ins Co (see above)
Marcia L. Sher: admin

APPLICATION INFORMATION
Initial Approach: *Initial Contact:* brief letter or proposal *Include Information On:* description of the organization, list of officers, statement of goals and objectives, locations and scope of activities, project description, project's financial need, result expected including evaluation methods, current budget, annual report, sources of funding, and copy of IRS Code Section 501(c)(3) tax-exempt letter *Deadlines:* before October 1

Restrictions on Giving: Does not contribute to individuals or any individual benefit, political organizations, candidates for political office, religious organizations for nonsecular purposes, social clubs, or labor organizations for political or organizational purposes.

GRANTS ANALYSIS
Total Grants: $747,000
Typical Range: $1,000 to $3,000 and $5,000 to $25,000
Disclosure Period: fiscal year ending November 30, 1994

Note: Figures are for foundation grants only. Recent grants are derived from a fiscal 1994 partial grants list.

RECENT GRANTS

General

15,000	Washington University, St. Louis, MO — AIDS research
10,000	University of Missouri School of Medicine, Columbia, MO — AIDS research

---

Green Foundation, Allen P. and Josephine B.

CONTACT
Walter G. Staley
Secretary-Treasurer
Allen P. and Josephine B. Green Fdn.
PO Box 523
Mexico, MO 65265
(314) 581-5568

FINANCIAL SUMMARY
Recent Giving: $398,700 (1993); $550,800 (1989); $500,600 (1988)
Assets: $6,483,660 (1993); $10,925,042 (1989); $9,265,298 (1988)
EIN: 43-6030135

CONTRIBUTIONS SUMMARY
Donor(s): the late Allen P. Green, the late Mrs. Allen P. Green

Typical Recipients: • *Arts & Humanities:* Historic Preservation, Libraries, Museums/Galleries, Performing Arts • *Civic & Public Affairs:* Botanical Gardens/Parks, Housing • *Education:* Agricultural Education, Colleges & Universities, Student Aid,

Vocational & Technical Education • *Environment:* General • *Health:* Children's Health/Hospitals, Diabetes, Mental Health • *Religion:* Churches, Religious Organizations, Religious Welfare • *Science:* Scientific Centers & Institutes • *Social Services:* Child Welfare, Community Service Organizations, Family Services, People with Disabilities, Recreation & Athletics, Senior Services, Youth Organizations

Grant Types: capital, conference/seminar, emergency, endowment, fellowship, project, scholarship, and seed money
Geographic Distribution: focus on the Mexico, MO, area

GIVING OFFICERS
Arthur D. Bond III: dir
Christopher Samuel Bond: dir *B* St Louis MO 1939 *ED* Princeton Univ BA 1960; Univ VA LLB 1963 *CURR EMPL* senator: MO *NONPR AFFIL* chmn: Midwestern Govs Conf, Rep Govs Assn
Robert R. Collins: dir
Susan Green Foote: dir
Martha S. Marks: dir
James F. McHenry: dir
Robert McIntosh: dir
Walter G. Staley, Jr.: dir
Walter G. Stanley: secy, treas
George C. Willson III: pres
Robert A. Wood: dir

APPLICATION INFORMATION
Initial Approach: Send brief letter of inquiry describing program or project. There are no deadlines.

Restrictions on Giving: Does not support individuals.

PUBLICATIONS
Annual Report

GRANTS ANALYSIS
Total Grants: $398,700
Number of Grants: 44
Highest Grant: $25,700
Typical Range: $500 to $25,000
Disclosure Period: 1993

Note: Recent grants are derived from a 1993 Form 990.

RECENT GRANTS

General

25,700	Children's Trust Fund, St. Louis, MO — to employ an individual for fundraising
25,000	Englemann Mathematics and Science Institute — for classes for gifted students
25,000	Missouri Girls Town, St. Louis, MO — for renovation of the Pott Pavilion into an education-training center
20,000	Annie Malone Children and Family Service Center — Saturday Enrichment program
20,000	Edgewood Children's Center, St. Louis, MO — for Project Smooth Start for School

Jordan Charitable Foundation, Mary Ranken Jordan and Ettie A.

CONTACT
Fred E. Arnold
Chairman, Advisory Committee
Jordan and Ettie A. Jordan Charitable
Foundation
One Mercantile Ctr., Ste. 3400
St. Louis, MO 63101
(314) 425-2525

FINANCIAL SUMMARY
Recent Giving: $860,000 (1994 approx.);
$738,420 (1993); $1,001,120 (1990)
Assets: $17,417,448 (1994); $19,403,037
(1993); $16,114,293 (1990)
EIN: 43-6020554

CONTRIBUTIONS SUMMARY
Donor(s): The foundation was established
in 1957 by the late Mary Ranken Jordan
and Ettie A. Jordan.

Typical Recipients: • *Arts & Humanities:*
Arts Associations & Councils, Arts Funds,
Dance, Ethnic & Folk Arts, Historic Preser-
vation, History & Archaeology, Libraries,
Literary Arts, Museums/Galleries, Music,
Opera, Performing Arts, Public Broadcast-
ing, Theater • *Civic & Public Affairs:* Bo-
tanical Gardens/Parks, General,
Zoos/Aquariums • *Education:* Colleges &
Universities, Private Education (Precollege),
Secondary Education (Private), Secondary
Education (Public), Special Education, Voca-
tional & Technical Education • *Health:* Chil-
dren's Health/Hospitals, Diabetes,
Emergency/Ambulance Services, Hospitals
• *International:* International Relations • *Re-
ligion:* Churches, Ministries, Religious Wel-
fare • *Social Services:* Child Welfare,
Community Centers, Family Services,
Food/Clothing Distribution, Homes, People
with Disabilities, Scouts, United
Funds/United Ways, Volunteer Services,
YMCA/YWCA/YMHA/YWHA, Youth Or-
ganizations

Grant Types: capital and general support

Geographic Distribution: limited to Missouri, with emphasis on St. Louis

GIVING OFFICERS
Fred E. Arnold: chmn adv comm

W. Stanley Walch: mem adv comm *B* Se-
dalia MO 1934 *ED* Kenyon Coll AB 1956;
Univ MI JD 1959 *CORP AFFIL* dir: Central
St Diversified Corp; Morgan-Wrightmann
Supply Co, Orion Capital Corp, Precision
Stainless Co *NONPR AFFIL* dir: Downtown
St Louis Inc; mem: Am Bar Assn, Am Law
Inst, MO Bar Assn, St Louis Bar Assn; mem
campaign comm: Un Way St Louis *CLUB
AFFIL* Noonday

W. David Wells: mem adv comm

APPLICATION INFORMATION
Initial Approach:

The foundation requests applications be
made in writing.

The deadline for submitting proposals is December 31st.

Restrictions on Giving: The foundation
makes grants only to charitable organizations. The foundation does not make grants
to individuals or for endowment funds.

PUBLICATIONS
Application guidelines

GRANTS ANALYSIS
Total Grants: $738,420

Number of Grants: 66

Highest Grant: $100,000

Average Grant: $11,188

Typical Range: $1,000 to $20,000

Disclosure Period: 1993

Note: Recent grants are derived from a 1993
Form 990.

RECENT GRANTS

Library
3,500	St. Louis Mercantile Library, St. Louis, MO	

General
100,000	Washington University, St. Louis, MO	
50,000	Ranken Technical College, St. Louis, MO	
50,000	St. Louis Children's Hospital, St. Louis, MO	
45,000	Missouri Botanical Garden, St. Louis, MO	
40,000	Ranken-Jordan Children's Rehabilitation Center, St. Louis, MO	

Kansas City Southern Industries

Sales: $961.1 million
Employees: 174
Headquarters: Kansas City, MO
SIC Major Group: Business Services, Holding
& Other Investment Offices, Railroad
Transportation, and Security & Commodity
Brokers

CONTACT
Jan Armstrong
Assistant to the Vice President, Director
Community Relations
Kansas City Southern Industries
114 W 11th St.
Kansas City, MO 64105
(816) 556-0535

FINANCIAL SUMMARY
Fiscal Note: Company does not disclose
contributions figures.

CONTRIBUTIONS SUMMARY
Support goes to local education, human service, health, arts, and civic organizations.

Typical Recipients: • *Arts & Humanities:*
Arts Associations & Councils, Arts Centers,
Arts Festivals, Arts Funds, Arts Institutes,
Arts Outreach, Ballet, Community Arts,
Dance, Ethnic & Folk Arts, Film & Video,

General, Historic Preservation, History & Ar-
chaeology, Libraries, Literary Arts, Muse-
ums/Galleries, Music, Opera, Performing
Arts, Public Broadcasting, Theater, Visual
Arts • *Civic & Public Affairs:* African
American Affairs, Asian American Affairs,
Botanical Gardens/Parks, Business/Free En-
terprise, Chambers of Commerce, Civil
Rights, Community Foundations, Economic
Development, Economic Policy, Ethnic Or-
ganizations, General, Hispanic Affairs, Hous-
ing, Inner-City Development,
Municipalities/Towns, Native American Af-
fairs, Nonprofit Management, Parades/Festi-
vals, Philanthropic Organizations, Public
Policy, Safety, Urban & Community Affairs,
Women's Affairs, Zoos/Aquariums • *Educa-
tion:* Afterschool/Enrichment Programs, Ag-
ricultural Education, Arts/Humanities
Education, Business Education, Business-
School Partnerships, Colleges & Universi-
ties, Community & Junior Colleges,
Continuing Education, Economic Education,
Education Funds, Elementary Education
(Public), General, Literacy, Minority Educa-
tion, Preschool Education, Private Education
(Precollege), Public Education (Precollege),
Science/Mathematics Education, Secondary
Education (Private), Secondary Education
(Public), Social Sciences Education, Special
Education • *Environment:* General, Resource
Conservation, Wildlife Protection • *Health:*
Adolescent Health Issues, AIDS/HIV, Alzhe-
imers Disease, Arthritis, Cancer, Children's
Health/Hospitals, Clinics/Medical Centers,
Diabetes, Eyes/Blindness, General, Geriatric
Health, Health Organizations, Heart, Home-
Care Services, Hospices, Hospitals, Hospi-
tals (University Affiliated), Long-Term
Care, Medical Rehabilitation, Nursing Serv-
ices, Single-Disease Health Associations
• *Science:* General, Science Exhibits &
Fairs, Science Museums, Scientific Centers
& Institutes, Scientific Research • *Social
Services:* Animal Protection, At-Risk Youth,
Camps, Child Welfare, Community Centers,
Community Service Organizations, Counsel-
ing, Day Care, Delinquency & Criminal Re-
habilitation, Domestic Violence, Emergency
Relief, Family Planning, Family Services,
Food/Clothing Distribution, General,
Homes, People with Disabilities, Recreation
& Athletics, Refugee Assistance, Senior
Services, Sexual Abuse, Shelters/Homeless-
ness, Substance Abuse, United Funds/United
Ways, Volunteer Services,
YMCA/YWCA/YMHA/YWHA, Youth Or-
ganizations

Grant Types: capital, challenge, emergency, employee matching gifts, endowment, general support, multiyear/continuing
support, operating expenses, and project

Nonmonetary Support Types: donated
equipment, in-kind services, loaned employees, and loaned executives

Geographic Distribution: in headquarters
and operating communities

Operating Locations: LA (Shreveport), MO
(Kansas City)

CORP. OFFICERS
Paul Harry Henson: *B* Bennet NE 1925 *ED*
Univ NE BS 1948; Univ NE MS 1950 *CURR*

EMPL chmn: Kansas City Southern Industries *CORP AFFIL* dir: Armco, Duke Power Co, Hallmark Cards, Sprint Corp *NONPR AFFIL* mem: Eta Kappa Nu, Kappa Sigma, Sigma Tau, Sigma Xi; trust: Armed Forces Communs Electronics Assn, Childrens Mercy Hosp, Greater Kansas City Commun Fdn, Inst Electrical Electronics Engrs, Midwest Res Inst, Nelson-Atkins Mus Art, Tax Fdn, Univ MO (Kansas City), Univ NE Fdn, US Telephone Assn; vchmn: Press Natl Security Telecommunications Adv Comm *CLUB AFFIL* Eldorado, Kansas City, Kansas City CC, Masons, Old Baldy, River, Shriners

L.H. Rowland: *CURR EMPL* pres, ceo, dir: KS City Southern Indus

APPLICATION INFORMATION

Initial Approach: Send a brief letter of inquiry and a full proposal. Include a description of organization, amount requested, purpose of funds sought, recently audited financial statement, proof of tax-exempt status, and a list of the board of directors.

Restrictions on Giving: Does not support individuals, religious organizations for sectarian purposes, political or lobbying groups, or organizations outside operating areas.

GRANTS ANALYSIS

Typical Range: $1,000 to $2,500

Note: Recent grants are derived from a grants list provided by company in 1995.

RECENT GRANTS

General
Avila College
Boys and Girls Clubs, Kansas City, MO
Children's Center for the Visually Impaired, Kansas City, MO
Children's Mercy Hospital, Kansas City, MO
DeLaSalle Education Center

Kemper Foundation, William T.

CONTACT
William T. Kemper Foundation
Commerce Bank, Trustee
PO Box 13095
Kansas City, MO 64199-3095
(816) 234-2985
Note: The foundation does not list a specific contact person.

FINANCIAL SUMMARY
Recent Giving: $5,813,474 (fiscal 1993); $3,397,723 (fiscal 1991); $1,954,018 (fiscal 1990)

Assets: $146,625,811 (fiscal 1993); $128,593,821 (fiscal 1991); $111,511,244 (fiscal 1990)

Gifts Received: $1,860,457 (fiscal 1993); $112,035,121 (fiscal 1990)

Fiscal Note: In fiscal 1993, the foundation received contributions from the William T. Kemper Trust.

EIN: 43-6345116

CONTRIBUTIONS SUMMARY
Donor(s): The foundation was established in 1989, following the death of William T. Kemper . Kemper was associated with the former First National Bank of Independence, as their president, chairman, chairman of the executive committee, and director. He was involved in the development and improvement of downtown Kansas City and was active in social service and community organizations like the American Red Cross, Boy Scouts of America, and American Royal Association. He was an avid art collector and he founded the Charlotte Crosby Kemper Gallery at the Kansas City Art Institute, in memory of his mother. Kemper was associated with Commerce Bank of Kansas City by family ties, and gave the majority of his estate to the William T. Kemper Foundation, with Commerce Bank as co-trustee, at his death.

Typical Recipients: • *Arts & Humanities:* Arts Associations & Councils, Arts Institutes, Libraries, Museums/Galleries, Music, Opera, Public Broadcasting, Theater • *Civic & Public Affairs:* Botanical Gardens/Parks, Chambers of Commerce, Employment/Job Training, General, Law & Justice, Philanthropic Organizations, Urban & Community Affairs, Zoos/Aquariums • *Education:* Arts/Humanities Education, Colleges & Universities, General, Private Education (Precollege), Secondary Education (Public) • *Health:* Cancer, Children's Health/Hospitals, Clinics/Medical Centers, Eyes/Blindness, Health Organizations, Hospitals, Medical Research, Nursing Services • *Religion:* Churches, Dioceses, Jewish Causes, Religious Organizations, Religious Welfare • *Science:* Science Museums • *Social Services:* Child Welfare, Community Service Organizations, Homes, Scouts

Grant Types: general support, operating expenses, and project

Geographic Distribution: the Midwest, with a focus on Missouri

APPLICATION INFORMATION
Initial Approach:

All proposals and inquiries must be submitted in writing.

A complete proposal must include a brief project summary outlining the goals of the project and methods of achievement. A budget for the project, including additional sources of support, and a recent audited financial statement, must be submitted. Also include a timetable with highlighted objectives and methods of project evaluation, as well as uses of the requested funding and plans for financial stability at the expiration of the grant. A list of the organization's board of directors and the IRS determination letter, which states the organization's 509(a)(1) or 509(a)(2) status and also that the contribution is tax deductible under Section 170(c), is required.

There are no deadlines for proposals.

Restrictions on Giving: The foundation does not fund private foundations, individuals, tickets for benefits, exhibits, or other event activities, advertisements, endowment funds, politically partisan purposes, or research unrelated to current priorities. Although the foundation typically makes one-year grants, requests for up to five years of funding for special projects may be considered.

OTHER THINGS TO KNOW
Commerce Bank of Kansas City is the foundation's trustee.

PUBLICATIONS
Application guidelines brochure

GRANTS ANALYSIS
Total Grants: $5,813,474
Number of Grants: 275
Highest Grant: $400,000
Average Grant: $21,140
Typical Range: $15,000 to $50,000
Disclosure Period: fiscal year ending October 31, 1993
Note: Recent grants are derived from a fiscal 1993 Form 990.

RECENT GRANTS

General

400,000	Children's Mercy Hospital, Kansas City, MO
250,000	Missouri Botanical Garden, St. Louis, MO
250,000	Missouri Botanical Garden, St. Louis, MO
250,000	Research Medical Center, Kansas City, MO
200,000	Grace and Holy Trinity Cathedral, Kansas City, MO

Lichtenstein Foundation, David B.

CONTACT
Daniel B. Lichtenstein
President
David B. Lichtenstein Fdn.
PO Box 19740
St. Louis, MO 63144
(314) 966-0263

FINANCIAL SUMMARY
Recent Giving: $1,763,520 (1992); $327,235 (1989); $138,300 (1988)

Assets: $12,843,176 (1992); $8,131,769 (1989); $6,130,274 (1988)

Gifts Received: $1,813,742 (1988)
EIN: 43-6033786

CONTRIBUTIONS SUMMARY
Donor(s): the late David Lichtenstein

Typical Recipients: • *Arts & Humanities:* Arts Funds, General, Libraries • *Civic & Public Affairs:* General, Municipalities/Towns • *Education:* Colleges & Universities, Minority Education, Private Education (Precollege), Student Aid, Vocational & Technical Education • *Health:* Cancer, Children's Health/Hospitals, Diabetes, Health Organizations, Heart, Hospitals,

Medical Research, Mental Health, Preventive Medicine/Wellness Organizations • *International:* Missionary/Religious Activities • *Religion:* Churches, Jewish Causes, Religious Organizations, Religious Welfare • *Social Services:* Animal Protection, Child Welfare, Community Service Organizations, Family Services, Recreation & Athletics, United Funds/United Ways

Grant Types: general support

Geographic Distribution: limited to MO

GIVING OFFICERS
Bernard Chaitman, MD: dir

Kenneth Cohen: secy

Sheldon Cohen: trust

Arlene Frazier: dir

Wayne Frazier: dir

Allene N. Lichtenstein: vp

Daniel B. Lichtenstein: pres

W. Stefan Morovitz: dir

Bernard Reiss: dir

Craig K. Reiss, MD: dir

APPLICATION INFORMATION
Initial Approach: The foundation has no formal grant application procedure or application form. There are no deadlines.

GRANTS ANALYSIS
Total Grants: $1,763,520

Number of Grants: 135

Highest Grant: $209,199

Typical Range: $500 to $26,000

Disclosure Period: 1992

Note: Recent grants are derived from a 1992 Form 990.

RECENT GRANTS
Library
20,100	CASA Library

General
209,199	St. Louis University, St. Louis, MO
180,000	Jewish Hospital Dental Group, St. Louis, MO
121,550	Jewish Federation of St. Louis, St. Louis, MO
105,530	Southside Baptist Church, St. Louis, MO
76,100	Cardinal Glennon Children's Hospital, St. Louis, MO

Maritz Inc.
Sales: $1.4 billion
Employees: 5,500
Headquarters: Fenton, MO
SIC Major Group: Schools & Educational Services Nec

CONTACT
Sidwell Hutchins
Senior Vice President, Corporate Communications
Maritz Inc.
1375 N Highway Dr.
Fenton, MO 63099
(314) 827-2237

FINANCIAL SUMMARY
Recent Giving: $820,000 (1995 est.); $937,000 (1994 approx.); $900,000 (1993 approx.)

Fiscal Note: Company gives directly only. Above figures include nonmonetary support.

CONTRIBUTIONS SUMMARY
Typical Recipients: • *Arts & Humanities:* Arts Associations & Councils, Arts Funds, Arts Institutes, Community Arts, Dance, Ethnic & Folk Arts, Historic Preservation, Libraries, Museums/Galleries, Music, Opera, Performing Arts, Public Broadcasting, Theater, Visual Arts • *Civic & Public Affairs:* Business/Free Enterprise, Civil Rights, Economic Development, Employment/Job Training, Municipalities/Towns, Philanthropic Organizations, Public Policy, Women's Affairs, Zoos/Aquariums • *Education:* Colleges & Universities, Community & Junior Colleges, Economic Education, Elementary Education (Private), Literacy, Minority Education, Preschool Education, Public Education (Precollege) • *Environment:* General • *Health:* General, Hospitals, Mental Health • *Social Services:* Child Welfare, Delinquency & Criminal Rehabilitation, Domestic Violence, Emergency Relief, Food/Clothing Distribution, General, People with Disabilities, Shelters/Homelessness, Substance Abuse, United Funds/United Ways, Youth Organizations

Grant Types: award, capital, conference/seminar, emergency, employee matching gifts, general support, matching, and multiyear/continuing support

Note: Employee matching gift ratio: 1 to 1. The company also awards one-time grants.

Nonmonetary Support: $20,000 (1994); $150,000 (1993); $150,000 (1992)

Nonmonetary Support Types: donated equipment, donated products, in-kind services, loaned employees, and loaned executives

Geographic Distribution: headquarters and operating locations

Operating Locations: CA (Los Angeles), IL (Chicago), KS (Kansas City), MI (Detroit), MN (Minneapolis), MO (Fenton, St. Louis), NY (New York), TX (Dallas)

CORP. OFFICERS
David Lee Fleisher: *B* Battle Creek MI 1934 *ED* Univ MI 1956; Univ MI 1957 *CURR EMPL* cfo, sr exec vp: Maritz Inc

Sidwell D. Hutchins: *CURR EMPL* sr vp corp commun: Maritz Inc

William Edward Maritz: *B* St. Louis MO 1928 *ED* Princeton Univ BA 1950 *CURR EMPL* chmn, ceo, dir: Maritz Inc *CORP AFFIL* dir: Brown Group Inc, Centerre Bancorp, Petrolite Corp, Wetterau Inc; fdr, chmn bd: Laclede Landing Devel Corp *NONPR AFFIL* chmn, vp: Fair Fdn; dir: Am Youth Fdn, John Burroughs Sch, Camping Ed Fdn, Civic Progress, Commun Sch, Cystic Fibrosis, KETC, MO Botanical Gardens, Princeton Univ, St Lukes Hosp, Washington Univ *PHIL AFFIL* trust: George Warren Brown Foundation

Norman L. Schwesig: *CURR EMPL* pres: Maritz Inc

APPLICATION INFORMATION
Initial Approach: *Initial Contact:* brief letter of inquiry and a full proposal *Include Information On:* a description of organization, amount requested, purpose of funds sought, and recently audited financial statement *Deadlines:* none

Restrictions on Giving: Does not support individuals or religious organizations for sectarian purposes.

GRANTS ANALYSIS
Total Grants: $937,000*

Typical Range: $500 to $2,000

Disclosure Period: 1994

Note: Total grants figure is approximate.

May Department Stores Company, The / May Stores Foundation

Revenue: $12.22 billion
Employees: 113,000
Headquarters: St. Louis, MO
SIC Major Group: Department Stores and Shoe Stores

CONTACT
James Abrams
Vice President, Corporate Communications
The May Department Stores Company
611 Olive St.
St. Louis, MO 63101
(314) 342-6300

FINANCIAL SUMMARY
Recent Giving: $13,800,000 (1994 approx.); $10,213,791 (1992); $10,100,000 (1991 approx.)

Assets: $13,204,430 (1992); $20,047,487 (1990); $21,449,802 (1989)

Fiscal Note: Contributions are made directly and through the foundation.

EIN: 43-6028949

CONTRIBUTIONS SUMMARY
Typical Recipients: • *Arts & Humanities:* Arts Associations & Councils, Arts Centers, Arts Funds, Ballet, Community Arts, Ethnic & Folk Arts, Historic Preservation, Libraries, Museums/Galleries, Music, Performing Arts, Public Broadcasting, Theater • *Civic & Public Affairs:* African American Affairs, Civil Rights, Clubs, Economic Development, Employment/Job Training, General, Public Policy, Safety, Urban & Community Affairs, Zoos/Aquariums • *Education:* Business Education, Colleges & Universities, Continuing Education, Education Associations, Education Funds, Education Reform, Engineering/Technological Education, Literacy, Medical Education, Minority Education, Science/Mathematics Education, Student Aid • *Environment:* General • *Health:* AIDS/HIV, Cancer, Children's Health/Hospitals, Health Funds, Health Organizations, Heart, Hospitals, Multiple Scle-

rosis • *Religion:* Dioceses, Jewish Causes, Religious Organizations, Religious Welfare, Synagogues/Temples • *Science:* Scientific Centers & Institutes • *Social Services:* Child Welfare, Community Centers, Community Service Organizations, Counseling, People with Disabilities, Substance Abuse, United Funds/United Ways, Youth Organizations

Grant Types: capital, employee matching gifts, and operating expenses

Geographic Distribution: operating locations

Operating Locations: CA (Hollywood, Los Angeles), CO (Denver), CT (Hartford), DC, IN (Indianapolis), KS (Topeka), MA (Boston), MD (Baltimore), MO (St. Louis), NY (New York), OH (Cleveland), OR (Portland), PA (Pittsburgh), TX (Houston), VA (Richmond)

Note: Operates approximately 325 department stores and approximately 3,000 Payless ShoeSource stores. Also operates in 14 offices overseas.

CORP. OFFICERS
Richard L. Battram: *B* Oakland City IN 1934 *ED* Butler Univ BA 1960 *CURR EMPL* vchmn: May Dept Stores Co *CORP AFFIL* dir: Boatmens Bancshares Inc, Pet Inc *NONPR AFFIL* dir: St Louis Art Mus, St Louis Symphony Orchestra, St Lukes Hosp, Un Way St Louis *CLUB AFFIL* Old Warson CC, Round Table, St Louis

David Coakley Farrell: *B* Chicago IL 1933 *ED* Antioch Coll BA 1956 *CURR EMPL* chmn, ceo, dir: May Dept Stores Co *CORP AFFIL* dir: Emerson Electric Co, Emerson Purina Co, First Natl Bank St Louis *NONPR AFFIL* dir: Arts & Ed Fund Greater St Louis, Boy Scouts Am St Louis Area Counc, St Louis Symphony Soc; mem: Natl Retail Merchants Assn *CLUB AFFIL* Bogey, Duquesne, MD Athletic, Noonday, St Louis CC, Univ

Thomas A. Hays: *B* Cleveland OH 1932 *ED* Wabash Coll BA 1955 *CURR EMPL* dept chmn, dir: May Dept Stores Co *CORP AFFIL* dir: Mercantile Bancorp Inc, Mercantile Trust Co, Union Electric Co

Jan Rogers Kniffen: *B* Herrin IL 1948 *ED* Univ IL 1966-1968; Southern IL Univ BS 1968-1971; Lindenwood Coll MBA 1975-1978; St Louis Univ 1985 *CURR EMPL* sr vp, treas: May Dept Stores Co *CORP AFFIL* treas, dir: May Dept Stores Intl *NONPR AFFIL* adjunct prof, dir: Lindenwood Coll *CLUB AFFIL* Media

Jerome Thomas Loeb: *B* St Louis MO 1940 *ED* Tufts Univ BS 1962; Washington Univ MA 1964 *CURR EMPL* pres, cfo, dir: May Dept Stores Co *CORP AFFIL* dir: Centerre Trust Co *NONPR AFFIL* chmn: Jr Achievement; dir: Barnes-Jewish Inc/Christian Health Svcs; mem bd commnr: St Louis Sci Ctr; vchmn: Jewish Hosp St Louis, Jr Achievement MI Valley *CLUB AFFIL* Boone Valley GC, Westwood CC

GIVING OFFICERS
James Abrams: vp corp commun

Richard Alan Brickson: asst secy *B* Madison WI 1948 *ED* Wabash Coll BA 1970;

Georgetown Univ JD 1973 *CURR EMPL* vp, secy, sr couns: May Dept Stores Intl

Robert F. Cerulli: asst treas, dir

David Coakley Farrell: vp, dir *CURR EMPL* chmn, ceo, dir: May Dept Stores Co (see above)

Thomas A. Hays: vp, dir *CURR EMPL* dept chmn, dir: May Dept Stores Co (see above)

Jan Rogers Kniffen: vp, secy, treas, dir *CURR EMPL* sr vp, treas: May Dept Stores Co (see above)

Jerome Thomas Loeb: pres, dir *CURR EMPL* pres, cfo, dir: May Dept Stores Co (see above)

APPLICATION INFORMATION
Initial Approach: *Initial Contact:* letter *Include Information On:* description of the organization, amount requested, purpose for which funds are sought, recently audited financial statement, proof of tax-exempt status *Deadlines:* none

Restrictions on Giving: Foundation does not give to individuals.

GRANTS ANALYSIS
Total Grants: $10,213,791

Number of Grants: 3,202

Highest Grant: $700,000

Average Grant: $3,190

Typical Range: $1,000 to $5,000

Disclosure Period: 1992

Note: Recent grants are derived from a 1992 Form 990.

RECENT GRANTS
Library
35,000	Wadsworth Atheneum, Hartford, CT	

General
700,000	United Way
354,500	United Way
250,000	Washington University, St. Louis, MO
216,495	Older Adult Service and Information System (OASIS), St. Louis, MO
209,000	United Way

McGee Foundation

CONTACT
Joseph J. McGee, Jr.
Chairman
McGee Fdn.
4900 Main St., Ste. 717
Kansas City, MO 64112-2644
(816) 931-1515

FINANCIAL SUMMARY
Recent Giving: $308,625 (1993); $299,458 (1992); $209,750 (1991)

Assets: $7,513,437 (1993); $7,131,493 (1992); $6,890,564 (1991)

Gifts Received: $3,000 (1993); $3,000 (1992)

EIN: 44-6006285

CONTRIBUTIONS SUMMARY
Donor(s): the late Joseph J. McGee, the late Mrs. Joseph I. McGee, the late Frank McGee, the late Mrs. Frank McGee, the late Louis B. McGee, Old American Insurance Co., Thomas McGee and Sons, Joseph I. McGee, Jr.

Typical Recipients: • *Arts & Humanities:* Libraries, Museums/Galleries • *Civic & Public Affairs:* Clubs, General, Hispanic Affairs, Public Policy, Urban & Community Affairs • *Education:* Business Education, Colleges & Universities, Education Funds, Education Reform, General, Private Education (Precollege), Religious Education, Science/Mathematics Education, Secondary Education (Public), Special Education, Student Aid • *Health:* Cancer, Clinics/Medical Centers, Geriatric Health, Health Organizations, Home-Care Services, Hospices, Hospitals, Medical Rehabilitation, Prenatal Health Issues, Trauma Treatment • *International:* Missionary/Religious Activities • *Religion:* Churches, Missionary Activities (Domestic), Religious Organizations, Religious Welfare • *Social Services:* Camps, Child Welfare, Community Service Organizations, Food/Clothing Distribution, People with Disabilities, Senior Services, United Funds/United Ways, Youth Organizations

Grant Types: capital, general support, multiyear/continuing support, operating expenses, project, and scholarship

Geographic Distribution: limited to the greater Kansas City, MO, area

GIVING OFFICERS
Mrs. Bernard J. Duffy, Jr.: mem

Robert A. Long: mem

Joseph John McGee, Jr.: pres, chmn, mem, dir *B* Kansas City MO 1919 *ED* Georgetown Univ; Rockhurst Coll *NONPR AFFIL* dir: Menorah Med Ctr, Truman (Harry S) Library Inst, Truman Med Ctr; trust: Rockhurst Coll

Thomas F. McGee, Sr.: vchmn, mem, dir

Thomas R. McGee: treas, mem, dir *CURR EMPL* Old Am Ins Co

Thomas R. McGee, Jr.: mem

Edward J. Reardon: secy, mem, dir

APPLICATION INFORMATION
Initial Approach: Send a brief letter of inquiry. Include a description of organization, amount requested, purpose of funds sought, recently audited financial statement, and proof of tax-exempt status. There are no deadlines.

Restrictions on Giving: Primary support to greater metropolitan Kansas City area. Does not support visual and performing arts, preservation of historic places, or with exception of applied research, scholarly research projects and programs.

PUBLICATIONS
Annual Report (including application guidelines)

GRANTS ANALYSIS
Total Grants: $308,625

Number of Grants: 36

Highest Grant: $50,000

Typical Range: $1,000 to $5,000

Disclosure Period: 1993

Note: Recent grants are derived from a 1993 Form 990.

RECENT GRANTS
Library

10,000	Harry S. Truman Library for National and International Affairs, Independence, MO — upgrading of Museum and its exhibits	

General

50,000	Kansas City St. Joseph Diocese Central City School Fund, Kansas City, MO — need-based scholarships to disadvantaged children
50,000	Rockhurst College, Kansas City, MO — support of programs that focus on the Jesuit Mission, and Values
50,000	Rockhurst High School, Kansas City, MO — debt reduction
25,000	Rockhurst College, Kansas City, MO — strengthen undergraduate science, and graduate allied health education
15,000	Avila College, Kansas City, MO — operating expenses and student scholarships

Messing Family Charitable Foundation

Former Foundation Name: Roswell Messing, Jr., Charitable Foundation

CONTACT
Wilma E. Messing
Trustee
Messing Family Charitable Fdn.
30 Westwood Country Club
St. Louis, MO 63131
(314) 432-8898

FINANCIAL SUMMARY
Recent Giving: $128,115 (1993); $166,175 (1992); $168,999 (1990)

Assets: $2,442,637 (1993); $2,168,161 (1992); $1,904,581 (1990)

Gifts Received: $135,099 (1993); $102,296 (1990)

Fiscal Note: In 1993, contributions were received from Roswell Messing III ($34,884) and Wilma E. Messing ($100,215).

EIN: 43-6034863

CONTRIBUTIONS SUMMARY
Donor(s): Roswell Messing, Jr., Mrs. Roswell Messing, Jr.

Typical Recipients: • *Arts & Humanities:* Arts Associations & Councils, Dance, Libraries • *Civic & Public Affairs:* Urban & Community Affairs, Women's Affairs, Zoos/Aquariums • *Education:* Colleges & Universities, Medical Education, Private

Education (Precollege), Student Aid • *Health:* Hospitals, Medical Research, Single-Disease Health Associations • *Religion:* Jewish Causes, Religious Organizations, Religious Welfare, Synagogues/Temples • *Social Services:* Community Service Organizations, Substance Abuse, United Funds/United Ways, Youth Organizations

Grant Types: research and scholarship

Geographic Distribution: focus on St. Louis, MO

GIVING OFFICERS
Harold S. Goodman: trust *B* St Louis MO 1937 *ED* Univ MO AB 1960; Washington Univ LLB 1963; Washington Univ JD 1963 *CURR EMPL* ptnr: Gallop Johnson & Neuman *NONPR AFFIL* mem: Am Bar Assn, MO Bar Assn, Phi Delta Phi, St Louis Bar Assn, WA Univ Law Alumni Assn, Zeta Beta Tau; trust: Cystic Fibrosis Fdn

Noel M. Hefty: trust

Terrance Hefty: trust

Roswell Messing III: trust

Wilma E. Messing: trust

Arlene M. Naschke: trust

APPLICATION INFORMATION
Initial Approach: The foundation has no formal grant application procedure or application form. There are no deadlines.

GRANTS ANALYSIS
Total Grants: $128,115

Number of Grants: 88

Highest Grant: $35,000

Typical Range: $25 to $15,000

Disclosure Period: 1993

Note: Recent grants are derived from a 1993 Form 990. Number of grants and typical range do not include grants to individuals.

RECENT GRANTS
Library

1,200	St. Louis University, St. Louis, MO — library associates
1,000	Mary Institute, St. Louis, MO — Library Foundation

General

35,000	JCCA, St. Louis, MO
15,000	Mary Institute, St. Louis, MO
13,000	Jewish Federation, St. Louis, MO — St. Louis Jewish Light
5,000	Parkview Towers Fund, St. Louis, MO
5,000	United Hebrew Temple

Miller-Mellor Association

CONTACT
James L. Miller
Secretary and Treasurer
Miller-Mellor Association
708 E 47th St.
Kansas City, MO 64110
(816) 561-4307

FINANCIAL SUMMARY
Recent Giving: $81,415 (fiscal 1993); $80,480 (fiscal 1992); $92,870 (fiscal 1991)

Assets: $2,419,096 (fiscal 1993); $2,265,335 (fiscal 1992); $2,117,030 (fiscal 1991)

EIN: 44-6011906

CONTRIBUTIONS SUMMARY
Typical Recipients: • *Arts & Humanities:* Arts Associations & Councils, Community Arts, History & Archaeology, Libraries, Museums/Galleries, Music, Performing Arts, Public Broadcasting, Theater • *Civic & Public Affairs:* Community Foundations, General, Law & Justice, Municipalities/Towns, Safety, Urban & Community Affairs • *Education:* Colleges & Universities, Private Education (Precollege), Secondary Education (Private), Secondary Education (Public) • *Environment:* Wildlife Protection • *Health:* Emergency/Ambulance Services, Health Organizations, Hospitals, Nursing Services, Prenatal Health Issues, Preventive Medicine/Wellness Organizations • *Religion:* Churches, Dioceses, Religious Organizations, Religious Welfare • *Science:* Scientific Labs • *Social Services:* Child Welfare, Community Service Organizations, Delinquency & Criminal Rehabilitation, Family Planning, Food/Clothing Distribution, People with Disabilities, Recreation & Athletics, Shelters/Homelessness, United Funds/United Ways, Youth Organizations

Grant Types: general support

Geographic Distribution: focus on Kansas City, MO

GIVING OFFICERS
James L. Miller: secy, treas

JoZach Miller IV: pres

Helena Miller Norquist: vp

APPLICATION INFORMATION
Initial Approach: The foundation has no formal grant application procedure or application form. There are no deadlines.

GRANTS ANALYSIS
Total Grants: $81,415

Number of Grants: 72

Highest Grant: $6,000

Typical Range: $100 to $2,000

Disclosure Period: fiscal year ending June 30, 1993

Note: Recent grants are derived from a fiscal 1993 Form 990.

RECENT GRANTS
Library

250	Rockhurt College Library Guild, Kansas City, MO
150	Schlesinger Library, Boston, MA

General

6,000	St. Dominic's Roman Catholic Church, Oyster Bay, NY
6,000	St. Martha Catholic Church, Sarasota, FL
5,000	Catholic Diocese of Kansas City, St. Joseph, MO

4,000	Little Sisters of the Poor, Kansas City, MO
3,050	Visiting Nurse Association, Kansas City, MO

Morgan Charitable Residual Trust, W. and E.

CONTACT
W. and E. Morgan Charitable Residual Trust
c/o Citizens Bank and Trust
PO Box 70
Rockport, MO 64482
(816) 744-5333

FINANCIAL SUMMARY
Recent Giving: $133,250 (1993); $125,806 (1992); $59,412 (1991)

Assets: $3,046,946 (1993); $2,962,393 (1992); $2,846,567 (1991)

EIN: 43-6347180

CONTRIBUTIONS SUMMARY
Typical Recipients: • *Arts & Humanities:* History & Archaeology, Libraries • *Civic & Public Affairs:* Botanical Gardens/Parks, Clubs, General, Municipalities/Towns, Parades/Festivals, Safety • *Education:* Public Education (Precollege), Religious Education, Student Aid • *Health:* Emergency/Ambulance Services, Hospitals • *Religion:* Churches, Ministries, Religious Organizations, Religious Welfare • *Social Services:* Community Centers, Community Service Organizations, Crime Prevention, Recreation & Athletics

Grant Types: department and general support

Geographic Distribution: focus on MO

GIVING OFFICERS
Citizens Bank & Trust: trust

Jody Ellison: trust

Kay Gibson: trust

Tim Whelan: trust

APPLICATION INFORMATION
Initial Approach: The foundation has no formal grant application procedure or application form. There are no deadlines.

GRANTS ANALYSIS
Total Grants: $133,250

Number of Grants: 64

Highest Grant: $40,000

Typical Range: $500 to $2,000

Disclosure Period: 1993

Note: Recent grants are derived from a 1993 Form 990.

RECENT GRANTS

Library

3,000	Atchison County Library, Tarkio, MO — reference material
1,000	Atchison County Library, Tarkio, MO — audio visual for young children

General

40,000	Nishnabotna Drainage District, Nishnabotna, MO — interest from funds to be used for pump fuel
5,500	Watson Fire Department, Watson, MO — Watson honor roll students
5,000	Fairfax Community Hospital, Fairfax, MO — assist in Doctor's office space
5,000	Greenhill Cemetery Association, Greenhill, MO — paving road
3,000	Village of Watson, Watson, MO — Community Facility Improvement

Olin Foundation, Spencer T. and Ann W.

CONTACT
Warren M. Shapleigh
President
Spencer T. and Ann W. Olin Foundation
7701 Forsyth Blvd., Ste. 1040
St. Louis, MO 63105
(314) 727-6202

FINANCIAL SUMMARY
Recent Giving: $5,210,175 (1993); $4,912,100 (1992); $4,480,575 (1991)

Assets: $33,825,818 (1993); $37,184,013 (1992); $41,635,990 (1991)

Gifts Received: $916,350 (1993); $875,800 (1992); $836,950 (1991)

Fiscal Note: The foundation receives contributions from the Spencer T. Olin Charitable Lead Trust and the S. Truman Olin, Jr., Charitable Lead Trust

EIN: 37-6044148

CONTRIBUTIONS SUMMARY
Donor(s): The foundation was established in 1957 by the late Ann W. Olin and Spencer T. Olin, and receives distributions from the S. Truman Olin, Jr., Charitable Lead Trust and the Spencer T. Olin Charitable Lead Trust.

Typical Recipients: • *Arts & Humanities:* Arts Associations & Councils, Arts Funds, General, Historic Preservation, History & Archaeology, Libraries, Museums/Galleries, Music • *Civic & Public Affairs:* African American Affairs, Botanical Gardens/Parks, General, Nonprofit Management, Philanthropic Organizations, Professional & Trade Associations, Public Policy, Women's Affairs, Zoos/Aquariums • *Education:* Afterschool/Enrichment Programs, Business Education, Colleges & Universities, Community & Junior Colleges, Continuing Education, Economic Education, Education Associations, Education Reform, Minority Education, Private Education (Precollege), Public Education (Precollege), Science/Mathematics Education, Secondary Education (Private), Special Education, Student Aid, Vocational & Technical Education

• *Environment:* General, Resource Conservation • *Health:* Alzheimers Disease, Arthritis, Clinics/Medical Centers, Emergency/Ambulance Services, Hospitals, Nursing Services, Preventive Medicine/Wellness Organizations • *Science:* Scientific Centers & Institutes • *Social Services:* Day Care, Family Planning, Family Services, United Funds/United Ways, YMCA/YWCA/YMHA/YWHA, Youth Organizations

Grant Types: fellowship, general support, project, and research

Geographic Distribution: broad geographic distribution

GIVING OFFICERS
Mary Dell: trust

Eunice O. Higgins: secy, trust

William Waugh Higgins: trust *B* Worcester MA 1935 *ED* Amherst Coll BA 1957; Harvard Univ Grad Sch Bus Admin 1959 *CORP AFFIL* dir: Olin Corp

Marquita L. Kunce: asst treas

Rolla Mottaz: trust

John C. Pritzlaff: trust

Warren M. Shapleigh: pres, trust

Barbara O. Taylor: trust

F. Morgan Taylor: trust

J. Lester Willemetz: exec dir, treas

APPLICATION INFORMATION
Initial Approach:

Applicants should send a brief letter to the foundation's president.

The letter should include a brief description of the program or project for which funding is requested and the need for it; information about the total cost of the program or project; specific amount requested; list of other sources of funding and amount raised or expected to be secured; time frame in which the funds are to be expended; copy of the most recent financial statement with balance sheet and income and expense statement; and a copy of the IRS letter determining tax-exempt status.

Restrictions on Giving: The foundation reports that it is only considering proposals from those organizations where there is a history of past support; no new proposals are being accepted because of long term commitments, which the foundation is attending to in stages.

It is the general policy of the foundation not to make grants for endowment funds, deficit financing, or ordinary annual operating expenses; for secondary education, except in special cases and for projects where there is a history of past support; to provide funding for more than three consecutive years; to support projects which are substantially financed by public tax funds; to make grants to individuals or for individual scholarships; to fund conferences, seminars, workshops, travel, or exhibits; or to make grants to national health or welfare organizations, to churches for religious purposes, or to other private foundations or projects requiring expenditure responsibility.

GRANTS ANALYSIS
Total Grants: $5,210,175

Number of Grants: 34

Highest Grant: $1,500,000

Average Grant: $69,068*

Typical Range: $2,000 to $25,000 and $100,000 to $250,000

Disclosure Period: 1993

Note: The average grant figure excludes the two highest grants totaling $3,000,000. Recent grants are derived from a 1993 Form 990.

RECENT GRANTS

Library
1,500	Foundation Center, New York, NY

General
1,500,000	Cornell University, Ithaca, NY — for the Spencer T. and Ann W. Olin Graduate Fellowship Program Endowment
1,500,000	Washington University, St. Louis, MO — for the Spencer T. and Ann W. Olin Medical Scientist Fellowship Program Endowment
325,000	Nature Conservancy
225,000	John Burroughs School, St. Louis, MO
200,000	National Center for Effective Schools Research and Development, Madison, WI

Oppenstein Brothers Foundation

CONTACT
Sheila Rice
Program Officer
Oppenstein Brothers Foundation
PO Box 13095
Kansas City, MO 64199-3095
(816) 234-8671

FINANCIAL SUMMARY
Recent Giving: $835,000 (fiscal 1995 est.); $833,974 (fiscal 1994); $805,035 (fiscal 1993)

Assets: $19,500,000 (fiscal 1995 est.); $19,500,000 (fiscal 1994 approx.); $20,011,659 (fiscal 1993)

EIN: 43-6203035

CONTRIBUTIONS SUMMARY
Donor(s): The foundation was established in 1975 by the late Michael Oppenstein .

Typical Recipients: • *Arts & Humanities:* Arts Funds, Libraries, Museums/Galleries, Music, Opera, Theater • *Civic & Public Affairs:* Community Foundations, General, Hispanic Affairs, Housing, Philanthropic Organizations, Professional & Trade Associations, Women's Affairs, Zoos/Aquariums • *Education:* Colleges & Universities, Community & Junior Colleges, Economic Education, Education Funds, General, Private Education (Precollege), Public Education (Precollege), Science/Mathematics Education, Special Education • *Environment:* General • *Health:* AIDS/HIV, Children's Health/Hospitals, Clinics/Medical Centers, Emergency/Ambulance Services, Health Organizations, Heart, Hospices, Hospitals, Medical Rehabilitation, Mental Health, Single-Disease Health Associations • *International:* International Relations • *Religion:* Jewish Causes, Ministries, Religious Organizations, Religious Welfare • *Social Services:* Camps, Child Welfare, Community Centers, Community Service Organizations, Counseling, Family Planning, Family Services, Homes, People with Disabilities, Recreation & Athletics, Senior Services, Shelters/Homelessness, United Funds/United Ways, Volunteer Services, Youth Organizations

Grant Types: conference/seminar, emergency, general support, matching, operating expenses, project, and seed money

Geographic Distribution: limited to Kansas City, MO

GIVING OFFICERS
Mary Bloch: mem disbursement comm

Laura Kemper Fields: mem disbursement comm *PHIL AFFIL* secy, treas: David Woods Kemper Memorial Foundation

Roger Hurwitz: mem disbursement comm

John Morgan: chmn disbursement comm

Shelia Rice: program off

Estelle G. Sosland: mem disbursement comm *PHIL AFFIL* dir: Sosland Foundation

APPLICATION INFORMATION
Initial Approach:

The foundation requests applications be made in writing.

Written proposals should be submitted with two copies.

Proposals should be submitted three weeks prior to a board meeting.

The board generally meets bimonthly. Decisions are made within two to four months.

Restrictions on Giving: The foundation does not give to individuals, medical research, annual campaigns, building funds, scholarships, fellowships, medical equipment, endowment funds, or loans.

PUBLICATIONS
Informational brochure including application guidelines and a three-year report

GRANTS ANALYSIS
Total Grants: $805,035

Number of Grants: 88

Highest Grant: $70,000

Average Grant: $9,148

Typical Range: $1,000 to $12,500

Disclosure Period: fiscal year ending March 31, 1993

Note: Recent grants are derived from a fiscal 1993 grants list.

RECENT GRANTS

Library
10,000	Kansas City Public Library, Kansas City, MO

General
70,000	Children's Mercy Hospital, Kansas City, MO
40,000	Jewish Federation of Greater Kansas City, Overland Park, KS
40,000	Jewish Federation of Greater Kansas City, Overland Park, KS
25,000	Marilliac Center for Children, Kansas City, MO
20,000	Boy Scouts of America Heart of America Council, Kansas City, MO

Pettus Crowe Foundation

Headquarters: New York, NY

CONTACT
James A. Finch, III
Trustee
Pettus Crowe Fdn.
c/o Guaranty Trust Co.
7733 Forsyth, Ste. 900
Clayton, MO 63105
(314) 725-9055

FINANCIAL SUMMARY
Recent Giving: $119,750 (1993); $82,000 (1992); $62,500 (1991)

Assets: $2,351,976 (1993); $2,395,611 (1992); $2,370,841 (1991)

Gifts Received: $885 (1991)

EIN: 23-7025310

CONTRIBUTIONS SUMMARY
Donor(s): Irene Pettus-Crowe

Typical Recipients: • *Arts & Humanities:* Film & Video, Libraries • *Civic & Public Affairs:* Civil Rights, Gay/Lesbian Issues, General, Law & Justice, Native American Affairs, Philanthropic Organizations, Public Policy, Urban & Community Affairs, Women's Affairs • *Education:* Colleges & Universities, Legal Education • *Environment:* General, Resource Conservation • *Health:* AIDS/HIV, Health Organizations, Mental Health, Single-Disease Health Associations • *International:* Human Rights • *Religion:* Religious Organizations • *Social Services:* Animal Protection, Community Service Organizations, Sexual Abuse

Grant Types: general support

Geographic Distribution: national

GIVING OFFICERS
Dr. Irene Crowe: pres, treas

Mary Crowe: vp, asst treas

Phillippe Crowe Neilson: vp, asst treas

John R. Young: vp, asst treas *CURR EMPL* Cahill Gordon & Reindel *PHIL AFFIL* dir: G. Harold and Leila Y. Mathers Charitable Foundation

APPLICATION INFORMATION
Initial Approach: The foundation has no formal grant application procedure or application form. There are no deadlines.

GRANTS ANALYSIS
Total Grants: $119,750

Number of Grants: 21

Highest Grant: $41,000

Typical Range: $500 to $12,500

Disclosure Period: 1993

Note: Recent grants are derived from a 1993 Form 990.

RECENT GRANTS

Library

1,500	Foundation Center, New York, NY

General

41,000	Hastings Center, Briarcliff Manor, NY
12,500	Chronic Fatigue Immune Disfunction Syndrome Fund, San Francisco, CA
7,000	Center for Democratic Renewal and Education, Atlanta, GA
6,000	National Women's Law Center, Washington, DC
5,250	Mental Health Law Center

Pott Foundation, Herman T. and Phenie R.

CONTACT
James Collins
Member of Advisory Committee
Herman T. and Phenie R. Pott Foundation
PO Box 4503
Chesterfield, MO 63006-4503
(314) 537-0016

FINANCIAL SUMMARY
Recent Giving: $603,150 (1994); $690,900 (1990); $683,000 (1989)

Assets: $17,000,000 (1994 approx.); $13,742,758 (1990); $13,614,314 (1989)

EIN: 43-6041541

CONTRIBUTIONS SUMMARY
Donor(s): The foundation was established in 1963.

Typical Recipients: • *Arts & Humanities:* Historic Preservation, Libraries, Museums/Galleries, Opera • *Civic & Public Affairs:* Philanthropic Organizations, Zoos/Aquariums • *Education:* Colleges & Universities, Education Funds, Science/Mathematics Education • *Environment:* General • *Health:* Health Organizations, Hospitals, Medical Research, Mental Health • *Religion:* Churches, Religious Organizations • *Social Services:* Child Welfare, Community Service Organizations, Domestic Violence, Family Planning, Family Services, Food/Clothing Distribution, Homes, Shelters/Homelessness, United Funds/United Ways, Youth Organizations

Grant Types: multiyear/continuing support and operating expenses

Geographic Distribution: focus on Missouri, with an emphasis on St. Louis

GIVING OFFICERS
James Collins: mem adv comm

APPLICATION INFORMATION
Initial Approach:

The foundation requests applications be made in writing.

The foundation has no deadline for submitting proposals.

Restrictions on Giving: Grants are made only to organizations exempt under section 501(c)(3) of the IRS code. The foundation does not make grants to individuals.

GRANTS ANALYSIS
Total Grants: $690,900

Number of Grants: 123

Highest Grant: $40,000

Average Grant: $5,617

Typical Range: $500 to $12,000

Disclosure Period: 1990

Note: Recent grants are derived from a 1990 grants list.

RECENT GRANTS

Library

40,000	St. Louis Mercantile Library Association, St. Louis, MO
30,000	St. Louis Mercantile Library Association, St. Louis, MO

General

30,000	Grace Hill Settlement House, St. Louis, MO
30,000	Missouri Girls Town Foundation, Kingdom City, MO
30,000	Salvation Army Hope Center, St. Louis, MO
30,000	Washington University, St. Louis, MO
30,000	Washington University, St. Louis, MO

Pulitzer Publishing Co. / Pulitzer Publishing Co. Foundation

Revenue: $426.99 million
Employees: 2,950
Headquarters: St. Louis, MO
SIC Major Group: Newspapers, Radio Broadcasting Stations, and Television Broadcasting Stations

CONTACT
Ronald H. Ridgway
Secretary & Treasurer
Pulitzer Publishing Co. Foundation
900 N Tucker Blvd.
St. Louis, MO 63101
(314) 340-8000

FINANCIAL SUMMARY
Recent Giving: $535,000 (1995 est.); $546,000 (1994 approx.); $559,433 (1991)

Assets: $742,411 (1991); $772,079 (1989); $733,528 (1988)

Fiscal Note: Company gives through the foundation only. Above figures exclude non-monetary support. See "Other Things To Know" for more details.

EIN: 43-6052854

CONTRIBUTIONS SUMMARY
Typical Recipients: • *Arts & Humanities:* Arts Appreciation, Arts Associations & Councils, Arts Funds, Arts Institutes, Dance, Historic Preservation, Libraries, Museums/Galleries, Music, Opera, Public Broadcasting, Theater, Visual Arts • *Civic & Public Affairs:* Business/Free Enterprise, Civil Rights, Economic Development, Employment/Job Training, First Amendment Issues, Professional & Trade Associations • *Education:* Business Education, Colleges & Universities, Education Funds, International Exchange, Journalism/Media Education, Legal Education, Medical Education, Minority Education, Private Education (Precollege), Science/Mathematics Education, Student Aid • *Environment:* General • *Health:* Hospices, Hospitals, Mental Health, Single-Disease Health Associations • *International:* International Relations • *Religion:* Churches, Religious Organizations, Religious Welfare • *Social Services:* Child Welfare, Community Service Organizations, Emergency Relief, Family Planning, Family Services, Food/Clothing Distribution, Homes, Senior Services, United Funds/United Ways, Youth Organizations

Grant Types: capital, endowment, general support, project, and scholarship

Geographic Distribution: primarily in St. Louis, MO, metropolitan area

Operating Locations: AZ (Phoenix, Tucson), IN (Fort Wayne), KY (Louisville), LA (New Orleans), MO (St. Louis), NC (Winston-Salem), NE (Omaha), NM (Albuquerque), PA (Lancaster), SC (Greenville)

CORP. OFFICERS
Michael Edgar Pulitzer: *B* St Louis MO 1930 *ED* Harvard Univ AB 1951; Harvard Univ LLB 1954 *CURR EMPL* chmn, ceo: Pulitzer Publ Co *CORP AFFIL* pres, ceo, dir: Lerner Newspaper, Pulitzer Community Newspapers; pres, ceo, publ, editor, dir: Star Publ Co; vchmn, dir: KETV, KKLT-FM, KOAT, KTAR-AM, WDSU, WGAL, WLKY, WXII, WYFF *NONPR AFFIL* trust: St Louis Univ *CLUB AFFIL* Mountain Oyster, St Louis CC

Ronald H. Ridgway: *CURR EMPL* sr vp fin, dir: Pulitzer Publ Co *CORP AFFIL* sr vp fin, dir: St Louis Post Dispatch

Nicholas G. Tenniman IV: *CURR EMPL* vp newspaper oper: Pulitzer Publ Co

GIVING OFFICERS
David Lipman: dir *B* Springfield MO 1931 *ED* Univ MO *CURR EMPL* mng editor: St Louis Post Dispatch *CORP AFFIL* vp, dir: Pulitzer Productions *NONPR AFFIL* chmn: Intl Am Press Assn; chmn bd advs: Univ

MO Sch Journalism Natl Alumni Assn; dir: Mid-Am Press Inst, New Directions News; mem: Am Soc Newspaper Editors, Assn Press Mng Editors Assn, Football Writers Assn Am, Kappa Tau Alpha, MO Editors & Publs Assn, Omicron Delta Kappa, Sigma Delta Chi; vchmn, mem: MO Soc Newspaper Editors *CLUB AFFIL* Press St Louis

Joseph Pulitzer IV: dir

Michael Edgar Pulitzer: chmn, pres, ceo *CURR EMPL* chmn, ceo: Pulitzer Publ Co (see above)

Ronald H. Ridgway: secy, treas, dir *CURR EMPL* sr vp fin, dir: Pulitzer Publ Co (see above)

Nicholas G. Tenniman IV: dir *CURR EMPL* vp newspaper oper: Pulitzer Publ Co (see above)

William Franklin Woo: dir *B* Shanghai People's Republic of China 1936 *ED* Univ KS BA 1960 *CURR EMPL* editor: St Louis Post Dispatch

APPLICATION INFORMATION

Initial Approach: *Initial Contact:* brief letter or proposal *Include Information On:* description of the organization, amount requested, purpose for which funds are sought, recently audited financial statement, proof of tax-exempt status *Deadlines:* none

OTHER THINGS TO KNOW

Foundation receives contributions from KETV Television, Omaha, NE; KOAT Television, Albuquerque, NM; Phoenix Broadcasting Co., AZ; Pulitzer Broadcasting Co., St. Louis, MO; Pulitzer Publishing Co., St. Louis, MO; Star Publishing Co., Tucson, AZ; WGAL Television, Lancaster, PA; WPTA Television, Fort Wayne, IN; WXII Television, Winston-Salem, NC; and WYFF Television, Greenville, SC.

GRANTS ANALYSIS

Total Grants: $546,000*

Typical Range: $2,000 to $20,000

Disclosure Period: 1994

Note: Total grants figure is approximate. Recent grants are derived from a 1991 Form 990.

RECENT GRANTS

Library
1,500	Thomas Jefferson Library-UMSL, St. Louis, MO

General
90,500	United Way of Greater St. Louis, St. Louis, MO
50,000	Columbia University, New York, NY
20,000	Pennsylvania State University, University Park, PA
20,000	University of Arizona, Tucson, AZ
16,000	University of Missouri, Columbia, MO

Ralston Purina Co. / Ralston Purina Trust Fund

Revenue: $7.7 billion
Employees: 358,864
Headquarters: St. Louis, MO
SIC Major Group: Dog & Cat Food, Cereal Breakfast Foods, Prepared Feeds Nec, and Bread, Cake & Related Products

CONTACT

Fred H. Perabo
Secretary, Board of Control
Ralston Purina Trust Fund
Checkerboard Sq.
St. Louis, MO 63164
(314) 982-3234

FINANCIAL SUMMARY

Recent Giving: $1,971,025 (fiscal 1993); $2,080,225 (fiscal 1991); $2,300,000 (fiscal 1990 approx.)

Assets: $17,720,497 (fiscal 1993); $17,027,154 (fiscal 1991); $15,696,740 (fiscal 1989)

Gifts Received: $1,000,000 (fiscal 1993)

Fiscal Note: Above figures include trust fund contributions only. Company direct contributions total about $2.0 million annually.

EIN: 43-1209652

CONTRIBUTIONS SUMMARY

Typical Recipients: • *Arts & Humanities:* Arts Associations & Councils, Arts Centers, Historic Preservation, Libraries, Museums/Galleries, Music, Performing Arts, Public Broadcasting • *Civic & Public Affairs:* Business/Free Enterprise, Civil Rights, Employment/Job Training, Professional & Trade Associations, Public Policy, Urban & Community Affairs • *Education:* Arts/Humanities Education, Colleges & Universities, Education Funds, Medical Education, Minority Education, Private Education (Precollege), Science/Mathematics Education • *Environment:* General • *Health:* Health Policy/Cost Containment, Hospitals, Medical Research, Nursing Services • *International:* International Relations • *Religion:* Religious Organizations, Religious Welfare • *Science:* Scientific Centers & Institutes • *Social Services:* Child Welfare, Community Service Organizations, Delinquency & Criminal Rehabilitation, Family Planning, Food/Clothing Distribution, Homes, People with Disabilities, Recreation & Athletics, Senior Services, Shelters/Homelessness, Substance Abuse, United Funds/United Ways, Volunteer Services, Youth Organizations

Grant Types: capital, employee matching gifts, endowment, general support, and project

Nonmonetary Support Types: cause-related marketing & promotion, donated equipment, donated products, in-kind services, loaned employees, loaned executives, and workplace solicitation

Note: Value of nonmonetary support is not available.

Geographic Distribution: primarily St. Louis and company plant locations

Operating Locations: CA (Los Angeles, San Diego), CO (Denver), CT, IA (Davenport), KY (Louisville), MN (Minneapolis), MO (St. Louis), NY, OH (Cincinnati, Zanesville), TN (Memphis)

CORP. OFFICERS

Paul Harold Hatfield: *B* Topeka KS 1936 *ED* KS St Univ 1959 *CURR EMPL* vp: Ralston Purina Co *CORP AFFIL* ceo, pres: Protein Tech Intl Inc *NONPR AFFIL* dir: Japan-Am Soc, US/Yugoslavia Trade Econ Counc; mem: US/USSR Trade Econ Counc

W. Patrick McGinnis: *B* 1947 *CURR EMPL* vp: Ralston Purina Co

John H. Morris, Jr.: *B* Pittsburgh PA 1942 *ED* WV Univ 1964; Case Western Reserve Univ 1983 *CURR EMPL* vp corp strategic planning: Ralston Purina Co *CORP AFFIL* exec vp, dir: RPM Inc

William Paul Stiritz: *B* Jasper AR 1934 *ED* Northwestern Univ BS 1959; St Louis Univ MA 1968 *CURR EMPL* chmn, ceo, pres, dir: Ralston Purina Co *CORP AFFIL* dir: Angelica Corp, Ball Corp, Boatmens Bancshares Inc, Gen Am Life Ins Co, SC Johnson & Son Inc, May Dept Stores Co *NONPR AFFIL* dir: Grocery Mfrs Am, Washington Univ

GIVING OFFICERS

R. E. Bell: mem bd control

John H. Morris, Jr.: mem bd control *CURR EMPL* vp corp strategic planning: Ralston Purina Co (see above)

James Morton Neville: mem bd control *B* Minneapolis MN 1939 *ED* Univ MN BA 1961; Univ MN JD 1964 *CURR EMPL* vp gen couns: Ralston Purina Co *NONPR AFFIL* mem: Am Bar Assn, Am Corp Couns Assn, Am Soc Corp Secys, Hennepin County Bar Assn, MD Bar Assn, MN Bar Assn, Order Coif, Phi Delta Phi, Psi Upsilon, St Louis Bar Assn, Univ MN Law Sch Alumni Assn, US Supreme Ct Bar Assn *CLUB AFFIL* Ladue Racquet, MD Athletic, Noonday, Old Warson CC

Fred H. Perabo: secy bd control *CURR EMPL* dir commun aff: Ralston Purina Co

E. D. Richards: mem bd control

C. S. Sommer: mem bd control

APPLICATION INFORMATION

Initial Approach: *Initial Contact:* brief letter or proposal *Include Information On:* clear statement of the problem/need, accomplishments by a particular date, background on organization and staff that administer grant, general plan for postgrant evaluation, proof of 501(c)(3) status, amount requested, detailed program budget, copy of most recent financial statement, letter from board chairman or chief administrative officer endorsing proposal *Deadlines:* none

Restrictions on Giving: The fund does not support organizations unable to produce 501(c)(3) tax determination letters; individuals for other than educational purposes; religious or politically partisan causes; projects that require funding outside the United States or its possessions; loans or investment funds; veterans or fraternal organizations, unless they furnish services to the general public; tickets for dinners, benefits, exhibits, conferences, sports events, or other short-term activities; advertisements; underwriting of deficits or postevent funding; or research that is not action-oriented.

OTHER THINGS TO KNOW
Preference is given to projects that offer a maximum multiplier effect, a good basis for replication, and a prevention component.

GRANTS ANALYSIS
Total Grants: $1,971,025

Number of Grants: 47

Highest Grant: $500,000

Average Grant: $31,979*

Typical Range: $5,000 to $40,000

Disclosure Period: fiscal year ending August 31, 1993

Note: Figure for average grant excludes foundation's largest grant of $500,000. Recent grants are derived from a fiscal 1993 Form 990.

RECENT GRANTS

General
500,000	Washington University, St. Louis, MO
221,250	United Way Greater St. Louis, St. Louis, MO
221,250	United Way Greater St. Louis, St. Louis, MO
221,250	United Way Greater St. Louis, St. Louis, MO
200,000	St. Louis Science Center, St. Louis, MO

Shaw Foundation, Arch W.

CONTACT
William W. Shaw
Trustee
Arch W. Shaw Fdn.
Thomasville Rt. Box 60-B
Birch Tree, MO 65438
(417) 764-3701

FINANCIAL SUMMARY
Recent Giving: $640,000 (1993); $580,000 (1991); $411,000 (1990)

Assets: $2,806,295 (1993); $15,546,990 (1991); $9,262,888 (1990)

EIN: 36-6055262

CONTRIBUTIONS SUMMARY
Typical Recipients: • *Arts & Humanities:* Historic Preservation, History & Archaeology, Libraries, Museums/Galleries • *Civic & Public Affairs:* Botanical Gardens/Parks, Law & Justice, Women's Affairs, Zoos/Aquariums • *Education:* Arts/Humanities Education, Colleges & Universities, Environmental Education, Medical Education, Private Education (Precollege), Science/Mathematics Education • *Environment:* General, Resource Conservation • *Health:* Alzheimers Disease, Children's Health/Hos-

pitals, Clinics/Medical Centers, Diabetes, Emergency/Ambulance Services, Hospices, Hospitals, Medical Rehabilitation, Prenatal Health Issues • *International:* International Relief Efforts • *Religion:* Religious Welfare • *Social Services:* Child Welfare, Community Service Organizations, Family Services, Food/Clothing Distribution, People with Disabilities, United Funds/United Ways, Youth Organizations

Grant Types: general support

Geographic Distribution: focus on IL

GIVING OFFICERS
Arch W. Shaw II: trust

Bruce P. Shaw: trust

Roger D. Shaw, Jr.: trust

William W. Shaw: trust

APPLICATION INFORMATION
Initial Approach: Send brief letter of inquiry describing program or project. There are no deadlines.

Restrictions on Giving: Does not support individuals.

GRANTS ANALYSIS
Total Grants: $640,000

Number of Grants: 91

Highest Grant: $40,000

Typical Range: $1,000 to $15,000

Disclosure Period: 1993

Note: Recent grants are derived from a 1993 Form 990.

RECENT GRANTS

Library
10,000	Nantucket Athenaeum, Nantucket, MA

General
40,000	Prairie School, Racine, WI — endowment
25,000	New York University Medical Center, New York, NY — cancer center
20,000	Good Shepherd Hospital, Barrington, IL
20,000	Good Shepherd Hospital, Barrington, IL — building equipment
15,000	Joslin Diabetes Center, Boston, MA — endowment

Smith Foundation, Ralph L.

CONTACT
David P. Hias
Trust Officer
Ralph L. Smith Fdn.
c/o Boatmen's First National Bank of Kansas City
PO Box 419038
Kansas City, MO 64183
(816) 691-7481

FINANCIAL SUMMARY
Recent Giving: $780,000 (1993)

Assets: $16,304,636 (1993)

EIN: 44-6008508

CONTRIBUTIONS SUMMARY
Typical Recipients: • *Arts & Humanities:* Ethnic & Folk Arts, Libraries, Music, Public Broadcasting, Theater • *Civic & Public Affairs:* Community Foundations, Economic Development, Gay/Lesbian Issues, General, Hispanic Affairs, Housing, Municipalities/Towns, Native American Affairs, Public Policy, Women's Affairs • *Education:* Faculty Development, Private Education (Precollege), Science/Mathematics Education • *Environment:* Resource Conservation • *Health:* AIDS/HIV, Cancer, Children's Health/Hospitals, Single-Disease Health Associations • *International:* Foreign Educational Institutions, Health Care/Hospitals • *Religion:* Churches • *Social Services:* Big Brother/Big Sister, Community Service Organizations, Domestic Violence, Family Planning, Family Services, Shelters/Homelessness, Substance Abuse, Youth Organizations

Grant Types: general support

Geographic Distribution: focus on MO

GIVING OFFICERS
Harriet S. Denison: mgr

Anne S. Douthat: mgr

Carol Denison Santessar: mgr

Elizabeth Smith: mgr

Ralph L. Smith, Jr.: mgr

APPLICATION INFORMATION
Initial Approach: Send a brief letter of inquiry. Include a description of organization, amount requested, purpose of funds sought, recently audited financial statement, and proof of tax-exempt status.

GRANTS ANALYSIS
Total Grants: $780,000

Number of Grants: 138

Highest Grant: $58,500

Typical Range: $1,000 to $50,000

Disclosure Period: 1993

Note: Recent grants are derived from a 1993 Form 990.

RECENT GRANTS

Library
20,000	Honnold Mudd Library, Claremont, CA — support joint information exchange agreement with UCLA in collaboration with Caltech and Cal Poly
5,000	Ft. Jones Library, Ft. Jones, CA

General
58,500	Oregon Community Foundation, Portland, OR — for the Dension Family Foundation
35,000	Women's Foundation of Oregon, Portland, OR
25,000	Oregon Community Foundation, Portland, OR — for Women's Foundation of Oregon Fund

20,000	Caltech Division of Biology, Pasadena, CA — support research on the mind brain problem
20,000	University of Cambridge, Cambridge, England — support research on quantum theory of gravity and other topics

Stupp Foundation, Norman J.

CONTACT
John W. North
Trust Officer
Norman J. Stupp Fdn.
c/o Commerce Bank
8000 Forsyth Blvd.
Clayton, MO 63105
(314) 746-7220

FINANCIAL SUMMARY
Recent Giving: $589,370 (fiscal 1993); $531,249 (fiscal 1991); $509,708 (fiscal 1990)

Assets: $13,094,421 (fiscal 1993); $11,967,051 (fiscal 1991); $11,776,001 (fiscal 1990)

EIN: 43-6027433

CONTRIBUTIONS SUMMARY
Donor(s): the late Norman J. Stupp

Typical Recipients: • *Arts & Humanities:* Arts Centers, Arts Outreach, Historic Preservation, History & Archaeology, Libraries, Museums/Galleries, Music, Public Broadcasting • *Civic & Public Affairs:* African American Affairs, Botanical Gardens/Parks, Municipalities/Towns, Zoos/Aquariums • *Education:* Colleges & Universities, Community & Junior Colleges, Literacy, Medical Education, Private Education (Precollege), Science/Mathematics Education, Special Education, Vocational & Technical Education • *Health:* AIDS/HIV, Alzheimers Disease, Cancer, Children's Health/Hospitals, Emergency/Ambulance Services, Eyes/Blindness, Health Organizations, Hospitals, Medical Research • *Religion:* Religious Welfare • *Science:* Science Museums, Scientific Centers & Institutes • *Social Services:* Camps, Child Welfare, Community Service Organizations, Domestic Violence, Family Services, Food/Clothing Distribution, People with Disabilities, Substance Abuse, United Funds/United Ways, Youth Organizations

Grant Types: capital, endowment, operating expenses, project, research, and scholarship

Geographic Distribution: focus on St. Louis, MO

GIVING OFFICERS
Commerce Bank of St. Louis: trust

APPLICATION INFORMATION
Initial Approach: The foundation has no formal grant application procedure or application form. There are no deadlines.

GRANTS ANALYSIS
Total Grants: $589,370

Number of Grants: 39

Highest Grant: $83,333

Typical Range: $3,000 to $10,000

Disclosure Period: fiscal year ending June 30, 1993

Note: Recent grants are derived from a fiscal 1993 Form 990.

RECENT GRANTS
Library

3,000	St. Louis Mercantile Library, St. Louis, MO

General

83,333	Washington University, St. Louis, MO — endowed chair
50,000	Bethesda General Hospital, St. Louis University Eye Institute, St. Louis, MO
50,000	St. Louis University, Eye Institute, St. Louis, MO
30,000	St. Louis Science Center, St. Louis, MO
30,000	St. Louis Science Center, St. Louis, MO

Sunnen Foundation

CONTACT
Helen S. Sly
President and Director
Sunnen Foundation
7910 Manchester Ave.
St. Louis, MO 63143
(314) 781-2100

FINANCIAL SUMMARY
Recent Giving: $471,712 (1995); $2,276,650 (1994); $666,473 (1993)

Assets: $13,500,000 (1995 est.); $13,250,000 (1994); $15,514,000 (1993)

Gifts Received: $1,053 (1989)

Fiscal Note: In 1989, a gift was received from the Sunnen Foundation Trust.

EIN: 43-6029156

CONTRIBUTIONS SUMMARY
Donor(s): The Sunnen Foundation was established in Missouri in 1953 by Joseph Sunnen, founder of Sunnen Products Company, a manufacturer of high precision tools and gauges.

Typical Recipients: • *Arts & Humanities:* Historic Preservation, History & Archaeology, Libraries • *Civic & Public Affairs:* Clubs, Economic Policy, First Amendment Issues, General, Housing, Public Policy, Safety, Urban & Community Affairs, Women's Affairs • *Education:* Business Education, Colleges & Universities, Continuing Education, Economic Education, Medical Education, Private Education (Precollege), Special Education • *Health:* Children's Health/Hospitals, Emergency/Ambulance Services, Health Policy/Cost Containment, Health Organizations, Single-Disease Health Associations, Speech & Hearing • *Religion:* Religious Welfare, Social/Policy Issues • *Social Services:* At-Risk Youth, Camps, Child Welfare, Community Service Organizations, Day Care, Delinquency & Criminal Rehabilitation, Domestic Violence, Family Planning, Family Services, Food/Clothing Distribution, People with Disabilities, Senior Services, Shelters/Homelessness, Substance Abuse, Youth Organizations

Grant Types: project

Geographic Distribution: principally to national organizations

GIVING OFFICERS
Ruth Bailey: secy

James K. Berthold: vp, dir, asst treas *B* St. Louis MO 1938 *ED* Univ MO Rolla BS 1960; Washington Univ MBA 1962 *CURR EMPL* chmn, pres, dir: Sunnen Products Co *CORP AFFIL* dir: Citizens Natl Bank St Louis

C. Diane Boulware: dir *CURR EMPL* secy,treas: Sunnen Products Co

Esther S. Kreider: dir, fdr daughter

Paul Edward Slaten: treas, dir *B* Grafton IL 1933 *ED* IL Wesleyan Univ 1958; Washington Univ MBA 1960 *CURR EMPL* treas: Sunnen Products Co

Helen S. Sly: pres, dir, fdr daughter

APPLICATION INFORMATION
Initial Approach:

Initial contact should be in the form of a brief letter.

Applicants should submit five copies of the proposal and should include a full description of the project, the organization's qualifications to conduct the program, purpose for which grant is desired, rationale behind proposed project, outline of the solution and method of evaluation, total budget, and confirmation of tax-exempt status. A commitment must also be made to furnish final project results for the foundation's records.

The annual deadline for applications is August 1. The board meets in October to consider proposals.

Restrictions on Giving: With the exception of specific projects related to its areas of main concern, grants are not made to general fund-raising drives, religious bodies, educational institutions, environmental organizations, hospitals or medical charities, charities with broad based appeal, or to the arts. No scholarship, research, or travel grants are made to or for specific individuals.

GRANTS ANALYSIS
Total Grants: $2,276,650

Number of Grants: 25

Highest Grant: $1,250,000

Average Grant: $42,777*

Typical Range: $2,000 to $50,000

Disclosure Period: 1994

Note: Average grant figure excludes the highest grant of $1,250,000. Recent grants are derived from a 1995 list of approved grants.

RECENT GRANTS

Library
50,000	Missouri Botanical Gardens, St. Louis, MO — library automation and capital campaign
35,000	PP-St. Louis, St. Louis, MO — library and popular literature

General
50,000	Belle Center, St. Louis, MO — new facility capital campaign
40,000	Scottish Rite Clinic, St. Louis, MO — speech and language program
30,000	Religious Coalition for Reproduction Choice, St. Louis, MO — clergy counseling program
25,000	Planned Parenthood Alabama, AL — telephone system and colposcopy equipment
25,000	Rainbow Village, St. Louis, MO — first year of four-year pledge for endowment program

Swift Co. Inc., John S. / Swift Co. Inc. Charitable Trust, John S.

Employees: 550
Parent Company: J.S.S. Co. Inc.
Headquarters: Chicago, IL
SIC Major Group: Printing & Publishing

CONTACT
Brian Swift
President
John S. Swift Co. Inc.
1248 Research Dr.
Saint Louis, MO 63122
(314) 991-4300

FINANCIAL SUMMARY
Recent Giving: $119,500 (1993); $143,380 (1990); $42,130 (1989)

Assets: $1,822,990 (1993); $1,923,096 (1990); $1,430,492 (1989)

Gifts Received: $500,000 (1990)

Fiscal Note: In 1990, contributions were received from John S. Swift Co.

EIN: 43-6020812

CONTRIBUTIONS SUMMARY
Typical Recipients: • *Arts & Humanities:* Arts Centers, Arts Institutes, History & Archaeology, Libraries, Museums/Galleries, Public Broadcasting • *Civic & Public Affairs:* Zoos/Aquariums • *Education:* Colleges & Universities, Medical Education • *Environment:* General • *Health:* Children's Health/Hospitals, Hospitals, Medical Research • *Religion:* Churches, Religious Welfare • *Social Services:* Community Service Organizations, Scouts, Substance Abuse, United Funds/United Ways, Youth Organizations

Grant Types: challenge and general support

Geographic Distribution: primarily in MO and IL

Operating Locations: IL (Chicago), MO (St. Louis)

CORP. OFFICERS
Bryan Swift: *CURR EMPL* pres: John S Swift Co

GIVING OFFICERS
Mercantile Trust Co: trust

Ben Heckel: trust

Hampden M. Swift: trust

APPLICATION INFORMATION
Initial Approach: Send brief letter of inquiry. There are no deadlines.

GRANTS ANALYSIS
Total Grants: $119,500

Number of Grants: 40

Highest Grant: $100,000

Typical Range: $50 to $5,000

Disclosure Period: 1993

Note: Recent grants are derived from a 1993 Form 990.

RECENT GRANTS

General
100,000	John G. Shedd Aquarium, Chicago, IL
5,000	Eugene Hotchkiss Fund of Lake Forest College, Lake Forest, IL
1,000	Anti-Drug Abuse Education Fund, Chicago, IL
1,000	College of the Ozarks, Point Lookout, MO
1,000	Crusade of Mercy, Chicago, IL

Union Electric Co. / Union Electric Co. Charitable Trust

Revenue: $2.0 billion
Employees: 6,417
Headquarters: St. Louis, MO
SIC Major Group: Electric & Other Services Combined

CONTACT
Carlin Scanlan
Manager, Corporate Communications
Union Electric Co. Charitable Trust
1901 Chouteau Ave.
PO Box 149
St. Louis, MO 63166
(314) 554-2902

FINANCIAL SUMMARY
Recent Giving: $3,246,000 (1994); $2,300,351 (1993); $3,340,488 (1992)

Assets: $2,625,524 (1993); $905,000 (1992); $3,000,000 (1991)

Fiscal Note: Above figures include trust contributions, which totaled $2,700,000 in 1994, and direct giving, which totaled $546,000 in 1994. Above figures exclude nonmonetary support.

EIN: 43-6022693

CONTRIBUTIONS SUMMARY
Typical Recipients: • *Arts & Humanities:* Arts Associations & Councils, Arts Centers, Arts Festivals, Arts Funds, Arts Institutes, Dance, Historic Preservation, Libraries, Museums/Galleries, Music, Performing Arts, Theater, Visual Arts • *Civic & Public Affairs:* African American Affairs, Botanical Gardens/Parks, Economic Development, Housing, Safety, Urban & Community Affairs • *Education:* Business Education, Colleges & Universities, Community & Junior Colleges, Economic Education, Education Funds, Education Reform, Elementary Education (Private), Engineering/Technological Education, General, Minority Education, Private Education (Precollege), Public Education (Precollege), Science/Mathematics Education, Student Aid • *Environment:* General • *Health:* Emergency/Ambulance Services, Health Organizations • *Religion:* Dioceses, Jewish Causes, Ministries, Religious Organizations, Religious Welfare • *Science:* Scientific Centers & Institutes • *Social Services:* Child Welfare, Community Centers, Community Service Organizations, Counseling, Delinquency & Criminal Rehabilitation, Emergency Relief, Family Services, Food/Clothing Distribution, Homes, People with Disabilities, Recreation & Athletics, Scouts, Senior Services, Shelters/Homelessness, United Funds/United Ways, Volunteer Services, Youth Organizations

Grant Types: capital, employee matching gifts, general support, project, and scholarship

Note: Employee matching gift ratio: 1 to 1. Gifts are only matched to accredited colleges and universities.

Nonmonetary Support: $214,000 (1994); $167,000 (1993); $180,000 (1992)

Nonmonetary Support Types: donated equipment and loaned executives

Note: See "Other Things You Should Know" for further information. Requests for nonmonetary support are handled by Susan B. Martel, supervisor of corporate communications.

Geographic Distribution: near headquarters and operating locations

Operating Locations: IL, MO (Cape Girardeau, Jefferson City, Kirksville, St. Louis)

CORP. OFFICERS
M. Patricia Barrett: *CURR EMPL* vp corp commun: Un Electric Co

Joe Birk: *CURR EMPL* asst to gen couns & vp: Un Electric Co

Charles William Mueller: *B* Belleville IL 1938 *ED* St Louis Univ BSEE 1961; St Louis Univ MBA 1966 *CURR EMPL* chmn, pres, ceo: Un Electric Co *CORP AFFIL* dir: Assn Edison Illuminating Cos, Boatmens Natl Bank St Louis, Canterbury Entertainment Inc, Downtown St Louis Inc, Electric Energy Inc, Union Colliery Co *NONPR AFFIL* dir: Civic Progress, Municipal Theatre Assn, Regional Commerce & Growth Assn, St Louis Childrens Hosp, St Louis Sci Ctr;

mem: Inst Electrical Electronics Engrs; trust: Webster Univ *CLUB AFFIL* Bogey, MO Athletic, Oak Hill Tennis, St Clair CC, St Louis

GIVING OFFICERS
Charles William Mueller: trust *CURR EMPL* chmn, pres, ceo: Un Electric Co (see above)

Carlin Scanlan: mgr corp commun

APPLICATION INFORMATION
Initial Approach: *Initial Contact:* brief letter or full proposal and one copy on organization letterhead *Include Information On:* explanation of project for which funds are requested, statement of organization's purpose and services, fund-raising goal, amount sought, current status of fund raising for project, organization's current board-approved operating budget, audited financial statement for previous year, proof of tax-exempt status, roster of organization's governing board *Deadlines:* none

Restrictions on Giving: Does not support individuals, political organizations, or religious organizations for sectarian purposes.

The company never contributes electric or natural service.

OTHER THINGS TO KNOW
Items of salvage from company stock sometimes are donated to nonprofit organizations, including utility poles, office furnishings, and other surplus items. Organizations receiving such material must arrange pickup. Same general policies and procedures prevail with monetary contributions.

PUBLICATIONS
Community report

GRANTS ANALYSIS
Total Grants: $3,246,000*

Highest Grant: $640,000

Typical Range: $2,000 to $20,000

Disclosure Period: 1994

Note: Figures include direct and trust giving and exclude $214,000 in nonmonetary support. Recent grants are derived from a 1994 partial grants list.

RECENT GRANTS

General

640,000	United Way Greater St. Louis, St. Louis, MO
110,000	Washington University St. Louis, St. Louis, MO
100,000	Missouri Botanical Garden, St. Louis, MO
75,000	Provident Counseling, St. Louis, MO — for the support of Union Electric's Dollar More program
60,000	St. Vincent DePaul Society St. Louis, St. Louis, MO — for the support of Union Electric's Dollar More program

Van Evera Foundation, Dewitt

Former Foundation Name: Dewitt Caroline Van Evera Foundation

CONTACT
Margaretta Forrester
Co-Trustee
Dewitt Van Evera Fdn.
7811 Carondele, Ste. 102
Saint Louis, MO 63105
(612) 973-0067

FINANCIAL SUMMARY
Recent Giving: $127,000 (1993); $120,000 (1991); $116,000 (1990)

Assets: $2,721,349 (1993); $2,697,092 (1991); $2,384,469 (1990)

EIN: 87-6117907

CONTRIBUTIONS SUMMARY
Donor(s): the late Dewitt Van Evera, the late Caroline Irene Van Evera

Typical Recipients: • *Arts & Humanities:* Libraries, Public Broadcasting, Theater • *Education:* Colleges & Universities, Engineering/Technological Education, Private Education (Precollege), Science/Mathematics Education • *International:* Foreign Educational Institutions

Grant Types: capital, endowment, general support, operating expenses, and scholarship

Geographic Distribution: focus on MN, WI, and UT

GIVING OFFICERS
First Bank NA: corp trust

Margretta Forrester: co-trust

Laura J. Van Evera LaFond: co-trust

William P. Van Evera: adv *PHIL AFFIL* scholarship comm mem: Oscar Mitchell, Jr. Trust

William P. Van Evera: co-trust

APPLICATION INFORMATION
Initial Approach: Send brief letter of inquiry describing program. There are no deadlines.

Restrictions on Giving: Does not support individuals.

GRANTS ANALYSIS
Total Grants: $127,000

Number of Grants: 9

Highest Grant: $45,000

Typical Range: $3,000 to $30,000

Disclosure Period: 1993

Note: Recent grants are derived from a 1993 Form 990.

RECENT GRANTS

Library

10,000	Jessie F. Halley Memorial Library, Crosby, MN

General

45,000	Northland College, Ashland, WI
30,000	St. John's Preparatory School, Collegeville, MN
17,000	College of St. Benedict, St. Joseph, MN
5,000	Webster University, St. Louis, MO
3,000	International Education Consortium, St. Louis, MO

MONTANA

Montana Power Co. / MPCo/Entech Foundation

Revenue: $1.08 billion
Employees: 4,089
Headquarters: Butte, MT
SIC Major Group: Combination Utility Nec, Bituminous Coal & Lignite—Surface, Bituminous Coal—Underground, and Crude Petroleum & Natural Gas

CONTACT
Pamela K. Merrell
Vice President, Secretary
MPCo/Entech Fdn.
40 E Broadway
Butte, MT 59701
(406) 723-5454
Note: Pamela Merrell's extension is 72142.

FINANCIAL SUMMARY
Recent Giving: $591,985 (1994); $671,900 (1993); $361,977 (1992)

Assets: $285,128 (1993); $342,356 (1992); $186,832 (1991)

Gifts Received: $607,699 (1993); $509,433 (1992); $417,489 (1991)

Fiscal Note: Contributes through foundation only. In 1991, contributions were received from Montana Power Company. In 1992, contributions were received from Montana Power Company, Entech, Inc., and Independent Power Group, Inc.

EIN: 81-0432484

CONTRIBUTIONS SUMMARY
Typical Recipients: • *Arts & Humanities:* Arts Funds, Historic Preservation, History & Archaeology, Libraries, Museums/Galleries, Music • *Civic & Public Affairs:* General, Professional & Trade Associations • *Education:* Colleges & Universities, Community & Junior Colleges, Engineering/Technological Education, Private Education (Precollege), Science/Mathematics Education, Secondary Education (Public), Student Aid • *Health:* Cancer, Clinics/Medical Centers, Diabetes, Health Organizations, Hospitals • *International:* International Affairs • *Religion:* Religious Welfare • *Social Services:* Child Welfare, Community Centers, Community Service Organizations, Domestic Violence, Recreation & Athletics, United Funds/United Ways, Youth Organizations

Grant Types: capital, employee matching gifts, general support, multiyear/continuing support, project, and scholarship

Note: Employee matching gift ratio: 1 to 1.

Nonmonetary Support Types: donated equipment and donated products

Note: Estimated value of nonmonetary support is not available.

Geographic Distribution: primarily in areas of company operations

Operating Locations: AL, CO, MT (Billings, Bozeman, Butte, Colstrip, Great Falls, Helena, Missoula, Thompson Falls), TX (Jewitt), WA (Issaquah), WY (Rocky Butte)

CORP. OFFICERS

Daniel T. Berube: *B* 1934 *ED* Univ WA BSME 1964; MT Tech Univ MS 1972 *CURR EMPL* chmn, ceo, dir: MT Power Co *CORP AFFIL* chmn, ceo, dir: Altana Exploration Co; chmn, dir: Horizon Coal Svcs; pres, ceo, dir: Entech

Perry J. Cole: *B* Hayre MT 1957 *ED* Univ MT 1979; Univ MT 1980 *CURR EMPL* treas: MT Power Co

R. P. Gannon: *ED* Univ Notre Dame BA 1966; Univ MT JD 1969 *CURR EMPL* pres, dir: MT Power Co

Pamela K. Merrell: *B* Panguitch UT 1952 *ED* Univ UT 1974; Univ UT Law Sch *CURR EMPL* vp, secy: MT Power Co *CORP AFFIL* secy: Western Energy Inc; vp, secy: Entech Inc *NONPR AFFIL* mem: Am Bar Assn, Am Soc Corp Secys

John S. Miller: *CURR EMPL* contr: MT Power Co

Arthur K. Neill: *CURR EMPL* exec vp, dir: MT Power Co

Jerrold P. Pederson: *CURR EMPL* vp, cfo, dir: MT Power Co

GIVING OFFICERS

Daniel T. Berube: dir *CURR EMPL* chmn, ceo, dir: MT Power Co (see above)

Alan F. Cain: dir *CORP AFFIL* dir: MT Power Co

Perry J. Cole: treas *CURR EMPL* treas: MT Power Co (see above)

R. P. Gannon: dir *CURR EMPL* pres, dir: MT Power Co (see above)

Carl Lehrkind III: dir *B* 1939 *CURR EMPL* pres, dir: Lehrkinds *CORP AFFIL* dir: MT Power Co

Pamela K. Merrell: vp, secy *CURR EMPL* vp, secy: MT Power Co (see above)

John S. Miller: comptr *CURR EMPL* contr: MT Power Co (see above)

J. J. Murphy: dir

Arthur K. Neill: dir *CURR EMPL* exec vp, dir: MT Power Co (see above)

Jerrold P. Pederson: dir *CURR EMPL* vp, cfo, dir: MT Power Co (see above)

APPLICATION INFORMATION

Initial Approach: *Initial Contact:* write for a copy of the application guidelines and an application form *Deadlines:* before April 1, August 1, or December 1

Restrictions on Giving: The foundation does not support United Way umbrella or-

ganizations (except for capital funds), or fraternal, veterans', or similar organizations. Prefers to support capital fund drives rather than operating funds (except for organizations such as the United Way). No support to individuals or political or lobbying groups.

PUBLICATIONS

Annual report, including application guidelines

GRANTS ANALYSIS

Total Grants: $671,900

Number of Grants: 166

Highest Grant: $63,684

Average Grant: $4,048

Typical Range: $500 to $5,000

Disclosure Period: 1993

Note: Recent grants are derived from a 1993 Form 990; they are a list of approved grants.

RECENT GRANTS

General

960,240	Montana University System, Butte, MT — support academic excellence
79,907	United Way — fund raising campaign
40,000	Florence Crittenton Home Services, Charlotte, NC — capital contribution
40,000	Montana Tech Butte, Butte, MT — unrestricted contribution
32,000	Butte Central High School, Butte, MT — unrestricted contribution

NEBRASKA

Ameritas Life Insurance Corp. / Ameritas Charitable Foundation

Former Foundation Name: BLN Charitable Foundation
Employees: 607
Headquarters: Lincoln, NE
SIC Major Group: Insurance Carriers and Security & Commodity Brokers

CONTACT

JoAnn Martin
Senior Vice President, Controller, Chief Financial Officer
Ameritas Life Insurance Corp.
PO Box 81889
Lincoln, NE 68501
(402) 467-7706

FINANCIAL SUMMARY

Recent Giving: $230,512 (1993); $198,066 (1992); $180,358 (1990)

Assets: $2,789,277 (1993); $2,738,516 (1992); $2,128,163 (1990)

Gifts Received: $497,700 (1992); $760,575 (1989); $295,925 (1988)

Fiscal Note: In 1992, contributions were received from Ameritas Life Insurance Corp.

EIN: 36-3428705

CONTRIBUTIONS SUMMARY

Typical Recipients: • *Arts & Humanities:* Arts Associations & Councils, Dance, Libraries, Music, Public Broadcasting, Theater • *Civic & Public Affairs:* Clubs, Economic Development, Economic Policy, Employment/Job Training, General, Housing, Parades/Festivals, Professional & Trade Associations • *Education:* Business Education, Colleges & Universities, Economic Education, Health & Physical Education, Minority Education, Private Education (Precollege), Religious Education, Science/Mathematics Education • *Environment:* General • *Health:* AIDS/HIV, Hospitals, Medical Research, Research/Studies Institutes • *Religion:* Religious Organizations, Religious Welfare • *Social Services:* Community Service Organizations, Family Services, Food/Clothing Distribution, Homes, People with Disabilities, Senior Services, United Funds/United Ways, Youth Organizations

Grant Types: capital, general support, multiyear/continuing support, professorship, project, and research

Geographic Distribution: emphasis on Lincoln, NE

Operating Locations: NE (Lincoln)

CORP. OFFICERS

Lawrence J. Arth: *B* Lincoln NE 1943 *ED* Univ NE BBA 1965; Univ NE MA 1969 *CURR EMPL* chmn, pres, ceo, dir: Ameritas Life Ins Corp *CORP AFFIL* fellow: Fin Analysts Fed; mem: Fin Analysts, Omaha/Lincoln SOc; pres, dir: Ameritas Investment Advisors *CLUB AFFIL* Lincoln CC

JoAnn Martin: *CURR EMPL* sr vp, contr, cfo: Ameritas Life Ins Corp

GIVING OFFICERS

Lawrence J. Arth: vp, dir *CURR EMPL* chmn, pres, ceo, dir: Ameritas Life Ins Corp (see above)

JoAnn Martin: contr *CURR EMPL* sr vp, contr, cfo: Ameritas Life Ins Corp (see above)

William C. Smith: pres, dir

Neal E. Tyner: secy, treas, dir *B* Grand Island NE 1930 *ED* Univ NE BBA 1956 *CORP AFFIL* bd dirs audit comm: Spencer Foods; dir: Norwest Bank *NONPR AFFIL* bd govs: NE Wesleyan Univ; dir: Am Counc Life Ins; fellow: Chartered Fin Analysts; mem: NE Diplomats, Newcomer Soc US, Omaha/Lincoln Soc Fin Analysts, Pres Assn, Repbl Inner Circle; trust: Fordham Univ, Investment Banking Inst, Lincoln Fdn, Univ NE Fdn *CLUB AFFIL* Lincoln CC, Nebraska

APPLICATION INFORMATION

Initial Approach: The foundation requests applications be made in writing. Include a description of organization, amount requested, purpose of funds sought, recently audited financial statement, and proof of tax-exempt status.

GRANTS ANALYSIS
Total Grants: $230,512

Number of Grants: 41

Highest Grant: $50,500

Typical Range: $200 to $25,000

Disclosure Period: 1993

Note: Recent grants are derived from a 1993 Form 990.

RECENT GRANTS
General
50,500	United Way of Lincoln, Lincoln, NE
25,000	Nebraska Wesleyan University, Lincoln, NE
15,000	Madonna Centers, Lincoln, NE — capital campaign
15,000	Pius X School, Lincoln, NE — Embrace the Future campaign
10,000	Christian Urban Education Service, Omaha, NE — employability program

Farr Trust, Frank M. and Alice M.

CONTACT
James E. Koepke
Trustee
Frank M. and Alice M. Farr Trust
1101 12th St.
Aurora, NE 68818
(402) 694-3136

FINANCIAL SUMMARY
Recent Giving: $243,727 (1993); $387,884 (1990); $269,995 (1989)

Assets: $3,860,794 (1993); $3,545,121 (1990); $3,538,202 (1989)

EIN: 47-6144457

CONTRIBUTIONS SUMMARY
Typical Recipients: • *Arts & Humanities:* Historic Preservation, History & Archaeology, Libraries, Music • *Civic & Public Affairs:* Botanical Gardens/Parks, Clubs, Housing, Municipalities/Towns, Rural Affairs, Safety, Urban & Community Affairs • *Education:* Agricultural Education, Student Aid • *Health:* Alzheimers Disease, Health Organizations • *Social Services:* Community Centers, Community Service Organizations, Youth Organizations

Grant Types: capital, general support, and operating expenses

Geographic Distribution: limited to Hamilton County, NE

GIVING OFFICERS
James E. Koepke: trust

APPLICATION INFORMATION
Initial Approach: Send request for application form. Deadline is February 15.

GRANTS ANALYSIS
Total Grants: $243,727

Number of Grants: 17

Highest Grant: $60,179

Typical Range: $2,000 to $15,000

Disclosure Period: 1993

Note: Recent grants are derived from a 1993 Form 990.

RECENT GRANTS
General
53,500	Hamilton County Agricultural Society, Aurora, NE
50,000	Hamilton Manor Alzheimers Wing, Aurora, NE
15,000	Memorial Foundation, Houston, TX — cafeteria
10,000	Aurora Housing Development Corporation, Aurora, NE
10,000	Hamilton Community Foundation, Aurora, NE — Farr Rotary Scholarships

IBP, Inc. / IBP Foundation, Inc., The

Sales: $11.67 billion
Employees: 24,000
Headquarters: Dakota City, NE
SIC Major Group: Food & Kindred Products

CONTACT
Don Willoghby
Director, Community & Government Affairs
IBP, Inc.
PO Box 515
Dakota City, NE 68731
(402) 494-2061

FINANCIAL SUMMARY
Recent Giving: $204,000 (1993); $163,500 (1992); $143,946 (1990)

Assets: $2,204,882 (1993); $2,403,356 (1992); $2,239,596 (1990)

Gifts Received: $500,000 (1988)

EIN: 47-6014039

CONTRIBUTIONS SUMMARY
Typical Recipients: • *Arts & Humanities:* Libraries • *Civic & Public Affairs:* Employment/Job Training, General, Native American Affairs, Professional & Trade Associations, Rural Affairs, Safety, Urban & Community Affairs, Zoos/Aquariums • *Education:* Agricultural Education, Business Education, General, Public Education (Precollege) • *Health:* Health Organizations, Hospitals • *Social Services:* Child Welfare, Day Care, Food/Clothing Distribution, Recreation & Athletics, Volunteer Services, Youth Organizations

Grant Types: general support

Geographic Distribution: limited to Boise, ID; Columbus Junction, Council Bluffs, Denison, Sioux City, and Storm Lake, IA; Joslin, IL; Emporia and Garden City, KS; Luverne, MN; Dakota City, Lexington, Madison, South Sioux City, and West Point, NE; Amarillo, TX; and Pasco, WA

Operating Locations: NE (Dakota City)

CORP. OFFICERS
Robert L. Peterson: *B* NE 1932 *ED* Univ NE *CURR EMPL* chmn, pres, ceo: IBP Inc *CORP AFFIL* dir: Midwest Resources *CLUB AFFIL* Sioux City CC

GIVING OFFICERS
Lonnie O. Grigsby: dir *B* Cadiz KY 1939 *ED* Duke Univ AB 1962; Duke Univ JD 1964; Univ Louisville MBA 1972 *CURR EMPL* exec vp fin & admin, secy: IBP

Richard A. Jochum: off

Eugene D. Leman: dir *B* Peoria IL 1942 *ED* Univ IL 1964 *CURR EMPL* exec vp pork div: IBP *CORP AFFIL* dir: IBP *NONPR AFFIL* mem: Am Meat Inst

George S. Spencer: off, dir

Leon O. Trautwein: off

APPLICATION INFORMATION
Initial Approach: Application form required. There are no deadlines.

Restrictions on Giving: Grants are limited to the following areas: Boise, ID; Joslin, IL; Luverne, MN; Amarillo, TX; and Pasco, WA; as well as Columbus Junction, Denison, Perry, Sioux City, Storm Lake, and Waterloo, IA; Emporia and Garden City, KS; and Dakota City, Lexington, Madison, South Sioux City, and West Point, NE.

GRANTS ANALYSIS
Total Grants: $204,000

Number of Grants: 12

Highest Grant: $54,000

Typical Range: $1,500 to $50,000

Disclosure Period: 1993

Note: Recent grants are derived from a 1993 Form 990.

RECENT GRANTS
Library
1,500	Dakota City Library, Dakota City, NE

General
54,000	National Pork Producers Council
50,000	National Cattlemen's Association
30,000	Siouxland Soccer Field Complex, Siouxland, IA
20,000	Opportunities Unlimited, Sioux City, IA
14,000	National Future Farmers of America Foundation, Madison, WI

Kiewit Foundation, Peter

CONTACT
Lyn L. Wallin Ziegenbein
Executive Director and Secretary
Peter Kiewit Foundation
1200 Woodmen Tower
Farnam at Seventeenth
Omaha, NE 68102
(402) 344-7890

FINANCIAL SUMMARY
Recent Giving: $11,974,080 (fiscal 1992); $9,124,540 (fiscal 1991); $10,296,987 (fiscal 1989)

Assets: $240,000,519 (fiscal 1992); $226,581,831 (fiscal 1991); $206,745,435 (fiscal 1989)

Gifts Received: $2,800 (fiscal 1992); $7,535 (fiscal 1991); $2,001 (fiscal 1988)

EIN: 47-6098282

CONTRIBUTIONS SUMMARY
Donor(s): The Peter Kiewit Foundation was established in Nebraska in 1975 by the late Peter Kiewit (1900-1979), president of Peter Kiewit Sons, a construction company. He successively worked as a mason tender, hod carrier, and bricklayer for his family business during his summer vacations and throughout high school. He completed one year of study at Dartmouth College before entering the construction business full-time at the age of 19. After he joined the business, Mr. Kiewit began buying company stock from his brothers. When Mr. Kiewit assumed leadership in 1931, the company's total assets were less than $125,000. Hard work, dedication to the principle of good relations with owners and their representatives, the ability to recognize contracting opportunities, and a farsighted plan of rewarding key employees with stock ownership in the company made Peter Kiewit Sons a multi-million dollar firm and one of the largest construction companies in the world. The present foundation is the result of Mr. Kiewit's personal philanthropy, and has no affiliation with the Kiewit Company.

Mr. Kiewit was committed to "building the character of men and good things for a better, more meaningful world." His commitment extended to civil rights, as he believed that "the competitive construction business allows no room for prejudice in employment practices." In 1963, he headed the employment subcommittee of the Mayors Bi-Racial Committee in Omaha, and in 1967, the National Conference of Christians and Jews presented him with its Brotherhood Award.

Peter Kiewit was also committed to philanthropy. At the time of his death, he had contributed $15 million to various causes, and had pledged an additional $5 million. The foundation which bears his name is a continuing reflection of Peter Kiewit's philanthropic interests.

Typical Recipients: • *Arts & Humanities:* Arts Associations & Councils, Arts Funds, Historic Preservation, History & Archaeology, Libraries, Museums/Galleries, Music, Opera, Performing Arts, Theater • *Civic & Public Affairs:* Botanical Gardens/Parks, Economic Development, Employment/Job Training, Municipalities/Towns, Native American Affairs, Parades/Festivals, Philanthropic Organizations, Safety, Urban & Community Affairs, Zoos/Aquariums • *Education:* Colleges & Universities, Faculty Development, International Studies, Journalism/Media Education, Literacy, Minority Education, Preschool Education, Public Education (Precollege),

Science/Mathematics Education, Special Education, Student Aid • *Environment:* General, Resource Conservation • *Health:* AIDS/HIV, Emergency/Ambulance Services, Health Organizations, Hospitals, Nutrition • *Religion:* Religious Organizations, Religious Welfare • *Social Services:* Child Welfare, Community Centers, Community Service Organizations, Family Planning, Family Services, Food/Clothing Distribution, People with Disabilities, Recreation & Athletics, Senior Services, Shelters/Homelessness, United Funds/United Ways, Volunteer Services, Youth Organizations

Grant Types: capital, professorship, project, scholarship, and seed money

Geographic Distribution: Nebraska; the part of Iowa which is within a 100-mile radius of Omaha, NE; Sheridan, WY; and Rancho Mirage, CA

GIVING OFFICERS
Richard L. Coyne: trust

Ray L. Daniel: vchmn, trust *B* 1921

Robert B. Daugherty: chmn *B* 1922 *CURR EMPL* chmn, dir: Valmont Indus Inc *CORP AFFIL* dir: ConAgra Inc, FirsTier Fin Inc, Peter Kiewit Sons Inc, KN Energy *NONPR AFFIL* trust: Hastings Coll *PHIL AFFIL* pres: Valmont Foundation; off: ConAgra Foundation, Robert B. Daugherty Foundation

Marjorie H. Kiewit: trust

Peter Kiewit, Jr.: trust *B* 1926 *ED* Univ AZ BS; Univ AZ JD *CURR EMPL* of couns: Gallagher & Kennedy *CORP AFFIL* secy: Un Metro Materials *NONPR AFFIL* mem: Am Bar Assn

Lyn L. Wallin Ziegenbein: exec dir, secy *B* 1952 *ED* Univ KS BS 1974; Creighton Univ JD 1977

APPLICATION INFORMATION
Initial Approach:

Applicants should contact the executive director to obtain standard application forms. Personal interviews are not a part of the normal application process, and are not encouraged.

Grant applications should be submitted to the foundation's executive director at least 75 days prior to the board meeting at which consideration is desired.

The board of trustees meets in March, June, September, and December.

Restrictions on Giving: Organizations whose applications have been denied must wait one full year before resubmitting. Grants are made only on a matching fund basis, except in situations involving dire need where matching funds cannot be made available. The foundation will also consider granting seed money for innovative programs. Priority consideration is given to organizations which are not tax-supported. At least equal matching funds are required of organizations which are not tax-supported, and at least a three-to-one match is required of organizations which receive tax support. Any grants made for the purposes of capital construction are conditioned upon the actual completion of such improvement. Applicants are encouraged to develop other

sources of support for a particular project prior to approaching the foundation.

Restrictions on Giving: The foundation does not make grants to individuals or private, nonoperating foundations. The foundation generally does not consider support for endowment funds; elementary and secondary schools; churches and similar groups; or construction, renovation, or operations of normally tax-supported public facilities. A low priority is given to applications for normal operating budgets or contributions to annual fund-raising campaigns. No more than two applications from the same organization will be considered in any calendar year.

OTHER THINGS TO KNOW
Firstier Bank, N.A., Omaha serves as the corporate trustee for the foundation.

GRANTS ANALYSIS
Total Grants: $11,974,080

Number of Grants: 144

Highest Grant: $2,250,000

Average Grant: $43,433*

Typical Range: $15,000 to $50,000 and $100,000 to $200,000

Disclosure Period: fiscal year ending June 30, 1992

Note: The figure for the average grant figure excludes the three highest grants totaling $5,850,000. Recent grants are derived from a fiscal 1992 grants list.

RECENT GRANTS

Library

50,000	Beatrice Public Library Foundation, Beatrice, NE — to partially fund the construction of grantee's program facility
25,000	Central City Library Foundation, Central City, NE — to partially fund the construction of a new library facility
5,000	Arizona State University Foundation, Tempe, AZ — to partially fund the construction of a new library

General

2,250,000	Dartmouth College, Hanover, NH — for a cooperative and educational research program
1,600,000	Girls Incorporated of Omaha, Omaha, NE — to fund acquisition and renovation of Clifton Hills school for use as grantee's main program
1,000,000	Omaha Zoological Society, Omaha, NE — to partially fund the construction of a restaurant and education facility adjacent to the Lied Jungle
607,950	United Way of Midlands, Omaha, NE — for 1990-91 general fund drive campaign
300,000	Siouxland Foundation, Sioux City, IA — to provide a basic endowment to establish a community foundation

Norwest Bank Nebraska, N.A.

Employees: 800
Parent Company: Norwest Corporation
Headquarters: Omaha, NE
SIC Major Group: National Commercial Banks

CONTACT
Margaret Shugrue
Assistant Vice President and Director of
 Public Relations
Norwest Bank Nebraska
1919 Douglas St.
Omaha, NE 68102
(402) 536-2362

FINANCIAL SUMMARY
Recent Giving: $625,000 (1995 est.);
$700,000 (1994 approx.)

Fiscal Note: Company gives directly. Annual Giving Range: $500,000 to $750,000.

CONTRIBUTIONS SUMMARY
Typical Recipients: • *Arts & Humanities:*
Arts Associations & Councils, Arts Festivals, Arts Funds, Community Arts, Dance, Libraries, Music, Performing Arts, Theater, Visual Arts • *Civic & Public Affairs:* Economic Development, Housing, Philanthropic Organizations, Zoos/Aquariums • *Education:* Agricultural Education, Colleges & Universities, Community & Junior Colleges, Education Funds, Elementary Education (Private), Public Education (Precollege), Religious Education • *Health:* Health Organizations, Mental Health, Public Health, Single-Disease Health Associations • *Religion:* Religious Welfare • *Social Services:* Child Welfare, Community Centers, Counseling, Family Planning, Food/Clothing Distribution, Homes, People with Disabilities, Recreation & Athletics, United Funds/United Ways, Youth Organizations

Grant Types: general support

Nonmonetary Support Types: cause-related marketing & promotion, donated equipment, in-kind services, loaned employees, and loaned executives

Note: Value of non-monetary support was not available.

Geographic Distribution: operating communities

Operating Locations: NE (Omaha)

GIVING OFFICERS
Margaret Shugrue: *CURR EMPL* asst vp, dir (pub rels): Norwest Bank NE

APPLICATION INFORMATION
Initial Approach: *Initial Contact:* brief letter of inquiry *Include Information On:* a description of organization; proof of tax-exempt status; list of officers and board members; statement outlining the purpose, including timeline and evaluation methods; complete budget for organization or project, including breakdown of programs and administrative expenses; list of contributors and amounts received in current and past year; and a financial statement *Deadlines:* none

GRANTS ANALYSIS
Total Grants: $700,000

Disclosure Period: 1994

Note: Recent grants are derived from a 1991 grants list provided by the company.

RECENT GRANTS

Library
Hastings Library Foundation, Hastings, NE

General
AkSarBen Agricultural Youth Foundation, Omaha, NE
American Red Cross, Omaha, NE
Bellevue College, Bellevue, NE
Boy Scouts of America, Omaha, NE
Boystown National Institute, Omaha, NE

Pamida, Inc. / Pamida Foundation

Sales: $656.91 million
Employees: 6,971
Parent Company: Pamida Holdings Corp.
Headquarters: Omaha, NE
SIC Major Group: General Merchandise Stores

CONTACT
Bret Williams
Manager, Community Relations
Pamida, Inc.
PO Box 3856
Omaha, NE 68103-0856
(402) 339-2400

FINANCIAL SUMMARY
Recent Giving: $35,750 (fiscal 1994);
$59,546 (fiscal 1991); $70,575 (fiscal 1989)
Assets: $111,496 (fiscal 1994); $271,395 (fiscal 1991); $258,080 (fiscal 1989)
Gifts Received: $50,000 (fiscal 1991); $30,000 (fiscal 1989)
Fiscal Note: In 1991, contributions were received from Pamida.
EIN: 47-0656225

CONTRIBUTIONS SUMMARY
Typical Recipients: • *Arts & Humanities:*
Arts Funds, General, Libraries, Museums/Galleries • *Civic & Public Affairs:* Botanical Gardens/Parks, Clubs, Community Foundations, General, Parades/Festivals, Safety, Urban & Community Affairs • *Education:* Agricultural Education, Colleges & Universities, Elementary Education (Public), General, Private Education (Precollege), School Volunteerism, Student Aid • *Health:* Children's Health/Hospitals, Emergency/Ambulance Services, General, Geriatric Health, Health Funds, Hospitals • *Social Services:* Community Centers, Community Service Organizations, Crime Prevention, Food/Clothing Distribution, General, People with Disabilities, Recreation & Athletics, Senior Services, Substance Abuse, Veterans, Youth Organizations

Grant Types: challenge, conference/seminar, emergency, endowment, and general support

Geographic Distribution: in headquarters and operating communities

Operating Locations: IA, IL, KS, MI, MN, MO, MT, ND, NE, SD, WI, WY

CORP. OFFICERS
Steven S. Fishman: *CURR EMPL* pres, dir: Pamida

GIVING OFFICERS
Richard W. Ramm: pres, treas *B* Omaha NE 1949 *ED* Univ NE 1972 *NONPR AFFIL* mem: Am Inst CPAs, Natl Assn Accts

Frank Washburn: vp

Byron L. Wolff: vp

APPLICATION INFORMATION
Initial Approach: Send a brief letter of inquiry including a description of organization, amount requested, purpose of funds sought, and proof of tax-exempt status. There are no deadlines.

Restrictions on Giving: Does not support individuals, religious organizations for sectarian purposes, political or lobbying groups, or organizations outside operating areas.

OTHER THINGS TO KNOW
Grant making is suspended until 1995.

GRANTS ANALYSIS
Total Grants: $35,750

Number of Grants: 44

Highest Grant: $1,000

Typical Range: $250 to $1,000

Disclosure Period: fiscal year ending January 31, 1994

Note: Recent grants are derived from a fiscal 1994 Form 990.

RECENT GRANTS

Library
1,000   Benson Public Library, Benson, MN — software for public use

General
1,000   Beulah Swimming Pool Slide Project, Beulah, ND — swimming pool slide replacement
1,000   Cavalier Jaycees, Cavalier, ND — new heater system for public pool
1,000   Chariton Community Foundation, Chariton, IA — new school playground equipment
1,000   City of Bluffton Senioride, Bluffton, IN — assist in continued services for senior citizen transportation
1,000   City of Louisa, Louisa, KY — fire fighting equipment

Quivey-Bay State Foundation

CONTACT
Ted Cannon
Secretary-Treasurer
Quivey-Bay State Fdn.
1515 E 20th St.
Scottsbluff, NE 69361
(308) 635-3701

FINANCIAL SUMMARY
Recent Giving: $163,150 (fiscal 1994); $161,200 (fiscal 1992); $147,932 (fiscal 1990)

Assets: $2,936,322 (fiscal 1994); $2,751,749 (fiscal 1992); $2,359,916 (fiscal 1990)

EIN: 47-6024159

CONTRIBUTIONS SUMMARY
Donor(s): M. S. Oulvey, Mrs. M. S. Quivey

Typical Recipients: • *Arts & Humanities:* Arts Centers, Historic Preservation, History & Archaeology, Libraries, Music • *Civic & Public Affairs:* Clubs, Economic Development, Urban & Community Affairs, Zoos/Aquariums • *Education:* Colleges & Universities, Education Funds, Engineering/Technological Education, General, Public Education (Precollege), Religious Education, Student Aid • *Health:* Cancer, Children's Health/Hospitals, Clinics/Medical Centers, Emergency/Ambulance Services, Health Organizations, Kidney, Prenatal Health Issues, Respiratory • *International:* Health Care/Hospitals • *Religion:* Churches, Religious Organizations, Religious Welfare • *Science:* Science Museums • *Social Services:* Animal Protection, Camps, Child Welfare, Community Centers, Community Service Organizations, Day Care, Delinquency & Criminal Rehabilitation, Homes, People with Disabilities, Recreation & Athletics, Scouts, United Funds/United Ways, Volunteer Services, YMCA/YWCA/YMHA/YWHA, Youth Organizations

Grant Types: general support and scholarship

Geographic Distribution: focus on NE

GIVING OFFICERS
Ted Cannon: secy, treas

APPLICATION INFORMATION
Initial Approach: Send brief letter of inquiry describing program. Include a description of organization, amount requested, purpose of funds sought, recently audited financial statement, and proof of tax-exempt status. There are no deadlines.

Restrictions on Giving: Does not support individuals or provide funds for endowments.

GRANTS ANALYSIS
Total Grants: $163,150

Number of Grants: 57

Highest Grant: $15,000

Typical Range: $100 to $15,000

Disclosure Period: fiscal year ending January 31, 1994

Note: Recent grants are derived from a fiscal 1994 Form 990.

RECENT GRANTS

Library
1,500	Friends of the Mitchell Library

General
15,000	YMCA
15,000	YMCA — capitol improvements
12,000	Regional West Medical Center, Scottsbluff, NE
10,000	Boy Scouts of America
10,000	Camp Fire Girls, Ft. Worth, TX

Reynolds Foundation, Edgar

CONTACT
Fred M. Glade, Jr.
Chairman
Edgar Reynolds Fdn.
204 N Walnut St.
Grand Island, NE 68801
(308) 384-0957

FINANCIAL SUMMARY
Recent Giving: $244,142 (1993); $170,950 (1990); $225,450 (1989)

Assets: $4,966,757 (1993); $4,362,741 (1990); $4,262,690 (1989)

EIN: 47-0589941

CONTRIBUTIONS SUMMARY
Donor(s): the late Edgar Reynolds

Typical Recipients: • *Arts & Humanities:* Libraries, Museums/Galleries • *Civic & Public Affairs:* Botanical Gardens/Parks, Community Foundations, Philanthropic Organizations • *Education:* Colleges & Universities, Community & Junior Colleges, Education Funds • *Health:* Clinics/Medical Centers, Hospitals • *Religion:* Religious Welfare • *Social Services:* Child Welfare, Crime Prevention, People with Disabilities, Recreation & Athletics, United Funds/United Ways, Youth Organizations

Grant Types: capital, research, and scholarship

Geographic Distribution: focus on NE

GIVING OFFICERS
Fred M. Glade, Jr.: chmn, dir
Robert Mattke: dir
Frances Reynolds: secy, treas, dir
Harlan Speer: dir

APPLICATION INFORMATION
Initial Approach: Application form required. There are no deadlines.

PUBLICATIONS
Application Guidelines

GRANTS ANALYSIS
Total Grants: $244,142

Number of Grants: 17

Highest Grant: $55,300

Typical Range: $500 to $40,000

Disclosure Period: 1993

Note: Recent grants are derived from a 1993 Form 990.

RECENT GRANTS

Library
2,000	Sidney Public Library, Sidney, NE

General
55,300	College Park Fund, Grand Island, NE
40,000	Grand Island Soccer League Grant, Grand Island, NE
25,000	Central Community College, Grand Island, NE
18,600	St. Francis Medical Center, Grand Island, NE
17,250	Central Nebraska Goodwill, Grand Island, NE — debt retirement and rehab center

Valmont Industries, Inc. / Valmont Foundation

Revenue: $438.76 million
Employees: 3,984
Headquarters: Valley, NE
SIC Major Group: Lighting Equipment Nec, Farm Machinery & Equipment, and Transformers Except Electronic

CONTACT
Robert B. Daugherty
President
Valmont Foundation
PO Box 358
Valley, NE 68064
(402) 359-2201

FINANCIAL SUMMARY
Recent Giving: $336,143 (fiscal 1994); $263,933 (fiscal 1993); $263,750 (fiscal 1992)

Assets: $13,092 (fiscal 1994); $48,938 (fiscal 1993); $36,920 (fiscal 1992)

Gifts Received: $300,019 (fiscal 1994); $275,027 (fiscal 1993); $295,034 (fiscal 1992)

Fiscal Note: Contributes through foundation only. Contributions are received from Valmont Industries.

EIN: 36-2895245

CONTRIBUTIONS SUMMARY
Typical Recipients: • *Arts & Humanities:* Arts Associations & Councils, Ballet, General, Libraries, Museums/Galleries, Music, Public Broadcasting, Theater • *Civic & Public Affairs:* Botanical Gardens/Parks, Business/Free Enterprise, Clubs, Parades/Festivals, Professional & Trade Associations, Women's Affairs • *Education:* Agricultural Education, Business Education, Colleges & Universities, Community & Junior Colleges, Economic Education, Education Funds, Engineering/Technological Education, Minority Education, Student Aid

463

- *Environment:* Wildlife Protection
- *Health:* Arthritis, Children's Health/Hospitals, Hospitals, Kidney, Medical Rehabilitation, Nutrition, Single-Disease Health Associations • *Religion:* Religious Organizations, Religious Welfare • *Science:* Science Exhibits & Fairs • *Social Services:* Child Welfare, People with Disabilities, Recreation & Athletics, Senior Services, United Funds/United Ways, Youth Organizations

Grant Types: general support

Geographic Distribution: primarily in Nebraska; limited nationally

Operating Locations: CO (Ft. Collins), IL (Danville), IN (Elkhart), NE (Omaha, Valley), OK (Tulsa), TX (Brenham, El Paso), UT (Salt Lake City)

CORP. OFFICERS

Mogens C. Bay: *B* 1953 *CURR EMPL* pres, ceo: Valmont Indus Inc *CORP AFFIL* chmn, dir: Am Lighting Standards Corp

Robert B. Daugherty: *B* 1922 *CURR EMPL* chmn, dir: Valmont Indus Inc *CORP AFFIL* dir: ConAgra Inc, FirsTier Fin Inc, Peter Kiewit Sons Inc, KN Energy *NONPR AFFIL* trust: Hastings Coll *PHIL AFFIL* chmn: Peter Kiewit Foundation; off: ConAgra Foundation, Robert B. Daugherty Foundation

Terry James McClain: *B* Osmond NE 1948 *ED* Wayne St Univ 1970; Univ SD 1971 *CURR EMPL* vp, cfo: Valmont Indus Inc *CORP AFFIL* treas, dir: Valmont NW Inc *NONPR AFFIL* mem: Fin Execs Inst

GIVING OFFICERS

Robert B. Daugherty: pres *CURR EMPL* chmn, dir: Valmont Indus Inc *PHIL AFFIL* chmn: Peter Kiewit Foundation; off: ConAgra Foundation, Robert B. Daugherty Foundation (see above)

Thomas P. Egan, Jr.: off *B* 1948 *ED* Creighton Univ BSBA 1971; Creighton Univ JD 1973 *CURR EMPL* vp, corp couns, secy: Valmont Indus Inc *CORP AFFIL* secy, dir: Valmont Electric Inc, Valmont NW Inc; vp, dir: Am Lighting Standards Corp

Terry James McClain: dir *CURR EMPL* vp, cfo: Valmont Indus Inc (see above)

Brian C. Stanley: off *B* 1942 *CURR EMPL* vp: Valmont Indus Inc *CORP AFFIL* treas, dir: Valmont Electric Inc

APPLICATION INFORMATION

Initial Approach: *Initial Contact:* letter of solicitation *Deadlines:* none

GRANTS ANALYSIS

Total Grants: $336,143

Number of Grants: 65

Highest Grant: $65,000

Average Grant: $5,171

Typical Range: $250 to $7,000

Disclosure Period: fiscal year ending February 28, 1994

Note: Recent grants are derived from a fiscal 1994 Form 990.

RECENT GRANTS

General

65,000	United Way of the Midlands, Omaha, NE
25,000	Creighton University, Omaha, NE
20,000	Aksarben Agriculture Youth Foundation, Omaha, NE
20,000	Boy Scouts of America Mid-America Council, Kansas City, MO
20,000	Fremont Family YMCA, Fremont, NE

NEVADA

Cord Foundation, E. L.

CONTACT
William O. Bradley
Trustee
E. L. Cord Foundation
200 Court St.
Reno, NV 89501
(702) 323-0373

FINANCIAL SUMMARY
Recent Giving: $2,880,610 (1994); $2,679,289 (1992); $2,604,800 (1991)

Assets: $57,831,193 (1992); $58,233,082 (1991); $55,712,907 (1990)

EIN: 36-6072793

CONTRIBUTIONS SUMMARY
Donor(s): The foundation was established in 1962 by the late E. L. Cord .

Typical Recipients: • *Arts & Humanities:* Arts Associations & Councils, Arts Centers, Dance, Historic Preservation, History & Archaeology, Libraries, Museums/Galleries, Music, Opera, Performing Arts, Public Broadcasting, Theater • *Civic & Public Affairs:* Botanical Gardens/Parks, General, Hispanic Affairs, Law & Justice, Legal Aid, Women's Affairs • *Education:* Business Education, Colleges & Universities, Community & Junior Colleges, Elementary Education (Public), Engineering/Technological Education, Legal Education, Medical Education, Private Education (Precollege), Public Education (Precollege), Science/Mathematics Education, Secondary Education (Public), Student Aid • *Environment:* Research • *Health:* Children's Health/Hospitals, Diabetes, Emergency/Ambulance Services, Hospitals, Single-Disease Health Associations • *Religion:* Churches, Religious Welfare • *Science:* Scientific Labs • *Social Services:* Child Welfare, Community Service Organizations, Counseling, Domestic Violence, Food/Clothing Distribution, People with Disabilities, Recreation & Athletics, Scouts, Shelters/Homelessness, Substance Abuse, United Funds/United Ways, YMCA/YWCA/YMHA/YWHA, Youth Organizations

Grant Types: general support

Geographic Distribution: national, with an emphasis on Nevada

GIVING OFFICERS
William O. Bradley: trust

Thomas Patrick Ford: trust *B* Wausau WI 1918 *ED* Univ Notre Dame PhB 1940; Harvard Univ LLB 1947 *CLUB AFFIL* Everglades, Madison Beach, River *PHIL AFFIL* dir, mem legal comm, chmn & mem dirs grant program comm: W. M. Keck Foundation

APPLICATION INFORMATION
Initial Approach:

The foundation requests applicants write the foundation for application procedures.

Applications are accepted throughout the year and held until the next meeting of the board of trustees.

PUBLICATIONS
Informational brochure

GRANTS ANALYSIS
Total Grants: $2,880,610

Number of Grants: 88

Highest Grant: $250,000

Average Grant: $32,734

Typical Range: $5,000 to $50,000

Disclosure Period: 1994

Note: Recent grants are derived from a list of approved grants for 1994.

RECENT GRANTS

Library

30,000	University of Nevada Reno Savitt Medical Library, Reno, NV
25,000	White Pine County Public Library

General

100,000	University of Nevada College of Education, Reno, NV
90,000	University of Nevada Reno College of Human and Community Sciences, Reno, NV
75,000	Boys and Girls Club of Truckee Meadows, Reno, NV
75,000	National Council of Juvenile and Family Court Judges, Reno, NV
75,000	Truckee Meadows Boys and Girls Club, Reno, NV

Hawkins Foundation, Robert Z.

CONTACT
William H. Wallace, Jr.
Chairman
Robert Z. Hawkins Foundation
One E Liberty St., Ste. 509
Reno, NV 89501
(702) 786-1105

FINANCIAL SUMMARY
Recent Giving: $900,000 (1995 est.); $900,000 (1994 approx.); $600,000 (1993 approx.)

Assets: $16,500,000 (1995 est.); $16,500,000 (1994 approx.); $16,500,000 (1993 approx.)

Gifts Received: $948,018 (1991)

Fiscal Note: In 1991, contributions were received from the trust fund of Kathryn Ackley Hawkins.

EIN: 88-0162645

CONTRIBUTIONS SUMMARY
Donor(s): The foundation was established in 1980 by the Kathryn Ackley Hawkins Trust.

Typical Recipients: • *Arts & Humanities:* Libraries, Music, Public Broadcasting • *Civic & Public Affairs:* Business/Free Enterprise, Housing • *Education:* Business Education, Colleges & Universities, Community & Junior Colleges, Engineering/Technological Education, Public Education (Precollege), Secondary Education (Public) • *Health:* Children's Health/Hospitals, Long-Term Care • *Religion:* Religious Organizations, Religious Welfare • *Social Services:* Animal Protection, Child Welfare, Community Service Organizations, Counseling, Family Services, Food/Clothing Distribution, People with Disabilities, Recreation & Athletics, United Funds/United Ways, Youth Organizations

Grant Types: project

Geographic Distribution: limited to northern Nevada; focus on Reno

GIVING OFFICERS
Carolyn Bernard: trust

Prince A. Hawkins: trust

Bill A. Ligon: trust

William H. Wallace, Jr.: chmn *B* Senatobia MS 1933 *ED* Univ IL PhD; Univ MS BBA; Univ MS MBA

APPLICATION INFORMATION
Initial Approach:

The foundation requests applications be made in writing.

The foundation has no deadline for submitting proposals.

Restrictions on Giving: The foundation reports that grants are restricted to organizations within the state of Nevada that have tax-exempt status and operate for charitable and humanitarian purposes. The foundation does not make grants to individuals.

OTHER THINGS TO KNOW
The Bank of Nevada acts as a corporate trustee for the foundation.

GRANTS ANALYSIS
Total Grants: $442,425

Number of Grants: 79

Highest Grant: $34,950

Average Grant: $5,224*

Typical Range: $1,000 to $6,000

Disclosure Period: 1992

Note: Average grant figure excludes highest grant of $34,950. Recent grants are derived from a 1992 Form 990.

RECENT GRANTS
Library
5,000   Friends of Washoe County Library, Reno, NV — assistance grant

General
21,000   American Animal Assistance Society, Reno, NV — assistance grant
20,000   Assistance League, Reno, NV — assistance grant
20,000   Truckee Meadows Boys and Girls Club, Sparks, NV — assistance grant
20,000   University of Nevada Reno School of Engineering, Reno, NV — educational
20,000   YMCA, Reno, NV — religious

May Foundation, Wilbur

CONTACT
Anita May Rosenstein
President
Wilbur May Foundation
c/o Suellen Fulstone
Woodburn & Widge
One E First St., Ste. 1600
Reno, NV 89505
Note: The foundation does not list a phone number.

FINANCIAL SUMMARY
Recent Giving: $1,637,425 (fiscal 1994); $1,036,000 (fiscal 1992); $1,407,200 (fiscal 1991)

Assets: $35,569,548 (fiscal 1994); $34,989,502 (fiscal 1992); $34,537,985 (fiscal 1991)

EIN: 94-3126741

CONTRIBUTIONS SUMMARY
Donor(s): The Wilbur May Foundation was established in California in 1951. Mr. Wilbur May died in 1982.

Typical Recipients: • *Arts & Humanities:* Dance, Libraries, Visual Arts • *Civic & Public Affairs:* Law & Justice, Municipalities/Towns, Public Policy • *Education:* Agricultural Education, Colleges & Universities • *Health:* Health Organizations, Hospitals, Medical Rehabilitation, Medical Research, Single-Disease Health Associations • *Social Services:* Delinquency & Criminal Rehabilitation, Emergency Relief, Food/Clothing Distribution, Homes, People with Disabilities, Recreation & Athletics, United Funds/United Ways, Youth Organizations

Grant Types: capital, general support, operating expenses, and research

Geographic Distribution: generally in Reno, NV, and Southern California, primarily the Los Angeles area

GIVING OFFICERS
Aaron Clark: vp

Suellen Fulstone: vp, legal counsel

Dee May: vp

Anita May Rosenstein: pres

Mary Turner: secy

APPLICATION INFORMATION
Initial Approach:

Applicants should send a letter of proposal to the foundation.

The foundation reports no deadlines for applications or specific restrictions on funding for organizations.

The board generally meets in August to review proposals. Funding notification generally occurs after the meeting.

Restrictions on Giving: The foundation does not make grants to individuals.

GRANTS ANALYSIS
Total Grants: $1,637,425

Number of Grants: 66

Highest Grant: $670,425

Average Grant: $14,877*

Typical Range: $5,000 to $20,000

Disclosure Period: fiscal year ending May 31, 1994

Note: The average grant figure excludes the largest grant of $670,425. Recent grants are derived from a fiscal 1992 Form 990.

RECENT GRANTS
Library
20,000   Nevada County Library

General
500,000   Washoe County Parks and Recreation, Washoe, NV
75,000   Jules Stein Eye Institute, Los Angeles, CA
50,000   Annie Malone Children's Home, St. Louis,
50,000   Western Cardiac Foundation, Los Angeles, CA
50,000   YWCA

PriMerit Bank / PriMerit Bank Charitable Foundation

Sales: $229.6 million
Employees: 600
Parent Company: Southwest Gas Corp.
Headquarters: Las Vegas, NV
SIC Major Group: Depository Institutions and Nondepository Institutions

CONTACT
Dan J. Cheever
President, Chief Executive Officer
PriMerit Bank
3300 W Sahara Ave.
Las Vegas, NV 89102
(702) 362-5555

FINANCIAL SUMMARY
Fiscal Note: Annual Giving Range: less than $100,000

EIN: 88-0223637

CONTRIBUTIONS SUMMARY

Typical Recipients: • *Arts & Humanities:* Arts Outreach, General, Historic Preservation, Libraries, Museums/Galleries • *Civic & Public Affairs:* Economic Development, Employment/Job Training, General, Urban & Community Affairs • *Education:* Afterschool/Enrichment Programs, Business-School Partnerships, Colleges & Universities, Community & Junior Colleges, Continuing Education, Education Associations, Elementary Education (Public), General, Public Education (Precollege), Secondary Education (Public) • *Health:* Adolescent Health Issues, General, Hospices • *Social Services:* At-Risk Youth, Camps, Community Centers, Community Service Organizations, Delinquency & Criminal Rehabilitation, Domestic Violence, Family Planning, Family Services, General, Shelters/Homelessness, Substance Abuse, United Funds/United Ways, Youth Organizations

Grant Types: challenge, employee matching gifts, general support, multiyear/continuing support, and project

Nonmonetary Support Types: donated equipment, loaned employees, and loaned executives

Geographic Distribution: only in headquarters area

Operating Locations: NV (Boulder City, Carson City, Gardnerville, Henderson, Las Vegas, Reno, Sparks)

CORP. OFFICERS

Dan J. Cheever: *CURR EMPL* pres, ceo, dir: PriMerit Bank

Harry E. Hinderliter: *CURR EMPL* chief admin off, corp secy, chief counc: PriMerit Bank

Bernadette M. Mashas: *CURR EMPL* cfo, treas: PriMerit Bank

GIVING OFFICERS

Dan J. Cheever: pres *CURR EMPL* pres, ceo, dir: PriMerit Bank (see above)

APPLICATION INFORMATION

Initial Approach: Send a brief letter of inquiry and a full proposal. Include a description of organization, amount requested, purpose of funds sought, recently audited financial statement, and proof of tax-exempt status.

Restrictions on Giving: Does not support individuals, religious organizations for sectarian purposes, political or lobbying groups, or organizations outside operating areas.

GRANTS ANALYSIS

Typical Range: $1,000 to $2,500

Note: Recent grants are derived from a grants list provided by company in 1994.

RECENT GRANTS

General
Assistance League/Operation School Bell, Las Vegas, NV
CARE Chest of Sierra Nevada, Reno, NV
Children's Cabinet, Reno, NV
HELP of Southern Nevada, Las Vegas, NV

Las Vegas Natural History Museum, Las Vegas, NV

Sierra Pacific Resources / Sierra Pacific Resources Charitable Foundation

Revenue: $528.08 million
Employees: 1,840
Headquarters: Reno, NV
SIC Major Group: Electric, Gas & Sanitary Services, Holding & Other Investment Offices, and Real Estate

---

CONTACT
Vida Dietz
Administrator
Sierra Pacific Resources Charitable Foundation
PO Box 30150
Reno, NV 89520

FINANCIAL SUMMARY

Recent Giving: $236,600 (1993); $259,770 (1992); $165,459 (1989)

Assets: $269,542 (1992); $146,479 (1989)

Gifts Received: $209,730 (1992); $310,205 (1989)

Fiscal Note: In 1992, contributions were received from Sierra Pacific Resources.

EIN: 88-0244735

CONTRIBUTIONS SUMMARY

Typical Recipients: • *Arts & Humanities:* Arts Centers, Arts Funds, Community Arts, General, Libraries, Museums/Galleries, Music, Opera, Public Broadcasting, Theater • *Civic & Public Affairs:* African American Affairs, Business/Free Enterprise, Clubs, Economic Development, General, Municipalities/Towns, Parades/Festivals, Professional & Trade Associations, Safety • *Education:* Agricultural Education, Business Education, Colleges & Universities, Community & Junior Colleges, General, Legal Education, Public Education (Precollege), Religious Education • *Environment:* General • *Health:* Children's Health/Hospitals, Diabetes, Heart, Hospitals, Mental Health, Respiratory, Single-Disease Health Associations • *Religion:* Jewish Causes, Religious Welfare • *Science:* Scientific Research • *Social Services:* Camps, Community Service Organizations, Delinquency & Criminal Rehabilitation, Family Planning, General, People with Disabilities, United Funds/United Ways, Youth Organizations

Grant Types: general support

Geographic Distribution: in headquarters and operating communities, including northern NV and northeastern CA

Operating Locations: NV (Reno)

CORP. OFFICERS
Walter M. Higgins: *CURR EMPL* chmn, pres, ceo, dir: Sierra Pacific Resources

GIVING OFFICERS
Vida Dietz: admin
Rosemary Flores: dir

APPLICATION INFORMATION

Initial Approach: Send a brief letter of inquiry. Include a description of organization, amount requested, purpose of funds sought, and proof of tax-exempt status. There are no deadlines.

Restrictions on Giving: The foundation does not make grants to individuals. Does not fund scholarships; does not sponsor or fund athletic or sporting events/ teams; does not fund relious organizations.

GRANTS ANALYSIS

Total Grants: $259,770

Number of Grants: 258

Highest Grant: $100,000

Typical Range: $50 to $10,000

Disclosure Period: 1992

Note: Recent grants are derived from a 1992 Form 990.

RECENT GRANTS

Library

750	Library of Congress, Washington, DC

General

100,000	University of Nevada Reno Foundation, Reno, NV
10,000	Desert Research Institute, Seabrook, TX
9,375	United Way of Northern Nevada, Reno, NV
9,375	United Way of Northern Nevada, Reno, NV
9,375	United Way of Northern Nevada, Reno, NV

Wiegand Foundation, E. L.

CONTACT
Kristen A. Avansino
President and Executive Director
E. L. Wiegand Foundation
Wiegand Center
165 W Liberty St.
Reno, NV 89501
(702) 333-0310

FINANCIAL SUMMARY

Recent Giving: $3,800,000 (fiscal 1995 est.); $3,950,065 (fiscal 1994); $4,266,185 (fiscal 1993)

Assets: $82,000,000 (fiscal 1995 est.); $82,000,000 (fiscal 1994 approx.); $83,253,674 (fiscal 1993)

Gifts Received: $40,000 (fiscal 1995 est.); $106,783 (fiscal 1994); $53,600 (fiscal 1993)

EIN: 94-2839372

CONTRIBUTIONS SUMMARY

Donor(s): Edwin L. Wiegand was born in Dover, OH, in 1891. He experimented with electricity as a boy and concluded that the use of electricity for heating afforded the most important growth potential for the future. In 1915, he obtained his first patent on a metal-sheathed, refractory-insulated electric heating element, and two years later founded the Edwin L. Wiegand Company in Pittsburgh. In a small room with one employee, he manufactured the first successful resistance heating units. Under the trade name "Chromalox," Mr. Wiegand developed and manufactured heating elements for home appliances and industrial uses that are still the heart of many electric appliances today. In 1968, he merged his company with Emerson Electric Company of St. Louis, MO. He moved to Reno, NV, in 1971 and became an active participant in Miami Oil Producers, especially in their development of oil and gas properties. He served on the Miami board until his death at the age of 88.

The foundation was established in 1982 for general charitable purposes. To foster the religious beliefs of E.L. Wiegand, a part of the annual grants are made to Roman Catholic charitable institutions.

Typical Recipients: • *Arts & Humanities:* Ballet, Libraries, Museums/Galleries, Music, Performing Arts, Public Broadcasting • *Civic & Public Affairs:* Civil Rights, Law & Justice, Legal Aid, Public Policy • *Education:* Arts/Humanities Education, Business Education, Colleges & Universities, Elementary Education (Private), Legal Education, Medical Education, Private Education (Precollege), Religious Education, Science/Mathematics Education, Secondary Education (Private), Secondary Education (Public) • *Health:* Cancer, Children's Health/Hospitals, Clinics/Medical Centers, Diabetes, Heart, Hospitals, Long-Term Care, Medical Research • *International:* International Affairs • *Religion:* Dioceses, Religious Organizations, Religious Welfare • *Science:* Science Museums • *Social Services:* Camps, Community Service Organizations, Special Olympics, YMCA/YWCA/YMHA/YWHA, Youth Organizations

Grant Types: project

Geographic Distribution: Nevada, California, Oregon, Idaho, Utah, Arizona, District of Columbia, and New York City

GIVING OFFICERS

Kristen A. Avansino: pres, exec dir

Raymond C. Avansino, Jr.: chmn, trust *B* 1944 *CURR EMPL* pres, coo, dir: Hilton Hotels Corp

James T. Carrico: treas

Frank Joseph Fahrenkopf, Jr.: trust *B* Brooklyn NY 1939 *ED* Univ NV BA 1962; Univ CA Berkeley JD 1965 *CURR EMPL* ptnr: Hogan & Hartson *NONPR AFFIL* bd dir: Natl Endowment Democracy; chmn: Natl Judical Coll Counc Future; co-chmn: Commn Natl Political Conventions, Natl Commn Presidential Debates; dep chmn: Intl Democracy Union; faculty mem: Natl Judicial Coll; mem: Alpha Tau Omega, Am Bar Assn, Am Judicature Soc, Am Trial Lawyers Assn, Barristers Club NV, Commercial Law League Am, Execs Assn Reno, Natl Assn Gaming Attys, Northern NV Trial Lawyers Assn, Washoe County Bar Assn; vchmn: Ctr Democratic

Harvey C. Fruehauf, Jr.: trust *B* Grosse Pointe Park MI 1929 *ED* Univ MI 1952 *CURR EMPL* pres, dir: HCF Enterprises *CORP AFFIL* chmn: Miami Oil Producers; dir: Georgia Pacific Corp; pres, treas, dir: HCF Realty *PHIL AFFIL* pres, dir: Fruehauf Foundation

Mario Joseph Gabelli: trust *B* New York NY 1942 *ED* Fordham Univ BS 1965; Columbia Univ MBA 1967 *CURR EMPL* fdr, chmn: Gabelli & Co *CORP AFFIL* chmn: Lynch Corp; chmn, ceo: Gabelli Funds; chmn, pres, ceo: Gabelli Equity Trust; dir: Balfour Maclaine Corp, Gabelli Intl Ltd, US Home Health Care Corp *NONPR AFFIL* mem: Entertainment Analysts NY, NY Soc Auto Analysts, NY Soc Security Analysts; mem, dir: Columbia Univ Alumni Assn; trust: Fordham Prep Sch *PHIL AFFIL* pres, dir: Gabelli Foundation

Joanne C. Hildahl: vp (grants program)

Michael J. Melarkey: vp, secy *PHIL AFFIL* secy: Bretzlaff Foundation

APPLICATION INFORMATION
Initial Approach:

Applicants must submit a letter of inquiry describing the organization and the proposed request.

Proposals must be submitted with an original Application for Grant form, a description of the project, an itemized budget for the project, project starting date and schedule, qualifications of key personnel, a brief history of the institution, a list of officers and their affiliations, the name of any employee or officer of the foundation who is associated with the applicant, a copy of the IRS tax-exempt determination letter, a copy of current documentary evidence from the organization's state classifying the applicant as tax-exempt, a copy of the most recent 990, current audited financial statements, current interim financial statements, a financial budget for the current year, a statement of the applicant's major sources of support for the last five years, and an indication of how the program will be evaluated upon its completion.

Letters of inquiry are accepted throughout the year. Upon receiving the Application for Grant Form, applicants are notified of deadlines.

The board usually meets three times a year, generally in February, June and October.

Restrictions on Giving: Grants will not be given for the following purposes: endowments; debt retirement or operating deficits; general, ordinary, and normal operations or their extension, including the repair and maintenance of facilities; emergency funding; general fundraising events, appeals, campaigns, dinners, or mass mailings; loans; distribution of funds to beneficiaries; the influence of legislation or elections; multi-year grants, production of documentaries, publications, films, or media presentations; religious institutions for the construction or restoration of buildings; or to institutions

that have been in existence for less than five years; federal, state, or local government agencies or institutions; institutions supported by public tax funds; institutions served by the United Way; or individuals.

OTHER THINGS TO KNOW

There are specific geographic restrictions for program areas. Education grants are made in Nevada, California, Oregon, Idaho, Utah, and Arizona. Health and medical research grants are made in Nevada, California, Oregon, Idaho, Utah, and Arizona. Public affairs grants are made in Nevada, California, Washington, DC, and New York City. Civic and community affairs grants are made in Nevada and California. Arts and cultural affairs grants are made in Nevada and California.

A portion of the foundation's fund balance is held as a special fund for the benefit of Roman Catholic charitable organizations.

PUBLICATIONS

Informational booklet avaliable upon request

GRANTS ANALYSIS

Total Grants: $3,950,065

Number of Grants: 89

Highest Grant: $196,000

Average Grant: $44,383

Typical Range: $5,000 to $100,000

Disclosure Period: fiscal year ending October 31, 1994

Note: Recent grants are derived from a fiscal 1993 Form 990.

RECENT GRANTS

Library
55,000	School of the Sacred Heart, San Francisco, CA — library automation equipment
36,400	St. Mary of the Valley School, Beaverton, OR — library automation; equipment

General
360,000	YMCA of the Sierra, Reno, NV — Wiegand Youth Center expansion
119,000	Washington Legal Foundation, Washington, DC — conference center furnishings
115,000	Santa Clara University, Santa Clara, CA — media center equipment
109,250	Georgetown University, Washington, DC — E.L. Wiegand Distinguished Visitor
107,430	Loyola Marymount University, Los Angeles, CA — science laboratory renovation

NEW HAMPSHIRE

Bean Foundation, Norwin S. and Elizabeth N.

CONTACT
Norwin S. and Elizabeth N. Bean Fdn.
c/o NH Charitable Fund
PO Box 1335
Concord, NH 03302-1335
(603) 225-6641

FINANCIAL SUMMARY
Recent Giving: $364,532 (1993); $402,850 (1992); $319,172 (1990)
Assets: $10,492,212 (1993); $10,141,309 (1992); $8,382,945 (1990)
EIN: 02-6013381

CONTRIBUTIONS SUMMARY
Donor(s): the late Norwin S. Bean, the late Elizabeth N. Bean

Typical Recipients: • *Arts & Humanities:* Arts Associations & Councils, Arts Centers, Arts Festivals, Arts Institutes, Arts Outreach, Community Arts, History & Archaeology, Libraries, Museums/Galleries, Music, Performing Arts, Theater • *Civic & Public Affairs:* Employment/Job Training, General, Housing, Municipalities/Towns, Native American Affairs, Philanthropic Organizations, Urban & Community Affairs, Women's Affairs • *Education:* Arts/Humanities Education, Colleges & Universities, Education Reform, Faculty Development, Preschool Education, Private Education (Precollege), School Volunteerism, Science/Mathematics Education, Secondary Education (Private), Secondary Education (Public) • *Environment:* General, Resource Conservation • *Health:* AIDS/HIV, Cancer, Children's Health/Hospitals, Clinics/Medical Centers, Health Organizations, Mental Health, Nursing Services, Prenatal Health Issues • *Religion:* Religious Welfare • *Social Services:* At-Risk Youth, Big Brother/Big Sister, Child Welfare, Community Service Organizations, Counseling, Delinquency & Criminal Rehabilitation, Family Services, Food/Clothing Distribution, People with Disabilities, Shelters/Homelessness, Substance Abuse, United Funds/United Ways, YMCA/YWCA/YMHA/YWHA, Youth Organizations

Grant Types: conference/seminar, emergency, general support, loan, project, scholarship, and seed money

Geographic Distribution: limited to Amherst and Manchester, NH

GIVING OFFICERS
Peter F. Bergen: trust

Carol J. Descoteaux: trust *B* Nashua NH 1948 *ED* Norte Dame Coll BA 1970; Boston Coll MEd 1974; Univ Notre Dame MA 1984; Univ Notre Dame PhD 1985 *CORP AFFIL* mem: Am Assn Univ Women, Coll Theology Soc Am, NH Women Higher Ed,

NH Womens Forum, Soc Christian Ethics *NONPR AFFIL* mem: Am Academy Rel, Catholic Med Ctr, Un Way Manchester; pres: Fed Holy Cross Colls, Notre Dame Col; treas: NH Coll & Univ Counc; trust: Kings Coll, NH Higher Ed Assistance Fdn

Thomas J. Donavan: trust

John Roy McLane, Jr.: trust *B* Manchester NH 1916 *CURR EMPL* dir: McLane Graf Raulerson & Middleton *NONPR AFFIL* dir: Palace Theatre Trust; mem: Am Bar Assn, Manchester Bar Assn, NH Bar Assn

James A. Shanahan, Jr.: trust *PHIL AFFIL* trust: McIninch Foundation

APPLICATION INFORMATION
Initial Approach: Include a description of organization, amount requested, purpose of funds sought, recently audited financial statement, and proof of tax-exempt status. Send a brief letter of inquiry. Deadlines are December 1, April 1, and September 1 for meetings in February, June, and November.

Restrictions on Giving: Does not support individuals or provide funds for scholarships.

PUBLICATIONS
Annual Report, Informational Brochure (including application guidelines)

GRANTS ANALYSIS
Total Grants: $364,532
Number of Grants: 34
Highest Grant: $100,000
Typical Range: $5,000 to $10,000
Disclosure Period: 1993
Note: Recent grants are derived from a 1993 Form 990.

RECENT GRANTS
Library
4,380   Amherst Town Library, Amherst, NH — to purchase and install on-line phone access catalogs to replace the card catalog system

General
40,000   Manchester Community Health Center, Manchester, NH — to purchase capital equipment for the new facility
35,000   Manchester Neighborhood Housing Services, Manchester, NH — for operating support to continue revitalization efforts in the center city neighborhood
28,600   New Hampshire Charitable Foundation, Concord, NH — for annual support to affiliated trusts, general programming, and activities which strengthen philanthorophy in New Hampshire
20,000   New Hampshire Community Loan Fund, Concord, NH — to establish the Families in Transition program as an

independent nonprofit organization serving homeless women and children
17,500   New Hampshire Charitable Foundation, Concord, NH — to support the capital campaign for a new building

Cogswell Benevolent Trust

CONTACT
David P. Goodwin
Trustee
Cogswell Benevolent Trust
1001 Elm St.
Manchester, NH 03101
(603) 622-4013

FINANCIAL SUMMARY
Recent Giving: $619,915 (1993); $367,256 (1992); $421,215 (1991)
Assets: $13,734,592 (1993); $12,464,703 (1992); $11,925,812 (1991)
EIN: 02-0235690

CONTRIBUTIONS SUMMARY
Donor(s): the late Leander A. Cogswell

Typical Recipients: • *Arts & Humanities:* Community Arts, History & Archaeology, Libraries, Museums/Galleries, Music, Public Broadcasting, Theater • *Civic & Public Affairs:* Botanical Gardens/Parks, Ethnic Organizations, Housing, Urban & Community Affairs • *Education:* Arts/Humanities Education, Colleges & Universities, Minority Education, Private Education (Precollege), Science/Mathematics Education, Secondary Education (Private), Student Aid • *Environment:* General, Resource Conservation • *Health:* AIDS/HIV, Children's Health/Hospitals, Emergency/Ambulance Services, Eyes/Blindness, Hospitals, Long-Term Care, Mental Health, Prenatal Health Issues, Research/Studies Institutes • *Religion:* Churches, Religious Welfare • *Social Services:* Child Welfare, Community Service Organizations, Family Services, People with Disabilities, Shelters/Homelessness, United Funds/United Ways, Youth Organizations

Grant Types: endowment, general support, and operating expenses

Geographic Distribution: focus on NH Trust restricted by will to donate 90 percent of funds within New Hampshire

GIVING OFFICERS
David P. Goodwin: trust
Mark Northridge: trust
Theodore Wadleigh: trust

APPLICATION INFORMATION
Initial Approach: Send brief letter of inquiry describing program or project. Include a description of organization, amount requested, purpose of funds sought, recently audited financial statement, and proof of tax-exempt status. There are no deadlines.

Restrictions on Giving: Donates 90 percent of grants within New Hampshire.

GRANTS ANALYSIS

Total Grants: $619,915

Number of Grants: 86

Highest Grant: $50,000

Typical Range: $600 to $50,000

Disclosure Period: 1993

Note: Recent grants are derived from a 1992 Form 990.

RECENT GRANTS

Library

5,000	New Hampshire State Library, NH — video equipment

General

50,000	University of New Hampshire Foundation, Manchester, NH — Honors program challenge
40,000	Manchester Neighborhood Housing Services - to revitilize Manchester center city, Manchester, NH
28,000	United Way, Manchester, NH
20,000	Healthy Baby Fund, Manchester, NH
15,000	Havenwood Heritage Heights, Concord, NH — rugs, furniture

Dingman Foundation, Michael D.

CONTACT

Alan M. Renfrew
Vice President and Assistant Secretary
Michael D. Dingman Fdn.
One Liberty Ln.
Hampton, NH 03842
(603) 926-5911

FINANCIAL SUMMARY

Recent Giving: $700,000 (1993); $229,750 (1992); $1,403,580 (1990)

Assets: $7,154,413 (1993); $5,167,040 (1992); $4,250,506 (1990)

Gifts Received: 1,130,810 (1993); $96,000 (1992); $3,021,615 (1990)

Fiscal Note: In 1993, contributions were received from Michael D. Dingman ($1,058,810), Lincolnshire, Inc. ($24,000), Winthrop, Inc. ($24,000), and Chatam, Inc. ($24,000).

EIN: 94-3080164

CONTRIBUTIONS SUMMARY

Typical Recipients: • *Arts & Humanities:* History & Archaeology, Libraries, Museums/Galleries, Music, Theater • *Civic & Public Affairs:* Housing, Legal Aid, Public Policy, Safety, Zoos/Aquariums • *Education:* Business Education, Colleges & Universities, Private Education (Precollege) • *Environment:* General • *Health:* Clinics/Medical Centers, Emergency/Ambulance Services, Eyes/Blindness, Health Organizations, Hospices, Hospitals, Medical Research, Single-Disease Health Associations • *International:* Foreign Educational Institutions, Health Care/Hospitals • *Religion:* Churches, Religious Organizations, Religious Welfare • *Social Services:* Animal Protection, Camps, Crime Prevention, Volunteer Services, Youth Organizations

Grant Types: department and general support

Geographic Distribution: national

GIVING OFFICERS

Edwin H. Danenhauer: asst secy

Elizabeth T. Dingman: vp

Michael David Dingman: pres *B* New Haven CT 1931 *ED* Univ MD *CURR EMPL* chmn, ceo: Gen Chem Group *PHIL AFFIL* dir, ptnr: Chatam Inc.; trust: John A. Hartford Foundation; dir: Devonshire Trust; dir, ptnr: Lincolnshire; dir: Henley Manufacturing Charitable Foundation

Barbara A. Prina: secy

Alan M. Renfrew: vp, asst secy

APPLICATION INFORMATION

Initial Approach: Send a brief letter of inquiry. There are no deadlines.

GRANTS ANALYSIS

Total Grants: $700,000

Number of Grants: 44

Highest Grant: $206,000

Typical Range: $1,000 to $10,000

Disclosure Period: 1993

Note: Recent grants are derived from a 1993 Form 990.

RECENT GRANTS

Library

2,000	Jackson Memorial Library, Jackson, NH

General

100,000	Aspen Institute, Queenstown, MD
50,000	First Presbyterian Church, Jasper, IN
50,000	St. Georges School, Middletown, RI
42,500	Hun School, Princeton, NJ
40,000	Berwick Academy, Exeter, NH

Fuller Foundation

CONTACT

John T. Bottomley
Executive Director
Fuller Fdn.
PO Box 461
Rye Beach, NH 03871
(603) 964-8998

FINANCIAL SUMMARY

Recent Giving: $401,200 (1993); $409,660 (1992); $394,795 (1991)

Assets: $10,463,214 (1993); $9,885,649 (1992); $9,475,226 (1991)

EIN: 04-2241130

CONTRIBUTIONS SUMMARY

Donor(s): the late Alvan T. Fuller, Sr.

Typical Recipients: • *Arts & Humanities:* Historic Preservation, Libraries, Music, Performing Arts • *Civic & Public Affairs:* General, Philanthropic Organizations • *Education:* Engineering/Technological Education, Leadership Training, Private Education (Precollege) • *Environment:* General • *Health:* AIDS/HIV, Cancer • *Social Services:* Family Services, Food/Clothing Distribution, Scouts

Geographic Distribution: focus on Boston, MA, and the immediate seacoast area of NH

GIVING OFFICERS

Miranda Fuller Bocko: trust

John T. Bottomley: exec dir, trust

Lydia Fuller Bottomley: trust

Stephen D. Bottomley: trust

Anne Fuller Donovan: trust

Peter Fuller: trust *B* Boston MA 1923 *ED* Harvard Univ *CURR EMPL* chmn, pres: Cadillac Automobile Co Boston *CORP AFFIL* pres, dir: Fuller Enterprises

Peter Fuller, Jr.: trust

James D. Henderson: trust

Hope Halsey Swasey: trust

Samuel S. Talbot: trust

Melinda F. Vanden Heuvel: trust

APPLICATION INFORMATION

Initial Approach: Send cover letter and full proposal. Include a description of organization, amount requested, purpose of funds sought, recently audited financial statement, and proof of tax-exempt status. Deadlines are March 15, July 15, and December 15

Restrictions on Giving: Does not support individuals or provide funds for publications or conferences.

PUBLICATIONS

Application Guidelines.

GRANTS ANALYSIS

Total Grants: $401,200

Number of Grants: 134

Highest Grant: $15,000

Typical Range: $100 to $15,000

Disclosure Period: 1993

Note: Recent grants are derived from a 1993 Form 990.

RECENT GRANTS

Library

5,000	Boston Public Library, Boston, MA

General

15,000	Bridge Over Troubled Waters, Boston, MA — outreach
15,000	Syracuse Cancer, Syracuse, NY
10,000	Bridge Over Troubled Waters, Boston, MA — capital
10,000	FCD Foundation, Needham, MA
10,000	Southfield

Hunt Foundation, Samuel P.

CONTACT
Therese A. Benoit
Vice President
Samuel P. Hunt Fdn.
c/o First NH Investment Services Corp.
PO Box 150
Manchester, NH 03105
(603) 634-6779

FINANCIAL SUMMARY

Recent Giving: $385,960 (fiscal 1993); $272,677 (fiscal 1991); $388,862 (fiscal 1990)

Assets: $8,455,166 (fiscal 1993); $8,094,581 (fiscal 1991); $6,188,761 (fiscal 1990)

Gifts Received: $636 (fiscal 1991)

EIN: 02-6004471

CONTRIBUTIONS SUMMARY

Donor(s): the late Samuel P. Hunt

Typical Recipients: • *Arts & Humanities:* Arts Associations & Councils, Arts Centers, Arts Institutes, Community Arts, Historic Preservation, History & Archaeology, Libraries, Museums/Galleries, Music, Opera, Performing Arts, Theater • *Civic & Public Affairs:* Housing, Urban & Community Affairs • *Education:* Colleges & Universities, Environmental Education, International Studies, Private Education (Precollege), Science/Mathematics Education, Secondary Education (Public) • *Environment:* Resource Conservation • *Health:* Children's Health/Hospitals, Hospitals, Medical Rehabilitation, Medical Research, Nursing Services, Single-Disease Health Associations • *Religion:* Churches, Religious Welfare • *Science:* Scientific Centers & Institutes • *Social Services:* Community Service Organizations, Domestic Violence, Family Services, Homes, People with Disabilities, Recreation & Athletics, Scouts, Senior Services, United Funds/United Ways, Youth Organizations

Grant Types: capital, conference/seminar, emergency, general support, multiyear/continuing support, project, research, and seed money

Geographic Distribution: limited to NH

GIVING OFFICERS

First NH Bank: trust

Douglas A. McIninch: trust *PHIL AFFIL* trust: McInich Scholarship Fund

Ralph A. McIninch: trust *B* Manchester NH 1912 *ED* Harvard Univ BS 1934; Rutgers Univ Stonier Sch Banking 1938 *CURR EMPL* chmn: First NH Bank NA *CORP AFFIL* dir: Amoskeag Industires, First Bank Mortgage, Laconia Peoples Natl Bank & Trust Co, NH Ins Co; treas: dir: First NH

Bank NA *NONPR AFFIL* dir: Federated Arts Manchester, NH Indus Devel Authority; mem: Manchester Chamber Commerce; mem exec bd: Boy Scouts Am; treas: Manchester Inst Arts Sciences; trust: City Manchester Cemetery Trust Funds, Gale Home, Manchester City Library; trust emeritus: Colby-Sawyer Coll *PHIL AFFIL* pres, treas, trust: McIninch Foundation; co-trust: Samuel P. Hunt Foundation

James C. Tyrie: trust

APPLICATION INFORMATION

Initial Approach: Send brief letter of inquiry describing program or project. Include a description of organization, amount requested, purpose of funds sought, recently audited financial statement, and proof of tax-exempt status. Deadlines are March 1 and September 1.

Restrictions on Giving: Does not support individuals or provide funds for scholarships or fellowships.

PUBLICATIONS
Program policy statement, Application Guidelines

GRANTS ANALYSIS

Total Grants: $385,960

Number of Grants: 118

Highest Grant: $25,000

Typical Range: $1,000 to $10,000

Disclosure Period: fiscal year ending September 30, 1993

Note: Recent grants are derived from a fiscal 1993 Form 990.

RECENT GRANTS

Library

12,500	Manchester Historic Association, Manchester, NH — salary support for librarian
12,500	Manchester Historic Association, Manchester, NH — salary support for librarian

General

25,000	Boy Scouts of America Daniel Webster Council, Portsmouth, NH — Bridge funding for at-risk youth
25,000	Boy Scouts of America Daniel Webster Council, Portsmouth, NH — Bridge funding for at-risk youth
20,000	Manchester Boys and Girls Club, Manchester, NH
16,000	New Hampshire Association for the Blind, Concord, NH
15,000	Boy Scouts of America Daniel Webster Council, Portsmouth, NH — purchase mountain bikes and kayaks

Kingsbury Corp. / Kingsbury Fund

Employees: 450
Headquarters: Keene, NH
SIC Major Group: Industrial Machinery & Equipment

CONTACT
James E. O'Neil
Vice President, Manufacturing
Kingsbury Corp.
PO Box 2020
Keene, NH 03431-2059
(603) 352-5212

FINANCIAL SUMMARY

Recent Giving: $147,590 (1993); $122,105 (1992); $154,377 (1991)

Assets: $3,113,783 (1993); $2,845,940 (1992); $2,747,296 (1991)

Gifts Received: $20,000 (1993); $20,000 (1992); $19,800 (1991)

Fiscal Note: In 1992, contributions were received from Kingsbury Corporation.

EIN: 02-6004465

CONTRIBUTIONS SUMMARY

Typical Recipients: • *Arts & Humanities:* Arts Appreciation, Arts Associations & Councils, Arts Centers, Arts Festivals, Arts Funds, Community Arts, Dance, Ethnic & Folk Arts, Historic Preservation, History & Archaeology, Libraries, Museums/Galleries, Music, Opera, Performing Arts, Public Broadcasting, Theater, Visual Arts • *Civic & Public Affairs:* Clubs, Economic Development, General, Parades/Festivals, Safety, Urban & Community Affairs • *Education:* Arts/Humanities Education, Business Education, Colleges & Universities, Community & Junior Colleges, Continuing Education, Education Funds, Engineering/Technological Education, General, International Studies, Private Education (Precollege), Science/Mathematics Education, Student Aid, Vocational & Technical Education • *Environment:* Air/Water Quality, General • *Health:* Cancer, Children's Health/Hospitals, Clinics/Medical Centers, Health Organizations, Heart, Hospices • *Religion:* Religious Welfare • *Science:* Observatories & Planetariums • *Social Services:* Animal Protection, Community Centers, Community Service Organizations, Crime Prevention, Day Care, Emergency Relief, Food/Clothing Distribution, General, Recreation & Athletics, Scouts, Senior Services, Special Olympics, Substance Abuse, United Funds/United Ways, Volunteer Services, Youth Organizations

Grant Types: employee matching gifts, general support, multiyear/continuing support, operating expenses, project, scholarship, and seed money

Nonmonetary Support Types: donated equipment, donated products, in-kind services, and loaned employees

Geographic Distribution: Grants are awarded in headquarters and operating communities.

Operating Locations: NH (Keene)

CORP. OFFICERS
Walter M. Burkart: *CURR EMPL* chmn, dir: Kingsbury Corp

James L. Koontz: *CURR EMPL* pres, ceo, dir: Kingsbury Corp

GIVING OFFICERS
John S. Cookson: trust

Charles J. Hanrahan: trust

James L. Koontz: trust *CURR EMPL* pres, ceo, dir: Kingsbury Corp (see above)

Priscilla K. Maynard: trust

James E. O'Neil: trust

Jeffrey M. Toner: trust

APPLICATION INFORMATION
Initial Approach: The foundation has no formal grant application procedure or application form. There are no deadlines.

Restrictions on Giving: Limited to Cheshire County, NH.

OTHER THINGS TO KNOW
Provides scholarships for higher education to the children of employees.

GRANTS ANALYSIS
Total Grants: $147,590

Number of Grants: 151*

Highest Grant: $20,000

Typical Range: $25 to $1,000

Disclosure Period: 1993

Note: Recent grants are derived from a 1993 Form 990.

RECENT GRANTS
Library
4,000   Keene Public Library, Keene, NH — final pledge payment/Library campaign

General
8,000   Cedarcrest Final Pledge Payment — construction campaign
8,000   Dartmouth-Hitchcock Medical Center, Lebanon, NH — final pledge payment/Looking Forward campaign
7,554   Monadnock United Way, Keene, NH — final quarterly payment 1992-93 campaign
7,554   Monadnock United Way, Keene, NH — quarterly payment
7,554   Monadnock United Way, Keene, NH — quarterly payment

Mascoma Savings Bank / Mascoma Savings Bank Foundation

Sales: $18.66 million
Employees: 85
Headquarters: Lebanon, NH
SIC Major Group: Depository Institutions

CONTACT
Clark Griffiths
Chairman
Mascoma Savings Bank
c/o Mascoma Savings Bank
PO Box 435
Lebanon, NH 03766
(603) 448-3650

FINANCIAL SUMMARY
Recent Giving: $62,150 (1993); $57,820 (1992); $42,375 (1990)

Assets: $1,315,333 (1993); $1,290,798 (1992); $1,125,943 (1990)

EIN: 22-2816632

CONTRIBUTIONS SUMMARY
Typical Recipients: • *Arts & Humanities:* General, Libraries, Opera, Public Broadcasting • *Civic & Public Affairs:* General • *Education:* Colleges & Universities, General, Public Education (Precollege), Science/Mathematics Education, Student Aid • *Environment:* Air/Water Quality, Energy • *Health:* Cancer, Emergency/Ambulance Services, General • *Social Services:* Child Welfare, Community Service Organizations, General, Recreation & Athletics, Scouts, Senior Services, Youth Organizations

Grant Types: capital, general support, and project

Nonmonetary Support Types: donated equipment

Geographic Distribution: operating communities

Operating Locations: NH (Lebanon)

CORP. OFFICERS
Stephen Christy: *CURR EMPL* pres, ceo: Mascoma Savings Bank

Clark Griffiths: *CURR EMPL* chmn: Mascoma Savings Bank

GIVING OFFICERS
Charter Trust Company: trust

Reuben D. Cole: secy

Clark Griffiths: trust *CURR EMPL* chmn: Mascoma Savings Bank (see above)

Jean Kennedy: trust

Jacqueline A. Lary: trust

William Maloy: trust

APPLICATION INFORMATION
Initial Approach: Send a brief letter of inquiry. Include a description of organization, amount requested, purpose of funds sought, recently audited financial statement, and proof of tax-exempt status. Deadlines are April 1 and October 1.

GRANTS ANALYSIS
Total Grants: $62,150

Number of Grants: 21

Highest Grant: $5,000

Typical Range: $400 to $3,000

Disclosure Period: 1993

Note: Recent grants are derived from a 1993 Form 990.

RECENT GRANTS
Library
3,000   Mascome Regional High School — to support funding for a multimedia work station for the library/media center

General
5,000   Lebanon College, Lebanon, PA — to support funding of computer science program update
2,500   David's House, Hanover, NH — to help with relocation of David's House, a home-away-from-home for families with children being treated at Dartmouth-Hitchcock Medical Center
2,000   Enfield Fast Squad, Enfield, CT — to replace aging communication equipment in ambulance
2,000   Grafton County Senior Citizens Council Inc, Lebanon, NH
2,000   Lebanon School District, Lebanon, PA — to support funding of the 1993-94 school year bio-search project, documenting memory

Monadnock Paper Mills / Verney Foundation, Gilbert

Sales: $30.0 million
Employees: 250
Headquarters: Bennington, NH
SIC Major Group: Paper Mills

CONTACT
Richard G. Verney
Chief Executive Officer
Monadnock Paper Mills
Antrim Rd.
Bennington, NH 03442
(603) 588-3311

FINANCIAL SUMMARY
Recent Giving: $91,895 (1993); $39,905 (1992); $45,995 (1991)

Assets: $1,868,401 (1993); $1,692,873 (1992); $1,585,821 (1991)

Gifts Received: $150,000 (1993); $150,000 (1992); $50,000 (1991)

Fiscal Note: In 1993, contributions were received from Monadnock Paper Mills.

EIN: 02-6007363

CONTRIBUTIONS SUMMARY

Typical Recipients: • *Arts & Humanities:* Arts Associations & Councils, Arts Centers, Arts Funds, Arts Outreach, Community Arts, History & Archaeology, Libraries, Literary Arts, Museums/Galleries, Music, Performing Arts, Public Broadcasting • *Civic & Public Affairs:* General, Native American Affairs, Urban & Community Affairs, Women's Affairs • *Education:* Agricultural Education, Leadership Training, Private Education (Precollege), Science/Mathematics Education • *Environment:* General, Resource Conservation, Wildlife Protection • *Health:* Diabetes, Hospices, Hospitals • *Religion:* Churches, Religious Organizations • *Social Services:* Animal Protection, Domestic Violence, Family Services, Youth Organizations

Grant Types: general support

Geographic Distribution: focus on MA and NH

Operating Locations: NH (Bennington)

CORP. OFFICERS

Richard G. Verney: *B* Providence RI 1946 *ED* Brown Univ 1968 *CURR EMPL* chmn, ceo, dir: Monadnock Paper Mills

GIVING OFFICERS

Diane V. Greenway: trust

E. Geoffrey Verney: trust

Richard G. Verney: pres, dir *CURR EMPL* chmn, ceo, dir: Monadnock Paper Mills (see above)

APPLICATION INFORMATION

Initial Approach: The foundation has no formal grant application procedure or application form. There are no deadlines.

GRANTS ANALYSIS

Total Grants: $91,895

Number of Grants: 46

Highest Grant: $31,000

Typical Range: $50 to $10,000

Disclosure Period: 1993

Note: Recent grants are derived from a 1993 Form 990.

RECENT GRANTS

Library
1,000	Nantucket Athenaeum, Nantucket, MA

General
31,000	St. George's School
10,000	Running Strong for American Indian Youth
2,600	All Saints Parish, Manchester, NH
2,500	Monadnock Community Hospital, Petersborough, NH
1,200	Harris Center for Conservation Education, Hancock, NH

472

Putnam Foundation

CONTACT
David F. Putnam
Trustee
Putnam Fdn.
150 Congress St.
Keene, NH 03431
(603) 352-2448

FINANCIAL SUMMARY
Recent Giving: $313,610 (fiscal 1993); $369,957 (fiscal 1992); $287,090 (fiscal 1991)

Assets: $4,987,224 (fiscal 1993); $4,837,780 (fiscal 1992); $4,484,729 (fiscal 1991)

Gifts Received: $19,360 (fiscal 1993); $84,122 (fiscal 1992); $4,989 (fiscal 1991)

Fiscal Note: In 1993, contributions were received from Markem Class C Stock ($19,360).

EIN: 02-6011388

CONTRIBUTIONS SUMMARY
Donor(s): David F. Putnam

Typical Recipients: • *Arts & Humanities:* Arts Associations & Councils, Community Arts, Dance, Ethnic & Folk Arts, Historic Preservation, History & Archaeology, Libraries, Museums/Galleries, Music, Public Broadcasting, Theater • *Civic & Public Affairs:* Botanical Gardens/Parks, Business/Free Enterprise, General, Hispanic Affairs, Housing, Municipalities/Towns, Philanthropic Organizations, Professional & Trade Associations, Urban & Community Affairs • *Education:* Arts/Humanities Education, Colleges & Universities, Education Funds, Engineering/Technological Education, General, International Studies, Leadership Training, Minority Education, Private Education (Precollege), Secondary Education (Public), Student Aid • *Environment:* Air/Water Quality, General, Resource Conservation • *Health:* Clinics/Medical Centers, Emergency/Ambulance Services, Health Organizations, Hospitals • *International:* International Relations, Missionary/Religious Activities • *Religion:* Churches, Religious Organizations, Religious Welfare • *Social Services:* Community Service Organizations, Recreation & Athletics, Scouts, United Funds/United Ways, YMCA/YWCA/YMHA/YWHA, Youth Organizations

Grant Types: capital and general support

Geographic Distribution: limited to NH

GIVING OFFICERS
David F. Putnam: trust

James A. Putnam: trust *CURR EMPL* vp, dir: Markem Corp

Rosamond P. Putnam: trust

APPLICATION INFORMATION
Initial Approach: Send a brief letter of inquiry. Include a description of organization, amount requested, purpose of funds sought, recently audited financial statement, and

proof of tax-exempt status. There are no deadlines.

Restrictions on Giving: Awards are limited to historical preservation, cultural enhancement, and ecological maintenance.

GRANTS ANALYSIS
Total Grants: $313,610

Number of Grants: 478

Highest Grant: $75,000

Typical Range: $500 to $10,000

Disclosure Period: fiscal year ending October 31, 1993

Note: Recent grants are derived from a fiscal 1993 Form 990.

RECENT GRANTS
Library
10,000	Library Campaign, Kenne, NH — Keene Public Library
500	Church of Jesus Christ of Latter-Day Saints Family History Library

General
25,000	Augustus St. Gaudens Memorial — Advised Fund
16,600	Dublin School, Dublin, OH
10,000	Dartmouth-Hitchcock Medical Center, Lebanon, NH
8,400	Dublin School, Dublin, OH
7,500	Franklin Pierce College, Rindge, NH

Smith Charitable Foundation, Lou and Lutza

CONTACT
Charles A. DeGrandpre
Trustee
Lou and Lutza Smith Charitable Fdn.
c/o New Hampshire Charitable Fund
One S St., PO Box 1335
Concord, NH 03301
(603) 436-2818

FINANCIAL SUMMARY
Recent Giving: $233,300 (1993); $537,530 (1992); $504,330 (1990)

Assets: $2,299,141 (1993); $2,583,656 (1992); $3,300,752 (1990)

EIN: 23-7162940

CONTRIBUTIONS SUMMARY
Donor(s): Lutza Smith, Louis Smith Marital Trust

Typical Recipients: • *Arts & Humanities:* Arts Associations & Councils, Arts Centers, Historic Preservation, History & Archaeology, Libraries, Music, Public Broadcasting • *Civic & Public Affairs:* Employment/Job Training, Housing, Safety, Urban & Community Affairs, Women's Affairs • *Education:* Agricultural Education, General, Private Education (Precollege), Student Aid • *Environment:* General • *Health:* Children's Health/Hospitals, Hospitals, Long-Term Care, Mental Health, Nursing Services, Prenatal Health Issues • *Religion:* Ministries

• *Science:* Scientific Centers & Institutes
• *Social Services:* At-Risk Youth, Big Brother/Big Sister, Child Welfare, Community Centers, Community Service Organizations, Domestic Violence, Family Services, Food/Clothing Distribution, Homes, People with Disabilities, Senior Services, Shelters/Homelessness, Substance Abuse, United Funds/United Ways, Youth Organizations

Grant Types: capital and project

Geographic Distribution: focus on NH

GIVING OFFICERS
Charles A. DeGrandpre: trust

Louise K. Newman: trust

Kathleen M. Robinson: trust

APPLICATION INFORMATION
Initial Approach: The foundation requests applications be made in writing. Include a description of organization, amount requested, purpose of funds sought, recently audited financial statement, and proof of tax-exempt status. Deadlines are February 1, May 1, August 1, and November 1.

PUBLICATIONS
Informational Brochure (including application guidelines)

GRANTS ANALYSIS
Total Grants: $233,300

Number of Grants: 23

Highest Grant: $125,000

Typical Range: $2,000 to $100,000

Disclosure Period: 1993

Note: Recent grants are derived from a 1993 Form 990. Number of grants and typical range do not include matching grants.

RECENT GRANTS
General
125,000	University of New Hampshire Foundation, Durham, NH — for renovation of the former dairy buildings into the Lou and Lutza Smith Equine Science Center, a research teaching and conference facility
100,000	Derryfield School, Manchester, NH — establish scholarship to provide tuition assistance to students in Summerbridge Manchester program
20,000	New Hampshire Community Loan Fund, Concord, NH — for continued support of the families in transition program
15,000	Circle Program, Plymouth, NH — for startup of residential camp and year-round support services for girls
15,000	Dover Group Home — for capital campaign to relocate the residential program for abused and neglected adolescent girls

Unitrode Corp.

Revenue: $86.92 million
Employees: 750
Headquarters: Billerica, MA
SIC Major Group: Electronic & Other Electrical Equipment and Industrial Machinery & Equipment

CONTACT
S. Kelley MacDonald
Vice President, Corp. Communication
Unitrode Corp.
7 Continental Blvd.
Merrimack, NH 03054
(603) 429-8770

FINANCIAL SUMMARY
Recent Giving: $25,000 (1993 est.)

CONTRIBUTIONS SUMMARY
Company reports that 40% of contributions are allocated to civic and public affairs; 30% to education; 20% to arts and humanities; and 10% to health and human services.

Volunteerism: Company actively promotes volunteerism, and employee-sponsored requests are given priority.

Typical Recipients: • *Arts & Humanities:* Arts Centers, Arts Festivals, Community Arts, General, Libraries, Museums/Galleries, Music, Performing Arts, Theater, Visual Arts • *Civic & Public Affairs:* Chambers of Commerce, Community Foundations, General, Law & Justice, Municipalities/Towns, Parades/Festivals, Professional & Trade Associations, Safety, Urban & Community Affairs • *Education:* Afterschool/Enrichment Programs, Business Education, Business-School Partnerships, Colleges & Universities, Community & Junior Colleges, Continuing Education, Economic Education, Education Funds, Elementary Education (Public), Engineering/Technological Education, General, Public Education (Precollege), Science/Mathematics Education, Secondary Education (Public), Social Sciences Education, Special Education, Vocational & Technical Education • *Health:* Adolescent Health Issues, Children's Health/Hospitals, General, Home-Care Services, Hospices, Hospitals, Speech & Hearing • *Science:* General, Science Exhibits & Fairs, Science Museums, Scientific Centers & Institutes • *Social Services:* At-Risk Youth, Camps, Child Welfare, Community Centers, Community Service Organizations, Counseling, Day Care, Delinquency & Criminal Rehabilitation, Domestic Violence, General, People with Disabilities, Recreation & Athletics, Refugee Assistance, Senior Services, Sexual Abuse, Shelters/Homelessness, Substance Abuse, United Funds/United Ways, Volunteer Services, Youth Organizations

Grant Types: award, capital, challenge, conference/seminar, general support, operating expenses, and scholarship

Nonmonetary Support Types: donated equipment and in-kind services

Geographic Distribution: in headquarters and operating communities

Operating Locations: CA (San Jose), NC (Cary), NH (Merrimack)

CORP. OFFICERS
Robert L. Gable: *B* Baltimore MD 1930 *ED* Univ MD 1952; Univ MD Sch Bus Admin 1953 *CURR EMPL* chmn, pres, ceo, dir: Unitrode Corp *CORP AFFIL* chmn: NH Savings Bank Corp, Rockingham County Trust Co; dir: Apollo Computer, Fin Concepts, H K Webster Co, Symbolics Inc *NONPR AFFIL* vchmn: Outward Bound

Cosmo S. Trapani: *CURR EMPL* exec vp, cfo: Unitrode Corp

APPLICATION INFORMATION
Initial Approach: Send a brief letter of inquiry. Include a a description of organization, amount requested, purpose of funds sought, and proof of tax-exempt status. There are no deadlines.

Restrictions on Giving: Does not support individuals, religious organizations for sectarian purposes, or political or lobbying groups.

GRANTS ANALYSIS
Typical Range: $50 to $1,000

Note: Recent grants are derived from a grants list provided by company in 1995.

RECENT GRANTS
General
Home and Hospice, Merrimack, NH
Merrimack Schools, Merrimack, NH
Merrimack Youth Association, Merrimack, NH
Museum of Science, Boston, MA
United Way, Nashua, NH

NEW JERSEY

AlliedSignal Inc. / AlliedSignal Foundation Inc.

Revenue: $12.81 billion
Employees: 86,400
Headquarters: Morris Township, NJ
SIC Major Group: Aircraft Engines & Engine Parts, Industrial Inorganic Chemicals Nec, Plastics Materials & Resins, and Organic Fibers—Noncellulosic

CONTACT
Alan S. Painter
Vice President & Executive Director Corporate Affairs
AlliedSignal Foundation Inc.
PO Box 2245
Morristown, NJ 07962-2245
(201) 455-5876
Note: The company's World Wide Web address is http://www.os.kcp.com/home/ascorp.html"

FINANCIAL SUMMARY
Recent Giving: $10,000,000 (1995 est.); $10,000,000 (1994); $10,000,000 (1993 approx.)

Assets: $627 (1993); $627 (1992); $326,267 (1991)

Gifts Received: $8,982,188 (1993); $8,881,324 (1992)

Fiscal Note: Figures include foundation and direct giving. Foundation giving totaled $9,000,000 in 1994 and $8,982,188 in 1993. Direct giving is reserved for programs that do not qualify for tax-exempt status. Also included above is $1.0 million in contributions made annually from budgets of other company departments. Above figures exclude nonmonetary support. The foundation receives gifts from AlliedSignal.

EIN: 22-2416651

CONTRIBUTIONS SUMMARY
Typical Recipients: • *Arts & Humanities:* Arts Associations & Councils, Arts Centers, Arts Institutes, Community Arts, Dance, Historic Preservation, Libraries, Museums/Galleries, Music, Opera, Performing Arts, Public Broadcasting, Theater • *Civic & Public Affairs:* African American Affairs, Chambers of Commerce, Economic Development, Employment/Job Training, General, Housing, Law & Justice, Professional & Trade Associations, Public Policy, Safety, Urban & Community Affairs, Women's Affairs • *Education:* Arts/Humanities Education, Business Education, Business-School Partnerships, Colleges & Universities, Community & Junior Colleges, Continuing Education, Education Funds, Education Reform, Elementary Education (Public), Engineering/Technological Education, Faculty Development, General, Health & Physical Education, International Exchange, Legal Education, Literacy, Medical Education, Minority Education, Private Education (Precollege), Public Education (Precollege), Science/Mathematics Education, Social Sciences Education, Special Education, Student Aid • *Environment:* General • *Health:* Cancer, Children's Health/Hospitals, Clinics/Medical Centers, Diabetes, Geriatric Health, Health Organizations, Heart, Hospitals, Medical Rehabilitation, Medical Research, Multiple Sclerosis, Nursing Services, Single-Disease Health Associations, Transplant Networks/Donor Banks • *International:* International Affairs • *Religion:* Churches, Dioceses, Jewish Causes, Ministries, Religious Welfare • *Science:* Scientific Centers & Institutes • *Social Services:* At-Risk Youth, Child Welfare, Community Centers, Community Service Organizations, Counseling, Delinquency & Criminal Rehabilitation, Domestic Violence, Family Services, Food/Clothing Distribution, Homes, People with Disabilities, Recreation & Athletics, Senior Services, Sexual Abuse, Shelters/Homelessness, Substance Abuse, United Funds/United Ways, Volunteer Services, Youth Organizations

Grant Types: capital, department, and employee matching gifts

Note: Employee matching gift ratio: 1 to 1.

Nonmonetary Support Types: donated equipment

Note: Estimated value of nonmonetary support is not available.

Geographic Distribution: principally near operating locations

Operating Locations: AL (Greenville), AZ (Phoenix, Tempe, Tucson), CA (Los Angeles, San Diego, Sylmar, Torrance), CT (Cheshire), DC, FL (Ft. Lauderdale, Jacksonville), IL (Des Plaines, Metropolis), IN (South Bend), KS (Lawrence, Olathe), LA (Baton Rouge, Geismar), MD (Columbia, Towson), MI (Boyne City, Southfield, St. Joseph, Troy), MO (Kansas City), NC (Charlotte, Moncure, Rocky Mount), NJ (Eatontown, Morris Township, Morristown, Teterboro), NY (Hoosick Falls), OH (Elyria, Fostoria, Greenville), OK (Catoosa), PA (Philadelphia, Pottsville, South Montrose), RI (East Providence, Phillipsdale), SC (Columbia, Sumter), TN (Cleveland, Jackson, Knoxville), UT (Clearfield), VA (Chesterfield, Hopewell, Petersburg)

CORP. OFFICERS
Lawrence Arthur Bossidy: *B* Pittsfield MA 1935 *ED* Colgate Univ BA 1957 *CURR EMPL* chmn, ceo, dir: AlliedSignal Inc *CORP AFFIL* chmn: Gen Electric Capital Corp; dir: Merck & Co Inc; vchmn, dir: Employers Reins Corp, Gen Electric Commun & Svcs, Gen Electric Fin Svcs, Gen Electric Indus & Power Sys, Gen Electric Investment Corp, Gen Electric Lighting, Gen Electric Motors, Kidder Peabody & Co Inc, Ladd Petroleum Corp *NONPR AFFIL* mem: Bus Counc, Bus Roundtable

Peter Michael Kreindler: *B* Liberty NY 1945 *ED* Harvard Univ BA 1967; Harvard Univ JD 1971 *CURR EMPL* sr vp, gen couns: AlliedSignal Inc

GIVING OFFICERS
Isaac Ruben Barpal: dir *B* Argentina 1940 *ED* CA St Univ BSEE 1967; Univ CA Santa Barbara PhDEE 1970 *NONPR AFFIL* fellow: Inst Electrical Electronics Engrs; mem: Indus Res Inst, Inst Electrical Electronics Engrs Engg Mgmt Soc; mem adv counc: CA Polytech St Univ Sch Engg

John William Barter III: dir *B* Mobile AL 1946 *ED* Spring Hill Coll BS 1968; Tulane Univ MBA 1973 *CURR EMPL* exec vp: AlliedSignal Inc *CORP AFFIL* dir: BMC Software Inc *NONPR AFFIL* trust: Spring Hill Coll, Tri-County Scholarship Fund

Lawrence Arthur Bossidy: chmn, dir *CURR EMPL* chmn, ceo, dir: AlliedSignal Inc (see above)

Daniel Patrick Burnham: dir *B* Birmingham MI 1946 *ED* Xavier Univ BS 1968; Univ NH MBA 1970 *CURR EMPL* pres: AlliedSignal Aerospace Co *CORP AFFIL* chmn: Intl Turbine Engine Co; dir: Light Helicopter Turbines Engg Co, Normalair Garrett Ltd UK; exec vp: AlliedSignal Inc *NONPR AFFIL* bd gov: Aerospace Indus Assn Am

Ken Cole: secy

Nancy Garvey: treas

Peter Michael Kreindler: pres, dir *CURR EMPL* sr vp, gen couns: AlliedSignal Inc (see above)

Alan S. Painter: vp, exec dir

Frederick M. Poses: dir *B* 1942 *ED* NY Univ BBA 1965 *CURR EMPL* exec vp: AlliedSignal Inc

Donald J. Redlinger: dir *CURR EMPL* sr vp human resources: AlliedSignal Inc

James E. Sierk: dir *B* Warsaw NY 1938 *ED* Rutgers Univ 1960; Rensselaer Polytech Inst 1964 *CURR EMPL* AlliedSignal Inc

APPLICATION INFORMATION
Initial Approach: *Initial Contact:* brief letter *Include Information On:* description of the organization, including name, address, primary mission, and contact person; description of proposed project; amount of grant request, including plans for implementation and benefits expected; copy of 501(c)(3) exemption letter; budget information (i.e. annual report, audited financial statement, proposed project budget); list of board members; list of other corporate support; and any additional information that may be helpful *Deadlines:* applications taken from June to September *Note:* Requests from community-based organizations should be submitted through local plants or facilities. Requests from national organizations and colleges and universities should be directed to the foundation itself.

Restrictions on Giving: Generally does not support member agencies of the United Way, individuals, political or lobbying groups, religious organizations for sectarian purposes, dinners or special events, fraternal organizations, or goodwill advertising.

The foundation only funds organizations with tax-exempt status.

OTHER THINGS TO KNOW
The foundation also sponsors a number of programs, including matching gifts for active employees and directors of AlliedSignal; Challenge 2000 Program, which has donated almost $500,000 since its inception in 1991 to innovative K-12 programs to improve literacy and science and match skills; Targeted University Program, which awards $100,000 grants to universities that conduct research on technologies key to AlliedSignal's business activities; and a number of scholarship programs for employee children.

PUBLICATIONS
AlliedSignal Contributions Program

GRANTS ANALYSIS
Total Grants: $8,982,188

Number of Grants: 720*

Highest Grant: $399,000

Average Grant: $12,475*

Typical Range: $1,000 to $20,000

Disclosure Period: 1993

Note: Number of grants and average grant figures are approximates. Above figures represent foundation giving only. Recent grants are derived from a 1993 Form 990.

RECENT GRANTS

General

399,000	United Way of Los Angeles, Region IV, Los Angeles, CA
355,000	United Way of Tri-State, New York, NY
200,900	South Bend Community School Corporation, South Bend, IN — math-science program for at-risk students, grades K-6
150,000	American Chemical Society, Washington, DC — campaign for chemistry, last of five payments on $500,000 pledge
140,000	United Way Valley of the Sun, Phoenix, AZ

Barker Foundation, J.M.R.

CONTACT
Robert R. Barker
President
J.M.R. Barker Fdn.
85 Livingston Ave.
Roseland, NJ 07068-1785
(212) 371-6777

FINANCIAL SUMMARY
Recent Giving: $598,500 (1993); $500,700 (1992); $591,500 (1991)

Assets: $14,744,745 (1993); $13,029,620 (1992); $14,106,199 (1991)

EIN: 13-6268289

CONTRIBUTIONS SUMMARY
Donor(s): the late James M. Barker, the late Margaret R. Barker, Robert R. Barker

Typical Recipients: • *Arts & Humanities:* Community Arts, Libraries, Literary Arts, Museums/Galleries, Music, Performing Arts, Public Broadcasting • *Civic & Public Affairs:* General, Nonprofit Management, Philanthropic Organizations, Public Policy, Urban & Community Affairs • *Education:* Colleges & Universities, Engineering/Technological Education, Legal Education, Minority Education, Private Education (Precollege), Public Education (Precollege), School Volunteerism • *Environment:* General, Resource Conservation, Wildlife Protection • *Health:* Health Funds, Hospitals • *International:* International Environmental Issues, International Relations, International Relief Efforts • *Religion:* Jewish Causes • *Science:* Science Museums, Scientific Centers & Institutes, Scientific Labs • *Social Services:* Community Service Organizations, Family Planning, Family Services, Refugee Assistance, United Funds/United Ways, Volunteer Services, Youth Organizations

Grant Types: capital, endowment, general support, multiyear/continuing support, operating expenses, project, and research

Geographic Distribution: focus on the New York, NY, and Boston, MA, area

GIVING OFFICERS
Ann S. Barker: dir

Elizabeth S. Barker: vp, dir

James R. Barker: vp, dir *B* Cleveland OH 1935 *ED* Columbia Univ BA 1957; Harvard Univ MBA 1963 *CURR EMPL* vchmn, co-owner: Mormac Marine Group *CORP AFFIL* chmn, dir: Interlake Steamship Co; dir: Gen Telephone & Electronics, TW Holdings *NONPR AFFIL* bd visitors: Columbia Univ; mem: Am Bur Shipping; mem bus adv bd: Northwestern Univ; trust: Stamford Hosp

Robert R. Barker: pres, dir

Dr. William Benjamin Barker: dir *B* Stamford CT 1947 *ED* Harvard Univ 1969-1975 *CURR EMPL* pres: BBN Advanced Computers *CORP AFFIL* gen ptnr: Barker (Robert R) & Co; pres: BBN Advanced Computers

Margaret Barker Clark: dir

Robert P. Conner: treas, dir *B* New Bedford MA 1948 *ED* Boston College BS 1970; Pace Univ MS 1977 *CURR EMPL* sr vp: J&W Seligman & Co *CORP AFFIL* dir: CRB Broadcasting Corp *NONPR AFFIL* mem: Alpha Sigma Nu, Am Inst CPAs, Beta Gamma Sigma, NY St Soc CPAs

John W. Holman, Jr.: dir *PHIL AFFIL* chmn, dir: Hyde and Watson Foundation

Maureen A. Hopkins: secy, adm

Richard D. Kahn: asst secy, dir *B* New York NY 1931 *ED* Harvard Univ AB 1952; Harvard Univ JD 1955 *CURR EMPL* couns: Debevoise & Plimpton *NONPR AFFIL* dir: Concerned Citizens Montauk, Group S Fork, JMR Barker Fdn; mem: New York City Bar Assn, Phi Beta Kappa

Dwight E. Lee: vp, dir

Donna Rosario: asst treas

APPLICATION INFORMATION
Initial Approach: Send a brief letter of inquiry. Include a description of organization, amount requested, purpose of funds sought, recently audited financial statement, and proof of tax-exempt status. Deadline is November 1.

GRANTS ANALYSIS
Total Grants: $598,500

Number of Grants: 33

Highest Grant: $135,000

Typical Range: $3,000 to $10,000

Disclosure Period: 1993

Note: Recent grants are derived from a 1993 Form 990.

RECENT GRANTS

General

135,000	American Museum of Natural History, New York, NY
125,000	Harvard University, Cambridge, MA
65,000	Stamford Hospital Foundation, Stamford, CT
50,000	Jackson Laboratory, Bar Harbor, ME
50,000	Massachusetts Institute of Technology, Cambridge, MA

Beck Foundation, Elsie E. and Joseph W.

CONTACT
J. Keegan
Secretary
Elsie E. and Joseph W. Beck Fdn.
1129 Broad St.
Shrewsbury, NJ 07701
(201) 389-0330

FINANCIAL SUMMARY
Recent Giving: $286,000 (1993); $286,000 (1992); $231,000 (1990)

Assets: $4,885,738 (1993); $4,652,468 (1992); $4,248,655 (1990)

EIN: 23-7246078

CONTRIBUTIONS SUMMARY
Donor(s): the late Elsie Beck

Typical Recipients: • *Arts & Humanities:* Libraries • *Civic & Public Affairs:* General, Law & Justice • *Education:* Business Education, Colleges & Universities, General, Legal Education, Private Education (Precollege), Public Education (Precollege), Secondary Education (Private), Student Aid • *Religion:* Churches, Missionary Activities (Domestic), Religious Organizations, Religious Welfare • *Social Services:* Community Service Organizations, People with Disabilities, Scouts, Youth Organizations

Grant Types: scholarship

Geographic Distribution: focus on NJ

GIVING OFFICERS
John P. Keegan: secy *B* 1927 *PHIL AFFIL* vp, treas, trust: Charles Edison Fund

Frank E. Walsch, Jr.: pres

Joseph W. Walsch: vp

C. Nelson Winget: treas

APPLICATION INFORMATION
Initial Approach: Send brief letter of inquiry describing program or project. Include a description of organization, amount requested, purpose of funds sought, recently audited financial statement, and proof of tax-exempt status. There are no deadlines.

Restrictions on Giving: Does not support individuals.

GRANTS ANALYSIS
Total Grants: $286,000

Number of Grants: 18

Highest Grant: $40,000

Typical Range: $1,000 to $30,000

Disclosure Period: 1993

Note: Recent grants are derived from a 1993 Form 990.

RECENT GRANTS

Library

40,000	Seton Hall University, West Orange, NJ — for restricted Library Room

General

30,000	St. Vincent's Academy, Newark, NJ
25,000	Seton Hall Prep, West Orange, NJ — for capital program
25,000	University of Notre Dame, Notre Dame, IN — for restricted scholarship program
20,000	St. Bonaventure University, St. Bonaventure, NY
18,500	Seton Hall Prep, West Orange, NJ

Brady Foundation

CONTACT
James C. Brady, Jr.
President
Brady Fdn.
PO Box 351
Gladstone, NJ 07934
(908) 234-1900

FINANCIAL SUMMARY
Recent Giving: $232,500 (1993); $225,660 (1992); $146,000 (1990)

Assets: $6,437,292 (1993); $6,892,943 (1992); $6,293,029 (1990)

EIN: 13-6167209

CONTRIBUTIONS SUMMARY
Donor(s): the late Helen M. Cutting, Nicholas Brady

Typical Recipients: • *Arts & Humanities:* Arts Associations & Councils, Ballet, Dance, Libraries, Museums/Galleries, Music, Public Broadcasting • *Civic & Public Affairs:* General, Municipalities/Towns, Philanthropic Organizations, Safety, Urban & Community Affairs • *Education:* Arts/Humanities Education, Private Education (Precollege) • *Environment:* Air/Water Quality, General, Resource Conservation, Watershed, Wildlife Protection • *Health:* Alzheimers Disease, Cancer, Clinics/Medical Centers, Emergency/Ambulance Services, Health Funds, Health Organizations, Hospitals, Medical Research, Mental Health, Prenatal Health Issues, Single-Disease Health Associations • *Religion:* Churches • *Science:* Scientific Centers & Institutes • *Social Services:* Big Brother/Big Sister, Camps, Child Welfare, People with Disabilities, Recreation & Athletics, Scouts, United Funds/United Ways, Youth Organizations

Grant Types: general support

Geographic Distribution: focus on NJ

GIVING OFFICERS
James C. Brady, Jr.: pres, treas, trust

Nicholas Frederick Brady: trust *B* New York NY 1930 *ED* Yale Univ BA 1952; Harvard Univ MBA 1954 *NONPR AFFIL* trust: Boys Club Newark *CLUB AFFIL* Bond NY, Links, Lunch *PHIL AFFIL* trust: Darby Foundation

Anderson Fowler: trust

Karen Wisnosky: secy

APPLICATION INFORMATION
Initial Approach: The foundation requests applications be made in writing. There are no deadlines.

GRANTS ANALYSIS
Total Grants: $232,500

Number of Grants: 43

Highest Grant: $25,000

Typical Range: $250 to $25,000

Disclosure Period: 1993

Note: Recent grants are derived from a 1993 Form 990.

RECENT GRANTS

General

25,000	Gladstone Equestrian Association, Peapack, NJ
25,000	Grayson Jockey Club Research Foundation, New York, NY
20,000	BCGN Life Camp, Newark, NJ
20,000	Matheny School, Peapack, NJ
15,000	Morristown Memorial Health Foundation, Morristown, NJ

Bunbury Company

CONTACT
Samuel W. Lambert III
President
Bunbury Company
169 Nassau St.
Princeton, NJ 08542
(609) 683-1414

FINANCIAL SUMMARY
Recent Giving: $660,964 (1993 est.); $652,175 (1992); $544,700 (1991)

Assets: $14,150,000 (1993 est.); $15,570,716 (1992); $16,045,003 (1991)

EIN: 13-6066172

CONTRIBUTIONS SUMMARY
Donor(s): The foundation was incorporated in New York by the late Dean Mathey .

Typical Recipients: • *Arts & Humanities:* Ballet, Dance, History & Archaeology, Libraries, Museums/Galleries, Music, Public Broadcasting, Theater • *Civic & Public Affairs:* Community Foundations, Hispanic Affairs, Nonprofit Management, Philanthropic Organizations, Professional & Trade Associations, Women's Affairs • *Education:* Colleges & Universities, International Exchange, Private Education (Precollege), Special Education • *Environment:* Air/Water Quality, General • *Health:* AIDS/HIV, Clinics/Medical Centers, Emergency/Ambulance Services, Hospitals, Medical Research • *Religion:* Religious Organizations • *Social Services:* At-Risk Youth, Domestic Violence, Family Planning, Family Services, Food/Clothing Distribution, Homes, People with Disabilities, Recreation & Athletics, Senior Services, Shelters/Homelessness, Substance Abuse, Youth Organizations

Grant Types: general support

Geographic Distribution: most grants are distributed in the Princeton, NJ, area to a lesser degree in Vermont

GIVING OFFICERS
Charles B. Atwater: dir *CORP AFFIL* treas, secy: Grafton Village Cheese Co *PHIL AFFIL* vp, secy: Windham Foundation

James Richard Cogan: treas, dir *B* Jersey City NJ 1928 *ED* Yale Univ BA 1950; Columbia Univ LLB 1953 *CURR EMPL* ptnr: Walter Conston Alexander & Green PC *CORP AFFIL* chmn bd: Grafton Village Cheese Co; pres, dir: S Forest Co *NONPR AFFIL* dir: Aging Am, Am Friends Plantin-Moretus Mus, Corp Relief Widows & Children Clergymen, Village Nursing Home NY; mem: Am Bar Assn, Am Coll Probate Couns, Assn Bar City New York, NY County Lawyers Assn; trust: Charlotte Palmer Phillips Fdn *CLUB AFFIL* mem: Salmagundi Artists, Yale *PHIL AFFIL* chmn: Windham Foundation

Samuel Waldron Lambert III: pres, trust *B* New York NY 1938 *CURR EMPL* mng ptnr: Drinker Biddle & Reath *CORP AFFIL* dir: Chem Bank NJ, Peterson Guides *NONPR AFFIL* dir: Curtis W McGraw Fdn; mem: Am Bar Assn, NJ Bar Assn, Princeton Bar Assn *PHIL AFFIL* secy, treas, trust: Curtis W. McGraw Foundation; trust: Winslow Foundation; vp, trust: Windham Foundation

William McGuigan: asst treas

Stephan A. Morse: dir *B* 1947 *CORP AFFIL* pres, admin, dir: Grafton Village Cheese Co *PHIL AFFIL* pres, ceo: Windham Foundation

Robert M. Olmsted: dir

Barbara L. Ruppert: asst secy

Edward Joseph Toohey: vp, dir *B* Jersey City NY 1930 *ED* Yale Univ BA 1953 *CURR EMPL* first vp: Merrill Lynch Pierce Fenner & Smith *CORP AFFIL* dir: New York City Ballet *NONPR AFFIL* dir: New York City Ballet; vchmn: Peddie Sch *CLUB AFFIL* Canoe Brook CC, Georgetown, Sky, Univ, Yale *PHIL AFFIL* trust: Windham Foundation

Charles C. Townsend, Jr.: secy, dir

William Bigelow Wright: dir *B* Rutland VT 1924 *ED* Princeton Univ AB *CURR EMPL* chmn: Marble Fin Corp *CORP AFFIL* chmn: Marble Bank *NONPR AFFIL* first vp, treas, dir: 10th Mountain Div Assn NE Chap; pres: Princeton Alumni Assn VT; trust, treas: Green Mountain Coll; vp, treas, dir: Windham Fdn *CLUB AFFIL* Ivy, Princeton *PHIL AFFIL* vp, treas, trust: Windham Foundation

Edward R. Zuccaro: dir *CORP AFFIL* clerk: Ad Sanel Inc; secy, treas: Hoveys Shops Inc

APPLICATION INFORMATION
Initial Approach:

The foundation requests applications be made in writing.

Applicants should submit written proposals including a description of the project, the approximate budget, and other funding sources. In addition, the foundation requests a balance sheet, income statement of the applying organization, and an IRS tax-exempt status letter.

The foundation has no deadline for submitting proposals. Submit proposals at least one month before a board meeting for consideration.

The board meets in February, May, July, and October.

Restrictions on Giving: The foundation does not make grants to individuals, or for building funds, fellowships, or loans.

OTHER THINGS TO KNOW
The foundation is affiliated with the Windham Foundation in Grafton, VT.

PUBLICATIONS
Annual report and application guidelines

GRANTS ANALYSIS
Total Grants: $652,175

Number of Grants: 139

Highest Grant: $25,000

Average Grant: $4,692

Typical Range: $1,000 to $5,000

Disclosure Period: 1992

Note: Recent grants are derived from a 1992 grants list.

RECENT GRANTS

General
25,000	Experiment in International Living, Brattleboro, VT
25,000	Pingry School, Martinsville, NJ
25,000	Stuart Country Day School, Princeton, NJ
25,000	Stuart Country Day School, Princeton, NJ
10,000	Hun School of Princeton, Princeton, NJ

Cape Branch Foundation

CONTACT
Gretchen Johnson
Director, Trustee
Cape Branch Fdn.
c/o Danser, Balaam and Frank
5 Independence Way
Princeton, NJ 08540
(609) 987-0300

FINANCIAL SUMMARY
Recent Giving: $129,450 (1993); $283,000 (1992); $210,000 (1990)

Assets: $12,121,298 (1993); $10,388,704 (1992); $10,400,196 (1991)

EIN: 22-6054886

CONTRIBUTIONS SUMMARY

Typical Recipients: • *Arts & Humanities:* Arts Associations & Councils, Libraries, Museums/Galleries • *Education:* Arts/Humanities Education, Colleges & Universities, Private Education (Precollege), Secondary Education (Private), Student Aid • *Environment:* Air/Water Quality, General, Resource Conservation, Watershed • *Health:* AIDS/HIV, Hospitals • *Social Services:* Recreation & Athletics, Youth Organizations

Grant Types: capital, general support, and research

Geographic Distribution: focus on NJ

GIVING OFFICERS

Gordon O. Danser: trust

Gretchen W. Johnson: dir, trust

James Lawrence Johnson: dir *B* Vernon TX 1927 *ED* TX Tech Univ BBA 1949 *CURR EMPL* chmn emeritus: GTE Corp *CORP AFFIL* dir: Bloomington Unlimited, British Columbia Telecommunications, First Fed Savings & Loan Assn, Mutual Life Ins Co NY *NONPR AFFIL* dir: IL Telephone Assn, McLean County Assn Commerce Indus; mem: Fin Execs Inst, Natl Assn Accts, Wesleyan Assocs, Wesleyan Univ; mem adv counc: IL St Univ Coll Bus; trust, mem adv counc: Mennonite Hosp *CLUB AFFIL* Bloomington CC, Crestwicke CC, Woodway CC

APPLICATION INFORMATION

Initial Approach: Send brief letter of inquiry describing program or project. Include a description of organization, amount requested, purpose of funds sought, recently audited financial statement, and proof of tax-exempt status. There are no deadlines.

GRANTS ANALYSIS
Total Grants: $129,450

Number of Grants: 6

Highest Grant: $80,000

Typical Range: $450 to $25,000

Disclosure Period: 1993

Note: Recent grants are derived from a 1993 Form 990.

RECENT GRANTS

Library
5,000	Clarence Dillon Public Library Project 91, Bedminster, NJ — for new building fund

General
80,000	Gladstone Equestrian Association, Gladstone, NJ
25,000	Massachusetts General Hospital Neurolinguistics Lab, Boston, MA — for Neurolinguistics Lab Fund and precursor program
10,000	Upper Raritan Watershed Association, Gladstone, NJ
	— for conservation of natural resources
450	First Avenue School, Newark, NJ — for busing

Church & Dwight Co., Inc.

Sales: $507.65 million
Employees: 1,096
Headquarters: Princeton, NJ
SIC Major Group: Soap & Other Detergents, Alkalies & Chlorine, Industrial Inorganic Chemicals Nec, and Polishes & Sanitation Goods

CONTACT
Jean M. Reince
Manager, Community Relations
Church & Dwight Co., Inc.
469 N Harrison St.
Princeton, NJ 08543-5297
(609) 683-5900

FINANCIAL SUMMARY
Recent Giving: $300,000 (1993 approx.); $300,000 (1991 approx.); $175,000 (1990 approx.)

Fiscal Note: Company gives directly.

CONTRIBUTIONS SUMMARY
Typical Recipients: • *Arts & Humanities:* Community Arts, Historic Preservation, Libraries, Museums/Galleries, Music, Public Broadcasting • *Civic & Public Affairs:* Urban & Community Affairs • *Education:* Agricultural Education, Arts/Humanities Education, Business Education, Colleges & Universities • *Environment:* General • *Health:* Emergency/Ambulance Services, Health Funds, Health Organizations, Hospitals, Medical Research, Mental Health • *Science:* Scientific Organizations • *Social Services:* Animal Protection, Community Service Organizations, Emergency Relief, Food/Clothing Distribution, United Funds/United Ways, Youth Organizations

Grant Types: employee matching gifts and research

Nonmonetary Support Types: donated equipment, donated products, in-kind services, loaned employees, and loaned executives

Geographic Distribution: primarily in New Jersey

Operating Locations: NJ (Princeton)

Note: Company also operates in Canada and the United Kingdom.

CORP. OFFICERS
Anthony P. Deasey: *B* Brighton England 1949 *CURR EMPL* vp, cfo: Church & Dwight Co Inc *NONPR AFFIL* mem: Inst Chartered Accts

Dwight Church Minton: *B* North Hills NY 1934 *ED* Yale Univ BA 1959; Stanford Univ Grad Sch Bus Admin MBA 1961 *CURR EMPL* chmn, ceo: Church & Dwight Co Inc *CORP AFFIL* dir: Chem Bank NJ, Crane Corp, First Brands Corp, Medusa Cement Corp *NONPR AFFIL* dir: Greater Yellowstone Coalition; mem: Chem Mfrs Assn, Grocery Mfrs Am; trust: Morehouse Coll *CLUB AFFIL* Lotos, Racquet & Tennis, Seawan-haka Corinthian YC, Yale

GIVING OFFICERS
Jean M. Reince: *CURR EMPL* mgr commun rels: Church & Dwight Co Inc

APPLICATION INFORMATION
Initial Approach: *Initial Contact:* letter of inquiry and full proposal *Include Information On:* description of the organization, amount requested, purpose of funds sought, recently audited financial statements, and proof of tax-exempt status *Deadlines:* none

Restrictions on Giving: Does not support individuals, religious organizations for sectarian purposes, or political or lobbying groups.

CPC International Inc.

Revenue: $7.42 billion
Employees: 35,000
Headquarters: Englewood Cliffs, NJ
SIC Major Group: Wet Corn Milling, Cheese—Natural & Processed, Canned Specialties, and Canned Fruits & Vegetables

---

CONTACT
Patricia Biale
Manager, Personnel Services
CPC International, Inc.
International Plz.
PO Box 8000
Englewood Cliffs, NJ 07632
(201) 894-2521

FINANCIAL SUMMARY
Recent Giving: $2,587,000 (1995 est.); $2,653,000 (1994 approx.); $2,420,000 (1993 approx.)

Fiscal Note: Company gives directly, through a decentralized contributions program. Above figures represent cash contributions and matching gifts made through company's central operations only. Company also gives through its divisions (see notes in "Their Priorities" and "Other Things You Should Know"). Above figures include nonmonetary support.

CONTRIBUTIONS SUMMARY
Typical Recipients: • *Arts & Humanities:* Arts Associations & Councils, Arts Centers, Arts Festivals, Arts Funds, Community Arts, Dance, Ethnic & Folk Arts, Historic Preservation, Libraries, Museums/Galleries, Music, Performing Arts, Public Broadcasting, Theater • *Civic & Public Affairs:* Business/Free Enterprise, Civil Rights, Economic Development, Employment/Job Training, Law & Justice, Municipalities/Towns, Professional & Trade Associations, Public Policy, Safety, Urban & Community Affairs, Zoos/Aquariums • *Education:* Business Education, Colleges & Universities, Community & Junior Colleges, Economic Education, Education Associations, Faculty Development, International Exchange, International Studies, Literacy, Minority Education, Private Education (Prec-

ollege), Public Education (Precollege), Science/Mathematics Education, Student Aid • *Environment:* General • *Health:* Health Policy/Cost Containment, Health Funds, Health Organizations, Hospitals, Medical Research, Mental Health, Nursing Services, Single-Disease Health Associations • *International:* International Peace & Security Issues, International Relations • *Social Services:* Child Welfare, Community Centers, Community Service Organizations, Domestic Violence, Family Services, People with Disabilities, Refugee Assistance, Senior Services, Substance Abuse, United Funds/United Ways, Youth Organizations

Grant Types: employee matching gifts, general support, project, research, scholarship, and seed money

Note: Company matches employee gifts to all nonprofit organizations except fraternal organizations or organizations concerned with religion or politics.

Nonmonetary Support: $12,700,000 (1994); $7,200,000 (1992); $15,000,000 (1991)

Nonmonetary Support Types: donated equipment, donated products, and in-kind services

Note: Estimated value of nonmonetary support was $7.2 million in 1992 (see note to "Their Priorities"). This support is not included in above figures.

Geographic Distribution: principally near operating locations and to national organizations, with limited support to international organizations

Operating Locations: AR, CA, IL (Argo), IN, MA, MD, NC, NJ (Englewood Cliffs, Fairfield, Newark, Totowa), PA, PR, RI, WA, WI

CORP. OFFICERS
Charles Richard Shoemate: *B* La Harpe IL 1939 *ED* Western IL Univ BS 1962; Univ Chicago MBA 1973 *CURR EMPL* chmn, pres, ceo: CPC Intl Inc *CORP AFFIL* dir: Cigna Corp *NONPR AFFIL* dir: Ams Soc, Grocery Mfrs Am; mem: Bus Roundtable, Comm Econ Devel, Conf Bd

GIVING OFFICERS
Richard P. Bergeman: chmn contributions comm *CURR EMPL* vp human resources: CPC Intl Inc

Patricia Biale: mem contributions comm *CURR EMPL* mgr pers services: CPC Intl Inc

Charles Feldberg: *CURR EMPL* mem contributions comm: CPC Intl Inc

James E. Healey: mem contributions comm *B* New York NY 1941 *ED* Pace Univ 1964 *CURR EMPL* comptr: CPC Intl Inc *CORP AFFIL* dir: Interchange Fin Svcs Corp, Interchange St Bank

John B. Meagher: mem contributions comm *B* New York NY 1936 *ED* Georgetown Univ BA 1958; Fordham Univ Law Sch JD 1966 *CURR EMPL* secy: CPC Intl Inc

APPLICATION INFORMATION
Initial Approach: *Initial Contact:* letter and proposal to Patricia Biale at above ad-

dress *Include Information On:* cover letter should include reason for request, specific amount sought, and name of contact person; proposal should include purpose and history of organization, objectives for coming year, client population and geographic scope, current board membership, projected income and expenses for current year, audited financial statement of previous year, proof of tax-exempt status, list of current supporters *Deadlines:* none; committee meets six times per year

Restrictions on Giving: Company does not support individuals; political, fraternal, or religious organizations; or goodwill advertising and special events.

OTHER THINGS TO KNOW
Company also sponsors the CPC Education Foundation, which awards scholarships to children of employees.

Company also makes contributions through its Best Foods, Corn Wet Milling, and international divisions. In 1992, the company reports its baking division gave approximately $7.0 million, primarily in day old bread; harvest division, $2.0 million; and food unit, $300,000. Giving figures for international divisions not available.

GRANTS ANALYSIS
Total Grants: $2,471,000

Typical Range: $1,000 to $5,000

Disclosure Period: 1994

Darby Foundation

CONTACT
Katherine D. Brady
Trustee
Darby Fdn.
c/o Summit Bank
40 Beechwood Rd.
Summit, NJ 07901

FINANCIAL SUMMARY
Recent Giving: $124,400 (1993); $135,667 (1992); $176,009 (1991)

Assets: $2,079,069 (1993); $2,025,087 (1992); $2,056,209 (1991)

EIN: 13-6212178

CONTRIBUTIONS SUMMARY
Donor(s): Nicholas F. Brady

Typical Recipients: • *Arts & Humanities:* Historic Preservation, Libraries, Museums/Galleries, Performing Arts, Theater • *Civic & Public Affairs:* Botanical Gardens/Parks, Clubs, Public Policy, Safety, Zoos/Aquariums • *Education:* Colleges & Universities, General, Private Education (Precollege), Student Aid • *Environment:* General, Resource Conservation • *Health:* Clinics/Medical Centers, Emergency/Ambulance Services, Eyes/Blindness, Hospitals, Medical Research, Research/Studies Institutes, Single-Disease Health Associations • *International:* Foreign Educational Institutions • *Religion:* Churches • *Social Services:* Child Welfare, Community Service Organizations, Domestic Violence, Food/Clothing Distribution, Senior Services, Shelters/Homelessness, United Funds/United Ways, Youth Organizations

Grant Types: general support

Geographic Distribution: focus on Northeast

GIVING OFFICERS

Katherine D. Brady: trust

Nicholas Frederick Brady: trust *B* New York NY 1930 *ED* Yale Univ BA 1952; Harvard Univ MBA 1954 *NONPR AFFIL* trust: Boys Club Newark *CLUB AFFIL* Bond NY, Links, Lunch *PHIL AFFIL* trust: Brady Foundation

APPLICATION INFORMATION

Initial Approach: Send a brief letter of inquiry. There are no deadlines.

GRANTS ANALYSIS

Total Grants: $124,400

Number of Grants: 22

Highest Grant: $50,000

Typical Range: $500 to $10,000

Disclosure Period: 1993

Note: Recent grants are derived from a 1993 Form 990.

RECENT GRANTS

Library

50,000	Bush Presidential Library Foundation, TX — educational

General

10,000	Boys and Girls Club, Newark, NJ
10,000	St. Malachy's Catholic Church, NY — operational
5,000	Iona Senior Services, Washington, DC — operational
5,000	Trappe Volunteer Fire Department, Trappe, MD — operational
5,000	US Kids, Washington, DC — educational

Dodge Foundation, Geraldine R.

CONTACT

Scott McVay
Executive Director
Geraldine R. Dodge Foundation
163 Madison Ave.
PO Box 1239
Morristown, NJ 07962-1239
(201) 540-8442

FINANCIAL SUMMARY

Recent Giving: $10,921,097 (1993); $9,656,483 (1992); $9,196,455 (1991)

Assets: $199,184,930 (1993); $177,856,708 (1992); $175,738,210 (1991)

Gifts Received: $15,000 (1993); $30,000 (1992)

Fiscal Note: In 1992, the foundation received gifts from the Sealed Air Corporation, New York Community Trust, Bristol Myers Corporation, New Jersey Bell, and Schumann Fund for New Jersey. In 1993, the foundation received gifts from Victoria Foundation.

EIN: 23-7406010

CONTRIBUTIONS SUMMARY

Donor(s): The Geraldine R. Dodge Foundation was established in 1974 in accordance with the will of the late Geraldine R. Dodge , who died in 1973. She was the daughter of William Rockefeller (a former president of Standard Oil) and the niece of John D. Rockefeller. Her husband Marcellus Hartley Dodge was chairman of the Remington Arms Co. Mrs. Dodge, an avid dog breeder and pet lover, also established an animal shelter at her death.

Typical Recipients: • *Arts & Humanities:* Arts Appreciation, Arts Associations & Councils, Arts Centers, Arts Festivals, Arts Outreach, Community Arts, Dance, History & Archaeology, Libraries, Literary Arts, Museums/Galleries, Music, Opera, Performing Arts, Public Broadcasting, Theater, Visual Arts • *Civic & Public Affairs:* Public Policy, Urban & Community Affairs, Women's Affairs • *Education:* Arts/Humanities Education, Colleges & Universities, Education Associations, Education Reform, Elementary Education (Private), Elementary Education (Public), Engineering/Technological Education, Environmental Education, Faculty Development, Gifted & Talented Programs, International Exchange, International Studies, Medical Education, Minority Education, Private Education (Precollege), Public Education (Precollege), Science/Mathematics Education, Secondary Education (Public) • *Environment:* Air/Water Quality, Energy, General, Protection, Resource Conservation, Wildlife Protection • *Health:* Medical Research • *International:* Health Care/Hospitals, International Development • *Science:* Science Museums, Scientific Centers & Institutes • *Social Services:* Animal Protection, Domestic Violence, Family Planning, Family Services, Shelters/Homelessness, Youth Organizations

Grant Types: challenge, general support, operating expenses, and project

Geographic Distribution: national, with emphasis on New Jersey

GIVING OFFICERS

Robert Hayes Burns Baldwin: chmn, trust

Barbara Knowles Debs: trust *B* Eastham MA 1931 *ED* Vassar Coll BA 1953; Radcliffe Coll 1956-1958; Harvard Univ PhD 1967 *NONPR AFFIL* dir: Intl Fdn Art Res; mem: Am Counc Ed, Coll Art Assn, Counc Foreign Rels, Phi Beta Kappa, Renaissance Soc Am, Young Audiences; pres, ceo, dir: NY Historical Soc; trust: Comm Econ Devel, NY Law Sch *CLUB AFFIL* Century, Cosmopolitan, Hundred Westchester

Vera DuMont: asst to dir

Christopher J. Elliman: trust

Cynthia Evans: trust

Henry Upham Harder: trust

John Lloyd Huck: trust *B* Brooklyn NY 1922 *ED* PA St Univ BS 1946 *NONPR AFFIL* trust: Morristown Meml Health Fdn *CLUB AFFIL* Morris County GC, Pipers Landing GC, Stuart FL YC & CC

Robert Le Buhn: pres, trust *CURR EMPL* pres: Instoria Inc/Providentia Ltd

Nancy D. Lindsay: trust

Scott McVay: exec dir *PHIL AFFIL* trust: W. Alton Jones Foundation

Paul J. O'Donnell: trust

John Yingling: chief adm, fin off

APPLICATION INFORMATION
Initial Approach:

Grant requests should be addressed to Scott McVay, Executive Director.

Grant requests should begin with a one-page summary of the project, followed by no more than six pages of the main body of the application. The proposal should describe the project and the need for it, the qualifications and past accomplishments of the sponsoring organization, how the project is to proceed and who is to carry it out, a time frame and budget, the benefits to be gained and for whom, and the plans for evaluating and funding the project in the future. Also included should be a recent financial statement, together with the names and occupations of the trustees of the organization, as well as IRS confirmation of tax-exempt status. The foundation requests that the proposal be presented in an environmentally sensitive manner. Proposals should use two-sided copies without binders or plastic packaging. No faxed proposals are accepted and the foundation prefers that express mail carriers not be used.

Requests should be submitted on or before one of the following deadlines: December 15 for animal welfare and local projects in Morris County, March 15 for precollegiate education, June 15 for the arts, and September 15 for public issues.

The board of trustees meets four times yearly. It considers pre-collegiate education in March, the arts in June, local projects and the welfare of animals in September, and public issues in December.

Restrictions on Giving: The foundation does not consider grants for higher education, health, and religion. Grants usually are not made for capital programs, equipment purchases, endowment funds, or deficit operations. Grants typically are not made to individuals, scholarship funds, or to organizations that distribute funds to other organizations.

OTHER THINGS TO KNOW

In 1992, the foundation decided to report grants in the same year in which they are approved, to reflect more accurately the trustees' decisions. Previously, grants were reported in the same year in which the cash payment was made.

Grant recipients are asked to make periodic progress reports, and at the termination of a grant, to submit a narrative report and an accounting of all disbursements. It is customary for an organization, whether it is funded or not, to wait one year before submitting another proposal.

PUBLICATIONS

Annual report

GRANTS ANALYSIS
Total Grants: $10,921,097
Number of Grants: 494
Highest Grant: $150,000
Average Grant: $22,107
Typical Range: $10,000 to $100,000
Disclosure Period: 1993

Note: Recent grants are derived from a 1993 Form 990.

RECENT GRANTS

General

150,000 Planned Parenthood Federation of America, New York, NY — this grant supports PPFA's Public Impact programs, focused on preventing teen pregnancies and promoting sexuality education

145,000 American Association for Gifted Children, Durham, NC — provide $1,000 awards for 141 presidential scholars, all of whom are graduating high school seniors, representing 50 states, the District of Columbia, and the territories

125,000 Summer Educational Opportunity Award for Principals, Morristown, NJ — 25 grants of $5,000 each were offered to public school principals in 1993; an additional grant of $1,000 each was given to each respective school district to assist with expenses associated with the grant.

125,000 Summer Educational Opportunity Awards, Morris County, NJ — since 1985, this foundation initiative has recognized the need for teachers to be supported professionally in pursuing educational dreams during the summer

110,000 Earthwatch, Watertown, MA — enable 45 New Jersey teachers over the next three summers to expand their horizons on summer research expeditions in selected tropical rain forest environments

Dow Jones & Company, Inc. / Dow Jones Foundation

Sales: $1.93 billion
Employees: 10,000
Headquarters: New York, NY
SIC Major Group: Newspapers

CONTACT
Leonard E. Doherty
Administrative Officer
Dow Jones Fdn.
PO Box 300
Princeton, NJ 08543
(609) 520-5143

FINANCIAL SUMMARY
Recent Giving: $2,300,000 (1995 est.); $2,300,000 (1994 approx.); $2,300,000 (1993 approx.)

Assets: $2,000,000 (1995 est.); $3,130,023 (1994); $2,074,491 (1993)

Gifts Received: $1,500,000 (1993); $500,000 (1992)

Fiscal Note: Above figures include giving from the Dow Jones Foundation ($1,473,825 in 1994), direct giving, and nonmonetary support.

EIN: 13-6070158

CONTRIBUTIONS SUMMARY
Typical Recipients: • *Arts & Humanities:* History & Archaeology, Libraries, Museums/Galleries, Music • *Civic & Public Affairs:* Economic Policy, First Amendment Issues, General, Hispanic Affairs, Native American Affairs, Professional & Trade Associations, Urban & Community Affairs, Women's Affairs • *Education:* Colleges & Universities, Education Associations, Journalism/Media Education, Minority Education, Student Aid • *Health:* Clinics/Medical Centers, Hospitals • *International:* International Organizations, International Relations • *Social Services:* Child Welfare, Family Services, People with Disabilities, United Funds/United Ways, Volunteer Services

Grant Types: general support

Geographic Distribution: mainly near operating locations and to national organizations

Operating Locations: AZ (Sun City), CA (Palo Alto, Riverside, Santa Cruz), CO (Denver), CT (Danbury), FL (Orlando), GA (LaGrange), IA (Des Moines), IL (Highland, Naperville), KY (Ashland), MA (Beverly, Boston, Chicopee Falls, Fall River, Gloucester, Hyannis, Nantucket, New Bedford, Newburyport, Peabody), MD (White Oak), MI (Traverse City), MN (Mankato), MO (Joplin), NC (Charlotte), NH (Exeter, Hampton), NJ (Jersey City, Princeton, South Brunswick), NY (Campbell Hall, Ithaca, Middletown, New York, Oneonta, Plattsburgh, Port Jervis), OH (Bowling Green), OR (Medford), PA (Grove City, Sharon, Stroudsburg, Sunbury), TX (Beaumont, Dallas), VA (Ashland), WA (Federal Way)

Note: Also operates internationally.

CORP. OFFICERS
Kenneth L. Burenga: *B* Somerville NJ 1944 *ED* Rider Coll BS 1970 *CURR EMPL* pres, coo, dir: Dow Jones & Co Inc *CORP AFFIL* dir: Dow Jones Courier, Ottaway Newspapers Inc; gen mgr: Wall St Journal

Peter Robert Kann: *B* New York NY 1942 *ED* Harvard Univ BA 1964 *CURR EMPL* chmn, ceo, publ, dir: Dow Jones & Co Inc *CORP AFFIL* chmn, bd dirs, pub: Wall St Journal *NONPR AFFIL* dir: Group Expansion; mem: Inst Advanced Study, Pulitzer Prize Bd; trust: Asia Soc *CLUB AFFIL* Spee

Roger May: *CURR EMPL* dir corp rels: Dow Jones & Co Inc

James Haller Ottaway, Jr.: *B* Binghamton NY 1938 *ED* Yale Univ BA 1960 *CURR EMPL* sr vp, dir: Dow Jones & Co Inc *CORP AFFIL* chmn, dir: Ottaway Newspapers Inc *NONPR AFFIL* mem: Am Newspaper Publs Assn, Am Soc Newspaper Editors; trust: Am Sch Classical Studies Athens, Stormling Art Ctr *PHIL AFFIL* don, pres, trust: Nicholas B. Ottaway Foundation

GIVING OFFICERS
Bettina Bancroft: mem adv comm *B* 1941 *CORP AFFIL* dir: Dow Jones & Co Inc

Nicole Bourgois: mem adv comm

Jane Bancroft Cook: chmn adv comm *B* 1912 *CORP AFFIL* dir: Dow Jones & Co Inc

Leonard Edward Doherty: mem adv comm, admin off *B* Lowell MA 1940 *ED* Merrimack Coll BBA 1962 *CURR EMPL* treas, asst secy: Dow Jones & Co Inc *CORP AFFIL* asst treas, asst secy: Natl Delivery Svc Inc; treas, dir: Dow Jones Telerate Inc *NONPR AFFIL* mem: Am Inst CPAs, Inst Newspaper Contrs & Fin Offs, Intl Newspaper Fin Execs, NJ Soc CPAs

Peter Robert Kann: mem adv comm *CURR EMPL* chmn, ceo, publ, dir: Dow Jones & Co Inc (see above)

James Haller Ottaway, Jr.: mem adv comm *CURR EMPL* sr vp, dir: Dow Jones & Co Inc *PHIL AFFIL* don, pres, trust: Nicholas B. Ottaway Foundation (see above)

APPLICATION INFORMATION
Initial Approach: *Initial Contact:* brief letter or proposal *Include Information On:* outline of proposed purpose of grant, proof of tax-exempt status *Deadlines:* September

Restrictions on Giving: Does not currently support medical and scientific research or cultural activities.

OTHER THINGS TO KNOW
Foundation has policy of considering contributions to institutions and causes where there has been a history of active participation and support by company employees.

Foundation reports U.S. Trust Co. of New York as corporate trustee.

In 1993, Dow Jones Foundation donated $400,000 to the Dow Jones Newspaper Fund, a program which supports journalism education for minority high school and college students. Also provides internships and fellowships.

GRANTS ANALYSIS
Total Grants: $1,444,350

Number of Grants: 134

Highest Grant: $400,000

Average Grant: $10,779

Typical Range: $1,000 to $20,000

Disclosure Period: 1993

Note: Above figures are for foundation only. Recent grants are derived from a 1993 Form 990.

RECENT GRANTS

Library

6,000	Princeton Public Library, Princeton, NJ

General

400,000	Dow Jones Newspaper Fund, New York, NY
233,000	National Merit Scholarship Corporation, Evanston, IL
55,000	United Way of Pioneer Valley, Springfield, MA
55,000	United Way of Tri-State, New York, NY
40,000	Kirby Potter Fund, New York, NY

Fund for New Jersey

CONTACT
Mark M. Murphy
Executive Director and Secretary
Fund for New Jersey
Kilmer Sq.
65 Church St., Ste. 200
New Brunswick, NJ 08901
(908) 220-8656

FINANCIAL SUMMARY
Recent Giving: $1,500,000 (1995 est.); $1,500,000 (1994 approx.); $1,476,725 (1993)

Assets: $36,000,000 (1995 est.); $36,322,000 (1994); $35,437,010 (1993)

Gifts Received: $8,465 (1993)

Fiscal Note: In 1993, the foundation received a grant from the Kellogg Foundation.

EIN: 22-1895028

CONTRIBUTIONS SUMMARY
Donor(s): The fund was established in 1969 by the family of the late Mr. and Mrs. Charles F. Wallace of Westfield, NJ, to "maximize contributions to social improvements." Mr. Charles Wallace declined naming any specific purpose for the fund, stating that only individuals living in and currently aware of existing problems in the community could decide the best use of its fund. The orginal board of trustees was then augmented with well-informed individuals of standing in the community who could contribute meaningfully to board deliberations.

Typical Recipients: • *Arts & Humanities:* Libraries • *Civic & Public Affairs:* Community Foundations, Economic Development, Hispanic Affairs, Housing, Law & Justice, Municipalities/Towns, Nonprofit Management, Philanthropic Organizations, Professional & Trade Associations, Public Policy, Rural Affairs, Urban & Community Affairs, Women's Affairs • *Education:* Arts/Humanities Education, Colleges & Universities, Education Associations, Education Reform, Public Education (Precollege), Science/Mathematics Education • *Environment:* Air/Water Quality, General, Protection, Resource Conservation, Watershed • *Health:* AIDS/HIV, Health Organizations, Hospitals • *Social Services:* Child Welfare, Community Service Organizations, Domestic Violence, Family Services, United Funds/United Ways

Grant Types: conference/seminar, general support, multiyear/continuing support, project, research, and seed money

Geographic Distribution: focus on New Jersey

GIVING OFFICERS
Candace McKee Ashmun: trust

Ann L. Auerbach: trust

William Oliver Baker: trust *B* Chestertown MD 1915 *ED* Washington Coll BS 1935; Princeton Univ PhD 1938 *CURR EMPL* dir: Summit Trust Co *CORP AFFIL* dir: Gen Am Investors Co, Health Effects Inst *NONPR AFFIL* adv coun: Special Libraries Assn; chmn emeritus: Rockefeller Univ; chmn telecommuns bd: US Dept State; co-chmn natl counc: Am Assn Advancement Science; dir: Counc Library Resources, EDUCOM, Health Effects Inst; fellow: Am Academy Arts Sciences, Am Inst Chemists, Am Physical Soc, Franklin Inst; mem: Am Chem Soc, Am Philosophical Soc, Carnegie Forum Ed Science Tech & Econ, Dirs Indus Res, Indus Res Inst, Natl Academy Engg, Natl Academy Sciences, Omicron Delta Kappa, Phi Lambda Upsilon, Sigma Xi; mem adv counc: Fed Emergency Mgmt Adv Bd, NJ Regional Med Library; mem bd overseers: Univ PA Coll Engg Applied Science; mem counc: Marconi Fellowships; mem exec comm: NJ Bd Higher Ed; mem science adv bd: Natl Security Agency; mem, vchmn: NJ Commn Science & Tech; mem visiting comm sciences & math: Drew Univ; trust: Charles Babbage Inst *CLUB AFFIL* Cosmos, Princeton Northwestern NJ; hon mem: Chemists NY *PHIL AFFIL* trust: General Motors Cancer Research Foundation, Fund for Innovation and Public Service; dir: Harry Frank Guggenheim Foundation; chmn emeritus: Andrew W. Mellon Foundation

John W. Cornwall: trust *PHIL AFFIL* trust: Fund for Innovation and Public Service

Joseph C. Cornwall: chmn, treas, trust *PHIL AFFIL* chmn, treas, trust: Fund for Innovation and Public Service

Dickinson Richards Debevoise: trust *B* Orange NJ 1924 *ED* Williams Coll BA 1948; Columbia Univ LLB 1951 *NONPR AFFIL* fellow: Am Bar Fdn; judge: US District Ct NJ; mem: Am Bar Assn, Am Judicature Soc, Am Law Inst, Assn Fed Bar St NJ, Essex County Bar Assn, Fed Bar Assn, NJ Bar Assn; trust: Hosp Ctr Orange NJ *PHIL AFFIL* trust: Fund for Innovation and Public Service

John Joseph Gibbons: vp, trust *B* Newark NJ 1924 *ED* Holy Cross Coll BS 1947; Harvard Univ LLB 1950 *NONPR AFFIL* adjunct prof: Duke Univ, Rutgers Univ, Seton Hall Univ, Suffolk Univ; fellow: Am Bar Fdn; mem: Am Bar Assn, Essex County Bar Assn, Holy Cross Coll Gen Alumni Assn, NJ Bar Assn; prof constitutional law: Seton Hall Univ; trust: Holy Cross Coll, Practicing Law Inst *PHIL AFFIL* trust: Fund for Innovation and Public Service

Carol Head: asst treas

Gustav Heningburg: trust *PHIL AFFIL* trust: Fund for Innovation and Public Service

Leonard Lieberman: trust *B* Elizabeth NJ 1929 *ED* Yale Univ BA 1950; Columbia Univ JD 1953 *CORP AFFIL* dir: Celestial Seasonings, Consolidated Cigar Corp, Outlet Commun, Perfect Fit Indus, Republic NY Corp, Russell-Stanley Corp, Sonic Indus, Super D Drugs, Van Dusen Airport Svcs *NONPR AFFIL* chmn: NJ Academy Aquatic Sciences; chmn, trust: Ctr Analysis Pub Issues; dir: Newark Performing Arts Corp; hon pres, trust: Newark Beth Israel Med Ctr; mem: Food Mktg Inst, NJ Comm Regional Plan Assn, Partnership NJ; mem couns NJ aff: Princeton Univ Counc NJ Aff; mem NJ comm, dir: Regional Plan Assn; trust: Boys & Girls Clubs Newark, NJ Ctr Performing Arts, Victim Svc Agency *CLUB AFFIL* Essex County, Harvard New York City

Gordon A. MacInnes: trust

Mark M. Murphy: secy, exec dir *PHIL AFFIL* exec dir: Fund for Innovation and Public Service

Clement A. Price: trust

Mary S. Strong: trust *PHIL AFFIL* trust: Fund for Innovation and Public Service

Richard J. Sullivan: pres, trust *B* Green Bay WI 1949 *CURR EMPL* exec vp: Fleishman-Hillard *NONPR AFFIL* mem: Pub Rels Soc Am *CLUB AFFIL* Natl Press *PHIL AFFIL* pres, trust: Fund for Innovation and Public Service, Environmental Endowment for New Jersey

Jane W. Thorne: trust *PHIL AFFIL* trust: Fund for Innovation and Public Service

APPLICATION INFORMATION
Initial Approach:

Applicants should send a proposal that includes a one page cover sheet to the fund.

The one page cover sheet should include the following: amount requested; a one or two sentence description of the problem or need addressed by the proposed project; a one or two sentence description of the proposed activity and what it is expected to accomplish; and the mailing address and telephone number of the organization and the contact person. The fund encourages applicants to submit in the body of their proposal whatever information they feel is important for consideration. However, all proposals must be accompanied by a copy of the applicant's IRS tax exemption letter, the names and affiliations of the board of directors, and a budget showing projected sources of income and anticipated expenditures.

There are no application deadlines.

The board of trustees meets four times a year. The fund does not specify a time frame for making a decision concerning a specific application or notifying applicants of the board's decision.

Restrictions on Giving: The fund stresses that it only makes grants to organizations which have applied for or have been granted tax-exempt status under Section 501(c)(3) of Internal Revenue Code. The fund does not accept applications for support of individuals, nor for capital projects including acquisition, mortgage retirement, revovation, or equipment. In general, the fund will not support day care centers, drug treatment programs, land acquisitions, health care delivery, scholarships, or curricular changes in educational institutions.

PUBLICATIONS
Annual rcport includes application guidelines

GRANTS ANALYSIS
Total Grants: $1,476,725

Number of Grants: 50

Highest Grant: $110,000

Average Grant: $29,535

Typical Range: $20,000 to $50,000

Disclosure Period: 1993

Note: Recent grants are derived from a 1993 Form 990.

RECENT GRANTS

Library

2,000	Foundation Center, New York, NY

General

110,000	Associated New Jersey Environmental Commission, Mendham, NC — state plan
75,000	Early Childhood Facilities Fund, Pennington, NJ — planning
75,000	New Community Corporation, Newark, NJ — director
75,000	Walt Whitman Center of Rutgers, Newark, NJ
70,000	University Heights Science Park, Newark, NJ — planning

High Foundation

CONTACT
High Fdn.
c/o High Industries Scholarship Program
Princeton, NJ 08541

FINANCIAL SUMMARY
Recent Giving: $329,400 (fiscal 1992); $320,583 (fiscal 1991); $313,683 (fiscal 1990)

Assets: $2,399,857 (fiscal 1992); $2,710,435 (fiscal 1991); $2,052,439 (fiscal 1990)

Gifts Received: $75,000 (fiscal 1992); $500,000 (fiscal 1991); $250,000 (fiscal 1990)

Fiscal Note: In fiscal 1992, contributions were received from High Industries, Inc.

EIN: 23-2149972

CONTRIBUTIONS SUMMARY
Typical Recipients: • *Arts & Humanities:* Arts Centers, Community Arts, Historic Preservation, Libraries, Music, Performing Arts, Theater • *Civic & Public Affairs:* Ethnic Organizations, Housing, Parades/Festivals, Professional & Trade Associations • *Education:* Arts/Humanities Education, Colleges & Universities, Education Funds, Minority Education, Private Education (Precollege), Religious Education, Student Aid • *Health:* Children's Health/Hospitals, Hospitals • *Religion:* Churches, Religious Organizations, Religious Welfare • *Social Services:* Community Service Organizations, United Funds/United Ways, Youth Organizations

Grant Types: general support and scholarship

GIVING OFFICERS
Calvin G. High: trust

APPLICATION INFORMATION
Initial Approach: The foundation has no formal grant application procedure or application form.

GRANTS ANALYSIS
Total Grants: $329,400

Number of Grants: 29

Highest Grant: $150,000

Typical Range: $500 to $5,000

Disclosure Period: fiscal year ending August 31, 1992

Note: Recent grants are derived from a fiscal 1992 Form 990.

RECENT GRANTS

Library

150,000	Elizabethtown College, Elizabethtown, PA — library
1,000	Lancaster County Library, Lancaster, PA — operating expenses

General

20,000	Messiah College, Grantham, PA — operating expenses
20,000	Spanish American Civic Association, Lancaster, PA — building renovation
17,500	Lancaster Area Habitat for Humanity, Lancaster, PA — operating expenses
14,000	Educational Testing Service, Princeton, NJ — scholarships
10,000	Boys and Girls Club of Lancaster, Lancaster, PA — camping facility

Hoffmann-La Roche Inc. / Hoffmann-La Roche Foundation

Sales: $3.0 billion
Employees: 18,000
Parent Company: Roche Holdings AG
Headquarters: Nutley, NJ
SIC Major Group: Pharmaceutical Preparations, Medicinals & Botanicals, and Medical Laboratories

CONTACT
Vivian Beatle
Director, Community Affairs
Hoffmann-La Roche Inc.
340 Kingsland St.
Nutley, NJ 07110-1199
(201) 235-5000

FINANCIAL SUMMARY
Recent Giving: $734,086 (1993); $882,750 (1992); $702,916 (1991)

Assets: $28 (1993); $28 (1992); $28 (1991)

Gifts Received: $734,086 (1993); $882,750 (1992)

Fiscal Note: Figures for foundation only. Company administers direct giving program but does not release contributions figures. Above figures exclude nonmonetary support. In 1993, the foundation received funds from Hoffmann-La Roche.

EIN: 22-6063790

CONTRIBUTIONS SUMMARY
Typical Recipients: • *Arts & Humanities:* Libraries • *Civic & Public Affairs:* Community Foundations, Philanthropic Organizations, Professional & Trade Associations, Zoos/Aquariums • *Education:* Colleges & Universities, Education Funds, Medical Education, Minority Education, Science/Mathematics Education • *Environment:* General, Wildlife Protection • *Health:* Children's Health/Hospitals, Health Organizations, Hospitals, Medical Research, Medical Training, Mental Health • *International:* Health Care/Hospitals, International Relations • *Religion:* Churches • *Science:* Science Museums, Scientific Centers & Institutes, Scientific Labs, Scientific Organizations • *Social Services:* Animal Protection, People with Disabilities, Substance Abuse

Grant Types: employee matching gifts, fellowship, research, and seed money

Nonmonetary Support Types: donated equipment, donated products, and in-kind services

Note: Value of nonmonetary support is unavailable.

Geographic Distribution: concentrated in New Jersey

Operating Locations: NC (Burlington), NJ (Belleville, Belvidere, Montclair, Nutley, Paramus, Raritan, Totowa)

CORP. OFFICERS
Irwin Lerner: *CURR EMPL* chmn, dir: Hoffmann-La Roche Inc *CORP AFFIL* dir:

Roche Biomed Labs; pres, dir: HLR Svc
Corp

Patrick J. Zenner: *B* 1948 *ED* Creighton
Univ BSBA 1969; Fairleigh Dickinson Univ
MBA *CURR EMPL* ceo, pres, dir: Hoffmann-
La Roche Inc

GIVING OFFICERS
Vivian Beatle: admin dir *CURR EMPL* dir
commun aff: Hoffmann-La Roche Inc

Harold Frederick Boardman, Jr.: trust *B*
Darby PA 1939 *ED* Trinity Coll BS 1961;
George Washington Univ JD 1964; Duke
Univ Advanced Mgmt Program 1988 *CURR
EMPL* vp, secy, gen couns, dir: Hoffmann-
La Roche Inc *CORP AFFIL* secy, dir: HLR
Svc Corp, Roche Biomed Labs *NONPR AF-
FIL* mem: Am Bar Assn, Am Corp Couns
Assn, DC Bar Assn, HI Bar Assn, NJ Bar
Assn, NJ Corp Couns Assn, Pharmaceutical
Mfrs Assn *CLUB AFFIL* Orange Lawn Ten-
nis

Ronald G. Kuntzman: trust *B* Brooklyn
NY 1933 *ED* CUNY Brooklyn Coll BS
1955; George Washington Univ MS 1957;
George Washington Univ PhD 1962 *NONPR
AFFIL* adjunct: Roche Inst Molecular Biol-
ogy; adjunct prof: Rutgers Univ Coll Phar-
macy; mem: Am Acad Arts & Sci, Am Assn
Advancement Sci, Am Coll Neuropsycho-
pharmacology, Am Soc Biological Chem,
Am Soc Pharmacology Experimental Thera-
peutics, George Washington Univ Alumni
Assn, Sigma Xi, Soc Toxicology

Irwin Lerner: trust *CURR EMPL* chmn,
dir: Hoffmann-La Roche Inc (see above)

Martin F. Stadler: trust *B* Hungary 1942
ED Rutgers Univ BS 1970; Fairleigh Dickin-
son Univ MBA 1974 *CURR EMPL* sr vp fin,
human resources & admin, dir: Hoffmann-
La Roche Inc *CORP AFFIL* dir: Roche
Biomed Labs; vp fin, dir: HLR Svc Corp

APPLICATION INFORMATION
Initial Approach: *Initial Contact:* for the
foundation, a brief letter or proposal; for direct corporate grants, a completed application form *Include Information On:* type of
scientific and medical research in the bios-
ciences together with a short paragraph outlining the proposed research *Deadlines:* for
the foundation, there are no deadlines; for direct corporate grants, applications are reviewed February 15, May 15, August 15,
and November 15 *Note:* Proposals from site
communities must be approved by plant managers before submission to foundation office.

Restrictions on Giving: Foundation grants
generally are limited to scientific and medical research at the post-doctoral level at major universities and teaching hospitals.

The foundation does not provide scholarships, gifts for capital campaigns, endowment funds, or grants to individuals.

Also not funded are political organizations;
veteran's organizations, unless projects are
in the interests of the general community; labor groups; member organizations of agencies funded by the company; or "goodwill"
advertising.

OTHER THINGS TO KNOW
Preference is given to organizations located
within the state of New Jersey and sites of
Hoffmann-La Roche. Preference is also
given to local chapters of national health organizations. National headquarters of health
organizations are rarely funded.

PUBLICATIONS
Guidelines

GRANTS ANALYSIS
Total Grants: $734,086
Number of Grants: 22
Highest Grant: $100,000
Average Grant: $33,368
Typical Range: $2,000 to $30,000
Disclosure Period: 1993

Note: Fiscal information represents foundation only. Recent grants are derived from a
1993 Form 990.

RECENT GRANTS
Library
10,000   Friends of the National
         Library of Medicine,
         Washington, DC

General
100,000 Independent College Fund of
         New Jersey, Summit, NJ
100,000 Puerto Rico Community
         Foundation, Hato Rey, PR
52,100   University of Medicine and
         Dentistry of New Jersey
         Foundation, Newark, NJ
50,000   Cold Spring Harbor
         Laboratory, Cold Spring
         Harbor, NY
50,000   ILSI Research Foundation,
         Washington, DC

Holzer Memorial Foundation, Richard H.

CONTACT
Erich Holzer
Secretary, Treasurer
Richard H. Holzer Memorial Fdn.
120 Sylvan Ave.
Englewood Cliffs, NJ 07632
(201) 947-8810

FINANCIAL SUMMARY
Recent Giving: $240,577 (1993); $195,459
(1992); $210,051 (1991)
Assets: $3,387,854 (1993); $3,050,474
(1992); $2,708,531 (1991)
Gifts Received: $220,709 (1993); $172,717
(1992); $165,500 (1991)
Fiscal Note: In 1993, major contributions
were received from Chickmaster International Inc. ($100,000), Eva Holzer Charita-
ble Lead Trust ($120,659), and Victor
Koenig ($50).
EIN: 23-7014880

CONTRIBUTIONS SUMMARY
Donor(s): Erich Holzer

Typical Recipients: • *Arts & Humanities:*
Arts Associations & Councils, Arts Centers,
Community Arts, Dance, Libraries, Muse-
ums/Galleries, Music, Opera, Performing
Arts, Public Broadcasting, Theater • *Civic &
Public Affairs:* General • *Education:* Busi-
ness Education, Colleges & Universities,
Gifted & Talented Programs, Minority Edu-
cation, Private Education (Precollege), Stu-
dent Aid • *Health:* Cancer, Health
Organizations, Hospitals, Medical Rehabili-
tation, Medical Research • *Religion:*
Churches, Jewish Causes, Religious Organizations, Synagogues/Temples • *Social Services:* Community Centers, Community
Service Organizations, Counseling, Homes

Grant Types: general support

Geographic Distribution: focus on Northeast

GIVING OFFICERS
Erich Holzer: secy, treas
Eva Holzer: vp
Vivian Holzer: pres

APPLICATION INFORMATION
Initial Approach: Send brief letter describing program. There are no deadlines.

GRANTS ANALYSIS
Total Grants: $240,577
Number of Grants: 40
Highest Grant: $33,000
Typical Range: $250 to $5,000
Disclosure Period: 1993

Note: Recent grants are derived from a 1993
Form 990.

RECENT GRANTS
Library
300   Demarest Public Library,
         Demarest, NJ

General
30,000   Solomon Schechter Day
         School, New York, NY
26,300   University of Vermont,
         Burlington, VT
25,000   Jewish Theological Seminary,
         New York, NY
16,667   Jewish Museum, New York,
         NY
15,000   PVH Foundation, New York,
         NY

Huber Foundation

CONTACT
Lorraine Barnhart
Assistant Secretary and Executive Director
Huber Foundation
PO Box 277
Rumson, NJ 07760
(908) 872-2322

FINANCIAL SUMMARY
Recent Giving: $1,454,900 (1993 approx.);
$1,455,600 (1992 approx.); $1,284,500
(1991 approx.)

Assets: $30,991,901 (1993); $29,382,777 (1992); $28,144,477 (1991)

Gifts Received: $12,333 (1993); $76,000 (1992); $178,900 (1991)

Fiscal Note: The foundation receives contributions from the estate of C. G. Huber.

EIN: 21-0737062

CONTRIBUTIONS SUMMARY

Donor(s): The Huber Foundation was established in 1949 in New Jersey. Since then, the foundation has received personal contributions from various members of the Huber family.

Typical Recipients: • *Arts & Humanities:* Libraries • *Civic & Public Affairs:* African American Affairs, Civil Rights, General, Philanthropic Organizations, Professional & Trade Associations, Public Policy, Urban & Community Affairs, Women's Affairs • *Education:* Colleges & Universities • *Environment:* General • *Health:* Clinics/Medical Centers, Health Organizations, Hospitals • *International:* Health Care/Hospitals • *Religion:* Social/Policy Issues • *Social Services:* Family Planning

Grant Types: general support and project

Geographic Distribution: emphasis on national organizations and regional affiliates

GIVING OFFICERS

Lorraine Barnhart: asst secy, exec dir, trust *PHIL AFFIL* exec dir: Freed Foundation

Jennifer Curry: trust

David G. Huber: vp, trust

Hans A. Huber: pres, trust

Michael W. Huber: secy, trust *B* 1926 *CURR EMPL* chmn, dir: JM Huber Corp

Julia Ann Nagy: treas

Christopher W. Seely: trust

Catherine Weiss: trust

APPLICATION INFORMATION
Initial Approach:

Applications should take the form of a typewritten letter.

Letters of application should describe the proposed project, and include a budget for the project, and proof of the applicant's tax-exempt status.

There are no application deadlines. The trustees meet four times a year. The dates for these meetings are not fixed.

Restrictions on Giving: Grants are made only to tax-exempt organizations. The foundation does not consider grants to individuals, foreign organizations, capital campaigns, scholarships, endowment funds, research, or international projects.

PUBLICATIONS
Annual report

GRANTS ANALYSIS
Total Grants: $1,454,900

Number of Grants: 42

Highest Grant: $215,000

Average Grant: $34,640

Typical Range: $5,000 to $43,000

Disclosure Period: 1993

Note: Recent grants are derived from a 1993 Form 990.

RECENT GRANTS

Library

1,500	Foundation Center, New York, NY

General

215,000	Planned Parenthood Federation of America, New York, NY
110,000	Alan Guttmacher Institute, New York, NY
100,000	American Civil Liberties Union Foundation, New York, NY
100,000	Center for Reproductive Law and Policy, New York, NY
80,000	National Abortion Rights Action League Foundation, Washington, DC

Hyde and Watson Foundation

CONTACT
Robert W. Parsons, Jr.
President
Hyde and Watson Foundation
437 Southern Blvd.
Chatham Township, NJ 07928
(201) 966-6024

FINANCIAL SUMMARY
Recent Giving: $3,000,000 (1995 est.); $2,900,000 (1994 approx.); $2,479,730 (1993)

Assets: $62,300,000 (1994 est.); $66,305,688 (1993); $58,000,000 (1992 approx.)

EIN: 22-2425725

CONTRIBUTIONS SUMMARY
Donor(s): The Hyde and Watson Foundation was formed in 1983 through the consolidation of the Lillia Babbitt Hyde Foundation and the John Jay and Eliza Jane Watson Foundation.

Lillia Babbitt Hyde formed the Lillia Babbitt Hyde Foundation in 1924 to augment her many charitable contributions in fields such as medical research, health care, and education. John Jay Watson made his money from the rubber and tire industry. After his death in 1939, Eliza Jane Watson , his wife, established the John Jay and Eliza Jane Watson Foundation to continue their philanthropic works.

For more efficient management, the two foundations merged. The board of directors of the Hyde and Watson Foundation follows the principles and guidelines of the late benefactors.

Typical Recipients: • *Arts & Humanities:* Historic Preservation, History & Archaeology, Libraries, Museums/Galleries, Music, Opera, Performing Arts, Theater, Visual

Arts • *Civic & Public Affairs:* Botanical Gardens/Parks, Economic Development, Employment/Job Training, General, Hispanic Affairs, Nonprofit Management, Philanthropic Organizations, Safety • *Education:* Arts/Humanities Education, Colleges & Universities, Engineering/Technological Education, International Studies, Medical Education, Private Education (Precollege), Public Education (Precollege), Religious Education, Science/Mathematics Education, Special Education • *Environment:* Air/Water Quality, General, Resource Conservation • *Health:* Cancer, Children's Health/Hospitals, Clinics/Medical Centers, Emergency/Ambulance Services, Eyes/Blindness, Health Organizations, Hospitals, Medical Rehabilitation, Medical Research, Prenatal Health Issues, Single-Disease Health Associations, Speech & Hearing • *Religion:* Churches, Religious Organizations, Religious Welfare, Seminaries • *Science:* Science Museums, Scientific Labs • *Social Services:* Child Welfare, Community Centers, Community Service Organizations, Day Care, Family Services, Food/Clothing Distribution, Homes, People with Disabilities, Substance Abuse, YMCA/YWCA/YMHA/YWHA, Youth Organizations

Grant Types: capital and research

Geographic Distribution: restricted to the United States; primarily metropolitan New York City and Essex, Union, and Morris counties in New Jersey

GIVING OFFICERS
Nancy A. Allocco: grants adm, asst secy

Loretta J. Becht: asst secy

Hunter W. Corbin: vp, dir

H. Corbin Day: treas, dir *B* Orange NJ 1937 *ED* Brown Univ BA 1959; Univ PA MBA 1963 *CURR EMPL* gen ptnr: Goldman Sachs & Co *CORP AFFIL* chmn, ceo, dir: Jemison Investment Co; chmn, dir: Jemison Industries, Jemison Lumber Co, Southwest Stainless *PHIL AFFIL* trust: Day Family Foundation, Stephen and Barbara Friedman Foundation

Ada M. Dougherty: asst secy

Joseph G. Engel: dir emeritus

William V. Engel: dir *PHIL AFFIL* pres, trust: Union Foundation; exec dir, trust: E. J. Grassmann Trust

David Ferguson: dir

John W. Holman, Jr.: chmn, dir

G. Morrison Hubbard, Jr.: dir emer

Caryl A. Lethbridge: asst secy

John G. MacKechnie: dir *B* Newark NJ 1909 *ED* Dartmouth Coll BA 1931; Harvard Univ LLB 1934 *CURR EMPL* chmn, dir: New Jersey Mfr Co

Robert W. Parsons, Jr.: pres, prin off, dir

Roger B. Parsons: vp, secy, dir

Kate B. Wood: dir

APPLICATION INFORMATION
Initial Approach:

A preliminary application in the form of a letter should be sent to the foundation. Appeals will be considered only if submitted by an appropriate officer of the organization, acting on behalf of the management.

The letter should concisely describe the purpose of the project, list the organization's board of directors, and indicate the project's other major supporters. In addition, copies indicating IRS 501(c)(3) and 509(a) status must be included.

Preliminary letter should be received by February 15 for the spring meetings and September 15 for the fall meetings.

Due to the large volume of proposed projects, not all letters may be answered; although, an effort will be made to respond to each one.

Restrictions on Giving: The foundation does not make grants to individuals nor to applicants located outside the United States. Requests for endowment or operating support or from fiscal agents are not likely to receive favorable responses.

OTHER THINGS TO KNOW
The foundation reports that it also provides investment advice and board and volunteer services to nonprofit organizations.

The foundation reports that it is affiliated with the Charles E. and Joy C. Pettinos Foundation in New Jersey.

PUBLICATIONS
Annual report

GRANTS ANALYSIS
Total Grants: $2,479,730

Number of Grants: 204

Highest Grant: $100,000

Average Grant: $12,155

Typical Range: $3,000 to $20,000

Disclosure Period: 1993

Note: Recent grants are derived from a 1993 Form 990.

RECENT GRANTS

Library

25,000	Foundation at New Jersey Institute of Technology, Newark, NJ — purchase of technical journal abstracts in electronic format and software to increase efficiency and capacity of library services and educational programs
15,000	Kean College of New Jersey Foundation, Union, NJ — alteration and modernization of library facility

General

100,000	Foundation of the University of Medicine and Dentistry of New Jersey, Newark, NJ — establishment of a molecular biology laboratory including purchase of necessary equipment for an expanded comprehensive neuro- and multiple-trauma research center
75,000	Market Street Mission, Morristown, NJ — essential

	alterations and modernization of facility to ensure compliance with fire and safety standards
50,000	Pingry Corporation, Martinsville, NJ — essential alteration and modernization of Short Hills Campus
50,000	Summit Speech School, Summit, NJ — essential alterations and improvements and relocation to new facilities to expand program for hearing-impaired children
35,000	Waterford Institute, Provo, UT — development of a computer-based reading program to help solve reading problems of disadvantaged students

International Foundation

CONTACT
Edward A. Holmes
Grants Chairman
International Foundation
1700 Rt. 23 N
Ste. 170
Wayne, NJ 07470
(615) 598-0894

FINANCIAL SUMMARY
Recent Giving: $850,000 (1995 est.); $920,500 (1994); $1,006,000 (1993)

Assets: $23,883,000 (1994); $22,609,813 (1992); $21,552,453 (1991)

EIN: 13-1962255

CONTRIBUTIONS SUMMARY
Typical Recipients: • *Arts & Humanities:* Arts Funds, Libraries • *Civic & Public Affairs:* Business/Free Enterprise, Economic Development, Employment/Job Training, Legal Aid, Native American Affairs, Philanthropic Organizations • *Education:* Agricultural Education, Colleges & Universities, Religious Education • *Environment:* General, Resource Conservation • *Health:* Clinics/Medical Centers, Emergency/Ambulance Services, Health Funds, Hospitals, Medical Rehabilitation, Medical Training, Nutrition, Single-Disease Health Associations • *International:* Foreign Arts Organizations, Foreign Educational Institutions, Health Care/Hospitals, International Development, International Environmental Issues, International Organizations, International Relief Efforts, Missionary/Religious Activities • *Religion:* Missionary Activities (Domestic), Religious Welfare • *Social Services:* Family Planning, Food/Clothing Distribution, Homes, People with Disabilities, Refugee Assistance

Grant Types: project and seed money

Geographic Distribution: only international

GIVING OFFICERS
David S. Bate: vp, trust *B* Montclair NJ 1918 *ED* Hamilton Coll AB; Harvard Univ LLB *CURR EMPL* ptnr: Booth Bate Greico & Briody *PHIL AFFIL* secy, treas, trust: Florence and John Schumann Foundation

John D. Carrico II: asst secy, asst treas

Duncan William Clark, MD: trust *B* New York NY 1910 *ED* Fordham Univ AB 1932 *CORP AFFIL* mem: Governors Adv Couns AIDS NY St Health *NONPR AFFIL* chmn: Pub Health Comm; diplomate: Am Bd Internal Medicine, Am Bd Preventive Medicine; dir: Med Health Res Assn; fellow: Am Coll Physicians, Am Coll Preventive Medicine, Am Pub Health Assn, NY Academy Medicine; mem: Alpha Omega Alpha, Am Assn Advancement Science, Am Med Assn, Assn Teachers Preventive Medicine, Commn Protect Our Childrens Teeth, Conf Profs Preventive Medicine, Harvey Soc, Intl Epidemiological Assn, NY Academy Sciences, NY Pub Health Assn; mem, del: NY St Med Soc; prof emeritus: St Univ NY Coll Medicine; trust, chmn pub health comm: Kings County Med Soc

Gary Dicovitsky: chmn fdn comm

J. Carter Hammel: trust

Edward A. Holmes: grants chmn, trust

Frank H. Madden: pres, trust

Dr. William M. McCormack: trust

APPLICATION INFORMATION
Initial Approach:

The foundation requests applications be made in writing.

Written proposals should include a statement from the IRS of the organization's not-for-profit status, a brief overview of the proposal, the amount requested, a brief background of the organization, a statement of the problem addressed by the project, a plan of operation, the beneficiaries of the project, the methods of evaluating the project, a budget, and a list of sources of other funding applied for or received. The foundation also requests applicants include a self-addressed stamped envelope.

Proposals are accepted throughout the year.

The board begins to consider grants in January, but approval may be given at any of the quarterly meetings. In general, funding is not available until November.

Restrictions on Giving: The foundation does not make grants to individuals. The foundation does not support endowment funds, operating budgets, scholarships, fellowships, matching gifts, video productions, conferences, or loans.

PUBLICATIONS
Informational brochure including application guidelines

GRANTS ANALYSIS
Total Grants: $920,500

Number of Grants: 74

Highest Grant: $35,000

Average Grant: $12,439

Typical Range: $5,000 to $20,000

Disclosure Period: 1994

Note: Recent grants are derived from a 1992 Form 990.

RECENT GRANTS

General

35,000	MAP International, Brunswick, GA — medical, training, leadership, and nutrition in Bolivia
30,000	Concern America, Santa Ana, CA — medical and health training in Honduras
29,000	Planned Parenthood of New England, Burlington, VT — medical training of nurses and midwives in Uganda
25,000	Africare, Washington, DC — medical
25,000	Africare, Washington, DC — medical and essential drug distribution in Ghana

Jaydor Corp. / Jaydor Foundation, The

Sales: $100.0 million
Employees: 350
Headquarters: Millburn, NJ
SIC Major Group: Wholesale Trade—Nondurable Goods

CONTACT
Michael Silverman
Trustee
Jaydor Foundation
16 Bleeker St.
Millburn, NJ 07041
(201) 379-1234

FINANCIAL SUMMARY
Recent Giving: $99,865 (fiscal 1993); $69,562 (fiscal 1992); $69,069 (fiscal 1990)
Assets: $4,990 (fiscal 1993); $12,851 (fiscal 1992); $18,194 (fiscal 1990)
Gifts Received: $92,000 (fiscal 1993); $72,000 (fiscal 1992); $72,000 (fiscal 1990)
Fiscal Note: In fiscal 1993, contributions were received from the Taylor Corp.
EIN: 22-6067078

CONTRIBUTIONS SUMMARY
Typical Recipients: • *Arts & Humanities:* General, Libraries, Museums/Galleries, Music, Performing Arts, Visual Arts • *Civic & Public Affairs:* Botanical Gardens/Parks, Business/Free Enterprise, Community Foundations, Economic Development, General, Hispanic Affairs, Housing, Municipalities/Towns, Parades/Festivals, Philanthropic Organizations, Professional & Trade Associations, Urban & Community Affairs • *Education:* Business Education, Colleges & Universities, General, Minority Education, Private Education (Precollege), Student Aid • *Environment:* Air/Water Quality • *Health:* Cancer, Children's Health/Hospitals, Diabetes, Emergency/Ambulance Services, Eyes/Blindness, General, Health Organizations, Heart, Hospitals, Medical Rehabilitation, Mental Health, Multiple Sclerosis, Prenatal Health Issues, Single-Disease Health Associations • *International:* Foreign Educational Institutions • *Religion:* Churches, General, Jewish Causes, Religious Organizations, Social/Policy Issues, Synagogues/Temples • *Social Services:* Child Abuse, Community Service Organizations, Delinquency & Criminal Rehabilitation, Domestic Violence, Family Services, Food/Clothing Distribution, General, People with Disabilities, Recreation & Athletics, Scouts, United Funds/United Ways, Veterans, Youth Organizations

Grant Types: general support

Geographic Distribution: giving primarily in NJ

Operating Locations: NJ (Millburn)

CORP. OFFICERS
Barry S. Silverman: *CURR EMPL* chmn, dir: Jaydor Corp

Michael D. Silverman: *CURR EMPL* pres, dir: Jaydor Corp

GIVING OFFICERS
Barry S. Silverman: trust *CURR EMPL* chmn, dir: Jaydor Corp (see above)

Jeffrey Silverman: trust

Michael D. Silverman: trust *CURR EMPL* pres, dir: Jaydor Corp (see above)

APPLICATION INFORMATION
Initial Approach: Send a brief letter of inquiry. Include a description of organization, amount requested, and purpose of funds sought.

Restrictions on Giving: The foundation does not make grants to individuals.

GRANTS ANALYSIS
Total Grants: $99,865
Number of Grants: 65
Highest Grant: $52,000
Typical Range: $100 to $10,000
Disclosure Period: fiscal year ending August 31, 1993

Note: Recent grants are derived from a fiscal 1993 grants list. Number of grants and typical range do not include miscellaneous contributions of $1,914.

RECENT GRANTS

General

52,000	United Jewish Appeal of Metrowest, Newark, NJ
12,500	Temple B'nai Abraham
10,000	Henry H. Kessler Foundation, West Orange, NJ
6,000	Federation of Jewish Agencies of Atlantic County, Northfield, NJ
1,136	March of Dimes

Jockey Hollow Foundation

CONTACT
Betsy S. Michel
President and Secretary
Jockey Hollow Fdn.
PO Box 462
Bernardsville, NJ 07924

FINANCIAL SUMMARY
Recent Giving: $823,409 (fiscal 1994); $715,600 (fiscal 1993); $657,042 (fiscal 1992)

Assets: $11,748,470 (fiscal 1994); $12,048,483 (fiscal 1993); $11,105,535 (fiscal 1992)

Gifts Received: $206,000 (fiscal 1994); $206,000 (fiscal 1993); $206,000 (fiscal 1992)

Fiscal Note: In fiscal 1994, contributions were received from the BBS Charitable Trust 1 and 2.

EIN: 22-1724138

CONTRIBUTIONS SUMMARY
Donor(s): Carl Shirley, Mrs. Carl Shirley

Typical Recipients: • *Arts & Humanities:* Arts Associations & Councils, Ethnic & Folk Arts, Historic Preservation, History & Archaeology, Libraries, Museums/Galleries, Music, Theater • *Civic & Public Affairs:* African American Affairs, General, Safety, Urban & Community Affairs • *Education:* Colleges & Universities, Education Funds, Medical Education, Minority Education, Private Education (Precollege), Secondary Education (Private), Student Aid • *Environment:* General, Resource Conservation • *Health:* Clinics/Medical Centers, Emergency/Ambulance Services, Health Funds, Health Organizations, Hospitals, Medical Research, Nursing Services, Trauma Treatment • *Religion:* Churches • *Social Services:* Child Welfare, Community Centers, Community Service Organizations, Domestic Violence, Family Planning, Family Services, Shelters/Homelessness, United Funds/United Ways, Youth Organizations

Grant Types: general support and scholarship

Geographic Distribution: focus on CT, NJ, and MA

GIVING OFFICERS
Joanne S. Forkner: vp, trust

Betsy S. Michel: pres, secy, trust

Clifford Lloyd Michel: vp, treas, trust *B* New York NY 1939 *ED* Princeton Univ AB 1961; Yale Univ JD 1964 *CURR EMPL* ptnr: Cahill Gordon & Reindel *CORP AFFIL* dir: Alliance Capital Mgmt Mutual Funds, Faber-Castell Corp, Placer Dome Inc, Wenonah Devel Co *NONPR AFFIL* dir: Morristown Meml Hosp, St Marks Sch; mem: Am Bar Assn, Am Soc Intl Law, Fed Bar Assn, NY Bar Assn, NY County Lawyers Assn

Betsy B. Shirley: vp, trust

Carl Shirley: vp, trust

APPLICATION INFORMATION
Initial Approach: Send a brief letter of inquiry. Include a description of organization, amount requested, purpose of funds sought, recently audited financial statement, and proof of tax-exempt status. There are no deadlines.

GRANTS ANALYSIS
Total Grants: $823,409

Number of Grants: 99

Highest Grant: $130,000

Typical Range: $50 to $95,000

Disclosure Period: fiscal year ending March 31, 1994

Note: Recent grants are derived from a fiscal 1994 Form 990.

RECENT GRANTS

Library

75,000	Yale University, New Haven, CT — Beinecke Rare Book and Manuscript Library
26,000	Bernardsville Public Library, Bernardsville, NJ
25,000	Nantucket Athenaeum, Nantucket, MA

General

130,000	Phillips Academy, Andover, MA
95,000	Morristown Memorial Health Foundation, Morristown, NJ
50,000	Morristown Neighborhood House, Morristown, NJ
38,000	Bernardsville Area Scholarship Assistance, Bernardsville, NJ
32,500	Cambridge College, Cambridge, MA

Kirby Foundation, F. M.

CONTACT
F. M. Kirby II
President
F. M. Kirby Foundation
17 DeHart St.
PO Box 151
Morristown, NJ 07963-0151
(201) 538-4800

FINANCIAL SUMMARY
Recent Giving: $9,000,000 (1995 est.); $8,500,000 (1994 approx.); $8,968,743 (1993)

Assets: $250,000,000 (1995 est.); $240,000,000 (1994 approx.); $269,025,549 (1993)

EIN: 51-6017929

CONTRIBUTIONS SUMMARY
Donor(s): The Kirby Foundation was established by the late Fred M. Kirby (1861-1940). In 1912, Mr. Kirby merged his interest in a chain of variety stores with F. W. Woolworth Company. He was a trustee of Lafayette College and a director of Wilkes-Barre Hospital, Wilkes-Barre YMCA, and the Wyoming Seminary. Mr. Kirby's son, Allan P. Kirby, was also a major contributor to the foundation, endowing it with approximately $10 million in Alleghany Corporation stock through his will in 1973. The Kirby family's fortune also stems from holdings in such companies as Alleghany Corporation, Investors Diversified Services, and Pittston Company.

Typical Recipients: • *Arts & Humanities:* Arts Associations & Councils, Arts Festivals, Community Arts, History & Archaeology, Libraries, Museums/Galleries, Opera, Performing Arts, Public Broadcasting • *Civic & Public Affairs:* Civil Rights, Philanthropic Organizations, Professional & Trade Associations, Public Policy, Urban & Community Affairs • *Education:* Business Education, Colleges & Universities, Education Associations, Education Funds, Elementary Education (Private), International Exchange, International Studies, Journalism/Media Education, Medical Education, Private Education (Precollege), Religious Education, Science/Mathematics Education, Special Education, Student Aid • *Environment:* Air/Water Quality, General, Resource Conservation • *Health:* AIDS/HIV, Alzheimers Disease, Arthritis, Cancer, Emergency/Ambulance Services, Eyes/Blindness, Geriatric Health, Health Funds, Heart, Hospices, Hospitals, Medical Rehabilitation, Nursing Services, Respiratory, Single-Disease Health Associations • *International:* Health Care/Hospitals, International Affairs • *Religion:* Churches, Religious Organizations, Religious Welfare • *Science:* Science Museums • *Social Services:* At-Risk Youth, Child Welfare, Community Centers, Community Service Organizations, Domestic Violence, Family Planning, Family Services, Food/Clothing Distribution, People with Disabilities, Recreation & Athletics, Shelters/Homelessness, Substance Abuse, United Funds/United Ways, Youth Organizations

Grant Types: capital, general support, and project

Geographic Distribution: geographic areas where the Kirby family has lived and worked, primarily New Jersey, Pennsylvania, and North Carolina; some national funding

GIVING OFFICERS
Thomas J. Bianchini: secy, treas

Alice Kirby Horton: dir

Fred Morgan Kirby II: pres *B* Wilkes Barre PA 1919 *ED* Lafayette Coll BA 1942; Harvard Univ MBA 1947 *CURR EMPL* chmn, mem exec comm: Alleghany Corp *CORP AFFIL* dir: Affirmative Ins Co, Am Express Co, Chicago Title Ins Co, Chicago Title & Trust Co, Insura Property & Casualty Ins Co, Sacramento Savings Bank, Shelby Fin Corp, Shelby Ins Co, Shelby Life Ins Co; dir, chmn exec comm: Cyclops Indus; dir, mem exec comm: Pittston Co, Woolworth Corp *NONPR AFFIL* mem: Zeta Psi *CLUB AFFIL* Hounds, Racquet & Tennis, Spring Valley, Treyburn CC, Westmoreland CC, World Trade

Fred Morgan Kirby III: dir

Jefferson W. Kirby: dir

S. Dillard Kirby: dir

Walker D. Kirby: vp, dir

Paul B. Mott, Jr.: exec dir

APPLICATION INFORMATION
Initial Approach:

Two or three page proposals should be sent to the foundation. There is no formal application form.

Proposals should identify the directors or trustees and principal officers of the applicant organization; describe the organization, its purpose, its project, and the project's budget; and include IRS proof of tax-exempt status, with a statement certifying that it is not a private foundation.

Proposals are considered throughout the year. Proposals received after October 31 are filed for consideration in the following year.

The foundation does not grant interviews to grant applicants. Unsuccessful applicants do not receive notification.

Restrictions on Giving: The foundation does not fund organizations which have applied for tax-exempt status, but have not as yet received it; organizations outside the IRS regulations; groups which pass on funds to other non-exempt organizations or activities; or public foundations. No grants are made to individuals, fund-raising events such as benefits, charitable dinners, or sporting events. No loans or pledges are made.

OTHER THINGS TO KNOW
Grants usually are reflective of personal interest by one or more members of the Kirby family.

PUBLICATIONS
Information brochure

GRANTS ANALYSIS
Total Grants: $15,097,375

Number of Grants: 299*

Highest Grant: $5,000,000

Average Grant: $33,884*

Typical Range: $5,000 to $50,000

Disclosure Period: 1992

Note: The average grant excludes the highest grant of $5,000,000. The number of grants and the average grant figures are approximate. Recent grants are derived from a 1992 grants list.

RECENT GRANTS

Library

150,000	Morristown and Morris Township Library Foundation, Morristown, NJ — to replenish reserve fund

General

5,000,000	Scheie Eye Institute, Philadelphia, PA — to establish and name the F. M. Kirby Center for Molecular Ophthalmology
1,500,000	Lafayette College, Easton, PA — reserved for future decision

1,125,000	YMCA of Madison Area, Madison, NJ — to renovate and rename the F. M. Kirby Children's Center
1,000,000	Lawrenceville School, Lawrenceville, NJ — reserved for future decision
1,000,000	Summit Speech School, Summit, NJ — to name the new Summit speech school building

Klipstein Foundation, Ernest Christian

CONTACT
Marion C. White
Secretary
Ernest Christian Klipstein Fdn.
Village Rd.
New Vernon, NJ 07976
(201) 538-4445

FINANCIAL SUMMARY
Recent Giving: $117,940 (1993); $103,465 (1992); $71,525 (1990)

Assets: $3,675,195 (1993); $3,016,890 (1992); $2,140,262 (1990)

EIN: 22-6028529

CONTRIBUTIONS SUMMARY
Donor(s): Kenneth H. Klipstein

Typical Recipients: • *Arts & Humanities:* Arts Associations & Councils, Arts Funds, Community Arts, Libraries, Museums/Galleries, Music, Opera, Public Broadcasting, Theater • *Civic & Public Affairs:* Safety, Urban & Community Affairs • *Education:* Colleges & Universities, Engineering/Technological Education, Legal Education, Private Education (Precollege), Public Education (Precollege) • *Environment:* Air/Water Quality, General, Resource Conservation, Watershed • *Health:* AIDS/HIV, Children's Health/Hospitals, Clinics/Medical Centers, Emergency/Ambulance Services, Health Organizations, Hospitals, Medical Research, Research/Studies Institutes • *International:* International Organizations • *Religion:* Churches, Jewish Causes, Religious Organizations • *Science:* Scientific Labs • *Social Services:* Animal Protection, Community Centers, Community Service Organizations, Family Planning, Homes, Recreation & Athletics, Scouts, United Funds/United Ways, Youth Organizations

Grant Types: general support

Geographic Distribution: focus on CA, MA, and NJ

GIVING OFFICERS
David J. Klipstein: pres

Kenneth H. Klipstein II: vp

Constance M. Tebinka: treas

Marion C. White: secy

APPLICATION INFORMATION
Initial Approach: The foundation has no formal grant application procedure or application form. There are no deadlines.

GRANTS ANALYSIS
Total Grants: $117,940

Number of Grants: 79

Highest Grant: $20,000

Typical Range: $100 to $1,000

Disclosure Period: 1993

Note: Recent grants are derived from a 1993 Form 990.

RECENT GRANTS
Library

500	La Jolla Country Day School, La Jolla, CA — Lower School Library
250	Joint Free Public Library of Chester Borough and Chester Township, Chester, NJ
200	Rancho Santa Fe Library Guild, Rancho Santa Fe, CA

General

20,000	La Jolla Country Day School, La Jolla, CA
20,000	Massachusetts Institute of Technology, Cambridge, MA — capital campaign
15,000	Morristown Memorial Hospital Health Foundation, Morristown, NJ
6,000	La Jolla Country Day School, La Jolla, CA
5,500	Rutgers Preparatory School, Somerset, NJ

Lazarus Charitable Trust, Helen and Charles

CONTACT
Charles Lazarus
Trustee
Helen and Charles Lazarus Charitable Trust
c/o Toys 'R' Us
461 From Rd.
Paramus, NJ 07652

FINANCIAL SUMMARY
Recent Giving: $211,464 (fiscal 1993); $133,874 (fiscal 1991); $89,380 (fiscal 1990)

Assets: $3,043,808 (fiscal 1993); $2,712,829 (fiscal 1991); $2,779,174 (fiscal 1990)

EIN: 13-3360876

CONTRIBUTIONS SUMMARY
Donor(s): Charles Lazarus

Typical Recipients: • *Arts & Humanities:* Community Arts, Dance, History & Archaeology, Libraries, Museums/Galleries, Music, Public Broadcasting • *Civic & Public Affairs:* Clubs, General, Municipalities/Towns, Urban & Community Affairs • *Education:* Colleges & Universities, Private Education (Precollege) • *Environment:* General, Resource Conservation • *Health:* AIDS/HIV, Cancer, Clinics/Medical Centers, Diabetes, Emergency/Ambulance Services, Health Organizations, Hospices, Hospitals, Medical Research, Mental Health, Multiple Sclerosis, Single-Disease Health Associations • *International:* Human Rights • *Religion:* Jewish Causes, Religious Organizations • *Social Services:* Community Centers, Community Service Organizations, Family Planning, Food/Clothing Distribution, Recreation & Athletics, Youth Organizations

Grant Types: general support

Geographic Distribution: focus on NY and Washington, DC

GIVING OFFICERS
Charles Lazarus: trust *B* Washington DC 1923 *CURR EMPL* chmn, dir: Toys R Us *CORP AFFIL* dir: Automatic Data Processing, Wal Mart Stores

APPLICATION INFORMATION
Initial Approach: Send brief letter describing program. There are no deadlines.

GRANTS ANALYSIS
Total Grants: $211,464

Number of Grants: 59

Highest Grant: $30,000

Typical Range: $100 to $10,000

Disclosure Period: fiscal year ending May 31, 1993

Note: Recent grants are derived from a fiscal 1993 Form 990.

RECENT GRANTS
Library

2,000	New York Public Library, New York, NY

General

30,000	New York Hospital Department of Psychology, New York, NY
29,000	Sidwell Friends, Washington, DC
25,255	Dalton School, New York, NY
25,000	Geoffrey Funds, Paramus, NJ
25,000	United Jewish Appeal Federation, New York, NY

Lipton, Thomas J. / Lipton Foundation, Thomas J.

Sales: $1.02 billion
Employees: 4,600
Parent Company: Unilever, United States
Headquarters: New York, NY
SIC Major Group: Food & Kindred Products

CONTACT
Helen Siegle
Administrator
Thomas J. Lipton Fdn.
800 Sylvan Ave.
Englewood Cliffs, NJ 07632
(201) 894-7778

FINANCIAL SUMMARY
Recent Giving: $1,107,157 (1992); $927,742 (1991); $939,298 (1990)

Assets: $73,175 (1992); $184,939 (1991); $112,188 (1990)

Gifts Received: $993,750 (1992)

Fiscal Note: All contributions are made through the foundation. Company official reports that the contributions budget was cut by 60% in 1994. In 1992, Calvin Klein Cosmetic Corp. donated 21,200 shares of Colgate-Palmolive stock to the foundation.

EIN: 22-6063094

CONTRIBUTIONS SUMMARY
Typical Recipients: • *Arts & Humanities:* Arts Associations & Councils, Arts Centers, Arts Festivals, Dance, Historic Preservation, Libraries, Museums/Galleries, Music, Performing Arts, Public Broadcasting, Theater • *Civic & Public Affairs:* Business/Free Enterprise, Civil Rights, Economic Development, Law & Justice, Legal Aid, Philanthropic Organizations, Public Policy, Safety, Urban & Community Affairs, Women's Affairs, Zoos/Aquariums • *Education:* Business Education, Colleges & Universities, Community & Junior Colleges, Economic Education, Education Associations, Education Funds, Health & Physical Education, Legal Education, Literacy, Medical Education, Minority Education, Science/Mathematics Education • *Environment:* General • *Health:* Health Funds, Health Organizations, Hospices, Hospitals, Medical Rehabilitation, Medical Research, Medical Training, Mental Health, Nutrition, Single-Disease Health Associations • *International:* International Relations • *Science:* Scientific Organizations • *Social Services:* Community Centers, Community Service Organizations, Emergency Relief, Family Planning, Food/Clothing Distribution, People with Disabilities, Recreation & Athletics, Substance Abuse, United Funds/United Ways, Volunteer Services, Youth Organizations

Grant Types: employee matching gifts and general support

Geographic Distribution: primarily near corporate headquarters and plant locations

Operating Locations: CA (Los Angeles, Santa Cruz), FL (Jacksonville), IA (Sioux City), NJ (Englewood Cliffs, Fairfield, Flemington, Moonachie), PA (Harrisburg, Independence), VA (Suffolk)

CORP. OFFICERS
William K. Godfrey: *B* Litchfield IL 1933 *ED* St Louis Univ 1957; St Meinrad Coll *CURR EMPL* vp, mem exec comm, dir: Thomas J Lipton Co *NONPR AFFIL* mem: Am Compensation Assn, Am Soc Pers Admin, Natl Assn Mfrs

David E. Grein: *CURR EMPL* sr vp fin, cfo, dir: Thomas J Lipton Co

Blaine R. Hess: *B* Hershey PA 1932 *CURR EMPL* pres, ceo, dir: Thomas J Lipton Co

James Reid: *CURR EMPL* exec vp, gen mng oper, dir: Thomas J Lipton Co

William J. Sellitti: *CURR EMPL* vp, contr: Thomas J Lipton Co

David Willard St. Clair: *B* Erie PA 1933 *ED* Yale Univ BA 1955; Harvard Univ JD 1960 *CURR EMPL* sr vp law & admin: Thomas J Lipton Co

GIVING OFFICERS
William K. Godfrey: trust *CURR EMPL* vp, mem exec comm, dir: Thomas J Lipton Co (see above)

David E. Grein: sr vp, treas *CURR EMPL* sr vp fin, cfo, dir: Thomas J Lipton Co (see above)

Blaine R. Hess: pres, trust *CURR EMPL* pres, ceo, dir: Thomas J Lipton Co (see above)

James Reid: exec vp *CURR EMPL* exec vp, gen mng oper, dir: Thomas J Lipton Co (see above)

William J. Sellitti: vp, contr *CURR EMPL* vp, contr: Thomas J Lipton Co (see above)

Helen Siegle: admin

David Willard St. Clair: vp, secy *CURR EMPL* sr vp law & admin: Thomas J Lipton Co (see above)

APPLICATION INFORMATION
Initial Approach: *Initial Contact:* write for guidelines; then a letter or proposal *Include Information On:* description of the organization and its purpose, amount requested, purpose for which funds are sought, recently audited financial statement, proof of tax-exempt status, list of current sponsors and amount each contributes, past record of support, description of programs offered and their geographical scope, annual report, name of agency executive and phone number, methods to be used for evaluating program or project *Deadlines:* budget is established at the beginning of each year; to be included in this year's budget, submit no later than December of the prior year; some late applications are approved if proposal meets requirements and funds are available; many are held over to the next year *Note:* Currently funded organizations wishing continued support should send letter by end of year with updated information.

Restrictions on Giving: Does not support individuals, dinners, tours, or special events.

Restricted from supporting international giving where funds will be spent overseas.

PUBLICATIONS
Guidelines

GRANTS ANALYSIS
Total Grants: $927,742

Number of Grants: 485

Highest Grant: $70,000

Average Grant: $1,913

Typical Range: $500 to $5,000 and $10,000 to $20,000

Disclosure Period: 1991

Note: Recent grants are derived from a 1991 Form 990.

RECENT GRANTS
Library

6,000	New York Public Library, New York, NY

General

70,000	Rutgers University College of Pharmacy, New Brunswick, NJ
53,360	National Merit Scholarship
50,000	We Will Rebuild
40,000	Rutgers University Center for Advancement, New Brunswick, NJ
25,000	Green Bay Packers Foundation, Green Bay, WI — Boys/Girls Club

Maneely Fund

CONTACT
James E. O'Donnell
President
Maneely Fund
900 Haddon Ave., Ste. 432
Collingswood, NJ 08108
(609) 854-5400

FINANCIAL SUMMARY
Recent Giving: $118,790 (1993); $102,025 (1992); $117,435 (1991)

Assets: $3,322,775 (1993); $3,245,056 (1992); $3,159,285 (1991)

EIN: 23-1569917

CONTRIBUTIONS SUMMARY
Donor(s): the late Edward F. Maneely

Typical Recipients: • *Arts & Humanities:* Ballet, History & Archaeology, Libraries, Museums/Galleries, Music, Opera, Public Broadcasting • *Civic & Public Affairs:* Botanical Gardens/Parks, Clubs, Economic Development, General, Public Policy, Safety • *Education:* Arts/Humanities Education, Business Education, Colleges & Universities, Education Funds, General, Legal Education, Preschool Education, Private Education (Precollege), Religious Education, Student Aid • *Health:* Emergency/Ambulance Services, Health Organizations, Hospices, Hospitals, Long-Term Care, Medical Research, Single-Disease Health Associations • *Religion:* Churches, Religious Organizations, Religious Welfare • *Social Services:* At-Risk Youth, Child Welfare, Community Service Organizations, Delinquency & Criminal Rehabilitation, Domestic Violence, Family Planning, Family Services, Homes, United Funds/United Ways, Youth Organizations

Grant Types: general support

Geographic Distribution: focus on PA

GIVING OFFICERS
Elizabeth J. Boylan: vp

Marie E. Dooner: secy

James E. O'Donnell: pres, treas

APPLICATION INFORMATION
Initial Approach: Send a brief letter of inquiry. Include a description of organization, amount requested, purpose of funds sought, recently audited financial statement, and proof of tax-exempt status. There are no deadlines.

GRANTS ANALYSIS

Total Grants: $118,790

Number of Grants: 62

Highest Grant: $20,000

Typical Range: $250 to $4,000

Disclosure Period: 1993

Note: Recent grants are derived from a 1993 Form 990.

RECENT GRANTS

Library
1,000	Immaculata College, Immaculata, PA — library construction

General
5,000	Penn Northwest Development Corporation, Greenville, PA — perpetuation of the economic development of Mercer County
4,000	Catholic Life 2000, Philadelphia, PA — general support
4,000	Institute of American Universities, Aix-En-Provence, France — to support Marchuz School Minibus fund for school transportation
3,000	Children's House, Gladwyne, PA — teachers enrichment and childrens cultural enrichment programs
3,000	Roman Catholic High School, Philadelphia, PA — scholarship fund

Martini Foundation, Nicholas

CONTACT
Nancy L. DeLuca
Executive Administrator
Nicholas Martini Fdn.
1064 Pompton Ave., Rte. 23
Cedar Grove, NJ 07009
(201) 890-1899

FINANCIAL SUMMARY
Recent Giving: $733,231 (1993); $0 (1992); $6,750 (1991)

Assets: $9,722,803 (1993); $6,329,789 (1992); $5,300,435 (1991)

Gifts Received: $3,550,961 (1993); $5,161,497 (1991)

Fiscal Note: In 1993, contributions were received from the estate of Nicholas Martini.

EIN: 22-2756049

CONTRIBUTIONS SUMMARY
Donor(s): the late Nicholas Martini

Typical Recipients: • *Arts & Humanities:* Dance, History & Archaeology, Libraries • *Civic & Public Affairs:* Clubs, General, Hispanic Affairs, Public Policy • *Education:* Colleges & Universities, Gifted & Talented Programs, Journalism/Media Education, Preschool Education, Private Education (Precollege), Secondary Education (Public), Vocational & Technical Education • *Health:* Cancer, Emergency/Ambulance Services, Health Organizations, Heart, Hospitals, Mental Health • *International:* Missionary/Religious Activities • *Religion:* Churches, Dioceses, Religious Welfare • *Social Services:* At-Risk Youth, Child Welfare, Community Service Organizations, Day Care, Family Services, Homes, People with Disabilities, Recreation & Athletics, Senior Services, Youth Organizations

Grant Types: general support

Geographic Distribution: giving primarily in Passaic, Essex, and Bergen counties, NJ

GIVING OFFICERS
William J. Martini: trust

Fannie Rosta: trust

Marie Salanitri: trust

APPLICATION INFORMATION
Initial Approach: Send brief letter of inquiry. There are no deadlines.

Restrictions on Giving: Does not provide grants to individuals.

GRANTS ANALYSIS
Total Grants: $733,231

Number of Grants: 91

Highest Grant: $324,000

Typical Range: $500 to $5,000

Disclosure Period: 1993

Note: Recent grants are derived from a 1993 Form 990.

RECENT GRANTS

Library
7,500	Belleville Public Library, Belleville, NJ
2,500	Bloomfield Public Library, Bloomfield, NJ
2,000	Glen Ridge Public Library, Glen Ridge, NJ

General
324,000	Archdiocese of Newark, Newark, NJ
25,000	Boys and Girls Club of Clifton, Clifton, NJ
20,000	Caucus New Jersey, Montclair, NJ
15,000	Barnert Hospital Foundation, Paterson, NJ
15,000	Frainese Society

Merck & Co. / Merck Co. Foundation

Revenue: $14.96 billion
Employees: 47,100
Headquarters: Rahway, NJ
SIC Major Group: Medicinals & Botanicals, Poultry Hatcheries, Prepared Feeds Nec, and Industrial Inorganic Chemicals Nec

CONTACT
John R. Taylor
Executive Vice President
Merck Co. Fdn.
One Merck Dr.
PO Box 100
Whitehouse Station, NJ 08889-0100
(908) 423-2042
Note: Mr. Taylor is the contact for foundation and direct gifts.

FINANCIAL SUMMARY
Recent Giving: $21,000,000 (1994 approx.); $11,574,970 (1993); $12,246,910 (1992)

Assets: $56,253,000 (1993 approx.); $7,691,983 (1992); $20,000,000 (1991)

Gifts Received: $11,573,445 (1993); $11,251,243 (1992)

Fiscal Note: Figures represent foundation giving only. Company also contributes directly. Approximate value of 1994 cash contributions include direct corporate giving and foundation giving. Above figures exclude nonmonetary support. The foundation receives contributions from Merck & Co.

EIN: 22-6028476

CONTRIBUTIONS SUMMARY
Typical Recipients: • *Arts & Humanities:* Arts Centers, Libraries, Museums/Galleries, Music, Performing Arts, Public Broadcasting, Theater • *Civic & Public Affairs:* Botanical Gardens/Parks, General, Hispanic Affairs, Professional & Trade Associations, Public Policy, Safety, Urban & Community Affairs, Women's Affairs • *Education:* Business Education, Colleges & Universities, Community & Junior Colleges, Economic Education, Education Associations, Education Funds, Engineering/Technological Education, Faculty Development, General, Health & Physical Education, International Exchange, Journalism/Media Education, Medical Education, Minority Education, Public Education (Precollege), Science/Mathematics Education • *Environment:* General, Resource Conservation • *Health:* Cancer, Children's Health/Hospitals, Clinics/Medical Centers, Emergency/Ambulance Services, Geriatric Health, Health Policy/Cost Containment, Health Organizations, Heart, Hospitals, Medical Research, Medical Training, Research/Studies Institutes • *International:* Foreign Educational Institutions, Health Care/Hospitals, International Affairs, International Relations • *Science:* Science Exhibits & Fairs, Scientific Centers & Institutes, Scientific Labs, Scientific Organizations • *Social Services:* Child Welfare, Community Service Organizations, Day

Care, Family Services, Senior Services, Substance Abuse, United Funds/United Ways, Youth Organizations

Grant Types: department, employee matching gifts, fellowship, and project

Nonmonetary Support: $55,000,000 (1994); $40,000,000 (1993); $45,000,000 (1992)

Nonmonetary Support Types: donated products

Note: Nonmonetary support is not included in above figures and generally consists of product donations to humanitarian relief overseas and treatment of health problems in Eastern European and Third World countries. See "Other Things To Know" for more details.

Geographic Distribution: principally near operating locations and nationally

Operating Locations: CA (San Diego), CT (Preston, Southport), DE (Wilmington), FL (Miami), GA (Fairburn), KS (Lawrence), MA (Newton), MO (St. Louis), NH (Walpole), NJ (Elmwood Park, Fairlawn, Iselin, Montvale, Rahway, Whitehouse Station, Woodbridge), OK (Okmulgee), PA (Danville, Ft. Washington, North Versailles, West Point)

CORP. OFFICERS

Raymond V. Gilmartin: *B* Washington DC 1941 *ED* Un Coll BS 1963; Harvard Univ MBA 1968 *CURR EMPL* chmn, pres, ceo: Merck & Co Inc *CORP AFFIL* pres, dir: Merck Holdings Inc *NONPR AFFIL* dir: Trust Valley Hosp, Un Way Bergen County; exec bd, vp: Boy Scouts Am Bergen Counc; mem: Health Indus Mfrs Assn

GIVING OFFICERS

Clarence Allen Abramson: secy *B* Ft Worth TX 1932 *ED* Univ TX BBA 1952; Univ TX JD 1954 *CURR EMPL* vp, sec: Merck & Co Inc *CORP AFFIL* dir: Handy & Harmon Inc; fdr: Poly Pharmaceuticals Inc; pres: Health Care Ventures Intl *NONPR AFFIL* adv: Inst Circadian Physiology; chmn: Merck Political Action Comm; mem: Am Bar Assn, NJ Bar Assn, NY Bar Assn, PA Bar Assn, TX Bar Assn; mem adv bd: Southwestern Legal Fdn; trust: Commun Health Law Project

Albert David Angel: pres *B* Brooklyn NY 1937 *ED* CUNY Brooklyn Coll 1957; Yale Univ Law Sch 1960

Michael Gerard Atieh: treas *B* Paterson NJ 1953 *ED* Upsala Coll BA 1975 *CURR EMPL* vp pub aff: Merck & Co Inc *NONPR AFFIL* mem: Am Inst CPAs, NJ Soc CPAs

Horace Brewster Atwater, Jr.: trust *B* Minneapolis MN 1931 *ED* Princeton Univ AB 1952; Stanford Univ MBA 1954 *CURR EMPL* chmn, ceo, dir: Gen Mills Inc *CORP AFFIL* dir: Gen Electric Co, Merck & Co Inc, Natl Broadcasting Co; mem intl counc: JP Morgan & Co *NONPR AFFIL* adv bd mem: Whitney Mus Am Art; dir: Am Pub Radio; mem: Bus Counc; mem adv counc: Stanford Univ Grad Sch Bus; mem bd: MN Bus Partnership, Walker Art Ctr; mem policy comm: Bus Roundtable *PHIL AFFIL* chmn, trust: General Mills Foundation;

chmn mems, chmn bd trusts: General Mills Fdn; trust: Merck Co Fdn *CLUB AFFIL* Woodhill CC

William Gordon Bowen, PhD: trust *B* Cincinnati OH 1933 *ED* Denison Univ BA 1955; Princeton Univ PhD 1958 *CORP AFFIL* dir: Am Express Co, Merck & Co Inc, Readers Digest Assn Inc, Rockefeller Group Inc *NONPR AFFIL* mem: Am Econ Assn, Counc Foreign Rels, Indus Rels Res Assn, Phi Beta Kappa; mem bd regents: Smithsonian Inst; trust: Denison Univ *CLUB AFFIL* Univ *PHIL AFFIL* pres, trust: Andrew W. Mellon Foundation; dir: Lila Wallace-Reader's Digest Fund, DeWitt Wallace-Reader's Digest Fund

Brenda D. Colatrella: asst secy

Carolyne Kahle Davis, PhD: trust *B* Penn Yan NY 1932 *ED* Johns Hopkins Univ BS 1954; Syracuse Univ MS 1965; Syracuse Univ PhD 1972 *CURR EMPL* consult: Ernst & Young LLP *CORP AFFIL* dir: Beckman Inst, Merck & Co Inc, Pharmaceutical Mktg Svcs Inc, Prudential Ins Co Am, Sci Applications Intl Corp *NONPR AFFIL* assoc trust: Univ PA Med Ctr; dir: Natl Mus Health & Med; mem: Natl League Nursing, Phi Delta Kappa, Sigma Theta Tau *PHIL AFFIL* trust: Prudential Foundation

Lloyd Charles Elam, MD: trust *B* Little Rock AR 1928 *ED* Roosevelt Univ BS 1950; Univ WA MD 1957 *CORP AFFIL* dir: Merck & Co Inc *PHIL AFFIL* trust: Alfred P. Sloan Foundation

Charles Errol Exley, Jr.: trust *B* Detroit MI 1929 *ED* Wesleyan Univ BA 1952; Columbia Univ MBA 1954 *CORP AFFIL* dir: Banc One Corp, Merck & Co Inc, Owens-Corning Fiberglas Corp *CLUB AFFIL* Brook, Dayton Racquet, Grosse Pointe, Miami Valley Hunt & Polo, Moraine CC, Ocean Reef, Question *PHIL AFFIL* trust: Andrew W. Mellon Foundation

Charles R Hogen, Jr.: exec vp

John J. Horan: trust *B* Staten Island NY 1920 *ED* Manhattan Coll AB 1940; Columbia Univ LLB 1946 *CORP AFFIL* dir: Atrix Laboratories, Merck & Co Inc, Myriad Genetics Inc, Patho Genesis Corp *NONPR AFFIL* mem: Pharmaceutical Mfrs Assn *PHIL AFFIL* trust: Robert Wood Johnson Foundation

Shuang R. Huang: vp

Albert Wall Merck: trust *B* New York NY 1920 *ED* Harvard Univ AB 1943; Harvard Univ MBA 1947; Rutgers Univ 1968 *CORP AFFIL* dir: Merck & Co Inc *PHIL AFFIL* mem: Merck Family Fund

Ruben Frederick Mettler: trust *B* Shafter CA 1924 *ED* Stanford Univ 1941; CA Inst Tech BSEE 1944; CA Inst Tech MS 1947; CA Inst Tech PhD 1949 *CORP AFFIL* dir: BankAm Corp, Merck & Co Inc, TRW Inc *NONPR AFFIL* adv: Counc Japan-US Econ Rels; chmn bd trusts: CA Inst Tech; dir: Japan Soc, Natl Action Counc Minorities Engg; fellow: Am Inst Aeronautics Astronautics, Inst Electrical Electronics Engrs; mem: Bus Counc, Bus Roundtable, Eta Kappa Nu, Natl Acad Engg, Sci Res Soc Am, Sigma Xi, Tau Beta Pi, Theta Xi; trust: Cleveland Clinic Fdn, Comm Econ Devel, Conf Bd

Richard Starr Ross: trust *B* Richmond IN 1924 *ED* Harvard Univ 1942-1944; Harvard Univ MD 1947 *CORP AFFIL* dir: Merck & Co Inc, Waverly Press *NONPR AFFIL* dean emeritus med faculty: Johns Hopkins Univ Sch Med; dir: Wellcome Res Lab; fellow: Am Coll Cardiology; mem: Alpha Omega Alpha, Am Clinical & Climatological Assn, Am Coll Physicians, Am Fed Clinical Res, Am Heart Assn, Am Physiological Soc, Am Soc Clinical Investigation, Assn Am Physicians, Assn Univ Cardiologists, Boylston Med Soc, Heart Assn MD, Inst Med, Sigma Xi; physician, dir: Johns Hopkins Hosp Frances Scott Key Med Ctr *CLUB AFFIL* mem: Century Assn, Elkridge, Interurban, Peripatetic

John R. Taylor: exec vp

Pindaros Roy Vagelos: chmn, trust, don *B* Westfield NJ 1929 *ED* Univ PA AB 1950; Columbia Univ MD 1954 *CORP AFFIL* dir: PepsiCo, Prudential Ins Co Am, TRW Inc *NONPR AFFIL* chmn sci adv bd: Ctr Advanced Biotech & Med; dir: Inst Intl Econ, Metro Opera Assn, Natl Fdn Biomed Res, NJ Ctr Performing Arts; mem: Adv Comm Trade Policy Negotiations, Am Acad Arts & Sci, Am Chem Soc, Am Soc Biological Chem, Bus Counc, Bus Roundtable, Natl Acad Sci Inst Med; trust: Rockefeller Univ, Univ PA *PHIL AFFIL* trust: Danforth Foundation

Dennis Weatherstone: trust *B* London England 1930 *ED* Northwestern Polytech Inst 1946-1949 *CORP AFFIL* chmn, ceo: Morgan Guaranty Trust Co NY; dir: Gen Motors Corp, Merck & Co Inc *NONPR AFFIL* dir: Inst Intl Econ; mem: Assn Reserve City Bankers, British Am Chamber Commerce, Bus Roundtable, Counc Foreign Rels; pres, trust: Royal Coll Surgeons Fdn; vchmn: Bus Counc; vp: Intl Monetary Conf *CLUB AFFIL* Econ *PHIL AFFIL* mem adv comm: Morgan Guaranty Trust Co. NY Charitable Trust

APPLICATION INFORMATION

Initial Approach: *Initial Contact:* brief letter *Include Information On:* brief summary of project and planned objectives, means for accomplishing the goal, project budget, sources of funding; full proposal should include description of the organization and proof of tax-exempt status *Deadlines:* none

Restrictions on Giving: Does not support individuals; political, labor, or sectarian groups; endowments; or publications. Except within foundation programs, grants are not given for scholarships or fellowships.

As a rule, does not provide operating support except through United Way contributions.

OTHER THINGS TO KNOW

Foundation sponsors numerous established programs. For this reason, many grants are made on the initiative of the foundation.

The company also makes gifts for activities such as continuing education programs in medicine and pharmacy, public education in health awareness, and memberships in professional and business organizations, which do not qualify as charitable under the Internal Revenue Code.

Raymond V. Gilmartin will assume the chairmanship of the company in November 1994, when Dr. P. Roy Vagelos retires.

PUBLICATIONS
Contributions report

GRANTS ANALYSIS
Total Grants: $11,574,970

Number of Grants: 320

Highest Grant: $1,999,077

Average Grant: $36,172

Typical Range: $2,500 to $50,000

Disclosure Period: 1993

Note: Total grants amount reflects foundation giving only. Recent grants are derived from a 1993 Form 990.

RECENT GRANTS

General
1,999,077	Merck Institute for Science Education, Whitehouse Station, NJ
360,000	United Way of Union County, Elizabeth, NJ
235,099	American Federation for Aging Research, New York, NY
215,900	North Penn United Way, Lansdale, PA
210,000	American College of Cardiology, Bethesda, MD

Nabisco Foods Group / Nabisco Foundation Trust

Employees: 29,000
Parent Company: RJR Nabisco, Inc.
Headquarters: Parsippany, NJ
SIC Major Group: Cookies & Crackers, Cheese—Natural & Processed, Cereal Breakfast Foods, and Prepared Flour Mixes & Doughs

CONTACT
Henry Sandbach
Vice President, Public Relations
Nabisco Fdn. Trust
7 Campus Dr.
Parsippany, NJ 07054
(201) 682-7098

FINANCIAL SUMMARY
Recent Giving: $1,500,000 (1995 est.); $1,350,000 (1994 approx.); $1,717,331 (1993)

Assets: $6,247,028 (1993); $7,440,012 (1992); $8,693,852 (1991)

Fiscal Note: Above figures represent foundation giving only. Company also sponsors a limited direct giving program. Above figures exclude nonmonetary support.

EIN: 13-6042595

CONTRIBUTIONS SUMMARY
Typical Recipients: • *Arts & Humanities:* Arts Funds, Community Arts, Dance, Libraries, Museums/Galleries, Performing Arts,

Public Broadcasting, Theater • *Civic & Public Affairs:* Business/Free Enterprise, Clubs, Economic Development, General, Professional & Trade Associations, Rural Affairs • *Education:* Business Education, Business-School Partnerships, Colleges & Universities, Education Funds, Elementary Education (Private), General, Medical Education, Private Education (Precollege), Public Education (Precollege), Student Aid • *Health:* Health Organizations, Hospitals, Nutrition • *Religion:* Jewish Causes, Religious Welfare • *Science:* Scientific Centers & Institutes • *Social Services:* Child Welfare, Food/Clothing Distribution, Recreation & Athletics, United Funds/United Ways, Youth Organizations

Grant Types: capital, employee matching gifts, general support, and scholarship

Nonmonetary Support Types: donated equipment and donated products

Note: Value of nonmonetary contributions is not available.

Geographic Distribution: areas where Nabisco Brands maintains corporate facilities

Operating Locations: NJ (Parsippany)

CORP. OFFICERS
Joseph W. Farrelly: *CURR EMPL* sr vp, chief information off: Nabisco Foods Group

H. John Greeniaus: *CURR EMPL* chmn, ceo: Nabisco Foods Group

GIVING OFFICERS
Robert K. Devries: mem admin comm *ED* George Washington Univ Law Sch 1969-1971 *CURR EMPL* asst secy, dir: Nabisco Intl SA

John Frederick Manfredi: mem admin comm *B* New York NY 1940 *ED* Yale Univ 1958-1961; Columbia Univ BA 1967 *CURR EMPL* sr vp external & govt aff: Nabisco Brands Inc *NONPR AFFIL* chmn: Intl Chamber Commerce; chmn comm mktg & advertising: US Counc Intl Bus; mem: Arthur W Page Soc, Intl Pub Rels Assn, Pub Rels Soc Am, US Olympic Comm; mem, dir: Intl Advertising Assn; pres: Intl Food Info Counc *CLUB AFFIL* Natl Press, Wiseman

Henry A. Sandbach: mem admin comm *CURR EMPL* vp pub rels: Nabisco Brands Inc

APPLICATION INFORMATION
Initial Approach: *Initial Contact:* brief letter or proposal *Include Information On:* description of the organization, amount requested, purpose for which funds are sought, recently audited financial statement, proof of tax-exempt status *Deadlines:* none

GRANTS ANALYSIS
Total Grants: $1,717,331

Number of Grants: 91

Highest Grant: $148,000

Average Grant: $18,872

Typical Range: $2,000 to $30,000

Disclosure Period: 1993

Note: Recent grants are derived from a 1993 Form 990.

RECENT GRANTS

General
148,000	United Way Morris County, Morristown, NJ — human services
145,000	Liberty Science Center, Jersey City, NJ — education
60,000	Desert Hospital Foundation, Palm Springs, CA — health
60,000	United Way Crusade of Mercy, Chicago, IL — human services
55,000	United Way Desert, Palm Springs, CA — human services

National Westminster Bank New Jersey

Assets: $6.12 billion
Employees: 3,300
Parent Company: National Westminster Bancorp Inc.
Headquarters: Jersey City, NJ
SIC Major Group: Holding & Other Investment Offices, Security & Commodity Brokers, and National Commercial Banks

CONTACT
Chris Cameris
Senior Vice President
National Westminster Bank New Jersey
10 Exchange Pl. Center
Jersey City, NJ 07302
(201) 547-7572

FINANCIAL SUMMARY
Recent Giving: $525,000 (1992 approx.); $525,000 (1991 approx.); $585,000 (1990)

Fiscal Note: All contributions are made directly by the company.

CONTRIBUTIONS SUMMARY
Typical Recipients: • *Arts & Humanities:* Arts Associations & Councils, Arts Centers, Arts Festivals, Community Arts, Dance, Ethnic & Folk Arts, Historic Preservation, Libraries, Museums/Galleries, Music, Performing Arts, Public Broadcasting, Theater • *Civic & Public Affairs:* Business/Free Enterprise, Civil Rights, Economic Development, Employment/Job Training, Law & Justice, Professional & Trade Associations, Public Policy, Safety, Urban & Community Affairs, Women's Affairs • *Education:* Business Education, Colleges & Universities, Community & Junior Colleges, Economic Education, Education Associations, Elementary Education (Private), Engineering/Technological Education, Faculty Development, International Exchange, International Studies, Literacy, Minority Education, Private Education (Precollege), Science/Mathematics Education, Student Aid • *Environment:* General • *Health:* Health Funds, Hospitals, Medical Research, Mental Health, Single-Disease Health Associations • *International:* International Relations • *Religion:* Religious Organizations, Religious Welfare • *Science:* Scientific Organizations • *Social Services:* Child Welfare, Community Centers, Commu-

nity Service Organizations, Delinquency & Criminal Rehabilitation, Domestic Violence, Family Services, People with Disabilities, Refugee Assistance, Senior Services, Substance Abuse, United Funds/United Ways, Volunteer Services, Youth Organizations

Grant Types: capital, challenge, conference/seminar, employee matching gifts, general support, research, and scholarship

Geographic Distribution: near headquarters and operating locations only

Operating Locations: NJ (Jersey City)

CORP. OFFICERS

John A. Petts: *B* 1940 *CURR EMPL* pres, ceo, dir: Natl Westminster Bancorp NJ *CORP AFFIL* sr exec vp, cfo, dir: Natl Westminster Bancorp

John Tugwell: *B* 1940 *CURR EMPL* chmn: Natl Westminster Bancorp NJ *CORP AFFIL* chmn: Natl Westminster Bancorp NJ, Natl Westminster Bank USA; chmn, ceo: Natl Westminster Bancorp; chmn, pres: Natwest Holdings Inc

GIVING OFFICERS

Chris Cameris: *CURR EMPL* sr vp corp aff: Natl Westminster Bancorp NJ

APPLICATION INFORMATION

Initial Approach: *Initial Contact:* brief letter *Include Information On:* description of the organization, amount requested, purpose for which funds are sought, recently audited financial statement, and proof of tax-exempt status *Deadlines:* none

GRANTS ANALYSIS

Total Grants: $525,000*

Typical Range: $1,000 to $5,000

Disclosure Period: 1992

Note: Total grants figure is approximate.

New Jersey Natural Gas Co. / New Jersey Resources Foundation

Revenue: $390.0 million
Employees: 784
Parent Company: New Jersey Resources Corp.
Headquarters: Wall, NJ
SIC Major Group: Natural Gas Distribution

CONTACT
Tom Kononowitz
Vice President
New Jersey Resources Foundation
PO Box 1464
Wall, NJ 07719
(908) 938-1134
Note: The company is located at 1415 Wyckoff Rd., Wall NJ 07719.

FINANCIAL SUMMARY
Recent Giving: $238,000 (fiscal 1995 est.); $240,000 (fiscal 1994 approx.); $253,632 (fiscal 1993)

Assets: $43,903 (fiscal 1993); $66,176 (fiscal 1992)

Gifts Received: $230,659 (fiscal 1993); $224,221 (fiscal 1992)

Fiscal Note: Company gives through the foundation only. Above figures exclude nonmonetary support. In fiscal 1993, contributions were received from New Jersey Natural Gas Co.

EIN: 22-2835065

CONTRIBUTIONS SUMMARY
Typical Recipients: • *Arts & Humanities:* General, Libraries • *Civic & Public Affairs:* African American Affairs, General, Philanthropic Organizations, Public Policy, Safety, Urban & Community Affairs • *Education:* Colleges & Universities, Community & Junior Colleges, Education Funds, General, Minority Education, Public Education (Precollege) • *Environment:* General • *Health:* Cancer, Clinics/Medical Centers, Emergency/Ambulance Services, General, Health Organizations, Hospitals, Prenatal Health Issues, Single-Disease Health Associations • *Religion:* Social/Policy Issues • *Social Services:* Child Welfare, Community Centers, Family Services, General, People with Disabilities, Scouts, Substance Abuse, United Funds/United Ways, YMCA/YWCA/YMHA/YWHA

Grant Types: general support and matching

Nonmonetary Support Types: donated equipment and loaned employees

Geographic Distribution: donations generally limited to company's service area, including part of Morris County, NJ, and all of Monmouth and Ocean counties, NJ

Operating Locations: NJ (Wall)

CORP. OFFICERS
Laurence M. Downes: *B* Ridgefield NJ 1957 *ED* OH St Univ 1972 *CURR EMPL* pres, ceo: NJ Natural Gas Co *NONPR AFFIL* mem: Am Gas Assn, Fin Execs Inst, Natl Investor Rels Inst

GIVING OFFICERS
Laurence M. Downes: treas *CURR EMPL* pres, ceo: NJ Natural Gas Co (see above)

Oleta J. Harden: secy *CURR EMPL* sr vp, secy, gen coun: NJ Natural Gas Co

Thomas J. Kononowitz: vp *CURR EMPL* sr vp mktg & consumer svc: NJ Natural Gas Co

APPLICATION INFORMATION
Initial Approach: *Initial Contact:* letter of inquiry *Include Information On:* statement of purpose, amount requested, description of constituency served, proof of tax-exempt status *Deadlines:* none

GRANTS ANALYSIS
Total Grants: $253,632

Number of Grants: 126*

Highest Grant: $30,225

Average Grant: $2,013*

Typical Range: $50 to $2,500

Disclosure Period: fiscal year ending September 30, 1993

Note: Recent grants are derived from a fiscal 1993 Form 990. Number of grants and average grant figures do not include match-

ing gifts through the foundation's "Gift of Warmth" program.

RECENT GRANTS

Library

650	Monmouth College Library Association, W. Long Branch, NJ

General

30,225	United Way
11,350	Monmouth College, W. Long Branch, NJ
7,500	Georgian Court College
6,127	New Jersey Natural Gas — donated gas grill
6,000	Cancer Care of New Jersey, NJ

Newcombe Foundation, Charlotte W.

CONTACT
Janet A. Fearon
Executive Director
Charlotte W. Newcombe Foundation
35 Park Pl.
Princeton, NJ 08542
(609) 924-7022

FINANCIAL SUMMARY
Recent Giving: $1,720,000 (1995); $1,690,000 (1994 est.); $1,539,200 (1993)

Assets: $33,500,000 (1995 est.); $33,250,000 (1994); $33,880,125 (1993)

EIN: 23-2120614

CONTRIBUTIONS SUMMARY
Donor(s): The Charlotte W. Newcombe Foundation is a private foundation created under the will of Mrs. Newcombe, who died in 1979, and leaving a fortune in excess of $34 million. In her will, Mrs. Newcombe nominated five trustees, charged them with the creation of a scholarship foundation to bear her name, and funded the foundation with half of her residual estate.

The Charlotte W. Newcombe Foundation was chartered in Pennsylvania in November 1979, and opened its administrative offices in Princeton, NJ, in January 1980.

Typical Recipients: • *Arts & Humanities:* Libraries • *Civic & Public Affairs:* Community Foundations • *Education:* Colleges & Universities, Community & Junior Colleges, Continuing Education, Education Funds, Student Aid

Grant Types: fellowship and scholarship

Geographic Distribution: national; scholarships for mature women and students with disabilities are available only to colleges and universities in Pennsylvania, New Jersey, Maryland, Delaware, Washington, DC, and New York City

GIVING OFFICERS
Robert M. Adams: trust

K. Roald Bergethon: trust *ED* DePauw Univ AB 1938; Cornell Univ MA 1940; Cornell Univ PhD 1945 *CORP AFFIL* dir: Am

Home Product Corp; ed consultant: Easton Inc *NONPR AFFIL* mem: Alpha Phi Omega, Phi Beta Kappa, Phi Eta Sigma, Phi Kappa Phi, Phi Theta Pi, Sigma Delta Chi; mem bd dirs: Project Easton; pres emeritus: Lafayette Coll *CLUB AFFIL* Cornell, Northampton CC

Sallie G. Campbell: assoc dir

Janet A. Fearon: exec dir, trust

Aaron E. Gast: trust

Millard E. Gladfelter: trust emeritus

Thomas Parvin Glassmoyer: trust *B* Reading PA 1915 *ED* Ursinus Coll AB 1936; Univ PA LLB 1939 *CURR EMPL* couns: Schnader Harrison Segal & Lewis *CORP AFFIL* secy, dir: Lawrence McFadden Co *NONPR AFFIL* chmn exec comm: Ursinus Coll; fellow: PA Bar Fdn; lecturer: NY Univ Inst Fed Taxation; mem: Am Bar Assn, Fed Bar Assn, Judge Advocates Assn, Lawyers Club, Natl Assn Coll Univ Attys, Order Arrow, Order of Coif, PA Bar Assn, PA Folklife Soc, Philadelphia Bar Assn, Quakertown Historical Soc, US Golf Assn; trust: Bernard G Segal Fdn *CLUB AFFIL* Manorlu, Mfrs GC & CC, Union League

APPLICATION INFORMATION
Initial Approach:

Prospective applicant institutions should send a letter or telephone the foundation. For fellowships, applicants should request applications by mid-November from the Woodrow Wilson National Fellowship Foundation, CN 5281, Princeton, NJ 08543-5281. Information on the scholarships will be sent to qualifying schools who call or write the foundation. Scholarships for students with disabilities and scholarships for mature women applicants can obtain application materials from June through October.

Deadlines for returning completed applications are November 1 for students with disabilities and mature women scholarships and mid-December for fellowships. No deadlines are listed the scholarhips at Presbyterian colleges.

Applicants for students with disabilities and mature women scholarships will be notified in May about scholarships that will be funded in July. Applicants for fellowships will be notified in April for fellowships that begin in June or September.

Restrictions on Giving: The foundation only supports colleges and universities through scholarships and fellowships for under-graduate and graduate students; no aid is available for post-doctoral fellowships. Scholarships are not granted for publicly supported two-year colleges. In the program for mature women, no grants are made to professional schools. A college or university may apply for funding in only one of these two scholarship programs. No grants are given to individuals, community organizations, or for staffing, program development, or building funds. No loans are made.

PUBLICATIONS
Annual report

GRANTS ANALYSIS
Total Grants: $1,539,200

Number of Grants: 56

Highest Grant: $587,950

Average Grant: $17,295*

Typical Range: $1,750 to $45,000

Disclosure Period: 1993

Note: Average grant figure excludes a single grant for $587,950, the total amount given in Doctoral Dissertation Fellowships. Recent grants are derived from a 1993 annual report.

RECENT GRANTS
General

45,000	Gallaudet University, Washington, DC — scholarships
40,000	New York University, New York, NY — scholarships
32,000	University of Maryland, College Park, MD — scholarships
31,000	Pennsylvania State University, University Park, PA — scholarships
29,000	Davis and Elkins College, Elkins, WV — scholarships

Prudential Insurance Co. of America, The / Prudential Foundation

Revenue: $36.94 billion
Employees: 74,067
Headquarters: Newark, NJ
SIC Major Group: Life Insurance, Accident & Health Insurance, and Fire, Marine & Casualty Insurance

CONTACT
Thomas P. Scanlan
Secretary
Prudential Foundation
Prudential Plz.
751 Broad St.
15th Fl.
Newark, NJ 07102-3777
(201) 802-7354

FINANCIAL SUMMARY
Recent Giving: $18,000,000 (1995 est.); $17,939,631 (1994); $16,599,151 (1993)

Assets: $140,677,000 (1994); $136,696,000 (1993); $125,703,000 (1992)

Fiscal Note: Above figures are for foundation only and include all programs. Figure for 1994 includes $2,445,104 in matching gifts to education, $3,181,506 to the United Way, and $508,500 in grants given by the Prudential Community Champions program. Above figures exclude nonmonetary support.
EIN: 22-2175290

CONTRIBUTIONS SUMMARY
Typical Recipients: • *Arts & Humanities:* Arts Associations & Councils, Arts Centers, Arts Funds, Arts Institutes, Community Arts, Historic Preservation, Libraries, Museums/Galleries, Music, Opera, Performing Arts, Public Broadcasting • *Civic & Public*

Affairs: Botanical Gardens/Parks, Business/Free Enterprise, Civil Rights, Economic Development, Economic Policy, Employment/Job Training, Hispanic Affairs, Law & Justice, Legal Aid, Municipalities/Towns, Nonprofit Management, Professional & Trade Associations, Public Policy, Safety, Urban & Community Affairs, Women's Affairs • *Education:* Arts/Humanities Education, Business Education, Colleges & Universities, Community & Junior Colleges, Continuing Education, Economic Education, Education Associations, Education Funds, Education Reform, Elementary Education (Private), Elementary Education (Public), Faculty Development, General, Health & Physical Education, Journalism/Media Education, Legal Education, Literacy, Medical Education, Minority Education, Preschool Education, Private Education (Precollege), Public Education (Precollege), Religious Education, Science/Mathematics Education, Special Education, Student Aid • *Environment:* General • *Health:* AIDS/HIV, Children's Health/Hospitals, Clinics/Medical Centers, Emergency/Ambulance Services, Geriatric Health, Health Policy/Cost Containment, Health Organizations, Hospitals, Medical Rehabilitation, Medical Training, Mental Health • *Religion:* Religious Welfare • *Social Services:* At-Risk Youth, Child Welfare, Community Centers, Community Service Organizations, Counseling, Day Care, Delinquency & Criminal Rehabilitation, Emergency Relief, Family Planning, Family Services, Food/Clothing Distribution, Homes, People with Disabilities, Recreation & Athletics, Senior Services, Shelters/Homelessness, Substance Abuse, United Funds/United Ways, Volunteer Services, Youth Organizations

Grant Types: employee matching gifts and general support

Note: Employee matching gift ratio: 1.5 to 1 for private colleges and universities. Employee matching gift ratio: 1 to 1 for all other eligible institutions.

Nonmonetary Support: $2,500,000 (1993); $327,000 (1992); $5,300,000 (1991)

Nonmonetary Support Types: donated equipment, in-kind services, loaned employees, and loaned executives

Note: Contact for nonmonetary support is Gina Esteves.

Geographic Distribution: near operating locations, with special emphasis on New Jersey and the city of Newark; also nationally

Operating Locations: AR (Little Rock), AZ (Phoenix, Scottsdale), CA (Fresno, Irvin, Los Angeles, Pleasanton, Sacramento, Sunnyvale, Van Gury, Westlake Village, Woodland Hills), DC, FL (Coral Gables, Deerfield Beach, Fort Lauderdale, Jacksonville, Maitland, Orlando, Tampa Bay), GA (Atlanta), IL (Chicago, Des Plaines, Downers Grove), IN (Indianapolis), LA (Monroe, New Orleans), MA (Boston), MI (Southfield), MN (Minneapolis), MO (Creve Coere), MS (Greenville), NC (Charlotte), NE (Kearny, Omaha), NJ (Chatham, Holmdel, Iselin, Newark, Parsippany, Pleasantville), NY

(New York), OH (Cincinnati, Columbus, Mansfield), OK (Oklahoma City, Tulsa), PA (Fort Washington, Horsham, Philadelphia), TN (Memphis, Nashville), TX (Austin, Bellaire, Dallas, Houston, San Antonio), VA (Richmond), WA (Tri Cities), WY (Casper)

CORP. OFFICERS
James Robert Gillen: *B* New York NY 1937 *ED* Harvard Univ AB 1959; Harvard Univ LLB 1965 *CURR EMPL* sr vp, gen couns: Prudential Ins Co Am *NONPR AFFIL* mem: Am Bar Assn, Assn Life Ins Counc, NJ Bar Assn; mem bd trustees: Columbia Inst Investor Project; trust: NJ Shakespeare Festival *CLUB AFFIL* Harvard, Newark

Mark B. Grier: *CURR EMPL* cfo: Prudential Ins Co Am

Garnett Lee Keith, Jr.: *B* Atlanta GA 1935 *ED* GA Inst Tech BS 1957; Harvard Univ MBA 1962 *CURR EMPL* vchmn: Prudential Ins Co Am *CORP AFFIL* chmn: Prudential Funding Corp; dir: AEA Investors Inc, Pruco Inc, SuperValu Stores Inc *NONPR AFFIL* mem: Inst Chartered Fin Analysts; trust: Drew Univ; trust, mem bd pensions: Un Presbyterian Church USA *CLUB AFFIL* Harvard

Dorothy Kaplan Light: *B* Alden IA 1937 *ED* Univ IA BA 1959; Univ IA JD 1961 *CURR EMPL* vp, secy: Prudential Ins Co Am *CORP AFFIL* dir: NJ Resources *NONPR AFFIL* dir: Ctr Analysis Pub Issues; mem: Am Soc Corp Secys; mem natl adv bd: Leadership Am; vchmn: One To One NJ Fdn

Edward Donald Zinbarg: *B* New York NY 1934 *ED* City Univ NY BBA 1954; Univ PA MBA 1955; NY Univ PhD 1959 *CURR EMPL* sr vp investments: Prudential Ins Co Am *CORP AFFIL* dir: Pruco Inc, Prudential Reins Co *NONPR AFFIL* mem: Am Fin Assn, NY Soc Security Analysts; mem investment comm: Un Way Essex & W Hudson NJ; mem, trust: Oheb Shalom Congregation; trust: Trenton St Coll

GIVING OFFICERS
Peter Bushyeager: program off health & human svcs

Lisle C. Carter, Jr.: trust

Gabriella M. Coleman: pres

Carolyne Kahle Davis, PhD: trust *B* Penn Yan NY 1932 *ED* Johns Hopkins Univ BS 1954; Syracuse Univ MS 1965; Syracuse Univ PhD 1972 *CURR EMPL* consult: Ernst & Young LLP *CORP AFFIL* dir: Beckman Inst, Merck & Co Inc, Pharmaceutical Mktg Svcs Inc, Prudential Ins Co Am, Sci Applications Intl Corp *NONPR AFFIL* assoc trust: Univ PA Med Ctr; dir: Natl Mus Health & Med; mem: Natl League Nursing, Phi Delta Kappa, Sigma Theta Tau *PHIL AFFIL* trust: Merck Co. Foundation

James Robert Gillen: trust *CURR EMPL* sr vp, gen couns: Prudential Ins Co Am (see above)

Jon F. Hanson: trust *CURR EMPL* chmn: Hampshire Mgmt Co *CORP AFFIL* dir: Prudential Ins Co Am; mem bd: NJ Sports & Expo Authority

Elizabeth Kilickiran: program off bus & civic

Dorothy Kaplan Light: chmn *CURR EMPL* vp, secy: Prudential Ins Co Am (see above)

Marijane Lundt: program off Focus on Children

Paul Gerard O'Leary: vp *B* Boston MA 1935 *ED* Harvard Univ AB 1956; Univ PA MBA 1958 *CURR EMPL* vp portfolio mgmt: Prudential Investment Corp *NONPR AFFIL* mem: Am Nuclear Insurers, Assn Ins & Fin Analysts, Boston Latin Sch Alumni Assn, Ins Inst Hwy Safety, Inst Chartered Fin Analysts, NY Property Ins Underwriting Assn, NY Soc Security Analysts *CLUB AFFIL* Harvard NJ, Indian Trail, Upper Ridgewood Tennis

Donald E. Procknow: trust *B* Madison SD 1923 *ED* Univ WI BSEE 1947 *CORP AFFIL* dir: CPC Corp, Ingersoll-Rand Co, Prudential Ins Co Am *NONPR AFFIL* mem: Tau Beta Pi; trust: Drew Univ

Mary Puryear: program off culture & the arts

Arthur F. Ryan: trust *B* Brooklyn NY 1942 *ED* Providence Coll BA 1963; Am Univ *CURR EMPL* pres, coo: Chase Manhattan Bank NA Inc *CORP AFFIL* chmn: Prudential Ins Co Am; dir: Depository Trust Co; exec vp, dir: Chase Natl Corp Svcs; pres, chmn: Chase Manhattan Banking Corp, Chase Manhattan Natl Holding Co; pres, coo: Chase Manhattan Corp *NONPR AFFIL* mem: Am Bankers Assn *PHIL AFFIL* trust: Chase Manhattan Foundation

Thomas P. Scanlan: secy

James J. Straine: treas

Monika Vazirani: program off ed

Edward Donald Zinbarg: trust *CURR EMPL* sr vp investments: Prudential Ins Co Am (see above)

APPLICATION INFORMATION
Initial Approach: *Initial Contact:* application form, may submit descriptive letter with application form *Include Information On:* proof of tax-exempt status; latest audited financial statement and Form 990; description of the organization and geographic scope; type, amount, and duration of request; description, expected results, evaluative criteria, and itemized budget of project; names and affiliations of board members, compensation, and number of meetings held; number, compensation, and qualifications of employees and volunteers; breakdown of current funding sources and list of other sources being approached; and statement that periodic reports will be furnished *Deadlines:* none *Note:* Every proposal will receive a response. The Prudential requests that no fax applications or videotapes be sent. Organizations may contact the foundation concerning the status of their proposal after 30 days.

Restrictions on Giving: In general, grants are not made to veterans, labor, religious, political, fraternal, or athletic groups, except when program benefits or provides services to the community at large; individuals; organizations that do not have 501(c)(3) status; general operating support for single-disease health organizations, except local AIDS groups; goodwill advertising; or fundraising events.

OTHER THINGS TO KNOW
The foundation has shifted its emphasis in recent years; top priority categories will receive increased funding. In particular, greater emphasis will be on stabilization of health care costs and focus on children. Also, special attention will be paid to organizations in New Jersey, especially Newark, and the four regional headquarters cities of Philadelphia, PA; Jacksonville, FL; Minneapolis, MN; and Los Angeles, CA.

GRANTS ANALYSIS
Total Grants: $11,794,521

Number of Grants: 718*

Highest Grant: $315,000

Average Grant: $16,427*

Typical Range: $1,000 to $20,000

Disclosure Period: 1994

Note: Fiscal information for general foundation grants only. Number of grants and average grants exclude matching gifts to education, contributions to United Ways, and grants through the Prudential Champions Awards Program. Recent grants are derived from a 1993 annual report.

RECENT GRANTS
Library
275,000   American Library Association, Chicago, IL — link health clinics and libraries to reach at-risk parents and their babies through Born to Read demonstration project

General
200,000   Early Childhood Facilities Fund of New Jersey, Newark, NJ — create financial intermediary that will assist Head Start and other childcare programs in improving, expanding, and operating facilities

200,000   University of Medicine and Dentistry of New Jersey, Newark, NJ — Newark women and children grant program

182,000   Association for Children of New Jersey, Invest In Children, Newark, NJ — program to enhance WIC services; support for the Childhood Health Access project

165,000   Life Underwriter Training Council, Bethesda, MD — general support

160,000   Children's Defense Fund, Washington, DC — educate national policymakers and leaders on child poverty, its costs and potential solutions

Public Service Electric & Gas Co.

Parent Company: Public Service Enterprise Group Inc.
Revenue: $5.91 billion
Parent Employees: 11,857
Headquarters: Newark, NJ
SIC Major Group: Electric & Other Services Combined

CONTACT
Ed Skwirut
General Manager, Corporate Contributions
Public Service Electric and Gas Co.
80 Park Plz.
PO Box 570
Newark, NJ 07101
(201) 430-8660

FINANCIAL SUMMARY
Recent Giving: $3,200,000 (1995 est.); $3,000,000 (1994 approx.); $3,500,000 (1993 approx.)

Fiscal Note: Company gives directly. Above figures exclude nonmonetary support.

CONTRIBUTIONS SUMMARY
Typical Recipients: • *Arts & Humanities:* Arts Centers, Arts Funds, Historic Preservation, Libraries, Museums/Galleries, Performing Arts, Public Broadcasting, Theater • *Civic & Public Affairs:* Economic Development, Employment/Job Training, Housing, Law & Justice, Professional & Trade Associations, Public Policy, Safety, Urban & Community Affairs, Women's Affairs • *Education:* Business Education, Colleges & Universities, Community & Junior Colleges, Elementary Education (Private), Engineering/Technological Education, Minority Education, Private Education (Precollege), Public Education (Precollege), Science/Mathematics Education • *Environment:* General • *Health:* Emergency/Ambulance Services, Hospitals • *Science:* Science Exhibits & Fairs, Scientific Centers & Institutes • *Social Services:* Child Welfare, Community Service Organizations, Counseling, Delinquency & Criminal Rehabilitation, Food/Clothing Distribution, People with Disabilities, Recreation & Athletics, Senior Services, Substance Abuse, United Funds/United Ways, Youth Organizations

Grant Types: capital, challenge, employee matching gifts, general support, project, scholarship, and seed money

Nonmonetary Support Types: donated equipment, donated products, in-kind services, and loaned executives

Note: Value of nonmonetary support is unavailable.

Geographic Distribution: primarily in service area; education grants awarded nationally

Operating Locations: NJ (Camden, Elizabeth, Jersey City, New Brunswick, Newark, Paramus, Paterson, Ridgewood, Trenton)

Note: Also operates in the Virgin Islands.

CORP. OFFICERS
E. James Ferland: *B* Boston MA 1942 *ED* Univ ME BSME 1964; Univ New Haven MBA 1979 *CURR EMPL* chmn, pres, ceo: Pub Svc Enterprise Group Inc *CORP AFFIL* dir: Commun Energy Alternatives Inc, Energy Devel Corp, First Fidelity Bancorp, First Fidelity Bank NA, Foster Wheeler Corp, Gasdel Pipeline Sys Inc, Hartford Steam Boiler Inspection & Ins Co, Pub Svc Resources Corp *NONPR AFFIL* dir: Am Nuclear Energy Counc, Electric Power Res Inst, Mulberry St Urban Renewal Corp, NJ Utilities Assn

GIVING OFFICERS
Ed Skwirut: gen mgr corp contributions

APPLICATION INFORMATION
Initial Approach: *Initial Contact:* letter accompanied by full proposal *Include Information On:* description of the organization and project, budget, and proof of tax-exempt status *Deadlines:* none

Restrictions on Giving: Does not support individuals, member agencies of united funds, political or lobbying groups, or religious organizations for sectarian purposes.

PUBLICATIONS
Corporate responsiblity report

GRANTS ANALYSIS
Total Grants: $3,000,000*

Typical Range: $1,000 to $5,000

Disclosure Period: 1994

Note: Total grants figure is approximate. Recent grants are derived from a 1993 grants list.

RECENT GRANTS

General

125,000	Community Agencies Corporation of New Jersey, Newark, NJ	
125,000	Princeton Center Leadership Training, Lawrenceville, NJ	

Read Foundation, Charles L.

CONTACT
Rodger H. Herrigel
Secretary
Charles L. Read Fdn.
374 Millburn Ave.
Millburn, NJ 07841
(201) 379-5850

FINANCIAL SUMMARY
Recent Giving: $129,500 (1993); $138,250 (1992); $149,150 (1991)

Assets: $3,187,120 (1993); $2,994,120 (1992); $2,984,734 (1991)

EIN: 22-6053510

CONTRIBUTIONS SUMMARY
Donor(s): Charles L. Read

Typical Recipients: • *Arts & Humanities:* Dance, Historic Preservation, History & Archaeology, Libraries, Music, Performing Arts, Theater • *Civic & Public Affairs:* Employment/Job Training, General, Housing, Professional & Trade Associations, Rural Affairs, Safety • *Education:* Colleges & Universities, Education Funds, Private Education (Precollege), Public Education (Precollege), Religious Education, School Volunteerism, Student Aid • *Environment:* General, Watershed • *Health:* Children's Health/Hospitals, Emergency/Ambulance Services, Eyes/Blindness, Health Organizations, Hospices, Hospitals, Long-Term Care, Medical Research, Mental Health, Speech & Hearing • *International:* Missionary/Religious Activities • *Religion:* Churches, Jewish Causes, Religious Organizations, Religious Welfare • *Social Services:* Camps, Child Welfare, Community Centers, Community Service Organizations, Day Care, Homes, Recreation & Athletics, Shelters/Homelessness, United Funds/United Ways, YMCA/YWCA/YMHA/YWHA, Youth Organizations

Grant Types: general support

Geographic Distribution: focus on NJ and NY

GIVING OFFICERS
Richard Eisenberg: vp

Saul Eisenberg: treas

Fred Herrigel III: pres

Rodger H. Herrigel: secy

APPLICATION INFORMATION
Initial Approach: Send a brief letter of inquiry. Include a description of organization, amount requested, purpose of funds sought, recently audited financial statement, and proof of tax-exempt status. There are no deadlines.

GRANTS ANALYSIS
Total Grants: $129,500

Number of Grants: 80

Highest Grant: $20,000

Typical Range: $500 to $2,500

Disclosure Period: 1993

Note: Recent grants are derived from a 1993 Form 990.

RECENT GRANTS

Library

2,500	Louise Adelia Read Memorial Library, Hancock, NY	
2,000	Library of Chathams, Chatham, NJ	
1,500	Albert F Totman Library, Phippsburg, ME	
1,000	Bogue Banks Library, Pine Knoll Shores, NC	

General

20,000	Trust and Agency Fund Hancock Central School, Hancock, NY	
5,000	Daughters of Israel, West Orange, NJ	
5,000	Fairview Lakes Camps YMCA, Stillwater, NJ	
5,000	Southside Hospital, Bayshore, NY	
4,500	Drew University, Madison, NJ	

Rhone-Poulenc Inc.

Sales: $2.2 billion
Employees: 9,000
Parent Company: Rhone-Poulenc S.A.
Headquarters: Princeton, NJ
SIC Major Group: Chemicals & Allied
  Products, Food & Kindred Products, and
  Rubber & Miscellaneous Plastics Products

CONTACT
George Palmer
Vice President, Communications
Rhone-Poulenc Inc.
CN5266
Princeton, NJ 08543-5266
(908) 297-0100

FINANCIAL SUMMARY
Fiscal Note: Company does not disclose
contributions figures.

CONTRIBUTIONS SUMMARY
Rhone-Poulenc Inc. has no set giving priorities; rather it handles requests on a case-by-case basis. Past recipients have fallen mainly in the areas of arts and social services. Cultural support goes to dance, music, the performing arts, libraries, museums, and galleries. Social services funding includes community service and youth organizations and sports teams. Funds programs for the disabled, the elderly, and drug and alcohol rehabilitation. Also gives to education, including public (precollege) schools. Contributes to hospitals and single-disease health associations such as the American Heart Association and the Cancer Society. Company is planning activities for Eden School in Princeton.

Volunteerism: Plans for a corporate volunteerism program are underway.

Typical Recipients: • *Arts & Humanities:* Dance, Libraries, Museums/Galleries, Music, Performing Arts • *Education:* Public Education (Precollege) • *Health:* Hospitals, Single-Disease Health Associations • *Social Services:* Community Service Organizations, People with Disabilities, Senior Services, Substance Abuse, Youth Organizations

Grant Types: employee matching gifts and general support

Geographic Distribution: principally near operating locations and to national organizations

Operating Locations: CT, NC, NJ, OR, SC, TN, TX, WA

CORP. OFFICERS
Thomas F. Kirk: *CURR EMPL* sr vp, cfo: Rhone-Poulenc

Peter J. Neff: *CURR EMPL* pres, ceo, coo, dir: Rhone-Poulenc

GIVING OFFICERS
Gus Karageorge: *CURR EMPL* intl communs specialist: Rhone-Poulenc

APPLICATION INFORMATION
Initial Approach: A brief letter of inquiry may be submitted at any time and should include a description of the organization, proof of tax-exempt status, and the purpose for which funds are sought, along with the amount requested.

Restrictions on Giving: Does not give to religious organiztions for sectarian purposes, or to civic and public affairs.

Subsidiaries administer independent giving programs.

Does not provide nonmonetary support.

OTHER THINGS TO KNOW
Rhone-Poulenc operates in 23 states.

Sandy Hill Foundation

CONTACT
Maria Sapol
Sandy Hill Fdn.
330 S St., PO Box 1975
Morristown, NJ 07962-1975
(201) 540-9020

FINANCIAL SUMMARY
Recent Giving: $1,616,755 (fiscal 1993); $1,307,538 (fiscal 1992); $1,170,955 (fiscal 1990)

Assets: $11,018,549 (fiscal 1993); $11,147,483 (fiscal 1992); $11,591,114 (fiscal 1990)

Gifts Received: $1,828,750 (fiscal 1990); $5,849,843 (fiscal 1989)

Fiscal Note: Fiscal 1990 contribution received from Frank E. Walsh, Jr.

EIN: 22-2668774

CONTRIBUTIONS SUMMARY
Donor(s): the donor is Frank E. Walsh, Jr., president and director of the foundation

Typical Recipients: • *Arts & Humanities:* Arts Funds, History & Archaeology, Libraries • *Civic & Public Affairs:* Community Foundations, Employment/Job Training, General, Philanthropic Organizations, Urban & Community Affairs • *Education:* Arts/Humanities Education, Colleges & Universities, Education Associations, Education Funds, Education Reform, Legal Education, Private Education (Precollege), Secondary Education (Private), Student Aid • *Health:* AIDS/HIV, Cancer, Clinics/Medical Centers, Health Organizations, Hospices, Hospitals, Medical Research, Single-Disease Health Associations • *International:* International Relief Efforts • *Religion:* Dioceses, Religious Organizations, Religious Welfare, Seminaries • *Social Services:* At-Risk Youth, Child Welfare, Community Service Organizations, Domestic Violence, Emergency Relief, Food/Clothing Distribution, Homes, People with Disabilities, Recreation & Athletics, Shelters/Homelessness, United Funds/United Ways, Youth Organizations

Grant Types: capital, general support, multiyear/continuing support, operating expenses, and scholarship

Geographic Distribution: primarily NJ

GIVING OFFICERS
Frank E. Walsh III: vp

Frank E. Walsh, Jr.: vp *B* 1941 *CURR EMPL* chmn, ptnr: Wesray Capital Corp *CORP AFFIL* dir: Dyersburg Fabrics, Harding Svc Corp, Heekin Can, Lincoln Foodservice Products, Outlet Broadcasting, Outlet Communs, Triple C Acquisition Corp *PHIL AFFIL* dir: MCJ Foundation

Jeffrey R. Walsh: vp, asst treas, secy

Joseph Walsh: pres

Mary D. Walsh: treas

Meghan Walsh: vp

APPLICATION INFORMATION
Initial Approach: The foundation has no formal grant application procedure or application form. There are no deadlines.

GRANTS ANALYSIS
Total Grants: $1,616,755

Number of Grants: 110

Highest Grant: $399,864

Typical Range: $1,000 to $10,000

Disclosure Period: fiscal year ending July 31, 1993

Note: Recent grants are derived from a fiscal 1993 Form 990.

RECENT GRANTS

Library

399,864	Seton Hall University, South Orange, NJ — library	

General

210,000	Lehigh University, Bethlehem, PA — general fund	
210,000	University of Vermont, Burlington, VT — general fund	
100,000	Seton Hall Preparatory School, South Orange, NJ — general fund	
66,667	Archdiocese of Newark, Newark, NJ — general fund	
50,000	Immaculata College, Immaculata, PA — general fund	

Schenck Fund, L. P.

CONTACT
Patrick Clark
Vice President
L. P. Schenck Fund
c/o Midlantic National Bank
41 Oak St.
Ridgewood, NJ 07450
(201) 652-8499

FINANCIAL SUMMARY
Recent Giving: $436,176 (fiscal 1993); $416,627 (fiscal 1992); $440,175 (fiscal 1991)

Assets: $8,627,289 (fiscal 1993); $8,466,332 (fiscal 1992); $8,027,294 (fiscal 1991)

EIN: 22-6040581

CONTRIBUTIONS SUMMARY
Donor(s): the late Lillian Pitkin Schenck

Typical Recipients: • *Arts & Humanities:* Arts Centers, Community Arts, Libraries, Museums/Galleries, Music, Theater • *Civic & Public Affairs:* Urban & Community Affairs • *Education:* Public Education (Precollege) • *Environment:* General • *Health:* Cancer, Emergency/Ambulance Services, Hospitals, Mental Health • *Religion:* Religious Welfare • *Social Services:* At-Risk Youth, Child Welfare, Community Centers, Community Service Organizations, Day Care, Family Planning, Family Services, Food/Clothing Distribution, People with Disabilities, Substance Abuse, Volunteer Services, Youth Organizations

Grant Types: capital, general support, operating expenses, and project

Geographic Distribution: limited to the Englewood, NJ, area

GIVING OFFICERS

Midatlantic National Bank: trust

Mary P. Oenslager: trust

Elizabeth N. Thatcher: trust

APPLICATION INFORMATION

Initial Approach: Send a brief letter of inquiry. Include a description of organization, amount requested, purpose of funds sought, recently audited financial statement, and proof of tax-exempt status. Deadline is August 1.

GRANTS ANALYSIS

Total Grants: $436,176

Number of Grants: 29

Highest Grant: $55,250

Typical Range: $2,000 to $20,000

Disclosure Period: fiscal year ending August 31, 1993

Note: Recent grants are derived from a fiscal 1993 Form 990.

RECENT GRANTS

Library
11,276	Englewood Public Library, Englewood, NJ

General
55,250	Social Service Federation, Leonard Johnson Day Nursery, Englewood, NJ
50,000	Youth Consultation Services, Holley House, Newark, NJ
40,000	Community Centers for Mental Health, Englewood, NJ
35,000	Friendship House, Hackensack, NJ
20,000	Englewood Hospital, Englewood, NJ

Schering-Plough Corp. / Schering-Plough Foundation

Revenue: $4.65 billion
Employees: 21,600
Headquarters: Madison, NJ
SIC Major Group: Pharmaceutical Preparations, Biological Products Except Diagnostic, and Toilet Preparations

CONTACT
Rita Sacco
Assistant Secretary
Schering-Plough Fdn.
1 Giralda Farms
Madison, NJ 07940-1000
(201) 822-7412
Note: Contact for information on direct contributions is Joan Henderson at (201) 822-7000

FINANCIAL SUMMARY
Recent Giving: $2,968,424 (1993); $2,827,338 (1992); $3,168,669 (1991)

Assets: $18,294,715 (1993); $17,591,836 (1992); $17,333,918 (1991)

Gifts Received: $1,500,000 (1993); $1,500,000 (1992); $1,500,000 (1991)

Fiscal Note: Company gives through foundation (about 75%) and directly (about 25%). Figure for 1993 represents foundation giving only and includes $448,123 in matching gifts to educational institutions, foundations, hospitals, and associations. The foundation receives gifts from the Schering-Plough Corp.

EIN: 22-1711047

CONTRIBUTIONS SUMMARY
Typical Recipients: • *Arts & Humanities:* Arts Associations & Councils, Arts Centers, Arts Festivals, Community Arts, Dance, General, Historic Preservation, Libraries, Museums/Galleries, Music, Performing Arts, Theater • *Civic & Public Affairs:* Civil Rights, Community Foundations, Economic Development, Hispanic Affairs, Nonprofit Management, Philanthropic Organizations, Professional & Trade Associations, Public Policy, Zoos/Aquariums • *Education:* Arts/Humanities Education, Business Education, Colleges & Universities, Education Associations, Education Funds, Engineering/Technological Education, Faculty Development, Health & Physical Education, Literacy, Medical Education, Minority Education, Private Education (Precollege), Science/Mathematics Education, Student Aid • *Health:* Cancer, Clinics/Medical Centers, Hospitals, Long-Term Care, Medical Research, Medical Training, Public Health, Single-Disease Health Associations, Transplant Networks/Donor Banks • *International:* Health Care/Hospitals, International Peace & Security Issues, International Relations • *Religion:* Churches, Religious Welfare • *Science:* Scientific Labs, Scientific Research • *Social Services:* Child Welfare, Family Services, Substance Abuse, United Funds/United Ways, Youth Organizations

Grant Types: capital, employee matching gifts, fellowship, general support, professorship, research, scholarship, and seed money

Nonmonetary Support Types: donated equipment, donated products, in-kind services, and loaned employees

Note: Value of nonmonetary support is unavailable. See "Other Things To Know" for more details.

Geographic Distribution: emphasizes locations in which corporation has major facilities, and national organizations

Operating Locations: AR (Little Rock), CA (La Mirada, Palo Alto, San Leandro), FL (Miami, Pembroke Pines), GA (Chamblee, Chatsworth), IL (Alsip, Chicago, Des Plaines, Niles), NE (Elkhorn, Omaha), NJ (Allentown, Bloomfield, Carteret, Cream Ridge, Kenilworth, Lafayette, Liberty Corner, Madison, Maplewood, Union), NY, PR (Hato Rey, Las Piedres, Manati), TN (Cleveland, Memphis), TX (Irving)

Note: Also operates in Mississauga, Ontario, Canada, and Pointe Claire, Quebec, Canada.

CORP. OFFICERS
Donald Ransford Conklin: *B* Bound Brook NJ 1936 *ED* Williams Coll BA 1958; Rutgers Univ MBA 1961; Harvard Univ Advanced Mgmt Program 1970 *CURR EMPL* exec vp: Schering-Plough Corp *CORP AFFIL* dir: Cytotherapeutics Inc, Vertex Pharmaceuticals; pres: Schering-Plough Healthcare Products; vp, dir: Schering Corp, Schering Overseas Ltd *NONPR AFFIL* dir: Mt Kemble Hosp

Richard Jay Kogan: *B* New York NY 1941 *ED* CUNY BA 1963; NY Univ MBA 1968 *CURR EMPL* pres, coo, dir: Schering-Plough Corp *CORP AFFIL* chmn, pres: Schering Corp; dir: Gen Signal Corp, Natl Westminster Bancorp, Rite Aid Corp *NONPR AFFIL* chmn, trust: Food Drug Law Inst; dir: Accts Network Am; mem bd overseers: NY Univ Stern Sch Bus; treas, dir: Pharmaceutical Mfrs Assn; trust: St Barnabas Med Ctr

GIVING OFFICERS
David Edmond Collins: trust, mem *B* Oak Park IL 1934 *ED* Univ Notre Dame BA 1956; Harvard Univ LLB 1959 *CURR EMPL* pres, dir: Schering-Plough Healthcare Products *NONPR AFFIL* chmn: Independent Coll Fund; mem: Am Bar Assn, Assn Gen Couns, Commn Future Independent Higher Ed NJ, NJ Bar Assn, NJ Chamber Commerce; mem adv counc: Univ Notre Dame Law Sch; trust: Fairleigh Dickinson Univ

Donald Ransford Conklin: trust *CURR EMPL* exec vp: Schering-Plough Corp (see above)

Hugh Alfred D'Andrade: trust *B* Metuchen NJ 1938 *ED* Rutgers Univ BA 1961; Columbia Univ LLB 1964 *CURR EMPL* exec vp admin: Schering-Plough Corp *CORP AFFIL* chmn: DNAX Res Inst Molecular Cell Biology; dir: Autoimmune, Molecular Devices Corp *NONPR AFFIL* dir: Biotech Indus Org; mem: Am Bar Assn, NJ Bar Assn; mem bd overseers: NJ Inst Tech Fdn; mem bd visit: Columbia Univ Law Sch; trust: Drew Univ

Harold Russell Hiser, Jr.: trust *B* Decatur IL 1931 *ED* Princeton Univ BSE 1953 *CURR EMPL* exec vp fin: Schering-Plough Corp *CORP AFFIL* dir: ReCapital Corp *NONPR AFFIL* treas, dir: Overlook Hosp Assn; trust: Patriot Group Investment Trust

Richard Jay Kogan: trust, mem *CURR EMPL* pres, coo, dir: Schering-Plough Corp (see above)

Allan Stanford Kushen: pres *B* Chicago IL 1929 *ED* Univ Miami BBA 1952; NY Univ LLB 1955 *CURR EMPL* sr vp pub aff: Schering-Plough Corp *CORP AFFIL* dir, mem adv comm: Allendale Ins Co *NONPR AFFIL* assoc law: Am Coll Legal Med; dir: Pub Aff Counc; mem: Am Bar Assn, FL Bar Assn, NJ Bar Assn, NY Bar Assn, Phi Delta Phi; trust: Food & Drug Law Inst, Kean Coll, Morris Mus Arts Sci, Newark Mus; trust, pres: Arts Counc Morris Area

Robert Peter Luciano: trust *B* New York NY 1933 *ED* City Coll NY BBA 1954; Univ MI JD 1958 *CORP AFFIL* dir: AlliedSignal Inc, Bank NY Co Inc, CR Bard Inc, Merrill Lynch & Co Inc *NONPR AFFIL* dir: Natl Assn Mfrs, NJ Chamber Commerce, Un Way Tri-St; mem: Am Bar Assn, NY Bar Assn *CLUB AFFIL* Econ, Sky, Union League

Joseph S. Roth: secy

Rita Sacco: asst secy

Jack L. Wyszomierski: treas *B* 1955 *ED* Carnegie-Mellon Univ BS 1977; Carnegie-Mellon Univ MS 1978 *CURR EMPL* vp, treas: Schering-Plough Corp *CORP AFFIL* vp, treas: Schering Corp

APPLICATION INFORMATION
Initial Approach: *Initial Contact:* letter or proposal on organization letterhead *Include Information On:* specific purpose for which funding is sought, background information on requesting organization, major programs and services rendered, proof of tax-exempt status, latest audited financial statement, program budget (if application relates to specific activity); supporting material (including annual report) is desirable *Deadlines:* requests must be received before February 1 or July 1 (foundation board meets twice annually in March and October) *Note:* Requests that do not include the information above will be returned to applicants.

Restrictions on Giving: Grants are not made to individuals.

OTHER THINGS TO KNOW
Occasionally makes product donations, primarily to assist efforts of U.S. organizations working in developing countries. Surplus equipment is made available to organizations in operating communities.

Foundation historically pays grants for annual support in the fourth quarter of the year.

GRANTS ANALYSIS
Total Grants: $2,520,301

Number of Grants: 118

Highest Grant: $100,000

Average Grant: $21,358

Typical Range: $50 to $1,000 and $5,000 to $50,000

Disclosure Period: 1993

Note: Total grants figure is for the foundation only. Total grants, number of grants, and average grant exclude matching gifts, which totaled $448,123 in 1993. Recent grants are derived from a 1993 Form 990.

RECENT GRANTS

General

100,000	Puerto Rico Community Foundation, Hato Rey, PR
95,000	University of Michigan School of Pharmacy, Ann Arbor, MI
69,451	National Merit Scholarship Corporation, Evanston, IL
60,000	Pharmaceutical Manufacturers Association Foundation, Washington, DC
50,000	Fordham University, Bronx, NY

Schumann Fund for New Jersey

CONTACT
Julie A. Keenan
Executive Director
Schumann Fund for New Jersey
21 Van Vleck St
Montclair, NJ 07042
(201) 509-9883
Note: The foundation shares its office with the Florence and John Schumann Foundation.

FINANCIAL SUMMARY
Recent Giving: $903,295 (1993); $1,108,100 (1992); $1,193,111 (1991)

Assets: $28,524,930 (1993); $25,255,625 (1992); $21,099,234 (1991)

EIN: 52-1556076

CONTRIBUTIONS SUMMARY
Donor(s): The foundation was established in 1988 by the Florence and John Schumann Foundation.

Typical Recipients: • *Arts & Humanities:* Libraries, Public Broadcasting • *Civic & Public Affairs:* Community Foundations, Economic Development, Hispanic Affairs, Housing, Nonprofit Management, Public Policy, Urban & Community Affairs • *Education:* Afterschool/Enrichment Programs, Colleges & Universities, Education Associations, Education Reform, Elementary Education (Private), Elementary Education (Public), Environmental Education, Faculty Development, General, Preschool Education, Private Education (Precollege), Public Education (Precollege), Special Education • *Environment:* Air/Water Quality, General, Resource Conservation • *Health:* Diabetes, Prenatal Health Issues, Single-Disease Health Associations • *Religion:* Churches, Religious Welfare • *Social Services:* Child Welfare, Community Service Organizations, Day Care, Emergency Relief, Family Services, Shelters/Homelessness, Volunteer Services, YMCA/YWCA/YMHA/YWHA, Youth Organizations

Grant Types: multiyear/continuing support and project

Geographic Distribution: New Jersey, with a focus on Essex County

GIVING OFFICERS
Aubin Z. Ames: chmn, trust

Leonard S. Coleman: trust

Christopher J. Daggett: trust *CURR EMPL* William E. Simon & Sons

Andrew Christian Halvorsen: secy, trust *B* Englewood NJ 1946 *ED* Brown Univ AB 1968; Univ PA MBA 1972 *CURR EMPL* pres, cfo, dir: Beneficial Corp

George R. Harris: vchmn, trust

Julie A. Keenan: exec dir

Alan Rosenthal: trust

Donald Malcolm Wilson: trust *B* Glen Ridge NJ 1925 *ED* Yale Univ BA 1948 *CURR EMPL* publ: Business Central NJ *NONPR AFFIL* dir: Ctr Analysis Pub Issues, Solomon R. Guggenheim Mus; mem: Counc Foreign Rels; mem adv counc: Edward R Murrow Ctr, Tufts Univ *CLUB AFFIL* Century Assn, Fed City

APPLICATION INFORMATION
Initial Approach:

Applicants should submit a written proposal.

The propsal should include a detailed description of the proposed project and the plan for accomplishment. The proposal should be accompanied by a copy of the organization's latest financial statement, an expense budget which specifically identifies all sources of income, the project's time frame and future funding plans, and a copy of the organization's IRS tax-exempt determination letter.

Proposals should be submitted before January 15, April 15, August 15, or October 15, which is approximately six weeks before the following board meeting.

The board meets four times a year in March, June, October, and December. The foundation indicates that action on proposals may be reserved for a later quarter, but it will reply as promptly as possible as to the status of all requests.

Restrictions on Giving: In general, the fund does not accept applications for capital campaigns, annual giving, endowment, direct support of individuals, or local programs in counties other than Essex.

PUBLICATIONS
Annual report including application guidelines

GRANTS ANALYSIS
Total Grants: $903,295

Number of Grants: 58

Highest Grant: $65,000

Average Grant: $15,574

Typical Range: $10,000 to $50,000

Disclosure Period: 1993

Note: Recent grants are derived from a 1993 Form 990.

RECENT GRANTS

Library
2,500	Montclair Public Library, Montclair, NJ — trustee grant

General
65,000	Partnership for New Jersey, Trenton, NJ — conduct and publicize a study of the efficiency and educational results in the Union Township public schools
50,000	Chad School, Newark, NJ — operating and development support for independent nursery, elementary, and junior high school
50,000	Early Childhood Facilities Fund, Newark, NJ — assist Head Start and child care programs in providing quality facilities for current and expansion needs
45,000	Unified Vailsburg Services Organization, Vailsburg, NJ — child care, meals on wheels, administrative support
37,500	Industrial Areas Foundation, Newark, NJ — initiate a church-based community organizing effort in Newark

Schwartz Foundation, Arnold A.

CONTACT
Edward D. Kunzman
President
Arnold A. Schwartz Fdn.
c/o Bivona, Cohen, Kunzman, Coley, et al.
15 Mountain Blvd.
Warren, NJ 07060
(201) 757-7800

FINANCIAL SUMMARY
Recent Giving: $195,650 (fiscal 1993); $185,240 (fiscal 1992); $172,300 (fiscal 1991)

Assets: $4,420,774 (fiscal 1993); $4,210,336 (fiscal 1992); $3,977,606 (fiscal 1991)

EIN: 22-6034152

CONTRIBUTIONS SUMMARY
Donor(s): the late Arnold A. Schwartz

Typical Recipients: • *Arts & Humanities:* Libraries • *Civic & Public Affairs:* Clubs, Employment/Job Training, General, Housing • *Education:* Colleges & Universities, Gifted & Talented Programs, Private Education (Precollege), Special Education • *Environment:* Wildlife Protection • *Health:* Cancer, Children's Health/Hospitals, Clinics/Medical Centers, Emergency/Ambulance Services, Eyes/Blindness, Health Organizations, Hospitals, Mental Health, Multiple Sclerosis, Single-Disease Health Associations • *Religion:* Jewish Causes, Religious Organizations, Religious Welfare • *Social*

Services: Camps, Child Welfare, Community Service Organizations, Counseling, Day Care, Family Services, Food/Clothing Distribution, People with Disabilities, Recreation & Athletics, Shelters/Homelessness, United Funds/United Ways, Volunteer Services, YMCA/YWCA/YMHA/YWHA, Youth Organizations

Grant Types: general support

Geographic Distribution: focus on northern NJ

GIVING OFFICERS
Victor DiLeo: trust

Louis Harding: vp

Edward D. Kunzman: pres

Steven Kunzman: secy, treas

David Lackland: trust

Robert Shapiro: trust

Kenneth Turnbull: trust

APPLICATION INFORMATION
Initial Approach: Send brief letter describing program. Include a description of organization, amount requested, purpose of funds sought, recently audited financial statement, and proof of tax-exempt status. Deadline is September 30.

Restrictions on Giving: Does not support individuals or provide funds for endowments.

GRANTS ANALYSIS
Total Grants: $195,650

Number of Grants: 54

Highest Grant: $20000

Typical Range: $1,000 to $5,000

Disclosure Period: fiscal year ending November 30, 1993

Note: Recent grants are derived from a fiscal 1993 Form 990.

RECENT GRANTS

Library
10,000	Matheny School, Peapack, NJ — operating funds for library
9,800	A.A. Schwartz Memorial, Dunellen, NJ — update computer Children's Library

General
20,000	Muhlenberg Hospital, Plainfield, NJ — equipment center fetal systems
10,000	Deborah Hospital Foundation, Brown Mills, NJ — renovate facility
10,000	McAuley School for Exceptional Children, Watchung, NJ — purchase equipment
6,000	American Red Cross, Plainfield, NJ — to continue programs
5,000	Dunellen Fish, Middlesex, NJ — for food and clothing for poor and needy

Seton Leather Co. / Seton Co. Foundation

Headquarters: Newark, NJ

CONTACT
Dianne Fedor
Seton Leather Co.
849 Broadway
Newark, NJ 07104
(201) 485-4800

FINANCIAL SUMMARY
Recent Giving: $82,440 (1993); $71,510 (1991)

Assets: $850,279 (1993); $954,122 (1991)

EIN: 22-6029254

CONTRIBUTIONS SUMMARY
Typical Recipients: • *Arts & Humanities:* Libraries, Music, Public Broadcasting • *Civic & Public Affairs:* Clubs, General, Safety, Women's Affairs • *Education:* Colleges & Universities, Education Funds, General, Legal Education, Literacy, Medical Education, Private Education (Precollege), Secondary Education (Private) • *Environment:* Air/Water Quality, Resource Conservation • *Health:* Cancer, Hospices, Hospitals, Medical Rehabilitation, Mental Health, Multiple Sclerosis • *Religion:* Churches, Jewish Causes, Religious Welfare, Social/Policy Issues • *Science:* Scientific Labs • *Social Services:* At-Risk Youth, Child Welfare, Community Service Organizations, Family Planning, Recreation & Athletics, Scouts, Special Olympics, United Funds/United Ways, Youth Organizations

Grant Types: general support

Geographic Distribution: focus on CT, MA, MI, NJ, and NY

GIVING OFFICERS
Robert DeMajistre: trust

Philip D. Kaltenbacher: trust *CURR EMPL* chmn, ceo, dir: Seton Co

APPLICATION INFORMATION
Initial Approach: Send a brief letter of inquiry. Include a description of organization, amount requested, purpose of funds sought, recently audited financial statement, and proof of tax-exempt status. There are no deadlines.

GRANTS ANALYSIS
Total Grants: $82,440

Number of Grants: 79

Highest Grant: $6,000

Typical Range: $25 to $1,000

Disclosure Period: 1993

Note: Recent grants are derived from a 1993 Form 990.

RECENT GRANTS

Library
500	Saxton Community Library, Saxton, PA

General

6,000	Boys and Girls Club of Southeast Michigan, Detroit, MI
6,000	St. Benedict's Preparatory School, Newark, NJ
5,000	Boy Scouts of America Essex Council
5,000	Marthas Vineyard Hospital Foundation, Martha's Vineyard, MA
5,000	Rutgers University, New Brunswick, NJ

Simon Foundation, William E. and Carol G.

CONTACT
William E. Simon
Chairman
William E. and Carol G. Simon Foundation
c/o William E. Simons & Sons
310 South St., PO Box 1913
Morristown, NJ 07962-1913
(201) 898-0293

FINANCIAL SUMMARY
Recent Giving: $2,800,000 (1995 est.); $2,700,000 (1994 approx.); $1,239,844 (1993)

Assets: $11,000,000 (1995 est.); $10,800,000 (1994 approx.); $17,253,261 (1993)

Gifts Received: $6,244,753 (1993); $621,781 (1992); $416,400 (1991)

Fiscal Note: In 1993, the foundation received gifts from William E. and Carol G. Simon.

EIN: 13-6217788

CONTRIBUTIONS SUMMARY
Donor(s): The William E. and Carol G. Simon Foundation was established in the mid 1980s by William E. Simon, former secretary of the treasury under former Presidents Richard Nixon and Gerald Ford.

Mr. Simon was born in 1927 in Paterson, NJ, went to Newark Academy, then Lafayette College where he graduated in 1951 with a bachelor's degree in government and law. He went right to work on Wall Street, specializing in government securities and municipal bonds. He rose to become a senior partner in Salomon Brothers, a large investment firm where his annual salary is estimated to have been between $2 million and $3 million in 1971 and 1972.

He left Wall street in 1972 when he was appointed as the deputy secretary of the treasury under George Schultz. One year later, Mr. Simon was named the administrator of the Federal Energy Office where, as the "energy czar," he coordinated the country's energy policy during the energy crisis. He left that post to become the secretary of the treasury in 1974 where he served until 1977, when he left government service.

Before he began his government service, Mr. Simon had placed in a blind trust his assets which had declined about 60% in value. Once back in private life, Mr. Simon began to rebuild his personal wealth by establishing his own network of consultancies and corporate relationships. He combined his economic expertise with his recent government service to negotiate financial opportunities with the largest companies in the country. He joined a dozen or so blue-chip corporate and philanthropic boards including Xerox Corporation and the John M. Olin Foundation.

In 1981, Mr. Simon and Ray Chambers founded Wesray Corporation, an investment and banking firm that specialized in leveraged buyouts. The company became one of the the largest private companies in the country with sales of $1.8 billion in 1983. Today, Mr. Simon directs his own company, William E. Simon and Sons, located in Morristown, NJ. His personal fortune was estimated to be approximately $300 million in 1991.

Mr. Simon's accomplishments reflect a personal philosophy of hard work and a belief in the free enterprise system. His associates have described him as a nonstop worker who can regularly put in 18-hour days. He authored two books including "A Time for Truth" an account of his Washington, DC, experiences and conservative economics, which was a bestseller for 30 weeks. He donated the proceeds to his alma mater, Lafayette College in Easton, PA. He has served on or is currently serving on the boards of more than 60 charitable organizations. He has received more than 50 awards, and he is a member of more than 20 clubs across the country.

He married the former Carol Girard in 1950. The couple has seven children: William E. Simon, Jr., John P. Simon, Mary Beth Simon Streep, Carol Leigh Simon Porges, Aimee Simon Bloom, Julie Ann Simon, and Johanna Katrina Simon. The nine members of the family serve as officers or directors of the William E. and Carol Simon Foundation.

Typical Recipients: • *Arts & Humanities:* Arts Associations & Councils, Arts Funds, Dance, Historic Preservation, Libraries, Museums/Galleries, Music • *Civic & Public Affairs:* Business/Free Enterprise, Civil Rights, First Amendment Issues, General, Housing, Municipalities/Towns, Philanthropic Organizations, Professional & Trade Associations, Public Policy, Safety, Urban & Community Affairs, Women's Affairs • *Education:* Arts/Humanities Education, Business Education, Colleges & Universities, Community & Junior Colleges, Education Associations, Education Funds, Legal Education, Private Education (Precollege), Religious Education, Special Education, Student Aid • *Environment:* Resource Conservation • *Health:* Cancer, Clinics/Medical Centers, Health Funds, Health Organizations, Hospices, Hospitals, Multiple Sclerosis, Nursing Services, Public Health, Single-Disease Health Associations • *International:* International Affairs, International Organizations, International Peace & Security Issues, International Relations, International Relief Efforts • *Religion:* Churches, Dioceses, Religious Organizations, Religious Welfare • *Science:* Scientific Research • *Social Services:* Animal Protection, At-Risk Youth, Child Welfare, Community Centers, Community Service Organizations, Family Planning, Family Services, Food/Clothing Distribution, Homes, People with Disabilities, Recreation & Athletics, Shelters/Homelessness, Substance Abuse, United Funds/United Ways, Veterans, Youth Organizations

Grant Types: capital, endowment, general support, operating expenses, and scholarship

Geographic Distribution: nationally, with emphasis on the Northeast particularly New York and New Jersey

GIVING OFFICERS
Aimee Simon Bloom: dir

Carol Leigh Simon Porges: dir

Carol G. Simon: pres, dir

J. Peter Simon: vp, secy, dir *B* 1927 *CURR EMPL* pres, dir: Wesaire

Johanna K. Simon: dir

Julie A. Simon: dir *B* 1950 *CURR EMPL* vp, dir: Human Kinetics Publs

William Edward Simon: chmn, dir *B* Paterson NJ 1927 *ED* Lafayette Coll BA 1952 *CURR EMPL* chmn, pres: William E Simon & Sons *CORP AFFIL* co-chmn: WSPG Intl Los Angeles; dir: Castleton, Pompano Pk Reality, Wellsford Group; mem adv bd: Washington Times *NONPR AFFIL* bd govs: Natl Counc Recording Blind, NY Hosp, Hugh O'Brian Youth Fdn, Ronald Reagan Presidential Fdn; chmn: Commun Fdn, Newark Academy, Richard Nixon Presidential Library & Birthplace Fdn; chmn adv bd: Teachers Am; chmn bd trusts: US Olympic Fdn; chmn investment comm: US Air Force Academy; co chmn, dir: Endowment Comm Covenant House; contributor: NJ St Caddy Scholarship Fund, US Golf Assn; dir: Am Friends Covent Garden, Atlantic Counc US, Boys Harbor, Catholic Big Bros, Citizens Against Govt Waste, Citizens Network Foreign Affs, Courage Fdn, Covenant House, Intl Fdn Ed & Self-Help, Kissinger Assoc, Natl Football Fdn & Hall Fame, Royal Ballet, Sequoia Inst, Space Studies Inst, World Cup 94 Organizing Comm; dir, mem budget & finance: Gerald R Ford Fdn; hon chmn: Comm Preservation Treasury Bldg, Inst Ed Aff; hon chmn fundraising: YMCA Morris Ctr; hon co-chmn: Liberty Park Fdn, Natl Fitness Fdn, Suffolk County Vietnam Veterans Meml Commn, US Fitness Academy Campaign; hon trust: Adelphi Univ, Newark Boys Chorus Sch; mem: Amwell Valley Conservancy, Assn NJ Rifle & Pistol Club, Cardinals Comm Laity, Counc Foreign Rels, Explorers Club, Friendly Sons St Patrick, Intl Comm Human Dignity, John B Kelly Jr Meml Boathouse Restoration Comm, Mont Pelerin Soc, Ambassador John O G Moore Scholarship Fund, Morality Media, Natl Counc Recording Blind, PA Soc, Pilgrims US, Villa Taverna Soc; mem adv bd: Action Inst, Am Rep Pacific Security Res Inst, Catholics Committed Support Pope, Ctr Christianity & Common Good, John D J Moore Scholarship Fund, Pacific Security

Res Inst, Pvt Sector Initiatives Fdn, SAIL Adventures Learning, Univ Dallas Ctr Intl Mgmt Ed, Univ Southern CA Sch Bus Admin, US Assn Blind Athletes, Womens Sports Fdn; mem adv bd, secy, treas: Jesse Owens Fdn; mem adv counc: Consumer Alert; mem bd overseers: Exec Counc Foreign Diplomats, Stanford Univ Hoover Inst War Revolution Peace; mem chmn comm: Natl Counc Alcoholism & Drug Dependence; mem comm: Cardinals Comm Laity; mem counc: Templeton Coll; mem exec bd, admin comm, fin comm: US Olympic Comm; mem exec comm: Bretton Woods Comm, Daytop Village; mem fed adv bd: Commn Preservation Treasury Bldg; mem hon comm: Womens Econ Roundtable; mem inaugural adv bd: Gene Autry Western Heritage Mus; mem intl adv bd: Intl Ctr Disabled; mem intl councillors: Ctr Strategic & Intl Studies; mem natl adv bd: Sudden Infant Death Syndrome Alliance; mem natl counc trust: Freedoms Fdn Valley Forge; mem natl steering comm: Jefferson Energy Fdn; mem policy counc: Tax Fdn; mem visiting comm: St Univ NY Stony Brook Marine Science Res Ctr; prin: Counc Excellence Govt; trust: Animal Med Ctr, Asia Soc, Boston Univ, Hillsdale Coll, George C Marshall Res Fdn, Natl Investors Hall Fame; trust emeritus: Lafayette Coll; trust, mem exec comm: Order Malta; trust, mem fin comm: Heritage Fdn; trust, mem investment comm, mem exec adv counc: Univ Rochester Simon Grad Sch Bus Admin *CLUB AFFIL* Alfalfa, Balboa Bay, Bond of NY, Brook Forum, CC CO, Commonwealth CA, Gulf Stream GC, Robert Trent Jones Intl GC, Links, Lyford Cay, Madison Sq Garden, Maidstone, Maui CC, Merdham Valley Gun, Morris County GC, Municipal Bond NY, New York Athletic, New York YC, Oahu CC, River, Rolling Rock, Sherriffs Jury, Waialae CC *PHIL AFFIL* pres, trust, mem exec comm: John M. Olin Foundation; chmn: William E. Simon Foundation; secy: Mayo Foundation

Mary B. Simon Streep: dir

APPLICATION INFORMATION
Initial Approach:

Applications to the foundation should be made in writing and include a copy of the requesting organization's IRS determination letter.

OTHER THINGS TO KNOW
In 1990, the foundation received $40,000 worth of ENSR Corporation stock from William E. Simon.

GRANTS ANALYSIS
Total Grants: $1,239,844

Number of Grants: 309

Highest Grant: $166,667

Average Grant: $4,012

Typical Range: $250 to $5,000 and $10,000 to $50,000

Disclosure Period: 1993

Note: Recent grants are derived from a 1993 Form 990.

RECENT GRANTS
Library

30,000	Richard Nixon Library and Birthplace, Yorba Linda, CA
20,000	Richard Nixon Library, Yorba Linda, CA — endowment fund

General

166,667	Archdiocese of New York, New York, NY — scholarship fun
150,000	University of Vermont, Burlington, VT — scholarship fund
73,000	Adelphi University, New York, NY — endowment fund
71,000	Manhattanville College, Purchase, NY — endowment fund
50,000	Gerald R. Ford Foundation, Ann Arbor, MI — endowment fund

Snyder Foundation, Harold B. and Dorothy A.

CONTACT
Audrey Snyder
Executive Director
Harold B. and Dorothy A. Snyder Fdn.
PO Box 671
Moorestown, NJ 08057
(609) 273-9745

FINANCIAL SUMMARY
Recent Giving: $275,000 (fiscal 1992); $210,237 (fiscal 1990); $179,926 (fiscal 1989)

Assets: $7,582,013 (fiscal 1992); $6,779,258 (fiscal 1990); $5,520,840 (fiscal 1989)

Gifts Received: $160,229 (fiscal 1991); $6,805 (fiscal 1990); $322,948 (fiscal 1989)

Fiscal Note: In 1991, contributions were received from Audrey Snyder ($1,625), Arline Critese ($595), Ethlyn Allison ($600), Holly Roeck ($200), Bernard Professional Center ($6,765), and the estate of Harold B. Snyder.

EIN: 22-2316043

CONTRIBUTIONS SUMMARY
Donor(s): the late Harold B. Snyder, Sr.

Typical Recipients: • *Arts & Humanities:* History & Archaeology, Libraries • *Civic & Public Affairs:* Community Foundations, Employment/Job Training, General, Housing, Nonprofit Management, Professional & Trade Associations, Urban & Community Affairs • *Education:* Preschool Education, Private Education (Precollege), Religious Education, Science/Mathematics Education • *Health:* Children's Health/Hospitals, Health Organizations, Hospitals, Single-Disease Health Associations • *Religion:* Churches, Religious Organizations, Religious Welfare • *Social Services:* Community Service Organizations, Family Services, Homes, People with Disabilities, Shelters/Homelessness, Youth Organizations

Grant Types: general support, loan, multi-year/continuing support, operating expenses, project, and seed money

Geographic Distribution: focus on the Union County, NJ, area

GIVING OFFICERS
Ethelyn Allison: trust

Arline Snyder Cortese: trust

Lillian Palumbo: trust

Audrey Snyder: exec dir, trust

Phyllis Johnson Snyder: trust

APPLICATION INFORMATION
Initial Approach: Send a brief letter of inquiry. 5 copies. There are no deadlines.

Restrictions on Giving: Limited to Union County Institutions.

OTHER THINGS TO KNOW
Provides scholarships to residents of New Jersey entering the Presbytarian Ministry, nursing, and the building construction industry.

GRANTS ANALYSIS
Total Grants: $275,000

Number of Grants: 34

Highest Grant: $43,000

Typical Range: $100 to $6,000

Disclosure Period: fiscal year ending September 30, 1992

Note: Recent grants are derived from a Fiscal 1992 Form 990. Information listed does not include scholarships.

RECENT GRANTS
Library

3,640	Kenilworth Public Library
1,000	Foundation Center

General

43,000	Community United Methodist Church
20,500	Muhlenberg Foundation
15,000	Cerebral Palsy League of Union County
15,000	Elizabethport Presbyterian Center
10,000	Summit Speech School

South Branch Foundation

CONTACT
Peter S. Johnson
South Branch Fdn.
c/o Gillen and Johnson
PO Box 477
Somerville, NJ 08876
(201) 722-6400

FINANCIAL SUMMARY
Recent Giving: $410,000 (1990); $480,000 (1989); $440,500 (1988)

Assets: $9,326,940 (1990); $9,853,370 (1989); $7,978,014 (1988)

EIN: 22-6029434

CONTRIBUTIONS SUMMARY

Donor(s): J. Seward Johnson, J. Seward Charitable Trust

Typical Recipients: • *Arts & Humanities:* Arts Centers, Community Arts, Dance, Historic Preservation, Libraries, Music, Public Broadcasting • *Civic & Public Affairs:* Civil Rights, Zoos/Aquariums • *Education:* Arts/Humanities Education, Colleges & Universities • *Environment:* General • *Social Services:* Animal Protection, Community Service Organizations

Grant Types: fellowship, multiyear/continuing support, project, research, and scholarship

Geographic Distribution: focus on NY, NJ, and MA

GIVING OFFICERS

Jennifer Johnson Duke: dir *B* 1941 *CURR EMPL* co-owner: Gallery Applied Arts

Esther U. Johnson: trust

James Lawrence Johnson: trust *B* Vernon TX 1927 *ED* TX Tech Univ BBA 1949 *CURR EMPL* chmn emeritus: GTE Corp *CORP AFFIL* dir: Bloomington Unlimited, British Columbia Telecommunications, First Fed Savings & Loan Assn, Mutual Life Ins Co NY *NONPR AFFIL* dir: IL Telephone Assn, McLean County Assn Commerce Indus; mem: Fin Execs Inst, Natl Assn Accts, Wesleyan Assocs, Wesleyan Univ; mem adv counc: IL St Univ Coll Bus; trust, mem adv counc: Mennonite Hosp *CLUB AFFIL* Bloomington CC, Crestwicke CC, Woodway CC

John Duncan Mack: trust *B* New York NY 1924 *ED* St Johns Annapolis Coll 1948; Harvard Univ 1950 *CURR EMPL* pres Carter Products: Carter-Wallace *CORP AFFIL* dir: Cuisinarts

APPLICATION INFORMATION

Initial Approach: Send cover letter and full proposal. Deadline is December 31.

Restrictions on Giving: Does not support individuals.

GRANTS ANALYSIS

Total Grants: $410,000

Number of Grants: 32

Highest Grant: $150,000

Typical Range: $1,000 to $10,000

Disclosure Period: 1990

Note: Recent grants are derived from a 1990 Form 990.

RECENT GRANTS

General

150,000	Matheny School, Peapack, NJ
125,000	Nature Conservancy, Pottersville, NJ
100,000	Massachusetts Audubon Society, Lincoln, MA
50,000	Juilliard School, New York, NY
10,000	Vermont Studio School, Johnson, VT

Subaru of America Inc. / Subaru of America Foundation

Sales: $1.72 billion
Employees: 1,132
Parent Company: Fuji Heavy Industries, Ltd.
Headquarters: Cherry Hill, NJ
SIC Major Group: Wholesale Trade—Durable Goods

CONTACT

Sandra Capell
Foundation Administrator
Subaru of America Foundation
Subaru Plz.
PO Box 6000
Cherry Hill, NJ 08034-6000
(609) 488-5099

FINANCIAL SUMMARY

Recent Giving: $151,405 (1993); $203,529 (1992); $244,923 (1991)

Assets: $543,713 (1993); $678,399 (1992); $853,805 (1991)

Fiscal Note: Figures for foundation only and do not include company direct giving.

EIN: 22-2531774

CONTRIBUTIONS SUMMARY

Typical Recipients: • *Arts & Humanities:* Arts Associations & Councils, Arts Centers, Arts Outreach, Ballet, Dance, History & Archaeology, Libraries, Music, Theater • *Civic & Public Affairs:* Nonprofit Management, Safety • *Education:* Afterschool/Enrichment Programs, Education Reform, Elementary Education (Public), Faculty Development, International Exchange, Literacy, Minority Education, Private Education (Precollege), Science/Mathematics Education, Special Education • *Environment:* Resource Conservation • *Health:* AIDS/HIV, Cancer, Children's Health/Hospitals, Emergency/Ambulance Services, Medical Rehabilitation, Trauma Treatment • *International:* International Affairs • *Science:* Science Museums • *Social Services:* At-Risk Youth, Child Abuse, Child Welfare, Community Service Organizations, Counseling, Crime Prevention, Day Care, Domestic Violence, Family Planning, Family Services, Food/Clothing Distribution, People with Disabilities, Substance Abuse, United Funds/United Ways, YMCA/YWCA/YMHA/YWHA, Youth Organizations

Grant Types: employee matching gifts and project

Geographic Distribution: primarily supports organizations immediately surrounding company's Cherry Hill, NJ, headquarters; to a lesser degree, foundation supports organizations in regional office locations: Aurora, CO; Addison, IL; Moorestown, NJ; Austell, GA; and Portland, OR

CORP. OFFICERS

Y. Fujiki: *CURR EMPL* chmn, ceo, dir: Subaru of Am

George T. Muller: *CURR EMPL* pres, coo, dir: Subaru Am

GIVING OFFICERS

Sandra E. Capell: admin

Tom Gibson: trust

Takeshi Higurashi: vp, trust

Kazuhiro Miyake: trust *CURR EMPL* exec vp, dir: Subaru Am

George T. Muller: pres, trust *CURR EMPL* pres, coo, dir: Subaru Am (see above)

Joseph T. Scharff: secy, treas, trust

APPLICATION INFORMATION

Initial Approach: The foundation issues annual Requests for Proposals (RFP) notices. Each RFP sets forth specific criteria including applicable dates as well as the issue(s) to be addressed. Only proposals received in response to a RFP will be accepted. Initial inquiries to the foundation should be a brief letter of inquiry. Send a 10, self-addressed unstamped envelope to the foundation to receive a copy of "Policies and Guidelines." Procedures for receiving future RFPs are contained in the policies brochure.

Restrictions on Giving: Because foundation prefers to fund grass-roots organizations, it will not consider grants to organizations that have fund balances in excess of two years of current operating budget.

Grants are limited to organizations that are tax-exempt under Section 501(c)(3). Organizations that the foundation trustees prefer not to fund include, but are not limited to, the following: individuals; veterans, fraternal, and/or labor organizations; government agencies; direct support of churches, religious groups, or sectarian groups; social, membership, or other groups that serve the special interests of their constituency; advertising in charitable publications; sponsorhip of special events or athletic activities; capital campaigns; political organizations, campaigns, or candidates running for public office; organizations that benefit individuals or groups outside the U.S.; and organizations which, in policy or practice, discriminate against a person or group on the basis of age, political affiliation, race, national origin, ethnicity, gender, religious belief, disability, or sexual orientation.

Foundation does not donate vehicles.

OTHER THINGS TO KNOW

As a general rule, national organizations are not eligible for foundation funds. However, small grants may be considered to organizations that impact foundation or corporate goals. Decisions will be at the sole discretion of the foundation staff, contributions committee, and trustees.

Eligibility for employee matching gifts includes nonprofit institutions/organizations located in the United States that are recognized by the Internal Revenue Service as tax-exempt under Section 501(c)(3), excluding religious, political, or fraternal organizations.

503

Recipients of grants are expected to submit a written evaluation or report concerning the impact of their project in the community.

Only proposals received in response to a RFP are accepted. The foundation does not accept unsolicited funding requests. Only one proposal per organization will be considered within any 12-month period. The foundation makes no multiyear grants, although it may consider to renew support of a project. However, all funding requests must be submitted annually in response to a RFP.

PUBLICATIONS
Policies and Guidelines, Requests for Proposals (RFPs)

GRANTS ANALYSIS
Total Grants: $151,405

Number of Grants: 72

Highest Grant: $7,542

Typical Range: $50 to $4,000

Disclosure Period: 1993

Note: Number of grants and average grant figures do not include employee matching gifts. Foundation released new guidelines in 1994. Recent grants are derived from a 1990 Form 990.

RECENT GRANTS

General
7,542	United Way of Camden County, Camden, NJ — annual contribution of 18 dollars/employee on behalf of SFS/SDA's 419 employees
7,000	Children's Literacy Institute, Philadelphia, PA — for follow-up training sessions at Sumner and Forest Hills Schools
5,000	New Jersey Academy for Aquatic Sciences, Camden, NJ — annual corporate membership
5,000	Planned Parenthood/Greater Camden Area, Camden, NJ — towards the construction of a new facility in Camden, New Jersey
4,500	Larc School, Bellmawr, NJ — purchase of two computers for Adult Basic Skills program

Sullivan Foundation, Algernon Sydney

CONTACT
William E. Bardusch, Jr.
President
Algernon Sydney Sullivan Fdn.
53 Maple Ave.
Morristown, NJ 07963-0398
(201) 539-3100

FINANCIAL SUMMARY
Recent Giving: $549,600 (1993); $549,350 (1992); $549,350 (1991)

Assets: $10,827,574 (1993); $10,993,075 (1992); $11,075,443 (1991)

Gifts Received: $32,876 (1993); $25,000 (1992); $15,000 (1991)

Fiscal Note: In 1993, contributions were received from the estate of Vera H. Armstrong.

EIN: 13-6084596

CONTRIBUTIONS SUMMARY
Donor(s): the late Mrs. Algernon Sydney Sullivan, the late George Hammond Sullivan, the late Zilph P. Devereaux

Typical Recipients: • *Arts & Humanities:* Libraries • *Civic & Public Affairs:* Urban & Community Affairs • *Education:* Colleges & Universities, Elementary Education (Private), Private Education (Precollege) • *Environment:* Air/Water Quality • *Health:* Cancer, Hospitals, Nursing Services, Respiratory • *Religion:* Religious Welfare • *Social Services:* Child Welfare, Community Service Organizations, People with Disabilities

Grant Types: scholarship

Geographic Distribution: focus on the Southeast

GIVING OFFICERS
William E. Bardusch, Jr.: pres, trust

Charles W. Cook: secy, trust

Nancy Cortner: trust

Walter Grey Dunnington, Jr.: trust *B* New York NY 1927 *ED* Univ VA BA 1948; Univ VA LLB 1950 *CORP AFFIL* dir: Brittainia Indus Ltd *NONPR AFFIL* bd govs: NY Hosp; mem: Am Bar Assn, Assn Bar City New York, NY St Bar Assn; trust: Boys Club NY, Woodberry Forest Sch *CLUB AFFIL* Brook, Natl Golf Links Am, Racquet & Tennis, Somerset Hills CC *PHIL AFFIL* trust: Seth Sprague Educational and Charitable Foundation

Hiram B. Ely, Jr.: trust

R. Bruce McBratney: trust

Myles C. Morrison III: vp, trust

Frederick L. Redpath: treas, trust

Darla J. Wilkinson: trust

Gray Williams, Jr.: trust

APPLICATION INFORMATION
Initial Approach: Send brief letter of inquiry describing program or project. There are no deadlines.

Restrictions on Giving: Does not support individuals.

GRANTS ANALYSIS
Total Grants: $549,600

Number of Grants: 25

Highest Grant: $29,500

Typical Range: $10,000 to $29,500

Disclosure Period: 1993

Note: Recent grants are derived from a 1993 Form 990.

RECENT GRANTS

Library
17,250	Davis and Elkins College, Elkins, WV

General
29,500	Berea College, Berea, KY
21,750	Randolph-Macon College, Ashland, VA
20,250	Hampden-Sydney College, Hampden-Sydney, VA
20,250	University of the South Sewanee, Sewanee, TN
19,250	Alice Lloyd College, Pippa Passes, KY

Turrell Fund

CONTACT
E. Belvin Williams
Executive Director and Secretary
Turrell Fund
21 Van Vleck St.
Montclair, NJ 07042
(201) 783-9358

FINANCIAL SUMMARY
Recent Giving: $4,325,361 (1993); $4,187,159 (1992); $4,289,192 (1991)

Assets: $97,912,802 (1993); $98,929,930 (1992); $82,751,580 (1990)

Gifts Received: $4,575 (1989)

EIN: 22-1551936

CONTRIBUTIONS SUMMARY
Donor(s): The Turrell Fund was established in 1935 by Herbert Turrell and Margaret Turrell. Mr. Turrell was associated with Parke, Davis and Co. and American Home Products. The foundation has some of its assets in the latter company. Since its inception, the Turrell Fund has aided children and youth, a major interest of the Turrells during their lifetimes. Although the foundation originally was empowered to make grants to organizations in New York, New Jersey, and Vermont, the trustees have phased out giving in New York.

Typical Recipients: • *Arts & Humanities:* Libraries, Music • *Civic & Public Affairs:* Economic Development, Employment/Job Training, Hispanic Affairs, Housing • *Education:* Afterschool/Enrichment Programs, Arts/Humanities Education, Colleges & Universities, Education Associations, Education Funds, Education Reform, Elementary Education (Private), General, Literacy, Medical Education, Minority Education, Preschool Education, Private Education (Precollege), Public Education (Precollege), Secondary Education (Public), Special Education, Student Aid • *Health:* AIDS/HIV, Clinics/Medical Centers • *International:* International Organizations • *Religion:* Religious Welfare • *Social Services:* At-Risk Youth, Child Welfare, Community Centers, Community Service Organizations, Counseling, Day Care, Family Planning, Family Services, Food/Clothing Distribution, General, People with Disabilities, Recreation & Athletics, Scouts, Substance Abuse, Volunteer Services, YMCA/YWCA/YMHA/YWHA, Youth Organizations

Grant Types: capital, challenge, general support, project, scholarship, and seed money

Geographic Distribution: New Jersey and
Vermont

GIVING OFFICERS

Paul J. Christiansen: trust *B* Orange NJ
1906 *ED* Rutgers Univ LLB 1927 *CURR
EMPL* ptnr: Christiansen Jube & Keegan
PHIL AFFIL pres, trust: Charles Edison
Fund

Ann G. Dinse: trust

Carl Gustaf Fjellman: trust *B* Cedar Rapids IA 1919 *ED* Augustana Coll BA 1941;
Augustana Theological Seminary BD 1945;
Drew Univ PhD 1955

Robert H. Grasmere: pres, trust

Frank Joseph Hoenemeyer: chmn, trust

Larry Prendergast: trust

Vivian B. Shapiro: trust

E. Belvin Williams: exec dir, secy, trust *ED*
Columbia Univ MA; Columbia Univ MS;
Columbia Univ PhD; Denver Univ

Sonyia Woloshyn: trust, treas

APPLICATION INFORMATION
Initial Approach:

Organizations that meet the foundation's
geographic requirements and provide direct
services for children and youth should submit a brief letter on offical letterhead to the
executive director.

The letter should describe the project, include a project budget, and be sent on the organization's letterhead, signed by an official
on behalf of the governing board. If the request meets eligibility requirements, a more
complete proposal will be requested. Information should include background on the organization, identification of board members,
and staff qualifications; financial report, current budget, and project costs; copy of IRS
letter granting tax exemption; and a description of project, its purpose, and its relation
to other activities of the organization.

The fall deadline is September 1, and the
spring deadline is February 1. For organizations that have previously received grants
from the Turrell Fund, the deadlines are October 1 and March 1.

Proposals are screened by the grant committee, which then recommends selected proposals to the board of trustees for consideration
and action. Evaluative criteria include evidence of need, organizational resources to
meet the need, evidence of local support,
prospects for future support, and plans for
evaluation of the project. A visit by a fund
representative may precede the final decision. Notice of the board's decision is sent
out in late December and in late May. Progress reports and a final accounting of the
use of funds is required of all grant recipients.

Restrictions on Giving: The fund does not
encourage requests for support of cultural activities; and will not fund advocacy, research, endowment funds, grants to
individuals, and most hospital and health
care services.

PUBLICATIONS
Annual report

GRANTS ANALYSIS
Total Grants: $4,325,361
Number of Grants: 162
Highest Grant: $441,344
Average Grant: $26,700
Typical Range: $10,000 to $35,000
Disclosure Period: 1993

Note: Recent grants are derived from a 1993
Form 990.

RECENT GRANTS

Library
25,000   Greensboro Free Library,
Greensboro, VT —
children's room and staffing

General
441,344   Turrell Scholarship Program,
W. Orange, NJ —
scholarships
145,000   King Street Area Youth
Program, Burlington, VT —
capital campaign
75,000   National Council on
Alcoholism and Drug
Dependence, Montclair, NJ
— TIGS program
75,000   Salvation Army New Jersey
Divisional Headquarters,
Union, NJ — program
support in Newark
60,000   YMCA, E. Orange, NJ —
program support

Union Camp Corporation /
Union Camp Charitable
Trust

Revenue: $3.39 billion
Employees: 18,646
Headquarters: Wayne, NJ
SIC Major Group: Paper Mills, Forest
Products, Sawmills & Planing
Mills—General, and Reconstituted Wood
Products

CONTACT
Sydney N. Phin
Director, Human Resources
Union Camp Corporation
1600 Valley Rd.
Wayne, NJ 07470
(201) 628-2248

FINANCIAL SUMMARY
Recent Giving: $2,500,000 (1995 est.);
$2,500,000 (1994 approx.); $2,226,560
(1993)
Assets: $551,978 (1993); $1,220,862
(1992); $1,641,007 (1991)
Gifts Received: $1,500,000 (1993);
$1,600,000 (1992)
Fiscal Note: Figures represent foundation
contributions only. Company also sponsors
limited direct giving program. Above figures exclude nonmonetary support. Foundation receives contributions from the Union
Camp Corporation.
EIN: 13-6034666

CONTRIBUTIONS SUMMARY
Typical Recipients: • *Arts & Humanities:*
Arts Associations & Councils, Arts Festivals, Arts Funds, Community Arts, Ethnic &
Folk Arts, Historic Preservation, Libraries,
Literary Arts, Museums/Galleries, Music,
Public Broadcasting, Visual Arts • *Civic &
Public Affairs:* Business/Free Enterprise,
Economic Development, Economic Policy,
Employment/Job Training, General, Law &
Justice, Legal Aid, Municipalities/Towns,
Professional & Trade Associations, Public
Policy, Safety, Urban & Community Affairs,
Women's Affairs, Zoos/Aquariums • *Education:* Agricultural Education, Business Education, Colleges & Universities, Community
& Junior Colleges, Continuing Education,
Economic Education, Education Associations, Education Funds, Elementary Education (Private), Engineering/Technological
Education, Faculty Development, Legal Education, Literacy, Medical Education, Minority Education, Preschool Education, Private
Education (Precollege), Public Education
(Precollege), Religious Education, Science/Mathematics Education, Secondary
Education (Public), Social Sciences Education, Special Education, Student Aid • *Environment:* Air/Water Quality, General,
Resource Conservation • *Health:* Clinics/Medical Centers, Emergency/Ambulance
Services, Geriatric Health, Health Funds,
Health Organizations, Hospices, Hospitals,
Medical Rehabilitation, Medical Research,
Medical Training, Mental Health, Nursing
Services, Single-Disease Health Associations • *Religion:* Churches, Religious Organizations, Religious Welfare,
Synagogues/Temples • *Science:* Science Exhibits & Fairs, Scientific Organizations • *Social Services:* Child Welfare, Community
Centers, Community Service Organizations,
Counseling, Day Care, Delinquency &
Criminal Rehabilitation, Domestic Violence,
Emergency Relief, Family Planning, Family
Services, Homes, People with Disabilities,
Recreation & Athletics, Senior Services,
Shelters/Homelessness, Substance Abuse,
United Funds/United Ways, Volunteer Services, Youth Organizations

Grant Types: capital, employee matching
gifts, endowment, fellowship, general support, multiyear/continuing support, research,
and scholarship

Nonmonetary Support: $20,000 (1990);
$20,000 (1989); $20,000 (1988)

Nonmonetary Support Types: donated
products and loaned employees

Note: Nonmonetary support in the form of
donated land also is given, but no estimate
is available. A. Withington is the contact for
nonmonetary support.

Geographic Distribution: principally near
operating locations and to national organizations

Operating Locations: AL (Birmingham,
Chapman, Cullman, Decatur, Montgomery,
Opelika, Prattville, Thorsby), AR (Conway,
Monticello), CA (Hanford, Stockton), CO
(Denver), CT (Newtown), FL (Eaton Park,
Jacksonville, Lakeland), GA (Atlanta, Folkston, Forest Park, Griffin, Meldrim, Merid-

ian, Savannah, Statesboro, Tifton, Tucker, Valdosta, Waycross), IA (Sibley), IL (Chicago, Normal), IN (Seymour), KY (Shelbyville), LA (Lafayette), MA (Auburn), ME (Auburn), MI (Flint, Kalamazoo), MO (Kansas City, St. Louis), MS (Houston), NC (Asheville, Greensboro, Raleigh, Reidsville, Seaboard), NJ (Clifton, Englewood, Montvale, Moonachie, Morristown, Norwood, Princeton, Trenton, Wayne), OH (Centerville, Cleveland, Dover, Franklin), PA (Hazelton, Lancaster, Washington), SC (Eastover, Spartanburg, Sumter), TN (Morristown), TX (Carrollton, Denton, Edinburgh, Houston, Orange, San Antonio), VA (Franklin, Richmond), WI (Tomah)

CORP. OFFICERS

Jerry Hunter Ballengee: *B* Martinsville VA 1937 *ED* VA Polytech Inst & St Univ BSME 1962; Xavier Univ MBA 1974 *CURR EMPL* exec vp, dir: Union Camp Corp *NONPR AFFIL* mem: Paper Indus Mgmt Assn; mem, dir: Tech Assn Pulp & Paper Indus

Russell W. Boekenheide: *B* St Louis MO 1930 *ED* Blackburn Coll BA 1952 *CURR EMPL* sr vp: Union Camp Corp *NONPR AFFIL* adv bd: Univ SC Riegel & Emory Human Resources Res Ctr; mem: Am Forest & Paper Assn; mem empl & labor rels comm: Am Paper Inst; trust: Blackburn Coll, NJ Independent Coll Fund *CLUB AFFIL* Indian Trail

William Craig McClelland: *B* Orange NJ 1934 *ED* Princeton Univ AB 1952; Harvard Univ MBA 1965 *CURR EMPL* chmn, ceo: Union Camp Corp *CORP AFFIL* dir: Allegheny Ludlum Corp, PNC Fin Corp, Quaker St Oil Refining Corp; sr vp, dir: Intl Paper Co *NONPR AFFIL* chmn: PA St Univ Counc Fellows Behrend Campus; corporator: Hamot Med Ctr, St Vincent Health Ctr; dir: Am Paper Inst

Sydney N. Phin: *CURR EMPL* dir human resources: Union Camp Corp

James M. Reed: *B* New Sharon IA 1933 *ED* Simpson Coll BSBA 1954 *CURR EMPL* vchmn, cfo: Union Camp Corp *CORP AFFIL* dir: Martin Marietta Materials Inc; vchmn, dir: Bush Boake Allen Inc

GIVING OFFICERS

Russell W. Boekenheide: trust *CURR EMPL* sr vp: Union Camp Corp (see above)

Sydney N. Phin: trust *CURR EMPL* dir human resources: Union Camp Corp (see above)

James M. Reed: trust *CURR EMPL* vchmn, cfo: Union Camp Corp (see above)

APPLICATION INFORMATION

Initial Approach: *Initial Contact:* brief letter or proposal *Include Information On:* description of the organization, amount requested, purpose for which funds are sought, recently audited financial statement, proof of tax-exempt status *Deadlines:* none

GRANTS ANALYSIS

Total Grants: $2,226,560

Number of Grants: 1,625*

Highest Grant: $235,355

Average Grant: $13,678

Typical Range: $500 to $15,000

Disclosure Period: 1993

Note: Recent grants are derived from a 1993 Form 990.

RECENT GRANTS

Library

50,000	University of Virginia Darden School of Business, Charlottesville, VA — Camp Library	
25,000	City of Franklin Library Fund, Franklin, VA	

General

235,355	United Way of the Coastal Empire, Savannah, GA	
55,000	Rider College, Laurenceville, NJ — Science Building capital fund	
40,000	United Way of Augusta County, Prattville, AL	
38,640	United Way of the Midlands, Columbia, SC	
32,000	Allegro Productions, Boca Raton, FL — science screen reports	

Van Houten Memorial Fund

Former Foundation Name: Van Houten Charitable Trust

CONTACT

James S. Hohn
Vice President
Van Houten Memorial Fund
c/o First Fidelity Bank, N.A.
765 Broad St.
Newark, NJ 07102
(201) 430-4533

FINANCIAL SUMMARY

Recent Giving: $620,000 (fiscal 1995 est.); $733,602 (fiscal 1994); $1,046,131 (fiscal 1993)

Assets: $14,940,000 (fiscal 1995 est.); $14,932,000 (fiscal 1994); $14,583,622 (fiscal 1993)

EIN: 22-6311438

CONTRIBUTIONS SUMMARY

Donor(s): The foundation was established in 1979 by the late Stella C. Van Houten .

Typical Recipients: • *Arts & Humanities:* Libraries • *Civic & Public Affairs:* Philanthropic Organizations, Urban & Community Affairs • *Education:* Colleges & Universities, Medical Education, Private Education (Precollege), Special Education • *Health:* Cancer, Children's Health/Hospitals, Clinics/Medical Centers, Geriatric Health, Hospitals, Hospitals (University Affiliated), Medical Rehabilitation, Medical Research, Mental Health, Multiple Sclerosis, Prenatal Health Issues, Respiratory, Single-Disease Health Associations • *Religion:* Churches, Religious Welfare • *Social Services:* Camps, Child Welfare, Day Care, Family Planning, Homes, Scouts, Youth Organizations

Grant Types: capital, project, and seed money

Geographic Distribution: Bergen and Passaic counties, NJ, only; except children's programs are funded statewide

GIVING OFFICERS

James Samonte Hohn: contact *B* New York NY 1946 *ED* City Univ NY BA 1969; Fairleigh Dickinson Univ MBA 1982 *CURR EMPL* vp: First Fidelity Bank NA NJ *CORP AFFIL* admin: Ohl Trust *NONPR AFFIL* admin: Mills Fdn, Talcott Fund; adv: Seton Hall Univ Ctr Pub Svc; mem: Counc NJ Grantmakers, Natl Comm Planned Giving; pres: Ed Fdn Chesters; trust: William Limmer Fdn *CLUB AFFIL* Chester Lions

APPLICATION INFORMATION

Initial Approach:

The fund requests application be made in writing.

Proposals are accepted throughout the year. Proposals must be received no later than February 1 for review in March; May 1 for review in June; August 1 for review in September; and November 1 for review in December.

Restrictions on Giving: The fund does not make grants to individuals, churches, or political organizations, or for general operating needs or endowments. The fund does not make loans; it also does not make grants outside of New Jersey.

OTHER THINGS TO KNOW

First Fidelity Bank, N.A., in Newark, NJ, is the fund's corporate trustee.

PUBLICATIONS

Application guidelines

GRANTS ANALYSIS

Total Grants: $733,602

Number of Grants: 21

Highest Grant: $150,000

Average Grant: $25,000*

Typical Range: $10,000 to $50,000

Disclosure Period: fiscal year ending November 30, 1994

Note: Average grant figure was supplied by the fund. Recent grants are derived from a 1993 grants list.

RECENT GRANTS

General

134,910	University of Medicine and Dentistry of New Jersey Foundation, Newark, NJ	
75,000	St. Joseph's Hospital and Medical Center Foundation, Paterson, NJ	
70,240	Henry H. Kessler Foundation, West Orange, NJ — Kessler Institute for Rehabilitation	
70,240	Henry H. Kessler Foundation, West Orange, NJ — Kessler Institute for Rehabilitation	
66,032	University of Medicine and Dentistry Foundation, Newark, NJ	

NEW MEXICO

Maddox Foundation, J. F.

CONTACT
Robert D. Socolofsky
Vice President, Finance and Administration
J. F. Maddox Foundation
PO Box 2588
Hobbs, NM 88241
(505) 393-6338

FINANCIAL SUMMARY

Recent Giving: $4,000,000 (fiscal 1995 est.); $4,208,418 (fiscal 1994); $3,762,348 (fiscal 1993)

Assets: $92,500,000 (fiscal 1995 est.); $91,514,739 (fiscal 1994); $91,358,252 (fiscal 1993)

Gifts Received: $9,760 (fiscal 1991); $425,212 (fiscal 1990); $14,772,299 (fiscal 1989)

Fiscal Note: In fiscal 1989, the foundation received gifts totaling $14,740,121 from the Mabel S. Maddox Trust and $32,177 from the estate of Mabel S. Maddox. The fiscal 1991 contribution came from the Louise Scofield Gordon Trust.

EIN: 75-6023767

CONTRIBUTIONS SUMMARY

Donor(s): The foundation was established in 1963 by the late J. F. Maddox and the late Mabel S. Maddox .

Typical Recipients: • *Arts & Humanities:* General, Libraries, Museums/Galleries, Music • *Civic & Public Affairs:* Botanical Gardens/Parks, Hispanic Affairs, Professional & Trade Associations • *Education:* Arts/Humanities Education, Colleges & Universities, Education Reform, Private Education (Precollege), Public Education (Precollege) • *Health:* Cancer, Emergency/Ambulance Services • *Religion:* Churches, Jewish Causes, Religious Organizations • *Social Services:* Child Welfare, Community Service Organizations, Day Care, Food/Clothing Distribution, General, Homes, Recreation & Athletics, Shelters/Homelessness, Substance Abuse, United Funds/United Ways, Youth Organizations

Grant Types: capital, endowment, general support, operating expenses, and scholarship

Geographic Distribution: no geographic restrictions, with preference to New Mexico and West Texas

GIVING OFFICERS
Harry H. Lynch: dir

Don Maddox: vp

James M. Maddox: pres

Robert J. Reid: exec vp

Robert D. Socolofsky: vp fin & admin

APPLICATION INFORMATION
Initial Approach:

Potential applicants should submit a preliminary letter briefly describing the applicant's organization and proposed project.

The foundation will request further information if the initial contact is considered to fall within the scope of the foundation.

Applications may be submitted at any time.

Restrictions on Giving: The foundation does not ordinarily approve grants for individuals, operating budgets, other foundations, or endowment funds.

PUBLICATIONS

Application guidelines

GRANTS ANALYSIS
Total Grants: $3,762,348

Number of Grants: 96

Highest Grant: $1,048,357

Average Grant: $28,568*

Typical Range: $500 to $5,000 and $10,000 to $100,000

Disclosure Period: fiscal year ending June 30, 1993

Note: The average grant excludes the largest grant of $1,048,357. Recent grants are derived from a fiscal 1993 Form 990.

RECENT GRANTS

Library
218,651	Tatum Public Library, Tatum, NM
105,000	Eunice Public Library, Eunice, NM

General
1,048,357	Lea County Good Samaritan Village, Hobbs, NM
539,000	Texas Tech University, Lubbock, TX
350,000	New Mexico Christian Children's Home, Portales, NM
300,000	Community Services Center, Portales, NM
300,000	New Mexico Boys and Girls Ranch Foundation, Albuquerque, NM

McCune Charitable Foundation, Marshall and Perrine D.

CONTACT
S. J. Sanchez
Trustee
Marshall and Perrine D. McCune Charitable Fdn.
123 E. Marcy St., Ste. 201
Santa Fe, NM 87501
(505) 983-8300

FINANCIAL SUMMARY
Recent Giving: $3,809,292 (1993)

Assets: $84,268,794 (1993)

Gifts Received: $2,600 (1993)

EIN: 85-0375622

CONTRIBUTIONS SUMMARY

Typical Recipients: • *Arts & Humanities:* Arts Associations & Councils, Libraries, Literary Arts, Museums/Galleries, Opera, Public Broadcasting • *Civic & Public Affairs:* Business/Free Enterprise, Community Foundations, Economic Development, General, Hispanic Affairs, Housing, Legal Aid, Municipalities/Towns, Native American Affairs • *Education:* Colleges & Universities, Community & Junior Colleges, General, Preschool Education, Public Education (Precollege), Secondary Education (Public) • *Health:* AIDS/HIV, Clinics/Medical Centers, Hospices, Hospitals • *Religion:* Religious Welfare • *Social Services:* Big Brother/Big Sister, Child Welfare, Community Service Organizations, Family Services, Food/Clothing Distribution, United Funds/United Ways, Youth Organizations

Grant Types: general support

Geographic Distribution: focus on NM

GIVING OFFICERS

James M. Edwards: mem *B* Champaign IL 1931 *ED* Univ IL BA 1953; Inst Des Science Politiques 1955; Yale Univ 1960 *CURR EMPL* ptnr: Cravath Swaine & Moore *PHIL AFFIL* mem distribution comm, don nephew: McCune Foundation; mem dispensing comm: John R. McCune Charitable Trust

Owen Lopez: exec dir

Sara McCune Losinger: chmn *PHIL AFFIL* mem dispensing comm: John R. McCune Charitable Trust

John R. McCune VI: mem

APPLICATION INFORMATION

Initial Approach: Send a brief letter of inquiry. Include a description of organization, amount requested, purpose of funds sought, recently audited financial statement, and proof of tax-exempt status.

GRANTS ANALYSIS

Total Grants: $3,809,292

Number of Grants: 186

Highest Grant: $500,000

Typical Range: $100 to $250,000

Disclosure Period: 1993

Note: Recent grants are derived from a 1993 Form 990.

RECENT GRANTS

Library

20,000	Mora County Community Library, Mora, NM

General

500,000	Tulane University, New Orleans, LA
80,000	La Nueva Vida, Santa Fe, NM
79,218	La Familia Medical Center, Santa Fe, NM
75,000	Ayudantes, Santa Fe, NM
65,000	Hospice Center, Santa Fe, NM

Public Service Co. of New Mexico / PNM Foundation

Revenue: $873.88 million
Employees: 2,656
Headquarters: Albuquerque, NM
SIC Major Group: Electric, Gas & Sanitary Services

CONTACT
Judy Zanotti
President
PNM Foundation
Alvarado Square
Albuquerque, NM 87158
(505) 241-2675

FINANCIAL SUMMARY
Recent Giving: $177,077 (1994); $161,519 (1993); $144,014 (1992)

Assets: $4,541,279 (1993); $4,353,502 (1992); $4,283,576 (1991)

Gifts Received: $91,806 (1988)

EIN: 85-0309005

CONTRIBUTIONS SUMMARY
Typical Recipients: • *Arts & Humanities:* Arts Centers, Ethnic & Folk Arts, History & Archaeology, Libraries, Museums/Galleries, Music, Public Broadcasting • *Civic & Public Affairs:* African American Affairs, Business/Free Enterprise, Community Foundations, Employment/Job Training, General, Hispanic Affairs, Women's Affairs • *Education:* Colleges & Universities, Education Funds, Education Reform, Engineering/Technological Education, Faculty Development, General, Minority Education, Public Education (Precollege), Student Aid • *Health:* Health Organizations, Hospices, Hospitals • *Social Services:* Community Service Organizations, Day Care, Youth Organizations

Grant Types: award, employee matching gifts, endowment, general support, matching, multiyear/continuing support, and seed money

Nonmonetary Support Types: donated equipment, in-kind services, loaned employees, and loaned executives

Geographic Distribution: primarily in NM

Operating Locations: NM (Albuquerque)

CORP. OFFICERS
Max H. Maerki: *CURR EMPL* sr vp, cfo: Public Svc Co NM

Benjamin F. Montoya: *CURR EMPL* pres, ceo: Pub Svc Co NM

GIVING OFFICERS
John Tryon Ackerman: dir *B* Cleveland OH 1941 *ED* Univ NM 1968; NM St Univ 1971 *CORP AFFIL* dir: First Interstate Bank, Paragon Resources *NONPR AFFIL* mem: Am Mgmt Assn, Natl Soc Professional Engrs

Barbara Barsky: secy, treas, dir

William Real: vp, dir

Judy Zanotti: pres, dir

APPLICATION INFORMATION
Initial Approach: Application form required. Send letter requesting guidelines and form. While there are no deadlines, the board of directors meets quarterly to review and approve proposals for funding.

Restrictions on Giving: Grants are not given to or for sectarian or religious organizations, programs, or activities; testimonial dinners, fund-raising events or advertising; payments of loans, interest, taxes, or debt retirement; individuals; endowments; programs or projects that duplicate existing services and/or programs; operational and maintenance expenses (except for seed money or pilot projects); or United Way agencies except for capital projects not normally funded by United Way gifts.

PUBLICATIONS
Grant policies and application guidelines (including application form)

GRANTS ANALYSIS
Total Grants: $161,519

Number of Grants: 70

Highest Grant: $20,000

Typical Range: $5,000 to $15,000

Disclosure Period: 1993

Note: Recent grants are derived from a 1993 Form 990.

RECENT GRANTS

Library

10,000	Navajo Nation Museum and Library Fund, Window Rock, AZ — for general support

General

20,000	Albuquerque Community Foundation, Albuquerque, NM — for general support
15,000	Eastern New Mexico University, Portales, NM — for Distinguished Education award
8,000	New Mexico Highlands University, Las Cruces, NM — for support of Kennedy Hall
7,500	Casa Esperanza, Albuquerque, NM — for general support
5,560	Women's Community Association, Albuquerque, NM — for general support

NEW YORK

Achelis Foundation

CONTACT
Joseph S. Dolan
Secretary and Executive Director
Achelis Foundation
767 Third Ave, 4th Fl
New York, NY 10017
(212) 644-0322

FINANCIAL SUMMARY
Recent Giving: $1,000,000 (1995 est.); $1,000,000 (1994 approx.); $914,852 (1993)

Assets: $23,000,000 (1995 est.); $22,797,499 (1994 approx.); $23,730,968 (1993)

Gifts Received: $1,500 (1993); $7,500 (1992); $270,243 (1990)

Fiscal Note: In 1990, the foundation received $270,243 from a Trust under the will of Elisabeth Achelis. In 1992, the foundation received $7,500 from a Trust under the will of Elisabeth Achelis. In 1993, the foundation received $1,500 from a Trust under the will of Elisabeth Achelis.

EIN: 13-6022018

CONTRIBUTIONS SUMMARY
Donor(s): The foundation was established in 1940, with funds donated by the late Elisabeth Achelis . Born in Brooklyn Heights in 1880, Miss Achelis was active with many social and charitable causes until her death in 1974. The Achelis Foundation is affiliated with the Bodman Foundation and it reports that they share some officers.

Typical Recipients: • *Arts & Humanities:* Ballet, Dance, Libraries, Museums/Galleries, Music, Opera, Theater • *Civic & Public Affairs:* Botanical Gardens/Parks, Economic Development, Employment/Job Training, Ethnic Organizations, General, Housing, Nonprofit Management, Public Policy, Urban & Community Affairs, Zoos/Aquariums • *Education:* Afterschool/Enrichment Programs, Arts/Humanities Education, Education Funds, Elementary Education (Private), Literacy, Medical Education, Minority Education, Preschool Education, Private Education (Precollege), Social Sciences Education, Special Education, Student Aid • *Environment:* Air/Water Quality, Resource Conservation • *Health:* AIDS/HIV, Cancer, Children's Health/Hospitals, Clinics/Medical Centers, Emergency/Ambulance Services, Health Funds, Health Organizations, Hospitals, Medical Rehabilitation, Medical Training, Mental Health, Nursing Services, Outpatient Health Care, Speech & Hearing • *Religion:* Religious Organizations, Religious Welfare • *Science:* Science Museums, Scientific Centers & Institutes, Scientific Labs, Scientific Research • *Social Services:* At-Risk Youth, Child Welfare, Community Centers, Community Service Organizations, Counseling, Day Care, Domestic Violence, Family Services, Food/Clothing Distribu-

tion, People with Disabilities, Recreation &
Athletics, Scouts, Senior Services, Shel-
ters/Homelessness, Substance Abuse, Youth
Organizations

Grant Types: capital, endowment, general
support, multiyear/continuing support, operating expenses, and scholarship

Geographic Distribution: primarily New
York City

GIVING OFFICERS
Harry Wesley Albright, Jr.: trust *B* Albany
NY 1925 *ED* Yale Univ BA 1949; Cornell
Univ LLB 1952 *CURR EMPL* couns: Patter-
son Belknap Webb & Tyler *CORP AFFIL*
chmn bd: Battery Pk City Authority; chmn
emeritus: Dime Savings Bank NY; dir: Com-
mun Lending Corp, Intl Life Investors Ins
Co; pres: Thrift Inst Adv Counc Fed Re-
serve Bd *NONPR AFFIL* chmn: Marymount
Coll; dir: Pratt Inst; mem: Am Bar Assn,
Assn Bar City New York, NY St Bar Assn,
NY St Commn Judicial Nomination Ct Ap-
peals; mem greater NY adv bd: Salvation
Army; mem regional panel selection comm:
White House Fellows *CLUB AFFIL* Sleepy
Hollow, Stockbridge GC

Mary B. Braga: trust

Walter Joseph Patrick Curley, Jr.: trust *B*
Pittsburgh PA 1922 *ED* Yale Univ BA 1944;
Harvard Univ MBA 1948; Univ Oslo 1948
CORP AFFIL pres, dir: Curley Land Co
NONPR AFFIL mem bd govs: Foreign Pol-
icy Assn

Joseph S. Dolan: exec dir, secy *PHIL AF-
FIL* exec dir, secy: Bodman Foundation

Anthony Drexel Duke: trust *B* New York
NY 1918 *ED* Princeton Univ 1941 *NONPR
AFFIL* Battle Normandy Mus, Duke Univ,
Pom Pret Sch, US Naval Academy; chmn,
pres, fdr: Boys Harbor; mem: Natl Comm
Am Foreign Policy, Save the Children
CLUB AFFIL Beaver Dam, Maidstone,
Mashomack, Piping Rock, Racquet & Ten-
nis, River *PHIL AFFIL* trust: Bodman Foun-
dation

Peter Frelinghuysen: trust *B* New York NY
1916 *CURR EMPL* atty: Morris & McVeigh
CORP AFFIL secy: K O A Holdings Inc
NONPR AFFIL First vchmn: NY Eye Ear Infirmary *PHIL AFFIL* trust: Bodman Foundation; vp, dir: Frelinghuysen Foundation

John N. Irwin III: first vp, trust *B* 1954 *ED*
Princeton Univ 1976 *CURR EMPL* vp, mng
dir, dir: Hillside Indus Inc *PHIL AFFIL* first
vp, trust: Bodman Foundation; trust: Mrs.
Giles Whiting Foundation; mem adv bd:
Thomas J. Watson Foundation

Leslie Lenkowsky, PhD: trust *PHIL AFFIL*
trust: Bodman Foundation

Marguerite S. Nichols, MD: trust *PHIL AF-
FIL* trust: Bodman Foundation

Russell Parsons Pennoyer: second vp, trust
B New York NY 1951 *ED* Harvard Univ BA
1974; Columbia Univ Sch Law JD 1982
CURR EMPL sr vp, gen counc & secy: Am
Exploration Co *CORP AFFIL* dir: Westerly
Film-Video Inc; sr vp, secy, gen couns:
Amex Oil Co *NONPR AFFIL* fellow: Pier-
pont Morgan Library; mem: Am Bar Assn,
Assn Bar City New York, Rockefeller Univ

Counc; trust: St Bernards Sch *PHIL AFFIL*
second vp: Bodman Foundation

Mary Stone Phipps: trust *NONPR AFFIL*
mem-at-large, dir: Girl Scout Counc Greater
NY *PHIL AFFIL* trust: Bodman Foundation
CLUB AFFIL Colony, Links, Long Island
Wyandanch, Meadow Brook, Pilgrims, Pip-
ing Rock, Somerset

Guy G. Rutherfurd: pres, treas, trust *B*
New York NY 1913 *ED* Princeton Univ BA
1938; Univ VA LLB 1942 *CURR EMPL*
ptnr: Morris & McVeigh *NONPR AFFIL*
mem: Assn Bar City New York, NY Bar
Assn; vp, dir: Lenox Hill Neighborhood
Assn *PHIL AFFIL* pres, treas, trust: Bodman
Foundation

APPLICATION INFORMATION
Initial Approach:

The foundation does not provide an application form. Grant requests should be sent by
letter (no more than two pages), one copy
only, with the signature of an appropriate officer. Personal interviews are arranged when
additional information would be helpful.

Organizations with which the foundation
may not be familiar should include a statement of history and purpose, scope of current activities, list of board members and
key personnel, proof of tax-exempt status,
project or purpose for which funds are
sought, and financial data (budget and
audited financial statements) for both the organization and the project itself. Proposals
should not exceed five pages.

Applications may be submitted any time during the year. The foundation's board meets
in May, September, and December, and
holds special meetings whenever warranted.

The trustees review all requests for funds
from staff recommendations and make all decisions on grant applications. Organizations
requesting support must be aware that the
foundation can respond affirmatively to only
a small number of the many applications received each year.

Restrictions on Giving: Grants usually are
not authorized for travel, writing, conferences, or films. The foundation does not engage directly in research or experimental
projects. From time to time, grant aid may
be extended to independent schools, colleges, and universities. The foundation does
not make loans, nor does it make grants to
individuals.

OTHER THINGS TO KNOW
The foundation also offers proposal writing
assistance and seminars/workshops.

PUBLICATIONS
Biennial report

GRANTS ANALYSIS
Total Grants: $914,852

Number of Grants: 63

Highest Grant: $30,000

Average Grant: $14,521

Typical Range: $10,000 to $30,000

Disclosure Period: 1993

Note: Recent grants are derived from a 1993
Form 990.

RECENT GRANTS
Library
15,000   New York Society Library,
New York, NY

General
30,000   ICD International Center for
the Disabled, New York, NY
25,000   American Museum of Natural
History, New York, NY
25,000   Inner-City Scholarship Fund,
New York, NY
20,000   Boys Brotherhood Republic of
New York, New York, NY
20,000   Boys Harbor/The Harbor for
Girls and Boys, New York,
NY

Air France
Employees: 950
Headquarters: New York, NY
SIC Major Group: Transportation by Air

CONTACT
Graham Hotchkiss
Director, Corporate Communications
Air France
142 W 57th St.
New York, NY 10019
(212) 830-4000

CONTRIBUTIONS SUMMARY
Air France gives only nonmonetary support
in the form of airplane tickets. While the
company has no set contributions policy and
considers each request on a case-by-case basis, it prefers to support organizations and
programs which promote French culture and
history, as well as the French language.
Typical recipients include art museums, cultural and language exchange programs, music, dance, and fashion design programs and
competitions. Other recipients include public broadcasting, civic affairs (international
affairs and professional and trade associations), health (hospitals, medical research,
pediatric health, and single-disease health associations), religious organizations, scientific organizations, and child welfare
programs. While most contributions decisions are made by the headquarters office,
each gateway sales office makes recommendations regarding possible recipients in its
area, for approval by general manager.

Typical Recipients: • *Arts & Humanities:*
Dance, Historic Preservation, Libraries, Mu-
seums/Galleries, Music, Performing Arts,
Public Broadcasting, Theater • *Civic & Public Affairs:* Professional & Trade Associations • *Education:* International Studies
• *Health:* Hospitals, Medical Research, Single-Disease Health Associations • *International:* International Relations • *Religion:*
Religious Organizations • *Science:* Scientific Organizations • *Social Services:* Child
Welfare

Nonmonetary Support Types: donated
products

Geographic Distribution: generally near
"gateway" cities from which Air France

flies to Europe: New York, NY; Boston, MA; Philadelphia, PA; Washington, DC; Miami, FL; Houston, TX; Chicago, IL; San Francisco, CA; and Los Angeles, CA

Operating Locations: CA, DC, FL, IL, MA, NY (New York), PA, TX

CORP. OFFICERS
Joel Lunot: *CURR EMPL* vp, gen mgr: Air France

GIVING OFFICERS
Nils Peyron: dir *CURR EMPL* asst to vp, gen mgr USA: Air France

APPLICATION INFORMATION
Initial Approach: Initial letter may be submitted at any time to Mr. Jim Ferri or to the nearest Air France local sales office. While applications are accepted throughout the year, fall is generally best for funding during the following year. Include a description of the organization, number of tickets requested, purpose for which tickets are sought, and the type and level of exposure (advertisements, press releases, etc.) which Air France will gain from making the contribution.

Restrictions on Giving: Compagnie Nationale Air France in Paris has its own contributions program.

While Air France has no set restrictions on its giving, the company generally prefers to support those organizations whose image is compatible with its own.

GRANTS ANALYSIS
Typical Range: $1,000 to $2,500

AKC Fund

CONTACT
Ann Brownell Sloane
Administrator
AKC Fund
165 E 72nd St.
New York, NY 10021
(212) 737-1011

FINANCIAL SUMMARY
Recent Giving: $163,000 (1993); $168,000 (1992); $168,500 (1991)

Assets: $3,883,649 (1993); $3,679,899 (1992); $3,714,201 (1991)

Gifts Received: $100 (1991)

EIN: 13-6091321

CONTRIBUTIONS SUMMARY
Donor(s): members of the Childs and Lawrence families

Typical Recipients: • *Arts & Humanities:* Ballet, Historic Preservation, History & Archaeology, Libraries, Music, Public Broadcasting • *Civic & Public Affairs:* Economic Development, General, Urban & Community Affairs, Women's Affairs • *Education:* Colleges & Universities, International Studies, Minority Education, Preschool Education,

Private Education (Precollege) • *Environment:* General, Resource Conservation, Wildlife Protection • *Health:* Health Organizations, Hospitals, Medical Research, Mental Health, Prenatal Health Issues, Single-Disease Health Associations • *Religion:* Churches • *Science:* Science Museums • *Social Services:* Camps, Family Planning, Recreation & Athletics, Senior Services, United Funds/United Ways, YMCA/YWCA/YMHA/YWHA, Youth Organizations

Grant Types: capital, general support, multiyear/continuing support, and professorship

Geographic Distribution: national, with giving in CT, DC, NY, OR, VT, and VT

GIVING OFFICERS
Edward C. Childs: dir

Hope S. Childs: secy

John W. Childs: treas *PHIL AFFIL* chmn bd mgrs: Jane Coffin Childs Memorial Fund for Medical Research

Anne Childs Collins: dir

Barbara Childs Lawrence: pres

J. Vinton Lawrence: dir

Jane L. Mali: dir

Mrs. James M. Preston: dir

Jenny Childs Preston: dir

Susannah C. L. Wood: dir

APPLICATION INFORMATION
Initial Approach: Send a brief letter of inquiry. Include a description of organization, amount requested, purpose of funds sought, recently audited financial statement, and proof of tax-exempt status. There are no deadlines.

PUBLICATIONS
Annual Report

GRANTS ANALYSIS
Total Grants: $163,000

Number of Grants: 59

Highest Grant: $30,000

Typical Range: $500 to $2,000

Disclosure Period: 1993

Note: Recent grants are derived from a 1993 Form 990.

RECENT GRANTS
General

30,000	Jane Coffin Childs Memorial Fund for Medical Research, New Haven, CT
20,000	Foxcroft School, Middleburg, VA
15,000	Sheridan School, Washington, DC
6,000	Norfolk Community Playground, Norfolk, VA
5,500	Nature Conservancy Connecticut Chapter, Middletown, CT

Alavi Foundation of New York

Former Foundation Name: Mostazafan Foundation of New York
Headquarters: New York, NY

CONTACT
Mohammad Geramian
President
Alavi Fdn. of New York
500 Fifth Ave., 39th Fl.
New York, NY 10110
(212) 944-8333
Note: Other contacts for the Alavi Foundation of New York are Pari Fardi for the student scholarship loan program and Ali Aliabadi for the book distribution program. Both of these contacts are at the above address and telephone number.

FINANCIAL SUMMARY
Recent Giving: $1,124,602 (fiscal 1993); $1,925,095 (fiscal 1992); $2,292,597 (fiscal 1991)

Assets: $62,418,935 (fiscal 1993); $62,002,787 (fiscal 1992); $62,280,801 (fiscal 1991)

Gifts Received: $26,409 (fiscal 1993); $107,846 (fiscal 1991)

EIN: 23-7345978

CONTRIBUTIONS SUMMARY
Donor(s): The foundation was incorporated in 1973 by Bank Melli of Iran.

Typical Recipients: • *Arts & Humanities:* Libraries, Public Broadcasting • *Civic & Public Affairs:* African American Affairs, Ethnic Organizations, General, Safety • *Education:* Colleges & Universities, Community & Junior Colleges, Medical Education, Private Education (Precollege), Religious Education • *Environment:* Air/Water Quality • *Health:* Arthritis, Cancer, Children's Health/Hospitals, Heart, Hospitals, Multiple Sclerosis, Single-Disease Health Associations • *International:* Foreign Educational Institutions, Health Care/Hospitals, International Peace & Security Issues, International Relief Efforts, Missionary/Religious Activities • *Religion:* Religious Organizations, Seminaries • *Social Services:* Community Centers

Grant Types: endowment, multiyear/continuing support, project, and scholarship

Geographic Distribution: national and international

GIVING OFFICERS
Hoshang Ahmadi: vp, dir

Ali Aliabadi: book distr program contact

Alireza Ebrahimi: secy

Pari Fardi: scholarship program contact

Mohammad Geramian: pres

Mehdi Hodjat: dir

Naser Hossein Mardi: dir of philanthropy *CURR EMPL* dir philathrophy: Bank Melli Iran

Abbas Mirakhor: treas
Mohammad Pirayandeh: dir

APPLICATION INFORMATION
Initial Approach:

The foundation requests applicants contact the foundation for a formal application form.

The foundation has no deadline for submitting proposals.

The board meets annually.

OTHER THINGS TO KNOW
The foundation is endowed with a 36-story Fifth Avenue office building, which has a mortgage secured by Bank Melli of Iran.

PUBLICATIONS
Application form

GRANTS ANALYSIS
Total Grants: $1,124,602
Number of Grants: 13
Highest Grant: $491,000
Average Grant: $86,508
Typical Range: $500 to $316,000
Disclosure Period: fiscal year ending March 31, 1993

Note: Recent grants are derived from a fiscal 1993 Form 990. Numer of grants and typical range do not inclue grants for individual student scholarships.

RECENT GRANTS
Library
500 New York Public Library, New York, NY

General
493,100 Islamic Education Center, Potomac, MD
316,000 Muslim Community School, Potomac, MD
60,000 Islamic Seminary of New Jersey, NJ
40,000 Islamische Wissen Akademie
21,000 Brooklyn Mosque, Brooklyn, NY

Alexander Foundation, Joseph

CONTACT
Robert M. Weintraub
Vice President, Director
Joseph Alexander Foundation
400 Madison Ave., Ste. 906
New York, NY 10017
(212) 355-3688

FINANCIAL SUMMARY
Recent Giving: $690,000 (fiscal 1995 est.); $690,000 (fiscal 1994 est.); $754,000 (fiscal 1993)
Assets: $15,500,000 (fiscal 1995 est.); $15,000,000 (fiscal 1994 est.); $15,588,492 (fiscal 1993)
Gifts Received: $1,619 (fiscal 1990)

Fiscal Note: In fiscal 1990, contributions were received from the trust of Joseph Alexander.
EIN: 51-0175951

CONTRIBUTIONS SUMMARY
Donor(s): The foundation was established in 1960 by the late Joseph Alexander.

Typical Recipients: • *Arts & Humanities:* Arts Centers, Arts Institutes, Historic Preservation, History & Archaeology, Libraries, Museums/Galleries, Performing Arts, Public Broadcasting • *Civic & Public Affairs:* Clubs, Philanthropic Organizations, Urban & Community Affairs, Women's Affairs • *Education:* Colleges & Universities, Education Funds, Gifted & Talented Programs, Legal Education, Literacy, Medical Education, Private Education (Precollege), Science/Mathematics Education, Student Aid • *Health:* AIDS/HIV, Cancer, Children's Health/Hospitals, Diabetes, Emergency/Ambulance Services, Eyes/Blindness, Geriatric Health, Health Organizations, Hospitals, Medical Rehabilitation, Medical Research, Mental Health, Nursing Services, Single-Disease Health Associations, Transplant Networks/Donor Banks, Trauma Treatment • *International:* Foreign Arts Organizations, Foreign Educational Institutions, Health Care/Hospitals, International Peace & Security Issues, International Relations, Missionary/Religious Activities • *Religion:* Jewish Causes, Religious Organizations, Synagogues/Temples • *Science:* Science Museums • *Social Services:* Child Welfare, Community Service Organizations, Day Care, Family Planning, Family Services, Homes, People with Disabilities, Senior Services, Substance Abuse, United Funds/United Ways, Youth Organizations

Grant Types: capital, conference/seminar, endowment, general support, project, research, and scholarship

Geographic Distribution: national, with emphasis on New York, NY

GIVING OFFICERS
Arthur S. Alfert: pres, dir
Alfred Mackler: dir
Harvey A. Mackler: dir *CURR EMPL* exec vp: Gibraltar Corp Am
Helen Mackler: treas, dir
Robert M. Weintraub: vp, dir

APPLICATION INFORMATION
Initial Approach:

The foundation requests applications be made in writing.

The foundation has no deadline for submitting proposals.

The board meets on a regular basis.

Restrictions on Giving: The foundation does not make grants to individuals.

PUBLICATIONS
Financial statement

GRANTS ANALYSIS
Total Grants: $754,000
Number of Grants: 79
Highest Grant: $50,000

Average Grant: $9,544
Typical Range: $2,000 to $10,000
Disclosure Period: fiscal year ending October 31, 1993
Note: Recent grants are derived from a fiscal 1993 Form 990.

RECENT GRANTS
Library
50,000 Bar Ilan University, New York, NY — for Joseph Alexander library

General
50,000 Yeshiva University, New York, NY — Joseph Alexander science education enhancement program at Stern/Yeshiva college
25,000 American Jewish Congress, New York, NY
25,000 Genesis Foundation, New York, NY — lecture series
25,000 Salk Institute, San Diego, CA — AIDS research
25,000 University of Pennsylvania, Philadelphia, PA — Jewish studies program fund

Allen Brothers Foundation

CONTACT
Allen Brothers Fdn.
711 Fifth Ave.
New York, NY 10022
(212) 832-8000

FINANCIAL SUMMARY
Recent Giving: $200,000 (1993); $10,000 (1992); $35,000 (1991)
Assets: $2,597,935 (1993); $2,501,296 (1992); $2,509,168 (1991)
EIN: 13-3202281

CONTRIBUTIONS SUMMARY
Typical Recipients: • *Arts & Humanities:* Libraries, Museums/Galleries • *Education:* Colleges & Universities, Medical Education, Private Education (Precollege) • *Environment:* Resource Conservation • *Health:* Cancer, Medical Research • *International:* Foreign Educational Institutions, International Relief Efforts • *Religion:* Jewish Causes, Religious Organizations • *Social Services:* Community Service Organizations, Recreation & Athletics

Grant Types: general support
Geographic Distribution: focus on NY

GIVING OFFICERS
Herbert A. Allen, Sr.: pres *B* New York NY 1908 *ED* Ithaca Coll DCS *CURR EMPL* mng ptnr: Allen & Co *CORP AFFIL* dir emeritus: Irvine Co *NONPR AFFIL* trust, vp: Hackley Sch *CLUB AFFIL* Bal Harbour, Deepdale GC, Indian Creek GC, Marks, Saratoga Golf & Polo, Surf *PHIL AFFIL* trust: Frances Allen Foundation
Paul A. Gould: vp

Irwin H. Kramer: vp

James W. Quinn: asst secy *B* Bronxville NY 1945 *ED* Univ Notre Dame AB 1967; Fordham Univ JD 1971 *CURR EMPL* ptnr: Weil Gotshal & Manges *NONPR AFFIL* mem: Amer Bar Assn, Assn Bar City NY

Robert H. Werbel: secy

APPLICATION INFORMATION
Initial Approach: The foundation has no formal grant application procedure or application form. There are no deadlines.

GRANTS ANALYSIS
Total Grants: $200,000

Number of Grants: 9

Highest Grant: $50,000

Typical Range: $10,000 to $25,000

Disclosure Period: 1993

Note: Recent grants are derived from a 1993 Form 990.

RECENT GRANTS

General

50,000	Stanford University, Stanford, CA	
25,000	International Rescue Committee, New York, NY	
25,000	Leukemia Society of America, New York, NY	
25,000	Nature Conservancy Silver Creek Preserve, Sun Valley, ID	
25,000	University of California Los Angeles Foundation, Los Angeles, CA	

Allyn Foundation

CONTACT
Marie Infanger
Executive Director
Allyn Fdn.
RD No. 1
Cayuga, NY 13034
(315) 252-7618

FINANCIAL SUMMARY
Recent Giving: $255,139 (1993); $237,000 (1992); $196,025 (1991)

Assets: $5,353,231 (1993); $5,344,676 (1992); $5,390,245 (1991)

Gifts Received: $130,000 (1993); $150,000 (1992); $160,000 (1991)

Fiscal Note: In 1993, contributions were received from Welch Allyn, Inc.

EIN: 15-6017723

CONTRIBUTIONS SUMMARY
Donor(s): the late William N. Allyn and William Allyn, Inc.

Typical Recipients: • *Arts & Humanities:* Historic Preservation, Libraries, Museums/Galleries, Music, Public Broadcasting, Theater • *Civic & Public Affairs:* African American Affairs, Community Foundations, Economic Development, Ethnic Organizations, Housing, Public Policy, Safety • *Edu-*

cation: Colleges & Universities, Community & Junior Colleges, Education Funds, Literacy, Minority Education, Private Education (Precollege), Public Education (Precollege), Special Education, Student Aid • *Health:* Alzheimers Disease, Cancer, Children's Health/Hospitals, Clinics/Medical Centers, Emergency/Ambulance Services, Hospitals, Hospitals (University Affiliated), Long-Term Care, Medical Research, Single-Disease Health Associations • *International:* Missionary/Religious Activities • *Religion:* Churches, Religious Welfare • *Science:* Science Museums, Scientific Centers & Institutes • *Social Services:* Camps, Day Care, Family Planning, Family Services, Food/Clothing Distribution, People with Disabilities, Recreation & Athletics, Scouts, Substance Abuse, YMCA/YWCA/YMHA/YWHA, Youth Organizations

Grant Types: capital, fellowship, research, and scholarship

Geographic Distribution: focus on Onondaga and Cayuga counties, NY

GIVING OFFICERS
Dawn Allyn: asst secy, dir

Eric R. Allyn: dir

Janet J. Allyn: asst treas, dir

Laura A. Allyn: dir

Lew F. Allyn: vp, dir

W. Scott Allyn: dir

William Finch Allyn: vp, dir *B* Auburn NY 1935 *ED* Dartmouth Coll BA 1958 *CURR EMPL* pres: Welch Allyn *CORP AFFIL* dir: Niagara Mohawk Power Corp, Oneida Silver, Ontario Bank, Syracuse Res Corp *NONPR AFFIL* trust: Commun Gen Hosp *CLUB AFFIL* Skaneateles CC *PHIL AFFIL* dir: Fred L. Emerson Foundation, Inc.

William G. Allyn: pres, dir

Tasha Falcone: dir

Marie W. Infanger: exec dir, secy, treas, dir

Margaret M. O'Connell: dir

Elsa A. Soderberg: dir

Peter Soderberg: dir

Robert C. Soderberg: dir

Wilbur L. Townsend: dir

Charles S. Tracy: dir

APPLICATION INFORMATION
Initial Approach: Send a brief letter of inquiry. Include a description of organization, amount requested, purpose of funds sought, recently audited financial statement, and proof of tax-exempt status. There are no deadlines.

PUBLICATIONS
Application Guidelines

GRANTS ANALYSIS
Total Grants: $255,139

Number of Grants: 51

Highest Grant: $25,000

Typical Range: $1,000 to $10,000

Disclosure Period: 1993

Note: Recent grants are derived from a 1993 Form 990.

RECENT GRANTS

Library

6,000	Skaneateles Library Association, Skaneateles, NY	
3,000	Seymour Library, Seymour, NY	
2,455	Weedsport Free Library, Weedsport, NY — building fund	

General

25,000	YWCA of Cortland, Cortland, NY — coalition for children	
20,000	Planned Parenthood, Syracuse, NY	
16,667	E. John Gavras Center, Syracuse, NY	
16,667	Faatz-Crofut Home for Elderly, Syracuse, NY	
15,000	Independent College Fund, Syracuse, NY	

Altman Foundation

CONTACT
John S. Burke
President
Altman Foundation
220 E 42nd St., Ste. 411
New York, NY 10017
(212) 682-0970

FINANCIAL SUMMARY
Recent Giving: $6,100,000 (1994 est.); $5,988,900 (1993); $5,477,650 (1992)

Assets: $140,000,000 (1994 est.); $144,688,816 (1993); $137,698,012 (1992)

EIN: 13-1623879

CONTRIBUTIONS SUMMARY
Donor(s): The Altman Foundation was established in 1913 in New York under the will of Benjamin Altman . The founder of the B. Altman & Company department store bequeathed his ownership of the company to the foundation to support charitable and educational institutions in New York.

Colonel Michael Friedsam succeeded Mr. Altman as president of the foundation until his death in 1931. He was succeeded by John S. Burke, who in turn was succeeded by his son, John S. Burke, Jr., the current president.

Typical Recipients: • *Arts & Humanities:* Arts Associations & Councils, Arts Outreach, History & Archaeology, Libraries, Museums/Galleries • *Civic & Public Affairs:* Botanical Gardens/Parks, Economic Development, Employment/Job Training, Housing, Safety, Urban & Community Affairs, Women's Affairs, Zoos/Aquariums • *Education:* Arts/Humanities Education, Colleges & Universities, Elementary Education (Private), General, Literacy, Medical Education, Minority Education, Private Education (Precollege), Special Education, Student Aid • *Health:* AIDS/HIV, Cancer, Children's Health/Hospitals, Clinics/Medical Centers, Geriatric Health, Health Funds, Health Organizations, Hospitals, Outpatient Health Care • *Religion:* Jewish Causes, Religious Organizations, Religious Welfare, Seminaries • *Social Services:* Big Brother/Big Sister, Child Welfare, Community Centers, Community Service Organizations, Day Care, Domestic Violence, Family Services, People with Disabilities, Recreation & Athletics, Senior Services, Shelters/Homelessness, Youth Organizations

Grant Types: project

Geographic Distribution: New York State, with emphasis on the five boroughs of New York City

GIVING OFFICERS
Marion C. Baer: secy

John S. Burke: pres, trust *B* New York NY 1923

Thomas C. Burke: vp, trust *B* New York NY 1924

John P. Casey: treas *B* NY 1945 *ED* City Univ NY Bernard M Baruch Coll 1971 *CORP AFFIL* dir: Energy Tech Intl Corp *NONPR AFFIL* treas: Union League; trust: Franciscan Svcs; vchmn, dir: St Agnes Hospital

Bernard Finkelstein: trust *B* New York NY 1930 *CURR EMPL* ptnr: Paul Weiss Rifkind Wharton & Garrison

Jane B. O'Connell: trust *NONPR AFFIL* treas: Female Academy Sacred

Karen L. Rosa: vp, exec dir

Maurice A. Selinger, Jr.: trust

Julie V. Shea: trust

John W. Townsend IV: trust *CORP AFFIL* asst exec dir, asst sec: Boettcher Foundation

Victor D. Ziminsky, Jr.: trust

APPLICATION INFORMATION
Initial Approach:

Grant requests should be in letter form and no longer than three pages.

Applicants must describe the project for which funds are being solicited, and include proof of tax-exempt status, most recent financial statement, budget, and a list of officers or trustees. The Altman Foundation accepts the New York area common grant application form.

The foundation reports no application deadlines.

Restrictions on Giving: No grants are made to individuals.

OTHER THINGS TO KNOW
The foundation occasionally initiates discretionary grants and offers ongoing support to organizations that have received previous funding.

PUBLICATIONS
General guidelines and application procedure brochure

GRANTS ANALYSIS
Total Grants: $6,100,000*

Number of Grants: 164*

Highest Grant: $300,000

Average Grant: $37,288*

Typical Range: $25,000 to $100,000

Disclosure Period: 1994

Note: Grants analysis was provided by the foundation. Recent grants are derived from a 1993 Form 990.

RECENT GRANTS

Library

100,000	New York Public Library, New York, NY	

General

300,000	St. Vincents Hospital and Medical Center of New York, New York, NY
100,000	Bronx-Lebanon Hospital New Directions Fund, Bronx, NY — for Bronx-Lebanon Hospital Center
100,000	Catholic Charities, Archdiocese of New York, New York, NY
100,000	Catholic Home Bureau, New York, NY
100,000	Children's Storefront Foundation, New York, NY

Altschul Foundation

CONTACT
Susan Rothstein-Schwimmer
President and Trustee
Altschul Fdn.
1740 Broadway
New York, NY 10019
(212) 489-8230

FINANCIAL SUMMARY
Recent Giving: $243,150 (fiscal 1993); $518,700 (fiscal 1992); $282,450 (fiscal 1991)

Assets: $11,717,336 (fiscal 1993); $11,855,143 (fiscal 1992); $8,640,031 (fiscal 1991)

EIN: 13-6400009

CONTRIBUTIONS SUMMARY
Donor(s): the late Louis Altschul, the late Jeanette Cohen Altschul

Typical Recipients: • *Arts & Humanities:* Community Arts, Libraries, Music • *Civic & Public Affairs:* Chambers of Commerce, General, Law & Justice, Public Policy • *Education:* Colleges & Universities • *Health:* AIDS/HIV, Alzheimers Disease, Cancer, Emergency/Ambulance Services, Eyes/Blindness, Health Organizations, Hospitals, Long-Term Care, Medical Rehabilitation, Medical Research, Multiple Sclerosis, Nursing Services, Single-Disease Health Associations, Transplant Networks/Donor Banks • *International:* Foreign Educational Institutions, Missionary/Religious Activities • *Religion:* Jewish Causes, Religious Organizations, Religious Welfare • *Social Services:* Community Service Organizations, People with Disabilities, Recreation & Athletics, Senior Services, United Funds/United Ways, Youth Organizations

Grant Types: general support

Geographic Distribution: focus on New York City, NY

GIVING OFFICERS
Valerie Aspinwall: trust

Vivian C. Reichman: secy, treas, trust

Louis Rothstein: vp, trust

Phyllis Rothstein-Doniger: trust

Susan Rothstein-Schwimmer: pres, trust

APPLICATION INFORMATION
Initial Approach: Send brief letter of inquiry describing program or project. There are no deadlines.

GRANTS ANALYSIS
Total Grants: $243,150

Number of Grants: 31

Highest Grant: $200,000

Typical Range: $200 to $15,000

Disclosure Period: fiscal year ending June 30, 1993

Note: Recent grants are derived from a fiscal 1993 Form 990.

RECENT GRANTS

Library

250	New York Public Library, New York, NY

General

200,000	South Palm Beach County Jewish Federation, Palm Beach, FL
15,000	Leukemia Society of America, New York, NY
7,500	Cancer Research Institute for Gar Reichman Foundation
3,000	Anti-Defamation League, New York, NY
2,000	City of Hope, Los Angeles, CA

AMETEK, Inc. / AMETEK Foundation

Sales: $732.2 million
Employees: 6,100
Headquarters: Paoli, PA
SIC Major Group: Motors & Generators, Cold-Finishing of Steel Shapes, Process Control Instruments, and Measuring & Controlling Devices Nec

CONTACT
Robert W. Yannarell
Secretary and Treasurer
AMETEK Fdn.
410 Park Ave.
New York, NY 10022
(212) 935-8640

FINANCIAL SUMMARY
Recent Giving: $850,000 (1995 est.); $850,000 (1994 approx.); $793,220 (1993)

Assets: $5,924,992 (1993); $5,118,826 (1992); $4,741,305 (1991)

Gifts Received: $650,000 (1993); $650,000 (1992)

Fiscal Note: Above figures are for the foundation only. Company also offers direct gifts. Estimate of this support is not available. The foundation receives contributions from AMETEK, Inc.

EIN: 13-6095939

CONTRIBUTIONS SUMMARY

Typical Recipients: • *Arts & Humanities:* Arts Centers, Ballet, Dance, Ethnic & Folk Arts, Historic Preservation, Libraries, Museums/Galleries, Music • *Civic & Public Affairs:* Professional & Trade Associations, Safety, Urban & Community Affairs, Zoos/Aquariums • *Education:* Colleges & Universities, Education Associations, Education Funds, Elementary Education (Private), Engineering/Technological Education, Literacy, Medical Education, Private Education (Precollege), Science/Mathematics Education, Student Aid, Vocational & Technical Education • *Environment:* General, Resource Conservation • *Health:* Cancer, Health Funds, Health Organizations, Hospitals, Medical Rehabilitation, Medical Research, Mental Health • *Religion:* Jewish Causes, Ministries • *Science:* Scientific Centers & Institutes • *Social Services:* Child Welfare, Homes, People with Disabilities, Senior Services, Shelters/Homelessness, United Funds/United Ways, Youth Organizations

Grant Types: general support and research

Geographic Distribution: to national organizations and near plant locations

Operating Locations: CA (Fresno, Simi Valley), CT (Wallingford), DE (Newark, Wilmington), FL (Bartow, Largo), IL (Skokie), KY (Wurtland), MA (Wilmington), NC (Graham, Rock Creek Township), NY (New York), OH (Cambridge, Kent, Wapakoneta), PA (Allentown, Chadds Ford, Eighty-four, Feasterville, Nesquehoning, Paoli, Pittsburgh, Sellersville), WA (Redmond), WI (Racine, Sheboygan)

CORP. OFFICERS

Walter Elwood Blankley: *B* Philadelphia PA 1935 *CURR EMPL* chmn, dir: AMETEK Inc *NONPR AFFIL* mem: Aluminum Extruders Counc, World Aff Counc; mem adv bd: Am Soc Mechanical Engrs

William C. Cleary: *CURR EMPL* dir investor rels: AMETEK Inc

Roger K. Derr: *B* 1932 *ED* Kent St Univ BA 1958; Kent St Univ MBA 1963 *CURR EMPL* exec vp, coo: AMETEK Inc *CORP AFFIL* pres: Ametek Aerospace Products

John J. Molinelli: *CURR EMPL* sr vp, cfo: AMETEK Inc

GIVING OFFICERS

Walter Elwood Blankley: pres, dir *CURR EMPL* chmn, dir: AMETEK Inc (see above)

Lewis George Cole: dir *B* New York NY 1931 *ED* Univ PA BS 1951; Yale Univ LLB 1954 *CURR EMPL* admin ptnr: Stroock & Stroock & Lavan *CORP AFFIL* dir: AMETEK Inc *NONPR AFFIL* mem: Am Bar Assn, Assn Bar City New York, Beta Gamma Sigma, NY Bar Assn, Order Coif

Helmut N. Friedlaender: dir *CORP AFFIL* chmn, fin adv: Am Securities Corp; dir: AMETEK Inc

Elizabeth Rosenwald Varet: vp, dir *ED* Harvard Univ AB 1965 *CORP AFFIL* dir: Am Securities Corp, AMETEK Inc, Ketema Corp *PHIL AFFIL* vp, dir: William Rosenwald Family Fund; chmn: American Charitable Fund; vp, dir: William and Mary Rosenewald Foundation, American Philanthropic Foundation

Robert W. Yannarell: secy, treas *B* 1933 *ED* St Josephs Univ BS 1962 *CURR EMPL* secy: AMETEK Inc *CORP AFFIL* treas: Ametek Aerospace Products

APPLICATION INFORMATION

Initial Approach: *Initial Contact:* brief letter or proposal *Include Information On:* description of the organization, amount requested, purpose for which funds are sought, recently audited financial statement, and proof of tax-exempt status *Deadlines:* March 1 for April meeting, or by October 1 for November meeting

Restrictions on Giving: Does not give to political or lobbying groups.

GRANTS ANALYSIS

Total Grants: $793,220

Number of Grants: 117

Highest Grant: $100,000

Average Grant: $6,780

Typical Range: $1,000 to $10,000

Disclosure Period: 1993

Note: Recent grants are derived from a 1993 Form 990.

RECENT GRANTS

General

100,000	United Jewish Appeal, New York, NY — for general welfare	
33,680	National Merit Scholarship Corporation, Evanston, IL — for education	
25,000	Albert Einstein College of Medicine of Yeshiva University, New York, NY — for medical research and care	
25,000	Memorial Sloan-Kettering Cancer Center, New York, NY — for medical research and care	
22,000	Fox Chase Cancer Center, Philadelphia, PA — for medical research and care	

Anderson Foundation

CONTACT

Bertha A. Greenlee
President
Anderson Fdn.
PO Box 3251
Elmira, NY 14902
(607) 734-0296

FINANCIAL SUMMARY

Recent Giving: $152,416 (fiscal 1994); $171,570 (fiscal 1993); $121,240 (fiscal 1992)

Assets: $2,623,657 (fiscal 1994); $2,657,942 (fiscal 1993); $2,018,292 (fiscal 1992)

EIN: 16-6024689

CONTRIBUTIONS SUMMARY

Donor(s): Jane G. Anderson, the late Douglas G. Anderson

Typical Recipients: • *Arts & Humanities:* Community Arts, Historic Preservation, History & Archaeology, Libraries, Museums/Galleries, Music, Opera, Performing Arts, Public Broadcasting • *Civic & Public Affairs:* Community Foundations, Employment/Job Training, Housing, Urban & Community Affairs • *Education:* Colleges & Universities, Gifted & Talented Programs, Literacy, Preschool Education • *Environment:* Resource Conservation • *Health:* Long-Term Care, Multiple Sclerosis, Nursing Services • *Religion:* Religious Welfare • *Social Services:* Camps, Child Welfare, Community Centers, Community Service Organizations, Food/Clothing Distribution, Senior Services, Substance Abuse, United Funds/United Ways, Volunteer Services, Youth Organizations

Grant Types: general support, operating expenses, and scholarship

Geographic Distribution: focus on Elmira, NY

GIVING OFFICERS

Bertha A. Greenlee: pres, trust

J. Philip Hunter: secy

Robert T. Jones: trust

Jane G. Joralemon: vp, trust

Kenneth A. Tifft: asst secy, trust

E. William Whittaker: treas, trust

Ethel A. Whittaker: vp, trust

Charles A. Winding: trust, vp

APPLICATION INFORMATION

Initial Approach: The foundation has no formal grant application procedure or application form. There are no deadlines.

GRANTS ANALYSIS

Total Grants: $152,416

Number of Grants: 24

Highest Grant: $27,000

Typical Range: $1,245 to $25,000

Disclosure Period: fiscal year ending April 30, 1994

Note: Recent grants are derived from a fiscal 1994 Form 990.

RECENT GRANTS

Library

20,000	Steele Memorial Library, Elmira, NY — for reading material	

General

15,000	Bethany Retirement Center, Horsehead, NY — for the activities room	
12,500	United Way, Elmira, NY — for general support	
5,000	County of Chemung Summer Cohesion Program, Elmira, NY — for general support	

| 5,000 | Economic Opportunity Program, Elmira, NY — for Second Place East program |
| 5,000 | Literacy Volunteers of America, Elmira, NY — for general support |

Arkell Hall Foundation

CONTACT
Joseph A. Santangelo
Vice President, Treasurer, Administrator
Arkell Hall Foundation
66 Montgomery St.
Canajoharie, NY 13317
(518) 673-5417

FINANCIAL SUMMARY
Recent Giving: $500,000 (fiscal 1995 est.); $500,000 (fiscal 1994 approx.); $1,672,915 (fiscal 1993)

Assets: $39,000,000 (fiscal 1995 est.); $39,000,000 (fiscal 1994 approx.); $44,008,469 (fiscal 1993)

EIN: 14-1343077

CONTRIBUTIONS SUMMARY
Donor(s): The foundation was established in 1948 by the late Mrs. F. E. Barbour .

Typical Recipients: • *Arts & Humanities:* Arts Centers, Libraries, Museums/Galleries • *Civic & Public Affairs:* Botanical Gardens/Parks, Housing, Legal Aid, Municipalities/Towns, Philanthropic Organizations, Urban & Community Affairs • *Education:* Colleges & Universities, Community & Junior Colleges, Engineering/Technological Education, International Exchange, Legal Education, Medical Education, Minority Education, Public Education (Precollege), Religious Education, Science/Mathematics Education, Student Aid • *Health:* Cancer, Children's Health/Hospitals, Clinics/Medical Centers, Emergency/Ambulance Services, Health Funds, Heart, Hospitals, Long-Term Care, Medical Research, Single-Disease Health Associations • *International:* International Relief Efforts • *Religion:* Churches, Religious Organizations, Religious Welfare • *Social Services:* Animal Protection, Big Brother/Big Sister, Community Centers, Community Service Organizations, Counseling, Domestic Violence, Family Services, Food/Clothing Distribution, People with Disabilities, Recreation & Athletics, Scouts, Senior Services, Youth Organizations

Grant Types: capital, project, and scholarship

Geographic Distribution: limited to the Canajoharie, NY, area

GIVING OFFICERS
James R. Dern: trust

Joyce G. Dresser: trust

Frances L. Howard: asst secy, trust

Ferdinand C. Kaiser: vp, secy, trust

Joseph A. Santangelo: vp, treas, admin *B* Norristown PA 1954 *ED* Drexel Univ 1977

CURR EMPL treas: FPA Corp *CORP AFFIL* treas: Orleans Corp; vp: Orleans Construction Corp

Edward W. Shineman, Jr.: pres, trust *B* Canajoharie NY 1915 *ED* Cornell Univ AB 1937 *CORP AFFIL* bd dir: Fenimore Asset Mgmt; dir: Taconic Farms *NONPR AFFIL* mem: Fin Execs Inst, Natl Assn Accts; mem emeritus counc: Cornell Univ

Charles J. Tallent: trust

Robert H. Wille: vp, treas, trust

Charles E. Wright: trust

APPLICATION INFORMATION
Initial Approach:

Applications should be sent in full proposal form. The foundation has no specific application form.

Grant proposals should include a one- to three-page statement describing, in order, how the project will significantly impact the target community, the organization, the organization's staff, the organization's goals, the problem to be addressed, how the proposal addresses the problem, and the funding amount requested; documentation providing financial background on the organization and the proposal, including overall expense and revenue budgets and other funding sources; and an official IRS determination letter documenting the organization's tax-exempt status.

All required information must be received by September 15.

Initial review of requests is performed upon receipt. Results are forwarded to the applicant within one month. Qualifying requests are then reviewed and acted upon by the foundation's trustees in October or November, with notification and distribution (if awarded) by November 30.

Restrictions on Giving: Grants or loans are not made to individuals or to organizations for the express use or benefit of any individual. The most important requirement for funding is significant direct impact in the Western Montgomery County, NY community. Projects or organizations with large service areas (such as national or regional) will not qualify for funding, nor will projects in which the target community is not the primary focus of activity. Grants are made on a single-year basis only. A grant application is valid only in the year in which it is received. Grants are not made to individuals, or for multi-year commitments, travel, conferences, or loans.

PUBLICATIONS
Grant program guidelines

GRANTS ANALYSIS
Total Grants: $1,672,915

Number of Grants: 70

Highest Grant: $1,200,500

Average Grant: $6,749*

Typical Range: $500 to $15,000

Disclosure Period: fiscal year ending November 30, 1993

Note: The highest grant of $1,200,500 was not included in the average grant figure. Recent grants are derived from a fiscal 1993 Form 990.

RECENT GRANTS
General

1,200,500	Arkell Center, Canajoharie, NY — building program for this center that provides services and living facilities for senior citizens
65,000	Amsterdam Memorial Hospital Foundation Pediatrics Department, Amsterdam, NY — expanded services
65,000	St. Mary's Hospital Foundation — capital campaign gift
50,000	Canajoharie Central School, Canajoharie, NY — Barbour scholarships
27,250	Canajoharie Community Services, Canajoharie, NY — facility repairs and improvements

Arnhold Foundation

CONTACT
Henry H. Arnhold
President
Arnhold Fdn.
19 Rector St., Ste. 2400
New York, NY 10006

FINANCIAL SUMMARY
Recent Giving: $306,000 (1993); $149,818 (1992)

Assets: $8,602,658 (1993); $7,080,261 (1992)

Gifts Received: $807,218 (1993); 3,104,341 (1992)

EIN: 13-3456684

CONTRIBUTIONS SUMMARY
Typical Recipients: • *Arts & Humanities:* Arts Funds, Arts Outreach, Ballet, Libraries, Museums/Galleries, Music, Opera • *Civic & Public Affairs:* Botanical Gardens/Parks, General, Parades/Festivals • *Education:* Arts/Humanities Education, Private Education (Precollege) • *Environment:* General • *Health:* Clinics/Medical Centers, Emergency/Ambulance Services, Hospitals, Nursing Services • *International:* International Affairs • *Religion:* Jewish Causes • *Social Services:* Animal Protection, Community Service Organizations, Food/Clothing Distribution, Youth Organizations

Grant Types: general support

Geographic Distribution: New York City metropolitan area

GIVING OFFICERS
Henry H. Arnhold: pres

John P. Arnhold: secy, treas

APPLICATION INFORMATION
Initial Approach: Send a brief letter of inquiry and a full proposal. Include a description of organization. There are no deadlines.

GRANTS ANALYSIS
Total Grants: $306,000

Number of Grants: 148

Highest Grant: $50,000

Typical Range: $50 to $50,000

Disclosure Period: 1993

Note: Recent grants are derived from a 1993 Form 990.

RECENT GRANTS

Library

1,250	New York Public Library, New York, NY

General

12,000	Julliard School, New York, NY
10,000	Sociey for the Prevention of Cruelty to Animals, New York, NY
5,000	American Red Cross Disaster Relief Fund, New York, NY — Hurricane
5,000	Food for Needy, New York, NY
5,000	Trinity School, New York, NY

ASDA Foundation

CONTACT
Guido Goldman
Director
ASDA Fdn.
499 Deer Ave., 26th Flr.
New York, NY 10022
(212) 688-4010

FINANCIAL SUMMARY
Recent Giving: $60,000 (1993)

Assets: $9,172,851 (1993)

EIN: 52-1319624

CONTRIBUTIONS SUMMARY
Typical Recipients: • *Arts & Humanities:* Libraries • *Civic & Public Affairs:* General, Urban & Community Affairs • *Education:* Colleges & Universities, International Studies • *Health:* Alzheimers Disease, Cancer • *International:* International Organizations, International Relations • *Religion:* Jewish Causes, Religious Welfare • *Social Services:* Child Welfare

Grant Types: general support and research

Geographic Distribution: no geographic restrictions

GIVING OFFICERS
Alain De Gunzburg: dir

Charles De Gunzburg: dir

Jean De Gunzburg: dir

Guido Goldman: dir *NONPR AFFIL* dir: Harvard Univ Ctr European Studies *PHIL AFFIL* trust: German Marshall Fund of the United States

Ken Musen: asst secy

Kevin Penn: secy

Lynne Rodriguez: treas

B. Lance Sauerteig: dir

APPLICATION INFORMATION
Initial Approach: The foundation has no formal grant application procedure or application form. There are no deadlines.

GRANTS ANALYSIS
Total Grants: $60,000

Number of Grants: 1

Highest Grant: $60,000

Disclosure Period: 1993

Note: Recent grants are derived from a 1993 Form 990.

RECENT GRANTS

Library

500	New York Public Library, New York, NY — general support

General

350,000	Harvard University Center for European Studies, Cambridge, MA — general support
350,000	Harvard University Center for European Studies, Cambridge, MA — general support
160,700	Samuel and Daidye Bronfman Family Foundation, Montreal, Quebec, Canada — general support
160,700	Samuel and Saidye Bronfman Family Foundation, Montreal, Canada — general support
150,000	University of Michigan, Ann Arbor, MI — chemotherapy research

Astor Foundation, Vincent

CONTACT
Linda Gillies
Director
Vincent Astor Foundation
405 Park Ave., Rm. 1703
New York, NY 10022
(212) 758-4110

FINANCIAL SUMMARY
Recent Giving: $1,000,000 (1995 est.); $1,603,500 (1994); $1,343,200 (1993)

Assets: $23,000,000 (1995 est.); $22,900,000 (1994 approx.); $25,227,091 (1993)

EIN: 23-7167124

CONTRIBUTIONS SUMMARY
Donor(s): The foundation was established in 1948 by the late Vincent Astor . A descendant of John Jacob Astor, who launched the family fortune in fur and tea trading and New York City real estate, Vincent Astor was engaged in many business activities during his career, especially investments, real estate operations, and hotels. When he died in 1959, Vincent Astor's will stipulated that half of his $127 million estate go to the foundation. His widow, Brooke Astor, is the foundation's president.

Typical Recipients: • *Arts & Humanities:* Arts Associations & Councils, Arts Centers, Arts Outreach, Historic Preservation, History & Archaeology, Libraries, Museums/Galleries, Opera, Public Broadcasting, Theater • *Civic & Public Affairs:* African American Affairs, Botanical Gardens/Parks, Economic Development, Employment/Job Training, General, Housing, Urban & Community Affairs, Zoos/Aquariums • *Education:* Afterschool/Enrichment Programs, Colleges & Universities, Literacy, Public Education (Precollege), Science/Mathematics Education, Student Aid • *Environment:* General, Resource Conservation, Wildlife Protection • *Health:* Clinics/Medical Centers, Hospitals (University Affiliated) • *International:* International Relations • *Religion:* Churches, Religious Welfare, Synagogues/Temples • *Science:* Science Museums • *Social Services:* Animal Protection, At-Risk Youth, Child Welfare, Community Centers, Community Service Organizations, Day Care, People with Disabilities, Recreation & Athletics, Shelters/Homelessness, Substance Abuse

Grant Types: capital, general support, and project

Geographic Distribution: primarily New York City metropolitan area

GIVING OFFICERS
Roberta Brooke Russell Astor: pres, trust *B* Portsmouth NH 1903 *NONPR AFFIL* mem: Asia Soc, China Soc, Japan Soc, Municipal Art Soc, Natl Park Fdn, Navy League US, Venerable Order St John Jerusalem; mem bd overseers: Cornell Univ; mem corp bd: Astor Home Children; trust: Marconi Intl Fellowship Counc, Sleepy Hollow Restorations; trust emeritus, chmn visual comm dept Asian Art: Metro Mus Art; trust, hon chmn, mem devel comm, mem exec comm: NY Pub Library; trust, mem conservation comm, mem exec comm: NY Zoological Soc; trust, mem exec comm: Rockefeller Univ, WNET Channel 13; trust, mem exec comm, mem counc fellows: Pierpont Morgan Library *CLUB AFFIL* Board Room, Century Assn, Coffee House, Colony, Grolier, Knickerbocker, New York YC, Pilgrims, River, Sleepy Hollow CC

Henry Christensen III: trust *B* Jersey City NJ 1944 *ED* Yale Univ BA 1966; Harvard Univ JD 1969 *CURR EMPL* chmn: Prospect Pk Alliance *CORP AFFIL* mem: NY State Bar Assn; ptnr: Assoc Sullivan & Cromwell *NONPR AFFIL* secy, dir: Freedom Inst; trust: Am Fund Tate Gallery; vp, dir: Am Friends Whitechapel Art Gallery Fdn *PHIL AFFIL* vp, secy: Odysseus Foundation; vp: Dunlevy Milbank Foundation

Thomas R. Coolidge: trust *B* Boston MA 1934 *CURR EMPL* pres: Coolidge & Co

Henry N. Ess III: trust *B* Kansas City MO 1921

Peter P. M. Gates: secy *PHIL AFFIL* secy: Andy Warhol Foundation for the Visual Arts

Linda Gillies: dir, trust

Anthony D. Marshall: vp, trust

Peter S. Paine: adv trust *B* Willsboro NY 1909

Richard S. Perkins: adv trust *B* Milton MA 1910

Howard Phipps, Jr.: trust *B* 1934 *PHIL AF-FIL* dir: Edward John Noble Foundation; don: Howard Phipps Family Charitable Foundation; trust: Perkin Fund, Howard Phipps Foundation

John Pierrepont: trust

Fergus Reid III: treas, trust *B* 1932 *CURR EMPL* chmn, secy, dir: Lumelite Corp

APPLICATION INFORMATION

Initial Approach:

Initial letters of inquiry should be sent to the foundation's director.

Letters of inquiry should describe the proposed project and the sponsoring agency, and include a budget and a list of other sources of funding. Proposals should also include the organization's most recent audited financial statement, Form 990, and a copy of the IRS determination letter of tax-exempt (and not a private foundation) status.

There are no formal deadlines for submitting letters.

The review of and decision on any pending application depends upon the number and nature of other applications and the availability of funds. If a request falls within the foundation's guidelines and appears to have a reasonable chance for funding, a meeting will be arranged and the foundation will request more detailed information. The trustees meet to consider grant applications in May, October, and December. Because of the many requests directed to the foundation, the review process can take several months.

Restrictions on Giving: As a rule, the foundation does not support programs involving mental health, medicine, private schools, research or advocacy.

OTHER THINGS TO KNOW

The foundation expects to receive concise written reports about projects for which grants are given, as well as financial accountings for the expenditure of funds.

PUBLICATIONS

Annual report

GRANTS ANALYSIS

Total Grants: $1,603,500

Number of Grants: 92

Highest Grant: $250,000

Average Grant: $17,429

Typical Range: $10,000 to $25,000

Disclosure Period: 1994

Note: Recent grants are derived from a 1993 Form 990.

RECENT GRANTS

Library

25,000	Bank Street College of Education, New York, NY — toward small libraries for the Partners for Success program
25,000	Fund for New York City Public Education, New York, NY — toward the library media center at the Education Complex at JHS 99 in Manhattan
25,000	Fund for Public Schools, New York, NY — toward renovation and purchase of books and equipment for the library at Manhattan Comprehensive Night High School
25,000	New York Public Library, Astor, Lenox and Tilden Foundation, New York, NY — toward opening the research library on Mondays
5,000	New York Public Library, Astor, Lenox and Tilden Foundation, New York, NY — general support

General

125,000	New York Zoological Society/The Wildlife Conservation Society, New York, NY — toward the Ecology Education Center on Astor Court
100,000	Animal Medical Center, New York, NY — toward the capital campaign
50,000	Partnership for the Homeless, New York, NY — toward Furnish a Future, a furniture distribution program for formerly homeless people
30,000	Lenox Hill Neighborhood Association, New York, NY — toward "Transitions," a program to identify and assist chronic homeless substance abusers living in the New York City subway system
25,000	American Museum of Natural History, New York, NY — toward education programming for the museum's new Hall of Biology and Evolution

AT&T Corp. / AT&T Foundation

Revenue: $75.09 billion
Employees: 308,700
Headquarters: Basking Ridge, NJ
SIC Major Group: Radiotelephone Communications, Telephone Communications Except Radiotelephone, and Communications Services Nec

CONTACT

Laura M. Abbott
Secretary
AT&T Foundation
1301 Avenue of the Americas
Rm. 3124
New York, NY 10019
(212) 841-4747
Note: Timothy J. McClimon, Vice President, International Programs, is the contact person regarding international contributions. The

company's World Wide Web address is http://www.att.com

FINANCIAL SUMMARY

Recent Giving: $49,871,000 (1995 est.); $48,096,000 (1994 approx.); $44,973,475 (1993)

Assets: $124,600,000 (1994 approx.); $129,000,000 (1993 approx.); $120,000,000 (1992 approx.)

Fiscal Note: Above figures include foundation and direct giving. Foundation contributions totaled $35,880,000 in 1994. The 1993 figure includes $32.2 million in foundation gifts, $7.8 million in regional and direct contributions, $7.0 million in nonmonetary support, and international giving.

EIN: 13-3166495

CONTRIBUTIONS SUMMARY

Typical Recipients: • *Arts & Humanities:* Arts Associations & Councils, Arts Centers, Arts Festivals, Dance, Museums/Galleries, Music, Opera, Performing Arts, Theater, Visual Arts • *Civic & Public Affairs:* African American Affairs, Civil Rights, Economic Development, Economic Policy, Employment/Job Training, Hispanic Affairs, Housing, Nonprofit Management, Professional & Trade Associations, Public Policy, Urban & Community Affairs, Women's Affairs • *Education:* Business Education, Colleges & Universities, Education Associations, Education Funds, Education Reform, Engineering/Technological Education, Faculty Development, International Exchange, Medical Education, Minority Education, Public Education (Precollege), Science/Mathematics Education, Secondary Education (Public), Student Aid • *Environment:* General • *Health:* Children's Health/Hospitals, Emergency/Ambulance Services, Hospitals, Speech & Hearing • *International:* International Relations • *Social Services:* Child Welfare, Community Service Organizations, Day Care, Emergency Relief, Family Services, People with Disabilities, Substance Abuse, United Funds/United Ways, Youth Organizations

Grant Types: award, conference/seminar, employee matching gifts, fellowship, and multiyear/continuing support

Note: Employee matching gift ratio: 1 to 1 for tax-deductible gifts. The Matching Gifts Program funds higher educational and cultural institutions with grants from $25 to $10,000 and a maximum of $50,000 per organization. The foundation also sponsors the AT&T CARES program which provides grants to organizations where employees volunteer at least 50 hours of time.

Nonmonetary Support: $7,000,000 (1993); $9,900,000 (1992); $22,100,000 (1991)

Nonmonetary Support Types: cause-related marketing & promotion, donated products, in-kind services, and loaned executives

Note: The company does not accept unsolicited requests for nonmonetary support. See "Other Things To Know" for more details. The contact for nonmonetary support is M. Jo-Ann Greene, director, AT&T University Equipment Donation Program.

517

Geographic Distribution: near operating locations and to national organizations

Operating Locations: CA (Los Angeles, San Francisco), CO (Denver), DC, FL (Jacksonville, Largo, Miami, Orlando), GA (Atlanta), IL (Chicago), MA (Boston), NJ (Basking Ridge, Berkeley Heights, Middletown, Morristown, Murray Hill, Whippany), NY (New York), OH (Dayton), PA (Philadelphia)

CORP. OFFICERS

Robert Eugene Allen: *B* Joplin MO 1935 *ED* Wabash Coll BA 1957; Harvard Univ Grad Sch Bus Admin 1965 *CURR EMPL* chmn, ceo, dir: AT&T *CORP AFFIL* dir: Bristol-Myers Squibb Co, Fed Reserve Bank NY, PepsiCo *NONPR AFFIL* bd govs: Un Way Am; dir: Am Sch Devel Corp, Bus Counc NY, Japan Soc; mem: Bus Roundtable, Natl Assn Wabash Men; trust: Wabash Coll *CLUB AFFIL* Baltusrol GC, Bay Head YC, Burning Tree, CC FL, Congressional CC, Short Hills

Marilyn Laurie: *B* New York NY *ED* Barnard Coll BA 1959; Pace Univ MBA 1975 *CURR EMPL* sr vp pub rels & employee commun: AT&T *NONPR AFFIL* co-fdr: Environmental Action Coalition; dir: New York City Ballet, New York City Pub Ed Fund; mem: Pub Rels Soc Am; mem, dir: Catalyst; pres, mem: Arthur W Page Soc; trust: NJ Symphony

GIVING OFFICERS

Laura M. Abbott: secy, commun dir

Curtis R. Artis: trust

Harry S. Bennett: trust

Martina Bradford: trust

Gerald J. Butters: trust

W. Frank Cobbin, Jr.: trust *CURR EMPL* vp fin: Am Transtech

Melvin Irwin Cohen: trust *B* New York NY 1936 *ED* MA Inst Tech SB 1957; MA Inst Tech SM 1958; Rensselaer Polytech Inst PhD 1965 *CURR EMPL* vp res effectiveness: AT&T Bell Labs *NONPR AFFIL* fellow: Inst Electrical Electronics Engrs, Optical Soc Am; mem: Am Assn Advancement Sci; mem exec bd: Anderson Ctr Innovation Undergrad Ed; mem panel natl standards & tech program: Natl Res Counc; mem sci policy bd: Rutgers Univ; recruiter, mem dept advbd: Rensselaer Polytech Inst

Gary Doran: vp policy & admin

Mirian M. Graddick: trust

John C. Guerra, Jr.: trust

Sarah Jepsen: exec dir

Marilyn Laurie: chmn, trust *CURR EMPL* sr vp pub rels & employee commun: AT&T (see above)

Reynold Levy: trust *B* 1945 *ED* Hobart Coll BA 1966; Univ VA MA 1968; Columbia Univ JD 1973; Univ VA PhD 1973 *NONPR AFFIL* dir: Am Counc Arts, Consortium Advancement Higher Ed, Independent Sector; mem: Oi Gamma Mu *PHIL AFFIL* mem bd: Nathan Cummings Foundation

Judith A. Maynes: trust *CURR EMPL* asst gen coun: AT&T

Gail J. McGovern: trust

Ray M. Robinson: trust

Yvonne M. Shepard: trust

Lola Signom: trust *PHIL AFFIL* pres: AT&T Global Information Solutions Foundation

Kent M. Takeda: trust

Sara A. Tucker: trust

Thomas C. Wajnert: trust *B* Evergreen Park IL 1943 *ED* IL Inst Tech BS 1965; Southern Methodist Univ MBA 1966 *CURR EMPL* pres, ceo, chmn: AT&T Capital Corp *CORP AFFIL* chmn: AT&T Automotive Svcs, AT&T Commercial Fin Corp, AT&T Sys Leasing Corp; chmn, ceo: AT&T Capital Holdings, AT&T Credit Holdings; dir: AT&T Universal Card Svcs *NONPR AFFIL* dir: Wharton Ctr for Fin Inst

Doreen S. Yochum: trust

APPLICATION INFORMATION

Initial Approach: *Initial Contact:* obtain biennial report and giving guidelines; address letter of inquiry (preferably no more than three pages) to foundation secretary for requests that are national in scope; regional requests should be directed to local AT&T contributions managers listed in the guidelines and biennial report *Include Information On:* description of the organization; statement relating purpose to interests and priorities of foundation; summary of purpose for which grant is sought and proof of need; operating budget for current year showing anticipated sources of revenue and expenses (if project support sought, include a detailed budget for the project); and proof of 501(c)(3) status *Deadlines:* none

Restrictions on Giving: Foundation does not make grants to individuals; organizations that practice discrimination; political organizations, campaigns, or lobbying groups; religious groups for sectarian purposes; operating expenses or capital campaigns of local health and human service organizations other than hospitals; endowments or memorials; building projects; local chapters of national organizations; sports teams or athletic events; or goodwill advertising, banquets, or other fund-raising events.

OTHER THINGS TO KNOW

Company suggests that giving guidelines be obtained and read before sending in applications for grants. Guidelines may be obtained by either calling (903) 636-3898, sending a fax message to (904) 636-1674 or writing AT&T Foundation, Dept. BR, PO Box 45284, Jacksonville, FL 32232-5284.

The company's nonmonetary support program provides AT&T computer laboratories to selected colleges and universities. This is an invitational program not open to unsolicited requests.

Foundation officers not listed above because of limited space are Robert E. Angelica, treas; Liz Jackson, asst secy; Lawrence M. Unrein, asst treas; Marilyn Reznick, vp (ed programs); Milton J. Little, vp (health & human services programs); Suzanne Sato, vp (arts & culture program); Jerry Carter, program mgr (ed programs); Claire Spencer,

program mgr (health & human services programs); Valerie D'Antonio, program mgr (art & culture program); Marcy Chapin, dir (community involvement programs); and Elaine Anacker, staff associate (matching gifts programs).

PUBLICATIONS

Corporate citizenship biennial report, guidelines

GRANTS ANALYSIS

Total Grants: $35,880,000

Number of Grants: 604*

Highest Grant: $1,835,000

Average Grant: $34,500*

Typical Range: $5,000 to $50,000*

Disclosure Period: 1994

Note: Figures represent foundation giving. Number of grants, average grant, and typical grant range do not include matching gifts. Recent grants are derived from a 1994 partial grants list.

RECENT GRANTS

General

895,000   Families and Work Institute, New York, NY — a three-year grant to support the pilot program EQUIP's transition to the implementation stage, in which local EQUIP teams will conduct quality audits, carry out improvement plans, and continue to build awareness about early-childhood care

500,000   Cultural Transactions: The Global Art of Latin America — a five-year grant to support the opening of a multi-media exhibition representing 27 artists from 11 countries at six museums in Mexico, Venezuela, Columbia, and Brazil

150,000   Committee for Economic Development, New York, NY — a two-year grant for the completion of a policy statement on inner-city problems and for a study of the global economy

100,000   Egleston Children's Hospital at Emory University/Center for Child Advocacy, Atlanta, GA — to support research leading to improvement in the quality of prenatal care in Georgia, develop a campaighn to reduce infant mortality and publish the study's results

60,000   Instituto Tecnologico Y De Estudios Superiores De Monterrey — a two-year grant to support the development of a graduate research program in telecommunications at ITESM's Center of

Electronics and
Telecommunications

Atran Foundation

CONTACT
Diane Fischer
Corporate Secretary
Atran Foundation
23-25 E 21st St., 3rd Fl.
New York, NY 10010
(212) 505-9677

FINANCIAL SUMMARY
Recent Giving: $685,000 (fiscal 1995 est.);
$685,000 (fiscal 1994 approx.); $667,555
(fiscal 1993)

Assets: $14,500,000 (fiscal 1995 est.);
$14,500,000 (fiscal 1994 approx.);
$15,903,591 (fiscal 1993)

EIN: 13-5566548

CONTRIBUTIONS SUMMARY
Donor(s): The foundation was incorporated
in 1945 by the late Frank Z. Atran .

Typical Recipients: • *Arts & Humanities:*
Historic Preservation, Libraries, Muse-
ums/Galleries, Public Broadcasting • *Civic
& Public Affairs:* African American Affairs,
Botanical Gardens/Parks, Economic Policy,
Law & Justice, Philanthropic Organizations,
Professional & Trade Associations, Public
Policy, Women's Affairs, Zoos/Aquariums
• *Education:* Colleges & Universities, Educa-
tion Reform, International Studies, Medical
Education, Minority Education, Religious
Education, Social Sciences Education • *Envi-
ronment:* General • *Health:* Clinics/Medical
Centers, Emergency/Ambulance Services,
Geriatric Health, Hospitals, Long-Term
Care, Medical Research • *International:* Hu-
man Rights, International Peace & Security
Issues, Missionary/Religious Activities • *Re-
ligion:* Jewish Causes, Religious Organiza-
tions, Synagogues/Temples • *Social
Services:* Child Welfare, Community Serv-
ice Organizations, Homes, People with Disabilities, Senior Services, Special Olympics,
United Funds/United Ways, Youth Organizations

Grant Types: conference/seminar, emergency, endowment, general support, matching, multiyear/continuing support, project,
research, scholarship, and seed money

Geographic Distribution: focus on New
York

GIVING OFFICERS
Max Atran: pres, dir

Diane Fischer: corp secy, dir

William Stern: vp

APPLICATION INFORMATION
Initial Approach:

The foundation requests a proposal in writing.

Proposals should include the nature of the
project, its objectives including its useful-
ness, a program or plan for achieving the objectives, and an estimate of time to carry out
the program. The foundation also requests
an itemized budget showing the total cost of
the project, any contributions by the applicant or others, and the amount requested
from the foundation. Applicants should include whether and how the results of the project will be disseminated, and a copy of the
ruling granting federal tax exemption.

The deadline for submitting proposals is September 30.

OTHER THINGS TO KNOW
Recipients are expected to forward periodic
progress reports, and upon termination of
the project, to submit a final report detailing
the statements of disbursements. Funds not
expended are required to be returned to the
foundation.

PUBLICATIONS
Application guidelines

GRANTS ANALYSIS
Total Grants: $667,555

Number of Grants: 52

Highest Grant: $150,000

Average Grant: $12,838

Typical Range: $250 to $15,000

Disclosure Period: fiscal year ending November 30, 1993

Note: Recent grants are derived from a fiscal 1993 Form 990.

RECENT GRANTS

Library
3,000	New York Public Library, New York, NY

General
150,000	Albert Einstein College of Medicine of Yeshiva University, Bronx, NY
80,000	Jewish Labor Committee, New York, NY
75,000	United Jewish Appeal, Israel Emergency Fund, New York, NY
75,000	Yivo Institute for Jewish Research, New York, NY
45,000	Columbia University in the City of New York, New York, NY

Avery Arts Foundation, Milton and Sally

CONTACT
Sally M. Avery
President
Milton and Sally Avery Arts Fdn.
300 Central Park W.
New York, NY 10024

FINANCIAL SUMMARY
Recent Giving: $184,800 (1993); $169,050
(1992)

Assets: $3,993,656 (1993); $3,675,463
(1992)

EIN: 13-3093638

CONTRIBUTIONS SUMMARY

Typical Recipients: • *Arts & Humanities:*
Arts Associations & Councils, Arts Centers,
Arts Funds, Arts Institutes, Community
Arts, Dance, General, Historic Preservation,
Libraries, Literary Arts, Museums/Galleries,
Music, Public Broadcasting, Visual Arts
• *Civic & Public Affairs:* African American
Affairs, General, Urban & Community Af-
fairs, Women's Affairs • *Education:*
Arts/Humanities Education, Colleges & Uni-
versities, Private Education (Precollege) • *In-
ternational:* Foreign Arts Organizations,
Foreign Educational Institutions • *Religion:*
Jewish Causes • *Social Services:* Commu-
nity Service Organizations

Grant Types: general support

Geographic Distribution: primarily New
England and NY

GIVING OFFICERS

Sally M. Avery: pres

March A. Cavanaugh: trust

APPLICATION INFORMATION

Initial Approach: Send a brief letter of inquiry and a full proposal. Include a description of organization. There are no deadlines.

GRANTS ANALYSIS

Total Grants: $184,800

Number of Grants: 40

Highest Grant: $50,000

Typical Range: $1,000 to $5,000

Disclosure Period: 1993

Note: Recent grants are derived from a 1993
Form 990.

RECENT GRANTS

Library
2,700	New York Public Library, New York, NY

General
50,000	Bard College, Annandale-on-Hudson, NY
20,000	Pitzer College, Claremont, CA
15,400	New York Studio School, New York, NY
10,000	University of Arts of Philadelphia, Philadelphia, PA
5,000	Skowhegan School of Painting and Sculpture, New York, NY

519

Avon Products, Inc. / Avon Products Foundation, Inc.

Revenue: $4.32 billion
Employees: 29,700
Headquarters: New York, NY
SIC Major Group: Toilet Preparations, Costume Jewelry, and Drugs, Proprietaries & Sundries

CONTACT
Glenn S. Clarke
President
Avon Products Foundation, Inc.
9 W 57th St.
New York, NY 10019
(212) 546-6731

FINANCIAL SUMMARY
Recent Giving: $2,000,000 (1994 est.); $1,977,755 (1993); $1,488,749 (1992)

Assets: $56,817 (1993); $58,985 (1992); $67,111 (1991)

Gifts Received: $2,000,000 (1993); $1,500,000 (1992)

Fiscal Note: All cash contributions are made through the foundation. Above figures exclude nonmonetary support. Contributions are received from Avon Products, Inc.

EIN: 13-6128447

CONTRIBUTIONS SUMMARY
Typical Recipients: • *Arts & Humanities:* Arts Associations & Councils, Arts Centers, Arts Festivals, Arts Funds, Arts Institutes, Community Arts, Ethnic & Folk Arts, Libraries, Museums/Galleries, Music, Opera, Performing Arts, Public Broadcasting, Theater • *Civic & Public Affairs:* Business/Free Enterprise, Civil Rights, Economic Development, Economic Policy, Employment/Job Training, Law & Justice, Legal Aid, Public Policy, Urban & Community Affairs, Women's Affairs, Zoos/Aquariums • *Education:* Arts/Humanities Education, Business Education, Colleges & Universities, Economic Education, Education Funds, Literacy, Medical Education, Minority Education, Special Education, Student Aid • *Environment:* General • *Health:* Emergency/Ambulance Services, Health Funds, Health Organizations, Hospices, Hospitals, Medical Rehabilitation, Medical Research, Mental Health, Single-Disease Health Associations • *International:* International Development • *Religion:* Religious Welfare • *Social Services:* Animal Protection, At-Risk Youth, Child Welfare, Community Centers, Community Service Organizations, Delinquency & Criminal Rehabilitation, Family Services, Food/Clothing Distribution, People with Disabilities, Recreation & Athletics, Senior Services, Shelters/Homelessness, Substance Abuse, United Funds/United Ways, Volunteer Services, Youth Organizations

Grant Types: capital, employee matching gifts, and scholarship

Nonmonetary Support: $9,000,000 (1993); $3,000,000 (1988); $3,500,000 (1987)

Nonmonetary Support Types: donated equipment, donated products, and in-kind services

Note: Products are distributed through a partnership with Gifts In Kind.

Geographic Distribution: near headquarters and operating locations

Operating Locations: CA (Los Angeles, Pasadena, Santa Monica), DE (Newark), GA (Atlanta), IL (Glenview, Morton Grove), NY (New York, Rye, Suffern), OH (Springdale), PR

CORP. OFFICERS
Gail Blanke: *B* 1941 *CURR EMPL* sr vp pub aff: Avon Products Inc

Margo R. Long: *CURR EMPL* vp: Avon Products Inc

James Edward Preston: *B* Cleveland OH 1933 *ED* Northwestern Univ BS 1955; Temple Univ *CURR EMPL* chmn, ceo: Avon Products Inc *CORP AFFIL* dir: FW Woolworth Co *NONPR AFFIL* chmn: Direct Selling Ed Fdn; dir: Am Womens Econ Devel Corp, Bus Counc NY, Cosmetic Toiletry Fragrance Assn; dir, treas: Fragrance Fdn; mem adv bd: Salvation Army Greater NY

Edward Joseph Robinson: *B* White Plains NY 1940 *ED* Iona Coll BBA 1962 *CURR EMPL* pres, coo, dir: Avon Products Inc *NONPR AFFIL* mem: Am Inst CPAs, NY Soc CPAs; trust: Iona Coll *CLUB AFFIL* Metro, NY Athletic, Winged Foot CC

GIVING OFFICERS
Gail Blanke: vp *CURR EMPL* sr vp pub aff: Avon Products Inc (see above)

Glenn S. Clarke: pres, dir

Maria Montoya: dir

James Edward Preston: vp, dir *CURR EMPL* chmn, ceo: Avon Products Inc (see above)

APPLICATION INFORMATION
Initial Approach: *Initial Contact:* national organizations forward two-page letter to foundation; local and regional organizations located near company locations, send request to personnel manager (addresses available in foundation's Information & Guidelines brochure) *Include Information On:* purpose, aims, and programs of organization; annual report; list of board members; copy of IRS tax-exemption letter; list of other corporate contributors; need or problem and manner in which grant will be used; number of people and geographic area served; evaluative criteria; program budget and amount requested *Deadlines:* none

Restrictions on Giving: Foundation does not support individual member agencies of united funds; loan or endowment programs; fraternal, political, or lobbying groups; religious groups for sectarian purposes; dinners or special events; goodwill advertising; or individuals, except through scholarship programs.

OTHER THINGS TO KNOW
Avon also supports research into alternatives to the use of animal testing in new product development.

Company encourages active employee volunteerism.

Foundation prefers faxes rather than telephone solicitations.

PUBLICATIONS
Information and Guidelines Brochure

GRANTS ANALYSIS
Total Grants: $1,847,960
Number of Grants: 69
Highest Grant: $500,000
Average Grant: $19,823*
Typical Range: $500 to $25,000
Disclosure Period: 1993

Note: Figures exclude $118,448 in scholarships and $11,347 in matching gifts. Average Grant figure excludes highest grant. Recent grants are derived from a 1993 Form 990.

RECENT GRANTS

General

159,100	National Merit Scholarship Corporation, Evanston, IL
100,000	YWCA, Nashville, TN
77,500	Business and Professional Women
76,000	United Way
75,000	United Negro College Fund, New York, NY

Badgeley Residuary Charitable Trust, Rose M.

CONTACT
Eleanor D. Kress
Administrative Vice President
Rose M. Badgeley Residuary Charitable Trust
c/o Marine Midland Bank, N.A.
250 Park Ave., 4th Fl.
New York, NY 10177
(212) 503-2786

FINANCIAL SUMMARY
Recent Giving: $597,500 (fiscal 1993); $687,500 (fiscal 1992); $631,500 (fiscal 1991)

Assets: $14,345,521 (fiscal 1992); $13,049,400 (fiscal 1991); $12,662,399 (fiscal 1990)

Gifts Received: $135,890 (fiscal 1992); $84,908 (fiscal 1991); $161,928 (fiscal 1990)

Fiscal Note: The trust receives gifts from a trust under the will of Rose M. Badgeley.

EIN: 13-6744781

CONTRIBUTIONS SUMMARY
Donor(s): The trust was established in 1977, with the late Rose M. Badgeley as donor under her will.

Typical Recipients: • *Arts & Humanities:* Libraries, Music, Opera, Performing Arts • *Civic & Public Affairs:* Employment/Job Training, Housing • *Education:* Colleges & Universities • *Health:* Health Organizations, Hospitals, Medical Research, Single-Disease Health Associations • *Religion:* Religious

Welfare • *Social Services:* Child Welfare, Community Service Organizations, Counseling, Food/Clothing Distribution, Homes, People with Disabilities, Senior Services, Shelters/Homelessness, Substance Abuse, Youth Organizations

Grant Types: capital, general support, project, and research

Geographic Distribution: primarily New York metropolitan area

GIVING OFFICERS
John J. Duffy, Esq.: dir, trust *PHIL AFFIL* secy, dir: James T. Lee Foundation

Eleanor D. Kress: admin, vp

APPLICATION INFORMATION
Initial Approach:

Letters of inquiry should be directed to the chairman of the trust's grants committee at Marine Midland Bank.

The trust has no standard application form. However, requests should include current financial statements, list of board members and patrons, operating budget, and proof of tax-exempt status.

Applications must be postmarked no earlier than December 1 and no later than March 15.

OTHER THINGS TO KNOW
Marine Midland Bank serves as the corporate trustee for the foundation.

GRANTS ANALYSIS
Total Grants: $597,500

Number of Grants: 37

Highest Grant: $65,000

Average Grant: $16,149

Typical Range: $5,000 to $30,000

Disclosure Period: fiscal year ending January 31, 1993

Note: Recent grants are derived from a fiscal 1993 grants list.

RECENT GRANTS

Library
5,000	Queens Library, Flushing, NY — plays for teenagers to focus on cross-cultural awareness and enhanced literacy

General
65,000	New York Hospital Cornell Medical Center, New York, NY — for the Dr. Mary Allen Engle Division of Pediatric Cardiology
60,000	Skin Cancer Foundation, New York, NY — continuing funding for research into vaccine to prevent malignant melanoma
50,000	Iona College, New Rochelle, NY — endowment funding
50,000	Rockefeller University, New York, NY — continued funding for research for the study of Synapsin II
25,000	Catholic Charities of the Archdiocese of New York, New York, NY

Baker Trust, George F.

CONTACT
Rocio Suarez
Executive Director
George F. Baker Trust
767 Fifth Ave., Ste. 2850
New York, NY 10153
(212) 755-1890

FINANCIAL SUMMARY
Recent Giving: $4,533,544 (1992); $1,289,733 (1991); $1,537,400 (1990)

Assets: $28,600,925 (1992); $27,420,528 (1991); $21,515,162 (1990)

EIN: 13-6056818

CONTRIBUTIONS SUMMARY
Donor(s): The trust was established in 1937 by the late George F. Baker , chairman of the First National Bank of New York.

Typical Recipients: • *Arts & Humanities:* Arts Appreciation, Ballet, Historic Preservation, History & Archaeology, Libraries, Museums/Galleries, Music, Performing Arts • *Civic & Public Affairs:* Clubs, Philanthropic Organizations, Public Policy, Safety, Urban & Community Affairs • *Education:* Business Education, Colleges & Universities, Engineering/Technological Education, International Studies, Private Education (Precollege), Special Education, Student Aid • *Environment:* Air/Water Quality, General, Resource Conservation, Wildlife Protection • *Health:* Children's Health/Hospitals, Diabetes, Emergency/Ambulance Services, Hospitals, Medical Rehabilitation, Medical Research • *International:* Human Rights • *Religion:* Churches, Religious Welfare • *Science:* Scientific Research • *Social Services:* At-Risk Youth, Community Service Organizations, Family Planning, People with Disabilities, Recreation & Athletics, Substance Abuse, Youth Organizations

Grant Types: capital, endowment, general support, professorship, project, and scholarship

Geographic Distribution: national, with emphasis on New York City

GIVING OFFICERS
Anthony K. Baker: trust

George F. Baker III: trust

Kane K. Baker: trust

Rocio Suarez: exec dir

APPLICATION INFORMATION
Initial Approach:

Applicants should send a brief description of the proposed project. There is no formal application form.

The initial letter should outline the proposed project, include the amount requested, list other sources of funding, and be signed by an authorized officer.

Board meetings are held in June and November. Applications may be sent any time.

Notification of grant approval occurs within six months following proposal receipt. No notice is sent to those applicants who do not receive funding.

Restrictions on Giving: No grants are made to individuals, or for scholarships, capital or endowment funds, fellowships, loans, or special projects.

OTHER THINGS TO KNOW
Citibank, N.A. is listed as a corporate trustee of the foundation.

PUBLICATIONS
Annual report

GRANTS ANALYSIS
Total Grants: $4,533,554

Number of Grants: 51

Highest Grant: $3,000,000

Average Grant: $30,671*

Typical Range: $5,000 to $60,000

Disclosure Period: 1992

Note: Average grant figure excludes the foundation's highest grant totaling $3,000,000. Recent grants are derived from a 1992 Form 990.

RECENT GRANTS

Library
3,000,000	Dartmouth University, Hanover, NH — for renovation and improvement of the Baker Library and for support for programs of the Baker and Berry library facilities
50,000	Society for the Preservation of Long Island Antiquities, Setauket, NY — for an annex to the Cold Spring Harbor Library

General
250,000	Harvard University, Cambridge, MA — for the endowment of the George F. Baker Full Professorship in Russian/Soviet Studies at the Faculty of Arts and Sciences
200,000	Harvard University Graduate School of Business Administration, Cambridge, MA — support of new fitness and recreational sports facility
100,000	New York Zoological Society, New York, NY — to be applied to the Wildlife Crisis Campaign
60,000	Rollins College, Winter Park, FL — for the environmental studies program and the establishment of the "Baker Center for Environmental Studies"
60,000	Trinity College, Hartford, CT — for a new academic building to be used for the computing center, engineering and computer science, and mathematics departments

Baldwin Foundation, David M. and Barbara

CONTACT
David M. Baldwin
President
David M. and Barbara Baldwin Fdn.
c/o McGrath, Doyle, & Phair
150 Broadway
New York, NY 10038
(212) 571-2300

FINANCIAL SUMMARY
Recent Giving: $190,930 (fiscal 1993); $137,090 (fiscal 1992); $130,670 (fiscal 1991)

Assets: $3,525,754 (fiscal 1993); $3,257,901 (fiscal 1992); $2,644,803 (fiscal 1991)

Gifts Received: $302,800 (fiscal 1992)

Fiscal Note: In fiscal 1992, contributions were received from David M. Baldwin.

EIN: 13-3391384

CONTRIBUTIONS SUMMARY
Donor(s): David M. Baldwin

Typical Recipients: • *Arts & Humanities:* Dance, Libraries, Performing Arts, Public Broadcasting, Theater • *Civic & Public Affairs:* Botanical Gardens/Parks, Clubs, Community Foundations, General, Safety, Urban & Community Affairs, Women's Affairs • *Education:* Colleges & Universities, General, Private Education (Precollege), Secondary Education (Private), Student Aid • *Environment:* General • *Health:* AIDS/HIV, Alzheimers Disease, Cancer, Clinics/Medical Centers, Diabetes, Emergency/Ambulance Services, Eyes/Blindness, Health Organizations, Heart, Hospices, Hospitals, Hospitals (University Affiliated), Medical Research, Mental Health, Prenatal Health Issues, Research/Studies Institutes, Single-Disease Health Associations • *International:* Human Rights, International Relief Efforts, Missionary/Religious Activities • *Religion:* Churches, Religious Organizations, Religious Welfare • *Social Services:* Child Welfare, Community Service Organizations, Family Planning, General, People with Disabilities, Recreation & Athletics, Shelters/Homelessness, Substance Abuse, United Funds/United Ways, YMCA/YWCA/YMHA/YWHA, Youth Organizations

Grant Types: general support

Geographic Distribution: focus on NJ, NY, and PA

GIVING OFFICERS
Barbara Baldwin: vp, trust

David M. Baldwin: trust, pres

Nicholas Jacangelo: treas *PHIL AFFIL* vp: Jessie Smith Noyes Foundation

APPLICATION INFORMATION
Initial Approach: Send brief letter describing program. Include a description of organization, amount requested, purpose of funds sought, recently audited financial statement, and proof of tax-exempt status. There are no deadlines.

GRANTS ANALYSIS
Total Grants: $190,930

Number of Grants: 49

Highest Grant: $100,000

Typical Range: $50 to $25,000

Disclosure Period: fiscal year ending November 30, 1993

Note: Recent grants are derived from a fiscal 1993 Form 990.

RECENT GRANTS

General
100,000	PMI Strang Clinic
25,000	Skidmore College, Saratoga Springs, NY
11,700	American Paralysis Association, Springfield, NJ
5,250	Christ Church in Short Hills, Short Hills, NJ
5,000	Environmental Learning Center, Vero Beach, FL

Bank of New York Company, Inc.

Revenue: $4.25 billion
Employees: 13,847
Headquarters: New York, NY
SIC Major Group: Bank Holding Companies and State Commercial Banks

CONTACT
Patricia D. Stuebe
Assistant Vice President
Bank of New York Company, Inc.
48 Wall St.
10th Fl.
New York, NY 10286
(212) 495-1730

FINANCIAL SUMMARY
Recent Giving: $4,680,000 (1995 est.); $3,672,000 (1994); $3,200,000 (1993)

Fiscal Note: All contributions are made directly by the company.

CONTRIBUTIONS SUMMARY
Typical Recipients: • *Arts & Humanities:* Arts Appreciation, Arts Associations & Councils, Arts Centers, Historic Preservation, Libraries, Literary Arts, Museums/Galleries, Music, Opera, Performing Arts, Public Broadcasting • *Civic & Public Affairs:* Business/Free Enterprise, Civil Rights, Economic Development, Housing, Zoos/Aquariums • *Education:* Education Associations, Elementary Education (Private), Minority Education, Private Education (Precollege) • *Environment:* General • *Health:* Health Organizations, Hospitals, Nursing Services, Single-Disease Health Associations • *Social Services:* Child Welfare, Community Service Organizations, Family Services, Shelters/Homelessness, Substance Abuse, United Funds/United Ways, Volunteer Services, Youth Organizations

Grant Types: award, capital, conference/seminar, emergency, employee matching gifts, endowment, fellowship, general support, and multiyear/continuing support

Note: Employee matching gift ratio: 1 to 1.

Geographic Distribution: most grants restricted to company operating areas in the state of New York, New Jersey, and Delaware

Operating Locations: CA, CT, DE (Newark), FL, NJ, NY (Harrison, New York, Utica)

CORP. OFFICERS
John Carter Bacot: *B* Utica NY 1933 *ED* Hamilton Coll AB 1955; Cornell Univ LLB 1958 *CURR EMPL* chmn, ceo: Bank NY Co Inc *CORP AFFIL* dir: Atlantic Reinsurance Co, Bank NY Intl Corp, Centennial Ins Co, Home Life Ins Co; trust: Atlantic Mutual Ins Co *NONPR AFFIL* chmn bd trusts: Hamilton Coll; chmn, trust: NY Clearing House Assn; dir: Assn Bank Holding Cos, Downtown-Lower Manhattan Assn, Philharmonic Symphony Soc NY; mem: Assn Reserve City Bankers, Counc Foreign Rels, New York City Partnership, NY Bar Assn, Pilgrims US; vchmn, dir: Un Way New York City *CLUB AFFIL* Econ NY, Links, Montclair GC, Union *PHIL AFFIL* mem fin comm, dir: Josiah Macy, Jr. Foundation

Alan Richard Griffith: *B* Mineola NY 1941 *ED* Lafayette Coll BA 1964; CUNY MBA 1971 *CURR EMPL* sr exec vp, vchmn: Bank NY Co Inc *NONPR AFFIL* trust: Amyotrophic Lateral Sclerosis Assn, Nature Conservancy *CLUB AFFIL* Univ NY

Thomas A. Renyi: *B* Passaic NJ 1946 *ED* Rutgers Univ BA 1967; Rutgers Univ MBA 1968 *CURR EMPL* pres, dir: Bank NY Co Inc

GIVING OFFICERS
Patricia D. Stuebe: *CURR EMPL* asst vp: Bank NY Co Inc

APPLICATION INFORMATION
Initial Approach: *Initial Contact:* letter with proposal attached *Include Information On:* goals and financial statement for organization and project; tax identification number *Deadlines:* none, but prefers to receive proposals in the fall *Note:* Regional branches have discretionary budgets for contributions to local nonprofits. The headquarters office handles requests from statewide groups.

Restrictions on Giving: *Company does not support religious or political organizations or individuals.

OTHER THINGS TO KNOW
Majority of recipients are organizations the company traditionally supports, though policy does not restrict first-time requests.

GRANTS ANALYSIS
Total Grants: $3,672,000

Typical Range: $1,000 to $10,000

Disclosure Period: 1994

Note: Recent grants are derived from a 1992 grants list.

RECENT GRANTS

Library
New York Public Library, New York, NY

General
52 Association for the Handicapped
African American Men of Westchester, White Plains, NY
Anderson School, Stratsburg, NY
Arden Hill Hospital, Goshen, NY
Asian Americans for Equality, New York, NY

Bankers Trust Company / BT Foundation

Employees: 12,500
Parent Company: Bankers Trust New York Corp.
Revenue: $7.5 billion
Headquarters: New York, NY
SIC Major Group: State Commercial Banks

CONTACT
Page Chapman III
President
BT Foundation
280 Park Ave., Fl. 19 W
New York, NY 10017
(212) 454-3500

FINANCIAL SUMMARY
Recent Giving: $8,700,000 (fiscal 1995 est.); $8,706,853 (fiscal 1994); $7,422,452 (fiscal 1993)

Assets: $21,795 (fiscal 1991)

Fiscal Note: Totals include contributions from the BT Foundation, direct corporate giving, domestic subsidiary giving, and international subsidiary giving. In 1994, foundation giving totaled $6,706,853, direct corporate giving totaled $838,500, domestic subsidiary giving totaled $61,500, and international subsidiary giving totaled $1,100,000.

EIN: 13-3321736

CONTRIBUTIONS SUMMARY
Typical Recipients: • *Arts & Humanities:* Libraries, Literary Arts, Museums/Galleries, Opera, Performing Arts • *Civic & Public Affairs:* Economic Policy, Employment/Job Training, General, Public Policy, Urban & Community Affairs, Women's Affairs • *Education:* Business Education, Colleges & Universities, Minority Education, Public Education (Precollege), Science/Mathematics Education • *Environment:* General • *Health:* Hospitals • *International:* International Relations • *Social Services:* Community Service Organizations, United Funds/United Ways, Youth Organizations

Grant Types: capital, challenge, employee matching gifts, general support, operating expenses, and project

Note: Employee matching gift ratio: 2 to 1.

Nonmonetary Support Types: donated equipment

Note: The company donates furniture and computers; the value of such support is not available.

Geographic Distribution: primarily New York City; also in company operating locations in the United States and overseas

Operating Locations: CA (Los Angeles), CT (Greenwich), DE (Wilmington), FL (West Palm Beach), IL (Chicago), ME (Harborside), NJ (Jersey City), NY (New York), OR (Portland), TN (Nashville), TX (Houston)

CORP. OFFICERS
Douglas B. Kidd: *CURR EMPL* mgr dir pub aff: Bankers Trust Co

Charles Steadman Sanford, Jr.: *B* Savannah GA 1936 *ED* Univ GA BA 1958; Univ PA Wharton Sch MBA 1960 *CURR EMPL* chmn: Bankers Trust NY Corp *CORP AFFIL* chmn: Bankers Trust Co; dir: JC Penney Co Inc, Mobil Corp *NONPR AFFIL* dir: Counc Fin Aid Ed; mem: Assn Reserve City Bankers, Bus Counc, Bus Roundtable, Counc Foreign Rels; overseer: Univ PA Wharton Sch Bus; trust: Comm Econ Devel, Univ GA Fdn

GIVING OFFICERS
Robert Blank: secy

Page Chapman III: pres, dir

Gary S. Hattem: treas

Margaret P. Johnson: vp

Sandra West: asst secy

APPLICATION INFORMATION
Initial Approach: *Initial Contact:* brief letter and proposal *Include Information On:* brief statement of purpose of organization, amount being requested, and purpose for which funds are sought; IRS determination letter of 501(c)(3) status; tax ID number; current overall budget and project budget; most recently audited form 990; report on the percentage of support derived from corporations, foundations, government agencies, membership, and earned income; list of current corporate and foundation support and level of support; list of all directors and trustees; if a renewal, a brief report on the use of the previous grant *Deadlines:* none

Restrictions on Giving: Bankers Trust does not support individuals, religious work of churches or sectarian organizations; fraternal, political, or veterans organizations; United Way recipients unless they provide a fund-raising waiver; endowment campaigns; legal advocacy; or areas outside programmatic foci such as elderly and senior citizen projects, animal welfare, national organizations concerned with a specific disease, and non-U.S.-targeted economic development. The foundation does not loan staff members for clerical assistance during fund-raising drives.

OTHER THINGS TO KNOW
The bank's Volunteer Assistance Fund allows employees to secure grants of up to $5000 for specific projects to benefit groups in which they serve as volunteers.

GRANTS ANALYSIS
Total Grants: $8,706,853

Typical Range: $10,000 to $75,000

Disclosure Period: fiscal year ending November 30, 1994

Note: Recent grants are derived from a fiscal 1993 annual report.

RECENT GRANTS
General
125,000	Local Initiatives Support Corporation, New York, NY
100,000	Fund for New York City Public Education, New York, NY
94,700	Sponsors for Educational Opportunities, New York, NY
83,000	Clearpool School, New York, NY
75,000	Abyssinian Development Corporation, New York, NY

Barth Foundation, Theodore H.

CONTACT
Irving P. Berelson
President
The Theodore H. Barth Foundation
45 Rockefeller Plaza, 20th Fl.
New York, NY 10111
Note: The foundation does not list a phone number.

FINANCIAL SUMMARY
Recent Giving: $907,913 (1993); $910,300 (1992); $731,225 (1991)

Assets: $20,916,501 (1993); $19,550,934 (1992); $18,924,739 (1991)

EIN: 13-6103401

CONTRIBUTIONS SUMMARY
Donor(s): The foundation was incorporated in 1953 by the late Theodore H. Barth .

Typical Recipients: • *Arts & Humanities:* Ballet, Dance, Libraries, Literary Arts, Museums/Galleries, Music, Opera, Performing Arts, Public Broadcasting, Visual Arts • *Civic & Public Affairs:* Botanical Gardens/Parks, Community Foundations, Economic Development, Legal Aid, Urban & Community Affairs, Zoos/Aquariums • *Education:* Arts/Humanities Education, Colleges & Universities, Education Reform, General, Legal Education, Science/Mathematics Education, Special Education • *Environment:* Air/Water Quality, General, Resource Conservation • *Health:* Clinics/Medical Centers, Health Funds, Health Organizations, Hospices, Hospitals, Nursing Services, Research/Studies Institutes, Single-Disease Health Associations, Speech & Hearing, Transplant Networks/Donor Banks • *International:* Foreign Arts Organizations • *Religion:* Churches, Religious Welfare • *Science:* Science Museums • *Social Services:* At-Risk Youth, Child Welfare, Community Centers, Community Service Organizations, Day Care, Family Services, Food/Clothing Distribution, People with Disabilities, Shelters/Homelessness, United Funds/United Ways, Youth Organizations

Grant Types: general support

Geographic Distribution: primarily New York and Massachusetts

GIVING OFFICERS

Irving P. Berelson: pres, treas, dir *B* 1916 *CURR EMPL* secy, dir: Barden Corp *CORP AFFIL* ptnr: Parker Chapin Flattau & Klimpl *NONPR AFFIL* pres-emeritus, dir: New York League Hard Hearing

Thelma D. Berelson: secy, dir

APPLICATION INFORMATION

Initial Approach:

The foundation requests a general letter of interest.

The foundation has no deadline for submitting proposals.

Restrictions on Giving: The foundation does not make grants to individuals.

GRANTS ANALYSIS

Total Grants: $907,913

Number of Grants: 107

Highest Grant: $100,000

Average Grant: $8,485

Typical Range: $1,000 to $25,000

Disclosure Period: 1993

Note: Recent grants are derived from a 1993 Form 990.

RECENT GRANTS

Library

25,000	New York Public Library, New York, NY — charitable

General

62,500	New York League for the Hard of Hearing, New York, NY — charitable
50,000	Tobey Health Systems, Wareham, MA — medical
32,500	Church of the Good Shepherd, Wareham, MA — religious
26,000	New York Law School, New York, NY — educational
25,000	Harvard Law School Fund, Cambridge, MA — educational

Bay Foundation

CONTACT

Robert W. Ashton
Executive Director and Secretary
Bay Foundation
17 W 94th St.
New York, NY 10025
(212) 663-1115

FINANCIAL SUMMARY

Recent Giving: $473,866 (1993); $491,166 (1992); $472,905 (1991)

Assets: $12,020,546 (1993); $11,179,388 (1992); $10,991,577 (1991)

EIN: 13-5646283

CONTRIBUTIONS SUMMARY

Donor(s): The Bay Foundation was established in 1950 by Charles Ulrick Bay and his wife, Josephine Bay. In his early years

as an entreprenuer, Charles U. Bay founded a company which specialized in the production and marketing of surgical bandages. His later interests included enterprises in the petroleum and securities industries. Following World War II, Mr. Bay was appointed U.S. Ambassador to Norway, a post he occupied for seven years.

After Mr. Bay's death, Josephine Bay became chairman of the board of American Export Lines and the first female president of a New York Stock Exchange member firm.

Typical Recipients: • *Arts & Humanities:* Arts Associations & Councils, Arts Centers, Film & Video, General, Historic Preservation, History & Archaeology, Libraries, Literary Arts, Museums/Galleries, Public Broadcasting, Theater • *Civic & Public Affairs:* Botanical Gardens/Parks, General, Municipalities/Towns, Native American Affairs, Zoos/Aquariums • *Education:* Arts/Humanities Education, Colleges & Universities, Education Reform, Elementary Education (Public), Engineering/Technological Education, Environmental Education, Private Education (Precollege), Public Education (Precollege), Science/Mathematics Education, Special Education • *Environment:* General, Resource Conservation, Wildlife Protection • *Health:* Medical Rehabilitation, Single-Disease Health Associations • *International:* International Environmental Issues, International Peace & Security Issues, International Relief Efforts • *Religion:* Religious Organizations, Religious Welfare • *Science:* Science Museums, Scientific Centers & Institutes, Scientific Labs, Scientific Research • *Social Services:* At-Risk Youth, Child Welfare, Community Centers, Community Service Organizations, Family Services, General, Youth Organizations

Grant Types: general support, project, and research

Geographic Distribution: national, with some preference for the East Coast

GIVING OFFICERS

Robert W. Ashton: exec dir, secy *B* Memphis TN 1937 *ED* Univ MI BA 1960; Vanderbilt Univ LLB 1964 *NONPR AFFIL* bd dirs: St Matthew's & St Timothy's Neighborhood Ctr; mem: Am Bar Assn, Assn Bar City New York, NY State Bar Assn; treas, dir: St Lukes Orchestra *PHIL AFFIL* exec dir: Paul (Josephine Bay and C Michael) Foundation; treas, dir: Wheeler Foundation

Frederick Bay: chmn, dir *PHIL AFFIL* pres, exec dir: Josephine Bay Paul and C. Michael Paul Foundation

Christopher Bay-Hansen: dir

Daniel Anthony Demarest: treas, dir *B* Plainfield NJ 1924 *ED* Harvard Univ AB 1948; Harvard Univ LLB 1951 *NONPR AFFIL* mem: Assn Bar City New York, Phi Beta Kappa *PHIL AFFIL* secy, treas: Josephine Bay Paul and C. Michael Paul Foundation; dir: Paul (Josephine Bay and C Michael) Foundation *CLUB AFFIL* Knickerbocker NY

Hans A. Ege: vp, dir *PHIL AFFIL* vp: Josephine Bay Paul and C. Michael Paul Foundation

Synnova Bay Hayes: pres, dir *PHIL AFFIL* chmn, dir: Josephine Bay Paul and C. Michael Paul Foundation

APPLICATION INFORMATION

Initial Contact: A letter of solicitation should be sent to the foundation's executive director.

Include Information On: Applicants should submit a brief description of the program for which grants are being sought, including objectives, budget, list of additional sources of support, and proof of tax-exempt status.

Deadlines: Letters may be submitted anytime. Proposals must be received by March 15 for the spring meeting; by September 1 for the fall meeting; and by December 15 for the winter meeting.

Review Process: The foundation has a six-member board of directors which decides on proposals.

Restrictions on Giving: Funding is not available for individuals, building campaigns, or nonpublicly supported charities.

OTHER THINGS TO KNOW

The foundation reports that first time grants generally fall within the $2,000 to $6,000 range.

PUBLICATIONS

Annual report

GRANTS ANALYSIS

Total Grants: $473,866

Number of Grants: 110

Highest Grant: $40,000

Average Grant: $4,308

Typical Range: $2,000 to $10,000

Disclosure Period: 1993

Note: Recent grants are derived from a 1993 Form 990.

RECENT GRANTS

Library

4,000	New York Public Library, New York, NY

General

30,000	Tufts University, Medford, MA
25,000	First Nations Development Institute, Falmouth, VA
25,000	Marylhurst College, Marylhurst, OR
25,000	University of Oklahoma Returning Gift Foundation, Norman, OK
15,000	Vanderbilt University, Nashville, TN

Benenson Foundation, Frances and Benjamin

CONTACT
Charles B. Benenson
President
Francis and Benjamin Benenson Foundation
708 Third Ave., 28th Fl.
New York, NY 10017
(212) 867-0990

FINANCIAL SUMMARY
Recent Giving: $1,200,000 (fiscal 1995 est.); $1,200,000 (fiscal 1994 est.); $804,915 (fiscal 1993)

Assets: $24,000,000 (fiscal 1995 est.); $24,000,000 (fiscal 1994 est.); $21,398,619 (fiscal 1993)

Gifts Received: $687,500 (fiscal 1993); $1,156,484 (fiscal 1992); $187,500 (fiscal 1991)

Fiscal Note: In 1993, contributions were received from the Dollar Land Syndicate.

EIN: 13-3267113

CONTRIBUTIONS SUMMARY
Donor(s): The foundation was established in 1983 by Charles B. Benenson.

Typical Recipients: • *Arts & Humanities:* Arts Associations & Councils, Arts Centers, Arts Institutes, Ethnic & Folk Arts, Film & Video, General, Libraries, Museums/Galleries, Opera, Performing Arts, Public Broadcasting, Theater • *Civic & Public Affairs:* General, Municipalities/Towns, Professional & Trade Associations, Urban & Community Affairs • *Education:* Colleges & Universities, Elementary Education (Private), Minority Education, Private Education (Precollege), Secondary Education (Public), Social Sciences Education, Student Aid • *Health:* AIDS/HIV, Cancer, Children's Health/Hospitals, Clinics/Medical Centers, Diabetes, Emergency/Ambulance Services, Health Organizations, Hospitals, Single-Disease Health Associations • *International:* Foreign Arts Organizations, Foreign Educational Institutions, International Relations, International Relief Efforts, Missionary/Religious Activities • *Religion:* Jewish Causes, Religious Organizations, Religious Welfare, Synagogues/Temples • *Science:* Scientific Organizations • *Social Services:* Child Welfare, Community Centers, Community Service Organizations, General, People with Disabilities, Recreation & Athletics, Shelters/Homelessness, Substance Abuse, United Funds/United Ways, Youth Organizations

Grant Types: emergency and general support

Geographic Distribution: focus on New York, NY

GIVING OFFICERS
Charles Benjamin Benenson: pres *B* New York NY 1913 *ED* Yale Univ BA 1930 *CURR EMPL* pres: Benenson Realty Co *CORP AFFIL* dir: Loews Corp *NONPR AFFIL* dir: Un Cerebral Palsy Assn; pres: Citizens Tax Counc; vp: Natl Realty Comm

PHIL AFFIL dir: Realty Foundation New York

Anthony J. Dinome: secy, treas

Emanuel Labin: vp

APPLICATION INFORMATION
Initial Approach:
The foundation requests applications be made in writing.

The foundation reports that the purpose of the grant and the amount must be stated in the proposal.

The foundation has no deadline for submitting proposals. 2 The foundation reports that it considers all proposals.

Restrictions on Giving: The foundation does not make grants to individuals.

GRANTS ANALYSIS
Total Grants: $804,915

Number of Grants: 90

Highest Grant: $200,000

Average Grant: $8,944

Typical Range: $1,000 to $65,000

Disclosure Period: fiscal year ending November 30, 1993

Note: Recent grants are derived from a 1993 Form 990.

RECENT GRANTS

Library

50,000	New York Public Library, New York, NY	

General

200,000	Yale University, New Haven, CT
100,000	United Jewish Appeal, New York, NY
50,000	Johns Hopkins University, Baltimore, MD
25,000	Duke University, Durham, NC
20,000	American Associates of Ben-Gurion University, New York, NY

Benetton Services Corp.

Sales: $3.2 million
Employees: 16
Headquarters: New York, NY
SIC Major Group: Apparel & Other Textile Products

CONTACT
Peter Fressola
Director of Communications
Benetton Retail Corporation
55 E 59th St.
New York, NY 10022
(212) 593-0290

FINANCIAL SUMMARY
Fiscal Note: Annual Giving Range: approximately $100,000

CONTRIBUTIONS SUMMARY
Company declined to provide information on charitable contributions.

Typical Recipients: • *Arts & Humanities:* Dance, Historic Preservation, Libraries, Museums/Galleries, Performing Arts • *Education:* Colleges & Universities, Private Education (Precollege), Public Education (Precollege) • *Health:* Hospitals, Medical Research, Single-Disease Health Associations • *Science:* Scientific Organizations • *Social Services:* Community Service Organizations, Domestic Violence, People with Disabilities, Refugee Assistance, Substance Abuse, United Funds/United Ways, Youth Organizations

Grant Types: general support

Nonmonetary Support Types: donated products

Geographic Distribution: no geographic restrictions

Operating Locations: NC, NY (New York)

CORP. OFFICERS
Luciano Benetton: *B* Treviso Italy 1935 *CURR EMPL* pres, dir: Benetton *CORP AFFIL* dir: Eliodona Publs

Carlo Tunioli: *CURR EMPL* vp, gen mgr: Benetton

GIVING OFFICERS
Peter Fressola: *CURR EMPL* commun dir: Benetton

APPLICATION INFORMATION
Initial Approach: Initial letter may be submitted at any time, but September is generally best. Applications should include a description of the organization, amount requested, and purpose for which funds are sought.

Restrictions on Giving: Benetton does not support political or lobbying groups.

GRANTS ANALYSIS
Typical Range: $10,000 to $25,000

Bingham Second Betterment Fund, William

CONTACT
William Bingham Second Betterment Fund
330 Madison Ave., Rm. 3500
New York, NY 10017
(212) 557-7700
Note: Inquiries should be sent to the attention of Maria Shasransky at the offices of Davidson Dawson & Clark, located at the address listed above.

FINANCIAL SUMMARY
Recent Giving: $1,100,000 (1994 est.); $1,100,565 (1993); $1,100,000 (1992)

Assets: $28,143,093 (1993); $26,754,763 (1992); $26,684,268 (1991)

EIN: 13-6072625

CONTRIBUTIONS SUMMARY
Typical Recipients: • *Arts & Humanities:* Arts Associations & Councils, General, History & Archaeology, Libraries, Museums/Galleries • *Civic & Public Affairs:* Chambers of Commerce, Community Foun-

dations, Employment/Job Training, General, Housing, Law & Justice, Municipalities/Towns, Philanthropic Organizations, Public Policy, Urban & Community Affairs, Women's Affairs • *Education:* Agricultural Education, Arts/Humanities Education, Colleges & Universities, Education Funds, Education Reform, Faculty Development, General, Health & Physical Education, Leadership Training, Literacy, Private Education (Precollege) • *Environment:* Air/Water Quality, General, Resource Conservation, Wildlife Protection • *Health:* Cancer, Clinics/Medical Centers, Diabetes, Health Funds, Health Organizations, Home-Care Services, Long-Term Care, Preventive Medicine/Wellness Organizations • *Religion:* Ministries • *Social Services:* Child Welfare, Community Service Organizations, Counseling, Family Planning, Family Services, Food/Clothing Distribution, Homes, Recreation & Athletics, Substance Abuse, Youth Organizations

Grant Types: capital, endowment, and general support

Geographic Distribution: Maine only

GIVING OFFICERS
William M. Throop, Jr.: trust

William B. Winship: trust

Carolyn S. Wollen: trust *CURR EMPL* vp, dir: Gould Academy

APPLICATION INFORMATION
Initial Approach:

The foundation requests applications be made in writing.

Proposals should include information about the organization, the purpose of the grant, and the amount requested for the project. In addition, the foundation requests a copy of the IRS letter confirming the organization's tax-exempt status.

Proposals should be submitted by the last day of February, May, August, and November.

Restrictions on Giving: The foundation does not make grants to individuals.

OTHER THINGS TO KNOW
The United States Trust Company of New York is the fund's corporate trustee.

GRANTS ANALYSIS
Total Grants: $1,100,565

Number of Grants: 47

Highest Grant: $100,000

Average Grant: $23,416

Typical Range: $5,000 to $25,000

Disclosure Period: 1993

Note: Recent grants are derived from a 1993 Form 990.

RECENT GRANTS

Library
12,000	MSAD 3 Trout Foundation — library project

General
100,000	University of New England, Biddeford, ME
82,485	Maine Community Foundation, Portland, ME
75,000	University of Maine at Farmington, Farmington, ME
61,800	Gould Academy, Bethel, ME
45,000	Maine-Dartmouth Family Practice Residency, Portland, ME

Blum Foundation, Edna F.

CONTACT
Jean L. Stern
Trustee
Edna F. Blum Foundation
Cradle Rock Rd.
Box 145
Pound Ridge, NY 10576
(914) 764-0451

FINANCIAL SUMMARY
Recent Giving: $187,700 (fiscal 1993); $137,000 (fiscal 1992); $149,999 (fiscal 1991)

Assets: $3,712,168 (fiscal 1993); $4,011,121 (fiscal 1992); $3,288,013 (fiscal 1991)

Gifts Received: $866,768 (fiscal 1991); $1,812,946 (fiscal 1990)

EIN: 13-3563460

CONTRIBUTIONS SUMMARY
Typical Recipients: • *Arts & Humanities:* Libraries, Museums/Galleries, Music, Theater • *Civic & Public Affairs:* Housing, Urban & Community Affairs • *Education:* Medical Education, Private Education (Precollege) • *Health:* Emergency/Ambulance Services, Home-Care Services • *Religion:* Religious Welfare • *Social Services:* Child Welfare, Community Service Organizations, Family Planning, People with Disabilities, Shelters/Homelessness, Youth Organizations

Grant Types: general support and project

Geographic Distribution: primarily New York City

GIVING OFFICERS
Jean L. Stern: trust

Robert A. Stern: trust

APPLICATION INFORMATION
Initial Approach: Send for application form. There are no deadlines.

GRANTS ANALYSIS
Total Grants: $187,700

Number of Grants: 14

Highest Grant: $30,000

Typical Range: $3,000 to $10,000

Disclosure Period: fiscal year ending July 31, 1993

Note: Recent grants are derived from a Fiscal 1993 Form 990.

RECENT GRANTS

Library
15,000	New York Public Library, New York, NY

General
28,000	Planned Parenthood, White Plains, NY
25,000	Visions, New York, NY
23,000	Children's Aid Society, New York, NY
19,250	Salvation Army, New York, NY
17,750	Hamilton Madison House, New York, NY

Bobst Foundation, Elmer and Mamdouha

CONTACT
Mamdouha S. Bobst
President
Elmer and Mamdouha Bobst Foundation
c/o Elmer Holmes Bobst Library, New York Univ./
70 Washington Sq. S
New York, NY 10012
(212) 998-2440

FINANCIAL SUMMARY
Recent Giving: $1,474,245 (1993); $1,374,150 (1992); $1,374,490 (1991)

Assets: $30,438,114 (1993); $32,621,836 (1992); $32,239,877 (1991)

Gifts Received: $30,630 (1993); $157,000 (1992)

Fiscal Note: In fiscal 1993, the foundation received cash from the terminated trust of Dorothy Kelly.

EIN: 13-2616114

CONTRIBUTIONS SUMMARY
Donor(s): The foundation was established in 1968 by the late Elmer H. Bobst .

Typical Recipients: • *Arts & Humanities:* History & Archaeology, Libraries, Museums/Galleries, Music, Opera, Performing Arts, Public Broadcasting • *Civic & Public Affairs:* Botanical Gardens/Parks, Community Foundations, Economic Development, Ethnic Organizations, General, Philanthropic Organizations • *Education:* Colleges & Universities • *Environment:* Resource Conservation • *Health:* AIDS/HIV, Cancer, Clinics/Medical Centers, Health Organizations, Heart, Hospices, Hospitals, Single-Disease Health Associations • *International:* Foreign Educational Institutions, Health Care/Hospitals, International Organizations, International Relief Efforts • *Religion:* Churches, Dioceses, Religious Organizations, Religious Welfare • *Social Services:* Animal Protection, Big Brother/Big Sister, Community Service Organizations, Crime Prevention, Food/Clothing Distribution, Recreation & Athletics, Youth Organizations

Grant Types: general support and research

Geographic Distribution: New York, NY, and Israel

GIVING OFFICERS
Farouk as-Sayid: dir

Mamdouha S. Bobst: pres, treas, dir

Raja Kabbani: dir

Arthur Joseph Mahon: secy *B* New York
NY 1934 *ED* Manhattan Coll BA 1955; NY
Univ JD 1958 *CURR EMPL* ptnr: Mudge
Rose Guthrie Alexander & Ferron *NONPR
AFFIL* bd dirs: Un Way Intl; chmn planned
giving comm: Archdiocese NY; dir: Skin
Disease Soc; mem: Assn Bar City New
York, DC Bar Assn, FL Bar Assn, Noel Fdn,
NY Bar Assn; mem comm trust & estate gift
plans: Rockefeller Univ; mem joint bd: NY
Hosp-Cornell Med Ctr; pres; dir: Royal Soc
Medicine Fdn; trust: Manhattan Coll; vchmn
bd overseers: Cornell Univ Med Coll *CLUB
AFFIL* India House, Sky *PHIL AFFIL* dir:
New York Society for the Advancement of
Cutaneous Biology and Medicine; trust:
Adrian and Jessie Archbold Charitable Trust

Mary French Rockefeller: dir *B* New York
NY 1910 *PHIL AFFIL* mem distribution
comm: NY Community Trust

Milton Curtiss Rose: dir *B* Cleveland OH
1904 *ED* Williams Coll AB 1927; Harvard
Univ LLB 1930 *CURR EMPL* ptnr: Mudge
Rose Guthrie Alexander & Ferrow *NONPR
AFFIL* bd dir vp sec: Mario Negri Inst Fdn;
bd overseers emeritus: Simons Rock; dir:
Royal Soc Medicine Fdn; life trust: Pfeiffer
Coll; mem: Am Bar Assn, Assn Bar City
New York, NY Bar Assn, NY County Law-
yers Assn; treas, dir: Margaret Kendrick
Blodgett Fdn; trust: Shaker Commun *CLUB
AFFIL* Century Assn, Grolier, Univ; mem:
Garret, Lenox

APPLICATION INFORMATION
Initial Approach:

The foundation requests applications be
made in writing.

The foundation requests applications include
information on the organization and the purpose of the grant.

The foundation has no deadline for submitting proposals.

Restrictions on Giving: The foundation
does not make grants to individuals.

PUBLICATIONS
Annual report and informational brochure including application guidelines.

GRANTS ANALYSIS
Total Grants: $1,474,245
Number of Grants: 47
Highest Grant: $900,000
Average Grant: $10,539*
Typical Range: $1,000 to $25,000
Disclosure Period: 1993

Note: Average grant figure excludes the two
highest grants totalling $1 million. Recent
grants are derived from a 1993 Form 990.

RECENT GRANTS

General
900,000	Animal Medical Center, New York, NY	
100,000	New York University, New York, NY	
80,000	Moslum Hospital Tripoli	
70,000	American Society for Beirut, New York, NY	
50,000	American Cancer Service, New York, NY	

Bodman Foundation

CONTACT
Joseph S. Dolan
Secretary and Executive Director
Bodman Foundation
767 Third Ave.
Fourth Floor
New York, NY 10017
(212) 644-0322

FINANCIAL SUMMARY
Recent Giving: $1,500,000 (1995 est.);
$1,500,000 (1994); $1,875,000 (1993)

Assets: $40,000,000 (1995 est.);
$39,234,069 (1994); $43,178,307 (1993)

EIN: 13-6022016

CONTRIBUTIONS SUMMARY
Donor(s): The Bodman Foundation was organized in 1945 by George M. Bodman , a
senior partner in the New York City brokerage firm of Cyrus J. Lawrence and Sons.
Both Mr. Bodman, who died in 1950, and
his wife, Louise C. Bodman, who died five
years later, were active in civic and charitable causes in New York City and Monmouth
County, NJ, during their lifetimes.

Typical Recipients: • *Arts & Humanities:*
Dance, Libraries, Museums/Galleries, Mu-
sic, Opera, Performing Arts • *Civic & Public
Affairs:* Asian American Affairs, Botanical
Gardens/Parks, Economic Development, Em-
ployment/Job Training, Housing, Nonprofit
Management, Philanthropic Organizations,
Public Policy, Urban & Community Affairs,
Zoos/Aquariums • *Education:* Arts/Humani-
ties Education, Colleges & Universities,
Education Reform, Elementary Education
(Private), Elementary Education (Public),
General, Medical Education, Minority Edu-
cation, Preschool Education, Private Educa-
tion (Precollege), Public Education
(Precollege), School Volunteerism, Sci-
ence/Mathematics Education, Special Educa-
tion, Student Aid • *Environment:* Air/Water
Quality, General, Resource Conservation,
Wildlife Protection • *Health:* Cancer, Clin-
ics/Medical Centers, Emergency/Ambulance
Services, Eyes/Blindness, Health Funds,
Health Organizations, Hospices, Hospitals,
Medical Rehabilitation, Medical Research,
Speech & Hearing • *International:* Interna-
tional Affairs • *Religion:* Religious Welfare
• *Science:* Science Museums, Scientific
Labs, Scientific Research • *Social Services:*
Child Welfare, Community Centers, Commu-
nity Service Organizations, Counseling, Do-
mestic Violence, Family Services,
Food/Clothing Distribution, Homes, People
with Disabilities, Recreation & Athletics,
Scouts, Senior Services, Shelters/Homeless-
ness, Substance Abuse, Youth Organizations

Grant Types: capital, endowment, general
support, multiyear/continuing support, and
scholarship

Geographic Distribution: primarily metropolitan New York City, and Monmouth
County, NJ

GIVING OFFICERS
Harry Albright: trust

Mary A. Braga: trust

Joseph S. Dolan: exec dir, secy *PHIL AF-
FIL* exec dir, secy: Achelis Foundation

Anthony Drexel Duke: trust *B* New York
NY 1918 *ED* Princeton Univ 1941 *NONPR
AFFIL* Battle Normandy Mus, Duke Univ,
Pom Pret Sch, US Naval Academy; chmn,
pres, fdr: Boys Harbor; mem: Natl Comm
Am Foreign Policy, Save the Children
CLUB AFFIL Beaver Dam, Maidstone,
Mashomack, Piping Rock, Racquet & Ten-
nis, River *PHIL AFFIL* trust: Achelis Foun-
dation

Peter Frelinghuysen: trust *B* New York NY
1916 *CURR EMPL* atty: Morris & McVeigh
CORP AFFIL secy: K O A Holdings Inc
NONPR AFFIL First vchmn: NY Eye Ear Infirmary *PHIL AFFIL* trust: Achelis Foundation; vp, dir: Frelinghuysen Foundation

John N. Irwin III: first vp, trust *B* 1954 *ED*
Princeton Univ 1976 *CURR EMPL* vp, mng
dir, dir: Hillside Indus Inc *PHIL AFFIL* first
vp, trust: Achelis Foundation; trust: Mrs.
Giles Whiting Foundation; mem adv bd:
Thomas J. Watson Foundation

Leslie Lenkowsky, PhD: trust *PHIL AFFIL*
trust: Achelis Foundation

Marguerite S. Nichols, MD: trust *PHIL AF-
FIL* trust: Achelis Foundation

Russell Parsons Pennoyer: second vp *B*
New York NY 1951 *ED* Harvard Univ BA
1974; Columbia Univ Sch Law JD 1982
CURR EMPL sr vp, gen counc & secy: Am
Exploration Co *CORP AFFIL* dir: Westerly
Film-Video Inc; sr vp, secy, gen couns:
Amex Oil Co *NONPR AFFIL* fellow: Pier-
pont Morgan Library; mem: Am Bar Assn,
Assn Bar City New York, Rockefeller Univ
Counc; trust: St Bernards Sch *PHIL AFFIL*
second vp, trust: Achelis Foundation

Mary Stone Phipps: trust *NONPR AFFIL*
mem-at-large, dir: Girl Scout Counc Greater
NY *PHIL AFFIL* trust: Achelis Foundation
CLUB AFFIL Colony, Links, Long Island
Wyandanch, Meadow Brook, Pilgrims, Pip-
ing Rock, Somerset

Mary Caslin Ross: exec dir, secy *B* New
York NY 1953 *ED* St Johns Univ BA 1975;
Manhattanville Coll MA 1986 *NONPR AF-
FIL* dir: Philanthropy Roundtable; lecturer:
New Sch Fundraising Inst; mem: Cold
Spring Harbor Fish Hatchery; vp, trust: ICD
Intl Ctr Disabled

Guy G. Rutherfurd: pres, treas, trust *B*
New York NY 1913 *ED* Princeton Univ BA
1938; Univ VA LLB 1942 *CURR EMPL*
ptnr: Morris & McVeigh *NONPR AFFIL*
mem: Assn Bar City New York, NY Bar
Assn; vp, dir: Lenox Hill Neighborhood
Assn *PHIL AFFIL* pres, treas, trust: Achelis
Foundation

APPLICATION INFORMATION
Initial Approach:

The foundation has no standard application
form. Proposals should be made in writing
and sent to the foundation. Introductory letters should be no longer than two pages.

527

All requests should include the history, purpose, and financial statement of the applying organization, as well as descriptions of current activities and programs. In addition, grant requests should contain names of board members, personnel involved in the project, purpose of the request, amount needed, and financial data or IRS information supporting the organization's tax-exempt status. Proposals should not exceed five pages.

Applications may be submitted anytime.

The foundation's trustees meet in May, September, and December to decide on grant requests. When the board makes final decisions on grants, it takes into account the recommendations of its professional staff. Personal interviews and site visits are arranged when necessary.

Restrictions on Giving: Two-year grants are given occasionally. No grants or loans are made to individuals. Generally, grant requests for conferences, travel, films, and publications are discouraged. The foundation generally will not fund national health and mental health organizations, performing arts groups, museums, or research and experimental projects. The foundation prefers to support well-established organizations.

OTHER THINGS TO KNOW

The foundation shares office space and staff with the Achelis Foundation, New York, NY.

PUBLICATIONS
Biennial report

GRANTS ANALYSIS

Total Grants: $1,500,000*

Number of Grants: 56*

Highest Grant: $70,000*

Average Grant: $26,786

Typical Range: $15,000 to $50,000

Disclosure Period: 1994

Note: Figures were supplied by the foundation. Recent grants are derived from a 1993 Form 990.

RECENT GRANTS

General
70,000	Children's Aid Society, New York, NY
60,000	Inner-City Scholarship Fund, New York, NY
50,000	American Museum of Natural History, New York, NY
50,000	ICD-International Center for the Disabled, New York, NY
50,000	National Center for Disability Services, Albertson, NY

Booth Ferris Foundation

CONTACT
Robert J. Murtagh
Trustee
Booth Ferris Foundation
c/o Morgan Guaranty Trust Company of New York
60 Wall St., 46th Fl.
New York, NY 10260
(212) 809-1630

FINANCIAL SUMMARY
Recent Giving: $6,400,000 (1994 est.); $6,024,000 (1993); $6,897,000 (1992)

Assets: $165,101,340 (1993); $155,294,016 (1992); $151,924,900 (1991)

EIN: 13-6170340

CONTRIBUTIONS SUMMARY
Donor(s): The foundation began operations in 1957, through trusts established by Mrs. Chancie Ferris Booth (d. 1957) and from the estate of Willis H. Booth (d. 1958). The combined trusts created the Booth Ferris Foundation in 1964. For many years, Willis Booth served as vice president of Guaranty Trust Company (now Morgan Guaranty Trust Company), and acted as trustee for many different corporations.

Typical Recipients: • *Arts & Humanities:* Arts Funds, Arts Institutes, Ballet, Film & Video, Libraries, Literary Arts, Museums/Galleries, Music, Public Broadcasting, Theater • *Civic & Public Affairs:* Asian American Affairs, Botanical Gardens/Parks, Economic Development, Employment/Job Training, General, Housing, Municipalities/Towns, Nonprofit Management, Professional & Trade Associations, Urban & Community Affairs, Women's Affairs • *Education:* Arts/Humanities Education, Business Education, Colleges & Universities, Education Funds, Education Reform, Engineering/Technological Education, Faculty Development, General, Private Education (Precollege), Science/Mathematics Education, Social Sciences Education, Vocational & Technical Education • *Environment:* Air/Water Quality, General • *Health:* Children's Health/Hospitals, Emergency/Ambulance Services, Eyes/Blindness, Health Organizations, Hospitals, Research/Studies Institutes • *International:* International Peace & Security Issues • *Religion:* Ministries, Religious Organizations, Religious Welfare, Seminaries • *Science:* Science Museums • *Social Services:* Child Welfare, Community Centers, Community Service Organizations, Day Care, Family Planning, Family Services, Food/Clothing Distribution, People with Disabilities, Recreation & Athletics, Shelters/Homelessness, Substance Abuse, Youth Organizations

Grant Types: capital and project

Geographic Distribution: national, with emphasis on New York City

GIVING OFFICERS
Robert J. Murtagh: trust

APPLICATION INFORMATION
Initial Approach:

A grant proposal should be sent to the foundation office.

In addition to a grant proposal, applicants should send an annual report and financial data, including a current budget and the most recent audited financial statement.

The trustees meet every two to three months. Grant proposals may be submitted any time.

Restrictions on Giving: The foundation does not give support to organizations operating outside the United States, individuals, federated campaigns, educational institutions for scholarships and fellowships for unrestricted endowments, to social service and cultural programs outside the New York City metropolitan area, or for specific diseases and disabilities, or individual research.

OTHER THINGS TO KNOW
Interviews will be granted only after proposals are received and in cases in which the trustees deem it will be helpful. The foundation tries to inform applicants promptly if there is a possibility for funding.

Morgan Guaranty Trust Company of New York serves as corporate trustee for the foundation.

PUBLICATIONS
Annual report

GRANTS ANALYSIS
Total Grants: $6,024,000

Number of Grants: 107

Highest Grant: $150,000

Average Grant: $56,299

Typical Range: $15,000 to $150,000

Disclosure Period: 1993

Note: Recent grants are derived from a 1993 Form 990.

RECENT GRANTS

Library
100,000	Bronx Educational Services, Bronx, NY — library renovations
100,000	Brooklyn Historical Society, Brooklyn, NY — library modernization
100,000	Heritage College, Toppenish, WA — construction of library and learning center
100,000	New York Public Library, New York, NY — restorations of the reference collections
50,000	Johns Hopkins University, Baltimore, MD — library acquisitions

General
150,000	Fund for New York City Public Education, New York, NY — new visions program
150,000	Goddard Riverside Community Center, New York, NY — OPTIONS program
100,000	American Red Cross, Washington, DC — Mississippi River Flood Relief

| 100,000 | Appalachian Ministries Resource Center, S. Charleston, WV — educational resource center |
| 100,000 | Carleton College, Northfield, MN — construction math and computer science building |

Bowne Foundation, Robert

CONTACT
Dianne Kangisser
Executive Director
Robert Bowne Fdn.
345 Hudson St.
New York, NY 10014
(212) 924-5500

FINANCIAL SUMMARY
Recent Giving: $499,700 (1993); $457,550 (1992); $412,500 (1991)

Assets: $10,479,565 (1993); $9,495,385 (1992); $8,855,594 (1991)

Gifts Received: $75,000 (1993); $75,000 (1992); $310,981 (1991)

Fiscal Note: In 1993, contributions were received from Thomas O. Stanley ($50,000) and Bowne of New York City ($25,000).

EIN: 13-2620393

CONTRIBUTIONS SUMMARY
Donor(s): Edmund A. Stanley, Jr., and members of the Stanley family

Typical Recipients: • *Arts & Humanities:* Arts Associations & Councils, General, History & Archaeology, Libraries, Museums/Galleries • *Civic & Public Affairs:* Economic Development, Employment/Job Training, General, Hispanic Affairs, Housing, Municipalities/Towns, Philanthropic Organizations, Public Policy, Urban & Community Affairs, Women's Affairs • *Education:* Arts/Humanities Education, Colleges & Universities, General, Literacy, Science/Mathematics Education, Special Education, Vocational & Technical Education • *Religion:* Churches, Religious Organizations, Religious Welfare • *Social Services:* At-Risk Youth, Child Welfare, Community Centers, Community Service Organizations, Family Services, Recreation & Athletics, Shelters/Homelessness, Youth Organizations

Grant Types: general support, multi-year/continuing support, operating expenses, project, and seed money

Geographic Distribution: primarily New York, NY, especially the boroughs outside Manhattan

GIVING OFFICERS
Douglas F. Bauer: secy, treas *B* Lackawanna NY 1942 *ED* Princeton Univ AB 1964; Harvard Univ JD 1967 *CURR EMPL* secy, gen coun: Bowne & Co *NONPR AFFIL* couns: Friends of Princeton Univ Lib; mem: Am Bar Assn, Am Soc Corp Secys, Fellows Pierpont Morgan, Natl Assn Corp Dirs, NY Bar Assn, NY City Bar Assn; vp,trust: Bowne (Robert) House Historical Soc *CLUB AFFIL* Grolier, Princeton

Suzanne Carothers: trust

Dianne Kangisser: vp, exec dir, trust

Richard Harvey Koontz: trust *B* Bedford PA 1940 *ED* PA St Univ BS 1962 *CURR EMPL* pres, ceo, dir: Bowne & Co

Rosa N. Lavergne: trust

Edmund Allport Stanley, Jr.: pres, chmn, trust *B* New York NY 1924 *ED* Princeton Univ AB 1949 *CURR EMPL* chmn exec comm: Bowne & Co *PHIL AFFIL* pres, exec dir, trust: Town Creek Foundation

Jennifer Stanley: vp, trust *PHIL AFFIL* vp: Town Creek Foundation

Franz von Ziegesar: vp, trust *B* Sao Paulo Brazil 1924 *ED* Yale Univ BA 1948 *CURR EMPL* chmn, ceo, dir: Bowne & Co *CORP AFFIL* dir: Southeastern Indus, Zarn Inc

APPLICATION INFORMATION
Initial Approach: First send letter requesting guidelines. There are no deadlines. Decisions are made within three months.

Restrictions on Giving: Does not support religious organizations, primary or secondary schools, colleges or universities, except when some aspect of their work is an integral part of a program supported by the foundation. Also does not support individuals, capital campaigns, or endowments.

PUBLICATIONS
Informational Brochure

GRANTS ANALYSIS
Total Grants: $499,700

Number of Grants: 32

Highest Grant: $48,000

Typical Range: $3,000 to $44,500

Disclosure Period: 1993

Note: Recent grants are derived from a 1993 Form 990.

RECENT GRANTS

General

48,000	Research Foundation of City University of New York, New York, NY — for Institute for Literacy Studies
44,500	Research Foundation of City University of New York, New York, NY — for Literacy Assistance Center
40,500	Brooklyn in Touch Information Center, Brooklyn, NY
32,000	Project Reach Youth, New York, NY
25,000	Academy for Educational Development, Washington, DC

Bristol-Myers Squibb Company / Bristol-Myers Squibb Foundation Inc.

Revenue: $11.98 billion
Employees: 49,500
Headquarters: New York, NY
SIC Major Group: Pharmaceutical Preparations, Food Preparations Nec, Surgical & Medical Instruments, and Manufacturing Industries Nec

CONTACT
Cindy Johnson
Grants Administrator
Bristol-Myers Squibb Foundation, Inc.
345 Park Ave.
New York, NY 10154
(212) 546-4331
Note: Requests also may be addressed to Mr. John L. Damonti, vice president, Bristol-Myers Squibb Foundation, at the same address. Mr. Damonti's telephone number is (212) 546-4566.

FINANCIAL SUMMARY
Recent Giving: $24,968,741 (1995 est.); $24,873,192 (1994); $22,175,636 (1993)

Assets: $2,320,620 (1993); $2,841,710 (1992); $11,090,316 (1991)

Gifts Received: $12,000,000 (1993); $2,000,000 (1992)

Fiscal Note: Above figures include donations by company, foundation, subsidiaries and divisions. Above figures exclude nonmonetary support. In 1993, foundation giving totaled $12,606,155. In 1992, gifts were received from Bristol-Myers Squibb Co. staff ($625,416) and E. R. Squibb & Sons ($468,268). Additional funds were received from subsidiaries.

EIN: 13-3127947

CONTRIBUTIONS SUMMARY
Typical Recipients: • *Arts & Humanities:* Arts Associations & Councils, Arts Centers, Arts Funds, Arts Institutes, Arts Outreach, Historic Preservation, Libraries, Museums/Galleries, Music, Opera, Performing Arts, Public Broadcasting, Theater • *Civic & Public Affairs:* African American Affairs, Botanical Gardens/Parks, Business/Free Enterprise, Economic Development, Employment/Job Training, General, Housing, Law & Justice, Professional & Trade Associations, Public Policy, Safety, Urban & Community Affairs, Zoos/Aquariums • *Education:* Business Education, Colleges & Universities, Education Funds, Education Reform, Medical Education, Minority Education, Private Education (Precollege), Student Aid • *Environment:* Air/Water Quality, General • *Health:* AIDS/HIV, Cancer, Children's Health/Hospitals, Diabetes, Emergency/Ambulance Services, Health Organizations, Heart, Hospitals, Medical Rehabilitation, Medical Research, Medical Training, Nutrition • *International:* Foreign Educational Institutions, International Organizations, International Relations • *Religion:* Jewish Causes, Religious Welfare

• *Science:* Scientific Research • *Social Services:* Community Service Organizations, Food/Clothing Distribution, People with Disabilities, Shelters/Homelessness, Substance Abuse, United Funds/United Ways, Youth Organizations

Grant Types: employee matching gifts, general support, project, and research

Note: Employee matching gift ratio: 1 to 1. Since 1977, the company has committed more than $45 million through the Unrestricted Medical Research Grants Programs. Grant and awards are made to renowned research institutions for research in cancer, neuroscience, cardiovascular, nutrition, orthopedics, pain and infectious diseases.

Nonmonetary Support Types: donated products

Note: Value of nonmonetary support is unavailable. Contact local operating facilities for local nonmonetary giving. Contact Frank Cifuni at the Edison, NJ, facility for international product requests.

Geographic Distribution: principally near operating locations, nationally and internationally

Operating Locations: CT (Stamford, Wallingford), IN (Evansville, Warsaw), NC (Greensboro, Morrisville), NJ (Cranbury, Hillside, New Brunswick, Plainsboro, Princeton, Skillman), NY (Buffalo, New York, Syracuse), PR (Barceloneta, Mayaguez, Humacao), WA (Seattle)

CORP. OFFICERS

Richard Lee Gelb: *B* New York NY 1924 *ED* Yale Univ BA 1945; Harvard Univ MBA 1950 *CURR EMPL* chmn: Bristol-Myers Squibb Co *CORP AFFIL* dir: Bessemer Securities Corp, NY Life Ins Co, NY Times Co *NONPR AFFIL* charter trust: Phillips Acad Andover; dir: Lincoln Ctr Performing Arts; mem: Bus Counc, Bus Roundtable, Counc Foreign Rels; ptnr: New York City Partnership; trust: Comm Econ Devel, NY Racing Assn; vchmn bd overseers: Meml Sloan Kettering Cancer Ctr; vchmn, trust: New York City Police Fdn *PHIL AFFIL* chmn, don: Lawrence M. Gelb Foundation; dir: New York Times Co. Foundation

Charles Andreas Heimbold, Jr.: *B* Newark NJ 1933 *ED* Villanova Univ BA 1954; Hague Acad Intl Law 1959; Univ PA LLB 1960; NY Univ LLM 1966 *CURR EMPL* pres, ceo, dir: Bristol-Myers Squibb Co *CORP AFFIL* sr vp: Teck Corp *NONPR AFFIL* chmn bd overseers: Univ PA Law Sch; dir: Health Indus Mfrs Assn, Phoenix House; mem: Assn Bar City New York, Assn Professional Engrs, Canadian Inst Mining & Metallurgy; mem bd visit: Friends Biddle Law Lib; trust: Intl House, Sarah Lawrence Coll *CLUB AFFIL* Riverside YC

Michael F. Mee: *B* 1943 *ED* Bentley Coll 1966; Univ MN MBA *CURR EMPL* sr vp, cfo: Bristol-Myers Squibb Co

John Skule: *CURR EMPL* vp: Bristol-Myers Squibb Co

GIVING OFFICERS

John L. Damonti: vp corp contributions

Richard Lee Gelb: chmn, dir *CURR EMPL* chmn: Bristol-Myers Squibb Co *PHIL AFFIL* chmn, don: Lawrence M. Gelb Foundation; dir: New York Times Co. Foundation (see above)

Cindy Johnson: grants admin

Claire Payawal: mgr

APPLICATION INFORMATION

Initial Approach: *Initial Contact:* brief letter or proposal *Include Information On:* brief statement of history, goals, and accomplishments to date; amount requested; purpose for which funds are sought; list of current funding sources; recently audited financial statement; current year's operating budget; current annual report; list of board members; proof of tax-exempt status; most recent IRS Form 990 *Deadlines:* by October 1; organizations should not submit more than one grant application in a 12-month period

Restrictions on Giving: The foundation does not support individuals; political, fraternal, social, or veterans organizations; religious or sectarian activities, unless they benefit entire community; organizations funded through federated campaigns; endowments; or courtesy advertising.

In general, grants for specific public broadcasting programs or films are not considered.

GRANTS ANALYSIS

Total Grants: $12,606,155

Number of Grants: 1,624

Highest Grant: $2,000,000

Average Grant: $5,000*

Typical Range: $1,000 to $10,000

Disclosure Period: 1993

Note: Figures are for foundation only. Average grant figure was provided by the company. Recent grants are derived from a 1993 Form 990.

RECENT GRANTS

Library

25,000	New York Public Library, New York, NY

General

2,000,000	Princeton University Trustees, Princeton, NJ
520,000	United Way Tri-State, New York, NY
245,383	National Merit Scholarship Corporation, Evanston, IL
225,000	Morehouse School of Medicine, Atlanta, GA
200,000	New American Schools Development Corporation, Arlington, VA

Brooks Foundation, Gladys

CONTACT
Jessica L. Rutledge
Administrative Assistant
Gladys Brooks Foundation
226 7th St., Ste. 101
Garden City, NY 11530
(516) 746-6103

FINANCIAL SUMMARY
Recent Giving: $1,000,000 (1995 est.); $1,000,000 (1994 approx.); $1,000,000 (1993 approx.)

Assets: $25,000,000 (1995 est.); $25,000,000 (1994 approx.); $25,000,000 (1993 approx.)

EIN: 13-2955337

CONTRIBUTIONS SUMMARY
Donor(s): The foundation was established in 1981 by the late Gladys Brooks Thayer .

Typical Recipients: • *Arts & Humanities:* Libraries, Museums/Galleries • *Civic & Public Affairs:* General • *Education:* Business Education, Colleges & Universities, Medical Education, Secondary Education (Private) • *Health:* Children's Health/Hospitals, Hospitals, Medical Research, Single-Disease Health Associations • *International:* Missionary/Religious Activities • *Religion:* Religious Organizations • *Science:* Observatories & Planetariums • *Social Services:* People with Disabilities, Youth Organizations

Grant Types: capital, endowment, and scholarship

Geographic Distribution: limited to Connecticut, Delaware, Maine, Massachusetts, New Hampshire, New Jersey, New York, Pennsylvania, Rhode Island, and Vermont

GIVING OFFICERS
James J. Daly: mem bd govs
Harman Hawkins: chmn bd govs
Thomas O. Morris: mem bd govs
Jessica L. Rutledge: admin asst

APPLICATION INFORMATION
Initial Approach:

The foundation requests applicants obtain a formal application form from the foundation.

The deadline for submitting formal applications is June 1.

Restrictions on Giving: As a matter of policy, the foundation will make grants only to private, publicly supported, nonprofit, tax-exempt organizations. Grant applications will only be considered if outside funding (including governmental) is not available; or, if the project will be largely funded by the grant and will not be part of a larger project; or, if the funds will be used for capital projects, including equipment or endowments. In addition, grant applications will only be considered for major expenditures, generally between $50,000 and $100,000. The board follows the practice of determining, at the beginning of each calendar year, a limited scope of activities for which it will consider grant applications for that year.

The foundation does not make grants to individuals or to support research projects.

PUBLICATIONS
Program policy statement and an annual report including application guidelines

GRANTS ANALYSIS
Total Grants: $1,018,700

Number of Grants: 23

Highest Grant: $100,000

Average Grant: $44,291

Typical Range: $5,000 to $50,000

Disclosure Period: 1992

Note: Recent grants are derived from a 1992 Form 990.

RECENT GRANTS

Library
10,000	Oceanic Free Library, Rumson, NJ
5,000	Friends of the Shelter Island Public Library Society, Shelter Island, NY

General
100,000	Colby College, Waterville, ME
100,000	College of Physicians and Surgeons of Columbia University, New York, NY
100,000	National Center for Disability Services, Albertson, NY
100,000	Presbyterian Hospital in the City of New York, New York, NY
100,000	Riverview Foundation, Rumson, NJ

Burchfield Foundation, Charles E.

CONTACT
John E. Palmer
Attorney
Charles E. Burchfield Fdn.
c/o Cohen & Swados
70 Niagara St.
Buffalo, NY 14202
(716) 856-4600

FINANCIAL SUMMARY
Recent Giving: $121,500 (1993); $112,000 (1992); $1,869,775 (1991)

Assets: $2,223,664 (1993); $2,367,692 (1992); $2,373,263 (1991)

Gifts Received: $235,000 (1993)

Fiscal Note: In 1993, contributions were received in form of paintings.

EIN: 16-6073522

CONTRIBUTIONS SUMMARY
Donor(s): the late Charles E. Burchfield

Typical Recipients: • *Arts & Humanities:* Arts Centers, Arts Institutes, History & Archaeology, Libraries, Museums/Galleries, Music • *Civic & Public Affairs:* General, Law & Justice, Safety • *Education:* Colleges & Universities, Education Funds, Private Education (Precollege), Religious Educa-

tion, Secondary Education (Private), Student Aid • *Health:* Clinics/Medical Centers, Medical Research, Respiratory, Single-Disease Health Associations • *Religion:* Bible Study/Translation, Churches, Ministries, Religious Organizations, Religious Welfare • *Social Services:* Child Welfare, Community Centers, Community Service Organizations, Day Care, United Funds/United Ways, Youth Organizations

Grant Types: capital, multiyear/continuing support, operating expenses, and scholarship

Geographic Distribution: focus on NY, CA, and DE

GIVING OFFICERS
C. Arthur Burchfield: pres, dir

Violet P. Burchfield: dir

George Hill: dir

Sally B. Hill: vp, dir

Phyllis S. Mustain: dir

Robert D. Mustain: trust, secy

APPLICATION INFORMATION
Initial Approach: Send brief letter describing program. There are no deadlines.

PUBLICATIONS
Annual Report

GRANTS ANALYSIS
Total Grants: $121,500

Number of Grants: 76

Highest Grant: $190,220

Typical Range: $1,000 to $69,000

Disclosure Period: 1993

Note: Recent grants are derived from a 1993 Form 990.

RECENT GRANTS

General
190,220	Lutheran Film Association, New York, NY
170,800	Lutheran High School Association, Maspeth, NY
132,000	Amarillo Wesley Community Center, Amarillo, TX
125,120	Child
122,587	Popper-Keizer Advanced School, Santa Cruz, CA

Burden Foundation, Florence V.

CONTACT
Eliza Rossman
Executive Director
Florence V. Burden Foundation
10 E. 53rd St., 32nd Floor
New York, NY 10022
(212) 872-1150

FINANCIAL SUMMARY
Recent Giving: $688,113 (1993); $831,368 (1992); $612,206 (1991)

Assets: $12,904,685 (1993); $14,464,543 (1992); $12,556,052 (1991)

Gifts Received: $300 (1992)

EIN: 13-6224125

CONTRIBUTIONS SUMMARY
Donor(s): The foundation was established by Florence Vanderbilt Burden in 1967, two years before her death. Mrs. Burden had been involved in philanthropic activities throughout her life. Her son, William A. M. Burden, managed the foundation until 1973 when a full-time executive director was employed. Several members of the Burden family continue to serve on the foundation's board.

Typical Recipients: • *Arts & Humanities:* Arts Centers, Ballet, Dance, Libraries, Performing Arts, Public Broadcasting, Theater • *Civic & Public Affairs:* Employment/Job Training, General, Law & Justice, Public Policy, Urban & Community Affairs, Women's Affairs • *Education:* Colleges & Universities, Community & Junior Colleges, Education Reform, General, Literacy, Private Education (Precollege), Public Education (Precollege), Secondary Education (Private), Student Aid • *Environment:* Air/Water Quality • *Health:* AIDS/HIV, Alzheimers Disease, Clinics/Medical Centers, Geriatric Health, Health Organizations, Hospices, Hospitals, Long-Term Care, Single-Disease Health Associations, Transplant Networks/Donor Banks • *Religion:* Churches, Religious Welfare, Social/Policy Issues • *Social Services:* Child Welfare, Community Service Organizations, Crime Prevention, Delinquency & Criminal Rehabilitation, Domestic Violence, Family Planning, Family Services, Senior Services, Substance Abuse, Youth Organizations

Grant Types: project, research, and seed money

Geographic Distribution: national, with emphasis on New York

GIVING OFFICERS
Carter Burden: dir, mem exec comm

Edward P. H. Burden: dir, co-chair

Floebelle F. Burden: dir

Jean Prussing Burden: dir *B* Waukegan IL 1901 *ED* Univ Chicago BA 1936 *NONPR AFFIL* mem: Academy Am Poets, Authors Guild, Poetry Soc Am

Margaret L. Burden: dir, don daughter

Norah M. Burden: dir

Ordway Partridge Burden: vp, dir *B* New York NY 1944 *ED* Harvard Univ AB 1966; Harvard Univ MBA 1968; Harvard Univ Law Sch 1969-1971 *CURR EMPL* ptnr: William Am Burden Co *NONPR AFFIL* chmn, fdr, mem: Law Enforcement Assistance Fdn; fdr, chmn, mem: Natl Law Enforcement Counc; mem: Intl Assn Chiefs Police, Natl Sheriffs Assn; mem, dir: Natl Crime Prevention Counc; mem natl sponsoring comm: Natl Law Enforcement Officers Meml Fund *CLUB AFFIL* mem: Capitol Hill, Metropolitan

S. Carter Burden III: dir

Susan L. Burden: secy, treas, dir

Wendy Burden: dir

William A. M. Burden IV: dir

Frederick C. Childs: dir

Margaret Burden Childs: co-chair, dir

Barbara Reynolds Greenberg: exec dir *B* Boston MA 1947 *ED* Boston Univ BA 1974; Univ CT MSW 1974 *NONPR AFFIL* bd dir: NY Regional Assn Grantmakers; mem: Am Soc Aging; mem adv comm: Washington Bus Group Health

Florence C. MacDonald: dir

Eliza Rossman: exec dir

APPLICATION INFORMATION
Initial Approach:

Applicants should begin the grant-seeking process by requesting an annual report and then submitting a brief concept paper of not more than five pages.

Ideally, the concept paper will include a description of the problem, the project goals, objectives, and implementation plan. The paper should also outline the ways in which the project is innovative and will advance knowledge and practice or change public policy, how success will be evaluated, and the amount of funding needed.

The foundation reports no application deadlines.

If the foundation can consider funding the project, it will send the applicant a grant application. If not, the foundation will notify the applicant in writing.

The foundation evaluates each grant application, paying special attention to the caliber and competence of the people who will carry out the project, ways to evaluate its success, and the feasibility and cost of disseminating results. The foundation plays an active role in helping to shape grant applications in order to increase their productivity. Members of the board of directors often visit the prospective grantee before awarding a grant.

Restrictions on Giving: The foundation does not normally consider endowments or grants to individuals. The foundation does not provide funding for general support, operating expenses, or building construction costs.

OTHER THINGS TO KNOW
The foundation reports that it also makes grants for applied research and demonstration, and dissemination and replication grants.

PUBLICATIONS
Annual report

GRANTS ANALYSIS
Total Grants: $688,113

Number of Grants: 85

Highest Grant: $41,000

Average Grant: $8,095

Typical Range: $2,000 to $15,000

Disclosure Period: 1993

Note: Recent grants are derived from a 1993 Form 990.

RECENT GRANTS
General
41,000   National Crime Prevention Council, Washington, DC

40,000   Hetrick-Martin Institute, New York, NY

38,826   Brookdale Center on Aging, New York, NY

35,000   Survivors of Domestic Abuse, New York, NY

31,844   Chelsea School Department/Chelsea High School, Chelsea, MA

Calder Foundation, Louis

CONTACT
Barbara Sommer
Grant Program Manager
Louis Calder Foundation
230 Park Ave., Rm. 1525
New York, NY 10169
(212) 687-1680

FINANCIAL SUMMARY
Recent Giving: $4,260,000 (fiscal 1994); $5,222,600 (fiscal 1993); $5,174,750 (fiscal 1992)

Assets: $123,419,053 (fiscal 1993); $115,297,278 (fiscal 1992); $112,637,738 (fiscal 1991)

EIN: 13-6015562

CONTRIBUTIONS SUMMARY
Donor(s): The foundation was established in 1951 by Louis Calder . Mr. Calder, who was chairman of the board of Perkins-Goodwin Co., died in 1963. The foundation was funded by gifts from Mr. Calder during his lifetime and later by a residuary bequest in his will.

Typical Recipients: • *Arts & Humanities:* Arts Outreach, Libraries, Public Broadcasting • *Civic & Public Affairs:* Housing, Urban & Community Affairs • *Education:* Afterschool/Enrichment Programs, Arts/Humanities Education, Colleges & Universities, Elementary Education (Private), Leadership Training, Literacy, Minority Education, Private Education (Precollege), Public Education (Precollege), Special Education, Student Aid • *Health:* AIDS/HIV, Children's Health/Hospitals, Heart, Research/Studies Institutes • *Religion:* Churches, Religious Welfare • *Social Services:* Community Service Organizations, Family Services, Recreation & Athletics, YMCA/YWCA/YMHA/YWHA, Youth Organizations

Grant Types: challenge, general support, and project

Geographic Distribution: New York City

GIVING OFFICERS
Paul R. Brenner: trust *B* Yonkers NY 1942 *CURR EMPL* ptnr, atty: Kelley Drye & Warren

Peter D. Calder: trust *ED* Univ RI BA 1974; Univ RI MA 1977

Barbara Sommer: grants program mgr

APPLICATION INFORMATION
Initial Approach:

The foundation has no formal application form. Applicants should send a proposal, after determining suitability of request.

Proposals should consist of a one- to three-page letter with a concise statement of the purpose of the grant and the amount. The letter should be accompanied by a copy of IRS 501(c)(3) determination letter; brief description of the organization's history and activities; current list of organization members, trustees, directors, and officers; latest audited financial report; detailed project or organization budget; and an accounting of other foundation support. The foundation now accepts the New York Area Common Application Form.

Applications should be submitted no later than five months prior to the end of the applicant's fiscal year or by March 31, depending on which date is the earliest.

The trustees have no set schedule of meetings. Decisions are based upon the nature of the proposal, availability of funding, and the applicant's fiscal year.

Restrictions on Giving: Grants are not made to individuals, private foundations, government organizations, or publicly operated educational and medical institutions. Grants for endowments, building funds, capital development, and grants payable over several years are made occasionally.

OTHER THINGS TO KNOW
Chemical Bank Company is listed as a trustee of the foundation.

PUBLICATIONS
Annual report, grant guidelines

GRANTS ANALYSIS
Total Grants: $4,260,000

Number of Grants: 126

Highest Grant: $200,000

Average Grant: $33,813

Typical Range: $10,000 to $50,000

Disclosure Period: fiscal year ending October 31, 1994

Note: Recent grants are derived from a fiscal 1993 form 990.

RECENT GRANTS
Library
150,000   New York Public Library, New York, NY — final payment of a $500,000 grant to "adopt" the Sedgwick Branch Libary at 176th Street and University Avenue in the Bronx and support is renovation and reconstruction

General
250,000   Duke University, Durham, NC — final installment of a $250,000 two-for-one challenge grant to establish a $1,000,000 nonathletic scholarship endowment fund for students from the city of New York who show high academic promise and whose

250,000 Manhattan College, New York, NY — first installment of a $250,000 two-for-one challenge grant to establish a $750,000 nonathletic scholarship endowment fund for students from the city of New York who show high academic promise and whose families have demonstrated an acute financial need

200,000 Rockefeller University, New York, NY — support of the heart disease research

125,000 Fordham University, New York, NY — a one-to-one challenge grant not to exceed $125,000 to meet additional construction costs of the renovation of the Calder Center in Armonk

100,000 Clark University, Worcester, MA — first installment of a $250,000 two-for-one challenge grant to establish a $750,000 nonathletic scholarship endowment fund for students from the city of New York who show high academic promise and whose families have demonstrated an acute financial need

Canon U.S.A., Inc.

Sales: $4.0 billion
Employees: 5,000
Headquarters: Lake Success, NY
SIC Major Group: Industrial Machinery & Equipment, Instruments & Related Products, and Wholesale Trade—Durable Goods

CONTACT
David Farr
Senior Vice President, General Manager
Canon U.S.A., Inc.
One Canon Plz.
Lake Success, NY 11042
(516) 488-6700

CONTRIBUTIONS SUMMARY
Philanthropic program has traditionally not advertised its contributions activities. However, it is active in supporting community organizations in its headquarters area. In addition, company is a major sponsor of the PBS series "Innovation" and the Greater Hartford Open. With Hewlett-Packard, company has sponsored the Clean Earth Campaign, which recycles toner cartridges. See "Other Things" for more information.

Typical Recipients: • *Arts & Humanities:* Arts Centers, Historic Preservation, Libraries, Museums/Galleries, Performing Arts, Public Broadcasting • *Civic & Public Affairs:* Municipalities/Towns, Urban & Community Affairs, Women's Affairs • *Education:* Colleges & Universities, Elementary Education (Private) • *Health:* Health Organizations, Medical Research

• *Religion:* Religious Organizations • *Social Services:* Community Service Organizations, People with Disabilities, United Funds/United Ways, Youth Organizations

Nonmonetary Support Types: donated equipment and donated products
Operating Locations: NY (Lake Success)

CORP. OFFICERS
Ryuzaburo Kaku: *CURR EMPL* chmn: Canon USA
Haruo Murase: *CURR EMPL* pres, ceo: Canon USA

GIVING OFFICERS
David Farr: *CURR EMPL* sr vp, gen mgr corp commun: Canon USA

APPLICATION INFORMATION
Initial Approach: Send a brief introductory letter.

OTHER THINGS TO KNOW
Canon U.S.A. sponsors a "Clean Earth Campaign" in conjunction with the National Wildlife Federation and the Nature Conservancy. The program has several purposes: it helps to keep the environment clean by encouraging customers to return used toner cartridges to the company, free of charge, instead of disposing them in the trash; it conserves industrial resources by utilizing the recyclable portion of the cartridge to create new ones; and it helps to protect wildlife and the environment, because the National Wildlife Federation and the Nature Conservancey share equally a $1-per-cartridge contribution from Canon. For more information, contact Canon U.S.A., Inc., at 1-800-962-2708.

Carnahan-Jackson Foundation

CONTACT
David H. Carnahan
Trustee
Carnahan-Jackson Fdn.
PO Box 3326
Jamestown, NY 14702-3326
(716) 483-1015

FINANCIAL SUMMARY
Recent Giving: $740,301 (fiscal 1993); $531,116 (fiscal 1991); $533,146 (fiscal 1990)
Assets: $10,550,343 (fiscal 1993); $9,782,113 (fiscal 1991); $9,489,630 (fiscal 1990)
EIN: 16-6151608

CONTRIBUTIONS SUMMARY
Donor(s): the late Katharine J. Carnahan

Typical Recipients: • *Arts & Humanities:* Libraries • *Civic & Public Affairs:* Municipalities/Towns • *Education:* Colleges & Universities, Medical Education, Public Education (Precollege) • *Environment:* General • *Health:* Hospitals • *Religion:* Churches • *Social Services:* Child Welfare, Community Centers, Community Service Or-

ganizations, People with Disabilities, United Funds/United Ways, Youth Organizations
Grant Types: capital, general support, project, scholarship, and seed money
Geographic Distribution: focus on Chautauqua County, NY

GIVING OFFICERS
Fleet Trust Co: trust
David H. Carnahan: trust

APPLICATION INFORMATION
Initial Approach: Send a brief letter of inquiry. Include a description of organization, amount requested, purpose of funds sought, recently audited financial statement, and proof of tax-exempt status.
Restrictions on Giving: Does not support individuals.

PUBLICATIONS
Application guidelines, grants list

GRANTS ANALYSIS
Total Grants: $740,301
Typical Range: $3,000 to $15,000
Disclosure Period: fiscal year ending July 31, 1993
Note: Recent grants are derived from a fiscal 1991 Form 990. No grants list was provided 1993.

RECENT GRANTS
Library
12,035 James Prendergast Library Association, Jamestown, NY

General
120,000 Chautauqua Institution, Chautauqua, NY
45,000 Jamestown Audubon Society, Jamestown, NY
30,000 United Way, Jamestown, NY
25,000 YMCA, Jamestown, NY
20,000 Davis and Elkins College, Elkins, WV

Carnegie Corporation of New York

CONTACT
Dorothy Wills Knapp
Secretary
Carnegie Corporation of New York
437 Madison Ave.
New York, NY 10022
(212) 371-3200

FINANCIAL SUMMARY
Recent Giving: $55,000,000 (fiscal 1995 est.); $53,500,000 (fiscal 1994 approx.); $51,870,145 (fiscal 1993)
Assets: $1,140,000,000 (fiscal 1994); $1,170,000,000 (fiscal 1993); $1,051,666,391 (fiscal 1992)
EIN: 13-1628151

CONTRIBUTIONS SUMMARY
Donor(s): Andrew Carnegie was born in Scotland in 1835. He moved to the United

States 13 years later, beginning work as a bobbin boy in a cotton mill. After holding various jobs with Western Union and the Pennsylvania Railroad, Carnegie resigned in 1865 to establish his own business enterprises and eventually organized the Carnegie Steel Company. At the turn of the century, he sold his major Pittsburgh steel company to J. P. Morgan for $400 million.

Carnegie was one of the first wealthy Americans to believe that the well-to-do had a moral responsibility to assist the less fortunate. Carnegie's personal philanthropy began in his thirties with a large gift to his hometown of Dunfermline, Scotland. One of his earliest interests was the establishment of free public libraries throughout the United States, a cause to which he donated over $56 million. Other interests included adult education and education in the fine arts. Over the years, Carnegie established seven philanthropic and educational organizations in the United States, and several more in Europe to carry out these and other programs. In the United States, he established the Carnegie Foundation for the Advancement of Teaching, the Carnegie Institute (Pittsburgh), the Carnegie Mellon University (formed by the 1967 merger of the Mellon Institute and the Carnegie Institute of Technology), the Carnegie Endowment for International Peace, and the Carnegie Institution of Washington. Overseas, Mr. Carnegie established the Carnegie Trust for the Universities of Scotland to assist students and fund expansion and research, and the Carnegie Dunfermline and United Kingdom Trusts to improve social conditions in his native town, and the wellbeing of the people of Great Britain and Ireland through aid to community service, arts and crafts, and leadership training. Mr. Carnegie also established hero funds in the United States, the United Kingdom, and Europe to recognize heroic acts performed in peaceful occupations. In all, Mr. Carnegie's gifts and bequests totaled over $350 million.

Typical Recipients: • *Arts & Humanities:* Libraries, Public Broadcasting • *Civic & Public Affairs:* African American Affairs, Asian American Affairs, Economic Development, Hispanic Affairs, Law & Justice, Legal Aid, Native American Affairs, Nonprofit Management, Philanthropic Organizations, Professional & Trade Associations, Public Policy, Urban & Community Affairs, Women's Affairs • *Education:* Afterschool/Enrichment Programs, Colleges & Universities, Education Associations, Education Reform, Elementary Education (Public), General, Health & Physical Education, International Studies, Legal Education, Literacy, Medical Education, Minority Education, Preschool Education, Public Education (Precollege), Science/Mathematics Education, Secondary Education (Public), Special Education • *Environment:* General • *Health:* Adolescent Health Issues, Children's Health/Hospitals, Clinics/Medical Centers, Health Policy/Cost Containment, Health Organizations, Medical Research, Mental Health, Prenatal Health Issues, Public

Health • *International:* Foreign Educational Institutions, Health Care/Hospitals, Human Rights, International Affairs, International Development, International Organizations, International Peace & Security Issues, International Relations, Missionary/Religious Activities, Trade • *Science:* Scientific Centers & Institutes, Scientific Organizations • *Social Services:* At-Risk Youth, Child Welfare, Community Service Organizations, Crime Prevention, Day Care, Family Planning, Family Services, Substance Abuse, Volunteer Services, Youth Organizations

Grant Types: general support, project, research, and seed money

Geographic Distribution: national, many British Commonwealth nations, and Mexico

GIVING OFFICERS
Richard I. Beattie: trust, mem fin & admin comm *B* New York NY 1939 *CURR EMPL* ptnr: Simpson Thatcher & Bartlett *PHIL AFFIL* dir: Henry R. Kravis Foundation

Richard Celeste: trust

James Pierpont Comer: trust, mem nominating comm *B* East Chicago IN 1934 *ED* IN Univ AB 1956; Howard Univ MD 1960; Univ MI MS 1964 *CORP AFFIL* dir: CT Energy Corp; trust: CT Savings Bank *NONPR AFFIL* assoc dean: Yale Univ Sch Medicine; co-dir: Greater New Haven Black Family Roundtable; consult: Joint Commn Mental Health Children, Natl Commn Causes Prevention Violence, Natl Inst Mental Health; dir: Natl Counc Effective Schs, Yale Afro-Am House; dir sch devel program: Yale Child Study Ctr; mem: Alpha Omega Alpha, Alpha Phi Alpha, Am Academy Child Adolescent Psychiatry, Am Academy Child Psychiatry, Am Orthopsychiatric Assn, Am Psychiatric Assn, Black Coalition New Haven, Black Psychiatrists Am, NAACP, Natl Med Assn, Natl Mental Health Assn; mem ad hoc adv comm: CT Res Commn; mem adv comm adolescent pregnancy prevention: Childrens Defense Fund; mem adv counc: Natl Comm Citizens Ed; mem professional adv counc: Natl Assn Mental Health; pupil svcs: Baldwin-King Sch Project; trust: Albertus Magnus Coll, CT St Univ, Dixwell Soul Station

Eugene H. Cota-Robles: vchmn, trust, nominating comm

Barbara Denning Finberg: exec vp, program chmn (special projects) *B* Pueblo CO 1929 *ED* Stanford Univ BA 1949; Am Univ Beirut MA 1951 *NONPR AFFIL* dir: Consortium Advancement Pvt Higher Ed, Hole Wall Gang Camp Fund, Indus Sector, Investor Responsibility Res Ctr; mem: Am Ed Res Assn, Counc Foreign Rels, Soc Res Child Devel; mem adv comm: Radcliffe Coll Henry A Murray Res Ctr *CLUB AFFIL* Cosmopolitan

Jeanmarie Conte Grisi: treas *B* Queens NY 1958 *ED* St Johns Univ BS 1980 *NONPR AFFIL* mem: Am Inst CPAs

David A. Hamburg: pres, trust, mem nominating comm *B* Evansville IN 1925 *ED* IN Univ MD 1947 *CURR EMPL* pres: Carnegie Corp *NONPR AFFIL* dir: Mt Sinai Hosp, Rockefeller Univ; mem: Alpha Omega Al-

pha, Am Academy Arts Sciences, Am Assn Advancement Science, Am Psychiatric Assn, Am Psychosomatic Soc, Assn Res Nervous Mental Diseases, Natl Academy Sciences, Phi Beta Kappa; mem exec panel adv comm: Chief Naval Opers; sr adv: Ctr Social Policy Studies Israel; trust: Am Mus Natural History, Stanford Univ

Caryl Parker Haskins: hon trust, mem fin & admin comm *B* Schenectady NY 1908 *ED* Yale Univ PhB 1930; Harvard Univ PhD 1935 *CURR EMPL* pres, res dir, dir: Haskins Labs *NONPR AFFIL* adv trust: Rand Corp; fellow: Am Academy Arts Sciences, Am Assn Advancement Science, Am Physical Soc, Entomology Soc Am, Pierpont Morgan Library, Royal Entomology Soc; hon trust comm res & exploration: Natl Geographic Soc; mem: Am Philosophical Soc, Asia Soc, Audubon Soc, Biophysics Soc, British Assn Advancement Science, Delta Sigma Rho, Faraday Soc, Inst Intl Strategic Studies, Japan Soc, Linnean Soc, Metro Mus Art, Natl Academy Sciences, NY Academy Sciences, NY Botanical Garden, NY Zoological Soc, Omicron Delta Kappa, Phi Beta Kappa, Royal Soc Arts, Sigma Xi, WA Academy Sciences; mem bd visitors: Tulane Univ; mem counc: Am Mus Natural History; mem counc, trust: Woods Hole Oceanographic Inst; mem, mem counc: Save-the-Redwoods League; mem visitors comm: Harvard Univ, Johns Hopkins Univ; regent emeritus: Smithsonian Inst; trust: Asia Fdn, Counc Library Resources, Natl Humanities Ctr, Wildlife Preservation Trust Intl *CLUB AFFIL* Century, Cosmos, Lawn, Metropolitan, Mohawk, Somerset, St Botolph, Yale

Maria Teresa Thierstein Simoes-Ferreira Heinz: trust, mem nominating comm *B* Mozambique 1938 *ED* Univ Witwatersrand *NONPR AFFIL* chmn: Natl Counc Families & Television; trust: Yale Art Gallery; vchmn: Environmental Defense Fund *CLUB AFFIL* Bohemian, Fox Chapel GC, Pittsburgh GC *PHIL AFFIL* chmn: Heinz Family Foundation; trust: Howard Heinz Endowment, Winslow Foundation

James A. Johnson: trust, mem fin & admin comm *B* Benson MN 1943 *ED* Univ MN BA 1965; Princeton Univ MA 1968 *CURR EMPL* chmn, ceo, dir: Fed Natl Mortgage Assn *PHIL AFFIL* chmn: Fannie Mae Foundation

Helene Lois Kaplan: dir, mem fin & admin comm *B* New York NY 1933 *ED* Barnard Coll AB 1953; NY Univ JD 1967 *CURR EMPL* of couns: Skadden Arps Slate Meagher & Flom *CORP AFFIL* dir: Chem Bank, Chem Banking Corp, May Dept Stores, Met Life Ins Co, Mobil Corp, NYNEX Corp, Verde Exploration Ltd; ptnr: New York City Partnership; trust: Mitre Corp *NONPR AFFIL* chmn: Barnard Coll; dir: Catskill Ctr Conservation & Devel; mem: Am Academy Arts Sciences, Am Bar Assn, Am Philosophical Soc, Assn Bar City New York, Bretton Woods Comm, Carnegie Commn Science Tech & Govt, Carnegie Counc Adolescent Devel, Century Assn, Counc Foreign Rels, NY St Bar Assn, NY St Govs Task Force Life Law, Womens Forum; mem counc: Rockefeller Univ; trust: Am

Mus Natural History, Inst Advanced Studies, Mt Sinai Hosp Med Ctr, Mt Sinai Med Sch, Olive Free Library *CLUB AFFIL* Coffee House, Cosmopolitan *PHIL AFFIL* trust: John Simon Guggenheim Memorial Foundation; secy, dir: Golden Family Foundation; dir: Commonwealth Fund; trust: J. Paul Getty Trust

Thomas H. Kean: trust *B* New York NY 1935 *ED* Columbia Univ MA; Princeton Univ AB *CORP AFFIL* dir: Beneficial Corp *NONPR AFFIL* bd dir: World Wildlife Fund/Conservation Fdn; pres: Drew Univ *PHIL AFFIL* trust: Robert Wood Johnson Foundation

Dorothy Wills Knapp: secy

Vincent A. Mai: trust *CURR EMPL* pres, dir: AEA Investors *CORP AFFIL* ceo, dir: SOLA Holdings; pres, dir: PLI Investors (De Corp) *NONPR AFFIL* pres, dir: Friends Academy

Shirley M. Malcom: trust

Cynthia E Merritt: assoc secy

Newton Norman Minow: chmn, trust, mem fin & admin comm *B* Milwaukee WI 1926 *ED* Northwestern Univ BA 1949; Northwestern Univ JD 1950 *CURR EMPL* of couns: Sidley & Austin *CORP AFFIL* dir: AON Corp, Chicago Pacific Corp, Encyclopaedia Britannica, Foote Cone & Belding Commun, Manpower Inc, Sara Lee Corp, Tribune Co; mem intl adv bd: Pan Am World Airways *NONPR AFFIL* dir: Annenberg Washington Program; fellow: Am Bar Fdn; hon chmn, trust: Chicago Ed Television; lecturer: Northwestern Univ Medhill Sch Journalism; life trust: Chicago Symphony Orchestral Assn, Northwestern Univ; mem: Am Bar Assn, Chicago Bar Assn, IL Bar Assn, Northwestern Univ Alumni Assn; trust: Mayo Fdn, Univ Notre Dame *CLUB AFFIL* Century, Chicago, Commercial, Econ, Standard *PHIL AFFIL* treas, secy: J. Ira and Nicki Harris Foundation; vp, asst secy: Tiny Tiger Foundation

Henry James Muller: trust, mem nominating comm *B* Garmisch-Partenkirchen Germany 1947 *ED* Stanford Univ BA 1968 *CURR EMPL* mng editor: Time Magazine *NONPR AFFIL* mem, dir: Am Soc Magazine Editors; trust, faculty mem: Stanford Univ

Condoleezza Rice: trust *B* Birmingham AL 1955 *ED* Univ Denver BA 1974; Univ Notre Dame PhD 1981; Univ Notre Dame MA *CORP AFFIL* consultant: ABC News *NONPR AFFIL* dir: Soviet & Eastern European Affs; fellow: Hoover Inst; mem: Counc Foreign Rels, Natl Counc Humanities

Patricia L. Rosenfield: program chmn (human resources in developing countries)

David C. Speedie III: program chmn preventing deadly conflict

Vivien Stewart: program chmn (education & development of youth)

Laurence Alan Tisch: trust, mem fin & admin comm *B* New York NY 1923 *ED* NY Univ BS 1942; Univ PA MA 1943; Harvard Univ Law Sch *CURR EMPL* chmn, pres, ceo, dir: CBS Inc *CORP AFFIL* ceo, dir: Loews Corp; chmn: CNA Fin Corp; dir: Automatic Data Processing, Bulova Corp,

Getty Oil Co, RH Macy & Co Inc, NY Stock Exchange, Petrie Stores Corp *NONPR AFFIL* chmn bd trustees: NY Univ; dir: Un Jewish Appeal Fed Jewish Philanthropies NY; mem: Counc Foreign Rels, Mayors Comm Pub-Pvt Partnerships; trust: Metro Mus Art, NY Pub Lib *PHIL AFFIL* trust: Loews Foundation; sr vp, don: Tisch Foundation

Wilma S. Tisch: trust *PHIL AFFIL* dir, don wife: Tisch Foundation

APPLICATION INFORMATION
Initial Approach:

The corporation does not have application forms. Initial contact should be by letter.

The initial proposal should be a brief written statement describing the project's aims, methods, personnel, and the amount of financial support required. Corporation officers will request supplementary information or a personal discussion when necessary. The endorsement of the administrative head of the requesting institution need not be sent with the initial proposal, but it will be required before a favorable recommendation is made to the corporation's trustees.

There is no deadline for proposals.

Corporation officers consider each project. If they decide to evaluate a project for funding, a more developed project proposal will be requested.

Restrictions on Giving: The foundation does not operate scholarship, fellowship, or travel grant programs; it does not make grants for basic operating expenses, endowments, or facilities of educational or human services institutions; nor does it make program-related investments.

PUBLICATIONS
Annual report; general information pamphlet; "Carnegie Quarterly"

GRANTS ANALYSIS
Total Grants: $51,870,145

Number of Grants: 275*

Highest Grant: $1,665,700*

Average Grant: $188,619*

Typical Range: $25,000 to $300,000

Disclosure Period: fiscal year ending September 30, 1993

Note: Number of grants, average grant, and highest grant figures are based on a partial grants list. Number of grants and average grant are approximate. Recent grants are derived from a fiscal 1994 partial grants list.

RECENT GRANTS

Library
180,000　　Commission on Preservation and Access, Washington, DC — over 19 months, toward a study of the implications of technological developments for higher education and scholarly communication, with the University of Michigan School of Information and Library Studies

General

1,200,000	Project on Ethnic Relations — over two years, toward a project on ethnic conflict in Eastern Europe
900,000	Aspen Institute, Washington, DC — toward support of the Congressional International Program
800,000	Carnegie Endowment for International Peace, Washington, DC — over two years, toward projects on nonproliferation and regional security
700,000	Children's Defense Fund, Washington, DC — over three years, toward support of violence prevention, health, and child care projects
700,000	Quality Education for Minorities Network, Washington, DC

Carvel Foundation, Thomas and Agnes

CONTACT
Robert Davis
President
Thomas and Agnes Carvel Foundation
35 E Grassy Sprain Rd.
Yonkers, NY 10710
(914) 793-7300

FINANCIAL SUMMARY
Recent Giving: $1,000,000 (fiscal 1994 est.); $1,164,500 (fiscal 1993); $822,830 (fiscal 1992)

Assets: $17,000,000 (fiscal 1994 est.); $17,500,000 (fiscal 1993 approx.); $17,537,105 (fiscal 1992)

EIN: 13-2879673

CONTRIBUTIONS SUMMARY
Donor(s): The foundation was established in 1976 by Agnes Carvel and the late Thomas Carvel . The foundation also reports that it is affiliated with the International Institute of Health Foods, Inc.

Typical Recipients: • *Arts & Humanities:* Libraries, Museums/Galleries, Public Broadcasting • *Education:* Colleges & Universities, Elementary Education (Public), Special Education • *Health:* Children's Health/Hospitals, Clinics/Medical Centers, Emergency/Ambulance Services, Hospitals, Medical Research, Nutrition, Single-Disease Health Associations, Transplant Networks/Donor Banks • *Religion:* Dioceses • *Social Services:* Community Centers, Community Service Organizations, Recreation & Athletics, United Funds/United Ways

Grant Types: capital and general support

Geographic Distribution: New York, with a focus on Westchester County

GIVING OFFICERS

Robert H. Abplanalp: dir *B* 1922 *ED* Villanova Coll *CURR EMPL* chmn, pres, dir: Precision Valve Corp

Mildred Arcadipane: vp, secy, dir

Brendan T. Byrne: dir *CURR EMPL* treas, dir: New Jersey Sports & Exposition Authority

Agnes Carvel: chmn, dir

Robert Davis: pres, dir

William E. Griffin: dir *B* 1936 *CURR EMPL* pres: Griffin Litsen Coogan & Venaruso *CORP AFFIL* chmn, dir: Hudson Valley Holding Corp, Hudson Valley Natl Bank; secy, dir: Precision Valve Corp

Ann McHugh: vp, treas, dir

Salvador Molella: vp, dir

Malcolm Wilson: dir *B* New York NY 1914 *ED* Fordham Univ BA 1933; Fordham Univ LLB 1936 *CURR EMPL* of couns: Kent Hazzard Jaeger Wilson Freeman & Greer *CORP AFFIL* dir: Colin Svc Sys, Shearson Lehman Bros, Shearson Lehman Hutton Holdings *NONPR AFFIL* dir: Archdiocese NY, Catholic Youth Org, Farmers Mus, NY St Historical Assn; mem: Am Bar Assn, Ancient Order Hibernians, NY Farm Bur, NY St Bar Assn, Soc Friendly Sons St Patrick, Westchester County Bar Assn; trust: Natl Conf Christians & Jews *PHIL AFFIL* dir: Clark Foundation

APPLICATION INFORMATION

Initial Approach:

The foundation requests applications be made in writing.

The foundation requests that the application be supported by any additional information that may seem necessary.

Proposals should be submitted by October 1.

GRANTS ANALYSIS

Total Grants: $1,164,500

Number of Grants: 7

Highest Grant: $540,000

Average Grant: $104,083*

Typical Range: $75,000 to $150,000

Disclosure Period: fiscal year ending November 30, 1993

Note: Average grant excludes the highest grant of $540,000. Recent grants are derived from a fiscal 1993 grants list.

RECENT GRANTS

Library

150,000	Ardsley Public Library, Ardsley, NY — for the Thomas and Agnes Carvel Foundation Children's Library

General

540,000	St. Josephs Hospital — for the Thomas and Agnes Carvel Foundation Family Health Center
150,000	Yonkers Public Schools, Yonkers, NY — playgrounds
108,500	New York Blood Center, New York, NY — for the Thomas and Agnes Carvel
100,000	Foundation Bone Marrow Transplantation Research Project
	Archodiocese of Newark, Newark, NJ — for the Thomas and Agnes Carvel Foundation Children's Scholarship Fund
75,000	St. Agnes Hospital — for the Thomas and Agnes Carvel Foundation Children's Rehabilitation Center

---

CBS, Inc. / CBS Foundation

Revenue: $3.71 billion
Employees: 6,000
Headquarters: New York, NY
SIC Major Group: Television Broadcasting Stations and Radio Broadcasting Stations

CONTACT

Kathryn L. Edmundson
President, CBS Fdn.
The CBS Charitable Contributions Office
CBS, Inc.
51 W 52nd St.
New York, NY 10019
(212) 975-5791
Note: The company's World Wide Web address is http://www.cbs.com

FINANCIAL SUMMARY

Recent Giving: $1,455,137 (1993 approx.); $1,580,828 (1992); $1,627,750 (1991)

Assets: $9,893,977 (1993); $6,158,859 (1992); $7,512,176 (1991)

Gifts Received: $4,850,000 (1993); $727,728 (1990); $819,634 (1989)

Fiscal Note: Above figures are for foundation giving only and include matching gifts. CBS gives directly through their Corporate Contributions Program. Above figures exclude nonmonetary support.

EIN: 13-6099759

CONTRIBUTIONS SUMMARY

Typical Recipients: • *Arts & Humanities:* Dance, Ethnic & Folk Arts, History & Archaeology, Libraries, Museums/Galleries, Performing Arts, Theater • *Civic & Public Affairs:* Asian American Affairs, Economic Development, Ethnic Organizations, Hispanic Affairs, Native American Affairs, Nonprofit Management, Professional & Trade Associations, Safety, Urban & Community Affairs • *Education:* Colleges & Universities, Education Associations, Education Funds, Engineering/Technological Education, Faculty Development, General, Journalism/Media Education, Minority Education, Private Education (Precollege), Secondary Education (Public), Student Aid • *Health:* General, Research/Studies Institutes • *International:* International Affairs, International Peace & Security Issues • *Religion:* Churches, Religious Welfare • *Social Services:* Community Service Organizations, Day Care, Food/Clothing Distribution, United Funds/United Ways, Youth Organizations

Grant Types: employee matching gifts, general support, multiyear/continuing support, operating expenses, project, and scholarship

Nonmonetary Support Types: in-kind services

Geographic Distribution: primarily in areas of company operations, including New York, NY; Philadelphia, PA; Los Angeles, CA; Chicago, IL; Miami, FL; and St. Louis, MO; and to national programs

Operating Locations: CA (Los Angeles, San Francisco, Studio City), DC, FL (Miami, St. Petersburg), IL (Chicago), MA (Boston), MI (Detroit), MN (Minneapolis), MO (St. Louis), NY (New York), PA (Philadelphia), TX (Dallas, Fort Worth, Houston), WI (Green Bay)

Note: CBS Television Network operates 14 divisions in operating locations.

CORP. OFFICERS

Laurence Alan Tisch: *B* New York NY 1923 *ED* NY Univ BS 1942; Univ PA MA 1943; Harvard Univ Law Sch *CURR EMPL* chmn, pres, ceo, dir: CBS Inc *CORP AFFIL* ceo, dir: Loews Corp; chmn: CNA Fin Corp; dir: Automatic Data Processing, Bulova Corp, Getty Oil Co, RH Macy & Co Inc, NY Stock Exchange, Petrie Stores Corp *NONPR AFFIL* chmn bd trustees: NY Univ; dir: Un Jewish Appeal Fed Jewish Philanthropies NY; mem: Counc Foreign Rels, Mayors Comm Pub-Pvt Partnerships; trust: Metro Mus Art, NY Pub Lib *PHIL AFFIL* trust: Loews Foundation; sr vp, don: Tisch Foundation; trust, mem fin & admin comm: Carnegie Corporation of New York

GIVING OFFICERS

Michel Christian Bergerac: dir *B* Biarritz France 1932 *ED* Sorbonne Univ MA 1953; Univ CA Los Angeles MBA 1955 *CURR EMPL* chmn, ceo: MC Bergerac & Co *CORP AFFIL* dir: CBS Inc, ICN Pharmaceuticals, Intl Telecharge, Topps Co *NONPR AFFIL* trust: NY Zoological Soc

Joseph Castellano: secy

Kathryn L. Edmundson: pres

Henry Alfred Kissinger: dir *B* Fuerth Germany 1923 *ED* Harvard Univ AB 1950; Harvard Univ MA 1952; Harvard Univ PhD 1954 *CURR EMPL* fdr, chmn: Kissinger Assocs *NONPR AFFIL* mem: Am Acad Arts & Sci, Am Political Sci Assn, Counc Foreign Rels, Phi Beta Kappa; trust: Metro Mus Art *CLUB AFFIL* Bohemian San Francisco, Century, Metro DC, River New York City *PHIL AFFIL* chmn, dir: William S. Paley Foundation

Louis J. Rauchenberger, Jr.: treas

Linda Richter: asst treas

Franklin Augustine Thomas: dir *B* Brooklyn NY 1934 *ED* Columbia Univ BA 1956; Columbia Univ LLB 1963 *CORP AFFIL* dir: Aluminum Co Am, AT&T, CBS Inc, Citicorp/Citibank NA, Cummins Engine Co Inc

Preston Robert Tisch: chmn, dir *B* Brooklyn NY 1926 *ED* Bucknell Univ 1943-1944; Univ MI BA 1948 *CURR EMPL* pres, coceo: Loews Corp *CORP AFFIL* chmn: 48th St & 8th Ave Corp; chmn, dir: Loews Hotels Inc; dir: Bulova Corp, CBS Inc, Hasbro Inc,

Pathogenesis Corp, Rite Aid Corp; dir, chmn exec comm: CNA Fin Corp; owner, co-chmn & ceo: NY Football Giants Inc *NONPR AFFIL* chmn: New York City Partnership; chmn emeritus: NY Convention & Visit Bur; mem: Govs Bus Adv Counc NY, Quadrennial Comm Exec Legislative Judicial Salaries, Sigma Alpha Mu, Travel Indus Assn Am; mem travel tourism adv bd: US Dept Commerce; trust: NY Univ, Sales Mktg Execs Greater NY *CLUB AFFIL* Century CC, Harrison, Rye Racquet *PHIL AFFIL* trust: Loews Foundation; pres, don: Tisch Foundation

APPLICATION INFORMATION

Initial Approach: *Initial Contact:* one- to two- page letter of inquiry; do not send a full proposal *Include Information On:* description of the organization, its activities, and goals for the year; statement of purpose for which the funds are requested, proposed amount, and the expected outcome; budget for organization; attach separately or include in the letter: the program or project for which grant is requested, including a list of other sources of support; a list of applicant's board of directors or trustees; and organization's tax status designation under the Internal Revenue Code *Deadlines:* none

Restrictions on Giving: Company only supports charitable organizations with IRS 501(c)(3) tax-exempt status.

Does not support projects that are directly associated with the internal operations of divisions of CBS; organizations via advertisements in journals; endowment or capital costs, including construction, renovation, and/or equipment; internal programs and institutions; or individuals.

PUBLICATIONS
CBS Charitable Contributions Program

GRANTS ANALYSIS
Total Grants: $1,285,319

Number of Grants: 100

Highest Grant: $333,000

Average Grant: $12,853

Typical Range: $2,500 to $15,000

Disclosure Period: 1993

Note: Figures exclude $256,887 in matching grants. Grants to educational institutions range between $10,000 and $25,000. Recent grants are derived from a 1993 Form 990.

RECENT GRANTS

General

104,750	Center for Strategic Communication, Washington, DC
90,000	Foundation for Independent Higher Education, Stamford, CT
50,000	University of Michigan Burton R. Benjamin Fellowship, Ann Arbor, MI
30,000	Mt. St. Mary's College, Los Angeles, CA
25,000	Los Angeles Regional Foodbank, Los Angeles, CA

Central Hudson Gas & Electric Corp.

Revenue: $517.37 million
Employees: 1,327
Headquarters: Poughkeepsie, NY
SIC Major Group: Electric, Gas & Sanitary Services

CONTACT
Joseph J. DeVirgilio, Jr.
Vice President, Human Resources
Central Hudson Gas & Electric Corp.
284 S Ave.
Poughkeepsie, NY 12601
(914) 452-2000

FINANCIAL SUMMARY
Recent Giving: $250,000 (1991); $267,165 (1990)

CONTRIBUTIONS SUMMARY
Typical Recipients: • *Arts & Humanities:* Arts Associations & Councils, Arts Funds, Historic Preservation, Libraries, Performing Arts • *Civic & Public Affairs:* Economic Development, Housing, Philanthropic Organizations, Professional & Trade Associations • *Education:* Colleges & Universities, Science/Mathematics Education • *Health:* Hospices, Hospitals, Mental Health • *Science:* Science Exhibits & Fairs • *Social Services:* Child Welfare, Community Centers, Community Service Organizations, Domestic Violence, Food/Clothing Distribution, Homes, Senior Services, Shelters/Homelessness, United Funds/United Ways, Volunteer Services, Youth Organizations

Grant Types: capital and matching

Nonmonetary Support Types: donated equipment, loaned employees, and loaned executives

Geographic Distribution: corporate operating locations

Operating Locations: NY (Poughkeepsie)

CORP. OFFICERS
Paul J. Ganci: *B* New York NY 1938 *ED* Rensselaer Polytech Inst 1960; Union Coll 1969 *CURR EMPL* pres, coo, dir: Central Hudson Gas & Electric Corp *CORP AFFIL* dir: Mid Hudson Pattern Progress

John E. Mack III: *B* Poughkeepsie NY 1934 *ED* Siena Coll 1956; Siena Coll 1966 *CURR EMPL* chmn, ceo, dir: Central Hudson Gas & Electric Corp *CORP AFFIL* dir: NY Business Devel Corp *NONPR AFFIL* mem: Am Gas Assn, Edison Electric Inst, NY Gas Assn, NY Power Pool

Howard C. St. John: *CURR EMPL* vchmn, dir: Central Hudson Gas & Electric Corp

APPLICATION INFORMATION
Initial Approach: Send brief letter of inquiry, including a description of the organization, amount requested, purpose of funds sought, recently audited financial statements, and proof of tax-exempt status. There are no deadlines.

Restrictions on Giving: Does not support individuals, religious organizations for sec-

tarian purposes, organizations outside the company's service territory, or political or lobbying groups.

Chapman Charitable Corporation, Howard and Bess

CONTACT
Peter M. Dunn
Secretary and General Counsel
Howard and Bess Chapman Charitable Corporation
160 Main St.
Oneida, NY 13421-1675
Note: The foundation's books are in the care of Oneida Valley National Bank, Oneida, NY.

FINANCIAL SUMMARY
Recent Giving: $131,583 (fiscal 1993); $148,583 (fiscal 1992); $112,333 (fiscal 1991)

Assets: $2,555,593 (fiscal 1993); $2,459,263 (fiscal 1992); $2,449,481 (fiscal 1991)

Gifts Received: $586,846 (fiscal 1991); $1,711,860 (fiscal 1990)

Fiscal Note: In fiscal 1991, contributions were received from the estate of Howard Chapman.

EIN: 16-1373396

CONTRIBUTIONS SUMMARY
Donor(s): the donor is the estate of Howard Chapman

Typical Recipients: • *Arts & Humanities:* Arts Associations & Councils, Libraries • *Civic & Public Affairs:* General • *Education:* Colleges & Universities, Education Funds, General, Student Aid • *Health:* Hospitals • *Religion:* Churches • *Social Services:* Community Service Organizations, Food/Clothing Distribution, Senior Services, United Funds/United Ways, YMCA/YWCA/YMHA/YWHA, Youth Organizations

Grant Types: capital, general support, and scholarship

Geographic Distribution: focus on Oneida, NY, area

GIVING OFFICERS
Peter M. Dunn, Esq.: secy, gen coun

Robert H. Fearon, Jr.: vp

John G. Haskell: pres

Dr. Steven Schneeweiss: treas

Rowland Stevens: trust

APPLICATION INFORMATION
Initial Approach: Send a brief letter of inquiry. Include a description of organization, amount requested, purpose of funds sought, recently audited financial statement, and proof of tax-exempt status. There are no deadlines.

GRANTS ANALYSIS
Total Grants: $131,583

Number of Grants: 12

Highest Grant: $20,000

Typical Range: $2,000 to $5,000

Disclosure Period: fiscal year ending October 31, 1993

Note: Recent grants are derived from a fiscal 1993 Form 990.

RECENT GRANTS

Library

20,000	Oneida Library Building Fund, Oneida, NY — unrestricted
1,000	Sherrill Kenwood Free Library, Sherrill, NY — unrestricted

General

10,000	Cazenovia College, Cazenovia, NY — unrestricted
7,333	Tri-Valley YMCA, Oneida, NY — construct YMCA in Oneida
5,000	Christ Church, Sherrill, NY — unrestricted
5,000	Community Memorial Hospital, Hamilton, NY — unrestricted
5,000	Idyllic Foundation, Oneida, NY — unrestricted

Charina Foundation

CONTACT

Richard L. Menschel
President, Treasurer
Charina Fdn.
85 Broad St.
New York, NY 10004
(212) 902-6897

FINANCIAL SUMMARY

Recent Giving: $626,185 (fiscal 1993); $606,093 (fiscal 1992); $602,332 (fiscal 1991)

Assets: $13,048,442 (fiscal 1993); $12,215,238 (fiscal 1992); $11,987,716 (fiscal 1991)

EIN: 13-3050294

CONTRIBUTIONS SUMMARY

Donor(s): Richard L. Menschel, The Menschel Foundation

Typical Recipients: • *Arts & Humanities:* Arts Centers, Film & Video, Historic Preservation, History & Archaeology, Libraries, Museums/Galleries, Music, Performing Arts, Theater • *Civic & Public Affairs:* Botanical Gardens/Parks, Community Foundations, Economic Development, General, Housing, Philanthropic Organizations, Urban & Community Affairs • *Education:* Business Education, Colleges & Universities, Minority Education, Private Education (Precollege), Student Aid • *Environment:* Air/Water Quality, General • *Health:* Cancer, Hospitals, Medical Research, Single-Disease Health Associations • *International:*

International Relief Efforts • *Religion:* Jewish Causes, Religious Organizations, Synagogues/Temples • *Social Services:* Child Welfare, Community Centers, Community Service Organizations, Day Care, People with Disabilities, Scouts, Senior Services, Youth Organizations

Grant Types: endowment, general support, and scholarship

Geographic Distribution: focus on NY

GIVING OFFICERS

Richard Lee Menschel: pres, treas, dir *B* New York NY 1934 *ED* Syracuse Univ BS 1955; Harvard Univ MBA 1959 *CURR EMPL* ptnr: Goldman Sachs & Co *CORP AFFIL* dir: Kieckhefer Assocs *PHIL AFFIL* trust: Margaret T. Morris Foundation; dir: Horace W. Goldsmith Foundation

Ronay Menschel: secy, dir

Eugene P. Polk: dir *PHIL AFFIL* admin off, trust: J. W. Kieckhefer Foundation; trust: Margaret T. Morris Foundation

APPLICATION INFORMATION

Initial Approach: Send a brief letter of inquiry. Include a description of organization, amount requested, purpose of funds sought, recently audited financial statement, and proof of tax-exempt status.

Restrictions on Giving: Does not support individuals.

GRANTS ANALYSIS

Total Grants: $626,185

Number of Grants: 224

Highest Grant: $100,000

Typical Range: $500 to $10,000

Disclosure Period: fiscal year ending August 31, 1993

Note: Recent grants are derived from a fiscal 1993 Form 990.

RECENT GRANTS

Library

20,000	Pierpont Morgan Library, New York, NY
3,400	Pierpont Morgan Library, New York, NY
2,500	New York Public Library, New York, NY

General

100,000	Federation of Jewish Philanthropies, New York, NY
33,000	Harvard College, Cambridge, MA
25,000	Harvard University, Cambridge, MA
25,000	Nightingale-Bamford Scholarship Fund, New York, NY
22,500	Cornell University, Ithaca, NY

Chase Manhattan Bank, N.A. / Chase Manhattan Foundation

Employees: 31,108
Parent Company: Chase Manhattan Corporation
Revenue: $11.18 billion
Headquarters: New York, NY
SIC Major Group: National Commercial Banks

CONTACT

David S. Ford
Vice President & Director of Philanthropy
Chase Manhattan Bank, NA
One Chase Manhattan Plz.
9th Fl.
New York, NY 10081
(212) 552-7556
Note: See "Other Things To Know" for more details. The company's World Wide Web address is http://www.llnl.gov/fstc/chase_manhattan.html"

FINANCIAL SUMMARY

Recent Giving: $9,076,320 (1993); $8,843,973 (1992); $8,006,170 (1991)

Assets: $1,121,694 (1993); $1,008,004 (1992); $1,003,400 (1991)

Gifts Received: $250,000 (1993)

Fiscal Note: Total contributions figures include both foundation and direct giving. In 1993, direct giving totaled $8,931,717; foundation giving, $144,603. Above figures exclude contributions by international subsidiaries and contributions by U.S. business units ($2,615,155). Above figures exclude nonmonetary support. In 1993, the foundation received funds from Chase Manhattan Bank.

EIN: 23-7049738

CONTRIBUTIONS SUMMARY

Typical Recipients: • *Arts & Humanities:* Arts Appreciation, Arts Associations & Councils, Arts Centers, Arts Festivals, Arts Funds, Community Arts, Dance, Ethnic & Folk Arts, Libraries, Literary Arts, Museums/Galleries, Music, Opera, Performing Arts, Public Broadcasting, Theater, Visual Arts • *Civic & Public Affairs:* Asian American Affairs, Botanical Gardens/Parks, Business/Free Enterprise, Civil Rights, Economic Development, Economic Policy, Employment/Job Training, General, Housing, Law & Justice, Legal Aid, Municipalities/Towns, Nonprofit Management, Philanthropic Organizations, Professional & Trade Associations, Public Policy, Rural Affairs, Safety, Urban & Community Affairs, Women's Affairs • *Education:* Business Education, Business-School Partnerships, Colleges & Universities, Economic Education, Education Associations, Education Funds, Education Reform, Elementary Education (Private), Engineering/Technological Education, Faculty Development, General, Health & Physical Education, International Studies, Literacy, Minority Education, Preschool Education, Private Education (Precollege), Public Education (Precollege),

Science/Mathematics Education, Special Education, Student Aid • *Environment:* General, Wildlife Protection • *Health:* Children's Health/Hospitals, Eyes/Blindness, Geriatric Health, Health Policy/Cost Containment, Health Organizations, Hospitals, Medical Rehabilitation, Public Health, Transplant Networks/Donor Banks • *International:* Foreign Educational Institutions, Health Care/Hospitals, International Affairs, International Development, International Peace & Security Issues, International Relations • *Religion:* Dioceses, Jewish Causes, Religious Welfare • *Science:* Science Museums, Scientific Centers & Institutes, Scientific Organizations • *Social Services:* At-Risk Youth, Child Welfare, Community Centers, Community Service Organizations, Counseling, Day Care, Delinquency & Criminal Rehabilitation, Domestic Violence, Emergency Relief, Family Planning, Family Services, Food/Clothing Distribution, Homes, People with Disabilities, Recreation & Athletics, Senior Services, Shelters/Homelessness, Substance Abuse, United Funds/United Ways, Volunteer Services, YMCA/YWCA/YMHA/YWHA, Youth Organizations

Grant Types: award, capital, challenge, department, employee matching gifts, fellowship, general support, multiyear/continuing support, operating expenses, professorship, and project

Nonmonetary Support: $373,251 (1993); $355,929 (1992); $2,124,911 (1991)

Nonmonetary Support Types: donated equipment and in-kind services

Note: Company donates equipment and surplus furniture, and supplies *pro bono* printing.

Geographic Distribution: primarily near headquarters and operating locations; also nationally and internationally

Operating Locations: AZ (Phoenix), CA (Los Angeles, San Diego, San Francisco), CT, DE (Newark, Wilmington), FL (Boca Raton, Miami, Palm Beach, St. Petersburg, Tampa), IL (Chicago), MD (Baltimore), NY (New York, Rochester), TX (Dallas, Houston)

Note: Also operates internationally in Europe, Middle East, Africa, Asia, Australia, and throughout the Western Hemisphere.

CORP. OFFICERS

Richard James Boyle: *B* Brooklyn NY 1943 *ED* Coll Holy Cross 1965; NY Univ 1969 *CURR EMPL* vchmn, dir: Chase Manhattan Corp *CORP AFFIL* pres: Chase Commercial Corp; pres, ceo: LTV Aerospace & Defense Co; vchmn: Chase Manhattan Bank NA Inc *NONPR AFFIL* dir: Regional Planning Assn, Regis High Sch, St Vincent Hosp, YMCA Greater NY; mem: Urban Land Trust *CLUB AFFIL* Baltusrol GC, Beacon Hill

Thomas Goulet Labrecque: *B* Long Branch NJ 1938 *ED* Villanova Univ BA 1960; Am Univ 1962-1964; NY Univ 1965 *CURR EMPL* chmn, ceo, dir: Chase Manhattan Corp *CORP AFFIL* chmn, ceo, dir: Chase Manhattan Bank NA Inc; dir: AMAX Inc

NONPR AFFIL dir: Am Bankers Assn, Assn Reserve City Bankers, Fund NY Pub Ed, NY Chamber Commerce Indus, Un Way New York City, Un Way Tri-St; mem: Bus Counc, Bus Higher Ed Forum, Bus Roundtable, Counc Foreign Rels, Cystic Fibrosis Res Devel Counc, Intl Monetary Conf, New York City Partnership; mem bd visit: Duke Univ Fuqua Sch Bus; mem exec comm: Partnership Quality Ed; treas: Un Negro Coll Fund; trust: Brookings Inst, Central Pk Conservancy

Arjun K. Mathruni: *B* 1945 *CURR EMPL* exec vp, cfo: Chase Manhattan Corp

Michael Urkowitz: *B* Bronx NY 1943 *ED* City Univ NY BE 1965; City Univ NY MME 1967 *CURR EMPL* exec vp: Chase Manhattan Bank *CORP AFFIL* chmn: Participants Trust Co; dir: CEDEL SA, Depository Trust Co; sector exec: Chase InfoServ Intl *NONPR AFFIL* mem: Pi Tau Sigma, Tau Beta Pi; mem adv bd: New York City Salvation Army

James W. Zeigon: *CURR EMPL* exec vp: Chase Manhattan Bank NA Inc

GIVING OFFICERS

Donald L. Boudreau: vp, trust *B* White Plains NY 1940 *ED* Pace Univ 1970 *CURR EMPL* exec vp: Chase Manhattan Bank NA Inc *CORP AFFIL* chmn: Chase Natl Bank CT, NY Switch Corp; exec vp: Chase Manhattan Bank *NONPR AFFIL* chmn: Marymount Coll

Richard James Boyle: trust *CURR EMPL* vchmn, dir: Chase Manhattan Corp (see above)

Robert Royal Douglass: trust *B* Binghamton NY 1931 *ED* Dartmouth Coll BA 1953; Cornell Univ LLB 1959 *CURR EMPL* vchmn: Chase Manhattan Bank NA Inc *CORP AFFIL* dir: Gryphon Inc, Home Holdings, HRE Properties; exec vp: Chase Natl Corp Svcs; vchmn: Chase Manhattan Banking Corp *NONPR AFFIL* chmn exec comm, dir: Downtown-Lower Manhattan Assn; mem: Am Bar Assn, Counc Foreign Rels, NY Bar Assn; mem bd editors: NY Law Journal; trust: Dartmouth Coll, Mus Modern Art *CLUB AFFIL* Blind Brook, Century Assn, Harbor, Round Hill, World Trade Ctr

Anson Wright Elliott: vp, trust *B* New Orleans LA 1935 *ED* Princeton Univ BA 1957; LA St Univ MA 1964 *CURR EMPL* exec vp corp commun group: Chase Manhattan Bank NA Inc *NONPR AFFIL* dir: Bus-Indus Political Action Comm, Manhattan Inst Pub Policy Res; mem govt rels counc: Am Bankers Assn *CLUB AFFIL* Blind Brook, Econ NY, Police Athletic League, Siwanoy CC

Michael Patrick Esposito, Jr.: trust *B* Hackensack NJ 1939 *ED* Univ Notre Dame BBA 1961; NY Univ MBA 1967 *CURR EMPL* cfo, chief corp compliance contr & administration: Chase Manhattan Corp *CORP AFFIL* dir: Exel Ins Co; exec vp: Chase Manhattan Bank NA Inc *NONPR AFFIL* mem: Bank Admin Inst, Fin Execs Inst, Inst Mgmt Execs, Natl Assn Accts

John B. Evans: asst secy, asst treas

Hughlyn F. Fierce: trust *B* New York NY 1935 *ED* Morgan St Univ AB; NY Univ

MBA *CORP AFFIL* chmn, dir: Chase Bank AZ *NONPR AFFIL* mem: Am Chamber Commerce

David S. Ford: vp, dir

Robert D. Hunter: trust

Thomas Goulet Labrecque: pres *CURR EMPL* chmn, ceo, dir: Chase Manhattan Corp (see above)

Maria Elena Lagomasino: trust

Thomas C. Lynch: trust *CURR EMPL* exec vp: Chase Manhattan Bank

Arjun K. Mathruni: trust *CURR EMPL* exec vp, cfo: Chase Manhattan Corp (see above)

Arthur F. Ryan: trust *B* Brooklyn NY 1942 *ED* Providence Coll BA 1963; Am Univ *CURR EMPL* pres, coo: Chase Manhattan Bank NA Inc *CORP AFFIL* chmn: Prudential Ins Co Am; dir: Depository Trust Co; exec vp, dir: Chase Natl Corp Svcs; pres, chmn: Chase Manhattan Banking Corp, Chase Manhattan Natl Holding Co; pres, coo: Chase Manhattan Corp *NONPR AFFIL* mem: Am Bankers Assn *PHIL AFFIL* trust: Prudential Foundation

Susan Wylie Schoon: trust *B* Brooklyn IA 1948 *ED* NY Univ MBA; Univ IA BA

John Vincent Scicutella: trust *B* New York NY 1949 *ED* Fordham Univ 1971; Columbia Univ 1979 *CURR EMPL* exec vp oper & sys: Chase Manhattan Bank NA Inc

L. Edward Shaw, Jr.: trust *B* Elmira NY 1944 *ED* Georgetown Univ 1966; Yale Univ 1969 *CURR EMPL* exec vp, gen coun: Chase Manhattan Bank NA Inc *NONPR AFFIL* mem: Assn Bar City New York, Phi Beta Kappa *CLUB AFFIL* Winged Foot GC

Deborah L. Talbot: trust

Michael Urkowitz: trust *CURR EMPL* exec vp: Chase Manhattan Bank (see above)

James W. Zeigon: trust *CURR EMPL* exec vp: Chase Manhattan Bank NA Inc (see above)

APPLICATION INFORMATION

Initial Approach: *Initial Contact:* brief letter or proposal *Include Information On:* brief statement of history, goals, and accomplishments; synopsis of current activities; purpose or objective of proposal; amount requested; proof of 501(c)(3) status; current budget showing anticipated expenses and income; current funding sources (and donations); most recently audited financial statement; most recent annual report; number of staff and name and title of highest paid staff member; and list of board of directors *Deadlines:* October 1, but prefers that applications be submitted in January or June

Restrictions on Giving: Does not support member organizations of the United Way; religious, fraternal, or veterans organizations; political or lobbying groups; dinners, special events, or goodwill advertising; endowment purposes; or individuals except under National Merit Scholarship Program, Educational Testing Service, or Chase Manhattan Foundation.

OTHER THINGS TO KNOW

Chase Manhattan's corporate responsibility program is guided by the Corporate Responsibility Committee, whose members also serve as trustees of the foundation. Contributions to United States and international organizations are made by the Chase Manhattan Bank; however, contributions to upstate New York organizations generally are made by Chase Lincoln First Bank. Contributions to organizations either headquartered outside the continental United States or for programs abroad generally are made by the Chase Manhattan Foundation. Foundation may make grants to foreign-based organizations that have never applied for or received an IRS tax-exempt ruling if applicant organization provides information sufficient to prove that it is a charitable, educational, or scientific organization within the meaning of Section 501(c)(3).

The foundation decided in 1991 to discontinue the scholarship program once existing grants have expired. In 1993, scholarship awards totaled $44,603.

Community-based nonprofit 501(c)(3) organizations located in New York City, Long Island, Dutchess County, Orange County, Putnam County, Rockland County, or Westchester County are eligible for the Neighborhood Grants Program, which provides funds for projects in culture and the arts, education, health and human services, and housing and economic development. The application deadline is mid-February. Chase currently has ten contribution committees to review proposals for grants in their states. Contacts are the following:

— Patrick J. Radigan, Vice President
Chase Bankcard Services
100 W University-5th Fl.
Tempe, AZ 85281
— Raquel Castro, Manager, Contributions Committee
Chase National Corporate Services
801 S Grande Ave.-16th Fl.
Los Angeles, CA 90017
— Beth Culotta, Vice President, Marketing
Chase Manhattan Bank of Connecticut
999 Broad St.-2 Fl.
Bridgeport, CT 06604
— David C. Blank, Second Vice President
Chase Manhattan Bank (USA) NA
802 Delaware Ave. Wilmington, DE 19801
— Peter Arps, CRA Officer
Chase Manhattan Bank of Florida
6698 68th Ave. N
Pinnellas Park, FL 34665
— Kristin Zuidema, Manager Contribution Committee
Chase Manhattan of Illinois
1420 Kensington Rd., Ste. 116
Oakbrook, IL 60521
— Kevin Dwyer, Executive Vice President/CFO
Tray & Nichols
PO Box 4025
Monroe, LA 71211-4025

— Jacqueline G. King, Assistant Vice President
Chase Manhattan Bank of Maryland
10 E Baltimore St.
Baltimore, MD 21202
— Barbara Burns, Vice President, Public Affairs
Chase Manhattan Bank-Upstate
1 Lincoln First Sq.-CS5
Rochester, NY 14643
— Lora T. Vesel, Manager, Contributions Committee
Chase National Corporate Services
One Houston Ctr.
909 Fannin 30th Fl.
Houston, TX 77010

International contact for programs and projects outside of the United States are the following:

Latin America and Canada
— David S. Ford, Vice President
Chase Manahattan Bank
1 Chase Manhattan Plz., 9th Fl.
New York, NY 10081

Europe/Africa/Middle East
— Larry L. Wallace, Vice President
Chase Manhattan Bank
PO Box 440
Woolgate House, Coleman St.
London EC2P 2HD
England

Asia/Pacific
— Christopher I. Burrows, Vice President
Chase Manhattan Bank
12/f World Trade Center
280 Gloucester Rd.
Causeway Bay
Hong Kong

GRANTS ANALYSIS

Total Grants: $144,603

Highest Grant: $25,000

Typical Range: $1,000 to $5,000 and $10,000 to $20,000

Disclosure Period: 1993

Note: Above figures represent foundation giving only. Recent grants are derived from a 1993 Form 990.

RECENT GRANTS

General

1,100,000	United Way of Tri-State, Tri-State, NY	
108,000	United Way of Greater Rochester, Rochester, NY — housing and homeless programs	
50,000	Manhattan Bowery Corporation, New York, NY — Fresh Start	
50,000	YMCA of Greater New York, New York, NY — capital campaign	
40,000	American Museum of Natural History, New York, NY — Moveable Museum	

Chazen Foundation

CONTACT

Jerome A. Chazen
Trustee
Chazen Fdn.
c/o Nathan Berkman and Co.
29 Broadway, Rm. 2800
New York, NY 10006-3296
(212) 269-4141

FINANCIAL SUMMARY

Recent Giving: $316,777 (1993); $1,615,100 (1992); $3,404,283 (1991)

Assets: $9,891,240 (1993); $14,129,624 (1992); $12,207,181 (1991)

Gifts Received: $489,855 (1993); $2,021,000 (1992)

Fiscal Note: In 1993, contributions were received from Jerome and Simona Chazen.

EIN: 13-3229474

CONTRIBUTIONS SUMMARY

Donor(s): Jerome A. Chazen

Typical Recipients: • *Arts & Humanities:* Arts Associations & Councils, Arts Centers, Arts Funds, Community Arts, Ethnic & Folk Arts, Libraries, Museums/Galleries, Music, Opera, Performing Arts, Public Broadcasting, Theater • *Civic & Public Affairs:* Civil Rights, General, Hispanic Affairs, Public Policy, Urban & Community Affairs, Women's Affairs • *Education:* Arts/Humanities Education, Business Education, Colleges & Universities, General, Private Education (Precollege), Social Sciences Education • *Environment:* Air/Water Quality, Forestry • *Health:* AIDS/HIV, Arthritis, Cancer, Emergency/Ambulance Services, Eyes/Blindness, Hospitals, Medical Research, Prenatal Health Issues • *International:* Foreign Arts Organizations, International Relations, Missionary/Religious Activities • *Religion:* Jewish Causes, Religious Organizations, Religious Welfare, Synagogues/Temples • *Social Services:* Animal Protection, Camps, Child Welfare, Community Centers, Community Service Organizations, Counseling, Emergency Relief, Family Planning, Family Services, Recreation & Athletics, Shelters/Homelessness, United Funds/United Ways, Volunteer Services, YMCA/YWCA/YMHA/YWHA, Youth Organizations

Grant Types: capital

Geographic Distribution: focus on New York, NY

GIVING OFFICERS

Jerome A. Chazen: trust *B* New York NY 1927 *ED* Univ WI BA 1948; Columbia Univ MBA 1950 *CURR EMPL* co-fdr, chmn, dir: Liz Claiborne *NONPR AFFIL* dir: Ed Fdn, Fashion Inst Tech, Rockland Ctr Arts,

Shenkar Coll Fashion & Textiles *PHIL AF-FIL* trust: Liz Claiborne Foundation

Simona A. Chazen: trust

APPLICATION INFORMATION
Initial Approach: Send brief letter of inquiry describing program or project. There are no deadlines.

GRANTS ANALYSIS
Total Grants: $316,777

Number of Grants: 62

Highest Grant: $60,375

Typical Range: $500 to $6,000

Disclosure Period: 1993

Note: Recent grants are derived from a 1993 Form 990.

RECENT GRANTS

Library

300	South Orange Public Library, South Orange, NY

General

45,000	United Jewish Appeal Federation of Rockland County, New York, NY
25,450	SLE Foundation, New York, NY
25,000	Volunteer Counseling Service of Rockland County, Rockland, NY
6,000	Rockland YM-YWHA, Rockland, NY
5,680	Temple Beth Torah, New York, NY

Cheatham Foundation, Owen

CONTACT
Celeste C. Weisglass
President
Owen Cheatham Fdn.
435 E 52nd St.
New York, NY 10022
(212) 753-4733

FINANCIAL SUMMARY
Recent Giving: $335,877 (1993); $350,305 (1992); $350,000 (1991)

Assets: $6,776,976 (1993); $6,792,942 (1992); $6,814,279 (1991)

EIN: 13-6097798

CONTRIBUTIONS SUMMARY
Donor(s): the late Gwen Robertson Cheatham, the late Celeste W. Cheatham

Typical Recipients: • *Arts & Humanities:* Arts Funds, Arts Institutes, Ballet, Community Arts, Dance, Libraries, Museums/Galleries, Music, Opera, Public Broadcasting, Theater • *Education:* Colleges & Universities, Private Education (Precollege) • *Environment:* General • *Health:* Clinics/Medical Centers, Hospices, Hospitals, Medical Research, Mental Health, Single-Disease Health Associations • *International:* Foreign Educational Institutions, International Or-

ganizations • *Religion:* Jewish Causes, Religious Organizations, Synagogues/Temples • *Social Services:* Animal Protection, At-Risk Youth, Community Service Organizations, Recreation & Athletics, Shelters/Homelessness, Substance Abuse, United Funds/United Ways

Grant Types: operating expenses, project, and scholarship

Geographic Distribution: focus on NY

GIVING OFFICERS
MacDonald Budd: dir

Ilse C. Meckauer: secy, dir

Celeste C. Weisglass: pres, dir

Stephen S. Weisglass: vp, treas, dir

APPLICATION INFORMATION
Initial Approach: Include a description of organization, amount requested, purpose of funds sought, recently audited financial statement, and proof of tax-exempt status. Must be on organizations stationery. There are no deadlines.

GRANTS ANALYSIS
Total Grants: $335,877

Number of Grants: 100

Highest Grant: $25,375

Typical Range: $100 to $10,000

Disclosure Period: 1993

Note: Recent grants are derived from a 1993 Form 990.

RECENT GRANTS

General

25,375	Graham-Windham Services, New York, NY
23,654	American Council for Drug Education, New York, NY
20,165	Choate Rosemary Hall, Wallingford, CT
20,000	Vanderbilt University, Nashville, TN
10,000	Free Synagogue of Flushing, Flushing, NY

Christian Dior New York, Inc.

Sales: $4.7 million
Employees: 55
Headquarters: New York, NY
SIC Major Group: Apparel & Accessory Stores, Holding & Other Investment Offices, and Wholesale Trade—Nondurable Goods

CONTACT
Diane Schwartz
Director, Advertising
Christian Dior New York, Inc.
712 Fifth Ave., 37th Fl.
New York, NY 10019
(212) 582-0500

FINANCIAL SUMMARY
Fiscal Note: Company does not disclose contributions figures.

CONTRIBUTIONS SUMMARY
Christian Dior provides a broad range of support but its first priority is the humanities. Company also supports education through donations to fashion schools, mainly in the New York City area.

Typical Recipients: • *Arts & Humanities:* Art History, Arts Appreciation, Arts Associations & Councils, Arts Centers, Arts Festivals, Arts Funds, Arts Institutes, Arts Outreach, Ballet, Community Arts, Dance, Ethnic & Folk Arts, Film & Video, General, Historic Preservation, History & Archaeology, Libraries, Literary Arts, Museums/Galleries, Music, Opera, Performing Arts, Public Broadcasting, Theater, Visual Arts • *Education:* Colleges & Universities, Education Associations, General, International Studies • *Health:* AIDS/HIV, Cancer, General, Single-Disease Health Associations, Speech & Hearing • *Social Services:* General, People with Disabilities, Youth Organizations

Grant Types: general support

Nonmonetary Support Types: donated products

Geographic Distribution: in the New York City area and to national organizations

Operating Locations: NY (New York)

CORP. OFFICERS
Michael Burke: *CURR EMPL* exec vp, dir: Christian Dior New York

Philippe Soussand: *CURR EMPL* treas, admin vp fin: Christian Dior NY

Philippe Vindry: *CURR EMPL* pres, dir: Christian Dior New York

GIVING OFFICERS
Diane Schwartz: *CURR EMPL* dir advertising: Christian Dior NY

APPLICATION INFORMATION
Initial Approach: Send a brief letter or proposal, including a description of the organization and purpose of grant.

CIBC Wood Gundy

Sales: $11.23 million
Employees: 800
Headquarters: New York, NY
SIC Major Group: Depository Institutions

CONTACT
Katherine S. Griffith
Managing Director, Corporate Communications USA
Canadian Imperial Bank of Commerce U.S.
425 Lexington Ave., 8th Fl.
New York, NY 10017
(212) 856-4029

FINANCIAL SUMMARY
Recent Giving: $250,000 (1994); $250,000 (1993)

CONTRIBUTIONS SUMMARY
Company reports contributions activities are designed to fulfill the requirements under

the community reinvestment act. Priorities are housing and economic development.

Volunteerism: Company is currently developing an employee volunteer program.

Typical Recipients: • *Arts & Humanities:* Libraries • *Civic & Public Affairs:* Chambers of Commerce, Economic Development, Employment/Job Training, General, Housing, Inner-City Development, Legal Aid, Municipalities/Towns, Urban & Community Affairs • *Education:* Business Education • *Health:* General • *International:* General • *Religion:* General • *Science:* General • *Social Services:* General, United Funds/United Ways, YMCA/YWCA/YMHA/YWHA

Grant Types: capital, general support, loan, operating expenses, project, and seed money

Nonmonetary Support Types: donated equipment and in-kind services

Geographic Distribution: focus on New York, NY

Operating Locations: CA (Los Angeles, San Francisco), GA (Atlanta), IL (Chicago), NY (New York), TX (Houston)

CORP. OFFICERS

Al Flood: *CURR EMPL* chmn, ceo: Canadian Imperial Bank Commerce

GIVING OFFICERS

Katherine S. Griffith: *CURR EMPL* mng dir: CIBC Wood Gundy

APPLICATION INFORMATION

Initial Approach: Send a brief letter of inquiry and a full proposal. Include a description of organization, amount requested, purpose of funds sought, recently audited financial statement, and proof of tax-exempt status.

Restrictions on Giving: Does not support individuals, religious organizations for sectarian purposes, political or lobbying groups, or organizations outside operating areas.

GRANTS ANALYSIS

Typical Range: $1,000 to $2,500

Note: Recent grants are derived from a grants list provided by company in 1995.

RECENT GRANTS

Library
New York Public Library, New York, NY

General
Banana Kelly
Greater Jamaica Development Corporation
Housing Partnership Development
  Corporation, New York, NY
Local Initiatives Support Corporation
Neighborhood Housing Services, New York,
  NY

Citibank

Revenue: $31.65 billion
Employees: 88,500
Headquarters: New York, NY
SIC Major Group: Bank Holding Companies
  and National Commercial Banks

CONTACT

Paul Michael Ostergard
Vice President, Director, Corporate
  Contributions & Civic Responsibility
Citibank, N.A.
850 Third Ave., 13th Fl., Zone 10
New York, NY 10043
(212) 559-0170
Note: The company's World Wide Web
address is http://www.citicorp.com.

FINANCIAL SUMMARY

Recent Giving: $26,000,000 (1995 est.);
$23,000,000 (1994 approx.); $22,113,621
(1993)

Fiscal Note: Totals include contributions by domestic and foreign subsidiaries, which total $3 million to $4 million annually, and matching gifts. International giving figures are included in the above figures.

CONTRIBUTIONS SUMMARY

Typical Recipients: • *Arts & Humanities:* Arts Appreciation, Arts Associations & Councils, Arts Centers, Arts Festivals, Arts Funds, Arts Institutes, Dance, Ethnic & Folk Arts, Historic Preservation, Libraries, Museums/Galleries, Music, Opera, Performing Arts, Public Broadcasting, Theater • *Civic & Public Affairs:* Business/Free Enterprise, Civil Rights, Economic Development, Economic Policy, Employment/Job Training, Nonprofit Management, Public Policy, Urban & Community Affairs, Women's Affairs, Zoos/Aquariums • *Education:* Arts/Humanities Education, Business Education, Colleges & Universities, Community & Junior Colleges, Continuing Education, Economic Education, Education Associations, Education Funds, Elementary Education (Private), International Exchange, International Studies, Literacy, Minority Education, Private Education (Precollege), Public Education (Precollege), Science/Mathematics Education, Special Education • *Environment:* General • *Health:* Emergency/Ambulance Services, Health Policy/Cost Containment, Health Organizations, Hospices, Hospitals, Medical Research, Single-Disease Health Associations • *International:* Foreign Educational Institutions, Health Care/Hospitals, International Peace & Security Issues, International Relations • *Social Services:* Child Welfare, Community Centers, Community Service Organizations, Day Care, Emergency Relief, Family Services, Food/Clothing Distribution, Homes, People with Disabilities, Shelters/Homelessness, United Funds/United Ways, Volunteer Services, Youth Organizations

Grant Types: employee matching gifts, general support, and project

Note: Employee matching gift ratio: 1 to 1.

Geographic Distribution: in New York City and near operating locations

Operating Locations: CA (Los Angeles, Oakland, San Diego, San Francisco), CO (Denver), CT (Stamford), DC, DE (New Castle), FL (Miami, Tampa), GA (Atlanta), IL (Chicago), MA (Boston), MD (Hagerstown, Silver Spring), MO (St. Louis), NJ, NM, NV, NY (New York), OR, PA, SD (Sioux Falls), TX (Dallas, Houston), VA, WA (Seattle)

Note: Parent company and subsidiaries operate in 40 states, the District of Columbia, and 90 countries.

CORP. OFFICERS

Pei-Yuan Chia: *B* Hong Kong Taiwan 1939 *ED* Tunghai Univ BA 1961; Univ PA MBA 1965 *CURR EMPL* vchmn: Citibank NA *CORP AFFIL* vchmn: Citicorp *NONPR AFFIL* dir: Comm 100; trust: China Inst Am

Paul John Collins: *B* West Bend WI 1936 *ED* Univ WI BBA 1958; Harvard Univ MBA 1961 *CURR EMPL* vchmn: Citicorp *CORP AFFIL* dir: Kimberly-Clark Corp; vchmn: Citibank NA *NONPR AFFIL* trust: China Inst Am, Hosp Special Surgery, NY Philharmonic, Univ WI Fdn *CLUB AFFIL* River

John Shepard Reed: *B* Chicago IL 1939 *ED* Washington & Jefferson Coll BA 1959; MA Inst Tech MS 1965 *CURR EMPL* chmn, ceo, dir: Citicorp *CORP AFFIL* chmn, ceo: Citibank NA; dir: Monsanto Co, Philip Morris Cos Inc, Un Techs Corp *NONPR AFFIL* chmn: Coalition Svc Indus; mem: Bus Roundtable, Ctr Advanced Study Behavioral Sci; mem bd govs: Meml Sloan-Kettering Cancer Ctr; trust: MA Inst Tech, NY Blood Ctr, RAND Corp; vchmn: Am Soc, Bus Counc *PHIL AFFIL* trust: Russell Sage Foundation; dir: Spencer Foundation

William Reginald Rhodes: *B* New York NY 1935 *ED* Brown Univ BA 1957 *CURR EMPL* vchmn: Citibank NA *CORP AFFIL* mem adv comm: Export-Import Bank US; vchmn: Citicorp *NONPR AFFIL* chmn US secy: Venezuela-US Bus Counc; dir: Ams Soc, Booth Meml Hosp, New York City Partnership, NY Hosp, Pvt Export Funding Corp; mem: Bankers Assn Foreign Trade, Counc Foreign Rels, Reserve City Bankers Assn, Venezuela-Am Chamber Commerce; mem exec comm: Bretton Woods Comm; off: Order Francisco Miranda, Order Merito Trabajo; trust: Counc Ams, Northfield MT Hermon Sch; vchmn: Inst Intl Fin

Herman Onno Ruding: *B* Breda Netherlands 1939 *ED* Erasmus Univ/Netherlands Sch Econ MA 1964; Erasmus Univ/Netherlands Sch Econ PhD 1969 *CURR EMPL* vchmn: Citicorp *NONPR AFFIL* mem: Christian Democratic Alliance, Comm Monetary Union Europe, Trilateral Commn

GIVING OFFICERS

Alan Okada: *CURR EMPL* vp health programs: Citicorp *CORP AFFIL* vp health programs: Citibank NA

Paul Michael Ostergard: *B* Akron OH 1939 *ED* Univ Madrid 1959-1960; Case Western Reserve Univ AB 1961; Univ MI JD 1964; Harvard Univ MPA 1969 *CURR EMPL* vp, dir corp contributions: Citibank

NA *CORP AFFIL* dir: Inst Ed Leadership Bd, Penn Towers Inc, Pullman Co; vp, dir: Clearfield Bituminous Coal Corp *NONPR AFFIL* dir: Jr Achievement NY; mem: Lowndes County Pub Sch Improvement Comm, Natl Hispanic Scholarship Comm, OH Bar Assn, Omicron Delta Kappa, Phi Beta Kappa; mem adv comm: League Women Voters; mem bd: Am Counc Arts; mem corp adv counc: Am Red Cross; mem exec comm: Harvard Univ Alumni Assn; task force leader: Un Way Am *CLUB AFFIL* Atrium, Harvard

Peter C. Thorp: *CURR EMPL* vp univ rels: Citicorp *CORP AFFIL* vp univ rels: Citibank NA

APPLICATION INFORMATION

Initial Approach: *Initial Contact:* contact local contributions committee listed in Citicorp Contributions and Guidelines (New York metropolitan neighborhood groups should contact local Citibank manager for Citigrant forms) *Include Information On:* brief statement of history, goals, and accomplishments; purpose and objective of proposal; current annual report; amount requested; proof of tax-exempt status; current year's budget showing anticipated expenses and income; IRS 501(c)(3) Tax Exempt Form; list of funding sources and amounts contributed; most recently audited financial statement; list of governing board members; and list of accrediting agencies, when appropriate *Deadlines:* small requests handled regularly; other requests have various deadlines available from the contact person *Note:* Many contributions committees use a proposal application form, available from local contact person if necessary.

Restrictions on Giving: The company does not support individuals; political causes or candidates; religious, veterans, or fraternal organizations, unless project significantly benefits entire community; fund-raising dinners, benefits, or events; or advertising.

OTHER THINGS TO KNOW

The company generally prefers to support specific, one-year programs in areas of charitable interest.

Potential for combination with volunteers, in-kind services, or other direct Citibank involvement is frequently a deciding factor in grant decisions.

Citibank also makes housing, small business, and student loans; is involved with programs to hire minority youth and to pay summer interns at community nonprofit organizations; provides technical assistance; and encourages employees to participate in the matching gifts program.

In February 1991, Prince Alwaleed Bin Talal of Saudi Arabia invested $590 million in Citicorp, acquiring at least 10% of company.

PUBLICATIONS

Public Responsibility at Citibank 1992, Citicorp contributions and guidelines

GRANTS ANALYSIS
Total Grants: $22,113,621
Number of Grants: 519*
Highest Grant: $499,708
Average Grant: $20,349*
Typical Range: $2,500 to $25,000
Disclosure Period: 1993

Note: Number of grants and average grant exclude $5,064,200 in matching gifts and $6,488,463 in contributions by domestic and foreign subsidiaries. Recent grants are derived from a 1992 annual report.

RECENT GRANTS

General

375,912	DePaul University, Chicago, IL — Smarter Schools Program
375,912	Federal City Council, Washington, DC — Smarter Schools Program
250,000	United Negro College Fund, New York, NY — Campaign 2000: An Investment in America's future
200,000	The Door, New York, NY — Unity High School
187,956	Dade Public Education Fund, Miami, FL — Smarter Schools Program, Broward County

City National Bank and Trust Co. / City National Bank Foundation

Sales: $7.0 million
Employees: 70
Headquarters: Hastings, NE
SIC Major Group: Depository Institutions

CONTACT
William N. Smith
City National Bank and Trust Co.
12 N Main St.
Gloversville, NY 12078
(518) 773-7911

FINANCIAL SUMMARY
Recent Giving: $38,733 (1993); $14,700 (1991)
Assets: $33,672 (1993); $5,920 (1991)
Gifts Received: $40,000 (1993); $12,000 (1991)
Fiscal Note: In 1993, contributions were received from City National Bank and Trust Co.
EIN: 22-2816974

CONTRIBUTIONS SUMMARY
Typical Recipients: • *Arts & Humanities:* Libraries • *Civic & Public Affairs:* Clubs, Housing, Municipalities/Towns, Safety, Urban & Community Affairs • *Education:* Literacy, School Volunteerism • *Health:* Cancer, Emergency/Ambulance Services, Heart, Hospices, Respiratory • *Religion:* Jewish Causes, Religious Welfare • *Social Services:* Animal Protection, Child Welfare, Family Services, United Funds/United Ways, YMCA/YWCA/YMHA/YWHA

Grant Types: general support

Geographic Distribution: focus on Gloversville, NY

CORP. OFFICERS

Michael J. Frank: *CURR EMPL* comptr, vp: City National Bank and Trust Co

Owen J. McDougal, Jr.: *CURR EMPL* chmn: City National Bank and Trust Co

Norman Nackerud: *CURR EMPL* ceo, pres: City National Bank and Trust Co

William N. Smith: *CURR EMPL* pres, dir: City National Bank and Trust Co

GIVING OFFICERS

Clark Easterly: trust

Leon Finkle: trust

Brian Hanaburgh: trust

Richard E. Hathaway: trust

Theodore E. Hoye, Jr.: trust

Robert L. Maider: trust

John C. Miller: trust

George A. Morgan: trust

Frank E. Perrella: trust

Paul E. Smith: trust

William N. Smith: pres, trust *CURR EMPL* pres, dir: City National Bank and Trust Co (see above)

James W. St. Thomas: trust

APPLICATION INFORMATION

Initial Approach: Send a brief letter of inquiry. Include a description of organization, amount requested, purpose of funds sought, recently audited financial statement, and proof of tax-exempt status. There are no deadlines.

GRANTS ANALYSIS
Total Grants: $38,733
Number of Grants: 27
Highest Grant: $13,000
Typical Range: $500 to $5,000
Disclosure Period: 1993

Note: Recent grants are derived from a 1993 Form 990.

RECENT GRANTS

Library

100	Friends of Gloversville Free Library, Gloversville, NY

General

13,000	United Way of Fulton County, Gloversville, NY	
5,000	Family Counseling Center, Gloversville, NY	
5,000	Family Counseling Center, Gloversville, NY	
5,000	Gloversville YWCA, Gloversville, NY	
3,000	Gloversville Holiday Christmas Lights, Gloversville, NY	

Claiborne and Art Ortenberg Foundation, Liz

Former Foundation Name: Ortenberg Foundation

CONTACT

Liz Claiborne and Art Ortenberg Foundation
650 Fifth Ave.
10th Fl.
New York, NY 10019
(212) 333-2536
Note: The foundation does not list a contact person.

FINANCIAL SUMMARY

Recent Giving: $1,333,907 (fiscal 1994); $1,943,989 (fiscal 1993); $1,671,520 (fiscal 1992)

Assets: $37,327,203 (fiscal 1994); $35,586,613 (fiscal 1993); $34,874,734 (fiscal 1992)

Gifts Received: $750,000 (fiscal 1994); $750,000 (fiscal 1993 approx.); $30,000 (fiscal 1992)

Fiscal Note: In fiscal 1991, the foundation received $13,921,250 worth of Liz Claiborne, Inc., stock from the trustees and donors of the foundation, Arthur and Elisabeth Claiborne Ortenberg. In fiscal 1992, the foundation received $30,000 in cash from Arthur and Elisabeth C. Orthenberg. In fiscal 1993, the foundation received personal funds from Liz Claiborne and Art Ortenberg.

EIN: 13-3200329

CONTRIBUTIONS SUMMARY

Donor(s): The foundation was established in 1984 by Arthur Ortenberg and Elisabeth Claiborne Ortenberg, who founded Liz Claiborne, Inc., the largest seller of women's sportswear in department stores.

The couple started the clothing company in 1976 with an initial investment of $250,000. They contributed $50,000 themselves and borrowed $200,000 from family and friends. The company had sales of $1.4 billion in 1990. Mr. Ortenberg and Ms. Claiborne are no longer on the board of directors of Liz Claiborne, Inc. They no longer hold Liz Clairborne, Inc., stock.

Mrs. Ortenberg was born in Brussels in 1929 while her father, a banker from New Or-
leans, was posted overseas. She attended the Art School in Brussels in 1947 and the Academie des Beaux Arts in Paris in 1948, where she studied painting. She decided to remain in the United States when she won a Harper's Bazaar design contest while she was vacationing in New Orleans in 1949. She is a direct descendant of William C. C. Claiborne, Louisiana's governor during the War of 1812.

Mrs. Ortenberg made a name for herself as a designer in New York at Jonathan Logan, where she spent sixteen years designing moderately priced junior dresses. Elisabeth Claiborne and Arthur Ortenberg were married in 1957. They both had children by a previous marriage. He has two children and she has one, Alexander G. Schultz.

Typical Recipients: • *Arts & Humanities:* Arts Centers, Arts Funds, Libraries, Museums/Galleries, Public Broadcasting • *Civic & Public Affairs:* Botanical Gardens/Parks, Economic Development, Economic Policy, Ethnic Organizations, General, Philanthropic Organizations, Urban & Community Affairs • *Education:* Colleges & Universities, Elementary Education (Private), Private Education (Precollege), Science/Mathematics Education • *Environment:* Air/Water Quality, Forestry, General, Resource Conservation, Wildlife Protection • *Health:* Health Organizations, Single-Disease Health Associations • *International:* Health Care/Hospitals, International Environmental Issues, International Peace & Security Issues • *Science:* Science Museums, Scientific Labs • *Social Services:* Animal Protection, Family Planning, People with Disabilities, Youth Organizations

Grant Types: general support

Geographic Distribution: nationally; internationally, principally to the Third World

GIVING OFFICERS

James Murtaugh: program dir

Arthur Ortenberg: don, trust, dir *B* 1926

Elisabeth Claiborne Ortenberg: don, dir, trust *B* Brussels Belgium 1929 *ED* Art Sch Brussels 1948-1949; Academie Nice (France) 1950 *NONPR AFFIL* dir: Counc Am Fashion Designers, Fire Island Lighthouse Restoration Comm; guest lecturer: Fashion Inst Tech, Parsons Sch Design; mem: Fashion Group

Mary Pearl: dir

David Quammen: dir

David Western: dir

APPLICATION INFORMATION

Initial Approach:

Send brief letter of inquiry. All requests must be in writing.

Applicants should include a brief description of the project, the amount requested, and the contact person in charge of the project.
The foundation does not list any application deadlines for proposals.

GRANTS ANALYSIS

Total Grants: $1,333,907

Number of Grants: 99

Highest Grant: $352,853

Average Grant: $13,474

Typical Range: $1,000 to $25,000

Disclosure Period: fiscal year ending January 31, 1994

Note: Recent grants are derived from a fiscal 1994 Form 990.

RECENT GRANTS

Library

2,000	Scarsdale Public Library, Scarsdale, NY	

General

352,853	Workshop on Community-Based Conservation — to provide an important and easily accessible source of material for planners, managers, aid organizations, and conservationists	
287,500	Wildlife Conservation Society, Washington, DC	
152,300	World Wildlife Fund, Washington, DC	
107,000	Nature Conservancy, New York, NY	
76,806	Missouri Botanical Garden, St. Louis, MO	

Clark Foundation

CONTACT

Joseph H. Cruickshank
Secretary
Clark Foundation
30 Wall St.
New York, NY 10005
(212) 269-1833

FINANCIAL SUMMARY

Recent Giving: $10,918,442 (fiscal 1994); $7,874,691 (fiscal 1993); $9,634,951 (fiscal 1992)

Assets: $292,999,378 (fiscal 1994); $290,381,369 (fiscal 1993); $264,654,849 (fiscal 1992)

Gifts Received: $2,872,500 (fiscal 1993); $951,829 (fiscal 1992); $16,500 (fiscal 1991)

Fiscal Note: Gifts received in fiscal 1991 came from the Glider Foundation. Source of 1992 gift is unknown. In fiscal 1993, the foundation received $2,842,500 from the estate of Stephen C. Clark, Jr., $20,000 from the Stephen C. Clark, Jr. Charitable Trust, and $10,000 from the Glider Foundation.

EIN: 13-5616528

CONTRIBUTIONS SUMMARY

Donor(s): The Clark Foundation was established in 1931 in New York by members of the Clark family, including Edwin Severin Clark, Stephen Carlton Clark , and Frederick Ambrose Clark. The donors were heirs to the Clark family fortune, which originated in the 1800s with Edward Clark, a Cooperstown lawyer who was one of the founders of the Singer Company. The foundation has made major contributions to the residents of Cooperstown through gifts of a museum, a hospital affiliated with Columbia University, a community recreation center, and a college scholarship program for local students. In 1973, the foundation merged with the Scriven Foundation, another Clark endowment. The foundation is governed by a thirteen-member board of directors, including two members of the Clark family.

Typical Recipients: • *Arts & Humanities:* Ballet, Libraries, Museums/Galleries, Music, Opera, Performing Arts, Public Broadcasting • *Civic & Public Affairs:* Civil Rights, Economic Development, Employment/Job Training, Housing, Legal Aid, Nonprofit Management, Professional & Trade Associations, Urban & Community Affairs, Women's Affairs, Zoos/Aquariums • *Education:* Afterschool/Enrichment Programs, Arts/Humanities Education, Colleges & Universities, Education Funds, Education Reform, Elementary Education (Private), Elementary Education (Public), General, Medical Education, Minority Education, Private Education (Precollege), Public Education (Precollege), Student Aid, Vocational & Technical Education • *Environment:* Air/Water Quality, General, Wildlife Protection • *Health:* Cancer, Emergency/Ambulance Services, Health Funds, Hospitals, Kidney, Medical Training, Outpatient Health Care • *Religion:* Religious Welfare • *Social Services:* At-Risk Youth, Child Welfare, Community Centers, Community Service Organizations, Delinquency & Criminal Rehabilitation, Family Planning, Family Services, Homes, People with Disabilities, Recreation & Athletics, Senior Services, Shelters/Homelessness, Substance Abuse, United Funds/United Ways, Volunteer Services, Youth Organizations

Grant Types: general support

Geographic Distribution: primarily Cooperstown, NY, and New York City

GIVING OFFICERS

Kent L. Barwick: dir *B* 1941 *CURR EMPL* vp, dir: 457 Madison Ave Corp

Jane Forbes Clark: pres, don daughter, dir *B* 1956 *CURR EMPL* chwm: Clark Estates *NONPR AFFIL* chmn, dir: Farmers Mus; pres, dir: Am Horse Shows Assn, Clara Welch Thanksgiving Home; vp, dir: US Equestrian Team *PHIL AFFIL* pres, dir: Fernleigh Foundation

Leonard S. Coleman, Jr.: dir

Joseph H. Cruickshank: secy *PHIL AFFIL* secy, dir: Fernleigh Foundation

William Maxwell Evarts, Jr.: dir *B* New York NY 1925 *ED* Harvard Univ AB 1949; Harvard Univ LLB 1952 *CURR EMPL* ptnr: Winthrop Stimson Putnam & Roberts *NONPR AFFIL* dir: NY St Nature Conservancy, Scenic Hudson, Trust Pub Land, Un Hosp Fund; mem: Am Bar Assn, Assn Bar City New York; mem distr comm: NY Commun Trust *PHIL AFFIL* dir: New York Community Trust

Gates H. Hawn: dir

Archie F. MacAllaster: dir

Mrs. Edward B. McMenamin: dir

Kevin S. Moore: treas, dir *CURR EMPL* cfo, vp, dir: Clark Estates *NONPR AFFIL* treas, dir: Clara Welch Thanksgiving Home, Farmers Mus *PHIL AFFIL* treas, dir: Fernleigh Foundation

Anne Labouisse Peretz: dir *B* 1939 *CURR EMPL* co-owner: The New Republic *NONPR AFFIL* fdr: The Family Ctr

Edward William Stack: vp, dir *B* Rockville Centre NY 1935 *ED* Pace Univ BBA 1956 *CURR EMPL* pres, dir: Clark Estates *CORP AFFIL* pres, dir: Leatherstocking Corp; secy, treas, dir: New Republic *NONPR AFFIL* mem: Down Town Assn; pres, chmn: Natl Baseball Hall Fame & Mus; secy, trust: NY St Historical Assn; trust: Baseball Am Fdn; trust, treas: Bethany Deaconess Soc; vchmn, dir: Farmers Mus; vchmn, trust: Mary Imogene Bassett Hosp *CLUB AFFIL* Downtown Assn, Mohican *PHIL AFFIL* vp, bd dirs: Nourse Foundation; trust: Baseball Am Foundation; vp, dir: Fernleigh Foundation

John Hoyt Stookey: dir *B* New York NY 1930 *ED* Amherst Coll BA 1952; Columbia Univ BS 1955 *CURR EMPL* chmn, ceo, pres, dir: Quantum Chem Corp *CORP AFFIL* affil: QFB; dir: Chesapeake Corp, Rexham Corp, Riegel Textile Corp; trust: US Trust Co NY *NONPR AFFIL* dir: Assn Better NY; fdr, pres: Berkshire Boys Choir; mem: Alpha Pi Mu, Counc Foreign Rels, Delta Kappa Epsilon; mem adv bd: Grosvenor Neighborhood House; trust: Bio-Energy Counc, Boston Symphony Orchestra, Coll Human Svcs, Counc Ams *CLUB AFFIL* Century Assn, Ctr Harbor YC, Downtown Assn, Lenox, Metropolitan Opera, Pequot YC, Pinnacle, Union, Weston Gun *PHIL AFFIL* dir: Robert Sterling Clark Foundation

Clifton Reginald Wharton, Jr.: dir *B* Boston MA 1926 *NONPR AFFIL* deputy secy: US Dept State; mem: Am Agricultural Econ Assn, Assn Asian Studies, Natl Academy Ed *CLUB AFFIL* CC Cooperstown NY, Univ

Malcolm Wilson: dir *B* New York NY 1914 *ED* Fordham Univ BA 1933; Fordham Univ LLB 1936 *CURR EMPL* of couns: Kent Hazzard Jaeger Wilson Freeman & Greer *CORP AFFIL* dir: Colin Svc Sys, Shearson Lehman Bros, Shearson Lehman Hutton Holdings

NONPR AFFIL dir: Archdiocese NY, Catholic Youth Org, Farmers Mus, NY St Historical Assn; mem: Am Bar Assn, Ancient Order Hibernians, NY Farm Bur, NY St Bar Assn, Soc Friendly Sons St Patrick, Westchester County Bar Assn; trust: Natl Conf Christians & Jews *PHIL AFFIL* dir: Thomas and Agnes Carvel Foundation

APPLICATION INFORMATION
Initial Approach:

Applicants should send a preliminary letter to the foundation.

The letter should include a description of the project, amount requested, audited financial report, budget, and proof of tax-exempt status. If the foundation is interested in the project, further information will be requested.

There are no deadlines for submitting letters of request. The foundation's board of directors meets in October and May and at other times during the year. The grants committee, however, meets more frequently.

The grants committee has the authority to approve some grants, but its general function is to make recommendations to the board of directors concerning grant requests. Decisions usually are made by the entire board.

Restrictions on Giving: No grants are given for deficit financing, matching gifts, or loans.

PUBLICATIONS
Program policy statement, application guidelines

GRANTS ANALYSIS
Total Grants: $7,874,691*

Number of Grants: 122

Highest Grant: $178,750

Average Grant: $37,121*

Typical Range: $10,000 to $50,000

Disclosure Period: fiscal year ending June 30, 1993

Note: Figures include $3,345,883 that was divided among scholarships, the Susan V. Clark Fund, the Friends Fund, the St. Timothy's Fund, and the Alfred C. Clark Gymnasium. The number of grants and average grant figures exclude scholarship funding. Recent grants are derived from a fiscal 1993 Form 990.

RECENT GRANTS
General

178,750	United Way of New York City, New York, NY
150,000	Long Island University, Brookville, NY
150,000	St. Luke's - Roosevelt Hospital Center, New York, NY
149,075	East Harlem Employment Service, New York, NY
125,000	Friends Council on Education, Philadelphia, PA

Coleman Foundation, George E.

CONTACT
Denis Loncto
Trustee
George E. Coleman Fdn.
c/o Neville, Rodie and Shaw
200 Madison Ave.
New York, NY 10016
(212) 727-1440

FINANCIAL SUMMARY
Recent Giving: $525,600 (1993); $477,000 (1992); $384,000 (1990)

Assets: $7,072,470 (1993); $6,368,271 (1992); $4,568,677 (1990)

EIN: 13-3025258

CONTRIBUTIONS SUMMARY
Donor(s): the late George E. Coleman, Jr.

Typical Recipients: • *Arts & Humanities:* Historic Preservation, History & Archaeology, Libraries, Museums/Galleries, Music • *Civic & Public Affairs:* Economic Policy, General, Municipalities/Towns, Philanthropic Organizations, Public Policy, Urban & Community Affairs, Zoos/Aquariums • *Education:* Colleges & Universities, Education Funds, General, International Studies, Journalism/Media Education, Private Education (Precollege), Secondary Education (Private) • *Environment:* General, Resource Conservation, Wildlife Protection • *International:* International Environmental Issues, International Peace & Security Issues, International Relations • *Religion:* Churches, Religious Organizations, Religious Welfare • *Social Services:* Youth Organizations

Grant Types: general support and research

Geographic Distribution: focus on NY, PA, and Washington, DC

GIVING OFFICERS
Denis Loncto: trust

Daniel Oliver: trust

Louise Oliver: trust *PHIL AFFIL* dir: William H. Donner Foundation

APPLICATION INFORMATION
Initial Approach: The foundation has no formal grant application procedure or application form. There are no deadlines.

GRANTS ANALYSIS
Total Grants: $525,600

Number of Grants: 40

Highest Grant: $135,000

Typical Range: $1,000 to $20,000

Disclosure Period: 1993

Note: Recent grants are derived from a 1993 Form 990.

RECENT GRANTS
General

135,000	Centre for European Defense and Strategic Studies
87,500	Heritage Foundation, Washington, DC
39,000	American Enterprise Institute for Public Policy Research, Washington, DC
35,000	Corporation for Maintaining Editorial Diversity in America, Boston, MA
30,000	Andrew Oliver Trust, New York, NY

Coltec Industries, Inc. / Coltec Industries Charitable Foundation, Inc.

Former Foundation Name: Colt Industries Charitable Foundation
Sales: $1.33 billion
Employees: 10,000
Parent Company: Coltec Holdings, Inc.
Headquarters: New York, NY
SIC Major Group: Internal Combustion Engines Nec, Tires & Inner Tubes, Gaskets, Packing & Sealing Devices, and Laminated Plastics Plate & Sheet

CONTACT
Terry Bellew
Secretary
Coltec Industries Charitable Fdn.
430 Park Ave.
New York, NY 10022
(212) 940-0400

FINANCIAL SUMMARY
Recent Giving: $329,850 (fiscal 1993); $276,580 (fiscal 1992); $308,495 (fiscal 1991)

Assets: $3,072 (fiscal 1993); $3,057 (fiscal 1992); $5,051 (fiscal 1991)

Gifts Received: $330,000 (fiscal 1993); $277,000 (fiscal 1992); $305,000 (fiscal 1991)

Fiscal Note: Above figures represent foundation giving only. Above figures exclude nonmonetary support. In fiscal 1993, contributions were received from Garlock, Inc.

EIN: 25-6057849

CONTRIBUTIONS SUMMARY
Typical Recipients: • *Arts & Humanities:* Arts Centers, Film & Video, Libraries, Performing Arts • *Civic & Public Affairs:* Business/Free Enterprise, Economic Development, Economic Policy, Legal Aid, Nonprofit Management, Philanthropic Organizations • *Education:* Colleges & Universities, Education Funds, Engineering/Technological Education • *Health:* Health Funds, Health Organizations, Hospices, Hospitals, Medical Research, Medical Training • *Science:* Scientific Organizations • *Social Services:* Community Centers, Shelters/Homelessness, United Funds/United Ways, Youth Organizations

Grant Types: general support

Geographic Distribution: nationally where company has plants or facilities

Operating Locations: AR (Pine Bluff), CA (Burbank), CT (Naugatuck, West Hartford), IA (West Des Moines), IL (Quincy), IN (Hammond), KY (Bowling Green), MA (Peabody), MI (Troy, Warren), MO (Water Valley), NC (Greensboro), NJ (Thorofare), NY (New York, Palmyra, Rochester), OK (Sallisaw), PA (Newtown), TN (Lexington), TX (Ft. Worth, Longview), WI (Beloit)

CORP. OFFICERS
Terry Bellew: *CURR EMPL* secy: Coltec Indus

Salvatore James Cozzolino: *B* New Haven CT 1924 *ED* St Johns Univ BBA 1950 *CURR EMPL* vchmn, dir: Coltec Indus *CORP AFFIL* dir: Crucible Materials Corp, Mariner Institutional Funds, Mariner Tax-Free Institutional Funds

Anthony Joseph DiBuono: *B* New York NY 1930 *ED* St Johns Univ BA 1951; St Johns Univ LLB 1954; St Johns Univ LLM 1955 *CURR EMPL* exec vp, secy, chief legal off: Coltec Indus *CORP AFFIL* secy: Coltec Holdings, Coltec Holdings; vp, secy: Garlock Inc, Walbar Inc *NONPR AFFIL* mem: Am Bar Assn *CLUB AFFIL* mem: Univ

John W. Guffey, Jr.: *B* Zanesville OH 1938 *ED* Youngstown St Univ 1962; Kent St Univ 1964 *CURR EMPL* chmn, ceo, pres, dir: Coltec Indus *CORP AFFIL* pres, dir: Garlock Inc

David Israel Margolis: *B* New York NY 1930 *ED* City Univ NY BA 1950; City Univ NY MBA 1952; NY Univ 1952-1955 *CURR EMPL* prin, dir: Coltec Indus *CORP AFFIL* chmn: Walbar Inc; chmn, ceo, dir: Garlock Inc; dir: Burlington Indus Inc, Offitbank *NONPR AFFIL* bd overseers: NY Univ Stern Sch Bus; mem: Counc Foreign Rels; trust: Presbyterian Hosp NY City

GIVING OFFICERS
Salvatore James Cozzolino: vp, treas, dir *CURR EMPL* vchmn, dir: Coltec Indus (see above)

Anthony Joseph DiBuono: vp, secy, dir *CURR EMPL* exec vp, secy, chief legal off: Coltec Indus (see above)

John J. Ennis: asst treas *CURR EMPL* asst treas: Garlock Inc

Julius Levinson: asst treas *B* New York NY 1925 *ED* City Univ NY 1947; Harvard Univ 1950 *CURR EMPL* vp taxes: Coltec Indus *NONPR AFFIL* mem: Tax Execs Inst; mem tax comm: Am Bar Assn; mem tax counc: Mfrs Alliance Productivity Innovation

David Israel Margolis: pres, dir *CURR EMPL* prin, dir: Coltec Indus (see above)

Donald E. O'Keefe: asst secy

William D. Rudolph: asst secy

APPLICATION INFORMATION
Initial Approach: *Initial Contact:* written proposal *Include Information On:* description of program, amount requested, and proof of tax-exempt status *Deadlines:* submission deadline is during the fourth quarter of the calender year

Restrictions on Giving: Company stresses location of nonprofit or program in communities and states in which company has plants or facilities.

GRANTS ANALYSIS
Total Grants: $329,850

Number of Grants: 110
Highest Grant: $36,500
Average Grant: $2,999
Typical Range: $1,000 to $5,000
Disclosure Period: fiscal year ending June 30, 1993

Note: Recent grants are derived from a fiscal 1993 Form 990.

RECENT GRANTS

Library
7,000   New York Public Library, New York, NY

General
36,500   United Way of Capital Area Fund, West Hartford, CT
29,000   United Way of Wayne County, Newark, NY
20,000   Stateline United Way, Beloit, WI
16,000   United Way of Los Angeles, Van Nuys, CA
15,000   United Way of Central Iowa, Des Moines, IA

Continental Corp. / Continental Corp. Foundation

Revenue: $5.16 billion
Employees: 16,200
Headquarters: New York, NY
SIC Major Group: Holding Companies Nec, Personal Credit Institutions, Accident & Health Insurance, and Insurance Agents, Brokers & Service

CONTACT
David Vidal
Assistant Vice President
Continental Corp. Fdn.
180 Maiden Ln., 12th Fl.
New York, NY 10038
(212) 440-7729

FINANCIAL SUMMARY
Recent Giving: $3,500,000 (1995 est.); $3,000,000 (1994 approx.); $2,204,421 (1993)

Assets: $26,340,931 (1993); $26,178,095 (1991); $25,207,612 (1990)

Fiscal Note: All contributions are made through the foundation. Above figures include general grants, scholarships, matching gifts, nonmonetary support, and grants made through the Employee Assistance Program.

EIN: 13-6090280

CONTRIBUTIONS SUMMARY
Typical Recipients: • *Arts & Humanities:* Arts Associations & Councils, Arts Centers, Arts Funds, Arts Institutes, Community Arts, Dance, Ethnic & Folk Arts, Historic Preservation, Libraries, Museums/Galleries, Music, Performing Arts, Public Broadcasting, Theater, Visual Arts • *Civic & Public Affairs:* African American Affairs, Business/Free Enterprise, Economic Development, Economic Policy, Housing, Law & Justice, Legal Aid, Municipalities/Towns, Professional & Trade Associations, Public Policy, Safety, Urban & Community Affairs, Zoos/Aquariums • *Education:* Arts/Humanities Education, Business Education, Colleges & Universities, Economic Education, Education Funds, Minority Education, Religious Education, Student Aid • *Environment:* General • *Health:* Emergency/Ambulance Services, Health Funds, Health Organizations, Hospitals, Medical Research, Single-Disease Health Associations • *International:* Foreign Educational Institutions, International Relations • *Religion:* Jewish Causes • *Social Services:* Child Welfare, Community Centers, Community Service Organizations, Delinquency & Criminal Rehabilitation, Family Services, Homes, People with Disabilities, Recreation & Athletics, Scouts, Shelters/Homelessness, Special Olympics, Substance Abuse, United Funds/United Ways, Youth Organizations

Grant Types: employee matching gifts, project, and seed money

Nonmonetary Support: $85,000 (1993)

Nonmonetary Support Types: cause-related marketing & promotion

Note: Nonmonetary support is provided by both the company and the foundation in the form of technical support in marketing for selected grants.

Geographic Distribution: primarily New York City; also gives nationally with emphasis on corporate locations

Operating Locations: CA (Los Angeles), FL (Miami), IL (Chicago), MI (Southfield), NJ (Cranbury), NY (New York), OH (Columbus)

Note: Also has operations in Bermuda, Canada, Greece, Guatemala, and the United Kingdom.

CORP. OFFICERS
John Pierre Mascotte: *B* Ft Wayne IN 1939 *ED* St Josephs Coll BA 1961; St Josephs Coll BS 1961; Univ VA LLB 1964 *CURR EMPL* chmn, ceo, dir: Continental Corp *CORP AFFIL* chmn: Boston Old Colony Ins Co, Buckeye Union Ins Co, Continental Ins Co, Fidelity and Casualty Co NY, Firemens Ins Co Newark, Franklin National-Ben Ins, Glen Falls Ins Co, Niagara Fire Ins Co, Pacific Ins Co; dir: Bus Mens Assurance Co Am, Chem Bank, Chem Banking Corp, Continental Ins Co Newark, Hallmark Cards Inc *NONPR AFFIL* chmn: Am Ins Assn *PHIL AFFIL* dir: Hall Family Foundation

GIVING OFFICERS
William Shepard Gibson: vp, secy *B* Brooklyn NY 1933 *ED* Univ IL BS 1954; Univ IL JD 1959 *CURR EMPL* vp, dir govt & pub aff: Continental Corp *CORP AFFIL* chmn: Continental PAC; vp: Fidelity & Casualty Co NY *NONPR AFFIL* dir: Lower Manhattan Cultural Counc; mem: Am Bar Assn, IL Bar Assn, Intl Assn Ins Counc, NY Bar Assn, NY Med Malpractice Ins Assoc, NY Motor Vehicle Accident Indemnity Corp

Irvine O. Hockaday, Jr.: trust *B* Ludington MI 1936 *ED* Princeton Univ AB 1958; Univ MI LLB 1961; Univ MI JD 1961 *CURR*

EMPL pres, ceo: Hallmark Cards Inc *CORP AFFIL* dir: Continental Corp, Dow Jones & Co Inc, Ford Motor Co; pres: Ctr Fixture Oper; pres, ceo, dir: Hallmark Cards Inc *NONPR AFFIL* adv trust: Middlebury Coll; mem: Midwest Res Inst; trust: Aspen Inst *CLUB AFFIL* Kansas City CC *PHIL AFFIL* dir: Hall Family Foundation

John Edward Jacob: trust *B* Trout LA 1934 *ED* Howard Univ BA 1957; Howard Univ MS 1963 *CORP AFFIL* dir: Coca-Cola Enterprises Inc, Continental Corp, LTV Corp, Natl Westminster Bancorp, NYNEX NY; exec vp, chief commun off, dir: Anheuser-Busch Cos Inc *NONPR AFFIL* chmn emeritus, trust: Howard Univ; dir: Bennett Coll, Eisenhower Fdn, Independent Sector, Jr Achievement, Local Initiatives Support Corp, Natl Conf Christians Jews, Natl Pk Fdn; mem: Acad Certified Social Workers, Natl Assn Social Workers; pres, ceo: Natl Urban League

Daniel A. Lemole: asst secy

John Pierre Mascotte: chmn, pres, trust *CURR EMPL* chmn, ceo, dir: Continental Corp *PHIL AFFIL* dir: Hall Family Foundation (see above)

Charles A. Parker: vp *B* Columbus NJ 1934 *ED* Univ CO BS 1956; Univ VA 1967 *CURR EMPL* exec vp, dir: Continental Corp *CORP AFFIL* chmn: Continental Asset Mgmt; exec vp, dir: Continental Ins Co, Fidelity & Casualty Co NY, Glen Falls Ins Co

Louis Edwin Smart, Jr.: trust *B* Columbus OH 1923 *ED* Harvard Univ AB 1947; Harvard Univ JD 1949 *CURR EMPL* couns: Hughes Hubbard & Reed *CORP AFFIL* dir: Continental Corp, Flagstar Cos Inc, Flagstar Holdings Corp, Sonat Inc, Southern Natural Resources, TW Svcs Inc *NONPR AFFIL* mem: Am Bar Assn, NY County Lawyers Assn, Phi Beta Kappa, Sigma Alpha Epsilon; trust: Comm Econ Devel, Conf Bd *CLUB AFFIL* Harvard, Marco Polo

Steven James Smith: exec vp *B* Ft Wayne IN 1945 *ED* Univ MI BA 1967; Harvard Univ MBA 1970 *CURR EMPL* exec vp, off chmn: Continental Corp *CORP AFFIL* exec vp, dir: Continental Ins Co, Fidelity & Casualty Co NY, Glen Falls Ins Co *NONPR AFFIL* dir: Ins Info Inst; mem: Am Soc CLUs; pres, mem: Chatam Sch Bd; trust: Intl Ctr Photography

David Vidal: asst vp

Francis Thomas Vincent, Jr.: trust *B* Waterbury CT 1938 *ED* Williams Coll BA 1960; Yale Univ LLB 1963 *NONPR AFFIL* mem: Phi Beta Kappa; trust: Carleton Coll, Hotchkiss Sch *CLUB AFFIL* Belle Haven, NY Athletic, Univ

Anne Wexler: trust *B* New York NY 1930 *ED* Skidmore Coll BA 1951 *CURR EMPL* chmn govt rels & pub affs couns: Wexler Reynolds Harrison & Schule Inc *CORP AFFIL* chmn: Wexler Group; dir: Am Cyanamid Co, Continental Corp, Dreyfus Index Funds, New England Electric Sys; sr vp: Hill & Knowlton Inc *NONPR AFFIL* bd advs: Carter Ctr, Emory Univ; bd dirs: Ctr Natl Policy; bd visitors: Univ MD Sch Pub Aff; mem: Comm 200, Counc Foreign Rels,

Natl Womens Forum; mem visit comm: Harvard Univ John F Kennedy Sch Govt

APPLICATION INFORMATION

Initial Approach: *Initial Contact:* letter *Include Information On:* description and objectives of organization; description of project, including why it is important and what it is expected to achieve; total budget for program and of amount requested; funding already committed or expected; size and composition of community to be served; timetable for project; names of officers and key staff members; list of names and primary professional affiliations of board members; proof of tax-exempt status; most recently audited financial statement; list of funding sources; and description of how organization will acknowledge assistance from the Continental Foundation *Deadlines:* none; most grants are issued toward year end *Note:* Application materials will not be returned to applicants.

Restrictions on Giving: The foundation will not support individuals (except through its scholarship program); religious or professional groups; basic academic or scientific research; athletic events or sponsorship; endowments or capital campaigns; organizations established to influence legislation or specific elections; annual operating support fund drives; social functions or advertising in commemorative journals, yearbooks, or special events publications; organizations that discriminate on the basis of race, religion, sex, or national origin; or religious, fraternal, or veterans organizations.

OTHER THINGS TO KNOW

In 1995, the company reported that it planned to merge with CNA Insurance of Chicago. At publication time, the merger had not yet been confirmed.

Grantee organizations must submit a yearly report to the foundation.

Long-term contributions are contingent upon satisfactory progress made during the preceding year.

Proposals are reviewed annually. In general, the foundation does not make multi-year commitments.

PUBLICATIONS

Continental Corp. Foundation Guidelines; *Continental People Care*

GRANTS ANALYSIS

Total Grants: $2,204,421*

Number of Grants: 486*

Highest Grant: $350,000

Average Grant: $4,536*

Typical Range: $100 to $5,000

Disclosure Period: 1993

Note: Total grants, number of grants, and average grant figures include scholarships, matching gifts, and grants paid through the Employee Assistance Program. Recent grants are derived from a 1993 Form 990.

RECENT GRANTS

Library
100,000	New York Public Library, New York, NY
5,000	New York Public Library Schomburg Center, New York, NY

General
230,000	United Way of Tri-State, Tri-State, NY
200,000	Local Initiatives Support Corporation, Hartford, CT
188,583	National Merit Scholarship Corporation, Evanston, IL
57,519	United Way of Franklin County, Columbus, OH
50,000	Aspen Institute, Aspen, CO

Cooperman Foundation, Leon and Toby

CONTACT
Leon Cooperman
Trustee
Leon and Toby Cooperman Fdn.
c/o Goldman Sachs and Co., 85 Broad St.
New York, NY 10004
(212) 902-6897

FINANCIAL SUMMARY
Recent Giving: $221,950 (fiscal 1994); $173,762 (fiscal 1993)

Assets: $7,021,297 (fiscal 1994); $4,573,580 (fiscal 1993)

Gifts Received: $2,054,890 (fiscal 1994)

Fiscal Note: In fiscal 1994, contributions were received from Toby F. Cooperman, and Leon G. Cooperman.

EIN: 13-3102941

CONTRIBUTIONS SUMMARY
Typical Recipients: • *Arts & Humanities:* Dance, General, Libraries • *Civic & Public Affairs:* Economic Development, General, Public Policy • *Education:* Business Education, Colleges & Universities, General, Preschool Education • *Health:* AIDS/HIV, Cancer, Children's Health/Hospitals, Clinics/Medical Centers, Hospitals, Prenatal Health Issues, Single-Disease Health Associations • *International:* Health Care/Hospitals, International Environmental Issues, Missionary/Religious Activities • *Religion:* Churches, Jewish Causes, Religious Welfare • *Social Services:* At-Risk Youth, Child Welfare, Family Services, United Funds/United Ways, Youth Organizations

Grant Types: general support

Geographic Distribution: primarily the East Coast

GIVING OFFICERS
Leon Cooperman: trust

Michael S. Cooperman: trust

Toby F. Cooperman: trust

Wayne M. Cooperman: trust

APPLICATION INFORMATION
Initial Approach: Send a brief letter of inquiry and a full proposal. Include a description of organization, amount requested, purpose of funds sought, and proof of tax-exempt status.

GRANTS ANALYSIS
Total Grants: $221,950

Number of Grants: 64

Highest Grant: $50,000

Typical Range: $250 to $10,000

Disclosure Period: fiscal year ending January 31, 1994

Note: Recent grants are derived from a fiscal 1994 Form 990.

RECENT GRANTS

General
50,000	Columbia University Graduate School of Business, New York, NY
25,000	Crohn's and Colitis Foundation, New York, NY
20,000	St. Barnabas Medical Center, Livingston, NJ
15,000	Brown University, Providence, RI
10,000	Associated Jewish Charities, Baltimore, MD

Cornell Trust, Peter C.

CONTACT
Joseph H. Morey, Jr.
Trustee
Peter C. Cornell Trust
c/o Fiduciary Services, Inc.
120 Delaware Ave., Ste. 430
Buffalo, NY 14202-2783
(716) 854-1244

FINANCIAL SUMMARY
Recent Giving: $456,000 (fiscal 1993); $474,133 (fiscal 1992); $514,500 (fiscal 1991)

Assets: $4,183,225 (fiscal 1993); $4,201,047 (fiscal 1992); $4,335,457 (fiscal 1991)

EIN: 95-1660344

CONTRIBUTIONS SUMMARY
Donor(s): the late Peter C. Cornell, M.D.

Typical Recipients: • *Arts & Humanities:* Arts Outreach, History & Archaeology, Libraries, Music, Public Broadcasting, Theater • *Civic & Public Affairs:* African American Affairs, Municipalities/Towns, Safety, Urban & Community Affairs, Zoos/Aquariums • *Education:* Arts/Humanities Education, Colleges & Universities, Continuing Education, Education Funds, Education Reform, Legal Education, Literacy, Medical Education, Minority Education, Private Education (Precollege), Special Education • *Health:* Alzheimers Disease, Children's Health/Hospitals, Clinics/Medical Centers, Emergency/Ambulance Services, Health Organizations, Hospices, Hospitals, Long-Term Care, Nursing Services, Single-Disease Health Associations • *Religion:* Churches, Ministries, Religious Organizations, Religious Welfare, Seminaries • *Sci-*

ence: Science Museums, Scientific Organizations • *Social Services:* Child Welfare, Community Service Organizations, Family Planning, Family Services, Food/Clothing Distribution, People with Disabilities, Senior Services, Substance Abuse, United Funds/United Ways, Youth Organizations

Grant Types: capital, emergency, general support, multiyear/continuing support, operating expenses, and seed money

Geographic Distribution: focus on Buffalo and Erie County, NY

GIVING OFFICERS

Wende Alford: trust

S. Douglas Cornell: trust

Joseph H. Morey, Jr.: trust

APPLICATION INFORMATION

Initial Approach: Send cover letter and full proposal. Include a description of organization, amount requested, purpose of funds sought, recently audited financial statement, and proof of tax-exempt status. The deadline is October 1.

Restrictions on Giving: Does not provide loans or support individuals, demonstration projects, publications, or conferences.

PUBLICATIONS

Application Guidelines

GRANTS ANALYSIS

Total Grants: $456,000

Number of Grants: 66

Highest Grant: $80,000

Typical Range: $1,000 to $10,000

Disclosure Period: fiscal year ending September 30, 1993

Note: Recent grants are derived from a fiscal 1993 Form 990.

RECENT GRANTS

General
80,000	University at Buffalo Foundation, Buffalo, NY — final payment on grant
35,000	Lifelong Learning Center, Austin, TN — seventh payment
33,000	United Way of Buffalo, Buffalo, NY — operating funds
25,000	Hospice Buffalo, Buffalo, NY — final payment on grant
20,000	Millard Fillmore Hospital, Buffalo, NY — capital campaign

Corning Incorporated / Corning Incorporated Foundation

Revenue: $4.79 billion
Employees: 39,000
Headquarters: Corning, NY
SIC Major Group: Pressed & Blown Glass Nec, Nonferrous Wiredrawing & Insulating, Telephone & Telegraph Apparatus, and Laboratory Apparatus & Furniture

CONTACT
Kristin A. Swain
President
Corning Incorporated Fdn.
Main Plant, LB-02-1
Corning, NY 14831
(607) 974-8746
Note: Alternative phone number is (607) 974-8749. An alternative contact is Karen C. Martin, program supervisor.

FINANCIAL SUMMARY
Recent Giving: $2,397,820 (1994 approx.); $2,624,453 (1993); $2,239,674 (1992)

Assets: $2,829,446 (1993); $2,861,308 (1992); $2,845,967 (1991)

Gifts Received: $2,648,412 (1993)

Fiscal Note: Company gives primarily through foundation. Above figures include nonmonetary support.

EIN: 16-6051394

CONTRIBUTIONS SUMMARY
Typical Recipients: • *Arts & Humanities:* Arts Associations & Councils, Arts Outreach, Community Arts, Historic Preservation, Libraries, Museums/Galleries, Music, Performing Arts, Public Broadcasting, Visual Arts • *Civic & Public Affairs:* Community Foundations, Economic Development, Employment/Job Training, Municipalities/Towns, Professional & Trade Associations, Public Policy, Urban & Community Affairs, Women's Affairs • *Education:* Business Education, Business-School Partnerships, Colleges & Universities, Education Reform, Engineering/Technological Education, Faculty Development, Minority Education, Public Education (Precollege), Science/Mathematics Education, Student Aid • *Environment:* General • *Health:* Emergency/Ambulance Services, Hospitals (University Affiliated) • *Social Services:* Family Planning, Recreation & Athletics, Scouts, United Funds/United Ways, Youth Organizations

Grant Types: employee matching gifts and project

Note: Employee matching gift ratio: 1 to 1.

Nonmonetary Support Types: loaned executives

Note: Nonmonetary support is provided by the company.

Geographic Distribution: principally near operating locations; international giving is restricted to U.S.-based organizations with an international focus

Operating Locations: CA (Chatsworth, San Fernando), IL (Clinton), KY (Harrodsburg), NC (Hickory, Wilmington), NJ (Teterboro), NY (Big Flats, Canton, Corning, Erwin, Horseheads, Oneonta), OH (Cincinnati, Greenville), PA (Charleroi, Greencastle, State College), VA (Blacksburg, Danville, Vienna, Waynesboro), WI (Madison), WV (Martinsburg, Parkersburg)

CORP. OFFICERS
Chesley Peter Washburn Booth: *B* Huntington NY 1939 *ED* Harvard Univ AB 1961; Harvard Univ JD 1965 *CURR EMPL* sr vp devel: Corning Inc *NONPR AFFIL* mem: Assn Bar City New York *CLUB AFFIL* Univ

Van C. Campbell: *B* Charleston WV 1938 *ED* Cornell Univ BA 1960; Harvard Univ MBA 1963 *CURR EMPL* vchmn admin & fin: Corning Inc *CORP AFFIL* dir: Armstrong World Indus, Chase Lincoln First Bank NA, Corning Intl Corp, Corning Lab Svcs Inc, Dow Corning Corp, Gen Signal Corp, Pittsburgh-Corning Corp; vchmn: Corning Glass Works *NONPR AFFIL* trust: Corning Glass Works Fdn

David Allen Duke: *B* Salt Lake City UT 1935 *ED* Univ UT BS 1957; Univ UT MS 1959; Univ UT PhD 1962 *CURR EMPL* vchmn tech, dir: Corning Inc *CORP AFFIL* dir: Armco Inc, Ciba Corning Diagnostics Corp, Corning Inc, Corning Intl Corp, Dow Corning Corp, Siecor Corp, Siecor GmbH *NONPR AFFIL* mem: Am Ceramic Soc, Natl Acad Engg

Kenneth W. Freeman: *B* White Plains NY 1950 *ED* Bucknell Univ 1972; Harvard Univ 1976 *CURR EMPL* pres, coo: Corning Asahi Video Products Co *CORP AFFIL* dir: Dow Corning Corp; exec vp: Corning Inc

Norman E. Garrity: *B* Homestead PA 1941 *ED* Bucknell Univ 1962; Bucknell Univ 1963 *CURR EMPL* exec vp: Corning Inc

James Richardson Houghton: *B* Corning NY 1936 *ED* Harvard Univ AB 1958; Harvard Univ MBA 1962 *CURR EMPL* chmn, ceo, dir: Corning Inc *CORP AFFIL* chmn, pres: Corning Glass Intl, Corning Intl Corp; dir: CBS Inc, Dow Corning Corp, Metro Life Ins Co, JP Morgan & Co, Owens-Corning Fiberglas Corp *NONPR AFFIL* mem: Bus Comm Arts New York City, Bus Roundtable, Counc Foreign Rels; mem bus counc: Trilateral Commn; trust: Bus Counc NY, Corning Mus Glass, Metro Mus Art, Pierpont Morgan Lib *PHIL AFFIL* vp, trust: Houghton Foundation, Houghton Foundation *CLUB AFFIL* Augusta Natl GC, Brookline CC, Corning CC, Harvard, Laurel Valley GC, Links, River, Rolling Rock, Tarratine, Univ

Martin Rome: *CURR EMPL* dir pub aff: Corning Inc

GIVING OFFICERS
Roger G. Ackerman: trust *B* Peterson NJ 1938 *ED* Rutgers Univ 1960; Rutgers Univ 1962 *CURR EMPL* pres, coo, dir: Corning Inc *CORP AFFIL* dir: Corning Intl Corp, Dow Corning Corp, MA Mutual Life Ins Co, Pittsburgh Corning Corp, Pittston Co, Siecor Corp *NONPR AFFIL* mem exec comm: Natl Assn Mfrs

Chesley Peter Washburn Booth: trust *CURR EMPL* sr vp devel: Corning Inc (see above)

Lindsay W. Brown: treas *CURR EMPL* asst treas, dir: Corning Mus Glass

Thomas Scharman Buechner: trust *B* New York NY 1926 *ED* Princeton Univ 1945; Ecole des Beaux Arts 1946; Institut voor Pictologie 1947; Univ Paris 1947 *CORP AFFIL* consult: Corning Glass Works; dir: Corning Hilton Hotel *NONPR AFFIL* dir: Brooklyn Mus, Market St Restoration Agency; mem: Brooklyn Inst Arts & Sci, Natl Collection Fine Arts; mem faculty art sch: Bild-Werk Fravenau Germany; pres: Corning Mus Glass; trust: Chemung County Performing Arts, Corning Glass Works Fdn, Pilchuck Fdn, Rockwell Mus, Tiffany Fdn *CLUB AFFIL* Century Assn

Van C. Campbell: trust *CURR EMPL* vchmn admin & fin: Corning Inc (see above)

David Allen Duke: trust *CURR EMPL* vchmn tech, dir: Corning Inc (see above)

Kenneth W. Freeman: trust *CURR EMPL* pres, coo: Corning Asahi Video Products Co (see above)

Norman E. Garrity: trust *CURR EMPL* exec vp: Corning Inc (see above)

M. Ann Gosnell: asst secy *CURR EMPL* asst secy, dir: Corning Intl Corp *CORP AFFIL* asst secy, dir: Corning Enterprises Inc

Sandra L. Helton: chmn, trust *B* Paintsville KY 1949 *ED* Univ KY BS 1971; MA Inst Tech MBA 1977 *CURR EMPL* sr vp, treas: Corning Inc *CORP AFFIL* vp, treas: Corning Glass Works; vp, treas, dir: Corning Intl Corp *NONPR AFFIL* dir: Arnot Hosp Fdn; dir, mem fin comm: Clemens Performing Arts Ctr; mem bus comm: Metro Mus Art; pres bd dirs: Rockwell Mus; treas, dir: Corning Mus Glass

James Richardson Houghton: trust *CURR EMPL* chmn, ceo, dir: Corning Inc *PHIL AFFIL* vp, trust: Houghton Foundation (see above)

John W. Loose: trust *B* Hartford CT 1942 *ED* Earlham Coll BA 1964 *CURR EMPL* chmn, ceo: Corning Vitro Corp *CORP AFFIL* chmn: Revere Ware Corp; dir: Polaroid Corp; pres, ceo: Corning Consumer Products Co

Karen C. Martin: program supvr

Arthur John Peck, Jr.: secy *B* Trenton NJ 1940 *ED* Yale Univ BA 1962; Washington & Lee Univ LLB 1968 *CURR EMPL* secy: Corning Inc *CORP AFFIL* secy, dir: Corning Intl Corp *NONPR AFFIL* asst secy, dir: Corning Mus Glass

Richard E. Rahill: trust *B* 1934 *CURR EMPL* pres, dir: Corning Enterprises Inc

James M. Ramich: trust *CURR EMPL* pres: Corning Japan KK

Jan H. Suwinski: trust *B* Buffalo NY 1941 *ED* Cornell Univ BME 1964; Cornell Univ MBA 1965 *CURR EMPL* exec vp optp-electronics: Corning Inc *CORP AFFIL* chmn: Siecor Corp

Kristin A. Swain: pres

William Casper Ughetta: trust *B* New York NY 1933 *ED* Princeton Univ AB 1954; Har-

vard Univ LLB 1959 *CURR EMPL* sr vp, gen couns: Corning Inc *CORP AFFIL* dir: Chemung Canal Trust Co, Corning Europe Inc, Corning France, Corning Hilton Inn, Hazleton Labs Corp, Metpath, Siecor Corp; sr vp, gen couns: Corning Glass Works; vp, gen couns, dir: Corning Intl Corp *NONPR AFFIL* dir: Boy Scouts Am; mem: Am Bar Assn, Am Corp Couns Assn, Assn Bar City New York, NY Bar Assn; off: Corning Glass Works Fdn; secy, dir: Corning Mus Glass; trust: Corning Commun Coll *CLUB AFFIL* Corning CC, Princeton, Univ

APPLICATION INFORMATION
Initial Approach: *Initial Contact:* brief letter *Include Information On:* project's purpose, details on how its objectives are to be attained and evaluated, latest financial statement and itemized project budget, other potential and secured sources of support, description of the organization, list of officers and board members, amount requested, date when funds are needed, project timetable, proof of tax-exempt status, and an explanation of how the request meets foundation's goals. *Deadlines:* none

Restrictions on Giving: Grants are not made to individuals; political parties, campaigns, or causes; labor or veterans organizations; religious groups; fraternal orders; united fund member agencies; or for fund-raising dinners, special events, or goodwill advertising.

OTHER THINGS TO KNOW
Foundation prefers to support projects that not only are innovative but benefit the most persons over the longest period of time.

PUBLICATIONS
Guidelines

GRANTS ANALYSIS
Total Grants: $2,397,820

Number of Grants: 209*

Highest Grant: $235,000

Average Grant: $7,696*

Typical Range: $1,000 to $2,500

Disclosure Period: 1994

Note: Number of grants and average grant figures exclude matching gifts. Recent grants are derived from a 1994 grants list.

RECENT GRANTS

General

235,000	United Way of Chemung and Steuben Counties, Corning, NY —for general program support
44,000	Corning City School District, Painted Post, NY —for curriculum enrichment
37,500	Elmira College, Elmira, NY —for building/renovation project
33,000	Cornell University, Ithaca, NY —for Center for the Environment
30,000	University Medical Center Corporation, Tucson, AZ —for Child Life Program

Cosmair, Inc.
Sales: $1.3 billion
Employees: 500
Headquarters: Clark, NJ
SIC Major Group: Chemicals & Allied Products

CONTACT
Joan Lasker
Vice President, Corp. Public Relations
Cosmair, Inc.
575 Fifth Ave.
New York, NY 10017
(212) 984-4105

FINANCIAL SUMMARY
Fiscal Note: Company does not disclose contributions figures.

CONTRIBUTIONS SUMMARY
Priorities are various social services and health programs, which receive over half of total contributions. Arts and civic organizations are next highest priority. Company also sponsors educational matching grants program. Company reports the majority of giving is for business-related charitable events.

Typical Recipients: • *Arts & Humanities:* Dance, Ethnic & Folk Arts, General, Historic Preservation, Libraries, Literary Arts, Museums/Galleries, Music, Opera, Performing Arts, Public Broadcasting, Theater, Visual Arts • *Civic & Public Affairs:* General, Housing, Philanthropic Organizations, Urban & Community Affairs • *Education:* General • *Health:* General, Hospitals, Medical Research, Nursing Services, Single-Disease Health Associations • *Religion:* Churches, General, Missionary Activities (Domestic), Religious Organizations, Synagogues/Temples • *Science:* General • *Social Services:* Animal Protection, Child Welfare, Emergency Relief, General, Senior Services, Shelters/Homelessness, Substance Abuse, United Funds/United Ways, Volunteer Services, Youth Organizations

Nonmonetary Support Types: donated products

Geographic Distribution: New York and New Jersey metropolitan area

Operating Locations: NJ, NY

CORP. OFFICERS
Roger Dolden: *CURR EMPL* sr vp fin, cfo: Cosmair

Lindsay Owen-Jones: *CURR EMPL* chmn, dir: Cosmair

Guy Peyrelongue: *CURR EMPL* pres, ceo, dir: Cosmair

Michel Somnolet: *CURR EMPL* coo, exec vp, dir: Cosmair

GIVING OFFICERS
Joan Lasker: *CURR EMPL* vp corp pub rels: Cosmair

APPLICATION INFORMATION
Initial Approach: Send a proposal, including a description of organization, amount requested, and purpose of funds sought.

Restrictions on Giving: Does not support individuals or political or lobbying groups.

GRANTS ANALYSIS
Typical Range: $1,000 to $5,000

Cowles Charitable Trust

CONTACT
Mary Croft
Secretary and Treasurer
Cowles Charitable Trust
630 Fifth Ave., Ste. 1612
New York, NY 10111
(212) 765-6262
Note: Faxed proposals are not accepted.

FINANCIAL SUMMARY
Recent Giving: $995,300 (1993); $991,750 (1992); $900,650 (1991)

Assets: $18,099,844 (1993); $17,020,877 (1992); $15,858,715 (1991)

Gifts Received: $1,039,802 (1986)

EIN: 13-6090295

CONTRIBUTIONS SUMMARY
Donor(s): The trust was established in 1948 with funds contributed by Gardner Cowles, Jr. Mr. Cowles, along with his father, Gardner Cowles, Sr., and brother, John Cowles, built a media empire which included the *Des Moines Register*, the *Evening Tribune*, the *Minneapolis Star*, *Look Magazine*, and radio and television stations. In 1985, the Des Moines Register and Tribune Company, owned primarily by the Cowles, sold its newspapers to Gannett Company for $260 million. Cowles Media of Minneapolis, MN, a private corporation, is owned almost entirely by descendants of John Cowles, Sr.

Typical Recipients: • *Arts & Humanities:* Arts Appreciation, Arts Associations & Councils, Arts Centers, Arts Funds, Arts Institutes, Community Arts, Dance, General, Historic Preservation, History & Archaeology, Libraries, Museums/Galleries, Music, Opera, Performing Arts, Public Broadcasting, Visual Arts • *Civic & Public Affairs:* African American Affairs, Botanical Gardens/Parks, Civil Rights, Clubs, Employment/Job Training, General, Legal Aid, Urban & Community Affairs, Women's Affairs, Zoos/Aquariums • *Education:* Arts/Humanities Education, Colleges & Universities, Faculty Development, Literacy, Minority Education, Private Education (Precollege), Social Sciences Education • *Environment:* General • *Health:* AIDS/HIV, Cancer, Clinics/Medical Centers, Emergency/Ambulance Services, Health Organizations, Hospitals, Medical Research, Mental Health, Single-Disease Health Associations • *International:* Foreign Educational Institutions • *Religion:* Religious Welfare • *Science:* Scientific Centers & Institutes • *Social Services:* Animal Protection, Child Welfare, Community Centers, Community Service Organizations, Counseling, Crime Prevention, Delinquency & Criminal Rehabilitation, Emergency Relief,

Family Planning, Family Services, Food/Clothing Distribution, People with Disabilities, Senior Services, Shelters/Homelessness, Substance Abuse, United Funds/United Ways, Volunteer Services, Youth Organizations

Grant Types: capital, emergency, endowment, general support, operating expenses, and project

Geographic Distribution: national, with emphasis in New York City

GIVING OFFICERS
Charles Cowles: trust *B* Santa Monica CA 1941 *ED* Stanford Univ 1959-1965 *CURR EMPL* pres, dir: Charles Cowles Gallery *NONPR AFFIL* chmn, trust: NY Studio Sch; mem: Art Dealers Assn Am

Gardner Cowles III: pres, trust *PHIL AFFIL* trust: Gardner Cowles Charitable Foundation

Jan Streate Cowles: trust *B* Berkeley CA 1918

Mary Croft: secy, treas

Lois Cowles Harrison: trust

Kate Cowles Nichols: trust

Virginia Cowles Schroth: trust

APPLICATION INFORMATION
Initial Approach:

Applicants should send seven copies of a full proposal to the trust.

A brief letter of application should be included along with proposal. The letter should describe the organization, its history, and scope of current activities. It should also include a description of the project; explanation of the need for the project; statement of its objectives or goals; timetable; and a statement of the project's overall cost including a detailed list of additional sources of project support. If the letter of application is submitted by someone other than the chief executive officer, a separate letter for organization's chief executive officer should be included.

Proposals should include a project budget, as well as a list of the organization's governing body and its officers, showing business, professional and community affiliations. Also to be included is one copy of the most recent letter from the Internal Revenue Service determining the organization's current tax-exempt status under both sections 501(c)(3) and 509 of the Internal Revenue Code. The foundation also needs one copy of the organization's most recent audited financial statement and other supporting documents if they supplement but do not substitute for the essential information specified for inclusion in the letter of application. Videos and other special supplementary material cannot be returned to applicants. Proposal materials need not be bound, inserted in protective sleeves or prepared in notebooks, etc.

Any eligible request that arrives too late for one meeting will be placed on the agenda of the following meeting. Proposals must be received at the trust offices by 5 p.m. on the following dates to be included on the agendas noted: December 1 - January agenda;

March 1 - April agenda; June 1 - July agenda; and September 1 October agenda.

The board meets in January, April, July, and October to review proposals. The trust will notify, in writing, all grant applicants generally within two weeks of a board meeting.

Restrictions on Giving: No contributions are made to individuals. The trust will also not consider more than one application from any one organization within a 12 month period. The trust also does not consider applications from any nonprofit receiving a multiyear grant until payment of that grant is completed.

PUBLICATIONS
Annual report and guidelines

GRANTS ANALYSIS
Total Grants: $995,300

Number of Grants: 185

Highest Grant: $75,000

Average Grant: $5,380

Typical Range: $500 to $10,000

Disclosure Period: 1993

Note: Recent grants are derived from a 1993 Form 990

RECENT GRANTS

Library
20,000	Forest Avenue Library
10,000	New York Public Library, New York, NY

General
50,000	New York Studio School of Drawing, Painting, and Sculpture, New York, NY
50,000	Tampa Bay Research Institute, Tampa Bay, FL
38,000	Planned Parenthood of Central Florida, Orlando, FL
30,000	National Council on Crime and Delinquency, San Francisco, CA
30,000	Palmer Trinity School

Crary Foundation, Bruce L.

CONTACT
Richard W. Lawrence, Jr.
President
Bruce L. Crary Fdn.
PO Box 396
Elizabethtown, NY 12932
(518) 873-6496

FINANCIAL SUMMARY
Recent Giving: $282,929 (fiscal 1994); $295,526 (fiscal 1993); $290,896 (fiscal 1992)

Assets: $6,194,546 (fiscal 1994); $6,564,123 (fiscal 1993); $6,644,467 (fiscal 1992)

EIN: 23-7366844

CONTRIBUTIONS SUMMARY
Donor(s): Crary Public Trust, the late Bruce L. Crary

Typical Recipients: • *Arts & Humanities:* Arts Centers, Historic Preservation, History & Archaeology, Libraries • *Civic & Public Affairs:* Urban & Community Affairs • *Education:* Community & Junior Colleges, Secondary Education (Private) • *Environment:* General • *Health:* Emergency/Ambulance Services, Hospices, Hospitals, Mental Health • *Social Services:* Animal Protection, Community Service Organizations, Domestic Violence, Family Planning

Grant Types: general support and scholarship

Geographic Distribution: for higher education scholarships: limited to Clinton, Essex, Franklin, Hamilton, and Warren counties, NY; for educational and social service agencies: Essex County, NY

GIVING OFFICERS
G. Gordon Davis, Esq.: secy, trust

Janet Decker: gov

Euphemia V. Hall: vp, trust

Richard Wesley Lawrence, Jr.: pres, trust *B* New York NY 1909 *ED* Princeton Univ BS 1931; Columbia Univ LLB 1934 *CURR EMPL* pres, dir: Conservation Mgmt *CORP AFFIL* vp, dir: Umont Mining Inc *NONPR AFFIL* chmn: Commnr Edns Comm on Reference & Res, Lib Resources; dir: New York Parks & Conservation Assn; hon mem: New York Lib Assn; mem: Govs Commnr on Future of Adirondacks in the 21st Century; pres: Crary Ed Fdn; trust: NY St Historical Assn *CLUB AFFIL* Ausable, Essex County Hist Soc, Explorers, Princeton, Union League

Meredith Prime: trust *PHIL AFFIL* trust: David A. Weir, Jr. Family Foundation

Arthur Savage: treas, trust *PHIL AFFIL* trust: Adirondack Historical Association; dir: George W. Perkins Memorial Foundation

APPLICATION INFORMATION
Initial Approach: The foundation has no formal grant application procedure or application form. There are no deadlines. Student aid applications should include information regarding financial need, cost of institution of choice, scholastic information, and high school achievement. Deadline for student aid is March 31.

Restrictions on Giving: Limited to charitable organizations in Essex County, NY. Student Aid is limited to Clinton, Essex, Franklin, Hamilton, and Warren County, NY.

OTHER THINGS TO KNOW
Provides scholarships to individuals for higher education.

GRANTS ANALYSIS
Total Grants: $282,929

Number of Grants: 562*

Highest Grant: $9,709

Typical Range: $100 to $3,000

Disclosure Period: fiscal year ending June 30, 1994

Note: Recent grants are derived from a fiscal 1994 Form 990. Number of grants is approximate.

RECENT GRANTS
Library

500	Foundation Center, New York, NY

General

8,453	Hand House, Elizabethtown, NY — for meetings and conferences of community organizations
3,000	Citizen's Domestic Violence Program, Elizabethtown, NY
1,000	Boquet River Association, Elizabethtown, NY
1,000	Elizabethtown Community Hospital, Elizabethtown, NY — Hale memorial grant
750	Northern Adirondack Planned Parenthood, Plattsburgh, NY

CS First Boston Corporation / CS First Boston Foundation Trust

Former Foundation Name: First Boston Foundation Trust
Employees: 4,040
Parent Company: CS First Boston, Inc.
Headquarters: New York, NY
SIC Major Group: Security Brokers & Dealers

CONTACT
Larry Reno
Vice President
CS First Boston Foundation Trust
55 E 52nd St.
New York, NY 10055
(212) 909-4571

FINANCIAL SUMMARY
Recent Giving: $557,500 (1994 approx.); $1,336,266 (1993); $1,192,629 (1992)

Assets: $305,694 (1993); $326,725 (1992); $281,604 (1991)

Gifts Received: $1,318,085 (1993); $1,244,975 (1992)

Fiscal Note: Company gives directly and through the foundation. Figures are for foundation only. Company is a private firm that does not reveal its direct giving figures. Above figures exclude nonmonetary support. In 1994, the foundation cancelled its employee matching gifts program. In 1993, the foundaiton received contributions from CS First Boston Corporation.

EIN: 04-6059692

CONTRIBUTIONS SUMMARY
Typical Recipients: • *Arts & Humanities:* Arts Associations & Councils, Arts Centers, Arts Funds, Arts Institutes, Dance, Libraries, Museums/Galleries, Music, Opera, Performing Arts, Public Broadcasting, Theater • *Civic & Public Affairs:* African American Affairs, Botanical Gardens/Parks, Business/Free Enterprise, Civil Rights, Economic Development, Economic Policy, General, Municipalities/Towns, Professional & Trade Associations, Public Policy, Urban & Community Affairs, Women's Affairs • *Education:* Business Education, Colleges

& Universities, Continuing Education, Economic Education, Education Funds, Education Reform, Engineering/Technological Education, Minority Education, Preschool Education, Private Education (Precollege), Public Education (Precollege), Special Education • *Environment:* Air/Water Quality • *Health:* Cancer, Children's Health/Hospitals, Clinics/Medical Centers, Emergency/Ambulance Services, Medical Research, Mental Health, Single-Disease Health Associations, Transplant Networks/Donor Banks • *International:* Health Care/Hospitals, International Relations • *Religion:* Religious Welfare • *Social Services:* At-Risk Youth, Child Welfare, Community Centers, Community Service Organizations, People with Disabilities, Recreation & Athletics, Shelters/Homelessness, Special Olympics, United Funds/United Ways, Volunteer Services, YMCA/YWCA/YMHA/YWHA, Youth Organizations

Grant Types: general support

Note: The foundation also awards minigrants.

Nonmonetary Support Types: donated equipment and workplace solicitation

Note: Value of noncash donations is not available.

Geographic Distribution: nationally and near operating locations

Operating Locations: NY (New York), PR (Hato Rey)

Note: Maintains offices in principal cities throughout the United States.

CORP. OFFICERS
John M. Hennessy: *B* 1936 *ED* Harvard Univ; MA Inst Tech *CURR EMPL* ceo: CS First Boston Corp *CORP AFFIL* dir: Corning Inc

Ruedi Stalder: *B* Solothurn Switzerland 1940 *CURR EMPL* cfo, mem exec bd: CS First Boston Corp *CORP AFFIL* dir: CS First Boston Corp NY USA, CS First Boston Ltd Zug, CS First Boston Pacific Inc; mem exec bd: CS Holding Zurich

Maynard Joy Toll, Jr.: *B* Los Angeles CA 1942 *ED* Stanford Univ BA 1963; Johns Hopkins Univ MA 1965; Johns Hopkins Univ PhD 1970 *CURR EMPL* dir mktg & corp contributions: CS First Boston Corp *NONPR AFFIL* mem: Counc Foreign Rels *CLUB AFFIL* Anglers NY, Links, Vineyard Haven YC

Allen D. Wheat: *CURR EMPL* pres, coo: CS First Boston Corp

GIVING OFFICERS
Becky Barfield-Johnson: trust

William Bowden: trust *CURR EMPL* gen couns: CS First Boston Corp

Adrian R. T. Cooper: trust *CURR EMPL* mng dir: CS First Boston Corp

Ken Miller: vchmn *CURR EMPL* vchmn: CS First Boston Corp *CORP AFFIL* dir: Kinder-Care Learning Ctrs, Viacom Inc

David C. O'Leary: chmn, trust

Douglas L. Paul: trust

Larry Reno: vp *CURR EMPL* vp, dir corp contributions: First Boston Corp

Ruedi Stalder: trust *CURR EMPL* cfo, mem exec bd: CS First Boston Corp (see above)

Maynard Joy Toll, Jr.: trust *CURR EMPL* dir mktg & corp contributions: CS First Boston Corp (see above)

APPLICATION INFORMATION
Initial Approach: *Initial Contact:* brief letter requesting guidelines *Include Information On:* description of the organization, amount requested, purpose for which funds are sought, recently audited financial statement, proof of tax-exempt status, and list of board members *Deadlines:* none

Restrictions on Giving: Foundation does not give to political or religious groups, or member agencies of united funds.

OTHER THINGS TO KNOW
In 1994, the company reported that it has changed its name. The company was formerly known as First Boston Inc. The company is now known as CS First Boston Corp. Additionally, the company's trust has changed its name from First Boston Foundation Trust to CS First Boston Foundation Trust.

PUBLICATIONS
Guidelines

GRANTS ANALYSIS
Total Grants: $557,400

Number of Grants: 105

Highest Grant: $100,000

Average Grant: $5,309

Typical Range: $1,000 to $10,000

Disclosure Period: 1994

Note: Recent grants are derived from a 1993 Form 990.

RECENT GRANTS
Library
20,000	New York Public Library, New York, NY

General
100,000	Covenant House, New York, NY
40,141	Pride First Corporation, New York, NY
25,000	Americas Society, Washington, DC
25,000	United Way of Tri-State, Tri-State, NY
20,000	Carnegie Mellon University, Pittsburgh, PA

Culver Foundation, Constans

CONTACT
Robert Rosenthal
Vice President
Constans Culver Fdn.
c/o Chemical Bank
270 Park Ave.
New York, NY 10017
(212) 270-9109

FINANCIAL SUMMARY
Recent Giving: $249,150 (1993); $259,200 (1992); $259,100 (1990)

Assets: $5,044,527 (1993); $4,860,495 (1992); $4,424,411 (1990)

EIN: 13-6048059

CONTRIBUTIONS SUMMARY
Donor(s): the late Erne Constans Culver

Typical Recipients: • *Arts & Humanities:* Arts Centers, Community Arts, History & Archaeology, Libraries, Museums/Galleries, Music, Opera, Performing Arts, Theater • *Civic & Public Affairs:* Botanical Gardens/Parks, Economic Development, General, Public Policy, Urban & Community Affairs, Zoos/Aquariums • *Education:* Arts/Humanities Education, Colleges & Universities, General, Minority Education, Private Education (Precollege), Student Aid • *Environment:* General • *Health:* Emergency/Ambulance Services, Hospitals • *International:* International Development • *Religion:* Churches, Jewish Causes, Religious Organizations, Religious Welfare • *Science:* Science Museums • *Social Services:* At-Risk Youth, Child Welfare, Community Service Organizations, Family Services, Homes, People with Disabilities, Recreation & Athletics, United Funds/United Ways, YMCA/YWCA/YMHA/YWHA, Youth Organizations

Grant Types: general support and multi-year/continuing support

Geographic Distribution: focus on NY

GIVING OFFICERS
Chemical Bank: trust

Pauline May Herd: trust

Victoria Prescott Herd: trust

APPLICATION INFORMATION
Initial Approach: The foundation has no formal grant application procedure or application form. There are no deadlines.

GRANTS ANALYSIS
Total Grants: $249,150

Number of Grants: 110

Highest Grant: $22,500

Typical Range: $500 to $5,000

Disclosure Period: 1993

Note: Recent grants are derived from a 1993 Form 990.

RECENT GRANTS
Library
3,000	Brooklyn Public Library, Brooklyn, NY
2,500	New York Public Library, New York, NY

General
22,500	Third Church of Christ Scientist, New York, NY
5,000	Brooklyn Botanic Garden, Brooklyn, NY
5,000	Episcopal Church Foundation, New York, NY
5,000	Grace Church Building Fund, New York, NY
5,000	Melmark Home, Berwyn, PA

Cummings Foundation, James H.

CONTACT
William J. McFarland
Executive Director and Secretary
James H. Cummings Foundation
1807 Elmwood Avenue, Rm. 112
Buffalo, NY 14207
(716) 874-0040

FINANCIAL SUMMARY
Recent Giving: $539,079 (fiscal 1994); $631,844 (fiscal 1993); $708,818 (fiscal 1992)

Assets: $14,823,968 (fiscal 1993); $14,281,808 (fiscal 1992); $13,217,155 (fiscal 1991)

EIN: 16-0864200

CONTRIBUTIONS SUMMARY
Donor(s): The James H. Cummings Foundation was established in 1962, under the will of James H. Cummings . Mr. Cummings was a prominent manufacturer of pharmaceuticals with operations in Buffalo, NY, and Toronto, Ontario.

Typical Recipients: • *Arts & Humanities:* History & Archaeology, Libraries, Music, Public Broadcasting • *Civic & Public Affairs:* Clubs, Employment/Job Training, General, Municipalities/Towns, Urban & Community Affairs • *Education:* Colleges & Universities, Community & Junior Colleges, General, Minority Education, Private Education (Precollege), Secondary Education (Public), Special Education, Student Aid • *Health:* Cancer, Children's Health/Hospitals, Clinics/Medical Centers, Geriatric Health, Health Organizations, Heart, Hospices, Hospitals, Medical Research, Medical Training, Respiratory • *International:* Health Care/Hospitals • *Religion:* Churches, Jewish Causes, Religious Organizations, Religious Welfare • *Science:* Science Museums • *Social Services:* Camps, Community Service Organizations, Family Services, Food/Clothing Distribution, General, Homes, People with Disabilities, Recreation & Athletics, United Funds/United Ways, Youth Organizations

Grant Types: capital, project, and research

Geographic Distribution: support limited to the cities of Buffalo, NY; Toronto, Ontario; and Hendersonville, NC

GIVING OFFICERS
Kenneth M. Alford, MD: vp, dir

William George Gisel: pres, dir *B* Jamestown NY 1916 *ED* Miami Univ 1937 *CORP AFFIL* dir: Devon Group, Niagara Share Corp, Reeves Brothers; trust: Gold Dome Savings Bank, Western NY Savings Bank *NONPR AFFIL* comr: Niagara Frontier Transportation Authority; mem: Natl Defense Transportation Assn, Natl Security Indus Assn

Robert James Armstrong Irwin: treas, dir *B* Buffalo NY 1927 *ED* Colgate Univ BA 1949; Babson Inst Fin 1953 *CURR EMPL*

pres, ceo, dir: Niagara Share Corp *CORP AFFIL* dir: Kleinwort Benson Investment Strategies, St Joe Paper Co; dir, dep chmn: ASA Ltd; mem dirs adv counc: Mfrs & Traders Trust Co; mem inst invest comm: Nat Assn of Security Dealers *NONPR AFFIL* chmn: Buffalo Med Fdn; dir: Boys Club Western NY; mem: NY St Comptrs Investment Adv Comm; trust: Grosvenor Soc, Old Ft Niagara Assn, Ridley Coll Scholarship Fund, St Barnabas Coll Fdn *CLUB AFFIL* Buffalo, Canoe, Mid Day, Royal Canadian YC, Saturn, University *PHIL AFFIL* trust: Baird Foundation

William J. McFarland: exec dir, secy

John Patrick Naughton, MD: dir *B* West Nanticoke PA 1933 *ED* Cameron St Coll AA 1952; St Louis Univ BS 1954; OK Univ MD 1958 *NONPR AFFIL* dean, prof: St Univ NY Buffalo Sch Medicine; dir: Natl Exercise Heart Disease Project; fellow: Am Coll Cardiology, Am Coll Chest Physicians, Am Coll Physicians, Am Coll Sports Medicine

Robert S. Scheu: dir *PHIL AFFIL* vp, trust: Western New York Foundation

John N. Walsh, Jr.: dir

APPLICATION INFORMATION
Initial Approach:

A preliminary letter or telephone inquiry concerning the foundation's policies is encouraged.

Seven copies of a formal proposal (limited to two pages) should be submitted. The proposal should include: the name and address of the organization; short history of the agency, with specific purpose, amount requested, and expected goals of the project; project budget; other sources being approached for funding; any other essential facts, including when the grant would be needed. Also include seven copies of the organization's most recently audited financial statement, list of current directors, and IRS tax-exemption certification letter. Canadian organizations should submit tax-exemption certification from the Department of National Revenue, Ottawa. The application should be signed by an officer of the organization.

The board of directors meets in March, June, September, and December. To be considered at the next meeting, a proposal should be received no later than the middle of the month preceding a board meeting.

Restrictions on Giving: Grants, including scholarships and fellowships, are not made to individuals. Grants are not made for operating expenses, deficit financing, contingency reserves, or endowments, or to national health organizations.

OTHER THINGS TO KNOW
The foundation asks recipient organizations to submit progress reports and, at the termination of the grant, file an accounting of how the funds were disbursed, with an evaluation of the result. Unexpended funds must be returned to the foundation.

PUBLICATIONS
Annual report and guidelines

GRANTS ANALYSIS
Total Grants: $539,079

Number of Grants: 21

Highest Grant: $150,000

Average Grant: $25,670

Typical Range: $5,000 to $50,000

Disclosure Period: fiscal year ending May 31, 1994

Note: Recent grants are derived from a fiscal 1994 annual report.

RECENT GRANTS
Library
235	Buffalo and Erie County Public Library, Buffalo, NY

General
150,000	University at Buffalo Foundation, Buffalo, NY
83,000	Buffalo General Hospital, Buffalo, NY
35,000	Baycrest Centre for Geriatric Care, Buffalo, NY
28,000	United Way of Buffalo and Erie County, Buffalo, NY
25,000	Blue Ridge Community Health Service, Buffalo, NY

Curtice-Burns Foods, Inc. / Curtice-Burns/Pro-Fac Foundation

Sales: $878.63 million
Employees: 5,000
Parent Company: Agway, Inc.
Headquarters: Rochester, NY
SIC Major Group: Canned Fruits & Vegetables, Canned Specialties, Frozen Fruits & Vegetables, and Frozen Specialties Nec

CONTACT
Marilyn T. Helmer
Vice President
Curtice-Burns/Pro-Fac Foundation
PO Box 681
Rochester, NY 14603
(716) 383-1850

FINANCIAL SUMMARY
Recent Giving: $300,000 (fiscal 1995 est.); $339,420 (fiscal 1994); $299,472 (fiscal 1993)

Assets: $135,728 (fiscal 1994); $468,180 (fiscal 1993); $417,445 (fiscal 1992)

Gifts Received: $300,000 (fiscal 1993)

Fiscal Note: Company gives through foundation only. Above figures exclude nonmonetary support. In fiscal 1993, contributions were received from Curtice-Burns Foods Inc.

EIN: 16-6071142

CONTRIBUTIONS SUMMARY
Typical Recipients: • *Arts & Humanities:* Arts Associations & Councils, Arts Centers, Community Arts, Libraries, Museums/Galleries, Music, Performing Arts, Public Broadcasting, Theater • *Civic & Public Affairs:* Business/Free Enterprise, Civil

Rights, Clubs, Community Foundations, Economic Development, Employment/Job Training, General, Housing, Rural Affairs, Safety, Urban & Community Affairs, Women's Affairs • *Education:* Agricultural Education, Business Education, Colleges & Universities, Community & Junior Colleges, Education Funds, Literacy, Minority Education, Special Education, Student Aid • *Environment:* General, Resource Conservation • *Health:* Children's Health/Hospitals, Clinics/Medical Centers, Emergency/Ambulance Services, Geriatric Health, Health Organizations, Heart, Hospices, Hospitals, Medical Rehabilitation, Mental Health, Nursing Services, Public Health, Single-Disease Health Associations • *Science:* Science Museums • *Social Services:* Animal Protection, Child Welfare, Community Centers, Community Service Organizations, Delinquency & Criminal Rehabilitation, Domestic Violence, Emergency Relief, Family Planning, Family Services, Food/Clothing Distribution, Homes, People with Disabilities, Recreation & Athletics, Scouts, Senior Services, Shelters/Homelessness, Substance Abuse, United Funds/United Ways, Veterans, Volunteer Services, Youth Organizations

Grant Types: capital, general support, operating expenses, project, and scholarship

Nonmonetary Support: $120,000 (fiscal 1989)

Nonmonetary Support Types: donated products

Note: Nonmonetary support requests are handled individually by each division.

Geographic Distribution: near headquarters and operating locations

Operating Locations: CO (Denver), GA (Montezuma), IA (Cedar Rapids, Des Moines, Mitchellville, Wall Lake), IL (Collinsville, Ridgeway), IN (Mount Summit), MI (Benton Harbor, Coloma, Fennville, Fenville, Sodus), NE (North Bend), NJ (Clifton, Newark, Vineland), NY (Alton, Barker, Bergen, Brockport, Gorham, LeRoy, Leicester, Lyons, Oakfield, Phelps, Red Creek, Rochester, Rushville, Shortsville, South Dayton, Waterport), OH (Cincinnati, Lodi), OR (Albany, Cornelius, Portland), PA (Berlin), TN (Cordova), TX (Alamo), WA (Auburn, Enumclaw, Mount Vernon, Seattle, Spokane, Tacoma)

CORP. OFFICERS
Roy A. Myers: *B* 1931 *CURR EMPL* exec vp, dir: Curtice-Burns Foods Inc

Bea Slizewski: *CURR EMPL* dir corp communs: Curtice-Burns Foods Inc

GIVING OFFICERS
Robert V. Call, Jr.: chmn, trust

Virginia Ford: trust *CORP AFFIL* dir: Curtice-Burns Foods Inc

Marilyn T. Helmer: vp

George Rowcliffe: trust

APPLICATION INFORMATION
Initial Approach: *Initial Contact:* brief letter or proposal *Include Information On:* description of the organization, amount requested, purpose for which funds are

sought, recently audited financial statement, and proof of tax-exempt status *Deadlines:* September through May

Restrictions on Giving: Contributions generally are not made to individuals, political groups, dinners or special events, fraternal organizations, goodwill advertising, denominational religious activities, or for sectarian purposes.

GRANTS ANALYSIS
Total Grants: $339,420

Number of Grants: 243

Highest Grant: $25,000

Average Grant: $1,397

Typical Range: $500 to $5,000

Disclosure Period: fiscal year ending June 30, 1994

Note: Recent grants are derived from a fiscal 1994 grants list.

RECENT GRANTS

Library
2,500   Southwest Michigan Library Co-op, Paw Paw, MI — annual operating support

General
25,000   United Way of Greater Rochester, Rochester, NY — annual fund drive

24,000   United Way Greater Rochester, Rochester, NY — annual fund drive

15,000   United Way of Pierce County, Tacoma, WA — annual operating support

10,000   Blossomland United Way, Benton Harbor, MI — annual operating support

10,000   United Way Pierce County, Tacoma, WA — purchase of a new building

Daily News / Daily News Foundation

Sales: $62.0 million
Employees: 1,600
Parent Company: dba Daily News
Headquarters: New York, NY
SIC Major Group: Printing & Publishing

CONTACT
John Campi
Promotions
Daily News
450 W 33rd St., 3rd Fl.
New York, NY 10001
(212) 210-2100

FINANCIAL SUMMARY
Recent Giving: $157,450 (1992); $139,350 (1991); $260,350 (1990)

Assets: $4,466,483 (1992); $4,352,538 (1991); $3,658,684 (1990)

Gifts Received: $2,611 (1991)

EIN: 13-6161525

CONTRIBUTIONS SUMMARY
Typical Recipients: • *Arts & Humanities:* Arts Associations & Councils, Arts Centers, Arts Funds, Arts Outreach, Community Arts, Libraries, Museums/Galleries, Music, Performing Arts, Public Broadcasting, Theater, Visual Arts • *Civic & Public Affairs:* Botanical Gardens/Parks, Economic Development, General, Hispanic Affairs, Housing, Municipalities/Towns, Public Policy, Zoos/Aquariums • *Education:* Colleges & Universities, Education Funds, Private Education (Precollege), Special Education • *Environment:* Resource Conservation • *Health:* Hospitals, Long-Term Care, Medical Research • *Religion:* Religious Organizations, Religious Welfare • *Social Services:* Child Welfare, Community Service Organizations, Food/Clothing Distribution, People with Disabilities, United Funds/United Ways, Volunteer Services, Youth Organizations

Grant Types: general support

Operating Locations: CA (Woodland Hills)

CORP. OFFICERS
Fred Drasner: *CURR EMPL* pres, ceo, dir: US News & World Report

Mortimer Benjamin Zuckerman: *B* Montreal Canada 1937 *ED* McGill Univ BA 1957; McGill Univ LLB 1961; Harvard Univ LLM 1962; Univ PA MBA 1962 *CURR EMPL* co-fdr, chmn: Boston Properties Co *CORP AFFIL* owner, chmn, editor-in-chief, dir: US News & World Report; owner, chmn, pres: Atlantic Monthly Co *NONPR AFFIL* adv bd: Ctr Strategic Intl Studies, Univ PA Wharton Sch; dir: Tennis Hall Fame, Wolf Trap Fdn *PHIL AFFIL* dir: Natl. Book Foundation, Natl Book Foundation *CLUB AFFIL* Harmonie

GIVING OFFICERS
Patrick J. Austin: asst secy, treas, dir

Paul A. Bissonette: vp, dir

Gail Busby: secy

Michael Eigner: pres, dir

Raymond Gardella: vp, dir

Gerald P. McCarthy: dir

L. Clark Morehouse III: dir

Kathleen S. M. Shepherd: dir

Richard Stone: dir

APPLICATION INFORMATION
Initial Approach: Send a brief letter of inquiry. Include a description of organization, amount requested, purpose of funds sought, recently audited financial statement, and proof of tax-exempt status. There are no deadlines.

GRANTS ANALYSIS
Total Grants: $157,450

Number of Grants: 48

Highest Grant: $10,000

Typical Range: $750 to $5,000

Disclosure Period: 1992

Note: Recent grants are derived from a 1992 Form 990.

RECENT GRANTS

Library
5,000   New York Public Library, New York, NY

General
10,000   Foundation for Minority Interests in Media, New York, NY

5,000   Art Education for the Blind, New York, NY

5,000   Central Park Conservancy, New York, NY

5,000   Children's Express, New York, NY

5,000   Hospital Audiences, New York, NY

Dana Charitable Trust, Eleanor Naylor

CONTACT
The Eleanor Naylor Dana Charitable Trust
c/o Trustees
38th Floor
375 Park Ave.
New York, NY 10152
(212) 754-2890
Note: All correspondence should be addressed to the trustees. The trust does not report a specific contact person.

FINANCIAL SUMMARY
Recent Giving: $3,250,000 (fiscal 1995 est.); $3,250,000 (fiscal 1994 approx.); $2,927,303 (fiscal 1993)

Assets: $6,650,000 (fiscal 1995 est.); $6,650,000 (fiscal 1994 approx.); $6,145,022 (fiscal 1993)

Gifts Received: $4,197,096 (fiscal 1994 est.); $4,197,096 (fiscal 1993); $4,197,100 (fiscal 1992)

Fiscal Note: In 1993, contributions were received from a Trust established by Eleanor N. Dana.

EIN: 13-2992855

CONTRIBUTIONS SUMMARY
Donor(s): The trust was established in 1979 by the late Eleanor Naylor Dana . Mrs. Dana was the wife of Charles A. Dana (also deceased), an attorney and New York State legislator who founded Dana Corporation. The Danas established the Charles A. Dana Foundation in 1950.

Typical Recipients: • *Arts & Humanities:* Arts Centers, Arts Festivals, Ballet, Dance, General, Libraries, Music, Opera, Performing Arts, Theater • *Education:* Arts/Humanities Education, Colleges & Universities, Medical Education, Private Education (Precollege) • *Health:* AIDS/HIV, Cancer, Children's Health/Hospitals, Clinics/Medical Centers, Diabetes, Hospitals, Medical Research, Transplant Networks/Donor Banks • *International:* Health Care/Hospitals, International Affairs, International Development • *Religion:* Churches • *Science:* Scientific Research • *Social Services:* Family Planning

Grant Types: general support and project

Geographic Distribution: emphasis on the East Coast, with primary focus on New York City area

GIVING OFFICERS

Robert Alan Good, MD: trust *B* Crosby MN 1922 *ED* Univ MN BA 1944; Univ MN MB 1946; Univ MN PhD 1947; Univ MN MD 1947 *CURR EMPL* physician-in-chief: All Childrens Hospital *CORP AFFIL* cons: Merck & Co; mem expert adv panel immunology: World Health Org *NONPR AFFIL* fellow: Academy Multidisciplinary Res, Am Academy Arts & Sciences, Am Assn Advancement Science, Am Coll Allergy & Immunology, NY Academy Sciences; foreign adv: Academy Med Sciences; mem: Alpha Omega Alpha, Am Assn Anatomists, Am Assn History Medicine, Am Assn Immunologists, Am Assn Pathologists, Am Assn Univ Profs, Am Clinical & Climatological Assn, Am Fed Clinical Res, Am Pediatric Soc, Am Rheumatism Assn, Am Soc Clinical Investigation, Am Soc Experimental Pathology, Am Soc Microbiology, Am Soc Transplant Surgeons, Assn Am Physicians, Central Clinical Res, Detroit Surgical Assn, FL Govs Task Force AIDS, Harvey Soc, Infectious Diseases Soc Am, Intl Academy Pathology, Intl Soc Blood Transfusion, Intl Soc Experimental Hematology, Intl Soc for Transplantation Biology, Intl Soc Immunopharmacology, Intl Soc Nephrology, Minneapolis Pediatric Soc, MN St Med Assn, Natl Academy Sciences, Natl Academy Sciences Inst Medicine, Northwest Pediatric Soc, Phi Beta Kappa, Practitioners Soc, Reticuloendothelial Soc, Sigma Xi, Soc Experimental Biology & Medicine, Soc Pediatric Res, Transplantion Soc, Western Soc Immunologists; mem adv comm: Bone Marrow Transplant Registry; mem bd dirs: Natl Marrow Donors Program; prof dept pediatrics: Univ S FL

David Joseph Mahoney: trust *B* Bronx NY 1923 *ED* Univ PA BS 1945; Columbia Univ 1946-1947; Manhattan Coll LLD *CURR EMPL* chmn, ceo: David Mahoney Ventures *CORP AFFIL* dir: The Dreyfus Corp, Lone Star Indus, Natl Health Laboratories, NYNEX Corp *NONPR AFFIL* chmn: Am Health Fdn, Phoenix House; dir: Natl Urban League; hon mem: Boys Club NY Alumni Assn; mem: Young Pres Org; trust: Tuskegee Inst, Univ PA *PHIL AFFIL* pres: David J. Mahoney Foundation; chmn bd dirs, mem investment & other comms: Charles A. Dana Foundation

Carlos Dupre Moseley: trust *B* Laurens SC 1914 *ED* Duke Univ BA 1935; Philadelphia Conservatory Music 1941-1944 *NONPR AFFIL* chmn emeritus: Philharmonic Symphony Soc NY; mem: Mu Phi Epsilon, Phi Beta Kappa, Phi Eta Sigma, Phi Kappa Lambda; trust: Converse Coll *CLUB AFFIL* Century Assn, Piedmont *PHIL AFFIL* vp, dir: Fan Fox and Leslie R. Samuels Foundation; dir: Charles A. Dana Foundation

A. J. Signorile: treas, trust

Robert Edward Wise, MD: trust *B* Pittsburgh PA 1918 *ED* Univ Pittsburgh BS 1941; Univ MD MD 1943 *CORP AFFIL* dir:

Bay St Skills Corp *NONPR AFFIL* chmn, trust: Lahey Clinic Hosp; clinical prof radiology: Boston Univ Med Sch; corporator: New England Deaconess Hosp; mem: Am Coll Radiology, Am Med Assn, Eastern Radiological Soc, MA Med Soc, MA Radiological Soc, New England Roentgen Ray Soc, Radiological Soc N Am; mem bd dirs: Pk St Corp; trust: Boston Ballet, Boston Pk Opera Assn *CLUB AFFIL* Algonquin, Atlantis GC, Braeburn CC, Kennebunk River, La-Coquille, Webhannet GC

APPLICATION INFORMATION
Initial Approach:

Initial inquiries should be submitted as a brief letter of intent, not to exceed one thousand words. Selected applicants will be invited to submit detailed proposals.

OTHER THINGS TO KNOW
In general, biomedical research grants are limited to no more than three years and must not exceed $100,000. Performing arts grants must not exceed $100,000 and must show: anticipated benefit and long-range potential as a result of grant; stature of organization; need for the grant; and financial viability.

PUBLICATIONS
Informational brochure

GRANTS ANALYSIS
Total Grants: $2,927,303

Number of Grants: 116

Highest Grant: $100,000

Average Grant: $25,235

Typical Range: $1,000 to $100,000

Disclosure Period: fiscal year ending May 31, 1993

Note: Recent grants are derived from a fiscal 1993 Form 990.

RECENT GRANTS

Library

50,000	Boston Medical Library, Boston, MA	

General

100,000	Beth Israel Hospital, Boston, MA — Harvard Medical School
100,000	Harvard Medical School, Cambridge, MA
100,000	Harvard Medical School, Cambridge, MA
100,000	Harvard University, Cambridge, MA
100,000	Harvard University, Cambridge, MA

Dana Foundation, Charles A.

CONTACT
Stephen A. Foster
Executive Vice President
Charles A. Dana Foundation
745 Fifth Ave., Ste. 700
New York, NY 10151
(212) 223-4040

Note: Contact addresses for information on the Dana Awards are the following: Office of the President, The New School for Social Research, 66 W 12th St., New York, NY 10011; or, c/o Dr. Eve Marder, Dept. of Biology, Brandeis University, 415 S St., Waltham MA 02154.

FINANCIAL SUMMARY
Recent Giving: $12,606,213 (1993); $6,114,483 (1992); $4,224,915 (1991)

Assets: $238,648,541 (1993); $222,308,576 (1992); $209,690,603 (1991)

Fiscal Note: In 1992, the foundation appropriated a total of $16,682,933 in grants and awards. The figure above reflects the grant money that was actually paid to awardees.

EIN: 06-6036761

CONTRIBUTIONS SUMMARY
Donor(s): Charles A. Dana and Eleanor N. Dana (both deceased) established the foundation in 1950. Mr. Dana was an attorney, New York State legislator, founder of Dana Corporation, and philanthropist. He served as president of the foundation from 1950 to 1966. He shaped the foundation's programs and principles until his death in 1975.

Typical Recipients: • *Arts & Humanities:* History & Archaeology, Libraries, Museums/Galleries, Music, Performing Arts, Public Broadcasting • *Civic & Public Affairs:* Municipalities/Towns, Professional & Trade Associations, Public Policy, Zoos/Aquariums • *Education:* Arts/Humanities Education, Colleges & Universities, Education Reform, Elementary Education (Private), Engineering/Technological Education, Faculty Development, General, Legal Education, Medical Education, Minority Education, Private Education (Precollege), Public Education (Precollege), Science/Mathematics Education, Social Sciences Education, Student Aid • *Environment:* General • *Health:* AIDS/HIV, Cancer, Clinics/Medical Centers, Geriatric Health, Health Organizations, Hospitals, Medical Research, Medical Training, Mental Health • *Science:* Scientific Centers & Institutes, Scientific Labs • *Social Services:* Day Care, People with Disabilities, Substance Abuse, Volunteer Services

Grant Types: conference/seminar, general support, project, and research

Geographic Distribution: United States, no international giving

GIVING OFFICERS
Dr. Edward C. Andrews, Jr.: dir, mem budget comm *B* Rockland ME 1925 *ED* Middlebury Coll AB 1946; Johns Hopkins Univ MD 1951 *CURR EMPL* pres: ME Med Ctr *CORP AFFIL* dir: Chittenden Trust Co, Med Mutual Ins Co, Ventrex Laboratory *NONPR AFFIL* dir: VT Higher Ed Counc; mem: Am Hosp Assn, Assn Am Med Colls, ME Hosp Assn, Portland Chamber Commerce; prof pathology: Univ VT *PHIL AFFIL* trust: Robert Wood Johnson Foundation

Wallace Lawrence Cook: dir, chmn investment comm *B* New York NY 1939 *ED* Harvard Univ AB 1961; Univ VA LLB 1964 *CURR EMPL* investment counselor: Rockefeller & Co *NONPR AFFIL* mem: Am Bar

Assn, New York City Bar Assn, NY Bar
Assn

Walter G. Corcoran: vp bd dirs, mem investment comm *B* Waterbury CT 1922 *ED*
Tulane Univ BBA 1945; Bentley Coll

Charles A. Dana, Jr.: chmn audit comm,
dir, mem budget comm *B* New York NY
1915 *ED* Princeton Univ 1937 *NONPR AF-
FIL* trust: Mus City New York, NY Univ
Med Ctr, Skowhegan Sch Art

Stephen A. Foster: exec vp

James H. French: hon dir *ED* Univ Edinburgh

Barbara E. Gill: vp

David Joseph Mahoney: chmn bd dirs,
mem investment & other comms *B* Bronx
NY 1923 *ED* Univ PA BS 1945; Columbia
Univ 1946-1947; Manhattan Coll LLD
CURR EMPL chmn, ceo: David Mahoney
Ventures *CORP AFFIL* dir: The Dreyfus
Corp, Lone Star Indus, Natl Health Laborato-
ries, NYNEX Corp *NONPR AFFIL* chmn:
Am Health Fdn, Phoenix House; dir: Natl
Urban League; hon mem: Boys Club NY
Alumni Assn; mem: Young Pres Org; trust:
Tuskeegee Inst, Univ PA *PHIL AFFIL* pres:
David J. Mahoney Foundation; trust:
Eleanor Naylor Dana Charitable Trust

Donald Baird Marron: dir, mem invest-
ment comm *B* Goshen NY 1934 *ED* Baruch
Coll 1956 *CURR EMPL* chmn, ceo, dir:
PaineWebber Group Inc *CORP AFFIL*
chmn, ceo: PaineWebber Inc; co-fdr, dir:
Data Resources *NONPR AFFIL* dir: Bus
Comm Arts, New York City Partnership;
mem: Counc Foreign Rels, Govs Sch & Bus
Alliance Task Force, Pres Commn Arts &
Humanities; mem bd overseers: Meml Sloan
Kettering Cancer Ctr; vchmn: Mus Modern
Art *CLUB AFFIL* River *PHIL AFFIL* trust:
Donald B. & Catherine C. Marron Founda-
tion, PaineWebber Foundation

Carlos Dupre Moseley: dir *B* Laurens SC
1914 *ED* Duke Univ BA 1935; Philadelphia
Conservatory Music 1941-1944 *NONPR AF-
FIL* chmn emeritus: Philharmonic Sym-
phony Soc NY; mem: Mu Phi Epsilon, Phi
Beta Kappa, Phi Eta Sigma, Phi Kappa
Lambda; trust: Converse Coll *CLUB AFFIL*
Century Assn, Piedmont *PHIL AFFIL* trust:
Eleanor Naylor Dana Charitable Trust; vp,
dir: Fan Fox and Leslie R. Samuels Founda-
tion

L. Guy Palmer II: mem bd dirs, mem investment comm *B* New York NY

William L. Safire: dir *B* New York NY
1929 *CURR EMPL* columnist: NY Times

Clark M. Whittemore, Jr.: secy-treas bd
dirs, chmn budget comm *ED* Harvard Univ
AB; Univ VA LLB

APPLICATION INFORMATION
Initial Approach:

Applicants should send a brief letter of inquiry (no longer than two pages).

Letters should include the following: the specific need and approach proposed; congru-
ence of the project with the interests and
grant-making guidelines of the foundation;
capabilities of the institution to implement
the proposal; qualifications of the proposed

director of the project; and the estimated
cost and proposed methods of financing the
project, including the institution's intended
contribution.

The board of directors meets in April, June,
and October to consider grant proposals.

Applications for Charles A. Dana Awards
are by nomination only. Completion of an
application form is not required for other
types of grants. The foundation acknowledges receipt of proposals and grants interviews with applicants after a proposal letter
has passed review. Supporting materials
should not be submitted until requested.

Restrictions on Giving: Requests from organizations outside the United States or organizations that conduct activities outside
the United States are not considered for
grants. Aside from the Dana Awards, grants
are not made directly to individuals. The
foundation generally declines requests to
support operating funds of professional organizations. Requests for endowment and
support for facilities generally are not accepted, although they are not excluded. The
grantees are expected to share the cost of
the project or raise funds.

OTHER THINGS TO KNOW
The Charles A. Dana Awards for Pioneering
Achievements in Health and Education program was initiated in 1986 "to spotlight innovative ideas in health and education that
had demonstrated their value but not yet
achieved their full potential. The purpose of
the awards is to speed dissemination of
those ideas to individuals and institutions
who might benefit from them. The directors
authorize up to five awards annually of
$50,000 each, stipulating that divisions of
the awards between health and education
should correspond to the quality of the nominations in each field.

"The Dana Awards are intended to reflect
and reinforce the Foundation's grant programs. Awards in education currently span
the spectrum from pre-school through adult
continuing education. Awards in health target advances in fundamental or clinical neuroscience that promise progress in the
diagnosis, treatment, or prevention of disorders that afflict human beings."

The foundation has created nominating committees in health and education chaired respectively by Samuel O. Thier, MD,
president of Brandeis University, and
Jonathan Fanton, president of the New
School for Social Research. These committees forward their nominations for consideration by the Dana Awards Jury.

PUBLICATIONS
Annual report and quarterly newsletter

GRANTS ANALYSIS
Total Grants: $12,606,213

Number of Grants: 55

Highest Grant: $5,167,080

Average Grant: $137,762*

Typical Range: $20,000 to $250,000

Disclosure Period: 1993

Note: Average grant figure excludes the
highest grant of $5,167,080. Recent grants
are derived from a 1993 annual report.

RECENT GRANTS
Library
100,000	Syracuse University, Syracuse, NY — special collections of the university's library
75,000	Library of Congress/National Institute of Mental Health, Washington, DC — enhancing the "Decade of the Brain" lecture series
50,000	New York Public Library, New York, NY — to convert records into machine-readable form

General
5,167,080	Dana Farber Cancer Institute, Boston, MA — Dana Division of Human Cancer Genetics
939,783	Dana Alliance for Brain Initiatives, New York, NY — public education campaign on neuroscience research
750,000	Central Park Conservancy, New York, NY — creation of a "Discovery Center" in Central Park
670,000	Cold Spring Harbor Laboratory, Cold Spring Harbor, NY — Dana Consortium on the Genetic Basis of Manic-Depressive Illness
323,000	Harvard Medical School, Cambridge, MA — Dana Consortium on Memory Loss and Aging

Davenport-Hatch Foundation

CONTACT
Laura Weisenfluh
Contact
Davenport-Hatch Foundation
c/o Fleet Investment Services
45 East Ave.
Rochester, NY 14638
(716) 546-9822

FINANCIAL SUMMARY
Recent Giving: $900,000 (fiscal 1994 est.);
$793,342 (fiscal 1993); $907,600 (fiscal
1992)

Assets: $19,500,000 (fiscal 1994 est.);
$21,594,134 (fiscal 1993); $19,658,413 (fiscal 1992)

Gifts Received: $4569 (fiscal 1992);
$12,492 (fiscal 1991)

EIN: 16-6027105

CONTRIBUTIONS SUMMARY
Donor(s): The foundation was established
in 1952 by the late Augustus Hatch .

Typical Recipients: • *Arts & Humanities:* Historic Preservation, History & Archaeology, Libraries, Museums/Galleries, Music, Public Broadcasting, Theater • *Civic & Public Affairs:* Employment/Job Training, Housing, Urban & Community Affairs • *Education:* Business Education, Colleges & Universities, Community & Junior Colleges, Elementary Education (Private), Engineering/Technological Education, Literacy, Medical Education, Private Education (Precollege), Science/Mathematics Education, Secondary Education (Private) • *Health:* Cancer, Clinics/Medical Centers, Emergency/Ambulance Services, Health Organizations, Hospices, Hospitals, Kidney, Long-Term Care, Medical Rehabilitation, Medical Research, Multiple Sclerosis, Nursing Services, Single-Disease Health Associations • *International:* International Peace & Security Issues • *Religion:* Churches, Jewish Causes, Religious Organizations, Religious Welfare • *Science:* Science Museums, Scientific Centers & Institutes • *Social Services:* Child Welfare, Day Care, Family Planning, Family Services, Homes, People with Disabilities, Recreation & Athletics, Scouts, United Funds/United Ways, Volunteer Services, YMCA/YWCA/YMHA/YWHA, Youth Organizations

Grant Types: capital, multiyear/continuing support, project, and scholarship

Geographic Distribution: focus on the Rochester, NY, area

GIVING OFFICERS
Robert J. Brinkman: dir

William L. Ely: dir *B* 1940 *ED* Syracuse Univ BS 1958-1962 *CURR EMPL* pres-treas, dir: Sloan & Co Inc

Helen H. Heller: secy, treas, dir

A. Thomas Hildebrandt: dir

Austin E. Hildebrandt: pres, dir

Elizabeth H. Hildebrandt: dir

John Ross: dir

David H. Taylor: vp, dir *B* 1944 *CURR EMPL* pres, treas, dir: Hart Taylor Lincoln Mercury

Douglas F. Taylor: dir *CURR EMPL* vp, secy, dir: Hart Taylor Lincoln Mercury

Hart Taylor: dir *B* 1913 *CURR EMPL* chmn, dir: Hart Taylor Lincoln Mercury

Laura Weisenfluh: contact

APPLICATION INFORMATION
Initial Approach:

The foundation has no formal grant procedure or grant application form.

The foundation has no deadline for submitting proposals.

Restrictions on Giving: The foundation does not make grants to individuals.

GRANTS ANALYSIS
Total Grants: $793,342

Number of Grants: 64

Highest Grant: $45,000

Average Grant: $12,396

Typical Range: $2,500 to $25,000

Disclosure Period: fiscal year ending May 31, 1993

Note: Recent grants are derived from a fiscal 1993 Form 990.

RECENT GRANTS
Library
5,000	Rochester Toy Library, Rochester, NY — site renovation and expansion

General
45,000	United Way, Rochester, NY — Red Cross campaign
40,000	University of Rochester, Rochester, NY — capital campaign
40,000	University of Rochester, Rochester, NY — University Campaign for the 90s
30,000	Boy Scouts of America Otetiana Council, Rochester, NY — Camp Cutler campaign
25,000	Hillside Children's Center, Rochester, NY — school building campaign

Delavan Foundation, Nelson B.

CONTACT
Gary Shultz
Trust Officer
Nelson B. Delavan Fdn.
c/o Chase Manhattan Bank, N.A.
5 Seneca St.
Geneva, NY 14456
(315) 781-0280

FINANCIAL SUMMARY
Recent Giving: $224,815 (fiscal 1993); $229,200 (fiscal 1992); $189,950 (fiscal 1991)

Assets: $4,315,222 (fiscal 1993); $4,353,853 (fiscal 1992); $4,267,081 (fiscal 1991)

EIN: 16-6260274

CONTRIBUTIONS SUMMARY
Typical Recipients: • *Arts & Humanities:* Arts Institutes, Historic Preservation, Libraries, Music, Performing Arts • *Civic & Public Affairs:* Public Policy • *Education:* Colleges & Universities • *Environment:* General • *Health:* Emergency/Ambulance Services, Health Organizations, Hospitals • *Religion:* Churches, Religious Organizations • *Social Services:* Animal Protection, Community Service Organizations, Counseling, Family Planning, Family Services, Senior Services

Grant Types: operating expenses

Geographic Distribution: focus on NY, preference for the Seneca Falls region

GIVING OFFICERS
Chase Manhattan Bank, NA: trust

APPLICATION INFORMATION
Initial Approach: The foundation requests applications be made in writing. Include a description of organization, amount requested, purpose of funds sought, recently audited financial statement, and proof of tax-exempt status. There are no deadlines.

GRANTS ANALYSIS
Total Grants: $224,815

Number of Grants: 29

Highest Grant: $12,500

Typical Range: $1,000 to $5,000

Disclosure Period: fiscal year ending March 31, 1993

Note: Recent grants are derived from a fiscal 1993 Form 990.

RECENT GRANTS
Library
1,000	Geneva Free Library, Geneva, NY

General
12,500	Washington Humane Society, Washington, DC
10,000	American Red Cross, Seneca County Chapter, Seneca, NY
4,000	Planned Parenthood of the Finger Lakes, Geneva, NY
1,000	Environmental Data Research Institute
500	New York Chiropractic College, New York, NY

Delaware North Co., Inc.

Sales: $1.0 billion
Employees: 40,000
Headquarters: Buffalo, NY
SIC Major Group: Holding Companies Nec, Eating Places, Real Estate Agents & Managers, and Racing Including Track Operations

CONTACT
Samuel L. Gifford II
Vice President, Public Affairs
Delaware North Co., Inc.
438 Main St.
Buffalo, NY 14202
(716) 858-5270

FINANCIAL SUMMARY
Recent Giving: $500,000 (1995 est.); $500,000 (1994 approx.); $500,000 (1993)

Fiscal Note: Company gives directly.

CONTRIBUTIONS SUMMARY
Typical Recipients: • *Arts & Humanities:* Arts Associations & Councils, Arts Centers, Arts Festivals, Arts Institutes, Community Arts, Historic Preservation, Libraries, Museums/Galleries, Music, Opera, Performing Arts, Public Broadcasting, Theater • *Civic & Public Affairs:* Business/Free Enterprise, Civil Rights, Economic Development, Economic Policy, Professional & Trade Associations, Urban & Community Affairs, Zoos/Aquariums • *Education:* Business Education, Colleges & Universities, Community

& Junior Colleges, Economic Education, Elementary Education, Elementary Education (Private), Minority Education, Private Education (Precollege) • *Environment:* General • *Health:* Hospitals, Medical Research, Single-Disease Health Associations • *International:* International Peace & Security Issues, International Relations • *Social Services:* Animal Protection, Community Centers, Emergency Relief, People with Disabilities, Shelters/Homelessness, Substance Abuse

Grant Types: award, capital, challenge, emergency, endowment, general support, operating expenses, professorship, research, and scholarship

Nonmonetary Support Types: donated equipment, donated products, in-kind services, loaned employees, and workplace solicitation

Geographic Distribution: headquarters and operating locations

Operating Locations: NY (Buffalo)

Note: Company operates in 38 states.

CORP. OFFICERS

Jeremy Maurice Jacobs: *B* 1940 *ED* Harvard Univ Advanced Mgmt Program 1979; SUNY Buffalo *CURR EMPL* chmn, dir: DE North Cos

Jeremy Maurice Jacobs, Jr.: *B* 1962 *ED* Georgetown Univ; Univ PA Wharton Sch MBA *CURR EMPL* sr exec vp: DE North Cos

Louis M. Jacobs: *B* 1961 *ED* Harvard Univ; Harvard Univ MBA *CURR EMPL* sr exec vp: DE North Cos

Richard T. Stephens: *CURR EMPL* pres, dir: DE North Cos

GIVING OFFICERS

Samuel L. Gifford II: *B* Burlington VT 1935 *ED* Syracuse Univ 1968 *CURR EMPL* vp commun: DE North Cos *CORP AFFIL* pres, dir: Gifford & Gifford, Si Li Goose Indus

APPLICATION INFORMATION

Initial Approach: *Initial Contact:* letter *Include Information On:* a description of organization, amount requested, purpose of funds sought, and proof of tax-exempt status *Deadlines:* by September for requests for the following year *Note:* Budget is completed in October. The company also recommends that along with proposals applicants send an invoice to aid the giving program financial office, especially if those requests are over a two year period.

Restrictions on Giving: Does not support individuals, religious organizations for sectarian purposes, or noncharitable groups.

Diamond Foundation, Aaron

CONTACT
Vincent McGee
Executive Director
Aaron Diamond Foundation
1270 Avenue of the Americas, Ste. 2624
New York, NY 10020
(212) 757-7680
Note: Information and application packets for the Aaron Diamond Foundation Postdoctoral Research Fellowships are available by mail or phone from Ellen L. Rautenberg, Program Director, Aaron Diamond Foundation Postdoctoral Research Fellowships, 5 Penn Plz., Rm. 308, New York, NY 10001, (212) 613-2525.

FINANCIAL SUMMARY
Recent Giving: $22,500,000 (1995 est.); $22,348,901 (1994); $20,551,610 (1993)
Assets: $45,900,000 (1995 est.); $45,890,960 (1994); $44,702,000 (1993)
Gifts Received: $4,935,163 (1991); $330,602 (1990); $648,131 (1989)
Fiscal Note: Gifts received are distributions from the estate of Aaron Diamond.
EIN: 13-2678431

CONTRIBUTIONS SUMMARY
Donor(s): The foundation was established in 1955, with the late Aaron Diamond as donor. In the year before his death (by heart attack in 1984), Aaron and Irene Diamond had begun to draw up plans to support New York City projects. They concentrated on medical research, minority education, and culture. They also determined that the foundation should have a functional life of ten years after its major funding was in place.

Following Mr. Diamond's death, the foundation was reorganized to meet its new responsibilities under the leadership of Irene Diamond, president, with a reorganized board of directors and a small staff.

Typical Recipients: • *Arts & Humanities:* Arts Appreciation, Ballet, Dance, History & Archaeology, Libraries, Museums/Galleries, Music, Opera, Performing Arts • *Civic & Public Affairs:* Civil Rights, Ethnic Organizations, First Amendment Issues, Legal Aid, Public Policy, Urban & Community Affairs, Women's Affairs • *Education:* Arts/Humanities Education, Colleges & Universities, Education Associations, Education Reform, Engineering/Technological Education, Faculty Development, Health & Physical Education, Literacy, Minority Education, Preschool Education, Public Education (Precollege), Secondary Education (Public), Student Aid • *Health:* AIDS/HIV, Children's Health/Hospitals, Health Organizations, Home-Care Services, Medical Research, Outpatient Health Care • *International:* Human Rights • *Social Services:* Community Centers, Family Services, Substance Abuse, Youth Organizations

Grant Types: general support, project, and research

Geographic Distribution: New York City

GIVING OFFICERS
Robert Louis Bernstein: vp, dir *B* New York NY 1923 *ED* Harvard Univ BS 1944 *CURR EMPL* publ-at-large, adv trade publ div: John Wiley & Sons *NONPR AFFIL* chmn: US Helsinki Watch; dir: Am Book Publ; mem: Africa Watch, Ams Watch, Asia Watch, Assn Am Publs, Counc Foreign Rels, Middle East Watch, NY Univ Soc Fellows; mem adv comm: Carter-Menil Human Rights Fdn *CLUB AFFIL* Century Assn, Century CC, Univ

Noreen Morrison Clark: dir *B* Glasgow Scotland 1943 *ED* Univ UT BS 1965; Columbia Univ MA 1972; Columbia Univ MPhil 1975; Columbia Univ PhD 1976 *NONPR AFFIL* adjunct prof health admin: Columbia Univ Sch Pub Health; assoc: Synergos Inst; bd dir: Freedom From Hunger Fdn; dir: Am Lung Assn, Family Care Intl; editor: Health Ed Quarterly; fellow: Soc Pub Health Ed; mem: Am Pub Health Assn, Am Thoracic Soc, Counc Foreign Rels, Intl Union Health Ed, Pi Sigma Alpha, Soc Behavioral Medicine; mem coordinating comm: Natl Asthma Ed Program; prin investigator: Natl Insts Health; prof, chmn health behavior & ed dept: Univ MI Sch Public Health *PHIL AFFIL* mem exec comm, dir: Freedom from Hunger Foundation

Adrian W. DeWind: dir *B* Chicago IL 1913 *CURR EMPL* atty, ptnr: Paul Weiss Rifkind Wharton & Garrison

Irene Diamond: pres, dir *B* Pittsburgh PA 1910 *NONPR AFFIL* dir: Aaron Diamond AIDS Res Ctr; mem: Film Soc Lincoln Ctr, Fund Free Expression, Sundance Inst, Young Concert Artists

David N. Dinkins: dir *B* Trenton NJ 1927 *ED* Brooklyn Law Sch JD; Howard Univ BA *NONPR AFFIL* mem: Black-Jewish Coalition, Counc Black Elected Dems NY, NAACP, Natl Conf Black Lawyers, Urban League Greater NY

Marian Wright Edelman: dir *B* Bennettsville SC 1939 *ED* Univ Paris 1958-1959; Spelman Coll BA 1960; Yale Univ LLB 1963 *NONPR AFFIL* dir: Citizens Constitutional Concerns, City Lights, Ctr Law Social Policy, Leadership Conf Civil Rights, NAACP Legal Defense Ed Fund, Natl Alliance Bus, Parents As Teachers Natl Ctr; mem: Natl Commn Children; mem adv bd: Hampshire Coll; mem adv counc: Martin Luther King Jr Meml Ctr; pres, fdr: Childrens Defense Fund; trust: Joint Ctr Political Studies, Martin Luther King Jr Meml Ctr, March Dimes, Spelman Coll; US comm: UN Children's Fund *PHIL AFFIL* dir: Aetna Foundation; trust: Skadden, Arps, Slate, Meagher & Flom Fellowship Foundation

Alfred Gellhorn, MD: dir *B* St Louis MO 1913 *ED* Amherst Coll 1930-1932; Washington Univ MD 1937 *NONPR AFFIL* bd regents: Natl Library Medicine; diplomate: Am Bd Internal Medicine; dir: Inst Cancer Res; dir med aff: NY St Dept Health; mem: Am Assn Cancer Res, Am Coll Physicians, Am Soc Biological Chems, Assn Am Physicians, Coll Physicians Philadelphia, Natl Academy Sciences Inst Medicine, NY

County Med Soc, Soc Clinical Investigation; visiting prof: Albert Einstein Coll Medicine

Vartan Gregorian: dir *B* Tabriz Iran 1934 *ED* Coll Armenien 1955; Stanford Univ BA 1958; Stanford Univ PhD 1964 *NONPR AFFIL* chmn bd visitors: City Univ NY Grad Sch Univ Ctr, NY Pub Library; dir: Boston Univ Inst Advanced Study, Trinity Sch; mem: Am Acad Medicine, Am Assn Advancement Slavic Studies, Am Historical Assn, Am Library Assn, Am Philosophical Soc, Counc Foreign Rels, Intl Fed Library Assn, Intl League Human Rights, Mid-East Studies Assn, Natl Humanities Faculty; pres: Brown Univ; prof: New Sch Social Res; prof history: NY Univ *CLUB AFFIL* Grolier, Round Table *PHIL AFFIL* trust: J. Paul Getty Trust

Howard H. Hiatt, MD: dir *B* Patchogue NY 1925 *ED* Harvard Univ MD 1948 *NONPR AFFIL* mem: Alpha Omega Alpha, Am Academy Arts Sciences, Am Soc Clinical Investigation, Assn Am Physicians, Natl Academy Sciences Inst Medicine; prof: Harvard Univ Med Sch, Sch Pub Health; sr physician: Brigham & Womens Hosp

Peter Kimmelman: treas, dir *B* New York NY 1944 *ED* Univ PA Wharton Sch 1966; Harvard Univ JD 1969 *CURR EMPL* pres: Peter Kimmelman Asset Mgmt Co *CORP AFFIL* chmn credit review comm, mem exec comm, dir: Republic Natl Bank NY; dir: Manhattan Savings Bank; dir, mem exec comm: Republic NY Corp; exec vp, dir: Diamond Admin Off Inc, Aaron Diamond Realty Corp

Vincent McGee: exec dir *PHIL AFFIL* dir: Hunt Alternatives Fund, Helen Hunt Alternatives Fund; trust: Baker Foundation

Ellen L. Rautenberg: program dir

APPLICATION INFORMATION
Initial Approach:

Letters of request should be addressed to the foundation's executive director.

Letters should be accompanied by two copies of a short proposal giving a history of the project; goals to be achieved; methods, budget, and schedule for implementation; copy of the applicant's most recent annual financial statement; list of board members and financial supporters; and a copy of the organization's IRS determination letter of tax-exempt status.

There are no deadlines for submitting requests; the board meets regularly throughout the year to consider proposals.

The foundation will respond to each applicant in writing and may request additional materials or a meeting.

Restrictions on Giving: The foundation reports that at the end of 1996 it will be disolved.

OTHER THINGS TO KNOW

The foundation often supports groups that are "recognized leaders in their particular field, and then works with these groups to generate special initiatives in minority education. Two examples of such cooperative effort are the Foundation's Guidance and Nursing Initiatives." To start a "renaissance of research in New York, the foundation, in 1990, established the Aaron Diamond Foundation Postdoctoral Research Fellowship Program. Starting in 1990 and going through 1994, the foundation will award five three-year investigatorships each year, three in biomedical research and two in health science, social medicine or behaviorial medicine research."

The foundation reported in 1995 that by the end of 1996 the foundation will be disolved.

PUBLICATIONS

Annual report

GRANTS ANALYSIS

Total Grants: $21,966,520

Number of Grants: 466

Highest Grant: $2,000,000

Average Grant: $47,138

Typical Range: $25,000 to $100,000

Disclosure Period: 1992

Note: Recent grants are derived from a 1993 parital grants list.

RECENT GRANTS

General

234,480	Montefiore Medical Center, Bronx, NY — for renewed support for research on 1) the natural history of HIV infection in intravenous drug users and 2) transmission of HIV from infected mothers to infants
150,000	Bank Street College of Education, New York, NY — final renewed support of the Principals Institute
150,000	New York City Public Schools, New York, NY — for renewed support for the expanded HIV/AIDS education program, including condom availability, of the board of education
75,000	American Foundation for AIDS Research, New York, NY — for support for the evaluation of the New York City Syringe Exchange Program
75,000	Capital District Center for Drug Abuse Research and Treatment, Albany, NY — final renewed support for the development and utilization of new drugs for treating drug addiction

Dillon Dunwalke Trust, Clarence and Anne

CONTACT
Crosby R. Smith
Trustee
Clarence and Anne Dillon Dunwalke Trust
1330 Ave. of the Americans, 27th Flr.
New York, NY 10019
(212) 515-8340

FINANCIAL SUMMARY
Recent Giving: $997,300 (fiscal 1993)
Assets: $20,252,093 (fiscal 1993)
EIN: 23-7043773

CONTRIBUTIONS SUMMARY
Typical Recipients: • *Arts & Humanities:* Ballet, Libraries, Music • *Civic & Public Affairs:* Community Foundations, General, Housing, Public Policy • *Education:* Colleges & Universities, Private Education (Precollege), Student Aid • *Environment:* General, Resource Conservation, Wildlife Protection • *Health:* Emergency/Ambulance Services, Geriatric Health, Prenatal Health Issues • *International:* International Relations, International Relief Efforts • *Religion:* Churches • *Social Services:* Recreation & Athletics, United Funds/United Ways, Youth Organizations

Grant Types: general support and scholarship

Geographic Distribution: national, with focus on Washington, DC, ME, MO, and NY

GIVING OFFICERS
Philip D. Allen: trust *PHIL AFFIL* vp, dir: Bedminster Fund

Douglas Collins: trust

Frances Collins: trust

Phyllis Dillon Collins: trust

C. Douglas Dillon: trust

Dorothy A. Dillon Eweson: trust *CORP AFFIL* vp: Apollo Muses *NONPR AFFIL* hon trust: Upper Raritan Watershed Assoc; mem: Opera Music Theatre Intl; vp: Am Federation Aging Res *PHIL AFFIL* pres, dir: Bedminster Fund; trust: Clarence and Anne Dillon Dunwalke Trust, Clarence & Anne Dillon Dunwalke Trust

Joan M. Frost: trust

David H. Peipers: trust *PHIL AFFIL* vp, dir: Bedminster Fund

Crosby R. Smith: trust

Martin C. Zetterberg: trust

APPLICATION INFORMATION
Initial Approach: The foundation has no formal grant application procedure or application form. There are no deadlines.

Restrictions on Giving: The foundation does not make grants to individuals.

GRANTS ANALYSIS
Total Grants: $997,300

Number of Grants: 69

Highest Grant: $500,000

Typical Range: $1,000 to $25,000

Disclosure Period: fiscal year ending June 30, 1993

Note: Recent grants are derived from a Fiscal 1993 Form 990.

RECENT GRANTS

Library

500,000 Clarence Dillon Public Library, Bedminster, NJ — annual operating needs

5,000 Friends of Alice L. Pendleton Library, Islesboro, ME — toward the cost of a new library addition

General

50,000 Brookings Institution, Washington, DC — support of the research project

35,000 NMSU Development Fund Corporation, Northeast Missouri State University, Kirksville, MO — support of research project

30,000 American University, Washington, DC — toward the Charles Collidge Parlin scholarship fund

25,000 American Federation for Aging Research, New York, NY — annual operating needs

25,000 Asphalt Green, New York, NY — toward the swim center campaign

Dodge Foundation, Cleveland H.

CONTACT
Phyllis M. Criscuoli
Administrative Director and Treasurer
Cleveland H. Dodge Foundation
670 W 247th St.
Bronx, NY 10471
(718) 543-1220

FINANCIAL SUMMARY
Recent Giving: $1,671,601 (1993); $1,693,925 (1992); $1,043,070 (1991)

Assets: $32,433,502 (1993); $32,821,229 (1992); $32,310,175 (1991)

EIN: 13-6015087

CONTRIBUTIONS SUMMARY
Donor(s): The Dodge Foundation was established in 1917 by Cleveland Hoadley Dodge, whose father headed Phelps Dodge Corporation, a copper company.

Typical Recipients: • *Arts & Humanities:* Arts Associations & Councils, Arts Outreach, History & Archaeology, Libraries, Museums/Galleries, Performing Arts • *Civic & Public Affairs:* Botanical Gardens/Parks, Clubs, Employment/Job Training, General, Nonprofit Management, Philanthropic Organizations, Public Policy, Urban & Community Affairs, Zoos/Aquariums • *Education:*

Arts/Humanities Education, Colleges & Universities, Education Reform, Elementary Education (Public), General, International Exchange, International Studies, Minority Education, Private Education (Precollege), Public Education (Precollege), School Volunteerism, Science/Mathematics Education, Student Aid • *Environment:* Air/Water Quality, General, Wildlife Protection • *Health:* Emergency/Ambulance Services, Health Organizations, Nursing Services • *International:* Foreign Educational Institutions, International Affairs, International Organizations, International Peace & Security Issues, International Relations • *Religion:* Churches, Religious Welfare • *Science:* Science Museums • *Social Services:* Child Welfare, Community Centers, Community Service Organizations, Emergency Relief, Family Planning, Family Services, People with Disabilities, Recreation & Athletics, Senior Services, Shelters/Homelessness, Volunteer Services, YMCA/YWCA/YMHA/YWHA, Youth Organizations

Grant Types: capital, endowment, general support, matching, multiyear/continuing support, operating expenses, and project

Geographic Distribution: concentration in metropolitan New York, NY; some giving in Arizona, New Mexico, and the Northeast

GIVING OFFICERS
Phyllis M. Criscuoli: admin dir, treas

Cleveland Earl Dodge, Jr.: pres, chmn exec comm, mem fin comm, dir *B* New York NY 1922 *ED* Princeton Univ BSME 1943 *CURR EMPL* pres, treas, dir: Intl Dodge Inc *CORP AFFIL* dir: Banded Hub Corp, Centennial Ins Co, Display Sys, Key Bank NA, Phelps Dodge Corp; pres, dir: Cleeland Corp, Dodge Machine Co; trust: Atlantic Mutual Ins Co *NONPR AFFIL* mem: Princeton Engg Assn, Princeton Rowing Assn; trust: Bennington Mus, Springfield Coll, Thousand Island Shipyard Mus, YMCA Retirement Fund *CLUB AFFIL* Berkshire Tennis, Kiwanis, Laurentian Lodge, Princeton, San San Bay GC, Taconic GC

David S. Dodge: mem exec comm, dir *NONPR AFFIL* chmn, dir: Near E Fdn *PHIL AFFIL* chmn, dir: Near East Foundation

Margaret Dodge Garrett: dir emerita

Robert Garrett: chmn fin comm, dir *B* Morristown NJ 1937 *ED* Princeton Univ AB 1959; Harvard Univ MBA 1965 *PHIL AFFIL* trust: Wenner-Gren Foundation for Anthropological Research, Abell Foundation

Alfred Hunt Howell: vp, mem exec & fin comms, dir *B* Wyoming OH 1912 *ED* Princeton Univ AB 1934; Columbia Univ MA, MPhil 1978 *NONPR AFFIL* chmn bd trusts, mem exec comm: YMCAs NY St; dir: Near East Coll Assn; hon trust, emeritus dir: YMCA Greater NY; mem: Am Oriental Soc, Medieval Academy Am; trust: AUB Fdn, Frick Collection, Sophia Am Schs; trust emeritus: Am Univ Beirut, YMCAs Natl Counc

Gilbert Kerlin: secy, mem exec & fin comms, dir *B* Camden NJ 1909 *ED* Harvard Univ 1933; Trinity Coll 1936 *CURR EMPL*

of couns: Shearman & Sterling *CORP AFFIL* chmn: Exmin Corp, Guerlain Inc, Silver Resources Corp; chmn bd, chmn exec comm: N Central Oil Corp; chmn, dir: N Central Intl; dir: Brunswick Mining & Smelting Corp, Hicks Dome Corp, Silver Jacket Corp, Wave Hill; pres, dir: PI Corp, Winward Oil & Gas Corp; secy, dir: Christiani & Nielsen Corp, Malher Mining Co; vp, dir: Goelet Corp, RI Corp

William Dodge Rueckert: mem exec & fin comms, dir *ED* Univ NH 1977

Ingrid R. Warren: mem exec comm, dir

Mary Rea Weidlein: dir

APPLICATION INFORMATION
Initial Approach:

To apply for a grant, organizations may send a brief letter to the foundation's administrative director and treasurer. There are no application forms.

Letters of application should describe the proposed project and include a budget. After a preliminary review, a detailed proposal may be requested.

Applications should be submitted prior to January, April, and October 15. The board of directors meets in June to determine dates for the other annual board meetings.

At one of the annual board meetings, the directors review the activities of recipient organizations to ensure that they are "being maintained at a satisfactory level." The remainder of the yearly income is disbursed in the form of one-time grants for capital campaigns and special projects.

Restrictions on Giving: The foundation does not make loans or grants to individuals. Low priority is given to cultural organizations, such as museums, libraries, or exhibitions; and to research institutes, preparatory schools, colleges, and universities. The foundation generally does not fund medical research or health care and training, and it is not interested in managing programs or projects of unestablished organizations.

OTHER THINGS TO KNOW
"To encourage the descendants of the Founder to take an interest in philanthropy, the Foundation matches, to a limited extent, their individual grants made to agencies in which they are actively involved."

PUBLICATIONS
Annual report

GRANTS ANALYSIS
Total Grants: $1,671,601

Number of Grants: 88*

Highest Grant: $400,000

Average Grant: $16,442*

Typical Range: $2,000 to $20,000

Disclosure Period: 1993

Note: Average grant figure and number of grants exclude matching grants totaling $224,700. Recent grants are derived from a 1993 Form 990.

RECENT GRANTS

Library
10,000	New York Public Library, New York, NY — for Lifelong Learning Collection of the Branch Libraries
5,000	New York Public Library, New York, NY

General
400,000	YMCA of Greater New York, New York, NY — for second installment of a $1,000,000 grant for Endowment for Youth
100,000	New York Botanical Garden, Bronx, NY — toward a $600,000 grant for Children's Adventure project
50,000	Kingsbridge Heights Community Center, Bronx, NY — for capital campaign
50,000	New York Zoological Society, Bronx, NY — for second installment of a $100,000 grant for Wildlife Crisis campaign
50,000	Teach for America, New York, NY

Donner Foundation, William H.

CONTACT
William T. Alpert
Senior Program Officer
William H. Donner Foundation
500 Fifth Ave., Ste. 1230
New York, NY 10110
(212) 719-9290

FINANCIAL SUMMARY
Recent Giving: $2,600,000 (fiscal 1995 est.); $2,877,000 (fiscal 1994); $2,058,836 (fiscal 1993)

Assets: $65,903,000 (fiscal 1994); $73,436,463 (fiscal 1993); $65,645,000 (fiscal 1992)

EIN: 23-1611346

CONTRIBUTIONS SUMMARY
Donor(s): William H. Donner was born in Columbus, IN, in 1864. In his twenties, he took over and made a success of a family-owned grain mill. Before he was 30, Donner profited from his investments in real estate, having realized that the recent discovery of natural gas in Indiana would bring new industry to the area. He used these profits to start the National Tin Plate Company of North Anderson, IN. He later sold his tin plate investments to the American Tin Plate Company. William Donner, along with the Mellon brothers and Clay Frick, helped start the Union Steel Company. The company merged with the Sharon Steel Company in 1902, and was subsequently purchased by the U.S. Steel Corporation. He later became president of Cambria Steel Company, and chairman of the board of the Pennsylvania

Steel Company. His final business venture was the establishment of the Donner Steel Company in Buffalo, NY.

Having lost his eldest son to cancer, Mr. Donner devoted much of his time and resources to cancer research. He established the International Cancer Research Foundation in 1932. Following his retirement from business, Mr. Donner spent much of his time in Montreal, where he supported neurological research efforts. In 1950, he established the Donner Canadian Foundation. William H. Donner died in Montreal in 1953. The William H. Donner Foundation was established in 1961 with an endowment originally donated by William H. Donner for the International Cancer Research Institute.

Typical Recipients: • *Arts & Humanities:* Arts Centers, Arts Outreach, Film & Video, Libraries, Museums/Galleries, Public Broadcasting • *Civic & Public Affairs:* African American Affairs, Business/Free Enterprise, Chambers of Commerce, Civil Rights, Economic Development, Economic Policy, Employment/Job Training, General, Professional & Trade Associations, Public Policy, Urban & Community Affairs • *Education:* Business Education, Business-School Partnerships, Colleges & Universities, Education Associations, Education Reform, Elementary Education (Public), General, International Studies, Literacy, Private Education (Precollege) • *Environment:* General • *Health:* Adolescent Health Issues, Clinics/Medical Centers, Geriatric Health, Hospitals, Mental Health, Prenatal Health Issues • *International:* Foreign Educational Institutions, Human Rights, International Affairs, International Development, International Environmental Issues, International Organizations, International Peace & Security Issues, International Relations, International Relief Efforts • *Science:* Scientific Centers & Institutes, Scientific Organizations • *Social Services:* Food/Clothing Distribution, People with Disabilities, Shelters/Homelessness, Youth Organizations

Grant Types: project

Geographic Distribution: principally to national organizations

GIVING OFFICERS
William T. Alpert: sr program off

James Balog: dir *B* Vintondale PA 1928 *ED* PA St Univ 1950; Rutgers Univ 1958 *CURR EMPL* chmn: Lambert Brussels Capital Corp *CORP AFFIL* chmn: 1838 Investment Advs; dir: AL Labs, Coast US Properties, Transatlantic Holdings

Peter B. Cannell: dir *B* Glen Ridge NJ 1926 *CURR EMPL* pres: Peter B Cannell & Co

James Vincent Capua: pres *B* Ossining NY 1949 *ED* Univ Rochester BA 1971; Univ Chicago MA 1972; Univ Chicago PhD 1976 *NONPR AFFIL* mem: Am Soc Marine Artists, New York City Comm Bicentennial US Constitution

Alexander Donner: dir

Robert Donner, Jr.: vp, asst treas

Timothy E. Donner: dir

John Jacob Hagenbuch: dir *B* Park Forest IL 1951 *ED* Princeton Univ AB 1974; Stanford Univ MBA 1978 *CURR EMPL* gen partner: Hellman & Friedman *CORP AFFIL* dir: Am Pres Co, Eagle Indus Inc, Great Am Investment & Mgmt Inc, Story First Commun Inc *NONPR AFFIL* bd gov: San Francisco Symphony, Town Sch Boys *CLUB AFFIL* Burlingame CC, CA Tennis, Pacific-Union, Villa Taverna

Peter Lawson Johnson: dir

Louise Oliver: dir *PHIL AFFIL* trust: George E. Coleman Foundation

William D. Roosevelt: treas *B* 1932 *CORP AFFIL* off: Heonig & Strock

Deborah Donner Roy: dir

Monica Winsor Washburn: dir

Wilcomb Edward Washburn: dir *B* Ottawa KS 1925 *ED* Dartmouth Coll AB 1948; Harvard Univ MA 1951; Harvard Univ PhD 1955 *NONPR AFFIL* fellow: Am Anthropological Assn; historian: Smithsonian Inst Am Studies; mem: Am Antiquarian Soc, Am Soc Ethnohistory, Am Studies Assn, Columbia Historical Soc, MA Historical Assn, Org Am Historians, Soc History Discoveries

Curtin Winsor III: dir

Curtin Winsor, Jr.: secy, dir

APPLICATION INFORMATION
Initial Approach:

To apply for a grant, an organization should send a pre-proposal letter to the foundation.

The letter should describe the project, the organization's objectives, and include a tentative budget for the project. If the project is of interest to the foundation, a formal application will be requested.

Formal proposals should describe the background of the project; the organization's qualifications to deal with the problem or proposed project; a clear, concise description of the activities of the proposed project, including objectives, anticipated results, time schedule, evaluation plan, how results will be disseminated, other sources of support, and plans for future support; a line item budget; proof of tax-exempt status; a copy of the organization's latest financial statements; names and resumes of project's principal staff; and names, addresses, and telephone numbers of four people able to comment on the proposed project. Six copies of the proposal should be submitted.

Trustees meet in January, May, and September to consider formal proposals. Applications must be received by October 15, March 1, and July 1 to meet the review dates.

Notification of status of proposals usually takes place by the end of the month in which a board meeting takes place. Evaluative criteria include the impact of the project, potential for it to serve as a model, the applicant's ability to carry out the project, and its conformity to foundation priorities.

Restrictions on Giving: The foundation does not fund construction or renovation of buildings, capital campaigns, annual charitable drives, individuals, research and travel, operating deficits, loans, scientific or medical research, or indirect costs. The foundation generally does not support more than one project of a given organization, and discourages requests for continuation of existing grants.

OTHER THINGS TO KNOW
The foundation is closely associated with the Donner Canadian Foundation in Toronto, Canada. In addition to its grant-making activities, the foundation also provides operating services for small foundations.

PUBLICATIONS
Annual report

GRANTS ANALYSIS
Total Grants: $2,877,000

Number of Grants: 26

Highest Grant: $272,500

Average Grant: $110,000*

Typical Range: $20,000 to $150,000

Disclosure Period: fiscal year ending October 31, 1994

Note: The average grant figure was supplied by the foundation. Recent grants are derived from a fiscal 1993 Form 990.

RECENT GRANTS

Library
5,000	Foundation Center, New York, NY — partial support for Foundation Giving

General
233,694	Johns Hopkins University, Baltimore, MD
185,000	Producers Incorporated for Television
185,000	Producers Incorporated for Television, Columbia, SC — support for a pilot television series introducing new ideas and voices to William F. Buckley's Firing Line
137,500	Pacific Basin Research Institute, Santa Barbara, CA
137,500	Pacific Basin Research Institute, Rockville, MD — support for the development of a market strategy for Vietnam

Dreyfus Foundation, Jean and Louis

CONTACT
Edmee de Montmollin Firth
Executive Director
Jean & Louis Dreyfus Foundation
c/o Decker, Hubbard, and Weldon
30 Rockefeller Plz., Ste. 4340
New York, NY 10112
(212) 581-7575

FINANCIAL SUMMARY
Recent Giving: $850,000 (1995 est.); $850,000 (1994 approx.); $851,650 (1993)

Assets: $18,500,000 (1995 est.); $18,400,000 (1994 approx.); $18,480,182 (1993)

Gifts Received: $28,938 (1989); $875,000 (1988)

EIN: 13-2947180

CONTRIBUTIONS SUMMARY
Donor(s): The foundation was incorporated in 1978 by the late Louis Dreyfus .

Typical Recipients: • *Arts & Humanities:* Arts Associations & Councils, Arts Centers, Arts Institutes, Arts Outreach, Libraries, Literary Arts, Museums/Galleries, Music, Opera, Theater • *Civic & Public Affairs:* Economic Development, General, Hispanic Affairs, Housing, Municipalities/Towns, Public Policy, Urban & Community Affairs, Women's Affairs • *Education:* After-school/Enrichment Programs, Arts/Humanities Education, Colleges & Universities, General, Literacy, Medical Education, Private Education (Precollege) • *Health:* AIDS/HIV, Alzheimers Disease, Cancer, Clinics/Medical Centers, Geriatric Health, Health Funds, Hospitals, Medical Training, Mental Health, Nursing Services • *International:* Foreign Educational Institutions, Health Care/Hospitals, International Organizations • *Social Services:* At-Risk Youth, Child Welfare, Community Centers, Community Service Organizations, Crime Prevention, Delinquency & Criminal Rehabilitation, Family Planning, Food/Clothing Distribution, Scouts, Senior Services, Shelters/Homelessness, Substance Abuse, Youth Organizations

Grant Types: general support and project

Geographic Distribution: eastern United States, focus on New York, NY

GIVING OFFICERS
Edmee de Montmollin Firth: exec dir

Nicholas L. D. Firth: pres

Thomas J. Hubbard: secy *NONPR AFFIL* chmn, dir: Metro Opera Guild

Thomas Joseph Sweeney, Jr.: vp, treas *B* New York NY 1923 *ED* NY Univ BA 1947; Columbia Univ JD 1949 *CURR EMPL* of couns: Decker Hubbard & Welden *CORP AFFIL* dir: Engelhard Hanovia *NONPR AFFIL* dir: WR Kenan Fund; mem: NY St Bar Assn; trust: Para-Educator Fdn *PHIL AFFIL* trust: Pinkerton Foundation; co-trust: Sidney and Judith Kranes Charitable Trust

APPLICATION INFORMATION
Initial Approach:

The foundation requests applications be made in writing and sent to Edmee de Montmollin Firth.

Written applications should include an outline of the proposed project, a statement of its significance, and the proposed budget. The foundation also requests that the applicant submit ruling letters from the IRS showing that the applicant has a tax-exempt status under section 501(c)(3), and the applicant's classification under sections 509 and 4942(j)(3) as a public charity, private operating foundation, or private foundation other than an operating foundation.

The foundation has no deadline for submitting proposals.

Applications are normally considered at the board's spring meeting. Post-grant requirements include submission of complete reports outlining the progress made on an annual basis and a statement of income and expenditures. The grantee shall permit representatives of the foundation to visit the premises of the grantee for review. The foundation also requests that the grantee inform the foundation of any public announcements involving the grant, or any change of circumstances involving the organization's tax-exempt status. Failure to comply with any provisions set forth by the foundation may result in a request for repayment to the foundation or discontinuance of payment by the foundation.

Restrictions on Giving: The foundation reports that preference for grants is given to established institutions of the arts and medicine. The foundation does not make grants to individuals.

GRANTS ANALYSIS
Total Grants: $851,650

Number of Grants: 60

Highest Grant: $70,000

Average Grant: $14,194

Typical Range: $5,000 to $20,000

Disclosure Period: 1993

Note: Recent grants are derived from a 1993 grants list.

RECENT GRANTS

Library
10,000	Brooklyn Public Library, Brooklyn, NY

General
70,000	Third Street Music School Settlement, New York, NY
40,000	Johns Hopkins CTY
30,000	Brookdale Center on Aging, New York, NY
25,000	Center to Prevent Handgun Violence, Washington, DC
20,000	Alianza Dominicana, New York, NY

Dreyfus Foundation, Max and Victoria

CONTACT
Lucy Gioia
Office Administrator
Max and Victoria Dreyfus Foundation
50 Main St., Ste. 1000
White Plains, NY 10606
(914) 682-2008

FINANCIAL SUMMARY
Recent Giving: $2,000,000 (1995 est.); $1,497,500 (1994); $1,507,400 (1993)

Assets: $49,000,000 (1994 approx.); $52,487,009 (1993); $48,206,126 (1992)

EIN: 13-1687573

CONTRIBUTIONS SUMMARY

Donor(s): The foundation was established in New York in 1965 by the late Victoria Dreyfus . When Mrs. Dreyfus died in 1976, her assests were bequeathed to the foundation. Mrs. Dreyfus was the wife of the late Max Dreyfus, a leading figure in the music publishing business and one of the founding members of ASCAP.

Typical Recipients: • *Arts & Humanities:* Arts Appreciation, Arts Associations & Councils, Arts Festivals, Arts Outreach, Ballet, Community Arts, Dance, Historic Preservation, Libraries, Literary Arts, Museums/Galleries, Music, Opera, Performing Arts, Public Broadcasting, Theater, Visual Arts • *Civic & Public Affairs:* Community Foundations, Employment/Job Training, Law & Justice, Legal Aid, Municipalities/Towns, Native American Affairs, Nonprofit Management, Parades/Festivals, Philanthropic Organizations, Safety, Urban & Community Affairs, Zoos/Aquariums • *Education:* Agricultural Education, Arts/Humanities Education, Colleges & Universities, Education Associations, Engineering/Technological Education, Environmental Education, General, Legal Education, Medical Education, Minority Education, Private Education (Precollege), Public Education (Precollege), Science/Mathematics Education, Secondary Education (Private), Secondary Education (Public), Special Education, Student Aid, Vocational & Technical Education • *Environment:* General, Wildlife Protection • *Health:* Cancer, Emergency/Ambulance Services, Hospices, Hospitals, Hospitals (University Affiliated), Medical Rehabilitation, Medical Research, Mental Health, Single-Disease Health Associations • *Religion:* Churches, Religious Welfare • *Social Services:* Animal Protection, Child Welfare, Community Service Organizations, Counseling, Crime Prevention, Day Care, Delinquency & Criminal Rehabilitation, Family Planning, Family Services, Food/Clothing Distribution, People with Disabilities, Recreation & Athletics, Senior Services, Shelters/Homelessness, Substance Abuse, Volunteer Services, Youth Organizations

Grant Types: general support, project, and research

Geographic Distribution: national

GIVING OFFICERS

Lucy Gioia: off adm

Nancy E. Oddo: vp, dir

David Jerome Oppenheim: chmn, dir *NONPR AFFIL* mem: Am Fed Arts, Counc Fine Arts Deans, Natl Soc Literature & Arts Intl, NY St Arts Deans, Soc Fellows; mem bd dirs: Am Stefan Wolpe Soc, Film Soc Lincoln Ctr, Town Hall Fdn, Young Audiences

Norman S. Portenoy: vp, dir

Winifred Riggs Portenoy: pres, dir

Mary P. Surrey: secy, treas, dir

APPLICATION INFORMATION
Initial Approach:

Applicants should send a letter request, not exceeding three pages.

The letter should include an outline of the project, a copy of an IRS tax-exempt determination letter, and budget sheet for project/program.

Board reviews applications every four months. Deadlines are March 30, July 30, and November 30.

Restrictions on Giving: The foundation does not support individuals or international organizations.

OTHER THINGS TO KNOW

The foundation moved its offices in April 1994 from New York, NY, to White Plains, NY.

GRANTS ANALYSIS

Total Grants: $1,507,400

Number of Grants: 254

Highest Grant: $40,000

Average Grant: $5,000*

Typical Range: $1,000 to $10,000

Disclosure Period: 1993

Note: Average grant was supplied by the foundation. Recent grants are derived from a 1993 Form 990.

RECENT GRANTS

Library

10,000	Kutztown University, Kutztown, PA — library expansion	
10,000	Village of Tuckahoe, Tuckahoe, NY — library expansion/community programs	

General

35,000	Mt. Vernon College, Washington, DC — educational	
25,000	Anderson College, Anderson, SC — building fund	
25,000	Angel View Crippled Children's Foundation, Desert Hot Springs, CA — building support	
25,000	Foundation for the Retarded Children of the Desert, Palm Desert, CA — transportation/vehicle	
25,000	Iona Senior Services, Washington, DC	

Dula Educational and Charitable Foundation, Caleb C. and Julia W.

CONTACT
Gale Fitch
Senior Trust Officer
Caleb C. and Julia W. Dula Educational and Charitable Foundation
c/o Chemical Bank
270 Park Ave., 21st Fl.
New York, NY 10017
(212) 270-9066

FINANCIAL SUMMARY
Recent Giving: $1,250,000 (1995 est.); $1,250,000 (1994 approx.); $1,017,000 (1993)

Assets: $28,900,000 (1995 est.); $28,900,000 (1994 approx.); $26,123,590 (1993)

EIN: 13-6045790

CONTRIBUTIONS SUMMARY
Donor(s): The foundation was established in 1939 by the late Julia W. Dula .

Typical Recipients: • *Arts & Humanities:* Arts Funds, Historic Preservation, History & Archaeology, Libraries, Museums/Galleries, Music, Opera, Theater • *Civic & Public Affairs:* Botanical Gardens/Parks, Clubs, First Amendment Issues, General, Public Policy, Urban & Community Affairs, Zoos/Aquariums • *Education:* Agricultural Education, Colleges & Universities, Health & Physical Education, Medical Education, Private Education (Precollege), Special Education • *Environment:* General, Resource Conservation, Wildlife Protection • *Health:* Cancer, Children's Health/Hospitals, Diabetes, Emergency/Ambulance Services, Health Organizations, Hospitals, Nursing Services, Single-Disease Health Associations • *Religion:* Churches, Religious Organizations • *Science:* Science Museums • *Social Services:* Animal Protection, Child Welfare, Day Care, Family Services, People with Disabilities, Senior Services, Shelters/Homelessness, United Funds/United Ways, Youth Organizations

Grant Types: operating expenses

Geographic Distribution: primarily New York and Missouri

GIVING OFFICERS
Gale Fitch: contact *CURR EMPL* sr trust off: Chemical Bank

Margaret C. Taylor: trust

Julia P. Wightman: trust

Orrin S. Wightman III: trust

APPLICATION INFORMATION
Initial Approach:

The foundation has no formal grant application procedure or application form.

The trustees generally meet twice a year, in Spring and again in late Fall, to consider the distribution of funds to various applicants. Proposals must be sent to the trustees by February for the Fall meeting and by August for the October meeting.

Restrictions on Giving: Grants are made only to tax-exempt organizations. The foundation does not support individuals or make loans.

GRANTS ANALYSIS
Total Grants: $1,017,000

Number of Grants: 98

Highest Grant: $100,000

Average Grant: $10,377

Typical Range: $1,000 to $15,000

Disclosure Period: 1993

Note: Recent grants are derived from a 1993 Form 990.

RECENT GRANTS

Library

100,000	Pierpont Morgan Library, New York, NY
100,000	Pierpont Morgan Library, New York, NY
10,000	St. Louis Public Library, St. Louis, MO

General

50,000	Missouri Botanical Garden, St. Louis, MO
50,000	Missouri Botanical Garden, St. Louis, MO
50,000	National Fish and Wildlife Foundation, Washington, DC
25,000	Duke University, Durham, NC
15,000	Austen Riggs Center, Stockbridge, MA

Dun & Bradstreet Corp. / Dun & Bradstreet Corp. Foundation, Inc.

Revenue: $4.89 billion
Employees: 52,400
Headquarters: New York, NY
SIC Major Group: Credit Reporting Services, Book Publishing, Miscellaneous Publishing, and Advertising Nec

CONTACT
Juliann Gill
Administrator
Dun & Bradstreet Corp. Foundation, Inc.
299 Park Ave.
New York, NY 10171
(212) 593-6746
Note: The company's World Wide Web address is http://www.dnb.com

FINANCIAL SUMMARY
Recent Giving: $3,879,613 (1993); $3,750,553 (1992); $3,431,265 (1991)

Assets: $7,836,982 (1993); $11,631,038 (1992); $14,014,243 (1991)

Fiscal Note: All contributions are made through the foundation.

EIN: 13-6148188

CONTRIBUTIONS SUMMARY
Typical Recipients: • *Arts & Humanities:* Arts Associations & Councils, Arts Centers, Historic Preservation, Libraries, Museums/Galleries, Performing Arts, Public Broadcasting • *Civic & Public Affairs:* African American Affairs, Business/Free Enterprise, Civil Rights, Economic Policy, Law & Justice, Municipalities/Towns, Professional & Trade Associations, Public Policy, Urban & Community Affairs • *Education:* Business Education, Colleges & Universities, Education Associations, Education Funds, Literacy, Minority Education, Student Aid • *Health:* AIDS/HIV, Cancer, Emergency/Ambulance Services, Health Organizations, Hospitals, Mental Health, Single-Disease Health Associations • *Science:* Scientific Centers & Institutes • *Social Services:* Child Welfare, Community Service Organizations, Food/Clothing Distribution, People with Disabilities, Recreation & Athletics, United Funds/United Ways, Youth Organizations

Grant Types: employee matching gifts and general support

Geographic Distribution: nationwide

Operating Locations: AL (Huntsville), CA (Garden Grove, Los Angeles, Menlo Park, Orange, San Jose), CT (Norwalk, Stamford, Wilton), DC, FL (Dunedin), GA (Atlanta), IA (Clinton), IL (Chicago, Lincolnshire, Northbrook, Schaumburg), MA (Framingham, Lexington), MD (Baltimore, Rockville), NE (Omaha), NJ (Berkeley Heights, Murray Hill, Parsippany, Totowa), NY (New York, Purchase, Rochester), PA (Newtown Square, Plymouth Meeting, West Norrington), TX (Irving), WI (Fond du Lac)

CORP. OFFICERS
Charles Worthington Moritz: *B* Washington DC 1936 *ED* Yale Univ BA 1958 *CURR EMPL* chmn: Dun & Bradstreet Corp *NONPR AFFIL* mem: Am Mgmt Assn, Bus Roundtable, Direct Mktg Assn, Sales & Mktg Execs Greater NY *CLUB AFFIL* Blind Brook CC, Econ, Johns Island, Natl Golf Links Am, Pine Valley, Wee Burn CC

Robert Evan Weissman: *B* New Haven CT 1940 *ED* Babson Coll BS 1964 *CURR EMPL* pres, ceo, dir: Dun & Bradstreet Corp *CORP AFFIL* dir: State St Boston Corp *NONPR AFFIL* chmn: Assn Data Processing Svc Org; mem: Info Tech Assn Am, Inst Electrical Electronics Engrs, Inst Mgmt Accts, Natl Assn Accts, Soc Mfg Engrs; mem bus roundtable: US-Japan Bus Counc; vchmn: Babson Coll

GIVING OFFICERS
Edwin A. Bescherer, Jr.: trust *B* Brooklyn NY 1933 *ED* Purdue Univ BS 1955 *CURR EMPL* exec vp fin, cfo: Dun & Bradstreet Corp *CORP AFFIL* dir: R H Donnelley Corp, Dun & Bradstreet Plan Svcs Inc *NONPR AFFIL* mem: Fin Execs Inst

William Hobart Buchanan, Jr.: asst secy *B* Summit NJ 1937 *ED* Princeton Univ AB 1959; Harvard Univ LLB 1963 *CURR EMPL* vp law: Dun & Bradstreet Corp *CORP AFFIL* secy, dir: Dun & Bradstreet Plan Svcs Inc; sr vp, chief legal couns, secy: R H Donnelly Corp *NONPR AFFIL* dir: Am Soc

Corp Execs; mem: Am Bar Assn, Am Soc Corp Secys, Assn Bar City New York, NY Bar Assn *CLUB AFFIL* New Canaan Field, Princeton

Philip C. Danford: treas *B* Columbus OH 1944 *ED* Villanova Univ BS 1967; Harvard Univ 1969 *CURR EMPL* vp, treas: Dun & Bradstreet Corp *CORP AFFIL* treas: D&B Shared Svcs Inc, AC Nielsen Co

William O. Frohlich: vp

Juliann Gill: admin

Alan J. Klutch: comptr *B* 1944 *ED* CUNY BBA 1967; St Johns Univ MBA 1971 *CURR EMPL* vp fin planning: Dun & Bradstreet Corp *CORP AFFIL* vp: AC Nielsen Co

Daniel S. Miller: asst treas

Dennis N. Pidherny: asst treas

Virginia Simone: secy

Robert Evan Weissman: trust *CURR EMPL* pres, ceo, dir: Dun & Bradstreet Corp (see above)

APPLICATION INFORMATION
Initial Approach: *Initial Contact:* brief letter or proposal *Include Information On:* description of the organization, amount requested, purpose for which funds are sought, recently audited financial statement, and copy of IRS Code Section 501(c)(3) tax-exempt status *Deadlines:* October for grants to be made in following year

Restrictions on Giving: Foundation does not make grants for dinners or special events, fraternal organizations, political or lobbying groups, religious organizations for sectarian purposes, goodwill advertising, or individuals.

Foundation will not consider organizations without an IRS 501(c)(3) tax exempt status.

GRANTS ANALYSIS
Total Grants: $3,879,613

Number of Grants: 285*

Highest Grant: $317,100

Average Grant: $4,543*

Typical Range: $500 to $10,000

Disclosure Period: 1993

Note: The figures for average grant and number of grants exclude $2,584,858 in matching gifts. Recent grants are derived from a 1993 Form 990.

RECENT GRANTS

Library

5,000	New York Public Library, New York, NY

General

317,100	United Way Tri-State, New York, NY
57,900	United Way Tri-State, New York, NY
50,000	Metropolitan Crusade of Mercy/United Way, Chicago, IL
37,500	Columbia University, New York, NY
31,593	National Merit Scholarship Corporation, Evanston, IL

Eastman Kodak Company / Eastman Kodak Charitable Trust

Revenue: $16.86 billion
Employees: 137,750
Headquarters: Rochester, NY
SIC Major Group: Photographic Equipment &
   Supplies, Plastics Materials & Resins,
   Cellulosic Manmade Fibers, and Organic
   Fibers—Noncellulosic

CONTACT
Essie L. Calhoun
President
Eastman Kodak Charitable Trust
343 State St.
Rochester, NY 14650-0517
(716) 724-1980
Note: Ms. Calhoun is director of community
relations and contributions for the company.
The company's World Wide Web address is
http://www.kodak.com

FINANCIAL SUMMARY
Recent Giving: $9,800,000 (1995 est.);
$13,200,000 (1994); $15,700,000 (1993)
Assets: $2,853,311 (1994); $5,051,593
(1993); $18,865,189 (1991)
Gifts Received: $15,590 (1993);
$20,075,000 (1990)
Fiscal Note: Figures include direct gifts and
charitable trust contributions. Above figures
exclude nonmonetary support.
EIN: 16-6015274

CONTRIBUTIONS SUMMARY
Typical Recipients: • *Arts & Humanities:*
Arts Associations & Councils, Arts Funds,
Libraries, Museums/Galleries, Music, Performing Arts • *Civic & Public Affairs:* Afri-
can American Affairs, Botanical
Gardens/Parks, Business/Free Enterprise,
Economic Policy, Employment/Job Train-
ing, General, Housing, Professional & Trade
Associations, Public Policy, Urban & Com-
munity Affairs • *Education:* Business Educa-
tion, Colleges & Universities, Community &
Junior Colleges, Education Funds, Educa-
tion Reform, Engineering/Technological
Education, General, Health & Physical Education, Minority Education, Public Education (Precollege), Religious Education,
Science/Mathematics Education, Special
Education, Student Aid • *Environment:* General • *Health:* Clinics/Medical Centers,
Emergency/Ambulance Services, Health Organizations, Medical Rehabilitation, Mental
Health • *International:* Foreign Arts Organizations, Health Care/Hospitals, International
Environmental Issues • *Religion:* Jewish
Causes, Religious Welfare • *Science:* Science Museums, Scientific Centers & Institutes, Scientific Organizations • *Social
Services:* Child Welfare, Community Service Organizations, Family Services, People
with Disabilities, United Funds/United
Ways, Youth Organizations

Grant Types: capital, department, fellowship, general support, multiyear/continuing
support, research, and scholarship

Nonmonetary Support: $16,500,000
(1994); $77,000 (1993); $5,000,000 (1991)
Nonmonetary Support Types: donated
equipment and donated products
Note: The company also donates property.
Nonmonetary support in 1994 was a donation of land in California and product donations. Nonmonetary support budget is
separate from the corporate giving budget.

Geographic Distribution: education grants
made nationwide; others made in main corporate locations

Operating Locations: CO (Windsor), IL
(Lincoln), KS (McPherson), NJ (Belle
Mead), NY (Rensselaer, Rochester), PA
(Myerstown), PR

CORP. OFFICERS
George Myles Cordell Fisher: *B* Anna IL
1940 *ED* Univ IL BS 1962; Brown Univ MS
1964; Brown Univ PhD 1966 *CURR EMPL*
chmn, pres, ceo: Eastman Kodak Co
NONPR AFFIL dir: Natl Merit Scholarship
Fdn, Univ IL Fdn; mem: Inst Electrical &
Electronics Engrs; trust: Brown Univ

GIVING OFFICERS
Essie L. Calhoun: pres *CURR EMPL*
admin, asst commun rels & contributions:
Eastman Kodak Co

APPLICATION INFORMATION
Initial Approach: *Initial Contact:* brief letter or proposal *Include Information On:* description of the organization, amount
requested, purpose for which funds are
sought, recently audited financial statement,
and proof of tax-exempt status *Deadlines:*
none

Restrictions on Giving: The trust does not
consider the following organizations or purposes: dinners or special events, fraternal organizations, goodwill advertising, member
agencies of united funds, political or lobbying groups, religious organizations, individuals, or sectarian purposes.

OTHER THINGS TO KNOW
Charitable trust generally does not solicit
funding requests.

PUBLICATIONS
Kodak Contributions: Investing in Tomorrow

GRANTS ANALYSIS
Total Grants: $13,200,000
Typical Range: $5,000 to $20,000 and
$50,000 to $100,000
Disclosure Period: 1994
Note: Recent grants are derived from a 1993
annual report.

RECENT GRANTS
Library
50,000	New York Public Library, New York, NY — Schomberg Center for Research in Black Culture

General
921,250	United Way of Greater Rochester, Rochester, NY
825,000	United Way of Greater Rochester, Rochester, NY
825,000	United Way of Greater Rochester, Rochester, NY
825,000	United Way of Greater Rochester, Rochester, NY
500,000	World Wildlife Fund, Washington, DC — Windows on the Wild Program

Edmonds Foundation, Dean S.

CONTACT
Marjorie Thompson
Dean S. Edmonds Fdn.
c/o The Bank of New York
48 Wall St.
New York, NY 10286
(212) 527-3733

FINANCIAL SUMMARY
Recent Giving: $79,000 (1993); $85,500
(1992); $102,500 (1990)
Assets: $2,168,131 (1993); $2,102,655
(1992); $1,896,836 (1990)
EIN: 13-6161381

CONTRIBUTIONS SUMMARY
Typical Recipients: • *Arts & Humanities:*
Historic Preservation, History & Archaeol-
ogy, Libraries, Museums/Galleries, Music,
Opera, Performing Arts, Public Broadcasting
• *Civic & Public Affairs:* Clubs, General,
Philanthropic Organizations, Professional &
Trade Associations, Safety, Women's Af-
fairs • *Education:* Business Education, Col-
leges & Universities,
Engineering/Technological Education, Medi-
cal Education, Private Education (Precol-
lege), Science/Mathematics Education,
Student Aid • *Health:* Children's Health/Hos-
pitals, Diabetes, Hospitals • *International:*
Foreign Educational Institutions • *Science:*
Scientific Organizations • *Social Services:*
Community Service Organizations

Grant Types: general support

Geographic Distribution: no geographic restrictions

GIVING OFFICERS
The Bank of New York: trust
Dean S. Edmonds III: trust

APPLICATION INFORMATION
Initial Approach: Send brief letter describing program. There are no deadlines.

GRANTS ANALYSIS
Total Grants: $79,000
Number of Grants: 39
Highest Grant: $7,000
Typical Range: $1,000 to $5,000
Disclosure Period: 1993
Note: Recent grants are derived from a 1993
Form 990.

RECENT GRANTS
Library
3,000	University of North Carolina Library, Chapel Hill, NC —

	rare books and writing collection project
1,000	Friends of the Libraries of Boston University, Boston, MA
500	Library of the Boston Athenaeum, Boston, MA

General

6,000	Trustees of Boston University, Boston, MA
5,000	Boca Raton Community Hospital, Boca Raton, FL
5,000	EAA Aviation Foundation, Oshkosh, WI
4,000	Association of Childhood Education International
3,000	Boston University School of Medicine, Boston, MA — Ruth Levine Fund

Emerson Foundation, Inc., Fred L.

CONTACT
Ronald D. West
Executive Director and Secretary
Fred L. Emerson Foundation, Inc.
PO Box 276
Auburn, NY 13021
(315) 253-9621

FINANCIAL SUMMARY
Recent Giving: $2,588,865 (1993);
$2,411,459 (1992); $2,268,143 (1991)

Assets: $56,269,770 (1993); $54,195,752 (1992); $54,081,818 (1991)

Gifts Received: $1,000 (1989)

EIN: 15-6017650

CONTRIBUTIONS SUMMARY
Donor(s): The foundation was established in 1932 by the late Fred L. Emerson . Mr. Emerson was president of Dunn and McCarthy, Inc., a manufacturer of women's shoes in Auburn, NY.

Typical Recipients: • *Arts & Humanities:* Arts Associations & Councils, Arts Centers, Arts Festivals, Arts Institutes, Dance, Historic Preservation, History & Archaeology, Libraries, Museums/Galleries, Music, Performing Arts, Theater • *Civic & Public Affairs:* Economic Development, General, Municipalities/Towns, Parades/Festivals, Safety • *Education:* Business Education, Colleges & Universities, Community & Junior Colleges, Private Education (Precollege), Science/Mathematics Education, Student Aid • *Environment:* Air/Water Quality • *Health:* Cancer, Emergency/Ambulance Services, Eyes/Blindness, Health Organizations, Hospices, Hospitals, Medical Rehabilitation, Medical Research, Single-Disease Health Associations • *Religion:* Churches, Religious Welfare • *Social Services:* Animal Protection, Child Welfare, Community Service Organizations, Homes, Recreation & Athletics, Senior Services, Shelters/Homelessness, United Funds/United Ways, Youth Organizations

Grant Types: capital, challenge, endowment, general support, matching, project, research, and scholarship

Geographic Distribution: primarily Auburn, Cayuga County, and central New York

GIVING OFFICERS
William Finch Allyn: dir *B* Auburn NY 1935 *ED* Dartmouth Coll BA 1958 *CURR EMPL* pres: Welch Allyn *CORP AFFIL* dir: Niagara Mohawk Power Corp, Oneida Silver, Ontario Bank, Syracuse Res Corp *NONPR AFFIL* trust: Commun Gen Hosp *CLUB AFFIL* Skaneateles CC *PHIL AFFIL* vp, dir: Allyn Foundation

David L. Emerson: vp, dir

Kristen D. Emerson: dir

Lori L. Emerson: dir

Peter J. Emerson: pres

W. Gary Emerson: asst treas, dir

Anthony D. Franceschelli: treas, dir

Dr. J. David Hammond: dir

Ronald D. West: exec dir, secy, dir *PHIL AFFIL* dir: D.E. French Foundation

APPLICATION INFORMATION
Initial Approach:

Applicants should send a proposal in letter form to the foundation.

Proposals should detail the project for which support is sought. Attachments should include copies of current financial statements, a list of other sources of support, and a copy of the IRS determination letter of tax-exempt status.

Proposals should be received no later than one month prior to board meetings scheduled in early June and December.

Most major grants are made in early December. Meetings may be arranged with the foundation's grants officers if the applicant's program falls within the foundation's areas of interest.

Restrictions on Giving: The foundation does not make grants to individuals or for deficit financing or loans. The foundation prefers not to fund operating expenses.

PUBLICATIONS
Application guidelines

GRANTS ANALYSIS
Total Grants: $2,588,865

Number of Grants: 55

Highest Grant: $425,500

Average Grant: $47,070

Typical Range: $1,000 to $100,000

Disclosure Period: 1993

Note: Recent grants are derived from a 1993 Form 990.

RECENT GRANTS

Library

50,000	Seymour Library, Auburn, NY — building renovation
10,000	Hazard Library, Poplar Ridge, NY — cellar renovation
9,650	Aurora Library, Aurora, NY — Morgan Opera House Renovation Project
3,000	Foundation Center, Washington, DC — information services
3,000	Skaneateles Library Association, Skaneateles, NY — annual appeal

General

425,500	Faatkz Crofut Home for the Elderly, Auburn, NY — renovations
350,000	E. John Garvas Center, Auburn, NY — renovations
200,000	Hobart and William Smith Colleges, Geneva, NY — teaching and learning endowment
125,000	LeMoyne College, Syracuse, NY — annual fund
116,436	United Way of Cayuga County, Auburn, NY — annual support

Erpf Fund, Armand G.

CONTACT
Sue E. Van de Bovenkamp
President
Armand G. Erpf Fund
640 Park Ave.
New York, NY 10021
(212) 872-7725

FINANCIAL SUMMARY
Recent Giving: $431,963 (fiscal 1993); $393,725 (fiscal 1992); $353,452 (fiscal 1991)

Assets: $7,637,589 (fiscal 1993); $7,303,365 (fiscal 1992); $6,803,572 (fiscal 1991)

Gifts Received: $146,874 (fiscal 1993); $139,642 (fiscal 1992); $137,386 (fiscal 1991)

Fiscal Note: In fiscal 1993, contributions were received from ERPF Charitable Trust.

EIN: 13-6085594

CONTRIBUTIONS SUMMARY
Donor(s): the late Armand G. Erpf

Typical Recipients: • *Arts & Humanities:* Arts Associations & Councils, Arts Centers, Arts Institutes, Ballet, Community Arts, Dance, Historic Preservation, Libraries, Museums/Galleries, Music, Opera, Public Broadcasting, Theater • *Civic & Public Affairs:* Botanical Gardens/Parks, Economic Development, Ethnic Organizations, General, Zoos/Aquariums • *Education:* Arts/Humanities Education, Colleges & Universities, General, International Studies, Private Education (Precollege) • *Environment:* General, Resource Conservation, Wildlife Protection • *Health:* Hospitals • *International:* Foreign Educational Institutions, International Development, International Environmental Issues, International Organizations, International Peace &

Security Issues, International Relations, International Relief Efforts • *Religion:* Religious Organizations • *Science:* Science Museums, Scientific Labs • *Social Services:* Child Welfare, Youth Organizations

Grant Types: general support

Geographic Distribution: focus on NY

GIVING OFFICERS

Gina Caimi: secy

Douglas Campbell: exec vp, trust

Armand B. Erpf: dir

Cornelia A. Erpf: dir

Henry B. Hyde: dir

Carl L. Kempner: treas, trust

Roger D. Stone: dir *PHIL AFFIL* dir: Cintas Foundation

Sue E. Van de Bovenkamp: pres, dir

APPLICATION INFORMATION

Initial Approach: The foundation has no formal grant application procedure or application form. There are no deadlines.

GRANTS ANALYSIS

Total Grants: $431,963

Number of Grants: 113

Highest Grant: $75,000

Typical Range: $100 to $63,500

Disclosure Period: fiscal year ending November 30, 1993

Note: Recent grants are derived from a fiscal 1992 Form 990.

RECENT GRANTS

Library
13,750	Peirpont Morgan Library, New York, NY	
10,000	New York Public Library, New York, NY	
1,100	Atheneum, Philadelphia, PA	

General
75,250	New York Zoological Society, New York, NY	
57,050	World Wildlife Fund, Washington, DC	
28,533	Asia Society, New York, NY	
16,000	International Wilderness Leadership Society, Ft. Collins, CO	
10,000	American Museum of Natural History, New York, NY	

Ettinger Foundation

CONTACT

Richard P. Ettinger, Jr.
President, Trustee
Ettinger Fdn.
665 Fifth Ave.,
New York, NY 10022

FINANCIAL SUMMARY

Recent Giving: $599,420 (1992); $637,495 (1991); $609,865 (1990)

Assets: $14,647,791 (1992); $14,071,670 (1991); $11,534,208 (1990)

Gifts Received: $44,572 (1991)

Fiscal Note: In 1991, contributions were received from Richard Ettinger ($18,662), Sharon Ettinger ($10,200), Elaine P. Hapgood ($10,210), Lynn P. Babicka ($3,000), and Rocco Landesman ($2,500).

EIN: 06-6038938

CONTRIBUTIONS SUMMARY

Donor(s): members of the Ettinger family

Typical Recipients: • *Arts & Humanities:* Arts Associations & Councils, Libraries, Literary Arts, Music, Theater • *Civic & Public Affairs:* General, Housing, Native American Affairs, Rural Affairs, Women's Affairs • *Education:* Colleges & Universities, Education Funds, General, International Studies, Literacy, Minority Education, Private Education (Precollege), Public Education (Precollege), Social Sciences Education • *Environment:* General • *Health:* Arthritis, Hospices, Hospitals, Medical Research, Single-Disease Health Associations • *International:* Health Care/Hospitals, International Environmental Issues, International Relations • *Religion:* Churches • *Science:* Scientific Organizations • *Social Services:* Child Welfare, Community Service Organizations, Counseling, Family Planning, Family Services, Food/Clothing Distribution, Recreation & Athletics, Shelters/Homelessness, Youth Organizations

Grant Types: scholarship

GIVING OFFICERS

Lynn P. Babicka: trust *PHIL AFFIL* pres, trust: Educational Foundation of America

Richard P. Ettinger, Jr.: pres, trust *B* New York NY 1922 *ED* Dartmouth Coll AB 1944; Whittier Coll PhD 1973 *CURR EMPL* chmn, dir: HDL Communs *CORP AFFIL* dir: Prentice-Hall *NONPR AFFIL* mem: Belmont Chamber Commerce, Sons Am Revolution, Stanford Sailing Assn, US Yacht Racing Assn; treas, dir: Native Am Prep Sch; trust: Natl Fitness Fdn *CLUB AFFIL* Indian Harbor YC, Newport Harbor YC *PHIL AFFIL* trust: Educational Foundation of America

Sharon W. Ettinger: trust *PHIL AFFIL* dir: Educational Foundation of America

Elaine P. Hapgood: vp, trust *PHIL AFFIL* trust: Educational Foundation of America

Rocco Landesman: trust

John P. Powers: trust *PHIL AFFIL* dir: Educational Foundation of America

APPLICATION INFORMATION

Initial Approach: Send brief letter of inquiry describing program or project. There are no deadlines.

Restrictions on Giving: Does not support individuals or provide loans, general support, or endowments.

GRANTS ANALYSIS

Total Grants: $599,420

Number of Grants: 140

Highest Grant: $10,000

Typical Range: $1,000 to $5,000

Disclosure Period: 1992

Note: Recent grants are derived from a 1992 Form 990.

RECENT GRANTS

General
10,000	American Indian Graduate Center	
10,000	Association of American Indian Affairs	
10,000	Haven	
10,000	Hospice by the Sea, Boca Raton, FL	
10,000	Lighthawk	

Evans Foundation, T. M.

CONTACT

Luciano F. Cerrone
Secretary, Treasurer
T. M. Evans Fdn.
250 Pk. Ave.
New York, NY 10177
(212) 557-5575

FINANCIAL SUMMARY

Recent Giving: $296,600 (1992); $209,500 (1991); $1,031,000 (1990)

Assets: $4,880,586 (1992); $5,028,295 (1991); $4,450,462 (1990)

EIN: 25-6012086

CONTRIBUTIONS SUMMARY

Donor(s): Thomas Mellon Evans

Typical Recipients: • *Arts & Humanities:* General, Historic Preservation, History & Archaeology, Libraries, Literary Arts, Museums/Galleries, Opera • *Civic & Public Affairs:* Botanical Gardens/Parks, Employment/Job Training, General, Urban & Community Affairs, Zoos/Aquariums • *Education:* Colleges & Universities, Medical Education, Private Education (Precollege) • *Environment:* General • *Health:* Cancer, Clinics/Medical Centers, Hospitals, Medical Research, Mental Health, Single-Disease Health Associations • *Religion:* Churches, Religious Organizations • *Science:* Scientific Organizations • *Social Services:* Community Centers, Day Care, Youth Organizations

Grant Types: capital, emergency, general support, multiyear/continuing support, operating expenses, and research

Geographic Distribution: focus on NY

GIVING OFFICERS

Luciano F. Cerrone: secy, treas

Betty B. Evans: trust

Edward Parker Evans: trust *B* Pittsburgh PA 1942 *ED* Yale Univ BA 1964; Harvard Univ MBA 1967 *CURR EMPL* chmn: K-III Holdings *CORP AFFIL* dir: Fasig-Tipton Co; owner: Spring Hill Farm VA *NONPR AFFIL* mem: Andover Devel Bd *PHIL AFFIL* trust: Edward P. Evans Foundation

Thomas M. Evans: pres, trust *B* Pittsburgh PA 1910 *ED* Yale Univ BA 1931 *CURR EMPL* pres, dir: Evans & Co *CORP AFFIL* chmn exec comm: HK Porter Co; dir: Fansteel *NONPR AFFIL* dir: Childrens Village; trust: Hirshhorn Mus *CLUB AFFIL* Brook, Colony, Cosmopolitan, Edgeworth, Maidstone, New York YC, Pittsburgh, River, Turf & Field

Thomas M. Evans, Jr.: trust

APPLICATION INFORMATION
Initial Approach: The foundation has no formal grant application procedure or application form. There are no deadlines.

GRANTS ANALYSIS
Total Grants: $296,600

Number of Grants: 33

Highest Grant: $80,000

Typical Range: $500 to $10,000

Disclosure Period: 1992

Note: Recent grants are derived from a 1992 Form 990.

RECENT GRANTS

Library
| 2,000 | Pierpont Morgan Library, New York, NY |

General
80,000	New York University Medical Center, New York, NY
50,000	Carnegie Mellon University, Pittsburgh, PA
20,000	Fountain House, New York, NY
20,000	Greenwich Hospital, Greenwich, CT
18,650	Round Hill Community Church, Greenwich, CT

Everett Charitable Trust

CONTACT
Everett Charitable Trust
c/o Fleet Trust Co.
120 Genesee St.
Auburn, NY 13201

FINANCIAL SUMMARY
Recent Giving: $109,074 (1993); $121,044 (1992); $102,294 (1991)

Assets: $2,073,714 (1993); $1,987,983 (1992); $1,959,237 (1991)

Gifts Received: $1,725 (1992); $98 (1991)

EIN: 15-6018093

CONTRIBUTIONS SUMMARY
Typical Recipients: • *Arts & Humanities:* Arts Associations & Councils, Arts Centers, Libraries, Music, Performing Arts • *Education:* Colleges & Universities, Community & Junior Colleges • *Health:* Hospitals • *International:* Human Rights • *Religion:* Churches • *Social Services:* Animal Protection, Child Welfare, Community Service Organizations, Recreation & Athletics, Scouts, United Funds/United Ways, YMCA/YWCA/YMHA/YWHA, Youth Organizations

Grant Types: general support and scholarship

Geographic Distribution: focus on Cayuga County, NY

GIVING OFFICERS
Fleet Trust Company: trust

APPLICATION INFORMATION
Initial Approach: Send a brief letter of inquiry. Include a description of organization, amount requested, purpose of funds sought, recently audited financial statement, and proof of tax-exempt status. Deadline is November 1.

GRANTS ANALYSIS
Total Grants: $109,074

Number of Grants: 20

Highest Grant: $47,216

Typical Range: $1,000 to $10,943

Disclosure Period: 1993

Note: Recent grants are derived from a 1993 Form 990.

RECENT GRANTS

Library
| 15,000 | Seymour Library, Seymour, NY |
| 2,000 | Weedsport Free Library, Weedsport, NY |

General
47,216	United Way of Cayuga County, Auburn, NY
10,943	Westminster Presbyterian Church, Westminster, NY
5,472	First Presbyterian Church of Springport, Springport, NY
5,472	YMCA-WEIU, Auburn, NY
5,471	United Way of Cayuga County, Auburn, NY

Feil Foundation, Louis and Gertrude

CONTACT
Louis Feil
Secretary-Treasurer
Louis and Gertrude Feil Fdn.
370 Seventh Ave., Ste. 618
New York, NY 10001
(212) 563-6557

FINANCIAL SUMMARY
Recent Giving: $315,880 (fiscal 1993); $385,969 (fiscal 1992); $259,055 (fiscal 1991)

Assets: $4,835,940 (fiscal 1993); $4,942,000 (fiscal 1992); $4,919,055 (fiscal 1991)

EIN: 13-2958414

CONTRIBUTIONS SUMMARY
Donor(s): Louis Feil

Typical Recipients: • *Arts & Humanities:* Arts Centers, Libraries • *Civic & Public Affairs:* Civil Rights, General, Housing, Philanthropic Organizations • *Education:* Colleges & Universities, Education Funds, Legal Education, Medical Education, Private Education (Precollege), Religious Education, Student Aid • *Health:*

Clinics/Medical Centers, Geriatric Health, Home-Care Services, Hospitals, Hospitals (University Affiliated), Medical Research, Single-Disease Health Associations, Speech & Hearing • *International:* International Organizations, Missionary/Religious Activities • *Religion:* Jewish Causes, Religious Organizations, Religious Welfare, Social/Policy Issues • *Social Services:* Community Centers, Crime Prevention, People with Disabilities, Scouts

Grant Types: general support

Geographic Distribution: focus on New York, NY

GIVING OFFICERS
Gertrude Feil: pres, dir

Jeffrey Feil: vp, dir

Louis Feil: secy, treas, dir

APPLICATION INFORMATION
Initial Approach: Send brief letter of inquiry describing program or project. There are no deadlines.

GRANTS ANALYSIS
Total Grants: $315,880

Number of Grants: 65

Highest Grant: $50,000

Typical Range: $50 to $5,000

Disclosure Period: fiscal year ending June 30, 1993

Note: Recent grants are derived from a fiscal 1993 Form 990.

RECENT GRANTS

Library
| 500 | New York Public Library, New York, NY |
| 500 | New York Public Library, New York, NY |

General
50,000	Albert Einstein College of Medicine of Yeshiva University, New York, NY
50,000	Gurwin Jewish Geriatric Center, Commack, NY
35,000	New York Hospital Cornell Medical Center, New York, NY
30,000	United Jewish Appeal, New York, NY
25,000	Feil Scholarship Cornell, Ithaca, NY

Fife Foundation, Elias and Bertha

CONTACT
Bernard Fife
President
Elias and Bertha Fife Fdn.
37-18 Northern Blvd.
Long Island City, NY 11101
(718) 392-0200

FINANCIAL SUMMARY

Recent Giving: $87,850 (fiscal 1994); $177,205 (fiscal 1993); $195,400 (fiscal 1992)

Assets: $3,654,489 (fiscal 1994); $3,771,394 (fiscal 1993); $2,734,123 (fiscal 1992)

Gifts Received: $40,000 (fiscal 1994); $80,000 (fiscal 1993); $60,000 (fiscal 1992)

EIN: 11-6035634

CONTRIBUTIONS SUMMARY

Donor(s): members of the Fife family, Standard Motor Products

Typical Recipients: • *Arts & Humanities:* History & Archaeology, Libraries, Museums/Galleries, Public Broadcasting • *Civic & Public Affairs:* Community Foundations, Employment/Job Training, General, Public Policy, Urban & Community Affairs • *Education:* Colleges & Universities, Faculty Development, Private Education (Precollege), School Volunteerism • *Health:* Cancer, Children's Health/Hospitals, Emergency/Ambulance Services, Eyes/Blindness, Health Organizations, Hospitals, Hospitals (University Affiliated), Medical Research, Multiple Sclerosis, Prenatal Health Issues, Single-Disease Health Associations • *Religion:* Jewish Causes, Religious Organizations, Synagogues/Temples • *Science:* Science Museums • *Social Services:* Child Welfare, Community Centers, Community Service Organizations, Family Planning, Family Services, People with Disabilities, Recreation & Athletics, Scouts

Grant Types: general support

Geographic Distribution: focus on Northeast

GIVING OFFICERS

Arlene R. Fife: dir

Bernard Fife: pres, dir *B* 1915 *ED* NY Univ BS *CURR EMPL* co-chmn, co-ceo, dir: Standard Motor Products

Nathaniel L. Sills: secy, treas, dir *CURR EMPL* co-chmn, co-ceo, dir: Standard Motor Products

Ruth Sills: dir

APPLICATION INFORMATION

Initial Approach: Send brief letter of inquiry describing program or project. Include a description of organization, amount requested, purpose of funds sought, recently audited financial statement, and proof of tax-exempt status. There are no deadlines.

GRANTS ANALYSIS

Total Grants: $87,850

Number of Grants: 112

Highest Grant: $20,000

Typical Range: $100 to $15,000

Disclosure Period: fiscal year ending April 30, 1994

Note: Recent grants are derived from a fiscal 1994 Form 990.

RECENT GRANTS

Library

2,500	Brookline Public Library, Brookline, MA
300	New York Public Library, New York, NY

General

20,000	United Jewish Appeal Federation, New York, NY
15,000	United Jewish Appeal Federation, New York, NY
15,000	United Jewish Appeal Federation, New York, NY
3,000	North Shore University Hospital, Manhasset, NY
2,000	New York Urban Coalition, New York, NY

Fink Foundation

CONTACT

Romie Shapiro
President
Fink Fdn.
654 Madison Ave.
New York, NY 10021
(212) 935-1900

FINANCIAL SUMMARY

Recent Giving: $173,000 (1993); $165,500 (1992); $137,350 (1991)

Assets: $2,276,582 (1993); $2,285,034 (1992); $2,316,547 (1991)

EIN: 13-6135438

CONTRIBUTIONS SUMMARY

Donor(s): David Fink, Nathan Fink

Typical Recipients: • *Arts & Humanities:* Libraries, Museums/Galleries, Music • *Civic & Public Affairs:* Women's Affairs • *Education:* Colleges & Universities, Community & Junior Colleges, Faculty Development, Legal Education, Minority Education, Private Education (Precollege), Public Education (Precollege) • *Health:* Health Organizations, Hospices, Hospitals, Long-Term Care • *International:* Foreign Arts Organizations, Foreign Educational Institutions, Health Care/Hospitals, Missionary/Religious Activities • *Religion:* Jewish Causes, Religious Organizations, Synagogues/Temples • *Social Services:* Camps, Community Service Organizations, Family Services, Homes, People with Disabilities, Senior Services

Grant Types: general support

Geographic Distribution: focus on New York, NY

GIVING OFFICERS

David M. Levitan: vp *B* Tver Lithuania 1915 *ED* Northwestern Univ BS 1936; Northwestern Univ MA 1937; Univ Chicago PhD 1940; Columbia Univ JD 1948 *CURR EMPL* coun: Hahn & Hessen *NONPR AFFIL* fellow: Am Coll Trust & Estate Couns; mem: Am Bar Assn, Am Law Inst, Am Political Science Assn, Am Soc Intl Law, New York City Bar Assn, NY Bar Assn

Romie Shapiro: pres

APPLICATION INFORMATION

Initial Approach: Include a description of organization, amount requested, purpose of funds sought, recently audited financial statement, and proof of tax-exempt status. There are no deadlines.

GRANTS ANALYSIS

Total Grants: $173,000

Number of Grants: 54

Highest Grant: $20,000

Typical Range: $500 to $5,000

Disclosure Period: 1993

Note: Recent grants are derived from a 1993 Form 990.

RECENT GRANTS

General

20,000	American Committee for Sharre Zedek Hospital, New York, NY
10,000	Benjamin N. Cardozo School of Law of Yeshiva University, New York, NY
10,000	Friends of Bezalel Academy, New York, NY
10,000	Hadassah Hospice, New York, NY
7,500	Jewish Theological Seminary, New York, NY

Fischbach Foundation

CONTACT

Jerome Fischbach
President
Fischbach Fdn.
Timber Trail
Rye, NY 10580

FINANCIAL SUMMARY

Recent Giving: $101,500 (1993); $95,555 (1992); $133,425 (1991)

Assets: $2,905,010 (1993); $2,604,125 (1992); $2,612,231 (1991)

Gifts Received: $2,000 (1993); $2,000 (1992); $1,500 (1991)

EIN: 23-7416874

CONTRIBUTIONS SUMMARY

Donor(s): members of the Fischbach family

Typical Recipients: • *Arts & Humanities:* Dance, Libraries, Museums/Galleries, Music, Opera, Public Broadcasting • *Civic & Public Affairs:* Urban & Community Affairs, Women's Affairs • *Education:* Arts/Humanities Education, Colleges & Universities, Engineering/Technological Education, General, Minority Education, Private Education (Precollege), Religious Education, Science/Mathematics Education • *Environment:* Air/Water Quality • *Health:* Cancer, Clinics/Medical Centers, Diabetes, Emergency/Ambulance Services, Eyes/Blindness, Hospitals, Medical Rehabilitation, Medical Research, Single-Disease Health Associations • *International:* Foreign Arts Organizations, Health Care/Hospitals, Missionary/Religious Activities • *Religion:* Jewish Causes, Religious Organizations, Religious Welfare • *Social Services:* Child Welfare, Community Centers, Community Service Organizations, Food/Clothing Distribution, United Funds/United Ways, Youth Organizations

Grant Types: general support

Geographic Distribution: focus on NY; some giving in Israel

GIVING OFFICERS
Jerome Fischbach: pres

Beatrice Levinson: secy

APPLICATION INFORMATION
Initial Approach: Send brief letter describing program. There are no deadlines.

GRANTS ANALYSIS
Total Grants: $101,500

Typical Range: $200 to $10,000

Disclosure Period: 1993

Note: Recent grants are derived from a 1992 Form 990. Grants list for 1993 was incomplete.

RECENT GRANTS

General

10,000	Juvenile Diabetes Foundation, New York, NY
10,000	Rensselaer Polytechnic Institute, Rochester, NY
10,000	United Hospital Medical Center, Portchester, NY
10,000	United Jewish Appeal Federation, New York, NY
5,000	American Society for Technion, New York, NY

Forbes Inc. / Forbes Foundation

Sales: $150.0 million
Employees: 500
Headquarters: New York, NY
SIC Major Group: Book Publishing

CONTACT
Leonard H. Yablon
President
Forbes Foundation
60 5th Ave.
New York, NY 10011
(212) 620-2248

FINANCIAL SUMMARY
Recent Giving: $2,115,214 (1993); $2,086,305 (1992); $1,674,005 (1991)

Assets: $15,671 (1993); $55,952 (1992); $267,987 (1991)

Gifts Received: $2,070,720 (1993)

Fiscal Note: All contributions are made through the foundation. In 1993, contributions were received from Forbes, Inc.

EIN: 23-7037319

CONTRIBUTIONS SUMMARY
Typical Recipients: • *Arts & Humanities:* Arts Associations & Councils, Arts Centers, Arts Funds, Dance, Ethnic & Folk Arts, Historic Preservation, History & Archaeology,

Libraries, Literary Arts, Museums/Galleries, Music, Opera, Public Broadcasting, Theater • *Civic & Public Affairs:* Civil Rights, Economic Development, Economic Policy, Housing, Legal Aid, Nonprofit Management, Professional & Trade Associations, Public Policy, Safety, Urban & Community Affairs, Zoos/Aquariums • *Education:* Colleges & Universities, Education Associations, Education Reform, Medical Education, Minority Education, Private Education (Precollege), Public Education (Precollege), Science/Mathematics Education, Student Aid • *Environment:* General, Wildlife Protection • *Health:* AIDS/HIV, Cancer, Clinics/Medical Centers, Emergency/Ambulance Services, Health Organizations, Hospices, Hospitals, Medical Research, Mental Health, Nursing Services, Single-Disease Health Associations • *International:* Foreign Educational Institutions, International Affairs, International Peace & Security Issues, International Relations, International Relief Efforts • *Religion:* Churches, Jewish Causes, Religious Organizations, Religious Welfare • *Social Services:* Child Welfare, Community Centers, Community Service Organizations, Family Planning, Family Services, Homes, Recreation & Athletics, Senior Services, Substance Abuse, United Funds/United Ways, Volunteer Services, Youth Organizations

Grant Types: capital, endowment, and general support

Geographic Distribution: giving is primarily in the New York, NY, area

Operating Locations: CT (Hartford), NY (New York)

CORP. OFFICERS
James J. Dunn: *B* New York NY 1920 *ED* Manhattan Coll BBA 1941 *CURR EMPL* vchmn, dir: Forbes Inc *CLUB AFFIL* Blind Brook, Everglades, Jupiter Hills, Laurel Valley, Winged Foot GC

Christopher Forbes: *B* Morristown NJ 1950 *ED* Princeton Univ BA 1972 *CURR EMPL* vchmn, corp secy, dir: Forbes Inc *NONPR AFFIL* bd advs: Princeton Univ Art Mus; chmn: Am Friends English Heritage; dir: British Inst US, Friends NJ St Mus, Historic Hudson Valley, Newark Mus, NY Historical Soc, Victorian Soc Am; mem: Cultural & Historical Commun; mem adv comm: Mus Fine Arts; mem counc: Am Mus Britain, Heritage London Trust Appeal; mem pres counc: Mus City New York; natl trust: Baltimore Mus Art; vchmn bus comm: Metro Mus Art *CLUB AFFIL* Brook, Century CC, Essex Fox Hounds, Grolier, Knickerbocker, Natl Arts, Salmagundi, Turf

Malcolm Stevenson Forbes, Jr.: *B* Morristown NJ 1947 *ED* Princeton Univ BA 1970; Heidelberg Coll LittD *CURR EMPL* pres: Forbes Inc *CORP AFFIL* chmn: Forbes Newspapers; dir: Am Heritage, Fiji Forbes, Forbes Investors Adv Inst, Forbes Trinchera, Princeton Univ Investment Co, Sangre de Cristo Ranches; ed in chief: Forbes Magazine *NONPR AFFIL* mem adv counc: Princeton Univ Econ Dept; mem bd overseers: Meml Sloan-Kettering Cancer Ctr; trust: Fdn Student Commun, Ronald

Reagan Pres Fdn; trust, pres bd trusts: Brooks Sch

GIVING OFFICERS
Christopher Forbes: vp *CURR EMPL* vchmn, corp secy, dir: Forbes Inc (see above)

Malcolm Stevenson Forbes, Jr.: pres *CURR EMPL* pres: Forbes Inc (see above)

Leonard Harold Yablon: secy-treas *B* New York NY 1929 *ED* Long Island Univ BS 1950; CUNY MBA 1969 *CURR EMPL* exec vp, dir: Forbes Inc *CORP AFFIL* pres: Forbes Trinchera; pres, dir: Fiji Forbes, Forbes Europe, Sangre de Cristo Ranches; vp, dir: Forbes Investors Adv Inst, Forbes Investors Adv Inst

APPLICATION INFORMATION
Initial Approach: *Initial Contact:* brief letter or proposal *Include Information On:* description of the organization, amount requested, purpose for which funds are sought, recently audited financial statement, and proof of tax-exempt status *Deadlines:* January

GRANTS ANALYSIS
Total Grants: $2,115,214

Number of Grants: 556

Highest Grant: $500,000

Average Grant: $3,804

Typical Range: $100 to $5,000

Disclosure Period: 1993

Note: Recent grants are derived from a 1993 Form 990.

RECENT GRANTS

Library

10,000	Ronald Reagan Presidential Foundation, Simi Valley, CA
5,000	John F. Kennedy Library Foundation, Boston, MA

General

500,000	Brown University, Providence, RI
100,000	Memorial Sloan-Kettering Cancer Center, New York, NY
75,000	Brooks School, North Andover, MA
50,000	Far Hills Country Day School, Far Hills, NJ
50,000	Margaret Thatcher Foundation, Washington, DC

Ford Foundation

CONTACT
Barron M. Tenny
Vice President, Secretary, and General Counsel
Ford Foundation
320 E 43rd St.
New York, NY 10017
(212) 573-5000

FINANCIAL SUMMARY

Recent Giving: $262,938,000 (fiscal 1994); $285,780,000 (fiscal 1993); $261,998,000 (fiscal 1992)

Assets: $6,600,562,000 (fiscal 1994); $6,938,849,000 (fiscal 1993); $6,470,503,000 (fiscal 1992)

Gifts Received: $65,703 (fiscal 1989)

EIN: 13-1684331

CONTRIBUTIONS SUMMARY

Donor(s): The Ford Foundation was established in 1936 by Henry Ford , who founded Ford Motor Company in 1903, and his son, Edsel Ford. The late Henry Ford II (d. 1987), chairman of Ford Motor Company and a son of Edsel Ford, served on the foundation's board from 1943 until 1976. Under his tenure, the foundation evolved from a Michigan charity into a worldwide institutional philanthropy. Today, the foundation no longer has ties to the Ford family or company.

Typical Recipients: • *Arts & Humanities:* Arts Associations & Councils, Arts Centers, Dance, Ethnic & Folk Arts, Film & Video, Historic Preservation, Libraries, Music, Performing Arts, Public Broadcasting, Theater • *Civic & Public Affairs:* African American Affairs, Business/Free Enterprise, Civil Rights, Community Foundations, Economic Development, Economic Policy, Employment/Job Training, First Amendment Issues, Hispanic Affairs, Housing, Law & Justice, Municipalities/Towns, Native American Affairs, Nonprofit Management, Philanthropic Organizations, Public Policy, Rural Affairs, Urban & Community Affairs, Women's Affairs • *Education:* Agricultural Education, Arts/Humanities Education, Colleges & Universities, Community & Junior Colleges, Continuing Education, Economic Education, Education Associations, Education Funds, Education Reform, Faculty Development, General, International Studies, Literacy, Minority Education, Public Education (Precollege), Science/Mathematics Education, Social Sciences Education • *Environment:* Air/Water Quality, General, Resource Conservation • *Health:* AIDS/HIV, Health Organizations, Medical Research, Nutrition, Public Health • *International:* Foreign Arts Organizations, Foreign Educational Institutions, Health Care/Hospitals, Human Rights, International Affairs, International Development, International Environmental Issues, International Organizations, International Peace & Security Issues, International Relations, International Relief Efforts, Trade • *Religion:* Religious Organizations, Religious Welfare • *Science:* Scientific Centers & Institutes, Scientific Organizations • *Social Services:* At-Risk Youth, Child Welfare, Community Service Organizations, Delinquency & Criminal Rehabilitation, Family Planning, Family Services, Refugee Assistance, Substance Abuse, United Funds/United Ways, Youth Organizations

Grant Types: conference/seminar, endowment, fellowship, general support, loan, professorship, project, research, and seed money

Geographic Distribution: nationally and internationally

GIVING OFFICERS

Susan Vail Berresford: pres *B* New York NY 1943 *ED* Vassar Coll 1961-1963; Radcliffe Coll BA 1965 *CORP AFFIL* dir: Chase Manhattan Corp *NONPR AFFIL* adv comm: Ctr Global Partnership; trust: Hermine & Robert Popper Fdn

Robert Coles: consult *B* Boston MA 1929 *ED* Harvard Univ AB 1950; Columbia Univ MD 1954 *CURR EMPL* research psychiatrist: Harvard Univ Health Svcs *CORP AFFIL* bd editors: Parents Choice; contributing editor: Am Poetry Rev, Aperture, Lit & Medicine, New Oxford Review, New Republic; editor: Children & Youth Services Revision; mem editorial bd: Child Psychiatry Human Devel, Grants Magazine, Integrated Ed, Intl Journal Family Therapy, Jouranl Ed, Journal Am Culture, Learning Magazine, Review Books & Religion *NONPR AFFIL* adv: Ctr Southern Folklore; bd editors: Parents Choice; consult: Appalachian Volumes, Univ MS Ctr Study Southern Culture; consult supt dept psychiatry: Cambridge Hosp MA; dir: Am Freedom Hunger Fdn, Am Parents Comm, Duke Univ Documentary Studies, Reading Is Fundamental, Smithsonian Inst; fellow: Am Academy Arts & Sciences, Davenport Coll, Inst Soc Ethics & Life Sciences, Yale Univ; lecturer, prof: Harvard Univ; mem: Academy Psychoanalysis, Am Orthopsychiatric Assn, Am Psychiatric Assn, Natl Adv Comm Farm Labor, Natl Org Migrant Children; mem adv comm: Natl Indian Ed Assn; mem adv counc: Ams Childrens Relief, Martin Luther King Jr Ctr Nonviolent Social Change; mem natl adv bd: Foxfire Fund; mem natl adv comm: AL Citizens Responsive Pub TV; mem natl adv counc: Rural Am; mem natl comm: Ed Young Children; trust: Austen Riggs Fdn, Robert F Kennedy Action Corps, Robert F Kennedy Meml Fdn, MS Inst Early Childhood Ed, Twentieth Century Fund; visiting prpub policy: Duke Univ *PHIL AFFIL* trust: Lyndhurst Foundation; consult: Edna McConnell Clark Foundation, Rockefeller Foundation

Nancy P. Feller: assoc gen counc, dir legal svcs

Frances Daly Fergusson: trust *B* Boston MA 1944 *ED* Wellesley Coll BA 1965; Harvard Univ MA 1966; Harvard Univ PhD 1973 *CORP AFFIL* dir: Marine Midland Bank *NONPR AFFIL* pres: Vassar Coll; trust: Historic Hudson Valley, Mayo Fdn

Kathryn Scott Fuller: trust *B* New York NY 1946 *ED* Brown Univ BA 1968; Univ TX JD 1976 *NONPR AFFIL* mem: DC Bar Assn, Zonta Intl; pres, ceo: World Wildlife Fund

Barry D. Gaberman: dep vp

Nicholas M. Gabriel: treas, comptr, dir fin svcs

Diane L. Galloway-May: asst secy

Robert D. Haas: trust *B* San Francisco CA 1942 *ED* Univ CA Berkeley BA 1964; Harvard Univ MBA 1968 *CURR EMPL* chmn, ceo, dir: Levi Strauss Assocs Inc *CORP AFFIL* chmn, ceo: Levi Strauss & Co *PHIL AFFIL* pres, dir: Levi Strauss Foundation;

trust, don son: Evelyn and Walter Haas, Jr. Fund

Christopher Anthony Hogg: trust *B* London England 1936 *ED* Trinity Coll Oxford 1960; Harvard Univ 1962 *CURR EMPL* chmn: Courtaulds PLC *CORP AFFIL* chmn: Courtaulds Textiles PLC, Reuters Holdings PLC; dir: Bank England

Vernon Eulion Jordan, Jr.: trust *B* Atlanta GA 1935 *ED* DePauw Univ BA 1957; Howard Univ JD 1960 *CURR EMPL* sr ptnr: Akin Gump Strauss Hauer & Feld *CORP AFFIL* dir: Am Express Co, Bankers Trust Co, Bankers Trust NY Corp, Corning Glass Works, Dow Jones & Co, JCPenney, RJR Nabisco Inc, Revlon Group, Ryder Sys, Sara Lee Corp, Union Carbide Corp, Xerox Corp *PHIL AFFIL* dir: Taconic Foundation

David Todd Kearns: trust *B* Rochester NY 1930 *ED* Univ Rochester BS 1952 *CORP AFFIL* dir: Chase Manhattan Bank, Chase Manhattan Corp, Crum & Forster, Dayton Hudson Corp, Fuji Xerox Co, Rank Xerox Ltd, Ryder Sys, Time-Warner, Westmark Sys *NONPR AFFIL* bd visitors: Duke Univ Fuqua Sch Bus; chmn: United Way Tri St; dir: Univ Rochester; mem: Am Philosophical Assn, Bus Roundtable, Counc Foreign Rels, Pres Ed Policy Adv Comm; trust: Natl Urban League

Wilma Pearl Mankiller: trust *B* Stilwell OK 1945 *ED* San Bruno Coll 1973; San Francisco St Coll 1973-1975; Flaming Rainbow Coll BA 1977; Univ AR 1979 *NONPR AFFIL* dir: OK Academy St Goals, OK Indus Devel Commn; mem: Cherokee Country Dem Womens Club, Natl Cong Am Indians, Natl Tribal Chmns Assn; mem exec bd: Counc Energy Resource Tribes; pres: Inter-Tribal Counc

Luis Guerrero Nogales: trust *B* Madera CA 1943 *ED* San Diego St Univ BA 1966; Stanford Univ JD 1969 *CURR EMPL* pres: Nogales Ptnrs *CORP AFFIL* dir: Bank CA San Francisco *NONPR AFFIL* dir: Stanford Univ Ctr Pub Svc

Olusegun Obasanjo: trust

Dorothy Sattes Ridings: trust *B* Charleston WV 1939 *ED* Randolph-Macon Womens Coll 1957-1959; Northwestern Univ BSJ 1961; Univ NC MA 1968 *CURR EMPL* pres, publ: Bradenton Herald *NONPR AFFIL* trust: Louisville Presbyterian Theological Seminary, Manatee Commun Coll *PHIL AFFIL* dir: Benton Foundation

Henry Brewer Schacht: chmn bd *B* Erie PA 1934 *ED* Yale Univ BS 1956; Harvard Univ MBA 1962 *CURR EMPL* chmn, ceo: Cummins Engine Co Inc *CORP AFFIL* dir: Aluminum Co Am, AT&T, CBS Inc, Chase Manhattan Bank NA Inc, Chase Manhattan Corp *NONPR AFFIL* dir: Bus Enterprise Trust, Bus Roundtable; mem: Bus Counc, Counc Foreign Rels, Harvard Univ Grad Sch Bus Admin Assocs, Mgmt Execs Soc, Tau Beta Pi; sr mem: Conf Bd; trust: Brookings Inst, Comm Econ Devel, Yale Corp *PHIL AFFIL* vchmn, dir: Cummins Engine Foundation

Linda B. Strumpf: vp, chief investment off

Monkombu S. Swaminathan: trust

Ratan Naval Tata: trust *B* Bombay India *ED* Cornell Univ; Harvard Univ Grad Sch Bus Admin *CURR EMPL* chmn: Tata Group *NONPR AFFIL* mem: Asia Soc, E-W Ctr, Intl Counc Prince Wales Bus Leaders Forum; trust: JRD Tata Trust, Natl Fdn India

Barron M. Tenny: vp, secy, gen couns

APPLICATION INFORMATION
Initial Approach:

Domestic applications and inquiries should be sent to the foundation's vice president and secretary. International applicants should direct their proposals to the resident representatives, who are listed in the foundation's annual report.

The foundation does not use application forms. Applications should include objectives and methodology, qualifications of personnel and institutions involved, institution's affirmative action policy and record, and an estimated budget.

There are no deadlines for submitting requests.

A professional staff evaluates grant applications and recommends proposals for approval.

Restrictions on Giving: The foundation limits its grants to efforts likely to have wide effect. It does not make grants for purely personal or local needs, routine operating costs of institutions, programs for which government support is readily available, or for religious activities.

PUBLICATIONS
Annual report, Current Interests of the Ford Foundation, Ford Foundation Report, and numerous reports

GRANTS ANALYSIS
Total Grants: $262,938,000

Number of Grants: 1,524*

Highest Grant: $5,000,000

Average Grant: $172,000*

Typical Range: $43,500 to $244,000

Disclosure Period: fiscal year ending September 30, 1993

Note: Number of grants and average grant figures are approximate and exclude program-related investments totaling $15,644,750. Recent grants are derived from a fiscal 1994 partial grants list.

RECENT GRANTS

Library

450,000	Foundation Center, New York, NY — three-year supplement, for general support
300,000	American Association for the Advancement of Science, Washington, DC — over three years, to test CD-ROM technology for accessing bibliographic data bases in three African university libraries

General

7,000,000	Urban Institute, Washington, DC — over five years, to

	help meet the institute's endowment goal of $25 million
2,000,000	Structured Employment Economic Development Corporation (SEEDCO), New York, NY — three-year supplement, to expand community revitalization projects at historically black colleges and universities
1,800,000	Center on Addiction and Substance Abuse, New York, NY — supplement over 22 months, for a research program that tests comprehensive, community-based services aimed at preventing drug use among at-risk youth
1,800,000	Joint Center for Political Economic Studies, Washington, DC — two-year supplement, for research, analysis, and dissemination activities on public policies affecting African Americans, national economic policy, and the military
1,650,000	Aspen Institute, Queenstown, MD — three-year supplement, for the institute's Nonprofit Sector Research Fund, which promotes the study of philanthropy and the nonprofit sector

---

Freeman Charitable Trust, Samuel

CONTACT
Anne Smith-Ganey
Assistant Vice President
Samuel Freeman Charitable Trust
c/o U.S. Trust Company of New York
114 W 47th St.
New York, NY 10036-1532
(212) 852-3683

FINANCIAL SUMMARY
Recent Giving: $1,003,230 (1993); $1,273,743 (1992); $1,408,678 (1991)

Assets: $27,557,611 (1992); $28,773,603 (1991); $24,190,847 (1990)

EIN: 13-6803465

CONTRIBUTIONS SUMMARY
Donor(s): The trust was established in 1981 by the late Samuel Freeman .

Typical Recipients: • *Arts & Humanities:* Arts Associations & Councils, Ballet, Dance, Libraries, Museums/Galleries, Music, Opera, Performing Arts, Public Broadcasting, Theater • *Civic & Public Affairs:* Business/Free Enterprise, Municipalities/Towns, Philanthropic Organizations, Public Policy, Safety, Urban & Community Affairs • *Education:* Arts/Humanities Education, Colleges & Universities, Education As-

sociations, International Exchange, Legal Education, Minority Education, Private Education (Precollege), Public Education (Precollege) • *Environment:* Resource Conservation • *Health:* AIDS/HIV, Cancer, Clinics/Medical Centers, Eyes/Blindness, Single-Disease Health Associations • *International:* International Relations • *Religion:* Churches, Jewish Causes • *Social Services:* Community Service Organizations, Family Planning, People with Disabilities, Shelters/Homelessness, Youth Organizations

Grant Types: general support, matching, and operating expenses

Geographic Distribution: mid-Atlantic United States

GIVING OFFICERS
William E. Murray: trust *B* 1926 *CURR EMPL* chmn bd-ceo, dir: East Bay Company Ltd

Anne L. Smith-Ganey: asst vp *CURR EMPL* asst vp: US Trust Co NY *PHIL AFFIL* asst vp, contact: Seth Sprague Educational and Charitable Foundation; dir: Marie and John Zimmermann Fund; contact: Oliver S. and Jennie R. Donaldson Charitable Trust

APPLICATION INFORMATION
Initial Approach:

The trust requests a two-page proposal.

The proposal should include a budget, the most recent audit report, and an IRS determination letter.

The trust has no deadline for submitting proposals.

Restrictions on Giving: The trust does not make grants to individuals or private entities.

OTHER THINGS TO KNOW
The trust lists the United States Trust Company of New York as a corporate trustee.

PUBLICATIONS
Program policy statement

GRANTS ANALYSIS
Total Grants: $1,003,230

Number of Grants: 79

Highest Grant: $200,000

Average Grant: $12,699

Typical Range: $1,000 to $25,000

Disclosure Period: 1993

Note: Recent grants are derived from a 1993 grants list.

RECENT GRANTS

Library

2,500	Harry S. Truman Library Institute, Independence, MO

General

200,000	Cold Spring Harbor Laboratory Cancer Research Institute, Cold Spring Harbor, NY
100,000	Marymount Manhattan College, New York, NY
60,000	St. Paul's School, Concord, NH
50,000	Holmes Research, Charleston, SC

50,000   University of South Carolina, Columbia, SC

French Foundation, D.E.

CONTACT
J. Douglas Pedley
President, Director
D.E. French Fdn.
120 Genessee St., Rm. 503
Auburn, NY 13021
(315) 253-9321

FINANCIAL SUMMARY
Recent Giving: $173,800 (1993); $173,700 (1992)

Assets: $3,373,745 (1993); $3,230,210 (1992)

EIN: 16-6052246

CONTRIBUTIONS SUMMARY
Typical Recipients: • *Arts & Humanities:* Arts Centers, Libraries, Museums/Galleries • *Civic & Public Affairs:* Employment/Job Training, General, Housing • *Education:* Community & Junior Colleges, Elementary Education (Public), Medical Education, Private Education (Precollege), Secondary Education (Public), Special Education, Student Aid • *Health:* Hospitals, Long-Term Care, Medical Rehabilitation • *Religion:* Churches, Religious Welfare • *Social Services:* Animal Protection, Camps, Community Centers, People with Disabilities, Recreation & Athletics, Scouts, Senior Services, United Funds/United Ways, YMCA/YWCA/YMHA/YWHA, Youth Organizations

Grant Types: capital and general support

Geographic Distribution: upstate New York

GIVING OFFICERS
Caryl W. Adams: secy

Frederick J. Atkins: dir

James P. Costello: dir

Burke W. Drummond: dir

Walter M. Lowe: dir

J. Douglas Pedley: pres, dir

Ronald D. West: dir *PHIL AFFIL* exec dir, secy, dir: Fred L. Emerson Foundation, Inc.

APPLICATION INFORMATION
Initial Approach: The foundation has no formal grant application procedure or application form. There are no deadlines.

GRANTS ANALYSIS
Total Grants: $173,800

Number of Grants: 80

Highest Grant: $16,000

Typical Range: $100 to $10,000

Disclosure Period: 1993

Note: Recent grants are derived from a 1993 Form 990.

RECENT GRANTS
Library
7,000	Seymour Library Association, Auburn, NY	
7,000	Seymour Library Foundation, Auburn, NY — new handicap wing	
6,000	Weedsport Free Library, Weedsport, NY	
6,000	Weedsport Free Library, Weedsport, NY — building fund	

General
16,000	Mercy Health and Rehabilitation Center, Auburn, NY
15,000	Town of Owasco, Owasco, NY — playground
13,000	Auburn Memorial Hospital, Auburn, NY
10,000	Faatz-Crofut Home for the Elderly, Auburn, NY
10,000	Mercy Health and Rehabilitation Center, Auburn, NY

Frese Foundation, Arnold D.

CONTACT
James S. Smith
President and Treasurer
Arnold D. Frese Fdn.
30 Rockefeller Plaza, Ste. 1938
New York, NY 10112
(212) 757-6626

FINANCIAL SUMMARY
Recent Giving: $1,480,992 (1993); $1,415,000 (1992); $1,522,500 (1991)

Assets: $11,193,039 (1993); $11,159,132 (1992); $10,728,175 (1991)

EIN: 13-6212507

CONTRIBUTIONS SUMMARY
Donor(s): the late Arnold D. Frese

Typical Recipients: • *Arts & Humanities:* Arts Associations & Councils, General, Libraries, Museums/Galleries, Music, Performing Arts • *Civic & Public Affairs:* General, Women's Affairs • *Education:* Colleges & Universities, Legal Education, Private Education (Precollege), Public Education (Precollege) • *Environment:* Air/Water Quality, General • *Health:* Cancer, Clinics/Medical Centers, Hospitals, Prenatal Health Issues • *International:* Human Rights, International Peace & Security Issues • *Religion:* Churches, Religious Welfare • *Social Services:* Community Centers, Family Services, Food/Clothing Distribution, People with Disabilities, Recreation & Athletics, United Funds/United Ways, Youth Organizations

Grant Types: general support

Geographic Distribution: focus on New York, NY, and Greenwich, CT

GIVING OFFICERS
Hector G. Dowd: secy

Ines Frese: chmn, trust

Henry D. Mercer, Jr.: trust

Emil Mosbacher, Jr.: trust *B* White Plains NY 1922 *ED* Dartmouth Coll BA 1943 *CORP AFFIL* dir: Amax Gold, Avon Products, Chemical Bank, Chubb Corp, Fed Ins Co, Vigilant Ins Co *NONPR AFFIL* mem: Independent Petroleum Assn Am, Pilgrims US, US Seniors Golf Assn, US Yacht Racing Assn; mem bd overseers: Hoover Inst; trust: Lenox Hill Hosp *PHIL AFFIL* pres, dir: Emil Mosbacher, Jr. Foundation

James S. Smith: pres, treas

APPLICATION INFORMATION
Initial Approach: Send a brief letter of inquiry. Include a description of organization, amount requested, purpose of funds sought, recently audited financial statement, and proof of tax-exempt status. There are no deadlines.

GRANTS ANALYSIS
Total Grants: $1,480,992

Number of Grants: 44

Highest Grant: $550,000

Typical Range: $1,000 to $200,000

Disclosure Period: 1993

Note: Recent grants are derived from a 1993 Form 990.

RECENT GRANTS
General
550,000	Harvard College, Cambridge, MA
110,000	Memorial Sloan-Kettering Cancer Center, New York, NY
79,982	Presbyterian Hospital, New York, NY
51,000	Greenwich Hospital Association, Greenwich, CT
50,000	Greenwich Academy, Greenwich, CT

Fribourg Foundation

CONTACT
Dwight C. Coffin
Secretary
Fribourg Fdn.
277 Pk. Ave., 50th Fl.
New York, NY 10172
(212) 207-5571

FINANCIAL SUMMARY
Recent Giving: $384,100 (1993); $505,900 (1992); $274,730 (1990)

Assets: $1,754,673 (1993); $2,019,616 (1992); $2,223,804 (1990)

Gifts Received: $250,000 (1990)

Fiscal Note: In 1990, contributions were received from Continental Grain Company.

EIN: 13-6159195

CONTRIBUTIONS SUMMARY
Donor(s): Michel Fribourg, Lucienne Fribourg Arrow Steamship Co., Continental Grain Co.

Typical Recipients: • *Arts & Humanities:* Arts Associations & Councils, Arts Centers, Arts Festivals, Arts Outreach, Community Arts, General, Historic Preservation, History & Archaeology, Libraries, Museums/Galleries, Music, Opera, Performing Arts, Theater • *Civic & Public Affairs:* Botanical Gardens/Parks, Ethnic Organizations, General, Housing • *Education:* Arts/Humanities Education, Colleges & Universities, International Studies, Medical Education, Private Education (Precollege) • *Environment:* Resource Conservation • *Health:* Cancer, Children's Health/Hospitals, Geriatric Health, Health Organizations, Hospitals, Medical Research, Single-Disease Health Associations, Transplant Networks/Donor Banks • *International:* Foreign Arts Organizations, Foreign Educational Institutions, International Organizations, International Peace & Security Issues, International Relations, International Relief Efforts, Missionary/Religious Activities • *Religion:* Jewish Causes, Religious Organizations, Synagogues/Temples • *Science:* Science Museums • *Social Services:* Child Welfare, Community Service Organizations, Delinquency & Criminal Rehabilitation, Family Services, Recreation & Athletics, Shelters/Homelessness, United Funds/United Ways, Youth Organizations

Grant Types: general support

Geographic Distribution: focus on New York, NY

GIVING OFFICERS
Dwight C. Coffin: secy *PHIL AFFIL* vp, secy, dir: Continental Grain Foundation

Gerald Frenchman: vp *PHIL AFFIL* vp: Continental Grain Foundation

Mary Ann Fribourg: mem, dir

Michel Fribourg: pres, mem, dir *B* 1913 *CURR EMPL* chmn, dir: Continental Grain Co *PHIL AFFIL* pres, dir: Continental Grain Foundation

David G. Friiedman: asst secy

Bernard Steinweg: mem, dir

Lawrence Weppler: vp, dir

Daniel J. Willet: treas *PHIL AFFIL* treas: Continental Grain Foundation

APPLICATION INFORMATION
Initial Approach: Send brief letter describing program. Include a description of organization, amount requested, purpose of funds sought, recently audited financial statement, and proof of tax-exempt status. There are no deadlines.

GRANTS ANALYSIS
Total Grants:

Number of Grants: 135

Highest Grant: $50,000

Typical Range: $100 to $30,000

Disclosure Period: 1994

Note: Recent grants are derived from a 1994 Form 990.

RECENT GRANTS
Library
1,200   New York Public Library, New York, NY

General
50,000	Trinity School, New York, NY
35,000	Cornell University Medical Center Department of Medicine, New York, NY
30,000	American Friends of Tel Aviv University, Silver Spring, MD
30,000	French Institute/Alliance Francaise, New York, NY
30,000	New York University, New York, NY

Fuld Health Trust, Helene

CONTACT
Arlene J. Snyder
Grants Office Administrator
Helene Fuld Health Trust
405 Lexington Ave., 26th Fl.
New York, NY 10174
(212) 973-6859
Note: Applicants may also contact Robert C. Miller, counsel for the trust.

FINANCIAL SUMMARY
Recent Giving: $4,752,530 (fiscal 1993); $6,719,283 (fiscal 1992); $3,734,540 (fiscal 1991)

Assets: $89,152,085 (fiscal 1993); $86,541,253 (fiscal 1992); $85,595,682 (fiscal 1991)

EIN: 13-6309307

CONTRIBUTIONS SUMMARY
Donor(s): The trust is the outgrowth of the former Helene Fuld Health Foundation, established in 1935 by the late Dr. Leonard Felix Fuld (1883-1965) and his sister in memory of their mother. The Helene Fuld Health Trust succeeded the original foundation in 1969.

Typical Recipients: • *Arts & Humanities:* Libraries • *Education:* Colleges & Universities, Community & Junior Colleges, Education Reform, Engineering/Technological Education, Medical Education, Science/Mathematics Education • *Health:* Clinics/Medical Centers, Health Organizations, Hospitals, Nursing Services • *International:* Foreign Educational Institutions, Health Care/Hospitals

Grant Types: capital

Geographic Distribution: national

GIVING OFFICERS
Jayne M. Kurzman: couns *PHIL AFFIL* vp, dir: Hurford Foundation

Robert C. Miller: couns *ED* Bucknell Univ BS 1965; Stanford Univ MS 1966 *CORP AFFIL* dir: MA Tech Park *NONPR AFFIL* dir: Bucknell Sch Eng; mem: Inst Electrical Electronics Engrs

Arlene J. Snyder: grants off admin

APPLICATION INFORMATION
Initial Approach:
The trust provides an official application form, which is updated each year, and available in August. Initial contact should be in the form of a letter requesting an application form.

A proposal should list the amount of money needed, the purpose for which funds will be used, the school's background, proof of tax-exempt status, approval of its nursing program under the laws of the jurisdiction in which it is organized and operates, and nursing licensure examination results for each of the last three years (showing the number of candidates who took each examination, the percentage who passed on their first testing, and the mean score). Additional information may be requested.

Applications must be received by October 31 for consideration. The board meets in March, June, September, and December, but reviews applications only in March.

Applicants are notified by June 1.

Restrictions on Giving: Grants are made only to state-approved nursing schools which are tax-exempt, accredited, and affiliated with one or more accredited hospitals. They must also have graduated at least three classes of nursing students. No grants are made for operating or personnel expenses. Apart from longstanding exceptions, grants are not made for scholarships or financial aid. The trust generally makes grants for projects which can be funded and completed within one year. Requests for construction funds are not favored, as they often require an extended commitment and a larger amount than typical trust grants.

OTHER THINGS TO KNOW
First-time grants generally do not exceed $35,000.

The trust reports that it also sponsors conferences, seminars, workshops, and offers proposal writing assistance.

The Marine Midland Bank is the trust's corporate trustee.

GRANTS ANALYSIS
Total Grants: $4,554,111*

Number of Grants: 163

Highest Grant: $421,875

Average Grant: $27,939

Typical Range: $20,000 to $70,000

Disclosure Period: fiscal year ending September 30, 1993

Note: Total grants figure excludes $198,419 for the Fuld Fellowship Program. Recent grants are derived from a fiscal 1993 Form 990.

RECENT GRANTS
General
421,875	Helene Fuld School for Nursing, Camden, NJ — to purchase classroom furniture and for scholarships
261,842	University of Colorado, Boulder, CO — to implement model curriculum project
100,000	University of Texas San Antonio, San Antonio, TX — to purchase CAI and IAV equipment

86,990	Southeastern Louisiana University, Hammond, LA — to purchase IAV and CAI equipment
79,603	Fairfield University, Fairfield, CT — to purchase CAI and IAV equipment and to renovate ITS lab

---

Gebbie Foundation

CONTACT
John D. Hamilton
President and Director
Gebbie Foundation
308 Hotel Jamestown Office Bldg.
PO Box 1277
Jamestown, NY 14702-1277
(716) 487-1062

FINANCIAL SUMMARY
Recent Giving: $2,800,000 (fiscal 1995 est.); $2,650,492 (fiscal 1994); $6,860,521 (fiscal 1993)

Assets: $54,000,000 (fiscal 1995 est.); $54,569,658 (fiscal 1994); $51,754,659 (fiscal 1993)

EIN: 16-6050287

CONTRIBUTIONS SUMMARY
Donor(s): The foundation was established and initially funded by Miss Marion Gebbie and Mrs. Geraldine Gebbie Bellinger in memory of their parents, the late Frank and Harriet Louise Hubbell Gebbie. Frank Gebbie was one of the developers (with Gail Borden) of condensed milk, and a founder of the Mohawk Condensed Milk Company.

Typical Recipients: • *Arts & Humanities:* Arts Funds, Historic Preservation, History & Archaeology, Libraries, Music, Opera, Performing Arts, Public Broadcasting • *Civic & Public Affairs:* Community Foundations, Economic Development, Housing, Municipalities/Towns, Professional & Trade Associations, Urban & Community Affairs • *Education:* Business-School Partnerships, Colleges & Universities, Community & Junior Colleges, Education Funds, Education Reform, Environmental Education, Literacy, Minority Education, Private Education (Precollege), Public Education (Precollege), Student Aid • *Environment:* Air/Water Quality, General, Resource Conservation, Watershed • *Health:* Children's Health/Hospitals, Heart, Hospices, Hospitals, Medical Research, Nursing Services, Prenatal Health Issues, Research/Studies Institutes • *Religion:* Churches, Religious Welfare • *Science:* Scientific Centers & Institutes • *Social Services:* Child Welfare, Community Service Organizations, Counseling, Domestic Violence, Family Services, Homes, People with Disabilities, Substance Abuse, United Funds/United Ways, YMCA/YWCA/YMHA/YWHA, Youth Organizations

Grant Types: capital, general support, loan, matching, multiyear/continuing support, operating expenses, and project

Geographic Distribution: Jamestown/Chautauqua County, NY

GIVING OFFICERS
Dianne L. Eisenhardt: asst treas, asst secy

Myron B. Franks: vp, dir

Charles T. Hall: treas, dir

John D. Hamilton: pres, dir *B* Pavilion NY *ED* Hamilton Coll AB 1922 *NONPR AFFIL* trust: Chautauqua Inst, Jamestown Commun Coll

Rhoe B. Henderson III: dir

Dr. Lillian V. Ney: dir

Bertram B. Parker: dir

Geraldine M. Parker: dir

William I. Parker: secy, dir

Paul W. Sandberg: dir

APPLICATION INFORMATION
Initial Approach:

The initial means of contact is a letter of inquiry addressed to the president of the foundation.

The letter should contain a brief statement of the need for funds and enough factual information to enable the staff to determine whether or not the application falls within the foundation's areas of preferred interest or warrants consideration as a special project.

If the request falls into the foundation's geographical and interest areas, further information will be solicited including a formal application, IRS tax-determination letter, most recent audited financial statements, and most recent Form 990.

Although proposals may be submitted at any time, they must reach the foundation by January 1, for the March meeting; May 1, for the July meeting; and by September 1, for the November meeting.

A voluntary board of directors operates the foundation.

Restrictions on Giving: The foundation encourages appplicants to obtain funding from more than one source. No grants are made to individuals. Neither are they available to sectarian or religious organizations; however, traditional support is an exception. Special projects may be supported, but funds are not usually available for general support, endowment purposes, or national appeals.

OTHER THINGS TO KNOW
Progress reports on grants made, and annual audits of the grant program or agency, are requested. The foundation also suggests that programs seek funding from other sources.

GRANTS ANALYSIS
Total Grants: $2,650,492

Number of Grants: 73

Highest Grant: $500,000

Average Grant: $36,308

Typical Range: $5,000 to $30,000 and $50,000 to $100,000

Disclosure Period: fiscal year ending September 30, 1994

Note: Recent grants are derived from a 1994 grants list.

RECENT GRANTS
Library
25,000	Patterson Library of Westfield, Westfield, NY — toward new handicap accessible entrance project
21,000	Chautauqua-Cattaraugus Library System, Chautauqua, NY — renewal of Book Plan and Subscriptions to School Library Journal
19,895	James Prendergast Free Library, Jamestown, NY — toward purchase of books and other materials for Children's Department
7,500	Foundation Center of New York, New York, NY — toward annual support over three years

General
500,000	Jamestown Community College, Jamestown, NY — toward capital construction and renovations
300,000	United Way of Southern Chautauqua County, Jamestown, NY — toward the 1993 annual campaign goal
250,000	Jamestown Community College, Jamestown, NY — toward construction and renovations over three years
200,000	Jamestown Community College, Jamestown, NY — matching grant for scholarships over five years
115,000	Jamestown Community College, Jamestown, NY — to continue programs at Jamestown Community Schools over three years

---

Gifford Charitable Corporation, Rosamond

CONTACT
Dean A. Lesilinski
Executive Director
Rosamond Gifford Charitable Corporation
731 James St., Rm. 404
Syracuse, NY 13203
(315) 474-2489

FINANCIAL SUMMARY
Recent Giving: $670,500 (1995 est.); $670,512 (1994 approx.); $732,015 (1993)

Assets: $18,500,000 (1995 est.); $18,172,779 (1994 approx.); $18,358,979 (1993)

EIN: 15-0572881

CONTRIBUTIONS SUMMARY
Donor(s): The corporation was incorporated in 1954 by the late Rosamond Gifford .

Typical Recipients: • *Arts & Humanities:* Libraries, Museums/Galleries, Performing Arts, Public Broadcasting, Theater • *Civic & Public Affairs:* Clubs, Housing, Legal Aid, Municipalities/Towns, Urban & Community Affairs • *Education:* Arts/Humanities Education, Business Education, Colleges & Universities, Literacy, Public Education (Precollege) • *Health:* Alzheimers Disease, Emergency/Ambulance Services, Health Organizations, Heart, Hospices, Hospitals, Kidney, Medical Research, Mental Health, Single-Disease Health Associations • *Religion:* Jewish Causes, Religious Organizations, Religious Welfare, Social/Policy Issues • *Science:* Scientific Centers & Institutes, Scientific Organizations • *Social Services:* Animal Protection, Child Welfare, Community Centers, Community Service Organizations, Family Services, Food/Clothing Distribution, Homes, People with Disabilities, Recreation & Athletics, Senior Services, Sexual Abuse, Shelters/Homelessness, Substance Abuse, United Funds/United Ways, Youth Organizations

Grant Types: capital, project, research, and seed money

Geographic Distribution: limited to organizations serving the residents of Syracuse and Onondaga counties, NY

GIVING OFFICERS
Suzan L. Anderson: asst secy, trust

Nancy H. Calhoun: asst secy, trust

Robert F. Dewey: pres, trust

Dean A. Lesilinski: exec dir

John H. Lynch: secy, trust

Roger L. MacDonald: vp, treas, trust

Donald M. Mills: asst treas, trust

APPLICATION INFORMATION
Initial Approach:

Applicants should write to the corporation to request an application form.

There are no deadlines for submitting proposals.

Restrictions on Giving: The corporation does not make grants to individuals, or for endowment funds, continuing support, deficit financing, land acquisition, matching gifts, scholarships, fellowships, or loans.

PUBLICATIONS
Application guidelines, program policy statement, and multi-year report.

GRANTS ANALYSIS
Total Grants: $732,015

Number of Grants: 22

Highest Grant: $97,500

Average Grant: $33,273

Typical Range: $5,000 to $50,000

Disclosure Period: 1993

Note: Recent grants are derived from a 1993 Form 990.

RECENT GRANTS
Library
16,360	Fayetteville Free Library, Fayetteville, NY

General
97,500	United Way of Central New York, Syracuse, NY — 1993 program
55,000	Rescue Mission Alliance of Syracuse, Syracuse, NY
55,000	Salvation Army, Syracuse Area Services, Syracuse, NY
50,000	Consortium for Children's Services, Syracuse, NY
50,000	Discovery Center of Science and Technology, Syracuse, NY

Gilman Foundation, Howard

CONTACT
Howard Gilman
President
The Howard Gilman Foundation
111 W 50th St.
New York, NY 10020
(212) 246-3300

FINANCIAL SUMMARY

Recent Giving: $2,800,000 (fiscal 1995 est.); $2,801,943 (fiscal 1994); $2,221,126 (fiscal 1993)

Assets: $35,000,000 (fiscal 1995 est.); $35,291,538 (fiscal 1994); $31,300,268 (fiscal 1993)

Gifts Received: $6,500,000 (fiscal 1994); $1,500,000 (fiscal 1993); $6,000,000 (fiscal 1992)

Fiscal Note: In fiscal 1994, contributions were received from Gilman Securities Corporation. In fiscal 1993, gifts were received from Gilman Investment Company.

EIN: 13-3097486

CONTRIBUTIONS SUMMARY

Donor(s): The foundation was incorporated in 1981 by Gilman Investment Co. and Gilman Paper Co.

Typical Recipients: • *Arts & Humanities:* Arts Appreciation, Arts Funds, Ballet, Dance, Ethnic & Folk Arts, Film & Video, Libraries, Museums/Galleries, Music, Opera, Performing Arts, Theater • *Civic & Public Affairs:* Civil Rights, Employment/Job Training, General, Municipalities/Towns, Professional & Trade Associations, Public Policy, Urban & Community Affairs, Women's Affairs • *Education:* Arts/Humanities Education, Colleges & Universities, Literacy • *Environment:* General • *Health:* AIDS/HIV, Clinics/Medical Centers, Health Organizations, Hospitals, Hospitals (University Affiliated), Single-Disease Health Associations • *International:* Foreign Arts

Organizations, Health Care/Hospitals, Human Rights, International Affairs, International Development, International Peace & Security Issues • *Religion:* Religious Organizations, Synagogues/Temples • *Science:* Science Museums • *Social Services:* Community Service Organizations, Crime Prevention, Food/Clothing Distribution, Shelters/Homelessness

Grant Types: general support

Geographic Distribution: some national and international; focus on New York City, NY

GIVING OFFICERS

Bernard D. Bergreen: dir *B* 1923 *ED* NY Univ AB 1943; Columbia Univ LLB 1948 *CURR EMPL* pres, dir: Gilman Investment Co *CORP AFFIL* fdr: Bernard D Bergreen PC *NONPR AFFIL* mem: Am Bar Assn, Assn Bar City New York, NY St Bar Assn

Howard L. Gilman: pres, dir *B* 1925 *CURR EMPL* chmn, dir: Gilman Investment Co *CORP AFFIL* chmn bd, dir: St Marys Railroad Co; chmn, ceo, dir: Gilman Paper Co *PHIL AFFIL* pres: Gilman Paper Co. Foundation

Sylvia P. Gilman: dir *B* 1902

APPLICATION INFORMATION
Initial Approach:

The foundation has no formal grant application procedure or application form.

The foundation has no deadline for submitting proposals.

Restrictions on Giving: The foundation generally awards grants to religious, charitable, scientific, literary, and educational organizations, including the encouragement of the arts and the prevention of cruelty to children and animals.

GRANTS ANALYSIS
Total Grants: $2,801,943

Number of Grants: 123

Highest Grant: $1,050,000

Average Grant: $14,360*

Typical Range: $500 to $15,000

Disclosure Period: fiscal year ending April 30, 1994

Note: Average grant figure excludes the highest grant of $1,050,000. Recent grants are derived from a fiscal 1993 Form 990.

RECENT GRANTS

General
700,000	Cornell University Medical Center, New York, NY
176,083	Center for Democracy, Washington, DC
131,000	New York University Medical center, New York, NY
65,000	Human Rights Watch, New York, NY
61,500	Learning Thru Art, New York, NY

Givenchy Corp.

Employees: 9
Headquarters: New York, NY
SIC Major Group: Wholesale
    Trade—Nondurable Goods

CONTACT
Kevin Curry
Vice President
Givenchy Corp.
21 E 75th St.
New York, NY 10021
(212) 772-0677

FINANCIAL SUMMARY
Fiscal Note: Annual Giving Range: less than $100,000

CONTRIBUTIONS SUMMARY
Givenchy's cash contributions budget is very small. The majority of support is given through donated products, valued at between $2,000 and $2,500. Givenchy-designed and tailored clothing and jewelry are given to charities directly or donated to special fund-raising events.

Typical Recipients: • *Arts & Humanities:* Ballet, Libraries, Museums/Galleries, Opera, Performing Arts • *Civic & Public Affairs:* Gay/Lesbian Issues, Safety • *Education:* Colleges & Universities • *Health:* Adolescent Health Issues, Cancer, Diabetes, General, Single-Disease Health Associations • *International:* Foreign Arts Organizations, Foreign Educational Institutions

Grant Types: general support

Nonmonetary Support Types: donated products

Note: Also Givenchy does fashion shows where the price of seats ($50 to $100) goes to local charity.

Geographic Distribution: no geographic restrictions

Operating Locations: GA, NY (New York)

GIVING OFFICERS
Kevin Curry: *CURR EMPL* vp: Givenchy Corp

APPLICATION INFORMATION
Initial Approach: The company supports preselected organizations and does not accept unsolicited requests for funds.

Restrictions on Giving: Does not support political or lobbying groups.

GRANTS ANALYSIS
Typical Range: $2,500 to $5,000

RECENT GRANTS
Library
Winston Churchill Memorial Library, Fulton, MO
General
AIDS Resource Center, New York, NY
American Heart Association, Atlanta, GA
Arts for the Aging, Washington, DC
Colbert Foundation, New York, NY
New York City Ballet, New York, NY

Glanville Family Foundation

CONTACT
Nancy H. Glanville
President
Glanville Family Fdn.
c/o Lazard Freres and Co.
One Rockefeller Plz.
New York, NY 10020
(212) 632-6507

FINANCIAL SUMMARY
Recent Giving: $19,000 (fiscal 1994); $932,634 (fiscal 1993); $698,133 (fiscal 1992)

Assets: $900,940 (fiscal 1994); $891,722 (fiscal 1993); $1,192,725 (fiscal 1992)

Gifts Received: $500,000 (fiscal 1993); $344,752 (fiscal 1992); $2,175,412 (fiscal 1990)

Fiscal Note: In fiscal 1993, contributions were received from Nancy Hart Glanville ($500,000).

EIN: 13-3284981

CONTRIBUTIONS SUMMARY
Donor(s): James W. Glenville, Nancy H. Glanville

Typical Recipients: • *Arts & Humanities:* Libraries, Museums/Galleries • *Civic & Public Affairs:* Community Foundations, General • *Education:* Colleges & Universities, Engineering/Technological Education, Private Education (Precollege), Religious Education, Science/Mathematics Education • *Environment:* General • *Health:* Cancer, Eyes/Blindness, Hospices, Medical Research • *International:* International Development • *Religion:* Churches, Seminaries • *Science:* Science Museums • *Social Services:* Community Service Organizations, Family Planning, Family Services, Recreation & Athletics, Substance Abuse, United Funds/United Ways, Youth Organizations

Grant Types: general support

Geographic Distribution: giving in CA, CT, DC, and PA

GIVING OFFICERS
Charles D. Glanville: dir

John Glanville: vp, dir

Nancy H. Glanville: pres, dir

Robert E. Glanville: dir *B* Binghamton NY 1950 *ED* State Univ NY BA 1972; Cornell Univ JD 1976 *CURR EMPL* ptnr: Phillips, Lytle, Hitchcock, et al *NONPR AFFIL* mem: Am Bar Assn, Am Gas Assn, Erie County Bar Assn, NY State Bar Assn

Thomas Glanville: vp, dir

Howard V. Sontag: secy, treas *PHIL AFFIL* secy, treas: Steven L. Rattner and P. Maureen White Foundation

APPLICATION INFORMATION
Initial Approach: Send brief letter of inquiry describing program or project. There are no deadlines.

GRANTS ANALYSIS
Total Grants: $19,000

Number of Grants: 10

Highest Grant: $11,000

Typical Range: $500 to $1,500

Disclosure Period: fiscal year ending June 30, 1994

Note: Recent grants are derived from a fiscal 1994 Form 990.

RECENT GRANTS
General

11,000	M.D. Anderson Cancer Center, Houston, TX
1,500	Rice University, Houston, TX
1,000	Hotchkiss School, Lakesville, CT
1,000	Loomis Chaffee School, Windsor, CT
1,000	Rainbow Connection, Rohester, MI

Gleason Foundation

Former Foundation Name: Gleason Memorial Fund

CONTACT
John Kodweis
Vice President of Administration
Gleason Memorial Fund
1000 University Ave.
PO Box 22970
Rochester, NY 14692-2970
(716) 461-8159

FINANCIAL SUMMARY
Recent Giving: $3,400,000 (1994); $3,053,000 (1993); $2,722,120 (1992)

Assets: $70,000,000 (1994); $68,000,000 (1993); $69,510,821 (1992)

Gifts Received: $11,396,774 (1989)

Fiscal Note: In 1989, due to a merger with the Gleason Fund, the Gleason Memorial Fund received the book value of the former fund's assets.

EIN: 16-6023235

CONTRIBUTIONS SUMMARY
Donor(s): Formerly known as the Emmet Blakeney Gleason Memorial Fund, the fund was incorporated in 1959 in New York by the late Miriam Blakeney Gleason in memory of her son. In 1961, it was merged with the J. E. and Eleanor Gleason Trust to form the Gleason Memorial Fund.

Typical Recipients: • *Arts & Humanities:* General, Historic Preservation, Libraries, Literary Arts, Museums/Galleries, Music, Public Broadcasting, Theater • *Civic & Public Affairs:* African American Affairs, Botanical Gardens/Parks, Economic Development, Employment/Job Training, General, Housing, Public Policy, Urban & Community Affairs • *Education:* Business Education, Colleges & Universities, Community & Junior Colleges, Engineering/Technological Education, Minority Education, Religious Education, Student Aid • *International:* Foreign Educational Institutions • *Science:* Science Museums • *Social Services:* Child Welfare, Community Centers, People with Disabilities, Senior Services, Shelters/Homelessness, United Funds/United Ways, Volunteer Services, Youth Organizations

Grant Types: capital, general support, project, research, and scholarship

Geographic Distribution: primarily metropolitan Rochester, NY

GIVING OFFICERS
Dr. Edward C. Atwater: dir

James S. Gleason: pres, dir *B 1934 ED* Princeton Univ 1955; Univ Rochester MBA 1973 *CURR EMPL* pres, ceo, dir: Gleason Works *CORP AFFIL* chmn, pres, ceo, dir: Gleason Corp; ptnr: Hinman Howard & Kattell; vp, treas, dir: Alliance Tool Corp *PHIL AFFIL* dir: Gleason Works Foundation

Janis F. Gleason: dir

Ralph E. Harper: secy, treas, dir *B Batavia NY 1933 ED* Univ Rochester 1956; George Washington Univ JD 1967 *CURR EMPL* vp, secy, couns: Gleason Corp *CORP AFFIL* secy: Gleason Works *NONPR AFFIL* secy, treas, dir: Gleason Meml Fund *PHIL AFFIL* secy, treas, dir: Gleason Works Foundation

Gary Kimmett: dir

John B. Kodweis: vp admin, dir *B 1941 ED* John Carroll Univ BS 1963; Univ Rochester MBA 1971 *CURR EMPL* vp: Gleason Corp *CORP AFFIL* vp admin-human resources: Gleason Works

Albert Wendell Moore: dir *B Norwood MA 1934 ED* Clarkson Coll Tech 1959; Univ Rochester 1970 *CORP AFFIL* dir: Gleason Corp *NONPR AFFIL* pres, dir: Assn Mfg Tech

Sterling L. Weaver: chmn, dir *ED* Amherst Coll BA 1953; Columbia Univ JD 1956 *CURR EMPL* ptnr: Nixon Hargrave Devans & Doyle *NONPR AFFIL* mem: Am Bar Assn; mem exec comm (tax section): NY Bar Assn

APPLICATION INFORMATION
Initial Approach:

Applicants should send a proposal to the Gleason Memorial Fund.

The proposal should include a history and background of the organization; explanation of the project; amount requested; project budget and time schedule; names of board of directors and responsible staff; detailed financial statements for current and two previous years; a list of present funding sources; and a copy of IRS 501(c)(3) or 509(a).

There are no deadlines for submitting requests.

The board meets quarterly. Final notification occurs after board meetings.

Restrictions on Giving: Generally no funding is made for United Way-supported agencies. No grants are made to individuals. Grants are limited to metropolitan Rochester, New York.

OTHER THINGS TO KNOW
The foundation changed its name from the Gleason Memorial Fund to the Gleason Foundation.

PUBLICATIONS
Application guidelines

GRANTS ANALYSIS
Total Grants: $2,722,120

Number of Grants: 127

Highest Grant: $450,000

Average Grant: $21,434

Typical Range: $5,000 to $40,000

Disclosure Period: 1992

Note: Recent grants are derived from a 1992 Form 990.

RECENT GRANTS

Library

50,000	Rundel Library Foundation, Rochester, NY

General

450,000	Rochester Museum and Science Center, Rochester, NY
279,659	Ohio State University, Columbus, OH
250,000	Rochester Institute of Technology, Rochester, NY
250,000	United Neighborhood Centers, Rochester, NY
178,000	United Way, Rochester, NY

Goldie-Anna Charitable Trust

CONTACT
Kenneth L. Stein
Trustee
Goldie-Anna Charitable Trust
99 Park Ave.
New York, NY 10016
(212) 818-9600

FINANCIAL SUMMARY
Recent Giving: $345,800 (1992); $278,960 (1990); $258,575 (1988)

Assets: $10,870,805 (1992); $8,883,797 (1990); $9,401,537 (1988)

EIN: 13-2897474

CONTRIBUTIONS SUMMARY
Typical Recipients: • *Arts & Humanities:* Arts Associations & Councils, Libraries, Music, Public Broadcasting • *Civic & Public Affairs:* General, Legal Aid, Philanthropic Organizations • *Education:* Colleges & Universities, Legal Education, Medical Education, Minority Education, Private Education (Precollege), Student Aid • *Environment:* Air/Water Quality • *Health:* Hospices, Hospitals, Medical Research, Prenatal Health Issues • *International:* Missionary/Religious Activities • *Religion:* Churches, Jewish Causes, Religious Organizations, Religious Welfare, Synagogues/Temples • *Social Services:* At-Risk Youth, Child Welfare, Community Service Organizations, Food/Clothing Distribution, People with Disabilities, Shelters/Homelessness, United Funds/United Ways, Youth Organizations

Grant Types: endowment and scholarship

Geographic Distribution: focus on the New York, NY, metropolitan area

GIVING OFFICERS
Julius Greenfield: trust

Kenneth L. Stein: trust

APPLICATION INFORMATION
Initial Approach: Send cover letter and full proposal. Deadline is November 30.

Restrictions on Giving: Emphasis on aid to qualified organizations dealing with indigent, elderly and disadvantaged, and medical/research and education.

GRANTS ANALYSIS
Total Grants: $345,800

Number of Grants: 108

Highest Grant: $152,000

Typical Range: $500 to $5,000

Disclosure Period: 1992

Note: Recent grants are derived from a 1992 Form 990.

RECENT GRANTS

Library

7,000	Branigan Memorial Library
1,750	New York Public Library, New York, NY

General

152,000	American Friends of Hebrew University, New York, NY
35,000	University of Pennsylvania Graduation School Education, Philadelphia, PA
10,000	University of Pennsylvania Dissemenation Award, Philadelphia, PA
7,000	Bet Torah, New York, NY
5,000	Chappaqua Summer Scholarship Program

Goldsmith Foundation, Horace W.

CONTACT
James C. Slaughter, Esq.
Chief Executive Officer and Director
Horace W. Goldsmith Foundation
375 Park Ave.
Ste. 1602
New York, NY 10152
(212) 308-9832

FINANCIAL SUMMARY
Recent Giving: $18,000,000 (1994 est.); $17,363,122 (1993); $16,923,055 (1992)

Assets: $386,915,373 (1993); $419,478,483 (1992); $420,962,614 (1991)

Gifts Received: $965,000 (1993)

Fiscal Note: In 1993, gifts were received from the Trust f/b/o Grace R. Goldsmith.

EIN: 13-6107758

CONTRIBUTIONS SUMMARY
Donor(s): The foundation was established in 1955. The donor was the late Horace W. Goldsmith .

Typical Recipients: • *Arts & Humanities:* Arts Associations & Councils, Arts Centers, Arts Festivals, Arts Funds, Arts Institutes, Ballet, Community Arts, Dance, Film & Video, Libraries, Museums/Galleries, Music, Opera, Performing Arts, Public Broadcasting, Theater, Visual Arts • *Civic & Public Affairs:* Botanical Gardens/Parks, Civil Rights, Economic Development, General, Law & Justice, Legal Aid, Zoos/Aquariums • *Education:* Arts/Humanities Education, Business Education, Colleges & Universities, Education Funds, Education Reform, Elementary Education (Public), General, Health & Physical Education, Legal Education, Medical Education, Private Education (Precollege), School Volunteerism, Science/Mathematics Education, Social Sciences Education, Special Education • *Environment:* General • *Health:* AIDS/HIV, Cancer, Clinics/Medical Centers, Geriatric Health, Heart, Hospitals, Hospitals (University Affiliated), Medical Rehabilitation, Medical Research, Nursing Services, Public Health, Research/Studies Institutes, Single-Disease Health Associations • *International:* Foreign Arts Organizations, Foreign Educational Institutions, Health Care/Hospitals, International Organizations, International Relations, International Relief Efforts, Missionary/Religious Activities • *Religion:* Churches, Jewish Causes • *Science:* Science Museums, Scientific Centers & Institutes • *Social Services:* At-Risk Youth, Child Welfare, Community Service Organizations, Crime Prevention, Day Care, Delinquency & Criminal Rehabilitation, Family Planning, Family Services, People with Disabilities, Recreation & Athletics, Senior Services, Shelters/Homelessness, Substance Abuse, Volunteer Services, Youth Organizations

Grant Types: challenge, endowment, general support, and multiyear/continuing support

Geographic Distribution: no geographic restrictions; emphasis on the New York City metropolitan area

GIVING OFFICERS

Richard Lee Menschel: dir *B* New York NY 1934 *ED* Syracuse Univ BS 1955; Harvard Univ MBA 1959 *CURR EMPL* ptnr: Goldman Sachs & Co *CORP AFFIL* dir: Kieckhefer Assocs *PHIL AFFIL* trust: Margaret T. Morris Foundation; pres, treas, dir: Charina Foundation

Robert Benjamin Menschel: dir *B* New York NY 1929 *ED* NY Univ 1951-1953; Syracuse Univ BS 1951 *CURR EMPL* ptnr: Goldman Sachs & Co *NONPR AFFIL* dir: Parks Counc, YM-YWHA; dir, mem fin & budget comm: NY Pub Library; mem: Investment Assn NY; mem exec bd: Am Jewish Comm NY; pres bd trust, mem exec comm: Dalton Sch; trust: Guild Hall, Mus Modern Art; trust, mem exec comm: Montefiore Hosp Med Ctr, Syracuse Univ; vp, dir: YMHA Emanu-El Midtown *CLUB AFFIL* City Athletic, Dunes Racquet, India House *PHIL AFFIL* pres, treas: Robert and Joyce Menschel Foundation

James C. Slaughter: ceo, dir

Thomas R. Slaughter: dir
William A. Slaughter: dir

APPLICATION INFORMATION
Initial Approach:

Applicants should send a letter of inquiry to the foundation.

Prospective applicants may send written inquiries any time.

The foundation's board of directors meets eight times a year to initiate and review grants.

GRANTS ANALYSIS
Total Grants: $17,363,122

Number of Grants: 317

Highest Grant: $1,106,615

Average Grant: $54,773

Typical Range: $25,000 to $150,000

Disclosure Period: 1993

Note: Recent grants are derived from a 1993 Form 990.

RECENT GRANTS

Library

367,000	Pierpont Morgan Library, New York, NY	
125,000	New York Public Library, New York, NY	

General

1,106,615	Kivel Geriatric Center, New York, NY	
600,000	Hospital for Special Surgery, New York, NY	
500,000	Harvard University, Cambridge, MA	
300,000	Harvard School of Public Health, Cambridge, MA	
300,000	Jerusalem Foundation, New York, NY	

Goodstein Family Foundation, David

CONTACT
Robert Goodstein
President
David Goodstein Family Fdn.
60 E 42nd St., Ste. 823
New York, NY 10165-0823
(212) 687-9515

FINANCIAL SUMMARY
Recent Giving: $1,892,030 (fiscal 1992); $220,950 (fiscal 1990); $252,171 (fiscal 1989)

Assets: $3,795,180 (fiscal 1992); $4,919,031 (fiscal 1990); $4,383,052 (fiscal 1989)

EIN: 13-6094685

CONTRIBUTIONS SUMMARY
Donor(s): members of the Goodstein family and family-related businesses

Typical Recipients: • *Arts & Humanities:* General, History & Archaeology, Libraries, Museums/Galleries • *Civic & Public Affairs:*

Professional & Trade Associations • *Education:* Colleges & Universities, Medical Education, Private Education (Precollege), Science/Mathematics Education • *Health:* Diabetes, Emergency/Ambulance Services, Hospices, Hospitals, Medical Research • *Religion:* Jewish Causes, Religious Organizations, Religious Welfare, Synagogues/Temples • *Social Services:* Community Service Organizations, Food/Clothing Distribution, Shelters/Homelessness, United Funds/United Ways

Grant Types: capital, emergency, general support, multiyear/continuing support, and scholarship

Geographic Distribution: focus on NY

GIVING OFFICERS
Robert Goodstein: pres

Jeanne Goodwin: secy

Ivan Kushen: treas

Marilyn Kushen: vp, dir

APPLICATION INFORMATION
Initial Approach: Send cover letter and full proposal. There are no deadlines.

Restrictions on Giving: Does not support individuals or provide loans or matching gifts.

GRANTS ANALYSIS
Total Grants: $1,892,030

Number of Grants: 5

Highest Grant: $630,010

Typical Range: $1,000 to $630,010

Disclosure Period: fiscal year ending February 28, 1992

Note: Recent grants are derived from a fiscal 1992 grants list.

RECENT GRANTS

General

630,010	American Society for Technion, New York, NY	
630,010	Hadassah, Westchester, NY	
630,010	United Jewish Appeal Federation of Jewish Philanthropies, Westchester, NY	
1,000	Committee to Protect Journalists, New York, NY	
1,000	United Way, Chicago, IL	

Gordon/Rousmaniere/Roberts Fund

CONTACT
Mary G. Roberts
Trustee
Gordon/Rousmaniere/Roberts Fund
10 Hanover Sq.
New York, NY 10005
(212) 510-4690

FINANCIAL SUMMARY
Recent Giving: $3,000,000 (1995 est.); $3,000,000 (1994 approx.); $3,100,000 (1993 approx.)

Assets: $14,500,000 (1995 est.);
$14,300,000 (1994 approx.); $14,300,000
(1993 approx.)

EIN: 13-3257793

CONTRIBUTIONS SUMMARY

Donor(s): The foundation was established
in 1985 by Albert H. Gordon.

Typical Recipients: • *Arts & Humanities:*
Libraries, Museums/Galleries, Music • *Civic
& Public Affairs:* Public Policy • *Education:*
Arts/Humanities Education, Colleges & Uni-
versities, Medical Education, Private Educa-
tion (Precollege) • *Environment:* General
• *Health:* Hospitals, Single-Disease Health
Associations • *International:* International
Relations • *Religion:* Churches • *Social Serv-
ices:* Emergency Relief, Recreation & Ath-
letics, Youth Organizations

Grant Types: general support

Geographic Distribution: focus on New
York, Massachusetts, and Connecticut

GIVING OFFICERS
Mary G. Roberts: trust

APPLICATION INFORMATION
Initial Approach:

The foundation requests applications be
made in writing.

The written application should include an
outline of the purpose of the grant.

The foundation has no deadline for submitting proposals.

Restrictions on Giving: The foundation
does not make grants to individuals.

GRANTS ANALYSIS
Total Grants: $3,106,650

Number of Grants: 87

Highest Grant: $600,000

Average Grant: $29,147*

Typical Range: $2,000 to $30,000

Disclosure Period: 1991

Note: Average grant figure does not include
the highest grant of $600,000. Recent grants
are derived from a 1991 grants list.

RECENT GRANTS

Library

25,000	Geneva Free Library, Geneva, NY
25,000	Geneva Free Library, Geneva, NY
5,000	Grolier Club Library Fund, New York, NY

General

600,000	Harvard University, Cambridge, MA
300,000	Asphalt Green, New York, NY
250,000	Harvard School of Public Health, Cambridge, MA
150,000	YWCA, New York, NY
125,000	Harvard Crimson Trust II, Cambridge, MA

Gould Foundation, The Florence

Former Foundation Name: Florence J.
Gould Foundation

CONTACT
John R. Young
President
The Florence Gould Foundation
c/o Cahill Gordon and Reindel
80 Pine St.
New York, NY 10005
(212) 701-3400

FINANCIAL SUMMARY
Recent Giving: $5,685,603 (1992);
$4,628,586 (1991); $3,587,638 (1990)

Assets: $76,440,522 (1992); $76,302,202
(1991); $67,833,784 (1990)

Gifts Received: $6,494 (1992); $7,456
(1991); $10,799 (1990)

Fiscal Note: The foundation receives contributions from trusts under the will of
Florence J. Gould.

EIN: 13-6176855

CONTRIBUTIONS SUMMARY
Donor(s): The foundation was established
in 1957 by Florence J. Gould.

Typical Recipients: • *Arts & Humanities:*
Arts Centers, Dance, General, Historic Pres-
ervation, Libraries, Museums/Galleries, Music, Performing Arts, Public Broadcasting,
Theater, Visual Arts • *Civic & Public Affairs:* General, Law & Justice, Philanthropic
Organizations • *Education:* Arts/Humanities
Education, Colleges & Universities, Continu-
ing Education, Engineering/Technological
Education, International Exchange, Interna-
tional Studies • *Environment:* General
• *Health:* Clinics/Medical Centers • *Interna-
tional:* Foreign Arts Organizations, Foreign
Educational Institutions, Health Care/Hospi-
tals, International Organizations, Interna-
tional Peace & Security Issues, International
Relations • *Science:* Scientific Labs • *Social
Services:* People with Disabilities

Grant Types: conference/seminar, department, endowment, general support, and research

Geographic Distribution: national; and
France

GIVING OFFICERS
Walter Conway Cliff: asst treas, asst secy,
dir *B* Detroit MI 1932 *ED* Univ Detroit BS
1955; Univ Detroit LLB 1955; NY Univ
LLM 1956 *CURR EMPL* pres: Walter C
Cliff PC *CORP AFFIL* ptnr: Cahill Gordon
& Reindel *NONPR AFFIL* mem: Am Bar
Assn, Assn Bar City New York, NY Bar
Assn *CLUB AFFIL* Downtown, Stockbridge
GC *PHIL AFFIL* vp, secy, asst treas, dir:
Geoffrey C. Hughes Foundation

Daniel Pomeroy Davison: vp, treas, dir *B*
New York NY 1925 *ED* Yale Univ BA
1949; Harvard Univ JD 1952 *CURR EMPL*
chmn: Christie Manson & Woods International Inc *CORP AFFIL* dir: Atlantic Cos,
Burlington Northern, Christies Intl Publ Li-

ability Co, Discount Corp NY, Dusco, US-
Trust Corp *NONPR AFFIL* trust: Cooper Union, Nature Conservancy

Daniel Leopold Wildenstein: vp, dir *B* Ver-
rieres-le-Buisson France 1917 *CURR EMPL*
chmn, pres: Wildenstein & Co *CORP AFFIL*
exec dir: Wildenstein Arte *NONPR AFFIL*
fdr: Am Inst France; mem: French Chamber
Commerce

John R. Young: pres *CURR EMPL* Cahill
Gordon & Reindel *PHIL AFFIL* dir: G.
Harold and Leila Y. Mathers Charitable
Foundation

APPLICATION INFORMATION
Initial Approach:

No particular form of application is required.

There are no deadlines for requests; applications are accepted throughout the year.

GRANTS ANALYSIS
Total Grants: $5,685,603

Number of Grants: 103

Highest Grant: $1,614,052

Average Grant: $39,917*

Typical Range: $5,000 to $100,000

Disclosure Period: 1992

Note: The average grant figure excludes the
largest grant of $1,614,052. Recent grants
are derived from a 1992 Form 990.

RECENT GRANTS

Library

75,000	New York Public Library, New York, NY
50,000	American Library in Paris, Paris, France
30,000	Wadsworth Atheneum, Hartford, CT

General

333,333	American Hospital of Paris Foundation, New York, NY
325,735	French Institute Alliance Francaise, New York, NY
220,000	Friends of Vieilles Maisons Francaises
132,175	Mt. Sinai Medical Center, New York, NY
100,000	Academie des Beaux Arts

Greenwall Foundation

CONTACT
William C. Stubing
President
Greenwall Foundation
2 Park Ave., 24th Fl.
New York, NY 10016-9301
(212) 679-7266

FINANCIAL SUMMARY
Recent Giving: $2,416,350 (1995 est.);
$2,215,802 (1994); $2,016,148 (1993)

Assets: $66,749,405 (1995 est.);
$63,570,862 (1994); $67,699,404 (1993)

Gifts Received: $5,100 (1993); $9,000
(1992); $5,500 (1990)

Fiscal Note: The foundation received the following contributions from the estate of Frank K. Greenwall: $19,832,094 in 1986, $127,136 in 1987, and $112,489 in 1989.

EIN: 13-6082277

CONTRIBUTIONS SUMMARY

Donor(s): Frank Greenwall and his wife, Anna Alexander Greenwall , established the foundation in 1949. Anna Alexander Greenwall's father owned a company called National Gum and Mica. In 1920, Frank Greenwall joined the company, which became National Starch and Chemical Corporation in 1959. Mr. Greenwall was chairman and chief executive of the adhesives, resins, and specialty chemical business.

The foundation was originally named the Susan Greenwall Foundation in memory of the Greenwall's daughter. Its focus was on bone cancer research, the disease which took Susan's life at age 16. Frank and Anna were joined as donors to the foundation by their daughter, Nancy Greenwall, and their close friends and colleagues, Alfred A. Halden and Elias D. Cohen.

In 1981, after the deaths of both Anna and Nancy, the name of the foundation was changed to the Greenwall Foundation to honor the deceased family members. Frank Greenwall, the last surviving founder, died in 1985.

Typical Recipients: • *Arts & Humanities:* Arts Associations & Councils, Arts Funds, Arts Outreach, Ballet, Dance, Ethnic & Folk Arts, General, Historic Preservation, History & Archaeology, Libraries, Museums/Galleries, Music, Opera, Performing Arts, Theater, Visual Arts • *Civic & Public Affairs:* Botanical Gardens/Parks, General, Law & Justice, Professional & Trade Associations, Public Policy • *Education:* Arts/Humanities Education, Colleges & Universities, Education Associations, Education Funds, Education Reform, Engineering/Technological Education, General, Medical Education, Minority Education, Private Education (Precollege), Public Education (Precollege), Science/Mathematics Education • *Health:* Clinics/Medical Centers, Diabetes, Health Organizations, Hospitals, Medical Research, Public Health • *Science:* Scientific Centers & Institutes, Scientific Labs, Scientific Research • *Social Services:* Community Service Organizations, Volunteer Services, Youth Organizations

Grant Types: project and research

Geographic Distribution: primarily in New York for arts and humanities; to national organizations for medical research and education

GIVING OFFICERS
Chester Billings, Jr.: dir

George Bugliarello, MD: dir *B* Trieste Italy 1927 *ED* Univ Padua Italy DEngl 1951; Univ MN MS 1954; MA Inst Tech DSc 1959 *CORP AFFIL* dir: Comtech Corp, Long Island Lighting Co, Lord Corp *NONPR AFFIL* alumni rep visitors comm civil engg: MA Inst Tech; bd visitors: Duke Univ Sch Engg; chmn, mem: High Tech Task Fork, Mayors Commn Science & Tech;

fellow: Am Assn Advancement Science, Am Soc Engg Ed, NY Academy Music; mem: Intl Assn Hydraulic Res, N Atlantic Treaty Org Adv Comm Science Stability Program, Natl Academy Engg, Natl Medal Tech Nomination Evaluation Comm, Natl Res Counc, New York City Publ Pvt Adv Group Math Ed, NY Academy Medicine, NY Academy Sciences, NY Partnership; mem adv comm: Tech & Environment; trust: ANSER, Natl Assn Science Tech & Soc *PHIL AFFIL* trust: Teagle Foundation

George Francis Cahill, Jr.: chmn *B* New York NY 1927 *ED* Yale Univ BS 1949; Columbia Univ MD 1953; Harvard Univ MA 1966 *NONPR AFFIL* fellow: Am Academy Arts Sciences, Am Assn Advancement Science; mem: Am Clinical Climatological Assn, Am Diabetes Assn, Am Physiological Soc, Am Soc Clinical Investigation, Assn Am Physicians, Endocrine Soc, Natl Commn Diabetes; mem res training commn: Natl Insts Health; prbiological sciences: Dartmouth Coll; prof medicine emeritus: Harvard Univ *CLUB AFFIL* Siasconset Casino

Christine Karen Cassel, MD: dir *B* Minneapolis MN 1945 *ED* Univ Chicago AB 1967; Univ MA MD 1976 *NONPR AFFIL* assoc prof medicine: Univ Chicago; diplomate: Am Bd Internal Medicine; fellow: Am Coll Physicians, Am Geriatrics Soc; mem: Soc Health Human Values; pres, mem, dir: Physicians Social Responsibility

Donald Jordan Donahue: dir *B* Brooklyn NY 1924 *ED* Georgetown Univ BA 1947; NY Univ MBA 1951 *CURR EMPL* chmn: Magma Copper Co *CORP AFFIL* dir: Couns Cash Reserve Fund, Couns Tandem Securities Fund, GEV Corp, Greenwall Fed, Natl Starch & Chem Co, Northeast Utilities, Signet Star Holdings Inc; treas, dir: Nacohah Holding Corp *CLUB AFFIL* Blind Brook CC, Greenwich CC, Jupiter Hills GC, Loblolly Pines GC, Univ

Beatrix Ann Hamburg, MD: dir *B* Jacksonville FL 1923 *ED* Vassar Coll AB 1944; Yale Univ MD 1948 *NONPR AFFIL* mem: Academy Res Behavioral Medicine, Natl Academy Sciences Inst Medicine, Phi Beta Kappa, Soc Adolescent Medicine, Soc Study Social Biology; mem comm behavior & soc: Natl Academy Sciences; prof psychiatry & pediatrics: Mt Sinai Med Sch

Rosmarie E. Homberger: secy

Fredrica Jarcho: program off

Edward M. Kresky: dir

Edith Levett: secy emerita

Andrew Alexander MacGrath: dir

C. Richard MacGrath: treas, dir *B* East Orange NJ 1921 *ED* Princeton Univ AB 1943 *NONPR AFFIL* dir: Hosp Special Surgery, Skowhegan Sch Painting Sculpture; mem: Huguenot Soc, Order Magna Carta, Soc Cincinatti, Soc Colonial Wars, Sons Am Revolution, St Nicholas Soc *CLUB AFFIL* Dublin Lake, Hugenot Soc, Kane Lodge, Mid Ocean, Princeton, River, SAR, Soc Cin, Soc Colonial Wars, St Nich Soc

Francis Fowler MacGrath: dir

Susan Abigail MacGrath: dir

Carl Braun Menges: dir *B* New York NY 1930 *ED* Hamilton Coll BA 1951; Harvard Univ MBA 1953 *CURR EMPL* vchmn, mng dir: Donaldson Lufkin & Jenrette *CORP AFFIL* chmn, pres, ceo: Wood Struthers & Winthrop; pres, chmn: Winthrop Focus Fund; treas: G-Tech Corp *NONPR AFFIL* dir: Boys Club NY, Med Indemnity Assurance Corp; trust: Hamilton Coll, Hosp Special Surgery *CLUB AFFIL* Bond NY, Leash, Long Island Wyandanch, Maidstone, Natl Golf Links Am, Regency Whist, Union

Joseph George Perpich, MD: dir *B* Hibbing MN 1941 *ED* Univ MN BA 1963; Univ MN MD 1966; Georgetown Univ JD 1974 *NONPR AFFIL* diplomate: Am Bd Psychiatry Neurology; fellow: Am Psychiatric Assn; mem: Alpha Omega Alpha, Am Assn Advancement Science, Am Bar Assn, Am Intellectual Property Law Assn, Bar DC Ct Appeals; mem adv bd: Am Bd Internal Medicine, Tech Soc Intl Journal; mem editorial bd: Biotechnology Law Report *PHIL AFFIL* vp grants & special programs: Howard Hughes Medical Institute

Oscar Melick Ruebhausen: chmn emeritus *B* New York NY 1912 *ED* Dartmouth Coll AB 1934; Yale Univ LLB 1937 *NONPR AFFIL* chmn: Commn Coll Retirement; mem: Am Bar Assn, Assn Bar City New York, Counc Foreign Rels, NY St Bar Assn, Order Coif, Phi Beta Kappa, Rockefeller Univ Counc, Sigma Phi Epsilon, Yale Law Sch Assn; mem adv counc: Carnegie Commn Science Tech & Govt; mem natl comm: US-China Rels *CLUB AFFIL* Century, Hemisphere, Rancho Sante Fe Assn, River, Rockefeller Ctr

Richard L. Salzer: vp, dir *B* New York NY 1922 *ED* Purdue Univ 1942 *CURR EMPL* sr vp: Seligman & Latz

Dr. Richard L. Salzer, Jr.: dir

Stephen Stamas: vchmn, dir *B* Salem MA 1931 *ED* Harvard Univ AB 1953; Oxford Univ BPhil 1955; Harvard Univ PhD 1957 *CURR EMPL* investment exec: Wincrest Ptnrs *CORP AFFIL* dir: BNY Hamilton Funds *NONPR AFFIL* chmn: Philharmonic Symphony Soc NY; dir: Enterprise Fdn; mem: Academy Political Science, Phi Beta Kappa; mem, bd dirs: Am Counc Germany, Counc Foreign Rels; pres, trust: Am Ditchley Fdn; trust: Am Assembly, Columbia Univ, Marlboro Sch Music, NY Pub Library, Rockefeller Univ; vchmn: Lincoln Ctr Performing Arts *CLUB AFFIL* Century Assn, Harvard, Manursing Island

William C. Stubing: pres, dir

William S. Vaun, MD: vp, dir

APPLICATION INFORMATION
Initial Approach:

The foundation does not have an application form or a standard outline for proposals. Initial letter should describe the program, objectives, amount requested, and qualifications of organization and project directors.

If interested, the foundation will request additional information such as financial statements, itemized budget, tax-exempt status letter, and other relevant material.

Applications must be received by February 1 for consideration at the spring board meeting, or by August 1 for the autumn meeting. The foundation gives special attention to proposals demonstrating innovative approaches.

Restrictions on Giving: The foundation generally will not fund private foundations, endowment campaigns, or individuals. Arts organizations that have received contributions from the foundation for three consecutive years are not eligible for renewals until at least a full year elapses without foundation support.

PUBLICATIONS
Annual report

GRANTS ANALYSIS
Total Grants: $2,016,148
Number of Grants: 89
Highest Grant: $150,000
Average Grant: $22,653
Typical Range: $5,000 to $25,000
Disclosure Period: 1993

Note: Recent grants are derived from a 1993 Form 990.

RECENT GRANTS

General

150,000	Stanford University, Stanford, CA
103,551	National Center for State Courts, New York, NY
94,221	Mt. Sinai Medical Center, New York, NY
87,500	New York University, New York, NY
75,728	University of Chicago, Chicago, IL

Greve Foundation, William and Mary

CONTACT
Anthony C. M. Kiser
President
William and Mary Greve Foundation
630 Fifth Ave., Ste., 1750
New York, NY 10111
(212) 307-7850

FINANCIAL SUMMARY
Recent Giving: $829,990 (1992); $825,397 (1991); $583,299 (1990)
Assets: $25,946,263 (1992); $26,461,128 (1991); $21,074,232 (1990)
EIN: 13-6020724

CONTRIBUTIONS SUMMARY
Donor(s): The William and Mary Greve Foundation was incorporated in New York in 1964 with funds donated by the late Mary P. Greve . The principal of the Mary P. Greve Trust and the William M. Greve Trust for Mary P. Greve was designated to the foundation by Mrs. Greve during her lifetime. After her death in 1975, the assets of these trusts were transferred to the foundation. The foundation's chairman, John W. Kiser III, and president, Anthony C. M. Kiser, are grandsons of Mrs. Greve.

Typical Recipients: • *Arts & Humanities:* Arts Associations & Councils, Arts Institutes, Arts Outreach, Ballet, General, Historic Preservation, Libraries, Literary Arts, Music, Theater • *Civic & Public Affairs:* Botanical Gardens/Parks, Economic Development, Nonprofit Management, Public Policy, Rural Affairs, Urban & Community Affairs, Women's Affairs, Zoos/Aquariums • *Education:* Arts/Humanities Education, Colleges & Universities, Engineering/Technological Education, Preschool Education, Private Education (Precollege) • *Environment:* General • *International:* International Affairs, International Peace & Security Issues, International Relations • *Social Services:* At-Risk Youth, People with Disabilities

Grant Types: conference/seminar, general support, research, and seed money

Geographic Distribution: national, with some emphasis on New York

GIVING OFFICERS
Anthony C. M. Kiser: pres, dir
John W. Kiser III: chmn
James W. Sykes, Jr.: dir
John J. Tommaney: secy, dir

APPLICATION INFORMATION
Initial Approach:

Applicants should send a brief letter.

Letters of application must include a brief description of the purpose for funding, amount needed, and a detailed budget of how the grant will be used. The qualifications of the organization and its management, and a copy of IRS tax-exempt status letter must accompany the letter.

Applicants may submit proposals any time.

The foundation does not use application forms. All applicants will be notified if their grant request has been approved or rejected, or if additional information is needed.

Restrictions on Giving: No grants are made to individuals, or for scholarships, fellowships, or loans.

PUBLICATIONS
Application guidelines

GRANTS ANALYSIS
Total Grants: $829,990
Number of Grants: 51
Highest Grant: $95,000
Average Grant: $16,274
Typical Range: $2,000 to $30,000
Disclosure Period: 1992

Note: Recent grants are derived from a 1992 Form 990.

RECENT GRANTS

Library

15,000	New York Public Library, New York, NY

General

75,000	Center for the Study of Soviet Changes, New York, NY
40,000	Broad Jump Prep for Prep, New York, NY
40,000	Center for Post-Soviet Studies, New York, NY
39,700	Studio in a School, New York, NY
35,000	University of Missouri, New York, NY

Griffis Foundation

CONTACT
Hughes Griffis
President
Griffis Fdn.
c/o Pulsifer and Hutner Inc.
14 Wall St.
New York, NY 10005
(212) 577-8400

FINANCIAL SUMMARY
Recent Giving: $316,606 (1992); $333,611 (1991); $203,943 (1990)
Assets: $7,997,920 (1992); $8,043,357 (1991); $8,240,731 (1990)
EIN: 13-5678764

CONTRIBUTIONS SUMMARY
Donor(s): the late Stanton Griffis, Nixon Griffis

Typical Recipients: • *Arts & Humanities:* Arts Associations & Councils, Arts Centers, Dance, Libraries, Museums/Galleries, Music • *Civic & Public Affairs:* Botanical Gardens/Parks, General, Municipalities/Towns, Philanthropic Organizations, Zoos/Aquariums • *Education:* Colleges & Universities, Private Education (Precollege) • *Health:* Cancer, Emergency/Ambulance Services, Hospices, Hospitals, Medical Research, Single-Disease Health Associations • *International:* Human Rights • *Religion:* Religious Welfare • *Social Services:* Family Services, United Funds/United Ways, Youth Organizations

Grant Types: general support

Geographic Distribution: focus on NY, CT, and FL

GIVING OFFICERS
Alexander Dmitrieff: dir
Hughes Griffis: pres, dir
Elizabeth Nye: vp, dir
Patricia M. Shippee: dir
Sharon Tripp: dir

APPLICATION INFORMATION
Initial Approach: The foundation has no formal grant application procedure or application form. There are no deadlines.

PUBLICATIONS
Program policy statement, application guidelines

GRANTS ANALYSIS
Total Grants: $316,606
Number of Grants: 85
Highest Grant: $22,400

Typical Range: $100 to $10,000

Disclosure Period: 1992

Note: Recent grants are derived from a 1992 Form 990.

RECENT GRANTS

General

20,000	Freedom Institute, New York, NY
20,000	St. Thomas More Playgroup
15,000	Lenox Hill Hospital, New York, NY
10,000	Lawrence Memorial Hospital, Lawrence, MA
10,000	Memorial Sloan-Kettering Cancer Society, New York, NY

Guardian Life Insurance Company of America

Revenue: $6.13 billion
Employees: 5,315
Headquarters: New York, NY
SIC Major Group: Life Insurance, Savings Institutions Except Federal, and Accident & Health Insurance

CONTACT
Karen Dickinson
Assistant Corporate Secretary
Guardian Life Insurance Company of America
201 Park Ave. S
New York, NY 10003
(212) 598-7499

FINANCIAL SUMMARY
Recent Giving: $697,800 (1995 est.); $608,735 (1994); $527,751 (1993)

Fiscal Note: Company gives directly since December 1992. See "Other Things To Know" for more details.

CONTRIBUTIONS SUMMARY
Typical Recipients: • *Arts & Humanities:* Arts Centers, Community Arts, Historic Preservation, Libraries, Museums/Galleries, Music, Opera, Performing Arts, Public Broadcasting, Theater • *Civic & Public Affairs:* Business/Free Enterprise, Economic Development, Economic Policy, Law & Justice, Safety, Urban & Community Affairs, Zoos/Aquariums • *Education:* Arts/Humanities Education, Business Education, Colleges & Universities, Community & Junior Colleges, Economic Education, Education Funds, Literacy • *Health:* Health Policy/Cost Containment, Hospices, Medical Research, Single-Disease Health Associations • *Social Services:* Food/Clothing Distribution, Substance Abuse, United Funds/United Ways, Youth Organizations

Grant Types: employee matching gifts and general support

Note: Employee matching gift ratio: 1 to 1.

Geographic Distribution: in headquarters and operating communities

Operating Locations: NY (New York), PA, WA, WI

CORP. OFFICERS
Arthur Vincent Ferrara: *B* New York NY 1930 *ED* Coll Holy Cross BS 1952 *CURR EMPL* chmn, ceo, pres: Guardian Life Ins Co Am *CORP AFFIL* chmn: Guardian Asset Mgmt Corp, Guardian Baillie Gifford Ltd; pres, chmn, ceo: Guardian Ins & Annuity Co; trust: Guardian Life Trust, Guardian Life Welfare Trust *NONPR AFFIL* dir: 14th St Un Sq Local Devel Corp; mem: Am Counc Life Ins, Am Soc Certified Life Underwriters, Golden Key Soc Certified Life Underwriters, Natl Life Underwriters, New York City Assn Life Underwriters, Westchester Life Underwriters Assn; mem, pres counc: Coll Holy Cross; secy-treas, dir: Life Ins Counc NY

Peter Lounsbery Hutchings: *B* New York NY 1943 *ED* Yale Univ BA 1964 *CURR EMPL* exec vp, cfo: Guardian Life Ins Co Am *CORP AFFIL* dir: Guardian Ins & Annuity Co, Guardian Investors Svcs Corp *NONPR AFFIL* dir: 14th St Bus Improvement District; fellow: Soc Actuaries; mem: Actuarial Soc Greater NY, Am Acad Actuaries

Joseph Dudley Sargent: *B* Philadelphia PA 1937 *ED* Fairfield Univ AB 1959 *CURR EMPL* pres, dir: Guardian Life Ins Co Am *NONPR AFFIL* dir: Life Ins Mktg & Res Inst; mem: Natl Assn Life Underwriters

GIVING OFFICERS
Karen Dickinson: *CURR EMPL* asst corp secy: Guardian Life Ins Co Am

APPLICATION INFORMATION
Initial Approach: *Initial Contact:* brief letter of inquiry *Include Information On:* a description of the organization; amount requested and purpose of funds sought; recently audited financial statement; and proof of tax-exempt status *Deadlines:* none

Restrictions on Giving: Does not support individuals, religious organizations for sectarian purposes, or political or lobbying groups.

OTHER THINGS TO KNOW
The Guardian Life Charitable Trust was terminated in December 1993.

GRANTS ANALYSIS
Total Grants: $608,735

Typical Range: $1,000 to $2,500

Disclosure Period: 1994

Guggenheim Foundation, Harry Frank

CONTACT
Joel Wallman
Program Officer
Harry Frank Guggenheim Foundation
527 Madison Ave., 15th Fl.
New York, NY 10022-4304
(212) 644-4909

FINANCIAL SUMMARY
Recent Giving: $1,800,000 (1994 est.); $2,000,000 (1993 approx.); $1,532,588 (1992)

Assets: $52,000,000 (1994 est.); $50,000,000 (1993 approx.); $49,242,001 (1992)

EIN: 13-6043471

CONTRIBUTIONS SUMMARY
Donor(s): The foundation was established in 1929 by the late Harry Frank Guggenheim .

Typical Recipients: • *Arts & Humanities:* Ethnic & Folk Arts, History & Archaeology, Libraries, Museums/Galleries • *Civic & Public Affairs:* Professional & Trade Associations, Safety • *Education:* Colleges & Universities, General, International Studies, Medical Education, Science/Mathematics Education, Social Sciences Education • *Environment:* General • *Health:* Health Funds, Medical Research • *International:* Foreign Educational Institutions • *Religion:* Jewish Causes, Religious Organizations • *Science:* Scientific Research • *Social Services:* People with Disabilities, United Funds/United Ways

Grant Types: research

Geographic Distribution: no geographic restrictions

GIVING OFFICERS
William Oliver Baker: dir *B* Chestertown MD 1915 *ED* Washington Coll BS 1935; Princeton Univ PhD 1938 *CURR EMPL* dir: Summit Trust Co *CORP AFFIL* dir: Gen Am Investors Co, Health Effects Inst *NONPR AFFIL* adv coun: Special Libraries Assn; chmn emeritus: Rockefeller Univ; chmn telecommuns bd: US Dept State; co-chmn natl counc: Am Assn Advancement Science; dir: Counc Library Resources, EDUCOM, Health Effects Inst; fellow: Am Academy Arts Sciences, Am Inst Chemists, Am Physical Soc, Franklin Inst; mem: Am Chem Soc, Am Philosophical Soc, Carnegie Forum Ed Science Tech & Econ, Dirs Indus Res, Indus Res Inst, Natl Academy Engg, Natl Academy Sciences, Omicron Delta Kappa, Phi Lambda Upsilon, Sigma Xi; mem adv counc: Fed Emergency Mgmt Adv Bd, NJ Regional Med Library; mem bd overseers: Univ PA Coll Engg Applied Science; mem counc: Marconi Fellowships; mem exec comm: NJ Bd Higher Ed; mem science adv bd: Natl Security Agency; mem, vchmn: NJ Commn Science & Tech; mem visiting comm sciences & math: Drew Univ; trust: Charles Babbage Inst *CLUB AFFIL* Cosmos, Princeton Northwestern NJ; hon mem: Chemists NY *PHIL AFFIL* trust: General Motors Cancer Research Foundation, Fund for Innovation and Public Service, Fund for New Jersey; chmn emeritus: Andrew W. Mellon Foundation

Josiah Bunting III: dir

Peyton S. Cochran, Jr.: dir *CURR EMPL* sr vp, dir: Rouse Co of St Louis *CORP AFFIL* sr vp, dir: Rouse Co of NJ Inc, Salem Mall

Karen Colvard: program off

James Burrows Edwards: dir *B* Hawthorne FL 1927 *ED* Coll Charleston BS 1950; Univ Louisville DMD 1955; Coll Charleston

LittD 1975; Francis Marion Coll D Hum 1978 *CORP AFFIL* dir: Brendles Inc, Encyclopaedia Britannica, IMO Indus, Natl Data Corp, Phillips Petroleum Co, SC Natl Bank, SCANA Corp, WMX TechS; mem adv bd: Norfolk Southern Corp *NONPR AFFIL* dir: William Benton Fdn, Pi Kappa Phi Fdn; fellow: Intl Coll Dentists; mem: Am Coll Dentists, Am Dental Assn, Am Hellenic Progressive Assn, Am Soc Oral & Maxillofacial Surgeons, Coastal District Dental Soc, Fed Dentaire Intl, Chalmers J Lyons Academy Oral Surgery, Navy League US, SC Dental Soc, SC Soc Oral & Maxillofacial Surgeons, Southeastern Soc Oral Maxillofacial Surgeons; pres: Med Univ SC *CLUB AFFIL* Anepa, Masons, Rotary

George J. Fountaine: dir

Donald Redfield Griffin: dir *B* Southampton NY 1915 *ED* Harvard Univ BS 1938; Harvard Univ MA 1940; Harvard Univ PhD 1942 *NONPR AFFIL* assoc: Mus Comparative Zoology; mem: Am Academy Arts Sciences, Am Ornithologists Union, Am Philosophical Soc, Am Physiological Soc, Am Soc Naturalists, Am Soc Zoologists, Ecological Soc Am, Natl Academy Sciences, Phi Beta Kappa, Sigma Xi; prof emeritus: Rockefeller Univ

James McNaughton Hester: pres, dir *B* Chester PA 1924 *ED* Princeton Univ BA 1945; Oxford Univ BA 1950; Oxford Univ PhD 1955 *CORP AFFIL* dir: Union Carbide Corp *NONPR AFFIL* dir: Alliance Fund; mem: Assn Am Rhodes Scholars, Counc Foreign Rels *CLUB AFFIL* Century Assn, Knickerbocker, Pretty Brook Tennis, Univ *PHIL AFFIL* dir: Robert Lehman Foundation

Joseph A. Koenigsberger: treas

Carol Langstaff: dir

Peter Orman Lawson-Johnston: chmn, dir *B* New York NY 1927 *ED* Univ VA 1951 *CURR EMPL* sr ptnr: Guggenheim Brothers *CORP AFFIL* chmn, dir: Zemex Corp; dir: Counc US Italy, Feldspar Corp, McGraw-Hill, Natl Review; ltd ptnr emeritus: Alexander Brown & Sons; pres, dir: Elgerbar Corp *NONPR AFFIL* mem adv bd: Jeffersonian Restoration *CLUB AFFIL* Bedens Brook, Brook, Carolina Plantation Soc, Century Assn, Edgartown Reading Room, Edgartown YC, Green Spring Valley Hunt, Island, Links, Medical, Nassau Gun, Pilgrims, Pretty Brook Tennis, River, Seminole GC, US Seniors Golf Assn, Yeamans Hall *PHIL AFFIL* pres, trust: Solomon R. Guggenheim Foundation

Theodore Davidge Lockwood: dir *B* Hanover NH 1924 *ED* Trinity Coll BA 1948; Princeton Univ MA 1950; Princeton Univ PhD 1952 *NONPR AFFIL* dir: Ars Publica; dir adv counc: Audubon Soc; mem: Assn Am Colls, Greater Hartford Chamber Commerce, Phi Beta Kappa, Pi Gamma Mu; mem Nepal adv comm: World Wildlife Fund; pres: Armand Hammer Un World Coll Am

Alan Jay Parrish Pifer: dir *B* Boston MA 1921 *ED* Emmanuel Coll 1947-1948; Harvard Univ AB 1947 *CORP AFFIL* dir: McGraw-Hill, Technoserve *NONPR AFFIL* chmn, pres: Southport Inst Policy Analysis;

dir: Bus Counc Effective Literacy, US-S Africa Leader Exchange Program; fellow: Am Academy Arts Sciences, Royal Soc Arts; fellow, fdr: African Studies Assn; mem: Am Assn Higher Ed, Counc Foreign Rels, Pilgrims US; trust: Univ Bridgeport *CLUB AFFIL* Century, Harvard

Floyd Ratliff: dir *B* La Junta CO 1919 *ED* CO Coll BA 1947; Brown Univ MS 1949; Brown Univ PhD 1950 *NONPR AFFIL* dir: Esperanza; fellow: Am Assn Advancement Science; mem: Am Inst Physics, Am Philosophical Soc, Am Psychological Assn, Am Psychological Soc, Asia Soc, China Inst Am, Intl Brain Res Org, Japan Soc, Manhattan Philosophical Soc, Oriental Ceramic Soc, Phi Beta Kappa, Sigma Xi; prof emeritus: Rockefeller Univ

Lois Dickson Rice: dir *B* Portland ME 1933 *ED* Columbia Univ 1954-1955; Radcliffe Coll AB 1954 *CORP AFFIL* dir: Chesapeake & Potomac Telephone Co, Firestone Tire & Rubber Co, Hartford Steam Boiler Inspection & Ins Co, Intl Multifoods, McGraw-Hill, Shawmut Natl Corp *NONPR AFFIL* dir: Joint Ctr Political & Econ Studies, Potomac Inst, Reading Is Fundamental; guest scholar: Brookings Inst Program Econ Studies; mem: Phi Beta Kappa, Urban Inst; overseer: Dartmouth Coll Tuck Sch Mgmt; trust: George Washington Univ *CLUB AFFIL* Cosmos

Rudy Lamont Ruggles, Jr.: dir *B* Evanston IL 1938 *ED* Harvard Univ BA 1960; Harvard Univ MBA 1966 *CURR EMPL* ptnr: Philadelphia Mgmt Consulting Group *NONPR AFFIL* dir: Danbury Hosp; mem: Inst Intl Strategic Studies, North Am Soc Corp Planning, US China Bus Counc; mem bd visitors: Georgetown Univ Sch Languages Linguistics; mem parents comm: St Pauls Sch; mng dir: New China Group; trust: New Canaan Country Sch *CLUB AFFIL* Explorers, Harvard, Silver Spring CC

Roger W. Straus: dir *B* New York NY 1917 *ED* Univ MO BJ 1939 *CURR EMPL* fdr, pres: Farrar Strauss & Giroux *CORP AFFIL* dir, ceo: Univ MO Press *PHIL AFFIL* trust emeritus: John Simon Guggenheim Memorial Foundation

Joan G. Van De Maele: dir

Joel Wallman: program off

William C. Westmoreland: dir

Mary-Alice Yates: secy

APPLICATION INFORMATION
Initial Approach:

Application form required. Submit six copies of a typewritten application in English to the foundation.

Applications should include a description of the project in plain English and its relevance to human dominance, aggression, and violence, a curricula vita and lists of relevant publications for the principal investigator and all professional personnel, an IRS tax-exempt determination letter if proposal is submitted by an institution, and a budget in dollars with justification of each item.

Deadlines are August 1 and February 1.

Applications are reviewed twice a year and final decisions are made by the board of directors at its meetings in December and June. Applicants will be informed promptly by letter of the board's decision.

Restrictions on Giving: The fondation will not accept applications for the support of meetings and conferences or travel costs for participants. The foundation ordinarily makes awards in the range of $15,000 to $35,000 a year for one or two years. The foundation provides grants for post-doctoral research projects and a Dissertation Fellowship program to support individuals during the writing of their Ph.D. thesis.

PUBLICATIONS
Biennial report, application guidelines

GRANTS ANALYSIS
Total Grants: $1,121,855*

Number of Grants: 46*

Highest Grant: $103,514

Average Grant: $22,077*

Typical Range: $15,000 to $35,000

Disclosure Period: 1992

Note: The figures for total grants, number of grants, and average grant exclude $410,733 in grants paid to individuals. Recent grants are derived from a 1992 Form 990.

RECENT GRANTS

Library

1,000	Foundation Center, New York, NY — general use

General

103,514	Harry Frank Guggenheim Foundation Publication Program, New York, NY — To Publish "Understanding Violence," a Review of Research Related to Violence, Aggression, and Dominance"
44,977	Duke University Department of Cultural Anthropology, Durham, NC — "Cultural Redefinition of Peace and Violence: The Invention and Diffusion of Gandhian Nonviolent Revolution"
34,975	American Institute of Physics, New York, NY — "The History of Peace Among Democracies"
34,951	University of Southern California, Los Angeles, CA — "Criminal Violence and Mental Illness in a Birth Cohort"
34,890	University of Virginia, Charlottesville, VA — "Assessment of Instrumental and Reactive Aggression in Violent Criminal Defendants"

Guttman Foundation, Stella and Charles

CONTACT
Elizabeth Olofson
Executive Director
The Stella & Charles Guttman Foundation
445 Park Ave., 19th Fl.
New York, NY 10022
(212) 371-7082

FINANCIAL SUMMARY
Recent Giving: $1,703,674 (1993); $679,800 (1992); $1,304,500 (1991)

Assets: $32,855,434 (1993); $30,558,515 (1992); $29,086,428 (1991)

EIN: 13-6103039

CONTRIBUTIONS SUMMARY
Donor(s): The foundation was incorporated in 1959 by the late Charles Guttman and the late Stella Guttman .

Typical Recipients: • *Arts & Humanities:* Dance, Libraries, Museums/Galleries, Music, Public Broadcasting • *Civic & Public Affairs:* Employment/Job Training, Public Policy, Urban & Community Affairs • *Education:* Colleges & Universities, Education Associations, Education Funds, Elementary Education (Public), Health & Physical Education, Medical Education, Minority Education, Public Education (Precollege), Religious Education, Special Education, Student Aid • *Environment:* Air/Water Quality, General • *Health:* AIDS/HIV, Alzheimers Disease, Cancer, Diabetes, Hospitals, Medical Research, Public Health, Single-Disease Health Associations • *International:* International Relations, International Relief Efforts, Missionary/Religious Activities • *Religion:* Jewish Causes, Religious Organizations, Religious Welfare • *Social Services:* Camps, Child Welfare, Community Centers, Community Service Organizations, Family Planning, Homes, People with Disabilities, Recreation & Athletics, Senior Services, United Funds/United Ways, Youth Organizations

Grant Types: capital, general support, operating expenses, and project

Geographic Distribution: focus on the New York, NY, metropolitan area

GIVING OFFICERS
Charles S. Brenner: dir

Edgar H. Brenner: vp, dir *B* New York NY 1930 *ED* Carleton Coll BA 1951; Yale Univ JD 1954 *NONPR AFFIL* mem: Am Bar Assn, DC Bar Assn; natl dir: Behavioral Law Ctr *CLUB AFFIL* mem: Explorers, Yale

Robert S. Gassman: treas, dir

Peter A. Herbert: dir

Elizabeth Olofson: exec dir

Abraham Rosenberg: pres, dir *PHIL AFFIL* pres, treas: Sunny and Abe Rosenberg Foundation

Sonia Rosenberg: secy, dir *PHIL AFFIL* vp, secy: Sunny and Abe Rosenberg Foundation

Ernest Rubenstein: dir

APPLICATION INFORMATION
Initial Approach:

The foundation requests applications be made in writing with complete details.

The foundation has no deadline for submitting proposals.

Restrictions on Giving: The foundation does not make grants to religious organizations for religious purposes, public interest litigation, anti-vivisectionist causes, individuals, or for foreign travel or study.

PUBLICATIONS
Informational brochure including application guidelines

GRANTS ANALYSIS
Total Grants: $679,800

Number of Grants: 73

Highest Grant: $100,000

Average Grant: $9,312

Typical Range: $2,000 to $15,000

Disclosure Period: 1992

Note: Recent grants are derived from a 1992 Form 990.

RECENT GRANTS

Library

6,000	New York Public Library, New York, NY — toward general support

General

100,000	United Jewish Appeal Federation of Jewish Philanthropies of New York, New York, NY — in support of Operation Exodus
35,000	Educational Alliance, New York, NY — general support
25,000	Clearpool — in conjunction with the Edwin Gould Foundation for Children; Clearpool, a residential summer camp in Carmel, NY, is collaborating with Bedford-Stuyvesant School District 16 to create a model year-round K-8 grade school with campuses at both locations
25,000	Henry Street Settlement, New York, NY — in support of Phase II of the settlement's capital campaign
25,000	Stella and Charles Guttman Breast Diagnostic Institute, New York, NY — general support

Hagedorn Fund

CONTACT
Robert C. Rosenthal
Vice President
Hagedorn Fund
c/o Chemical Bank
270 Park Ave., 23rd Fl.
New York, NY 10017
(212) 270-9107

FINANCIAL SUMMARY
Recent Giving: $1,305,000 (1995 est.); $1,305,000 (1994 est.); $1,290,000 (1993 est.)

Assets: $20,500,000 (1995 est.); $20,400,000 (1994 est.); $20,300,000 (1993 est.)

EIN: 13-6048718

CONTRIBUTIONS SUMMARY
Donor(s): The foundation was established in 1953 by the late William Hagedorn .

Typical Recipients: • *Arts & Humanities:* Libraries • *Civic & Public Affairs:* Botanical Gardens/Parks, Women's Affairs • *Education:* Colleges & Universities, Community & Junior Colleges, Legal Education, Minority Education, Private Education (Precollege), Religious Education, Student Aid • *Environment:* Resource Conservation • *Health:* AIDS/HIV, Arthritis, Cancer, Clinics/Medical Centers, Diabetes, Emergency/Ambulance Services, Eyes/Blindness, Health Policy/Cost Containment, Health Organizations, Heart, Hospices, Hospitals, Medical Rehabilitation, Mental Health • *International:* Health Care/Hospitals • *Religion:* Churches, Religious Welfare, Seminaries, Synagogues/Temples • *Social Services:* Child Welfare, Community Service Organizations, Counseling, Family Planning, Family Services, Food/Clothing Distribution, General, People with Disabilities, Recreation & Athletics, Shelters/Homelessness, United Funds/United Ways, YMCA/YWCA/YMHA/YWHA, Youth Organizations

Grant Types: capital, general support, operating expenses, and scholarship

Geographic Distribution: Northeastern United States, with a focus on New York, NY

GIVING OFFICERS
William J. Fischer, Jr.: trust

Charles B. Lauren: trust

Robert C. Rosenthal: vp *B* New Rochelle NY 1933 *ED* Bucknell Univ 1955 *CURR EMPL* pres, dir: Absolute Coatings

APPLICATION INFORMATION
Initial Approach:

The foundation has no formal grant application procedure or application form.

The foundation has no deadline for submitting proposals.

Restrictions on Giving: The foundation does not make grants to individuals, or for continuing support, seed money, emergency funds, deficit financing, endowment funds, matching gifts, scholarships, fellowships, research, special projects, publications, conferences, or loans.

GRANTS ANALYSIS
Total Grants: $1,335,000
Number of Grants: 120
Highest Grant: $90,000
Average Grant: $11,125
Typical Range: $1,000 to $15,000
Disclosure Period: 1992

Note: Recent grants are derived from a 1992 Form 990.

RECENT GRANTS

Library
25,000	New York Public Library, New York, NY

General
90,000	Wells College, Aurora, NY
30,000	St. Matthews Church, New York, NY
25,000	Children Aid Society, New York, NY
25,000	Hospice of Martin, Martin, NY
25,000	Immaculate Conception Church, New York, NY

Handy and Harman Foundation

Income: $781.04 million
Employees: 4,826
SIC Major Group: Chemicals & Allied Products, Primary Metal Industries, and Transportation Equipment

CONTACT
Richard N. Daniel
Chief Executive Officer
Handy & Harman
250 Park Ave.
New York, NY 10177
(212) 661-2400

FINANCIAL SUMMARY
Recent Giving: $151,317 (1994); $148,455 (1993); $163,275 (1992)
Assets: $31,739 (1993); $29,248 (1992); $41,164 (1991)
Gifts Received: $150,000 (1992); $150,000 (1991); $150,000 (1990)
EIN: 23-7408431

CONTRIBUTIONS SUMMARY
Typical Recipients: • *Arts & Humanities:* Arts Centers, Community Arts, General, Libraries, Museums/Galleries, Public Broadcasting • *Civic & Public Affairs:* Botanical Gardens/Parks, Business/Free Enterprise, Clubs, Community Foundations, Economic Development, Economic Policy, Employment/Job Training, General, Inner-City Development, Law & Justice, Legal Aid, Public Policy, Safety, Urban & Community Affairs, Zoos/Aquariums • *Education:* Arts/Humanities Education, Business Education, Colleges & Universities, Economic

Education, Education Funds, Engineering/Technological Education, General, Legal Education, Medical Education, Minority Education, Public Education (Precollege), Secondary Education (Public) • *Health:* Arthritis, Cancer, Children's Health/Hospitals, Clinics/Medical Centers, Diabetes, Eyes/Blindness, General, Health Organizations, Heart, Home-Care Services, Hospitals, Hospitals (University Affiliated), Medical Training, Nursing Services • *International:* International Affairs • *Religion:* Dioceses, General • *Social Services:* Camps, Community Centers, Community Service Organizations, Domestic Violence, Emergency Relief, General, Recreation & Athletics, Substance Abuse, United Funds/United Ways, Youth Organizations

Grant Types: general support

Geographic Distribution: principally near operating locations and to national organizations

Operating Locations: CT (Fairfield, South Windsor), IN (Bedford, Carmel, Evansville), MA (North Attleboro), MD (Cockeysville), MI (Auburn Hills), NJ (Willingboro), NY (New York, Oriskany, Rye), OH (Dover), OK (Tulsa), PA (Norristown), WI (Cudahy)

GIVING OFFICERS
Richard N. Daniel: pres, dir *B* Brooklyn NY 1935 *ED* St Johns Univ BBA 1957; Univ PA Wharton Sch MBA 1959 *CURR EMPL* chmn, ceo, dir: Handy & Harman

Richard N. Daniel: pres, dir *CURR EMPL* chmn, ceo, dir: Handy & Harman (see above)

Paul E. Dixon: secy

Frank E. Grzelecki: off *CURR EMPL* pres, coo: Handy & Harman

Stephen B. Mudd: vp, dir *B* Jefferson City MO 1932 *ED* St Louis Univ 1954 *CURR EMPL* vp, treas: Handy & Harman *NONPR AFFIL* mem: Am Inst CPAs, Fin Execs Inst

APPLICATION INFORMATION
Initial Approach: Requests should be in writing on organization's letterhead. Include a description of organization, amount requested, and proof of tax-exempt status. There are no deadlines.

Restrictions on Giving: Does not support individuals, religious organizations for sectarian purposes, political or lobbying groups, or organizations outside operating areas.

GRANTS ANALYSIS
Total Grants: $148,455
Number of Grants: 206
Highest Grant: $27,000
Typical Range: $100 to $9,000
Disclosure Period: 1993

Note: Recent grants are derived from a 1993 Form 990.

RECENT GRANTS

General
27,000	United Way Tri-State, New York, NY
25,000	United Way Eastern Fairfield County, Fairfield, CT
9,000	United Way of Greater Milwaukee, Milwaukee, WI
6,000	United Way of Tuscarawas County, New Philadelphia, PA
4,000	Tax Foundation, Washington, DC

Hanson Industries North America / Hanson White Foundation

Sales: $14.61 billion
Employees: 80,000
Parent Company: Hanson PLC
Headquarters: New York, NY
SIC Major Group: Inorganic Pigments, Residential Lighting Fixtures, Commercial Lighting Fixtures, and Construction Machinery

CONTACT
Isabel Cardin
Director, Special Projects
Hanson Industries North America
410 Park Ave., 20th Fl.
New York, NY 10022
(212) 759-8477

FINANCIAL SUMMARY
Recent Giving: $375,000 (1994 approx.); $315,450 (1993); $324,900 (1992)
Assets: $23,351 (1993); $63,941 (1992)
Gifts Received: $275,000 (1993); $350,000 (1992)
Fiscal Note: Company gives through the foundation only. In 1993, contributions were received from H.M. Anglo American Ltd.
EIN: 16-6039441

CONTRIBUTIONS SUMMARY
Typical Recipients: • *Arts & Humanities:* History & Archaeology, Libraries, Theater • *Civic & Public Affairs:* Clubs, Economic Development, Employment/Job Training, Philanthropic Organizations, Public Policy, Urban & Community Affairs • *Education:* Colleges & Universities, Education Funds, Education Reform, Environmental Education, General, International Exchange, Medical Education, Minority Education, Public Education (Precollege), Student Aid • *Health:* AIDS/HIV, Alzheimers Disease, Cancer, Children's Health/Hospitals, Diabetes, Eyes/Blindness, Hospitals, Medical Research, Multiple Sclerosis, Single-Disease Health Associations, Speech & Hearing, Transplant Networks/Donor Banks • *International:* Foreign Educational Institutions, International Organizations, International Relief Efforts • *Science:* Science Museums, Scientific Labs • *Social Services:* Child Welfare, Community Service Organizations, Domestic Violence, Family Services, People with Disabilities, Substance Abuse, United Funds/United Ways, Veterans

Grant Types: general support

Geographic Distribution: principally near operating locations and to national organizations

Operating Locations: AL, AZ, CA, FL, IN, MD, MI, MO, MS, NJ, NY, OK, PA, RI, TX, WA, WV

CORP. OFFICERS
Isabel Cardin: *CURR EMPL* dir special projects: Hanson Indus N Am

Robert E. Lee: *CURR EMPL* sr vp, coo: Hanson Indus N Am

John E. Lushefski: *CURR EMPL* sr vp, cfo: Hanson Indus N Am

GIVING OFFICERS
Steven C. Barre: asst secy

G. H. Hempstead III: vp, secy *CURR EMPL* sr vp, secy, gen coun: Hanson Indus N Am

Robert E. Lee: vp, treas *CURR EMPL* sr vp, coo: Hanson Indus N Am (see above)

Dorothy E. Sander: vp *CURR EMPL* vp admin & benefits: Hanson Indus N Am

APPLICATION INFORMATION
Initial Approach: *Initial Contact:* letter of inquiry *Include Information On:* a description of organization and proof of tax-exempt status *Deadlines:* none

Restrictions on Giving: Does not support religious organizations for sectarian purposes or political or lobbying groups.

GRANTS ANALYSIS
Total Grants: $315,450

Number of Grants: 52

Highest Grant: $100,000

Average Grant: $6,066

Typical Range: $2,000 to $25,000

Disclosure Period: 1993

Note: Recent grants are derived from a 1993 Form 990.

RECENT GRANTS

Library

100,000	Ronald Reagan Presidential Foundation, Washington, DC — for general support
5,000	Recording for the Blind, Princeton, NJ — to provide recorded and computerized textbooks and library services to the blind
5,000	Recording for the Blind, Princeton, NJ —to provide recorded and computerized textbooks and library services to the blind
5,000	Winston Churchill Memorial and Library, Fulton, MO —for restoration of memorial and library building
5,000	Winston Churchill Memorial and Library in the US Westminister College in Fulton, Missouri, Fulton, MO — for restoration of memorial and library building

General

25,000	Children's Diabetes Foundation, Denver, CO — to further programs of care and research on behalf of those afflicted with diabetes
25,000	Children's Diabetes Foundation, Denver, CO —to further programs of care and research on behalf of those afflicted with diabetes
25,000	United Nations International Children Educational Foundation, New York, NY — to support a full range of child survival and developmental programs
25,000	United Nations International Children Educational Foundation, New York, NY —to support a full range of child survival and developmental programs
25,000	United Negro College Fund, New York, NY — to help African Americans overcome the cultural and financial obstacles to a higher education

---

HarperCollins Publishers Inc.

Sales: $750.0 million
Employees: 3,500
Parent Company: News Corp., Ltd.
Headquarters: New York, NY
SIC Major Group: Printing & Publishing

CONTACT
Karen Berberich
Administrative Assistant
HarperCollins Publishers Inc.
10 E 53rd St.
New York, NY 10022
(212) 207-7555

FINANCIAL SUMMARY
Fiscal Note: Company does not disclose contributions figures.

CONTRIBUTIONS SUMMARY
HarperCollins has no set program description, but generally limits its giving to "publishing-related" projects in its areas of operation.

Typical Recipients: • *Arts & Humanities:* Ethnic & Folk Arts, Libraries, Literary Arts • *Civic & Public Affairs:* First Amendment Issues, Women's Affairs • *Education:* General, Literacy, Minority Education • *Social Services:* Community Service Organizations, Family Services, Volunteer Services

Grant Types: employee matching gifts and general support

Nonmonetary Support Types: donated products and workplace solicitation

Note: Workplace solicitation is United Way only.

Geographic Distribution: principally near operating locations and to national organizations

Operating Locations: CA, IL, MI, NY (New York), PA

CORP. OFFICERS
William Baker: *B* Brooklyn NY 1935 *ED* St Johns Univ Brooklyn BBA 1957; Lace Univ MBA 1967 *CURR EMPL* group vp, cao: HarperCollins Publs *NONPR AFFIL* mem: Am Inst Certified Pub Accts, Fin Execs Inst, Masons *CLUB AFFIL* mem: University

George Craig: *CURR EMPL* pres, ceo, dir: HarperCollins Publs *CORP AFFIL* dir: News Corp Ltd *NONPR AFFIL* mem, dir: Assn Am Pubs; mem ed adv bd: Pubs Weekly Intl

Neil Topham: *CURR EMPL* group vp, cfo, dir: HarperCollins Publs

GIVING OFFICERS
Karen Berberich: *CURR EMPL* admin asst: HarperCollins Publs

Barbara Hufham: *CURR EMPL* sr vp, human resources: HarperCollins Publs

APPLICATION INFORMATION
Initial Approach: Initial letter and proposal, addressed to Karen Berberich, may be submitted at any time and should include a description of the organization, amount requested, purpose for which funds are sought, a recently audited financial statement, and proof of tax-exempt status.

Restrictions on Giving: Does not support fraternal organizations, individuals, member agencies of united funds, political or lobbying groups, or religious organizations for sectarian purposes.

GRANTS ANALYSIS
Total Grants:

Disclosure Period: 1994

Note: Recent grants are derived from a grants list provided by company in 1995. Grant size varies.

RECENT GRANTS

Library
Friends of Libraries USA, Chicago, IL
New York Public Library, New York, NY

General
National Center for Family Literacy, Louisville, KY
New York City School Volunteer Program, New York, NY
Parents Choice Foundation, Waban, MA
Publishing Institute, Denver, CO
Women's National Book Association, Chatsworth, CA

Harriman Foundation, Gladys and Roland

CONTACT
William F. Hibberd
Secretary
Gladys and Roland Harriman Foundation
63 Wall St., 13th Fl.
New York, NY 10005
(212) 493-8182

FINANCIAL SUMMARY

Recent Giving: $4,752,842 (1993); $4,434,899 (1992); $4,353,324 (1991)

Assets: $99,490,110 (1993); $94,115,419 (1992); $99,136,422 (1991)

Gifts Received: $1,200,000 (1993); $1,200,000 (1992); $1,200,000 (1991)

Fiscal Note: The foundation receives funds from the trusts of Gladys F. and E. Roland Harriman.

EIN: 51-0193915

CONTRIBUTIONS SUMMARY

Donor(s): The foundation was established in 1966 by the late Gladys Harriman and Roland Harriman. Their trusts continue to support the foundation.

Typical Recipients: • *Arts & Humanities:* Ballet, Historic Preservation, History & Archaeology, Libraries, Museums/Galleries, Public Broadcasting • *Civic & Public Affairs:* Economic Development, Employment/Job Training, General, Public Policy, Urban & Community Affairs • *Education:* Colleges & Universities, Elementary Education (Public), Engineering/Technological Education, Medical Education, Private Education (Precollege), Public Education (Precollege), Secondary Education (Private), Student Aid • *Environment:* Air/Water Quality, General, Resource Conservation • *Health:* Cancer, Clinics/Medical Centers, Diabetes, Emergency/Ambulance Services, Geriatric Health, Health Organizations, Hospitals, Medical Research, Speech & Hearing • *International:* Foreign Educational Institutions • *Religion:* Seminaries • *Science:* Science Museums • *Social Services:* Big Brother/Big Sister, Child Welfare, Community Service Organizations, Domestic Violence, Family Services, Substance Abuse, Youth Organizations

Grant Types: general support

Geographic Distribution: nationally, with an emphasis on New York, NY

GIVING OFFICERS

William J. Corcoran: treas *PHIL AFFIL* treas: Mary W. Harriman Foundation, Mary H. Rumsey Foundation

Thomas F. Dixon: dir

Terrence Michael Farley: dir *B* New York NY 1930 *ED* City Coll NY BBA 1955 *CURR EMPL* mng ptnr: Brown Brothers Harriman & Co *CORP AFFIL* dir: Atlantic Reinsurance Co, Centennial Ins Co; trust: Atlantic Mutual Ins Co, Overlook Hosp Fdn *CLUB AFFIL* Echo Lake CC, India House, Links, Univ, Wianno

Elbridge Thomas Gerry: pres, dir *B* New York NY 1908 *ED* Harvard Univ BA 1931 *CURR EMPL* ptnr: Brown Brothers Harriman & Co *CORP AFFIL* dir: Doubleday & Co; ptnr: Gerry Bros & Co *PHIL AFFIL* dir: Mary W. Harriman Foundation

Elbridge Thomas Gerry, Jr.: dir *B* New York NY 1933 *ED* Harvard Univ AB 1955 *CURR EMPL* ptnr: Brown Brothers Harriman & Co *CORP AFFIL* chmn: Instoria; chmn, dir: Providentia Ltd; dir: Royal Ins Co, Union Pacific Corp *NONPR AFFIL*

pres: NY Society; treas: Hall Fame Trotter *PHIL AFFIL* treas, trust: Brown Brothers Harriman & Co. Undergraduate Fund

William F. Hibberd: secy *PHIL AFFIL* secy: Mary W. Harriman Foundation; trust: Irving Hansen Memorial Foundation; dir: J. Homer Butler Foundation

Edward Harriman Northrop: dir *B* New York NY 1943 *ED* Dartmouth Coll BA 1966; Univ VA MBA 1971 *CURR EMPL* chmn: Xicom Inc *PHIL AFFIL* dir: Mary W. Harriman Foundation

William Rich III: vp *CURR EMPL* pres: Middleburg Mgmt Corp *CORP AFFIL* chmn: Princeton-New York Investors *PHIL AFFIL* vp: Mary W. Harriman Foundation

APPLICATION INFORMATION

Initial Approach:

Applicants should submit a written proposal.

Proposals should be typed and include the organization's history and details of its program.

There are no application deadlines.

Restrictions on Giving: There are no restrictions or limitations on grants.

OTHER THINGS TO KNOW

The foundation shares office space and members of the board of directors with the Mary W. Harriman Foundation, New York, NY.

GRANTS ANALYSIS

Total Grants: $4,752,842

Number of Grants: 88

Highest Grant: $750,000

Average Grant: $54,010

Typical Range: $10,000 to $75,000

Disclosure Period: 1993

Note: Recent grants are derived from a 1993 Form 990.

RECENT GRANTS

Library

105,000	Tuxedo Park Library, Tuxedo Park, NY
35,000	New York Public Library, New York, NY

General

750,000	New York Hospital Cornell Medical Center, New York, NY
270,000	Columbia University, New York, NY
265,000	Arden Hill Foundation, Goshen, NY
265,000	Good Samaritan Hospital, Suffern, NY
187,500	Children's Family Center of Idaho, Boise, ID

Harriman Foundation, Mary W.

CONTACT

William F. Hibberd
Secretary
Mary W. Harriman Foundation
63 Wall St., 13th Fl.
New York, NY 10005
(212) 493-8182

FINANCIAL SUMMARY

Recent Giving: $913,000 (1995 est.); $913,000 (1994 approx.); $952,200 (1993)

Assets: $23,000,000 (1995 est.); $23,000,000 (1994 approx.); $21,930,312 (1993)

EIN: 23-7356000

CONTRIBUTIONS SUMMARY

Donor(s): The Mary W. Harriman Foundation was established in New York in 1925 and incorporated in 1973, with funds donated by the late Mary W. Harriman , wife of Union Pacific Railroad magnate and financier Edward Henry Harriman.

Typical Recipients: • *Arts & Humanities:* Ballet, Film & Video, History & Archaeology, Libraries, Museums/Galleries, Music, Performing Arts, Public Broadcasting • *Civic & Public Affairs:* Botanical Gardens/Parks, Clubs, Public Policy • *Education:* Colleges & Universities, Education Associations, Faculty Development, General, International Studies, Medical Education, Private Education (Precollege), Public Education (Precollege), Religious Education, School Volunteerism, Secondary Education (Private) • *Environment:* General, Wildlife Protection • *Health:* AIDS/HIV, Cancer, Children's Health/Hospitals, Emergency/Ambulance Services, Hospices, Hospitals, Mental Health • *International:* International Affairs, International Relations • *Science:* Science Museums • *Social Services:* Counseling, Family Planning, Family Services, People with Disabilities, Recreation & Athletics, Volunteer Services, Youth Organizations

Grant Types: department, general support, project, and research

Geographic Distribution: primarily New York City metropolitan area

GIVING OFFICERS

William J. Corcoran: treas *PHIL AFFIL* treas: Gladys and Roland Harriman Foundation, Mary H. Rumsey Foundation

Mary A. Fisk: dir

Elbridge Thomas Gerry: dir *B* New York NY 1908 *ED* Harvard Univ BA 1931 *CURR EMPL* ptnr: Brown Brothers Harriman & Co *CORP AFFIL* dir: Doubleday & Co; ptnr: Gerry Bros & Co *PHIL AFFIL* pres, dir: Gladys and Roland Harriman Foundation

William F. Hibberd: secy *PHIL AFFIL* secy: Gladys and Roland Harriman Foundation; trust: Irving Hansen Memorial Foundation; dir: J. Homer Butler Foundation

Kathleen H. Mortimer: pres, dir *PHIL AFFIL* chmn counc: Foundation for Child Development

Edward Harriman Northrop: dir *B* New York NY 1943 *ED* Dartmouth Coll BA 1966; Univ VA MBA 1971 *CURR EMPL* chmn: Xicom Inc *PHIL AFFIL* dir: Gladys and Roland Harriman Foundation

William Rich III: vp *CURR EMPL* pres: Middleburg Mgmt Corp *CORP AFFIL* chmn: Princeton-New York Investors *PHIL AFFIL* vp: Gladys and Roland Harriman Foundation

APPLICATION INFORMATION
Initial Approach:

Applicants should submit a written proposal.

Proposals should be typed and include the organization's history and details of its program.

There are no deadlines for submitting proposals.

OTHER THINGS TO KNOW
The foundation shares office space and members of the board of directors with the Gladys and Roland Harriman Foundation.

GRANTS ANALYSIS
Total Grants: $952,200

Number of Grants: 108

Highest Grant: $50,000

Average Grant: $8,817

Typical Range: $1,000 to $25,000

Disclosure Period: 1993

Note: Recent grants are derived from a 1993 Form 990.

RECENT GRANTS

General

50,000	American Assembly, New York, NY
50,000	Kennan Institute for Advanced Russian Studies, Washington, DC
35,000	Boys Club of New York, New York, NY
30,000	Bennington College, Bennington, VT
30,000	Scenic Hudson, Poughkeepsie, NY

Hartford Foundation, John A.

CONTACT
Richard S. Sharpe
Program Director
John A. Hartford Foundation
55 E 59th St.
New York, NY 10022-1178
(212) 832-7788

FINANCIAL SUMMARY
Recent Giving: $13,650,000 (1994 approx.); $12,082,976 (1993); $11,300,483 (1992)

Assets: $350,000,000 (1994 approx.); $339,301,353 (1993); $304,106,083 (1992)

Gifts Received: $50,000 (1988); $2,100,000 (1986)

Fiscal Note: In 1986, the foundation received bequests totaling $2,100,000 from the estate of Loretta D. Ehrgott.

EIN: 13-1667057

CONTRIBUTIONS SUMMARY
Donor(s): The John A. Hartford Foundation was established in 1929 by the late John A. Hartford (d. 1951) and George L. Hartford Jr. (d. 1957). The donors were the sons of George Huntington Hartford who, with George F. Gilman, founded the Great Atlantic and Pacific Tea Company in 1869 (which became the A&P foodstore chain). Upon their father's death in 1917, George Hartford, Jr. became chairman of the company, and John Hartford, the president. The brothers left the bulk of their estates to the foundation. Although the foundation formerly held a great deal of A&P stock, its holdings have been diversified and its portfolio no longer contains A&P stock.

Typical Recipients: • *Arts & Humanities:* Arts Associations & Councils, Ethnic & Folk Arts, Libraries • *Civic & Public Affairs:* Nonprofit Management, Philanthropic Organizations, Professional & Trade Associations, Public Policy • *Education:* Colleges & Universities, Medical Education, Minority Education, Private Education (Precollege) • *Health:* Clinics/Medical Centers, Geriatric Health, Health Policy/Cost Containment, Health Funds, Health Organizations, Hospitals, Long-Term Care, Medical Rehabilitation, Medical Research, Medical Training, Research/Studies Institutes • *Religion:* Religious Welfare • *Social Services:* At-Risk Youth, Community Service Organizations, People with Disabilities, Volunteer Services, Youth Organizations

Grant Types: project

Geographic Distribution: national

GIVING OFFICERS
Richard A. Cramer: trust

Michael David Dingman: trust *B* New Haven CT 1931 *ED* Univ MD *CURR EMPL* chmn, ceo: Gen Chem Group *PHIL AFFIL* pres: Michael D. Dingman Foundation; dir, ptnr: Chatam Inc.; dir: Devonshire Trust; dir, ptnr: Lincolnshire; dir: Henley Manufacturing Charitable Foundation

Stephen Carstairs Eyre: exec dir, treas *B* New York NY 1922 *ED* Yale Univ 1947; Pace Univ 1981 *CORP AFFIL* chmn: Locust Valley Cemetery Assn; dir: Faircom Inc, Prudential Global Fund, Prudential Pacific Growth Fund, Prudential Short-Term Global Fund; pres: Delmonico Plaza Condominium; treas: Soc St Johnland, St Johnland Nursing Home; trust: Pace Univ, Prudential US Govt Fund *NONPR AFFIL* chmn: Locust Valley Cemetary Assn; chmn exec comm, dir: Intl House; treas, dir: Soc St Johnland; trust: Pace Univ

James Duncan Farley: chmn, trust *B* Chicago IL 1926 *ED* Georgetown Univ BS 1949 *CORP AFFIL* dir: Moore Corp *NONPR AFFIL* trust: Georgetown Univ *CLUB AFFIL* Birnham Wood GC, Cypress Point, Loblolly Pines GC, Los Angeles CC, Round Hill, The Valley, Wequetonsing GC *PHIL AFFIL* trust: Marie G. Dennett Foundation

Samuel R. Gische: fin dir, contr *B* 1953 *ED* Queens Coll 1975; NY Univ MBA 1983

Alexander Mellon Laughlin: trust *ED* Yale Univ BA 1949 *CURR EMPL* investment broker: Deltec Securities Corp

Robert Henry Mulreany: secy, trust *B* Brooklyn NY 1915 *ED* NY Univ LLB 1940 *CURR EMPL* of couns: DeForest & Duer *CORP AFFIL* pres, trust: Provident Loan Soc *NONPR AFFIL* mem: Am Bar Assn, Assn Bar City New York *CLUB AFFIL* Bay Head YC, Downtown Assn, Echo Lake CC, Univ *PHIL AFFIL* trust: Smith Richardson Foundation

Charles E. Murphy, Jr.: vchmn, trust *CURR EMPL* sr ptnr: Whitman & Ransom

Nuala Pell: trust

Thomas A. Reynolds, Jr.: trust

Richard S. Sharpe: program dir

Norman Hans Volk: vchmn, trust *B* New York NY 1935 *ED* Valparaiso Univ BA 1957; Marquette Univ MA 1959 *CURR EMPL* pres: Chamberlain & Steward Assoc *CORP AFFIL* trust: John Hartford Fnd *CLUB AFFIL* Doubles, Univ, Univ Glee NY

Kathryn Dineen Wriston: trust *B* Syracuse NY *ED* Univ Geneva 1958-1959; Smith Coll BA 1960; Univ MI LLB 1963 *CORP AFFIL* bd: Rand Inst for Civil Justive; bd dir: AICPA, Am Arbitration Assn, Ctrs for Pub Resources, John A. Hartford Fnd, Northwestern Mutual Life Ins Co, Santa Fe Energy Resources; chmn: Presidents Commn White House Fellows *NONPR AFFIL* bd dir: Am Arbitration Assn; bd overseers: Rand Inst Civil Justice; bdd dir: Ctrs Pub Resources; dir: Am Inst CPAs, Fin Accounting Fdn; mem: Am Bar Assn, Assn Bar City New York, Fin Womens Assn, Natl Assn Accts, NY County Lawyers Assn, State Bar Assn; mem visiting comm: Univ MI Law Sch; vp: Practicing Law Inst

APPLICATION INFORMATION
Initial Approach:

Applicants are requested to describe the proposed activity in a letter of inquiry. Initial inquiries should be made at least six months before funding is needed.

Applicants should submit concise project descriptions and proposals outlining the nature and importance of the problem to be addressed; specific solution to be designed or evaluated; ways the proposed solution differs from other projects addressing the same problem; what unique contributions the project will make; criteria for measuring the project's success; relevant experience and expertise of key personnel; and the amount of funds needed. Preference will be given to projects that seek to demonstrate and evaluate specific innovative solutions to clearly defined problems.

Applicants may submit proposals any time. Although the foundation requires no formal application, it expects applicants to be familiar with the guidelines and interests of the foundation. Current program guidelines may be obtained by contacting the foundation. The proposed project will be reviewed by members of the foundation's staff and possibly by outside reviewers. Results of this review will be sent within approximately one month.

Restrictions on Giving: Grants are made only to organizations with tax-exempt status under IRS section 501(c)(3) and which are not private foundations under sections 509(a) or 170(c)(1). No grants are given to individuals. Support is not provided for general research. Rarely will the foundation support projects for longer than three years.

PUBLICATIONS
Annual report

GRANTS ANALYSIS
Total Grants: $10,819,066*

Number of Grants: 75

Highest Grant: $932,260

Average Grant: $144,254

Typical Range: $50,000 to $300,000

Disclosure Period: 1993

Note: Total grants figure excludes $288,100 in matching grants and $975,810 in foundation-administered projects. Total giving figure is $12,082,976. Recent grants are derived from a 1993 annual report.

RECENT GRANTS

Library

20,000	New York Public Library Astor, Lenox and Tilden Foundation, New York, NY
8,000	Foundation Center, New York, NY

General

932,260	National Business Coalition on Health, Washington, DC — "Expanding the Community Health Reform Movement"
637,986	American Federation for Aging Research (AFAR), New York, NY — "Medical Student Geriatric Scholars Program"
564,045	California Pacific Medical Center, San Francisco, CA — "Senior Care Connections"
398,900	Institute for Healthcare Improvement, Boston, MA — core support
387,275	Interfaith Health Care Ministries, Providence, RI — "Aging 2000: Systemic Change in Care for the Elderly in Rhode Island"

Hatch Charitable Trust, Margaret Milliken

CONTACT
Donna Daniels
Vice President
Margaret Milliken Hatch Charitable Trust
c/o The Bank of New York
706 Madison Ave.
New York, NY 10021
(212) 527-3729

FINANCIAL SUMMARY
Recent Giving: $1,890,000 (fiscal 1993); $421,582 (fiscal 1992); $3,087,059 (fiscal 1991)

Assets: $3,633,402 (fiscal 1993); $4,964,925 (fiscal 1992); $5,110,926 (fiscal 1991)

Gifts Received: $95,799 (fiscal 1990)

EIN: 13-6330533

CONTRIBUTIONS SUMMARY
Donor(s): the late Margaret Milliken Hatch

Typical Recipients: • *Arts & Humanities:* General, Libraries • *Civic & Public Affairs:* Zoos/Aquariums • *Education:* Colleges & Universities, Education Funds, Medical Education, Minority Education, Science/Mathematics Education, Student Aid • *Health:* Cancer, Clinics/Medical Centers, Hospitals • *International:* International Affairs, International Development • *Religion:* Churches, Religious Welfare • *Social Services:* Animal Protection, Senior Services, United Funds/United Ways, YMCA/YWCA/YMHA/YWHA, Youth Organizations

Grant Types: emergency and general support

Geographic Distribution: focus on NY and CT

GIVING OFFICERS
Bank of New York: trust

Rakia I. Hatch: trust

Richard L. Hatch: trust

APPLICATION INFORMATION
Initial Approach: Send brief letter of inquiry describing program or project. There are no deadlines.

Restrictions on Giving: Does not support individuals.

GRANTS ANALYSIS
Total Grants: $1,890,000

Number of Grants: 13

Highest Grant: $1,010,000

Typical Range: $1,000 to $850,000

Disclosure Period: fiscal year ending October 31, 1993

Note: Recent grants are derived from a fiscal 1993 Form 990.

RECENT GRANTS

General

1,010,000	Columbia Presbyterian Medical Center, New York,

	NY — Hatch Professorship Chair
850,000	Rockefeller University, New York, NY — renovation of McEwen Lab and Research Facility
6,000	Cancer Research Institute, New York, NY
6,000	Near East Foundation, New York, NY
3,000	Ladies Christian Union, New York, NY

Hauser Foundation

CONTACT
Rita Hauser
Manager
Hauser Fdn.
712 Fifth Ave.
New York, NY 10021
(212) 956-3645

FINANCIAL SUMMARY
Recent Giving: $374,501 (fiscal 1993); $244,800 (fiscal 1992); $106,180 (fiscal 1990)

Assets: $13,028,803 (fiscal 1993); $6,698,245 (fiscal 1992); $5,797,850 (fiscal 1990)

Gifts Received: $6,231,000 (fiscal 1993); $5,500,000 (fiscal 1990)

Fiscal Note: In fiscal 1993, contributions were received from Gustave and Rita Hauser.

EIN: 11-0016142

CONTRIBUTIONS SUMMARY
Typical Recipients: • *Arts & Humanities:* Arts Institutes, Libraries, Museums/Galleries, Music, Opera, Visual Arts • *Civic & Public Affairs:* Civil Rights, Clubs, General, Professional & Trade Associations, Public Policy, Urban & Community Affairs, Women's Affairs • *Education:* International Studies, Legal Education, Private Education (Precollege), Social Sciences Education • *Environment:* General • *Health:* AIDS/HIV, Research/Studies Institutes • *International:* Foreign Educational Institutions, Human Rights, International Affairs, International Development, International Organizations, International Peace & Security Issues, International Relations • *Religion:* Jewish Causes • *Science:* Scientific Centers & Institutes • *Social Services:* Family Services, Food/Clothing Distribution, Refugee Assistance, Substance Abuse, YMCA/YWCA/YMHA/YWHA

Grant Types: general support

Geographic Distribution: focus on New York, NY

GIVING OFFICERS
Gustave Hauser: vp

Rita Hauser: mgr

APPLICATION INFORMATION
Initial Approach: Send a brief letter of inquiry. There are no deadlines.

GRANTS ANALYSIS
Total Grants: $374,501

Number of Grants: 71

Highest Grant: $151,800

Typical Range: $100 to $50,000

Disclosure Period: fiscal year ending November 30, 1993

Note: Recent grants are derived from a fiscal 1993 Form 990.

RECENT GRANTS

Library

600	Gunn Memorial Library, Washington Depot, CT

General

151,800	Council on Foreign Relations, New York, NY
50,000	Graduate Institute of International Studies
50,000	International Peace Academy, New York, NY
15,000	Environmental Law Institute, Washington, DC
11,000	Human Rights Watch, New York, NY

Hazen Foundation, Edward W.

CONTACT
Barbara Taveras
Executive Director
Edward W. Hazen Foundation
60 Madison Ave., Rm. 1110
New York, NY 10010
(212) 889-3034

FINANCIAL SUMMARY
Recent Giving: $665,000 (1995 est.); $577,088 (1994); $321,788 (1993)

Assets: $17,000,000 (1995 est.); $16,900,000 (1994 approx.); $16,788,901 (1993)

EIN: 06-0646671

CONTRIBUTIONS SUMMARY
Donor(s): The foundation was incorporated in 1925 by the late Edward Warriner Hazen , the late Helen Russell Hazen , the late Lucy Abigail Hazen , and the late Mary Hazen Arnold .

Typical Recipients: • *Arts & Humanities:* Arts Funds, Arts Outreach, Libraries, Music, Public Broadcasting • *Civic & Public Affairs:* African American Affairs, Asian American Affairs, Community Foundations, Employment/Job Training, Gay/Lesbian Issues, General, Hispanic Affairs, Housing, Law & Justice, Legal Aid, Native American Affairs, Nonprofit Management, Philanthropic Organizations, Professional & Trade Associations, Public Policy, Rural Affairs, Safety, Urban & Community Affairs, Women's Affairs, Zoos/Aquariums • *Education:* Education Funds, Education Reform, General, Leadership Training, Legal Education, Minority Education, Private Education (Precollege), Public Education (Precollege), School Volunteerism, Science/Mathematics Education • *Environment:* Air/Water Quality, General, Resource Conservation • *Health:* AIDS/HIV, Medical Research, Mental Health, Single-Disease Health Associations • *International:* Foreign Arts Organizations, Human Rights, International Affairs, International Environmental Issues, International Relations • *Religion:* Churches, Ministries, Religious Organizations, Religious Welfare • *Science:* Scientific Labs • *Social Services:* At-Risk Youth, Child Welfare, Community Service Organizations, Crime Prevention, Delinquency & Criminal Rehabilitation, Family Services, Food/Clothing Distribution, Homes, Refugee Assistance, Shelters/Homelessness, United Funds/United Ways, YMCA/YWCA/YMHA/YWHA, Youth Organizations

Grant Types: project and seed money

Geographic Distribution: national

GIVING OFFICERS
Arlene Adler: vchmn *CURR EMPL* vp: Citibank NA *PHIL AFFIL* dir: Citibank Employees Foundation

Carol Anastasio: secy, trust

Mary Lothrop Bundy: chwm, trust *ED* Radcliffe Coll 1946; City Univ Hunter Coll MSW 1980 *CORP AFFIL* dir: Corning Inc *NONPR AFFIL* mem: Assn Certified Social Workers, Forum Women Dirs, Natl Assn Social Workers, Phi Beta Kappa *PHIL AFFIL* dir: Foundation for Child Development

Earl Durham: trust

Lewis M. Feldstein: treas, trust *B* 1941

Barbara K. Hatton: trust

Barbara Taveras: exec dir

APPLICATION INFORMATION
Initial Approach:

Applicants should send a brief letter of inquiry to the foundation. The letter should highlight the goals, approach, target population, duration, and total cost of the project for which funding is sought.

If the foundation staff feel that the goals of the project address the foundation's mission and the approach is a sound one, they will mail applicants a formal application. The application should be prepared in compliance with instructions supplied by the foundation. Two copies should be submitted.

Deadlines for applications are January 15 and July 15 for review at the spring and fall board meetings, respectively.

The trustees meet twice each year to set foundation policy and make grants. Because the trustees review more proposals than they can fund, neither the request for a formal application nor a recommendation to the trustees guarantees funding.

Restrictions on Giving: The foundation does not consider requests for endowments or buildings, deficits, individual scholarships or fellowships, or schools or school districts.

PUBLICATIONS
Annual report and informational brochure including application guidelines

GRANTS ANALYSIS
Total Grants: $577,088

Number of Grants: 58

Highest Grant: $50,000

Average Grant: $9,950

Typical Range: $1,000 to $25,000

Disclosure Period: 1994

Note: Recent grants are derived from a 1994 partial grants list.

RECENT GRANTS

Library

1,000	Foundation Center, New York, NY

General

50,000	Southern Echo, Jackson, MS — a two-year grant to support development and implementation of a community organizing and training program designed to strengthen the Southern Initiative of the Algebra Project
25,000	Action for Grassroots Empowerment and Neighborhood Development, Los Angeles, CA — to support the Agenda for Action Among Youth project, a youth organizing and training initiative designed to involve at-risk youth in the process of rebuilding Los Angeles
25,000	Advocates for Children of New York City, Long Island City, NY — to support implementation of a parent organizing and training program focused on Chapter 1 compliance and systemwide reform
25,000	Alabama Arise, Montgomery, AL — to allow organization to intensify its citizens' education and advocacy efforts around educational reform in Alabama
25,000	Citizens Planning and Housing Association, Baltimore, MD — toward the Community Schools Initiative

Hearst Foundation, William Randolph

CONTACT
Robert M. Frehse, Jr.
Executive Director and Vice President
William Randolph Hearst Foundation
888 Seventh Ave., 45th Fl.
New York, NY 10106-0057
(212) 586-5404
Note: Applicants headquartered east of the Mississippi River should mail appeals to the New York office. Applicants headquartered west of the Mississippi River should mail

appeals to Thomas Eastham, Western Director, Hearst Foundations, 90 New Montgomery St., Ste. 1212, San Francisco, CA 94105. The California office telephone number is (415) 543-0400.

FINANCIAL SUMMARY
Recent Giving: $19,742,000 (1994); $13,505,000 (1993); $11,958,500 (1992)

Assets: $358,428,051 (1992); $350,260,000 (1991); $297,339,230 (1990)

Fiscal Note: Giving figures previous to 1994 reflect grants approved. Giving figure for 1994 reflects grants paid during 1994.

EIN: 13-6019226

CONTRIBUTIONS SUMMARY
Donor(s): The William Randolph Hearst Foundation was founded in 1948 by publisher and philanthropist William Randolph Hearst . Its original name, the California Charities, was changed soon after Mr. Hearst's death in 1951. Mr. Hearst founded the Hearst Corporation, a private media empire which included the *San Francisco Examiner* and other newspapers, book and magazine publishing, and television and radio broadcasting. All Hearst Corporation stock is now owned by trusts for the benefit of the surviving sons and grandchildren of William Randolph Hearst. The foundation is an independent private philanthropy operating separately from the Hearst Corporation.

Typical Recipients: • *Arts & Humanities:* Arts Centers, Ballet, Libraries, Museums/Galleries, Music, Opera, Performing Arts • *Civic & Public Affairs:* Employment/Job Training, Hispanic Affairs, Native American Affairs, Nonprofit Management, Safety • *Education:* Arts/Humanities Education, Business Education, Colleges & Universities, Engineering/Technological Education, Faculty Development, Literacy, Medical Education, Minority Education, Private Education (Precollege), Religious Education, Science/Mathematics Education, Secondary Education (Private), Special Education, Student Aid • *Health:* Cancer, Children's Health/Hospitals, Geriatric Health, Health Funds, Health Organizations, Hospitals, Medical Rehabilitation, Medical Research, Medical Training, Prenatal Health Issues, Transplant Networks/Donor Banks • *Religion:* Dioceses, Religious Welfare, Seminaries • *Science:* Scientific Labs, Scientific Organizations • *Social Services:* At-Risk Youth, Child Welfare, Community Service Organizations, Counseling, Family Services, People with Disabilities, Recreation & Athletics, Senior Services, Shelters/Homelessness, Substance Abuse, Volunteer Services, Youth Organizations

Grant Types: endowment, general support, project, and scholarship

Geographic Distribution: United States and its possessions

GIVING OFFICERS
Frank Anthony Bennack, Jr.: vp, dir *B* San Antonio TX 1933 *ED* Univ MD 1954-1956; St Marys Univ 1956-1958 *CURR EMPL* ceo, pres, dir: Hearst Corp *CORP AFFIL* chmn, dir: Huron Publ Co; dir: Am

Home Products Corp, Chem Bank, Discount Corp NY *NONPR AFFIL* chmn: Mus Broadcasting, Newspaper Assn Am; hon trust: Witte Meml Mus; mem: Greater San Antonio Chamber Commerce, TX Daily Newspaper Assn; mem bd govs: NY Hosp; trust: Our Lady Lake Coll

Mayra Cedem: grants admin

John G. Conomikes: vp, dir *CURR EMPL* vp, dir: Hearst Corp

Ralph Cuomo: treas *PHIL AFFIL* treas: Hearst Foundation

Richard Emmet Deems: vp, dir *B* New York NY 1913 *CURR EMPL* dir, mem fin comm, mem exec comm: Hearst Corp

Thomas Eastham: vp, western dir *B* Attleboro MA 1923 *ED* Northwestern Univ 1952 *PHIL AFFIL* vp, western dir: Hearst Foundation

Robert M. Frehse, Jr.: vp, exec dir *PHIL AFFIL* exec dir, vp: Hearst Foundation

George Randolph Hearst, Jr.: vp, dir *B* San Francisco CA 1927 *CURR EMPL* vp: Hearst Corp

John Randolph Hearst, Jr.: vp, dir *B* 1934

Randolph Apperson Hearst: dir *B* New York NY 1915 *ED* Harvard Univ 1933-1934 *CURR EMPL* chmn, dir: Hearst Corp

William R. Hearst III: vp, dir *B* Washington DC 1949 *ED* Harvard Univ AB 1972 *CURR EMPL* publ: San Francisco Examiner

Jodie King: asst secy *CURR EMPL* asst secy: Eastern News Distributors *PHIL AFFIL* asst secy: Hearst Foundation

Joseph Kingsbury-Smith: vp, dir *B* New York NY 1908 *ED* Univ London 1928 *CURR EMPL* vp, dir: Hearst Corp *CORP AFFIL* natl editor, sr reporter: Hearst Newspapers *NONPR AFFIL* trust: Fordham Univ, Hearst Family Estate *PHIL AFFIL* vp, dir: Hearst Foundation

Harvey L. Lipton: vp, dir *B* Brooklyn NY 1925 *ED* NY Univ 1948; St Johns Univ LLB 1951 *CURR EMPL* vp, secy, gen coun, dir: Hearst Corp *PHIL AFFIL* vp, dir, secy: Hearst Foundation

Gilbert Charles Maurer: vp, dir *B* New York NY 1928 *ED* St Lawrence Univ AB 1950; Harvard Univ MBA 1952 *CURR EMPL* exec vp, dir: Hearst Corp *PHIL AFFIL* vp, dir: Hearst Foundation

Raymond Joseph Petersen: vp, dir *B* West Orange NJ 1919 *CURR EMPL* exec vp, dir: Hearst Magazines *CORP AFFIL* publ, dir: Good Housekeeping Magazine *NONPR AFFIL* dir: Boys & Girls Clubs Madison Sq, Natl Crime Prevention Counc; hon adv: Children Alcoholics Fdn; mem chmn comm: Un Cerebral Palsy Campaign; mem, dir: Am Advertising Fed; vp, dir: Un Svc Org Metro NY *PHIL AFFIL* vp, dir: Hearst Foundation

APPLICATION INFORMATION
Initial Approach:

The foundation does not have a formal application form. Applicants should submit proposals in letter form. The foundation also accepts the New York Area Common Application Form.

Letters should include a brief description of the objectives of the proposed program, amount requested, budget, brief history of the organization, names and primary affiliations of officers and board members, most recent audited financial report, current year's operating budget, and list of other sources of funding. A copy of the IRS determination letter, certifying that applicant is tax-exempt under section 501(c)(3) and "not a private foundation" under section 509(a) under the IRS code, is also required.

Applications are accepted throughout the year. Board meetings are held in March, June, September, and December. Only fully documented appeals will be considered.

Meetings are arranged between foundation staff and applicants only if serious consideration of the appeal is anticipated.

Restrictions on Giving: Grants from the foundation must be used for charitable purposes by tax-exempt organizations; they may not be used for political purposes. The foundation does not purchase tickets, tables, or advertising for fund-raising events, or give grants to individuals or loan funds.

OTHER THINGS TO KNOW
Organizations should be listed in the current IRS Cumulative List of Tax-Exempt Organizations (publication 78). If an organization has been omitted from this publication, further documentation as to tax-exempt status will be required. Catholic Church organizations should be listed in the current Official Catholic Directory.

The William Randolph Hearst Foundation and the Hearst Foundation, Inc., are independent private philanthropies operating separately from the Hearst Corporation. Charitable goals of the two foundations are essentially the same. For economy, they are administered as one and only one proposal need be submitted.

PUBLICATIONS
Application guidelines

GRANTS ANALYSIS
Total Grants: $13,887,000*

Number of Grants: 267*

Highest Grant: $1,000,000

Average Grant: $52,011*

Typical Range: $15,000 to $60,000

Disclosure Period: 1994

Note: Above figures exclude $575,000 in journalism awards, $930,000 in Senate Youth Program Scholarships, and $4,350,000 in grants approved prior to 1994 but paid during 1994. Total contributions, including these categories, is $19,742,000. Recent grants are derived from a partial 1994 grants list.

RECENT GRANTS
General
1,000,000	New York Hospital, New York, NY — capital campaign
200,000	Howard University, Washington, DC — to establish endowments for

200,000	visiting professionals in the Department of Journalism
	Ohio University Foundation, Athens, OH — to establish endowments for visiting professionals in the Department of Journalism
200,000	University of Colorado at Boulder, Boulder, CO — to establish endowments to support visiting professionals in their schools of journalism
200,000	University of Kansas, Lawrence, KS — to establish endowments to support visiting professionals in their schools of journalism

Hebrew Technical Institute

CONTACT
Anita Goldberg
Trust Officer
Hebrew Technical Institute
c/o Murphy, O'Connor & Co.
60 E 42nd St.
New York, NY 10065-3698
(212) 736-2284

FINANCIAL SUMMARY
Recent Giving: $269,346 (1992); $282,701 (1991); $262,829 (1990)

Assets: $3,178,024 (1992); $3,273,745 (1991); $3,200,065 (1990)

Gifts Received: $16,434 (1992); $13,925 (1991); $18,769 (1990)

Fiscal Note: In 1992, contributions were received from Henry Sterne Trust.

EIN: 13-5562240

CONTRIBUTIONS SUMMARY
Typical Recipients: • *Arts & Humanities:* Libraries • *Civic & Public Affairs:* Housing, Women's Affairs • *Education:* Arts/Humanities Education, Colleges & Universities • *Environment:* General, Resource Conservation • *Religion:* Jewish Causes, Religious Organizations • *Science:* Scientific Centers & Institutes, Scientific Organizations • *Social Services:* Community Service Organizations, Youth Organizations

Grant Types: general support

Geographic Distribution: focus on NY

GIVING OFFICERS
Catherine H. Behrend: dir

Lawrence A. Benenson: dir

Seth Dubin: dir

Irving Lipkowitz: dir

John R. Menke: dir

Herbert A. Raiser: pres, dir

Hyman B. Ritchin: dir

Mrs. Frederick Rose: dir

Robert Rosenthal, Esq.: dir

Bruce D. Schlechter: treas, dir

APPLICATION INFORMATION
Initial Approach: Send brief letter of inquiry describing program. There are no deadlines.

GRANTS ANALYSIS
Total Grants: $269,346

Number of Grants: 10

Highest Grant: $52,500

Typical Range: $15,000 to $40,000

Disclosure Period: 1992

Note: Recent grants are derived from a 1992 Form 990.

RECENT GRANTS

Library

20,000	New York Public Library, New York, NY

General

52,500	New York Hall of Science, New York, NY
40,000	Cooper Union for the Advancement of Science and Art, New York, NY
31,376	New York University Conservation Center, New York, NY
31,000	Columbia University, New York, NY
27,000	American Society for Technion, New York, NY

Heckscher Foundation for Children

CONTACT
Virginia Sloane
President
Heckscher Foundation for Children
17 E 47th St.
New York, NY 10017
(212) 371-7775

FINANCIAL SUMMARY
Recent Giving: $1,790,829 (1993); $1,667,285 (1992); $1,722,749 (1991)

Assets: $33,290,239 (1993); $33,122,968 (1992); $32,943,573 (1991)

EIN: 13-1820170

CONTRIBUTIONS SUMMARY
Donor(s): August Heckscher , who died in 1941, was the donor of the Heckscher Foundation for Children, which was established in 1921. Mr. Heckscher made his fortune in mining and New York City real estate. He first demonstrated his interest in the welfare of children in New York City in the early twentieth century, when he donated a building and the land on which it stood to a children's home.

Typical Recipients: • *Arts & Humanities:* Arts Centers, Arts Institutes, Arts Outreach, Dance, Ethnic & Folk Arts, Historic Preservation, History & Archaeology, Libraries, Museums/Galleries, Music, Opera, Performing Arts, Public Broadcasting, Theater • *Civic & Public Affairs:* Botanical Gardens/Parks, Clubs, Economic Development, General, Hispanic Affairs, Housing, Philanthropic Organizations, Public Policy, Urban & Community Affairs, Zoos/Aquariums • *Education:* Arts/Humanities Education, Colleges & Universities, Education Associations, Elementary Education (Private), Medical Education, Minority Education, Preschool Education, Private Education (Precollege), Public Education (Precollege), Student Aid • *Environment:* General • *Health:* Cancer, Children's Health/Hospitals, Clinics/Medical Centers, Emergency/Ambulance Services, Health Organizations, Hospitals, Medical Rehabilitation, Medical Research, Mental Health, Nursing Services, Preventive Medicine/Wellness Organizations, Single-Disease Health Associations, Transplant Networks/Donor Banks • *Religion:* Churches, Jewish Causes, Religious Welfare • *Social Services:* Big Brother/Big Sister, Camps, Child Welfare, Community Centers, Community Service Organizations, Day Care, Delinquency & Criminal Rehabilitation, Family Planning, Family Services, People with Disabilities, Recreation & Athletics, Scouts, Shelters/Homelessness, Substance Abuse, Volunteer Services, Youth Organizations

Grant Types: capital, general support, and project

Geographic Distribution: primarily New York City

GIVING OFFICERS
William D. Hart, Jr.: couns, trust *B* 1918 *ED* Yale Univ AB 1940; Harvard Univ LLB 1947 *CURR EMPL* vp, dir: N Shore Corp *CORP AFFIL* ptnr: Whitman & Ransom; vp, treas, dir: Park Lexington Co

Richard N. Kerst: trust

Elinor Kruch: trust

Carole Landman: trust

John D. MacNeary: vp, trust

Gail Meyers: trust

John M. O'Mara: trust *B* OH *ED* Princeton Univ BA 1950; Univ VA LLB 1953 *CURR EMPL* first vp: White Weld & Co

Fred Obser: trust

Howard Grant Sloane: trust *B* 1922 *CURR EMPL* pres, dir: N Shore Corp *CORP AFFIL* pres, dir: Park Lexington Co

Virginia Sloane: pres, trust

Arthur J. Smadbeck: trust *CURR EMPL* vp, dir: Park Lexington Co *CORP AFFIL* vp, treas, dir: N Shore Corp

Mina Smadbeck: trust

Paul Smadbeck: trust *CURR EMPL* vp, dir: Park Lexington Co *CORP AFFIL* vp, dir: N Shore Corp

APPLICATION INFORMATION
Initial Approach:

Applicants should send a letter to the foundation.

Proposals should contain a concise statement of the program or project, amount of funding requested, a brief background of the organization, a budget for the program, a list of board officers, donor list for the past twelve months, and a copy of the IRS tax-determination letter.

The foundation reports no application deadlines.

PUBLICATIONS
Application guidelines

GRANTS ANALYSIS
Total Grants: $1,790,829

Number of Grants: 164

Highest Grant: $140,000

Average Grant: $10,920

Typical Range: $100 to $25,000

Disclosure Period: 1993

Note: Recent grants are derived from a 1993 Form 990.

RECENT GRANTS

General

140,000	Juilliard School, New York, NY
100,000	New York Hospital Cornell Medical Center, New York, NY — for Pediatric Imaging Center
75,000	Brooklyn Bureau of Community Service, Brooklyn, NY
75,000	City Parks Foundation, New York, NY — for the citywide Disabled Playground Project at Asser Levy Park
64,000	Jewish Child Care Association of New York, New York, NY

Hill Foundation, Sandy

CONTACT
Floyd Rourke
Trustee
Sandy Hill Fdn.
PO Box 30
Hudson Falls, NY 12839
(518) 747-5805

FINANCIAL SUMMARY
Recent Giving: $359,042 (fiscal 1993)

Assets: $7,670,359 (fiscal 1993)

EIN: 14-6018954

CONTRIBUTIONS SUMMARY
Typical Recipients: • *Arts & Humanities:* Arts Associations & Councils, History & Archaeology, Libraries, Literary Arts, Museums/Galleries, Music, Performing Arts • *Civic & Public Affairs:* Botanical Gardens/Parks, Chambers of Commerce, General, Hispanic Affairs, Native American Affairs, Parades/Festivals, Urban & Community Affairs • *Education:* Colleges & Universities, Education Funds, Literacy, Private Education (Precollege), Public Education (Precollege), Science/Mathematics Education, Student Aid • *Environment:* General, Wildlife Protection • *Health:* AIDS/HIV, Cancer, Clinics/Medical Centers, Emergency/Ambulance Services, Heart, Hospitals • *Religion:* Churches, Religious Welfare, Synagogues/Temples • *Social Services:* Ani-

mal Protection, Child Welfare, Community Service Organizations, Counseling, Family Services, People with Disabilities, Recreation & Athletics, Scouts, United Funds/United Ways, Veterans, Volunteer Services, YMCA/YWCA/YMHA/YWHA, Youth Organizations

Grant Types: general support

Geographic Distribution: focus on greater Hudson Falls, NY, area

GIVING OFFICERS
Nancy Juckett Brown: trust

Floyd H. Rourke: trust

APPLICATION INFORMATION
Initial Approach: Request application form. Deadline in April 1.

GRANTS ANALYSIS
Total Grants: $359,042

Number of Grants: 111

Highest Grant: $110,038

Typical Range: $100 to $3,000

Disclosure Period: fiscal year ending August 31, 1993

Note: Recent grants are derived from a fiscal 1993 Form 990.

RECENT GRANTS

Library

1,000	Hudson Falls Free Library Association, Hudson Falls, NY

General

110,038	Adirondack Samaritan Counseling Center, Hudson Falls, NY
110,038	Adirondack Samaritan Counseling Center, Hudson Falls, NY
25,000	University of Maine Pulp and Paper Foundation, Orono, ME
25,000	University of Maine Pulp and Paper Foundation, Orono, ME
25,000	YMCA Capital Fund, Glens Falls, NY

Hillman Family Foundation, Alex

CONTACT
Rita K. Hillman
President
Alex Hillman Family Foundation
630 Fifth Ave.
New York, NY 10111
(212) 265-3115

FINANCIAL SUMMARY
Recent Giving: $1,045,786 (1993); $956,761 (1992); $970,380 (1991)

Assets: $48,105,334 (1993); $48,544,650 (1992); $57,539,766 (1991)

Gifts Received: $15,277 (1993); $10,868 (1992); $13,010 (1991)

Fiscal Note: In 1992 and 1993, contributions were received from Rita Hillman.

EIN: 13-2560546

CONTRIBUTIONS SUMMARY
Donor(s): The foundation was incorporated in 1966 by Rita K. Hillman and the late Alex L. Hillman .

Typical Recipients: • *Arts & Humanities:* Arts Associations & Councils, Arts Funds, Community Arts, Dance, Film & Video, Historic Preservation, Libraries, Museums/Galleries, Music, Performing Arts, Public Broadcasting, Theater, Visual Arts • *Civic & Public Affairs:* General, Public Policy, Urban & Community Affairs • *Education:* Arts/Humanities Education, Colleges & Universities, Medical Education, Private Education (Precollege) • *Health:* Emergency/Ambulance Services, Hospitals, Nursing Services • *International:* Foreign Arts Organizations, Health Care/Hospitals • *Religion:* Jewish Causes, Religious Organizations, Synagogues/Temples • *Social Services:* Community Service Organizations, Crime Prevention, Food/Clothing Distribution, People with Disabilities, Recreation & Athletics

Grant Types: operating expenses

Geographic Distribution: focus on the New York, NY, metropolitan area

GIVING OFFICERS
William M. Griffin: vp, dir

Alex Hillman: dir

Rita K. Hillman: pres, dir *B* New York NY 1912 *ED* NY Univ 1929-1932 *NONPR AFFIL* chmn: Intl Ctr Photography; mem: Am Friends Israel Mus, Metro Mus Art; vchmn: Brooklyn Academy Music

James Stewart Marcus: dir *B* New York NY 1929 *ED* Harvard Univ AB 1951; Harvard Univ MBA 1953 *CURR EMPL* ltd ptnr: Goldman Sachs & Co *CORP AFFIL* dir: Am Biltrite, Kellwood Co *NONPR AFFIL* chmn bd: Metro Opera Assn; mem: Century Assn, Phi Beta Kappa; mem exec commn: Lincoln Ctr Performing Arts; trust: Am Composers Orchestra, Guild Hall, Lenox Hill Hosp, Regenstrief Fdn *CLUB AFFIL* Metropolitan Opera *PHIL AFFIL* dir: H. Frederick Krimendahl II Foundation

Ahrin Mishan: dir

Harold L. Schiff: secy, treas, dir

William Spiro: dir

APPLICATION INFORMATION
Initial Approach:

The foundation requests applications be made in writing.

Written proposals should include the purpose of the funds and other information or material relevant and descriptive of the proposed project.

The foundation has no deadline for submitting proposals.

Restrictions on Giving: The foundation makes grants to organizations involved in education, the arts, and nursing.

Restrictions on Giving: The foundation does not make grants to individuals.

PUBLICATIONS
Annual report

GRANTS ANALYSIS
Total Grants: $1,045,786

Number of Grants: 30

Highest Grant: $442,051

Average Grant: $5,806*

Typical Range: $250 to $10,000

Disclosure Period: 1993

Note: The average grant figure excludes four grants totaling $894,836. Recent grants are derived from a 1992 Form 990.

RECENT GRANTS

General

442,051	University of Pennsylvania School of Nursing, Philadelphia, PA
225,000	Philips Beth Israel School of Nursing, New York, NY
120,500	Lenox Hill Hospital, New York, NY
100,000	New York University School of Nursing, New York, NY
11,150	International Center of Photography, New York, NY

Hino Diesel Trucks (U.S.A.)

Sales: $44.48 million
Employees: 44
Headquarters: Orangeburg, NY
SIC Major Group: Wholesale Trade—Durable Goods

CONTACT
Frank Merz
Manager, Finance & Administration
Hino Diesel Trucks (U.S.A)
25 Corporate Dr.
Orangeburg, NY 10962
(914) 365-1400

FINANCIAL SUMMARY
Fiscal Note: Annual Giving Range: less than $25,000

CONTRIBUTIONS SUMMARY
Limited support to local community organizations; information not disclosed.

Typical Recipients: • *Arts & Humanities:* Libraries • *Social Services:* Substance Abuse, Volunteer Services, Youth Organizations

Grant Types: capital

Geographic Distribution: headquarters and operating communities

GIVING OFFICERS
Barbara Aubin: *CURR EMPL* human resources admin: Hino Diesel Trucks (USA)

APPLICATION INFORMATION
Applications not encouraged.

Homeland Foundation

CONTACT
E. Lisk Wyckoff, Jr.
President
Homeland Foundation
230 Park Ave.
New York, NY 10017
(212) 949-0949

FINANCIAL SUMMARY
Recent Giving: $815,600 (fiscal 1993); $1,026,372 (fiscal 1992); $903,288 (fiscal 1991)

Assets: $77,413,178 (fiscal 1993); $74,342,915 (fiscal 1992); $73,434,198 (fiscal 1991)

Gifts Received: $257,970 (fiscal 1993); $816,828 (fiscal 1992); $1,050,000 (fiscal 1991)

Fiscal Note: In 1992, contributions were received from a private estate.

EIN: 13-6113816

CONTRIBUTIONS SUMMARY
Donor(s): The foundation was incorporated in 1938. In fiscal 1990, the foundation's assets grew to more than $75 million under a trust established by the late Chauncey Stillman .

Typical Recipients: • *Arts & Humanities:* Dance, Historic Preservation, Libraries, Museums/Galleries, Music, Opera • *Civic & Public Affairs:* General, Housing, Law & Justice, Public Policy • *Education:* Colleges & Universities, Education Associations, Education Funds, General, Minority Education, Private Education (Precollege), Religious Education, Secondary Education (Private), Student Aid • *Health:* Cancer, Hospitals • *International:* Foreign Arts Organizations, Health Care/Hospitals, Human Rights, International Peace & Security Issues, Missionary/Religious Activities • *Religion:* Churches, Dioceses, Missionary Activities (Domestic), Religious Organizations, Religious Welfare, Seminaries • *Social Services:* Camps, Child Welfare, Community Service Organizations, Family Planning, Family Services, Food/Clothing Distribution, Youth Organizations

Grant Types: general support and scholarship

Geographic Distribution: most grants are disbursed in New York metropolitan area; however, grants are made nationally and internationally

GIVING OFFICERS
Father Rafael F. Caamano: trust

Monseigneur Eugene V. Clark: vp, secy, trust

Patricia P. Donahoe: program dir

Lucy Fleming-McGrath: trust

Thomas Roepe: trust

Carl Schmitt: trust

Charles Scribner III: vp, trust *B* Washington DC 1951 *ED* Princeton Univ AB 1973; Princeton Univ MFA 1975; Princeton Univ PhD 1977 *CURR EMPL* vp: Macmillan Publ Co *NONPR AFFIL* bd advs: Wethersfield Inst; dir: Metro Opera Guild; mem: Assn Princeton Univ Press, Coll Art Assn; mem adv counc univ library: Princeton Univ; trust: Princeton Univ Press *CLUB AFFIL* Ivy, Piping Rock, Racquet & Tennis

E. Lisk Wyckoff, Jr.: pres, treas, trust *ED* Duke Univ BA 1955; Univ MI JD 1960 *CURR EMPL* ptnr: Kelley Drye & Warren *NONPR AFFIL* fellow: Am Coll Probate Couns; lecturer: Practicing Law Inst; mem: Am Bar Assn, Intl Bar Assn, Intl Fiscal Assn, New York City Bar Assn, NY Bar Assn; pres, dir: Wyckoff House Assn; trust: NY Historical Soc, Soc Preservation Long Island Antiquities

APPLICATION INFORMATION
Initial Approach:

The foundation has no standard application form. The foundation reports that a letter to the president of the foundation is sufficient.

Include a concise statement of the purpose of the grant requested and a specific amount requested. Each grant proposal, signed by an officer of the organization, should also be accompanied with a brief description of the nature, history, and activities of the application; a budget for the project, program, or organization, as applicable, with a board resolution approving the budget; a statement of other sources of funding to applicant or to the project and the purpose and amounts of their commitments; and a list of the names and addresses of board members and offices of the applicant.

The letter should be accompanied by a copy of the U.S. Internal Revenue Service letter of determination confirming applicant's tax status as an exempt organization and, in addition, that the organization is not a private foundation. If the organization is Catholic, include a copy of the organization's inclusion in the Kenedy Official Catholic Directory. The foundation also requires a signed statement by an officer of the organization that the IRS has not revoked or changed or threatened to revoke or change the applicant's present or any prior determination of its tax status or, when applicabale, that the United States Catholic Conference has not advised the applicant that it will or that it is considering deleting the applicant's listing in the Official Catholic Directory.

September 10 is the deadline for a mid-November board decision; January 31 is the deadline for a mid-March board decision.

The foundation requires a report on a grant made indicating how the applicant used the grant together with dates and expenditure responsibility.

Restrictions on Giving: Grants are not made to individuals, private foundations, or governmental organizations. Grants for endowments, building funds, and capital development are made only on the basis of a special interest.

GRANTS ANALYSIS
Total Grants: $815,600

Number of Grants: 71

Highest Grant: $160,000

Average Grant: $11,487

Typical Range: $2,000 to $20,000

Disclosure Period: fiscal year ending April 30, 1993

Note: Recent grants are derived from a fiscal 1993 Form 990.

RECENT GRANTS

Library

50,000	Roman Athenaeum Foundation, New Rochelle, NY — operating expenses
35,500	Thomas Aquinas College, Santa Paula, CA — equipment for new library
10,000	New York Public Library, New York, NY — conservation program

General

160,000	Thomas More College, Merrimade, NH — operating expenses
80,000	Vatican Museums — tapestry project
50,000	Camp Wethersfield, Yonkers, NY — operating expenses
30,500	International Institute for Culture, Drexell Hill, PA — summer program in Germany and seminar on faith/culture
25,000	Cornell Cooperative Extension, Millbrook, NY — future harvest program

Hopkins Foundation, Josephine Lawrence

CONTACT

Josephine Lawrence Hopkins Fdn.
61 Broadway, Ste. 2912
New York, NY 10006
(212) 480-0400
Note: Foundation does not list a contact person.

FINANCIAL SUMMARY

Recent Giving: $195,500 (1993); $177,400 (1992); $219,325 (1991)

Assets: $3,280,627 (1993); $3,204,640 (1992); $3,268,132 (1991)

EIN: 13-6277593

CONTRIBUTIONS SUMMARY

Donor(s): the late Josephine H. Graeber

Typical Recipients: • *Arts & Humanities:* Arts Centers, Community Arts, Libraries, Literary Arts, Music, Performing Arts, Public Broadcasting • *Civic & Public Affairs:* Clubs, General, Professional & Trade Associations, Zoos/Aquariums • *Education:* Colleges & Universities, Private Education (Precollege), Science/Mathematics Education, Secondary Education (Private) • *Environment:* Air/Water Quality, General, Resource Conservation • *Health:* Children's Health/Hospitals, Emergency/Ambulance Services, Geriatric Health, Health Organizations, Hospitals, Medical Research • *International:* Missionary/Religious Activities • *Religion:* Churches, Religious Organizations, Religious Welfare • *Social Services:* Animal Protection, Child Welfare, Community Centers, Community Service Organizations, Counseling, People with Disabilities, Recreation & Athletics, Youth Organizations

Grant Types: general support

Geographic Distribution: focus on NY

GIVING OFFICERS

Vera L. Colage: vp, dir

Lee Harrison Corbin: dir, asst secy, asst treas

William P. Hurley: dir, asst secy, asst treas

Ivan Obolensky: pres, treas, dir *B* London England 1925 *ED* Yale Univ AB 1947 *CURR EMPL* sr vp: Josephthal & Co *CORP AFFIL* gen ptnr: Astor Capital Mgmt Assocs; sr vp: Josephthal & Co *NONPR AFFIL* dir: Childrens Blood Fdn, NY Hosp

Meredith N. Stiles, Jr.: vp, asst treas, secy, dir

Susan H. Whitmore: vp, dir

APPLICATION INFORMATION

Initial Approach: The foundation has no formal grant application procedure or application form. Deadline is October 1.

Restrictions on Giving: Does not support individuals or provide loans.

GRANTS ANALYSIS

Total Grants: $195,500

Typical Range: $1,500 to $10,000

Disclosure Period: 1993

Note: Grants list for 1993 was incomplete. Recent grants are derived from a 1992 Form 990.

RECENT GRANTS

General

250,000	Bouverie Audubon Preserve — to establish and maintain a chair in Biology

Howard and Bush Foundation

CONTACT

Deborah Byers
Contact Person
Howard and Bush Foundation
2 Belle Ave.
Troy, NY 12180
(518) 271-1134

FINANCIAL SUMMARY

Recent Giving: $428,000 (1993); $329,627 (1992); $622,731 (1991)

Assets: $3,675,156 (1993); $3,624,000 (1992); $3,624,855 (1991)

Gifts Received: $170,050 (1993); $2,448 (1990); $2,219 (1989)

EIN: 06-6059063

CONTRIBUTIONS SUMMARY

Donor(s): The Howard and Bush Foundation was established by Edith Mason Howard (1861-1949) and Julia Howard Bush (1872-1962), daughter and granddaughter, respectively, of James L. Howard, an original stockholder and director of Travelers Insurance Company.

Edith Howard was born and raised in Hartford, CT, and was particularly interested in local Baptist religious and social service organizations. Julia Bush's interests were centered in Troy, NY, and included Presbyterian organizations, Emma Willard School, and Russell Sage College.

Typical Recipients: • *Arts & Humanities:* Arts Associations & Councils, Arts Centers, Dance, General, Historic Preservation, History & Archaeology, Libraries, Music, Performing Arts, Public Broadcasting • *Civic & Public Affairs:* African American Affairs, Botanical Gardens/Parks, Business/Free Enterprise, Economic Development, General, Housing, Law & Justice, Legal Aid, Municipalities/Towns, Safety, Urban & Community Affairs • *Education:* Arts/Humanities Education, Colleges & Universities, Elementary Education (Public), Literacy, Minority Education, Private Education (Precollege), Public Education (Precollege) • *Health:* AIDS/HIV, Health Organizations, Hospitals, Medical Rehabilitation • *Religion:* Ministries, Religious Organizations, Religious Welfare • *Social Services:* Community Centers, Community Service Organizations, Recreation & Athletics, Senior Services, Youth Organizations

Grant Types: challenge and project

Geographic Distribution: Rensselaer County, NY

GIVING OFFICERS

Donald C. Bowes: dir

Sarah H. Catlin: pres, dir, trust

David S. Haviland: dir, trust *B* Rome NY 1942 *NONPR AFFIL* mem: Am Inst Archts, Assn Collegiate Schs, Counc Ed Facility Planners, NY St Assn Architects, Project Mgmt Inst; mem facilities comm: Albany Med Ctr; prof architecture: Rensselaer Polytech Univ; treas: Architectural Res Ctrs Consortium; trust: Rensselaer Newman Fdn, Troy Music Hall; vis prof: Univ Reading Un Kingdom

Margaret Mochon: dir, trust

David W. Parmelee: trust *PHIL AFFIL* trust, treas: Jacob L. and Lewis Fox Foundation

APPLICATION INFORMATION

Initial Contact: Guidelines are sent upon request.

Include Information On: Concept papers should include purpose of the organization, name and phone number of contact person, brief description of the proposed project, and financial information.

Deadlines: Deadlines for submitting concept papers are January 15, May 15, and September 15.

Note: The foundation ordinarily does not make grants to government agencies;

597

churches or schools not associated with the founders, except for nondenominational community projects; organizations that have received grants from the foundation within the past two years; operating deficits; endowment funds; municipalities or other tax-supported institutions; reserve or revolving funds; or to individuals.

OTHER THINGS TO KNOW

In 1991, the foundation contributed approximately $4 million, about half of the foundation's assets, to the Hartford Foundation for Public Giving. The funds supported approximately 27 advised grants made by the Hartford Foundation's main fund and created two permanent funds—Tomlinson Fund for Philanthropy and Endowment Fund for Architecture Conservancy of Hartford. Both are administered by the Hartford Foundation.

PUBLICATIONS

Annual report

GRANTS ANALYSIS

Total Grants: $428,000

Number of Grants: 22

Highest Grant: $50,000

Typical Range: $5,000 to $45,000

Disclosure Period: 1993

Note: Recent grants are derived from a from a 1993 Form 990.

RECENT GRANTS

General

50,000	Committee on Economic Opportunity	
45,000	Troy Rehabilitation and Improvement Program, Troy, NY	
35,000	Barn Raisers	
23,500	Center for Law and Justice, Albany, NY	
21,000	Urban League of Albany, Albany, NY	

Hoyt Foundation, Stewart W. and Willma C.

CONTACT

Judith C. Peckham
Executive Director
Stewart W. and Willma C. Hoyt Foundation
105-107 Court St.,
Ste. 400
Binghamton, NY 13901
(607) 722-6706

FINANCIAL SUMMARY

Recent Giving: $410,942 (1993); $140,410 (1992); $344,898 (1991)

Assets: $13,770,441 (1992); $14,249,265 (1991); $12,640,628 (1990)

Fiscal Note: See note in "Other Things You Should Know."

EIN: 22-3209342

CONTRIBUTIONS SUMMARY

Donor(s): The foundation was established in 1970 by late Willma C. Hoyt .

Typical Recipients: • *Arts & Humanities:* Arts Associations & Councils, Arts Centers, Arts Funds, Arts Outreach, Community Arts, Libraries, Music, Opera, Performing Arts, Theater • *Civic & Public Affairs:* General, Housing, Municipalities/Towns, Philanthropic Organizations, Professional & Trade Associations, Urban & Community Affairs, Zoos/Aquariums • *Education:* Arts/Humanities Education, Education Associations, Health & Physical Education, Leadership Training, Literacy, Preschool Education, Private Education (Precollege), Student Aid • *Environment:* Air/Water Quality • *Health:* Alzheimers Disease, Children's Health/Hospitals, Emergency/Ambulance Services, Health Organizations, Heart, Home-Care Services, Hospitals, Mental Health • *Religion:* Churches, Jewish Causes, Religious Welfare • *Social Services:* Community Centers, Community Service Organizations, Counseling, Day Care, Delinquency & Criminal Rehabilitation, Family Planning, Family Services, General, People with Disabilities, Recreation & Athletics, Scouts, Senior Services, Substance Abuse, Youth Organizations

Grant Types: capital, general support, matching, operating expenses, project, and seed money

Geographic Distribution: limited to Broome County, NY

GIVING OFFICERS

Denise M. Balkas: dir

John M. Keeler: dir *B* 1933 *ED* Hamilton Coll AB 1955; Cornell Univ LLB 1961 *CURR EMPL* mng ptnr: Hinman Howard & Kattell *NONPR AFFIL* mem: Broome County Bar Assn, NY St BAr Assn

Fannie R. Linder: bd mem

Albert Mamary: dir

Judith C. Peckham: exec dir

William Rincker: secy, treas, dir *B* 1930 *CURR EMPL* pres, ceo: Binghamton Savings Bank

John F. Russell: chmn, dir

Jacqueline Visser: bd mem

APPLICATION INFORMATION

Initial Contact: The foundation requests letters or calls of inquiry before submitting a full proposal.

Include Information On: Formal proposals should include information about the applying organization, the project, and the finances for the project. The foundation requests the following information concerning the organization; a copy of a letter from the IRS recognizing charitable tax-exempt status, a copy of the most recent audited financial statements, a copy of the budget for current fiscal year, a current list of the board of directors and their affiliations, a copy of the most recent annual report, the organizations bylaws and organizational chart, and the most recent filed 990 form. Information about the project should include a brief narrative explaining need met by project and

plans for procedure, and job descriptions and qualifications of the personnel responsible for the project. Information concerning project finances should include a copy of the budget, showing breakdown of expenses, as well as earned and contributed income; and a list of sources from other funds received. A summary sheet should also be included and can be obtained from the foundation office.

Deadlines: Formal proposals should be submitted by February 1, June 1, and October 1.

Review Process: The board meets in January, March, May, July, September, and November. Grants may be considered at the May and September meetings. Applicants should check with the foundation before submitting proposals for these months. Grants are not awarded at the January meeting.

Restrictions on Giving: The foundation reports it does not make grants to individuals, churches, religious organizations, annual campaigns, deficit financing, general endowments, research, or publications.

OTHER THINGS TO KNOW

"The Hoyt Foundation formerly operated as a trust. Pursuant to the trust agreement, the foundation was incorporated and all the net assets which totaled $12,763,072 were transferred to the corporation at the end of December 31, 1993. The Foundation will operate in the corporate form in essentially the same manner as it has in the past and the trust has been terminated. "

GRANTS ANALYSIS

Total Grants: $410,942

Number of Grants: 42

Highest Grant: $95,000

Average Grant: $9,784

Typical Range: $2,000 to $25,000

Disclosure Period: 1993

Note: Recent grants are derived from a 1993 Form 990.

RECENT GRANTS

Library

4,222	Four County Library, Binghamton, NY — automation of graphic system	
3,161	Broome County Public Library, Binghamton, NY — CD collection	
1,000	Deposit Free Library, Deposit, NY — computer for patron use	

General

30,000	Broome County Child Development Council, Binghamton, NY — assistance in development/improvement of day care in Broome County	
22,207	Binghamton Area Girls Softball Association, Binghamton, NY — construction of softball complex	
20,000	Boys and Girls Club of Binghamton, Binghamton,	

	NY — construction of teen center
17,500	Broome Community College Foundation, Binghamton, NY — scholarships to Broome County students
15,000	Action for Older Persons, Binghamton, NY — emergency cash flow loan

Hugoton Foundation

CONTACT
Joan K. Stout
President
Hugoton Foundation
900 Park Ave.
New York, NY 10021
(212) 734-5447

FINANCIAL SUMMARY
Recent Giving: $1,091,750 (1993); $1,425,000 (1992); $1,346,000 (1990)

Assets: $30,773,712 (1993); $30,320,280 (1992); $26,920,568 (1990)

EIN: 34-1351062

CONTRIBUTIONS SUMMARY
Donor(s): The foundation was established in 1981 by the late Wallace Gilroy .

Typical Recipients: • *Arts & Humanities:* Libraries, Music, Performing Arts • *Civic & Public Affairs:* Botanical Gardens/Parks • *Education:* Business Education, Colleges & Universities, Medical Education, Private Education (Precollege), Science/Mathematics Education, Secondary Education (Private), Student Aid • *Environment:* Resource Conservation • *Health:* Alzheimers Disease, Cancer, Children's Health/Hospitals, Clinics/Medical Centers, Emergency/Ambulance Services, Geriatric Health, Health Organizations, Heart, Hospitals, Medical Research, Mental Health, Nursing Services, Single-Disease Health Associations, Transplant Networks/Donor Banks • *Religion:* Churches, Dioceses, Religious Organizations, Religious Welfare • *Social Services:* Animal Protection, Child Welfare, Food/Clothing Distribution, Homes, People with Disabilities, Senior Services

Grant Types: project and research

Geographic Distribution: focus on New York, NY, and Miami, FL

GIVING OFFICERS
Frank S. Fejes: dir

Jean C. Stout: treas, dir

Joan K. Stout: pres, mng dir

Joan M. Stout: secy, dir

John K. Stout: dir

Ray E. Stout III: vp, dir

APPLICATION INFORMATION
Initial Approach:

The foundation requests applications be made in writing.

Written request must include description of organization, proof of tax-exempt status, brief statement of need, date request is needed by, and a detailed cost analysis. Requests should not exceed three pages.

Requests are received and reviewed within the calendar year.

GRANTS ANALYSIS
Total Grants: $1,091,750

Number of Grants: 51

Highest Grant: $200,000

Average Grant: $21,407

Typical Range: $2,000 to $25,000

Disclosure Period: 1993

Note: Recent grants are derived from a 1993 Form 990.

RECENT GRANTS
Library

5,000	Fund for Public Schools, Brooklyn, NY — school library modernization
5,000	New York Public Library, New York, NY — research

General

200,000	Lenox Hill Hospital, New York, NY — ambulatory surgical center
175,000	Mt. Sinai Medical Center, Miami Beach, FL
100,000	Columbia University Trustees, New York, NY — MRI center
65,000	University of Miami, Miami, FL — training lab computers
50,000	Hospital for Special Surgery, New York, NY — spine fellowship

Hulbert Foundation, Nila B.

CONTACT
Henry L. Hulbert
Trustee
Nila B. Hulbert Fdn.
6 Ford Ave.
Oneonta, NY 13820
(607) 432-6720

FINANCIAL SUMMARY
Recent Giving: $128,000 (1993); $118,150 (1992)

Assets: $3,629,107 (1993); $3,310,948 (1992)

Gifts Received: $14,021 (1992)

EIN: 23-7039996

CONTRIBUTIONS SUMMARY
Typical Recipients: • *Arts & Humanities:* Libraries, Music • *Civic & Public Affairs:* Philanthropic Organizations • *Education:* Colleges & Universities, Public Education (Precollege) • *Health:* Hospices, Hospitals • *Religion:* Religious Organizations, Religious Welfare • *Social Services:* Family Services, Recreation & Athletics, United Funds/United Ways, YMCA/YWCA/YMHA/YWHA, Youth Organizations

Grant Types: general support

Geographic Distribution: focus on Oneonta, NY

GIVING OFFICERS
Henry L. Hulbert: trust *PHIL AFFIL* mgr, trust: Riley J. and Lillian N. Warren and Beatrice W. Blanding Foundation

J. Burton Hulbert: trust

William H. Hulbert: trust

APPLICATION INFORMATION
Initial Approach: Send a brief letter of inquiry and a full proposal. Include a description of organization. Deadline in September 30.

GRANTS ANALYSIS
Total Grants: $128,000

Number of Grants: 20

Highest Grant: $25,000

Typical Range: $500 to $20,000

Disclosure Period: 1993

Note: Recent grants are derived from a 1993 Form 990.

RECENT GRANTS
Library

19,000	Huntington Memorial Library, Oneonta, NY

General

25,000	A.O. Fox Memorial Hospital Foundation, Oneonta, NY
20,000	Hartwick College, Oneonta, NY
10,000	Catskill Area Hospice, Oneonta, NY
10,000	National Soccer Hall of Fame, Oneonta, NY
8,000	A.O. Fox Memorial Hospital Chaplaincy Foundation, Oneonta, NY

Hultquist Foundation

CONTACT
Thomas J. Flowers
President
Hultquist Fdn.
c/o Price, Miller, Evans and Flowers
Fenton Bldg.
Jamestown, NY 14701
(716) 664-7414

FINANCIAL SUMMARY
Recent Giving: $548,996 (fiscal 1992); $390,087 (fiscal 1991); $509,239 (fiscal 1990)

Assets: $11,880,096 (fiscal 1992); $11,132,736 (fiscal 1991); $5,360,520 (fiscal 1990)

Gifts Received: $71,359 (fiscal 1992)

Fiscal Note: In fiscal 1992, contributions were received from estate of Jane H. Pearson.

EIN: 16-0907729

CONTRIBUTIONS SUMMARY

Typical Recipients: • *Arts & Humanities:* Arts Associations & Councils, Arts Funds, Historic Preservation, Libraries, Music • *Civic & Public Affairs:* Urban & Community Affairs • *Education:* Colleges & Universities, Community & Junior Colleges, Education Funds • *Health:* Hospitals • *Religion:* Religious Welfare • *Social Services:* Child Welfare, Community Service Organizations, Homes, United Funds/United Ways, Youth Organizations

Grant Types: general support

Geographic Distribution: focus on Chautauqua County, NY

GIVING OFFICERS

Thomas J. Flowers: pres, dir

Charles H. Price: vp, dir

Robert F. Rohm, Jr.: secy, treas, dir

William L. Wright: vp, dir

APPLICATION INFORMATION

Initial Approach: Send brief letter of inquiry describing program or project. Deadlines are June 1 and December 1

GRANTS ANALYSIS

Total Grants: $548,996

Number of Grants: 15

Highest Grant: $300,000

Typical Range: $2,000 to $10,000

Disclosure Period: fiscal year ending June 30, 1992

Note: Recent grants are derived from a fiscal 1992 Form 990.

RECENT GRANTS

Library

49,422	James Prendergast Library Association, Jamestown, NY

General

300,000	Jamestown Community College, Jamestown, NY
50,000	Chautauqua Area Girl Scout Council, Jamestown, NY
34,459	Lutheran Social Services, Jamestown, NY
25,000	Chautauqua Institution, Chautauqua, NY
14,500	United Way, Jamestown, NY

Icahn Foundation, Carl C.

CONTACT

Gail Golden
Secretary
Icahn & Co.
100 S Bedford Rd.
Mt. Kisco, NY 10549
(914) 242-4010

FINANCIAL SUMMARY

Recent Giving: $147,174 (fiscal 1993); $655,629 (fiscal 1992); $790,263 (fiscal 1991)

Assets: $12,610,164 (fiscal 1993); $12,081,782 (fiscal 1992); $12,641,499 (fiscal 1991)

EIN: 13-3091588

CONTRIBUTIONS SUMMARY

Donor(s): Carl C. Icahn

Typical Recipients: • *Arts & Humanities:* Arts Associations & Councils, Community Arts, History & Archaeology, Libraries, Museums/Galleries, Music, Opera, Performing Arts, Public Broadcasting • *Civic & Public Affairs:* Civil Rights, Community Foundations, Municipalities/Towns, Philanthropic Organizations • *Education:* Arts/Humanities Education, Colleges & Universities, General, Private Education (Precollege) • *Environment:* General • *Health:* Alzheimers Disease, Cancer, Diabetes, Health Organizations, Hospitals, Medical Research, Mental Health, Multiple Sclerosis, Single-Disease Health Associations • *International:* International Environmental Issues, International Relief Efforts • *Religion:* Jewish Causes • *Social Services:* Child Welfare, Community Service Organizations, Counseling, Day Care, Domestic Violence, People with Disabilities, Recreation & Athletics, Refugee Assistance, Substance Abuse, United Funds/United Ways, Youth Organizations

Grant Types: general support

Geographic Distribution: focus on New York, NY

GIVING OFFICERS

Gail Golden: secy, treas

Carl Celian Icahn: pres, dir *B* Queens NY 1936 *ED* Princeton Univ BA 1957; NY Univ Sch Medicine *CURR EMPL* chmn, ceo, dir: Icahn & Co *CORP AFFIL* chmn, ceo, dir: ACF Indus Inc; chmn, pres: Icahn Holding Corp; chmn, pres, ceo: Trans World Airlines; dir: Fairchild Corp *PHIL AFFIL* pres, treas: ACF Foundation

Liba Icahn: dir, treas

Robert T. Osborne: coo

APPLICATION INFORMATION

Initial Approach: Send brief letter of inquiry describing program or project. There are no deadlines.

GRANTS ANALYSIS

Total Grants: $147,174

Number of Grants: 24

Highest Grant: $50,000

Typical Range: $250 to $40,000

Disclosure Period: fiscal year ending November 30, 1993

Note: Recent grants are derived from a fiscal 1993 Form 990.

RECENT GRANTS

General

50,000	Rippowam Cisqua School, Bedford, NY
40,000	New York Hospital Cornell Medical Center, New York, NY
10,000	American Civil Liberties Union Children's Rights Project, New York, NY
8,500	Yivo Institute for Jewish Research, New York, NY
5,000	Guild Hall Academy of Arts, East Hampton, NY

International Business Machines Corp. / IBM International Foundation

Revenue: $64.05 billion
Employees: 235,000
Headquarters: Armonk, NY
SIC Major Group: Computer Peripheral Equipment Nec, Computer Storage Devices, Telephone & Telegraph Apparatus, and Carbon Paper & Inked Ribbons

CONTACT

Paula W. Baker
Director, Corporate Support Plans and Programs
International Business Machines Corp.
Old Orchard Rd.
Armonk, NY 10504
800-426-3333

Note: Another number for Paula W. Baker is (914) 765-6420. The company also recently established the IBM International Foundation. See "Other Things To Know" for more details. The company's World Wide Web address is http://www.ibm.com

FINANCIAL SUMMARY

Recent Giving: $68,000,000 (1995 est.); $64,800,000 (1994 approx.); $92,100,000 (1993 approx.)

Fiscal Note: Total contributions figure includes value of nonmonetary support (see below). The area and site locations are given a discretionary budget to use from the worldwide budget. Above figures do not include foundation giving.

CONTRIBUTIONS SUMMARY

Typical Recipients: • *Arts & Humanities:* Arts Associations & Councils, Arts Centers, Arts Funds, Arts Institutes, Community Arts, Dance, Ethnic & Folk Arts, Historic Preservation, Libraries, Museums/Galleries, Music, Opera, Performing Arts, Public Broadcasting, Theater, Visual Arts • *Civic & Public Affairs:* Civil Rights, Employment/Job Training, Public Policy, Urban & Community Affairs, Women's Affairs, Zoos/Aquariums • *Education:* Colleges & Universities, Community & Junior Colleges, Education Associations, Engineering/Technological Education, Faculty Development, Literacy, Minority Education, Private Education (Precollege), Public Education (Precollege), Science/Mathematics Education, Special Education • *Environment:* General • *Health:* Health Policy/Cost Containment, Health Organizations, Hospitals, Mental Health, Single-Disease Health Associations • *International:* Foreign Educational Institutions, Health Care/Hospitals, International Peace & Security Issues • *Science:* Science

Exhibits & Fairs, Scientific Organizations • *Social Services:* Child Welfare, Community Service Organizations, Delinquency & Criminal Rehabilitation, Emergency Relief, Family Services, People with Disabilities, Senior Services, Substance Abuse, United Funds/United Ways, Volunteer Services, Youth Organizations

Grant Types: capital, employee matching gifts, fellowship, general support, matching, multiyear/continuing support, and research

Note: Employee matching gift ratio: 1 to 1. There is a maximum of $5,000 per donor per institution, up to $10,000 in gifts per calendar year. Matching for retired employees is on a .50 to 1 ratio. An equipment match option is available on a 1.5 to 1 basis for active employees and .75 to 1 for retirees for colleges and universities receiving more than $5,000 and hospitals receiving more than $2,500.

Nonmonetary Support: $37,600,000 (1994); $32,500,000 (1993); $39,300,000 (1992)

Nonmonetary Support Types: donated equipment, in-kind services, loaned employees, and loaned executives

Note: Total contributions figures include donations of cash, equipment, and other resources. Nonmonetary support generally accounts for about one-third of contributions.

Geographic Distribution: nationally, internationally, and in areas where company operates

Operating Locations: AZ (Tucson), CA (San Jose), CO (Boulder), CT (Norwalk, Southbury, Stamford), DC, FL (Boca Raton, Tampa), GA (Atlanta), IL (Chicago, Oak Brook, Springfield), KY (Lexington), MD (Bethesda, Gaithersburg), MN (Rochester), NC (Charlotte, Raleigh), NJ (Dayton, Montvale), NY (Armonk, East Fishkill, Endicott, Hopewell Junction, Kingston, New York, Oswego, Poughkeepsie, Somers, Tarrytown, White Plains, Yorktown Heights), TX (Austin, Dallas, Houston), VA (Manassas), VT (Burlington)

CORP. OFFICERS
Louis Vincent Gerstner, Jr.: *B* Mineola NY 1942 *ED* Dartmouth Coll BA 1963; Harvard Univ MBA 1965 *CURR EMPL* chmn, ceo: Intl Bus Machines Corp *CORP AFFIL* dir: AT&T, Bristol-Myers Squibb Co, Caterpillar Inc, Jewel Cos, NY Times Co, Shearson Lehman Hutton Holdings *NONPR AFFIL* dir: Am-China Soc, Greenwich Boys Club Assn, Intl Mgmt Inst Fdn, Japan Soc, Lincoln Ctr Performing Arts; mem: Bus Counc, Bus Higher Ed Forum, Bus Roundtable, Counc Foreign Rels, Grocery Mfrs Am, Natl Cancer Adv Bd, New York City Partnership, Next Century Schs Fdn; trust: NY Pub Lib; trust, adv bd: Ctr Strategic & Intl Studies; vchmn, dir: New Am Schs Devel Corp

David B. Kalis: *CURR EMPL* vp commun: Intl Bus Machines Corp *PHIL AFFIL* dir: RJR Nabisco Foundation

Joan Mockler: *CURR EMPL* mgr, corp support admin: Intl Bus Machines Corp

GIVING OFFICERS
Paula W. Baker: vp *CURR EMPL* dir corp support plans & programs: Intl Bus Machines Corp

Stanley S. Litow: pres *CURR EMPL* dir corp support programs: Intl Bus Machines Corp

APPLICATION INFORMATION
Initial Approach: *Initial Contact:* local community organizations should contact local branch office; national and international organizations should contact the IBM director of corporate support programs *Include Information On:* a statement fully describing the mission of the organization, the amount requested, and purpose of the contribution; name and telephone number of the project contact; description of solution proposed and how IBM technology will be incorporated; current annual report, audited financial statement or form 990, and IRS 501(c)(3) ruling; project budget with anticipated sources of income (state amount expected to be raised from business sources); list of current contributions from business (name of firm and amount) for general support and/or special projects; names of officers and directors/trustees with business affiliation where appropriate; plan to measure results; equipment requests must also indicate commitment to care and retain items as well as how they will be used *Deadlines:* none

Restrictions on Giving: Does not support individuals; political, labor, religious, fraternal organizations; sports groups; or organizations without tax-exempt status. Also does not fund operating cost requests from United Way member organizations; raffles or telethons; auctions; capital campaigns; construction; or endowments and scholarships. Company generally does not underwrite conferences or symposia.

OTHER THINGS TO KNOW
National and international organizations should contact the IBM Director of Corporate Support Programs at the above address and telephone number.

The IBM International Foundation (IIF) provides the organizational structure and funding vehicle to facilitate the implementation of the new strategy and initiatives of the company both in the U.S. and worldwide.

PUBLICATIONS
Corporate Support Programs Guidelines and Reinventing Education Guidelines

GRANTS ANALYSIS
Total Grants: $68,400,000*

Disclosure Period: 1994

Note: Total grants figure is an approximate. Recent grants are derived from a 1993 grants list.

RECENT GRANTS
General

2,800,000	Florida Atlantic University, Boca Raton, FL — for engineering education
2,250,000	Purdue University, West Lafayette, IN
2,228,383	University of Miami, Miami, FL
1,300,000	Miami-Dade Community College, Miami, FL — for computers and software
1,200,000	Auburn University, AL — for computer equipment

International Paper Co. / International Paper Co. Foundation

Revenue: $14.96 billion
Employees: 72,500
Headquarters: Purchase, NY
SIC Major Group: Paperboard Mills, Miscellaneous Nonmetallic Minerals, Reconstituted Wood Products, and Wood Products Nec

CONTACT
Sandra C. Wilson
Vice President
International Paper Co. Fdn.
Two Manhattanville Rd.
Purchase, NY 10577
(914) 397-1503
Note: In communities where company maintains facilities, contact mill or plant manager, or communications, human resources, or public affairs manager.

FINANCIAL SUMMARY
Recent Giving: $2,800,000 (1995 est.); $2,600,000 (1994 approx.); $2,532,753 (1993)

Assets: $40,000,000 (1995); $41,262,265 (1993); $39,905,243 (1992)

Gifts Received: $158,390 (1993); $154,097 (1992)

Fiscal Note: Above figures represent foundation contributions only. Company also gives directly; direct contributions were about $3 million in 1993.

EIN: 13-6155080

CONTRIBUTIONS SUMMARY
Typical Recipients: • *Arts & Humanities:* Arts Associations & Councils, Arts Centers, Arts Festivals, Arts Funds, Dance, Historic Preservation, Libraries, Museums/Galleries, Music, Opera, Public Broadcasting, Theater • *Civic & Public Affairs:* General, Municipalities/Towns, Zoos/Aquariums • *Education:* Agricultural Education, Business Education, Colleges & Universities, Economic Education, Elementary Education (Private), Engineering/Technological Education, General, Literacy, Minority Education, Private Education (Precollege), Public Education (Precollege), Science/Mathematics Education, Secondary Education (Public) • *Environment:* General • *Health:* Clinics/Medical Centers, Emergency/Ambulance Services, Health Organizations, Hospitals • *Religion:* Dioceses, Religious Organizations • *Social Services:* Child Welfare, Community Centers, Community Service Organizations, Day Care, Family Services, Food/Clothing Distribution, General, Senior

Services, Shelters/Homelessness, Substance Abuse, Volunteer Services, Youth Organizations

Grant Types: employee matching gifts, general support, matching, and project

Note: Employee matching gift ratio: 2 to 1, for employee gifts up to $200 each year; 1 to 1 for gifts over $200. The minimum gift the foundation will match is $25, the maximum amount is $6,000 per employee per year.

Nonmonetary Support Types: donated equipment, donated products, and workplace solicitation

Note: Contact local facility for nonmonetary requests. Estimated value not is available and is not included in figures above.

Geographic Distribution: mainly in areas where company facilities are located, and limited giving to national organizations

Operating Locations: AL (Mobile, Selma), AR (Camden, Gurdon, Pine Bluff), CA (Ukiah), FL (Panama City), IL (Chicago), LA (Bastrop, Mansfield, Pineville, Springhill), MA (Springfield, Walpole), ME (Jay), MS (Moss Point, Natchez, Vicksburg), NY (Binghamton, Corinth, Oswego, Purchase, Ticonderoga), OH (Springdale, Wooster), OR (Gardiner), PA (Erie, Lewisburg, Lock Haven, Towanda), SC (Georgetown, Haig Point), TN (Memphis), TX (Dallas, Houston, Texarkana), WI (De Pere, Fond Du Luc, Green Bay, Kaukauna, Menasha)

CORP. OFFICERS
John A. Georges: *B* El Paso TX 1931 *ED* Univ IL BS 1951; Drexel Univ MS 1958 *CURR EMPL* chmn, ceo: Intl Paper Co *CORP AFFIL* dir: NY Stock Exchange *NONPR AFFIL* dir: Fed Reserve Bank NY; mem: Bus Roundtable, Pres Comm Environmental Quality; mem pres counc: Tulane Univ; trust: Drexel Univ, Pub Policy Inst Bus Counc NY St *CLUB AFFIL* NY YC

James Patrick Melican, Jr.: *B* Worcester MA 1940 *ED* Fordham Univ BA 1962; Harvard Univ JD 1965; MI St Univ MBA 1971 *CURR EMPL* exec vp: Intl Paper Co *CORP AFFIL* dir: Scitex Corp Ltd *NONPR AFFIL* chmn fin & mgmt policy comm: Natl Assn Mfrs; mem: Am Bar Assn, Am Law Inst, Assn Bar City New York, NY Bar Assn

Mark A. Suwyn: *B* Denver CO 1942 *ED* Hope Coll BS 1964; WA St Univ PhD 1967 *CURR EMPL* exec vp, forest & special products: Intl Paper Co *CORP AFFIL* dir: Scitex Co

GIVING OFFICERS
John A. Georges: dir *CURR EMPL* chmn, ceo: Intl Paper Co (see above)

James Walter Guedry: pres *B* Morgan City LA 1941 *ED* Georgetown Univ AB 1962; Univ Brussels 1962-1963; Univ VA LLB 1966 *CURR EMPL* assoc gen couns, corp secy, staff vp: Intl Paper Co *NONPR AFFIL* mem: Assn Bar City New York

Marianne Larsen: mgr contribution programs

James Patrick Melican, Jr.: dir *CURR EMPL* exec vp: Intl Paper Co (see above)

Joyce Nelson: treas

Ann Marie Ryan: secy

Mark A. Suwyn: dir *CURR EMPL* exec vp, forest & special products: Intl Paper Co (see above)

Sandra C. Wilson: vp admin, dir *B* 1949

APPLICATION INFORMATION
Initial Approach: *Initial Contact:* request application form from local facility; send to manager of local International Paper Co. facility, or to Sandra C. Wilson, if in her locality *Include Information On:* brief background of organization, including board of directors; concise description of program and objectives; audited financial statement; IRS tax-exemption letter; current funding sources and specific amounts; current annual report; and program budget, including amount requested *Deadlines:* check with local facilities for local deadlines; if submitting directly to foundation, applications are accepted from January 1 through March 1

Restrictions on Giving: Does not support individuals; programs for gifted students; general operating expenses; endowments; capital expenses for cultural, civic, or educational institutions; veterans or labor groups; athletic organizations; religious, political, or lobbying groups; organizations located outside of or whose contributed funds go outside of the United States and its territories; tables at charitable functions or courtesy advertising; organizations which discriminate on the basis of sex, race, or creed; or groups that do not have 501(c)3 tax-exempt status.

GRANTS ANALYSIS
Total Grants: $2,532,753

Number of Grants: 1,520

Highest Grant: $50,500

Average Grant: $1,666

Typical Range: $1,000 to $5,000

Disclosure Period: 1993

Note: Above figures are for foundation giving only. Recent grants are derived from a 1994 approved grants list.

RECENT GRANTS
Library

6,000	Public Library of Selma-Dallas County

General

95,000	National Council on Economic Education, New York, NY
50,000	United Negro College Fund, New York, NY
25,000	Southeastern Consortium for Minorities in Engineering, Atlanta, GA
20,000	LADS
15,000	Earth Focus

Ittleson Foundation

CONTACT
Anthony C. Wood
Executive Director

Ittleson Foundation
645 Madison Ave., 16th Fl.
New York, NY 10022
(212) 838-5010

FINANCIAL SUMMARY
Recent Giving: $1,197,499 (1993); $1,230,184 (1992); $1,318,559 (1991)

Assets: $18,319,759 (1993); $18,196,330 (1992); $18,475,505 (1991)

Gifts Received: $175,000 (1992); $375,000 (1989)

Fiscal Note: In 1989 and 1992, the foundation received contributions from the estate of Nancy S. Ittleson.

EIN: 51-0172757

CONTRIBUTIONS SUMMARY
Donor(s): The Ittleson Foundation was established in New York in 1932 by the late Henry Ittleson , founder and past chairman of C.I.T. Financial Corporation. After his death in 1948, the foundation received a substantial bequest from his estate. Mr. Ittleson's widow, Blanche F. Ittleson, former trustee of the foundation (until her death in 1975), directed the focus of the foundation toward health and welfare, particularly mental health care and research.

Typical Recipients: • *Arts & Humanities:* Arts Associations & Councils, Arts Centers, Arts Outreach, Film & Video, Libraries, Museums/Galleries, Opera, Public Broadcasting • *Civic & Public Affairs:* Chambers of Commerce, Civil Rights, Gay/Lesbian Issues, General, Housing, Law & Justice, Legal Aid, Minority Business, Nonprofit Management, Philanthropic Organizations, Professional & Trade Associations, Public Policy, Safety, Urban & Community Affairs, Women's Affairs • *Education:* Arts/Humanities Education, Colleges & Universities, Education Associations, Education Reform, Elementary Education (Private), Environmental Education, Faculty Development, Private Education (Precollege), Social Sciences Education • *Environment:* Air/Water Quality, General, Resource Conservation, Wildlife Protection • *Health:* AIDS/HIV, Cancer, Children's Health/Hospitals, Geriatric Health, Health Organizations, Hospitals, Mental Health, Public Health, Research/Studies Institutes, Single-Disease Health Associations • *International:* International Environmental Issues • *Religion:* Churches, Jewish Causes • *Social Services:* At-Risk Youth, Child Welfare, Community Service Organizations, Counseling, Crime Prevention, Delinquency & Criminal Rehabilitation, Family Services, Food/Clothing Distribution, People with Disabilities, Senior Services, Shelters/Homelessness, United Funds/United Ways, Volunteer Services, Youth Organizations

Grant Types: general support, multi-year/continuing support, project, research, and seed money

Geographic Distribution: national

GIVING OFFICERS
Henry Anthony Ittleson: chmn, pres, dir *B* New York NY 1937 *ED* Brown Univ BA 1960 *CURR EMPL* exec special projects:

CIT Group *CORP AFFIL* chmn: Travent Ltd; dir: Osborn Communs Corp *NONPR AFFIL* bd fellows: Brown Univ; mem: Phi Gamma Delta; trust: Boys Club NY, Brooks Sch *CLUB AFFIL* Brown Univ, Garden Gods CO, Long Island Wyandanch, Meadow, Regency Whist

Marianne S. Ittleson: dir

Lionel I. Pincus: dir *B* Philadelphia PA 1931 *ED* Univ PA BA 1953; Columbia Univ Bus Sch MBA 1956 *CURR EMPL* chmn, ceo, dir: EM Warburg Pincus & Co *CORP AFFIL* chmn: Counsellors Tandem Securities; chmn, ceo: Warburg Pincus Couns, Warburg Pincus Ventures; dir: Christians Intl, Commun Newspapers, Journal Co, Journal News, Mattel, Mellon Bank Corp, NH Acquisition Corp; mng dir: Warburg Pincus Capital Co, Warburg Pincus Investors *NONPR AFFIL* mem: Counc Foreign Rels; trust: Am Sch Ballet, Citizens Budget Commn, Columbia Univ, Montefiore Hosp Med Ctr *CLUB AFFIL* Meadow *PHIL AFFIL* pres: Pincus Family Fund; vp: Hera Foundation

Lawrence Sneag: treas

Pamela Syrmis: vp, dir

Victor Syrmis, MD: dir *B* 1943

Anthony C. Wood: exec dir

APPLICATION INFORMATION
Initial Approach:

Applicants should send the foundation an introductory letter.

Grant requests should include a description of the organization and project for which funds are sought, organization's budget, an annual report, if available, and evidence of tax-exempt status.

The deadlines for requests are April 1 for the spring meeting, and September 1 for the fall meeting.

The foundation does not supply application forms. Grant requests are reviewed on a continuing basis. If the grant proposal fits within the foundation's current scope of interest, additional information will be required. All grant requests are acknowledged upon receipt and interviews may be requested after the initial letter review. The board of directors meets in May and December. Final notification of funding is given within three months. If the foundation declines a proposal, applicants must wait at least one year before reapplying for any purpose.

Restrictions on Giving: The foundation generally does not provide funding for general support, capital building projects, endowments, grants to individuals, scholarships, fellowships, or internships (except as part of a program), biomedical research, or continuing support to existing programs. Support also is not given to programs of direct service to individuals with only a local focus or constituency. Funding is provided to pilot programs or for the start-up of a truly innovative service when there is a credible plan for national impact and dissemination. The foundation does not make international grants.

OTHER THINGS TO KNOW
The foundation reports that it supports pilot programs or the start-up of new services when:

the service or project is truly innovative

there are practical plans for evaluation

there appears to be an audience for the results, and

there is a credible plan for dissemination to those audiences.

PUBLICATIONS
Annual report

GRANTS ANALYSIS
Total Grants: $1,197,499

Number of Grants: 86*

Highest Grant: $400,000

Average Grant: $12,529*

Typical Range: $50 to $2,500 and $5,000 to $50,000

Disclosure Period: 1993

Note: Number of grants and average grants figures exclude $120,000 in individual scholarships. Recent grants are derived from a 1993 Form 990.

RECENT GRANTS

Library

1,750	Foundation Center, New York, NY

General

400,000	Brown University, Providence, RI — expand the environmental studies program
55,000	Fortune Society, New York, NY — support of their model job development program for HIV-positive symptomatic ex-offenders
50,000	Brooks School, North Andover, MA
50,000	Hetrick-Martin Institute, New York, NY — one-time grant to support the training of child welfare administrators and social workers in mainstream agencies on working with lesbian, gay, and bisexual youth and tolerance training for other youth served by these agencies
50,000	University of Pennsylvania, Philadelphia, PA — support an applied research project to be conducted by integrating three years of homeless shelter registry data with mental health and AIDS data bases in Philadelphia and New York

JM Foundation

CONTACT
Chris K. Olander
Executive Director and Assistant Treasurer
JM Foundation
60 E 42nd St., Ste. 1651
New York, NY 10165
(212) 687-7735

FINANCIAL SUMMARY
Recent Giving: $1,000,000 (1995 est.); $1,272,800 (1994); $2,110,325 (1993)

Assets: $20,000,000 (1995 est.); $20,000,000 (1994 approx.); $22,206,907 (1993)

EIN: 13-6068340

CONTRIBUTIONS SUMMARY
Donor(s): Jeremiah Milbank was engaged throughout his life in philanthropic activities. Mr. Milbank was born in New York City on January 24, 1887. After graduating from Yale University in 1909, Mr. Milbank established his own investment firm in 1916. A believer in free enterprise, Mr. Milbank was a director of several companies and had long-term investments in private corporations.

Mr. Milbank's belief that persons with disabilities could lead independent and meaningful lives was to become a subject of major national importance. His conviction that the Red Cross was a viable organization led him to found the Red Cross Institution for Crippled Soldiers and Sailors in 1917. This was the first American organization to address the needs of physically disabled veterans. In 1919, he founded the Institute for the Crippled and Disabled (ICD). It was at this Institute that vocational education, medical service, and psychosocial support were integrated to form a new comprehensive rehabilitation approach for people with physical disabilities.

In 1928, Mr. Milbank founded and financed the International Committee for the Study of Infantile Paralysis. As a result of this active interest in the subject of polio, President Roosevelt asked him to be the acting chairman of the organization that preceded the National Foundation for Infantile Paralysis.

Mr. Milbank personally contributed to a collaborative effort with Metropolitan Life Insurance Company to finance a research project to combat diptheria. In addition, he worked with President Hoover to form the Boys and Girls Clubs of America, and served as its treasurer for 25 years. Mr. Milbank also had personal interests in recovering and converting acres of swampland in South Carolina for agricultural use. His spiritual beliefs led to his financing the first film on the life of Jesus Christ, Cecil B. DeMille's "King of Kings." Mr. Milbank died on March 22, 1972.

Typical Recipients: • *Arts & Humanities:* General, Libraries, Public Broadcasting • *Civic & Public Affairs:* African American Affairs, Business/Free Enterprise, Civil

Rights, Economic Policy, Employment/Job Training, General, Housing, Law & Justice, Native American Affairs, Philanthropic Organizations, Professional & Trade Associations, Public Policy, Safety, Urban & Community Affairs • *Education:* Arts/Humanities Education, Business Education, Education Associations, Education Reform, Journalism/Media Education, Medical Education, Minority Education, Private Education (Precollege) • *Health:* Cancer, Clinics/Medical Centers, Geriatric Health, Health Policy/Cost Containment, Health Organizations, Heart, Hospitals, Medical Rehabilitation, Medical Research, Prenatal Health Issues, Public Health • *Religion:* Religious Organizations, Social/Policy Issues • *Social Services:* Child Welfare, Crime Prevention, Family Planning, Family Services, People with Disabilities, Scouts, Substance Abuse, Volunteer Services, Youth Organizations

Grant Types: project, research, and seed money

Geographic Distribution: no geographic restrictions

GIVING OFFICERS
Mrs. H. Lawrence Bogert: vp, dir

Jeremiah Milbank Bogert: dir *B* New York NY 1941 *ED* Yale Univ BA 1963; Univ CT MBA 1973 *CURR EMPL* chmn bd, dir: James C Edwards & Co Inc *CORP AFFIL* ptnr: Mason B Starring & Co Ltd *PHIL AFFIL* vp, treas, trust: Woodland Foundation

Jack Brauntuch: special couns, treas

Lynn R. Bruhn: asst secy

William Lee Hanley, Jr.: treas, dir

Jeremiah Milbank III: dir *CORP AFFIL* dir: Intl Minerals & Chems Corp

Jeremiah Milbank, Jr.: pres, dir *B* New York NY 1920 *ED* Yale Univ BA 1942; Harvard Univ MBA 1948 *CURR EMPL* pres: Cypress Woods Corp *CORP AFFIL* dir: IMCERA Group, Intl Minerals & Chems Corp *NONPR AFFIL* chmn: Boys & Girls Clubs Am; chmn emeritus: Boys & Girls Club Greenwich; hon pres: Intl Ctr Disabled; trust: Madison Ctr Ed Aff *CLUB AFFIL* Brook, River, Round Hill *PHIL AFFIL* vp, trust: Evelyn Sharp Foundation

Peter C. Morse: dir

Chris K. Olander: exec dir, asst treas

Michael Sanger: dir

Daniel Gleason Tenney, Jr.: secy, dir *B* New York NY 1913 *ED* Yale Univ BA 1935; Yale Univ LLB 1938 *CURR EMPL* ptnr: Milbank Tweed Hadley & McCloy

APPLICATION INFORMATION
Initial Approach:

The foundation invites written proposals. The foundation requests that applicants do not send video or audio tapes unless requested.

The proposal should contain a brief summary of the proposed project of one page or less; vitae of author, researcher, or project officer, if applicable; need for support, including background; objectives; time period; key staff; project budget; evaluation plan;

annual report and/or descriptive brochure; most recent audited financial statement; list of governing board members; copy of IRS 501(c)(3) tax-exemption letter; list of organization supporters and amounts, current funders of the proposed project, and grant makers with whom proposals are pending; and the expected outcome or results.

The foundation has no deadline for submitting proposals.

The foundation does not have a printed application form or a rigid format for requests. Applicants will be notified of a decision within three to four weeks. Proposals that are consistent with the capacity and interests of the foundation are examined further, and forwarded to the directors who meet in January, May, and October.

Restrictions on Giving: The foundation usually declines to support general operating funds, capital campaigns, or annual appeals. The foundation does not provide grants to individuals, international projects, arts, music, theater, dinner events, equipment such as computers and biomedical devices, government agencies, public schools, or endowment funds.

OTHER THINGS TO KNOW
The foundation assists potential grantees in a variety of ways including but not limited to: fundraising, networking, and proposal writing. The foundation also collaborates with like-minded foundations.

GRANTS ANALYSIS
Total Grants: $1,272,800

Number of Grants: 65

Highest Grant: $175,000

Average Grant: $19,582

Typical Range: $10,000 to $35,000

Disclosure Period: 1994

Note: Recent grants are derived from a 1993 annual report.

RECENT GRANTS
General

200,000	Boys and Girls Clubs of America, New York, NY — to support Outreach Two Million, a three-year plan to serve 2,000,000 disadvantaged youngsters nationwide by 1994, final payment of a two-year grant
200,000	ICD-International Center for the Disabled, New York, NY — toward the 75th Anniversary fundraising campaign, final payment of a four-year, $1 million challenge grant
60,000	Philanthropy Roundtable, Indianapolis, IN — in support of educational programs for foundations, corporations, trust and estate officers, and individual donors
51,150	Memorial Sloan-Kettering Cancer Center, New York, NY — to establish a

collaborative outpatient rehabilitation program between Sloan-Kettering and the International Center for the Disabled

50,000   Ronald Reagan Presidential Foundation, Simi Valley, CA — toward research, educational forums, and publications on domestic issues, final payment of a two-year grant

Johnson Charitable Trust, Keith Wold

CONTACT
R. W. Johnson IV
Principal Manager
Keith Wold Johnson Charitable Trust
c/o Johnson Co.
630 Fifth Ave.
New York, NY 10111
(212) 872-7903

FINANCIAL SUMMARY
Recent Giving: $151,000 (1993); $134,000 (1992); $111,500 (1990)

Assets: $3,388,940 (1993); $3,166,654 (1992); $2,565,602 (1990)

EIN: 11-2845826

CONTRIBUTIONS SUMMARY
Typical Recipients: • *Arts & Humanities:* Libraries, Public Broadcasting • *Civic & Public Affairs:* Zoos/Aquariums • *Education:* Colleges & Universities • *Health:* Health Organizations, Nursing Services • *Religion:* Religious Welfare • *Social Services:* Food/Clothing Distribution

Grant Types: general support

Geographic Distribution: focus on NY and NJ

GIVING OFFICERS
Christopher W. Johnson: trust

Elizabeth Ross Johnson: trust

Robert Wood Johnson IV: trust, prin mgr *NONPR AFFIL* trust: WNET-TV; trust, secy: NY Zoological Soc *PHIL AFFIL* pres, dir: Willard T. C. Johnson Foundation; co-chmn capital campaign: Juvenile Diabetes Foundation

APPLICATION INFORMATION
Initial Approach: The foundation has no formal grant application procedure or application form. There are no deadlines.

GRANTS ANALYSIS
Total Grants: $151,000

Number of Grants: 2

Highest Grant: $150,000

Disclosure Period: 1993

Note: Recent grants are derived from a 1993 Form 990.

RECENT GRANTS

Library
1,000   Clarence Dillon Public Library

Johnson Foundation, Willard T. C.

CONTACT
Robert W. Johnson IV
President and Director
Willard T. C. Johnson Foundation
c/o The Johnson Co.
630 Fifth Ave., Ste. 1510
New York, NY 10111
(212) 332-7500

FINANCIAL SUMMARY
Recent Giving: $1,503,000 (1992); $1,455,000 (1991); $893,500 (1990)
Assets: $37,392,352 (1992); $33,218,171 (1991); $30,920,723 (1990)
Gifts Received: $1,124,456 (1992); $188 (1991); $659,855 (1990)
Fiscal Note: In 1990, contributions were received from Keith W. Johnson.
EIN: 13-2993310

CONTRIBUTIONS SUMMARY
Donor(s): The foundation was incorporated in 1979 by the late Willard T.C. Johnson and the late Keith W. Johnson .

Typical Recipients: • *Arts & Humanities:* Libraries, Opera • *Civic & Public Affairs:* African American Affairs, Business/Free Enterprise, Parades/Festivals • *Education:* Education Funds • *Health:* AIDS/HIV, Diabetes, Emergency/Ambulance Services, Hospitals • *Science:* Scientific Centers & Institutes • *Social Services:* Family Planning, Senior Services, Youth Organizations

Grant Types: general support
Geographic Distribution: primarily New York City and New Jersey

GIVING OFFICERS
Robert Wood Johnson IV: pres, dir *NONPR AFFIL* trust: WNET-TV; trust, secy: NY Zoological Soc *PHIL AFFIL* trust, prin mgr: Keith Wold Johnson Charitable Trust; co-chmn capital campaign: Juvenile Diabetes Foundation

Robert J. Mortimer: vp, secy

APPLICATION INFORMATION
Initial Approach:
The foundation has no formal grant application procedure or application form.

The foundation has no deadline for submitting proposals.

Restrictions on Giving: Grants are made to organizations listed under section 501(c)(3) of the IRS code. The foundation does not make grants to individuals.

GRANTS ANALYSIS
Total Grants: $1,503,000
Number of Grants: 8
Highest Grant: $850,000

Average Grant: $93,286*
Typical Range: $10,000 to $125,000
Disclosure Period: 1992
Note: Average grant figure does not include a single grant of $850,000. Recent grants are derived from a 1992 Form 990.

RECENT GRANTS
General
850,000   Juvenile Diabetes Foundation International, New York, NY
250,000   Black Youth Organization, Newark, NJ
150,000   Planned Parenthood Association of Mercer Area, Mercer, NJ
78,000   Pediatric AIDS Foundation, Los Angeles, CA
30,000   Fund for Aging Services, New York, NY

Johnson & Higgins

Revenue: $933.0 million
Employees: 8,200
Headquarters: New York, NY
SIC Major Group: Insurance Agents, Brokers & Service

CONTACT
Christine Meehan
Vice President
Johnson & Higgins
125 Broad St.
New York, NY 10004
(212) 574-7061

FINANCIAL SUMMARY
Recent Giving: $3,500,000 (1995 est.); $3,200,000 (1994 approx.); $3,200,000 (1993)

Fiscal Note: Company gives directly. Above figures exclude nonmonetary support.

CONTRIBUTIONS SUMMARY
Typical Recipients: • *Arts & Humanities:* Arts Appreciation, Arts Associations & Councils, Arts Centers, Arts Festivals, Arts Funds, Arts Institutes, Community Arts, Dance, Ethnic & Folk Arts, Historic Preservation, Libraries, Literary Arts, Museums/Galleries, Music, Opera, Performing Arts, Public Broadcasting, Theater, Visual Arts • *Civic & Public Affairs:* Business/Free Enterprise, Civil Rights, Economic Development, Economic Policy, Law & Justice, Professional & Trade Associations, Public Policy, Safety, Urban & Community Affairs, Zoos/Aquariums • *Education:* Arts/Humanities Education, Business Education, Colleges & Universities, Community & Junior Colleges, Continuing Education, Economic Education, Education Associations, Education Funds, Elementary Education (Private), Engineering/Technological Education, Faculty Development, Health & Physical Education, Literacy, Medical Education, Minority Education, Preschool Education, Private Education (Precollege), Public Education (Precollege), Science/Mathematics Education, Social Sciences Education, Special

Education, Student Aid • *Environment:* General • *Health:* Emergency/Ambulance Services, Geriatric Health, Health Policy/Cost Containment, Health Organizations, Hospices, Hospitals, Medical Rehabilitation, Medical Research, Medical Training, Mental Health, Nursing Services, Nutrition, Public Health, Single-Disease Health Associations • *Social Services:* Child Welfare, Community Service Organizations, People with Disabilities, Senior Services, Substance Abuse, United Funds/United Ways, Volunteer Services, Youth Organizations

Grant Types: capital, challenge, employee matching gifts, general support, and project

Nonmonetary Support: $150,000 (1988)

Nonmonetary Support Types: donated equipment

Note: Estimated value of nonmonetary support is less than $50,000 annually.

Geographic Distribution: no geographic restrictions

Operating Locations: AK (Anchorage), AL (Birmingham), AZ (Phoenix), CA (Costa Mesa, Los Angeles, Riverside, San Diego, San Francisco, San Jose), CO (Denver), CT (Hartford, Stamford), DC, DE (Wilmington), FL (Miami), GA (Atlanta), HI (Honolulu), ID (Boise), IL (Chicago), KY (Louisville), LA (New Orleans), MA (Boston), MD (Baltimore), ME (Portland), MI (Grand Rapids, Jackson), MN (Minneapolis), MO (St. Louis), NC (Charlotte), NJ (Parsippany), NV (Las Vegas), NY (New York), OH (Cincinnati, Cleveland, Columbus), OK (Tulsa), OR (Portland), PA (Philadelphia, Pittsburgh), SC (Charleston), TN (Nashville), TX (Austin, Dallas, Houston), UT (Salt Lake City), VA (Richmond, Roanoke), WA (Seattle)

Note: Johnson & Higgins operates 48 offices nationwide and 54 offices outside the United States.

CORP. OFFICERS
Richard A. Nielsen: *B* 1937 *ED* Univ MI *CURR EMPL* pres, coo, dir: Johnson & Higgins *CORP AFFIL* exec vp, dir: Johnson & Higgins Washington DC

David A. Olsen: *B* Brooklyn NY 1937 *ED* Bowdoin Coll BA 1959 *CURR EMPL* chmn, ceo, dir: Johnson & Higgins *NONPR AFFIL* dir: New York City Partnership, Un Way Am; dir corp congress: NY Pub Lib; mem: Natl Assn Ins Brokers, Psi Upsilon; mem bd overseers: Bowdoin Coll; vchmn, treas: S St Seaport Mus *CLUB AFFIL* Econ NY, Explorers

GIVING OFFICERS
Christine Meehan: *CURR EMPL* vp: Johnson & Higgins

APPLICATION INFORMATION
Initial Approach: *Initial Contact:* letter or brief proposal *Include Information On:* description of the organization, amount requested, purpose for which funds are sought, recently audited financial statement, and proof of tax-exempt status *Deadlines:* in the fall

Restrictions on Giving: Company does not support individuals; political, lobbying, religious, or fraternal organizations; goodwill advertising or benefit events; or member agencies of united funds.

GRANTS ANALYSIS
Total Grants: $3,200,000*

Typical Range: $2,500 to $5,000

Disclosure Period: 1994

Note: Total grants figure is approximate.

Jones Foundation, Daisy Marquis

CONTACT
Roger L. Gardner
President and Trustee
Daisy Marquis Jones Foundation
500 Granite Bldg.
130 E Main St.
Rochester, NY 14604-1620
(716) 263-3331

FINANCIAL SUMMARY
Recent Giving: $900,000 (1995 est.); $555,000 (1994 approx.); $1,324,780 (1993)

Assets: $22,500,000 (1995 est.); $22,215,000 (1994 approx.); $23,702,231 (1993)

Gifts Received: $420,496 (1990); $4,128 (1989); $26,500 (1988)

Fiscal Note: The foundation has received gifts from Leo M. Lyons, its chairman.

EIN: 23-7000227

CONTRIBUTIONS SUMMARY
Donor(s): "The Daisy Marquis Jones Foundation is a not-for-profit, private foundation created in 1968 by the late Daisy Marquis Jones . Daisy Marquis Jones was born in Pennsylvania and came to Rochester around 1909. She married Nelson Jones, a Himrod dairy farmer in the 1940s. The years they operated the dairy farm together formed the basis for her special interest in Yates County. She gave her Himrod farmhouse to the fledgling volunteer fire department and continued to support them in building a firehouse and purchasing equipment. After her husband's death in 1961 she returned to Rochester. Daisy was a shrewd investor and an astute businesswoman. She had the admiration and respect of the bankers and brokers of the downtown area, but was little known in the community until after her death in 1971. She left a multi-million dollar estate to the Foundation she had set up three years before her death."

Typical Recipients: • *Arts & Humanities:* Arts Outreach, Dance, General, Libraries, Literary Arts, Music, Public Broadcasting, Visual Arts • *Civic & Public Affairs:* African American Affairs, Botanical Gardens/Parks, Civil Rights, General, Housing, Law & Justice, Legal Aid, Municipalities/Towns, Nonprofit Management, Philanthropic Organizations, Public Policy, Safety, Urban & Community Affairs, Women's Affairs • *Education:* Arts/Humanities Education, Colleges & Universities, Community &

Junior Colleges, General, Health & Physical Education, Literacy, Medical Education, Preschool Education, Science/Mathematics Education, Secondary Education (Public), Special Education • *Health:* Adolescent Health Issues, AIDS/HIV, Alzheimers Disease, Children's Health/Hospitals, Clinics/Medical Centers, Emergency/Ambulance Services, Geriatric Health, Health Organizations, Hospitals, Medical Rehabilitation, Mental Health, Nursing Services, Nutrition, Outpatient Health Care • *Religion:* Religious Organizations, Religious Welfare • *Science:* Science Museums, Scientific Centers & Institutes, Scientific Organizations • *Social Services:* Child Welfare, Community Centers, Day Care, Delinquency & Criminal Rehabilitation, Domestic Violence, Family Planning, Family Services, Food/Clothing Distribution, Homes, People with Disabilities, Recreation & Athletics, Senior Services, Shelters/Homelessness, YMCA/YWCA/YMHA/YWHA, Youth Organizations

Grant Types: capital, challenge, general support, matching, project, and seed money

Geographic Distribution: Monroe and Yates counties, NY

GIVING OFFICERS
Roger L. Gardner: pres, trust

Leo M. Lyons: chmn, trust

Pearl W. Rubin: adv, trust

Sydney R. Rubin: gen couns

Donald W. Whitney: trust

APPLICATION INFORMATION
Initial Approach:

A short letter of inquiry should be sent to the foundation.

The letter should describe the project, list the amount requested, and include an intended starting date. If the foundation is interested in the proposal, an application form will be sent. The form should include a detailed program description, work plan, qualifications of staff, itemized program budget, plans for evaluation, and coordination with related organizations and programs.

There are no deadlines for applications, but early submission of requests is encouraged.

A decision generally takes two to three months. The board usually meets monthly, except during July and August, to review proposals.

Restrictions on Giving: The foundation does not make grants in the following areas: arts, endowments, local chapters of national health-related organizations, private schools, religious projects, research, scholarships, and projects by or for individuals.

OTHER THINGS TO KNOW
Marine Midland Bank serves as corporate trustee for the foundation.

PUBLICATIONS
Annual report

GRANTS ANALYSIS
Total Grants: $1,324,780

Number of Grants: 126

Highest Grant: $125,000

Average Grant: $10,514

Typical Range: $2,500 to $30,000

Disclosure Period: 1993

Note: Recent grants are derived from a 1993 Form 990.

RECENT GRANTS
General

125,000	Park Ridge Foundation, Rochester, NY
100,000	Rushville Health, Rushville, NY
70,000	Visiting Nurse Service of Rochester, Rochester, NY
62,500	Park Ridge Foundation, Rochester, NY
62,500	Park Ridge Foundation, Rochester, NY

Joy Family Foundation

CONTACT
Marsha J. Sullivan
Trustee
Joy Family Foundation
107-111 Goundry St.
North Tonawanda, NY 14120
(716) 692-6665

FINANCIAL SUMMARY
Recent Giving: $197,636 (1993); $182,598 (1992); $140,838 (1991)

Assets: $4,100,246 (1993); $3,880,454 (1992); $3,505,420 (1991)

Gifts Received: $181,311 (1993); $370,000 (1992); $2,870,597 (1990)

Fiscal Note: In 1993, contributions were received from Paul W. Joy ($130,297) and Mrs. Joan H. Joy ($51,014).

EIN: 16-6335211

CONTRIBUTIONS SUMMARY
Donor(s): the donor is Paul W. Joy, the foundation's trustee

Typical Recipients: • *Arts & Humanities:* Historic Preservation, Libraries, Music • *Civic & Public Affairs:* General, Housing, Law & Justice, Women's Affairs, Zoos/Aquariums • *Education:* Business Education, Colleges & Universities, Community & Junior Colleges, Faculty Development, General, Literacy, Private Education (Precollege), Secondary Education (Private), Special Education • *Health:* Children's Health/Hospitals, Hospices, Hospitals • *Religion:* Churches, Religious Organizations, Religious Welfare • *Social Services:* At-Risk Youth, Community Centers, Community Service Organizations, Counseling, Day Care, Family Services, Food/Clothing Distribution, People with Disabilities, Recreation & Athletics, Substance Abuse, United Funds/United Ways, Youth Organizations

Grant Types: capital, department, and general support

Geographic Distribution: Erie and Niagara counties, NY

GIVING OFFICERS
Joan H. Joy: trust
Paul W. Joy: trust, don
Stephen T. Joy: trust
Paula Joy Reinhold: trust
Marsha Joy Sullivan: trust

APPLICATION INFORMATION
Initial Approach: Request application form. There are no deadlines.

GRANTS ANALYSIS
Total Grants: $197,636
Number of Grants: 22
Highest Grant: $25,600
Typical Range: $300 to $20,000
Disclosure Period: 1993

Note: Recent grants are derived from a 1993 Form 990.

RECENT GRANTS
General
25,600	Children's Hospital, Buffalo, NY
20,000	Court Appointed Special Advocates, Buffalo, NY
15,839	Family and Children's Services, Niagara Falls, NY
15,000	Language Development Program, Buffalo, NY
14,050	St. Mary's School for the Deaf, Buffalo, NY

Julia R. and Estelle L. Foundation

CONTACT
Richard L. Wolf
Vice President
Julia R. and Estelle L. Foundation
3600 Marine Midland Ctr.
Buffalo, NY 14203
(716) 856-9490

FINANCIAL SUMMARY
Recent Giving: $2,598,750 (1993); $2,323,480 (1992); $2,345,000 (1991)
Assets: $38,597,737 (1993); $33,036,932 (1992); $31,676,787 (1991)
Gifts Received: $575,283 (1993); $734,043 (1992); $10,319,994 (1991)
Fiscal Note: In 1991, the foundation received $10,319,994 from various trusts including a $9,287,374 gift from the R. John Oishei Trust A. In 1992, the foundation received gifts from John R. Oishei Trusts, the John R. Oishei Appreciation Charitable Trust, and the Insurance Trust of Sarah Nathan. In 1993, the foundation received gifts from the John R. Oishei Appreciation Charitable Trust and the John R. Oishei Trust f/b/o R. John Oishei.
EIN: 16-0874319

CONTRIBUTIONS SUMMARY
Donor(s): The Julia R. and Estelle L. Foundation was founded in New York in 1941, with contributions by the Peter C. Cornell Trust and the late John R. Oishei. The foundation receives continuing support from the John R. Oishei Appreciation Trust.

Typical Recipients: • *Arts & Humanities:* Arts Institutes, History & Archaeology, Libraries, Music, Public Broadcasting, Theater • *Civic & Public Affairs:* Zoos/Aquariums • *Education:* Colleges & Universities, Private Education (Precollege), Secondary Education (Private), Secondary Education (Public), Special Education • *Health:* Children's Health/Hospitals, Emergency/Ambulance Services, Hospices, Hospitals, Long-Term Care, Medical Research • *Religion:* Churches, Dioceses, Religious Welfare, Seminaries • *Social Services:* Animal Protection, Child Welfare, Family Services, Food/Clothing Distribution, People with Disabilities, Scouts, Senior Services, United Funds/United Ways, YMCA/YWCA/YMHA/YWHA, Youth Organizations

Grant Types: general support, project, and research

Geographic Distribution: primarily Buffalo and the greater western New York State area

GIVING OFFICERS
Patricia O. Colby: mem
Carl E. Larson: vp
Albert R. Mugel: vp, secy, treas, dir *B* 1917 *ED* Univ Buffalo Law Sch LLB 1941 *CURR EMPL* ptnr: Jaeckle Fleischmann & Mugel *NONPR AFFIL* mem: Am Bar Assn, Erie County Bar Assn, NY St Bar Assn
Julian R. Oishei: mem
Rupert Warren: pres, dir *B* Lincoln NE 1908 *ED* Univ NE 1928; Harvard Univ LLB 1931 *NONPR AFFIL* fellow: Am Bar Fdn
Richard Lloyd Wolf: vp, dir *B* Hamlin NY 1935 *ED* US Naval Academy BS 1960; Northwestern Univ JD 1966; Univ Rochester Grad Sch Mgmt 1981-1983 *CURR EMPL* chmn, pres, ceo: Trico Products Corp *CORP AFFIL* dir: Chase Lincoln First Bank, FIAMM Technologies; pres, dir: Trico Holding Co *NONPR AFFIL* mem: NY St Bar Assn; mem, dir: Buffalo Chamber Commerce *CLUB AFFIL* Buffalo

APPLICATION INFORMATION
Initial Approach:
Prospective applicants should send a preliminary letter of inquiry to the foundation. There are no formal application procedures.
The letter should contain the following information: a concise statement of the program or project, the amount of funding requested, a brief description of the nature and activities of the applicant, proof of tax-exempt status, and a list of officers and directors of the organizations.
There are no deadlines.
In general, annual distribution of funds is in December.
Restrictions on Giving: The foundation reports that its support is limited to the Buffalo, NY, metropolitan area except for a few national organizations. Additionally, the foundation does not make grants for operating expenses or scholarships. Private founda-

tions and individuals are also not eligible for funding.

GRANTS ANALYSIS
Total Grants: $2,598,750
Number of Grants: 138
Highest Grant: $150,000
Average Grant: $18,832
Typical Range: $3,000 to $30,000
Disclosure Period: 1993

Note: Recent grants are derived from a 1993 Form 990.

RECENT GRANTS
Library
100,000	Buffalo and Erie County Public Library, Buffalo, NY

General
150,000	Catholic Charities Appeal, Buffalo, NY
125,000	Canisius College, Buffalo, NY
105,000	United Way of Buffalo and Erie County, Buffalo, NY
100,000	Effective Parenting Information for Children, Buffalo, NY
100,000	Hospice Buffalo, Buffalo, NY

Jurzykowski Foundation, Alfred

CONTACT
Bluma D. Cohen
Executive Director, Vice President
Alfred Jurzykowski Foundation
21 E 40th St.
New York, NY 10016
(212) 689-2460

FINANCIAL SUMMARY
Recent Giving: $1,199,954 (1993); $1,435,122 (1992); $1,032,299 (1991)
Assets: $21,870,807 (1993); $20,950,395 (1992); $21,427,629 (1991)
EIN: 13-6192256

CONTRIBUTIONS SUMMARY
Donor(s): The foundation was incorporated in 1960 by the late Alfred Jurzykowski.

Typical Recipients: • *Arts & Humanities:* Arts Outreach, Ethnic & Folk Arts, Libraries, Museums/Galleries, Music, Performing Arts, Theater • *Civic & Public Affairs:* Employment/Job Training, Ethnic Organizations, Philanthropic Organizations, Public Policy, Zoos/Aquariums • *Education:* Colleges & Universities, Education Funds, Faculty Development, International Exchange, International Studies, Literacy, Minority Education, Private Education (Precollege), Science/Mathematics Education, Secondary Education (Public), Student Aid • *Environment:* General, Resource Conservation • *Health:* Cancer, Children's Health/Hospitals, Clinics/Medical Centers, Health Organizations, Hospices, Hospitals • *International:* Foreign Arts Organizations, Health Care/Hospitals, Human Rights, International

Affairs, International Development, International Environmental Issues, International Organizations, International Relations, International Relief Efforts • *Religion:* Religious Organizations, Religious Welfare, Synagogues/Temples • *Science:* Scientific Centers & Institutes • *Social Services:* Big Brother/Big Sister, Child Welfare, Delinquency & Criminal Rehabilitation, Family Planning, Family Services, Food/Clothing Distribution, People with Disabilities, Shelters/Homelessness, United Funds/United Ways, Youth Organizations

Grant Types: fellowship, general support, multiyear/continuing support, project, and seed money

Geographic Distribution: focus on Poland, Brazil, and New York, NY, metropolitan area

GIVING OFFICERS
Bluma D. Cohen: vp, exec dir, mgr, trust

Karin Falencki: trust

M. Christine Jurzykowski: secy, treas, trust *B* New York NY 1949 *ED* Boston Univ BA 1968 *PHIL AFFIL* pres: Crystal Channel Foundation

Yolande Jurzykowski: exec vp, trust *PHIL AFFIL* pres: Rafael Foundation

William Pyka, MD: trust

APPLICATION INFORMATION
Initial Approach:

The foundation requests applications be made in writing.

Applications must include a statement of the purposes and objectives of the organization, an explanation of the current financial needs, a project budget and any other sources of support, a copy of the most recent audited financial statement, and a formal statement from the IRS as to the organization's tax-exempt status and that it is not a private foundation. Applicants are encouraged to include any other information that might be helpful in reaching a decision.

The foundation has no deadline for submitting proposals.

Restrictions on Giving: The foundation does not make grants to individuals, or for endowment funds or loans.

PUBLICATIONS
Application guidelines

GRANTS ANALYSIS
Total Grants: $1,133,954*

Number of Grants: 49*

Highest Grant: $141,500

Average Grant: $23,142*

Typical Range: $3,000 to $30,000

Disclosure Period: 1993

Note: The figures for total of grants, number of grants, and average grant exclude fifteen scholarship grants totaling $66,000. Recent grants are derived from a 1993 Form 990.

RECENT GRANTS

Library
141,500	Committee for the Blind of Poland, New York, NY —

	for construction of library at the Institute for the Blind at Laski, Poland
10,000	New York Public Library, New York, NY — in support of research libraries
3,000	Foundation Center, New York, NY — general support

General
120,000	Kosciuszko Foundation, New York, NY — in support of Polish scholarship/grants
100,000	Conservation International Foundation, Washington, DC — to support specific programs of their Brazilian biodiversity conservation initiatives
88,125	Ashoka, Arlington, VA — in support of 10 Brazilian fellows identified as innovators in the areas of working with street children and the environment
40,000	Global Fund for Women, Menlo Park, CA — to support specific programs focusing on women's economic autonomy in Brazil
40,000	New York Medical College, Valhalla, NY — fellowship program for visiting Polish scientists and pathologists at the College's Department of Pathology

---

Kaplan Fund, J. M.

CONTACT
J. M. Kaplan Fund
30 Rockefeller Plz., Ste. 4250
New York, NY 10112
(212) 767-0630
Note: The fund does not list a specific contact person.

FINANCIAL SUMMARY
Recent Giving: $5,000,000 (fiscal 1995 est.); $4,100,000 (fiscal 1994); $2,500,000 (fiscal 1993 approx.)

Assets: $95,000,000 (fiscal 1995 est.); $95,000,000 (fiscal 1994); $92,000,000 (fiscal 1993 approx.)

Gifts Received: $6,243 (fiscal 1987)

EIN: 13-6090286

CONTRIBUTIONS SUMMARY
Donor(s): Jacob Merrill Kaplan (1891-1987) established the fund in 1945 with proceeds from the Welch Grape Juice Company, which he headed for many years. His daughter, Joan K. Davidson, was president of the fund between 1977 and 1993. Mr. Kaplan worked imaginatively in responding to human need and the improvement of American social service institutions. Today, Mr. Kaplan's ideas and values govern the work of the fund, as they have for over forty years.

Typical Recipients: • *Arts & Humanities:* Arts Festivals, Film & Video, Historic Preservation, History & Archaeology, Libraries, Literary Arts, Museums/Galleries • *Civic & Public Affairs:* Botanical Gardens/Parks, Employment/Job Training, Hispanic Affairs, Housing, Public Policy, Rural Affairs • *Education:* Elementary Education (Public), Secondary Education (Private), Secondary Education (Public) • *Environment:* Air/Water Quality, General, Resource Conservation • *Health:* AIDS/HIV, Children's Health/Hospitals • *International:* Human Rights, International Relief Efforts • *Religion:* Churches • *Social Services:* Child Welfare, Family Planning, Family Services, Food/Clothing Distribution, Senior Services

Grant Types: general support, project, and seed money

Geographic Distribution: primarily New York

GIVING OFFICERS
Bradford Davidson: trust

Elizabeth Davidson: co-chp

John Matthew Davidson: secy, trust

Peter W. Davidson: trust *B* 1959 *ED* Stanford Univ BA 1981; Harvard Univ MBA 1986 *CURR EMPL* gen ptnr: El Diario Assoc

Caio Fonseca: trust

Elizabeth K. Fonseca: vp, trust

Isabel Fonseca: trust

Quina Fonseca: trust

Mary E. Kaplan: vp, trust

Richard D. Kaplan: co-chmn, trust

Henry Ng: secy, dir *B* 1953 *ED* NY Univ BA 1974; Univ Chicago 1976

APPLICATION INFORMATION
Initial Approach:

Initial inquiries by telephone or brief letter are preferred.

If the project is appropriate, the fund will send an application checklist for the remaining materials including the following: budgets, sources of income, lists of board and staff members, IRS tax-exempt determination letter and Form 990, and other supporting documents.

Requests are considered between March 1 and Ocotber 15. Music requests are considered only in September.

The foundation is reviewing its application procedures and guidelines. Applicants should contact the foundation directly for new procedures and guidelines.

GRANTS ANALYSIS
Total Grants: $4,100,000

Number of Grants: 150

Highest Grant: $250,000

Average Grant: $27,333

Typical Range: $10,000 to $50,000

Disclosure Period: fiscal year ending November 30, 1994

Note: Recent grants are derived from a fiscal 1992 annual report.

RECENT GRANTS

Library

75,000   Mid-York Library System, Utica, NY — toward the purchase of a new bookmobile that will replace an unreliable older one, to improve the only library service for 90,000 people in Madison, Oneida, and Herkimer counties in North County of New York state

65,000   NYSERNET for Project GAIN (Global Access Information Network), Syracuse, NY — a pilot community information system to enable rural libraries in New York State to broaden their services through innovative telecommunications technologies

60,000   Blue Mountain Center National Library Support Project, Blue Mountain Lake, NY — to develop a campaign to raise public awareness of the importance of public libraries on local, state, and national levels; to organize multiple constituencies in support of public libraries

General

275,000   Center for Educational Innovation (Manhattan Institute for Policy Research), New York, NY — to enable the Center to provide its educational expertise to the East Brooklyn Congregations that, with Rev. Johnny Ray Youngblood's leadership, are establishing two new high schools

159,000   Beaverkill Conservancy, New York, NY — for their Special Projects Fund, which supports efforts to enhance and protect the natural and built environment of New York city and state

133,000   New School for Social Research, New York, NY — for the final installment of the fund's commitment as a sponsor of the Environmental Simulation Center at the New School

105,000   Community Research Initiative on AIDS, New York, NY — to conduct clinical trials of promising new AIDS therapies in New York City's only community-based research facility that works directly with local doctors and their AIDS patients

100,000   Center for Independent Thought, New York, NY — for "Critical Review," their quarterly journal of "classical liberal thought," to enable them to establish a firm financial footing

Kaplun Foundation, Morris J. and Betty

CONTACT
Zvi Levavy
President
Morris J. and Betty Kaplun Fdn.
225 W 34th St.
New York, NY 10122
(212) 594-8155

FINANCIAL SUMMARY
Recent Giving: $111,023 (fiscal 1993); $123,287 (fiscal 1992); $113,600 (fiscal 1991)

Assets: $3,326,852 (fiscal 1993); $3,229,320 (fiscal 1992); $3,163,617 (fiscal 1991)

EIN: 13-6096009

CONTRIBUTIONS SUMMARY
Donor(s): the late Morris J. Kaplun

Typical Recipients: • *Arts & Humanities:* Libraries, Literary Arts, Theater • *Civic & Public Affairs:* Civil Rights, General • *Education:* Arts/Humanities Education, Colleges & Universities, Education Funds, General, Literacy, Private Education (Precollege), Religious Education • *Health:* Health Organizations, Hospitals, Medical Research, Prenatal Health Issues, Single-Disease Health Associations • *International:* Foreign Educational Institutions, International Relations, Missionary/Religious Activities • *Religion:* Jewish Causes, Religious Organizations, Religious Welfare • *Social Services:* Child Welfare, Community Service Organizations, Delinquency & Criminal Rehabilitation, Family Services, Homes, People with Disabilities, Senior Services, United Funds/United Ways, Youth Organizations

Grant Types: general support and research

Geographic Distribution: focus on New York, NY

GIVING OFFICERS
Gloria Isakower: vp

Zvi Levavy: pres

Lawrence Marin: vp

Moshe Sheinbaum: vp

APPLICATION INFORMATION
Initial Approach: Send brief letter of inquiry describing program. There are no deadlines.

GRANTS ANALYSIS
Total Grants: $111,023

Typical Range: $500 to $5,000

Disclosure Period: fiscal year ending August 31, 1993

Note: Recent grants are derived from a fiscal 1992 Form 990.

RECENT GRANTS

General

28,913   Essay Contest, New York, NY

10,000   American Friends of Hebrew University, New York, NY

7,000   American Association Bikur Cholim Hospital/Jerusalem, New York, NY

6,000   Medical Development for Israel, New York, NY — medical

6,000   National Tay Sachs and Allied Diseases Association, Brookline, MA

Kaufmann Foundation, Henry

CONTACT
Jeffrey A. Horwitz
Secretary
Henry Kaufmann Fdn.
1585 Broadway
New York, NY 10036
(212) 969-3299

FINANCIAL SUMMARY
Recent Giving: $1,794,000 (1993); $2,211,105 (1992); $1,213,020 (1991)

Assets: $2,768,086 (1993); $4,428,251 (1992); $6,374,401 (1991)

EIN: 13-6034179

CONTRIBUTIONS SUMMARY
Donor(s): the late Henry Kaufmann

Typical Recipients: • *Arts & Humanities:* Arts Centers, Arts Outreach, Libraries, Museums/Galleries, Theater • *Civic & Public Affairs:* Housing, Municipalities/Towns, Urban & Community Affairs • *Education:* Arts/Humanities Education, Colleges & Universities, Education Associations, Education Reform, Literacy, Medical Education, Private Education (Precollege), Public Education (Precollege) • *Environment:* General • *Health:* AIDS/HIV, Cancer, Hospitals, Long-Term Care, Mental Health, Prenatal Health Issues, Single-Disease Health Associations • *International:* International Affairs, International Organizations • *Religion:* Jewish Causes, Religious Organizations, Religious Welfare • *Social Services:* Camps, Child Welfare, Community Centers, Community Service Organizations, Counseling, Family Planning, Family Services, Homes, People with Disabilities, Senior Services, YMCA/YWCA/YMHA/YWHA, Youth Organizations

Grant Types: general support

Geographic Distribution: focus on the New York, NY, and Pittsburgh, PA, metropolitan areas

GIVING OFFICERS
Leonard Nathan Block: vp, dir *B* Brooklyn NY 1911 *ED* Univ PA BS 1933 *CURR EMPL* sr chmn: Block Drug Co *NONPR AFFIL* dir: Fed Jewish Philanthropies *CLUB AFFIL* Harmonie, Hollywood GC, Ocean

Beach *PHIL AFFIL* pres: Adele and Leonard Block Foundation

Mitchell A. Drossman: asst secy

William Theodore Golden: treas, dir *B* New York NY 1909 *ED* Harvard Univ 1930-1931; Univ PA AB 1930; Columbia Univ MA 1979 *CORP AFFIL* dir: Block Drug Co, Gen Am Investors Co, Verde Exploration Ltd *NONPR AFFIL* chmn, mem gov counc: NY Univ Courant Inst Mathematical Sciences; chmn, trust: Am Mus Natural History; co-chmn: Carnegie Commn Science Tech & Govt; dir: Columbia Univ Grad Faculties Alumni; fellow, treas, dir: Am Assn Advancement Science; mem: Am Academy Arts Sciences, Am Philosophical Soc, Counc Foreign Rels, History Science Soc, Marine Biological Lab Woods Hole MA, Natl Academy Pub Admin; mem adv counc: Columbia Univ Sch Gen Studies; mem bd govs: NY Academy Sciences; mem bd overseers: Univ PA Sch Arts & Sciences; mem bd visitors: City Univ NY Grad Sch & Univ Ctr; mem counc: Rockefeller Univ; mem visiting comm astronomy: Harvard Univ, Princeton Univ; pub mem: Hudson Inst; secy, trust: Carnegie Inst, Carnegie Inst; treas, dir: Am Assn Advancement Science; treas, trust: Hebrew Free Loan Soc; trust: Catskill Ctr Conservation Devel, Neuroscience Res Fdn, Univ PA Press; trust emeritus: Haskins Laboratories, Natl Humanities Ctr; trust, vchmn: Barnard Coll; vchmn: Mayors Commn Science Tech, Mt Sinai Med Ctr, Scientists Inst Pub Information; vchmn, trust: Am Trust British Library, City Univ NY Mt Sinai Sch Medicine, Mt Sinai Hosp *CLUB AFFIL* Army Navy, Century Assn, City Midday, Cosmos *PHIL AFFIL* pres, dir: Golden Family Foundation; vp, treas, dir: Olive Bridge Fund; dir: Arthur Ross Foundation

Philip J. Hirsh: dir

Jeffrey A. Horwitz: secy

Arnold Levine: dir

Charles Looker: dir *PHIL AFFIL* secy: C. L. C. Kramer Foundation; pres, dir: Kathryn and Gilbert Miller Fund

Frederick Phineas Rose: dir *B* New York NY 1923 *ED* Yale Univ BCE 1944 *CURR EMPL* chmn: Rose Assocs *CORP AFFIL* dir: Consolidated Edison Co NY, Home Life Ins Co; mem publs comm: Commentary Magazine *NONPR AFFIL* dir: Lincoln Ctr Performing Arts, Metro Mus Art, New York City Partnership, Rockefeller Univ; fellow: Yale Univ; hon chmn: Federation Jewish Philanthropies NY; mem: Century Assn; trust: Aspen Inst Humanistic Studies, Citizens Budget Comm, Manhattan Inst Pub Policy, Philharmonic Symphony Soc *PHIL AFFIL* pres, dir: Frederick P. and Sandra P. Rose Foundation, Frederick P. and Sandra P. Rose Foundation, Frederick P & Sandra P Rose Foundation *CLUB AFFIL* Beach Point YC, Century CC

John W. Wolf, Sr.: dir

APPLICATION INFORMATION
Initial Approach: Send a brief letter of inquiry. There are no deadlines.

PUBLICATIONS
Annual report

GRANTS ANALYSIS
Total Grants: $1,794,000

Number of Grants: 36

Highest Grant: $360,000

Typical Range: $1,000 to $50,000

Disclosure Period: 1993

Note: Recent grants are derived from a 1993 Form 990.

RECENT GRANTS

General
360,000	Jewish Community Center of Pittsburgh, Pittsburgh, PA
250,000	Hebrew Free Loan Society, New York, NY
250,000	Jewish Board of Family and Children's Services, New York, NY
100,000	Jewish Community Centers Association, New York, NY
100,000	Riverdale YM-YWHA, Riverdale, NY

Kaye, Scholer, Fierman, Hays & Handler / Kaye Foundation

Revenue: $55.0 million
Employees: 640
Headquarters: New York, NY
SIC Major Group: Legal Services

CONTACT
Peter Faber
Chairman
Kaye, Scholer, Fierman, Hays & Handler
425 Park Ave.
New York, NY 10022
(212) 836-8000

FINANCIAL SUMMARY
Recent Giving: $135,000 (fiscal 1993); $90,500 (fiscal 1992); $225,500 (fiscal 1991)

Assets: $735 (fiscal 1993); $2,566 (fiscal 1992); $2,363 (fiscal 1991)

Gifts Received: $135,000 (fiscal 1993); $90,580 (fiscal 1992); $222,000 (fiscal 1991)

EIN: 23-7161546

CONTRIBUTIONS SUMMARY
Typical Recipients: • *Arts & Humanities:* General, Libraries • *Civic & Public Affairs:* Civil Rights, General, Law & Justice, Legal Aid, Professional & Trade Associations, Public Policy • *Education:* General • *Health:* General • *Social Services:* General, United Funds/United Ways

Grant Types: general support

Geographic Distribution: primarily in NY

CORP. OFFICERS
Peter Faber: *CURR EMPL* chmn: Kaye Scholer Fierman Hays & Handler

Milton E. Handler: *CURR EMPL* sr ptnr: Kaye, Scholer, Fierman Hays & Handler

Clifford Hook: *CURR EMPL* cfo: Kaye Scholer Fierman Hays & Handler

Michael Krames: *CURR EMPL* chmn exec comm: Kaye Scholer Fierman Hays & Handler

Andrew McDonald: *CURR EMPL* ptnr: Kaye Scholer Fierman Hays & Handler

GIVING OFFICERS
Peter M. Fishbein: trust *B* New York NY 1934 *ED* Dartmouth Coll BA 1955; Harvard Univ JD 1958 *CURR EMPL* ptnr: Kaye Scholer Fierman Hays & Handler *NONPR AFFIL* fellow: Am Bar Fdn, Am Coll Trial Lawyers; mem: Am Bar Assn, Assn Bar City New York

Fred N. Fishman: trust *B* New York NY 1925 *ED* Harvard Univ SB 1946; Harvard Univ LLB 1948 *CURR EMPL* special couns: Kaye Scholer Fierman Hays & Handler *NONPR AFFIL* bd overseers: Comm Univ Resources; fellow: Am Bar Fdn; mem: Am Bar Assn, Am Law Inst, Assn Bar City New York, Harvard Law Sch Assn, Legal Aid Soc, NY St Bar Assn, Phi Beta Kappa; mem steering comm: Campaign for Harvard Law Sch; trust, dir: Lawyers Comm civil Rights Under Law *CLUB AFFIL* Harvard

David Klingsberg: trust

Sheldon Oliensis: trust

Stanley D. Robinson: trust

Sidney Silberman: trust

APPLICATION INFORMATION
Initial Approach: The foundation has no formal grant application procedure or application form. There are no deadlines

GRANTS ANALYSIS
Total Grants: $135,000

Number of Grants: 1

Highest Grant: $135,000

Disclosure Period: fiscal year ending November 30, 1993

Note: Recent grants are derived from a fiscal 1993 Form 990.

RECENT GRANTS

General
135,000	Legal Aid Society, New York, NY

Kennedy Foundation, Ethel

CONTACT
Ethel K. Marran
President and Treasurer
Ethel Kennedy Fdn.
Box 82
Cold Spring Harbor, NY 11724
(516) 367-4817

FINANCIAL SUMMARY
Recent Giving: $251,200 (1992); $190,000 (1991); $226,900 (1990)

Assets: $4,667,113 (1992); $5,411,360
(1991); $3,637,386 (1990)

EIN: 11-2768682

CONTRIBUTIONS SUMMARY
Typical Recipients: • *Arts & Humanities:*
Arts Centers, Libraries, Museums/Galleries,
Public Broadcasting, Theater • *Civic & Public Affairs:* Economic Development, Employment/Job Training, Ethnic Organizations,
General, Housing, Women's Affairs • *Education:* Colleges & Universities, Education
Funds, Minority Education, Private Education (Precollege), Student Aid • *Environment:* Air/Water Quality, General, Resource
Conservation • *Health:* Arthritis, Cancer,
Health Organizations, Hospitals, Medical
Research, Single-Disease Health Associations • *International:* Health Care/Hospitals,
Human Rights • *Religion:* Religious Welfare
• *Social Services:* At-Risk Youth, Camps,
Child Welfare, Community Centers, Community Service Organizations, Family Planning, Family Services, Food/Clothing
Distribution, Homes, People with Disabilities, Senior Services, Shelters/Homelessness, United Funds/United Ways, Youth
Organizations

Grant Types: general support

Geographic Distribution: focus on NY

GIVING OFFICERS
Elizabeth Marran: vp

Ethel K. Marran: pres, treas

Laura Marran: secy

APPLICATION INFORMATION
Initial Approach: The foundation requests
applications be made in writing. Include a
description of organization, amount requested, purpose of funds sought, recently
audited financial statement, and proof of tax-exempt status. There are no deadlines.

Restrictions on Giving: Does not support
individuals.

GRANTS ANALYSIS
Total Grants: $251,200

Number of Grants: 68

Highest Grant: $50,000

Typical Range: $500 to $5,000

Disclosure Period: 1992

Note: Recent grants are derived from a 1992
Form 990.

RECENT GRANTS

Library
1,000	East Hampton Library, E. Hampton, NY

General
50,000	Planned Parenthood, Amarillo, MN
31,000	Family Service League, Waterloo, IA
20,000	Phillips Exeter Academy, Andover, MA
15,500	Hamilton College, Clinton, NY
10,000	Arthritis Foundation of New York, New York, NY

Klock and Lucia Klock Kingston Foundation, Jay E.

Former Foundation Name: Kingston Foundation

CONTACT
Jay E. Klock and Lucia Klock Kingston Fdn.
c/o Key Trust Co.
267 Wall St.
Kingston, NY 12401
(518) 486-8388
Note: Foundation does not list a phone number
or a contact person.

FINANCIAL SUMMARY
Recent Giving: $250,867 (1993); $247,000
(1992); $291,213 (1991)

Assets: $4,233,982 (1993); $4,195,434
(1992); $4,224,521 (1991)

EIN: 14-6038479

CONTRIBUTIONS SUMMARY
Typical Recipients: • *Arts & Humanities:*
Libraries, Music, Performing Arts • *Civic &
Public Affairs:* Economic Development,
Safety, Urban & Community Affairs • *Education:* Business Education, Community &
Junior Colleges, Literacy, Student Aid
• *Health:* Cancer, Children's Health/Hospitals, Health Organizations, Heart, Hospices,
Hospitals, Medical Research, Mental Health
• *Religion:* Churches, Religious Welfare •
Science: Scientific Centers & Institutes • *Social Services:* Child Welfare, Community
Service Organizations, Homes, People with
Disabilities, Scouts, Substance Abuse,
United Funds/United Ways,
YMCA/YWCA/YMHA/YWHA, Youth Organizations

Grant Types: general support

Geographic Distribution: limited to Kingston and Ulster counties, NY

GIVING OFFICERS
Key Trust Company: trust

APPLICATION INFORMATION
Initial Approach: Send a brief letter of inquiry. Deadline is the end of each quarter.

Restrictions on Giving: Limited to Kingston and Ulster City, NY.

GRANTS ANALYSIS
Total Grants: $250,867

Number of Grants: 30

Highest Grant: $12,000

Typical Range: $1,000 to $5,000

Disclosure Period: 1993

Note: Recent grants are derived from a 1993
Form 990.

RECENT GRANTS

Library
7,500	Kingston Area Library
7,500	Kingston Area Library

General
12,000	YMCA of Kingston and Ulster County — balance of 1993 building fund pledge
11,000	United Way of Ulster County, Kingston, NY
10,000	Boys and Girls Club of Kingston
10,000	Children's Home of Kingston
7,500	Ulster Association for Retarded Citizens

Klosk Fund, Louis and Rose

CONTACT
Margaret M. Peterson
Trust Officer
Louis and Rose Klosk Fund
c/o Chemical Bank
270 Park Ave.
New York, NY 10017
(212) 270-4731

FINANCIAL SUMMARY
Recent Giving: $140,500 (1993); $126,000
(1992); $153,000 (1991)

Assets: $4,366,465 (1993); $4,189,352
(1992); $4,236,525 (1991)

EIN: 13-6328994

CONTRIBUTIONS SUMMARY
Donor(s): the late Louis Klosk

Typical Recipients: • *Arts & Humanities:*
Libraries, Music, Opera • *Civic & Public Affairs:* General, Women's Affairs • *Education:* Colleges & Universities, Medical
Education, Private Education (Precollege),
Science/Mathematics Education • *Health:*
Clinics/Medical Centers, Geriatric Health,
Hospitals, Kidney, Medical Research, Multiple Sclerosis, Single-Disease Health Associations • *International:* International
Relations, Missionary/Religious Activities •
Religion: Jewish Causes, Religious Organizations, Synagogues/Temples • *Social Services:* Child Abuse, Community Service
Organizations, Domestic Violence, Homes,
People with Disabilities, Senior Services,
United Funds/United Ways

Grant Types: general support

Geographic Distribution: focus on NY

GIVING OFFICERS
Chemical Bank: trust

Barry Cooper: trust

Nathan Cooper: trust

APPLICATION INFORMATION
Initial Approach: The foundation has no
formal grant application procedure or application form. There are no deadlines.

GRANTS ANALYSIS
Total Grants: $140,500

Number of Grants: 37

Highest Grant: $12,500

Typical Range: $1,000 to $5,000

Disclosure Period: 1993

Note: Recent grants are derived from a 1993 Form 990.

RECENT GRANTS

Library
1,500	New York Public Library, New York, NY — charitable contribution

General
12,500	Columbia University College of Physicians and Surgeons, New York, NY — charitable contribution
12,500	Cornell University Medical College, New York, NY — charitable contribution
12,500	Cornell University Medical College, New York, NY — charitable contribution
6,000	Hadassah, Jerusalem, Israel — charitable contribution
6,000	United Jewish Appeal, New York, NY — charitable contribution

Kornfeld Foundation, Emily Davie and Joseph S.

CONTACT
John F. White
President
Emily Davie and Joseph S. Kornfeld Fdn.
c/o Patterson, Belviar, Webb and Tyler
30 Rockefeller Plz.
New York, NY 10112
(212) 598-2500

FINANCIAL SUMMARY
Recent Giving: $966,763 (1993)
Assets: $22,754,413 (1993)
EIN: 13-3042360

CONTRIBUTIONS SUMMARY
Typical Recipients: • *Arts & Humanities:* Libraries • *Civic & Public Affairs:* Philanthropic Organizations, Public Policy • *Education:* Colleges & Universities, Education Reform, General, Medical Education, Minority Education • *Health:* Adolescent Health Issues, Clinics/Medical Centers, Hospitals (University Affiliated) • *International:* Human Rights • *Social Services:* Community Service Organizations

Grant Types: general support

Geographic Distribution: focus on NY

GIVING OFFICERS
Christopher C. Angell: secy, treas, dir
Harriet H. Warren: dir
William J. Welch: vp, dir
John F. White: pres, dir

APPLICATION INFORMATION
Initial Approach: Send a brief letter of inquiry. Include a description of organization, amount requested, purpose of funds sought, recently audited financial statement, and proof of tax-exempt status.

GRANTS ANALYSIS
Total Grants: $966,763
Number of Grants: 16
Highest Grant: $300,000
Typical Range: $1,100 to $140,000
Disclosure Period: 1993

Note: Recent grants are derived from a 1993 Form 990.

RECENT GRANTS

Library
20,000	Tuxedo Park Library, Tuxedo, NY

General
300,000	Center for Biomedical Ethics of University of Virginia, Charlottesville, VA
140,000	Center for Collaborative Education, New York, NY
110,719	Mt. Sinai School of Medicine, New York, NY
104,905	Columbia University Externship Program in Human Rights and Health Care, New York, NY
75,000	Memorial Sloan-Kettering Center, New York, NY

Kress Foundation, Samuel H.

CONTACT
Lisa M. Ackerman
Vice President
Samuel H. Kress Foundation
174 E 80th St.
New York, NY 10021
(212) 861-4993

FINANCIAL SUMMARY
Recent Giving: $3,000,000 (fiscal 1995 est.); $3,167,041 (fiscal 1994); $3,315,920 (fiscal 1993)

Assets: $67,000,000 (fiscal 1995 est.); $66,745,241 (fiscal 1994); $70,687,139 (fiscal 1993)

Gifts Received: $10,000 (fiscal 1989)

Fiscal Note: In 1989, the Kress Foundation fiscal year was changed from August 31 to June 30.

EIN: 13-1624176

CONTRIBUTIONS SUMMARY
Donor(s): The Samuel H. Kress Foundation was established in 1929, with three brothers, Samuel H. Kress (1863-1955), Claude W. Kress (1876-1940), and R. H. Kress (1877-1963), as donors. Samuel H. Kress, a native Pennsylvanian, was the founder of the S. H. Kress and Company stores. Although Samuel was known for his extensive collection of Italian Renaissance art, the brothers expanded the Kress Collection to contain works of European masters in a variety of mediums. This vast collection of more than 3,000 pieces was eventually donated to 50 museums in 38 states. Samuel was a trustee of the Metropolitan Museum of Art and the National Gallery of Art, which received a significant portion of his art collection and named him as a Founding Benefactor.

Typical Recipients: • *Arts & Humanities:* Arts Associations & Councils, Arts Funds, Arts Institutes, Historic Preservation, History & Archaeology, Libraries, Museums/Galleries • *Civic & Public Affairs:* General, Professional & Trade Associations, Urban & Community Affairs • *Education:* Arts/Humanities Education, Colleges & Universities, International Studies • *International:* Foreign Arts Organizations, Foreign Educational Institutions, International Organizations, International Peace & Security Issues • *Religion:* Religious Organizations • *Social Services:* Community Service Organizations

Grant Types: conference/seminar, fellowship, professorship, project, and research

Geographic Distribution: no geographic restrictions

GIVING OFFICERS
Lisa M. Ackerman: vp *B* 1960

William Banks Bader: secy, treas, trust *B* Atlantic City NJ 1931 *ED* Pomona Coll BA 1953; Princeton Univ MA 1960; Princeton Univ PhD 1964 *CURR EMPL* sr vp: SRI Intl-Menlo Park *NONPR AFFIL* adjunct prof: Georgetown Univ; dir: Am Ditchley Fdn, Am Inst Contemporary German Studies, Intl Res Exchanges Bd; mem: Counc Foreign Rels, Inst Intl Strategic Studies *CLUB AFFIL* Cosmos

Daniel N. Belin: vchmn, trust *PHIL AFFIL* trust: Ahmanson Foundation

Inmaculada De Habsburgo: trust

Lyman Field, Esq.: trust *B* Kansas City MO 1914 *ED* Univ KS AB 1936; Harvard Univ LLB 1939 *CURR EMPL* ptnr: Field Gentry & Benjamin *NONPR AFFIL* adv bd: Spencer Mus Art, Univ KS; bd dir: Cross Fdn, Kansas City Soc Western Art; chmn adv comm: Univ MO Kansas City Cockefair Chair Continuing Ed; chmn, mem: Thomas Hart Benton Homestead Meml Adv Commn MO; mem: Am Bar Assn, Am Judicature Soc, Intl Assn Ins Couns, Kansas City Bar Assn, Lawyers Assn Kansas City, MO Bar Assn, Nelson-Atkins Mus Art, Soc Fellows, Univ MO Kansas City Univ Assocs; trust: Thomas Hart Benton & Rita P Benton Trust, Conservatory Music Kansas City *CLUB AFFIL* Carriage, Kansas City CC, Univ *PHIL AFFIL* trust: George E. and Annette Cross Murphy Charitable Fund

John C. "Jack" Fontaine: chmn, trust *ED* Univ MI BA 1953; Harvard Univ LLB 1956 *CURR EMPL* ptnr: Hughes Hubbard & Reed *CORP AFFIL* exec vp: Knight-Ridder Inc

Victoria Newhouse: trust

Marilyn Perry: pres, trust *B* 1940 *ED* Univ NC 1970

William Clarke Wescoe, MD: trust emer *B* Allentown PA 1920 *ED* Muhlenberg Coll BS 1941; Cornell Univ MD 1944 *CORP AFFIL* dir: NY Stock Exchange, Phillips Petroleum Co *NONPR AFFIL* fellow: Am Coll Physicians; mem: Alpha Omega Alpha, Alpha Tau Omega, Am Soc Pharmacology & Experimental Therapeutics, Nu Sigma Nu, Phi Beta Kappa, Sigma Xi

APPLICATION INFORMATION
Initial Approach:

Applicants should contact the foundation by letter.

Letters should include a description of the project, budget summarizing major anticipated expenses, background information on the principal investigator, and proof of tax-exempt status.

Proposals for projects within the standard funding programs may be submitted any time. Application deadline for research fellowships in art history is November 30; application deadline for fellowships in art conservation is February 28.

Restrictions on Giving: The foundation does not support art history programs below the predoctoral level or the purchase of works of art. No grants are given to artists, operating budgets, annual campaigns, endowments, deficit financing, capital funds, films, or loans.

OTHER THINGS TO KNOW

Application forms for fellowships in art history and conservation are required. Applications are to be addressed: Fellowship Administrator, Samuel H. Kress Foundation, 174 E 80th Street, New York, NY 10021.

PUBLICATIONS
Annual report

GRANTS ANALYSIS

Total Grants: $3,167,041

Number of Grants: 300*

Highest Grant: $152,000

Average Grant: $7,000*

Typical Range: $1,000 to $30,000

Disclosure Period: fiscal year ending June 30, 1994

Note: Figures for average grant and number of grants were supplied by the foundation. Recent grants are derived from a 1993 form 990.

RECENT GRANTS

General
75,000	University of Kansas at Spencer, Spencer, KS
50,000	Harvard University Center, Cambridge, MA
50,000	University of Kansas at Spencer, Spencer, KS
40,000	International Research and Exchange, Princeton, NJ
37,500	Architect Institute of America

Lake Placid Education Foundation

CONTACT
John S. Lansing
Executive Director
Lake Placid Education Fdn.
157 Saranac Ave.
Lake Placid, NY 12946
(518) 523-4933

FINANCIAL SUMMARY
Recent Giving: $237,427 (fiscal 1994)
Assets: $10,653,418 (fiscal 1994)
Gifts Received: $17,545 (fiscal 1994)
EIN: 51-0243919

CONTRIBUTIONS SUMMARY
Typical Recipients: • *Arts & Humanities:* Libraries • *Civic & Public Affairs:* Philanthropic Organizations • *Education:* Literacy, Science/Mathematics Education

Grant Types: general support

Geographic Distribution: focus on NY

GIVING OFFICERS
Henry M. Bonner: dir
Fred E. Brown: dir
William J. Bumsted: dir
Frederick C. Calder: vp
Philip G. Cole: secy
Walter W. Curley: pres
W. John Friedlander: dir
George G. Hart: dir
Gardner F. Landon: dir
John S. Lansing: exec dir
James M. O'Brien: dir
Peter F. Roland: dir
Edward W. Scudder: treas
Thomas N. Stainback: dir
Henry Uihlein II: dir

APPLICATION INFORMATION
Initial Approach: The foundation has no formal grant application procedure or application form. There are no deadlines.

GRANTS ANALYSIS
Total Grants: $237,427
Number of Grants: 22
Highest Grant: $17,545
Typical Range: $1,000 to $35,000
Disclosure Period: fiscal year ending June 30, 1994
Note: Recent grants are derived from a fiscal 1994 Form 990.

RECENT GRANTS

Library
17,545	Longlake Library — for library books

General
5,000	Literacy Volunteers of America, Elizabethtown, NY — for support for literacy program

2,500	Wilmington Cooper Memorial, Wilmington, NY — for computers
2,500	Wilmington Cooper Memorial, Wilmington, NY — for reading program
1,000	Reason Foundation, Los Angeles, CA — for educational studies program
1,000	Wilmington Cooper Memorial, Wilmington, NY — for general support

Lang Foundation, Eugene M.

CONTACT
Christine Hermanek
Contact
Eugene M. Lang Foundation
122 E 42nd St., 3rd Fl.
New York, NY 10168
(212) 687-4741

FINANCIAL SUMMARY
Recent Giving: $2,444,445 (1994 approx.); $3,886,397 (1993); $1,237,020 (1992)
Assets: $27,747,240 (1993); $28,694,480 (1992); $27,416,249 (1991)
Gifts Received: $15,000 (1991)
EIN: 13-6153412

CONTRIBUTIONS SUMMARY
Donor(s): The foundation was established in 1968 by Eugene M. Lang. Mr. Lang is the founder and president of REFAC Technology Development Corporation, which licences and promotes new technologies. He is most well-known for his offer to pay college tuition for a sixth-grade class at New York City's P.S. 121, which he attended as a youth. The I Have a Dream Foundation offers programs to motivate disadvantaged grade school students to attend college by offering scholarships, reading materials, support groups, and counseling services.

Typical Recipients: • *Arts & Humanities:* Libraries, Museums/Galleries, Music, Opera, Performing Arts, Public Broadcasting, Theater • *Civic & Public Affairs:* Botanical Gardens/Parks, Law & Justice, Philanthropic Organizations, Urban & Community Affairs, Women's Affairs • *Education:* Arts/Humanities Education, Colleges & Universities, Education Funds, Legal Education, Minority Education, Private Education (Precollege), Public Education (Precollege), Student Aid • *Health:* Clinics/Medical Centers, Health Organizations, Hospitals, Medical Rehabilitation, Mental Health • *International:* International Peace & Security Issues, International Relief Efforts • *Religion:* Churches, Jewish Causes, Religious Welfare • *Science:* Science Museums • *Social Services:* Child Welfare, Community Service Organizations, Family Services, Recreation & Athletics, Shelters/Homelessness, Youth Organizations

Grant Types: general support and scholarship

Geographic Distribution: primarily New York, NY, but no geographic restrictions

GIVING OFFICERS

Christine Hermanek: contact

David Lang: trust

Eugene Michael Lang: don, trust *B* New York NY 1919 *ED* Swarthmore Coll BA 1938; Columbia Univ Bus Sch MS 1940 *CURR EMPL* fdr, chmn, ceo: Refac Tech Devel Corp *CORP AFFIL* dir: Alexanders, Gough Econ Inc, Three Five Sys, Toshniwal-Sperry Ltd *NONPR AFFIL* chmn emeritus: Swarthmore Coll; dir: Columbia Univ Grad Sch Bus, Mannes Coll Music; mem: Licensing Exec Soc; mng dir: New York City Opera Assn; vchmn, trust: New Sch Social Res *CLUB AFFIL* Century CC, University *PHIL AFFIL* fdr, hon chmn, trust: I Have A Dream Foundation

Jane Lang: trust

Stephen Lang: trust

Theresa Lang: trust *B* Hochhausen Germany 1952 *ED* Fordham Univ BA 1974; Univ CA Los Angeles MBA 1982 *CURR EMPL* dir investment banking: Merrill Lynch & Co

APPLICATION INFORMATION

Initial Approach:

The foundation does not have a formal application. Grant requests should be submitted in letter form.

There are no deadlines for applications.

GRANTS ANALYSIS

Total Grants: $3,886,397

Number of Grants: 90

Highest Grant: $2,510,200

Average Grant: $15,463*

Typical Range: $250 to $25,000

Disclosure Period: 1993

Note: The average grant figure excludes the foundation's highest grant totaling $2,510,200. Recent grants are derived from a 1992 Form 990.

RECENT GRANTS

Library
1,000	New York Public Library, New York, NY

General
505,000	Columbia University, New York, NY
367,425	Swarthmore College, Swarthmore, PA
72,500	Rockefeller University, New York, NY
41,500	University of Pennsylvania Law School, Philadelphia, PA
25,000	Bard College, Annandale-on-Hudson, NY

Lasdon Foundation

CONTACT
Jeffrey S. Lasdon
Vice President
Lasdon Fdn.
10 Rockefeller Plaza
New York, NY 10020
(212) 977-8420

FINANCIAL SUMMARY
Recent Giving: $137,425 (fiscal 1993); $114,425 (fiscal 1992); $168,990 (fiscal 1991)

Assets: $3,160,291 (fiscal 1993); $3,045,514 (fiscal 1992); $2,952,423 (fiscal 1991)

EIN: 13-1739997

CONTRIBUTIONS SUMMARY
Donor(s): the late W. S. Lasdon, the late Stanley S. Lasdon, the late I. S. Lasdon, the late M. S. Lasdon

Typical Recipients: • *Arts & Humanities:* Ballet, Libraries, Music, Opera, Public Broadcasting • *Civic & Public Affairs:* Civil Rights • *Education:* Colleges & Universities, Medical Education • *Environment:* Air/Water Quality • *Health:* Adolescent Health Issues, Cancer, Clinics/Medical Centers, Eyes/Blindness, Geriatric Health, Hospitals, Medical Research, Mental Health, Single-Disease Health Associations • *International:* Foreign Educational Institutions, International Relations, Missionary/Religious Activities • *Religion:* Jewish Causes, Religious Organizations, Religious Welfare, Synagogues/Temples • *Social Services:* Animal Protection, Child Welfare, Homes, People with Disabilities, Senior Services, Shelters/Homelessness, Youth Organizations

Grant Types: general support, multi-year/continuing support, and research

Geographic Distribution: focus on NY

GIVING OFFICERS
Gene S. Lasdon: vp, dir

Jeffrey S. Lasdon: vp, dir

Mildred D. Lasdon: vp, dir *PHIL AFFIL* pres: William and Mildred Lasdon Foundation

APPLICATION INFORMATION
Initial Approach: Send brief letter of inquiry describing program. There are no deadlines.

Restrictions on Giving: Limited to medical services, performing arts, and higher education.

GRANTS ANALYSIS
Total Grants: $137,425

Number of Grants: 39

Highest Grant: $25,000

Typical Range: $100 to $25,000

Disclosure Period: fiscal year ending November 30, 1993

Note: Recent grants are derived from a fiscal 1993 Form 990.

RECENT GRANTS

Library
1,000	New York Hospital Patient's Library, New York, NY
100	New York Hospital Patient's Library, New York, NY

General
25,000	Cornell Medical Center, New York, NY — recreational grant/Adolescent Development program
25,000	Long Island University School of Pharmacy, Brookville, NY
25,000	State of Israel Bonds, New York, NY — contributed to UJA
15,000	New York Hospital Cornell Medical Center, New York, NY — research grant
10,000	United Jewish Appeal Federation, New York, NY

Lasdon Foundation, William and Mildred

CONTACT
Mildred D. Lasdon
President
William and Mildred Lasdon Fdn.
575 Madison Ave., 10th Flr.
New York, NY 10022
(212) 935-3916

FINANCIAL SUMMARY
Recent Giving: $268,395 (1993)

Assets: $10,077,239 (1993)

Gifts Received: $10,000 (1993)

Fiscal Note: In 1993, contributions were received from Mildred D. Lasdon.

EIN: 23-7380362

CONTRIBUTIONS SUMMARY
Typical Recipients: • *Arts & Humanities:* Arts Associations & Councils, Ballet, Film & Video, Libraries, Museums/Galleries, Music, Opera, Performing Arts, Public Broadcasting, Theater • *Civic & Public Affairs:* General • *Education:* Arts/Humanities Education, Colleges & Universities, Medical Education • *Health:* Cancer, Clinics/Medical Centers, Hospitals, Nursing Services • *International:* Missionary/Religious Activities • *Religion:* Jewish Causes, Seminaries • *Social Services:* Youth Organizations

Grant Types: general support

Geographic Distribution: focus on NY

GIVING OFFICERS
Bonnie Eletz: vp

Nanette L. Laitman: secy, treas

Mildred D. Lasdon: pres *PHIL AFFIL* vp, dir: Lasdon Foundation

Cathy Sorkin: vp

APPLICATION INFORMATION
Initial Approach: The foundation has no formal grant application procedure or application form.

GRANTS ANALYSIS
Total Grants: $268,395

Number of Grants: 111

Highest Grant: $150,000

Typical Range: $100 to $12,500

Disclosure Period: 1993

Note: Recent grants are derived from a 1993 Form 990.

RECENT GRANTS

Library

1,250	New York Public Library, New York, NY
700	New York Public Library, New York, NY

General

150,000	University School of Nova University
5,000	Congregation Emanu El, New York, NY
5,000	Congregation Emanu El, New York, NY
5,000	Jewish Theological Seminary of America, New York, NY
2,000	Manhattan School of Music, New York, NY

Lauder Foundation

CONTACT
Barbara E. Capri
Administrator
Lauder Foundation
767 Fifth Ave.
New York, NY 10153
(212) 572-4426

FINANCIAL SUMMARY
Recent Giving: $600,000 (fiscal 1995 est.); $650,000 (fiscal 1994 approx.); $614,990 (fiscal 1993)

Assets: $7,625,000 (fiscal 1995 est.); $7,600,000 (fiscal 1994 approx.); $7,696,848 (fiscal 1993)

Gifts Received: $255,000 (fiscal 1993); $500 (fiscal 1988); $1,500 (fiscal 1986)

Fiscal Note: In fiscal 1993, the foundation received gifts from Estee Lauder, Inc. ($250,000) and the Permanent Label Corporation ($5,000).

EIN: 13-6153743

CONTRIBUTIONS SUMMARY
Donor(s): The Lauder Foundation was incorporated in New York in 1962, with funds donated by the Lauder family. Estee Lauder and her husband, Joseph H. Lauder, founded the cosmetics firm, Estee Lauder, in 1946. Most of the company stock is still owned by members of the Lauder family, including Estee Lauder's two sons, Ronald S. Lauder and Leonard A. Lauder.

Typical Recipients: • *Arts & Humanities:* Art History, Arts Associations & Councils, Arts Centers, Ballet, Dance, Historic Preservation, Libraries, Museums/Galleries, Music, Theater • *Civic & Public Affairs:* Botanical Gardens/Parks, Ethnic Organiza-

tions, General, Professional & Trade Associations, Public Policy, Zoos/Aquariums • *Education:* Arts/Humanities Education, Colleges & Universities, Literacy • *Environment:* General • *Health:* Cancer, Clinics/Medical Centers, Eyes/Blindness, Health Funds, Heart, Hospitals, Medical Research • *International:* Foreign Arts Organizations, International Peace & Security Issues, International Relief Efforts • *Religion:* Jewish Causes, Religious Welfare • *Science:* Science Museums • *Social Services:* Family Services, Homes, People with Disabilities, Recreation & Athletics, Senior Services, Youth Organizations

Grant Types: general support

Geographic Distribution: primarily New York City

GIVING OFFICERS
Barbara E. Capri: admin

Estee Lauder: pres *B* Queens NY 1908 *CURR EMPL* chmn: Estee Lauder *CORP AFFIL* chmn, dir: Aramis Inc, EJL Corp

Leonard Alan Lauder: secy-treas *B* New York NY 1933 *ED* Univ PA BS 1954 *CURR EMPL* pres, ceo: Estee Lauder *CORP AFFIL* dir: US Trust Corp *NONPR AFFIL* bd govs: Joseph H Lauder Inst Mgmt Intl Studies; founding mem: Whitney Mus Am Art Natl Comm; mem: Chief Execs Org, Foreign Policy Assn, French-Am Chamber Commerce US, Natl Comm Am Foreign Policy, World Bus Counc; pres: Whitney Mus Am Art; trust: Aspen Inst Humanistic Studies, Univ PA

Ronald Stephen Lauder: vp *B* New York NY 1944 *ED* Univ Paris 1964; Univ PA BS 1965 *CURR EMPL* ptnr: RS Lauder Gaspar & Co *CORP AFFIL* dir: EJL Corp, Estee Lauder; exec vp, dir: McGinnis Inc; secy-treas, dir: McNational Inc *NONPR AFFIL* trust: Mt Sinai Med Ctr, Mus Modern Art *PHIL AFFIL* don, pres, trust: Ronald S. Lauder Foundation; pres, dir: Ronald S. Lauder Foundation; don, pres, trust: Lauder (Ronald S) Foundation

APPLICATION INFORMATION
Initial Contact: Prospective applicants should send a letter to the foundation.

Include Information On: The letter should describe the organization and the project for which funds are sought.

Deadlines: There are no deadlines for submitting requests and no application forms.

Review Process: Applicants will be notified of a decision four to eight weeks after the letter has been received. The board meets as required.

Restrictions on Giving: No grants are given to individuals.

GRANTS ANALYSIS
Total Grants: $614,990

Number of Grants: 77

Highest Grant: $100,000

Average Grant: $7,987

Typical Range: $1,000 to $25,000

Disclosure Period: fiscal year ending November 30, 1993

Note: Recent grants are derived from a fiscal 1993 Form 990.

RECENT GRANTS

Library

2,000	New York Public Library, New York, NY

General

100,000	United Jewish Appeal, New York, NY
50,000	American Museum of Natural History, New York, NY
50,000	Aspen Institute, Queenstown, MD
50,000	US Holocaust Memorial Museum, Washington, DC
27,600	Central Park Conservancy, New York, NY

Lemberg Foundation

CONTACT
John Usdan
Treasurer
Lemberg Fdn.
60 E 42nd St., Rm. 1814
New York, NY 10165
(212) 682-9595

FINANCIAL SUMMARY
Recent Giving: $605,121 (1993); $462,347 (1991); $260,858 (1990)

Assets: $13,442,290 (1993); $12,110,027 (1991); $10,311,604 (1990)

Gifts Received: $500 (1991)

EIN: 13-6082064

CONTRIBUTIONS SUMMARY
Donor(s): the late Samuel Lemberg

Typical Recipients: • *Arts & Humanities:* Arts Associations & Councils, Arts Centers, Community Arts, Dance, Historic Preservation, Libraries, Museums/Galleries, Music, Opera, Performing Arts, Public Broadcasting, Theater, Visual Arts • *Civic & Public Affairs:* Botanical Gardens/Parks, General • *Education:* Arts/Humanities Education, Colleges & Universities, Education Funds, Literacy, Minority Education, Private Education (Precollege), Religious Education, Science/Mathematics Education, Student Aid • *Health:* Clinics/Medical Centers, Health Organizations, Hospitals, Hospitals (University Affiliated), Medical Research • *International:* Foreign Arts Organizations • *Religion:* Jewish Causes, Religious Organizations, Synagogues/Temples • *Social Services:* Animal Protection, Child Welfare, Community Service Organizations, Family Services, People with Disabilities, United Funds/United Ways, YMCA/YWCA/YMHA/YWHA

Grant Types: capital, endowment, fellowship, project, research, and scholarship

Geographic Distribution: focus on New York, NY

GIVING OFFICERS
Adam Usdan: secy

John Usdan: treas

Suzanne Usdan: pres

APPLICATION INFORMATION

Initial Approach: Send brief letter of inquiry describing program or project. There are no deadlines.

Restrictions on Giving: No grants for matching gifts.

GRANTS ANALYSIS

Total Grants: $605,121

Number of Grants: 74

Highest Grant: $161,000

Typical Range: $25 to $125,250

Disclosure Period: 1993

Note: Recent grants are derived from a 1993 Form 990.

RECENT GRANTS

Library

2,500	New York Public Library, New York, NY

General

161,000	USDAN Center
125,250	Brandeis University, Waltham, MA
75,000	United Jewish Appeal Federation, New York, NY
50,000	Wesleyan University, Middletown, CT
30,700	Jewish Museum, New York, NY

Lenna Foundation, Reginald A. and Elizabeth S.

CONTACT

Reginald A. Lenna
Reginald A. and Elizabeth S. Lenna Fdn.
Fenton Bldg., Rm. 401
Jamestown, NY 14701
(716) 483-1151

FINANCIAL SUMMARY

Recent Giving: $142,100 (1992)

Assets: $3,493,637 (1992)

EIN: 11-2800733

CONTRIBUTIONS SUMMARY

Typical Recipients: • *Arts & Humanities:* Arts Funds, Libraries, Music • *Civic & Public Affairs:* Community Foundations, Urban & Community Affairs • *Education:* Colleges & Universities, General • *Health:* Emergency/Ambulance Services, Hospices • *Social Services:* Community Centers, Recreation & Athletics, Youth Organizations

Grant Types: general support

Geographic Distribution: primarily Jamestown, NY, area

GIVING OFFICERS

Francis B. Grow: dir

John D. Hamilton: dir *B* Pavilion NY *ED* Hamilton Coll AB 1922 *NONPR AFFIL* trust: Chautauqua Inst, Jamestown Commun

Coll *PHIL AFFIL* pres, dir: Gebbie Foundation

Elizabeth S. Lenna: dir

Reginald A. Lenna: dir

Samuel P. Price: dir

APPLICATION INFORMATION

Initial Approach: Send a brief letter of inquiry and a full proposal. Include purpose of funds sought, amount requested, a description of organization, and proof of tax-exempt status. There are no deadlines.

GRANTS ANALYSIS

Total Grants: $142,100

Number of Grants: 15

Highest Grant: $85,000

Typical Range: $200 to $15,000

Disclosure Period: 1992

Note: Recent grants are derived from a 1992 Form 990.

RECENT GRANTS

Library

4,800	James Prendergast Library, Jamestown, NY — general operations
200	Lakewood Library, Lakewood, NY — general operations

General

85,000	Chautauqua Foundation, Chautauqua, NY — ESL building
15,000	Chautauqua Striders, Jamestown, NY — general operations
10,000	Hospice, Jamestown, NY — general operations
3,000	Chaut Region Community Foundation, Jamestown, NY — eco dev fund
1,100	Reg Lenna Civic Center, Jamestown, NY — general operations

Liberman Foundation, Bertha and Isaac

CONTACT

Jeffrey Klein
President
Bertha and Isaac Liberman Fdn.
480 Pk. Ave.
New York, NY 10022

FINANCIAL SUMMARY

Recent Giving: $275,500 (fiscal 1993); $249,000 (fiscal 1992); $271,375 (fiscal 1991)

Assets: $4,390,605 (fiscal 1993); $4,390,729 (fiscal 1992); $4,952,644 (fiscal 1991)

EIN: 13-6119056

CONTRIBUTIONS SUMMARY

Donor(s): the late Isaac Liberman

Typical Recipients: • *Arts & Humanities:* Libraries, Museums/Galleries • *Education:*

Colleges & Universities, Private Education (Precollege), Secondary Education (Private) • *Environment:* General • *Health:* Hospitals, Prenatal Health Issues, Single-Disease Health Associations • *Religion:* Jewish Causes, Religious Organizations • *Social Services:* Community Service Organizations, Delinquency & Criminal Rehabilitation, Youth Organizations

Grant Types: general support

Geographic Distribution: focus on NY

GIVING OFFICERS

Jeffrey Klein: pres

Joan K. Lieberman: trust

APPLICATION INFORMATION

Initial Approach: Send brief letter of inquiry describing program or project. There are no deadlines.

Restrictions on Giving: Does not support individuals.

GRANTS ANALYSIS

Total Grants: $249,000

Number of Grants: 14

Highest Grant: $67,500

Typical Range: $1,000 to $20,000

Disclosure Period: fiscal year ending July 1, 1992

Note: Recent grants are derived from a fiscal 1992 Form 990.

RECENT GRANTS

Library

25,000	New York Public Library, New York, NY

General

67,500	92nd Street YM-YWHA, New York, NY
50,000	Mt. Sinai Medical Center, New York, NY
24,000	New York University, New York, NY
20,000	Lab School of Washington, Washington, DC
10,000	United Jewish Appeal, New York, NY

Link, Jr. Foundation, George

CONTACT

Bernard F. Joyce
Vice President, Secretary, and Director
George Link, Jr. Foundation
c/o Emmet, Marvin & Martin
120 Broadway, Ste. 3200
New York, NY 10271
(212) 422-2974

FINANCIAL SUMMARY

Recent Giving: $1,984,750 (1993); $1,949,900 (1992); $1,713,500 (1991)

Assets: $28,073,872 (1993); $26,860,347 (1992); $26,420,712 (1991)

Gifts Received: $93,431 (1993); $456,559 (1992); $150,000 (1991)

Fiscal Note: In 1989, the foundation received $100,000 from the estate of George Link, Jr. In 1991, the foundation received $150,000 from a donor the foundation did not identify. In 1992, the foundation received a $456,559 donation from an unidentified source. In 1993, the foundation received $93,431 from the estate of George Link, Jr.

EIN: 13-3041396

CONTRIBUTIONS SUMMARY

Donor(s): The foundation was established in 1980 by the late George Link, Jr.

Typical Recipients: • *Arts & Humanities:* Arts Associations & Councils, Arts Centers, Ethnic & Folk Arts, Libraries, Museums/Galleries, Theater • *Civic & Public Affairs:* Law & Justice, Safety • *Education:* Arts/Humanities Education, Colleges & Universities, Community & Junior Colleges, Education Funds, Legal Education, Medical Education, Private Education (Precollege), Religious Education, Secondary Education (Private), Secondary Education (Public), Special Education, Student Aid • *Health:* Clinics/Medical Centers, Health Funds, Health Organizations, Heart, Hospitals, Medical Research, Mental Health, Single-Disease Health Associations • *International:* Health Care/Hospitals, International Organizations • *Religion:* Churches, Missionary Activities (Domestic), Religious Organizations, Religious Welfare, Seminaries • *Social Services:* At-Risk Youth, Child Welfare, Family Services, Homes, People with Disabilities, Senior Services, Shelters/Homelessness, Volunteer Services, Youth Organizations

Grant Types: capital, endowment, fellowship, general support, and scholarship

Geographic Distribution: primarily New York and New Jersey

GIVING OFFICERS

Michael J. Catanzaro: vp, treas, dir

Coleman F. Clougherty: vp, dir

Bernard F. Joyce: vp, secy, dir

Eleanor Irene Higgins Link: chmn

Robert Emmett Link: vchmn, dir

APPLICATION INFORMATION
Initial Approach:

An letter of inquiry should be sent to Michael J. Catanzaro.

No application deadlines are reported.

GRANTS ANALYSIS
Total Grants: $1,984,750

Number of Grants: 128

Highest Grant: $120,000

Average Grant: $15,506

Typical Range: $5,000 to $25,000

Disclosure Period: 1993

Note: Recent grants are derived from a 1993 grants list.

RECENT GRANTS

Library
13,000	Friends of the Clifton Public Library, Clifton, NJ

General
120,000	St. Vincents Hospital and Medical Center of New York, New York, NY
100,000	John F. Kennedy Medical Center Foundation, Edison, NJ
100,000	St. Francis Hospital, Jersey City, NJ
70,000	Church and Friary of St. Francis of Assisi, New York, NY
61,000	Felician College, Lodi, NJ

Littauer Foundation, Lucius N.

CONTACT
William Lee Frost
President
Lucius N. Littauer Foundation
60 E 42nd St., Ste. 2910
New York, NY 10165
(212) 697-2677
Note: Applicants may also contact Pamela Ween Brumberg, Program Officer.

FINANCIAL SUMMARY
Recent Giving: $1,300,000 (1995 est.); $1,225,026 (1994); $1,146,957 (1993)

Assets: $21,300,000 (1995 est.); $21,300,000 (1994 approx.); $22,000,000 (1993 approx.)

Fiscal Note: 1994 figures were granted from January 1 to September 30, 1994.

EIN: 13-1688027

CONTRIBUTIONS SUMMARY
Donor(s): The foundation was established by Lucius N. Littauer in 1929. The late Mr. Littauer was president of Littauer Brothers, a family-owned glove manufacturing company, and president or director of several public utilities, and transportation and banking firms. He also served as a U.S. congressman.

Mr. Littauer was an active philanthropist. Aside from the charitable activities of the Littauer Foundation, he donated over $2.25 million to Harvard University for the Littauer Center and Graduate School in Public Administration, and established the Nathan Littauer Hospital in Gloversville, NY.

Typical Recipients: • *Arts & Humanities:* Arts Outreach, Ethnic & Folk Arts, Historic Preservation, History & Archaeology, Libraries, Literary Arts, Museums/Galleries, Music • *Civic & Public Affairs:* Botanical Gardens/Parks, Philanthropic Organizations • *Education:* Colleges & Universities, Education Funds, Engineering/Technological Education, International Studies, Legal Education, Medical Education, Private Education (Precollege), Religious Education, School Volunteerism • *Environment:* General • *Health:* Geriatric Health, Health Organizations, Hospitals • *International:* Foreign Arts Organizations, Foreign Educational Institutions, Health Care/Hospitals, International Organizations, International Relations, Missionary/Religious Activities • *Religion:* Jewish Causes, Religious Organizations, Religious Welfare • *Social Services:* Community Centers, Family Services, Senior Services

Grant Types: challenge, conference/seminar, endowment, general support, project, and research

GIVING OFFICERS
Charles Berlin: dir *B* Boston MA 1936 *ED* Hebrew Coll 1956; Harvard Univ AB 1958; Hebrew Coll 1959; Harvard Univ PhD 1963; Simmons Coll MLS 1964 *NONPR AFFIL* consult: Emory Univ, Univ FL, Univ TX; head Judaica div: Harvard Coll; mem: Assn Jewish Libraries; mem, exec secy: Assn Jewish Studies; trust: Hebrew Coll

Berthold Bilski: dir

William Lee Frost: pres, treas, dir *B* Larchmont NY 1926 *ED* Harvard Univ BA 1947; Yale Univ LLB 1951; Harvard Univ MPA 1958 *CORP AFFIL* dir: Overseas Shipholding Group *NONPR AFFIL* chmn: Jewish Telegraphic Agency, PEF Israel Endowment; hon curator Judaica: Harvard Coll Library; mem: Assn Bar City New York, Harvard Alumni Assn, NY County Bar Assn, NY St Bar Assn, State NY Pub Health Counc; trust: Collegiate Sch

George Harris: asst secy, asst treas, dir

Henry A. Lowet: vp, secy, dir

Peter J. Solomon: dir *B* New York NY 1938 *ED* Harvard Univ BA 1960; Harvard Univ MBA 1963 *CURR EMPL* chmn, ceo: Peter J Solomon Co Ltd *PHIL AFFIL* trust: Peter and Linda Solomon Foundation

APPLICATION INFORMATION
Initial Approach:

Applications should be sent in complete proposal form.

Include a project description, budget, timetable, name of person in charge of project, resumes of key personnel, and proof of tax exemption.

The officers and directors meet as needed to decide on grants. Proposals may be submitted throughout the year.

Restrictions on Giving: Grants are seldom made for endowments (except for book funds), operating budgets, or capital projects.

GRANTS ANALYSIS
Total Grants: $1,225,026

Number of Grants: 142

Highest Grant: $175,000

Average Grant: $8,627

Typical Range: $1,000 to $10,000

Disclosure Period: 1994

Note: Recent grants are derived from a partial 1994 grants list.

RECENT GRANTS

Library
175,000	Harvard College Library, Cambridge, MA — addition to endowment, sixth payment
75,000	Friends of Harvard-Radcliffe Hillel, Cambridge, MA —

50,000	for the Judah J. Shapiro Library in Rosovsky Hall, second installment American Friends of Hebrew University, New York, NY — Jewish National and University Library project to microfilm the Jewish Press Collection in the Russian State Library, second and final payment
10,000	New York Public Library, New York, NY — renewed support for Microcomputer Page Project at branch libraries

General

25,000	Abraham Joshua Heschel School, New York, NY — endowment
25,000	Columbia University, New York, NY — Yiddish studies program and scholarship support for graduate students
25,000	Nathan Littauer Hospital — in honor of its Centennial
25,000	National Foundation for Jewish Culture, New York, NY — Doctoral Dissertation fellowship in Jewish studies endowment, first of two installments
25,000	National Foundation for Jewish Culture, New York, NY — Doctoral Dissertation Fellowship Program

Liz Claiborne, Inc. / Liz Claiborne Foundation

Sales: $2.2 billion
Employees: 7,000
Headquarters: New York, NY
SIC Major Group: Women's/Misses' Outerwear Nec, Women's/Misses' Blouses & Shirts, Women's/Misses' Dresses, and Women's/Misses' Suits & Coats

CONTACT
Melanie Lyons
Director
Liz Claiborne Fdn.
1441 Broadway Ave.
New York, NY 10018
(212) 626-5424

FINANCIAL SUMMARY
Recent Giving: $1,681,179 (1993); $1,490,740 (1992); $1,492,233 (1991)

Assets: $17,883,222 (1993); $16,099,505 (1992); $12,678,805 (1990)

Gifts Received: $1,179,329 (1993); $1,604,179 (1992)

Fiscal Note: All contributions made through the foundation. Above figures exclude non-monetary support.

EIN: 13-3060673

CONTRIBUTIONS SUMMARY
Typical Recipients: • *Arts & Humanities:* Arts Associations & Councils, Arts Centers, Community Arts, Libraries, Museums/Galleries, Music, Opera, Public Broadcasting • *Civic & Public Affairs:* Employment/Job Training, Urban & Community Affairs, Zoos/Aquariums • *Education:* Arts/Humanities Education, Colleges & Universities, Education Funds, Medical Education, Preschool Education, Private Education (Precollege), Public Education (Precollege), Secondary Education (Private) • *Environment:* General • *Health:* AIDS/HIV, Cancer, Clinics/Medical Centers, Eyes/Blindness, Hospitals, Prenatal Health Issues, Single-Disease Health Associations • *Religion:* Jewish Causes, Religious Welfare • *Social Services:* Camps, Child Welfare, Community Service Organizations, Day Care, Domestic Violence, Emergency Relief, Family Services, Food/Clothing Distribution, Recreation & Athletics, Senior Services, Youth Organizations

Grant Types: challenge, employee matching gifts, general support, and project

Geographic Distribution: New York City and Hudson County, NJ

Operating Locations: NJ (North Bergen, Secaucus), NY (New York)

CORP. OFFICERS
Robert Bernard: *CURR EMPL* sr vp intl sales: Liz Claiborne

Jerome A. Chazen: *B* New York NY 1927 *ED* Univ WI BA 1948; Columbia Univ MBA 1950 *CURR EMPL* co-fdr, chmn, dir: Liz Claiborne *NONPR AFFIL* dir: Ed Fdn, Fashion Inst Tech, Rockland Ctr Arts, Shenkar Coll Fashion & Textiles *PHIL AFFIL* trust: Chazen Foundation

Harvey L. Falk: *B* 1934 *ED* NY Univ 1955 *CURR EMPL* pres, vchmn: Liz Claiborne *CORP AFFIL* vchmn, pres: LCI Holdings Inc, Liz Claiborne Cosemetics Inc, Liz Claiborne Foreign Holdings Inc, RTVCH Holdings Inc

Joseph Allen McNeary: *B* New York NY 1948 *ED* Georgetown Univ BA 1969 *CURR EMPL* sr vp: Liz Claiborne *NONPR AFFIL* mem exec bd: Brooklyn Bus Commun Svcs *CLUB AFFIL* Heights Casino

GIVING OFFICERS
Robert Bernard: mem grantmaking comm *CURR EMPL* sr vp intl sales: Liz Claiborne (see above)

Jerome A. Chazen: trust *CURR EMPL* co-fdr, chmn, dir: Liz Claiborne *PHIL AFFIL* trust: Chazen Foundation (see above)

Harvey L. Falk: mem grantmaking comm *CURR EMPL* pres, vchmn: Liz Claiborne (see above)

Melanie Lyons: dir, mem grantmaking comm

Jay M. Margolis: mem grantmaking comm *B* New York NY 1949 *ED* Queens Coll BA 1971 *CURR EMPL* chmn: Pepe Jeans USA Inc *CORP AFFIL* vchmn: Liz Claiborne Cosemetics Inc, RTVCH Holdings Inc *NONPR AFFIL* mem bd: Fathers Day/Mothers Day Counc *CLUB AFFIL* City Athletic

Joseph Allen McNeary: mem grantmaking comm *CURR EMPL* sr vp: Liz Claiborne (see above)

Nancy Rogers: mem grantmaking comm

APPLICATION INFORMATION
Initial Approach: *Initial Contact:* brief letter or proposal *Include Information On:* description of project and organization; amount requested; other sources of funding; current budgetary information (income and expenses); evaluation plan for project; audited financial statement; and proof of tax-exempt status *Deadlines:* none

Restrictions on Giving: Does not support endowments, capital campaigns, individuals, fraternal, or veterans organizations; programs based or operating outside the United States; research; professional meetings or symposia; media projects; technical assistance; or dinners, special events, or goodwill advertising.

GRANTS ANALYSIS
Total Grants: $1,681,179

Number of Grants: 180

Highest Grant: $246,600

Average Grant: $8,014*

Typical Range: $500 to $10,000

Disclosure Period: 1993

Note: Average grant figure excludes highest grant figure. Recent grants are derived from a 1993 Form 990.

RECENT GRANTS
Library

13,000	New York Public Library, New York, NY
10,000	Library of Congress Madison, Madison, WI

General

150,000	United Jewish Appeal Federation, New York, NY
92,000	National Alliance of Breast Cancer Organizations, New York, NY
53,000	Clearpool, New York, NY
40,000	KIDS of North Jersey, NJ
36,250	New York Zoological Society, Bronx, NY

Loews Corporation / Loews Foundation

Revenue: $13.51 billion
Employees: 27,100
Headquarters: New York, NY
SIC Major Group: Holding Companies Nec, Cigarettes, Life Insurance, and Fire, Marine & Casualty Insurance

CONTACT
Roy Edward Posner
Senior Vice President, Chief Financial Officer
Loews Fdn.
667 Madison Ave.
New York, NY 10021
(212) 545-2950

FINANCIAL SUMMARY
Recent Giving: $2,365,717 (1993);
$2,314,235 (1992); $1,510,270 (1991)

Assets: $86,979 (1993); $23,459 (1992);
$52,884 (1991)

Gifts Received: $2,430,000 (1993)

Fiscal Note: Company gives through the
foundation only. Above figures exclude nonmonetary support. In 1993, Foundation received contributions from Loews
Corporation and its subsidiaries.

EIN: 13-6082817

CONTRIBUTIONS SUMMARY
Typical Recipients: • *Arts & Humanities:*
Arts Associations & Councils, Dance, His-
toric Preservation, Libraries, Museums/Gal-
leries, Music, Performing Arts, Theater
• *Civic & Public Affairs:* African American
Affairs, Botanical Gardens/Parks, Economic
Development, Municipalities/Towns, Profes-
sional & Trade Associations, Safety, Urban
& Community Affairs, Women's Affairs,
Zoos/Aquariums • *Education:* Arts/Humani-
ties Education, Colleges & Universities,
Education Reform, General, Public Educa-
tion (Precollege), Social Sciences Education, Student Aid • *Environment:* General
• *Health:* AIDS/HIV, Cancer, Children's
Health/Hospitals, Diabetes, Emergency/Am-
bulance Services, Hospitals, Medical Research, Multiple Sclerosis, Nutrition,
Single-Disease Health Associations • *International:* Human Rights, International Peace
& Security Issues, International Relief Efforts • *Religion:* Jewish Causes • *Social Services:* Child Welfare, Community Service
Organizations, People with Disabilities, Recreation & Athletics, United Funds/United
Ways, Volunteer Services, Youth Organizations

Grant Types: employee matching gifts, general support, and scholarship

Note: Scholarships are provided for children
of Loews Corporation through the National
Merit Scholarship Corp.

Nonmonetary Support: $50,000 (1992)

Nonmonetary Support Types: donated
products

Note: Occasional donation of hotel rooms
and watches.

Geographic Distribution: primarily New
York, also in operating locations

Operating Locations: AZ (Tucson), CA
(San Diego, Santa Monica), CO (Denver),
DC (Washington), IL (Chicago), LA (New
Iberia), MD (Annapolis), NC (Greensboro),
NY (Maspeth, New York, Orangeburg,
Woodside), PA (Lancaster, West Willow),
TN (Nashville), TX (Alice, Dallas, Hous-
ton), VA (Danville)

CORP. OFFICERS
Roy Edward Posner: *B* Chicago IL 1933
ED Univ IL BS 1951-1953; Harvard Univ
Grad Sch Bus Admin 1976 *CURR EMPL* sr
vp, cfo: Loews Corp *CORP AFFIL* consult:
NY Football Giants Inc; dir: Bulova Italy
SPA, Bulova Sys & Instruments Corp, GF
Corp, Loews Hotels Monaco, Loews Intl
Svcs, Taj Mahal Holding Corp; sr vp, cfo,
dir: Loews Hotels Holding Corp; sr vp, dir:

48th St & 8th Ave Corp, Loews NY Hotel
Inc; sr vp fin, dir: Loews Tucson Hotel Inc
NONPR AFFIL mem: Am Hotel & Motel
Assn, Am Inst CPAs, Fin Execs Inst, IL Soc
CPAs, Ins Acct & Statistics Assn, Intl Hospi-
tality Acct Assoc, NY Soc CPAs, Tri
County Golf Assn; mem editorial comm:
Uniform Sys Accounting Hotels; meme:
Delta Tau Delta *CLUB AFFIL* Alpine CC

Laurence Alan Tisch: *B* New York NY
1923 *ED* NY Univ BS 1942; Univ PA MA
1943; Harvard Univ Law Sch *CURR EMPL*
chmn, pres, ceo, dir: CBS Inc *CORP AFFIL*
ceo, dir: Loews Corp; chmn: CNA Fin Corp;
dir: Automatic Data Processing, Bulova
Corp, Getty Oil Co, RH Macy & Co Inc, NY
Stock Exchange, Petrie Stores Corp *NONPR
AFFIL* chmn bd trustees: NY Univ; dir: Un
Jewish Appeal Fed Jewish Philanthropies
NY; mem: Counc Foreign Rels, Mayors
Comm Pub-Pvt Partnerships; trust: Metro
Mus Art, NY Pub Lib *PHIL AFFIL* sr vp,
don: Tisch Foundation; trust, mem fin &
admin comm: Carnegie Corporation of New
York

Preston Robert Tisch: *B* Brooklyn NY
1926 *ED* Bucknell Univ 1943-1944; Univ
MI BA 1948 *CURR EMPL* pres, co-ceo:
Loews Corp *CORP AFFIL* chmn: 48th St &
8th Ave Corp; chmn, dir: Loews Hotels Inc;
dir: Bulova Corp, CBS Inc, Hasbro Inc,
Pathogenesis Corp, Rite Aid Corp; dir,
chmn exec comm: CNA Fin Corp; owner, co-
chmn & ceo: NY Football Giants Inc
NONPR AFFIL chmn: New York City Part-
nership; chmn emeritus: NY Convention &
Visit Bur; mem: Govs Bus Adv Counc NY,
Quadrennial Comm Exec Legislative Judi-
cial Salaries, Sigma Alpha Mu, Travel Indus
Assn Am; mem travel tourism adv bd: US
Dept Commerce; trust: NY Univ, Sales
Mktg Execs Greater NY *CLUB AFFIL* Cen-
tury CC, Harrison, Rye Racquet *PHIL AF-
FIL* chmn, dir: CBS Foundation; pres, don:
Tisch Foundation

GIVING OFFICERS
John J. Kenny: secy, treas, trust *B* Jersey
City NJ 1938 *ED* NY Univ 1965; St Johns
Univ Sch Law 1972 *CURR EMPL* treas:
Loews Corp *CORP AFFIL* treas: Loews Ho-
tels Inc; treas, dir: 48th St & 8th Ave Corp

Roy Edward Posner: trust *CURR EMPL* sr
vp, cfo: Loews Corp (see above)

Laurence Alan Tisch: trust *CURR EMPL*
chmn, pres, ceo, dir: CBS Inc *PHIL AFFIL*
sr vp, don: Tisch Foundation; trust, mem fin
& admin comm: Carnegie Corporation of
New York (see above)

Preston Robert Tisch: trust *CURR EMPL*
pres, co-ceo: Loews Corp *PHIL AFFIL*
chmn, dir: CBS Foundation; pres, don:
Tisch Foundation (see above)

APPLICATION INFORMATION
Initial Approach: *Initial Contact:* by letter;
no phone calls *Include Information On:* description of the organization and project,
budget, proof of tax exemption *Deadlines:*
none *Note:* Applications for employee-related sponsorships are available from the
foundation.

Restrictions on Giving: Foundation does
not make grants to individuals.

OTHER THINGS TO KNOW
All charitable giving is through the foundation. Subsidiaries do not make grants independent of Loews Foundation, except for
CNA Insurance Co. (see separate entry for
details), which is affiliated with CNA Financial Corp., a Loews Corp. joint venture.

GRANTS ANALYSIS
Total Grants: $2,365,717

Number of Grants: 67*

Highest Grant: $625,000

Average Grant: $24,819*

Typical Range: $1,000 to $10,000 and
$10,000 to $500,000

Disclosure Period: 1993

Note: The figures for number of grants and
average grant exclude $21,116 in matching
gifts and $56,710 in scholarships. Average
grant figure also excludes the foundation's
highest grant of $625,000. Recent grants are
derived from a 1993 Form 990.

RECENT GRANTS
Library
100,000	New York Public Library, New York, NY	

General
625,000	United Jewish Appeal Federation, New York, NY
250,000	Mt. Sinai Children's Center Foundation, New York, NY
150,000	Montefiore Medical Center, New York, NY
126,000	Gay Men's Health Crisis, New York, NY
62,500	AIDS Project Los Angeles, Los Angeles, CA

Long Island Lighting Co.

Revenue: $2.88 billion
Employees: 6,600
Headquarters: Hicksville, NY
SIC Major Group: Electric, Gas & Sanitary
Services

CONTACT
Suzanne M. Halpin
Director, Media & Community Relations
Long Island Lighting Co.
175 E Old Country Rd.
Hicksville, NY 11801
(516) 545-5068

CONTRIBUTIONS SUMMARY
Typical Recipients: • *Arts & Humanities:*
Arts Associations & Councils, Arts Centers,
Arts Festivals, Arts Funds, Community Arts,
Ethnic & Folk Arts, Historic Preservation,
Libraries, Literary Arts, Museums/Galleries,
Music, Opera, Performing Arts, Public
Broadcasting, Theater, Visual Arts • *Civic &
Public Affairs:* Economic Development, Em-
ployment/Job Training, Nonprofit Manage-
ment, Professional & Trade Associations,
Safety, Urban & Community Affairs,

Women's Affairs, Zoos/Aquariums • *Education:* Business Education, Colleges & Universities, Community & Junior Colleges, Continuing Education, Elementary Education (Private), Engineering/Technological Education, Faculty Development, Literacy, Minority Education, Public Education (Precollege), Science/Mathematics Education, Social Sciences Education, Special Education • *Environment:* General • *Health:* Geriatric Health, Nutrition, Single-Disease Health Associations • *Science:* Science Exhibits & Fairs, Scientific Centers & Institutes, Scientific Organizations • *Social Services:* Community Centers, Family Services, Food/Clothing Distribution, People with Disabilities, Senior Services, Shelters/Homelessness, United Funds/United Ways, Volunteer Services, Youth Organizations

Nonmonetary Support Types: donated equipment, in-kind services, loaned employees, loaned executives, and workplace solicitation

Geographic Distribution: service area

Operating Locations: NY (Hicksville)

CORP. OFFICERS
William J. Catacosinos: *CURR EMPL* chmn, ceo: Long Island Lighting Co

James T. Flynn: *CURR EMPL* coo: Long Island Lighting Co

APPLICATION INFORMATION
Initial Approach: Send inquiry letter.

Lowenstein Foundation, Leon

CONTACT
Robert Austin Bendheim
President
Leon Lowenstein Foundation
126 E 56th St., 28th Fl.
New York, NY 10022
(212) 319-0670

FINANCIAL SUMMARY
Recent Giving: $2,613,825 (1993); $3,141,425 (1992); $2,632,850 (1990)

Assets: $81,601,592 (1993); $78,332,148 (1992); $62,806,931 (1990)

Gifts Received: $2,441,585 (1992)

Fiscal Note: In 1992, the foundation received funding from the Elizabeth Rose Newman and Leon Lowenstein Trust dated 2/9/62, the Elizabeth Rose Newman and Leon Lowenstein Trust dated 1/13/47, and the Josephine Lowenstein Trust.

EIN: 13-6015951

CONTRIBUTIONS SUMMARY
Donor(s): The foundation was established in 1941, with the late Leon Lowenstein as donor. Mr. Lowenstein's fortune stemmed from M. Lowenstein Corporation, a textile firm, now a subsidiary of Springs Industries.

Typical Recipients: • *Arts & Humanities:* History & Archaeology, Libraries, Museums/Galleries, Performing Arts, Public

Broadcasting • *Civic & Public Affairs:* General, Philanthropic Organizations, Zoos/Aquariums • *Education:* Business Education, Colleges & Universities, Education Reform, Elementary Education (Private), Medical Education, Minority Education, Private Education (Precollege), Public Education (Precollege), Special Education, Student Aid • *Health:* Cancer, Clinics/Medical Centers, Emergency/Ambulance Services, Eyes/Blindness, Health Organizations, Hospitals, Medical Research, Nursing Services, Single-Disease Health Associations • *Religion:* Jewish Causes, Religious Welfare • *Science:* Science Museums • *Social Services:* At-Risk Youth, Big Brother/Big Sister, Child Welfare, Community Centers, Emergency Relief, Family Services, Food/Clothing Distribution, People with Disabilities, Recreation & Athletics, Substance Abuse, United Funds/United Ways, Volunteer Services, YMCA/YWCA/YMHA/YWHA, Youth Organizations

Grant Types: general support

Geographic Distribution: emphasis on New York City metropolitan area

GIVING OFFICERS
John M. Bendheim: vp *B* New York NY 1918 *CURR EMPL* dir: M Lowenstein Corp

John M. Bendheim, Jr.: dir

Robert Austin Bendheim: pres *B* New York NY 1916 *ED* Princeton Univ AB 1937; Harvard Univ 1942 *CURR EMPL* chmn, ceo: M Lowenstein Corp

Lynn Bendheim-Thurman: dir

Bernard R. Rapaport: secy, treas *B* New York NY 1919 *ED* Cornell Univ 1939; Cornell Univ JD 1941 *CURR EMPL* secy, treas, gen coun, dir: M Lowenstein Corp

John Frederic Van Gorder: exec dir *B* Jacksonville FL 1943 *ED* Dover Coll 1961; Dartmouth Coll AB 1965; Air Force Inst Tech 1967-1968; George Washington Univ MS 1973; Fordham Univ Sch Law JD 1981 *NONPR AFFIL* adv comm: Toshiba Am Fdn; mem: Alpha Delta Phi, Am Bar Assn, DC Jaycees, Intl Jaycees, New York City Jaycees, NJ Bar Assn, Soc Mayflower Descendents, Sons Am Revolution, Student Bar Assn, Tabernacle Repbl Club, US Jaycees *CLUB AFFIL* Lions, Masons, Toastmasters

Thomas H. Wright, Jr.: dir *B* 1918 *CURR EMPL* chmn, treas, dir: Wright Chem

APPLICATION INFORMATION
Initial Approach:

Applications should be in letter form.

There are no deadlines for submitting requests.

GRANTS ANALYSIS
Total Grants: $2,613,825

Number of Grants: 110

Highest Grant: $509,000

Average Grant: $23,762

Typical Range: $1,000 to $25,000 and $50,000 to $100,000

Disclosure Period: 1993

Note: Recent grants are derived from a 1993 Form 990.

RECENT GRANTS
Library

10,000	Greenwich Library, Greenwich, CT
6,000	New York Public Library, New York, NY

General

509,000	Princeton University, Princeton, NJ
275,000	Greenwich Hospital Association, Greenwich, CT
250,000	Columbia University College of Physicians and Surgeons, New York, NY
250,000	Duke University, Durham, NC
250,000	White Plains Hospital Medical Center, White Plains, NY

Lurcy Charitable and Educational Trust, Georges

CONTACT
Seth E. Frank
Trustee
Georges Lurcy Charitable and Educational Trust
125 W 55th St.
New York, NY 10019
(212) 424-8000

FINANCIAL SUMMARY
Recent Giving: $675,883 (fiscal 1992); $638,620 (fiscal 1989); $637,873 (fiscal 1987)

Assets: $17,837,886 (fiscal 1992); $15,675,544 (fiscal 1989); $15,110,480 (fiscal 1987)

EIN: 13-6372044

CONTRIBUTIONS SUMMARY
Donor(s): The foundation was established by the late Georges Lurcy .

Typical Recipients: • *Arts & Humanities:* Arts Associations & Councils, Libraries, Museums/Galleries, Opera, Public Broadcasting • *Education:* Colleges & Universities, International Exchange, International Studies, Minority Education, Private Education (Precollege), Science/Mathematics Education • *Health:* Single-Disease Health Associations • *International:* Foreign Educational Institutions, International Peace & Security Issues • *Religion:* Religious Organizations • *Social Services:* Family Planning

Grant Types: fellowship

Geographic Distribution: national

GIVING OFFICERS
Alan S. Bernstein: trust

Daniel Lewis Bernstein: trust *B* Durham NC 1937 *ED* Amherst Coll AB 1959; Harvard Univ LLB 1962 *CURR EMPL* ptnr: Mannheimer Swartling *CORP AFFIL* secy, dir: NJ Automatic Door Inc *NONPR AFFIL* mem: Am Bar Assn, Bar Assn NY City, Intl Bar Assn

George Lurcy Bernstein: trust
Seth E. Frank: trust
Sidney O. Friedman: trust

APPLICATION INFORMATION
Initial Contact: Universities are requested to recommend a candidate for its fellowship. Applicants from France must apply to the FrancoAmerican Commission for Educational Exchange. Applicants cannot apply directly to the foundation.

Deadlines: The foundation has no deadline for submitting proposals.

GRANTS ANALYSIS
Total Grants: $675,883

Number of Grants: 42

Highest Grant: $90,000

Average Grant: $14,290*

Typical Range: $2,000 to $15,000

Disclosure Period: fiscal year ending June 30, 1992

Note: Average grant figure does not include the highest grant of $90,000. Recent grants are derived from a fiscal 1992 Form 990.

RECENT GRANTS
Library

4,000	Newberry Library

General

90,000	University of Chicago, Chicago, IL
87,000	University of North Carolina, Chapel Hill, NC
61,825	Harvard University, Cambridge, MA
59,500	Brookings Institute, Washington, DC
52,272	Columbia University, New York, NY

Macy & Co., Inc., R.H.

Sales: $6.97 billion
Employees: 51,000
Headquarters: New York, NY
SIC Major Group: Department Stores

CONTACT
Edward Jay Goldberg
Vice President, Consumer Affairs
R.H. Macy & Co.
151 W 34th St., 20th Fl.
New York, NY 10001
(212) 494-5568

FINANCIAL SUMMARY
Recent Giving: $3,000,000 (1990 approx.); $3,281,000 (1989); $2,698,000 (1988)

Fiscal Note: All contributions are made directly by the company. Above figures exclude nonmonetary support.

CONTRIBUTIONS SUMMARY
Typical Recipients: • *Arts & Humanities:* Arts Associations & Councils, Arts Centers, Arts Festivals, Arts Funds, Arts Institutes, Community Arts, Dance, Historic Preservation, Libraries, Literary Arts, Museums/Gal-leries, Music, Opera, Performing Arts, Public Broadcasting, Visual Arts • *Civic & Public Affairs:* Business/Free Enterprise, Civil Rights, Economic Policy, Employment/Job Training, Law & Justice, Legal Aid, Professional & Trade Associations, Public Policy, Safety, Urban & Community Affairs, Women's Affairs, Zoos/Aquariums • *Education:* Business Education, Colleges & Universities, Community & Junior Colleges, Continuing Education, Economic Education, Education Funds, Legal Education, Medical Education, Minority Education, Private Education (Precollege), Social Sciences Education, Special Education • *Health:* Emergency/Ambulance Services, Health Funds, Health Organizations, Hospitals, Medical Rehabilitation, Medical Research, Medical Training, Mental Health, Public Health • *Social Services:* Child Welfare, Community Centers, Community Service Organizations, Counseling, Delinquency & Criminal Rehabilitation, Emergency Relief, Homes, People with Disabilities, Recreation & Athletics, Senior Services, Substance Abuse, United Funds/United Ways, Volunteer Services, Youth Organizations

Grant Types: employee matching gifts, general support, and project

Geographic Distribution: company operating locations

Operating Locations: CA (Los Angeles, Newark, San Francisco, San Jose, San Leandro, Sunnyvale), GA (Decatur), KS (Mission), NJ (Cranford, East Brunswick, Lawrenceville, Paramus), NY (Bay Shore, Brooklyn, New York)

CORP. OFFICERS
Rudolph John Borneo: *B* Brooklyn NY 1941 *ED* Monmouth Coll BBA 1964 *CURR EMPL* pres: RH Macy & Co Inc *CORP AFFIL* pres, dir: Bullocks, Macys CA; sr vp, dir merchandising: Bambergers

Mark S. Handler: *B* Chicago IL 1933 *ED* Roosevelt Univ BS 1957; NY Univ MS 1958; Univ IL *CURR EMPL* exec dir: RH Macy & Co Inc

Myron Edward Ullman III: *B* Youngstown OH 1946 *ED* Univ Cincinnati BS 1969; Harvard Univ Inst Ed Mgmt 1977 *CURR EMPL* chmn, ceo: RH Macy & Co Inc *CORP AFFIL* dir: Mercy Unlimited Inc; vchmn: Mercy Ships Intl *NONPR AFFIL* dir: Brunswick Sch, Lincoln Ctr Devel, Mothers Choice Hong Kong, Univ Cincinnati Fdn; exec comm, dir: St Vincent Hosp; mem: Delta Tau Delta, White House Fellows Alumni Assn; vchmn, mem exec comm: Natl Retail Fed; vp: Univ Cincinnati Alumni Assn *CLUB AFFIL* Econ

GIVING OFFICERS
Edward Jay Goldberg: *CURR EMPL* vp consumer aff: RH Macy & Co Inc

APPLICATION INFORMATION
Initial Approach: *Initial Contact:* letter and proposal *Include Information On:* description of the organization, amount requested, purpose for which funds are sought, recently audited financial statement, last year's operating budget, list of major corporate contributors, copy of IRS determination letter *Deadlines:* none

OTHER THINGS TO KNOW
Although the company is now in Chapter 11, it is continuing its contributions. However, requests are being reviewed more carefully.

The company's objective is to donate 1% of pretax earnings to charitable activities.

At the time of publication, Macy's and Federated Department Stores were involved in discussions concerning a possible merger.

GRANTS ANALYSIS
Typical Range: $500 to $5,000

Mailman Family Foundation, A. L.

CONTACT
Luba H. Lynch
Executive Director and Secretary
A. L. Mailman Family Foundation
707 Westchester Ave.
White Plains, NY 10604
(914) 681-4448

FINANCIAL SUMMARY
Recent Giving: $899,633 (1993); $886,967 (1992); $844,340 (1991)

Assets: $21,096,187 (1993); $20,166,864 (1992); $19,975,983 (1991)

Gifts Received: $5,052 (1993); $15,000 (1992); $1,960,547 (1991)

Fiscal Note: In 1992, contributions were received from Patricia Lieberman ($10,000), and Marilyn Segal ($5,000). In 1991, gifts were received from Debra J. Segal Trust ($5,000), Patricia Lieberman ($5,000), estate of Alice Mailman,($1,945,529), and Marilyn Segal ($5,000).

EIN: 51-0203866

CONTRIBUTIONS SUMMARY
Donor(s): The foundation was created by the late Abraham L. Mailman and the Mailman Foundation, Inc.

Typical Recipients: • *Arts & Humanities:* Arts Centers, Libraries, Museums/Galleries, Performing Arts • *Civic & Public Affairs:* Civil Rights, Community Foundations, Hispanic Affairs, Housing, Law & Justice, Professional & Trade Associations, Public Policy, Urban & Community Affairs, Women's Affairs, Zoos/Aquariums • *Education:* Colleges & Universities, Continuing Education, Education Reform, General, Medical Education, Preschool Education, Public Education (Precollege) • *Health:* Cancer, Children's Health/Hospitals, Clinics/Medical Centers, Health Organizations, Mental Health, Prenatal Health Issues, Research/Studies Institutes • *International:* Health Care/Hospitals • *Religion:* Jewish Causes, Social/Policy Issues • *Social Services:* Child Welfare, Community Service Organizations, Crime Prevention, Day Care, Delinquency & Criminal Rehabilitation, Domestic Violence, Family Planning, Family

Services, People with Disabilities, Shelters/Homelessness, United Funds/United Ways, Youth Organizations

Grant Types: matching, project, research, and seed money

Geographic Distribution: national

GIVING OFFICERS

Betty S. Bardige: trust *CURR EMPL* stockholder, dir: Puritan Investment Corp

Jonathan R. Gordon: trust

Jay B. Langner: trust *B* 1930 *ED* Univ PA Wharton Sch 1950; Univ PA BS *CURR EMPL* chmn, pres, ceo, dir: Hudson Gen Corp *CORP AFFIL* pres, dir: Hudson Aviation Svc Del

Patricia S. Leiberman: trust *CURR EMPL* stockholder, dir: Puritan Investment Corp

Luba H. Lynch: exec dir, secy *B* Regensburg Germany 1947 *ED* Royal Conservatory Music Toronto AA 1967; Univ Toronto BA 1968 *NONPR AFFIL* bd mem: Viola W Bernard Fdn, Family Resource Coalition, NY Regional Assn Grantmakers; mem: Am Orthopsychiatric Assn, Natl Assn Ed Young Children

Wendy S. Masi: trust *CURR EMPL* stockholder, dir: Puritan Investment Corp

Marilyn Mailman Segal: chmn, trust *B* Utica NY 1927 *ED* Wellesley Coll BA 1948; McGill Univ BS 1949; Nova Univ PhD 1970 *CORP AFFIL* stockholder, dir: Puritan Investment Corp *NONPR AFFIL* chmn natl visiting comm: Univ Miami Sch Nursing; dean: Nova Univ Family Sch Ctr; mem: Am Psychological Assn, Delta Kappa Gamma, Soc Res Child Devel; trust: Univ Miami

Richard D. Segal: pres, trust *CURR EMPL* stockholder, dir: Puritan Investment Corp

Donna Tookmanian: treas *CURR EMPL* secy, dir: Puritan Investment Corp

APPLICATION INFORMATION
Initial Approach:

All potential applicants are encouraged to write a short letter describing their ideas before writing a full proposal. A budget and a brief description of the project should be included in the initial letter. If the proposed project is of interest to the foundation, the applicant will be invited to send a full proposal.

The full grant application should include the following: a two-page summary of the proposal; information about the applicant organization; a statement of need for the proposed project; a description of the project and the rationale for its approach; a description of the evaluation plan; the qualifications of the organization and staff; a project budget, showing committed and anticipated funds; the organization's current operating budget; a list of board members and/or advisors; letters of support from the board and collaborating organizations; and a copy of the organization's IRS tax-exempt certification.

Proposals are due by October 15 for January review and by March 15 for June review.

The directors of the foundation meet twice a year to set policy and to authorize grants.

Grants of $50,000 or more must be authorized at two consecutive board meetings.

Restrictions on Giving: The foundation does not give grant support for ongoing direct services, general operating expenses, individuals, capital expenditures, or endowment campaigns.

OTHER THINGS TO KNOW
The foundation reports that they also conduct seminars and workshops.

PUBLICATIONS
Annual report including application guidelines

GRANTS ANALYSIS
Total Grants: $899,633

Number of Grants: 93

Highest Grant: $60,000

Average Grant: $9,673

Typical Range: $500 to $10,000

Disclosure Period: 1993

Note: Recent grants are derived from a 1993 Form 990.

RECENT GRANTS

General

60,000	Nova University, Ft. Lauderdale, FL — family center	
50,000	Families and Work Institute, New York, NY — Florida Quality Improvement Study	
50,000	Montefiore Medical Center, Bronx, NY — pediatric facilities	
50,000	South Broward Hospital District, Hollywood, FL — pediatric oncology	
49,792	Save the Children, Child Care Support Center, Altanta, GA — PSP Replication project	

Mailman Foundation

CONTACT
Phyllis Mailman
President
Mailman Fdn.
150 E 58th St.
New York, NY 10155
(212) 421-3131

FINANCIAL SUMMARY
Recent Giving: $825,256 (1992); $566,656 (1991); $500,902 (1990)

Assets: $18,054,157 (1992); $16,291,756 (1991); $4,672,209 (1990)

Gifts Received: $414,738 (1992); $9,141,063 (1991); $410,000 (1990)

Fiscal Note: In 1992, contributions were received from Joseph S. Mailman Trust.

EIN: 13-6161556

CONTRIBUTIONS SUMMARY
Donor(s): the late Joseph L. Mailman and the late Abraham L. Mailman

Typical Recipients: • *Arts & Humanities:* Arts Centers, Arts Funds, Arts Institutes, Dance, Libraries, Museums/Galleries, Opera, Performing Arts, Public Broadcasting, Theater • *Civic & Public Affairs:* Botanical Gardens/Parks, General, Native American Affairs, Philanthropic Organizations, Professional & Trade Associations, Urban & Community Affairs, Zoos/Aquariums • *Education:* Colleges & Universities, Medical Education, Minority Education, Private Education (Precollege), Secondary Education (Private), Student Aid • *Environment:* Wildlife Protection • *Health:* AIDS/HIV, Clinics/Medical Centers, Hospitals, Medical Research, Mental Health, Nursing Services, Research/Studies Institutes • *International:* Foreign Arts Organizations, Health Care/Hospitals, Human Rights, International Environmental Issues, Missionary/Religious Activities • *Religion:* Churches, Jewish Causes, Religious Organizations, Synagogues/Temples • *Social Services:* Child Welfare, Community Service Organizations, Crime Prevention, Emergency Relief, Family Services, Food/Clothing Distribution, People with Disabilities, Shelters/Homelessness, United Funds/United Ways, Youth Organizations

Grant Types: general support

Geographic Distribution: focus on NY

GIVING OFFICERS
Joseph V. Hastings: secy, treas

Joshua L. Mailman: vp, trust

Phyllis Mailman: pres, trust

Joan M. Wolfe: vp, asst secy

Judson Wolfe: vp, trust

APPLICATION INFORMATION
Initial Approach: The foundation reports it only makes contributions to preselected charitable organizations.

Restrictions on Giving: Does not support individuals.

PUBLICATIONS
Annual Report

GRANTS ANALYSIS
Total Grants: $825,256

Number of Grants: 70

Highest Grant: $250,000

Typical Range: $200 to $120,000

Disclosure Period: 1992

Note: Recent grants are derived from a 1992 Form 990.

RECENT GRANTS

General

250,000	McLean Hospital Mailman Research Center	
120,000	United Jewish Appeal Federation, New York, NY	
100,000	Threshold Foundation, San Francisco, CA	
25,000	Business for Social Responsibility, New York, NY	
25,000	Congregation B'nai Jeshurun, Short Hills, NJ	

Mandeville Foundation

CONTACT
Hubert T. Mandeville
President
Mandeville Fdn.
230 Park Ave.
New York, NY 10169
(212) 697-4785

FINANCIAL SUMMARY
Recent Giving: $402,851 (1993); $377,905 (1992); $422,768 (1991)

Assets: $2,590,372 (1993); $2,723,595 (1992); $2,933,657 (1991)

EIN: 06-6043343

CONTRIBUTIONS SUMMARY
Donor(s): Ernest W. Mandeville

Typical Recipients: • *Arts & Humanities:* Arts Associations & Councils, Community Arts, Ethnic & Folk Arts, General, Historic Preservation, History & Archaeology, Libraries, Museums/Galleries, Music, Theater • *Civic & Public Affairs:* General, Public Policy, Safety • *Education:* Colleges & Universities, Education Associations, Faculty Development, Medical Education, Minority Education, Preschool Education, Private Education (Precollege), Student Aid • *Environment:* Air/Water Quality, General, Resource Conservation • *Health:* Cancer, Clinics/Medical Centers, Emergency/Ambulance Services, Heart, Hospitals, Medical Research, Single-Disease Health Associations • *International:* Foreign Educational Institutions, International Organizations, International Relations • *Religion:* Churches • *Social Services:* Animal Protection, Camps, Child Welfare, Community Service Organizations, Recreation & Athletics, Youth Organizations

Grant Types: general support

Geographic Distribution: focus on NY and CT

GIVING OFFICERS
Maurice C. Greenbaum: secy, dir *B* Detroit MI 1918 *ED* Wayne St Univ BA 1938; Univ MI JD 1941; NY Univ LLM 1948 *CURR EMPL* couns: Rosenman & Colin *CORP AFFIL* dir: Entotech, Novo Nordisk Biochem, Novo Nordisk Bioindustrials, Scrambler, Wigwam Productions *NONPR AFFIL* assoc trust: N Shore Univ Hosp; dir: World Rehab Fund *PHIL AFFIL* secy: Rosenstiel Foundation

Meredith H. Hollis: dir

Hubert T. Mandeville: pres, treas, dir

Matthew T. Mandeville: dir

P. Kempton Mandeville: vp, dir

APPLICATION INFORMATION
Initial Approach: The foundation has no formal grant application procedure or application form. There are no deadlines.

GRANTS ANALYSIS
Total Grants: $402,851
Number of Grants: 49

Highest Grant: $138,537
Typical Range: $500 to $15,000
Disclosure Period: 1993
Note: Recent grants are derived from a 1993 Form 990.

RECENT GRANTS
Library
1,000	Pequot Library, Southport, CT

General
138,537	Up with People, Tucson, AZ
59,167	Westover School, Middlebury, CT
49,385	Ridley College
27,589	St. Barnabas College, New York, NY
20,000	Episcopal Academy, Merion, PA

Markle Foundation, John and Mary R.

CONTACT
Tracie Sullivan
Grants Manager
John and Mary R. Markle Foundation
75 Rockefeller Plz., Ste. 1800
New York, NY 10019-6908
(212) 489-6655

FINANCIAL SUMMARY
Recent Giving: $2,939,089 (fiscal 1994); $3,402,532 (fiscal 1993); $5,563,753 (fiscal 1992)

Assets: $107,551,483 (fiscal 1994); $109,076,441 (fiscal 1993); $104,435,226 (fiscal 1992)

Gifts Received: $42,610 (fiscal 1991)

Fiscal Note: In fiscal 1991, the foundation received a gift from a trust fund for the benefit of Emily Markle Bannard, which was established by John Markle.

EIN: 13-1770307

CONTRIBUTIONS SUMMARY
Donor(s): The founder, John Markle (1858-1933), was born in Hazleton, PA, and graduated from Lafayette College in 1880 with a degree in mining engineering. When he returned home after college, John Markle took over his father's mining operations (G. B. Markle and Company) in Hazleton, and implemented technical improvements. His achievements culminated in a $1 million investment in a drainage tunnel that opened up the flooded Jeddo Coal Fields, which Mr. Markle had the foresight to acquire when they were nearly worthless.

In 1902, Mr. Markle moved to New York, where he engaged in a variety of business enterprises that substantially increased his fortune. In later years, he engaged in philanthropic activities. He built a dormitory for the McAuley Water Street Mission, and a hotel for working women in Greenwich Village. Mr. Markle also made a gift of $900,000 to the department of mining engineering at his alma mater, Lafayette College, of which he was also a trustee.

He established the foundation in 1927 with an initial endowment of $3 million, which later increased to approximately $16 million by the terms of his will.

Typical Recipients: • *Arts & Humanities:* Film & Video, Historic Preservation, Libraries, Public Broadcasting • *Civic & Public Affairs:* General, Nonprofit Management, Professional & Trade Associations, Public Policy • *Education:* Colleges & Universities • *International:* International Organizations, International Relations • *Social Services:* Senior Services

Grant Types: project and research

Geographic Distribution: no geographic restrictions; principally gives to national organizations

GIVING OFFICERS
Michael Lewis Ainslie: dir *B* Johnson City TN 1943 *ED* Vanderbilt Univ BA 1965; Harvard Univ MBA 1968 *CURR EMPL* ceo, pres: Sothebys Holdings *NONPR AFFIL* dir: NY Landmarks Conservancy, Young Pres Org; mem adv bd: Friends Vieilles Maisons Francaises, Univ VA; trust: Vanderbilt Univ; vchmn: Graham-Windham *CLUB AFFIL* Bucks, Bucks, Bucks, Meadow, Meadow, Meadow, Metro, Metro, Metropolitan, Queens, Queens, Queens, River, River, River

David Odell Beim: dir *B* Minneapolis MN 1940 *ED* Stanford Univ BA 1963; Oxford Univ BPhil 1965 *CORP AFFIL* chmn, pres, mem exec comm: Wave Hill *NONPR AFFIL* mem: Counc Foreign Rels; prof: Columbia Univ; trust: Outward Bound

Lewis W. Bernard: dir *CURR EMPL* chmn: Classroom Inc *CORP AFFIL* dir: Morgan Stanley Group *NONPR AFFIL* trust: Am Mus Natural History, Central Pk Conservancy, Columbia Univ Teachers Coll, Ed Broadcasting Corp *PHIL AFFIL* don, pres, treas: Mariposa Foundation

Edith C. Bjornson: program off

Karen D. Byers: dir fin oper

Catherine H. Clark: program assoc

Raymond C. Clevenger III: dir *B* Tokeka KS 1937 *ED* Yale Univ BA 1959 *CURR EMPL* ptnr: Wilmer Cutler & Pickering

Ronald Daniel: dir *B* Hartford CT 1930 *ED* Wesleyan Univ BA 1952; Harvard Univ MBA 1954

Stephen W. Fillo: dir *PHIL AFFIL* treas: Stony Brook Foundation

Joel Lawrence Fleishman: dir *B* Fayetteville NC 1934 *ED* Univ NC AB 1955; Univ NC JD 1959; Univ NC MA 1959; Yale Univ LLM 1960 *NONPR AFFIL* chmn: Ctr Documentary Studies; co-dir: Ctr Communs & Journalism; dir: Am Alliance Rights & Responsibilities; mem: Assn Pub Policy Analysis Mgmt, Natl Academy Pub Admin, Order Golden Fleece; sr prof law: Duke Univ; trust: Artscroll Mesorah Fdn, Ruth K Broad Fdn Biomedical Res, Dillard Univ, Jewish Theological Seminary; trust emeritus: Urban Inst *PHIL AFFIL* mem: Kathleen Price and Joseph M. Bryan Family Foundation *CLUB*

AFFIL Century Assn, Metropolitan, Univ, Yale

John Gaines Heimann: dir *B* New York NY 1929 *ED* Syracuse Univ BA 1950 *CURR EMPL* chmn global fin insts group: Merrill Lynch & Co *CORP AFFIL* dir: Merrill Lynch Intl Bank *NONPR AFFIL* chmn: N Am Natl Planning Assn, NY St Superintendents Adv Comm Trans-Natl Banking Insts; dir: Am Ditchley Fdn; dir, treas: Group Thirty; gov: Atlantic Wharton Sch; lecturer: Columbia Univ, Harvard Univ, NY Univ; lecturer, mem adv bd: Yale Univ; mem: British-N Am Comm, Citizens Comm Affordable Housing, Fishman-Davidson Ctr Study Svc Sector, New York City Housing Partnership; special adv gov: Temporary Comm Banking Ins Fin Reform; trust: Fin Accounting Fdn, Hampshire Coll *CLUB AFFIL* F St DC

Gertrude Geraldine Michelson: chmn, dir *B* Jamestown NY 1925 *ED* PA St Univ BA 1945; Columbia Univ LLB 1947 *CORP AFFIL* dir: Chubb Corp, Gen Electric Co, Goodyear Tire & Rubber Co, RH Macy & Co Inc, Quaker Oats Co, Stanley Works; gov: Am Stock Exchange Inc; trust emeritus: Rand Corp *NONPR AFFIL* chmn emeritus bd trust: Columbia Univ; dir: Better Bus Bur Metro NY, Work Am Inst; life trust: Spelman Coll; mem: New York City Partnership, Womens Forum; mem adv counc: Catalyst; mem, exec comm, vchmn: New York City Chamber Commerce; trust: Interracial Counc Bus Opportunity; vchmn: New York City Partnership *CLUB AFFIL* Econ *PHIL AFFIL* chmn: Helena Rubinstein Foundation

Dolores E. Miller: secy

Lloyd N. Morrisett: pres, dir *B* Oklahoma City OK 1929 *ED* Oberlin Coll BA 1951; Yale Univ PhD 1956

Diana T. Murray: dir

Stanley S. Shuman: dir *B* Cambridge MA 1935 *ED* Harvard Univ BA 1956; Harvard Univ JD 1959; Harvard Univ MBA 1961 *CURR EMPL* exec vp, mng dir: Allen & Co *CORP AFFIL* dir: Bayou Steel Corp, Global Asset Mgmt, Hudson Gen Corp, News Am Holdings, News Corp Ltd, Sesac Inc; mem: Fin Control Bd New York City; dir: GHS Inc *NONPR AFFIL* chmn adv bd: Duke Univ Inst Policy Sciences & Pub Aff; hon trust: Dalton Sch; mem: Am Bar Assn; trust: Carnegie Hall, Channel 13 WNET, Natl Pub Radio Fdn, NY Law Sch *CLUB AFFIL* City Athletic, E Hampton Tennis, Harvard Boston, Harvard NY, Quaker Ridge GC

Tracie L. Sullivan: grants mgr

George B. Weiksner: dir *B* Boulder CO 1944 *ED* Princeton Univ BS 1966; Stanford Univ MBA 1970; Stanford Univ JD *CURR EMPL* managing dir: First Boston Corp *NONPR AFFIL* mem: Am Bar Assn, Counc Foreign Rels, NY Bar Assn; trust: Riverdale Country Sch *CLUB AFFIL* Econ

APPLICATION INFORMATION
Initial Approach:

Potential grantees should submit a letter of inquiry.

Letters should describe the project, purpose for which aid is sought, resources needed, personnel involved, and methods to be used.

There are no deadlines for funding requests. The board meets in November, March, and June to make final decisions on grants and to decide on policy.

A professional staff screens and evaluates grant requests for the board. If the request falls within the foundation's specific areas of interest, the foundation will request a proposal, which will provide a complete description of the project and a detailed budget.

Restrictions on Giving: Grants are not made outside the area of mass communications or for endowments, buildings, or individual scholarships. Funds are rarely awarded for production of films, radio, or television programs.

OTHER THINGS TO KNOW

The foundation reports that it also makes program-related investments.

PUBLICATIONS

Annual report, information brochure

GRANTS ANALYSIS

Total Grants: $2,939,089

Number of Grants: 45

Highest Grant: $1,748,775*

Average Grant: $65,313

Typical Range: $10,000 to $75,000 and $125,000 to $225,000

Disclosure Period: fiscal year ending June 30, 1994

Note: The highest grant figure is from 1993. Recent grants are derived from a fiscal 1993 annual report.

RECENT GRANTS

Library

8,000	Foundation Center, New York, NY — for 1992 membership and general support

General

1,748,775	Cable News Network (CNN)
605,000	SeniorNet
164,165	Markle Foundation-Sponsored Project, New York, NY — election project 1992
152,767	Carnegie Mellon University, School of Computer Science, Pittsburgh, PA — to continue research on computer-based models of cognition and interactive media
150,000	University of Pennsylvania, Philadelphia, PA

Marsh & McLennan Companies, Inc.

Revenue: $3.43 billion
Employees: 25,600
Headquarters: New York, NY
SIC Major Group: Insurance Agents, Brokers & Service, Investors Nec, and Management Consulting Services

CONTACT
Gloria Chin
Contributions Administrator
Marsh & McLennan Companies, Inc.
1166 Avenue of the Americas
New York, NY 10036
(212) 345-5645

FINANCIAL SUMMARY
Recent Giving: $4,700,000 (1993 approx.); $4,300,000 (1992 approx.); $4,300,000 (1991 approx.)

Fiscal Note: Company gives directly. Each subsidiary makes contribution decisions independently. Above figures exclude nonmonetary support.

CONTRIBUTIONS SUMMARY
Typical Recipients: • *Arts & Humanities:* Arts Associations & Councils, Arts Centers, Arts Institutes, Dance, Historic Preservation, Libraries, Museums/Galleries, Music, Opera, Performing Arts, Public Broadcasting, Theater • *Civic & Public Affairs:* Business/Free Enterprise, Civil Rights, Economic Development, Economic Policy, Public Policy, Women's Affairs, Zoos/Aquariums • *Education:* Business Education, Elementary Education (Private), Minority Education, Private Education (Precollege) • *Environment:* General • *Social Services:* Child Welfare, Community Service Organizations, Recreation & Athletics, Substance Abuse, United Funds/United Ways

Grant Types: employee matching gifts and general support

Nonmonetary Support Types: donated equipment and in-kind services

Note: Value of nonmonetary support is unknown but includes office furniture and equipment, as well as professional consulting services.

Geographic Distribution: nationally

Operating Locations: NY (New York)

Note: Operates more than 200 offices in 80 countries.

CORP. OFFICERS
Alexander John Court Smith: *B* Glasgow Scotland 1934 *CURR EMPL* chmn: Marsh & McLennan Cos Inc *CORP AFFIL* trust: Putnam Convertible Income Growth Trust, George Putnam Fund Boston, Putnam High Income Govt Trust, Putnam High Yield Trust, Putnam Investors Fund, Putnam Option Income Trust, Putnam Option Income Trust II, Putnam Voyager Fund *NONPR AFFIL* trust: Central Pk Conservancy, Employee Benefit Res Inst *CLUB AFFIL* Apawanis, Caledonian, Racquet & Tennis, Royal Canadian YC

Philip L. Wroughton: *CURR EMPL*
vchmn, dir: Marsh & McLennan Cos Inc

GIVING OFFICERS
Gloria Chin: *CURR EMPL* contributions
admin: Marsh & McLennan Cos Inc

APPLICATION INFORMATION
Initial Approach: *Initial Contact:* formal
proposal *Include Information On:* description of the organization, its history, and its
purpose; proof of tax-exempt status; summary of project or program for which support is requested and amount requested;
copy of most recent annual report and list of
board members *Deadlines:* none

Restrictions on Giving: Does not support
organizations which promote political or religious ideologies, fraternal or professional
organizations, individuals, tax-supported
groups, operating expenses of member agencies of united funds, or organizations that do
not have tax-exempt status.

GRANTS ANALYSIS
Total Grants: $4,700,000*
Disclosure Period: 1993
Note: Total grants figure is approximate.

Marx Foundation, Virginia and Leonard

CONTACT
Virginia Marx
President
Virginia and Leonard Marx Fdn.
18 Heathcote Rd.
Scarsdale, NY 10583
(212) 557-1400

FINANCIAL SUMMARY
Recent Giving: $608,350 (1993); $598,250
(1992); $389,600 (1991)
Assets: $7,656,690 (1993); $6,456,710
(1992); $5,330,195 (1991)
Gifts Received: $1,386,430 (1993);
$1,372,581 (1992); $444,698 (1991)
Fiscal Note: In 1993, major contributions
were received from Leonard and Virginia
Marx ($1,000,000), Dollar Land Syndicate
($207,727), and Guest Realty Co., Inc.
($40,000).
EIN: 13-6162557

CONTRIBUTIONS SUMMARY
Donor(s): Leonard Marx and Virginia Marx
Typical Recipients: • *Arts & Humanities:*
Arts Funds, Historic Preservation, History &
Archaeology, Libraries, Museums/Galleries,
Music, Public Broadcasting, Theater • *Civic
& Public Affairs:* General, Philanthropic Or-
ganizations • *Education:* Colleges & Univer-
sities, Community & Junior Colleges
• *Health:* Mental Health, Research/Studies
Institutes • *Religion:* Jewish Causes, Relig-
ious Organizations, Religious Welfare • *So-
cial Services:* Camps, Child Welfare, Family
Planning, Family Services, United
Funds/United Ways, Youth Organizations

Grant Types: general support
Geographic Distribution: focus on New
York, NY

GIVING OFFICERS
Leonard Marx: vp, trust *B* New York NY
1932 *ED* Yale Univ 1954; Harvard Univ
1956 *CURR EMPL* pres, dir: Merchants Natl
Properties

Virginia Marx: pres, trust

APPLICATION INFORMATION
Initial Approach: Send brief letter of inquiry describing program or project. There
are no deadlines.

GRANTS ANALYSIS
Total Grants: $608,350
Number of Grants: 22
Highest Grant: $250,000
Typical Range: $1,000 to $10,000
Disclosure Period: 1993
Note: Recent grants are derived from a 1993
Form 990.

RECENT GRANTS

Library
26,600	Westchester Library System, Westchester, NY	
5,000	New York Public Library, New York, NY	

General
250,000	Westchester Community College, Westchester, NY	
150,000	Teachers College of Columbia, New York, NY	
100,000	United Jewish Appeal Federation, New York, NY	
10,000	Jewish Board of Family and Children's Services, New York, NY	
10,000	Sarah Lawrence College, Bronxville, NY	

Mather Fund, Richard

CONTACT
Stephen E. Chase
Trustee
Richard Mather Fund
c/o Key Trust Co.
221 S Warren St.
Syracuse, NY 13202
(315) 470-5223

FINANCIAL SUMMARY
Recent Giving: $129,050 (1993); $144,337
(1992); $152,907 (1991)
Assets: $3,069,673 (1993); $2,769,591
(1992); $2,736,142 (1991)
Gifts Received: $14,290 (1993); $15,942
(1992); $19,957 (1991)
Fiscal Note: In 1993, contributions were re-
ceived from Hosmer Trust.
EIN: 15-6018423

CONTRIBUTIONS SUMMARY
Donor(s): the late Flora Mather Hosmer, the
late R. C. Hosmer, Jr., Hosmer Descendants
Trust

Typical Recipients: • *Arts & Humanities:*
Arts Associations & Councils, Community
Arts, General, Libraries, Museums/Galler-
ies, Music, Opera, Public Broadcasting,
Theater • *Civic & Public Affairs:* Community Foundations, Municipalities/Towns,
Public Policy • *Education:* Colleges & Universities, Literacy, Private Education (Precollege) • *International:* International
Organizations • *Religion:* Missionary Activities (Domestic), Religious Welfare • *Science:* Scientific Centers & Institutes • *Social
Services:* Camps, Child Welfare, Community Service Organizations, Family Planning, Family Services, United Funds/United
Ways, Youth Organizations

Grant Types: endowment, general support,
and project

Geographic Distribution: focus on central
NY, with emphasis on Syracuse

GIVING OFFICERS
Stephen E. Chase: trust

S. Sterling McMillan: trust

Gay M. Pomeroy: trust

Elizabeth H. Schaefer: trust

APPLICATION INFORMATION
Initial Approach: The foundation requests
applications be made in writing. Include a
description of organization, amount requested, purpose of funds sought, recently
audited financial statement, and proof of tax-
exempt status. There are no deadlines.

Restrictions on Giving: Limited to central
New York cultural fields.

PUBLICATIONS
Informational Brochure (Application Guidelines)

GRANTS ANALYSIS
Total Grants: $129,050
Highest Grant: $25,000
Typical Range: $1,000 to $7,500
Disclosure Period: 1993
Note: Recent grants are derived from a 1993
Form 990.

RECENT GRANTS

Library
5,000	Cazenovia Public Library

General
25,000	City of New York Community Foundation
6,700	United Way of Central New York, Syracuse, NY
6,500	International Center of Syracuse, Syracuse, NY
5,000	Oakwood Cemeteries of Syracuse, Syracuse, NY

Mathis-Pfohl Foundation

CONTACT
James M. Pfohl
President
Mathis-Pfohl Fdn.
5-46 46th Ave.
Long Island City, NY 11101
(718) 784-4800

FINANCIAL SUMMARY
Recent Giving: $198,525 (fiscal 1993); $184,635 (fiscal 1992); $181,685 (fiscal 1991)

Assets: $4,608,923 (fiscal 1993); $4,303,782 (fiscal 1992); $3,994,214 (fiscal 1991)

Gifts Received: $15,000 (fiscal 1993); $22,543 (fiscal 1992); $5,000 (fiscal 1991)

Fiscal Note: In fiscal 1993, contributions were received from James M. Pfohl ($10,000) and Plastic Center ($5,000).

EIN: 11-6013764

CONTRIBUTIONS SUMMARY
Donor(s): members of the Pfohl family and associated companies

Typical Recipients: • *Arts & Humanities:* Ballet, Community Arts, Historic Preservation, History & Archaeology, Libraries, Museums/Galleries, Music, Opera, Public Broadcasting • *Civic & Public Affairs:* General, Zoos/Aquariums • *Education:* Arts/Humanities Education, Colleges & Universities, Education Funds, Education Reform, Legal Education, Private Education (Precollege), Public Education (Precollege), Secondary Education (Private), Secondary Education (Public) • *Environment:* Air/Water Quality • *Health:* Health Organizations, Hospitals, Mental Health, Single-Disease Health Associations • *International:* International Relations • *Religion:* Churches, Religious Organizations, Religious Welfare • *Science:* Science Museums • *Social Services:* Child Welfare, Community Service Organizations, Homes, Youth Organizations

Grant Types: general support and scholarship

Geographic Distribution: giving in IA, MA, NC, and NY

GIVING OFFICERS
James M. Pfohl: pres

APPLICATION INFORMATION
Initial Approach: Send brief letter of inquiry describing program or project. There are no deadlines.

GRANTS ANALYSIS
Total Grants: $198,525
Number of Grants: 81
Highest Grant: $25,000
Typical Range: $100 to $12,000
Disclosure Period: fiscal year ending November 30, 1993

Note: Recent grants are derived from a fiscal 1993 Form 990.

RECENT GRANTS
General

25,000	Duke University Parents Fund, Durham, NC
12,000	Loras College, Dubuque, IA
10,000	Harvard Law School, Cambridge, MA
10,000	Partnership for Quality Education, New York, NY
5,000	Annual Stewardship Appeal

MBIA Inc.

Revenue: $428.98 million
Employees: 293
Headquarters: Armonk, NY
SIC Major Group: Insurance Carriers Nec

CONTACT
Arlene Altomare
Vice President
MBIA Inc.
113 King St.
Armonk, NY 10504
(914) 273-4545

FINANCIAL SUMMARY
Recent Giving: $540,000 (1995 est.); $500,000 (1994 approx.); $415,000 (1993 approx.)

Fiscal Note: Company gives directly. Above figures exclude nonmonetary support.

CONTRIBUTIONS SUMMARY
Typical Recipients: • *Arts & Humanities:* Arts Associations & Councils, General, Historic Preservation, Libraries, Museums/Galleries, Performing Arts • *Civic & Public Affairs:* Employment/Job Training, General, Housing, Municipalities/Towns, Women's Affairs • *Education:* Business Education, Colleges & Universities, Elementary Education (Private), General, Legal Education • *Health:* General, Geriatric Health, Health Organizations, Medical Research, Single-Disease Health Associations • *Social Services:* Community Centers, Community Service Organizations, Counseling, Day Care, Family Planning, Family Services, Food/Clothing Distribution, General, Homes, People with Disabilities, Recreation & Athletics, Senior Services, Shelters/Homelessness, Substance Abuse, Volunteer Services, Youth Organizations

Grant Types: emergency, employee matching gifts, and general support

Note: Employee matching gift ratio: 2 to 1 for $25 to $1000. Employee matching gift ratio: 1 to 1 for $1001, to a max of $1500. The total amount matched from both employee and spouse may not exceed $1,500 per year.

Nonmonetary Support: $50,000 (1995)

Nonmonetary Support Types: donated equipment and in-kind services

Note: The company also offers the use of its auditorium.

Geographic Distribution: generally in tri-state area, but exceptions do occur

Operating Locations: NY (Armonk)

CORP. OFFICERS
David Holland Elliott: *B* Hartford CT 1941 *ED* Yale Univ BA 1964; Boston Univ LLB 1967 *CURR EMPL* chmn, ceo: MBIA Inc *CORP AFFIL* ceo: Municipal Bond Ins Assn Corp

Arthur M. Warren: *B* Peterborough NH 1935 *ED* Harvard Coll 1956; Harvard Univ Grad Sch Bus Admin 1962 *CURR EMPL* sr vp, cfo: MBIA Inc

GIVING OFFICERS
Arlene S. Altomare: *CURR EMPL* vp: MBIA Inc

APPLICATION INFORMATION
Initial Approach: *Initial Contact:* letter of inquiry *Include Information On:* a description of organization, amount requested, purpose of funds sought, recently audited financial statement, and proof of tax-exempt status *Deadlines:* none *Note:* After initial contact, company will send a formal funding profile application. The funding profile should include a description of the project needing funds; a needs assessment, including community needs and number of people served; importance and timeliness, including total budget and if the project needs continued support; the area served; and list of any MBIA employees involved. Attachments should include annual financial audits and IRS Form 990 from the most recent three years.

Restrictions on Giving: The company does not support individuals, religious organizations for sectarian purposes, or political or lobbying groups.

GRANTS ANALYSIS
Typical Range: $2,500 to $7,500*

Note: Company provided typical grant range figures. report based on: dg

RECENT GRANTS

General
Alzheimer's Disease and Related Disorders Association, White Plains, NY
College Careers, White Plains, NY
Food Patch, White Plains, NY
League of Women Voters, White Plains, NY
Learning Foundation, Westchester, NY

McCann Foundation

CONTACT
John J. Gartland, Jr.
President
McCann Foundation
35 Market St.
Poughkeepsie, NY 12601
(914) 452-3085

FINANCIAL SUMMARY
Recent Giving: $1,400,000 (1995 est.); $1,400,000 (1994 approx.); $1,389,958 (1993)

Assets: $26,000,000 (1995 est.);
$26,000,000 (1994 approx.); $26,000,000
(1993)
EIN: 14-6050628

CONTRIBUTIONS SUMMARY

Donor(s): The McCann Foundation was established in New York in 1969 following the death of James J. McCann , the foundation's benefactor. Mr. McCann, a grain merchant, was a lifetime resident of Poughkeepsie, NY. He owned and operated a feed and grain store; however, he amassed his fortune through shrewd understanding of and success with the stock market. His deep ties with the Catholic Church underlie one of the main focuses of the McCann Foundation.

Typical Recipients: • *Arts & Humanities:* Historic Preservation, History & Archaeology, Libraries, Music, Performing Arts, Public Broadcasting • *Civic & Public Affairs:* Community Foundations, Employment/Job Training, Housing, Law & Justice, Municipalities/Towns, Nonprofit Management, Philanthropic Organizations, Professional & Trade Associations, Safety, Zoos/Aquariums • *Education:* Colleges & Universities, Community & Junior Colleges, Continuing Education, Education Funds, Environmental Education, Legal Education, Private Education (Precollege), Secondary Education (Private), Student Aid • *Environment:* Resource Conservation • *Health:* Children's Health/Hospitals, Hospitals • *International:* Missionary/Religious Activities • *Religion:* Churches, Dioceses, Religious Organizations, Religious Welfare • *Social Services:* Animal Protection, Community Centers, Community Service Organizations, Day Care, Emergency Relief, People with Disabilities, Recreation & Athletics, Senior Services, Shelters/Homelessness, United Funds/United Ways, Volunteer Services, Youth Organizations

Grant Types: capital, fellowship, multi-year/continuing support, project, and scholarship

Geographic Distribution: limited to Poughkeepsie, NY, and Dutchess County, NY

GIVING OFFICERS

Richard V. Corbally: secy, dir

William L. Gardner, Jr.: vp, dir

John J. Gartland, Jr.: pres, dir

Michael G. Gartland: asst secy, dir *CURR EMPL* vchmn, secy: Hastings Health Sys

Dr. Dennis J. Murray: dir *B* Los Angeles CA 1946 *ED* CA St Univ BA 1968; Univ Southern CA MA 1970; Univ Southern CA PhD 1975

APPLICATION INFORMATION

Initial Approach:

The foundation has no formal application guidelines or forms. Letters of inquiry or application should be addressed to the trustees.

Applications should include purpose for grant and amount requested.

There are no fixed deadlines, but applications should be received as far in advance as

possible before trustees' meetings in January and July.

Trustees consider all proposals at board of trustees' meetings.

Restrictions on Giving: The foundation makes no grants to individuals or for operating budgets, emergency funds, endowment funds, deficit financing, matching gifts, or loans.

OTHER THINGS TO KNOW

The McCann Foundation and the James J. McCann Charitable Trust are separate legal entities which act as a single unit. Most of the assets are held in the trust. For convenience, the activities of both organizations are referred to as the McCann Foundation.

GRANTS ANALYSIS

Total Grants: $1,389,958

Number of Grants: 84

Highest Grant: $488,874

Average Grant: $16,547

Typical Range: $500 to $50,000

Disclosure Period: 1993

Note: Recent grants are derived from a 1993 annual report.

RECENT GRANTS

General

488,874	St. Peter's Parish, Hyde Park, NY — for construction and equipment
150,000	Culinary Institute of America, Hyde Park, NY — purchase of property
148,350	Mid-Hudson Civic Center, Poughkeepsie, NY — toward debt obligation
116,336	St. Peter's Parish, Hyde Park, NY — for architectural planning, engineering, land, and environmental surveys
94,559	Mid-Hudson Civic Center, Poughkeepsie, NY — for management, equipment, and capital repairs

McGonagle Foundation, Dextra Baldwin

CONTACT
David O. Spanier
President
Dextra Baldwin McGonagle Fdn.
40 Crossing at Blind Brook
Purchase, NY 10577
(914) 694-3498

FINANCIAL SUMMARY

Recent Giving: $477,975 (1993); $443,900 (1992); $460,075 (1991)

Assets: $8,337,256 (1993); $8,156,426 (1992); $7,988,756 (1991)

EIN: 13-6219236

CONTRIBUTIONS SUMMARY

Donor(s): the late Mrs. Dextra Baldwin McGonagle

Typical Recipients: • *Arts & Humanities:* Art History, Arts Associations & Councils, Community Arts, History & Archaeology, Libraries, Museums/Galleries, Music, Opera, Performing Arts • *Civic & Public Affairs:* Botanical Gardens/Parks, General, Legal Aid, Municipalities/Towns, Philanthropic Organizations, Public Policy, Zoos/Aquariums • *Education:* Colleges & Universities, Legal Education, Medical Education, Preschool Education, Private Education (Precollege), Science/Mathematics Education • *Environment:* General • *Health:* Cancer, Clinics/Medical Centers, Emergency/Ambulance Services, Hospices, Hospitals, Hospitals (University Affiliated), Medical Research, Mental Health, Prenatal Health Issues, Research/Studies Institutes, Single-Disease Health Associations • *International:* Foreign Educational Institutions, International Organizations, Missionary/Religious Activities • *Religion:* Jewish Causes, Religious Organizations, Religious Welfare, Synagogues/Temples • *Science:* Science Museums, Scientific Centers & Institutes • *Social Services:* Child Welfare, Community Service Organizations, Family Services, People with Disabilities, Senior Services, United Funds/United Ways, Youth Organizations

Grant Types: capital, endowment, general support, research, and seed money

Geographic Distribution: focus on NY and CA

GIVING OFFICERS

David B. Spanier: pres, dir

Helen G. Spanier: vp, secy, treas, dir

Maury L. Spanier: chmn, dir *B* New York NY 1916 *ED* City Univ NY 1936 *CURR EMPL* chmn emeritus: Un Aircraft Products *CORP AFFIL* chmn exec comm: Baldwin Investment Co

APPLICATION INFORMATION

Initial Approach: The foundation has no formal grant application procedure or application form. There are no deadlines.

GRANTS ANALYSIS

Total Grants: $477,975

Number of Grants: 80

Highest Grant: $114,500

Typical Range: $100 to $3,000

Disclosure Period: 1993

Note: Recent grants are derived from a 1993 Form 990.

RECENT GRANTS

Library

500	Foundation Library Center, New York, NY

General

114,500	Beth Israel Foundation, New York, NY
75,000	University of North Dakota, Grand Forks, ND
50,200	White Plains Medical Center, White Plains, NY
35,400	Purchase College Foundation, Purchase, NY

20,000   American Committee for
          Weizmann Institute of
          Science, New York, NY

McGraw-Hill, Inc. / McGraw-Hill Foundation

Revenue: $2.76 billion
Employees: 13,393
Headquarters: New York, NY
SIC Major Group: Book Publishing,
  Newspapers, Periodicals, and Miscellaneous
  Publishing

CONTACT
Susan A. Wallman
Vice President
McGraw-Hill Foundation
1221 Avenue of the Americas
New York, NY 10020
(212) 512-6113

FINANCIAL SUMMARY
Recent Giving: $2,200,000 (1994 approx.);
$2,156,012 (1993); $2,193,452 (1992)

Assets: $109,205 (1993); $48,399 (1992);
$24,096 (1991)

Fiscal Note: Company provides cash support primarily through the foundation, but it also provides direct corporate contributions of approximately $300,000 annually (not included in above figures). Above figures exclude nonmonetary support.

EIN: 13-2955464

CONTRIBUTIONS SUMMARY
Typical Recipients: • *Arts & Humanities:* Arts Centers, Libraries, Museums/Galleries, Performing Arts, Public Broadcasting
• *Civic & Public Affairs:* Civil Rights, First Amendment Issues, Law & Justice, Women's Affairs • *Education:* Education Associations, Minority Education, Student Aid
• *Health:* Health Organizations • *Social Services:* Substance Abuse, United Funds/United Ways, Volunteer Services

Grant Types: employee matching gifts and general support

Note: Employee matching gift ratio: 2 to 1.

Nonmonetary Support: $4,362,000 (1993); $6,216,000 (1992); $3,200,000 (1991)

Nonmonetary Support Types: donated products

Geographic Distribution: principally near operating locations, with emphasis on New York City, and on national organizations

Operating Locations: CA (Bakersfield, Berkeley, Los Angeles, Monterey, San Diego, San Francisco), CO (Colorado Springs, Denver, Englewood), DC (Washington), GA (Atlanta), IL (Chicago), IN (Indianapolis), MA (Boston, Lexington), MN (Minneapolis), NH (Peterborough), NJ (Delran, Highstown), NY (Buffalo, New York), OH (Columbus, Westerville), PA (Blue Ridge Summit, Plymouth Meeting), WA (Seattle)

CORP. OFFICERS
Joseph Lewis Dionne: *B* Montgomery AL 1933 *ED* Hofstra Univ BA 1955; Hofstra

Univ MS 1957; Columbia Univ EdD 1965 *CURR EMPL* chmn, ceo: McGraw-Hill Inc *CORP AFFIL* dir: Equitable Life Ins Am, Harris Corp, Sprint Corp, US Telecommuns Ins *NONPR AFFIL* mem: Kappa Delta Pi, Phi Alpha Theta, Phi Delta Kappa; trust: Hofstra Univ *CLUB AFFIL* Blind Brook CC, Woodway CC

Harold Whittlesey "Terry" McGraw III: *B* Summit NJ 1948 *ED* Tufts Univ BA 1972; Univ PA Wharton Sch MBA 1976 *CURR EMPL* pres, coo, dir: McGraw-Hill Inc *CORP AFFIL* chmn: McGraw-Hill Securities Trading Inc, Standard & Poors Compustat Svcs Inc, Tower Group Intl; chmn, dir: Standard & Poors Securities; chmn, pres, ceo: Standard & Poors Corp; pres: McGraw-Hill Fin Svcs Co *NONPR AFFIL* dir: Brunswick Sch, Hartley House

Donald S. Rubin: *B* Chicago IL 1934 *ED* Univ Miami AB 1956; Columbia Univ *CURR EMPL* sr vp investor rels: McGraw-Hill Inc

GIVING OFFICERS
Frank Joseph Kaufman: vp, dir *B* New York NY 1944 *ED* Hamilton Coll BA 1966; Harvard Univ JD 1972 *CURR EMPL* sr vp taxes: McGraw-Hill Inc *NONPR AFFIL* mem: Phi Beta Kappa

Robert Nathan Landes: vp, dir *B* New York NY 1930 *ED* Columbia Univ AB 1952; Columbia Univ LLB 1954 *CURR EMPL* exec vp, secy, gen couns: McGraw-Hill Inc *CORP AFFIL* dir: Standard & Poors Corp *NONPR AFFIL* dir: Greenwich House Inc; mem: Am Bar Assn, Am Soc Corp Secys, Assn Bar City New York, Columbia Coll Alumni Assn, Columbia Univ Law Sch Alumni Assn, Intl Bar Assn, Magazine Publs Assn, NY Bar Assn, NY County Bar Assn, Soc Columbia Grads; mem legal aff comm: Assn Am Publs; trust: Lawyers Comm Civil Rights Under Law *CLUB AFFIL* Pelham CC, Pelican Bay, Vineyards CC

Barbara A. Munder: pres, dir *B* New York NY 1945 *ED* Elmira Coll 1967; NY Univ 1980 *CURR EMPL* sr vp, exec asst to chmn: McGraw-Hill Inc

Frank Dennis Penglase: vp, treas *B* Sherman TX 1940 *ED* Stanford Univ BA 1962; Columbia Univ MBA 1966 *CURR EMPL* sr vp, treas: McGraw-Hill Inc *CORP AFFIL* dir: Westminster Homeowners Inc; mem: NY Treas Group; treas: Standard & Poors Compustat Svcs Inc, Standard & Poors Corp; vp, dir: Tower Group Intl *NONPR AFFIL* alumni bd: Columbia Univ Bus Sch; exec vp, dir: Natl Assn Corp Treas; mem: Fin Execs Inst

Thomas John Sullivan: vp, dir *B* Jersey City NJ 1935 *ED* St Peters Coll BS 1957; Seton Hall Univ JD 1969 *CURR EMPL* exec vp admin: McGraw Hill Inc *NONPR AFFIL* mem: Am Bar Assn, Fin Execs Inst, Inst Mgmt Accts, Natl Assn Accts, NJ Bar Assn

Susan A. Wallman: vp, secy *CURR EMPL* vp: McGraw-Hill Inc

APPLICATION INFORMATION
Initial Approach: *Initial Contact:* brief letter or proposal *Include Information On:* brief background of your organization including its goals and objectives, staff and outside directors; a concise description of the program and objectives for which funds are sought; a copy of most recent audited financial statement and annual report; current year's budget and the sources from which funding is derived; the budget for the program for which you support is sought, and the sum requested; and evidence of your public charity status under the U.S. Internal Revenue Code. *Deadlines:* none; board meets quarterly to make grant decisions

Restrictions on Giving: Foundation does not support political activities or organizations established to influence legislation; individuals; publication of books, magazines, or films; member organizations of United Way funds; sectarian or religious organizations; conferences, trips, or tours; endowment funds; loans; or institutions and agencies clearly outside McGraw-Hill's primary geographic concerns and interests.

Foundation does not subscribe to tables or tickets for charitable events, sponsor courtesy advertisements, or pledge support for walk-a-thons or similar activities.

OTHER THINGS TO KNOW
Foundation sometimes requests meetings with prospective recipients.

Grants are not renewed automatically; new requests must be submitted each year, accompanied by a current, audited financial statement, Form 990, and proof of tax-exempt status.

Foundation does not directly administer programs it supports, but recipients are asked to submit periodic reports on, and evaluation of, progress and an annual financial report.

GRANTS ANALYSIS
Total Grants: $1,167,214*

Number of Grants: 181*

Highest Grant: $99,702

Average Grant: $6,449*

Typical Range: $5,000 to $10,000

Disclosure Period: 1993

Note: Total grants, number of grants, and average grant figures do not include the employee matching gifts totaling $988,798. Recent grants are derived from a 1993 Form 990.

RECENT GRANTS
Library
25,000   New York Public Library, New
          York, NY

General
99,702   National Merit Scholarship
          Corporation, Evanston, IL
85,000   United Way of Tri-State, New
          York, NY
85,000   United Way of Tri-State, New
          York, NY
50,000   Salvation Army of Greater
          New York, New York, NY
30,000   Columbia University
          Knight-Baghot Fellowship,
          New York, NY

Mellon Foundation, Andrew W.

CONTACT
Richard Ekman
Secretary
Andrew W. Mellon Foundation
140 E 62nd St.
New York, NY 10021
(212) 838-8400

FINANCIAL SUMMARY
Recent Giving: $118,200,000 (1994);
$93,989,549 (1993); $95,865,156 (1992)

Assets: $2,200,000,000 (1994 est.);
$2,330,432,410 (1993); $2,184,968,873
(1992)

Gifts Received: $49,212 (1989)

Fiscal Note: The 1989 contribution is from
the estate of Margaret Meehan.

EIN: 13-1879954

CONTRIBUTIONS SUMMARY
Donor(s): The Andrew W. Mellon Foundation is the product of the 1969 consolidation
of two previously independent foundations:
the Avalon Foundation, established by Ailsa
Mellon Bruce , and the Old Dominion Foundation, established by her brother, Paul Mellon. As the children of Pittsburgh financier
Andrew W. Mellon, Paul and Ailsa inherited
one of the nation's largest fortunes, including substantial holdings in the Mellon National Bank and Trust Co., Gulf Oil Corp.,
Aluminum Co. of America, Koppers Co.,
and Carborundum Co. The foundation received additional funds from the estate of
Mrs. Ailsa Mellon Bruce upon her death in
1969.

Typical Recipients: • *Arts & Humanities:*
Arts Associations & Councils, Dance, His-
toric Preservation, Libraries, Literary Arts,
Museums/Galleries, Music, Opera, Perform-
ing Arts, Theater • *Civic & Public Affairs:*
Botanical Gardens/Parks, Economic Policy,
Hispanic Affairs, Nonprofit Management,
Public Policy, Zoos/Aquariums • *Education:*
Arts/Humanities Education, Colleges & Uni-
versities, Continuing Education, Economic
Education, Education Associations, Educa-
tion Reform, Engineering/Technological
Education, Environmental Education, Fac-
ulty Development, General, International
Studies, Legal Education, Literacy, Medical
Education, Minority Education, Sci-
ence/Mathematics Education, Social Sci-
ences Education • *Environment:* General,
Research, Resource Conservation • *International:* Foreign Arts Organizations, Foreign
Educational Institutions, Health Care/Hospi-
tals, International Affairs, International Development, International Environmental
Issues, International Peace & Security Issues, International Relations, Trade • *Science:* Scientific Centers & Institutes,
Scientific Organizations, Scientific Research • *Social Services:* Family Planning

Grant Types: challenge, endowment, fellowship, general support, multiyear/continu-
ing support, project, and research

Geographic Distribution: national

GIVING OFFICERS
William Gordon Bowen, PhD: pres, trust *B*
Cincinnati OH 1933 *ED* Denison Univ BA
1955; Princeton Univ PhD 1958 *CORP AF-
FIL* dir: Am Express Co, Merck & Co Inc,
Readers Digest Assn Inc, Rockefeller Group
Inc *NONPR AFFIL* mem: Am Econ Assn,
Counc Foreign Rels, Indus Rels Res Assn,
Phi Beta Kappa; mem bd regents: Smith-
sonian Inst; trust: Denison Univ *CLUB AF-
FIL* Univ *PHIL AFFIL* trust: Merck Co.
Foundation; dir: Lila Wallace-Reader's Di-
gest Fund, DeWitt Wallace-Reader's Digest
Fund

Richard Ekman: secy *B* New York NY
1945 *ED* Harvard Univ AB 1966; Harvard
Univ AM 1967; Harvard Univ PhD 1972
NONPR AFFIL mem editorial bd: Liberal
Ed; mem natl adv comm: Rackham Advance-
ment Counc Univ MI, Yale New Haven
Teachers Inst; trust: Collegiate Sch *CLUB
AFFIL* Harvard

Charles Errol Exley, Jr.: trust *B* Detroit
MI 1929 *ED* Wesleyan Univ BA 1952; Co-
lumbia Univ MBA 1954 *CORP AFFIL* dir:
Banc One Corp, Merck & Co Inc, Owens-
Corning Fiberglas Corp *CLUB AFFIL*
Brook, Dayton Racquet, Grosse Pointe, Mi-
ami Valley Hunt & Polo, Moraine CC,
Ocean Reef, Question

Hanna Holborn Gray, PhD: trust *B* Heidelberg Germany 1930 *ED* Bryn Mawr Coll AB
1950; Harvard Univ PhD 1957; Yale Univ
MA 1971 *CORP AFFIL* dir: Ameritech
Corp, Atlantic Richfield Co, Cummins Engine Co Inc, JP Morgan & Co, Morgan Guaranty Trust Co *NONPR AFFIL* bd overseers:
Marlboro Sch Music; bd regents: Smithsonian Inst; dir: Chicago Counc Foreign
Rels; fellow: Am Acad Arts & Sci; hon fellow: Oxford Univ, St Anns Coll; mem: Am
Philosophical Soc, Natl Acad Ed, Phi Beta
Kappa, Renaissance Soc Am; mem bd overseers: Harvard Univ; prof: Univ Chicago;
trust: Bryn Mawr Coll *PHIL AFFIL* trust:
Howard Hughes Medical Institute

Timothy Mellon: trust *B* Pittsburgh PA
1942 *ED* Yale Univ BA 1964; Yale Univ
Sch Art & Architecture MCP 1966 *CURR
EMPL* chmn, ceo, dir: Guilford Transporta-
tion Indus *CORP AFFIL* dir: Boston & ME
Corp, Geostar Corp; treas, dir: Perma Treat
Corp *PHIL AFFIL* pres, trust: Sachem Fund

W. Taylor Reveley III: trust *B* Churchville
VA 1943 *ED* Princeton Univ AB 1965; Univ
VA JD 1968 *CURR EMPL* pntr: Hunton &
Williams *NONPR AFFIL* bd dirs: Pres-
bytarian Church Fdn, Richmond Symphony,
VA Historical Soc, VA Mus Fdn; bd dirs,
mem: Princeton Assn VA; mem: Am Bar
Assn, Am Judicature Soc, Am Soc Intl Law,
DC Bar Assn, Order Coif, Raven Soc, Rich-
mond Bar Assn, VA Bar Assn; pres, dir:
Presbytarian Outlook Fdn Book Svc; trust:
Princeton Univ, Union Theological Semi-
nary *CLUB AFFIL* CC Virginia, Downtown,
Knickerbocker

Frank Harold Trevor Rhodes: trust *B* War-
wickshire England 1926 *ED* Univ Birmingham BS 1948; Univ Birmingham PhD 1950

Charles Andrew Ryskamp: trust *B* East
Grand Rapids MI 1928 *ED* Calvin Coll AB
1950; Yale Univ MA 1951; Yale Univ PhD
1956 *NONPR AFFIL* assoc trust: William
Blake Trust; comm honor, mem: Assn Inter-
nationali de Bibliophilie; dir: Giannalisa Fel-
trinelli Fdn; mem: Academy Am Poets, Am
Antiquarian Soc, Assn Art Mus Dirs, Bibli-
ographical Soc Am, Cowper Soc, Keats-
Shelley Assn Am, Museums Counc New
York City; mem adv bd: Skowhegan Sch
Painting & Sculpture; mem adv counc:
Princeton Univ Art Mus; mem bd mgrs:
Yale Univ Lewis Walpole Library; mem
counc: Columbia Univ Dept Art Archaeol-
ogy; mem natl comm: Drawing Soc; pres:
Master Drawings Assn; prof: Princeton
Univ; trust: Amon Carter Mus Western Art,
Corning Mus Glass; visiting comm: Metro
Mus Art *PHIL AFFIL* trust: John Simon
Guggenheim Memorial Foundation; vp, dir:
Gerard B. Lambert Memorial Foundation;
dir: Frederick R. Koch Foundation *CLUB
AFFIL* Century Assn, Elizabethan, Grolier,
Lotos, Pilgrims, Roxburghe

Eileen Scott: treas, asst secy

T. Dennis Sullivan: vp fin

John Cunningham Whitehead: chmn, trust
B Evanston IL 1922 *ED* Haverford Coll BA
1943; Harvard Univ MBA 1947 *CURR
EMPL* chmn: AEA Investors *NONPR AFFIL*
chmn: Asia Soc, Intl House, Intl Rescue
Comm, UN Nations Assn US Am, Youth Un-
derstanding; chmn emeritus: Brookings Inst;
mem: Counc Foreign Rels; pres: Boy Scouts
America NY Counc; trust: Haverford Coll,
Lincoln Ctr Theater, Outward Bound, Rocke-
feller Univ; trust counc: Natl Gallery Art
CLUB AFFIL F St DC, Links, Met, Univ

Harriet Zuckerman: vp *B* New York NY
1937 *ED* Vassar Coll AB 1958; Columbia
Univ PhD 1965 *CORP AFFIL* dir: Annual
Reviews; mem editorial bd: Scientometrics
NONPR AFFIL mem: Am Academy Arts &
Sciences, Counc Foreign Rels, Soc Social
Studies Science; mem adv bd: Inst Scientific
Information, Social Science Citation Index;
prof: Columbia Univ; trust: Ctr Advanced
Study Behavioral Sciences *CLUB AFFIL*
Cosmopolitan

APPLICATION INFORMATION
Initial Approach:

The foundation does not have application
forms. A letter of request is sufficient.

The letter should state the need, the nature,
and the amount of the request and the justification for it. Evidence of classification by
the IRS should be included. Supplementary
exhibits may be submitted.

The foundation accepts requests throughout
the year.

Restrictions on Giving: The foundation
does not award fellowships or give grants to
individuals. It does not make grants to primarily local organizations.

PUBLICATIONS
Annual report

GRANTS ANALYSIS
Total Grants: $118,200,000

Number of Grants: 361

Highest Grant: $15,000,000

Average Grant: $327,400*

Typical Range: $50,000 to $750,000

Disclosure Period: 1994

Note: The average grant was provided by the foundation. Recent grants are derived from a 1993 Form 990.

RECENT GRANTS

Library

1,450,000	Frick Collection, New York, NY — matching endowment for use by the Frick Art Reference Library in support of its cataloging activities
1,200,000	Southern Education Foundation, Atlanta, GA — for use over four years in support of a program to strengthen the libraries of leading private Black colleges
1,188,000	Mt. Holyoke College, South Hadley, MA — for use over three years toward development of the Czech and Slovak Library Information Network
1,150,000	Southern Education Foundation, Atlanta, GA — to strengthen libraries of leading private black colleges
951,000	Marie Curie Sklodowska University, Lublin, Poland — for use over three years toward costs of automating the libraries of the Lublin Consortium

General

6,280,000	Woodrow Wilson National Fellowship, Princeton, NJ — in support of the programs of Mellon fellowships
2,010,000	United Negro College Fund, New York, NY — for an undergraduate fellowship program to increase the number of minority students who enroll in Ph.D. programs in the arts and sciences
1,300,000	Social Science Research Council, New York, NY — for use over three years in support of a program of research and training on international migration and its impact on American society
1,200,000	Population Council, New York, NY — for use over two years by its Center for Biomedical Research in support of contraceptive development
1,200,000	United Negro College Fund, New York, NY — for a program to increase the number of minority scholars holding doctorates in the arts and sciences

---

Memton Fund

CONTACT
Daphne W. White
President
Memton Fund
527 Madison Ave., 15th Flr.
New York, NY 10022
(212) 682-2783

FINANCIAL SUMMARY
Recent Giving: $238,900 (1993); $212,600 (1992); $297,250 (1991)

Assets: $7,893,952 (1993); $7,012,423 (1992); $6,796,163 (1991)

EIN: 13-6096608

CONTRIBUTIONS SUMMARY
Donor(s): the late Albert G. Milbank, the late Charles M. Cauldwell

Typical Recipients: • *Arts & Humanities:* Ballet, Community Arts, Dance, Libraries, Museums/Galleries, Music, Performing Arts, Public Broadcasting, Theater • *Civic & Public Affairs:* Botanical Gardens/Parks, Business/Free Enterprise, Philanthropic Organizations, Professional & Trade Associations, Public Policy, Women's Affairs, Zoos/Aquariums • *Education:* Colleges & Universities, Legal Education, Literacy, Private Education (Precollege), Secondary Education (Private), Student Aid • *Environment:* General, Resource Conservation • *Health:* AIDS/HIV, Children's Health/Hospitals, Clinics/Medical Centers, Hospices, Hospitals, Long-Term Care, Medical Rehabilitation, Nursing Services • *International:* Foreign Arts Organizations, Health Care/Hospitals • *Religion:* Churches • *Science:* Scientific Centers & Institutes • *Social Services:* Animal Protection, Community Service Organizations, Crime Prevention, Family Services, People with Disabilities, Recreation & Athletics, Scouts, United Funds/United Ways, Youth Organizations

Grant Types: capital, endowment, general support, and scholarship

Geographic Distribution: primarily in the Northeast

GIVING OFFICERS
Lillian I. Daniels: secy

Elenita M. Drumwright: dir

Robert V. Edgar: dir

Marjorie M. Farrar: dir

Olivia Farrar-Wellman: dir

Ellen White Levy: dir

David M. Milbank: dir

Michelle R. Milbank: dir

Samuel L. Milbank: dir

Daphne M. White: pres, dir

APPLICATION INFORMATION
Initial Approach: Send a brief letter of inquiry. Include a description of organization, amount requested, purpose of funds sought, recently audited financial statement, and proof of tax-exempt status. There are no deadlines.

Restrictions on Giving: Does not support individuals.

GRANTS ANALYSIS
Total Grants: $238,900

Number of Grants: 110

Highest Grant: $12,000

Typical Range: $500 to $10,000

Disclosure Period: 1993

Note: Recent grants are derived from a 1993 Form 990.

RECENT GRANTS

Library

5,000	New York Public Library, New York, NY

General

12,000	Boy Scouts of America National Area Council, Washington, DC
10,000	Princeton University, Princeton, NJ
7,500	Bryn Mawr College campaign for Bryn Mawr, Bryn Mawr, PA
5,000	Alumnae Fund of Smith College, Northampton, MA
5,000	Center for National Independence in Politics, Coravllis, OR

Mercury Aircraft / Mercury Aircraft Foundation

Sales: $65.0 million
Employees: 700
Headquarters: Hammondsport, NY

CONTACT
Gregory Hintz
Treasurer
Mercury Aircraft
17 Wheeler Ave.
Hammondsport, NY 14840
(607) 569-4200

FINANCIAL SUMMARY
Recent Giving: $145,575 (1992); $50,904 (1991); $47,164 (1989)

Assets: $1,232,878 (1992); $1,252,342 (1991); $982,561 (1989)

Gifts Received: $55,000 (1992); $33,000 (1991); $33,000 (1989)

EIN: 16-6028162

CONTRIBUTIONS SUMMARY
Typical Recipients: • *Arts & Humanities:* Arts Associations & Councils, Libraries, Museums/Galleries • *Civic & Public Affairs:* Clubs, Economic Development, Safety, Urban & Community Affairs • *Education:* Colleges & Universities • *Health:* Cancer,

Emergency/Ambulance Services, Health Organizations, Hospitals, Respiratory • *Religion:* Churches, Religious Welfare • *Science:* Scientific Centers & Institutes, Scientific Organizations • *Social Services:* Animal Protection, Family Planning, Homes, People with Disabilities, United Funds/United Ways, Youth Organizations

Grant Types: capital and general support

Geographic Distribution: giving primarily in western NY

Operating Locations: NY (Hammondsport)

CORP. OFFICERS
Joseph F. Meade III: *CURR EMPL* pres, dir: Mercury Aircraft

GIVING OFFICERS
Joseph F. Meade, Jr.: trust

Lawrence D. Murray, Jr.: trust

Donald R. Searle: trust

APPLICATION INFORMATION
Initial Approach: The foundation has no formal grant application procedure or application form. There are no deadlines.

GRANTS ANALYSIS
Total Grants: $145,575

Number of Grants: 44

Highest Grant: $100,000

Typical Range: $100 to $6,000

Disclosure Period: 1992

Note: Recent grants are derived from a 1992 Form 990.

RECENT GRANTS
Library

200	Pulteney Free Library

General

6,000	Alfred University, Alfred, NY
6,000	Keuka College, Keuka Park, NY — community associates campaign
5,000	J. F. Meade Memorial Science Fund
5,000	Keuka College, Keuka Park, NY — centennial campaign
3,500	United Way of Central Steuben County, Bath, NY

Merrill Lynch & Co., Inc. / Merrill Lynch & Co. Foundation Inc.

Revenue: $18.23 billion
Employees: 40,100
Headquarters: New York, NY
SIC Major Group: Holding Companies Nec and Security Brokers & Dealers

CONTACT
Westina L. Matthews
Vice President, Philanthropic Programs
Merrill Lynch & Co.
World Headquarters, South Tower
World Financial Ctr.
225 Liberty St., 6th floor
New York, NY 10080-6106
(212) 236-4319

Note: The contact for special events is Linda Federici, vice president, special events. Organizations outside of the greater New York area should contact local Merrill Lynch offices for information.

FINANCIAL SUMMARY
Recent Giving: $16,500,000 (1995 est.); $16,972,779 (1993); $12,267,974 (1992)

Assets: $33,478,762 (1993); $25,751,381 (1992); $21,245,629 (1990)

Gifts Received: $7,206,475 (1993); $6,603,422 (1992)

Fiscal Note: Above figures include direct giving, foundation giving, and matching gifts. In 1993, company and its subsidiaries contributed $9,639,064; the foundation contributed $7,333,715; and the foundation matched $5,160,750 in employee gifts. Above figures exclude nonmonetary support.

EIN: 13-6139556

CONTRIBUTIONS SUMMARY
Typical Recipients: • *Arts & Humanities:* Arts Centers, History & Archaeology, Libraries, Museums/Galleries, Music, Performing Arts, Public Broadcasting, Theater • *Civic & Public Affairs:* African American Affairs, Botanical Gardens/Parks, Business/Free Enterprise, Civil Rights, Community Foundations, Economic Development, Employment/Job Training, General, Housing, Public Policy, Women's Affairs, Zoos/Aquariums • *Education:* Business Education, Colleges & Universities, Economic Education, Education Reform, Literacy, Minority Education, Student Aid • *Health:* AIDS/HIV, Cancer, Clinics/Medical Centers, Emergency/Ambulance Services, Geriatric Health, Health Organizations, Hospitals, Medical Research, Single-Disease Health Associations, Transplant Networks/Donor Banks • *International:* Foreign Educational Institutions, International Peace & Security Issues, International Relations, International Relief Efforts • *Religion:* Religious Welfare • *Science:* Scientific Centers & Institutes, Scientific Labs • *Social Services:* At-Risk Youth, Child Welfare, Community Centers, Emergency Relief, Food/Clothing Distribution, People with Disabilities, Recreation & Athletics, Senior Services, Shelters/Homelessness, Substance Abuse, Youth Organizations

Grant Types: capital, conference/seminar, employee matching gifts, general support, and scholarship

Note: Corporation also underwrites special events.

Nonmonetary Support Types: donated equipment

Note: Company donates equipment when available. Value of nonmonetary support is unavailable.

Geographic Distribution: primarily in areas where Merrill Lynch & Co. maintains offices with priority given to organizations in greater New York metropolitan area; also to national organizations

Operating Locations: NY (New York)

CORP. OFFICERS
Stephen Lawrence Hammerman: *B* New York NY 1938 *ED* Univ PA BS 1959; NY Univ LLB 1962 *CURR EMPL* vchmn: Merrill Lynch & Co Inc *CORP AFFIL* gen counsel: Merrill Lynch Pierce Fenner & Smith; mem: NY Stock Exchange *NONPR AFFIL* mem: Securities Indus Assn; mem, investment comm chmn: Assn Bar City New York

Daniel P. Tully: *B* 1932 *ED* St Johns Univ BBA 1953 *CURR EMPL* chmn, pres, ceo, coo: Merrill Lynch & Co Inc *CORP AFFIL* chmn, pres, dir: Merrill Lynch Pierce Fenner & Smith; dir: NY Stock Exchange *NONPR AFFIL* dir: Fairfield Univ, NY Racing Assn *PHIL AFFIL* trust: Daniel P. and Grace I. Tully Charitable Trust

Roger M. Vasey: *B* 1935 *ED* Univ MO BS 1958; Univ Chicago MBA 1970 *CURR EMPL* exec vp, sr adv: Merrill Lynch & Co Inc *CORP AFFIL* exec vp, dir: Merrill Lynch Pierce Fenner & Smith

GIVING OFFICERS
Paul W. Critchlow: vp, trust *CURR EMPL* sr vp commun: Merrill Lynch & Co Inc

John A. Fitzgerald: vp, trust

Stephen Lawrence Hammerman: trust *CURR EMPL* vchmn: Merrill Lynch & Co Inc (see above)

Thomas J. Lombardi: treas, trust *PHIL AFFIL* treas: Magowan Family Foundation

Westina L. Matthews: secy, trust *B* Chillicothe OH 1948 *ED* Univ Dayton BS 1970; Univ Dayton MS 1974; Univ Chicago PhD 1980 *CURR EMPL* vp phil programs: Merrill Lynch & Co Inc *NONPR AFFIL* dir: Coalition 100 Black Women; mem: Assn Black Fdns, Middle St Assn, NY Regional Assn Grantmakers

Matthew Morgan McKenna: vp, trust *B* 1950 *ED* Hamilton Coll BA 1972; Georgetown Univ JD 1975; Georgetown Univ LLM 1978 *CURR EMPL* vp taxes: PepsiCo *NONPR AFFIL* mem: Am Bar Assn, Assn Bar City New York, NY Bar Assn; trust: Mt St Marys Coll

Daniel P. Tully: vp *CURR EMPL* chmn, pres, ceo, coo: Merrill Lynch & Co Inc *PHIL AFFIL* trust: Daniel P. and Grace I. Tully Charitable Trust (see above)

Roger M. Vasey: pres *CURR EMPL* exec vp, sr adv: Merrill Lynch & Co Inc (see above)

Patrick Walsh: trust

APPLICATION INFORMATION
Initial Approach: *Initial Contact:* brief letter; if outside greater New York area, apply directly to local branch office *Include Information On:* description and background of organization, amount requested, purpose for which funds are sought, duration of project, plan to evaluate the use of the funds, copy of 501(c)(3) tax exemption letter, list of governing board members, most recent annual audited financial statement, current financial statement, and current operating budget *Deadlines:* none

Restrictions on Giving: The company will not make grants to the following: individuals; fraternal, social or athletic organizations; religious organizations or government agencies (for operating support); political parties, groups, or candidates; local affiliates of national organizations; or organizations that serve a very limited geographic area.

The company will not make grants for the reduction of an operating deficit or to liquidate a debt.

OTHER THINGS TO KNOW
Merrill Lynch & Co. underwrites cultural events, in addition to cash grants, especially in geographic areas where the company has a major presence.

The company sponsors an Employee Community Involvement Program, giving grants of $100 to $500 to community organizations for specific projects assisted by employees of the company.

The company will consider support of capital needs when the specific project submitted has distinctive importance or the promise of a unique contribution to the field.

Since the company has a predetermined limit on multiyear commitments, grants usually are of a one-year duration. Requests for continuing support are considered using the company's priorities for the proposed grant year.

PUBLICATIONS
Merrill Lynch 1993 Philanthropic Programs

GRANTS ANALYSIS
Total Grants: $16,972,779
Number of Grants: 10,875
Highest Grant: $250,000
Average Grant: $1,561
Typical Range: $5,000 to $10,000
Disclosure Period: 1993
Note: Recent grants are derived from a 1993 Form 990.

RECENT GRANTS
Library
25,000	Fairfield University, Fairfield, CT — Nylesius Library automation, second payment of a $100,000 pledge
25,000	New York Public Library, New York, NY — research libraries

General
250,000	Massachusetts General Hospital, Boston, MA — Merrill Lynch Cardiology Research Award, first payment of a $1 million pledge
200,000	Central Park Conservancy, New York, NY — capital campaign, final payment of a $500,000 pledge
150,000	Boy Scouts of America Greater New York Councils, New York, NY — Cub World/Camp Alpine, second of three payments of a $500,000 pledge
150,000	Partnership for a Quality Education, New York, NY —

	final payment of a $500,000 pledge
125,000	Daytop Village Foundation, New York, NY — final payment of a $500,000 pledge

---

Metropolitan Life Insurance Co. / Metropolitan Life Foundation

Revenue: $22.25 billion
Employees: 44,000
Headquarters: New York, NY
SIC Major Group: Life Insurance and Pension, Health & Welfare Funds

---

CONTACT
Sibyl C. Jacobson
President
Metropolitan Life Foundation
One Madison Ave.
New York, NY 10010
(212) 578-6272

FINANCIAL SUMMARY
Recent Giving: $13,310,049 (1994); $9,989,132 (1993); $10,088,722 (1992)

Assets: $99,516,568 (1993); $100,103,026 (1992); $103,479,914 (1991)

Fiscal Note: Above figures include direct and foundation giving. Foundation giving in 1994 totaled $10,585,208 and in 1993 totaled $7,906,429. Above figures exclude nonmonetary support.

EIN: 13-2878224

CONTRIBUTIONS SUMMARY
Typical Recipients: • *Arts & Humanities:* Arts Associations & Councils, Arts Centers, Arts Institutes, Ballet, Dance, Ethnic & Folk Arts, Historic Preservation, Libraries, Museums/Galleries, Music, Opera, Performing Arts, Public Broadcasting, Theater • *Civic & Public Affairs:* African American Affairs, Business/Free Enterprise, Civil Rights, Economic Development, Economic Policy, Employment/Job Training, Housing, Professional & Trade Associations, Public Policy, Safety, Urban & Community Affairs, Women's Affairs, Zoos/Aquariums • *Education:* Arts/Humanities Education, Business Education, Colleges & Universities, Community & Junior Colleges, Economic Education, Education Reform, Health & Physical Education, Literacy, Medical Education, Minority Education, Science/Mathematics Education, Student Aid • *Health:* AIDS/HIV, Children's Health/Hospitals, Health Policy/Cost Containment, Health Funds, Health Organizations, Hospitals, Medical Research, Medical Training, Nursing Services, Nutrition, Transplant Networks/Donor Banks • *International:* Foreign Arts Organizations, Foreign Educational Institutions, International Organizations • *Social Services:* Child Welfare, Counseling, Delinquency & Criminal Rehabilitation, Family Services, Food/Clothing Distribution, Homes, Shelters/Homelessness, Sub-

stance Abuse, United Funds/United Ways, Volunteer Services, Youth Organizations

Grant Types: employee matching gifts, general support, project, research, scholarship, and seed money

Note: Employee matching gift ratio: 1 to 1. Also sponsors scholarships for employee children.

Nonmonetary Support: $128,694 (1987)

Nonmonetary Support Types: donated equipment, in-kind services, loaned employees, and loaned executives

Note: The value of nonmonetary support is unavailable. The company also offers select use of facilities by nonprofits.

Geographic Distribution: special consideration to communities in which Metropolitan has a major presence, and to programs that are national in scope

Operating Locations: NY (New York)

Note: Company is licensed to operate in all 50 states, the District of Columbia, Puerto Rico, and Canada.

CORP. OFFICERS
Ted Athanassiades: *B* 1939 *ED* Princeton Univ 1961; Brooklyn Polytech Inst BS 1963 *CURR EMPL* pres, coo: Metro Life Ins Co *CORP AFFIL* chmn: Metro Property & Casulty Ins

Harry Paul Kamen: *B* Montreal Canada 1933 *ED* Univ PA AB 1954; Harvard Univ LLB 1957 *CURR EMPL* chmn, ceo: Metro Life Ins Co *CORP AFFIL* chmn, pres: Metro Tower Corp; dir: Banco Santander, Bethlehem Steel Corp *NONPR AFFIL* bd overseers: Univ PA Sch Arts & Sci; chancellors, adv counc: SUNY; chmn: Am Law Inst, Assn Bar City New York, Counc Bus Law Secys; dir: New York City Partnership Bus Counc; mem: Am Arbitration Assn, Am Bar Assn, Am Counc Life Ins, Assn Life Ins Counc, New York County Lawyers Assn, NY Chamber Commerce, Phi Beta Kappa; mem adv bd: Univ PA Inst Law & Econs; mem pres counc: NY Acad Sci; trust: Comm Econ Devel, Smith Coll; vchmn: John F Kennedy Ctr Corp Fund *CLUB AFFIL* Hampton Tennis, Harvard

Catherine Amelia Rein: *B* Lebanon PA 1943 *ED* PA St Univ BA 1965; NY Univ JD 1968 *CURR EMPL* exec vp admin svcs: Metro Life Ins Co *CORP AFFIL* dir: Broadmoor Housing Inc, Corning Inc, Gen Pub Utilities Corp, Inroads NY City Inc *NONPR AFFIL* mem: Am Bar Assn, Assn Bar City New York; trust, dir: Natl Urban League

Arthur G. Typermass: *B* New York NY 1937 *ED* Wesleyan Univ AB 1957; Columbia Univ MBA 1959 *CURR EMPL* sr vp, treas: Metro Life Ins Co *CORP AFFIL* chmn, ceo: Metlife Holdings Inc; treas, dir: Corp Health Strategies Inc *NONPR AFFIL* dir: Pueblo Intl; mem: Inst Chartered Fin Analysts, NY Soc Security Analysts; trust: YMCA Retirement Plan

GIVING OFFICERS
John J. Creedon: dir *B* New York NY 1924 *ED* NY Univ BS 1952; NY Univ LLB 1955 *CORP AFFIL* dir: Albany Life Assurance Co Ltd, Banco Santander, Melville Corp,

NYNEX Corp, Rockwell Intl Corp, Sonat Inc, Union Carbide Corp *NONPR AFFIL* dir: NY Univ Law Ctr Fdn; mem: Am Law Inst, Assn Bar City New York, Assn Life Ins Counc, Bus Counc NY, NY Bar Assn, NY Chamber Commerce *PHIL AFFIL* pres, treas, dir: John J. Creedon Foundation

Robert J. Crimmins: chmn, dir *B* 1938 *CURR EMPL* exec vp engg: Metro Life Ins Co

William Thomas Friedewald, MD: dir *B* New York NY 1939 *ED* Univ Notre Dame BS 1960; Yale Univ MD 1963 *CURR EMPL* chief med dir: Metro Life Ins Co

Sibyl C. Jacobson: pres, ceo, dir *CURR EMPL* vp: Metro Life Ins Co

John Daniel Moynahan, Jr.: dir *B* Chicago IL 1935 *ED* Univ Notre Dame BA 1957 *CURR EMPL* exec vp: Metro Life Ins Co

Catherine Amelia Rein: dir *CURR EMPL* exec vp admin svcs: Metro Life Ins Co (see above)

Vincent P. Reusing: dir

Arthur G. Typermass: treas, dir *CURR EMPL* sr vp, treas: Metro Life Ins Co (see above)

APPLICATION INFORMATION
Initial Approach: *Initial Contact:* brief letter *Include Information On:* description of the organization (legal name, history, activities, purpose, and governing board), purpose for which grant is requested, amount requested and list of other sources of financial support, most recently audited financial statement, copy of IRS determination letter indicating 501(c)(3) tax-exempt status, and Form 990; requests for funds to support a specific project or program should include fully defined need, objective, benefits, plans (including time frame and evaluative criteria), staff, and budget *Deadlines:* none; requests reviewed throughout year *Note:* If request falls under foundation guidelines and program priorities, organization may be asked to provide more complete information before a decision is made.

Restrictions on Giving: Grants are not made to individuals; private foundations; hospital capital fund campaigns; organizations receiving support from United Ways; organizations whose activities are mainly international; local chapters of national organizations; disease-specific organizations; organizations primarily engaged in patient care or direct treatment; drug treatment centers or community health clinics; elementary or secondary schools; endowments; courtesy advertising or festival participation; or religious, fraternal, political, athletic, social, or veterans organizations.

OTHER THINGS TO KNOW
In 1993, the foundation's Social Investment Program committed $13,856,250 million in loans. These loans expand the foundation's ability to reach urban neighborhoods by making investments in projects that address significant social needs but do not meet all of the company's regular investment criteria.

Occasionally, foundation establishes particular areas of interest for emphasis within a program area. When this is done, foundation actively seeks opportunites for providing grants and may issue requests for proposals. Grant renewals are not automatic and cannot be guaranteed from year to year.

PUBLICATIONS
Contributions report

GRANTS ANALYSIS
Total Grants: $9,989,132
Number of Grants: 445*
Highest Grant: $1,500,000
Average Grant: $1,000*
Typical Range: $5,000 to $10,000
Disclosure Period: 1993

Note: Number of grants and average grant figures exclude more than 600 matching gifts. Recent grants are derived from a 1993 contributions report.

RECENT GRANTS
Library
20,000	New York Public Library, New York, NY

General
700,000	United Way of Tri-State, Tri-State, NY
648,440	United Ways
635,237	Health and Safety Education Program
550,000	Awards for Medical Research
280,000	Economic Policy Institute, Washington, DC

Millbrook Tribute Garden

CONTACT
George T. Whalen, Jr.
Trustee
Millbrook Tribute Garden
PO Box AC
Millbrook, NY 12545
(914) 677-3434

FINANCIAL SUMMARY
Recent Giving: $889,000 (fiscal 1993); $923,200 (fiscal 1992); $938,000 (fiscal 1990)
Assets: $15,393,305 (fiscal 1993); $16,156,636 (fiscal 1992); $18,255,751 (fiscal 1990)
EIN: 14-1340079

CONTRIBUTIONS SUMMARY
Typical Recipients: • *Arts & Humanities:* Art History, Arts Associations & Councils, Libraries, Public Broadcasting • *Civic & Public Affairs:* Clubs, General, Municipalities/Towns • *Education:* Colleges & Universities, Environmental Education, Literacy, Private Education (Precollege), Secondary Education (Public), Student Aid • *Environment:* General, Resource Conservation, Wildlife Protection • *Health:* Hospitals • *Religion:* Churches, Religious Organizations, Religious Welfare • *Social Services:* Animal Protection, Child Welfare, Community Service Organizations, Homes, Recreation &

Athletics, Scouts, Senior Services, Volunteer Services, Youth Organizations
Grant Types: capital and general support
Geographic Distribution: limited to Millbrook, NY

GIVING OFFICERS
Felicitas S. Thorne: vp

Oakleigh Thorne: vp, secy *PHIL AFFIL* vp, secy: Oakleigh L. Thorne Foundation

Oakleigh Thorne: vp, secy *PHIL AFFIL* vp, secy: Oakleigh L. Thorne Foundation (see above)

Oakleigh Blakeman Thorne: pres, trust *B* Santa Barbara CA 1932 *ED* Harvard Univ BA 1954 *CURR EMPL* chmn, dir: Commerce Clearing House *CORP AFFIL* chmn: CCH Computax; dir: Bank Millbrook; pres: CT Corp Sys, Legal Information Svcs *PHIL AFFIL* chmn, pres, treas, dir: Oakleigh L. Thorne Foundation; pres: Oakleigh L. Thorne Foundation; chmn, pres, dir *CLUB AFFIL* Brook, Racquet & Tennis

Vincent N. Turletes: trust

George T. Whalen, Jr.: trust *CURR EMPL* pres, dir: Bank Millbrook

Robert W. Whalen: trust

APPLICATION INFORMATION
Initial Approach:

The foundation requests applications be made in writing.

Written proposals should include supporting materials explaining the purpose of the request and a financial statement.

The foundation has no deadline for submitting proposals.

Restrictions on Giving: The foundation makes grants only to public charities under section 509(a)(1),(2), and (3) of the IRS code. The foundation does not make grants to individuals.

GRANTS ANALYSIS
Total Grants: $889,000
Number of Grants: 31
Highest Grant: $200,000
Average Grant: $28,677
Typical Range: $1,000 to $35,000
Disclosure Period: fiscal year ending September 30, 1993

Note: Recent grants are derived from a fiscal 1993 Form 990.

RECENT GRANTS
Library
20,000	Millbrook Free Library, Millbrook, NY

General
200,000	Dutchess Day School, Millbrook, NY
115,000	Grace Episcopal Church, Millbrook, NY
115,000	Millbrook School, Millbrook, NY
110,000	Sharon Hospital, Sharon, CT
50,000	Institute of Ecosystem Studies, Millbrook, NY

Miller Fund, Kathryn and Gilbert

CONTACT
Charles Looker
President
Kathryn and Gilbert Miller Fund
c/o Proskauer, Rose, Goetz & Mendelsohn
1585 Broadway
New York, NY 10036
(212) 969-3000

FINANCIAL SUMMARY
Recent Giving: $206,667 (fiscal 1994); $252,565 (fiscal 1993); $327,500 (fiscal 1992)

Assets: $1,218,128 (fiscal 1994); $1,402,202 (fiscal 1993); $1,544,266 (fiscal 1992)

Gifts Received: $550 (fiscal 1993)

Fiscal Note: In 1993, contributions were received from Mr. Charles Looker, Esquire.

EIN: 13-6121254

CONTRIBUTIONS SUMMARY
Donor(s): the late Kathryn B. Miller

Typical Recipients: • *Arts & Humanities:* Arts Associations & Councils, Arts Centers, Ballet, Community Arts, Libraries, Music, Opera, Performing Arts, Public Broadcasting, Theater • *Civic & Public Affairs:* Law & Justice, Legal Aid • *Education:* Colleges & Universities, Elementary Education (Public), Medical Education, Private Education (Precollege) • *Health:* Alzheimers Disease, Cancer, Hospitals, Single-Disease Health Associations • *Religion:* Jewish Causes • *Social Services:* Child Welfare, Community Service Organizations, People with Disabilities, Senior Services, United Funds/United Ways, Youth Organizations

Grant Types: research

Geographic Distribution: focus on NY

GIVING OFFICERS
Philip J. Hirsch: vp, treas, dir

Charles Looker: pres, dir *PHIL AFFIL* dir: Henry Kaufmann Foundation; secy: C. L. C. Kramer Foundation

Jerold Zieselman: secy, dir

APPLICATION INFORMATION
Initial Approach: The foundation has no formal grant application procedure or application form. There are no deadlines.

GRANTS ANALYSIS
Total Grants: $206,667

Number of Grants: 24

Highest Grant: $17,000

Typical Range: $1,000 to $20,000

Disclosure Period: fiscal year ending March 31, 1994

Note: Recent grants are derived from a fiscal 1994 Form 990.

RECENT GRANTS
General

15,000	Columbia University, New York, NY
10,000	Alzheimers Disease and Related Disorders Association, New York, NY
10,000	United Jewish Appeal Federation, New York, NY
5,000	Dalton School, New York, NY
5,000	Dana Farber Cancer Institute, Boston, MA

Mitsubishi International Corp. / Mitsubishi International Corp. Foundation

Sales: $11.84 billion
Employees: 1,035
Parent Company: Mitsubishi Corp.
Headquarters: New York, NY
SIC Major Group: Wholesale Trade—Durable Goods and Wholesale Trade—Nondurable Goods

CONTACT
Martha Gellens
Manager, Public Relations
Mitsubishi International Corp.
520 Madison Ave.
New York, NY 10022
(212) 605-2082

FINANCIAL SUMMARY
Recent Giving: $25,000 (1993); $0 (1992)

Assets: $806,275 (1993); $805,545 (1992)

Gifts Received: $39,075 (1993); $835,650 (1992)

Fiscal Note: In 1993, contributions were received from the Mitsubishi International Corp.

EIN: 13-3676166

CONTRIBUTIONS SUMMARY
Typical Recipients: • *Arts & Humanities:* Community Arts, Ethnic & Folk Arts, Libraries, Museums/Galleries, Performing Arts, Public Broadcasting, Theater • *Civic & Public Affairs:* Economic Development, Employment/Job Training, Public Policy, Urban & Community Affairs • *Education:* Business Education, Economic Education, Education Associations, International Exchange, International Studies • *Health:* Medical Research • *International:* International Relations • *Social Services:* Community Centers, Community Service Organizations, Senior Services, Youth Organizations

Grant Types: general support, project, and research

Nonmonetary Support Types: donated products

Geographic Distribution: preference given to projects where offices are located

CORP. OFFICERS
M. Numagushi: *CURR EMPL* pres, ceo, dir: Mitsubishi Intl Corp

GIVING OFFICERS
James E. Brumm: pres *B* San Antonio TX 1941 *ED* CA St Univ AB 1965; Columbia Univ LLB 1968 *CURR EMPL* exec vp, gen couns, dir: Mitsubishi Intl Corp *CORP AFFIL* dir: Brunei Coldgas *NONPR AFFIL* chmn comm intl trade, mem: Assn Bar City NY; mem: Am Bar Assn; trust: Spuyten Duyvil Nursery Sch *CLUB AFFIL* Nippon, Univ

Audrey G. Cohen: secy

Richard Epstein: treas

Judith E. Friedman: asst secy

Tetsuo Kamimura: chmn bd

Masaharu Masuyama: exec dir

Mitsutake Okano: dir

APPLICATION INFORMATION
Initial Approach: Send inquiry letter of less than three pages at any time; applications should include a description of the organization, amount requested, purpose for which funds are sought, a recently audited financial statement, and proof of tax-exempt status.

GRANTS ANALYSIS
Total Grants: $25,000

Number of Grants: 1

Highest Grant: $25,000

Disclosure Period: 1993

Note: Recent grants are derived from a 1993 Form 990.

Mnuchin Foundation

CONTACT
Robert E. Mnuchin
Principal Manager
Mnuchin Fdn.
85 Broad St.
New York, NY 10004
(212) 902-6897

FINANCIAL SUMMARY
Recent Giving: $490,342 (fiscal 1993); $487,820 (fiscal 1991); $228,938 (fiscal 1990)

Assets: $3,889,315 (fiscal 1993); $4,074,016 (fiscal 1991); $4,359,543 (fiscal 1990)

Gifts Received: $535,116 (fiscal 1990); $700,000 (fiscal 1989)

EIN: 13-3050751

CONTRIBUTIONS SUMMARY
Donor(s): Robert E. Mnuchin

Typical Recipients: • *Arts & Humanities:* Arts Associations & Councils, Community Arts, Dance, Ethnic & Folk Arts, Film & Video, Libraries, Museums/Galleries, Music, Opera, Performing Arts, Theater • *Civic & Public Affairs:* Civil Rights, General, Municipalities/Towns, Philanthropic Organizations, Women's Affairs • *Education:*

Colleges & Universities, Private Education (Precollege) • *Health:* AIDS/HIV, Eyes/Blindness, Hospitals, Medical Research, Single-Disease Health Associations • *International:* Foreign Arts Organizations, Missionary/Religious Activities • *Religion:* Jewish Causes, Religious Organizations, Synagogues/Temples • *Social Services:* Community Service Organizations, Counseling, Domestic Violence, Food/Clothing Distribution, Shelters/Homelessness, Substance Abuse

Grant Types: general support

Geographic Distribution: focus on NY

GIVING OFFICERS
Eugene Mercy, Jr.: trust *PHIL AFFIL* pres, dir: Sue and Eugene Mercy, Jr. Foundation

Adrian Mnuchin: trust

Robert E. Mnuchin: prin mgr, secy, trust *CURR EMPL* gen ptnr: Goldman Sachs & Co *PHIL AFFIL* secy, dir: Sue and Eugene Mercy, Jr. Foundation

APPLICATION INFORMATION
Initial Approach: Send brief letter of inquiry describing program or project. There are no deadlines.

GRANTS ANALYSIS
Total Grants: $490,342

Number of Grants: 72

Highest Grant: $90,500

Typical Range: $100 to $5,000

Disclosure Period: fiscal year ending April 30, 1993

Note: Recent grants are derived from a fiscal 1993 Form 990.

RECENT GRANTS
General

50,000	United Jewish Appeal Federation, New York, NY
35,000	Barnard College, New York, NY
25,000	United Jewish Appeal Federation, New York, NY
10,000	National Victim Center, New York, NY
10,000	Seth Israel Foundation, New York, NY

Monell Foundation, Ambrose

CONTACT
George Rowe, Jr.
President
Ambrose Monell Foundation
1 Rockefeller Plz., Ste. 301
New York, NY 10020
(212) 586-0700

FINANCIAL SUMMARY
Recent Giving: $8,581,000 (1993); $7,210,000 (1992); $7,056,000 (1991)

Assets: $173,459,205 (1993); $167,684,586 (1992); $170,557,121 (1991)

EIN: 13-1982683

CONTRIBUTIONS SUMMARY
Donor(s): The Ambrose Monell Foundation was established in 1952. Funds for its incorporation were donated by Mrs. Maude Monell Vetlesen. Ambrose Monell, who died in 1921, served as president of International Nickel Company.

Typical Recipients: • *Arts & Humanities:* Arts Funds, Ballet, Libraries, Museums/Galleries, Music, Opera, Performing Arts, Public Broadcasting • *Civic & Public Affairs:* Botanical Gardens/Parks, Employment/Job Training, Legal Aid, Public Policy • *Education:* Arts/Humanities Education, Colleges & Universities, Education Associations, Health & Physical Education, Medical Education, Minority Education, Private Education (Precollege), Public Education (Precollege) • *Health:* AIDS/HIV, Alzheimers Disease, Arthritis, Cancer, Emergency/Ambulance Services, Eyes/Blindness, Geriatric Health, Hospitals, Medical Rehabilitation, Medical Research, Mental Health, Research/Studies Institutes, Speech & Hearing • *International:* Health Care/Hospitals, International Peace & Security Issues • *Religion:* Jewish Causes • *Science:* Science Museums, Scientific Centers & Institutes, Scientific Research • *Social Services:* Animal Protection, Delinquency & Criminal Rehabilitation, Homes, Scouts, YMCA/YWCA/YMHA/YWHA, Youth Organizations

Grant Types: capital, endowment, general support, multiyear/continuing support, and research

Geographic Distribution: national, with emphasis on the New York City metropolitan area

GIVING OFFICERS
Eugene Philip Grisanti: dir *B* Buffalo NY 1929 *ED* Coll Holy Cross AB 1951; Boston Univ LLB 1953; Harvard Univ LLM 1954 *CURR EMPL* chmn, pres, dir: Intl Flavors & Fragrances *NONPR AFFIL* dir: Cosmetic Toiletry Fragrance Assn, Fragrance Fdn *CLUB AFFIL* Larchmont YC, Univ, Winged Foot CC *PHIL AFFIL* pres: IFF Foundation Inc.; dir: G. Unger Vetlesen Foundation

George Rowe, Jr.: pres *B* Ossining NY 1922 *ED* Yale Univ AB 1943; Columbia Univ LLB 1948 *CURR EMPL* mem: Fulton Duncombe & Rowe *PHIL AFFIL* pres: G. Unger Vetlesen Foundation

Henry G. Walter, Jr.: dir *B* New York NY 1910 *ED* Columbia Univ BA 1931; Columbia Univ LLB 1934

APPLICATION INFORMATION
Initial Approach:

Applicant should send a brief letter to the foundation.

Letters should include an outline of the proposed project and explain the reason funding is needed.

The board meets on December 1.

GRANTS ANALYSIS
Total Grants: $8,581,000

Number of Grants: 75

Highest Grant: $1,500,000

Average Grant: $114,413

Typical Range: $25,000 to $50,000 and $100,000 to $250,000

Disclosure Period: 1993

Note: Recent grants are derived from a 1993 Form 990.

RECENT GRANTS
Library

100,000	New York Public Library, New York, NY

General

1,500,000	Harvard School of Public Health, Cambridge, MA — research immunology
650,000	Carnegie Institution of Washington, Washington, DC
600,000	McNell Chemical Senses Center, Philadelphia, PA
470,000	Massachusetts General Hospital Cancer Society, Boston, MA
350,000	Institute for Advanced Study, Princeton, NJ

Morgan & Company, J.P. / Morgan Charitable Trust, J.P.

Revenue: $11.91 billion
Employees: 15,745
Headquarters: New York, NY
SIC Major Group: State Commercial Banks, Investment Advice, Functions Related to Deposit Banking, and Security Brokers & Dealers

CONTACT
Roberta A. Ruocco
Vice President, Community Relations & Public Affairs
J.P. Morgan & Company
60 Wall St.
New York, NY 10260
(212) 648-9673
Note: Elizabeth Herbst, Community Relations & Public Affairs, is the contact for international contributions. The company's World Wide Web address is http://www.jpmorgan.com

FINANCIAL SUMMARY
Recent Giving: $13,775,000 (1995 est.); $13,882,187 (1994); $14,026,579 (1993)

Assets: $34,000,000 (1995 est.); $34,122,188 (1994); $36,660,614 (1993)

Gifts Received: $11,128,610 (1994); $8,709,741 (1993)

Fiscal Note: Above totals represent foundation contributions, direct giving by the company, and domestic and international subsidiary giving. Above figures exclude nonmonetary support. The trust receives contributions from J.P. Morgan & Company.

EIN: 13-6037931

CONTRIBUTIONS SUMMARY

Typical Recipients: • *Arts & Humanities:* Arts Associations & Councils, Arts Funds, Arts Outreach, Ballet, Dance, History & Archaeology, Libraries, Museums/Galleries, Music, Opera, Performing Arts, Public Broadcasting, Theater, Visual Arts • *Civic & Public Affairs:* African American Affairs, Botanical Gardens/Parks, Business/Free Enterprise, Economic Development, Employment/Job Training, Hispanic Affairs, Housing, Law & Justice, Legal Aid, Municipalities/Towns, Nonprofit Management, Rural Affairs, Urban & Community Affairs, Women's Affairs, Zoos/Aquariums • *Education:* Arts/Humanities Education, Business Education, Colleges & Universities, Faculty Development, Literacy, Medical Education, Minority Education, Public Education (Precollege), Science/Mathematics Education, Student Aid, Vocational & Technical Education • *Environment:* Air/Water Quality, General • *Health:* Cancer, Clinics/Medical Centers, Emergency/Ambulance Services, Geriatric Health, Health Policy/Cost Containment, Health Organizations, Hospitals, Transplant Networks/Donor Banks • *International:* Foreign Arts Organizations, Foreign Educational Institutions, Human Rights, International Affairs, International Development, International Peace & Security Issues, International Relations, International Relief Efforts • *Religion:* Religious Welfare • *Science:* Science Museums • *Social Services:* At-Risk Youth, Child Welfare, Community Centers, Community Service Organizations, Counseling, Crime Prevention, Day Care, Domestic Violence, Family Planning, Family Services, Food/Clothing Distribution, People with Disabilities, Recreation & Athletics, Senior Services, Sexual Abuse, Shelters/Homelessness, Volunteer Services, YMCA/YWCA/YMHA/YWHA, Youth Organizations

Grant Types: capital, employee matching gifts, general support, and multiyear/continuing support

Note: Employee matching gift ratio: 1 to 1. Trust also funds project support. The Volunteer Involvement Fund provides contributions of $100 to $1,000 to organizations where employees volunteer that would not normally be funded by corporate contributions.

Nonmonetary Support Types: donated equipment

Note: Value of nonmonetary support is not available. Nonmonetary support is provided by the company. Contact for nonmonetary support is Kim Persaud with Community Relations and Public Affairs.

Geographic Distribution: primarily New York City; supports some programs nationally and internationally

Operating Locations: CA (Los Angeles, San Francisco), DE (Wilmington), FL (Palm Beach), IL (Chicago), NY (New York), TX (Houston)

CORP. OFFICERS

Elizabeth R. Herbst: *CURR EMPL* assoc dir commun rels, pub rels: JP Morgan & Co

Roberto G. Mendoza: *B* Cuba 1945 *ED* Yale Univ BA 1967; Harvard Univ MBA 1974 *CURR EMPL* vchmn: JP Morgan & Co

Kurt F. Viermetz: *B* Augsburg Bavaria Germany 1939 *ED* Heilig Kreuz Coll 1957 *CURR EMPL* vchmn: JP Morgan & Co *CORP AFFIL* vchmn: Morgan Guaranty Trust Co *NONPR AFFIL* mem: Am Chamber Commerce Germany

Rodney B. Wagner: *B* 1931 *CURR EMPL* vchmn: JP Morgan & Co

Douglas Alexander Warner III: *B* Cincinnati OH 1946 *ED* Yale Univ BA 1968 *CURR EMPL* chmn, pres, ceo: JP Morgan & Co *CORP AFFIL* dir: Anheuser-Busch Cos Inc, Gen Electric Co; pres: Morgan Guaranty Trust Co NY *NONPR AFFIL* mem: Assn Reserve City Bankers; mem bd overseers: Meml Sloan-Kettering Cancer Ctr; trust: Cold Spring Harbor Laboratory, Pierpont Morgan Lib *CLUB AFFIL* Links River, Meadowbrook

GIVING OFFICERS

Karen A. Erdos: *CURR EMPL* vp commun rels & pub aff: JP Morgan & Co

Edward L. Jones: *CURR EMPL* vp commun rels & pub aff: JP Morgan & Co

Roberta A. Ruocco: *CURR EMPL* vp commun rels & pub aff: JP Morgan & Co

Hildy J. Simmons: *CURR EMPL* mng dir commun rels & pub aff: JP Morgan & Co *PHIL AFFIL* vp: Emma A. Sheafer Charitable Trust

Gloria P. Turner: *CURR EMPL* vp commun rels & pub aff: JP Morgan & Co

APPLICATION INFORMATION

Initial Approach: *Initial Contact:* written request for application form *Include Information On:* goals of organization, including a statement on the segment of the population to which grant is to be directed; latest annual report, if available; brief history of organization; brief description of programs and accomplishments in last year; list of directors or trustees and their affiliations, senior staff members, and number of full staff; recently audited financial statement; current budget, including sources of projected income; budget for next fiscal year, if available; list of foundation and corporate supporters and other sources of income; copy of 501(c)(3) letter; recent Form 990; a brief description of the specific project for which funds are requested; and plan for measuring the effectiveness of project *Deadlines:* anytime prior to September 15 to be considered in that calendar year *Note:* Two copies of application form should accompany grant requests.

Restrictions on Giving: Does not support individuals, religious organizations for sec-

tarian purposes, chemical dependency programs, specific disability or single-disease health associations other than AIDS programs, political or lobbying groups, scholarly research, scholarships, or fellowships.

OTHER THINGS TO KNOW

J.P. Morgan & Co. matches contributions of its employees, retired employees, bank directors, and any eligible person's spouse dollar-for-dollar. Gifts of cash, securities, and real estate are matched in six giving categories of giving—culture, education, environmental concerns, health care, human services, and international affairs. Minimum gift matched is $25. Maximum combined giving total matched is $8,000 per calendar year.

GRANTS ANALYSIS

Total Grants: $8,101,290*
Number of Grants: 440*
Highest Grant: $425,000
Average Grant: $18,412*
Typical Range: $5,000 to $25,000
Disclosure Period: 1994

Note: Figures for total grants, number of grants, and average grant exclude matching gifts of $3,246,935 and domestic and international subsidiary giving of $2,533,962. Above figures do include trust giving of $7,044,930 and corporate giving of $1,056,360. Recent grants are derived from a 1994 grants list.

RECENT GRANTS

Library
210,000 — Pace University, White Plains, NY — for first payment of $50,000 grant for the Center for Academic Excellence and $185,000 start-up grant for the College Library Usage Project

General
425,000 — New York University, New York, NY — for first payment of $650,000 grant for the Professional Development Laboratory Program and $100,000 grant for the Reading Recovery Program
107,500 — Bank Street College of Education, New York, NY — for final payment of $100,000 capital grant and $75,000 for the Principals Institute/Leadership Center
100,000 — Classroom, New York, NY — for their professional development program
100,000 — Food for Survival, New York, NY — for final payment of $100,000 general support grant and $50,000 special holiday season grant
100,000 — Primary Care Development Corporation, New York, NY — for final payment of $20,000 startup grant for this

planning, development, and
financing intermediary
organization

Morgan Stanley & Co., Inc. / Morgan Stanley Foundation

Employees: 9,300
Parent Company: Morgan Stanley Group, Inc.
Revenue: $9.37 billion
Headquarters: New York, NY
SIC Major Group: Security Brokers & Dealers
and Commodity Contracts Brokers & Dealers

CONTACT
Patricia Schaefer
Vice President
Morgan Stanley Foundation
1251 Avenue of the Americas
39th Fl.
New York, NY 10020
(212) 703-6610

FINANCIAL SUMMARY
Recent Giving: $2,100,000 (1993 approx.);
$1,800,000 (1992); $1,800,000 (1991)

Assets: $13,000,000 (1992); $9,360,514
(1990); $9,196,192 (1989)

Fiscal Note: Although company gives both
directly and through the foundation, there is
no formal program for direct contributions,
and company does not solicit applications
for direct support. Above figures exclude
nonmonetary support.

EIN: 13-6155650

CONTRIBUTIONS SUMMARY
Typical Recipients: • *Arts & Humanities:*
Arts Institutes, Ballet, Dance, Historic Preservation, Libraries, Museums/Galleries, Performing Arts, Public Broadcasting, Visual
Arts • *Civic & Public Affairs:* Economic De-
velopment, Employment/Job Training, Hispanic Affairs, Housing, Zoos/Aquariums
• *Education:* Arts/Humanities Education,
Business Education, Colleges & Universities, Engineering/Technological Education,
Minority Education, Public Education (Precollege), Special Education • *Environment:*
Air/Water Quality, General, Wildlife Protection • *Health:* AIDS/HIV, Cancer, Children's Health/Hospitals, Home-Care
Services, Hospitals, Medical Rehabilitation
• *Social Services:* At-Risk Youth, Community Service Organizations, Emergency Re-
lief, Family Planning, Family Services,
Food/Clothing Distribution, Homes, Recreation & Athletics, Scouts, Shelters/Homeless-
ness, United Funds/United Ways, Volunteer
Services, YMCA/YWCA/YMHA/YWHA,
Youth Organizations

Grant Types: employee matching gifts and
general support

Note: The employee matching gift program
matches grants made to secondary schools,
colleges, and universities only. Gifts must
be at least $50.

Nonmonetary Support Types: donated
equipment

Note: Estimated value of nonmonetary support is not available and is not included in
figures above. Patricia Doyle, grants administrator, is the contact at the above address
for nonmonetary support.

Geographic Distribution: primarily New
York City; San Francisco, Los Angeles, and
Chicago branches

Operating Locations: CA (Los Angeles,
San Francisco), IL (Chicago), NY (New
York)

CORP. OFFICERS
Richard B. Fisher: *B* Philadelphia PA 1936
ED Princeton Univ BA 1957; Harvard Univ
MBA 1962 *CURR EMPL* chmn, mng dir:
Morgan Stanley Group *NONPR AFFIL* dir:
Ministers & Missionaries Benefit Bd Am
Baptist Churches; trust: Carnegie Corp NY,
Historic Hudson Valley, Princeton Univ, Ur-
ban Inst *CLUB AFFIL* Blind Brook CC,
Links, Natl Golf Links Am, Rockaway Hunt-
ing

Mary Stubbs: *CURR EMPL* corp commun:
Morgan Stanley & Co

GIVING OFFICERS
Kenneth de Regt: trust *CURR EMPL* vp,
dir: Morgan Stanley Market Products

Deborah A. DeCatis: trust

Patricia Doyle: grants admin

Robert F. Gartland: trust *CURR EMPL*
pres, dir: MS Securities Svcs Inc

Elaine LaRoche: trust

William M. Lewis: trust

James Runde: chmn *B* Sparta WI 1946 *ED*
Marquette Univ 1969; George Washington
Univ 1973

Patricia Schaefer: vp

John Hill Tucker Wilson: trust *B* Charlotte
NC 1934 *ED* Princeton Univ BA 1956; Har-
vard Univ MBA 1960 *CURR EMPL* mng dir:
Morgan Stanley & Co *NONPR AFFIL* chmn:
Settlement Coll Readiness; dir: Environ-
mental Defense Fund, Union Settlement
Assn; mem bd visit: Univ NC Sch Bus;
trust: Brunswick Sch, Greenwich Hosp Assn
CLUB AFFIL Field, Links, Round Hill

APPLICATION INFORMATION
Initial Approach: *Initial Contact:* contact
the foundation for an application form *Include Information On:* description of the organization, amount requested, purpose for
which funds are sought, recently audited financial statement, proof of tax-exempt
status, list of board members and their affiliations *Deadlines:* none

Restrictions on Giving: Generally, does not
make grants to individuals; national organizations; goodwill advertising; dinners or special events; political or fraternal
organizations; member agencies of united
funds; religious organizations; organizations
concerned with specific disease research;
capital or building campaigns; or public or
private schools.

PUBLICATIONS
Program guidelines and grants listing

GRANTS ANALYSIS
Total Grants: $2,100,000*

Typical Range: $2,500 to $10,000

Disclosure Period: 1993

Note: Total grants figure is approximate. Recent grants are derived from a 1993 annual
report.

RECENT GRANTS
Library
Los Angeles Public Library, Los Angeles, CA
— for the arts

General
Ada S. McKinley Community Services,
Chicago, IL — for social service
American-Italian Foundation for Cancer
Research, New York, NY — for free
mammograms for low-income women
Black Leadership Commission on AIDS, New
York, NY — for health care
Boy Scouts of America Greater New York
Councils, New York, NY — for social
service
Boys and Girls Clubs of Chicago, Chicago, IL
— for social service

Morris Foundation, William T.

CONTACT
Edward A. Antonelli
President, Chief Executive Officer, and
Director
William T. Morris Foundation
230 Park Ave., Ste. 622
New York, NY 10169-0622
(212) 986-8036
Note: Information on William T. Morris
Foundation Scholarships may be obtained by
contacting Robert Ripa at Wyoming Area
High School, Exeter, PA 18643.

FINANCIAL SUMMARY
Recent Giving: $1,570,000 (fiscal 1993);
$2,095,000 (fiscal 1991); $1,531,000 (fiscal
1989)

Assets: $44,553,565 (fiscal 1993);
$40,335,230 (fiscal 1991); $39,243,085 (fiscal 1989)

EIN: 13-1600908

CONTRIBUTIONS SUMMARY
Donor(s): The William T. Morris Founda-
tion was established in 1937, with the late
William T. Morris as donor.

Typical Recipients: • *Arts & Humanities:*
Arts Centers, Ballet, Dance, Historic Preser-
vation, History & Archaeology, Libraries,
Museums/Galleries, Music, Opera • *Civic &
Public Affairs:* Botanical Gardens/Parks, Ur-
ban & Community Affairs, Zoos/Aquariums
• *Education:* Arts/Humanities Education,
Colleges & Universities, Education Funds,
Medical Education • *Environment:*
Air/Water Quality, General, Resource Con-
servation • *Health:* Arthritis, Cancer, Clin-
ics/Medical Centers, Health Funds,
Hospitals, Medical Rehabilitation, Medical
Research, Respiratory • *Religion:* Religious
Welfare • *Science:* Science Museums • *So-*

cial Services: People with Disabilities, Recreation & Athletics, United Funds/United Ways, Youth Organizations

Grant Types: department, fellowship, general support, research, and scholarship

Geographic Distribution: emphasis on New York, Connecticut, and Pennsylvania

GIVING OFFICERS

Edward A. Antonelli: pres, ceo, dir

Bruce A. August: secy, dir

A. C. Laske, Jr.: treas, dir

Wilmot Fitch Wheeler, Jr.: vp, dir *B* Southport CT 1923 *ED* Yale Univ BA 1945; NY Univ postgrad 1947-1948 *CURR EMPL* chmn, dir: Jelliff Corp *CORP AFFIL* dir: Peoples Bank CT, Sormir Petroleum; trust: Peoples Mutual Holdings *NONPR AFFIL* bd dir: Wilmot Wheeler Fdn; trust: Am Farm Sch, Bridgeport Hosp *PHIL AFFIL* pres: Wilmot Wheeler Foundation *CLUB AFFIL* Fairfield CC, Sky, Yale

APPLICATION INFORMATION
Initial Approach:

Written proposals should be sent to the foundation.

There is no prescribed form of application.

There are no deadlines for submitting general proposals. Scholarship applications must be submitted by July 31.

OTHER THINGS TO KNOW
Scholarships are restricted to residents of West Pittston, PA. Scholarship application forms may be obtained by writing: Robert Ripa, Wyoming Area High School, Exeter, PA 18643.

GRANTS ANALYSIS
Total Grants: $2,079,000*

Number of Grants: 69

Highest Grant: $250,000

Average Grant: $26,897*

Typical Range: $10,000 to $50,000

Disclosure Period: fiscal year ending June 30, 1991

Note: Total grants figure excludes $16,000 in scholarships. Average grant figure excludes the foundation's highest grant of $250,000. Recent grants are derived from a fiscal 1991 grants list.

RECENT GRANTS

Library

50,000	New York Public Library, New York, NY

General

75,000	Bridgeport Hospital Foundation, Bridgeport, CT
75,000	St. Vincent's Medical Center Foundation, Bridgeport, CT
50,000	Assumption College, Worcester, MA
50,000	Boston College, Chestnut Hill, MA
50,000	Bowdoin College, Brunswick, ME

Moses Fund, Henry and Lucy

CONTACT
Henry Schneider
President
Henry and Lucy Moses Fund
c/o Moses and Singer
1301 Avenue of the Americas, 40th Fl.
New York, NY 10019
(212) 554-7800
Note: An additional contact is Irving Sitnick, secretary, located at the above address.

FINANCIAL SUMMARY
Recent Giving: $2,273,000 (1995 est.); $2,000,000 (1994 approx.); $1,771,770 (1993)

Assets: $2,100,000 (1995 est.); $2,100,000 (1994 approx.); $1,817,043 (1993)

Gifts Received: $2,170,000 (1995 est.); $2,000,000 (1994 approx.); $982,500 (1993)

Fiscal Note: The foundation receives contributions from the Henry and Lucy Moses Foundation Trust, the Henry L. Moses Trust, and the Lucy G. Moses Trust.

EIN: 13-6092967

CONTRIBUTIONS SUMMARY
Donor(s): The Henry and Lucy Moses Fund was established in New York in 1942 by Mr. Henry L. Moses and his wife, Lucy Moses. Mr. Moses, an attorney and banker, was a partner in the law firm of Moses and Singer. He also was chairman of the Public National Bank and Trust Company and, upon its merger with Bankers Trust Company, a director of that bank. Mr. Moses was a noted philanthropist, with a special interest in hospitals. He served as president and chairman of the board of Montefiore Hospital and as director of the planning commission of the Hospital Council of Greater New York and the United Hospital Fund.

Typical Recipients: • *Arts & Humanities:* Ballet, Dance, Libraries, Museums/Galleries, Music, Opera, Performing Arts, Public Broadcasting • *Civic & Public Affairs:* African American Affairs, Botanical Gardens/Parks, Civil Rights, Housing, Legal Aid, Philanthropic Organizations, Urban & Community Affairs, Zoos/Aquariums • *Education:* Arts/Humanities Education, Colleges & Universities, Education Associations, Literacy, Medical Education, Minority Education, School Volunteerism, Special Education, Student Aid • *Environment:* General • *Health:* Cancer, Clinics/Medical Centers, Health Organizations, Hospitals, Medical Research, Nursing Services, Single-Disease Health Associations • *International:* Foreign Educational Institutions • *Religion:* Jewish Causes, Religious Organizations, Religious Welfare • *Social Services:* Child Welfare, Community Centers, Community Service Organizations, Family Planning, Family Services, Food/Clothing Distribution, People with Disabilities, Recreation & Athletics, Senior

Services, Shelters/Homelessness, Volunteer Services, YMCA/YWCA/YMHA/YWHA

Grant Types: capital, endowment, general support, and operating expenses

Geographic Distribution: primarily New York City metropolitan area, some national funding

GIVING OFFICERS
Alfred W. Bressler: vp, treas, dir *B* New York NY 1905 *ED* City Univ NY BA 1925; Columbia Univ JD 1927 *CURR EMPL* ptnr: Moses & Singer

Joseph L. Fishman: vp, dir *CURR EMPL* ptnr: Moses & Singer

Henry Schneider: pres, dir *B* New York NY 1910 *ED* City Univ NY BA 1931; Columbia Univ JD 1934 *CURR EMPL* special coun: Moses & Singer

Irving Sitnick: secy, dir *CURR EMPL* ptnr: Moses & Singer

APPLICATION INFORMATION
Initial Approach:

Organizations contacting the fund should write a brief introductory letter.

Letters should describe the organization and the proposed project, and include proof of IRS tax-exempt status.

Restrictions on Giving: The foundation does not make grants to individuals, or for loans, film production, or travel.

OTHER THINGS TO KNOW
The foundation reported that it is closely affiliated with the Henry and Lucy Moses Foundation Trust, the Henry L. Moses Trust, and the Lucy G. Moses Trust. All are located in the state of New York.

New proposals are currently not being accepted. The foundation states that "the annual amount available for grants generally is committed to the activities supported in previous years by the foundation."

GRANTS ANALYSIS
Total Grants: $1,771,770

Number of Grants: 103

Highest Grant: $500,000

Average Grant: $17,202

Typical Range: $1,000 to $25,000

Disclosure Period: 1993

Note: Recent grants are derived from a 1993 Form 990.

RECENT GRANTS

Library

10,000	New York Public Library, New York, NY

General

500,000	United Jewish Appeal Federation of Jewish Philanthropies, New York, NY
100,000	Montefiore Medical Center, New York, NY
100,000	New York Zoological Society, Bronx, NY

| 100,000 | United Jewish Appeal Federation of Jewish Philanthropies, New York, NY |
| 50,000 | Central Park Conservancy, New York, NY |

Neuberger Foundation, Roy R. and Marie S.

CONTACT
Mary Piatuff
Director
Roy R. and Marie S. Neuberger Fdn.
605 Third Ave., 41st Fl.
New York, NY 10158

FINANCIAL SUMMARY
Recent Giving: $859,930 (1992); $744,525 (1991); $667,600 (1989)

Assets: $13,025,778 (1992); $12,603,916 (1991); $10,835,614 (1989)

Gifts Received: $492,150 (1991); $1,148,750 (1989)

Fiscal Note: In 1991, contributions were received from Roy R. Neuberger.

EIN: 13-6066102

CONTRIBUTIONS SUMMARY
Donor(s): Roy R. Neuberger, Marie S. Neuberger

Typical Recipients: • *Arts & Humanities:* Arts Associations & Councils, Arts Centers, Dance, Ethnic & Folk Arts, General, Historic Preservation, Libraries, Museums/Galleries, Music, Performing Arts, Public Broadcasting • *Civic & Public Affairs:* African American Affairs, General, Urban & Community Affairs, Women's Affairs, Zoos/Aquariums • *Education:* Arts/Humanities Education, Colleges & Universities, Legal Education, Private Education (Precollege), Social Sciences Education • *Environment:* Resource Conservation • *Health:* Health Organizations, Hospitals, Medical Research, Nursing Services, Single-Disease Health Associations • *Religion:* Jewish Causes, Religious Organizations, Synagogues/Temples • *Social Services:* Community Service Organizations, People with Disabilities, United Funds/United Ways, Youth Organizations

Grant Types: general support

Geographic Distribution: focus on NY

GIVING OFFICERS
Ann N. Aceves: vp, dir

James Kaufman: secy

James A. Neuberger: vp, dir

Marie S. Neuberger: vp, dir

Roy R. Neuberger: pres, treas, dir *B* Bridgeport CT 1903 *ED* NY Univ *CURR EMPL* sr ptnr: Neuberger & Berman *CORP AFFIL* chmn: Guardian Mutual Fund *NONPR AFFIL* counc friends: Inst Fine Arts; dir: City Ctr Music Drama NY; dir coll ctr: Bard Coll; mem: Am Federation Arts, NY Soc Security Analysts Inst; mem collector's comm:

Natl Gallery Art; mem pres counc: Mus City NY; trust emeritus: Whitney Mus Am Art

Roy S. Neuberger: vp, dir

Mary Piatuff: dir

APPLICATION INFORMATION
Initial Approach: Send brief letter of inquiry describing program or project. There are no deadlines.

Restrictions on Giving: Does not support individuals.

GRANTS ANALYSIS
Total Grants: $859,930

Number of Grants: 168

Highest Grant: $350,000

Typical Range: $100 to $5,000

Disclosure Period: 1992

Note: Recent grants are derived from a 1992 Form 990.

RECENT GRANTS
Library

| 1,250 | New York Public Library, New York, NY |

General

350,000	Purchase College Foundation, Purchase, NY — R.R.N. Endowment Fund
250,000	Bryn Mawr College, Bryn Mawr, PA
50,000	United Jewish Appeal Federation of Jewish Philanthropies, New York, NY
15,000	Purchase College Foundation, Purchase, NY
15,000	United Jewish Appeal Federation of Jewish Philanthropies, New York, NY

New-Land Foundation

CONTACT
Robert Wolf
President
New-Land Foundation
1114 Avenue of the Americas, 46th fl.
New York, NY 10036
(212) 479-6000

FINANCIAL SUMMARY
Recent Giving: $1,466,862 (1993); $1,472,572 (1992); $1,822,553 (1991)

Assets: $23,598,223 (1993); $22,174,940 (1992); $19,387,434 (1991)

Gifts Received: $162,008 (1993); $2,899,992 (1992); $121 (1991)

Fiscal Note: The foundation receives contributions from the Gladys Lack Unit Trust under the will of Muriel Buttinger and from the estate of M. Buttinger. In 1992, the foundation received a gift of $365,702 from the Muriel Buttinger Trust and $2,534,290 from the Joseph Buttinger Trust. In 1993 the foundation received contribution from the estate of Joseph Buttinger.

EIN: 13-6086562

CONTRIBUTIONS SUMMARY
Donor(s): The New-Land Foundation was incorporated in 1941 in New York by Joseph Buttinger and Muriel Buttinger.

Typical Recipients: • *Arts & Humanities:* Arts Institutes, Arts Outreach, Libraries, Museums/Galleries, Music • *Civic & Public Affairs:* African American Affairs, Botanical Gardens/Parks, Civil Rights, Economic Development, Economic Policy, General, Hispanic Affairs, Law & Justice, Legal Aid, Native American Affairs, Professional & Trade Associations, Public Policy, Urban & Community Affairs, Women's Affairs • *Education:* Colleges & Universities, Education Associations, Education Funds, Education Reform, Engineering/Technological Education, Legal Education, Literacy, Medical Education, Minority Education, Science/Mathematics Education, Special Education • *Environment:* Air/Water Quality, Energy, General, Resource Conservation, Wildlife Protection • *Health:* Clinics/Medical Centers, Hospitals, Medical Research, Mental Health, Research/Studies Institutes • *International:* Health Care/Hospitals, Human Rights, International Development, International Organizations, International Peace & Security Issues, International Relations • *Religion:* Jewish Causes • *Social Services:* Child Welfare, Community Service Organizations, Family Planning, Homes, Senior Services, Volunteer Services, Youth Organizations

Grant Types: general support and project

Geographic Distribution: principally to national organizations

GIVING OFFICERS
Constance Harvey: vp, dir

Joan Harvey: dir

Joseph Harvey: dir

Thomas Hal Harvey: vp, dir *B* Aspen CO 1960 *ED* Stanford Univ BSE 1982; Stanford Univ MS 1984 *NONPR AFFIL* chmn bd: Inst Global Commun *PHIL AFFIL* trust: Joyce Mertz-Gilmore Foundation; dir: Energy Foundation

Anna Frank Loeb: dir

Renee Gerstler Schwartz: secy-treas, dir *B* Brooklyn NY 1933 *ED* Brooklyn Coll AB 1953; Columbia Univ LLB 1955 *CURR EMPL* atty, ptnr: Kronish Lieb Weiner & Hellman *NONPR AFFIL* mem: Assn Bar City New York

Albert Jay Solnit: dir *B* Los Angeles CA 1919 *ED* Univ CA BA 1940; Univ CA MA 1942; Univ CA MD 1943 *NONPR AFFIL* commnr: CT St Dept Mental Health; consult: Childrens Bur Health Ed & Welfare, Natl Inst Mental Health Div Mental Health Svc Program; mem: Am Academy Child & Adolescent Psychiatry, Am Academy Pediatrics, Am Assn Advancement Science, Am Assn Child Psychoanalysis, Am Orthopsychiatric Assn, Am Psychoanalytic Assn, Intl Assn Child & Adolescent Psychiatry, Intl Pediatric Soc, Intl Psychoanalytic Assn, Natl Academy Sciences Inst Medicine, NY Psychoanalytic Soc, Soc Professionals Child

Psychiatry; mem adv bd: Action Childrens TV; mem adv counc: Erikson Inst Early Childhood Ed; mem comm publs: Yale Univ Press; mem div med sciences: Natl Res Counc Assembly Life Sciences; mem editorial comm: Israel Annals Psychiatry Related Disciplines; natl adv: Children Magazine; train supervising analyst: NY Psychoanalytic Inst, Western New England Inst Psychoanalysis

Robert Wolf: pres *B* New York NY 1916 *ED* Harvard Univ BS 1937; Columbia Univ LLB 1957 *CURR EMPL* couns: Kronish Lieb Weiner & Hellman

APPLICATION INFORMATION
Initial Approach:

Initial contact should be in writing.

The foundation issues guidelines and application forms on written request. Organizations requesting support from the foundation should submit one copy of a full proposal. Information should include the intended purpose of the grant, and the applicant's tax-exempt determination letter.

Deadlines for proposals are February 1 and August 1.

Notification of the board's decision on positive responses only is sent approximately two weeks after the semi-annual board meetings.

Restrictions on Giving: No grants are given to individuals, and no loans are distributed. The foundation does not typically award grants for capital campaigns, publications, films, endowment campaigns, building compaigns, or conferences.

PUBLICATIONS
Application guidelines, application form

GRANTS ANALYSIS
Total Grants: $1,466,862

Number of Grants: 146

Highest Grant: $50,000

Average Grant: $10,047

Typical Range: $1,000 to $50,000

Disclosure Period: 1993

Note: Recent grants are derived from a 1993 Form 990.

RECENT GRANTS

Library
15,000	New York Public Library, New York, NY	

General
50,000	Anna Freud Foundation, New York, NY
40,000	Institute for Policy Studies, Washington, DC
35,000	Green Seal, Washington, DC
30,000	Children's Research Institute, Washington, DC
30,000	NAACP Legal Defense Education Fund, New York, NY

New York Life Insurance Co. / New York Life Foundation

Revenue: $12.06 billion
Employees: 9,000
Headquarters: New York, NY
SIC Major Group: Life Insurance

CONTACT
Carol J. Reuter
President and Executive Director
New York Life Foundation
51 Madison Ave.
New York, NY 10010
(212) 576-7000
Note: Ms. Reuter's extension is 7341.

FINANCIAL SUMMARY
Recent Giving: $2,475,426 (1992); $2,448,496 (1991); $2,299,078 (1989)

Assets: $40,245,825 (1992); $37,620,657 (1991); $38,549,617 (1989)

Gifts Received: $1,000,000 (1992)

Fiscal Note: Company gives through the foundation only.

EIN: 13-2989476

CONTRIBUTIONS SUMMARY
Typical Recipients: • *Arts & Humanities:* Arts Associations & Councils, Arts Centers, Historic Preservation, Libraries, Museums/Galleries, Music, Performing Arts, Public Broadcasting • *Civic & Public Affairs:* African American Affairs, Asian American Affairs, Business/Free Enterprise, Civil Rights, Economic Development, Economic Policy, Employment/Job Training, Law & Justice, Legal Aid, Nonprofit Management, Philanthropic Organizations, Professional & Trade Associations, Urban & Community Affairs, Women's Affairs, Zoos/Aquariums • *Education:* Arts/Humanities Education, Business Education, Colleges & Universities, Community & Junior Colleges, Education Associations, Education Funds, Health & Physical Education, Legal Education, Literacy, Medical Education, Minority Education, Religious Education • *Health:* AIDS/HIV, Emergency/Ambulance Services, Geriatric Health, Health Organizations, Hospitals, Medical Rehabilitation, Medical Research, Medical Training, Mental Health, Nursing Services, Single-Disease Health Associations • *Science:* Scientific Organizations • *Social Services:* Child Welfare, Community Centers, Community Service Organizations, Counseling, Day Care, Domestic Violence, Family Services, Food/Clothing Distribution, People with Disabilities, Recreation & Athletics, Senior Services, Shelters/Homelessness, Substance Abuse, United Funds/United Ways, Volunteer Services, Youth Organizations

Grant Types: capital, employee matching gifts, general support, project, and scholarship

Geographic Distribution: nationally

Operating Locations: CT (Greenwich), DE (Wilmington), GA (Marietta), NJ (Ft. Lee), NY (New York), TX (Austin, Dallas)

CORP. OFFICERS
George August William Bundschuh: *B* Yonkers NY 1933 *ED* Pace Univ BBA 1955; Columbia Univ Sch Bus Admin MS 1959 *CURR EMPL* pres, dir: NY Life Ins Co *NONPR AFFIL* mem: Inst Chartered Fin Analysts; trust: Pace Univ

Lee Morgan Gammill, Jr.: *B* New York NY 1934 *ED* Dartmouth Coll BA 1956 *CURR EMPL* exec vp, dir: NY Life Ins Co *CORP AFFIL* dir: NY Life Equity Corp, NY Life Realty Corp, NY Life Securities Corp; pres, dir: NY Life Ins & Annuity Corp *NONPR AFFIL* chmn: Life Ins Mktg & Res Assn; dir, mem exec comm: Life Underwriters Training Counc; mem: Gen Agents & Mgrs Assn, Natl Assn Life Underwriters *CLUB AFFIL* Bohemian, Lagunitas CC, Links, Pacific-Union

Harry George Hohn, Jr.: *B* New York NY 1932 *ED* NY Univ BS 1953; Fordham Univ JD 1956; NY Univ LLM 1959 *CURR EMPL* chmn, ceo, dir: NY Life Ins Co *CORP AFFIL* dir: Witco Corp *NONPR AFFIL* mem: Assn Life Ins Counc; trust: Am Coll, Fdn Independent Higher Ed, Life Off Mgmt Assn

Alice Theresa Kane: *B* New York NY 1948 *ED* Manhattanville Coll AB 1969; NY Univ Law Sch JD 1972 *CURR EMPL* exec vp, gen couns, secy: NY Life Ins Co *CORP AFFIL* vp, secy, dir: NYLife Inc *NONPR AFFIL* mem: Am Bar Assn, Assn Life Ins Counc

Michael John McLaughlin: *B* Cambridge MA 1944 *ED* Boston Coll AB 1965; NY Univ Law Sch JD 1968 *CURR EMPL* sr vp, deputy gen couns: NY Life Ins Co *NONPR AFFIL* mem: NY Bar Assn

Carol Joan Reuter: *B* Brooklyn NY 1941 *ED* St Johns Univ BA 1962 *CURR EMPL* corp vp: NY Life Ins Co *NONPR AFFIL* mem: Conf Bd; mem corp adv comm: Am Natl Red Cross, Un Coll Fund; mem corp assocs: Un Way Am; mem natl corp adv comm: Fdn Independent Higher Ed; vchmn, mem corp adv comm: Un Way Tri-St

GIVING OFFICERS
George August William Bundschuh: dir *CURR EMPL* pres, dir: NY Life Ins Co (see above)

Lee Morgan Gammill, Jr.: dir *CURR EMPL* exec vp, dir: NY Life Ins Co (see above)

Harry George Hohn, Jr.: chmn, dir *CURR EMPL* chmn, ceo, dir: NY Life Ins Co (see above)

Celia Holtzberg: treas

Alice Theresa Kane: dir *CURR EMPL* exec vp, gen couns, secy: NY Life Ins Co (see above)

Michael John McLaughlin: secy *CURR EMPL* sr vp, deputy gen couns: NY Life Ins Co (see above)

Carol Joan Reuter: pres *CURR EMPL* corp
vp: NY Life Ins Co (see above)

APPLICATION INFORMATION

Initial Approach: *Initial Contact:* brief letter and proposal *Include Information On:* list of officers and board members, brief background information on organization, description of current program, latest annual report and audited financial statement, concise description of program for which funds are sought, current budget and funding sources, proof of tax-exempt status, and list of corporate and foundation contributors during past 12 months *Deadlines:* none; board meets in March, June, September, December

Restrictions on Giving: In general, the foundation does not make grants to individuals; public educational institutions; sectarian or religious organizations; fraternal, social, professional, athletic, or veterans organizations; seminars, conferences or trips; preschool, primary, or secondary educational institutions; endowments, memorials, or capital campaigns; organizations that are members of United Ways already supported by the foundation; or foundations that are themselves grant-making bodies.

OTHER THINGS TO KNOW

The foundation requires periodic reports from all organizations that it supports.

In recent years, foundation has primarily supported AIDS and literacy organizations.

GRANTS ANALYSIS

Total Grants: $2,475,426

Number of Grants: 439

Highest Grant: $400,000

Average Grant: $5,639

Typical Range: $250 to $10,000

Disclosure Period: 1992

Note: Recent grants are derived from a 1992 Form 990.

RECENT GRANTS

General

400,000	United Way of Tri-State, New York, NY
253,937	American Red Cross, Washington, DC
250,000	Korean American Coalition, Los Angeles, CA
250,000	Los Angeles Urban League, Los Angeles, CA
100,000	Life and Health Insurance Medical Research Fund, Washington, DC

New York Mercantile Exchange / NYMEX Charitable Foundation

Sales: $76.34 million
Employees: 375
Headquarters: New York, NY
SIC Major Group: Security & Commodity Brokers

CONTACT
Madeline Boyd
Chairman
NYMEX Charitable Foundation
4 World Trade Ctr., 8th Fl.
New York, NY 10048
(212) 938-2899

FINANCIAL SUMMARY
Recent Giving: $280,750 (1994); $279,360 (1993); $94,000 (1992)

Assets: $357,099 (1992); $323,448 (1991)

Gifts Received: $175,000 (1992)

Fiscal Note: In 1992, contributions were received from New York Mercantile Exchange.

EIN: 13-3586378

CONTRIBUTIONS SUMMARY
Typical Recipients: • *Arts & Humanities:* Community Arts, General, Libraries, Museums/Galleries • *Civic & Public Affairs:* Community Foundations, Employment/Job Training, General, Housing, Inner-City Development • *Education:* Afterschool/Enrichment Programs, Elementary Education (Public), General, Medical Education • *Environment:* General • *Health:* General • *Religion:* General • *Social Services:* Camps, Community Centers, Counseling, Day Care, Delinquency & Criminal Rehabilitation, Domestic Violence, Emergency Relief, Family Services, Food/Clothing Distribution, General, People with Disabilities, Senior Services, Shelters/Homelessness, Substance Abuse, Youth Organizations

Grant Types: emergency, general support, project, research, scholarship, and seed money

Nonmonetary Support Types: donated equipment

Geographic Distribution: grants are awarded principally near operating locations and to national organizations

Operating Locations: NY (New York)

CORP. OFFICERS
Daniel Rappaport: *CURR EMPL* chmn, dir: New York Mercantile Exchange

R. Patrick Thompson: *CURR EMPL* pres, dir: New York Mercantile Exchange

APPLICATION INFORMATION
Initial Approach: Organizations seeking support must be sponsored by a member or by staff. Submit a full proposal. Include a description of organization, amount requested, purpose of funds sought, recently audited financial statement, and proof of tax-exempt status. Also attach a copy of most recent IRS Form 990.

Restrictions on Giving: Does not support individuals.

GRANTS ANALYSIS
Total Grants: $279,360

Typical Range: $2,500 to $7,500

Disclosure Period: 1993

Note: Recent grants list provided by company in 1993.

RECENT GRANTS

General
American Cancer Society, New York, NY
Auxilliary to Bellvue Hospital, New York, NY
Camelot Family Foundation, Staten Island, NY
Juvenile Diabetes, New York, NY
National Multiple Sclerosis Society, Hawthorne, NY

New York Stock Exchange, Inc. / New York Stock Exchange Foundation, Inc.

Revenue: $320.0 million
Employees: 1,447
Headquarters: New York, NY
SIC Major Group: Security & Commodity Exchanges

CONTACT
James E. Buck
Secretary
New York Stock Exchange Foundation, Inc.
11 Wall St., 6th Fl.
New York, NY 10005
(212) 656-2060

FINANCIAL SUMMARY
Recent Giving: $500,000 (1995 est.); $410,672 (1994); $428,152 (1993)

Assets: $7,792,000 (1994); $8,644,291 (1993); $8,213,491 (1992)

Gifts Received: $300,235 (1992)

EIN: 13-3203195

CONTRIBUTIONS SUMMARY
Typical Recipients: • *Arts & Humanities:* Arts Associations & Councils, Arts Centers, Community Arts, Libraries, Museums/Galleries, Music, Performing Arts, Public Broadcasting, Theater • *Civic & Public Affairs:* Economic Policy, Municipalities/Towns, Public Policy, Safety, Urban & Community Affairs • *Education:* Business Education, Business-School Partnerships, Colleges & Universities, Economic Education, Health & Physical Education, Legal Education, Medical Education, Student Aid • *Environment:* General • *Health:* Cancer, Hospitals • *Religion:* Religious Organizations, Religious Welfare • *Social Services:* At-Risk Youth, Camps, Community Service Organizations, Day Care, Food/Clothing Distribution, People with Disabilities, Shelters/Homelessness, United Funds/United Ways, Volunteer Services, Youth Organizations

Grant Types: employee matching gifts and general support

Geographic Distribution: focus on New York City

Operating Locations: NY (New York)

CORP. OFFICERS

Richard A. Grasso: *B* 1946 *ED* Harvard Univ Advanced Mgmt Program 1985; Pace Univ BS *CURR EMPL* chmn, ceo: NY Stock Exchange *CORP AFFIL* coodinator: Natl Securities Clearing Corp; coordinator: Depository Trust Co; dir: Securities Indus Automation Corp; overseer opers: NY Futures Exchange Inc

GIVING OFFICERS

Geoffrey Cyril Bible: dir *B* Canberra Australia 1937 *ED* Chartered Inst Mgmt Accts UK; Inst Chartered Accts Australia *CURR EMPL* pres, ceo, dir: Philip Morris Cos Inc *NONPR AFFIL* trust: Am Grad Sch Intl Mgmt

James E. Buck: secy *CURR EMPL* sr vp, secy: NY Stock Exchange *CORP AFFIL* secy, dir: NY Futures Exchange Inc

John L. Clendenin: dir *B* El Paso TX 1934 *ED* Northwestern Univ BA 1955 *CURR EMPL* chmn, ceo, pres: BellSouth Corp *CORP AFFIL* dir: Capital Holding Corp, Coca-Cola Enterprises Inc, Equifax, Kroger Co, Natl Svc Indus, NY Stock Exchange, Wachovia Corp; pub rep: Springs Indus Inc *NONPR AFFIL* chmn: Comm Econ Devel; mem natl exec bd: Boy Scouts Am, Jr Achievement; natl chmn: Natl Alliance Bus; trust: Conf Bd; trust, mem conf bd: Emory Univ, Tuskegee Univ, Univ GA Fdn *CLUB AFFIL* Breakers/Breakers W, Cherokee Town & CC, Commerce, Mid Am, Piedmont Driving

Benjamin Howell Griswold IV: dir *B* Baltimore MD 1940 *ED* Princeton Univ AB 1962; Harvard Univ MBA 1967 *CURR EMPL* chmn, dir: Alex Brown & Sons Inc *CORP AFFIL* chmn, dir, mng dir: Alex Brown & Sons *CLUB AFFIL* Links, MD

Keith R. Helsby: treas *B* Scranton PA 1944 *ED* Gettysburg Coll 1966 *CURR EMPL* vp fin, dir: NY Stock Exchange *CORP AFFIL* vp fin, dir: NY Futures Exchange Inc

A. James Jacoby: chmn *B* New York NY 1939 *ED* Cornell Univ AB 1959; NY Univ MBA 1962 *CURR EMPL* mng partner: Asiel & Co *CORP AFFIL* dir: NY Stock Exchange *NONPR AFFIL* mem: Natl Assn Securities Dealers, Securities Indus Assn *CLUB AFFIL* Bond

William R. Johnston: dir *CURR EMPL* mng dir: La Branche & Co

Deryck C. Maughan: dir *B* Consett England 1947 *ED* Univ London Kings Coll BA 1969; Stanford Univ MBA 1978 *CURR EMPL* chmn, ceo: Salomon Bros *CORP AFFIL* ceo, dir: Salomon Bros Holding Co; dir: Salomon Inc

APPLICATION INFORMATION

Initial Approach: *Initial Contact:* brief letter *Include Information On:* description of program *Deadlines:* none

GRANTS ANALYSIS

Total Grants: $428,152

Number of Grants: 29*

Highest Grant: $100,000

Average Grant: $13,811*

Typical Range: $2,500 to $15,000

Disclosure Period: 1993

Note: Number of grants and average grant figures exclude $27,629 in matching gifts. Recent grants are derived from a 1993 Form 990.

RECENT GRANTS

Library

2,500	New York Public Library, New York, NY — educational

General

100,000	New York Infirmary Beekman Downtown Hospital, New York, NY — charitable
72,850	United Way Tri-State, New York, NY — charitable
36,000	Junior Achievement of New York, New York, NY — educational
11,673	Murray Bergtraum Business Advisory Council, New York, NY — educational
11,500	New York City Partnership Foundation, New York, NY — charitable

New York Times Company / New York Times Co. Foundation

Revenue: $2.35 billion
Employees: 10,100
Headquarters: New York, NY
SIC Major Group: Newspapers, Periodicals, Radio Broadcasting Stations, and Television Broadcasting Stations

CONTACT

Arthur Gelb
President
New York Times Co. Fdn.
229 W 43rd St.
New York, NY 10036
(212) 556-1091

FINANCIAL SUMMARY

Recent Giving: $4,688,434 (1993); $4,697,514 (1992); $4,924,149 (1991)

Assets: $1,811,081 (1993); $1,680,904 (1991); $2,197,159 (1990)

Fiscal Note: Contributions are primarily made through the foundation. Included in the giving figure is a matching-gifts program totalling $838,617 in 1993.

EIN: 13-6066955

CONTRIBUTIONS SUMMARY

Typical Recipients: • *Arts & Humanities:* Arts Centers, Arts Festivals, Arts Institutes, Arts Outreach, Ballet, Community Arts, Dance, Ethnic & Folk Arts, Film & Video, Historic Preservation, History & Archaeology, Libraries, Literary Arts, Museums/Galleries, Music, Opera, Performing Arts, Public Broadcasting, Theater • *Civic & Public Affairs:* Botanical Gardens/Parks, Eco-

nomic Development, Employment/Job Training, First Amendment Issues, Housing, Professional & Trade Associations, Safety, Urban & Community Affairs, Women's Affairs • *Education:* Colleges & Universities, Community & Junior Colleges, Engineering/Technological Education, Journalism/Media Education, Leadership Training, Legal Education, Literacy, Minority Education, Private Education (Precollege), Public Education (Precollege), Science/Mathematics Education, Special Education, Student Aid • *Environment:* Air/Water Quality, General, Wildlife Protection • *International:* Foreign Arts Organizations, Foreign Educational Institutions • *Science:* Science Museums • *Social Services:* Community Service Organizations, Delinquency & Criminal Rehabilitation, Food/Clothing Distribution, General, Homes, Recreation & Athletics, Senior Services, Substance Abuse, United Funds/United Ways, Volunteer Services, YMCA/YWCA/YMHA/YWHA, Youth Organizations

Grant Types: employee matching gifts, fellowship, general support, project, research, and scholarship

Note: Employee matching gift ratio: 1.5 to 1.

Geographic Distribution: concentration on greater New York area and localities served by affiliates of company; also some national and international activities

Operating Locations: AL (Florence, Gadsden, Huntsville, Tuscaloosa), AR (Ft. Smith), CA (Santa Barbara, Santa Rosa), CT (Trumbull), FL (Avon Park, Fernandina Beach, Gainesville, Lake City, Lakeland, Leesburg, Marco Island, Ocala, Palatka, Sarasota, Sebring), GA (Atlanta), IL (Moline), KY (Harlan, Madisonville, Middlesboro), LA (Houma, Opelousas, Thibodaux), MA (Billerica, Boston), ME (Kennebunk, Madison), MS (Booneville, Corinth), NC (Hendersonville, Lenoir, Lexington, Wilmington), NJ (Carlstadt, Cherry Hill, Edison), NY (New York), PA (Avoca), RI (Newport), SC (Spartanburg), TN (Dyersburg, Memphis, Tazewell)

CORP. OFFICERS

Lance Roy Primis: *B* Brooklyn NY 1946 *ED* Univ WI BA 1968 *CURR EMPL* pres, coo: NY Times Co *NONPR AFFIL* mem: Am Assn Advertising Agencies, Cosmetic Toiletry Fragrance Assn, Intl Newspaper Promotion Assn, Natl Sales Assn, Proprietary Assn; mem, chmn natl advertiser rels comm: Intl Newspaper Advertisment Execs *CLUB AFFIL* NJ Advertising

Arthur Ochs Sulzberger, Jr.: *B* New York NY 1951 *ED* Tufts Univ BA 1974; Harvard Univ Grad Sch Bus Admin 1985 *CURR EMPL* publ: NY Times Co *NONPR AFFIL* dir: NC Outward Bound Sch, Times Sq Bus Improvement District

GIVING OFFICERS

John Fellows Akers: dir *B* Boston MA 1934 *ED* Yale Univ BS 1956 *CORP AFFIL* dir: NY Times Co, PepsiCo, Springs Indus Inc *NONPR AFFIL* mem bd govs: Un Way Am; trust: CA Inst Tech, Metro Mus Art

Laura J. Corwin: secy *B* Cambridge MA 1945 *ED* Brown Univ AB 1966; Univ PA MA 1967; Univ PA PhD 1970; Yale Univ JD 1975 *CURR EMPL* corp couns, secy: NY Times Co *CORP AFFIL* secy, dir: Golf Digest/Tennis Inc, Sarasota Herald-Tribune Co *NONPR AFFIL* mem: Am Bar Assn, Am Corp Couns Assn, Assn Bar City New York, Phi Beta Kappa

Arthur Gelb: pres, dir *B* New York NY 1924 *ED* NY Univ BA 1946 *NONPR AFFIL* chmn: Intl Newspaper Coalition, NY Pub Lib; commander: Order Arts & Letters France; counc mem: Alliance New Am Musicals; mem adv bd: Columbia Journalism Review, Natl Arts Journalism Program, NY Univ Ireland House; trust: IN Jounalists Fdn *CLUB AFFIL* Century *PHIL AFFIL* trust: Arthur and Linda Gelb Charitable Foundation

Richard Lee Gelb: dir *B* New York NY 1924 *ED* Yale Univ BA 1945; Harvard Univ MBA 1950 *CURR EMPL* chmn: Bristol-Myers Squibb Co *CORP AFFIL* dir: Bessemer Securities Corp, NY Life Ins Co, NY Times Co *NONPR AFFIL* charter trust: Phillips Acad Andover; dir: Lincoln Ctr Performing Arts; mem: Bus Counc, Bus Roundtable, Counc Foreign Rels; ptnr: New York City Partnership; trust: Comm Econ Devel, NY Racing Assn; vchmn bd overseers: Meml Sloan Kettering Cancer Ctr; vchmn, trust: New York City Police Fdn *PHIL AFFIL* chmn, don: Lawrence M. Gelb Foundation; chmn, dir: Bristol-Myers Squibb Foundation Inc.

Louis Vincent Gerstner, Jr.: dir *B* Mineola NY 1942 *ED* Dartmouth Coll BA 1963; Harvard Univ MBA 1965 *CURR EMPL* chmn, ceo: Intl Bus Machines Corp *CORP AFFIL* dir: AT&T, Bristol-Myers Squibb Co, Caterpillar Inc, Jewel Cos, NY Times Co, Shearson Lehman Hutton Holdings *NONPR AFFIL* dir: Am-China Soc, Greenwich Boys Club Assn, Intl Mgmt Inst Fdn, Japan Soc, Lincoln Ctr Performing Arts; mem: Bus Counc, Bus Higher Ed Forum, Bus Roundtable, Counc Foreign Rels, Grocery Mfrs Am, Natl Cancer Adv Bd, New York City Partnership, Next Century Schs Fdn; trust: NY Pub Lib; trust, adv bd: Ctr Strategic & Intl Studies; vchmn, dir: New Am Schs Devel Corp

David L. Gorham: sr vp, treas *B* Salt Lake City UT 1932 *ED* Univ UT BS 1955; Univ CA Berkeley MBA 1968 *CURR EMPL* sr vp, cfo: NY Times Co *CORP AFFIL* treas, dir: Sarasota Herald-Tribune Co; vp, dir: Houma Courier Newspaper Corp; vp, secy, dir: Daily Leesbury Commercial Inc; vp, treas, dir: Cruising World Publs *NONPR AFFIL* mem: Am Inst CPAs, CA Soc CPAs; mem adv comm: Univ UT; mem adv comm dean bus sch: Univ CA Berkeley

Marian Sulzberger Heiskell: dir *B* New York NY 1918 *ED* Frobeleague Kindergarten Training Sch 1941 *CORP AFFIL* dir: Merck & Co Inc, NY Times Co; trust parks counc: Consolidated Edison Co NY *NONPR AFFIL* bd mgrs, exec comm: NY Botanical Garden; chmn: Counc Environment New York City; co-chmn: We Care About NY;

dir: Audubon Soc, New York City Partnership, Regional Planning Assn; mem: St Pk & Recreation Comm City New York *PHIL AFFIL* pres, dir: Sulzberger Foundation

A. Leon Higginbotham, Jr.: dir *B* Trenton NJ 1928 *ED* Purdue Univ 1944-1946; Antioch Coll BA 1949; Yale Univ LLB 1952 *CURR EMPL* of couns: Paul Weiss Rifkind Wharton & Garrison *CORP AFFIL* dir: NY Times Co *NONPR AFFIL* prof: Harvard Univ John F Kennedy Sch Govt

Walter Edward Mattson: vchmn, dir *B* Erie PA 1932 *ED* Univ ME BS 1955; Northeastern Univ AS 1959 *CORP AFFIL* dir: NY Times Co *NONPR AFFIL* dir natl counc: Northeastern Univ; mem, vchmn (production mgmt comm): Am Newspaper Publs Assn

George Barber Munroe: dir *B* Joliet IL 1922 *ED* Dartmouth Coll AB 1943; Harvard Univ LLB 1949; Oxford Univ BA 1951; Oxford Univ MA 1956 *CURR EMPL* dir: NY Life Ins Co *CORP AFFIL* dir: NY Life Ins Co, NY Times Co, Phelps Dodge Corp, Santa Fe Pacific Gold Corp *NONPR AFFIL* assoc: Am Inst Mining Metallurgical Petroleum Engrs; dir: Acad Political Sci; mem: Am Bar Assn, Counc Foreign Rels, Mining & Metallurgical Soc Am; trust: Dartmouth Coll; trust, chmn fin comm: Metro Mus Art; vchmn, dir: NY Intl Festival Arts *CLUB AFFIL* Bridgehampton, Century, River, Sky, Univ

Donald M. Stewart: dir *CORP AFFIL* dir: Campbell Soup Co, NY Times Co *NONPR AFFIL* pres, dir: Coll Entrance Examination Bd

Judith P. Sulzberger: dir *CORP AFFIL* dir: NY Times Co *PHIL AFFIL* vp, dir: Sulzberger Foundation

Cyrus Roberts Vance: dir *B* Clarksburg WV 1917 *ED* Yale Univ BA 1939; Yale Univ LLB 1942 *CURR EMPL* ptnr: Simpson Thatcher & Bartlett *CORP AFFIL* dir: Gen Dynamics Corp, NY Times Co *NONPR AFFIL* chmn: Am Ditchley Fdn; chmn, mem: Japan Soc; fellow: Am Coll Trial Lawyers; mem: Am Bar Assn, Assn Bar City New York, Counc Foreign Rels, Independent Comm Disarmament Security Issues, NY St Comm Govt Integrity, NY St Judicial Comm Minorities; trust: Aspen Inst Humanistic Studies, Mayo Fdn, NY Presbyterian Hosp

Solomon Brown Watson IV: vp *B* Salem NJ 1944 *ED* Howard Univ BA 1966; Harvard Univ JD 1971 *CURR EMPL* vp, gen couns: NY Times Co *CORP AFFIL* secy, dir: Cruising World Publs *NONPR AFFIL* dir: Agent Orange Asst Fund, Am Arbitration Assn, Jobs Youth, Legal Aid Soc, Veterans Adv Bd; mem: Am Bar Assn, Am Soc Corp Secys, Assn Bar City New York, MA Bar Assn; mem legal aff comm: Newspaper Assn Am

APPLICATION INFORMATION

Initial Approach: *Initial Contact:* brief letter *Include Information On:* description of the organization, amount requested, purpose for which funds are sought, recently audited

financial statement, proof of tax-exempt status, and other potential sources of support *Deadlines:* January or July; board of directors meets at least twice annually *Note:* The foundation discourages investment of excessive time and money in preparation of requests and proposals; simple statement of purpose, need, and fiscal condition are sufficient. Appeals for grants should be addressed to the president.

Restrictions on Giving: Does not support individuals; sectarian religious organizations; health-, drug-, or alcohol-related programs; fraternal organizations; dinners or special events; goodwill advertising; or political or lobbying groups.

OTHER THINGS TO KNOW

The company also administers the New York Times Neediest Cases Fund, which raise about $5 million annually for organizations that respond to urban needs such as hunger and homelessness.

GRANTS ANALYSIS

Total Grants: $4,688,434

Number of Grants: 430*

Highest Grant: $250,000

Average Grant: $11,715

Typical Range: $1,000 to $15,000

Disclosure Period: 1993

Note: number of grants does not include matching gifts. Recent grants are derived from a 1993 annual report.

RECENT GRANTS

Library

55,000	New York Public Library, New York, NY — $25,000 is for U.S. Newspaper Project
25,000	University of Scranton, Scranton, PA — Governor William Scranton Heritage Library
17,500	Pierpont Morgan Library, New York, NY — gallery guide and public programs for "Guttenberg and the Genesis of Printing" exhibition
15,000	Chamber Music Society of Lincoln Center, New York, NY — free student concerts at public library

General

100,000	Community Court — pilot project in Times Square area
75,000	American Museum of Natural History, New York, NY — "Electronic Newpaper" project in new Hall of Human Biology and Evolution
75,000	Fresh Air Fund, New York, NY
70,000	United Way of Tri-State, Tri-State, NY
50,000	Columbia University Graduate School of Journalism, New York, NY — project to research establishing a Ph.D. program

Nias Foundation, Henry

CONTACT
Albert J. Rosenberg
President
Henry Nias Foundation
Ste. 226
540 W Boston Post Rd.
Mamaroneck, NY 10543
(407) 969-9707

FINANCIAL SUMMARY
Recent Giving: $625,000 (fiscal 1995 est.); $625,000 (fiscal 1994); $617,500 (fiscal 1993)

Assets: $15,000,000 (fiscal 1995 est.); $15,000,000 (fiscal 1994); $15,467,434 (fiscal 1993)

EIN: 13-6075785

CONTRIBUTIONS SUMMARY
Donor(s): The foundation was incorporated in 1955 by the late Henry Nias .

Typical Recipients: • *Arts & Humanities:* Arts Institutes, Arts Outreach, Ballet, Community Arts, Film & Video, Libraries, Museums/Galleries, Music, Opera, Performing Arts, Public Broadcasting • *Civic & Public Affairs:* Clubs, General, Urban & Community Affairs • *Education:* Colleges & Universities, Medical Education, Social Sciences Education • *Health:* Clinics/Medical Centers, Geriatric Health, Health Organizations, Hospitals, Long-Term Care, Medical Rehabilitation, Single-Disease Health Associations, Speech & Hearing • *International:* International Peace & Security Issues, Missionary/Religious Activities • *Religion:* Jewish Causes, Ministries, Religious Organizations, Religious Welfare • *Science:* Science Museums • *Social Services:* Child Welfare, Community Service Organizations, Family Planning, General, People with Disabilities, Recreation & Athletics, Senior Services, Shelters/Homelessness, United Funds/United Ways, YMCA/YWCA/YMHA/YWHA, Youth Organizations

Grant Types: general support and multi-year/continuing support

Geographic Distribution: New York City only

GIVING OFFICERS
Richard J. Edelman: asst secy

Stanley Edelman, MD: chmn

Charles D. Fleischman: vp, treas

Albert J. Rosenberg: pres

William F. Rosenberg: vp, secy

Beth R. Zweibel: dir

APPLICATION INFORMATION
Initial Approach:

The foundation reports there are no special requirements for preliminary applications other than stating the nature of the activity.

The deadline for submitting proposals is August.

GRANTS ANALYSIS
Total Grants: $617,500

Number of Grants: 55

Highest Grant: $33,000

Average Grant: $11,227

Typical Range: $3,000 to $15,000

Disclosure Period: fiscal year ending November 30, 1993

Note: Recent grants are derived from a fiscal 1993 grants list.

RECENT GRANTS

Library

9,000	New York Public Library, New York, NY

General

33,000	Jewish Community Center of Bensonhurst, Bensonhurst, NY
30,000	Jewish Home and Hospital for the Aged, New York, NY
25,000	Catholic Charities, New York, NY — archdiocese of New York inner-city scholarship fund
25,000	Educational Alliance Homeless Residence Program, New York, NY
25,000	Fedcap Rehabilitation Services, New York, NY — impairment and loss of facilities

Noble Foundation, Edward John

CONTACT
Noble Smith
Executive Director
Edward John Noble Foundation
32 E 57th St.
New York, NY 10022-2513
(212) 759-4212

FINANCIAL SUMMARY
Recent Giving: $3,409,746 (1993); $3,887,032 (1992); $3,859,901 (1991)

Assets: $112,385,797 (1993); $106,708,348 (1992); $105,867,985 (1991)

EIN: 06-1055586

CONTRIBUTIONS SUMMARY
Donor(s): The foundation was established in Connecticut in 1940 by the late Edward John Noble . Successful in confectionery manufacturing and commercial broadcasting, Mr. Noble was chairman of the board of Beechnut Lifesavers, and chairman of the finance committee of American Broadcasting Company and Paramount Theaters. He created the American Broadcasting Company from National Broadcasting Company's Blue Network, which he had purchased.

Typical Recipients: • *Arts & Humanities:* Arts Associations & Councils, Arts Centers, Arts Festivals, Arts Funds, Arts Outreach, Historic Preservation, History & Archaeology, Libraries, Museums/Galleries, Music, Opera, Performing Arts • *Civic & Public Affairs:* Botanical Gardens/Parks, Economic Development, Nonprofit Management, Philanthropic Organizations, Urban & Community Affairs, Zoos/Aquariums • *Education:* Arts/Humanities Education, Colleges & Universities, Education Associations, Environmental Education, Faculty Development, Health & Physical Education, Medical Education, Minority Education, Private Education (Precollege), School Volunteerism, Science/Mathematics Education, Secondary Education (Public), Special Education • *Environment:* General, Resource Conservation, Wildlife Protection • *Health:* Cancer, Health Organizations, Hospitals, Medical Research, Medical Training, Trauma Treatment • *International:* Health Care/Hospitals, International Environmental Issues, International Relations • *Science:* Science Museums, Scientific Organizations • *Social Services:* Child Welfare, Community Centers, Counseling, Family Planning, Family Services, Senior Services, Volunteer Services, Youth Organizations

Grant Types: capital, general support, and project

Geographic Distribution: the Northeast, primarily New York; limited support elsewhere

GIVING OFFICERS
Shirley M. Crowell: secy

Frank Y. Larkin: vchmn, dir

June Noble Larkin: chmn, pres, dir *B* New York NY 1922 *ED* Sarah Lawrence Coll BA 1944 *NONPR AFFIL* chmn, trust: Juilliard Sch Music; mem: Natl Soc Colonial Dames St NY; mem bd dirs: Lincoln Ctr Performing Arts; vchmn, trust: Mus Modern Art *CLUB AFFIL* Colony New York City, Sulgrave

Howard Phipps, Jr.: dir *B* 1934 *PHIL AFFIL* trust: Vincent Astor Foundation; don: Howard Phipps Family Charitable Foundation; trust: Perkin Fund, Howard Phipps Foundation

Frank P. Piskor: dir

David S. Smith, Jr.: dir

Noble Smith: exec dir

Carroll Livingston Wainwright, Jr.: dir *B* New York NY 1925 *ED* Yale Univ AB 1949; Harvard Univ LLB 1952 *CURR EMPL* ptnr: Milbank Tweed Hadley & McCloy *CORP AFFIL* trust: US Trust Corp *NONPR AFFIL* mem: Am Bar Assn, Am Coll Trust & Estate Couns, Assn Bar City New York, NY St Bar Assn; mem gov bd: NY Commun Trust; trust: Am Mus Natural History; trust, pres: Boys Club NY; trust, vchmn: Cooper Union Advancement Science Art *CLUB AFFIL* Downtown, Maidstone, River, Union

APPLICATION INFORMATION
Initial Approach:

Applicants should send a brief letter to the foundation describing the project. The foundation reports that supporting materials are not necessary with an initial request. Additional information will be requested as needed.

There are no deadlines for applications.

All requests are reviewed and answered as soon as possible. If interested, the foundation will request further information and a meeting, if appropriate. If proposals are considered for grants, the applicants will be notified promptly of the directors' action.

Restrictions on Giving: The foundation generally does not consider support for buildings or equipment; publications, performances, films or television projects; or individuals.

PUBLICATIONS
Annual report

GRANTS ANALYSIS
Total Grants: $3,409,746

Number of Grants: 83

Highest Grant: $589,500

Average Grant: $41,081

Typical Range: $10,000 to $50,000

Disclosure Period: 1993

Note: Recent grants are derived from a 1992 Form 990.

RECENT GRANTS

Library
42,570	New York Public Library, New York, NY — Music Division's work-study project for Juilliard graduate students

General
589,500	St. Catherine's Island Foundation, Midway, GA — support for research and conservation programs
420,000	New York Zoological Society, Bronx, NY — continued support of the Wildlife Survival Center on St. Catherine's Island, GA
191,735	American Museum of Natural History, New York, NY — first year for collections management and archaeological research program
185,751	American Museum of Natural History, New York, NY — final year of Creek Indian archaeological study
150,000	Worldwatch Institute, Washington, DC

Normandie Foundation

CONTACT
Andrew E. Norman
President, Treasurer
Normandie Fdn.
147 E 48th St.
New York, NY 10017
(212) 230-9800

FINANCIAL SUMMARY
Recent Giving: $104,000 (1993); $115,200 (1991); $158,300 (1990)

Assets: $2,146,375 (1993); $2,029,409 (1991); $1,809,420 (1990)

Gifts Received: $89,828 (1993); $49,841 (1991)

Fiscal Note: In 1993, contributions were received from Andrew E. Norman.

EIN: 13-6213564

CONTRIBUTIONS SUMMARY
Donor(s): Andrew E. Norman, The Aaron E. Norman Fund

Typical Recipients: • *Arts & Humanities:* Arts Centers, Community Arts, History & Archaeology, Libraries, Museums/Galleries, Performing Arts, Public Broadcasting • *Civic & Public Affairs:* Civil Rights, General, Philanthropic Organizations, Public Policy • *Education:* Colleges & Universities, Education Funds, Legal Education • *Environment:* Air/Water Quality, General, Resource Conservation • *Health:* Hospitals • *International:* Human Rights, International Environmental Issues, International Organizations, International Peace & Security Issues, International Relations, International Relief Efforts • *Science:* Scientific Centers & Institutes, Scientific Labs, Scientific Research • *Social Services:* Child Welfare, Community Service Organizations, Emergency Relief, Family Planning, Food/Clothing Distribution, Recreation & Athletics, United Funds/United Ways, Youth Organizations

Grant Types: general support

Geographic Distribution: focus on Rockland County and New York, NY, and Barnstable County, MA

GIVING OFFICERS
Nancy Norman Lassalle: vp, secy *PHIL AFFIL* vp, dir: Norman Foundation

Andrew E. Norman: pres, treas *B* New York NY 1930 *ED* Harvard Univ BA 1951; Harvard Univ JD 1954 *PHIL AFFIL* chmn: Norman Foundation

Helen D. Norman: vp

APPLICATION INFORMATION
Initial Approach: Send brief letter of inquiry describing program. There are no deadlines.

GRANTS ANALYSIS
Total Grants: $104,000

Number of Grants: 27

Highest Grant: $25,000

Typical Range: $100 to $20,000

Disclosure Period: 1993

Note: Recent grants are derived from a 1993 Form 990.

RECENT GRANTS

Library
1,000	New York Public Library, New York, NY
500	Palisades Free Library, New York, NY

General
25,000	American Civil Liberties Union Foundation, New York, NY

20,000	Africa Fund, New York, NY
15,000	International Rescue Committee, New York, NY
10,000	International Society for Ecology and Culture, Berkeley, CA
5,500	Woods Hole Oceanographic, Woods Hole, MA

NYNEX Corporation / NYNEX Corporate Philanthropy and Foundation

Revenue: $13.3 billion
Employees: 76,164
Headquarters: New York, NY
SIC Major Group: Telephone Communications Except Radiotelephone

CONTACT
Suzanne A. DuBose
Director, Philanthropy
NYNEX Corporate Philanthropy and Foundation
1095 Avenue of the Americas, Rm. 3003
New York, NY 10036
800-360-7955

FINANCIAL SUMMARY
Recent Giving: $19,400,000 (1994 approx.); $18,400,000 (1993 approx.); $3,750,000 (1992 approx.)

Assets: $43,702,288 (1993); $42,865,110 (1992); $31,960,000 (1989)

Gifts Received: $3,000,000 (1992)

Fiscal Note: The company gives directly, through the foundation, and through other NYNEX family companies. Figures for 1993 and 1994 include foundation giving, direct corporate donations, and contributions made through major NYNEX family companies. Above figures exclude nonmonetary support. The foundation received contributions in 1992 from NYNEX Corp.

EIN: 13-3319048

CONTRIBUTIONS SUMMARY
Typical Recipients: • *Arts & Humanities:* Arts Outreach, Performing Arts, Public Broadcasting • *Civic & Public Affairs:* Business/Free Enterprise, Economic Development, Employment/Job Training, Urban & Community Affairs • *Education:* Business Education, Colleges & Universities, Economic Education, Engineering/Technological Education, Medical Education, Minority Education, Preschool Education, Science/Mathematics Education • *Health:* Health Policy/Cost Containment • *Science:* Science Exhibits & Fairs • *Social Services:* At-Risk Youth, Food/Clothing Distribution, People with Disabilities, Senior Services, United Funds/United Ways

Grant Types: employee matching gifts and project

Nonmonetary Support: $1,300,000 (1994); $75,000 (1989); $50,000 (1988)

Nonmonetary Support Types: donated products, in-kind services, and loaned employees

Geographic Distribution: company operating locations and to some national organizations

Operating Locations: MA (Boston, Lynn, Marshfield), NY (New York, Pearl River, White Plains), TN (Nashville)

CORP. OFFICERS

William Charles Ferguson: *B* Detroit MI 1930 *ED* Albion Coll BA 1952 *CURR EMPL* chmn, ceo: Nynex Corp *CORP AFFIL* dir: CPC Intl Inc, GenRe Corp, Marine Midland Banks Inc *NONPR AFFIL* chmn bd trust: Albion Coll; dir: New York City Partnership, NY St Bus Counc, Un Way Tri-St; mem: Conf Bd, NY Govs Adv Bd, NY Govs Counc Fiscal & Econ Priorities

Frederic V. Salerno: *B* New York NY 1943 *ED* Manhattan Coll BSEE 1965; Adelphi Univ MBA *CURR EMPL* vchmn fin & bus devel: NYNEX Corp *CORP AFFIL* dir: Avnet Inc, Bear Stearns Cos Inc, Orange & Rockland Utilities Inc, Viacom Inc; pres, dir: NYNEX Worldwide Svcs Group *NONPR AFFIL* dir: Long Island Philharmonic; mem: Ave Ams Assn

Ivan G. Seidenberg: *B* New York NY 1946 *ED* CUNY BS 1972; Pace Univ MBA 1980 *CURR EMPL* pres, coo: NYNEX Corp *CORP AFFIL* dir: AlliedSignal Inc, Melville Corp, Scholastic Corp, Scholastic Inc; pres, dir: Telesector Resources Group Inc *NONPR AFFIL* dir: US Telephone Assn; mem: Rockland Bus Counc

GIVING OFFICERS

Alfred F. Boschulte: mem contributions comm *B* 1943 *CURR EMPL* vp marketing: NYNEX Corp *CORP AFFIL* pres, dir: NYNEX MBL Commun Co

Geoffrey B. Cooke: exec dir, mem contributions comm *CURR EMPL* mng dir: NYNEX NY

Morrison Des. Webb: secy, dir

Suzanne A. DuBose: vp, programs

William F. Heitmann: vp, treas

Donald B. Reed: pres, dir *B* Winthrop MA 1944 *ED* VA Military Inst BA 1966 *CURR EMPL* pres, ceo: NYNEX New England *CORP AFFIL* chmn: US First; dir: Paul Revere Corp, Telesector Resources Group Inc

Casimir S. Skrzypczak: mem contributions comm *B* New York NY 1941 *ED* Villanova Univ 1963; Hofstra Univ 1970 *CURR EMPL* pres, dir: NYNEX Sci & Tech Inc *CORP AFFIL* chmn: Alliance Telecommun Indus Solutions; dir: Battery Ventures, Bell Commun Res; vp: Telesector Resources Group Inc *NONPR AFFIL* dir: Polytech Univ

Matthew J. Stover: chmn contributions comm *B* Palo Alto CA 1955 *ED* Yale Univ BA 1976; Univ VA 1987 *CURR EMPL* pres: NYNEX Info Resources Co *NONPR AFFIL* dir: Computer & Commun Indus Assn, Legal Aid Soc, Natl Assn Mfrs, Yellow Page Publs Assn; mem: Am Mgmt Assn, Conf Bd, Counc Excellence Govt, Intl Assn Bus Commun, Natl Advertising Review Bd, Natl Comm US-China Rels, Arthur W Page Soc,

Pub Rels Soc Am; mem svcs policy adv comm: US Trade Rep; trust: Comm Econ Devel *CLUB AFFIL* Yale

APPLICATION INFORMATION

Initial Approach: *Initial Contact:* proposal, following established guidelines *Include Information On:* amount requested; action proposed, methods of implementation, and expected results; ability to meet community needs; timetable; budget; qualifications of person responsible for project; anticipated cooperation with other community organizations; proposed method of accountability; other sources of support; proof of tax-exempt status; copy of Form 990; copy of annual budget and audited financial statements from the previous two years; organizational information, including board of directors and corporate officers; evidence of competent leadership, active participation by governing board, and effective use of volunteers; list of current contributors and amounts; description of the organization, its history, and its areas of growth, as well as a statement of objectives and an overview of long-range plans *Deadlines:* none

Restrictions on Giving: Does not support individuals; organizations that are not tax-exempt; religious organizations, unless the particular program will benefit a large portion of a community and does not duplicate the work of other agencies; political causes, candidates, organizations, or campaigns; organizations that discriminate on the basis of race, sex, or religion; fraternal organizations; organizations whose primary purpose is to influence legislation; special occasion or goodwill advertising; endowment; or operating expenses of organizations supported by the United Way.

OTHER THINGS TO KNOW

Contact addresses for NYNEX family companies are:

New England Staff Director
125 High St., Rm. 1215
Boston, MA 02110
New York Staff Director
1095 Avenue of the Americas, Rm. 4126
New York, NY 10036

PUBLICATIONS

Corporate responsibility report

GRANTS ANALYSIS

Total Grants: $2,752,962

Number of Grants: 51

Highest Grant: $462,930

Average Grant: $53,980

Typical Range: $30,000 to $100,000

Disclosure Period: 1993

Note: Above figures are for the NYNEX Foundation only. Recent grants are derived from a 1993 Form 990.

RECENT GRANTS

General

462,930	National Science Teachers Association, Washington, DC — scholarships
400,000	United Way
100,000	National Park Foundation, New York, NY — national park service rangers
85,000	Lesley College, Cambridge, MA — Project Best
65,000	Global Kids — learning component

O'Connor Foundation, A. Lindsay and Olive B.

CONTACT

Donald F. Bishop II
President
A. Lindsay and Olive B. O'Connor Foundation
PO Box D
Hobart, NY 13788
(607) 538-9248
Note: Foundation accepts phone calls on Monday, Wednesday, and Friday from 8 a.m. to 12 p.m.

FINANCIAL SUMMARY

Recent Giving: $1,400,000 (1995 est.); $1,350,770 (1994 approx.); $1,500,480 (1993)

Assets: $37,500,000 (1995 est.); $37,600,800 (1994); $35,500,800 (1993)

EIN: 16-6063485

CONTRIBUTIONS SUMMARY

Donor(s): The foundation was established in 1965 by the late Olive B. O'Connor .

Typical Recipients: • *Arts & Humanities:* Arts Associations & Councils, Arts Centers, Arts Institutes, Historic Preservation, History & Archaeology, Libraries, Museums/Galleries, Music, Theater • *Civic & Public Affairs:* Botanical Gardens/Parks, Economic Development, Housing, Law & Justice, Municipalities/Towns, Philanthropic Organizations, Professional & Trade Associations, Safety, Zoos/Aquariums • *Education:* Agricultural Education, Community & Junior Colleges, Education Funds, Education Reform, Elementary Education (Private), Health & Physical Education, Legal Education, Medical Education, Public Education (Precollege), Student Aid • *Environment:* General, Resource Conservation • *Health:* Hospices, Hospitals, Single-Disease Health Associations • *Religion:* Religious Organizations • *Social Services:* Community Centers, Community Service Organizations, Day Care, People with Disabilities, United Funds/United Ways, Youth Organizations

Grant Types: capital, endowment, general support, operating expenses, project, and scholarship

Geographic Distribution: focus on Delaware County, NY, and contiguous rural counties in upstate New York, which include Broome, Chenango, Greene, Otsego, Schoharie, Sullivan, and Ulster counties

GIVING OFFICERS

Donald F. Bishop II: pres, mem adv comm

Robert L. Bishop: secy, mem adv comm

Robert L. Bishop II: chmn, mem adv comm

Charlotte Bishop Hill: vchwm, mem adv comm

William J. Murphy: mem adv comm

Eugene E. Peckham: mem adv comm *CURR EMPL* ptnr: Hinman Howard & Kattell *PHIL AFFIL* secy: Dr. G. Clifford and Florence B. Decker Foundation

APPLICATION INFORMATION
Initial Approach:
Contact the foundation for an application form.

In addition to the information required on the application, the foundation requires applicants to provide proof of tax-exempt status under IRS section 501(c)(3) or proof that the applicant is a unit of the government. It is preferred, but not required, to have sketches or drawings submitted on legal size or smaller paper. In almost all cases, a site visit will be arranged after the full application has been filed. Grant proposals for less than $10,000 must meet the conditions that follow: the focus shall be on rural projects, recipient of a grant cannot re-apply for three years for the same project, and there is a required dollar-for-dollar match, which is raised after the date of the grant approval letter from the foundation.

Deadlines are the first day of every month; advisory committee meets monthly to consider grants less than $5,000 and requires those applications to be filed by the first of each month.

Board usually meets in June and October. Applicants are usually notified within two weeks after semiannual meetings.

Restrictions on Giving: As a general rule, the foundation will not make grants for meeting annual operating expenditures or retiring existing debts, and prefers to make grants of a non-recurring nature.

PUBLICATIONS
Program policy statement, grant application

GRANTS ANALYSIS
Total Grants: $1,764,377

Number of Grants: 132

Highest Grant: $600,000

Average Grant: $13,367

Typical Range: $5,000 to $15,000

Disclosure Period: 1992

Note: Recent grants are derived from a 1992 Form 990.

RECENT GRANTS
General
600,000	Village of Hobart, Hobart, NY — rebuilding sewer system
150,000	Village of Hobart, Hobart, NY — water and sewer project
75,000	Broome Community College, Binghamton, NY — health science center
37,200	Delaware County Planning Board, Delhi, NY — TPAS programs
35,000	Catskill Center for Conservation and Development, Arkville, NY — fulltime Main Street manager

Ohrstrom Foundation

CONTACT
George F. Ohrstrom
President
Ohrstrom Foundation
540 Madison Ave.
New York, NY 10022
(212) 759-5380

FINANCIAL SUMMARY
Recent Giving: $900,000 (fiscal 1994 approx.); $900,000 (fiscal 1993 approx.); $910,260 (fiscal 1992)

Assets: $24,000,000 (fiscal 1994 approx.); $24,000,000 (fiscal 1993 approx.); $23,419,252 (fiscal 1992)

EIN: 54-6039966

CONTRIBUTIONS SUMMARY
Donor(s): The foundation was incorporated in 1953 by members of the Ohrstrom family.

Typical Recipients: • *Arts & Humanities:* Arts Centers, Libraries, Museums/Galleries • *Civic & Public Affairs:* Business/Free Enterprise, Municipalities/Towns, Philanthropic Organizations, Urban & Community Affairs, Zoos/Aquariums • *Education:* Agricultural Education, Colleges & Universities, Education Funds, Elementary Education (Private), Private Education (Precollege), Public Education (Precollege), Religious Education, Science/Mathematics Education • *Environment:* General • *Health:* Hospices, Hospitals, Medical Research, Single-Disease Health Associations • *International:* International Peace & Security Issues • *Religion:* Churches • *Social Services:* Animal Protection, Child Welfare, Community Centers, Community Service Organizations, Counseling, People with Disabilities, Recreation & Athletics, Substance Abuse, Youth Organizations

Grant Types: capital, endowment, matching, multiyear/continuing support, operating expenses, and seed money

Geographic Distribution: nationally, with a focus on Virginia

GIVING OFFICERS
Magalen Ohrstrom Bryant: trust *B* 1928 *CORP AFFIL* chmn: Tara Wildlife Mgmt Svcs; dir: Carlisle Cos, Dover Corp, O'Sullivan Corp

Palma Cifu: treas

George F. Ohrstrom: pres

George Lewis Ohrstrom, Jr.: chmn, dir *B* 1928 *ED* Princeton Univ 1950 *CURR EMPL* ptnr: GL Ohrstrom & Co *CORP AFFIL* dir: Burnley Corp, Carlisle Cos, Dover Corp,

Harrow Products; vp, dir: Chronicle Horse, Harrow Corp, Harrow Indus, Vistan Corp; vp, secy: Leach Corp *NONPR AFFIL* mem founding comm: Marion du Pont Scott Esquire Med Ctr *PHIL AFFIL* pres: Little River Foundation

APPLICATION INFORMATION
Initial Approach:
Applicants should send a written proposal to the foundation.

The proposal should include a concise description of the project and the applying organization's tax identification number.

Proposals should be submitted by the end of May.

The foundation will generally make decisions on proposals by the end of June, and will not contact organizations if a project has been denied funding.

Restrictions on Giving: The foundation does not make loans, or support individuals, deficit financing, scholarships, fellowships, research, special projects, conferences, or publications.

GRANTS ANALYSIS
Total Grants: $910,260

Number of Grants: 123

Highest Grant: $206,000

Average Grant: $5,773*

Typical Range: $1,000 to $6,000

Disclosure Period: fiscal year ending May 31, 1992

Note: The average grant figure excludes the highest grant of $206,000. Recent grants are derived from a fiscal 1992 grants list.

RECENT GRANTS
Library
5,000	National Sporting Library, Middleburg, VA

General
206,000	Little River Foundation, The Plains, VA
150,000	Hill School Capital Campaign
124,000	Little River Foundation, The Plains, VA
30,000	International Cancer Alliance
25,000	Greater Yellowstone Coalition, Bozeman, MT

Olin Foundation, F. W.

CONTACT
Lawrence W. Milas
President
F. W. Olin Foundation
780 Third Ave., Ste. 3403
New York, NY 10017
(212) 832-0508
Note: Applicants also must send a copy of the application letter to William B. Horn, vice president, at the foundation's Minneapolis office, 821 Marquette Avenue, 2700 Foshay Tower, Minneapolis, MN 55402, (612) 341-2581.

FINANCIAL SUMMARY

Recent Giving: $20,500,000 (1995 est.); $20,105,000 (1994 approx.); $9,652,215 (1993)

Assets: $306,700,000 (1995 est.); $305,705,598 (1994 approx.); $317,180,977 (1993)

EIN: 13-1820176

CONTRIBUTIONS SUMMARY

Donor(s): The F. W. Olin Foundation was established in New York in 1938 by Franklin W. Olin , and was funded entirely by Mr. Olin and his wife, Mary Olin. Mr. Olin, who died in 1953, founded the Olin Corporation, a large manufacturing and processing firm.

Typical Recipients: • *Arts & Humanities:* Libraries • *Education:* Business Education, Colleges & Universities, Science/Mathematics Education

Grant Types: capital and general support

Geographic Distribution: national; no specific geographic restrictions

GIVING OFFICERS

William B. Horn: vp, dir

Lawrence William Milas: pres, dir *B* Milwaukee WI 1935 *ED* Babson Coll BSBA 1958; Columbia Univ LLB 1963 *CURR EMPL* ptnr, of couns: Baer Marks & Upham *NONPR AFFIL* mem: Am Bar Assn, Assn Bar City New York, NY St Bar Assn *CLUB AFFIL* Northport YC, Princeton *PHIL AFFIL* vp: George D. Smith Fund

William B. Norden, Esq.: secy, counc, dir *PHIL AFFIL* secy, treas, dir: Samuel and Rae Eckman Charitable Foundation

William J. Schmidt: treas, dir

APPLICATION INFORMATION

Initial Approach:

Applications should be in letter form, and not more than five pages. All applications should be addressed to Lawrence W. Milas, president, at the New York City office, with a copy directed to William B. Horn, vice president, at the Minneapolis, MN, office.

The letter should describe the proposed building including its size, cost, the reasons it is needed, and the programs it will house. The goals, enrollment, academic quality, and financial condition, of the applying institution should be described, as well as the expected impact of the building.

Although detailed plans are not required, the program and cost estimates for the proposed facility should be fully developed including construction, loose furnishings and equipment, and architect's fees. Estimated gross square feet of the building and a description of any special architectural features should also be included.

Applications may be submitted in January or September. Only one application per calendar year will be accepted.

The foundation selects a small number of proposals from the applications filed in that year and examines and studies these proposals. Those who are not selected may reapply. All applicants will be notified of their status by March of the following year. It is possible that the only foundation response to those applicants who meet the guidelines will be a brief acknowledgement. Institutions within the foundation's guidelines may be granted a meeting. The foundation discourages requests for meetings between November 1 and January 31 with representatives of institutions which have submitted grant applications.

Restrictions on Giving: Grants are not made for additions to and renovations of existing buildings (unless under the special grants policy); to repay indebtness incurred to construct buildings; physical education facilities; student centers; administrative space; social service buildings; institutions whose survival is questionable; schools which clearly have no difficulty in funding their building needs from other sources; institutions which have not attempted or succeeded in gaining a satisfactory level of financial support from their alumni, trustees, and friends in annual fund drives and capital campaigns; requests for immediate grants; institutions which require faculty members to espouse a particular religious doctrine or position; and institutions which require students to accept or adhere to a particular religious belief or practice. The foundation does not make grants when the costs are shared with any other donor; it will only make grants for the total cost of new facilities.

The foundation considers cost to be all expenses associated with constructing and equipping the building within the area bounded by a perimeter line five feet out from the building's foundation, as well as the architect's fees. Landscaping, extension of utility lines beyond five feet from the building, land acquisition costs, the cost of demolishing existing buildings, and endowment to maintain the new building are not costs included in the grant amount.

OTHER THINGS TO KNOW

The largest grant to date has been $6.3 million. In addition, emphasis is placed on buildings for undergraduate use; however, the foundation will consider proposals for graduate facilities.

The foundation generally makes annual commitments to support two new buildings.

PUBLICATIONS

Statement of grant policies and procedures, which includes a list of recent foundation grants

GRANTS ANALYSIS

Total Grants: $9,652,215

Number of Grants: 10

Highest Grant: $4,085,000

Average Grant: $965,222

Typical Range: $100,000 to $1,600,000

Disclosure Period: 1993

Note: Recent grants are derived from a 1993 grants list.

RECENT GRANTS

Library

125,715	Drury College, Springfield, MO — library building construction
5,000	Foundation Center, New York, NY — general purposes

General

4,085,000	Alfred University, Alfred, NY — business administration, building construction
1,658,000	DePauw University, Greencastle, IN — science building construction
1,457,000	Connecticut College, New London, CT — science building construction
1,051,500	Harvey Mudd College, Claremont, CA — science building construction
970,000	Denison University, Granville, OH — math and physical science building construction

Osborn Charitable Trust, Edward B.

CONTACT

Howard Feller
Trust Officer
Edward B. Osborn Charitable Trust
c/o U.S. Trust Co. of New York
114 W 47th St.
New York, NY 10038
(212) 852-1000

FINANCIAL SUMMARY

Recent Giving: $214,250 (fiscal 1993); $207,050 (fiscal 1991); $236,255 (fiscal 1990)

Assets: $4,827,108 (fiscal 1993); $4,222,024 (fiscal 1991); $3,769,886 (fiscal 1990)

EIN: 13-6071296

CONTRIBUTIONS SUMMARY

Donor(s): Edward B. Osborn

Typical Recipients: • *Arts & Humanities:* Arts Centers, Ballet, Dance, Libraries, Museums/Galleries, Music, Opera, Performing Arts • *Civic & Public Affairs:* Botanical Gardens/Parks, General, Zoos/Aquariums • *Education:* Colleges & Universities, Private Education (Precollege) • *Environment:* General • *Health:* Cancer, Diabetes, Hospices, Hospitals, Medical Research, Nursing Services, Single-Disease Health Associations • *International:* International Relations • *Religion:* Churches • *Social Services:* Family Planning, Food/Clothing Distribution, Substance Abuse, Youth Organizations

Grant Types: general support

Geographic Distribution: focus on NY and FL

GIVING OFFICERS

U.S. Trust Company of New York: trust

APPLICATION INFORMATION
Initial Approach: Send brief letter of inquiry describing program or project. There are no deadlines.

GRANTS ANALYSIS
Total Grants: $214,250

Number of Grants: 50

Highest Grant: $20,000

Typical Range: $1,000 to $17,250

Disclosure Period: fiscal year ending October 31, 1993

Note: Recent grants are derived from a fiscal 1993 Form 990.

RECENT GRANTS

Library

10,000	New York Public Library, New York, NY

General

20,000	Planned Parenthood Association, New York, NY
17,250	Central Park Conservancy, New York, NY
10,000	Margaret Thatcher Foundation, Washington, DC
10,000	Memorial Sloan-Kettering Cancer Center, New York, NY
10,000	Orentrich Foundation

Osceola Foundation

CONTACT
Walter Beinecke, Jr.
Director
Osceola Foods Employee Educational Fund, Inc
c/o Osceola Foods, Inc
51 E 42nd St., Ste. 1601
New York, NY 10017
(212) 697-9840

FINANCIAL SUMMARY
Recent Giving: $146,300 (1993); $128,034 (1992); $181,131 (1991)

Assets: $2,544,090 (1993); $2,538,019 (1992); $2,643,040 (1991)

Gifts Received: $2,303 (1991); $5,000 (1990)

EIN: 13-6094234

CONTRIBUTIONS SUMMARY
Donor(s): Katherine Sperry Beinecke Trust

Typical Recipients: • *Arts & Humanities:* General, Historic Preservation, History & Archaeology, Libraries, Museums/Galleries, Performing Arts, Theater • *Civic & Public Affairs:* Urban & Community Affairs • *Education:* Arts/Humanities Education, Colleges & Universities, Elementary Education (Private), Private Education (Precollege) • *Environment:* General, Resource Conservation • *Health:* Hospitals • *Religion:* Churches • *Social Services:* Crime Prevention, Delinquency & Criminal Rehabilitation

Grant Types: general support and scholarship

Geographic Distribution: national, with focus on MA

GIVING OFFICERS
Perry Ashley: secy, dir

Deborah B. Beale: dir

Walter Beinecke III: dir

Walter Beinecke, Jr.: dir *B* 1918 *CURR EMPL* chmn: Nantucket Electric Co *CORP AFFIL* dir: Context Indus

Paul Billings: pres

Barbara B. Collar: treas, dir

Harry Keatts: dir

Dalton Lynch: secy

Ann B. Oliver: pres, dir

APPLICATION INFORMATION
Initial Approach: Send brief letter of inquiry describing program or project. Deadline is prior to end of year.

GRANTS ANALYSIS
Total Grants: $146,300

Number of Grants: 15

Highest Grant: $26,000

Typical Range: $50 to $24,700

Disclosure Period: 1993

Note: Recent grants are derived from a 1993 Form 990.

RECENT GRANTS

General

26,000	Nantucket Cottage Hospital, Nantucket, MA
24,700	University of Florida Foundation, Gainesville, FL
20,000	Bonny Doon Presbyterian Church, Bonny Doon, CA
19,000	Mannes College, New York, NY
15,000	Mt. Vernon College, Washington, DC

Overbrook Foundation

CONTACT
Sheila McGoldrick
Corresponding Secretary
Overbrook Foundation
521 Fifth Ave., Rm. 1501
New York, NY 10175
(212) 661-8710

FINANCIAL SUMMARY
Recent Giving: $3,294,253 (1993); $3,167,357 (1992); $2,844,139 (1991)

Assets: $77,467,208 (1993); $76,113,154 (1992); $73,027,739 (1991)

Gifts Received: $28,796 (1993); $537,700 (1992); $26,700 (1991)

Fiscal Note: The estate of Helen G. Altschul contributes to the foundation.

EIN: 13-6088860

CONTRIBUTIONS SUMMARY
Donor(s): The Overbrook Foundation was incorporated in New York in 1948 by Mr. Frank Altschul, Mrs. Frank Altschul and their three children. Frank Altschul was the chairman of General American Investors Company, a New York City investment company now chaired by his son, Arthur Altschul.

Typical Recipients: • *Arts & Humanities:* Arts Associations & Councils, Arts Centers, Arts Festivals, Arts Institutes, Dance, Historic Preservation, History & Archaeology, Libraries, Museums/Galleries, Music, Opera, Public Broadcasting, Theater • *Civic & Public Affairs:* Botanical Gardens/Parks, Civil Rights, Community Foundations, Economic Development, Economic Policy, Employment/Job Training, First Amendment Issues, General, Law & Justice, Legal Aid, Nonprofit Management, Philanthropic Organizations, Professional & Trade Associations, Public Policy, Safety, Urban & Community Affairs, Zoos/Aquariums • *Education:* Arts/Humanities Education, Colleges & Universities, Education Associations, Education Funds, International Exchange, Legal Education, Literacy, Minority Education, Private Education (Precollege), Social Sciences Education • *Environment:* General, Resource Conservation • *Health:* AIDS/HIV, Emergency/Ambulance Services, Health Organizations, Hospices, Hospitals, Medical Research, Nursing Services, Single-Disease Health Associations • *International:* Health Care/Hospitals, Human Rights, International Environmental Issues, International Organizations, International Peace & Security Issues, International Relations, International Relief Efforts • *Religion:* Churches, Jewish Causes, Religious Welfare • *Social Services:* Animal Protection, Child Welfare, Community Centers, Community Service Organizations, Counseling, Crime Prevention, Emergency Relief, Family Planning, Food/Clothing Distribution, Homes, People with Disabilities, Recreation & Athletics, Senior Services, Shelters/Homelessness, Substance Abuse, United Funds/United Ways, Volunteer Services, Youth Organizations

Grant Types: endowment, general support, multiyear/continuing support, project, and scholarship

Geographic Distribution: national, with emphasis on New York metropolitan area and Connecticut

GIVING OFFICERS
Arthur Goodhart Altschul: pres, treas, dir *B* New York NY 1920 *ED* Yale Univ AB 1943 *CURR EMPL* ltd ptnr: Goldman Sachs Group LP *CORP AFFIL* chmn, dir: Gen Am Investors Co; dir: Assoc Dry Goods Corp, Boswell Energy Corp, Sunbelt Energy Corp, Wicat Sys *NONPR AFFIL* chmn: Intl Fdn Art Res; chmn bd trusts: Barnard Coll; fellow: Metro Mus Art; mem: Counc Foreign Rels; mem distribution comm: NY Commun Trust; mem gov bd: Yale Univ Art Gallery; mem natl bd: Smithsonian Assocs *CLUB AFFIL* Century CC, Cosmopolitan, Downtown *PHIL AFFIL* vp, dir: Edith and Herbert Lehman Foundation; trust: John L. Weinberg Foundation, Whitehead Foundation; dir: New York Community Trust

Emily H. Altschul: dir

Stephen F. Altschul: dir

Julie Graham: dir

Michelle C. Graham: dir

Robert C. Graham, Jr.: dir

Frances L. Labaree: dir

Robert Labaree: dir

Margaret A. Lang: vp, dir

M. Sheila McGoldrick: corresponding secy

APPLICATION INFORMATION
Initial Approach:

Applicants should send a letter to the foundation.

The letter should give a description of the project, the organization and its activities, and should include a copy of the IRS determination letter of tax-exempt status.

Applications are accepted any time. The board usually meets in April and November.

Notification of a decision will be given within eight weeks.

Restrictions on Giving: No grants are given to individuals.

GRANTS ANALYSIS
Total Grants: $3,294,253

Number of Grants: 272

Highest Grant: $270,000

Average Grant: $12,111

Typical Range: $1,000 to $50,000

Disclosure Period: 1993

Note: Recent grants are derived from a 1993 Form 990.

RECENT GRANTS

General

270,000	Barnard College, New York, NY
126,760	Planned Parenthood of New York City, New York, NY
104,500	Choate Rosemary Hall, Wallingford, CT
102,800	Middlebury College, Middlebury, VT
100,000	Fund for Free Expression

PaineWebber / PaineWebber Foundation

Revenue: $2.9 billion
Employees: 12,784
Parent Company: PaineWebber Group, Inc.
Headquarters: New York, NY
SIC Major Group: Holding Companies Nec and Security Brokers & Dealers

CONTACT
Elaine Conti
Trustee
PaineWebber Foundation
1285 Ave. of the Americas
New York, NY 10019
(212) 713-2808

FINANCIAL SUMMARY
Recent Giving: $415,000 (1994 approx.); $330,683 (1993); $298,750 (1992)

Assets: $14,209,325 (1993); $11,966,513 (1992); $8,486,634 (1991)

Gifts Received: $1,941,091 (1993); $2,870,885 (1992); $1,873,040 (1991)

Fiscal Note: Company gives through the foundation. In 1993, major contributions were received from Wellfleet Financial ($448,156) and Ensco ($965,986).

EIN: 04-6032804

CONTRIBUTIONS SUMMARY
Typical Recipients: • *Arts & Humanities:* Arts Associations & Councils, Arts Centers, Libraries, Museums/Galleries, Music, Theater • *Civic & Public Affairs:* Community Foundations, General, Municipalities/Towns, Women's Affairs • *Education:* Business Education, Colleges & Universities, Education Associations, Education Reform, Legal Education, Minority Education, Private Education (Precollege), Student Aid • *Environment:* General • *Health:* AIDS/HIV, Cancer, Children's Health/Hospitals, Diabetes, Emergency/Ambulance Services, Hospitals, Medical Research, Single-Disease Health Associations, Transplant Networks/Donor Banks • *International:* International Development, International Relief Efforts • *Religion:* Churches, Dioceses, Jewish Causes, Ministries, Religious Organizations, Religious Welfare • *Social Services:* Animal Protection, At-Risk Youth, Child Welfare, Community Service Organizations, Counseling, Day Care, Family Services, Food/Clothing Distribution, General, Shelters/Homelessness, Substance Abuse, YMCA/YWCA/YMHA/YWHA, Youth Organizations

Grant Types: general support and research

Geographic Distribution: focus on New York, NY

Operating Locations: MA (Boston), MD (Columbia), NY (New York), TX (Houston)

CORP. OFFICERS
John A. Bult: *CURR EMPL* chmn: PaineWebber Intl

Joseph J. Grano, Jr.: *B* Hartford CT 1948 *CURR EMPL* pres: PaineWebber Inc

Donald Baird Marron: *B* Goshen NY 1934 *ED* Baruch Coll 1956 *CURR EMPL* chmn, ceo, dir: PaineWebber Group Inc *CORP AFFIL* chmn, ceo: PaineWebber Inc; co-fdr, dir: Data Resources *NONPR AFFIL* dir: Bus Comm Arts, New York City Partnership; mem: Counc Foreign Rels, Govs Sch & Bus Alliance Task Force, Pres Commn Arts & Humanities; mem bd overseers: Meml Sloan Kettering Cancer Ctr; vchmn: Mus Modern Art *CLUB AFFIL* River *PHIL AFFIL* trust: Donald B. & Catherine C. Marron Foundation; dir, mem investment comm: Charles A. Dana Foundation

GIVING OFFICERS
Elaine Conti: trust

Paul B. Guenther: trust *B* New York NY 1940 *ED* Fordham Univ 1962; Columbia Univ 1964 *CURR EMPL* pres: PaineWebber Inc *CORP AFFIL* dir: Globalome Plus Fund, PaineWebber Group Inc, PaineWebber Mutual Funds, PaineWebber Trust Co

Donald Baird Marron: trust *CURR EMPL* chmn, ceo, dir: PaineWebber Group Inc *PHIL AFFIL* trust: Donald B. & Catherine C. Marron Foundation; dir, mem investment comm: Charles A. Dana Foundation (see above)

APPLICATION INFORMATION
Initial Approach: *Initial Contact:* send brief typewritten letter of inquiry on organization's letterhead *Include Information On:* a description of organization, amount requested, and proof of tax-exempt status *Deadlines:* December 1

GRANTS ANALYSIS
Total Grants: $330,683

Number of Grants: 71

Highest Grant: $100,000

Average Grant: $4,658

Typical Range: $1,000 to $10,000

Disclosure Period: 1993

Note: Recent grants are derived from a 1993 Form 990.

RECENT GRANTS

Library

25,000	New York Public Library, NY
8,333	Rafael Hernandez Colon Library

General

100,000	United Negro College Fund, New York, NY
30,000	Inner-City Schools of Archdiocese of New York, New York, NY
15,000	Pediatric AIDS Foundation, Los Angeles, CA
10,000	Center for Addiction and Substance Abuse
10,000	Frost Valley YMCA, Claryville, NY

Paley Foundation, William S.

CONTACT
Patrick S. Gallagher
Executive Director
William S. Paley Foundation
1 E 53rd St., Ste. 1400
New York, NY 10022
(212) 888-2520

FINANCIAL SUMMARY
Recent Giving: $2,900,000 (1995 est.); $2,810,640 (1994); $2,714,000 (1993)

Assets: $70,500,000 (1995 est.); $70,550,000 (1994 approx.); $70,426,498 (1993)

Gifts Received: $108,691 (1992); $474,139 (1991); $47,615,299 (1990)

Fiscal Note: In 1991 and 1992, gifts were received from the estate of William S. Paley.

EIN: 13-6085929

CONTRIBUTIONS SUMMARY
Donor(s): The foundation was established in 1936 by the late William S. Paley (1901-

1990), the founder and former chairman of CBS. He bequeathed more than $40 million to the foundation from his estimated personal fortune of $460 million.

Mr. Paley, a native of Chicago, began his college education at the University of Chicago but earned his bachelor's of science degree from the University of Pennsylvania in 1922. He also received honorary PhDs from Ithaca College, University of Southern California, Adelphi University, Bates College, University of Pennsylvania, Brown University, Pratt Institute, Dartmouth College, and Columbia University, where he served as a trustee from 1950 to 1973.

Mr. Paley lived in New York City, home to two of his favorite charities, the Museum of Broadcasting, which he founded in 1976, and the Museum of Modern Art, where he served as chairman from 1972 to 1985. In his will, he left his valuable private art collection to the museum.

Mr. Paley, divorced from his first wife, married Barbara (Babe) Cushing in 1947. Barbara Paley died in 1978. Jeffrey Hearst and Hillary Hearst Byers are his two children from his first marriage to the former Dorothy Hart Hearst. He has two stepchildren by his second marriage, Amanda Ross and Stanley Mortimer, III, and two children, Kate C. Paley and William C. Paley, who currently serve as officers of the foundation.

Typical Recipients: • *Arts & Humanities:* Arts Associations & Councils, Dance, Libraries, Museums/Galleries • *Civic & Public Affairs:* Professional & Trade Associations, Public Policy, Zoos/Aquariums • *Education:* Colleges & Universities, International Studies, Literacy, Medical Education • *Health:* Hospices, Hospitals • *International:* Foreign Arts Organizations, Foreign Educational Institutions • *Religion:* Religious Organizations • *Social Services:* Youth Organizations

Grant Types: general support, multiyear/continuing support, professorship, and scholarship

Geographic Distribution: focus on New York, NY

GIVING OFFICERS
Patrick S. Gallagher: exec dir *NONPR AFFIL* vp, treas: Mus TV Radio *PHIL AFFIL* trust: Goldie Paley Foundation

George Joseph Gillespie III: dir *B* New York NY 1930 *ED* Georgetown Univ AB 1952; Harvard Univ LLB 1955 *CURR EMPL* ptnr: Cravath Swaine & Moore *CORP AFFIL* dir: Fund Am, Washington Post Co *NONPR AFFIL* dir, chmn emeritus: Natl Multiple Sclerosis Soc; mem: Am Bar Assn, Assn Bar City New York; pres, dir: Boys & Girls Club Madison Sq; secy: Mus Broadcasting, Mus TV Radio; trust, treas: Hoover Inst *CLUB AFFIL* Am YC, Century, Falmouth CC, Prouts Neck CC, Winged Foot GC *PHIL AFFIL* asst secy, asst treas, trust: John M. and Mary A. Joyce Foundation; pres, trust: Pinkerton Foundation; secy, dir: Arthur Ross Foundation; mem adv comm: Edward E. Ford Foundation; treas, secy, trust, mem exec comm: John M. Olin Foundation; trust: J & AR Foundation

Sidney W. Harl: vp, dir

Henry Alfred Kissinger: chmn, dir *B* Fuerth Germany 1923 *ED* Harvard Univ AB 1950; Harvard Univ MA 1952; Harvard Univ PhD 1954 *CURR EMPL* fdr, chmn: Kissinger Assocs *NONPR AFFIL* mem: Am Acad Arts & Sci, Am Political Sci Assn, Counc Foreign Rels, Phi Beta Kappa; trust: Metro Mus Art *CLUB AFFIL* Bohemian San Francisco, Century, Metro DC, River New York City *PHIL AFFIL* dir: CBS Foundation

Arthur L. Liman: dir *B* New York NY 1932 *ED* Harvard Univ AB 1954; Yale Univ LLB 1957 *CURR EMPL* ptnr: Paul Weiss Rifkind Wharton & Garrison *CORP AFFIL* dir: Continental Grain Co, Equitable Life Assurance Soc US *NONPR AFFIL* chmn: Mayors Comm Appointments; chmn, dir: Legal Action Ctr; dir: Harvard Univ; fellow: Am Bar Fdn, Am Coll Trial Lawyers; mem: Am Bar Assn, Harvard Univ Lawyers Comm Civil Rights Under Bd Overseers, NY Bar Assn; mem, exec comm: Assn Bar City New York

John S. Minary: dir *PHIL AFFIL* trust: Goldie Paley Foundation

Daniel L. Mosley: secy, treas *PHIL AFFIL* mem adv bd: Thomas J. Watson Foundation

Kate C. Paley: dir

William Cushing Paley: vp, dir *B* 1948 *CURR EMPL* pres, vp, dir: VM Devel *CORP AFFIL* exec vp, dir: Texwipe Co

Phillip A. Raspe: asst secy, asst treas

APPLICATION INFORMATION
Initial Approach:

Proposals should be made in writing.

The foundation reports that no particular application form is required, but full financial information should be disclosed.

There are no deadlines for forwarding proposals.

Restrictions on Giving: The foundation does not make grants to individuals.

GRANTS ANALYSIS
Total Grants: $1,550,000

Number of Grants: 4

Highest Grant: $1,300,000

Average Grant: $83,333*

Typical Range: $5,000 to $100,000

Disclosure Period: 1992

Note: The average grant figure excludes a single grant of $1,300,000. Recent grants are derived from a 1992 Form 990.

RECENT GRANTS

Library
30,000   New York Public Library, New York, NY — general program

General
50,000   Jerusalem Foundation, New York, NY — Paley Art Center

Palisades Educational Foundation

CONTACT
Ralph F. Anthony
President
Palisades Educational Fdn.
665 Fifth Ave., 2nd Fl.
New York, NY 10022
(212) 688-5151

FINANCIAL SUMMARY
Recent Giving: $198,000 (1993); $175,500 (1992); $280,000 (1991)

Assets: $4,981,847 (1993); $5,053,371 (1992); $4,970,706 (1991)

EIN: 51-6015053

CONTRIBUTIONS SUMMARY
Donor(s): Prentice-Hall

Typical Recipients: • *Arts & Humanities:* Arts Associations & Councils, General, Libraries, Music • *Civic & Public Affairs:* Native American Affairs • *Education:* Arts/Humanities Education, Business Education, Colleges & Universities, Community & Junior Colleges, Education Associations, Education Funds, Medical Education, Minority Education, Private Education (Precollege), Student Aid • *Health:* Cancer, Clinics/Medical Centers, Hospitals, Medical Research, Prenatal Health Issues, Single-Disease Health Associations • *Religion:* Religious Welfare • *Science:* Science Museums • *Social Services:* At-Risk Youth, Child Welfare, Community Service Organizations, Family Services, Homes, Recreation & Athletics, Scouts, Senior Services, Shelters/Homelessness, Volunteer Services, Youth Organizations

Grant Types: multiyear/continuing support, operating expenses, and scholarship

Geographic Distribution: focus on areas of company operations, with emphasis on northern NJ, NY, and southern CT

GIVING OFFICERS
Frederick W. Anthony: secy

Ralph F. Anthony: pres, dir

Gerald J. Dunworth: treas

Colin Gunn: dir *PHIL AFFIL* asst secy, gov: Lucy Pang Yoa Chang Foundation

Donald A. Schaefer: vp, dir

APPLICATION INFORMATION
Initial Approach: Send brief letter of inquiry describing program or project. There are no deadlines.

GRANTS ANALYSIS
Total Grants: $198,000

Number of Grants: 32

Highest Grant: $15,000

Typical Range: $1,000 to $10,000

Disclosure Period: 1993

Note: Recent grants are derived from a 1993 Form 990.

RECENT GRANTS

General

15,000	Johns Hopkins Medical Center, Baltimore, MD — for scholarship aid for the School of Medicine
12,500	Colgate University, Hamilton, NY — for general education fund
10,000	Contact, We Care, Westfield, NJ — for general support
10,000	Covenant House, New York, NY — for aid for homeless children
10,000	Cushing Academy, Ashburnham, MA — for Native American Preparatory School

Palisano Foundation, Vincent and Harriet

CONTACT
Charles J. Palisano
Trustee
Vincent and Harriet Palisano Fdn.
PO Box 538
Orchard Park, NY 14127
(716) 832-2010

FINANCIAL SUMMARY
Recent Giving: $210,000 (fiscal 1994); $206,500 (fiscal 1993); $191,482 (fiscal 1992)

Assets: $4,171,380 (fiscal 1994); $4,198,138 (fiscal 1992); $4,079,846 (fiscal 1991)

EIN: 16-6052186

CONTRIBUTIONS SUMMARY
Donor(s): the late Vincent H. Palisano, the late Harriet A. Paisano

Typical Recipients: • *Arts & Humanities:* Libraries, Public Broadcasting • *Civic & Public Affairs:* General • *Education:* Colleges & Universities, General, Private Education (Precollege), Religious Education, Secondary Education (Private), Secondary Education (Public), Special Education, Student Aid • *Religion:* Churches, Dioceses, Religious Organizations, Religious Welfare • *Social Services:* Senior Services

Grant Types: scholarship

Geographic Distribution: focus on the Buffalo, NY, ar

GIVING OFFICERS
James M. Beardsley: trust

Charles J. Palisano: trust

Joseph S. Palisano: trust

APPLICATION INFORMATION
Initial Approach: Send brief letter of inquiry describing program or project. There are no deadlines.

GRANTS ANALYSIS
Total Grants: $210,000

Number of Grants: 36

Highest Grant: $55,000

Typical Range: $1,500 to $20,000

Disclosure Period: fiscal year ending May 31, 1994

Note: Recent grants are derived from a fiscal 1994 Form 990.

RECENT GRANTS

General

55,000	Canisius College, Buffalo, NY — for Palisano Religious Vocation program
20,000	Canisius College, Buffalo, NY — for added funding Palisano Religious Vocational program
20,000	Hilbert College, Hamburg, NY — for equipment
20,000	Trocaire College, Buffalo, NY — for equipment
10,000	Diocese of Buffalo, Buffalo, NY — for Daybreak Television productions to produce half-hour video

Park Foundation

CONTACT
Park Fdn.
Terrace Hill
Ithaca, NY 14850
(607) 272-9020

FINANCIAL SUMMARY
Recent Giving: $49,227 (1993); $63,823 (1991)

Assets: $5,761,122 (1993); $5,953,986 (1991)

Gifts Received: $830,000 (1991)

Fiscal Note: In 1991, contributions were received from RHP, Inc.

EIN: 16-6071043

CONTRIBUTIONS SUMMARY
Typical Recipients: • *Arts & Humanities:* Arts Associations & Councils, Libraries, Museums/Galleries • *Civic & Public Affairs:* Business/Free Enterprise, Economic Development, General • *Education:* Colleges & Universities, Education Funds, General, Private Education (Precollege) • *Health:* Cancer, Diabetes, Eyes/Blindness, Hospitals, Medical Rehabilitation • *International:* Foreign Arts Organizations, Missionary/Religious Activities • *Religion:* Churches, Missionary Activities (Domestic) • *Science:* Scientific Labs • *Social Services:* Community Service Organizations, United Funds/United Ways

Grant Types: general support

Geographic Distribution: primarily Ithaca, NY, and Chattanooga, TN, areas; some grants in the South

GIVING OFFICERS
Adelaide P. Gomer: dir

Dorothy D. Park: pres, dir *CURR EMPL* chmn, secy, dir: Park Communications

APPLICATION INFORMATION
Initial Approach: Send a brief letter of inquiry and a full proposal. Include a description of organization and purpose of funds sought. There are no deadlines.

GRANTS ANALYSIS
Total Grants: $49,227

Number of Grants: 31

Highest Grant: $6,600

Typical Range: $100 to $6,500

Disclosure Period: 1993

Note: Recent grants are derived from a 1993 Form 990.

RECENT GRANTS

Library

1,000	Tompkins County Public Library, Ithaca, NY

General

6,600	United Way, Chattanooga, TN
6,500	United Way of Tompkins County, Ithaca, NY
5,000	Boyce Thompson Institute for Plant Research, Ithaca, NY
5,000	United Way Services, Richmond, VA
3,250	First Presbyterian Church, Ithaca, NY

Parshelsky Foundation, Moses L.

CONTACT
Tony B. Berk
Trustee
Moses L. Parshelsky Fdn.
26 Ct. St.
Brooklyn, NY 11242
(718) 875-8883

FINANCIAL SUMMARY
Recent Giving: $240,350 (1993); $240,300 (1992); $278,350 (1991)

Assets: $5,846,433 (1993); $5,680,659 (1992); $5,581,088 (1991)

EIN: 11-1848260

CONTRIBUTIONS SUMMARY
Donor(s): Moses L. Parshelsky

Typical Recipients: • *Arts & Humanities:* Arts Associations & Councils, Arts Institutes, Dance, Libraries, Museums/Galleries, Music, Performing Arts • *Civic & Public Affairs:* General, Philanthropic Organizations • *Education:* Colleges & Universities, Religious Education • *Health:* Cancer, Clinics/Medical Centers, Geriatric Health, Health Funds, Hospitals, Medical Research, Respiratory, Single-Disease Health Associations • *Religion:* Jewish Causes, Religious Organizations • *Social Services:* Camps, Community Centers, Community Service Organizations, Family Planning, Family Services, Food/Clothing Distribution, People with Disabilities, Recreation & Athletics, Senior Services,

YMCA/YWCA/YMHA/YWHA, Youth Organizations

Grant Types: general support

Geographic Distribution: focus on Brooklyn and Queens, NY

GIVING OFFICERS

Tony B. Berk: trust

Josephine B. Krinsky: trust

Robert Daniel Krinsky: trust *B* Brooklyn NY 1937 *ED* Antioch Coll BA 1957 *CURR EMPL* pres: Segal (Martin E) Co *NONPR AFFIL* corporator: Columbia Univ Sch Social Work; mem: Am Academy Actuaries, Assn Private Pension Welfare Plans, Natl Dance Inst, Soc Actuaries; trust: Antioch Univ

APPLICATION INFORMATION

Initial Approach: Send a brief letter of inquiry. Include a description of organization, amount requested, purpose of funds sought, recently audited financial statement, and proof of tax-exempt status. Deadline is May 31.

Restrictions on Giving: Limited to Brooklyn and Queens in New York, NY.

GRANTS ANALYSIS

Total Grants: $240,350

Number of Grants: 51

Highest Grant: $27,500

Typical Range: $1,000 to $20,000

Disclosure Period: 1993

Note: Recent grants are derived from a 1993 Form 990.

RECENT GRANTS

Library
2,000	New York Public Library, New York, NY — in support of Jewish Division

General
27,500	Brookdale Hospital and Medical Center, Brookdale, NY
25,000	Metropolitan Jewish Geriatric Center, Brooklyn, NY — for upkeep and improvement of Parshelsky Foundation
17,500	VISIONS/Services for the Blind and Visually Impaired, New York, NY — year-end
10,000	Brookdale Hospital and Medical Center, Brookdale, NY — surgery department
10,000	Camp Vacamas Association, New York, NY — children's camp activities

Penguin Books USA, Inc. / Worthy Causes Foundation

Sales: $275.0 million
Employees: 1,000
Parent Company: Pearson plc
Headquarters: New York, NY
SIC Major Group: Printing & Publishing

CONTACT
Derek Smith
Executive Vice President
Penguin Books USA, Inc.
375 Hudson St.
New York, NY 10014
(212) 366-2000
Note: The Worthy Causes Foundation is located at 702 South Michigan St., South Bend, IN 46601. The contact is Rev. Dave Schlauer, President, Ave Maria Press.

FINANCIAL SUMMARY
Recent Giving: $6,023 (fiscal 1992); $8,001 (fiscal 1991); $1,600 (fiscal 1990)

Assets: $515,637 (fiscal 1992); $445,353 (fiscal 1991); $313,737 (fiscal 1990)

Gifts Received: $50,000 (fiscal 1992); $114,625 (fiscal 1991)

Fiscal Note: Figures above for foundation only. Company primarily gives directly; however, it does not disclose contributions figures. In fiscal 1992, contributions were received from The Distributors.

EIN: 35-1704631

CONTRIBUTIONS SUMMARY
Typical Recipients: • *Arts & Humanities:* Arts Festivals, Arts Outreach, Community Arts, Libraries • *Civic & Public Affairs:* Community Foundations, General, Philanthropic Organizations, Urban & Community Affairs, Women's Affairs • *Education:* Afterschool/Enrichment Programs, General • *Health:* General

Grant Types: general support

Nonmonetary Support Types: donated products

Geographic Distribution: nationally

Operating Locations: NY (New York)

CORP. OFFICERS
Marvin Brown: *CURR EMPL* pres: Penguin Books USA

Peter Mayer: *B* London England 1936 *ED* Columbia Coll grad; Oxford Univ grad *CURR EMPL* ceo, chmn: Penguin Books USA

Derek Smith: *CURR EMPL* exec vp: Penguin Books USA

GIVING OFFICERS
Bernard Kilbride: vp

Michael Raymond: secy, treas

Rev. Dave Schlauer, SSC: pres

Ray Turner: exec dir

APPLICATION INFORMATION
Initial Approach: Send a full proposal. Include description of the organization and project, type of books requested, and how

they will be used. Attach a recently audited financial statement and proof of tax-exempt status.

Restrictions on Giving: Does not support individuals or political or lobbying groups.

OTHER THINGS TO KNOW
Company primarily donates excess inventory. The Worthy Causes Foundation is a small foundation established by one of Penguin's distributors.

GRANTS ANALYSIS
Total Grants: $6,023

Number of Grants: 4

Highest Grant: $2,272

Typical Range: $750 to $2,272

Disclosure Period: fiscal year ending January 31, 1992

Note: Recent grants are derived from a fiscal 1992 Form 990. Grants represent Worthy Causes Foundation contributions only.

RECENT GRANTS

General
2,272	Basic Adult Education
2,000	Cleveland Center for Research in Child Development, Cleveland, OH
1,000	Multicultural Publishers Exchange
750	South Bend Indiana School Corporation, S. Bend, IN

Pfizer, Inc. / Pfizer Foundation

Revenue: $8.28 billion
Employees: 40,500
Headquarters: New York, NY
SIC Major Group: Pharmaceutical Preparations, Medicinals & Botanicals, Industrial Organic Chemicals Nec, and Surgical & Medical Instruments

CONTACT
Paula Luff
Associate Manager, Corp. Philanthropy
Pfizer Inc
235 E 42nd St.
New York, NY 10017-5755
(212) 573-1758

FINANCIAL SUMMARY
Recent Giving: $41,000,000 (1994); $29,400,000 (1993); $22,739,960 (1992)

Assets: $6,900,870 (1992); $3,589,470 (1990); $2,986,631 (1989)

Fiscal Note: Figures include all types of giving. Company gives directly (about 34% of total contributions), through the foundation (about 2%), and nonmonetarily (about 63%). Each division is responsible for its respective contributions budget.

EIN: 13-6083839

CONTRIBUTIONS SUMMARY
Typical Recipients: • *Arts & Humanities:* Arts Associations & Councils, Arts Centers, Arts Funds, Dance, Historic Preservation,

History & Archaeology, Libraries, Museums/Galleries, Music, Opera, Performing Arts, Public Broadcasting, Theater • *Civic & Public Affairs:* Botanical Gardens/Parks, Business/Free Enterprise, Civil Rights, Economic Development, Economic Policy, Employment/Job Training, Housing, Law & Justice, Legal Aid, Municipalities/Towns, Professional & Trade Associations, Public Policy, Safety, Urban & Community Affairs, Women's Affairs, Zoos/Aquariums • *Education:* Business Education, Business-School Partnerships, Colleges & Universities, Community & Junior Colleges, Economic Education, Education Associations, Education Funds, Education Reform, Elementary Education (Private), Elementary Education (Public), Engineering/Technological Education, Faculty Development, International Exchange, International Studies, Legal Education, Literacy, Medical Education, Minority Education, Private Education (Precollege), Public Education (Precollege), Science/Mathematics Education, Student Aid • *Environment:* General, Resource Conservation • *Health:* Adolescent Health Issues, Emergency/Ambulance Services, Geriatric Health, Health Organizations, Hospices, Hospitals, Medical Rehabilitation, Medical Research, Mental Health, Single-Disease Health Associations, Transplant Networks/Donor Banks • *International:* Foreign Arts Organizations, Foreign Educational Institutions, Health Care/Hospitals, International Development, International Peace & Security Issues, International Relations • *Science:* Science Museums, Scientific Centers & Institutes, Scientific Labs • *Social Services:* Child Welfare, Community Centers, Community Service Organizations, Counseling, Delinquency & Criminal Rehabilitation, Emergency Relief, Family Services, Food/Clothing Distribution, People with Disabilities, Recreation & Athletics, Senior Services, Shelters/Homelessness, Substance Abuse, United Funds/United Ways, Volunteer Services, Youth Organizations

Grant Types: capital, employee matching gifts, general support, multiyear/continuing support, operating expenses, professorship, project, research, and scholarship

Note: Employee matching gift ratio: 1 to 1.

Nonmonetary Support: $25,900,000 (1994); $9,351,860 (1992); $317,378 (1990)

Nonmonetary Support Types: donated equipment, donated products, in-kind services, and workplace solicitation

Note: Nonmonetary contributions include donations of medicine and equipment to emergency relief and disaster aid. See "Other Things To Know" for more details.

Geographic Distribution: nationally and in communities where Pfizer and its subsidiaries operate; some emphasis on New York City

Operating Locations: CO (Boulder), CT (Groton), IN (Terre Haute), MN (Minnetonka), NJ (Rutherford), NY (Brooklyn, New York), PR (Barceloneta), TN (Memphis)

Note: Also operates major facilities worldwide in the United Kingdom, France, Germany, Japan, Brazil, India, Ireland, Mexico, Argentina, Spain, and South Korea, and Puerto Rico.

CORP. OFFICERS
Edward Cushing Bessey: *B* Portland ME 1934 *ED* Dartmouth Coll AB; Dartmouth Coll MBA *CURR EMPL* vchmn: Pfizer Inc *CORP AFFIL* dir: GP Fin Corp; pres, dir: US Pharmaceuticals Group *NONPR AFFIL* bd dir: Un Svc Org Metro NY, Un Way Tri-St; mem natl adv comm: Agency Health Care Policy Res *CLUB AFFIL* Woodway

C. L. Clemente: *CURR EMPL* sr vp corp aff: Pfizer Inc

Terence Joseph Gallagher: *B* New York NY 1934 *ED* Manhattan Coll BA 1955; Harvard Univ JD 1958 *CURR EMPL* vp corp gov, asst secy: Pfizer Inc *CORP AFFIL* secy, dir: Adforce Inc, Quigley Co *NONPR AFFIL* dir: Am Soc Corp Secys, Calvary Hosp Fund; mem: NY Bar Assn; mem, chmn corp counc comm: Am Bar Assn; trust: Bus Adv Counc Fed Reports

James Richard Gardner: *B* Wellsville NY 1944 *ED* US Military Acad BS 1966; Princeton Univ 1968; Long Island Univ MBA 1977; Princeton Univ PhD 1977; US Army War Coll 1989 *CURR EMPL* vp corp investor rels: Pfizer Inc *NONPR AFFIL* chmn: Natl Eagle Scout Assn New York City; colonel: USAR; dir: Boy Scouts Am Greater NY Counc; head: US Army Political & Military Aff Div; mem: N Am Soc Corp Planning, Phi Kappa Phi, Planning Forum; mem adv comm: Princeton Univ Dept Astrophysical Sci; mem adv counc: Princeton Univ Ctr Intl Studies; mem, dir: W Point Soc NY; mem faculty: US Army Command Gen Staff Coll

Henry A. McKinnell: *B* 1942 *CURR EMPL* cfo, exec vp: Pfizer Inc

William Campbell Steere, Jr.: *B* Ann Arbor MI 1936 *ED* Stanford Univ BA 1959; Univ CA Santa Barbara *CURR EMPL* chmn, pres, ceo: Pfizer Inc *CORP AFFIL* dir: CT Mutual Life Ins Co, Fed Reserve Bank NY, Minerals Techs, Texaco Inc *NONPR AFFIL* chmn: Pharmaceutical Mfrs Assn; dir: Bus Counc; mem: Am Soc Corp Execs, US Counc Intl Bus; trust: NY Botanical Garden *CLUB AFFIL* NY YC, Univ *PHIL AFFIL* dir: Connecticut Mutual Life Foundation

GIVING OFFICERS
Terence Joseph Gallagher: secy, dir *CURR EMPL* vp corp gov, asst secy: Pfizer Inc (see above)

James Richard Gardner: vp *CURR EMPL* vp corp investor rels: Pfizer Inc (see above)

Kevin Keating: treas *CURR EMPL* treas, dir: Pfizer Overseas Inc

Robert Albert Wilson: pres *B* Jamestown NY 1936 *ED* Colgate Univ BA 1959; Sch Advanced Intl Studies (Italy) 1960; Johns Hopkins Univ MA 1961 *CURR EMPL* vp pub aff: Pfizer Inc *NONPR AFFIL* chmn adv comm: Fdn Higher Ed; dir: Natl Health Counc; exec comm: Religion Am Life; mem: Am Acad Political Sci, Phi Beta Kappa, Pub Rels Soc Am; steering comm: Pharmacists Mfg Assn Pub Aff *CLUB AFFIL* Colgate, Riverside YC

APPLICATION INFORMATION
Initial Approach: *Initial Contact:* brief letter or proposal *Include Information On:* description of the organization; amount requested; purpose for which funds are sought; recently audited financial statement or annual report; list of board members, trustees, and officers; other corporate supporters; proof of tax-exempt status *Deadlines:* none; contributions committee meets regularly to consider proposals

Restrictions on Giving: In 1994, the foundation reported that it is currently not accepting applications for funding. All requests should be directed to the company's corporate philanthropy programs.

Does not support individuals; veterans, political, fraternal, labor, or sectarian religious organizations; anti-business organizations; private foundations; organizations not tax-exempt; or independent agencies that duplicate work of United Way member agencies.

Both the company and the foundation only consider applicants meeting requirements of Internal Revenue Code Section 501(c)(3); foundation requires that applicants also meet requirements of Section 509(a)(1), (2), or (3).

OTHER THINGS TO KNOW
Generally, the company sponsors local organizations in company operating communities.

Gives special consideration to programs at which employees volunteer.

Disaster aid generally dispensed through established international relief organizations. Contact operating divisions for information on nonmonetary support, and contact the corporate office for product donations.

GRANTS ANALYSIS
Total Grants: $41,000,000

Typical Range: $1,000 to $15,000

Disclosure Period: 1994

Note: Grants analysis includes grants paid through the foundation and the company. Recent grants are derived from a 1994 partial grants list.

RECENT GRANTS
General
150,000   United Negro College Fund, New York, NY

Pforzheimer Foundation, Carl and Lily

CONTACT
Carl H. Pforzheimer III
President
Carl and Lily Pforzheimer Foundation
650 Madison Ave., 23rd Fl.
New York, NY 10022
(212) 223-6500

FINANCIAL SUMMARY
Recent Giving: $2,003,057 (1993); $1,473,498 (1992); $2,800,719 (1991)

Assets: $38,969,688 (1993); $37,816,271 (1992); $37,766,466 (1991)

EIN: 13-5624374

CONTRIBUTIONS SUMMARY

Donor(s): The foundation was established in 1942 by Carl H. Pforzheimer. Many members of the family serve as officers or directors of the foundation.

Typical Recipients: • *Arts & Humanities:* Arts Associations & Councils, Arts Centers, Arts Institutes, Community Arts, Dance, Film & Video, Historic Preservation, Libraries, Literary Arts, Museums/Galleries, Music, Opera, Performing Arts, Public Broadcasting, Theater, Visual Arts • *Civic & Public Affairs:* Community Foundations, Professional & Trade Associations, Public Policy, Urban & Community Affairs • *Education:* Arts/Humanities Education, Colleges & Universities, Community & Junior Colleges, Education Associations, General, Literacy, Private Education (Precollege), Secondary Education (Public) • *Health:* Clinics/Medical Centers, Emergency/Ambulance Services, Hospitals, Nursing Services • *International:* Foreign Arts Organizations, International Affairs • *Science:* Scientific Organizations • *Social Services:* Child Welfare, Community Service Organizations

Grant Types: general support

Geographic Distribution: national, with a focus on New York, NY

GIVING OFFICERS

Nancy P. Aronson: dir

Richard Watrous Couper: dir *B* Binghamton NY 1922 *ED* Hamilton Coll AB 1947; Harvard Univ AM 1948 *CORP AFFIL* dir: Security Mutual Life Ins Co; trust: Episcopal Divinity Sch, Equitable Funds, Hudson River Trust *NONPR AFFIL* charter trust: Hamilton Coll; mem: Am Historical Assn, Org Am Historians, Phi Beta Kappa; mem, trust: NY St Historical Assn; pres emeritus: New York City Pub Library, Woodrow Wilson Natl Fellowship Fdn *CLUB AFFIL* Century Assn, Ft Schuyler, Harvard, Lotos, Nassau, Pretty Brook Tennis, Sadaquada GC *PHIL AFFIL* chmn, trust: Link Foundation

Anthony L. Ferranti: comptr

George L. K. Frelinghuysen: asst treas, dir

Mary Kitabjian: asst secy

Carl Howard Pforzheimer III: pres, treas, dir *B* 1936 *ED* Harvard Univ MBA 1963 *CURR EMPL* Carl H Pforzheimer & Co *NONPR AFFIL* chmn bd, dir: Visiting Nurse Svc NY

Carl Howard Pforzheimer, Jr.: hon chmn, dir *B* New York NY 1907 *ED* Harvard Univ AB 1928; Harvard Univ MBA 1930 *CURR EMPL* sr ptnr: Pforzheimer & Co (Carl H) *CORP AFFIL* pres, dir: Petroleum & Trading Corp *NONPR AFFIL* counc mem: Rockefeller Univ; hon dir: Harvard Univ Alumni Assn; hon fellow: Signet Soc; hon life bd mem: Natl Civic League; hon trust: Boys Club NY, Horace Mann Sch, Mt Sinai Med Ctr; mem: Am Assn Commun Jr Colls, NY Chamber Commerce Indus; mem emeritus: NY St Bd Regents; treas: Citizens Forum

Self Govt *CLUB AFFIL* Ambassador, Army & Navy, Century Assn, City Midday, Grolier, Harvard, Union Boat, Union Interaille, Willoughby CC

Carol K. Pforzheimer: dir

Gary M. Pforzheimer: dir

Martin Franklin Richman: secy *B* Newark NJ 1930 *ED* St Lawrence Univ BA 1950; Harvard Univ LLB 1953 *CURR EMPL* mem firm: Lord Day & Lord Barrett Smith *NONPR AFFIL* fellow: Am Bar Fdn, NY Bar Fdn; mem: Am Bar Assn, Am Law Inst, Assn Bar City New York, Fed Bar Assn, NY County Lawyers Assn, NY St Bar Assn; vchmn, trust: St Lawrence Univ

Alison A. Sherman: dir

APPLICATION INFORMATION
Initial Approach:

Send full outline of the project.

There is no formal application form, but proposals should include financial information.

There are no deadlines for submitting proposals.

The board meets quarterly in April, June, October, and December. Notification usually occurs following the meeting.

Restrictions on Giving: The foundation does not make grants to individuals or for bricks and mortar projects.

GRANTS ANALYSIS
Total Grants: $2,003,057

Number of Grants: 36

Highest Grant: $400,000

Average Grant: $55,640

Typical Range: $20,000 to $100,000

Disclosure Period: 1993

Note: Recent grants are derived from a 1993 Form 990.

RECENT GRANTS

Library
98,465	New York Public Library, New York, NY
50,000	Library Foundation of Martin County, Stuart, FL

General
400,000	Radcliffe College, Cambridge, MA
234,500	Mt. Sinai Medical Center, New York, NY
100,000	Bank Street College of Education, New York, NY
100,000	Harvard University, Cambridge, MA
100,000	Henry Street Settlement, New York, NY

Phipps Foundation, Howard

CONTACT
A. Power, Jr.
Howard Phipps Fdn.
c/o Bessemer Trust Co.
630 Fifth Ave.
New York, NY 10111

FINANCIAL SUMMARY
Recent Giving: $1,689,000 (fiscal 1993); $1,656,500 (fiscal 1991); $2,292,805 (fiscal 1990)

Assets: $7,101,000 (fiscal 1993); $6,633,254 (fiscal 1991); $6,527,862 (fiscal 1990)

Gifts Received: $1,528,545 (fiscal 1993); $1,528,545 (fiscal 1991); $1,528,545 (fiscal 1990)

Fiscal Note: In fiscal 1993, contributions were received from Harriett Phipps Charitable Trust.

EIN: 22-6095226

CONTRIBUTIONS SUMMARY
Donor(s): the late Harriet Phipps

Typical Recipients: • *Arts & Humanities:* Historic Preservation, Libraries, Museums/Galleries, Music • *Civic & Public Affairs:* Botanical Gardens/Parks, Economic Development, Zoos/Aquariums • *Education:* Colleges & Universities, Private Education (Precollege), Secondary Education (Public) • *Environment:* General, Resource Conservation, Wildlife Protection • *Health:* Long-Term Care • *International:* Missionary/Religious Activities • *Religion:* Churches • *Science:* Science Museums • *Social Services:* Animal Protection, Family Planning, Food/Clothing Distribution, Scouts, Youth Organizations

Grant Types: general support

Geographic Distribution: focus on New York, NY

GIVING OFFICERS
Bessemer Trust Co: trust

Howard Phipps, Jr.: trust *B* 1934 *PHIL AFFIL* dir: Edward John Noble Foundation; trust: Vincent Astor Foundation; don: Howard Phipps Family Charitable Foundation; trust: Perkin Fund

Anne Phipps Sidamon-Eristoff: trust *B* New York NY 1932 *ED* Bryn Mawr Coll BA 1954 *NONPR AFFIL* dir: Am Mus Natural History, Greenacre Fdn, Highland Falls Pub Library, Mus Hudson Highlands; dir-at-large: Black Rock Forest Consortium; dir, secy: US Conservation Fdn, World Wildlife Fund *PHIL AFFIL* don: Howard Phipps Family Charitable Foundation, Howard Phipps Family Charitable Foundation *CLUB AFFIL* Century Assn, Colony, Cosmopolitan, Knickerbocker, Long Island Wyandarch, Natl Soc Colonial Dames, Racquet & Tennis

APPLICATION INFORMATION
Initial Approach: Send brief letter of inquiry describing program or project. There are no deadlines.

GRANTS ANALYSIS
Total Grants: $1,689,000

Number of Grants: 49

Highest Grant: $350,000

Typical Range: $5,000 to $25,000

Disclosure Period: fiscal year ending June 30, 1993

Note: Recent grants are derived from a fiscal 1993 Form 990.

RECENT GRANTS

Library

25,000	Harvard University Library, Cambridge, MA
25,000	Pierpont Morgan Library, New York, NY
10,000	Highland Falls Public Library, Highland Falls, NY

General

350,000	American Museum of Natural History, New York, NY
350,000	New York Zoological Society, Bronx, NY
100,000	Old Westbury Gardens, Old Westbury, NY
100,000	Phipp's Community Development Corporation, New York, NY
75,000	Girl Scout Council of Greater New York, New York, NY

Piankova Foundation, Tatiana

CONTACT
Mildred Brinn
President, Treasurer, Director
Tatiana Piankova Fdn.
570 Park Ave.
New York, NY 10021
(212) 758-7764

FINANCIAL SUMMARY
Recent Giving: $123,150 (fiscal 1992); $118,700 (fiscal 1991); $109,700 (fiscal 1990)

Assets: $2,811,215 (fiscal 1992); $2,604,319 (fiscal 1991); $2,605,773 (fiscal 1990)

EIN: 13-3142090

CONTRIBUTIONS SUMMARY
Donor(s): Susan Polachek

Typical Recipients: • *Arts & Humanities:* Arts Associations & Councils, Arts Institutes, Ballet, Community Arts, Dance, Libraries, Museums/Galleries, Music, Opera, Performing Arts, Theater, Visual Arts • *Civic & Public Affairs:* General, Urban & Community Affairs • *Education:* Arts/Humanities Education, Medical Education, Private Education (Precollege) • *Health:* Cancer, Health Organizations, Hospices, Hospitals, Medical Research • *International:* Foreign Arts Organizations, Foreign Educational Institutions, International Organizations • *Religion:* Churches • *Science:* Science Museums • *Social Services:* Child Welfare, Community Service Organizations, Counseling, Family Services, People with Disabilities, Recreation & Athletics, Senior Services, Youth Organizations

Grant Types: general support

GIVING OFFICERS
Mildred Cunningham Brinn: pres, treas, dir *PHIL AFFIL* pres, treas, dir: L and L Foundation

APPLICATION INFORMATION
Initial Approach: Send a brief letter of inquiry. There are no deadlines.

GRANTS ANALYSIS
Total Grants: $123,150

Number of Grants: 35

Highest Grant: $25,000

Typical Range: $100 to $5,000

Disclosure Period: fiscal year ending July 31, 1992

Note: Recent grants are derived from a fiscal 1992 Form 990.

RECENT GRANTS

Library

200	Rogers Memorial Library

General

10,000	Lacoure School of the Arts, New York, NY
10,000	Youth Counseling League, New York, NY
9,000	Skowhegan School of Painting and Sculpture, New York, NY
5,500	National Academy of Design, New York, NY
5,500	Southampton Hospital, Southampton, NY

Porter Foundation, Mrs. Cheever

CONTACT
Alton E. Peters
Director
Mrs. Cheever Porter Fdn.
c/o Kelley, Drye and Warren
101 Pk. Ave.
New York, NY 10178

FINANCIAL SUMMARY
Recent Giving: $246,250 (fiscal 1994); $242,250 (fiscal 1993); $209,900 (fiscal 1991)

Assets: $2,829,715 (fiscal 1994); $3,049,702 (fiscal 1993); $2,952,801 (fiscal 1991)

EIN: 13-6093181

CONTRIBUTIONS SUMMARY
Typical Recipients: • *Arts & Humanities:* Arts Associations & Councils, Arts Centers, Ballet, Libraries, Museums/Galleries, Opera, Theater • *Civic & Public Affairs:* Botanical Gardens/Parks, General, Municipalities/Towns, Public Policy, Urban & Community Affairs, Zoos/Aquariums • *Education:* Colleges & Universities, Medical Education, Private Education (Precollege) • *Environment:* Air/Water Quality, General, Wildlife Protection • *Health:* Cancer, Clinics/Medical Centers, Hospitals, Prenatal Health Issues • *Religion:* Religious Welfare • *Social Services:* Animal Protection, Community Service Organizations, Homes, People with Disabilities, Youth Organizations

Grant Types: general support

Geographic Distribution: giving in MA and NY

GIVING OFFICERS
Alton E. Peters: dir

Edgar Scott, Jr.: dir

Clifford E. Starkins: dir

APPLICATION INFORMATION
Initial Approach: Send brief letter describing program. There are no deadlines.

GRANTS ANALYSIS
Total Grants: $246,250

Number of Grants: 48

Highest Grant: $85,000

Typical Range: $250 to $25,000

Disclosure Period: fiscal year ending June 30, 1994

Note: Recent grants are derived from a fiscal 1993 Form 990.

RECENT GRANTS

Library

2,000	New York Public Library, New York, NY
2,000	New York Society Library, New York, NY

General

55,000	Tufts University, Medford, MA
30,000	Goodwill Industries of Greater New York, New York, NY
10,000	Cornell University Veterinary School, Ithaca, NY
10,000	University of Pennsylvania School of Veterinary Medicine, Philadelphia, PA
9,500	Huntington Townwide Fund

Price Foundation, Louis and Harold

CONTACT
Harold Price
Chairman
Louis and Harold Price Foundation
654 Madison Ave., Ste. 2005
New York, NY 10021
(212) 753-0240
Note: Applicants may also contact Mrs. Rosemary Guidone, executive vice president, at the above address.

FINANCIAL SUMMARY
Recent Giving: $1,536,184 (1992); $1,450,661 (1991); $1,934,589 (1990)

Assets: $69,000,000 (1992 approx.); $39,316,165 (1990); $42,589,346 (1989)

EIN: 13-6121358

CONTRIBUTIONS SUMMARY
Donor(s): The Louis and Harold Price Foundation was established in 1951 by the late Louis Price and Harold Price.

Typical Recipients: • *Arts & Humanities:* Arts Associations & Councils, Libraries • *Civic & Public Affairs:* Civil Rights, First Amendment Issues, Housing, Law & Justice,

Philanthropic Organizations • *Education:* Business Education, Colleges & Universities, Religious Education • *Environment:* General • *Health:* Hospitals, Medical Rehabilitation, Medical Research, Mental Health, Single-Disease Health Associations • *International:* International Development, International Peace & Security Issues, International Relief Efforts • *Religion:* Churches, Religious Welfare, Synagogues/Temples • *Social Services:* Animal Protection, Child Welfare, Community Centers, Counseling, Emergency Relief, Food/Clothing Distribution, Senior Services, United Funds/United Ways, Youth Organizations

Grant Types: endowment, operating expenses, project, and scholarship

Geographic Distribution: primarily in metropolitan New York and Los Angeles; also in Israel

GIVING OFFICERS

Gloria W. Appel: trust

George Asch: trust

David Gerstein: trust

Rosemary Guidone: exec vp, asst treas, asst secy, trust

Harold Price: chmn, treas, trust

Pauline Price: vp, secy, trust

Linda Vitti: trust

APPLICATION INFORMATION
Initial Approach:

Prospective applicants should send a letter of inquiry or one copy of a full proposal to the foundation.

Applicants may submit proposals any time; there are no deadlines for requests.

The board generally meets in February, May, and as required. Final notification takes place in one to three months. Receipt of proposals is acknowledged, and the foundation grants interviews with applicants when deemed necessary.

Restrictions on Giving: The foundation does not give grants to individuals or for building funds.

GRANTS ANALYSIS
Total Grants: $1,536,184

Number of Grants: 126

Highest Grant: $1,011,300

Average Grant: $2,192

Typical Range: $100 to $1,000 and $10,000 to $37,000

Disclosure Period: 1992

Note: Recent grants are derived from a 1992 grants list.

RECENT GRANTS
General

1,011,300	Price Institute for Entrepreneurial Studies, New York, NY	
140,000	Israel Emergency Fund, Beverly Hills, CA	
100,000	Sara Lee Foundation, Chicago, IL	
35,000	United Jewish Fund (State of Israel Bonds), Miami, FL	

30,000	United Jewish Fund, Los Angeles, CA	

Prospect Hill Foundation

CONTACT
Constance Eiseman
Executive Director
Prospect Hill Foundation
420 Lexington Ave., Ste. 3020
New York, NY 10170-0087
(212) 370-1144

FINANCIAL SUMMARY
Recent Giving: $2,200,000 (fiscal 1995 est.); $2,080,800 (fiscal 1994); $2,111,130 (fiscal 1993)

Assets: $43,500,000 (fiscal 1994 approx.); $43,500,000 (fiscal 1993 approx.); $43,505,856 (fiscal 1992)

Gifts Received: $208,638 (fiscal 1991); $1,567,487 (fiscal 1987); $1,461,911 (fiscal 1986)

Fiscal Note: In 1987, contributions derived from trusts established by Carrie Sperry Beinecke, Frederick W. Beinecke, and William S. Beinecke. In 1989, the foundation changed its fiscal year from a calendar year to one ending June 30.

EIN: 13-6075567

CONTRIBUTIONS SUMMARY
Donor(s): The Prospect Hill Foundation was established in 1960. William S. Beinecke, the foundation's donor and president, was chairman of Sperry & Hutchinson Company of New York City. In 1983, the foundation merged with the Frederick W. Beinecke Fund, which was established by his parents, Frederick and Carrie Sperry Beinecke.

Typical Recipients: • *Arts & Humanities:* Ballet, Historic Preservation, Libraries, Museums/Galleries, Music, Theater • *Civic & Public Affairs:* Botanical Gardens/Parks, Public Policy, Women's Affairs, Zoos/Aquariums • *Education:* Colleges & Universities, Legal Education, Minority Education, Private Education (Precollege), Student Aid • *Environment:* Air/Water Quality, General, Resource Conservation, Wildlife Protection • *Health:* Emergency/Ambulance Services, Hospitals • *International:* Health Care/Hospitals, International Environmental Issues, International Peace & Security Issues, International Relations • *Religion:* Ministries • *Science:* Science Museums • *Social Services:* Family Planning

Grant Types: capital, challenge, department, general support, matching, project, and scholarship

Geographic Distribution: nationally, with emphasis on New York

GIVING OFFICERS
Robert Barletta: treas *CURR EMPL* treas, dir: Antaeus Enterprises Inc

Elizabeth G. Beinecke: vp, dir

Frederick William Beinecke: vp, dir *B* Stamford CT 1943 *ED* Yale Univ BA 1966; Univ VA JD 1972; Harvard Univ PMD 1977 *CURR EMPL* pres, dir: Antaeus Enterprises Inc *CORP AFFIL* dir: Nature Food Ctrs, RehabClinics *NONPR AFFIL* mem: Assn Bar City New York; trust: NY Zoological Soc, Phillips Academy, Trudeau Inst *CLUB AFFIL* Clove Valley, Hollenbeck, River, Sky, Yale *PHIL AFFIL* pres, dir: Sperry Fund

John B. Beinecke: vp, dir *CURR EMPL* vp, secy, dir: Antaeus Enterprises Inc *NONPR AFFIL* pres, dir: Beaumont (Vivian) Theater Inc

William S. Beinecke: don, pres, dir *B* New York NY 1914 *ED* Yale Univ BA 1936; Columbia Univ LLB 1940 *CURR EMPL* co-fdr: Casey Beinecke & Chase *CORP AFFIL* dir: Antaeus Enterprises Inc *NONPR AFFIL* chmn: Hudson River Fdn Scientific Environmental Res; mem: Counc Foreign Rels; mem bd mgrs: NY Botanical Garden *CLUB AFFIL* Baltusrol GC, Bohemian, Eastward Ho CC, Gulf Stream GC, Sky, Yale Univ *PHIL AFFIL* vp, dir: Sperry Fund

Constance Eiseman: exec dir, secy

Frances Beinecke Elston: dir

Nettie Foskett: adm

Sarah Beinecke Richardson: dir

APPLICATION INFORMATION
Initial Approach:

Letters of request (no more than three pages) should be submitted to the foundation (in duplicate) in accordance with requirements listed in the Grants and Guidelines brochure.

Letters should summarize the organization's history and goals; project for which funding is sought; contribution of the project to other work in the field or to the organization's own development; the organization's total budget and staff size; project budget; and a list of the organization's board of directors. If the foundation is interested in the proposal, more information will be requested.

Grant requests may be submitted anytime. The foundation's directors meet three or four times a year.

All material is reviewed by the executive director and one or more board members. Response generally is provided within four weeks. Whenever possible, applicants will be visited by a representative of the foundation before it acts on a proposal.

Restrictions on Giving: The foundation does not consider grants for individuals, scholarly research, or sectarian religious activities. It favors project support over general support requests. Proposals from arts, cultural, and educational institutions should be upon invitation only. The foundation requires a final narrative and financial report from each application.

Proposals for education or the arts are by invitation only.

PUBLICATIONS
Grants and guidelines brochure (should be requested before letter of request is submitted)

GRANTS ANALYSIS
Total Grants: $2,080,800

Number of Grants: 98

Highest Grant: $180,000

Average Grant: $21,226

Typical Range: $10,000 to $30,000

Disclosure Period: fiscal year ending June 30, 1994

Note: Recent grants are derived from a 1994 fiscal grants list.

RECENT GRANTS
Library
50,000	New York Botanical Garden, New York, NY — second installment of $250,000 grant for construction of a library
25,000	New York Public Library, New York, NY — toward conservation laboratory

General
100,000	New York Zoological Society Wildlife Conservation Society, Bronx, NY — fifth and sixth installments of $500,000 commitment to the Crisis Fund for Vanishing Wildlife to endow field staff positions
60,000	Yale University, New Haven, CT — first payment of $750,000 grant for the Campaign for Yale
50,000	American Museum of Natural History, New York, NY — fourth installment of $250,000 toward restoration of murals by Charles Knight
50,000	American Red Cross, Washington, DC — for relief to victims of flooding in the Midwest
50,000	American Red Cross, Washington, DC — for relief to victims of flooding in the Midwest

Prudential Securities, Inc. / Prudential Securities Foundation

Sales: $180.0 million
Employees: 16,000
Parent Company: Prudential Insurance Co. of America
Headquarters: New York, NY
SIC Major Group: Security Brokers & Dealers

CONTACT
Elizabeth A. Longley
Vice President, Corporate Affairs
Prudential Securities Foundation
One Seaport Plz.
New York, NY 10292
(212) 214-4884
Note: An alternate contact is Bruno Bissetta, Vice President and Treasurer, Prudential

Securities Foundations, 100 Gold St., New York, NY 10292.

FINANCIAL SUMMARY
Recent Giving: $890,430 (fiscal 1994); $645,948 (fiscal 1992); $446,190 (fiscal 1991)

Assets: $371,174 (fiscal 1993); $36,867 (fiscal 1992); $31,786 (fiscal 1990)

Gifts Received: $1,242,499 (fiscal 1993); $530,000 (fiscal 1989)

Fiscal Note: Company gives through the foundation only.

EIN: 13-6193023

CONTRIBUTIONS SUMMARY
Typical Recipients: • *Arts & Humanities:* Libraries, Museums/Galleries, Music, Performing Arts, Theater • *Civic & Public Affairs:* Business/Free Enterprise, Civil Rights, Economic Development, Housing, Law & Justice, Zoos/Aquariums • *Education:* Colleges & Universities, Education Associations, Literacy • *Environment:* General • *Health:* Health Organizations, Hospitals, Mental Health, Single-Disease Health Associations • *International:* International Peace & Security Issues • *Religion:* Churches, Religious Organizations, Synagogues/Temples • *Social Services:* Community Service Organizations, People with Disabilities, Senior Services, Shelters/Homelessness, United Funds/United Ways, Youth Organizations

Grant Types: emergency and general support

Nonmonetary Support Types: in-kind services

Geographic Distribution: focus on New York

Operating Locations: IL (Chicago), MA (Boston), NJ (Newark), NY (New York)

CORP. OFFICERS
Bruno George Bissetta: *B* New York NY 1934 *ED* NY Univ 1956 *CURR EMPL* first vp: Prudential Securities Inc *NONPR AFFIL* mem: Am Inst CPAs, Natl Assn Accts

Howard Atwood Knight: *B* Providence RI 1942 *ED* Williams Coll BA 1963; Yale Univ JD 1966 *CURR EMPL* pres: Prudential Securities Inc *CORP AFFIL* chmn, ceo, pres: Avalon Corp; dir: First Australia Fund, First Australia Prime Income Fund, Hicks Muse & Co Inc, Paringa Mining & Exploration Co, Prudential Securities Group, Saugatuck Capital Corp, Scandinavian Broadcasting Sys *NONPR AFFIL* dir: VT Alpine Racing Assn; mem: Am Assn Petroleum Geologists, Am Bar Assn, Petroleum Soc NY, Soc Petroleum Engrs *CLUB AFFIL* Bond, Econ, Links, Racquet & Tennis, Wee Burn CC

Leland B. Paton: *B* Worcester MA 1943 *CURR EMPL* pres capital markets, dir, mem exec comm: Prudential Securities Inc *CORP AFFIL* dir: Chicago Bd Options Exchange, Prudential Securities Group; exchange off: Am Stock Exchange Inc; mem: NY Stock Exchange *NONPR AFFIL* mem: Am Mktg Assn *CLUB AFFIL* Apawanis, Bond, Harvard, Long Cove, Mid-Ocean

Loren Schechter: *CURR EMPL* exec vp, secy, gen couns, dir: Prudential Securities Group

Hardwick Simmons: *B* Baltimore MD 1940 *ED* Harvard Univ BA 1962; Harvard Univ MBA 1966 *CURR EMPL* pres, ceo, dir: Prudential Securities Inc *CORP AFFIL* ceo, dir: Prudential Capital & Investment Svcs, Prudential Properties; pres, ceo, dir: Prudential Securities Group *NONPR AFFIL* dir: Chicago Bd Options Exchange *CLUB AFFIL* Bond

Robert Cushing Winters: *B* Hartford CT 1931 *ED* Yale Univ BA 1953; Boston Univ MBA 1963 *CURR EMPL* chmn, dir: Prudential Securities Inc *CORP AFFIL* chmn, ceo: Prudential Ins Co Am; pres, dir: Pruco Inc *NONPR AFFIL* chmn: Greater Newark Chamber Commerce; dir: Regional Planning Assn; fellow, dir: Soc Actuaries; mem: Am Acad Actuaries, Am Counc Life Ins, Bus Counc, Bus Roundtable, Life Off Mgmt Assn, NJ Chamber Commerce, Partnership NJ, Sigma Xi

GIVING OFFICERS
Bruno George Bissetta: vp, treas *CURR EMPL* first vp: Prudential Securities Inc (see above)

Lisa J. Finnell: asst secy

Alan D. Hogan: vp *B* 1935 *CURR EMPL* exec vp, dir: Prudential Securities Group *CORP AFFIL* pres admin group, dir: Prudential Securities Inc

Howard Atwood Knight: pres *CURR EMPL* pres: Prudential Securities Inc (see above)

Elizabeth A. Longley: vp corp aff

Nathalie P. Maio: vp, secy

Loren Schechter: vp *CURR EMPL* exec vp, secy, gen couns, dir: Prudential Securities Group (see above)

APPLICATION INFORMATION
Initial Approach: *Initial Contact:* brief letter describing program *Deadlines:* none

GRANTS ANALYSIS
Total Grants: $890,430

Number of Grants: 81

Highest Grant: $275,000

Average Grant: $10,993

Typical Range: $1,000 to $15,000

Disclosure Period: fiscal year ending January 31, 1994

Note: Recent grants are derived from a fiscal 1994 Form 990.

RECENT GRANTS
Library
35,000	New York Public Library, New York, NY

General
275,000	United Way Tri-State, New York, NY
35,000	New York City Partnership Foundation, New York, NY
30,000	New York Downtown Hospital, New York, NY
25,330	National Merit Scholarship Corporation, Evanston, IL

| 25,000 | Central Park Wildlife Center, New York, NY |

Raymond Corp. / Raymond Foundation

Revenue: $148.73 million
Employees: 1,195
Headquarters: Binghamton, NY
SIC Major Group: Industrial Machinery & Equipment

CONTACT
Terri Brant
Assistant Executive Secretary
Raymond FdN
PO Box 1736
Greene, NY 13778
(607) 656-2311

FINANCIAL SUMMARY
Recent Giving: $71,104 (1992); $79,248 (1991); $34,000 (1990)
Assets: $2,495,853 (1992); $1,578,984 (1991); $1,349,530 (1990)
Gifts Received: $11,560 (1992); $56,798 (1991); $34,650 (1990)
Fiscal Note: In 1992, contributions were received from the Raymond Corporation.
EIN: 16-6047847

CONTRIBUTIONS SUMMARY
Typical Recipients: • *Arts & Humanities:* Arts Associations & Councils, Historic Preservation, History & Archaeology, Libraries, Public Broadcasting • *Civic & Public Affairs:* Business/Free Enterprise, Chambers of Commerce, Clubs, Employment/Job Training, General, Municipalities/Towns, Parades/Festivals, Public Policy, Rural Affairs, Safety, Urban & Community Affairs, Zoos/Aquariums • *Education:* Business Education, Colleges & Universities, Education Associations, Education Funds, General, Literacy, Private Education (Precollege), Public Education (Precollege), Secondary Education (Private) • *Health:* Children's Health/Hospitals, Emergency/Ambulance Services, Eyes/Blindness, Health Organizations, Hospitals, Kidney, Respiratory, Single-Disease Health Associations • *International:* Missionary/Religious Activities • *Religion:* Religious Welfare • *Science:* Science Museums • *Social Services:* Animal Protection, Child Welfare, Community Service Organizations, Day Care, Recreation & Athletics, United Funds/United Ways, Volunteer Services, Youth Organizations
Grant Types: capital, matching, and project
Geographic Distribution: limited to areas of company operations in NY and CA
Operating Locations: NY (Binghamton), VI (St. Thomas)

CORP. OFFICERS
Robert T. Cline: *B* Binghamton NY 1941 *ED* Cornell Univ 1964; State Univ NY 1967 *CURR EMPL* vp org & planning: Crowley Foods

Ross K. Colquhoun: *CURR EMPL* pres, ceo, dir: Raymond Corp

George G. Raymond, Jr.: *B* Brooklyn NY 1921 *ED* Cornell Univ 1942 *CURR EMPL* chmn, dir: Raymond Corp *CORP AFFIL* chmn: Raymond Indus Equipment Ltd; dir: GN Johnston Equipment Co Ltd, Natl Bank & Trust Co of Norwich NY, Rath & Strong, Security Mutual Life Ins Co, Tier Parts Warehousing

GIVING OFFICERS
James F. Barton: chmn
Terri Brant: asst exec secy
Patrick J. McManus: treas
Richard Najarian: trust
George G. Raymond, Jr.: trust *CURR EMPL* chmn, dir: Raymond Corp (see above)
Jean C. Raymond: trust
Stephen S. Raymond: vchmn
George G. Raymond III: exec secy
John Riley: trust
Jeanette L. Williamson: trust
Lee J. Wolf: trust *B* Allenton WI 1915 *ED* WI St Coll 1940; Marquette Univ 1947 *CURR EMPL* dir: Raymond Corp
Madeleine R. Young: trust

APPLICATION INFORMATION
Initial Approach: Send a brief letter of inquiry. Include a description of organization, amount requested, purpose of funds sought, recently audited financial statement, and proof of tax-exempt status. There are no deadlines.

PUBLICATIONS
Application Guidelines

GRANTS ANALYSIS
Total Grants: $71,104
Number of Grants: 43
Highest Grant: $10,000
Typical Range: $30 to $10,000
Disclosure Period: 1992
Note: Recent grants are derived from a 1992 Form 990.

RECENT GRANTS
Library
| 10,000 | Moore Memorial Library |

General
10,000	Catholic Charities, New York, NY
8,000	Greene Lions Club Park, Greene, NY
5,000	Broome-Chenango Alternative High School, Binghamton, NY
5,000	Good Shepherd Fairview Home
4,235	Gilbertsville Central School System, Gilbertsville, NY

Reed Foundation

CONTACT
J. Sinclair Armstrong
Secretary and Assistant Treasurer
Reed Foundation
444 Madison Ave., Ste. 2901
New York, NY 10022-6902
(212) 223-1330

FINANCIAL SUMMARY
Recent Giving: $750,000 (1995 est.); $733,401 (1994 approx.); $881,846 (1993)
Assets: $10,250,000 (1995 est.); $9,918,764 (1994 approx.); $10,278,287 (1993)
EIN: 13-1990017

CONTRIBUTIONS SUMMARY
Donor(s): Founded by the late Samuel Rubin, the Reed Foundation operated as a private foundation for thirty-five years under the name of the Samuel Rubin Foundation. In December 1985, the foundation made arrangements to distribute half of its assets to a separate, unaffiliated foundation. The name of the original foundation was then changed to the Reed Foundation.

Samuel Rubin (1901-1978) was founder of the Spanish Trading Corporation and Faberge Perfumes. He was a founder of the New York University Bellevue Medical Center; chairman of the advisory board of Fordham Hospital; president of the American-Israel Cultural Foundation and the American Symphony Orchestra; and a trustee of the New York Medical Center, Sydenham Hospital, and the Spoleto Festival.

Typical Recipients: • *Arts & Humanities:* Arts Associations & Councils, Arts Centers, Arts Festivals, Arts Funds, Community Arts, Film & Video, General, Historic Preservation, Libraries, Literary Arts, Museums/Galleries, Music, Performing Arts, Theater • *Civic & Public Affairs:* Civil Rights, Community Foundations, Legal Aid, Philanthropic Organizations, Professional & Trade Associations, Urban & Community Affairs • *Education:* Arts/Humanities Education, Colleges & Universities, International Exchange, Legal Education, Medical Education, Private Education (Precollege) • *Health:* Medical Research, Research/Studies Institutes • *International:* Foreign Educational Institutions, International Relations • *Social Services:* Community Service Organizations

Grant Types: general support and project
Geographic Distribution: broad geographic distribution; emphasis on New York

GIVING OFFICERS
James Sinclair Armstrong: secy, asst treas *B* New York NY 1915 *ED* Harvard Univ AB 1938; Harvard Univ JD 1941; Northwestern Univ 1942-1944; Northwestern Univ 1946-1948 *CURR EMPL* of couns: Whitman & Ransom *NONPR AFFIL* chmn: English Speaking Union US, Natl Inst Social Sciences; dir: Laymens Club; mem: Am Law Inst, Am Soc Venerable Order St John Jeru-

salem, Assn Bar City New York, Harvard Law Sch Assn, Huguenot Soc Am, Navy League US, NY Historical Soc, NY Soc Libraries, Pilgrims US, Practicing Law Inst, Soc Colonial Wars, St Nicholas Soc City New York; mem, chmn standing comm: St Andrews Soc St NY; trust emeritus: Gunnery Sch; vchmn, intl counc: English Speaking Union Commonwealth; vestryman: L'Eglise Francaise du St Esprit *CLUB AFFIL* mem: Ch Club of NY, Chevy Chase, Edgartown Reading Room, Edgartown Yacht, Harvard, NY Yacht, Thursday Evening, Union, Washington Court, Washington Court Garden Club

Jane Lockhart Gregory Rubin: treas *B* Richmond VA 1944 *ED* Vassar Coll BA 1965; Columbia Univ JD 1975; NY Univ LLM 1984 *CURR EMPL* of couns: Lankenau Kovner & Kurtz *NONPR AFFIL* adv bd: VT Studio Ctr; mem: Am Arbitration Assn, Assn Bar City New York

Reed Rubin: pres

APPLICATION INFORMATION

Initial Contact: Applicants should send a letter of request, describing the project to be funded. If the project is of interest to the board of directors, a proposal will be requested.

Include Information On: Proposals should give a detailed description of the project, including its administration, operation, budget, and other sources of funding. Also required are copies of the most recent 990 Form and tax-exempt status letter from the IRS.

Deadlines: There are no deadlines for application. The board meets on a flexible schedule approximately once every two months.

Review Process: The board of directors is capable of acting quickly on proposals, and applicants can expect immediate acknowledgement of receipt and a decision within two months.

Restrictions on Giving: No grants are given to individuals.

GRANTS ANALYSIS

Total Grants: $881,846

Number of Grants: 20

Highest Grant: $305,000

Average Grant: $44,923*

Typical Range: $1,000 to $30,000

Disclosure Period: 1993

Note: The foundation provided the average grant figure. Recent grants are derived from a 1993 Form 990.

RECENT GRANTS

Library

1,000	Foundation Center, New York, NY

General

305,000	Research Institute for the Study of Man, New York, NY
200,000	Harvard Law School, Cambridge, MA
30,000	Yale University School of Medicine, New Haven, CT
25,000	Yale University, New Haven, CT
20,000	American Trust for Oxford University, Oxford, England

Reicher Foundation, Anne and Harry J.

CONTACT

Leonard Zalkin
Vice President, Treasurer
Anne and Harry J. Reicher Fdn.
1173-A Second Ave., Box 363
New York, NY 10021
(212) 599-0500

FINANCIAL SUMMARY

Recent Giving: $742,600 (1993); $723,200 (1992); $1,040,000 (1991)

Assets: $4,321,454 (1993); $4,694,360 (1992); $5,249,827 (1991)

Gifts Received: $107,082 (1993); $1,764,509 (1991)

Fiscal Note: In 1993, contributions were received from the estate of Sydell Markelson.

EIN: 13-6115086

CONTRIBUTIONS SUMMARY

Typical Recipients: • *Arts & Humanities:* Historic Preservation, Libraries, Museums/Galleries • *Civic & Public Affairs:* Civil Rights, Housing, Municipalities/Towns, Philanthropic Organizations, Public Policy, Women's Affairs • *Education:* Business-School Partnerships, Colleges & Universities, Education Funds, General, Religious Education • *Environment:* General, Resource Conservation • *Health:* AIDS/HIV, Cancer, Children's Health/Hospitals, Clinics/Medical Centers, Geriatric Health, Health Organizations, Hospices, Hospitals, Medical Research, Nursing Services, Single-Disease Health Associations • *International:* Foreign Arts Organizations, Human Rights, International Development, Missionary/Religious Activities • *Religion:* Jewish Causes, Religious Organizations, Social/Policy Issues, Synagogues/Temples • *Science:* Science Museums • *Social Services:* Community Service Organizations, Family Planning, People with Disabilities, Senior Services

Grant Types: general support

Geographic Distribution: focus on the greater New York, NY, metropolitan area

GIVING OFFICERS

Rabbi Bulfour Brickner: secy

Harold Lamberg: pres

Leonard Zalkin: vp, treas

APPLICATION INFORMATION

Initial Approach: The foundation reports it only makes contributions to preselected charitable organizations.

Restrictions on Giving: Does not support individuals.

GRANTS ANALYSIS

Total Grants: $742,600

Number of Grants: 44

Highest Grant: $250,000

Typical Range: $1,000 to $125,000

Disclosure Period: 1993

Note: Recent grants are derived from a 1993 Form 990.

RECENT GRANTS

General

250,000	Hospital for Joint Diseases Orthopaedic Institute, New York, NY
125,000	Settlement Housing Fund, New York, NY
50,000	St. Lukes-Roosevelt Hospital Center, New York, NY
46,000	Stephen Wise Free Synagogue, New York, NY
35,000	Halom House, Cincinnati, OH

Republic NY Corp.

Revenue: $2.55 billion
Employees: 4,800
Headquarters: New York, NY
SIC Major Group: Bank Holding Companies

CONTACT

J. Phillip Burgess
Vice President, Director of Corporate Communications
Republic New York Corp.
452 Fifth Ave.
New York, NY 10018
(212) 525-6597

FINANCIAL SUMMARY

Recent Giving: $1,000,000 (1991 approx.); $1,000,000 (1990 approx.); $1,000,000 (1989 approx.)

Fiscal Note: All contributions are made directly by the company. Above figures exclude nonmonetary support.

CONTRIBUTIONS SUMMARY

Typical Recipients: • *Arts & Humanities:* Dance, Libraries, Museums/Galleries, Music, Opera, Performing Arts, Public Broadcasting, Theater • *Civic & Public Affairs:* Economic Development, Employment/Job Training, Housing, Public Policy, Zoos/Aquariums • *Education:* Colleges & Universities, Faculty Development, Minority Education, Religious Education • *Social Services:* Community Service Organizations, Food/Clothing Distribution, People with Disabilities, Senior Services, Shelters/Homelessness, Substance Abuse, Youth Organizations

Grant Types: employee matching gifts, general support, multiyear/continuing support, and project

Nonmonetary Support Types: donated equipment and in-kind services

Note: Estimate is not available for value of nonmonetary support.

Geographic Distribution: principally in the New York metropolitan area

Operating Locations: CA (Beverly Hills, Los Angeles), FL (Miami), NC (Charlotte), NY (New York)

CORP. OFFICERS

Cyril S. Dwek: *B* Kobe Japan 1936 *ED* Univ PA Wharton Sch BS 1958 *CURR EMPL* vchmn: Republic NY Corp *CORP AFFIL* vchmn: Republic Natl Bank NY *NONPR AFFIL* bd adv: Brazilian Inst Bus Programs, Pace Univ; vp: Brazilian Am Chamber Commerce *CLUB AFFIL* Racing de France

Ernest Ginsberg: *B* Syracuse NY 1931 *ED* Syracuse Univ BA 1953; Syracuse Univ JD 1955; Georgetown Univ LLM 1963 *CURR EMPL* vchmn, dir: Republic NY Corp *CORP AFFIL* Republic Bank CA NA, Republic Bank Savings; dir: Republic Natl Bank NY, Safra Corp *NONPR AFFIL* bd visit: Syracuse Univ Coll Law; dir: Bankers Roundtable, Intl Fin Conf, Washington Fin Forum Ltd; mem: Am Bankers Assn, Am Bar Assn, NY Bar Assn, NY St Bankers Assn, Phi Delta Phi, Phi Sigma Delta; vchmn: Roundabout Theatre Co

Jeffrey Craig Keil: *B* West Orange NJ 1943 *ED* Univ PA 1965; Harvard Univ MBA 1968 *CURR EMPL* pres, dir: Republic NY Corp *CORP AFFIL* chmn: Republic Bank CA NA, Safra Bank NA; vchmn: Republic Natl Bank NY

Margit Mason: *CURR EMPL* corp commun analyst: Republic NY Corp

John A. Pancetti: *B* 1930 *CURR EMPL* chmn, ceo, pres: Republic Bank Savings *CORP AFFIL* dir: Republic Natl Bank NY; vchmn: Republic NY Corp

Vito S. Portera: *B* 1942 *ED* St Johns Univ 1965 *CURR EMPL* vchmn: Republic NY Corp *CORP AFFIL* chmn: Republic Intl Bank NY; treas, dir: Safra Corp CA; vchmn: Republic Natl Bank NY

Dov C. Schlein: *B* Haifa Israel 1947 *ED* CUNY 1970 *CURR EMPL* vchmn: Republic Natl Bank NY *CORP AFFIL* vchmn: Republic NY Corp *NONPR AFFIL* mem: Am Inst CPAs, Comex NY

Walter Herman Weiner: *B* Brooklyn NY 1930 *ED* Univ MI BA 1952; Univ MI JD 1953 *CURR EMPL* chmn, ceo: Republic NY Corp *CORP AFFIL* chmn, ceo: Republic Natl Bank NY; dir: Manhattan Savings Bank, Safra Republic Holdings SA *NONPR AFFIL* bd visit: Univ MI Law Sch; mem: Am Bankers Assn, Am Bar Assn, Assn Bar City New York, NY Bar Assn, NY Holocaust Meml Commn; treas, dir: Bryant Pk Restoration Corp, Intl Sephardic Ed Fdn; trust: Guild Hall

GIVING OFFICERS

J. Phillip Burgess: *CURR EMPL* vp, dir corp commun: Republic NY Corp

James LoGatto: *CURR EMPL* sr vp, mem contr comm: Republic Natl Bank NY

Joseph Rhatigan: *CURR EMPL* vp: Republic Natl Bank NY

Phyllis Rosenblum: first vp *CURR EMPL* first vp: Republic Natl Bank NY

APPLICATION INFORMATION

Initial Approach: *Initial Contact:* letter *Include Information On:* background and budget of organization, range of support sought, purpose of contribution, list of board/organization officers, and proof of tax-exempt status *Deadlines:* none

Restrictions on Giving: Program does not support political or lobbying groups or veterans organizations.

OTHER THINGS TO KNOW

Company reported that it is making no new grants for calendar year 1995.

GRANTS ANALYSIS

Total Grants: $1,000,000

Typical Range: $100 to $2,000

Disclosure Period: 1991

Reynolds Foundation, Christopher

CONTACT

Andrea Panaritis
Executive Director
Christopher Reynolds Foundation
121 E 61st St.
New York, NY 10021
(212) 838-2920

FINANCIAL SUMMARY

Recent Giving: $1,317,313 (fiscal 1994); $1,363,311 (fiscal 1993); $1,388,882 (fiscal 1992)

Assets: $23,852,084 (fiscal 1994); $23,579,969 (fiscal 1993); $21,467,248 (fiscal 1992)

EIN: 13-6129401

CONTRIBUTIONS SUMMARY

Donor(s): The foundation was incorporated in 1952 by the late Libby Holman Reynolds .

Typical Recipients: • *Arts & Humanities:* Libraries • *Civic & Public Affairs:* Asian American Affairs, General • *Education:* Colleges & Universities, International Exchange, International Studies, Private Education (Precollege), Student Aid • *International:* Foreign Arts Organizations, Foreign Educational Institutions, Health Care/Hospitals, International Affairs, International Development, International Environmental Issues, International Organizations, International Peace & Security Issues, International Relations, International Relief Efforts, Missionary/Religious Activities • *Religion:* Churches, Religious Organizations • *Social Services:* Veterans

Grant Types: conference/seminar, multi-year/continuing support, project, and research

Geographic Distribution: focus on U.S. organizations working in Indochina (Vietnam, Laos, and Cambodia)

GIVING OFFICERS

John R. Boettiger: dir

Jack Clareman: secy, treas, dir

Suzanne Derrer: dir

Michael Kahn: pres, dir

Andrea Panaritis: exec dir

Gratia Stevens: program off

APPLICATION INFORMATION
Initial Approach:

The foundation does not use a formal grant application form.

Proposals should include specific objectives, detailed estimated budgets, qualifications of the organizations and individuals involved, and proof of tax-exempt status from the IRS. Six copies of the application are required.

Restrictions on Giving: The foundation does not make grants for building funds, medical research, educational or religious institutions (except in relation to research on subjects that fall within the scope of the foundation's current interests), or general operating or overhead expenses (except for newly organized entities whose objectives fall within the areas of the foundation's current interests).

PUBLICATIONS

Multi-year report including application guidelines

GRANTS ANALYSIS

Total Grants: $1,317,313

Number of Grants: 44

Highest Grant: $265,000

Average Grant: $29,939

Typical Range: $5,000 to $50,000

Disclosure Period: fiscal year ending January 31, 1994

Note: Recent grants are derived from a fiscal 1994 Form 990.

RECENT GRANTS

Library

10,000	Cornell University, Ithaca, NY — Cambodia library project
1,500	Foundation Center, New York, NY — general purposes

General

251,742	Harvard Institute of International Development, Cambridge, MA — Project Thirty (economic program - vietnam)
214,044	Harvard Institute of International Development, Cambridge, MA — Indochina program for 1993
75,000	Center for National Policy, US, Washington, DC — delegation of influential persons in Vietnam and Cambodia
67,500	PACT — Vietnamese-American Volunteer Youth Project and Conference
65,000	Center for National Policy, US, Washington, DC — reorienting US assistance policy in Cambodia

Rich Products Corporation / Rich Family Foundation

Sales: $940.0 million
Employees: 7,000
Headquarters: Buffalo, NY
SIC Major Group: Frozen Specialties Nec, Frozen Fruits & Vegetables, and Frozen Bakery Products Except Bread

CONTACT
David A. Rich
Executive Director
Rich Family Foundation
1150 Niagara St.
Buffalo, NY 14213
(716) 878-8000

FINANCIAL SUMMARY
Recent Giving: $400,000 (1995 est.); $350,000 (1994 approx.); $334,875 (1992)

Assets: $1,205,001 (1992); $1,029,009 (1991); $815,559 (1990)

Gifts Received: $420,000 (1992); $380,000 (1991); $240,000 (1990)

Fiscal Note: Contributes through foundation only. In 1991, contributions were received from Rich Products Corporation.

EIN: 16-6026199

CONTRIBUTIONS SUMMARY
Typical Recipients: • *Arts & Humanities:* Arts Associations & Councils, Arts Centers, Arts Institutes, Historic Preservation, History & Archaeology, Libraries, Museums/Galleries, Music, Performing Arts, Public Broadcasting • *Civic & Public Affairs:* Economic Development, Professional & Trade Associations, Urban & Community Affairs, Zoos/Aquariums • *Education:* Business Education, Colleges & Universities, Continuing Education, Legal Education, Private Education (Precollege), Special Education, Student Aid • *Health:* Children's Health/Hospitals, Health Organizations, Hospitals, Multiple Sclerosis, Prenatal Health Issues, Single-Disease Health Associations • *Religion:* Churches, Dioceses, Jewish Causes, Religious Organizations, Religious Welfare • *Social Services:* Child Welfare, Community Centers, Community Service Organizations, Family Services, Food/Clothing Distribution, Recreation & Athletics, United Funds/United Ways, Youth Organizations

Grant Types: general support

Geographic Distribution: primarily in Buffalo, NY

Operating Locations: CA (Escalon), GA (St. Simons Island), NJ (Vineland), NY (Buffalo), OH (Columbus, Dayton, Hilliard), TN (Gallatin)

CORP. OFFICERS
David A. Rich: *B* Buffalo NY 1944 *ED* Bradley Univ 1970 *CURR EMPL* secy, dir: Rich Products Corp *CORP AFFIL* dir: Rich Commun Corp

Janet W. Rich: *B* 1914 *CURR EMPL* vp, dir: Rich Products Corp

Robert E. Rich, Jr.: *B* 1941 *ED* Univ Rochester MBA; Williams Coll *CURR EMPL* pres, dir: Rich Products Corp *NONPR AFFIL* vchmn, dir: Buffalo Sabres Hockey Club

Robert E. Rich, Sr.: *B* Buffalo NY 1913 *ED* Univ Buffalo 1935 *CURR EMPL* fdr, chmn, dir: Rich Products Corp *CORP AFFIL* chmn: Buffalo Bisons; owner: Wilber Farms Dairy

GIVING OFFICERS
David A. Rich: exec dir *CURR EMPL* secy, dir: Rich Products Corp (see above)

Janet W. Rich: asst secy *CURR EMPL* vp, dir: Rich Products Corp (see above)

Robert E. Rich, Jr.: secy *CURR EMPL* pres, dir: Rich Products Corp (see above)

Robert E. Rich, Sr.: pres, treas *CURR EMPL* fdr, chmn, dir: Rich Products Corp (see above)

APPLICATION INFORMATION
Initial Approach: *Initial Contact:* formal letter of request *Deadlines:* none

GRANTS ANALYSIS
Total Grants: $334,875

Number of Grants: 155

Highest Grant: $100,000

Average Grant: $2,160

Typical Range: $100 to $2,500

Disclosure Period: 1992

Note: Recent grants are derived from a 1992 Form 990.

RECENT GRANTS

Library
1,000	Friends of Linebaugh Library

General
100,000	University of Buffalo Foundation, Buffalo, NY
50,000	Dioceses of Western New York, Buffalo, NY
25,000	Greater Buffalo Development Foundation, Buffalo, NY
10,000	Redbone
9,000	United Way of Buffalo and Erie County, Buffalo, NY

Richardson Charitable Trust, Anne S.

CONTACT
Stephen Bois
Anne S. Richardson Charitable Trust
c/o Chemical Bank
270 Park AVe., 21st Flr.
New York, NY 10117
(212) 270-9443

FINANCIAL SUMMARY
Recent Giving: $318,500 (fiscal 1993); $523,500 (fiscal 1991); $520,500 (fiscal 1990)

Assets: $10,399,940 (fiscal 1993); $9,196,173 (fiscal 1991); $9,095,480 (fiscal 1990)

EIN: 13-6192516

CONTRIBUTIONS SUMMARY
Donor(s): the late Anne S. Richardson

Typical Recipients: • *Arts & Humanities:* Historic Preservation, Libraries, Museums/Galleries, Music, Opera, Performing Arts, Public Broadcasting • *Civic & Public Affairs:* Botanical Gardens/Parks, Clubs, Economic Development, Public Policy, Women's Affairs • *Education:* Arts/Humanities Education, Colleges & Universities, Private Education (Precollege) • *Environment:* General, Resource Conservation • *Health:* Cancer, Children's Health/Hospitals, Heart, Hospices, Hospitals, Single-Disease Health Associations • *International:* International Organizations • *Religion:* Churches, Religious Organizations, Religious Welfare • *Social Services:* Child Welfare, Counseling, Domestic Violence, Family Planning, Family Services, Scouts, Senior Services, Substance Abuse, United Funds/United Ways, Youth Organizations

Grant Types: general support

Geographic Distribution: focus on CT and NY

GIVING OFFICERS
Chemical Bank: trust

APPLICATION INFORMATION
Initial Approach: Send brief letter of inquiry describing program or project. Include a description of organization, amount requested, purpose of funds sought, recently audited financial statement, and proof of tax-exempt status. There are no deadlines.

Restrictions on Giving: Does not support individuals or provide endowment funds, scholarships, or loans.

GRANTS ANALYSIS
Total Grants: $318,500

Number of Grants: 48

Highest Grant: $20,000

Typical Range: $1,000 to $15,000

Disclosure Period: fiscal year ending July 31, 1993

Note: Recent grants are derived from a fiscal 1993 Form 990.

RECENT GRANTS

Library
10,000	New York Public Library, New York, NY

General
20,000	Yale University, New Haven, CT — fifth and final payment
15,000	Caramoor Garden Guild, Katonah, NY
10,000	Connecticut College, New London, CT
10,000	International Center in New York, New York, NY
10,000	Memorial Sloan-Kettering Cancer Center, New York, NY

RJR Nabisco Inc. / RJR Nabisco Foundation

Revenue: $15.77 billion
Employees: 120,334
Parent Company: Kohlberg Kravis Roberts & Co.
Headquarters: New York, NY
SIC Major Group: Holding Companies Nec, Ice Cream & Frozen Desserts, Pickles, Sauces & Salad Dressings, and Frozen Specialties Nec

CONTACT
JoEllen M. Shiffman
Director of Philanthropy
RJR Nabisco Fdn.
1301 Avenue of the Americas
New York, NY 10019
(212) 258-5600
Note: Applications should be addressed to JoEllen Shiffman at 1455 Pennsylvania Avenue, Washington, DC 20004. The phone number is 202-626-7270.

FINANCIAL SUMMARY
Recent Giving: $14,024,533 (1993); $45,000,000 (1992); $35,000,000 (1991 approx.)

Assets: $59,855,310 (1993); $32,041,000 (1992); $74,710,666 (1991)

Fiscal Note: Figures represent foundation giving only. Above figures include nonmonetary support.

EIN: 58-1681920

CONTRIBUTIONS SUMMARY
Typical Recipients: • *Arts & Humanities:* Arts Associations & Councils, Arts Centers, Community Arts, Dance, Historic Preservation, Libraries, Museums/Galleries, Music, Performing Arts, Public Broadcasting • *Civic & Public Affairs:* Botanical Gardens/Parks, Business/Free Enterprise, Chambers of Commerce, General, Professional & Trade Associations, Public Policy, Rural Affairs, Urban & Community Affairs, Women's Affairs • *Education:* Agricultural Education, Arts/Humanities Education, Business Education, Business-School Partnerships, Colleges & Universities, Education Reform, Elementary Education (Private), Elementary Education (Public), Engineering/Technological Education, Faculty Development, General, International Exchange, Medical Education, Minority Education, Preschool Education, Private Education (Precollege), Public Education (Precollege), Science/Mathematics Education, Secondary Education (Private), Secondary Education (Public), Special Education, Student Aid • *Health:* Hospitals, Medical Research • *International:* International Relations, International Relief Efforts • *Social Services:* Child Welfare, Community Service Organizations, People with Disabilities, Recreation & Athletics, United Funds/United Ways, Volunteer Services, Youth Organizations

Grant Types: capital, challenge, department, employee matching gifts, fellowship, general support, operating expenses, project, research, and scholarship

Note: Matching gifts are for arts and education only.

Nonmonetary Support: $4,000,000 (1989); $6,600,000 (1988); $6,400,000 (1987)

Nonmonetary Support Types: donated equipment, donated products, in-kind services, and workplace solicitation

Note: Estimated value of nonmonetary support was more than $4,000,000 in 1989. Noncash support consists primarily of product donations to Second Harvest food bank.

Geographic Distribution: nationally, with an emphasis near major operating facilities

Operating Locations: CA (San Leandro), DC, NC (Winston-Salem), NJ (East Hanover, Parsippany), NY (Bronx, New York), PR (Guaynabo), WI (Wrightstown)

Note: Listed above are major operating locations only. Company also operates throughout the United States and internationally.

CORP. OFFICERS
Charles Michel Harper: *B* Lansing MI 1927 *ED* Purdue Univ BSME 1949; Univ Chicago MBA 1950 *CURR EMPL* chmn, ceo: RJR Nabisco Inc *CORP AFFIL* dir: Burlington Northern Inc, EI du Pont de Nemours & Co, Peter Kiewit Sons Inc, Norwest Corp, Valmont Indus Inc *NONPR AFFIL* dir: Bus Roundtable, Creighton Univ, Joslyn Art Mus; gov: Ak-Sar-Ben; mem: Beta Theta Pi, Omaha Chamber Commerce, Univ NE Lincoln Coll Bus Admin Alumni Assn, US Chamber Commerce; trust: Bishop Clarkson Meml Hosp, Comm Econ Devel

George Rosenberg Roberts: *B* Houston TX 1943 *ED* Claremont Mens Coll BA 1966; Univ CA Hastings Coll JD 1969 *CURR EMPL* ptnr: Kohlberg Kravis Roberts & Co *CORP AFFIL* beneficial owner: ConAgra Inc, Fred Meyer Inc; dir: BCI Holdings Corp, Duracell, Duracell Holdings Corp, Houdaille Indus, Lily-Tulip Inc, Malone & Hyde, Marley Co, NI Indus, Owens-IL Inc, RJR Nabisco Capital Corp, RJR Nabisco Holdings Corp, RJR Nabisco Holdings Group, Sargent Indus, Stop & Shop Cos Inc, Stop & Shop Holdings, Stop & Shop Supermarket Holding Co, Storer Commun, Walter Indus; dir, beneficial owner: Autozone, Duracell Intl, Idex Corp, Safeway Inc, Union TX Petroleum Holdings *PHIL AFFIL* don, vp, secy-treas: Roberts Foundation; don, trust: Roberts April 1988 Foundation, Roberts April 1988 Foundation *CLUB AFFIL* Menlo Circus, Olympic, San Francisco Tennis

Roger Dale Semerad: *B* Troy NY 1940 *ED* Un Coll BA 1962 *CURR EMPL* sr vp: RJR Nabisco Inc *NONPR AFFIL* dir: Bryce Harlow Fdn, Hudson Inst, Madison Ctr Ed Aff; treas: New Am Schs Devel Corp *PHIL AFFIL* dir: Bruce Harlow Foundation *CLUB AFFIL* Metro

Robert Francis Sharpe, Jr.: *B* Long Branch NJ 1952 *ED* DePauw Univ BA 1975; Purdue Univ BSE 1975; Wake Forest Univ JD 1978 *CURR EMPL* vp, asst gen couns: RJR Nabisco Inc *CORP AFFIL* vp, asst gen couns: RJR Nabisco Holdings Corp *NONPR*

AFFIL dir: Lewisville Fire Dept; mem: Am Bar Assn, Am Corp Couns Assn, Atlanta Bar Assn, Forsyth County Bar Assn

GIVING OFFICERS
William Apostolides: asst treas

Richard R. Beattie: dir

David B. Kalis: dir *CURR EMPL* vp commun: Intl Bus Machines Corp

Henry R. Kravis: dir *B* Tulsa OK 1944 *ED* Claremont Mens Coll BA 1967; Columbia Univ Sch Bus Admin MBA 1969 *CURR EMPL* ptnr: Kohlberg Kravis Roberts & Co *CORP AFFIL* dir: Beatrice Co, Duracell, Duracell Holdings Corp, LB Foster Co, Hillsborough Holdings Corp, Houdaille Indus, Malone & Hyde, Marley Co, Owens-IL Inc, RJR Nabisco Capital Corp, RJR Nabisco Holdings Corp, RJR Nabisco Holdings Group, RJR Nabisco Inc, Safeway Inc, Stop & Shop Cos Inc, Union TX Petroleum Holdings, Walter Indus *NONPR AFFIL* chmn: WNET-TV/Channel 13; dir: Central Pk Conservancy, Mt Sinai Med Ctr, New York City Ballet, Spence Sch *PHIL AFFIL* chmn, pres, dir: Henry R. Kravis Foundation; dir: Vail Valley Foundation; trust: Kravis April 1988 Foundation; dir: Vail Valley Foundation

H. Colin McBride: secy

Thomas M. Sansone: asst treas

W. Read Smith: asst secy

APPLICATION INFORMATION
Initial Approach: *Initial Contact:* preliminary letter *Include Information On:* proposed project, including analysis of purpose, need, goals, timetable for completion, and evaluative criteria; background information on organization, including governing board and qualifications of proposed leaders; financial information, including evidence of tax-exempt status, latest audited financial statement, and budget; list of other sources of funding and plan for future support *Deadlines:* none

Restrictions on Giving: Does not support athletic groups, social clubs, fraternal or veterans organizations; labor or political organizations; educational institutions already supported through fundraising organizations such as the United Negro College Fund or the Independent College Fund; sectarian or denominational religious groups; marathons or similar sports events; endowments or revolving funds; courtesy advertising or raffle tickets; conferences, workshops, seminars or trips; and production or distribution of audio-visual materials.

GRANTS ANALYSIS
Total Grants: $14,024,533*

Number of Grants: 114

Highest Grant: $900,000

Average Grant: $123,022

Typical Range: $20,000 to $500,000

Disclosure Period: 1993

Note: Total grants figure is for the foundation only and includes funding for the Next Century Schools program, which totaled $6,392,091 in 1993 and funding for the matching gifts program, which totaled

$2,841,611 in that same year. Recent grants are derived from a 1993 Form 990.

RECENT GRANTS

Library
500,000   New York Public Library Schomburg Center, New York, NY — library projects

General
900,000   Bowman Gray School of Medicine, Winston-Salem, NC — capital campaign
470,000   Next Century Schools Replication Grants
401,897   North Carolina Tobacco Foundation, Raleigh, NC — agriculture and science program
377,350   University of Kentucky, Lexington, KY — agriculture and science program
337,490   National Merit Scholarship Corporation, Evanston, IL

Robinson-Broadhurst Foundation

CONTACT
David R. Hillson
Executive Director
Robinson-Broadhurst Fdn.
PO Box 160
Stamford, NY 12167-0160
(607) 652-2508

FINANCIAL SUMMARY
Recent Giving: $1,457,130 (fiscal 1994); $757,396 (fiscal 1993)

Assets: $25,418,666 (fiscal 1994); $26,598,949 (fiscal 1993)

Gifts Received: $1,582,930 (fiscal 1993)

Fiscal Note: In fiscal 1993, contributions were received from Anna Broadhurst ($84,042) and R. Avery Robinson ($1,498,888).

EIN: 22-2558699

CONTRIBUTIONS SUMMARY
Typical Recipients: • *Arts & Humanities:* Arts Centers, History & Archaeology, Libraries, Museums/Galleries, Music, Public Broadcasting • *Civic & Public Affairs:* Botanical Gardens/Parks, General, Municipalities/Towns, Safety, Urban & Community Affairs • *Education:* Community & Junior Colleges, General, Private Education (Precollege), Public Education (Precollege), Secondary Education (Public), Student Aid • *Health:* Clinics/Medical Centers, Emergency/Ambulance Services, Health Funds, Health Organizations, Hospices • *Religion:* Churches, Religious Welfare • *Social Services:* Camps, Child Welfare, Day Care, Family Planning, Recreation & Athletics, Scouts, Senior Services, Youth Organizations

Grant Types: capital, general support, and project

Geographic Distribution: focus on Stamford, CT; Worcester, NY; and Winchendon, MA

GIVING OFFICERS
David R. Hillson: exec dir, secy
Charles McKenzie: trust
Martin A. Parks: trust
Winnie M. Robinson: pres, trust

APPLICATION INFORMATION
Initial Approach: Request application form. Deadlines are December 31 and May 1.

GRANTS ANALYSIS
Total Grants: $1,457,130
Number of Grants: 56
Highest Grant: $387,049
Typical Range: $327 to $325,000
Disclosure Period: fiscal year ending April 30, 1994

Note: Recent grants are derived from a fiscal 1994 Form 990.

RECENT GRANTS

Library
13,337   Village of Stamford, Stamford, NY — library

General
387,049   Stamford Health Care Society, Stamford, NY — building construction
325,000   Wendell P. Clark Memorial, Winchendon, MA — capital improvement and operations
116,058   Village of Stamford, Stamford, NY — capital improvement
100,000   Southwestern Otsego Health Center, Worcester, NY — capital improvement
50,000   Winchendon Health Foundation, Winchendon, MA — capital improvements

Robinson Fund, Maurice R.

CONTACT
Marian I. Steffens
Secretary
Maurice R. Robinson Fund
555 Broadway
New York, NY 10012
(212) 635-1987

FINANCIAL SUMMARY
Recent Giving: $375,211 (fiscal 1994); $220,724 (fiscal 1993); $239,115 (fiscal 1992)

Assets: $8,461,602 (fiscal 1994); $9,077,784 (fiscal 1993); $7,465,214 (fiscal 1992)

Gifts Received: $49,980 (fiscal 1993); $40,000 (fiscal 1992); $1,034,880 (fiscal 1991)

Fiscal Note: In fiscal 1993, contributions were received from Scholastic, Inc. ($48,980) and Scott Newman Foundation ($1,000).

EIN: 13-6161094

CONTRIBUTIONS SUMMARY
Donor(s): Maurice R. Robinson, Florence L. Robinson

Typical Recipients: • *Arts & Humanities:* Arts Associations & Councils, Arts Centers, Arts Festivals, Arts Funds, Arts Institutes, Community Arts, History & Archaeology, Libraries, Literary Arts, Museums/Galleries, Music • *Civic & Public Affairs:* Civil Rights, Economic Development, Employment/Job Training, General, Professional & Trade Associations, Public Policy • *Education:* Arts/Humanities Education, Colleges & Universities, Education Funds, Education Reform, Faculty Development, Journalism/Media Education, Private Education (Precollege), Public Education (Precollege), Social Sciences Education • *Health:* Hospitals • *International:* International Affairs • *Religion:* Churches, Ministries, Religious Organizations • *Science:* Observatories & Planetariums • *Social Services:* Child Welfare, Community Service Organizations, Family Services

Grant Types: general support

Geographic Distribution: national, with focus on NY

GIVING OFFICERS
Katherine Carsky: trust
Claudia Cohl: pres, trust
Ernest B. Fleishman: trust *CURR EMPL* sr vp ed & corp rels: Scholastic
Marian I. Steffens: secy
Barbara D. Sullivan, Esq: trust

APPLICATION INFORMATION
Initial Approach: Send a brief letter of inquiry. Include a description of organization, amount requested, purpose of funds sought, recently audited financial statement, and proof of tax-exempt status. There are no deadlines.

GRANTS ANALYSIS
Total Grants: $375,211
Number of Grants: 24
Highest Grant: $200,000
Typical Range: $500 to $26,500
Disclosure Period: fiscal year ending March 31, 1994

Note: Recent grants are derived from a fiscal 1994 Form 990.

RECENT GRANTS

General
26,500   Constitutional Rights Foundation, Los Angeles, CA
19,011   Trinity College Campus Ministry Program
11,500   Life Resources
11,000   Reach Out and Read/Boston City Hospital, Boston, MA
10,000   Columbia School of Journalism, New York, NY

Rockefeller Fund, David

CONTACT
Marnie Pillsbury
Executive Director
David Rockefeller Fund
1290 Ave. of the Americas
New York, NY 10104
(212) 373-4200

FINANCIAL SUMMARY
Recent Giving: $138,100 (1993); $127,500 (1992); $136,625 (1990)
Assets: $3,390,906 (1993); $3,025,494 (1992); $2,650,189 (1990)
Gifts Received: $3,000,000 (1989)
EIN: 13-3533359

CONTRIBUTIONS SUMMARY
Donor(s): The donor is David Rockefeller, Jr., the foundation's president.

Typical Recipients: • *Arts & Humanities:* Historic Preservation, History & Archaeology, Libraries, Museums/Galleries, Music, Public Broadcasting • *Civic & Public Affairs:* Economic Development, Housing, Municipalities/Towns, Parades/Festivals, Safety, Urban & Community Affairs • *Education:* Colleges & Universities, Private Education (Precollege) • *Environment:* General, Resource Conservation • *Health:* Hospitals, Nursing Services, Prenatal Health Issues, Public Health • *Religion:* Churches, Missionary Activities (Domestic), Religious Welfare • *Science:* Scientific Labs • *Social Services:* Community Service Organizations, Counseling, Day Care, Family Planning, Family Services, Homes, Recreation & Athletics, United Funds/United Ways, YMCA/YWCA/YMHA/YWHA, Youth Organizations

Grant Types: general support

Geographic Distribution: initially limited to the Seal Harbor, ME, and Pocantico, NY, communities

GIVING OFFICERS
Colin G. Cambell: dir

Peggy Dulany: dir

Neva R. Goodwin: pres, dir *B* New York NY 1944 *ED* Radcliffe Coll AB 1966; Radcliffe Coll MPA 1982; Boston Univ PhD 1987 *NONPR AFFIL* exec dir: Tufts Univ Ctr Study Global Devel Change *PHIL AFFIL* trust: Rockefeller Brothers Fund; pres, dir: Island Foundation

Christopher J. Kennan: dir

Marnie Pillsbury: exec dir

Richard E. Salomon: secy, treas, dir *PHIL AFFIL* dir: Richard and Edna Salomon Foundation

APPLICATION INFORMATION
Initial Approach: The fund reports that in its first few years of operation, it expects to limit its grant-making program to tax-exempt organizations which are located in the Seal Harbor, ME, and Pocantico, NY, communities. There are no deadlines for applications for funds, and no particular application form is used.

GRANTS ANALYSIS
Total Grants: $138,100
Number of Grants: 66
Highest Grant: $25,000
Typical Range: $250 to $15,000
Disclosure Period: 1993
Note: Recent grants are derived from a 1993 Form 990.

RECENT GRANTS
General

10,000	United Way of the Tarrytowns, Tarrytown, NY
8,000	Mt. Desert Public Health Nursing Association, Northeast Harbor, ME
5,000	College of Atlantic, Bar Harbor, ME
5,000	Jackson Laboratory, Bar Harbor, ME
5,000	Marymount College Tarrytown, Tarrytown, NY

Rohatyn Foundation, Felix and Elizabeth

Former Foundation Name: Felix G. Rohatyn Foundation

CONTACT
Felix G. Rohatyn
President
Felix and Elizabeth Rohatyn Fdn.
c/o Lazard Freres & Co.
One Rockefeller Plz.
New York, NY 10020
(212) 632-6507

FINANCIAL SUMMARY
Recent Giving: $1,202,804 (1993); $1,193,350 (1992); $993,905 (1991)
Assets: $4,017,852 (1993); $4,000,998 (1992); $4,421,672 (1991)
Gifts Received: $1,004,310 (1993); $500,000 (1992); $400,000 (1991)
Fiscal Note: In 1993, contributions were received from Felix G. Rohatyn.
EIN: 23-7015644

CONTRIBUTIONS SUMMARY
Donor(s): Felix G. Rohatyn

Typical Recipients: • *Arts & Humanities:* Arts Associations & Councils, Arts Centers, Arts Funds, Ballet, Community Arts, Dance, History & Archaeology, Libraries, Museums/Galleries, Music, Opera, Public Broadcasting, Theater, Visual Arts • *Civic & Public Affairs:* Botanical Gardens/Parks, General, Municipalities/Towns, Public Policy, Urban & Community Affairs, Women's Affairs • *Education:* Colleges & Universities, Education Funds, Education Reform, Elementary Education (Private), Literacy, Minority Education, Private Education (Prec-

ollege), Public Education (Precollege), Secondary Education (Private), Special Education, Student Aid • *Health:* Cancer, Emergency/Ambulance Services, Eyes/Blindness, Hospitals, Medical Research, Single-Disease Health Associations • *International:* Foreign Arts Organizations, Human Rights, International Organizations, International Relations, International Relief Efforts, Missionary/Religious Activities • *Religion:* Churches, Jewish Causes, Religious Welfare • *Social Services:* Child Welfare, Community Centers, Community Service Organizations, People with Disabilities, Youth Organizations

Grant Types: general support

Geographic Distribution: focus on the New York, NY, area

GIVING OFFICERS
Vivien Stiles Duffy: exec dir

Melvin L. Heinemen: secy, treas, dir

Elizabeth Rohatyn: vp, dir

Felix George Rohatyn: pres *B* Vienna Austria 1928 *ED* Middlebury Coll BS 1948 *CURR EMPL* ptnr: Lazard Freres & Co *CORP AFFIL* dir: Howmet Turbine Components Corp, MCA, Schlumberger Ltd

APPLICATION INFORMATION
Initial Approach: Send brief letter of inquiry describing program or project. There are no deadlines.

GRANTS ANALYSIS
Total Grants: $1,202,804
Number of Grants: 134
Highest Grant: $365,000
Typical Range: $250 to $336,000
Disclosure Period: 1993
Note: Recent grants are derived from a 1993 Form 990.

RECENT GRANTS
Library

50,000	New York Public Library, New York, NY — unrestricted

General

106,000	Fund for New York City Education/Waterford Institute, New York, NY — unrestricted
63,200	Grand Street Settlement House, New York, NY — unrestricted
32,500	I Have A Dream Foundation, New York, NY — scholarship fund
30,000	LHNA/Lenox Hill Neighborhood Association, New York, NY — unrestricted
20,000	Presbyterian Hospital, New York, NY — Psoriasis and Cutaneous Cancer Center

Rose Foundation, Billy

CONTACT
Terri C. Mangino
Executive Director and Assistant Secretary
Billy Rose Foundation
805 Third Ave.
New York, NY 10022
(212) 349-4141

FINANCIAL SUMMARY
Recent Giving: $1,022,500 (1993);
$1,257,000 (1992); $1,334,500 (1991)

Assets: $9,794,323 (1993); $9,072,336
(1992); $9,112,402 (1991)

Gifts Received: $5,000 (1993)

Fiscal Note: In fiscal year 1993, the foundation recieved $5,000 from J.R. Cherry, an officer and director of the foundation.

EIN: 13-6165466

CONTRIBUTIONS SUMMARY
Donor(s): The Billy Rose Foundation was incorporated in 1958 by Billy Rose . During his lifetime, Mr. Rose's interests included theatrical production, songwriting, the stock market, real estate investments, and art collecting. His activities in the stock market accounted for much of the fortune he had amassed by the time of his death in 1966. His will provided for a bequest of more than $10 million to the foundation.

Typical Recipients: • *Arts & Humanities:* Arts Associations & Councils, Arts Centers, Arts Festivals, Arts Funds, Arts Institutes, Arts Outreach, Ballet, Dance, Ethnic & Folk Arts, Film & Video, General, Historic Preservation, Libraries, Museums/Galleries, Music, Opera, Performing Arts, Public Broadcasting, Theater, Visual Arts • *Civic & Public Affairs:* Botanical Gardens/Parks, General, Philanthropic Organizations, Public Policy • *Education:* Arts/Humanities Education, Business Education, Colleges & Universities, Education Associations, Education Reform, General, Legal Education • *Environment:* General • *Health:* Cancer, Health Organizations, Hospitals, Medical Rehabilitation, Medical Research, Nursing Services, Single-Disease Health Associations • *International:* Foreign Arts Organizations • *Religion:* Jewish Causes, Religious Organizations, Religious Welfare • *Social Services:* Community Centers, Family Planning, Youth Organizations

Grant Types: general support and project

Geographic Distribution: emphasis on New York City

GIVING OFFICERS
Arthur Cantor: pres, dir *B* Boston MA 1920

James R. Cherry: chmn, dir, treas

Terri C. Mangino: exec dir, asst secy

Edward J. Walsh, Jr.: secy, asst treas

Charles Wohlstetter: pres, dir *B* 1910 *CURR EMPL* chmn, dir: Contel Corp *CORP AFFIL* dir: New Court Asset Mgmt, Tesoro Petroleum Corp; vchmn: GTE Corp *NONPR AFFIL* chmn: Inst Ed Affs; chmn adv panel: US Information Agency Intl Cultural & Ed Exchange; mem: Am Enterprise Inst, Counc World Communs, French Academy Wine; mem adv counc: Rockefeller Univ; natl ambassador: Salk Inst; reg chmn: Pres Commn White House Fellowships; trust: Fdn Res Medicine & Biology, Freedoms Fdn Valley Forge; vchmn, trust: John F Kennedy Ctr Performing Arts, Natl Symphony Orchestra Assn

APPLICATION INFORMATION
Initial Approach:

Applications should be submitted in the form of a letter to the foundation.

The letter should summarize the need for support and include the amount of the request. A copy of the IRS determination letter of tax-exempt status and any recent publicity articles should also be included.

There are no deadlines for submitting letters of request.

GRANTS ANALYSIS
Total Grants: $1,022,500

Number of Grants: 85

Highest Grant: $325,000

Average Grant: $8,304*

Typical Range: $2,500 to $20,000

Disclosure Period: 1993

Note: Average grant figure excludes the highest grant of $325,000. Recent grants are derived from a 1993 Form 990.

RECENT GRANTS
General

325,000	American Friends of Israel Museum, New York, NY	
50,000	American Enterprise Institute for Public Policy Research, Washington, DC	
40,000	Rockefeller University, New York, NY	
25,000	National Foundation for Facial Reconstruction, New York, NY	
20,000	Convent of the Sacred Heart, New York, NY	

Rosen Foundation, Joseph

CONTACT
Abraham A. Rosen
President
Joseph Rosen Fdn.
PO Box 334, Lenox Hill Sta.
New York, NY 10021
(212) 249-1550

FINANCIAL SUMMARY
Recent Giving: $537,436 (fiscal 1993);
$454,141 (fiscal 1992); $478,043 (fiscal 1991)

Assets: $12,979,870 (fiscal 1993);
$13,001,328 (fiscal 1992); $12,335,513 (fiscal 1991)

Gifts Received: $50,000 (fiscal 1993);
$25,000 (fiscal 1992); $55,000 (fiscal 1991)

Fiscal Note: In fiscal 1993, contributions were received from Ira Belfer.

EIN: 13-6158412

CONTRIBUTIONS SUMMARY
Typical Recipients: • *Arts & Humanities:* Arts Institutes, Community Arts, Libraries, Museums/Galleries, Opera, Performing Arts, Public Broadcasting, Theater • *Civic & Public Affairs:* Botanical Gardens/Parks, General, Zoos/Aquariums • *Education:* Arts/Humanities Education, Colleges & Universities, Legal Education, Medical Education, Private Education (Precollege) • *Environment:* General, Wildlife Protection • *Health:* AIDS/HIV, Cancer, Clinics/Medical Centers, Hospitals, Medical Research, Single-Disease Health Associations • *International:* Foreign Arts Organizations, Human Rights, International Organizations, Missionary/Religious Activities • *Religion:* Jewish Causes, Religious Organizations, Synagogues/Temples • *Science:* Science Museums • *Social Services:* Community Centers, People with Disabilities, Youth Organizations

Grant Types: general support

Geographic Distribution: focus on Northeast

GIVING OFFICERS
Irving S. Bobrow: vp, asst treas

Abraham A. Rosen: pres, dir

Jonathan P. Rosen: vp, secy, dir

Miriam Rosen: treas, dir

APPLICATION INFORMATION
Initial Approach: The foundation reports it only makes contributions to preselected charitable organizations.

GRANTS ANALYSIS
Total Grants: $537,436

Number of Grants: 215*

Highest Grant: $60,100

Typical Range: $100 to $50,000

Disclosure Period: fiscal year ending June 30, 1993

Note: Recent grants are derived from a fiscal 1993 Form 990. Number of grants is approximate.

RECENT GRANTS
Library

3,000	New York Public Library, New York, NY	

General

60,100	Amherst College Alumni Fund, Amherst, MA	
60,000	Greater Hartford Jewish Community Center, West Hartford, CT	
50,000	Hartford Jewish Federation, Hartford, CT	
50,000	Harvard Medical School, Cambridge, MA	
15,000	American ORT Federation, New York, NY	

Rubin Foundation, Samuel

CONTACT
Cora Weiss
President
Samuel Rubin Foundation
777 United Nations Plz.
New York, NY 10017
(212) 697-8945

FINANCIAL SUMMARY
Recent Giving: $644,402 (fiscal 1993);
$660,900 (fiscal 1992); $794,750 (fiscal
1991)

Assets: $12,837,707 (fiscal 1993);
$12,299,690 (fiscal 1992); $11,788,594 (fiscal 1991)

Gifts Received: $30,000 (fiscal 1993);
$157,500 (fiscal 1986)

Fiscal Note: In 1993, the foundation received a gift from an anonymous donor.

EIN: 13-6164671

CONTRIBUTIONS SUMMARY
Donor(s): The Samuel Rubin Foundation
was incorporated in New York in 1949 from
funds donated by the late Samuel Rubin .
Mr. Rubin was the founder of Faberge. He
also was a founder of the New York University Bellevue Medical Center and the American Symphony Orchestra.

Typical Recipients: • *Arts & Humanities:*
Arts Associations & Councils, Arts Centers,
Arts Funds, Community Arts, Film & Video,
Libraries, Literary Arts, Museums/Galleries,
Performing Arts, Public Broadcasting, Theater • *Civic & Public Affairs:* Botanical Gardens/Parks, Business/Free Enterprise, Civil
Rights, Community Foundations, Economic
Policy, Employment/Job Training, General,
Housing, Nonprofit Management, Philanthropic Organizations, Public Policy, Safety,
Urban & Community Affairs, Women's Affairs • *Education:* Arts/Humanities Education, Colleges & Universities, Education
Associations, Education Funds, Education
Reform, Health & Physical Education, International Studies, Legal Education, Science/Mathematics Education • *Environment:*
Air/Water Quality • *Health:* Hospitals, Medical Research • *International:* International
Affairs, International Development, International Environmental Issues, International
Organizations, International Peace & Security Issues, International Relations, International Relief Efforts • *Religion:* Jewish
Causes, Religious Welfare • *Science:* Scientific Centers & Institutes • *Social Services:*
Homes, Shelters/Homelessness, Veterans

Grant Types: general support and project

Geographic Distribution: national and international

GIVING OFFICERS
Charles L. Mandelstam: secy *CURR EMPL*
Dornbush Mensch Mandelstam & Silverman
NY City

Cora Weiss: pres

Daniel Weiss: dir

Judy Weiss: vp

Peter Weiss: treas *B* Vienna Austria 1925
ED St Johns Coll AB 1949; Yale Univ JD
1952

Tamara Weiss: dir

APPLICATION INFORMATION
Initial Approach:

The foundation has no formal application
procedures. Applicants should submit a proposal in writing.

A proposal must describe in detail the organization and the project. Include a budget
and tax-exempt status letter.

There are no deadlines for applying.

The board of directors meets three times a
year. However limited funds and recurring
commitments restrict the board's grant making ability.

Restrictions on Giving: The foundation
does not award grants for building funds,
scholarships, or to individuals.

PUBLICATIONS
Program policy statement

GRANTS ANALYSIS
Total Grants: $644,402

Number of Grants: 85

Highest Grant: $100,000

Average Grant: $7,581

Typical Range: $1,000 to $10,000

Disclosure Period: fiscal year ending June
30, 1993

Note: Recent grants are derived from a fiscal 1993 Form 990.

RECENT GRANTS
Library
2,500   Meiklejohn Civil Liberties Library, Berkeley, CA

General
100,000   Institute for Policy Studies, Washington, DC — for Transnational Institute
100,000   Institute for Policy Studies, Washington, DC — for Transnational Institute
50,000   Center for Constitutional Rights, New York, NY — legal
25,000   Downtown Community Television Center, New York, NY
25,000   Hampshire College, Amherst, MA

Rubinstein Foundation, Helena

CONTACT
Diane Moss
President
Helena Rubinstein Foundation
405 Lexington Ave., 15th Fl.
New York, NY 10174
(212) 986-0806

FINANCIAL SUMMARY
Recent Giving: $4,300,000 (fiscal 1994
est.); $4,033,158 (fiscal 1993); $4,050,781
(fiscal 1992)

Assets: $34,223,125 (fiscal 1994 est.);
$34,173,997 (fiscal 1993); $33,177,354 (fiscal 1992)

EIN: 13-6102666

CONTRIBUTIONS SUMMARY
Donor(s): The foundation was created in
1953 by businesswoman Helena Rubinstein .
Ms. Rubinstein was born in Poland in 1871,
and at the age of twenty she began her cosmetics business with one product, a face
cream. Her cosmetics empire expanded to
London in 1902, to Paris in 1906, and to
New York in 1912. During her lifetime she
accumulated significant collections of African sculptures, modern paintings and sculptures, Oriental and Oceanic art, and
Egyptian antiques. The foundation was a major beneficiary of her legacy when she died
in 1965.

Typical Recipients: • *Arts & Humanities:*
Arts Festivals, Arts Outreach, Ballet, Dance,
Libraries, Museums/Galleries, Music, Performing Arts, Public Broadcasting, Theater,
Visual Arts • *Civic & Public Affairs:* Employment/Job Training, Housing, Public Policy • *Education:* Arts/Humanities Education,
Colleges & Universities, Education Reform,
Literacy, Medical Education, Minority Education, Preschool Education, Science/Mathematics Education, Student Aid • *Health:*
AIDS/HIV, Cancer, Geriatric Health, Health
Organizations, Hospitals, Medical Rehabilitation, Medical Research, Medical Training,
Nursing Services, Prenatal Health Issues,
Public Health, Single-Disease Health Associations • *International:* Foreign Arts Organizations, Health Care/Hospitals,
International Affairs, International Relief Efforts • *Religion:* Jewish Causes • *Social Services:* Child Welfare, Counseling, Day Care,
Family Planning, Family Services, Recreation & Athletics, Shelters/Homelessness,
Substance Abuse, United Funds/United
Ways, Youth Organizations

Grant Types: endowment, fellowship, general support, multiyear/continuing support,
operating expenses, research, scholarship,
and seed money

Geographic Distribution: primarily New
York, NY; minimal support nationally and
internationally

GIVING OFFICERS
Robert S. Friedman: secy, treas

Oscar Kolin: pres emeritus

Gertrude Geraldine Michelson: chmn *B*
Jamestown NY 1925 *ED* PA St Univ BA
1945; Columbia Univ LLB 1947 *CORP AFFIL* dir: Chubb Corp, Gen Electric Co,
Goodyear Tire & Rubber Co, RH Macy &
Co Inc, Quaker Oats Co, Stanley Works;
gov: Am Stock Exchange Inc; trust emeritus: Rand Corp *NONPR AFFIL* chmn emeritus bd trust: Columbia Univ; dir: Better Bus
Bur Metro NY, Work Am Inst; life trust:
Spelman Coll; mem: New York City Partnership, Womens Forum; mem adv counc: Catalyst; mem, exec comm, vchmn: New York

City Chamber Commerce; trust: Interracial Counc Bus Opportunity; vchmn: New York City Partnership *CLUB AFFIL* Econ *PHIL AFFIL* chmn, dir: John and Mary R. Markle Foundation

Diane Moss: pres, ceo

Robert Moss: dir

Martin Eli Segal: dir *B* Vitebsk Union of Soviet Socialist Republics 1916 *CURR EMPL* chmn emeritus: Martin E Segal Co *NONPR AFFIL* adv trust: Am-Scandinavian Fdn; bd adv: Library Am; bd visitors: City Univ NY Grad Sch & Univ Ctr; chmn: NY Intl Festival Arts; chmn emeritus: Lincoln Ctr Performing Arts; dir: Am Pub Radio; founding mem publs comm: Pub Interest; mem: Natl Bd Young Audiences; mem visitors comm: Harvard Univ Sch Pub Health; pres emeritus: Film Soc Lincoln Ctr; trust emeritus: Inst Advanced Studies *CLUB AFFIL* Century, City Athletic, Players

Louis E. Slesin: dir *PHIL AFFIL* vp: Roy and Niuta Titus Foundation

Suzzanne Slesin: dir *PHIL AFFIL* vp: Roy and Niuta Titus Foundation

APPLICATION INFORMATION
Initial Approach:

There is no application form. Organizations seeking funding should submit a letter rather than make telephone inquiries.

Written proposals must outline the project, describe goals, provide a budget, state the amount requested, list other funding sources, and give a succinct history of the organization.

Proposals are accepted throughout the year.

Every proposal is acknowledged by letter. Additional information may be requested if the proposal is of interest to the foundation. A meeting or site visit may be arranged by the foundation. Funding decisions are made in May and November. Grants are not renewed automatically, but are considered on the basis of evaluation of reports, site visits, priorities, and the availability of funds.

Restrictions on Giving: Grants are made only to tax-exempt nonprofit organizations. Scholarship and fellowship grants are made directly to institutions. General operating grants are made, but the foundation prefers to support specific projects or programs. The foundation does not support individuals, film or video projects, endowments, capital campaigns, loans, or emergency funds. Funding is limited by present and long-term commitments and fiscal constraints.

PUBLICATIONS
Annual report

GRANTS ANALYSIS
Total Grants: $4,033,158

Number of Grants: 225

Highest Grant: $300,000

Average Grant: $17,925

Typical Range: $5,000 to $25,000

Disclosure Period: fiscal year ending May 31, 1993

Note: Recent grants are derived from a fiscal 1993 annual report.

RECENT GRANTS
Library
60,000 American Friends of Tel Aviv Museum of Art, New York, NY — renovation of the Helena Rubinstein Art Library

50,000 American Friends of Tel Aviv Museum of Art, New York, NY — book, periodical, microfilm, and equipment purchases for the Helena Rubinstein Art Library

General
300,000 US Holocaust Memorial Museum Campaign, Washington, DC — endowment of the cinema in the museum's cultural and conference center in memory of Helena Rubinstein

242,000 United Jewish Appeal Federation of Jewish Philanthropies of New York, New York, NY — general support

104,000 New York University Medical Center, Department of Obstetrics and Gynecology, New York, NY — establishment of clinic and research program for postmenopausal women

100,000 Parsons School of Design, New York, NY — establishment of the Oscar Kolin fellowship fund for outstanding students in the Master of Fine Arts in Painting program

100,000 Whitney Museum of American Art, New York, NY — fellowship endowment and annual fellowships for the Independent Study Program providing curatorial training for college and graduate students

Rudin Foundation

CONTACT
Susan H. Rapaport
Administrator
Rudin Fdn.
345 Pk. Ave.
New York, NY 10154
(212) 407-2400

FINANCIAL SUMMARY
Recent Giving: $1,054,747 (1993); $965,996 (1992); $978,369 (1991)

Assets: $631,899 (1993); $985,722 (1992); $1,063,155 (1991)

Gifts Received: $716,000 (1993); $884,500 (1992); $1,134,500 (1991)

Fiscal Note: In 1992, major contributions were received from 945 Fifth Ave., Inc. ($221,000), Pine-Water Garage Inc.

($333,600), 415 Madison Inc. ($87,400), and 355 Lexington, Inc. ($63,200).

EIN: 13-6113064

CONTRIBUTIONS SUMMARY
Donor(s): Jack Rudin and Lewis Rudin

Typical Recipients: • *Arts & Humanities:* Arts Associations & Councils, Dance, Libraries, Museums/Galleries, Music, Performing Arts, Theater • *Civic & Public Affairs:* Botanical Gardens/Parks, Business/Free Enterprise, Economic Development, General, Law & Justice, Municipalities/Towns, Parades/Festivals, Philanthropic Organizations, Public Policy, Urban & Community Affairs, Women's Affairs, Zoos/Aquariums • *Education:* Arts/Humanities Education, Business Education, Colleges & Universities, Minority Education, Private Education (Precollege), Secondary Education (Public) • *Health:* Clinics/Medical Centers, Health Organizations, Hospitals, Long-Term Care, Medical Research, Single-Disease Health Associations, Speech & Hearing • *Religion:* Churches, Jewish Causes, Religious Organizations, Religious Welfare, Synagogues/Temples • *Social Services:* Child Welfare, Community Centers, Community Service Organizations, Crime Prevention, Delinquency & Criminal Rehabilitation, Food/Clothing Distribution, Recreation & Athletics, Senior Services, Substance Abuse, United Funds/United Ways, Volunteer Services, Youth Organizations

Grant Types: general support

Geographic Distribution: focus on New York, NY

GIVING OFFICERS
Beth Rudin DeWoody: vp, dir *PHIL AFFIL* vp, dir: Samuel and May Rudin Foundation, Louis and Rachel Rudin Foundation

David B. Levy: treas, dir

John Lewin: dir

Jack Rudin: pres, dir *B* 1924 *CURR EMPL* chmn: Rudin Mgmt Co *NONPR AFFIL* head: New York City Marathon Comm; planning comm: Celebration Arts *PHIL AFFIL* pres, dir: Samuel and May Rudin Foundation, Louis and Rachel Rudin Foundation

Lewis Rudin: exec vp, dir *B* 1927 *CURR EMPL* pres, dir: Rudin Mgmt Co *CORP AFFIL* ptnr: 345 Park Co *NONPR AFFIL* chmn: Assn Better NY *PHIL AFFIL* exec vp, secy, treas, dir: Samuel and May Rudin Foundation; secy, dir: Louis and Rachel Rudin Foundation

John Sills: dir

Richard C. Snider: secy, dir

Jeffrey Steinman: dir

Lewis Steinman: dir *PHIL AFFIL* dir: Louis and Rachel Rudin Foundation

Adelaide Rudin Zisson: dir

APPLICATION INFORMATION
Initial Approach: Send a brief letter of inquiry. Include a description of organization, amount requested, purpose of funds sought, recently audited financial statement, and proof of tax-exempt status. There are no deadlines.

GRANTS ANALYSIS

Total Grants: $1,054,747

Number of Grants: 159

Highest Grant: $400,000

Typical Range: $500 to $100,000

Disclosure Period: 1993

Note: Recent grants are derived from a 1993 Form 990.

RECENT GRANTS

Library

55,000	New York Public Library, New York, NY

General

400,000	United Jewish Appeal Federation of New York, New York, NY
100,000	United Jewish Appeal Federation of Jewish Philanthropies, New York, NY
20,000	United Cerebral Palsy of New York City, New York, NY
15,000	American Jewish Congress, New York, NY
15,000	Anti-Defamation League, New York, NY

Salomon Inc.

Revenue: $6.27 billion

Employees: 8,900

Headquarters: New York, NY

SIC Major Group: Investment Offices Nec, Security Brokers & Dealers, Commodity Contracts Brokers & Dealers, and Investment Advice

CONTACT

Jane E. Heffner
Vice President, Corporate Communications
Salomon Inc.
7 World Trade Ctr.
New York, NY 10048
(212) 783-7434

FINANCIAL SUMMARY

Recent Giving: $3,800,000 (1995 est.); $5,000,000 (1994 approx.); $3,800,000 (1993 approx.)

Fiscal Note: All giving is through the company. See "Other Things To Know" for more details.

EIN: 13-3388259

CONTRIBUTIONS SUMMARY

Typical Recipients: • *Arts & Humanities:* Ballet, Historic Preservation, Libraries, Museums/Galleries, Music, Opera, Performing Arts, Public Broadcasting, Theater, Visual Arts • *Civic & Public Affairs:* Economic Development, Employment/Job Training, Law & Justice, Legal Aid, Women's Affairs, Zoos/Aquariums • *Education:* Arts/Humanities Education, Business Education, Economic Education, Elementary Education (Private), Literacy, Minority Education, Public Education (Precollege) • *Health:* Hospitals, Medical Research, Single-Disease

Health Associations • *Science:* Scientific Centers & Institutes • *Social Services:* Delinquency & Criminal Rehabilitation, Emergency Relief, Family Planning, Food/Clothing Distribution, Recreation & Athletics, Substance Abuse, Youth Organizations

Grant Types: employee matching gifts, general support, and operating expenses

Note: Employee matching gift ratio: 1 to 1.

Geographic Distribution: nationally, with emphasis on cities where company operates

Operating Locations: CA (Los Angeles, San Francisco), CT (Westport), GA (Atlanta), IL (Chicago), MA (Boston), NY (New York), TX (Dallas)

CORP. OFFICERS

Robert Edwin Denham: *B* Dallas TX 1945 *ED* Univ TX BA 1966; Harvard Univ MA 1968; Harvard Univ JD 1971 *CURR EMPL* chmn, ceo: Salomon Inc *NONPR AFFIL* adv bd of pres: CA St Univ; co-chmn subcounc: Capital Allocation Competitiveness Policy Counc; dir: Exec Leadership Fdn; mem: Am Bar Assn, CA Bar Assn, Los Angeles County Bar Assn, Pres Clinton Bipartisan Commn Entitlements; trust: Cathedral Corp Diocese Los Angeles, Natural Resources Defense Counc, Polytech Sch Pasadena *CLUB AFFIL* City Los Angeles

Andrew J. Hall: *B* 1951 *CURR EMPL* chmn, ceo: Salomon Phibro Div Inc *CORP AFFIL* exec vp, dir: Salomon Inc

Deryck C. Maughan: *B* Consett England 1947 *ED* Univ London Kings Coll BA 1969; Stanford Univ MBA 1978 *CURR EMPL* chmn, ceo: Salomon Bros *CORP AFFIL* ceo, dir: Salomon Bros Holding Co; dir: Salomon Inc *PHIL AFFIL* dir: New York Stock Exchange Foundation, Inc.

GIVING OFFICERS

Jane E. Heffner: *CURR EMPL* vp corp contributions: Salomon Bros

APPLICATION INFORMATION

Initial Approach: *Initial Contact:* brief letter or proposal *Include Information On:* proof of tax-exempt status *Deadlines:* none

Restrictions on Giving: Fraternal organizations, political or lobbying groups, or groups for sectarian purposes are not considered for contributions.

OTHER THINGS TO KNOW

The company responds to all funding requests addressed to either of its two main segments: Salomon Brothers or the Phibro Division of Salomon.

The company, which disbursed $596,201 through its foundation in 1992, reports all contributions are now provided directly by the company.

GRANTS ANALYSIS

Total Grants: $3,800,000*

Number of Grants: 420

Highest Grant: $100,000

Average Grant: $2,500*

Typical Range: $1,000 to $5,000

Disclosure Period: 1993

Note: Total grants figure is approximate. Average grant figure was provided by the company. Recent grants are derived from a 1992 partial grants list.

RECENT GRANTS

Library

10,000	Chicago Public Library, Chicago, IL
10,000	Chicago Public Library, Chicago, IL

General

20,000	New York Downtown Hospital, New York, NY
20,000	New York Downtown Hospital, New York, NY
5,000	St. Louis Science Center, St. Louis, MO
5,000	St. Louis Science Center, St. Louis, MO
3,000	Planned Parenthood of New York City, New York, NY

Salomon Foundation, Richard and Edna

CONTACT

R. M. Schleicher
Vice President, Treasurer
Richard and Edna Salomon Fdn.
45 Rockefeller Plz.
New York, NY 10111
(212) 903-1216

FINANCIAL SUMMARY

Recent Giving: $440,950 (1993); $547,685 (1992); $609,250 (1990)

Assets: $2,437,516 (1993); $2,567,369 (1992); $2,537,892 (1990)

EIN: 13-6163521

CONTRIBUTIONS SUMMARY

Donor(s): Richard B. Salomon

Typical Recipients: • *Arts & Humanities:* Arts Associations & Councils, Arts Centers, Arts Institutes, Ethnic & Folk Arts, Film & Video, Libraries, Museums/Galleries, Performing Arts, Public Broadcasting • *Civic & Public Affairs:* Botanical Gardens/Parks, Business/Free Enterprise, Civil Rights, General, Housing, Professional & Trade Associations, Urban & Community Affairs, Women's Affairs • *Education:* Colleges & Universities, Education Funds, Literacy, Private Education (Precollege), Social Sciences Education, Special Education • *Environment:* Air/Water Quality • *Health:* AIDS/HIV, Alzheimers Disease, Cancer, Health Organizations, Hospitals, Medical Research, Nursing Services, Respiratory, Single-Disease Health Associations • *International:* Human Rights, International Peace & Security Issues, International Relations • *Religion:* Jewish Causes • *Social Services:* Community Service Organizations, Family Planning, People with Disabilities, Shelters/Homelessness, United Funds/United Ways

Grant Types: general support

Geographic Distribution: focus on New York, NY

GIVING OFFICERS

Merwin Lewis: secy *PHIL AFFIL* vp, dir: Sylvan and Ann Oestreicher Foundation

Richard B. Salomon: pres, dir *B* New York NY 1912 *ED* Brown Univ PhB 1932; Brown Univ LLD 1972 *CORP AFFIL* managing ptnr: Riverbank Assocs *NONPR AFFIL* chancellor emeritus: Brown Univ; dir: Common Cause; trust: Lincoln Ctr Performing Arts; vchmn: NY Pub Library

Richard E. Salomon: dir *PHIL AFFIL* secy, treas, dir: David Rockefeller Fund

Raymond M. Schleicher: vp, treas, dir

APPLICATION INFORMATION

Initial Approach: Send brief letter of inquiry describing program or project. There are no deadlines.

GRANTS ANALYSIS

Total Grants: $440,950

Number of Grants: 44

Highest Grant: $50,000

Typical Range: $1,000 to $40,000

Disclosure Period: 1993

Note: Recent grants are derived from a 1993 Form 990.

RECENT GRANTS

Library

25,000	New York Public Library, New York, NY
7,000	Library of America, New York, NY

General

40,000	Brown University, Providence, RI
40,000	Institute for East-West Studies, New York, NY
20,000	Fund for Free Expression, New York, NY
20,000	Rockefeller University, New York, NY
12,500	BENS Education Fund, New York, NY

Sasco Foundation

CONTACT
Uwe Lindner
Vice President
Sasco Fdn.
270 Pk. Ave.
New York, NY 10017
(212) 270-9452

FINANCIAL SUMMARY

Recent Giving: $229,000 (1992); $226,375 (1991); $213,000 (1989)

Assets: $5,367,007 (1992); $5,318,432 (1991); $4,494,759 (1989)

EIN: 13-6046567

CONTRIBUTIONS SUMMARY

Donor(s): the late Leila E. Riegel, Katherine R. Emory

Typical Recipients: • *Arts & Humanities:* Historic Preservation, History & Archaeology, Libraries, Music, Public Broadcasting • *Civic & Public Affairs:* Botanical Gardens/Parks, General, Public Policy, Urban & Community Affairs, Women's Affairs, Zoos/Aquariums • *Education:* Colleges & Universities, Private Education (Precollege) • *Environment:* General, Resource Conservation • *Health:* Cancer, Emergency/Ambulance Services, Hospitals, Medical Research, Nursing Services • *International:* Health Care/Hospitals • *Religion:* Churches • *Science:* Science Museums • *Social Services:* Animal Protection, Child Welfare, Community Service Organizations, Family Planning, Family Services, Food/Clothing Distribution, United Funds/United Ways, Volunteer Services, Youth Organizations

Grant Types: general support

Geographic Distribution: focus on NY, CT, and ME

GIVING OFFICERS
Chemical Bank: trust

APPLICATION INFORMATION

Initial Approach: Send cover letter and full proposal. Deadline is November 30.

GRANTS ANALYSIS

Total Grants: $229,000

Number of Grants: 52

Highest Grant: $10,000

Typical Range: $500 to $5,000

Disclosure Period: 1992

Note: Recent grants are derived from a 1992 Form 990.

RECENT GRANTS

Library

2,000	Pequot Library Association, Southport, CT
1,000	Foundation Center, New York, NY

General

10,000	American Red Cross — disaster relief fund
10,000	Central Park Conservancy, New York, NY
10,000	Landmark Volunteers, Concord, MA
10,000	Planned Parenthood
10,000	US Committee

Scherman Foundation

CONTACT
Sandra Silverman
Executive Director
The Scherman Foundation
16 E 52nd St., Ste. 601
New York, NY 10022-5306
(212) 832-3086

FINANCIAL SUMMARY

Recent Giving: $4,000,000 (1995 approx.); $3,385,700 (1994); $4,177,303 (1993)

Assets: $70,000,000 (1995 est.); $67,000,000 (1994 approx.); $72,686,569 (1993)

EIN: 13-6098464

CONTRIBUTIONS SUMMARY

Donor(s): The Scherman Foundation was established in 1941 by members of the Scherman family, including the late Harry Scherman. Mr. Scherman, who died in 1969, was one of the founders of the Book-of-the-Month Club. During his lifetime, Mr. Scherman served as a director of the National Bureau of Economic Research and as a trustee of the Mannes College of Music.

Typical Recipients: • *Arts & Humanities:* Ballet, Dance, Libraries, Literary Arts, Museums/Galleries, Music, Opera, Performing Arts, Public Broadcasting, Theater, Visual Arts • *Civic & Public Affairs:* African American Affairs, Botanical Gardens/Parks, Civil Rights, Economic Development, Economic Policy, Employment/Job Training, Hispanic Affairs, Housing, Law & Justice, Legal Aid, Municipalities/Towns, Professional & Trade Associations, Public Policy, Urban & Community Affairs, Women's Affairs, Zoos/Aquariums • *Education:* Arts/Humanities Education, Colleges & Universities, Education Associations, Education Reform, General, International Studies, School Volunteerism • *Environment:* General, Resource Conservation • *Health:* AIDS/HIV, Health Organizations • *International:* Health Care/Hospitals, Human Rights, International Development, International Environmental Issues, International Organizations, International Relief Efforts, Missionary/Religious Activities • *Religion:* Jewish Causes, Social/Policy Issues • *Science:* Science Museums, Scientific Organizations • *Social Services:* Child Welfare, Community Service Organizations, Domestic Violence, Family Planning, Family Services, Food/Clothing Distribution, Senior Services, Shelters/Homelessness, Volunteer Services, Youth Organizations

Grant Types: challenge, general support, multiyear/continuing support, and operating expenses

Geographic Distribution: national, with emphasis on metropolitan New York City for the arts and social welfare programs

GIVING OFFICERS

Hillary Brown: dir

Helen W. Edey: dir *PHIL AFFIL* trust: Edey Foundation

David Forgan Freeman: treas *B* Chicago IL 1918 *ED* Princeton Univ AB 1940; Yale Univ LLB 1947

Archibald R. Murray: dir *B* 1933 *ED* Howard Univ BA 1954; NY Law Sch 1988; Fordham Univ 1992 *NONPR AFFIL* exec dir, chief atty: Legal Aid Soc; mem: Am Bar Assn, NY St Bar Assn; trust: Fordham Univ; vestry mem: St Philips Church

Axel G. Rosin: chmn, dir

Katharine S. Rosin: secy, dir

Anthony M. Schulte: dir

Sandra Silverman: exec dir, asst secy

Karen R. Sollins: pres, dir

Marcia T. Thompson: dir

APPLICATION INFORMATION
Initial Approach:

There are no application forms. Applicants should submit a brief letter outlining the purpose for which funds are sought.

Include a budget, recent financial statement listing sources of support, evidence of tax-exempt status, and names of members of the board of directors and of key personnel.

There are no deadlines for submitting proposals.

Applications which fall within the scope of interests of the foundation are considered and acted upon by the board at its meetings. The board meets four times a year; dates of the meetings are not fixed.

Restrictions on Giving: The foundation generally excludes from consideration all applications requesting grants for individuals, colleges, universities, or professional schools. The foundation generally does not fund in the area of health; nor does it support individual performances, film, or video production.

PUBLICATIONS

Annual report; statement of policy and procedures

GRANTS ANALYSIS
Total Grants: $4,177,303

Number of Grants: 135

Highest Grant: $130,000

Average Grant: $30,943

Typical Range: $10,000 to $35,000

Disclosure Period: 1993

Note: Recent grants are derived from a 1993 Form 990.

RECENT GRANTS

Library
100,000	New York Public Library, New York, NY

General
130,000	United Jewish Appeal Federation of Jewish Philanthropies, New York, NY
100,000	NAACP Legal Defense and Educational Fund, New York, NY
100,000	Planned Parenthood of New York City, New York, NY
90,000	Partnership for the Homeless, New York, NY
90,000	Population Action International, Washington, DC — public education program and special projects fund

Schiff Foundation, Dorothy

Former Foundation Name: The Pisces Foundation

CONTACT
Adele Hall Sweet
President
Dorothy Schiff Fdn.
53 E 66th St.
New York, NY 10021
(212) 270-4723

FINANCIAL SUMMARY
Recent Giving: $421,000 (1993); $461,000 (1992); $401,500 (1990)

Assets: $9,206,421 (1993); $9,171,816 (1992); $8,249,840 (1990)

Gifts Received: $49,500 (1993); $102,031 (1987)

EIN: 13-6018311

CONTRIBUTIONS SUMMARY
Donor(s): the late Dorothy Schiff, New York Post Corp.

Typical Recipients: • *Arts & Humanities:* Arts Associations & Councils, History & Archaeology, Libraries, Museums/Galleries, Public Broadcasting • *Civic & Public Affairs:* Clubs, Economic Development, General, Municipalities/Towns, Professional & Trade Associations, Public Policy, Urban & Community Affairs • *Education:* Colleges & Universities, Engineering/Technological Education, Medical Education, Minority Education, Private Education (Precollege), Public Education (Precollege), School Volunteerism, Secondary Education (Private), Social Sciences Education • *Environment:* General, Resource Conservation • *Health:* AIDS/HIV, Cancer, Hospitals, Medical Research, Prenatal Health Issues, Single-Disease Health Associations • *Science:* Scientific Centers & Institutes • *Social Services:* At-Risk Youth, Child Welfare, Community Centers, Community Service

Organizations, Family Planning, Family Services, People with Disabilities, Refugee Assistance, Shelters/Homelessness, Youth Organizations

Grant Types: general support

Geographic Distribution: focus on NY

GIVING OFFICERS
Mortimer W. Hall: treas

Sarah-Ann Kramarsky: secy

Adele Hall Sweet: pres

APPLICATION INFORMATION
Initial Approach: Send brief letter of inquiry describing program or project. There are no deadlines.

GRANTS ANALYSIS
Total Grants: $421,000

Number of Grants: 37

Highest Grant: $30,000

Typical Range: $2,500 to $25,000

Disclosure Period: 1993

Note: Recent grants are derived from a 1993 Form 990.

RECENT GRANTS

Library
25,000	New York Public Library, New York, NY
25,000	New York Public Library Department of Rare Books, New York, NY

General
30,000	Memorial Sloan-Kettering Cancer Center, New York, NY
25,000	East Harlem School at Exodus House, New York, NY
25,000	Woods Hole Research Center, Woods Hole, MA
20,000	New School for Social Research, New York, NY
20,000	Planned Parenthood of New York City, New York, NY

Schlumberger Ltd. / Schlumberger Foundation

Revenue: $6.71 billion
Employees: 51,000
Parent Company: Schlumberger Ltd., Paris, France
Headquarters: New York, NY
SIC Major Group: Oil & Gas Field Services Nec, Oil & Gas Field Machinery, and Instruments to Measure Electricity

CONTACT
Arthur W. Alexander
Secretary-Treasurer
Schlumberger Foundation
277 Park Ave.
New York, NY 10172-0266
(212) 350-9455

Note: The company's World Wide Web address is http://www.slb.com

FINANCIAL SUMMARY

Recent Giving: $845,184 (1993); $940,977 (1992); $762,101 (1991)

Assets: $17,582,240 (1993); $18,003,561 (1992); $18,833,582 (1991)

Fiscal Note: All contributions are made through the foundation.

EIN: 23-7033142

CONTRIBUTIONS SUMMARY

Typical Recipients: • *Arts & Humanities:* Arts Centers, Ballet, Dance, Ethnic & Folk Arts, Historic Preservation, Libraries, Literary Arts, Museums/Galleries, Opera, Public Broadcasting, Theater • *Civic & Public Affairs:* Botanical Gardens/Parks, Economic Development, Legal Aid, Minority Business, Nonprofit Management, Professional & Trade Associations, Women's Affairs • *Education:* Arts/Humanities Education, Colleges & Universities, Economic Education, Education Associations, Engineering/Technological Education, Faculty Development, International Studies, Medical Education, Minority Education, Science/Mathematics Education, Special Education, Student Aid • *Environment:* General, Resource Conservation • *Health:* Alzheimers Disease, Eyes/Blindness, Hospitals, Medical Research, Single-Disease Health Associations • *International:* Foreign Educational Institutions • *Science:* Science Museums, Scientific Centers & Institutes • *Social Services:* Community Service Organizations, Food/Clothing Distribution, People with Disabilities, Shelters/Homelessness, Youth Organizations

Grant Types: capital, fellowship, general support, professorship, project, research, and scholarship

Geographic Distribution: nationally to education; other contributions concentrated in New York City area

Operating Locations: CA (Mountain View, Oxnard, San Jose), CT (Bridgeport), GA (Atlanta, Norcross), MI (Ann Arbor), NY (Elmsford, New York, Syosset), OR (Medford), PA (Archbold), TX (Dallas, Houston, Sugarland)

Note: Company maintains operations throughout the world.

CORP. OFFICERS

Dugald Euan Baird: *B* Aberdeen Scotland 1937 *ED* Aberdeen Univ 1955; Cambridge Univ BA 1960 *CURR EMPL* chmn, ceo: Schlumberger Ltd

Roland Genin: *B* Thuilley France 1927 *ED* Arts et Metiers 1949 *CURR EMPL* vchmn, dir: Schlumberger Ltd

GIVING OFFICERS

Arthur W. Alexander: secy-treas *CURR EMPL* vp, dir pers: Schlumberger Ltd

John D. Ingram: vp

George Hiram Jewell: dir *B* Ft. Worth TX 1922 *ED* Univ TX BA 1942; Univ TX LLB 1950 *CURR EMPL* couns: Baker & Botts *CORP AFFIL* dir: Bank SW Houston, Pogo Producing Co, Schlumberger Ltd, SW Bancshares *NONPR AFFIL* Phi Beta Kappa, Phi Delta Phi; fellow: Am Bar Fdn, Am Coll Tax Counc; mem: Am Bar Assn, Order Coif; mem adv counc: Univ TX Coll Natural Sci; trust: TX Childrens Hosp *CLUB AFFIL* Coronado CC, Eldorado CC, Houston CC, Old Baldy CC

Pierre Marcel Schlumberger: dir *B* 1943 *ED* Yale Univ BA 1963; Southern Methodist Univ LLD 1966 *CLUB AFFIL* Argyle *PHIL AFFIL* secy, dir: Menil Foundation

Roy Ray Shourd: pres *B* East St Louis IL 1927 *ED* Univ MO 1950 *CURR EMPL* exec vp drilling & products: Schlumberger Ltd *NONPR AFFIL* mem: Am Petroleum Inst

APPLICATION INFORMATION

Initial Approach: *Initial Contact:* brief letter or proposal *Include Information On:* description of the organization, amount requested, purpose for which funds are sought, recently audited financial statement, and proof of tax-exempt status *Deadlines:* none

GRANTS ANALYSIS

Total Grants: $845,184

Number of Grants: 87

Highest Grant: $50,000

Average Grant: $9,715

Typical Range: $1,000 to $10,000

Disclosure Period: 1993

Note: Recent grants are derived from a 1993 Form 990.

RECENT GRANTS

General
50,000	Houston Museum of Natural Science, Houston, TX — for the arts
25,000	Georgia Institute of Technology Visualization, Atlanta, GA
23,350	Central Park Conservancy, New York, NY
20,000	Colorado School of Mines, Golden, CO — for Borehole Technologies
20,000	Rice University Seismic Data Processing, Houston, TX

Schmitt Foundation, Kilian J. and Caroline F.

CONTACT
Gary J. Lindsay
Secretary-Treasurer
Kilian J. and Caroline F. Schmitt Fdn.
349 W. Commercial St.
East Rochester, NY 14445
(716) 264-0030

FINANCIAL SUMMARY

Recent Giving: $291,473 (fiscal 1994)

Assets: $8,142,290 (fiscal 1994)

EIN: 22-3087449

CONTRIBUTIONS SUMMARY

Typical Recipients: • *Arts & Humanities:* Libraries, Public Broadcasting • *Civic & Public Affairs:* Clubs • *Education:* Colleges & Universities, Engineering/Technological Education, Student Aid • *Health:* Children's Health/Hospitals, Home-Care Services, Kidney, Speech & Hearing • *International:* International Organizations • *Religion:* Churches • *Social Services:* Camps, Community Service Organizations, People with Disabilities, Senior Services

Grant Types: general support

Geographic Distribution: focus on NY

GIVING OFFICERS

James R. Dray: dir

Leon Fella: dir

Robert H. Fella: pres

Alfred Hallenbeck: dir

Roger D. Lathan: dir

Gary J. Lindsay: secy, treas

Michael Walker: vp

APPLICATION INFORMATION

Initial Approach: Send a brief letter of inquiry. Include a description of organization, amount requested, purpose of funds sought, recently audited financial statement, and proof of tax-exempt status.

GRANTS ANALYSIS
Total Grants: $291,473

Number of Grants: 23

Highest Grant: $160,000

Typical Range: $500 to $60,000

Disclosure Period: fiscal year ending February 28, 1994

Note: Recent grants are derived from a fiscal 1994 Form 990.

RECENT GRANTS

Library
500	Rochester Toy Library, Rochester, NY

General
160,000	University of Rochester, Rochester, NY — endowed professorship
60,000	Nazareth College, Rochester, NY — endowed professorship
30,000	Roberts Wesleyan College, Rochester, NY — capital campaign
10,000	Camp Good Days and Special Times, Mendon, NY — special international program for sick children
10,000	University of Rochester, Rochester, NY — symposium

Schwartz Fund for Education and Health Research, Arnold and Marie

CONTACT
Marie D. Schwartz
President
Arnold and Marie Schwartz Fund for
Education and Health Research
465 Pk. Ave.
New York, NY 10022

FINANCIAL SUMMARY
Recent Giving: $362,180 (fiscal 1994); $553,378 (fiscal 1993); $499,725 (fiscal 1992)

Assets: $5,416,914 (fiscal 1994); $5,694,025 (fiscal 1993); $5,596,180 (fiscal 1992)

EIN: 23-7115019

CONTRIBUTIONS SUMMARY

Donor(s): Arnold Schwartz Charitable Trust.

Typical Recipients: • *Arts & Humanities:* Arts Associations & Councils, Arts Festivals, Arts Institutes, Ballet, Dance, Ethnic & Folk Arts, Historic Preservation, History & Archaeology, Libraries, Museums/Galleries, Music, Opera, Performing Arts, Public Broadcasting • *Civic & Public Affairs:* Botanical Gardens/Parks, Clubs, General, Housing, Law & Justice, Parades/Festivals, Public Policy, Safety, Women's Affairs, Zoos/Aquariums • *Education:* Arts/Humanities Education, Colleges & Universities, Health & Physical Education, Medical Education • *Environment:* General • *Health:* Cancer, Emergency/Ambulance Services, Health Organizations, Hospitals, Hospitals (University Affiliated), Medical Research, Single-Disease Health Associations • *International:* Foreign Educational Institutions, Human Rights, Missionary/Religious Activities • *Religion:* Bible Study/Translation,

Churches, Jewish Causes, Ministries, Religious Organizations, Religious Welfare, Synagogues/Temples • *Social Services:* Child Welfare, Community Service Organizations, Family Services, Recreation & Athletics, Youth Organizations

Grant Types: general support

Geographic Distribution: focus on the New York, NY, area

GIVING OFFICERS
Sylvia Kassel: dir

Ruth Kerstein: secy, dir

Nellie J. McDonald: dir

Marie D. Schwartz: pres

APPLICATION INFORMATION
Initial Approach: Send brief letter of inquiry describing program or project. There are no deadlines.

GRANTS ANALYSIS
Total Grants: $362,180

Number of Grants: 77

Highest Grant: $156,500

Typical Range: $50 to $50,000

Disclosure Period: fiscal year ending March 31, 1994

Note: Recent grants are derived from a 1994 Form 990.

RECENT GRANTS

General
156,500	New York University, New York, NY — donation
12,200	Police Athletic League, New York, NY — donation
6,000	American New Women's Foundation, Washington, DC — donation
6,000	Arnold and Marie Schwartz Fund, Brooklyn, NY — donation
5,500	Cumberland College, Williamsburg, KY — donation

Seagram & Sons, Inc., Joseph E. / Bronfman Foundation, Samuel

Sales: $3.9 billion
Employees: 16,200
Headquarters: New York, NY
SIC Major Group: Distilled & Blended Liquors, Canned Fruits & Vegetables, Wines, Brandy & Brandy Spirits, and Bottled & Canned Soft Drinks

CONTACT
William K. Friedman
Vice President & Trustee
Joseph E. Seagram & Sons, Inc.
375 Park Ave.
New York, NY 10152
(212) 572-7516

FINANCIAL SUMMARY
Recent Giving: $10,000,000 (1994 est.); $6,061,582 (1993); $5,633,175 (1992)

Assets: $10,031,054 (1993); $8,019,527 (1992); $12,307,375 (1991)

Gifts Received: $7,711,374 (1993); $1,828,416 (1992)

Fiscal Note: Company and subsidiaries give through foundation only. Sales companies may give individually, but such grants must be approved by the foundation. In 1993, contributions were received from Seagram Distillers Charitable Trust ($4,691,007), Edgar M. Bronfman ($1,000,000), Joseph E. Seagram & Sons, Inc. ($2,000,000), Louisville Crown Co. ($5,000), and Price Waterhouse ($5,000); miscellaneous donations totaling $10,367 were also received.

EIN: 13-6084708

CONTRIBUTIONS SUMMARY
Typical Recipients: • *Arts & Humanities:* Arts Centers, Libraries, Museums/Galleries, Public Broadcasting • *Civic & Public Affairs:* African American Affairs, Business/Free Enterprise, Civil Rights, Legal Aid, Public Policy • *Education:* Business Education, Colleges & Universities, Minority Education, Religious Education, Student Aid • *Health:* Medical Research • *International:* Foreign Educational Institutions, International Organizations, International Peace & Security Issues, International Relations, Missionary/Religious Activities • *Religion:* Jewish Causes, Religious Organizations • *Social Services:* Emergency Relief, Substance Abuse, Youth Organizations

Grant Types: challenge, employee matching gifts, fellowship, general support, professorship, and research

Nonmonetary Support Types: donated products

Note: Value of nonmonetary support is unavailable and is not included above.

Geographic Distribution: primarily New York City

Operating Locations: CA (Los Angeles), FL (Bradenton, Tampa), IL (Des Plaines), IN (Lawrenceburg), KY (Louisville), MD (Baltimore), NY (New York), OH (Cleveland)

CORP. OFFICERS
Edgar Miles Bronfman: *B* Montreal Quebec Canada 1929 *ED* Williams Coll 1946-1949; McGill Univ BA 1951 *CURR EMPL* chmn: Joseph E Seagram & Sons Inc *CORP AFFIL* chmn, ceo, dir: Seagram Co Ltd; dir: EI du Pont de Nemours & Co *NONPR AFFIL* bd delegates: Un Am Hebrew Congregation; chmn: Am Jewish Comm; chmn planning comm, mem adv counc: Columbia Univ Sch Intl Pub Aff; chmn, pres: World Jewish Congress; chmn, trust: Bnai Brith Anti-Defamation League NY; dir: Am Technician Soc, US-USSR Trade Econ Counc, Weizmann Inst; mem: Bus Comm Arts, Counc Econ Devel, Counc Foreign Rels, Ctr

Intl-Am Rels, Foreign Policy Assn, Hundred Years Assn NY, Un Jewish Appeal; mem bd overseers: Bnai Brith Intl Trust; pres: N Am Consortium Free Market Study

Edgar Miles Bronfman, Jr.: *B* 1955 *CURR EMPL* pres, ceo, dir: Joseph E Seagram & Sons Inc *CORP AFFIL* pres, ceo, dir: JE Seagram Corp

William K. Friedman: *CURR EMPL* vp corp aff: Joseph E Seagram & Sons Inc

GIVING OFFICERS
Stephen Edward Banner: trust *B* New York NY 1938 *ED* Harvard Univ LLB; Yale Univ BA *CURR EMPL* sr exec vp, dir: Seagram Co Ltd *CORP AFFIL* sr exec vp, dir: JE Seagram Corp, Joseph E Seagram & Sons Inc *NONPR AFFIL* lecturer: Practicing Law Inst; mem: Assn Bar City New York

Charles R. Bronfman: trust

Edgar Miles Bronfman: chmn, trust *CURR EMPL* chmn: Joseph E Seagram & Sons Inc (see above)

Edgar Miles Bronfman, Jr.: trust *CURR EMPL* pres, ceo, dir: Joseph E Seagram & Sons Inc (see above)

Samuel Bronfman II: pres, trust *B* 1954 *CURR EMPL* pres, chmn, ceo: Sterling Vineyards Inc *CORP AFFIL* pres, dir: Domaine Nunn Inc

Claire Cullen: secy *CURR EMPL* dir corp philanthropy: Joseph E Seagram & Sons Inc

William K. Friedman: trust *CURR EMPL* vp corp aff: Joseph E Seagram & Sons Inc (see above)

Patricia Glazer: trust *CURR EMPL* dir pub aff: Joseph E Seagram & Sons Inc

David G. Sacks: trust

APPLICATION INFORMATION
Initial Approach: *Initial Contact:* letter *Include Information On:* reason for requesting support, amount needed, and proof of tax-exempt status *Deadlines:* none *Note:* Further information will be requested if foundation is interested.

Restrictions on Giving: Does not support individuals.

GRANTS ANALYSIS
Total Grants: $6,061,582

Number of Grants: 33

Highest Grant: $1,004,600

Typical Range: $20,000 to $1,000,000

Disclosure Period: 1993

Note: Number of grants and typical range do not include contributions under $20,000, totaling $532,813 in 1993. Recent grants are derived from a 1993 Form 990.

RECENT GRANTS
Library

95,000	Bronfman Library, New York, NY

General

1,004,600	World Jewish Congress, New York, NY
1,000,000	Bronfman Center for Jewish Life, New York, NY
800,000	United Jewish Appeal, New York, NY
500,000	Canadian Centre for Architecture
460,000	Bronfman Youth Fellowships, New York, NY

Seneca Foods Corp. / Seneca Foods Foundation

Sales: $290.0 million
Employees: 1,336
Headquarters: Pittsford, NY
SIC Major Group: Apparel & Other Textile Products, Food & Kindred Products, and Transportation by Air

CONTACT
Kraig Kayser
President and CEO
Seneca Foods Foundation
1162 Pittsford-Victor Rd.
Pittsford, NY 14534
(716) 385-9500

FINANCIAL SUMMARY
Recent Giving: $76,750 (fiscal 1993); $86,468 (fiscal 1992); $89,017 (fiscal 1991)

Assets: $1,742,880 (fiscal 1993); $1,585,397 (fiscal 1992); $1,965,009 (fiscal 1991)

EIN: 22-2996324

CONTRIBUTIONS SUMMARY
Typical Recipients: • *Arts & Humanities:* Arts Associations & Councils, General, Libraries, Museums/Galleries, Music, Performing Arts, Public Broadcasting • *Civic & Public Affairs:* Chambers of Commerce, Clubs, General, Housing, Parades/Festivals, Professional & Trade Associations, Safety, Urban & Community Affairs, Zoos/Aquariums • *Education:* Agricultural Education, Business Education, Colleges & Universities, Community & Junior Colleges, General, Private Education (Precollege), Student Aid • *Environment:* Wildlife Protection • *Health:* Cancer, Children's Health/Hospitals, Diabetes, Emergency/Ambulance Services, General, Health Organizations, Heart, Hospitals, Medical Rehabilitation, Multiple Sclerosis, Prenatal Health Issues • *Religion:* Churches, Jewish Causes • *Social Services:* Camps, Child Welfare, Community Service Organizations, Delinquency & Criminal Rehabilitation, Family Services, General, People with Disabilities, Recreation & Athletics, Scouts, Special Olympics, Substance Abuse, United Funds/United Ways, Veterans, YMCA/YWCA/YMHA/YWHA, Youth Organizations

Grant Types: general support

Geographic Distribution: headquarters and operating locations

Operating Locations: MN (Rochester), NY (Marion, Pittsford)

CORP. OFFICERS
Kraig H. Kayser: *CURR EMPL* pres, ceo: Seneca Foods Corp

Frederick W. Leick: *B* Lakewood OH 1943 *ED* Case Western Reserve Univ 1967 *CURR EMPL* pres, ceo: Seneca Foods Corp

GIVING OFFICERS
Devra A. Bevona: asst secy, treas

Kraig H. Kayser: pres, ceo, dir *CURR EMPL* pres, ceo: Seneca Foods Corp (see above)

Susan W. Stuart: dir

Jeffrey L. Van Riper: secy

Arthur S. Wolcott: chmn, dir

APPLICATION INFORMATION
Initial Approach: The foundation has no formal grant application procedure or application form. There are no deadlines.

GRANTS ANALYSIS
Total Grants: $76,750

Number of Grants: 65

Highest Grant: $25,000

Typical Range: $100 to $17,690

Disclosure Period: fiscal year ending July 31, 1993

Note: Recent grants are derived from a fiscal 1993 Form 990.

RECENT GRANTS
General

25,000	Cornell University, Ithaca, NY
17,690	United Way Fund
2,500	Camp Good Days, Cayuga, NY
2,500	New York Special Olympics, New York, NY
2,000	Al Sigl Center, Rochester, NY

Shubert Foundation

CONTACT
Vicki Reiss
Executive Director
Shubert Foundation
234 W 44th St.
New York, NY 10036
(212) 944-3777

FINANCIAL SUMMARY
Recent Giving: $6,032,650 (fiscal 1994); $5,400,500 (fiscal 1993); $3,558,000 (fiscal 1992)

Assets: $124,725,000 (fiscal 1994 approx.); $149,277,109 (fiscal 1993); $119,244,000 (fiscal 1992)

Gifts Received: $134,000 (fiscal 1994 approx.); $140,553 (fiscal 1993); $150,000 (fiscal 1992)

Fiscal Note: The foundation receives contributions from the estate and trust of Lee Shubert under his will.

EIN: 13-6106961

CONTRIBUTIONS SUMMARY

Donor(s): The Shubert Foundation was established in 1945 as the Sam S. Shubert Foundation by Lee Shubert and Jacob J. Shubert , in memory of their brother. The name was changed to the Shubert Foundation in 1971. The brothers contributed annually to the foundation. The foundation's funds were increased significantly by funds received from the estate of Lee Shubert in 1970 and from the estate of Jacob J. Shubert in 1972. The foundation is the sole shareholder of the Shubert Organization, which owns and operates the Shubert theaters.

Typical Recipients: • *Arts & Humanities:* Arts Associations & Councils, Ballet, Dance, General, Libraries, Music, Opera, Performing Arts, Theater • *Education:* Arts/Humanities Education, Colleges & Universities • *Health:* Clinics/Medical Centers • *Religion:* Jewish Causes

Grant Types: general support

Geographic Distribution: to national organizations only

GIVING OFFICERS

Bernard B. Jacobs: pres *B* New York NY 1916 *ED* NY Univ BA 1937; Columbia Univ JD 1940 *CURR EMPL* pres: Shubert Org *NONPR AFFIL* vp, dir: League NY Theaters Producers

John Werner Kluge: vp *B* Chemnitz Germany 1914 *ED* Columbia Univ BA 1937 *CURR EMPL* chmn, dir: Metromedia Co *CORP AFFIL* chmn: Metpon Acquisition; chmn, dir: LDDS Communs, Pon Holding Corp; chmn, pres, dir: Benole Holdings Corp, Kluge Finkelstein & Co, Metbenale Holdings Corp; chmn, treas: Kluge & Co, Tri-Suburban Broadcasting Corp; chmn, treas, pres: Silver City Sales Co; dir: Belding Hemingway Co, Chock Full O Nuts, Just One Break Inc, Marriott-Hot Shoppes, Natl Bank MD, Waldorf Astoria Corp *NONPR AFFIL* bd gov: NY Coll Osteopathic Medicine; dir: Brand Names Fdn; mem: Advertising Club Washington, Advertising Counc New York City, Grocery Mfrs Reps Washington, Grocery Wheels Washington, Natl Assn Radio TV Broadcasters, Natl Food Brokers Assn, Natl Sugar Brokers Assn, Washington Bd Trade, Washington Food Brokers Assn; pres, chmn exec comm, dir: Un Cerebral Palsy Assn; treas: Preventive Medicine Inst; trust: Miliken Univ Strang Clinic *PHIL AFFIL* chmn, don: Kluge Foundation *CLUB AFFIL* Army & Navy, Broadcasters, Columbia Assocs, Figure Skating, Marco Polo, Metropolitan, Natl Capitol Skeet & Trap, Olympic, University

D. S. Moynihan: program dir

Vicki Reiss: exec dir

Gerald Schoenfeld: chmn *B* 1924 *ED* Univ IL BS 1947; NY Univ LLB 1949 *CURR EMPL* chmn, dir: Shubert Org

Lee J. Seidler: treas *B* Newark NJ 1935 *ED* Columbia Coll BA 1956; Columbia Univ MS 1957; Columbia Univ PhD 1965 *CURR EMPL* special assoc dir: Bear Stearns & Co *CORP AFFIL* dir: Players Intl, Shubert Org, Synthetics Indus

Michael Ira Sovern: vp *B* New York NY 1931 *ED* Columbia Univ AB 1953; Columbia Univ LLB 1955 *CORP AFFIL* dir: AT&T, Chem Bank, GNY Ins Group, Orion Pictures Corp, Shubert Org *NONPR AFFIL* dir: Asian Cultural Counc, NAACP Legal Defense Ed Fund; fellow: Am Academy Arts Sciences; mem: Am Arbitration Assn, Am Bar Assn, Am Law Inst, Bar Assn City New York, Counc Foreign Rels, Natl Academy Arbitrators, NJ Bd Mediation Panel Arbitration, Pulitzer Prize Bd; mem panel arbitrators: Fed Mediation Conciliation Svc *CLUB AFFIL* Econ *PHIL AFFIL* dir: Jerome L. Greene Foundation

Irving M. Wall: secy, dir

APPLICATION INFORMATION
Initial Approach:

All requests must be submitted on the foundation's application form.

Applicants must include audited financial statements for the most recent fiscal year and a copy of 501(c)(3) tax-exemption status letter. The audited financial statement should include a comparative statement to the prior year.

Applications are available after September 1, and must be received no later than December 1 to qualify for a grant.

The foundation uses various criteria in the evaluation of an applicant's program. Performing theater and dance organizations are evaluated with respect to their contribution to their discipline as a whole. Larger, well-established organizations are expected to demonstrate their continued ability to develop and produce significant additions to their discipline. Smaller organizations are evaluated with respect to their size and resources. Both types of organizations are evaluated in terms of their effectiveness in reaching audiences. Arts-related organizations are evaluated on the importance and value of their work as demonstrated by past and current performance. Evidence of financial responsibility is also an important factor in the evaluation process.

College and university drama departments are evaluated in terms of their ability to develop and educate new talent. The role that the school takes in theatrical innovation is considered. Preference is given to private universities.

Non-arts-related organizations are sometimes allocated support, but they must possess unique attributes which demonstrate their deservedness. Organizations improving the urban environment in which theaters op-

erate are accorded preference. All grants are announced and disbursed in the late spring of each year.

Restrictions on Giving: The foundation does not provide funds for audience devlopment, direct subsidies for reduced admission price, captial campaigns, brick and mortar projects, or to individuals. Grants are not made to community foundations or other conduit orgazniations. The foundation reports that it does not provide seed money or grants to newly created organizations. Groups with budgets of less than $150,000 should contact the foundation before submitting an application.

PUBLICATIONS
Annual report

GRANTS ANALYSIS

Total Grants: $6,032,650

Number of Grants: 216

Average Grant: $27,929

Typical Range: $5,000 to $50,000

Disclosure Period: fiscal year ending May 31, 1994

Note: The highest grant figure for 1994 was unavailable. Recent grants are derived from a fidcal 1993 grants list.

RECENT GRANTS

Library
250,000	Columbia University, New York, NY — Sovern Library	

General
100,000	Columbia University, New York, NY — presidential scholars program	
100,000	Tisch School of the Arts, New York, NY	
75,000	United Jewish Appeal Federation of Jewish Philanthropies, New York, NY	
45,000	Brooklyn Academy of Music, Brooklyn, NY	
30,000	New York University Medical Center, New York, NY	

Slifka Foundation, Joseph and Sylvia

CONTACT
Sylvia Slifka
Vice President
Joseph and Sylvia Slifka Fdn.
477 Madison Ave.
New York, NY 10022
(212) 753-5766

FINANCIAL SUMMARY

Recent Giving: $881,313 (fiscal 1993); $940,610 (fiscal 1992); $312,660 (fiscal 1991)

Assets: $3,406,942 (fiscal 1993); $3,412,585 (fiscal 1992); $3,661,002 (fiscal 1991)

Gifts Received: $500,000 (fiscal 1993); $380,000 (fiscal 1992); $806,915 (fiscal 1991)

Fiscal Note: In fiscal 1993, contributions were received from Sylvia Slifka.

EIN: 13-6106433

CONTRIBUTIONS SUMMARY

Typical Recipients: • *Arts & Humanities:* Arts Associations & Councils, Libraries, Museums/Galleries, Music, Performing Arts, Public Broadcasting • *Civic & Public Affairs:* Botanical Gardens/Parks, General, Urban & Community Affairs • *Education:* Colleges & Universities, Medical Education, Minority Education, Private Education (Precollege), Student Aid • *Environment:* Air/Water Quality, General, Resource Conservation • *Health:* AIDS/HIV, Cancer, Children's Health/Hospitals, Clinics/Medical Centers, Eyes/Blindness, Geriatric Health, Heart, Hospitals, Medical Research • *International:* Foreign Arts Organizations, Missionary/Religious Activities • *Religion:* Jewish Causes, Religious Organizations, Religious Welfare, Synagogues/Temples • *Social Services:* Animal Protection, Big Brother/Big Sister, Child Welfare, Community Centers, Community Service Organizations, Family Planning, Family Services, Food/Clothing Distribution, Homes, People with Disabilities, Recreation & Athletics, United Funds/United Ways, Youth Organizations

Grant Types: general support and research

Geographic Distribution: focus on New York, NY

GIVING OFFICERS

Alan B. Slifka: treas *B* New York NY 1929 *ED* Yale Univ 1951; Harvard Univ 1953 *CURR EMPL* mng ptnr: Slifka (Alan B) & Co/Halycon Partnerships *CORP AFFIL* dir: Pall Corp *PHIL AFFIL* pres, treas: Alan B. Slifka Foundation

Barbara S. Slifka: secy, trust

Sylvia Slifka: vp

APPLICATION INFORMATION

Initial Approach: The foundation requests applications be made in writing. Include a description of organization, amount requested, purpose of funds sought, recently audited financial statement, and proof of tax-exempt status. There are no deadlines.

GRANTS ANALYSIS

Total Grants: $881,313

Number of Grants: 79

Highest Grant: $500,000

Typical Range: $100 to $100,000

Disclosure Period: fiscal year ending October 31, 1993

Note: Recent grants are derived from a fiscal 1993 Form 990.

RECENT GRANTS

Library
1,000	New York Public Library, New York, NY

General
500,000	Yale University, New Haven, CT
100,000	Congregation Emanu-El, New York, NY
100,000	United Jewish Appeal Federation, New York, NY
50,000	Abraham Fund, New York, NY
10,000	Congregation Emanu-El, New York, NY

Sloan Foundation, Alfred P.

CONTACT
Ralph E. Gomory
President
Alfred P. Sloan Foundation
630 Fifth Ave., Ste. 2550
New York, NY 10111
(212) 649-1649

FINANCIAL SUMMARY

Recent Giving: $31,016,702 (1993); $32,625,776 (1992); $28,561,076 (1991)

Assets: $849,741,304 (1993); $775,698,874 (1992); $727,641,989 (1991)

Gifts Received: $274,667 (1992); $243,356 (1990)

Fiscal Note: In 1992, contributions were in the form of refunds from prior year grants.

EIN: 13-1623877

CONTRIBUTIONS SUMMARY

Donor(s): Alfred Pritchard Sloan, Jr., was born in New Haven, CT, on May 23, 1875. After graduating with a degree in electrical engineering from the Massachusetts Institute of Technology in 1892, he began his career with the Hyatt Roller Bearing Company in Newark, NJ. He became president of the company at the age of 24.

In 1916, the company merged with the United Motors Company, and two years later became part of the General Motors Company. Alfred Sloan was elected president in 1923; and subsequently served as chief executive officer for twenty-three years until 1946. In 1937, he was elected chairman of GM. He resigned the chairmanship in 1956, remaining honorary chairman until his death in 1966. He established the Alfred P. Sloan Foundation in 1934.

Typical Recipients: • *Arts & Humanities:* Arts Associations & Councils, Libraries, Museums/Galleries, Public Broadcasting • *Civic & Public Affairs:* Business/Free Enterprise, Community Foundations, Economic Policy, Philanthropic Organizations, Professional & Trade Associations, Public Policy • *Education:* Arts/Humanities Education, Business Education, Colleges & Universities, Community & Junior Colleges, Economic Education, Education Associations, Engineering/Technological Education, Faculty Development, General, International Exchange, International Studies, Minority Education, Science/Mathematics Education, Social Sciences Education • *International:* Health Care/Hospitals, International Affairs, International Organizations, International Relations • *Science:* General, Scientific Centers & Institutes, Scientific Organizations, Scientific Research • *Social Services:* Family Services, People with Disabilities, Substance Abuse

Grant Types: conference/seminar, department, fellowship, multiyear/continuing support, project, and research

Geographic Distribution: national

GIVING OFFICERS

Lucy Peters Wilson Benson: trust *B* New York NY 1927 *ED* Smith Coll BA 1949; Smith Coll MA 1955 *CURR EMPL* pres: Benson & Assocs *CORP AFFIL* dir: Commun Satellite Corp, Dreyfus Convertible Securities Fund, Dreyfus Fund, Dreyfus Liquid Assets, Dreyfus Third Century Fund, Dreyfus US Guaranteed Money Fund, Gen Re Corp, Grumman Corp *NONPR AFFIL* dir: Catalyst, Intl Exec Svc Corps, Logistics Mgmt Inst; mem: Am Civil Liberties Union, Counc Foreign Rels, Inst Intl Strategic Studies, Jersey Wildlife Preservation Trust Channel Islands, NAACP, Natl Academy Pub Admin, Trilateral Commn, Un Nations Assn, Urban League; mem visiting comm: Harvard Univ John F Kennedy Sch Govt; trust: Lafayette Coll; vchmn: Citizens Network Foreign Affs

Stewart Fred Campbell: fin vp, secy *B* St Louis MO 1931 *ED* Lehigh Univ BS 1954; NY Univ MBA 1961 *CORP AFFIL* dir: Pocono Hotels Corp *NONPR AFFIL* trust, pres: Meml Home Upper Montclair *CLUB AFFIL* Montclair GC, Rockefeller Ctr, Skytop

Hirsh Cohen: vp

Lloyd Charles Elam, MD: trust *B* Little Rock AR 1928 *ED* Roosevelt Univ BS 1950; Univ WA MD 1957 *CORP AFFIL* dir: Merck & Co Inc *PHIL AFFIL* trust: Merck Co. Foundation

S. Parker Gilbert: trust, mem *B* New York NY 1933 *ED* Yale Univ BA 1956

Ralph Edward Gomory: pres, trust, mem exec & investment comms *B* Brooklyn Heights NY 1929 *ED* Cambridge Univ Kings Coll 1950-1951; Williams Coll BA 1950; Cambridge Univ Kings Coll PhD 1954 *CORP AFFIL* dir: Ashland Oil, Bank NY, Lexmark Intl, Washington Post Co *NONPR AFFIL* fellow: Am Academy Arts & Sciences, Am Philosophical Soc, Econometric Soc; mem: Counc Foreign Rels, Natl Academy Engg, Natl Academy Sciences

Howard Wesley Johnson: commission trust, chmn exec comm, mem investment comm *B* Chicago IL 1922 *ED* Central Coll BA 1943; Univ Chicago MA 1947 *CORP AFFIL* dir: Champion Intl Corp, EI du Pont de Nemours & Co, John Hancock Mutual Life Ins Co, JP Morgan & Co, Morgan Guaranty Trust Co *NONPR AFFIL* fellow: Am Academy Arts & Sciences, Am Assn Advancement Science; mem: Am Philosophical Soc, Counc Foreign Rels, Phi Gamma Delta; mem-at-large: Boy Scouts Am; mem corp: Mus Science Boston, Woods Hole Oceanographic Inst; trust: Boston Mus Fine Arts; trust emeritus: Wellesley Coll *CLUB AFFIL* Century Assn New York City, Commercial, St Botolph, Tavern, Univ New York City

Howard H. Kehrl: trust *B* Detroit MI 1923 *ED* IL Inst Tech BS 1944; Univ Notre Dame MSME 1948

Donald Newton Langenberg: trust *B* Devils Lake ND 1932 *ED* IA St Univ BS 1953; Univ CA Los Angeles MS 1955; Univ CA Berkeley PhD 1959 *NONPR AFFIL* chancellor: Univ MD Adelphi; fellow: Am Assn Advancement Science, Am Physical Soc; mem: Sigma Xi

Cathleen Synge Morawetz: trust, mem audit comm *B* Toronto Canada 1923 *ED* Univ Toronto BA 1945; MA Inst Tech SM 1946; NY Univ PhD 1951 *NONPR AFFIL* fellow: Am Assn Advancement Science; mem: Am Academy Arts & Sciences, Am Mathematical Soc, Natl Academy Sciences, Soc Indus Applied Math; prof, dir: NY Univ Courant Inst Mathematical Sciences

Frank D. Press: trust, mem exec comm *B* Brooklyn NY 1924 *ED* City Univ NY BS 1944; Columbia Univ MA 1946; Columbia Univ PhD 1949 *NONPR AFFIL* foreign mem: Academy Sciences USSR; mem: Am Academy Arts & Sciences, Am Assn Univ Profs, Am Geophysical Union, Am Philosophical Soc, French Academy Sciences, Legion Honor, Natl Academy Pub Admin, Natl Academy Sciences, Natl Science Bd, Royal Soc, Seismological Soc Am, Soc Exploration Geophysicists; mem counc: Geological Soc Am; mem lunar & planetary missions bd: Natl Aeronautics Space Admin; mem US delegation: Nuclear Test Ban Negotiations

Lewis Thompson Preston: trust, chmn audit comm *B* New York NY 1926 *ED* Harvard Univ 1951 *CURR EMPL* pres: Intl Bank Reconstruction & Devel *CORP AFFIL* bd overseers: Coll Retirement Equity Fund, Teachers Insurance & Annuity Assn; dir: Anheuser-Busch Cos, British Petroleum Co, Fed Reserve Bank NY, Gen Electric Co, LAir Liquide; mem intl adv bd: Allianz A G *NONPR AFFIL* dir: Urban Fdn USA; mem: Assn Reserve City Bankers, Counc Foreign Rels *CLUB AFFIL* Bedford Golf & Tennis, Brook, Pilgrims, River

Harold Tafler Shapiro: trust, mem exec & investment comms *B* Montreal Canada 1935 *ED* McGill Univ B Commerce 1956; Prince-

ton Univ PhD 1964 *CORP AFFIL* mem tech adv counc: Ford Motor Co *NONPR AFFIL* dir: Natl Bur Econ Res; fellow: Am Academy Arts & Sciences; mem: Am Philosophical Soc, Natl Academy Sciences Inst Medicine; pres: Princeton Univ; trust: Interlochen Ctr Arts, Univ Res Assn

Roger B. Smith: trust *B* Columbus OH 1925 *ED* Univ MI BBA 1947; Univ MI MBA 1949 *CORP AFFIL* dir: Citicorp, Gen Motors Corp, Intl Paper Corp, Johnson & Johnson, PepsiCo *NONPR AFFIL* mem: Bus Counc *CLUB AFFIL* Bloomfield Hills CC, Detroit, Detroit Athletic, Links, Orchard Lake CC *PHIL AFFIL* chmn, trust: General Motors Cancer Research Foundation

Robert Metron Solow: trust *B* Brooklyn NY 1924 *ED* Harvard Univ BA 1947; Harvard Univ MA 1949; Harvard Univ PhD 1951 *NONPR AFFIL* fellow: Am Academy Arts Sciences; mem: Am Assn Advancement Science; prof econ: MA Inst Tech; trust: Woods Hole Oceanographic Inst; trust, chmn: Ctr Advanced Study Behavioral Sciences *PHIL AFFIL* dir: Energy Foundation

APPLICATION INFORMATION
Initial Approach:

The foundation advises applicants to send a brief letter of inquiry to determine whether a project or organization falls within funding guidelines. Letters of application should be addressed to the foundation's president.

There are no standard application forms. A letter of application should include details about the applicant and the proposed project, and information regarding the cost and duration of the work. Excluding recognized institutions of higher education, new organizations must provide tax-status information.

The foundation has no deadlines for applications.

Grants of $30,000 or less are made throughout the year by foundation officers. Larger grants are approved by the trustees, who meet four times annually. The foundation screens proposals for technical feasibility and competence, social relevance, financial stability, and for their relation to the foundation's interests.

Restrictions on Giving: Foundation interests do not include primary or secondary education, religion, creative or performing arts, medical research, health care, or humanities. Grants will not be made for endowments, buildings, or equipment. Grants are rarely made for general support or for activities outside the United States. The foundation's program in public management has been terminated.

PUBLICATIONS
Annual report

GRANTS ANALYSIS
Total Grants: $31,016,702

Number of Grants: 300

Highest Grant: $3,500,000*

Average Grant: $103,389

Typical Range: $10,000 to $50,000 and $100,000 to $500,000

Disclosure Period: 1993

Note: The highest grant figure is from 1992. Recent grants are derived from a 1994 partial grants list.

RECENT GRANTS

General

1,656,570	Harvard University, Cambridge, MA — for a research center for the apparel and textile industry
1,518,530	University of California San Francisco, San Francisco, CA — to establish centers for theoretical neurobiology
1,437,040	University of California Institute of Technology, Pasadena, CA — to establish centers for theoretical neurobiology
1,387,453	Salk Institute, San Diego, CA — to establish centers for theoretical neurobiology
1,266,050	Brandeis University, Waltham, MA — to establish centers for theoretical neurobiology

Smeal Foundation, Mary Jean and Frank P.

CONTACT
Frank P. Smeal
Trustee
Goldman, Sachs & Co.
85 Broad St.
New York, NY 10004
(212) 902-6897

FINANCIAL SUMMARY
Recent Giving: $735,620 (fiscal 1994); $939,083 (fiscal 1993); $310,128 (fiscal 1992)

Assets: $1,445,454 (fiscal 1994); $1,150,466 (fiscal 1993); $1,789,323 (fiscal 1992)

Gifts Received: $895,995 (fiscal 1994); $200,000 (fiscal 1993)

Fiscal Note: In fiscal 1994, contributions were received from Frank P. Smeal.

EIN: 13-3318167

CONTRIBUTIONS SUMMARY
Donor(s): Frank P. Smeal

Typical Recipients: • *Arts & Humanities:* Historic Preservation, Libraries, Museums/Galleries, Performing Arts, Theater • *Civic & Public Affairs:* Economic Development, Economic Policy, General, Native American Affairs, Philanthropic Organizations, Safety, Urban & Community Affairs • *Education:* Colleges & Universities, Private Education (Precollege), Student Aid • *Health:* Children's Health/Hospitals, Clinics/Medical Centers, Emergency/Ambulance Services, Geriatric Health, Health Organizations, Hospitals, Kidney, Mental Health, Pre-natal Health Issues • *International:* International Organizations, International Peace & Security Issues • *Religion:* Jewish Causes • *Social Services:* Child Welfare, Community Service Organizations, Delinquency & Criminal Rehabilitation, People with Disabilities, Scouts, Senior Services, Shelters/Homelessness, Substance Abuse, United Funds/United Ways, Youth Organizations

Grant Types: general support and scholarship

Geographic Distribution: focus on the Northeast

GIVING OFFICERS

Frank P. Smeal: trust *B* Sykesville PA 1918 *ED* PA St Univ 1942 *CURR EMPL* ltd ptnr: Goldman Sachs & Co *NONPR AFFIL* dir: Citizens Budget Comm NY

Mary Jean Smeal: trust

APPLICATION INFORMATION

Initial Approach: Send brief letter of inquiry describing program or project. There are no deadlines.

Restrictions on Giving: Does not support individuals or provide loans.

GRANTS ANALYSIS

Total Grants: $735,620

Number of Grants: 41

Highest Grant: $250,000

Typical Range: $500 to $100,000

Disclosure Period: fiscal year ending February 28, 1994

Note: Recent grants are derived from a fiscal 1994 Form 990.

RECENT GRANTS

General
250,000	Citizens Budget Commission, New York, NY
100,000	Boy Scouts of America Greater New York Council, New York, NY
100,000	Boy Scouts of America Greater New York Council, New York, NY
100,000	Dartmouth-Hitchcock Medical Center, Lebanon, NH — 2nd installment
26,500	Pennsylvania State University, University Park, PA — DuBois building fund

Snow Foundation, John Ben

CONTACT
Vernon F. Snow
President
John Ben Snow Fdn.
PO Box 376
Pulaski, NY 13142
(908) 654-5704

FINANCIAL SUMMARY
Recent Giving: $193,975 (fiscal 1994); $198,625 (fiscal 1993); $180,065 (fiscal 1992)

Assets: $4,844,122 (fiscal 1994); $5,031,872 (fiscal 1993); $4,891,492 (fiscal 1992)

EIN: 13-6112704

CONTRIBUTIONS SUMMARY
Donor(s): the late John Ben Snow

Typical Recipients: • *Arts & Humanities:* Arts Associations & Councils, Historic Preservation, Libraries, Literary Arts, Museums/Galleries • *Civic & Public Affairs:* Housing, Nonprofit Management, Philanthropic Organizations, Professional & Trade Associations • *Education:* Colleges & Universities, Elementary Education (Private), Legal Education, Literacy, Preschool Education, Private Education (Precollege), Public Education (Precollege), Student Aid • *Environment:* General • *Health:* Health Organizations, Hospitals, Public Health • *Religion:* Churches, Religious Organizations • *Social Services:* Child Welfare, Community Service Organizations, People with Disabilities, Youth Organizations

Grant Types: capital, fellowship, project, and scholarship

Geographic Distribution: limited to central NY, with focus on Oswego County

GIVING OFFICERS
Allen R. Malcolm: pres *PHIL AFFIL* trust: John Ben Snow Memorial Trust

Rollan D. Melton: vp *PHIL AFFIL* trust: John Ben Snow Memorial Trust

Royle Melton: mem

David H. Snow: vp, treas

Dr. Vernon F. Snow: dir *PHIL AFFIL* trust: John Ben Snow Memorial Trust

APPLICATION INFORMATION
Initial Approach: The foundation requests applications be made in writing. Include a description of organization, amount requested, purpose of funds sought, recently audited financial statement, and proof of tax-exempt status. Deadline is April 15.

Restrictions on Giving: Does not support individuals.

PUBLICATIONS
Annual Report (including application guidelines)

GRANTS ANALYSIS
Total Grants: $193,975

Typical Range: $5,000 to $15,000

Disclosure Period: fiscal year ending March 31, 1994

Note: Recent grants are derived from a fiscal 1993 Form 990. No grants list was provided for fiscal 1994.

RECENT GRANTS

Library
5,000	Friends of Tompkins County Public Library, Ithaca, NY
4,000	Pulaski Public Library, Pulaski, NY
2,000	Foundation Center, New York, NY

General
20,500	Syracuse University, Maxwell School, Syracuse, NY
15,000	Northfield Mt. Hermon School, E. Northfield, MA
15,000	PROP, Pulaski, NY
15,000	Syracuse University, School Press Institute, Syracuse, NY
10,150	Independent Sector, Washington, DC

Snow Memorial Trust, John Ben

CONTACT
Vernon F. Snow
Trustee
John Ben Snow Memorial Trust
847 James St., Ste. 107
Syracuse, NY 13203
(315) 298-6401

FINANCIAL SUMMARY
Recent Giving: $969,300 (1994); $928,750 (1993); $1,022,985 (1992)

Assets: $20,000,000 (1994 approx.); $20,189,522 (1993); $19,817,218 (1992)

EIN: 13-6633814

CONTRIBUTIONS SUMMARY
Donor(s): The trust was incorporated in 1948 by the late John Ben Snow . John Ben Snow was born and raised in Pulaski, NY, a small village north of Syracuse. He graduated from New York University in 1904 and began employment at the Woolworth organization. A man of vision, he was attracted to mass-market sales and introduced innovative retailing techniques. He rose rapidly through the ranks of Woolworth from stock boy to corporate director, initially in New York, and finally in Great Britain, where he accumulated a small fortune through hard work, saving, and wise investments. After retiring from Woolworth's in 1939, Mr. Snow devoted the remainder of his life to building the Speidel chain of newspapers and publishing the "Western Horseman." He was fond of animals, especially horses, and enjoyed racing, fox hunting, polo, and range riding. Throughout his life, John Ben Snow shared his wealth with relatives, friends, business associates, and fellow Pulaskians. He gave generously and freely to those persons and causes he cherished. He preferred to invest in people, especially the young, by making financial assistance available. He also believed in improving the quality of life in Pulaski and its environs.

Typical Recipients: • *Arts & Humanities:*
Arts Associations & Councils, Arts Centers,
Arts Outreach, Ethnic & Folk Arts, Historic
Preservation, History & Archaeology, Li-
braries, Museums/Galleries, Public Broad-
casting, Theater • *Civic & Public Affairs:*
Community Foundations, General, Law &
Justice, Municipalities/Towns, Native
American Affairs, Philanthropic Organiza-
tions, Professional & Trade Associations,
Safety, Women's Affairs • *Education:*
Arts/Humanities Education, Business Educa-
tion, Colleges & Universities, Community &
Junior Colleges, Economic Education, Edu-
cation Funds, Faculty Development, Gen-
eral, Journalism/Media Education, Legal
Education, Medical Education, Minority
Education, Private Education (Precollege),
Student Aid • *Environment:* General, Re-
source Conservation • *Health:* Cancer, Geriatric Health, Health Funds, Hospitals,
Medical Research • *Religion:* Churches • *Science:* Science Museums, Scientific Organizations • *Social Services:* Community Service
Organizations, Day Care, Delinquency &
Criminal Rehabilitation, General, People
with Disabilities,
YMCA/YWCA/YMHA/YWHA, Youth Or-
ganizations

Grant Types: fellowship, matching, project,
research, scholarship, and seed money

Geographic Distribution: focus on eastern
United States

GIVING OFFICERS
Allen R. Malcolm: trust *PHIL AFFIL* pres:
John Ben Snow Foundation

Rollan D. Melton: trust *PHIL AFFIL* vp:
John Ben Snow Foundation

Dr. Vernon F. Snow: trust *PHIL AFFIL* dir:
John Ben Snow Foundation

APPLICATION INFORMATION
Initial Approach:

The trust requests applications be made in
writing.

The deadline for submitting proposals is
April 15.

The trustees meet once a year, usually in
June.

Restrictions on Giving: The present trustees prefer to give challenge and matching
grants, pilot programs, and seed funding.

Restrictions on Giving: The trust does not
make grants to individuals, government
agencies, endowment funds, religious organizations, or unspecified projects.

PUBLICATIONS
Annual report, including application guidelines

GRANTS ANALYSIS
Total Grants: $969,300

Number of Grants: 48

Highest Grant: $75,000

Average Grant: $20,194

Typical Range: $5,000 to $25,000

Disclosure Period: 1994

Note: Recent grants are derived from a 1994
annual report.

RECENT GRANTS
Library
15,000	New Jersey Historical Society, Newark, NJ — renovation of historic building for museum and library	
6,000	Village of Pulaski, Pulaski, NY — maintenance of library and meeting rooms	

General
75,000	New York University School of Law, New York, NY — funding of Root-Tilden-Snow Scholarship Program	
75,000	New York University Stern School of Business, New York, NY — support for undergraduate scholarships in business	
75,000	Syracuse University, Syracuse, NY — construction of seminar room in Eggers Hall	
57,500	New York Law School, New York, NY — funding of Snow Scholarships in law	
52,000	Pulaski Central School, Pulaski, NY — scholarship awards for college-bound high school students	

Solow Foundation

CONTACT
Sheldon H. Solow
President
Solow Fdn.
9 W 57th St.
New York, NY 10019-2601
(212) 751-1100

FINANCIAL SUMMARY
**Recent Giving: $662,017 (fiscal
1993); $382,785 (fiscal 1992);
$274,001 (fiscal 1990)**
Assets: $7,989,832 (fiscal 1993);
$7,962,408 (fiscal 1992); $7,576,339 (fiscal
1990)

EIN: 13-2950685

CONTRIBUTIONS SUMMARY
Donor(s): Sheldon H. Solow

Typical Recipients: • *Arts & Humanities:*
Arts Associations & Councils, Arts Centers,
Community Arts, Ethnic & Folk Arts, Librar-
ies, Museums/Galleries, Music, Performing
Arts, Theater • *Civic & Public Affairs:* Afri-
can American Affairs, Botanical Gar-
dens/Parks, General, Law & Justice,
Municipalities/Towns, Philanthropic Organi-
zations, Professional & Trade Associations,
Public Policy, Urban & Community Affairs
• *Education:* Arts/Humanities Education,
Colleges & Universities, Education Associa-
tions, Education Reform, General, Medical
Education, Religious Education, Social Sciences Education, Student Aid • *Environ-
ment:* Air/Water Quality • *Health:*
Clinics/Medical Centers, Heart, Hospitals,

Multiple Sclerosis, Single-Disease Health
Associations • *International:* Foreign Arts
Organizations, International Development,
International Organizations, Missionary/Re-
ligious Activities • *Religion:* Churches, Jew-
ish Causes • *Social Services:* Child Welfare,
Community Service Organizations, General,
Recreation & Athletics, Scouts, Substance
Abuse, United Funds/United Ways, Youth
Organizations

Grant Types: general support

Geographic Distribution: focus on New
York, NY

GIVING OFFICERS
Steven Cherniak: treas

Leonard Lazarus: secy

Sheldon Henry Solow: don, pres *B* 1928
PHIL AFFIL pres, treas: Sheldon H. Solow
Foundation

Rosalie S. Wolff: vp

APPLICATION INFORMATION
Initial Approach: The foundation has no
formal grant application procedure or application form. There are no deadlines.

GRANTS ANALYSIS
Total Grants: $662,017

Number of Grants: 63

Highest Grant: $250,000

Typical Range: $250 to $100,000

Disclosure Period: fiscal year ending October 31, 1993

Note: Recent grants are derived from a fiscal 1993 Form 990.

RECENT GRANTS
Library
25,000	New York Public Library, New York, NY	

General
100,000	United Jewish Appeal Federation, New York, NY — capital campaign	
20,000	Jewish Museum, New York, NY	
15,000	Rebny Foundation, New York, NY	
10,000	American Friends of Israel Philharmonic Orchestra, New York, NY	
10,000	American School of Classical Studies, New York, NY	

Sprague Educational and Charitable Foundation, Seth

CONTACT
Maureen O. Augusciak
Senior Vice President
Seth Sprague Educational and Charitable
  Foundation
U.S. Trust Company of New York
114 W. 47th St.
New York, NY 10036
(212) 852-3686

Note: Anne L. Smith-Ganey, assistant vice president, may also be contacted for information. The foundation lists an additional number: 212-852-3683.

FINANCIAL SUMMARY
Recent Giving: $1,705,000 (1992); $1,819,500 (1991); $1,556,500 (1990)

Assets: $40,864,561 (1992); $41,082,406 (1991); $36,831,033 (1990)

EIN: 13-6071886

CONTRIBUTIONS SUMMARY
Donor(s): Established in 1939 by Seth Sprague , the Sprague Educational and Charitable Foundation is administered by its trustees and the United States Trust Company of New York. All of the trustees were either associates of Mr. Sprague or familiar with his philanthropic pursuits.

Seth Sprague was a graduate of Norwich Academy and a lifetime employee of F. H. Foster and Company, a Boston cotton processing corporation of which he eventually became president. Mr. Sprague died in 1941.

Typical Recipients: • *Arts & Humanities:* Arts Funds, Arts Institutes, Ballet, Dance, Ethnic & Folk Arts, General, Historic Preservation, History & Archaeology, Libraries, Literary Arts, Museums/Galleries, Music, Opera, Performing Arts, Public Broadcasting, Theater • *Civic & Public Affairs:* Botanical Gardens/Parks, Business/Free Enterprise, Economic Development, Employment/Job Training, Ethnic Organizations, General, Law & Justice, Professional & Trade Associations, Public Policy, Urban & Community Affairs, Women's Affairs, Zoos/Aquariums • *Education:* Arts/Humanities Education, Colleges & Universities, Community & Junior Colleges, Education Associations, Education Funds, International Studies, Journalism/Media Education, Legal Education, Medical Education, Minority Education, Private Education (Precollege), Public Education (Precollege), Religious Education, Special Education, Student Aid • *Environment:* General, Resource Conservation • *Health:* Emergency/Ambulance Services, Geriatric Health, Health Funds, Health Organizations, Hospices, Hospitals, Medical Rehabilitation, Medical Research, Medical Training, Mental Health, Nursing Services, Single-Disease Health Associations • *Religion:* Churches, Religious Welfare • *Science:* Scientific Centers & Institutes, Scientific Labs • *Social Services:* Animal Protection, At-Risk Youth, Child Welfare, Community Centers, Community Service Organizations, Counseling, Delinquency & Criminal Rehabilitation, Domestic Violence, Family Planning, Family Services, People with Disabilities, Recreation & Athletics, Senior Services, Shelters/Homelessness, Substance Abuse, Volunteer Services, Youth Organizations

Grant Types: general support and operating expenses

Geographic Distribution: nationally, with a primary focus on New York and Massachusetts

GIVING OFFICERS
Maureen O. Augusciak: contact person *CURR EMPL* sr vp: US Trust Co NY

Walter Grey Dunnington, Jr.: trust *B* New York NY 1927 *ED* Univ VA BA 1948; Univ VA LLB 1950 *CORP AFFIL* dir: Brittainia Indus Ltd *NONPR AFFIL* bd govs: NY Hosp; mem: Am Bar Assn, Assn Bar City New York, NY St Bar Assn; trust: Boys Club NY, Woodberry Forest Sch *CLUB AFFIL* Brook, Natl Golf Links Am, Racquet & Tennis, Somerset Hills CC *PHIL AFFIL* trust: Algernon Sydney Sullivan Foundation

Arline Ripley Greenleaf: trust

Jacqueline DeNeuflize Simpkins: trust

Anne L. Smith-Ganey: asst vp, contact *CURR EMPL* asst vp: US Trust Co NY *PHIL AFFIL* dir: Marie and John Zimmermann Fund; contact: Oliver S. and Jennie R. Donaldson Charitable Trust; asst vp: Samuel Freeman Charitable Trust

APPLICATION INFORMATION
Initial Approach:

Initial contact should be a written request.

Applications should include a summary (two pages), budget, audited financial statement, and an IRS determination letter.

The board of directors meets in March, June, September, and November. Deadlines for applications are April 15 and October 1. Grants are made in June and December.

Restrictions on Giving: The foundation does not give grants for research or capital expenditures. In addition, the foundation does not make grants to individuals or for organizations located outside the United States.

GRANTS ANALYSIS
Total Grants: $1,705,000

Number of Grants: 417

Highest Grant: $48,000

Average Grant: $4,089

Typical Range: $1,000 to $5,000

Disclosure Period: 1992

Note: Recent grants are derived from a 1992 Form 990.

RECENT GRANTS
Library
5,000	South Yarmouth Library Association, S. Yarmouth, MA	

General
48,000	Woodberry Forest School, Woodberry Forest, VA	
30,000	Birth Right Forces, Bath, ME	
20,000	Atlantic Challenge Foundation, Rockport, ME	
20,000	Atlantic Challenge Foundation, Rockport, ME	
20,000	Riley School, Glen Cove, ME	

Starr Foundation

CONTACT
Ta Chun Hsu
President and Director
Starr Foundation
70 Pine St.
New York, NY 10270
(212) 770-6882

FINANCIAL SUMMARY
Recent Giving: $40,150,209 (1993); $40,436,495 (1992); $33,034,519 (1991)

Assets: $893,216,217 (1993); $893,229,359 (1992); $780,052,477 (1991)

Gifts Received: $283,373 (1993); $290,023 (1992); $2,000,023 (1991)

Fiscal Note: In 1990, the foundation received $4,000,000 from the estate of Howard L. Kleinoeder and $1,500 from John S. Galinato. In 1991, 1992, and 1993, the foundation received gifts from the estate of Howard L. Kleinoeder.

EIN: 13-6151545

CONTRIBUTIONS SUMMARY
Donor(s): Cornelius Vander Starr (1892-1968) established the foundation in New York in 1955. Mr. Starr attended the University of California, and passed the California Bar exam at age 21. After serving in World War I, he resided in China and established the Asia Life and American Asiatic Life Insurance Companies. By the 1930s, his insurance activities and investments in real estate and automobiles extended throughout the Far East. After World War II, he renamed the companies the American Life Insurance Company. At the time of his death, his operations expanded to a group of 100 insurance companies in about 130 countries. Since the 1970s, the foundation has received considerable donations of stock from the corporate directors of American International Group.

Typical Recipients: • *Arts & Humanities:* Arts Associations & Councils, Arts Centers, Arts Festivals, Arts Funds, Arts Institutes, Dance, Ethnic & Folk Arts, Historic Preservation, History & Archaeology, Libraries, Museums/Galleries, Music, Opera, Performing Arts, Public Broadcasting, Theater • *Civic & Public Affairs:* Botanical Gardens/Parks, Civil Rights, Economic Development, Economic Policy, Employment/Job Training, Ethnic Organizations, Law & Justice, Nonprofit Management, Philanthropic Organizations, Public Policy, Rural Affairs, Women's Affairs, Zoos/Aquariums • *Education:* Afterschool/Enrichment Programs, Arts/Humanities Education, Business Education, Colleges & Universities, Economic Education, Education Associations, Education Reform, Health & Physical Education, International Exchange, International Studies, Journalism/Media Education, Legal Education, Medical Education, Minority Education, Private Education (Precollege), Public Education (Precollege), Religious Education, Science/Mathematics Education, Special Education, Student Aid • *Environ-*

ment: General • *Health:* AIDS/HIV, Cancer, Emergency/Ambulance Services, Geriatric Health, Health Organizations, Hospices, Hospitals, Medical Research, Medical Training, Nursing Services, Single-Disease Health Associations, Transplant Networks/Donor Banks • *International:* Foreign Arts Organizations, Foreign Educational Institutions, Health Care/Hospitals, International Affairs, International Development, International Organizations, International Peace & Security Issues, International Relations, International Relief Efforts, Trade • *Religion:* Churches, Jewish Causes, Religious Welfare • *Social Services:* Child Welfare, Community Centers, Community Service Organizations, Counseling, Crime Prevention, Emergency Relief, Family Planning, Family Services, Food/Clothing Distribution, People with Disabilities, Recreation & Athletics, Refugee Assistance, Senior Services, Shelters/Homelessness, Substance Abuse, Youth Organizations

Grant Types: capital, emergency, endowment, general support, multiyear/continuing support, professorship, project, and scholarship

Geographic Distribution: national and international, with emphasis on metropolitan New York City

GIVING OFFICERS
Marion I. Breen: vp, dir

Houghton Freeman: dir *B* Peking People's Republic of China 1921 *ED* Wesleyan Univ BA 1943 *CURR EMPL* dir: Am Intl Group *CORP AFFIL* chmn: Am Intl Underwriters, China Am Ins Co; dir: CV Starr & Co, Starr Intl Co

Ida E. Galler: secy

Maurice Raymond Greenberg: chmn bd, dir *B* New York NY 1925 *ED* Univ Miami BA 1948; NY Univ Law Sch JD 1950 *CURR EMPL* chmn: Am Intl Group *CORP AFFIL* chmn: N Am Mgrs Inc; chmn bd govs: NY Hosp; chmn, dir: AIG Risk Mgmt, Am Intl Aviation Agency, Am Intl Group Data Ctr, NHIG Holding Corp, Transatlantic Holdings, Transatlantic Reinsurance Co; dir: Am Home Assurance Co, Am Intl Reinsurance Co, Natl Union Fire Ins Co Pittsburgh; dir, dep chmn: Fed Reserve Bank NY; pres, ceo, dir: C V Starr & Co *NONPR AFFIL* mem: Coalition Svc Indus, Counc Foreign Rels, Foreign Policy Assn, Hoover Inst, New York City Partnership, NY Bar Assn, Police Athletic League, Sigma Alpha Mu, US-ASEAN Bus Adv Counc, US-USSR Trade Econ Counc; pres adv comm: Ctr Strategic Intl Studies *PHIL AFFIL* chmn, dir: Maurice R. and Corinne Greenberg Foundation

Ta Chun Hsu: pres, dir

Edwin Alfred Grenville Manton: dir *B* Essex England 1909 *ED* London Univ 1925-1927 *CURR EMPL* sr adv, dir: Am Intl Group *CORP AFFIL* chmn: Am Intl MAR Agency NY; dir: AIV Ins Co, Am Home Assurance Co, Birmingham Fire & Ins Co PA; hon dir: CV Starr & Co; vchmn, dir: Starr Tech Risks Agency *NONPR AFFIL* trust: St Lukes-Roosevelt Hosp; vp: St Georges Soc *CLUB AFFIL* City, Mid Day, Salmagundi,

Williams *PHIL AFFIL* trust: Manton Foundation

John Joseph Roberts: dir *B* Montreal Canada 1922 *ED* Princeton Univ BA 1945 *CURR EMPL* chmn, ceo, dir: Am Intl Underwriters *CORP AFFIL* dir: Adams Express Co, Petroleum & Resources Corp, SICO, CV Starr & Co, Starr Intl Co, Starr Tech Risks Agency; vchmn, dir: Am Intl Group *NONPR AFFIL* chmn: Bus Counc Intl Understanding; chmn intl corp counc: Columbia Univ Sch Intl & Pub Affs; chmn US sect: Hungarian US Bus Counc; mem: Counc Foreign Rels; trust: Counc Ams, Juilliard Sch Music, Mason Early Ed Fdn *CLUB AFFIL* Brook, Downtown, India House, Nassau, Racquet & Tennis, Union

Ernest Edward Stempel: dir *B* New York NY 1916 *ED* Manhattan Coll AB 1938; Fordham Univ LLB 1946; NY Univ LLM 1949; NY Univ DJS 1951 *CURR EMPL* vchmn, dir: Am Intl Group *CORP AFFIL* chmn, dir: Am Intl Co, Am Intl Ins Co, Am Intl Reinsurance Co, Australian Am Assurance Co, Phillipine Am Life Ins Co; dir: AIG Life Ins Co, Am Intl Life Assurance Co, Am Intl Reinsurance Co, Am Intl Underwriters, Am Life Ins Co, DE Am Life Ins Co, La Interamericana, Mt Mansfield Co, Pacific Union Assurance Co, Seguros Interamericana SA, Seguros Venezuela, CV Starr & Co, Underwriters Adjustment Co; pres, dir: Starr Intl Co *NONPR AFFIL* mem: Am Bar Assn, NY Bar Assn *CLUB AFFIL* Coral Beach, Marco Polo, Mid Ocean, Riddells Bay Golf & CC, Royal Bermuda YC

Frank R. Tengi: treas

Gladys R. Thomas: vp

APPLICATION INFORMATION
Initial Approach:

Applications should be submitted in writing. There are no formal application forms.

Include a description of organization, amount requested, purpose of funds sought, recently audited financial statement, and proof of tax-exempt status.

There are no deadlines for submitting proposals.

OTHER THINGS TO KNOW
Grants to individuals are limited to four scholarship programs. Those programs are the Starr Foundation Scholarship Program for "American International" Children (U.S.), the Starr Foundation Scholarship Program for "American International" Children (overseas), the Brewster Starr Scholarship Program, and the Lower Manhattan Starr Scholarship Program.

PUBLICATIONS
Annual report

GRANTS ANALYSIS
Total Grants: $40,150,209

Number of Grants: 385

Highest Grant: $6,250,000

Average Grant: $72,194*

Typical Range: $10,000 to $50,000 and $100,000 to $250,000

Disclosure Period: 1993

Note: The average grant figure excludes two grants totaling $12,500,000. Recent grants are derived from a 1993 Form 990.

RECENT GRANTS

Library

1,000,000	New York Public Library, New York, NY — challenge grant met for Center for Japan-US Business and Economic Studies at New York University
1,000,000	Yale University, New Haven, CT — third installment of five-year grant totaling $5 million in support of renovation and redesign of the Sterling Library Reference Center
500,000	Bush Presidential Library Foundation, University College Station, TX — to help establish the George Bush Presidential Library Foundation at Texas A&M University
500,000	New York Public Library, New York, NY — second payment of three-year grant totaling $1.5 million in support of the new Science, Industry, and Business Library
350,000	Nixon, Richard, Library, and Birthplace Foundation, Yorba Linda, CA — first payment of three-year grant totaling $1 million to endow Chair in Sino-US Relations

General

6,250,000	New York Hospital, New York, NY — fourth payment of five-year grant totaling $20 million in support of New York Hospital's Major Modernization Campaign
1,000,000	Council on Foreign Relations, New York, NY — first payment of four-year grant totaling $4 million to endow International Affairs Fellowship Program
1,000,000	United Negro College Fund, New York, NY — first payment of five-year grant totaling $5 million in support of Campaign 2000
625,000	Cornell University Medical College, New York, NY — first payment of four-year grant totaling $2.5 million to fund study of neurological disabilities in the elderly
515,000	State Bureau of Cultural Relics, Beijing, People's Republic of China — fund to purchase Tong Ting Panels and reinstallation in the Summer Palace in Beijing as a cultural relic of the Chinese people

Steele-Reese Foundation

CONTACT
William T. Buice III
Co-Trustee
Steele-Reese Foundation
c/o Davidson, Dawson and Clark
330 Madison Ave., 35th Fl.
New York, NY 10017
(212) 557-7700
Note: Southern Appalachia applicants should address inquiries to Dr. John R. Bryden, 760 Malabu Dr., Lexington, KY 40502. Northwest applicants should address inquiries to: Mrs. Christine N. Brady, PO Box 7263, Boise, ID 83707. High school seniors in Lemhi and Custer Counties, ID, are invited to apply for foundation undergraduate scholarships through their schools.

FINANCIAL SUMMARY
Recent Giving: $1,447,000 (fiscal 1995 est.); $1,056,905 (fiscal 1994); $1,569,248 (fiscal 1993)

Assets: $30,460,000 (fiscal 1994 approx.); $31,776,721 (fiscal 1993); $30,798,610 (fiscal 1992)

EIN: 13-6034763

CONTRIBUTIONS SUMMARY
Donor(s): The foundation was established in 1955 by Eleanor Steele Reese , whose father Charles Steele was a partner of J.P. Morgan. Eleanor Steele was born in New York City in 1893. After pursuing a career as an opera singer and recitalist in Europe and the United States for two decades, she moved to the western United States. She met and married Emmet P. Reese in 1941. At the time of their marriage, he and Eleanor bought and operated a small working ranch near Shoup, ID. In the mid-1950s, they moved to a large ranch in Salmon, ID, which they operated until a few years before her death in 1977. Emmet P. Reese died in 1982. The original trustees of the foundation were Sidney W. Davidson and J.P. Morgan & Co., Inc.

Typical Recipients: • *Arts & Humanities:* Historic Preservation, History & Archaeology, Libraries, Literary Arts • *Civic & Public Affairs:* Civil Rights, Community Foundations, Employment/Job Training, Legal Aid, Municipalities/Towns, Philanthropic Organizations, Rural Affairs, Urban & Community Affairs • *Education:* Colleges & Universities, Education Associations, Education Reform, Private Education (Precollege), Public Education (Precollege), Student Aid • *Environment:* General, Resource Conservation • *Health:* AIDS/HIV, Clinics/Medical Centers, Heart, Hospices, Hospitals, Single-Disease Health Associations, Transplant Networks/Donor Banks • *Religion:* Religious Welfare • *Science:* Science Museums, Scientific Centers & Institutes • *Social Services:* Child Welfare, Community Service Organizations, Counseling, Family Planning, Food/Clothing Distribution, Homes, People with Disabilities,

Senior Services, Shelters/Homelessness, Substance Abuse, Youth Organizations

Grant Types: endowment, general support, and scholarship

Geographic Distribution: primarily Southern Appalachia, particularly Kentucky; and the Northwest, particularly Idaho and surrounding states

GIVING OFFICERS
William T. Buice III: co-trust

Robert T. H. Davidson: co-trust *PHIL AFFIL* trust: Harry Wilson Loose Trust, The Bingham Trust

APPLICATION INFORMATION
Initial Approach:

Applicants should review the foundation's policy and criteria, available upon request, in detail. If a proposal seems warranted, applicants should write a succinct factual letter of no more than several pages. Any brief printed material that is pertinent to an application should also be included.

There are no application deadlines.

The officers meet as necessary to review proposals. Grant installments are generally paid in February and August of each year.

Restrictions on Giving: No grants are made to individuals, virtually none for research or planning, and few for construction. The foundation seeks grantees which have "special experience in their fields, unusually talented staff, an imaginative and courageous approach toward pursuing their goals, or some other essential quality." The foundation generally does not fund projects where its funds would be the major contribution or where evidence of strong community support is lacking. Other preferred qualities include teamwork and financial responsibility. In addition, the foundation "avoids organizations which seem to pivot on a single manager who could not be replaced with smooth continuity."

OTHER THINGS TO KNOW
Morgan Guaranty Trust Company of New York serves as the corporate trustee for the foundation.

The individual trustees share the responsibility for grant determination. To reduce overhead costs, the foundation does not maintain an office or a full-time staff. Trustees are assisted with grant decisions in Southern Appalachia by Dr. John R. Bryden of Lexington, KY; in the Northwest by Mrs. Christine N. Brady of Carmen, ID.

PUBLICATIONS
Annual report includes detailed grant application information

GRANTS ANALYSIS
Total Grants: $1,056,905

Number of Grants: 39

Highest Grant: $100,000

Average Grant: $27,100

Typical Range: $10,000 to $50,000

Disclosure Period: fiscal year ending August 31, 1994

Note: Recent grants are derived from a fiscal 1993 Form 990.

RECENT GRANTS
Library

5,000	Chouteau County Free Library Foundation, Ft. Benton, MT

General

275,072	Gonzaga University, Spokane, WA
100,075	Pacific Lutheran University, Tacoma, WA
100,000	Christ School, Arden, SC
100,000	Davidson College, Davidson, NC
77,000	Bear Lake Memorial Hospital, Mon Pelier, ID

Steinbach Fund, Ruth and Milton

CONTACT
John Klingenstein
President
Ruth and Milton Steinbach Fund
c/o Wertheim Schroder Holdings, Inc.
787 Seventh Ave.
New York, NY 10019-6016
(212) 492-6190

FINANCIAL SUMMARY
Recent Giving: $700,000 (fiscal 1993); $652,797 (fiscal 1992); $200,000 (fiscal 1991)

Assets: $17,230,739 (fiscal 1993); $16,025,273 (fiscal 1992); $15,815,614 (fiscal 1991)

Gifts Received: $7,000,000 (fiscal 1990)

Fiscal Note: In 1990, contributions were received from Ruth A. Steinbach.

EIN: 13-6028785

CONTRIBUTIONS SUMMARY
Donor(s): the late Milton Steinbach

Typical Recipients: • *Arts & Humanities:* Libraries, Museums/Galleries • *Education:* Business Education, Colleges & Universities, Medical Education, Private Education (Precollege), Special Education • *Health:* Clinics/Medical Centers, Hospitals, Medical Research, Single-Disease Health Associations • *Religion:* Religious Organizations • *Science:* Science Museums, Scientific Centers & Institutes • *Social Services:* People with Disabilities, United Funds/United Ways

Grant Types: general support and research

Geographic Distribution: focus on NY

GIVING OFFICERS
Kenneth H. Fields: asst treas

Frederick Adler Klingenstein: vp, secy, dir *B* New York NY 1931 *ED* Harvard Univ Grad Sch Bus Admin 1953-1954; Yale Univ BA 1953 *CURR EMPL* chmn: Klingenstein Fields & Co *NONPR AFFIL* chmn: Mt Sinai Med Ctr; trust: Am Mus Natural History *PHIL AFFIL* don son, vp, secy, dir: Esther A. and Joseph Klingenstein Fund

John Klingenstein: pres, treas, dir *CURR EMPL* gen ptnr: Klingenstein Fields & Co *PHIL AFFIL* don son, pres, treas, dir: Esther A. and Joseph Klingenstein Fund

Patricia D. Klingenstein: dir

Sharon L. Klingenstein: dir

APPLICATION INFORMATION
Initial Approach: Send brief letter of inquiry describing program or project. There are no deadlines.

GRANTS ANALYSIS
Total Grants: $700,000

Number of Grants: 13

Highest Grant: $100,000

Typical Range: $25,000 to $100,000

Disclosure Period: fiscal year ending October 31, 1993

Note: Recent grants are derived from a fiscal 1993 Form 990.

RECENT GRANTS

Library
25,000	New York Public Library, New York, NY

General
100,000	Harvard Medical School, Cambridge, MA
100,000	Johns Hopkins University, Baltimore, MD
100,000	Lighthouse for Blind, New York, NY
100,000	Stanford University, Stanford, CA
50,000	American Museum of Natural History, New York, NY

Sulzberger Foundation

CONTACT
Marian S. Heiskell
President
Sulzberger Foundation
229 W 43rd St.
New York, NY 10036
(212) 556-1750

FINANCIAL SUMMARY
Recent Giving: $1,100,000 (1995 est.); $1,021,750 (1994 approx.); $1,002,700 (1993)

Assets: $21,700,000 (1995 est.); $21,560,000 (1994 approx.); $21,681,993 (1993)

Gifts Received: $28,953 (1990); $1,500,000 (1989); $1,547,490 (1988)

Fiscal Note: In 1990, contributions were received from the Sarah Christy Trust.

EIN: 13-6083166

CONTRIBUTIONS SUMMARY
Donor(s): The foundation was incorporated in 1956 by the late Arthur Hays Sulzberger and the late Iphigene Ochs Sulzberger .

Typical Recipients: • *Arts & Humanities:* Arts Associations & Councils, Arts Funds, Historic Preservation, History & Archaeol-
ogy, Libraries, Literary Arts, Museums/Galleries, Music, Opera, Public Broadcasting, Theater • *Civic & Public Affairs:* Botanical Gardens/Parks, Clubs, Economic Development, General, Municipalities/Towns, Philanthropic Organizations, Professional & Trade Associations, Safety, Zoos/Aquariums • *Education:* Colleges & Universities, Education Funds, Elementary Education (Private), General, International Studies, Journalism/Media Education, Medical Education, Minority Education, Private Education (Precollege), Public Education (Precollege), School Volunteerism, Student Aid • *Environment:* General, Resource Conservation, Wildlife Protection • *Health:* AIDS/HIV, Clinics/Medical Centers, Hospitals, Medical Research, Single-Disease Health Associations • *International:* Foreign Educational Institutions, International Environmental Issues, International Organizations • *Religion:* Jewish Causes, Religious Organizations, Synagogues/Temples • *Science:* Science Museums, Scientific Organizations • *Social Services:* Community Service Organizations, Crime Prevention, Family Planning, Recreation & Athletics, Shelters/Homelessness, United Funds/United Ways, Youth Organizations

Grant Types: capital, conference/seminar, emergency, endowment, fellowship, general support, operating expenses, professorship, project, scholarship, and seed money

Geographic Distribution: national

GIVING OFFICERS
Marian Sulzberger Heiskell: pres, dir *B* New York NY 1918 *ED* Frobeleague Kindergarten Training Sch 1941 *CORP AFFIL* dir: Merck & Co Inc, NY Times Co; trust parks counc: Consolidated Edison Co NY *NONPR AFFIL* bd mgrs, exec comm: NY Botanical Garden; chmn: Counc Environment New York City; co-chmn: We Care About NY; dir: Audubon Soc, New York City Partnership, Regional Planning Assn; mem: St Pk & Recreation Comm City New York *PHIL AFFIL* dir: New York Times Co. Foundation

Frederick T. Mason: asst secy, asst treas

Arthur Ochs Sulzberger, Sr.: vp, sec, treas, dir *B* New York NY 1926 *ED* Columbia Univ BA 1951 *CURR EMPL* chmn, ceo, dir: NY Times Co *CORP AFFIL* chmn, dir: Gadsden Times; dir: Times Printing Co *NONPR AFFIL* chmn, trust: Metro Mus Art; dir: Bur Newspaper Advertising; mem: Sons Am Revolution; trust emeritus: Columbia Univ *CLUB AFFIL* Century CC, Explorers, Metropolitan, Overseas Press *PHIL AFFIL* chmn, dir: New York Times Co. Foundation

Judith P. Sulzberger: vp, dir *CORP AFFIL* dir: NY Times Co *PHIL AFFIL* dir: New York Times Co. Foundation

APPLICATION INFORMATION
Initial Approach:

The foundation has no formal grant application procedure or application form.

The foundation has no deadline for submitting proposals.

Restrictions on Giving: The foundation makes grants only to public charities described in IRS section 501(c)(3). No grants
are made to individuals, or for matching gifts or loans.

GRANTS ANALYSIS
Total Grants: $1,002,700

Number of Grants: 196

Highest Grant: $86,500

Average Grant: $5,116

Typical Range: $500 to $10,000

Disclosure Period: 1993

Note: Recent grants are derived from a 1993 Form 990.

RECENT GRANTS

General
86,500	Council on the Environment of New York City, New York, NY
54,900	Rainforest Alliance, New York, NY
50,000	American Foundation for AIDS Research, New York, NY
45,600	Duke University, Durham, NC
35,000	Jewish Campus Life Fund, New York, NY

Swiss Bank Corp.

Employees: 1,500
Headquarters: New York, NY
SIC Major Group: Depository Institutions

CONTACT
Joan Moschello
Director
Swiss Bank Corp.
PO Box 395
Church St. Station
New York, NY 10008
(212) 574-3000

CONTRIBUTIONS SUMMARY
Program supports all traditional categories of giving: arts and humanities, civic and public affairs, education, health, and social services.

Typical Recipients: • *Arts & Humanities:* Arts Centers, Arts Funds, Dance, Ethnic & Folk Arts, Historic Preservation, Libraries, Museums/Galleries, Music, Performing Arts, Theater • *Civic & Public Affairs:* Zoos/Aquariums • *Education:* Colleges & Universities, Private Education (Precollege) • *Health:* Hospitals, Single-Disease Health Associations • *Social Services:* United Funds/United Ways, Youth Organizations

Grant Types: general support

Geographic Distribution: in the eight cities with operating branches: New York, Miami, Atlanta, Chicago, Houston, Dallas, San Francisco, and Los Angeles

Operating Locations: CA, FL, GA, IL, NY (New York), TX

CORP. OFFICERS
Walter G. Frehner: *CURR EMPL* pres, gen mgr: Swiss Bank Corp

Franz Galliker: *CURR EMPL* chmn: Swiss Bank Corp

GIVING OFFICERS
Joan Moschello: dir

APPLICATION INFORMATION
Initial Approach: Send a letter any time including a description of the organization, amount and purpose of funds sought, recently audited financial statement, and proof of tax-exempt status.

Restrictions on Giving: Does not support individuals, member agencies of united funds, political or lobbying groups, or religious organizations for sectarian purposes.

GRANTS ANALYSIS
Typical Range: $1,000 to $5,000

Taconic Foundation

CONTACT
Jane Lee Eddy
Executive Director and Secretary
Taconic Foundation
745 Fifth Avenue, Ste. 1608
New York, NY 10151
(212) 758-8673

FINANCIAL SUMMARY
Recent Giving: $765,000 (1995 est.); $765,000 (1994 approx.); $765,000 (1993 approx.)

Assets: $21,500,000 (1995 est.); $21,500,000 (1994 approx.); $21,500,000 (1993 approx.)

Gifts Received: $112,699 (1988); $278,791 (1985)

Fiscal Note: The 1988 gift of $112,699 was the remainder of the interest matured under the will of Stephen Currier.

EIN: 13-1873668

CONTRIBUTIONS SUMMARY
Donor(s): The Taconic Foundation was established in 1958 by the late Mr. Stephen R. Currier and Mrs. Audrey Currier, the former Audrey Mellon Bruce. She was the daughter of Ailsa Mellon, who was the sister of Paul Mellon and the daughter of Andrew Mellon. Mr. and Mrs. Currier, who were lost in the Caribbean on an airplane flight in 1967, left a fund having a current market value of approximately $15 million to carry on their charitable activities.

Typical Recipients: • *Arts & Humanities:* Libraries • *Civic & Public Affairs:* African American Affairs, Asian American Affairs, Civil Rights, Economic Development, Employment/Job Training, Housing, Law & Justice, Philanthropic Organizations, Public Policy, Urban & Community Affairs • *Education:* Colleges & Universities, Education Associations, Education Funds, Literacy, Minority Education, Private Education (Precollege), School Volunteerism • *Health:* Children's Health/Hospitals • *International:* Health Care/Hospitals, International Relations • *Religion:* Churches • *Social Services:*

Child Welfare, Community Service Organizations, Counseling, Family Planning, Shelters/Homelessness, Youth Organizations

Grant Types: general support and project

Geographic Distribution: national, with emphasis on New York City

GIVING OFFICERS
Sheila M. Bautz: asst treas

Jane Lee Eddy: exec dir, secy, trust

John Gerald Simon: pres, treas, trust *B* New York NY 1928 *ED* Harvard Univ AB 1950; Yale Univ LLB 1953 *NONPR AFFIL* mem: Phi Beta Kappa; trust: Fdn Ctr; trust, secy: Potomac Inst; vchmn: Cooperative Assistance Fund

APPLICATION INFORMATION
Initial Approach:

Prospective applicants should send a letter to the foundation.

The letter should briefly describe the intended project. If the foundation is interested, one copy of a proposal will be requested.

The board meets four to six times a year, and there are no deadlines for submitting requests.

Final notification comes within two to three months.

Restrictions on Giving: No grants are given for higher education, art and cultural programs, mass media, crime and justice, health, medicine, mental health, ecology and the environment, individual economic development projects, or local community programs outside New York City. The foundation also makes no grants to individuals or to building or endowment funds. It rarely makes grants for research or loans.

PUBLICATIONS
Biennial report

GRANTS ANALYSIS
Total Grants: $585,988
Number of Grants: 42
Highest Grant: $300,000
Average Grant: $13,952
Typical Range: $5,000 to $20,000
Disclosure Period: 1992

Note: Recent grants are derived from a 1992 Form 990.

RECENT GRANTS
Library
5,000	Foundation Center, New York, NY — special gifts campaign
2,000	Foundation Center, New York, NY — support of general program

General
300,000	Smokey House Project, Danby, VT — support of general program
36,000	Potomac Institute, Washington, DC — support of general program
35,000	Business and Professional People for the Public Interest, Chicago, IL —

	support of national Gautreaux implementation
25,000	Enterprise Foundation, Columbia, MD — support of the New York City program
25,000	Public Education Association, New York, NY — support of general program

Taylor Foundation, Fred and Harriett

CONTACT
Fred and Harriett Taylor Fdn.
c/o Chase Manhattan Bank, N.A.
PO Box 1412
Rochester, NY 14603
(716) 258-5317

FINANCIAL SUMMARY
Recent Giving: $365,138 (1993); $362,696 (1992); $459,600 (1990)

Assets: $7,384,443 (1993); $7,116,337 (1992); $6,299,820 (1990)

EIN: 16-6205365

CONTRIBUTIONS SUMMARY
Donor(s): the late Fred C. Taylor

Typical Recipients: • *Arts & Humanities:* Libraries, Museums/Galleries • *Civic & Public Affairs:* Clubs, General, Municipalities/Towns, Safety, Urban & Community Affairs, Women's Affairs • *Education:* Colleges & Universities, Education Funds, Public Education (Precollege) • *Health:* Cancer, Children's Health/Hospitals, Emergency/Ambulance Services, Health Organizations, Heart, Hospitals, Medical Research, Single-Disease Health Associations • *International:* Health Care/Hospitals • *Religion:* Churches • *Social Services:* Animal Protection, Child Welfare, Community Service Organizations, Food/Clothing Distribution, People with Disabilities, Recreation & Athletics, United Funds/United Ways, Youth Organizations

Grant Types: general support and research

Geographic Distribution: limited to the Hammondsport, NY, area

GIVING OFFICERS
Chase Manhatten Bank: trust

APPLICATION INFORMATION
Initial Approach: The foundation has no formal grant application procedure or application form. There are no deadlines.

GRANTS ANALYSIS
Total Grants: $365,138
Typical Range: $2,000 to $33,087
Disclosure Period: 1993

Note: Recent grants are derived from a 1992 Form 990. Grants list for 1993 was incomplete.

RECENT GRANTS
Library
3,128	Hammondsport Public Library, Hammondsport, NY

General

75,000	Independent College Fund of New York, New York, NY
64,360	Ira Davenport Memorial Hospital, NY
32,180	Hammondsport Board of Education, Hammondsport, NY
25,774	Hammondsport Beautification Committee, Hammondsport, NY
22,526	Boy Scouts of America Five River Council, NY

Teagle Foundation

CONTACT
Richard W. Kimball
Chief Executive Officer and President
The Teagle Foundation
10 Rockefeller Plz., Rm. 920
New York, NY 10020-1903
(212) 373-1970

FINANCIAL SUMMARY
Recent Giving: $5,100,000 (fiscal 1995 est.); $5,109,647 (fiscal 1994); $4,748,031 (fiscal 1993)

Assets: $109,000,000 (fiscal 1995 est.); $107,198,354 (fiscal 1994); $105,852,520 (fiscal 1993)

Gifts Received: $275 (fiscal 1991)

EIN: 13-1773645

CONTRIBUTIONS SUMMARY
Donor(s): The Teagle Foundation was established in 1944 by the late Walter C. Teagle , former president and chairman of the Standard Oil Company (New Jersey), now Exxon Corporation. The foundation's assets also come from bequests from Mr. Teagle's wife, Rowena Lee Teagle , and their son, Walter C. Teagle, Jr.

Typical Recipients: • *Arts & Humanities:* Libraries • *Education:* Arts/Humanities Education, Colleges & Universities, Community & Junior Colleges, Education Associations, Engineering/Technological Education, Faculty Development, Medical Education, Religious Education, Science/Mathematics Education, Student Aid • *Health:* Hospitals • *Social Services:* Community Service Organizations, United Funds/United Ways, Youth Organizations

Grant Types: challenge, general support, multiyear/continuing support, project, and seed money

Geographic Distribution: national, with limited giving in Canada

GIVING OFFICERS
James C. Anderson: treas, contr

Donald M. Cox: chmn, dir

Richard W. Kimball: ceo, pres, dir

Margaret B. Sullivan: secy

APPLICATION INFORMATION
Initial Approach:

Applicants should submit a brief preliminary letter to the foundation. Applications for the Exxon scholarship program are available within Exxon.

The letter should describe the grant seeker and outline the scope and purpose of the proposed grant.

Applications may be submitted at any time.

If initial evoluation is favorable, a more detailed proposal will be requested. The board meets in November, February, and May to review requests.

Restrictions on Giving: The foundation does not support two-year institutions or, except for the Exxon Scholarship Program and its nursing program, public ones. It makes no grants to individuals and no grants for scholarships except for its Exxon and foundation sponsored scholarship program. It does not make grants for building funds, seminars or lectureships, the arts, research, primary or secondary schools, or community service organizations outside New York City. It does not fund college-based programs for precollege youth, including partnerships with public school systems. Activities of U.S.-based organizations which take place outside the U.S. are also not funded.

PUBLICATIONS
Annual report

GRANTS ANALYSIS
Total Grants: $5,109,647*

Number of Grants: 241

Highest Grant: $150,000

Typical Range: $20,000 to $65,000

Disclosure Period: fiscal year ending May 31, 1994

Note: Total grants figure comprises payments to 156 colleges and universities for scholarships awarded under the Exxon scholarship program and 85 grants to institutions of higher education, community service organizations, and foundation-related organizations, representing in the aggregate, 98% of the foundation's grant expenditures. The average grant figure is not applicable. Recent grants are derived from a fiscal 1993 annual report.

RECENT GRANTS

Library

50,000	College of St. Scholastica, Duluth, MN — to respond to the special needs of disadvantaged, nontraditional and minority students; to help faculty pursue advance degrees; and to enhance library resources
50,000	Greenville College, Greenville, IL — for programs to improve retention of high-risk students; to enhance library holdings for academic computing hardware and software; and to help increase alumni giving

25,000	Graduate Theological Union, Berkeley, CA — for its library automation project

General

150,000	Cornell University, Ithaca, NY — toward endowment of the Walter C. Teagle Director of Freshman Writing Seminars
92,000	Council of Independent Colleges, Washington, DC — for a faculty/administrator exchange program between United Negro College Fund colleges and other CIC member colleges
91,000	North Carolina Agricultural and Technical State University, Greensboro, NC — nursing education
90,000	Hampton University, Hampton, VA — nursing education
90,000	Otterbein College, Westerville, OH — nursing education

Texaco Inc. / Texaco Foundation

Revenue: $33.76 billion
Employees: 38,000
Headquarters: White Plains, NY
SIC Major Group: Lubricating Oils & Greases, Crude Petroleum & Natural Gas, Drilling Oil & Gas Wells, and Oil & Gas Exploration Services

CONTACT
Carl Barry Davidson
President
Texaco Foundation
2000 Westchester Ave.
White Plains, NY 10650
(914) 253-4000
Note: Mr. Davidson's extension is 4669.

FINANCIAL SUMMARY
Recent Giving: $12,000,000 (1994 approx.); $11,831,399 (1993); $11,595,425 (1992)

Assets: $36,314,975 (1991); $48,600,000 (1989)

Fiscal Note: Figures reflect foundation giving only. In 1993, company gave $12.2 million in direct grants.

EIN: 13-3007516

CONTRIBUTIONS SUMMARY
Typical Recipients: • *Arts & Humanities:* Arts Associations & Councils, Arts Festivals, Arts Funds, Ballet, Community Arts, Dance, History & Archaeology, Libraries, Museums/Galleries, Music, Opera, Performing Arts • *Civic & Public Affairs:* African American Affairs, Botanical Gardens/Parks, Business/Free Enterprise, Civil Rights, Economic Development, Economic Policy, Employment/Job Training, Housing, Law & Justice, Legal Aid, Municipalities/Towns, Public Policy, Safety, Urban & Community Affairs, Women's Affairs, Zoos/Aquariums • *Education:* Business Education, Colleges

& Universities, Community & Junior Colleges, Education Associations, Education Funds, Engineering/Technological Education, General, International Studies, Medical Education, Minority Education, Public Education (Precollege), Science/Mathematics Education, Secondary Education (Public), Special Education, Student Aid • *Environment:* General • *Health:* Children's Health/Hospitals, Diabetes, Emergency/Ambulance Services, Hospices, Hospitals, Medical Rehabilitation, Medical Research, Medical Training, Public Health, Transplant Networks/Donor Banks • *International:* Foreign Educational Institutions, Health Care/Hospitals, International Affairs, International Development, International Relations, International Relief Efforts • *Religion:* Jewish Causes • *Science:* Science Museums, Scientific Centers & Institutes, Scientific Labs, Scientific Organizations, Scientific Research • *Social Services:* Community Service Organizations, Delinquency & Criminal Rehabilitation, People with Disabilities, Recreation & Athletics, Senior Services, Substance Abuse, United Funds/United Ways, Volunteer Services, Youth Organizations

Grant Types: department, employee matching gifts, fellowship, project, research, and scholarship

Note: Employee matching gift ratio: 2 to 1 for the first $1,000 and 1 to 1 thereafter up to $20,000.

Geographic Distribution: national organizations and organizations near operating locations

Operating Locations: CA (Los Angeles, Universal City), CO (Denver), FL (Coral Gables), KS (El Dorado), LA (New Orleans), NY (White Plains), OK (Tulsa), PR (San Juan), TX (Austin, Bellaire, Houston, Port Arthur, Port Neches)

CORP. OFFICERS

Alfred Charles DeCrane, Jr.: *B* Cleveland OH 1931 *ED* Univ Notre Dame BA 1953; Georgetown Univ JD 1959 *CURR EMPL* chmn, ceo: Texaco Inc *CORP AFFIL* dir: CIGNA Corp, CPC Intl Inc, Dean Witter Discover & Co *NONPR AFFIL* dir: Am Petroleum Inst; mem: Am Bar Assn; trust: Conf Bd, Counc Econ Devel, Univ Notre Dame

Elizabeth Patience Smith: *B* New York NY 1949 *ED* Bucknell Univ BA 1971; Georgetown Univ JD 1976 *CURR EMPL* vp investor rels & shareholder svcs: Texaco Inc *NONPR AFFIL* dir: Westchester Ed Coalition; mem: Investor Rels Inst, Natl Investor Rels Inst, NY Bar Assn, Petroleum Investors Rels Assn; mem bd trust: Marymount Coll

GIVING OFFICERS

John Doss Ambler: dir *B* Buena Vista VA 1934 *ED* VA Polytech Inst & St Univ BS 1956 *CURR EMPL* vp: Texaco Inc *CORP AFFIL* dir: Caltex Petroleum Corp, Texaco Trinidad; pres: Texaco Europe

Michael N. Ambler: gen tax couns *CURR EMPL* gen tax couns: Texaco Refining &

Mktg *CORP AFFIL* gen tax couns: TRMI Holdings Inc

John Brademas: chmn *B* Mishawaka IN 1927 *ED* Harvard Univ BA 1949; Oxford Univ PhD 1954 *CORP AFFIL* dir: NYNEX Corp, Texaco Inc *NONPR AFFIL* bd adv: Carnegie Counc Ethics & Intl Aff, Carter Ctr, Emory Univ, Trilateral Commn; chmn: Natl Adv Comm Fighting Back; dir: Acad Ed Devel, Am Counc Arts, Aspen Inst, Athens Coll, Berlitz Intl Inc, Counc Aid Ed, Alexander S Onassis Pub Benefit Fdn; mem: Am Legion, Ctr Natl Policy, Natl Adv Counc Pub Svc, Natl Commn Financing Post-Secondary Ed, NY Govs Counc Fiscal & Econ Priorities, Phi Beta Kappa, Smithsonian Inst Natl Bd; trust: Spelman Coll *CLUB AFFIL* Ahepa, Masons

C. A. Brooks: asst secy

John J. Coppinger, Jr.: asst comptr

David C. Crikelair: treas *CORP AFFIL* treas: TRMI Holdings Inc

William James Crowe, Jr.: dir *B* La Grange KY 1925 *ED* US Naval Acad BS 1946; Stanford Univ MA 1956; Princeton Univ PhD 1965 *CORP AFFIL* dir: Gen Dynamics Corp, Merrill Lynch & Co Inc, Norfolk Southern Corp, Pfizer Inc, Texaco Inc *NONPR AFFIL* couns: Ctr Strategic & Intl Studies; mem: Am Political Sci Assn, Intl Studies Assn, Phi Delta Phi, Phi Gamma Delta, US Naval Inst; prof: Univ OK

Carl Barry Davidson: pres, dir *B* Trenton NJ 1933 *ED* Rutgers Univ AB 1954; Rutgers Univ LLB 1957 *CURR EMPL* vp, corp secy: Texaco Inc *CORP AFFIL* secy: Texaco Refining & Mktg, TRMI Holdings Inc; secy, dir: Four Star Oil & Gas Co, vp, secy, dir: Texaco Gas Mktg Inc *NONPR AFFIL* mem: Am Soc Corp Secys

George H. Eaton: comptr *CORP AFFIL* vp: Texaco Overseas Holdings Inc

Dr. Franklyn Green Jenifer: trust *ED* Howard Univ 1965; Univ MD PhD 1970 *CORP AFFIL* dir: Texaco Inc *NONPR AFFIL* pres: Univ TX

J. David Keough: asst treas

Robert E. Koch: vp

Regina Longo: asst secy

Maria Mike-Mayer: secy

Robert C. Oelkers: dir *CURR EMPL* vp: Western Sts Petroleum Assn *CORP AFFIL* sr vp: Texaco Refining & Mktg

Elizabeth Patience Smith: dir *CURR EMPL* vp investor rels & shareholder svcs: Texaco Inc (see above)

John E. Tuohy: gen couns

R. W. Ulrich: treas *CORP AFFIL* treas, dir: Four Star Oil & Gas Co, Texaco Caribbean Inc; vp, treas: Texaco Refining & Mktg

APPLICATION INFORMATION

Initial Approach: *Initial Contact:* cover letter highlighting the following: description, timetable, and objectives of project; reason why Texaco is appropriate donor; amount requested; any prior history of Texaco funding; Texaco operations in vicinity; part played in applicant's organization by Texaco employee or director volunteers; descrip-

tion of how Texaco's support will be acknowledged *Include Information On:* background in the form of enclosures describing the following: budget for project or event with reasonable breakdown of costs and sources already committed or expected; size and composition of the population to be served by the project; explanation of how efforts do not duplicate those of other agencies or institutions in the same or related fields; instrument and method of evaluating success; description of overall purpose and objectives of organization; list of names and primary professional affiliations of members of organization's board of trustees; copy of IRS Code Section 501(c)(3) tax-exempt status; most recently audited financial statement; organization's general funding sources by category and, if available, a list of contributors and the size of their contributions *Deadlines:* none *Note:* If of local or regional scope, apply directly to Community Relations Committee at local plant.

Restrictions on Giving: The foundation generally does not provide funds for unrestricted operating support or capital campaigns. Giving is directed more toward specific activities, programs, and events.

The foundation normally does not support individuals; private foundations; non tax-exempt organizations; social functions, commemorative journals or meetings; religious, fraternal, social, or veterans organizations; political or partisan organizations or candidates; endowments; organizations attempting to influence legislation or elections or that carry on any voter-registration drives.

GRANTS ANALYSIS

Total Grants: $11,831,399

Number of Grants: 478

Highest Grant: $851,659

Average Grant: $24,752

Typical Range: $1,000 to $5,000 and $10,000 to $25,000

Disclosure Period: 1993

Note: Recent grants are derived from a 1993 grands list.

RECENT GRANTS

Library

25,000	Bradford Memorial Library, El Dorado, KS

General

1,807,810	United Funds — nationwide
851,659	Texaco Foundation Scholarship Program
200,000	United Negro College Fund, New York, NY
191,000	Texaco Star Academic Challenge Program
106,400	Texas A&M University Department of Petroleum Engineering, College Station, TX

The New Yorker Magazine, Inc.

Sales: $1.0 million
Employees: 400
Parent Company: Advance Magazine
  Publishers, Inc.
Headquarters: New York, NY
SIC Major Group: Printing & Publishing

CONTACT
Steven Thomas Florio
President
The New Yorker Magazine, Inc.
20 W 43rd St.
New York, NY 10036-7440
(212) 536-5400

FINANCIAL SUMMARY
Fiscal Note: Company does not disclose
contributions figures.

CONTRIBUTIONS SUMMARY
Typical Recipients: • *Arts & Humanities:*
Arts Appreciation, Arts Associations &
Councils, Arts Centers, Arts Festivals, Arts
Funds, Arts Institutes, Community Arts,
Dance, Ethnic & Folk Arts, General, His-
toric Preservation, Libraries, Literary Arts,
Museums/Galleries, Music, Opera, Perform-
ing Arts, Public Broadcasting, Theater, Vis-
ual Arts • *Civic & Public Affairs:* Civil
Rights, First Amendment Issues, General,
Law & Justice, Legal Aid, Women's Affairs, Zoos/Aquariums • *Education:* Arts/Hu-
manities Education, Colleges &
Universities, Education Associations, Education Funds, Elementary Education (Private),
General, Journalism/Media Education, Literacy, Medical Education, Minority Educa-
tion, Preschool Education, Public Education
(Precollege), Science/Mathematics Educa-
tion, Special Education • *Health:* Emer-
gency/Ambulance Services, General,
Geriatric Health, Health Policy/Cost Con-
tainment, Health Funds, Health Organiza-
tions, Hospices, Hospitals, Medical
Rehabilitation, Medical Research, Medical
Training, Mental Health, Nursing Services,
Nutrition, Public Health, Single-Disease
Health Associations • *International:* Health
Care/Hospitals • *Science:* Observatories &
Planetariums, Scientific Centers & Insti-
tutes, Scientific Organizations • *Social Serv-
ices:* Child Welfare, Community Service
Organizations, Domestic Violence, Family
Planning, Family Services, Food/Clothing
Distribution, General, People with Disabili-
ties, Refugee Assistance, Senior Services,
Shelters/Homelessness, Substance Abuse,
United Funds/United Ways, Volunteer Serv-
ices, Youth Organizations

Grant Types: award, employee matching
gifts, general support, multiyear/continuing
support, and scholarship

Nonmonetary Support Types: donated
equipment

Geographic Distribution: primarily headquarters area

Operating Locations: NY (New York)

APPLICATION INFORMATION
Initial Approach: Send a brief letter of inquiry and a full proposal. Include a description of organization, amount requested,
purpose of funds sought, and proof of tax-exempt status. There are no deadlines.

Restrictions on Giving: Does not support
individuals, religious organizations for sectarian purposes, or political or lobbying
groups.

GRANTS ANALYSIS
Typical Range: $50 to $1,000

Thompson Co., J. Walter / Thompson Co. Fund, J. Walter

Income: $6.2 billion
Employees: 6,600
Parent Company: WPP Group plc
Headquarters: New York, NY
SIC Major Group: Business Services

CONTACT
Nancy Fitzpatrick
Secretary and Director
J. Walter Thompson Co. Fund
466 Lexington Ave.
New York, NY 10017
(212) 210-8000
Note: Contact's extension number is 7508.

FINANCIAL SUMMARY
Recent Giving: $211,676 (fiscal 1993);
$162,607 (fiscal 1992); $92,818 (fiscal 1991)
Assets: $1,517,394 (fiscal 1993);
$1,074,833 (fiscal 1992); $1,017,104 (fiscal
1991)
EIN: 13-6020644

CONTRIBUTIONS SUMMARY
Typical Recipients: • *Arts & Humanities:*
Arts Centers, Ballet, Dance, General, Libraries, Museums/Galleries, Music, Opera, Performing Arts, Theater • *Civic & Public
Affairs:* African American Affairs, Busi-
ness/Free Enterprise, Economic Development, Ethnic Organizations, General,
Municipalities/Towns, Professional & Trade
Associations, Safety • *Education:* Arts/Hu-
manities Education, Colleges & Universi-
ties, Education Funds, Education Reform,
Engineering/Technological Education, Gen-
eral, International Exchange, Private Educa-
tion (Precollege), Social Sciences
Education, Student Aid • *Environment:* Re-
source Conservation • *Health:* Cancer, Dia-
betes, Medical Research, Single-Disease
Health Associations • *Religion:* Jewish
Causes, Religious Organizations • *Science:*
Scientific Research • *Social Services:* Child
Welfare, Community Centers, General,
Scouts, United Funds/United Ways, Youth
Organizations

Grant Types: employee matching gifts and
general support

Nonmonetary Support Types: in-kind services, loaned employees, loaned executives,
and workplace solicitation

Geographic Distribution: internationally
Operating Locations: CA (Los Angeles,
San Francisco), GA (Atlanta), IL (Chicago),
MI (Detroit), NY (New York)

CORP. OFFICERS
Chris Jones: *CURR EMPL* co-pres: J Walter Thompson Co

Burton J. Manning: *B* 1931 *CURR EMPL*
chmn, ceo: J Walter Thompson Co World-
wide *NONPR AFFIL* dir: Adult Ed Fdn, Natl
Assn Depressive Illness, Players Co; trust:
Neuroscis Inst, New Sch Social Res *CLUB
AFFIL* mem: Lotus

Peter A. Schweitzer: *B* Chicago IL 1939
ED Univ Michigan BA 1961; Western Michi-
gan Univ MBA 1967 *CURR EMPL* co-pres:
J Walter Thompson Co

Lewis J. Trencher: *CURR EMPL* coo, cfo:
J Walter Thompson Co

GIVING OFFICERS
Nancy Fitzpatrick: secy, dir *CURR EMPL*
ptnr, secy: J Walter Thompson Co

Burton J. Manning: pres, dir *CURR EMPL*
chmn, ceo: J Walter Thompson Co Worldwide (see above)

Donna Matteo: treas

Susan Mirsky: vp, dir

Lewis J. Trencher: chmn, dir *CURR EMPL*
coo, cfo: J Walter Thompson Co (see above)

APPLICATION INFORMATION
Initial Approach: Send a brief proposal. Include a description of organization, amount
requested, purpose of funds sought, and
proof of tax-exempt status. There are no
deadlines.

Restrictions on Giving: Does not support
individuals, religious organizations for sectarian purposes, or political or lobbying
groups.

GRANTS ANALYSIS
Total Grants: $211,676

Number of Grants: 150

Highest Grant: $50,000

Typical Range: $1,000 to $10,000

Disclosure Period: fiscal year ending November 30, 1993

Note: Recent grants are derived from a fiscal 1993 Form 990.

RECENT GRANTS

Library

25,000	Duke University Libraries, Durham, NC
1,000	New York Public Library, New York, NY

General

50,000	United Way of New York City, New York, NY
10,000	New York City Partnership, New York, NY
7,500	Advertising Council, New York, NY
4,125	Advertising Council, New York, NY
3,630	National Merit Scholarship Corporation, Evanston, IL

Thorne Foundation

CONTACT
Miriam A. Thorne
President
Thorne Fdn.
435 E 52nd St.
New York, NY 10022
(212) 758-2425

FINANCIAL SUMMARY
Recent Giving: $213,349 (1993); $323,865 (1992); $463,954 (1991)

Assets: $1,863,793 (1993); $1,922,319 (1992); $2,206,527 (1991)

EIN: 13-6109955

CONTRIBUTIONS SUMMARY
Donor(s): the late Landon K. Thorne, the late Julia L. Thorne

Typical Recipients: • *Arts & Humanities:* Arts Institutes, Film & Video, Historic Preservation, History & Archaeology, Libraries, Museums/Galleries, Performing Arts, Public Broadcasting, Theater • *Civic & Public Affairs:* Botanical Gardens/Parks, Community Foundations, General, Municipalities/Towns, Urban & Community Affairs, Zoos/Aquariums • *Education:* Colleges & Universities, International Studies, Private Education (Precollege), Secondary Education (Private) • *Environment:* Resource Conservation • *Health:* Cancer, Clinics/Medical Centers, Emergency/Ambulance Services, Health Organizations, Hospitals, Hospitals (University Affiliated), Medical Rehabilitation, Medical Research, Research/Studies Institutes, Respiratory, Speech & Hearing • *International:* Foreign Educational Institutions, International Peace & Security Issues • *Religion:* Religious Organizations, Religious Welfare • *Science:* Science Museums • *Social Services:* Child Welfare, Community Service Organizations, Family Services, Homes, People with Disabilities, United Funds/United Ways, YMCA/YWCA/YMHA/YWHA, Youth Organizations

Grant Types: general support

Geographic Distribution: focus on NY

GIVING OFFICERS
John B. Jessup: secy *PHIL AFFIL* co-trust: Elizabeth T. Wheeler Trust

David H. Thorne: vp

Miriam A. Thorne: pres

APPLICATION INFORMATION
Initial Approach: Send brief letter of inquiry describing program. Include a description of organization, amount requested, purpose of funds sought, recently audited financial statement, and proof of tax-exempt status. There are no deadlines.

GRANTS ANALYSIS
Total Grants: $213,349

Number of Grants: 83

Highest Grant: $25,000

Typical Range: $50 to $25,000

Disclosure Period: 1993

Note: Recent grants are derived from a 1993 Form 990.

RECENT GRANTS

Library
25,000	Pierpont Morgan Library, New York, NY
2,000	New York Public Library, New York, NY

General
25,000	American University in Cairo, New York, NY
25,000	National Foundation for Facial Reconstruction, New York, NY
20,000	Manhattan Eye, Ear, and Throat Hospital, New York, NY
15,000	Business Executives for National Security, Washington, DC
15,000	YMCA-YWCA Camping Services

Titus Foundation, Roy and Niuta

CONTACT
Lester Dembitzer
Secretary-Treasurer
Roy and Niuta Titus Fdn.
1790 Broadway, Rm. 705
New York, NY 10019
(212) 265-5340

FINANCIAL SUMMARY
Recent Giving: $284,750 (fiscal 1993)

Assets: $6,219,368 (fiscal 1993)

EIN: 13-2832086

CONTRIBUTIONS SUMMARY
Typical Recipients: • *Arts & Humanities:* Arts Associations & Councils, Community Arts, Dance, Film & Video, History & Archaeology, Libraries, Museums/Galleries, Performing Arts, Theater • *Civic & Public Affairs:* Civil Rights, Economic Development, General, Urban & Community Affairs, Women's Affairs • *Education:* Arts/Humanities Education, Private Education (Precollege) • *Environment:* Air/Water Quality • *Health:* AIDS/HIV, Children's Health/Hospitals, Diabetes, Eyes/Blindness, Health Organizations, Nursing Services, Transplant Networks/Donor Banks • *International:* Foreign Arts Organizations, International Relief Efforts • *Religion:* Jewish Causes, Synagogues/Temples • *Science:* Science Museums • *Social Services:* Child Welfare, Community Service Organizations, Food/Clothing Distribution, Youth Organizations

Grant Types: general support

Geographic Distribution: focus on New York, NY

GIVING OFFICERS
Lester Dembitzer: secy, treas *PHIL AFFIL* secy, treas: Atsuko Chiba Foundation, Andrew and Irma Hilton Foundation, George and Joyce Wein Foundation

Louis E. Slesin: vp *PHIL AFFIL* dir: Helena Rubinstein Foundation

Suzanne Slesin: vp *PHIL AFFIL* dir: Helena Rubinstein Foundation

Niuta Titus: pres

APPLICATION INFORMATION
Initial Approach: Send a brief letter of inquiry and a full proposal. Include a description of organization and proof of tax-exempt status. There are no deadlines.

GRANTS ANALYSIS
Total Grants: $284,750

Number of Grants: 90

Highest Grant: $25,000

Typical Range: $200 to $25,000

Disclosure Period: fiscal year ending September 30, 1993

Note: Recent grants are derived from a fiscal 1993 Form 990.

RECENT GRANTS

Library
5,000	New York Public Library, New York, NY
5,000	New York Public Library, New York, NY

General
25,000	AFTAM, New York, NY
25,000	AFTAM, New York, NY
25,000	Dalton School, New York, NY
25,000	Dalton School, New York, NY
25,000	Wilmer Institute, Baltimore, MD

Travelers Inc. / Travelers Foundation

Former Foundation Name: Primerica Foundation
Revenue: $18.5 billion
Employees: 16,650
Headquarters: New York, NY
SIC Major Group: Short-Term Business Credit, State Commercial Banks, Personal Credit Institutions, and Miscellaneous Business Credit Institutions

CONTACT
Dee Topol
President
The Travelers Foundation
388 Greenwich St.
New York, NY 10013
(212) 816-8884
Note: Ms. Topol is the contact for the New York City area and for national organizations. Ms. Patricia R. Byrne, Grants Manager, is an additional contact for these areas. Organizations located outside the New York City area should contact the nearest office of the Travelers Group.

FINANCIAL SUMMARY

Recent Giving: $10,000,000 (1995 est.);
$9,206,248 (1994); $5,001,794 (1993)

Assets: $4,525,873 (1993); $2,600,906
(1991); $2,500,000 (1990)

Fiscal Note: The 1994 total includes
$3,601,634 in general grants, $4,691,394
from local contributions programs, $642,170
from the Volunteer Incentive Program, and
$271, 050 in gifts for events and dinners.
The 1993 figure includes $4,077,569 in foundation giving and $924,225 in direct corporate giving.

EIN: 13-6161154

CONTRIBUTIONS SUMMARY

Typical Recipients: • *Arts & Humanities:*
Arts Associations & Councils, Arts Centers,
Arts Outreach, Ballet, Community Arts,
Dance, History & Archaeology, Libraries,
Museums/Galleries, Music, Opera, Performing Arts, Theater, Visual Arts • *Civic & Public Affairs:* Botanical Gardens/Parks,
Business/Free Enterprise, Economic Development, Employment/Job Training, Housing, Municipalities/Towns,
Parades/Festivals, Public Policy, Women's
Affairs • *Education:* Afterschool/Enrichment Programs, Arts/Humanities Education,
Business Education, Colleges & Universities, Economic Education, Education Funds,
Education Reform, General, Literacy, Medical Education, Preschool Education, Private
Education (Precollege), Public Education
(Precollege), Secondary Education (Public)
• *Environment:* General, Resource Conservation • *Health:* AIDS/HIV, Cancer, Children's Health/Hospitals, Clinics/Medical
Centers, Health Organizations, Hospitals,
Hospitals (University Affiliated), Prenatal
Health Issues, Preventive Medicine/Wellness Organizations • *International:* Missionary/Religious Activities • *Religion:* Jewish
Causes, Religious Organizations, Religious
Welfare, Seminaries • *Social Services:* Child
Abuse, Child Welfare, Community Centers,
Community Service Organizations, Day
Care, Domestic Violence, Family Services,
Food/Clothing Distribution, Scouts, Shelters/Homelessness, Substance Abuse, United
Funds/United Ways, Youth Organizations

Grant Types: general support and project

Note: The Volunteer Incentive Program provides grants of up to $1,500 to organizations
where employees volunteer their time.

Geographic Distribution: near headquarters and operating locations only

Operating Locations: DE (Wilmington),
GA (Duluth), MD (Baltimore), NY (New
York), TX (Fort Worth, Houston)

Note: Travelers has branch offices throughout the U.S. Its main business subsidiaries
include: Smith Barney Shearson; Primerica
Financial Services; Commerical Credit Co.;
American Capital Management & Research;
RCM; Transport Life Insurance Co.;
Primerica Bank; and Gulf Insurance Co.;
and The Travelers Insurance Companies.

CORP. OFFICERS

James R. Dimon: *B* NY 1956 *ED* Tufts
Univ BA 1978; Harvard Univ Grad Sch Bus

Admin MBA 1982 *CURR EMPL* pres, cfo,
coo, dir: Travelers NY Inc *CORP AFFIL*
exec vp, cfo: Commercial Credit Co

Robert Irving Lipp: *B* 1938 *ED* Williams
Coll 1960; Harvard Univ MBA 1963; NY
Univ JD 1969 *CURR EMPL* vchmn, group
chief exec, dir: Travelers Inc *CORP AFFIL*
ceo, pres, dir: Travelers Ins Group; chmn:
Phoenix Ins Co; dir: Greater NY Fund; exec
vp: Commercial Credit Co *NONPR AFFIL*
dir: New York City Ballet; trust: Jackie Robinson Fdn

Mary McDermott: *CURR EMPL* sr vp pub
aff: Travelers Inc

Charles O. Prince III: *B* 1950 *ED* Univ
Southern CA BA 1971; Univ Southern CA
MA 1975; Univ Southern CA JD 1975
CURR EMPL sr vp, sec, gen couns: Travelers Inc *CORP AFFIL* sr vp, secy, gen couns:
Commercial Credit Co

Sanford I. Weill: *B* Brooklyn NY 1933 *ED*
Cornell Univ BA 1955 *CURR EMPL* chmn,
ceo: Travelers Inc *CORP AFFIL* chmn, pres,
ceo: Commercial Credit Co; dir: Am Central
Mgmt & Res, IDS Mutual Funds Group
NONPR AFFIL chmn: Carnegie Hall, New
York City Temporary Commn Early Childhood & Child Care Programs; dir: Baltimore
Symphony Orchestra; fdr: Acad Fin; mem:
Bus Roundtable, NY Soc Security Analysts;
mem bd overseers: Cornell Univ Med Coll;
mem bus comm: Mus Modern Art; mem
joint bd: NY Hosp; vchmn adv counc: Cornell Univ Johnson Grad Sch Mgmt *CLUB
AFFIL* Century CC, Cornell, Harmonie

GIVING OFFICERS

Mark Amhein: asst secy

Patricia Byrne: grants mgr

James R. Dimon: trust *CURR EMPL* pres,
cfo, coo, dir: Travelers NY Inc (see above)

Robert Irving Lipp: vp, treas *CURR EMPL*
vchmn, group chief exec, dir: Travelers Inc
(see above)

Charles O. Prince III: sec, trust *CURR
EMPL* sr vp, sec, gen couns: Travelers Inc
(see above)

Dee Topol: pres, trust

Sanford I. Weill: chmn bd of trust *CURR
EMPL* chmn, ceo: Travelers Inc (see above)

APPLICATION INFORMATION

Initial Approach: *Initial Contact:* one to
three page preliminary proposal *Include Information On:* description of nature and purpose of organization; name, title, address,
and phone number of contact person; description of project to be funded (include objectives, target groups, needs, activities,
budget, and timespan); copy of IRS tax-exempt letter; recent financial information, including a recently audited financial
statement, list of recent contributors, and an
annual report, if available; list of organization's governing board; description of staff;
and proof that organization and services are
not discriminatory in any way *Deadlines:*
none

Restrictions on Giving: The foundation
does not support individuals; political organizations; religious bodies; labor organiza-

tions; agencies whose sole purpose is social
or recreational; and professional marketing
or trade organizations.

The following activities are not eligible for
support: courtesy advertising; special
events; books, magazines, or articles in professional journals; or fund-raising activities
such as benefits, charitable dinners or sporting events.

The foundation does not support capital or
endowment fund drives, except under special circumstances with a waiver from the
foundation's board of directors, nor general
operating funds for member agencies of
United Way in areas where The Travelers or
its affiliates give to those united fund drives.

OTHER THINGS TO KNOW

Effective 12/31/93 The Travelers Company
was merged into the Primerica Corporation.
Primerica, as the surviving corporation of
this merger, has changed its name to The
Travelers Inc.

The name of the Primerica Foundation has
been changed to The Travelers Foundation
effective 1/1/94. The entity formerly known
as The Travelers Companies Foundation has
ceased to be independent and has become
part of The Travelers Foundation.

GRANTS ANALYSIS

Total Grants: $9,206,248*

Number of Grants: 2,957

Highest Grant: $1,000,000

Average Grant: $3,113

Typical Range: $1,000 to $20,000

Disclosure Period: 1994

Note: Figures reflect foundation and direct
corporate giving. Total grants include
$8,415,921 in foundation giving and
$790,327 in direct corporate contributions.
Recent grants are derived from a 1994
grants list.

RECENT GRANTS

Library

15,000	Wadsworth Atheneum, Hartford, CT

General

1,000,000	United Way of the Capital Area, Hartford, CT
900,000	Cornell University Medical College, New York, NY — for general operating support
360,000	Doctor Ronald E. McNair Foundation, Atlanta, GA
350,000	National Academy Foundation, New York, NY — for education
250,000	Hartford Foundation for Public Giving, Hartford, CT — for early childhood education and care

Tuch Foundation, Michael

CONTACT
Eugene Tuck
President
Michael Tuch Fdn.
122 E 42nd St., No. 2905
New York, NY 10168
(212) 986-9083

FINANCIAL SUMMARY
Recent Giving: $435,988 (1993); $293,724 (1991); $292,932 (1990)

Assets: $5,908,555 (1993); $6,046,526 (1991); $5,494,950 (1990)

Gifts Received: $59,867 (1993); $63,412 (1991); $27,078 (1990)

Fiscal Note: In 1993, contributions were received from Eugene Tuch.

EIN: 13-6002848

CONTRIBUTIONS SUMMARY
Donor(s): the late Michael Tuch

Typical Recipients: • *Arts & Humanities:* Arts Festivals, Community Arts, Libraries, Museums/Galleries, Music, Opera, Theater • *Civic & Public Affairs:* Urban & Community Affairs, Zoos/Aquariums • *Education:* Arts/Humanities Education, Colleges & Universities, School Volunteerism • *Environment:* Air/Water Quality, General • *Health:* AIDS/HIV • *Religion:* Jewish Causes, Religious Organizations • *Social Services:* Child Welfare, Community Service Organizations, Food/Clothing Distribution, People with Disabilities, Recreation & Athletics, United Funds/United Ways, YMCA/YWCA/YMHA/YWHA, Youth Organizations

Grant Types: fellowship, project, and scholarship

Geographic Distribution: focus on New York, NY

GIVING OFFICERS
Martha Rozete: vp

Eugene Tuck, Esq.: pres, trust

Jonathan S. Tuck: trust

APPLICATION INFORMATION
Initial Approach: Send cover letter and full proposal. Include a description of organization, amount requested, purpose of funds sought, recently audited financial statement, and proof of tax-exempt status. There are no deadlines.

Restrictions on Giving: Does not support individuals.

GRANTS ANALYSIS
Total Grants: $435,988

Number of Grants: 95

Highest Grant: $24,000

Typical Range: $100 to $17,808

Disclosure Period: 1993

Note: Recent grants are derived from a 1993 Form 990.

RECENT GRANTS
Library
17,808   Brooklyn Public Library, Brooklyn, NY

General
24,000   City Harvest, New York, NY
15,000   92nd Street Y, New York, NY
15,000   New York City Foodbank Food for Survival, New York, NY
10,000   God's Love We Deliver, New York, NY
10,000   New York City School Volunteer Program, New York, NY

Unilever United States, Inc. / Unilever Foundation

Sales: $6.95 billion
Employees: 200
Parent Company: Unilever N.V. and Unilever P.L.C
Headquarters: New York, NY
SIC Major Group: Business Services Nec

CONTACT
John T. Gould, Jr.
Director, Corporate Affairs
Unilever United States, Inc.
Lever House, 390 Park Ave.
New York, NY 10022
(212) 906-4685

FINANCIAL SUMMARY
Recent Giving: $1,000,000 (1994 est.); $1,280,821 (1993); $1,069,260 (1992)

Assets: $331,539 (1993); $387,641 (1992); $287,797 (1991)

Gifts Received: $1,206,425 (1993); $1,148,836 (1992); $547,182 (1991)

Fiscal Note: Figures include foundation contributions only. Above figures exclude nonmonetary support. The Unilever United States Foundation gives on behalf of Unilever, Unilever Research U.S., Leverr Brothers, and Vanden Bergh Foods Co. In 1993, the foundation received 21,400 shares of Colgate Palmolive stock, worth $1,206,425, from Calvin Klein Cosmetics.

EIN: 13-6122117

CONTRIBUTIONS SUMMARY
Typical Recipients: • *Arts & Humanities:* Arts Centers, Arts Institutes, Libraries, Museums/Galleries, Music, Performing Arts, Public Broadcasting, Theater • *Civic & Public Affairs:* African American Affairs, Botanical Gardens/Parks, Business/Free Enterprise, Civil Rights, Economic Development, Economic Policy, Employment/Job Training, Municipalities/Towns, Nonprofit Management, Professional & Trade Associations, Public Policy, Safety, Urban & Community Affairs, Zoos/Aquariums • *Education:* Agricultural Education, Business Education, Business-School Partnerships, Colleges & Universities, Economic Education, Education Associations, Elementary Education (Private), Engineering/Techno-logical Education, International Studies, Literacy, Minority Education, Private Education (Precollege), Public Education (Precollege), Science/Mathematics Education, Student Aid • *Environment:* General • *Health:* Children's Health/Hospitals, Health Organizations, Hospitals, Single-Disease Health Associations, Trauma Treatment • *Science:* Science Museums, Scientific Organizations • *Social Services:* Community Centers, Community Service Organizations, Day Care, Food/Clothing Distribution, People with Disabilities, Senior Services, Shelters/Homelessness, Substance Abuse, United Funds/United Ways, Youth Organizations

Grant Types: emergency, employee matching gifts, and general support

Nonmonetary Support Types: cause-related marketing & promotion, donated equipment, and donated products

Note: Value of nonmonetary support is unavailable.

Geographic Distribution: primarily in communities where company has major facilities

Operating Locations: CA, CT (Clinton, Greenwich), FL (Jacksonville), GA, IN, MD, MO, NJ (Englewood Cliffs), NY (New York), PR

CORP. OFFICERS
Richard A. Goldstein: *B* Boston MA 1942 *ED* Univ MA BBA 1963; Harvard Univ 1968; Boston Univ LLM *CURR EMPL* pres, ceo; dir: Unilever US Inc

John T. Gould, Jr.: *B* Brunswick ME 1938 *ED* Bowdoin Coll 1960 *CURR EMPL* dir corp aff: Unilever US Inc *NONPR AFFIL* dir: Natl Press Fdn, Pub Aff Counc; mem: Arthur W Page Soc, Pub Rels Soc Am *CLUB AFFIL* Natl Press, Overseas Press

GIVING OFFICERS
John T. Gould, Jr.: vp *CURR EMPL* dir corp aff: Unilever US Inc (see above)

Thomas J. Hoolihan: secy

Clarence Lewis Roberts, Jr.: treas *B* Bryn Mawr PA 1934 *ED* Yale Univ 1956; Am Univ 1962 *CURR EMPL* asst treas: Unilever US Inc

T. Keith Rowland: dir

Walter Mark Volpi: dir *B* New York NY 1946 *ED* St Johns Univ BA 1968; St Johns Univ JD 1974 *CURR EMPL* sr vp, gen couns: Lever Bros *NONPR AFFIL* mem: Am Bar Assn, Am Law Inst, Assn Bar City New York, St Bar Assn

APPLICATION INFORMATION
Initial Approach: *Initial Contact:* letter or proposal on organization's letterhead and signed by its chief executive officer *Include Information On:* the grant's purpose, background information on the organization, the most recent annual report, a copy of the current operating budget, proof of tax-exempt status *Deadlines:* none; budget is determined annually in February

Restrictions on Giving: The foundation does not support research activities; organizations or programs of international scope; labor organizations; veterans groups for fraternal/social purposes; project underwriting;

purchase of advertising in benefit publications or for support of benefit events; political activities; capital campaigns (other than hospitals in communities where company employees are concentrated); organizations which espouse religious philosophies; operating funds of member agencies of United Way; individuals; or scholarships, except through the National Merit Scholarship Program.

GRANTS ANALYSIS
Total Grants: $1,280,821

Number of Grants: 307

Highest Grant: $88,030

Average Grant: $4,172

Typical Range: $1,000 to $5,000

Disclosure Period: 1993

Note: Recent grants are derived from a 1993 Form 990.

RECENT GRANTS

Library

10,000	New York Public Library, New York, NY

General

88,030	National Merit Scholarship Corporation, Evanston, IL
35,000	United Way of Tri-State, Tri-State, NY
32,000	Stevens Institute of Technology Education Program, Hoboken, NJ
25,000	Lake Area United Way, Griffith, IN
18,000	Eco Sense II

Uris Brothers Foundation

CONTACT
Alice Paul
Executive Director and Secretary
Uris Brothers Foundation
300 Park Ave.
New York, NY 10022
(212) 355-7080

FINANCIAL SUMMARY
Recent Giving: $1,575,380 (fiscal 1994); $1,560,970 (fiscal 1993); $1,450,874 (fiscal 1992)

Assets: $21,808,002 (fiscal 1994); $22,656,487 (fiscal 1993); $25,930,385 (fiscal 1992)

EIN: 13-6115748

CONTRIBUTIONS SUMMARY
Donor(s): The foundation was established in 1956 in New York by Percy Uris and Harold Uris , then co-owners of Uris Brothers Building Corporation of New York. During the building boom of the 1920s, the brothers ranked among the country's foremost builders of hotels and large apartment and office buildings. Their investment building firm remained successful until the Depression. By the 1970s, however, Uris Building's assets rose to $350 million.

Percy Uris, the elder brother and a trustee of Columbia University, died in 1971. Harold Uris died in 1982.

Typical Recipients: • *Arts & Humanities:* Arts Associations & Councils, Arts Centers, Libraries, Music, Opera, Performing Arts, Public Broadcasting • *Civic & Public Affairs:* Botanical Gardens/Parks, Economic Development, Employment/Job Training, Housing, Law & Justice, Legal Aid, Urban & Community Affairs, Zoos/Aquariums • *Education:* Arts/Humanities Education, Faculty Development, Legal Education, Literacy, Medical Education, Preschool Education, Special Education • *Health:* Emergency/Ambulance Services, Heart, Speech & Hearing • *Religion:* Jewish Causes, Religious Welfare • *Social Services:* Camps, Child Welfare, Community Centers, Community Service Organizations, Counseling, Day Care, Domestic Violence, Family Planning, Family Services, Food/Clothing Distribution, Senior Services, Shelters/Homelessness, Substance Abuse, Volunteer Services, Youth Organizations

Grant Types: capital, general support, loan, multiyear/continuing support, and project

Geographic Distribution: primarily New York City; limited support elsewhere

GIVING OFFICERS
Robert H. Abrams: dir

Robert L. Bachner: asst secy, dir *PHIL AFFIL* dir: Robert I. Wishnick Foundation

Jane Bayard: vp, dir

Bernard Fisher: dir

Benjamin Gessula: treas *B* 1921

Susan Halpern: pres, dir

Alice Paul: exec dir, secy

Linda Sanger: vp, dir

Ruth Uris: chmn, dir

APPLICATION INFORMATION
Initial Approach:

A letter and a brief proposal is the recommended form of initial contact.

Letter of inquiry should include a description of the applicant organization, specific project, and budget.

There are no application deadlines. The board of directors meets quarterly.

Restrictions on Giving: The foundation is primarily interested in organizations within New York City. Grants are not made to individuals, for endowment funds, films, or studies. The foundation does not make loans to individuals.

OTHER THINGS TO KNOW
Besides making grants, the foundation provides technical assistance to grantees on fund raising and program development.

GRANTS ANALYSIS
Total Grants: $1,575,380

Number of Grants: 87

Highest Grant: $100,000

Average Grant: $18,108

Typical Range: $5,000 to $50,000

Disclosure Period: fiscal year ending October 31, 1994

Note: Recent grants are derived from a fiscal 1993 grants list.

RECENT GRANTS

Library

60,000	New York Public Library, New York, NY
50,000	Harvard Medical School Countway Library, Cambridge, MA

General

150,000	Community Partnership Development Corporation, New York, NY
100,000	Columbia University Graduate School of Business, New York, NY
75,000	Local Initiatives Support Corporation, New York, NY
75,000	Pratt Institute, Brooklyn, NY
75,000	SURDNA Foundation/CCRP-Multifunders Account

Utica National Insurance Group / Utica National Group Foundation

Premiums: $489.0 million
Employees: 1,450
Parent Company: Utica Mutual Insurance Co.
Headquarters: Utica, NY
SIC Major Group: Insurance Agents, Brokers & Service and Insurance Carriers

CONTACT
George P. Wardley III
Secretary
Utica National Group Foundation
PO Box 530
Utica, NY 13503
(315) 734-2521

FINANCIAL SUMMARY
Recent Giving: $149,545 (1993); $112,199 (1992); $78,154 (1991)

Assets: $2,022,265 (1993); $1,968,198 (1992); $1,930,108 (1991)

Gifts Received: $2,563 (1992); $1,000,000 (1991); $25,000 (1990)

Fiscal Note: In 1991, contributions were received from Utica Mutual Insurance Company.

EIN: 16-1313450

CONTRIBUTIONS SUMMARY
Typical Recipients: • *Arts & Humanities:* Arts Funds, Historic Preservation, Libraries, Museums/Galleries, Performing Arts, Public Broadcasting • *Civic & Public Affairs:* Economic Development, General, Legal Aid, Municipalities/Towns, Urban & Community Affairs • *Education:* Preschool Education • *Health:* Children's Health/Hospitals, Emergency/Ambulance Services, Health Organizations, Hospitals, Long-Term Care, Medical Research, Mental Health, Single-Disease Health Associations • *Religion:* Churches, Religious Welfare • *Science:* Science Muse-

ums • *Social Services:* Community Service Organizations, Family Services, Food/Clothing Distribution, People with Disabilities, Scouts, Shelters/Homelessness, Special Olympics, United Funds/United Ways, YMCA/YWCA/YMHA/YWHA, Youth Organizations

Grant Types: employee matching gifts and general support

Geographic Distribution: focus on NY

Operating Locations: NY (Utica)

CORP. OFFICERS
W. Craig Heston: *B* Philadelphia PA 1935 *CURR EMPL* chmn, ceo, dir: Utica Natl Corp Group

GIVING OFFICERS
Alfred E. Calligaris: dir

Edward W. Duffy: dir

John G. Haehl: dir

W. Craig Heston: pres, dir *CURR EMPL* chmn, ceo, dir: Utica Natl Corp Group (see above)

Herbert P. Ladds, Jr.: dir

David R. Newcomb: dir

Randall H. Pakula: dir

Robert L. Tarnow: dir *B* Rochester NY 1924 *ED* Oberlin Coll AB 1949 *CURR EMPL* chmn, dir: Goulds Pumps *CORP AFFIL* dir: Bausch & Lomb, Norstar Bancorp, Raymond Corp, Utica Mutual Ins

George P. Wardley III: secy

John R. Zapisek: treas, dir

APPLICATION INFORMATION
Initial Approach: Request application form. Deadlines are the first 15 days of each calendar quarter.

Restrictions on Giving: Limited to the greater Utica area.

GRANTS ANALYSIS
Total Grants: $149,545

Number of Grants: 22

Highest Grant: $63,000

Typical Range: $2,000 to $10,000

Disclosure Period: 1993

Note: Recent grants are derived from a 1993 Form 990.

RECENT GRANTS
Library
2,598	Mid-York Library System, Utica, NY — two computers	

General
63,000	United Way of Greater Utica, Utica, NY
10,000	St. Francis DeSales Church, Utica, NY
7,500	Utica Head Start, Utica, NY — construction of new center
5,900	YWCA, Utica, NY — paging system used in rape crisis
5,000	Association for Retarded Citizens, Utica, NY — production of video tape

van Ameringen Foundation

CONTACT
Henry P. van Ameringen
President and Chief Executive Officer
van Ameringen Foundation
509 Madison Ave.
New York, NY 10022
(212) 758-6221

FINANCIAL SUMMARY
Recent Giving: $3,015,552 (1993); $2,415,664 (1992); $1,682,487 (1991)

Assets: $43,027,741 (1993); $42,605,651 (1992); $42,100,266 (1991)

EIN: 13-6125699

CONTRIBUTIONS SUMMARY
Donor(s): The van Ameringen Foundation was established in 1950 by Arnold Louis van Ameringen , chairman of International Flavors and Fragrances. Mr. van Ameringen died in 1966, leaving his family to continue his lifetime work in the field of mental health.

Typical Recipients: • *Arts & Humanities:* Arts Associations & Councils, Arts Outreach, Libraries, Museums/Galleries, Public Broadcasting • *Civic & Public Affairs:* Economic Development, Housing, Municipalities/Towns, Urban & Community Affairs, Women's Affairs • *Education:* Colleges & Universities, Leadership Training, Science/Mathematics Education, Special Education • *Health:* AIDS/HIV, Cancer, Children's Health/Hospitals, Clinics/Medical Centers, Geriatric Health, Hospitals, Mental Health, Preventive Medicine/Wellness Organizations • *International:* International Affairs • *Religion:* Churches, Religious Welfare • *Social Services:* At-Risk Youth, Child Welfare, Community Service Organizations, Counseling, Day Care, Domestic Violence, Family Services, People with Disabilities, Senior Services, Shelters/Homelessness, Substance Abuse, Veterans, Youth Organizations

Grant Types: general support, multi-year/continuing support, project, research, and seed money

Geographic Distribution: Northeastern United States

GIVING OFFICERS
Lily van Ameringen Auchincloss: vp

Alexandra Herzan: dir

Kenneth Kind: dir

Patricia Kind: dir

Henry van Ameringen: pres, ceo, treas *B* 1931 *CORP AFFIL* dir: Intl Flavors & Fragrances *PHIL AFFIL* trust, don: Hedwig van Ameringen Foundation

Mrs. A. L. van Ameringen: hon chmn

Henry G. Walter, Jr.: dir *B* New York NY 1910 *ED* Columbia Univ BA 1931; Columbia Univ LLB 1934

APPLICATION INFORMATION
Initial Approach:

Applications may be sent to the foundation and addressed to the president. Although a concise statement of the aims and significance of a proposed project is sufficient, the foundation prefers to receive a full proposal.

Proposals must include a concise cover letter containing a description of the nature and purpose of the proposed project, major activities planned, amount requested, and a description of the organization itself. The proposal, not exceeding five pages, should include an outline of program design and anticipated accomplishments during the proposed grant period; statement indicating the qualifications of the organization to complete the proposed project; statement of how the program will be evaluated; and a budget marking all anticipated expenditures, income, and sources of income. Each application must additionally contain a copy of the IRS letter indicating tax-exempt status; recent financial statement (preferably audited); current operating budget; list of the directors and officers; and the most recent annual report. Relevant documents, publications, or articles may be included.

The board meets in March, June, and November. Applications should be submitted two months in advance of the scheduled meeting at which funding decisions are made.

Grant recipients are notified in writing shortly after the board decision. Grant recipients are expected to submit periodic progress reports and a final report indicating financial activity and evaluated results.

Restrictions on Giving: The foundation does not fund any programs for mental retardation, physical disabilities, or drug and alcohol problems. No grants are given to individuals, for capital or endowment funds, to areas outside the mental health field, for annual fund-raising drives, or in support of international organizations or activities. Grants are made only to charitable organizations that are tax-exempt under section 501(c)(3) of the IRS code.

OTHER THINGS TO KNOW
Short-term funding is favored over long-range commitments, although occasional multi-year grants are approved. Interviews may be arranged only after a proposal has been submitted.

PUBLICATIONS
Annual report and program and application guidelines

GRANTS ANALYSIS
Total Grants: $3,015,552

Number of Grants: 76

Highest Grant: $123,645

Average Grant: $39,678

Typical Range: $10,000 to $50,000

Disclosure Period: 1993

Note: Recent grants are derived from a 1993 Form 990.

RECENT GRANTS
Library
33,000	New York Public Library Astor, Lenox, and the Tilden	

Foundations, New York, NY
— general book fund

General

123,645 Life Force Women Fighting
AIDS, Brooklyn, NY —
training volunteers to lead
prevention education groups
at clinics and hospitals, in
street outreach, home
progress, prisons, and schools

120,000 Wediko Children's Services,
Boston, MA — grant for
fund-raising personnel,
curriculum development, and
engineering and architectural
planning in the expansion of
this year-round program for
emotionally disturbed
children

100,000 Alliance for the Mentally Ill
of Greene County/North
River Gallery Empowerment
Center, Catskill, NY — staff
salaries and purchasing a van
in the expansion of outreach
and services at this center
for the recovering mentally
ill, serving Greene and
Columbia counties

80,000 Fountain House, New York,
NY — grant for continued
support of the van
Ameringen Center for
Education and Research

80,000 International Association of
Psycho-Social Rehabilitation
Services/New York
Association of Psychiatric
Rehabilitation Services,
Albany, NY — grant for
startup costs of an Albany
office of NYAPRS, which
would protect and expand
the clubhouses for the
recovering mentally ill in
New York

Vernon Fund, Miles Hodsdon

CONTACT
Robert C. Thomson, Jr.
President
Miles Hodsdon Vernon Fund
49 Beekman Ave.
North Tarrytown, NY 10591
(914) 631-4534

FINANCIAL SUMMARY
Recent Giving: $284,050 (1993); $196,580 (1992); $208,060 (1991)

Assets: $5,964,089 (1993); $5,940,219 (1992); $5,636,639 (1991)

Gifts Received: $165,000 (1992)

Fiscal Note: In 1992, contributions were received from the proceeds from Trust U/W Miles Hodsdon Vernon F/B/O Frances S. Vernon.

EIN: 13-6076836

CONTRIBUTIONS SUMMARY
Donor(s): the late Miles Hodsdon Vernon, Martha Hodsdon Kinney, and Louise Hodsdon

Typical Recipients: • *Arts & Humanities:* History & Archaeology, Libraries, Music, Public Broadcasting • *Education:* Colleges & Universities, General, Medical Education, Science/Mathematics Education, Student Aid • *Health:* Cancer, Clinics/Medical Centers, Diabetes, Emergency/Ambulance Services, Health Organizations, Hospitals, Long-Term Care, Medical Research, Mental Health, Nursing Services, Single-Disease Health Associations, Trauma Treatment • *Religion:* Religious Welfare • *Social Services:* Camps, Child Welfare, Community Service Organizations, Day Care, Family Services, Food/Clothing Distribution, People with Disabilities, Senior Services, Shelters/Homelessness, United Funds/United Ways, YMCA/YWCA/YMHA/YWHA, Youth Organizations

Grant Types: research and scholarship

Geographic Distribution: national, with focus on NY

GIVING OFFICERS
Dennis M. Fitzgerald: vp, secy, dir

Eleanor C. Thomson: dir

Robert C. Thomson, Jr.: pres, treas, dir

Gertrude Whalen: asst treas, dir

APPLICATION INFORMATION
Initial Approach: Send cover letter and full proposal. There are no deadlines.

GRANTS ANALYSIS
Total Grants: $284,050

Number of Grants: 44

Highest Grant: $49,000

Typical Range: $1,000 to $30,000

Disclosure Period: 1993

Note: Recent grants are derived from a 1993 Form 990.

RECENT GRANTS

General

49,000 Camp Spears-Eljabar YMCA,
Dirgmans Ferry, PA — cabin
renovations and aid for
youth programs

30,000 Columbia University College
of Physicians and Surgeons,
New York, NY —
encephalitis research aid

30,000 Wolfeboro Area Children's
Center, Wolfeboro, NY —
aid for child care programs

25,000 Aquinas High School,
Lacrosse, WI — scholarship
aid and educational supplies

20,000 Tarrytown and Northern
Tarrytown YMCA,
Tarrytown, NY — aid for
equipment and programs

Vetlesen Foundation, G. Unger

CONTACT
George Rowe, Jr.
President
G. Unger Vetlesen Foundation
One Rockefeller Plaza
Ste. 301
New York, NY 10020
(212) 586-0700

FINANCIAL SUMMARY
Recent Giving: $2,213,873 (1993); $2,413,818 (1992); $2,155,349 (1991)

Assets: $46,231,895 (1993); $48,033,475 (1992); $53,175,742 (1991)

EIN: 13-1982695

CONTRIBUTIONS SUMMARY
Donor(s): The foundation was established in 1955 by the late George Unger Vetlesen .

Typical Recipients: • *Arts & Humanities:* Libraries • *Civic & Public Affairs:* General, Professional & Trade Associations, Public Policy, Zoos/Aquariums • *Education:* Colleges & Universities, Education Funds, International Studies, Medical Education, School Volunteerism, Science/Mathematics Education, Student Aid • *Environment:* General, Resource Conservation, Wildlife Protection • *International:* Foreign Arts Organizations, International Organizations, International Peace & Security Issues, International Relations • *Religion:* Churches • *Science:* Scientific Centers & Institutes, Scientific Labs, Scientific Organizations, Scientific Research • *Social Services:* Recreation & Athletics, Volunteer Services

Grant Types: general support

Geographic Distribution: no geographic restrictions, with emphasis on New York and Massachusetts

GIVING OFFICERS
Eugene Philip Grisanti: dir *B* Buffalo NY 1929 *ED* Coll Holy Cross AB 1951; Boston Univ LLB 1953; Harvard Univ LLM 1954 *CURR EMPL* chmn, pres, dir: Intl Flavors & Fragrances *NONPR AFFIL* dir: Cosmetic Toiletry Fragrance Assn, Fragrance Fdn *CLUB AFFIL* Larchmont YC, Univ, Winged Foot CC *PHIL AFFIL* dir: Ambrose Monell Foundation; pres: IFF Foundation Inc.

Joseph C. Hart: secy

George Rowe, Jr.: pres *B* Ossining NY 1922 *ED* Yale Univ AB 1943; Columbia Univ LLB 1948 *CURR EMPL* mem: Fulton Duncombe & Rowe *PHIL AFFIL* pres: Ambrose Monell Foundation

Henry G. Walter, Jr.: dir *B* New York NY 1910 *ED* Columbia Univ BA 1931; Columbia Univ LLB 1934

APPLICATION INFORMATION
Initial Approach:

Applicants should submit a simple letter outlining program or project to be funded, and amount of funding requested.

Applications will be accepted at any time.

GRANTS ANALYSIS
Total Grants: $2,213,873

Number of Grants: 23

Highest Grant: $500,000

Average Grant: $57,803*

Typical Range: $5,000 to $50,000 and $100,000 to $500,000

Disclosure Period: 1993

Note: Average grant figure does not include two grants totaling $1,000,000. Recent grants are derived from a 1993 Form 990.

RECENT GRANTS

Library

100,000	Pierpont Morgan Library, New York, NY

General

500,000	Lamont-Doherty Geological Observatory, New York, NY
500,000	Scripps Oceanographic Institute, La Jolla, CA — Global Exchange program
400,000	Woods Hole Oceanographic Institute, Woods Hole, MA
250,000	Marine Biological Laboratory, Woods Hole, MA
100,000	University of Pennsylvania School of Veterinary Medicine, Philadelphia, PA

Vogler Foundation, Laura B.

CONTACT
D. Donald D'Amato
President, Director
Laura B. Vogler Fdn.
PO 610508
Bayside, NY 11361

FINANCIAL SUMMARY
Recent Giving: $142,450 (fiscal 1993); $152,748 (fiscal 1992)

Assets: $4,270,323 (fiscal 1993); $4,003,960 (fiscal 1992)

EIN: 11-6022241

CONTRIBUTIONS SUMMARY
Typical Recipients: • *Arts & Humanities:* Arts Outreach, Libraries, Museums/Galleries • *Civic & Public Affairs:* Employment/Job Training, Legal Aid • *Education:* Afterschool/Enrichment Programs, Secondary Education (Public) • *Health:* AIDS/HIV, Emergency/Ambulance Services, Home-Care Services, Long-Term Care, Nursing Services • *Religion:* Ministries, Religious Welfare • *Science:* Science Museums • *Social Services:* Community Centers, Food/Clothing Distribution, People with Disabilities, Recreation & Athletics, Senior Services, Shelters/Homelessness, YMCA/YWCA/YMHA/YWHA, Youth Organizations

Grant Types: general support

Geographic Distribution: focus on NY

GIVING OFFICERS
D. Donald D'Amato: pres, dir

Lawrence L. D'Amato: treas, dir

Max Kupferberg: dir

Stanley C. Pearson: dir

Robert T. Waldbauer: dir

Karen M. Yost: dir

APPLICATION INFORMATION
Initial Approach: Send a brief letter of inquiry and a full proposal. Include a description of organization, purpose of funds sought, amount requested, and proof of tax-exempt status.

GRANTS ANALYSIS
Total Grants: $142,450

Number of Grants: 56

Highest Grant: $5,000

Typical Range: $1,000 to $5,000

Disclosure Period: fiscal year ending October 31, 1993

Note: Recent grants are derived from a fiscal 1993 Form 990.

RECENT GRANTS

Library

2,500	Brooklyn Public Library, Brooklyn, NY — stimulating the interest of youngsters in their local libraries

General

5,000	Flushing YMCA, Flushing, NY
5,000	For our Children and Us, Hicksville, NY — free legal clinics
3,500	All Hallows High School, Bronx, NY — offering inner-city students an education
3,500	Binding Together, New York, NY — job training and employment
3,500	Good Shepherd Services, New York, NY — help youngsters with substance and drug abuse problems

---

Wallace-Reader's Digest Fund, DeWitt

CONTACT
M. Christine DeVita
President
DeWitt Wallace-Reader's Digest Fund
2 Park Ave., 23rd Fl.
New York, NY 10016
(212) 251-9700

FINANCIAL SUMMARY
Recent Giving: $40,726,265 (1993); $73,102,761 (1992); $33,443,295 (1991)

Assets: $1,010,511,922 (1993); $1,133,982,206 (1992); $1,088,044,858 (1991)

Gifts Received: $375,430 (1993); $7,273 (1992); $7,158 (1991)

EIN: 13-6183757

CONTRIBUTIONS SUMMARY
Donor(s): The fund's donor, DeWitt Wallace (1889-1981) was born in St. Paul, MN. His father was president of Macalester College, where Mr. Wallace studied for two years before transfering to the University of California at Berkeley. In 1922, Mr. Wallace and his wife, Lila Acheson Wallace , founded Reader's Digest with $5,000 in borrowed money. Upon his retirement in 1972, Reader's Digest was the world's most widely read magazine. "He was particularly interested in young people and education, and that continues to be reflected in the Fund's current grant program."

Typical Recipients: • *Arts & Humanities:* Libraries • *Civic & Public Affairs:* Employment/Job Training, Hispanic Affairs, Nonprofit Management, Professional & Trade Associations • *Education:* Colleges & Universities, Community & Junior Colleges, Education Associations, Education Funds, Education Reform, Faculty Development, General, Minority Education, Preschool Education, Private Education (Precollege), Public Education (Precollege), Student Aid, Vocational & Technical Education • *Social Services:* At-Risk Youth, Child Welfare, Youth Organizations

Grant Types: general support, multi-year/continuing support, project, scholarship, and seed money

Geographic Distribution: no geographic restrictions and principally to national organizations

GIVING OFFICERS
William Gordon Bowen, PhD: dir *B* Cincinnati OH 1933 *ED* Denison Univ BA 1955; Princeton Univ PhD 1958 *CORP AFFIL* dir: Am Express Co, Merck & Co Inc, Readers Digest Assn Inc, Rockefeller Group Inc *NONPR AFFIL* mem: Am Econ Assn, Counc Foreign Rels, Indus Rels Res Assn, Phi Beta Kappa; mem bd regents: Smithsonian Inst; trust: Denison Univ *CLUB AFFIL* Univ *PHIL AFFIL* pres, trust: Andrew W. Mellon Foundation; trust: Merck Co. Foundation; dir: Lila Wallace-Reader's Digest Fund

Jessica Chao: vp *PHIL AFFIL* vp: Lila Wallace-Reader's Digest Fund

M. Christine DeVita: pres, dir *CORP AFFIL* dir: Readers Digest Assn Inc *PHIL AFFIL* pres, dir: Lila Wallace-Reader's Digest Fund

George V. Grune: chmn, dir *B* White Plains NY 1929 *ED* Duke Univ BA 1952; Univ FL 1955-1956 *CORP AFFIL* chmn, ceo, dir: Travel Pubs; chmn, dir: RD Pubs; dir: Avon Products, Chem Bank, CPC Intl, Fed Dept Stores *NONPR AFFIL* dir: Boys Club Am; mem bd overseers, bd mgrs: Counc Fin Aid Ed, Counc Foreign Rels, Inst France, Meml Sloan-Kettering Cancer Ctr, NY Pub Library Counc Conservators; mem conf bd, dir: Metro Opera Assn; mem policy comm: Bus Roundtable; natl leaders fellow: YMCA; trust: Duke Univ, Metro Mus Art, NY Zoological Soc, Outward Bound USA, Rollins Coll Roy E Crummer Grad Sch Bus; vchmn: Conf Bd *CLUB AFFIL* Blind Brook CC, CC North Carolina, Fairfield Beach, Jupiter Hills, Patterson GC, Ponte Vedra, Sawgrass,

Sky, Union League *PHIL AFFIL* chmn, dir: Lila Wallace-Reader's Digest Fund

Melvin Robert Laird: dir *B* Omaha NE 1922 *ED* Carleton Coll BA 1942 *CURR EMPL* sr counsellor natl & intl affs: Readers Digest Assn Inc *CORP AFFIL* bd dirs: Commun Satellite Corp, IDS Mutual Fund Group, Martin Marietta Corp, Metro Life Ins Co, Northwest Airlines, Phillips Petroleum Co, Science Applications Intl Corp *NONPR AFFIL* bd dir: Airlie Fdn; bd dirs: Boys Clubs Am, George Washington Univ, Laird Youth Leadership Fdn, World Rehab Fund; mem: Am Inst CPAs, Am Legion, Military Order Purple Heart, Veterans Foreign Wars; trust: John F Kennedy Ctr Performing Arts *PHIL AFFIL* dir: Lila Wallace-Reader's Digest Fund *CLUB AFFIL* Augusta Natl GC, Burning Tree, Lodge Mason

Robert D. Nagel: treas *PHIL AFFIL* treas: Lila Wallace-Reader's Digest Fund

Jane Bryant Quinn: program dir *B* Niagara Falls NY 1939 *ED* Middlebury Coll BA 1960 *CURR EMPL* contributing editor: Newsweek *CORP AFFIL* contributing fin columnist: Womens Day; syndicated fin columnist: Washington Post Writers Group *NONPR AFFIL* mem: Phi Beta Kappa

Laraine S. Rothenberg: dir *PHIL AFFIL* dir: Lila Wallace-Reader's Digest Fund

James P. Schadt: dir *B* Saginaw MI 1938 *ED* Northwestern Univ BA 1960 *CURR EMPL* pres, ceo, dir: Readers Digest Assn Inc *CORP AFFIL* ceo, dir: RD Publ Inc *NONPR AFFIL* chmn advocacy comm: Northwestern Univ Coll Arts & Sci; mem: Food Mktg Inst, Grocery Mfrs Am, Natl Soft Drink Assn; trust: Leukemia Soc Am *PHIL AFFIL* dir: Lila Wallace-Reader's Digest Fund; chmn, dir: Reader's Digest Foundation

Walter Vincent Shipley: mem, dir *B* Newark NJ 1935 *ED* NY Univ BS 1961; Harvard Univ Grad Sch Bus Admin 1976 *CURR EMPL* chmn, ceo: Chem Banking Corp *CORP AFFIL* chmn, dir: TX Commerce Bancshares Inc; dir: Champion Intl Corp, NYNEX Corp, Readers Digest Assn Inc *NONPR AFFIL* dir: Assn Reserve City Bankers, Lincoln Ctr Performing Arts, New York City Partnership, NY Chamber Commerce Indus, Un Way Tri-St; mem: Bus Counc, Bus Roundtable, Counc Foreign Rels, English Speaking Union, Japan Soc, Pilgrims US; pres, dir: Goodwill Indus Greater NY; trust: NY Univ *CLUB AFFIL* Augusta Natl GC, Baltusrol GC, Blind Brook CC, Links *PHIL AFFIL* mem, dir: Lila Wallace-Reader's Digest Fund

Cecil Jesse Silas: dir *B* Miami FL 1932 *ED* GA Tech Univ BS 1954 *CORP AFFIL* dir: First Natl Bank Tulsa, Readers Digest Assn Inc *NONPR AFFIL* chmn: Am Petroleum Inst; dir: Boys Club Am, Bus-Indus Political Action Comm, Ethics Resource Ctr, Jr Achievement, OK Fdn Excellence, OK Res Fdn, Regional Med Devel Fdn; mem: Am Counc Ed, Atlantic Counc US, Conf Bd, Counc Foreign Rels, US Chamber Commerce; trust: Bluestem Regional Med Devel Fdn, GA Tech Fdn *PHIL AFFIL* trust: Frank

Phillips Foundation; dir: Lila Wallace-Reader's Digest Fund

APPLICATION INFORMATION
Initial Approach:

Initial approach should be through a brief letter of inquiry of no more than two pages. The fund requests that video tapes not be sent.

The initial letter should describe the organization, proposed project and its goal, and include an estimated budget of the project and the portion of the budget requiring funding. If the request falls within fund interests, a formal proposal with detailed information will be requested.

There are no proposal deadlines.

The board meets four times a year to consider proposals. Proposals will be reviewed for the potential contribution to the field, the organization's ability to produce and sustain the proposed projects, plans for documenting both process and results, and the financial stability of the organization.

Restrictions on Giving: Areas currently outside giving guidelines include health and medical services or research; scholarly research; capital campaigns, including but not limited to, buildings and endowments; religious, fraternal, or veterans organizations; and private foundations or individuals.

OTHER THINGS TO KNOW
The fund is closely affiliated with the Lila Wallace Reader's Digest Fund.

The fund has become more national and less local in its grant making. Generally, the fund does not make grants under $100,000 or grants for long-term annual support of an organization. Multiyear funding will be considered relative to specific needs and the potential of a particular project. The fund will increasingly be initiating projects internally.

PUBLICATIONS
Annual report includes application guidelines

GRANTS ANALYSIS
Total Grants: $40,726,265

Number of Grants: 82

Highest Grant: $7,713,037

Average Grant: $496,662

Typical Range: $100,000 to $600,000

Disclosure Period: 1993

Note: Recent grants are derived from a 1993 grants list.

RECENT GRANTS

Library
2,838,000   American Library Association, Chicago, IL — over four years to serve as the central coordinator of the National Library Power Program

1,222,000   Chattanooga-Hamilton County Public Education Foundation, Chattanooga, TN — over three years to implement Library Power in 26 elementary and middle

schools that serve 11,400 students

1,222,000   Lincoln Public Schools Foundation, Lincoln, NE — over three years to implement Library Power in 36 elementary and middle schools that service 23,200 students

1,219,700   Dade Public Education Fund, Miami, FL — over three years to implement Library Power in 30 elementary and middle schools that serve 28,000 students

1,219,600   Public Education Coalition, Denver, CO — over three years to implement Library Power in 30 elementary and middle schools in four Denver-area districts, serving 19,000 students

General
7,713,037   Wellesley School-Age Child Care Project, Wellesley, MA — over four years and eight months to establish Wellesley's School-Aged Child Care Project (WSACP) as project manager for the new Community School-Age Child Care Initiative

3,296,464   Kansas State University, Manhattan, KS — over three years to implement Counseling for High Skills: VoTech Career Options

3,000,000   Public/Private Ventures, Philadelphia, PA — over five years to launch WORK-PLUS

2,685,165   Greater New York Hospital Foundation, New York, NY — over five years to support the implementation of Walks of Life, an employment preparation program for youth in two New York City public high schools and some of their "feeder" junior high and elementary schools

2,653,983   Bay State Skills Corporation, Boston, MA — over five years to support the Communities and Schools for Career Success initiative

Wallace-Reader's Digest Fund, Lila

CONTACT
M. Christine DeVita
President
Lila Wallace-Reader's Digest Fund
2 Park Ave., 23rd Fl.
New York, NY 10016
(212) 251-9700

FINANCIAL SUMMARY
Recent Giving: $33,405,891 (1993); $40,048,145 (1992); $32,675,042 (1991)

Assets: $773,370,314 (1994); $855,569,785 (1992); $821,550,514 (1991)

Gifts Received: $5,733 (1993); $44,805 (1992); $55,658 (1991)

EIN: 13-6086859

CONTRIBUTIONS SUMMARY

Donor(s): The late Lila Wallace and her late husband, DeWitt Wallace, founded Reader's Digest magazine in 1922 in New York City. The company has grown to be a leading global publisher and direct-mail marketer of magazines, books, music, and video products. Lila Wallace was a social worker who established innovative programs in conjunction with the YMCA and the U.S. Department of Labor. She also was interested in the arts and supported various museums, performing arts organizations, and programs to beautify the environment.

She and her husband established four charitable foundations to support their interests. In 1987, the DeWitt Wallace Fund, L.A.W. Fund, Lakeview Fund, and High Winds Fund were merged into two funds known as the DeWitt Wallace-Reader's Digest Fund and the Lila Wallace-Reader's Digest Fund.

Typical Recipients: • *Arts & Humanities:* Arts Appreciation, Arts Associations & Councils, Arts Centers, Arts Festivals, Arts Funds, Arts Institutes, Arts Outreach, Community Arts, Dance, Ethnic & Folk Arts, History & Archaeology, Libraries, Literary Arts, Museums/Galleries, Music, Opera, Performing Arts, Theater, Visual Arts • *Civic & Public Affairs:* Botanical Gardens/Parks, Professional & Trade Associations, Zoos/Aquariums • *Education:* Arts/Humanities Education, Literacy

Grant Types: project

Geographic Distribution: no geographic restrictions and principally to national organizations

GIVING OFFICERS

William Gordon Bowen, PhD: dir *B* Cincinnati OH 1933 *ED* Denison Univ BA 1955; Princeton Univ PhD 1958 *CORP AFFIL* dir: Am Express Co, Merck & Co Inc, Readers Digest Assn Inc, Rockefeller Group Inc *NONPR AFFIL* mem: Am Econ Assn, Counc Foreign Rels, Indus Rels Res Assn, Phi Beta Kappa; mem bd regents: Smithsonian Inst; trust: Denison Univ *CLUB AFFIL* Univ *PHIL AFFIL* pres, trust: Andrew W. Mellon Foundation; trust: Merck Co. Foundation; dir: DeWitt Wallace-Reader's Digest Fund

Jessica Chao: vp *PHIL AFFIL* vp: DeWitt Wallace-Reader's Digest Fund

M. Christine DeVita: pres, dir *CORP AFFIL* dir: Readers Digest Assn Inc *PHIL AFFIL* pres, dir: DeWitt Wallace-Reader's Digest Fund

George V. Grune: chmn, dir *B* White Plains NY 1929 *ED* Duke Univ BA 1952; Univ FL 1955-1956 *CORP AFFIL* chmn, ceo, dir: Travel Pubs; chmn, dir: RD Pubs; dir: Avon Products, Chem Bank, CPC Intl, Fed Dept Stores *NONPR AFFIL* dir: Boys Club Am; mem bd overseers, bd mgrs: Counc Fin Aid Ed, Counc Foreign Rels, Inst France, Meml Sloan-Kettering Cancer Ctr, NY Pub Library

Counc Conservators; mem conf bd, dir: Metro Opera Assn; mem policy comm: Bus Roundtable; natl leaders fellow: YMCA; trust: Duke Univ, Metro Mus Art, NY Zoological Soc, Outward Bound USA, Rollins Coll Roy E Crummer Grad Sch Bus; vchmn: Conf Bd *CLUB AFFIL* Blind Brook CC, CC North Carolina, Fairfield Beach, Jupiter Hills, Patterson GC, Ponte Vedra, Sawgrass, Sky, Union League *PHIL AFFIL* chmn, dir: DeWitt Wallace-Reader's Digest Fund

Melvin Robert Laird: dir *B* Omaha NE 1922 *ED* Carleton Coll BA 1942 *CURR EMPL* sr counsellor natl & intl affs: Readers Digest Assn Inc *CORP AFFIL* bd dirs: Commun Satellite Corp, IDS Mutual Fund Group, Martin Marietta Corp, Metro Life Ins Co, Northwest Airlines, Phillips Petroleum Co, Science Applications Intl Corp *NONPR AFFIL* bd dir: Airlie Fdn; bd dirs: Boys Clubs Am, George Washington Univ, Laird Youth Leadership Fdn, World Rehab Fund; mem: Am Inst CPAs, Am Legion, Military Order Purple Heart, Veterans Foreign Wars; trust: John F Kennedy Ctr Performing Arts *PHIL AFFIL* dir: DeWitt Wallace-Reader's Digest Fund *CLUB AFFIL* Augusta Natl GC, Burning Tree, Lodge Mason

Robert D. Nagel: treas *PHIL AFFIL* treas: DeWitt Wallace-Reader's Digest Fund

Laraine S. Rothenberg: dir *PHIL AFFIL* dir: DeWitt Wallace-Reader's Digest Fund

James P. Schadt: dir *B* Saginaw MI 1938 *ED* Northwestern Univ BA 1960 *CURR EMPL* pres, ceo, dir: Readers Digest Assn Inc *CORP AFFIL* ceo, dir: RD Publ Inc *NONPR AFFIL* chmn advocacy comm: Northwestern Univ Coll Arts & Sci; mem: Food Mktg Inst, Grocery Mfrs Am, Natl Soft Drink Assn; trust: Leukemia Soc Am *PHIL AFFIL* dir: DeWitt Wallace-Reader's Digest Fund; chmn, dir: Reader's Digest Foundation

Walter Vincent Shipley: mem, dir *B* Newark NJ 1935 *ED* NY Univ BS 1961; Harvard Univ Grad Sch Bus Admin 1976 *CURR EMPL* chmn, ceo: Chem Banking Corp *CORP AFFIL* chmn, ceo, dir: TX Commerce Bancshares Inc; dir: Champion Intl Corp, NYNEX Corp, Readers Digest Assn Inc *NONPR AFFIL* dir: Assn Reserve City Bankers, Lincoln Ctr Performing Arts, New York City Partnership, NY Chamber Commerce Indus, Un Way Tri-St; mem: Bus Counc, Bus Roundtable, Counc Foreign Rels, English Speaking Union, Japan Soc, Pilgrims US; pres, dir: Goodwill Indus Greater NY; trust: NY Univ *CLUB AFFIL* Augusta Natl GC, Baltusrol GC, Blind Brook CC, Links *PHIL AFFIL* mem, dir: DeWitt Wallace-Reader's Digest Fund

Holly Sidford: program dir

Cecil Jesse Silas: dir *B* Miami FL 1932 *ED* GA Tech Univ BS 1954 *CORP AFFIL* dir: First Natl Bank Tulsa, Readers Digest Assn Inc *NONPR AFFIL* chmn: Am Petroleum Inst; dir: Boys Club Am, Bus-Indus Political Action Comm, Ethics Resource Ctr, Jr Achievement, OK Fdn Excellence, OK Res Fdn, Regional Med Devel Fdn; mem: Am Counc Ed, Atlantic Counc US, Conf Bd,

Counc Foreign Rels, US Chamber Commerce; trust: Bluestem Regional Med Devel Fdn, GA Tech Fdn *PHIL AFFIL* trust: Frank Phillips Foundation; dir: DeWitt Wallace-Reader's Digest Fund

APPLICATION INFORMATION
Initial Approach:

Initial approach should be a letter of no more than three pages.

The letter should describe the organization, proposed project and its goal, and include an estimated total budget for the project, and the relationship between the goals of the project and the mission of the Lila Wallace-Reader's Digest Fund. If the request falls within fund interests, a formal proposal with detailed information will be requested.

There are no proposal deadlines.

The board meets three times a year to consider proposals. Proposals will be reviewed for their potential contribution to the field, the organization's ability to produce the proposed project, the financial stability of the organization, and the potential furthering of the fund's goals.

Restrictions on Giving: Grants generally are not given to individuals, religious organizations, fraternal or veterans' groups, or private foundations.

OTHER THINGS TO KNOW
The fund generally will not make grants under $50,000, or for long-term annual support of an organization. The fund is closely affiliated with the DeWitt Wallace-Reader's Digest Fund.

PUBLICATIONS
Annual report includes application guidelines

GRANTS ANALYSIS
Total Grants: $33,405,891

Number of Grants: 126

Highest Grant: $4,000,000

Average Grant: $265,126

Typical Range: $100,000 to $500,000

Disclosure Period: 1993

Note: Recent grants are derived from a 1994 partial grants list.

RECENT GRANTS

General

800,000 Austin Parks Foundation (Texas) and Trust for Public Land (San Francisco) — over four years to develop parks in east and southeast Austin, TX, and encourage community involvement in the development

590,307 Arts International, New York, NY — over four years to send up to 24 visual artists from the US to work and study at Claude Monet's historic gardens in Giverny, France

520,500 San Francisco Foundation — over four years for park and community garden projects in Oakland's Fruitvale and

463,300	Flatlands neighborhoods and to develop portions of a mile-long corridor in West Oakland, CA, into park space Trust for Public Land, San Francisco, CA — over four years to develop the Gwynns Falls Trail, a 14-mile greenway through West Baltimore
460,300	Trust for Public Land, San Francisco, CA — over four years to develop several playground and neighborhood parks and a neighborhood greenway

Warner Fund, Albert and Bessie

CONTACT
Lewis Steel
Trustee
Albert and Bessie Warner Foundation
c/o Funding Exchange
666 Broadway Ste. 300
New York, NY 10012
(516) 725-0145

FINANCIAL SUMMARY
Recent Giving: $215,725 (1993); $209,900 (1992); $186,501 (1991)

Assets: $4,610,003 (1993); $4,573,740 (1992); $4,554,890 (1991)

EIN: 13-6095213

CONTRIBUTIONS SUMMARY
Typical Recipients: • *Arts & Humanities:* Arts Funds, Dance, Libraries, Museums/Galleries, Public Broadcasting, Theater • *Civic & Public Affairs:* Civil Rights, General, Nonprofit Management, Philanthropic Organizations, Public Policy, Urban & Community Affairs • *Education:* Colleges & Universities, Legal Education • *Environment:* Air/Water Quality, General, Resource Conservation • *Health:* Hospices, Hospitals, Mental Health • *Religion:* Religious Organizations • *Social Services:* Child Welfare, Community Service Organizations, Delinquency & Criminal Rehabilitation, Youth Organizations

Grant Types: general support

Geographic Distribution: focus on New York, NY

GIVING OFFICERS
Arthur J. Steel: trust

Kitty Steel: trust

Lewis M. Steel: trust

Ruth M. Steel: trust

APPLICATION INFORMATION
Initial Approach: Send brief letter of inquiry describing program or project. There are no deadlines.

GRANTS ANALYSIS
Total Grants: $215,725

Number of Grants: 25

Highest Grant: $75,000

Typical Range: $500 to $72,500

Disclosure Period: 1993

Note: Recent grants are derived from a 1993 Form 990.

RECENT GRANTS
Library
1,000	Rogers Memorial Library, Southampton, NY

General
75,000	Funding Exchange, New York, NY
72,500	Funding Exchange, New York, NY
15,000	Institute for Policy Studies, Washington, DC
10,000	Institute for Policy Studies, Washington, DC
10,000	Institute for Public Affairs, Washington, DC

Warren and Beatrice W. Blanding Foundation, Riley J. and Lillian N.

CONTACT
Henry L. Hulbert
Manager
Riley J. and Lillian N. Warren and Beatrice W. Blanding Fdn.
Six Ford Ave.
Oneonta, NY 13820
(607) 432-6720

FINANCIAL SUMMARY
Recent Giving: $174,000 (1993); $174,550 (1992); $189,000 (1991)

Assets: $6,040,568 (1993); $5,614,797 (1992); $5,612,847 (1991)

EIN: 23-7203341

CONTRIBUTIONS SUMMARY
Donor(s): Beatrice W. Blanding

Typical Recipients: • *Arts & Humanities:* Libraries, Music • *Civic & Public Affairs:* Employment/Job Training, General • *Education:* Colleges & Universities, Literacy, Private Education (Precollege), Religious Education • *Health:* Hospices, Hospitals • *Religion:* Churches, Religious Organizations • *Social Services:* Community Service Organizations, People with Disabilities, Recreation & Athletics, United Funds/United Ways

Grant Types: general support

Geographic Distribution: focus on Oneonta, NY

GIVING OFFICERS
Robert A. Harlem: trust

Henry L. Hulbert: mgr, trust *PHIL AFFIL* trust: Nila B. Hulbert Foundation

APPLICATION INFORMATION
Initial Approach: Send brief letter of inquiry describing program or project. The deadline is November 1.

GRANTS ANALYSIS
Total Grants: $174,000

Number of Grants: 20

Highest Grant: $75,000

Typical Range: $1,000 to $15,000

Disclosure Period: 1993

Note: Recent grants are derived from a 1993 Form 990.

RECENT GRANTS
Library
10,000	Huntington Memorial Library, Oneonta, NY

General
75,000	St. Marys School, Oneonta, NY
15,000	A.O. Fox Memorial Hospital Chaplaincy Foundation, Oneonta, NY
15,000	Hartwick College, Oneonta, NY
10,000	National Soccer Hall of Fame, Oneonta, NY
10,000	Siena College, Loudonville, NY

Weezie Foundation

CONTACT
Robert Schwecherl
Secretary, Treasurer, and Trustee
Weezie Foundation
c/o Morgan Guaranty Trust Co. of New York
9 W 57th St.
New York, NY 10019
(212) 826-7607
Note: The alternate contact is Charles Davidson. The number listed above is for Mr. Davidson at Morgan Guaranty Trust Co. of New York.

FINANCIAL SUMMARY
Recent Giving: $1,000,000 (1995 est.); $1,000,000 (1994 approx.); $836,700 (1993)

Assets: $17,000,000 (1995 est.); $17,000,000 (1994 approx.); $17,350,272 (1993)

EIN: 13-6090903

CONTRIBUTIONS SUMMARY
Donor(s): The foundation was established in 1961 by the late Adelaide T. Corbett .

Typical Recipients: • *Arts & Humanities:* Libraries • *Civic & Public Affairs:* General, Urban & Community Affairs • *Education:* Agricultural Education, Arts/Humanities Education, Colleges & Universities, Community & Junior Colleges, Education Associations, General, Medical Education, Private Education (Precollege), Religious Education, Science/Mathematics Education, Student Aid • *Environment:* General • *Health:* Clinics/Medical Centers, Hospitals, Mental Health • *Religion:* Churches, Ministries, Religious Organizations • *Science:* Scientific Labs • *Social Services:* Community Service Organizations, Counseling, Family Services, Homes, People with Disabilities, Recreation

& Athletics, Substance Abuse, Youth Organizations

Grant Types: general support

Geographic Distribution: focus on northeastern United States

GIVING OFFICERS

D. Nelson Adams, Esq.: mem adv comm *CURR EMPL* atty: Davis Polk & Wardwell *PHIL AFFIL* trust: Bugher Foundation

Adelrick Benziger, Jr.: mem adv comm

Thomas W. Carroll: adv

James F. Dolan: secy, treas, dir, adv *B* Orange NJ 1930 *ED* Seton Hall Univ BS 1950; Columbia Univ LLB 1953 *CURR EMPL* ptnr: Davis Polk & Wardwell *PHIL AFFIL* secy, dir: Coral Reef Foundation

Mrs. William H. Hays III: mem adv comm

H. S. Graham McBride: adv

Robert Schwecherl: secy, treas, trust

Charles H. Theriot: mem adv comm

APPLICATION INFORMATION
Initial Approach:

The foundation requests applications be made in writing.

OTHER THINGS TO KNOW
The foundation lists Morgan Guaranty Trust Company of New York as a corporate trustee.

GRANTS ANALYSIS
Total Grants: $836,700

Number of Grants: 27

Highest Grant: $100,000

Average Grant: $30,989

Typical Range: $10,000 to $50,000

Disclosure Period: 1993

Note: Recent grants are derived from a 1993 Form 990.

RECENT GRANTS

Library

100,000	Nantucket Atheneum Building, Nantucket, MA

General

100,000	St. Marks School, Southborough, MA
60,000	Miss Porter's School, Farmington, CT
50,000	Fay School, Southborough, MA
50,000	Metrowest Medical Center, Nantucket, MA
50,000	Nantucket Boys and Girls Club, Nantucket, MA

Weil, Gotshal and Manges Foundation

CONTACT
Jesse D. Wolff
Treasurer
Weil, Gotshal and Manges Fdn.
767 Fifth Ave.
New York, NY 10153
(212) 310-8000

FINANCIAL SUMMARY
Recent Giving: $1,366,760 (1993); $920,750 (1990); $1,067,655 (1988)

Assets: $3,738,172 (1993); $3,358,323 (1990); $2,824,950 (1989)

Gifts Received: $1,500,000 (1992); $1,300,000 (1990); $1,500,000 (1988)

Fiscal Note: In 1992, contributions were received from Weil, Gotshal & Manges.

EIN: 13-3158325

CONTRIBUTIONS SUMMARY
Donor(s): Robert Todd Lang, Ira M. Millstein, and Harvey R. Miller

Typical Recipients: • *Arts & Humanities:* Arts Centers, Dance, History & Archaeology, Libraries, Museums/Galleries, Performing Arts, Public Broadcasting • *Civic & Public Affairs:* African American Affairs, Botanical Gardens/Parks, Business/Free Enterprise, Economic Policy, Law & Justice, Legal Aid, Municipalities/Towns, Public Policy, Women's Affairs • *Education:* Arts/Humanities Education, Colleges & Universities, Legal Education • *Environment:* General • *Health:* AIDS/HIV, Emergency/Ambulance Services, Medical Research, Prenatal Health Issues, Single-Disease Health Associations, Transplant Networks/Donor Banks • *International:* Human Rights, International Affairs, International Relations • *Religion:* Jewish Causes, Religious Organizations • *Social Services:* At-Risk Youth, Camps, Community Service Organizations, Emergency Relief, Family Planning, Family Services, Shelters/Homelessness, United Funds/United Ways, Youth Organizations

Grant Types: general support

Geographic Distribution: focus on NY

GIVING OFFICERS
Robert Todd Lang: chmn, dir *B* New York NY 1924 *ED* Yale Univ 1945 *CURR EMPL* partner: Weil Gotschal & Manges *NONPR AFFIL* mem: Am Bar Assn

Harvey R. Miller: secy, dir

Ira M. Millstein: pres, dir *B* New York NY 1926 *ED* Columbia Univ BS 1947; Columbia Univ LLB 1949 *CORP AFFIL* ptnr: Weil Gotschal & Manges *NONPR AFFIL* adjunct prof, dir: Columbia Univ Grad Sch Bus; chmn bd advs: Columbia Univ Ctr Law Econ Studies; mem: Am Bar Assn, NY Bar Assn; prof: Columbia Univ Ctr Law & Econ Studies; vchmn bd overseers: Albert Einstein Coll Medicine

Jesse D. Wolff: treas, dir *B* Minneapolis MN 1913 *ED* Dartmouth Coll BA 1935; Harvard Univ JD 1938 *CURR EMPL* couns: Weil Gotshal & Manges *CORP AFFIL* mem adv bd: Sothebys Holdings *NONPR AFFIL* mem: Am Bar Assn, Judge Adv Gen Assn; trust Greater NY chapter: Am Red Cross

APPLICATION INFORMATION
Initial Approach: Send brief letter of inquiry describing program or project. The deadline is November 1.

GRANTS ANALYSIS
Total Grants:

Number of Grants: 98

Highest Grant: $550,000

Typical Range: $500 to $5,000

Disclosure Period: 1992

Note: Recent grants are derived from a 1992 Form 990.

RECENT GRANTS

General

550,000	United Jewish Appeal Federation of Jewish Philanthropies, New York, NY
225,000	Legal Aid Society, New York, NY
140,000	United Way, New York, NY
20,000	New York Legal Assistance, New York, NY
15,000	Central Park Conservancy, New York, NY

Weinstein Foundation, J.

CONTACT
Max L. Shulman
President
J. Weinstein Fdn.
Rockridge Farm, Rte. 52
Carmel, NY 10512
(914) 225-7647

FINANCIAL SUMMARY
Recent Giving: $258,190 (1993); $203,835 (1992); $147,908 (1991)

Assets: $5,205,868 (1993); $6,308,771 (1992); $4,274,720 (1991)

Gifts Received: $50,000 (1993); $50,000 (1992); $50,000 (1991)

EIN: 11-6003595

CONTRIBUTIONS SUMMARY
Donor(s): the late Joe Weinstein and J. W. Mays

Typical Recipients: • *Arts & Humanities:* Libraries, Museums/Galleries • *Civic & Public Affairs:* General, Safety, Urban & Community Affairs • *Education:* Colleges & Universities, Medical Education, Private Education (Precollege), Special Education • *Health:* Cancer, Eyes/Blindness, Health Organizations, Hospitals, Hospitals (University Affiliated), Research/Studies Institutes, Single-Disease Health Associations • *International:* Foreign Arts Organizations, Foreign Educational Institutions, International Peace & Security Issues, Missionary/Religious Activities • *Religion:* Jewish Causes, Religious Organizations, Synagogues/Temples • *Science:* Scientific Centers & Institutes • *Social Services:* Animal Protection, At-Risk Youth, Camps, Child Welfare, Community Service Organizations, People with Disabilities, Recreation & Athletics, Senior Services, Youth Organizations

Grant Types: endowment, general support, and multiyear/continuing support

Geographic Distribution: focus on NY

GIVING OFFICERS

Lloyd J. Shulman: vp, dir *CURR EMPL* pres, dir: JW Mays

Max L. Shulman: pres, dir *B* New York NY 1908 *ED* City Univ NY 1924; Natl Univ 1930 *CURR EMPL* chmn, dir: JW Mays *CORP AFFIL* chmn, pres: Weinstein Enterprises *NONPR AFFIL* pres: Weinstein Fdn *CLUB AFFIL* mem: Harmonie Rotary

Sylvia W. Shulman: vp, dir

APPLICATION INFORMATION

Initial Approach: The foundation has no formal grant application procedure or application form. There are no deadlines.

GRANTS ANALYSIS

Total Grants: $258,190

Number of Grants: 42

Highest Grant: $87,000

Typical Range: $200 to $50,000

Disclosure Period: 1993

Note: Recent grants are derived from a 1993 Form 990.

RECENT GRANTS

Library
2,000	Kent Public Library, Carmel, NY

General
87,000	American Committee for Weizmann Institute of Science, New York, NY
50,000	Brookdale Center on Aging at Hunter College, Brookdale, NY
31,500	American Friends of Israel Museum, New York, NY
25,000	American Committee for Shenkar College in Israel, New York, NY
15,300	Women's League for Israel, New York, NY

Wendt Foundation, Margaret L.

CONTACT
Robert J. Kresse
Secretary and Trustee
Margaret L. Wendt Foundation
40 Fountain Plz., Ste. 277
Buffalo, NY 14202-2220
(716) 855-2146

FINANCIAL SUMMARY
Recent Giving: $3,563,336 (fiscal 1994); $2,067,422 (fiscal 1993); $1,616,294 (fiscal 1992)

Assets: $58,978,257 (fiscal 1994); $59,060,185 (fiscal 1993); $57,166,160 (fiscal 1992)

EIN: 16-6030037

CONTRIBUTIONS SUMMARY
Donor(s): The Margaret L. Wendt Foundation was established in 1955, with funds donated by the late Margaret L. Wendt . The assets of the foundation more than doubled in the period between 1975 and 1980 because of the final distribution of Miss Wendt's bequest.

Typical Recipients: • *Arts & Humanities:* Arts Associations & Councils, Arts Centers, Arts Outreach, Ballet, Dance, Historic Preservation, Libraries, Literary Arts, Museums/Galleries, Music, Opera, Public Broadcasting, Theater • *Civic & Public Affairs:* Economic Development, Employment/Job Training, Housing, Urban & Community Affairs, Women's Affairs, Zoos/Aquariums • *Education:* Arts/Humanities Education, Colleges & Universities, Education Reform, Faculty Development, Private Education (Precollege), Public Education (Precollege), Science/Mathematics Education, Special Education, Student Aid • *Environment:* Air/Water Quality, General, Wildlife Protection • *Health:* AIDS/HIV, Alzheimers Disease, Children's Health/Hospitals, Emergency/Ambulance Services, Health Funds, Health Organizations, Hospices, Hospitals, Medical Research, Mental Health, Nursing Services, Single-Disease Health Associations • *International:* Foreign Arts Organizations, International Organizations • *Religion:* Churches, Ministries, Religious Organizations, Religious Welfare, Seminaries • *Science:* Science Museums, Scientific Centers & Institutes • *Social Services:* Animal Protection, Child Welfare, Community Centers, Community Service Organizations, Counseling, Day Care, Family Services, Homes, People with Disabilities, Substance Abuse, United Funds/United Ways, YMCA/YWCA/YMHA/YWHA, Youth Organizations

Grant Types: capital, challenge, general support, operating expenses, project, research, and seed money

Geographic Distribution: primarily Buffalo, and Western New York

GIVING OFFICERS
Robert J. Kresse: secy, trust *CURR EMPL* ptnr: Hiscock & Barclay

Ralph William Loew: trust *B* Columbus OH 1907 *ED* Capital Univ AB 1928; Hamma Divinity Sch MDiv 1931; Wittenberg Univ DD 1947 *NONPR AFFIL* trust: Chautauqua Inst

Thomas D. Lunt: trust

APPLICATION INFORMATION
Initial Approach:

Applicants should send four copies of a letter of request.

Letters should include a description of the applicant organization, need or problem to be addressed, outline of the proposed project including total budget, specific amount requested, list of the board of directors, audited financial statements for the last three years, and the most recent copy of the organization's IRS determination letter of tax-exempt status.

Submit applications one month prior to the foundation's quarterly meetings.

Restrictions on Giving: The foundation does not make grants to individuals.

GRANTS ANALYSIS
Total Grants: $3,563,336

Number of Grants: 107

Highest Grant: $300,000

Average Grant: $33,302

Typical Range: $4,000 to $50,000

Disclosure Period: fiscal year ending January 31, 1994

Note: Recent grants are derived from a fiscal 1994 Form 990.

RECENT GRANTS

Library
50,000	Library Foundation of Buffalo and Erie County, Buffalo, NY — completion of the Mark Twain Room in the main library and Lafayette Square
30,000	St. Bonaventure University, St. Bonaventure, NY — to increase library holdings in the humanities

General
300,000	Children's Hospital of Buffalo Foundation, Buffalo, NY — pediatric intensive care and trauma center project
250,000	Hopevale, Hamburg, NY — toward improvements to the facility
200,000	Hospice Buffalo, Buffalo, NY — construction of a centralized hospice health care campus
105,644	University of Buffalo, Buffalo, NY — construction of laboratory and equipment for neurosurgical endovascular research
100,000	Buffalo Museum of Science, Buffalo, NY — establishment of Science Education Center

Western New York Foundation

CONTACT
Welles V. Moot, Jr.
President
Western New York Fdn.
1402 Main Seneca Bldg.
Buffalo, NY 14203
(716) 847-6440

FINANCIAL SUMMARY
Recent Giving: $213,694 (fiscal 1993); $238,735 (fiscal 1992); $212,000 (fiscal 1991)

Assets: $5,535,618 (fiscal 1993); $5,535,999 (fiscal 1992); $5,356,293 (fiscal 1991)

EIN: 16-0845962

CONTRIBUTIONS SUMMARY
Donor(s): the late Welles V. Moot

Typical Recipients: • *Arts & Humanities:* Arts Associations & Councils, Community Arts, General, Historic Preservation, Libraries, Music, Performing Arts, Public Broadcasting, Theater • *Civic & Public Affairs:* Botanical Gardens/Parks, Business/Free Enterprise, Municipalities/Towns, Urban & Community Affairs, Zoos/Aquariums • *Education:* Colleges & Universities, Elementary Education (Private), Private Education (Precollege), Public Education (Precollege), Student Aid • *Health:* Children's Health/Hospitals, Health Organizations, Hospices, Hospitals • *International:* International Affairs, International Organizations • *Social Services:* Child Welfare, Community Centers, Community Service Organizations, Day Care, Family Services, People with Disabilities, Substance Abuse, United Funds/United Ways, Volunteer Services, Youth Organizations

Grant Types: capital, conference/seminar, emergency, endowment, loan, project, and seed money

Geographic Distribution: limited to the 8th Judicial District of NY (Erie, Niagara, Genesee, Wyoming, Allegany, Cattaraugus, and Chautauqua counties)

GIVING OFFICERS
Cecily M. Johnson: vp, trust
Trudy A. Mollenberg: trust
Andrew Moot: trust
John R. Moot: secy, trust
Richard Moot: treas, trust
Welles V. Moot, Jr.: pres, trust
Robert S. Scheu: vp, trust *PHIL AFFIL* dir: James H. Cummings Foundation
John N. Walsh III: trust

APPLICATION INFORMATION
Initial Approach: Send brief letter of inquiry describing program or project. Include a description of organization, amount requested, purpose of funds sought, recently audited financial statement, and proof of tax-exempt status. There are no deadlines.

Restrictions on Giving: Does not support individuals.

PUBLICATIONS
Annual Report

GRANTS ANALYSIS
Total Grants: $213,694
Number of Grants: 22
Highest Grant: $40,000
Typical Range: $550 to $50,000
Disclosure Period: fiscal year ending July 31, 1993

Note: Recent grants are derived from a fiscal 1993 Form 990.

RECENT GRANTS
Library
10,000   Pavilion Public Library, Pavilion, NY — for renovation of library

74   Buffalo and Erie County Public Library, Buffalo, NY — for microfiche cards

General
30,000   Nichols School, Buffalo, NY — endowment for summer internship program
25,000   World University Games 1993, Buffalo, NY — to assist in administering and marketing
20,000   Blind Association of Western New York, Buffalo, NY — to upgrade present computer system
15,000   Federation of Neighborhood Centers, Buffalo, NY — for centennial
12,500   Hospice Foundation, Buffalo, NY — for extended grant

WestLB New York Branch

Headquarters: New York, NY
SIC Major Group: Depository Institutions

CONTACT
Gerard Barton
Vice President
WestLB New York Branch
1211 Ave. of the Americas
New York, NY 10036
(212) 852-6000

FINANCIAL SUMMARY
Fiscal Note: Annual Giving Range: $50,000 annually

CONTRIBUTIONS SUMMARY
Program is unstructured and fluid. All requests are forwarded to the headquarters office in Dusseldorf for approval.

Typical Recipients: • *Arts & Humanities:* Libraries, Museums/Galleries, Music • *Civic & Public Affairs:* Professional & Trade Associations • *Education:* Private Education (Precollege) • *Social Services:* United Funds/United Ways

Grant Types: general support

Geographic Distribution: only in the New York metropolitan area

Operating Locations: NY

CORP. OFFICERS
John Paul Garber: *CURR EMPL* joint chmn N Am: WestLB NY Branch

GIVING OFFICERS
Gerard Barton: *CURR EMPL* vp: WestLB NY Branch

APPLICATION INFORMATION
Initial Approach: Send letter, preferably in November, including a description of the organization, amount requested, and purpose of funds sought. All requests are forwarded to Dusseldorf for approval at the end of the year.

Westvaco Corporation / Westvaco Foundation Trust

Revenue: $2.61 billion
Employees: 14,440
Headquarters: New York, NY
SIC Major Group: Paper Mills, Pulp Mills, Paperboard Mills, and Corrugated & Solid Fiber Boxes

CONTACT
Roger Holmes
Secretary, Contributions Committee
Westvaco Corporation
299 Park Ave.
New York, NY 10171
(212) 318-5288

FINANCIAL SUMMARY
Recent Giving: $1,300,000 (fiscal 1995 est.); $1,300,000 (fiscal 1994 approx.); $1,299,473 (fiscal 1993)

Assets: $6,800,000 (fiscal 1995 est.); $6,800,000 (fiscal 1994 approx.); $6,232,740 (fiscal 1993)

Gifts Received: $1,100,000 (fiscal 1993)

Fiscal Note: Company gives primarily through the foundation. Local managers administer small discretionary budgets, cumulatively disbursing about $350,000 annually. This support is not included in above figures. All grants in fiscal 1993 were matching gifts. Above figures exclude nonmonetary support.

EIN: 13-6021319

CONTRIBUTIONS SUMMARY
Typical Recipients: • *Arts & Humanities:* Arts Centers, Historic Preservation, Libraries, Museums/Galleries, Performing Arts, Theater • *Civic & Public Affairs:* Business/Free Enterprise, Civil Rights, Economic Development, Economic Policy, Employment/Job Training, Nonprofit Management, Professional & Trade Associations, Public Policy, Safety, Urban & Community Affairs, Women's Affairs, Zoos/Aquariums • *Education:* Business Education, Colleges & Universities, Community & Junior Colleges, Continuing Education, Education Associations, Education Funds, Elementary Education (Private), International Studies, Literacy, Medical Education, Minority Education, Religious Education, Science/Mathematics Education • *Environment:* General • *Health:* Health Funds, Health Organizations, Hospitals, Medical Rehabilitation, Medical Research, Single-Disease Health Associations • *International:* International Relations • *Social Services:* Animal Protection, Community Service Organizations, Counseling, People with Disabilities, Recreation & Athletics, Substance Abuse, United Funds/United Ways, Youth Organizations

Grant Types: capital, challenge, employee matching gifts, endowment, general support, and multiyear/continuing support

Note: Employee matching gift ratio: 1 to 1.5. Contributions from eligible employees are matched, with a minimum of $25 to a maximim of $2,000 per calendar year.

Geographic Distribution: near headquarters and operating locations only

Operating Locations: CA (Los Angeles, San Francisco), CT (Enfield, Meridian), DE (Newark), FL (Mulberry), GA (Atlanta, Columbus), IL (Chicago), IN (Indianapolis), KY (Wickliffe), LA (DeRidder, New Orleans), MA (Springfield), MD (Baltimore, Luke), NC (Gastonia), NY (Buffalo, New York), OH (Cleveland, Eaton), PA (Tyrone, Williamsburg), SC (Cameron, Cameron, Charleston, Summerville), TN (Cleveland), TX (Dallas), VA (Covington, Richmond), WV (Rupert)

CORP. OFFICERS
William S. Beaver: *B* 1951 *ED* Dickinson Coll BA 1973; Harvard Univ MBA 1978 *CURR EMPL* treas: Westvaco Corp *CORP AFFIL* treas, dir: Westvaco Devel Corp

George E. Cruser: *B* Princeton NJ 1930 *ED* Juniata Coll BA 1952; Univ PA Wharton Sch MBA 1954 *CURR EMPL* sr vp fin, dir: Westvaco Corp *CORP AFFIL* sr vp, dir: Westvaco Devel Corp

David Lincoln Luke III: *B* Tyrone PA 1923 *ED* Yale Univ BA 1945 *CURR EMPL* chmn, dir: Westvaco Corp *CORP AFFIL* chmn, dir: Cold Spring Harbor Laboratory; dir: BF Goodrich Co, Clupak, Grumman Corp, Irving Bank Corp, Irving Trust Co, McGraw-Hill Inc, NY Stock Exchange *NONPR AFFIL* dir: Ventures Ed; mem: Am Paper Inst, Inst Paper Sci Tech; trust emeritus: Hotchkiss Sch *CLUB AFFIL* Colony, Links, Megantic Fish & Game, Piping Rock, River *PHIL AFFIL* dir, mem exec comm: Josiah Macy, Jr. Foundation

John Anderson Luke, Jr.: *B* NY 1949 *ED* Lawrence Univ BA 1971; Univ PA Wharton Sch MBA 1979 *CURR EMPL* pres, ceo, dir: Westvaco Corp *CORP AFFIL* adv dir: Arkwright Mutual Ins Co *NONPR AFFIL* dir: ACCION Intl, Am Soc, Counc Ams; dir, exec comm mem: Am Paper Inst; gov: UN Assn; mem: Am Forest Paper Assn; trust: Lawrence Univ *CLUB AFFIL* Univ

GIVING OFFICERS
William S. Beaver: trust *CURR EMPL* treas: Westvaco Corp (see above)

George E. Cruser: trust *CURR EMPL* sr vp fin, dir: Westvaco Corp (see above)

APPLICATION INFORMATION
Initial Approach: *Initial Contact:* brief letter or proposal *Include Information On:* description of the organization, amount requested, purpose for which funds are sought, and proof of tax-exempt status *Deadlines:* none; best time of year is July *Note:* Program is decentralized; recommended procedure is to apply through company operating units, rather than directly to the foundation.

GRANTS ANALYSIS
Total Grants: $1,299,473

Number of Grants: 175

Highest Grant: $75,000

Average Grant: $7,426

Typical Range: $1,000 to $5,000

Disclosure Period: fiscal year ending September 30, 1993

Note: Recent grants are derived from a fiscal 1991 Form 990.

RECENT GRANTS

General

75,000	United Way
70,107	United Way of Tri-State, New York, NY
65,000	County United Way
50,000	National Geographic Education Foundation, Washington, DC
35,000	Cold Spring Harbor Laboratory, Cold Spring Harbor, NY

Wiley & Sons, Inc., John

Sales: $294.28 million
Employees: 1,680
Headquarters: New York, NY
SIC Major Group: Printing & Publishing

CONTACT
Deborah Wiley
Vice President
John Wiley & Sons, Inc.
605 Third Ave.
New York, NY 10158
(212) 850-6000

FINANCIAL SUMMARY
Recent Giving: $189,000 (fiscal 1995); $180,000 (fiscal 1994); $113,000 (fiscal 1993)

CONTRIBUTIONS SUMMARY
Company reports that 44% of contributions are allocated to business-related organizations, including libraries, literary councils, and first ammendment organizations; 30% to arts and humanities; 22% to education; and 2% each to health and human services and civic and public affairs.

Volunteerism: Company promotes volunteerism through a structured corporate volunteer program and a ServiceMatch program.

Typical Recipients: • *Arts & Humanities:* Ballet, Dance, Libraries, Museums/Galleries, Opera, Performing Arts, Public Broadcasting, Theater • *Civic & Public Affairs:* Botanical Gardens/Parks, Civil Rights, First Amendment Issues, Zoos/Aquariums • *Education:* Arts/Humanities Education, Business Education, Colleges & Universities, Community & Junior Colleges, Continuing Education, Education Associations, Education Funds, Elementary Education (Private), Elementary Education (Public), General, Legal Education, Literacy, Medical Education, Minority Education, Preschool Education, Private Education (Precollege), Public Education (Precollege), Secondary Education (Private), Secondary Education (Public) • *Environment:* Resource Conservation, Wildlife Protection • *Health:* AIDS/HIV, Mental Health • *International:* Human Rights • *Science:* Science Museums, Scientific Organizations • *Social Services:* Emergency Relief, Shelters/Homelessness

Nonmonetary Support Types: donated products and workplace solicitation

Geographic Distribution: headquarters area

Operating Locations: NY (New York)

CORP. OFFICERS
Charles R. Ellis: *CURR EMPL* pres, ceo, dir: John Wiley & Sons

Deborah Wiley: *CURR EMPL* vp: John Wiley & Sons

W. Bradford Wiley II: *CURR EMPL* chmn, dir: John Wiley & Sons

APPLICATION INFORMATION
Initial Approach: Send brief letter of inquiry, including a description of the organization, amount requested, purpose of funds sought, and proof of tax-exempt status. There are no deadlines.

Restrictions on Giving: Does not support individuals, film projects, religious organizations for sectarian purposes, or political or lobbying groups.

OTHER THINGS TO KNOW
Contributions to education are made primarily through matching gift program.

GRANTS ANALYSIS
Typical Range: $1,000 to $2,500

Note: Recent grants are derived from a grants list provided by company in 1995.

RECENT GRANTS

Library
New York Public Library, New York, NY

General
American Geographical Society, New York, NY
Children of Bellevue, New York, NY
Human Rights Watch, New York, NY
Literacy Volunteers of New York City, New York, NY
National Book Foundation, New York, NY

Wilson Foundation, H. W.

CONTACT
Leo M. Weins
President, Treasurer
H. W. Wilson Fdn.
950 University Ave.
Bronx, NY 10452
(718) 588-8400

FINANCIAL SUMMARY
Recent Giving: $509,717 (fiscal 1993); $524,117 (fiscal 1992); $487,091 (fiscal 1991)

Assets: $9,141,278 (fiscal 1993); $8,828,759 (fiscal 1992); $8,512,273 (fiscal 1991)

EIN: 23-7418062

CONTRIBUTIONS SUMMARY
Donor(s): the late H. W. Wilson, the late Mrs. H. W. Wilson, the H. W. Wilson Co.

Typical Recipients: • *Arts & Humanities:* Arts Associations & Councils, Historic Preservation, History & Archaeology, Libraries, Museums/Galleries, Public Broadcasting • *Civic & Public Affairs:* Botanical Gardens/Parks, Legal Aid, Nonprofit Management, Public Policy, Urban & Community Affairs, Zoos/Aquariums • *Education:* Colleges & Universities, Community & Junior Colleges, Literacy, Student Aid • *Environment:* General, Resource Conservation • *Health:* Eyes/Blindness, Hospitals • *International:* Foreign Educational Institutions, Health Care/Hospitals, International Affairs, International Organizations • *Religion:* Religious Welfare • *Science:* Science Museums • *Social Services:* Community Centers, Community Service Organizations, Crime Prevention, Delinquency & Criminal Rehabilitation, People with Disabilities, Substance Abuse

Grant Types: research and scholarship

Geographic Distribution: national, with giving in CA, DC, IL, NY, and PA

GIVING OFFICERS
James Humphrey III: vp, dir *CORP AFFIL* dir: Wilson (HW) Co

Rutherford David Rogers: dir *B* Jesup IA 1915 *ED* Univ Northern IA BA 1936; Columbia Univ MA 1937; Columbia Univ BS 1938; Univ Northern IA LittD 1977 *CORP AFFIL* dir: Wilson (HW) Co *NONPR AFFIL* fdr, chmn: Res Libraries Group; fellow: Am Academy Arts Sciences; mem: Am Assn Univ Profs, Am Librarians Assn, Assn Res Libraries, Bibliographical Soc Am; univ librarian emeritus: Stanford Univ

Leo M. Weins: pres, treas, dir *B* Racine WI 1912 *ED* Loyola Univ 1936; Univ Chicago 1938; Northwestern Univ 1947 *CURR EMPL* pres, treas, dir: HW Wilson Co *NONPR AFFIL* gov: Foreign Policy Assn; mem: Am Antiquarian Soc, Am Librarians Assn

William Alexander Ziegler: secy, dir *B* New York NY 1924 *ED* Harvard Univ AB 1944; Harvard Univ JD 1949 *CORP AFFIL* consult: Sullivan & Cromwell; dir: Standard Commercial Corp, HW Wilson Co *NONPR AFFIL* dir: Engg Information, Foreign Policy Assn; mem: Am Bar Assn, New York City Bar Assn, NY Bar Assn; trust: Land Trust Darien *CLUB AFFIL* Harvard Fairfield County, Riverside CC, Wee Burn CC

APPLICATION INFORMATION
Initial Approach: Send brief letter of inquiry describing program or project. Include a description of organization, amount requested, purpose of funds sought, recently audited financial statement, and proof of tax-exempt status. There are no deadlines.

Restrictions on Giving: Focus on is on libraries.

GRANTS ANALYSIS
Total Grants: $509,717

Number of Grants: 55

Highest Grant: $48,000

Typical Range: $1,000 to $37,950

Disclosure Period: fiscal year ending November 30, 1993

Note: Recent grants are derived from a fiscal 1993 Form 990.

RECENT GRANTS

Library

48,000	International Federation of Library Associations
37,950	Urban Libraries Council, Evanston, IL
20,000	Northeast Document Conservation Center, Andover, MA
10,000	New York Public Library, New York, NY
10,000	Special Libraries Association, Washington, DC

General

20,000	Clarion University of Pennsylvania, Clarion, PA
16,667	University of California Riverside, Riverside, CA
10,000	Foreign Policy Association Endowment Fund, New York, NY
10,000	Kent State University, Kent, OH
10,000	New York Zoological Society, New York, NY

Winston Foundation, Norman and Rosita

CONTACT
Julian S. Perlman
Director
Norman and Rosita Winston Foundation
1740 Broadway
New York, NY 10019
(212) 757-0707

FINANCIAL SUMMARY
Recent Giving: $3,000,000 (1995 est.); $3,000,000 (1994 approx.); $3,072,480 (1993)

Assets: $60,000,000 (1995 est.); $60,000,000 (1994 approx.); $54,500,000 (1991 est.)

Gifts Received: $500,268 (1987)

Fiscal Note: In 1987, the foundation received a contribution of $500,268 from the estate of N. K. Winston.

EIN: 13-6161672

CONTRIBUTIONS SUMMARY
Donor(s): The foundation was established in 1954. Its donor was the late Norman K. Winston .

Typical Recipients: • *Arts & Humanities:* Arts Centers, Dance, Historic Preservation, Libraries, Museums/Galleries, Music, Opera, Theater, Visual Arts • *Civic & Public Affairs:* Civil Rights • *Education:* Colleges & Universities, Legal Education, Medical Education, Social Sciences Education • *Health:* Hospitals, Medical Research • *Religion:* Synagogues/Temples • *Social Services:* Recreation & Athletics, Senior Services

Grant Types: fellowship, general support, professorship, project, research, and scholarship

Geographic Distribution: principally New York

GIVING OFFICERS
Laurie Friedland: dir

Arthur Levitt, Jr.: emeritus *B* Brooklyn NY 1931 *ED* Williams Coll BA 1952 *CURR EMPL* chmn: Levitt Media Co *CORP AFFIL* chmn: New York City Econ Devel Corp; dir: BDM Holdings, First Empire St Corp, Shared Med Sys Corp; mem: Equitable Life Assurance Soc US; trust: E NY Savings Bank *NONPR AFFIL* bd dir: Solomon R. Guggenheim Fdn; chmn: Securities Exchange Commn, Special Adv Task Force Future Devel W Side Manhattan; mem: NY St Counc Arts; trust: Williams Coll

Julian S. Perlman: dir

Richard Rifkind: dir

Simon Hirsh Rifkind: dir emeritus *B* Meretz Russia 1901 *CURR EMPL* ptnr: Paul Weiss Rifkind Wharton & Garrison *NONPR AFFIL* mem: New York City Bar Assn, Phi Beta Kappa *CLUB AFFIL* Harmonie NY

APPLICATION INFORMATION
Initial Approach:

Proposals should be directed to Julian S. Perlman.

There is no prescribed form for applications.

There is no deadline for submitting proposals.

GRANTS ANALYSIS
Total Grants: $3,072,480

Number of Grants: 129

Highest Grant: $140,000

Average Grant: $23,818

Typical Range: $5,000 to $50,000

Disclosure Period: 1993

Note: Recent grants are derived from a 1992 grants list.

RECENT GRANTS

Library

25,000	New York Public Library, New York, NY

General

140,000	Jewish Theological Seminary of America, New York, NY
100,000	American Friends of Hebrew University, New York, NY
100,000	City College Simon H. Rifkind Center, New York, NY
100,000	Cornell University Medical College, New York, NY
100,000	Fordham University School of Law, New York, NY — Sidney C. Norris Chair of Law

Witco Corp. / Wishnick Foundation, Robert I.

Former Foundation Name: Witco Foundation
Revenue: $2.23 billion
Employees: 8,200
Headquarters: New York, NY
SIC Major Group: Lubricating Oils & Greases, Industrial Organic Chemicals Nec, Chemical Preparations Nec, and Asphalt Paving Mixtures & Blocks

CONTACT
William Wishnick
President, Director
Robert I. Wishnick Foundation
375 Park Ave.
New York, NY 10152
(212) 371-1844

FINANCIAL SUMMARY
Recent Giving: $700,000 (1995 est.); $650,000 (1994 approx.); $683,030 (1993)

Assets: $9,320,785 (1993); $9,637,765 (1992); $9,174,665 (1991)

Gifts Received: $31,569 (1992); $500,000 (1989); $18,106 (1988)

Fiscal Note: Contributes through foundation only. Above figures exclude nonmonetary support. In 1992, contributions were received from the Eli Wishnick Foundation.

EIN: 13-6068668

CONTRIBUTIONS SUMMARY
Typical Recipients: • *Arts & Humanities:* Arts Centers, Arts Festivals, Ballet, Dance, Libraries, Museums/Galleries, Music, Opera, Performing Arts, Theater, Visual Arts • *Civic & Public Affairs:* Civil Rights, Clubs, General, Law & Justice, Safety, Urban & Community Affairs, Women's Affairs • *Education:* Business Education, Colleges & Universities, Engineering/Technological Education, Medical Education, Preschool Education, Private Education (Precollege), Student Aid • *Health:* Cancer, Clinics/Medical Centers, Emergency/Ambulance Services, Hospitals, Single-Disease Health Associations • *Religion:* Churches, Jewish Causes, Religious Organizations, Religious Welfare, Synagogues/Temples • *Science:* Scientific Organizations • *Social Services:* Animal Protection, Camps, Child Welfare, Community Service Organizations, Family Planning, General, Homes, People with Disabilities, Recreation & Athletics, United Funds/United Ways, Youth Organizations

Grant Types: conference/seminar, endowment, fellowship, general support, research, and scholarship

Geographic Distribution: operating communities

Operating Locations: AL (Phenix City), CA (City of Industry, Commerce, Los Angeles, Oildale, Rancho Dominguez, Richmond, Santa Fe Springs), CT (Greenwich), FL (Jacksonville), IA (Spencer), IL (Blue Island, Chicago, Mapleton, Melrose Park), IN (Indianapolis), KS (Olathe), LA (Gretna, Harahan, Taft), MI (Highland Park), MS

(Philadelphia), NE (Omaha), NJ (Brainards, Newark, Oakland, Perth Amboy), NV (Las Vegas), NY (Beacon, Brooklyn, New York), OH (Dublin), OK (Ponca City), OR (Klamath Falls), PA (Bakerstown, Bradford, Petrolia, Trainer), TN (Memphis), TX (Fort Worth, Houston, LaPorte, Marshall, Marshall, Sunray), WA (Quincy), WI (Janesville)

CORP. OFFICERS
Denis Andreuzzi: *B* New York NY 1931 *ED* Columbia Univ BA 1953; NY Univ MBA 1958 *CURR EMPL* chmn exec comm, vchmn, pres, coo, dir: Witco Corp *CORP AFFIL* dir: Witco BV Holland *NONPR AFFIL* mem: Chem Mfrs Assn, IN Lubricant Mfrs Assn, Natl Petroleum Refiners Assn

GIVING OFFICERS
Robert L. Bachner: dir *PHIL AFFIL* asst secy, dir: Uris Brothers Foundation

Simeon Brinberg: dir

Lisa Wishnick: dir

William Wishnick: pres, dir *B* Brooklyn NY 1924 *ED* Univ TX BBA 1949; Carnegie Inst Tech *CURR EMPL* mem exec comm, dir: Witco Corp *CORP AFFIL* chmn: Aero Oil Co; chmn, dir: Continental Carbon Co *NONPR AFFIL* fellow: Polytech Inst NY; mem: Am Chem Soc, Am Petroleum Inst, NY Paint Varnish & Lacquer Assn, Salesmans Assn, Tau Delta Phi; trust: Carnegie-Mellon Univ, Mt Sinai Med Ctr *CLUB AFFIL* Chems, Harmonie *PHIL AFFIL* pres: Eli Wishnick Foundation

APPLICATION INFORMATION
Initial Approach: *Initial Contact:* brief letter *Include Information On:* description of program, amount of funds requested *Deadlines:* none

Restrictions on Giving: Foundation does not support individuals (except for employee-related scholarships) or matching gifts. Loans are not made.

OTHER THINGS TO KNOW
The foundation and corporation operate as separate entities.

The foundation will not be making any new grants until 1996.

GRANTS ANALYSIS
Total Grants: $683,030

Number of Grants: 129

Highest Grant: $140,000

Average Grant: $5,295

Typical Range: $1,000 to $10,000

Disclosure Period: 1993

Note: Recent grants are derived from a 1993 Form 990.

RECENT GRANTS

Library
10,000	Bradford Library Building Fund, Bradford, MA
4,400	Library of Israel

General
140,000	Mt. Sinai Hospital Five Year Pledge, New York, NY
25,000	Westchester Association for Retarded Citizens, White Plains, NY
20,000	Medical Center Foundation of Point Pleasant, Point Pleasant, NJ
17,000	Children's Hope Foundation, New York, NY
15,000	Carnegie Mellon University, Pittsburgh, PA

Woodward Fund

CONTACT
Samuel A. Curtis, Jr,
Administrator
Woodward Fund
c/o Fleet Trust Dept.
45 East Ave.
Rochester, NY 14638
(617) 346-2405

FINANCIAL SUMMARY
Recent Giving: $127,084 (fiscal 1993); $122,124 (fiscal 1992); $125,750 (fiscal 1991)

Assets: $2,473,262 (fiscal 1993); $2,428,555 (fiscal 1992); $2,297,275 (fiscal 1991)

Gifts Received: $1,828 (fiscal 1992)

EIN: 16-6064221

CONTRIBUTIONS SUMMARY
Donor(s): Florence S. Woodward

Typical Recipients: • *Arts & Humanities:* Art History, Arts Centers, Arts Funds, History & Archaeology, Libraries, Museums/Galleries, Music • *Civic & Public Affairs:* General, Housing, Legal Aid, Municipalities/Towns, Nonprofit Management, Women's Affairs, Zoos/Aquariums • *Education:* Colleges & Universities, International Exchange, Minority Education, Preschool Education, Private Education (Precollege), Public Education (Precollege), School Volunteerism, Secondary Education (Public) • *Environment:* General, Resource Conservation, Wildlife Protection • *Health:* Emergency/Ambulance Services, Health Organizations, Hospices, Hospitals, Medical Rehabilitation, Medical Research, Single-Disease Health Associations • *International:* Human Rights, International Development • *Religion:* Churches • *Science:* Science Museums • *Social Services:* Animal Protection, At-Risk Youth, Child Welfare, Community Service Organizations, Day Care, Domestic Violence, Family Planning, People with Disabilities, Recreation & Athletics, Shelters/Homelessness, YMCA/YWCA/YMHA/YWHA, Youth Organizations

Grant Types: general support and research

Geographic Distribution: focus on AZ and ME

GIVING OFFICERS
Fleet Trust Company: trust

Barbara W. Piel: dir

Reid T. Woodward: dir

Stephen S. Woodward: dir

William S. Woodward: dir

APPLICATION INFORMATION
Initial Approach: The foundation has no formal grant application procedure or application form. Send a brief letter of inquiry. There are no deadlines.

Restrictions on Giving: Does not support individuals.

GRANTS ANALYSIS
Total Grants: $127,084

Number of Grants: 44

Highest Grant: $10,000

Typical Range: $524 to $5,000

Disclosure Period: fiscal year ending November 30, 1993

Note: Recent grants are derived from a fiscal 1993 Form 990.

RECENT GRANTS

Library

4,000	Town of Guilford Memorial Library, Guilford, NC
524	Friends of Guilford Memorial Library, Guilford, ME

General

10,000	Heifer Project International, Little Rock, AR
5,000	Arizona Boys Ranch, Tucson, AZ
5,000	Carmel High School Padre Parents, Carmel, CA
5,000	Gompers Rehabilitation Center
5,000	Maine Audubon Society, Falmouth, ME — environmental centers project

Zenkel Foundation

CONTACT
Lois Zenkel
President
Zenkel Fdn.
15 W 53rd St.
New York, NY 10019
(212) 944-8811

FINANCIAL SUMMARY
Recent Giving: $254,067 (1993); $260,448 (1992); $245,096 (1991)

Assets: $5,055,973 (1993); $5,123,741 (1992); $4,883,919 (1991)

EIN: 13-3380631

CONTRIBUTIONS SUMMARY
Typical Recipients: • *Arts & Humanities:* Dance, Film & Video, General, Libraries, Museums/Galleries, Public Broadcasting, Theater, Visual Arts • *Civic & Public Affairs:* African American Affairs, General, Housing, Legal Aid, Municipalities/Towns • *Education:* Colleges & Universities, Medical Education, Student Aid • *Environment:* General, Resource Conservation, Wildlife Protection • *Health:* AIDS/HIV, Cancer, Children's Health/Hospitals, Hospitals, Medical Research, Single-Disease Health Associations, Speech & Hearing • *International:* Foreign Arts Organizations • *Religion:* Jewish Causes, Religious Organizations, Synagogues/Temples • *Social Services:* Community Service Organizations, Family Services, Food/Clothing Distribution, Homes, Recreation & Athletics, United Funds/United Ways, Youth Organizations

Grant Types: capital, general support, and scholarship

Geographic Distribution: focus on NY

GIVING OFFICERS
Bruce L. Zenkel: dir

Daniel R. Zenkel: secy, treas, dir

Gary B. Zenkel: dir

Lisa R. Zenkel: dir

Lois S. Zenkel: pres, dir

APPLICATION INFORMATION
Initial Approach: Send a brief letter of inquiry.

GRANTS ANALYSIS
Total Grants: $254,067

Number of Grants: 94

Highest Grant: $50,000

Typical Range: $100 to $40,000

Disclosure Period: 1993

Note: Recent grants are derived from a 1993 Form 990.

RECENT GRANTS

Library

1,250	New York Public Library, New York, NY

General

50,000	University of Michigan, Ann Arbor, MI
40,000	United Jewish Appeal Federation, New York, NY
20,000	Greenwich Hospital, Greenwich, CT
17,500	International Center of Photography, New York, NY
10,000	Greenwich Jewish Federation, Greenwich, CT

Zlinkoff Fund for Medical Research and Education, Sergei S.

CONTACT
Jerome J. Cohen
Secretary
Sergei S. Zlinkoff Fund for Medical Research and Education
c/o Carter, Ledyard & Milburn
2 Wall St.
New York, NY 10005
(212) 732-3200

FINANCIAL SUMMARY
Recent Giving: $308,700 (fiscal 1993); $297,500 (fiscal 1992); $235,000 (fiscal 1991)

Assets: $2,404,481 (fiscal 1993); $2,381,425 (fiscal 1992); $2,510,845 (fiscal 1991)

EIN: 13-6094651

CONTRIBUTIONS SUMMARY
Donor(s): Sergei S. Zlinkoff

Typical Recipients: • *Arts & Humanities:* Libraries • *Education:* Colleges & Universities, International Exchange, Medical Education • *Health:* Clinics/Medical Centers, Health Organizations, Hospitals, Outpatient Health Care • *International:* International Peace & Security Issues, Missionary/Religious Activities • *Religion:* Jewish Causes • *Social Services:* Family Planning, People with Disabilities

Grant Types: general support

Geographic Distribution: focus on NY

GIVING OFFICERS
Jerome J. Cohen: secy

Deborah L. Goldsmith: vp

Robert Goldstein, MD: vp

Milton Hamolsky, MD: pres

Sandra Z. Hamolsky: vp, dir

Ralph Emil Hansmann: vp, treas *B* Utica NY 1918 *ED* Hamilton Coll AB 1940; Harvard Univ MBA 1942 *CURR EMPL* investment assoc: Harold F Linder & William T Golden *CORP AFFIL* dir: First Eagle Fund Am, Schroder Capital Funds, Verde Exploration Ltd *NONPR AFFIL* life trust: Hamilton Coll; mem: Phi Beta Kappa; mem visitors comm: New Sch Grad Faculty; trust, treas: Inst Advanced Studies, NY Pub Library *CLUB AFFIL* City Midday, Ridgewood CC *PHIL AFFIL* treas, dir: Golden Family Foundation; asst secy: Olive Bridge Fund

Barbara Lipkin: vp

John O. Lipkin, MD: vp

Mack Lipkin, Jr.,MD: vp *B* New York NY 1943 *ED* Harvard Univ AB 1965; Harvard Univ MD 1970 *CORP AFFIL* editor: Frontiers Primary Med *NONPR AFFIL* assoc prof medicine: NY Univ Sch Medicine; fellow: NY Academy Medicine; mem: Am Assn Advancement Science, Am Psychosomatic Soc, Intl Epidemiology Assn, North Am Primary Care Res Group, Phi Beta Kappa, Primary Care Internal Medicine, Soc Gen Internal Medicine, Task Force Doctor & Patient

Ellen Parker: vp

APPLICATION INFORMATION
Restrictions on Giving: Does not support individuals.

GRANTS ANALYSIS
Total Grants: $308,700

Number of Grants: 16

Highest Grant: $45,000

Typical Range: $5,000 to $30,000

Disclosure Period: fiscal year ending October 31, 1993

Note: Recent grants are derived from a fiscal 1993 Form 990.

RECENT GRANTS

Library

15,000	New York Public Library, New York, NY

General

45,000	New York University Medical Center, New York, NY
30,000	Ashoka, Arlington, VA
30,000	Planned Parenthood of New York City, New York, NY
26,500	Brown University School of Medicine, Providence, RI
25,000	Center for Research on Population and Security, Chapel Hill, NC

NORTH CAROLINA

Acme-McCrary Corp./Sapona Manufacturing Co. / Acme-McCrary and Sapona Foundation

Sales: $45.0 million
Employees: 900
Headquarters: Asheboro, NC
SIC Major Group: Textile Mill Products

CONTACT
Herold J. Weiler
President
Acme-McCrary and Sapona Foundation
PO Box 1287
Asheboro, NC 27203
(910) 625-2161

FINANCIAL SUMMARY
Recent Giving: $78,633 (1993); $87,848 (1990)

Assets: $736,239 (1993); $552,835 (1990)

Gifts Received: $50,000 (1993); $75,000 (1990)

Fiscal Note: In 1993, contributions were received from Sapona Manufacturing Co. Inc.

EIN: 56-6047739

CONTRIBUTIONS SUMMARY
Typical Recipients: • *Arts & Humanities:* General, Libraries, Music • *Civic & Public Affairs:* Chambers of Commerce, Civil Rights, General, Hispanic Affairs, Nonprofit Management, Zoos/Aquariums • *Education:* Colleges & Universities, General • *Environment:* Resource Conservation, Wildlife Protection • *Health:* General • *Religion:* Jewish Causes • *Social Services:* General

Grant Types: award and capital

Nonmonetary Support Types: loaned executives

Geographic Distribution: focus on NC

CORP. OFFICERS
Charles W. McCrary, Jr.: *CURR EMPL* chmn of bd, ceo, dir: Acme-McCrary Corp

GIVING OFFICERS
Charles W. McCrary, Jr.: vp *CURR EMPL* chmn of bd, ceo, dir: Acme-McCrary Corp (see above)

Bruce Patram: secy, treas

Harold J. Weiler: pres

APPLICATION INFORMATION
Initial Approach: Send a brief letter of inquiry and a full proposal. Include a description of organization, amount requested, purpose of funds sought, recently audited financial statement, and proof of tax-exempt status. There are no deadlines.

Restrictions on Giving: Does not support individuals or political or lobbying groups.

GRANTS ANALYSIS
Total Grants: $78,633

Number of Grants: 28

Highest Grant: $20,000

Typical Range: $100 to $16,000

Disclosure Period: 1993

Note: Recent grants are derived from a 1993 Form 990.

RECENT GRANTS

General

20,000	Randolph Hospital, Asheboro, NC
16,000	United Way of Randolph County, Asheboro, NC
15,000	First United Methodist Church, Asheboro, NC
11,000	Randolph-Asheboro YMCA, Asheboro, NC
5,000	Hospice of Randolph County, Asheboro, NC

Blue Bell, Inc. / Blue Bell Foundation

Revenue: $1.07 billion
Employees: 20,000
Parent Company: VF Corp.
Headquarters: Greensboro, NC
SIC Major Group: Men's/Boys' Trousers & Slacks, Knit Outerwear Mills, Men's/Boys' Suits & Coats, and Men's/Boys' Shirts

CONTACT
Charles Conklin
Secretary, Advisory Committee
Blue Bell Foundation
PO Box 21488
Greensboro, NC 27420
(910) 332-4106

FINANCIAL SUMMARY
Recent Giving: $200,000 (1994 approx.); $231,884 (1993); $325,840 (1992)

Assets: $4,018,570 (1992); $3,898,711 (1990)

Fiscal Note: Grants are made through foundation only.

EIN: 56-6041057

CONTRIBUTIONS SUMMARY
Typical Recipients: • *Arts & Humanities:* Arts Associations & Councils, Arts Festivals, Arts Funds, Community Arts, Historic Preservation, Libraries, Museums/Galleries, Music • *Civic & Public Affairs:* Botanical Gardens/Parks, Employment/Job Training, Housing, Municipalities/Towns, Public Policy, Urban & Community Affairs • *Education:* Agricultural Education, Business Education, Colleges & Universities, Community & Junior Colleges, Education Associations, Education Funds, Private Education (Precollege), Public Education (Precollege), Secondary Education (Public), Student Aid • *Health:* Cancer, Children's Health/Hospitals, Hospices, Hospitals, Medical Research, Single-Disease Health Associations • *Religion:* Churches, Jewish Causes, Ministries, Religious Organizations • *Science:* Scientific Centers & Institutes • *Social Services:* Child Welfare, Community Centers, Community Service Organizations, Counseling, Day Care, Food/Clothing Distribution, Homes, Recreation & Athletics, Substance Abuse, United Funds/United Ways, Youth Organizations

Grant Types: employee matching gifts and general support

Geographic Distribution: areas where company has facilities

Operating Locations: NC (Greensboro)

CORP. OFFICERS
Lawrence R. Pugh: *CURR EMPL* chmn, dir: VF Corp *CORP AFFIL* chmn: Blue Bell Inc

John Schamberger: *CURR EMPL* pres: Blue Bell Inc

GIVING OFFICERS
Charles Conklin: secy adv comm

Don P. Laws: mem adv comm

John Schamberger: mem adv bd *CURR EMPL* pres: Blue Bell Inc (see above)

APPLICATION INFORMATION
Initial Approach: *Initial Contact:* letter *Include Information On:* description of the organization; IRS tax determination letter; and amount requested *Deadlines:* none

Restrictions on Giving: The foundation does not support individuals. Grants are made to organizations that directly benefit the company's employees.

GRANTS ANALYSIS
Total Grants: $325,840

Number of Grants: 146*

Highest Grant: $21,960

Average Grant: $2,087*

Typical Range: $100 to $5,000

Disclosure Period: 1992

Note: Number of grants and average grant figures do not include 56 matching grants totaling $21,179. Recent grants are derived from a 1992 Form 990.

RECENT GRANTS

Library

2,500	Harriman Public Library, Harriman, TN

General

21,960	National Merit Scholarship Corporation, Evanston, IL
20,000	Monroe County Middle School, Rompkinsville, KY
12,500	Foundation for Greater Greensboro, Greensboro, NC
10,000	Chabad of St. Louis, St. Louis, MO
10,000	Guilford College, Greensboro, NC

Burlington Industries, Inc. / Burlington Industries Foundation

Sales: $2.1 billion
Employees: 23,400
Headquarters: Greensboro, NC
SIC Major Group: Broadwoven Fabric Mills—Cotton, Broadwoven Fabric Mills—Manmade, Broadwoven Fabric Mills—Wool, and Women's Hosiery Except Socks

CONTACT
Park R. Davidson
Executive Director
Burlington Industries Foundation
PO Box 21207
Greensboro, NC 27420-1207
(910) 379-2515

FINANCIAL SUMMARY
Recent Giving: $1,000,000 (fiscal 1995 est.); $958,813 (fiscal 1994); $891,179 (fiscal 1993)

Assets: $4,800,000 (fiscal 1995 est.); $5,458,010 (fiscal 1994); $6,333,672 (fiscal 1993)

Fiscal Note: Figures represent foundation giving only. Burlington Industries, Inc., also gives less than $50,000 annually through the public relations department. Contact Bryant Haskins, Manager, Community & Media Relations, for information. Above figures exclude nonmonetary support.

EIN: 56-6043142

CONTRIBUTIONS SUMMARY
Typical Recipients: • *Arts & Humanities:* Arts Associations & Councils, Arts Funds, Historic Preservation, Libraries, Museums/Galleries • *Civic & Public Affairs:* Business/Free Enterprise, Clubs, Employment/Job Training, Housing, Law & Justice, Safety, Urban & Community Affairs • *Education:* Business Education, Colleges & Universities, Community & Junior Colleges, Education Associations, Education Funds, Education Reform, Elementary Education (Public), Faculty Development, General, Minority Education, Private Education (Precollege), Public Education (Precollege), Science/Mathematics Education • *Health:*

AIDS/HIV, Health Organizations, Hospitals, Multiple Sclerosis, Single-Disease Health Associations • *International:* International Affairs • *Religion:* Jewish Causes, Ministries • *Social Services:* Community Centers, Community Service Organizations, Delinquency & Criminal Rehabilitation, Family Services, Recreation & Athletics, Substance Abuse, United Funds/United Ways, Youth Organizations

Grant Types: award, capital, employee matching gifts, and general support

Note: Employee matching gift ratio: 1 to 1, up to $5,000 for active employees and up to $1,000 for retired employees.

Nonmonetary Support: $250,000 (fiscal 1994); $200,000 (fiscal 1989); $300,000 (fiscal 1988)

Nonmonetary Support Types: donated equipment and donated products

Note: Bryant Haskins, Manager, Community & Media Relations, is the contact for nonmonetary gifts.

Geographic Distribution: primarily in North and South Carolina, Virginia, and near corporate operating locations

Operating Locations: AR, GA, MS, NC (Burlington, Greensboro), NY (New York), PA, SC, TN, TX, VA

Note: Operates in 10 states and 42 communities. Also has plants in Mexico.

CORP. OFFICERS
Park R. Davidson: *B* Keosauqua IA 1934 *ED* Univ IA 1955; Univ IA Law Sch 1957 *CURR EMPL* treas: Burlington Indus Inc

George W. Henderson III: *B* 1948 *ED* Univ NC 1970; Emory Univ 1974 *CURR EMPL* pres, coo, dir: Burlington Indus Inc *CORP AFFIL* dir: Halstead Indus Inc

J. Kenneth Lesley: *B* 1936 *ED* LA Coll BS 1959; GA St Univ MBA 1966 *CURR EMPL* vp personnel & pub rels: Burlington Indus Inc *CORP AFFIL* dir: B I Transportation

C. Winham: *CURR EMPL* dir pub aff: Burlington Indus Inc

GIVING OFFICERS
John C. Cowan, Jr.: trust

Park R. Davidson: exec dir, trust *CURR EMPL* treas: Burlington Indus Inc (see above)

Donald R. Hughes: trust *B* 1929 *ED* Harvard Univ MBA 1957 *CURR EMPL* vchmn, dir: Burlington Indus Inc

J. Kenneth Lesley: trust *CURR EMPL* vp personnel & pub rels: Burlington Indus Inc (see above)

Charles A. McLendon: trust

APPLICATION INFORMATION
Initial Approach: *Initial Contact:* brief letter or proposal *Include Information On:* description of the organization, including its aims and purpose; need and justification for program; evidence that organization and its programs are developed and have direction; information on organization's reputation, efficiency, management ability, financial status, and other income sources; proof that organization is tax-exempt and is not a pri-

vate foundation *Deadlines:* none *Note:* Foundation may request additional information.

Restrictions on Giving: Contributions generally are not made to national organizations; organizations that are not tax-exempt; fraternal, labor, or veterans organizations; churches; endowment funds; organizations supported through federated campaigns; private secondary schools; historic preservation projects; outdoor dramas; individuals; workshops, conferences, or seminars; production of films, documentaries, or other similar projects; operating expenses; political organizations, parties, or candidates; or medical research.

OTHER THINGS TO KNOW
In 1992, Burlington Industries, Inc., returned to its former publicly-held status.

GRANTS ANALYSIS
Total Grants: $958,813

Number of Grants: 172*

Highest Grant: $35,000

Average Grant: $4,110*

Typical Range: $500 to $10,000

Disclosure Period: fiscal year ending September 30, 1994

Note: Number of grants and average grant figures exclude 312 matching gifts totaling $209,175 and gifts to employees in distress totaling $42,750. Recent grants are derived from a fiscal 1993 grants list.

RECENT GRANTS

Library

20,000	Jesse Helms Center Foundation, Wingate, NC—build Helms Library and Museum

General

50,000	Philadelphia College of Textile and Science, Philadelphia, PA — campaign for textile
38,600	Mitchell Community College, Statesville, NC — project "LEAD"
20,000	Clemson University Foundation, Clemson, SC — for student center
20,000	Greensboro Day School, Greensboro, NC — building the future campaign
20,000	Greensboro Urban Ministry, Greensboro, NC — Project X

Chatham Manufacturing Co. / Chatham Foundation

Headquarters: Elkin, NC

CONTACT
David H. Cline
Secretary & Treasurer
Chatham Manufacturing Co.
c/o Chatham Foundation
PO Box 6201
Elkin, NC 28621
(919) 835-2211

FINANCIAL SUMMARY
Recent Giving: $123,000 (1993); $100,000 (1992)

Assets: $2,355,827 (1993); $2,853,591 (1992)

EIN: 56-0771852

CONTRIBUTIONS SUMMARY
Typical Recipients: • *Arts & Humanities:* Arts Associations & Councils, History & Archaeology, Libraries, Public Broadcasting • *Civic & Public Affairs:* General, Municipalities/Towns, Parades/Festivals • *Education:* Student Aid • *Health:* Emergency/Ambulance Services, Geriatric Health • *Religion:* Religious Welfare • *Social Services:* United Funds/United Ways

Grant Types: general support, matching, operating expenses, and scholarship

Geographic Distribution: focus on NC

GIVING OFFICERS
Alex Chatham, Jr.: mem

Barbara F. Chatham: vp

Lucy Hanes Chatham: pres *PHIL AFFIL* trust: John Motley Morehead Foundation

Mary Chatham: mem

Thomas L. Chatham: mem

David H. Cline: secy, treas

APPLICATION INFORMATION
Initial Approach: Send a brief letter of inquiry. Include a description of organization, amount requested, purpose of funds sought, recently audited financial statement, and proof of tax-exempt status.

GRANTS ANALYSIS
Total Grants: $123,000

Number of Grants: 15

Highest Grant: $25,000

Typical Range: $1,000 to $5,000

Disclosure Period: 1993

Note: Recent grants are derived from a 1993 Form 990.

RECENT GRANTS

Library
2,500	Elkin Public Library, Elkin, NC — for computer equipment
2,500	Jonesville-Arlington Public Library, Jonesville, NC — for computer equipment

General
25,000	Alleghany Fairgrounds, Sparta, NC
20,000	North Carolina Textile Foundation, Raleigh, NC — for outstanding balance due on Chatham Manufacturing Company pledge
15,000	Salem College, Winston-Salem, NC — for LHC Scholarship Fund
13,000	Town of Elkin, Elkin, NC — for Hollywood Cemetery landscaping project

5,000	Bowman Gray School of Medicine, Winston-Salem, NC — for J. Paul Sticht Center on Aging

Connemara Fund

CONTACT
Herrick Jackson
Trustee
Connemara Fund
PO Box 20124
Greensboro, NC 27420
(919) 274-5471

FINANCIAL SUMMARY
Recent Giving: $289,200 (fiscal 1992); $290,700 (fiscal 1990); $245,250 (fiscal 1989)

Assets: $6,638,306 (fiscal 1992); $6,534,617 (fiscal 1990); $6,929,858 (fiscal 1989)

EIN: 56-6096063

CONTRIBUTIONS SUMMARY
Donor(s): the late Mary R. Jackson

Typical Recipients: • *Arts & Humanities:* Libraries, Museums/Galleries, Public Broadcasting • *Civic & Public Affairs:* Civil Rights, Legal Aid, Zoos/Aquariums • *Education:* Colleges & Universities, Private Education (Precollege) • *Environment:* General • *Health:* Hospitals, Single-Disease Health Associations • *Religion:* Missionary Activities (Domestic) • *Social Services:* Child Welfare, United Funds/United Ways, Youth Organizations

Grant Types: general support and multi-year/continuing support

Geographic Distribution: focus on the New England area

GIVING OFFICERS
Herrick Jackson: trust

Robert W. Jackson: trust

Alison Jackson Van Dyk: trust

APPLICATION INFORMATION
Initial Approach: Send cover letter and full proposal. There are no deadlines.

Restrictions on Giving: Does not support individuals.

GRANTS ANALYSIS
Total Grants: $289,200

Number of Grants: 83

Highest Grant: $40,000

Typical Range: $1,000 to $5,000

Disclosure Period: fiscal year ending June 30, 1992

Note: Recent grants are derived from a fiscal 1992 Form 990.

RECENT GRANTS

General
40,000	Cultural Council Foundation, New York, NY
15,000	CATO Institute, Washington, DC

15,000	St. Luke's Foundation, New Canaan, CT
15,000	Windward School, White Plains, NY
10,000	Connecticut Fund for the Environment, New Haven, CT

Dalton Foundation, Harry L.

CONTACT
Mary Dalton
Director
Harry L. Dalton Fdn.
736 Wachovia Ctr.
Charlotte, NC 28205
(704) 332-5380

FINANCIAL SUMMARY
Recent Giving: $131,650 (fiscal 1992); $109,840 (fiscal 1991); $80,200 (fiscal 1989)

Assets: $2,973,749 (fiscal 1992); $2,687,926 (fiscal 1991); $2,283,694 (fiscal 1989)

EIN: 56-6061267

CONTRIBUTIONS SUMMARY
Typical Recipients: • *Arts & Humanities:* Community Arts, Historic Preservation, Libraries, Music, Performing Arts, Theater • *Civic & Public Affairs:* Zoos/Aquariums • *Education:* Colleges & Universities, Private Education (Precollege) • *Environment:* General • *Religion:* Churches • *Social Services:* Community Service Organizations, Recreation & Athletics, United Funds/United Ways, Youth Organizations

Grant Types: general support

GIVING OFFICERS
Elizabeth D. Brand: secy

Harry I. Dalton: dir, pres, treas

Mary E. Dalton: dir, vp

APPLICATION INFORMATION
Initial Approach: Send brief letter describing program. There are no deadlines.

GRANTS ANALYSIS
Total Grants: $131,650

Number of Grants: 32

Highest Grant: $43,100

Typical Range: $100 to $5,000

Disclosure Period: fiscal year ending July 31, 1992

Note: Recent grants are derived from a fiscal 1992 Form 990.

RECENT GRANTS

Library
10,000	Queens College Library, Charlotte, NC

General
43,100	Charlotte Country Day School, Charlotte, NC

25,000	Leighton Ford Foundation, Charlotte, NC
10,000	Queens College, Charlotte, NC
5,025	Duke University, Durham, NC
4,300	Agnes Scott College, Decatur, GA

Dover Foundation

Sales: $2.48 billion
Employees: 20,445

CONTACT
Hoyt Q. Bailey
President
Dover Foundation
PO Box 208
Shelby, NC 28151
(704) 487-8890

FINANCIAL SUMMARY
Recent Giving: $800,000 (fiscal 1995 est.); $822,000 (fiscal 1994); $800,000 (fiscal 1993 approx.)

Assets: $20,000,000 (fiscal 1995 est.); $17,000,000 (fiscal 1994 approx.); $20,000,000 (fiscal 1993)

Gifts Received: $483,544 (fiscal 1991)

Fiscal Note: In 1991, contributions were received from the estate of Charles I. Dover.

EIN: 56-0769897

CONTRIBUTIONS SUMMARY
Donor(s): The Dover foundation was founded in 1944 by John Randolph Dover, Jr. and Charles Irvin Dover for the purpose of assisting religious, charitable, scientific, literary, and educational organizations.

Typical Recipients: • *Arts & Humanities:* Libraries • *Education:* Colleges & Universities • *Health:* Health Funds, Hospices, Mental Health • *Religion:* Churches, Religious Organizations • *Social Services:* Community Service Organizations, Family Planning, Senior Services, United Funds/United Ways, Youth Organizations

Grant Types: multiyear/continuing support, operating expenses, and project

Geographic Distribution: almost exclusively North Carolina

GIVING OFFICERS
Hoyt Q. Bailey: pres

W. W. Gainey, Jr.: treas

Harvey B. Hamrick: secy

Kathleen D. Hamrick: vp

APPLICATION INFORMATION
Initial Approach:

A formal grant request may be submitted to the foundation by letter.

The applicant's proposal letter must include the following information: the full legal name of the organization; a brief description of the organization, its purpose, and program; the specific amount of money requested; a brief description of the purpose for which the grant would be used; a definite plan for the successful completion of the project; the signature of the principal of-ficer of the governing board; and the signature of the organization's chief administrative officer. Detailed supporting information about the program or project may be attached to the grant request. The applicant must also attach a copy of the organization's most recent tax exemption letter from the IRS and a list of the of the organization's board of directors. One copy of the proposal is sufficient.

The foundation board of directors meets four times a year to consider grant awards. These meetings are in January, April, July, and October. Deadlines for grant requests to be received by the foundation in order to be considered at the next meeting are: December 1, for the January meeting; March 1, for the April meeting; June 1, for the July meeting; and September 1, for the October meeting.

Restrictions on Giving: The foundation does not ordinarily make grants to political entities or for their activities, to individuals or their projects, advertising, newsletters, magazines, books, trips, tours, or to organizations whose principal activities take place outside the United States.

GRANTS ANALYSIS
Total Grants: $822,000

Number of Grants: 156

Highest Grant: $200,000

Average Grant: $5,269

Typical Range: $1,000 to $6,000

Disclosure Period: fiscal year ending August 31, 1994

Note: Recent grants are derived from a fiscal 1991 grants list.

RECENT GRANTS
Library

12,500	Cleveland Memorial Library, Shelby, NC

General

183,000	Gardner-Webb College, Boiling Springs, NC
50,000	Medical Foundation of North Carolina, Chapel Hill, NC
25,000	North Carolina State University, Raleigh, NC
17,000	Dover Baptist Church, Dover, NC
16,500	United Way, Shelby, NC

Duke Endowment

CONTACT
Jere W. Witherspoon
Executive Director
Duke Endowment
100 N Tryon St., Ste. 3500
Charlotte, NC 28202-4012
(704) 376-0291

FINANCIAL SUMMARY
Recent Giving: $50,000,000 (1995 est.); $50,500,000 (1994 approx.); $49,777,079 (1993)

Assets: $1,350,000,000 (1995 est.); $1,300,000,000 (1994 approx.); $1,425,000,000 (1993 approx.)

Gifts Received: $102,841 (1991)

EIN: 56-0529965

CONTRIBUTIONS SUMMARY
Donor(s): The Duke Endowment was established in 1924 by James Buchanan Duke (d. 1925) with a $40 million endowment. The Duke family derived its wealth from tobacco, textiles, and the development of hydroelectric power in North and South Carolina. The family tobacco business began shortly after the Civil War. In 1884, the small firm gambled on an innovation—automation—and the cottage industry grew into the American Tobacco Company with James Duke as president. The company was dissolved in 1911 when the Supreme Court upheld the Sherman Anti-Trust Act; but the Duke family had already turned their attention to hydroelectric power in 1905. This led to the founding of Duke Power Company in 1907. Mr. Duke also had business investments in texiles and blocks of shares of Aluminum Company of America.

During the family's years of prosperity, they generously contributed to orphanages, hospitals, the Methodist church, and Trinity College, which became Duke University when the Duke Endowment was founded.

The Duke Endowment is also closely affiliated with Angier B. Duke Memorial, NC, and Nanaline Duke Fund for Duke University, NC. Doris Duke , former trustee and late daughter of the donor, established the Doris Duke Charitable Foundation under her will. Ms. Duke died in April 1993.

Typical Recipients: • *Arts & Humanities:* Libraries • *Education:* Arts/Humanities Education, Colleges & Universities, Engineering/Technological Education, Faculty Development, International Studies, Minority Education, Religious Education, Science/Mathematics Education, Student Aid • *Health:* Adolescent Health Issues, AIDS/HIV, Alzheimers Disease, Cancer, Children's Health/Hospitals, Clinics/Medical Centers, Diabetes, Emergency/Ambulance Services, Geriatric Health, Health Policy/Cost Containment, Health Organizations, Heart, Home-Care Services, Hospices, Hospitals, Hospitals (University Affiliated), Long-Term Care, Medical Rehabilitation, Medical Research, Nursing Services, Nutrition, Outpatient Health Care, Prenatal Health Issues, Preventive Medicine/Wellness Organizations, Respiratory • *Religion:* Churches, Religious Organizations, Religious Welfare • *Social Services:* Child Welfare, Day Care, Family Planning, Family Services, Homes, People with Disabilities

Grant Types: capital, conference/seminar, emergency, endowment, fellowship, general support, operating expenses, professorship, project, research, and seed money

Geographic Distribution: North Carolina and South Carolina

GIVING OFFICERS
Dr. William G. Anlyan: trust *B* Alexandria Egypt 1925 *ED* Yale Univ BS 1945; Yale

Univ MD 1949 *CORP AFFIL* dir: Searle/Monsanto, Wachovia Bank *NONPR AFFIL* chancellor emeritus: Duke Univ; chmn counc commn on med aff: Yale Univ; chmn, mem bd visitors: Cornell Univ Med Coll; mem: Alpha Omega Alpha, Am Heart Assn, Am Med Assn, Am Surgical Assn, Assn Academy Health Ctrs, Assn Am Med Colls, Assn Am Med Colls, Coordinating Counc Med Ed, Counc Deans, Halsted Soc, Intl Cardiovascular Soc, Natl Academy Sciences Independent Res Roundtable, Natl Academy Sciences Inst Medicine, Phi Beta Kappa, Soc Clinical Surgery, Soc Med Admins, Soc Univ Surgeons, Soc Vascular Surgery, Southern Med Assn, Surgical Biology Club II, Allen O Whipple Surgical Soc; mem bd visitors: Stanford Univ; trust: Commn Future Structure Veterans Health Care *CLUB AFFIL* Rotary

Hugh McMaster Chapman: vchmn, trust *B* Spartanburg SC 1932 *ED* Univ NC BS 1955; Rutgers Univ Grad Sch Banking 1966 *CURR EMPL* chmn: NationsBank S *CORP AFFIL* chmn: NationsBank FL NA, NationsBank GA NA, NationsBank TN NA; dir: Inman Mills, SCANA Corp, Spartan Mills *NONPR AFFIL* trust: Thomas Jefferson Meml Fdn

John Hope Franklin: trust *B* Rentiesville OK 1915 *ED* Fisk Univ AB 1935; Harvard Univ AM 1936; Harvard Univ PhD 1941 *NONPR AFFIL* dir: DuSable Mus; fellow: Am Academy Arts & Sciences, Southern Historical Assn; mem: Am Assn Univ Profs, Am Historical Assn, Am Philosophical Soc, Am Studies Assn, Assn Study Negro Life & History, Org Am Historians, Phi Alpha Theta, Phi Beta Kappa

Richard Hampton Jenrette: trust *B* Raleigh NC 1929 *ED* Univ NC BA 1951; Harvard Univ MBA 1957 *CURR EMPL* chmn, ceo: Equitable Cos Inc *CORP AFFIL* chmn: Donaldson Lufkin & Jenrette; chmn, ceo: Equitable Life Assurance Soc US *NONPR AFFIL* chmn: Adv Counc Historic Preservation, Historic Hudson Valley; dir: Bus Fdn NC, White House Endowment Fund; mem: Inst Chartered Fin Analysts, NY Soc Security Analysts, Phi Beta Kappa, Securities Indus Assn; trust: Natl Trust Historic Preservation, NY Historical Soc, Univ NC *CLUB AFFIL* Brook, Carolina YC, Harvard, Links, Univ *PHIL AFFIL* pres, dir: Richard Hampton Jenrette Foundation; trust: Rockefeller Foundation

Mary Duke Trent Jones: trust *PHIL AFFIL* 2nd vchmn, asst secy, asst treas, trust: Mary Duke Biddle Foundation

Frank H. Kenan: trust emeritus *B* Atlanta GA 1912 *ED* Univ NC BS 1935 *CURR EMPL* chmn, treas, ceo, dir: Kenan Transport Co *CORP AFFIL* dir: Flagler Sys Inc, Kenan Oil Co *PHIL AFFIL* pres, dir: Kenan Family Foundation; trust: William R. Kenan, Jr. Charitable Trust, Randleigh Foundation Trust

Thomas Stephen Kenan III: trust *B* Durham NC 1937 *ED* Univ NC BA 1959 *PHIL AFFIL* secy, treas, trust, secy comm investments: Mary Duke Biddle Foundation; dir, vp, treas: Kenan Family Foundation; trust: William R. Kenan, Jr. Charitable Trust, Ran-

dleigh Foundation Trust *CLUB AFFIL* Breakers Beach & GC, Hope Valley CC, Treyburn GC & CC, Univ

Juanita Morris Kreps: trust *B* Lynch KY 1921 *ED* Berea Coll AB 1942; Duke Univ MA 1944; Duke Univ PhD 1948 *CORP AFFIL* chmn bd overseers: Teachers Ins & Annuity Assn; dir: Zurn Indus *NONPR AFFIL* chmn bd oversees: Coll Retirement Equities Fund; fellow: Am Academy Arts & Sciences, Gerontological Soc; mem: Am Assn Univ Profs, Am Assn Univ Women, Am Econ Assn, Natl Manpower Policy Task Force, Southern Econ Assn; mem exec comm: Indus Rels Res Assn; trust: Berea Coll

Thomas A. Langford: trust *B* Winston-Salem NC 1929 *ED* Davidson Coll AB 1951; Duke Univ BD 1954; Duke Univ PhD 1958 *NONPR AFFIL* adjunct prof: Duke Univ

William B. McGuire: trust emeritus

Charles F. Myers, Jr.: trust *B* Charleston WV 1911 *ED* Davidson Coll BA 1933; Harvard Univ 1935 *CORP AFFIL* dir: Richardson-Vicks

Russell M. Robinson II: trust *B* Charlotte NC 1932 *ED* Duke Univ Sch Law LLB 1956; Princeton Univ *CURR EMPL* ptnr: Robinson Bradshaw & Hinson *NONPR AFFIL* mem: Am Bar Assn, NC Bar Assn

James Cuthbert Self, Sr.: trust *B* Greenwood SC 1919 *ED* Citadel BS 1941 *CURR EMPL* chmn exec comm, dir: Greenwood Mills *CORP AFFIL* dir: Duke Power Co, Greenwood Motor Lines, SC Natl Bank; pres: Textile Investments Co *NONPR AFFIL* life mem bd trusts: Clemson Univ; mem: Am Textile Mfrs Inst, NY Cotton Exchange, SC Textile Mfrs Assn *CLUB AFFIL* Metropolitan *PHIL AFFIL* pres, trust: Self Foundation

Mary Duke Biddle Trent Semans: chmn, trust *B* New York NY *PHIL AFFIL* vchmn, chmn grants comm, don daughter: Mary Duke Biddle Foundation

Louis Cornelius Stephens, Jr.: vchmn, trust *B* Dunn NC 1921 *ED* Univ NC BS 1942; Harvard Univ MBA 1947 *CURR EMPL* pres, ceo, dir: Pilot Life Ins Co *CORP AFFIL* dir: Jefferson-Pilot Corp, Jefferson-Pilot Southern Fire Casuality Cos, Jefferson-Pilot Title Ins Co; pres, dir: JP Investment Mgmt Co; treas: JP Growth Fund *NONPR AFFIL* dir: Belmont Abbey Coll, Ecumenical Inst, NC Leadership Inst, Res Triangle Inst, Salem Coll Academy; dir excellence fund: Univ NC Greensboro

E. Craig Wall, Jr.: trust

Jere Wathen Witherspoon: exec dir *B* Shepherdstown WV 1932 *ED* Davidson Coll BS 1954; Washington Univ MHA 1961 *NONPR AFFIL* chmn, bd deacons: Myers Park Presbyterian Church; comm chmn: Mecklenburg County Area Mental Health Bd; comm chmn, dir: NC League Nursing; fellow: Am Coll Healthcare Execs; mem: Am Hosp Assn; mem study comm AIDS: Un Way; pres, dir: Hospice Charlotte; trust: Southeastern Counc Fdns; vp, dir: Hospice NC

APPLICATION INFORMATION
Initial Approach:

Applicants should mail a letter of inquiry describing the proposed project. Eligible requests will be referred to the appropriate program officer in education, health care, child care, or the rural Methodist church.

A program officer may request a full proposal, including project description, budget, funding sources, proof of tax-exempt status, audited financial statements, list of board members, and other pertinent information.

Applications may be submitted at any time. The board makes final decisions at its meetings which are held monthly.

Applications are screened by trustee committees and sent with recommendations to the full board. Letters of inquiry are usually answered within thirty days. If a meeting is desirable, the program officer will arrange it. It may take between two and six months for a final decision on a proposal.

OTHER THINGS TO KNOW
In addition to its grant-making activities, the endowment also sponsors conferences, seminars/workshops, and technical assistance consulting for eligible beneficiaries. The endowment's library is designated a Foundation Center cooperating collection. Their library is open to grantseekers daily, Monday through Friday. Grantsmanship seminars are also held for area nonprofits.

PUBLICATIONS
Annual report, general information brochure, and magazine (Issues)

GRANTS ANALYSIS
Total Grants: $50,500,000*
Number of Grants: 900*
Highest Grant: $2,898,427
Average Grant: $56,111*
Typical Range: $10,000 to $200,000
Disclosure Period: 1994

Note: The total grants, number of grants, and average grant figures are estimates provided by the endowment. Recent grants are derived from a partial 1994 grants list.

RECENT GRANTS

General

2,898,427	Hospitals in North Carolina and South Carolina — for reimbursement of $1 for each day of charity care rendered at 179 hospitals
1,318,000	Child Care Institutions in North Carolina and South Carolina — for general operating support to 46 organizations
1,000,000	Duke University Medical Center, Durham, NC — to construct the Medical Sciences Research Building, a 90,000 square-foot biomedical science research facility
750,000	Duke University Medical Center, Durham, NC — to support the Levine Science

250,000 | Research Center, a 170,000 square-foot facility for interdisciplinary research for the School of the Environment, the Department of Computer Science, and components of biomedical engineering

250,000 Alamance Health Services, Burlington, NC — to construct a single new hospital to replace both Alamance County and Alamance Memorial hospitals

Duke Power Co. / Duke Power Co. Foundation

Revenue: $4.48 billion
Employees: 18,274
Headquarters: Charlotte, NC
SIC Major Group: Electric Services

CONTACT
S. Dock Kornegay, Jr.
Executive Vice President
Duke Power Co. Foundation
422 S Church St.
PB-03-Q
Charlotte, NC 28242-0001
(704) 382-7200

FINANCIAL SUMMARY
Recent Giving: $6,300,000 (1995 est.); $6,300,000 (1994 approx.); $6,651,007 (1993)

Assets: $920,028 (1993); $6,427,748 (1992); $370,905 (1991)

Gifts Received: $1,028,747 (1993); $12,487,691 (1992); $6,236,620 (1990)

Fiscal Note: All contributions are made through the foundation. Above figures exclude nonmonetary support. In 1993, contributions were received from the Duke Power Company ($1,018,747) and Nantahala Power & Light Company ($10,000).

EIN: 58-1586283

CONTRIBUTIONS SUMMARY
Typical Recipients: • *Arts & Humanities:* Arts Associations & Councils, Arts Centers, Arts Festivals, Arts Funds, Community Arts, Dance, Ethnic & Folk Arts, Historic Preservation, Libraries, Museums/Galleries, Music, Opera, Performing Arts, Theater • *Civic & Public Affairs:* Business/Free Enterprise, Chambers of Commerce, Civil Rights, Economic Development, Housing, Legal Aid, Municipalities/Towns, Professional & Trade Associations, Public Policy, Rural Affairs, Safety, Urban & Community Affairs, Women's Affairs, Zoos/Aquariums • *Education:* Agricultural Education, Arts/Humanities Education, Business Education, Colleges & Universities, Economic Education, Education Associations, Education Funds, Elementary Education (Private), Engineering/Technological Education, General, Literacy, Minority Education, Private Education (Precollege), Public Education (Precollege), Religious Education, Sci-

ence/Mathematics Education, Social Sciences Education, Student Aid • *Environment:* General • *Health:* Emergency/Ambulance Services, Health Policy/Cost Containment, Health Organizations, Hospices, Hospitals, Mental Health, Nutrition, Single-Disease Health Associations • *International:* International Peace & Security Issues, International Relations • *Religion:* Ministries, Religious Welfare • *Science:* Science Exhibits & Fairs, Scientific Centers & Institutes, Scientific Organizations • *Social Services:* Animal Protection, Child Welfare, Community Centers, Community Service Organizations, Counseling, Emergency Relief, Family Planning, Family Services, Food/Clothing Distribution, People with Disabilities, Recreation & Athletics, Senior Services, Substance Abuse, United Funds/United Ways, Youth Organizations

Grant Types: capital, challenge, conference/seminar, employee matching gifts, endowment, general support, project, and scholarship

Nonmonetary Support Types: donated equipment, loaned executives, and workplace solicitation

Note: No estimate is available for value of nonmonetary support, and it is not included above. Nonmonetary support is provided by both the company and the foundation.

Geographic Distribution: mainly near headquarters and operating locations; organizations not located in North Carolina or South Carolina providing substantial benefits to these states may be considered

Operating Locations: DE (Wilmington), NC (Burlington, Chapel Hill, Charlotte, Durham, Gastonia, Greensboro, Hendersonville, Hickory, High Point, Rutherfordton, Salisbury, Winston-Salem), SC (Anderson, Greenville, Lancaster, Spartanburg)

CORP. OFFICERS
William Humphrey Grigg: *B* Shelby NC 1932 *ED* Duke Univ AB 1954; Duke Univ LLB 1958 *CURR EMPL* chmn, ceo: Duke Power Co *CORP AFFIL* dir: Aegis Ins Svcs, NationsFunds Inc; vp, dir: Church St Capital Corp *NONPR AFFIL* dir: Fdn Carolinas, Johnson C Smith Univ Res Triangle Pk, YMCA; mem: Am Bar Assn, NC Bar Assn; trust: Eugene M Cole Fdn, Methodist Home Aged, Pfeiffer Coll *CLUB AFFIL* Charlotte CC

Don E. Hatley: *CURR EMPL* vp pub aff: Duke Power Co

GIVING OFFICERS
William Humphrey Grigg: chmn *CURR EMPL* chmn, ceo: Duke Power Co (see above)

David Hauser: treas

S. Dock Kornegay: vp, exec dir

Robert S. Lilien: secy *B* Raleigh NC 1947 *ED* Duke Univ AB 1969; Univ NC JD 1975 *CURR EMPL* ptnr: Robinson Bradshaw & Hinson *NONPR AFFIL* mem: Am Bar Assn, AM Inst CPAs, NC Assn CPAs, NC Bar Assn, NC Bar Assn, Order Coif

S. L. Love: asst treas

Phyllis T. Simpson: asst secy

APPLICATION INFORMATION
Initial Approach: *Initial Contact:* brief letter or proposal *Include Information On:* description of the organization, amount requested, purpose for which funds are sought, recently audited financial statement, proof of tax-exempt status, list of other supporting corporations and levels of such support *Deadlines:* none

Restrictions on Giving: Foundation does not support individuals (except within scholarship programs); political candidates; hospitals supported by the Duke Endowment; single sectarian or denominational religious, veterans, or fraternal organizations; or projects, institutions, or organizations where the foundation would be the only donor. Foundation generally does not support organizations primarily supported through tax revenues or foundations whose contributions programs duplicate Duke Power Company Foundation contributions.

OTHER THINGS TO KNOW
The foundation has increased its limit on matching gifts to $12,000 a year per employee. The matching gift program is restricted to higher education, elementary education, and educational foundations.

GRANTS ANALYSIS
Total Grants: $6,651,007
Number of Grants: 1,116
Highest Grant: $400,000
Average Grant: $5,960
Typical Range: $500 to $15,000
Disclosure Period: 1993

Note: Recent grants are derived from a 1993 Form 990.

RECENT GRANTS
General
264,912 | Crisis Assistance Ministry, Charlotte, NC
250,500 | United Way of Central Carolinas, Charlotte, NC
154,503 | Crisis Control Ministry, Winston-Salem, NC
122,400 | Independent College Fund of North Carolina, Winston-Salem, NC
117,248 | Greensboro Urban Ministry, Greensboro, NC

Ferebee Endowment, Percy O.

CONTACT
Linda Tilley
Percy O. Ferebee Endowment
c/o Wachovia Bank of NC, NA
PO Box 3099
Winston-Salem, NC 27150
(919) 770-5372

FINANCIAL SUMMARY
Recent Giving: $71,840 (1993); $74,200 (1992); $143,881 (1990)

Assets: $2,673,577 (1993); $2,558,051 (1992); $2,156,197 (1990)

Gifts Received: $1,302 (1988)

EIN: 56-6118992

CONTRIBUTIONS SUMMARY
Donor(s): the late Percy Ferebee

Typical Recipients: • *Arts & Humanities:* Arts Associations & Councils, Libraries, Public Broadcasting • *Civic & Public Affairs:* Employment/Job Training, Municipalities/Towns, Urban & Community Affairs • *Education:* Private Education (Precollege), Secondary Education (Public), Student Aid • *Health:* Hospitals, Long-Term Care, Nutrition, Preventive Medicine/Wellness Organizations • *International:* International Relations • *Social Services:* Animal Protection, Community Service Organizations, Food/Clothing Distribution, Homes, Shelters/Homelessness

Grant Types: capital, emergency, and seed money

Geographic Distribution: focus on Cherokee, Clay, Graham, Jackson, Macon, and Swain counties, NC, and the Cherokee Indian Reservation

GIVING OFFICERS
Wachovia Bank of NC, NA: trust

Mrs. Frela Owl Beck: awards adv comm

Ty W. Burnette: awards adv comm

James Conely: awards adv comm

Maggie Alice Sandlin Crisp: awards adv comm

J. Smith Howell: awards adv comm

John Parris: chmn, awards adv comm

John Waldroup: awards adv comm

APPLICATION INFORMATION
Initial Approach: Application form required. Deadline is October 1.

OTHER THINGS TO KNOW
The foundation primarily provides scholarships to regional high school students to pursue higher education.

PUBLICATIONS
Informational brochure

GRANTS ANALYSIS
Total Grants: $71,840

Number of Grants: 4

Highest Grant: $12,500

Disclosure Period: 1993

Note: Recent grants are derived from a 1993 Form 990. Number of grants figure does not include scholarships to individuals.

RECENT GRANTS
General

12,500	Manna Food Bank, Asheville, NC — purchase of new warehouse
12,000	Town of Murphy Hospital Authority, Murphy, NC —
2,500	Murphy Medical Center, nursing home solarium Industrial Opportunities, Marble, NC

Fieldcrest Cannon Inc. / Fieldcrest Cannon Foundation

Former Foundation Name: Fieldcrest Foundation

Revenue: $1.0 billion

Employees: 17,407

Parent Company: Amoskeag Co.

Headquarters: Eden, NC

SIC Major Group: Broadwoven Fabric Mills—Cotton, Broadwoven Fabric Mills—Manmade, Finishing Plants—Cotton, and Finishing Plants—Manmade

CONTACT
C.C. Barnhardt, Jr.
Secretary
Fieldcrest Cannon Foundation
326 E Stadium Dr.
Eden, NC 27288
(910) 627-3046

FINANCIAL SUMMARY
Recent Giving: $635,280 (1992); $783,483 (1990); $868,219 (1989)

Assets: $1,993,650 (1992); $2,255,780 (1990); $2,348,422 (1989)

Gifts Received: $445,755 (1992)

Fiscal Note: All figures reflect foundation contributions only. Company does not reveal information on direct giving. In 1992, gifts were received from Fieldcrest Cannon Inc..

EIN: 56-6046659

CONTRIBUTIONS SUMMARY
Typical Recipients: • *Arts & Humanities:* Arts Associations & Councils, Arts Festivals, Libraries, Museums/Galleries, Music • *Civic & Public Affairs:* Employment/Job Training, Law & Justice, Professional & Trade Associations, Safety, Zoos/Aquariums • *Education:* Business Education, Colleges & Universities, Community & Junior Colleges, Education Funds, Elementary Education (Private), Public Education (Precollege), Science/Mathematics Education, Secondary Education (Public), Student Aid • *Environment:* General • *Health:* Cancer, Emergency/Ambulance Services, Health Organizations, Heart, Hospitals • *Religion:* Religious Welfare • *Social Services:* Child Welfare, Community Centers, Community Service Organizations, Delinquency & Criminal Rehabilitation, People with Disabilities, Recreation & Athletics, United Funds/United Ways, Volunteer Services, Youth Organizations

Grant Types: capital, operating expenses, project, and scholarship

Note: Scholarships are available only to children of employees.

Geographic Distribution: primarily to organizations in company plant communities

Operating Locations: AL (Phoenix City), CA, GA (Columbus, Lyerly), NC (Concord, Greensboro, Kannapolis, Laurel Hill, Salisbury, Smithfield), NY (New York), PA, SC (Belton, Landrum, York), TX, VA (Fieldale)

CORP. OFFICERS
James M. Fitzgibbons: *B* Boston MA 1934 *ED* Harvard Univ AB 1956; Harvard Univ PMD 1963 *CURR EMPL* chmn, ceo: Fieldcrest Cannon Inc *CORP AFFIL* chmn: Howes Leather Co; dir: Amoskeag Co, Barrett Resources Corp, Fiduciary Trust Co Boston, Lumber Mutual Ins Co; pres, dir: Downeast Securities Corp; trust: Boston Co Funds *NONPR AFFIL* dir: Boston Co Funds

Charles G. Horn: *B* Decatur IL 1939 *ED* Univ Southern CA BS 1963; Harvard Univ Advanced Mgmt Program 1981 *CURR EMPL* pres, coo: Fieldcrest Cannon Inc *CLUB AFFIL* Harvard CC

Chris L. Kametches: *B* Raleigh NC 1935 *ED* NC St Univ 1959; Univ VA 1972 *CURR EMPL* sr vp: Fieldcrest Cannon Inc *NONPR AFFIL* dir: NC Textile Mfrs Assn; mem: Am Textile Mfrs Inst; mem intl trade policy comm: Natl Cotton Counc Am

C. Edward Midgley, Jr.: *B* Yonkers NY 1937 *ED* Princeton Univ BA 1958; Harvard Univ MBA 1962 *CURR EMPL* vchmn: Fieldcrest Cannon Inc *CORP AFFIL* dir: AT Walker Corp, Bankers Trust Co; trust: Dumaine; vchmn: Amoskeag Co

Thomas Robert Staab: *B* Beaver Falls PA 1942 *ED* Univ Pittsburgh BBA 1964; Univ Pittsburgh MBA 1965 *CURR EMPL* vp fin, cfo: Fieldcrest Cannon Inc *CORP AFFIL* mem adv bd: Arkwright Mutual Ins Co *NONPR AFFIL* mem: Am Inst CPAs, Am Textile Mfrs Inst, NC Textile Mfrs Assn, PA Inst CPAs

GIVING OFFICERS
C. C. Barnhardt, Jr.: secy

Marion K. Doss: dir *B* Wildwood FL 1939 *ED* GA Inst Tech BS 1961; Univ GA LLB 1963 *CURR EMPL* vp, secy, gen couns: Fieldcrest Cannon Inc *NONPR AFFIL* mem: Am Bar Assn, Am Textile Mfrs Inst, Am Trial Lawyers Assn, Atlanta Bar Assn, Corp Counc Assn Greater Atlanta, Defense Res Inst, GA Assn Plaintiffs Trial Atty, GA Bar Assn, NC Bar Assn, NC Chamber Commerce, NC Trial Lawyers Assn, Rockingham County Bar Assn

W. F. Evans: dir

Kenneth William Fraser, Jr.: treas, dir *B* New York NY 1937 *ED* Cornell Univ BME 1960; NY Univ MBA 1968 *CURR EMPL* sr vp fin: Fieldcrest Cannon Inc *CORP AFFIL* dir: Branch Banking & Trust Co *NONPR AFFIL* mem: Fin Execs Inst; treas: YMCA Eden; trust: Morehead Meml Hosp *CLUB AFFIL* Rotary, Union League

Charles G. Horn: pres, dir *CURR EMPL* pres, coo: Fieldcrest Cannon Inc (see above)

Chris L. Kametches: vp, dir *CURR EMPL* sr vp: Fieldcrest Cannon Inc (see above)

Osborne L. Raines, Jr.: dir *B* Portsmouth VA 1941 *ED* VA Polytech Inst & St Univ BS 1963; Univ NC MBA 1964 *CURR EMPL* vp human rels: Fieldcrest Cannon Inc

J. J. Riley: dir

Thomas Robert Staab: asst treas *CURR EMPL* vp fin, cfo: Fieldcrest Cannon Inc (see above)

APPLICATION INFORMATION

Initial Approach: *Initial Contact:* organizations near company locations can submit form to management of local operation; other groups can forward form to company headquarters in Eden, NC *Include Information On:* IRS status; total amount organization is seeking, project to be funded, amounts pledged and received from other agencies; reason foundation has been chosen as funding source; and benefits project will have on company and its employees *Deadlines:* on calendar-year basis; generally cannot respond in current year to requests made after January 1; scholarship deadline: March 1; grants-in-aid: July 1

Restrictions on Giving: Recipients must be tax-exempt under 501(c)(3).

Formal presentations are not accepted.

GRANTS ANALYSIS

Total Grants: $635,280

Number of Grants: 81

Highest Grant: $179,980

Average Grant: $7,843

Typical Range: $500 to $10,000

Disclosure Period: 1992

Note: Fiscal information reflects foundation contributions only. Recent grants are derived from a 1992 Form 990.

RECENT GRANTS

Library

500	Chattoga County Georgia Library, Summerville, GA

General

179,980	Kannapolis North Carolina United Fund, Kannapolis, NC
67,000	YMCA, Eden, NC
36,000	Fieldcrest, Eden, NC — scholarships 1990
33,300	Fieldcrest, Eden, NC — scholarships 1989
30,600	Fieldcrest, Eden, NC — scholarships 1991

Finch Foundation, Doak

CONTACT
J. C. Dorety
Trustee
Doak Finch Fdn.
10 Welloskie Dr.
Thomasville, NC 27360
(704) 374-7581

FINANCIAL SUMMARY

Recent Giving: $152,000 (fiscal 1993); $207,300 (fiscal 1990); $190,300 (fiscal 1989)

Assets: $3,456,452 (fiscal 1993); $2,800,409 (fiscal 1990); $2,981,675 (fiscal 1989)

EIN: 56-6042823

CONTRIBUTIONS SUMMARY

Donor(s): the late Doak Finch

Typical Recipients: • *Arts & Humanities:* Arts Associations & Councils, Libraries • *Civic & Public Affairs:* General, Housing, Municipalities/Towns • *Education:* Community & Junior Colleges, Private Education (Precollege), Public Education (Precollege), Secondary Education (Public) • *Health:* Hospitals • *Religion:* Churches, Religious Welfare • *Social Services:* Child Welfare, Community Service Organizations, Crime Prevention, Food/Clothing Distribution, Homes, Recreation & Athletics, Substance Abuse, United Funds/United Ways, YMCA/YWCA/YMHA/YWHA, Youth Organizations

Grant Types: general support

Geographic Distribution: limited to the Thomasville, NC, area

GIVING OFFICERS

J. C. Dorety: trust

Helen Finch: trust

Richard J. Finch: trust

Jane F. Turner: trust

David R. Williams: trust

APPLICATION INFORMATION
Initial Approach: Send brief letter describing program. Deadline is February 1.

GRANTS ANALYSIS
Total Grants: $152,000

Number of Grants: 18

Highest Grant: $40,000

Typical Range: $2,000 to $30,000

Disclosure Period: fiscal year ending October 31, 1993

Note: Recent grants are derived from a fiscal 1993 Form 990.

RECENT GRANTS

General

40,000	Memorial United Methodist Church, Thomasville, NC
30,000	YMCA, Thomasville, NC
15,000	Thomasville Recreation, Thomasville, NC
10,000	Thomasville City Schools, Thomasville, NC
5,000	Children's Home Society, Thomasville, NC

Finch Foundation, Thomas Austin

CONTACT
Linda G. Tilley
Trustee
Thomas Austin Finch Fdn.
c/o Wachovia Bank of NC, N.A.
PO Box 3099
Winston-Salem, NC 27150-1022
(919) 770-5352

FINANCIAL SUMMARY
Recent Giving: $310,000 (1993); $351,000 (1992); $340,861 (1990)

Assets: 7,752,745 (1993); $7,484,912 (1992); $6,160,863 (1990)

EIN: 56-6037907

CONTRIBUTIONS SUMMARY
Donor(s): Ernestine L. Finch Mobley, Thomas Austin Finch, Jr.

Typical Recipients: • *Arts & Humanities:* Arts Associations & Councils, Libraries • *Civic & Public Affairs:* Community Foundations, Housing, Municipalities/Towns • *Education:* Colleges & Universities, Community & Junior Colleges, Private Education (Precollege), Public Education (Precollege), Secondary Education (Public) • *Health:* Hospitals • *Religion:* Churches, Religious Welfare • *Social Services:* Community Service Organizations, Crime Prevention, Domestic Violence, Food/Clothing Distribution, Senior Services, United Funds/United Ways, YMCA/YWCA/YMHA/YWHA, Youth Organizations

Grant Types: capital, general support, multi-year/continuing support, and operating expenses

Geographic Distribution: limited to Thomasville, NC, area

GIVING OFFICERS
Wachovia Bank of NC, NA: trust

Kermit Cloniger: trust

David Finch: chmn *B* Des Moines IA 1941 *ED* IA St Univ 1965; Univ Chicago MBA 1967 *CURR EMPL* exec vp pub & employee rels: Harris Trust & Savings Bank *CORP AFFIL* dir: Derivatives Markets Mgmt, Harris Bank Hindsdale, Harris Brokerage Svcs, Harris Futures Corp *NONPR AFFIL* mem: Corp Fiduciaries Assn IL; trust: Roosevelt Univ

John L. Finch: trust

Sumner Finch: trust

Meredith S. Person: trust

Linda G. Tilley: trust

APPLICATION INFORMATION
Initial Approach: Application form required. There are no deadlines.

Restrictions on Giving: Limited to the Thomasville, NC, area.

PUBLICATIONS
Informational Brochure (including application guidelines)

GRANTS ANALYSIS
Total Grants: $310,000

Number of Grants: 20

Highest Grant: $41,460

Typical Range: $2,000 to $10,000

Disclosure Period: 1993

Note: Recent grants are derived from a 1993 Form 990.

RECENT GRANTS

General

60,000	Westchester Academy, High Point, NC
41,460	Tom A. Finch Community YMCA, Thomasville, NC — endowment fund
30,000	Memorial United Methodist Church, Thomasville, NC
20,000	Community General Hospital of Thomasville, Thomasville, NC
20,000	Habitat for Humanity, Thomasville, NC

First Union Corp. / First Union Foundation

Revenue: $6.25 billion

Employees: 23,459

Headquarters: Charlotte, NC

SIC Major Group: Holding Companies Nec and Mortgage Bankers & Correspondents

CONTACT
Judith N. Allison

Vice President, Director Corporate Contributions

First Union Corp.

Two First Union Plz.

Charlotte, NC 28288-0143

(704) 374-6649

Note: The company's World Wide Web address is http://www.firstunion.com

FINANCIAL SUMMARY
Recent Giving: $8,600,000 (1995 est.); $7,475,846 (1994); $7,325,645 (1993)

Assets: $465,816 (1993); $431,113 (1992)

Gifts Received: $7,238,220 (1993)

Fiscal Note: Company gives primarily through the foundation. In 1994, foundation giving totaled approximately $6,447,000, and direct giving totaled about $1,029,000. In 1993, giving figure includes foundation matching gifts to educational institutions totaling $275,250. Above figures exclude nonmonetary support. In 1993, contributions were received from First Union Corp. ($6,800,000), Dominion Charitable Trust ($116,784.04), estate of York Cress ($97,500), Savannah Charitable Trust, (96,884.62), and miscellaneous contributions of less than $70,000.

EIN: 56-6288589

CONTRIBUTIONS SUMMARY
Typical Recipients: • *Arts & Humanities:* Arts Associations & Councils, Arts Centers, Arts Festivals, Arts Funds, Arts Institutes, Community Arts, Dance, Ethnic & Folk Arts, Historic Preservation, Libraries, Literary Arts, Museums/Galleries, Music, Opera, Performing Arts, Public Broadcasting, Theater, Visual Arts • *Civic & Public Affairs:* Business/Free Enterprise, Clubs, Economic Development, Economic Policy, Employment/Job Training, Hispanic Affairs, Housing, Municipalities/Towns, Philanthropic Organizations, Safety, Urban & Community Affairs, Zoos/Aquariums • *Education:* Agricultural Education, Arts/Humanities Education, Business Education, Colleges & Universities, Community & Junior Colleges, Continuing Education, Economic Education, Education Funds, Faculty Development, Legal Education, Literacy, Medical Education, Minority Education, Preschool Education, Public Education (Precollege), Science/Mathematics Education, Social Sciences Education, Special Education • *Environment:* General • *Health:* Children's Health/Hospitals, Emergency/Ambulance Services, Geriatric Health, Health Funds, Health Organizations, Hospices, Hospitals, Medical Rehabilitation, Mental Health, Research/Studies Institutes, Single-Disease Health Associations • *Religion:* Churches • *Science:* Observatories & Planetariums, Science Exhibits & Fairs, Science Museums, Scientific Centers & Institutes, Scientific Organizations • *Social Services:* Child Welfare, Community Centers, Community Service Organizations, Counseling, Day Care, Delinquency & Criminal Rehabilitation, Domestic Violence, Emergency Relief, Family Planning, Family Services, Food/Clothing Distribution, Homes, People with Disabilities, Senior Services, Shelters/Homelessness, Substance Abuse, United Funds/United Ways, Volunteer Services, Youth Organizations

Grant Types: capital, emergency, employee matching gifts, endowment, fellowship, general support, matching, and multiyear/continuing support

Note: Employee matching gift ratio: 1 to 1, for education only.

Nonmonetary Support Types: donated equipment, in-kind services, loaned employees, and loaned executives

Note: Value of nonmonetary support is not available.

Geographic Distribution: in headquarters and operating locations only

Operating Locations: DC, FL, GA, MD, NC (Charlotte), SC, TN, VA

CORP. OFFICERS
Edward Elliott Crutchfield, Jr.: *B* Detroit MI 1941 *ED* Davidson Coll BA 1963; Univ PA Wharton Sch MBA 1965 *CURR EMPL* chmn, ceo: First Union Corp *CORP AFFIL* dir: BellSouth Telecommun Inc, Bernhardt Furniture, Bernhardt Indus, Liberty Corp, Southern Bell Telephone Co, VF Corp; vchmn, dir: First Union Natl Bank *NONPR AFFIL* bd deacons: Myers Pk Presbyterian Church; bd mgrs: Charlotte Meml Hosp; bd visitors: Davidson Coll; dir: Charlotte Latin Sch, Salvation Army, Un Commun Svcs; mem: Am Bankers Assn, Am Textile Mfrs Assn, Am Textile Mfrs Inst, Assn Reserve City Bankers, Charlotte Chamber Commerce, NC Bankers Assn, Young Pres Org; trust: Mint Mus Art, Nature Conservancy NC *CLUB AFFIL* Charlotte CC, Charlotte City, Linville GC

John R. Georgius: *B* 1944 *ED* GA St Univ BBA 1967 *CURR EMPL* pres, dir: First Union Corp

GIVING OFFICERS
James A. Abbott: dir *B* Raleigh NC 1939 *ED* Univ NC BA 1961; Northwestern Univ Sch Mortgage Banking 1966 *CURR EMPL* pres, ceo: First Union Mortgage Corp *NONPR AFFIL* mem: Mortgage Bankers Assn, Mortgage Bankers Carolinas

Judith N. Allison: vp, dir corp contributions

Robert Atwood: dir *B* 1940 *ED* Univ NC BS 1958; Univ NC Law Sch LLB 1964 *CURR EMPL* exec vp, cfo: First Union Corp

Edward Elliott Crutchfield, Jr.: dir *CURR EMPL* chmn, ceo: First Union Corp (see above)

Frank H. Dunn, Jr.: dir *B* 1937 *ED* Univ NC MBA; Wake Forest Univ *CURR EMPL* chmn, ceo: First Un Natl Bank NC

Malcolm E. Everett III: dir *B* 1946 *ED* Univ GA *CURR EMPL* pres, dir: First Un Natl Bank NC

John R. Georgius: dir *CURR EMPL* pres, dir: First Union Corp (see above)

Don R. Johnson: dir

H. Burt Melton: dir *B* Henrietta NC 1942 *ED* Wake Forest Univ 1964 *CURR EMPL* exec vp: First Un Corp

Malcolm T. Murray, Jr.: dir

Alvin T. Sale: dir

APPLICATION INFORMATION
Initial Approach: *Initial Contact:* letter or proposal to local First Union city executive *Include Information On:* description of the organization (purpose, history, and current activities); current budget, including sources of income and audited financial report; list of key management and board of directors; relationship with company, including past contributions; description of program for which funding is sought (purpose, population served, plan of action and time frame, total funding needed and projected sources, amount requested from company, method of evaluation, and plans for continuance); and proof of tax-exempt status *Deadlines:* by September 1 for consideration in following year's budget

Restrictions on Giving: Capital grants made only when there is a community-wide fund-raising campaign that includes the entire business community. Commitments are for one year only, unless a multiyear pledge is made. Except for united fund drives and long-term pledges, grants are not made to the same organization for more than three consecutive years. Grants are made directly to community organizations for known projects, not to intermediary organizations for future projects.

No grants made to individuals; political causes or candidates; religious, veteran, or fraternal organizations; retirement homes or communities; organizations receiving support through a united fund (except for capital drives approved by capital funds board); organizations without 501(c)(3) tax-exempt status; dinners or special events; goodwill advertising; or national organizations, except through their local affiliates.

OTHER THINGS TO KNOW
Special consideration given to organizations or causes in which company employees are involved.

PUBLICATIONS
Corporate Contributions pamphlet

GRANTS ANALYSIS
Total Grants: $7,475,846

Number of Grants: 1,708

Average Grant: $4,377

Typical Range: $500 to $10,000

Disclosure Period: 1994

Note: Recent grants are derived from a 1993 Form 990.

RECENT GRANTS

Library

25,000	Belmont University, Nashville, TN

General

775,013	Davidson College, Davidson, NC
680,590	Johnson C. Smith University, Charlotte, NC
265,000	United Way Dade County, Miami, FL
228,300	We Will Rebuild, Miami, FL
200,000	South Carolina Aquarium, Charleston, SC

First Union National Bank of Florida

Assets: $27.77 billion
Employees: 7,835
Parent Company: First Union Corp.
Headquarters: Jacksonville, FL
SIC Major Group: National Commercial Banks

CONTACT
Jim Robertson
Vice President & Director, Marketing
First Union National Bank of Florida
301 S Tryon St. T-3
Charlotte, NC 28202
(904) 383-1400

FINANCIAL SUMMARY
Recent Giving: $2,100,000 (1994 est.); $2,100,000 (1993 approx.)

Fiscal Note: Company gives directly. Above figures exclude nonmonetary support.

CONTRIBUTIONS SUMMARY
Typical Recipients: • *Arts & Humanities:* Arts Associations & Councils, Arts Funds, General, Libraries, Museums/Galleries, Performing Arts, Public Broadcasting • *Civic & Public Affairs:* General, Housing • *Education:* Colleges & Universities, Continuing Education, Elementary Education (Private), General, Literacy, Public Education (Precollege) • *Environment:* General • *Health:* General, Health Organizations, Hospitals • *Social Services:* Community Service Organizations, General, Youth Organizations

Grant Types: employee matching gifts and general support

Nonmonetary Support Types: cause-related marketing & promotion, donated equipment, loaned employees, and loaned executives

Geographic Distribution: limited to Florida, with a focus on Jacksonville

Operating Locations: FL (Jacksonville)

CORP. OFFICERS
Byron E. Hodnett: *B* Langdale AL 1945 *ED* GA Inst Tech 1967; Univ NC Charlotte 1977 *CURR EMPL* chmn, ceo: First Un Natl Bank FL

GIVING OFFICERS
Jim Robertson: *CURR EMPL* vp, dir mktg: First Un Natl Bank FL

APPLICATION INFORMATION
Initial Approach: *Initial Contact:* clear and specific letter *Include Information On:* description of the organization, including purpose, history, and current activities; IRS letter showing 501(c)(3) status; current budget, including sources of income and audited financial statement; list of key management and board of directors; relationship with First Union, including contributions and volunteers; and description of program needing funding, including its purpose, population served, plan of action and time frame, total funding needed, projected sources for funding, amount requested from First Union, method of evaluation, and plans for continuance *Deadlines:* none

Restrictions on Giving: Does not support individuals, travel or conferences, political causes or candidates, organizations influencing legislation, religious organizations, veteran groups, fraternal organizations, retirement homes or communities, precollege private schools except through matching gifts program, United Way-supported organizations, and organizations other than tax-exempt as recognized by the IRS.

OTHER THINGS TO KNOW
First Union also operates giving programs in its Atlanta, GA; Charlotte, NC; Greenville, SC; Nashville, TN; and Roanoke, VA, offices. Requests in these areas should be sent to the corresponding location.

Capital grants are made only when a community-wide funding campaign involves the entire business community.

Grants will not be made for more than three consecutive years to one organization, except to United Way and multiyear commitments.

Grants are made directly to community organizations for known projects, and not to intermediary organizations for projects chosen in the future.

Special consideration is given to programs in which First Union employees volunteer, those that help children and youth in becoming self-sufficient adults, and those that help disadvantaged people overcome barriers.

PUBLICATIONS
Program brochure

Giles Foundation, Edward C.

CONTACT
Lucille P. Giles
President
Edward C. Giles Fdn.
PO Box 33056
Charlotte, NC 28233
(704) 376-1293

FINANCIAL SUMMARY
Recent Giving: $716,239 (1993); $655,268 (1992); $624,733 (1990)

Assets: $15,338,694 (1993); $15,982,410 (1992); $10,798,562 (1990)

EIN: 58-1450874

CONTRIBUTIONS SUMMARY
Donor(s): Lucille P. Giles

Typical Recipients: • *Arts & Humanities:* Libraries • *Civic & Public Affairs:* General, Philanthropic Organizations • *Health:* Health Organizations • *Religion:* Churches, Religious Organizations • *Social Services:* Community Service Organizations, Day Care, Food/Clothing Distribution, Homes, People with Disabilities, Shelters/Homelessness, United Funds/United Ways, Youth Organizations

Grant Types: general support and scholarship

Geographic Distribution: focus on NC

GIVING OFFICERS
Lucille P. Giles: pres

James Y. Preston: secy

APPLICATION INFORMATION
Initial Approach: Application form is required (include biographical, scholastic, extracurricular, civic, and financial information). Deadline is February 15.

Restrictions on Giving: Scholarship applicants must be descendents of employees of Caraustar Industries, Inc. and its subsidiaries.

PUBLICATIONS
Informational Brochure (including application guidelines)

GRANTS ANALYSIS
Total Grants: $716,239

Number of Grants: 2

Highest Grant: $490,000

Typical Range: $35,000 to $490,000

Disclosure Period: 1993

Note: Recent grants are derived from a 1993 Form 990.

RECENT GRANTS

General

490,000	Foundation for the Carolinas, Charlotte, NC
35,000	Hezekiah Alexander Fund

Glenn Foundation, Carrie C. and Lena V.

CONTACT
W. W. Dickson
Director
Carrie C. and Lena V. Glenn Fdn.
223 W Nash St.
Wilson, NC 27893

FINANCIAL SUMMARY
Recent Giving: $212,000 (fiscal 1992); $200,000 (fiscal 1991); $185,000 (fiscal 1990)

Assets: $5,045,855 (fiscal 1992); $5,007,300 (fiscal 1991); $4,118,218 (fiscal 1990)

EIN: 23-7140170

CONTRIBUTIONS SUMMARY
Typical Recipients: • *Arts & Humanities:* Libraries, Public Broadcasting • *Civic & Public Affairs:* Employment/Job Training • *Education:* Colleges & Universities, Literacy, Medical Education, Private Education (Precollege), Public Education (Precollege) • *Health:* Health Organizations, Hospices, Single-Disease Health Associations • *Religion:* Churches • *Social Services:* Child Welfare, Emergency Relief, Shelters/Homelessness, United Funds/United Ways

Grant Types: emergency and general support

Geographic Distribution: focus on Gaston County, NC

GIVING OFFICERS
Sarah Abernethy: dir

Hugh F. Bryant: dir

Dr. John Debvois: dir

Dr. W. W. Dickson: dir

Craig Fielding: dir

Alex Hall: dir

Judith M. Miller: dir

Elizabeth T. Stewart: dir

Mrs. John Stewart: dir

Dr. James G. Stuart: dir

Dr. Lonnie Waggoner: dir

APPLICATION INFORMATION
Initial Approach: Send brief letter of inquiry describing program or project. There are no deadlines.

GRANTS ANALYSIS
Total Grants: $212,000

Number of Grants: 24

Highest Grant: $18,500

Typical Range: $3,000 to $10,000

Disclosure Period: fiscal year ending September 30, 1992

Note: Recent grants are derived from a fiscal 1992 Form 990.

RECENT GRANTS

Library

12,000	Gaston-Lincoln Library, Wilson, NC

General

18,500	Hospice of Gaston County, Gastonia, NC
18,000	Crisis Assistance Ministry, Charlotte, NC
15,000	AIDS Council, Wilson, NC
15,000	Lees-McRae College, Banner Elk, NC
10,871	Discovery Place, Wilson, NC

Hanes Foundation, John W. and Anna H.

CONTACT
Joyce T. Adger
Vice President
John W. & Anna H. Hanes Foundation
c/o Wachovia Bank & Trust Co., N.A.
PO Box 3099
Winston-Salem, NC 27150
(910) 770-5274

FINANCIAL SUMMARY
Recent Giving: $672,001 (1991); $626,699 (1990); $527,833 (1989)

Assets: $16,169,347 (1991); $14,010,068 (1990); $14,412,034 (1989)

EIN: 56-6037589

CONTRIBUTIONS SUMMARY
Donor(s): The foundation was established in 1947.

Typical Recipients: • *Arts & Humanities:* Arts Institutes, Community Arts, Historic Preservation, Libraries, Museums/Galleries, Music, Performing Arts, Theater • *Civic & Public Affairs:* Municipalities/Towns, Zoos/Aquariums • *Education:* Arts/Humanities Education, Colleges & Universities, Private Education (Precollege), Religious Education • *Environment:* General • *Health:* Health Funds, Hospitals, Single-Disease Health Associations • *Religion:* Churches, Religious Organizations • *Social Services:* Homes, United Funds/United Ways, Youth Organizations

Grant Types: capital, emergency, endowment, matching, project, and research

Geographic Distribution: limit to North Carolina, with focus on Forsythe County and Winston-Salem

GIVING OFFICERS
Joyce T. Adger: vp

Frank Borden Hanes, Jr.: trust

Frank Borden Hanes, Sr.: trust *B* Winston-Salem NC 1920 *ED* Univ NC BA 1942 *PHIL AFFIL* vchmn, trust: John Motley Morehead Foundation

Ralph Philip Hanes, Jr.: trust *B* Winston-Salem NC 1926 *ED* Univ NC BA 1976-1977; Yale Univ BA 1979 *CURR EMPL* chmn emeritus: Hanes Cos *NONPR AFFIL* dir: Am Land Trust, Arena Stage, Jargon Soc, Potomac Appalachian Mt Club, Spoleto Festival; fdr: Am Counc Arts; mem: African Wildlife Soc, Am League Anglers, Appalachian Consortium, Appalachian Trail Conf, Izaak Walton League, N Am Mycological Assn, Natl Wildlife Federation, PA Academy Fine Arts, Royal Soc Arts, Southeastern Counc Fdns, Walpole Soc, Wilderness Soc; mem adv comm: Am Farmland Trust; mem intl counc: Mus Modern Art *CLUB AFFIL* Bohemian, Cane River, Century Assn, Currituck, Met, Peale Visual Arts, Roaring Gap, Yale

APPLICATION INFORMATION
Initial Approach:

Organizations should write to the foundation for a formal application.

The foundation's formal application includes the name and address of the organization requesting assistance; a contact person; a brief description of the organization, including a list of trustees; major goals and purposes; range and scope of programs; properties owned and rented; and date of founding. Applicants are also requested to attach a copy of the IRS certification indicating the organization's status as tax-exempt and as a private or public foundation. Information about the project should include a three-page outline of the project's scope and purpose, a desription of the geographic area to be served, the project budget, other sources of funding, and plans for future funding of the project.

Deadlines for submitting applications are March 15, June 15, September 15, and December 15.

The board reviews applications in January, April, July, and October.

Restrictions on Giving: Grants are disbursed to IRS designated tax-exempt section 501(c)(3) organizations only and must be public foundations. The foundation reports that in order for a request to receive adequate attention from the trustees, prospective applicants must complete an application form and adhere to foundation's established procedures. No grants are made to individuals or for operating expenses.

OTHER THINGS TO KNOW
Wachovia Bank and Trust Company, N.A., is the foundation's corporate trustee.

PUBLICATIONS
Program policy statement and application guidelines

GRANTS ANALYSIS
Total Grants: $672,001

Number of Grants: 41

Highest Grant: $166,667

Average Grant: $12,633*

Typical Range: $1,000 to $15,000

Disclosure Period: 1991

Note: Average grant figure does not include the highest grant of $166,667. Recent grants are derived from a 1991 grants list.

RECENT GRANTS

General

166,667	University of North Carolina at Chapel Hill, Chapel Hill, NC
100,000	North Carolina School of the Arts Foundation, Winston-Salem, NC
54,000	Eastern Carolina Exchange/Exchangette Child Abuse Prevention Center, Kinston, NC
50,000	Winston-Salem State University, Winston-Salem, NC
50,000	YMCA of Greater Winston-Salem, Winston-Salem, NC

Harvey Foundation, Felix

CONTACT
Felix Harvey
President
Felix Harvey Fdn.
901 Dewey St.
Kinston, NC 28501
(919) 523-4103

FINANCIAL SUMMARY
Recent Giving: $133,550 (fiscal 1992); $119,088 (fiscal 1991); $104,737 (fiscal 1990)

Assets: $2,503,646 (fiscal 1992); $2,113,882 (fiscal 1991); $1,739,995 (fiscal 1990)

Gifts Received: $108,000 (fiscal 1992); $112,000 (fiscal 1991); $81,000 (fiscal 1990)

Fiscal Note: In fiscal 1992, major contributions were received from Margaret B. Harvey ($29,000), C. Felix Harvey ($25,000), and Dixie-Denning Supply Company ($25,000).

EIN: 23-7038942

CONTRIBUTIONS SUMMARY
Donor(s): Felix Harvey, Margaret B. Harvey

Typical Recipients: • *Arts & Humanities:* Libraries, Music • *Civic & Public Affairs:* Botanical Gardens/Parks, General, Housing, Safety • *Education:* Business Education, Colleges & Universities, Community & Junior Colleges, Education Funds, Private Education (Precollege), Secondary Education (Public) • *Health:* Health Organizations, Single-Disease Health Associations, Trauma Treatment • *Religion:* Churches, Religious Organizations, Religious Welfare • *Science:* Scientific Centers & Institutes • *Social Services:* Community Service Organizations, Food/Clothing Distribution, Homes, Youth Organizations

Grant Types: general support

GIVING OFFICERS
Sunny Harvey Burrows: asst secy
Felix Harvey: pres
Margaret B. Harvey: treas
Ruth Heath: secy
John McNairy: vp
Leigh McNairy: vp

APPLICATION INFORMATION
Initial Approach: The foundation has no formal grant application procedure or application form. There are no deadlines.

GRANTS ANALYSIS
Total Grants: $133,550
Number of Grants: 28
Highest Grant: $26,000
Typical Range: $500 to $1,000
Disclosure Period: fiscal year ending August 31, 1992

Note: Recent grants are derived from a fiscal 1992 Form 990.

RECENT GRANTS

Library

1,000	Kinston Public Library, Kinston, NC

General

26,000	Queen Street Methodist Church, Charlotte, NC
23,300	UNC General Alumni, Chapel Hill, NC
17,350	Mt. Olive College, Mt. Olive, NC
15,000	Duke Fuqua School, Durham, NC
10,000	Jefferson Pilot Fund, Charlotte, NC

Hillsdale Fund

CONTACT
Ruth Forest
Secretary to Administrative Vice President
Hillsdale Fund
PO Box 20124
Greensboro, NC 27420
(910) 274-5471

FINANCIAL SUMMARY
Recent Giving: $970,000 (1993); $925,550 (1991); $806,100 (1990)

Assets: $26,686,685 (1993); $23,308,705 (1991); $18,572,390 (1990)

Gifts Received: $50,118 (1993); $1,514,360 (1991); $85,112 (1990)

Fiscal Note: In 1993, contributions were received from L.R. Jr. Charitable Lead Unitrust ($412,118) and Lunsford Richardson Jr. ($8,000).

EIN: 56-6057433

CONTRIBUTIONS SUMMARY
Donor(s): The fund was incorporated in 1963 by the L. Richardson family.

Typical Recipients: • *Arts & Humanities:* Arts Associations & Councils, Arts Centers, Arts Festivals, Dance, Film & Video, Historic Preservation, History & Archaeology, Libraries, Literary Arts, Museums/Galleries, Music, Opera, Performing Arts, Public Broadcasting • *Civic & Public Affairs:* Botanical Gardens/Parks, Ethnic Organizations, Housing, Municipalities/Towns, Public Policy, Safety • *Education:* Agricultural Education, Arts/Humanities Education, Colleges & Universities, Community & Junior Colleges, Elementary Education (Private), Health & Physical Education, Literacy, Private Education (Precollege), Public Education (Precollege), Religious Education, Student Aid • *Environment:* General, Resource Conservation • *Health:* AIDS/HIV, Alzheimers Disease, Cancer, Children's Health/Hospitals, Health Organizations, Hospices, Hospitals, Preventive Medicine/Wellness Organizations, Public Health • *International:* Missionary/Religious Activities • *Religion:* Churches, Ministries, Missionary Activities (Domestic), Religious Organizations, Religious Welfare, Seminaries • *Science:* Science Museums, Scientific Centers & Institutes • *Social Services:* At-Risk Youth, Child Welfare, Community Service Organizations, Counseling, Family Planning, Food/Clothing Distribution, Homes, People with Disabilities, Recreation & Athletics, Senior Services, Substance Abuse, United Funds/United Ways, YMCA/YWCA/YMHA/YWHA, Youth Organizations

Grant Types: general support

Geographic Distribution: primarily eastern United States, with a focus on North Carolina

GIVING OFFICERS
Sion A. Boney: admin vp, secy, treas, trust
Barbara Richardson Evans: dir
Ruth Forest: secy to admin vp
J. Peter Gallagher: trust
Margaret W. Gallagher: trust
Thomas H. Griggs: asst secy
Laurinda V. Lowenstein: trust
Louise Boney McCoy: trust
Beatrix W. Richardson: trust, don
Eudora L. Richardson: trust
Lunsford Richardson, Jr.: pres, trust *B* Greensboro NC 1924 *ED* Lehigh Univ 1946 *CURR EMPL* chmn: Richardson Corp Greensboro *PHIL AFFIL* mem bd govs: Smith Richardson Foundation
Lunsford Richardson Smith: dir
Molly R. Smith: trust
Richard G. Smith III: trust
Margaret R. White: trust

APPLICATION INFORMATION
Initial Approach:

Applicants should call or write for application form.

Applicants should include a copy of an IRS exemption letter with the proposal.

Deadlines for proposals are March 1 and September 1.

Restrictions on Giving: No grants are made to individuals or for operating budgets.

PUBLICATIONS
Application form

GRANTS ANALYSIS
Total Grants: $925,550

Number of Grants: 80

Highest Grant: $50,000

Average Grant: $11,569

Typical Range: $5,000 to $25,000

Disclosure Period: 1991

Note: Recent grants are derived from a 1991 Form 990.

RECENT GRANTS

General

50,000	Hollins College, Roanoke, VA
40,000	Gladney Fund, Ft. Worth, TX
35,000	Greensboro Independent Schools Corporation, Greensboro, NC
29,000	Building Together, Raleigh, NC
25,000	Canterbury School, Greensboro, NC

Janirve Foundation

CONTACT
Met R. Poston
Chairman of the Advisory Committee
The Janirve Foundation
PO Box 3276
82 Patton Ave.
Asheville, NC 28802
(704) 258-1877

FINANCIAL SUMMARY
Recent Giving: $2,315,700 (1994); $2,517,365 (1993); $1,801,654 (1991)

Assets: $47,036,746 (1994); $52,390,576 (1993); $55,313,204 (1991)

Gifts Received: $6,029,712 (1988)

Fiscal Note: In 1988, the foundation received contributions from the estate of Jeannett Reuter totaling $6,029,712.

EIN: 59-6147678

CONTRIBUTIONS SUMMARY
Donor(s): The Janirve Foundation was established by the late Irving J. Reuter , a General Motors executive, in 1964. Upon the death of his widow, Jeannett Reuter, in 1984, the foundation became active on a full-time basis.

In 1985, the foundation received $25 million from the estate of Irving and Jeannett Reuter . Financial records are kept in Palm Beach, FL, the location of the Reuter's residence. The grant-making office is located in Asheville, NC, where the Reuters kept a summer home.

Typical Recipients: • *Arts & Humanities:* Arts Associations & Councils, Arts Centers, History & Archaeology, Libraries, Museums/Galleries, Music, Public Broadcasting, Theater • *Civic & Public Affairs:* General, Housing, Law & Justice, Legal Aid, Urban & Community Affairs • *Education:* After-school/Enrichment Programs, Colleges &

Universities, Community & Junior Colleges, Education Associations, Education Reform, Leadership Training, Literacy, Private Education (Precollege), Special Education • *Environment:* Air/Water Quality, General, Resource Conservation • *Health:* Adolescent Health Issues, Clinics/Medical Centers, Geriatric Health, Health Organizations, Hospices, Hospitals, Preventive Medicine/Wellness Organizations • *Religion:* Ministries, Religious Welfare • *Social Services:* Animal Protection, Child Welfare, Community Centers, Community Service Organizations, Counseling, Day Care, Domestic Violence, Family Planning, Family Services, Food/Clothing Distribution, Homes, People with Disabilities, Scouts, Senior Services, YMCA/YWCA/YMHA/YWHA

Grant Types: capital and project

Geographic Distribution: North Carolina, South Carolina, and Florida

GIVING OFFICERS
E. Charles Dyson: mem adv comm

John W. Erichson: mem adv comm

Met R. Poston: chmn adv comm

James Woollcott: mem adv comm

Richard B. Wynne: mem adv comm

APPLICATION INFORMATION
Initial Approach:

Prospective applicants may call or write the foundation for an application.

Applicants should send a written proposal, no longer than three single-spaced pages, including a detailed description of the organization's activities, amount requested, grant purpose, financial information, and a list of governing members. Four copies of the proposal, with a completed application form and IRS tax exemption letter, should be sent to the foundation's office.

Proposals should be received by December 1 for the first quarter, by March 1 for the second quarter, by June 1 for the third quarter, and by September 1 for the fourth quarter.

Proposals are considered quarterly by a five-person advisory committee. Applicants will be notified of the committee's decision following the final meeting of the quarter.

Restrictions on Giving: The foundation does not make loans and does not make grants to individuals.

OTHER THINGS TO KNOW
All accepted applicants are expected to furnish a progress report(s) as well as a project completion report accounting for the use of the Janirve Foundation grant. The foundation makes single-year grants as opposed to multiple-year awards. It gives low priority to projects proposed by government groups or those operated primarily with tax funds.

First National Bank in Palm Beach, a division of First Union National Bank is a trustee of the foundation.

PUBLICATIONS
Application form, information sheet for applicants

GRANTS ANALYSIS
Total Grants: $2,315,700

Number of Grants: 86

Highest Grant: $250,000

Average Grant: $26,927

Typical Range: $5,000 to $50,000

Disclosure Period: 1994

Note: Recent grants are derived from a 1993 Form 990.

RECENT GRANTS

General

500,000	Lewis Rathbun Wellness Center, Asheville, NC
150,000	Pack Place Education, Arts and Sciences Center, Asheville, NC
75,000	Mountain Area Nutritional Needs Alliance, Asheville, NC
60,000	United Way of Asheville and Buncombe County, Asheville, NC
50,000	Mars Hill College, Mars Hill, NC

Martin Marietta Materials / Martin Marietta Philanthropic Trust

Sales: $452.91 million
Employees: 2,400
Headquarters: Raleigh, NC
SIC Major Group: Nonmetallic Minerals Except Fuels and Stone, Clay & Glass Products

CONTACT
John F. Long, Jr.
Vice President, Community Affairs and Government Relations
Martin Marietta Materials
PO Box 30013
Raleigh, NC 27622
(919) 781-4550
Note: Another contact address for the foundation is c/o First Union National Bank of NC, P.O. Box 3008, Raleigh, NC, 27602.

FINANCIAL SUMMARY
Recent Giving: $103,200 (1993); $86,250 (1992); $118,225 (1991)

Assets: $1,436,944 (1992); $1,483,256 (1991); $1,477,200 (1990)

EIN: 56-6035971

CONTRIBUTIONS SUMMARY
Typical Recipients: • *Arts & Humanities:* Arts Centers, Community Arts, General, Libraries, Museums/Galleries, Music • *Civic & Public Affairs:* Botanical Gardens/Parks, Chambers of Commerce, General, Philanthropic Organizations, Urban & Community Affairs, Zoos/Aquariums • *Education:* Business-School Partnerships, Colleges & Universities, Community & Junior Colleges, Education Funds, Elementary Education (Public), Engineering/Technological Education, General, Private Education (Precol-

lege), Public Education (Precollege), Science/Mathematics Education, Student Aid • *Environment:* Air/Water Quality, Resource Conservation, Wildlife Protection • *Health:* Clinics/Medical Centers, General, Hospitals, Multiple Sclerosis, Single-Disease Health Associations • *Religion:* Churches, Religious Welfare • *Science:* General, Science Museums, Scientific Centers & Institutes • *Social Services:* Child Welfare, Community Centers, Community Service Organizations, General, United Funds/United Ways, Youth Organizations

Grant Types: general support

Nonmonetary Support Types: donated products

Geographic Distribution: focus on NC

Operating Locations: CO (Denver, Littleton), FL (Orlando), LA (New Orleans), MD (Baltimore, Greenbelt, Hunt Valley), NC (Raleigh)

CORP. OFFICERS
Stephen P. Zelnak, Jr.: *CURR EMPL* pres, ceo: Martin Marietta Aggregates

GIVING OFFICERS
First Union National Bank: trust

Robert A. Bischoff: vp

William B. Harwood: exec dir

John F. Long, Jr.: dir

APPLICATION INFORMATION
Initial Approach: Send a brief letter of inquiry. Include a description of organization, amount requested, purpose of funds sought, recently audited financial statement, and proof of tax-exempt status. There are no deadlines.

Restrictions on Giving: Does not support individuals, religious organizations for sectarian purposes, political or lobbying groups, or organizations outside operating areas.

GRANTS ANALYSIS
Total Grants: $86,250

Number of Grants: 63

Highest Grant: $5,750

Typical Range: $600 to $1,500

Disclosure Period: 1992

Note: Recent grants are derived from a 1992 Form 990.

RECENT GRANTS
Library
1,000 Berkeley County Library Fund — for general fund support

General
5,750 Independent College Fund of North Carolina, Winston-Salem, NC — for support of 28 member colleges
5,000 Science Center of Iowa, Des Moines, IA — capital campaign
4,000 United Way — for general budget purposes
3,000 Breezy Hill Baptist Church — capital campaign

3,000 Carmel Junior High School — for state-of-the-art technology lab

Miller Brewing Company/North Carolina

Employees: 850
Headquarters: Eden, NC
SIC Major Group: Food & Kindred Products

CONTACT
Helen Dennison
Public Relations Manager
Miller Brewing Company/North Carolina
863 E Meadow Rd.
PO Box 3327
Eden, NC 27288
(910) 627-2167

FINANCIAL SUMMARY
Fiscal Note: Annual Giving Range: $100,000 to $250,000

CONTRIBUTIONS SUMMARY
Company reports 50% of contributions support the arts; 20% to education; 20% to health and human services; and 5% each to environmental and civic organizations.

Typical Recipients: • *Arts & Humanities:* Arts Appreciation, Arts Associations & Councils, Arts Festivals, Arts Funds, Arts Outreach, Community Arts, Dance, Ethnic & Folk Arts, General, Historic Preservation, Libraries, Museums/Galleries, Music, Performing Arts, Theater, Visual Arts • *Civic & Public Affairs:* African American Affairs, Business/Free Enterprise, Chambers of Commerce, Civil Rights, Clubs, Economic Development, Employment/Job Training, Ethnic Organizations, Gay/Lesbian Issues, General, Hispanic Affairs, Municipalities/Towns, Parades/Festivals, Philanthropic Organizations, Rural Affairs, Safety, Women's Affairs • *Education:* Afterschool/Enrichment Programs, Agricultural Education, Arts/Humanities Education, Business-School Partnerships, Colleges & Universities, Community & Junior Colleges, Elementary Education (Private), Engineering/Technological Education, General, Literacy • *Environment:* General, Resource Conservation, Wildlife Protection • *Health:* AIDS/HIV, Emergency/Ambulance Services, General, Health Policy/Cost Containment, Hospices, Nutrition • *International:* Health Care/Hospitals • *Science:* General • *Social Services:* Animal Protection, At-Risk Youth, Camps, Community Centers, Community Service Organizations, Counseling, Delinquency & Criminal Rehabilitation, Food/Clothing Distribution, General, Homes, Shelters/Homelessness, Substance Abuse, United Funds/United Ways

Grant Types: emergency, general support, and multiyear/continuing support

Nonmonetary Support Types: donated equipment, donated products, and loaned employees

Geographic Distribution: principally near operating locations and to national organizations

Operating Locations: NC (Eden)

CORP. OFFICERS
Patricia Henry: *CURR EMPL* plant mgr: Miller Brewing Co/NC

APPLICATION INFORMATION
Initial Approach: Send a brief letter of inquiry. Include a description of organization, amount requested, purpose of funds sought, and proof of tax-exempt status.

Restrictions on Giving: Does not support religious organizations for sectarian purposes or political or lobbying groups.

GRANTS ANALYSIS
Typical Range: $1,000 to $2,500

Note: Recent grants are derived from a grants list provided by comany in 1995.

RECENT GRANTS
General
Eden United Way, Eden, NC
Eden YMCA, Eden, NC
Junior Achievement of Eden, Eden, NC
Salvation Army After-School Program, Eden, NC

Moore & Sons, B.C. / Moore & Sons Foundation, B.C.

Sales: $100.0 million
Employees: 2,400
Headquarters: Wadesboro, NC
SIC Major Group: General Merchandise Stores

CONTACT
Carl E. Bennett
Vice President, Senior Officer
B.C. Moore & Sons
PO Drawer 72
Wadesboro, NC 28170
(205) 558-6717
Note: The company is located at 101 S Green St., Wadesboro, NC 28170 (704) 694-2171

FINANCIAL SUMMARY
Recent Giving: $70,000 (fiscal 1994); $67,050 (fiscal 1993); $47,550 (fiscal 1992)

Assets: $1,536,110 (fiscal 1994); $1,435,253 (fiscal 1993); $1,303,760 (fiscal 1992)

Gifts Received: $100,000 (fiscal 1993); $100,000 (fiscal 1992); $100,000 (fiscal 1990)

EIN: 56-6062082

CONTRIBUTIONS SUMMARY
Typical Recipients: • *Arts & Humanities:* Arts Associations & Councils, Arts Centers, Libraries, Performing Arts, Theater • *Civic & Public Affairs:* Botanical Gardens/Parks, General, Safety, Urban & Community Affairs • *Education:* Colleges & Universities, Education Funds, Minority Education, Religious Education, Secondary Education (Public), Vocational & Technical Education • *Environment:* Resource Conservation

• *Health:* Emergency/Ambulance Services, Hospices, Hospitals, Research/Studies Institutes • *Religion:* Churches, Ministries, Missionary Activities (Domestic), Religious Organizations, Religious Welfare • *Social Services:* Community Centers, People with Disabilities, Special Olympics, YMCA/YWCA/YMHA/YWHA

Grant Types: general support

Geographic Distribution: focus on the Southeast

Operating Locations: NC (Wadesboro)

CORP. OFFICERS
James C. Crawford, Jr.: *CURR EMPL* chmn, pres, dir: BC Moore & Sons

John R. Hartley: *CURR EMPL* cfo: BC Moore & Sons

GIVING OFFICERS
Benjamin M. Belcher, Jr.: pres *CURR EMPL* vp: Benjamin Moore & Co *PHIL AFFIL* pres: Benjamin Moore Educational Foundation

Carl E. Bennett: secy

William J. Fritz: treas *PHIL AFFIL* treas: Benjamin Moore Educational Foundation

Richard Roob: trust *CURR EMPL* chmn, dir: Benjamin Moore & Co *PHIL AFFIL* trust: Benjamin Moore Educational Foundation

Maurice C. Workman: trust *CURR EMPL* pres, dir: Benjamin Moore & Co *PHIL AFFIL* trust: Benjamin Moore Educational Foundation

APPLICATION INFORMATION
Initial Approach: Send brief letter describing program. There are no deadlines.

GRANTS ANALYSIS
Total Grants: $70,000

Number of Grants: 40

Highest Grant: $5,000

Typical Range: $200 to $5,000

Disclosure Period: fiscal year ending January 31, 1994

Note: Recent grants are derived from a fiscal 1994 Form 990.

RECENT GRANTS
Library
1,000   Brewton Public Library

General
5,000   Brevard College
5,000   Cheraw Community Park, Cheraw, SD
4,000   Alabama Independent Colleges, Birmingham, AL
4,000   Billy Graham Evangelical Association, Minneapolis, MN
4,000   Georgia Foundation for Independent Colleges, Atlanta, GA

National Gypsum Co. / National Gypsum Foundation, Inc.

Sales: $278.6 million
Employees: 2,600
Headquarters: Charlotte, NC
SIC Major Group: Engineering & Management Services, General Building Contractors, Paper & Allied Products, and Stone, Clay & Glass Products

CONTACT
Lori Thompson
Secretary
National Gypsum Foundation, Inc.
2001 Rexford Rd.
Charlotte, NC 28211
(704) 365-7300

FINANCIAL SUMMARY
Recent Giving: $200,000 (1993); $40,105 (1992); $130,000 (1991)

Assets: $0 (1992); $3,264,283 (1990); $4,061,309 (1989)

EIN: 34-6551614

CONTRIBUTIONS SUMMARY
Typical Recipients: • *Arts & Humanities:* Arts Associations & Councils, Arts Institutes, Ballet, Community Arts, Dance, Historic Preservation, Libraries, Museums/Galleries, Music, Opera, Performing Arts, Public Broadcasting, Theater • *Civic & Public Affairs:* Economic Development, General, Housing, Law & Justice, Nonprofit Management, Women's Affairs, Zoos/Aquariums • *Education:* Business Education, Colleges & Universities, Community & Junior Colleges, Legal Education, Literacy • *Health:* Emergency/Ambulance Services, Health Organizations, Hospitals, Medical Research, Single-Disease Health Associations • *Social Services:* Community Service Organizations, People with Disabilities, Substance Abuse, United Funds/United Ways, Youth Organizations

Grant Types: capital, challenge, emergency, employee matching gifts, and general support

Nonmonetary Support Types: donated products

Geographic Distribution: focus on NC

Operating Locations: NC (Charlotte)

Note: List includes division locations.

CORP. OFFICERS
Stephen Humphrey: *CURR EMPL* pres, ceo: Natl Gypsum Co

Robert Prokay: *CURR EMPL* vp, cfo: Natl Gypsum Co

GIVING OFFICERS
A. Cecil: pres, trust
Dick Dircher: trust
Lori Thompson: secy
Dave Walsh: vp, trust
Craig Weisbruch: trust

APPLICATION INFORMATION
Initial Approach: Send a brief letter of inquiry and a full proposal. Include a description of organization, amount requested, purpose of funds sought, and proof of tax-exempt status. There are no deadlines.

Restrictions on Giving: Company does not support individuals or political or lobbying groups.

GRANTS ANALYSIS
Total Grants: $40,105

Number of Grants: 54

Highest Grant: $7,500

Typical Range: $1,000 to $5,000

Disclosure Period: 1992

Note: Recent grants are derived from a 1992 Form 990.

RECENT GRANTS
Library
500   Southern Methodist University School of Law Library Fund, Dallas, TX — educational institution library fund

General
7,500   Presbyterian Hospital, Charlotte, NC — general support
2,000   Central Piedmont Community College, Charlotte, NC — educational institution general support
1,250   Relatives, Charlotte, NC — annual pledge
1,000   Junior Achievement, Charlotte, NC — annual fund drive
1,000   Queens College, Charlotte, NC — educational institution general support

Ottley Trust-Watertown, Marion W.

Former Foundation Name: Marian W. Ottley Trust-Watertown David, Helen, and Marian Woodward Fund-Watertown

CONTACT
E. Edward Thompson
Trustee
Marion W. Ottley Trust-Watertown
c/o Wachovia Bank of North Carolina, N.A.
Winston-Salem, NC 27150-1022
(919) 770-5252

FINANCIAL SUMMARY
Recent Giving: $464,816 (fiscal 1993); $377,900 (fiscal 1990); $370,919 (fiscal 1989)

Assets: $11,461,060 (fiscal 1993); $8,842,907 (fiscal 1990); $8,145,021 (fiscal 1989)

EIN: 58-6222005

CONTRIBUTIONS SUMMARY

Donor(s): the late Marian W. Ottley

Typical Recipients: • *Arts & Humanities:* Libraries, Music • *Education:* Colleges & Universities, Private Education (Precollege), Public Education (Precollege), Special Education • *Health:* Cancer, Health Organizations, Home-Care Services, Hospitals, Mental Health, Single-Disease Health Associations • *Religion:* Churches • *Social Services:* Camps, Child Welfare, Community Service Organizations, United Funds/United Ways, Youth Organizations

Grant Types: capital, endowment, and scholarship

Geographic Distribution: focus on CT

GIVING OFFICERS

M. Heminway Merriman II: trust

Edith Pelletier: trust

Alyce Thompson: secy

E. Edward Thompson: trust

APPLICATION INFORMATION

Initial Approach: Send brief letter of inquiry and full proposal (three copies). Include a description of organization, amount requested, purpose of funds sought, recently audited financial statement, and proof of tax-exempt status. Deadline is 30 days prior to board meetings. Board meets in June and December.

Restrictions on Giving: Does not support individuals.

GRANTS ANALYSIS

Total Grants: $464,816

Number of Grants: 23

Highest Grant: $83,333

Typical Range: $1,500 to $50,000

Disclosure Period: fiscal year ending May 31, 1993

Note: Recent grants are derived from a fiscal 1993 Form 990.

RECENT GRANTS

Library

10,000	Hodge Memorial Library, Roxbury, CT
1,000	Petersburgh Public Library, Petersburgh, NY

General

83,333	Taft School, Watertown, CT
83,333	Taft School, Watertown, CT
60,000	St. Margarets-Moternan School, Waterbury, CT
60,000	St. Margarets-Motternan School, Waterbury, CT
50,000	Children's Community School, Waterbury, CT

Reichhold Chemicals, Inc.

Sales: $765.59 million
Employees: 3,958
Headquarters: Research Triangle Park, NC
SIC Major Group: Chemicals & Allied Products, Rubber & Miscellaneous Plastics Products, and Wholesale Trade—Nondurable Goods

CONTACT

Stephen G. Brechbiel
Corporate Communications Manager
Reichhold Chemicals, Inc.
PO Box 13582
Research Triangle Park, NC 27709
(919) 990-7500

FINANCIAL SUMMARY

Fiscal Note: Annual Giving Range: $25,000 to $50,000

CONTRIBUTIONS SUMMARY

Company tries to divide contributions evenly between arts, education, and health and human services. Prefers to support organizations that directly affect company's employee base. Plants throughout the United States have discretionary spending budgets; large grants are approved by corporate headquarters.

Typical Recipients: • *Arts & Humanities:* Arts Funds, Libraries, Museums/Galleries, Music, Performing Arts • *Education:* Business Education, Colleges & Universities, Economic Education, Public Education (Precollege) • *Health:* Health Organizations, Hospitals, Single-Disease Health Associations • *Social Services:* Community Service Organizations, United Funds/United Ways, Youth Organizations

Grant Types: capital and employee matching gifts

Geographic Distribution: primarily headquarters area

CORP. OFFICERS

Phillip D. Ashkettle: *CURR EMPL* pres, ceo: Reichhold Chemicals

GIVING OFFICERS

Stephen G. Brechbiel: *CURR EMPL* corp communications mgr: Reichhold Chemicals

APPLICATION INFORMATION

Initial Approach: Send letter of inquiry including a description of the organization, need addressed, and amount requested. Plants can be contacted directly. Other subsidiaries of Dainippon administer independent programs.

Rixson Foundation, Oscar C.

CONTACT

Thomas J. Elliott, Sr.
President
Oscar C. Rixson Fdn.
307 Gregory Way
Hendersonville, NC 28739
(704) 891-5490

FINANCIAL SUMMARY

Recent Giving: $177,100 (1993); $175,400 (1992); $172,500 (1991)

Assets: $2,297,451 (1993); $2,375,765 (1992); $2,388,717 (1991)

Gifts Received: $57,108 (1993); $60,427 (1992); $53,767 (1991)

EIN: 13-6129767

CONTRIBUTIONS SUMMARY

Typical Recipients: • *Arts & Humanities:* Libraries • *Civic & Public Affairs:* Botanical Gardens/Parks, General, Public Policy • *Education:* Colleges & Universities, Private Education (Precollege), Religious Education • *International:* Foreign Educational Institutions, International Organizations, International Relations, International Relief Efforts, Missionary/Religious Activities • *Religion:* Bible Study/Translation, Ministries, Religious Organizations, Religious Welfare, Seminaries • *Social Services:* Camps, People with Disabilities, Youth Organizations

Grant Types: general support

Geographic Distribution: national and international

GIVING OFFICERS

Donald Dunkerton: dir

Nathan E. Dunkerton: vp, secy, dir

Thomas J. Elliot, Jr.: trust

Thomas J. Elliot, Sr.: pres, dir

James M. Gilbert: trust

Joseph Giordano: trust *B* New York NY 1932 *ED* PA Military Coll BSIE 1955 *CURR EMPL* sr vp, dir, chief tech off: Fedders Corp *CORP AFFIL* pres: Nycor; sr vp: Rotorex Corp *PHIL AFFIL* vp, dir: Giordano Foundation; vp: Salvatore Giordano Foundation

William R. Kusche: dir

Alan Mojounier: vp, treas, dir

Timothy C. Van Wyck: trust

Richard Yeskoo: trust

APPLICATION INFORMATION

Initial Approach: Send a brief letter of inquiry. Include a description of organization, amount requested, purpose of funds sought, recently audited financial statement, and proof of tax-exempt status. There are no deadlines.

OTHER THINGS TO KNOW

Provides grants to individuals for Christian missions.

GRANTS ANALYSIS

Total Grants: $177,100

Highest Grant: $2,500

Average Grant: 98*

Typical Range: $200 to $1,000

Disclosure Period: 1993

Note: Recent grants are derived from a 1993 Form 990.

RECENT GRANTS

General

2,000	Emanus Bible College
2,000	Emanus Correspondence School
1,500	Christian Mission in Many Lands
1,500	International Foundation, Washington, DC
1,500	Missionary Enterprises

Rose's Stores, Inc.

Sales: $1.21 billion

Employees: 18,000

Headquarters: Henderson, NC

SIC Major Group: Apparel & Accessory Stores, Eating & Drinking Places, General Merchandise Stores, and Miscellaneous Retail

CONTACT

Robert Gorham

Commun, Training, Quality Assurance Manager

Rose's Stores, Inc.

218-220 Garrett St.

PO Drawer 947

Henderson, NC 27536

(919) 430-2600

CONTRIBUTIONS SUMMARY

Typical Recipients: • *Arts & Humanities:* Arts Festivals, Community Arts, General, Libraries • *Civic & Public Affairs:* Business/Free Enterprise, Chambers of Commerce, Clubs, Community Foundations, Employment/Job Training, General, Nonprofit Management, Parades/Festivals, Philanthropic Organizations, Professional & Trade Associations, Rural Affairs, Safety, Urban & Community Affairs • *Education:* Business Education, Business-School Partnerships, Colleges & Universities, Continuing Education, Economic Education, Faculty Development, General, Literacy • *Health:* General, Health Organizations, Public Health • *Social Services:* Child Welfare, Community Centers, Community Service Organizations, Emergency Relief, Family Planning, Family Services, Food/Clothing Distribution, General, United Funds/United Ways, Volunteer Services, Youth Organizations

Nonmonetary Support Types: workplace solicitation

Note: Other: Donated Facilities

Operating Locations: NC (Henderson)

CORP. OFFICERS

R. Edward Anderson: *CURR EMPL* pres, ceo: Roses Stores

Jeanette Peters: *CURR EMPL* cfo: Roses Stores

APPLICATION INFORMATION

Restrictions on Giving: Does not support individuals, religious organizations for sectarian purposes, or organizations outside operating areas.

OTHER THINGS TO KNOW

Company emerged from Chapter 11 in early 1995. Contributions are limited.

Royal Group, Inc. / Royal Insurance Foundation

Parent Company: Westgate House Nominees Limited

Headquarters: Charlotte, NC

SIC Major Group: Holding Companies Nec

CONTACT

Linda Holland

Contact

Royal Insurance Foundation

9300 Arrowpoint Blvd.

Charlotte, NC 28201-1000

(704) 522-2057

FINANCIAL SUMMARY

Recent Giving: $474,800 (1995 est.); $474,800 (1994); $465,071 (1993)

Assets: $89,381 (1993); $75,133 (1992); $49,435 (1990)

Gifts Received: $475,000 (1993); $370,942 (1990); $353,478 (1989)

Fiscal Note: Contributes through foundation only. Above figures exclude nonmonetary support.

EIN: 56-1658178

CONTRIBUTIONS SUMMARY

Typical Recipients: • *Arts & Humanities:* Arts Appreciation, Arts Associations & Councils, Arts Centers, Community Arts, Dance, Ethnic & Folk Arts, General, Historic Preservation, Libraries, Museums/Galleries, Music, Opera, Performing Arts, Public Broadcasting, Theater, Visual Arts • *Civic & Public Affairs:* Business/Free Enterprise, Civil Rights, Economic Development, General, Housing, Safety • *Education:* Business Education, Colleges & Universities, Continuing Education, Education Funds, Elementary Education (Private), General, Literacy, Minority Education, Preschool Education, Private Education (Precollege), Public Education (Precollege) • *Environment:* General • *Health:* Emergency/Ambulance Services, General, Geriatric Health, Health Funds, Health Organizations, Hospices, Hospitals • *Social Services:* Child Welfare, Community Centers, Community Service Organizations, Counseling, Family Services, General, Homes, People with Disabilities, Refugee Assistance, Senior Services, Shelters/Homelessness, Substance Abuse, United Funds/United Ways, Volunteer Services, Youth Organizations

Grant Types: capital, employee matching gifts, general support, operating expenses, project, and scholarship

Note: Employee matching gift ratio: 1 to 1 for gifts to higher education only.

Nonmonetary Support: $25,000 (1994)

Nonmonetary Support Types: donated equipment, in-kind services, and workplace solicitation

Geographic Distribution: primarily in the headquarters area, but also through 30 field offices across the country

Operating Locations: CO, CT, FL, GA, IL, KS, MA, MD, ME, MI, NC (Charlotte), NH, NJ, NY, OH, PA, TX, UT, VA, WA

CORP. OFFICERS

Linda Holland: *CURR EMPL* dir commun rels: Royal Group Inc

Joyce W. Wheeler: *B* Durham NC 1951 *ED* Albright Coll 1973; Univ Houston Law Sch 1980 *CURR EMPL* secy: Royal Group Inc *CORP AFFIL* asst corp secy, dir: Royal Ins Co Am; corp secy, dir: Am & Foreign Ins Co, Globe Indemnity Co, Newark Ins Co, Royal Indemnity Inc, Royal Surplus Lines Ins Co, Safeguard Ins Co; corp secy, dir: Special Risks Ins Co; secy: Protected Settlements Inc, Royal Holdings Inc, Royal Specialty Underwriting Inc; secy, dir: BEI Svcs Inc, Shield Mgmt Inc; secy, treas: Risk Innovations Svc & Consult Inc, Royal Excess & Special Risks GA Inc, Royal Excess & Special Risks IL Inc, Royal Excess & Special Risks Ins Svcs Inc, Royal Excess & Special Risks TX Inc, US Transportation Underwriters Inc; secy, treas, dir: Charlotte Lloyds Inc, Crown & Shield Inc, RC Holding Inc; underwriter: Royal Lloyds TX

GIVING OFFICERS

Fred Dabney: dir

Linda Holland: contact *CURR EMPL* dir commun rels: Royal Group Inc (see above)

Philip Kline: treas, dir

Elizabeth McLaughlin: chmn

C. Ronald Riley: dir *CURR EMPL* sr vp, cfo, dir: Royal Ins Co Am

Joyce W. Wheeler: secy, dir *CURR EMPL* secy: Royal Group Inc (see above)

APPLICATION INFORMATION

Initial Approach: *Initial Contact:* write for application form *Include Information On:* completed application; what makes Royal Insurance an appropriate donor; list of current board of directors; schedule of board meetings; proof of IRS tax-exemption; and current financial statement *Deadlines:* none

Restrictions on Giving: Does not support individuals, religious organizations for sectarian purposes, political or lobbying groups, organizations outside operating areas, fraternal organizations, medical research, veterans organizations, broadcast fundraising, or endowments.

No funding may be secured through telephone solicitation or direct mail marketing. Contributions also will not be made to an organization solely because a company officer or employee is involved in fundraising efforts.

OTHER THINGS TO KNOW
The majority of contributions stay within the state of North Carolina and are decided upon at corporate headquarters. Field offices across the United States have autonomy to make smaller discretionary donations. At the headquarters, the board of directors meets quarterly to vote on all expenditures of over $2,500.

Capital funding requests are presented for consideration once per year at the annual meeting of the board of directors. Priority is given to industry-related projects.

PUBLICATIONS
Application guidelines

GRANTS ANALYSIS
Total Grants: $465,071

Number of Grants: 121

Highest Grant: $100,000

Average Grant: $3,844

Typical Range: $1,000 to $5,000

Disclosure Period: 1993

Note: Recent grants are derived from a 1993 Form 990.

RECENT GRANTS

Library

2,000	Insurance Library of Boston, Boston, MA

General

25,000	United Way Central Carolinas, Charlotte, NC — for first quarter payment on 1992-93 pledge
25,000	United Way Central Carolinas, Charlotte, NC — for fourth quarter payment on 1992-93 corporate pledge
25,000	United Way Central Carolinas, Charlotte, NC — for second quarter payment on 1992-93 pledge
25,000	United Way Central Carolinas, Charlotte, NC — for third quarter payment on 1992-93 corporate pledge
15,000	Johnson C. Smith University, Charlotte, NC — for capital campaign and endowed scholarship

Sara Lee Hosiery, Inc.

Employees: 5,500
Parent Company: Sara Lee Corp.
Parent Sales: $15.5 billion
Headquarters: Winston-Salem, NC
SIC Major Group: Women's Hosiery Except Socks

CONTACT
Larry Willard
Manager, General Accounting
Sara Lee Hosiery, Inc.
5650 University Pkwy.
Winston-Salem, NC 27105
(910) 519-3893

FINANCIAL SUMMARY
Recent Giving: $275,000 (1995 est.); $275,000 (1994 approx.); $350,000 (1992 approx.)

Fiscal Note: Company gives directly.

CONTRIBUTIONS SUMMARY
Typical Recipients: • *Arts & Humanities:* Arts Appreciation, Arts Associations & Councils, Arts Funds, Community Arts, Film & Video, Historic Preservation, Libraries, Literary Arts, Museums/Galleries, Music, Performing Arts, Public Broadcasting, Visual Arts • *Civic & Public Affairs:* Business/Free Enterprise, Civil Rights, Economic Development, General, Philanthropic Organizations, Urban & Community Affairs • *Education:* Business Education, Community & Junior Colleges, Education Funds, Elementary Education (Private), General, Literacy, Minority Education, Preschool Education, Private Education (Precollege) • *Environment:* General • *Health:* Emergency/Ambulance Services, General, Health Organizations, Hospices, Hospitals, Public Health • *Religion:* Churches • *Social Services:* Animal Protection, Child Welfare, Community Service Organizations, Counseling, Day Care, Domestic Violence, Emergency Relief, Family Services, Food/Clothing Distribution, General, People with Disabilities, Refugee Assistance, Senior Services, Shelters/Homelessness, Substance Abuse, United Funds/United Ways, Volunteer Services, Youth Organizations

Grant Types: award, capital, emergency, employee matching gifts, fellowship, general support, operating expenses, project, and seed money

Note: Employee matching gift ratio: 2 to 1 up to $1,000. Employee matching gift ratio: 1 to 1 from $1,000 to a maximum of $10,000.

Geographic Distribution: in headquarters and operating communities

Operating Locations: AK (Clarksville), CA (Cerritos, La Mirada), IL (Champaign), MS (Jackson, Olive Branch), NC (Rockingham, Winston-Salem, Yadkinville), NM (Mesilla), NV (Henderson), SC (Florence, Hartsville, Marion), VA (Salem)

CORP. OFFICERS
John Piazza: *CURR EMPL* pres: Sara Lee Hosiery Inc *CORP AFFIL* pres: Leggs Products Inc

Joseph Sardella: *CURR EMPL* cfo: Sara Lee Hosiery Inc

GIVING OFFICERS
Larry Willard: *CURR EMPL* mgr gen acct: Sara Lee Hosiery Inc

APPLICATION INFORMATION
Initial Approach: *Initial Contact:* letter of inquiry *Include Information On:* a description of organization, amount requested, purpose of funds sought, recently audited financial statement, and proof of tax-exempt status *Deadlines:* none

Restrictions on Giving: The company does not support national or statewide United Way recipients.

GRANTS ANALYSIS
Typical Range: $50 to $5,000

Sternberger Foundation, Tannenbaum

Former Foundation Name: Sigmund Sternberger Foundation

CONTACT
Robert O. Klepfer, Jr.
Foundation Manager
Tannenbaum Sternberger Fdn.
PO Box 3111
600 NCNB Bldg.
Greensboro, NC 27402
(919) 373-1500

FINANCIAL SUMMARY
Recent Giving: $416,380 (fiscal 1994); $613,689 (fiscal 1993); $636,664 (fiscal 1991)

Assets: $11,270,800 (fiscal 1994); $11,470,164 (fiscal 1993); $9,930,738 (fiscal 1991)

Gifts Received: $1,696 (fiscal 1994); $341,566 (fiscal 1993)

EIN: 56-6045483

CONTRIBUTIONS SUMMARY
Donor(s): the late Sigmund and Rosa Sternberger Williams

Typical Recipients: • *Arts & Humanities:* Arts Associations & Councils, Arts Centers, Arts Festivals, Community Arts, Historic Preservation, Libraries, Music, Theater • *Civic & Public Affairs:* African American Affairs, General, Housing, Law & Justice, Parades/Festivals, Public Policy • *Education:* Colleges & Universities, Community & Junior Colleges, Education Funds, Student Aid • *Health:* Alzheimers Disease, Mental Health, Nutrition • *Religion:* Churches, Ministries, Religious Welfare, Synagogues/Temples • *Social Services:* Child Welfare, Community Service Organizations, Day Care, Family Services, Homes, People with Disabilities, Senior Services, United Funds/United Ways, Youth Organizations

Grant Types: capital, general support, and scholarship

Geographic Distribution: focus on Guilford County, NC

GIVING OFFICERS
Howard Ernest Carr: dir *B* Johnson City TN 1908 *ED* E TN State Univ BS 1929; Duke Univ MEd 1935; Univ NC 1938-1939 *CURR EMPL* Jefferson Standard Life Ins Co *NONPR AFFIL* dir: Cancer Soc; mem: Greensboro Assn Life Underwriters, Greensboro Chamber of Commerce, Natl Assn Life Underwriters, North Carolina Leaders Club; mem adv comm: Guilford Coll *CLUB AFFIL* Kiwanis, Mason

Rabbi Richard Harkavy: dir

Robert O. Klepfer, Jr.: mgr, dir

Charles M. Reid: secy, treas, dir

Jeanne L. Tannenbaum: dir

Leah Louise B. Tannenbaum: chmn

Nancy B. Tannenbaum: dir

Sigmund Tannenbaum: dir

Susan M. Tannenbaum: dir

APPLICATION INFORMATION
Initial Approach: Send letter requesting application form. There are no deadlines.

PUBLICATIONS
Application Guidelines

GRANTS ANALYSIS
Total Grants: $416,380

Number of Grants: 52

Highest Grant: $33,333

Typical Range: $1,000 to $30,000

Disclosure Period: fiscal year ending March 31, 1994

Note: Recent grants are derived from a fiscal 1994 Form 990. Number of grants and typical range do not include scholarships to individuals.

RECENT GRANTS

General

106,000	Duke University, Durham, NC — scholarships
81,667	Greensboro Urban Ministry, Greensboro, NC
50,000	Natural Science Center Drug and Nutrition Exhibits, Greensboro, NC
50,000	University of North Carolina School of Social Works, Raleigh, NC
26,821	Court Watch of North Carolina, Greensboro, NC

Thomasville Furniture Industries / Thomasville Furniture Industries Foundation

Sales: $438.0 million
Employees: 8,000
Parent Company: Armstrong World Industries, Inc.
Headquarters: Thomasville, NC
SIC Major Group: Furniture & Fixtures

CONTACT
Vickie Holder
Office Administrator
Thomasville Furniture Industries
PO Box 339
Thomasville, NC 27360
(910) 472-4000

FINANCIAL SUMMARY
Recent Giving: $250,000 (1994); $250,000 (1993); $240,128 (1992)

Assets: $3,601,645 (1992); $3,248,376 (1990); $3,381,806 (1989)

EIN: 56-6047870

CONTRIBUTIONS SUMMARY
Typical Recipients: • *Arts & Humanities:* Arts Associations & Councils, Community

Arts, Libraries, Museums/Galleries, Music, Performing Arts, Theater • *Civic & Public Affairs:* General, Housing • *Education:* Colleges & Universities, Community & Junior Colleges, Education Funds, Minority Education, Public Education (Precollege), Secondary Education (Public), Student Aid • *Health:* Hospitals, Medical Research • *Religion:* Religious Welfare • *Science:* Scientific Centers & Institutes • *Social Services:* Child Welfare, Community Centers, Community Service Organizations, Family Services, Recreation & Athletics, United Funds/United Ways, Youth Organizations

Grant Types: general support

Nonmonetary Support Types: donated products

Geographic Distribution: focus on NC

Operating Locations: MS (Fayette), NC (Statesville, Thomasville), TN (Johnson City), VA (Appomattox, Brookneal, Carysbrook)

CORP. OFFICERS
Vickie L. Holder: *CURR EMPL* off admin: Thomasville Furniture Indus

Frederick B. Starr: *CURR EMPL* pres, ceo, dir: Thomasville Furniture Indus

GIVING OFFICERS
Wachovia Bank of NC, NA: trust

Ronald G. Berrier: trust

Charles O. Gordon: trust

Vickie L. Holder: admin comm *CURR EMPL* off admin: Thomasville Furniture Indus (see above)

Frederick B. Starr: chmn *CURR EMPL* pres, ceo, dir: Thomasville Furniture Indus (see above)

APPLICATION INFORMATION
Initial Approach: Send a brief letter of inquiry and a full proposal. Include a a description of organization, amount requested, purpose of funds sought, and proof of tax-exempt status. There are no deadlines.

Restrictions on Giving: Does not support individuals, religious organizations for sectarian purposes, political or lobbying groups, or organizations outside operating areas.

GRANTS ANALYSIS
Total Grants: $240,128

Number of Grants: 50

Highest Grant: $25,000

Typical Range: $1,000 to $5,000

Disclosure Period: 1992

Note: Recent grants are derived from a 1992 Form 990. Information listed does not include scholarships.

RECENT GRANTS

Library

20,000	Davidson County Library Foundation, Thomasville, NC

General

25,000	Community General Hospital, Thomasville, NC
7,925	City of Lenoir, Lenoir, NC — aquatic and fitness center

7,500	City of Hope, Duarte, CA
7,500	Independent College Fund, Winston-Salem, NC
7,500	United Negro College Fund, Salisbury, NC

Van Every Foundation, Philip L.

CONTACT
Zean Jamison, Jr.
Executive Director
Philip L. Van Every Foundation
c/o Lance, Inc.
PO Box 32368
Charlotte, NC 28232
(704) 554-1421

FINANCIAL SUMMARY
Recent Giving: $1,700,000 (1995 est.); $1,600,000 (1994 approx.); $1,569,708 (1993)

Assets: $26,000,000 (1995 est.); $25,000,000 (1994 approx.); $23,000,000 (1993 approx.)

Gifts Received: $13,413 (1988); $14,530 (1987)

Fiscal Note: In 1988, the foundation received a $13,413 contribution from Lance, Inc. of Charlotte, NC.

EIN: 56-6039337

CONTRIBUTIONS SUMMARY
Donor(s): The foundation was established in 1961 by Philip Van Every.

Typical Recipients: • *Arts & Humanities:* Arts Associations & Councils, Historic Preservation, Libraries, Museums/Galleries • *Civic & Public Affairs:* Business/Free Enterprise, Housing, Municipalities/Towns, Philanthropic Organizations, Safety, Zoos/Aquariums • *Education:* Colleges & Universities, Education Associations, Education Funds, Public Education (Precollege) • *Environment:* General • *Health:* Hospices, Hospitals, Medical Research, Single-Disease Health Associations • *Religion:* Churches, Religious Organizations, Religious Welfare • *Social Services:* Child Welfare, Community Service Organizations, Homes, Recreation & Athletics, Shelters/Homelessness, United Funds/United Ways, Youth Organizations

Grant Types: general support, research, and scholarship

Geographic Distribution: primarily North Carolina

GIVING OFFICERS
J. William Disher: mem bd admns *B* Charlotte NC 1933 *ED* Wake Forest Univ 1959 *CURR EMPL* chmn, ceo: Lance Inc *CORP AFFIL* dir: First Union Natl Bank-Charlotte *PHIL AFFIL* dir: Lance Foundation

Thomas Borland Harack: mem bd adms *B* Durham NC 1946 *CURR EMPL* vp, secy, treas, mem bd dirs: Lance Inc

Zean Jamison, Jr.: exec dir *B* Gastonia NC 1932 *ED* Belmont Abbey Coll 1959 *CURR*

EMPL dir human resources: Lance Inc *PHIL AFFIL* dir: Lance Foundation

William B. Meacham: mem bd admins *CURR EMPL* vp acquisitions & subsidiaries, dir: Lance Inc *PHIL AFFIL* dir: Lance Foundation

Albert Frazier Sloan: mem bd admins *B* Charlotte NC 1929 *ED* Presbyterian Coll 1955; Univ NC 1969 *CORP AFFIL* dir: Lance Inc *PHIL AFFIL* dir: Lance Foundation

Paul Stroup: mem bd adms

APPLICATION INFORMATION
Initial Approach:

The foundation lists no specific application procedures.

There are no application deadlines.

Restrictions on Giving: The foundation reports no restrictions or limitations on giving.

OTHER THINGS TO KNOW
NationsBank of North Carolina serves as corporate trustee for the foundation.

GRANTS ANALYSIS
Total Grants: $1,452,652

Number of Grants: 123

Highest Grant: $125,000

Average Grant: $9,939*

Typical Range: $5,000 to $50,000

Disclosure Period: 1991

Note: The average figure excludes two grants totaling $250,000. Recent grants are derived from a 1991 Form 990.

RECENT GRANTS

General
125,000	Charlotte-Mecklenburg Hospital, Charlotte, NC
125,000	Charlotte-Mecklenburg Hospital, Charlotte, NC
100,000	Hope Haven
75,000	Willingway Foundation
50,000	Florence Crittenton Services, Charlotte, NC

Wachovia Bank of North Carolina, N.A. / Wachovia Foundation, Inc.

Employees: 5,123
Parent Company: Wachovia Corporation
Assets: $36.52 billion
Headquarters: Winston-Salem, NC
SIC Major Group: Bank Holding Companies and National Commercial Banks

CONTACT
Ed Loflin
Assistant Treasurer
Wachovia Bank of North Carolina, N.A.
301 N Main St.
PO Box 3099
Winston-Salem, NC 27150
(910) 770-5000

FINANCIAL SUMMARY
Recent Giving: $4,692,000 (1994 approx.); $4,602,590 (1993); $3,486,753 (1992)

Assets: $10,342,411 (1993); $9,593,039 (1992); $8,937,180 (1991)

Gifts Received: $5,090,003 (1993)

Fiscal Note: All contributions are made by the bank or its holding company, Wachovia Corporation, but they pass through the Wachovia Foundation. Company stresses that the bank and the company are the only decision-making bodies; foundation is merely the funding vehicle. See also Wachovia Bank of Georgia, N.A. Above figures exclude nonmonetary support.

EIN: 58-1485946

CONTRIBUTIONS SUMMARY
Typical Recipients: • *Arts & Humanities:* Arts Associations & Councils, Arts Centers, Arts Festivals, Arts Funds, Community Arts, Dance, Historic Preservation, Libraries, Museums/Galleries, Opera, Performing Arts, Public Broadcasting • *Civic & Public Affairs:* African American Affairs, Business/Free Enterprise, Civil Rights, Economic Development, General, Municipalities/Towns, Philanthropic Organizations, Professional & Trade Associations, Urban & Community Affairs, Women's Affairs, Zoos/Aquariums • *Education:* Agricultural Education, Business Education, Business-School Partnerships, Colleges & Universities, Community & Junior Colleges, Economic Education, Education Funds, Elementary Education (Private), Private Education (Precollege), Public Education (Precollege), Science/Mathematics Education • *Environment:* General • *Health:* Emergency/Ambulance Services, Health Funds, Health Organizations, Hospices, Hospitals, Respiratory • *International:* International Peace & Security Issues • *Religion:* Religious Welfare • *Science:* Scientific Centers & Institutes • *Social Services:* Child Welfare, Community Centers, Community Service Organizations, Day Care, Delinquency & Criminal Rehabilitation, Family Planning, Family Services, Food/Clothing Distribution, People with Disabilities, Recreation & Athletics, Senior Services, Substance Abuse, United Funds/United Ways, Youth Organizations

Grant Types: capital, challenge, employee matching gifts, endowment, and general support

Nonmonetary Support: $100,000 (1992)

Nonmonetary Support Types: loaned executives

Note: Contact local bank office for nonmonetary support.

Geographic Distribution: primarily in North Carolina, South Carolina, and Georgia

Operating Locations: NC (Ahoskie, Andrews, Asheboro, Asheville, Aurora, Bayboro, Belhaven, Belmont, Bethel, Burlington, Chapel Hill, Charlotte, Durham, Eden, Elizabeth City, Elizabethtown, Fayetteville, Gastonia, Goldsboro, Greensboro, Greenville, Hendersonville, Hickory, High Point, Jacksonville, Kernersville, Kinston, Laurinburg, Lumberton, Marshall, More-

head, Morgantown, Murphy, New Bern, Raleigh, Reidsville, Robersonville, Rocky Mount, Salisbury, Statesville, Thomasville, Vanceboro, Washington, Williamston, Wilmington, Winston-Salem)

Note: Company operates in 87 communities in North Carolina.

CORP. OFFICERS
Leslie Mayo Baker, Jr.: *B* Brunswick MD 1942 *ED* Univ Richmond BA 1964; Univ VA MBA 1969 *CURR EMPL* pres, ceo, dir: Wachovia Corp *CORP AFFIL* chmn, dir: Wachovia Bank NC NA; dir: Wachovia Mortgage Co; trust: Carolina Medicorp Inc *NONPR AFFIL* chmn: Wake Forest Univ; mem: Am Bankers Assn, Salvation Army Boys Club Counc

Clyatt E. Loflin, Jr.: *CURR EMPL* trust off: Wachovia Corp

Ed Loflin: *CURR EMPL* asst treas: Wachovia Bank NC NA

J. Walter McDowell: *B* 1951 *ED* Univ NC BS 1973 *CURR EMPL* pres, ceo, dir: Wachovia Bank NC NA *CORP AFFIL* exec vp: Wachovia Corp

G. Joseph Prendergast: *B* 1945 *ED* Pace Univ MBA; Wesleyan Univ BA *CURR EMPL* exec vp: Wachovia Corp *CORP AFFIL* chmn, dir: First Natl Bank Atlanta *PHIL AFFIL* pres: Wachovia Foundation of Georgia; dir: David, Helen, Marian Woodward Fund-Atlanta, Atlanta Foundation

GIVING OFFICERS
Leslie Mayo Baker, Jr.: dir *CURR EMPL* pres, ceo, dir: Wachovia Corp (see above)

Anthony Lloyd Furr: vp *B* Albemarle NC 1944 *ED* Univ NC 1968; Am Grad Sch Intl Mgmt 1969 *CORP AFFIL* dir: Wachovia Intl Banking Corp *NONPR AFFIL* pres, mem exec comm, dir: Bankers Assn Foreign Trade

J. Walter McDowell: dir *CURR EMPL* pres, ceo, dir: Wachovia Bank NC NA (see above)

G. Joseph Prendergast: dir *CURR EMPL* exec vp: Wachovia Corp *PHIL AFFIL* pres: Wachovia Foundation of Georgia; dir: David, Helen, Marian Woodward Fund-Atlanta, Atlanta Foundation (see above)

William R. Spencer: dir *B* 1940

Gary Thompson: dir

APPLICATION INFORMATION
Initial Approach: *Initial Contact:* requests should be sent to officer in charge of nearest branch bank *Include Information On:* description of the organization, amount requested, purpose for which funds are sought, recently audited financial statement, proof of tax-exempt status, list of contributors *Deadlines:* none

Restrictions on Giving: Does not support individuals, political or lobbying groups, good will advertising, or religious organizations for sectarian purposes.

GRANTS ANALYSIS
Total Grants: $3,486,753
Number of Grants: 324
Highest Grant: $500,000
Average Grant: $10,762
Typical Range: $1,000 to $20,000

Disclosure Period: 1992

Note: Figures exclude nonmonetary support. Recent grants are derived from a 1992 Form 990.

RECENT GRANTS

General

500,000	North Carolina Central University, Durham, NC
200,000	University of North Carolina Chapel Hill, Chapel Hill, NC
200,000	Winston-Salem State University, Winston-Salem, NC — centennial campaign
182,000	United Funds of Winston-Salem, Winston-Salem, NC
150,000	Salem College and Academy, Winston-Salem, NC

NORTH DAKOTA

Myra Foundation

CONTACT
Edward C. Gillig
President
Myra Fdn.
PO Box 13536
Grand Forks, ND 53208
(701) 775-9420

FINANCIAL SUMMARY
Recent Giving: $207,782 (1993); $200,216 (1990); $169,429 (1989)

Assets: $2,724,057 (1993); $2,603,743 (1990); $653,002 (1989)

EIN: 45-0215088

CONTRIBUTIONS SUMMARY
Donor(s): the late John E. Myra

Typical Recipients: • *Arts & Humanities:* Community Arts, Dance, Historic Preservation, Libraries, Music, Performing Arts, Theater • *Education:* Colleges & Universities, Public Education (Precollege) • *Social Services:* Animal Protection, Child Welfare, Community Service Organizations, Senior Services, Shelters/Homelessness, Youth Organizations

Grant Types: general support and scholarship

Geographic Distribution: limited to Grand Forks County, ND

GIVING OFFICERS
Edward C. Gillig: pres

Robert F. Hanson: secy, treas

Hilda Johnson: vp

APPLICATION INFORMATION
Initial Approach: Send brief letter describing program. There are no deadlines.

Restrictions on Giving: Does not support individuals.

PUBLICATIONS
Informational Brochure (including Application Guidelines).

GRANTS ANALYSIS
Total Grants: $207,782

Typical Range: $1,000 to $10,000

Disclosure Period: 1993

Note: Recent grants are derived from a 1993 Form 990. No grants list was provided for 1993.

RECENT GRANTS

General

27,000	University of North Dakota, Grand Forks, ND — scholarships
25,000	YMCA, Grand Forks, ND
12,000	Red River Valley Gymnastics, Grand Forks, ND — gymnastics equipment
12,000	Shelter for Homeless, Grand Forks, ND — renovation of shelter
9,129	Listen Drop-In Center, Grand Forks, ND — computer system and other improvements

OHIO

Amcast Industrial Corp. / Amcast Industrial Foundation

Sales: $222.64 million
Employees: 2,172
Headquarters: Dayton, OH
SIC Major Group: Fabricated Metal Products, Miscellaneous Manufacturing Industries, Primary Metal Industries, and Stone, Clay & Glass Products

CONTACT
Phyllis Naylor
Director, Corporate Communications
Amcast Industrial Corp.
7887 Washington Village Dr.
Dayton, OH 45459
(513) 291-7000

FINANCIAL SUMMARY
Recent Giving: $132,665 (fiscal 1993); $134,618 (fiscal 1991); $125,774 (fiscal 1990)

Assets: $347,004 (fiscal 1991); $395,247 (fiscal 1990); $585,603 (fiscal 1989)

Gifts Received: $25,000 (fiscal 1991); $25,000 (fiscal 1990)

Fiscal Note: In 1991, contributions were received from Amcast Industrial Corp.

EIN: 31-6016458

CONTRIBUTIONS SUMMARY
Typical Recipients: • *Arts & Humanities:* Arts Centers, Arts Funds, Arts Institutes, General, Libraries, Performing Arts • *Civic & Public Affairs:* Chambers of Commerce, Community Foundations, Economic Development, General, Housing, Inner-City Development, Public Policy, Safety, Urban & Community Affairs, Women's Affairs • *Education:* Colleges & Universities, Community & Junior Colleges, General • *Health:* AIDS/HIV, Alzheimers Disease, Cancer, Children's Health/Hospitals, General, Health Organizations, Heart, Hospices • *Social Services:* Community Centers, Emergency Relief, Family Planning, General, Senior Services, Shelters/Homelessness, United Funds/United Ways, Youth Organizations

Grant Types: capital, challenge, emergency, employee matching gifts, multiyear/continuing support, project, research, and scholarship

Geographic Distribution: Dayton, OH

Operating Locations: AR (Fayetteville), CA (Rancho Cucamonga), IN (Elkhart, Gas City, Geneva, Richmond), OH (Dayton), WI (Cedarburg)

Note: List includes division and plant locations.

CORP. OFFICERS
Michael R. Higgins: *CURR EMPL* treas: Amcast Industrial Crop

Leo William Ladehoff: *B* Gladbrook IA 1932 *ED* Univ IA BS 1957 *CURR EMPL* chmn, ceo, dir: Amcast Indus Corp *CORP AFFIL* dir: Hobart Brothers Co, Krug Intl Corp, Soc Corp *NONPR AFFIL* mem: Am Defense Preparedness Assn, Am Foundrymens Assn, Dayton Area Chamber Commerce, Newcomen Soc North Am, Soc Automotive Engrs, Univ IA Alumni Assn

Phyllis Naylor: *CURR EMPL* dir corp comm: Amcast Indus Corp

GIVING OFFICERS
Leo William Ladehoff: pres, trust *CURR EMPL* chmn, ceo, dir: Amcast Indus Corp (see above)

Phyllis Naylor: asst secy *CURR EMPL* dir corp comm: Amcast Indus Corp (see above)

APPLICATION INFORMATION
Initial Approach: Send a brief letter of inquiry. Include a description of organization, amount requested, purpose of funds sought, and proof of tax-exempt status. There are no deadlines.

Restrictions on Giving: Does not support individuals, religious organizations for sectarian purposes, political or lobbying groups, organizations outside operating areas, or schools, except in certain situations.

PUBLICATIONS
Operating Guidelines

GRANTS ANALYSIS
Total Grants: $134,618
Number of Grants: 80
Highest Grant: $8,000
Typical Range: $100 to $5,000

Disclosure Period: fiscal year ending August 31, 1991

Note: Recent grants are derived from a fiscal 1991 Form 990.

RECENT GRANTS

General

8,000	City of Kettering, Kettering, OH — Lincoln Park
8,000	United Way, Dayton, OH
7,400	Wright State University Foundation, Dayton, OH
5,000	Dayton Area Chamber of Commerce, Dayton, OH
5,000	Miami Valley Health Foundation, Dayton, OH

Andersons, The / Anderson Foundation

Sales: $776.0 million
Employees: 2,400
Headquarters: Maumee, OH
SIC Major Group: Cash Grains Nec, Grain & Field Beans, Farm Supplies, and Business Services Nec

CONTACT
Beverly J. Lange
Secretary to Chairman
Anderson Fdn.
PO Box 119
Maumee, OH 43537
(419) 891-6404

FINANCIAL SUMMARY
Recent Giving: $969,000 (1995 est.); $733,000 (1994 approx.); $502,701 (1993)

Assets: $5,103,879 (1993); $4,694,879 (1992); $4,474,819 (1991)

Gifts Received: $520,847 (1993); $209,153 (1992)

Fiscal Note: Above figures are for the foundation only. The company offers a small amount of direct gifts. Individual company departments make contributions from corporate funds. Contact Thomas H. Anderson, foundation chairman, for more details. See "Other Things To Know" for more details. The foundation receives yearly contributions from The Andersons.

EIN: 34-6528868

CONTRIBUTIONS SUMMARY
Typical Recipients: • *Arts & Humanities:* Arts Associations & Councils, Arts Centers, Historic Preservation, History & Archaeology, Libraries, Museums/Galleries, Music, Opera, Public Broadcasting • *Civic & Public Affairs:* Clubs, Municipalities/Towns, Public Policy, Urban & Community Affairs, Zoos/Aquariums • *Education:* Agricultural Education, Business Education, Colleges & Universities, Education Associations, Education Funds, Literacy, Minority Education, Private Education (Precollege), Secondary Education (Private) • *Environment:* General • *Health:* Clinics/Medical Centers, Emergency/Ambulance Services, Medical Research, Mental Health, Single-Disease

Health Associations • *Religion:* Churches, Ministries, Religious Organizations, Religious Welfare • *Social Services:* Animal Protection, Child Welfare, Community Centers, Community Service Organizations, Family Services, Food/Clothing Distribution, People with Disabilities, Recreation & Athletics, Refugee Assistance, Senior Services, United Funds/United Ways, Youth Organizations

Grant Types: capital, employee matching gifts, general support, project, and seed money

Note: Employee matching gift ratio: 1 to 1.

Geographic Distribution: near operating locations, including plant locations

Operating Locations: IL (Champaign), IN (Delphi, Dunkirk, Frankfort), MI (Albion, Potterville, Webberville, White Pigeon), OH (Maumee, Toledo)

CORP. OFFICERS
Thomas Harold Anderson: *B* Toledo OH 1924 *CURR EMPL* chmn, dir: Andersons Mgmt Corp *CORP AFFIL* chmn: Andersons *NONPR AFFIL* chmn: Toledo Area Chamber Commerce; pres, dir: Intl Ctr Preservation Wild Animals *CLUB AFFIL* Rotary

Joanne Kapnick: *CURR EMPL* dir pub aff: Andersons Mgmt Corp

GIVING OFFICERS
Andrew T. Anderson: trust

Charles D. Anderson: trust *B* Detroit MI 1931 *ED* MI Sch Mines 1953 *CURR EMPL* chmn, pres: Anderson Tool Sales *CORP AFFIL* chmn: ATD Tools Corp

Jeffrey W. Anderson: trust

Richard Paul Anderson: trust *B* Toledo OH 1929 *ED* MI St Univ BS 1953 *CORP AFFIL* dir: Centerior Energy Corp, First MS Corp, Toledo Edison Co; ltd ptnr, ceo: Andersons *NONPR AFFIL* chmn support counc: OH Agricultural Res & Devel Ctr; dir: Childrens Svcs, Pub Broadcasting Fdn, St Lukes Hosp; trust: Univ Toledo Corp *CLUB AFFIL* Rotary

Thomas Harold Anderson: chmn, trust *CURR EMPL* chmn, dir: Andersons Mgmt Corp (see above)

John P. Kraus: trust

Beverly J. Lange: contact *CURR EMPL* secy chmn: Andersons Mgmt Corp

Ruth M. Miller: trust

APPLICATION INFORMATION
Initial Approach: *Initial Contact:* brief letter of inquiry, not more than five pages *Include Information On:* description of the organization, including organization's purpose and objectives; amount requested; purpose of funds sought; the need, including population served; recently audited financial statements; proof of tax-exempt status; list of officers and directors; and list of major donors *Deadlines:* at least three weeks before quarterly board meeting

Restrictions on Giving: Does not support individuals, or political or lobbying groups. Also not funded are endowment funds, church building or operating funds, or build-

ing or operating funds for elementary schools.

Generally, does not serve as major, or sole, funder of project.

OTHER THINGS TO KNOW
The foundation's major donor is The Andersons, but foundation representative reports that its activities are separate. The company does offer a very limited amount of direct giving in its headquarters area.

GRANTS ANALYSIS
Total Grants: $502,701
Number of Grants: 172
Highest Grant: $165,200
Average Grant: $2,923
Typical Range: $50 to $5,000
Disclosure Period: 1993

Note: Recent grants are derived from a 1993 Form 990.

RECENT GRANTS
General

165,200	United Way Toledo, Toledo, OH
61,050	University of Toledo, Toledo, OH
50,000	Center of Science and Industry, Toledo, OH
35,934	Central City Ministries, Toledo, OH
18,614	United Way Franklin County, Columbus, OH

Andrews Foundation

CONTACT
Richard S. Tomer
President
Andrews Fdn.
925 Euclid Ave., Ste. 1525
Cleveland, OH 44115-1407
(216) 621-3215

FINANCIAL SUMMARY
Recent Giving: $238,700 (1993); $169,200 (1992); $249,838 (1991)

Assets: $6,852,474 (1993); $6,500,515 (1992); $5,456,099 (1991)

EIN: 34-6515110

CONTRIBUTIONS SUMMARY
Donor(s): the late Mrs. Matthew Andrews

Typical Recipients: • *Arts & Humanities:* Arts Centers, Ballet, Community Arts, General, Libraries, Museums/Galleries, Music, Performing Arts, Theater • *Civic & Public Affairs:* Economic Development, Employment/Job Training, General, Law & Justice, Municipalities/Towns, Parades/Festivals, Urban & Community Affairs • *Education:* Colleges & Universities, Minority Education, Private Education (Precollege), Public Education (Precollege), Secondary Education (Private), Student Aid • *Health:* Clinics/Medical Centers, Emergency/Ambulance Services, Health Organizations, Heart • *Religion:* Religious Organizations, Religious

Welfare, Seminaries • *Science:* Science Museums • *Social Services:* Child Welfare, Community Service Organizations, Delinquency & Criminal Rehabilitation, Domestic Violence, People with Disabilities, Substance Abuse, United Funds/United Ways, Veterans, Youth Organizations

Grant Types: capital, endowment, and general support

Geographic Distribution: limited to northeastern OH

GIVING OFFICERS
Barbara J. Baxter: vp, trust

Laura S. Baxter: asst secy, treas, trust

James Howard Dempsey, Jr.: secy, trust *B* Cleveland OH 1916 *ED* Yale Univ BA 1938; Yale Univ LLB 1941 *CURR EMPL* gen ptnr: Squire Sanders & Dempsey *NONPR AFFIL* mem: Am Bar Assn, Cleveland Bar Assn, OH Bar Assn; trust: Univ Hosps *CLUB AFFIL* Chagrin Valley Hunt, Kirtland, Pepper Pike, Tavern, Union *PHIL AFFIL* secy, trust: Marguerite M. Wilson Foundation

Richard S. Tomer: pres, trust

APPLICATION INFORMATION
Initial Approach: Include a description of organization, amount requested, purpose of funds sought, recently audited financial statement, and proof of tax-exempt status. There are no deadlines.

GRANTS ANALYSIS
Total Grants: $238,700

Number of Grants: 32

Highest Grant: $40,000

Typical Range: $1,000 to $25,000

Disclosure Period: 1993

Note: Recent grants are derived from a 1993 Form 990 and includes future commitments.

RECENT GRANTS

Library
225,000	College of Wooster, Wooster, OH — Andrews Library Council Campaign

General
50,000	St. Bernadette Church, Westlake, OH — Jewel Tomer Scholarship Fund
45,000	Betty Ford Renewal Center, Palm Springs, CA — Patient Assistance Fund
40,000	Gilmour Academy, Gates Mills, OH — endowment fund Matthew A. Baxter Middle School
40,000	Magnificat High School, Rocky River, OH — Convent construction and renovation
40,000	Ursuline Nuns, Cleveland, OH — St. Angela Health Care Center construction

Ashtabula Foundation

CONTACT
Ashtabula Fdn.
PO Drawer A
Ashtubula, OH 44004
(216) 993-2222

FINANCIAL SUMMARY
Recent Giving: $439,197 (1993)

Assets: $10,842,214 (1993)

Gifts Received: $2,291 (1993)

EIN: 34-6538130

CONTRIBUTIONS SUMMARY
Typical Recipients: • *Arts & Humanities:* History & Archaeology, Libraries • *Civic & Public Affairs:* Economic Development, Housing, Urban & Community Affairs • *Education:* Colleges & Universities, Public Education (Precollege) • *Health:* Alzheimers Disease, Clinics/Medical Centers, Heart, Prenatal Health Issues • *Religion:* Churches, Religious Welfare • *Social Services:* Camps, Child Welfare, Community Centers, Community Service Organizations, People with Disabilities, Recreation & Athletics, United Funds/United Ways, YMCA/YWCA/YMHA/YWHA

Grant Types: general support and scholarship

Geographic Distribution: focus on OH

GIVING OFFICERS
Wilbur L. Anderson: trust

Roy H. Bean: trust

Dr. Jerome Bockway: trust

Thad Hague: trust

Douglas A. Hedberg: trust

Eleanor A. Jammal: vp, trust

Robert E. Martin, Jr.: secy, treas

Glen W. Warner: trust

Barbara P. Wiese: trust

Dr. William C. Zweier: pres, trust

APPLICATION INFORMATION
Initial Approach: Request application form. Contact foundation for deadlines.

GRANTS ANALYSIS
Total Grants: $439,197

Number of Grants: 35

Highest Grant: $100,000

Typical Range: $11 to $38,460

Disclosure Period: 1993

Note: Recent grants are derived from a 1993 Form 990. Number of grants and typical range do not include scholarships totaling $18,500.

RECENT GRANTS

Library
30,000	Ashtabula County District Library, Ashtabula, OH — NOLA Regional Library participation
11	Kingsville Public Library, Kingsville, OH

General
100,000	Civic Development Corporation, Ashtabula, OH
38,460	Ashtabula County Public Boards of Education, Jefferson, OH — Thurgood Marshall Family Resource Center
30,910	Ashtabula County Medical Center, Ashtabula, OH
30,497	YMCA, Ashtabula, OH
30,000	Ashtabula United Way, Ashtabula, OH

Bank One, Youngstown, NA

Employees: 550
Parent Company: Banc One Corp.
Headquarters: Youngstown, OH
SIC Major Group: Depository Institutions

CONTACT
Albert A. Matasy, CRA
Senior Vice President
Bank One, Youngstown, NA
6 Federal Plz. W
Youngstown, OH 44503
(216) 744-5041

FINANCIAL SUMMARY
Recent Giving: $275,000 (1994)

Fiscal Note: Annual contribution figures are between $100,000 and $250,000.

CONTRIBUTIONS SUMMARY
Company reports that 50% of contributions support health and human services; 11%, civic and public affairs; 10%, arts and humanities; and 9%, economic development.

Typical Recipients: • *Arts & Humanities:* Arts Centers, Arts Festivals, Arts Funds, Arts Institutes, Ballet, Community Arts, Ethnic & Folk Arts, General, Libraries, Museums/Galleries, Music, Opera, Performing Arts, Theater • *Civic & Public Affairs:* African American Affairs, Asian American Affairs, Business/Free Enterprise, Civil Rights, Community Foundations, Economic Development, Ethnic Organizations, General, Hispanic Affairs, Housing, Inner-City Development, Native American Affairs, Nonprofit Management, Parades/Festivals, Urban & Community Affairs, Women's Affairs • *Education:* Arts/Humanities Education, Business Education, Colleges & Universities, Economic Education, Elementary Education (Public), General, Literacy, Minority Education • *Environment:* General • *Health:* Alzheimers Disease, Arthritis, Cancer, Children's Health/Hospitals, General, Health Organizations, Heart, Hospices, Hospitals, Kidney, Mental Health, Multiple Sclerosis, Preventive Medicine/Wellness Organizations, Speech & Hearing • *International:* Trade • *Social Services:* At-Risk Youth, Community Centers, Community Service Organizations, Day Care, Family Planning, General, Homes, People with Disabilities, Senior Services, Shelters/Homelessness, United Funds/United Ways, Volunteer Services, Youth Organizations

Grant Types: award, capital, challenge, general support, project, scholarship, and seed money

Nonmonetary Support Types: cause-related marketing & promotion, donated equipment, in-kind services, loaned employees, loaned executives, and workplace solicitation

Geographic Distribution: Grants are awarded in headquarters and operating communities.

Operating Locations: OH (Youngstown)

CORP. OFFICERS
Donald Cagigas: *CURR EMPL* chmn, ceo, dir: Bank One Youngstown NA

Arthur Carina: *CURR EMPL* cfo: Bank One Youngstown NA

APPLICATION INFORMATION
Initial Approach: Send a brief letter of inquiry which includes a description of organization, amount requested, purpose of funds sought, and proof of tax-exempt status. Also include whether or not organization is affiliated with the United Way.

Restrictions on Giving: Does not support individuals, religious organizations for sectarian purposes, political or lobbying groups, or organizations outside operating areas.

GRANTS ANALYSIS
Typical Range: $500 to $10,000

Barry Corp., R. G. / Barry Foundation

Revenue: $101.17 million
Employees: 2,400
Headquarters: Columbus, OH
SIC Major Group: Leather & Leather Products and Wholesale Trade—Nondurable Goods

---

CONTACT
Darla Price
Human Resources
R.G. Barry Corp.
PO Box 129
Columbus, OH 43216
(614) 864-6400

FINANCIAL SUMMARY
Recent Giving: $290,878 (1993); $7,300 (1991); $84,000 (1990)

Assets: $6,873 (1993); $315 (1991); $8,278 (1990)

Gifts Received: $297,274 (1993); $216,525 (1990)

Fiscal Note: In 1993, contributions were received from the R.G. Barry Corp.

EIN: 31-6051086

CONTRIBUTIONS SUMMARY
Typical Recipients: • *Arts & Humanities:* Arts Centers, Arts Funds, Arts Institutes, Ballet, Community Arts, Dance, Ethnic & Folk Arts, General, Libraries, Museums/Galleries, Music, Opera, Performing Arts, Public Broadcasting, Theater • *Civic & Public*

Affairs: Business/Free Enterprise, Community Foundations, Economic Development, General, Urban & Community Affairs • *Education:* Colleges & Universities, Community & Junior Colleges, Education Associations, General, Religious Education • *Health:* Diabetes, General, Health Funds, Health Organizations, Medical Research, Single-Disease Health Associations • *International:* International Affairs, Missionary/Religious Activities • *Religion:* Churches, Jewish Causes, Religious Organizations, Religious Welfare, Synagogues/Temples • *Social Services:* Child Welfare, Community Centers, Community Service Organizations, Family Services, General, People with Disabilities, Scouts, Senior Services, United Funds/United Ways, Youth Organizations

Grant Types: general support

Nonmonetary Support Types: donated products

Geographic Distribution: provides grants nationally

Operating Locations: OH (Pickerington)

CORP. OFFICERS
Richard L. Burrell: *B* Union City OH 1933 *ED* Miami Univ BS 1955; Xavier Univ MBA 1965 *CURR EMPL* vp fin: RG Barry Corp *CORP AFFIL* dir: Lord, Sullivan, Yoder, Worthington, Ohio, ZeeMed Svcs *NONPR AFFIL* mem: Fin Execs Inst

Gordon Zacks: *B* Terre Haute IN 1933 *ED* OH St Univ BA 1955 *CURR EMPL* pres, ceo, dir: RG Barry Corp *NONPR AFFIL* hon chmn: Un Jewish Appeal; mem: Am Mgmt Assn, Chief Execs Org, Natl Repbl Senatorial Comm

GIVING OFFICERS
Richard L. Burrell: treas *CURR EMPL* vp fin: RG Barry Corp (see above)

William Edward Ellis, Jr.: secy, trust *B* Statesville NC 1949 *ED* NC St Univ 1973; Univ NC *CURR EMPL* exec vp mktg: Monex Resources

Harvey M. Krueger: trust *B* Jersey City NJ 1929 *ED* Columbia Coll 1951; Columbia Univ 1953 *CURR EMPL* mng dir: Shearson Lehman Brothers *CORP AFFIL* dir: Ampal Corp, Automatic Data Processing, Manhattan Indus, RG Barry Corp

Florence Melton: chmn, trust

Gordon Zacks: pres, trust *CURR EMPL* pres, ceo, dir: RG Barry Corp (see above)

APPLICATION INFORMATION
Initial Approach: Send a brief letter of inquiry. Include a description of organization, amount requested, purpose of funds sought, and proof of tax-exempt status. There are no deadlines.

Restrictions on Giving: Does not support individuals, religious organizations for sectarian purposes, or political or lobbying groups.

PUBLICATIONS
Financial Statements

GRANTS ANALYSIS
Total Grants: $290,878
Number of Grants: 25

Highest Grant: $166,666
Typical Range: $100 to $30,000
Disclosure Period: 1993

Note: Recent grants are derived from a 1993 Form 990.

RECENT GRANTS
Library
30,000	Ronald Reagan Presidential Foundation, Simi Valley, CA — Presidential Library Education

General
166,666	Columbus Jewish Federation, Columbus, OH — Jewish Community programs
30,000	American Friends of the Shalom Hartman Institute, Englewood, NJ — endowment fund
18,535	United Way of Franklin County, Columbus, OH — local community fund
14,276	United Way of the Concho Valley, San Angelo, TX — local community fund
6,000	LifeCare Alliance, Columbus, OH — programs for the elderly

---

Battelle Memorial Institute

Sales: $854.0 million
Employees: 8,400
Headquarters: Columbus, OH
SIC Major Group: Commercial Physical Research

CONTACT
Barbara A. Sills
Director, Community Relations
Battelle Memorial Institute
505 King Ave.
Columbus, OH 43201
(614) 424-7980

FINANCIAL SUMMARY
Recent Giving: $1,756,186 (1993); $1,900,000 (1990); $1,200,000 (1989)

Fiscal Note: Company gives directly.

CONTRIBUTIONS SUMMARY
Typical Recipients: • *Arts & Humanities:* Arts Associations & Councils, Community Arts, Dance, Libraries, Museums/Galleries, Music, Opera, Performing Arts, Public Broadcasting, Theater • *Civic & Public Affairs:* Business/Free Enterprise, Economic Development, Employment/Job Training, Professional & Trade Associations, Zoos/Aquariums • *Education:* Business Education, Colleges & Universities, Community & Junior Colleges, Economic Education, Elementary Education (Private), Engineering/Technological Education, Faculty Development, Literacy, Medical Education, Minority Education, Public Education (Precollege), Science/Mathematics Education • *Health:* Geriatric Health, Health Policy/Cost Containment, Hospitals, Medical

Research, Nursing Services, Nutrition, Single-Disease Health Associations • *Social Services:* Child Welfare, Family Planning, Family Services, People with Disabilities, Recreation & Athletics, Senior Services, Substance Abuse, United Funds/United Ways, Youth Organizations

Grant Types: capital, challenge, conference/seminar, endowment, and general support

Nonmonetary Support: $432,000 (1990); $390,000 (1988)

Nonmonetary Support Types: donated equipment, loaned employees, and loaned executives

Note: Noncash requests may also be referred to Ms. Sills.

Geographic Distribution: giving is near headquarters and operating locations only

Operating Locations: OH (Columbus), WA (Richland)

Note: Also operates internationally.

CORP. OFFICERS

Douglas Eugene Olesen: *B* Tonasket WA 1939 *ED* Univ WA BS 1962; Univ WA MS 1963; Univ WA PhD 1972 *CURR EMPL* pres, ceo: Battelle Meml Inst *CORP AFFIL* dir: Fed Reserve Bank Cleveland *NONPR AFFIL* dir: OH St Univ Fdn; mem: Columbus Area Chamber Commerce, OH Chamber Commerce; trust: Capital Univ, Columbus Mus Art, Columbus 1992 Comm, Columbus Symphony Orchestra, Columbus Zoo, INROADS/Columbus, Riverside Hosp Fdn, Un Way Franklin

Willis Sheridan White, Jr.: *B* Portsmouth VA 1926 *ED* VA Polytech Inst & St Univ BS 1948; MA Inst Tech MS 1958 *CURR EMPL* trust, chmn: Battelle Meml Inst *CORP AFFIL* dir: Bank NY Co Inc *NONPR AFFIL* dir: Riverside Methodist Hosp; mem: Eta Kappa Nu, Inst Electrical Electronics Engrs, Natl Acad Engg, Omicron Delta Kappa

GIVING OFFICERS

Barbara A. Sills: *B* Lancaster OH 1946 *CURR EMPL* dir commun rels: Battelle Meml Inst

APPLICATION INFORMATION

Initial Approach: *Initial Contact:* phone call or letter requesting an appointment for an informal meeting *Include Information On:* description of the organization; amount requested; purpose for which funds are sought; recently audited financial statement; and proof of tax-exempt status *Deadlines:* none

Restrictions on Giving: Does not support fraternal organizations, goodwill advertising, individuals, political or lobbying groups, or religious organizations.

GRANTS ANALYSIS

Total Grants: $1,756,186

Typical Range: $1,000 to $2,500

Disclosure Period: 1993

Note: Recent grants are derived from a 1990 grants list.

Bingham Foundation, William

CONTACT
Laura C. Hitchcock Gilbertson
Director
William Bingham Foundation
1250 Leader Bldg.
Cleveland, OH 44114
(216) 781-3275

FINANCIAL SUMMARY
Recent Giving: $1,676,014 (1993); $1,301,016 (1992); $1,295,062 (1991)

Assets: $32,904,595 (1993); $30,799,000 (1992); $23,099,000 (1991)

Gifts Received: $1,000 (1993); $1,000 (1992); $2,000 (1990)

EIN: 34-6513791

CONTRIBUTIONS SUMMARY
Donor(s): The William Bingham Foundation was incorporated in 1955 by Elizabeth Bingham Blossom , in memory of her brother, William Bingham II.

Initially, the foundation contributed to a wide variety of organizations in education, the arts, health, and welfare in the Cleveland area. After the death of Mrs. Blossom in 1970, the foundation continued this traditional giving under the leadership of her daughter, Mary Blossom Lee, (d. 1976), and her daughter-in-law, Emily E. Blossom. The current trustees are grandchildren of the founder.

Typical Recipients: • *Arts & Humanities:* Arts Appreciation, Arts Associations & Councils, Arts Centers, Arts Funds, Ballet, Dance, Libraries, Literary Arts, Museums/Galleries, Public Broadcasting, Theater, Visual Arts • *Civic & Public Affairs:* Economic Development, Nonprofit Management, Professional & Trade Associations • *Education:* Arts/Humanities Education, Colleges & Universities, Education Associations, Elementary Education (Public), Environmental Education, Faculty Development, General, Gifted & Talented Programs, International Exchange, International Studies, Preschool Education, Private Education (Precollege), Public Education (Precollege), Secondary Education (Private), Special Education, Student Aid • *Environment:* Air/Water Quality, General, Resource Conservation, Watershed, Wildlife Protection • *Health:* Clinics/Medical Centers, Diabetes, Hospitals, Multiple Sclerosis • *International:* International Environmental Issues, Missionary/Religious Activities • *Science:* Science Museums, Scientific Labs, Scientific Organizations • *Social Services:* Animal Protection, Camps, Child Welfare, Community Service Organizations, Domestic Violence, People with Disabilities, Recreation & Athletics, Shelters/Homelessness, Substance Abuse, Youth Organizations

Grant Types: capital, challenge, conference/seminar, general support, matching, project, and scholarship

Geographic Distribution: United States only; preference for communities in which trustees reside

GIVING OFFICERS
Thomas F. Allen: secy *PHIL AFFIL* treas, trust: George S. Dively Foundation; treas, asst secy, trust: Weatherhead Foundation; asst secy: 2714 Foundation; treas, asst secy: Spahr Family Foundation

C. Bingham Blossom: trust, chmn investment comm treas

C. Perry Blossom: trust

Dudley S. Blossom: trust

Laurel Blossom: trust

Robin Dunn Blossom: trust

Benjamin Gale: trust

Thomas H. Gale: trust

Thomas V. Gale: trust

Mary E. Gale-Holweger: vp, trust

Laura C. Hitchcock Gilbertson: dir

Elizabeth Blossom Heffernan: pres, trust

APPLICATION INFORMATION
Initial Approach:

Requests should be submitted in the form of a one- to two-page letter; no other attachments or documentation should be included.

The initial letter should outline the nature of the project, budget requirements, and the amount requested.

The initial request may be submitted any time.

If the project corresponds with the foundation's interests, the executive director or a trustee may request a meeting or a full proposal. If the foundation requests a full grant proposal, the proposal must be submitted two months before the next meeting of the board of trustees, usually held in May and October. The trustees act on full grant applications, when requested, at these semi-annual meetings.

Restrictions on Giving: The foundation encourages applicants to seek additional funding sources and asks applicants to inform the foundation of other grants received. The foundation expects a grantee to report at least annually on the progress of its program, and to account for funds at the completion of the grant period.

Restrictions on Giving: Grants ordinarily do not exceed one year in duration. The foundation does not make grants to individuals for fellowships, scholarships, or research projects. No funding is extended to individuals or organizations outside the United States.

PUBLICATIONS
Annual report

GRANTS ANALYSIS
Total Grants: $1,676,014

Number of Grants: 38

Highest Grant: $275,000

Average Grant: $31,973*

Typical Range: $5,000 to $50,000

Disclosure Period: 1993

Note: Average grant figure excludes two grants totaling $525,000. Recent grants are derived from a 1993 Form 990.

RECENT GRANTS

Library

20,000   Palm Beach County Library Association, W. Palm Beach, FL — for 1994 support of BookFest of the Palm Beaches, a book fair promoting literacy, literature, and reading

5,000   Foundation Center, New York, NY — for general operating support of the Cleveland Field office

General

250,000   Yale University, New Haven, CT — to create an endowment fund for the Studies in the Environment Program of Yale's Institute for Biospheric Studies

200,000   Environmental Defense Fund, New York, NY — for the global climate change program

100,000   Kent School, Chestertown, MD — for the school's capital and endowment campaign

100,000   Malone College, Canton, OH — for construction of the college's Centennial Center

50,000   Climate Institute, Washington, DC — general operating support

---

Borden, Inc. / Borden Foundation, Inc.

Revenue: $6.49 billion
Employees: 41,900
Headquarters: New York, NY
SIC Major Group: Cheese—Natural & Processed, Ice Cream & Frozen Desserts, Dry, Condensed & Evaporated Dairy Products, and Fluid Milk

CONTACT

Judith Barker
President
Borden Foundation, Inc.
180 East Broad St.
Columbus, OH 43215-3799
(614) 225-2025

FINANCIAL SUMMARY

Recent Giving: $2,457,269 (1993); $2,335,681 (1992); $2,430,091 (1991)

Assets: $33,394 (1993); $34,334 (1992); $31,500 (1991)

Gifts Received: $2,755,000 (1993); $2,675,000 (1992)

Fiscal Note: Cash contributions are disbursed through the foundation; the corpora-

tion also provides noncash support. Above figures exclude nonmonetary support.

EIN: 13-6089941

CONTRIBUTIONS SUMMARY

Typical Recipients: • *Arts & Humanities:* Arts Associations & Councils, Arts Centers, Arts Institutes, Ballet, Community Arts, Dance, Historic Preservation, Libraries, Museums/Galleries, Music, Opera, Performing Arts, Theater • *Civic & Public Affairs:* African American Affairs, Business/Free Enterprise, Civil Rights, Clubs, Community Foundations, Economic Development, Economic Policy, Ethnic Organizations, Hispanic Affairs, Law & Justice, Municipalities/Towns, Nonprofit Management, Parades/Festivals, Philanthropic Organizations, Professional & Trade Associations, Public Policy, Urban & Community Affairs, Women's Affairs • *Education:* Business Education, Colleges & Universities, Continuing Education, Education Associations, Education Funds, Engineering/Technological Education, General, Literacy, Minority Education, Private Education (Precollege), Public Education (Precollege), Science/Mathematics Education, Special Education, Student Aid • *Environment:* General • *Health:* AIDS/HIV, Cancer, Eyes/Blindness, Hospitals, Medical Research, Mental Health, Prenatal Health Issues, Single-Disease Health Associations • *International:* International Relations • *Religion:* Churches, Religious Organizations, Religious Welfare • *Science:* Scientific Organizations • *Social Services:* At-Risk Youth, Child Welfare, Community Service Organizations, Family Services, Food/Clothing Distribution, Homes, People with Disabilities, Recreation & Athletics, Scouts, Shelters/Homelessness, United Funds/United Ways, Volunteer Services, Youth Organizations

Grant Types: challenge, department, employee matching gifts, and general support

Nonmonetary Support: $1,800,000 (1990); $1,800,000 (1989); $500,000 (1988)

Nonmonetary Support Types: donated products and in-kind services

Note: Value of nonmonetary support is not available.

Geographic Distribution: preference given to locations where Borden Inc. maintains facilities

Operating Locations: AL (Birmingham), AZ, CA (Anaheim, Los Angeles), CO (Denver), FL (St. Augustine, Winter Haven), GA, IL (Bellwood, Chicago, Elk Grove Village, Schaumburg, Westchester), IN (Ft. Wayne, Indianapolis), KS (Lenexa), KY, LA (Geismar, Harahan, Lafayette), MA (Haverhill, Lowell, North Andover), MD (Baltimore), ME (Orchard Beach), MI (Warren), MN (Minneapolis, St. Paul), MO (Liberty, St. Louis), MS, NC (Goldsboro), NE (Omaha), NJ (Fair Lawn, Merchantville, Mountainside), NY (Bainbridge, Buffalo, Glen Cove, New York), OH (Cincinnati, Columbus), OR, PA (Berwick, Carnegie), PR, SC (Beaufort, Greenville), TN (Memphis),

TX (Austin, Dallas, Houston), UT (Kaysville), VA (Bristol), WA (Bellvue, Kent), WI (Milwaukee), WV (Charleston)

CORP. OFFICERS

Robert Kidder: *CURR EMPL* chmn: Borden Inc

Ervin Richard Shames: *B* Des Moines IA 1940 *ED* Univ FL BSBA 1962; Harvard Univ MBA 1966 *CURR EMPL* pres, ceo, coo, dir: Borden Inc *CORP AFFIL* dir: First Brands Corp *NONPR AFFIL* bd visit: Duke Univ Fuqua Sch Bus, Northeastern Univ Coll Bus Admin; dir: Harvard Univ Grad Sch Bus Admin Alumni Assn

GIVING OFFICERS

Judith Barker: pres *B* Burlington NC 1941 *ED* Franklin Univ; OH St Univ *CURR EMPL* vp social responsibility: Borden Inc *NONPR AFFIL* dir: Better Bus Bur Fdn, Columbus Airport Authority, Columbus Commn Ethics Values, Greater Columbus Arts Counc, OH St Univ Hosps, Pub-Pvt Ventures; mem: NY Contributions Adv Group; mem adv bd: OH St Univ Sch Home Econs; mem Afro-Am adv bd: Columbus Mus Art; mem corp adv comm: Philanthropic Adv Svc

Richard Hays Byrd: treas *B* Wheeling WV 1939 *ED* MI St Univ BA 1960; MI St Univ MBA 1961 *CURR EMPL* asst treas: Borden Inc *CORP AFFIL* asst treas: Borden Chem and Plastics *NONPR AFFIL* secy, treas: Central OH Fire Mus; trust: Better Bus Bureau Central OH, Columbus Area Chamber Commerce, Perry Township Franklin County OH *CLUB AFFIL* Athletic Columbus, York Lodge 563 F & Am Box 15, Masons, Shriners

Anthony S. D'Amato: chmn *B* Brooklyn NY 1930 *ED* Polytech Inst Brooklyn BS 1952 *CORP AFFIL* dir: Bank NY Co Inc; pres: Borden Chem Co *NONPR AFFIL* mem: Am Chem Soc

H. C. Doughty, Jr.: secy

Frankie Nowlin: exec dir

APPLICATION INFORMATION

Initial Approach: *Initial Contact:* preliminary letter of inquiry to the foundation* *Include Information On:* full proposals must include responses, in numerical order, to the following: (1) name, affiliation, address, and phone number of organization and its contact person; (2) how long organization has existed and geographical area and number of people served; (3) principal staff and board of trustees, and how often board meets; (4) members of board associated with or employed by organization and whether the board has authorized grant request; (5) amount of compensation, if any, for board members; (6) current sources of income, with percentages, for the past three years; (7) amount and percentage of total income expended for fund-raising, program, administrative, and general operations; (8) copy of IRS tax exemption letter, current financial statement, and most recent financial audit; (9) information on Philanthropic Advisory

Service rating; (10) description of the organization's affiliations; (11) purpose of project or request, including whether problem area to be addressed is a special project or part of general operating support; (12) why organization should be the vehicle of support for project and how this project will benefit recipients and total community; (13) how project will be carried out; (14) principal project staff, with brief summaries of education and work experience; (15) distinguishing characteristics of this project from others in the same field; (16) proposed budget; (17) amount requested and time frame for disbursement; (18) percentage of total budget supplied by government, if any; (19) all organizations to be approached for funding of project and amounts requested from each; (20) organizations that have committed support and at what levels; (21) how project will be sustained after foundation support is completed; (22) what review and evaluation procedures will determine success of project *Deadlines:* none; review may take three to six months *Note:* Borden Foundation publishes detailed guidelines for format and content of formal grant applications.

Restrictions on Giving: Foundation does not support individuals; endowments; memberships; lobbying organizations; conferences, workshops, or seminars; building or renovation; journal advertisements; political activities or organizations; organizations deriving major support from government funding; or organizations that discriminate in any way consistent with national equal opportunity policies.

OTHER THINGS TO KNOW
All contributions by Borden, Inc., awarded through Borden Foundation, Inc.

Foundation requires status reports on the success of project.

GRANTS ANALYSIS
Total Grants: $2,457,269

Number of Grants: 218

Highest Grant: $202,500

Average Grant: $11,272

Typical Range: $1,000 to $10,000

Disclosure Period: 1993

Note: The figure for Number of Grants is an estimate. Recent grants are derived from a 1993 Form 990.

RECENT GRANTS

General

202,500	United Negro College Fund, New York, NY
184,800	United Way of Franklin County, Columbus, OH
102,500	ASPIRA Association, Washington, DC
100,000	Arthur James Cancer Hospital and Research Foundation
100,000	Children's Defense Fund, Washington, DC

BP America Inc.

Sales: $15.0 billion
Employees: 25,000
Parent Company: BP America Holdings Limited
Headquarters: Cleveland, OH
SIC Major Group: Holding Companies Nec

CONTACT
W. B. Doggett
Director, Communications & Community Relations
BP America Inc.
200 Public Sq., 40-N
Cleveland, OH 44114
(216) 586-5552

FINANCIAL SUMMARY
Recent Giving: $7,000,000 (1995 est.); $8,000,000 (1994); $9,128,664 (1993)

Fiscal Note: Company gives directly.

CONTRIBUTIONS SUMMARY
Typical Recipients: • *Arts & Humanities:* Arts Associations & Councils, Arts Centers, Arts Institutes, Community Arts, Dance, Historic Preservation, Libraries, Museums/Galleries, Music, Opera, Performing Arts, Public Broadcasting, Theater • *Civic & Public Affairs:* Economic Development, Public Policy, Urban & Community Affairs, Women's Affairs • *Education:* Arts/Humanities Education, Colleges & Universities, Engineering/Technological Education, Minority Education, Public Education (Precollege), Science/Mathematics Education • *Environment:* General • *Health:* Health Organizations, Hospitals • *Social Services:* Community Centers, Community Service Organizations, United Funds/United Ways, Youth Organizations

Grant Types: award, capital, challenge, conference/seminar, employee matching gifts, matching, and multiyear/continuing support

Nonmonetary Support: $200,000 (1994)

Nonmonetary Support Types: donated equipment, in-kind services, loaned employees, and loaned executives

Note: Contact Shirley Simpson, contributions assistant, for more information about nonmonetary support. Above figures exclude nonmonetary support.

Geographic Distribution: in communities where company has significant operations

Operating Locations: AK (Anchorage), LA (Belle Chasse), NY (Niagara Falls), OH (Cleveland, Lima, Toledo), PA (Marcus Hook), TX (Green Lake, Houston), WA (Ferndale)

CORP. OFFICERS
Charles H. Bowman: *B* 1936 *ED* PA St Univ BS; TX A&M Univ MS; TX A&M Univ PhD *CURR EMPL* pres, ceo: BP Am Inc *CORP AFFIL* chmn, pres, ceo: Standard Oil Co

Steven W. Percy: *B* 1946 *ED* Cleveland St Univ JD; Rensselaer Polytech Inst BA; Univ MI MBA *CURR EMPL* pres, ceo: BP Oil Co

CORP AFFIL exec vp, dir: BP Am Inc; pres, dir: BP Exploration & Oil Inc

GIVING OFFICERS
W. B. Doggett: *CURR EMPL* dir communs & commun rels: BP Am Inc

APPLICATION INFORMATION
Initial Approach: *Initial Contact:* in writing or by telephone; typewritten proposals (no more than five pages) should be sent to director of corporate contributions *Include Information On:* amount of funds requested, why they are needed, and how they will be used (if seeking general operating support or capital grant); plan for raising funds from other sources; community need to be addressed; goals and objectives, activities to be undertaken to meet objectives, with implementation schedule, plan for evaluation, reporting, and disseminating results and findings; brief description of the organization, including legal name, history, mission, and activities; names and qualifications of persons administering and managing the organization; list of officers and directors of organization; copy of organization's most recently audited financial statement; organizational budget listing expenses and income; project budget, listing sources of committed and pending financial support; list of corporations and foundations that contributed to organization during previous year; copy of most recent Form 990; and proof of tax-exempt status *Deadlines:* none

Restrictions on Giving: Grants are not made to individuals or for religious purposes. BP America normally does not make grants to organizations in their first year of operation.

OTHER THINGS TO KNOW
BP America also sponsors a "Social Investment" program and committed $971,592 in 1993 to projects that restore neighborhoods and return a profit to the company.

BP America's contributions program includes BP Exploration (Anchorage, AK), BP Oil (Cleveland, OH), BP Chemicals (Cleveland, OH), BP Minerals America, BP Advanced Materials, Hitco Materials (Gardena, CA), BP Coal (USA) Inc. (Cleveland, OH) America, Old Ben Coal Co., BP Nutrition America (St. Louis, MO), and other companies.

For information about contributions outside of the U.S., contact a local BP office.

GRANTS ANALYSIS
Total Grants: $8,000,000

Number of Grants: 600

Highest Grant: $400,000

Average Grant: $10,000*

Typical Range: $1,000 to $10,000

Disclosure Period: 1994

Note: Company provided an approximate average grant figure. Recent grants are derived from a 1991 annual report.

RECENT GRANTS

General

1,435,085	United Way, Cleveland, OH — corporate pledge

500,000	Neighborhood Progress, Cleveland, OH
486,500	Cleveland Initiative for Education, Cleveland, OH — scholarship in escrow
345,000	United Way of Anchorage, Anchorage, AK — corporate pledge
276,000	Case Western Reserve University, Cleveland, OH

Calhoun Charitable Trust, Kenneth

CONTACT
Karen Krino
Trust Administrator
Kenneth Calhoun Charitable Trust
c/o Society National Bank
157 S Main St.
Akron, OH 44308
(216) 379-1647

FINANCIAL SUMMARY
Recent Giving: $274,116 (fiscal 1993); $297,983 (fiscal 1992); $247,487 (fiscal 1991)

Assets: $4,116,781 (fiscal 1993); $4,234,232 (fiscal 1992); $4,031,297 (fiscal 1991)

EIN: 34-1370330

CONTRIBUTIONS SUMMARY
Donor(s): the late Kenneth Calhoun

Typical Recipients: • *Arts & Humanities:* Ballet, Historic Preservation, History & Archaeology, Libraries, Museums/Galleries, Music, Performing Arts, Public Broadcasting, Theater • *Civic & Public Affairs:* Economic Development, Law & Justice, Zoos/Aquariums • *Education:* Colleges & Universities, Education Reform, General, Medical Education, Minority Education, Private Education (Precollege), Secondary Education (Private) • *Health:* Children's Health/Hospitals, Emergency/Ambulance Services, Health Organizations, Heart, Hospitals, Nursing Services • *Religion:* Churches, Ministries, Religious Organizations, Religious Welfare • *Social Services:* Child Welfare, Community Service Organizations, Domestic Violence, Family Services, Food/Clothing Distribution, People with Disabilities, Senior Services, Shelters/Homelessness, United Funds/United Ways, Youth Organizations

Grant Types: general support

Geographic Distribution: limited to the greater Akron, OH, area

GIVING OFFICERS
Society National Bank: trust

APPLICATION INFORMATION
Initial Approach: Send brief letter of inquiry describing program or project. Deadline is June 30.

GRANTS ANALYSIS
Total Grants: $274,116

Number of Grants: 81

Highest Grant: $35,000

Typical Range: $500 to $12,000

Disclosure Period: fiscal year ending July 31, 1993

Note: Recent grants are derived from a fiscal 1993 Form 990.

RECENT GRANTS
Library
| 1,000 | Alpha Library Committee, Akron, OH |

General
35,000	Akron General Development Foundation, Akron, OH
12,500	Furnace Street Mission Victim Assistance, Akron, OH
12,000	Akron City Hospital Foundation, Akron, OH
10,500	University of Akron Foundation, Akron, OH
10,000	Hanna Perkins School, Akron, OH

Cayuga Foundation

CONTACT
Gerald Miller
Vice President
Cayuga Fdn.
c/o Society Bank & Trust
PO Box 10099
Toledo, OH 43699-0099
(419) 259-8058

FINANCIAL SUMMARY
Recent Giving: $94,000 (1993); $82,000 (1991); $75,000 (1990)

Assets: $2,245,585 (1993); $2,013,416 (1991); $1,606,181 (1990)

EIN: 34-6504822

CONTRIBUTIONS SUMMARY
Typical Recipients: • *Arts & Humanities:* Community Arts, Libraries, Public Broadcasting • *Civic & Public Affairs:* Economic Development, General, Housing, Municipalities/Towns, Public Policy, Urban & Community Affairs • *Education:* Colleges & Universities, Elementary Education (Public), Minority Education, Preschool Education, Private Education (Precollege), Public Education (Precollege) • *Environment:* General, Wildlife Protection • *Health:* Cancer, Clinics/Medical Centers, Health Organizations, Hospitals, Long-Term Care • *International:* Human Rights, International Organizations, International Relations • *Religion:* Churches, Ministries, Religious Organizations • *Social Services:* Child Welfare, Community Service Organizations, Family Planning, Family Services, Recreation & Athletics, Scouts, United Funds/United Ways, Youth Organizations

Grant Types: capital, general support, and scholarship

Geographic Distribution: focus on Toledo, OH, and NY

GIVING OFFICERS
Society Bank & Trust: trust

Sandra Fritz: adv

Donald J. Keune: adv

Elizabeth M. Pfenninger: adv

APPLICATION INFORMATION
Initial Approach: Send brief letter describing program. Include a description of organization, amount requested, purpose of funds sought, recently audited financial statement, and proof of tax-exempt status. There are no deadlines.

GRANTS ANALYSIS
Total Grants: $94,000

Number of Grants: 32

Highest Grant: $5,875

Typical Range: $1,175 to $5,875

Disclosure Period: 1993

Note: Recent grants are derived from a 1993 Form 990.

RECENT GRANTS
Library
| 4,700 | Aurora Free Library Association, Aurora, NY — general |
| 1,175 | Weedsport Free Library, Weedsport, NY — general |

General
5,875	United Ministry, Union Springs, NY — religious
5,875	Village of Cayuga, Cayuga, NY — general
5,875	Wells College, Aurora, NY — educational
4,700	Aurora Preschool Center, Aurora, NY — general
4,700	Comfortcare of Cayuga County, Auburn, NY — medical

Centerior Energy Corp. / Centerior Energy Foundation

Revenue: $2.42 billion
Employees: 6,650
Headquarters: Cleveland, OH
SIC Major Group: Holding Companies Nec and Apartment Building Operators

CONTACT
Jackie K. Hauserman
Chairman Contributions Committee
Centerior Energy Foundation
P.O. Box 94661
Cleveland, OH 44101
(216) 479-4907

FINANCIAL SUMMARY
Recent Giving: $1,500,000 (1995 est.); $1,541,355 (1994); $1,615,947 (1993)

Assets: $18,604,254 (1993); $17,741,094 (1992); $18,000,000 (1991 approx.)

Fiscal Note: Above figures for foundation only. The Company also makes limited direct corporate gifts. Estimated budget for 1995 is $350,000. Contact Darlene Johnson, contributions coordinator, for more information at (216)449-4907. Above figures exclude nonmonetary support.

EIN: 34-6514181

CONTRIBUTIONS SUMMARY

Typical Recipients: • *Arts & Humanities:* Arts Appreciation, Arts Associations & Councils, Arts Centers, Arts Festivals, Arts Institutes, Dance, Historic Preservation, Libraries, Museums/Galleries, Music, Opera, Performing Arts, Theater • *Civic & Public Affairs:* Business/Free Enterprise, Civil Rights, Economic Development, Employment/Job Training, Law & Justice, Professional & Trade Associations, Public Policy, Urban & Community Affairs • *Education:* Arts/Humanities Education, Colleges & Universities, Community & Junior Colleges, Economic Education, Education Associations, Minority Education, Private Education (Precollege) • *Environment:* General • *Health:* Health Organizations, Hospitals, Medical Training, Mental Health • *Social Services:* Child Welfare, Community Centers, Community Service Organizations, Delinquency & Criminal Rehabilitation, People with Disabilities, Senior Services, Volunteer Services, Youth Organizations

Grant Types: capital, employee matching gifts, general support, multiyear/continuing support, and operating expenses

Note: Multiyear support is limited.

Nonmonetary Support Types: donated equipment, in-kind services, and loaned executives

Note: Nonmonetary support is provided by the company. Nonmonetary support contact is Darlene L. Johnson, contributions coordinator.

Geographic Distribution: exclusively in northeastern and northwestern Ohio: does not give out of service area

Operating Locations: OH (Independence)

CORP. OFFICERS

Robert J. Farling: *B* Cleveland OH 1936 *ED* Case Inst Tech BSEE 1958; Case Western Reserve Univ MBA 1965 *CURR EMPL* chmn, ceo, dir: Centerior Energy Corp *CORP AFFIL* dir: Natl City Bank Cleveland; pres, dir: Cleveland Electric Illuminating Co

Gerald J. Meyer: *CURR EMPL* corp commun dir: Centerior Energy Corp

GIVING OFFICERS

David M. Blank: treas

Murray Richard Edelman: vchmn *B* Trenton NJ 1939 *ED* Case Inst Tech BSEE 1958; Case Western Reserve Univ BMME 1961; Harvard Univ Advanced Mgmt Program 1987 *CURR EMPL* exec vp oper & engg: Centerior Svc Co

Robert J. Farling: chmn *CURR EMPL* chmn, ceo, dir: Centerior Energy Corp (see above)

Barbara A. Frastaci: asst treas

Jackie K. Hauserman: pres *CURR EMPL* vp admin: Cleveland Electric Illuminating Co

Gary M. Hawkinson: treas *B* Chicago IL 1948 *CURR EMPL* treas: Centerior Energy Corp *NONPR AFFIL* treas, trust: Lutheran Med Ctr Fdn *CLUB AFFIL* Cleveland Treas, Rotary

Terrence Gregory Linnert: vp *B* Cleveland OH 1946 *ED* Univ Notre Dame BSEE 1968; Cleveland St Univ JD 1975 *CURR EMPL* vp: Centerior Energy Corp

E. Lyle Pepin: secy *B* Cleveland OH 1941 *ED* Bowling Green St Univ 1963; MI St Univ 1965 *CURR EMPL* secy: Centerior Energy Corp *CORP AFFIL* secy: Cleveland Electric Illuminating Co, Toledo Edison Co

Janis T. Percio: asst secy

Robert A. Sliwinski: asst treas

David W. Whitehead: asst treas

APPLICATION INFORMATION

Initial Approach: *Initial Contact:* one- or two-page letter *Include Information On:* brief history and description of the organization, amount requested, purpose for which funds are sought, area served by the organization, the organization's contributions to the area, list of officers and trustees, recently audited financial statement, proof of tax-exempt status, and a copy of most current review by the Financial Support Review Committee of Greater Cleveland Growth Association *Deadlines:* none

Restrictions on Giving: Foundation only accepts grant requests from organizations located in northeastern and northwestern Ohio.

Does not provide grants to individuals or political organizations. Also does not provide grants for endowment funds, deficit financing, research, scholarships or fellowships, or loans.

OTHER THINGS TO KNOW

Foundation matches gifts of $25 to $5,000 from all regular full-time or retired employees. Gifts to secondary schools, local community colleges, four-year institutions, graduate and professional schools, seminaries, theological schools, and technical schools are eligible for matching funds. Approved cultural organizations in company's service areas are also eligible. Contributions are matched on a dollar-to-dollar basis. Some limitations apply.

Foundation makes contributions for Centerior Energy Corp. and its subsidiaries, Centerior Service Co., Cleveland Electric Illuminating Co., and Toledo Edison Co.

GRANTS ANALYSIS

Total Grants: $1,615,947

Number of Grants: 1,167

Highest Grant: $483,000

Average Grant: $1,385

Typical Range: $25 to $500 and $1,000 to $5,000

Disclosure Period: 1993

Note: Recent grants are derived from a 1993 Form 990.

RECENT GRANTS

General

483,000	United Way Greater Cleveland, Cleveland, OH
170,000	United Way Greater Toledo, Toledo, OH
144,010	Case Western Reserve University, Cleveland, OH
38,500	Lake County United Way
33,000	United Way Ashtabula County, Ashtabula, OH

Columbus Dispatch Printing Co. / Wolfe Associates, Inc.

Sales: $41.6 million
Employees: 603
Headquarters: Columbus, OH
SIC Major Group: Security & Commodity Brokers

CONTACT

A. Kenneth Pierce, Jr.
Vice President, Secretary & Treasurer
Wolfe Associates, Inc.
34 S Third St.
Columbus, OH 43215
(614) 461-5000

FINANCIAL SUMMARY

Recent Giving: $3,000,000 (fiscal 1995 est.); $1,234,903 (fiscal 1994); $2,515,352 (fiscal 1993)

Assets: $6,171,196 (fiscal 1994); $5,159,515 (fiscal 1993); $5,922,864 (fiscal 1992)

Gifts Received: $2,130,002 (fiscal 1994); $1,626,259 (fiscal 1993)

Fiscal Note: Company gives through foundation only. Above figures exclude nonmonetary support. In fiscal 1994, gifts were received form the Dispatch Printing Co., the Ohio Co., WBNS-TV, VideoIndiana, Inc., and Dispatch Consumer Services, Inc.

EIN: 23-7303111

CONTRIBUTIONS SUMMARY

Typical Recipients: • *Arts & Humanities:* Arts Associations & Councils, Arts Funds, Arts Institutes, Ballet, Dance, Historic Preservation, History & Archaeology, Libraries, Literary Arts, Museums/Galleries, Music, Opera, Performing Arts, Theater • *Civic & Public Affairs:* African American Affairs, Business/Free Enterprise, Chambers of Commerce, Community Foundations, Economic Development, Employment/Job Training, General, Housing, Law & Justice, Municipalities/Towns, Philanthropic Organizations, Safety, Zoos/Aquariums • *Education:* Business Education, Colleges & Universities, Economic Education, Education Associations, Education Funds, General, Literacy, Private Education (Precollege), Public Education (Precollege), Religious Education, Social Sciences Education, Student Aid • *Health:* Cancer, Children's Health/Hospitals, Emergency/Ambulance Services, General, Health Funds, Heart, Hospitals, Long-Term Care, Single-Disease Health Associations • *International:* International Relations • *Religion:* Churches, Jewish Causes, Ministries, Religious Welfare • *Social Services:* Animal Protection, Child Welfare, Community Centers, Community Service Organizations, Family Planning, Food/Clothing Distribution, People with Disabilities, Senior Services, Shelters/Homelessness, United Funds/United Ways, Youth Organizations

Grant Types: capital, conference/seminar, endowment, general support, project, and scholarship

Nonmonetary Support Types: in-kind services

Note: Value of nonmonetary support is not available.

Geographic Distribution: primarily central Ohio and other areas in which the corporate donors have a substantial presence

Operating Locations: OH (Columbus)

CORP. OFFICERS
John F. Wolfe: *B* 1944 *CURR EMPL* pub, pres, ceo, dir: Dispatch Printing Co *CORP AFFIL* pub, pres, ceo, dir: Columbus Dispatch Printing Co; vice chmn, dir: OH Co *PHIL AFFIL* co-trust: Robert F. and Edgar T. Wolfe Charitable Trust

GIVING OFFICERS
Nancy Wolfe Lane: vp

A. Kenneth Pierce, Jr.: vp, secy, treas

John F. Wolfe: pres *CURR EMPL* pub, pres, ceo, dir: Dispatch Printing Co *PHIL AFFIL* co-trust: Robert F. and Edgar T. Wolfe Charitable Trust (see above)

William C. Wolfe, Jr.: vp

APPLICATION INFORMATION
Initial Approach: *Initial Contact:* one- or two-page letter addressed to Wolfe Associates, Inc *Include Information On:* purpose of organization, population it serves, how funds are to be used, date of IRS tax-exempt letter, date of applicant's most recent Form 990 *Deadlines:* none *Note:* If initial inquiry is favorable, applicant organization may be required to submit a formal, detailed proposal. Information to include in full proposal is included in "Information for Grant Applicants," available from Wolfe Associates, Inc.

Restrictions on Giving: Foundation does not support individuals, public school systems, research and demonstration projects, publications, or conferences.

OTHER THINGS TO KNOW
Corporate donors to the foundation are the Dispatch Printing Company, the Ohio Company, WBNS TV Inc., and RadiOhio Inc.

Foundation gives priority to organizations that enhance or strengthen the nation's health care, educational, or economic systems on a regional or national basis.

Grants are not automatically renewable and current recipients must reapply annually for continued support.

Foundation may require annual progress reports and notice of any material modification to project during the funding year.

GRANTS ANALYSIS
Total Grants: $1,234,903

Number of Grants: 110

Highest Grant: $336,000

Average Grant: $11,226

Typical Range: $500 to $25,000

Disclosure Period: fiscal year ending June 30, 1994

Note: Recent grants are derived from a fiscal 1994 Form 990.

RECENT GRANTS
General

336,000	United Way of Franklin County, Columbus, OH — for 1993 campaign
200,000	Columbus Foundation Trilogy, Columbus, OH — for culture and the environment
76,666	Wellington School, Columbus, OH — for capital campaign
40,350	Children's Hospital Foundation, Columbus, OH — for health and medicine
40,000	Jack Nicklaus Private Operating Foundation, Palm Beach, FL — for culture and the environment

Crandall Memorial Foundation, J. Ford

CONTACT
R. J. Cristian
Attorney
J. Ford Crandall Memorial Fdn.
311 Mahoning Bank Bldg.
Youngstown, OH 44503
(216) 744-2125

FINANCIAL SUMMARY
Recent Giving: $214,108 (1993); $249,168 (1992); $230,379 (1991)

Assets: $4,203,877 (1993); $4,223,393 (1992); $4,311,000 (1991)

EIN: 34-6513634

CONTRIBUTIONS SUMMARY
Donor(s): the late J. Ford Crandall

Typical Recipients: • *Arts & Humanities:* Arts Associations & Councils, Community Arts, Historic Preservation, Libraries, Music • *Civic & Public Affairs:* Botanical Gardens/Parks, Economic Development • *Education:* Colleges & Universities, Private Education (Precollege), Student Aid • *Health:* Clinics/Medical Centers, Hospitals, Research/Studies Institutes • *Religion:* Churches, Missionary Activities (Domestic), Religious Organizations, Religious Welfare • *Social Services:* Child Welfare, Community Centers, Community Service Organizations, Counseling, Family Services, Senior Services, Shelters/Homelessness, Substance Abuse, United Funds/United Ways, Youth Organizations

Grant Types: capital, endowment, and scholarship

Geographic Distribution: limited to Mahoning County, OH

GIVING OFFICERS
Andrew G. Bresko: trust

Amy H. Gambrel: trust

William M. Marshall: trust

APPLICATION INFORMATION
Initial Approach: The foundation has no formal grant application procedure or application form. There are no deadlines.

Restrictions on Giving: Limited to Mahoning County, OH.

GRANTS ANALYSIS
Total Grants: $214,108

Number of Grants: 8

Highest Grant: $75,000

Typical Range: $1,275 to $60,000

Disclosure Period: 1993

Note: Recent grants are derived from a 1993 Form 990.

RECENT GRANTS
General

75,000	Mill Creek Park Foundation, Youngstown, OH — for capital improvement program
75,000	Mill Creek Park Foundation, Youngstown, OH — for public improvement program
60,000	Copeland Oaks Crandall Medical Center, Sebring, OH — for capital improvement program
50,000	Millcreek Child Development Center, Youngstown, OH — for capital improvement program
25,000	Millcreek Child Development Center, Youngstown, OH — for capital improvement program

Dater Foundation, Charles H.

CONTACT
Bruce A. Krone
Secretary
Charles H. Dater Fdn.
524 Walnut St.
Cincinnati, OH 45202
(513) 241-1234

FINANCIAL SUMMARY
Recent Giving: $222,000 (fiscal 1992); $228,400 (fiscal 1991); $186,275 (fiscal 1990)

Assets: $8,929,398 (fiscal 1992); $5,569,064 (fiscal 1991); $5,011,644 (fiscal 1990)

Gifts Received: $78,285 (fiscal 1992); $175,750 (fiscal 1991); $187,048 (fiscal 1990)

Fiscal Note: In fiscal 1992, contributions were received from Procter & Gamble ($56,000) and Lorillard ($22,285).

EIN: 31-1150951

CONTRIBUTIONS SUMMARY

Typical Recipients: • *Arts & Humanities:* Historic Preservation, History & Archaeology, Libraries, Museums/Galleries, Opera, Performing Arts, Public Broadcasting • *Civic & Public Affairs:* Clubs, Zoos/Aquariums • *Education:* Business Education, Private Education (Precollege), Student Aid • *Health:* Cancer, Children's Health/Hospitals, Hospitals, Multiple Sclerosis • *International:* International Peace & Security Issues • *Religion:* Religious Organizations, Religious Welfare • *Social Services:* Child Welfare, Community Service Organizations, Delinquency & Criminal Rehabilitation, Domestic Violence, Family Services, Food/Clothing Distribution, Homes, People with Disabilities, Recreation & Athletics, Shelters/Homelessness, United Funds/United Ways, Youth Organizations

Grant Types: capital, general support, multiyear/continuing support, project, scholarship, and seed money

Geographic Distribution: focus on the greater Cincinnati, OH, area

GIVING OFFICERS
Stanley J. Frank, Jr.: vp, trust

Bruce A. Krone: secy, trust

Paul W. Krone: pres, trust

David L. Olberding: treas, trust

John D. Silvati: vp, trust

APPLICATION INFORMATION
Initial Approach: Application form required. There are no deadlines.

Restrictions on Giving: Focus is on the children in the Tri-state area.

GRANTS ANALYSIS
Total Grants: $222,000
Number of Grants: 42
Highest Grant: $20,000

Typical Range: $1,000 to $10,000

Disclosure Period: fiscal year ending August 31, 1992

Note: Recent grants are derived from a fiscal 1992 Form 990.

RECENT GRANTS
Library
20,000   Public Library of Cincinnati and Hamilton County, Cincinnati, OH — for the Westwood Branch Library children's programs and services

General
20,000   YMCA Colerain Branch, Cincinnati, OH — expansion campaign

10,000   Cincinnati Zoo and Botanical Garden, Cincinnati, OH — purchase van for outreach program

10,000   Clovernook Center, Cincinnati, OH — purchase outdoor playground equipment for children

10,000   Santa Maria Community Services, Cincinnati, OH — activities and programs for disadvantaged children

10,000   Springer School, Cincinnati, OH — challenge campaign

Deuble Foundation, George H.

CONTACT
Andrew H. Deuble
Trustee
George H. Deuble Foundation
PO Box 2288
North Canton, OH 44720
(216) 494-4199

FINANCIAL SUMMARY
Recent Giving: $893,462 (1993); $840,019 (1992); $699,860 (1990)

Assets: $18,307,808 (1993); $17,863,288 (1992); $15,486,875 (1990)

EIN: 34-6500426

CONTRIBUTIONS SUMMARY
Donor(s): The foundation was established in 1947 by the late George H. Deuble .

Typical Recipients: • *Arts & Humanities:* Arts Centers, Arts Funds, Ballet, Community Arts, Historic Preservation, History & Archaeology, Libraries, Music, Performing Arts, Theater • *Civic & Public Affairs:* African American Affairs, Economic Development, Housing, Municipalities/Towns, Parades/Festivals, Urban & Community Affairs • *Education:* Business Education, Colleges & Universities, Education Funds, Education Reform, Legal Education, Medical Education, Private Education (Precollege), School Volunteerism, Student Aid • *Health:* Adolescent Health Issues, Children's Health/Hospitals, Emergency/Ambulance Services, Health Funds, Heart, Hospitals, Medical Research, Single-Disease Health Associations • *Religion:* Churches, Ministries, Religious Organizations, Religious Welfare • *Social Services:* Big Brother/Big Sister, Camps, Child Welfare, Community Centers, Community Service Organizations, Day Care, Family Planning, Family Services, Food/Clothing Distribution, Homes, People with Disabilities, Recreation & Athletics, Substance Abuse, United Funds/United Ways, YMCA/YWCA/YMHA/YWHA, Youth Organizations

Grant Types: capital, conference/seminar, emergency, endowment, loan, matching, and scholarship

Geographic Distribution: focus on the Stark County, OH, area

GIVING OFFICERS
Andrew H. Deuble: trust

Steven G. Deuble: trust *B* Canton OH 1947 *ED* OH Wesleyan Univ 1969 *CURR EMPL* ceo, dir: DCC Corp *CORP AFFIL* pres, dir: Massillon Plaque Co

Walter C. Deuble: pres, trust *B* 1921 *CURR EMPL* chmn bd, dir: DCC Corp

Charles A. Morgan: trust *B* 1947 *CURR EMPL* pres, dir: DCC Corp

APPLICATION INFORMATION
Initial Approach:

The foundation requests applications be made in writing.

Applicants should include a written proposal including an explanation for the request and the amount.

The foundation has no deadline for submitting proposals.

Restrictions on Giving: Grants are not made to individuals, or for operating budgets, seed money, deficit financing, general endowments, land acquisition, research, or publications. The foundation reports that grants are to go to any corporation, trust, community chest, fund, or foundation organized and operated exclusively for religious, charitable, educational, or philanthropic and benevolent purposes as defined by the Internal Revenue Code.

GRANTS ANALYSIS
Total Grants: $893,462

Number of Grants: 118

Highest Grant: $66,800

Average Grant: $7,572

Typical Range: $500 to $10,000

Disclosure Period: 1993

Note: Recent grants are derived from a 1993 Form 990.

RECENT GRANTS

General
66,800   Aultman Hospital, Canton, OH — equipment for cardiac care unit

50,000   Education Enhancement Partnership, Canton, OH — to finance education initiatives

50,000   Malone College, Canton, OH — capital drive for construction of the Centennial Center

32,180   Trinity United Church of Christ, Canton, OH — purchase of carillon

30,000   Canton Student Loan Foundation, Canton, OH — new student loans fund

Eaton Corporation / Eaton Charitable Fund

Revenue: $6.05 billion
Employees: 50,000
Headquarters: Cleveland, OH
SIC Major Group: Motor Vehicle Parts & Accessories, Mechanical Rubber Goods, Bolts, Nuts, Rivets & Washers, and Industrial Valves

CONTACT

Frederick B. Unger
Director, Community Affairs
Eaton Corporation
1111 Superior Ave., N.E.
Cleveland, OH 44114
(216) 523-4438

FINANCIAL SUMMARY

Recent Giving: $3,800,000 (1994 approx.); $3,400,000 (1993); $3,413,958 (1992)

Assets: $2,886,852 (1992); $3,087,000 (1991); $7,594,965 (1990)

Fiscal Note: In addition to the fund, company sponsors a direct giving program on the corporate and divisions levels. Divisions may make contributions of $500 or less independently of the headquarters office. This support, included in above figures, is estimated at $500,000 annually.

EIN: 34-6501856

CONTRIBUTIONS SUMMARY

Typical Recipients: • *Arts & Humanities:* Arts Associations & Councils, Arts Centers, Arts Festivals, Arts Funds, Ballet, Community Arts, Dance, Historic Preservation, Libraries, Museums/Galleries, Music, Opera, Performing Arts, Public Broadcasting, Theater, Visual Arts • *Civic & Public Affairs:* Business/Free Enterprise, Economic Development, Economic Policy, Employment/Job Training, Housing, Law & Justice, Legal Aid, Municipalities/Towns, Professional & Trade Associations, Public Policy, Rural Affairs, Safety, Urban & Community Affairs • *Education:* Business Education, Colleges & Universities, Community & Junior Colleges, Economic Education, Education Associations, Education Funds, Education Reform, Engineering/Technological Education, Minority Education, Private Education (Precollege), Public Education (Precollege), Religious Education, Science/Mathematics Education, Student Aid • *Environment:* General • *Health:* Cancer, Health Policy/Cost Containment, Health Funds, Health Organizations, Hospices, Hospitals, Single-Disease Health Associations • *International:* International Relations • *Religion:* Religious Welfare • *Social Services:* Child Welfare, Community Centers, Community Service Organizations, Counseling, Delinquency & Criminal Rehabilitation, Emergency Relief, Family Services, Food/Clothing Distribution, Homes, People with Disabilities, Recreation & Athletics, Senior Services, Shelters/Homelessness, United Funds/United Ways, Volunteer Services, Youth Organizations

Grant Types: capital, employee matching gifts, general support, and multiyear/continuing support

Nonmonetary Support: $23,264 (1990); $50,000 (1989); $50,000 (1988)

Nonmonetary Support Types: donated equipment, in-kind services, loaned employees, and loaned executives

Note: Contact person listed above also handles requests for nonmonetary support.

Geographic Distribution: corporate operating locations

Operating Locations: AL (Arab, Athens), CA (Costa Mesa, Culver City, El Segundo, Los Angeles, San Jose, Santa Clara, Westlake Village), CT (Danbury, New Haven), FL (Manatee, Sarasota), GA (Athens), IA (Belmond, Shenandoah, Spencer), IL (Carol Stream, Lincoln), IN (South Bend), KS (Hutchinson), KY (Bowling Green, Henderson), MA (Beverly, Danvers), MI (Detroit, Galesburg, Gladstone, Kalamazoo, Marshall, Saginaw, Southfield, Troy), MN (Eden Prairie), MO, NC (Arden, Fletcher, Kings Mountain, Laurinberg, Roxboro, Sanford, Selma), NE (Kearney), NJ (Whippany), NY (Deer Park, Farmingdale), OH (Cleveland, Lakewood, Marion, Massillon), OK (Shawnee), OR (Beaverton), SC (Westminster), TN (Cleveland, Humboldt, Shelbyville), TX (Austin), UT (Bountiful, Salt Lake City), WI (Kenosha, Milwaukee, Watertown), WY (Riverton)

CORP. OFFICERS

William E. Butler: *B* 1931 *ED* Univ IL BA 1956 *CURR EMPL* chmn, ceo: Eaton Corp

Stephen Roger Hardis: *B* New York NY 1935 *ED* Cornell Univ BA 1956; Princeton Univ Woodrow Wilson Sch Intl Pub Aff MPA 1960 *CURR EMPL* chmn, ceo: Eaton Corp *CORP AFFIL* dir: Nordson Corp, Progressive Cos, Soc Corp, Soc Natl Bank; treas: Sybron Corp; vp, treas, dir: AIL Sys Inc *NONPR AFFIL* mem: Fin Execs Inst, Phi Beta Kappa; trust: Cleveland Clinic, First Un Realty Trust

GIVING OFFICERS

Alexander Mac Donald Cutler: mem contributions comm *B* Milwaukee WI 1951 *ED* Yale Univ BA 1973; Dartmouth Coll MBA 1975 *CURR EMPL* pres, coo, dir: Eaton Corp *NONPR AFFIL* bd gov: Natl Electrical Mfrs Assn; class agent alumni fund: Loomis Chaffee Sch; dir: Cleveland Commn Higher Ed; mem: Yale Univ Alumni Assn; trust: Cleveland Play House, Mus Natural History Cleveland *CLUB AFFIL* Chagrin Valley Hunt

Gerald Lee Gherlein: mem contributions comm *B* Warren OH 1938 *ED* OH Wesleyan Univ 1956-1958; OH St Univ BS 1960; Univ MI JD 1963 *CURR EMPL* exec vp, gen couns: Eaton Corp *CORP AFFIL* dir: AIL Sys Inc; vp, dir: Eaton-Kenway Inc *NONPR AFFIL* mem: Am Bar Assn, Am Soc Corp Secys, Greater Cleveland Bar Assn, OH Bar Assn; trust: WVIZ Pub Television *CLUB AFFIL* Mayfield CC, Tavern, Union

John Wallace Hushen: chmn contributions comm *B* Detroit MI 1935 *ED* Wayne St Univ BA 1958 *CURR EMPL* vp corp aff: Ea-

ton Corp *NONPR AFFIL* mem: Assn Former Senate Aides, Bus-Govt Rels Counc, Senate Press Secys Assn; mem conf bd: Counc Pub Aff Execs, Mfg Alliance, Pub Aff Counc; trust: Citizens League Res Inst, YMCA *CLUB AFFIL* Capitol Hill, Detroit Press, Union

Carol S. Markey: mgr commun involvement

Tanga C. Perkins: admin corp contributions

John Stuart Rodewig: mem corp contributions comm *B* Westfield NJ 1933 *ED* Cornell Univ BEE 1956 *CURR EMPL* pres, coo, dir: Eaton Corp *CORP AFFIL* dir: Axles India Ltd, Eaton Ltd, Eaton Mfrs SA, Eaton SA, FKI PLC, Hayes Wheels Intl, Hounslow, St Nazaire *NONPR AFFIL* mem: Am Trucking Assn, Soc Automotive Engrs, Soc Motor Mfrs & Traders Europe; mem adv comm: Cornell Univ Coll Engg; mem corp counc: Cleveland Mus Art; mem exec com: Western Hwy Inst

Frederick Branson Unger: mem contributions comm *B* Lakewood OH 1940 *ED* OH St Univ 1963; Cleveland St Univ *CURR EMPL* dir commun aff: Eaton Corp

APPLICATION INFORMATION

Initial Approach: *Initial Contact:* brief letter or proposal *Include Information On:* description of the organization's history and purpose, copies of most recent financial statements and current budget, roster of officers and directors, listing of corporate donors and amounts, employee involvement with organization (if applicable), and copy of IRS determination letter *Deadlines:* none

Restrictions on Giving: Grants not awarded to religious, fraternal, or labor organizations, or to individuals.

OTHER THINGS TO KNOW

Employee contributions to educational and cultural institutions are matched on a two-for-one basis.

GRANTS ANALYSIS

Total Grants: $3,850,000

Typical Range: $1,000 to $25,000

Disclosure Period: 1994

Note: Recent grants are derived from a 1993 annual report.

RECENT GRANTS

General

109,000	Cleveland Initiative for Education, Cleveland, OH — Phase II
100,000	Cleveland Clinic Foundation, Cleveland, OH — deWindt Family Cancer Research Lab
62,500	Northcoast Fund, Cleveland, OH — minority entrepreneurship
59,400	Cleveland Initiative For Education, Cleveland, OH — Phase I
50,000	John Carroll University, University Heights, OH — capital campaign

Eaton Foundation, Cyrus

CONTACT
Henry W. Gulick
President
Cyrus Eaton Fdn.
24200 Chagrin Blvd., Ste. 233
Beachwood, OH 44122
(216) 360-9550

FINANCIAL SUMMARY
Recent Giving: $189,000 (1993); $49,250 (1992); $53,000 (1991)

Assets: $2,556,954 (1993); $2,615,906 (1992); $2,557,030 (1991)

EIN: 23-7440277

CONTRIBUTIONS SUMMARY
Typical Recipients: • *Arts & Humanities:* Arts Associations & Councils, Arts Centers, Arts Festivals, Arts Institutes, Community Arts, Dance, Historic Preservation, History & Archaeology, Libraries, Museums/Galleries, Music, Opera, Performing Arts, Public Broadcasting, Theater • *Civic & Public Affairs:* African American Affairs, Botanical Gardens/Parks, First Amendment Issues, Gay/Lesbian Issues, General, Municipalities/Towns, Public Policy, Urban & Community Affairs • *Education:* Arts/Humanities Education, Colleges & Universities, Community & Junior Colleges, General, International Studies, Private Education (Precollege), Student Aid • *Environment:* Resource Conservation • *Health:* Children's Health/Hospitals, Clinics/Medical Centers, Medical Research, Multiple Sclerosis, Single-Disease Health Associations • *International:* Foreign Educational Institutions, Health Care/Hospitals, International Peace & Security Issues • *Science:* Science Museums, Scientific Centers & Institutes • *Social Services:* Domestic Violence, Family Planning

Grant Types: endowment, general support, project, and seed money

Geographic Distribution: focus on Cleveland, OH

GIVING OFFICERS
Barring Coughlin: asst secy, trust *B* Wilkes-Barre PA 1913 *ED* Princeton Univ AB 1935; Harvard Univ JD 1938 *NONPR AFFIL* mem: Am Bar Assn, Am Law Inst, OH Bar Assn; trust: Gun Safety Inst *CLUB AFFIL* Adirondack League, Chagrin Valley Hunt, City, Edgewater YC, Princeton, Union

Mary Stephens Eaton: vp, trust

Henry W. Gulick: pres, trust

Ralph P. Higgins: treas, trust

Raymond Szabo: secy, trust

APPLICATION INFORMATION
Initial Approach: Send a brief letter of inquiry. Include a description of organization, amount requested, purpose of funds sought, recently audited financial statement, and proof of tax-exempt status. Deadline is October 31.

GRANTS ANALYSIS
Total Grants: $189,000

Number of Grants: 33

Highest Grant: $55,000

Typical Range: $500 to $16,700

Disclosure Period: 1993

Note: Recent grants are derived from a 1993 Form 990.

RECENT GRANTS

Library
500	Friends of Cleveland Public Library, Cleveland, OH

General
34,000	Cleveland Museum of Natural History, Cleveland, OH
17,000	Free Medical Clinic of Greater Cleveland, Cleveland, OH
12,500	Hathaway Brown School, Shaker Heights, OH
5,000	Case Western Reserve University, Cleveland, OH
5,000	Hitchcock House, Cleveland, OH

Evans Foundation, Thomas J.

CONTACT
J. Gilbert Reese
President
Thomas J. Evans Foundation
36 N Second St.
Newark, OH 43055-0764
(614) 349-3863

FINANCIAL SUMMARY
Recent Giving: $403,501 (fiscal 1993); $104,170 (fiscal 1992); $227,267 (fiscal 1991)

Assets: $15,713,930 (fiscal 1993); $15,276,480 (fiscal 1992); $14,293,898 (fiscal 1991)

EIN: 31-6055767

CONTRIBUTIONS SUMMARY
Donor(s): The foundation was established in 1965 by the late Thomas J. Evans .

Typical Recipients: • *Arts & Humanities:* Libraries, Museums/Galleries, Theater, Visual Arts • *Civic & Public Affairs:* Botanical Gardens/Parks, General, Municipalities/Towns • *Education:* Colleges & Universities, Education Reform, Elementary Education (Public), Public Education (Precollege), Student Aid • *Environment:* General • *Religion:* Churches, Ministries, Religious Organizations, Religious Welfare • *Social Services:* Recreation & Athletics, Youth Organizations

Grant Types: capital, general support, operating expenses, scholarship, and seed money

Geographic Distribution: focus on Licking County, OH

GIVING OFFICERS
John William Alford: chmn, trust *B* Baltimore MD 1912 *ED* DePauw Univ AB 1935

CURR EMPL chmn, dir: Park Natl Corp *CORP AFFIL* chmn, dir: Park Natl Bank; dir: Consolidated Computer Center, Contour Holdings, WE Schrider Co, Stocker & Sitler Oil Co *NONPR AFFIL* chmn: Thomas J Evans Fdn; chmn, mem, dir: OH Chamber Commerce; hon trust: Dawes Arboretum; life trust: Denison Univ; mem: Am Bankers Assn, Am Legion, Licking County Hosp Commn, Newark Chamber Commerce, OH Bankers Assn, Veterans Foreign Wars; mem adv bd: Salvation Army; trust: Methodist Theological *CLUB AFFIL* Capital, Columbus, Elks, Moundbuilders CC, Rotary

J. Gilbert Reese: pres, trust *B* 1926 *CURR EMPL* chmn bd, dir: First Fed Saving & Loan Assn.

Sarah R. Wallace: secy, trust *CURR EMPL* pres, dir: First Fed Saving & Loan Assn

APPLICATION INFORMATION
Initial Contact: The foundation has no formal grant application procedure or application form.

Deadlines: The foundation has no deadline for submitting proposals.

Restrictions on Giving: The foundation only gives grants to qualified charitable organizations and local governments. The foundation does not make grants to individuals.

GRANTS ANALYSIS
Total Grants: $403,501

Number of Grants: 13

Highest Grant: $128,604

Average Grant: $31,039

Typical Range: $5,000 to $38,000

Disclosure Period: fiscal year ending October 31, 1993

Note: Recent grants are derived from a fiscal 1993 Form 990.

RECENT GRANTS

General
128,604	City of Newark, Newark, OH — bridge and tunnel
50,000	Licking County Foundation, Newark, OH — COIC/University of Southern Ohio, bell tower
40,000	Call to College Fund, Newark, OH — scholarship fund
38,032	City of Newark, Newark, OH — blacktop basketball courts
33,333	Salvation Army, Newark, OH — building renovation

Firestone, Jr. Foundation, Harvey

CONTACT
Charles D'Arcy
Harvey Firestone, Jr. Fdn.
c/o Bank One Ohio Trust Co.
50 S Main St.
Akron, OH 44309
(216) 972-1872

FINANCIAL SUMMARY
Recent Giving: $670,000 (1993); $344,500 (1990); $125,000 (1989)

Assets: $14,137,528 (1993); $10,474,707 (1990); $10,240,855 (1989)

EIN: 34-1388254

CONTRIBUTIONS SUMMARY
Typical Recipients: • *Arts & Humanities:* Historic Preservation, History & Archaeology, Libraries, Music, Public Broadcasting • *Civic & Public Affairs:* Community Foundations, General • *Education:* Arts/Humanities Education, Colleges & Universities, Private Education (Precollege), Special Education • *Health:* Health Organizations, Hospitals, Nursing Services • *Religion:* Dioceses, Religious Organizations • *Social Services:* Child Welfare, Community Centers, Family Services, People with Disabilities, Recreation & Athletics, United Funds/United Ways, Youth Organizations

Grant Types: general support

Geographic Distribution: focus on the eastern US

GIVING OFFICERS
Bank One, Akron: trust

Anne F. Ball: trust

Martha F. Ford: trust *PHIL AFFIL* trust, mem: William and Martha Ford Fund

APPLICATION INFORMATION
Initial Approach: The foundation has no formal grant application procedure or application form. There are no deadlines.

GRANTS ANALYSIS
Total Grants: $670,000

Number of Grants: 48

Highest Grant: $280,000

Typical Range: $500 to $110,000

Disclosure Period: 1993

Note: Recent grants are derived from a 1993 Form 990.

RECENT GRANTS

Library
5,500	Greenwich Library, Greenwich, CT — general use

General
280,000	Henry Ford Health Systems, Detroit, MI — general use
110,000	Miss Porter's School, Farmington, CT — general use
35,000	Diocese of Bridgeport, Bridgeport, CT — general use
25,000	Princeton 2nd Century Fund, Rumson, NJ — general use
20,000	Family Center, Greenwich, CT — general use

Firman Fund

CONTACT
Neil A. Brown
Trustee
Firman Fund
1422 Euclid Ave., Ste. 1030
Cleveland, OH 44115
(216) 363-1030

FINANCIAL SUMMARY
Recent Giving: $484,117 (1993)

Assets: $8,514,511 (1993)

EIN: 34-6513655

CONTRIBUTIONS SUMMARY
Typical Recipients: • *Arts & Humanities:* History & Archaeology, Libraries, Museums/Galleries, Music, Opera, Public Broadcasting, Theater • *Civic & Public Affairs:* Botanical Gardens/Parks, Employment/Job Training, General, Municipalities/Towns, Women's Affairs • *Education:* Colleges & Universities, General, Medical Education, Private Education (Precollege), Science/Mathematics Education, Student Aid • *Environment:* General, Wildlife Protection • *Health:* Children's Health/Hospitals, Diabetes, Emergency/Ambulance Services, Eyes/Blindness, Medical Rehabilitation, Nursing Services, Speech & Hearing • *Science:* Science Museums, Scientific Research • *Social Services:* Child Welfare, Community Service Organizations, People with Disabilities, United Funds/United Ways, Volunteer Services

Grant Types: general support

Geographic Distribution: focus on OH

GIVING OFFICERS
N. A. Brown: trust *PHIL AFFIL* asst treas: Ireland Foundation

Pamela Firman: pres *PHIL AFFIL* trust: Cherokee Foundation

Royal Firman: trust

Carole M. Nowak: treas

Cindy Webster: trust *PHIL AFFIL* vp: Cherokee Foundation

APPLICATION INFORMATION
Initial Approach: Send a brief letter of inquiry. Include a description of organization, amount requested, purpose of funds sought, recently audited financial statement, and proof of tax-exempt status.

GRANTS ANALYSIS
Total Grants: $484,117

Number of Grants: 110

Highest Grant: $33,333

Typical Range: $50 to $30,000

Disclosure Period: 1993

Note: Recent grants are derived from a 1993 Form 990.

RECENT GRANTS

Library
5,000	Cleveland Medical Library Association, Cleveland, OH

General
33,333	Visiting Nurses Association, Cleveland, OH — capital campaign
30,000	Miss Hall's School, Pittsfield, MA — capital fund
30,000	University Hospitals, Cleveland, OH — Pediatric Hospital
27,500	Tall Timbers Research, Tallahassee, FL — Bobtail Quail research project
26,000	United Way Services, Cleveland, OH

Flowers Charitable Trust, Albert W. and Edith V.

CONTACT
Stephen C. Donatini
Trust Officer
Albert W. and Edith V. Flowers Charitable Trust
c/o Society National Bank
PO Box 9950
Canton, OH 44711-0950
(216) 489-5422

FINANCIAL SUMMARY
Recent Giving: $90,950 (1993); $867,000 (1992); $59,500 (1991)

Assets: $2,084,527 (1993); $1,945,661 (1992); $1,914,713 (1991)

EIN: 34-6608643

CONTRIBUTIONS SUMMARY
Donor(s): the late Albert W. Flowers, the late Edith V. Flowers

Typical Recipients: • *Arts & Humanities:* Arts Centers, Ballet, Historic Preservation, History & Archaeology, Libraries, Museums/Galleries, Music, Theater • *Civic & Public Affairs:* African American Affairs, Clubs, Economic Development, General, Municipalities/Towns • *Education:* Colleges & Universities, Private Education (Precollege), Public Education (Precollege), Student Aid • *Health:* Children's Health/Hospitals, Emergency/Ambulance Services • *International:* Missionary/Religious Activities • *Religion:* Bible Study/Translation, Churches, Religious Welfare • *Social Services:* Big Brother/Big Sister, Child Welfare, Community Centers, Community Service Organizations, Recreation & Athletics, Scouts, YMCA/YWCA/YMHA/YWHA, Youth Organizations

Grant Types: general support

Geographic Distribution: focus on Stark County, OH

GIVING OFFICERS
E. E. McCullough: trust

Albert Printz: trust

Ronald B. Tynan: chmn

APPLICATION INFORMATION
Initial Approach: Send brief letter describing program. Deadline is November 15.

Restrictions on Giving: Limited to organizations in Stark County.

GRANTS ANALYSIS

Total Grants: $90,950

Number of Grants: 29

Highest Grant: $25,000

Typical Range: $500 to $15,000

Disclosure Period: 1993

Note: Recent grants are derived from a 1993 Form 990.

RECENT GRANTS

General

25,000	St. Luke Lutheran Home, Canton, OH
15,000	Martin Luther Lutheran Church, Canton, OH
7,000	Holly Hills, Holly Hills, OH
5,000	Stark County Christian Academy, Canton, OH
4,000	Northwest Jackson Soccer Association, Canton, OH

Freedom Forge Corp. / Freedom Forge Foundation

Former Foundation Name: American Welding & Manufacturing Co. Foundation
Sales: $368.5 million
Employees: 2,000
Parent Company: Hoover Universal Inc.
Headquarters: Warren, OH
SIC Major Group: Fabricated Metal Products, Industrial Machinery & Equipment, and Transportation Equipment

CONTACT

Crystal L. Hudspeth
Senior Trust Officer
Freedom Forge Foundation
c/o Bank One Youngstown NA
PO Box 231
Warren, OH 44482-0231
(216) 841-7820

FINANCIAL SUMMARY

Recent Giving: $68,225 (1993); $49,582 (1992); $40,017 (1991)

Assets: $1,111,029 (1993); $0 (1992); $0 (1991)

EIN: 34-6516721

CONTRIBUTIONS SUMMARY

Typical Recipients: • *Arts & Humanities:* Arts Associations & Councils, Libraries, Music, Performing Arts, Public Broadcasting • *Civic & Public Affairs:* Clubs, Economic Development, Economic Policy, Municipalities/Towns, Professional & Trade Associations, Public Policy, Urban & Community Affairs • *Education:* Agricultural Education, Business Education, Colleges & Universi-

ties, Education Funds, Private Education (Precollege) • *Environment:* General, Resource Conservation, Wildlife Protection • *Health:* Cancer, Children's Health/Hospitals, Hospices, Hospitals, Kidney, Medical Research, Multiple Sclerosis, Prenatal Health Issues, Single-Disease Health Associations • *Religion:* Religious Welfare • *Science:* Science Exhibits & Fairs • *Social Services:* Community Service Organizations, Delinquency & Criminal Rehabilitation, People with Disabilities, Recreation & Athletics, Scouts, Special Olympics, Substance Abuse, United Funds/United Ways, Youth Organizations

Grant Types: general support

Geographic Distribution: focus on OH

Operating Locations: OH (Warren)

CORP. OFFICERS

James Spendiff: *CURR EMPL* pres: Freedom Forge Corp

GIVING OFFICERS

Bank One Ohio Trust Co., NA: trust

James Spindiff: trust

APPLICATION INFORMATION

Initial Approach: The foundation requests applications be made in writing. Include a description of organization, amount requested, purpose of funds sought, recently audited financial statement, and proof of tax-exempt status. There are no deadlines.

GRANTS ANALYSIS

Total Grants: $68,225

Number of Grants: 23

Highest Grant: $21,000

Disclosure Period: 1993

Note: Recent grants are derived from a 1993 Form 990.

RECENT GRANTS

Library

5,000	National Railroad Library Endowment, St. Louis, MO
1,000	Juniata Library Association, Lewistown, PA

General

21,000	United Way of Mifflin, Lewistown, PA
12,500	United Way of Trumbull County, Warren, OH
5,000	Pennsylvania State University, University Park, PA
4,300	United Way of Westmoreland County, Greensburg, PA
2,000	Belleville Mennonite School, Belleville, PA

French Oil Mill Machinery Co. / French Oil Mill Machinery Co. Charitable Trust

Sales: $24.0 million
Employees: 160
Headquarters: Piqua, OH
SIC Major Group: Industrial Machinery & Equipment

CONTACT

Joanne E. Townsend
Trust Officer
French Oil Mill Machinery Co.
c/o Fifth Third Bank
PO Box 703
Piqua, OH 45356-0703
(513) 778-4411

FINANCIAL SUMMARY

Recent Giving: $34,000 (fiscal 1994); $30,075 (fiscal 1993); $24,415 (fiscal 1992)

Assets: $471,656 (fiscal 1993); $471,955 (fiscal 1992); $444,798 (fiscal 1991)

EIN: 31-6024511

CONTRIBUTIONS SUMMARY

Typical Recipients: • *Arts & Humanities:* Arts Centers, Arts Festivals, Community Arts, General, Libraries • *Civic & Public Affairs:* Chambers of Commerce, Community Foundations, Economic Development, Employment/Job Training, General • *Education:* Afterschool/Enrichment Programs, Arts/Humanities Education, Colleges & Universities, Community & Junior Colleges, General, Religious Education • *Health:* Cancer, General, Heart, Hospices, Medical Rehabilitation, Respiratory • *Social Services:* Community Service Organizations, Family Planning, Food/Clothing Distribution, General, People with Disabilities, Recreation & Athletics, Senior Services, United Funds/United Ways, Youth Organizations

Grant Types: general support and seed money

Geographic Distribution: focus on Piqua, OH

Operating Locations: OH (Piqua)

CORP. OFFICERS

Daniel P. French, Jr.: *CURR EMPL* pres, ceo, dir: French Oil Mill Machinery Co

GIVING OFFICERS

Fifth Third Bank of Western Ohio: trust

APPLICATION INFORMATION

Initial Approach: Send a full proposal. Include a description of organization, amount requested, purpose of funds sought, and proof of tax-exempt status. There are no deadlines.

Restrictions on Giving: Does not support individuals, or political or lobbying groups.

GRANTS ANALYSIS

Total Grants: $30,075

Number of Grants: 44

Highest Grant: $10,000

Typical Range: $100 to $4,000

Disclosure Period: fiscal year ending November 30, 1993

Note: Recent grants are derived from a fiscal 1993 Form 990.

RECENT GRANTS

General

10,000	United Way
4,000	YMCA — capital improvement program
2,000	National Right to Work Legal Defense and Education Foundation, Springfield, VA
1,625	Hipple Cancer Research Center, Dayton, OH
1,000	Committee for Economic Development, Piqua, OH

Frisch's Restaurants Inc.

Former Foundation Name: Frisch Foundation

Revenue: $163.0 million

Employees: 6,700

Headquarters: Cincinnati, OH

SIC Major Group: Eating & Drinking Places, Holding & Other Investment Offices, Hotels & Other Lodging Places, and Wholesale Trade—Nondurable Goods

CONTACT

Louis J. Ullman

Senior Vice President, Finanace

Frisch's Restaurants Inc.

2800 Gilbert Ave.

Cincinnati, OH 45206

(513) 961-2660

FINANCIAL SUMMARY

Recent Giving: $1,215 (1993); $976 (1992); $204,203 (1991)

Assets: $10,996 (1993); $11,280 (1992); $11,321 (1991)

Fiscal Note: Company does not disclose contributions figures. Company foundation has been dissolved, and contributions are now made directly.

CONTRIBUTIONS SUMMARY

Initial Approach: Support goes to local education, human service, health, arts, and civic organizations.

Typical Recipients: • *Arts & Humanities:* Arts Associations & Councils, Arts Funds, Dance, Libraries, Museums/Galleries, Music, Performing Arts, Public Broadcasting • *Civic & Public Affairs:* Economic Development, Philanthropic Organizations, Professional & Trade Associations, Urban & Community Affairs, Women's Affairs, Zoos/Aquariums • *Education:* Arts/Humanities Education, Colleges & Universities, Economic Education • *Environment:* Air/Water Quality • *Health:* Alzheimers Disease, Cancer, Health Organizations, Heart, Hospices • *International:* International Relief Efforts • *Religion:* Religious Organizations, Synagogues/Temples • *Science:* Scientific Centers & Institutes • *Social Services:*

Community Service Organizations, Domestic Violence, United Funds/United Ways, Volunteer Services, Youth Organizations

Grant Types: general support, multi-year/continuing support, and operating expenses

Nonmonetary Support Types: cause-related marketing & promotion, donated equipment, donated products, and workplace solicitation

Geographic Distribution: Initial Approach: focus on OH, KY, and IN

Operating Locations: IN, KY, OH

CORP. OFFICERS

Marvin G. Fields: *CURR EMPL* sr vp, coo, dir: Frischs Restaurant

Craig F. Maier: *B* Cincinnati OH 1949 *ED* Trinity Coll 1971; Columbia Univ 1975 *CURR EMPL* pres, ceo: Frischs Restaurants

Jack Craig Maier: *B* St. Joseph MN 1925 *CURR EMPL* chmn: Frischs Restaurants *NONPR AFFIL* dir: Greater Cincinnati Charity Horse Show, Tri-State Horse Show Assn; mem: FL Restaurant Assn, Greater Cincinnati Restaurant Assn, KY Restaurant Assn, Natl Restaurant Assn, OH Restaurant Assn, Sigma Alpha Epsilon, Un Hunts Racing Assn *CLUB AFFIL* Kenwood CC, Masons, 100, Rotary

Louis J. Ullman: *CURR EMPL* sr vp, cfo: Frischs Restaurants

APPLICATION INFORMATION

Initial Approach: The foundation has no formal grant application procedure or application form. Submit a full proposal. Include a description of organization, amount requested, purpose of funds sought, and proof of tax-exempt status. There are no deadlines.

Restrictions on Giving: Does not support individuals, religious organizations for sectarian purposes, political or lobbying groups, or organizations outside operating areas.

Frohring Foundation, Paul and Maxine

CONTACT

William W. Falsgraf

Secretary

Paul and Maxine Frohring Fdn.

1900 E 9th St., Ste. 3200

Cleveland, OH 44114-3485

(216) 861-7376

FINANCIAL SUMMARY

Recent Giving: $539,500 (1993); $181,000 (1992); $158,000 (1991)

Assets: $4,053,740 (1993); $4,377,539 (1992); $5,393,980 (1991)

Gifts Received: $242,500 (1993)

Fiscal Note: In 1993, contributions were received from Paul R. Frohring.

EIN: 34-6513729

CONTRIBUTIONS SUMMARY

Typical Recipients: • *Arts & Humanities:* History & Archaeology, Libraries, Museums/Galleries, Opera • *Civic & Public Affairs:* Botanical Gardens/Parks, Employment/Job Training, Municipalities/Towns, Zoos/Aquariums • *Education:* Colleges & Universities, General, Minority Education, Private Education (Precollege) • *Health:* Hospitals, Long-Term Care, Nursing Services • *International:* Foreign Educational Institutions • *Religion:* Religious Welfare • *Social Services:* Community Service Organizations, Family Planning, People with Disabilities, Senior Services, Substance Abuse, Youth Organizations

Grant Types: general support

Geographic Distribution: focus on OH

GIVING OFFICERS

William Wendell Falsgraf: secy, trust *B* Cleveland OH 1933 *ED* Amherst Coll AB 1955; Case Western Reserve Univ JD 1958 *CURR EMPL* ptnr: Baker & Hostetler *NONPR AFFIL* chmn bd trusts: Hiram Coll; fellow: Am Bar Fdn, Am Coll Probate Couns; mem: Am Bar Assn, Amherst Coll Alumni Assn, Cleveland Bar Assn, OH Bar Assn, OH Bar Fdn; trust: Case Western Reserve Univ, Cleveland Health Mus *PHIL AFFIL* asst secy, trust: William O. and Gertrude Lewis Frohring Foundation

Paul Robert Frohring: pres, trust *B* Cleveland OH 1904 *ED* Case Inst Tech BS 1926; OH St Univ *CORP AFFIL* dir: Alco Standard, Am Home Products Corp, Cleveland Machine Controls, Horsburg & Scott, Irvin & Co, Newbury Indus *NONPR AFFIL* fellow: Garfield Soc, NY Academy Sciences; mem: Alpha Chi Sigma, Am Assn Advancement Science, Am Chem Soc, Am Dairy Science Assn, Am Oil Chem Soc, Navy League, Newcomen Soc, OH Academy Science, OH Soc, Pharmaceutical Mfrs Assn, Planned Parenthood; overseer: Case Western Reserve Univ; trust: FL Zoological Soc, Hiram Coll, John Cabot Univ; trust, hon chmn: Cleveland Health Ed Mus *CLUB AFFIL* Chagrin Valley Hunt, Commodore, Key Biscayne YC, Union *PHIL AFFIL* dir: Mercy Hospital Foundation

Elmer Jagow: trust

Paula Frohring Kushlan: trust

APPLICATION INFORMATION

Initial Approach: Send a brief letter of inquiry. Include a description of organization, amount requested, purpose of funds sought, recently audited financial statement, and proof of tax-exempt status. There are no deadlines.

Restrictions on Giving: Does not support individuals.

GRANTS ANALYSIS

Total Grants: $539,500

Number of Grants: 18

Highest Grant: $500,000

Typical Range: $1,000 to $10,000

Disclosure Period: 1993

Note: Recent grants are derived from a 1993 Form 990.

RECENT GRANTS

Library

1,000   Chagrin Falls Library, Chagrin Falls, OH — general support

General

500,000   John Cabot International College, Rome, Italy — general support

10,000   Hathaway Brown School, Shaker Heights, OH — general support

5,000   Garden Center, Cleveland, OH — general support

3,500   Zoological Society, Miami, FL — general support

2,500   Alcoholism Services of Cleveland, Cleveland, OH — general support

---

Frohring Foundation, William O. and Gertrude Lewis

CONTACT
William W. Falsgraf
Assistant Secretary
William O. and Gertrude Lewis Frohring Fdn.
3200 National City Ctr.
Cleveland, OH 44114
(216) 621-0200

FINANCIAL SUMMARY
Recent Giving: $226,600 (1993); $232,092 (1991); $210,950 (1990)

Assets: $5,109,659 (1993); $5,199,741 (1991); $4,160,642 (1990)

EIN: 34-6516526

CONTRIBUTIONS SUMMARY
Donor(s): the late William O. Frohring, the late Gertrude L. Frohring

Typical Recipients: • *Arts & Humanities:* Arts Institutes, Historic Preservation, History & Archaeology, Libraries, Museums/Galleries, Music, Opera, Performing Arts, Theater • *Civic & Public Affairs:* Botanical Gardens/Parks, General, Safety, Women's Affairs • *Education:* Arts/Humanities Education, Colleges & Universities, Education Funds, Preschool Education, Private Education (Precollege), Special Education, Student Aid • *Environment:* General • *Health:* Alzheimers Disease, Cancer, Eyes/Blindness, Geriatric Health, Hospices, Hospitals, Medical Research, Research/Studies Institutes, Single-Disease Health Associations • *International:* Foreign Arts Organizations, International Peace & Security Issues • *Religion:* Churches, Religious Welfare • *Science:* Science Museums • *Social Services:* Camps, Child Welfare, Community Service Organizations, People with Disabilities, Senior Services, Volunteer Services, YMCA/YWCA/YMHA/YWHA, Youth Organizations

Grant Types: capital, emergency, general support, multiyear/continuing support, operating expenses, scholarship, and seed money

Geographic Distribution: focus on Geauga, Lake, and Cuyahoga counties, OH

GIVING OFFICERS
William Wendell Falsgraf: asst secy, trust *B* Cleveland OH 1933 *ED* Amherst Coll AB 1955; Case Western Reserve Univ JD 1958 *CURR EMPL* ptnr: Baker & Hostetler *NONPR AFFIL* chmn bd trusts: Hiram Coll; fellow: Am Bar Fdn, Am Coll Probate Couns; mem: Am Bar Assn, Amherst Coll Alumni Assn, Cleveland Bar Assn, OH Bar Assn, OH Bar Fdn; trust: Case Western Reserve Univ, Cleveland Health Mus *PHIL AFFIL* secy, trust: Paul and Maxine Frohring Foundation

Glenn H. Frohring: chmn, trust

Lloyd W. Frohring: treas, trust

Elaine A. Szilagyi: secy, trust

APPLICATION INFORMATION
Initial Approach: Send brief letter of inquiry describing program or project. Include a description of organization, amount requested, purpose of funds sought, recently audited financial statement, and proof of tax-exempt status. There are no deadlines.

Restrictions on Giving: Does not support individuals.

GRANTS ANALYSIS
Total Grants: $226,600

Number of Grants: 53

Highest Grant: $100,000

Typical Range: $500 to $10,000

Disclosure Period: 1993

Note: Recent grants are derived from a 1993 Form 990.

RECENT GRANTS

Library

5,000   Newbury Local Schools Library Program, Newbury, OH

General

100,000   Corinne Dolan Alzheimers Center, Cleveland, OH

10,000   Hiram College, Hiram, OH

6,000   Baldwin-Wallace College, Berea, OH

6,000   Bowling Green State University, Bowling Green, KY

6,000   Eleanor B. Rainey Memorial Institute, Cleveland, OH

Gallagher Family Foundation, Lewis P.

CONTACT
Gilbert V. Kelling, Jr.
Secretary
Lewis P. Gallagher Family Fdn.
One Cascade Plz., Ste. 1220
Akron, OH 44308
(216) 253-2227

FINANCIAL SUMMARY
Recent Giving: $380,265 (1993); $266,661 (1992); $813,460 (1991)

Assets: $7,864,995 (1993); $6,788,157 (1992); $6,182,325 (1991)

Gifts Received: $917,936 (1993); $756,280 (1992); $769,513 (1991)

EIN: 34-1325313

CONTRIBUTIONS SUMMARY
Donor(s): Lewis P. Gallagher Family Charitable Income Trust

Typical Recipients: • *Arts & Humanities:* Libraries • *Education:* Colleges & Universities, Elementary Education (Private), Private Education (Precollege), Public Education (Precollege), Student Aid • *Health:* Health Policy/Cost Containment, Hospitals, Public Health • *International:* International Relations • *Religion:* Churches, Ministries, Missionary Activities (Domestic), Religious Organizations, Religious Welfare • *Social Services:* Child Welfare, Community Service Organizations, Food/Clothing Distribution, People with Disabilities, Recreation & Athletics, United Funds/United Ways, Youth Organizations

Grant Types: capital, general support, operating expenses, and scholarship

Geographic Distribution: focus on OH

GIVING OFFICERS
Monford D. Custer III: treas

Howard H. Fraser: pres

Gilbert V. Kelling, Jr.: secy

APPLICATION INFORMATION
Initial Approach: Send brief letter of inquiry describing program or project. The deadline is September 1.

Restrictions on Giving: Does not support individuals. Limited to organizations in Ohio, Maine, and Virginia.

GRANTS ANALYSIS
Total Grants: $380,265

Number of Grants: 14

Highest Grant: $50,000

Typical Range: $5,000 to $50,000

Disclosure Period: 1993

Note: Recent grants are derived from a 1993 Form 990.

RECENT GRANTS
Library

50,000   Shenandoah University, Winchester, VA — capital improvement Smith Library

General

50,000   Wheaton Christian Grammer School, Wheaton, IL — capital campaign

44,839   Child Evangelism Fellowship, Portland, ME — capital improvement; building construction challenge grant

25,000   Hospital Chaplaincy Services, Hampden, ME — general operations

25,000   Hudson School District, Hudson, OH — Barlow Scholarship Endowment Fund

20,000   Houghton College, Houghton, NY — scholarship for missionary children

GAR Foundation

CONTACT
Richard A. Chenoweth
Executive Director
GAR Foundation
50 S Main St.
PO Box 1500
Akron, OH 44309
(216) 376-5300

FINANCIAL SUMMARY
Recent Giving: $9,164,317 (1993); $6,641,470 (1992); $5,395,180 (1991)

Assets: $183,394,199 (1993); $212,152,515 (1992); $196,488,005 (1991)

EIN: 34-6577710

CONTRIBUTIONS SUMMARY
Donor(s): Galen Roush and his wife, Ruth C. Roush , established the GAR Foundation in 1967 in Ohio. Mr. Roush was a lawyer and the principal founder and chief executive of Roadway Express, one of the country's 25 largest transportation companies. Because they were raised in the Akron-northeastern Ohio area, the Roushes preferred to fund philanthropic organizations based in this section of Ohio. Mrs. Roush, an Oberlin College graduate, was interested in music, art, and education. As a result, the foundation gives significant support to arts and educational programs. Mr. Roush graduated from Hiram College and received his law degree from Case Western Reserve University. Both Mr. and Mrs. Roush firmly believed in the free enterprise system in which they had prospered. The foundation is endowed by their respective estates.

Typical Recipients: • *Arts & Humanities:* Arts Centers, Arts Festivals, Arts Institutes, Ballet, Community Arts, Historic Preservation, History & Archaeology, Libraries, Museums/Galleries, Music, Opera, Performing Arts, Public Broadcasting, Theater • *Civic & Public Affairs:* Botanical Gardens/Parks, Business/Free Enterprise, Community Foundations, Economic Development, Employment/Job Training, Housing, Municipalities/Towns, Urban & Community Affairs, Zoos/Aquariums • *Education:* Arts/Humanities Education, Business Education, Colleges & Universities, Education Associations, Education Funds, Education Reform, Elementary Education (Private), Faculty Development, General, Medical Education, Minority Education, Private Education (Precollege), Public Education (Precollege), Science/Mathematics Education, Secondary Education (Private), Student Aid • *Environment:* Wildlife Protection • *Health:* Alzheimers Disease, Children's Health/Hospitals, Emergency/Ambulance Services, Health Funds, Hospices, Hospitals, Mental Health, Multiple Sclerosis, Nursing Services • *Religion:* Churches, Religious Organizations, Religious Welfare • *Social Services:* Community Service Organizations, Day Care, Family Planning, Family Services, Food/Clothing Distribution, People with Disabilities, Recreation & Athletics, Senior Services, Shelters/Homelessness, Substance Abuse, United Funds/United Ways, YMCA/YWCA/YMHA/YWHA, Youth Organizations

Grant Types: capital, endowment, operating expenses, project, scholarship, and seed money

Geographic Distribution: Akron and the northeastern Ohio area

GIVING OFFICERS
Robert W. Briggs: co-trust

Margaret Carroll: secy

Richard A. Chenoweth: exec dir *PHIL AFFIL* trust: Burton D. Morgan Foundation

Joseph Mark Clapp: mem distribution comm *B* Greensboro NC 1936 *ED* Univ NC BS 1958 *CURR EMPL* chmn, pres, ceo, dir: Roadway Svcs *CORP AFFIL* chmn, dir: Roberts Express Inc *NONPR AFFIL* bd trusts: Akron City Hosp; mem: Regular Common Carrier Conf, Transportation Practitioners Assn; vp at large, mem: Am Trucking Assn *CLUB AFFIL* mem: Congressional CC, Fairlawn CC

Hugh Colopy: trust, mem distribution comm

G. James Roush: alternate mem distr comm

George C. Roush: alternate mem distr comm

Thomas W. Roush: alternate mem distr comm

John L. Tormey: mem distribution comm *B* 1913 *CURR EMPL* chmn, dir: Central Coated Products Inc *CORP AFFIL* pres, dir: Central Standard Co

Sally Roush Werner: mem distribution comm

Douglas A. Wilson: alternate mem distr comm *B* 1944 *ED* Univ PA BS 1966; Akron Univ JD 1975 *CURR EMPL* sr vp fin & planning, secy, cfo: Roadway Svcs *CORP AFFIL* secy: Roadway Express, Roadway Logistics Sys

Charles Francis Zodrow: mem distribution comm *B* Milwaukee WI 1922 *ED* Univ WI BBA 1948; Univ Akron JD 1958 *CURR EMPL* chmn, dir, ceo: Roadway Express *CORP AFFIL* dir: Soc Corp, Soc Natl Bank *NONPR AFFIL* mem: Am Bar Assn, Am Inst CPAs; mem, dir: Tax Counc; trust: Childrens Hosp Akron, John Carroll Univ; vp, dir: Am Trucking Assn

APPLICATION INFORMATION
Initial Approach:

Applicants should request and complete the foundation's application form.

Application information should include verification of tax-exempt status; detailed budget; latest IRS Form 990; description of general purposes and activities; list of members of governing board; other sources of funding; amount requested; and contact person's name.

The application should be submitted by February 15, May 15, August 15, and November 15. The distribution committee meets the second Thursday of February, May, August, and November.

Restrictions on Giving: Grants are made to endowment funds, particularly to those of educational institutions, including the endowment of chairs and scholarship funds. However, the foundation has strict guidelines on the means of memorializing endowment funds to ensure that the principal of an endowment grant is not used without the written consent of the GAR Foundation. Recipients of nonendowment grants must inform the foundation of the project's progress and completion, and provide a fiscal and program summary. Funds not used as designated must be returned to the foundation.

Restrictions on Giving: Ordinarily, grants are not made for general operating expenses not directly related to the grantee's purpose, to individuals, to other private nonoperating foundations, to mass appeal fund-raising drives, to national organizations, or for medical research.

OTHER THINGS TO KNOW
No grant is made for more than a calendar year. No grant will be renewed or made for a new project by the same grantee without a formal application being filed. Renewals cannot be guaranteed from year to year.

The foundation lists National City Bank as a co-trustee.

PUBLICATIONS
Application guidelines

GRANTS ANALYSIS
Total Grants: $9,164,317

Number of Grants: 170

Highest Grant: $1,250,000

Average Grant: $46,830*

Typical Range: $10,000 to $100,000

Disclosure Period: 1993

Note: The average grant figure excludes the largest grant of $1,250,000. Recent grants are derived from a 1993 Form 990.

RECENT GRANTS
Library

500,000   Hiram College, Hiram, OH — for library equipment and materials

75,000   Holy Family School, Stow, OH — toward replacement of the 6,500 library books lost in the July 31, 1992, flood

50,000   Mt. Vernon Nazarene College, Mt. Vernon, OH — for library equipment and materials

50,000   Wittenberg University, Springfield, OH — to the endowment fund of the humanities collection in its Thomas Library

40,000   Defiance College, Defiance, OH — to the restricted library endowment fund

General

1,250,000   University of Akron Foundation, Akron, OH —

$1 million to create the Lisle M. Buckingham Memorial Endowment Fund by the GAR Foundation, the income from which will be used for full scholarships for honors students for tuition and books based on merit and financial aid

1,132,500	Cleveland Foundation, Cleveland, OH — to meet outstanding challenge grants
752,000	Akron Community Foundation, Akron, OH — meet outstanding challenge grants and to establish endowment funds for local charities
250,000	Visiting Nurse Service, Akron, OH — $100,000 to be applied to construction costs and a challenge grant of $100,000 be authorized if applicant raises $200,000, all for endowment and toward the restricted endowment fund whose annual earnings can be used to provide services
240,000	Stark County Foundation, Canton, OH — to meet outstanding challenge grants

GenCorp Inc. / GenCorp Foundation, Inc.

Sales: $1.9 billion
Employees: 13,300
Headquarters: Akron, OH
SIC Major Group: Space Propulsion Units & Parts, Industrial Organic Chemicals Nec, Adhesives & Sealants, and Fabricated Rubber Products Nec

CONTACT
Theresa Carter
Communications Specialist
GenCorp Foundation, Inc.
175 Ghent Rd.
Fairlawn, OH 44333
(216) 869-4289

FINANCIAL SUMMARY
Recent Giving: $1,900,000 (fiscal 1995 est.); $1,768,438 (fiscal 1994); $1,704,245 (fiscal 1993)

Assets: $36,000,000 (fiscal 1995); $36,694,664 (fiscal 1994); $36,000,000 (fiscal 1993)

Fiscal Note: Above figures include foundation giving only. In 1994, the company gave $110,496 directly, and in 1993, it gave $163,780 directly. Above figures exclude nonmonetary support.

EIN: 34-6514223

CONTRIBUTIONS SUMMARY
Typical Recipients: • *Arts & Humanities:* Arts Institutes, Dance, Historic Preservation, Libraries, Museums/Galleries, Performing Arts, Public Broadcasting, Theater

• *Civic & Public Affairs:* Business/Free Enterprise, Economic Development, Economic Policy, Employment/Job Training, General, Municipalities/Towns, Professional & Trade Associations, Public Policy, Urban & Community Affairs, Women's Affairs, Zoos/Aquariums • *Education:* Business Education, Business-School Partnerships, Colleges & Universities, Community & Junior Colleges, Education Funds, Education Reform, Elementary Education (Private), Engineering/Technological Education, General, Literacy, Minority Education, Private Education (Precollege), Public Education (Precollege), Science/Mathematics Education, Student Aid • *Environment:* General • *Health:* Children's Health/Hospitals, Mental Health • *International:* International Affairs • *Science:* Scientific Centers & Institutes • *Social Services:* United Funds/United Ways, Volunteer Services, Youth Organizations

Grant Types: capital, challenge, emergency, employee matching gifts, general support, multiyear/continuing support, operating expenses, and project

Note: Employee matching gift ratio: 1 to 1, for contributions to education only.

Nonmonetary Support: $25,000 (fiscal 1993); $25,000 (fiscal 1992)

Nonmonetary Support Types: donated equipment and donated products

Geographic Distribution: near corporate operating locations

Operating Locations: AL (Huntsville), AR (Batesville, Ft. Smith), AZ (Phoenix), CA (Azusa, Chino, Downey, Los Angeles, Sacramento), CO (Colorado Springs), DC (Washington), GA (Dalton), IN (Evansville, Logansport, Marion, Peru, Rushville, Shelbyville, Wabash), MI (Ionia), MO (Berger, Cuba), MS (Columbus), NH (Salem), NJ (Hackensack, Pine Brook), NM (Socorro), NY (New York), OH (Akron, Fairlawn, Mogadore, Newcomerstown), PA (Jeanette), TN (Jonesboro), WI (Green Bay)

CORP. OFFICERS
Theresa Carter: *CURR EMPL* commun specialist: GenCorp Inc

Sam W. Hughes: *CURR EMPL* vp: Gencorp Inc

Rosemary Younts: *CURR EMPL* vp corp commun: GenCorp Inc

GIVING OFFICERS
Gary J. Goberville: trust

Russell Livigni: trust

Frederick J. Lucksinger: trust *CURR EMPL* vp, contr: GenCorp Inc

Rosemary Younts: trust *CURR EMPL* vp corp commun: GenCorp Inc (see above)

APPLICATION INFORMATION
Initial Approach: *Initial Contact:* request guidelines or write brief letter *Include Information On:* description of the organization, amount requested, purpose for which funds are sought, recently audited financial statement, and proof of tax-exempt status, list of GenCorp employees who currently volunteer with your organization, description of how

GenCorp Foundation's support will be recognized*Deadlines:* none

Restrictions on Giving: Foundation does not support individuals, endowments or loans, fraternal organizations, goodwill advertising, religious organizations for sectarian purposes, political organizations, research grants; organizations where there is a direct benefit to the trustees of the foundation, employees, or directors of the corporation; United Way member agencies, where the Foundation has already made a United Way grant in that calendar year.

Emphasis is placed on organizations in the communities where employees live and work.

GRANTS ANALYSIS
Total Grants: $1,767,413
Number of Grants: 356*
Highest Grant: $61,500
Average Grant: $4,219*
Typical Range: $1,000 to $10,000
Disclosure Period: fiscal year ending November 30, 1994

Note: Financial information for foundation only. Number of grants and average grant figures exclude matching gifts totaling $280,687. Recent grants are derived from a fiscal 1993 Form 990.

RECENT GRANTS

General

60,375	United Way Summit County, Akron, OH
60,000	University Hospitals of Cleveland, Cleveland, OH
41,200	United Way, Sacramento, CA
33,420	National Merit Scholarship Corporation, Evanston, IL
33,333	University of Massachusetts, Amherst, MA

Goodrich Co., The B.F. / Goodrich Foundation, Inc., B.F.

Sales: $1.82 billion
Employees: 14,701
Headquarters: Akron, OH
SIC Major Group: Plastics Materials & Resins, Alkalies & Chlorine, Synthetic Rubber, and Paints & Allied Products

CONTACT
Gary L. Habegger
President
The BFGoodrich Fdn.
3925 Embassy Pkwy.
Akron, OH 44333-1799
(216) 374-2000

FINANCIAL SUMMARY
Recent Giving: $2,236,147 (1995); $2,404,118 (1994); $2,087,231 (1993)

Assets: $14,312,474 (1995); $12,538,643 (1993); $12,126,908 (1992)

Fiscal Note: Company gives through foundation and directly through local manufacturing plants. In 1993, foundation giving was $881,202 and direct giving totaled $1,206,029. Above figures exclude nonmonetary support.

EIN: 34-1601879

CONTRIBUTIONS SUMMARY
Typical Recipients: • *Arts & Humanities:* Arts Centers, Community Arts, Dance, Historic Preservation, History & Archaeology, Libraries, Museums/Galleries, Music, Opera, Performing Arts, Public Broadcasting, Visual Arts • *Civic & Public Affairs:* Business/Free Enterprise, Economic Development, Economic Policy, Employment/Job Training, Law & Justice, Public Policy, Urban & Community Affairs, Women's Affairs • *Education:* Afterschool/Enrichment Programs, Business Education, Colleges & Universities, Community & Junior Colleges, Economic Education, Education Associations, Education Funds, Engineering/Technological Education, Minority Education, Science/Mathematics Education, Student Aid • *Health:* Emergency/Ambulance Services, Geriatric Health, Health Organizations, Hospitals • *Religion:* Religious Organizations • *Science:* Science Exhibits & Fairs, Scientific Centers & Institutes, Scientific Organizations • *Social Services:* Community Centers, Community Service Organizations, Emergency Relief, People with Disabilities, Recreation & Athletics, Senior Services, Substance Abuse, United Funds/United Ways, Youth Organizations

Grant Types: capital, employee matching gifts, and general support

Note: Matching gifts made to nonprofit, tax-exempt educational institutions and cultural organizations. Employee participants must be an alumnus, board member or faculty member of a nominated educational institution. Cultural institutions must be regional and the employee must reside in that region.

Nonmonetary Support: $128,000 (1990)

Nonmonetary Support Types: donated equipment

Geographic Distribution: foundation gives priority to organizations in Northeast Ohio; limited giving to national organizations: company gives near headquarters and operating locations

Operating Locations: AZ (Phoenix), CA (Long Beach), FL (Jacksonville), IL (Henry), IN, KY (Barbourville, Calvert City, Louisville), MA (Marlborough), MI (Grand Rapids), NJ (Pedricktown), OH (Akron, Avon Lake, Brecksville, Cleveland, Henry, Independence, Troy), TX (Austin, Deer Park, LaPorte), WA (Everett), WV (Grantsville, Union)

Note: Also operates in Canada, Europe, South America, and Australia.

CORP. OFFICERS
Nicholas James Calise: *B* New York NY 1941 *ED* Middlebury Coll AB 1962; Columbia Univ LLB 1965; Columbia Univ MBA *CURR EMPL* vp, assoc gen couns, secy: BF Goodrich Co *CORP AFFIL* secy: Arrowhead Indus Water; secy, asst treas: BF Goodrich Component Overhaul, Safeway Products Inc, Simmonds Precision Products; secy,

dir: BF Goodrich Flightsys Inc *NONPR AFFIL* life mem: Naval Reserve Assn, Reserve Offs Assn; mem: Am Bar Assn, Am Legion, Am Soc Corp Secys, Assn Bar City New York, Cleveland Bar Assn, CT Bar Assn, Judge Advocates Assn, Navy League US, NY Bar Assn, OH Bar Assn, US Naval Inst *CLUB AFFIL* Akron City, CC Hudson

Gary L. Habegger: *B* Decatur IN 1944 *ED* Seattle Pacific Univ 1966; Univ MI 1978 *CURR EMPL* vp pub aff: BF Goodrich Co *CORP AFFIL* vp: Simmonds Precision Products

Robert Jewell: *CURR EMPL* vp commun: BF Goodrich Co

Robert Allan McMillan: *B* Santa Barbara CA 1942 *ED* Univ CA Santa Barbara BS 1968; Univ CA Berkeley PhD 1972 *CURR EMPL* vp, treas: BF Goodrich Co *CORP AFFIL* treas: Arrowhead Indus Water, Safeway Products Inc, Simmonds Precision Products; treas, dir: BF Goodrich Flightsys Inc, Jet Electronics & Tech *NONPR AFFIL* mem: Conf Bus Economists, Fin Execs Inst, Natl Assn Bus Econ, Natl Assn Corp Treas; mem bus adv counc: Kent St Univ

John Doyle Ong: *B* Uhrichsville OH 1933 *ED* OH St Univ BA 1954; OH St Univ MA 1954; Harvard Univ LLB 1957 *CURR EMPL* chmn, ceo: BF Goodrich Co *CORP AFFIL* chmn, ceo: BF Goodrich Co; dir: Ameritech Corp, Asarco, Cooper Indus Inc, Kroger Co; pres: Tremco *NONPR AFFIL* chmn: Bus Roundtable; dir: Natl Alliance Bus; mem: Bus Counc, Chem Mfrs Assn, OH Bar Assn, Rubber Mfrs Assn; sr mem: Conf Bd; trust: Case Western Reserve Univ, Mus Arts Assn, Univ Chicago *CLUB AFFIL* Links, Ottawa Shooting, Portage CC, Rolling Rock, Union *PHIL AFFIL* trust: Sisler McFawn Foundation, Charles E. and Mabel M. Ritchie Memorial Foundation

GIVING OFFICERS
Nicholas James Calise: secy *CURR EMPL* vp, assoc gen couns, secy: BF Goodrich Co (see above)

Gary L. Habegger: pres *CURR EMPL* vp pub aff: BF Goodrich Co (see above)

Jon Vinton Heider: vp *B* Moline IL 1934 *ED* Univ WI AB 1956; Harvard Univ JD 1961; Harvard Univ Advanced Mgmt Program 1974 *CURR EMPL* exec vp, gen couns: BF Goodrich Co *CORP AFFIL* asst secy: Tremco Inc *NONPR AFFIL* mem: Akron Art Mus, Am Bar Assn, Am Law Inst, Assn Gen Couns, Un Way Summit County, Univ WI Fdn; trust: Akron City Hosp Fdn, Leadership Akron, St Thomas Fdn, St Thomas Med Ctr *CLUB AFFIL* Akron City, Bd Rm, Portage CC, Rolling Rock, Sky, Union

Robert Allan McMillan: treas *CURR EMPL* vp, treas: BF Goodrich Co (see above)

John Doyle Ong: chmn *CURR EMPL* chmn, ceo: BF Goodrich Co *PHIL AFFIL* trust: Sisler McFawn Foundation, Charles E. and Mabel M. Ritchie Memorial Foundation (see above)

Lois Sumegi: admin

D. Lee Tobler: vp *B* Provo UT 1933 *ED* Brigham Young Univ BA 1957; Northwestern Univ MBA 1958 *CURR EMPL* exec vp, cfo, dir: BF Goodrich Co *CORP AFFIL* dir: Tremco Inc *NONPR AFFIL* chmn: Akron Regulatory Devel Bd *CLUB AFFIL* Portage CC

APPLICATION INFORMATION
Initial Approach: *Initial Contact:* brief letter or proposal *Include Information On:* description of the organization; amount requested; purpose for which funds are sought; recently audited financial statement; proof of tax-exempt status *Deadlines:* by August

Restrictions on Giving: Company does not support individuals; dinners or special events; religious, fraternal, labor, political, or tax-supported organizations; operating costs of hospitals; educational institutions, except for specific needs; United Way recipients, except for capital needs; or national organizations, except for programs important to the company.

Generally grants will not be made to endowment funds, to other foundation, or to non tax-exempt organizations.

OTHER THINGS TO KNOW
BFGoodrich Foundation was established in January 1989. The foundation is the sole source of funding for organizations in Northeast Ohio and for national organizations. BFGoodrich manufacturing plants administer their own charitable giving budgets.

Foundation reports that its resources are committed for the next three to four years and it is not currently accepting applications for funding.

GRANTS ANALYSIS
Total Grants: $881,201

Number of Grants: 530

Highest Grant: $100,000

Average Grant: $1,663

Typical Range: $500 to $5,000

Disclosure Period: 1993

Note: Above figures are for foundation only and include matching gifts. In 1993, Company's direct giving was $1,174,529 for a total of $2,055,731. Recent grants are derived from a 1993 Form 990.

RECENT GRANTS
General
70,000	Akron University, Akron, OH
50,000	Case Western Reserve University Macromolecular Science Building, Cleveland, OH
30,000	Children's Hospital Medical Center, Boston, MA
30,000	Cleveland Museum of Natural History, Cleveland, OH
30,000	Ohio Foundation of Independent Colleges, Columbus, OH

Gould Electronics Inc. / Gould Foundation

Sales: $386.0 million
Employees: 4,500
Parent Company: Japan Energy Corp.
Headquarters: Eastlake, OH
SIC Major Group: Electronic & Other Electrical Equipment, Fabricated Metal Products, and Transportation Equipment

CONTACT
L. Joseph Huss
Vice President, Human Resources
Gould Electronics Inc.
35129 Curtis Blvd.
Eastlake, OH 44095
(216) 953-5000

FINANCIAL SUMMARY
Recent Giving: $168,637 (1993); $180,430 (1992); $189,291 (1991)

Assets: $2,547,147 (1993); $2,670,449 (1992); $2,897,843 (1991)

EIN: 34-6525555

CONTRIBUTIONS SUMMARY
Typical Recipients: • *Arts & Humanities:* Arts Funds, Ballet, Community Arts, General, Libraries, Museums/Galleries, Music, Performing Arts, Public Broadcasting, Theater • *Civic & Public Affairs:* African American Affairs, Business/Free Enterprise, Civil Rights, Economic Development, Employment/Job Training, General, Safety, Urban & Community Affairs, Women's Affairs • *Education:* Business Education, Colleges & Universities, Community & Junior Colleges, Education Reform, Engineering/Technological Education, General, Private Education (Precollege), Science/Mathematics Education • *Health:* Arthritis, Cancer, Children's Health/Hospitals, Clinics/Medical Centers, Diabetes, Emergency/Ambulance Services, General, Health Organizations, Heart, Hospices, Hospitals, Medical Research, Single-Disease Health Associations • *Religion:* Religious Welfare • *Science:* General, Science Museums, Scientific Organizations • *Social Services:* Child Welfare, Community Service Organizations, Crime Prevention, Domestic Violence, General, Homes, Shelters/Homelessness, United Funds/United Ways

Grant Types: employee matching gifts, research, and scholarship

Geographic Distribution: principally near operating locations and to national organizations

Operating Locations: AZ (Chandler), MA (Newburyport), MD (Millersville), OH (Eastlake, McConnelsville)

CORP. OFFICERS
C. David Ferguson: *CURR EMPL* pres, ceo, dir: Gould *CORP AFFIL* pres, ceo: Gould Electronics

GIVING OFFICERS
L. Joseph Huss: *CURR EMPL* vp human resources: Gould
J. L. Monaco: vp, treas

APPLICATION INFORMATION
Initial Approach: Application form required for scholarships. Deadline is January 31 of high school graduation year. For non-scholarship support, send a brief letter of inquiry. Include a description of organization, amount requested, purpose of funds sought, recently audited financial statement, and proof of tax-exempt status. Check with company for annual deadlines.

Restrictions on Giving: Does not support individuals, religious organizations for sectarian purposes, political or lobbying groups, or organizations outside operating areas.

GRANTS ANALYSIS
Total Grants: $168,637
Number of Grants: 90
Highest Grant: $42,125
Typical Range: $100 to $6,000
Disclosure Period: 1993
Note: Recent grants are derived from a 1993 Form 990.

RECENT GRANTS
General
16,329	United Way of Southeastern Idaho, Pocatello, ID
12,627	United Way of Lake County, Mentor, OH
5,552	United Way of Muskingum
5,000	National Foundation for Ileitis and Colitis, Beachwood, OH
3,328	United Way Services, Cleveland, OH

Griswold Foundation, John C.

CONTACT
Jacqueline G. Moore
President
John C. Griswold Fdn.
201 E Fifth St.
Cincinnati, OH 45202

FINANCIAL SUMMARY
Recent Giving: $162,000 (fiscal 1992); $116,000 (fiscal 1991); $116,000 (fiscal 1990)

Assets: $4,530,336 (fiscal 1992); $3,558,096 (fiscal 1991); $2,741,521 (fiscal 1990)

Gifts Received: $500,000 (fiscal 1992); $500,000 (fiscal 1991); $500,000 (fiscal 1990)

Fiscal Note: In 1992, contributions were received from the John C. Griswold Charitable Lead Trust.

EIN: 13-2978937

CONTRIBUTIONS SUMMARY
Donor(s): the late John C. Griswold

Typical Recipients: • *Arts & Humanities:* Libraries • *Civic & Public Affairs:* General, Public Policy • *Education:* Colleges & Universities, General, Medical Education, Private Education (Precollege) • *Environment:* General, Wildlife Protection • *Health:* Cancer, Children's Health/Hospitals, Hospitals • *Religion:* Churches, Jewish Causes • *Social Services:* Child Welfare, Domestic Violence, Youth Organizations

Grant Types: general support

GIVING OFFICERS
James R. Donnelley: vp, treas, trust *B* Chicago IL 1935 *ED* Dartmouth Coll BA 1957; Univ Chicago MBA 1962 *CURR EMPL* vchmn, chmn contributions comm: RR Donnelley & Sons Co *PHIL AFFIL* dir: Elliott and Ann Donnelley Foundation; mgr: Barker Welfare Foundation; don, pres, treas: Nina H. and James R. Donnelley Foundation; dir: Thomas E. II Donnelley Foundation

Henry W. Hobson: secy, trust *PHIL AFFIL* pres, trust: Thomas J. Emery Memorial

Jacqueline G. Moore: pres, trust

APPLICATION INFORMATION
Initial Approach: Send brief letter describing program. There are no deadlines.

GRANTS ANALYSIS
Total Grants: $162,000
Number of Grants: 15
Highest Grant: $66,000
Typical Range: $5,000 to $15,000
Disclosure Period: fiscal year ending November 30, 1992
Note: Recent grants are derived from a fiscal 1992 Form 990.

RECENT GRANTS
General
66,000	Millikin University, Decatur, IL
15,000	Greater Cincinnati Foundation, Cincinnati, OH
10,000	Archibald Rutledge Academy, McClellanville, SC
10,000	Children's Memorial Hospital, Chicago, IL
10,000	Good Shepard Lutheran School, Downey, CA

Hoover Foundation

CONTACT
Lawrence R. Hoover
Chairman
Hoover Foundation
101 E Maple St.
North Canton, OH 44720
(216) 499-9200

FINANCIAL SUMMARY
Recent Giving: $1,936,301 (1993); $1,735,114 (1992); $1,608,118 (1991)

Assets: $37,388,476 (1993); $35,939,729 (1992); $35,638,304 (1991)

Gifts Received: $332,500 (1993)

EIN: 34-6510994

CONTRIBUTIONS SUMMARY

Donor(s): The foundation was established in 1945 by members of the Hoover family.

Typical Recipients: • *Arts & Humanities:* Arts Centers, Arts Funds, Arts Institutes, Ballet, Historic Preservation, History & Archaeology, Libraries, Music, Public Broadcasting • *Civic & Public Affairs:* African American Affairs, Clubs, Economic Development, General, Municipalities/Towns, Philanthropic Organizations, Professional & Trade Associations, Safety, Urban & Community Affairs • *Education:* Business Education, Colleges & Universities, Economic Education, Education Funds, Education Reform, General, Minority Education, Private Education (Precollege), Public Education (Precollege), Secondary Education (Public), Student Aid • *Environment:* Forestry • *Health:* Health Funds, Health Organizations, Hospitals, Multiple Sclerosis, Respiratory • *Religion:* Ministries • *Social Services:* At-Risk Youth, Child Welfare, Community Centers, Community Service Organizations, Day Care, Family Planning, Family Services, Food/Clothing Distribution, Homes, People with Disabilities, Recreation & Athletics, Senior Services, Shelters/Homelessness, Substance Abuse, United Funds/United Ways, YMCA/YWCA/YMHA/YWHA, Youth Organizations

Grant Types: capital, general support, operating expenses, and scholarship

Geographic Distribution: focus on Stark County, OH; some grants in Florida

GIVING OFFICERS

Ronald Kent Bennington: trust *B* Circleville OH 1936 *ED* Kenyon Coll BA 1958; OH St Univ JD 1961 *CURR EMPL* ptnr: Black McCuskey Souers & Arbaugh *CORP AFFIL* secy, dir: OH Battery & Ignition Co *NONPR AFFIL* ambassador: OH Fdn Independent Colls; bd assocs: Union Coll; dir: Am Red Cross Canton; fundraising dir: Un Way Fund Drive; mem: Am Bar Assn, Leadership Canton, OH Bar Assn, Stark County Bar Assn; mem adv comm: Kenyon Coll; mem, fellow: Am Bar Fdn, OH St Bar Fdn; pres, mem: Eastern OH Football Officials Assn, Stark County Law Library Assn; steering comm: Pro Football Hall Fame; trust: Greater Canton Chamber Commerce, Malone Coll, Timken Mercy Med Ctr

Lawrence Richard Hoover: chmn, trust *B* Canton OH 1935 *ED* MA Inst Tech 1957 *CURR EMPL* vp: OH Power Co *CORP AFFIL* dir: Am Electric Power Svc Corp; vp: OH Power Co

Thomas H. Hoover: trust *B* 1921 *ED* Cornell Univ 1947 *CURR EMPL* pres: Stark Co Women's Clinic

Joyce U. Niffenegger: trust

Timothy D. Schiltz: trust

APPLICATION INFORMATION

Initial Approach:

The foundation does not publish a formal annual report, guidelines, or grant applications. Letters of request should be sent directly to the foundation.

Applicant must show proof of 501(c)(3) status.

There are no deadlines for submitting proposals.

Restrictions on Giving: The foundation primarily supports organizations located in the Stark County, Ohio, area. It does not make grants to individuals.

GRANTS ANALYSIS

Total Grants: $1,936,301

Number of Grants: 61

Highest Grant: $500,000

Average Grant: $31,743

Typical Range: $100 to $500 and $2,500 to $50,000

Disclosure Period: 1993

Note: Recent grants are derived from a 1993 Form 990.

RECENT GRANTS
General

500,000	North Canton Medical Foundation, N. Canton, OH — major expansion project
150,000	Education Enhancement Partnership, Canton, OH — funds for continuation of programs
130,000	United Way, Central Stark County, Canton, OH — , operating funds and community initiative program
108,000	Canton Country Day School, Canton, OH — major expansion program and matching funds program
93,840	YMCA of Canton, Canton, OH — major improvement project, youth physical fitness program, and new roof

Hoover Fund-Trust, W. Henry

CONTACT
Stephen C. Donatini
Trust Officer
W. Henry Hoover Fund-Trust
Society National Bank
PO Box 9950
Canton, OH 44711-0950
(216) 489-5422

FINANCIAL SUMMARY
Recent Giving: $174,800 (1993); $168,150 (1992); $163,250 (1991)

Assets: $3,763,665 (1993); $3,631,381 (1992); $3,615,984 (1991)

Gifts Received: $50,000 (1990)

EIN: 34-6573738

CONTRIBUTIONS SUMMARY
Donor(s): the late W. Henry Hoover

Typical Recipients: • *Arts & Humanities:* Arts Centers, Arts Funds, Arts Institutes, Historic Preservation, Libraries, Museums/Galleries • *Civic & Public Affairs:* Clubs, General, Urban & Community Affairs • *Education:* Colleges & Universities, Education Reform, Engineering/Technological Education, Minority Education, Private Education (Precollege) • *Environment:* Resource Conservation • *Health:* Cancer, Emergency/Ambulance Services, Heart, Respiratory • *International:* Health Care/Hospitals, International Relations • *Religion:* Churches, Religious Welfare • *Social Services:* Animal Protection, At-Risk Youth, Community Service Organizations, Scouts, United Funds/United Ways, YMCA/YWCA/YMHA/YWHA, Youth Organizations

Grant Types: general support

Geographic Distribution: focus on OH

GIVING OFFICERS
Society National Bank
trust

APPLICATION INFORMATION
Initial Approach: Send brief letter describing program. There are no deadlines.

GRANTS ANALYSIS
Total Grants: $174,800

Number of Grants: 34

Highest Grant: $25,000

Typical Range: $100 to $25,000

Disclosure Period: 1993

Note: Recent grants are derived from a 1993 Form 990.

RECENT GRANTS
Library

1,000	North Canton Library Association, North Canton, OH

General

25,000	Community Christian Church, Canton, OH
17,500	Frank and Edna Memorial Fund, Canton, OH
10,000	Boy Scouts of America, Canton, OH
10,000	Community Christian Church, Canton, OH
10,000	Ohio Wesleyan University, Delaware, OH

Humphrey Fund, George M. and Pamela S.

CONTACT
Jackie A. Horning
Secretary-Treasurer
George M. and Pamela S. Humphrey Fund
c/o Advisory Services, Inc.
1422 Euclid Ave., Ste. 1010
Cleveland, OH 44115-2078
(216) 363-6483

FINANCIAL SUMMARY

Recent Giving: $415,750 (1993); $383,450 (1992); $383,900 (1991)

Assets: $8,966,867 (1993); $8,934,125 (1992); $8,758,014 (1991)

EIN: 34-6513798

CONTRIBUTIONS SUMMARY

Donor(s): George M. Humphrey, the late Pamela S. Humphrey

Typical Recipients: • *Arts & Humanities:* Arts Associations & Councils, Historic Preservation, History & Archaeology, Libraries, Museums/Galleries, Music, Opera • *Civic & Public Affairs:* Botanical Gardens/Parks, Employment/Job Training, General, Philanthropic Organizations, Women's Affairs • *Education:* Colleges & Universities, Medical Education, Private Education (Precollege), Special Education, Student Aid • *Environment:* General, Resource Conservation, Wildlife Protection • *Health:* AIDS/HIV, Children's Health/Hospitals, Emergency/Ambulance Services, Eyes/Blindness, Hospitals, Hospitals (University Affiliated), Long-Term Care, Medical Rehabilitation, Medical Research, Multiple Sclerosis, Nursing Services, Single-Disease Health Associations, Speech & Hearing • *Religion:* Churches, Religious Welfare • *Science:* Science Museums, Scientific Centers & Institutes, Scientific Research • *Social Services:* Camps, Child Welfare, Community Service Organizations, Family Planning, Family Services, People with Disabilities, Recreation & Athletics, Senior Services, Substance Abuse, United Funds/United Ways, Volunteer Services

Grant Types: capital, emergency, endowment, general support, multiyear/continuing support, operating expenses, professorship, and research

Geographic Distribution: focus on OH

GIVING OFFICERS

Carol H. Butler: pres, trust

John G. Butler: vp, trust

Jackie A. Horning: secy, treas

Pamela B. Keefe: trust

APPLICATION INFORMATION

Initial Approach: Send brief letter of inquiry describing program or project prior to meetings in April, November, and December.

Restrictions on Giving: Does not support individuals or provide loans.

PUBLICATIONS

Annual Report

GRANTS ANALYSIS

Total Grants: $415,750

Number of Grants: 63

Highest Grant: $31,000

Typical Range: $500 to $25,000

Disclosure Period: 1993

Note: Recent grants are derived from a 1993 Form 990.

RECENT GRANTS

General

31,000	United Way Services of Cleveland, Cleveland, OH — unrestricted	
25,000	Hathaway Brown School, Shaker Heights, OH — capital campaign	
25,000	Phillips Osborne School, Painesville, OH — capital campaign	
25,000	Tall Timbers Research, Tallahassee, FL — quail research initiative	
25,000	University Circle, Cleveland, OH — endowment fund	

Ingalls Foundation, Louise H. and David S.

CONTACT

Louise Ingalls Brown
President and Trustee
Louise H. & David S. Ingalls Foundation
301 Tower E
20600 Chagrin Blvd.
Shaker Heights, OH 44122
(216) 921-6000

FINANCIAL SUMMARY

Recent Giving: $748,000 (1993); $630,334 (1992); $614,000 (1990)

Assets: $16,483,870 (1993); $15,185,760 (1992); $13,684,535 (1990)

EIN: 34-6516550

CONTRIBUTIONS SUMMARY

Donor(s): The foundation was incorporated in 1953 by Edith Ingalls Vignos, Louise Ingalls Brown, David S. Ingalls, Jr., Jane I. Davison, Anne I. Lawrence, the late Louise H. Ingalls , and the late David S. Ingalls .

Typical Recipients: • *Arts & Humanities:* Arts Centers, Arts Institutes, History & Archaeology, Libraries, Museums/Galleries, Music, Theater • *Civic & Public Affairs:* Employment/Job Training, Philanthropic Organizations, Urban & Community Affairs • *Education:* Arts/Humanities Education, Colleges & Universities, International Studies, Legal Education, Medical Education, Private Education (Precollege) • *Environment:* General, Resource Conservation, Wildlife Protection • *Health:* Eyes/Blindness, Health Organizations, Hospitals, Long-Term Care, Medical Rehabilitation, Nursing Services, Single-Disease Health Associations, Transplant Networks/Donor Banks • *International:* Foreign Educational Institutions • *Science:* Science Museums, Scientific Labs, Scientific Research • *Social Services:* Camps, Child Welfare, Community Centers, Community Service Organizations, Counseling, Family Planning, Recreation & Athletics, United Funds/United Ways, Youth Organizations

Grant Types: capital, endowment, project, and research

Geographic Distribution: focus on Ohio, Connecticut, Virginia, and New York

GIVING OFFICERS

Louise Ingalls Brown: pres, trust

Willard W. Brown: treas *CURR EMPL* chmn: Investors Computer Service

Jane I. Davidson: trust

Cynthia L. Ingalls: trust, secy

Anne I. Lawrence: trust

Edith Ingalls Vignos: vp, trust

Jane W. Watson: asst secy, asst treas

APPLICATION INFORMATION

Initial Approach:

The foundation has no formal grant application procedure or application form.

The foundation has no deadline for submitting proposals.

Restrictions on Giving: The foundation makes grants to public charities only. The foundation does not make grants to individuals.

GRANTS ANALYSIS

Total Grants: $748,000

Number of Grants: 29

Highest Grant: $118,000

Average Grant: $25,793

Typical Range: $10,000 to $25,000

Disclosure Period: 1993

Note: Recent grants are derived from a 1993 Form 990.

RECENT GRANTS

Library

5,000	Hanna Perkins School, Cleveland, OH — library archives	

General

118,000	Yale Law School, New Haven, CT — foreign comparative culture	
100,000	Kawken School, Gates Mills, OH — capital	
67,000	High Hopes Therapeutic Riding, Old Lyme, CT	
40,000	Jackson Laboratory, Bar Harbor, ME — capital	
25,000	American University of Cairo, New York, NY	

Jarson-Stanley and Mickey Kaplan Foundation, Isaac and Esther

Former Foundation Name: Isaac N. and Esther M. Jarson Charitable Trust

CONTACT

Stanley M. Kaplan
Trustee
Isaac and Esther Jarson-Stanley and Mickey Kaplan Fdn.
105 E Fourth St., Ste. 710
Cincinnati, OH 45202
(513) 721-5086

FINANCIAL SUMMARY

Recent Giving: $385,970 (1993); $170,716 (1992); $170,898 (1990)

Assets: $3,613,031 (1993); $3,722,430 (1992); $3,701,600 (1991)

EIN: 31-6033453

CONTRIBUTIONS SUMMARY

Typical Recipients: • *Arts & Humanities:* Arts Associations & Councils, Arts Centers, Arts Funds, Ballet, Community Arts, Dance, Historic Preservation, Libraries, Museums/Galleries, Music, Opera, Public Broadcasting, Theater • *Civic & Public Affairs:* African American Affairs, General, Philanthropic Organizations, Urban & Community Affairs • *Education:* Colleges & Universities, Education Funds, Engineering/Technological Education, Literacy, Medical Education, Minority Education, Private Education (Precollege), Public Education (Precollege), Secondary Education (Public), Student Aid • *Environment:* Air/Water Quality • *Health:* AIDS/HIV, Cancer, Children's Health/Hospitals, Diabetes, Emergency/Ambulance Services, Health Organizations, Hospices, Hospitals, Kidney, Medical Rehabilitation, Medical Research, Mental Health, Prenatal Health Issues, Preventive Medicine/Wellness Organizations, Single-Disease Health Associations • *International:* Foreign Arts Organizations, Health Care/Hospitals • *Religion:* Jewish Causes, Religious Organizations, Religious Welfare • *Social Services:* Animal Protection, At-Risk Youth, Child Welfare, Community Centers, Community Service Organizations, Emergency Relief, Food/Clothing Distribution, People with Disabilities, Shelters/Homelessness, United Funds/United Ways, Youth Organizations

Grant Types: general support

Geographic Distribution: focus on Cincinnati, OH

GIVING OFFICERS

Myran J. Kaplan: trust

Stanley Meisel Kaplan: trust *B* Cincinnati OH 1922 *ED* Univ Cincinnati BS 1943; Univ Cincinnati MD 1946; Inst Psychoanalysis 1962-1967 *CURR EMPL* prof, faculty dept psychiatry: University Cincinnati *NONPR AFFIL* chmn bd dirs: G&J Pepsi Cola; dir: Bonds for Israel, Cincinnati Ballet, Contemporary Arts Ctr OH, Friends Coll Conservatory Music; fellow: Am Psychiatric Assn; mem: Am Assn Univ Profs, Am Med Assn, Am Psychoanalytic Assn, Am Psychosomatic Soc, Sigma Xi; prof: Univ Cincinnati

APPLICATION INFORMATION

Initial Approach: Include a description of organization, amount requested, purpose of funds sought, recently audited financial statement, and proof of tax-exempt status. There are no deadlines.

Restrictions on Giving: Limited to the greater Cincinnati, OH, area.

GRANTS ANALYSIS

Total Grants: $385,970

Number of Grants: 69

Highest Grant: $150,000

Typical Range: $100 to $82,000

Disclosure Period: 1993

Note: Recent grants are derived from a 1993 Form 990.

RECENT GRANTS

Library

150,000	University of Cincinnati College of Medicine Library, Cincinnati, OH

General

82,000	Jewish Federation, Cincinnati, OH
25,600	Cincinnati Psychoanalytic Institute, Cincinnati, OH
12,600	American Cancer Society, Cincinnati, OH
11,000	United Way of Cincinnati, Cincinnati, OH
10,000	National Kidney Foundation, New York, NY

Kettering Fund

CONTACT

Richard F. Beach
Administrator
Kettering Fund
1440 Kettering Tower
Dayton, OH 45423
(513) 228-1021

FINANCIAL SUMMARY

Recent Giving: $3,500,000 (fiscal 1994 est.); $3,519,995 (fiscal 1993); $2,670,275 (fiscal 1992)

Assets: $70,000,000 (fiscal 1994 est.); $70,000,000 (fiscal 1993 approx.); $70,985,379 (fiscal 1992)

EIN: 31-6027115

CONTRIBUTIONS SUMMARY

Donor(s): The Kettering Fund was established in 1958 by Charles F. Kettering who died in the same year. Mr. Kettering was a principal stockholder in General Motors Corporation, which acquired his automotive engineering laboratory. Mr. Kettering's inventions include the modern automotive ignition system and the electric cash register. He worked with National Cash Register Company and General Motors, and organized Dayton Engineering Laboratories Company (Delco), Dayton Metal Products Company, and the Dayton-Wright Airplane Company. He was president of the Thomas A. Edison Foundation; co-founder of Moraine Park School; a trustee of Ohio State University, Antioch College, College of Wooster (OH), Miami University (OH), and Southern Research Institute; and a director of the Memorial Sloan-Kettering Institute of Cancer Research.

Typical Recipients: • *Arts & Humanities:* Arts Centers, Arts Festivals, Arts Funds, Arts Institutes, Community Arts, Historic Preservation, History & Archaeology, Libraries, Museums/Galleries, Music, Performing Arts, Public Broadcasting, Theater • *Civic & Public Affairs:* Botanical Gardens/Parks, Economic Development, Employment/Job Training, Hispanic Affairs, Law & Justice, Municipalities/Towns, Professional & Trade Associations, Rural Affairs, Urban & Community Affairs, Women's Affairs, Zoos/Aquariums • *Education:* Colleges & Universities, Education Associations, Education Funds, Engineering/Technological Education, General, Literacy, Private Education (Precollege) • *Environment:* General • *Health:* Clinics/Medical Centers, Emergency/Ambulance Services, Health Organizations, Hospitals, Nursing Services • *International:* International Development • *Religion:* Religious Welfare, Synagogues/Temples • *Science:* Science Museums • *Social Services:* Child Welfare, Community Service Organizations, Family Planning, Family Services, Homes, People with Disabilities, Senior Services, Youth Organizations

Grant Types: capital, challenge, endowment, general support, operating expenses, project, and research

Geographic Distribution: limited to Ohio, principally Dayton

GIVING OFFICERS

Richard F. Beach: admin *PHIL AFFIL* trust: Frank M. Tait Foundation

Susan K. Beck: mem distr comm, trust *PHIL AFFIL* vp, trust: Kettering Family Foundation

Virginia W. Kettering: trust *PHIL AFFIL* trust: Kettering Family Foundation

Jane K. Lombard: mem distr comm, trust *PHIL AFFIL* asst secy, asst treas: Kettering Family Foundation

Susan K. Williamson: mem distr comm, trust *PHIL AFFIL* trust: Kettering Family Foundation

APPLICATION INFORMATION

Initial Approach:

Proposals should be sent to the fund. No specific application form is required.

The proposal should include the amount requested, reason for request, description and dates of previous Kettering Fund support, names of other foundations which have given support, project and organization budget, and an audited financial statement.

Applications should be submitted by April 1 and September 1.

OTHER THINGS TO KNOW

The Kettering Fund is affiliated with the Kettering Family Foundation, which is located at the same address.

The fund lists Bank One Dayton, NA, as corporate trustee.

GRANTS ANALYSIS

Total Grants: $3,519,995

Number of Grants: 47

Highest Grant: $2,000,000

Average Grant: $33,043*

Typical Range: $5,000 to $50,000

Disclosure Period: fiscal year ending June 30, 1993

Note: The average grant figure excludes the highest grant of $2,000,000. Recent grants are derived from a fiscal 1993 grants list.

RECENT GRANTS

Library

1,000	Foundation Center, New York, NY

General

2,000,000	Kettering Medical Center, Kettering, OH
475,000	University of Dayton, Dayton, OH
250,000	GMI Engineering Management Institute, Flint, MI
100,000	Hathaway Brown School, Shaker Heights, OH
82,223	Mary Scott Nursing Center, Dayton, OH

Kilcawley Fund, William H.

CONTACT
William H. Kilcawley Fund
c/o National City Bank
PO Box 450
Youngstown, OH 44501
(216) 744-9000

FINANCIAL SUMMARY
Recent Giving: $229,500 (1993); $112,500 (1992); $292,000 (1991)

Assets: $2,221,102 (1993); $2,210,466 (1992); $2,108,738 (1991)

EIN: 34-6515643

CONTRIBUTIONS SUMMARY
Typical Recipients: • *Arts & Humanities:* Arts Centers, Arts Institutes, History & Archaeology, Libraries, Music, Performing Arts, Public Broadcasting • *Civic & Public Affairs:* General, Municipalities/Towns, Urban & Community Affairs • *Education:* Business Education, Colleges & Universities, Education Funds, Private Education (Precollege) • *Health:* AIDS/HIV, Children's Health/Hospitals, Health Organizations, Home-Care Services, Hospices, Research/Studies Institutes, Speech & Hearing • *Religion:* Churches, Religious Organizations, Religious Welfare • *Social Services:* Child Welfare, Community Service Organizations, Food/Clothing Distribution, People with Disabilities, Senior Services, United Funds/United Ways, Youth Organizations

Grant Types: capital and general support

Geographic Distribution: focus on OH

GIVING OFFICERS
Natl City Bank: trust

Anne K. Christman: trust

APPLICATION INFORMATION
Initial Approach: Send brief letter describing program. There are no deadlines.

Restrictions on Giving: Does not support individuals. Limited to Ohio.

GRANTS ANALYSIS
Total Grants: $229,500

Number of Grants: 17

Highest Grant: $25,000

Typical Range: $1,000 to $25,000

Disclosure Period: 1993

Note: Recent grants are derived from a 1993 Form 990.

RECENT GRANTS

Library

10,000	Public Library of Youngstown and Mahoning County, Youngstown, OH

General

25,000	NEOUCOM
25,000	Sisters of Charity of St. Augustine, Youngstown, OH
25,000	Ursuline Sisters of Motherhouse, Canfield, OH
25,000	Ursuline Sisters of Youngstown Beatitude House, Youngstown, OH
25,000	Ursuline Sisters of Youngstown Preschool Project, Youngstown, OH

Lennon Foundation, Fred A.

CONTACT
Fred A. Lennon
President
Fred A. Lennon Fdn.
29500 Solon Rd.
Solon, OH 44139
(216) 861-5000

FINANCIAL SUMMARY
Recent Giving: $1,889,100 (fiscal 1993); $7,136,655 (fiscal 1992); $4,701,060 (fiscal 1991)

Assets: $1,186,816 (fiscal 1993); $1,862,462 (fiscal 1992); $6,440,247 (fiscal 1991)

Gifts Received: $1,202,000 (fiscal 1993); $2,200,000 (fiscal 1992); $2,210,000 (fiscal 1991)

Fiscal Note: In fiscal 1993, contributions were received from Crawford Fitting Company.

EIN: 34-6572287

CONTRIBUTIONS SUMMARY
Typical Recipients: • *Arts & Humanities:* Arts Centers, Community Arts, Historic Preservation, Libraries, Museums/Galleries, Public Broadcasting • *Civic & Public Affairs:* Civil Rights, Economic Policy, General, Law & Justice, Legal Aid, Municipalities/Towns, Professional & Trade Associations, Public Policy, Safety, Urban & Community Affairs, Zoos/Aquariums • *Education:* Colleges & Universities, Economic Education, Education Funds, General, Minority Education, Private Education (Precollege), Religious Education, Secondary Education (Private), Secondary Education (Public), Student Aid • *Environment:* General • *Health:* Cancer, Children's Health/Hospitals, Clinics/Medical Centers, Diabetes, Eyes/Blindness, Heart, Hospices, Hospitals, Medical Research, Nursing Services, Public Health, Single-Disease Health Associations • *International:* International Relations • *Religion:* Churches, Religious Organizations, Religious Welfare, Seminaries • *Social Services:* Community Centers, Community Service Organizations, Crime Prevention, Food/Clothing Distribution, Homes, Substance Abuse, United Funds/United Ways, Youth Organizations

Grant Types: general support

Geographic Distribution: focus on OH

GIVING OFFICERS
F. J. Callahan: secy

A. P. Lennon: vp

Fred A. Lennon: pres

APPLICATION INFORMATION
Initial Approach: The foundation reports it only makes contributions to preselected charitable organizations.

GRANTS ANALYSIS
Total Grants: $1,889,100

Number of Grants: 152

Highest Grant: $200,000

Typical Range: $100 to $100,000

Disclosure Period: fiscal year ending November 30, 1993

Note: Recent grants are derived from a fiscal 1993 Form 990.

RECENT GRANTS

General

200,000	Vatican Observatory Foundation, Tucson, AZ
100,400	Gilmour Academy, Gates Mills, OH
100,000	Bishop James Quinn Scholarship Trust Fund, Cleveland, OH
100,000	Case Western Reserve University, Cleveland, OH
100,000	Friends of Ashbrook Center

Markey Charitable Fund, John C.

CONTACT
John R. Markey
President
John C. Markey Charitable Fund
PO Box 623
Bryan, OH 43506
(216) 638-1424

FINANCIAL SUMMARY
Recent Giving: $204,000 (fiscal 1994); $236,775 (fiscal 1993); $220,700 (fiscal 1992)

Assets: $3,592,897 (fiscal 1994); $3,785,432 (fiscal 1993); $3,716,104 (fiscal 1992)

EIN: 34-6572724

CONTRIBUTIONS SUMMARY

Donor(s): the late John C. Markey

Typical Recipients: • *Arts & Humanities:* Arts Associations & Councils, Arts Centers, Community Arts, History & Archaeology, Libraries, Museums/Galleries, Music, Opera, Public Broadcasting • *Civic & Public Affairs:* General, Parades/Festivals, Safety, Urban & Community Affairs, Women's Affairs • *Education:* Colleges & Universities, Elementary Education (Public), Engineering/Technological Education, Private Education (Precollege), Public Education (Precollege), Student Aid • *Environment:* Wildlife Protection • *Health:* Alzheimers Disease, Cancer, Clinics/Medical Centers, Emergency/Ambulance Services, Heart, Hospices, Hospitals, Nursing Services, Preventive Medicine/Wellness Organizations, Public Health • *International:* Health Care/Hospitals, International Peace & Security Issues • *Religion:* Churches, Ministries, Religious Organizations • *Social Services:* Animal Protection, Community Centers, Community Service Organizations, Domestic Violence, Family Planning, Homes, People with Disabilities, United Funds/United Ways, YMCA/YWCA/YMHA/YWHA, Youth Organizations

Grant Types: general support

Geographic Distribution: focus on OH

GIVING OFFICERS

Catherine M. Anderson: vp, treas, trust

L. W. Lisle: trust

John R. Markey: pres, treas, trust

Arthur S. Newcomer: secy, trust

APPLICATION INFORMATION

Initial Approach: Send brief letter of inquiry describing program. There are no deadlines.

GRANTS ANALYSIS

Total Grants: $204,000

Number of Grants: 91

Highest Grant: $21,000

Typical Range: $100 to $11,000

Disclosure Period: fiscal year ending June 30, 1994

Note: Recent grants are derived from a fiscal 1994 Form 990.

RECENT GRANTS

Library

5,000	Bryan Public Library, Bryan, OH
5,000	Frankfort City Library, Frankfort, MI
5,000	Sierra Madre Public Library, Sierra Madre, CA

General

21,000	Wesley United Methodist Church, Bryan, OH
11,000	Stanford University, Stanford, CA
10,000	Bowling Green State University, Bowling Green, OH
10,000	Defiance College, Defiance, OH

10,000	Texas A&M University, College Station, TX

Mather and William Gwinn Mather Fund, Elizabeth Ring

CONTACT

James D. Ireland III
President
Elizabeth Ring Mather and William Gwinn Mather Fund
850 Euclid Ave., Ste. 650
Cleveland, OH 44114
(216) 861-5341

FINANCIAL SUMMARY

Recent Giving: $951,576 (1993); $827,703 (1992); $848,137 (1991)

Assets: $9,075,618 (1993); $8,172,831 (1992); $7,957,984 (1991)

Gifts Received: $532,251 (1993); $569,618 (1992); $573,937 (1991)

Fiscal Note: In 1993, contributions were received from James D. Ireland III, Lucy I. Weller, Cornelia I. Hallinan, George R. Ireland, and United States Trust Company.

EIN: 34-6519863

CONTRIBUTIONS SUMMARY

Donor(s): the late Elizabeth Ring Mather

Typical Recipients: • *Arts & Humanities:* Arts Associations & Councils, Arts Institutes, Community Arts, Historic Preservation, History & Archaeology, Libraries, Museums/Galleries, Music, Opera, Public Broadcasting • *Civic & Public Affairs:* Botanical Gardens/Parks, Clubs, Community Foundations, Nonprofit Management, Philanthropic Organizations, Professional & Trade Associations, Urban & Community Affairs, Zoos/Aquariums • *Education:* Colleges & Universities, Legal Education, Medical Education, Private Education (Precollege), Public Education (Precollege), Student Aid • *Environment:* Air/Water Quality, General, Resource Conservation • *Health:* Cancer, Health Organizations, Hospitals, Medical Research, Nursing Services • *Science:* Science Museums • *Social Services:* Child Welfare, Community Service Organizations, Family Planning, Food/Clothing Distribution, People with Disabilities, Senior Services, United Funds/United Ways, Youth Organizations

Grant Types: capital, endowment, and general support

Geographic Distribution: focus on OH, with emphasis on the greater Cleveland area

GIVING OFFICERS

Theodore R. Colborn: secy, trust

Cornelia I. Hallinan: asst secy, trust

Cornelia W. Ireland: trust

George R. Ireland: treas, trust

James D. Ireland III: pres *CORP AFFIL* dir: Cleveland-Cliffs Inc

Jane J. Masters: asst secy, asst treas

R. Henry Norweb, Jr.: trust *PHIL AFFIL* trust: John Huntington Fund for Education

Lucy I. Weller: vp, trust

APPLICATION INFORMATION

Initial Approach: Send brief letter of inquiry describing program or project. There are no deadlines.

Restrictions on Giving: Does not support individuals or provide scholarships or loans.

GRANTS ANALYSIS

Total Grants: $951,576

Number of Grants: 43

Highest Grant: $626,189

Typical Range: $1,000 to $66,667

Disclosure Period: 1993

Note: Recent grants are derived from a 1993 Form 990.

RECENT GRANTS

Library

3,120	Library of American Landscape History, Amherst, MA — operations
3,000	Cleveland Medical Library Association, Cleveland, OH — renovations

General

626,189	University Circle, Cleveland, OH — operations
50,000	Holden Arboretum, Mentor, OH — Science Center
15,000	Cleveland Museum of Natural History, Cleveland, OH — operations
15,000	United Way Services, Cleveland, OH — operations
12,000	Kenyon College, Gambier, OH — operations

Mather Charitable Trust, S. Livingston

CONTACT

S. Sterling McMillan
Secretary
S. Livingston Mather Charitable Trust
803 Tower E.
20600 Chagrin Blvd.
Cleveland, OH 44122
(216) 942-6484

FINANCIAL SUMMARY

Recent Giving: $190,250 (1993); $162,250 (1992); $200,350 (1991)

Assets: $3,976,890 (1993); $3,902,951 (1992); $3,827,472 (1991)

Gifts Received: $1,766 (1993)

EIN: 34-6505619

CONTRIBUTIONS SUMMARY

Donor(s): the late S. Livingston Mather

Typical Recipients: • *Arts & Humanities:* Arts Associations & Councils, Arts Centers, Arts Institutes, General, Historic Preservation, History & Archaeology, Libraries, Museums/Galleries, Music, Opera, Performing

Arts, Public Broadcasting, Theater • *Civic & Public Affairs:* Botanical Gardens/Parks, Employment/Job Training, Urban & Community Affairs • *Education:* Afterschool/Enrichment Programs, Arts/Humanities Education, Colleges & Universities, Education Funds, Education Reform, Faculty Development, Medical Education, Minority Education, Private Education (Precollege), Public Education (Precollege), Student Aid • *Environment:* General, Resource Conservation • *Health:* AIDS/HIV, Clinics/Medical Centers, Emergency/Ambulance Services, Health Organizations, Hospices, Mental Health • *International:* Foreign Arts Organizations, International Affairs, International Organizations, International Peace & Security Issues, International Relations • *Religion:* Ministries, Religious Organizations • *Science:* Science Museums • *Social Services:* Camps, Child Abuse, Child Welfare, Community Centers, Community Service Organizations, Day Care, Domestic Violence, Family Planning, Family Services, Food/Clothing Distribution, Homes, Substance Abuse, United Funds/United Ways, Youth Organizations

Grant Types: general support

Geographic Distribution: focus on northeastern OH

GIVING OFFICERS
Society National Bank: trust

APPLICATION INFORMATION
Initial Approach: Send a brief letter of inquiry. Include a description of organization, amount requested, purpose of funds sought, recently audited financial statement, and proof of tax-exempt status. There are no deadlines.

Restrictions on Giving: Does not support individuals or provide deficit financing or loans. Limited to northeast Ohio.

PUBLICATIONS
Biennial report (including application guidelines)

GRANTS ANALYSIS
Total Grants: $190,250

Number of Grants: 55

Highest Grant: $32,000

Typical Range: $150 to $12,500

Disclosure Period: 1993

Note: Recent grants are derived from a 1993 Form 990.

RECENT GRANTS

General

32,000	United Way Services, Cleveland, OH — annual support
12,500	Hiram House, Chagrin Falls, OH — summer camperships
12,000	Goodrich-Gannett Neighborhood Center, Cleveland, OH — intergenerational art program
10,000	Child Guidance Center, Cleveland, OH — capital campaign pledge

10,000	Cleveland Museum of Natural History, Cleveland, OH — exhibition of Bodner art and Plains Indians

McDonald & Company Securities, Inc. / McDonald & Company Securities Foundation

Employees: 1,050
Parent Company: McDonald & Co. Investments, Inc.
Headquarters: Cleveland, OH
SIC Major Group: Security Brokers & Dealers

CONTACT
Thomas G. Clevidence
Secretary
McDonald & Company Securities Foundation
800 Superior Ave. Ste. 2100
Cleveland, OH 44114
(216) 443-2981

FINANCIAL SUMMARY
Recent Giving: $300,000 (fiscal 1995 est.); $286,107 (fiscal 1994); $152,266 (fiscal 1993)

Assets: $1,243,754 (fiscal 1994); $1,039,624 (fiscal 1993); $722,632 (fiscal 1992)

Gifts Received: $463,000 (fiscal 1994); $400,000 (fiscal 1993); $386,000 (fiscal 1992)

Fiscal Note: Above figures represent foundation giving only. In fiscal 1994, contributions were received from McDonald & Company Securities, Inc.

EIN: 34-1386528

CONTRIBUTIONS SUMMARY
Typical Recipients: • *Arts & Humanities:* Arts Associations & Councils, Arts Centers, Arts Festivals, Ballet, Community Arts, Ethnic & Folk Arts, Historic Preservation, Libraries, Museums/Galleries, Music, Opera, Performing Arts, Public Broadcasting, Theater, Visual Arts • *Civic & Public Affairs:* African American Affairs, Asian American Affairs, Business/Free Enterprise, Civil Rights, Community Foundations, Economic Development, Economic Policy, Employment/Job Training, Ethnic Organizations, General, Hispanic Affairs, Inner-City Development, Law & Justice, Philanthropic Organizations, Professional & Trade Associations, Urban & Community Affairs, Women's Affairs, Zoos/Aquariums • *Education:* Business Education, Colleges & Universities, Economic Education, Education Reform, Elementary Education (Public), General, Literacy, Minority Education, Public Education (Precollege), Student Aid • *Environment:* General, Wildlife Protection • *Health:* Children's Health/Hospitals, Emergency/Ambulance Services, General, Hospices, Hospitals, Medical Research, Mental Health, Multiple Sclerosis, Nursing Services, Single-Disease Health Associations, Speech & Hearing • *Religion:* Jewish

Causes, Religious Organizations, Religious Welfare • *Science:* Science Museums • *Social Services:* Animal Protection, At-Risk Youth, Camps, Child Welfare, Community Centers, Community Service Organizations, Counseling, Delinquency & Criminal Rehabilitation, Domestic Violence, Emergency Relief, Family Planning, Family Services, Food/Clothing Distribution, General, People with Disabilities, Recreation & Athletics, Senior Services, Sexual Abuse, Shelters/Homelessness, Substance Abuse, United Funds/United Ways, Youth Organizations

Grant Types: general support, multi-year/continuing support, operating expenses, project, and scholarship

Nonmonetary Support Types: cause-related marketing & promotion, in-kind services, loaned employees, and loaned executives

Geographic Distribution: in headquarters and operating communities

Operating Locations: AL (Anniston, Cottonton, Phenix City, Stevenson), CA (Buena Park), GA (Atlanta, Greenville, Smyrna), IL (Chicago, Godfrey, Springfield), IN (Indianapolis), MA (Cambridge, South Lee), MI (Escanaba), OH (Chillicothe, Cleveland), PA (Fairless Hills), TN (Kingsport), UT (Provo), VA (Charlottesville), WI (Menasha)

CORP. OFFICERS
Richard Clark: *CURR EMPL* mgr corp comm area: McDonald & Co Securities

Thomas G. Clevidence: *CURR EMPL* mng dir: McDonald & Co Securities

Robert T. Clutterbuck: *CURR EMPL* cfo, dir: McDonald & Co Securities

Thomas M. O'Donnell: *B* Cleveland OH 1936 *ED* Univ Notre Dame 1959; Univ PA MBA 1960 *CURR EMPL* chmn, ceo: McDonald & Co Securities *CORP AFFIL* dir: CID Equity Ptnr, Seaway Food Town Inc

Gordon A. Price: *B* Cleveland OH 1947 *CORP AFFIL* secy, treas: McDonald & Co Investments

William B. Summers, Jr.: *CURR EMPL* pres, ceo, dir: McDonald & Co Securities

GIVING OFFICERS
Thomas G. Clevidence: secy *CURR EMPL* mng dir: McDonald & Co Securities (see above)

Mark Filippell: trust

Dennis Golem: trust

Thomas McDonald: trust

John F. O'Brien: trust *CORP AFFIL* dir: McDonald & Co Securities

Thomas M. O'Donnell: chmn *CURR EMPL* chmn, ceo: McDonald & Co Securities (see above)

Gordon A. Price: treas (see above)

William B. Summers, Jr.: trust *CURR EMPL* pres, ceo, dir: McDonald & Co Securities (see above)

APPLICATION INFORMATION
Initial Approach: *Initial Contact:* brief letter of inquiry, followed by a full proposal *Include Information On:* description of the organization, amount requested, purpose for

751

which funds are sought, and proof of tax-exempt status *Deadlines:* none

Restrictions on Giving: Does not support individuals; religious organizations for sectarian purposes; political or lobbying groups; or organizations outside operating areas; athletic and sport related civic or national events such as the Olympics; causes that use tickets/lunches for fund raising; any sub-committee or auxiliary group of an organization to which a donation has already been made; secondary schools, both for annual support and capital programs. All recipients must be classified as a non-profit, tax exempt organization under the Internal Revenue Code. Generally support will be given to regional rather than national requests and most grants will be within the State of Ohio.

OTHER THINGS TO KNOW
To promote volunteerism, company encourages officers and employees to take specific positions with charitable organizations and provides financial support to organizations in which employees serve.

GRANTS ANALYSIS
Total Grants: $286,107

Number of Grants: 202

Highest Grant: $83,050

Typical Range: $250 to $2,000

Disclosure Period: fiscal year ending March 25, 1994

Note: Recent grants are derived from a fiscal 1994 Form 990.

RECENT GRANTS

General

83,050	Heart and Hand Foundation, Cleveland, OH — general fund
17,000	Great Lakes Museum of Science, Environment, and Technology, Cleveland, OH — general fund
15,000	Cleveland Initiative for Education, Cleveland, OH — general fund
15,000	United Way — general fund
10,000	Ohio Foundation of Independent Colleges, Columbus, OH — general fund

McFawn Trust No. 2, Lois Sisler

CONTACT
Sarah S. Wright
Lois Sisler McFawn Trust No. 2
3925 Embassy Parkway
Akron, OH 44333-1799
(216) 689-3043

FINANCIAL SUMMARY
Recent Giving: $508,306 (1993); $397,125 (1992); $781,033 (1991)

Assets: $13,058,754 (1993); $12,569,448 (1992); $12,172,061 (1991)

EIN: 34-6508111

CONTRIBUTIONS SUMMARY
Donor(s): Lois Sisler McFawn

Typical Recipients: • *Arts & Humanities:* Arts Associations & Councils, Arts Outreach, Ballet, Community Arts, Dance, General, Historic Preservation, History & Archaeology, Libraries, Museums/Galleries, Music, Performing Arts, Public Broadcasting, Theater • *Civic & Public Affairs:* Business/Free Enterprise, Clubs, Economic Development, Employment/Job Training, General, Housing, Nonprofit Management, Professional & Trade Associations, Urban & Community Affairs, Women's Affairs, Zoos/Aquariums • *Education:* Business Education, Colleges & Universities, General, Literacy, Private Education (Precollege), Science/Mathematics Education, Secondary Education (Private), Special Education • *Health:* AIDS/HIV, Arthritis, Cancer, Children's Health/Hospitals, Emergency/Ambulance Services, Eyes/Blindness, Hospitals, Medical Research, Mental Health, Nursing Services • *Religion:* Religious Welfare • *Science:* Science Museums, Scientific Centers & Institutes • *Social Services:* Big Brother/Big Sister, Camps, Child Welfare, Community Centers, Community Service Organizations, Counseling, Domestic Violence, Family Planning, Family Services, Food/Clothing Distribution, People with Disabilities, Refugee Assistance, Shelters/Homelessness, United Funds/United Ways, Volunteer Services, YMCA/YWCA/YMHA/YWHA, Youth Organizations

Grant Types: capital, general support, and research

Geographic Distribution: focus on the Akron, OH, area

GIVING OFFICERS
Society Natl Bank: trust

APPLICATION INFORMATION
Initial Approach: Send cover letter and full proposal. There are no deadlines.

Restrictions on Giving: Does not support individuals or provide loans.

PUBLICATIONS
Application Guidelines

GRANTS ANALYSIS
Total Grants: $508,306

Number of Grants: 38

Highest Grant: $50,000

Typical Range: $1,000 to $30,000

Disclosure Period: 1993

Note: Recent grants are derived from a 1993 Form 990.

RECENT GRANTS

General

50,000	University of Akron, Akron, OH
30,000	Children's Hospital Medical Center, Akron, OH
30,000	Visiting Nurse Service, Akron, OH
22,000	United Way of Summit County, Akron, OH
20,000	National Invention Center, Akron, OH

Mead Corporation, The / Mead Corp. Foundation

Revenue: $5.12 billion
Employees: 21,600
Headquarters: Dayton, OH
SIC Major Group: Paper Mills, Logging, Sawmills & Planing Mills—General, and Hardwood Dimension & Flooring Mills

CONTACT
Ronald F. Budzik
Executive Director
Mead Corp. Foundation
Courthouse Plz. NE
Dayton, OH 45463
(513) 495-3849

FINANCIAL SUMMARY
Recent Giving: $2,685,384 (1994); $3,672,000 (1993); $4,290,100 (1992)

Assets: $23,828,538 (1993); $21,825,562 (1991); $20,939,797 (1990)

Gifts Received: $2,000,000 (1993)

Fiscal Note: Company gives through direct and foundation gifts. In 1992, foundation contributions totaled $3,221,852. In 1993, foundation contributions totaled $2,545,163. The 1994 giving figure represents foundation giving only. In 1993, contributions were received form Mead Corp. ($2,000,000). Above figures exclude nonmonetary support.

EIN: 31-6040645

CONTRIBUTIONS SUMMARY
Typical Recipients: • *Arts & Humanities:* Arts Associations & Councils, Arts Centers, Arts Festivals, Arts Institutes, Community Arts, Dance, Historic Preservation, Libraries, Museums/Galleries, Music, Performing Arts, Public Broadcasting, Theater • *Civic & Public Affairs:* Business/Free Enterprise, Chambers of Commerce, Community Foundations, Economic Development, Municipalities/Towns, Philanthropic Organizations, Urban & Community Affairs, Women's Affairs • *Education:* Arts/Humanities Education, Colleges & Universities, Community & Junior Colleges, Economic Education, Education Associations, Education Funds, Engineering/Technological Education, Literacy, Minority Education, Public Education (Precollege), Science/Mathematics Education • *Health:* Emergency/Ambulance Services, Hospices • *International:* International Organizations • *Science:* Scientific Centers & Institutes • *Social Services:* Child Welfare, Community Service Organizations, Domestic Violence, Family Services, Food/Clothing Distribution, Shelters/Homelessness, United Funds/United Ways, Youth Organizations

Grant Types: capital, employee matching gifts, general support, and project

Note: Employee matching gift ratio: 1 to 1.

Nonmonetary Support: $731,000 (1990); $700,000 (1989); $600,000 (1988)

Nonmonetary Support Types: donated equipment, donated products, and in-kind services

Geographic Distribution: primarily in areas where Mead Corp. has operations

Operating Locations: AL (Birmingham, Cottonton, Phenix City, Stevenson), AR (Ft. Smith, Little Rock), AZ (Glendale, Phoenix, Tucson), CA (Bakersfield, Buena Park, Eureka, Fresno, Garden Grove, Los Angeles, National City, Sacramento, San Francisco, Santa Maria, Stockton), CO (Denver), FL (Ft. Myers, Jacksonville, Miami, Orlando, Tampa), GA (Atlanta, Columbus), HI (Honolulu), ID (Boise), IL (Chicago, Godfrey, Hillside), IN (Hartford City, Indianapolis), KY (Lexington, Louisville), MA (South Lee), MI (Detroit, Escanaba, Flint, Grand Rapids, Kalamazoo), MN (Minneapolis), MO (North Kansas City, St. Joseph, St. Louis), MT (Great Falls), NC (Charlotte, Raleigh), NV (Las Vegas), OH (Akron, Chilicothe, Cincinnati, Cleveland, Columbus, Dayton, Findlay, Miamisburg, Washington Court House), OK (Oklahoma City, Tulsa), OR (Portland), PA (Alexandria, Fairless Hills, Pittsburgh), SC (Spartanburg), TN (Chattanooga, Kingsport, Knoxville, Memphis, Nashville), TX (Garland), UT (Salt Lake City), VA (Charlottesville, Richmond), WA (Seattle, Spokane, Wenatchee), WI (Menasha)

Note: Also operates internationally.

CORP. OFFICERS

Steven Charles Mason: *B* Sarnia, Ontario Canada 1936 *ED* MA Inst Tech BS 1957 *CURR EMPL* chmn, ceo: Mead Corp *CORP AFFIL* dir: Duriron Co, PPG Indus Inc

GIVING OFFICERS

Betsy P. Bent: mem gov comm *CURR EMPL* vp Latin Am & legal admin: Mead Corp

Ronald F. Budzik: exec dir, vp *CURR EMPL* vp govt aff: Mead Corp

L. A. Horn: mem gov comm

Elias M. Karter: mem gov comm *B* 1940 *ED* Univ ME BS 1958; Univ ME MS 1962; Univ ME PHD 1964 *CURR EMPL* vp mfg tech: Mead Corp

R. W. Lane: mem gov comm

E. L. Miller: secy

Elizabeth L. Russo: mem gov comm *CURR EMPL* vp corp commun: Mead Corp

Kathryn Strawn: admin off

APPLICATION INFORMATION

Initial Approach: *Initial Contact:* brief letter or proposal to local Mead unit manager, for most requests; Dayton area organizations and educational institutions outside Mead communities should submit requests to foundation *Include Information On:* description and purpose of organization, amount requested, purpose for which funds are sought, list of board of directors and officers, re-

cently audited financial statement, proof of tax-exempt status, current budget, proposed use and benefits of support, explanation of project for which funds are sought, project budget, statement decribing how success of project will be measured, proposed funding sources, and number of people served *Deadlines:* none; distribution committee meets twice annually *Note:* Program policy statement and grant application guidelines are available upon request from the foundation.

Restrictions on Giving: Does not support individuals, labor or veterans organizations, religious or denominational organizations, political parties or candidates, or fraternal organizations.

OTHER THINGS TO KNOW

The Mead Corporation Foundation directs most of its philanthropy to the community level; national organizations receive limited funding.

Mead unit managers review local requests and are encouraged to adjust charitable priorities to meet local needs. Company actively encourages employee voluntarism.

GRANTS ANALYSIS

Total Grants: $2,545,163

Number of Grants: 900*

Highest Grant: $215,000

Average Grant: $2,828*

Typical Range: $100 to $10,000

Disclosure Period: 1993

Note: Number of grants and average grant figures are approximate. Recent grants are derived from a 1993 Form 990.

RECENT GRANTS

General

215,000	United Way Dayton Area, Dayton, OH
107,235	Miami University Foundation, Miami, FL
90,000	Russell County School System, Phenix City, AL
84,294	United Way Metropolitan Atlanta, Atlanta, GA
78,430	Barbour County Cooperative Extension Service, Philippi, WV

Morgan Foundation, Burton D.

CONTACT

John V. Frank
President
Burton D. Morgan Foundation
PO Box 1500
Akron, OH 44309-1500
(216) 258-6512

FINANCIAL SUMMARY

Recent Giving: $1,158,500 (1993); $541,700 (1992); $553,000 (1991)

Assets: $25,630,251 (1993); $23,455,589 (1992); $21,142,404 (1991)

Gifts Received: $1,500,000 (1993); $1,000,000 (1992); $500,000 (1991)

Fiscal Note: In 1992 and 1993, contributions were received from Burton D. Morgan.

EIN: 34-6598971

CONTRIBUTIONS SUMMARY

Donor(s): The foundation was established in 1967 by Burton D. Morgan.

Typical Recipients: • *Arts & Humanities:* Ballet, Dance, Historic Preservation, History & Archaeology, Libraries, Museums/Galleries, Music • *Civic & Public Affairs:* Botanical Gardens/Parks, Clubs, General, Municipalities/Towns, Nonprofit Management, Philanthropic Organizations, Professional & Trade Associations, Women's Affairs, Zoos/Aquariums • *Education:* Business Education, Colleges & Universities, Elementary Education (Public), General, Health & Physical Education, Private Education (Precollege), Public Education (Precollege), Religious Education, Science/Mathematics Education, Secondary Education, Secondary Education (Private), Secondary Education (Public), Student Aid • *Environment:* General • *Health:* Children's Health/Hospitals, Emergency/Ambulance Services, Hospices, Mental Health • *International:* Missionary/Religious Activities • *Religion:* Churches, Religious Organizations, Religious Welfare • *Social Services:* Child Welfare, Delinquency & Criminal Rehabilitation, Domestic Violence, Family Planning, Family Services, People with Disabilities, Recreation & Athletics, Senior Services, Shelters/Homelessness, United Funds/United Ways, Youth Organizations

Grant Types: capital, general support, scholarship, and seed money

Geographic Distribution: focus on Summit County, OH

GIVING OFFICERS

Weldon Wood Case: trust *B* Hudson OH 1921 *ED* OH Wesleyan Univ 1941

Richard A. Chenoweth: trust *PHIL AFFIL* exec dir: GAR Foundation

J. Martin Erbaugh: trust *B* 1948 *ED* Dennison Coll 1969-1973; Case Western Reserve Univ Law Sch 1973; Kent St Univ MBA 1978 *CURR EMPL* chmn bd pres, dir: Erbaugh Corp *CORP AFFIL* off: Coer Inc

John V. Frank: pres, trust *B* Cleveland OH 1936 *ED* Univ Miami FL BBA 1960 *CURR EMPL* pres: Summit Capital Mgmt Co *CORP AFFIL* councilman: City Akron *NONPR AFFIL* mem: Cleveland Soc Security Analysts, Counc Fdns Comm Legislation & Regulations; treas: Fairlawn Heights Assn; trust: Akron City Hosp Fdn, Howland Meml Fund *CLUB AFFIL* Hillsboro, Portage CC

Thomas G. Murdough: trust

APPLICATION INFORMATION

Initial Approach:

The foundation requests proposals be made in writing, not to exceed three pages.

The letter must give a clear and concise description of the purpose for the request. Attachments to the letter must include a copy of the IRS tax-determination letter, a separate nonprofit determination letter, a list of the current board of trustees, and a copy of the organization's most recent financial statement or audited report. Additional material may be submitted to supplement the application.

The deadlines for submitting proposals are May 15, September 15, and November 15.

The board meets three times per year. Requests that do not fall within the trustees' interests are declined within 30 days. Requests from the same organization can only be considered once every 12 months.

Restrictions on Giving: The foundation primarily makes grants to educational, research, mental health, and charitable organizations. The foundation does not make grants to individuals.

PUBLICATIONS
Application guidelines

GRANTS ANALYSIS
Total Grants: $1,158,500

Number of Grants: 35

Highest Grant: $500,000

Average Grant: $19,368*

Typical Range: $5,000 to $25,000

Disclosure Period: 1993

Note: Average grant excludes the highest grant of $500,000. Recent grants are derived from a 1993 Form 990.

RECENT GRANTS

Library
500	Foundation Center, Cleveland, OH

General
500,000	Purdue University, West Lafayette, IN — to establish and endow the Burton D. Morgan Endowment Venture Fund
275,000	Ashland University, Ashland, OH — toward the Burton D. Morgan Distinguished Chair in Business and Enterprise
50,000	Lynn University, Boca Raton, FL — to endow the Burton D. Morgan Scholarship Fund
50,000	Visiting Nurse Service, Akron, OH — for hospice care center building fund
25,000	Hiram College, Hiram, OH — for Presidential Discretionary Fund

Musson Charitable Foundation, R. C. and Katharine M.

CONTACT
Irving J. Musson, Jr.
Trustee
R. C. and Katharine M. Musson Charitable Fdn.
1188 Greenvale Ave.
Akron, OH 44313
(216) 864-5515

FINANCIAL SUMMARY
Recent Giving: $334,363 (fiscal 1994); $345,327 (fiscal 1993); $343,013 (fiscal 1992)

Assets: $3,724,530 (fiscal 1994); $4,146,699 (fiscal 1993); $4,023,536 (fiscal 1992)

EIN: 34-1549070

CONTRIBUTIONS SUMMARY
Donor(s): the late R. C. Musson

Typical Recipients: • *Arts & Humanities:* Arts Institutes, Ballet, History & Archaeology, Libraries, Music, Theater • *Civic & Public Affairs:* Economic Development, Employment/Job Training, General, Housing, Municipalities/Towns, Zoos/Aquariums • *Education:* Arts/Humanities Education, Colleges & Universities, Education Funds, Education Reform, General, Religious Education, Secondary Education (Public), Special Education • *Health:* Cancer, Children's Health/Hospitals, Diabetes, Health Organizations, Hospitals, Long-Term Care, Multiple Sclerosis, Nursing Services, Prenatal Health Issues • *International:* International Affairs • *Religion:* Churches, Jewish Causes, Ministries, Religious Organizations, Religious Welfare • *Social Services:* Big Brother/Big Sister, Child Welfare, Community Service Organizations, Counseling, Crime Prevention, Domestic Violence, Family Services, Food/Clothing Distribution, Homes, People with Disabilities, Scouts, Senior Services, Substance Abuse, United Funds/United Ways, Volunteer Services, YMCA/YWCA/YMHA/YWHA, Youth Organizations

Grant Types: general support

Geographic Distribution: focus on Summit County, OH

GIVING OFFICERS
Irvin J. Musson, Jr.: trust

Irvin J. Musson III: trust

Ben Segers: trust

Robert S. Segers: trust

APPLICATION INFORMATION
Initial Approach: Submit a narrative. There are no deadlines.

GRANTS ANALYSIS
Total Grants: $334,363

Number of Grants: 43

Highest Grant: $85,000

Typical Range: $500 to $33,000

Disclosure Period: fiscal year ending June 30, 1994

Note: Recent grants are derived from a fiscal 1994 Form 990.

RECENT GRANTS
General
85,000	Univeristy of Akron Musson Chair, Akron, OH — education
33,000	United Fund, Akron, OH — general
15,000	Multiple Sclerosis Society Friendly Visitor Program, Akron, OH — general
10,000	Akron Baptist Temple, Akron, OH — general
10,000	Children's Hospital, Akron, OH — general

Parker Hannifin Corp. / Parker Hannifin Foundation

Revenue: $2.57 billion
Employees: 26,730
Headquarters: Cleveland, OH
SIC Major Group: Valves & Pipe Fittings Nec, Fluid Power Cylinders & Actuators, Fluid Power Pumps & Motors, and Industrial Machinery Nec

CONTACT
Joseph D. Whiteman
Secretary and Trustee
Parker-Hannifin Foundation
17325 Euclid Ave.
Cleveland, OH 44112
(216) 531-3000

FINANCIAL SUMMARY
Recent Giving: $1,500,000 (fiscal 1995 est.); $1,413,257 (fiscal 1994); $1,485,954 (fiscal 1993)

Assets: $1,169,760 (fiscal 1994); $17,709 (fiscal 1993); $13,241 (fiscal 1992)

Gifts Received: $2,598,086 (fiscal 1994); $1,472,511 (fiscal 1993)

Fiscal Note: All giving is through the foundation. There are no standing assets. The average monthly value of assets, given in 1991, is $73,311.

EIN: 34-6555686

CONTRIBUTIONS SUMMARY
Typical Recipients: • *Arts & Humanities:* Arts Centers, Arts Institutes, Ballet, Historic Preservation, Libraries, Museums/Galleries, Music, Opera, Performing Arts, Theater • *Civic & Public Affairs:* Economic Development, Employment/Job Training, General, Municipalities/Towns, Parades/Festivals, Public Policy, Safety, Urban & Community Affairs, Zoos/Aquariums • *Education:* Business Education, Business-School Partnerships, Colleges & Universities, Community & Junior Colleges, Education Funds, Education Reform, Engineering/Technological Education, Minority Education, Secondary

Education (Public), Student Aid • *Health:* Emergency/Ambulance Services, Health Funds, Health Organizations, Hospitals, Medical Research, Mental Health, Outpatient Health Care • *Science:* Science Museums, Scientific Centers & Institutes • *Social Services:* Community Centers, Scouts, Senior Services, Shelters/Homelessness, Substance Abuse, United Funds/United Ways, Youth Organizations

Grant Types: capital, employee matching gifts, general support, and scholarship

Note: Scholarships are awarded through the "Merit Scholarship Program."

Geographic Distribution: nationally

Operating Locations: AL (Huntsville, Jacksonville), AZ (Tolleson), CA (City of Industry, Culver City, Irvine, Modesto, Moorpark, Santa Fe Springs), CO, FL (St. Augustine), GA (Atlanta), IL (Broadview, Des Plaines, Northbrook), IN (Lebanon), KS, KY (Lexington), MA (Lexington, Sharon, Waltham), ME (Gray, Portland), MI (Holt, Otsego, Oxford, Plymouth, Richland, Troy), MN (Eden Prairie, Minneapolis), MS (Batesville, Madison), NY (Brooklyn, Clyde, Lyons), OH (Akron, Avon, Cincinnati, Cleveland, Columbus, Dayton, Eastlake, Eaton, Elyria, Kent, Lewisburg, Metamora, Ravenna, St. Mary's, Wadsworth, Waverly, Wickliffe), OR (Portland), SC (Spartanburg), UT (Salt Lake City), WI (Grantsburg)

CORP. OFFICERS
Duane E. Collins: *B* 1936 *ED* Univ WI BSME *CURR EMPL* pres, ceo, dir: Parker-Hannifin Corp

Patrick Streeter Parker: *B* Cleveland OH 1929 *ED* Williams Coll BA 1951; Harvard Univ MBA 1953 *CURR EMPL* chmn: Parker-Hannifin Corp *NONPR AFFIL* trust: Case Western Reserve Univ, Woodruff Fdn *CLUB AFFIL* Country, Pepper Pike, Union *PHIL AFFIL* pres, dir: Arthur L. Parker Foundation; don, pres: Patrick S. Parker Foundation

Dennis W. Sullivan: *B* Chicago IL 1938 *ED* Purdue Univ BSME 1960; Case Western Reserve Univ MBA 1969 *CURR EMPL* exec vp, coo, dir: Parker-Hannifin Corp *CORP AFFIL* dir: Ferro Corp, Soc Natl Bank

GIVING OFFICERS
Duane E. Collins: vp, trust *CURR EMPL* pres, ceo, dir: Parker-Hannifin Corp (see above)

Patrick Streeter Parker: pres, trust *CURR EMPL* chmn: Parker-Hannifin Corp *PHIL AFFIL* pres, dir: Arthur L. Parker Foundation; don, pres: Patrick S. Parker Foundation (see above)

Joseph David Whiteman: secy, trust *B* Sioux Falls SD 1933 *ED* Univ MI BA 1955; Univ MI JD 1960 *CURR EMPL* vp, secy, gen couns: Parker-Hannifin Corp *NONPR AFFIL* dir: Great Lakes Theatre Festival, Judson Retirement Commun, St Lukes Hosp; mem: Am Bar Assn, Beta Theta Pi, Phi Delta Phi

APPLICATION INFORMATION
Initial Approach: *Initial Contact:* brief letter or proposal *Include Information On:* description of the organization, amount requested, purpose for which funds are sought, recently audited financial statement, proof of tax-exempt status *Deadlines:* none

GRANTS ANALYSIS
Total Grants: $1,413,257

Number of Grants: 376*

Highest Grant: $148,450

Average Grant: 3,387*

Disclosure Period: fiscal year ending June 30, 1994

Note: Number of grants and average grants exclude $139,608 in matching gifts. Recent grants are derived from a fiscal 1994 Form 990.

RECENT GRANTS

General

148,450	United Way Corporate, Cleveland, OH — for community fund
100,000	Provost's Scholarship in Engineering — for colleges and universities
36,000	Ohio Foundation of Independent Colleges, Columbus, OH — for colleges and universities
32,900	National Merit Scholarship Program, Cleveland, OH — for colleges and universities
30,000	Cleveland Tomorrow, Cleveland, OH — for civic purposes

Pollock Company Foundation, William B.

CONTACT
William B. Pollock Company Fdn.
c/o Bank One, Youngstown, N.A.
6 Federal Plz. W.
Youngstown, OH 44503
(216) 742-6741

FINANCIAL SUMMARY
Recent Giving: $206,600 (1993); $81,888 (1992); $76,025 (1991)

Assets: $1,990,633 (1993); $2,088,546 (1992); $2,079,366 (1991)

EIN: 34-6514078

CONTRIBUTIONS SUMMARY
Typical Recipients: • *Arts & Humanities:* Arts Institutes, Community Arts, Historic Preservation, History & Archaeology, Libraries, Music • *Civic & Public Affairs:* Business/Free Enterprise, Clubs, Economic Development, General, Public Policy • *Education:* Business Education, Colleges & Universities, Education Associations, Education Funds, Private Education (Precollege) • *Health:* Emergency/Ambulance Services, Health Organizations, Home-Care Services, Hospices, Hospitals, Nutrition • *Religion:* Jewish Causes, Religious Organizations, Religious Welfare • *Science:* Scientific Centers & Institutes • *Social Services:* Child Welfare, Community Service Organizations, Family Planning, People with Disabilities, Senior Services, Substance Abuse, United Funds/United Ways, Youth Organizations

Grant Types: general support

Geographic Distribution: focus on the Youngstown, OH, area

GIVING OFFICERS
Bank One of Youngstown, N.A.: trust

Franklin Bennett: trust

APPLICATION INFORMATION
Initial Approach: The foundation has no formal grant application procedure or application form. There are no deadlines.

GRANTS ANALYSIS
Total Grants: $206,600

Number of Grants: 18

Highest Grant: $111,000

Typical Range: $100 to $18,250

Disclosure Period: 1993

Note: Recent grants are derived from a 1993 Form 990.

RECENT GRANTS

General

111,000	Youngstown State University, Youngstown, OH
18,250	Youngstown/Mahoning Valley United Way, Youngstown, OH
17,000	Youngstown Foundation United Way, Youngstown, OH
10,000	Planned Parenthood Association, Youngstown, OH
7,000	Park Vista Life Care Fund, Youngstown, OH

Premier Industrial Corp. / Premier Industrial Foundation

Sales: $690.85 million
Employees: 3,300
Headquarters: Cleveland, OH
SIC Major Group: Polishes & Sanitation Goods, Chemical Preparations Nec, Hardware Nec, and Lubricating Oils & Greases

CONTACT
Virginia Levi
Associate Director
Premier Industrial Foundation
4500 Euclid Ave.
Cleveland, OH 44103
(216) 391-8300

FINANCIAL SUMMARY
Recent Giving: $2,000,000 (1995 est.); $1,904,084 (1994); $1,897,312 (1993)

Assets: $670,262 (1993); $2,232,694 (1992); $3,893,060 (1991)

Fiscal Note: Above figures reflect contributions by foundation, which handles all major giving. Above figures exclude nonmonetary support.

EIN: 34-6522448

CONTRIBUTIONS SUMMARY

Typical Recipients: • *Arts & Humanities:* Arts Associations & Councils, Arts Centers, Arts Institutes, Dance, Historic Preservation, History & Archaeology, Libraries, Museums/Galleries, Music, Opera, Performing Arts, Public Broadcasting, Theater • *Civic & Public Affairs:* African American Affairs, Community Foundations, Economic Development, Employment/Job Training, General, Philanthropic Organizations, Professional & Trade Associations, Safety, Urban & Community Affairs, Women's Affairs, Zoos/Aquariums • *Education:* Business Education, Colleges & Universities, Education Associations, Education Funds, Minority Education, Science/Mathematics Education, Student Aid • *Environment:* General • *Health:* AIDS/HIV, Eyes/Blindness, Health Organizations, Hospices, Hospitals, Nursing Services, Public Health • *International:* International Affairs • *Religion:* Jewish Causes, Religious Organizations, Religious Welfare • *Science:* Science Museums • *Social Services:* Child Welfare, Community Service Organizations, Domestic Violence, Emergency Relief, Food/Clothing Distribution, Homes, Recreation & Athletics, United Funds/United Ways, Volunteer Services, Youth Organizations

Grant Types: capital, general support, project, and scholarship

Geographic Distribution: primarily northeast Ohio with emphasis on Cleveland, and United Way organizations in ten cities where company divisions operate

Operating Locations: IL (Chicago), IN (Indianapolis), NY (Bohemia), OH (Cleveland, Wooster), SC (Gaffney)

CORP. OFFICERS

Bruce W. Johnson: *CURR EMPL* pres, dir: Premier Indus Corp

Jack N. Mandel: *B* Austria 1911 *ED* Fenn Coll 1930-1933; Cleveland Coll *CURR EMPL* chmn fin comm, dir: Premier Indus Corp *CORP AFFIL* chmn (fin comm), dir: MCM Electronics Inc *NONPR AFFIL* hon trust: Hebrew Univ; life trust: Cleveland Jewish Welfare Fdn, S Broward Jewish Fed; mem exec comm: Natl Conf Christians Jews; pres: Montefiore Home Aged; pres adv bd: Barry Univ; trust: FL Soc Blind, Tel Aviv Univ Mus Diaspora, Wood Hosp *CLUB AFFIL* Beachmont CC, Commede, Emerald Hills CC

Joseph C. Mandel: *B* 1913 *CURR EMPL* chmn exec comm, dir: Premier Indus Corp *CORP AFFIL* chmn exec comm, dir: MCM Electronics Inc; dir: D-A Lubricant Co *PHIL AFFIL* pres, trust: Joseph and Florence Mandel Foundation

Morton Leon Mandel: *B* Cleveland OH 1921 *ED* Case Western Reserve Univ 1939-1940; Pomona Coll 1943 *CURR EMPL* chmn, ceo, dir: Premier Indus Corp *CORP AFFIL* chmn, ceo, dir: MCM Electronics Inc *NONPR AFFIL* fdr: Clean Land OH, Cleveland Project MOVE, Cleveland Tomorrow; fdr, hon pres: Mid-Town Corridor, World Confed Jewish Commun Ctrs; hon pres: Natl Jewish Welfare Bd; life trust: Counc Jewish Feds, Jewish Commun Ctrs Cleveland, Jewish Commun Fed, Un Way Cleveland; trust: Case Western Reserve Univ, Cleveland Mus Art, Ctr Social Policy Studies, Un Way Am; trust emeritus: Mt Sinai Hosp Cleveland *PHIL AFFIL* trust: Morton and Barbara Mandel Foundation; secy, treas, trust: Jack N. and Lilyan Mandel Foundation

Philip Stuart Sims: *B* Cleveland OH 1927 *ED* Case Western Reserve Univ 1956 *CURR EMPL* vchmn, treas: Premier Indus Corp *PHIL AFFIL* trust: Joseph and Florence Mandel Foundation

GIVING OFFICERS

John Charles Colman: trust *B* Cleveland OH 1927 *ED* Cornell Univ 1949; Harvard Univ 1951 *CORP AFFIL* dir: Act II Jewelry Inc, Balmorhea Ranches Inc, DBA Sys Inc, Duplex Products Inc, Orion Capital Corp, Premier Indus Corp, Security Ins Co, Sesame Sys Ltd, Stein Health Svcs Inc

Virginia Levi: assoc dir

Joseph C. Mandel: trust *CURR EMPL* chmn exec comm, dir: Premier Indus Corp *PHIL AFFIL* pres, trust: Joseph and Florence Mandel Foundation (see above)

Morton Leon Mandel: trust *CURR EMPL* chmn, ceo, dir: Premier Indus Corp *PHIL AFFIL* trust: Morton and Barbara Mandel Foundation; secy, treas, trust: Jack N. and Lilyan Mandel Foundation (see above)

APPLICATION INFORMATION

Initial Approach: *Initial Contact:* brief letter or proposal; no formal application form is used *Include Information On:* description of project and justification for grant; amount and terms of request; pertinent financial information; IRS exemption status, including copy of exemption letter; if available, appraisal of the requesting organization by a standard-setting organization *Deadlines:* none

GRANTS ANALYSIS

Total Grants: $1,897,312

Number of Grants: 88

Highest Grant: $550,000

Average Grant: $15,486*

Typical Range: $500 to $20,000

Disclosure Period: 1993

Note: Fiscal information reflects foundation contributions only. Average grant figure excludes the highest grant. Recent grants are derived from a 1993 Form 990.

RECENT GRANTS

General

550,000	Premier Industrial Philanthropic Fund, Cleveland, OH	
500,100	Jewish Community Federation, Cleveland, OH	
246,584	Case Western Reserve University, Cleveland, OH	
169,000	United Way	
125,000	Neighborhood Progress, Cleveland, OH	

Reinberger Foundation

CONTACT

Robert N. Reinberger
Co-Director
Reinberger Foundation
27600 Chagrin Blvd.
Cleveland, OH 44122
(216) 292-2790

FINANCIAL SUMMARY

Recent Giving: $2,741,285 (1994); $2,674,940 (1993); $2,370,834 (1992)

Assets: $54,939,929 (1994); $60,123,327 (1993); $57,803,005 (1992)

Gifts Received: $4,836,859 (1988)

EIN: 34-6574879

CONTRIBUTIONS SUMMARY

Donor(s): The Reinberger Foundation was established in 1968 by Clarence T. Reinberger, a Cleveland businessman who developed the Automotive Parts Company and later became the chairman of Genuine Parts. Following Mr. Reinberger's death in 1968, the foundation received half of its current assets. The remainder of its assets were acquired following the death of Mr. Reinberger's wife, Louise Reinberger. The Reinbergers had no children; the foundation is directed by two of Mr. Reinberger's nephews.

Typical Recipients: • *Arts & Humanities:* Arts Associations & Councils, Arts Centers, Arts Festivals, Arts Institutes, Ballet, Historic Preservation, History & Archaeology, Libraries, Museums/Galleries, Music, Opera, Performing Arts, Public Broadcasting, Theater • *Civic & Public Affairs:* Botanical Gardens/Parks, Community Foundations, Nonprofit Management, Philanthropic Organizations, Professional & Trade Associations, Zoos/Aquariums • *Education:* Arts/Humanities Education, Colleges & Universities, Education Funds, Medical Education, Private Education (Precollege), Public Education (Precollege) • *Health:* Alzheimers Disease, Cancer, Children's Health/Hospitals, Clinics/Medical Centers, Health Organizations, Hospitals, Medical Research • *Religion:* Churches, Religious Welfare • *Science:* Science Museums • *Social Services:* Community Centers, Community Service Organizations, Family Planning, Family Services, Youth Organizations

Grant Types: capital, challenge, endowment, and general support

Geographic Distribution: primarily Cleveland and Columbus, OH

GIVING OFFICERS

Sara R. Dyer: trust

Karen R. Hooser: trust

Richard Heer Oman: secy *B* Columbus OH 1926 *ED* OH St Univ BA 1948; OH St Univ JD 1951 *NONPR AFFIL* fellow: OH St Bar Fdn; mem: Am Bar Assn, Am Coll Trust & Estate Couns, Columbus Bar Assn, OH St Bar Assn *CLUB AFFIL* Columbus, Kit Kat,

Rocky Fort Hunt & CC, Rotary, YC; mem: Nantucket

Robert N. Reinberger: co-dir, trust

William C. Reinberger: co-dir, trust

APPLICATION INFORMATION
Initial Approach:

There are no application forms or guidelines. Applicants should submit one copy of a full proposal.

Written applications should include a clear statement of purpose and a copy of the organization's exemption letter from the IRS. The foundation will request further information on proposals of interest.

There are no deadlines for proposals.

The board of directors meets in March, June, September, and December. The review process takes about six months. The board acknowledges the receipt of an application and may require an interview.

Restrictions on Giving: The foundation does not make grants to individuals.

GRANTS ANALYSIS
Total Grants: $2,370,834

Number of Grants: 58

Highest Grant: $166,667

Average Grant: $40,876

Typical Range: $5,000 to $50,000

Disclosure Period: 1992

Note: Recent grants are derived from a 1992 Form 990.

RECENT GRANTS

Library

100,000	Columbus Academy, Columbus, OH — second of $500 million grant for upper and lower libraries construction

General

100,000	Case Western Reserve University, Cleveland, OH — final installment for school of Medicine Biomedical Research Facility
100,000	Cleveland Clinic Foundation, Cleveland, OH — third of $600,000 grant to fund neurosciences group lab in the health sciences
100,000	Cleveland Museum of Natural History, Cleveland, OH — third installment of grant for new wing
100,000	Cleveland Zoological Society, Cleveland, OH — first payment of $500,000 commitment toward construction of education center
100,000	Holden Arboretum, Cleveland, OH — first payment of $500,000 commitment toward greenhouse/nursery research facility construction

Ritter Charitable Trust, George W. and Mary F.

CONTACT
Craig H. Shopneck
George W. and Mary F. Ritter Charitable Trust
c/o Society Bank & Trust
PO Box 10099
Toledo, OH 43699-0099
(419) 259-8763

FINANCIAL SUMMARY
Recent Giving: $229,514 (fiscal 1993); $242,808 (fiscal 1992); $264,650 (fiscal 1991)

Assets: $5,673,498 (fiscal 1993); $5,616,352 (fiscal 1992); $5,166,818 (fiscal 1991)

EIN: 34-6781636

CONTRIBUTIONS SUMMARY
Typical Recipients: • *Arts & Humanities:* Libraries, Museums/Galleries • *Civic & Public Affairs:* Clubs, General, Law & Justice • *Education:* Colleges & Universities, Student Aid • *Health:* Children's Health/Hospitals, Hospitals • *Religion:* Churches, Religious Organizations, Religious Welfare, Synagogues/Temples • *Social Services:* Community Service Organizations, Scouts, YMCA/YWCA/YMHA/YWHA, Youth Organizations

Grant Types: general support, operating expenses, and scholarship

Geographic Distribution: focus on the Toledo, OH, area

GIVING OFFICERS
Society National Bank: trust

Larry Firestine: mem scholarship selection comm

Edgar A. Gibson: mem scholarship selection comm

James D. Harvey: mem scholarship selection comm

Michael D. Wilkins: mem scholarship selection comm

APPLICATION INFORMATION
Initial Approach: Application form required. There are no deadlines.

GRANTS ANALYSIS
Total Grants: $229,514

Number of Grants: 26

Highest Grant: $33,878

Typical Range: $337 to $22,585

Disclosure Period: fiscal year ending November 30, 1993

Note: Recent grants are derived from a fiscal 1993 Form 990.

RECENT GRANTS

Library

22,585	Ritter Library, Vermillion, OH

General

33,878	Toledo Hospital, Toledo, OH

22,585	Baldwin-Wallace College, Berea, OH
17,857	Shrine Hospital for Crippled Children and Burn Institute, Toledo, OH
9,035	Flower Hospital, Sylvania, OH
9,035	St. Vincent Hospital, Toledo, OH

Ross Laboratories

Revenue: $1.5 billion
Employees: 2,400
Parent Company: Abbott Laboratories
Headquarters: Columbus, OH
SIC Major Group: Chemicals & Allied Products and Food & Kindred Products

CONTACT
Shirley Adkins
Communications Specialist
Ross Products Division
625 Cleveland Ave.
Columbus, OH 43215
(614) 624-7581

FINANCIAL SUMMARY
Fiscal Note: Company does not disclose contributions figures.

CONTRIBUTIONS SUMMARY
Support goes to local education, human service, health, arts, and civic organizations.

Typical Recipients: • *Arts & Humanities:* Arts Associations & Councils, Ballet, Community Arts, General, Libraries, Museums/Galleries, Opera, Theater • *Civic & Public Affairs:* Chambers of Commerce, Civil Rights, General, Inner-City Development, Philanthropic Organizations, Urban & Community Affairs, Zoos/Aquariums • *Education:* Colleges & Universities, Education Associations, Education Funds, General • *Environment:* Wildlife Protection • *Health:* AIDS/HIV, Alzheimers Disease, Cancer, Children's Health/Hospitals, General, Health Organizations, Hospitals, Hospitals (University Affiliated), Medical Research, Nutrition, Prenatal Health Issues • *Science:* General • *Social Services:* Animal Protection, Camps, Child Welfare, Community Centers, Community Service Organizations, Domestic Violence, Emergency Relief, Family Services, Food/Clothing Distribution, General, Homes, Senior Services, Shelters/Homelessness, United Funds/United Ways, Youth Organizations

Grant Types: general support, multi-year/continuing support, operating expenses, project, research, and scholarship

Nonmonetary Support Types: donated equipment and donated products

Geographic Distribution: in headquarters and operating communities

Operating Locations: OH (Columbus)

CORP. OFFICERS
Thomas McNally: *CURR EMPL* pres, Ross Products Div: Ross Laboratories

APPLICATION INFORMATION

Send a brief letter of inquiry. Include a description of organization, amount requested, purpose of funds sought, and proof of tax-exempt status.

Restrictions on Giving: Does not support individuals and religious organizations for sectarian purposes.

GRANTS ANALYSIS
Typical Range: $50 to $1,000

Sandusky International Inc. / Sandusky International Foundation

Sales: $21.0 million
Employees: 220
Headquarters: Sandusky, OH
SIC Major Group: Industrial Machinery & Equipment

CONTACT
R. A. Hargrave
Secretary-Treasurer
Sandusky International Inc.
615 W Market St., PO Box 5012
Sandusky, OH 44871-8012
(419) 626-5340

FINANCIAL SUMMARY
Recent Giving: $55,300 (1994); $70,350 (1993); $69,925 (1992)

Assets: $194,245 (1993); $257,504 (1992); $318,643 (1991)

Gifts Received: $200,000 (1991); $200,000 (1990); $150,000 (1989)

Fiscal Note: In 1991, contributions were received from Sandusky International Inc.

EIN: 34-6596951

CONTRIBUTIONS SUMMARY
Typical Recipients: • *Arts & Humanities:* Arts Associations & Councils, Community Arts, General, Libraries, Museums/Galleries, Music, Performing Arts, Theater • *Civic & Public Affairs:* Business/Free Enterprise, Clubs, Economic Development, General, Housing • *Education:* Business Education, Colleges & Universities, Education Funds, Elementary Education (Private), General, Private Education (Precollege), Public Education (Precollege), Science/Mathematics Education, Secondary Education (Private), Student Aid • *Health:* Cancer, General, Heart, Hospices • *Social Services:* Animal Protection, Camps, Child Welfare, Community Centers, Community Service Organizations, Domestic Violence, Food/Clothing Distribution, General, United Funds/United Ways, Volunteer Services, Youth Organizations

Grant Types: capital, challenge, and general support

Geographic Distribution: focus primarily on Sandusky, OH, area

Operating Locations: OH (Sandusky)

CORP. OFFICERS
Charles W. Rainger: *B* Cleveland OH 1933 *ED* Case Western Reserve Univ 1955 *CURR EMPL* pres, dir: Sandusky Intl *CORP AFFIL* chmn: Sandusky Ltd; dir: OH Edison Co, Third Natl Bank

GIVING OFFICERS
Carlos G. Alafita: trust

Richard A. Hall: trust

Richard A. Hargrave: trust

Charles W. Rainger: trust *CURR EMPL* pres, dir: Sandusky Intl (see above)

Daniel A. Scott: trust

APPLICATION INFORMATION
Initial Approach: Send a brief letter of inquiry and a full proposal. Include a description of organization, amount requested, purpose of funds sought, recently audited financial statement, and proof of tax-exempt status.

Restrictions on Giving: Does not support individuals, religious organizations for sectarian purposes, or political or lobbying groups.

GRANTS ANALYSIS
Total Grants: $70,350

Number of Grants: 26

Highest Grant: $18,600

Typical Range: $100 to $12,000

Disclosure Period: 1993

Note: Recent grants are derived from a 1993 Form 990.

RECENT GRANTS
General

12,000	United Way of Erie County, Sandusky, OH
7,500	Stein Hospice, Sandusky, OH
5,000	Greater Erie County Marketing Group, Sandusky, OH
5,000	Ohio Foundation of Independent Colleges, Columbus, OH
4,000	Sandusky High School Scholarship Fund, Sandusky, OH

Schlink Foundation, Albert G. and Olive H.

CONTACT
Robert A. Wiedemann
President
Albert G. and Olive H. Schlink Fdn.
401 Citizens National Bank Bldg.
Norwalk, OH 44857
(419) 668-8211

FINANCIAL SUMMARY
Recent Giving: $411,244 (1993); $393,891 (1992); $365,200 (1991)

Assets: $8,917,789 (1993); $8,407,396 (1992); $8,189,872 (1991)

EIN: 34-6574722

CONTRIBUTIONS SUMMARY
Typical Recipients: • *Arts & Humanities:* Libraries • *Civic & Public Affairs:* General • *Education:* Colleges & Universities • *Health:* Cancer, Diabetes, Eyes/Blindness, Hospices, Hospitals, Medical Rehabilitation, Medical Research, Research/Studies Institutes, Single-Disease Health Associations • *Religion:* Churches, Religious Welfare • *Science:* Science Museums • *Social Services:* Community Service Organizations, Food/Clothing Distribution, People with Disabilities, Senior Services, Shelters/Homelessness

Grant Types: general support and research

Geographic Distribution: focus on OH

GIVING OFFICERS
John D. Allton: treas, trust

Thomas Huff: trust

Curtis J. Koch: trust

Dorothy E. Wiedemann: vp, trust

Robert A. Wiedemann: pres, secy, trust

APPLICATION INFORMATION
Initial Approach: Include a description of organization, amount requested, purpose of funds sought, recently audited financial statement, and proof of tax-exempt status. There are no deadlines.

Restrictions on Giving: Does not support individuals.

GRANTS ANALYSIS
Total Grants: $411,244

Number of Grants: 16

Highest Grant: $155,000

Typical Range: $2,500 to $67,600

Disclosure Period: 1993

Note: Recent grants are derived from a 1993 Form 990.

RECENT GRANTS
Library

5,000	Cleveland Public Library, Cleveland, OH

General

155,000	Little Sisters of the Poor, Phoenix, AZ
67,600	American Diabetes Association, Cleveland, OH
38,500	Sight Center, Toledo, OH
26,500	St. Francis Rehabilitation Hospital, Green Springs, OH
25,000	Salk Institute for Biological Studies, San Diego, CA

Scott Fetzer Co. / Scott Fetzer Foundation

Revenue: $890.0 million
Employees: 13,000
Parent Company: Berkshire Hathaway Inc.
Headquarters: Westlake, OH
SIC Major Group: Electronic & Other Electrical Equipment, Fabricated Metal Products, Printing & Publishing, and Wholesale Trade—Durable Goods

CONTACT
Edie DeSantis
Vice President
Scott Fetzer Co.
28800 Clemens Rd.
Westlake, OH 44145
(216) 892-3000

FINANCIAL SUMMARY
Recent Giving: $229,586 (1993); $210,481 (1992); $257,387 (1990)

Assets: $764,089 (1993); $967,319 (1992); $1,256,160 (1990)

Gifts Received: $250,000 (1990)

Fiscal Note: In 1990, contributions were received from Scott and Fetzer Co.

EIN: 34-6596076

CONTRIBUTIONS SUMMARY
Typical Recipients: • *Arts & Humanities:* Arts Associations & Councils, Arts Centers, Community Arts, Libraries, Music, Performing Arts, Public Broadcasting, Theater • *Civic & Public Affairs:* Clubs, General, Legal Aid, Municipalities/Towns, Parades/Festivals, Urban & Community Affairs • *Education:* Business Education, Colleges & Universities, Economic Education, Education Associations, Education Funds, General, Secondary Education (Private) • *Health:* Arthritis, Children's Health/Hospitals, Health Funds, Health Organizations, Hospices, Hospitals, Medical Research, Prenatal Health Issues, Public Health, Single-Disease Health Associations • *International:* Foreign Educational Institutions • *Science:* Science Exhibits & Fairs • *Social Services:* Community Service Organizations, Food/Clothing Distribution, United Funds/United Ways, Volunteer Services, Youth Organizations

Grant Types: general support

Geographic Distribution: focus on OH

Operating Locations: OH (Westlake)

CORP. OFFICERS
Ralph Edward Schey: *B* Cleveland OH 1924 *ED* OH Univ 1948; Harvard Univ Bus A 1950 *CURR EMPL* chmn, ceo, dir: Scott Fetzer Co *CORP AFFIL* dir: Hauserman Co *PHIL AFFIL* pres, trust: Schey Foundation

GIVING OFFICERS
Timothy S. Guster: secy

C. L. Medford: vp

Ralph Edward Schey: chmn *CURR EMPL* chmn, ceo, dir: Scott Fetzer Co *PHIL AFFIL* pres, trust: Schey Foundation (see above)

Kenneth J. Semelsberger: pres *B* Marsteller PA 1936 *ED* OH St Univ BBA 1970; Cleveland St Univ MBA 1972 *CURR EMPL* pres, coo, dir: Scott Fetzer Co *CORP AFFIL* pres: Stahl Div Scott & Fetzer Co; production mgr: Holan Corp; Sales & Contracts mgr: Barth Cleve McNeil Corp

William W. T. Stephans: vp, treas

APPLICATION INFORMATION
Initial Approach: Send brief letter describing program. There are no deadlines.

GRANTS ANALYSIS
Total Grants: $229,586

Number of Grants: 126

Highest Grant: $50,000

Typical Range: $100 to $15,000

Disclosure Period: 1993

Note: Recent grants are derived from a 1993 Form 990.

RECENT GRANTS

Library

10,000	American Library Association, Chicago, IL
2,500	Canadian Library Association, Ottawa, Canada
1,500	Catholic Library Association, Haverford, PA

General

50,000	Cleveland Clinic Foundation, Cleveland, OH
15,000	Direct Selling Education Foundation, Washington, DC
12,500	Hospice, Mentor, OH
11,250	United Way, Cleveland, OH
11,250	United Way Services, Cleveland, OH

Scripps Co., E.W. / Scripps Howard Foundation

Sales: $1.21 billion
Employees: 11,500
Headquarters: Cincinnati, OH
SIC Major Group: Newspapers

CONTACT
Mary Lou Marusin
Executive Director
Scripps Howard Foundation
PO Box 5380
Cincinnati, OH 45201
(513) 977-3036

FINANCIAL SUMMARY
Recent Giving: $1,756,000 (1995 est.); $1,944,025 (1994); $895,650 (1993)

Assets: $28,000,000 (1995); $27,011,409 (1994); $17,918,804 (1993)

Fiscal Note: Above figures for foundation only. Company also makes contributions directly from corporate funds. Contact for this support is M. Denise Kuprionis, Corporate Secretary. Estimate of support is not available. Above figures exclude nonmonetary support.

EIN: 31-6025114

CONTRIBUTIONS SUMMARY
Typical Recipients: • *Arts & Humanities:* History & Archaeology, Libraries, Literary Arts, Theater • *Civic & Public Affairs:* African American Affairs, Economic Development, First Amendment Issues, Professional & Trade Associations, Public Policy, Women's Affairs • *Education:* Colleges & Universities, Engineering/Technological Education, Environmental Education, Journalism/Media Education, Legal Education, Literacy, Minority Education, Science/Mathematics Education, Secondary Education (Public), Student Aid, Vocational & Technical Education • *Environment:* General • *Science:* Science Museums

Grant Types: general support, project, and scholarship

Note: Scholarships are awarded to undergraduate students preparing for careers in the communications industry, primarily print and electronic journalism.

Nonmonetary Support Types: donated equipment

Note: Value of nonmonetary support is unavailable.

Geographic Distribution: nationally, with emphasis on operating locations

Operating Locations: AL (Birmingham), AZ (Phoenix), CA (Los Angeles, Redding, Sacramento, San Luis Obispo, South Gate, Thousand Oaks, Tulare, Ventura, Watsonville), CO (Denver, Longmont), DC, FL (Bonita Springs, Destin, Jupiter, Naples, Palm Beach, Port St. Lucie, Stuart, Tampa), GA (Rome), IN (Evansville), KY (Covington), MD (Baltimore), MI (Detroit), MO (Kansas City), NM (Albequerque), NY (New York), OH (Cincinnati, Cleveland), OK (Tulsa), SC, TN (Chattanooga, Knoxville, Memphis), TX (El Paso), VA, WA (Bremerton), WV

CORP. OFFICERS
Lawrence Arthur Leser: *B* Cincinnati OH 1935 *ED* Xavier Univ BS 1957 *CURR EMPL* chmn, ceo: EW Scripps Co *CORP AFFIL* dir: Evansville Courier Co Inc, Heekin Can Inc, KeyCorp Inc, Soc Natl Bank, Union Central Life Ins Co; mem natl adv bd: Chem Bank; pres, ceo, dir: Scripps Howard Broadcasting Co, Scripps Howard Inc; prin, dir: Memphis Publ Co *NONPR AFFIL* bd govs: Newspaper Assn Am; dir: Newspaper Advertising Bur

Gary Robinson: *CURR EMPL* vp: EW Scripps Co

GIVING OFFICERS
William Robert Burleigh: mem *B* Evansville IN 1935 *ED* Marquette Univ BS 1957 *CURR EMPL* exec vp, coo, dir: Scripps Howard Newspapers *CORP AFFIL* dir: Evansville Courier Co Inc; exec vp, dir: Scripps Howard Inc *NONPR AFFIL* mem: Alpha Sigma Nu, Am Soc Newspaper Editors *CLUB AFFIL* Cincinnati CC, Cincinnati Commercial, Cincinnati Literacy, Queen City *PHIL AFFIL* adv comm: Murray and Agnes Seasongood Good Government Foundation

John Hunter Burlingame: mem *B* Milwaukee WI 1933 *ED* Univ WI BS 1960; Univ

WI LLB 1963 *CURR EMPL* exec ptnr: Baker & Hostetler *CORP AFFIL* dir: EW Scripps Co, Scripps Howard Broadcasting Co, Scripps Howard Inc *NONPR AFFIL* mem: Am Bar Assn, Cleveland Bar Assn; trust: Edward W Scripps Trust *CLUB AFFIL* Pepper Pike, Shoreby, Soc Ctr, Union *PHIL AFFIL* trust: Mellen Foundation

Daniel J. Castellini: treas *B* 1940 *CURR EMPL* sr vp fin/admin: EW Scripps Co *CORP AFFIL* cfo, dir: Hall Sys Inc; secy, treas: Tampa Bay Television Inc; secy, treas, dir: Scripps Howard Broadcasting Co; sr vp fin/admin: Scripps Howard Inc; vp: Evansville Courier Co Inc; vp, dir: Monterey County Herald Co

Judy G. Clabes: trust *B* Henderson KY 1945 *ED* Univ KY BA 1967; ID St Univ pub admin 1984 *CORP AFFIL* dir: Huntington Bank Kenton County; pres, publ: Picture This! Books *NONPR AFFIL* chmn: Dinsmore Homestead Fdn; dir: KY Ctr Pub Issues, KY Ed Television Authority; fdr: First Amendment Ctr; mem: Am Soc Newspaper Editors, Natl Fed Press Women; pres: First Amendment Congress, Spiral Festival

Colleen Christner Conant: trust *B* Oklahoma City OK 1947 *ED* Oklahoma City Univ MusB 1970 *CURR EMPL* editor: Naples Daily News *NONPR AFFIL* mem: Am Soc Newspaper Editors, Assn Press Mng Editors Assn, Collier County Ed Fdn, FL Soc Newspaper Editors, Scripps Howard Mng Editors Assn *CLUB AFFIL* Forum Collier County, Rotary

F. Steve Crawford: trust *B* Cedar Rapids IA 1952 *ED* IA St Univ 1974 *CURR EMPL* vp: Grinnell Mutual Reinsurance Co *CORP AFFIL* dir: Grinnell Select Ins Co

Charlotte Moore English: trust

Pamela (Howard) Gumprecht: trust

Pam Howard: mem

David R. Huhn: mem *B* Cincinnati OH 1937 *CORP AFFIL* dir: EW Scripps Co, Scripps Howard Inc

Paul Frederick Knue: trust *B* Lawrenceburg IN 1947 *ED* Murray St Univ BS 1969 *CURR EMPL* editor: Cincinnati Post *NONPR AFFIL* mem: Am Soc Newspaper Editors, Assn Press Mng Editors Assn; trust: Assn Press Soc OH

M. Denise Kuprionis: secy *B* 1956 *CORP AFFIL* secy: Evansville Courier Co Inc, EW Scripps Co, Scripps Howard Inc; secy, asst treas: Tampa Bay Television Inc; secy, dir: Denver Publ Co, Hall Sys Inc, Monterey County Herald Co *NONPR AFFIL* mem: Am Soc Newspaper Editors

Lawrence Arthur Leser: mem *CURR EMPL* chmn, ceo: EW Scripps Co (see above)

Mary Lou Marusin: exec dir

Daniel Joseph Meyer: mem *B* Flint MI 1936 *ED* Purdue Univ BS 1958; IN Univ MBA 1963 *CURR EMPL* chmn, ceo, dir: Cincinnati Milacron Inc *CORP AFFIL* chmn, dir: Cincinnati Milacron Mktg Co; dir: Hubbell Inc, EW Scripps Co, Star Banc Corp *NONPR AFFIL* mem: Am Inst CPAs, Am Mgmt Assn *CLUB AFFIL* Kenwood CC

PHIL AFFIL pres: Cincinnati Milacron Foundation

Nicholas Biddle Paumgarten: mem *B* Philadelphia PA 1945 *ED* Univ PA BA 1967; Columbia Univ MBA 1971 *CURR EMPL* mng dir: JP Morgan & Co *CORP AFFIL* dir: EW Scripps Co, Scripps Howard Inc

Carole Philipps: trust

Sue Porter: trust

Gary Robinson: trust *CURR EMPL* vp: EW Scripps Co (see above)

Albert J. Schettelkotte: pres, ceo, trust, mem *B* Cheviot OH 1927 *CURR EMPL* sr vp: Scripps Howard Broadcasting Co

Charles Edward Scripps: mem *B* San Diego CA 1920 *ED* Coll William & Mary 1938-1940; Pomona Coll 1940-1941 *CURR EMPL* chmn, dir: Scripps Howard Broadcasting Co *CORP AFFIL* chmn: Sacramento Cable Television, Scripps Howard Inc, V Force Corp; dir: Star Banc Corp, Star Bank NA; trust: EW Scripps Trust *NONPR AFFIL* bd govs: Webb Sch; dir: Commun Improvement Corp Cincinnati; mem: CAP, Theta Delta Chi; mem natl bd adv: Salvation Army; trust: Freedoms Fdn

Marilyn Joy Scripps: trust

Paul K. Scripps: trust *CORP AFFIL* chmn, dir: John P Scripps Newspapers; dir: EW Scripps Co *PHIL AFFIL* trust: Ellen Browning Scripps Foundation; vp, dir: Quest for Truth Foundation; pres: John P. Scripps Foundation

Robert P. Scripps, Jr.: trust *CURR EMPL* dir: EW Scripps Co

Dan King Thomasson: trust *B* Shelbyville IN 1933 *ED* IN Univ BS 1956; CO Univ 1959 *CURR EMPL* editor: Scripps Howard News Svc *CORP AFFIL* vp: Scripps Howard Newspapers Cincinnati *NONPR AFFIL* mem: Am Soc Newspaper Editors, Sigma Delta Chi, White House Correspondents Assn; mem natl pub aff counc: IN Univ; pres: Raymond Clapper Fdn; trust: Franklin Coll *CLUB AFFIL* Gridiron, Natl Press, Univ WA, WA Golf & CC

APPLICATION INFORMATION

Initial Approach: *Initial Contact:* special grants applicants, send brief letter or proposal; for scholarship programs, submit a letter, stating college major and career goal by December 20 to receive scholarship application *Include Information On:* for special grants: brief description of project and expected results, line-item budget, amount requested, and proof of tax-exempt status *Deadlines:* special grant proposals are reviewed as received; completed scholarship application due February 25

Restrictions on Giving: Foundation discourages requests for grants which are not related to program areas described above. Generally declines to fund public causes, public radio and television, campus newspapers, governmental studies, seminars, operating funds, capital campaigns, annual appeals, and international projects. Grants normally not made to other private foundations.

Does not support dinners or special events, fraternal organizations, goodwill advertising, individuals, political or lobbying groups, or religious organizations for sectarian purposes.

PUBLICATIONS

Scripps Howard Foundation 1993 Progress Report, guidelines

GRANTS ANALYSIS

Total Grants: $1,944,025

Highest Grant: $157,000

Typical Range: $1,000 to $3,000

Disclosure Period: 1994

Note: Figures were provided by the foundation. Recent grants are derived from a 1993 Form 990.

RECENT GRANTS

Library

2,000	Broadcast Pioneers Educational Fund/Library, Washington, DC

General

125,925	University of Michigan, Ann Arbor, MI — Ted Scripps Environmental Fellows
100,000	Ohio University E.W. Scripps School of Journalism, Athens, OH
98,853	Literacy Grants
32,836	Indiana University R.W. Howard Seminar, Bloomington, IN
25,000	Rochester Institute of Technology, Rochester, NY — RPS Scholarships

Seaway Food Town, Inc.

Sales: $566.0 million
Employees: 4,500
Headquarters: Maumee, OH
SIC Major Group: Grocery Stores and Drug Stores & Proprietary Stores

CONTACT

Pat Nowak
Director Public Relations & Consumer Affairs
Seaway Food Town, Inc.
1020 Ford St.
Maumee, OH 43537
(419) 893-9401

FINANCIAL SUMMARY

Recent Giving: $500,000 (1995 est.); $469,000 (1994 approx.); $469,000 (1993 approx.)

Fiscal Note: Company makes direct contributions. Above figures include nonmonetary support.

CONTRIBUTIONS SUMMARY

Typical Recipients: • *Arts & Humanities:* Arts Appreciation, Arts Associations & Councils, Arts Centers, Arts Festivals, Community Arts, Ethnic & Folk Arts, Libraries, Museums/Galleries, Opera, Performing Arts, Public Broadcasting, Theater, Visual Arts

• *Civic & Public Affairs:* Philanthropic Organizations, Zoos/Aquariums • *Education:* Colleges & Universities, Elementary Education (Private), Literacy • *Health:* Geriatric Health, Health Organizations, Hospitals, Nutrition • *Religion:* Churches, Synagogues/Temples • *Science:* Science Exhibits & Fairs • *Social Services:* Child Welfare, Community Centers, Community Service Organizations, Domestic Violence, Food/Clothing Distribution, Recreation & Athletics, Shelters/Homelessness, Substance Abuse, Youth Organizations

Grant Types: multiyear/continuing support

Nonmonetary Support Types: cause-related marketing & promotion, donated equipment, donated products, in-kind services, and workplace solicitation

Geographic Distribution: only in headquarters area

Operating Locations: OH (Maumee, Toledo)

Note: Company operates 24 Food Town Supermarkets, 20 Food Town Plus Supermarkets, and 22 discount drug stores under the name of "Pharm."

CORP. OFFICERS
Richard B. Iott: *B* Columbus OH 1951 *ED* Hillsdale Coll *CURR EMPL* pres, dir: Seaway Food Town Inc

Wallace D. Iott: *CURR EMPL* chmn, ceo: Seaway Food Town Inc

GIVING OFFICERS
Pat Nowak: *CURR EMPL* dir pub rels & commun aff: Seaway Food Town Inc

APPLICATION INFORMATION
Initial Approach: *Initial Contact:* brief letter of inquiry and full proposal *Include Information On:* a description of organization, amount requested, purpose of funds sought, and proof of tax-exempt status *Deadlines:* one month in advance of date that funds are needed

Restrictions on Giving: Does not support individuals, political or lobbying groups, or organizations outside operating areas.

GRANTS ANALYSIS
Total Grants: $469,000*

Typical Range: $2,500 to $5,000

Disclosure Period: 1994

Note: Company reports that total grants figure is approximate.

RECENT GRANTS
General
American Heart Association, Toledo, OH
Easter Seals, Perrysburg, OH
Epilepsy Foundation, Toledo, OH
March of Dimes, Toledo, OH
National Family Service, Toledo, OH

Second Foundation

CONTACT
Phillip A. Ranney
Secretary
Second Foundation
1525 National City Bank Bldg.
Cleveland, OH 44114
(216) 696-4200

FINANCIAL SUMMARY
Recent Giving: $3,091,373 (1994); $8,217,262 (1993); $2,301,889 (1992)

Assets: $21,909,375 (1993); $28,022,833 (1992); $29,005,678 (1991)

EIN: 34-1436198

CONTRIBUTIONS SUMMARY
Donor(s): The foundation was established in 1984 by the 1525 Foundation.

Typical Recipients: • *Arts & Humanities:* Libraries, Museums/Galleries • *Civic & Public Affairs:* Community Foundations, General, Municipalities/Towns, Philanthropic Organizations, Women's Affairs • *Education:* Colleges & Universities, Private Education (Precollege) • *Environment:* General, Resource Conservation • *Health:* Health Funds, Hospitals, Hospitals (University Affiliated) • *Religion:* Religious Organizations, Religious Welfare • *Social Services:* Child Abuse, Child Welfare, Domestic Violence, Emergency Relief, Food/Clothing Distribution, YMCA/YWCA/YMHA/YWHA, Youth Organizations

Grant Types: endowment, general support, matching, multiyear/continuing support, operating expenses, and seed money

Geographic Distribution: focus on Cleveland, OH

GIVING OFFICERS
Phillip A. Ranney: secy, treas, dir *PHIL AFFIL* secy, treas: 1525 Foundation; secy: P. K. Ranney Foundation; counc, trust: Hugo H. and Mabel B. Young Foundation

Thelma G. Smith: pres, dir *PHIL AFFIL* vp: 1525 Foundation

APPLICATION INFORMATION
Initial Approach:

There are no formal grant application forms. Written applications should be sent to the foundation.

Written proposals should include a brief description of the organization, the purpose of the grant request, any applicable financial data, the names of other contributors to the project, and a copy of the organization's IRS tax-exempt letter.

The foundation has no deadlines for proposals.

The foundation's trustees meet frequently and will usually notify the organization one month after receipt of the proposal.

Restrictions on Giving: The foundation does not make loans and does not make grants to individuals.

GRANTS ANALYSIS
Total Grants: $8,217,262

Number of Grants: 13

Highest Grant: $7,556,857

Average Grant: $14,582*

Typical Range: $1,000 to $30,000

Disclosure Period: 1993

Note: Average grant figure excludes two high grants totaling $8,056,857. Recent grants are derived from a 1993 grants list.

RECENT GRANTS
Library
| 6,500 | Foundation Center, Cleveland, OH |
| 1,000 | Friends of Cleveland Public Library, Cleveland, OH |

General
7,556,857	Case Western Reserve University, Cleveland, OH
500,000	University Circle, Cleveland, OH
54,480	Berea College, Berea, KY
29,000	Bellflower Center for Prevention of Child Abuse, Cleveland, OH
25,000	Cleveland Recycling Center, Cleveland, OH

Slemp Foundation

CONTACT
John A. Reid
Trustee
Slemp Fdn.
c/o Star Bank, N.A.
Fifth & Walnut St.
Cincinnati, OH 45201
(513) 632-4579

FINANCIAL SUMMARY
Recent Giving: $566,108 (fiscal 1994); $497,909 (fiscal 1993); $597,597 (fiscal 1992)

Assets: $11,017,490 (fiscal 1994); $11,194,659 (fiscal 1993); $10,938,296 (fiscal 1992)

Gifts Received: $1,325 (fiscal 1994); $775 (fiscal 1993); $825 (fiscal 1992)

Fiscal Note: In fiscal 1994, contributions were received from Katherine MacMillan ($325), Tammy and Tommy Baker ($500), and Dr. David Kinsler ($500).

EIN: 31-6025080

CONTRIBUTIONS SUMMARY
Donor(s): the late C. Bascom Slemp

Typical Recipients: • *Arts & Humanities:* Arts Outreach, Community Arts, Libraries, Museums/Galleries, Music, Theater • *Civic & Public Affairs:* Clubs, Municipalities/Towns, Safety • *Education:* Agricultural Education, Arts/Humanities Education, Colleges & Universities, Community & Junior Colleges, General, Literacy, Private Education (Precollege), Public Education (Precollege), Science/Mathematics Education,

Secondary Education (Public), Student Aid • *Environment:* General • *Health:* Children's Health/Hospitals, Clinics/Medical Centers, Emergency/Ambulance Services • *Religion:* Religious Welfare • *Social Services:* Child Welfare, Community Service Organizations, People with Disabilities, Recreation & Athletics, Scouts, Youth Organizations

Grant Types: capital, emergency, endowment, scholarship, and seed money

Geographic Distribution: focus on TN and VA

GIVING OFFICERS
Star Bank, NA: trust

Campbell S. Edmonds: agent

Mary Virginia Edmonds: trust

John A. Reid: trust

Melissa Smith Sircy: trust

James Smith: trust

Nancey E. Smith: trust

APPLICATION INFORMATION
Initial Approach: Application forms provided for scholarship applicants. Deadline is October 1 for scholarships.

GRANTS ANALYSIS
Total Grants: $566,108

Number of Grants: 47

Highest Grant: $50,000

Typical Range: $100 to $25,000

Disclosure Period: fiscal year ending June 30, 1994

Note: Recent grants are derived from a fiscal 1994 Form 990. Number of grants and typical range do not include scholarships to individuals totaling $322,000.

RECENT GRANTS

Library
5,000	Lonesome Pine Regional Library, Wise, VA — toward the purchase of new cargo van
4,000	Lonesome Pine Library Literacy Project, Wise, VA — purchase of books for Literacy Project

General
50,000	Lee County High School, Jonesville, VA — final installment of pledge for auditorium
19,685	Appalachia Rescue Squad, Appalachia, VA — funds to purchase equipment and an ambulance
15,000	Appalachia Fire Department, Appalachia, VA
10,000	Lee County Public Schools, Jonesville, VA
10,000	Lee County Public Schools, Jonesville, VA — demonstration teaching project pledged

Smith Foundation, Kelvin and Eleanor

CONTACT
John L. Dampeer
Chairman, Treasurer, and Trustee
The Kelvin and Eleanor Smith Foundation
1100 Natl City Bank Bldg
Cleveland, OH 44114
(216) 566-5566

FINANCIAL SUMMARY
Recent Giving: $3,000,000 (fiscal 1995 est.); $2,800,000 (fiscal 1994 approx.); $2,671,100 (fiscal 1993)

Assets: $65,000,000 (fiscal 1995 est.); $62,000,000 (fiscal 1994 approx.); $61,124,490 (fiscal 1993)

Gifts Received: $2,098 (fiscal 1992); $14,920,981 (fiscal 1990); $713,436 (fiscal 1989)

Fiscal Note: In fiscal 1990 and 1992, gifts were received from the estate of Kelvin Smith.

EIN: 34-6555349

CONTRIBUTIONS SUMMARY
Donor(s): The foundation was established in 1955 by the late Kelvin Smith .

Typical Recipients: • *Arts & Humanities:* Arts Associations & Councils, Arts Centers, Arts Outreach, Historic Preservation, Libraries, Museums/Galleries, Music, Opera, Performing Arts, Public Broadcasting, Theater • *Civic & Public Affairs:* Botanical Gardens/Parks, Employment/Job Training, Public Policy • *Education:* Arts/Humanities Education, Colleges & Universities, Literacy, Private Education (Precollege), Public Education (Precollege), Special Education, Student Aid • *Environment:* General • *Health:* Clinics/Medical Centers, Eyes/Blindness, Health Organizations, Nursing Services • *International:* International Affairs • *Science:* Science Museums, Scientific Research • *Social Services:* Camps, Child Welfare, Community Service Organizations, Food/Clothing Distribution, People with Disabilities

Grant Types: general support and project

Geographic Distribution: focus on the greater Cleveland, OH area

GIVING OFFICERS
M. Roger Clapp: trust *PHIL AFFIL* pres: M. Roger and Anne Melby Clapp Foundation

John Lyell Dampeer: chmn, treas, trust *B* Cleveland OH 1916 *ED* Harvard Univ SB; Harvard Univ LLB *CURR EMPL* ptnr: Thompson Hine & Flory *CORP AFFIL* dir, secy: Van Dorn Co *NONPR AFFIL* mem: Am Bar Assn, Cleveland Bar Assn, OH Bar Assn, Phi Beta Kappa; vp, treas, dir: Sea Res Fdn *CLUB AFFIL* Kirtland CC, Union *PHIL AFFIL* trust: Kelvin Smith 1980 Charitable Trust; pres, treas, secy, trust: Marlboro 2465 Foundation

Michael D. Eppig, M.D.: trust

Andrew L. Fabens III: asst secy *B* Washington DC 1942 *ED* Yale Univ AB 1964; Univ Chicago JD 1967 *CURR EMPL* ptnr: Thompson Hine & Flory *NONPR AFFIL* fellow: Am Coll Trust & Estate Couns; mem: Cleveland Bar Assn, OH St Bar Assn; secy, dir: Sea Res Fdn; trust: Am McGregor Home, Bascom Little Fund *PHIL AFFIL* trust: Eleanor Armstrong Smith Charitable Fund

Ellen S. Mavec: secy, trust

Lucia S. Nash: vp, trust

Lincoln Reavis: trust *B* Cleveland OH 1933 *ED* Cornell Univ BA 1955; Harvard Univ JD 1959 *CURR EMPL* ptnr: Spieth Bell McCurdy & Newell *NONPR AFFIL* fellow: Am Coll Trust Estate Couns; mem: Am Bar Assn, Cleveland Bar Assn; trust: Hawken Sch, Holden Arboretum, Judson Retirement Commun, Univ Circle *CLUB AFFIL* mem: Rowfant, Tavern, Union *PHIL AFFIL* trust: Switzer Foundation

Cara S. Stirn: vp, trust

APPLICATION INFORMATION
Initial Approach:

An initial written application should be submitted to the foundation. Telephone inquiries are discouraged.

The application should identify the applicant and its tax status, the nature of the project, its budget requirements, and the amount and scope of the requested grant. If the project appears to be of interest, but additional information is required, the foundation will request such information before taking action on the application. Personal interviews may be scheduled by appointment in some instances.

There are no deadlines for submitting proposals.

Restrictions on Giving: Applicants must be tax-exempt under Sections 509(a)(1), (2), and (3) of the IRS. The foundation does not make grants to private foundations or to individuals. An applicant may make only one request in a twelve month period.

PUBLICATIONS
Application guidelines

GRANTS ANALYSIS
Total Grants: $2,671,100

Number of Grants: 34

Highest Grant: $1,700,000

Average Grant: $29,427*

Typical Range: $1,000 to $10,000 and $25,000 to $50,000

Disclosure Period: fiscal year ending October 31, 1993

Note: The average grant figure excludes the largest grant of $1,700,000. Recent grants are derived from a fiscal 1993 grants list.

RECENT GRANTS

Library
1,700,000	Case Western Reserve University, Cleveland, OH — Kelvin Smith Library

10,000	Cleveland Medical Library Association, Cleveland, OH — capital campaign
2,900	Foundation Center, Cleveland, OH

General

150,000	Hathaway Brown School, Shaker Heights, OH — capital campaign
55,000	Cleveland Society for the Blind, Cleveland, OH — land acquisition
33,500	Holden Arboretum, Mentor, OH — horticulture science center
17,200	Vocational Guidance Services, Cleveland, OH
15,000	Cleveland Museum of Natural History, Cleveland, OH

South Waite Foundation

CONTACT
Thomas P. Demeter
Trustee
South Waite Fdn.
c/o Society National Bank, Custodian
127 Public Square, Mail Code OH-01-27-1800
Cleveland, OH 44114-1306
(216) 689-1088

FINANCIAL SUMMARY
Recent Giving: $126,000 (1993); $134,000 (1992); $139,000 (1991)

Assets: $2,249,682 (1993); $2,261,148 (1992); $2,203,958 (1991)

EIN: 34-6526411

CONTRIBUTIONS SUMMARY
Donor(s): the late Francis M. Sherwin, Margaret H. Sherwin

Typical Recipients: • *Arts & Humanities:* Arts Associations & Councils, Historic Preservation, History & Archaeology, Libraries, Museums/Galleries, Music, Public Broadcasting • *Civic & Public Affairs:* Botanical Gardens/Parks, General • *Education:* Colleges & Universities, Health & Physical Education, Minority Education, Private Education (Precollege), Student Aid • *Environment:* General, Resource Conservation, Wildlife Protection • *Health:* Clinics/Medical Centers, Health Organizations, Hospitals, Medical Rehabilitation, Medical Research, Speech & Hearing • *International:* International Environmental Issues, International Organizations • *Science:* Science Museums, Scientific Centers & Institutes, Scientific Labs • *Social Services:* Community Service Organizations, Delinquency & Criminal Rehabilitation, Family Planning, People with Disabilities, Substance Abuse, United Funds/United Ways, YMCA/YWCA/YMHA/YWHA, Youth Organizations

Grant Types: capital, multiyear/continuing support, and operating expenses

Geographic Distribution: limited to the Cleveland, OH, area

GIVING OFFICERS
Society National Bank: trust

Sherman Dye: mem, trust *B* Portland OR 1915 *ED* Oberlin Coll AB 1937; Case Western Reserve Univ LLB 1940 *CURR EMPL* ptnr: Baker & Hostetler *NONPR AFFIL* chmn: First Baptist Church Greater Cleveland; mem: Am Bar Assn, Cleveland Bar Assn, Coll Club Cleveland, OH Bar Assn, Order Coif, Phi Delta Phi, Soc Benchers; mem, trust: Assn Continuing Ed; treas: Am Cancer Soc Cleveland

Donald W. Gruetner: trust, secy, treas

Brian Sherwin: trust, pres

Dennis Sherwin: mem

Margaret H. Sherwin: trust, vp

Peter Sherwin: mem

Peter Sherwin: mem (see above)

APPLICATION INFORMATION
Initial Approach: The foundation has no formal grant application procedure or application form. There are no deadlines.

GRANTS ANALYSIS
Total Grants: $126,000

Number of Grants: 31

Highest Grant: $12,000

Typical Range: $2,000 to $10,000

Disclosure Period: 1993

Note: Recent grants are derived from a 1993 Form 990.

RECENT GRANTS

General

12,000	United Way Services, Cleveland, OH — operations
10,000	Society for Rehabilitation, Mentor, OH — special MHS endowment
8,000	Alcoholism Services of Cleveland, Cleveland, OH — operating
8,000	Jackson Laboratory, Bar Harbor, ME — annual fund
7,000	Cleveland Clinic Foundation, Cleveland, OH — F.M. Sherwin radiology fund

Tait Foundation, Frank M.

CONTACT
Susan T. Rankin
Executive Director
Frank M. Tait Fdn.
Courthouse Plaza, S.W., 5th fl.
Dayton, OH 45402
(513) 222-2401

FINANCIAL SUMMARY
Recent Giving: $262,589 (1993); $269,225 (1992); $259,625 (1991)

Assets: $5,962,254 (1993); $5,837,530 (1992); $5,897,962 (1991)

EIN: 31-6037499

CONTRIBUTIONS SUMMARY
Donor(s): the late Frank M. Tait, the late Mrs. Frank M. Tait

Typical Recipients: • *Arts & Humanities:* Arts Associations & Councils, Arts Centers, Arts Institutes, Community Arts, Dance, Film & Video, Historic Preservation, Libraries, Museums/Galleries, Music, Opera, Performing Arts, Public Broadcasting, Theater, Visual Arts • *Civic & Public Affairs:* African American Affairs, Botanical Gardens/Parks, Chambers of Commerce, Community Foundations, Employment/Job Training, Housing, Municipalities/Towns, Nonprofit Management, Philanthropic Organizations, Professional & Trade Associations, Urban & Community Affairs • *Education:* Colleges & Universities, Education Funds, Education Reform, General, Secondary Education (Public) • *Environment:* General • *Health:* Health Funds, Health Organizations • *Science:* Science Museums • *Social Services:* At-Risk Youth, Child Welfare, Community Centers, Community Service Organizations, Counseling, Family Planning, Family Services, People with Disabilities, Scouts, United Funds/United Ways, YMCA/YWCA/YMHA/YWHA, Youth Organizations

Grant Types: general support

Geographic Distribution: focus on Montgomery County, OH

GIVING OFFICERS
Richard F. Beach: trust *PHIL AFFIL* admin: Kettering Fund

Peter Hans Forster: vp, trust *B* Berlin Germany 1942 *ED* Univ WI BS 1964; Brooklyn Law Sch JD 1972 *CURR EMPL* chmn: Dayton Power & Light Co *CORP AFFIL* chmn, ceo, pres: DPL Inc; dir: Amcast Indus Corp, Bank One Dayton, CH Gosiger Machinery Co, Comair Inc *NONPR AFFIL* dir: Miami Valley Hosp, Pub Ed Fund Gov Bd, Un Negro Coll Fund; mem: Am Bar Assn, Dayton Area Chamber Commerce, Dayton Bar Assn, Edison Electric Inst, OH Bar Assn; trust: Comm Econ Devel, Med Am Health Sys

Robert James Kegerreis: trust *B* Detroit MI 1921 *ED* OH State Univ BA 1943; OH State Univ BS 1943; OH State Univ PhD 1968; Univ Dayton PhD 1968 *CURR EMPL* consult: RJK Co *CORP AFFIL* dir: Bank One Dayton NA, Bank One Ohio Trust Co, DPL, Elder-Beerman Stores, Robbins & Meyers; exec vp: Spectra Group *NONPR AFFIL* exec dir: Arts Ctr Fdn *CLUB AFFIL* mem: Bicycle, Buz Fuz, Dayton City, Moraine CC, Pelican Bay CC

Susan T. Rankin: secy, treas, exec dir

Frederick W. Schantz: pres, trust

Alexander J. Williams: trust

APPLICATION INFORMATION
Initial Approach: Include a description of organization, amount requested, purpose of funds sought, recently audited financial statement, and proof of tax-exempt status. Deadlines are March 15, June 15, September 15, and December 15.

Restrictions on Giving: Limited to Montgomery County, OH. The foundation does not make grants to individuals.

GRANTS ANALYSIS
Total Grants: $262,589

Number of Grants: 45

Highest Grant: $30,009

Typical Range: $200 to $21,000

Disclosure Period: 1993

Note: Recent grants are derived from a 1993 Form 990.

RECENT GRANTS

Library

350	Foundation Center, Cleveland, OH — operating budget of Cleveland Library

General

30,009	Dayton Society of Natural History, Dayton, OH — Bieser Discovery Center
21,000	United Way of the Greater Dayton Area, Dayton, OH — Venture grant program
20,000	YWCA, Dayton, OH — capital campaign
7,500	Dayton Foundation, Dayton, OH — Human Services Education Fund
7,500	Goodwill Industries, Dayton, OH — literacy program expansion

Timken Foundation of Canton

CONTACT
Don D. Dickes
Secretary-Treasurer
Timken Foundation of Canton
236 Third St., S.W.
Canton, OH 44702
(216) 455-5281

FINANCIAL SUMMARY
Recent Giving: $7,500,000 (fiscal 1995 est.); $7,142,917 (fiscal 1994); $8,343,807 (fiscal 1993)

Assets: $160,000,000 (fiscal 1995 est.); $156,000,000 (fiscal 1994); $142,102,125 (fiscal 1993)

Gifts Received: $2,967,000 (fiscal 1988)

EIN: 34-6520254

CONTRIBUTIONS SUMMARY
Donor(s): The foundation was established in 1934. Donors are members of the Timken family. The Timken family fortune stems from Timken Company, a manufacturer of roller bearings and alloy steel.

Typical Recipients: • *Arts & Humanities:* Arts Centers, Arts Institutes, Historic Preservation, History & Archaeology, Libraries, Museums/Galleries, Theater • *Civic & Public Affairs:* Business/Free Enterprise, Chambers of Commerce, Economic Development, Housing, Municipalities/Towns, Parades/Festivals, Philanthropic Organizations • *Education:* Afterschool/Enrichment Programs, Colleges & Universities, Community & Junior Colleges, Education Funds, Education Reform, Minority Education, Private Education (Precollege), Public Education (Precollege), Student Aid • *Health:* Emergency/Ambulance Services, Hospitals • *International:* Foreign Arts Organizations, Foreign Educational Institutions, Health Care/Hospitals, International Organizations, International Peace & Security Issues, Missionary/Religious Activities • *Religion:* Religious Organizations • *Social Services:* Community Service Organizations, Day Care, Family Services, Food/Clothing Distribution, Recreation & Athletics, YMCA/YWCA/YMHA/YWHA, Youth Organizations

Grant Types: capital

Geographic Distribution: broad geographic distribution, with emphasis on Canton, OH; some international giving

GIVING OFFICERS
Don D. Dickes: secy, treas, trust

Ward J. Timken: pres, trust *B* 1942 *CURR EMPL* vp, dir: Timken Co *PHIL AFFIL* off: The Timken Company Charitable Trust; pres: Timken Co. Educational Fund

William Robert Timken: vp, trust

William Robert Timken, Jr.: vp, trust *B* Canton OH 1938 *ED* Stanford Univ BA 1960; Harvard Univ MBA 1962 *CURR EMPL* chmn, chmn exec comm, chmn fin comm, dir: Timken Co *CORP AFFIL* beneficial owner: Concurrent Computer Corp; dir: Diebold Inc, LA Land & Exploration Co, Trinova Corp *PHIL AFFIL* trust: Edith M. Timken Family Foundation; don, pres, trust: W. R. Timken Jr. Family Foundation; trust: Timken Family Charitable Trust

APPLICATION INFORMATION
Initial Approach:

Grant requests should be in writing.

No specific form of application is required; however, the application must include proof of tax-exempt status under Internal Revenue Code 501(c)(3).

There are no deadlines for application.

GRANTS ANALYSIS
Total Grants: $7,142,917

Number of Grants: 68

Highest Grant: $870,000

Average Grant: $100,000*

Typical Range: $5,000 to $400,000*

Disclosure Period: fiscal year ending September 30, 1994

Note: The average grant figure and the typical grant range were supplied by the foundation. Recent grants are derived from a fiscal 1993 Form 990.

RECENT GRANTS

Library

86,805	Read Education Trust, Braamfontein, Republic of South Africa — Read Library advisor

General

345,000	YMCA, Canton, OH — renovation of Residence Hall
250,000	Limestone College, Gaffney, SC — renovate buildings
180,000	Habitat for Humanity of Greater Canton, Canton, OH — construction and renovation of homes
150,000	Alliance Area Chamber of Commerce, Alliance, OH — Alliance Community Improvement Project
150,000	Dartmouth College, Hanover, NH — school leadership project

Van Wert County Foundation

CONTACT
Robert W. Games
Executive Secretary
Van Wert County Fdn.
101 1/2 E Main St.
Van Wert, OH 45891
(419) 238-1743

FINANCIAL SUMMARY
Recent Giving: $429,691 (1993); $545,943 (1991); $276,238 (1990)

Assets: $11,776,905 (1993); $10,152,048 (1991); $6,792,272 (1990)

Gifts Received: $661,663 (1993); $57,947 (1991); $19,905 (1990)

Fiscal Note: In 1993, contributions were received from the Rose R. and Ellis C. Lampe Fund ($11,,238), the Arnold J. Lippi Educational Trust ($328,000), the Gaylord and Eliza Saltzgaber Music Fund ($18,337), the Donald R. and Mary Pauline Neubrecht Scholarship Fund ($11,815), the Harold B. and Dorthea F. Cully Memorial Fund ($172,000), and the Walter W. James and Jennie L. Jones Memorial ($100,000); 11 other donors made contributions of less than $5,000.

EIN: 34-0907558

CONTRIBUTIONS SUMMARY
Donor(s): the late Charles F. Wassenberg, Gaylord Saltzgaber, the late John D. Ault, Kernan Wright, the late Richard L. Klein, the late Hazel Gleason, the late Constance Eirich

Typical Recipients: • *Arts & Humanities:* Arts Centers, Arts Institutes, Historic Preservation, History & Archaeology, Libraries, Museums/Galleries, Music, Performing Arts, Theater • *Civic & Public Affairs:* Botanical Gardens/Parks, Housing, Municipalities/Towns, Parades/Festivals, Safety • *Education:* Afterschool/Enrichment Programs, Agricultural Education, Arts/Humanities Education, General, Private Education (Precollege), Public Education (Precollege) • *Environment:* Resource Conservation • *Health:* Hospitals • *Religion:* Churches • *Social Services:* Animal Protection, Child Welfare,

Community Service Organizations, Day Care, Domestic Violence, People with Disabilities, Recreation & Athletics, United Funds/United Ways, YMCA/YWCA/YMHA/YWHA, Youth Organizations

Grant Types: general support and scholarship

Geographic Distribution: limited to Van Wert County, OH

GIVING OFFICERS
D. L. Brumback, Jr.: trust

William S. Derry: trust

Robert W. Games: exec secy

Bruce C. Kennedy: trust

Kenneth Koch: trust *ED* Univ PA 1976; OH St Univ 1979

Gaylord E. Leslie: trust

Watson Ley: trust

Paul W. Purmort, Jr.: trust

Charles F. Ross: trust

C. Allan Runser: trust

Donald C. Sutton: trust

Roger K. Thompson: trust *ED* Rensselaer Polytech Inst 1951 *CURR EMPL* pres: Kennedy Mfg Co

Sumner J. Walters: trust

Larry L. Wendel: vp

G. Dale Wilson: trust

Michael R. Zedaker: trust

APPLICATION INFORMATION
Initial Approach: Application forms and guidelines issued for scholarship program.

Restrictions on Giving: Does not provide loans.

PUBLICATIONS
Application Guidelines

GRANTS ANALYSIS
Total Grants: $429,691

Number of Grants: 63

Highest Grant: $31,850

Typical Range: $300 to $29,200

Disclosure Period: 1993

Note: Recent grants are derived from a 1993 Form 990. Number of grants and typical range do not include grants to individuals.

RECENT GRANTS
Library
10,000	Brombeck Library, Van Wert, OH — development of computer program
1,000	Antwerp Library, Antwerp, OH
1,000	Paulding County Library, Paulding, OH

General
29,200	YMCA, Van Wert, OH
29,200	YWCA, Van Wert, OH
16,674	Van Wert City Schools, Van Wert, OH — indigent children
13,000	Van Wert Extension Service, Van Wert, OH

8,460	Van Wert City Schools, Van Wert, OH — music department

Wean Foundation, Raymond John

CONTACT
Raymond J. Wean, Jr.
Chairman
Raymond John Wean Foundation
PO Box 760
Warren, OH 44482
(216) 394-5600

FINANCIAL SUMMARY
Recent Giving: $2,167,522 (1993); $2,667,093 (1992); $2,472,531 (1991)

Assets: $51,995,265 (1993); $50,092,965 (1992); $47,088,534 (1991)

Gifts Received: $1,325 (1989); $4,784,564 (1988)

Fiscal Note: In 1988, the foundation received a gift from the estate of Sara R. Wean of Warren, Ohio.

EIN: 34-6505038

CONTRIBUTIONS SUMMARY
Donor(s): Raymond J. Wean (1895-1980) established the foundation in 1949. Mr. Wean was chairman of Wean United and the Second National Bank of Warren, OH. He was also a trustee of the Community Chest of Palm Beach, American Institute of Economics, Trinity College, and Carnegie-Mellon University.

Typical Recipients: • *Arts & Humanities:* Arts Associations & Councils, Arts Centers, Arts Festivals, Arts Funds, Arts Institutes, Dance, Historic Preservation, Libraries, Literary Arts, Museums/Galleries, Music, Opera, Public Broadcasting, Theater • *Civic & Public Affairs:* Clubs, Economic Development, Employment/Job Training, Municipalities/Towns, Professional & Trade Associations, Public Policy, Safety, Urban & Community Affairs, Women's Affairs, Zoos/Aquariums • *Education:* Arts/Humanities Education, Colleges & Universities, Continuing Education, Education Associations, Education Funds, Faculty Development, Legal Education, Medical Education, Minority Education, Private Education (Precollege), Public Education (Precollege), Religious Education, Science/Mathematics Education, Student Aid • *Environment:* General • *Health:* Health Organizations, Hospices, Hospitals, Medical Rehabilitation, Mental Health, Nursing Services, Single-Disease Health Associations • *International:* International Relations • *Religion:* Churches, Religious Organizations, Religious Welfare • *Science:* Scientific Research • *Social Services:* Animal Protection, Child Welfare, Family Planning, Food/Clothing Distribution, Homes, People with Disabilities, Recreation & Athletics, Scouts, Senior Services, Substance Abuse, United Funds/United Ways, Youth Organizations

Grant Types: capital, department, endowment, general support, project, research, and scholarship

Geographic Distribution: national, emphasis on Ohio and the eastern states

GIVING OFFICERS
Roberta Fenwick: admin

Gordon B. Wean: mem bd adms

Raymond John Wean III: vchmn bd adms *B* 1948 *ED* Babson Coll BS 1973; Babson Coll BA 1973 *CURR EMPL* pres, dir: Danieli Wean

Raymond John Wean, Jr.: don, chmn bd adms *B* Warren OH 1921 *ED* Yale Univ BA 1943 *CURR EMPL* chmn: Wean Inc *CORP AFFIL* dir: Second Natl Bank Warren OH

APPLICATION INFORMATION
Initial Approach:

Applicants should send a letter of inquiry. There are no formal guidelines or application forms.

In the initial letter, applicants should include an outline of the proposed project and proof of tax exemption.

A four-member board of administrators makes all decisions regarding applications.

GRANTS ANALYSIS
Total Grants: $2,167,522

Number of Grants: 771

Highest Grant: $250,000

Average Grant: $2,811

Typical Range: $100 to $500 and $1,000 to $25,000

Disclosure Period: 1993

Note: Recent grants are derived from a 1993 Form 990.

RECENT GRANTS
Library
50,000	Blair Academy, Blairstown, NJ — library and faculty study

General
250,000	Miss Porter's School, Farmington, CT — 150th anniversary campaign student center
250,000	Palm Beach Day School, Palm Beach, FL — capital campaign
150,000	Pine Manor College, Chestnut Hill, MA — Class of '44 Special Gift Program
150,000	University School — Faculty Children's Educational Fund
75,000	Wooster School, Danbury, CT — capital campaign endowment

Wildermuth Foundation, E. F.

CONTACT
Homer W. Lee
Treasurer
E. F. Wildermuth Fdn.
1014 Dublin Rd.
Columbus, OH 43215-1116
(614) 487-0040

FINANCIAL SUMMARY
Recent Giving: $180,578 (1993); $178,611 (1992); $180,039 (1991)

Assets: $3,526,332 (1993); $3,373,398 (1992); $3,271,310 (1991)

Gifts Received: $35,000 (1989); $50,000 (1988)

EIN: 31-6050202

CONTRIBUTIONS SUMMARY
Typical Recipients: • *Arts & Humanities:* Ballet, Dance, History & Archaeology, Libraries, Music, Public Broadcasting • *Civic & Public Affairs:* General • *Education:* Arts/Humanities Education, Business Education, Colleges & Universities, Medical Education, Minority Education, Public Education (Precollege) • *Health:* Children's Health/Hospitals, Emergency/Ambulance Services, Health Organizations, Heart, Hospitals, Respiratory • *Religion:* Churches, Religious Organizations • *Social Services:* Animal Protection, Big Brother/Big Sister, Child Welfare, Community Service Organizations, People with Disabilities, United Funds/United Ways, Youth Organizations

Grant Types: general support

Geographic Distribution: focus on OH

GIVING OFFICERS
Karl Borton: trust

J. Patrick Campbell: trust

Genevieve Connable: secy, trust

H. Ward Ewalt: pres, trust

Bettie A. Kalb: vp, trust

Homer W. Lee: treas, trust *PHIL AFFIL* trust: Richard H. and Ann Shafer Foundation

Robert W. Lee: trust

David R. Patterson: asst to pres, trust

David T. Patterson: trust *PHIL AFFIL* treas: Mount Aloysius Foundation

Phillip N. Phillipson: trust

APPLICATION INFORMATION
Initial Approach: The foundation has no formal grant application procedure or application form. Include a description of organization, amount requested, purpose of funds sought, recently audited financial statement, and proof of tax-exempt status. Deadline is August 1.

Restrictions on Giving: Limited to Optometric education and visual research.

GRANTS ANALYSIS
Total Grants: $180,578

Number of Grants: 25

Highest Grant: $48,334

Typical Range: $100 to $36,144

Disclosure Period: 1993

Note: Recent grants are derived from a 1993 Form 990.

RECENT GRANTS
Library
1,000   Ohioan Library Association, Columbus, OH

General
48,334   Ohio State University College of Optometry, Columbus, OH
36,144   Wildermuth Memorial Church, Carroll, OH
25,000   Pennsylvania College of Optometry, Philadelphia, PA
9,000   Illinois College of Optometry, Chicago, IL
9,000   Pilot Dogs, Columbus, OH

Worthington Foods / Worthington Foods Foundation

Sales: $25.0 million
Employees: 480
Headquarters: Worthington, OH
SIC Major Group: Food & Kindred Products

CONTACT
Allan R. Butler
Trustee
Worthington Foods
825 Proprietors Rd.
Worthington, OH 43085
(614) 885-9511

FINANCIAL SUMMARY
Recent Giving: $24,300 (fiscal 1994); $29,000 (fiscal 1993); $32,000 (fiscal 1992)

Assets: $8,823 (fiscal 1994); $3,123 (fiscal 1993); $7,153 (fiscal 1992)

Gifts Received: $30,000 (fiscal 1994); $25,000 (fiscal 1993); $30,000 (fiscal 1992)

Fiscal Note: In fiscal 1994, contributions were received from Worthington Foods.

EIN: 31-1286538

CONTRIBUTIONS SUMMARY
Typical Recipients: • *Arts & Humanities:* History & Archaeology, Libraries • *Education:* Colleges & Universities, Education Funds, Health & Physical Education, Medical Education, Minority Education, Private Education (Precollege), Student Aid • *Health:* Adolescent Health Issues, Alzheimers Disease, Children's Health/Hospitals, Heart, Nutrition • *Religion:* Religious Organizations • *Social Services:* People with Disabilities

Grant Types: general support, project, and scholarship

Geographic Distribution: focus on CA and OH

CORP. OFFICERS
Allan R. Buller: *CURR EMPL* chmn, treas, dir: Worthington Foods

William T. Kirkwood: *CURR EMPL* cfo, vp fin, dir: Worthington Foods

Dale E. Twomley: *CURR EMPL* pres, ceo, dir: Worthington Foods

GIVING OFFICERS
Allan R. Buller: trust *CURR EMPL* chmn, treas, dir: Worthington Foods (see above)

George T. Harding: trust

George T. Harding IV: trust

Dale E. Twomley: trust *CURR EMPL* pres, ceo, dir: Worthington Foods (see above)

APPLICATION INFORMATION
Initial Approach: Send a brief letter of inquiry. Include a description of organization, amount requested, purpose of funds sought, recently audited financial statement, and proof of tax-exempt status. There are no deadlines.

GRANTS ANALYSIS
Total Grants: $24,300

Number of Grants: 8

Highest Grant: $10,000

Typical Range: $300 to $5,000

Disclosure Period: fiscal year ending April 30, 1994

Note: Recent grants are derived from a fiscal 1994 Form 990.

RECENT GRANTS
Library
1,000   Pacific Union College, Angwin, CA — library equipment

General
10,000   American Heart Association, Columbus, OH — support association activities
5,000   Andrews University, Berrien Springs, MI — congress on diet and nutrition
3,500   Harding Evans Foundation, Worthington, OH — building fund for care of children and adolescents
2,000   Kettering Medical Center Fund, Kettering, OH — education scholarship
1,500   Seventh Day Adventist Dietetic Association, Loma Linda, CA — education scholarship

---

Young Foundation, Hugo H. and Mabel B.

CONTACT
James S. Lingenfelter
Secretary-Treasurer
Hugo H. and Mabel B. Young Fdn.
c/o Farmers Bank
PO Box 179
Loudonville, OH 44842
(419) 994-4115

FINANCIAL SUMMARY
Recent Giving: $340,680 (fiscal 1994); $280,934 (fiscal 1993); $241,495 (fiscal 1992)

Assets: $4,049,012 (fiscal 1994); $4,326,670 (fiscal 1993); $4,159,779 (fiscal 1992)

EIN: 34-6560664

CONTRIBUTIONS SUMMARY
Typical Recipients: • *Arts & Humanities:* Community Arts, Libraries, Music • *Civic & Public Affairs:* Community Foundations, Economic Development, Professional & Trade Associations, Rural Affairs, Safety • *Education:* Private Education (Precollege), Public Education (Precollege), Student Aid • *Health:* Cancer, Clinics/Medical Centers, Health Organizations, Hospitals • *Social Services:* Community Service Organizations, People with Disabilities, Scouts, Senior Services, Youth Organizations

Grant Types: capital and scholarship

Geographic Distribution: focus on Ashland County, OH

GIVING OFFICERS
Robert Dubler: trust

James Dudte: pres, trust

Avery C. Hand, Jr.: trust

James S. Lingenfelter: secy, treas, trust

R. D. Mayer: vp, trust

Phillip A. Ranney: counc, trust *PHIL AFFIL* secy, treas: 1525 Foundation; secy: P. K. Ranney Foundation; secy, treas, dir: Second Foundation

APPLICATION INFORMATION
Initial Approach: Send a brief letter of inquiry. Include a description of organization, amount requested, purpose of funds sought, recently audited financial statement, and proof of tax-exempt status. There are no deadlines.

Restrictions on Giving: Does not support individuals or provide loans.

GRANTS ANALYSIS
Total Grants: $340,680

Number of Grants: 10

Highest Grant: $155,000

Typical Range: $2,500 to $96,230

Disclosure Period: fiscal year ending April 30, 1994

Note: Recent grants are derived from a fiscal 1994 Form 990.

RECENT GRANTS
Library

31,000	Loudonville Public Library, Loudonville, OH

General

155,000	Kettering Mohican Area Medical Center, Loudonville, OH
96,230	Loudonville-Perrysville School, Loudonville, OH
30,000	Mohican Area Growth Foundation, Loudonville, OH
8,000	Loudonville-Perrysville Scholarship, Loudonville, OH

5,950	West Holmes School, Loudonville, OH

OKLAHOMA

American Fidelity Corporation / American Fidelity Corporation Founders Fund

Sales: $355.99 million
Employees: 1,100
Headquarters: Oklahoma City, OK

CONTACT
Dortha Dever
Assistant Vice President
American Fidelity Corporation
2000 Classen Center
Oklahoma City, OK 73106
(405) 523-5372

FINANCIAL SUMMARY
Recent Giving: $246,167 (fiscal 1993); $234,556 (fiscal 1992); $259,762 (fiscal 1991)

Assets: $3,321,846 (fiscal 1993); $3,078,172 (fiscal 1992); $2,906,290 (fiscal 1991)

Gifts Received: $200,000 (fiscal 1993); $85,607 (fiscal 1992); $335,162 (fiscal 1991)

Fiscal Note: In fiscal 1993, contributions were received from the American Fidelity Assurance Co.

EIN: 73-1236059

CONTRIBUTIONS SUMMARY
Typical Recipients: • *Arts & Humanities:* Arts Associations & Councils, Arts Funds, Arts Institutes, Ballet, Historic Preservation, History & Archaeology, Libraries, Museums/Galleries, Music, Theater • *Civic & Public Affairs:* Community Foundations, Economic Development, General, Municipalities/Towns, Urban & Community Affairs, Zoos/Aquariums • *Education:* Business Education, Colleges & Universities, Community & Junior Colleges, Faculty Development, Private Education (Precollege), Public Education (Precollege), Science/Mathematics Education • *Environment:* Resource Conservation • *Health:* Arthritis, Clinics/Medical Centers, Heart, Hospitals, Single-Disease Health Associations • *Religion:* Churches, Ministries • *Science:* Science Museums • *Social Services:* Big Brother/Big Sister, Community Service Organizations, People with Disabilities, Recreation & Athletics, United Funds/United Ways, YMCA/YWCA/YMHA/YWHA, Youth Organizations

Grant Types: general support

Geographic Distribution: focus on OK

CORP. OFFICERS
Dortha Dever: *CURR EMPL* asst vp: Am Fidelity Corp

William E. Durrett: *CURR EMPL* chmn: Am Fidelity Corp

John Rex: *CURR EMPL* exec vp, cfo: Am Fidelity Corp

GIVING OFFICERS
Dortha Dever: secy *CURR EMPL* asst vp: Am Fidelity Corp (see above)

William E. Durrett: pres *CURR EMPL* chmn: Am Fidelity Corp (see above)

John Rex: treas *CURR EMPL* exec vp, cfo: Am Fidelity Corp (see above)

APPLICATION INFORMATION
Initial Approach: Send letter requesting application form.

GRANTS ANALYSIS
Total Grants: $246,167

Number of Grants: 130

Highest Grant: $37,522

Typical Range: $50 to $18,800

Disclosure Period: fiscal year ending June 30, 1993

Note: Recent grants are derived from a fiscal 1993 Form 990.

RECENT GRANTS
Library

5,000	Endowment Trust of Metro Library System, Oklahoma City, OK
5,000	Endowment Trust of Metro Library System, Oklahoma City, OK — urban/civic

General

37,522	United Way, Oklahoma City, OK
35,823	United Way, Oklahoma City, OK
20,000	Omniplex Science and Arts Museum, Oklahoma City, OK
18,000	Westminster Church, Oklahoma City, OK
12,155	Oklahoma City Public School Foundation, Oklahoma City, OK

Beatty Trust, Cordelia Lunceford

CONTACT
James R. Rodgers
Trustee
Cordelia Lunceford Beatty Trust
PO Box 514
Blackwell, OK 74631
(405) 363-3684

FINANCIAL SUMMARY
Recent Giving: $75,078 (1993); $72,803 (1992); $73,991 (1991)

Assets: $2,006,970 (1993); $1,912,699 (1992); $1,847,488 (1991)

EIN: 73-6094952

CONTRIBUTIONS SUMMARY

Typical Recipients: • *Arts & Humanities:* Libraries, Music • *Civic & Public Affairs:* Municipalities/Towns, Safety • *Education:* Agricultural Education, Colleges & Universities, Literacy, Private Education (Precollege), Public Education (Precollege), Religious Education, Secondary Education (Public) • *Social Services:* Community Service Organizations, People with Disabilities, Recreation & Athletics, Scouts, United Funds/United Ways, Youth Organizations

Grant Types: scholarship

Geographic Distribution: limited to Blackwell, OK

GIVING OFFICERS

James R. Rodgers: trust *PHIL AFFIL* trust: Cordelia Lee Beattie Foundation Trust

William W. Rodgers: trust *PHIL AFFIL* trust: Cordelia Lee Beattie Foundation Trust

APPLICATION INFORMATION

Initial Approach: The foundation has no formal grant application procedure or application form. There are no deadlines.

GRANTS ANALYSIS

Total Grants: $75,078

Number of Grants: 23

Highest Grant: $7,784

Typical Range: 300 to $7,784

Disclosure Period: 1993

Note: Recent grants are derived from a 1993 Form 990.

RECENT GRANTS

Library
1,000	Blackwell Public Library, Blackwell, OK — children's books

General
7,784	Anthonys Department Store, Blackwell, OK — Rotary Christmas party
6,500	Blackwell Youth Center, Blackwell, OK
6,300	Blackwell Baseball, Blackwell, OK
3,681	Blackwell Public Schools, Blackwell, OK — grant applications
3,500	Associated Charities, Blackwell, OK

Broadhurst Foundation

CONTACT
Ann Cassidy Baker
Chairman
Broadhurst Fdn.
401 S Boston, Ste. 100
Tulsa, OK 74103
(918) 584-0661

FINANCIAL SUMMARY
Recent Giving: $154,527 (1993); $162,523 (1992); $135,902 (1991)

Assets: $6,283,598 (1993); $6,138,802 (1992); $6,009,758 (1991)

EIN: 73-6061115

CONTRIBUTIONS SUMMARY
Donor(s): William Broadhurst

Typical Recipients: • *Arts & Humanities:* Arts Centers, Libraries, Museums/Galleries, Opera • *Civic & Public Affairs:* Zoos/Aquariums • *Education:* Colleges & Universities, Medical Education, Private Education (Precollege), Religious Education, Student Aid • *Health:* Eyes/Blindness, Medical Research, Respiratory, Single-Disease Health Associations • *Religion:* Churches, Religious Organizations, Seminaries • *Social Services:* Community Service Organizations, United Funds/United Ways, Youth Organizations

Grant Types: capital, fellowship, loan, multiyear/continuing support, research, scholarship, and seed money

Geographic Distribution: focus on the Midwest, particularly OK

GIVING OFFICERS
Ann Cassidy Baker: chmn
John Cassidy, Jr.: trust
Clint V. Cox: trust
Ernestine Broadhurst Howard: vchmn
Wishard Lemons: trust

APPLICATION INFORMATION
Initial Approach: Send brief letter of inquiry or full proposal. There are no deadlines.

Restrictions on Giving: Limited to educational, religious, and medical research institutions in the Midwest.

PUBLICATIONS
Annual Report

GRANTS ANALYSIS
Total Grants: $154,527
Number of Grants: 59
Highest Grant: $11,500
Typical Range: $100 to $10,000
Disclosure Period: 1993

Note: Recent grants are derived from a 1993 Form 990.

RECENT GRANTS

Library
4,350	City of Oxford, Oxford, KS — computer for city library

General
11,500	National Jewish Center for Immunology and Respiratory Medicine, Denver, CO — fellowship program
10,000	Holland Hall School, Tulsa, OK
10,000	Schepens Eye Research Institute, Boston, MA
10,000	Town and Country School, Tulsa, OK
7,500	Asbury Theological Seminary, Wilmore, KY — scholarship program

Collins Foundation, George and Jennie

CONTACT
Loreine C. Dietrich
Chairman
George and Jennie Collins Fdn.
c/o Collins and Weese
2627 E 21st St., Ste. 126
Tulsa, OK 74114-1710
(918) 742-5456

FINANCIAL SUMMARY
Recent Giving: $161,550 (1993); $107,656 (1991); $318,404 (1990)

Assets: $3,919,960 (1993); $3,437,309 (1990); $3,570,947 (1989)

EIN: 73-6093053

CONTRIBUTIONS SUMMARY
Donor(s): George F. Collins, Jr., Liberty Glass Co., and others

Typical Recipients: • *Arts & Humanities:* Community Arts, Libraries, Museums/Galleries • *Education:* Colleges & Universities, Education Funds • *Health:* Alzheimers Disease, Hospitals • *Religion:* Churches, Missionary Activities (Domestic), Religious Organizations, Religious Welfare • *Social Services:* Child Welfare, Community Service Organizations, Recreation & Athletics, Sexual Abuse, Shelters/Homelessness, United Funds/United Ways, YMCA/YWCA/YMHA/YWHA

Grant Types: capital and scholarship

Geographic Distribution: focus on OK

GIVING OFFICERS
Roger B. Collins: trust
Loreine C. Dietrich: chmn, trust *PHIL AFFIL* treas: George Fulton Collins, Jr. Foundation
Helen Jayne Henley: trust

APPLICATION INFORMATION
Initial Approach: Send brief letter of inquiry describing program or project. Include a description of organization, amount requested, purpose of funds sought, recently audited financial statement, and proof of tax-exempt status. There are no deadlines.

GRANTS ANALYSIS
Total Grants: $161,550
Number of Grants: 10
Highest Grant: $55,000
Typical Range: $1,000 to $25,000
Disclosure Period: 1993

Note: Recent grants are derived from a 1993 Form 990.

RECENT GRANTS

General
55,000	Day Center for the Homeless, Tulsa, OK — new building project
25,000	Baker University, Baldwin City, KS — renovation of Mabee Hall

25,000	St. Simeon's Episcopal Home, Tulsa, OK — building expansion for patients with Alzheimers and dementia related illnesses
21,050	Westside YMCA, Tulsa, OK — ropes course and building repairs
3,500	Cookson Hills Center, Cookson, OK — for copier and operation budget

Collins, Jr. Foundation, George Fulton

CONTACT
Fulton Collins
Chairman
George Fulton Collins, Jr. Fdn.
2627 E 21st St., Ste. 126
Tulsa, OK 74114-1710
(918) 742-5456

FINANCIAL SUMMARY
Recent Giving: $159,550 (1993); $102,000 (1991); $378,882 (1990)

Assets: $3,488,275 (1993); $3,398,646 (1991); $3,249,171 (1990)

EIN: 23-7008179

CONTRIBUTIONS SUMMARY
Typical Recipients: • *Arts & Humanities:* Community Arts, Libraries, Museums/Galleries • *Civic & Public Affairs:* Women's Affairs, Zoos/Aquariums • *Education:* Colleges & Universities, Private Education (Precollege) • *Health:* Emergency/Ambulance Services, Health Funds, Health Organizations • *Religion:* Churches, Religious Organizations, Religious Welfare • *Social Services:* Child Welfare, Community Service Organizations, Counseling, Food/Clothing Distribution, Recreation & Athletics, Sexual Abuse, Shelters/Homelessness, YMCA/YWCA/YMHA/YWHA

Grant Types: capital and scholarship

Geographic Distribution: focus on OK

GIVING OFFICERS
Fulton Collins: chmn *CURR EMPL* chmn, ceo, dir: Liberty Glass Co *PHIL AFFIL* don, trust: Fulton and Susie Collins Foundation

Loreine C. Dietrich: treas *PHIL AFFIL* chmn, trust: George and Jennie Collins Foundation

Frank M. Engle: secy *PHIL AFFIL* trust, vp: Howard E. Felt Foundation

APPLICATION INFORMATION
Initial Approach: Send cover letter and full proposal. Include a description of organization, amount requested, purpose of funds sought, recently audited financial statement, and proof of tax-exempt status. There are no deadlines.

GRANTS ANALYSIS
Total Grants: $159,550

Number of Grants: 11

Highest Grant: $55,000

Typical Range: $1,000 to $25,000

Disclosure Period: 1993

Note: Recent grants are derived from a 1993 Form 990.

RECENT GRANTS
General

55,000	Day Center for the Homeless, Tulsa, OK — new building project
25,000	Baker University, Baldwin City, KS — renovation of Mabee Hall
25,000	St. Simeon's Episcopal Home, Tulsa, OK — building addition for patients with Alzheimers and dementia
21,050	Westside YMCA, Tulsa, OK — ropes course and building repairs
2,500	Fellowship of Christian Athletes, Kansas City, MO — bus transportation to summer camp

Goddard Foundation, Charles B.

CONTACT
William R. Goddard, Jr.
Trustee
Charles B. Goddard Fdn.
PO Box 1485
Ardmore, OK 73402
(405) 226-6040

FINANCIAL SUMMARY
Recent Giving: $267,246 (fiscal 1994); 255,345 (fiscal 1993); $332,410 (fiscal 1992)

Assets: $5,508,755 (fiscal 1994); $6,144,069 (fiscal 1993); $5,739,472 (fiscal 1992)

EIN: 75-6005868

CONTRIBUTIONS SUMMARY
Donor(s): the late Charles B. Goddard

Typical Recipients: • *Arts & Humanities:* Historic Preservation, Libraries, Museums/Galleries, Performing Arts • *Civic & Public Affairs:* General, Law & Justice, Legal Aid, Parades/Festivals, Public Policy, Safety, Urban & Community Affairs, Zoos/Aquariums • *Education:* Colleges & Universities, Education Funds, Education Reform, Elementary Education (Private), Literacy, Private Education (Precollege), Public Education (Precollege), Science/Mathematics Education • *Environment:* Wildlife Protection • *Health:* Clinics/Medical Centers, Health Policy/Cost Containment, Health Organizations, Hospices, Hospitals, Medical Rehabilitation, Medical Research, Single-Disease Health Associations • *Religion:* Churches, Religious Welfare • *Science:* Scientific Centers & Institutes, Scientific Organizations • *Social Services:* Animal Protection, At-Risk Youth, Camps, Child Welfare, Community Service Organizations, Crime Prevention, Day Care,

Domestic Violence, Family Services, Homes, People with Disabilities, Scouts, Shelters/Homelessness, Substance Abuse, United Funds/United Ways, Youth Organizations

Grant Types: capital, emergency, general support, multiyear/continuing support, operating expenses, research, and seed money

Geographic Distribution: focus on southern OK and northern TX

GIVING OFFICERS
Elizabeth E. Cashman: trust

Ann G. Corrigan: trust

William R. Goddard: trust *CURR EMPL* chmn bd: Goddard Investments Co *PHIL AFFIL* trust: Samuel Roberts Noble Foundation

William R. Goddard, Jr.: trust *PHIL AFFIL* trust: Merrick Foundation

William M. Johns: trust

APPLICATION INFORMATION
Initial Approach: Send a brief letter of inquiry. There are no deadlines.

GRANTS ANALYSIS
Total Grants: $267,246

Number of Grants: 23

Highest Grant: $100,000

Typical Range: $100 to $50,000

Disclosure Period: fiscal year ending June 30, 1994

Note: Recent grants are derived from a fiscal 1994 Form 990. Number of grants and typical range do not include contributions of $25,746.

RECENT GRANTS
General

100,000	Oak Hall Episcopal School, Ardmore, OK — building campaign
80,000	Oak Hall Alphabetic Phonics Program, Ardmore, OK
50,000	Goddard Youth Camp Building Campaign, Sulphur, OK
50,000	Memorial Hospital of Southern Oklahoma, Ardmore, OK
40,000	Southwestern Medical Foundation, Dallas, TX

Harmon Foundation, Pearl M. and Julia J.

CONTACT
George L. Hangs, Jr.
Secretary-Treasurer
Pearl M. and Julia J. Harmon Foundation
PO Box 52568
Tulsa, OK 74152-0568
(918) 743-6191

FINANCIAL SUMMARY
Recent Giving: $1,200,000 (fiscal 1995 est.); $1,200,000 (fiscal 1994 approx.); $201,641 (fiscal 1993)

Assets: $25,000,000 (fiscal 1995 est.); $25,000,000 (fiscal 1994 approx.); $22,824,849 (fiscal 1993)

Gifts Received: $2,000 (fiscal 1993)

Fiscal Note: In October 1992, the foundation received a gift from Farris P. Saffa, Jr.

EIN: 73-6095893

CONTRIBUTIONS SUMMARY
Donor(s): The foundation was established in 1962 by the late Claude C. Harmon and the late Julia J. Harmon .

Typical Recipients: • *Arts & Humanities:* Arts Associations & Councils, General, History & Archaeology, Libraries, Museums/Galleries, Music, Opera • *Civic & Public Affairs:* Botanical Gardens/Parks, Employment/Job Training, General, Hispanic Affairs, Municipalities/Towns, Nonprofit Management, Parades/Festivals, Urban & Community Affairs • *Education:* Elementary Education (Private), Elementary Education (Public), General, Private Education (Precollege), Public Education (Precollege) • *Health:* Mental Health, Prenatal Health Issues • *Religion:* Churches, Dioceses, Ministries, Religious Organizations, Religious Welfare • *Social Services:* Community Service Organizations, Domestic Violence, Food/Clothing Distribution, Recreation & Athletics, Shelters/Homelessness, Volunteer Services, Youth Organizations

Grant Types: general support and loan

Geographic Distribution: focus on Tulsa, OK

GIVING OFFICERS
Catherine H. Frederick: trust

George L. Hangs, Jr.: secy, treas, trust

George L. Hangs, Sr.: chmn, trust

Jean M. Kuntz: trust

APPLICATION INFORMATION
Initial Approach:

Applicants should send a one-page letter of inquiry.

The foundation has no deadline for submitting proposals.

Restrictions on Giving: The foundation is restricted by Trust Agreement to charitable organizations in Oklahoma, Kansas, Texas, Arkansas, and New Mexico. The foundation does not fund evangelism or research, and it will not make grants to individuals or to support foundations.

OTHER THINGS TO KNOW
The foundation reports that, in addition to grant-making, it also provides the following services: conferences; seminars; workshops; meeting rooms; and desktop publishing for Tulsa, OK, charities.

PUBLICATIONS
Application guidelines

GRANTS ANALYSIS
Total Grants: $201,641

Number of Grants: 74

Highest Grant: $90,000

Average Grant: $1,529*

Typical Range: $500 to $5,000

Disclosure Period: fiscal year ending May 31, 1993

Note: Average grant figure excludes the highest gift of $90,000. Recent grants are derived from a 1993 Form 990.

RECENT GRANTS

General

90,000	Catholic Charities, Tulsa, OK
5,000	Catholic Charities, Tulsa, OK
5,000	City of Tulsa, Tulsa, OK
5,000	Emergency Infant Services, Tulsa, OK
5,000	First United Methodist Church of Nowata, Nowata, OK

Helmerich Foundation

CONTACT
Walter H. Helmerich III
Trustee
Helmerich Foundation
1579 E 21st St.
Tulsa, OK 74114
(918) 742-5531

FINANCIAL SUMMARY
Recent Giving: $2,240,000 (fiscal 1993); $2,183,406 (fiscal 1992); $2,082,945 (fiscal 1991)

Assets: $52,722,231 (fiscal 1993); $49,501,566 (fiscal 1992); $45,230,722 (fiscal 1991)

Gifts Received: $178,588 (fiscal 1990); $18,690,886 (fiscal 1989); $1,143,381 (fiscal 1988)

Fiscal Note: In 1990, contributions were received from W.H. Helmerich.

EIN: 73-6105607

CONTRIBUTIONS SUMMARY
Donor(s): The foundation was established in 1965 by the late W.H. Helmerich .

Typical Recipients: • *Arts & Humanities:* Ballet, History & Archaeology, Libraries, Museums/Galleries, Opera • *Civic & Public Affairs:* Botanical Gardens/Parks, Clubs, Women's Affairs, Zoos/Aquariums • *Education:* Colleges & Universities, Education Reform, Elementary Education (Public), Private Education (Precollege), Religious Education • *Environment:* General • *Health:* Children's Health/Hospitals, Clinics/Medical Centers, Eyes/Blindness, Health Organizations • *Religion:* Ministries, Religious Organizations, Religious Welfare • *Social Services:* Community Service Organizations, Crime Prevention, Domestic Violence, Family Services, Food/Clothing Distribution, Homes, People with Disabilities, Recreation & Athletics

Grant Types: capital and endowment

Geographic Distribution: limited to the Tulsa, OK, area

GIVING OFFICERS
Walter Hugo Helmerich III: trust *B* Tulsa OK 1923 *ED* Univ OK BA 1948; Harvard Univ MBA 1950 *CURR EMPL* chmn, dir: Helmerich & Payne *CORP AFFIL* chmn: Helmerich & Payne Ecuador, Helmerich & Payne Intl Drilling, Helmerich & Payne Venezuela; dir: Atwood Oceanics, Caterpillar Inc, Liberty Natl Bank & Trust OK City, Liberty Natl Bank & Trust Tulsa, Natural Gas Odorizing Inc, Whitman Corp; hon chmn: Banks Mid-Am; pres, dir: Helmerich & Payne Properties; trust: Northwestern Mutual Life Ins Co *NONPR AFFIL* chmn endowment drive: OK Fdn Excellence; dir: OK Health Sciences Fdn, OK Med Res Fdn; mem: Sigma Nu, World Bus Counc; mem, dir: Independent Petroleum Assn Am, Tulsa Chamber Commerce; trust: Chief Execs Forum, Hillcrest Med Ctr, Retina Res Fdn, Tulsa Psychiatric Ctr

APPLICATION INFORMATION
Initial Approach:

The foundation does not publish an annual report or an official grant application. Applicants should send request letters directly to foundation.

Restrictions on Giving: Future grants will be limited to the Tulsa area and will focus primarily on large capital needs. The foundation does not make grants to individuals, or for general support, annual campaigns, seed money, endowment funds, scholarships, matching gifts, fellowships, emergency funds, deficit financing, research, operating budgets, demonstration projects, conferences, publications, or loans.

PUBLICATIONS
Application guidelines and program policy statement

GRANTS ANALYSIS
Total Grants: $2,240,000

Number of Grants: 24

Highest Grant: $1,000,000

Average Grant: $53,913*

Typical Range: $30,000 to $100,000

Disclosure Period: fiscal year ending September 30, 1993

Note: Average grant figure excludes the highest grant of $1,000,000. Recent grants are derived from a fiscal 1993 Form 990.

RECENT GRANTS

General

250,000	Salvation Army, Tulsa, OK — capital funds drive
150,000	Oklahoma State University Foundation, Stillwater, OK — baseball stadium
100,000	Park Friends, Tulsa, OK — police camcorders
70,000	Boston Avenue United Methodist Church, Tulsa, OK — lighting improvements
62,500	Tulsa Education Fund, Tulsa, OK — elementary school capital improvements

Kerr Foundation

CONTACT
Robert Kerr, Jr.
President
Kerr Foundation
6301 N Western, Ste. 130
Oklahoma City, OK 73118
(405) 842-1510

FINANCIAL SUMMARY
Recent Giving: $650,000 (1995 est.);
$699,740 (1994 approx.); $433,477 (1993)

Assets: $25,000,000 (1995 est.);
$24,797,244 (1994); $23,843,508 (1993)

Gifts Received: $6,434 (1991); $5,868
(1990); $4,504 (1989)

Fiscal Note: The foundation receives contributions from various affiliated trusts.

EIN: 73-1256122

CONTRIBUTIONS SUMMARY
Donor(s): The foundation was established
in 1963, with the late Grayce B. Kerr Flynn
as donor.

Typical Recipients: • *Arts & Humanities:*
Arts Centers, Arts Festivals, Arts Funds,
Arts Institutes, Ballet, Libraries, Museums/Galleries • *Civic & Public Affairs:* Professional & Trade Associations, Safety,
Urban & Community Affairs • *Education:*
Colleges & Universities, Faculty Development, Literacy, Medical Education, Private
Education (Precollege), Public Education
(Precollege), Science/Mathematics Education, Secondary Education (Private), Secondary Education (Public) • *Environment:*
General • *Health:* Clinics/Medical Centers •
Science: Scientific Organizations • *Social
Services:* Community Service Organizations, Domestic Violence, Family Planning,
Food/Clothing Distribution, Youth Organizations

Grant Types: capital, department, endowment, operating expenses, project, and research

Geographic Distribution: Oklahoma (first
preference), Arkansas, Colorado, Kansas,
Missouri, New Mexico, and Texas; also
Washington, DC, if the organization directly
benefits the granting area

GIVING OFFICERS
Royce Mitchell Hammons: treas *B* Hallettsville TX 1945 *ED* Univ OK BBA 1969;
Southern Methodist Univ 1976; Stanford
Univ 1990 *CURR EMPL* pres, ceo, dir: OK
Bank *CORP AFFIL* pres, ceo, dir: First
Sooner Bancshares; trust: Hunziger Bros
NONPR AFFIL mem: OK Bankers Assn;
trust: Arthritis Fdn, Bone & Joint Hosp,
Oklahoma City Univ, Univ OK Assoc
Counc *CLUB AFFIL* Galveston CC, Oklahoma City Din, Oklahoma City GC & CC,
Quail Creek GC & CC, Whitehall

Lou C. Kerr: vp, secy

Robert Samuel Kerr, Jr.: pres *B* Ada OK
1926 *ED* Univ OK 1951; Univ OK 1955
CURR EMPL atty, sr ptnr: Kerr Irvine &
Rhodes *CORP AFFIL* dir: Bank OK, Kerr-

McGee Corp *NONPR AFFIL* mem: Am Bar
Assn

Sharon Kerr: trust

Steven Kerr: asst treas, trust

Ray Klein: trust

Elmer Boyd Staats: trust *B* Richfield KS
1914 *ED* McPherson Coll AB 1935; Univ
KS MA 1936; Univ MN PhD 1939 *CORP
AFFIL* dir: Computer Data Sys; mem pres
adv counc: Metro Life Ins Co *NONPR AF-
FIL* mem: Am Mgmt Assn, Am Soc Pub
Admin, Assn Govt Accts, Beta Gamma
Sigma, Natl Academy Pub Admin, Phi Beta
Kappa, Pi Sigma Alpha, Univ Chicago
Comm Pub Policy Studies; mem, dir: Am
Academy Political & Social Science; mem
visiting comm: Univ CA Los Angeles Grad
Sch Mgmt; trust, mem res policy comm,
econ devel comm: McPherson Coll *CLUB
AFFIL* Cosmos

APPLICATION INFORMATION
Initial Approach:

Applicants should request the foundation's
application forms.

Requests for funding should include a cover
letter with summary request, completed institutional profile and proposal summary
forms, copy of the IRS determination letter
of tax-exempt status, a proposal, and other
documentation appropriate to the request.

Applications should be received at least
forty-five days prior to quarterly trustee
meetings to allow time for review for consideration at the meetings.

Restrictions on Giving: The foundation
does not make grants to individuals.

PUBLICATIONS
Annual report

GRANTS ANALYSIS
Total Grants: $527,191

Number of Grants: 30

Highest Grant: $115,000

Average Grant: $17,573

Typical Range: $5,000 to $25,000

Disclosure Period: 1992

Note: Recent grants are derived from a 1992
Form 990.

RECENT GRANTS

Library
500	Grace M. Pickens Public Library	

General
115,000	Oklahoma City University, Oklahoma City, OK	
115,000	University of Oklahoma Foundation, Norman, OK	
103,900	New Mexico Military Institute, Roswell, NM	
30,000	Nature Conservancy, Arlington, VA	
25,000	Oklahoma City Metro Alliance for Safer Cities, Oklahoma City, OK	

Kirkpatrick Foundation

CONTACT
Marilyn B. Myers
Director and Assistant Secretary
Kirkpatrick Foundation
PO Box 268822
Oklahoma City, OK 73126
(405) 840-2882

FINANCIAL SUMMARY
Recent Giving: $1,300,000 (1995 est.);
$1,300,000 (1994 approx.); $1,243,595
(1993)

Assets: $30,000,000 (1995 est.);
$29,076,134 (1994); $29,038,010 (1993)

EIN: 73-0701736

CONTRIBUTIONS SUMMARY
Donor(s): The foundation was incorporated
in 1955 by Eleanor B. Kirkpatrick, John E.
Kirkpatrick, and Joan E. Kirkpatrick.

Typical Recipients: • *Arts & Humanities:*
Arts Associations & Councils, Arts Centers,
Arts Institutes, Ballet, Dance, Ethnic & Folk
Arts, Historic Preservation, Libraries, Museums/Galleries, Music, Opera, Performing
Arts, Theater • *Civic & Public Affairs:*
Asian American Affairs, Community Foundations, Economic Development, General,
Housing, Municipalities/Towns, Public Policy, Urban & Community Affairs,
Zoos/Aquariums • *Education:* Colleges &
Universities, General, International Studies,
Literacy, Private Education (Precollege),
Public Education (Precollege), Secondary
Education (Private) • *Health:* Children's
Health/Hospitals, Clinics/Medical Centers,
Emergency/Ambulance Services, Hospitals,
Medical Research, Single-Disease Health
Associations • *Religion:* Ministries, Religious Welfare • *Social Services:* Child Welfare, Community Service Organizations,
Domestic Violence, Family Planning, Family Services, Food/Clothing Distribution,
Recreation & Athletics, Senior Services,
United Funds/United Ways, Youth Organizations

Grant Types: capital, emergency, endowment, matching, operating expenses, project,
and seed money

Geographic Distribution: focus on the
Oklahoma City area

GIVING OFFICERS
John L. Belt: dir *CURR EMPL* secy, dir:
Am Bancorp OK

Ann Byrd: dir

Douglas R. Cummings: hon dir

James Gindling Harlow, Jr.: dir *B* Oklahoma City OK 1934 *ED* Univ OK BS 1957;
Univ OK 1959-1961 *CURR EMPL* chmn,
pres, ceo, dir: OK Gas & Electric Co *CORP
AFFIL* dir: Fleming Cos Inc, MA Mutual
Life Ins Co; dir, mem exec comm: Edison
Electric Inst *NONPR AFFIL* adv bd: St Anthony Hosp; chmn, trust: Univ OK Fdn; dir:
OK Chamber Commerce, OK St Fair; dir,
mem exec comm: Edison Electric Inst; mem:
OK Soc Security Analysts, Oklahoma City

Chamber Commerce, US Chamber Commerce; pres, mem bd consult: Kirkpatrick Ctr; trust: OK Zoological Soc, Oklahoma City Univ *CLUB AFFIL* Beacon, Econ, Mens Dinner, Oklahoma City GC & CC, Petroleum *PHIL AFFIL* pres, dir: Oklahoma Gas & Electric Co. Foundation

Dan Hogan: dir *B* 1933 *CURR EMPL* chmn, dir: Journal Record Publ Co

Christian Kirkpatrick Keesee: vp, dir *B* Oklahoma City OK 1961 *ED* Menlo Coll AA 1983; Pepperdine Univ 1984-1985; Harvard Univ 1985; Univ Central OK BS 1991 *CURR EMPL* pres, dir: Am Bancorp OK *CORP AFFIL* chmn, dir: Am Bank Trust Edmond *NONPR AFFIL* pres: City Arts Ctr; trust: Ballet OK, Inst Intl Ed, Oklahoma City Art Mus *CLUB AFFIL* Doubles, Oklahoma City GC & CC

Eleanor Blake Kirkpatrick: treas, dir *B* Mangum OK 1909 *ED* Smith Coll BA 1931 *CURR EMPL* ptnr: Kirkpatrick Oil Co *CORP AFFIL* ptnr: Kirkpatrick Oil & Gas *NONPR AFFIL* bd consult: Kirkpatrick Ctr; bd dirs: Oklahoma City Art Mus; co-fdr, hon pres: Alliance Francaise; mem: Oklahoma City Univ Socs *PHIL AFFIL* ptnr

Joan E. Kirkpatrick: pres, dir

John Elson Kirkpatrick: chmn, dir *B* Oklahoma City OK 1908 *ED* US Naval Academy BS 1931; Harvard Univ Grad Sch Bus Admin 1935-1936 *CURR EMPL* ptnr: Kirkpatrick Oil Co *CORP AFFIL* chmn emeritus: Banks Mid-Am; chmn emeritus, dir: Liberty Bancorp; ptnr: Kirkpatrick Oil & Gas *NONPR AFFIL* dir emeritus: OK Historical Soc; dir, life trust: Natl Cowboy Hall Fame Western Heritage Ctr; dir, pres: OK Ctr Science & Arts; fdr, dir: Oklahoma City Commun Fdn; hon chmn: Lyric Theatre OK, Omniplex; hon dir: OK St Fair; hon trust: Mercy Hosp; life dir: Oklahoma City Chamber Commerce; life trust: OK Zoological Soc; mem: Allied Arts Fdn, Asia Soc OK, Harvard Area Group, Indus Petroleum Assn, OK County Historical Soc, OK Heritage Assn; mem, life bd mem: Oklahoma City Art Mus; trust: Falcon Fdn *CLUB AFFIL* Econ, Mens Dinner, Oklahoma City Petroleum, Rotary *PHIL AFFIL* ptnr

Eleanor Johnson Maurer: secy, dir *B* Milan MO 1914 *ED* Stephens Coll 1930-1931; Southwestern St Univ 1932; Draughons Bus Coll 1933 *CURR EMPL* ceo: Kirkpatrick Oil Co *NONPR AFFIL* dir Oklahoma City chap: English Speaking Union; mem: Comm 200, Exec Women Intl; treas: Oklahoma City Commun Fdn; trust: OK Ctr Science & Arts

Dr. Anne Hodges Morgan: dir

Marilyn B. Myers: dir, asst secy

Charles E. Nelson: dir *B* 1944 *ED* OK St Univ 1965 *CURR EMPL* chmn, ceo, pres, dir: Liberty Bancorp *CORP AFFIL* chmn, pres, ceo: Liberty Bank & Trust Oklahoma City *PHIL AFFIL* dir, chmn, ceo: Liberty Foundation

George J. Records: dir *B* St. Louis MO 1934 *ED* Dartmouth Coll 1956 *CURR EMPL* chmn, pres: Midland Mortgage

Robert E. Torray: dir

APPLICATION INFORMATION
Initial Approach:

The foundation has no specific application forms.

Grant proposals should include the following information: a description of the general program, if an operating grant is requested; a description of the particular project, if a project grant is requested; a recent financial statement or audit; a general operating budget and a project budget, if appropriate; a list of the organization's board of directors, including the total amount of money contributed to the organization by directors, and the number of directors contributing; and a copy of the organization's IRS tax-exempt letter.

Grant proposals are due on the 15th of February, May, August, and November for consideration in March, June, September, and December, respectively.

The foundation's board of trustees makes funding decisions.

Restrictions on Giving: The foundation does not make grants to individuals. Health care, mental health, research, and religious programs are not ordinarily funded; school trips are never funded.

OTHER THINGS TO KNOW
The foundation reports an affiliation with the Oklahoma City Community Foundation.

PUBLICATIONS
Informational brochure

GRANTS ANALYSIS
Total Grants: $1,243,595

Number of Grants: 158

Highest Grant: $631,500

Average Grant: $7,871

Typical Range: $500 to $10,000

Disclosure Period: 1993

Note: Recent grants are derived from a 1993 Form 990.

RECENT GRANTS
General

631,500	Oklahoma City Community Foundation, Oklahoma City, OK
50,000	Southeast Area Health Center, Oklahoma City, OK
25,000	Ronald McDonald House, Oklahoma City, OK
22,000	Skyline Urban Ministry, Oklahoma City, OK
20,500	Oklahoma City Public Schools Foundation, Oklahoma City, OK

Lyon Foundation
Former Foundation Name: E. H. Lyon and Melody Lyon Foundation

CONTACT
James W. Connor
President
Lyon Foundation
PO Box 546
Bartlesville, OK 74005
(918) 336-0066

FINANCIAL SUMMARY
Recent Giving: $743,000 (1995 est.); $743,000 (1994 approx.); $408,970 (1993)

Assets: $16,105,000 (1995 est.); $16,105,000 (1994 approx.); $16,050,139 (1993)

Gifts Received: $90,385 (1993); $81,102 (1991); $85,990 (1990)

Fiscal Note: In 1993, contributions were received from E. H. Lyon Trust.

EIN: 23-7299980

CONTRIBUTIONS SUMMARY
Donor(s): The foundation was established in 1975 by the late E. H. Lyon and the late Melody Lyon .

Typical Recipients: • *Arts & Humanities:* Arts Festivals, Community Arts, Historic Preservation, Libraries, Museums/Galleries, Music • *Civic & Public Affairs:* Municipalities/Towns, Parades/Festivals, Safety • *Education:* Medical Education, Public Education (Precollege) • *Health:* Emergency/Ambulance Services, Geriatric Health, Health Organizations, Medical Rehabilitation, Mental Health, Nutrition • *Religion:* Churches, Religious Welfare • *Social Services:* Child Welfare, Community Centers, Community Service Organizations, People with Disabilities, Recreation & Athletics, Youth Organizations

Grant Types: capital

Geographic Distribution: focus on Bartlesville, OK

GIVING OFFICERS
Walter W. Allison: vp, asst treas

James W. Connor: pres

Don Donaldson: vp, asst secy

John F. Kane: treas

Larry G. Markel: asst secy

Charles W. Selby: secy, dir

APPLICATION INFORMATION
Initial Approach:

The foundation requests applications be made in writing.

Written proposals should include the amount requested and the purpose of the requested funds.

The foundation has no deadline for submitting proposals.

Restrictions on Giving: The foundation does not make grants to individuals.

GRANTS ANALYSIS
Total Grants: $408,970

Number of Grants: 15
Highest Grant: $111,921
Average Grant: $27,265
Typical Range: $5,000 to $50,000
Disclosure Period: 1993

Note: Recent grants are derived from a 1993 Form 990.

RECENT GRANTS

Library

100,000   Bartlesville Library Trust Authority, Bartlesville, OK — book endowment fund

General

111,921   Bartlesville Wesleyan College, Bartlesville, OK — establishment of nursing program

50,000   Salvation Army, Bartlesville, OK — addition-challenge grant

50,000   Westside Community Center, Bartlesville, OK — new building on existing land

30,000   Bartlesville Little League, Bartlesville, OK — lights and electrical work

14,000   Constantine Center, Pawhuska, OK — air conditioning for center

McCasland Foundation

CONTACT
Monica McCasland
Executive Director
McCasland Foundation
PO Box 400
Duncan, OK 73534
(405) 252-5580

FINANCIAL SUMMARY
Recent Giving: $1,457,652 (1993); $1,359,146 (1992); $1,216,244 (1991)

Assets: $31,593,363 (1993); $30,874,364 (1992); $26,832,317 (1991)

Gifts Received: $3,023 (1991); $812,329 (1990); $350,000 (1989)

Fiscal Note: In 1990, the foundation received contributions totaling $812,329 from the Mack Oil Company, Ellen Fullwood, and Gene Nelson. In 1991, the foundation received $3,023 from Ellen Fullwood.

EIN: 73-6096032

CONTRIBUTIONS SUMMARY
Donor(s): The foundation was established in 1952. The donors include members of the McCasland family as well as Mack Oil Company, where Thomas H. McCasland, Jr, a foundation trustee, serves as chairman and chief executive officer.

Typical Recipients: • *Arts & Humanities:* Arts Associations & Councils, Arts Centers, Arts Funds, Arts Institutes, Ethnic & Folk Arts, General, Historic Preservation, History & Archaeology, Libraries, Museums/Galleries, Music, Theater • *Civic & Public Affairs:* Botanical Gardens/Parks, Business/Free Enterprise, Clubs, General, Housing, Municipalities/Towns, Nonprofit Management, Philanthropic Organizations • *Education:* Arts/Humanities Education, Business Education, Colleges & Universities, Community & Junior Colleges, Education Associations, Education Funds, Education Reform, General, Literacy, Medical Education, Private Education (Precollege), Public Education (Precollege), Religious Education, Science/Mathematics Education, Special Education, Student Aid • *Environment:* Wildlife Protection • *Health:* Alzheimers Disease, Clinics/Medical Centers, Emergency/Ambulance Services, Health Organizations, Hospices, Hospitals, Medical Research, Single-Disease Health Associations • *International:* Foreign Educational Institutions • *Religion:* Churches, Ministries, Religious Organizations, Religious Welfare • *Science:* Science Exhibits & Fairs, Science Museums, Scientific Centers & Institutes, Scientific Organizations • *Social Services:* Child Welfare, Community Centers, Community Service Organizations, Emergency Relief, Family Services, People with Disabilities, Recreation & Athletics, Scouts, Senior Services, Shelters/Homelessness, Substance Abuse, United Funds/United Ways, Volunteer Services, YMCA/YWCA/YMHA/YWHA, Youth Organizations

Grant Types: capital, department, endowment, general support, multiyear/continuing support, operating expenses, project, and scholarship

Geographic Distribution: primarily Oklahoma

GIVING OFFICERS
Mary Frances Maurer: trust *CORP AFFIL* shareholder: Security Natl Bank & Trust

Monica McCasland: exec dir

Thomas H. McCasland, Jr.: trust *B* Duncan OK 1933 *ED* Univ OK BPOE 1956 *CURR EMPL* chmn, ceo: Mack Energy Co *CORP AFFIL* pres, dir: Investors Trust Co, M&M Supply Co, Thomas Drilling Co; vp, dir: Mack Oil Co

Mary F. Michaelis: trust

W. H. Phelps: trust

APPLICATION INFORMATION
Initial Approach:

Organizations should send a letter of proposal describing briefly the nature of the organization, the amount and purpose of the grant, names of contact persons, and proof of tax-exempt status. An application form is available, but the foundation reports that use of the form is optional.

There are no deadlines for requests.

The board of trustees generally meets on a quarterly basis. Applicants receive notification after the following board meeting.

GRANTS ANALYSIS
Total Grants: $1,457,652

Number of Grants: 124

Highest Grant: $100,000

Average Grant: $11,755

Typical Range: $1,000 to $20,000

Disclosure Period: 1993

Note: Recent grants are derived from a 1993 Form 990.

RECENT GRANTS

Library

10,000   Oklahoma University Foundation, Norman, OK — Bizzell Library

10,000   Western Plains Library System, Clinton, OK — children's library area

General

100,000   Oklahoma University Foundation, Norman, OK — Museum of Natural History Building Fund

100,000   Oklahoma University Foundation, Norman, OK — Oklahoma Museum of Natural History

75,000   Cameron University, Lawton, OK — science equipment

75,000   Oklahoma State University Foundation, Stillwater, OK — Laserscope KTP/532 Fiberoptic System

35,000   First Baptist Church, Duncan, OK — Peyton Johnson Fund

McMahon Foundation

CONTACT
James F. Wood
Director
McMahon Foundation
PO Box 2156
Lawton, OK 73502
(405) 355-4622

FINANCIAL SUMMARY
Recent Giving: $1,600,000 (fiscal 1995 est.); $483,009 (fiscal 1994); $882,773 (fiscal 1993)

Assets: $35,629,978 (fiscal 1994); $35,063,561 (fiscal 1993); $32,916,173 (fiscal 1992)

EIN: 73-0664314

CONTRIBUTIONS SUMMARY
Donor(s): The McMahon Foundation was established in Oklahoma in 1940, with funds donated by the estate of the late Eugene D. McMahon . The purpose of the foundation is to benefit the city of Lawton and Comanche County, OK.

Typical Recipients: • *Arts & Humanities:* Arts Institutes, Community Arts, Historic Preservation, History & Archaeology, Libraries, Museums/Galleries, Music • *Civic & Public Affairs:* Botanical Gardens/Parks, General, Municipalities/Towns, Professional & Trade Associations, Safety • *Education:* Colleges & Universities, Gifted & Talented Programs, Journalism/Media Education, Public Education (Precollege), Secondary Education (Private), Special Education, Student Aid, Vocational & Technical Education • *En-*

vironment: Wildlife Protection • *Health:* Hospices • *Religion:* Religious Welfare • *Social Services:* Community Service Organizations, Crime Prevention, Recreation & Athletics, United Funds/United Ways, Youth Organizations

Grant Types: capital, general support, project, and scholarship

Geographic Distribution: only Oklahoma; emphasis on the city of Lawton, and Comanche County

GIVING OFFICERS
Kenneth Bridges: trust

Ronald E. Cagle, MD: trust

Kenneth Easton: trust

Charles S. Graybill, MD: chmn, trust

Manville Redman: vchmn

Gale Sadler: secy, treas

Orville D. Smith: trust

James F. Wood: dir

APPLICATION INFORMATION
Initial Approach:

The foundation does not issue specific guidelines for applications. Send an initial letter of inquiry.

The initial letter should describe the nature of the organization and the purpose of the grant requested.

The board meets on the first Monday of each month.

Restrictions on Giving: The foundation does not make grants to recipients outside of Oklahoma.

GRANTS ANALYSIS
Total Grants: $483,009

Number of Grants: 20

Highest Grant: $300,000

Average Grant: $24,150

Typical Range: $4,000 to $40,000

Disclosure Period: fiscal year ending March 31, 1994

Note: Recent grants are derived from a fiscal 1994 Form 990.

RECENT GRANTS
Library
3,948   Comanche County Clerk, Lawton, OK — purchase video tapes and films for county school film library

General
100,000   Cameron University, Lawton, OK — scholarships

50,000   United Way of Lawton, Lawton, OK

35,630   Oklahoma Department of Public Safety, Oklahoma City, OK — replace roof on local highway patrol building

30,858   Lawton Public Schools, Lawton, OK — support special programs

30,720   Great Plains Vo-Tech Foundation, Lawton, OK — scholarships

Merrick Foundation

CONTACT
Frank W. Merrick
Trustee
Merrick Fdn.
PO Box 998
Ardmore, OK 73402
(405) 226-7000

FINANCIAL SUMMARY
Recent Giving: $242,350 (1993); $267,520 (1992); $241,457 (1991)

Assets: $7,135,611 (1993); $6,832,264 (1992); $6,668,368 (1991)

EIN: 73-6111622

CONTRIBUTIONS SUMMARY
Donor(s): the late Mrs. Frank W. Merrick

Typical Recipients: • *Arts & Humanities:* Arts Associations & Councils, Arts Funds, Arts Institutes, Historic Preservation, History & Archaeology, Libraries, Performing Arts • *Civic & Public Affairs:* African American Affairs, Chambers of Commerce, General, Public Policy, Urban & Community Affairs • *Education:* Colleges & Universities, Education Associations, Education Reform, Private Education (Precollege), Public Education (Precollege), Student Aid • *Health:* Clinics/Medical Centers, Diabetes, Emergency/Ambulance Services, Hospitals, Medical Research, Mental Health • *Religion:* Churches, Religious Organizations, Religious Welfare • *Science:* Science Museums, Scientific Centers & Institutes • *Social Services:* Child Welfare, Community Service Organizations, Day Care, Food/Clothing Distribution, People with Disabilities, Recreation & Athletics, Substance Abuse, United Funds/United Ways, YMCA/YWCA/YMHA/YWHA, Youth Organizations

Grant Types: capital and seed money

Geographic Distribution: focus on OK, with emphasis on southern OK

GIVING OFFICERS
Valda M. Buchanan: secy, trust

Michael A. Cawley: trust *PHIL AFFIL* pres, trust: Samuel Roberts Noble Foundation

Charles R. Coe, Jr.: trust

Elizabeth Merrick Coe: pres, trust

Ross M. Coe: trust

Ward I. Coe: trust

William R. Goddard, Jr.: trust *PHIL AFFIL* trust: Charles B. Goddard Foundation

Frank W. Merrick: trust

Robert B. Merrick: trust

Ward S. Merrick, Jr.: vp, trust

Jack D. Wilkes: trust

APPLICATION INFORMATION
Initial Approach: Send brief letter of inquiry describing program or project. There are no deadlines.

Restrictions on Giving: Does not support individuals.

GRANTS ANALYSIS
Total Grants: $242,350

Number of Grants: 34

Highest Grant: $50,000

Typical Range: $500 to $15,000

Disclosure Period: 1993

Note: Recent grants are derived from a 1993 Form 990.

RECENT GRANTS
Library
5,000   Ardmore Public Library, Ardmore, OK

General
50,000   Greater Ardmore Scholarship Foundation, Ardmore, OK

15,000   United Way of South Central Oklahoma, Ardmore, OK

14,750   Ardmore YWCA, Ardmore, OK

12,500   Oklahoma Medical Research Foundation, Oklahoma City, OK

11,000   Ardmore Chamber of Commerce Foundation, Ardmore, OK

Noble Foundation, Samuel Roberts

CONTACT
Michael A. Cawley
President and Trustee
Samuel Roberts Noble Foundation
PO Box 2180
Ardmore, OK 73402
(405) 223-5810

FINANCIAL SUMMARY
Recent Giving: $8,369,586 (fiscal 1994); $5,416,296 (fiscal 1993); $4,995,499 (fiscal 1992)

Assets: $581,301,116 (fiscal 1994); $567,300,000 (fiscal 1993); $383,579,000 (fiscal 1991 approx.)

Gifts Received: $876,819 (fiscal 1994); $449,000 (fiscal 1993); $1,000 (fiscal 1989)

EIN: 73-0606209

CONTRIBUTIONS SUMMARY
Donor(s): Lloyd Noble, an Oklahoma oilman who developed the Noble Drilling and Samedan Oil corporations, provided the funding to create the Samuel Roberts Noble Foundation in 1945. The foundation was named for Lloyd Noble's father. Six family members sit on the current board of trustees.

Typical Recipients: • *Arts & Humanities:* Arts Centers, Ethnic & Folk Arts, Historic Preservation, History & Archaeology, Libraries, Museums/Galleries, Performing Arts • *Civic & Public Affairs:* Botanical Gardens/Parks, Business/Free Enterprise, Economic Development, Economic Policy, Law & Justice, Legal Aid, Municipalities/Towns, Professional & Trade Associations, Public Policy, Rural Affairs, Urban & Community Affairs • *Education:* Agricultural Education,

Business Education, Colleges & Universities, Continuing Education, Economic Education, Education Funds, Faculty Development, General, Health & Physical Education, Journalism/Media Education, Private Education (Precollege), Public Education (Precollege), Science/Mathematics Education, Student Aid • *Environment:* General • *Health:* Cancer, Diabetes, Emergency/Ambulance Services, Health Policy/Cost Containment, Health Organizations, Hospices, Hospitals, Medical Rehabilitation, Medical Research, Mental Health, Research/Studies Institutes, Single-Disease Health Associations, Transplant Networks/Donor Banks • *International:* International Affairs, International Organizations • *Religion:* Churches, Religious Organizations, Religious Welfare • *Science:* Scientific Centers & Institutes, Scientific Organizations • *Social Services:* Child Welfare, Community Service Organizations, Family Planning, Homes, People with Disabilities, Recreation & Athletics, Shelters/Homelessness, Substance Abuse, Youth Organizations

Grant Types: capital, challenge, matching, project, research, and seed money

Geographic Distribution: Southwestern United States, primarily Oklahoma

GIVING OFFICERS
Elizabeth A. Aldridge: sec

Ann Noble Brown: trust *PHIL AFFIL* trust, secy, treas: Vivian Bilby Noble Foundation; trust: HBE Foundation

David R. Brown, MD: trust

Michael A. Cawley: pres, trust *PHIL AF-FIL* trust: Merrick Foundation

Vivian Noble DuBose: trust

Bob Geurin: asst secy-treas

William R. Goddard: trust *CURR EMPL* chmn bd: Goddard Investments Co *PHIL AFFIL* trust: Charles B. Goddard Foundation

Edward E. Noble: trust *B* Ardmore OK 1928 *ED* Univ OK BS Geology 1951

Mary Jane Noble: trust

Rusty Noble: trust

Larry Pulliam: vp, treas, cfo *B* 1948

John F. Snodgrass: trust

APPLICATION INFORMATION
Initial Approach:

A letter of inquiry should be sent to the foundation.

The letter should contain background information about the requesting organization, specific details about the proposed project, and the amount needed. The foundation will then send application forms as needed.

The trustees generally hold meetings in January, April, July, and October. Applications must be completed by December 1, March 1, June 1, and September 1 in order to be considered at the next meeting.

Applicants should expect a two- to four-month decision-making period.

Restrictions on Giving: The foundation prefers not to fund operational costs.

OTHER THINGS TO KNOW
The foundation reports that it also sponsors seminars and workshops.

PUBLICATIONS
Annual report

GRANTS ANALYSIS
Total Grants: $8,369,586*

Number of Grants: 95

Highest Grant: $2,786,467

Average Grant: $88,101

Typical Range: $5,000 to $100,000

Disclosure Period: fiscal year ending October 31, 1994

Note: Total grants includes $109,455 in scholarship funding for the children of employees and $83,838 in employee matching gifts. Recent grants are derived from a fiscal 1993 grants list.

RECENT GRANTS

Library
5,000	Foundation Center, New York, NY — operating budget

General
1,414,051	Oklahoma Medical Research Foundation, Oklahoma City, OK — biomedical research support
619,148	Salk Institute for Biological Studies, San Diego, CA — plant cell biology project
500,000	Scott and White Memorial Hospital, Temple, TX — Fastrac CT Scanner
450,000	Heritage Foundation, Washington, DC — operating budget
178,333	Salk Institute for Biological Studies, San Diego, CA — plant cell biology fellowships

OG&E Electric Services / Oklahoma Gas & Electric Co. Foundation

Sales: $1.45 billion
Employees: 2,492
Headquarters: Oklahoma City, OK
SIC Major Group: Electric Services

CONTACT
James G. Harlow, Jr.
President
Oklahoma Gas & Electric Co. Foundation
Box 321
Oklahoma City, OK 73101
(405) 553-3196

FINANCIAL SUMMARY
Recent Giving: $622,000 (1994 est.); $593,901 (1993); $625,575 (1992)

Assets: $1,198,332 (1993); $950,558 (1992); $929,030 (1991)

Gifts Received: $800,000 (1993)

Fiscal Note: Totals are for foundation only. Company also gives directly, about

$500,000 to $600,000 annually. Total company giving in 1994 is not available and is not included in figures above. Above figures exclude nonmonetary support.

EIN: 73-6093572

CONTRIBUTIONS SUMMARY
Typical Recipients: • *Arts & Humanities:* Arts Funds, Arts Institutes, Ethnic & Folk Arts, Historic Preservation, History & Archaeology, Libraries, Museums/Galleries, Music, Theater • *Civic & Public Affairs:* Community Foundations, Municipalities/Towns, Urban & Community Affairs, Zoos/Aquariums • *Education:* Business Education, Colleges & Universities, Community & Junior Colleges, Economic Education, Private Education (Precollege), Public Education (Precollege) • *Health:* Clinics/Medical Centers, Emergency/Ambulance Services, Health Organizations, Heart, Hospitals • *International:* International Affairs • *Science:* Science Museums • *Social Services:* Community Service Organizations, Emergency Relief, Family Planning, Family Services, People with Disabilities, Recreation & Athletics, Senior Services, Youth Organizations

Grant Types: capital, employee matching gifts, general support, and scholarship

Nonmonetary Support Types: loaned employees and loaned executives

Note: Nonmonetary support is provided by the company. Estimated value for support is not available.

Geographic Distribution: areas of corporate operations; primarily Oklahoma

Operating Locations: AR, OK (Oklahoma City)

CORP. OFFICERS
James Gindling Harlow, Jr.: *B* Oklahoma City OK 1934 *ED* Univ OK BS 1957; Univ OK 1959-1961 *CURR EMPL* chmn, pres, ceo, dir: OK Gas & Electric Co *CORP AFFIL* dir: Fleming Cos Inc, MA Mutual Life Ins Co; dir, mem exec comm: Edison Electric Inst *NONPR AFFIL* adv bd: St Anthony Hosp; chmn, trust: Univ OK Fdn; dir: OK Chamber Commerce, OK St Fair; dir, mem exec comm: Edison Electric Inst; mem: OK Soc Security Analysts, Oklahoma City Chamber Commerce, US Chamber Commerce; pres, mem bd consult: Kirkpatrick Ctr; trust: OK Zoological Soc, Oklahoma City Univ *CLUB AFFIL* Beacon, Econ, Mens Dinner, Oklahoma City GC & CC, Petroleum *PHIL AFFIL* dir: Kirkpatrick Foundation

GIVING OFFICERS
Irma B. Elliott: secy, treas *CURR EMPL* secy: OK Gas & Electric Co

James Gindling Harlow, Jr.: pres, dir *CURR EMPL* chmn, pres, ceo, dir: OK Gas & Electric Co *PHIL AFFIL* dir: Kirkpatrick Foundation (see above)

Patrick J. Ryan: vp, dir *B* Chicago IL 1938 *ED* Univ OK BS 1961 *CURR EMPL* exec vp, coo: OK Gas & Electric Co *NONPR AFFIL* dir: Commun Counc Oklahoma City, OK Philharmonic Soc, St Anthony Hosp Fdn, Un Way Oklahoma City; mem: Am Inst Mining Engrs, NSPE City, OK Chamber

Commerce, OK Soc Professional Engrs, Univ OK Assocs; mem bd visit: Univ OK Coll Engg *CLUB AFFIL* Oklahoma City GC & CC, Petroleum

A. M. Strecker: vp, dir *B* Seiling OK 1943 *ED* OK St Univ BSEE 1971 *CURR EMPL* vp, treas: OK Gas & Electric Co

APPLICATION INFORMATION
Initial Approach: *Initial Contact:* brief letter *Include Information On:* outline of the proposed project, amount requested, 501(c)(3) status *Deadlines:* none

Restrictions on Giving: Does not support fraternal organizations, individuals, political or lobbying groups, or religious organizations for sectarian purposes.

GRANTS ANALYSIS
Total Grants: $593,901

Number of Grants: 121

Highest Grant: $50,000

Average Grant: $4,908

Typical Range: $3,000 to $10,000

Disclosure Period: 1993

Note: Figures are for foundation only. Recent grants are derived from a 1993 Form 990.

RECENT GRANTS

Library
3,333	Metropolitan Library System Endowment Trust, Oklahoma City, OK

General
50,000	National Cowboy Hall of Fame, Oklahoma City, OK
50,000	Oklahoma Christian University of Science and Arts, Oklahoma City, OK
50,000	Oklahoma State University Foundation, Stillwater, OK
50,000	YMCA Second Century Campaign, Oklahoma City, OK
35,000	Oklahoma City University, Oklahoma City, OK

Oxy USA Inc. / Oxy USA Charitable Foundation

Former Foundation Name: Occidental Oil & Gas Charitable Foundation
Sales: $773.0 million
Employees: 1,450
Parent Company: Occidental Petroleum Corp.
Headquarters: Tulsa, OK
SIC Major Group: Crude Petroleum & Natural Gas

CONTACT
Ronald G. Peters
Director, Public Affairs
Oxy USA Inc.
PO Box 300
Tulsa, OK 74102
(918) 561-2212

FINANCIAL SUMMARY
Recent Giving: $650,000 (1995 est.); $588,555 (1994); $617,720 (1993)

Assets: $9,938,680 (1993); $9,748,222 (1991); $9,194,423 (1990)

Fiscal Note: Company gives primarily through the foundation. Above figures exclude nonmonetary support. Ronald G. Peters is the contact for direct giving through the public affairs department.

EIN: 13-6081799

CONTRIBUTIONS SUMMARY
Typical Recipients: • *Arts & Humanities:* Community Arts, Libraries, Museums/Galleries, Music, Opera, Theater • *Civic & Public Affairs:* Zoos/Aquariums • *Education:* Colleges & Universities, Community & Junior Colleges, Education Funds • *Environment:* General • *Health:* Hospices, Hospitals, Medical Rehabilitation, Mental Health, Single-Disease Health Associations • *Social Services:* Child Welfare, Community Service Organizations, Delinquency & Criminal Rehabilitation, Domestic Violence, Emergency Relief, Food/Clothing Distribution, People with Disabilities, Senior Services, Shelters/Homelessness, Substance Abuse, United Funds/United Ways

Grant Types: capital and general support

Nonmonetary Support: $100,000 (1994); $200,000 (1993); $100,000 (1992)

Nonmonetary Support Types: donated equipment and in-kind services

Note: Ronald G. Peters is the contact for nonmonetary support.

Geographic Distribution: near operating locations

Operating Locations: CO (Denver), OK (Oklahoma City, Tulsa), TX (Houston, Midland)

CORP. OFFICERS
James R. Niehaus: *B* 1944 *ED* Univ CA Davis BS 1966; Univ MN MS 1969 *CURR EMPL* pres, dir: Oxy Oil & Gas USA *CORP AFFIL* exec vp: Occidental Oil & Gas Corp; pres, dir: Oxy USA Inc

Tommy Lynn Nowell: *B* Wichita Falls TX 1947 *ED* E Central Univ BS 1974; Univ Tulsa MBA 1980 *CURR EMPL* vp fin, contr: OXY USA Inc *NONPR AFFIL* mem: Am Petroleum Inst, Petroleum Accts Soc; trust: Am Heart Assn Tulsa Metro Div, Union Pub Schs Ed Fdn

Charles A. Purser: *B* Tulsa OK 1940 *ED* Univ OK 1962; Univ OK 1965 *CURR EMPL* secy: Oxy USA Inc

GIVING OFFICERS
Read William Archibald: vp *B* Modesto CA 1941 *ED* Univ CA Berkeley 1964; Univ CA Berkeley 1973 *CURR EMPL* vp fin & admin, cfo: Rand Corp *CORP AFFIL* dir: Pier Restoration Corp *NONPR AFFIL* mem: Am Soc Pub Admin, Natl Contract Mgmt Assn, Opers Res Soc Am

L. Frank Frick: asst secy

C. Jolley: asst treas

James R. Niehaus: pres, trust *CURR EMPL* pres, dir: Oxy Oil & Gas USA (see above)

Tommy Lynn Nowell: treas, trust *CURR EMPL* vp fin, contr: OXY USA Inc (see above)

Ronald G. Peters: exec secy *B* Okmulgee OK 1931 *ED* Univ OK BBA 1957 *CURR EMPL* dir pub aff: Oxy USA Inc

Charles A. Purser: secy *CURR EMPL* secy: Oxy USA Inc (see above)

APPLICATION INFORMATION
Initial Approach: *Initial Contact:* brief letter or proposal *Include Information On:* description of the organization, amount requested, purpose for which funds are sought, recently audited financial statement, proof of tax-exempt status *Deadlines:* June through September

Restrictions on Giving: Does not support dinners or special events, fraternal organizations, goodwill advertising, individuals, political or lobbying groups, or religious organizations for sectarian purposes.

OTHER THINGS TO KNOW
Occidental Oil & Gas Corp. has changed its name to Oxy USA, Inc.

GRANTS ANALYSIS
Total Grants: $588,555

Number of Grants: 200

Highest Grant: $10,000

Average Grant: $1,000*

Typical Range: $500 to $1,500

Disclosure Period: 1994

Note: Company provided average grant figure. Recent grants are derived from a 1993 Form 990.

RECENT GRANTS

General
100,000	Tulsa Area United Way, Tulsa, OK — contribution
15,000	Salvation Army, Tulsa, OK — building fund
15,000	YMCA Metro Tulsa, Tulsa, OK — capital campaign contribution
10,160	National Merit Scholarship Corporation, Evanston, IL — contribution
10,000	St. John Medical Center Foundation, Tulsa, OK — building fund

Puterbaugh Foundation

CONTACT
Don C. Phelps
Managing Trustee
Puterbaugh Fdn.
PO Box 729
McAlester, OK 74502
(918) 426-1591

FINANCIAL SUMMARY
Recent Giving: $322,175 (1993); $278,083 (1992); $229,403 (1991)

Assets: $7,937,118 (1993); $7,568,723 (1992); $7,489,479 (1991)
EIN: 73-6092193

CONTRIBUTIONS SUMMARY
Donor(s): the late Jay Garfield Puterbaugh, the late Leela Oliver Puterbaugh

Typical Recipients: • *Arts & Humanities:* Arts Associations & Councils, History & Archaeology, Libraries, Literary Arts, Public Broadcasting • *Civic & Public Affairs:* Botanical Gardens/Parks, Clubs, Economic Development, Inner-City Development, Municipalities/Towns, Urban & Community Affairs • *Education:* Colleges & Universities, Economic Education, Literacy, Public Education (Precollege) • *Health:* Children's Health/Hospitals, Clinics/Medical Centers, Emergency/Ambulance Services, Health Organizations, Hospices, Hospitals, Medical Research, Nursing Services • *Religion:* Religious Welfare • *Science:* Scientific Centers & Institutes • *Social Services:* Child Welfare, Community Service Organizations, Crime Prevention, Family Planning, Family Services, Homes, People with Disabilities, Shelters/Homelessness, Substance Abuse, United Funds/United Ways, Youth Organizations

Grant Types: capital, endowment, general support, professorship, project, and scholarship

Geographic Distribution: focus on OK

GIVING OFFICERS
Frank G. Edwards: trust
Don C. Phelps: mng trust
Steven W. Taylor: trust
Norris J. Welker: trust

APPLICATION INFORMATION
Initial Approach: Send brief letter of inquiry describing program or project. Deadline is January 15 for payment in December.

Restrictions on Giving: Does not support individuals.

PUBLICATIONS
Financial Statement

GRANTS ANALYSIS
Total Grants: $322,175
Number of Grants: 31
Highest Grant: $37,500
Typical Range: $200 to $35,000
Disclosure Period: 1993

Note: Recent grants are derived from a 1993 Form 990.

RECENT GRANTS

Library
37,500	Oklahoma State University Foundation, Stillwater, OK — library program
500	McAlester Public Library, McAlester, OK

General
35,000	McAlester United Way, McAlester, OK
33,750	McAlester Public Schools Foundation, McAlester, OK
30,000	Oklahoma Independent Living Resource Center, Oklahoma City, OK — handicapped citizens self-support program
25,000	Hospice, McAlester, OK
25,000	Oklahoma Medical Research Foundation, Oklahoma City, OK

Reynolds Foundation, Donald W.

CONTACT
Donald E. Pray
Executive Director
Donald W. Reynolds Foundation
7130 S Lewis Ave.
Ste. 900
Tulsa, OK 74136
(918) 496-0033

FINANCIAL SUMMARY
Recent Giving: $7,399,462 (fiscal 1994); $1,699,637 (fiscal 1993); $391,378 (fiscal 1991)

Assets: $853,168,000 (fiscal 1994); $850,663,000 (fiscal 1993); $6,910,825 (fiscal 1991)

Gifts Received: $802,000,000 (fiscal 1993); $6,000,000 (fiscal 1988)

EIN: 71-6053383

CONTRIBUTIONS SUMMARY
Donor(s): The foundation was established in 1954 by Donald W. Reynolds, who owns Donrey Media Group that includes more than fifty daily newspapers, radio and television stations, and billboard and cable operations. In 1977, Mr. Reynolds signed over all his stock and assets to the foundation to assure continuity for the company. The foundation stands to inherit a business which Forbes magazine has estimated to be worth $950 million.

Mr. Reynolds graduated from the University of Missouri School of Journalism in 1927. He purchased his first newspaper in 1940 in Oklahoma. He lives in Las Vegas. Mr. Reynolds, eighty five, has three children and has been married three times. His children are not involved with the foundation.

Typical Recipients: • *Arts & Humanities:* Arts Associations & Councils, Arts Centers, Community Arts, Libraries, Museums/Galleries, Music, Theater • *Civic & Public Affairs:* Business/Free Enterprise, Clubs, Economic Development, First Amendment Issues, Hispanic Affairs, Legal Aid, Municipalities/Towns, Professional & Trade Associations, Urban & Community Affairs, Women's Affairs • *Education:* Business Education, Colleges & Universities, Education Associations, Education Funds, Literacy, Student Aid • *Environment:* General • *Health:* Emergency/Ambulance Services, Health Funds, Health Organizations, Hospitals, Single-Disease Health Associations • *Social Services:* Child Welfare, Community Service Organizations, Counseling, Family Services, Food/Clothing Distribution, Recreation & Athletics, Senior Services, Shelters/Homelessness, Substance Abuse, United Funds/United Ways, YMCA/YWCA/YMHA/YWHA, Youth Organizations

Grant Types: capital

Geographic Distribution: national

GIVING OFFICERS
Steve Anderson: trust

Keith Boman: trust

James C. Dailey: treas

John L. Goolsby: trust *B* 1941 *CURR EMPL* ceo, pres: Hughes Corp *CORP AFFIL* ceo, pres: Howard Hughes Properties Ltd Ptnr, Summa Devel Corp; ceo, pres, dir: Howard Hughes Realty Inc, Summa Corp

Barbara Hanna: trust

Darrell Loftin: trust

E. H. Patterson: vchmn, trust *B* 1931 *ED* Univ MS BBA 1955 *CURR EMPL* exec vp, cfo: Donrey Inc *CORP AFFIL* vp, dir: Scores Inc

Ross Pendergraft: vchmn, trust *B* 1925 *CURR EMPL* pres, dir: Scores Inc *CORP AFFIL* exec vp, coo, dir: Donrey Inc

Donald E. Pray: exec dir *PHIL AFFIL* trust: Grace and Franklin Bernsen Foundation

John Schlereth: trust

Fred Wesley Smith: chmn *B* Arkoma OK 1934 *ED* AR Polytech Coll *CURR EMPL* pres: Donrey Media Group *CORP AFFIL* dir: First Interstate Bank NV *NONPR AFFIL* mem: Sigma Delta Chi; mem exec bd: Boy Scouts Am Las Vegas; trust: Univ NV Las Vegas Fdn; trust, mem exec bd: Univ Ozarks

Joel R. Stubblefield: trust

APPLICATION INFORMATION
Initial Approach:

Initial requests should be submitted in writing, three pages or less, on the letterhead of the applying organization and signed by the chief executive officer or other authorized person.

Propsals should include the goals, purpose, and significance of the project, qualifications of persons responsible for carrying out the project, list of organization's officers, and a copy of the IRS taw-determination letter. Requests should contain finacial plans, including the amount of the grant requested, and total funds needed for the project.

Deadline for submission is August 1st.

The board meets in January and June. Foundation grants will be made on a competitive selection basis once each year at the June trustees' meeting.

PUBLICATIONS
Application guidelines

GRANTS ANALYSIS
Total Grants: $7,399,462
Number of Grants: 134
Highest Grant: $2,500,000
Average Grant: $36,838
Typical Range: $5,000 to $15,000

Disclosure Period: fiscal year ending June 30, 1994

Note: Average grant figure excludes highest grant of $2,500,000. Recent grants are derived from a fiscal 1993 Form 990.

RECENT GRANTS

Library
1,000	Friends of the Sherman Public Library, Sherman, TX

General
13,512	No Mans Land Senior Citizens Organization
10,000	Baylor University, Houston, TX
10,000	Casa Colina Foundation, Pomona, CA
10,000	Oklahoma State University, Stillwater, OK
7,500	Arkansas State University Foundation, Little Rock, AR — scholarship

Sarkeys Foundation

CONTACT
Cheri D. Cartwright
Executive Director
Sarkeys Foundation
116 S Peters, Rm. 219
Norman, OK 73069
(405) 364-3703

FINANCIAL SUMMARY
Recent Giving: $2,700,000 (fiscal 1995 est.); $2,659,391 (fiscal 1994); $2,750,018 (fiscal 1993)

Assets: $62,202,647 (fiscal 1993); $63,313,629 (fiscal 1992); $58,000,000 (fiscal 1991 approx.)

EIN: 73-0736496

CONTRIBUTIONS SUMMARY
Donor(s): The foundation was established in 1962, with S. J. Sarkeys as the donor.

Typical Recipients: • *Arts & Humanities:* Arts Associations & Councils, Arts Institutes, Ballet, Dance, History & Archaeology, Libraries, Museums/Galleries, Music, Opera, Performing Arts, Theater • *Civic & Public Affairs:* Asian American Affairs, Community Foundations, Economic Development, Employment/Job Training, General, Housing, Native American Affairs, Urban & Community Affairs, Zoos/Aquariums • *Education:* Agricultural Education, Arts/Humanities Education, Colleges & Universities, Education Reform, Engineering/Technological Education, General, Legal Education, Literacy, Medical Education, Private Education (Precollege), Public Education (Precollege), Science/Mathematics Education, Special Education, Student Aid • *Environment:* General, Resource Conservation • *Health:* AIDS/HIV, Alzheimers Disease, Health Organizations, Hospitals, Medical Rehabilitation, Single-Disease Health Associations • *International:* International Relations • *Religion:* Religious Organizations, Religious Welfare • *Science:* Science Museums • *Social Services:* Animal Protection, Big Brother/Big Sister, Child Abuse, Child Welfare, Community Service Organizations, Family Planning, Family Services, Food/Clothing Distribution, General, Homes, People with Disabilities, Scouts, Senior Services, Sexual Abuse, Shelters/Homelessness, Special Olympics, Substance Abuse, Youth Organizations

Grant Types: capital, challenge, professorship, project, and research

Geographic Distribution: Oklahoma

GIVING OFFICERS
Richard Bell: pres

Molly Boren: secy, treas, trust

Cheri D. Cartwright: exec dir, asst secy-treas

Richard Hefler: mgr

Jane Joyroe: vp, trust

Joseph W. Morris: trust

Robert Rennie: trust

Robert Rizley: secy-treas

Paul Frederick Sharp: trust *B* Kirksville MO 1918 *ED* Phillips Univ AB 1939; Univ MN PhD 1947 *NONPR AFFIL* dir: Cleveland County Red Cross, Cleveland County YMCA; mem: Phi Alpha Theta, Phi Beta Kappa, Phi Delta Kappa, Phi Kappa Phi, Pi Gamma Nu; pres: Univ OK

Preston Albert Trimble: trust *B* Salina OK 1930 *ED* Univ OK BA 1956; Univ OK LLB 1960 *NONPR AFFIL* bd regents: Natl Coll District Attorneys; chmn: OK Corrections Workshop; dir: Am Retarded Citizens, OK Univ Crisis Ctr; mem: Am Legion, Appellate Judges Conf, Cleveland County Bar Assn, Judicial Counc OK, Natl District Attorneys Assn, OK Bar Assn, OK District Attorneys Assn; mem planning comm: Natl Inst Crime Delinquency; trust: Natl Assn Pretrial Svc Agencies Resource Ctr *CLUB AFFIL* Lions

Terry West: trust

Lee Anne Wilson: trust

APPLICATION INFORMATION
Initial Approach:

Proposals should be single-spaced, unbound, stapled, and printed on only one side of white, 8 1/2- by 11-inch paper.

Proposals should contain the name, address, phone number, contact person, and brief history of the organization; copy of the IRS determination letter of tax-exempt status; names of principal officers, directors, and key staff; budget for the project including amount requested as well as other sources of support, including a list of all outstanding requests for funds; and a copy of organization's most recent audit, if available, or a financial report or organizational budget. Include a three- to four-page description of the project with a description of the organization's activities; problem or need project will address; outline of project including goals, objectives, activities, and timetable; geographical area and number of people to be served by project; description of similar projects; evaluation process; source of funds in operating budget and an indication of approximately what percentage of that budget is spent on fund raising; and plans for continuing project after grant ends.

Applications should be submitted by February 15 or August 15.

The trustees meet in January, April, July, and October. Grant proposals are considered at the April and October meetings. Organizations whose applications are accepted for inclusion on the agenda for the April or October meetings will be notified and required to submit additional copies of their proposals.

Restrictions on Giving: The foundation normally does not fund local programs appropriately financed within the community, or direct mail solicitations. The foundation makes no grants to individuals, nor does it take responsibility for permanent financing of a program.

PUBLICATIONS
Guidelines for proposals brochure

GRANTS ANALYSIS
Total Grants: $2,659,391

Number of Grants: 69

Highest Grant: $660,000

Average Grant: $38,542

Typical Range: $10,000 to $50,000

Disclosure Period: fiscal year ending November 30, 1994

Note: Recent grants are derived from a 1994 grants list.

RECENT GRANTS

General
12 and 12 Transition House, Oklahoma City, OK
Big Brothers and Big Sisters of Greater Oklahoma City, Oklahoma City, OK
Call Rape, Oklahoma City, OK
Cameron College Foundation, Lawton, OK
Child Abuse Network, Oklahoma City, OK

Share Trust, Charles Morton

CONTACT
B. Michael Carroll
Trustee
Charles Morton Share Trust
c/o Liberty National Bank and Trust Co.
PO Box 25848, Trust Dept.
Oklahoma City, OK 73125
(405) 231-6438

FINANCIAL SUMMARY
Recent Giving: $412,700 (fiscal 1994); $406,316 (fiscal 1993); $410,560 (fiscal 1992)

Assets: $8,636,851 (fiscal 1994); $8,817,705 (fiscal 1993); $8,990,674 (fiscal 1992)

EIN: 73-6090984

CONTRIBUTIONS SUMMARY

Donor(s): the late Charles Morton Share

Typical Recipients: • *Arts & Humanities:* Arts Institutes, Libraries, Museums/Galleries, Music • *Civic & Public Affairs:* Clubs, General, Municipalities/Towns, Parades/Festivals, Safety • *Education:* Colleges & Universities, Education Funds, Literacy, Public Education (Precollege) • *Health:* Clinics/Medical Centers, Diabetes, Hospitals, Medical Research • *Science:* Science Museums • *Social Services:* Community Service Organizations, Delinquency & Criminal Rehabilitation, People with Disabilities, Scouts, Youth Organizations

Grant Types: scholarship

Geographic Distribution: focus on OK

GIVING OFFICERS

Liberty National Bank: trust

J. R. Holder: trust

C. E. Johnson: trust

Gertrude Myers: trust

B. H. Thornton: trust

APPLICATION INFORMATION

Initial Approach: Send cover letter and full proposal. Include a description of organization, amount requested, purpose of funds sought, recently audited financial statement, and proof of tax-exempt status. There are no deadlines.

Restrictions on Giving: Does not support individuals.

GRANTS ANALYSIS

Total Grants: $412,700

Number of Grants: 13

Highest Grant: $200,000

Typical Range: $5,000 to $65,000

Disclosure Period: fiscal year ending June 30, 1994

Note: Recent grants are derived from a fiscal 1994 Form 990.

RECENT GRANTS

General

200,000	State of Oklahoma Department of Corrections, Tulsa, OK
65,000	City of Alva, Alva, OK
50,000	Alva Public Schools, Alva, OK
20,000	City of Waynoka, Waynoka, OK
19,000	Northwestern Oklahoma State University Foundation, Alva, OK

Williams Companies, The / Williams Companies Foundation, The

Revenue: $2.67 billion
Employees: 6,795
Headquarters: Tulsa, OK
SIC Major Group: Natural Gas Transmission, Refined Petroleum Pipelines, and Miscellaneous Business Credit Institutions

CONTACT

Hannah Davis Robson
Managing Director
The Williams Companies Foundation
PO Box 2400
Tulsa, OK 74102
(918) 588-2106
Note: The company's World Wide Web address is http://www.twc.com/twc

FINANCIAL SUMMARY

Recent Giving: $3,400,000 (1994 approx.); $3,000,000 (1993 approx.); $3,041,143 (1991)

Assets: $8,276,553 (1991); $7,497,508 (1990); $8,085,000 (1989)

Fiscal Note: Figures include direct and foundation contributions. 1991 figure also includes nonmonetary support.

EIN: 23-7413843

CONTRIBUTIONS SUMMARY

Typical Recipients: • *Arts & Humanities:* Arts Associations & Councils, Arts Centers, Arts Institutes, Dance, Historic Preservation, Libraries, Museums/Galleries, Music, Opera, Performing Arts, Theater • *Civic & Public Affairs:* Business/Free Enterprise, Economic Development, Housing, Law & Justice, Philanthropic Organizations, Professional & Trade Associations, Public Policy, Rural Affairs, Safety, Urban & Community Affairs, Women's Affairs, Zoos/Aquariums • *Education:* Business Education, Colleges & Universities, Community & Junior Colleges, Economic Education, Education Associations, Education Funds, Elementary Education (Private), Private Education (Precollege), Public Education (Precollege), Science/Mathematics Education • *Environment:* General • *Health:* Health Funds, Health Organizations, Hospitals, Single-Disease Health Associations • *International:* International Relations • *Science:* Science Exhibits & Fairs, Scientific Organizations • *Social Services:* Child Welfare, Community Service Organizations, Domestic Violence, Emergency Relief, Family Planning, Family Services, Homes, People with Disabilities, Recreation & Athletics, Shelters/Homelessness, Substance Abuse, United Funds/United Ways, Youth Organizations

Grant Types: capital, employee matching gifts, endowment, and general support

Nonmonetary Support: $61,081 (1989); $75,890 (1988)

Nonmonetary Support Types: in-kind services, loaned executives, and workplace solicitation

Geographic Distribution: exclusively in areas near company headquarters and operating locations

Operating Locations: KS, LA, MO (St. Louis), OK (Tulsa), UT (Salt Lake City), WY

CORP. OFFICERS

Keith E. Bailey: *B* Kansas City MO 1942 *ED* MO Sch Mines & Metallurgy BS 1964; Univ MO 1981 *CURR EMPL* chmn, pres, ceo, dir: Williams Cos *CORP AFFIL* chmn, dir: NW Pipeline Corp *NONPR AFFIL* mem: Am Petroleum Inst, Assn Oil Pipe Lines, Interstate Natural Gas Assn Am, Natl Assn Corrosion Engrs, Natl Soc Professional Engrs, Southern Gas Assn

John C. Baumgarner, Jr.: *CURR EMPL* sr vp corp devel plan: Williams Cos

David M. Higbee: *B* Cedar City UT 1944 *ED* Brigham Young Univ 1968; Univ Chicago 1971 *CURR EMPL* secy: Williams Cos

John Furman Lewis: *B* Ft Worth TX 1934 *ED* Rice Univ BA 1956; Univ TX 1962 *CURR EMPL* sr vp, gen coun: Williams Cos *NONPR AFFIL* mem: Am Bar Assn, Arts & Humanities Counc Tulsa, OH Bar Assn, OK Bar Assn, Southwestern Legal Fdn Intl Oil & Gas Ed Ctr, Tulsa County Bar Assn, TX Bar Assn; mem adv bd: Southwestern Legal Fdn Intl Comparative Law Ctr; mem, gen law comm: Am Petroleum Inst

GIVING OFFICERS

Keith E. Bailey: pres, dir *CURR EMPL* chmn, pres, ceo, dir: Williams Cos (see above)

John C. Baumgarner, Jr.: dir *CURR EMPL* sr vp corp devel plan: Williams Cos (see above)

David M. Higbee: secy, treas *CURR EMPL* secy: Williams Cos (see above)

John Furman Lewis: dir *CURR EMPL* sr vp, gen coun: Williams Cos (see above)

Hannah Davis Robson: mng dir

APPLICATION INFORMATION

Initial Approach: *Initial Contact:* brief letter and proposal (one copy) *Include Information On:* description of the organization, amount requested, purpose for which funds are sought, recently audited financial statement, and proof of tax-exempt status *Deadlines:* none (board meets in June and December)

Restrictions on Giving: Does not support fraternal organizations, goodwill advertising, individuals, political or lobbying groups, or religious organizations for sectarian purposes.

GRANTS ANALYSIS

Total Grants: $1,506,781*

Number of Grants: 281*

Highest Grant: $510,463

Average Grant: $3,558*

Typical Range: $1,000 to $10,000

Disclosure Period: 1991

Note: Financial information is for the foundation only and does not include direct gifts. The average grant figure excludes a single grant totaling $510,463. Recent grants are derived from a 1991 Form 990.

RECENT GRANTS

General
510,463	Tulsa Area United Way, Tulsa, OK
41,666	Tulsa Zoo Development, Tulsa, OK
33,334	Oklahoma State University Foundation, Stillwater, OK
33,334	University of Oklahoma Foundation, Norman, OK
33,333	Kansas University Endowment Association

Zarrow Foundation, Anne and Henry

CONTACT
Judith Z. Kishner
Director
Anne and Henry Zarrow Fdn.
PO Box 1530
Tulsa, OK 74101
(918) 587-3391

FINANCIAL SUMMARY
Recent Giving: $317,535 (1993); $498,550 (1992); $309,100 (1991)

Assets: $5,355,661 (1993); $4,035,529 (1992); $4,103,348 (1991)

Gifts Received: $1,300,000 (1993); $100,000 (1992)

Fiscal Note: In 1993, contributions were received from Henry H. Zarrow.

EIN: 73-1286874

CONTRIBUTIONS SUMMARY
Donor(s): Henry H. Zarrow

Typical Recipients: • *Arts & Humanities:* Arts Associations & Councils, Arts Institutes, Ballet, Community Arts, Historic Preservation, History & Archaeology, Libraries, Museums/Galleries, Opera • *Civic & Public Affairs:* General, Hispanic Affairs, Law & Justice, Municipalities/Towns, Urban & Community Affairs • *Education:* Minority Education, Private Education (Precollege), Public Education (Precollege), Secondary Education (Public), Student Aid • *Health:* Cancer, Clinics/Medical Centers, Hospitals, Medical Rehabilitation, Medical Research, Mental Health, Research/Studies Institutes, Speech & Hearing • *International:* Foreign Arts Organizations • *Religion:* Churches, Jewish Causes, Ministries, Religious Welfare, Synagogues/Temples • *Social Services:* Community Service Organizations, Day Care, Domestic Violence, Family Planning, Family Services, Food/Clothing Distribution, People with Disabilities, Senior Services, Sexual Abuse, Substance Abuse, United Funds/United Ways, YMCA/YWCA/YMHA/YWHA, Youth Organizations

Grant Types: emergency and general support

Geographic Distribution: focus on Tulsa, OK, area

GIVING OFFICERS
Robert H. Elliot: secy, dir

Judith Z. Kishner: dir

Robert A. Mulholland: treas, dir

Anne Zarrow: vp, dir

Henry H. Zarrow: pres, dir *CURR EMPL* pres, ceo: Sooner Pipe & Supply Corp *PHIL AFFIL* pres: Sooner Pipe & Supply Corporation Foundation

Stuart A. Zarrow: dir

APPLICATION INFORMATION
Initial Approach: Send a brief letter of inquiry.

Restrictions on Giving: Limited to organizations providing relief to the poor, distressed, or underprivileged in the Tulsa, OK, area.

GRANTS ANALYSIS
Total Grants: $317,535

Number of Grants: 49

Highest Grant: $40,000

Typical Range: $1,000 to $28,500

Disclosure Period: 1993

Note: Recent grants are derived from a 1993 Form 990.

RECENT GRANTS

General
40,000	Tulsa Center for Physically Limited, Tulsa, OK
28,500	National Rehabilitation Hospital, Washington, DC
20,000	Catholic Charities Diocese of Tulsa, Tulsa, OK
15,000	Neighbor for Neighbor, Tulsa, OK
10,000	Domestic Violence Intervention, Tulsa, OK

OREGON

Carpenter Foundation

CONTACT
Dunbar Carpenter
Treasurer
Carpenter Fdn.
711 E Main St., Ste. 10
Medford, OR 97504
(503) 772-5851

FINANCIAL SUMMARY
Recent Giving: $552,072 (fiscal 1994); $483,096 (fiscal 1993); $525,609 (fiscal 1992)

Assets: $11,566,833 (fiscal 1994); $11,929,478 (fiscal 1993); $10,716,451 (fiscal 1992)

Gifts Received: $1,000 (fiscal 1994); $1,000 (fiscal 1993); $1,000 (fiscal 1992)

EIN: 93-0491360

CONTRIBUTIONS SUMMARY
Donor(s): the late Helen Bundy Carpenter, the late Alfred S.V. Carpenter, Harlow Carpenter

Typical Recipients: • *Arts & Humanities:* Arts Associations & Councils, Arts Festivals, History & Archaeology, Libraries, Literary Arts, Museums/Galleries, Music, Opera, Performing Arts, Public Broadcasting, Theater • *Civic & Public Affairs:* Botanical Gardens/Parks, Employment/Job Training, General, Hispanic Affairs, Housing, Legal Aid, Municipalities/Towns, Native American Affairs, Parades/Festivals, Urban & Community Affairs • *Education:* Afterschool/Enrichment Programs, Colleges & Universities, Community & Junior Colleges, Education Funds, Faculty Development, Preschool Education, Secondary Education (Public), Student Aid • *Environment:* Resource Conservation • *Health:* Hospitals, Long-Term Care, Nursing Services • *Religion:* Religious Welfare • *Science:* Science Museums • *Social Services:* At-Risk Youth, Child Welfare, Community Centers, Community Service Organizations, Counseling, Day Care, Delinquency & Criminal Rehabilitation, Domestic Violence, Family Services, Food/Clothing Distribution, People with Disabilities, Recreation & Athletics, Senior Services, Shelters/Homelessness, Substance Abuse, United Funds/United Ways, YMCA/YWCA/YMHA/YWHA, Youth Organizations

Grant Types: operating expenses, research, scholarship, and seed money

Geographic Distribution: focus on Jackson and Josephine counties, OR

GIVING OFFICERS
Karen C. Allan: secy, trust

Barbara Bean: pub trust

Pat Blair: pub trust

Dunbar Carpenter: treas, trust

Jane H. Carpenter: pres, trust

William Duhaime: pub trust

William R. Moffat: trust

Brian Mostue: trust

Emily C. Mostue: vp, trust

Shirley Patton: pub trust

APPLICATION INFORMATION
Initial Approach: Send a brief letter of inquiry. Include a description of organization, amount requested, purpose of funds sought, recently audited financial statement, and proof of tax-exempt status. Deadlines are quarterly.

Restrictions on Giving: Does not support individuals. Limited to Jackson or Josephine Counties.

PUBLICATIONS
Application Guidelines, Annual Report

GRANTS ANALYSIS
Total Grants: $552,072

Number of Grants: 71

Highest Grant: $25,076

Typical Range: $500 to $20,000

Disclosure Period: fiscal year ending June 30, 1994

Note: Recent grants are derived from a fiscal 1994 Form 990.

RECENT GRANTS

General

25,076	OnTrack, Medford, OR — toward afterschool program for primary grade students in White City
20,000	SOSC, Ashland, OR — Faculty Development Scholarship Grant
15,000	Britt Festivals, Medford, OR — in support of Britt Classical Festival
15,000	CERVS, Medford, OR — toward a permanent facility
15,000	Nature Conservancy, Portland, OR — first of two payments toward acquisition of parcel at Lower Table Rock

Collins Foundation

CONTACT
William C. Pine
Vice President and Executive Director
Collins Foundation
1618 SW 1st Ave., Ste. 305
Portland, OR 97201-5708
(503) 227-7171

FINANCIAL SUMMARY
Recent Giving: $4,500,000 (1995 est.); $4,500,000 (1994 approx.); $5,054,000 (1993)

Assets: $106,000,000 (1995 est.); $106,000,000 (1994 approx.); $109,000,000 (1993)

Gifts Received: $573,715 (1990)

EIN: 93-6021893

CONTRIBUTIONS SUMMARY
Donor(s): The Collins Foundation was established in Oregon in 1947 by members of the Collins family. The Collins family is involved in the lumber and wood products industry. Family members serve on the board of directors of the Collins Pine Company.

Typical Recipients: • *Arts & Humanities:* Arts Associations & Councils, Arts Festivals, Dance, Historic Preservation, History & Archaeology, Libraries, Museums/Galleries, Music, Opera, Public Broadcasting, Theater • *Civic & Public Affairs:* Economic Development, Housing, Urban & Community Affairs • *Education:* Colleges & Universities, Education Funds, Legal Education, Private Education (Precollege), Science/Mathematics Education, Special Education, Student Aid • *Environment:* Air/Water Quality, General, Resource Conservation • *Health:* Alzheimers Disease, Emergency/Ambulance Services, Health Funds, Health Organizations, Hospices, Hospitals,

Trauma Treatment • *Religion:* Churches, Ministries, Religious Organizations, Religious Welfare • *Science:* Science Museums • *Social Services:* Child Welfare, Community Service Organizations, Day Care, Family Planning, Food/Clothing Distribution, Homes, People with Disabilities, Volunteer Services, Youth Organizations

Grant Types: capital, challenge, and general support

Geographic Distribution: Oregon only

GIVING OFFICERS
Timothy R. Bishop: treas *B* 1951 *ED* Univ OR BS 1974 *CURR EMPL* vp, treas: Collins Pine Co *PHIL AFFIL* trust: Collins-McDonald Trust Fund

Ralph Bolliger: vp, dir

Maribeth Wilson Collins: pres, dir *B* Portland OR 1918 *ED* Univ OR BA 1940 *CORP AFFIL* dir: Collins Holding Co, Collins Pine Co, Ostrander Construction Co *NONPR AFFIL* mem: Gamma Phi Beta; mem exec comm, secy, bd trusts: Willamette Univ *CLUB AFFIL* Intl, Univ, West Hills Racquet *PHIL AFFIL* trust: Collins Medical Trust

Grace Collins Goudy: fdr, vp, dir

William C. Pine: vp, exec dir

Cherida C. Smith: vp, trust

Thomas B. Stoel: secy *PHIL AFFIL* trust: Rose E. Tucker Charitable Trust; secy, dir: Wessinger Foundation

APPLICATION INFORMATION
Initial Approach:

Interested organizations should submit a written application to the foundation.

Applications must include the name of the charitable organization; date the grant is needed; budget; copy of IRS determination letter of tax-exempt status; description of project; list of the board of directors; estimated total funds required and amount needed from the foundation; anticipated sources of remaining funds; list of other contributors; and other sources being approached for funding.

Applications may be submitted any time.

Processing of applications requires four to six weeks.

Restrictions on Giving: The foundation does not give grants to individuals. The foundation only gives grants to organizations located in Oregon.

PUBLICATIONS
General information brochure

GRANTS ANALYSIS
Total Grants: $5,054,000

Number of Grants: 222

Highest Grant: $750,000

Average Grant: $22,766

Typical Range: $5,000 to $25,000

Disclosure Period: 1993

Note: Recent grants are derived from a 1992 Form 990.

RECENT GRANTS

Library

30,000	Cottin Gabel School, Portland, OR — new library, middle school
25,000	Mt. Angel Abbey and Seminary, St. Benedict, OR — library enhancement program

General

500,000	Willamette University, Salem, OR — Collins Legal Center
300,000	Lewis and Clark College, Portland, OR — signature program
250,000	Willamette University, Salem, OR — G. Herbert Smith scholarships
200,000	University of Portland, Portland, OR — endowed chair in science
150,000	St. Vincent Medical Foundation, Portland, OR — support Center of Excellence in Laser Medicine and Surgery

Collins Medical Trust

CONTACT
Nancy L. Helseth
Administrator
Collins Medical Trust
1618 S.W. First Ave., No. 300
Portland, OR 97201
(503) 227-1219

FINANCIAL SUMMARY
Recent Giving: $202,167 (fiscal 1993); $201,208 (fiscal 1992); $125,404 (fiscal 1991)

Assets: $4,168,623 (fiscal 1993); $3,920,625 (fiscal 1992); $3,514,801 (fiscal 1991)

EIN: 93-6021895

CONTRIBUTIONS SUMMARY
Typical Recipients: • *Arts & Humanities:* Libraries • *Education:* Education Funds, Health & Physical Education, Medical Education • *Health:* Health Policy/Cost Containment, Health Organizations, Hospices, Hospitals, Medical Research, Nursing Services, Single-Disease Health Associations • *Social Services:* Child Welfare, Family Services, Veterans

Grant Types: research and scholarship

Geographic Distribution: focus on OR

GIVING OFFICERS
Maribeth Wilson Collins: trust *B* Portland OR 1918 *ED* Univ OR BA 1940 *CORP AFFIL* dir: Collins Holding Co, Collins Pine Co, Ostrander Construction Co *NONPR AFFIL* mem: Gamma Phi Beta; mem exec comm, secy, bd trusts: Willamette Univ *CLUB AFFIL* Intl, Univ, West Hills Racquet *PHIL AFFIL* pres, dir: Collins Foundation

Truman W. Collins, Jr.: trust

Joseph F. Paquet: trust
James R. Patterson: trust

APPLICATION INFORMATION
Initial Approach: Send brief letter of inquiry describing program or project. There are no deadlines.

GRANTS ANALYSIS
Total Grants: $202,167

Number of Grants: 18

Highest Grant: $51,567

Typical Range: $5,000 to $50,000

Disclosure Period: fiscal year ending September 30, 1993

Note: Recent grants are derived from a fiscal 1993 Form 990.

RECENT GRANTS

Library

20,000	Mid-Columbia Health Foundation, The Dalles, OR — for library grant

General

51,567	Medical Research Foundation of Oregon, Portland, OR
43,600	Providence Medical Foundation, El Paso, TX
25,000	Linfield College School of Nursing, Linfield, OR — for JFP Scholarship Fund
25,000	Veterans Affairs Research Foundation
20,000	Oregon Health Sciences University Foundation, Portland, OR

First Interstate Bank of Oregon / First Interstate Bank of Oregon Charitable Foundation

Parent Company: First Interstate Bancorp
Assets: $53.3 billion
Parent Employees: 28,123
Headquarters: Portland, OR
SIC Major Group: National Commercial Banks

CONTACT
Harleen Katke
Administrator and Trustee
First Interstate Bank of Oregon Charitable Fdn.
PO Box 3131
Portland, OR 97208
(503) 225-2167

FINANCIAL SUMMARY
Recent Giving: $1,300,000 (1995); $1,375,000 (1994); $1,275,277 (1993)

Assets: $49,539 (1993); $1,301,549 (1992); $2,056,866 (1990)

Fiscal Note: Company gives directly and through the foundation.

EIN: 93-0836170

CONTRIBUTIONS SUMMARY
Typical Recipients: • *Arts & Humanities:* Arts Appreciation, Arts Associations & Councils, Arts Centers, Arts Festivals, Arts Funds, Arts Institutes, Ballet, Community Arts, Dance, History & Archaeology, Libraries, Museums/Galleries, Music, Opera, Performing Arts, Public Broadcasting, Theater • *Civic & Public Affairs:* Business/Free Enterprise, Community Foundations, Economic Policy, Employment/Job Training, Municipalities/Towns, Rural Affairs, Safety, Urban & Community Affairs • *Education:* After-school/Enrichment Programs, Agricultural Education, Business Education, Colleges & Universities, Community & Junior Colleges, Continuing Education, Economic Education, Education Funds, Health & Physical Education, Medical Education, Minority Education, Science/Mathematics Education, Special Education, Student Aid • *Environment:* General • *Health:* Clinics/Medical Centers, Health Funds, Health Organizations, Heart, Hospices, Hospitals, Medical Rehabilitation, Medical Research, Mental Health • *Religion:* Religious Organizations, Religious Welfare • *Science:* Science Museums • *Social Services:* Child Welfare, Community Centers, Community Service Organizations, Family Services, Food/Clothing Distribution, People with Disabilities, Senior Services, Shelters/Homelessness, Substance Abuse, United Funds/United Ways, Youth Organizations

Grant Types: capital, department, employee matching gifts, general support, project, and scholarship

Note: Company matches employee gifts of $25 to $3,000.

Nonmonetary Support Types: donated equipment, loaned employees, and loaned executives

Note: The contact person for nonmonetary donations is Floyd Bennett, Senior Vice President. Above figures exclude nonmonetary support.

Geographic Distribution: matching gifts to colleges and universities are given in OR, WA, ID, MT, and AK. all other giving is within the state of Oregon

Operating Locations: OR (Portland)

CORP. OFFICERS
James J. Curran: *B* 1939 *ED* Univ San Francisco BA 1961 *CURR EMPL* chmn, ceo: First Interstate Bank OR NA *CORP AFFIL* ceo, dir: First Interstate Bank WA NA

Andrew Gerlicher: *CURR EMPL* sr vp, mgr bank rel: First Interstate Bank NW Region *CORP AFFIL* exec vp: First Interstate Bank WA NA

Robert G. Murray: *B* Portland OR 1937 *ED* Portland St Univ 1962; Univ OR 1964 *CURR EMPL* exec vp: First Interstate Bank NW Region *CORP AFFIL* exec vp: Capital Mgmt Group *NONPR AFFIL* chmn: Marylhurst Coll; dir: Portland Chamber Commerce; fin chmn: Boy Scouts Am; mem: Am Bankers Assn, Am Inst Banking, Inst Chartered Fin Analysts; mem bus adv counc: OR St Univ; treas, trust: Med Res Fdn, William Temple House, Un Way OR, Waverly Childrens Home; trust: OR Commun Fdn

Janice J. Wilson: *B* Brunswick GA 1942 *CURR EMPL* area pres, dir: First Interstate Bank OR NA *CORP AFFIL* dir: First Interstate Devel Corp

GIVING OFFICERS
Robert Ames: trust *CORP AFFIL* dir: FIB OR

Janice Frater: trust

Andrew Gerlicher: trust *CURR EMPL* sr vp, mgr bank rel: First Interstate Bank NW Region (see above)

Harleen Katke: admin, trust *CURR EMPL* exec admin: First Interstate Bank NW Region *PHIL AFFIL* dir: First Interstate Bank of WA Foundation

Robert G. Murray: trust *CURR EMPL* exec vp: First Interstate Bank NW Region (see above)

Janice J. Wilson: trust *CURR EMPL* area pres, dir: First Interstate Bank OR NA (see above)

APPLICATION INFORMATION
Initial Approach: *Initial Contact:* brief letter or proposal *Include Information On:* description of the organization and its programs, amount requested and specific purpose for which funds are sought, other means of support, current financial statement, project budget (if applicable), proof of 501(c)(3) tax-exempt status, and list of organization's board of directors *Deadlines:* none

Restrictions on Giving: Foundation does not fund endowments, conferences, seminars, or similar events. Does not contribute to individuals; political candidates, committees, or organizations; fraternal groups; service clubs; goodwill advertising; dinners or special events; religious organizations or institutions; charitable foundations except those operating to support a single cause; or member agencies of the United Way.

OTHER THINGS TO KNOW
Size of foundation's contributions varies based on purpose, size of goal, and other features of solicitation.

GRANTS ANALYSIS
Total Grants: $1,275,277

Number of Grants: 350

Highest Grant: $339,000

Average Grant: $3,644

Typical Range: $100 to $5,000

Disclosure Period: 1993

Note: Recent grants are derived from a 1993 Form 990.

RECENT GRANTS

General

339,000	United Way Columbia-Willamette, Portland, OR
90,287	Oregon Independent College Foundation, Portland, OR
25,085	United Way Lane County, Eugene, OR
25,000	Neighborhood Economic Development Corporation
25,000	OHSU School of Nursing

Fohs Foundation

CONTACT
Rose Mary Cooper
Secretary and Treasurer
Fohs Fdn.
PO Box 1001
Roseburg, OR 97470
(503) 440-1587

FINANCIAL SUMMARY
Recent Giving: $586,250 (1992); $555,250 (1991); $293,500 (1990)

Assets: $9,754,145 (1992); $9,169,984 (1991); $8,036,511 (1990)

EIN: 74-6003165

CONTRIBUTIONS SUMMARY
Donor(s): the late F. Julius Fohs, the late Cora B. Fohs

Typical Recipients: • *Arts & Humanities:* Libraries, Opera • *Civic & Public Affairs:* Housing • *Education:* Agricultural Education, Colleges & Universities, Education Funds, Minority Education, Private Education (Precollege), Religious Education, Student Aid • *Environment:* General • *Health:* Health Organizations, Single-Disease Health Associations • *International:* Foreign Educational Institutions, International Development, International Peace & Security Issues, International Relations, Missionary/Religious Activities • *Religion:* Religious Organizations • *Social Services:* Camps, Child Welfare, Recreation & Athletics, Refugee Assistance, Senior Services, Youth Organizations

Grant Types: endowment and scholarship

GIVING OFFICERS
Rose Mary Cooper: secy, treas

Edward Sohn: trust

Frances F. Sohn: chmn

Fred Sohn: vchmn

Howard Sohn: trust

Ruth Sohn: trust

APPLICATION INFORMATION
Initial Approach: Send brief letter of inquiry describing program or project. There are no deadlines.

GRANTS ANALYSIS
Total Grants: $586,250

Number of Grants: 18

Highest Grant: $150,000

Typical Range: $5,000 to $50,000

Disclosure Period: 1992

Note: Recent grants are derived from a 1992 Form 990.

RECENT GRANTS

Library

20,000	New York Public Library, New York, NY

General

150,000	American Associates of Ben Gurion University, New York, NY — Jacob Blaustein Institute for Desert Research, plant adaptation research unit
100,000	American Associates of Ben Gurion University, New York, NY — absorption program
50,000	Operation Restoration, Washington, DC — Israeli immigrant housing
40,000	American Society for Technion, New York, NY — fund for Ethiopian absorption (manpower program)
40,000	David School, David, KY — building program

Hunt Charitable Trust, C. Giles

CONTACT
C. Giles Hunt Charitable Trust
c/o First Interstate Bank of Oregon, N.A.
PO Box 10566
Eugene, OR 97440-9983
(503) 225-2331

FINANCIAL SUMMARY
Recent Giving: $184,825 (1993); $226,172 (1992); $256,466 (1991)

Assets: $4,817,273 (1993); $4,711,312 (1992); $4,558,414 (1991)

EIN: 23-7428278

CONTRIBUTIONS SUMMARY
Donor(s): the late C. Giles Hunt

Typical Recipients: • *Arts & Humanities:* Arts Associations & Councils, Community Arts, Historic Preservation, History & Archaeology, Libraries • *Civic & Public Affairs:* Botanical Gardens/Parks, Clubs, General, Municipalities/Towns, Safety, Urban & Community Affairs • *Education:* Agricultural Education, Community & Junior Colleges, Literacy, Private Education (Precollege), Public Education (Precollege), Secondary Education (Private), Secondary Education (Public) • *Environment:* Wildlife Protection • *Health:* Clinics/Medical Centers, Emergency/Ambulance Services, Health Organizations, Hospitals, Prenatal Health Issues • *Religion:* Churches, Missionary Activities (Domestic), Religious Welfare • *Social Services:* Child Welfare, Community Centers, Community Service Organizations, Counseling, Crime Prevention, Day Care, Domestic Violence, Family Planning, Family Services, Food/Clothing Distribution, People with Disabilities, Recreation & Athletics, Scouts, Senior Services, Shelters/Homelessness, Substance Abuse, Volunteer Services, Youth Organizations

Grant Types: capital

Geographic Distribution: focus on Douglas County, OR

GIVING OFFICERS
First Interstate Bank of Oregon: trust

APPLICATION INFORMATION
Initial Approach: Send letter requesting application form. There are no deadlines.

PUBLICATIONS
Application Guidelines

GRANTS ANALYSIS
Total Grants: $184,825

Number of Grants: 51

Highest Grant: $15,000

Typical Range: $500 to $15,000

Disclosure Period: 1993

Note: Recent grants are derived from a 1993 Form 990.

RECENT GRANTS

Library

15,000	Douglas County Library Foundation, Roseburg, OR
4,000	Oakland Branch Library, Oakland, OR
3,000	C. Giles Hunt Memorial Library, Eugene, OR
3,000	Yoncalla Branch Library, Yoncalla, OR
2,500	Winston Branch Library, Winston, OR

General

100,900	Friendly Kitchen, Roseburg, OR
15,000	Boy Scouts of America Oregon Trails, Eugene, OR
12,500	City of Roseburg Stewart Park, Roseburg, OR
10,000	Roseburg Rescue Mission, Roseburg, OR
10,000	Umpqua Community Action Network, Roseburg, OR

Jackson Foundation

CONTACT
Robert H. Depew
Vice President
Jackson Foundation
c/o U.S. National Bank of Oregon
PO Box 3168
Portland, OR 97208
(503) 275-6564

FINANCIAL SUMMARY
Recent Giving: $400,000 (fiscal 1995 est.); $323,723 (fiscal 1994); $437,698 (fiscal 1993)

Assets: $11,000,000 (fiscal 1995 est.); $11,076,796 (fiscal 1994); $10,549,013 (fiscal 1993)

Gifts Received: $37,507 (fiscal 1985)

EIN: 93-6020752

CONTRIBUTIONS SUMMARY
Donor(s): The Jackson Foundation was established as a trust in Oregon in 1960, with funds bequeathed by Maria C. Jackson, widow of the former owner of the *Oregon Journal*.

Typical Recipients: • *Arts & Humanities:* Arts Associations & Councils, Arts Festivals, Arts Institutes, Ballet, Dance, Historic Preservation, History & Archaeology, Libraries, Museums/Galleries, Music, Opera, Performing Arts, Public Broadcasting, Theater • *Civic & Public Affairs:* Clubs, Hispanic Affairs, Housing, Legal Aid, Urban & Community Affairs, Women's Affairs, Zoos/Aquariums • *Education:* Colleges & Universities, Community & Junior Colleges, General, Preschool Education, Private Education (Precollege), Public Education (Precollege), Science/Mathematics Education, Student Aid • *Environment:* General, Resource Conservation • *Health:* Alzheimers Disease, Emergency/Ambulance Services, Health Funds, Health Organizations, Hospices, Hospitals, Medical Research, Mental Health, Public Health • *Religion:* Jewish Causes, Religious Organizations, Religious Welfare • *Social Services:* At-Risk Youth, Child Welfare, Community Centers, Community Service Organizations, Counseling, Day Care, Domestic Violence, Family Planning, Family Services, Food/Clothing Distribution, Homes, People with Disabilities, Recreation & Athletics, Scouts, Senior Services, Shelters/Homelessness, Substance Abuse, United Funds/United Ways, Volunteer Services, YMCA/YWCA/YMHA/YWHA, Youth Organizations

Grant Types: capital, endowment, matching, multiyear/continuing support, project, and research

Geographic Distribution: focus on OR

GIVING OFFICERS
US Natl Bank OR: co-trust

Milo E. Ornseth: co-trust

Julie Vigeland: co-trust

APPLICATION INFORMATION
Initial Contact: Prospective applicants should request an application form by telephone or brief letter. Proof of tax-exempt status under IRS Code Section 501(c)(3) is required.

Deadlines: The trustees meet in April, September, and December. Application deadlines are March 25, August 25, and November 25 for the following month's meeting. If the application is received after the deadline it will be considered at the next meeting. Applicants will be notified by letter two to three weeks after the meeting date.

Restrictions on Giving: No grants are made to individuals or for endowments.

OTHER THINGS TO KNOW
The foundation reports, "Funds requested for operating purposes, staff salaries and the like do not, generally, have the priority that funds for one-time, special projects or developmental projects enjoy."

PUBLICATIONS
Annual report

GRANTS ANALYSIS
Total Grants: $323,723

Number of Grants: 88

Highest Grant: $10,000

Typical Range: $1,000 to $10,000

Disclosure Period: fiscal year ending June 30, 1994

Note: Recent grants are derived from a fiscal 1994 Form 990.

RECENT GRANTS

General

10,000	Albina Ministerial Alliance, Albina, OR
10,000	American National Red Cross, Portland, OR
10,000	Oregon Coast Aquarium, Newport, OR — for two years
7,500	Boy Scouts of America, Portland, OR
7,500	Salvation Army, Portland, OR

JELD-WEN, Inc. / JELD-WEN Foundation

Sales: $1.0 million
Employees: 50
Headquarters: Klamath Falls, OR
SIC Major Group: Millwork

CONTACT
R.C. Wendt
Trustee
JELD-WEN Fdn.
PO Box 1329
Klamath Falls, OR 97601
(503) 882-3451

FINANCIAL SUMMARY
Recent Giving: $800,000 (1994); $739,331 (1992); $590,568 (1991)

Assets: $16,910,434 (1992); $15,882,483 (1991); $14,249,689 (1990)

Fiscal Note: Figures reflect foundation contributions only.

EIN: 93-6054272

CONTRIBUTIONS SUMMARY
Typical Recipients: • *Arts & Humanities:* Arts Associations & Councils, Arts Festivals, Libraries, Museums/Galleries • *Civic & Public Affairs:* Botanical Gardens/Parks, Business/Free Enterprise, Chambers of Commerce, Housing, Public Policy, Safety, Urban & Community Affairs, Women's Affairs • *Education:* Colleges & Universities, Community & Junior Colleges, Education Reform, Elementary Education (Public), Engineering/Technological Education, General, Preschool Education, Private Education (Precollege), Science/Mathematics Education • *Environment:* General, Wildlife Protection • *Health:* Emergency/Ambulance Services, Health Organizations, Hospices, Hospitals • *Religion:* Religious Welfare • *Science:* Science Museums • *Social Services:* At-Risk Youth, Child Welfare, Community Centers, People with Disabilities, Recreation & Athletics, United Funds/United Ways, Volunteer Services, Youth Organizations

Grant Types: capital, challenge, general support, project, scholarship, and seed money

Geographic Distribution: in communities with company plants, or areas where a significant number of company employees reside

Operating Locations: AZ (Flagstaff), IA (Grinnell), NC (Charlotte), OH (Mount Vernon), OR (Klamath Falls), PA (Ringtown)

CORP. OFFICERS
William Bernard Early: *B* Mexico MO 1936 *ED* Stanford Univ 1958; Harvard Univ 1964 *CURR EMPL* sr vp, asst secy, dir: JELD-WEN Inc *CORP AFFIL* sr vp, asst secy, dir: Bend Millwork Sys Inc *PHIL AFFIL* pres: Early Family Foundation

Richard L. Wendt: *B* 1931 *CURR EMPL* fdr, chmn: JELD-WEN Inc *CORP AFFIL* chmn: Bend Millwork Sys Inc, Marshall & Wells Co; chmn, dir: Trendwest Mgmt Co; pres, treas: Paxton Inc; vp, dir: Jordan Millwork Co, Wenco Distrs

Roderick C. Wendt: *B* 1954 *ED* Willamette Univ Law Sch JD 1980 *CURR EMPL* pres, dir: JELD-WEN Inc *CORP AFFIL* pres: 3 D Indus Inc; pres, dir: Jordan Millwork Co, Wenco Distr Inc; pres, treas, dir: Bend Millwork Sys Inc, Bend Millwork Systems; secy: Paxton Inc; secy, treas, dir: Trendwest Mgmt Co

Larry V. Wetter: *B* Rockwell City IA 1933 *ED* IA Univ Sci & Tech 1955 *CURR EMPL* vchmn: JELD-WEN Inc *CORP AFFIL* dir: Paxton Inc; exec vp, dir: Bend Millwork Sys Inc

GIVING OFFICERS
William Bernard Early: trust *CURR EMPL* sr vp, asst secy, dir: JELD-WEN Inc *PHIL AFFIL* pres: Early Family Foundation (see above)

Nancy Wendt: trust

Richard L. Wendt: trust *CURR EMPL* fdr, chmn: JELD-WEN Inc (see above)

Larry V. Wetter: trust *CURR EMPL* vchmn: JELD-WEN Inc (see above)

APPLICATION INFORMATION
Initial Approach: *Initial Contact:* obtain a request for funding application and mail completed form to the foundation address *Include Information On:* as indicated in the request for funding application *Deadlines:* none

Restrictions on Giving: Foundation does not fund projects related to religious purposes; proposals which duplicate government or private agency programs; projects which serve a very narrow segment of the community; proposals that the foundation feels are not clearly defined, not feasible, not cost effective, or inappropriate to meet existing needs.

Foundation generally discourages requests for annual support outside of United Way giving.

Rejected proposals may not be resubmitted during the same calendar year.

OTHER THINGS TO KNOW
The foundation may fund an outstanding organization more than once in a short period

of time, but is cautious not to let organizations become dependent on regular giving. The foundation requests that organizations refrain from calling unless it is imperative to the project.

GRANTS ANALYSIS
Total Grants: $800,000

Typical Range: $1,500 to $10,000

Disclosure Period: 1994

Note: Figures reflect foundation contributions only. Recent grants are derived from a 1992 Form 990.

RECENT GRANTS

Library

10,000	Klamath County Library, Klamath Falls, OR — update book collection
5,000	Regional Library Board, Hartselle, AL — purchase of children's books

General

53,000	United Way of Klamath Basin, Klamath Falls, OR
34,015	Sacred Heart School, Klamath Falls, OR — building renovation
28,400	United Community Fund Knox County, Mt. Vernon, OH
25,000	Deschutes County Children's Foundation, Bend, OR — pledge payment
25,000	Deschutes United Way, Bend, OR

Louisiana-Pacific Corp. / Louisiana-Pacific Foundation

Revenue: $3.03 billion
Employees: 13,000
Headquarters: Portland, OR
SIC Major Group: Sawmills & Planing Mills—General, Millwork, Hardwood Veneer & Plywood, and Softwood Veneer & Plywood

CONTACT
Pamela A. Selis
Trustee
Louisiana-Pacific Fdn.
111 SW Fifth Ave.
Portland, OR 97204
(503) 221-0800

FINANCIAL SUMMARY
Recent Giving: $1,500,000 (1995 est.); $1,500,000 (1994 approx.); $1,500,000 (1993)

Assets: $70,000 (1994 approx.); $42,772 (1993); $39,516 (1992)

Gifts Received: $1,240,000 (1992)

Fiscal Note: Company gives primarily through the foundation. It also makes contributions directly from corporate funds; direct gifts are not included in above total giving figures. Estimate for direct support is un-

available. Above figures exclude nonmonetary support.

EIN: 23-7268660

CONTRIBUTIONS SUMMARY
Typical Recipients: • *Arts & Humanities:* Libraries, Museums/Galleries, Music, Opera, Performing Arts • *Civic & Public Affairs:* Botanical Gardens/Parks, General, Housing, Urban & Community Affairs, Zoos/Aquariums • *Education:* Business Education, Colleges & Universities, Literacy, Private Education (Precollege), Public Education (Precollege), Science/Mathematics Education, Secondary Education (Public), Student Aid • *Environment:* General • *Health:* Children's Health/Hospitals, Emergency/Ambulance Services, Health Organizations, Heart, Hospices, Hospitals, Single-Disease Health Associations • *International:* International Environmental Issues • *Religion:* Religious Organizations, Religious Welfare • *Science:* Science Exhibits & Fairs, Science Museums • *Social Services:* At-Risk Youth, Child Welfare, Community Service Organizations, Emergency Relief, Family Services, Food/Clothing Distribution, Homes, People with Disabilities, Recreation & Athletics, Shelters/Homelessness, Substance Abuse, United Funds/United Ways, Youth Organizations

Grant Types: capital, emergency, general support, project, and scholarship

Note: Scholarships are for dependents of employees, community, civic, arts, health, youth, and medical science.

Nonmonetary Support Types: donated equipment and donated products

Note: The company provides some nonmonetary support. The value of this support is not available. Write Pamela A. Selis for information.

Geographic Distribution: primarily near headquarters and operating locations

Operating Locations: AK (Annette, Ketchikan), AL (Braggs, Eufaula, Evergreen, Hanceville, Lockhart), CA (Arcata, Big Lagoon, Chino, Ft. Bragg, Oroville, Red Bluff, Rocklin, Samoa, Ukiah, Willits), CO (Montrose, Walden), FL (Crestview, Marianna, Westbay), GA (Eatonton, Hazelhurst, Statesboro, Waynesboro), ID (Chilco, Hayden Lake, Moyie Springs, Post Falls, Priest River, Rexburg, Sandpoint), KS (Dodge City, Salina), LA (Bernice, Logansport, Urania, Winnfield), ME (Houlton), MI (Newberry, Sagola), MN (Two Harbors), MO (Fenton), MS (Grenada, Hattiesburg, Philadelphia, Purvis), MT (Belgrade, Deer Lodge, Libby, Missoula), NC (Henderson, Nashville, Pittsboro, Wilmington), NV (Fernley, Reno), OH (Barberton, Ottawa, Winesburg, Youngstown), OK (Tulsa), OR (Pilot Rock, Portland), RI (East Providence), TX (Bon Weir, Bon Weir, Carthage, Cleveland, Conroe, Corrigan, Dallas, Jasper, Kountze, Lufkin, New Waverly, Silsbee, Trinity), VA (Dungannon), WA (Tacoma, Walla Walla), WI (Hayward, Mellen, Tomahawk), WY (Saratoga)

CORP. OFFICERS
Anton Conrad Kirchhof: *B* Portland OR 1945 *CURR EMPL* secy, gen couns: LA-Pacific Corp *NONPR AFFIL* mem: Am Corp Couns Assn, Am Soc Corp Secys

Harry Angelo Merlo, Sr.: *B* Stirling City CA 1925 *ED* Univ CA Berkeley BS 1949 *CURR EMPL* chmn, pres, ceo, dir: LA-Pacific Corp *CORP AFFIL* chmn: Ketchikan Pulp Co, Kirby Forest Indus; chmn, pres: LP Canada Ltd; dir: Whitman Corp *NONPR AFFIL* chmn, dir: Am Acad Achievement; dir: Am Paper Inst, Horatio Alger Ctr, Natl Forest Products Assn, Salvation Army, World Forestry Ctr; mem: CA Redwood Assn; mem adv bd: Univ CA Bus Sch; trust: Goodwill Indus, Hugh OBrian Youth Fdn, OR Mus Sci Indus *PHIL AFFIL* pres, dir: Harry A. Merlo Foundation

GIVING OFFICERS
Anita T. Davis: trust

William L. Hebert: asst secy, treas *CURR EMPL* secy, treas, dir: Hanco Inc

Anton Conrad Kirchhof: secy *CURR EMPL* secy, gen couns: LA-Pacific Corp (see above)

Gary R. Maffei: trust *PHIL AFFIL* vp, treas, dir: Harry A. Merlo Foundation

Harry Angelo Merlo, Sr.: chmn, pres *CURR EMPL* chmn, pres, ceo, dir: LA-Pacific Corp *PHIL AFFIL* pres, dir: Harry A. Merlo Foundation (see above)

Pamela Anne Selis: vp, trust *B* Portland OR 1942 *CURR EMPL* dir corp commun: LA Pacific Corp

APPLICATION INFORMATION
Initial Approach: *Initial Contact:* brief letter of proposal *Include Information On:* description of the organization, amount requested, purpose for which funds are sought, recently audited financial statement, and proof of tax-exempt status *Deadlines:* none

GRANTS ANALYSIS
Total Grants: $1,500,000

Number of Grants: 321

Highest Grant: $156,000

Average Grant: $4,000

Typical Range: $500 to $5,000

Disclosure Period: 1994

Note: Recent grants are derived from a 1992 Form 990.

RECENT GRANTS

Library

5,000	Ronald Reagan Presidential Foundation, Simi Valley, CA
5,000	William K. Kohrs Memorial Library, Deer Lodge, MT

General

124,570	University of Portland, Portland, OR
100,000	Heart Institute at St. Vincent Hospital, Portland, OR
100,000	Oregon Museum of Science and Industry Capital Campaign, Portland, OR

| 100,000 | University of Portland, Portland, OR |
| 100,000 | World Forestry Center, Portland, OR |

Meyer Memorial Trust

CONTACT
Charles S. Rooks
Executive Director
Meyer Memorial Trust
1515 SW Fifth Ave., Ste. 500
Portland, OR 97201
(503) 228-5512

FINANCIAL SUMMARY
Recent Giving: $15,000,000 (fiscal 1995 est.); $10,310,940 (fiscal 1994); $16,727,700 (fiscal 1993)

Assets: $310,000,000 (fiscal 1995 est.); $304,249,724 (fiscal 1994); $286,055,173 (fiscal 1993)

EIN: 93-0806316

CONTRIBUTIONS SUMMARY
Donor(s): The trust is the residuary beneficiary of the estate of Fred G. Meyer, and was established in April 1982. Fred Meyer, who died in 1978, bequeathed the trust approximately two million shares of stock in Fred Meyer, Inc. Mr. Meyer was born in 1886 into a family of Brooklyn grocers. After working his way through the wheat fields of the Dakotas and Montana and the gold fields of Alaska, he moved to Portland, OR, in 1909. He then became successful at peddling coffee and managing a downtown street market. Later he invested all of his assets in an "all package" grocery store, and began a chain of stores throughout the Pacific Northwest. By 1979, his stores employed more than 13,000 people and had over $1 billion in annual sales.

Fred Meyer's wife of 41 years, Eva, was an integral part of this success. She managed several store departments in the early years and became a director and the secretary-treasurer of Fred Meyer, Inc.

Fred Meyer's life and career exemplified ingenuity, hard work, and a commitment to the communities where he built his stores. He introduced innovative marketing concepts to the Northwest, including the packaging of bulk goods, one-stop shopping, cash-and-carry purchasing, self-service drug stores, and other creative and convenient services. He also supported economic development of the Northwest. He bought local products whenever possible, and he fostered the production of new crops in the region. He helped finance new business ventures as well as some in danger of failing.

Typical Recipients: • *Arts & Humanities:* Arts Centers, Arts Festivals, Arts Outreach, Ballet, Dance, Ethnic & Folk Arts, Historic Preservation, History & Archaeology, Libraries, Museums/Galleries, Music, Opera, Performing Arts, Public Broadcasting, Theater, Visual Arts • *Civic & Public Affairs:* Asian American Affairs, Botanical Gar-

dens/Parks, Economic Development, Employment/Job Training, Ethnic Organizations, Hispanic Affairs, Housing, Law & Justice, Legal Aid, Municipalities/Towns, Native American Affairs, Nonprofit Management, Philanthropic Organizations, Public Policy, Rural Affairs, Safety, Urban & Community Affairs, Zoos/Aquariums • *Education:* Afterschool/Enrichment Programs, Arts/Humanities Education, Business-School Partnerships, Colleges & Universities, Community & Junior Colleges, Continuing Education, Education Reform, Elementary Education (Private), Elementary Education (Public), Environmental Education, Faculty Development, International Exchange, International Studies, Leadership Training, Medical Education, Minority Education, Preschool Education, Private Education (Precollege), Public Education (Precollege), School Volunteerism, Science/Mathematics Education, Secondary Education (Private), Special Education • *Environment:* Air/Water Quality, General, Protection, Resource Conservation, Watershed • *Health:* AIDS/HIV, Alzheimers Disease, Cancer, Children's Health/Hospitals, Clinics/Medical Centers, Geriatric Health, Health Policy/Cost Containment, Health Organizations, Hospices, Hospitals, Long-Term Care, Medical Rehabilitation, Medical Research, Medical Training, Mental Health, Nursing Services, Prenatal Health Issues, Public Health • *Religion:* Jewish Causes, Religious Organizations, Religious Welfare, Seminaries • *Science:* Science Museums, Scientific Centers & Institutes • *Social Services:* At-Risk Youth, Child Abuse, Child Welfare, Community Centers, Community Service Organizations, Day Care, Delinquency & Criminal Rehabilitation, Domestic Violence, Family Planning, Family Services, Food/Clothing Distribution, People with Disabilities, Recreation & Athletics, Refugee Assistance, Senior Services, Sexual Abuse, Shelters/Homelessness, Substance Abuse, YMCA/YWCA/YMHA/YWHA, Youth Organizations

Grant Types: capital, challenge, general support, project, and seed money

Geographic Distribution: Oregon; and Alaska, Idaho, Montana, Oregon, and Washington for the children at-risk program

GIVING OFFICERS
Travis Cross: trust *B* Salem OR 1927 *ED* Stanford Univ BA 1949

Pauline W. Lawrence: trust

Warne Harry Nunn: trust

Wayne G. Pierson: treas, contr

G. Gerald Pratt: trust

Oran B. Robertson: trust *B* Turner OR 1937 *CURR EMPL* chmn, ceo, dir: Fred Meyer Inc

Charles S. Rooks: exec dir

APPLICATION INFORMATION
Initial Approach:

A grant application guidelines packet should be requested before submitting a proposal. Also, there are specific guidelines for the

Children At Risk, Small Grants, and Support for Teacher Initiatives programs.

The applicant should submit a completed application cover sheet (part of the packet); the organization's legal name and address; name, title, address, and telephone number of the person in charge of the project; description of the organization, including a summary of its background and its qualifications in the area for which funds are sought; list of names and primary affiliations of the organization's board of directors; list of the organization's most recent financial statement; and a copy of the IRS tax-exemption letter. Only one copy of these materials should be submitted. The proposal itself should contain a statement from the chief operating officer that the project has been reviewed and recommended for submission by the governing board; description of the project and why it is important to undertake; description of the people, organizations, or groups expected to benefit from the project's outcome and the ways they would benefit; substantiation of the extent of need for these benefits; explanation of why the applicant organization is the appropriate one to conduct the project; description of the plan of action and a timetable for implementation; methods and criteria for assessing the project's effectiveness; qualifications of people involved in implementing the project; detailed descriptions of previous budgets, if the project is already in operation; detailed current budget for the project; description of other possible sources of support; and an explanation of how the project could be sustained after the period for which support has been requested.

Proposals may be submitted any time, except in the focused programs. Deadlines for the Children at Risk program are March 1 and September 1. The deadlines for the Small Grants program are January 15, April 15, July 15, and October 15. The deadlines for the Support for Teacher Initiatives program are April 1 and October 1.

If a proposal submitted under the General Purpose or Children at Risk guidelines passes a first review by the trustees, a staff member will contact the applicant for additional information. Final action on proposals passing first review will not be made less than four months after submission. If a proposal is outside the field of interest of the trust, notification is given within two months. An applicant will be notified shortly after a decision had been reached on a proposal. Under the Small Grants program, a final decision will normally be made about six weeks after a deadline; incomplete proposals will not be considered. Under the Support for Teacher Initiatives program guidelines, applications submitted for the October 1 deadline will be awarded in December; applications submitted for the April 1 deadline will be awarded in June.

Restrictions on Giving: The trust does not favor proposals seeking funds for direct grants, scholarships, or fellowships to individuals; endowments; general fund drives or annual appeals; general ongoing operating budgets; indirect or overhead costs (except as specifically and essentially related to the grant project); debt retirement or operational deficits; projects of sectarian or religious organizations whose principal benefit is for their own members; or propagandizing or influencing elections or legislation.

OTHER THINGS TO KNOW
Except under the Children at Risk Program, applications are invited only from Oregon and that part of Washington located within the greater Portland metropolitan area.

PUBLICATIONS
Annual report, grant application guidelines, program guidelines

GRANTS ANALYSIS
Total Grants: $10,310,940

Number of Grants: 171

Highest Grant: $1,000,000

Average Grant: $60,298

Typical Range: $50,000 to $150,000*

Disclosure Period: fiscal year ending March 31, 1994

Note: The typical range for the foundation's Small Grants Program is $6,000 to $7,500. Recent grants are derived from a fiscal 1994 grants list.

RECENT GRANTS

Library

550,000	Lewis and Clark College, Portland, OR — to renovate and expand the Aubrey Watzek Library
373,000	Marylhurst College, Marylhurst, OR — for improvements to the library building
256,500	University of Oregon, Eugene, OR — to expand public access to the Knight Library by renovating and upgrading the Technical Service Center and creating a union catalog by merging the bibliographic databases of the University of Oregon and several other state-supported colleges

General

1,000,000	Pacific Northwest Museum of Natural History, Ashland, OR — for the development of this new natural history museum
575,000	Oregon State University, Corvallis, OR — to support the construction of the Environmental Computing Center to house an advanced computer system and research team for the NASA Earth Observing System project
500,000	George Fox College, Newberg, OR — to support the construction of a new science building
500,000	Oregon Graduate Institute, Portland, OR — for building renovation and construction of the Center for Lifelong Learning, which will include dining facilities, classrooms, a campus center, office space, and meeting rooms
500,000	Oregon Museum of Science and Industry, Portland, OR — to launch a capital campaign to finance construction of a new state-of-the-art facility on the east bank of the Willamette River

---

Northwest Natural Gas Co.

Revenue: $358.72 million
Employees: 1,293
Headquarters: Portland, OR
SIC Major Group: Natural Gas Distribution

CONTACT
Sharon Khormooji
Senior Staff Assistant
Northwest Natural Gas Co.
220 NW 2nd Ave.
Portland, OR 97209
(503) 226-4211

FINANCIAL SUMMARY
Recent Giving: $500,000 (1995 est.); $500,000 (1994 approx.); $349,900 (1993)

Fiscal Note: Company gives through the Oregon Community Foundation.

CONTRIBUTIONS SUMMARY
Typical Recipients: • *Arts & Humanities:* Arts Appreciation, Arts Associations & Councils, Arts Centers, Arts Festivals, Arts Funds, Arts Institutes, Community Arts, Dance, Ethnic & Folk Arts, General, Historic Preservation, Libraries, Museums/Galleries, Music, Opera, Performing Arts, Public Broadcasting, Theater, Visual Arts • *Civic & Public Affairs:* Economic Development, General, Housing, Professional & Trade Associations, Urban & Community Affairs, Women's Affairs, Zoos/Aquariums • *Education:* Business Education, Colleges & Universities, Elementary Education (Private), General, Minority Education • *Health:* General, Health Organizations, Hospices, Hospitals, Medical Rehabilitation, Mental Health, Single-Disease Health Associations • *Science:* Science Exhibits & Fairs • *Social Services:* Animal Protection, Child Welfare, Community Centers, Counseling, Day Care, Delinquency & Criminal Rehabilitation, Food/Clothing Distribution, General, Homes, People with Disabilities, Senior Services, Shelters/Homelessness, Substance Abuse, United Funds/United Ways, Volunteer Services, Youth Organizations

Grant Types: capital, employee matching gifts, general support, multiyear/continuing support, operating expenses, project, research, scholarship, and seed money

Note: Employee matching gifts support the United Way.

Nonmonetary Support Types: donated equipment, donated products, in-kind services, loaned employees, and loaned executives

Note: Value of non-monetary support was not available.

Geographic Distribution: headquarters and operating locations

Operating Locations: OR (Newport, Portland)

CORP. OFFICERS
Bruce R. DeBolt: *CURR EMPL* sr vp fin, cfo: NW Natural Gas Co

Robert Louis Ridgley: *B* Fort Wayne IN 1934 *ED* Cornell Univ 1956; Harvard Univ 1959 *CURR EMPL* pres, ceo, dir: NW Natural Gas Co *CORP AFFIL* dir: Bohemia, Kaiser Permanente, US Bancorp

GIVING OFFICERS
Sharon Khormooji: sr staff asst *CURR EMPL* sr staff asst: NW Natural Gas Co

C. J. Rue: *B* Portland OR 1945 *ED* Pacific Lutheran Univ 1967; Willamette Univ Law Sch 1974 *CURR EMPL* secy, asst treas: NW Natural Gas Co

APPLICATION INFORMATION
Initial Approach: *Initial Contact:* brief letter of inquiry and full proposal *Include Information On:* description of the organization, amount requested, purpose for which funds are sought, and proof of tax-exempt status *Deadlines:* none

Restrictions on Giving: Does not support individuals, religious organizations for sectarian purposes, or political or lobbying groups.

Company will not accept proposals from organizations outside of company service areas.

GRANTS ANALYSIS
Total Grants: $500,000*

Typical Range: $100 to $5,000

Disclosure Period: 1994

Note: Total grants figure is approximate.

OCRI Foundation

CONTACT
Judith Anderson
Administrator
OCRI Fdn.
PO Box 1705
Lake Oswego, OR 97035
(503) 635-8010

FINANCIAL SUMMARY
Recent Giving: $247,576 (1993); $250,904 (1992); $270,010 (1991)

Assets: $4,387,228 (1992); $4,420,689 (1991); $4,033,559 (1990)

EIN: 23-7120564

CONTRIBUTIONS SUMMARY
Donor(s): members of the Lamb family

Typical Recipients: • *Arts & Humanities:* Arts Associations & Councils, Community Arts, History & Archaeology, Libraries, Literary Arts, Museums/Galleries, Music, Public Broadcasting, Theater • *Civic & Public*

Affairs: Clubs, General, Hispanic Affairs, Native American Affairs, Public Policy, Urban & Community Affairs • *Education:* Arts/Humanities Education, Colleges & Universities, Community & Junior Colleges, Continuing Education, General, Literacy, Private Education (Precollege) • *Environment:* General, Resource Conservation, Wildlife Protection • *Health:* Clinics/Medical Centers, Diabetes, Emergency/Ambulance Services, Health Organizations, Hospices, Hospitals • *International:* International Affairs, International Peace & Security Issues, International Relief Efforts, Missionary/Religious Activities • *Religion:* Churches, Ministries, Religious Organizations, Religious Welfare, Seminaries • *Science:* Science Museums • *Social Services:* At-Risk Youth, Camps, Child Welfare, Community Service Organizations, Day Care, Delinquency & Criminal Rehabilitation, Family Services, Food/Clothing Distribution, People with Disabilities, Recreation & Athletics, Shelters/Homelessness, Youth Organizations

Grant Types: emergency, general support, project, and seed money

Geographic Distribution: limited to OR

GIVING OFFICERS
Anita Lamb Bailey: chmn, dir

Dorothy Lamb: dir

F. Gilbert Lamb: treas, dir

Frank Lamb: dir

Helen Lamb: secy, dir

Maryann Lamb: dir

Paula L. Lamb: vchmn, dir

Peter Lamb: dir

APPLICATION INFORMATION
Initial Approach: Send brief letter of inquiry describing program or project. There are no deadlines.

Restrictions on Giving: Does not support individuals.

PUBLICATIONS
Annual Report

GRANTS ANALYSIS
Total Grants: $247,576

Number of Grants: 78

Highest Grant: $26,000

Typical Range: $100 to $20,000

Disclosure Period: 1993

Note: Recent grants are derived from a 1993 Form 990.

RECENT GRANTS
General

26,000	Whitman College Fund, Walla Walla, WA	
20,000	Albertson College, Caldwell, ID	
20,000	Wilderness Society, Washington, DC	
12,000	Portland Christian Schools, Portland, OR	
6,000	Idaho Conservation League, Boise, ID	

Pioneer Trust Bank, NA / Pioneer Trust Bank, NA, Foundation

Sales: $11.91 million
Employees: 50
Headquarters: Salem, OR
SIC Major Group: Depository Institutions

CONTACT
Michael S. Compton
Vice President & Trust Officer
Pioneer Trust Bank, NA
PO Box 2305
Salem, OR 97308
(503) 363-3136
Note: Contact's extension number is 15.

FINANCIAL SUMMARY
Recent Giving: $24,343 (1994); $24,250 (1993); $24,475 (1992)

Assets: $620,203 (1993); $593,581 (1992); $478,646 (1991)

Gifts Received: $91,650 (1992); $86,012 (1991)

Fiscal Note: In 1992, contributions were received from Pioneer Trust Bank Corporation.

EIN: 93-0881673

CONTRIBUTIONS SUMMARY
Typical Recipients: • *Arts & Humanities:* Arts Associations & Councils, General, History & Archaeology, Libraries, Museums/Galleries, Public Broadcasting, Theater, Visual Arts • *Civic & Public Affairs:* General, Municipalities/Towns, Urban & Community Affairs, Women's Affairs • *Education:* General • *Environment:* Resource Conservation • *Health:* Emergency/Ambulance Services, Eyes/Blindness, General, Health Organizations, Hospices, Hospitals • *Religion:* Missionary Activities (Domestic), Religious Welfare • *Social Services:* Animal Protection, Child Welfare, Community Service Organizations, Domestic Violence, Food/Clothing Distribution, General, People with Disabilities, Scouts, Special Olympics, United Funds/United Ways, YMCA/YWCA/YMHA/YWHA, Youth Organizations

Grant Types: challenge, emergency, general support, operating expenses, project, research, and seed money

Geographic Distribution: focus on OR

Operating Locations: OR (Salem)

CORP. OFFICERS
William Meier: *CURR EMPL* pres, ceo: Pioneer Trust Bank NA

GIVING OFFICERS
Pioneer Trust Bank, N.A.: trust

APPLICATION INFORMATION
Initial Approach: Send a brief letter of inquiry. Include a description of organization, amount requested, purpose of funds sought, recently audited financial statement, and proof of tax-exempt status. Deadline is September 15.

Restrictions on Giving: Limited to Salem, OR, and surrounding area.

GRANTS ANALYSIS
Total Grants: $24,250

Number of Grants: 34

Highest Grant: $2,000

Typical Range: $25 to $2,000

Disclosure Period: 1993

Note: Recent grants are derived from a 1993 Form 990.

RECENT GRANTS
Library

1,500	Salem Public Library Foundation, Salem, OR — endow two chairs	
25	Salem Public Library Foundation, Salem, OR	

General

2,000	Humane Society of the Willamette Valley, Salem, OR — building fund	
2,000	United Way, Salem, WA	
1,500	Mid-Valley Children's Guild, Salem, OR — building fund	
1,000	Assistance League of Salem, Salem, OR — Operation School Bell	
1,000	Marion Polk Food Share, Marion, OH	

Roseburg Forest Products Co. / Ford Family Foundation

Former Foundation Name: Kenneth W. Ford Foundation
Sales: $700.0 million
Employees: 3,360
Parent Company: RLC Industries Co.
Headquarters: Roseburg, OR
SIC Major Group: Softwood Veneer & Plywood, Sawmills & Planing Mills—General, and Reconstituted Wood Products

CONTACT
Ronald C. Parker
Treasurer
Ford Family Foundation
PO Box 1088
Roseburg, OR 97470
(503) 679-3311

FINANCIAL SUMMARY
Recent Giving: $4,368,913 (fiscal 1994); $3,607,992 (fiscal 1993); $2,760,477 (fiscal 1992)

Assets: $113,564,991 (fiscal 1994); $107,406,207 (fiscal 1993)

Gifts Received: $3,634,100 (fiscal 1993)

Fiscal Note: Company gives through the foundation. In fiscal 1993, contributions were received from Roseburg Forest Products.

EIN: 93-6026156

CONTRIBUTIONS SUMMARY

Typical Recipients: • *Arts & Humanities:* Arts Appreciation, Arts Associations & Councils, Arts Centers, Community Arts, Libraries, Music, Performing Arts, Theater • *Civic & Public Affairs:* Botanical Gardens/Parks, Employment/Job Training, General, Municipalities/Towns, Parades/Festivals, Safety • *Education:* Colleges & Universities, Community & Junior Colleges, Education Funds, Elementary Education (Private), Elementary Education (Public), General, Preschool Education, Private Education (Precollege), Public Education (Precollege), Religious Education, Science/Mathematics Education, Secondary Education (Private), Secondary Education (Public) • *Environment:* Air/Water Quality • *Health:* Adolescent Health Issues, Cancer, Children's Health/Hospitals, Clinics/Medical Centers, Emergency/Ambulance Services, General, Health Organizations, Mental Health, Prenatal Health Issues • *International:* International Environmental Issues • *Religion:* Religious Welfare • *Science:* General, Science Museums, Scientific Centers & Institutes • *Social Services:* Child Welfare, Community Centers, Community Service Organizations, Counseling, Crime Prevention, Day Care, Domestic Violence, Family Services, Food/Clothing Distribution, General, Homes, People with Disabilities, Recreation & Athletics, Scouts, Senior Services, Shelters/Homelessness, Substance Abuse, United Funds/United Ways, Volunteer Services, Youth Organizations

Grant Types: award, capital, challenge, emergency, general support, and multiyear/continuing support

Geographic Distribution: in headquarters and operating communities

Operating Locations: CA (Weed), OR (Roseburg)

CORP. OFFICERS

Kenneth W. Ford: *B* 1908 *CURR EMPL* chmn: Roseburg Forest Products Co *CORP AFFIL* chmn: RLC Indus, Roseburg Lumber Co

Ronald C. Parker: *CURR EMPL* cfo: Roseburg Forest Products Co

GIVING OFFICERS

Mike J. Morgan: asst treas

Ronald C. Parker: treas *CURR EMPL* cfo: Roseburg Forest Products Co (see above)

APPLICATION INFORMATION

Initial Approach: *Initial Contact:* send a full proposal *Include Information On:* a description of organization, amount requested, purpose of funds sought, and proof of tax-exempt status *Deadlines:* March 15 is the annual deadline for applications

Restrictions on Giving: The Ford Family Foundation only provides funding to charitable organizations and does not support individuals. The majority of their contributions fund organizations within Oregon and Northern California, but this is not a requirement to receive funding.

OTHER THINGS TO KNOW

Company is an original donor to the Ford Family Foundation.

GRANTS ANALYSIS

Total Grants: $4,368,913

Number of Grants: 92

Highest Grant: $580,936

Average Grant: $41,626*

Typical Range: $5,000 to $50,000

Disclosure Period: fiscal year ending April 30, 1994

Note: Average grant figure excludes highest grant. Recent grants are derived from a fiscal 1994 grants list.

RECENT GRANTS

Library
59,919　Douglas County Library System — for computer enhancement services for new library

General
580,936　College of the Siskiyous, Weed, CA — for computers
573,890　Umpqua Community College, Roseburg, OR — for child care facility
350,000　Oregon Independent College Foundation, Portland, OR — for general support
264,200　Douglas Education Service District, Roseburg, OR — for mental health therapists for Douglas County Schools
172,565　Sutherlin High School — for computers for instructional program

---

Siltec Corp.

Sales: $83.0 million
Employees: 700
Parent Company: Mitsubishi Materials Corp.
Headquarters: Salem, OR
SIC Major Group: Electronic & Other Electrical Equipment

CONTACT

Judy Nix
Vice President, Human Resources
Siltec Corp.
PO Box 7748
Salem, OR 97303-4199
(503) 371-0041

FINANCIAL SUMMARY

Fiscal Note: Annual Giving Range: less than $100,000

CONTRIBUTIONS SUMMARY

Suppport is primarily directed to community human service organizations. It is biased towards women's crisis and children-oriented nonprofit agencies.

Volunteerism: Company tracks hours of employee voluteerism. An "appreciation breakfast" is given annually in honor of its volunteers.

Typical Recipients: • *Arts & Humanities:* Arts Festivals, General, Historic Preservation, Libraries, Museums/Galleries, Music • *Civic & Public Affairs:* Community Foundations, Economic Development, General, Women's Affairs • *Education:* Afterschool/Enrichment Programs, Education Funds, Elementary Education (Public), General, Public Education (Precollege), Special Education • *Health:* Hospices • *Social Services:* Child Welfare, Community Centers, Domestic Violence, General, People with Disabilities, Recreation & Athletics, Shelters/Homelessness, Substance Abuse, United Funds/United Ways, Volunteer Services

Grant Types: multiyear/continuing support, operating expenses, project, and scholarship

Nonmonetary Support Types: donated equipment and loaned executives

Geographic Distribution: limited to operating locations

Operating Locations: OR (Salem)

CORP. OFFICERS

S. Masuda: *CURR EMPL* chmn: Siltec Corp

Stanley T. Myers: *CURR EMPL* pres, ceo: Siltec Corp

H. Uchida: *CURR EMPL* sr exec vp admin: Siltec Corp

GIVING OFFICERS

Stanley T. Myers: *CURR EMPL* pres, ceo: Siltec Corp (see above)

APPLICATION INFORMATION

Initial Approach: Submit a brief letter of inquiry. Include a description of the organization and purpose of funds sought. Does not support individuals, religious organizations for sectarian purposes, political or lobbying groups, or organization.

Restrictions on Giving: Does not support organizations outside operating area

GRANTS ANALYSIS

Typical Range: $1,000 to $2,500

RECENT GRANTS

General
D.A.R.E., Salem, OR — drug awareness program
Gilbert House Children's Museum, Salem, OR
Little League, Salem, OR — Basketball/Baseball/Soccer
Oregon School for the Deaf, Salem, OR
Salem Boys and Girls Club, Salem, OR

Tucker Charitable Trust, Rose E.

CONTACT

Thomas B. Stoel
Trustee
Rose E. Tucker Charitable Trust
900 SW Fifth Ave., 24th Fl.
Portland, OR 97204
(503) 224-3380

FINANCIAL SUMMARY

Recent Giving: $600,000 (fiscal 1995 est.); $594,107 (fiscal 1994); $726,016 (fiscal 1993)

Assets: $17,750,000 (fiscal 1995 est.); $17,768,420 (fiscal 1994); $17,239,680 (fiscal 1993)

EIN: 93-6119091

CONTRIBUTIONS SUMMARY

Donor(s): The trust was established in 1976 by the late Rose E. Tucker and the Max and Rose Tucker Foundation.

Typical Recipients: • *Arts & Humanities:* Arts Festivals, Arts Institutes, Dance, Film & Video, General, History & Archaeology, Libraries, Museums/Galleries, Music, Opera, Public Broadcasting, Theater • *Civic & Public Affairs:* Botanical Gardens/Parks, Civil Rights, Clubs, Economic Development, General, Housing, Law & Justice, Legal Aid, Native American Affairs, Public Policy, Urban & Community Affairs, Zoos/Aquariums • *Education:* Arts/Humanities Education, Colleges & Universities, Continuing Education, Education Funds, Health & Physical Education, Minority Education, Preschool Education, Private Education (Precollege), Science/Mathematics Education, Student Aid • *Environment:* Energy, General, Resource Conservation • *Health:* Alzheimers Disease, Clinics/Medical Centers, Emergency/Ambulance Services, Health Funds, Health Organizations, Hospitals, Mental Health, Single-Disease Health Associations • *International:* International Affairs • *Religion:* Jewish Causes, Religious Organizations, Religious Welfare • *Science:* Science Museums • *Social Services:* At-Risk Youth, Camps, Community Service Organizations, Counseling, Crime Prevention, Family Planning, Family Services, Food/Clothing Distribution, Scouts, Substance Abuse, United Funds/United Ways, YMCA/YWCA/YMHA/YWHA, Youth Organizations

Grant Types: capital, general support, operating expenses, project, and scholarship

Geographic Distribution: restricted to Oregon, with emphasis on Portland metropolitan area

GIVING OFFICERS

Milo Ormseth: trust *B* Wolf Point MT 1932 *ED* St Olaf Coll BA 1954; Harvard Univ LLB 1959 *CURR EMPL* ptnr: Stoel Rives Boley Jones & Grey *PHIL AFFIL* co-trust: Jackson Foundation

Thomas B. Stoel: trust *PHIL AFFIL* secy: Collins Foundation; secy, dir: Wessinger Foundation

APPLICATION INFORMATION

Initial Approach:

The trust has no formal grant application procedure or application form.

Restrictions on Giving: The trust does not make grants to individuals, program-related loans or investments, organizations which unfairly discriminate, or efforts to carry on propaganda or to influence legislation. No grants are made for fellowships, operating budgets, or debt reduction.

PUBLICATIONS

Application guidelines and annual report

GRANTS ANALYSIS

Total Grants: $594,107

Number of Grants: 120

Highest Grant: $35,000

Average Grant: $4,951

Typical Range: $1000 to $10,000

Disclosure Period: fiscal year ending June 30, 1994

Note: Recent grants are derived from a fiscal 1994 grants list.

RECENT GRANTS

Library

10,000	Marylhurst College, Marylhurst, OR — Schoe Library collection	

General

35,000	Willamette University, Salem, OR — sesquicentennial campaign	
30,000	Lewis and Clark College, Portland, OR — scholarships	
20,000	1,000 Friends of Oregon, Portland, OR — capital building project	
19,000	Portland State University, Portland, OR — honors, scholarships, and development	
18,000	Tucker-Maxon Oral School, Portland, OR — continuing support	

Wheeler Foundation

CONTACT

Samuel C. Wheeler
President
Wheeler Fdn.
1211 S.W. Fifth Ave., Ste. 2906
Portland, OR 97204-1911
(503) 228-0261

FINANCIAL SUMMARY

Recent Giving: $375,000 (1993); $339,000 (1992); $252,600 (1991)

Assets: $9,369,124 (1993); $8,030,882 (1992); $5,415,668 (1991)

Gifts Received: $882,108 (1992); $20,000 (1991); $20,000 (1990)

Fiscal Note: In 1992, contributions were received from Cornelia T. Wheeler ($872,108) and Coleman H. Wheeler ($10,000).

EIN: 93-0553801

CONTRIBUTIONS SUMMARY

Donor(s): the late Coleman H. Wheeler, Cornelia T. Wheeler

Typical Recipients: • *Arts & Humanities:* Arts Festivals, Historic Preservation, History & Archaeology, Libraries, Museums/Galleries, Music, Opera, Theater • *Civic & Public Affairs:* Botanical Gardens/Parks, Clubs, Community Foundations, Economic Development, General, Munici- palities/Towns, Public Policy • *Education:* Arts/Humanities Education, Colleges & Universities, Education Funds, General, Minority Education, Private Education (Precollege), Science/Mathematics Education, Secondary Education (Private) • *Environment:* Forestry, General • *Health:* Cancer, Clinics/Medical Centers, Emergency/Ambulance Services, Health Funds, Health Organizations, Hospitals • *International:* International Environmental Issues • *Religion:* Ministries, Religious Organizations, Religious Welfare, Seminaries • *Social Services:* Child Welfare, Community Service Organizations, Crime Prevention, Food/Clothing Distribution, Homes, People with Disabilities, Scouts, Senior Services, Substance Abuse, United Funds/United Ways, Youth Organizations

Grant Types: general support

Geographic Distribution: focus on OR

GIVING OFFICERS

Lil M. Hendrickson: asst secy

Charles B. Wheeler: vp, dir

Edward T. Wheeler: secy, dir

John C. Wheeler: vp, dir

Samuel C. Wheeler: pres, dir

Thomas K. Wheeler: treas, dir

APPLICATION INFORMATION

Initial Approach: Send brief letter of inquiry describing program or project. There are no deadlines.

Restrictions on Giving: Limited to Oregon. The foundation does not make grants to individuals.

GRANTS ANALYSIS

Total Grants: $375,000

Number of Grants: 85

Highest Grant: $40,000

Typical Range: $500 to $18,000

Disclosure Period: 1993

Note: Recent grants are derived from a 1993 Form 990.

RECENT GRANTS

Library

4,000	Mid-Columbia Health Foundation, The Dalles, OR	

General

33,000	George Fox College, Newberg, OR	
18,000	World Forestry Center, Portland, OR	
16,000	Boy Scouts of America, Portland, OR	
15,000	St. Vincent Medical Foundation, Portland, OR	
13,000	Lewis and Clark College, Portland, OR	

PENNSYLVANIA

Air Products and Chemicals, Inc. / Air Products Foundation

Revenue: $3.48 billion
Employees: 14,075
Headquarters: Allentown, PA
SIC Major Group: Industrial Gases, Industrial Inorganic Chemicals Nec, Cyclic Crudes & Intermediates, and Industrial Organic Chemicals Nec

CONTACT
William J. Kendrick
Chairman
Air Products Foundation
7201 Hamilton Blvd.
Allentown, PA 18195-1510
(610) 481-6349

FINANCIAL SUMMARY
Recent Giving: $965,103 (fiscal 1994); $3,400,000 (fiscal 1993 approx.); $3,200,000 (fiscal 1992 approx.)

Assets: $15,090,842 (fiscal 1994); $2,914,648 (fiscal 1993); $2,143,653 (fiscal 1991)

Gifts Received: $13,237,500 (fiscal 1994)

Fiscal Note: The 1994 figure represents foundation giving only. All other years include both foundation and direct corporate contributions. In 1993, foundation contributions totaled $150,000, and in 1991, they reached approximately $1,400,000. In 1994, the Foundation received contributions from the Prodair Corporation.

EIN: 23-2130928

CONTRIBUTIONS SUMMARY
Typical Recipients: • *Arts & Humanities:* Arts Festivals, Arts Funds, Community Arts, Dance, Historic Preservation, Libraries, Museums/Galleries, Music, Opera, Performing Arts, Public Broadcasting, Theater • *Civic & Public Affairs:* Business/Free Enterprise, Civil Rights, Economic Development, Economic Policy, Housing, Public Policy, Safety, Urban & Community Affairs, Women's Affairs • *Education:* Arts/Humanities Education, Business Education, Colleges & Universities, Economic Education, Education Associations, Education Funds, Education Reform, Engineering/Technological Education, General, Legal Education, Literacy, Minority Education, Science/Mathematics Education • *Environment:* Air/Water Quality, General, Resource Conservation • *Health:* Cancer, Emergency/Ambulance Services, Health Organizations, Heart, Multiple Sclerosis, Nutrition, Single-Disease Health Associations • *International:* International Peace & Security Issues • *Religion:* Religious Welfare • *Science:* Science Exhibits & Fairs • *Social Services:* Child Welfare, Community Service Organizations, Counseling, Day Care, Delinquency & Criminal Rehabilitation, Domestic Violence, Emergency Relief, Family Services, Food/Clothing Distribution, Homes, People with Disabilities, Recreation & Athletics, Scouts, Senior Services, Shelters/Homelessness, Substance Abuse, United Funds/United Ways, Volunteer Services, Youth Organizations

Grant Types: capital, employee matching gifts, general support, multiyear/continuing support, operating expenses, and project

Note: Matching gifts support higher education institutions and arts and culture organizations.

Nonmonetary Support: $325,000 (fiscal 1989); $250,000 (fiscal 1988); $350,000 (fiscal 1987)

Nonmonetary Support Types: donated equipment, in-kind services, and loaned employees

Note: Contact for nonmonetary support is Mary Jo Egervary, Community Relations Representative.

Geographic Distribution: near headquarters and operating locations

Operating Locations: AL (Birmingham), AR, AZ, CA (Long Beach, Los Angeles, Stockton), CO, CT (Preston), DE (Wilmington), FL (Orlando, Pace), GA, IL, IN (Bailly), KS (Wichita), KY (Calvert City), LA (New Orleans, St. Gabriel), NC (Charlotte), NJ (Paulsboro, South Brunswick), NY (Hempstead, Niagara Falls), OH (Cleveland), OK, OR, PA (Allentown, Hometown, Trexlertown, Wilkes-Barre), PR, RI (Cumberland), TX (Dallas, Garland, LaPorte, Pasadena), UT

CORP. OFFICERS
James H. Agger: *B* 1936 *ED* St Josephs Coll AB 1958; Univ PA JD 1961 *CURR EMPL* vp, secy, gen couns: Air Products & Chem Inc *NONPR AFFIL* mem: Am Bar Assn

Pierre Leonce Brian: *B* New Orleans LA 1930 *ED* LA St Univ BS 1951; MA Inst Tech ScD 1956 *CURR EMPL* vp engg, dir: Air Products & Chem Inc *CORP AFFIL* dir: TN Chem Co *NONPR AFFIL* mem: Am Chem Soc, Am Inst Chem Engrs, Natl Acad Engg, Royal Acad Engg

Leo J. Daley: *CURR EMPL* vp, treas: Air Products & Chem Inc

William J. Kendrick: *B* Boston MA 1932 *ED* Boston Coll BSBA 1956; New England Sch Law LLB 1959 *CURR EMPL* vp pub aff: Air Products & Chem Inc *CORP AFFIL* vchmn: Lehigh-Northampton Airport Authority

John Robert Lovett: *B* Norristown PA 1931 *ED* Ursinus Coll BS 1953; Univ DE MS 1955; Univ DE PhD 1957 *CURR EMPL* exec vp strategic planning & tech: Air Products & Chem Inc *NONPR AFFIL* dir, mem: Chem Mfrs Assn; mem: Am Chem Soc, Am Inst Chem Engrs, Inst Chem Engrs, Soc Chem Indus

Harold A. Wagner: *B* Oakland CA 1935 *ED* Stanford Univ BS 1957; Harvard Univ MBA 1963 *CURR EMPL* chmn, pres, ceo: Air Products & Chem Inc

Gerald Andrew White: *B* Long Island NY 1934 *ED* Villanova Univ BChemEngg 1957 *CURR EMPL* sr vp fin, cfo: Air Products & Chem Inc *NONPR AFFIL* mem: Am Inst Chem Engrs, Fin Execs Inst, Fin Execs Res Fdn, Tau Beta Pi

GIVING OFFICERS
James H. Agger: dir *CURR EMPL* vp, secy, gen couns: Air Products & Chem Inc (see above)

Pierre Leonce Brian: trust *CURR EMPL* vp engg, dir: Air Products & Chem Inc (see above)

R.G. Cherrington: secy

Leo J. Daley: vp, treas *CURR EMPL* vp, treas: Air Products & Chem Inc (see above)

Ruth Margaret Davis: trust *B* Sharpsville PA 1928 *ED* Am Univ BA 1950; Univ MD MA 1952; Univ MD PhD 1955 *CURR EMPL* pres: Pymatuning Group *CORP AFFIL* dir: Air Products & Chem Inc, Air Products & Chem Inc, BTG Inc, Premark Intl Inc, Prin Fin Group, Spring Corp; Dir: SSDS Inc; dir: Varian Assocs Inc *NONPR AFFIL* bd visit: Catholic Univ Am; dir: Ceridian Inc; fellow: Am Inst Aeronautics Astronautics, Soc Info Display; mem: Am Acad Arts & Sci, Am Assn Advancement Sci, Am Math Soc, Math Assn Am, Natl Acad Engg, Natl Acad Pub Admin, Phi Kappa Phi, Sigma Pi Sigma, Tau Beta Pi, Washington Philosophical Soc; trust: Inst Defense Analysts

William J. Kendrick: chmn *CURR EMPL* vp pub aff: Air Products & Chem Inc (see above)

Terry Robert Lautenbach: trust *B* Cincinnati OH 1938 *ED* Xavier Univ BS 1959 *CORP AFFIL* dir: Arkwright Mutual Ins Co, Loomis Sayles Mutual Funds, Melville Corp, Varian Assocs Inc; pres: World Trade Ams *NONPR AFFIL* dir: Xavier Univ *CLUB AFFIL* Tokeneke, Wee Burn

Walter Frederick Light: trust *B* Cobalt Canada 1923 *ED* Queens Coll BS 1949 *CURR EMPL* dir: Newtel Indus *CORP AFFIL* dir: Air Products & Chem Inc, Inco Ltd, Moore Corp Ltd, Newtel Enterprises, Northern Telecom Ltd, Procter & Gamble Co, Rockcliffe Res & Tech, Rolls Royce Indus Canada Inc, Royal Bank Canada, Shell Canada Ltd, SNC Group, Transtream Inc *NONPR AFFIL* fellow: Canada Acad Engg, Engg Inst Canada, Montreal Mus Fine Arts; mem: Assn Professional Engrs, Corp Engrs Quebec; mem assocs: Carleton Univ *CLUB AFFIL* Mt Royal York

L. G. Long: asst secy

John Robert Lovett: dir *CURR EMPL* exec vp strategic planning & tech: Air Products & Chem Inc (see above)

Cornelius Patrick Powell: pres *B* St Paul MN 1931 *ED* Univ MN BBA 1952; Wayne St Univ 1961 *CURR EMPL* vp taxes: Air Products & Chem Inc

Gerald Andrew White: dir *CURR EMPL* sr vp fin, cfo: Air Products & Chem Inc (see above)

APPLICATION INFORMATION
Initial Approach: *Initial Contact:* brief letter and one copy of full proposal *Include In-*

formation On: description of the organization, including history, activities, purpose, constituency served, and governing board; purpose of grant; details on how purpose will be achieved; total amount of fund-raising campaign; amount requested and, if the request is for a specific project, description of project with applicable budget; proof of tax-exempt status; copy of most recent Form 990; copy of operating budget for current fiscal year; and list of current contributions or commitments received from companies, foundations, and government bodies, including amounts *Deadlines:* none

Restrictions on Giving: Does not support fraternal organizations, labor groups, service clubs, individuals, operating funds for member agencies of the United Way, political or lobbying groups, religious organizations, veterans organizations, hospitals, or elementary or secondary schools.

OTHER THINGS TO KNOW

Company has participated in public/private ventures to rehabilitate abandoned and condemned properties in Allentown, PA.

At the time of publication, the foundation was not accepting any unsolicited requests for funds; as it is working with a predetermined budget.

GRANTS ANALYSIS

Total Grants: $612,699

Number of Grants: 256

Highest Grant: $261,095

Average Grant: $2,393

Typical Range: $500 to $5,000

Disclosure Period: fiscal year ending September 30, 1994

Note: Above figures represent foundation giving only and exclude $352,404 in matching gifts. Recent grants are derived from a 1994 Form 990.

RECENT GRANTS

General

261,095	United Way of the Greater Lehigh Valley, Bethlehem, PA —for health and welfare	
31,400	Lehigh County Velodrome, Emmaus, PA —for developmental cycling program	
20,000	Kid Peace, Bethlehem, PA —for third payment of three-year pledge	
12,500	University of Delaware, Newark, DE —for RISE program	
10,000	Gross Towers Emergency Fund, Bethlehem, PA —for health and welfare	

Allegheny Foundation

CONTACT
Joanne B. Beyer
President
Allegheny Foundation
Three Mellon Bank Ctr.
525 William Penn Pl., Ste. 3900
Pittsburgh, PA 15219-1708
(412) 392-2900

FINANCIAL SUMMARY
Recent Giving: $1,644,400 (1993); $7,673,800 (1992); $2,765,700 (1991)

Assets: $25,870,317 (1993); $27,633,176 (1992); $34,716,444 (1991)

Gifts Received: $130,375 (1993); $1,156,250 (1992); $5,849,686 (1991)

Fiscal Note: In 1991, 1992, and 1993, the foundation received contributions in the form of stock from Richard M. Scaife.

EIN: 25-6012303

CONTRIBUTIONS SUMMARY
Donor(s): Established in 1953 by Richard Mellon Scaife, the Allegheny Foundation makes grants mainly for the benefit of Pittsburgh and western Pennsylvania. Richard Scaife is the son of Sarah Mellon Scaife, and great grandson of Judge Thomas Mellon, founder of Mellon Bank.

Typical Recipients: • *Arts & Humanities:* Historic Preservation, History & Archaeology, Libraries, Museums/Galleries, Music, Opera • *Civic & Public Affairs:* Botanical Gardens/Parks, Business/Free Enterprise, Economic Development, Economic Policy, General, Housing, Legal Aid, Nonprofit Management, Professional & Trade Associations, Public Policy, Urban & Community Affairs • *Education:* Colleges & Universities, Economic Education, Education Associations, Education Funds, Education Reform, General, Leadership Training, Literacy, Private Education (Precollege), Public Education (Precollege), Science/Mathematics Education, Student Aid • *Environment:* Air/Water Quality, General, Resource Conservation • *Health:* Cancer • *International:* Health Care/Hospitals • *Religion:* Religious Welfare • *Science:* Scientific Organizations • *Social Services:* Animal Protection, Child Welfare, Community Service Organizations, Counseling, People with Disabilities, Recreation & Athletics, Senior Services, Youth Organizations

Grant Types: general support and project

Geographic Distribution: primarily western Pennsylvania

GIVING OFFICERS
Peter B. Bell: trust

Joanne B. Beyer: pres, trust *PHIL AFFIL* vp, secy, treas: Scaife Family Foundation

Ralph H. Goettler: trust

Doris O'Donnell: trust

Dorothy May Ross: asst treas

Margaret R. Scaife: trust

Richard Mellon Scaife: don, chmn *B* Pittsburgh PA 1932 *ED* Yale Univ 1950-1951; Univ Pittsburgh BA 1957 *CURR EMPL* owner, chmn, publ: Tribune Review Publ Co *CORP AFFIL* chmn, dir: T-R Printing & Publ Co; dir: Air Tool Parts & Svc Co, City Commun, First Boston, Parax Corp, Sierra Publ Co *NONPR AFFIL* bd regents: Pepperdine Univ; dir: Goodwill Indus, Historical Soc Western PA, Pennsylvanians Effective Govt, Pittsburgh History & Landmarks Fdn, Preservation Action; mem: Pittsburgh Zoological Pk Comm; trust: Brandywine Conservancy, Carnegie Inst, Deerfield Academy; vp, dir: Western PA Hosp *PHIL AFFIL* chmn, trust: Sarah Scaife Foundation; chmn, don: Carthage Foundation *CLUB AFFIL* Duquesne, Laurel Valley GC, Rolling Rock

Donald C. Sipp: treas *PHIL AFFIL* vp, treas: Sarah Scaife Foundation

Nathan Julius Stark: trust *B* Minneapolis MN 1920

George Weymouth: trust

Arthur P. Ziegler, Jr.: trust

APPLICATION INFORMATION
Initial Approach:

Initial contact should be by letter, signed by the organization's president or authorized representative. The letter should be approved by the organization's board of directors.

Funding requests should include a concise description of the specific project for which funds are sought, list of the organization's officers and directors and their qualifications, annual budget for the project and the organization, latest audited financial statement and annual report, and proof of tax-exempt status. The foundation may request additional information.

The annual meeting is held in December. Proposals are accepted throughout the year, and will be acted upon as soon as possible.

Restrictions on Giving: The foundation does not make grants to individuals, or for endowments, scholarships, or fellowships.

GRANTS ANALYSIS
Total Grants: $1,644,400

Number of Grants: 45

Highest Grant: $300,000

Average Grant: $36,542

Typical Range: $5,000 to $50,000

Disclosure Period: 1993

Note: Recent grants are derived from a 1993 Form 990.

RECENT GRANTS

Library

77,000	Carnegie Library of Homestead, Munhall, PA	
70,000	Extra Mile Education Foundation, Pittsburgh, PA — library facilities	
24,000	Braddock's Field Historical Society, Braddock, PA — restoration of Braddock Carnegie library	
20,000	Blairsville Library Association, Blairsville, PA	

General

300,000	Intercollegiate Studies Institute, Bryn Mawr, PA — school lecture program
125,000	American Legislative Exchange Council, Washington, DC — renewed operating support
120,900	Youth Opportunities Unlimited, Pittsburgh, PA — Fairywood projects
50,000	Extra Mile Education Foundation, Pittsburgh, PA — Crossroads scholarship fund
50,000	Free Enterprise Partnership, Pittsburgh, PA — operating support

Allegheny Ludlum Corp. / Allegheny Ludlum Foundation

Sales: $1.1 billion
Employees: 6,000
Headquarters: Pittsburgh, PA
SIC Major Group: Blast Furnaces & Steel Mills

CONTACT
Jon D. Walton
Vice President, Secretary and General Counsel
Allegheny Ludlum Corp.
1000 Six PPG Pl.
Pittsburgh, PA 15222
(412) 394-2836

FINANCIAL SUMMARY
Recent Giving: $769,023 (1995 est.); $1,584,204 (1994); $1,134,065 (1993)

Assets: $2,604,342 (1992); $2,963,170 (1990); $2,681,963 (1989)

Gifts Received: $500,000 (1992)

Fiscal Note: Above figures for foundation only. Company maintains small direct giving program, which disbursed $224,084 in 1993.

EIN: 25-6228755

CONTRIBUTIONS SUMMARY
Typical Recipients: • *Arts & Humanities:* Arts Centers, Arts Festivals, Dance, Historic Preservation, Libraries, Museums/Galleries, Music, Opera, Public Broadcasting, Theater • *Civic & Public Affairs:* Business/Free Enterprise, Chambers of Commerce, Economic Development, General, Law & Justice, Professional & Trade Associations, Urban & Community Affairs, Women's Affairs, Zoos/Aquariums • *Education:* Business Education, Colleges & Universities, Community & Junior Colleges, Economic Education, Education Associations, Education Funds, Engineering/Technological Education, Minority Education, Science/Mathematics Education, Student Aid • *Health:* Children's Health/Hospitals, Hospitals, Medical Rehabilitation, Mental Health, Nursing Services, Single-Disease Health Associations • *International:* International Relations • *Religion:* Churches, Ministries, Religious Welfare

• *Social Services:* Child Welfare, Community Centers, Community Service Organizations, Counseling, Family Services, Food/Clothing Distribution, Homes, People with Disabilities, Recreation & Athletics, Senior Services, Sexual Abuse, United Funds/United Ways, Youth Organizations

Grant Types: capital, employee matching gifts, and general support

Note: Matches gifts to secondary, composite secondary or elementary education, up to $500 per year. Matches gifts to colleges and universities up to $2,000 per year. Employee matching gift ratio: 1 to 1.

Geographic Distribution: near operating locations only, with emphasis on the Pittsburgh, PA, area

Operating Locations: CT (Wallingford, Waterbury), IL (Schaumburg), IN (New Castle), NY (Lockport), OK (Claremore), PA (Bagdad, Brackenridge, Leechburg, Natrona, Pittsburgh, Vandergrift, Washington)

CORP. OFFICERS
Robert P. Bozzone: *B* Glens Falls NY 1933 *ED* Rensselaer Polytech Inst BS 1955 *CURR EMPL* pres, ceo, dir: Allegheny Ludlum Corp *CORP AFFIL* dir: DQE Inc, Duquesne Light Co

James L. Murdy: *B* Aberdeen SD 1938 *ED* Loyola Univ BBA 1960 *CURR EMPL* sr vp fin, cfo, dir: Allegheny Ludlum Corp *CORP AFFIL* vp, dir: AII Acquisition Corp

GIVING OFFICERS
Robert P. Bozzone: trust *CURR EMPL* pres, ceo, dir: Allegheny Ludlum Corp (see above)

James L. Murdy: trust *CURR EMPL* sr vp fin, cfo, dir: Allegheny Ludlum Corp (see above)

Jon David Walton: trust *B* Clairton PA 1942 *ED* Purdue Univ BS 1964; Valparaiso Univ JD 1969 *CURR EMPL* vp gen coun, secy: Allegheny Ludlum Corp *NONPR AFFIL* chmn: Pittsburgh Youth Golf Fdn; dir: Three Rivers Young Peoples Orchestra; first vp, dir: Music Mt Lebanon; mem: Allegheny County Bar Assn, Am Arbitration Assn, Am Bar Assn, Am Corp Couns Assn, Licensing Execs Soc, PA Bar Assn, PA Chamber Bus Indus; mem fin comm: Allegheny County Reps; mem, vp regional group: Am Soc Corp Secys *CLUB AFFIL* Duquesne, Valley Brook CC

APPLICATION INFORMATION
Initial Approach: *Initial Contact:* brief letter or proposal *Include Information On:* history of organization, amount requested, purpose for which funds are sought, and proof of tax-exempt status *Deadlines:* none *Note:* Foundation prefers grant requests forwarded by operating locations with the recommendation of local corporate officers or employees.

Restrictions on Giving: Foundation does not make contributions to individuals or private foundations.

Contributions are made primarily in operating locations.

GRANTS ANALYSIS
Total Grants: $1,134,065
Number of Grants: 109
Highest Grant: $343,592
Average Grant: $10,404
Typical Range: $500 to $15,000
Disclosure Period: 1993

Note: Recent grants are derived from a 1992 Form 990.

RECENT GRANTS

Library

10,000	Community Library of Allegheny Valley, Tarentum, PA

General

343,592	United Way of Southwestern Pennsylvania, Pittsburgh, PA
48,333	Salvation Army, Pittsburgh, PA
38,177	United Way of Kiski Valley, Vandergrift, PA
30,000	Allegheny Valley Hospital Sponsoring Committee, Natrona Heights, PA
28,000	United Way of Meriden - Wallingford, Meriden, CT

Aluminum Co. of America / Alcoa Foundation

Sales: $9.06 billion
Employees: 65,600
Headquarters: Pittsburgh, PA
SIC Major Group: Aluminum Sheet, Plate & Foil, Industrial Inorganic Chemicals Nec, Primary Aluminum, and Aluminum Extruded Products

CONTACT
F. Worth Hobbs
President
Alcoa Fdn.
425 6th Avenue
Pittsburgh, PA 15219-1850
(412) 553-2348

FINANCIAL SUMMARY
Recent Giving: $12,300,000 (1995 est.); $12,300,000 (1994 approx.); $12,300,000 (1993)

Assets: $268,583,194 (1992); $266,986,603 (1991); $11,413,200 (1990)

Gifts Received: $4,251 (1992)

Fiscal Note: Company gives through foundation only. Above figures exclude nonmonetary support.

EIN: 25-1128857

CONTRIBUTIONS SUMMARY
Typical Recipients: • *Arts & Humanities:* Arts Associations & Councils, Arts Centers, Arts Festivals, Arts Funds, Arts Institutes, Ballet, Community Arts, Dance, Historic Preservation, History & Archaeology, Libraries, Literary Arts, Museums/Galleries, Music, Opera, Performing Arts, Public Broadcasting, Theater, Visual Arts • *Civic & Public Affairs:* African American Affairs,

793

Botanical Gardens/Parks, Business/Free Enterprise, Civil Rights, Economic Development, Economic Policy, Employment/Job Training, Housing, Law & Justice, Legal Aid, Municipalities/Towns, Philanthropic Organizations, Professional & Trade Associations, Public Policy, Safety, Urban & Community Affairs, Women's Affairs, Zoos/Aquariums • *Education:* Agricultural Education, Arts/Humanities Education, Business Education, Colleges & Universities, Community & Junior Colleges, Economic Education, Education Associations, Education Funds, Education Reform, Elementary Education (Private), Engineering/Technological Education, Faculty Development, General, International Exchange, International Studies, Journalism/Media Education, Legal Education, Literacy, Medical Education, Minority Education, Preschool Education, Private Education (Precollege), Public Education (Precollege), Science/Mathematics Education, Student Aid • *Environment:* General, Resource Conservation • *Health:* AIDS/HIV, Cancer, Children's Health/Hospitals, Emergency/Ambulance Services, Geriatric Health, Health Policy/Cost Containment, Health Funds, Health Organizations, Hospices, Hospitals, Medical Rehabilitation, Medical Research, Medical Training, Mental Health, Prenatal Health Issues, Single-Disease Health Associations, Speech & Hearing • *International:* Foreign Arts Organizations, Foreign Educational Institutions, Health Care/Hospitals, International Environmental Issues, International Organizations, International Peace & Security Issues, International Relations, International Relief Efforts • *Religion:* Jewish Causes, Religious Organizations, Religious Welfare • *Science:* Science Exhibits & Fairs, Science Museums, Scientific Organizations • *Social Services:* At-Risk Youth, Big Brother/Big Sister, Child Welfare, Community Centers, Community Service Organizations, Counseling, Day Care, Delinquency & Criminal Rehabilitation, Domestic Violence, Emergency Relief, Family Planning, Family Services, Food/Clothing Distribution, General, Homes, People with Disabilities, Recreation & Athletics, Senior Services, Shelters/Homelessness, Special Olympics, Substance Abuse, United Funds/United Ways, Volunteer Services, YMCA/YWCA/YMHA/YWHA, Youth Organizations

Grant Types: capital, challenge, department, employee matching gifts, fellowship, general support, research, scholarship, and seed money

Geographic Distribution: national and international (near corporate operating facilities)

Operating Locations: AL (Mobile), AR (Bauxite, Ft. Smith), AZ (Chandler), CA (Irvine, Monrovia, San Diego, Vernon), CO (Englewood), CT (Cromwell), FL (Clearwater, Coral Gables, Ft. Meade), GA (Atlanta, Tifton), IA (Davenport), IL (Princeville, Rantoul), IN (Crawfordsville, Evansville, Lafayette, Richmond), LA (Delhi, Lake Charles, Vidalia), MD (Baltimore), MI (Mattawan, Traverse City), MS (Drew, Hous-

ton, Olive Branch), NC (Badin, Charlotte, Graham), NY (Massena, Randolph, Valhalla), OH (Barberton, Cleveland, Dayton, Gettysburg, Miamisburg, New Vienna, North Royalton, Sidney, Springboro), OR (Phoenix), PA (Lebanon, New Kensington, Pittsburgh), SC (Gaffney, Spartanburg), TN (Alcoa, Nashville), TX (Denison, Point Comfort, Rockdale, San Antonio), UT (Springville), VA (Stuarts Draft), WA (Addy, Wenatchee)

CORP. OFFICERS

Peter Reese Bridenbaugh: *B* Franklin PA 1940 *ED* Lehigh Univ BSME 1962; Lehigh Univ MS 1966; MA Inst Tech PhD 1968 *CURR EMPL* exec vp, chief tech off: Aluminum Co Am *NONPR AFFIL* dir: Indus Res Inst; fellow: Am Soc Metals; mem: Am Inst Mechanical Engrs, Dirs Indus Res, Natl Assn Engg, PA St Res Fdn, Sigma Xi; mem visit comm: Carnegie-Mellon Univ, Lehigh Univ, Northwestern Univ, PA St Univ, Stanford Univ, Univ Pittsburgh, Univ VA *CLUB AFFIL* Duquesne, Fox Chapel GC

Paul Henry O'Neill: *B* St Louis MO 1935 *ED* Fresno St Coll AB 1960; IN St Univ MPA 1966 *CURR EMPL* chmn, ceo, dir: Aluminum Co Am *CORP AFFIL* chmn: Alcoa Composites Inc; dir: Gen Motors Corp, Manpower Demonstration Res Corp, Natl Westminster Bancorp; trust: Rand Corp *NONPR AFFIL* chmn: Pres Ed Policy Adv Comm; dir: Gerald R Ford Fdn; fellow: Natl Inst Pub Aff; mem adv comm: Harvard Univ

GIVING OFFICERS

Peter Reese Bridenbaugh: dir *CURR EMPL* exec vp, chief tech off: Aluminum Co Am (see above)

Kathleen W. Buechel: vp *NONPR AFFIL* vp, dir: YWCA

Kathleen R. Burgan: secy, treas

John Leroy Diederich: dir *CURR EMPL* pres, dir: NW Alloys Inc

Earnest Jonathan Edwards: dir *B* Pamplin VA 1938 *ED* VA St Coll 1961; Duquesne Univ 1975 *CURR EMPL* vp, contr: Aluminum Co Am *NONPR AFFIL* mem: Fin Execs Inst, Inst Mgmt Accts

Richard Lawrence Fischer: dir *B* Pittsburgh PA 1936 *ED* Univ Pittsburgh AB 1958; Univ Pittsburgh JD 1961; Georgetown Univ LLM 1965 *CURR EMPL* exec vp chmn counc, dir: Aluminum Co Am *NONPR AFFIL* dir: St Francis Health Sys Pittsburgh; mem: Allegheny County Bar Assn, Am Bar Assn; mem bd visit: Univ Pittsburgh Sch Law *CLUB AFFIL* Duquesne, Laurel Valley GC, Oakmont CC

F. Worth Hobbs: pres, dir *B* 1934

Ronald R. Hoffman: dir *B* Allentown PA 1934 *ED* Lehigh Univ *CURR EMPL* exec vp human resources & commun: Aluminum Co Am *CORP AFFIL* dir: Taylor Chair Co *NONPR AFFIL* bd dir: Lehigh Univ

Richard B. Kelson: dir

APPLICATION INFORMATION

Initial Approach: *Initial Contact:* initial letter of inquiry and proposal *Include Information On:* description of specific project, purpose, procedure to be followed (for re-

search requests), amount requested, budget information, list of other corporate and foundation donors; recently audited financial statement; and proof of tax-exempt status *Deadlines:* none; requests acknowledged upon receipt

Restrictions on Giving: In general, foundation does not fund the following: organizations or causes in states or countries where company does not have operating locations; political or lobbying groups; fraternal organizations; individuals (except the scholarship program for children of Alcoa employees); sectarian or religious groups for services limited to their members; endowments; trips or tours; student exchanges; golf outings; fundraising dinners; tickets, tables, or advertising for benefit purposes; or hospitals for capital campaigns (unless cost-effectiveness of total capital program can be clearly demonstrated).

Only organizations classified as public charities that are tax-exempt under the Internal Revenue Code are considered for grants.

OTHER THINGS TO KNOW
Recommendations from local Alcoa personnel are important in determining awards.

GRANTS ANALYSIS
Total Grants: $12,300,000

Number of Grants: 2,565

Average Grant: $4,795

Typical Range: $1,000 to $5,000 and $25,000 to $75,000

Disclosure Period: 1993

Note: Number of grants and average grant figures are approximate. Recent grants are derived from a 1993 Form 990.

RECENT GRANTS

Library
Belmont University, Nashville, TN —for Computer Science program and equipment
Evansville Association for the Blind, Evansville, IN —for parent-infant program and toy lending library
Grantmakers of Western Pennsylvania, Pittsburgh, PA —for establishment of Foundation Center Library at the Carnegie Library of Pittsburgh
Thorndale Independent School District, Thorndale, TX —for library, computer equipment, and software

General
Accreditation Board for Engineering and Technology, New York, NY —for Chandler, AZ, Unified School District Number 80 Science Screen Report
Adams County Association for Retarded Children, Natchez, MS
Adelphoi, Latrobe, PA —for Human Services Center construction
AIDS Resource Group of Evansville, Evansville, IN —for office equipment
Allegheny County League of Women Voters, Pittsburgh, PA

Ames Charitable Trust, Harriett

CONTACT
L. Dianne Lomonaco
Trust Administrator
Harriett Ames Charitable Trust
St. Davids Center, Ste. A-200
150 Radnor-Chester Rd.
St. Davids, PA 19087
(215) 341-9270

FINANCIAL SUMMARY
Recent Giving: $750,500 (1995 est.); $750,500 (1994); $750,000 (1993)

Assets: $10,925,545 (1995 est.); $10,925,545 (1994); $11,342,943 (1993)

EIN: 23-6286757

CONTRIBUTIONS SUMMARY
Donor(s): The Harriett Ames Charitable Trust was founded in New York in 1952, with funds donated by the late Mrs. Harriet Ames . She was the daughter of Moses Annenberg, who founded Triangle Publications. The trust is affiliated with the Lita Annenberg Hazen Charitable Trust, Polly Annenberg Levee Charitable Trust-Levee Trust, Polly Annenberg Levee Charitable Trust-Krancer Trust, Janet Hooker Charitable Trust, Esther Simon Charitable Trust, and the Annenberg Foundation, all located in Pennsylvania.

Typical Recipients: • *Arts & Humanities:* Arts Associations & Councils, Arts Centers, Arts Festivals, Community Arts, Film & Video, History & Archaeology, Libraries, Museums/Galleries, Music, Performing Arts, Theater, Visual Arts • *Civic & Public Affairs:* General, Philanthropic Organizations, Public Policy • *Education:* Arts/Humanities Education, Colleges & Universities, Legal Education, Medical Education, Private Education (Precollege) • *Environment:* Wildlife Protection • *Health:* Alzheimers Disease, Cancer, Clinics/Medical Centers, Diabetes, Eyes/Blindness, Health Funds, Health Organizations, Hospitals, Medical Research, Multiple Sclerosis, Research/Studies Institutes, Single-Disease Health Associations, Trauma Treatment • *International:* Human Rights, International Environmental Issues, International Organizations, International Relations • *Religion:* Jewish Causes, Religious Organizations, Synagogues/Temples • *Social Services:* Animal Protection, Child Welfare, Community Service Organizations, People with Disabilities, Recreation & Athletics, Senior Services

Grant Types: general support

Geographic Distribution: emphasis on New York State, with some national giving

GIVING OFFICERS
Walter H. Annenberg: trust *B* Milwaukee WI 1908 *ED* Univ PA Wharton Sch *PHIL AFFIL* trust: Polly Annenberg Levee Charitable Tr Tr A Krancer Tr; don, chmn, pres, trust: Annenberg Foundation; trust: Esther Simon Charitable Trust, Lita Annenberg Hazen Charitable Trust, Janet A. Hooker Charitable Trust, Evelyn A. J. Hall 1952 Charitable Trust

L. Dianne Lomonaco: trust admin *PHIL AF-FIL* trust admin: Lita Annenberg Hazen Charitable Trust, Esther Simon Charitable Trust

APPLICATION INFORMATION
Initial Approach:

The foundation does not have a standard application form. Interested parties should send a letter of inquiry to the foundation.

Requests for funding should include information about the applicant organization, description of the proposed project, amount requested, and proof of tax-exempt status.

Letters may be sent any time.

Restrictions on Giving: Grants are not given to individuals.

OTHER THINGS TO KNOW
The foundation does not encourage unsolicited grant proposals.

GRANTS ANALYSIS
Total Grants: $750,000

Number of Grants: 46

Highest Grant: $72,000

Average Grant: $16,304

Typical Range: $1,000 to $25,000

Disclosure Period: 1993

Note: Recent grants are derived from a 1993 Form 990.

RECENT GRANTS

Library

5,000	New York Public Library Astor and Lenox Tilden, New York, NY	

General

72,000	United Cerebral Palsy of New York, New York, NY	
62,500	Mt. Sinai Medical Center, New York, NY	
57,500	Lenox Hill Hospital, New York, NY	
52,500	Tufts College Trustees, Medford, MA	
50,000	Cornell University, Ithaca, NY	

AMP Incorporated / AMP Foundation

Revenue: $4.02 billion
Employees: 27,200
Headquarters: Harrisburg, PA
SIC Major Group: Electronic Connectors, Hand & Edge Tools Nec, Electrical Industrial Apparatus Nec, and Current-Carrying Wiring Devices

CONTACT
Merrill A. Yohe, Jr.
Chairman, Corporate Contributions Committee
AMP Incorporated
PO Box 3608 (176-042)
Harrisburg, PA 17105-3608
(717) 780-6708
Note: The company's World Wide Web address is http://www.amp.com

FINANCIAL SUMMARY
Recent Giving: $1,500,000 (1995 est.); $985,000 (1994 approx.); $868,775 (1993)

Assets: $14,260,466 (1993); $13,783,795 (1992); $13,437,975 (1991)

Fiscal Note: Company primarily makes contributions through the foundation.

EIN: 23-2022928

CONTRIBUTIONS SUMMARY
Typical Recipients: • *Arts & Humanities:* Arts Associations & Councils, Arts Funds, Libraries, Museums/Galleries, Music, Public Broadcasting, Theater • *Civic & Public Affairs:* Business/Free Enterprise, Civil Rights, Employment/Job Training, Municipalities/Towns, Safety, Urban & Community Affairs • *Education:* Colleges & Universities, Community & Junior Colleges, Education Associations, Engineering/Technological Education, Literacy, Minority Education, Private Education (Precollege), Public Education (Precollege), Science/Mathematics Education • *Environment:* General • *Health:* Cancer, Children's Health/Hospitals, Clinics/Medical Centers, Emergency/Ambulance Services, Health Organizations, Hospices, Hospitals, Single-Disease Health Associations • *Science:* Scientific Centers & Institutes • *Social Services:* Child Welfare, Community Service Organizations, Family Services, Food/Clothing Distribution, People with Disabilities, Recreation & Athletics, Shelters/Homelessness, United Funds/United Ways, Youth Organizations

Grant Types: capital, general support, matching, and operating expenses

Note: Employee matching gift ratio: 1 to 1, for general contributions; 2 to 1 for contributions to education, for first $100 of employee gift.

Geographic Distribution: within a 50-mile radius of Harrisburg, PA, and in operating locations

Operating Locations: AZ, CA, CT, DE, FL, GA, MA, NC (Charlotte, Gastonia, Greensboro, Winston-Salem), NJ, OR, PA (Harrisburg, Lancaster, Middletown, York), TX, VA (Roanoke)

CORP. OFFICERS
William Jeffrey Hudson, Jr.: *B* Chicago IL 1934 *ED* Cornell Univ 1957; Drexel Univ 1959-1961 *CURR EMPL* ceo, pres: AMP Inc *CORP AFFIL* dir: Carpenter Tech Corp; pres, ceo: AMP Packaging Sys *NONPR AF-FIL* dir: Harrisburg Hosp; mem: Am Chamber Commerce, Natl Assn Mfrs

James Earl Marley: *B* Marietta PA 1935 *ED* PA St Univ BS 1957; Drexel Inst MS 1963 *CURR EMPL* chmn, dir: AMP Inc *CORP AFFIL* chmn: AMP Packaging Sys; dir: Armstrong World Indus, Dauphin Deposit Bank & Trust Co, Harsco Corp; pres, coo: Precision Interconnect Corp; vchmn: Matrix Sci Corp *NONPR AFFIL* mem: Am Mgmt Assn, Am Soc Mechanical Engrs, Harrisburg Chamber Commerce, Inst Electrical & Electronics Engrs, Mfg Counc Machinery Allied Products Inst *CLUB AFFIL* mem: Harrisburg CC *PHIL AFFIL* dir: Josiah W. and Bessie H. Kline Foundation

GIVING OFFICERS
Philip George Guarneschelli: dir *B* Brooklyn NY 1932 *ED* Gettysburg Coll BA 1954; Dickinson Coll Law Sch JD 1959 *CURR EMPL* vp human resources: AMP Inc *CORP AFFIL* dir: Capital Blue Cross, Harrisburg Med Mgmt *NONPR AFFIL* bd overseers: Widener Univ Sch Law

Joseph Overbaugh: dir *CURR EMPL* treas: AMP Packaging Sys

Merrill A. Yohe, Jr.: chmn contributions comm *B* Hanover PA 1934 *ED* Gettysburg Coll AB 1958; Dickinson Coll Law LLB 1964 *CURR EMPL* vp pub affairs: AMP Inc *CORP AFFIL* secy, dir: Carroll Touch, Precision Interconnect Corp

Anthony Zettlemoyer: dir

APPLICATION INFORMATION
Initial Approach: *Initial Contact:* brief letter or proposal *Include Information On:* description of the organization and its purposes; list of governing board members; proof of IRS section 501(c)(3) status; current operating budget, other sources of general funding, audited financial statement and most recent IRS Form 990; purpose for which funds are sought, proposed project budget, other sources of project funding, amount requested, and statement of how project will be evaluated *Deadlines:* by mid-November for funding during the next calendar year

Restrictions on Giving: Foundation does not support organizations in geographic areas where AMP has few or no employees; individuals; private foundations; service clubs; international organizations; fraternal, social, labor, or veterans organizations; requests of a political nature; organizations or programs that pose a potential conflict of interest for AMP; or programs of churches or religious organizations that restrict participation to members.

Foundation may not support courtesy advertising; testimonial or fund raising dinners, loans or investments; capital campaigns or other fund raising of national organizations; general operating needs of united fund organizations.

GRANTS ANALYSIS
Total Grants: $868,775

Highest Grant: $114,150

Average Grant: $1,900*

Typical Range: $500 to $5,000

Disclosure Period: 1993

Note: Average grant figure provided by the company. Recent grants are derived from a 1993 Form 990.

RECENT GRANTS
General

114,150	United Way Capital Region, Harrisburg, PA
101,550	Massachusetts Institute of Technology, Cambridge, MA
29,394	Pennsylvania State University, University Park, PA
17,500	Gaudenzia, Harrisburg, PA
17,000	United Way Forsyth County, Winston-Salem, NC

Annenberg Foundation

CONTACT
Gail C. Levin
Senior Program Officer
The Annenberg Foundation
St. Davids Center, Ste. A-200
150 Radnor-Chester Rd.
St. Davids, PA 19087
(610) 341-9066

FINANCIAL SUMMARY
Recent Giving: $119,042,326 (fiscal 1995 est.); $416,642,530 (fiscal 1994); $136,595,763 (fiscal 1993)

Assets: $1,120,000,000 (fiscal 1995 est.); $1,260,773,264 (fiscal 1994); $1,654,401,774 (fiscal 1993)

Gifts Received: $548,509 (fiscal 1992); $495,256 (fiscal 1991); $552,747 (fiscal 1990)

Fiscal Note: The foundation receives gifts from the Esther Simon Trust.

EIN: 23-6257083

CONTRIBUTIONS SUMMARY
Donor(s): Walter H. Annenberg is the son of Moses Annenberg, who owned the *Philadelphia Inquirer* and the *Daily Racing Form*. Walter Annenberg took over the family business in 1940 and launched the very successful *TV Guide* in 1953. In 1970, he sold the *Philadelphia Inquirer* to Knight Ridder. Mr. Annenberg sold his other publications to Rubert Murdoch in 1988 for $3 billion. He is an avid art collector, and owns one of the most coveted art collections in the country.

The Annenberg Foundation is the successor corporation to the Annenberg School at Radnor, PA, established in 1958. Mr. Annenberg is also the sole trustee of several Annenberg family trusts including the J.A. Hooker Charitable Trust, the Evelyn A.J. Hall Charitable Trust, the Lita Hazen Charitable Trust, the Esther Simon Charitable

Trust, the Polly Annenberg Levee Charitable Trusts, and the Harriett Ames Charitable Trust. He also served as president of the corporate-sponsored M.L. Annenberg Foundation, which has ceased operations.

Mr. Annenberg has also been involved in several private philanthropic pursuits. In 1958, he founded and endowed the Annenberg School for Communication, a graduate school at the University of Pennsylvania. He also endowed the Annenberg School for Communication at the University of Southern California; and the Washington Program in Communications Policy Studies of Northwestern University. The Annenberg Foundation provides ongoing support to each of these institutions. Mr. Annenberg has also donated a library and a residence to his alma mater, the Peddie School; in 1983, the school received $12 million. He has given $3 million to the University of Pennsylvania for a performing arts center, $8 million to the University of California, and $10 million to Annenberg Center for Health Sciences, part of a subsidiary of the Eisenhower Medical Center. Mr. Annenberg has also given major gifts to the Episcopal Academy in Philadelphia, the State of Israel, the Metropolitan Museum of Art, and the Desert Museum in Palm Springs, which he built. In 1993, Mr Annenberg made several major gifts from his foundation, including a gift to the University of Pennsylvania to endow the Annenberg School for Communication and to establish a Center for Public Policy; a gift to the University of Southern California to establish the Anneberg Center for Communication; a contribution to The Peddie School for an endowment and scholarships; and a gift to Colonial Williamsburg Foundation for an education center, museum, and library.

In 1989, he told a Washington Post reporter that "Richard Nixon gave me the greatest honor of my life." In 1968, Nixon appointed Annenberg as Ambassador to the Court of St. James and he served in Great Britain until 1974. The former ambassador remains close to Nixon and other prominent Republicans, as well as the Royal Family.

Typical Recipients: • *Arts & Humanities:* Arts Appreciation, Arts Associations & Councils, Arts Centers, Arts Funds, Historic Preservation, Libraries, Museums/Galleries, Music, Opera, Public Broadcasting, Theater • *Civic & Public Affairs:* Legal Aid, Philanthropic Organizations, Professional & Trade Associations, Public Policy • *Education:* Arts/Humanities Education, Colleges & Universities, Community & Junior Colleges, Education Associations, Education Funds, Education Reform, General, International Studies, Journalism/Media Education, Literacy, Medical Education, Minority Education, Preschool Education, Private Education (Precollege), Public Education (Precollege), Religious Education, Science/Mathematics Education, Secondary Education (Private), Secondary Education (Public), Vocational & Technical Education • *Environment:* General, Resource Conservation, Wildlife Protection • *Health:* Cancer, Clinics/Medical Centers, Emergency/Ambulance Services, Health Funds, Health Organizations, Hospitals, Medical Research, Research/Studies Institutes • *International:* Foreign Educational Institutions, International Affairs, International Environmental Issues, International Organizations, International Relations, Missionary/Religious Activities • *Religion:* Churches, Dioceses, Jewish Causes, Ministries, Missionary Activities (Domestic), Religious Organizations, Religious Welfare, Social/Policy Issues, Synagogues/Temples • *Science:* Scientific Centers & Institutes, Scientific Organizations • *Social Services:* Animal Protection, Child Welfare, Crime Prevention, Family Planning, Family Services, People with Disabilities, Recreation & Athletics, Scouts, Substance Abuse, United Funds/United Ways, Volunteer Services, Youth Organizations

Grant Types: project

Geographic Distribution: principally to national organizations

GIVING OFFICERS
Leonore A. Annenberg: vchmn, vp

Wallis Annenberg: vp

Walter H. Annenberg: don, chmn, pres, trust *B* Milwaukee WI 1908 *ED* Univ PA Wharton Sch *PHIL AFFIL* trust: Polly Annenberg Levee Charitable Tr Tr A Krancer Tr, Esther Simon Charitable Trust, Lita Annenberg Hazen Charitable Trust, Janet A. Hooker Charitable Trust, Evelyn A. J. Hall 1952 Charitable Trust, Harriett Ames Charitable Trust

William J. Henrich, Jr.: secy *B* Philadelphia PA 1929 *ED* La Salle Univ BA 1950; Temple Univ JD 1956 *CURR EMPL* pres, gen couns, dir: Triangle Publs *CORP AFFIL* mem bd mgrs: Beneficial Savings Bank *NONPR AFFIL* mem: Am Bar Assn, Philadelphia Bar Assn; trust: LaSalle Univ, Univ PA Annenberg Sch Communs

Dr. Gail C. Levin: sr program off

APPLICATION INFORMATION
Initial Approach:

Applicants should submit a brief letter.

Letters should include a description of the organization requesting funds and a summary of the project for which requested funds would be used.

The review process takes up to six months.

Restrictions on Giving: The foundation reports that it does not support individuals, basic research, capital campaigns, construction projects, or operating expenses. It is also unwilling to offer long-term support of an organization or activity. Most health care grants are long-standing annuals.

OTHER THINGS TO KNOW
The Annenberg Fund, which was established by Walter Annenberg in 1951, has merged with the Annenberg Foundation.

GRANTS ANALYSIS
Total Grants: $416,642,530*

Number of Grants: 400

Highest Grant: $120,000,000

Average Grant: $200,000*

Typical Range: $5,000 to $200,000

Disclosure Period: fiscal year ending June 30, 1994

Note: Total grants figure excludes other operating and administrative expenses for charitable purposes. Average grant figure was supplied by the foundation and excludes the three highest grants totaling $340,000,000. Recent grants are derived from a fiscal 1993 Form 990.

RECENT GRANTS
Library
334,000	Richard Nixon Library and Birthplace Foundation, Yorba Linda, CA
50,000	Pierpont Morgan Library, New York, NY

General
10,000,000	New American Schools Development Corporation, Arlington, VA
7,879,832	University of Pennsylvania Trustees, Philadelphia, PA
5,000,000	United Jewish Appeal, New York, NY
5,000,000	United Negro College Fund, New York, NY
4,829,167	University of Southern California, Los Angeles, CA

Arcadia Foundation

CONTACT
Marilyn L. Steinbright
President
The Arcadia Foundation
105 E Logan St.
Norristown, PA 19401-3058
(610) 275-8460

FINANCIAL SUMMARY
Recent Giving: $2,046,553 (fiscal 1995 est.); $1,965,434 (fiscal 1994); $2,125,110 (fiscal 1993)

Assets: $35,550,000 (fiscal 1995 est.); $34,489,895 (fiscal 1994); $38,115,242 (fiscal 1993)

Gifts Received: $20,537,884 (fiscal 1990)

Fiscal Note: In fiscal 1990, the foundation received a gift of $20,537,884 from Edith C. Steinbright, director emeritus of the foundation.

EIN: 23-6399772

CONTRIBUTIONS SUMMARY
Donor(s): Edith C. Steinbright and Marilyn Lee Steinbright founded the Arcadia Foundation in Pennsylvania in 1964.

Typical Recipients: • *Arts & Humanities:* Arts Associations & Councils, Ballet, Historic Preservation, History & Archaeology, Libraries, Museums/Galleries, Music, Public Broadcasting, Theater • *Civic & Public Affairs:* Clubs, Housing, Philanthropic Organizations, Safety, Urban & Community Affairs, Zoos/Aquariums • *Education:* Arts/Humanities Education, Colleges & Universities, Community & Junior Colleges, Literacy, Medical Education, Private Education

(Precollege), Religious Education, Secondary Education (Private) • *Environment:* General, Wildlife Protection • *Health:* Arthritis, Diabetes, Emergency/Ambulance Services, Health Organizations, Hospices, Hospitals, Nursing Services • *Religion:* Churches, Jewish Causes, Religious Welfare • *Science:* Science Museums, Scientific Centers & Institutes, Scientific Organizations • *Social Services:* Animal Protection, Child Welfare, Food/Clothing Distribution, People with Disabilities, Senior Services, Youth Organizations

Grant Types: general support

Geographic Distribution: limited to Eastern Pennsylvania with zip codes of 18000 and 19000.

GIVING OFFICERS
Tanya Hashorva: vp

Edward L. Jones: dir

Harvey S. S. Miller: treas *B* Philadelphia PA 1948 *ED* Swarthmore Coll MBA 1970; Harvard Univ JD 1973 *CURR EMPL* pres, ceo, dir: Daltex Med Sciences *CORP AFFIL* vchmn, ceo, coo, dir: Energy Solutions; vp, curator, dir: Assoc Debvoise & Plimpton *NONPR AFFIL* bd overseers: Univ PA Sch Nursing; dir: Wildlife Preservation Trust Intl; mem: Am Bar Assn, Am Philosophical Soc, Assn Bar City New York, Athenaeum Assn, Collections Comm Historical Soc, Library Coll, Mayors Cultural Adv Counc, Phi Sigma Kappa, Philadelphia Art Alliance, Union League; trust: Philadelphia Mus Art, Univ PA; trust emeritus: Univ PA Inst Contemporary Art *CLUB AFFIL* Harvard, Swarthmore *PHIL AFFIL* trust: Milton and Sally Avery Arts Foundation

David P. Sandler: secy

Kathleen Shellington: dir

Marilyn L. Steinbright: don, pres

APPLICATION INFORMATION
Initial Approach:

Applicants should submit a succinct letter of proposal, no longer than two pages, to the foundation.

The letter should include a description of the organization, the amount of funding requested, how funds will be spent, and proof of the organization's tax-exempt status.

Proposals are accepted only between June 1 and August 15 for the following calendar year.

The board meets in September and November. Notification usually is given within three months.

Restrictions on Giving: Grants are not made for land acquisition, fellowships, conferences, publications, demonstration projects, deficit financing, dinners, special events, fraternal organizations, political or lobbying groups, or goodwill advertising. Grants are not given to individuals.

GRANTS ANALYSIS
Total Grants: $2,125,110

Number of Grants: 187

Highest Grant: $50,000

Average Grant: $11,364

Typical Range: $500 to $20,000

Disclosure Period: fiscal year ending September 30, 1993

Note: Recent grants are derived from a fiscal 1993 grants list.

RECENT GRANTS

General

50,000	Academy of Natural Sciences, Philadelphia, PA
50,000	Cedar Crest College, Allentown, PA
50,000	Franklin Institute, Philadelphia, PA
50,000	Pennsylvania Academy of the Fine Arts, Philadelphia, PA
50,000	Philadelphia Zoological Society, Philadelphia, PA

Aristech Chemical Corp. / Aristech Foundation

Sales: $800.0 million
Employees: 1,800
Parent Company: ACC Holdings Corporation
Headquarters: Pittsburgh, PA
SIC Major Group: Cyclic Crudes & Intermediates, Plastics Materials & Resins, Industrial Organic Chemicals Nec, and Unsupported Plastics Film & Sheet

CONTACT

David G. Higie
Executive Director
Aristech Fdn.
600 Grant St., Rm. 1170
Pittsburgh, PA 15219-2704
(412) 433-7828

FINANCIAL SUMMARY

Recent Giving: $334,056 (1994); $293,779 (1993); $365,930 (1992)

Assets: $444,100 (1994 approx.); $755,678 (1993); $1,016,437 (1992)

Gifts Received: $500,000 (1989)

Fiscal Note: Company gives directly and through the foundation. In 1989, contributions were received from Aristech Chemical Corp.

EIN: 25-6298142

CONTRIBUTIONS SUMMARY

Typical Recipients: • *Arts & Humanities:* Arts Associations & Councils, Arts Centers, Arts Institutes, Ballet, Dance, General, Libraries, Museums/Galleries, Music, Opera, Public Broadcasting • *Civic & Public Affairs:* Civil Rights, Economic Development, Economic Policy, Employment/Job Training, General, Professional & Trade Associations, Urban & Community Affairs • *Education:* Business Education, Colleges & Universities, Education Funds, Engineering/Technological Education, General, Science/Mathematics Education, Student Aid • *Environment:* General, Resource Conservation • *Health:* Emergency/Ambulance Services, Hospices, Single-Disease Health Associations • *Religion:* Religious Welfare • *Science:* Scientific Centers & Institutes, Sci-

entific Organizations • *Social Services:* Community Service Organizations, Family Services, Food/Clothing Distribution, People with Disabilities, Recreation & Athletics, United Funds/United Ways, Youth Organizations

Grant Types: capital, conference/seminar, emergency, employee matching gifts, endowment, general support, and multiyear/continuing support

Note: Employee matching gift ratio: 1 to 1. Matching grants are for higher education only and have a maximum limit of $3,000.

Geographic Distribution: focus on areas in which company has operations: Pennsylvania, West Virginia, Texas, Ohio

Operating Locations: KY, OH, PA (Pittsburgh), TX, WV

CORP. OFFICERS

Michael Egan: *CURR EMPL* sr vp, cfo: Aristech Chem Corp

Charles W. Hamilton: *B* 1940 *ED* Grove City Coll *CURR EMPL* pres, coo: Aristech Chem Corp *CORP AFFIL* pres, coo, dir: ACC Holdings Corp

Jiro Kamimura: *CURR EMPL* chmn, ceo: Aristech Chem Corp *CORP AFFIL* vchmn: ACC Holdings Corp

Mark K. McNally: *CURR EMPL* sr vp, gen couns: Aristech Chem Corp *NONPR AFFIL* treas, dir: PA Assn Blind

GIVING OFFICERS

David G. Higie: exec dir

Jiro Kamimura: trust *CURR EMPL* chmn, ceo: Aristech Chem Corp (see above)

APPLICATION INFORMATION

Initial Approach: *Initial Contact:* concise written proposal, one to two pages* *Include Information On:* need, objectives of program, plan of action, list of other organizations involved with similar programs, and how the proposed project is similar or different from those programs, a line-item budget for the project, the amount of funding requested, organization's budget with income sources, IRS tax exemption letter, and a list of board of directors *Deadlines:* November 30 *Note:* The proposal must be prepared and signed by an authorized executive of the tax-exempt organization.

Restrictions on Giving: The foundation does not make grants to individuals, religious organizations for sectarian purposes, hospitals, or political groups.

Grants generally are not awarded for conferences, seminars, symposia, travel purposes, or for the publishing of books, films, or television productions.

GRANTS ANALYSIS

Total Grants: $334,056

Number of Grants: 62

Highest Grant: $52,500

Average Grant: $5,388

Typical Range: $1,000 to $5,000

Disclosure Period: 1994

Note: Recent grants are derived from a 1993 grants list.

RECENT GRANTS

Library

1,000	Carnegie Library of Pittsburgh, Pittsburgh, PA — science and technology department

General

52,500	United Way Southwestern Pennsylvania, Pittsburgh, PA
15,000	Allegheny Conference on Community Development, Pittsburgh, PA
15,000	Boy Scouts of America Allegheny Trails Council, Pittsburgh, PA
12,500	Carnegie Mellon University, Pittsburgh, PA
10,000	Carlow College, Pittsburgh, PA

Armco Inc. / Armco Foundation

Sales: $1.66 billion
Employees: 11,500
Headquarters: Parsippany, NJ
SIC Major Group: Blast Furnaces & Steel Mills, Pottery Products Nec, Steel Wire & Related Products, and Cold-Finishing of Steel Shapes

CONTACT

Colette M. Hucko
Community Relations Supervisor
Armco Inc.
1 Oxford Centre
301 Grant St.
Pittsburgh, PA 15219-1415
(412) 255-9800

FINANCIAL SUMMARY

Recent Giving: $650,000 (1995 est.); $552,879 (1994); $691,372 (1993)

Assets: $10,000,000 (1995 est.); $9,701,872 (1994 approx.); $10,157,092 (1993)

Fiscal Note: Figures reflect foundation giving.

EIN: 31-6026565

CONTRIBUTIONS SUMMARY

Typical Recipients: • *Arts & Humanities:* Arts Appreciation, Arts Associations & Councils, Arts Centers, Arts Festivals, Arts Funds, Arts Institutes, Historic Preservation, History & Archaeology, Libraries, Museums/Galleries, Music, Opera, Performing Arts, Public Broadcasting, Theater • *Civic & Public Affairs:* Business/Free Enterprise, Chambers of Commerce, Civil Rights, Economic Development, Economic Policy, General, Housing, Law & Justice, Municipalities/Towns, Nonprofit Management, Professional & Trade Associations, Public Policy, Safety, Urban & Community Affairs, Women's Affairs • *Education:* Business Education, Colleges & Universities, Community & Junior Colleges, Economic Education, Education Associations, Education Funds, Engineering/Technological Education, General, Literacy, Medical Education, Minority Education, Science/Mathematics Education, Student Aid • *Environment:* General • *Health:* Emergency/Ambulance Services, Health Funds, Health Organizations, Hospices, Hospitals, Medical Rehabilitation, Medical Training, Nursing Services, Public Health, Single-Disease Health Associations, Trauma Treatment • *International:* International Relations • *Religion:* Religious Welfare • *Science:* Observatories & Planetariums • *Social Services:* Child Welfare, Community Centers, Community Service Organizations, People with Disabilities, Recreation & Athletics, Senior Services, United Funds/United Ways, Volunteer Services, Youth Organizations

Grant Types: capital, challenge, employee matching gifts, general support, project, scholarship, and seed money

Note: Scholarships given to employee children.

Geographic Distribution: areas where major company operations exist

Operating Locations: AL, AZ, CO, CT, DC, FL (Boca Raton, Wildwood), GA, HI, IA (Des Moines), IL, IN, KS (Overland Park), KY (Ashland), LA, MA, MD (Baltimore), ME, MI, MN, MO (Kansas City), MS, MT, NC, ND, NE, NH, NJ (Englewood Cliffs, Princeton), NY (New York), OH (Cincinnati, Columbus, Middletown, Zanesville), OK, OR (Albany, Portland), PA (Ambridge, Butler), RI, SC, SD, TN, TX (Conroe, Dallas, Gainesville, San Marcos, Sugarland, Tomball, Waco), UT, VA, VT, WA, WI (Cudahy, Milwaukee), WV, WY (Caspar)

Note: Major facilities, which receive most funds, are in Butler, PA; Kansas City, KS; and Baltimore, MD.

CORP. OFFICERS

James L. Bertsch: *B* Cincinati OH 1943 *ED* Xavier Univ BS 1965; Xavier Univ MBA 1969 *CURR EMPL* vp, treas: Armco Inc *CORP AFFIL* treas, dir: Douglas Dynamics Inc *NONPR AFFIL* mem: Fin Execs Inst, Natl Assn Corp Treas, Natl Assn Credit Mgmt

Gary R. Hildreth: *B* 1939 *CURR EMPL* vp, gen couns, secy: Armco Inc *CORP AFFIL* vp, secy, dir: Douglas Dynamics Inc

Colette M. Hucko: *CURR EMPL* commun rels supvr: Armco Inc

James Frederick Will: *B* Pittsburgh PA 1938 *ED* PA St Univ BSEE 1961; Duquesne Univ MBA 1972 *CURR EMPL* pres, ceo, dir: Armco Inc

GIVING OFFICERS

James L. Bertsch: treas *CURR EMPL* vp, treas: Armco Inc (see above)

Gary R. Hildreth: asst secy *CURR EMPL* vp, gen couns, secy: Armco Inc (see above)

John H. Ladish: trust *B* Milwaukee WI 1924 *ED* Univ WI 1948 *CORP AFFIL* dir: Armco Inc, Banc One Milwaukee NA, Banc One WI Corp *PHIL AFFIL* trust: Ladish Co. Foundation; pres, treas, dir: Herman W. Ladish Family Foundation, Ladish Malting Co. Foundation; treas, dir: Victor F. Braun Foundation

Richard A. Moore: asst contr

APPLICATION INFORMATION

Initial Approach: *Initial Contact:* brief letter *Include Information On:* description of the organization or project; its purpose and importance to community; amount requested; purpose for which funds are sought; amount being solicited from all sources; current contributors; current financial statement; proof of tax-exempt status; descriptive literature supporting request, if available; any Armco relationship to the organization *Deadlines:* none, although foundation is not actively soliciting proposals (see "Other Things You Should Know" below) *Note:* Organizations are encouraged to initially send a brief letter rather than a full proposal.

Restrictions on Giving: Foundation does not give to political organizations or campaigns; programs directly linked to company; general endowments or deficit reduction plans; international organizations; individuals; or religious or fraternal organizations.

Foundation generally does not give to elementary or secondary schools; hospital operating drives; national health organizations; or organizations that already receive funds from the United Way, which the foundation supports.

Foundation does not automatically renew grants for organizations with which it has worked in the past.

OTHER THINGS TO KNOW

Foundation's giving program has decreased sharply in the past several years due to financial conditions. Currently, the foundation is not actively soliciting proposals.

In 1992, Armco merged with Cyclops.

Armco Inc. and Kawasaki created the Armco Steel Company Foundation in 1989. Each contributed $2.5 million. This separate operation makes contributions in Ashland, KY and Middletown, OH and has approximately the same priorities as the Armco Foundation.

GRANTS ANALYSIS

Total Grants: $428,000*

Number of Grants: 84*

Highest Grant: $61,000

Average Grant: $5,095*

Typical Range: $1,000 to $25,000

Disclosure Period: 1994

Note: Total grants figure, number of grants, and average grant figure exclude $82,667 in scholarships, $34,412 in matching gifts, and $7,800 in volunteer support. Total foundation giving in 1994 was $552,879. Recent grants are derived from a 1993 grants list.

RECENT GRANTS

Library

10,000	Butler Public Library, Butler, PA

General

61,000	United Way Butler County, Butler, PA
32,000	United Way Heart of America, Kansas City, MO
30,000	United Way Southwestern Pennsylvania, Pittsburgh, PA
25,000	United Way Richland County, Mansfield, OH
20,000	Carnegie Mellon University, Pittsburgh, PA

Asplundh Foundation

CONTACT
E. Boyd Asplundh
Secretary and Treasurer
Asplundh Fdn.
708 Blair Mill Rd.
Willow Grove, PA 19090
(215) 784-4200

FINANCIAL SUMMARY
Recent Giving: $256,000 (1993); $265,684 (1992); $256,583 (1991)

Assets: $6,440,816 (1993); $5,850,431 (1992); $5,368,728 (1991)

Gifts Received: $100,000 (1993); $101,000 (1992); $100,500 (1991)

Fiscal Note: In 1993, contributions were received from the Asplundh Tree Expert Co.

EIN: 23-6297246

CONTRIBUTIONS SUMMARY
Donor(s): the late Carl H. Asplundh, Lester Asplundh

Typical Recipients: • *Arts & Humanities:* Historic Preservation, History & Archaeology, Libraries, Museums/Galleries, Music • *Civic & Public Affairs:* Botanical Gardens/Parks, Employment/Job Training, General, Rural Affairs, Safety, Zoos/Aquariums • *Education:* Colleges & Universities, Private Education (Precollege) • *Health:* AIDS/HIV, Cancer, Emergency/Ambulance Services, Health Organizations, Hospitals • *International:* Health Care/Hospitals, International Environmental Issues • *Religion:* Churches, Religious Organizations • *Science:* Science Museums, Scientific Organizations • *Social Services:* At-Risk Youth, Community Service Organizations, People with Disabilities, Recreation & Athletics, United Funds/United Ways, Youth Organizations

Grant Types: general support

Geographic Distribution: primarily in PA

GIVING OFFICERS
Barr E. Asplundh: vp, dir *B* Bryn Athyn PA 1927 *ED* PA St Univ 1952 *CURR EMPL* chmn: Asplundh Tree Expert Co

Carl H. J. Asplundh, Jr.: dir

Christopher R. Asplundh: pres, dir

E. Boyd Asplundh: secy, treas, dir

Paul S. Asplundh: dir

Robert H. Asplundh: dir

Scott M. Asplundh: dir

George E. Graham, Jr.: dir

APPLICATION INFORMATION
Initial Approach: Send a brief letter of inquiry. Include a description of organization,

amount requested, purpose of funds sought, recently audited financial statement, and proof of tax-exempt status. There are no deadlines.

GRANTS ANALYSIS
Total Grants: $256,000
Number of Grants: 74
Highest Grant: $152,000
Typical Range: $200 to $3,000
Disclosure Period: 1993
Note: Recent grants are derived from a 1993 Form 990.

RECENT GRANTS
Library
1,000	Bucks County Free Library, Doylestown, PA

General
152,000	Bryn Athyn Church of the New Jerusalem, Bryn Athyn, PA
13,000	General Church of the New Jerusalem, Bryn Athyn, PA
6,500	Immanuel Church of the New Jerusalem, Glenview, IL
6,500	Pittsburgh Society of the General Church, Natrona Heights, PA
6,000	Academy of the New Church, Bryn Athyn, PA

Baker Foundation, Dexter F. and Dorothy H.

CONTACT
Richard W. Shaffer
Trustee
Dexter F. and Dorothy H. Baker Foundation
c/o Stevens & Johnson
740 Hamilton Mall
Allentown, PA 18101
(215) 439-1451

FINANCIAL SUMMARY
Recent Giving: $242,100 (1993); $124,300 (1992); $105,900 (1991)
Assets: $6,119,118 (1993); $6,614,234 (1992); $3,440,315 (1991)
Gifts Received: $2,355,500 (1992); $564,206 (1991); $984,632 (1990)
Fiscal Note: In 1992, cash contributions were received from Dexter F. Baker ($800,000); 34,000 shares of Air Products & Chemical stock valued at $1,555,500 were contributed as well.
EIN: 23-2453230

CONTRIBUTIONS SUMMARY
Donor(s): the donors are Dexter F. and Dorothy H. Baker
Typical Recipients: • *Arts & Humanities:* Arts Associations & Councils, Arts Festivals, Ballet, Community Arts, Dance, Historic Preservation, History & Archaeology, Libraries, Museums/Galleries, Music, Opera, Performing Arts, Public Broadcasting, Theater • *Civic & Public Affairs:* Safety,

Women's Affairs • *Education:* Arts/Humanities Education, Colleges & Universities, Engineering/Technological Education, General, Student Aid • *Environment:* Resource Conservation • *Health:* Health Funds, Medical Rehabilitation • *Religion:* Churches, Religious Welfare • *Social Services:* Child Welfare, Food/Clothing Distribution, People with Disabilities, Recreation & Athletics, Scouts, United Funds/United Ways, Volunteer Services, YMCA/YWCA/YMHA/YWHA, Youth Organizations
Grant Types: general support
Geographic Distribution: primarily in the Lehigh Valley, PA

GIVING OFFICERS
Mellon Bank: trust

APPLICATION INFORMATION
Initial Approach: Request application form. There are no deadlines.

GRANTS ANALYSIS
Total Grants: $242,100
Number of Grants: 33
Highest Grant: $56,000
Typical Range: $250 to $50,000
Disclosure Period: 1993
Note: Recent grants are derived from a 1993 Form 990.

RECENT GRANTS
Library
20,000	Hellertown Library, Hellertown, PA

General
56,000	First Presbyterian Church of Allentown, Allentown, PA — support local church
30,000	Lehigh University, Bethlehem, PA — support Baker auditorium
10,100	Minsi Trails Council, Lehigh Valley, PA — support inner-city scouting program
5,000	Allentown Area Food Bank, Allentown, PA
5,000	Lehigh University, Bethlehem, PA — Baker scholarship program

Bard Foundation, Robert

CONTACT
Pat Kling
Robert Bard Fdn.
c/o Mellon Bank East NA
PO Box 7236 AIM 193 0224
Philadelphia, PA 19101-7236
(215) 553-2584

FINANCIAL SUMMARY
Recent Giving: $137,987 (fiscal 1994); $112,871 (fiscal 1993); $122,500 (fiscal 1992)

Assets: $2,967,911 (fiscal 1994); $3,034,808 (fiscal 1993); $2,834,128 (fiscal 1992)
EIN: 23-6806099

CONTRIBUTIONS SUMMARY
Typical Recipients: • *Arts & Humanities:* History & Archaeology, Libraries • *Civic & Public Affairs:* Clubs, General, Urban & Community Affairs • *Education:* Colleges & Universities, Private Education (Precollege), Public Education (Precollege) • *Health:* Emergency/Ambulance Services, Nursing Services • *Social Services:* Child Welfare, Community Service Organizations, Counseling, Family Services, Food/Clothing Distribution, People with Disabilities, United Funds/United Ways, Volunteer Services, YMCA/YWCA/YMHA/YWHA, Youth Organizations
Grant Types: general support
Geographic Distribution: emphasis on Royersford, PA

GIVING OFFICERS
Mellon Bank, N.A.: trust
Norman E. Donahue II: trust
Norman E. Donoghue II: trust *B* Coatsville PA 1944 *ED* William Coll BA 1966; Duke Univ JD 1969 *CURR EMPL* ptnr: Dechert Price & Rhoads *NONPR AFFIL* fellow: Intl Academy Trust & Estate Lawyers; legal couns, dir: Intl Visitors Counc Philadelphia; mem: Am Bar Assn; trust, legal couns, corp secy: Princess Grace Fdn

APPLICATION INFORMATION
Initial Approach: Send a brief letter of inquiry. Include a description of organization, total cost, name of contact person, and IRS determination letter. Deadline is April 1.

GRANTS ANALYSIS
Total Grants: $137,987
Number of Grants: 17
Highest Grant: $20,000
Typical Range: $2,000 to $12,000
Disclosure Period: fiscal year ending June 30, 1994
Note: Recent grants are derived from a fiscal 1994 Form 990.

RECENT GRANTS
Library
10,900	Spring City Free Public Library, Spring City, PA
6,000	Royersford Public Library, Royersford, PA

General
20,000	Family Services of Montgomery County, Morristown, PA — Meals on Wheels
12,000	Camphill Village, Kimberton, PA
10,087	Royersford Community Chest, Royersford, PA
10,000	Spring Ford Area School District Educational Foundation, Collegeville, PA — series of multicultural programs in 1994-95

| 10,000 | Spring Ford Counseling Services, Royersford, PA |

Barra Foundation

CONTACT
Robert L. McNeil, Jr.
President
Barra Foundation
8200 Flourtown Ave., Ste. 12
Wyndmoor, PA 19038
(215) 233-5115

FINANCIAL SUMMARY
Recent Giving: $2,026,392 (1993); $1,841,398 (1992); $1,741,397 (1991)

Assets: $32,860,815 (1993); $28,270,081 (1992); $28,415,504 (1991)

EIN: 23-6277885

CONTRIBUTIONS SUMMARY
Donor(s): The foundation was established in Delaware in 1963. The donor, Robert L. McNeil, Jr., currently serves as president, treasurer, and director of the foundation.

Typical Recipients: • *Arts & Humanities:* Arts Associations & Councils, Arts Centers, Arts Funds, Arts Institutes, Community Arts, Ethnic & Folk Arts, Historic Preservation, History & Archaeology, Libraries, Museums/Galleries, Performing Arts, Public Broadcasting, Theater • *Civic & Public Affairs:* Botanical Gardens/Parks, Civil Rights, Community Foundations, Economic Development, Employment/Job Training, General, Hispanic Affairs, Housing, Philanthropic Organizations, Urban & Community Affairs, Women's Affairs, Zoos/Aquariums • *Education:* Arts/Humanities Education, Colleges & Universities, Economic Education, Education Associations, Health & Physical Education, Medical Education, Minority Education, Private Education (Precollege), Religious Education, Science/Mathematics Education, Social Sciences Education • *Environment:* General, Resource Conservation • *Health:* Children's Health/Hospitals, Emergency/Ambulance Services, Health Organizations, Home-Care Services, Hospices, Hospitals, Medical Rehabilitation, Medical Research, Single-Disease Health Associations • *International:* International Relations, International Relief Efforts • *Religion:* Churches, Jewish Causes, Religious Organizations, Religious Welfare • *Science:* Scientific Centers & Institutes • *Social Services:* Animal Protection, Child Welfare, Community Service Organizations, Family Planning, Family Services, Food/Clothing Distribution, Homes, People with Disabilities, Senior Services, Shelters/Homelessness, United Funds/United Ways, Youth Organizations

Grant Types: general support and project

Geographic Distribution: primarily the Philadelphia, PA, area

GIVING OFFICERS
Frank R. Donahue, Jr.: secy, dir

Herman R. Hutchinson: dir *PHIL AFFIL* trust: Robert L. McNeil, Jr. 1986 Charitable Trust

Robert L. McNeil, Jr.: pres, treas, dir

William T. Tredennick: vp, dir *B* Johnstown PA 1906 *ED* Alfred Univ BS 1928 *CURR EMPL* pres, dir: Resco Products *NONPR AFFIL* dir: Refractories Inst; mem: Am Ceramic Soc, Am Iron & Steel Inst

APPLICATION INFORMATION
Initial Approach:

Send a one- to two-page letter of inquiry to the foundation.

Letters should describe the organization, the intended project, and a budget for the proposed project.

There are no deadlines for applications.

The board meets in December.

Restrictions on Giving: Grant recipients are required to send the foundation publications of studies.

Restrictions on Giving: The foundation does not give grants to individuals, for annual or capital campaigns, deficit drives, building or endowment funds, operating budgets, scholarships, fellowships, or programs in process. In addition, the foundation will not make loans.

PUBLICATIONS
Program policy statement

GRANTS ANALYSIS
Total Grants: $2,026,392

Number of Grants: 296

Highest Grant: $250,000

Average Grant: $6,846

Typical Range: $1,000 to $10,000

Disclosure Period: 1993

Note: Recent grants are derived from a 1993 Form 990.

RECENT GRANTS

Library
| 80,000 | Athenaeum of Philadelphia, Philadelphia, PA |
| 10,000 | Germantown Historical Society, Philadelphia, PA — library project |

General
250,000	Chestnut Hill Hospital HealthCare, Philadelphia, PA
81,000	Philadelphia College of Textiles and Science, Philadelphia, PA — computer textile design project
75,000	Philadelphia College of Pharmacy and Science, Philadelphia, PA — 1938 scholarship
50,000	Boys and Girls Club of Martin County, Hobe Sound, FL — building expansion
25,000	American Red Cross, Philadelphia, PA — blood center

Benedum Foundation, Claude Worthington

CONTACT
Paul R. Jenkins
President and Trustee
Claude Worthington Benedum Foundation
1400 Benedum-Trees Bldg.
Pittsburgh, PA 15222
(412) 288-0360

FINANCIAL SUMMARY
Recent Giving: $9,725,897 (1993); $6,836,329 (1992); $7,978,262 (1991)

Assets: $217,290,811 (1993); $199,212,916 (1992); $195,020,105 (1991)

EIN: 25-1086799

CONTRIBUTIONS SUMMARY
Donor(s): The foundation was established in 1944 by Michael Late Benedum and his wife, Sarah Lantz Benedum, as a memorial to their only child, Claude Worthington Benedum, who died at the age of 18 in World War I. Michael Benedum worked in the oil and gas business for most of his life. With Joe C. Trees, he started the Benedum-Trees Oil Company in 1900. From its initial success in Benedum's home state of West Virginia, the company grew to be international in scale. Mr. Benedum worked in all phases of the oil and gas business until his death in 1959 at the age of 90.

Typical Recipients: • *Arts & Humanities:* Arts Festivals, Arts Funds, Arts Outreach, Ballet, Dance, Film & Video, Historic Preservation, History & Archaeology, Libraries, Museums/Galleries, Music, Opera, Performing Arts, Theater • *Civic & Public Affairs:* Economic Development, Employment/Job Training, Housing, Public Policy, Rural Affairs, Urban & Community Affairs, Women's Affairs • *Education:* Colleges & Universities, Education Funds, Education Reform, Faculty Development, General, Leadership Training, Literacy, Medical Education, Private Education (Precollege), School Volunteerism, Science/Mathematics Education • *Environment:* Air/Water Quality, General, Resource Conservation • *Health:* Children's Health/Hospitals, Emergency/Ambulance Services, Health Organizations, Hospitals, Nursing Services, Nutrition, Preventive Medicine/Wellness Organizations, Public Health • *Religion:* Churches, Jewish Causes • *Social Services:* At-Risk Youth, Child Welfare, Community Service Organizations, Family Services, Food/Clothing Distribution, People with Disabilities, Senior Services, United Funds/United Ways, Youth Organizations

Grant Types: capital, project, research, and seed money

Geographic Distribution: West Virginia and Pittsburgh, PA

GIVING OFFICERS
Ralph J. Bean, Jr.: trust *B* Cumberland MD 1941 *ED* WV Univ 1963; Harvard Univ 1967 *CURR EMPL* pres: Hope Gas Inc

CORP AFFIL dir: First Natl Bank Morgantown, Huntington Natl Bank *PHIL AFFIL* trust: Consolidated Natural Gas System Foundation

G. Nicholas Beckwith III: trust *B* 1945 *ED* Brown Univ 1967 *CURR EMPL* pres-ceo, dir: Beckwith Machinery Co *CORP AFFIL* chmn: Shadyside Health Ed Res Corp; trust: Shady Side Academy; v chmn: Shadyside Hosp

Paul G. Benedum, Jr.: chmn, trust

William P. Getty: dir

Paul R. Jenkins: pres, trust

Robert Earl Maxwell: trust

Jennings Randolph: emeritus trust

Hulett C. Smith: emeritus trust *B* 1918 *CURR EMPL* vp, dir: Beckley Hosp

George A. Stinson: emeritus trust *B* Camden AR 1915 *ED* Northwestern Univ AB 1936; Columbia Univ JD 1939; WV Univ LLD *CURR EMPL* hon dir: Natl InterGroup *CORP AFFIL* dir: Birmingham Steel Co; trust emeritus: Mutual Life Ins Co NY *NONPR AFFIL* mem: Am Iron Steel Inst, Am Law Inst, Bus Counc, Intl Iron Steel Inst, Phi Beta Kappa; trust emeritus: Univ Pittsburgh *CLUB AFFIL* Duquesne, Gulf Stream GC, Laurel Valley GC, Links *PHIL AFFIL* treas, trust: Maurice Falk Medical Fund; trust: George C. Marshall Foundation

G. Randolph Worls: trust

APPLICATION INFORMATION
Initial Approach:

There is no standard application form. Applicants should submit a preliminary letter of inquiry.

Requests for funding should include a cover letter signed by the organization's chairman or president; title page containing the organization's address and phone number, name of executive director, name of individual responsible for project, desciption of project, and specific amount of support; background information about the sponsoring agency; project description including project's purpose, population served, geographic area served, need of project, methods of evaluation, additional sources of funding, timeline, and project activities; listing of staff including qualifications of key personnel; listing of officers and directors of organization including affiliations; total budget; recent audited financial statements; recent annual report; and IRS tax-determination letter.

Applications are accepted at any time.

The staff will review preliminary letters of inquiry to determine whether a full proposal should be submitted. Response is generally prompt. Proposals with significant individual merit are presented to the board of trustees for decisions.

Restrictions on Giving: The foundation does not support individuals, propaganda influencing legislation, political campaigning,

national health and welfare campaigns, medical research, or religious activities. The foundation also does not fund business development by individuals, deficit funding, annual appeals, individual public or private elementary or secondary schools, hospital construction or equipment purchases, individual or group travel, or publications including books or audiovisual materials unless already supported by the foundation.

OTHER THINGS TO KNOW

The foundation reports that it also provides seminars/workshops, proposal writing assistance, and technical assistance to nonprofits.

PUBLICATIONS

Periodic and interim reports; application guidelines

GRANTS ANALYSIS

Total Grants: $9,725,897

Number of Grants: 153

Highest Grant: $1,000,000

Average Grant: $57,407*

Typical Range: $10,000 to $75,000

Disclosure Period: 1993

Note: Average grant excludes the highest grant of $1,000,000. Recent grants are derived from a 1993 Form 990.

RECENT GRANTS

General

1,000,000	Conservation Fund, Arlington, VA — to establish a land acquisition fund as part of the implementation of a plan for the environmentally sustainable economic development of Canaan Valley and surrounding communities
559,373	West Virginia University Foundation, Morgantown, WV — Benedum Teacher Education Project
500,000	Shady Side Academy, Pittsburgh, PA — to assist the academy in meeting the major capital needs
260,000	West Virginia University Foundation, Morgantown, WV — emergency medicine physician assistants program and management assistance program for rural ambulance squads throughout West Virginia
250,000	Concord College Foundation, Athens, WV — scholarships linking students with community service

Berwind Corporation

Sales: $400.0 million
Employees: 2,645
Headquarters: Philadelphia, PA
SIC Major Group: Real Property Lessors Nec, Highway & Street Construction, Bridge, Tunnel & Elevated Highway, and Pharmaceutical Preparations

CONTACT
Mary LaRue
Chairperson, Contributions Committee
Berwind Corporation
3000 Centre Sq. West
1500 Market St.
Philadelphia, PA 19102
(215) 563-2800

FINANCIAL SUMMARY
Recent Giving: $800,000 (1995 est.); $800,000 (1994 approx.); $650,000 (1993)
Fiscal Note: Company gives directly.

CONTRIBUTIONS SUMMARY
Typical Recipients: • *Arts & Humanities:* Arts Institutes, General, Libraries, Museums/Galleries, Music, Performing Arts, Public Broadcasting, Theater • *Civic & Public Affairs:* General, Women's Affairs, Zoos/Aquariums • *Education:* Business Education, Colleges & Universities, General, Legal Education, Minority Education • *Environment:* General • *Health:* General, Hospitals • *Science:* Scientific Centers & Institutes • *Social Services:* Child Welfare, Community Centers, Delinquency & Criminal Rehabilitation, Family Planning, Food/Clothing Distribution, Senior Services, United Funds/United Ways

Grant Types: capital, employee matching gifts, general support, multiyear/continuing support, and operating expenses

Note: Employee matching gift ratio: 1 to 1, up to $1,000.

Nonmonetary Support Types: donated equipment

Geographic Distribution: only in headquarters area

Operating Locations: KY (Kimper, Pikeville), MA (Ashland, Sharon), MD (Easton), MI (Port Huron), NJ (Neptune), NY (Amherst), OR (Portland), PA (Hollidaysburg, King of Prussia, Philadelphia, Warminster, West Point, Windber), TN (La Vergne), WV (Charleston)

CORP. OFFICERS
C. Graham Berwind, Jr.: *B* Bryn Mawr PA 1928 *ED* Univ VT BA 1951; Harvard Univ MBA 1953 *CURR EMPL* chmn, pres, ceo: Berwind Corp

GIVING OFFICERS
Mary LaRue: chp contributions comm *CURR EMPL* secy: Berwind Corp

APPLICATION INFORMATION
Initial Approach: *Initial Contact:* letter of inquiry *Include Information On:* description of the organization, amount requested, purpose of funds sought, list of organizations

which support the work done by your organization, list of board of directors, and IRS 501(c)(3) tax-determination letter *Deadlines:* by November preceding the year organization wants funding

Restrictions on Giving: Does not support political or lobbying groups.

GRANTS ANALYSIS
Total Grants: $800,000

Typical Range: $1,000 to $2,500

Disclosure Period: 1994

RECENT GRANTS

General
Citizens Crime Commission, Philadelphia, PA
Hahnemann University Hospital, Philadelphia, PA
International House, Philadelphia, PA
Pikeville College, Pikeville, KY
St. Francis College, Altoona, PA

Bethlehem Steel Corp. / Bethlehem Steel Foundation

Revenue: $4.81 billion
Employees: 20,500
Headquarters: Bethlehem, PA
SIC Major Group: Blast Furnaces & Steel Mills, Bituminous Coal & Lignite—Surface, Blast Furnaces & Steel Mills, and Steel Wire & Related Products

CONTACT
James F. Kostecky
Director, Corporate Support Programs
Bethlehem Steel Corp.
Rm. 1711, Martin Tower, 1170 8th Ave.
Bethlehem, PA 18016
(610) 694-6940
Note: Mr. Kostecky is also executive director of the Bethlehem Steel Foundation.

FINANCIAL SUMMARY
Recent Giving: $942,280 (1994); $775,000 (1993); $1,000,000 (1992)

Gifts Received: $943,401 (1994); $773,384 (1993)

Fiscal Note: Company offers both direct and foundation gifts. In 1994, approximately $175,000 was given directly. This figure is not included in the above figures.

CONTRIBUTIONS SUMMARY
Typical Recipients: • *Arts & Humanities:* Arts Associations & Councils, Arts Festivals, Community Arts, Historic Preservation, History & Archaeology, Libraries, Museums/Galleries, Music, Performing Arts, Public Broadcasting, Theater, Visual Arts • *Civic & Public Affairs:* African American Affairs, Botanical Gardens/Parks, Business/Free Enterprise, Civil Rights, Community Foundations, Economic Development, Economic Policy, Employment/Job Training, General, Hispanic Affairs, Housing, Law & Justice, Legal Aid, Municipalities/Towns, Philanthropic Organizations, Professional & Trade Associations, Public Policy, Safety, Urban & Community Affairs

• *Education:* Arts/Humanities Education, Business Education, Business-School Partnerships, Colleges & Universities, Economic Education, Engineering/Technological Education, Legal Education, Literacy, Minority Education, Private Education (Precollege), Public Education (Precollege), Science/Mathematics Education • *Environment:* Air/Water Quality, General • *Health:* Emergency/Ambulance Services, Geriatric Health, Health Policy/Cost Containment, Health Organizations, Hospitals, Nursing Services, Nutrition, Public Health • *Science:* Scientific Centers & Institutes • *Social Services:* Child Welfare, Community Centers, Community Service Organizations, Counseling, Day Care, Delinquency & Criminal Rehabilitation, Domestic Violence, Emergency Relief, Family Services, Food/Clothing Distribution, People with Disabilities, Recreation & Athletics, Senior Services, Shelters/Homelessness, Substance Abuse, United Funds/United Ways, Volunteer Services, Youth Organizations

Grant Types: capital, general support, operating expenses, project, and research

Nonmonetary Support: $30,000 (1993); $30,000 (1992)

Nonmonetary Support Types: donated equipment, donated products, in-kind services, and workplace solicitation

Note: Workplace solicitation is for the United Way only. Reported value of yearly nonmonetary support is $30,000 or less. Above figures exclude nonmonetary support.

Geographic Distribution: headquarters and operating locations

Operating Locations: IN (Chesterton), MD (Sparrows Point), MN, NY (Lackawanna), OH (Walbridge), PA (Bethlehem, Johnstown, Monessen, Steelton), TX (Port Arthur), WV

Note: Company operates five plants in locations.

CORP. OFFICERS
Curtis Handley Barnette: *B* St Albans WV 1935 *ED* Univ Manchester 1956-1957; WV Univ AB 1956; Yale Univ JD 1962; Harvard Univ Advanced Mgmt Program 1975 *CURR EMPL* chmn, ceo, dir: Bethlehem Steel Corp *NONPR AFFIL* chmn: PA Bus Roundtable, WV Univ Fdn; dir: Am Iron & Steel Inst, Natl Legal Ctr Pub Interest, PA Soc, WLVT-TV, Yale Univ Law Sch Fund; mem: Am Bar Assn, Am Corp Secys Assn, Am Law Inst, Assn Gen Couns, Beta Alpha Theta, Beta Theta Pi, CT Bar Assn, DC Bar Assn, Fed Bar Assn, Northampton County Bar Assn, PA Bar Assn, PA Chamber Bus Indus, Phi Beta Kappa, Phi Delta Phi, US Admin Conf, WV Bar Assn; mem adv counc: Trade Policy & Negotions; mem policy comm: Bus Roundtable; trust: Lehigh Univ; vchmn: Fdn Drug-Free PA, Intl Iron & Steel Inst *CLUB AFFIL* Bethlehem, Blooming Grove Hunting & Fishing, Links, Loblolly Bay YC, Saucon Valley CC, Univ WA, Yale

Steven G. Donches: *CURR EMPL* vp pub aff: Bethlehem Steel Corp

Gary Lee Millenbruch: *B* Marysville KS 1937 *ED* KS St Univ BS 1959 *CURR EMPL* cfo, exec vp: Bethlehem Steel Corp *NONPR AFFIL* mem: Am Iron & Steel Inst, Fin Execs Inst

Roger Pratt Penny: *B* Buffalo NY 1936 *ED* Un Coll BA 1958 *CURR EMPL* pres, coo, dir: Bethlehem Steel Corp *CORP AFFIL* dir: Double G Coatings, Walbridge Coatings *NONPR AFFIL* mem: Am Iron & Steel Engrs, Am Iron & Steel Inst, Buffalo Chamber Commerce, Orchard Pk Chamber Commerce, Valparaiso Chamber Commerce; vp exploring: Boy Scouts Am Lehigh Valley *CLUB AFFIL* Buffalo Soccer, Sand Creek, Saucon Valley CC

GIVING OFFICERS
Steven G. Donches: pres *CURR EMPL* vp pub aff: Bethlehem Steel Corp (see above)

James Frank Kostecky: exec dir *B* Ephrata PA 1943 *ED* Villanova Univ BCE 1965; Carnegie-Mellon Univ MSCE 1967; Lehigh Univ MS 1971 *CURR EMPL* dir corp support programs: Bethlehem Steel Corp *CORP AFFIL* dir: Burnside Plantation Inc *NONPR AFFIL* adv: Un Way Northampton & Warren Counties; assoc dir: Northampton County Conservation District; chmn: Natl Eagle Scout Assn Lehigh Valley; mem: Am Iron & Steel Inst, Assn Iron & Steel Engrs; mem adv counc: Boy Scouts Am Lehigh Valley; mem corp comm: Allentown Mus Art *CLUB AFFIL* Saucon Valley CC

APPLICATION INFORMATION
Initial Approach: *Initial Contact:* brief letter and proposal *Include Information On:* a complete description of the organization and a statement of objectives; a description of the benefits and geographic area to be served; financial information, including an explanation of disbursements as well as contributions and other sources of revenue; plans for reporting and measuring results; amount requested, recently audited financial statements, and proof of tax-exempt status

Restrictions on Giving: Does not support organizations not exempt from taxation under Section 501(c)(3), individuals, religious organizations for sectarian purposes, political lobbying groups, or foreign institutions and organizations.

OTHER THINGS TO KNOW
The Bethlehem Steel Foundation was founded in 1993. Before 1993, contributions were given solely through Bethlehem Steel Corp.

GRANTS ANALYSIS
Total Grants: $942,280

Number of Grants: 108

Highest Grant: $215,000

Average Grant: $5,024*

Typical Range: $500 to $7,500

Disclosure Period: 1994

Note: Figures reflect foundation giving only. Average grant figure excludes the two highest grants totaling $409,750. Recent grants are derived from a 1994 annual report.

RECENT GRANTS

General

215,000	United Way of Central Maryland, Baltimore, MD
194,750	United Way of Greater Lehigh Valley, Bethlehem, PA
115,500	United Way of Porter County, Valparaiso, IN
75,000	United Way of Greater Johnstown, Johnstown, PA
39,505	St. Luke's Hospital, Fountain Hill, PA — in-kind gift of structural steel for new Education Pavilion

Betts Industries / Betts Foundation

Sales: $25.0 million
Employees: 200
Headquarters: Warren, PA
SIC Major Group: Electronic & Other Electrical Equipment, Fabricated Metal Products, Primary Metal Industries, and Transportation Equipment

CONTACT
Clifford Betts
Director, Human Resources
Betts Foundation
Box 888
Warren, PA 16365
(814) 723-1250

FINANCIAL SUMMARY
Recent Giving: $69,530 (1993); $151,288 (1992); $107,147 (1991)

Assets: $1,719,322 (1993); $1,688,700 (1992); $1,497,469 (1991)

Gifts Received: $15,000 (1993); $260,000 (1992); $35,100 (1991)

Fiscal Note: In 1993, contributions were received from Betts Industries, Inc.

EIN: 25-6035169

CONTRIBUTIONS SUMMARY
Typical Recipients: • *Arts & Humanities:* Arts Associations & Councils, Libraries, Music • *Civic & Public Affairs:* Business/Free Enterprise, Economic Development, General, Municipalities/Towns, Public Policy, Safety, Urban & Community Affairs, Women's Affairs • *Education:* Business Education, Colleges & Universities, Community & Junior Colleges, Economic Education, Education Funds, Engineering/Technological Education, Public Education (Precollege), Secondary Education (Private) • *Health:* Emergency/Ambulance Services, Health Organizations, Hospices • *Religion:* Churches, Religious Welfare • *Social Services:* Animal Protection, Camps, Child Welfare, Community Service Organizations, Day Care, Delinquency & Criminal Rehabilitation, Family Services, Homes, Recreation & Athletics, Senior Services, United Funds/United Ways, YMCA/YWCA/YMHA/YWHA, Youth Organizations

Grant Types: general support

Geographic Distribution: focus on Warren, PA

Operating Locations: PA (Warren)

CORP. OFFICERS
Richard T. Betts: *CURR EMPL* pres, dir: Betts Indus

GIVING OFFICERS
C. R. Betts: trust

I. R. Betts: trust

R. E. Betts: trust

Richard T. Betts: trust *CURR EMPL* pres, dir: Betts Indus (see above)

M. D. Hedges: trust

APPLICATION INFORMATION
Initial Approach: Send brief letter describing program. There are no deadlines.

GRANTS ANALYSIS
Total Grants: $69,530

Number of Grants: 47

Highest Grant: $15,285

Typical Range: $300 to $8,000

Disclosure Period: 1993

Note: Recent grants are derived from a 1993 Form 990.

RECENT GRANTS

Library

8,000	Warren Library Association, Warren, PA

General

15,285	United Fund of Warren County, Warren, PA
4,319	City of Warren, Warren, PA
3,500	St. Josephs Church
3,222	Task, Trenton, NJ
2,900	Youth Baseball/Softball Association, Warren, PA

Binney & Smith Inc.

Sales: $350.0 million
Employees: 2,157
Parent Company: Hallmark Cards Inc.
Headquarters: Easton, PA
SIC Major Group: Lead Pencils & Art Goods, Adhesives & Sealants, and Games, Toys & Children's Vehicles

CONTACT
Marta Boulos
Community Affairs Specialist
Binney & Smith Inc.
1100 Church Ln., Box 431
Easton, PA 18044-0431
(610) 253-6271

FINANCIAL SUMMARY
Recent Giving: $300,000 (1994 approx.); $300,000 (1993 approx.); $265,800 (1992 approx.)

Fiscal Note: Company gives directly.

CONTRIBUTIONS SUMMARY
Typical Recipients: • *Arts & Humanities:* Arts Appreciation, Arts Associations & Councils, Arts Centers, Arts Festivals, Arts Funds, Arts Institutes, Community Arts, Dance, Film & Video, Historic Preservation, Libraries, Literary Arts, Museums/Galleries, Music, Opera, Performing Arts, Public Broadcasting, Theater, Visual Arts • *Civic & Public Affairs:* Business/Free Enterprise, Civil Rights, Community Foundations, Economic Development, Economic Policy, First Amendment Issues, General, Hispanic Affairs, Philanthropic Organizations • *Education:* Afterschool/Enrichment Programs, Arts/Humanities Education, Business Education, Colleges & Universities, Community & Junior Colleges, Continuing Education, Economic Education, Education Associations, Education Funds, Elementary Education (Private), General, Literacy, Preschool Education, Private Education (Precollege), Public Education (Precollege), Secondary Education (Private), Secondary Education (Public), Social Sciences Education, Special Education, Student Aid • *Environment:* General, Wildlife Protection • *Health:* Children's Health/Hospitals, Emergency/Ambulance Services, General, Speech & Hearing • *International:* International Relations • *Social Services:* At-Risk Youth, Child Welfare, Community Centers, Domestic Violence, Family Services, General, Sexual Abuse, Shelters/Homelessness, United Funds/United Ways, Volunteer Services, Youth Organizations

Grant Types: capital, employee matching gifts, general support, multiyear/continuing support, scholarship, and seed money

Nonmonetary Support Types: donated equipment, donated products, in-kind services, and loaned executives

Note: Value of nonmonetary support is unavailable.

Geographic Distribution: Easton, PA, and Winfield, KS only

Operating Locations: KS (Winfield), PA (Easton)

CORP. OFFICERS
Richard Stephen Gurin: *B* Philadelphia PA 1940 *ED* Hamilton Coll BA 1962 *CURR EMPL* pres, ceo, chmn: Binney & Smith Inc *NONPR AFFIL* dir: Boy Scouts Am Minsi Trails Counc, Easton Econ Devel Corp, Northampton County Devel Corp, Preservation PA; gen campaign chmn: Un Way Northampton County; mem: Natl Comm Standards Arts; mem leadership counc: Natl Cultural Alliance; mem steering comm: Chief St Sch Off; trust: Lehigh Valley Partnership *CLUB AFFIL* Saucon Valley CC, Sorrento YC

Dean Rodenbough: *CURR EMPL* dir corp aff: Binney & Smith Inc

GIVING OFFICERS
Marta Boulos: *CURR EMPL* commun aff specialist: Binney & Smith Inc

APPLICATION INFORMATION
Initial Approach: *Initial Contact:* letter of inquiry *Include Information On:* description of the organization, amount requested, purpose of funds sought, recently audited financial statements, and proof of tax-exempt status *Deadlines:* must be received by Sep-

tember 1 prior to the year for which funding is sought

Restrictions on Giving: The company does not support individuals, individual scout groups, individual schools, religious organizations for sectarian purposes, or political or lobbying groups.

PUBLICATIONS
Informational brochure (including guidelines)

GRANTS ANALYSIS
Total Grants: $300,000*

Typical Range: $1,000 to $2,500

Disclosure Period: 1994

Note: Total grants figure is an approximate.

Binswanger Cos. / Binswanger Foundation

Sales: $500.0 million
Employees: 150
Headquarters: Philadelphia, PA
SIC Major Group: Real Estate

CONTACT
James J. Dunleavy
Director, Corporate Finance
Binswanger Cos.
Two Logan Sq., 4th Fl.
Philadelphia, PA 19103
(215) 448-6000

FINANCIAL SUMMARY
Recent Giving: $296,345 (1993); $183,805 (1992); $293,411 (1991)

Assets: $614,456 (1993); $891,060 (1992); $943,585 (1991)

Gifts Received: $25,000 (1992); $48,242 (1991); $177,374 (1990)

EIN: 23-6296506

CONTRIBUTIONS SUMMARY
Typical Recipients: • *Arts & Humanities:* Arts Associations & Councils, General, Historic Preservation, Libraries, Museums/Galleries, Music • *Civic & Public Affairs:* Botanical Gardens/Parks, Business/Free Enterprise, General, Urban & Community Affairs, Zoos/Aquariums • *Education:* Arts/Humanities Education, Business-School Partnerships, Colleges & Universities, Private Education (Precollege) • *Health:* Cancer, Hospitals, Medical Research, Single-Disease Health Associations • *International:* International Affairs, International Organizations, Missionary/Religious Activities • *Religion:* Jewish Causes, Religious Organizations, Social/Policy Issues • *Science:* Science Museums • *Social Services:* Child Welfare, Community Service Organizations, Day Care, Delinquency & Criminal Rehabilitation, Recreation & Ath-

letics, United Funds/United Ways, Youth Organizations

Grant Types: general support

Geographic Distribution: focus on PA

Operating Locations: PA (Philadelphia)

CORP. OFFICERS
Frank G. Binswanger, Jr.: *B* Philadelphia PA 1928 *ED* Wesleyan Univ 1950 *CURR EMPL* chmn, dir: Binswanger Co *NONPR AFFIL* mem: Soc Indus & Off Realtors; mem, dir: Chief Execs Org, World Bus Counc; trust: Fox Chase Cancer Ctr; trust emeritus: Wesleyan Univ

John K. Binswanger: *B* Philadelphia PA 1932 *ED* Wesleyan Univ 1954 *CURR EMPL* ceo: Binswanger Co *CORP AFFIL* chmn: Binswanger Mgmt Corp; pres: Binswanger Investment & Financing Div; treas, dir: Binswanger Corp-Southern Div

Michael J. Brennan: *CURR EMPL* cfo, treas: Binswanger Co

GIVING OFFICERS
David R. Binswanger: treas

Frank G. Binswanger III: secy

Frank G. Binswanger, Jr.: chmn, dir *CURR EMPL* chmn, dir: Binswanger Co (see above)

John K. Binswanger: pres *CURR EMPL* ceo: Binswanger Co (see above)

Robert B. Binswanger: vchmn

APPLICATION INFORMATION
Initial Approach: The foundation has no formal grant application procedure or application form. Contributions decisions are made in January. Organizations interested in applying for support should send a request, information and literature by November.

GRANTS ANALYSIS
Total Grants: $296,345

Number of Grants: 44

Highest Grant: $90,500

Typical Range: $300 to $75,500

Disclosure Period: 1993

Note: Recent grants are derived from a 1993 Form 990.

RECENT GRANTS
Library
1,250	Rosenbach Museum and Library, PA

General
70,000	Jewish Federation, Philadelphia, PA
40,000	United Way, Philadelphia, PA
10,000	Friends of Rittenhouse, Philadelphia, PA

5,150	Hospital of the University of Philadelphia, Philadelphia, PA
5,000	Boy Scouts of America, Philadelphia, PA

Bryn Mawr Trust Co.

Assets: $321.0 million
Employees: 199
Parent Company: Bryn Mawr Bank Corp.
Headquarters: Bryn Mawr, PA
SIC Major Group: Depository Institutions

CONTACT
Joe Smith
Marketing Officer
Bryn Mawr Trust Co.
801 Lancaster Ave.
Bryn Mawr, PA 19010
(610) 526-2384

FINANCIAL SUMMARY
Fiscal Note: Annual Giving Range: less than $100,000

CONTRIBUTIONS SUMMARY
Company reports 43% of contributions support civic and public affairs; 25%, health and human services; 20%, the arts; and 12%, education.

Typical Recipients: • *Arts & Humanities:* Arts Associations & Councils, Arts Centers, Arts Festivals, Arts Funds, Arts Institutes, Community Arts, General, Historic Preservation, Libraries, Museums/Galleries, Music, Opera, Performing Arts, Theater • *Civic & Public Affairs:* African American Affairs, Botanical Gardens/Parks, Business/Free Enterprise, Chambers of Commerce, Civil Rights, Community Foundations, Economic Development, Environmental Affairs (General), General, Housing, Inner-City Development, Municipalities/Towns, Parades/Festivals, Professional & Trade Associations, Zoos/Aquariums • *Education:* Arts/Humanities Education, Colleges & Universities, General • *Environment:* Air/Water Quality, Resource Conservation • *Health:* Arthritis, Cancer, Children's Health/Hospitals, Clinics/Medical Centers, Emergency/Ambulance Services, General, Geriatric Health, Heart, Home-Care Services, Hospices, Hospitals, Long-Term Care, Nursing Services, Prenatal Health Issues, Preventive Medicine/Wellness Organizations • *Social Services:* Community Centers, Community Service Organizations, Counseling, Day Care, Food/Clothing Distribution, General, Recreation & Athletics, Senior Services, Shelters/Homelessness, United Funds/United Ways, Volunteer Services, YMCA/YWCA/YMHA/YWHA

Grant Types: operating expenses and scholarship

Geographic Distribution: primarily headquarters area

Operating Locations: PA (Bryn Mawr, Havertown, Poole, Wayne, Wynnewood)

CORP. OFFICERS
Robert L. Stevens: *CURR EMPL* pres, dir: Bryn Mawr Trust Co

APPLICATION INFORMATION
Initial Approach: Send brief letter of inquiry. Include a description of organization, amount requested, purpose of funds sought, recently audited financial statement, and proof of tax-exempt status. There are no deadlines.

Restrictions on Giving: Does not support individuals, religious organizations for sectarian purposes, political or lobbying groups, or organizations outside operating areas.

GRANTS ANALYSIS
Typical Range: $100 to $1,000

RECENT GRANTS

General
Academy of Vocal Arts, Philadelphia, PA
American Red Cross, Radnor, PA
Bryn Mawr Beautification Plan, Bryn Mawr, PA
Main Line Chamber of Commerce, Wayne, PA
March of Dimes, Bryn Mawr, PA

Buhl Foundation

CONTACT
Doreen E. Boyce
President
Buhl Foundation
4 Gateway Ctr., Rm. No. 1325
Pittsburgh, PA 15222
(412) 566-2711

FINANCIAL SUMMARY
Recent Giving: $2,500,000 (fiscal 1995 est.); $2,148,350 (fiscal 1994); $1,852,550 (fiscal 1993)

Assets: $51,000,000 (fiscal 1995 est.); $50,341,323 (fiscal 1994); $45,990,942 (fiscal 1993)

EIN: 25-0378910

CONTRIBUTIONS SUMMARY
Donor(s): The Buhls, a German merchant family for nine generations, immigrated to Zelienople, PA, around 1800. The Buhls established a legacy of concerned citizenship in Pennsylvania, as evidenced by their last heir, Henry Buhl, Jr. Trained as a merchant, he and his friend, Russell H. Boggs, established a profitable dry goods store in 1869. As he neared the end of his life, Mr. Buhl considered the future of his fortune. Because he had no children or other direct heirs, he established the Buhl Foundation as a memorial to his wife, Louise C. Buhl, to benefit "the citizens of the City of Pittsburgh and the County of Allegheny, Pennsylvania" first and foremost where he lived and "engaged in business activities and formed friendships." Henry Buhl, Jr., died in 1927.

Typical Recipients: • *Arts & Humanities:* Arts Outreach, General, History & Archaeology, Libraries, Museums/Galleries, Music, Performing Arts • *Civic & Public Affairs:* Business/Free Enterprise, Economic Development, Employment/Job Training, Housing, Philanthropic Organizations, Urban & Community Affairs • *Education:* Arts/Humanities Education, Business Education, Colleges & Universities, Community & Junior Colleges, Education Associations, Education Funds, Elementary Education (Private), Literacy, Minority Education, Preschool Education, Private Education (Precollege), Public Education (Precollege), Science/Mathematics Education, Secondary Education (Private), Special Education, Vocational & Technical Education • *Religion:* Ministries, Religious Organizations, Religious Welfare • *Science:* Observatories & Planetariums, Scientific Centers & Institutes • *Social Services:* At-Risk Youth, Child Abuse, Child Welfare, Day Care, Delinquency & Criminal Rehabilitation, Food/Clothing Distribution, People with Disabilities, Recreation & Athletics, Scouts, Youth Organizations

Grant Types: project, research, and seed money

Geographic Distribution: southwestern Pennsylvania region, with emphasis on the Pittsburgh metropolitan area

GIVING OFFICERS
Doreen E. Boyce: pres, exec dir *CURR EMPL* pres, dir: Res for Better Schools *CORP AFFIL* secy, dir: Microbac Laboratories Inc *PHIL AFFIL* trust: Henry C. Frick Educational Commission

Francis B. Nimick, Jr.: chmn bd dir *NONPR AFFIL* vp, dir: Western PA Sch Deaf

William H. Rea: vchmn *B* Pittsburgh PA 1912 *CURR EMPL* dir: Colt Indus Inc *PHIL AFFIL* trust: Howard Heinz Endowment, Vira I. Heinz Endowment, Drue Heinz Trust; dir: Robert Gemmill Foundation Trust

Jean A. Robinson: treas

Katherine E. Schumacher: secy, asst treas

Albert Clarence Van Dusen: vchmn *B* Tampa FL 1915 *ED* Univ FL BS 1937; Univ FL AM 1938; Northwestern Univ PhD 1942 *NONPR AFFIL* dir: Am Japan Soc Pittsburgh, YMCA Pittsburgh; fellow: Am Psychological Assn, Am Psychological Soc, Intl Fdn Social Econ Devel, PA Psychological Assn; mem: Am Coll Pub Rels Assn, Am Pers Guidance Assn, Assn Deans Dir Summer Sessions, Beta Gamma Sigma, Beta Theta Pi, Eastern Psychological Assn, Friends Art Pittsburgh Schs, Intl Assn Applied Psychology, Intl Assn Sch Inst Admin, Intl Assn Schs & Insts Admin, Midwest Psychological Assn, PA Pub TV Network Comm, Phi Beta Kappa, Pittsburgh Psychological Assn, Professional Sch World Aff Comm, Sigma Xi, W PA Counc Econ Ed, Western PA Counc Econ Ed; trust: Un Way PA; vchmn bd trusts: Pittsburgh History Landmarks Fdn; vice chancellor emeritus,prof emeritus: Northwestern Univ *CLUB AFFIL* Duquesne, Univ Pittsburgh *PHIL AFFIL* trust: Henry C. Frick Educational Commission

APPLICATION INFORMATION
Initial Approach:

Applicants must send a letter of inquiry to the foundation. A formal proposal will be requested if the foundation is interested.

Formal proposals must include a statement of objectives for the project and the means by which they will be achieved, including staff qualifications and a timetable; proof of need for the project, its uniqueness in comparison to other work being done in a similar area, and the result anticipated; documentation of procedures for evaluation of anticipated results; itemized budget indicating resources required for the project, other possible funding sources, and the amount requested of them; general information about the applying agency including its name, address, telephone number, contact person, executive director, members of the board, brief history, mission, tax-exempt status, and ability to initiate and sustain the project; and a statement that the proposal has been approved for submission to the foundation by the executive director of the applying organization.

Organizations should submit proposals at least two months before consideration may be given by the board.

If the foundation is interested in the proposed project, an interview will be scheduled. Grant decisions are made at monthly board meetings.

Restrictions on Giving: Grants generally are not made for building funds, overhead costs, accumulated deficits, ordinary operating budgets, fundraising campaigns, loans, scholarships, fellowships, nationally funded organized groups, conferences, seminars (unless grant-related), propaganda, sectarian religious activities, or lobbying. Grants are not made to other foundations or to individuals.

OTHER THINGS TO KNOW
Grant recipients will be expected to confer with the foundation on schedules of grant payments, progress reports on program achievements, and an evaluation upon completion of the program.

PUBLICATIONS
Annual report, program guidelines and application procedures

GRANTS ANALYSIS
Total Grants: $2,148,350

Number of Grants: 47

Highest Grant: $381,250

Average Grant: $45,710

Typical Range: $10,000 to $100,000

Disclosure Period: fiscal year ending June 30, 1994

Note: Recent grants are derived from a fiscal 1994 annual report.

RECENT GRANTS

Library
183,000   Point Park College, Pittsburgh, PA — automation and networking for the Library Center

150,000	Mt. Aloysius College, Cresson, PA — library automation
25,000	Carnegie Institute, Pittsburgh, PA — county-wide public library planning study
10,000	Braddocks Field Historical Society, Braddock, PA — step and walkway replacement at Braddock Carnegie Library and Community Center
5,000	Pittsburgh Early Music Ensemble, Pittsburgh, PA — for support of programs teaching children about baroque music while in residence at the Carnegie Library of Pittsburgh

General

150,000	Carnegie Mellon University, Pittsburgh, PA — Journey to the Center of the Cell Project
131,000	Western Pennsylvania School for the Deaf, Pittsburgh, PA — interactive technology-based curriculum
125,000	Vintage, Pittsburgh, PA — development of personal care facilities at a day care center for the elderly
110,000	MPC Corporation, Pittsburgh, PA — for Common Knowledge: Pittsburgh; the Pittsburgh Public School District and the Pittsburgh Supercomputing Center have joined together toward a five-year project, partially funded by the National Science Foundation
100,000	Allegheny College, Meadville, PA — campuswide communication network

Carpenter Foundation, E. Rhodes and Leona B.

CONTACT
Joseph A. O'Connor, Jr.
Director
E. Rhodes and Leona B. Carpenter Foundation
PO Box 58880
Philadelphia, PA 19102-8880
(215) 963-5212

FINANCIAL SUMMARY
Recent Giving: $5,902,843 (1993); $3,600,668 (1991); $3,733,804 (1990)

Assets: $137,755,312 (1993); $111,343,783 (1991); $88,192,197 (1990)

Gifts Received: $2,000,000 (1993); $1,000,000 (1989); $1,000,000 (1988)

Fiscal Note: In 1993, the foundation received a gift of $2,000,000 form the estate of Leona B. Carpenter.

EIN: 51-0155772

CONTRIBUTIONS SUMMARY
Donor(s): The foundation was established in 1976 by the late E. Rhodes Carpenter and Leona B. Carpenter.

Typical Recipients: • *Arts & Humanities:* Arts Associations & Councils, Arts Centers, Arts Funds, Ballet, Community Arts, Dance, Libraries, Museums/Galleries, Music, Opera, Performing Arts, Public Broadcasting, Theater • *Civic & Public Affairs:* Botanical Gardens/Parks, Economic Development, General, Housing, Philanthropic Organizations • *Education:* Arts/Humanities Education, Colleges & Universities, Education Funds, Elementary Education (Private), International Studies, Medical Education, Public Education (Precollege), Religious Education, Secondary Education (Public) • *Environment:* General • *Health:* Emergency/Ambulance Services, Health Organizations, Hospices, Hospitals, Medical Rehabilitation, Nursing Services, Single-Disease Health Associations • *Religion:* Churches, Ministries, Religious Organizations, Religious Welfare • *Science:* Science Museums • *Social Services:* Child Welfare, Community Service Organizations, Day Care, Family Services, Food/Clothing Distribution, People with Disabilities, Shelters/Homelessness, Youth Organizations

Grant Types: capital, challenge, emergency, general support, project, and scholarship

Geographic Distribution: generally east of the Mississippi River with an emphasis on Virginia

GIVING OFFICERS
Ann B. Day: pres

Paul B. Day, Jr.: vp, secy, treas

Joseph A. O'Connor: dir

M. H. Reinhart: dir *CURR EMPL* pres: Carpenter ER Co

APPLICATION INFORMATION
Initial Approach:

Informal letter applications are sufficient.

The letter application should iclude a brief history of the purpose of the organization, the dollar amount requested, a description of the specific project or program for which the amount is being requested and a copy of the organization's ruling that it is a 509(a)(1) or (2) institution.

There are no deadlines.

Restrictions on Giving: Generally, the foundation will not consider grant requests to support private secondary education, nor will it as a general rule consider grant requests from large public charities, such as the Red Cross, American Cancer Society or United Fund. Also the foundation generally will not transfer funds from its endowment to the endowment of another organization. Grants are made for specific projects or programs. The foundation does not support individuals.

PUBLICATIONS
Application guidelines

GRANTS ANALYSIS
Total Grants: $5,902,843

Number of Grants: 78

Highest Grant: $1,500,000

Average Grant: $57,180*

Typical Range: $5,000 to $25,000 and $50,000 to $100,000

Disclosure Period: 1993

Note: Average grant figure excludes the largest grant of $1,500,000. Recent grants are derived from a 1993 grants list.

RECENT GRANTS
Library

1,500,000	Foundation of Temple Public Library, Temple, TX — purchase of building
150,000	Duke University Libraries, Durham, NC — renovation of conference room in Perkins Library
50,000	Morgan Library, New York, NY

General

750,000	Hampden-Sydney College, Hampden-Sydney, VA — part of the cost of construction of the third Carpenter House
325,000	Divinity School, Nashville, TN — scholarships
325,000	Divinity School, Nashville, TN — scholarships
187,967	Russellville Independent Schools, Russellville, KY — funding completion of computerized instructional system
174,600	Mary Baldwin College, Staunton, VA — support program in healthcare and ministry

Carpenter Technology Corp. / Carpenter Technology Corp. Foundation

Sales: $628.8 million
Employees: 3,697
Headquarters: Reading, PA
SIC Major Group: Blast Furnaces & Steel Mills

CONTACT
Robert W. Lodge
Vice President
Carpenter Technology Corp. Foundation
PO Box 14662
Reading, PA 19612-4662
(610) 208-2294
Note: The company is located at 101 W Bern St., Reading, PA.

FINANCIAL SUMMARY
Recent Giving: $390,000 (fiscal 1995 est.); $364,083 (fiscal 1994 approx.); $363,574 (fiscal 1993)

Assets: $373,569 (fiscal 1994); $319,431 (fiscal 1993); $475,376 (fiscal 1992)

Gifts Received: $200,000 (fiscal 1994); $400,000 (fiscal 1993); $400,000 (fiscal 1990)

Fiscal Note: Contributes through foundation only. Above figures exclude nonmonetary support. In 1994, contributions were received from Carpenter Technology Corporation.

EIN: 23-2191214

CONTRIBUTIONS SUMMARY

Typical Recipients: • *Arts & Humanities:* Arts Associations & Councils, Arts Festivals, Arts Institutes, Community Arts, History & Archaeology, Libraries, Museums/Galleries, Music, Performing Arts • *Civic & Public Affairs:* African American Affairs, Chambers of Commerce, Economic Development, Housing, Legal Aid, Parades/Festivals, Professional & Trade Associations, Public Policy, Safety • *Education:* Arts/Humanities Education, Business Education, Business-School Partnerships, Colleges & Universities, Community & Junior Colleges, Economic Education, Education Associations, Education Funds, Elementary Education (Private), Faculty Development, Minority Education, Science/Mathematics Education, Secondary Education (Private), Student Aid, Vocational & Technical Education • *Environment:* Air/Water Quality, General, Resource Conservation • *Health:* AIDS/HIV, Cancer, Emergency/Ambulance Services, Health Funds, Health Organizations, Heart, Hospitals • *International:* Foreign Educational Institutions • *Religion:* Churches, Jewish Causes, Religious Welfare • *Science:* Science Exhibits & Fairs • *Social Services:* Family Services, Food/Clothing Distribution, Homes, Shelters/Homelessness, Substance Abuse, United Funds/United Ways, YMCA/YWCA/YMHA/YWHA, Youth Organizations

Grant Types: capital, employee matching gifts, general support, and scholarship

Note: Employee matching gift ratio: 1 to 1. The foundation will match dollar for dollar to a yearly maximum of $3,000 per employee.

Nonmonetary Support Types: in-kind services and loaned employees

Note: The company provides an unspecified amount of nonmonetary support. For more information contact Robert W. Lodge (see above).

Geographic Distribution: principally near operating locations and to national organizations

Operating Locations: CA (El Cajon, San Diego), ME (Fryeburg), PA (Reading), SC (Orangeburg)

Note: List includes plant and division locations.

CORP. OFFICERS

Robert Willard Cardy: *B* Saginaw MI 1936 *ED* Univ Cincinnati BBA 1959 *CURR EMPL* chmn, pres, ceo, dir: Carpenter Tech Corp *CORP AFFIL* dir: Meridian Bancorp Inc; mem exec comm, dir: Specialty Steel Industry *NONPR AFFIL* dir: Reading Hosp & Med Ctr; mem adv bd: PA St Univ Berks Campus; vp, dir: Grace Commun

G. Walton Cottrell: *B* Auburn NY 1939 *ED* Cornell Univ BSME 1962; Cornell Univ

MBA 1963 *CURR EMPL* sr vp, cfo: Carpenter Tech Corp *NONPR AFFIL* dir: Cornell Univ Counc, Natl Assn Corp Treas; mem: Fin Execs Inst

William J. Pendleton: *CURR EMPL* dir corp aff: Carpenter Tech Corp

John Albert Schuler: *B* Pulaski VA 1942 *ED* Coll William & Mary BA 1964 *CURR EMPL* treas: Carpenter Tech Corp

GIVING OFFICERS

Robert Willard Cardy: pres *CURR EMPL* chmn, pres, ceo, dir: Carpenter Tech Corp (see above)

Robert W. Lodge: vp

John Albert Schuler: treas *CURR EMPL* treas: Carpenter Tech Corp (see above)

John Rider Welty: secy *B* Waynesboro PA 1948 *ED* Shippensburg Univ PA BA 1970; Am Univ JD 1975 *CURR EMPL* vp, secy, gen couns: Carpenter Tech Corp *NONPR AFFIL* dir: Conrad Weiser Area Sch District; mem: Alpha Phi Omega, Am Bar Assn, Am Corp Couns Assn, PA Bar Assn, PA Self Insurers Assn, Phi Alpha Delta; mem distr comm, vchmn: Boy Scouts Am Hawk Mountain Counc

APPLICATION INFORMATION

Initial Approach: *Initial Contact:* letter of inquiry *Include Information On:* name and address of contact person; description of the organization, including history and purpose; amount requested; purpose for which funds are sought; recently audited financial statement; proof of tax-exempt status; current annual budget with amount spent on program services, fund-raising, administration, and general operating expenses; detailed project budget; donor list indicating contributions received, pledged, or requested within the past year; history of past support; how project will be sustained upon completion of support; list of board of directors and their affiliations; goals and objectives of project; similiarity to or differences from other area projects; statement of need; and time frame for completion *Deadlines:* none

Restrictions on Giving: The foundation does not support individuals, political or lobbying groups, religious organizations for sectarian purposes, endowments, foundations that are primarily grant-making bodies, organizations outside the United States, organizations without 501(c)(3) status, or sports or athletics.

PUBLICATIONS

Corporate contributions program policy statement, including guidelines

GRANTS ANALYSIS

Total Grants: $364,083

Number of Grants: 575

Highest Grant: $123,000

Average Grant: $633

Typical Range: $250 to $5,000

Disclosure Period: fiscal year ending September 30, 1994

Note: Recent grants are derived from a Fiscal 1994 Form 990.

RECENT GRANTS

General

123,000	United Fund Reading, Reading, PA —capital campaign
16,000	Olivet Boys and Girls Club, Reading, PA —capital campaign
15,000	Lutheran Home at Topton, Topton, PA —capital campaign
13,770	National Merit Scholarships, Chicago, IL
10,000	Pennsylvania State University, University Park, PA —for Campaign for Hershey

Cassett Foundation, Louis N.

CONTACT

Malcolm B. Jacobson
Trustee
Louis N. Cassett Fdn.
One Penn Ctr., Ste. 335
1617 JFK Blvd.
Philadelphia, PA 19103
(215) 563-8886

FINANCIAL SUMMARY

Recent Giving: $303,850 (1993); $299,850 (1992); $366,800 (1991)

Assets: $6,994,112 (1993); $6,542,218 (1992); $6,396,854 (1991)

EIN: 23-6274038

CONTRIBUTIONS SUMMARY

Donor(s): the late Louis N. Cassett

Typical Recipients: • *Arts & Humanities:* Arts Centers, Arts Institutes, Community Arts, Historic Preservation, Libraries, Music, Performing Arts, Public Broadcasting, Theater • *Civic & Public Affairs:* Civil Rights, General, Public Policy, Zoos/Aquariums • *Education:* Arts/Humanities Education, Colleges & Universities, Legal Education • *Environment:* Resource Conservation • *Health:* Children's Health/Hospitals, Clinics/Medical Centers, Diabetes, Hospitals, Medical Research, Nutrition, Single-Disease Health Associations • *International:* Missionary/Religious Activities • *Religion:* Churches, Jewish Causes, Religious Organizations • *Social Services:* Community Service Organizations, Day Care, Family Planning, People with Disabilities, Senior Services, United Funds/United Ways

Grant Types: capital and general support

Geographic Distribution: focus on the northeastern U.S.

GIVING OFFICERS

Albert J. Elias: trust

Carol Gerstley-Hofheimer: trust

Malcolm Jacobson: trust

APPLICATION INFORMATION

.&~ **Initial Approach:** Send a brief letter of inquiry. Include a description of organization, amount requested, purpose of funds sought, recently audited financial statement, and proof of tax-exempt status. There are no deadlines.

Restrictions on Giving: Does not support individuals.

GRANTS ANALYSIS
Total Grants: $303,850

Number of Grants: 138

Highest Grant: $40,000

Typical Range: $500 to $15,000

Disclosure Period: 1993

Note: Recent grants are derived from a 1993 Form 990.

RECENT GRANTS

General

40,000	United Cerebral Palsy Association, Philadelphia, PA
15,000	Federation of Allied Jewish Appeal, Philadelphia, PA
8,250	United Way, Philadelphia, PA
5,150	Friends of Ronald McDonald House, Philadelphia, PA
5,000	Academy of Music Restoration Fund, Philadelphia, PA

CIGNA Corporation / CIGNA Foundation

Revenue: $18.39 billion
Employees: 50,624
Headquarters: Philadelphia, PA
SIC Major Group: Holding Companies Nec, Investment Advice, Life Insurance, and Fire, Marine & Casualty Insurance

CONTACT
Arnold W. Wright, Jr.
Executive Director
CIGNA Foundation
One Liberty Pl.
1650 Market St., 5th Floor
Philadelphia, PA 19192-1540
(215) 761-4881
Note: Mr. Wright is the contact for general inquiries. For information on giving in the specific areas of Philadelphia, PA; Hartford, CT; and for national organizations, see "Other Things You Should Know." The company's World Wide Web address is http://204.189.36.1/cigna

FINANCIAL SUMMARY
Recent Giving: $7,000,000 (1995 est.); $6,935,715 (1994); $7,087,612 (1993)

Assets: $2,662,605 (1992); $2,728,183 (1991); $2,300,000 (1990)

Fiscal Note: Above figures represent foundation contributions only. Company also makes limited direct contributions in the Philadelphia and Hartford areas.

EIN: 23-6261726

CONTRIBUTIONS SUMMARY
Typical Recipients: • *Arts & Humanities:* Arts Associations & Councils, Arts Festivals, History & Archaeology, Libraries, Mu-

seums/Galleries, Music, Opera, Public Broadcasting, Theater • *Civic & Public Affairs:* Chambers of Commerce, Economic Development, Hispanic Affairs, Professional & Trade Associations, Public Policy, Safety, Urban & Community Affairs, Women's Affairs, Zoos/Aquariums • *Education:* Arts/Humanities Education, Business Education, Colleges & Universities, Education Reform, Elementary Education (Private), Faculty Development, General, Legal Education, Literacy, Private Education (Precollege), Public Education (Precollege), Secondary Education (Public), Student Aid • *Health:* Health Organizations, Prenatal Health Issues • *Science:* Science Museums • *Social Services:* Child Welfare, Food/Clothing Distribution, United Funds/United Ways

Grant Types: employee matching gifts, operating expenses, project, and scholarship

Note: Employee matching gift ratio: 1 to 1

Nonmonetary Support: $150,000 (1989); $150,000 (1988); $169,970 (1987)

Nonmonetary Support Types: donated equipment

Note: The company provides nonmonetary support, the estimated value of which is not available. Contact the Purchasing department of the company's local operating unit for more information.

Geographic Distribution: primarily in greater Philadelphia, PA, and in the Hartford, CT, metropolitan area

Operating Locations: CT (Hartford), PA (Philadelphia)

CORP. OFFICERS
Wilson H. Taylor: *B* Hartford CT 1943 *ED* Trinity Coll BS 1964 *CURR EMPL* chmn, ceo: CIGNA Corp *NONPR AFFIL* chmn: Am Ins Assn; dir: Philadelphia Orchestra Assn; mem: Phi Beta Kappa

GIVING OFFICERS
Lawrence P. English: dir *B* 1940 *ED* Rutgers Univ BA 1963; George Washington Univ MBA 1974 *CURR EMPL* chmn: CIGNA Healthcare *CORP AFFIL* chmn: CIGNA Health Corp

James N. Mason: dir civic aff *CORP AFFIL* dir: CIGNA Corp

Arnold W. Wright, Jr.: exec dir

APPLICATION INFORMATION
Initial Approach: *Initial Contact:* one- or two-page letter *Include Information On:* description of the organization (including name, history, activities, purpose, and board members); description of program for which grant is requested; objectives and evaluative criteria; most recently audited financial statement; copy of IRS determination letter; copy of the most recent form 990 *Deadlines:* none; however, the foundation recommends that proposals be submitted by September 1 for funding in the next year

Restrictions on Giving: CIGNA Foundation generally will not provide funds to the following categories: individuals, political organizations, religious activities or organizations that are denominational or sectarian, organizations receiving substantial support

through United Way or other CIGNA-supported federated funding agencies, endowment drives or capital campaigns, hospital capital improvements or expansions, or single-disease research and treatment.

OTHER THINGS TO KNOW
National organizations and groups in the Philadelphia area should contact Ms. Carole Thompson, director, civic affairs at CIGNA Foundation, Two Liberty Place, 1601 Chestnut Street, P.O. Box 7716, Philadelphia, PA 19192-2060. In the greater Hartford area, requests should be directed to Mr. James N. Mason, director, civic affairs, CIGNA Foundation, 900 Cottage Grove Avenue W-A, Bloomfield, CT 06002.

PUBLICATIONS
Cigna Foundation Annual Report

GRANTS ANALYSIS
Total Grants: $6,935,715

Number of Grants: 210

Highest Grant: $725,000

Average Grant: $33,027

Typical Range: $5,000 to $10,000 and $10,000 to $725,000

Disclosure Period: 1994

Note: Recent grants are derived from a 1994 annual report.

RECENT GRANTS

Library

25,000	Wadsworth Atheneum, Hartford, CT —for education

General

725,250	United Way of Southeastern Pennsylvania, Philadelphia, PA —for health and human services
516,000	United Way, Montgomery, AL —for health and human services
500,000	United Way National, Philadelphia, PA —for health and human services
260,000	CIGNA Neighborhood School Partnership —for education
150,000	Children's Fund of Connecticut, Hartford, CT —for health and human services

Clapp Charitable and Educational Trust, George H.

CONTACT
George H. Clapp Charitable and Educational Trust
1 Mellon Bank Ctr.
Pittsburgh, PA 15258
(412) 234-4695

FINANCIAL SUMMARY
Recent Giving: $691,500 (fiscal 1992); $486,000 (fiscal 1991); $460,500 (fiscal 1990)

Assets: $13,842,994 (fiscal 1992);
$13,029,955 (fiscal 1991); $10,887,326 (fiscal 1990)

EIN: 25-6018976

CONTRIBUTIONS SUMMARY
Donor(s): the late George H. Clapp

Typical Recipients: • *Arts & Humanities:* History & Archaeology, Libraries, Museums/Galleries, Public Broadcasting • *Civic & Public Affairs:* Economic Development, Employment/Job Training, General, Safety • *Education:* Colleges & Universities, Education Funds, Education Reform, Legal Education, Minority Education, Private Education (Precollege), Public Education (Precollege) • *Environment:* General, Resource Conservation • *Health:* Cancer, Children's Health/Hospitals, Emergency/Ambulance Services, Eyes/Blindness, Health Organizations, Hospitals, Long-Term Care, Medical Rehabilitation, Medical Research, Multiple Sclerosis, Nursing Services, Single-Disease Health Associations • *International:* International Environmental Issues • *Religion:* Religious Organizations, Religious Welfare • *Science:* Scientific Centers & Institutes • *Social Services:* Child Welfare, Community Centers, Community Service Organizations, Family Planning, Food/Clothing Distribution, Sexual Abuse, Shelters/Homelessness, United Funds/United Ways, Youth Organizations

Grant Types: general support

Geographic Distribution: focus on the Pittsburgh, PA, area

GIVING OFFICERS
William Edward Collins: trust *B* Brooklyn NY 1932 *ED* St Peters Coll BS 1954; Fordham Univ MA 1956; Fordham Univ PhD 1959 *NONPR AFFIL* dir: Aviation Psychology Lab FAA Civil Aeromed Inst; fellow: Aerospace Human Factors Assn, Am Assn Advancement Science, Am Psychological Assn, Am Psychological Soc, NY Academy Sciences; fellow, assoc editor: Aerospace Med Assn; mem: Assn Aviation Psychologists, Barany Soc, Natl Academy Science, OK Psychological Assn; prof: Univ OK Health Sciences Ctr *PHIL AFFIL* trust: Redman Foundation

William A. Galbraith, Jr.: trust

APPLICATION INFORMATION
Initial Approach: Send brief letter of inquiry describing program or project; application form provided after initial contact. There are no deadlines.

GRANTS ANALYSIS
Total Grants: $691,500

Number of Grants: 51

Highest Grant: $30,000

Typical Range: $10,000 to $15,000

Disclosure Period: fiscal year ending September 30, 1992

Note: Recent grants are derived from a fiscal 1992 Form 990.

RECENT GRANTS
Library
15,000 Carnegie Library, Pittsburgh, PA

General
30,000 University of Pittsburgh, Pittsburgh, PA
20,000 Children's Hospital of Pittsburgh, Pittsburgh, PA
20,000 Marian Manor, Pittsburgh, PA
15,000 Allegheny Conference on Community Development, Pittsburgh, PA
15,000 American Cancer Society, Pittsburgh, PA

Clemens Markets Corp. / Clemens Foundation

Sales: $215.35 million
Employees: 1,900
Headquarters: Kulpsville, PA
SIC Major Group: Food Stores

CONTACT
Jack Clemens
Clemens Markets Corp.
1555 Bustard Rd.
Kulpsville, PA 19443
(215) 361-9000

FINANCIAL SUMMARY
Recent Giving: $111,470 (fiscal 1993); $124,447 (fiscal 1992)

Assets: $517,430 (fiscal 1993); $523,628 (fiscal 1992)

Gifts Received: $50,000 (fiscal 1993); $55,000 (fiscal 1992)

EIN: 23-1675035

CONTRIBUTIONS SUMMARY
Typical Recipients: • *Arts & Humanities:* Libraries • *Civic & Public Affairs:* Housing, Safety • *Education:* Colleges & Universities, Religious Education, Secondary Education (Private), Student Aid • *Health:* Children's Health/Hospitals, Geriatric Health, Hospitals, Medical Research, Mental Health • *International:* Missionary/Religious Activities • *Religion:* Bible Study/Translation, Churches, Jewish Causes, Religious Organizations, Religious Welfare, Seminaries • *Social Services:* Community Service Organizations, Family Services, Food/Clothing Distribution, Homes, United Funds/United Ways, YMCA/YWCA/YMHA/YWHA, Youth Organizations

Grant Types: capital, general support, and scholarship

Geographic Distribution: focus on PA

CORP. OFFICERS
James S. Clemens, Jr.: *CURR EMPL* pres, ceo, dir: Clemens Markets Corp

GIVING OFFICERS
Abram S. Clemens: pres

Jack Clemens: treas

Lillan H. Clemens: trust
Matilda S. Clemens: vp
Suzanne C. Harris: asst treas
Jill Clemens Kulp: trust
Jules Pearlstine: asst secy
R. Carl Rhoads: trust
Janice C. Tyson: secy

APPLICATION INFORMATION
Initial Approach: Send a brief letter of inquiry. Include a description of organization, amount requested, purpose of funds sought, recently audited financial statement, and proof of tax-exempt status. Deadline is November 1.

GRANTS ANALYSIS
Total Grants: $111,470

Number of Grants: 136*

Highest Grant: $6,800

Typical Range: $200 to $2,500

Disclosure Period: fiscal year ending September 30, 1993

Note: Recent grants are derived from a fiscal 1993 Form 990.

RECENT GRANTS
Library
1,000 Calvary Baptist Church Library

General
6,800 North Penn United Way, Kulpsville, PA
6,000 North Penn YMCA, PA — for building fund
5,000 First Baptist Church Lansdale, Lansdale, PA — for building fund
5,000 Grandview Hospital — first of five payments for chapel
3,500 Eastern Baptist College

Coen Family Foundation, Charles S. and Mary

CONTACT
Mona Thompson
Trustee
Charles S. and Mary Coen Family Fdn.
1100 W Chestnut St.
Washington, PA 15301
(412) 223-5500

FINANCIAL SUMMARY
Recent Giving: $399,450 (fiscal 1994); $266,994 (fiscal 1992); $246,725 (fiscal 1991)

Assets: $5,996,710 (fiscal 1994); $5,698,807 (fiscal 1992); $5,311,736 (fiscal 1991)

Gifts Received: $34,000 (fiscal 1994); $36,000 (fiscal 1992); $105,000 (fiscal 1991)

Fiscal Note: In fiscal 1994, contributions were received from the C. S. Coen Estate.

EIN: 25-6033877

CONTRIBUTIONS SUMMARY

Donor(s): the late C. S. Coen, the late Mary Coen, Charles R. Coen, C. S. Coen Land Co.

Typical Recipients: • *Arts & Humanities:* Libraries, Music • *Civic & Public Affairs:* General, Housing • *Education:* Colleges & Universities, Literacy, Minority Education, Private Education (Precollege) • *Environment:* Resource Conservation • *Health:* Children's Health/Hospitals, Clinics/Medical Centers, Hospices, Hospitals, Medical Research, Single-Disease Health Associations • *International:* Health Care/Hospitals • *Religion:* Churches, Religious Welfare • *Social Services:* Child Welfare, Community Service Organizations, Homes, People with Disabilities, Recreation & Athletics, Senior Services, Substance Abuse, United Funds/United Ways, Youth Organizations

Grant Types: general support

Geographic Distribution: focus on the Washington, PA, and the St. Mary's, WV, areas

GIVING OFFICERS

Mona Thompson: trust

Lawrence A. Withum, Jr.: trust

APPLICATION INFORMATION

Initial Approach: Send brief letter describing program. There are no deadlines.

Restrictions on Giving: Does not support individuals.

GRANTS ANALYSIS

Total Grants: $399,450

Number of Grants: 86

Highest Grant: $100,000

Typical Range: $100 to $45,000

Disclosure Period: fiscal year ending February 28, 1994

Note: Recent grants are derived from a fiscal 1994 Form 990.

RECENT GRANTS

Library
12,500	Citizens Library, Washington, PA	

General
100,000	Presbyterian Association on Aging, Oakmont, PA
30,000	Washington Hospital, Washington, PA
30,000	Wilson College, Chambersburg, PA
20,000	United Cerebral Palsy of Southwestern Pennsylvania, Washington, PA
20,000	Washington and Jefferson College, Washington, PA

Connelly Foundation

CONTACT
Victoria K. Flaville
Vice President and Secretary
Connelly Foundation
One Tower Bridge, Ste. 1450
West Conshohocken, PA 19428
(610) 834-3222

FINANCIAL SUMMARY
Recent Giving: $13,877,190 (1993); $16,249,469 (1992); $12,353,617 (1991)

Assets: $420,994,636 (1993); $411,829,099 (1992); $300,000,000 (1991 approx.)

EIN: 23-6296825

CONTRIBUTIONS SUMMARY
Donor(s): John F. Connelly and his wife, Josephine Connelly, established the Connelly Foundation in Pennsylvania in 1955. The foundation's assets consist largely of stock in Crown Cork & Seal Company, of which John Connelly was chairman from 1956 until his death in 1990. Mrs. Connelly is the chairman of the foundation's board of directors.

Typical Recipients: • *Arts & Humanities:* Arts Institutes, Arts Outreach, Historic Preservation, History & Archaeology, Libraries, Music, Opera, Performing Arts • *Civic & Public Affairs:* Economic Development, Housing, Public Policy, Urban & Community Affairs • *Education:* Arts/Humanities Education, Colleges & Universities, Education Associations, Elementary Education (Private), Engineering/Technological Education, Faculty Development, Leadership Training, Literacy, Medical Education, Private Education (Precollege), Public Education (Precollege), Religious Education, School Volunteerism, Science/Mathematics Education, Secondary Education (Private), Secondary Education (Public), Special Education, Student Aid, Vocational & Technical Education • *Environment:* General • *Health:* AIDS/HIV, Alzheimers Disease, Cancer, Children's Health/Hospitals, Clinics/Medical Centers, Emergency/Ambulance Services, Geriatric Health, Health Organizations, Heart, Hospices, Hospitals, Long-Term Care, Medical Rehabilitation, Nursing Services, Outpatient Health Care, Prenatal Health Issues, Preventive Medicine/Wellness Organizations, Research/Studies Institutes, Transplant Networks/Donor Banks • *International:* Foreign Educational Institutions, Health Care/Hospitals, International Relief Efforts, Missionary/Religious Activities • *Religion:* Churches, Dioceses, Ministries, Religious Organizations, Religious Welfare, Social/Policy Issues • *Science:* Science Museums, Scientific Centers & Institutes • *Social Services:* Child Abuse, Child Welfare, Community Service Organizations, Day Care, Domestic Violence, Family Planning, Food/Clothing Distribution, Homes, People with Disabilities, Recreation & Athletics, Shelters/Homelessness, Substance Abuse, United Funds/United Ways, Youth Organizations

Grant Types: capital, endowment, general support, project, and scholarship

Geographic Distribution: primarily Pennsylvania and the surrounding Delaware Valley, with emphasis on Philadelphia

GIVING OFFICERS
Reda Amiry: treas

William Joseph Avery: trust *B* Chicago IL 1940 *ED* Univ Chicago 1968 *CURR EMPL* chmn, pres, ceo, dir: Crown Cork & Seal Co

Lewis William Bluemle, Jr.: vp fin, trust *B* Williamsport PA 1921 *ED* Johns Hopkins Univ AB 1943; Johns Hopkins Univ MD 1946 *CORP AFFIL* dir: Teleflex; dir, mem exec comm: Mellon Bank E *NONPR AFFIL* fellow: Am Coll Physicians, Coll Physicians Philadelphia, Royal Coll Physicians Edinburgh; mem: Alpha Omega Alpha, Am Clinical & Climatological Assn, Am Soc Artificial Internal Organs, Am Soc Nephrology, Assn Academy Health Ctrs, Phi Beta Kappa, Philadelphia Assn Clinic Trails; mem adv bd Philadelphia chap: Physicians Social Responsibility; pres: Thomas Jefferson Univ

Christine C. Connelly: trust, don daughter

Daniele Connelly: trust

Thomas S. Connelly: trust, don son *B* 1945 *CURR EMPL* pres, dir: Connelly Containers

Judith C. Delouvrier: trust, don daughter

Philippe Delouvrier: trust *NONPR AFFIL* mem: Phi Beta Kappa *CLUB AFFIL* Knickerbocker

Thomas J. Farrell: trust

Victoria K. Flaville: vp, secy

Chester C. Hilinski: vp, trust, gen counc *B* Bethlehem PA 1917 *ED* Univ PA BS 1938; Univ PA JD 1941 *CURR EMPL* sr ptnr: Dechert Price & Rhoads *CORP AFFIL* dir: Connelly Containers, Crown Cork & Seal Co *NONPR AFFIL* mem: Am Bar Assn, PA Bar Assn, Philadelphia Bar Assn *CLUB AFFIL* Union League Philadelphia

Josephine C. Mandeville: ceo, pres, trust, don daughter

Owen A. Mandeville: trust *CURR EMPL* pres: Mandeville Ins Assocs Inc *CORP AFFIL* dir: Crown Cork & Seal Co

Christopher J. Riley: trust

Emily C. Riley: exec vp, trust, don daughter

Thomas A. Riley: trust

APPLICATION INFORMATION
Initial Approach:

The foundation does not provide application guidelines or forms. Initial contact should be in writing.

Proposals should include the following: a brief history of the applicant; description of the project, its goals and objectives; project budget and list of funding received through the date of application; applicant's most recent financial statement; and a copy of the IRS tax-determination letter.

There are no specific deadlines, but the foundation prefers applications submitted early in the year.

The board of directors meets six times a year with the annual meeting at the foundation's office on the last Monday in January. Proposals are not acknowledged upon receipt. The foundation does not grant interviews. Final notification takes four to six months.

Restrictions on Giving: The foundation does not make grants to individuals.

GRANTS ANALYSIS

Total Grants: $13,877,190

Number of Grants: 487

Highest Grant: $1,511,250

Average Grant: $28,495

Typical Range: $1,000 to $50,000

Disclosure Period: 1993

Note: Recent grants are derived from a 1993 Form 990.

RECENT GRANTS

Library

90,000	Vanderbilt University, Nashville, TN — funding of the Divinity School's Roman Catholic Studies Program for scholarships, faculty support, and library additions

General

1,511,250	LaSalle College High School, Wyndmoor, PA — fourth installment of 1990 pledge
1,000,000	Misericordia Hospital, Philadelphia, PA — toward pledge to implement maternity program
1,000,000	Villanova University, Villanova, PA — toward five-year pledge
536,500	Mercy Vocational High School, Philadelphia, PA — faculty endowment to bring salary and benefits to parity with diocesan package
500,000	Mercy International Centre, Dublin, Ireland — restoration of original House of Mercy in Dublin and development of endowment fund to maintain mission and preserve heritage

Consolidated Natural Gas Co. / Consolidated Natural Gas System Foundation

Revenue: $3.03 billion
Employees: 8,000
Headquarters: Pittsburgh, PA
SIC Major Group: Holding Companies Nec, Crude Petroleum & Natural Gas, Drilling Oil & Gas Wells, and Gas Transmission & Distribution

CONTACT

Sarah Banda Purvis
Manager
Consolidated Natural Gas System Foundation
CNG Tower
625 Liberty Ave.
Pittsburgh, PA 15222-3199
(412) 227-1185

Note: An alternative contact is Mr. Ray N. Ivey, Vice President and Executive Director, Consolidated Natural Gas System Foundation.

FINANCIAL SUMMARY

Recent Giving: $3,500,000 (1995 est.); $3,500,000 (1994 approx.); $3,105,703 (1993)

Assets: $835,728 (1995 est.); $835,728 (1994 approx.); $1,344,182 (1993)

Gifts Received: $3,475,000 (1993); $3,488,258 (1991)

Fiscal Note: Company contributes through foundation only. Above figures exclude non-monetary support. In 1993, the foundation received $1,050,000 from the East Ohio Gas Company, $1,100,000 from Peoples Natural Gas Company, $100,000 from Virginia Natural Gas Company, $50,000 from the River Gas Company, $100,000 from West Ohio Gas Company, $500,000 from CNG Producing Company, and $575,000 in cash and property from CNG Transmission Corporation.

EIN: 13-6077762

CONTRIBUTIONS SUMMARY

Typical Recipients: • *Arts & Humanities:* Arts Centers, Arts Festivals, Arts Institutes, Ballet, Dance, Historic Preservation, Libraries, Museums/Galleries, Music, Opera, Public Broadcasting, Theater • *Civic & Public Affairs:* Business/Free Enterprise, Economic Development, Housing, Municipalities/Towns, Public Policy, Urban & Community Affairs, Women's Affairs, Zoos/Aquariums • *Education:* Business Education, Colleges & Universities, Community & Junior Colleges, Economic Education, Education Funds, Elementary Education (Private), Elementary Education (Public), Engineering/Technological Education, Literacy, Minority Education, Public Education (Precollege), Science/Mathematics Education • *Environment:* General, Resource Conservation • *Health:* Clinics/Medical Centers, Emergency/Ambulance Services, Health Organizations, Hospitals • *Religion:* Religious Welfare • *Social Services:* Community Centers, Community Service Organizations, Counseling, Domestic Violence, Food/Clothing Distribution, Homes, People with Disabilities, Recreation & Athletics, Senior Services, United Funds/United Ways, Youth Organizations

Grant Types: award, capital, employee matching gifts, general support, and project

Note: Employee matching gift ratio: 1 to 1.

Nonmonetary Support Types: donated equipment

Note: Nonmonetary support is provided by both the foundation and the corporation. An estimate of nonmonetary support is not available.

Geographic Distribution: principally in company's service areas of western Pennsylvania, Ohio, Virginia, and West Virginia, but also in Louisiana, Oklahoma, and Washington, D.C., with limited national giving

Operating Locations: LA (New Orleans), OH (Cleveland, Lima, Marietta), PA (Pittsburgh), VA (Norfolk), WV (Clarksburg)

CORP. OFFICERS

George A. Davidson, Jr.: *B* Pittsburgh PA 1938 *ED* Univ Pittsburgh BS 1960 *CURR EMPL* chmn, ceo: Consolidated Natural Gas Co

Bill Fox: *CURR EMPL* pres VA Gas: Consolidated Natural Gas Co

Leonard Joseph Timms, Jr.: *B* Pittsburgh PA 1936 *ED* MA Inst Tech BS 1958; Salem Coll BS 1975 *CURR EMPL* pres, dir: CNG Transmission Corp *CORP AFFIL* dir: Consolidated Natural Gas Co, Empire Natl Bank *NONPR AFFIL* dir: Un Hosp Ctr; mem: Am Gas Assn, Interstate Natural Gas Assn Am, Southern Gas Assn

Stephen E. Williams: *B* 1949 *ED* Harvard Coll; Harvard Univ; WV Univ Coll Law *CURR EMPL* sr vp, gen couns: Consolidated Natural Gas Co

Roger Ellerton Wright: *B* Sewickley PA 1946 *ED* OH Wesleyan Univ 1968; Univ Pittsburgh Law Sch 1971 *CURR EMPL* pres: Peoples Natural Gas Co *NONPR AFFIL* mem: Am Bar Assn, Am Gas Assn

GIVING OFFICERS

Ralph J. Bean, Jr.: trust *B* Cumberland MD 1941 *ED* WV Univ 1963; Harvard Univ 1967 *CURR EMPL* pres: Hope Gas Inc *CORP AFFIL* dir: First Natl Bank Morgantown, Huntington Natl Bank *PHIL AFFIL* trust: Claude Worthington Benedum Foundation

William F. Fritsche, Jr.: trust

Russell R. Gifford: trust

David P. Hunt: trust

Ray N. Ivey: vp, exec dir *CURR EMPL* chmn pub aff: Consolidated Natural Gas Co

Sarah Banda Purvis: mgr, secy

Stephen E. Williams: *CURR EMPL* sr vp, gen couns: Consolidated Natural Gas Co (see above)

Roger Ellerton Wright: pres *CURR EMPL* pres: Peoples Natural Gas Co (see above)

APPLICATION INFORMATION

Initial Approach: *Initial Contact:* letter of inquiry *Include Information On:* description of the organization, including legal name, history, activities, and governing board; amount requested and list of other sources of funding; purpose for which funds are sought; recently audited financial statement; proof of tax-exempt status; and narrative statement describing the project's objectives, need addressed, impact on community, and method of accomplishing objectives *Deadlines:* none

Restrictions on Giving: Foundation does not support dinners or special events, fraternal organizations, goodwill advertising, individuals, member agencies of united funds, political or lobbying groups, or religious organizations for sectarian purposes.

Grants are limited to organizations which are tax exempt under section 501 (c)(3) of the IRS Code. Organizations involved in the activities listed above and located within Consolidated's service area receive consideration. Grants to organizations outside service areas are rare.

OTHER THINGS TO KNOW

Each operating company sets its own giving priorities.

Company reports nonmonetary support; however, types of support vary among regional operating companies, and value was not known at time of publication.

GRANTS ANALYSIS

Total Grants: $3,105,703

Number of Grants: 1,232

Highest Grant: $160,000

Average Grant: $2,521

Typical Range: $100 to $5,000

Disclosure Period: 1993

Note: Above figures include matching gifts totaling $249,783. Recent grants are derived from a 1993 Form 990.

RECENT GRANTS

General

160,000	Case Western Reserve University, Cleveland, OH
100,000	University of Pittsburgh, Pittsburgh, PA
100,000	West Virginia University Foundation, Morgantown, WV
75,000	United Way Services, Cleveland, OH
75,000	United Way Services, Cleveland, OH

Crawford Estate, E. R.

CONTACT

Francis E. Neish, Jr.
Trustee
E. R. Crawford Estate
Trust Fund "A", PO Box 487
McKeesport, PA 15134
(412) 672-6670

FINANCIAL SUMMARY

Recent Giving: $399,496 (1993); $432,268 (1992); $464,668 (1990)

Assets: $6,425,923 (1993); $6,349,597 (1992); $5,674,802 (1990)

EIN: 25-6031554

CONTRIBUTIONS SUMMARY

Donor(s): E. R. Crawford

Typical Recipients: • *Arts & Humanities:* General, Historic Preservation, History & Archaeology, Libraries, Literary Arts, Music, Theater • *Civic & Public Affairs:* Chambers of Commerce, Clubs, General, Philanthropic Organizations, Professional & Trade Associations, Women's Affairs • *Education:* Business Education, Colleges & Universities, Community & Junior Colleges, General, Gifted & Talented Programs, Literacy, Preschool Education, Student Aid • *Health:* Cancer, Children's Health/Hospitals, Diabetes, Health Organizations, Hospitals, Medical Research, Multiple Sclerosis, Single-Disease Health Associations • *Relig-*

ion: Churches, Religious Organizations, Religious Welfare, Synagogues/Temples • *Social Services:* Child Welfare, Community Service Organizations, Food/Clothing Distribution, Homes, Recreation & Athletics, United Funds/United Ways, YMCA/YWCA/YMHA/YWHA, Youth Organizations

Grant Types: operating expenses and scholarship

Geographic Distribution: focus on PA, with emphasis on Allegheny County

GIVING OFFICERS

William O. Hunter: trust

Francis E. Neish, Jr.: trust

George F. Young, Jr.: trust

APPLICATION INFORMATION

Initial Approach: Application form required for individuals. Send a brief letter of inquiry. Include a description of organization, amount requested, purpose of funds sought, recently audited financial statement, and proof of tax-exempt status. There are no deadlines.

GRANTS ANALYSIS

Total Grants: $399,496

Number of Grants: 100

Highest Grant: $45,000

Typical Range: $500 to $40,000

Disclosure Period: 1993

Note: Recent grants are derived from a 1993 Form 990. Number of grants and typical range do not include grants to individuals.

RECENT GRANTS

Library

40,000	Carnegie Free Library, McKeesport, PA

General

30,000	YMCA, McKeesport, PA
30,000	YWCA, McKeesport, PA
25,000	McKeesport Meals on Wheels, McKeesport, PA
20,000	South Hills Health System/Jefferson Hospital, Jefferson Boro, PA
15,000	Community College of Allegheny County, Pittsburgh, PA

Dentsply International Inc. / Dentsply International Foundation

Sales: $552.61 million
Employees: 4,340
Headquarters: York, PA
SIC Major Group: Instruments & Related Products

CONTACT

Marcus K. Dixon
Trustee
Dentsply International Inc.
570 W College Ave.
York, PA 17405
(717) 845-7511

FINANCIAL SUMMARY

Recent Giving: $185,774 (1993); $197,836 (1992); $181,234 (1990)

Assets: $247,130 (1993); $226,128 (1992); $261,185 (1990)

Gifts Received: $200,000 (1993); $226,128 (1992)

Fiscal Note: In 1993, contributions were received from Dentsply International Inc.

EIN: 23-6297307

CONTRIBUTIONS SUMMARY

Typical Recipients: • *Arts & Humanities:* Arts Funds, General, Historic Preservation, History & Archaeology, Libraries, Museums/Galleries, Performing Arts • *Civic & Public Affairs:* Botanical Gardens/Parks, Chambers of Commerce, Clubs, General, Hispanic Affairs, Safety • *Education:* Arts/Humanities Education, Business Education, Colleges & Universities, General, Health & Physical Education, Medical Education, Minority Education, Public Education (Precollege) • *Health:* AIDS/HIV, Cancer, Children's Health/Hospitals, Diabetes, General, Geriatric Health, Health Organizations, Heart, Hospices, Hospitals, Medical Research, Single-Disease Health Associations • *Religion:* Churches, Religious Organizations, Religious Welfare • *Social Services:* Animal Protection, At-Risk Youth, Child Welfare, Community Service Organizations, Day Care, Food/Clothing Distribution, People with Disabilities, Recreation & Athletics, Senior Services, United Funds/United Ways, YMCA/YWCA/YMHA/YWHA

Grant Types: award, capital, general support, multiyear/continuing support, and research

Nonmonetary Support Types: donated equipment and donated products

Geographic Distribution: provides grants throughout the United States

Operating Locations: DE (Milford), OH (Cincinnati, Maumee), PA (York)

Note: List includes division locations

CORP. OFFICERS

John C. Miles II: *B* Portland ME 1942 *ED* Lehigh Univ 1964; NY Univ 1971 *CURR EMPL* pres, coo, dir: Dentsply Intl

GIVING OFFICERS

J. Patrick Clark: secy

Marcus K. Dixon: trust *B* Baltimore MD 1945 *ED* Univ Baltimore 1966 *CURR EMPL* treas: Dentsply Intl

John C. Miles II: trust *CURR EMPL* pres, coo, dir: Dentsply Intl (see above)

Edward D. Yates: trust

APPLICATION INFORMATION

Initial Approach: The foundation has no formal grant application procedure or application form. There are no deadlines.

Restrictions on Giving: Does not support individuals, religious organizations for sectarian purposes, political or lobbying groups, or organizations outside operating areas.

OTHER THINGS TO KNOW
Provides grants for dental health and higher education.

GRANTS ANALYSIS
Total Grants: $185,774

Number of Grants: 54

Highest Grant: $31,000

Typical Range: $250 to $30,000

Disclosure Period: 1993

Note: Recent grants are derived from a 1993 Form 990.

RECENT GRANTS

General

31,000	York Hospital, York, PA — for community service
30,000	York Hospital Foundation, York, PA — for community service
25,250	American Fund for Dental Health, Chicago, IL — for expenses for continuing education
19,000	United Way of York County, York, PA — for community service
10,000	Health Education Center, York, PA — for community service

Douty Foundation

Former Foundation Name: Alfred and Mary Douty Foundation

CONTACT
Judith L. Bardes
Executive Director
Douty Fdn.
PO Box 540
Plymouth Meeting, PA 19462
(215) 585-6894

FINANCIAL SUMMARY
Recent Giving: $249,480 (1993); $222,915 (1992); $218,650 (1991)

Assets: $4,769,549 (1993); $4,778,361 (1992); $4,799,592 (1991)

Gifts Received: $123,694 (1989)

EIN: 23-6463709

CONTRIBUTIONS SUMMARY
Donor(s): the late Alfred Douty and the late Mary M. Douty

Typical Recipients: • *Arts & Humanities:* Arts Associations & Councils, Arts Centers, Dance, Libraries, Literary Arts, Museums/Galleries, Performing Arts, Theater • *Civic & Public Affairs:* Asian American Affairs, Botanical Gardens/Parks, Community Foundations, Economic Development, Employment/Job Training, General, Hispanic Affairs, Housing, Law & Justice, Safety, Urban & Community Affairs, Women's Affairs • *Education:* Arts/Humanities Education, Colleges & Universities, Education Funds, Elementary Education (Public), Medical Education, Minority Education, Preschool Education, Private Educa-

tion (Precollege), Public Education (Precollege), Special Education • *Environment:* General • *Health:* Adolescent Health Issues, AIDS/HIV, Children's Health/Hospitals, Health Organizations, Hospitals, Nursing Services, Prenatal Health Issues • *Religion:* Churches, Religious Organizations, Religious Welfare • *Social Services:* At-Risk Youth, Child Welfare, Community Service Organizations, Crime Prevention, Delinquency & Criminal Rehabilitation, Domestic Violence, Family Planning, Family Services, Homes, People with Disabilities, Senior Services, United Funds/United Ways, Volunteer Services, Youth Organizations

Grant Types: general support and seed money

Geographic Distribution: focus on the greater Philadelphia, PA, area

GIVING OFFICERS
Richard G. Alexander: trust

Judith L. Bardes: exec dir, trust *PHIL AFFIL* adm: Percival E. and Ethel Brown Foerderer Foundation; mgr: Adam and Maria Sarah Seybert Institution for Poor Boys and Girls

Norma Elias: trust

Thomas B. Harvey, Esq.: trust

Nancy J. Kirby: trust

Carrolle Perry: trust

APPLICATION INFORMATION
Initial Approach: Send a brief letter of inquiry. Include a description of organization, amount requested, purpose of funds sought, recently audited financial statement, and proof of tax-exempt status. Deadlines are February 15, April 15, and October 15.

PUBLICATIONS
Annual Report (including Application Guidelines)

GRANTS ANALYSIS
Total Grants: $249,480

Number of Grants: 79

Highest Grant: $10,000

Typical Range: $600 to $8,350

Disclosure Period: 1993

Note: Recent grants are derived from a 1993 Form 990.

RECENT GRANTS

General

10,000	Local Initiatives Support Corporation, Philadelphia, PA
8,350	Pennsylvania Partnership for Children, Philadelphia, PA
8,000	School District of Philadelphia, Philadelphia, PA — Hunter Elementary School
7,000	St. Christophers Hospital for Children, Philadelphia, PA
6,000	University of Pennsylvania, Philadelphia, PA — school of medicine academic programs

Dynamet, Inc. / Dynamet Foundation

Sales: $50.0 million
Employees: 270
Headquarters: Washington, PA
SIC Major Group: Nonferrous Rolling & Drawing Nec, Nonferrous Forgings, and Industrial Machinery Nec

CONTACT
Viola G. Taboni
Treasurer, Assistant Secretary, Trustee
Dynamet Foundation
195 Museum Rd.
Washington, PA 15301
(412) 228-2087

FINANCIAL SUMMARY
Recent Giving: $391,141 (1993); $380,766 (1992); $332,217 (1991)

Assets: $5,752,597 (1993); $5,149,411 (1992); $4,644,804 (1991)

Gifts Received: $500,000 (1993); $475,000 (1992); $2,000,000 (1991)

Fiscal Note: Contributes through foundation only. In 1993, contributions were received from Dynamet, Inc.

EIN: 25-6327217

CONTRIBUTIONS SUMMARY
Typical Recipients: • *Arts & Humanities:* Arts Institutes, History & Archaeology, Libraries, Museums/Galleries, Music, Opera, Performing Arts, Public Broadcasting, Theater • *Civic & Public Affairs:* Economic Development, Employment/Job Training, Philanthropic Organizations, Urban & Community Affairs, Zoos/Aquariums • *Education:* Colleges & Universities, Education Reform, Engineering/Technological Education, Religious Education, Special Education • *Health:* Cancer, Clinics/Medical Centers, Diabetes, Emergency/Ambulance Services, Eyes/Blindness, Health Organizations, Hospices, Kidney, Medical Rehabilitation, Medical Research, Single-Disease Health Associations • *International:* International Affairs, International Relations • *Religion:* Religious Welfare • *Science:* Scientific Research • *Social Services:* Camps, Community Centers, Community Service Organizations, Food/Clothing Distribution, Homes, People with Disabilities, Senior Services, Shelters/Homelessness, Substance Abuse, United Funds/United Ways, Youth Organizations

Grant Types: general support

Geographic Distribution: focus on Pennsylvania, with an emphasis on Pittsburgh

Operating Locations: PA (Washington)

CORP. OFFICERS
Robert J. Dickson: *CURR EMPL* cfo, vp fin: Dynamet Inc

Peter C. Rossin: *B* 1923 *ED* Lehigh Univ BA; Yale Univ ME *CURR EMPL* chmn, ceo, dir: Dynamet Inc

Peter N. Stephans: *CURR EMPL* pres, dir: Dynamet Inc

GIVING OFFICERS
Ada E. Rossin: trust

Peter C. Rossin: chmn, trust *CURR EMPL* chmn, ceo, dir: Dynamet Inc (see above)

Joan R. Stephans: trust

Peter N. Stephans: pres, trust *CURR EMPL* pres, dir: Dynamet Inc (see above)

Viola G. Taboni: treas, asst secy, trust *CURR EMPL* asst secy, treas: Dynamet Inc

J. Robert Van Kirk: secy, trust

APPLICATION INFORMATION
Initial Approach: *Initial Contact:* letter *Include Information On:* statement of charitable purpose of grant requested *Deadlines:* none

Restrictions on Giving: The foundation does not make grants to individuals or private foundations.

GRANTS ANALYSIS
Total Grants: $391,141

Number of Grants: 77

Highest Grant: $250,000

Average Grant: $1,857

Typical Range: $500 to $5,000

Disclosure Period: 1993

Note: Average grant excludes Highest Grant Figure of $250,000. Recent grants are derived from a 1993 Form 990.

RECENT GRANTS

Library
5,000	Citizen's Library Association of Washington Pennsylvania, Washington, PA — educational program

General
250,000	Washington and Jefferson College, Washington, PA — educational assistance
17,500	Family House, Pittsburgh, PA — charitable organizations for terminally ill patients
13,934	Boy Scouts of America, Pittsburgh, PA
12,500	United Cerebral Palsy of Southwestern Pennsylvania, Washington, DC — scientific research
8,333	Washington County Council on Economic Development, Washington, PA — council for economic growth for Washington County

Eberly Foundation

CONTACT
Robert E. Eberly, Sr.
President
Eberly Fdn.
PO Box 2023
Uniontown, PA 15401
(412) 437-7557

FINANCIAL SUMMARY
Recent Giving: $2,160,591 (1993); $779,088 (1992); $299,447 (1991)

Assets: $22,064,589 (1993); $20,820,768 (1992); $15,604,960 (1991)

Gifts Received: $1,650,000 (1993); $4,367,834 (1992); $2,262,011 (1991)

Fiscal Note: In 1993, contributions were received from Ruth Eberly Estate.

EIN: 23-7070246

CONTRIBUTIONS SUMMARY
Typical Recipients: • *Arts & Humanities:* Arts Outreach, Ethnic & Folk Arts, History & Archaeology, Libraries, Museums/Galleries, Music, Opera • *Civic & Public Affairs:* Botanical Gardens/Parks, Chambers of Commerce, Economic Development, Economic Policy, General, Municipalities/Towns, Public Policy, Safety, Urban & Community Affairs • *Education:* Colleges & Universities, Elementary Education (Public), Medical Education, Public Education (Precollege), Science/Mathematics Education • *Environment:* General • *Health:* Clinics/Medical Centers, Heart, Hospitals • *Science:* Scientific Centers & Institutes • *Social Services:* Camps, Community Centers, Community Service Organizations, People with Disabilities, Scouts, Youth Organizations

Grant Types: general support

Geographic Distribution: focus on PA

GIVING OFFICERS
Carolyn E. Blaney: trust

Ruth Ann Carter: trust

Jill Drost: trust

Paul O. Eberly: trust

Robert E. Eberly, Jr.: trust

Robert E. Eberly, Sr.: pres, treas *B* Greensboro PA 1918 *ED* PA St Univ BA 1939 *CURR EMPL* chmn: Eberly & Meade *CORP AFFIL* chmn: Chalk Hill Gas, Gallatin Natl Bank, Greystone Resources; dir: Integra Fin Corp *NONPR AFFIL* dir: Fayette Heritage, Penns Southwest Assn, Uniontown Indus Fund, WQED/WQEX-TV; mem: Greater Uniontown Chamber Commerce, Indepdendent Petroleum Assn, OH Oil Gas Assn, OK Independent Petroleum Assn, OK Oil Gas Assn, PA Geological Soc, PA Oil Gas Assn, Western PA Conservancy, WV Oil Gas Assn; treas: Campaign Penn St; trust emeritus: Uniontown Hosp Assn

Margaret E. George: trust

Patricia Hillman Miller: secy

Jacob D. Moore: trust

APPLICATION INFORMATION
Initial Approach: Send a brief letter of inquiry. Include a description of organization, amount requested, purpose of funds sought, recently audited financial statement, and proof of tax-exempt status. Deadline is August 1.

GRANTS ANALYSIS
Total Grants: $2,160,591

Number of Grants: 166

Highest Grant: $500,000

Typical Range: $70 to $115,630

Disclosure Period: 1993

Note: Recent grants are derived from a 1993 Form 990.

RECENT GRANTS

General
500,000	West Virginia University, Morgantown, WV — initial payment for Eberly College
115,630	Goodwill Industries, Uniontown, PA
100,000	Fay-Penn Economic Development Corporation, Uniontown, PA
100,000	Fay-Penn Economic Development Corporation, Uniontown, PA
100,000	Goodwill Industries, Uniontown, PA — recycling plant

Eccles Foundation, Ralph M. and Ella M.

CONTACT
R. Grant Carner
Trust Officer
Ralph M. and Ella M. Eccles Fdn.
c/o Integra Trust Co.
248 Seneca St.
Oil City, PA 16301
(814) 678-3546

FINANCIAL SUMMARY
Recent Giving: $107,280 (1993); $159,404 (1992); $133,288 (1991)

Assets: $2,760,201 (1993); $2,775,948 (1992); $2,831,506 (1991)

EIN: 23-7261807

CONTRIBUTIONS SUMMARY
Typical Recipients: • *Arts & Humanities:* Libraries • *Civic & Public Affairs:* Economic Development, Municipalities/Towns, Safety • *Education:* Colleges & Universities, Education Funds, Public Education (Precollege), School Volunteerism • *Health:* Clinics/Medical Centers, Hospitals, Prenatal Health Issues • *Religion:* Churches, Religious Welfare • *Social Services:* Community Service Organizations, Recreation & Athletics, Youth Organizations

Grant Types: capital, emergency, general support, multiyear/continuing support, and operating expenses

Geographic Distribution: limited to Union School District of Clarion County, PA

GIVING OFFICERS
Integra Trust Company: trust

APPLICATION INFORMATION
Initial Approach: Send brief letter describing program. There are no deadlines.

Restrictions on Giving: Limited to organizations serving Clarion County.

PUBLICATIONS
Application Guidelines

GRANTS ANALYSIS
Total Grants: $107,280

Number of Grants: 7

Highest Grant: $66,515

Typical Range: $2,000 to $16,947

Disclosure Period: 1993

Note: Recent grants are derived from a 1993 Form 990.

RECENT GRANTS

Library
66,515   Eccles-Lesher Memorial Library, Rimersburg, PA

General
16,947   Rimersburg Medical Center, Rimersburg, PA
9,444   Union School District, Rimersburg, PA — purchases and activities
6,000   Union Parent Teacher Organization, Rimersburg, PA — playground equipment
3,874   Borough of Rimersburg, Rimersburg, PA — sewage system lagoons
2,500   Sligo Little League, Sligo, PA — playing field

Eden Hall Foundation

CONTACT
Edward M. Pierson
General Manager
Eden Hall Foundation
600 Grant, Ste. 3232
Pittsburgh, PA 15219
(412) 642-6697

FINANCIAL SUMMARY
Recent Giving: $5,123,075 (1993); $5,520,000 (1992); $5,504,450 (1991)

Assets: $107,861,197 (1993); $123,390,164 (1992); $113,468,351 (1991)

EIN: 25-1384468

CONTRIBUTIONS SUMMARY
Donor(s): The Eden Hall Foundation was established in 1984 by Eden Hall Farm.

Typical Recipients: • *Arts & Humanities:* Arts Centers, Arts Outreach, Libraries, Music, Public Broadcasting • *Civic & Public Affairs:* Economic Development, General, Housing, Philanthropic Organizations, Urban & Community Affairs, Women's Affairs, Zoos/Aquariums • *Education:* Business Education, Colleges & Universities, Education Associations, Education Funds, Medical Education, Minority Education, Private Education (Precollege), Special Education, Student Aid • *Health:* Arthritis, Cancer, Children's Health/Hospitals, Clinics/Medical Centers, Emergency/Ambulance Services, Health Funds, Health Organizations, Hospitals, Medical Rehabilitation, Mental Health, Nursing Services, Single-Disease Health Associations • *Religion:* Religious Organizations, Religious Welfare • *Social Services:* Camps, Child Welfare, Community Centers, Community Service Organizations, Counseling, Day Care, Domestic Violence, Food/Clothing Distribution, Homes, People with Disabilities, Scouts, Senior Services, Shelters/Homelessness, Substance Abuse, United Funds/United Ways, YMCA/YWCA/YMHA/YWHA, Youth Organizations

Grant Types: capital, endowment, project, research, and scholarship

Geographic Distribution: primarily western Pennsylvania

GIVING OFFICERS
George C. Greer: dir *B* Sharon PA 1932 *ED* PA St Univ 1954; Univ PA Sch Law 1957 *CURR EMPL* vp org devel & admin: H J Heinz Co

John Mazur: dir

Edward M. Pierson: gen mgr

APPLICATION INFORMATION
Initial Approach:

Initial requests should be in letter form.

Requests should include the purpose of the applying organization, current financial statement including the organization's other sources of funding, specific purposes for which the grant is to be used, and proof of IRS tax-exempt status.

Organizations receiving funds must acknowledge receipt in writing, stating that the grant will be used for the purpose for which it was made. When the organization expends the funds, a written report giving details and verification of the expenditures is required by the foundation.

The foundation reports no application deadlines.

The board of directors usually meets quarterly to consider grant proposals. Applicants will receive notification of the board's decision.

Restrictions on Giving: Requests to cover operating expenses, accumulated deficits, and general fund-raising campaigns are discouraged. Grants are not made to individuals or private foundations.

OTHER THINGS TO KNOW
Interviews or site visits may be required for additional information and confirmation.

PUBLICATIONS
Application guidelines

GRANTS ANALYSIS
Total Grants: $5,123,075

Number of Grants: 63

Highest Grant: $1,040,000

Average Grant: $81,319

Typical Range: $20,000 to $100,000

Disclosure Period: 1993

Note: Recent grants are derived from a 1993 Form 990.

RECENT GRANTS

Library
75,000   Point Park College, Pittsburgh, PA — children's library costs
50,000   Saxonburg Area Library, Saxonburg, PA — purchase of building, renovations, and furnishings
35,000   Mars Area Public Library, Mars, PA — expand existing building
25,000   Carnegie Library of Homestead, Munhall, PA — renovations

General
1,040,000   Cumberland College, Williamsburg, KY — construction, furnishings, and interest
375,000   Extra Mile Education Foundation, Pittsburgh, PA — endowment fund
235,000   Wilson College, Chambersburg, PA — educational program
200,000   Berea College, Berea, KY — construction
200,000   Girl Scouts of Southwestern Pennsylvania, Pittsburgh, PA — upgrade camps and program center

Edgewater Steel Corp. / Edgewater Corp. Charitable Trust

Sales: $25.0 million
Employees: 500
Headquarters: Oakmont, PA
SIC Major Group: Fabricated Metal Products and Primary Metal Industries

CONTACT
Edgewater Corp. Charitable Trust
300 College Ave.
Oakmont, PA 15139
(412) 826-7340

FINANCIAL SUMMARY
Recent Giving: $24,000 (1993); $3,211 (1992); $28,958 (1991)

Assets: $362,254 (1993); $368,370 (1992); $353,876 (1991)

Gifts Received: $2,649 (1992)

Fiscal Note: In 1992, contributions were received from Edgewater Steel Corp.

EIN: 25-6022200

CONTRIBUTIONS SUMMARY
Typical Recipients: • *Arts & Humanities:* Community Arts, Libraries, Museums/Galleries, Music, Opera • *Civic & Public Affairs:* African American Affairs, Chambers of Commerce, Clubs, Economic Development, Economic Policy, General, Municipalities/Towns, Safety, Urban & Community Affairs • *Education:* Business Education, Literacy, Secondary Education (Public) • *Health:* Children's Health/Hospitals, Hospitals, Medical Rehabilitation • *Religion:* Religious Organizations • *Social Services:* Community Service Organizations, Crime Prevention, People with Disabilities, United Funds/United Ways, Youth Organizations

Grant Types: general support

Geographic Distribution: focus on PA

Operating Locations: PA (Oakmont)

GIVING OFFICERS
PNC Bank, NA: trust

APPLICATION INFORMATION
Initial Approach: Send brief letter describing program. Include a description of organization, amount requested, purpose of funds sought, recently audited financial statement, and proof of tax-exempt status. There are no deadlines.

GRANTS ANALYSIS
Total Grants: $24,000

Number of Grants: 26

Highest Grant: $9,000

Typical Range: $100 to $6,000

Disclosure Period: 1993

Note: Recent grants are derived from a 1993 Form 990.

RECENT GRANTS

Library

200	Springdale Free Public Library, Springdale, PA

General

9,000	United Way of Southwestern Pennsylvania, Pittsburgh, PA
6,000	Bunker Challenge, Oakmont, PA
1,000	Gateway Rehabilitation Center, Aliquippa, PA
1,000	Harmarville Rehabilitation Center, Pittsburgh, PA — for capital endowment fund
1,000	St. Margaret's Memorial Hospital Foundation, Pittsburgh, PA

Elf Atochem North America, Inc. / Elf Atochem North America Foundation

Revenue: $1.56 billion
Employees: 5,508
Parent Company: Elf Aquitaine, Inc.
Headquarters: Philadelphia, PA
SIC Major Group: Chemical & Fertilizer Mining Nec, Alkalies & Chlorine, Industrial Gases, and Industrial Inorganic Chemicals Nec

CONTACT
George L. Hagar
Executive Secretary
Elf Atochem North America Fdn.
2000 Market St.
Philadelphia, PA 19103
(215) 419-7653

FINANCIAL SUMMARY
Recent Giving: $1,000,000 (1995 est.); $1,200,000 (1994 approx.); $1,300,000 (1993 approx.)

Assets: $700,769 (1992); $1,204,493 (1991); $1,779,124 (1990)

Gifts Received: $780,000 (1992); $780,000 (1991)

Fiscal Note: Giving figures are for foundation only. The company also makes contributions directly from corporate funds. Contact Peter McCarthy, vice president, publc affairs for more information.

EIN: 23-6256818

CONTRIBUTIONS SUMMARY
Typical Recipients: • *Arts & Humanities:* Arts Centers, Ballet, Dance, Historic Preservation, Libraries, Museums/Galleries, Music, Opera, Performing Arts, Public Broadcasting, Theater • *Civic & Public Affairs:* Chambers of Commerce, Economic Development, Economic Policy, Employment/Job Training, Law & Justice, Professional & Trade Associations, Public Policy, Safety, Urban & Community Affairs, Zoos/Aquariums • *Education:* Arts/Humanities Education, Business Education, Colleges & Universities, Community & Junior Colleges, Economic Education, Education Reform, General, Minority Education, Private Education (Precollege), Science/Mathematics Education • *Environment:* General • *Health:* Emergency/Ambulance Services, Hospitals, Medical Rehabilitation, Medical Research • *Science:* Science Museums, Scientific Centers & Institutes • *Social Services:* Community Service Organizations, People with Disabilities, United Funds/United Ways, Youth Organizations

Grant Types: capital, employee matching gifts, general support, and scholarship

Note: Employee matching gift ratio: 1 to 1. Foundation reports that scholarships are for children of employees only.

Geographic Distribution: nationally, with emphasis on areas where Elf Atochem North America has operations

Operating Locations: AL (Mobile), CA (Los Angeles, Monrovia), GA, IL (Rosiclaren), KY (Calvert City, Carroloton), MI (Wyandotte), NY (Buffalo, Geneseo, Homer), OH (Delaware), OK (Pryor, Tulsa), OR (Portland), PA (Cornwells Heights, King of Prussia, Philadelphia), TX (Beaumont, Bryan, Seagraves), WA (Tacoma)

CORP. OFFICERS
Bernard Azoulay: *B* 1940 *ED* Ecole Polytechnique *CURR EMPL* pres, ceo: Elf Atochem N Am

Douglas Lynn Cox: *B* Des Moines IA 1945 *ED* Univ PA BS 1968; Univ PA Wharton Sch MBA 1973 *CURR EMPL* sr vp fin, cfo: Elf Atochem N Am *CORP AFFIL* cfo: Elf Atochem N Am DE *NONPR AFFIL* bd dirs: Big Bros/Big Sisters; bd govs: PA Econ League; class gift chmn: Univ PA; mem: Phi Kappa Sigma; pres, trust: Friends Select

Sch; treas: Old Pine St Presbyterian Church *CLUB AFFIL* Philadelphia Racquet

Peter John McCarthy: *B* Philadelphia PA 1943 *ED* LaSalle Coll 1964; Temple Univ *CURR EMPL* vp pub aff: Elf Atochem N Am *PHIL AFFIL* pres, treas: McCarthy Charities

GIVING OFFICERS
Douglas Lynn Cox: trust *CURR EMPL* sr vp fin, cfo: Elf Atochem N Am (see above)

Anthony Peter DeLuca: trust *B* Boston MA 1930 *ED* Lafayette Coll 1951; US Military Acad 1953; Shippensburg Univ PA 1972 *CURR EMPL* sr vp human resouces: Elf Atochem N Am

George L. Hagar: exec secy *CURR EMPL* exec secy: Elf Atochem N Am

Peter John McCarthy: trust *CURR EMPL* vp pub aff: Elf Atochem N Am *PHIL AFFIL* pres, treas: McCarthy Charities (see above)

APPLICATION INFORMATION
Initial Approach: *Initial Contact:* brief letter or proposal *Include Information On:* description of the organization, amount requested, purpose for which funds are sought, recently audited financial statement, proof of tax-exempt status *Deadlines:* none

Restrictions on Giving: The foundation generally does not support political or lobbying groups or member agencies of united funds.

No longer supports health concerns.

OTHER THINGS TO KNOW
In 1991, company changed its name to Elf Atochem North America from Atochem North America. The company was also formerly known as Pennwalt Corp.

GRANTS ANALYSIS
Total Grants: $1,312,909

Number of Grants: 1,000*

Highest Grant: $90,500

Average Grant: $1,313*

Typical Range: $100 to $5,000

Disclosure Period: 1992

Note: Number of grants and average grant figures are approximates. Recent grants are derived from a 1992 Form 990.

RECENT GRANTS

General

90,500	United Way of Southeastern Pennsylvania, Philadelphia, PA
90,500	United Way of Southeastern Pennsylvania, Philadelphia, PA
90,500	United Way of Southeastern Pennsylvania, Philadelphia, PA
58,500	United Way of Southeastern Pennsylvania, Philadelphia, PA
26,000	Calvert Area United Fund, Calvert, KY

Fair Oaks Foundation, Inc.

Former Foundation Name: Ampco-Pitts-burgh Foundation

CONTACT
Rose Hoover
Secretary
Fair Oaks Foundation, Inc.
600 Grant St., Ste. 4600
Pittsburgh, PA 15219
(412) 456-4418

FINANCIAL SUMMARY

Recent Giving: $367,959 (1993); $377,260 (1992); $397,640 (1991)

Assets: $6,002,634 (1993); $5,842,455 (1992); $5,872,585 (1991)

Gifts Received: $2,139,615 (1989)

EIN: 25-1576560

CONTRIBUTIONS SUMMARY

Donor(s): Pittsburg Forgings Foundation, Ampco-Pittsburg Foundation

Typical Recipients: • *Arts & Humanities:* Arts Centers, Arts Festivals, Ballet, Community Arts, History & Archaeology, Libraries, Museums/Galleries, Music, Opera, Public Broadcasting, Theater • *Civic & Public Affairs:* African American Affairs, Botanical Gardens/Parks, Civil Rights, Economic Development, General, Parades/Festivals, Safety, Urban & Community Affairs, Women's Affairs, Zoos/Aquariums • *Education:* Business Education, Colleges & Universities, Education Funds, Legal Education, Medical Education, Minority Education, Private Education (Precollege) • *Health:* Cancer, Children's Health/Hospitals, Emergency/Ambulance Services • *Religion:* Jewish Causes, Religious Organizations, Religious Welfare • *Social Services:* Community Centers, Community Service Organizations, Crime Prevention, Family Planning, People with Disabilities, Recreation & Athletics, Scouts, United Funds/United Ways, Youth Organizations

Grant Types: general support and scholarship

Geographic Distribution: focus on NY

GIVING OFFICERS

Louis Berkman: chmn, trust *B* Canton OH 1909 *CURR EMPL* pres, treas, dir: Louis Berkman Co *CORP AFFIL* chmn: Meyer Products, Orrville Products; chmn exec comm, dir: Ampco-Pittsburgh Corp; pres, dir: Follansbee Steel Corp, Parkersburg Steel Co *PHIL AFFIL* pres, treas, trust: Louis and Sandra Berkman Foundation

Marshall L. Berkman: pres, trust *B* Steubenville OH 1936 *ED* Harvard Univ AB 1958; Harvard Univ MBA 1960; Harvard Univ JD 1963 *CURR EMPL* chmn, ceo: Ampco-Pittsburgh Corp *CORP AFFIL* chmn, ceo: Ampco-Pittsburgh Corp; dir: Louis Berkman Co *PHIL AFFIL* vp, asst secy, asst treas, trust: Louis and Sandra Berkman Foundation

Rose Hoover: secy

Robert Arthur Paul: vp, trust *B* New York NY 1937 *ED* Cornell Univ AB 1959; Harvard Univ JD 1962; Harvard Univ MBA 1964 *CURR EMPL* pres-ceo, dir: Ampco-Pittsburgh Corp *CORP AFFIL* dir: Louis Berkman Realty Co, Follansbee Steel Corp, Integra Fin Corp, Northwestern Steel & Wire Co, Ribozyme Pharmaceuticals; dir, vp, asst secy, dir: Parkersburg Steel Corp; gen ptnr: Romar Trading Co; vchmn, dir: Buffalo Pumps Co, Union Electric Steel Corp; vp, asst secy, dir: Berkman (Louis) Co *NONPR AFFIL* mem: Am Bar Assn, MA Bar Assn, Soc Security Analysts; trust: H.L. and Louis Berkman Fdn, Cornell Univ, Presbyterian Univ Hosp; trust, treas: Ampco Pittsburgh Fdn *CLUB AFFIL* Concordia, Duquesne, Harvard, Harvard-Yale-Princeton, Pittsburgh Athletic *PHIL AFFIL* vp, trust: Louis and Sandra Berkman Foundation; treas: Jewish Healthcare Foundation of Pittsburgh

APPLICATION INFORMATION
Initial Approach: The foundation has no formal grant application procedure or application form. Deadline is November 1.

OTHER THINGS TO KNOW
Provides scholarships to individuals for higher education.

GRANTS ANALYSIS
Total Grants: $367,959

Number of Grants: 75

Highest Grant: $100,000

Typical Range: $100 to $50,000

Disclosure Period: 1993

Note: Recent grants are derived from a 1993 Form 990.

RECENT GRANTS

Library
500   Carnegie Free Library, Carnegie, PA — for general support

General
100,000   Cornell University Medical College, New York, NY — for support of educational programs
50,000   United Jewish Federation, Pittsburgh, PA — for support of programs
37,500   Harvard College, Cambridge, MA — for support of educational programs
35,000   Harvard Law School, Cambridge, MA — for support of educational programs
30,000   Harvard Business School, Cambridge, MA — for support of educational programs

First Fidelity Bank

Parent Company: First Fidelity Bancorporation
Income: $2.05 billion
Parent Employees: 10,630
Headquarters: Philadelphia, PA
SIC Major Group: Bank Holding Companies, National Commercial Banks, Mortgage Bankers & Correspondents, and Security Brokers & Dealers

CONTACT
David Newell
Senior Vice President, Public Affairs
First Fidelity Bank
123 S Broad St., Ste. 1242
Philadelphia, PA 19109
(215) 985-3090
Note: The company is located on Broad and Walnut Streets. Applicants may also contact Jean Konrad at (215) 985-7141 for information.

FINANCIAL SUMMARY
Recent Giving: $1,600,000 (1991); $1,100,000 (1990)

Fiscal Note: Company gives directly. Above figures exclude nonmonetary support.

CONTRIBUTIONS SUMMARY
Typical Recipients: • *Arts & Humanities:* Arts Appreciation, Arts Associations & Councils, Arts Centers, Arts Institutes, Community Arts, Dance, Ethnic & Folk Arts, Libraries, Literary Arts, Museums/Galleries, Music, Opera, Performing Arts, Public Broadcasting, Theater • *Civic & Public Affairs:* Business/Free Enterprise, Civil Rights, Economic Development, Employment/Job Training, Housing, Law & Justice, Legal Aid, Urban & Community Affairs, Women's Affairs, Zoos/Aquariums • *Education:* Arts/Humanities Education, Business Education, Colleges & Universities, Community & Junior Colleges, Economic Education, International Exchange, Literacy, Minority Education • *Health:* Geriatric Health, Hospices • *International:* International Relations • *Social Services:* Child Welfare, Community Centers, Community Service Organizations, Delinquency & Criminal Rehabilitation, Domestic Violence, Emergency Relief, Family Planning, Family Services, Food/Clothing Distribution, Homes, Recreation & Athletics, Senior Services, Shelters/Homelessness, Substance Abuse, United Funds/United Ways, Volunteer Services, Youth Organizations

Grant Types: capital, employee matching gifts, general support, multiyear/continuing support, operating expenses, and project

Note: The bank matches gifts by employees to four-year, degree-granting colleges and universities and related graduate schools and federated campaigns to a maximum of $1,500 annually and by retirees to $250 annually. The bank matches the first $500 on a two-to-one basis and from $501 to $1,500 on a one-to-one basis.

Nonmonetary Support Types: donated equipment and in-kind services

Note: Nonmonetary support is provided through the company. The estimated value of that support is unknown. For more information contact David Newell.

Geographic Distribution: primarily Pennsylvania and operating locations

Operating Locations: PA (Philadelphia)

CORP. OFFICERS

Peter C. Palmieri: *B* Newark NJ 1934 *ED* Univ Dayton 1963; Harvard Univ *CURR EMPL* vchmn, chief credit off: First Fidelity Bancorp *PHIL AFFIL* vchmn

Wolfgang Schoellkopf: *B* Stuttgart Germany 1932 *ED* Univ CA Berkeley 1956; Cornell Univ 1960 *CURR EMPL* vchmn, cfo: First Fidelity Bancorp *CORP AFFIL* chmn, ceo, cfo: First Fidelity Bank NA NY; ptnr: PMW Assocs LP *PHIL AFFIL* vchmn, cfo

Anthony Patrick Terracciano: *B* Bayonne NJ 1938 *ED* Fordham Univ MA; St Peters Coll BS *CURR EMPL* chmn, pres, ceo: First Fidelity Bancorp *CORP AFFIL* ceo, dir: First Fidelity Bank; chmn: First Fidelity Bank NA NJ; chmn, pres, ceo: Fidelity Intl Bank; dir: NJ Bell Telephone Co, Pitcairn Co *NONPR AFFIL* dir: Metro Newark Chamber Commerce, NJ Performing Arts Ctr, NY Philharmonic; mem: Counc Foreign Rels, NJ Bankers Assn; mem exec counc: Better Bus Bur; trust: Renaissance Newark Inc

GIVING OFFICERS

Jean Konrad: *CURR EMPL* vp pub aff: First Fidelity Bank NA

David Newell: *CURR EMPL* sr vp pub aff: First Fidelity Bancorp *CORP AFFIL* vp pub aff/govt: First Fidelity Bank NA NJ

APPLICATION INFORMATION

Initial Approach: *Initial Contact:* letter and full proposal *Include Information On:* description of the organization, record as a viable organization for at least three years, information about governing board serving without compensation and holding regular meetings, amount requested, purpose of funds sought, detailed annual budget translating program plans into financial terms, audited financial statement, and proof of 501(c)(3) status *Deadlines:* by September 1 *Note:* Applicants should keep grant requests to a single-page letter.

Restrictions on Giving: The company does not support individuals, religious organizations for sectarian purposes, political or lobbying groups, veterans or fraternal organizations other than projects which directly benefit the community, missionary activities abroad, organizations receiving government support, organizations that do not meet the Better Business Bureau's standard for charitable solicitations, organizations in violation of state or local government regulations, multi-year capital drive commitments, national philanthropies or organizations, or endowments.

The company also does not support human service agencies already receiving support from the United Way, annual operating budgets of hospitals, medical research, annual operating campaigns of individual four-year degree-granting colleges and universities and related graduate schools, or private or public secondary and elementary schools.

OTHER THINGS TO KNOW

Special attention is given to proposals which advance and promote the economic life of the primary market area, and those that offer the broadest benefit to the community.

Contributions that support specific neighborhoods or localities are made through local branch offices. Usually the amount is less than $100.

PUBLICATIONS

Application guidelines

GRANTS ANALYSIS

Typical Range: $1,000 to $2,500

Forest Oil Corp. / Glendorn Foundation

Revenue: $105.15 million
Employees: 187
Headquarters: Bradford, PA
SIC Major Group: Oil & Gas Extraction

CONTACT

William F. Higie
Manager
Glendorn Foundation
78 Main St.
Bradford, PA 16701
(814) 368-7171

FINANCIAL SUMMARY

Recent Giving: $191,000 (1993); $0 (1992); $134,500 (1991)

Assets: $4,003,749 (1993); $3,521,013 (1992); $2,621,702 (1991)

Gifts Received: $6,250 (1992); $27,100 (1991); $198,000 (1990)

Fiscal Note: In 1991, contributions were received from Forest Oil Corp.

EIN: 25-1024349

CONTRIBUTIONS SUMMARY

Typical Recipients: • *Arts & Humanities:* Arts Festivals, Dance, Historic Preservation, Libraries, Museums/Galleries, Music, Opera, Performing Arts, Theater • *Civic & Public Affairs:* Business/Free Enterprise, Economic Development, General, Philanthropic Organizations, Zoos/Aquariums • *Education:* Colleges & Universities, Literacy, Medical Education, Private Education (Precollege), Special Education • *Health:* Clinics/Medical Centers, Hospices, Hospitals, Medical Research • *Science:* Science Museums • *Social Services:* Animal Protection, People with Disabilities, Shelters/Homelessness, Substance Abuse, United Funds/United Ways

Grant Types: capital, endowment, general support, and research

Nonmonetary Support Types: donated equipment and workplace solicitation

Geographic Distribution: throughout the United States

Operating Locations: CO (Denver), PA (Branford)

Note: List includes division location

CORP. OFFICERS

Bulent A. Berilgen: *CURR EMPL* vp, coo, dir: Forest Oil Corp

Robert S. Boswell: *CURR EMPL* pres: Forest Oil Corp

William L. Dorn: *CURR EMPL* chmn, ceo, dir: Forest Oil Corp

GIVING OFFICERS

Clayton D. Chisum: trust

David F. Dorn: trust *B* 1924 *CURR EMPL* co-chmn, chmn exec comm, dir: Forest Oil Corp *PHIL AFFIL* trust: Glendorn Foundation

Frederick M. Dorn: trust

John C. Dorn: trust *B* 1927 *ED* Yale Univ 1950 *PHIL AFFIL* trust: Glendorn Foundation

Dale B. Grubb: trust

William F. Higie: secy, mgr *B* Bradford PA 1926 *ED* St Bonaventure Univ 1949; Dickinson Sch Law 1952 *CURR EMPL* vp, secy, coun, dir: Forest Oil Corp *CORP AFFIL* vp, secy, coun, dir: Forest Oil Corp *NONPR AFFIL* vchmn: Bradford Hosp *PHIL AFFIL* dir: Bradford Educational Foundation

APPLICATION INFORMATION

Initial Approach: Due to the backlog of proposed gifts, no solicitations from grantees are desired at this time.

GRANTS ANALYSIS

Total Grants: $191,000

Number of Grants: 7

Highest Grant: $60,000

Typical Range: $6,000 to $30,000

Disclosure Period: 1993

Note: Recent grants are derived from a 1993 Form 990.

RECENT GRANTS

General

60,000	University of Pittsburgh, Bradford, PA — for research and education
40,000	Harvard Medical School, Cambridge, MA — for neurological research
30,000	National Fragile X Foundation, Denver, CO — for research and education
25,000	Trinity School of Midland, Midland, TX — for building fund
20,000	Bradford Regional Medical Center, Bradford, PA — for building fund

Foster Charitable Trust

CONTACT
Bernard S. Mars
Trustee
Foster Charitable Trust
PO Box 67
Pittsburgh, PA 15220
(412) 981-1411

FINANCIAL SUMMARY
Recent Giving: $386,200 (1993); $355,429 (1992); $363,900 (1991)

Assets: $2,075,523 (1993); $2,172,246 (1992); $2,258,022 (1991)

Gifts Received: $96,166 (1992); $221,249 (1989); $468,967 (1988)

Fiscal Note: In 1992, contributions were received from Foster Industries, Inc.

EIN: 25-6064791

CONTRIBUTIONS SUMMARY
Donor(s): Foster Industries

Typical Recipients: • *Arts & Humanities:* Arts Associations & Councils, Arts Festivals, Arts Funds, Ballet, Ethnic & Folk Arts, Libraries, Museums/Galleries, Music, Opera, Public Broadcasting, Theater • *Civic & Public Affairs:* Philanthropic Organizations • *Education:* Colleges & Universities, Health & Physical Education, Legal Education, Private Education (Precollege) • *Health:* AIDS/HIV, Clinics/Medical Centers, Eyes/Blindness, Hospitals, Medical Rehabilitation, Medical Research, Research/Studies Institutes, Single-Disease Health Associations • *International:* Foreign Educational Institutions, Missionary/Religious Activities • *Religion:* Jewish Causes, Religious Organizations, Religious Welfare, Synagogues/Temples • *Science:* Scientific Centers & Institutes • *Social Services:* Child Welfare, Community Centers, Community Service Organizations, People with Disabilities, Substance Abuse, United Funds/United Ways, Youth Organizations

Grant Types: general support

Geographic Distribution: focus on PA

GIVING OFFICERS
J. R. Foster: trust

Jay L. Foster: trust

L. B. Foster II: trust

Bernard S. Mars: trust

P. S. Mars: trust

Milton Porter: trust *B* Charleroi PA 1911 *ED* Univ Pittsburgh BA 1932 *CURR EMPL* chmn exec comm, dir: Foster (LB) Co *NONPR AFFIL* chmn: Health Ed Ctr Pittsburgh; dir: Un Way Southwestern PA; dir emeritus: Carnegie-Mellon Univ; life dir: Montefiore Hosp Med Ctr; vp, dir: Pittsburgh Symphony Soc

APPLICATION INFORMATION
Initial Approach: Send brief typed letter of inquiry. Include a description of organization, amount requested, purpose of funds sought, recently audited financial statement, and proof of tax-exempt status. There are no deadlines.

GRANTS ANALYSIS
Total Grants: $386,200

Number of Grants: 44

Highest Grant: $100,000

Typical Range: $500 to $46,500

Disclosure Period: 1993

Note: Recent grants are derived from a 1993 Form 990.

RECENT GRANTS
Library
1,000   Carnegie Institute, Pittsburgh, PA — fellows fund

General
100,000   United Jewish Federation Annual Campaign, Pittsburgh, PA
46,500   Ben-Gurion University of the Negev, New York, NY
40,000   United Jewish Federation Exodus 90, Pittsburgh, PA
25,000   United Jewish Federation Renaissance, Pittsburgh, PA
20,000   Jewish Community Center of Pittsburgh, Pittsburgh, PA

Freeport Brick Co. / Freeport Brick Co. Charitable Trust

Sales: $25.0 million
Employees: 200
Headquarters: Freeport, PA
SIC Major Group: Industrial Machinery & Equipment and Stone, Clay & Glass Products

CONTACT
F. H. Laube III
President
Freeport Brick Co.
Drawer F
Freeport, PA 16229-0306
(412) 295-2111

FINANCIAL SUMMARY
Recent Giving: $30,930 (1993); $63,600 (1992); $49,506 (1991)

Assets: $588,448 (1993); $872,534 (1992); $930,468 (1991)

EIN: 25-6074334

CONTRIBUTIONS SUMMARY
Typical Recipients: • *Arts & Humanities:* Historic Preservation, Libraries • *Civic & Public Affairs:* Botanical Gardens/Parks, Law & Justice, Municipalities/Towns, Safety, Urban & Community Affairs, Zoos/Aquariums • *Education:* Student Aid • *Health:* Emergency/Ambulance Services, Health Organizations, Hospitals, Medical Research, Single-Disease Health Associations • *Social Services:* Community Service Organizations, Crime Prevention, Food/Clothing Distribution, Recreation & Athletics, Senior Services, United Funds/United Ways, Youth Organizations

Grant Types: general support

Geographic Distribution: focus on Freeport, PA

Operating Locations: PA (Freeport)

CORP. OFFICERS
F. H. Laube III: *CURR EMPL* pres: Freeport Brick Co

Edward L. Straughn: *CURR EMPL* pres: Freeport Brick Co

GIVING OFFICERS
F. H. Laube III: chmn *CURR EMPL* pres: Freeport Brick Co (see above)

Harry R. Laube: asst secy, asst treas

J. Terry Medovitch: treas

J. C. Overholt: vchmn, dir

APPLICATION INFORMATION
Initial Approach: The foundation requests applications be made in writing. There are no deadlines.

GRANTS ANALYSIS
Total Grants: $30,930

Number of Grants: 8*

Highest Grant: $25,000

Typical Range: $500 to $1,000

Disclosure Period: 1993

Note: Recent grants are derived from a 1993 Form 990. Number of grants figure does not include miscellaneous grants under $500.

RECENT GRANTS
Library
1,000   Freeport Area Library Association, Freeport, PA

General
25,000   Freeport Community Park Corporation, Freeport, PA — community recreation
1,000   Freeport Volunteer Fire department, Freeport, PA
1,000   Pennsylvania State Police, Kittanning, PA — youth education
1,000   Pittsburgh Youth Golf Foundation, Pittsburgh, PA — youth recreation
500   Armstrong Health and Education Foundation, Armstrong, PA — medical facility

Gershman Foundation, Joel

CONTACT
Joel Gershman
President
Joel Gershman Fdn.
1027 Pheasant Rd.
Rydal, PA 19046
(215) 923-9476

FINANCIAL SUMMARY
Recent Giving: $21,625 (fiscal 1993); $193,790 (fiscal 1992); $126,549 (fiscal 1991)

Assets: $3,644,987 (fiscal 1993); $3,555,041 (fiscal 1992); $3,613,268 (fiscal 1991)

EIN: 22-2529629

CONTRIBUTIONS SUMMARY

Donor(s): Joel Gershman

Typical Recipients: • *Arts & Humanities:* Arts Centers, Arts Institutes, Community Arts, Ethnic & Folk Arts, Historic Preservation, History & Archaeology, Libraries, Museums/Galleries, Music • *Civic & Public Affairs:* Botanical Gardens/Parks, Clubs, General, Public Policy, Urban & Community Affairs • *Education:* Arts/Humanities Education, Colleges & Universities • *Health:* AIDS/HIV, Cancer, Geriatric Health, Heart, Hospitals, Single-Disease Health Associations • *International:* International Affairs, Missionary/Religious Activities • *Religion:* Jewish Causes, Religious Organizations • *Social Services:* Community Centers, Community Service Organizations, Day Care, Delinquency & Criminal Rehabilitation, Family Planning, Family Services, Homes, Recreation & Athletics, Senior Services, United Funds/United Ways

Grant Types: general support

Geographic Distribution: focus on Philadelphia, PA

GIVING OFFICERS

Joel Gershman: pres

Philip Sheikman: secy, treas

APPLICATION INFORMATION

Initial Approach: The foundation has no formal grant application procedure or application form. There are no deadlines.

GRANTS ANALYSIS

Total Grants: $21,625

Number of Grants: 35

Highest Grant: $2,500

Typical Range: $10 to $2,500

Disclosure Period: fiscal year ending November 30, 1993

Note: Recent grants are derived from a fiscal 1993 Form 990.

RECENT GRANTS

General

2,225	Academy of Music, Philadelphia, PA
2,000	Variety Club of Philadelphia, Philadelphia, PA — Heart of the Variety Fund
1,000	Cornell University, Ithaca, NY
1,000	Friends of Rittenhouse Square, Philadelphia, PA
1,000	Les Dames d' Aspen, Limited, Aspen, CO

Giant Eagle, Inc. / Giant Eagle Foundation

Sales: $1.17 billion
Employees: 9,000
Headquarters: Pittsburgh, PA
SIC Major Group: Grocery Stores and Wholesale Trade—Nondurable Goods

CONTACT

Victoria Clites
Administrator
Giant Eagle Foundation
101 Kappa Dr.
Pittsburgh, PA 15238
(412) 963-6200

FINANCIAL SUMMARY

Recent Giving: $900,000 (fiscal 1995 est.); $820,000 (fiscal 1994 approx.); $798,827 (fiscal 1993)

Assets: $3,955,585 (fiscal 1994); $4,148,007 (fiscal 1993); $4,553,997 (fiscal 1992)

Gifts Received: $328,000 (fiscal 1991)

Fiscal Note: Above figures reflect both foundation and direct giving. In fiscal 1994, $335,013 was given through the foundation. Above figures exclude nonmonetary support. In fiscal 1991, contributions were received from Giant Eagle, Inc.

EIN: 25-6033905

CONTRIBUTIONS SUMMARY

Typical Recipients: • *Arts & Humanities:* Arts Centers, Arts Institutes, Ballet, Community Arts, Dance, History & Archaeology, Libraries, Museums/Galleries, Music, Opera, Performing Arts, Theater • *Civic & Public Affairs:* African American Affairs, Civil Rights, Clubs, Economic Development, Economic Policy, General, Law & Justice, Legal Aid, Municipalities/Towns, Philanthropic Organizations, Urban & Community Affairs, Women's Affairs, Zoos/Aquariums • *Education:* Business Education, Colleges & Universities, Education Funds, Elementary Education (Private), Faculty Development, Minority Education, Private Education (Precollege), Religious Education, Student Aid • *Environment:* General, Resource Conservation • *Health:* AIDS/HIV, Cancer, Children's Health/Hospitals, Emergency/Ambulance Services, Geriatric Health, Health Organizations, Hospitals, Kidney, Medical Rehabilitation, Medical Research, Prenatal Health Issues, Single-Disease Health Associations • *International:* International Organizations, Missionary/Religious Activities • *Religion:* Jewish Causes, Religious Organizations, Religious Welfare, Social/Policy Issues, Synagogues/Temples • *Science:* Scientific Centers & Institutes, Scientific Research • *Social Services:* At-Risk Youth, Big Brother/Big Sister, Child Welfare, Community Centers, Community Service Organizations, Counseling, Delinquency & Criminal Rehabilitation, Domestic Violence, Family Services, Food/Clothing Distribution, People with Disabilities, Recreation & Athlet-

ics, Scouts, Senior Services, Shelters/Homelessness, United Funds/United Ways, Youth Organizations

Grant Types: general support and research

Geographic Distribution: emphasis on Pittsburgh, PA

Operating Locations: PA (Pittsburgh)

CORP. OFFICERS

Irwin W. Porter: *B* 1912 *CURR EMPL* chmn: Giant Eagle Inc

David S. Shapira: *B* 1941 *ED* Oberlin Coll BA 1964; Stanford Univ MA 1966 *CURR EMPL* ceo, pres, dir: Giant Eagle Inc *CORP AFFIL* chmn, dir: Phar-Mor Inc; dir: Action Indus, Bell Telephone Co PA, Equitable Resources, Mellon Bank Corp; pres: Tamarkin Co Inc *PHIL AFFIL* trust: Action Industries Charitable Foundation, David S. and Karen A. Shapira Charitable Trust

GIVING OFFICERS

Gerald Chait: trust

Victoria Clites: admin

Stanley Moravitz: trust

Donald Plung: trust

Irwin W. Porter: trust *CURR EMPL* chmn: Giant Eagle Inc (see above)

David S. Shapira: trust *CURR EMPL* ceo, pres, dir: Giant Eagle Inc *PHIL AFFIL* trust: Action Industries Charitable Foundation, David S. and Karen A. Shapira Charitable Trust (see above)

Norman Weizenbaum: trust

APPLICATION INFORMATION

Initial Approach: *Initial Contact:* written proposal *Include Information On:* a description of organization, amount requested, purpose of funds sought, recently audited financial statement, and proof of tax-exempt status *Deadlines:* none

Restrictions on Giving: Does not support individuals or non 501(c)(3) organizations.

GRANTS ANALYSIS

Total Grants: $335,013

Number of Grants: 102

Highest Grant: $25,000

Average Grant: $3,284

Typical Range: $500 to $5,000

Disclosure Period: fiscal year ending August 31, 1994

Note: Figures represent foundation giving only. Recent grants are derived from a fiscal 1994 Form 990.

RECENT GRANTS

General

33,333	Jewish National Fund, Pittsburgh, PA
33,333	Jewish National Fund, Pittsburgh, PA —for first installment of a three-year pledge
25,000	Allegheny Conference on Community Development, Pittsburgh, PA
10,000	Friends of Israel Disabled War Veterans, New York, NY

821

10,000 —for final installment of a five-year pledge
Salvation Army, Pittsburgh, PA —for first installment of a five-year pledge

Giant Food Stores

Sales: $1.1 billion
Employees: 9,400
Parent Company: Ahold N.V.
Headquarters: Carlisle, PA
SIC Major Group: Food Stores

CONTACT
Sue Simmons
Contributions Coordinator
Giant Food Stores
PO Box 249
Carlisle, PA 17013
(717) 249-4000 Ext. 342

FINANCIAL SUMMARY
Fiscal Note: Annual Giving Range: $50,000 to $150,000

CONTRIBUTIONS SUMMARY
Giant Food Stores' highest priority is the support of life-sustaining charities. The company also supports other needs of the community, including both cultural and civic affairs.

Typical Recipients: • *Arts & Humanities:* Arts Associations & Councils, Historic Preservation, Libraries, Public Broadcasting • *Civic & Public Affairs:* Business/Free Enterprise, Civil Rights, Economic Development, Law & Justice, Municipalities/Towns, Safety, Urban & Community Affairs, Women's Affairs • *Education:* Colleges & Universities, Literacy, Minority Education, Student Aid • *Environment:* General • *Health:* Health Funds, Health Organizations, Hospitals, Medical Research, Mental Health, Single-Disease Health Associations • *Religion:* Religious Organizations • *Social Services:* Child Welfare, Community Centers, Community Service Organizations, Domestic Violence, Family Services, People with Disabilities, Senior Services, Substance Abuse, United Funds/United Ways, Youth Organizations

Grant Types: capital, general support, and seed money

Nonmonetary Support Types: donated equipment and donated products

Geographic Distribution: near headquarters and operating locations only

Operating Locations: MD, PA (Carlisle), VA, WV

CORP. OFFICERS
Allen Noddle: *CURR EMPL* pres, dir: Giant Food Stores

GIVING OFFICERS
Sue Simmons: *CURR EMPL* contributions coordinator: Giant Food Stores

APPLICATION INFORMATION
Initial Approach: Initial contact may be by letter or proposal at any time. Applications should include a description of the organization, amount requested, and purpose for which funds are sought; a recently audited financial statement and proof of tax-exempt status occasionally are requested.

OTHER THINGS TO KNOW
Does not support political or lobbying groups.

Giant Food Stores makes contributions to United Way agencies in each of the localities where it does business. It also supports some capital campaigns for participating agencies, but generally does not support United Way member agencies. Giant's local stores are free to support local individual fund-raising activities at the store manager's discretion and as limited by the individual store's budget.

Glosser Foundation, David A.

CONTACT
Lester Edelstein
President
David A. Glosser Fdn.
72 Messenger St.
Johnstown, PA 15902
(814) 535-7521

FINANCIAL SUMMARY
Recent Giving: $101,100 (fiscal 1994); $116,032 (fiscal 1993); $117,865 (fiscal 1992)

Assets: $2,311,169 (fiscal 1994); $2,390,103 (fiscal 1993); $2,368,558 (fiscal 1992)

EIN: 25-6066913

CONTRIBUTIONS SUMMARY
Donor(s): the late David A. Glosser

Typical Recipients: • *Arts & Humanities:* Arts Centers, Community Arts, History & Archaeology, Libraries, Museums/Galleries, Music, Performing Arts, Theater • *Civic & Public Affairs:* Community Foundations, Women's Affairs • *Education:* Education Funds, Preschool Education, Private Education (Precollege), Public Education (Precollege), Religious Education, Secondary Education (Public), Special Education, Student Aid • *Health:* Heart, Hospices, Multiple Sclerosis, Single-Disease Health Associations • *International:* Missionary/Religious Activities • *Religion:* Jewish Causes, Religious Organizations, Religious Welfare, Synagogues/Temples • *Social Services:* Child Welfare, Community Centers, Community Service Organizations, Delinquency & Criminal Rehabilitation, Family Planning, Scouts, Senior Services, United Funds/United Ways, YMCA/YWCA/YMHA/YWHA, Youth Organizations

Grant Types: general support

Geographic Distribution: focus on Johnstown, PA

GIVING OFFICERS
Lester Edelstein: pres, secy
Milton Friedman: dir
Lester Goldstein: dir
Robert Krantzer: treas

APPLICATION INFORMATION
Initial Approach: Send brief letter of inquiry describing program. Include a description of organization, amount requested, purpose of funds sought, recently audited financial statement, and proof of tax-exempt status. There are no deadlines.

Restrictions on Giving: Limited to charitable organizations in Pennsylvania.

GRANTS ANALYSIS
Total Grants: $101,100

Number of Grants: 32

Highest Grant: $70,000

Typical Range: $50 to $10,000

Disclosure Period: fiscal year ending June 30, 1994

Note: Recent grants are derived from a fiscal 1994 Form 990.

RECENT GRANTS

Library

10,000	David A. Glosser Memorial Library, Johnstown, PA
200	Beaverdale Public Library, Beaverdale, PA
200	Windber Public Library, Windber, PA

General

70,000	United Jewish Appeal Federation, Johnstown, PA
10,000	United Jewish Appeal Federation, Johnstown, PA — Soviet immigration
2,000	Beginnings Child Early Intervention, Johnstown, PA
2,000	Johnstown Central High School, Johnstown, PA
1,000	Beth Sholom Congregation, Johnstown, PA

Groome Beatty Trust, Helen D.

CONTACT
Patricia M. Kling
Trustee
Helen D. Groome Beatty Trust
c/o Mellon Bank
PO Box 7236
Philadelphia, PA 19101
(215) 553-3208

FINANCIAL SUMMARY
Recent Giving: $339,695 (fiscal 1992); $309,729 (fiscal 1990); $205,854 (fiscal 1989)

Assets: $6,848,972 (fiscal 1992); $5,451,492 (fiscal 1990); $5,660,379 (fiscal 1989)

Gifts Received: $2,002 (fiscal 1992)

Fiscal Note: In 1992, contributions were received from Helen Beatty Trust.

EIN: 23-6224798

CONTRIBUTIONS SUMMARY

Donor(s): Helen D. Groome Beatty

Typical Recipients: • *Arts & Humanities:* Arts Associations & Councils, Arts Centers, Community Arts, Historic Preservation, History & Archaeology, Libraries, Museums/Galleries, Music, Theater • *Civic & Public Affairs:* General, Housing, Public Policy • *Education:* Colleges & Universities, Public Education (Precollege) • *Environment:* General • *Health:* Home-Care Services, Hospitals, Long-Term Care, Nursing Services • *Religion:* Jewish Causes, Religious Organizations • *Science:* Scientific Centers & Institutes • *Social Services:* Child Welfare, Community Service Organizations, Domestic Violence, Homes, People with Disabilities, Senior Services, Shelters/Homelessness, United Funds/United Ways, Youth Organizations

Grant Types: capital

Geographic Distribution: focus on the Philadelphia, PA, metropolitan area

APPLICATION INFORMATION

Initial Approach: Send cover letter and full proposal. Deadline is April 15.

Restrictions on Giving: Does not support individuals.

PUBLICATIONS

Application Guidelines

GRANTS ANALYSIS

Total Grants: $339,695

Number of Grants: 131

Highest Grant: $10,375

Typical Range: $1,000 to $4,000

Disclosure Period: fiscal year ending September 30, 1992

Note: Recent grants are derived from a fiscal 1992 Form 990.

RECENT GRANTS

Library

3,000	Athenaeum, Philadelphia, PA
2,000	David Library of the America Revolution, Washington Crossing, PA

General

10,375	Jewish Federation of Greater Philadelphia, Philadelphia, PA
7,020	White/Williams Foundation, Philadelphia, PA
3,000	Academy of Natural Sciences, Philadelphia, PA
3,000	Big Sisters of Philadelphia, Philadelphia, PA
3,000	Friends Hospital, Philadelphia, PA

Grundy Foundation

CONTACT

Roland H. Johnson
Executive Director
Grundy Foundation
680 Radcliffe St.
PO Box 701
Bristol, PA 19007
(215) 788-5460

FINANCIAL SUMMARY

Recent Giving: $711,863 (1994); $773,614 (1993); $824,547 (1991)

Assets: $45,240,431 (1993); $42,761,003 (1991); $37,096,271 (1990)

Gifts Received: $35,104 (1993)

Fiscal Note: In 1993, the foundation received gifts from the Johnson Fund.

EIN: 23-1609243

CONTRIBUTIONS SUMMARY

Donor(s): The foundation was established in 1961 pursuant to the will of the late Joseph Ridgeway Grundy . Mr. Grundy was president of Grundy and Company (a linen manufacturer) and the Farmers National Bank of Bucks county. He was also appointed by the governor of Pennsylvania to an unexpired term in the U.S. Senate (1929-1930).

Typical Recipients: • *Arts & Humanities:* Arts Outreach, Ethnic & Folk Arts, Historic Preservation, History & Archaeology, Libraries, Museums/Galleries, Music, Theater • *Civic & Public Affairs:* Economic Development, Housing, Municipalities/Towns, Urban & Community Affairs • *Education:* Community & Junior Colleges, Education Funds, Preschool Education, Public Education (Precollege), Secondary Education (Public), Student Aid • *Environment:* General, Resource Conservation • *Health:* Cancer, Children's Health/Hospitals, Hospitals, Long-Term Care, Respiratory • *Social Services:* Community Service Organizations, Crime Prevention, Family Planning, Family Services, Food/Clothing Distribution, Homes, People with Disabilities, Recreation & Athletics, Scouts, Shelters/Homelessness, Substance Abuse, United Funds/United Ways, YMCA/YWCA/YMHA/YWHA, Youth Organizations

Grant Types: capital and project

Geographic Distribution: Bucks County, PA

GIVING OFFICERS

James M. Gassaway: trust

Roland H. Johnson: exec dir

John Knoell: trust

Leonard N. Snyder: trust

William Philler Wood: trust *B* Bryn Mawr PA 1927 *ED* Harvard Univ AB 1949; Harvard Univ JD 1955 *NONPR AFFIL* chmn exec comm: Philadelphia Mus Art *CLUB AFFIL* Knickerbocker, State In Schuykill *PHIL AFFIL* trust, secy: Louis L. Stott Foundation

APPLICATION INFORMATION

Initial Approach:

There are no application forms; a brief letter will suffice.

Applicants should outline the need for the grant. Additional information will be requested if necessary.

There are no deadlines for submitting requests.

Trustees meet monthly, except in August, to approve grants.

Restrictions on Giving: The foundation does not make grants to individuals, religious organizations for sectarian purposes, or political or lobbying groups.

OTHER THINGS TO KNOW

The foundation operates a museum and a library. Fidelity Bank is listed as a corporate trustee of the foundation.

GRANTS ANALYSIS

Total Grants: $773,614

Number of Grants: 48

Highest Grant: $100,000

Average Grant: $16,117

Typical Range: $2,500 to $30,000

Disclosure Period: 1993

Note: Recent grants are derived from a 1993 Form 990.

RECENT GRANTS

General

100,000	United Way of Bucks County, Fairless Hills, PA — core grant and challenge grant for Annual Fund Drive
50,000	Better Homes, Inc. of Bucks County, Bristol, PA — purchase and rehabilitate low-income housing (Towpath Apartments) in Morrisville
50,000	Bucks County Association of Retired and Senior Citizens, Bristol, PA — repairs to kitchen and dining room of Lower Bucks Activity Center
50,000	Lower Bucks Hospital, Bristol, PA — capital campaign; hospital expansion
36,000	Borough of Bristol, CZM, Bristol, PA — rehabilitate Mill Street Wharf structure

GSM Industrial / Gooding Group Foundation

Sales: $7.36 million
Employees: 85
Headquarters: Ephrata, PA
SIC Major Group: Fabricated Metal Products

CONTACT

John s. Gooding
GSM Industrial
345 S Reading Rd.
Ephrata, PA 17522
(717) 733-1241

FINANCIAL SUMMARY

Recent Giving: $14,850 (1993); $12,635 (1991)

Assets: $83,333 (1993); $55,870 (1991)

Gifts Received: $18,000 (1993)

Fiscal Note: In 1993, contributions were received from GSM Industrial ($12,000) and Gooding, Simpson, and Mackes ($6,000).

EIN: 23-2516754

CONTRIBUTIONS SUMMARY

Typical Recipients: • *Arts & Humanities:* Historic Preservation, Libraries, Museums/Galleries, Opera • *Civic & Public Affairs:* Employment/Job Training, General, Hispanic Affairs, Housing, Safety • *Education:* Business Education, Colleges & Universities, Secondary Education (Private), Student Aid, Vocational & Technical Education • *Health:* Cancer, Children's Health/Hospitals, Emergency/Ambulance Services, Heart, Hospices, Hospitals, Nursing Services • *Religion:* Bible Study/Translation, Churches, Religious Welfare • *Social Services:* Big Brother/Big Sister, Child Abuse, Day Care, Family Planning, Family Services, People with Disabilities, Recreation & Athletics, Scouts, United Funds/United Ways, YMCA/YWCA/YMHA/YWHA, Youth Organizations

Grant Types: general support

Geographic Distribution: focus on PA

CORP. OFFICERS

John S. Gooding: *CURR EMPL* chmn, dir: GSM Industrial

GIVING OFFICERS

Robert E. Burkholder: secy, treas

John S. Gooding: pres *CURR EMPL* chmn, dir: GSM Industrial (see above)

James K. Towers III: vp *CURR EMPL* pres, dir: GSM Industrial

APPLICATION INFORMATION

Initial Approach: Send a brief letter of inquiry. There are no deadlines.

GRANTS ANALYSIS

Total Grants: $14,850

Number of Grants: 48

Highest Grant: $2,000

Typical Range: $25 to $500

Disclosure Period: 1993

Note: Recent grants are derived from a 1993 Form 990.

RECENT GRANTS

Library
1,500   Ephrata Public Library, Ephrata, PA

General
2,000   Planned Parenthood, Lancaster, PA
1,500   St. Joseph Hospital Foundation, Lancaster, PA
1,030   Goldey Beacon College, Wilmington, DE

625   Martin Luther King, Jr. Memorial Scholarship, Lancaster, PA
525   American Cancer Society, Lancaster, PA

Hamilton Bank / Hamilton Bank Foundation

Employees: 1,350
Parent Company: CoreStates Financial Corp.
Headquarters: Lancaster, PA
SIC Major Group: National Commercial Banks

CONTACT

Eloise Aurand
Director Public Relations
Hamilton Bank Foundation
PO Box 3959
Lancaster, PA 17604
(717) 291-3508

FINANCIAL SUMMARY

Recent Giving: $650,000 (1995 est.); $650,000 (1994 approx.); $643,253 (1993)

Assets: $110,826 (1993); $106,514 (1992); $97,737 (1991)

Gifts Received: $636,100 (1993); $561,400 (1992); $553,262 (1989)

Fiscal Note: Contribution are received from Hamilton Bank.

EIN: 23-6444555

CONTRIBUTIONS SUMMARY

Typical Recipients: • *Arts & Humanities:* Arts Associations & Councils, Arts Centers, Arts Funds, Historic Preservation, Libraries, Museums/Galleries, Music, Opera, Performing Arts, Theater • *Civic & Public Affairs:* Civil Rights, Economic Development, Ethnic Organizations, Housing, Urban & Community Affairs • *Education:* Business Education, Colleges & Universities, Community & Junior Colleges, Education Associations, Minority Education, Private Education (Precollege), Religious Education, Student Aid • *Environment:* General • *Health:* Children's Health/Hospitals, Emergency/Ambulance Services, Hospices, Hospitals, Medical Research, Mental Health, Nursing Services, Single-Disease Health Associations • *Religion:* Churches, Missionary Activities (Domestic), Religious Organizations, Religious Welfare • *Science:* Science Museums • *Social Services:* Child Welfare, Community Service Organizations, Family Services, Homes, People with Disabilities, United Funds/United Ways, Youth Organizations

Grant Types: capital, employee matching gifts, general support, loan, multiyear/continuing support, operating expenses, project, and scholarship

Geographic Distribution: limited to Berks, Cumberland, Dauphin, Lancaster, Lebanon, and York counties, PA

Operating Locations: PA (Harrisburg, Lancaster, Lebanon, Reading, York)

CORP. OFFICERS

Paul Aupperle: *CURR EMPL* vp fin, cfo: Hamilton Bank

Eloise C. Aurand: *CURR EMPL* dir publ rels: Hamilton Bank

GIVING OFFICERS

Eloise C. Aurand: alternative contact person *CURR EMPL* dir publ rels: Hamilton Bank (see above)

APPLICATION INFORMATION

Initial Approach: *Initial Contact:* submit letter and completed questionnaire to Area Executive Officer; forms for questionnaires may be obtained by contacting local Area Executive Officer (see "Other Things You Should Know") *Deadlines:* no later than the Thursday prior to Board of Directors meeting; meetings are held on the second Monday of February, May, September, and November

Restrictions on Giving: Does not support organizations that do not have IRS 501(c)(3) status; veterans groups or fraternal orders; labor groups; political parties or candidates; individual churches or congregations; groups that contribute to areas outside of bank's operations; organizations which spend exorbitant amounts of money on fundraising, administration, and distribution; or campaigns conducted by religious denominations.

OTHER THINGS TO KNOW

Company publishes a community report, and has a printed list of guidelines available.

Area Executive Officers are at the following locations: Berks County- Robert A. Rupel, 515 Penn Street, Reading, PA, 19603-3410, (215) 320-8120; Cumberland and Dauphin Counties- James R. Adair, 222 Market Street, Harrisburg, PA, 17101-2117, (717) 234-2799; Lancaster County- Thomas H. Bamford, 100 North Queen Street, Lancaster, PA 17603-3834, (717) 291-3508; Lebanon County- Merritt J. Marks, Eighth and Cumberland Streets, Lebanon, PA 17042, (717) 274-1471; York County- Harry R. Zimmerman, 12 East Market Street, York, PA 17401-1206, (717) 771-5235.

Hamilton Bank acts as a corporate trustee.

GRANTS ANALYSIS

Total Grants: $643,253

Number of Grants: 166

Highest Grant: $60,525

Average Grant: $3,875

Typical Range: $500 to $10,000

Disclosure Period: 1993

Note: Recent grants are derived from a 1993 Form 990.

RECENT GRANTS

General
60,525   United Way, Lancaster, PA
42,500   United Way Berks, Reading, PA
40,350   United Way, York, PA
31,600   Tri-County United Way, Harrisburg, PA
16,750   United Way, Lebanon, PA

Harsco Corp. / Harsco Corp. Fund

Sales: $1.4 billion
Employees: 12,900
Headquarters: Camp Hill, PA
SIC Major Group: Valves & Pipe Fittings Nec, Asphalt Felts & Coatings, Minerals—Ground or Treated, and Truck & Bus Bodies

CONTACT
Robert G. Yocum
Secretary
Harsco Corp. Fund
PO Box 8888
Camp Hill, PA 17001-8888
(717) 763-7064

FINANCIAL SUMMARY
Recent Giving: $554,610 (1993); $539,575 (1992); $552,152 (1991)

Assets: $9,183,173 (1993); $9,101,044 (1992); $8,657,210 (1991)

Fiscal Note: Company gives through fund only.

EIN: 23-6278376

CONTRIBUTIONS SUMMARY
Typical Recipients: • *Arts & Humanities:* Arts Associations & Councils, Arts Centers, Community Arts, Dance, Historic Preservation, Libraries, Museums/Galleries, Music, Opera, Performing Arts, Public Broadcasting, Theater • *Civic & Public Affairs:* African American Affairs, Business/Free Enterprise, Civil Rights, Economic Development, Economic Policy, Employment/Job Training, Law & Justice, Legal Aid, Philanthropic Organizations, Professional & Trade Associations, Public Policy, Safety, Urban & Community Affairs • *Education:* Arts/Humanities Education, Business Education, Colleges & Universities, Community & Junior Colleges, Economic Education, Education Associations, Education Funds, General, Medical Education, Minority Education, Public Education (Precollege), Religious Education, Science/Mathematics Education, Student Aid • *Health:* Children's Health/Hospitals, Emergency/Ambulance Services, Health Organizations, Hospices, Hospitals, Medical Research, Mental Health, Single-Disease Health Associations • *Religion:* Religious Welfare • *Social Services:* Community Centers, Community Service Organizations, Day Care, Emergency Relief, Family Planning, Food/Clothing Distribution, Homes, People with Disabilities, Recreation & Athletics, Sexual Abuse, Shelters/Homelessness, Substance Abuse, United Funds/United Ways, Volunteer Services, Youth Organizations

Grant Types: capital, department, employee matching gifts, general support, research, and scholarship

Geographic Distribution: near headquarters and operating locations only

Operating Locations: AL (Birmingham, Leeds, Theodore), CA (Los Angeles, Madera, Pomona), CT (Hamden), FL (Plant City, Tampa), GA (Decatur, Jessup), IA (Bloom-

field, Des Moines), IL (Chicago, Elmhurst), IN (Gary, Highland), KY (Drakesboro), LA (Crowley), MA (Fitchburg), MD (Baltimore), MN (Fairmont), NC (Charlotte), NJ (Clark, Fort Lee, Union), NY (Lockport, Long Island City, New York), OH (Carlisle, Cleveland, Columbus, Kenton, Lansing, Marion, Marysville, West Jefferson), OK (Tulsa), PA (Butler, Camp Hill, Cheswick, East Stroudsburg, Harrisburg, York), SC (West Columbia), TN (Nashville), TX (Channelview, Houston, Mineral Wells), UT (West Jordan), WV (Moundsville)

Note: Also operates internationally; has over 270 facilities domestically and abroad.

CORP. OFFICERS
Derek C. Hathaway: *B* 1944 *ED* Aston Univ BS 1965 *CURR EMPL* chmn, pres, ceo: Harsco Corp

GIVING OFFICERS
Leonard A. Campanaro: treas *B* Philadelphia PA 1948 *ED* Temple Univ BBA 1970 *CURR EMPL* sr vp fin, cfo: Harsco Corp

Malcolm W. Gambill: pres, trust *B* Crumpler NC 1930

Derek C. Hathaway: vp, trust *CURR EMPL* chmn, pres, ceo: Harsco Corp (see above)

Robert F. Nation: trust *CORP AFFIL* dir: Harsco Corp *PHIL AFFIL* pres, dir: Josiah W. and Bessie H. Kline Foundation

Robert G. Yocum: secy

APPLICATION INFORMATION
Initial Approach: *Initial Contact:* brief letter or proposal; organizations in company operating locations should contact local divisions directly *Include Information On:* description of the organization, amount requested, purpose for which funds are sought, recently audited financial statement, proof of tax-exempt status *Deadlines:* none

Restrictions on Giving: Does not support dinners or special events, fraternal organizations, goodwill advertising, political or lobbying groups, religious organizations for sectarian purposes, or individuals.

The fund seldom makes grants to organizations with limited purposes or for special projects that do not receive wide public support.

GRANTS ANALYSIS
Total Grants: $554,610

Number of Grants: 98

Highest Grant: $131,690

Average Grant: $5,659

Typical Range: $100 to $6,000

Disclosure Period: 1993

Note: Recent grants are derived from a 1993 Form 990.

RECENT GRANTS
General
131,690	National Merit Scholarship Corporation, Evanston, IL
99,335	United Way
22,800	Goodwill Industries, Tulsa, OK
14,500	Pennsylvania Foundation for Independent Colleges, Harrisburg, PA
11,000	Bethesda Mission, Harrisburg, PA

Heinz Company, H. J. / Heinz Company Foundation, H. J.

Revenue: $7.04 billion
Employees: 37,700
Headquarters: Pittsburgh, PA
SIC Major Group: Canned Specialties, Canned Fruits & Vegetables, Frozen Specialties Nec, and Food Preparations Nec

CONTACT
Loretta M. Oken
Manager
H.J. Heinz Co. Fdn.
PO Box 57
Pittsburgh, PA 15230
(412) 456-5772

FINANCIAL SUMMARY
Recent Giving: $6,000,000 (1995 est.); $6,100,000 (1994 approx.); $6,159,311 (1993)

Assets: $3,210,404 (1993); $3,139,519 (1992); $3,752,020 (1991)

Gifts Received: $6,141,973 (1993); $5,103,015 (1992); $5,122,419 (1991)

Fiscal Note: All contributions are made through the foundation. In 1993, the foundation received $6,000,000 from the H.J. Heinz Company and $141,973 from various individuals.

EIN: 25-6018924

CONTRIBUTIONS SUMMARY
Typical Recipients: • *Arts & Humanities:* Arts Associations & Councils, Arts Centers, Arts Festivals, Arts Outreach, Ballet, Dance, Historic Preservation, History & Archaeology, Libraries, Literary Arts, Museums/Galleries, Music, Opera, Performing Arts, Public Broadcasting, Theater • *Civic & Public Affairs:* African American Affairs, Business/Free Enterprise, Civil Rights, Community Foundations, Economic Development, Economic Policy, Employment/Job Training, General, Housing, Law & Justice, Legal Aid, Professional & Trade Associations, Public Policy, Rural Affairs, Safety, Urban & Community Affairs, Women's Affairs, Zoos/Aquariums • *Education:* Agricultural Education, Arts/Humanities Education, Business Education, Colleges & Universities, Community & Junior Colleges, Continuing Education, Economic Education, Education Associations, Education Funds, General, Health & Physical Education, International Exchange, International Studies, Journalism/Media Education, Legal Education, Literacy, Medical Education, Minority Education, Private Education (Precollege), Public Education (Precollege), Religious Education, Science/Mathematics Education, Secondary Education (Private), Special Education, Student Aid • *Environment:* General • *Health:* AIDS/HIV, Children's Health/Hospitals, Health Organizations, Home-Care

Services, Hospices, Hospitals, Medical Rehabilitation, Medical Research, Nutrition, Single-Disease Health Associations
• *International:* Foreign Educational Institutions, Health Care/Hospitals, International Affairs, International Development, International Organizations, International Peace & Security Issues, International Relations, International Relief Efforts • *Religion:* Religious Organizations, Religious Welfare • *Science:* Scientific Organizations • *Social Services:* Animal Protection, Child Welfare, Community Centers, Community Service Organizations, Counseling, Delinquency & Criminal Rehabilitation, Family Planning, Family Services, Homes, People with Disabilities, Recreation & Athletics, Senior Services, Substance Abuse, United Funds/United Ways, Volunteer Services, Youth Organizations

Grant Types: capital, challenge, conference/seminar, employee matching gifts, endowment, fellowship, general support, project, and scholarship

Note: Foundation gives to scholarship funds only and does not give individual scholarships.

Geographic Distribution: where company maintains facilities

Operating Locations: AR (Clarksville), CA (Bakersfield, Chatsworth, Escalon, Long Beach, Stockton, Terminal Island, Torrance, Tracy), CT (Wethersfield), FL (Ft. Myers), IA (Keokuk, Muscatine), ID (Boise, Burley, Pocatello), KS (Lenexa), MI (Holland), MN (Perham), MS (Biloxi), NC (Charlotte), NE (Grand Island), NJ (Blackwood, Bridgeport), NY (Buffalo, Jericho, Long Island, Manhasset, New York), OH (Freemont, Mason, Massillon, Richfield, Washington Courthouse), OK (Vinita), OR (Eugene, Ontario), PA (Bloomsburg, Chambersburg, King of Prussia, Pittsburgh, West Chester), PR (Mayaguez), TX (Dallas, El Paso), VA (Winchester), WA (Spokane), WI (Ft. Atkinson, Plover, Rice Lake), WV (Weirton)

CORP. OFFICERS

Anthony John Francis O'Reilly: *B* Dublin Ireland 1936 *ED* Univ Bradford; Univ Coll Dublin *CURR EMPL* chmn, ceo, pres, dir: H J Heinz Co *CORP AFFIL* chmn: Atlantic Resources, Fitzwilton PLC, Independent Newspapers PLC; dir: Bankers Trust NY Corp, NY Stock Exchange, Ore-Ida Foods Inc, Star-Kist Foods, Washington Post Co; ptnr: Cawley Sheerin Wynne & Co *NONPR AFFIL* bd govs: Hugh OBrian Youth Fdn; chmn: Am Irish Fnd; chmn, ceo counc: Intl Life Sci Inst Nutrition Fdn; counc: Irish Mgmt Inst; dir: Exec Counc Foreign Diplomats, Georgetown Univ, Harvard Univ Grad Sch Bus Admin Assocs; fellow: British Inst Mgmt, Royal Soc Arts; mem: Inst Dirs Inc; mem counc: Rockefeller Univ; mem natl comm: Whitney Mus Am Art; secy, dir: Grocery Mfrs Am; sr bd dirs: Conf Bd; treas: Law Soc Ireland; trust: Comm Econ Devel, Pittsburgh Ballet Theatre, Univ Pittsburgh *CLUB AFFIL* Allegheny, Annabels, Bd Rm New York City, Duquesne, Fox Chapel GC, Kildare St, Les Ambassadeurs, The Links, Lyford Cay, Marks London, Pittsburgh GC,

Pittsburgh Press, Rolling Rock, St Stephen Green, Union League, Univ Dublin

David R. Williams: *B* London England 1943 *ED* Exeter Univ BA 1964 *CURR EMPL* sr vp fin, cfo, dir: H J Heinz Co *NONPR AFFIL* mem: Assn Chartered Accts UK, Assn Chartered Accts US, Fin Execs Inst

GIVING OFFICERS
Karyll A. Davis: trust

Anthony John Francis O'Reilly: chmn, trust *CURR EMPL* chmn, ceo, pres, dir: H J Heinz Co (see above)

Loretta M. Oken: mgr

S. Donald Wiley: vchmn, trust *B* Pittsburgh PA 1926 *ED* Westminster Coll 1950; Univ PA Sch Law 1953 *PHIL AFFIL* trust: Vira I. Heinz Endowment

David R. Williams: trust *CURR EMPL* sr vp fin, cfo, dir: H J Heinz Co (see above)

APPLICATION INFORMATION
Initial Approach: *Initial Contact:* brief letter or proposal *Include Information On:* description of the organization, amount requested, purpose for which funds are sought, recently audited financial statement, to whom and where program will be offered, how objectives will be accomplished, whether request is for one-time or ongoing project, how program evaluation will be made, list of board of directors, and proof of tax-exempt status *Deadlines:* none; board meets quarterly

Restrictions on Giving: The foundation does not support individuals; general scholarships, fellowships, or travel grants; political campaigns; or sectarian or religious organizations.

OTHER THINGS TO KNOW
The foundation gives priority to united funds, scholarship programs in food-related courses of study, grants for health-related facilities, and contributions to matching gifts programs.

GRANTS ANALYSIS
Total Grants: $6,159,311

Number of Grants: 1,232

Highest Grant: $400,000

Average Grant: $4,999

Typical Range: $100 to $1,000 and $5,000 to $20,000

Disclosure Period: 1993

Note: Recent grants are derived from a 1993 Form 990.

RECENT GRANTS

Library

200,000	Carnegie Institute, Pittsburgh, PA	
91,667	Carnegie Institute, Pittsburgh, PA	
30,000	Carnegie Institute, Pittsburgh, PA	

General

400,000	United Way Southwestern Pennsylvania, Pittsburgh, PA	

200,000	American Ireland Fund, Boston, MA	
200,000	Up With People, Tucson, AZ	
165,000	Carnegie Mellon University, Pittsburgh, PA	
150,000	American Ireland Fund, Boston, MA	

Heinz Endowment, Howard

CONTACT
Frank Tugwell
Executive Director
Howard Heinz Endowment
30 CNG Tower
625 Liberty Ave.
Pittsburgh, PA 15222-3199
(412) 281-5777

FINANCIAL SUMMARY
Recent Giving: $21,049,527 (1993); $22,047,718 (1992); $27,979,459 (1991)

Assets: $551,473,047 (1993); $679,392,746 (1992); $629,894,770 (1991)

EIN: 25-1064784

CONTRIBUTIONS SUMMARY
Donor(s): The endowment was established in 1941 under the provisions of the will of Howard Heinz , whose father, Henry J. Heinz, began the Heinz food processing company. A bequest from Howard Heinz's widow, Mrs. Elizabeth Rust Heinz , added to the foundation's assets in 1952. The late donors' interests are still reflected in the activities of the Heinz Endowment, and the organizations that Mr. Heinz specified in his will continue to receive support.

Typical Recipients: • *Arts & Humanities:* Arts Associations & Councils, Arts Festivals, Arts Institutes, Ballet, Dance, Film & Video, History & Archaeology, Libraries, Museums/Galleries, Music, Opera, Performing Arts, Public Broadcasting, Theater • *Civic & Public Affairs:* Community Foundations, Economic Development, Economic Policy, Employment/Job Training, General, Housing, Municipalities/Towns, Nonprofit Management, Philanthropic Organizations, Professional & Trade Associations, Urban & Community Affairs, Zoos/Aquariums • *Education:* Business Education, Colleges & Universities, Education Associations, Education Funds, Education Reform, Elementary Education (Private), Elementary Education (Public), Faculty Development, International Studies, Literacy, Medical Education, Minority Education, Private Education (Precollege), Public Education (Precollege), Science/Mathematics Education, Secondary Education (Public), Student Aid, Vocational & Technical Education • *Environment:* General • *Health:* Children's Health/Hospitals, Clinics/Medical Centers, Health Policy/Cost Containment, Hospitals, Medical Rehabilitation, Medical Research, Mental Health, Nursing Services, Nutrition, Prenatal Health Issues • *Science:* Scientific Centers & Institutes • *Social Services:* At-Risk Youth, Child Abuse, Child Welfare, Day Care, Domestic Violence, Family Planning, Family Services, Senior Services, Shelters/Homelessness, Substance Abuse, United Funds/United Ways, Volunteer Services, Youth Organizations

Grant Types: capital, endowment, general support, loan, operating expenses, project, and seed money

Geographic Distribution: Pittsburgh and Allegheny County, PA

GIVING OFFICERS
Frank V. Cabonet: trust

Andre T. Heinz: trust

Ann T. Heinz: trust

H. John Heinz IV: trust

Maria Teresa Thierstein Simoes-Ferreira Heinz: trust *B* Mozambique 1938 *ED* Univ Witwatersrand *NONPR AFFIL* chmn: Natl Counc Families & Television; trust: Yale Art Gallery; vchmn: Environmental Defense Fund *CLUB AFFIL* Bohemian, Fox Chapel GC, Pittsburgh GC *PHIL AFFIL* chmn: Heinz Family Foundation; trust: Winslow Foundation; trust, mem nominating comm: Carnegie Corporation of New York

Jack E. Kime: cfo, assoc dir, chief admin off *PHIL AFFIL* assoc dir, cfo, chief admin off: Vira I. Heinz Endowment

Howard McClintic Love: trust *B* Pittsburgh PA 1930 *ED* Colgate Univ 1952; Harvard Univ Grad Sch Bus Admin 1956 *CORP AFFIL* dir: Comsat Corp, Hamilton Oil Corp, Monsanto Co *CLUB AFFIL* Laurel Valley GC

Wendy Jacobus Mackenzie: trust *PHIL AFFIL* secy: Heinz Family Foundation

William H. Rea: trust *B* Pittsburgh PA 1912 *CURR EMPL* dir: Colt Indus Inc *PHIL AFFIL* vchmn: Buhl Foundation; trust: Vira I. Heinz Endowment, Drue Heinz Trust; dir: Robert Gemmill Foundation Trust

Frank Tugwell: exec dir *PHIL AFFIL* exec dir: Vira I. Heinz Endowment

APPLICATION INFORMATION
Initial Approach:

To be considered for a grant, the organization should submit a proposal.

The proposal should describe the need for the program, its objectives, staff and organizational qualifications for carrying it out, and other organizations involved in similar programs and how the proposed program is different. Also include the amount of funding requested, budgets for the organization and the project, the most recent audit, IRS determination letter, and a list of the board of directors.

Applications must be submitted no later than mid-February for spring consideration and mid-September for fall consideration.

The board of trustees meet twice annually, in the late spring and the late fall.

Restrictions on Giving: Grants for individual colleges and universities are limited to those located in Pittsburgh and Allegheny County, PA.

OTHER THINGS TO KNOW
A representative of Mellon Bank serves as a corporate trustee for the endowment.

PUBLICATIONS
Annual report

GRANTS ANALYSIS
Total Grants: $21,049,527

Number of Grants: 154

Highest Grant: $1,494,000

Average Grant: $136,685

Typical Range: $2,000 to $20,000 and $50,000 to $150,000

Disclosure Period: 1993

Note: Recent grants are derived from a 1993 Form 990.

RECENT GRANTS
Library
1,000,000 Carnegie Institute, Pittsburgh, PA — towards the capital campaign Second Century Fund

145,200 Carnegie Library of Pittsburgh, Homewood Branch, Pittsburgh, PA — to expand Project Beacon, an early intervention literacy program targeted to children 0-5

General
1,250,000 Forbes Fund, Pittsburgh, PA — towards the establishment of the Forbes Fund on a permanent basis

725,000 Pittsburgh Partnership for Neighborhood Development, Pittsburgh, PA — operating support

500,000 Heinz Family Foundation, Washington, DC — to provide funding that will be used to establish regional environmental education centers for teacher education

492,939 Children's Hospital of Philadelphia, Philadelphia, PA — to develop and support a clinical post-resident training experience to prepare pediatricians for academic careers in nutrition

400,000 Mon Valley Initiative, Homestead, PA — renewal of operating support

Heinz Endowment, Vira I.

CONTACT
Frank Tugwell
Executive Director
Vira I. Heinz Endowment
30 CNG Tower
625 Liberty Ave.
Pittsburgh, PA 15222
(412) 281-5777

FINANCIAL SUMMARY
Recent Giving: $10,439,119 (1993); $13,500,448 (1992); $6,715,326 (1991)

Assets: $276,609,256 (1993); $340,924,039 (1992); $314,919,993 (1991)

Gifts Received: $76,740,755 (1987); $3,871,097 (1985)

Fiscal Note: In 1987, the endowment received $76,740,755 from the estate of Vira I. Heinz.

EIN: 25-6235878

CONTRIBUTIONS SUMMARY
Donor(s): The Vira I. Heinz Endowment was established in 1986 as provided for in the will of Vira Ingham Heinz. Mrs. Heinz was the wife of Clifford Heinz, a son of Henry J. Heinz, founder of the Heinz food processing company. Mrs. Heinz was active in philanthropic and civic work in Pittsburgh for more than 50 years. She founded the Civic Light Opera, was president of the Pittsburgh Youth Symphony, and served on the boards of the Pittsburgh Opera, Chamber Music Society, and Symphony Society. She was a trustee of Chatham College and Carnegie-Mellon University, and a board member of Pittsburgh Children's Hospital. Mrs. Heinz was "deeply concerned that her funds continue to be made available to those in need, to those in distress, and to those whose talents and insights enrich all of our lives."

Typical Recipients: • *Arts & Humanities:* Arts Associations & Councils, Arts Centers, Arts Funds, Arts Outreach, Ballet, Community Arts, Dance, Ethnic & Folk Arts, Historic Preservation, History & Archaeology, Libraries, Museums/Galleries, Music, Opera, Performing Arts, Public Broadcasting, Theater • *Civic & Public Affairs:* African American Affairs, Business/Free Enterprise, Community Foundations, Economic Development, Economic Policy, Employment/Job Training, General, Housing, Municipalities/Towns, Parades/Festivals, Philanthropic Organizations, Professional & Trade Associations, Urban & Community Affairs, Zoos/Aquariums • *Education:* Arts/Humanities Education, Colleges & Universities, Community & Junior Colleges, Education Associations, Education Funds, Education Reform, Engineering/Technological Education, Faculty Development, Medical Education, Private Education (Precollege), Public Education (Precollege), Religious Education, School Volunteerism, Science/Mathematics Education, Secondary Education (Public), Student Aid • *Environment:* Forestry, General, Research, Resource Conservation, Watershed, Wildlife Protection • *Health:* Cancer, Children's Health/Hospitals, Geriatric Health, Health Policy/Cost Containment, Hospitals, Medical Research, Mental Health, Single-Disease Health Associations • *International:* International Affairs, International Organizations, Missionary/Religious Activities • *Religion:* Churches, Jewish Causes, Religious Organizations, Religious Welfare, Seminaries • *Science:* Scientific Centers & Institutes • *Social Services:* At-Risk Youth, Child Welfare, Community Service Organizations, Crime

Prevention, Day Care, Delinquency & Criminal Rehabilitation, Domestic Violence, Emergency Relief, Family Planning, Family Services, Food/Clothing Distribution, Homes, Recreation & Athletics, Senior Services, Sexual Abuse, Shelters/Homelessness, Substance Abuse, United Funds/United Ways, Volunteer Services, YMCA/YWCA/YMHA/YWHA, Youth Organizations

Grant Types: capital, endowment, general support, operating expenses, project, research, scholarship, and seed money

Geographic Distribution: primarily western Pennsylvania

GIVING OFFICERS

Jack E. Kime: assoc dir, cfo, chief admin off *PHIL AFFIL* cfo, assoc dir, chief admin off: Howard Heinz Endowment

William H. Rea: trust *B* Pittsburgh PA 1912 *CURR EMPL* dir: Colt Indus Inc *PHIL AFFIL* vchmn: Buhl Foundation; trust: Howard Heinz Endowment, Drue Heinz Trust; dir: Robert Gemmill Foundation Trust

John Thomas Ryan, Jr.: trust *B* Pittsburgh PA 1912 *ED* PA St Univ BS 1934; Harvard Univ MBA 1936 *CURR EMPL* chmn exec comm, dir: Mine Safety Appliances Co *CORP AFFIL* dir: QED Communs *NONPR AFFIL* mem: Am Chem Soc, Am Inst Mining Metallurgical Petroleum Engrs, Am Soc Mechanical Engrs, Am Soc Safety Engrs, Counc Foreign Rels, Natl Acad Sci, Natl Soc Petroleum Engrs, Phi Delta Theta, Pittsburgh Symphony Soc, Tau Beta Pi, Veterans Safety; mem exec comm, dir: Allegheny Conf Commun Devel; trust: Thomas A Edison Fdn; trust emeritus: Univ Notre Dame *CLUB AFFIL* Allegheny, Chicago, Duquesne, Fox Chapel GC, Knights Malta, Metro, NY YC, Pittsburgh GC, Rolling Rock, Union League, Univ

Frank Tugwell: exec dir *PHIL AFFIL* exec dir: Howard Heinz Endowment

James Mellon Walton: chmn *B* Pittsburgh PA 1930 *ED* Yale Univ BA 1953; Harvard Univ MBA *CURR EMPL* vchmn: MMC Group *PHIL AFFIL* trust: Sarah Scaife Foundation, Scaife Family Foundation; treas, trust: Carnegie Hero Fund; trust: Matthew T. Mellon Foundation

S. Donald Wiley: trust *B* Pittsburgh PA 1926 *ED* Westminster Coll 1950; Univ PA Sch Law 1953 *PHIL AFFIL* vchmn, trust: H. J. Heinz Company Foundation

APPLICATION INFORMATION
Initial Approach:

Grant requests may be submitted by letter or in the form of a full proposal.

A full proposal should describe the purpose of the grant, amount requested, procedures to be employed in administering the project or program, personnel involved, and a complete financial statement. If the endowment finds the project within its area of interest, the applicant will be asked to fill out a brief application form relevant to the proposed activity.

Grant applications should be submitted 60 days prior to the next meeting of the board of trustees.

The trustees meet in March and October.

Restrictions on Giving: No grants will be awarded for general endowment purposes. In exceptional cases, grant requests to endow limited and clearly defined purposes may be considered.

OTHER THINGS TO KNOW
A representative of Mellon Bank serves as a corporate trustee for the endowment.

PUBLICATIONS
Annual report

GRANTS ANALYSIS
Total Grants: $10,439,119

Number of Grants: 154

Highest Grant: $850,000

Average Grant: $67,787

Typical Range: $2,000 to $10,000 and $25,000 to $250,000

Disclosure Period: 1993

Note: Recent grants are derived from a 1993 Form 990.

RECENT GRANTS

Library

150,000	Carnegie Mellon University, Pittsburgh, PA — for the development of prototype to demonstrate new technology that will enhance learning through interactive video libraries
30,000	Braddock's Field Historical Society, Braddock, PA — for continued support of the Community Center at the Braddock Carnegie Library

General

750,000	Forbes Fund, Pittsburgh, PA — to establish the Forbes Fund on a permanent basis
500,000	Pittsburgh Partnership for Neighborhood Development, Pittsburgh, PA — for core operating support
400,000	Zoological Society of Pittsburgh, Pittsburgh, PA — for a new education complex and a children's zoo
347,923	Environmental Defense Fund, New York, NY — operating support for the design of the Center for Environmental Science and Economics
330,000	Mon Valley Education Consortium, McKeesport, PA — to support the operations of the Mon Valley Education Consortium

Heinz Trust, Drue

Former Foundation Name: H. J. and Drue Heinz Foundation Drue Heinz Foundation

CONTACT
Harry A. Thompson II
Manager
Drue Heinz Foundation
606 Oliver Bldg.
535 Smithfield St.
Pittsburgh, PA 15222
(412) 281-5737

FINANCIAL SUMMARY
Recent Giving: $9,025,714 (1993); $15,272,347 (1992); $10,581,696 (1991)

Assets: $29,105,785 (1993); $41,221,148 (1992); $51,181,348 (1991)

Gifts Received: $88,537 (1993); $887,945 (1992); $346,547 (1991)

Fiscal Note: In 1993, contributions were received from the H. J. Heinz Revocable Trust.

EIN: 25-6018930

CONTRIBUTIONS SUMMARY
Donor(s): The foundation was established in 1954.

Typical Recipients: • *Arts & Humanities:* Arts Associations & Councils, Arts Funds, Ballet, Community Arts, Dance, Historic Preservation, Libraries, Literary Arts, Museums/Galleries, Music, Public Broadcasting, Theater, Visual Arts • *Civic & Public Affairs:* Ethnic Organizations, General, Philanthropic Organizations, Professional & Trade Associations, Public Policy, Urban & Community Affairs, Women's Affairs, Zoos/Aquariums • *Education:* Colleges & Universities, Education Reform, Elementary Education (Private), Literacy, Private Education (Precollege) • *Environment:* Air/Water Quality, General • *Health:* AIDS/HIV, Cancer, Eyes/Blindness, Hospitals, Medical Rehabilitation, Medical Research, Single-Disease Health Associations • *International:* Foreign Arts Organizations, Foreign Educational Institutions, International Environmental Issues, International Organizations, International Peace & Security Issues, International Relations • *Religion:* Religious Organizations • *Social Services:* Child Welfare, Community Service Organizations, People with Disabilities, Scouts, Shelters/Homelessness, United Funds/United Ways, Youth Organizations

Grant Types: general support and project

Geographic Distribution: focus on Pittsburgh, PA, New York, NY, and the United Kingdom

GIVING OFFICERS
James F. Dolan: trust

Drue Maher Heinz: trust

William H. Rea: trust *B* Pittsburgh PA 1912 *CURR EMPL* dir: Colt Indus Inc *PHIL AFFIL* vchmn: Buhl Foundation; trust: Howard Heinz Endowment, Vira I. Heinz Endowment; dir: Robert Gemmill Foundation Trust

Harry A. Thompson II: mgr

APPLICATION INFORMATION
Initial Approach:

The foundation reports that all requests should be submitted by letter.

The foundation has no deadline for submitting proposals.

GRANTS ANALYSIS
Total Grants: $9,025,714

Number of Grants: 68

Highest Grant: $1,500,000

Average Grant: $30,273*

Typical Range: $10,000 to $100,000

Disclosure Period: 1993

Note: Average grant figure excludes five grants totaling $7,118, 500. Recent grants are derived from a 1993 Form 990.

RECENT GRANTS

Library

2,000	Folger Shakespeare Library, Washington, DC

General

1,476,500	American Associates of the Royal Academy Trust, New York, NY
1,438,000	American Associates of the Royal Academy Trust, New York, NY
25,000	British Schools and Universities Foundation, New York, NY
25,000	International Society Forum, Pittsburgh, PA
20,000	Lutrce Foundation, New York, NY

Henkel Corp.

Sales: $922.0 million
Employees: 3,150
Parent Company: Henkel of America
Headquarters: Gulph Mills, PA
SIC Major Group: Chemicals & Allied Products

CONTACT
William B. Read
Director, Human Resources
Henkel Corp.
The Triad, Ste. 200
2200 Renaissance Blvd.
Gulph Mills, PA 19406
(610) 270-8100

FINANCIAL SUMMARY
Fiscal Note: Annual Giving Range: $100,000 to $250,000

CONTRIBUTIONS SUMMARY
United Way accounts for approximately two-thirds of contributions budget. Of the remainder, education is supported through a single grant to the Independent Colleges and Universities Foundation. Health contributions, aside from those to united funds, go to local hospitals. Donations also support numerous organizations representing the arts and civic affairs.

Typical Recipients: • *Arts & Humanities:* Arts Centers, Dance, Historic Preservation, Libraries, Museums/Galleries, Music, Public Broadcasting, Theater • *Civic & Public Affairs:* Business/Free Enterprise, Civil Rights, Law & Justice, Municipalities/Towns, Safety, Women's Affairs, Zoos/Aquariums • *Education:* Colleges & Universities • *Health:* Hospitals • *International:* International Relations • *Social Services:* United Funds/United Ways

Grant Types: general support

Geographic Distribution: in headquarters community and statewide

Operating Locations: AZ, IL, MA, MI, NC, NJ, PA (Gulph Mills)

CORP. OFFICERS
William B. Read: *CURR EMPL* dir human resources: Henkel Corp

Hans-Dietrich Winkhaus: *CURR EMPL* chmn, dir: Henkel Corp

Dr. Harald P. Wulff: *CURR EMPL* pres, ceo, dir: Henkel Corp

GIVING OFFICERS
William Jenkins: *CURR EMPL* vp human resources: Henkel Corp

APPLICATION INFORMATION
Initial Approach: Send a brief letter of inquiry and a full proposal. Include a description of the organization, amount and purpose of funds sought, and proof of tax-exempt status.

Restrictions on Giving: *Program does not support political or religious organizations. Member agencies of united funds also will not be considered. *The division of Henkel Corp. in Arizona, Illinois, Michigan, North Caroline, New Jersey, and Pennsylvania have independent giving programs.

GRANTS ANALYSIS
Typical Range: $2,500 to $5,000

Hershey Foods Corp. / Hershey Foods Corp. Fund

Revenue: $3.6 billion
Employees: 13,700
Headquarters: Hershey, PA
SIC Major Group: Chocolate & Cocoa Products, Candy & Other Confectionery Products, and Macaroni & Spaghetti

CONTACT
Andrea Bowerman
Corporate Contributions Manager
Hershey Foods Corp. Fund
100 Crystal A Dr.
Hershey, PA 17033-0810
(717) 534-7574

FINANCIAL SUMMARY
Recent Giving: $4,000,000 (1995 est.); $3,800,000 (1994 approx.); $3,500,000 (1993 approx.)

Assets: $244,447 (1993); $139,702 (1992); $1,061,925 (1991)

Gifts Received: $2,400,000 (1993)

Fiscal Note: Above figures represent fund and direct giving. Above figures exclude nonmonetary support.

EIN: 23-6239132

CONTRIBUTIONS SUMMARY
Typical Recipients: • *Arts & Humanities:* Arts Associations & Councils, Libraries, Museums/Galleries, Theater • *Civic & Public Affairs:* Business/Free Enterprise, Community Foundations, Economic Development, Employment/Job Training, General • *Education:* Colleges & Universities, Community & Junior Colleges, Economic Education, Engineering/Technological Education, Literacy, Religious Education, Science/Mathematics Education • *Environment:* Resource Conservation • *Health:* Clinics/Medical Centers, Hospitals, Nutrition • *Science:* Scientific Centers & Institutes, Scientific Organizations • *Social Services:* Community Service Organizations, Food/Clothing Distribution, People with Disabilities, Substance Abuse, United Funds/United Ways, Volunteer Services

Grant Types: capital, employee matching gifts, endowment, general support, operating expenses, project, and research

Note: Employee matching gift ratio: 2 to 1, to colleges only.

Nonmonetary Support: $8,244,281 (1993); $4,563,456 (1991); $2,870,000 (1989)

Nonmonetary Support Types: cause-related marketing & promotion, donated products, and loaned executives

Note: Product donations usually total between $1,000,000 and $4,000,000 annually. The contact for noncash contributions is Harold Miller, Senior Account Representative, Customer Service. Loaned executives are for United Way only.

Geographic Distribution: strongly prefers areas where Hershey Foods maintains facilities

Operating Locations: CA (Fresno, Oakdale), CT (Naugatuck), KY (Louisville), MO (Kansas City), NE (Omaha), NM (Farmington), NY (Long Island City), PA (Hazleton, Hershey, Lancaster, Lebanon, Reading), VA (Stuarts Draft, Winchester)

CORP. OFFICERS
William N. Lehr, Jr.: *B* St Louis MO 1940 *ED* Univ Notre Dame BBA 1961; Georgetown Univ JD 1964 *CURR EMPL* sr vp, secy, assoc gen couns: Hershey Foods Corp *NONPR AFFIL* chmn bd: Harrisburg Metro Arts; comm mem: PA Econ Devel Partnership Labor-Mgmt Adv Comm; dir: Boy Scouts Am Keystone Area Counc, Capital Blue Cross, Harrisburg Allied Arts, PA Citizen Svc Project; mem: Am Bar Assn, Am Soc Corp Secys, Fin Execs Inst, Natl Assn Corp Dirs, Stockholder Rels Soc NY; mem exec comm: PA Econ League; vchmn: PA Milrite Counc *CLUB AFFIL* Rotary

Joseph P. Viviano: *B* Louisville KY 1938 *ED* Xavier Univ 1959 *CURR EMPL* pres, coo, dir: Hershey Foods Corp *NONPR AFFIL* dir: Chocolate Mfrs Assn, Natl Confectioners Assn; mem: Natl Assn Mfrs; mem productivity counc: Grocery Mfrs Am

Kenneth L. Wolfe: *B* 1939 *ED* Yale Univ BA 1961; Univ PA MBA 1967 *CURR EMPL* chmn, ceo: Hershey Foods Corp

GIVING OFFICERS

Joseph P. Viviano: trust *CURR EMPL* pres, coo, dir: Hershey Foods Corp (see above)

Kenneth L. Wolfe: trust *CURR EMPL* chmn, ceo: Hershey Foods Corp (see above)

APPLICATION INFORMATION

Initial Approach: *Initial Contact:* brief letter or proposal to fund; organizations situated outside the Hershey, PA area should direct requests to management of facility in their area *Include Information On:* description of the organization and its purpose, including specific project for which funding is requested; need for the project and/or organization and the population (number, type, area) served; past and expected sources of support; fund-raising activities/plans, project cost, and campaign goal; amount requested; list of board of directors and affiliations; any special state or federal tax credits that may accrue to donors; how organization relates to company interests; IRS determination letter *Deadlines:* none; decisions generally made monthly; 60-day lead time needed

Restrictions on Giving: Does not support fraternal, veterans, or labor organizations or, religious organizations or denominations for sectarian purposes.

Generally does not provide operating support to United Way-supported agencies or grants or scholarships to individuals.

PUBLICATIONS

Biennial report

GRANTS ANALYSIS

Total Grants: $2,300,134

Number of Grants: 770

Highest Grant: $125,000

Average Grant: $2,987

Typical Range: $1,000 to $20,000

Disclosure Period: 1993

Note: Above figures reflect fund giving only and do not include direct giving or nonmonetary support. Recent grants are derived from a 1993 Form 990.

RECENT GRANTS

General

125,000	Pennsylvania Association for the Blind, Harrisburg, PA
96,500	Hershey Foods Corporation Scholarship Program, Minneapolis, MN
75,000	Lady Keystone Open, Harrisburg, PA
60,000	Pennsylvania State University School of Education, University Park, PA
60,000	Pennsylvania State University School of Education, University Park, PA

Hillman Foundation

CONTACT

Ronald W. Wertz
President
Hillman Foundation
2000 Grant Bldg.
Pittsburgh, PA 15219
(412) 338-3466

FINANCIAL SUMMARY

Recent Giving: $2,924,825 (1993); $2,932,240 (1992); $2,796,950 (1991)

Assets: $54,521,684 (1993); $48,682,221 (1992); $35,612,083 (1991)

EIN: 25-6011462

CONTRIBUTIONS SUMMARY

Donor(s): The Hillman Foundation was established in 1951 by John Hartwell Hillman, Jr. , a transportation and coal industrialist. The Hillman Company, a private corporation, is a major venture capital firm, with additional holdings in real estate and manufacturing. Mr. Hillman, who died in 1981, intended the foundation to benefit the city of Pittsburgh where his business interests were centered. The Hillmans had seven children, one of whom is chairman of the foundation.

Typical Recipients: • *Arts & Humanities:* Arts Centers, History & Archaeology, Libraries, Museums/Galleries, Opera, Public Broadcasting, Theater • *Civic & Public Affairs:* Clubs, Economic Development, Employment/Job Training, General, Housing, Minority Business, Urban & Community Affairs, Zoos/Aquariums • *Education:* Arts/Humanities Education, Business Education, Colleges & Universities, Community & Junior Colleges, Education Reform, Faculty Development, Private Education (Precollege), Religious Education, Science/Mathematics Education, Social Sciences Education, Special Education, Student Aid • *Health:* Cancer, Health Organizations, Long-Term Care, Medical Rehabilitation, Outpatient Health Care, Research/Studies Institutes, Single-Disease Health Associations • *Religion:* Religious Organizations, Religious Welfare, Seminaries • *Science:* Science Museums • *Social Services:* Child Welfare, Community Service Organizations, Day Care, Delinquency & Criminal Rehabilitation, Domestic Violence, Family Planning, People with Disabilities, Recreation & Athletics, Scouts, Senior Services, Sexual Abuse, Shelters/Homelessness, Substance Abuse, United Funds/United Ways, YMCA/YWCA/YMHA/YWHA, Youth Organizations

Grant Types: capital, department, endowment, fellowship, general support, professorship, scholarship, and seed money

Geographic Distribution: focus on Pittsburgh and southwestern Pennsylvania

GIVING OFFICERS

H. Vaughan Blaxter III: secy, dir *B* 1943 *CURR EMPL* vp, dir, secy: Hillman Co *CORP AFFIL* vp, secy, dir: Hillman Proper-

ties *PHIL AFFIL* dir: Henry L. Hillman Foundation

Carl G. Grefenstette: vp, dir *B* Toledo OH 1927 *ED* Duquesne Univ 1950 *CURR EMPL* chmn, ceo, dir: Hillman Co *CORP AFFIL* dir: Pittsburgh Natl Bank, PNC Fin Corp *NONPR AFFIL* dir: Duquesne Univ; mem: Am Inst CPAs *PHIL AFFIL* vp, dir: Polk Foundation

Elsie H. Hillman: dir *NONPR AFFIL* adv: Shadyside Hosp Social Svc Bd

Henry Lea Hillman: chmn, dir, don son *B* Pittsburgh PA 1918 *ED* Princeton Univ AB 1941 *PHIL AFFIL* don, pres, dir: Henry L. Hillman Foundation; pres, dir: Polk Foundation

David H. Ross: treas, asst secy

Rebecca F. Semmer: secy

Lawrence M. Wagner: dir *CURR EMPL* pres, coo, dir: Hillman Coal & Coke Co *CORP AFFIL* exec vp, coo, dir: Hillman Co; vp, treas, dir: Hillman Mfg Co *NONPR AFFIL* treas: Polk Fnd

Ronald W. Wertz: pres *B* 1937 *PHIL AFFIL* pres: Henry L. Hillman Foundation; secy, dir: Polk Foundation; dir, secy: Audrey Hillman Fisher Foundation, Henry Lea Hillman, Jr. Foundation

APPLICATION INFORMATION

Initial Contact: There is no formal application form. The proposal should be presented in a cover letter which describes the program and its objectives, and specifies the amount requested.

Include Information On: The letter should convey justification for the request and must be signed by an authorized official of the organization. The request should include an annual budget, a listing of the organization's directors or trustees, detailed information about costs of the project for which funds are sought, and a time schedule (if appropriate). Applications also must provide proof of tax-exempt status, and indicate that any grant received from the foundation will be considered a "qualifying distribution" as defined in the Internal Revenue Code Section 4942(g) rather than a "taxable expenditure" as defined in the Internal Revenue Code Section 4945(d).

Deadlines: There are no deadlines for proposals. The board meets quarterly to consider applications.

Restrictions on Giving: The foundation does not make grants to individuals or to organizations outside the U.S.

OTHER THINGS TO KNOW

Recipients are expected to provide periodic Written reports concerning the project or program funded. The foundation will specify the timetable and contents of the reports when each contribution is made.

PUBLICATIONS

Annual report

GRANTS ANALYSIS

Total Grants: $2,924,825

Number of Grants: 65

Highest Grant: $300,000

Average Grant: $44,997

Typical Range: $10,000 to $75,000

Disclosure Period: 1993

Note: Recent grants are derived from a 1993 annual report.

RECENT GRANTS

Library

30,000	Point Park College, Pittsburgh, PA — five-year pledge, toward renovation of facility to establish Library Center
25,000	Kiskiminetas, Saltsburg, PA — four-year pledge, toward construction of John A. Pidgeon Library and Communications Center

General

200,000	Shadyside Hospital Foundation, Pittsburgh, PA — five-year pledge, toward relocation of Mary Hillman Jennings Radiation Oncology Center and purchase of equipment
110,600	Carnegie Museum of Natural History, Pittsburgh, PA — three-year pledge, toward purchase of mineral specimens and developing new and refurbishing existing mineral exhibits in Hillman Hall of Minerals and Gems
100,000	Pittsburgh Theological Seminary, Pittsburgh, PA — five-year pledge, toward endowment of the Hillman Professor of Urban Ministry/Director of Metro-Urban Ministry
100,000	Salvation Army, Pittsburgh, PA — five-year pledge — toward purchase, renovation, and expansion of facility for emergency disaster services and purchase of disaster-related equipment
81,000	St. Oddment's Academy, Pittsburgh, PA — three-year pledge, toward purchase of property for and construction of athletic field

Holt Family Foundation

CONTACT
Leon C. Holt, Jr.
Trustee
Holt Family Foundation
3003 Pkwy. Blvd.
Allentown, PA 18104-5384
(215) 481-7065

FINANCIAL SUMMARY
Recent Giving: $82,250 (1993); $49,500 (1991); $25,500 (1990)

Assets: $1,973,331 (1993); $959,872 (1991); $741,764 (1990)

Gifts Received: $180,000 (1993); $132,000 (1991); $455,500 (1990)

Fiscal Note: In 1993, contributions were received from Leon C. Holt, Jr.

EIN: 23-6906143

CONTRIBUTIONS SUMMARY
Typical Recipients: • *Arts & Humanities:* Libraries, Museums/Galleries • *Education:* Colleges & Universities, Private Education (Precollege) • *Environment:* Resource Conservation, Wildlife Protection • *Religion:* Churches

Grant Types: general support

GIVING OFFICERS
June W. Holt: trust

Leon C. Holt, Jr.: trust *B* Reading PA 1925 *ED* Lehigh Univ BA 1948; Univ PA LLB 1951 *CURR EMPL* vchmn, chief admin off, dir: Air Products & Chemicals *CORP AFFIL* dir: VF Corp; vchmn, chief admin off, dir: Air Products & Chemicals *NONPR AFFIL* dir: Lehigh County Un Fund; mem: Allentown Chamber Commerce, Am Bar Assn, New York City Bar Assn, Tunkhannock Creek Assn; mem adv bd: Univ PA Inst Law Econ; mem exec comm: Machinery Allied Products Inst; trust: Allentown Art Mus, Comm Econ Devel, Pool (Dorothy Rider) Health Care Trust

Richard W. Holt, Jr.: trust

Deborah Holt Weil: trust

APPLICATION INFORMATION
Initial Approach: The foundation reports no specific application guidelines. Send a brief letter of inquiry, including statement of purpose, amount requested, and proof of tax-exempt status. There are no deadlines.

GRANTS ANALYSIS
Total Grants: $82,250

Number of Grants: 15

Highest Grant: $40,000

Typical Range: $250 to $3,500

Disclosure Period: 1993

Note: Recent grants are derived from a 1993 grants list.

RECENT GRANTS

Library

1,000	Allentown Public Library, Allentown, PA

General

17,500	University of Pennsylvania, Philadelphia, PA
9,000	Lehigh University, Bethlehem, PA
3,500	Church of the Mediator, Allentown, PA
2,500	Cornell University, Ithaca, NY
2,000	Moravian Academy, Bethlehem, PA

Hopwood Charitable Trust, John M.

CONTACT
Bruce Bickel
Vice President and Manager
John M. Hopwood Charitable Trust
c/o Charitable and Endowment Management
PNC Bank
One Oliver Plz., 27th Fl.
Pittsburgh, PA 15265
(412) 762-3412

FINANCIAL SUMMARY
Recent Giving: $687,678 (1994 approx.); $680,050 (1993); $707,647 (1992)

Assets: $14,504,707 (1994 approx.); $14,627,613 (1993); $15,817,825 (1992)

Gifts Received: $250,000 (1990)

Fiscal Note: In 1990, contributions were received from Mary Hopwood.

EIN: 25-6022634

CONTRIBUTIONS SUMMARY
Donor(s): The trust was established in 1948 by the late John M. Hopwood .

Typical Recipients: • *Arts & Humanities:* Arts Centers, Ballet, Dance, Libraries, Museums/Galleries, Music, Opera, Public Broadcasting, Theater • *Civic & Public Affairs:* Housing, Parades/Festivals, Urban & Community Affairs, Zoos/Aquariums • *Education:* Colleges & Universities, Community & Junior Colleges, Literacy, Medical Education, Private Education (Precollege), Public Education (Precollege), Student Aid • *Environment:* General, Resource Conservation • *Health:* Cancer, Children's Health/Hospitals, Emergency/Ambulance Services, Health Organizations, Hospices, Hospitals, Kidney, Long-Term Care, Medical Rehabilitation, Multiple Sclerosis, Nursing Services, Single-Disease Health Associations • *Religion:* Churches, Religious Welfare • *Social Services:* Big Brother/Big Sister, Community Service Organizations, Domestic Violence, Family Services, Homes, People with Disabilities, Recreation & Athletics, Senior Services, United Funds/United Ways, Youth Organizations

Grant Types: endowment, matching, and project

Geographic Distribution: focus on western Pennsylvania (75%) and Florida (25%)

GIVING OFFICERS
Bruce Bickel: trust off *CORP AFFIL* vp, gen mgr: PNC Bank

William T. Hopwood: trust

APPLICATION INFORMATION
Initial Approach:

The trust requests applications be made in writing.

There are no deadlines.

Restrictions on Giving: The trust reports grants are made only to corporations or organizations operated exclusively for religious, charitable, scientific, literary, or educational purposes.

OTHER THINGS TO KNOW
The PNC Bank acts as a corporate trustee for the John M. Hopwood Charitable Trust.

GRANTS ANALYSIS
Total Grants: $680,050

Number of Grants: 78

Highest Grant: $50,000

Average Grant: $8,719

Typical Range: $2,000 to $10,000

Disclosure Period: 1993

Note: Recent grants are derived from a 1993 Form 900.

RECENT GRANTS

Library
40,000	Citizens Library, Washington, PA

General
50,000	Shadyside Hospital Foundation, Pittsburgh, PA
35,000	Washington Hospital, Washington, PA
30,000	La Roche College, Pittsburgh, PA
30,000	Spina Bifida Association of Western Pennsylvania, Pittsburgh, PA
30,000	St. Clair Hospital Foundation, Pittsburgh, PA

Hoyt Foundation

CONTACT
Linda Pierog
Administrator
Hoyt Fdn.
101 E Washington St.
New Castle, PA 16101
(412) 652-5511

FINANCIAL SUMMARY
Recent Giving: $421,796 (fiscal 1992); $486,191 (fiscal 1990); $502,563 (fiscal 1989)

Assets: $10,302,248 (fiscal 1992); $9,683,159 (fiscal 1990); $8,951,770 (fiscal 1989)

EIN: 25-6064468

CONTRIBUTIONS SUMMARY
Donor(s): the late May Emma Hoyt, Alex Crawford Hoyt

Typical Recipients: • *Arts & Humanities:* Arts Institutes, Community Arts, Dance, Historic Preservation, Libraries, Performing Arts • *Civic & Public Affairs:* Business/Free Enterprise, General, Parades/Festivals, Urban & Community Affairs, Zoos/Aquariums • *Education:* Colleges & Universities, Student Aid • *Health:* Cancer, Children's Health/Hospitals, Emergency/Ambulance Services, Heart • *Religion:* Churches • *Social Services:* Animal Protection, Camps, Child Welfare, Community Centers, Community Service Organizations, Family Services,

Recreation & Athletics, Shelters/Homelessness, United Funds/United Ways, Youth Organizations

Grant Types: capital, general support, multiyear/continuing support, and seed money

Geographic Distribution: limited to residents of, or organizations located in Lawrence County, PA

GIVING OFFICERS
Thomas J. O'Shane: pres

John W. Sant: dir

Steve Warner: trust

APPLICATION INFORMATION
Initial Approach: Application form required. Deadlines are July 15 and December 15 for scholarships.

GRANTS ANALYSIS
Total Grants: $421,796

Number of Grants: 30

Highest Grant: $100,000

Typical Range: $500 to $10,000

Disclosure Period: fiscal year ending October 31, 1992

Note: Figures above do not include scholarships to individuals. Recent grants are derived from a fiscal 1992 Form 990.

RECENT GRANTS

Library
22,000	New Castle Public Library, New Castle, PA

General
100,000	Westminster College, New Wilmington, PA
35,000	Human Service Center, New Castle, PA
30,000	Girl Scouts of America Council Beaver-Castle, New Castle, PA
30,000	Lawrence County United Way, New Castle, PA
30,000	Westminister College, New Wilmington, PA

Hulme Charitable Foundation, Milton G.

CONTACT
Helen C. Hulme
Trustee
Milton G. Hulme Charitable Fdn.
519 Frick Bldg.
Pittsburgh, PA 15219
(412) 281-2007

FINANCIAL SUMMARY
Recent Giving: $248,000 (1993); $224,500 (1992); $205,000 (1991)

Assets: $5,094,879 (1993); $4,806,711 (1992); $4,595,050 (1991)

EIN: 25-6062896

CONTRIBUTIONS SUMMARY
Donor(s): Glove, Inc. and MacGregor

Typical Recipients: • *Arts & Humanities:* Ballet, Community Arts, Historic Preservation, History & Archaeology, Libraries, Museums/Galleries, Music, Opera, Performing Arts, Public Broadcasting, Theater • *Civic & Public Affairs:* Business/Free Enterprise, General • *Education:* Colleges & Universities, Private Education (Precollege), Special Education, Student Aid • *Environment:* Resource Conservation • *Health:* Children's Health/Hospitals, Emergency/Ambulance Services, Geriatric Health, Hospices, Hospitals, Medical Rehabilitation, Nursing Services, Single-Disease Health Associations • *Religion:* Churches, Ministries, Religious Organizations, Religious Welfare • *Science:* Scientific Centers & Institutes • *Social Services:* Child Welfare, Community Centers, Community Service Organizations, Family Planning, Family Services, Food/Clothing Distribution, Homes, People with Disabilities, Recreation & Athletics, Scouts, Senior Services, Shelters/Homelessness, United Funds/United Ways, Youth Organizations

Grant Types: general support

Geographic Distribution: focus on PA

GIVING OFFICERS
Natalie H. Curry: trust

Aura R. Hulme: trust

Helen C. Hulme: trust

Jocelyn H. MacConnell: trust

Helen H. Shoup: trust

APPLICATION INFORMATION
Initial Approach: Include a description of organization, amount requested, purpose of funds sought, recently audited financial statement, and proof of tax-exempt status. Deadline is June 30.

GRANTS ANALYSIS
Total Grants: $248,000

Number of Grants: 45

Highest Grant: $15,000

Typical Range: $1,000 to $15,000

Disclosure Period: 1993

Note: Recent grants are derived from a 1993 Form 990.

RECENT GRANTS

Library
5,000	Carnegie Library for the Blind and Physically Handicapped, Pittsburgh, PA

General
15,000	Salvation Army, Philadelphia, PA
15,000	Shadyside Hospital Foundation, Pittsburgh, PA
13,500	Shadyside Academy, Pittsburgh, PA
13,500	Winchester-Thurston School, Pittsburgh, PA
10,000	Shadyside Presbyterian Church, Pittsburgh, PA

Hunt Foundation

CONTACT
Torrence M. Hunt, Jr.
President
Hunt Fdn.
One Bigelow Sq., Ste. 630
Pittsburgh, PA 15219
(412) 234-4640

FINANCIAL SUMMARY
Recent Giving: $1,451,653 (fiscal 1994); $453,690 (fiscal 1993); $593,373 (fiscal 1992)

Assets: $0 (fiscal 1994); $14,093,061 (fiscal 1993); $14,048,628 (fiscal 1992)

EIN: 25-6018925

CONTRIBUTIONS SUMMARY
Donor(s): the late Roy A. Hunt, and members of the Hunt family

Typical Recipients: • *Arts & Humanities:* Arts Funds, Community Arts, Dance, Film & Video, Historic Preservation, History & Archaeology, Libraries, Museums/Galleries, Music, Opera, Performing Arts, Public Broadcasting, Theater • *Civic & Public Affairs:* Botanical Gardens/Parks, Civil Rights, Clubs, Economic Development, General, Public Policy, Urban & Community Affairs, Women's Affairs • *Education:* Colleges & Universities, Community & Junior Colleges, General, Private Education (Precollege), Science/Mathematics Education, Social Sciences Education • *Environment:* General, Resource Conservation, Wildlife Protection • *Health:* AIDS/HIV, Cancer, Children's Health/Hospitals, Clinics/Medical Centers, Health Organizations, Hospitals, Medical Rehabilitation, Medical Research, Mental Health, Single-Disease Health Associations • *International:* Foreign Arts Organizations, Foreign Educational Institutions, International Development, International Organizations, International Peace & Security Issues, International Relations, International Relief Efforts • *Religion:* Churches, Ministries • *Social Services:* Animal Protection, Camps, Child Welfare, Community Centers, Community Service Organizations, Day Care, Family Planning, Family Services, Homes, People with Disabilities, Recreation & Athletics, Substance Abuse, United Funds/United Ways, Youth Organizations

Grant Types: capital, endowment, and general support

Geographic Distribution: focus on the Pittsburgh, PA, and Boston, MA, areas

GIVING OFFICERS
Mellon Bank NA: corp trust

Dr. Susan Hunt Hollingsworth: trust *PHIL AFFIL* trust: Roy A. Hunt Foundation

Andrew McQ. Hunt: trust *PHIL AFFIL* trust: Roy A. Hunt Foundation

Christopher M. Hunt, MD: trust *PHIL AFFIL* trust: Roy A. Hunt Foundation

Daniel Kilner Hunt: trust *PHIL AFFIL* trust: Roy A. Hunt Foundation

Helen M. Hunt: trust *PHIL AFFIL* trust: Roy A. Hunt Foundation

John B. Hunt: trust *PHIL AFFIL* trust: Roy A. Hunt Foundation

Dr. Richard M. Hunt: trust *PHIL AFFIL* trust, don son: Roy A. Hunt Foundation

Dr. Roy A. Hunt III: trust *PHIL AFFIL* trust: Roy A. Hunt Foundation

Torrence M. Hunt, Jr.: pres, trust *B* 1948 *CURR EMPL* vp, dir: Elmhurst Corp *PHIL AFFIL* pres, trust: Roy A. Hunt Foundation

Torrence M. Hunt: trust *CORP AFFIL* dir: Alcoa Aluminum; vp, dir: Allegheny Cemetery *PHIL AFFIL* trust, don son: Roy A. Hunt Foundation

William Edward Hunt: trust *B* Columbus OH 1921 *ED* OH St Univ BA 1943; OH St Univ MD 1945 *CORP AFFIL* vp, dir: Elmhurst Corp *NONPR AFFIL* consulting staff: Childrens Hosp; mem: Academy Medicine Columbus & Franklin County, Alpha Omega Alpha, Am Academy Neurological Surgeons, Am Assn Neurological Surgeons, Am Coll Surgeons, Am Med Assn, Am Surgical Assn, Central OH Neuropsychiatric Assn, Cong Neurological Surgeons, Interurban Neurosurgical Soc, Intl Assn Study Pain, Neurosurgical Soc Am, OH St Med Assn, OH St Neurosurgical Soc, Pan-Am Med Assn, Phi Beta Kappa, Royal Soc Medicine, Sigma Xi, Soc Intl Chirurgie, Soc Neurological Surgeons, Soc Neuroscience, World Fed Neurosurgical Soc *PHIL AFFIL* trust: Roy A. Hunt Foundation

Marion M. Hunt-Badiner: trust *PHIL AFFIL* trust: Roy A. Hunt Foundation

Rachel M. Hunt Knowles: trust *PHIL AFFIL* trust: Roy A. Hunt Foundation

APPLICATION INFORMATION
Initial Approach: Send brief letter of inquiry describing program and requesting application guidelines.

GRANTS ANALYSIS
Total Grants: $1,451,653

Number of Grants: 168*

Highest Grant: $958,958

Typical Range: $250 to $10,000

Disclosure Period: fiscal year ending May 31, 1994

Note: Recent grants are derived from a fiscal 1994 Form 990.

RECENT GRANTS
Library
10,000	Carnegie Library of Pittsburgh, Pittsburgh, PA

General
958,958	Carnegie Mellon University, Pittsburgh, PA — endowment for Botanical Institute
10,000	Children's Oncology Services, Brookline, MA — operating support
10,000	Community of Mindful Living, Berkeley, CA — operating support
10,000	St. Paul's School, Concord, ME — annual fund
9,000	Dartmouth College, Hanover, NH — operating support

Hunt Foundation, Roy A.

CONTACT
Torrence M. Hunt, Jr.
President and Trustee
Roy A. Hunt Foundation
One Bigelow Sq., Ste. 630
Pittsburgh, PA 15219-3030
(412) 281-8734

FINANCIAL SUMMARY
Recent Giving: $950,641 (fiscal 1993 est.); $660,110 (fiscal 1992); $616,065 (fiscal 1991)

Assets: $31,405,897 (fiscal 1992); $28,638,854 (fiscal 1991); $26,370,812 (fiscal 1990)

EIN: 25-6105162

CONTRIBUTIONS SUMMARY
Donor(s): The Roy A. Hunt Foundation was established in 1966, with funds bequeathed by Roy A. Hunt, former president and chairman of the executive committee of Alcoa. Mr. Hunt was an alumnus of Shady Side Academy and Yale University, and a trustee of the Carnegie Institute of Technology (now Carnegie-Mellon University). Each of these institutions traditionally receives support from the foundation.

Mr. Hunt and his wife founded the Hunt Institute for Botanical Documentation at Carnegie-Mellon in 1961. This institute was formed to receive and supervise Mrs. Hunt's large botanical collections, and remains a substantial recipient of the foundation's annual grants. The late Mr. Hunt and members of his family also set up the Hunt Foundation in 1951.

Typical Recipients: • *Arts & Humanities:* Arts Centers, Arts Festivals, Dance, Historic Preservation, History & Archaeology, Libraries, Museums/Galleries, Music, Public Broadcasting, Theater • *Civic & Public Affairs:* Clubs, Native American Affairs, Philanthropic Organizations, Urban & Community Affairs, Zoos/Aquariums • *Education:* Agricultural Education, Colleges & Universities, International Exchange, Private Education (Precollege), Science/Mathematics Education, Social Sciences Education • *Environment:* General • *Health:* Alzheimers Disease, Children's Health/Hospitals, Hospitals, Medical Rehabilitation, Mental Health, Single-Disease Health Associations • *International:* International Relations • *Science:* Science Museums • *Social Services:* Camps, United Funds/United Ways, Youth Organizations

Grant Types: capital, general support, and operating expenses

Geographic Distribution: primarily Pittsburgh, PA, and Boston, MA

GIVING OFFICERS
Dr. Susan Hunt Hollingsworth: trust *PHIL AFFIL* trust: Hunt Foundation

Andrew McQ. Hunt: trust *PHIL AFFIL* trust: Hunt Foundation

Christopher M. Hunt, MD: trust *PHIL AFFIL* trust: Hunt Foundation

Daniel Kilner Hunt: trust *PHIL AFFIL* trust: Hunt Foundation

Helen M. Hunt: trust *PHIL AFFIL* trust: Hunt Foundation

John B. Hunt: trust *PHIL AFFIL* trust: Hunt Foundation

Dr. Richard M. Hunt: trust, don son *PHIL AFFIL* trust: Hunt Foundation

Dr. Roy A. Hunt III: trust *PHIL AFFIL* trust: Hunt Foundation

Torrence M. Hunt: trust, don son *CORP AFFIL* dir: Alcoa Aluminum; vp, dir: Allegheny Cemetery *PHIL AFFIL* trust: Hunt Foundation

Torrence M. Hunt, Jr.: pres, trust *B* 1948 *CURR EMPL* vp, dir: Elmhurst Corp *PHIL AFFIL* pres, trust: Hunt Foundation

William Edward Hunt: trust *B* Columbus OH 1921 *ED* OH St Univ BA 1943; OH St Univ MD 1945 *CORP AFFIL* vp, dir: Elmhurst Corp *NONPR AFFIL* consulting staff: Childrens Hosp; mem: Academy Medicine Columbus & Franklin County, Alpha Omega Alpha, Am Academy Neurological Surgeons, Am Assn Neurological Surgeons, Am Coll Surgeons, Am Med Assn, Am Surgical Assn, Central OH Neuropsychiatric Assn, Cong Neurological Surgeons, Interurban Neurosurgical Soc, Intl Assn Study Pain, Neurosurgical Soc Am, OH St Med Assn, OH St Neurosurgical Soc, Pan-Am Med Assn, Phi Beta Kappa, Royal Soc Medicine, Sigma Xi, Soc Intl Chirurgie, Soc Neurological Surgeons, Soc Neuroscience, World Fed Neurosurgical Soc *PHIL AFFIL* trust: Hunt Foundation

Marion M. Hunt-Badiner: trust *PHIL AFFIL* trust: Hunt Foundation

Rachel M. Hunt Knowles: trust *PHIL AFFIL* trust: Hunt Foundation

APPLICATION INFORMATION
Initial Approach:

Applicants should send a brief proposal to the foundation.

Proposal should include the following: description of the organization, list of board members, annual budget, amount of grant requested, description of project, and IRS letter of 501(c)(3) determination.

Deadlines are April 15 for June meeting, and September 15 for November meeting.

GRANTS ANALYSIS
Total Grants: $660,110

Number of Grants: 118

Highest Grant: $200,000*

Average Grant: $5,594

Typical Range: $1,000 to $10,000

Disclosure Period: fiscal year ending May 31, 1992

Note: The highest grant figure was supplied by the foundation. Recent grants are derived from a fiscal 1992 grant list.

834

RECENT GRANTS
Library
5,000   Harvard University Library, Cambridge, MA

General
50,000   Carnegie-Mellon University Hunt Institute, Pittsburgh, PA — operation support for Botanical Institute

50,000   Carnegie-Mellon University Hunt Institute, Pittsburgh, PA — operation support for Botanical Institute

50,000   Carnegie-Mellon University Hunt Institute, Pittsburgh, PA — operation support for Botanical Institute

50,000   Carnegie-Mellon University Hunt Institute, Pittsburgh, PA — operation support for Botanical Institute

15,000   Oberlin College, Oberlin, OH — annual fund

Huston Charitable Trust, Stewart

CONTACT
Louis J. Beccaria
Executive Director
Stewart Huston Charitable Trust
76 S First Ave.
Coatesville, PA 19320
(610) 384-2666

FINANCIAL SUMMARY
Recent Giving: $756,725 (fiscal 1993); $820,388 (fiscal 1992); $635,629 (fiscal 1991)

Assets: $17,274,736 (fiscal 1993); $15,861,062 (fiscal 1992); $15,375,716 (fiscal 1991)

Gifts Received: $12,908,574 (fiscal 1990)

EIN: 23-2612599

CONTRIBUTIONS SUMMARY
Donor(s): The foundation was established in 1990 in accordance with provisions left by Stewart Huston (d. 1971) in his will. He is the great-grandson of Rebecca Lukens, member of the founding family of Lukens Iron and Steel, Inc., of Coatesville, PA.

Typical Recipients: • *Arts & Humanities:* Dance, Historic Preservation, Libraries, Museums/Galleries, Music, Theater • *Civic & Public Affairs:* Philanthropic Organizations, Public Policy, Urban & Community Affairs • *Education:* Arts/Humanities Education, Colleges & Universities, Continuing Education, Literacy, Private Education (Precollege), Public Education (Precollege), Religious Education, Science/Mathematics Education, Special Education, Student Aid • *Health:* AIDS/HIV, Medical Rehabilitation, Mental Health • *International:* Missionary/Religious Activities • *Religion:* Churches, Ministries, Missionary Activities (Domestic), Religious Organizations, Relig-

ious Welfare, Social/Policy Issues • *Science:* Scientific Centers & Institutes • *Social Services:* Child Abuse, Child Welfare, Community Centers, Community Service Organizations, Delinquency & Criminal Rehabilitation, Emergency Relief, Family Planning, Family Services, Homes, Recreation & Athletics, Senior Services, Shelters/Homelessness, Substance Abuse, Volunteer Services, YMCA/YWCA/YMHA/YWHA, Youth Organizations

Grant Types: capital, general support, operating expenses, project, and scholarship

Geographic Distribution: Pennsylvania and Georgia

GIVING OFFICERS
Louis J. Beccaria: exec dir

Samuel A. Cann: trust

Charles Lukens Huston III: trust *B* Dayton OH 1934 *ED* Spring Garden Coll 1956; Univ VA *CURR EMPL* vp: Lukens *PHIL AFFIL* dir: Huston Foundation

Louis N. Seltzer: trust

APPLICATION INFORMATION
Initial Approach:

Contact the foundation to request an application form.

Applications should include name, address, tax identification number, purpose and activity of organization, geographic area, amount requested, proposed use of funds, other sources of funds, and a copy of the applicant's IRS tax-exempt determination letter.

Applications are accepted at any time; notices of approval, rejection, or requests for additional information are sent out semiannually in June and December.

PUBLICATIONS
Application form

GRANTS ANALYSIS
Total Grants: $756,725

Number of Grants: 94

Highest Grant: $60,000

Average Grant: $8,050

Typical Range: $1,000 to $10,000

Disclosure Period: fiscal year ending June 30, 1993

Note: Recent grants are derived from a fiscal 1993 Form 990.

RECENT GRANTS
Library
5,000   Eastern College, St. Davids, PA — to increase the library's holdings for students preparing for careers in Christian service

General
25,000   Bridges for Peace, Stillwater, OK — to support the Jerusalem Center building program and Operation Ezra

21,000   Georgia Baptist Children's Homes and Family Ministries, Bexley, GA — to repair and refurbish Bryce Cottage

20,000	International Christian Embassy Jerusalem-USA, Washington, DC — to purchase a dual cab Volkswagen truck
20,000	Salvation Army, Savannah, GA — to support the women's rehab program and to enhance men's and children's programs
18,000	Calvary Baptist Day School, Savannah, GA — purchase equipment/software to set up a science/math computer lab

Huston Foundation

CONTACT
Susan B. Heilman
Administrative Assistant
Huston Foundation
Ste. 910, One Tower Bridge
100 Front St.
West Conshohocken, PA 19428
(610) 832-4949

FINANCIAL SUMMARY
Recent Giving: $2,366,000 (1994 est.); $1,200,000 (1993 approx.); $1,221,467 (1992)

Assets: $35,676,000 (1993); $37,963,091 (1992); $31,208,348 (1991)

EIN: 23-6284125

CONTRIBUTIONS SUMMARY
Donor(s): The foundation was established in 1957 by the late Charles Lukens Huston, Jr. and the late Ruth Huston .

Typical Recipients: • *Arts & Humanities:* Arts Institutes, Historic Preservation, Libraries, Museums/Galleries, Music, Performing Arts, Theater • *Civic & Public Affairs:* Law & Justice, Municipalities/Towns, Philanthropic Organizations, Public Policy • *Education:* Colleges & Universities, Legal Education, Literacy, Medical Education, Private Education (Precollege), Religious Education, Student Aid • *Environment:* General • *Health:* Children's Health/Hospitals, Clinics/Medical Centers, Emergency/Ambulance Services, Eyes/Blindness, Health Organizations, Hospices, Hospitals, Medical Rehabilitation • *International:* Missionary/Religious Activities • *Religion:* Bible Study/Translation, Churches, Ministries, Missionary Activities (Domestic), Religious Organizations, Religious Welfare • *Science:* Scientific Centers & Institutes • *Social Services:* At-Risk Youth, Child Welfare, Community Service Organizations, Counseling, Family Planning, Family Services, Food/Clothing Distribution, Sexual Abuse, Shelters/Homelessness, United Funds/United Ways, Youth Organizations

Grant Types: capital, general support, operating expenses, and project

Geographic Distribution: eastern United States; emphasis on Pennsylvania

GIVING OFFICERS
Dorothy C. Hamilton: treas, asst secy

Mrs. Richard L. Hansen: vp, dir

Susan B. Heilman: admin asst

Charles Lukens Huston III: dir *B* Dayton OH 1934 *ED* Spring Garden Coll 1956; Univ VA *CURR EMPL* vp: Lukens *PHIL AFFIL* trust: Stewart Huston Charitable Trust

Nancy G. Huston: pres

Eleanor H. Lashley: dir

APPLICATION INFORMATION
Initial Approach:

The foundation requests a letter outlining the project.

Applicants should submit proposals by April 1 and October 1.

Restrictions on Giving: The foundation reports grants are made to religious, charitable, scientific, literary, and educational organizations. No grants are made to individuals, or for research, fellowships, or loans.

PUBLICATIONS
Annual report, informational brochure, and application guidelines

GRANTS ANALYSIS
Total Grants: $1,221,467

Number of Grants: 172

Highest Grant: $50,000

Average Grant: $7,102

Typical Range: $1,500 to $15,000

Disclosure Period: 1992

Note: Recent grants are derived from a 1992 Form 990.

RECENT GRANTS

Library

| 26,000 | Biblical Theological Seminary, Hatfield, PA — build library |
| 15,000 | Hampden-Sydney College, Hampden-Sydney, VA — to help meet the cost of completion of reclassification from Dewey Decimal System to Library of Congress and conversion of bibliographic records to machine readable format |

General

30,000	English Language Institute of China, San Dimas, CA — recruit, train, and send professional Christian teachers to China to teach English
30,000	Esperanza Health Center, Philadelphia, PA — helping the Hispanic community with all phases of health care
25,000	Walk Thru the Bible Ministries, Atlanta, GA — multiyear payment of $50,000 a year for Project Teach
20,000	Choices Pregnancy Options Center, Bensalem, PA —

| | salary for two part-time people |
| 20,000 | English Language Institute of China, San Dimas, CA — general support |

Independence Foundation

CONTACT
Theodore K. Warner, Jr.
President
Independence Foundation
2500 Philadelphia National Bank Bldg.
Philadelphia, PA 19107-3493
(215) 563-8105

FINANCIAL SUMMARY
Recent Giving: $4,299,113 (1994); $4,764,986 (1993); $4,027,173 (1992)

Assets: $81,279,563 (1994 approx.); $84,604,000 (1993); $91,133,080 (1992)

EIN: 23-1352110

CONTRIBUTIONS SUMMARY
Donor(s): The Independence Foundation was established in 1932 by William H. Donner , but was originally named the International Cancer Research Foundation. In 1962, the foundation was split to form the William H. Donner Foundation and the Independence Foundation. Mr. Donner (1864-1953) was chairman of the Pennsylvania Steel Company and the Otis Hidden Company, and president of Union Steel Company, Cambria Steel Company, and Donner Steel Company. He was also a founder of the towns of Donora and Monessen, PA.

Typical Recipients: • *Arts & Humanities:* Arts Centers, Arts Institutes, Ballet, Film & Video, General, History & Archaeology, Libraries, Museums/Galleries, Music, Opera, Public Broadcasting, Theater • *Civic & Public Affairs:* Botanical Gardens/Parks, Clubs, General, Law & Justice, Public Policy, Rural Affairs, Urban & Community Affairs • *Education:* Arts/Humanities Education, Colleges & Universities, Faculty Development, General, International Studies, Medical Education, Private Education (Precollege), Student Aid • *Environment:* Wildlife Protection • *Health:* Clinics/Medical Centers, Emergency/Ambulance Services, Health Organizations, Medical Rehabilitation, Medical Research, Nursing Services, Preventive Medicine/Wellness Organizations • *International:* International Relations • *Religion:* Religious Welfare • *Science:* Science Museums • *Social Services:* Child Welfare, Community Service Organizations, Family Planning, United Funds/United Ways

Grant Types: endowment, general support, and scholarship

Geographic Distribution: restricted to Pennsylvania, with primary concentration in Philadelphia

GIVING OFFICERS
Phyllis W. Beck: chmn *B* Bronx NY 1927 *ED* Brown Univ AB 1949; Temple Univ JD

1967 *NONPR AFFIL* bd consultants: Villanova Law Sch; bd overseers: Univ PA Sch Nursing; dir: Natl Bd Med Examiners, PA Humanities Counc, Presbyterian Hosp Philadelphia; mem: Am Bar Fdn, Am Law Inst; pres: Ctr Cognitive Therapy; vp: Montgomery County Emergency Svcs

Frederick H. Donner: vp, dir

Robert J. LaRocca: vp

Susan E. Sherman: secy-treas, dir

Theodore Kugler Warner, Jr.: pres, dir *B* Philadelphia PA 1909 *ED* Univ PA AB 1931; Univ PA LLB 1934 *CURR EMPL* couns: Harper & Driver *NONPR AFFIL* mem: Am Bar Assn, Am Law Inst, Natl Tax Assn, Order of Coif, PA Bar Assn, Tau Kappa Epsilon *CLUB AFFIL* Aronimink GC, Golf, Masons, Union League

APPLICATION INFORMATION
Initial Approach:

The foundation does not have standard application forms. Six copies of a brief letter should be sent.

The letter of application should include a description of the project for which funds are sought, anticipated results, budget of estimated project costs, and an estimated time frame over which funds will be required. Applicants must also provide proof of tax-exempt status, including whether the organization is considered by the IRS to be a private foundation.

Applications must be received by September 30.

If an application is within the scope of the foundation's interests, the board of directors may grant interviews.

Restrictions on Giving: The foundation usually does not give support to building and development projects; or grants-in-aid for travel, research, or publication.

PUBLICATIONS
Annual report

GRANTS ANALYSIS
Total Grants: $4,299,113

Number of Grants: 151

Highest Grant: $300,000

Average Grant: $28,471

Typical Range: $5,000 to $100,000 and $100,000 to $250,000

Disclosure Period: 1994

Note: Recent grants are derived from a 1993 grants list.

RECENT GRANTS

Library
35,000	Free Library of Philadelphia, Philadelphia, PA
10,000	Library Company of Philadelphia, Philadelphia, PA

General
400,000	Community College of Philadelphia School of Nursing, Philadelphia, PA — endowed nursing chair
400,000	LaSalle University School of Nursing, Philadelphia, PA — nursing chair
400,000	Temple University, Philadelphia, PA — endowed nursing chair
400,000	University of Pennsylvania School of Nursing, Philadelphia, PA — endowed nursing chair
250,000	Cognitive Therapy, Philadelphia, PA — endowment

Integra Bank of Uniontown

Employees: 221
Parent Company: Integra Financial Corp.
Headquarters: Uniontown, PA
SIC Major Group: Depository Institutions

CONTACT
John Buchanan
President and Chief Executive Officer
Integra Bank of Uniontown
2 W Main St.
Uniontown, PA 15401
(412) 439-3254

FINANCIAL SUMMARY
Recent Giving: $75,000 (1994)

CONTRIBUTIONS SUMMARY
Company reports that 34% of contributions support health and human services; 28% support the arts and humanities; 25% support civic and public affairs; and 13% support education. The company also has been a leader in supporting a county-wide healthcare needs assessment.

Volunteerism: Integra actively promotes volunteerism, and employee achievements are recognized in a weekly corporate newsletter.

Typical Recipients: • *Arts & Humanities:* Arts Outreach, Ballet, Dance, General, Historic Preservation, History & Archaeology, Libraries, Museums/Galleries, Music, Opera, Performing Arts, Theater • *Civic & Public Affairs:* Botanical Gardens/Parks, Economic Development, Employment/Job Training, General, Housing, Municipalities/Towns, Safety • *Education:* After-school/Enrichment Programs, Arts/Humanities Education, Colleges & Universities, Economic Education, Education Reform, General • *Health:* Cancer, Emergency/Ambulance Services, Eyes/Blindness, General, Heart, Home-Care Services, Hospices, Hospitals, Speech & Hearing • *Social Services:* Camps, General, People with Disabilities, Recreation & Athletics, United Funds/United Ways

Grant Types: capital, emergency, employee matching gifts, multiyear/continuing support, operating expenses, project, scholarship, and seed money

Nonmonetary Support Types: donated equipment and loaned employees

Geographic Distribution: primarily headquarters area

Operating Locations: PA (Uniontown)

CORP. OFFICERS
John Buchanan: *CURR EMPL* pres, ceo, dir: Integra BankSouth

APPLICATION INFORMATION
Initial Approach: Send a full proposal. Include a description of organization, amount requested, purpose of funds sought, and proof of tax-exempt status.

Restrictions on Giving: Does not support individuals, religious organizations for sectarian purposes, or political or lobbying groups.

GRANTS ANALYSIS
Typical Range: $1,000 to $2,500

Note: Recent grants are derived from a grants list provided by company in 1995.

RECENT GRANTS

General
American Heart Association, Uniontown, PA
Bedford County Regional Campus, Everett, PA
Cities in Schools in Fayette County, Uniontown, PA
Friends of George C. Marshall, Uniontown, PA
Goodwill Industries of Fayette County, Uniontown, PA

Jennings Foundation, Mary Hillman

CONTACT
Paul Euwer, Jr.
Director
Mary Hillman Jennings Foundation
One PNC Plaza, Ste. 2325
Fifth Ave. & Wood St.
Pittsburgh, PA 15222
(412) 566-2510

FINANCIAL SUMMARY
Recent Giving: $1,456,120 (1992); $1,352,375 (1991); $1,283,475 (1990)

Assets: $30,461,157 (1992); $29,022,223 (1991); $24,287,127 (1990)

EIN: 23-7002091

CONTRIBUTIONS SUMMARY
Donor(s): The foundation was established in 1968 by the late Mary Hillman Jennings.

Typical Recipients: • *Arts & Humanities:* History & Archaeology, Libraries, Opera, Public Broadcasting, Theater • *Civic & Public Affairs:* Economic Development, General, Housing, Parades/Festivals, Urban & Community Affairs, Zoos/Aquariums • *Education:* Colleges & Universities, Community & Junior Colleges, Education Funds, Education Reform, Elementary Education (Public), Private Education (Precollege), Public Education (Precollege), Social Sciences Education • *Health:* Alzheimers Disease, Cancer, Children's Health/Hospitals, Health Organizations, Hospitals, Medical Rehabilitation, Medical Research • *Religion:* Churches, Jewish Causes, Religious Welfare • *Social Services:* Camps, Domestic Violence, Emergency Relief, Family Planning, People with Disabilities, Sexual Abuse, United Funds/United Ways, Youth Organizations

Grant Types: endowment, general support, and seed money

Geographic Distribution: primarily Pittsburgh and surrounding areas

GIVING OFFICERS
Paul Euwer, Jr.: dir *NONPR AFFIL* vp-treas, dir: Allegheny Valley Sch

Christina W. Jennings: dir

Evan D. Jennings: pres

Irving A. Wechsler: treas

Andrew L. Weil: secy

APPLICATION INFORMATION
Initial Approach:

Applicants should submit a letter of proposal.

The letter should describe the organization, the amount requested, and the intended use of the grant.

The deadlines for submitting requests are May 15 and November 15.

The foundation's board of trustees meets twice a year to consider grant applications.

GRANTS ANALYSIS
Total Grants: $1,456,120

Number of Grants: 142

Highest Grant: $100,000

Average Grant: $10,254

Typical Range: $1,000 to $50,000

Disclosure Period: 1992

Note: Recent grants are derived from a 1992 Form 990.

RECENT GRANTS
Library

100,000	Carnegie Second Century Fund, Pittsburgh, PA

General

60,000	Allegheny Valley School, Coraopolis, PA
50,000	Avon Old Farms School, Avon, CT — Jennings Faculty Fund
50,000	Eye and Ear Institute of Pittsburgh, Pittsburgh, PA
50,000	Special Hurricane Relief Fund at Ocean Reef, Key Largo, FL
35,000	United Way of Allegheny County, Pittsburgh, PA

Jewish Healthcare Foundation of Pittsburgh

CONTACT
Karen Wolk Feinstein, PhD
President
Jewish Healthcare Foundation of Pittsburgh
Ctr. City Tower, Ste. 2550
650 Smithfield St.
Pittsburgh, PA 15222
(412) 261-1400

FINANCIAL SUMMARY
Recent Giving: $4,200,000 (1995 est.); $4,091,000 (1994); $3,174,591 (1993)

Assets: $90,000,000 (1995 est.); $88,000,000 (1994); $88,793,046 (1993)

EIN: 25-1624347

CONTRIBUTIONS SUMMARY
Donor(s): In 1990, Presbyterian University Hospital, which is located in Pittsburgh, PA, endowed a $75 million foundation as a healthcare resource after assuming control of Montefiore Hospital, which was also located in Pittsburgh.

Typical Recipients: • *Arts & Humanities:* Libraries, Theater • *Civic & Public Affairs:* African American Affairs, General, Public Policy • *Education:* Medical Education, Public Education (Precollege) • *Environment:* Air/Water Quality • *Health:* Adolescent Health Issues, AIDS/HIV, Alzheimers Disease, Cancer, Children's Health/Hospitals, Clinics/Medical Centers, Geriatric Health, Health Policy/Cost Containment, Health Funds, Health Organizations, Home-Care Services, Hospitals, Hospitals (University Affiliated), Kidney, Long-Term Care, Medical Research, Mental Health, Nutrition, Prenatal Health Issues, Public Health, Transplant Networks/Donor Banks • *International:* Health Care/Hospitals • *Religion:* Jewish Causes, Religious Welfare, Social/Policy Issues • *Social Services:* Child Welfare, Crime Prevention, Day Care, Domestic Violence, Family Services, Food/Clothing Distribution, People with Disabilities, Senior Services, Substance Abuse, United Funds/United Ways, Volunteer Services, YMCA/YWCA/YMHA/YWHA, Youth Organizations

Grant Types: matching and project

Geographic Distribution: western Pennsylvania

GIVING OFFICERS
Robert J. Feidner: fin off

Karen Wolk Feinstein, PhD: pres *B* 1945

William K. Lieberman: vchmn

Nancy Lionts: sr program off

Leon Netzer: vchmn *B* 1923 *ED* Univ Pittsburgh *CURR EMPL* pres: Fed Alloy Corp *CORP AFFIL* pres, dir: Nicroloy Co Inc

Robert Arthur Paul: treas *B* New York NY 1937 *ED* Cornell Univ AB 1959; Harvard Univ JD 1962; Harvard Univ MBA 1964 *CURR EMPL* pres-ceo, dir: Ampco-Pittsburgh Corp *CORP AFFIL* dir: Louis Berkman Realty Co, Follansbee Steel Corp, Integra Fin Corp, Northwestern Steel & Wire Co, Ribozyme Pharmaceuticals; dir, vp, asst secy, dir: Parkersburg Steel Corp; gen ptnr: Romar Trading Co; vchmn, dir: Buffalo Pumps Co, Union Electric Steel Corp; vp, asst secy, dir: Berkman (Louis) Co *NONPR AFFIL* mem: Am Bar Assn, MA Bar Assn, Soc Security Analysts; trust: H.L. and Louis Berkman Fdn, Cornell Univ, Presbyterian Univ Hosp; trust, treas: Ampco Pittsburgh Fdn *CLUB AFFIL* Concordia, Duquesne, Harvard, Harvard-Yale-Princeton, Pittsburgh Athletic *PHIL AFFIL* vp,

trust: Louis and Sandra Berkman Foundation, Fair Oaks Foundation, Inc.

Kenneth T. Segel: program off

David Shapiro: chmn *NONPR AFFIL* chmn, dir: Un Jewish Fed Greater Pittsburgh

APPLICATION INFORMATION
Initial Approach:

Applicants should send four copies of a preliminary letter of intent that does not exceed six pages.

The letter should include a budget, list of board of directors, IRS tax-determination letter, name and address of contact person, institutional and personnel qualifications, the most recent auditor's report (if available), and recent financial statements showing amounts and sources of current income. In addition, the proposal should describe the problem; partnerships; a timetable; program objectives; proposed intervention; anticipated outcome; innovative aspects; likelihood of success; long-term plans; and community education, research, and/or evaluation components.

Proposals should arrive at the foundation at least a month and preferably six weeks before board meetings.

The board meets three times a year in April, August, and December.

Restrictions on Giving: Generally, the foundation does not fund organizations without IRS tax-exempt status, organizations outside western Pennsylvania, programs without a health-care component, general operations, endowment programs, capital needs, operating deficits, debt retirement, political campaigns, scholarships, fellowships, individual research, and individual travel.

OTHER THINGS TO KNOW
Foundation also provides conferences, proposal writing assistance, convening, and technical assistance in planning.

PUBLICATIONS
Annual report including application guidelines, newsletter "Branches"

GRANTS ANALYSIS
Total Grants: $4,091,000*

Number of Grants: 76*

Highest Grant: $750,000*

Average Grant: $52,600*

Typical Range: $10,000* to $300,000

Disclosure Period: 1994

Note: Figures for total grants, number of grants, average grant, highest grant, and typical grant are approximate. Recent grants are derived from a 1993 grants list.

RECENT GRANTS
General

750,000	United Jewish Federation, Pittsburgh, PA — support health care for the underserved in the Jewish community
205,000	Chemical Dependency Grant, Pittsburgh, PA — support second year of chemical dependency program at

	Taylor Allderdice and Mt. Lebanon high schools
200,000	Exodus, Pittsburgh, PA — meet the health care needs of Soviet immigrants
179,115	United Jewish Federation Continuum of Care Phase I, Pittsburgh, PA — pan and implement a comprehensive system for Jewish elders
179,115	United Jewish Federation Continuum of Care Phase II, Pittsburgh, PA — plan and implement a comprehensive system for Jewish elders

Justus Trust, Edith C.

CONTACT
Stephen Kosak
Trust Officer
Edith C. Justus Trust
35 Fisher Ave.
Oil City, PA 16301
(814) 677-5085

FINANCIAL SUMMARY
Recent Giving: $184,437 (1993); $165,440 (1992); $216,085 (1991)

Assets: $3,930,923 (1993); $3,994,032 (1992); $4,019,759 (1991)

EIN: 25-6031057

CONTRIBUTIONS SUMMARY
Donor(s): the late Edith C. Justus

Typical Recipients: • *Arts & Humanities:* Arts Associations & Councils, History & Archaeology, Libraries, Museums/Galleries, Opera, Theater • *Civic & Public Affairs:* Botanical Gardens/Parks, Economic Development, Employment/Job Training, General, Housing, Municipalities/Towns, Safety, Urban & Community Affairs • *Education:* Agricultural Education, General, Private Education (Precollege) • *Environment:* General • *Health:* Health Organizations, Nursing Services • *Religion:* Churches, Religious Welfare • *Social Services:* Community Service Organizations, Family Services, Senior Services, United Funds/United Ways, YMCA/YWCA/YMHA/YWHA, Youth Organizations

Grant Types: general support

Geographic Distribution: focus on Venango County, PA, with emphasis on Oil City

GIVING OFFICERS
Integra Trust Company: trust

APPLICATION INFORMATION
Initial Approach: Send a brief letter of inquiry. Include a description of organization, amount requested, purpose of funds sought, recently audited financial statement, and proof of tax-exempt status. There are no deadlines.

Restrictions on Giving: Limited to Venango County, PA.

PUBLICATIONS
Application Guidelines

GRANTS ANALYSIS
Total Grants: $184,437

Number of Grants: 24

Highest Grant: $50,000

Typical Range: $500 to $20,000

Disclosure Period: 1993

Note: Recent grants are derived from a 1993 Form 990.

RECENT GRANTS
Library

20,000	Oil City Library, Oil City, PA
4,000	Oil City Library 1993 Personnel Funding Assistance, Oil City, PA

General

50,000	Oil City Community Development Corporation, Oil City, PA
20,000	Community Services of Venango County, Oil City, PA
17,500	Franklin YMCA, Franklin, PA
15,000	Allegheny Valley Trails Association, Franklin, PA
15,000	Venango County 911 System, Franklin, PA

Kardon Foundation, Samuel and Rebecca

CONTACT
Emanuel S. Kardon
President
Samuel and Rebecca Kardon Fdn.
117 S. 17th St.
Philadelphia, PA 19103
(215) 561-6633

FINANCIAL SUMMARY
Recent Giving: $415,830 (1993)

Assets: $8,144,140 (1993)

EIN: 23-6278123

CONTRIBUTIONS SUMMARY
Typical Recipients: • *Arts & Humanities:* Arts Associations & Councils, Arts Outreach, Libraries, Museums/Galleries, Music, Opera • *Civic & Public Affairs:* General • *Education:* Arts/Humanities Education, Colleges & Universities, Legal Education, Medical Education, Private Education (Precollege) • *Health:* Alzheimers Disease, Cancer, Heart, Hospitals, Medical Rehabilitation, Medical Research • *International:* International Affairs, Missionary/Religious Activities • *Religion:* Jewish Causes, Religious Welfare, Synagogues/Temples • *Social Services:* Community Service Organizations, General, People with Disabilities, Scouts, United Funds/United Ways, YMCA/YWCA/YMHA/YWHA

Grant Types: general support

Geographic Distribution: focus on PA

GIVING OFFICERS
Emanuel S. Kardon: pres, trust

APPLICATION INFORMATION
Initial Approach: Send a brief letter of inquiry. Include a description of organization, amount requested, purpose of funds sought, recently audited financial statement, and proof of tax-exempt status.

GRANTS ANALYSIS
Total Grants: $415,830

Number of Grants: 44

Highest Grant: $100,000

Typical Range: $200 to $64,000

Disclosure Period: 1993

Note: Recent grants are derived from a 1993 Form 990.

RECENT GRANTS
Library

5,000	Free Library of Philadelphia, Philadelphia, PA

General

100,000	Alzheimers Disease and Related Disorders Association, Chicago, IL
64,000	Kardon Institute of Music for the Handicapped, Philadelphia, PA
50,000	Moss Rehabilitation Hospital, Philadelphia, PA
34,125	Settlement Music School, Philadelphia, PA
25,000	Jewish Federation, Philadelphia, PA

Kavanagh Foundation, T. James

CONTACT
Brenda S. Brooks
Principal Manager
T. James Kavanagh Fdn.
PO Box 609
Broomall, PA 19008
(610) 356-0743

FINANCIAL SUMMARY
Recent Giving: $236,065 (1993); $228,863 (1992); $221,518 (1991)

Assets: $7,744,267 (1993); $6,975,524 (1992); $6,767,130 (1991)

EIN: 23-6442981

CONTRIBUTIONS SUMMARY
Donor(s): T. James Kavanagh

Typical Recipients: • *Arts & Humanities:* Ballet, Libraries, Music, Opera, Performing Arts, Theater • *Civic & Public Affairs:* Botanical Gardens/Parks, Safety • *Education:* Colleges & Universities, Elementary Education (Public), Private Education (Precollege), Religious Education, Secondary Education (Private), Student Aid • *Health:* Emergency/Ambulance Services, Health Organizations, Hospices, Long-Term Care, Medical Research, Single-Disease Health Associations • *Religion:* Churches, Missionary Activities (Domestic), Religious Organizations, Religious Welfare • *Social Services:* Camps, Community Service Organizations, Food/Clothing Distribution, Shelters/Homelessness, United Funds/United Ways, Youth Organizations

Grant Types: capital, emergency, general support, multiyear/continuing support, operating expenses, project, and research

Geographic Distribution: focus on PA

GIVING OFFICERS
Frank J. Brooks: trust

Louis J. Esposito: trust

Thomas E. Kavanagh: trust

APPLICATION INFORMATION
Initial Approach: Include a description of organization, amount requested, purpose of funds sought, recently audited financial statement, and proof of tax-exempt status.

PUBLICATIONS
Application Guidelines

GRANTS ANALYSIS
Total Grants: $236,065

Number of Grants: 128

Highest Grant: $15,000

Typical Range: $500 to $8,000

Disclosure Period: 1993

Note: Recent grants are derived from a 1993 Form 990.

RECENT GRANTS

Library
4,000	Kennedy Christian High School, Hermitage, PA — new computers with CD drives for the school library
2,000	Newtown Public Library, Newtown Square, PA — purchase books and other library materials

General
15,000	St. Josephs School, Sharon, PA — learning assistance program
10,000	St. Francis Xavier Church, PA — improve church property and aid needy students in parish school
5,000	Notre Dame Church, Hermitage, PA — funds to help young people participate in retreats, conferences and conventions, duplicating equipment and educational materials
5,000	Sharon Regional Health System, Sharon, PA
5,000	St. Albans Episcopal Church, Newtown Square, PA — building fund

Kline Foundation, Josiah W. and Bessie H.

CONTACT
Harry R. Bughman
Secretary
Josiah W. and Bessie H. Kline Foundation
42 Kline Village
Harrisburg, PA 17104
(717) 232-0266

FINANCIAL SUMMARY
Recent Giving: $684,450 (1993); $760,450 (1992); $924,820 (1991)

Assets: $21,590,715 (1993); $20,675,249 (1992); $20,424,140 (1991)

EIN: 23-6245783

CONTRIBUTIONS SUMMARY
Donor(s): The foundation was incorporated in 1952 by the late Josiah W. Kline and the late Bessie H. Kline .

Typical Recipients: • *Arts & Humanities:* Arts Associations & Councils, Historic Preservation, History & Archaeology, Libraries, Museums/Galleries, Music, Opera, Performing Arts, Public Broadcasting, Theater • *Civic & Public Affairs:* Botanical Gardens/Parks, Employment/Job Training, Housing, Professional & Trade Associations, Public Policy, Safety • *Education:* Colleges & Universities, Community & Junior Colleges, General, Legal Education, Literacy, Minority Education, Religious Education, Science/Mathematics Education • *Health:* Alzheimers Disease, Cancer, Children's Health/Hospitals, Clinics/Medical Centers, Emergency/Ambulance Services, Health Organizations, Heart, Hospices, Hospitals, Medical Research, Multiple Sclerosis, Outpatient Health Care, Public Health, Single-Disease Health Associations • *Social Services:* Child Welfare, Community Centers, Community Service Organizations, Family Planning, Food/Clothing Distribution, People with Disabilities, Shelters/Homelessness, Special Olympics, Substance Abuse, United Funds/United Ways, Volunteer Services, YMCA/YWCA/YMHA/YWHA, Youth Organizations

Grant Types: endowment, general support, matching, operating expenses, research, and scholarship

Geographic Distribution: limited to central Pennsylvania

GIVING OFFICERS
William D. Boswell: dir

Harry R. Bughman: secy, mgr, dir

Jeffrey John Burdge: dir *B* London England 1922 *ED* Youngstown St Univ *CURR EMPL* dir: Harsco Corp

Richard E. Jordan: vp, dir *PHIL AFFIL* dir: Donald B. and Dorothy L. Stabler Foundation

William Joseph King: treas, dir *B* Philadelphia PA 1929 *ED* Univ PA Wharton Sch 1954; La Salle Univ MBA 1979 *CURR*

EMPL chmn, ceo: Dauphin Deposit Corp *CORP AFFIL* dir: Hempt Bros, Millers Mutual Ins Co

James Earl Marley: dir *B* Marietta PA 1935 *ED* PA St Univ BS 1957; Drexel Inst MS 1963 *CURR EMPL* chmn, dir: AMP Inc *CORP AFFIL* chmn: AMP Packaging Sys; dir: Armstrong World Indus, Dauphin Deposit Bank & Trust Co, Harsco Corp; pres, coo: Precision Interconnect Corp; vchmn: Matrix Sci Corp *NONPR AFFIL* mem: Am Mgmt Assn, Am Soc Mechanical Engrs, Harrisburg Chamber Commerce, Inst Electrical & Electronics Engrs, Mfg Counc Machinery Allied Products Inst *CLUB AFFIL* mem: Harrisburg CC

Robert F. Nation: pres, dir *CORP AFFIL* dir: Harsco Corp *PHIL AFFIL* trust: Harsco Corp. Fund

Samuel D. Ross, Jr.: trust *B* 1933 *ED* Susquehanna Univ *CURR EMPL* pres, ceo, dir: Med Svc Assn PA

David A. Smith: dir *PHIL AFFIL* trust: Rose Law Firm Charitable Trust

John C. Tuten: dir

APPLICATION INFORMATION
Initial Approach:

The foundation requests applications be made in writing.

Written applications should include the name, location, and purpose of the organization requesting assistance, and the use and amount of funding needed.

The foundation has no deadline for submitting proposals.

Restrictions on Giving: The foundation only makes grants to tax-exempt charities. The foundation does not support individuals, endowment funds, operating budgets, special projects, publications, conferences, fellowships, or loans.

GRANTS ANALYSIS
Total Grants: $684,450

Number of Grants: 45

Highest Grant: $150,000

Average Grant: $12,147*

Typical Range: $1,000 to $50,000

Disclosure Period: 1993

Note: Average grant excludes largest grant of $150,000. Recent grants are derived from a 1992 Form 990.

RECENT GRANTS

Library
50,000	Elizabethtown College, Elizabethtown, PA — construction of new library
10,000	Dauphin County Library System, Harrisburg, PA — building expansion
10,000	Franklin and Marshall College, Lancaster, PA — construction of science library
2,500	West Shore Public Library, Camp Hill, PA — computer equipment

General

150,000	Polyclinic Medical Center, Harrisburg, PA — expansion and renovations
80,000	Lebanon Valley College, Annville, PA — construction sports center
50,000	Dickinson College, Carlisle, PA — land development
50,000	Gettysburg College, Gettysburg, PA — renovations of athletic complex
50,000	Messiah College, Grantham, PA — construction of academic center

Knoll Group

Sales: $500.0 million
Employees: 3800
Parent Company: Westinghouse Electric Corp.
Headquarters: East Greenville, PA
SIC Major Group: Furniture & Fixtures

CONTACT
Tom Every
Manager Financial Services
Knoll Group
Water St.
East Greenville, PA 18041
(215) 679-7991

FINANCIAL SUMMARY
Fiscal Note: Annual Giving Range: $250,000 to $500,000

CONTRIBUTIONS SUMMARY
Support goes to local education, human service, health, arts, and civic organizations.

Typical Recipients: • *Arts & Humanities:* Arts Centers, Arts Festivals, Arts Institutes, General, Libraries, Museums/Galleries, Performing Arts • *Civic & Public Affairs:* Chambers of Commerce, Economic Development, General, Parades/Festivals, Philanthropic Organizations • *Education:* General, Private Education (Precollege) • *Environment:* Air/Water Quality, Resource Conservation, Wildlife Protection • *Health:* Adolescent Health Issues, AIDS/HIV, Arthritis, Cancer, Children's Health/Hospitals, Diabetes, Emergency/Ambulance Services, General, Medical Rehabilitation, Multiple Sclerosis, Prenatal Health Issues, Respiratory • *International:* Foreign Educational Institutions, Health Care/Hospitals • *Science:* General, Science Exhibits & Fairs, Science Museums, Scientific Centers & Institutes • *Social Services:* Community Centers, Community Service Organizations, General, People with Disabilities, Recreation & Athletics, United Funds/United Ways, Volunteer Services, YMCA/YWCA/YMHA/YWHA, Youth Organizations

Grant Types: award, employee matching gifts, endowment, and scholarship

Nonmonetary Support Types: cause-related marketing & promotion and donated products

Geographic Distribution: principally near operating locations and to national organizations

Operating Locations: MI (Grand Rapids, Muskegon), PA (East Greenville)

Note: Also operates in Toronto, Canada.

CORP. OFFICERS
Barry McCabe: *CURR EMPL* contr: Knoll Group

Burton B. Staniar: *CURR EMPL* chmn, ceo, dir: Knoll Group

APPLICATION INFORMATION
Initial Approach: Send a brief letter of inquiry. Include a a description of organization, amount requested, and purpose of funds sought.

Restrictions on Giving: Does not support religious organizations for sectarian purposes or political or lobbying groups.

OTHER THINGS TO KNOW
Company subsidiary Shaw Walker Co., now know as Knoll Co. in Muskegon, MI, was is an original donor to the L.C. & Margaret Walker Foundation.

GRANTS ANALYSIS
Typical Range: $10 to $1,000

Note: Recent grants are derived from a grants list provided by company in 1995.

RECENT GRANTS

General
AIDS Project LA
American Red Cross, MI
Hospital for Sick Children, Toronto, Canada
March of Dimes
Museum of Science and Industry, Chicago, IL

Kunkel Foundation, John Crain

CONTACT
Hasbrouck S. Wright
Executive Trustee
John Crain Kunkel Fdn.
1400 Market St., Ste. 203
Camp Hill, PA 17011
(717) 763-1784

FINANCIAL SUMMARY
Recent Giving: $656,020 (1993); $298,500 (1991); $83,500 (1990)

Assets: $9,648,983 (1993); $9,257,381 (1991); $8,324,697 (1990)

EIN: 23-7026914

CONTRIBUTIONS SUMMARY
Typical Recipients: • *Arts & Humanities:* Arts Associations & Councils, Arts Funds, Ballet, Community Arts, History & Archaeology, Libraries, Museums/Galleries, Public Broadcasting • *Civic & Public Affairs:* Botanical Gardens/Parks, Clubs, Housing, Municipalities/Towns, Zoos/Aquariums • *Education:* Colleges & Universities, Medical Education, Private Education (Precollege), Secondary Education (Private)

• *Health:* Cancer, Health Organizations, Mental Health, Single-Disease Health Associations • *Religion:* Churches • *Social Services:* Community Service Organizations, Family Planning, Family Services, Substance Abuse, United Funds/United Ways, Youth Organizations

Grant Types: general support and project

Geographic Distribution: focus on PA

GIVING OFFICERS
W. Minster Kunkel: trust

K. R. Stark: trust

Hasbrouck S. Wright: exec trust

APPLICATION INFORMATION
Initial Approach: Send brief letter of inquiry describing program or project. There are no deadlines.

GRANTS ANALYSIS
Total Grants: $656,020

Number of Grants: 23

Highest Grant: $368,920

Typical Range: $100 to $100,000

Disclosure Period: 1993

Note: Recent grants are derived from a 1993 Form 990.

RECENT GRANTS

Library

10,000	Camp Hill Public Library, Camp Hill, PA

General

368,920	City of Harrisburg, Harrisburg, PA — memorial park
100,000	Franklin and Marshall College, Lancaster, PA
25,000	Planned Parenthood Association, Harrisburg, PA
12,500	Trinity High School, Camp Hill, PA
10,000	Aces, Harrisburg, PA

LamCo. Communications / LamCo. Foundation

Headquarters: Williamsport, PA

CONTACT
Andrew Stabler
Chairman
LamCo. Foundation
460 Market St., Ste. 310
Williamsport, PA 17701
(717) 323-2252

FINANCIAL SUMMARY
Recent Giving: $13,100 (1994); $7,250 (1992); $13,500 (1990)

Assets: $329,318 (1992); $288,493 (1990); $279,086 (1989)

Gifts Received: $10,000 (1989)

Fiscal Note: In 1989, contributions were received from LamCo. Communications.

EIN: 24-6012727

CONTRIBUTIONS SUMMARY

Typical Recipients: • *Arts & Humanities:* Art History, Arts Appreciation, Community Arts, General, Libraries, Museums/Galleries, Public Broadcasting • *Civic & Public Affairs:* Chambers of Commerce, Community Foundations, Economic Development, General, Housing, Inner-City Development, Urban & Community Affairs, Women's Affairs • *Education:* Business Education, Colleges & Universities, Economic Education, General, Medical Education • *Environment:* Air/Water Quality • *Health:* Alzheimers Disease, Cancer, Diabetes, Eyes/Blindness, General, Medical Research, Preventive Medicine/Wellness Organizations • *International:* Health Care/Hospitals, Missionary/Religious Activities • *Religion:* Churches, General, Religious Organizations, Religious Welfare • *Science:* General, Science Museums, Scientific Centers & Institutes • *Social Services:* Camps, Community Centers, Community Service Organizations, Emergency Relief, Family Services, General, Homes, United Funds/United Ways

Grant Types: award, capital, emergency, employee matching gifts, endowment, fellowship, general support, operating expenses, project, and scholarship

Geographic Distribution: focus on PA

Operating Locations: PA (Williamsport)

CORP. OFFICERS

Marshal R. Noecker: *CURR EMPL* pres, ceo: LamCo Communs

GIVING OFFICERS

Howard Lamade: dir

J. Robert Lamade: dir

James S. Lamade: dir

Andrew Stabler: chmn, dir

APPLICATION INFORMATION

Initial Approach: Send a full proposal. Include a description of organization, amount requested, and purpose of funds sought. There are no deadlines.

Restrictions on Giving: Does not support organizations outside operating areas.

GRANTS ANALYSIS

Total Grants: $7,250

Number of Grants: 7

Highest Grant: $1,500

Typical Range: $500 to $1,000

Disclosure Period: 1992

Note: Recent grants are derived from a 1992 Form 990.

RECENT GRANTS

General
1,500	American Rescue Workers, Williamsport, PA	
1,500	Foundation for Independent Colleges, Harrisburg, PA	
1,500	Salvation Army, Williamsport, PA	
1,000	Hope Enterprises, Williamsport, PA	
750	Shepherd of the Streets, Williamsport, PA	

Laurel Foundation

CONTACT
Donna M. Panazzi
Executive Director and Secretary
Laurel Foundation
Three Gateway Ctr., 6 North
Pittsburgh, PA 15222
(412) 765-2400

FINANCIAL SUMMARY
Recent Giving: $1,036,995 (1994); $980,520 (1993); $857,980 (1992)

Assets: $23,344,853 (1993); $22,979,408 (1991); $18,853,333 (1990)

EIN: 25-6008073

CONTRIBUTIONS SUMMARY
Donor(s): The foundation was incorporated in 1951 by Cordelia S. May.

Typical Recipients: • *Arts & Humanities:* Arts Associations & Councils, Arts Funds, Arts Outreach, Community Arts, Dance, Ethnic & Folk Arts, Film & Video, Historic Preservation, History & Archaeology, Libraries, Literary Arts, Museums/Galleries, Music, Opera, Public Broadcasting, Theater • *Civic & Public Affairs:* Business/Free Enterprise, Civil Rights, Economic Development, General, Philanthropic Organizations, Professional & Trade Associations, Public Policy, Rural Affairs, Urban & Community Affairs, Women's Affairs, Zoos/Aquariums • *Education:* Colleges & Universities, Education Associations, Education Funds, General, Literacy, Social Sciences Education, Student Aid • *Environment:* General, Resource Conservation, Wildlife Protection • *Health:* Emergency/Ambulance Services, Health Funds, Hospitals, Medical Research • *International:* Health Care/Hospitals, International Development, International Environmental Issues, International Relations • *Religion:* Religious Welfare • *Science:* Scientific Research • *Social Services:* Child Welfare, Community Service Organizations, Counseling, Family Planning, Family Services, General, Homes, People with Disabilities, Senior Services, United Funds/United Ways, Volunteer Services, Youth Organizations

Grant Types: general support

Geographic Distribution: focus on western Pennsylvania

GIVING OFFICERS
Mrs. John F. Kraft, Jr.: vp, trust

Cordelia Scaife May: chmn, trust, don *B* Pittsburgh PA 1928 *ED* Univ Pittsburgh *CORP AFFIL* Roldiva

Roger F. Meyer: vp, treas *B* 1936 *CORP AFFIL* pres, dir: Laurel Asset Group *CLUB AFFIL* St Clair CC

Donna M. Panazzi: exec dir, secy

Curtis S. Scaife: trust

Thomas Schmidt: trust *B* York PA 1930 *ED* Princeton Univ AB 1952; VA Theological Seminary MDiv 1955; St Univ NY PhD 1971 *CURR EMPL* exec vp, secy: Johnson Schmidt Assocs *CORP AFFIL* sr gen educa-

tor: Intl Bank Reconstruction & Devel *NONPR AFFIL* dir: St Univ NY Buffalo Alumni Assn; mem: Counc Chief St Sch Offs, Intl Assn Applied Social Scientists, Intl Soc Ed Planners; mem legis comm: Am Assn St Colls & Univs, St Higher Ed Exec Offs Assn

APPLICATION INFORMATION
Initial Approach:

Applicants are not encouraged to send letters of inquiry. Those with questions about whether their organization or project falls within the foundation's guidelines should call the foundation directly.

The foundation has no specific application forms. Applicants should send a letter addressed to the executive director with the following information, either in the body of the letter or in accompanying documentation: a proposal summary including the specific purpose of the requested grant and the amount requested; a narrative including organizational information (with a brief description, fewer than 300 words, of the applying organization and its mission and a brief summary, fewer than 300 words, of the project or—if the request is for unrestricted funds—of the organization's goals for the period of time during which the funds will be used), the key staff who will be involved, the timetable for the project's implementation, and the constituency or target population to be served or addressed; and a discussion of the expected results and how success will be defined and measured. The full proposal should also include a list of the board of directors; a current operating budget and annual financial statements for the past two years; a list of any major contributors, with amounts, and a summary of the balance of contributions; the names of the organization's executive staff and the total number of paid staff; an annual report, if available; and an IRS determination letter.

Formal submission deadlines are April 15 and October 15 for consideration at trustee meetings held in June and December, respectively. Applicants are encouraged to submit applications early, however, as applications received late in the cycle necessarily receive less intensive review.

Proposals are acknowledged promptly and applicants are advised of the meeting at which their request will be considered. Every effort is made to consider all proposals which have been timely submitted, but occasionally it is necessary to hold a request over until the following meeting. If this occurs, applicants are promptly advised and given an opportunity to revise or withdraw their request, as appropriate.

Restrictions on Giving: Social welfare and cultural organizations whose service areas fall outside the greater Pittsburgh area ordinarily are not funded. The foundation does not accept proposals from individuals. Large and popular organizations usually are not considered for funding.

PUBLICATIONS
Annual report and application guidelines

GRANTS ANALYSIS

Total Grants: $980,520

Number of Grants: 53

Highest Grant: $50,000

Average Grant: $18,500

Typical Range: $3,000 to $25,000

Disclosure Period: 1993

Note: Recent grants are derived from a 1993 grants list.

RECENT GRANTS
Library

25,000	Margaret Thatcher Foundation, Washington, DC — support an eight-week training program for ten Russian professional librarians
15,000	Carnegie Library of Homestead, Munhall, PA — support for purchase of computer equipment

General

50,000	American Farmland Trust, Washington, DC — support their Florida initiative
45,000	The Carnegie, Pittsburgh, PA — support Powdermill Nature Reserve
40,000	Marlboro Press — support to establish, staff, and maintain office in Brattleboro, VT
35,000	University of Maryland, College Park, MD — support George LaNoue's writing at the University of Maryland regarding affirmative action
30,000	Student Conservation Association, Charlestown, NH — three-year support

Lebanon Mutual Insurance Co. / Lebanon Mutual Foundation

Sales: $7.22 million
Employees: 31
Headquarters: Cleona, PA
SIC Major Group: Insurance Carriers

CONTACT
Roland Rissinger
President
Lebanon Mutual Insurance Co.
PO Box 2005
137 W Penn Ave.
Cleona, PA 17042
(717) 272-6655

FINANCIAL SUMMARY
Recent Giving: $14,260 (1993); $13,535 (1991); $6,125 (1989)

Assets: $250,196 (1993); $262,895 (1991); $178,600 (1989)

Gifts Received: $36,314 (1991); $3,200 (1989)

Fiscal Note: In 1991, contributions were received from Lebanon Mutual Insurance Company.

EIN: 22-2521649

CONTRIBUTIONS SUMMARY
Typical Recipients: • *Arts & Humanities:* Historic Preservation, Libraries, Performing Arts • *Civic & Public Affairs:* Clubs, General, Philanthropic Organizations, Public Policy • *Education:* Colleges & Universities, Education Associations, Secondary Education (Public) • *Environment:* General • *Health:* Hospitals • *Social Services:* United Funds/United Ways, YMCA/YWCA/YMHA/YWHA

Grant Types: general support

Geographic Distribution: giving limited to the Lebanon, PA area

Operating Locations: PA (Cleona)

CORP. OFFICERS
Samuel G. Kurtz: *CURR EMPL* chmn, dir: Lebanon Mutual Ins Co

Roland Rissinger: *CURR EMPL* pres, dir: Lebanon Mutual Ins Co

GIVING OFFICERS
Richard M. Bartlett: dir

Milton Garrison: dir

John Gerdes: dir

Darwin Glick: dir

Samuel B. Kurtz: dir

Samuel G. Kurtz: dir *CURR EMPL* chmn, dir: Lebanon Mutual Ins Co (see above)

Joseph Lauck: dir

Warren Lewis: dir

William Schadler: dir

Mark H. Tice: dir

Mark R. Tice: dir

APPLICATION INFORMATION
Initial Approach: The foundation has no formal grant application procedure or application form. There are no deadlines.

GRANTS ANALYSIS
Total Grants: $14,260

Number of Grants: 6

Highest Grant: $5,000

Typical Range: $35 to $5,000

Disclosure Period: 1993

Note: Recent grants are derived from a 1993 Form 990.

RECENT GRANTS

Library

500	Annville Free Library, Annville, PA

General

5,000	HACC, Harrisburg, PA
5,000	YMCA, Lebanon, PA
2,000	United Way, Lebanon, PA
1,000	Lebanon Valley College, Annville, PA
250	AC Chemical People, Annville, PA

Lebovitz Fund

CONTACT
Herbert C. Lebovitz
Treasurer
Lebovitz Fund
3050 Tremont St.
Allentown, PA 18104
(215) 820-5053

FINANCIAL SUMMARY
Recent Giving: $103,229 (fiscal 1994); 93,864 (fiscal 1993); $178,262 (fiscal 1991)

Assets: $2,168,754 (fiscal 1994); $2,166,732 (fiscal 1993); $1,833,266 (fiscal 1991)

Gifts Received: $9,480 (fiscal 1994); $8,573 (fiscal 1993)

Fiscal Note: In fiscal 1994, contributions were received from Peter Lebovitz.

EIN: 23-6270079

CONTRIBUTIONS SUMMARY
Typical Recipients: • *Arts & Humanities:* Arts Associations & Councils, Arts Centers, Community Arts, Libraries, Museums/Galleries, Music, Opera, Public Broadcasting, Theater • *Civic & Public Affairs:* General, Municipalities/Towns, Public Policy, Safety, Women's Affairs • *Education:* Colleges & Universities, Engineering/Technological Education, Private Education (Precollege), Secondary Education (Private), Student Aid • *Environment:* General, Wildlife Protection • *Health:* Children's Health/Hospitals, Health Organizations, Hospitals, Medical Research, Single-Disease Health Associations • *Religion:* Jewish Causes, Religious Organizations, Synagogues/Temples • *Science:* Science Museums • *Social Services:* Child Welfare, Community Service Organizations, Family Services, Food/Clothing Distribution, Recreation & Athletics, United Funds/United Ways

Grant Types: general support

Geographic Distribution: focus on MI

GIVING OFFICERS
Jonathan Javitch: dir

Clara H. Lebovitz: pres

Herbert C. Lebovitz: treas

James Lebovitz: dir

Beth Ann Segal: secy

APPLICATION INFORMATION
Initial Approach: Send brief letter describing program. There are no deadlines.

GRANTS ANALYSIS
Total Grants: $103,229

Number of Grants: 103

Highest Grant: $10,150

Typical Range: $20 to $10,000

Disclosure Period: fiscal year ending July 31, 1994

Note: Recent grants are derived from a fiscal 1994 Form 990.

RECENT GRANTS

General

10,150	Johns Hopkins University, Baltimore, MD — medical
10,000	Jewish Federation, Allentown, PA — religious
9,250	Federation of Jewish Services, Minneapolis, MN — religious
5,000	Cedar Crest Rodale Aquatic Center, Allentown, PA — social welfare
5,000	Columbia University Trustees, New York, NY — education

Lehigh Portland Cement Co. / Lehigh Portland Cement Charitable Trust

Sales: $300.0 million
Employees: 1,800
Parent Company: Heidelberger Zement A.G.
Headquarters: Allentown, PA
SIC Major Group: Furniture & Fixtures and Stone, Clay & Glass Products

CONTACT

Jeffry H. Brozyna
Vice President and Gen. Counsel
Lehigh Portland Cement Co.
7660 Imperial Way
Allentown, PA 18195
(610) 366-4681

FINANCIAL SUMMARY

Recent Giving: $178,563 (1994); $180,931 (1993); $171,470 (1992)

Assets: $427,333 (1993); $563,943 (1992); $771,789 (1990)

EIN: 23-6291364

CONTRIBUTIONS SUMMARY

Typical Recipients: • *Arts & Humanities:* Arts Funds, Historic Preservation, Libraries, Music, Performing Arts, Public Broadcasting • *Civic & Public Affairs:* General, Urban & Community Affairs, Zoos/Aquariums • *Education:* Business Education, Business-School Partnerships, Colleges & Universities, Community & Junior Colleges, Continuing Education, Economic Education, Education Funds, Elementary Education (Public), Engineering/Technological Education, General, Literacy, Preschool Education, Private Education (Precollege), Public Education (Precollege), Science/Mathematics Education, Secondary Education (Public), Special Education, Student Aid, Vocational & Technical Education • *Environment:* General • *Health:* Cancer, Children's Health/Hospitals, Emergency/Ambulance Services, General, Health Organizations, Heart, Hospices, Hospitals, Transplant Networks/Donor Banks • *Social Services:* At-Risk Youth, Child Welfare, Community Service Organizations, Counseling, Day Care, Domestic Violence, Emergency Relief, Family Services, General, People with Disabilities, Recreation & Athletics, Sexual Abuse, Shelters/Homelessness, Substance Abuse, United Funds/United Ways, Youth Organizations

Grant Types: employee matching gifts and general support

Geographic Distribution: focus on PA

Operating Locations: AL (Leeds), FL (Marianna), IA (Mason City), IN (Buffington, Mitchell), MD (Union Bridge, Woodsboro), NY (Cementon), PA (Allentown, York), TX (Waco)

Note: List includes plant locations.

CORP. OFFICERS

Richard Kline: *CURR EMPL* pres: Lehigh Portland Cement Co

GIVING OFFICERS

Fidelity Bank: trust

Jeffry H. Brozyna: trust *CURR EMPL* vp, gen couns: Lehigh Portland Cement Co

Helmut Leube: trust

Frank Ronald Snyder II: trust *B* Minersville PA 1939 *ED* Lehigh Univ 1962; Lehigh Univ MBA 1970 *CURR EMPL* vp, treas, contr: Lehigh Portland Cement Co *NONPR AFFIL* mem: Fin Execs Inst

Peter B. Tait: trust

APPLICATION INFORMATION

Initial Approach: Send a brief letter of inquiry. Include a a description of organization, amount requested, purpose of funds sought, and proof of tax-exempt status. Company prefers for applications to be submitted in the last quarter of the year.

Restrictions on Giving: Limited to the geographical areas in which the company has a place of business. Company's main focus is on education.

GRANTS ANALYSIS

Total Grants: $180,931

Number of Grants: 345*

Highest Grant: $10,000

Typical Range: $50 to $5,000

Disclosure Period: 1993

Note: Recent grants are derived from a 1993 Form 990. Number is approximate.

RECENT GRANTS

General

10,000	United Way of North Central Iowa, Mason City, IA — for general support
8,000	United Way of Greater Lehigh, Lehigh, PA — for general support
4,725	North Iowa Area Community College, IA — for educational purposes
4,700	United Way of Central Maryland, Baltimore, MD — for general support
3,924	North Iowa Area Community College, IA — for educational purposes

Levitt Foundation

CONTACT

Robert Appel
Treasurer
Levitt Fdn.
One Liberty Pl.
1650 Market St., Ste. 4900
Philadelphia, PA 19103

FINANCIAL SUMMARY

Recent Giving: $338,250 (fiscal 1994); $141,250 (fiscal 1993); $308,000 (fiscal 1992)

Assets: $9,772,899 (fiscal 1994); $9,335,400 (fiscal 1993); $8,371,300 (fiscal 1992)

EIN: 13-6128226

CONTRIBUTIONS SUMMARY

Donor(s): Levitt and Sons, the late Abraham Levitt, the late Alfred Levitt, William Levitt

Typical Recipients: • *Arts & Humanities:* Arts Appreciation, Arts Funds, History & Archaeology, Libraries, Museums/Galleries, Music, Opera • *Civic & Public Affairs:* African American Affairs, Economic Development, General, Housing, Legal Aid, Philanthropic Organizations, Urban & Community Affairs • *Education:* Arts/Humanities Education, Colleges & Universities, International Studies, Private Education (Precollege) • *Health:* Hospitals (University Affiliated), Mental Health, Prenatal Health Issues • *Religion:* Dioceses, Jewish Causes, Religious Organizations • *Science:* Science Museums, Scientific Centers & Institutes • *Social Services:* Child Welfare, Community Centers, Community Service Organizations, Day Care, Domestic Violence, Family Planning, Family Services, United Funds/United Ways

Grant Types: general support

Geographic Distribution: focus on NY and PA

GIVING OFFICERS

Robert J. Appel: treas, trust

Prudence Brown: trust

Dr. Farrell Jones: pres, trust

Stephen J. Mathes: secy, trust

May W. Newburger: trust

APPLICATION INFORMATION

Initial Approach: Send brief letter of inquiry describing program or project. There are no deadlines.

Restrictions on Giving: Does not support individuals.

GRANTS ANALYSIS

Total Grants: $338,250

Number of Grants: 21

Highest Grant: $100,000

Typical Range: $500 to $79,900

Disclosure Period: fiscal year ending April 30, 1994

Note: Recent grants are derived from a fiscal 1994 Form 990.

RECENT GRANTS

Library
| 2,000 | Port Washington Library, Port Washington, NY |

General
100,000	Henry Street Settlement, New York, NY
79,900	Bank Street College of Education, New York, NY
50,000	Mt. Holyoke College, South Hadley, MA
5,000	Chestnut Hill Academy, Philadelphia, PA
5,000	United Jewish Appeal Federation, New York, NY

Love Foundation, George H. and Margaret McClintic

CONTACT
George H. and Margaret McClintic Love Fdn.
Mellon Bank, N.A.
One Mellon Bank Ctr., Rm. 3815
Pittsburgh, PA 15258
(412) 234-4695

FINANCIAL SUMMARY
Recent Giving: $770,000 (1993); $369,000 (1992); $390,600 (1991)

Assets: $4,755,648 (1993); $5,175,980 (1992); $5,249,530 (1991)

Gifts Received: $56,967 (1993); $56,967 (1992); $284,467 (1991)

Fiscal Note: In 1993, contributions were received from the Charitable Trust No. 2.

EIN: 25-6018655

CONTRIBUTIONS SUMMARY
Donor(s): George H. Love

Typical Recipients: • *Arts & Humanities:* Community Arts, Libraries, Music • *Civic & Public Affairs:* General, Urban & Community Affairs, Women's Affairs • *Education:* Colleges & Universities, Private Education (Precollege), Public Education (Precollege), Religious Education • *Health:* Children's Health/Hospitals, Hospices, Hospitals, Medical Research, Single-Disease Health Associations • *Religion:* Churches, Religious Welfare • *Social Services:* Child Welfare, Community Service Organizations, Food/Clothing Distribution, People with Disabilities, Shelters/Homelessness, United Funds/United Ways, Youth Organizations

Grant Types: capital and general support

Geographic Distribution: national

GIVING OFFICERS
Mellon Bank, N.A.: trust

Howard McClintic Love: dir *B* Pittsburgh PA 1930 *ED* Colgate Univ 1952; Harvard Univ Grad Sch Bus Admin 1956 *CORP AFFIL* dir: Comsat Corp, Hamilton Oil Corp, Monsanto Co *CLUB AFFIL* Laurel Valley GC

APPLICATION INFORMATION
Initial Approach: Send brief letter of inquiry describing program. Include a description of organization, amount requested, purpose of funds sought, recently audited financial statement, and proof of tax-exempt status. There are no deadlines.

GRANTS ANALYSIS
Total Grants: $770,000

Number of Grants: 14

Highest Grant: $600,000

Typical Range: $1,000 to $60,000

Disclosure Period: 1993

Note: Recent grants are derived from a 1993 Form 990.

RECENT GRANTS

Library
| 5,000 | Carnegie Second Century Fund, Pittsburgh, PA |

General
600,000	Presbyterian Hospital, Pittsburgh, PA
60,000	Calvary Episcopal Church, Pittsburgh, PA
50,000	United Way of Southwest Pennsylvania, Pittsburgh, PA
17,000	Bank Street College of Education, New York, NY
12,000	Horizon Hospice Endowment, Chicago, IL

McCormick Trust, Anne

CONTACT
Larry A. Hartman
Trustee
Anne McCormick Trust
c/o Dauphin Deposit Bank and Trust
PO Box 2961
Harrisburg, PA 17105-2961
(717) 255-2045

FINANCIAL SUMMARY
Recent Giving: $96,500 (1993); $173,000 (1992); $229,297 (1991)

Assets: $5,301,148 (1993); $4,952,838 (1992); $4,709,886 (1991)

EIN: 23-6471389

CONTRIBUTIONS SUMMARY
Typical Recipients: • *Arts & Humanities:* Arts Associations & Councils, Dance, History & Archaeology, Libraries, Museums/Galleries, Music, Opera • *Civic & Public Affairs:* Botanical Gardens/Parks, General, Municipalities/Towns • *Education:* Colleges & Universities, Community & Junior Colleges, Education Funds, Medical Education • *Health:* Arthritis, Cancer, Clinics/Medical Centers, Emergency/Ambulance Services, Heart, Hospitals, Medical Research, Multiple Sclerosis, Single-Disease Health Associations • *Religion:* Churches • *Social Services:* Community Service Organizations, Emergency Relief, Family Services, Food/Clothing Distribution, People with Disabilities, Special Olympics, United Funds/United Ways, YMCA/YWCA/YMHA/YWHA, Youth Organizations

Grant Types: general support

Geographic Distribution: focus on PA

GIVING OFFICERS
Dauphin Deposit Bank & Trust Co.: trust

Larry A. Hartman: trust

APPLICATION INFORMATION
Initial Approach: Include a description of organization, amount requested, purpose of funds sought, recently audited financial statement, and proof of tax-exempt status. There are no deadlines.

Restrictions on Giving: Limited to Dauphin, Cumberland, Perry, York, and Franklin Counties of PA.

GRANTS ANALYSIS
Total Grants: $96,500

Number of Grants: 29

Highest Grant: $15,000

Typical Range: $500 to $10,000

Disclosure Period: 1993

Note: Recent grants are derived from a 1993 Form 990.

RECENT GRANTS

General
15,000	United Way of the Capital Region, Harrisburg, PA — for charitable purposes
10,000	Family and Children's Services, Camp Hill, PA
10,000	Harrisburg Area Community College, Harrisburg, PA — for charitable purposes, final pledge payment
6,000	American Cancer Society, Harrisburg, PA — for medical purposes
5,000	Messiah College, Grantham, PA — for educational purposes, first pledge payment

McCune Charitable Trust, John R.

CONTACT
Martha J. Perry
Managing Director
John R. McCune Charitable Trust
1104 Commonwealth Building
316 Fourth Ave.
Pittsburgh, PA 15222
(412) 644-7796

FINANCIAL SUMMARY
Recent Giving: $3,318,400 (fiscal 1994); $3,100,000 (fiscal 1993 approx.); $2,038,500 (fiscal 1992)

Assets: $72,960,148 (fiscal 1994); $75,000,000 (fiscal 1993 approx.); $72,623,460 (fiscal 1992)

EIN: 25-6160722

CONTRIBUTIONS SUMMARY
Donor(s): The trust was established in 1972 with funds donated by the late John R. McCune IV. The trust reports that it is affiliated with the McCune Foundation, which is also located in Pittsburgh, PA.

Typical Recipients: • *Arts & Humanities:* Arts Associations & Councils, History & Archaeology, Libraries, Public Broadcasting • *Civic & Public Affairs:* Business/Free Enterprise, Employment/Job Training, Nonprofit Management, Philanthropic Organizations, Public Policy, Urban & Community Affairs • *Education:* Arts/Humanities Education, Colleges & Universities, Education Funds, Elementary Education (Public), Private Education (Precollege), Religious Education, Special Education • *Environment:* General, Resource Conservation • *Health:* Children's Health/Hospitals, Clinics/Medical Centers, Health Funds, Health Organizations, Hospitals, Medical Research, Mental Health, Multiple Sclerosis, Prenatal Health Issues, Public Health, Research/Studies Institutes, Single-Disease Health Associations • *International:* International Relations • *Religion:* Ministries, Religious Organizations, Religious Welfare, Seminaries • *Science:* Scientific Research • *Social Services:* Child Welfare, Community Service Organizations, Counseling, Family Services, Homes, People with Disabilities, Recreation & Athletics, Substance Abuse, Volunteer Services, YMCA/YWCA/YMHA/YWHA, Youth Organizations

Grant Types: capital, general support, and project

Geographic Distribution: focus on western Pennsylvania

GIVING OFFICERS
Janet McCune Edwards Anti: mem dispensing comm

Molly McCune Cathey: mem dispensing comm

David L. Edwards: mem dispensing comm

James M. Edwards: mem dispensing comm *B* Champaign IL 1931 *ED* Univ IL BA 1953; Inst Des Science Politiques 1955; Yale Univ 1960 *CURR EMPL* ptnr: Cravath Swaine & Moore *PHIL AFFIL* mem distribution comm, don nephew: McCune Foundation; mem: Marshall and Perrine D. McCune Charitable Foundation

John H. Edwards: mem dispensing comm

Michael M. Edwards: mem dispensing comm

Carrie McCune Katigan: mem dispensing comm

Laurie M. Lewis: mem dispensing comm

Sara McCune Losinger: mem dispensing comm *PHIL AFFIL* chmn: Marshall and Perrine D. McCune Charitable Foundation

Martha J. Perry: mng dir *PHIL AFFIL* mng dir: McCune Foundation

APPLICATION INFORMATION
Initial Approach:

Applicants should submit a written inquiry, that is no more than two pages, to the trust.

The inquiry should include the following: project description, including budget; amount of funding requested; copy of IRS tax-determination letter verifying the applicant's status as a nonprofit organization.

Application deadline is Feruary 1.

The dispensing committee meets annually in June to authorize grants.

Restrictions on Giving: The trust does not make grants to individuals nor pledges beyond one year.

OTHER THINGS TO KNOW
Integra Trust Company, N.A., serves as a corporate trustee of the foundation.

Although the John R. McCune Charitable Trust and the McCune Foundation are co-housed, share staff and have overlapping board members, they operate as separate organizations with unique missions.

GRANTS ANALYSIS
Total Grants: $3,318,400

Number of Grants: 99

Highest Grant: $300,000

Average Grant: $33,519

Typical Range: $5,000 to $25,000 and $50,000 to $110,000

Disclosure Period: fiscal year ending November 30, 1994

Note: Recent grants are derived from a fiscal 1994 grants list.

RECENT GRANTS

General
300,000	Mercy Health Center, Oklahoma City, OK
110,000	North Care Mental Health Center, Oklahoma City, OK
100,000	Casady School, Oklahoma City, OK
100,000	Contact Telephone Helpline, Oklahoma City, OK
100,000	Goodwill Industries of Pittsburgh, Pittsburgh, PA

McFeely-Rogers Foundation

CONTACT
James R. Okonak
Executive Director
McFeely-Rogers Fdn.
PO Box 110
Latrobe, PA 15650
(412) 537-5588

FINANCIAL SUMMARY
Recent Giving: $487,580 (1993); $471,174 (1992); $533,259 (1991)

Assets: $13,480,749 (1993); $12,847,872 (1992); $12,220,638 (1991)

EIN: 25-1120947

CONTRIBUTIONS SUMMARY
Donor(s): the late James H. Rogers, the late Nancy K. McFeely, the late Nancy M. Rogers

Typical Recipients: • *Arts & Humanities:* Libraries, Museums/Galleries, Music, Theater • *Civic & Public Affairs:* African American Affairs, General, Municipalities/Towns, Philanthropic Organizations, Professional & Trade Associations, Zoos/Aquariums • *Education:* Colleges & Universities, Education Funds, Literacy, Minority Education, Private Education (Precollege), Public Education (Precollege), Student Aid • *Environment:* General • *Health:* Children's Health/Hospitals, Emergency/Ambulance Services, Health Organizations, Hospitals • *International:* International Relations • *Religion:* Churches, Religious Organizations, Religious Welfare • *Social Services:* At-Risk Youth, Camps, Community Service Organizations, Family Services, People with Disabilities, Recreation & Athletics, Scouts, Senior Services, United Funds/United Ways, YMCA/YWCA/YMHA/YWHA, Youth Organizations

Grant Types: capital, emergency, endowment, general support, multiyear/continuing support, operating expenses, and scholarship

Geographic Distribution: focus on the Latrobe and Pittsburgh, PA, areas

GIVING OFFICERS
William P. Barker: trust

Nancy R. Crozier: vp, trust

Grant F. Neely: treas, trust

Douglas R. Nowicki: trust

James R. Okonak: exec dir, secy, trust

Fred McFeely Rogers: pres *B* Latrobe PA 1928 *ED* Rollins Coll MusB 1951; Pittsburgh Theological Seminary MDiv 1962 *CURR EMPL* exec producer, host: Mister Rogers' Neighborhood *NONPR AFFIL* chmn child devel & mass media forum: White House Conf on Children; mem: Esther Island Preserve Assn, Luxor Ministerial Assn

James B. Rogers: trust

APPLICATION INFORMATION
Initial Approach: Send brief letter describing program. Include a description of organization, amount requested, purpose of funds sought, recently audited financial statement, and proof of tax-exempt status. Deadlines are April 15 and November 1.

Restrictions on Giving: Does not support individuals. Limited to the Latrobe, PA, area.

PUBLICATIONS
Application Guidelines

GRANTS ANALYSIS
Total Grants: $487,580

Number of Grants: 79

Highest Grant: $93,500

Typical Range: $250 to $50,260

Disclosure Period: 1993

Note: Recent grants are derived from a 1993 Form 990.

RECENT GRANTS

Library
20,000	Adams Memorial Library, Latrobe, PA — for endowment fund

7,500	Adams Memorial Library, Latrobe, PA — for Children's Library
1,000	Adams Memorial Library, Latrobe, PA — for collections additions

General

93,500	Latrobe Foundation, Latrobe, PA — for neighborhood playground
50,260	Latrobe Area Hospital, Latrobe, PA — for capital campaign nursery
33,000	Family Communication, Pittsburgh, PA — for special projects fund
30,000	Latrobe Foundation, Latrobe, PA — for pool capital improvement fund
22,000	Latrobe Foundation, Latrobe, PA — for pool and park fund

McKenna Foundation, Katherine Mabis

CONTACT
Linda Boxx
Secretary
Katherine Mabis McKenna Foundation
PO Box 186
Latrobe, PA 15650
(412) 537-6901

FINANCIAL SUMMARY
Recent Giving: $1,100,000 (1995 est.); $1,100,000 (1994 approx.); $1,100,000 (1993 approx.)

Assets: $20,400,000 (1995 est.); $20,400,000 (1994 approx.); $20,400,000 (1993 approx.)

Gifts Received: $118,455 (1991); $63,894 (1990); $44,028 (1989)

Fiscal Note: In 1991, contributions were received from the estate of Katherine Mabis McKenna.

EIN: 23-7042752

CONTRIBUTIONS SUMMARY
Donor(s): The foundation was incorporated in 1969 by the late Katherine M. McKenna .

Typical Recipients: • *Arts & Humanities:* Historic Preservation, Libraries, Museums/Galleries, Music, Public Broadcasting • *Civic & Public Affairs:* Economic Development, Municipalities/Towns, Philanthropic Organizations • *Education:* Colleges & Universities, Education Associations, Literacy, Private Education (Precollege) • *Environment:* General • *Health:* Hospitals, Single-Disease Health Associations • *Science:* Science Exhibits & Fairs • *Social Services:* United Funds/United Ways, Youth Organizations

Grant Types: capital, endowment, general support, project, scholarship, and seed money

Geographic Distribution: limited to eastern Westmoreland County, PA

GIVING OFFICERS
Linda McKenna Boxx: secy, dir

T. William Boxx: treas *PHIL AFFIL* secy, treas, off: Philip M. McKenna Foundation

Alex George McKenna: chmn, dir *B* Crafton PA 1914 *ED* Carnegie Inst Tech 1938 *CURR EMPL* dir: Kennametal *NONPR AFFIL* dir: Latrobe Hosp Assn, WQED/WQEX-TV; mem: Commonwealth Fdn Pub Policy Alternatives, PA Chamber Commerce, Pennsylvanians Effective Govt *CLUB AFFIL* Latrobe CC, Rolling Rock, University *PHIL AFFIL* chmn, off: Philip M. McKenna Foundation

Wilma F. McKenna: vchmn, dir

Zan McKenna Rich: dir

APPLICATION INFORMATION
Initial Approach:

The foundation does not have a specific application form.

All requests should briefly describe the requesting organization and the particular project for which funding is sought. Proposals should include budgets for both the organization and the project, a list of donors and trustees or directors, the organization's IRS tax-exempt letter, and its most recent audited financial statements.

Restrictions on Giving: The foundation does not support individuals, matching funds, or loans.

PUBLICATIONS
Program policy statement

GRANTS ANALYSIS
Total Grants: $1,081,560

Number of Grants: 59

Highest Grant: $112,000

Average Grant: $18,332

Typical Range: $1,500 to $25,000

Disclosure Period: 1991

Note: Recent grants are derived from a 1991 grants list.

RECENT GRANTS

Library

4,000	Adams Memorial Library, Latrobe, PA

General

112,000	Greensburg Garden and Civic Center, Greensburg, PA
100,000	Latrobe Area Hospital, Latrobe, PA
100,000	YMCA, Ligonier, PA
65,000	Philip M. McKenna Foundation, Latrobe, PA
60,000	University of Pittsburgh, Greensburg, PA

McKenna Foundation, Philip M.

CONTACT
T. William Boxx
Secretary-Treasurer
Philip M. McKenna Foundation
PO Box 186
Latrobe, PA 15650
(412) 537-6901

FINANCIAL SUMMARY
Recent Giving: $1,550,000 (1995 est.); $1,550,000 (1994 approx.); $1,875,230 (1993)

Assets: $16,000,000 (1995 est.); $16,000,000 (1994 approx.); $13,604,848 (1993)

Gifts Received: $200,000 (1993); $65,000 (1991)

Fiscal Note: In 1991 and 1993, gifts were received from the Katherine H. McKenna Foundation.

EIN: 25-6082635

CONTRIBUTIONS SUMMARY
Donor(s): The foundation was incorporated in 1967 by the late Philip M. McKenna .

Typical Recipients: • *Arts & Humanities:* Arts Centers, Libraries, Museums/Galleries, Public Broadcasting, Theater • *Civic & Public Affairs:* Business/Free Enterprise, Civil Rights, Economic Policy, Law & Justice, Legal Aid, Public Policy • *Education:* Business Education, Colleges & Universities, Continuing Education, Economic Education, Education Funds, Journalism/Media Education, Legal Education, Religious Education, Science/Mathematics Education, Student Aid • *Health:* Hospitals, Research/Studies Institutes • *International:* International Relations • *Religion:* Social/Policy Issues • *Science:* Science Museums, Scientific Centers & Institutes • *Social Services:* Family Services, Food/Clothing Distribution, United Funds/United Ways, Youth Organizations

Grant Types: capital, operating expenses, research, scholarship, and seed money

Geographic Distribution: focus on southwestern Pennsylvania for community and civic programs; grants to national organizations for public policy

GIVING OFFICERS
T. William Boxx: secy, treas, off *PHIL AFFIL* treas: Katherine Mabis McKenna Foundation

Richard M. Larry: dir *PHIL AFFIL* treas: Carthage Foundation; pres, trust: Sarah Scaife Foundation

Alex George McKenna: chmn, off *B* Crafton PA 1914 *ED* Carnegie Inst Tech 1938 *CURR EMPL* dir: Kennametal *NONPR AFFIL* dir: Latrobe Hosp Assn, WQED/WQEX-TV; mem: Commonwealth Fdn Pub Policy Alternatives, PA Chamber Commerce, Pennsylvanians Effective Govt *CLUB AFFIL* Latrobe CC, Rolling Rock,

University *PHIL AFFIL* chmn, dir: Katherine Mabis McKenna Foundation

Donald C. McKenna: vchmn

Norbert Tail: trust

APPLICATION INFORMATION
Initial Approach:

Applicants must write a letter to the foundation in order to receive a copy of application guidelines.

Restrictions on Giving: The foundation does not make grants to individuals, or for matching gifts or loans.

GRANTS ANALYSIS
Total Grants: $1,875,230

Number of Grants: 69

Highest Grant: $500,000

Average Grant: $27,177

Typical Range: $5,000 to $30,000

Disclosure Period: 1993

Note: Recent grants are derived from a 1993 Form 990.

RECENT GRANTS

Library

50,000	Center for Economic and Policy Education, Fairfax, VA — library automation pledge
16,750	Capital Research Center, Washington, DC — research library
10,000	Adams Memorial Library, Latrobe, PA — collection development pledge

General

500,000	Claremont McKenna College, Claremont, CA — Phillip M. McKenna Professorship pledge
335,000	Claremont McKenna College, Claremont, CA — DCM Achievement Awards pledge
85,000	Commonwealth Foundation of Public Policy Alternatives, Harrisburg, PA
85,000	Intercollegiate Studies Institute, Philadelphia, PA
80,000	Heritage Foundation, Washington, DC — McKenna Fellow

McLean Contributionship

CONTACT
William L. McLean III
Chairman and Trustee
McLean Contributionship
945 Haverford Rd.
Bryn Mawr, PA 19010
(610) 527-6330

FINANCIAL SUMMARY
Recent Giving: $1,200,000 (1995 est.); $1,200,000 (1994 approx.); $1,256,000 (1993)

Assets: $25,000,000 (1995 est.); $25,000,000 (1994 approx.); $25,919,450 (1993)

Gifts Received: $12,007 (1993); $10,149 (1991); $52,265 (1990)

Fiscal Note: In 1993, contributions were received from Independence Communications, Inc. ($10,000) and William McLean III ($2,007).

EIN: 23-6396940

CONTRIBUTIONS SUMMARY
Donor(s): The foundation was established in 1951 by Robert McLean, the late William L. McLean, Jr. , and Bulletin Co.

Typical Recipients: • *Arts & Humanities:* Arts Associations & Councils, Dance, Historic Preservation, Libraries, Museums/Galleries, Music, Performing Arts • *Civic & Public Affairs:* Botanical Gardens/Parks, Business/Free Enterprise, Clubs, Economic Development, Employment/Job Training, General, Urban & Community Affairs, Women's Affairs, Zoos/Aquariums • *Education:* Agricultural Education, Colleges & Universities, Education Funds, Education Reform, Literacy, Minority Education, Private Education (Precollege), Science/Mathematics Education • *Environment:* Air/Water Quality, General, Resource Conservation, Wildlife Protection • *Health:* Children's Health/Hospitals, Diabetes, Geriatric Health, Hospitals, Long-Term Care, Medical Rehabilitation, Medical Research, Public Health, Single-Disease Health Associations, Transplant Networks/Donor Banks • *International:* International Environmental Issues • *Religion:* Churches, Religious Welfare • *Science:* Scientific Centers & Institutes, Scientific Organizations • *Social Services:* Community Centers, Community Service Organizations, Day Care, Family Planning, Homes, People with Disabilities, Recreation & Athletics, Senior Services, United Funds/United Ways, Youth Organizations

Grant Types: capital, conference/seminar, and seed money

Geographic Distribution: focus on the Philadelphia, PA, metropolitan area

GIVING OFFICERS
Jean Bodine: trust

R. Jean Brownlee: trust

John Henry Buhsmer: pres, secy, trust *B* Wilkes-Barre PA 1932 *ED* Kings Coll BA 1956 *CURR EMPL* vp, dir: Independent Pubs *CORP AFFIL* pres, ceo: Newsnet

Charles E. Catherwood: treas *B* 1946 *ED* PA St Univ BS 1969; PA St Coll *CURR EMPL* vp, treas: Independent Pubs *CORP AFFIL* secy, dir: Finger Lakes Printing Co; treas, dir: Commun, Telegraph Publ Co

Joseph K. Gordon: trust *B* Philadelphia PA 1925 *ED* Princeton Univ 1948; Univ PA Sch Law 1951 *CURR EMPL* chmn, dir: Main Line Health *CORP AFFIL* chmn: Main Line Health; couns: Montgomery McCracken Walker & Rhoads; dir: Independent Pubs, PNC Bank

William L. McLean III: chmn, trust *B* Philadelphia PA 1927 *ED* Princeton Univ

BA 1949 *CURR EMPL* pres, dir: Finger Lakes Printing Co

APPLICATION INFORMATION
Initial Approach:

The foundation requests applications be made in writing.

Written applications should describe the project, include a budget and timetable, and list other sources for funding. Attachments to the application should include a financial statement for the most recent fiscal year and evidence of the organization's tax-exempt status. A list of officers and directors also is requested. The recipient of the grant is expected to submit periodic reports to the foundation.

Proposals are accepted throughout the year.

The foundation reports that trustees meet several times per year.

PUBLICATIONS
Application guidelines

GRANTS ANALYSIS
Total Grants: $1,256,000

Number of Grants: 73

Highest Grant: $75,000

Average Grant: $17,205

Typical Range: $1,000 to $25,000

Disclosure Period: 1993

Note: Recent grants are derived from a 1993 Form 990.

RECENT GRANTS

Library

50,000	Episcopal Academy, Merion Campus, Merion, PA — equip a library/resource center and implement a program in environmental studies
50,000	Library Company of Philadelphia, Philadelphia, PA — endowment of two cataloguing positions
20,000	Athenaeum of Philadelphia, Philadelphia, PA — building project

General

75,000	University of Pennsylvania, Philadelphia, PA — women's studies
70,000	Hospital of the University of Pennsylvania, Rodebaugh Diabetes Center, Philadelphia, PA — purchase equipment
50,000	Center for Alternative Learning, Bryn Mawr, PA — support activities
50,000	Nature Conservancy, Philadelphia, PA — establish a Stewardship endowment fund
50,000	Pennsylvania Horticultural Society, Philadelphia, PA — offset the losses due to snow storm at the flower show

McShain Charities, John

CONTACT
Mary McShain
President
John McShain Charities
540 N 17th St.
Philadelphia, PA 19130
(215) 564-2322

FINANCIAL SUMMARY
Recent Giving: $2,427,190 (fiscal 1994); $2,427,190 (fiscal 1993); $2,221,291 (fiscal 1992)

Assets: $56,084,331 (fiscal 1994); $54,873,056 (fiscal 1992); $53,430,177 (fiscal 1991)

EIN: 23-6276091

CONTRIBUTIONS SUMMARY
Donor(s): The foundation was established in Pennsylvania in 1949 with funds donated by John McShain of John McShain, Inc. Mr. McShain, a prominent builder, restored the White House during the Truman administration.

Typical Recipients: • *Arts & Humanities:* Arts Associations & Councils, Libraries, Museums/Galleries • *Education:* Arts/Humanities Education, Colleges & Universities, Education Funds, General, Private Education (Precollege), Religious Education, Secondary Education (Private), Student Aid, Vocational & Technical Education • *Health:* Clinics/Medical Centers, Health Organizations, Hospitals, Long-Term Care • *International:* International Affairs • *Religion:* Churches, Religious Organizations, Religious Welfare

Grant Types: general support, project, and scholarship

Geographic Distribution: primarily Philadelphia area; some national grants

GIVING OFFICERS
Henry B. Fitzpatrick: trust
Sister Pauline Mary: trust
Patricia J. McFillin: trust
Mary McShain: pres, dir
William L. Shinners: vp
Mary K. Tompkins: secy-treas

APPLICATION INFORMATION
Initial Approach:

Prospective applicants should send a letter of inquiry and state the purpose for which funds are sought.

There are no formal application procedures or deadlines.

Restrictions on Giving: Applicant organizations must be IRS approved, and organized and operated exclusively for religious, charitable, scientific, or educational purposes.

GRANTS ANALYSIS
Total Grants: $2,427,190
Number of Grants: 136
Highest Grant: $250,000
Average Grant: $17,847

Typical Range: $1,000 to $25,000
Disclosure Period: fiscal year ending March 31, 1994

Note: Recent grants are derived from a fiscal 1994 Form 990.

RECENT GRANTS

Library
100,000	Hagley Museum and Library, Wilmington, DE
20,000	Hagley Museum and Library, Wilmington, DE

General
250,000	Sisters of Mercy of the Americas, Silver Spring, MD
250,000	St. Josephs Preparatory School, Philadelphia, PA
200,000	Rosemont College, Rosemont, PA
100,000	Catholic University of America, Washington, DC
100,000	Rosemont College, Rosemont, PA

Mellon Family Foundation, R. K.

CONTACT
Robert B. Burr, Jr.
Secretary and Director
R.K. Mellon Family Foundation
PO Box 2930
Pittsburgh, PA 15230
(412) 392-2800

FINANCIAL SUMMARY
Recent Giving: $1,414,250 (1993); $1,389,075 (1992); $1,313,200 (1991)

Assets: $34,907,329 (1993); $31,035,467 (1992); $31,249,821 (1991)

EIN: 25-1356145

CONTRIBUTIONS SUMMARY
Donor(s): The R.K. Mellon Family Foundation was established in 1978 after the merger of the Loyalhanna, Rachelwood, Cassandra Mellon Henderson, and Landfall Foundations. The four predecessor foundations were created, respectively, by donors Richard P. Mellon, the late Constance B. Mellon, Cassandra Mellon Milbury, and Seward Prosser Mellon, all children of Richard King Mellon. Richard King Mellon was the chairman of Mellon National Bank from 1946 to 1966 and a director of Alcoa and Gulf Oil. R.K. Mellon was also governor and president of T. Mellon and Sons. He handled his family's financial empire until his death in 1970.

Typical Recipients: • *Arts & Humanities:* Arts Funds, Arts Institutes, History & Archaeology, Libraries, Museums/Galleries, Music • *Civic & Public Affairs:* Botanical Gardens/Parks, Philanthropic Organizations, Professional & Trade Associations, Safety, Urban & Community Affairs, Zoos/Aquariums • *Education:* Colleges & Universities, Education Funds, Education Reform, Medi-

cal Education, Private Education (Precollege), Science/Mathematics Education, Student Aid • *Environment:* General, Resource Conservation, Wildlife Protection • *Health:* Emergency/Ambulance Services, Health Funds, Hospitals, Medical Research, Medical Training • *International:* International Organizations • *Religion:* Churches • *Science:* Scientific Centers & Institutes, Scientific Research • *Social Services:* Community Service Organizations, Delinquency & Criminal Rehabilitation, Emergency Relief, Homes, People with Disabilities, Recreation & Athletics, Youth Organizations

Grant Types: general support, multi-year/continuing support, operating expenses, and research

Geographic Distribution: primarily in Pittsburgh and Western Pennsylvania

GIVING OFFICERS
Robert B. Burr, Jr.: secy, dir *PHIL AFFIL* asst treas: Richard King Mellon Foundation

Lawrence S. Busch: asst treas

Andrew Wray Mathieson: trust *B* Pittsburgh PA 1928 *ED* Bucknell Univ BS 1950; Carnegie Mellon Univ MS 1952 *CURR EMPL* exec vp: Richard K Mellon & Sons *CORP AFFIL* dir: Gen Re Corp, Gen Reinsurance (Europe), INDSPEC Chemical Corp, Mellon Bank Corp, Mellon Natl Corp *NONPR AFFIL* dir: St Margaret Meml Hosp; treas: Allegheny Conf Commun Devel; trust: Shady Side Academy *CLUB AFFIL* Duquesne, Fox Chapel GC, Laurel Valley GC, Links, Rolling Rock, Univ New York City *PHIL AFFIL* trust: Richard King Mellon Foundation

Seward Prosser Mellon: don, trust *B* Chicago IL 1942 *ED* Susquehanna Univ BA 1965 *CURR EMPL* pres: Richard K Mellon & Sons Ligonier *CORP AFFIL* dir: Mellon Bank Corp, Mellon Bank NA, Mellon Natl Corp *NONPR AFFIL* chmn real estate comm, chmn fin and exec comm: Valley Sch Ligonier; life mem: Western PA Conservancy; mem: Phi Mu Delta; pres: Loyalhanna Assn *PHIL AFFIL* pres, chmn exec comm, trust: Richard King Mellon Foundation *CLUB AFFIL* Duquesne, Lake Nona, Laurel Valley GC, Rolling Rock, Rolling Rock Hunt, Vintage

Arthur D. Miltenberger: vp *PHIL AFFIL* treas: Richard King Mellon Foundation

George H. Taber: chmn, trust *B* 1938 *NONPR AFFIL* chmn: Presbyterian-Univ Hosp *PHIL AFFIL* vp, dir, trust: Richard King Mellon Foundation

John Turcik: treas

Mason Walsh, Jr.: trust *B* Philadelphia PA 1935 *ED* PA St Univ BS 1957; Harvard Univ LLB 1960 *CURR EMPL* sr vp, gen counc: Richard K Mellon & Sons *NONPR AFFIL* trust: Am Farmland Trust, Childrens Hosp Pittsburgh *PHIL AFFIL* trust: Richard King Mellon Foundation

Michael B. Watson: asst secy *PHIL AFFIL* secy: Richard King Mellon Foundation

APPLICATION INFORMATION
Initial Approach:

Applicants should send a letter or a formal statement from the senior administrative officer to the foundation.

There is no specific application form. The letter should include a two-page overview of the organization, the proposed project, and the problem it addresses. Include additional information on the organization's background, its purpose, goals, the population it serves, and the names and affiliations of its board of directors. A description of the project's operation, qualifications of individuals involved, methods of project evaluation, and a timetable is also necessary. Send a statement of other sources of project support, as well as an explanation of how the project will be financed at the expiration of the proposed grant. A current operating budget and a projected budget for the year(s) in which the funding is requested, a copy of the IRS determination letter indicating tax-exempt status under Section 509(a) and 501(c)(3), and audited financial statements for the most recent two years, must be submitted. Include any printed material on the organization, such as annual reports or catalogs, if available.

Proposals should be received prior to April 1 and October 1.

The board of trustees meets twice a year, usually in June and December.

Restrictions on Giving: Proposals are not considered unless accompanied by a copy of IRS classification. The foundation does not give to individuals or to conduit organizations which pass on funds to other organizations.

GRANTS ANALYSIS
Total Grants: $1,414,250
Number of Grants: 70
Highest Grant: $100,000
Average Grant: $20,204
Typical Range: $5,000 to $25,000
Disclosure Period: 1992

Note: Recent grants are derived from a 1993 Form 990.

RECENT GRANTS

Library

60,000	Pierpont Morgan Library, New York, NY — expansion of the photography laboratory
50,000	Somerset House Art History Foundation, Philadelphia, PA — fellowships for American graduates to attend the Courtauld Institute and support the Witt and Conway libraries
25,000	Ligonier Valley Library Association, Ligonier, PA — upgrade and enhance the library's technological capabilities

General

100,000	Conservation Fund, Arlington, VA
75,000	Susquehanna University, Selinsgrove, PA — environmental sciences

program; toward the presidential discretionary fund for excellence

50,000	Chesapeake Bay Foundation, Annapolis, MD — campaign for William B. Mullins and environmental education center at Smith Island
50,000	Falmouth Academy, Falmouth, MA — school's endowment and building campaign
50,000	Ruffed Grouse Society, Grand Rapids, MI — forest habitat development work

Mellon Foundation, Richard King

CONTACT
George H. Taber
Vice President and Director
Richard King Mellon Foundation
PO Box 2930
Pittsburgh, PA 15230-2930
(412) 392-2800

FINANCIAL SUMMARY
Recent Giving: $38,408,438 (1993); $36,721,855 (1992); $44,957,129 (1991)
Assets: $1,095,840,415 (1993); $986,947,968 (1992); $825,346,987 (1991)
EIN: 25-1127705

CONTRIBUTIONS SUMMARY
Donor(s): The Richard King Mellon Foundation was established in 1947 by Richard King Mellon , son of Richard Beatty Mellon, and nephew of Andrew Mellon. Mr. Mellon, a lieutenant general in the United States Army Reserve, managed his family's many interests from the 1930s until his death on June 3, 1970. He served as president of the Mellon National Bank and chairman of the board of Mellon National Bank and Trust Company. He was also a director of many of the companies closely linked to the Mellon family, including the Aluminum Company of America and Gulf Oil Corporation. Mr. Mellon played a leading role in the movement to revitalize Pittsburgh and was active in civic and philanthropic affairs in Pittsburgh and Ligonier, PA. He married Constance Mary Prosser, who served as the foundation's chairman of the board of trustees from its inception in 1947 until her death in 1980.

Typical Recipients: • *Arts & Humanities:* Arts Centers, Arts Institutes, Ballet, Community Arts, Dance, Historic Preservation, History & Archaeology, Libraries, Museums/Galleries, Music, Opera, Performing Arts, Public Broadcasting, Theater • *Civic & Public Affairs:* Business/Free Enterprise, Economic Development, Economic Policy, Employment/Job Training, General, Housing, Law & Justice, Professional & Trade Associations, Rural Affairs, Urban & Community Affairs, Zoos/Aquariums • *Education:* Afterschool/Enrichment Programs, Agricultural Education, Arts/Humanities

Education, Business Education, Colleges & Universities, Community & Junior Colleges, Economic Education, Education Associations, Education Funds, Education Reform, Elementary Education (Private), Elementary Education (Public), Environmental Education, Gifted & Talented Programs, Literacy, Medical Education, Minority Education, Private Education (Precollege), Public Education (Precollege), Science/Mathematics Education, Special Education, Student Aid • *Environment:* Air/Water Quality, General, Protection, Resource Conservation, Wildlife Protection • *Health:* AIDS/HIV, Cancer, Children's Health/Hospitals, Clinics/Medical Centers, Emergency/Ambulance Services, Geriatric Health, Health Policy/Cost Containment, Health Organizations, Hospices, Hospitals, Long-Term Care, Medical Research, Medical Training, Mental Health, Single-Disease Health Associations • *International:* International Environmental Issues, International Relief Efforts • *Religion:* Churches, Jewish Causes, Religious Organizations, Religious Welfare, Synagogues/Temples • *Science:* Scientific Centers & Institutes • *Social Services:* Child Welfare, Community Centers, Community Service Organizations, Day Care, Family Planning, Family Services, Food/Clothing Distribution, Homes, People with Disabilities, Recreation & Athletics, Scouts, Senior Services, Sexual Abuse, Shelters/Homelessness, Substance Abuse, United Funds/United Ways, Volunteer Services, YMCA/YWCA/YMHA/YWHA, Youth Organizations

Grant Types: capital, general support, professorship, project, and scholarship

Geographic Distribution: Pittsburgh, PA, and western Pennsylvania; nationally for conservation programs

GIVING OFFICERS
Robert B. Burr, Jr.: asst treas *PHIL AFFIL* secy, dir: R. K. Mellon Family Foundation

Andrew Wray Mathieson: trust *B* Pittsburgh PA 1928 *ED* Bucknell Univ BS 1950; Carnegie Mellon Univ MS 1952 *CURR EMPL* exec vp: Richard K Mellon & Sons *CORP AFFIL* dir: Gen Re Corp, Gen Reinsurance (Europe), INDSPEC Chemical Corp, Mellon Bank Corp, Mellon Natl Corp *NONPR AFFIL* dir: St Margaret Meml Hosp; treas: Allegheny Conf Commun Devel; trust: Shady Side Academy *CLUB AFFIL* Duquesne, Fox Chapel GC, Laurel Valley GC, Links, Rolling Rock, Univ New York City *PHIL AFFIL* trust: R. K. Mellon Family Foundation

Richard Prosser Mellon: chmn, trust *B* Chicago IL 1939 *ED* Univ Pittsburgh 1958-1960 *NONPR AFFIL* corporator: Western PA Sch Blind; dir: Ducks Unlimited *CLUB AFFIL* Duquesne, Laurel Valley GC, Links, Links, Natl Steeplechase & Hunt Assn, Rolling Rock, Rolling Rock Westmoreland Hunt

Seward Prosser Mellon: pres, chmn exec comm, trust *B* Chicago IL 1942 *ED* Susquehanna Univ BA 1965 *CURR EMPL* pres: Richard K Mellon & Sons Ligonier *CORP AFFIL* dir: Mellon Bank Corp, Mellon Bank NA, Mellon Natl Corp *NONPR AFFIL* chmn real estate comm, chmn fin and exec comm: Valley Sch Ligonier; life mem: Western PA Conservancy; mem: Phi Mu Delta; pres: Loyalhanna Assn *PHIL AFFIL* don, trust: R. K. Mellon Family Foundation *CLUB AFFIL* Duquesne, Lake Nona, Laurel Valley GC, Rolling Rock, Rolling Rock Hunt, Vintage

Arthur D. Miltenberger: treas *PHIL AFFIL* vp: R. K. Mellon Family Foundation

Arthur M. Scully, Jr.: trust *CURR EMPL* vp, dir: Allegheny Cemetery *CLUB AFFIL* Laurel Valley GC

George H. Taber: vp, dir, trust *B* 1938 *NONPR AFFIL* chmn: Presbyterian-Univ Hosp *PHIL AFFIL* chmn, trust: R. K. Mellon Family Foundation

Mason Walsh, Jr.: trust *B* Philadelphia PA 1935 *ED* PA St Univ BS 1957; Harvard Univ LLB 1960 *CURR EMPL* sr vp, gen counc: Richard K Mellon & Sons *NONPR AFFIL* trust: Am Farmland Trust, Childrens Hosp Pittsburgh *PHIL AFFIL* trust: R. K. Mellon Family Foundation

Michael B. Watson: secy *PHIL AFFIL* asst secy: R. K. Mellon Family Foundation

APPLICATION INFORMATION
Initial Approach:

Initial contact should be by letter.

Applicants should contact the foundation and request a copy of their application form, which should accompany all proposals. Proposals should include an executive summary describing the sponsoring organization, proposed project, and the problems it seeks to address. Background information on the requesting organization should include its history, purpose, goals, the types of programs it offers, and the names and affiliations of members of the board. Financial information must include a current operating budget, a projected budget for the term in which the funding is requested, and audited financial statements for the most recent two years. A copy of the latest IRS determination letter of tax-exempt status under sections 501(c)(3) and 509(a) is required. Information on the proposed project should include its specific purpose and objective, budget, and timetable. A description of the proposed methods of operation and evaluation, and the qualifications of the individuals who will conduct the undertaking. A statement of other sources of support for the project should also be included, with an explanation of how the project will be financed at the expiration of the proposed grant. Supporting printed material, including annual reports, pamphlets, and brochures, may be included.

Proposals should be submitted by April 1 and October 1 to be considered at the next meeting of the board of trustees.

The board of trustees meets twice a year, usually in June and December.

Restrictions on Giving: The foundation will not consider requests on behalf of individuals, and normally does not consider requests for grants to conduit organizations which pass on funds to other organizations. The foundation does not make grants outside the United States.

PUBLICATIONS
Annual report, fact sheet

GRANTS ANALYSIS
Total Grants: $53,864,944*

Number of Grants: 181

Highest Grant: $1,500,000

Average Grant: $270,423*

Typical Range: $50,000 to $500,000

Disclosure Period: 1993

Note: The total grants figure includes $15,456,506 in program-related investments to the foundation's American Land Conservation program. Average grant figure excludes four individual grants of $1,500,000 each. Recent grants are derived from a 1993 Form 990.

RECENT GRANTS

Library

250,000	Point Park College, Pittsburgh, PA — capital campaign support for Bank Center Library
100,000	Carnegie Library of Pittsburgh, Pittsburgh, PA — to fund Family Literacy Program
70,000	Carnegie Library of Pittsburgh, Pittsburgh, PA — three-year operational support for Children's Programming Initiative

General

1,500,000	Carnegie Mellon University, Pittsburgh, PA — support for Center for the Neural Basis of Cognition
1,500,000	Salvation Army, Pittsburgh, PA — campaign to improve countywide facilities
1,500,000	University of Pennsylvania, Pittsburgh, PA — support of Center for the Neural Basis of Cognition
1,500,000	University of Pennsylvania, Pittsburgh, PA — to endow professorship in the neuroscience
1,000,000	Allegheny Council to Improve Our Neighborhoods-Housing, Pittsburgh, PA — recapitalize development fund

Mengle Foundation, Glenn and Ruth

CONTACT
D. Edward Chaplin
Executive Vice President
Glenn and Ruth Mengle Fdn.
First Commonwealth Trust Co.
PO Box 1046
DuBois, PA 15801
(814) 371-0660

FINANCIAL SUMMARY
Recent Giving: $449,550 (1993); $450,199 (1992); $438,381 (1991)

Assets: $9,633,828 (1993); $9,834,506 (1992); $9,976,228 (1991)

EIN: 25-6067616

CONTRIBUTIONS SUMMARY
Donor(s): the late Glenn A. Mengle, the late Ruth E. Mengle Blake

Typical Recipients: • *Arts & Humanities:* Arts Funds, Libraries, Museums/Galleries, Public Broadcasting • *Civic & Public Affairs:* Clubs, General, Municipalities/Towns, Philanthropic Organizations, Professional & Trade Associations, Urban & Community Affairs • *Education:* Colleges & Universities, Education Funds, Leadership Training, Science/Mathematics Education, Special Education, Student Aid • *Environment:* Air/Water Quality, General, Resource Conservation • *Health:* Children's Health/Hospitals, Clinics/Medical Centers, Hospitals, Long-Term Care, Nursing Services • *Religion:* Churches, Religious Organizations, Religious Welfare • *Social Services:* Child Welfare, Community Centers, Community Service Organizations, Family Services, Homes, People with Disabilities, Recreation & Athletics, Scouts, United Funds/United Ways, YMCA/YWCA/YMHA/YWHA, Youth Organizations

Grant Types: general support and scholarship

Geographic Distribution: limited to the Brockway, Dubois, and Erie, PA, areas

GIVING OFFICERS
First Commonwealth Trust Company: trust

DeVere L. Sheesley: trust

Devere Lamar Sheesley, Jr.: trust *B* DuBois PA 1938 *ED* Bucknell Univ AB 1961; Univ PA Wharton Sch MBA 1967 *CURR EMPL* cfo: Brockway *CORP AFFIL* cfo: Brockway Inc *NONPR AFFIL* dir: YMCA DuBois PA; mem: Am Mgmt Assn, North Am Soc Corp Planners; vp, trust: Maple Ave Hosp

APPLICATION INFORMATION
Initial Approach: Send cover letter and full proposal. Include a description of organization, amount requested, purpose of funds sought, recently audited financial statement, and proof of tax-exempt status. Deadline is September 1.

GRANTS ANALYSIS
Total Grants: $449,550

Number of Grants: 39

Highest Grant: $61,000

Typical Range: $1,000 to $56,101

Disclosure Period: 1993

Note: Recent grants are derived from a 1993 Form 990.

RECENT GRANTS

Library

25,000	Mengle Memorial Library, Brockway, PA — for 1993 grant

20,000	Mengle Memorial Library, Brockway, PA — for 1993 grant
2,500	DuBois Public Library, DuBois, PA — for 1993 grant

General

61,000	DuBois Regional Medical Center, DuBois, PA — for 1993 grant
56,101	Boy Scouts of America, DuBois, PA — for 1993 grant
38,000	DuBois Area YMCA, DuBois, PA — for 1993 grant
25,000	Mengle Scholarship Fund, DuBois, PA — for 1993 grant National Merit and DuBois Educational Foundation
22,000	Greater Erie YMCA, Erie, PA — for 1993 grant

Merck & Co. Human Health Division

Sales: $10.5 billion
Employees: 47,100
Parent Company: Merck & Co., Inc.
Headquarters: West Point, PA
SIC Major Group: Medicinals & Botanicals, Poultry Hatcheries, Prepared Feeds Nec, and Industrial Inorganic Chemicals Nec

CONTACT
Gregory Reaves
Manager, Public Affairs
Merck & Co. Human Health Division
PO Box 4
West Point, PA 19486
(215) 652-3517

FINANCIAL SUMMARY
Recent Giving: $280,000 (1995 est.); $350,000 (1994 approx.); $350,000 (1993 approx.)

Fiscal Note: Company gives directly. Company departments also give contributions. Contact John Taylor, Executive Vice President, Merck Company Foundation or see separate entry for more details about parent company contributions. Above figures exclude nonmonetary support.

CONTRIBUTIONS SUMMARY
Typical Recipients: • *Arts & Humanities:* Community Arts, Libraries, Museums/Galleries, Performing Arts • *Civic & Public Affairs:* Business/Free Enterprise, Economic Development, Housing, Safety, Zoos/Aquariums • *Education:* Colleges & Universities, Elementary Education (Private), Public Education (Precollege), Science/Mathematics Education • *Health:* Health Policy/Cost Containment, Hospitals, Public Health • *Science:* Science Exhibits & Fairs, Scientific Centers & Institutes, Scientific Organizations • *Social Services:* Community Service Organizations, People with Disabilities, Shelters/Homelessness, Youth Organizations

Grant Types: general support

Nonmonetary Support Types: donated equipment, donated products, and in-kind services

Geographic Distribution: in operating communities

Operating Locations: PA (West Point)

CORP. OFFICERS
David W. Anstice: *CURR EMPL* pres: Merck & Co Inc Human Health Div US

Richard Lane: *CURR EMPL* pres: Merck & Co Human Health Div

GIVING OFFICERS
Gregory Reaves: *CURR EMPL* mgr pub affs: Merck & Co Human Health Div

APPLICATION INFORMATION
Initial Approach: *Initial Contact:* brief letter of inquiry requesting community support program guidelines; if applicable, submit a letter *Include Information On:* a description of the background and goals of the organization if organization is new to Merck; if Merck funding has been received in the past, a description and justification for the current project, including measurable objectives, current status, and people or area served *Deadlines:* February 15, May 15, August 15, November 15 *Note:* All requests must be in writing. Form letters will not be considered. Enclose the following information with request: a copy of tax-exempt status; an audit, if available; an operating budget and interim financial statement; a list of officers and directors and their outside affiliations; other available materials such as an annual report; a budget and timetable for the project; the method for evaluating results; and other sources of funding received and organizations to be solicited.

Restrictions on Giving: Grants will not be made to individuals; endowment funds; organizations that are not tax-exempt; political, veteran, labor, or sectarian groups; or community organizations that lack Merck employee participation as volunteers.

OTHER THINGS TO KNOW
Company administers a divisional budget separate from the Merck Co. Foundation (see separate entry). Requests for major support are coordinated with the Merck Co. Foundation, with hospitals, colleges, and science education priorities.

PUBLICATIONS
Program guidelines

GRANTS ANALYSIS
Total Grants: $350,000*

Typical Range: $500 to $15,000

Disclosure Period: 1994

Note: Total grants figure is approximate.

Miller Charitable Foundation, Howard E. and Nell E.

CONTACT
Bruce Bickel
Vice President
Howard E. and Nell E. Miller Charitable Fdn.
c/o PNC Bank
Trust Department
Pittsburgh, PA 15265
(412) 762-3502

FINANCIAL SUMMARY
Recent Giving: $80,250 (fiscal 1994); $279,250 (fiscal 1993); $348,800 (fiscal 1992)

Assets: $5,239,326 (fiscal 1994); $5,258,619 (fiscal 1993); $4,947,269 (fiscal 1992)

Gifts Received: $131,620 (fiscal 1993); $12,481 (fiscal 1992)

Fiscal Note: In fiscal 1993, contributions were received from the Nell L. Miller Estate.

EIN: 25-6305933

CONTRIBUTIONS SUMMARY
Donor(s): the late Nellie E. Miller

Typical Recipients: • *Arts & Humanities:* Arts Associations & Councils, Arts Festivals, Community Arts, Ethnic & Folk Arts, Libraries, Music, Opera, Theater • *Civic & Public Affairs:* General, Housing, Municipalities/Towns, Professional & Trade Associations • *Education:* Colleges & Universities, Education Funds, Literacy • *Health:* Emergency/Ambulance Services, Hospices, Hospitals • *Religion:* Religious Organizations, Religious Welfare • *Social Services:* Community Service Organizations, Family Services, Homes, People with Disabilities, Recreation & Athletics, Senior Services, YMCA/YWCA/YMHA/YWHA, Youth Organizations

Grant Types: general support

Geographic Distribution: focus on Pittsburgh, PA

GIVING OFFICERS
PNC Bank-Trust Dept.: trust

Samuel P. Delisi: trust

Thomas M. Mulroy: trust

APPLICATION INFORMATION
Initial Approach: Send brief letter of inquiry. There are no deadlines.

Restrictions on Giving: Limited to charitable, religious, scientific, literary or educational organizations.

GRANTS ANALYSIS
Total Grants: $80,250

Number of Grants: 11

Highest Grant: $15,000

Typical Range: $500 to $15,000

Disclosure Period: fiscal year ending May 31, 1994

851

Note: Recent grants are derived from a fiscal 1994 Form 990.

RECENT GRANTS

General

15,000	Breachmenders, Pittsburgh, PA
15,000	Cross Trainers, Pittsburgh, PA
10,000	Extra Mile Education Foundation, Pittsburgh, PA
7,500	Beginning with Books, Pittsburgh, PA — for gift book program
5,000	Circle C Group Homes, Pittsburgh, PA

Mine Safety Appliances Co. / Mine Safety Appliances Co. Charitable Foundation

Sales: $429.22 million
Employees: 4,600
Headquarters: Pittsburgh, PA
SIC Major Group: Surgical Appliances & Supplies and Process Control Instruments

CONTACT
James E. Herald
Secretary
Mine Safety Appliances Co. Charitable Foundation
PO Box 426
Pittsburgh, PA 15230
(412) 967-3000

FINANCIAL SUMMARY
Recent Giving: $500,000 (1995 est.); $500,000 (1994 approx.); $600,000 (1992 approx.)

Assets: $0 (1991); $4,272,900 (1990); $5,115,428 (1989)

Fiscal Note: Company gives through foundation only. Above figures exclude nonmonetary support.

EIN: 25-6023104

CONTRIBUTIONS SUMMARY
Typical Recipients: • *Arts & Humanities:* Arts Centers, Arts Festivals, Dance, Libraries, Museums/Galleries, Music, Opera, Performing Arts, Public Broadcasting, Theater • *Civic & Public Affairs:* Economic Development, Professional & Trade Associations, Public Policy, Safety, Urban & Community Affairs, Zoos/Aquariums • *Education:* Business Education, Colleges & Universities, Community & Junior Colleges, Economic Education, Education Associations, Education Funds, Engineering/Technological Education, Minority Education, Science/Mathematics Education • *Environment:* General • *Health:* Health Funds, Health Organizations, Hospitals, Medical Rehabilitation, Mental Health, Single-Disease Health Associations • *Religion:* Religious Welfare • *Science:* Observatories & Planetariums, Scientific Centers & Institutes • *Social Services:* Child Welfare, Community Service Organizations, Emergency Relief, Family Services, People with Disabilities, Recreation & Athletics, United Funds/United Ways, Youth Organizations

Grant Types: capital, conference/seminar, general support, and project

Geographic Distribution: primarily in Pittsburgh, PA, and in other areas where company has operations

Operating Locations: MD (Baltimore), PA (Evans City, Pittsburgh), RI (Esmond)

Note: Also operates internationally.

CORP. OFFICERS
James E. Herald: *CURR EMPL* vp fin: Mine Safety Appliances Co

John Thomas Ryan III: *B* Pittsburgh PA 1943 *ED* Univ Notre Dame AB 1965; Harvard Univ MBA 1969 *CURR EMPL* chmn, pres, ceo, dir: Mine Safety Appliances Co *CORP AFFIL* dir: Auergesellschaft GmbH, Penns SW *NONPR AFFIL* dir: Catholic Youth Assn Pittsburgh, Mercy Hosp Fdn; mem: Am Mining Congress, New York City Counc Foreign Rels; mem adv counc: Univ Notre Dame Coll Bus Admin

John Thomas Ryan, Jr.: *B* Pittsburgh PA 1912 *ED* PA St Univ BS 1934; Harvard Univ MBA 1936 *CURR EMPL* chmn exec comm, dir: Mine Safety Appliances Co *CORP AFFIL* dir: QED Communs *NONPR AFFIL* mem: Am Chem Soc, Am Inst Mining Metallurgical Petroleum Engrs, Am Soc Mechanical Engrs, Am Soc Safety Engrs, Counc Foreign Rels, Natl Acad Sci, Natl Soc Petroleum Engrs, Phi Delta Theta, Pittsburgh Symphony Soc, Tau Beta Pi, Veterans Safety; mem exec comm, dir: Allegheny Conf Commun Devel; trust: Thomas A Edison Fdn; trust emeritus: Univ Notre Dame *CLUB AFFIL* Allegheny, Chicago, Duquesne, Fox Chapel GC, Knights Malta, Metro, NY YC, Pittsburgh GC, Rolling Rock, Union League, Univ *PHIL AFFIL* trust: Vira I. Heinz Endowment

GIVING OFFICERS
James E. Herald: secy *CURR EMPL* vp fin: Mine Safety Appliances Co (see above)

APPLICATION INFORMATION
Initial Approach: *Initial Contact:* brief letter or proposal *Include Information On:* description of the organization, amount requested, purpose for which funds are sought, recently audited financial statement, proof of tax-exempt status *Deadlines:* none

Restrictions on Giving: Foundation does not award scholarships or provide grants to individuals.

GRANTS ANALYSIS
Total Grants: $500,000*

Typical Range: $1,000 to $5,000

Disclosure Period: 1994

Note: Total grants figure is approximate. Recent grants are derived from a 1991 Form 990.

RECENT GRANTS

Library

1,000	Carnegie Library of Pittsburgh, Pittsburgh, PA

General

112,500	United Way of Southwestern Pennsylvania, Pittsburgh, PA
25,000	St. Margaret Memorial Hospital, Pittsburgh, PA
20,000	Allegheny Conference of Community Development, Pittsburgh, PA
20,000	Children's Hospital of Pittsburgh, Pittsburgh, PA
11,000	United Way of Butler County, Butler, PA

Murphy Co. Foundation, G.C.

CONTACT
Edwin W. Davis
Secretary
G.C. Murphy Co. Foundation
211 Oberdick Dr.
McKeesport, PA 15135
(412) 751-6649

FINANCIAL SUMMARY
Recent Giving: $171,700 (1992); $139,200 (1990); $159,520 (1989)

Assets: $3,459,750 (1992); $3,002,408 (1990); $3,127,531 (1989)

EIN: 25-6028651

CONTRIBUTIONS SUMMARY
Typical Recipients: • *Arts & Humanities:* History & Archaeology, Libraries, Music • *Civic & Public Affairs:* Chambers of Commerce, Economic Development, Housing, Municipalities/Towns, Urban & Community Affairs, Women's Affairs • *Education:* Business Education, Colleges & Universities • *Health:* Cancer, Health Organizations, Hospitals, Mental Health, Single-Disease Health Associations • *Religion:* Churches, Ministries, Religious Welfare • *Social Services:* Child Welfare, Community Service Organizations, Food/Clothing Distribution, Homes, United Funds/United Ways, Youth Organizations

Grant Types: general support

Geographic Distribution: southeastern Allegheny County, with emphasis on McKeesport, PA

GIVING OFFICERS
Edwin W. Davis: secy, dir

Alice J. Hajduk: dir

Thomas F. Hudak: pres, dir

Mrs. Martha M. Lewis: dir

Robert T. Messner: dir *B* McKeesport PA 1938 *ED* Dartmouth Coll 1960; Univ PA 1963 *CURR EMPL* vp, secy, gen couns: Dollar Bank *NONPR AFFIL* mem: Am Bar Assn, Am Corp Counc Assn, Am Soc Corp Secys

APPLICATION INFORMATION
Initial Approach: The foundation requests applications be made in writing. Include a description of organization, amount requested, purpose of funds sought, recently

audited financial statement, and proof of tax-exempt status. There are no deadlines.

OTHER THINGS TO KNOW
The G.C. Murphy Co. Foundation is independently administered and is not affiliated with G.C. Murphy Co. or McCrory Corp.

GRANTS ANALYSIS
Total Grants: $171,700

Number of Grants: 27

Highest Grant: $20,500

Typical Range: $1,000 to $15,000

Disclosure Period: 1992

Note: Recent grants are derived from a 1992 Form 990.

RECENT GRANTS

Library
8,000	Carnegie Library, Pittsburgh, PA

General
20,500	YMCA of McKeesport, McKeesport, PA
15,000	McKeesport Boys and Girls Club, McKeesport, PA
12,500	Auberle Home, McKeesport, PA
10,000	Assumption Church, McKeesport, PA
10,000	Greater Pittsburgh Community Food Bank, Pittsburgh, PA

Mutual Assurance Co. / Mutual Assurance Co. Charitable Trust

Sales: $60.44 million
Employees: 238
Headquarters: Philadelphia, PA
SIC Major Group: Insurance Carriers

CONTACT
Glenmede Trust Co.
229 S 18th St.
Philadelphia, PA 19103
(215) 925-0609
Note: Inquiries regarding the foundation should be directed to the Glenmede Trust Co., Attention: Trust Administration. The Mutual Assurance Co. is located at 414 Walnut St., Philadelphia, PA 19106, 215/925-0609.

FINANCIAL SUMMARY
Recent Giving: $89,121 (1993); $90,300 (1992)

Assets: $24,976 (1993); $109,384 (1992)

EIN: 23-6214828

CONTRIBUTIONS SUMMARY
Typical Recipients: • *Arts & Humanities:* History & Archaeology, Libraries, Museums/Galleries, Music, Opera, Public Broadcasting, Theater • *Civic & Public Affairs:* Clubs, Economic Development, Economic Policy, Employment/Job Training, Ethnic Organizations, General, Municipalities/Towns, Public Policy, Safety, Urban &

Community Affairs, Women's Affairs, Zoos/Aquariums • *Education:* Arts/Humanities Education, Business Education, Colleges & Universities, Engineering/Technological Education, International Exchange, Private Education (Precollege), Secondary Education (Public), Special Education, Student Aid • *Health:* Health Organizations, Hospitals • *International:* International Affairs • *Religion:* Religious Welfare, Social/Policy Issues • *Science:* Science Museums, Scientific Centers & Institutes • *Social Services:* Crime Prevention, Family Services, Recreation & Athletics, United Funds/United Ways, Volunteer Services, YMCA/YWCA/YMHA/YWHA

Grant Types: general support

Geographic Distribution: limited primarily to the Philadelphia, PA, area

CORP. OFFICERS
Paul M. Ingersoll: *CURR EMPL* chmn: Mutual Assurance Co

GIVING OFFICERS
Morris Cheston, Jr.: trust *CURR EMPL* chmn bd: PA Zoological Garden

Daniel F. Clough: trust *CURR EMPL* pres, ceo: Mutual Assurance Co

Walter L. Foulke: trust

Dr. William S. Gaiter: trust

Robert Drew Harrison: trust *B* Des Moines IA 1923 *ED* Harvard Univ SB 1945; Harvard Univ MBA 1948 *CORP AFFIL* dir: Central Philadelphia Devel Corp, Exec Suc Corps of DE Valley, US Golf Mgmt; mng ptnr, dir: US Golf Mgmt Ptnrs *CLUB AFFIL* Golf, Merion, Merion Cricket, Union

Paul M. Ingersoll: trust *CURR EMPL* chmn: Mutual Assurance Co (see above)

Jane G. Pepper: trust

Vivian O'Gara Weyerhaeuser Piasecki: trust *PHIL AFFIL* pres, dir: F. K. and Vivian O'Gara Weyerhauser Foundation; don: Weyerhaeuser Family Foundation

John A. H. Shober: trust

Edward Starr III: trust

APPLICATION INFORMATION
Initial Approach: Send a brief letter of inquiry. Include a description of organization, amount requested, purpose of funds sought, recently audited financial statement, and proof of tax-exempt status. There are no deadlines.

Restrictions on Giving: No grants for operating expenses, except to the United Fund of Philadelphia.

GRANTS ANALYSIS
Total Grants: $89,121

Number of Grants: 75

Highest Grant: $15,000

Typical Range: $50 to $10,511

Disclosure Period: 1993

Note: Recent grants are derived from a 1993 Form 990.

RECENT GRANTS

Library
550	Library of Philadelphia, Philadelphia, PA

General
15,000	United Way of Southeastern Pennsylvania, Philadelphia, PA
10,511	United Way of Franklin County, Shippensburg, PA
3,200	Pennsylvania Horticultural Society, Philadelphia, PA
2,700	Greater Philadelphia Urban Affairs Coalition, Philadelphia, PA
2,500	Central Philadelphia Development, Philadelphia, PA

National Forge Co. / National Forge Foundation

Sales: $85.0 million
Employees: 1,100
Headquarters: Irvine, PA
SIC Major Group: Fabricated Metal Products, Industrial Machinery & Equipment, and Primary Metal Industries

CONTACT
Bill Bailey
Director, Human Resources
National Forge Co.
One Front St.
Irvine, PA 16329
(814) 563-7522

FINANCIAL SUMMARY
Recent Giving: $87,605 (1993); $150,500 (1992); $46,500 (1991)

Assets: $286,905 (1993); $324,716 (1992); $360,579 (1991)

Gifts Received: $40,000 (1993); $70,000 (1991); $150,000 (1989)

Fiscal Note: In 1993, contributions were received from National Forge Company.

EIN: 25-6067621

CONTRIBUTIONS SUMMARY
Typical Recipients: • *Arts & Humanities:* General, Libraries, Music, Performing Arts, Theater • *Civic & Public Affairs:* Economic Development, General • *Education:* Colleges & Universities, Education Funds, Faculty Development, General • *Health:* General, Health Organizations, Hospices, Hospitals, Long-Term Care, Public Health • *International:* International Development • *Religion:* Religious Welfare • *Social Services:* Family Services, General, Recreation & Athletics, United Funds/United Ways

Grant Types: general support, matching, and operating expenses

Geographic Distribution: focus on PA

Operating Locations: MA (Andover), PA (Irvine)

CORP. OFFICERS

Maurice J. Cashman: *CURR EMPL* vp, dir: Natl Forge Co

Roger Clark: *CURR EMPL* chmn, pres, ceo, dir: Natl Forge Co

GIVING OFFICERS

Maurice J. Cashman: treas *CURR EMPL* vp, dir: Natl Forge Co (see above)

John G. Koedel, Jr.: secy, dir *B* Pittsburgh PA 1937 *ED* Washington & Lee Univ BS 1959 *CURR EMPL* vp, cfo: Natl Forge Co *CORP AFFIL* dir: Integra Fin, Mitchell Shackleton & Co Ltd, Natl Forge Europe NV *NONPR AFFIL* mem: Masons

John H. Morse: vp, dir *B* Estherville IA 1910 *ED* St Univ IA BA 1930; Harvard Univ MBA 1932; Yale Univ Law JD 1935

Robert O. Wilder: pres, dir *B* Warren PA 1927 *ED* Yale Univ 1951 *CORP AFFIL* pres: Forest Property Owners Assn *NONPR AFFIL* mem: Am Bar Assn, Phi Beta Kappa, Phi Gamma Delta

APPLICATION INFORMATION

Initial Approach: The foundation has no formal grant application procedure or application form. There are no deadlines.

Restrictions on Giving: Limited to communities where company has facilities.

GRANTS ANALYSIS

Total Grants: $87,605

Number of Grants: 7

Highest Grant: $39,125

Typical Range: $500 to $25,000

Disclosure Period: 1993

Note: Recent grants are derived from a 1993 Form 990.

RECENT GRANTS

Library
25,000	Warren Library Fund, Warren, PA — support library operations

General
39,125	United Way of Warren County, Warren, PA
15,000	World Leisure and Recreation, Ottawa, Canada — growth and development of recreation and leisure movement
5,000	Community Care, Warren, PA — health care services
2,000	Foundation for Independent Colleges, Mechanicsburg, PA — better communication and understanding between business community and independent higher education
980	Southern Christian Leadership, Atlanta, GA — nonviolent campaign against racial aggression

Neville Chemical Co.

Employees: 490
Headquarters: Pittsburgh, PA
SIC Major Group: Chemicals & Allied Products, Rubber & Miscellaneous Plastics Products, and Wholesale Trade—Nondurable Goods

CONTACT

L. Van V. Dauler, Jr.
Chairman, President
Neville Chemical Co.
2800 Neville Rd.
Pittsburgh, PA 15225-1496
(412) 331-4200

CONTRIBUTIONS SUMMARY

Typical Recipients: • *Arts & Humanities:* Libraries

Operating Locations: PA (Pittsburgh)

CORP. OFFICERS

L. Van V. Dauler, Jr.: *B* Pittsburgh PA 1943 *ED* Yale Univ BA 1966; Univ PA MBA 1968 *CURR EMPL* chmn, pres, dir: Neville Chem Co *CORP AFFIL* dir: Nevcin Polymers; pres, chmn: Vitae Investment Co; pres, dir: Nevco

RECENT GRANTS

Library
Carnegie Library of Pittsburgh, Pittsburgh, PA

Patterson Charitable Fund, W. I.

CONTACT

Robert B. Shust
Trustee
W. I. Patterson Charitable Fund
407 Oliver Bldg.
Pittsburgh, PA 15222
(412) 281-5580

FINANCIAL SUMMARY

Recent Giving: $116,676 (fiscal 1994); $123,178 (fiscal 1991); $124,424 (fiscal 1990)

Assets: $3,177,849 (fiscal 1994); $3,084,868 (fiscal 1991); $2,811,980 (fiscal 1990)

EIN: 25-6028639

CONTRIBUTIONS SUMMARY

Donor(s): the late W. I. Patterson

Typical Recipients: • *Arts & Humanities:* Historic Preservation, Libraries, Music, Opera, Public Broadcasting • *Civic & Public Affairs:* Employment/Job Training • *Education:* Colleges & Universities, Education Funds, Legal Education • *Health:* Arthritis, Cancer, Children's Health/Hospitals, Hospitals, Medical Research, Single-Dis-

ease Health Associations • *International:* Health Care/Hospitals • *Religion:* Ministries, Religious Welfare • *Social Services:* Big Brother/Big Sister, Child Welfare, Community Service Organizations, Food/Clothing Distribution, Homes, People with Disabilities, Shelters/Homelessness, United Funds/United Ways, Youth Organizations

Grant Types: capital, emergency, general support, multiyear/continuing support, operating expenses, and research

Geographic Distribution: focus on Allegheny County, PA

GIVING OFFICERS

Martin L. Moore, Jr.: trust

Robert B. Shust: trust

Lester K. Wolf: trust

APPLICATION INFORMATION

Initial Approach: Send brief letter describing program. Include a description of organization, amount requested, purpose of funds sought, recently audited financial statement, and proof of tax-exempt status. Deadline is June 30.

Restrictions on Giving: Does not support individuals.

GRANTS ANALYSIS

Total Grants: $116,676

Number of Grants: 52

Highest Grant: $23,335

Typical Range: $1,000 to $3,000

Disclosure Period: fiscal year ending July 31, 1994

Note: Recent grants are derived from a fiscal 1994 Form 990.

RECENT GRANTS

Library
23,335	Carnegie Library of Pittsburgh, Pittsburgh, PA
2,000	Christian Education for the Blind, Ft. Worth, TX — library ministry to blind persons

General
3,000	Foundation for Independent Colleges, Harrisburg, PA — area college support
3,000	Greater Pittsburgh Guild for the Blind, Bridgeville, PA — blind training program
3,000	Make-A-Wish Foundation of Western Pennsylvania, Pittsburgh, PA — programs for children with life threatening illnesses
3,000	Pittsburgh Mercy Foundation, Pittsburgh, PA — community hospital
3,000	Salvation Army, Pittsburgh, PA — international charity

PECO Energy Company

Revenue: $4.04 billion
Employees: 9,660
Headquarters: Philadelphia, PA
SIC Major Group: Electric, Gas & Sanitary
    Services

CONTACT
Linda Roth
Manager, Corporate Contributions
PECO Energy Company
2301 Market St.
Philadelphia, PA 19101
(215) 841-4124

FINANCIAL SUMMARY
Recent Giving: $3,000,000 (1995 est.);
$3,200,000 (1994 approx.); $3,200,000
(1993 approx.)
Fiscal Note: Company gives directly.

CONTRIBUTIONS SUMMARY
Typical Recipients: • *Arts & Humanities:*
Arts Funds, Dance, Ethnic & Folk Arts, Libraries, Music, Opera • *Civic & Public Affairs:* Housing, Law & Justice, Urban &
Community Affairs • *Education:* Business
Education, Colleges & Universities, Community & Junior Colleges, Education Funds,
General, Public Education (Precollege) • *Environment:* General • *Health:* Hospitals • *Social Services:* Child Welfare, United
Funds/United Ways

Grant Types: capital and operating expenses

Nonmonetary Support Types: donated
equipment, in-kind services, loaned employees, and loaned executives

Note: Estimated value of nonmonetary support is not available.

Geographic Distribution: in Bucks, Chester, Montgomery, Deleware, and York counties in Pennsylvania

Operating Locations: NJ (Hancock's
Bridge), PA (Bristol Township, Chester, Eddystone, Falls Township, Limerick Township, New Florence, Peach Bottom
Township, Philadelphia, Phoenixville,
Shelocta)

CORP. OFFICERS
Gwendolyn S. King: *CURR EMPL* sr vp,
corp pub aff: PECO Energy Co
Corbin Asahel McNeill, Jr.: *B* Santa Fe
NM 1939 *ED* Naval Nuclear Power Sch
1962-1963; US Naval Acad BS 1962; Univ
CA Berkeley 1975-1976; Syracuse Univ
1983-1984 *CURR EMPL* pres, coo, dir:
PECO Energy Co *CORP AFFIL* dir: Leadership Inc *NONPR AFFIL* dir: Am Gas Assn,
Am Nuclear Energy Counc, Drexel Univ,
Nuclear Utility Mgmt Resources Counc;
mem: Am Nuclear Soc, Electrical Assn
Philadelphia
Joseph F. Paquette, Jr.: *B* Norwood MS
1934 *ED* Yale Univ BS 1956 *CURR EMPL*
chmn, ceo: PECO Energy Co

GIVING OFFICERS
Linda Roth: *CURR EMPL* mgr corp contributions: PECO Energy Co

APPLICATION INFORMATION
Initial Approach: *Initial Contact:* brief letter *Include Information On:* description of
the organization, amount requested, list of
organization's board of directors, and copy
of 501(c)(3) letter of determination *Deadlines:* none

GRANTS ANALYSIS
Total Grants: $3,200,000*
Disclosure Period: 1994

Note: Total giving figure is an approximation.

Penn Foundation, William

CONTACT
Harry E. Cerino
President
William Penn Foundation
1630 Locust St.
Philadelphia, PA 19103
(215) 732-5114

FINANCIAL SUMMARY
Recent Giving: $35,767,692 (1993);
$35,684,155 (1992); $30,549,447 (1991)
Assets: $563,556,011 (1993); $528,382,523
(1992); $551,000,000 (1991)
Gifts Received: $12,521,876 (1993);
$11,739,000 (1992); $11,570,000 (1991)
EIN: 23-1503488

CONTRIBUTIONS SUMMARY
Donor(s): The William Penn Foundation
was established in 1945 by Otto Haas (1872-
1960) and his wife, Phoebe. Mr. Haas immigrated to the United States from Germany at
the turn of the century. He helped develop
and market an innovative leather tanning
process which proved to be highly popular
in the United States and later in South America. He built a career based on his expertise
in industrial chemicals. His wife, Phoebe
Waterman Haas , was born in North Dakota,
educated at Vassar, and was an astronomer.
In 1945, Otto and Phoebe Haas established
the Phoebe Waterman Foundation. Reflecting the founders' postwar concerns, grants
were used to fund European relief, provide
scholarships for fatherless children, and support medical and educational institutions.
When Otto Haas died in 1960, the foundation received the bulk of his estate. Mrs.
Haas continued adding funds to the foundation until her death in 1967. In 1970, the
name of the foundation was changed to the
Haas Community Foundation. In 1974, it
was renamed the William Penn Foundation,
reflecting its close ties to Philadelphia.

Typical Recipients: • *Arts & Humanities:*
Arts Associations & Councils, Arts Centers,
Arts Festivals, Arts Funds, Arts Institutes,
Ballet, Community Arts, Dance, Ethnic &
Folk Arts, Historic Preservation, Libraries,
Literary Arts, Museums/Galleries, Music,
Opera, Performing Arts, Public Broadcasting, Theater, Visual Arts • *Civic & Public
Affairs:* Botanical Gardens/Parks, Clubs,
Economic Development, Employment/Job

Training, Hispanic Affairs, Housing, Professional & Trade Associations, Urban & Community Affairs, Women's Affairs,
Zoos/Aquariums • *Education:* Arts/Humanities Education, Colleges & Universities,
Community & Junior Colleges, Elementary
Education (Private), Engineering/Technological Education, Minority Education, Preschool Education, Public Education
(Precollege), Science/Mathematics Education, Social Sciences Education • *Environment:* General, Resource Conservation
• *Health:* Geriatric Health, Health Organizations, Prenatal Health Issues, Public Health
• *Religion:* Religious Welfare • *Social Services:* Child Welfare, Community Centers,
Community Service Organizations, Counseling, Day Care, Domestic Violence, Family
Planning, Family Services, Homes, Recreation & Athletics, Senior Services, United
Funds/United Ways, Volunteer Services,
Youth Organizations

Grant Types: capital, multiyear/continuing
support, and project

Geographic Distribution: mostly restricted
to regional giving; some national and international giving

GIVING OFFICERS
Eric Ronald Aird: vp (fin), treas *B*
Glenolden PA 1936 *ED* Drexel Univ 1960
CURR EMPL exec vp fin & admin, secy,
treas, dir: Franklin Inst *NONPR AFFIL* dir:
Friends Logan Sq Fdn; secy, treas, trust: Bartol Res Fdn
Kenneth S. Brecher: pres, dir
Harry E. Cerino: pres
Ida K. Chen: dir *PHIL AFFIL* dir: Samuel
S. Fels Fund
Gloria Twine Chisum: dir
C. Richard Cox: sr program off
Graham Stanley Finney: dir *B* Greenwich
CT 1930 *ED* Washington & Lee Univ 1948-
1949; Yale Univ BA 1952; Harvard Univ
MPA 1954 *CURR EMPL* sr ptnr: Conservation Co *CLUB AFFIL* mem: Yale *PHIL AFFIL* trust: Adam and Maria Sarah Seybert
Institution for Poor Boys and Girls
David W. Haas: chmn, dir
Frederick R. Haas: dir
Janet F. Haas: vchwm, dir
John O. Haas: dir
Melinda A. Haas: dir *B* Victoria TX 1964
ED TX Lutheran Coll BBA 1986; Univ
Houston MS 1989 *CURR EMPL* sr acct:
Scott & Co *NONPR AFFIL* mem: Inst Mgmt
Accts, Natl Assn Female Execs
Nancy B. Haas: dir
William D. Haas: dir
Phoebe A. Haddon: dir
Barbara H. Hanrahan: dir
Philip C. Herr II: dir *PHIL AFFIL* trust:
John C. and Chara C. Haas Charitable Trust
Stephanie Naidoff: dir
Helen Davis Picher: program off
Edmund Benjamin Spaeth, Jr.: dir *B*
Washington DC 1920 *ED* Harvard Univ AB
1942; Harvard Univ LLB 1948 *CURR EMPL*
of couns: Pepper Hamilton & Scheetz

NONPR AFFIL dir: Ctr Professionalism, Curtis Inst Music, Pub Interest Law Ctr Philadelphia; fellow: Am Bar Fdn; mem: Am Bar Assn, Am Judicature Soc, Am Law Inst, Order Coif, PA Bar Assn, Phi Beta Kappa, Philadelphia Bar Assn; sr fellow: Univ PA Law Sch; trust: Lewis M Stevens Conf Trust

Anita Arrow Summers: dir *B* New York NY 1925 *ED* Hunter Coll BA 1945; Univ Chicago MA 1947 *CORP AFFIL* dir, chmn audit comm: Meridian Bancorp *NONPR AF-FIL* mem: Am Econ Assn, Assn Pub Policy & Mgmt; mem, subcom: Educational Governance; prof: Univ PA Wharton Sch; res policy counc: Comm Econ Devel New York City

Fasaha M. Traylor: program off

Cathy M. Weiss: program off

Nancy K. Zimmerman: program off

APPLICATION INFORMATION
Initial Approach:

Applications will not be considered unless submitted in writing. Visits to the foundation and contacts with members of the board or staff are strongly discouraged. A single copy of a proposal, in writing, is sufficient.

The proposal should include a one-page summary outline; information about the agency making the request; description of the proposed project; complete financial information; copy of the IRS determination letter of tax-exempt status; list of officers and directors of the organization making the application; copy of the most recent annual report; and a copy, audited if available, of the most recent financial statement.

There are no formal deadlines for funding requests.

All proposals are reviewed by the foundation staff to determine whether they fall within its areas of interest and current funding priorities. Those meeting the criteria are then subject to further study and investigation; some may then be submitted to the board of directors for consideration.

Restrictions on Giving: No grants are made to institutions which unfairly discriminate on the basis of race, creed, or sex. No grants are made to individuals or to support sectarian religious activities; or for scholarships, fellowships, or travel; lobbying or legislative activities; programs concerned with a particular disease; addiction treatment; recreational programs; or films. The foundation does not make loans or provide funds to be redistributed at an organization's discretion.

PUBLICATIONS
Annual report, grant application procedures

GRANTS ANALYSIS
Total Grants: $35,767,692

Number of Grants: 271*

Highest Grant: $3,000,000

Average Grant: $131,993*

Typical Range: $10,000 to $200,000

Disclosure Period: 1993

Note: Number of grant and average grant figures exclude discretionary and matching

gifts. Recent grants are derived from a 1994 partial grants list.

RECENT GRANTS
Library

35,000	Library Company of Philadelphia, Philadelphia, PA — for the increased costs of publishing the "Philadelphia Almanac and Citizen's Manual"	
17,000	Civil War Library and Museum, Philadelphia, PA — for an exhibition on women and the Civil War	

General

556,654	Health Promotion Council of Southeastern Pennsylvania, Philadelphia, PA — over three years to expand the Health Literacy Project, in which health care procedures, issues, and preventive measures such as mammograms are described simply for people with low reading skills	
500,000	Christ Church Hospital, Philadelphia, PA — to provide independent living for senior citizens	
500,000	Trust for Public Land, Morristown, NJ — over two years for the Barnegat Bay Initiative	
500,000	YMCA of Philadelphia and Vicinity, Philadelphia, PA — to expand day care facilities at three branches	
450,000	Philadelphia Corporation for Aging, Philadelphia, PA — for a capital improvement project	

Pennsylvania Dutch Co. / Pennsylvania Dutch Co. Foundation

Sales: $20.53 million
Employees: 200
Headquarters: Mount Holly Springs, PA
SIC Major Group: Food & Kindred Products

CONTACT
Lincoln A. Warrell
Secretary, Principal Manager
Pennsylvania Dutch Co.
408 n Baltimore Avenue
Mount Holly Springs, PA 17065
(717) 486-3496

FINANCIAL SUMMARY
Recent Giving: $42,380 (fiscal 1992); $50,800 (fiscal 1991); $32,297 (fiscal 1990)

Assets: $55,582 (fiscal 1992); $69,040 (fiscal 1991); $1,709 (fiscal 1990)

Gifts Received: $27,000 (fiscal 1992); $116,229 (fiscal 1991); $21,742 (fiscal 1990)

Fiscal Note: In fiscal 1992, contributions were received from the Pennsylvania Dutch Co., Inc.

EIN: 23-2022526

CONTRIBUTIONS SUMMARY
Typical Recipients: • *Arts & Humanities:* Ballet, History & Archaeology, Libraries, Public Broadcasting • *Civic & Public Affairs:* Economic Policy, Employment/Job Training • *Education:* Agricultural Education, Business Education, Colleges & Universities, Education Associations, Education Funds, Engineering/Technological Education, General, Public Education (Precollege), Student Aid • *Health:* Hospitals • *International:* Foreign Educational Institutions, International Organizations • *Religion:* Churches, Ministries, Religious Welfare • *Science:* Science Exhibits & Fairs • *Social Services:* Food/Clothing Distribution, Shelters/Homelessness, Substance Abuse, Youth Organizations

Grant Types: general support

Geographic Distribution: giving primarily in PA

Operating Locations: PA (Mount Holly Springs)

CORP. OFFICERS
Richard P. Billman: *CURR EMPL* pres, dir: PA Dutch Co

Lincoln A. Warrell: *CURR EMPL* chmn, ceo, dir: PA Dutch Co

GIVING OFFICERS
Lincoln A. Warrell: secy, mgr *CURR EMPL* chmn, ceo, dir: PA Dutch Co (see above)

APPLICATION INFORMATION
Initial Approach: Applications not accepted. The foundation reports it supports preselected organizations.

GRANTS ANALYSIS
Total Grants: $42,380

Number of Grants: 23

Highest Grant: $25,000

Typical Range: $100 to $1,000

Disclosure Period: fiscal year ending October 31, 1992

Note: Recent grants are derived from a fiscal 1992 Form 990.

RECENT GRANTS
General

25,000	Brian Bex Report, Hagerstown, IN — scholarship fund	
4,000	Safe Harbor, Carlisle, PA — capital fund campaign for homeless	
2,700	Brian Bex Report, Hagerstown, IN — educational material	
2,500	Pennsylvania State University, University Park, PA — college of engineering fund	
1,000	Competitive Enterprises Institute, Washington, DC — support of free enterprise system	

Peters Foundation, Charles F.

CONTACT
Joanna M. Mayo
Trust Officer
Integra Trust Co.
300 Fourth Ave.
Pittsburgh, PA 15278
(412) 355-4810

FINANCIAL SUMMARY
Recent Giving: $86,000 (1993); $102,750 (1992); $125,772 (1991)

Assets: $2,266,470 (1993); $2,322,783 (1992); $2,324,564 (1991)

EIN: 25-6070765

CONTRIBUTIONS SUMMARY
Donor(s): Charles F. Peters

Typical Recipients: • *Arts & Humanities:* Libraries, Music • *Civic & Public Affairs:* Clubs • *Education:* Colleges & Universities, Private Education (Precollege) • *Health:* Hospitals • *Religion:* Churches, Religious Organizations, Religious Welfare • *Social Services:* Community Service Organizations, Homes, United Funds/United Ways, YMCA/YWCA/YMHA/YWHA, Youth Organizations

Grant Types: general support

Geographic Distribution: focus on PA

GIVING OFFICERS
Integra Trust Company: trust

William H. Balter, Esq.: admin

Herman A. Haase: admin

J. Charles Peterson: admin

Peters Schoeller: off

Robert A. Stone: admin

APPLICATION INFORMATION
Initial Approach: Send brief letter describing program. There are no deadlines.

GRANTS ANALYSIS
Total Grants: $86,000

Number of Grants: 113

Highest Grant: $3,000

Typical Range: $250 to $2,000

Disclosure Period: 1993

Note: Recent grants are derived from a 1993 Form 990.

RECENT GRANTS
Library

1,000	Carnegie Free Library of McKeesport, McKeesport, PA

General

3,000	Pennsylvania State University McKeesport Campus, McKeesport, PA
2,000	Pennsylvania State University McKeesport Campus, McKeesport, PA
2,000	Salvation Army, McKeesport, PA
1,000	All Souls Episcopal Church, North Versailles, PA
1,000	Auberle Home, McKeesport, PA

Pew Charitable Trusts

CONTACT
Deidra A. Lyngard
Communications Manager
Pew Charitable Trusts
One Commerce Sq.
2005 Market St., Ste. 1700
Philadelphia, PA 19103-7017
(215) 575-9050

Note: The Trusts urges applicants to send letters of inquiry directly to the responsible program staff member in each area of interest if possible. Organizations can contact the Trusts for *New Sources: A Directory of Experts* for a list of staff members.

FINANCIAL SUMMARY
Recent Giving: $184,757,247 (1995 est.); $172,815,600 (1994); $166,624,400 (1993)

Assets: $3,454,991,739 (1994 approx.); $3,512,044,823 (1993); $3,300,000,000 (1992 approx.)

Fiscal Note: The figures for recent giving represents grants approved for that year.

EIN: 23-6299309

CONTRIBUTIONS SUMMARY
Donor(s): The Pew Charitable Trusts is the collective name for the seven individual charitable trusts established by the two sons and two daughters of Joseph N. Pew, the founder of the Sun Oil Company. The first of the trusts, the Pew Memorial Trust, was founded in 1948. Smaller trusts were subsequently established to fund the Pews' personal philanthropic interests. Those included within the Pew Charitable Trusts are the Pew Memorial Trust; J. Howard Pew Freedom Trust; Mabel Pew Myrin Trust; J. N. Pew, Jr., Charitable Trust; Medical Trust; Mary Anderson Trust; and Knollbrook Trust. Because there is overlap in the areas that the seven trusts support, they share a single set of guidelines to establish eligibility for funding. Grant funds are allocated from the individual trusts based on their funding priorities.

John Howard Pew , the second son of Joseph N. Pew, was born in 1882 in Bradford, PA. Following graduation from Grove City College in 1900, and after taking several advanced courses at the Massachusetts Institute of Technology, he joined the Sun Oil Company. He and his brother, Joseph N. Pew, Jr. , assumed control of the company in 1912 after their father's death. His personal trust, established in 1957, supports organizations and institutions embodying the values of hard work, Christian values, free enterprise, and access to opportunity for all individuals. He also assisted numerous organizations dedicated to improving the qual-

ity of life in Philadelphia. J. Howard Pew died in 1971.

Mary Ethel Pew , the third child of Joseph N. Pew, was born in 1884 in Pittsburgh, PA. After graduating from Bryn Mawr College in 1906, she remained in Philadelphia where the Pew family relocated from Pittsburgh. Following her mother's death from cancer, Mary Ethel Pew devoted her resources to the support of cancer research and health care both as a volunteer and a board member for various institutions. She became particularly interested in Philadelphia's Lankenau Hospital and Institute for Cancer Research. She also funded various Philadelphia cultural, educational, and social service organizations. The Medical Trust was established in 1979 through her will.

Joseph Newton Pew, Jr. , the youngest son of Joseph N. Pew, was born in 1886 in Pittsburgh, PA. After graduating with a degree in mechanical engineering from Cornell University in 1908, he worked briefly in the administrative offices of Sun Oil before leaving to learn the business from the ground up as an oilman in Illinois and as a roadlayer in South America. In 1912, upon his father's death, he became a vice president of the company. During his years at Sun, Mr. Pew focused his energies on designing new methods and products for the company. His contributions to educational and charitable institutions reflected his belief in free political expression, equal opportunity, and the free market system. The J. N. Pew, Jr., Charitable Trust was established from his estate following his death in 1963.

Mabel Pew Myrin , the youngest daughter of Joseph N. Pew, was born in 1889 in Pittsburgh, PA. Married in 1919, she and her husband, H. Alarik W. Myrin, moved to Argentina where they managed ranch property and developed mineral resources. After returning to the United States in the 1930s, they dedicated themselves to improving educational methods, aiding the handicapped, and preserving soil fertility. Mrs. Myrin strongly supported both the Waldorf educational method which takes a holistic approach to teaching, and the Camphill movement which applies Waldorf methods to the care and education of the handicapped. She also served as a trustee or board member for many institutions. The Mabel Pew Myrin Trust was established in 1957 to improve the human condition through support to the arts, education, health, and human services. She died in 1972.

Typical Recipients: • *Arts & Humanities:* Arts Festivals, Arts Funds, Arts Outreach, Dance, Ethnic & Folk Arts, Historic Preservation, History & Archaeology, Libraries, Museums/Galleries, Music, Opera, Performing Arts, Public Broadcasting, Theater, Visual Arts • *Civic & Public Affairs:* Business/Free Enterprise, Clubs, Economic Development, Employment/Job Training, First Amendment Issues, Housing, Public Policy, Rural Affairs, Urban & Community Affairs • *Education:* Arts/Humanities Education, Colleges & Universities, Education Associations, Elementary Education (Private), Faculty Development, General, International

Exchange, International Studies, Journalism/Media Education, Literacy, Medical Education, Minority Education, Private Education (Precollege), Public Education (Precollege), Religious Education, Science/Mathematics Education • *Environment:* Energy, Forestry, General, Resource Conservation • *Health:* Adolescent Health Issues, AIDS/HIV, Cancer, Children's Health/Hospitals, Emergency/Ambulance Services, Geriatric Health, Health Policy/Cost Containment, Health Organizations, Home-Care Services, Nutrition, Prenatal Health Issues, Public Health • *International:* Foreign Arts Organizations, Foreign Educational Institutions, Health Care/Hospitals, Human Rights, International Affairs, International Development, International Environmental Issues, International Organizations, International Peace & Security Issues, International Relations, International Relief Efforts, Missionary/Religious Activities, Trade • *Religion:* Churches, Jewish Causes, Ministries, Religious Organizations, Religious Welfare, Seminaries, Social/Policy Issues • *Science:* Scientific Centers & Institutes, Scientific Organizations, Scientific Research • *Social Services:* Child Welfare, Community Service Organizations, Domestic Violence, Family Planning, Family Services, Refugee Assistance, Senior Services, Substance Abuse, United Funds/United Ways, Volunteer Services, Youth Organizations

Grant Types: challenge, general support, project, research, and seed money

Geographic Distribution: nationally, with a special commitment to Philadelphia, PA; some international giving

GIVING OFFICERS

Susan W. Catherwood: dir *CURR EMPL* dir: Glenmede Trust Co *PHIL AFFIL* mgr: Ludwick Institute

Robert Galbraith Dunlop: dir *B* Boston MA 1909 *ED* Univ PA Wharton Sch BS 1931 *CORP AFFIL* dir: Glenmede Trust Co, Sun Co *NONPR AFFIL* mem: Beta Gamma Sigma, Sigma Phi Epsilon; trust: Univ PA

Thomas W. Langfitt, MD: dir *B* 1927 *CURR EMPL* pres, ceo: Glenmede Trust Co *CORP AFFIL* ceo, pres, dir: Glenmede Trust Co *NONPR AFFIL* secy, dir: Am Philosophical Soc

Deidra A. Lyngard: commun mgr

Robert Emmett McDonald: dir *B* Red Wing MN 1915 *ED* Univ MN BEE 1940; Univ Chicago 1942; Univ MN BBA *CORP AFFIL* dir: Genmede Trust Co *NONPR AFFIL* mem: Eta Kappa Nu, Tau Beta Pi *CLUB AFFIL* Acacia, Philadelphia CC, Union League

J. Howard Pew II: dir *CORP AFFIL* dir: Glenmede Trust Co

Joseph N. Pew IV, MD: dir *CORP AFFIL* dir: Glenmede Trust Co

Richard F. Pew: dir

Robert Anderson Pew: dir *B* Philadelphia PA 1936 *ED* Princeton Univ 1954-1956; Temple Univ BS 1959; MA Inst Tech MS 1970 *CURR EMPL* pres: Helios Capital Corp *CORP AFFIL* dir: Glenmede Corp,

Glenmede Trust Co *NONPR AFFIL* hon mem: Am Hosp Assn; mem, trust, chmn: Aircraft Owners Pilots Assn; trust: Temple Univ; trust, vchmn: Bryn Mawr Coll, Childrens Hosp Fdn Philadelphia *CLUB AFFIL* Acorn, Aviation CC, Courts, Merion Cricket, NE Harbor Fleet, Philadelphia Aviation CC, Seal Harbor, Union League

William Chase Richardson, PhD: dir *B* Passaic NJ 1940 *ED* Trinity Coll BA 1962; Univ Chicago MBA 1964; Univ Chicago PhD 1971 *CORP AFFIL* dir: Glenmede Trust Co *NONPR AFFIL* fellow: Am Pub Health Assn; mem: Natl Academy Sciences Inst Medicine; pres: Johns Hopkins Univ *PHIL AFFIL* trust: Henry J. Kaiser Family Foundation; pres, ceo: W. K. Kellogg Foundation

Rebecca Webster Rimel: pres, dir *CORP AFFIL* exec vp, dir: Glenmede Trust Co *NONPR AFFIL* adv counc: Natl Inst Neurosurgery Disorders Stroke; bd dir: Fdn Ctr, Independent Sector, Sunny von Bulow Coma Head Trauma Res Fdn; mem: Am Academy Nursing, Am Assn Neurosurgical Nurses, Am Nurses Assn, Am Pub Health Assn, Emergency Dept Nurses Assn, VA St Nurses Assn

APPLICATION INFORMATION

Initial Approach:

Initially, a brief letter of inquiry summarizing the proposal is suggested. If the proposal falls within funding priorities and guidelines of the Trusts, an application package will be provided with further instructions.

The inquiry should summarize the project for which support is sought. This should fit within guidelines for funding. Letters should include a description of the organization, nature of work and a brief history of achievements, especially as they relate to issue to be addressed; a statement of the problem to be addressed and an explanation of how it will be addressed; brief description of anticipated achievements or outcomes; description of time frame of proposed activities; estimated costs for the project or activity; and what is being requested from the Trusts. Full proposals are not encouraged without an initial contact with the staff.

Applications may be submitted throughout the year.

Letters of inquiry are reviewed by the appropriate program staff and grant seekers will be notified either by telephone or letter whether a request meets the funding criteria and guidelines of the program. If the request is of interest to the Trusts, the applicant will be asked to submit a full proposal, and an application package will be forwarded for completion. If the proposal is approved for funding, the applicant will be notified by letter within four to six weeks of a board meeting. The board of trustees meets in March, June, September, and December.

Restrictions on Giving: Prospective applicants are encouraged to request a copy of the Trusts' annual program guidelines and procedures pamphlet that provides detailed information on areas of interest to the Trusts, as well as funding restrictions.

Restrictions on Giving: In general, the Trusts do not provide funding for capital funds, endowments, debt reduction, general operations, library acquisitions, or individuals.

OTHER THINGS TO KNOW

The Glenmede Trust Company manages the funds and serves as trustee. In 1986, it reorganized the seven Trusts into one division for purposes of grant making and administration.

Although the Trusts have an interdisciplinary grants fund for propsals that fit within the guidelines of two or more programs, this status is determined by program officers at the Trusts. Applicants should apply to the program that suits their proposal.

The Trusts report that they offer occasional seminars and workshops on how to apply for grants to special programs, as well as communications and strategic planning assistance to selected grantees.

The Trusts discontinued their $60 million Children's Initiative in the spring of 1994. The program, which began in 1992, was discontinued because state collaborators were unable to project how much money they could contribute to the project. The project's aim was to create family centers where clients of state health and social services could receive all their services under one roof.

PUBLICATIONS

Annual report, guidelines and procedures, contact directory, and history of the Trusts

GRANTS ANALYSIS

Total Grants: $158,002,536*

Number of Grants: 529*

Highest Grant: $7,500,000*

Average Grant: $326,684*

Typical Range: $200,000* to $500,000

Disclosure Period: 1994

Note: The analysis was provided by the Trusts and represents grants paid in 1994. Recent grants are derived from a 1994 partial grants list.

RECENT GRANTS

General

4,450,000   Nature Conservancy, Arlington, VA — to design, develop, and operate four model conservation lodges in the United States and Caribbean

1,250,000   Cooperative Development Services Fund, Madison, WI — for a project to increase the demand for and supply of organic food in the upper Midwest

1,050,000   Philadelphia Foundation, Philadelphia, PA — to help Frankford Group Ministry and its partners stabilize and preserve Philadelphia's Frankford neighborhood, including revitalization of commercial areas and housing

1,040,000   United Way of Southeastern Pennsylvania, Philadelphia, PA — for the 1994 annual campaign, the Community Services Division, and the Jewish Federation of Greater Philadelphia

1,000,000   Children's Hospital Foundation, Philadelphia, PA — to furnish and equip a new pediatric research building at Children's Hospital of Philadelphia

Phillips Charitable Trust, Dr. and Mrs. Arthur William

CONTACT
William J. McFate
Trustee
Dr. and Mrs. Arthur William Phillips
  Charitable Trust
229 Elm St., P. O. Box 316
Oil City, PA 16301
(814) 676-2736

FINANCIAL SUMMARY
Recent Giving: $296,744 (fiscal 1994); $409,000 (fiscal 1991); $631,579 (fiscal 1990)

Assets: $10,866,850 (fiscal 1994); $9,826,223 (fiscal 1991); $9,621,852 (fiscal 1990)

EIN: 25-6201015

CONTRIBUTIONS SUMMARY
Donor(s): the late Arthur William Phillips

Typical Recipients: • *Arts & Humanities:* Libraries, Museums/Galleries • *Civic & Public Affairs:* Urban & Community Affairs • *Education:* Colleges & Universities, Education Associations, Education Funds, Minority Education, Secondary Education (Private), Student Aid • *Health:* Cancer, Children's Health/Hospitals, Health Organizations, Heart, Hospitals, Nursing Services, Single-Disease Health Associations • *Religion:* Churches, Religious Welfare • *Social Services:* Child Welfare, Community Service Organizations, People with Disabilities, Scouts, YMCA/YWCA/YMHA/YWHA, Youth Organizations

Grant Types: project

Geographic Distribution: focus on northwestern PA

GIVING OFFICERS
Judge William E. Breene: trust

William J. McFate: trust

APPLICATION INFORMATION
Initial Approach: Send cover letter and full proposal (three copies). Include a description of organization, amount requested, purpose of funds sought, recently audited financial statement, and proof of tax-exempt status. There are no deadlines.

GRANTS ANALYSIS
Total Grants: $296,744

Number of Grants: 24

Highest Grant: $50,000

Typical Range: $3,249 to $50,000

Disclosure Period: fiscal year ending September 30, 1994

Note: Recent grants are derived from a fiscal 1994 Form 990.

RECENT GRANTS
Library
5,000   Sarah Stewart Bovard Memorial Library, Tionesta, PA — assist in construction of building addition

General
50,000   Pennsylvania State University, Erie, PA

50,000   Pennsylvania State University, Erie, PA — balance scholarship

25,000   Visiting Nurses Association of Venango County, Oil City, PA — assist in upgrading current computer system

18,000   Venango Christian High School, Oil City, PA — purchase nine passenger van

16,625   YMCA, Oil City, PA — replacement and repairs projects

Pitt-Des Moines Inc. / Pitt-Des Moines Inc. Charitable Trust

Revenue: $400.0 million
Employees: 2,100
Headquarters: Pittsburgh, PA
SIC Major Group: Fabricated Metal Products, General Building Contractors, Special Trade Contractors, and Wholesale Trade—Durable Goods

CONTACT
W. R. Jackson
Trustee
Pitt-Des Moines Inc. Charitable Trust
3400 Grand Ave.
Pittsburgh, PA 15225-1582
(412) 331-3000

FINANCIAL SUMMARY
Recent Giving: $65,000 (1994); $60,000 (1993); $84,340 (1991)

Assets: $1,174,722 (1991); $1,100,697 (1989)

EIN: 25-6032139

CONTRIBUTIONS SUMMARY
Typical Recipients: • *Arts & Humanities:* Arts Centers, Community Arts, General, Historic Preservation, Libraries, Museums/Galleries, Opera, Public Broadcasting • *Civic & Public Affairs:* African American Affairs, Botanical Gardens/Parks, Business/Free Enterprise, Civil Rights, Economic Policy, General, Philanthropic Organizations, Public Policy, Urban & Community Affairs • *Education:* Colleges & Universities, Education Associations, Education Funds, General, Minority Education • *Environment:* General, Resource Conservation • *Health:* General, Hospitals • *International:* General, International Peace & Security Issues, Missionary/Religious Activities • *Religion:* General, Religious Organizations • *Science:* General • *Social Services:* Camps, Community Service Organizations, Emergency Relief, General, United Funds/United Ways, Youth Organizations

Geographic Distribution: focus on PA

Operating Locations: PA (Pittsburgh)

CORP. OFFICERS
P. O. Elbert: *CURR EMPL* chmn, dir: Pitt-Des Moines

W. W. McKee: *CURR EMPL* pres, ceo, dir: Pitt-Des Moines

GIVING OFFICERS
R. A. Byers: trust

P. O. Elbert: trust *CURR EMPL* chmn, dir: Pitt-Des Moines (see above)

W. R. Jackson: trust

APPLICATION INFORMATION
Initial Approach: Send a brief letter of inquiry. Include a copy of IRS-approved letter confirming 501(c)(3) status. There are no deadlines.

Restrictions on Giving: Does not support individuals.

GRANTS ANALYSIS
Total Grants: $84,340

Number of Grants: 51

Highest Grant: $25,000

Typical Range: $250 to $2,500

Disclosure Period: 1991

Note: Recent grants are derived from a 1991 Form 990.

RECENT GRANTS
General
25,000   Hurricane Allen St. Lucia Rebuilding Fund, New York, NY

8,000   United Way, Des Moines, IA

6,000   United Way, Pittsburgh, PA

5,000   Allegheny Trails Council, Pittsburgh, PA

4,000   Carnegie Institute Second Century Fund, Pittsburgh, PA

Pittsburgh Child Guidance Foundation

CONTACT
Judith M. Davenport
Secretary, Trustee
Pittsburgh Child Guidance Fdn.
Essex House, Ste. L-3
Pittsburgh, PA 15206
(412) 362-6203

FINANCIAL SUMMARY
Recent Giving: $179,456 (1993); $157,803 (1992); $143,543 (1991)

Assets: $4,243,054 (1993); $4,061,642 (1992); $3,873,287 (1991)

Gifts Received: $500 (1991)

EIN: 25-0965465

CONTRIBUTIONS SUMMARY

Typical Recipients: • *Arts & Humanities:* Arts Centers, Libraries • *Civic & Public Affairs:* Botanical Gardens/Parks, Housing, Nonprofit Management, Urban & Community Affairs • *Education:* Afterschool/Enrichment Programs, Elementary Education (Private), Literacy • *Health:* Children's Health/Hospitals, Medical Research, Mental Health, Prenatal Health Issues, Single-Disease Health Associations • *Religion:* Religious Organizations • *Social Services:* Big Brother/Big Sister, Child Abuse, Child Welfare, Community Service Organizations, Delinquency & Criminal Rehabilitation, Family Planning, Family Services, Food/Clothing Distribution, Homes, Recreation & Athletics, Sexual Abuse, Shelters/Homelessness, Substance Abuse, United Funds/United Ways, Youth Organizations

Grant Types: project and research

Geographic Distribution: limited to western PA, northern WV, and eastern OH

GIVING OFFICERS

Brigitte Alexander: exec dir

Alan A. Axelson: treas

Eileen H. Christman: trust

Nancy E. Curry: trust *B* Brockway PA 1931 *ED* Grove City Coll BA 1952; Univ Pittsburgh MEd 1956; Univ Pittsburgh PhD 1972 *NONPR AFFIL* mem: Am Assoc Univ Prof, Am Psychoanalytic Assn, Am Psychological Assn, Natl Assn Ed Young Children

Judith M. Davenport: trust, secy

Mona N. Generett: trust

Munro J. Grant: trust, pres

David B. Hartmann, MD: trust

Jeffrey S. Herzog: trust

Caroline B. Hunt: trust

James Patrick Kelly, Jr.: trust *B* Brooklyn NY 1933 *ED* US Naval Academy BS 1955; Univ Houston 1968-1969 *NONPR AFFIL* mem: Assn Retarded Citizens Pittsburgh, Mensa; pres: Comm Ed & Recreational Redevelopment Area Santa Ana; pres fdn bd: CA St Univ Los Angeles

Don A. Linzer: trust

Regis Murrin: trust *B* Erie PA 1930 *ED* Univ Notre Dame BA 1952; Harvard Univ JD 1959; Temple Univ LLM 1968 *CURR EMPL* ptnr: Reed Smith Shaw & McClay *NONPR AFFIL* mem: Edwin Sorin Soc, PA Bar Assn; trust: Pittsburgh Oratory

Victor J. Papale: trust

Marie Ford Reilly: trust

APPLICATION INFORMATION

Initial Approach: Contact foundation before submitting a proposal. Deadlines are March 1, June 1, and November 1.

PUBLICATIONS

Informational Brochure (including Application Guidelines), Application Guidelines, Informational Brochure, grants list

GRANTS ANALYSIS

Total Grants: $179,456

Number of Grants: 17

Highest Grant: $66,980

Typical Range: $500 to $27,345

Disclosure Period: 1993

Note: Recent grants are derived from a 1993 Form 990.

RECENT GRANTS

Library
500	Grantmakers of Western Pennsylvania, Pittsburgh, PA — establish a foundation center at Carnegie library to assist local grant seekers to identify potential grantors

General
66,980	Community Human Services Corporation, Pittsburgh, PA — replicate the program, Families Facing the Future in Bedford Dwellings, Pittsburgh
27,345	Arsenal Family and Children's Center, Pittsburgh, PA — conduct two programs for children ages zero to three
10,318	Allegheny Singer Research Institute, Pittsburgh, PA — research grant to evaluate the Family Growth Center Pilot Project which supports young mothers with first-born babies
10,000	Family Resources, Pittsburgh, PA — replicate an existing successful program, From Birth to Five, in two new communities by training volunteers to conduct the program
10,000	Mental Health Association of Beaver County, Monaca, PA — support the position of an advocate for children with severe emotional problems

Plankenhorn Foundation, Harry

CONTACT
Abram M. Snyder
Treasurer
Harry Plankenhorn Fdn.
R.D. 2
Cogan Station, PA 17728

FINANCIAL SUMMARY

Recent Giving: $192,352 (1993); $204,163 (1992); $236,507 (1991)

Assets: $4,689,199 (1993); $4,266,381 (1992); $3,917,271 (1991)

Gifts Received: $300 (1993); $300 (1992); $300 (1991)

Fiscal Note: In 1993, contributions were received from Ruth Askoy ($100) and Timothy Sander ($200).

EIN: 24-6023579

CONTRIBUTIONS SUMMARY

Donor(s): the late Harry Plankenhorn

Typical Recipients: • *Arts & Humanities:* Libraries • *Civic & Public Affairs:* General, Housing, Law & Justice, Urban & Community Affairs • *Education:* Agricultural Education • *Health:* Cancer, Emergency/Ambulance Services, Heart, Hospitals, Mental Health, Multiple Sclerosis, Preventive Medicine/Wellness Organizations, Respiratory, Single-Disease Health Associations • *Religion:* Churches, Religious Welfare • *Social Services:* Camps, Child Welfare, Community Centers, Community Service Organizations, Counseling, Emergency Relief, Family Services, People with Disabilities, Shelters/Homelessness, United Funds/United Ways, YMCA/YWCA/YMHA/YWHA, Youth Organizations

Grant Types: general support

Geographic Distribution: focus on Lycoming County, PA

GIVING OFFICERS

Rev. Bruce Druckenmiller: trust

Barbara Ertel: trust

Phillis Feese: trust

Fred A. Foulkrod: vp

Charles F. Greevy III: pres

W. Herbert Poff III: trust

Carolyn Seifert: trust

Carl H. Sump: dir, secy

Abram M. Synder: dir, treas

Lucinda A. Wagner: trust

Eleanor W. Whiting: asst treas

APPLICATION INFORMATION

Initial Approach: Send brief letter describing program. There are no deadlines.

Restrictions on Giving: Limited to Lycoming County, PA.

GRANTS ANALYSIS

Total Grants: $192,352

Number of Grants: 22

Highest Grant: $80,000

Typical Range: $1,000 to $45,000

Disclosure Period: 1993

Note: Recent grants are derived from a 1993 Form 990.

RECENT GRANTS

General
80,000	North Central Sight Services, Williamsport, PA — building fund
45,000	New Covenant United Church of Christ, Williamsport, PA — emergency fund
10,000	American Rescue Workers, Williamsport, PA — offset deficit in general operating fund

| 10,000 | Family Life Institute of Northeast Pennsylvania, Williamsport, PA — family wellness project |
| 10,000 | Salvation Army, Williamsport, PA |

PNC Bank, N.A. / PNC Bank Foundation

Former Foundation Name: Pittsburgh National Bank Foundation
Parent Company: PNC Bank Corp
Parent Employees: 22,000
Headquarters: Pittsburgh, PA
SIC Major Group: Bank Holding Companies and National Commercial Banks

CONTACT
Mia Hallett
Program Officer
PNC Bank Fdn.
One Oliver Plz., 27th Fl.
Pittsburgh, PA 15222
(412) 762-7076

FINANCIAL SUMMARY
Recent Giving: $2,082,287 (1993); $2,060,466 (1992); $2,026,162 (1991)
Assets: $32,781,937 (1993); $8,350,693 (1992); $5,744,355 (1991)
Gifts Received: $25,000,000 (1993); $4,164,772 (1992)
Fiscal Note: Giving is through the foundation only. The foundation receives contributions from PNC Bank Corp.
EIN: 25-1202255

CONTRIBUTIONS SUMMARY
Typical Recipients: • *Arts & Humanities:* Arts Associations & Councils, Arts Centers, Arts Festivals, Community Arts, Historic Preservation, History & Archaeology, Libraries, Literary Arts, Museums/Galleries, Music, Opera, Performing Arts, Public Broadcasting, Theater • *Civic & Public Affairs:* African American Affairs, Business/Free Enterprise, Economic Development, Employment/Job Training, General, Housing, Legal Aid, Parades/Festivals, Philanthropic Organizations, Professional & Trade Associations, Safety, Urban & Community Affairs, Zoos/Aquariums • *Education:* Colleges & Universities, Community & Junior Colleges, Education Associations, Education Funds, General, Literacy, Private Education (Precollege) • *Health:* Cancer, Children's Health/Hospitals, Health Organizations, Hospices, Hospitals, Long-Term Care, Medical Rehabilitation, Single-Disease Health Associations • *Religion:* Ministries, Religious Welfare • *Science:* Scientific Centers & Institutes • *Social Services:* Child Welfare, Community Centers, Community Service Organizations, Delinquency & Criminal Rehabilitation, Domestic Violence, Family Services, Food/Clothing Distribution, People with Disabilities, Recreation & Athletics, Senior Services, Shelters/Homelessness,

United Funds/United Ways, Youth Organizations
Grant Types: capital, employee matching gifts, general support, and multiyear/continuing support
Geographic Distribution: areas served by PNC Bank Corp. and affiliates
Operating Locations: PA (Blairsville, California, Cannonsburg, Charleroi, Connellsville, Elizabeth, Homestead, Indiana, McDonald, McKees Rocks, Pittsburgh, Sewickley, Somerset, Springdale, Washington)
Note: Operates in 114 locations in southwestern Pennsylvania.

CORP. OFFICERS
D. Paul Beard: *CURR EMPL* sr vp, contr: PNC Bank Corp
Edward Vincent Randall, Jr.: *B* Waterbury CT 1932 *ED* Brown Univ 1956 *CURR EMPL* sr exec vp: PNC Bank NA *NONPR AFFIL* chmn: Am Mgmt Assn, Pittsburgh Partnership Neighborhood Devel *CLUB AFFIL* Duquesne CC, St Clair CC
James Edward Rohr: *B* Cleveland OH 1948 *ED* Univ Notre Dame BA 1970; OH St Univ MBA 1972 *CURR EMPL* chmn: PNC Bank Corp Assn *CORP AFFIL* dir: Allegheny Ludlum Corp, Pvt Export Funding Corp; dir, pres: PNC Bank Corp; pres: PNC Fin Corp *NONPR AFFIL* dir: Allegheny Trails Counc, Am Cancer Soc Greater Pittsburgh Unit, Boy Scouts Am, Carnegie-Mellon Univ, Pittsburgh Cultural Trust, Shadyside Hosp, St Vincent Coll, Un Way Am; mem: Allegheny Conf, Am Bankers Assn, Bankers Roundtable, PA Bus Roundtable, Robert Morris Assocs, Young Pres Org; mem adv bd: Natl Flag Fdn, Salvation Army

GIVING OFFICERS
D. Paul Beard: treas, secy distr comm *CURR EMPL* sr vp, contr: PNC Bank Corp (see above)
Mia Hallett: program off
Thomas R. Moore: secy, couns
Edward Vincent Randall, Jr.: chmn distribution comm *CURR EMPL* sr exec vp: PNC Bank NA (see above)

APPLICATION INFORMATION
Initial Approach: *Initial Contact:* brief letter or proposal *Include Information On:* description of the organization, amount requested, purpose for which funds are sought, recently audited financial statement, proof of tax-exempt status, and list of officers and directors *Deadlines:* July

Restrictions on Giving: Foundation does not award scholarships or make grants to individuals.

OTHER THINGS TO KNOW
The company changed its name from Pittsburgh National Bank to PNC Bank, N.A. and the foundation from Pittsburgh National Bank Foundation to PNC Bank Foundation.

GRANTS ANALYSIS
Total Grants: $2,082,287
Number of Grants: 333
Highest Grant: $558,000

Average Grant: $6,253
Typical Range: $500 to $10,000
Disclosure Period: 1993
Note: Recent grants are derived from a 1993 Form 990.

RECENT GRANTS
General
558,000	United Way Southwestern Pennsylvania, Pittsburgh, PA — general contribution
66,666	Pittsburgh Partnership for Neighborhood Development, Pittsburgh, PA — general contribution
65,000	University of Pittsburgh, Pittsburgh, PA — general contribution
50,000	Community College of Allegheny County, Pittsburgh, PA — general contribution
50,000	Penn's Southwest Association, Pittsburgh, PA — general contribution

PPG Industries, Inc. / PPG Industries Foundation

Revenue: $6.33 billion
Employees: 32,300
Headquarters: Pittsburgh, PA
SIC Major Group: Paints & Allied Products, Alkalies & Chlorine, Plastics Materials & Resins, and Industrial Organic Chemicals Nec

CONTACT
Roslyn Rosenblatt
Executive Director
PPG Industries Fdn.
1 PPG Pl.
Pittsburgh, PA 15272
(412) 434-2962

FINANCIAL SUMMARY
Recent Giving: $4,000,000 (1995 est.); $3,850,406 (1994 approx.); $3,969,361 (1993)
Assets: $2,470,425 (1993); $5,961,455 (1992); $8,244,556 (1991)
Gifts Received: $213,499 (1993); $178,745 (1992); $5,143,167 (1991)
Fiscal Note: Above represents foundation only. Company also has limited direct giving, principally to Pittsburgh charities, under the Pennsylvania Neighborhood Assistance Act. Above figures exclude nonmonetary support. The foundation receives contributions from PPG Industries in the form of cash and administrative services.
EIN: 25-6037790

CONTRIBUTIONS SUMMARY
Typical Recipients: • *Arts & Humanities:* Arts Associations & Councils, Arts Festivals, Community Arts, Dance, Historic Preservation, Libraries, Literary Arts, Museums/Galleries, Music, Opera, Performing Arts, Public Broadcasting • *Civic & Pub-*

lic Affairs: Botanical Gardens/Parks, Business/Free Enterprise, Civil Rights, Economic Development, Economic Policy, Employment/Job Training, Housing, Law & Justice, Municipalities/Towns, Public Policy, Safety, Urban & Community Affairs, Women's Affairs • *Education:* Business Education, Business-School Partnerships, Colleges & Universities, Economic Education, Education Associations, Education Funds, Engineering/Technological Education, Faculty Development, Minority Education, Private Education (Precollege), Public Education (Precollege), Science/Mathematics Education, Student Aid • *Environment:* General • *Health:* Clinics/Medical Centers, Health Policy/Cost Containment, Health Organizations, Hospitals, Long-Term Care, Medical Rehabilitation, Mental Health, Nursing Services, Single-Disease Health Associations • *International:* International Relations • *Science:* Observatories & Planetariums, Science Exhibits & Fairs, Scientific Centers & Institutes, Scientific Organizations • *Social Services:* Child Welfare, Community Centers, Community Service Organizations, Day Care, Food/Clothing Distribution, Homes, People with Disabilities, Senior Services, United Funds/United Ways, Volunteer Services, Youth Organizations

Grant Types: capital, employee matching gifts, general support, operating expenses, and project

Note: Foundation matches gifts to eligible institutions, including higher education, private secondary schools, cultural organizations, hospitals, special education, and disaster relief. Minimum gift matched $25; maximum gift is $10,000 per institution. Total limit is $20,000 per year per donor.

Nonmonetary Support: $213,499 (1993)

Nonmonetary Support Types: in-kind services

Note: non-monetary support contributed in the form of administrative services

Geographic Distribution: nationally, with emphasis on corporate operating locations; special interest in Pittsburgh, PA, area

Operating Locations: AR (El Dorado), KS (Lenexa), LA (Lake Charles), OH (Cleveland, Delaware), PA (Pittsburgh), WI (Oak Creek), WV (Natrium)

CORP. OFFICERS
Jerry Edward Dempsey: *B* Landrum SC 1932 *ED* Clemson Univ BSME 1954; GA St Univ MBA 1968 *CURR EMPL* chmn, ceo: PPG Indus Inc *CORP AFFIL* dir: Brand Cos, Chem Waste Mgmt, Navistar Intl Corp, Wheelabrator Techs, WMX Techs Inc *NONPR AFFIL* chmn: Mid Am Comm; chmn deans adv bd: Clemson Univ Sch Engg; mem fdn bd, mem pres adv counc: Clemson Univ; trust: Adler Planetarium *CLUB AFFIL* Chicago, Econ Chicago, Execs Breakfast Chicago, Execs Breakfast Oak Brook, Greenville CC, Melrose, Univ Chicago

Robert D. Duncan: *B* Monroe LA 1939 *ED* Harvard Univ AMP; LA Tech Univ BS *CURR EMPL* exec vp: PPG Indus Inc

GIVING OFFICERS
Peter P. Bihuniak: mem screening comm

Rae R. Burton: mem screening comm

David C. Cannon, Jr.: mem screening comm

Russell L. Crane: vp human resources *CURR EMPL* vp human resources: PPG Indus Inc

Robert D. Duncan: chmn, dir *CURR EMPL* exec vp: PPG Indus Inc (see above)

Ernest A. Hahn: mem screening comm

Raymond W. LeBoeuf: vp, dir *B* Chicago IL 1946 *ED* Northwestern Univ BA 1967; Univ IL MBA 1970 *CURR EMPL* exec vp fin: PPG Indus Inc *NONPR AFFIL* mem: Fin Execs Inst

Roslyn Rosenblatt: exec dir *CURR EMPL* exec vp: PPG Indus Inc

Sue Sloan: secy

K. F. Sullivan: mem screening comm

APPLICATION INFORMATION
Initial Approach: *Initial Contact:* one- to two-page letter to foundation if organizations are located in Pittsburgh area or are national in scope; organizations serving communities where PPG facilities are located should direct inquiries to local PPG agent *Include Information On:* brief outline of purpose of organization; organization's mission statement; population it serves, including project benefit; grant's purpose; project summary; schedule of implementation; methods of evaluation; most recent audited financial statement; financial analysis for the project; list of board and their affiliations; and proof of tax-exempt status *Deadlines:* none; requests are reviewed year-round

Restrictions on Giving: No grant application for less than $100 will be considered. Foundation does not support operating funds of United Way agencies; political activities or organizations; individuals; advertising in benefit publications; direct student scholarships; sectarian groups for religious purposes; telephone solicitations; special events; or fraternal organizations.

OTHER THINGS TO KNOW
To ensure sensitivity to local needs in PPG plant communities, foundation has developed a local agent system. Approximately 40 company managers, most of whom live in PPG plant communities, have been designated as local agents for the foundation. Once a year agents recommend a budget for contributions in their communities to a screening committee for presentation to the foundation board.

PUBLICATIONS
Foundation annual report

GRANTS ANALYSIS
Total Grants: $3,075,575

Number of Grants: 627

Highest Grant: $440,000

Average Grant: $4,905

Typical Range: $1,000 to $10,000

Disclosure Period: 1993

Note: Figures exclude $893,786 in matching gifts. Recent grants are derived from a 1993 annual report.

RECENT GRANTS
General
440,000	United Way Southwest Pennsylvania, Pittsburgh, PA — for operating support
333,110	National Merit Scholarship Corporation, Evanston, IL — for scholarships
50,000	Allegheny County Community College, Pittsburgh, PA — for capital campaign
50,000	Carnegie Mellon University, Pittsburgh, PA — for chemistry
50,000	University of Pittsburgh, Pittsburgh, PA — for Third Century

Quaker Chemical Corp. / Quaker Chemical Foundation

Sales: $195.0 million
Employees: 936
Headquarters: Conshohocken, PA
SIC Major Group: Chemical Preparations Nec, Wood Preserving, Plastics Materials & Resins, and Soap & Other Detergents

CONTACT
Mary Lou McClain
Corporate Administrative Assistant
Quaker Chemical Corp.
Elm and Lee Sts.
Conshohocken, PA 19428
(610) 832-4119

FINANCIAL SUMMARY
Recent Giving: $387,093 (fiscal 1994); $390,000 (fiscal 1993); $426,183 (fiscal 1992)

Assets: $276,143 (fiscal 1994); $298,991 (fiscal 1992); $313,547 (fiscal 1991)

Gifts Received: $397,000 (fiscal 1994); $402,000 (fiscal 1992); $378,000 (fiscal 1991)

Fiscal Note: Contributes through foundation only. Above figures exclude nonmonetary support. In fiscal 1994, contributions were received from the Quaker Chemical Corporation.

EIN: 23-6245803

CONTRIBUTIONS SUMMARY
Typical Recipients: • *Arts & Humanities:* Arts Centers, Arts Funds, Arts Outreach, Community Arts, Historic Preservation, Libraries, Museums/Galleries, Music, Opera, Performing Arts • *Civic & Public Affairs:* Employment/Job Training, Urban & Community Affairs, Women's Affairs, Zoos/Aquariums • *Education:* Colleges & Universities, Private Education (Precollege), Special Education, Student Aid, Vocational & Technical Education • *Environment:* General • *Health:* Health Organizations, Hospitals, Medical Re-

search, Nursing Services, Nutrition, Single-Disease Health Associations • *International:* International Relations • *Social Services:* Child Welfare, Community Service Organizations, Counseling, Food/Clothing Distribution, Homes, People with Disabilities, Recreation & Athletics, Sexual Abuse, United Funds/United Ways, Volunteer Services, Youth Organizations

Grant Types: employee matching gifts and general support

Note: Employee matching gift ratio: 2 to 1, up to $250; 1 to 1, from $250 to $1000.

Nonmonetary Support Types: loaned employees and loaned executives

Geographic Distribution: primarily in operating areas

Operating Locations: CA (Fontana, Placentia, Pomona, South El Monte), DE (Wilmington), GA (Savannah), MI (Detroit), OK (Sapulpa), PA (Conshohocken, King of Prussia, Philadelphia), TX (Conroe, Fort Worth)

CORP. OFFICERS

Sigismundus W. W. Lubsen: *B* 1943 *ED* Erasmus Univ 1969; Columbia Univ MBA 1971 *CURR EMPL* pres, ceo: Quaker Chem Corp

GIVING OFFICERS

Katherine N. Coughenour: trust

Edwin J. Delattre: trust *CORP AFFIL* dir: Quaker Chem Corp

Alan J. Keyser: trust

Kathleen Mague: secy

Mary Lou McClain: secy *CURR EMPL* corp admin asst: Quaker Chem Corp

Karl Henry Spaeth: chmn, trust *B* Philadelphia PA 1929 *ED* Haverford Coll AB 1951; Oxford Univ 1955; Harvard Univ JD 1958 *CURR EMPL* vp, secy: Quaker Chem Corp *CORP AFFIL* secy: AC Products Inc, Gen Chem Inc, Multi-Chem Products Inc, Quaker Construction Products Inc, Quaker Petro Chemicals Co, Quaker Sealants & Coatings Co, Selby Battersby Co; secy, dir: Quaker Chem Corp-DE *NONPR AFFIL* bd overseers: Univ PA Univ Mus; dir: Central Philadelphia Devel Corp, Chestnut Hill Acad, Opera Co Philadelphia; dir, secy-treas: Edmond B Spaeth Clinical Res Fdn; intl adv comm: Philadelphia First Partnership Econ Devel; mem: Am Soc Corp Secys, Comm 70, Montgomery Bar Assn, PA Bar Assn, Philadelphia Comm Foreign Rels *CLUB AFFIL* Philadelphia, Philadelphia Cricket

J. Everett Wick: trust

Jane Williams: trust

APPLICATION INFORMATION

Initial Approach: *Initial Contact:* request guidelines from foundation *Deadlines:* application must be received no later than April 20

Restrictions on Giving: Distributions limited to geographic locations where the corporation has operations in the United States.

GRANTS ANALYSIS

Total Grants: $387,093

Number of Grants: 215

Highest Grant: $6,000

Average Grant: $1,800

Typical Range: $400 to $2,500

Disclosure Period: fiscal year ending June 30, 1994

Note: Figures include matching gifts totalling $86,400. Recent grants are derived from a fiscal 1994 grants list.

RECENT GRANTS

Library
2,500 William Jeanes Memorial Library, Lafayette Hill, PA — for civic and community purposes

General
6,000 Emory University, Atlanta, GA — for employee scholarship
6,000 University of California Regents, Oakland, CA — for employee scholarship
4,834 Tennessee Technological University, Cookeville, TN — for employee scholarship
4,500 University of Pennsylvania, Philadelphia, PA — for community scholarship
4,000 Carnegie Mellon University, Pittsburgh, PA — for employee scholarship

Reidler Foundation

CONTACT
Diana L. James
Secretary-Treasurer
Reidler Fdn.
c/o Hazleton National Bank
Broad and Laurel Sts.
Hazleton, PA 18201
(717) 459-4251

FINANCIAL SUMMARY
Recent Giving: $215,000 (fiscal 1992); $200,000 (fiscal 1991); $185,000 (fiscal 1990)

Assets: $5,606,611 (fiscal 1992); $5,362,193 (fiscal 1991); $4,732,926 (fiscal 1990)

Gifts Received: $19,825 (fiscal 1992); $28,219 (fiscal 1991); $25,313 (fiscal 1989)

Fiscal Note: In 1991, contributions were received from Dr. Howard D. and Mrs. Ann B. Fegan.

EIN: 24-6022888

CONTRIBUTIONS SUMMARY
Donor(s): John W. Reidler

Typical Recipients: • *Arts & Humanities:* History & Archaeology, Libraries, Music, Public Broadcasting • *Civic & Public Affairs:* General, Zoos/Aquariums • *Education:* Colleges & Universities, Education Funds, Secondary Education (Private), Student Aid • *Environment:* Resource Conservation, Wildlife Protection • *Health:* Cancer, Children's Health/Hospitals, Clinics/Medical Centers, Emergency/Ambulance Services, Hospitals, Multiple Sclerosis, Nursing Services • *International:* International Development, International Peace & Security Issues • *Religion:* Churches, Religious Welfare • *Social Services:* Child Welfare, Community Service Organizations, Delinquency & Criminal Rehabilitation, Family Planning, Family Services, Food/Clothing Distribution, People with Disabilities, Senior Services, United Funds/United Ways, Youth Organizations

Grant Types: general support

Geographic Distribution: focus on the Ashland and Hazleton, PA, areas

GIVING OFFICERS

Ann B. Fegan: pres

Howard D. Fegan: dir

Eugene C. Fish: dir *CURR EMPL* chmn, secy, dir: Eastern Foundry Co

Robert K. Gicking: vp *B* Hazleton PA 1931 *ED* Lafayette Coll 1952 *CURR EMPL* pres, dir: Hazleton Natl Bank *CORP AFFIL* pres: First Valley Corp

Diana L. James: secy, treas

Carl J. Reidler: dir

Paul G. Reidler: pres emeritus

APPLICATION INFORMATION

Initial Approach: Send brief letter of inquiry describing program or project. There are no deadlines.

Restrictions on Giving: Does not support individuals.

GRANTS ANALYSIS

Total Grants: $215,000

Number of Grants: 68

Highest Grant: $21,000

Typical Range: $500 to $15,000

Disclosure Period: fiscal year ending October 31, 1992

Note: Recent grants are derived from a fiscal 1992 Form 990.

RECENT GRANTS

Library
6,500 Hazleton Area Public Library, Hazleton, PA

General
21,000 Ashland Trusts, Ashland, PA — Helping Hand
15,000 Susquehanna University, Selingsgrove, PA — scholarships grants

15,000	Trinity Evangelical Lutheran Church Endowment
10,750	Lebanon Valley College, Annville, PA
10,500	Geisinger Foundation, Danville, PA

Rockwell International Corporation / Rockwell International Corporation Trust

Revenue: $11.2 billion
Employees: 77,028
Headquarters: Seal Beach, CA
SIC Major Group: Electronic & Other Electrical Equipment, Fabricated Metal Products, Industrial Machinery & Equipment, and Rubber & Miscellaneous Plastics Products

CONTACT
William R. Fitz
Assistant Secretary
Rockwell International Corporation Trust
625 Liberty Ave.
Pittsburgh, PA 15222-3123
(412) 565-5803
Note: Mr. Fitz is the contact for the Pittsburgh area and for national organizations. Local organizations outside the Pittsburgh area should contact the manager of the nearest Rockwell facility for further information. The company's World Wide Web address is http://www.rockwell.com

FINANCIAL SUMMARY
Recent Giving: $10,700,000 (fiscal 1995 est.); $10,300,000 (fiscal 1994 approx.); $10,400,000 (fiscal 1993 approx.)

Assets: $3,900,058 (fiscal 1994); $12,000,000 (fiscal 1993 est.); $13,000,000 (fiscal 1992 approx.)

Gifts Received: $8,500,000 (fiscal 1994); $8,000,000 (fiscal 1993)

Fiscal Note: Figures include giving by Rockwell International Corporation Trust, Rockwell International Canadian Trust, Rockwell International Corporation United Kingdom Trust, and direct giving by Rockwell International Corporation and its wholly owned subsidiaries. In 1994, direct giving totaled $1.5 million. Above figures exclude nonmonetary support. The foundation receives gifts from Rockwell International Corporation.

EIN: 25-1072431

CONTRIBUTIONS SUMMARY
Typical Recipients: • *Arts & Humanities:* Arts Associations & Councils, Arts Centers, Arts Festivals, Arts Funds, Arts Institutes, Community Arts, Dance, Historic Preservation, History & Archaeology, Libraries, Museums/Galleries, Music, Opera, Performing Arts, Public Broadcasting, Theater • *Civic & Public Affairs:* African American Affairs, Business/Free Enterprise, Chambers of Commerce, Civil Rights, Economic Development, Economic Policy, Employment/Job Training, Hispanic Affairs, Housing, Law &

Justice, Legal Aid, Nonprofit Management, Professional & Trade Associations, Public Policy, Safety, Urban & Community Affairs, Women's Affairs, Zoos/Aquariums • *Education:* Business Education, Colleges & Universities, Community & Junior Colleges, Continuing Education, Economic Education, Education Associations, Education Funds, Education Reform, Engineering/Technological Education, Faculty Development, General, Literacy, Minority Education, Public Education (Precollege), Science/Mathematics Education, Special Education, Student Aid • *Environment:* General • *Health:* Cancer, Children's Health/Hospitals, Emergency/Ambulance Services, Health Policy/Cost Containment, Health Organizations, Hospices, Hospitals, Medical Rehabilitation, Mental Health, Single-Disease Health Associations • *International:* International Affairs, International Peace & Security Issues, International Relations • *Religion:* Dioceses, Jewish Causes • *Science:* Science Exhibits & Fairs, Scientific Centers & Institutes, Scientific Organizations • *Social Services:* Child Welfare, Community Service Organizations, Counseling, Delinquency & Criminal Rehabilitation, Domestic Violence, Emergency Relief, Family Services, People with Disabilities, Recreation & Athletics, Shelters/Homelessness, Substance Abuse, United Funds/United Ways, Volunteer Services, YMCA/YWCA/YMHA/YWHA, Youth Organizations

Grant Types: capital, department, employee matching gifts, endowment, fellowship, general support, and multiyear/continuing support

Note: Company matches employee gifts on a one-to-one basis to accredited colleges and accredited public and private elementary and high schools. Company will match gifts of more than $25 to a maximum of $10,000 per employee per year.

Nonmonetary Support: $600,000 (fiscal 1995); $3,500,000 (fiscal 1993)

Nonmonetary Support Types: donated equipment, donated products, and in-kind services

Note: Contact William R. Fitz or nearest Rockwell facility for information or requests of nonmonetary support.

Geographic Distribution: where company maintains facilities; nationally to education

Operating Locations: CA (Anaheim, Canoga Park, Downey, El Segundo, Los Angeles, Santa Barbara, Seal Beach), IL (Chicago, Downers Grove), MA (Waltham), MI (Troy), OH (Highland Heights), PA (Pittsburgh), PR, TX (Richardson), WI (Milwaukee)

CORP. OFFICERS
W. Michael Barnes: *CURR EMPL* sr vp fin & planning, cfo: Rockwell Intl Corp

Donald Ray Beall: *B* Beaumont CA 1938 *ED* San Jose St Univ BS 1960; Univ Pittsburgh MBA 1961 *CURR EMPL* chmn, ceo: Rockwell Intl Corp *CORP AFFIL* dir: Amoco Corp, Times Mirror Co *NONPR AFFIL* mem: Am Inst Aeronautics & Astronau-

tics, Beta Gamma Sigma, Bus Counc, Bus Higher Ed Forum, Bus Roundtable, Chief Execs Org, Comm Econ Devel, Defense Policy Adv Comm Trade, Navy League US, Sigma Alpha Epsilon, Young Pres Org; mem bd overseers: Univ CA Irvine; trust: CA Inst Tech, Ctr Strategic Intl Studies *PHIL AFFIL* pres: Beall Family Foundation

Kent March Black: *B* Carrollton IL 1939 *ED* Univ IL BSEE 1962 *CURR EMPL* exec vp, coo: Rockwell Intl Corp *CORP AFFIL* adv comm: Natl Security Telecommun *NONPR AFFIL* dir: Assn Higher Ed N TX, Dallas County Commun Coll District Fdn Inc; mem: Aerospace Indus Assn Am, Natl Mgmt Assn, Naval Aviation Indus Counc; mem adv bd: Univ IL Coll Engg; mem devel bd: Univ TX Dallas; mem exec bd: Boy Scouts Am Circle Ten Counc

Donald H. Davis, Jr.: *B* 1939 *ED* TX A&M Univ BSME 1962; TX A&M Univ MBA 1963 *CURR EMPL* exec vp, coo: Rockwell Intl Corp

Thomas L. Gunckel II: *CURR EMPL* sr vp res & engg: Rockwell Intl Corp

Sam Frank Iacobellis: *B* Fresno CA 1929 *ED* CA St Univ Fresno BSME 1952; Univ CA Los Angeles MS 1963 *CURR EMPL* exec vp major programs: Rockwell Intl Corp *CORP AFFIL* dir: Rohr Inc *NONPR AFFIL* fellow: Am Inst Aeronautics & Astronautics; mem: Soc Mfg Engrs *CLUB AFFIL* Bel Air CC

Clayton M. Jones: *CURR EMPL* sr vp govt oper & intl: Rockwell Intl Corp

Richard R. Mau: *B* Des Moines IA 1931 *ED* Univ IA 1954 *CURR EMPL* sr vp commun: Rockwell Intl Corp

GIVING OFFICERS
W. Michael Barnes: mem trust comm *CURR EMPL* sr vp fin & planning, cfo: Rockwell Intl Corp (see above)

Donald Ray Beall: mem trust comm *CURR EMPL* chmn, ceo: Rockwell Intl Corp *PHIL AFFIL* pres: Beall Family Foundation (see above)

Donald H. Davis, Jr.: mem trust comm *CURR EMPL* exec vp, coo: Rockwell Intl Corp (see above)

William R. Fitz: asst secy *CURR EMPL* mgr contributions & commun rels: Rockwell Intl Corp

Thomas L. Gunckel II: mem trust comm *CURR EMPL* sr vp res & engg: Rockwell Intl Corp (see above)

Richard R. Mau: mem trust comm *CURR EMPL* sr vp commun: Rockwell Intl Corp (see above)

APPLICATION INFORMATION
Initial Approach: *Initial Contact:* brief letter or proposal *Include Information On:* description of the organization, amount requested, purpose for which funds are sought, recently audited financial statement, proof of tax-exempt status, list of other funding sources *Deadlines:* none

Restrictions on Giving: Does not support individuals, fraternal organizations, political or lobbying groups, goodwill advertising, or religious organizations for sectarian purposes.

GRANTS ANALYSIS
Total Grants: $8,406,240*

Number of Grants: 2,775*

Highest Grant: $675,000*

Average Grant: $3,029*

Typical Range: $1,000 to $10,000

Disclosure Period: fiscal year ending September 30, 1994

Note: Figures for total grants, number of grants, average grant, and highest grant reflect foundation giving only. Number of grants is approximate. Recent grants are derived from a fiscal 1994 Form 990.

RECENT GRANTS

General

675,000	United Way Los Angeles, Los Angeles, CA
250,000	New American Schools Development Corporation, Arlington, VA
189,200	United Way of Chicago, Chicago, IL
114,040	National Merit Scholarship Corporation, Evanston, IL
100,000	California Institute of Technology, Pasadena, CA

Rohm & Haas Co.

Revenue: $3.53 billion

Employees: 13,000

Headquarters: Philadelphia, PA

SIC Major Group: Industrial Organic Chemicals Nec, Plastics Materials & Resins, Agricultural Chemicals Nec, and Plastics Products Nec

CONTACT
Delbert S. Payne

Manager, Corporate Social Investment

Rohm & Haas Co.

100 Independence Mall W

Philadelphia, PA 19106

(215) 592-2863

Note: The company's World Wide Web address is http://www.rohmhaas.com

FINANCIAL SUMMARY
Recent Giving: $4,300,000 (1992 approx.); $4,300,000 (1991); $4,300,000 (1990)

Fiscal Note: Company gives directly. Above figures exclude nonmonetary support.

CONTRIBUTIONS SUMMARY
Typical Recipients: • *Arts & Humanities:* Arts Appreciation, Arts Associations & Councils, Arts Festivals, Arts Funds, Arts Institutes, Community Arts, Dance, Ethnic & Folk Arts, Historic Preservation, Libraries, Museums/Galleries, Music, Opera, Performing Arts, Public Broadcasting, Theater • *Civic & Public Affairs:* Business/Free Enterprise, Civil Rights, Economic Development, Employment/Job Training, Housing, Law & Justice, Nonprofit Management, Urban & Community Affairs, Zoos/Aquariums

• *Education:* Agricultural Education, Arts/Humanities Education, Business Education, Colleges & Universities, Community & Junior Colleges, Economic Education, Education Associations, Education Funds, Engineering/Technological Education, Faculty Development, Literacy, Minority Education, Preschool Education, Private Education (Precollege), Public Education (Precollege), Science/Mathematics Education, Special Education, Student Aid • *Environment:* General • *Health:* Emergency/Ambulance Services, Geriatric Health, Health Policy/Cost Containment, Health Organizations, Hospices, Hospitals, Medical Rehabilitation, Medical Research, Mental Health, Nursing Services, Public Health • *Science:* Science Exhibits & Fairs, Scientific Centers & Institutes, Scientific Organizations • *Social Services:* Child Welfare, Community Centers, Community Service Organizations, Emergency Relief, Family Services, Food/Clothing Distribution, Homes, People with Disabilities, Recreation & Athletics, Senior Services, Shelters/Homelessness, Substance Abuse, United Funds/United Ways, Volunteer Services, Youth Organizations

Grant Types: capital, challenge, department, employee matching gifts, fellowship, general support, project, scholarship, and seed money

Nonmonetary Support: $260,000 (1991); $140,000 (1990); $300,000 (1988)

Nonmonetary Support Types: donated equipment, donated products, in-kind services, loaned employees, and loaned executives

Note: Company sponsored employee volunteer programs include Dollars For Doers and Volunteer Recognition Programs.

Geographic Distribution: primarily in communities where employees live and company has facilities; limited support to national organizations

Operating Locations: CA (Carson, Hayward, Irvine, La Mirada, Newark), CT (Kensington), IL (Chicago Heights, Illiopolis, Kankakee, Lemont), KY (Louisville), MA (Marlboro), NC (Charlotte), PA (Bellefonte, Bristol, Philadelphia, Spring House), TN (Knoxville), TX (Bayport, Houston)

CORP. OFFICERS
John Patrick Mulroney: *B* Philadelphia PA 1935 *ED* Univ PA BS 1957; Univ PA MS 1959 *CURR EMPL* pres, coo, dir: Rohm & Haas Co *CORP AFFIL* dir: Aluminum Co Am, Teradyne Inc *NONPR AFFIL* mem: Acad Natural Sci, Am Chem Soc, Am Inst Chem Engrs, Greater Philadelphia Chamber Commerce, Soc Chem Indus, Univ PA; pres: Opera Co NY

James Lawrence Wilson: *B* Rosedale MS 1936 *ED* Vanderbilt Univ BSME 1958; Harvard Univ MBA 1963 *CURR EMPL* chmn, ceo: Rohm & Haas Co *CORP AFFIL* dir: Shipley Co, Vanguard Group Mutual Funds; mem: Cummins Engine Co Inc *NONPR AFFIL* chmn: Phil High School Acad; mem: Pres Export Counc; trust: Culver Ed Fdn, Vanderbilt Univ

GIVING OFFICERS
Delbert S. Payne: *CURR EMPL* mgr corp social investment: Rohm & Haas Co

APPLICATION INFORMATION
Initial Approach: *Initial Contact:* proposal *Include Information On:* organization's name and purpose, length of service, funding sources, current objectives and priorities, proof of tax-exempt status, descriptive literature as available (project outlines, programs, brochures, etc.) *Deadlines:* none

Restrictions on Giving: Company does not support fraternal organizations, political or lobbying groups, religious organizations for sectarian purposes, or individuals.

OTHER THINGS TO KNOW
Community activity guidelines set by corporate management; individual plants determine scope of program and specific activities.

Rohm and Haas tries to channel employees into community activities supported by company.

Contributions are not awarded on the basis of indefinitely continuing or unquestioned support. Even when multiyear pledges are made, Rohm and Haas retains right to terminate support if appropriate.

Rohm and Haas occasionally provides seed money grants, usually as an outright gift or in the form of a matching or challenge grant.

GRANTS ANALYSIS
Typical Range: $1,000 to $5,000

Note: Company did not disclose recent grants.

Scaife Family Foundation

CONTACT
Joanne B. Beyer

Vice President

Scaife Family Foundation

3 Mellon Bank Ctr.

525 William Penn Pl., Ste. 3900

Pittsburgh, PA 15219-1708

(412) 392-2900

FINANCIAL SUMMARY
Recent Giving: $6,607,100 (1992); $5,970,950 (1991); $4,691,142 (1990)

Assets: $114,906,427 (1992); $115,858,659 (1991); $86,901,937 (1990)

Gifts Received: $12,536,475 (1991); $12,505,805 (1990); $8,938,325 (1989)

Fiscal Note: The foundation receives gifts from the trust for the grandchildren of Sarah Mellon Scaife.

EIN: 25-1427015

CONTRIBUTIONS SUMMARY
Donor(s): The Scaife Family Foundation was established in 1983 by the late Sarah Mellon Scaife (d. 1965) by the conditions of a trust she provided for her grandchildren. She was the sister of Richard King Mellon, daughter of Richard B. Mellon, and granddaughter of Judge Thomas Mellon,

who founded the family's banking and investment fortune.

Typical Recipients: • *Arts & Humanities:* Historic Preservation, Libraries, Public Broadcasting • *Civic & Public Affairs:* Botanical Gardens/Parks, Economic Policy, Housing, Law & Justice, Municipalities/Towns, Parades/Festivals, Philanthropic Organizations, Public Policy, Safety, Urban & Community Affairs, Women's Affairs • *Education:* Business Education, Colleges & Universities, Economic Education, Education Funds, Education Reform, Elementary Education (Public), Literacy, Medical Education, Private Education (Precollege), Science/Mathematics Education, Special Education, Student Aid • *Health:* Children's Health/Hospitals, Eyes/Blindness, Health Funds, Health Organizations, Hospices, Hospitals, Medical Rehabilitation, Medical Research, Mental Health, Prenatal Health Issues, Single-Disease Health Associations • *Religion:* Churches, Religious Organizations, Religious Welfare • *Social Services:* Child Welfare, Community Centers, Counseling, Delinquency & Criminal Rehabilitation, Family Planning, Family Services, Food/Clothing Distribution, People with Disabilities, Senior Services, Shelters/Homelessness, Substance Abuse, Youth Organizations

Grant Types: capital, conference/seminar, department, general support, operating expenses, project, and scholarship

Geographic Distribution: focuses on Pittsburgh and western Pennsylvania areas

GIVING OFFICERS
J. Nicholas Beldecos: vp, secy-treas

Joanne B. Beyer: vp, secy, treas *PHIL AFFIL* pres, trust: Allegheny Foundation

Donald A. Collins: trust

Sanford B. Ferguson: pres

David N. Scaife: co-chmn, trust

Jennie K. Scaife: co-chmn, trust

James Mellon Walton: trust *B* Pittsburgh PA 1930 *ED* Yale Univ BA 1953; Harvard Univ MBA *CURR EMPL* vchmn: MMC Group *PHIL AFFIL* trust: Sarah Scaife Foundation; chmn: Vira I. Heinz Endowment; treas, trust: Carnegie Hero Fund; trust: Matthew T. Mellon Foundation

Joseph C. Walton: trust

APPLICATION INFORMATION
Initial Approach:

Initial inquiries to the foundation should be in letter form signed by the organization's president, or authorized representative, and have the approval of the organization's board of directors.

The letter should include a concise description of the specific program for which funds are requested. Additional information must include a budget for the program and for the organization, the latest audited financial statement, annual report, list of the board of directors, and a copy of the organization's current IRS tax exemption ruling under section 501(c)(3). Additional information may be requested if needed for further evaluation.

Requests may be submitted at any time, but the foundation normally considers grants in June and December.

The foundation promises that requests will be acted upon as expeditiously as possible.

Restrictions on Giving: The foundation does not make loans and will not consider grants to individuals.

PUBLICATIONS
Annual report

GRANTS ANALYSIS
Total Grants: $6,607,100

Number of Grants: 119

Highest Grant: $1,000,000

Average Grant: $55,522

Typical Range: $30,000 to $75,000

Disclosure Period: 1992

Note: Recent grants are derived from a 1992 Form 990.

RECENT GRANTS

Library

1,000,000	Carnegie, Pittsburgh, PA — Second Century fund

General

300,000	American Society of Addiction Medicine, Washington, DC — physical examination and certification in addiction medicine
300,000	Free Congress Research and Education Foundation, Washington, DC — national empowerment television
250,000	American Alliance for Rights and Responsibilities, Washington, DC — grassroots drug enforcement assistance and national registry of alcohol victims
225,000	Housing Opportunities, McKeesport, PA — operating support and revolving loan fund
202,640	Heritage Foundation, Washington, DC — healthcare reform program

Sharon Steel Corp. / SharonSteel Foundation

Sales: $500.0 million
Employees: 3,000
Parent Company: Sharon Specialty Steel, Inc.
Headquarters: Farrell, PA
SIC Major Group: Coal Mining, Fabricated Metal Products, Primary Metal Industries, and Wholesale Trade—Durable Goods

CONTACT
Sharon Steel Corp.
PO Box 270
Farrell, PA 16121
(412) 983-6336

FINANCIAL SUMMARY
Recent Giving: $35,200 (1993); $265,550 (1992); $102,750 (1991)

Assets: $2,798,940 (1993); $2,784,838 (1992); $2,969,185 (1991)

EIN: 25-6063133

CONTRIBUTIONS SUMMARY
Typical Recipients: • *Arts & Humanities:* Arts Institutes, Community Arts, Libraries, Music, Opera, Performing Arts, Public Broadcasting, Theater • *Civic & Public Affairs:* Botanical Gardens/Parks, Business/Free Enterprise, Clubs, Economic Development, General, Municipalities/Towns, Professional & Trade Associations • *Education:* Colleges & Universities, Private Education (Precollege) • *Health:* Health Funds, Hospitals, Medical Research, Single-Disease Health Associations • *Religion:* Religious Organizations, Religious Welfare • *Social Services:* Child Welfare, Community Service Organizations, Recreation & Athletics, United Funds/United Ways, Youth Organizations

Grant Types: general support

Geographic Distribution: focus on PA

Operating Locations: PA (Farrell)

CORP. OFFICERS
Wolfgang Jansen: *CURR EMPL* co-chmn: Sharon Steel Corp

Walter Sieckman: *CURR EMPL* co-chmn, ceo: Sharon Steel Corp

GIVING OFFICERS
John D. Fry: trust

Christian L. Oberbeck: trust

Malvin Gustav Sander: trust *B* Pittsburgh PA 1946 *ED* Bucknell Univ BS 1967; Duquesne Univ JD 1972 *CURR EMPL* sr vp, gen couns, secy: Sharon Steel Corp *CORP AFFIL* mem: Am Bar Assn, Am Trial Lawyers Assn, Coalition Empl through Exports, PA Bar Assn *NONPR AFFIL* mem: Delta Theta Phi

APPLICATION INFORMATION
Initial Approach: The foundation has no formal grant application procedure or application form. Include a description of organization, amount requested, purpose of funds sought, recently audited financial statement, and proof of tax-exempt status. There are no deadlines.

OTHER THINGS TO KNOW
The company remained in Chapter 11 bankruptcy as of July 1995. Charitable contributions were severely curtailed.

GRANTS ANALYSIS
Total Grants: $265,550

Number of Grants: 20

Highest Grant: $100,000

Typical Range: $500 to $40,000

Disclosure Period: 1992

Note: Recent grants are derived from a 1992 Form 990.

RECENT GRANTS

Library
1,000 Farrell City Library

General
100,000 United Way of Mercer County
40,000 United Way of Mercer County
24,000 United Steelworkers of America
20,000 Sharon Regional Health System Development Fund
20,000 United Way of Mercer County

Sheary for Charity, Edna M.

CONTACT
Edna M. Sheary for Charity
c/o Mellon Bank, N.A.
PO Box 346
Lewisburg, PA 17837
(717) 523-1230

FINANCIAL SUMMARY
Recent Giving: $583,524 (fiscal 1994)
Assets: $2,770,128 (fiscal 1994); $3,116,575 (fiscal 1993)
EIN: 25-1695940

CONTRIBUTIONS SUMMARY
Typical Recipients: • *Arts & Humanities:* Libraries, Museums/Galleries, Music • *Civic & Public Affairs:* General, Legal Aid, Urban & Community Affairs, Women's Affairs • *Education:* Colleges & Universities, Private Education (Precollege) • *Health:* Cancer, Emergency/Ambulance Services, Health Organizations, Hospitals, Research/Studies Institutes • *Religion:* Churches, Ministries, Religious Welfare • *Social Services:* Camps, Community Service Organizations, Day Care, Family Services, People with Disabilities

Geographic Distribution: focus on PA

APPLICATION INFORMATION
Initial Approach: Send a brief letter of inquiry. Include a description of organization, amount requested, purpose of funds sought, recently audited financial statement, and proof of tax-exempt status. Deadline is April 1.

GRANTS ANALYSIS
Total Grants: $583,524
Number of Grants: 26
Highest Grant: $102,655
Typical Range: $3,585 to $100,000
Disclosure Period: fiscal year ending May 31, 1994
Note: Recent grants are derived from a fiscal 1994 Form 990.

RECENT GRANTS

Library
5,050 Public Library of Union County, Lewisburg, PA — operational

General
102,655 Evangelical Community Hospital, Lewisburg, PA — building
100,000 Camp Mt. Luther Corporation, Lewisburg, PA — building
60,000 Union/Snyder Association for Retarded Citizens, Selinsgrove, PA — building
42,000 Family Life Institute of North Central, Williamsport, PA — operational
29,108 Susquehanna Council, Williamsport, PA — equipment

Sheppard Foundation, Lawrence B.

CONTACT
Charlotte S. Devan
President
Lawrence B. Sheppard Fdn.
c/o Buchen, Wise & Dorr
126 Carlisle St.
Hanover, PA 17331
(717) 637-2160

FINANCIAL SUMMARY
Recent Giving: $60,845 (fiscal 1993); $88,000 (fiscal 1992); $176,000 (fiscal 1989)
Assets: $1,352,002 (fiscal 1993); $2,677,721 (fiscal 1992); $2,535,491 (fiscal 1990)
EIN: 23-6251690

CONTRIBUTIONS SUMMARY
Donor(s): Lawrence B. Sheppard

Typical Recipients: • *Arts & Humanities:* History & Archaeology, Libraries, Museums/Galleries • *Civic & Public Affairs:* General, Municipalities/Towns, Urban & Community Affairs • *Education:* Colleges & Universities, Private Education (Precollege), Secondary Education (Private), Secondary Education (Public) • *Health:* Cancer, Children's Health/Hospitals, Emergency/Ambulance Services, Health Organizations, Hospitals, Medical Research, Nursing Services, Single-Disease Health Associations • *Religion:* Churches • *Social Services:* Child Welfare, Counseling, General, People with Disabilities, Shelters/Homelessness, Special Olympics, United Funds/United Ways, YMCA/YWCA/YMHA/YWHA, Youth Organizations

Grant Types: capital and general support

Geographic Distribution: focus on the Hanover, PA, area

GIVING OFFICERS
Charlotte S. Devan: vp
Lawrence S. Devan: dir
W. Todd Devan: dir
Donald Dorr: dir

APPLICATION INFORMATION
Initial Approach: Include a description of organization, amount requested, purpose of funds sought, recently audited financial statement, and proof of tax-exempt status. Deadline is October 31.

GRANTS ANALYSIS
Total Grants: $60,845
Number of Grants: 22
Highest Grant: $20,845
Typical Range: $1,000 to $7,000
Disclosure Period: fiscal year ending November 30, 1993
Note: Recent grants are derived from a fiscal 1993 Form 990.

RECENT GRANTS

Library
1,500 Hanover Public Library, Hanover, PA — computer

General
7,000 Hanover Area YMCA, Hanover, PA
5,000 Delone Catholic High School Challenge Gift
3,000 Visiting Nurse Association, York, PA
2,500 Clearview Terrace II, Hanover, PA
2,000 American Cancer Society, Hanover, PA — Hanover Branch

Smith Memorial Fund, Ethel Sergeant Clark

CONTACT
Camie Morrison
Vice President
Ethel Sergeant Clark Smith Memorial Fund
c/o Corestates Bank, N.A.
PO Box 7558
Philadelphia, PA 19101
(215) 973-2792

FINANCIAL SUMMARY
Recent Giving: $574,225 (fiscal 1994); $232,200 (fiscal 1992); $421,400 (fiscal 1991)
Assets: $12,109,893 (fiscal 1994); $11,852,378 (fiscal 1992); $11,284,806 (fiscal 1991)
EIN: 23-6648857

CONTRIBUTIONS SUMMARY
Donor(s): the late Ethel Sergeant Clark Smith

Typical Recipients: • *Arts & Humanities:* Arts Centers, Community Arts, Historic Preservation, Libraries, Music • *Civic & Public Affairs:* Housing • *Education:* Colleges & Universities • *Environment:* General • *Health:* Health Organizations • *Religion:* Religious Organizations • *Social Services:* Child Welfare, Community Centers, Community Service Organizations, Domestic Violence, People with Disabilities, United Funds/United Ways, Youth Organizations

Grant Types: capital, emergency, general support, multiyear/continuing support, operating expenses, project, research, scholarship, and seed money

Geographic Distribution: limited to Delaware County, PA

GIVING OFFICERS
Corestates Bank, N.A.: trust

APPLICATION INFORMATION
Initial Approach: Send cover letter and full proposal. Include a description of organization, amount requested, purpose of funds sought, recently audited financial statement, and proof of tax-exempt status. Deadlines are March 1 and September 1 for completed proposals.

Restrictions on Giving: Does not support individuals or provide loans.

PUBLICATIONS
Multi-year report (including Application Guidelines)

GRANTS ANALYSIS
Total Grants: $574,225

Typical Range: $2,500 to $15,000

Disclosure Period: fiscal year ending May 31, 1994

Note: Recent grants are derived from a fiscal 1992 Form 990. Grants list for fiscal 1994 was not included in the Form 990.

RECENT GRANTS

Library
10,000	Marble Public Library, Broomall, PA	

General
30,000	Widener University, Chester, PA
25,000	Delco Blind/Sight Center, Chester, PA
25,000	Domestic Abuse Project of Delaware County, Media, PA
25,000	Media-Providence Friends School, Media, PA
20,000	Better Housing for Chester, Chester, PA

SmithKline Beecham Corp. / SmithKline Beecham Foundation

Sales: $4.75 billion
Employees: 30,500
Parent Company: SmithKline Beecham PLC
Headquarters: Philadelphia, PA
SIC Major Group: Pharmaceutical Preparations, Prepared Feeds Nec, and Medical Laboratories

CONTACT
Elizabeth A. Tyson
Chairperson
SmithKline Beecham Foundation
One Franklin Plz.
PO Box 7929
Philadelphia, PA 19101
(215) 751-3574

FINANCIAL SUMMARY
Recent Giving: $1,200,000 (1995 est.); $3,800,000 (1994 approx.); $4,915,406 (1993)

Assets: $1,510,737 (1993); $1,509,345 (1992); $1,649,506 (1991)

Gifts Received: $5,151,500 (1993); $4,426,251 (1992); $4,399,795 (1991)

Fiscal Note: Company gives directly and through the foundation. Above giving figures are for the foundation only. In 1993, foundation giving totaled $3,903,835, and matching gifts totaled $1,011,571. Above figures exclude nonmonetary support. Foundation receives contributions from SmithKline Beecham Corporation.

EIN: 23-2120418

CONTRIBUTIONS SUMMARY
Typical Recipients: • *Arts & Humanities:* Ballet, History & Archaeology, Libraries, Museums/Galleries, Music, Opera, Theater • *Civic & Public Affairs:* Economic Policy, Municipalities/Towns, Philanthropic Organizations, Professional & Trade Associations, Public Policy, Urban & Community Affairs, Women's Affairs, Zoos/Aquariums • *Education:* Business Education, Colleges & Universities, Medical Education, Private Education (Precollege), Science/Mathematics Education, Student Aid • *Health:* Cancer, Emergency/Ambulance Services, Health Funds, Health Organizations, Long-Term Care, Single-Disease Health Associations • *International:* Foreign Educational Institutions • *Science:* Scientific Centers & Institutes, Scientific Labs • *Social Services:* Substance Abuse, Youth Organizations

Grant Types: employee matching gifts and project

Note: Employee matching gift ratio: 1 to 1.

Geographic Distribution: where company has major facilities

Operating Locations: PA (Philadelphia, Pittsburgh)

CORP. OFFICERS
Jean-Pierre Garnier: *B* 1947 *CURR EMPL* exec vp: Smithkline Beecham Corp

James Hill: *CURR EMPL* sr vp, corp aff: SmithKline Beecham Corp

Jan Leschley: *CURR EMPL* chmn: Smithkline Beecham PLC *CORP AFFIL* vp pharmaceuticals dir, dir: Smithkline Beecham Corp

GIVING OFFICERS
John Dent: dir

James Hill: dir *CURR EMPL* sr vp, corp aff: SmithKline Beecham Corp (see above)

Henry J. King: treas

W. Vickery Stoughton: dir *B* Peoria IL 1946 *ED* St Louis Univ BS 1968; Univ Chicago MBA 1973 *CURR EMPL* pres, ceo, dir: Smithkline Beecham Clinical Labs *CORP AFFIL* dir: Sun Life Assurance Co *NONPR AFFIL* fellow: Am Coll Hosp Admin

Elizabeth A. Tyson: chmn

J. B. Ziegler: dir

APPLICATION INFORMATION
Initial Approach: *Initial Contact:* letter of no more than two pages to foundation chair-

person *Include Information On:* a one-paragraph description of the organization; one-paragraph summaries of the proposed project or program, and the project's principal objective; the amount requested; and the relevancy of the project to SmithKline Beecham's giving priorities and how the proposed program reflects those priorities *Deadlines:* none

Restrictions on Giving: Foundation does not support capital campaigns, chairs, endowments, general operating expenses, deficit financing, debt retirement, conferences, symposia, individuals, fundraising events, and associated advertising.

PUBLICATIONS
Guidelines sheet

GRANTS ANALYSIS
Total Grants: $3,903,835

Number of Grants: 185

Highest Grant: $500,000

Average Grant: $21,102

Typical Range: $1,000 to $75,000

Disclosure Period: 1993

Note: Above analysis excludes matching gifts totaling $1,011,571. Recent grants are derived from a 1993 Form 990.

RECENT GRANTS

General
500,000	Charities Funds Transfers, Alexandria, VA
500,000	University of Pennsylvania Trustees, Philadelphia, PA
500,000	University of Pennsylvania Trustees, Philadelphia, PA
400,000	American Association of Colleges of Pharmacy, Bethesda, MD
250,000	Temple University, Philadelphia, PA

Snayberger Memorial Foundation, Harry E. and Florence W.

CONTACT
Harry E. and Florence W. Snayberger Memorial Fdn.
c/o Pennsylvania National Bank and Trust Co.
One S Ctr. St.
Pottsville, PA 17901
(717) 622-4200

FINANCIAL SUMMARY
Recent Giving: $174,713 (fiscal 1994); $178,786 (fiscal 1993); $229,000 (fiscal 1992)

Assets: $3,779,026 (fiscal 1994); $3,918,392 (fiscal 1993); $3,790,626 (fiscal 1992)

EIN: 23-2056361

CONTRIBUTIONS SUMMARY
Donor(s): the late Harry E. Snayberger

Typical Recipients: • *Arts & Humanities:* Arts Associations & Councils, Libraries, Music • *Civic & Public Affairs:* Municipalities/Towns, Safety • *Health:* Children's Health/Hospitals • *Religion:* Churches, Religious Welfare • *Social Services:* Day Care, People with Disabilities, Recreation & Athletics, Scouts, Substance Abuse, YMCA/YWCA/YMHA/YWHA, Youth Organizations

Grant Types: scholarship

Geographic Distribution: limited to Schuylkill County, PA

GIVING OFFICERS
Pennslyvania National Bank & Trust Co.: trust

APPLICATION INFORMATION
Initial Approach: Send letter requesting application form. Deadline is February 26.

OTHER THINGS TO KNOW
Provides scholarships to individuals for higher education.

GRANTS ANALYSIS
Total Grants: $174,713

Number of Grants: 221

Highest Grant: $1,500

Typical Range: $100 to $2,500

Disclosure Period: fiscal year ending March 31, 1994

Note: Recent grants are derived from a fiscal 1994 Form 990.

RECENT GRANTS
Library
| 500 | Schuylkill Haven Free Public Library, Schuylkill Haven, PA |

General
1,500	Boy Scouts of America Hawk Mountain Council, Hawk Mountain, PA
1,500	First United Methodist Church, Asheboro, NC
1,000	Dennis Reichert Family Fire Disaster
1,000	YWCA
500	Alcohol/Drug Help Others, Pottsville, PA — prevention/education

Sordoni Foundation

CONTACT
Benjamin Badman, Jr.
Executive Vice President
Sordoni Fdn.
45 Owen St.
Forty Fort, PA 18704
(717) 283-1211

FINANCIAL SUMMARY
Recent Giving: $194,700 (fiscal 1992); $1,048,562 (fiscal 1991); $589,833 (fiscal 1990)

Assets: $6,553,518 (fiscal 1992); $6,310,814 (fiscal 1991); $7,538,907 (fiscal 1990)

Gifts Received: $51,025 (fiscal 1992); $47,000 (fiscal 1991); $170,667 (fiscal 1990)

EIN: 24-6017505

CONTRIBUTIONS SUMMARY
Donor(s): the late Andrew J. Sordoni, Sr., the late Andrew J. Sordoni, Jr., Andrew J. Sordoni III, the late Mrs. Andrew J. Sordoni, Sr., the late Mrs. Andrew J. Sordoni, Jr., Mrs. Andrew J. Sordoni III

Typical Recipients: • *Arts & Humanities:* Community Arts, Libraries, Museums/Galleries, Music, Public Broadcasting, Theater • *Civic & Public Affairs:* Economic Development, General, Municipalities/Towns, Public Policy, Urban & Community Affairs • *Education:* Colleges & Universities, Education Funds, Vocational & Technical Education • *Health:* Health Organizations, Hospitals, Medical Research • *Religion:* Religious Organizations • *Social Services:* Child Welfare, Family Services, Youth Organizations

Grant Types: capital, endowment, general support, multiyear/continuing support, project, and seed money

Geographic Distribution: focus on northeastern PA

GIVING OFFICERS
Richard Allen: dir *PHIL AFFIL* vp: R. E. and Joan S. Allen Foundation

Rev. Jule Ayers: dir

Benjamin Badman, Jr.: exec vp, dir

Ruth Hitchner: asst secy

Dr. Roy E. Morgan: dir *B* Nanticoke PA 1908 *ED* PA St Univ BA 1931; PA St Univ MA 1935 *CURR EMPL* pres: WY Valley Broadcasting Co *CORP AFFIL* treas: Ra-Tel Realty Co *NONPR AFFIL* chmn emeritus exec comm: ABC Radio Network Affiliates Comm; dir: Econ Devel Counc Northeastern PA; mem pres counc: Kings Coll; trust: Hosp Assn PA

Patrick Solano: dir

Andrew John Sordoni III: pres *B* Pratt KS 1943 *ED* Notre Dame Univ 1961-1964; Kings Coll BA 1967 *CURR EMPL* chmn, dir: Sordoni Construction Svcs *CORP AFFIL* chmn: Commonwealth Telephone Co, Evergreen Capital Corp, Mercom, Pub Svc Enterprises PA, Whiteman Tower; dir: Harsco Corp, Sordoni Enterprises *NONPR AFFIL* dir: PA Chamber Bus Indus, Pennsylvanians Effective Govt, Valley Med Ctr Geisinger WY, WVIA; mem: NJ Jazz Soc, PA Jazz Soc *CLUB AFFIL* Friars, Sons Desert NY, Westmoreland CC

Stephen Sordoni: asst treas *B* 1948 *CURR EMPL* vp, secy: Sordoni Enterprises *CORP AFFIL* secy: Sordoni Construction Svcs, Whiteman Tower

Susan F. Sordoni: dir

William James Umphred, Sr.: dir *B* Wilkes-Barre PA 1928 *ED* Wilkes Coll 1952 *CORP AFFIL* dir: Franklin Fed Savings & Loan Assn, PA Millers Mutual Ins co

APPLICATION INFORMATION
Initial Approach: Send brief letter of inquiry describing program or project. There are no deadlines.

Restrictions on Giving: Does not support individuals or provide scholarships.

GRANTS ANALYSIS
Total Grants: $194,700

Number of Grants: 30

Highest Grant: $43,000

Typical Range: $100 to $5,000

Disclosure Period: fiscal year ending July 31, 1992

Note: Recent grants are derived from a fiscal 1992 Form 990.

RECENT GRANTS
Library
| 1,000 | Osterhout Free Library, Wilkes-Barre, PA |
| 500 | Hoyt Library, Kingston, PA |

General
15,000	Geisinger Foundation, Danville, PA
5,000	Committee for Economic Growth, Wilkes-Barre, PA
2,000	Family Service Association of Wyoming Valley, Wilkes-Barre, PA
1,000	John Heinz Institute, Scranton, PA
1,000	Johnson Technical Institute, Scranton, PA

Spang & Co. / Spang and Co. Charitable Trust

Sales: $100.0 million
Employees: 1,200
Headquarters: Butler, PA
SIC Major Group: Electronic & Other Electrical Equipment and Stone, Clay & Glass Products

CONTACT
C. R. Dorsch
Vice President, Finance
Spang & Co.
PO Box 751
Butler, PA 16003-0751
(412) 287-8781

FINANCIAL SUMMARY
Recent Giving: $82,074 (1993); $80,501 (1992); $73,611 (1991)

Assets: $1,580,838 (1993); $1,250,962 (1992); $976,877 (1991)

Gifts Received: $313,225 (1993); $314,580 (1992); $15,365 (1991)

Fiscal Note: In 1993, contributions were received from Spang & Co. ($300,000) and the employees of Spang & Co. ($13,225).

EIN: 25-6020192

CONTRIBUTIONS SUMMARY
Typical Recipients: • *Arts & Humanities:* Ballet, Libraries, Music, Opera, Public Broadcasting, Theater • *Civic & Public Af-*

fairs: Economic Policy, General, Safety • *Education:* Colleges & Universities, Medical Education, Private Education (Precollege), Special Education • *Health:* Children's Health/Hospitals, Hospitals, Hospitals (University Affiliated), Kidney, Medical Research, Single-Disease Health Associations • *Science:* Scientific Centers & Institutes • *Social Services:* Animal Protection, Camps, Child Welfare, Community Service Organizations, Delinquency & Criminal Rehabilitation, Domestic Violence, Food/Clothing Distribution, People with Disabilities, Recreation & Athletics, United Funds/United Ways, Volunteer Services, Youth Organizations

Grant Types: general support

Geographic Distribution: focus on PA

Operating Locations: PA (Butler)

CORP. OFFICERS
Frank E. Rath: *CURR EMPL* chmn, dir: Spang & Co

Frank E. Rath, Jr.: *CURR EMPL* pres, dir: Spang & Co

Robert A. Rath: *CURR EMPL* vchmn, dir: Spang & Co

GIVING OFFICERS
Frank E. Rath, Jr.: trust *CURR EMPL* pres, dir: Spang & Co (see above)

APPLICATION INFORMATION
Initial Approach: Send a brief letter of inquiry. Include a description of organization, amount requested, purpose of funds sought, recently audited financial statement, and proof of tax-exempt status. Deadline is 90 days before the end of the calendar quarter.

GRANTS ANALYSIS
Total Grants: $82,074

Number of Grants: 58

Highest Grant: $20,000

Typical Range: $100 to $20,000

Disclosure Period: 1993

Note: Recent grants are derived from a 1993 Form 990.

RECENT GRANTS

Library
2,000	Booneville Library, Booneville, AR	
2,000	Butler Public Library, Butler, PA	
500	Carnegie Institute, Pittsburgh, PA	

General
20,000	Johns Hopkins University Hospital/Brady Institute, Baltimore, MD	
20,000	United Way of Butler County, Butler, PA	
10,000	Presbyterian University Hospital, Pittsburgh, PA	
5,000	Easter Seal Society, Butler, PA	
1,494	Children's Hospital, Pittsburgh, PA	

Speyer Foundation, Alexander C. and Tillie S.

CONTACT
A. C. Speyer, Jr.
Manager, Trustee
Alexander C. and Tillie S. Speyer Fdn.
1202 Benedum Trees Bldg.
Pittsburgh, PA 15222
(412) 281-7225

FINANCIAL SUMMARY
Recent Giving: $182,550 (1992); $152,135 (1991); $167,639 (1990)

Assets: $3,779,320 (1992); $3,710,891 (1991); $3,424,008 (1990)

EIN: 25-6051650

CONTRIBUTIONS SUMMARY
Donor(s): members of the Speyer family

Typical Recipients: • *Arts & Humanities:* Arts Associations & Councils, Arts Centers, Arts Festivals, Arts Institutes, Community Arts, Ethnic & Folk Arts, General, Libraries, Museums/Galleries • *Civic & Public Affairs:* Botanical Gardens/Parks, Civil Rights, General • *Education:* Arts/Humanities Education, Colleges & Universities, Education Funds, Education Reform, General, Private Education (Precollege), Public Education (Precollege) • *Environment:* Air/Water Quality, General, Resource Conservation • *Health:* Emergency/Ambulance Services • *International:* Health Care/Hospitals, International Relations • *Religion:* Churches, Jewish Causes, Religious Organizations, Religious Welfare, Synagogues/Temples • *Science:* Scientific Centers & Institutes • *Social Services:* Community Service Organizations, Delinquency & Criminal Rehabilitation, Family Planning, Food/Clothing Distribution, Homes, People with Disabilities, United Funds/United Ways

Grant Types: general support

GIVING OFFICERS
Alexander C. Speyer, Jr.: mgr, trust *B* 1916 *CORP AFFIL* pres, treas: Parsons Coal Co *PHIL AFFIL* trust: Dorothy Richard Starling Foundation

Darthea Speyer: trust

APPLICATION INFORMATION
Initial Approach: The foundation has no formal grant application procedure or application form. There are no deadlines.

GRANTS ANALYSIS
Total Grants: $182,550

Number of Grants: 78

Highest Grant: $20,000

Typical Range: $150 to $10,000

Disclosure Period: 1992

Note: Recent grants are derived from a 1992 Form 990.

RECENT GRANTS

General
20,000	Carnegie Mellon University, Pittsburgh, PA	
13,000	United Jewish Federation, Pittsburgh, PA	
10,000	Rodef Shalom, Pittsburgh, PA	
10,000	United Way, Pittsburgh, PA	
8,000	New York Times Neediest Cases Fund, New York, NY	

Stabler Foundation, Donald B. and Dorothy L.

CONTACT
William King
Chairman, Board of Trustees
Donald B. and Dorothy L. Stabler Fdn.
c/o Dauphin Deposit Bank and Trust Co.
213 Market St.
Harrisburg, PA 17105
(717) 255-2121

FINANCIAL SUMMARY
Recent Giving: $456,100 (1992); $532,525 (1991); $471,980 (1990)

Assets: $6,814,575 (1992); $6,795,507 (1991); $6,429,083 (1990)

Gifts Received: $58,200 (1992); $138,500 (1991); $422,800 (1990)

Fiscal Note: In 1992, contributions were received from Donald B. and Dorothy L. Stabler ($58,000) and William J. King ($200).

EIN: 23-6422944

CONTRIBUTIONS SUMMARY
Donor(s): Stabler Companies

Typical Recipients: • *Arts & Humanities:* Libraries, Music, Public Broadcasting • *Civic & Public Affairs:* Clubs, General • *Education:* Colleges & Universities, Community & Junior Colleges, Education Funds, Legal Education, Medical Education, Private Education (Precollege), Public Education (Precollege), Student Aid • *Health:* Clinics/Medical Centers, Heart, Hospices, Hospitals, Prenatal Health Issues • *Religion:* Churches, Religious Organizations, Religious Welfare • *Social Services:* Child Welfare, Community Service Organizations, Food/Clothing Distribution, People with Disabilities, Senior Services, Substance Abuse, United Funds/United Ways, Volunteer Services, Youth Organizations

Grant Types: capital, endowment, general support, multiyear/continuing support, operating expenses, professorship, and scholarship

Geographic Distribution: focus on PA

GIVING OFFICERS
Richard E. Jordan: dir *PHIL AFFIL* vp, dir: Josiah W. and Bessie H. Kline Foundation

William Joseph King: chmn, trust *B* Philadelphia PA 1929 *ED* Univ PA Wharton Sch 1954; La Salle Univ MBA 1979 *CURR EMPL* chmn, ceo: Dauphin Deposit Corp *CORP AFFIL* dir: Hempt Bros, Millers Mutual Ins Co

David Schaper: dir

Frank A. Sinon: secy, trust

Richard Zimmerman: dir

APPLICATION INFORMATION
Initial Approach: Send brief letter of inquiry describing program or project. There are no deadlines.

GRANTS ANALYSIS
Total Grants: $456,100

Number of Grants: 68

Highest Grant: $100,000

Typical Range: $500 to $10,000

Disclosure Period: 1992

Note: Recent grants are derived from a 1992 Form 990.

RECENT GRANTS

Library
10,000	Elizabethtown College, Elizabethtown, PA — library fund
1,000	Dauphin County Library System, Harrisburg, PA — general

General
100,000	Woods School, Langhorne, PA — general
50,000	Harrisburg Area Community College, Harrisburg, PA — telecommunications center at Stabler Hall
50,000	Lehigh University, Bethlehem, PA — Stabler scholarship fund
45,000	Catholic Diocese of Allentown, Allentown, PA — scholarship fund
45,000	Catholic Diocese of Harrisburg, Harrisburg, PA — scholarship fund

Stackpole-Hall Foundation

CONTACT
William C. Conrad
Executive Secretary
Stackpole-Hall Foundation
44 S Saint Marys St.
St. Marys, PA 15857
(814) 834-1845

FINANCIAL SUMMARY
Recent Giving: $851,638 (1994); $656,511 (1993); $769,115 (1992)

Assets: $18,338,838 (1994); $20,067,947 (1993); $19,551,306 (1992)

EIN: 25-6006650

CONTRIBUTIONS SUMMARY
Donor(s): The Stackpole-Hall Foundation was established as a trust in Pennsylvania in 1951, with funds donated by the late L. G. Hall , J. H. Stackpole, Mrs. Adelaide Stackpole, and by Harrison C. Stackpole. James Hall Stackpole (1902-1964), son of Harrison C. Stackpole and the former Sallie Hall, was chairman of Stackpole Carbon Company. A portion of the foundation's funds is restricted by the donors through specific bequests to designated religious organizations.

Typical Recipients: • *Arts & Humanities:* Arts Associations & Councils, Historic Preservation, History & Archaeology, Libraries, Music • *Civic & Public Affairs:* Economic Development, Employment/Job Training, Municipalities/Towns, Nonprofit Management, Professional & Trade Associations, Urban & Community Affairs • *Education:* Colleges & Universities, Education Associations, General, Medical Education, Minority Education, Private Education (Precollege), Science/Mathematics Education, Secondary Education (Private) • *Environment:* General • *Health:* Emergency/Ambulance Services, Hospices, Hospitals, Mental Health, Nursing Services • *Religion:* Churches, Dioceses, Religious Organizations, Religious Welfare • *Social Services:* Community Centers, Family Planning, People with Disabilities, Recreation & Athletics, Scouts, Substance Abuse, United Funds/United Ways, Volunteer Services, Youth Organizations

Grant Types: capital, general support, project, and seed money

Geographic Distribution: focus on Elk County, PA, area

GIVING OFFICERS
William C. Conrad: exec secy

Douglas R. Dobson: trust *CURR EMPL* vchmn, dir: Stackpole Corp

Helen Hall Drew: trust

Lyle G. Hall: trust *B* 1929 *ED* Yale Univ 1948-1951; Harvard Univ 1969; Boston Univ BS 1975; Episcopal Divinity Sch M 1978 *CURR EMPL* chmn, ceo: Stackpole Corp *NONPR AFFIL* mem diocesan counc: Episcopal Church Diocese Erie; rector: trust: Church Home Soc, Dana Hall Sch, Episcopal Divinity Sch

J. M. Hamlin Johnson: trust *B* Ridgeway PA 1925 *ED* Grove City Coll BS 1949; PA St Univ 1969 *CORP AFFIL* dir: Hamlin Bank & Trust Co, Stackpole Corp; ptnr, treas: J & B Co *NONPR AFFIL* dir: Un Fund St Mary; dir, treas: ELCAM Vocational Rehab Ctr; mem: Natl Assn Accts; trust: A Kaul Meml Hosp *CLUB AFFIL* Kiwanis, St Marys CC

Alexander Sheble-Hall: trust

Harrison Clinton Stackpole: chmn, trust *B* Ridgeway PA 1914 *ED* Yale Univ

R. Dauer Stackpole: trust

APPLICATION INFORMATION
Initial Approach:

Applicants should telephone the foundation before submitting a request. After initial inquiry, a brief letter may be sent. If the board is interested in a project, it will request a more complete proposal.

Applicants should include a history of the organization, description of the proposed project, proposed budget, most recent financial statement, evidence of need for the project, and organizational staff list.

The board meets in February, May, August, and December. Proposals should be received by January, April, July, or November.

Restrictions on Giving: No grants are made to individuals.

PUBLICATIONS
Annual report

GRANTS ANALYSIS
Total Grants: $656,511

Number of Grants: 71

Highest Grant: $150,000

Average Grant: $9,247

Typical Range: $1,000 to $9,250 and $30,000 to $50,000

Disclosure Period: 1993

Note: Recent grants are derived from a 1993 Form 990.

RECENT GRANTS

Library
2,654	St. Marys Public Library, St. Marys, PA — summer job program

General
150,000	Elk County Development Foundation, St. Marys, PA — provide low interest loans for job creation
48,604	Grace Episcopal Church, Ridgway, PA
37,388	Episcopal Diocese of Northwest Pennsylvania, Erie, PA
26,090	Drug and Alcohol Abuse Services, Port Allegheny, PA — elementary school pilot program
25,000	Episcopal Divinity School, Cambridge, MA — funding for AGE program

Staunton Farm Foundation

CONTACT
Patricia MacDonald
Administrative Assistant
Staunton Farm Foundation
Center City Tower, Ste. 240
650 Smithfield St.
Pittsburgh, PA 15222
(412) 281-8020

FINANCIAL SUMMARY
Recent Giving: $1,000,000 (1995 est.); $1,000,000 (1994 approx.); $1,000,000 (1993 approx.)

Assets: $28,134,354 (1992); $27,603,590 (1991); $22,497,072 (1990)

Gifts Received: $5,428 (1987)

EIN: 25-0965573

CONTRIBUTIONS SUMMARY
Donor(s): The Staunton Farm Foundation was established in Pennsylvania in 1937, with funds donated by Mrs. Matilda S. McCready (born Matilda Staunton Craig). Mrs. McCready's original wish was that funds from the foundation would be used to erect a home for the mentally ill. However,

her estate lacked the necessary funds for such an undertaking.

Mrs. McCready realized her original intentions may not always be practical and stated, "In the event that advances in medical sciences or in social conditions render carrying on of the home...impractical, the directors of Staunton Farm may, with the consent of Orphan's Court of Allegheny County, PA, change its character so as to suit the needs of the times, keeping always in view the effort to alleviate the conditions of the sick and unfortunate."

Typical Recipients: • *Arts & Humanities:* Libraries • *Civic & Public Affairs:* Professional & Trade Associations, Women's Affairs • *Education:* Afterschool/Enrichment Programs, Colleges & Universities, Literacy, Medical Education • *Health:* AIDS/HIV, Children's Health/Hospitals, Health Funds, Health Organizations, Hospitals, Medical Rehabilitation, Mental Health • *Religion:* Churches, Jewish Causes, Ministries, Religious Welfare • *Social Services:* Child Welfare, Community Service Organizations, Counseling, Crime Prevention, Delinquency & Criminal Rehabilitation, Domestic Violence, Emergency Relief, Family Services, Recreation & Athletics, Senior Services, Sexual Abuse, Shelters/Homelessness, Substance Abuse, United Funds/United Ways, YMCA/YWCA/YMHA/YWHA, Youth Organizations

Grant Types: project

Geographic Distribution: Southwestern Pennsylvania

GIVING OFFICERS
Albert H. Burchfield III: pres, dir *B* 1931 *CURR EMPL* chmn, secy, dir: Bridge Products

G. L. Craig: dir

Howard K. Foster: dir

Rev. David C. Frederick: dir

Andrea Q. Griffiths: dir

Nancy E. Gruner: dir

Carolyn S. Hammer: dir

Alexander A. Henkels, Jr.: dir

Marilyn Ingalls: vp

Hope S. Linge: dir

Patricia MacDonald: admin asst

Barbara Robinson: secy/treas

Thomas L. Wentling, Jr.: dir

APPLICATION INFORMATION
Initial Approach:

A letter of inquiry should be sent describing the organization and proposed project. After initial review, prospective grantees may be asked to make a formal application for consideration by the Foundation's Project Committee.

Formal applications are due in the middle of January, April, July and October. Prospective grantees should plan accordingly.

Restrictions on Giving: The foundation does not usually contribute to general operating support, endowment funds, building campaigns, conferences, or grants to individuals. Exceptions have been made in situations

where the conduct of the project is directly dependent upon altered or new facilities.

OTHER THINGS TO KNOW
In 1987, to mark the 50th anniversary of the foundation, a chair of professor of Pediatrics and Psychiatry was endowed at the University of Pittsburgh Medical Center.

PUBLICATIONS
Guidelines

GRANTS ANALYSIS
Total Grants: $454,678*

Number of Grants: 24*

Highest Grant: $88,450*

Average Grant: $18,945*

Typical Range: $5,000* to $50,000

Disclosure Period: 1992

Note: The grants analysis figures are based on grants paid in 1992. Recent grants are derived from a 1993 list of grants approved.

RECENT GRANTS
General

1,500,000	University of Pittsburgh, Pittsburgh, PA — over six years, for professor of pediatrics and psychiatry
280,000	United Way of Allegheny County, Pittsburgh, PA — over three years, McKeesport and Hill collaboratives
204,800	Light of Life Ministries, Pittsburgh, PA — toward the Resident Counseling Component
188,158	Women's Center and Shelter, Pittsburgh, PA — over three years, integrated domestic violence intervention
150,000	Riverview Children's Center, Pittsburgh, PA — over three years, for expansion of mental health services

Steinman Foundation, James Hale

Headquarters: Lancaster, PA

CONTACT
Dennis A. Getz, Jr.
Secretary
James Hale Steinman Fdn.
8 W King St.
Lancaster, PA 17603
(717) 291-8607

FINANCIAL SUMMARY
Recent Giving: $699,752 (1992); $439,649 (1991); $449,275 (1990)

Assets: $9,592,467 (1992); $8,886,638 (1991); $7,589,485 (1990)

Gifts Received: $640,000 (1992); $440,000 (1991); $740,000 (1990)

Fiscal Note: In fiscal 1992, contributions were received from Lancaster Newspapers, Inc. ($360,000), Intelligencer Printing Co.

($160,000), and Delmarva Broadcasting Co. ($120,000).

EIN: 23-6266377

CONTRIBUTIONS SUMMARY
Donor(s): the late James Hale Steinman, the late Louise Steinman von Hess, Lancaster Newspapers, Inc.

Typical Recipients: • *Arts & Humanities:* Arts Associations & Councils, Community Arts, Historic Preservation, History & Archaeology, Libraries, Museums/Galleries, Music, Opera • *Civic & Public Affairs:* Botanical Gardens/Parks, Ethnic Organizations, General, Municipalities/Towns, Parades/Festivals, Philanthropic Organizations, Public Policy • *Education:* Afterschool/Enrichment Programs, Arts/Humanities Education, Colleges & Universities, Education Associations, Private Education (Precollege), Secondary Education (Private), Student Aid • *Health:* Cancer, Clinics/Medical Centers, Emergency/Ambulance Services, Eyes/Blindness, Heart, Hospitals, Medical Research, Multiple Sclerosis, Single-Disease Health Associations • *Religion:* Churches, Religious Organizations, Religious Welfare • *Social Services:* Community Service Organizations, Family Planning, People with Disabilities, United Funds/United Ways, Youth Organizations

Grant Types: capital, general support, and scholarship

Geographic Distribution: focus on Lancaster, PA

GIVING OFFICERS
John M. Buckwalter: trust *B* Lancaster PA 1931 *ED* Franklin & Marshall Coll 1952; Harvard Univ Sch Bus Admin 1954 *CURR EMPL* pres, dir: Lancaster Newspapers *CORP AFFIL* dir: Hamilton Bank, Intelligencer Printing Co *PHIL AFFIL* trust: John Frederick Steinman Foundation

Jack S. Gerhart: trust *PHIL AFFIL* trust: John Frederick Steinman Foundation

Dennis A. Getz, Jr.: secy, trust *CURR EMPL* vp, contr: Lancaster Newspapers *PHIL AFFIL* secy, trust: John Frederick Steinman Foundation

Caroline N. Hill: trust *CORP AFFIL* dir: Intelligencer Printing Co, Lancaster Newspapers Inc

Hale S. Krasne: trust *CORP AFFIL* dir: Intelligencer Printing Co, Lancaster Newspapers Inc

Caroline S. Nunan: chmn, trust *CORP AFFIL* dir: Intelligencer Printing Co, Lancaster Newspapers Inc

Willis Weidman Shenk: treas, trust *B* Manheim PA 1915 *CURR EMPL* chmn, dir: Lancaster Newspapers *CORP AFFIL* chmn: Delmarva Broadcasting Co, Steinman Mgmt Corp; chmn, dir: Intelligencer Printing Co *PHIL AFFIL* treas: John Frederick Steinman Foundation

Beverly R. Steinman: vchmn, trust *CORP AFFIL* dir: Intelligencer Printing Co, Lancaster Newspapers Inc

APPLICATION INFORMATION
Initial Approach: Application form available for employee-related scholarships. Deadline for scholarships is February 28 of senior year of high school.

GRANTS ANALYSIS
Total Grants: $699,752

Number of Grants: 41

Highest Grant: $483,056

Typical Range: $250 to $25,000

Disclosure Period: 1992

Note: Recent grants are derived from a 1992 Form 990.

RECENT GRANTS

Library
1,000	Lancaster County Library, Lancaster, PA

General
41,500	United Fund, Lancaster, PA
26,000	Linden Hall, Lancaster, PA
25,000	Pennsylvania Academy of Music, Lancaster, PA
7,500	Lancaster Boys and Girls Club, Lancaster, PA
5,000	Lancaster Celebration 250, Lancaster, PA

Steinman Foundation, John Frederick

CONTACT
Jay H. Wenrich
Secretary
John Frederick Steinman Fdn.
8 W King St.
Lancaster, PA 17608

FINANCIAL SUMMARY
Recent Giving: $515,460 (1992); $505,750 (1991); $477,533 (1990)

Assets: $13,279,572 (1992); $12,516,565 (1991); $10,850,484 (1990)

Gifts Received: $160,000 (1992); $160,000 (1991); $160,000 (1990)

Fiscal Note: In 1992, contributions were received from Intelligencer Printing Company.

EIN: 23-6266378

CONTRIBUTIONS SUMMARY
Donor(s): the late John Frederick Steinman, the late Shirley W. Steinman, Lancaster Newspapers, Inc.

Typical Recipients: • *Arts & Humanities:* Arts Appreciation, Arts Associations & Councils, Arts Festivals, Community Arts, General, History & Archaeology, Libraries, Literary Arts, Museums/Galleries, Music, Opera • *Civic & Public Affairs:* Employment/Job Training, General, Municipalities/Towns, Parades/Festivals, Public Policy • *Education:* Arts/Humanities Education, Business Education, Colleges & Universi-

ties, General, Literacy, Private Education (Precollege), Religious Education, Secondary Education (Private) • *Environment:* Air/Water Quality • *Health:* Clinics/Medical Centers, Hospices, Hospitals, Medical Research, Mental Health, Single-Disease Health Associations • *Religion:* Churches, Religious Organizations, Religious Welfare • *Social Services:* Community Service Organizations, Day Care, Family Planning, People with Disabilities, Sexual Abuse, Shelters/Homelessness, United Funds/United Ways, Youth Organizations

Grant Types: capital, fellowship, and general support

Geographic Distribution: focus on PA, with emphasis on the Lancaster area

GIVING OFFICERS

John M. Buckwalter: trust *B* Lancaster PA 1931 *ED* Franklin & Marshall Coll 1952; Harvard Univ Sch Bus Admin 1954 *CURR EMPL* pres, dir: Lancaster Newspapers *CORP AFFIL* dir: Hamilton Bank, Intelligencer Printing Co *PHIL AFFIL* trust: James Hale Steinman Foundation

Jack S. Gerhart: trust *PHIL AFFIL* trust: James Hale Steinman Foundation

Dennis A. Getz, Jr.: secy, trust *CURR EMPL* vp, contr: Lancaster Newspapers *PHIL AFFIL* secy, trust: James Hale Steinman Foundation

Henry Pildner, Jr.: trust *CORP AFFIL* dir: Intelligencer Printing Co

Willis Weidman Shenk: treas *B* Manheim PA 1915 *CURR EMPL* chmn, dir: Lancaster Newspapers *CORP AFFIL* chmn: Delmarva Broadcasting Co, Steinman Mgmt Corp; chmn, dir: Intelligencer Printing Co *PHIL AFFIL* treas, trust: James Hale Steinman Foundation

Pamela M. Thye: chmn, trust *CORP AFFIL* dir: Intelligencer Printing Co

Jay H. Wenrich: secy

APPLICATION INFORMATION
Initial Approach: Application for fellowship program available upon request. The deadline is February 1.

GRANTS ANALYSIS
Total Grants: $515,460

Number of Grants: 82

Highest Grant: $75,000

Typical Range: $500 to $25,000

Disclosure Period: 1992

Note: Recent grants are derived from a 1992 Form 990.

RECENT GRANTS

Library
1,500	Lancaster County Library, Lancaster, PA

General
75,000	Elizabethtown College, Elizabeth, PA

45,000	Girls Club of Lancaster, Lancaster, PA
41,500	United Fund, Lancaster, PA
25,000	Linden Hall, Lititz, PA
25,000	Messiah College, Grantham, PA

Strawbridge Foundation of Pennsylvania II, Margaret Dorrance

CONTACT
Diana S. Wister
President
Margaret Dorrance Strawbridge Fdn of Pennsylvania II
125 Strafford Ave., Ste. 108
Wayne, PA 19087
(215) 688-9260

FINANCIAL SUMMARY
Recent Giving: $343,389 (1993); $289,683 (1992); $266,380 (1991)

Assets: $2,909,586 (1993); $3,222,220 (1992); $3,376,865 (1991)

Gifts Received: $164,939 (1993); $126,520 (1992); $108,954 (1991)

Fiscal Note: In 1993, contributions were received from the trusts of Diana S. Norris.

EIN: 23-2371943

CONTRIBUTIONS SUMMARY
Donor(s): Margaret Dorrance Strawbridge Foundation

Typical Recipients: • *Arts & Humanities:* Arts Associations & Councils, Community Arts, Historic Preservation, History & Archaeology, Libraries, Museums/Galleries, Music, Performing Arts, Public Broadcasting • *Civic & Public Affairs:* Botanical Gardens/Parks, Clubs, Community Foundations, General, Public Policy, Safety, Urban & Community Affairs, Zoos/Aquariums • *Education:* Agricultural Education, Arts/Humanities Education, Colleges & Universities, Private Education (Precollege), Student Aid • *Environment:* General, Resource Conservation • *Health:* Cancer, Children's Health/Hospitals, Emergency/Ambulance Services, Hospices, Hospitals, Medical Rehabilitation, Medical Research, Prenatal Health Issues, Single-Disease Health Associations • *Religion:* Churches • *Science:* Scientific Centers & Institutes, Scientific Labs • *Social Services:* Animal Protection, Child Welfare, Community Service Organizations, Delinquency & Criminal Rehabilitation, Family Planning, People with Disabilities, Recreation & Athletics, Senior Services, Substance Abuse

Grant Types: general support, multi-year/continuing support, operating expenses, and research

Geographic Distribution: focus on the eastern U.S., especially PA and FL

GIVING OFFICERS
Diana S. Wister: pres *B* 1939 *PHIL AFFIL* co-trust: Dorrance Foundation, Dorrance Foundation

APPLICATION INFORMATION
Initial Approach: The foundation has no formal grant application procedure or application form. There are no deadlines.

Restrictions on Giving: Does not support individuals or provide loans.

GRANTS ANALYSIS
Total Grants: $343,389

Number of Grants: 76

Highest Grant: $41,289

Typical Range: $100 to $25,000

Disclosure Period: 1993

Note: Recent grants are derived from a 1993 Form 990.

RECENT GRANTS
Library

6,000	Agnes Irwin School, Rosemont, PA
2,000	Northeast Harbor Library, Northeast Harbor, ME

General

41,289	Groton School, Groton, MA
25,000	US International Sailing Association, Newport, RI
15,000	Pennsylvania Horticultural Society, Philadelphia, PA
15,000	Planned Parenthood Association, West Palm Beach, FL
12,500	Hospice Guild of Palm Beach, Palm Beach, FL

Superior Tube Co. / Superior-Pacific Fund, Inc.

Employees: 800
Headquarters: Wynnewood, PA
SIC Major Group: Steel Pipe & Tubes

CONTACT
Paul E. Kelly, Jr.
President
Superior-Pacific Fund, Inc.
Seven Wynnewood Rd.
Wynnewood, PA 19096
(610) 649-3210

FINANCIAL SUMMARY
Recent Giving: $520,427 (1993); $513,788 (1992); $527,524 (1991)

Assets: $13,794,858 (1993); $13,045,750 (1992); $12,402,442 (1991)

Fiscal Note: Contributes through foundation only.

EIN: 23-6298237

CONTRIBUTIONS SUMMARY
Typical Recipients: • *Arts & Humanities:* Community Arts, History & Archaeology, Libraries, Music, Opera, Public Broadcasting, Theater • *Civic & Public Affairs:* Bo-

tanical Gardens/Parks, Economic Policy, Minority Business, Professional & Trade Associations, Public Policy, Urban & Community Affairs • *Education:* Business Education, Colleges & Universities, Education Funds, Education Reform, Private Education (Precollege), Secondary Education (Private), Student Aid • *Environment:* Resource Conservation • *Health:* Cancer, Clinics/Medical Centers, Eyes/Blindness, Heart, Hospitals, Long-Term Care • *International:* International Affairs, International Relations • *Religion:* Churches, Religious Organizations • *Science:* Scientific Centers & Institutes • *Social Services:* Community Service Organizations, Senior Services, United Funds/United Ways, Youth Organizations

Grant Types: general support and scholarship

Note: Scholarships awarded to children of Superior Tube Company employees only.

Geographic Distribution: focus on Pennsylvania

Operating Locations: PA (Wynnewood)

CORP. OFFICERS
Donald C. Reilly: *B* Wilson PA 1950 *ED* Rider Coll 1973; CUNY 1974 *CURR EMPL* pres, ceo: Superior Tube Co *NONPR AFFIL* mem: Am Tube Assn, Steel Svc Ctr Inst

GIVING OFFICERS
Paul Edward Kelly, Jr.: dir *B* 1948 *CURR EMPL* pres, dir: Cawsl Corp *CORP AFFIL* secy, dir: Anchor/Darling Valve Co, Pressure Products Indus; vp, secy, dir: Anchor/Darling Indus Inc

APPLICATION INFORMATION
Initial Approach: *Initial Contact:* for grants, submit brief letter; for scholarships, written request for application guidelines *Include Information On:* brief description of program *Deadlines:* for grants, any time; for scholarships, completed application must be submitted by January 4.

Restrictions on Giving: Foundation makes scholarship awards to children of employees of Superior Tube Company only.

GRANTS ANALYSIS
Total Grants: $506,677*

Number of Grants: 85*

Highest Grant: $150,000

Average Grant: $5,961*

Typical Range: $1,000 to $10,000

Disclosure Period: 1993

Note: Total grants, number of grants, and average grant figures exclude 16 scholarships to individuals totaling $13,750. Recent grants are derived from a 1993 Form 990.

RECENT GRANTS
Library

3,000	Athenaeum, Philadelphia, PA

General

150,000	St. Joseph's Preparatory School, Philadelphia, PA

90,000	Bryn Mawr Hospital, Bryn Mawr, PA
45,000	Academy of Vocal Arts, Philadelphia, PA
30,750	Ursinus College, Collegeville, PA
27,913	United Fund of Southeastern Pennsylvania, Philadelphia, PA

Teleflex Inc. / Teleflex Foundation

Sales: $666.8 million
Employees: 8,000
Headquarters: Limerick, PA
SIC Major Group: Electronic & Other Electrical Equipment, Fabricated Metal Products, Industrial Machinery & Equipment, and Rubber & Miscellaneous Plastics Products

CONTACT
Robert Bertschey
Director, Training
Teleflex Inc.
155 S Limerick Rd.
Limerick, PA 19468
(610) 948-5100

FINANCIAL SUMMARY
Recent Giving: $195,607 (1993); $212,148 (1992)

Assets: $604,742 (1993); $348,133 (1992)

Gifts Received: $379,875 (1993); $200,000 (1992)

EIN: 23-2104782

CONTRIBUTIONS SUMMARY
Typical Recipients: • *Arts & Humanities:* Arts Associations & Councils, Arts Centers, Arts Funds, Arts Institutes, Ballet, Community Arts, Dance, Ethnic & Folk Arts, Historic Preservation, History & Archaeology, Libraries, Literary Arts, Museums/Galleries, Music, Opera, Performing Arts, Theater • *Civic & Public Affairs:* Asian American Affairs, Botanical Gardens/Parks, Business/Free Enterprise, General, Professional & Trade Associations, Urban & Community Affairs, Women's Affairs, Zoos/Aquariums • *Education:* Colleges & Universities, Private Education (Precollege) • *Environment:* Air/Water Quality • *Health:* Children's Health/Hospitals, Emergency/Ambulance Services, Hospices, Hospitals • *International:* International Affairs, International Organizations • *Religion:* Jewish Causes • *Science:* Observatories & Planetariums, Science Museums • *Social Services:* Child Welfare, Community Centers, Community Service Organizations, General, People with Disabilities, Recreation & Athletics, Substance Abuse, United Funds/United Ways, Volunteer Services, Youth Organizations

Grant Types: employee matching gifts and general support

Geographic Distribution: in headquarters and operating communities

Operating Locations: CA (Compton, Oxnard), CT (Suffield, Windsor), FL (Boynton Beach, Sarasota), MI (Hillsdale), NH (Jaffrey), OH (Van Wert), PA (King of Prussia, Limerick, North Wales, Plymouth Meeting), TX (Sugar Land), UT (Spanish Fork)

Note: Sermatech International Inc. operates 4 plants in locations.

CORP. OFFICERS
Robert Bertschey: *CURR EMPL* dir training: Teleflex

Lennox K. Black: *B* Montreal Canada 1930 *ED* Royal Naval Coll 1949; McGill Univ BC 1952 *CURR EMPL* chmn, ceo, dir: Teleflex *CORP AFFIL* chmn, ceo: Penn VA Corp; dir: Envirite Corp, Pep Boys, Quaker Chem Corp, TFX Engg, Westmoreland Coal Co

David S. Boyer: *CURR EMPL* pres: Teleflex

Harold L. Zuber, Jr.: *CURR EMPL* vp, cfo: Teleflex

GIVING OFFICERS
Robert Bertschey: treas *CURR EMPL* dir training: Teleflex (see above)

Lennox K. Black: pres *CURR EMPL* chmn, ceo, dir: Teleflex (see above)

Bennie Groff: secy

APPLICATION INFORMATION
Initial Approach: The foundation has no formal grant application procedure or application form. There are no deadlines.

GRANTS ANALYSIS
Total Grants: $195,607

Typical Range: $25 to $6,000

Disclosure Period: 1993

Note: Recent grants are derived from a 1992 Form 990. Grants list for 1993 was incomplete.

RECENT GRANTS
General

5,000	North Pennsylvania Valley Boys and Girls Club, Lansdale, PA
5,000	Philadelphia Zoological Gardens, Philadelphia, PA
5,000	Society of Automotive Engineers, Warrendale, PA
4,500	Jeffrey-Bridge Pride Award Fund, Jeffrey, MN
3,500	International House of Philadelphia, Philadelphia, PA

Trees Charitable Trust, Edith L.

CONTACT
James M. Ferguson III
Contact
Edith L. Trees Charitable Trust
c/o PNC Bank
Investment Management and Trust Division
One Oliver Plz., 29th Fl.
Pittsburgh, PA 15265-0970
(412) 762-3808

FINANCIAL SUMMARY
Recent Giving: $1,729,284 (1993); $1,328,271 (1992); $1,159,721 (1991)

Assets: $34,744,364 (1993); $33,030,817 (1992); $32,310,916 (1991)

Gifts Received: $1,781,026 (1993); $353,661 (1992); $2,159,451 (1991)

Fiscal Note: In 1991 and 1992, contributions were received from the Edith L. Trees Trust.

EIN: 25-6026443

CONTRIBUTIONS SUMMARY
Donor(s): The charitable trust received funds from the Edith L. Trees Trust. The late Edith Lehm Trees married the late Joe Clifton Trees in January 1929. Joe Trees, an oil and gas businessman, worked for the Benedum Trees Oil Company in western Pennsylvania and served as a trustee for the University of Pittsburgh.

Typical Recipients: • *Arts & Humanities:* Libraries • *Civic & Public Affairs:* Employment/Job Training, General, Philanthropic Organizations, Public Policy, Urban & Community Affairs • *Education:* Preschool Education, Private Education (Precollege), Public Education (Precollege), Special Education • *Health:* Health Organizations, Mental Health • *Social Services:* Camps, Child Welfare, Community Service Organizations, Homes, People with Disabilities, Recreation & Athletics

Grant Types: capital, department, endowment, and general support

Geographic Distribution: primarily in Pittsburgh, PA

GIVING OFFICERS
Murray Eagan: trust

James M. Ferguson III: contact

APPLICATION INFORMATION
Initial Approach:

Organizations should submit a written application.

The application should detail services provided by the organization, financial information for the previous three years, and a copy of IRS exemption letter.

The deadline is November 15.

Restrictions on Giving: The trust gives only to organizations "for the benefit of mentally-retarded children, or to corporations, associations or agencies organized and operated for that purpose." The trust does not provide grants to individuals.

OTHER THINGS TO KNOW
The PNC Bank of Pittsburgh, PA, is the trust's corporate trustee.

GRANTS ANALYSIS
Total Grants: $1,729,284

Number of Grants: 29

Highest Grant: $250,000

Average Grant: $45,899*

Typical Range: $20,000 to $50,000 and $100,000 to $250,000

Disclosure Period: 1993

Note: The average grant excludes the trust's two highest grants totaling $490,000. Recent grants are derived from a 1993 Form 990.

RECENT GRANTS
Library

25,500	California University of Pennsylvania, Foundation for California University of Pennsylvania, California, PA — video/CD library; computer equipment

General

250,000	Verland Foundation, Sewickley, PA — endowment
240,000	ARC Allegheny County, Pittsburgh, PA — camping sessions and respite services
150,000	St. Peters Child Development Centers, Pittsburgh, PA — salary and pension plan expense
118,478	Clelian Heights Schools, Greensburg, PA — remove and replace boilers and pumps, refurbish playground
85,000	Life Service Systems, Greensburg, PA — general

Trexler Trust, Harry C.

CONTACT
Thomas H. Christman
Secretary to the Trustees
Harry C. Trexler Trust
33 S Seventh St., Ste. 205
Allentown, PA 18101
(610) 434-9645

FINANCIAL SUMMARY
Recent Giving: $2,644,573 (fiscal 1994); $1,926,387 (fiscal 1992); $1,755,347 (fiscal 1991)

Assets: $69,017,782 (fiscal 1994); $69,825,825 (fiscal 1992); $64,319,581 (fiscal 1991)

Gifts Received: $5,881 (fiscal 1992); $6,822 (fiscal 1990); $4,903 (fiscal 1989)

Fiscal Note: The trust received a contribution in fiscal 1990 from the Harry C. Trexler Fund.

EIN: 23-1162215

CONTRIBUTIONS SUMMARY
Donor(s): The trust was established in 1934, with Harry C. Trexler and Mary M. Trexler as donors. Mr. Trexler was president of Trexler Lumber Company (Allentown, PA) and chairman of Lehigh Portland Cement Company and Bell Telephone Company of Pennsylvania. He was a trustee of Allentown State Hospital, Sacred Heart Hospital (Allentown), St. Luke's Hospital, Lehigh University, Franklin and Marshall College, and Muhlenberg College.

The Trexler will stipulated that one-half of the trust's income be distributed to charitable organizations which serve the benefit of mankind in Lehigh County, one-fourth be paid to the City of Allentown for parks, and one-fourth be added to the foundation's investment assets.

Typical Recipients: • *Arts & Humanities:* Arts Associations & Councils, Arts Festivals, Dance, Historic Preservation, History & Archaeology, Libraries, Museums/Galleries, Music, Opera, Performing Arts, Theater • *Civic & Public Affairs:* Botanical Gardens/Parks, Hispanic Affairs, Housing, Municipalities/Towns, Women's Affairs • *Education:* Arts/Humanities Education, Business Education, Colleges & Universities, Community & Junior Colleges, Economic Education, Literacy, Science/Mathematics Education, Special Education, Student Aid • *Environment:* General, Resource Conservation • *Health:* Long-Term Care, Medical Rehabilitation, Nursing Services • *Religion:* Churches, Dioceses, Religious Welfare • *Social Services:* Child Welfare, Community Centers, Community Service Organizations, Crime Prevention, People with Disabilities, Recreation & Athletics, Scouts, Senior Services, Shelters/Homelessness, YMCA/YWCA/YMHA/YWHA, Youth Organizations

Grant Types: capital, challenge, and general support

Geographic Distribution: Allentown and Lehigh County, PA, only

GIVING OFFICERS

Dexter Farrington Baker: trust *B* Worcester MA 1927 *ED* Lehigh Univ BS 1950; Lehigh Univ MBA 1957 *CURR EMPL* chmn, ceo, dir: Air Products & Chem *CORP AFFIL* dir: AMP Inc, Eastman Chem Co *NONPR AFFIL* bd assocs: Muhlenberg Coll; dir, mem exec comm: Natl Assn Mfrs; mem: Am Inst Chem Engrs, Am Mgmt Assn, Lehigh Univ Asa Packer Soc, Theta Chi; trust: Lehigh Univ

Philip I. Berman: trust *B* Pennsburg PA 1915 *CURR EMPL* pres: Philip I Berman/DBA Fleetways *CORP AFFIL* chmn, ceo: Homecare USA; underwriting mem: Lloyds London *NONPR AFFIL* adv bd mgrs, mem compensaation comm: Univ PA Morris Arboretum; bd govs: Shenkar Coll Fashion Textiles; chmn: PA St Pub TV Network Commn; dir: Am Friends Hebrew Univ, Lehigh Valley Ed TV-Channel 39, Pennsylvanians Effective Govt; exec bd: Boy Scouts Am Lehigh County Counc; exec comm: Philadelphia Mus Art; fellow: Culinary Inst Am, Metro Mus Art, PA Academy Fine Arts; intl bd: Hebrew Univ; mem: Am Assn Museums, Am Fed Arts, Am Retail Fed, Beta Gamma Sigma, Counc Consumer Information, Explorers Club NY, Metro Opera Guild, Polar Soc, Soc Automotive Engrs; natl bd: Am Jewish Comm; pres, dir: Allentown Symphony Assn, PA Indus Devel Corp, World Jewish Congress *PHIL AFFIL* pres: Philip and Murial Berman Foundation *CLUB AFFIL* Berkleigh CC, Breakers CC, Club World Trade Ctr, First Defenders, Safari, Union League; mem: Rancho Mirage CC

Thomas H. Christman: secy to trust

Carl John William Hessinger: trust *B* Allentown PA 1915 *ED* Muhlenberg Coll BPh

1937; Univ PA LLB 1940 *CURR EMPL* pres: Allen Title Co *NONPR AFFIL* mem: PA Land Title Assn, Philadelphia Skating & Humane Soc *CLUB AFFIL* mem: Lehigh CC, Penquin Figure Skating

Katherine Stephanoff: trust

Richard K. White: trust

APPLICATION INFORMATION
Initial Approach:

Grant requests should be in letter form.

Letters should state the purpose for which funds are sought, the amount requested, and the anticipated public benefit. Proposals should also include a copy of the organization's articles of incorporation and by-laws, proof of IRS nonprofit status, most recent financial statements, an operating budget, a list of other sources of project support, and detailed program descriptions with current client statistics.

Applications must be received prior to January 31 for funding consideration.

Trustees meet on the third Tuesday of every month to discuss applications. In these meetings the trustees familiarize themselves with an organization's stated purposes and structure. They also subjectively compare organizations seeking funds, preferring to fund the organization demonstrating a more compelling benefit to the local community.

OTHER THINGS TO KNOW
The foundation reports that it also offers proposal writing assistance.

PUBLICATIONS
Annual report

GRANTS ANALYSIS
Total Grants: $2,644,573

Number of Grants: 100

Highest Grant: $594,709

Average Grant: $26,446

Typical Range: $5,000 to $50,000

Disclosure Period: fiscal year ending March 31, 1994

Note: Recent grants are derived from a fiscal 1994 Form 990.

RECENT GRANTS
Library

66,000	Allentown Public Library, Allentown, PA — cost of addition
33,000	Allentown Public Library, Allentown, PA — budgetary support
33,000	Lehigh County Community College, Allentown, PA — computerization of the library

General

594,709	City of Allentown, Allentown, PA — for the improvement, extension, and maintenance of all city parks
77,000	County of Lehigh, Allentown, PA — for campaign to construct the Sports Field of Lehigh County
75,000	Cedar Crest College, Allentown, PA — scholarships
70,000	Boy Scouts of America Minsi Trails Council, Allentown, PA — for capital improvements to camp Trexler
61,118	Lehigh County Conference of Churches, Allentown, PA — toward purchase of leasehold interest in Alliance Hall

Union Pacific Corp. / Union Pacific Foundation

Revenue: $8.14 billion
Employees: 233
Headquarters: Bethlehem, PA
SIC Major Group: Holding Companies Nec, Metal Mining Services, Crude Petroleum & Natural Gas, and Oil & Gas Exploration Services

CONTACT
Judy L. Swantak
President, Secretary, Trustees
Union Pacific Foundation
Martin Tower
8th & Eaton Ave.
Bethlehem, PA 18018
(610) 861-3225

FINANCIAL SUMMARY
Recent Giving: $7,500,000 (1995 est.); $7,700,000 (1994 approx.); $7,167,100 (1993)

Assets: $2,004,802 (1993); $1,835,000 (1992); $1,031,353 (1990)

Gifts Received: $7,200,000 (1993)

Fiscal Note: Company gives only through the foundation. Contributions are expected to remain at the current level.

EIN: 13-6406825

CONTRIBUTIONS SUMMARY
Typical Recipients: • *Arts & Humanities:* Arts Associations & Councils, Arts Funds, Ballet, Dance, Historic Preservation, Libraries, Museums/Galleries, Music, Opera, Performing Arts, Public Broadcasting, Theater • *Civic & Public Affairs:* Business/Free Enterprise, Economic Development, Professional & Trade Associations, Public Policy • *Education:* Agricultural Education, Business Education, Colleges & Universities, Community & Junior Colleges, Economic Education, Education Funds, Engineering/Technological Education, Faculty Development, Literacy, Minority Education, Special Education, Student Aid • *Environment:* General, Wildlife Protection • *Health:* Alzheimers Disease, Cancer, Children's Health/Hospitals, Clinics/Medical Centers, Emergency/Ambulance Services, Health Organizations, Hospices, Hospitals, Medical Rehabilitation, Mental Health, Prenatal Health Issues • *Religion:* Religious Organizations • *Social Services:* Child Welfare, Community Centers, Community Service Organizations, Domestic Violence, Family

Services, Food/Clothing Distribution, Homes, People with Disabilities, Recreation & Athletics, Scouts, Senior Services, Shelters/Homelessness, Substance Abuse, United Funds/United Ways, YMCA/YWCA/YMHA/YWHA, Youth Organizations

Grant Types: capital, challenge, employee matching gifts, general support, and project

Note: Employee matching gift ratio: 2 to 1 for educational institutions and 1 to 1 for cultural institutions.

Geographic Distribution: in communities served by Union Pacific's operating companies, principally in the western United States

Operating Locations: AR, CA, CO, ID, IL, KS, LA, MO, NE (Omaha), NV, OK, OR, PA (Bethlehem), TX (Ft. Worth), UT, WA

CORP. OFFICERS
Ursula Farrell Fairbairn: *B* Newark NJ 1943 *ED* Upsala Coll BA 1965; Harvard Univ MA 1966 *CURR EMPL* sr vp human resources: Union Pacific Corp *CORP AFFIL* dir: Armstrong World Indus, Menasha Corp, VF Corp *NONPR AFFIL* dir: Historic Bethlehem Inc, Labor Policy Assn; mem: Women Execs St Govt; mem adv bd: Catalyst; mem (adv counc human resources): Conf Bd; mem employee rels comm: Bus Roundtable; secy: Comm 200 *CLUB AFFIL* Saucon Valley CC

L. White Matthews III: *B* Ashland KY 1945 *ED* Hampden-Sydney Coll BS 1967; Univ VA MBA 1970 *CURR EMPL* cfo, exec vp fin, dir: Union Pacific Corp *CORP AFFIL* cfo: MO Pacific RR Co; cfo, dir: Union Pacific Holdings Inc; dir: MO Pacific Corp, Overnite Transportation Co, Royal Ins Group, Union Pacific Resources Co, USPCI Inc; mem (natl adv bd): Chem Bank NY; vp fin: Union Pacific Aviation Co *NONPR AFFIL* dir: Moravian Acad, Moravian Coll; mem counc fin execs: Conf Bd; trust: Centerland Fund

Judy L. Swantak: *B* Bryn Mawr PA 1955 *CURR EMPL* vp, secy: Union Pacific Corp *CORP AFFIL* secy: Union Pacific Aviation Co, Union Pacific Realty Co, Union Pacific Resources Co, Union Pacific RR Co; secy, dir: MO Pacific Corp; vp, secy, dir: Union Pacific Holdings Inc *NONPR AFFIL* mem: Am Soc Corp Secys

Carl W. von Bernuth: *B* New York NY 1944 *ED* Yale Univ BA 1966; Yale Univ Law Sch LLB 1969 *CURR EMPL* sr vp, gen couns: Union Pacific Corp *CORP AFFIL* dir: Overnite Transportation Co, Union Pacific Aviation Co, Union Pacific Realty Co, Union Pacific Resources Co, USPCI Inc; vp, chief legal off: Union Pacific Holdings Inc *NONPR AFFIL* dir: Univ PA Inst Law & Econs

GIVING OFFICERS
Richard K. Davidson: trust *B* Allen KS 1942 *ED* Washburn Univ BA 1965 *CURR EMPL* chmn, ceo, dir: Union Pacific RR Co *CORP AFFIL* chmn, ceo, dir: MO Pacific RR Co; dir: CA Energy Co *CLUB AFFIL* Happy Hollow

Andrew Lindsay Lewis, Jr.: chmn *B* Philadelphia PA 1931 *ED* Haverford Coll BS

1953; Harvard Univ MBA 1955 *CURR EMPL* chmn, pres, ceo: Union Pacific Corp *CORP AFFIL* dir: Am Express Co, AT&T, Ford Motor Co, FPL Group Inc, Gulfstream Aerospace Corp, Rockefeller Group Inc; pres, dir: MO Pacific Corp *NONPR AFFIL* mem natl exec bd: Boy Scouts Am *CLUB AFFIL* Bohemian, Philadelphia, Saucon Valley CC, Sunnybrook GC *PHIL AFFIL* pres, don: Lilliput Foundation

Barbara C. Myers: mgr *CURR EMPL* asst secy: Union Pacific Corp

Judy L. Swantak: pres, secy, trust *CURR EMPL* vp, secy: Union Pacific Corp (see above)

Carl W. von Bernuth: gen couns *CURR EMPL* sr vp, gen couns: Union Pacific Corp (see above)

APPLICATION INFORMATION
Initial Approach: *Initial Contact:* letter *Include Information On:* description of the organization, purpose for which funds are sought *Deadlines:* formal application form, supplied by the foundation after receipt of initial inquiry, must be submitted by August 15 for consideration for the following year's budget (board meets annually in January)

Restrictions on Giving: Does not support organizations not eligible for tax-exempt status under Section 501(c)(3) of the Internal Revenue Service Code; specialized national health or welfare organizations other than through United Way; political organizations; organizations engaged in influencing legislation; religious organizations that are sectarian or denominational in purpose; veterans organizations, labor groups, social clubs, or fraternal organizations; individuals; dinners or special events; goodwill advertising; or grant-making organizations, except allied arts funds and independent college associations. Only reviews requests for support of capital projects from organizations funded by United Way.

GRANTS ANALYSIS
Total Grants: $7,167,100

Number of Grants: 800

Highest Grant: $230,000

Average Grant: $8,959

Typical Range: $1,000 to $30,000

Disclosure Period: 1993

Note: Recent grants are derived from a 1993 Form 990.

RECENT GRANTS

Library

31,250	University of Arkansas Little Rock Foundation, Little Rock, AR — establish a Hershel H. Friday Library Endowment Fund and name a courtroom in the new Little Rock Center in Mr. Friday's honor
25,000	Salt Lake Community College, Salt Lake City, UT — establish a learning resource center at the new library
15,000	Moravian Academy, Bethlehem, PA — unrestricted

General

230,000	United Way of Midlands, Omaha, NE
140,000	United Way of Metropolitan Tarrant County, Ft. Worth, TX
130,000	United Way of Greater St. Louis, St. Louis, MO
80,000	American National Red Cross, Washington, DC
75,000	United Negro College Fund, New York, NY — capital campaign/endowment fund

USX Corporation / USX Foundation

Revenue: $16.79 billion
Employees: 44,605
Headquarters: Pittsburgh, PA
SIC Major Group: Coal Mining, Metal Mining, Oil & Gas Extraction, and Primary Metal Industries

CONTACT
James L. Hamilton III
General Manager
USX Fdn.
USX Tower
600 Grant St., Rm. 2640
Pittsburgh, PA 15219-4776
(412) 433-5237

FINANCIAL SUMMARY
Recent Giving: $4,249,179 (fiscal 1994); $6,378,490 (fiscal 1993); $6,178,778 (fiscal 1992)

Assets: $1,336,024 (fiscal 1994); $928,591 (fiscal 1993); $6,999,299 (fiscal 1992)

Fiscal Note: USX gives only through its foundation. Above figures exclude nonmonetary support.

EIN: 13-6093185

CONTRIBUTIONS SUMMARY
Typical Recipients: • *Arts & Humanities:* Arts Associations & Councils, Arts Centers, Arts Festivals, Ballet, Dance, Historic Preservation, History & Archaeology, Libraries, Museums/Galleries, Music, Opera, Performing Arts, Public Broadcasting, Theater • *Civic & Public Affairs:* Business/Free Enterprise, Community Foundations, Employment/Job Training, General, Law & Justice, Professional & Trade Associations, Public Policy, Urban & Community Affairs • *Education:* Arts/Humanities Education, Business Education, Colleges & Universities, Community & Junior Colleges, Economic Education, Education Associations, Engineering/Technological Education, Minority Education, Public Education (Precollege), Science/Mathematics Education • *Environment:* General • *Health:* Health Organizations, Medical Rehabilitation, Mental Health, Single-Disease Health Associations, Trauma Treatment • *Religion:* Religious

Welfare • *Science:* Scientific Organizations • *Social Services:* At-Risk Youth, Community Centers, Community Service Organizations, Delinquency & Criminal Rehabilitation, People with Disabilities, Senior Services, Substance Abuse, United Funds/United Ways, Youth Organizations

Grant Types: capital, employee matching gifts, general support, operating expenses, project, and scholarship

Note: Matching grants are awarded for education only.

Geographic Distribution: U.S., with emphasis on communities where USX Corp. and its subsidiaries operate

Operating Locations: AL (Chickasaw, Fairfield), GA (Atlanta), IL (Joliet), IN (Gary), MN (Duluth), OH (Conneaut, Findlay), PA (Dravosburg, Monroeville, Pittsburgh), TX (Dallas, Garland, Houston, Wichita Falls), WV

CORP. OFFICERS

Charles Albert Corry: *B* Cincinnati OH 1932 *ED* Univ Cincinnati BS 1955; Univ Cincinnati JD 1959 *CURR EMPL* chmn, ceo, dir: USX Corp *CORP AFFIL* dir: Delhi Gas Pipeline Corp, Marathon Oil Co, Mellon Bank Corp, Mellon Bank NA, Transtar Inc, TX Oil & Gas Corp *NONPR AFFIL* dir: Natl Assn Mfrs, UN Way Southern PA; mem: Am Bar Assn, Am Iron Steel Inst, Fin Execs Inst, Machinery Allied Products Inst, N Am Soc Corp Planning, OH Bar Assn, PA Chamber Commerce; trust: Carnegie-Mellon Univ, Presbyterian Univ Hosp, Univ Pittsburgh; vchmn, dir: PA Chamber Bus Indus *CLUB AFFIL* Duquesne, Laurel Valley GC, Rolling Rock, St Clair CC

Gretchen R. Haggerty: *B* 1955 *ED* Case Western Reserve Univ BS; Duquesne Univ JD *CURR EMPL* vp, treas: USX Corp

GIVING OFFICERS

Victor Gene Beghini: trust *B* Greensboro PA 1934 *ED* PA St Univ BS 1956; Harvard Univ 1974 *CURR EMPL* pres, dir: Marathon Oil Co *CORP AFFIL* dir: Baker Hughes Inc, Texas Oil & Gas Corp; vchmn Marathon Group: USX Corp *NONPR AFFIL* chmn: Natural Gas Supply Assn; dir: Am Petroleum Inst, Boy Scouts Am Sam Houston Area Counc, Natl Petroleum Counc; mem: Mid-Continent Oil Gas Assn, Soc Petroleum Engrs; mem bus adv comm: Northwestern Univ Transportation Ctr

M. Sharon Cassidy: asst secy

Charles Albert Corry: chmn, trust *CURR EMPL* chmn, ceo, dir: USX Corp (see above)

James H. Fix: asst comptr

Patricia P. Funaro: program admin

Gary Allen Glynn: vp (investments) *B* Springfield VT 1946 *ED* Univ VT BS 1968; Univ PA MBA 1970 *CURR EMPL* pres: US Steel Co *NONPR AFFIL* chmn fin comm: Gen Svcs Bd Alcoholic Anonymous; mem: Assn Investment Mgmt & Res, Fin Execs Inst, Soc Security Analysts *CLUB AFFIL* Drones, Econ, Metro, Metro Opera, Tuxedo

James L. Hamilton III: gen mgr

John A. Hammerschmidt: asst secy

Robert M. Hernandez: cfo *B* Pittsburgh PA 1944 *ED* Univ Pittsburgh AB 1966; Univ PA Wharton Sch MBA 1968 *CURR EMPL* exec vp fin, cfo, dir: USX Corp *CORP AFFIL* chmn: RMI Titanium Co; dir: Am Casualty Excess Ltd, Corp Offs Dirs Assurance Ltd

Lewis B. Jones: vp, contr *B* 1943 *ED* OK St Univ BA 1966 *CURR EMPL* vp, comptr: USX Corp

David A. Lynch: asst secy

John T. Mills: tax couns *CURR EMPL* vp taxes: USX Corp

Peter Black Mulloney: pres, trust *B* Boston MA 1932 *ED* Yale Univ BA 1954 *CURR EMPL* vp, asst chmn: USX Corp *NONPR AFFIL* mem: Am Iron Steel Inst, Intl Iron & Steel Inst; mem adv bd, secy: Salvation Army Pittsburgh; vchmn: World Aff Counc Pittsburgh *CLUB AFFIL* Army & Navy, Duquesne, Harvard-Yale-Princeton

John L. Richmond: asst treas

Dan D. Sandman: gen couns, secy *B* 1949 *ED* OH St Univ BA 1970; OH St Univ JD 1973 *CURR EMPL* gen couns, secy: USX Corp

Thomas J. Usher: trust *B* 1942 *ED* Univ Pittsburgh BS; Univ Pittsburgh MS; Univ Pittsburgh PhD *CURR EMPL* chmn, ceo: USX Corp US Steel Group

Louis A. Valli: trust *B* Nemacolin PA 1932 *ED* Univ Pittsburgh BBA 1954 *CURR EMPL* sr vp employee rels: USX Corp

APPLICATION INFORMATION

Initial Approach: *Initial Contact:* one- or two-page letter *Include Information On:* description of project and its goals; a copy of the organization's Internal Revenue Service certification of tax-exempt status under Section 501(c)(3) of Internal Revenue Code; a copy of the organization's current budget and its most recent audited financial report; a full description of the project and its goals; the estimated cost of the project and the amount requested, with explanation of the need for funds in relation to the total requirements of the project and available resources; a statement of sources of aid in hand (if any) and the amount of committed support; a statement of sources of anticipated aid, i.e., prospective contributers that have been solicited and the amounts requested and/or prospective contributers still to be solicited; a list of the organization's chief executives and members of the Board of Directors/Trustees; the signature of an authorized executive of the tax-exempt organization; and a signed statement of approval by the chief executive of the parent organization if the application originates in a subdivision of such entity.*Deadlines:* by January 15 for public, cultural, and scientific requests; by April 15 for aid to education; by July 15 for social services and medical/health requests *Note:* Requests for personal interviews and site visits are accommodated as Foundation staff schedules permit.

Restrictions on Giving: The foundation does not award grants to individuals or to religious organizations for religious purposes.

Additionally, grants are not awarded for economic development projects; conferences, seminars or symposia; travel; exhibits; special events; fund-raising events; publication of papers, books or magazines; or production of films, videotapes or other audiovisual materials.

OTHER THINGS TO KNOW

Company also includes leasing and financial services; mining; mineral resources management.

PUBLICATIONS

Foundation annual report

GRANTS ANALYSIS

Total Grants: $2,821,960*

Number of Grants: 245*

Average Grant: $11,518*

Typical Range: $1,000 to $25,000

Disclosure Period: fiscal year ending November 30, 1994

Note: Recent grants are derived from a 1993 annual report. The figures for total grants, number of grants and average grant exclude 1,784 matching gifts totaling $988,819 and 150 scholarships totaling $438,400.

RECENT GRANTS

Library
Pleasant Hills Public Library, Pittsburgh, PA

General
American Legislative Exchange Council, Washington, DC
American Spectator Educational Foundation, Arlington, VA
American Trauma Society, Upper Marlboro, MD
Annapolis Center for Environmental Quality, Annapolis, MD
ARC-Allegheny Foundation, Pittsburgh, PA

Warwick Foundation

CONTACT

Warwick Fdn.
108 W Ct. St.
Doylestown, PA 18901
(215) 348-3199

FINANCIAL SUMMARY

Recent Giving: $258,700 (1993); $225,200 (1992); $168,700 (1991)

Assets: $5,101,545 (1993); $4,886,306 (1992); $4,766,922 (1991)

EIN: 23-6230662

CONTRIBUTIONS SUMMARY

Donor(s): Helen H. Gemmill, Kenneth Gemmill

Typical Recipients: • *Arts & Humanities:* Arts Centers, Historic Preservation, History & Archaeology, Libraries, Museums/Galleries, Music, Opera, Public Broadcasting • *Civic & Public Affairs:* Botanical Gardens/Parks, Clubs, Professional & Trade Associations, Zoos/Aquariums • *Education:* Agricultural Education, Arts/Humanities

Education, Colleges & Universities, Community & Junior Colleges, Legal Education, Private Education (Precollege), Religious Education, Special Education, Student Aid • *Environment:* General, Resource Conservation • *Health:* Emergency/Ambulance Services, Hospitals • *Religion:* Churches, Religious Welfare, Seminaries • *Science:* Science Museums, Scientific Centers & Institutes, Scientific Organizations • *Social Services:* Community Service Organizations, People with Disabilities, Shelters/Homelessness, United Funds/United Ways, YMCA/YWCA/YMHA/YWHA, Youth Organizations

Grant Types: operating expenses and scholarship

Geographic Distribution: focus on the Bucks County and Philadelphia, PA, areas

GIVING OFFICERS
Helen H. Gemmill: trust

William K. Gemmill: secy

APPLICATION INFORMATION
Initial Approach: The foundation has no formal grant application procedure or application form. There are no deadlines.

OTHER THINGS TO KNOW
Provides scholarships to students for higher education.

GRANTS ANALYSIS
Total Grants: $258,700

Number of Grants: 50

Highest Grant: $100,000

Typical Range: $500 to $10,000

Disclosure Period: 1993

Note: Recent grants are derived from a 1993 Form 990.

RECENT GRANTS

Library
2,000	Philadelphia Free Library, Philadelphia, PA
1,000	Athenaeum of Philadelphia, Philadelphia, PA

General
100,000	Neshaminy Warwick Presbyterian Church, Warminster, PA
10,000	Bryn Mawr College, Bryn Mawr, PA
10,000	Camp Pasquaney, Concord, NH — scholarships for Pennsylvanians
10,000	Princeton Theological Seminary, Princeton, NJ — scholarship
10,000	Princeton University, Princeton, NJ — scholarship

Waters Charitable Trust, Robert S.

CONTACT
Barbara K. Robinson
Vice President
Robert S. Waters Charitable Trust
Three Mellon Bank Ctr.
Pittsburgh, PA 15230
(412) 234-5784

FINANCIAL SUMMARY
Recent Giving: $116,500 (1993); $409,500 (1992); $267,250 (1991)

Assets: $4,404,516 (1993); $4,307,176 (1992); $4,573,390 (1991)

EIN: 25-6018986

CONTRIBUTIONS SUMMARY
Donor(s): the late Robert S. Waters

Typical Recipients: • *Arts & Humanities:* Arts Centers, Community Arts, Historic Preservation, History & Archaeology, Libraries, Museums/Galleries, Music • *Civic & Public Affairs:* General • *Education:* Colleges & Universities, Education Funds, General, Literacy, Medical Education, Private Education (Precollege) • *Environment:* Air/Water Quality, General, Resource Conservation, Wildlife Protection • *Health:* Hospitals • *Religion:* Religious Welfare • *Social Services:* Family Services, Homes, People with Disabilities, Shelters/Homelessness, United Funds/United Ways

Grant Types: general support

Geographic Distribution: focus on PA

GIVING OFFICERS
Mellon Bank, N.A.: trust

John Phillips Davis, Jr.: trust *B* Pittsburgh PA 1925 *ED* Harvard Univ AB 1947; Harvard Univ JD 1950 *CURR EMPL* couns: Reed Smith Shaw & McClay *CORP AFFIL* dir: Bloom Engg Co, Firth Stirling, Pittsburgh Gage & Supply Co *NONPR AFFIL* dir: Carnegie Mus Art, Historic Soc Western PA; mem: Allegheny County Bar Assn, Am Bar Assn, Am Law Inst, PA Bar Assn; trust: Shady Side Academy

APPLICATION INFORMATION
Initial Approach: Send letter requesting application form. There are no deadlines.

GRANTS ANALYSIS
Total Grants: $116,500

Number of Grants: 21

Highest Grant: $50,000

Typical Range: $2,000 to $5,000

Disclosure Period: 1993

Note: Recent grants are derived from a 1993 Form 990.

RECENT GRANTS

Library
4,000	Cambria Free Library, Johnstown, PA — educational

General
5,238	Western Pennsylvania Hospital, Pittsburgh, PA — Hazel Gearhart nurses scholarship fund
5,000	Family Social Services, Johnstown, PA
5,000	Harmarville Foundation, Pittsburgh, PA
4,500	Conamough Valley Hospital, Johnstown, PA
4,500	Mercy Hospital, Johnstown, PA

Wells Foundation, Franklin H. and Ruth L.

CONTACT
Miles J. Gibbons
Exec. Dir
Franklin H. and Ruth L. Wells Fdn.
PO Box 2961
Mechanicsburg, PA 17105-2961
(717) 255-2046

FINANCIAL SUMMARY
Recent Giving: $528,534 (1994); $525,510 (1992); $419,964 (1991)

Assets: $5,195,403 (1994); $5,341,769 (1992); $5,190,430 (1991)

Gifts Received: $97,324 (1994); $195,898 (1992); $195,267 (1991)

Fiscal Note: In fiscal 1994, contributions were received from Ruth L. Wells Annuity Trust.

EIN: 22-2541749

CONTRIBUTIONS SUMMARY
Donor(s): Ruth L. Wells Annuity Trust, Frank Wells Marital Trust

Typical Recipients: • *Arts & Humanities:* Arts Associations & Councils, Community Arts, History & Archaeology, Libraries, Museums/Galleries, Music, Opera, Theater • *Civic & Public Affairs:* Community Foundations, Employment/Job Training, General, Housing, Urban & Community Affairs • *Education:* Colleges & Universities, Community & Junior Colleges, Education Funds, Literacy, Medical Education, Minority Education, Private Education (Precollege), Science/Mathematics Education • *Environment:* Wildlife Protection • *Health:* Cancer, Health Organizations, Hospitals, Medical Research, Mental Health • *Religion:* Religious Organizations • *Science:* Science Museums • *Social Services:* Community Service Organizations, Domestic Violence, Family Planning, Family Services, Food/Clothing Distribution, People with Disabilities, Scouts, Substance Abuse, United Funds/United Ways, Volunteer Services, Youth Organizations

Grant Types: capital, emergency, project, and seed money

Geographic Distribution: focus on Dauphin, Cumberland, and Perry counties, PA

GIVING OFFICERS
Dauphin Deposit Bank & Trust Co: trust

Clifford S. Charles: comm mem
Gladys R. Charles: mem
Ellen R. Cramer: comm mem
William Cramer: comm mem

APPLICATION INFORMATION
Initial Approach: Send brief letter of inquiry describing program or project. Include a description of organization, amount requested, purpose of funds sought, recently audited financial statement, and proof of tax-exempt status. There are no deadlines.

Restrictions on Giving: Does not provide support for religious activities, operating expenses, endowments, or debts.

GRANTS ANALYSIS
Total Grants:

Highest Grant: $25,000

Typical Range: $5,000 to $25,000

Disclosure Period: 1993

Note: Recent grants are derived from a 1993 Form 990.

RECENT GRANTS

General
200,000	Tri-State University, Angola, IN — construction of theater and building
100,000	Allegheny College, Meadville, PA — construction costs for Hall of Biology
25,000	South Central Pennsylvania Food Bank, Steelton, PA — construction of warehouse and office facility
25,000	Youth Enhancement Services, Harrisburg, PA — operating expenses
15,000	Commonwealth Service Corps, Harrisburg, PA — intern coordinator

Williams Charitable Trust, John C.

CONTACT
Bruce Bickel
Vice President
John C. Williams Charitable Trust
c/o PNC Bank National Assn.
Pittsburgh, PA 15265
(412) 762-3502

FINANCIAL SUMMARY
Recent Giving: $159,129 (1993); $151,070 (1992); $150,000 (1991)

Assets: $5,054,616 (1993); $4,945,296 (1992); $4,804,924 (1991)

Gifts Received: $5,142 (1991)

EIN: 25-6024153

CONTRIBUTIONS SUMMARY
Donor(s): the late John C. Williams

Typical Recipients: • *Arts & Humanities:* Historic Preservation, Libraries, Music

• *Civic & Public Affairs:* General, Housing, Municipalities/Towns • *Education:* Colleges & Universities • *Health:* Clinics/Medical Centers, Emergency/Ambulance Services, Hospitals, Research/Studies Institutes • *Religion:* Ministries, Religious Organizations • *Social Services:* Community Service Organizations, Family Planning, Family Services, Homes, Youth Organizations

Grant Types: capital and general support

Geographic Distribution: limited to Steubenville, OH, and Weirton, WV

GIVING OFFICERS
Pittsburgh National Bank: trust

APPLICATION INFORMATION
Initial Approach: Send a brief letter of inquiry. Include a description of organization, amount requested, purpose of funds sought, recently audited financial statement, and proof of tax-exempt status. There are no deadlines.

Restrictions on Giving: Limited to the Weirton, WV, and Steubenville, OH, area.

PUBLICATIONS
Application Guidelines

GRANTS ANALYSIS
Total Grants: $159,129

Number of Grants: 10

Highest Grant: $30,000

Typical Range: $2,500 to $25,000

Disclosure Period: 1993

Note: Recent grants are derived from a 1993 Form 990.

RECENT GRANTS

General
30,000	Neighborhood House, Steubenville, OH
25,000	Urban Mission Ministries, Weirton, WV
20,000	American Red Cross, Steubenville, OH
20,000	Family Service Association of Steubenville, Steubenville, OH
10,000	Lamp Ministries, Weirton, WV

Wood Foundation of Chambersburg, PA

CONTACT
C. O. Wood III
Trustee
Wood Fdn of Chambersburg, PA
273 Lincoln Way E.
Chambersburg, PA 17201

FINANCIAL SUMMARY
Recent Giving: $380,930 (1993); $348,287 (1992); $271,742 (1991)

Assets: $7,146,507 (1993); $6,906,534 (1992); $6,773,734 (1991)

EIN: 25-1607838

CONTRIBUTIONS SUMMARY
Donor(s): Max Zimmer

Typical Recipients: • *Arts & Humanities:* Arts Associations & Councils, Arts Festivals, General, History & Archaeology, Libraries, Museums/Galleries, Music, Theater • *Civic & Public Affairs:* Chambers of Commerce, Community Foundations, Economic Development, Employment/Job Training, General, Housing, Legal Aid, Municipalities/Towns, Safety, Women's Affairs • *Education:* Colleges & Universities, Education Funds, Elementary Education (Public), General, Private Education (Precollege), Public Education (Precollege) • *Environment:* General • *Health:* Cancer, Children's Health/Hospitals, Heart, Hospices, Hospitals, Long-Term Care, Mental Health, Single-Disease Health Associations • *Religion:* Churches, Religious Welfare • *Social Services:* Camps, Community Service Organizations, Counseling, Family Services, Food/Clothing Distribution, Scouts, Shelters/Homelessness, United Funds/United Ways, YMCA/YWCA/YMHA/YWHA, Youth Organizations

Grant Types: general support

Geographic Distribution: giving primarily in Chambersburg and Franklin counties, Pennsylvania

GIVING OFFICERS
Emilie W. Myers: trust

Charles O. Wood III: trust *PHIL AFFIL* trust: Charles O. III and Miriam M. Wood Foundation

David S. Wood: trust

Miriam M. Wood: trust *PHIL AFFIL* trust: Charles O. III and Miriam M. Wood Foundation

APPLICATION INFORMATION
Initial Approach: The foundation has no formal grant application procedure or application form. There are no deadlines.

Restrictions on Giving: Limited to Chambersburg and Franklin Counties, PA.

GRANTS ANALYSIS
Total Grants: $380,930

Number of Grants: 68

Highest Grant: $76,356

Typical Range: $300 to $50,000

Disclosure Period: 1993

Note: Recent grants are derived from a 1993 Form 990.

RECENT GRANTS

Library
3,500	Fulton County Library, McConnellsburg, PA — reference and nonfiction books and educational videos
2,500	Coyle Free Library, Chambersburg, PA

General

76,356	Cumberland Valley Mental Health, Chambersburg, PA — deck installation
50,000	Mercersburg Academy, Mercersburg, PA
20,000	Chambersburg Hospital Health Services, Chambersburg, PA
20,000	Community Foundation of the Eastern Shore, Salisbury, MD
16,667	Easter Seal Society, Chambersburg, PA

Wyomissing Foundation

CONTACT
Alfred G. Hemmerich
Secretary
Wyomissing Foundation
1015 Penn Ave., Ste. 201
Wyomissing, PA 19610
(610) 376-7494

FINANCIAL SUMMARY
Recent Giving: $860,000 (1995 est.); $800,000 (1994); $612,025 (1993)

Assets: $18,600,000 (1995 est.); $18,500,000 (1994); $17,397,678 (1993)

EIN: 23-1980570

CONTRIBUTIONS SUMMARY
Donor(s): The foundation was incorporated in 1929 by the late Ferdinand Thun and members of the Thun family.

Typical Recipients: • *Arts & Humanities:* Arts Institutes, Ballet, Historic Preservation, History & Archaeology, Libraries, Museums/Galleries, Music, Public Broadcasting, Theater • *Civic & Public Affairs:* Economic Development, Economic Policy, Housing, Law & Justice, Parades/Festivals, Philanthropic Organizations, Public Policy, Zoos/Aquariums • *Education:* Arts/Humanities Education, Business Education, Colleges & Universities, Community & Junior Colleges, Education Reform, Literacy, Special Education • *Environment:* Air/Water Quality, General, Resource Conservation, Wildlife Protection • *Health:* AIDS/HIV, Emergency/Ambulance Services, Hospitals, Medical Rehabilitation, Nursing Services • *International:* International Affairs, International Relations • *Religion:* Jewish Causes, Religious Organizations, Religious Welfare • *Science:* Scientific Centers & Institutes • *Social Services:* Community Centers, Community Service Organizations, Counseling, Crime Prevention, Family Planning, Homes, People with Disabilities, Scouts, Senior Services, United Funds/United Ways, YMCA/YWCA/YMHA/YWHA, Youth Organizations

Grant Types: capital, emergency, multiyear/continuing support, operating expenses, and seed money

Geographic Distribution: focus primarily on Berks County, PA, and contiguous counties

GIVING OFFICERS
Thomas A. Beaver: trust *CURR EMPL* ptnr: Reinsel & Co

Victoria F. Guthrie: trust

Frederick Douglass Hafer: trust *B* West Reading PA 1941 *ED* Drexler Inst Tech 1959-1962 *CURR EMPL* pres, dir: Metro Edison Co *CORP AFFIL* dir: GPU Nuclear Corp, GPU Svc Corp, Meridian Bancorp, Meridian Bank, Reading Electric & Power Co, Utilities Mutual Ins Co *NONPR AFFIL* dir: Berks Festivals, Kutztown Univ Fdn, Leadership PA, Reading Hosp & Med Ctr; mem: Berks County Chamber Commerce, Mfrs Assn Berks County, PA Electrica Assn

Alfred G. Hemmerich: secy *CURR EMPL* ret pres: Green Hills Mgmt Co

Sidney D. Kline, Jr.: trust

Timothy Lake: trust

Marlin Miller, Jr.: trust *B* 1932 *ED* Alfred Univ BS 1954; Harvard Univ MBA 1956 *CURR EMPL* fdr, pres, ceo, dir: Arrow Intl *CORP AFFIL* dir: Endovations Inc *NONPR AFFIL* chmn: Reading Hosp & Med Ctr; trust: Alfred Univ

Paul Robert Roedel: pres, trust *B* Millville NJ 1927 *ED* Rider Coll BS 1949 *CURR EMPL* pres, dir: Carpenter Tech Corp *CORP AFFIL* dir: Gen Pub Utilities Corp, PH Glatfelter Co, Meridian Bancorp, Stainless Steel Industry US *NONPR AFFIL* bd dirs, treas: Reading Ctr City Devel Fund; dir: Boy Scouts Am Hawk Mountain Counc, Childrens Home Reading, PA 2000 Ed Coalition; trust: Gettysburg Coll

Lewis C. Scheffey, Jr.: trust *PHIL AFFIL* trust: Turkeybush Foundation

David L. Thun: vp, trust *B* 1937 *CURR EMPL* ceo, chmn bd, treas: Magnatech Intl Inc *CORP AFFIL* off: EPM Corp

Peter Thun: trust

APPLICATION INFORMATION
Initial Approach:

The foundation requests applications be made in writing.

The foundation has no deadline for submitting proposals.

Restrictions on Giving: The foundation does not make grants to individuals, or for endowments, deficit financing, land acquisition, publications, conferences, scholarships, fellowships, or loans.

PUBLICATIONS
Application guidelines, annual report, program policy statement, and financial statement

GRANTS ANALYSIS
Total Grants: $800,000

Number of Grants: 45

Highest Grant: $150,000

Average Grant: $17,778

Typical Range: $1,000 to $25,000

Disclosure Period: 1994

Note: Recent grants are derived from a 1993 Form 990.

RECENT GRANTS

Library

50,000	Williams College, Williamstown, PA — library endowment, fourth and final installment
25,000	Foundation for Reading Area Community College, Reading, PA — support of Library Learning Resource Center
25,000	Wyomissing Public Library, Wyomissing, PA — in honor of Margaret T. Fry, fourth and final installment

General

83,000	United Way of Berks County, Reading, PA — 1993 annual campaign
70,000	Berks Festivals, Reading, PA — sponsor of 1993 Sparks River Days
50,000	Olivet Boys Club, Reading, PA — improvements to existing facilities and erect a new building
50,000	Pennsylvania State University, Reading, PA — Berks Campus building, fourth and final installment
25,000	Berks Education Coalition, Wyomissing, PA — education improvement initiative

---

RHODE ISLAND

Allendale Insurance Co. / Allendale Insurance Foundation

Sales: $330.58 million
Employees: 1,214
Headquarters: Johnston, RI
SIC Major Group: Surety Insurance

CONTACT
Robert R. Gardner
Senior Vice President of Finance, and Treasurer
Allendale Insurance Foundation
PO Box 7500
Johnston, RI 02919
(401) 275-3000
Note: Janis McGuirl is Mr. Gardner's secretary. Corporation is located at 1301 Atwood Ave., Johnston, RI 02919.

FINANCIAL SUMMARY
Recent Giving: $700,000 (1995 est.); $680,494 (1994); $698,001 (1993)

Assets: $3,040,000 (1995); $3,141,827 (1994); $3,857,888 (1993)

Gifts Received: $1,000 (1993)

EIN: 22-2773230

CONTRIBUTIONS SUMMARY

Typical Recipients: • *Arts & Humanities:* Arts Centers, Arts Funds, Arts Institutes, Historic Preservation, Libraries, Museums/Galleries, Music, Performing Arts, Public Broadcasting, Theater • *Civic & Public Affairs:* Community Foundations, Law & Justice, Legal Aid, Municipalities/Towns, Philanthropic Organizations, Professional & Trade Associations, Public Policy, Urban & Community Affairs, Women's Affairs, Zoos/Aquariums • *Education:* Business Education, Colleges & Universities, Community & Junior Colleges, Elementary Education (Private), General, Literacy, Medical Education, Minority Education, Private Education (Precollege), Public Education (Precollege), Religious Education, Secondary Education (Private), Special Education, Student Aid • *Environment:* General • *Health:* Emergency/Ambulance Services, Health Organizations, Hospices, Hospitals, Medical Research, Mental Health, Nursing Services, Single-Disease Health Associations • *International:* International Relations • *Religion:* Religious Welfare • *Science:* Scientific Organizations • *Social Services:* Animal Protection, Child Welfare, Community Centers, Community Service Organizations, Day Care, Family Services, Food/Clothing Distribution, Homes, People with Disabilities, Shelters/Homelessness, United Funds/United Ways, Volunteer Services, Youth Organizations

Grant Types: employee matching gifts

Note: Employee matching gift ratio: 2 to 1 for education gifts. Employee matching gift ratio: 1 to 1 for civic and cultural gifts.

Geographic Distribution: nationwide, with emphasis on Rhode Island

Operating Locations: RI (Providence)

CORP. OFFICERS

John Joseph Carey: *B* Streator IL 1928 *ED* Univ Notre Dame 1952 *CURR EMPL* chmn: Allendale Assocs Inc *CORP AFFIL* chmn, ceo: Appalachian Ins Co, FM Affiliated Ins Co, New Providence Corp; dir: ESCO Electronics Corp *NONPR AFFIL* bd govs: Natl Assn Independent Insurers

Shivan Sivaswamy Subramaniam: *B* Madras India 1949 *ED* Birla Inst Tech BE 1970; Polytech Inst Brooklyn MS 1972; MA Inst Tech SM 1978 *CURR EMPL* pres, ceo, dir: Allendale Mutual Ins Co *CORP AFFIL* pres, ceo, dir: Allendale Assocs Inc, New Providence Corp; pres, dir: Appalachian Ins Co, FM Affiliated Ins Co *NONPR AFFIL* dir: RI Group Health Assn; mem: Fin Execs Inst, Natl Assn Corp Treas

GIVING OFFICERS

Norman D. Baker, Jr.: dir *PHIL AFFIL* trust: Horace A. Kimball and S. Ella Kimball Foundation

John Joseph Carey: dir *CURR EMPL* chmn: Allendale Assocs Inc (see above)

Robert R. Gardner: sr vp finance, treas *B* 1937 *CURR EMPL* treas, dir: Allendale Assocs Inc *CORP AFFIL* vp, treas, dir: Appalachian Ins Co, FM Affiliated Ins Co, New Providence Corp

Shivan Sivaswamy Subramaniam: dir *CURR EMPL* pres, ceo, dir: Allendale Mutual Ins Co (see above)

APPLICATION INFORMATION

Restrictions on Giving: Generally, the foundation will not match gifts to churches, seminaries, or purely sectarian organizations; political organizations; or to endowment funds.

OTHER THINGS TO KNOW

Allendale Insurance Co. offers only employee matching gifts. For education, the company matching gifts ratio is 2:1. For other IRS 501(c)(3) organizations, the foundation matching ratio is 1:1.

Allendale Insurance will match donations up to $3,000 per person per calendar year. Minimum donation matched is $25.

Company publishes a program pamphlet.

GRANTS ANALYSIS

Total Grants: $680,494

Number of Grants: 847

Highest Grant: $206,936

Average Grant: $803

Typical Range: $25 to $6,000

Disclosure Period: 1994

Note: Recent grants are derived from a 1993 Form 990.

RECENT GRANTS

General

182,474	United Way of Southeastern New England, Providence, RI — charitable
20,000	Campaign Fund — charitable
12,000	St. Louis University, St. Louis, MO — charitable
9,672	Rhode Island Public Expenditure Council, Providence, RI — charitable
7,600	United Way of Southeastern New England, Providence, RI — charitable

Champlin Foundations

CONTACT
David A. King
Executive Director
Champlin Foundations
410 S Main St.
Providence, RI 02903
(401) 421-3719

FINANCIAL SUMMARY
Recent Giving: $12,000,000 (1995 est.); $11,207,195 (1994); $13,032,592 (1993)

Assets: $300,000,000 (1995 est.); $290,501,150 (1994); $294,250,000 (1993)

Gifts Received: $750 (1991); $144,870 (1990); $100,000 (1989)

EIN: 51-6010168

CONTRIBUTIONS SUMMARY
Donor(s): The Champlin Foundation Trust was established in 1932 in Delaware by George S. Champlin (d. 1980), Hope C. Neaves (d. 1987), and Florence C. Hamilton (d. 1970). They founded the Second Champlin Foundation Trust in 1947. In 1975, George S. Champlin founded the Third Champlin Foundation.

Typical Recipients: • *Arts & Humanities:* Historic Preservation, History & Archaeology, Libraries, Museums/Galleries • *Civic & Public Affairs:* Employment/Job Training, Municipalities/Towns, Philanthropic Organizations, Safety, Urban & Community Affairs, Zoos/Aquariums • *Education:* Arts/Humanities Education, Colleges & Universities, Private Education (Precollege), Public Education (Precollege), Secondary Education (Public), Vocational & Technical Education • *Environment:* General, Resource Conservation • *Health:* Clinics/Medical Centers, Emergency/Ambulance Services, Health Organizations, Hospices, Hospitals, Medical Rehabilitation, Nursing Services, Transplant Networks/Donor Banks • *Religion:* Churches, Religious Welfare • *Science:* Science Museums • *Social Services:* Animal Protection, Child Welfare, Community Centers, Community Service Organizations, Crime Prevention, Family Planning, Food/Clothing Distribution, Homes, Recreation & Athletics, Scouts, Senior Services, United Funds/United Ways, YMCA/YWCA/YMHA/YWHA, Youth Organizations

Grant Types: capital

Geographic Distribution: almost exclusively Rhode Island

GIVING OFFICERS
Francis C. Carter: chmn distribution comm, mem investigating comm

John Gorham: mem distribution comm, mem investigating comm

Louis R. Hampton: mem distr comm *B* Hartford CT 1920 *ED* Univ RI 1942 *CURR EMPL* chmn exec comm, dir: Providence Energy Corp *CORP AFFIL* chmn: Newport Am, Providence Gas Co; dir: RI Blue Cross & Blue Shield

Earl W. Harrington, Jr.: mem distr comm

Robert W. Kenyon: mem distribution comm

David A. King: exec dir, mem distribution & investigating comms

Norma B. LaFreniere: secy distribution comm

John W. Linnell: mem distribution comm

APPLICATION INFORMATION
Initial Approach:

Applicants should send a one-page letter.

The letter should include a description of the project and its intended purpose, costs, amount requested, an accounting of other fund-raising efforts, and a listing of other sources of available funds. An applicant should also submit copies of its IRS 501(c)(3) exemption and 509(a) letters.

Requests should be submitted between April 1 and August 31. The distribution committees meet annually in November to accept or reject grant recommendations. Funds are distributed in December. The foundations report that funds are seldom available for applications filed at the last minute.

After acknowledging a request, the foundations may request additional information concerning fund-raising efforts. The foundations like to see fund-raising plans with some favorable results. If fund-raising is not totally sucessful, the foundations are interested in what parts of the project will proceed and the costs. Mortgage status and evidence of ability to pay for increased operating costs may also be requested.

Site visits by members of the investigating committee are scheduled between May 1 and September 30. Committee members prefer to meet with the chief of operations, selected staff members, and the treasurer in a very informal manner. Prepared speeches and slide shows should be omitted.

Restrictions on Giving: Grants are not awarded on a continuing basis, but applicants may qualify annually. Grants are not made for program or operating expenses. No grants are awarded to individuals.

OTHER THINGS TO KNOW
PNC Bank-Delaware serves as the corporate trustee for all of the Champlin Foundations.

GRANTS ANALYSIS
Total Grants: $11,207,195
Number of Grants: 193
Highest Grant: $1,300,000
Average Grant: $58,068
Typical Range: $15,000 to $70,000
Disclosure Period: 1994

Note: Recent grants are derived from a 1994 grants list.

RECENT GRANTS
Library
200,000	Providence Public Library, Providence, RI
98,950	North Kingstown Free Library, North Kingstown, RI
80,000	Narragansett Public Library, Narragansett, RI
76,950	Consortium of Rhode Island Academic and Research Libraries, Providence, RI
63,540	Newport Public Library, Newport, RI

General
1,300,000	Nature Conservancy, Providence, RI
550,000	Brown University, Providence, RI
371,870	YMCA of Greater Providence, Providence, RI
318,787	University of Rhode Island Foundation, Providence, RI
200,000	Bradley Hospital, Providence, RI

Citizens Bank of Rhode Island / Citizens Charitable Foundation

Headquarters: Providence, RI
SIC Major Group: State Commercial Banks

CONTACT
D. Faye Sanders
Senior Vice President
Citizens Charitable Fdn.
One Citizens Plaza
Providence, RI 02903-1339
(401) 456-7285

FINANCIAL SUMMARY
Recent Giving: $594,625 (1993); $430,650 (1992); $606,450 (1991)

Assets: $1,113,933 (1993); $1,024,563 (1992); $981,988 (1991)

Gifts Received: $597,518 (1993); $443,032 (1992); $441,024 (1991)

Fiscal Note: Recent grants are derived from a 1993 Form 990. In 1993, contributions were received from Citizens Savings Bank ($319,373), Citizens Trust Company ($274,373), and the River Rescue Fund ($3,772).

EIN: 05-6022653

CONTRIBUTIONS SUMMARY
Typical Recipients: • *Arts & Humanities:* Arts Centers, Arts Funds, Arts Institutes, Libraries, Museums/Galleries • *Civic & Public Affairs:* African American Affairs, General, Housing, Philanthropic Organizations, Urban & Community Affairs, Zoos/Aquariums • *Education:* Business Education, Colleges & Universities, Economic Education, Education Associations, Education Funds, Medical Education, Private Education (Precollege), Secondary Education (Public), Student Aid • *Health:* Emergency/Ambulance Services, Health Organizations, Hospitals, Medical Rehabilitation, Medical Research, Single-Disease Health Associations • *Religion:* Jewish Causes, Religious Organizations, Religious Welfare • *Social Services:* Camps, Child Welfare, Community Centers, Community Service Organizations, Day Care, Family Services, Food/Clothing Distribution, Homes, Senior Services, Substance Abuse, United Funds/United Ways, Youth Organizations

Grant Types: general support

Nonmonetary Support Types: cause-related marketing & promotion, donated equipment, and loaned employees

Geographic Distribution: focus on Rhode Island

Operating Locations: RI (Providence)

CORP. OFFICERS
Herbert W. Cummings: *B* 1935 *ED* Brown Univ Sch Savings Banking; Fairleigh Dickinson Univ *CURR EMPL* vchmn: Citizens Bank *CORP AFFIL* chmn, ceo: Citizens Bank MA; exec vp, dir: Citizens Corp; vchmn: Citizens Fin Group

James R. Dorsey: *CURR EMPL* dir corp aff: Citizens Bank *CORP AFFIL* sr vp: Citizens Fin Group

Lawrence K. Fish: *CURR EMPL* chmn, ceo: Citizens Bank

Mark J. Formica: *B* 1948 *CURR EMPL* pres: Citizens Bank *CORP AFFIL* pres, ceo, dir: Citizens Savings Bank; pres, dir: Citizens Trust Co

GIVING OFFICERS
Herbert W. Cummings: trust *CURR EMPL* vchmn: Citizens Bank (see above)

James R. Dorsey: trust *CURR EMPL* dir corp aff: Citizens Bank (see above)

Lawrence K. Fish: trust *CURR EMPL* chmn, ceo: Citizens Bank (see above)

Mark J. Formica: trust *CURR EMPL* pres: Citizens Bank (see above)

D. Faye Sanders: sr vp

APPLICATION INFORMATION
Initial Approach: *Initial Contact:* written proposal *Include Information On:* description of agency, its purpose, history, and programs; summary of need, amount requested, and description of agencies providing similar services; financial data on organization, such as independent audit, budget with sources of income, breakdown of expenditures by program, administration, and personnel; brief explanation why Citizens Charitable Foundation would be an appropriate donor; list of board of directors; copy of IRS tax-determination letter; and copy of affirmative action/equal opportunity policy *Deadlines:* none

Restrictions on Giving: The foundation does not award grants to the following: member agencies of federated organizations, including United Way agencies, except for major capital campaigns; government and quasi-governmental agencies and organizations including commissions and task forces; local affiliates of national health organizations; agencies outside the foundation's geographic area; labor, fraternal and veterans organizations, and programs or projects of a political nature. The foundation also does not provide funding to individuals, religious bodies, operating deficits, annual campaigns, conferences or seminars, endowments, general operating support, research projects, trips and tours, loans, or advertising and fund-raising activities.

OTHER THINGS TO KNOW
All organizations requesting funding must agree to evaluation procedures including on-site visits and community interviews. The foundation may request periodic reports from organizations receiving funding.

The foundation will not contribute in excess of 1% of the total goal to capital fund campaigns. Generally, payments are made within a three- to five-year period in order to eliminate an accumulation of substantial pledges in future years.

PUBLICATIONS
Annual report with application guidelines

GRANTS ANALYSIS
Total Grants: $594,625
Number of Grants: 56
Highest Grant: $193,000
Average Grant: $7,302*
Typical Range: $1,000 to $5,000
Disclosure Period: 1993

Note: Average grant figure does not include the largest grant of $193,000. Recent grants are derived from a 1993 grants list.

RECENT GRANTS

General

193,000	United Way Southeastern New England, Providence, RI
40,000	Miriam Hospital, Providence, RI
31,000	University of Rhode Island, Kingston, RI — River Rescue Project
30,000	Elmwood Neighborhood Housing Services, Providence, RI
25,000	St. Joseph's Hospital, Reading, PA

Clarke Trust, John

CONTACT
Wilbur Nelson, Jr.
Trustee
John Clarke Trust
c/o Rhode Island Hospital Trust National Bank
1 Hospital Trust Pl.
Providence, RI 02903
(401) 278-8700

FINANCIAL SUMMARY
Recent Giving: $158,890 (1993); $107,200 (1992); $145,499 (1991)

Assets: $2,345,406 (1993); $3,037,713 (1992); $3,040,862 (1991)

EIN: 05-6006062

CONTRIBUTIONS SUMMARY
Typical Recipients: • *Arts & Humanities:* Libraries, Music, Theater • *Civic & Public Affairs:* African American Affairs, General, Municipalities/Towns, Urban & Community Affairs, Women's Affairs • *Education:* Colleges & Universities, Education Funds, Engineering/Technological Education, General, Medical Education, Private Education (Precollege), Religious Education • *Health:* Health Organizations, Hospitals, Nursing Services • *Religion:* Churches, Ministries, Religious Organizations, Religious Welfare • *Science:* Science Museums • *Social Services:* Camps, Child Welfare, Community Centers, Community Service Organizations, Family Services, Scouts, Shelters/Homelessness, YMCA/YWCA/YMHA/YWHA

Grant Types: general support

Geographic Distribution: focus on RI

GIVING OFFICERS
RI Hospital Trust National Bank: trust

William G. Corcoran: trust

Wilbur Nelson, Jr.: trust

APPLICATION INFORMATION
Initial Approach: The foundation has no formal grant application procedure or application form. There are no deadlines.

GRANTS ANALYSIS
Total Grants: $158,890

Number of Grants: 69

Highest Grant: $10,000

Typical Range: $1,000 to $5,500

Disclosure Period: 1993

Note: Recent grants are derived from a 1993 Form 990.

RECENT GRANTS

Library

5,000	Providence Public Library, Providence, RI

General

10,000	Canonicus Camp and Conference Center, Providence, RI
10,000	New Visions for Newport City, Newport City, RI
8,800	Community Preparatory School, Providence, RI
5,000	Choices, Providence, RI
5,000	YWCA of Greater Rhode Island, Providence, RI

Cranston Print Works Company / Cranston Foundation

Sales: $275.0 million
Employees: 1,600
Headquarters: Cranston, RI
SIC Major Group: Finishing Plants—Cotton, Textile Machinery, and Paper Industries Machinery

CONTACT
Carolyn Lake
Administrator
Cranston Foundation
1381 Cranston St.
Cranston, RI 02920
(401) 943-4800

FINANCIAL SUMMARY
Recent Giving: $345,000 (fiscal 1995); $344,298 (fiscal 1994); $393,583 (fiscal 1993)

Assets: $461,011 (fiscal 1994); $557,625 (fiscal 1993); $702,695 (fiscal 1992)

Gifts Received: $230,906 (fiscal 1994); $226,255 (fiscal 1993); $236,068 (fiscal 1992)

Fiscal Note: Contributes through foundation only.

EIN: 05-6015348

CONTRIBUTIONS SUMMARY
Typical Recipients: • *Arts & Humanities:* Ethnic & Folk Arts, History & Archaeology, Libraries • *Civic & Public Affairs:* Safety • *Education:* Arts/Humanities Education, Colleges & Universities, Community & Junior Colleges, Minority Education, Science/Mathematics Education, Student Aid • *Health:* Hospitals • *Religion:* Jewish Causes, Religious Welfare • *Social Services:* Community Service Organizations, United Funds/United Ways, Youth Organizations

Grant Types: general support

Geographic Distribution: nationally, with a focus on areas where company has operations

Operating Locations: MA (Webster), NC (Fletcher), NY (New York), RI (Cranston)

CORP. OFFICERS
Leo C. Driscoll: *CURR EMPL* vp human resources: Cranston Print Works Co

Nancy Kirsch: *CURR EMPL* gen couns: Cranston Print Works Co

Carolyn Lake: *CURR EMPL* admin: Cranston Print Works Co

Robert Mandeville: *B* Woonsocket RI 1943 *ED* Bryant Coll 1963 *CURR EMPL* cfo, secy, treas: Cranston Print Works Co *CORP AFFIL* secy, treas, cfo: Cranston Intl Sales Corp, Cranston Trucking Co

Anthony J. Palazzo: *B* 1946 *ED* Nichols Coll MA 1970; Nichols Coll BS *CURR EMPL* vp textile oper: Cranston Print Works Co

Frederic Lincoln Rockefeller: *B* New York NY 1921 *ED* Yale Univ 1947 *CURR EMPL* chmn: Cranston Print Works Co *CORP AFFIL* dir: Chubb Corp, Howe Furniture Co *NONPR AFFIL* dir: Am Textile Mfrs Inst, Textile Distr Assn

George Whitcomb Shuster: *B* Trenton NJ 1946 *ED* Yale Univ 1967; Yale Univ Law Sch 1973 *CURR EMPL* pres, ceo, dir: Cranston Print Works Co *NONPR AFFIL* dir: Kent County Meml Hosp

GIVING OFFICERS
William Aniszewski: trust

Leo C. Driscoll: trust *CURR EMPL* vp human resources: Cranston Print Works Co (see above)

Cathy Giarusso: trust

Nancy Kirsch: trust *CURR EMPL* gen couns: Cranston Print Works Co (see above)

Carolyn Lake: admin *CURR EMPL* admin: Cranston Print Works Co (see above)

Robert Mandeville: trust *CURR EMPL* cfo, secy, treas: Cranston Print Works Co (see above)

Anthony J. Palazzo: trust *CURR EMPL* vp textile oper: Cranston Print Works Co (see above)

Frederic Lincoln Rockefeller: trust *CURR EMPL* chmn: Cranston Print Works Co (see above)

George Whitcomb Shuster: trust *CURR EMPL* pres, ceo, dir: Cranston Print Works Co (see above)

J. Wright: trust *CURR EMPL* vp diversified oper: Cranston Print Works Co

APPLICATION INFORMATION
Initial Approach: *Initial Contact:* letter *Include Information On:* details of project; budget information; organization's management structure, purpose, operation, and goals; copy of IRS classification letter; and recent financial statements *Deadlines:* must be submitted by August 30 *Note:* Requests received after April 15 will be held until the beginning of the new fiscal year on September 1.

Restrictions on Giving: The foundation only makes contributions to domestic organizations which have been ruled by the IRS as tax exempt under Section 501(c)(3) of the Internal Revenue Code.

GRANTS ANALYSIS
Total Grants: $344,298
Number of Grants: 118
Highest Grant: $14,598
Average Grant: $2,918
Typical Range: $100 to $3,000
Disclosure Period: fiscal year ending June 30, 1994
Note: Recent grants are derived from a fiscal 1994 Form 990.

RECENT GRANTS

Library
2,000   Providence Public Library, Providence, RI — operating funds

General
14,598   University of Rhode Island, Kingston, RI — scholarship to dependent child of donor employee
12,000   United Way Henderson County, Hendersonville, NC — operating funds
12,000   United Way of New York City, New York, NY — operating funds
12,000   United Way Southeastern New England, Providence, RI — operating funds
12,000   United Way Webster/Dudley, Webster, MA — operating funds

Dimeo Construction Co.

Sales: $1.0 million
Employees: 200
Headquarters: Providence, RI
SIC Major Group: Business Services, Engineering & Management Services, General Building Contractors, and Special Trade Contractors

CONTACT
Laurie Searles
Office Manager
Dimeo Construction Co.
75 Chapman St.
Providence, RI 02905
(401) 781-9800

FINANCIAL SUMMARY
Recent Giving: $100,000 (1991); $100,000 (1990)

CONTRIBUTIONS SUMMARY
Typical Recipients: • *Arts & Humanities:* Arts Appreciation, Arts Associations & Councils, Arts Centers, Arts Festivals, Community Arts, Historic Preservation, Libraries, Museums/Galleries, Music, Opera, Performing Arts, Theater • *Civic & Public Affairs:* Economic Development, Housing, Municipalities/Towns, Safety, Women's Affairs, Zoos/Aquariums • *Education:* Arts/Humanities Education, Business Education, Colleges & Universities, Community & Junior Colleges, Continuing Education, Economic Education • *Health:* Health Funds, Health Organizations, Hospitals, Mental Health, Nutrition, Single-Disease Health Associations • *International:* International Peace & Security Issues • *Religion:* Churches, Religious Organizations, Synagogues/Temples • *Social Services:* Animal Protection, Child Welfare, Community Centers, Community Service Organizations, Counseling, Family Planning, Senior Services, Substance Abuse

Grant Types: general support

Nonmonetary Support Types: in-kind services, loaned executives, and workplace solicitation

Geographic Distribution: primarily RI

Operating Locations: RI (Providence)

CORP. OFFICERS
Kevin Currier: *CURR EMPL* cfo: Dimeo Construction Co

Bradford S. Dimeo: *CURR EMPL* vp, dir: Dimeo Construction Co

Thomas P. Dimeo: *B* 1930 *ED* Brown Univ BA 1952 *CURR EMPL* chmn, pres, dir: Dimeo Enterprises *CORP AFFIL* ceo: Dimeo Construction Co; chmn: Dimeo Enterprises; dir: Old Stone Bank, Providence Mutual Fire Ins Co *NONPR AFFIL* dir: YMCA Greater Providence; mem corp: RI Hosp; trust: Cathedral St John Divine, Johnson Wales Coll

APPLICATION INFORMATION
Initial Approach: Send brief letter of inquiry, including a description of the organization, amount requested, purpose of funds sought, recently audited financial statements, and proof of tax-exempt status. There are no deadlines.

Restrictions on Giving: Does not support individuals.

Fleet Financial Group, Inc. / Fleet Charitable Trust

Former Foundation Name: Fleet/Norstar Charitable Trust
Employees: 25,200
Income: $4.68 billion
Headquarters: Providence, RI
SIC Major Group: Holding & Other Investment Offices and National Commercial Banks

CONTACT
Sheila McDonald
Secretary
Fleet Charitable Trust
111 Westminster St.
Providence, RI 02903
(401) 278-6242

FINANCIAL SUMMARY
Recent Giving: $2,500,000 (1995 est.); $2,200,000 (1994 approx.); $2,517,105 (1993)

Assets: $37,834,823 (1993); $37,487,386 (1992); $36,373,738 (1991)

Fiscal Note: Above figures are for the trust only and do not include direct contributions or nonmonetary support.

EIN: 05-6007619

CONTRIBUTIONS SUMMARY
Typical Recipients: • *Arts & Humanities:* Arts Centers, Community Arts, Dance, Ethnic & Folk Arts, Historic Preservation, Libraries, Museums/Galleries, Music, Performing Arts, Theater, Visual Arts • *Civic & Public Affairs:* Civil Rights, Economic Development, Housing, Safety, Urban & Community Affairs, Women's Affairs, Zoos/Aquariums • *Education:* Arts/Humanities Education, Colleges & Universities, Community & Junior Colleges, Economic Education, Education Funds, Legal Education, Literacy, Minority Education, Private Education (Precollege), Public Education (Precollege), Science/Mathematics Education, Student Aid • *Health:* AIDS/HIV, Cancer, Children's Health/Hospitals, Clinics/Medical Centers, Hospitals, Medical Research, Research/Studies Institutes • *Religion:* Religious Welfare • *Social Services:* Child Welfare, Community Centers, People with Disabilities, Shelters/Homelessness, Substance Abuse, United Funds/United Ways, Youth Organizations

Grant Types: capital, challenge, employee matching gifts, project, and scholarship

Note: Employee matching gift ratio: 1 to 1.

Nonmonetary Support Types: cause-related marketing & promotion and donated equipment

Geographic Distribution: primarily within areas where parent company maintains a major business presence

Operating Locations: CA (Long Beach), CT (Haddam, Hartford), FL (Miami), GA (Atlanta), MA (Boston), ME (Portland), NH (Nashua), NY (Albany, Buffalo, Garden City, Long Island, New York, Rochester, Syracuse, Westbury), RI (Providence), SC (Columbia), WI (Milwaukee)

CORP. OFFICERS
Robert J. Higgins: *B* Providence RI 1945 *ED* Univ RI BA 1967 *CURR EMPL* vchmn: Fleet Fin Group Inc *CORP AFFIL* chmn: Fleet Natl Bank; chmn, ceo: Fleet Bank Natl Assn; dir: Fleet Precious Metals Inc *NONPR AFFIL* mem: Assn Reserve City Bankers; trust: RI Philharmonic Orchestra, Trinity Repertory Co

J. Terrence Murray: *B* Woonsocket RI 1939 *ED* Harvard Univ BA 1962 *CURR EMPL* chmn, pres, ceo: Fleet Fin Group Inc *CORP AFFIL* chmn, ceo: Fleet Fin Corp; chmn, dir: Fleet Natl Bank; dir: AT Cross Co, Fed Reserve Bank Boston, St Mutual Assurance Co Am, Stop & Shop Cos Inc *NONPR AFFIL* dir: Am Bankers Assn, Assn Reserve City Bankers, Harvard Univ Alumni Assn; trust: Brown Univ, RI Sch Design

GIVING OFFICERS
Marc C. Leslie: legal couns *CURR EMPL* secy, dir: Fleet Precious Metals Inc

Sheila McDonald: secy

J. Terrence Murray: mem *CURR EMPL* chmn, pres, ceo: Fleet Fin Group Inc (see above)

APPLICATION INFORMATION
Initial Approach: *Initial Contact:* letter *Include Information On:* description and purpose of organization; amount requested and total amount needed; specific purpose for which funds are sought; recently audited financial statement and proof of tax-exempt status; and any other appropriate supporting materials *Deadlines:* none; committee meets quarterly

Restrictions on Giving: Does not support political or lobbying groups, fraternal organizations, individuals, goodwill advertising, dinners or special events, or groups located outside of areas where Fleet Financial Group operates.

OTHER THINGS TO KNOW
In 1991, parent company Fleet Financial Group acquired the Bank of New England Corp., which was subsequently renamed Fleet Bank of Massachusetts. The Bank of New England Corp. Foundation was dissolved; the giving program of Fleet Bank of Massachusetts is now merged with that of Fleet Charitable Trust.

GRANTS ANALYSIS
Total Grants: $2,517,105

Number of Grants: 636

Highest Grant: $400,000

Average Grant: $3,958

Typical Range: $1,000 to $10,000 and $10,000 to $100,000

Disclosure Period: 1993

Note: Above figures include matching grants. Recent grants are derived from a 1993 Form 990.

RECENT GRANTS
General

400,000	United Way
115,000	United Way Northeastern New York, Albany, NY
115,000	United Way Northeastern New York, Albany, NY
100,000	Brown University, Providence, RI
100,000	New Children's Hospital, Jacksonville, FL

Hasbro Inc. / Hasbro Charitable Trust Inc.

Revenue: $2.67 billion
Employees: 10,000
Headquarters: Pawtucket, RI
SIC Major Group: Games, Toys & Children's Vehicles

CONTACT
Mary Louise Fazzano
Director
Hasbro Charitable Trust Inc.
1027 Newport Ave.
Pawtucket, RI 02862

(401) 727-5429
Note: Trust does not accept faxed proposals.

FINANCIAL SUMMARY
Recent Giving: $1,100,000 (fiscal 1995 est.); $1,074,809 (fiscal 1994 approx.); $1,310,240 (fiscal 1993)

Assets: $2,337,426 (fiscal 1993); $2,928,763 (fiscal 1992); $3,540,205 (fiscal 1991)

Gifts Received: $750,000 (fiscal 1993); $600,000 (fiscal 1992)

Fiscal Note: Company gives primarily through the foundation (see "Other Things You Should Know" and "Other Support" notes). Figures for 1993 include $24,740 in matching gifts to higher education. Above figures exclude nonmonetary support. The trust receives contributions from Hasbro Inc.

EIN: 22-2538470

CONTRIBUTIONS SUMMARY
Typical Recipients: • *Arts & Humanities:* Arts Centers, Libraries, Music, Performing Arts • *Civic & Public Affairs:* African American Affairs, Housing, Minority Business, Municipalities/Towns, Public Policy, Women's Affairs, Zoos/Aquariums • *Education:* Business Education, Colleges & Universities, Economic Education, Education Funds, General, Literacy, Private Education (Precollege) • *Environment:* Air/Water Quality • *Health:* Clinics/Medical Centers, Geriatric Health, Hospitals, Prenatal Health Issues, Research/Studies Institutes • *International:* International Affairs • *Religion:* Ministries, Religious Welfare • *Social Services:* Child Welfare, Community Service Organizations, Family Planning, Family Services, Food/Clothing Distribution, Refugee Assistance, Sexual Abuse, Shelters/Homelessness, United Funds/United Ways, Volunteer Services, Youth Organizations

Grant Types: employee matching gifts and project

Note: Employee matching gift ratio: 1 to 1. Matching gifts are made only for higher educational purposes.

Nonmonetary Support: $500,000 (fiscal 1992); $250,000 (fiscal 1990); $300,000 (fiscal 1988)

Nonmonetary Support Types: donated products

Note: Company donates toys nationally to direct service organizations that provide services around the clock for children (see "Other Things You Should Know").

Geographic Distribution: headquarters and operating locations only

Operating Locations: MA (Springfield), NJ (Northvale), NY, OH, PA, RI (Pawtucket), SC, TX, VT, WA

CORP. OFFICERS
Alan Geoffrey Hassenfeld: *B* Providence RI 1948 *ED* Univ PA BA 1970 *CURR EMPL* chmn, pres, ceo, dir: Hasbro Inc *CORP AFFIL* chmn: Hasbro Canada; dir: Milton Bradley Co *NONPR AFFIL* dir: Foster Parents Plan, Intl House RI, Jewish Commun Ctr, Jewish Fed RI, Parents Anonymous, Toy Mfrs Am; mem: RI Air

Adv Task Force; mem exec comm: Deerfield Acad Alumni Assn; overseer: Univ PA Sch Arts & Sci; trust: Brown Univ, Miriam Hosp *PHIL AFFIL* vp, secy, treas: Hassenfeld Foundation

GIVING OFFICERS
Mary Louise Fazzano: dir

Alan Geoffrey Hassenfeld: pres *CURR EMPL* chmn, pres, ceo, dir: Hasbro Inc *PHIL AFFIL* vp, secy, treas: Hassenfeld Foundation (see above)

Donald M. Robbins: asst secy *B* Woonsocket RI 1935 *ED* Brandeis Univ 1953-1955; Univ MI AB 1957; Boston Univ LLB 1960 *CURR EMPL* sr vp, secy, gen couns: Hasbro Inc *CORP AFFIL* secy, dir: Playskool Inc; vp, secy: Playskool Baby Inc *NONPR AFFIL* chmn: Israel Bonds St RI; dir: Big Bros RI, Miriam Hosp, New England Legal Fdn; mem: Am Bar Assn, Am Soc Corp Secys, Assn Corp Counc, MA Bar Assn, RI Bar Assn; vp: Jewish Fed RI

Alfred J. Verrecchia: treas, trust *B* Providence RI 1943 *ED* Univ RI BS 1967; Univ RI MBA 1972 *CURR EMPL* coo domestic toys, dir: Hasbro Inc *NONPR AFFIL* chmn: Bradley Hosp

APPLICATION INFORMATION
Initial Approach: *Initial Contact:* by phone only, then an application will be sent *Include Information On:* statement of purpose and objectives; history of organization's programs; list of board and staff, as well as record of financial commitment by board for proposed project; annual operating budget for organization and for year in which grant will occur; recently audited financial statement; description of program for which funds are requested, including its budget; amount requested; copy of tax-exempt determination letter; list of other corporations and foundations approached and level of financial support requested or received *Deadlines:* prior to July 1 for consideration in current year *Note:* Telephone trust to request guidelines.

Restrictions on Giving: From time to time unusual or special projects will alter the grant review process.

Cash contributions are limited to operating locations. Does not support religious organizations, individuals, political organizations, scholarships, loans, endowments, goodwill advertising, fund raisers, sponsorship of recreational activities, or research.

OTHER THINGS TO KNOW
Hasbro also sponsors the Hasbro Children's Foundation, which contributes about $2,000,000 annually to health, social services, and educational programs for children under the age of 12. Contact is Eve Weiss, Executive Director, Hasbro Children's Foundation, 32 W 23rd Street, New York, NY 10010, (212) 645-2400.

Toy requests should be submitted by October 1. If an organization receives toys for 2 consecutive years, company follows with a 2 year hiatus. No participation in fundraisers, give-a-ways, or incentives. Toys go to supervised playrooms in organizations which provide direct services to children, especially shelters and child life departments of hospitals. Donates only to 501(c)(3) organizations within the U.S. Policy holds for Hasbro and is subsidiaries: Milton Bradley, Playskool, Tonka, Kenner, and Parker.

GRANTS ANALYSIS
Total Grants: $1,310,240

Number of Grants: 73*

Highest Grant: $519,000

Average Grant: $8,146*

Typical Range: $500 to $10,000

Disclosure Period: fiscal year ending December 26, 1993

Note: Number of grants and average grant figures exclude matching gifts totaling $24,740. Average grant figure also excludes the highest grant of $519,000. Recent grants are derived from a 1993 Form 990.

RECENT GRANTS

General

519,000	Rhode Island Hospital, Providence, RI
150,000	United Way of Southeastern New England, Providence, RI
93,750	RX for Reading, Los Angeles, CA
50,000	Miriam Hospital Foundation, Providence, RI
48,720	Children's Action Network Children's Defense Fund, Boston, MA

Hassenfeld Foundation

CONTACT
Alan G. Hassenfeld
Secretary-Treasurer
Hassenfeld Fdn.
1027 Newport Ave.
Pawtucket, RI 02861
(401) 431-8697

FINANCIAL SUMMARY
Recent Giving: $1,332,339 (1993); $1,102,930 (1992); $1,200,954 (1991)

Assets: $15,837,178 (1993); $15,172,180 (1992); $5,877,345 (1991)

Gifts Received: $418,921 (1993); $7,470,180 (1992); $626,867 (1991)

Fiscal Note: In 1993, contributions were received from the Stephen Hassenfeld Charitable Trust ($250,000), Boris Freiman ($157,921), Henry Orenstein ($10,000), and Fujio Maezman ($1,000).

EIN: 05-6015373

CONTRIBUTIONS SUMMARY
Donor(s): Hasbro, Inc., and members of the Hassenfeld family

Typical Recipients: • *Arts & Humanities:* Historic Preservation, Libraries, Museums/Galleries • *Civic & Public Affairs:* General, Philanthropic Organizations • *Education:* Colleges & Universities, Education Associations • *Health:* Children's

Health/Hospitals • *International:* International Relations, Missionary/Religious Activities • *Religion:* Churches, Jewish Causes, Religious Organizations, Synagogues/Temples

Grant Types: general support

Geographic Distribution: focus on Northeast

GIVING OFFICERS
Ellen Block: secy

Alan Geoffrey Hassenfeld: vp, secy, treas *B* Providence RI 1948 *ED* Univ PA BA 1970 *CURR EMPL* chmn, pres, ceo, dir: Hasbro Inc *CORP AFFIL* chmn: Hasbro Canada; dir: Milton Bradley Co *NONPR AFFIL* dir: Foster Parents Plan, Intl House RI, Jewish Commun Ctr, Jewish Fed RI, Parents Anonymous, Toy Mfrs Am; mem: RI Air Adv Task Force; mem exec comm: Deerfield Acad Alumni Assn; overseer: Univ PA Sch Arts & Sci; trust: Brown Univ, Miriam Hosp *PHIL AFFIL* pres: Hasbro Charitable Trust Inc.

Sylvia K. Hassenfeld: pres *CURR EMPL* vp corp aff, dir: Hasbro Bradley *NONPR AFFIL* pres, dir: Hassenfeld Fdn

APPLICATION INFORMATION
Initial Approach: The foundation reports it only makes contributions to preselected charitable organizations.

GRANTS ANALYSIS
Total Grants: $1,332,339

Number of Grants: 27

Highest Grant: $420,000

Typical Range: $1,000 to $200,000

Disclosure Period: 1993

Note: Recent grants are derived from a 1993 Form 990.

RECENT GRANTS

Library

1,000	Providence Public Library, Providence, RI

General

420,000	Jewish Federation of Rhode Island, Providence, RI
200,000	University of Pennsylvania, Philadelphia, PA
150,000	Johns Hopkins University, Baltimore, MD
118,699	Jerusalem Foundation, New York, NY
97,390	American Jewish Joint Distribution Committee, New York, NY

Jaffe Foundation

CONTACT
Holly Seagrove
Trustee
Jaffe Fdn.
300 Richmond St.
Providence, RI 02903
(401) 421-2920

FINANCIAL SUMMARY
Recent Giving: $491,156 (fiscal 1994); $588,814 (fiscal 1993); $500,125 (fiscal 1992)

Assets: $4,206,258 (fiscal 1994); $4,695,747 (fiscal 1993); $5,089,446 (fiscal 1992)

Gifts Received: $15,371 (fiscal 1994); $10,000 (fiscal 1991)

Fiscal Note: In fiscal 1994, contributions were received from Edwin A. Jaffe.

EIN: 04-6049261

CONTRIBUTIONS SUMMARY
Donor(s): the late Meyer Jaffe, Edwin A. Jaffe

Typical Recipients: • *Arts & Humanities:* Arts Centers, Dance, Libraries, Museums/Galleries, Music, Opera, Public Broadcasting, Theater • *Civic & Public Affairs:* African American Affairs, Economic Policy, General, Urban & Community Affairs • *Education:* Arts/Humanities Education, Colleges & Universities, Community & Junior Colleges, International Studies, Private Education (Precollege) • *Environment:* General • *Health:* Health Organizations, Hospices, Hospitals, Medical Research, Nursing Services, Single-Disease Health Associations • *International:* Foreign Arts Organizations, Human Rights, International Peace & Security Issues, Missionary/Religious Activities • *Religion:* Jewish Causes, Religious Organizations, Religious Welfare, Synagogues/Temples • *Social Services:* Community Service Organizations, Family Planning, Food/Clothing Distribution, People with Disabilities, Sexual Abuse, United Funds/United Ways, Youth Organizations

Grant Types: general support

Geographic Distribution: focus on MA

GIVING OFFICERS
Donna Jaffe Fishbein: trust

David S. Greer: trust *B* Brooklyn NY 1925 *ED* Univ Notre Dame BS 1948; Univ Chicago MD 1953; Brown Univ MA (hon) 1975; Southeastern Mass Univ LHD (hon) 1981 *NONPR AFFIL* dir: Assn Home Health Agencies; master: Am Coll Physicians; mem: Am Congress Rehab Medicine, Gerontological Soc, Govs Task Force, Inst Medicine, Inst Mental Health RI, Intl Physicians for Prevention Nuclear War, Intl Soc Rehab Medicine, RI Med Soc; prof community health: Brown Univ

Edwin A. Jaffe: chmn

Lola Jaffe: vchmn

Robert Jaffe: trust

Holly Seagrove: trust

APPLICATION INFORMATION
Initial Approach: Send a brief letter of inquiry. Include a description of organization, amount requested, purpose of funds sought, recently audited financial statement, and proof of tax-exempt status. There are no deadlines.

Restrictions on Giving: Does not support individuals.

PUBLICATIONS

Mission statement, including general guidelines

GRANTS ANALYSIS

Total Grants: $491,156

Number of Grants: 48

Highest Grant: $77,000

Typical Range: $100 to $52,500

Disclosure Period: fiscal year ending June 30, 1994

Note: Recent grants are derived from a fiscal 1994 Form 990.

RECENT GRANTS

General

77,000	Brandeis University, Waltham, MA
65,000	Brown University, Providence, RI
42,817	Miriam Hospital, Providence, RI
35,000	Economic Policy Institute, Washington, DC
25,000	Fall River United Jewish Appeal, Fall River, MA

Kimball Foundation, Horace A. Kimball and S. Ella

CONTACT

Thomas F. Black III
President
Horace A. Kimball and S. Ella Kimball Fdn.
c/o The Washington Trust Co.
23 Broad St.
Westerly, RI 02891
(401) 348-1200

FINANCIAL SUMMARY

Recent Giving: $152,000 (fiscal 1992); $167,500 (fiscal 1991); $208,100 (fiscal 1990)

Assets: $3,956,177 (fiscal 1992); $3,674,594 (fiscal 1991); $3,525,223 (fiscal 1990)

EIN: 05-6006130

CONTRIBUTIONS SUMMARY

Donor(s): the late H. Earle Kimball

Typical Recipients: • *Arts & Humanities:* Libraries, Performing Arts, Theater • *Civic & Public Affairs:* General, Municipalities/Towns, Safety, Women's Affairs • *Education:* Colleges & Universities, Private Education (Precollege) • *Environment:* General, Resource Conservation • *Health:* Health Organizations, Long-Term Care, Medical Research, Public Health, Single-Disease Health Associations • *Religion:* Religious Welfare • *Social Services:* Animal Protection, Camps, Child Welfare, Community Service Organizations, Day Care, Food/Clothing Distribution, Shelters/Homelessness, Youth Organizations

Grant Types: emergency, general support, and seed money

Geographic Distribution: limited to RI

GIVING OFFICERS

Norman D. Baker, Jr.: trust *PHIL AFFIL* dir: Allendale Insurance Foundation

Thomas F. Black III: pres, trust

Dexter Clarke: secy, treas, trust

APPLICATION INFORMATION

Initial Approach: The foundation has no formal grant application procedure or application form. There are no deadlines.

Restrictions on Giving: Limited to Rhode Island institutions.

GRANTS ANALYSIS

Total Grants: $152,000

Number of Grants: 22

Highest Grant: $20,000

Typical Range: $2,000 to $10,000

Disclosure Period: fiscal year ending September 30, 1992

Note: Recent grants are derived from a fiscal 1992 Form 990.

RECENT GRANTS

Library

10,000	Memorial and Library Association of Westerly
5,000	John Carter Brown Library
3,000	Langworthy Public Library

General

20,000	John Hope Settlement House
15,000	St. Mary's Home for Children
10,000	Camp Davis
10,000	Central Adult Day Care Services
10,000	Nature Conservancy Rhode Island Field Office, RI

Providence Gas Co.

Gross Operating Earnings: $205.82 million
Employees: 593
Parent Company: Providence Energy Corp.
Headquarters: Providence, RI
SIC Major Group: Holding & Other Investment Offices and Real Estate

CONTACT

Helen Toohey
Director, Community Relations
Providence Gas Co.
100 Weybosset St
Providence, RI 02903
(401) 272-5040

FINANCIAL SUMMARY

Fiscal Note: Annual Giving Range: $1,000,000 to $5,000,000

CONTRIBUTIONS SUMMARY

Typical Recipients: • *Arts & Humanities:* Arts Appreciation, Arts Associations & Councils, Arts Festivals, General, Libraries, Museums/Galleries, Music, Opera, Performing Arts, Visual Arts • *Civic & Public Affairs:* Civil Rights, Economic Development, General, Housing, Urban & Community Affairs • *Education:* Colleges & Universities, Community & Junior Colleges, Economic Education, General, Health & Physical Edu-

cation, Private Education (Precollege), Public Education (Precollege), Science/Mathematics Education • *Environment:* General • *Health:* General • *Social Services:* Community Service Organizations, Food/Clothing Distribution, General, Shelters/Homelessness, Substance Abuse, United Funds/United Ways, Youth Organizations

Grant Types: capital, employee matching gifts, general support, and operating expenses

Nonmonetary Support Types: donated equipment, in-kind services, loaned executives, and workplace solicitation

Operating Locations: MA (North Attleboro), RI (Providence)

CORP. OFFICERS

James H. Dodge: *CURR EMPL* chmn, ceo, pres, dir: Providence Energy Corp

APPLICATION INFORMATION

Initial Approach: Send letter of inquiry including a description of organization, amount requested, purpose of funds sought, and proof of tax-exempt status.

Providence Journal Company / Providence Journal Charitable Foundation

Sales: $262.0 million
Employees: 3,700
Headquarters: Providence, RI
SIC Major Group: Television Broadcasting Stations, Newspapers, and Cable & Other Pay Television Services

CONTACT

John Columbo
Trustee
Providence Journal Charitable Foundation
75 Fountain St.
Providence, RI 02902
(401) 277-7514

FINANCIAL SUMMARY

Recent Giving: $850,000 (1994 est.); $868,114 (1993); $765,476 (1992)

Assets: $7,543,433 (1993); $5,793,305 (1992); $2,778,898 (1991)

Gifts Received: $3,515,353 (1992)

Fiscal Note: Company gives through foundation only. Above figures exclude nonmonetary support. In 1992, gifts were received from Colony Communications.

EIN: 05-6015372

CONTRIBUTIONS SUMMARY

Typical Recipients: • *Arts & Humanities:* Arts Appreciation, Arts Associations & Councils, Arts Centers, Ballet, Historic Preservation, Libraries, Museums/Galleries, Music, Performing Arts, Public Broadcasting, Theater • *Civic & Public Affairs:* African American Affairs, Community Foundations, Economic Development, General, Housing, Municipalities/Towns, Parades/Festivals, Professional & Trade Associations,

Women's Affairs • *Education:* Arts/Humanities Education, Business Education, Colleges & Universities, Education Funds, Literacy, Private Education (Precollege), Public Education (Precollege) • *Environment:* General, Resource Conservation • *Health:* Emergency/Ambulance Services, Health Organizations, Hospices, Hospitals, Single-Disease Health Associations • *International:* International Affairs • *Religion:* Churches, Religious Welfare • *Social Services:* Child Welfare, Community Centers, Family Planning, People with Disabilities, Senior Services, Sexual Abuse, Substance Abuse, United Funds/United Ways, Youth Organizations

Grant Types: capital, general support, multiyear/continuing support, scholarship, and seed money

Nonmonetary Support: $10,000 (1990); $10,000 (1989); $10,000 (1988)

Nonmonetary Support Types: donated equipment and in-kind services

Geographic Distribution: throughout Rhode Island and nearby Massachusetts

Operating Locations: RI (Providence)

CORP. OFFICERS
Stephen Hamblett: *B* Nashua NH 1934 *ED* Harvard Coll 1957 *CURR EMPL* chmn, ceo: Providence Journal Co

GIVING OFFICERS
John Columbo: trust

Stephen Hamblett: trust *CURR EMPL* chmn, ceo: Providence Journal Co (see above)

APPLICATION INFORMATION
Initial Approach: *Initial Contact:* brief letter or proposal *Include Information On:* mission statement, amount requested, other sources of funding, proof of tax-exempt status, recent financial statements, list of board of directors *Deadlines:* none

GRANTS ANALYSIS
Total Grants: $868,114

Number of Grants: 38

Highest Grant: $208,000

Average Grant: $17,841*

Typical Range: $5,000 to $40,000

Disclosure Period: 1993

Note: Average Grant figure was calculated excluding the Highest Grant figure. Recent grants are derived from a 1993 Form 990.

RECENT GRANTS
Library
10,000	Providence Public Library, Providence, RI
5,000	Salve Regina University Library, Providence, RI

General
208,000	United Way of Southeastern New England, Providence, RI
80,000	Rhode Island Hospital, Providence, RI
41,500	Providence College, Providence, RI
40,000	Miriam Hospital, Providence, RI
30,000	International Institute of Rhode Island, Providence, RI

Textron, Inc. / Textron Charitable Trust

Revenue: $9.68 billion
Employees: 56,000
Headquarters: Providence, RI
SIC Major Group: Aircraft Parts & Equipment Nec, Greeting Cards, Blankbooks & Looseleaf Binders, and Toilet Preparations

CONTACT
Elizabeth W. Monahan
Contributions Coordinator, Secretary
Textron Charitable Trust
PO Box 878
Providence, RI 02901
(401) 457-2430

FINANCIAL SUMMARY
Recent Giving: $2,900,000 (1995 est.); $2,900,000 (1994 approx.); $2,900,000 (1993)

Assets: $10,814,603 (1992); $12,206,827 (1991); $12,715,514 (1990)

Fiscal Note: Company gives through charitable trust only. Above figures exclude nonmonetary support.

EIN: 25-6115832

CONTRIBUTIONS SUMMARY
Typical Recipients: • *Arts & Humanities:* Arts Appreciation, Arts Associations & Councils, Arts Centers, Arts Funds, Arts Institutes, Community Arts, Dance, Historic Preservation, Libraries, Museums/Galleries, Music, Opera, Performing Arts, Public Broadcasting, Theater • *Civic & Public Affairs:* Business/Free Enterprise, Civil Rights, Economic Development, Economic Policy, Employment/Job Training, Law & Justice, Legal Aid, Municipalities/Towns, Professional & Trade Associations, Public Policy, Safety, Urban & Community Affairs, Women's Affairs, Zoos/Aquariums • *Education:* Arts/Humanities Education, Business Education, Colleges & Universities, Community & Junior Colleges, Economic Education, Education Associations, Education Funds, Engineering/Technological Education, International Studies, Legal Education, Medical Education, Minority Education, Private Education (Precollege), Public Education (Precollege), Science/Mathematics Education, Student Aid • *Environment:* General • *Health:* Health Policy/Cost Containment, Health Organizations, Hospices, Hospitals, Single-Disease Health Associations • *International:* International Relations • *Religion:* Religious Welfare • *Science:* Science Exhibits & Fairs, Scientific Centers & Institutes • *Social Services:* Child Welfare, Community Centers, Community Service Organizations, Counseling, Emergency Relief, Family Planning, Food/Clothing Distribution, People with Disabilities, Recreation & Athletics, Refugee Assistance, Senior Serv-

ices, Shelters/Homelessness, Substance Abuse, United Funds/United Ways, Volunteer Services, Youth Organizations

Grant Types: capital, employee matching gifts, general support, and scholarship

Geographic Distribution: primarily in areas where company operates

Operating Locations: AL (Huntsville), CA (Anaheim, Irvine, Santa Ana, Santa Fe Springs, Valencia), CT (Newington, Stratford), FL (Cocoa, Orlando), GA (Americus, Augusta), IL (Harvard, Rockford), IN (Angola, Berne, Elwood, Pendleton, Vevay), LA (New Orleans), MA (Danvers, Lowell, Wilmington, Winchester, Worcester), MI (Ann Arbor, Detroit, Holland, Melvindale, Muskegon, Owosso, Traverse City, Walled Lake, Warren, Wyandotte, Zeeland), MN (St. Paul), NC (Charlotte, Hickory, Swannanoa), NH (Dover, Portsmouth), NY (Niagara Falls), OH (Blufton, Cincinnati, Cleveland, Fostoria, Greenville, Lima), PA (Williamsport), RI (Providence), SC (Greer), TN (Athens, Cookeville, Nashville), TX (Fort Worth, Houston), VT (Springfield), WI (Racine)

CORP. OFFICERS
Edward C. Arditte: *CURR EMPL* vp commun, risk mgmt: Textron Inc

James Franklin Hardymon: *B* Maysville KY 1934 *ED* Univ KY BSCE 1956; Univ KY MSCE 1958 *CURR EMPL* chmn, ceo: Textron Inc *CORP AFFIL* chmn: Davidson Interiors Textron, Micromatic Oper; chmn, pres, ceo: Avco Corp; pres, ceo: Compressor Components Textron *NONPR AFFIL* mem: Disciples Christ

Robert McWade: *CURR EMPL* dir corp commun: Textron Inc

GIVING OFFICERS
Elizabeth W. Monahan: contributions coordinator, secy contributions comm

APPLICATION INFORMATION
Initial Approach: *Initial Contact:* brief letter or proposal *Include Information On:* statement of purposes and objectives of the organization; history of the programs of the organization; list of the organization's officers, board of directors, and staff; annual operating budget for the organization for the year in which the project will occur; audited financial statements for the most recently completed year; description of the program or project that is the subject of the proposal and how it relates to the needs of the community; budget for the program or project that is the subject of the proposal; dollar level of support requested; copy of tax-exempt determination letter from the Internal Revenue Service; list of other sources approached for financial assistance and amounts received *Deadlines:* none

Restrictions on Giving: Does not support individuals, including political candidates; endowment funds; educational or hospital capital or operating expenses; requests intended to reduce operating deficits; fundraising appeals from churches, seminaries, or other religious organizations; operating funds of United Way member agencies; or organizations that are not 501(c)(3) tax-exempt.

OTHER THINGS TO KNOW
Grant recipients are required to complete a post-grant application form and adhere to terms of the grant. A fiscal and program summary must be submitted upon completion of the project.

Officer titles are likely to change.

Rhode Island Hospital Trust National Bank serves as a corporate trustee of the trust.

GRANTS ANALYSIS
Total Grants: $2,900,000

Typical Range: $1,000 to $5,000

Disclosure Period: 1994

Note: Recent grants are derived from a 1994 partial grants list.

RECENT GRANTS

General
1,100,000	Providence College, Providence, RI

SOUTH CAROLINA

Bowater Incorporated

Sales: $1.35 billion
Employees: 6,400
Headquarters: Greenville, SC
SIC Major Group: Paper Mills, Sawmills & Planing Mills—General, Pulp Mills, and Coated & Laminated Paper Nec

CONTACT
Robert D. Leahy
Vice President, Corporate Relations
Bowater Incorporated
55 E Camperdown Way
PO Box 1028
Greenville, SC 29602
(803) 282-9559

FINANCIAL SUMMARY
Recent Giving: $452,000 (1994); $765,561 (1993); $803,879 (1992)

Fiscal Note: Company gives directly. Above figures include nonmonetary support.

CONTRIBUTIONS SUMMARY
Typical Recipients: • *Arts & Humanities:* Arts Associations & Councils, Arts Centers, Community Arts, Libraries, Music, Performing Arts, Public Broadcasting • *Civic & Public Affairs:* Economic Development, Urban & Community Affairs • *Education:* Business Education, Colleges & Universities, Community & Junior Colleges, Continuing Education, Economic Education, Engineering/Technological Education, Minority Education • *Environment:* General • *Health:* Health Organizations, Hospitals • *Social Services:* United Funds/United Ways, Youth Organizations

Grant Types: capital, employee matching gifts, and general support
Note: Employee matching gift ratio: 1 to 1.

Nonmonetary Support: $21,500 (1993)

Nonmonetary Support Types: donated products

Geographic Distribution: in headquarters and operating communities

Operating Locations: AL (Albertville), IL (Moline), ME (Millinocket), SC (Catawba, Greenville), TN (Calhoun)

Note: Company also operates in Halifax, Nova Scotia (Canada)

CORP. OFFICERS
Robert Charles Lancaster: *B* Dover TN 1946 *ED* Southern IL Univ BS 1968 *CURR EMPL* sr vp, cfo: Bowater Inc *CORP AFFIL* asst contr: ACF Indus; sr mgr: Price Waterhouse

GIVING OFFICERS
Michelle Day: *CURR EMPL* mgr internal commun: Bowater Inc

Robert D. Leahy: *B* 1952 *ED* Johns Hopkins Univ MA; Loyola Univ BA *CURR EMPL* vp corp rels: Bowater Inc

APPLICATION INFORMATION
Initial Approach: *Initial Contact:* letter of inquiry *Include Information On:* a description of the organization, amount requested, purpose of funds sought, recently audited financial statement, and IRS tax-determination letter *Deadlines:* none *Note:* Requests for large contributions should be sent by July 31 for budget considerations.

Restrictions on Giving: Does not support individuals, religious organizations for sectarian purposes, or political or lobbying groups.

If the organization requesting a donation is supported by a united fund or if an agency which the contributions committee believes should be a member of a united fund, company will not make a donation.

OTHER THINGS TO KNOW
Each company division has its own contributions budget, with varying application procedures.

PUBLICATIONS
Bowater Incorporated Criteria for Corporate Giving

GRANTS ANALYSIS
Total Grants: $765,561

Typical Range: $250 to $1,000

Disclosure Period: 1993

Chapin Foundation of Myrtle Beach, South Carolina

CONTACT
Harold D. Clardy
Chairman
Chapin Fdn of Myrtle Beach, South Carolina

PO Box 2568
Myrtle Beach, SC 29577
(803) 448-4885

FINANCIAL SUMMARY
Recent Giving: $791,610 (fiscal 1992); $1,274,691 (fiscal 1991); $815,808 (fiscal 1990)

Assets: $8,954,422 (fiscal 1992); $8,967,186 (fiscal 1991); $8,036,756 (fiscal 1990)

EIN: 56-6039453

CONTRIBUTIONS SUMMARY
Donor(s): S. B. Chapin

Typical Recipients: • *Arts & Humanities:* Libraries • *Religion:* Churches, Religious Organizations, Synagogues/Temples • *Social Services:* Community Service Organizations, Youth Organizations

Grant Types: operating expenses

Geographic Distribution: limited to the Myrtle Beach, SC, area

GIVING OFFICERS
Harold D. Clardy: chmn, dir

Claude M. Epps, Jr.: secy, dir

Ruth T. Gore: dir

Harold Hartshorne, Jr.: dir

APPLICATION INFORMATION
Initial Approach: Send a brief letter of inquiry. Include tax exempt status. There are no deadlines.

Restrictions on Giving: general Myrtle Beach, SC, area

GRANTS ANALYSIS
Total Grants: $791,610

Number of Grants: 50

Highest Grant: $200,000

Typical Range: $3,000 to $20,000

Disclosure Period: fiscal year ending July 31, 1992

Note: Recent grants are derived from a fiscal 1992 Form 990.

RECENT GRANTS

Library
70,000	Chapin Memorial Library

General
200,000	Trinity Episcopal Church
65,000	Mt. Olive African Methodist, Mount Olive, NC
65,000	YMCA
50,000	First Baptist Church
50,000	St. John The Baptist

Close Foundation

Former Foundation Name: Francis Ley Springs Foundation

CONTACT
Charles A. Bundy
President
Close Fdn.
PO Drawer 460
Lancaster, SC 29721

(803) 286-2192

FINANCIAL SUMMARY
Recent Giving: $619,974 (1993); $618,173 (1992); $618,300 (1991)

Assets: $11,272,123 (1993); $9,824,537 (1992); $10,927,571 (1991)

Gifts Received: $50,450 (1993); $10,350 (1991); $30,200 (1990)

Fiscal Note: In 1993, contributions were received from Crandell C. Bowles ($50,050); six other donors made contributions of $150 or less each.

EIN: 23-7013986

CONTRIBUTIONS SUMMARY
Donor(s): members of the Springs and Close families.

Typical Recipients: • *Arts & Humanities:* Historic Preservation, History & Archaeology, Libraries, Performing Arts, Public Broadcasting • *Civic & Public Affairs:* Economic Development, General, Philanthropic Organizations, Public Policy • *Education:* Arts/Humanities Education, Business Education, Colleges & Universities, Community & Junior Colleges, Elementary Education (Private), Legal Education, Private Education (Precollege), Public Education (Precollege), Science/Mathematics Education, Vocational & Technical Education • *Environment:* General • *Health:* Emergency/Ambulance Services, Hospitals, Mental Health • *Religion:* Churches • *Science:* Scientific Organizations • *Social Services:* People with Disabilities, Recreation & Athletics, Substance Abuse, United Funds/United Ways, Youth Organizations

Grant Types: capital, conference/seminar, general support, loan, professorship, and seed money

Geographic Distribution: focus on Lancaster County, Chester Township of Chester County, and Fort Mill Township, SC; also some support in NC

GIVING OFFICERS
Crandall Close Bowles: vp, treas, dir *B* 1948 *CURR EMPL* pres: Springs Co *CORP AFFIL* dir: Duke Power Co, Richmond Fed Reserve Bank, Springs Indus; dir SC bd: SC Natl Bank *PHIL AFFIL* dir: Springs Foundation

James Bradley: dir *CORP AFFIL* dir: Springs Co *PHIL AFFIL* dir: Springs Foundation

Charles Alan Bundy: pres, dir *B* Cheraw SC 1930 *ED* Wofford Coll BA 1951 *NONPR AFFIL* dir: Elliott White Spring Meml Hosp; mem: Counc Fdns, Lancaster County Chamber Commerce *CLUB AFFIL* Rotary *PHIL AFFIL* pres, dir: Springs Foundation

Anne Springs Close: chmn, dir *PHIL AFFIL* don, chwm, dir: Springs Foundation

Derick Springsteen Close: dir *PHIL AFFIL* dir: Springs Foundation

Elliott Springs Close: dir *PHIL AFFIL* dir: Springs Foundation

Hugh William Close, Jr.: dir *PHIL AFFIL* vp, dir: Springs Foundation

Katherine Anne Close: dir *PHIL AFFIL* dir: Springs Foundation

Leroy Springs Close: dir *B* 1950 *CURR EMPL* pres: Sandlapper Fabrics *PHIL AFFIL* dir: Springs Foundation

Patricia Close: dir

Frances Close Hart: dir *PHIL AFFIL* dir: Springs Foundation

R. Carl Hubbard: dir

APPLICATION INFORMATION
Initial Approach: Send cover letter and full proposal. Include a description of organization, amount requested, purpose of funds sought, recently audited financial statement, and proof of tax-exempt status.

PUBLICATIONS
Annual Report

GRANTS ANALYSIS
Total Grants: $619,974

Number of Grants: 27

Highest Grant: $225,000

Typical Range: $400 to $50,000

Disclosure Period: 1993

Note: Recent grants are derived from a 1993 Form 990.

RECENT GRANTS

General

225,000	Leroy Springs and Company, Ft. Mill, SC — preschool/fitness center	
50,000	Wofford College, Spartanburg, SC	
40,000	York Technical College, York, PA — child development center	
30,000	Clemson University, Clemson, SC	
30,000	University of South Carolina, Columbia, SC — Business Partnership Foundation	

Colonial Life & Accident Insurance Co.

Income: $432.83 million
Employees: 1,195
Parent Company: Colonial Companies, Inc.
Headquarters: Columbia, SC
SIC Major Group: Insurance Agents, Brokers & Service

CONTACT
Robert Staton
Chairman
Colonial Life & Accident Insurance Co.
1200 Colonial Life Blvd.
PO Box 1365
Columbia, SC 29202
(803) 798-7000

FINANCIAL SUMMARY
Recent Giving: $500,000 (1994 est.); $500,000 (1993 approx.)

Fiscal Note: Company gives directly. Above figures include nonmonetary support.

CONTRIBUTIONS SUMMARY
Typical Recipients: • *Arts & Humanities:* Arts Appreciation, Arts Associations & Councils, Arts Centers, Arts Festivals, Arts Institutes, Community Arts, Dance, Ethnic & Folk Arts, Historic Preservation, Libraries, Museums/Galleries, Music, Opera, Performing Arts, Theater, Visual Arts • *Civic & Public Affairs:* Business/Free Enterprise, Economic Development, Economic Policy, Employment/Job Training, Housing, Law & Justice, Legal Aid, Nonprofit Management, Philanthropic Organizations, Professional & Trade Associations, Safety, Zoos/Aquariums • *Education:* Agricultural Education, Arts/Humanities Education, Business Education, Colleges & Universities, Community & Junior Colleges, Economic Education, International Exchange, International Studies, Private Education (Precollege), Public Education (Precollege), Student Aid • *Environment:* General • *Health:* Emergency/Ambulance Services, Geriatric Health, Health Policy/Cost Containment, Hospices, Hospitals, Medical Research, Medical Training, Mental Health, Nursing Services, Public Health, Single-Disease Health Associations • *Social Services:* Animal Protection, Child Welfare, Community Centers, Community Service Organizations, Counseling, Day Care, Delinquency & Criminal Rehabilitation, Domestic Violence, Emergency Relief, Family Planning, Family Services, Food/Clothing Distribution, Homes, People with Disabilities, Recreation & Athletics, Refugee Assistance, Senior Services, Substance Abuse, United Funds/United Ways, Volunteer Services, Youth Organizations

Grant Types: general support

Nonmonetary Support: $63,000 (1993)

Nonmonetary Support Types: donated equipment, in-kind services, loaned employees, and loaned executives

Geographic Distribution: primarily SC

Operating Locations: SC (Columbia)

CORP. OFFICERS
Paul Hoot Clifton, Jr.: *B* Ft Wayne IN 1947 *ED* Univ SC BA 1971; Harvard Univ Grad Sch Bus Admin 1983 *CURR EMPL* pres: Colonial Life & Accident Ins Co *NONPR AFFIL* dir: SC St Mus; mem: Am Soc Pers Admin, Columbia Art Assn, Columbia Forum, Columbia Pers Assn, Risk Ins Mgmt Soc, SE Pers Assn, Southern Pension Conf; mem human resources counc: Life Off Mgmt Assn

Stephen G. Hall: *CURR EMPL* coo: Colonial Life & Accident Ins Co

Robert Emmett Staton: *B* Suffolk VA 1946 *CURR EMPL* chmn: Colonial Life & Accident Ins Co

GIVING OFFICERS
Edwina Cames: *CURR EMPL* commun svc admin: Colonial Life & Accident Ins Co

APPLICATION INFORMATION
Initial Approach: *Initial Contact:* brief letter of inquiry *Include Information On:* description of the organization, amount requested, purpose of funds sought, recently

audited financial statements, and proof of tax-exempt status *Deadlines:* none

Restrictions on Giving: The company does not support beauty contests, fashion shows, adversarial groups, individuals, religious organizations for sectarian purposes, or political or lobbying groups.

GRANTS ANALYSIS
Total Grants: $500,000*

Typical Range: $1,000 to $2,500

Disclosure Period: 1993

Note: Total grants figure is approximate.

Fuller Foundation, C. G.

CONTACT
Pamela E. Pastol
Asst. Vice President and Trust Officer
C. G. Fuller Fdn.
c/o NationsBank of SC
PO Box 221513
Columbia, SC 29222
(803) 929-5920

FINANCIAL SUMMARY
Recent Giving: $148,649 (1993); $140,200 (1991); $156,403 (1989)

Assets: $3,011,033 (1993); $2,948,949 (1991); $2,629,141 (1989)

Gifts Received: $3,250 (1993); $13,000 (1991)

Fiscal Note: In 1991, contributions were received from Barnwell County ($2,000), Bennetsville Historical Society ($10,000), and Carol M. Bryant ($1,000).

EIN: 57-6050492

CONTRIBUTIONS SUMMARY
Donor(s): the late Cornell G. Fuller

Typical Recipients: • *Arts & Humanities:* History & Archaeology, Libraries • *Education:* Colleges & Universities, Private Education (Precollege) • *Health:* Cancer, Medical Research, Single-Disease Health Associations • *Religion:* Churches, Religious Organizations, Religious Welfare • *Social Services:* Child Welfare, Domestic Violence, Homes, Senior Services, Shelters/Homelessness

Grant Types: capital and scholarship

Geographic Distribution: limited to SC

GIVING OFFICERS
Victor B. John: trust

Clinton Lemon: trust

APPLICATION INFORMATION
Initial Approach: Application form required. There are no deadlines.

GRANTS ANALYSIS
Total Grants: $148,649

Number of Grants: 12

Highest Grant: $108,649

Typical Range: $1,400 to $7,500

Disclosure Period: 1993

Note: Recent grants are derived from a 1993 Form 990.

RECENT GRANTS
Library

6,500	Barnwell County Library, Barnwell, SC
2,500	Richland County Public Library, Columbia, SC

General

7,500	Center for Cancer Treatment, Columbia, SC
6,000	Epworth Children's Home, Columbia, SC
4,100	Bethlehem Baptist Church, Columbia, SC
3,000	Heathwood Hall Episopal School, Columbia, SC
2,500	Barnwell County Office of Aging, Barnwell, SC

Gregg-Graniteville Foundation

CONTACT
Joan F. Phibbs
Administrator and Secretary-Treasurer
Gregg-Graniteville Foundation
PO Box 418
Graniteville, SC 29829
(803) 663-7552

FINANCIAL SUMMARY
Recent Giving: $600,000 (1995 est.); $600,000 (1994 approx.); $234,991 (1993)

Assets: $14,000,000 (1995 est.); $14,000,000 (1994 approx.); $15,999,770 (1993)

EIN: 57-0314400

CONTRIBUTIONS SUMMARY
Donor(s): "The Gregg-Graniteville Foundation was established in 1941 in honor of William Gregg to carry out his philosophy of genuine concern for people, their betterment and their well-being."

Typical Recipients: • *Arts & Humanities:* Arts Associations & Councils, Ballet, Dance, Libraries, Museums/Galleries, Music, Opera, Performing Arts • *Civic & Public Affairs:* Clubs, Economic Development, Economic Policy, General, Rural Affairs, Safety, Urban & Community Affairs, Women's Affairs • *Education:* Business Education, Colleges & Universities, Community & Junior Colleges, Economic Education, Education Funds, Elementary Education (Private), Elementary Education (Public), General, Health & Physical Education, Minority Education, Public Education (Precollege), Secondary Education (Public), Vocational & Technical Education • *Health:* Cancer, Geriatric Health, Health Organizations, Hospitals, Hospitals (University Affiliated), Medical Rehabilitation, Mental Health, Research/Studies Institutes, Single-Disease Health Associations • *Religion:* Churches, Religious Organizations, Religious Welfare • *Science:* Scientific Organizations • *Social Services:* Camps, Community Centers, Community Service Organizations, Domestic Violence, Food/Clothing Distribution, Peo-

ple with Disabilities, Recreation & Athletics, Senior Services, Youth Organizations

Grant Types: capital, project, and scholarship

Geographic Distribution: Aiken County, SC, and Richmond County, GA

GIVING OFFICERS
Robert Morrall Bell: vp, dir *B* Graniteville SC 1936 *ED* Univ SC AB 1958; Univ SC LLB 1965 *CURR EMPL* sr ptnr: Bell & Surasky *NONPR AFFIL* mem: Aiken County Bar Assn, Am Bar Assn, Am Trial Lawyers Assn, Kappa Sigma Kappa, Phi Delta Phi, SC Bar Assn, SC Trial Lawyers Assn, Shriners, Tau Kappa Alpha *CLUB AFFIL* Masons

John W. Cunningham: vp, bd mem, dir

Jerry Ray Johnson: pres, bd mem, dir *B* Savannah GA 1926 *ED* Univ SC BSME 1950

Carl W. Littlejohn, Jr.: dir, bd mem

William C. Lott: dir, bd mem *B* Johnston SC 1914 *ED* Citadel BA 1935

Joan F. Phibbs: secy, treas, admin

James A. Randall: dir, bd mem

J. Paul Reeves: vp, bd mem, dir

Robert P. Timmerman: bd mem, dir *B* Warrenville SC 1920 *ED* Clemson Univ BA 1941 *CURR EMPL* dir: Graniteville Co *CORP AFFIL* chmn: C H Patrick & Co; chmn, ceo: Graniteville Intl Sales; dir: McCampbell Co Ltd (Tokyo Japan), Textile Hall Corp *NONPR AFFIL* chmn: Commun Svcs

APPLICATION INFORMATION
Initial Approach:

Send grant requests to the foundation.

Include a brief description of sponsoring organization, need to be addressed, financial resources available, constituency served by the grant, most recent audited financial statement or current operating budget, and a copy of the IRS tax exemption letter.

Submit applications at any time.

Applications are reviewed at the foundation office before presentation to the board of directors. Applicants are notified of the board's decision following regular meetings held bimonthly.

Restrictions on Giving: Other than scholarships, no grants are made to individuals. Grants are restricted to organizations operating in Georgia and South Carolina. The foundation does not provide grants for operating budgets.

PUBLICATIONS
Annual report

GRANTS ANALYSIS
Total Grants: $156,775*

Number of Grants: 34*

Highest Grant: $50,000

Average Grant: $4,611*

Typical Range: $1,000 to $15,000

Disclosure Period: 1993

Note: Figures exclude $78,216 given in scholarships to individuals. Total giving is $234,991. Recent grants are derived from a 1993 Form 990.

RECENT GRANTS

General

50,000	Clemson University Foundation, Clemson, SC
15,000	Independent Colleges and Universities of South Carolina, Columbia, SC
10,000	First Baptist Church, Vaucluse, SC
10,000	University Health Care Foundation, Augusta, GA
6,000	Georgia Foundation for Independent Colleges, Atlanta, GA

Self Foundation

CONTACT
Frank J. Wideman III
Executive Director
The Self Foundation
Drawer 1017
Greenwood, SC 29648
(803) 941-4036

FINANCIAL SUMMARY
Recent Giving: $1,496,000 (1994 est.); $1,298,834 (1993); $1,145,882 (1992)

Assets: $31,000,000 (1994 est.); $30,195,924 (1993); $30,000,000 (1992 approx.)

EIN: 57-0400594

CONTRIBUTIONS SUMMARY
Donor(s): The Self Foundation was founded in 1942 by the late James C. Self . Mr. Self was the founder of Greenwood Mills in Greenwood, SC. The original purpose of the foundation was to construct a hospital for Greenwood County. This mission was realized on November 1, 1951. At the time of the hospital's dedication, Mr. Self remarked that it was, "a debt of gratitude to the community that has been good to me."

Typical Recipients: • *Arts & Humanities:* Historic Preservation, Libraries, Museums/Galleries, Opera, Theater • *Civic & Public Affairs:* Nonprofit Management, Professional & Trade Associations, Safety • *Education:* Arts/Humanities Education, Colleges & Universities, Education Funds, Leadership Training, Private Education (Precollege), Public Education (Precollege), Science/Mathematics Education, Vocational & Technical Education • *Health:* Clinics/Medical Centers, Heart, Home-Care Services, Hospitals • *Science:* Scientific Centers & Institutes • *Social Services:* Community Service Organizations, Family Services, Senior Services, Sexual Abuse, Youth Organizations

Grant Types: capital, challenge, and project

Geographic Distribution: South Carolina, with emphasis on Greenwood area

GIVING OFFICERS
William B. Allin: treas

Joseph M. Anderson: trust

Virginia S. Brennan: trust *CORP AFFIL* dir: Greenwood Mills

Carroll H. Brooks: trust

R. Boykin Curry, Jr.: trust

Lynn W. Hodge: trust *B* 1947 *CURR EMPL* pres, ceo, dir: Un Fin Corp SC *CORP AFFIL* pres-ceo, dir: Un Savings Bank

J. C. Self III: trust

James Cuthbert Self, Sr.: pres, trust *B* Greenwood SC 1919 *ED* Citadel BS 1941 *CURR EMPL* chmn exec comm, dir: Greenwood Mills *CORP AFFIL* dir: Duke Power Co, Greenwood Motor Lines, SC Natl Bank; pres: Textile Investments Co *NONPR AFFIL* life mem bd trusts: Clemson Univ; mem: Am Textile Mfrs Inst, NY Cotton Exchange, SC Textile Mfrs Assn *CLUB AFFIL* Metropolitan *PHIL AFFIL* trust: Duke Endowment

Dr. Sally E. Self: trust

William Matthews Self: secy *B* 1948 *CURR EMPL* pres: Greenwood Mills *CORP AFFIL* dir: SC Natl Bank, SC Natl Corp; pres, dir: Lindale Mfg Co

Paul E. Welder: trust *B* Kansas City MO 1943 *ED* Univ VA 1965 *CURR EMPL* exec vp fin, dir: Greenwood Mills *CORP AFFIL* dir: Crescent-Greenwood, Jeantex Saca

Frank J. Wideman III: exec dir

APPLICATION INFORMATION
Initial Approach:
There are no application forms. A written proposal must be submitted.

Proposals must include a description of the organization's objectives and activities, its leadership, the project for which support is sought, and an implementation plan. Applicants also must include a copy of the organization's latest budget with income sources, a copy of IRS tax-exempt determination letter, and the most recent financial statement.

Proposals must be received by March 1, June 1, September 1, or December 1. Trustees meet the third week of March, June, September, and December. Late applications are held for consideration at the next meeting.

The trustees prefer to fund those organizations that have the financial potential to sustain projects on a continuing basis after funding.

Restrictions on Giving: No grants are made to individuals or for loans. The foundation also refrains from making recurring grants.

OTHER THINGS TO KNOW
In addition to making grants, the foundation also provides conferences and seminars.

PUBLICATIONS
Annual report

GRANTS ANALYSIS
Total Grants: $1,298,834

Number of Grants: 23

Highest Grant: $568,500

Average Grant: $56,471

Typical Range: $15,000 to $60,000

Disclosure Period: 1993

Note: Recent grants are derived from a 1993 Form 990.

RECENT GRANTS

General

568,500	J.C. Self Institute of Human Genetics, Greenwood, SC — assist with capital campaign to build a research institute to prevent birth defects and mental retardation
125,000	Greenwood Methodist Home, Greenwood, SC — assist with the cost of rehabilitating the Health Center (challenge grant)
100,000	Cambridge Academy, Greenwood, SC — assist with capital campaign to build classrooms and arts center (challenge grant)
75,000	Medical University of South Carolina, Charleston, SC — purchase an advanced two dimensional echocardiography and Doppler echocardiography device for outpatient clinical care facility within the Gazes Cardiac Research Institute
66,667	Independent Colleges and Universities of South Carolina, Columbia, SC — conduit for grant to Erskine College to assist with Campus Master Plan for computers (challenge grant)

Springs Foundation

CONTACT
Charles A. Bundy
President
Springs Foundation
PO Drawer 460
Lancaster, SC 29721
(803) 286-2196
Note: The foundation is located at 104 E Springs St., Lancaster, SC.

FINANCIAL SUMMARY
Recent Giving: $1,250,000 (1995 est.); $1,341,655 (1994 approx.); $1,461,468 (1993)

Assets: $25,238,370 (1993); $21,902,331 (1992); $20,342,234 (1991)

Gifts Received: $850 (1993)

EIN: 57-0426344

CONTRIBUTIONS SUMMARY
Donor(s): Colonel Elliott White Springs (1896-1959) was the founder of Springs Industries, one of the largest textile manufacturers in the United States. He established the foundation, formerly called the Elliott White Springs Foundation, in 1942. His wife, Frances Ley Springs , continued her husband's philanthropic interests through her work at the foundation. "Her estate provided the means for expanded philanthropic work over a wider geographic area. Those

funds began what is now called the Close Foundation."

Typical Recipients: • *Arts & Humanities:* Arts Associations & Councils, Community Arts, Libraries • *Civic & Public Affairs:* Botanical Gardens/Parks, Clubs, Economic Development, Employment/Job Training, Housing, Law & Justice, Municipalities/Towns, Safety • *Education:* Arts/Humanities Education, Business-School Partnerships, Colleges & Universities, Education Funds, Elementary Education (Public), Medical Education, Public Education (Precollege), Secondary Education (Public), Student Aid • *Environment:* General • *Health:* Cancer, Clinics/Medical Centers, Emergency/Ambulance Services, Health Organizations, Hospitals, Mental Health, Prenatal Health Issues • *Religion:* Churches, Religious Welfare • *Social Services:* Child Welfare, Community Service Organizations, Crime Prevention, Delinquency & Criminal Rehabilitation, Recreation & Athletics, Scouts, Substance Abuse, United Funds/United Ways, Youth Organizations

Grant Types: capital, challenge, endowment, project, and seed money

Geographic Distribution: Lancaster County, Chester Township of Chester County, and Fort Mill Township of York County, SC

GIVING OFFICERS
Crandall Close Bowles: dir *B* 1948 *CURR EMPL* pres: Springs Co *CORP AFFIL* dir: Duke Power Co, Richmond Fed Reserve Bank, Springs Indus; dir SC bd: SC Natl Bank *PHIL AFFIL* vp, treas, dir: Close Foundation

James Bradley: dir *CORP AFFIL* dir: Springs Co *PHIL AFFIL* dir: Close Foundation

Charles Alan Bundy: pres, dir *B* Cheraw SC 1930 *ED* Wofford Coll BA 1951 *NONPR AFFIL* dir: Elliott White Spring Meml Hosp; mem: Counc Fdns, Lancaster County Chamber Commerce *CLUB AFFIL* Rotary *PHIL AFFIL* pres, dir: Close Foundation

Anne Springs Close: don, chwm, dir *PHIL AFFIL* chmn, dir: Close Foundation

Derick Springsteen Close: dir *PHIL AFFIL* dir: Close Foundation

Elliott Springs Close: dir *PHIL AFFIL* dir: Close Foundation

Hugh William Close, Jr.: vp, dir *PHIL AFFIL* dir: Close Foundation

Katherine Anne Close: dir *PHIL AFFIL* dir: Close Foundation

Leroy Springs Close: dir *B* 1950 *CURR EMPL* pres: Sandlapper Fabrics *PHIL AFFIL* dir: Close Foundation

Pat Close: dir

Frances Close Hart: dir *PHIL AFFIL* dir: Close Foundation

R. C. Hubbard: dir

APPLICATION INFORMATION
Initial Approach:

Initial contact should take the form of a brief letter.

Letters should provide a brief statement of need.

Proposals are due by March 1 and November 1.

The president researches the proposal for merit, eligibility, and priority status. Recommendations are then presented to the board for approval. The board meets in April and November.

OTHER THINGS TO KNOW
The foundation is affiliated with the Close Foundation, also located in Lancaster, SC.

There is an interest-free student loan program available for students in Lancaster, Chester, and Fort Mill, SC, that are attending four-year colleges in South Carolina.

PUBLICATIONS
Annual report

GRANTS ANALYSIS
Total Grants: $1,461,468

Number of Grants: 47

Highest Grant: $725,000

Average Grant: $31,095

Typical Range: $1,000 to $50,000

Disclosure Period: 1993

Note: Recent grants are derived from a 1993 Form 990.

RECENT GRANTS
Library
15,000	Chester County Library, Chester, SC

General
725,000	Leroy Springs and Company, Ft. Mill, SC — maintenance
300,000	Leroy Springs and Company, Ft. Mill, SC — Springmaid Beach $4 million project
70,763	Elliott White Springs Memorial Hospital, Lancaster, SC — pneumatic tube delivery system
55,000	Lancaster County Healthy Mothers Healthy Babies Coalition, Lancaster, SC
31,687	Lancaster County School District, Lancaster, SC — school assistance programs

Stevens Foundation, John T.

CONTACT
Steve William, Sr.
President
John T. Stevens Fdn.
PO Box 158
Kershaw, SC 29067
(803) 432-6117

FINANCIAL SUMMARY
Recent Giving: $227,112 (fiscal 1994); $199,938 (fiscal 1991); $150,470 (fiscal 1990)

Assets: $4,754,739 (fiscal 1994); $3,953,259 (fiscal 1991); $3,803,300 (fiscal 1990)

EIN: 57-6005554

CONTRIBUTIONS SUMMARY
Donor(s): John T. Stevens

Typical Recipients: • *Arts & Humanities:* Arts Associations & Councils, Arts Centers, History & Archaeology, Libraries, Performing Arts • *Civic & Public Affairs:* Clubs, Municipalities/Towns, Safety • *Education:* Elementary Education (Public), Medical Education, Private Education (Precollege), Public Education (Precollege), Secondary Education (Public) • *Environment:* Resource Conservation • *Health:* Emergency/Ambulance Services, Health Organizations, Hospitals, Prenatal Health Issues • *Religion:* Churches • *Social Services:* Community Service Organizations, Crime Prevention, Domestic Violence, Recreation & Athletics, Scouts, United Funds/United Ways, Youth Organizations

Grant Types: general support

Geographic Distribution: focus on SC

GIVING OFFICERS
Virginia Davidson: asst secy

Mattie Seegars: secy

Douglas Williams: vp

Steve Williams, Jr.: treas

Steve L. Williams, Sr.: pres

APPLICATION INFORMATION
Initial Approach: Send brief letter of inquiry describing program or project. Include a description of organization, amount requested, purpose of funds sought, recently audited financial statement, and proof of tax-exempt status.

GRANTS ANALYSIS
Total Grants: $227,112

Number of Grants: 44

Highest Grant: $35,000

Typical Range: $100 to $20,000

Disclosure Period: fiscal year ending May 31, 1994

Note: Recent grants are derived from a fiscal 1994 Form 990.

RECENT GRANTS
General
35,000	Kershaw Cemetery Perpetual Care Trustees, Kershaw, SC
20,000	Health Sciences Foundation-Medical University
17,775	Town of Kershaw, Kershaw, SC
10,000	Heath Springs Baptist Church, Heath Springs, SC
10,000	Kershaw Second Baptist Church, Kershaw, SC

Symmes Foundation, F. W.

CONTACT
Gerald Lane
F. W. Symmes Fdn.
c/o Wachovia Bank, Trust Dept.
1401 Maine St.
Columbia, SC 29226-9365
(803) 765-3677

FINANCIAL SUMMARY
Recent Giving: $435,000 (fiscal 1994);
$633,500 (fiscal 1992); $468,800 (fiscal
1990)

Assets: $10,782,327 (fiscal 1993);
$9,488,315 (fiscal 1992); $8,385,832 (fiscal
1990)

EIN: 57-6017472

CONTRIBUTIONS SUMMARY
Donor(s): the late F.W. Symmes

Typical Recipients: • *Arts & Humanities:*
Arts Centers, Historic Preservation, Librar-
ies, Performing Arts, Theater • *Civic & Pub-
lic Affairs:* Municipalities/Towns, Urban &
Community Affairs • *Education:* Colleges &
Universities, Literacy • *Environment:* Gen-
eral • *Health:* Clinics/Medical Centers, Hos-
pitals • *Religion:* Churches, Ministries,
Religious Welfare • *Social Services:*
Food/Clothing Distribution, Homes,
YMCA/YWCA/YMHA/YWHA

Grant Types: capital and project

Geographic Distribution: focus on Greenville, SC

GIVING OFFICERS
Wachovia Trust Dept.: corp trust

William H. Orders: trust

Eleanor Welling: trust

F. McKinnon Wilkinson: trust

APPLICATION INFORMATION
Initial Approach: Send brief letter of inquiry describing program or project. Include
a description of organization, amount requested, purpose of funds sought, recently
audited financial statement, and proof of tax-
exempt status. There are no deadlines.

Restrictions on Giving: Does not support
individuals.

PUBLICATIONS
Application Guidelines, Informational Brochure

GRANTS ANALYSIS
Total Grants: $435,000

Number of Grants: 11

Highest Grant: $100,000

Typical Range: $2,500 to $50,000

Disclosure Period: fiscal year ending
March 31, 1994

Note: Recent grants are derived from a fiscal 1994 Form 990.

RECENT GRANTS
Library
| 50,000 | Greenville County Library, Greenville, SC |

General
100,000	YMCA Camp Greenville-Mulligan PJT, Greenville, SC
50,000	Greenville Free Medical Clinic, Greenville, SC
50,000	Salvation Army, Greenville, SC
50,000	United Ministries, Greenville, SC
37,500	Miracle Hill Ministries, Greenville, SC

TENNESSEE

Ansley Foundation, Dantzler Bond

CONTACT
Kim Williams
Trust Officer
Dantzler Bond Ansley Fdn.
c/o Third National Bank
PO Box 305110
Nashville, TN 37230-5110
(615) 748-7194

FINANCIAL SUMMARY
Recent Giving: $272,500 (fiscal 1994);
$268,500 (fiscal 1992); $246,500 (fiscal
1991)

Assets: $7,307,800 (fiscal 1994);
$6,783,132 (fiscal 1992); $6,452,231 (fiscal
1991)

EIN: 59-2111990

CONTRIBUTIONS SUMMARY
Donor(s): the late Mildred B. Ansley

Typical Recipients: • *Arts & Humanities:*
Historic Preservation, Libraries, Muse-
ums/Galleries, Music • *Civic & Public Af-
fairs:* General, Law & Justice, Legal Aid,
Municipalities/Towns, Zoos/Aquariums
• *Education:* Colleges & Universities, Legal
Education, Medical Education, Private Edu-
cation (Precollege) • *Health:* Cancer, Chil-
dren's Health/Hospitals, Health
Organizations, Medical Research, Mental
Health, Respiratory, Single-Disease Health
Associations • *Religion:* Churches, Minis-
tries, Missionary Activities (Domestic), Re-
ligious Organizations, Religious Welfare •
Social Services: Child Welfare, Community
Service Organizations, Counseling, Family
Services, General, Homes, People with Dis-
abilities, Recreation & Athletics, Scouts,
Special Olympics, Substance Abuse, United
Funds/United Ways,
YMCA/YWCA/YMHA/YWHA, Youth Or-
ganizations

Grant Types: capital and general support

Geographic Distribution: focus on Nashville, TN

GIVING OFFICERS
Third National Bank: trust

APPLICATION INFORMATION
Initial Approach: Send letter of inquiry.
Deadline is May 31.

GRANTS ANALYSIS
Total Grants: $272,500

Number of Grants: 44

Highest Grant: $50,000

Typical Range: $100 to $22,500

Disclosure Period: fiscal year ending April
30, 1994

Note: Recent grants are derived from a fiscal 1994 Form 990.

RECENT GRANTS
Library
| 1,900 | Brentwood Academy Duncan Library, Nashville, TN |
| 1,000 | Vanderbilt University, Nashville, TN — for Jean and Alexander Heard Library |

General
50,000	United Way, Nashville, TN
22,500	Montgomery Bell Academy, Nashville, TN
10,000	Fannie Battle Day Home, Nashville, TN
10,000	Sarah Cannon Cancer Foundation, Nashville, TN
10,000	YMCA, Nashville, TN

Benwood Foundation

CONTACT
Jean McDaniel
Executive Director
Benwood Foundation
1600 American National Bank Bldg.
736 Market St.
Chattanooga, TN 37402
(615) 267-4311

FINANCIAL SUMMARY
Recent Giving: $3,000,000 (1995 est.);
$3,392,000 (1994 approx.); $6,660,626
(1993)

Assets: $68,000,000 (1995 est.);
$68,000,000 (1994); $70,608,525 (1993)

EIN: 62-0476283

CONTRIBUTIONS SUMMARY
Donor(s): The donor of the Benwood Foundation was George T. Hunter . At the time
of his death in 1950, he was chairman of the
board of the Coca-Cola Bottling Company
(Thomas, Inc.). Mr. Hunter's uncle, Benjamin F. Thomas, was one of the founders of
the Coca-Cola bottling industry. Most of
Mr. Hunter's holdings in the bottling company were bequeathed to the foundation.

Typical Recipients: • *Arts & Humanities:*
Arts Associations & Councils, Arts Funds,
Ballet, General, Libraries, Museums/Galler-

ies, Music, Opera, Performing Arts, Theater • *Civic & Public Affairs:* Chambers of Commerce, Community Foundations, Economic Development, Parades/Festivals • *Education:* Business Education, Colleges & Universities, Continuing Education, Education Associations, Education Funds, Education Reform, Elementary Education (Private), Legal Education, Private Education (Precollege), Public Education (Precollege), Secondary Education (Private) • *Environment:* Air/Water Quality, General, Resource Conservation • *Health:* Clinics/Medical Centers, Health Organizations, Mental Health • *Religion:* Religious Organizations, Religious Welfare, Social/Policy Issues • *Science:* Science Exhibits & Fairs • *Social Services:* Child Welfare, Community Service Organizations, Family Services, Food/Clothing Distribution, Recreation & Athletics, Senior Services, Substance Abuse, United Funds/United Ways, Youth Organizations

Grant Types: challenge and project

Geographic Distribution: primarily Tennessee, principally Chattanooga

GIVING OFFICERS
Sebert Brewer, Jr.: chmn, trust

E. Y. Chapin III: pres, trust

Jean McDaniel: exec dir

Susan R. Randolph: secy, treas

Robert J. Sudderth, Jr.: vp, trust *B* Chattanooga TN 1942 *CURR EMPL* exec off: Am Natl Bank & Trust Co *CORP AFFIL* dir: Dixie Yarns

APPLICATION INFORMATION
Initial Approach:

A two-page letter requesting an application form should be sent to the foundation.

The letter should include the amount needed and an explanation of project for which funding is sought. Also include proof of tax exemption, a list of officers, and budget information.

The board of trustees meets quarterly in the months of January, April, July, and October to consider applications. Applications must be received by the twenty-fifth of the month preceding the meeting at which consideration is desired.

The board looks favorably on proposals for projects dealing with education, health, the humanities, religion, and social welfare, particularly in and around Chattanooga. The trustees reserve the right to delay final decision on grant requests for a two-month period.

Restrictions on Giving: The foundation does not provide gifts to endowments or continuing operating support.

GRANTS ANALYSIS
Total Grants: $6,660,626

Number of Grants: 151

Highest Grant: $1,200,000

Average Grant: $29,937*

Typical Range: $1,000 to $10,000 and $25,000 to $100,000

Disclosure Period: 1993

Note: The average grant figure excludes the two highest grants totaling $2,200,000. Recent grants are derived from a 1992 Form 990.

RECENT GRANTS
Library
25,000   Chattanooga-Hamilton County Library, Chattanooga, TN

General
620,000   McCallie School, Chattanooga, TN
375,000   Siskin Memorial Foundation
355,000   Baylor School Hugh Huddleston, Chattanooga, TN
330,000   Girls Preparatory School, Chattanooga, TN
250,000   Orange Grove Center, Chattanooga, TN

Bridgestone/Firestone, Inc. / Bridgestone/Firestone Trust Fund, The

Employees: 40,000
Parent Company: Bridgestone Corp.
Parent Sales: $5.1 billion
Headquarters: Nashville, TN
SIC Major Group: Tires & Inner Tubes, Fabricated Rubber Products Nec, and Tires & Tubes

CONTACT
Bernice Csaszar
Administrator
Bridgestone/Firestone, Inc.
50 Century Blvd.
Nashville, TN 37214
(615) 872-1415

FINANCIAL SUMMARY
Recent Giving: $1,730,426 (1993); $1,570,227 (1992); $1,585,162 (1991)

Assets: $15,369,587 (1993); $14,834,760 (1992); $13,909,015 (1991)

Fiscal Note: Above figures are for the foundation only. Above figures exclude nonmonetary support.

EIN: 34-6505181

CONTRIBUTIONS SUMMARY
Typical Recipients: • *Arts & Humanities:* Arts Associations & Councils, Arts Institutes, Community Arts, Dance, Historic Preservation, Libraries, Museums/Galleries, Music, Public Broadcasting, Theater • *Civic & Public Affairs:* Business/Free Enterprise, Civil Rights, Economic Development, Employment/Job Training, General, Housing, Law & Justice, Professional & Trade Associations, Public Policy, Urban & Community Affairs, Zoos/Aquariums • *Education:* Agricultural Education, Business Education, Colleges & Universities, Economic Education, Education Funds, Engineering/Technological Education, International Studies, Medical Education, Minority Education, Public Education (Precollege), Religious Education, Science/Mathematics Education, Special Education, Student Aid • *Environ-*

ment: General • *Health:* Children's Health/Hospitals, Health Organizations, Hospitals, Medical Research, Single-Disease Health Associations • *Religion:* Ministries • *Science:* Scientific Centers & Institutes, Scientific Organizations • *Social Services:* Child Welfare, Community Centers, Community Service Organizations, Emergency Relief, Family Planning, Family Services, People with Disabilities, Recreation & Athletics, Substance Abuse, United Funds/United Ways, Volunteer Services, Youth Organizations

Grant Types: capital, challenge, employee matching gifts, general support, operating expenses, project, scholarship, and seed money

Nonmonetary Support Types: cause-related marketing & promotion and in-kind services

Note: Value of noncash support is unavailable.

Geographic Distribution: near headquarters and operating locations only

Operating Locations: AR (Prescott, Russellville), IA (Des Moines), IL (Bloomington, Decatur, Rolling Meadows), IN (Indianapolis, Noblesville), LA (Lake Charles), NC (Gastonia, King Mountain, Wilson), OK (Oklahoma City), TN (LaVergie, Morrison, Nashville), TX (Ft. Stockton, Orange), VA (Hopewell)

Note: Also operate in Canada, Mexico, Europe, South and Central America, Liberia, and Singapore.

CORP. OFFICERS
Masatoshi Ono: *B* 1937 *ED* Kumamoto Univ Japan BS 1959 *CURR EMPL* ceo, dir: Bridgestone/Firestone Inc

GIVING OFFICERS
Bernice Csaszar: admin

Trevor C. Hoskins: chmn *CURR EMPL* vp pub aff: Bridgestone/Firestone Inc

APPLICATION INFORMATION
Initial Approach: *Initial Contact:* brief letter or proposal; organizations in communities where Bridgestone/Firestone operates should write to local plant manager *Include Information On:* description of the organization; amount requested; purpose for which funds are sought; recently audited financial statement; and proof of tax-exempt status *Deadlines:* none

Restrictions on Giving: Recipients must have 501(c)(3) status and must operate in accordance with the principle of equal opportunity. Grants do not support groups that discriminate, partisan political organizations, or sectarian religious organizations.

OTHER THINGS TO KNOW
In 1992, the company relocated its corporate headquarters from Akron, OH, to Nashville, TN.

In 1989, Bridgestone U.S.A., Inc., merged with Firestone Tire & Rubber Co. to become Bridgestone/Firestone, Inc., a wholly owned subsidiary of Bridgestone Corp. of Japan.

Although Bridgestone/Firestone, Inc., is now privately owned, company intends to main-

tain giving levels and priorities established
in prior years.

PUBLICATIONS
Guidelines

GRANTS ANALYSIS
Total Grants: $1,730,426

Number of Grants: 672*

Highest Grant: $221,820

Average Grant: $2,575*

Typical Range: $100 to $5,000

Disclosure Period: 1993

Note: The figures for average grant and
number of grants are approximate. Recent
grants are derived from a 1993 Form 990.

RECENT GRANTS

General

221,820	National Merit Scholarship Corporation, Evanston, IL
100,000	Akron Golf Charities Foundation, Akron, OH
100,000	American Truck Stop Foundation, Alexandria, VA
50,253	National 4-H Council, Chevy Chase, MD
42,000	United Way Central Iowa, Des Moines, IA

Christy-Houston Foundation

CONTACT
James R. Arnhart
Executive Director
Christy-Houston Foundation
1296 Dow St.
Murfreesboro, TN 37130
(615) 898-1140

FINANCIAL SUMMARY
Recent Giving: $3,000,000 (fiscal 1995
est.); $2,846,276 (fiscal 1994); $3,034,497
(fiscal 1993)

Assets: $62,000,000 (fiscal 1995 est.);
$62,984,672 (fiscal 1994); $61,767,838 (fiscal 1993)

Gifts Received: $536,630 (fiscal 1991);
$82,816 (fiscal 1990); $1,740,731 (fiscal 1988)

Fiscal Note: In 1991, a contribution was received from the Middle Tennessee Medical Center.

EIN: 62-1280998

CONTRIBUTIONS SUMMARY
Donor(s): The foundation was established
in 1987 with funding from the sale of a hospital.

Typical Recipients: • *Arts & Humanities:*
Libraries, Music • *Education:* Colleges &
Universities, Medical Education, Student
Aid • *Health:* Health Organizations, Hospices, Hospitals • *Social Services:* Scouts,
YMCA/YWCA/YMHA/YWHA, Youth Organizations

Grant Types: capital

Geographic Distribution: Rutherford
County, TN

GIVING OFFICERS
James R. Arnhart: exec dir

Granville S. R. Bouldin: dir

Henry King Butler: dir

Ed Delbridge: dir

Ed Elam: dir

Larry N. Haynes: dir

John S. Holmes, Jr.: dir

William H. Huddleston: off

Louis C. Jennings: dir

Roger C. Maples: dir

Hubert McCullough: dir

Edward E. Miller, Jr.: dir

Matt B. Murfree III: dir

Myers B. Parsons: dir

APPLICATION INFORMATION
Initial Approach:

Interested organizations should contact the
foundation for application information and
forms.

All applicants will be requested to provide
the following information: the name and address of the applicant; specific geographic
target area; affiliations with any other organization; list of any other organizations
doing the same or similar work in geographic area; a statement explaining how future funding for the project will be handled.
The applicant will also be requested to submit a program description which includes
the objectives and purposes of the project, a
planned method for evaluation, and the
amount of funding requested with an explanation of why funding from the Christy-
Houston foundation is needed. Along with
the application, organizations will be required to attach a copy of their most recent
determination letter from the IRS, a copy of
their most recent Form 990, a list of governing board members and their affiliations, a
list of any officers or paid staff, identity of
other sources of funding currently solicited,
and a copy of their most recent financial
statement together with a line-item operating budget incidental to the proposed project.

Applications are accepted at any time.

All applications are evaluated on individual
merit, and final approval is determined by
the board of directors which meets quarterly
during the months of June, September, December and March. Replies to applications
are made in the quarter following the one in
which they were considered.

Restrictions on Giving: The foundation
does not support organizations that do not
have tax-exempt status, legislative or lobbying efforts, religious organizations or endeavors, veterans organizations, any
program supported with tax funds, or payment to physicians or surgeons except for
radical or extraordinary treatment.

PUBLICATIONS
Application form

GRANTS ANALYSIS
Total Grants: $2,846,276

Number of Grants: 8

Highest Grant: $1,295,276

Average Grant: $355,785

Typical Range: $300,000 to $1,000,000

Disclosure Period: fiscal year ending April
30, 1994

Note: Recent grants are derived from a fiscal 1994 Form 990.

RECENT GRANTS

Library

50,000	City of Lavergne, Lavergne, TN — for public library building

General

1,295,276	Middle Tennessee State University, Murfreesboro, TN — for nursing department classroom building
1,000,000	YMCA, Murfreesboro, TN — for new building
300,000	Boys and Girls Club, Murfreesboro, TN — to purchase land for new building
120,000	Community Helpers, Murfreesboro, TN — for prescription drugs for the indigent
50,000	Boy Scouts of America, Murfreesboro, TN — for camp/endowment campaign

---

Clarkson Foundation, Jeniam

CONTACT
Charlotte Giannini
Executive Director
Jeniam Clarkson Fdn.
3030 Poplar Ave.
Memphis, TN 38111
(901) 325-4341

FINANCIAL SUMMARY
Recent Giving: $177,750 (1993)

Assets: $6,620,910 (1993)

Gifts Received: $437,500 (1993)

Fiscal Note: In 1993, contributions were received from Andrew M. and Carole G. Clarkson.

EIN: 62-1516244

CONTRIBUTIONS SUMMARY
Typical Recipients: • *Arts & Humanities:*
Arts Associations & Councils, History & Archaeology, Libraries, Museums/Galleries,
Music, Performing Arts • *Civic & Public Affairs:* General • *Education:* Private Education (Precollege) • *Environment:* Wildlife
Protection • *Health:* Arthritis, Children's

Health/Hospitals • *Religion:* Churches, Religious Welfare • *Social Services:* Community Service Organizations, Family Services

Grant Types: general support

Geographic Distribution: focus on CT and TN

GIVING OFFICERS

Andrew Macbeth Clarkson: trust *B* Glasgow Scotland 1937 *ED* Oxford Univ BA 1960; McGill Univ 1961; Harvard Univ MBA 1966; Oxford Univ MA 1980 *CURR EMPL* dir, secy, treas: Autozone *CORP AFFIL* dir: Flynn Indus, Royal Furniture *CLUB AFFIL* Crescent, Field, Harvard

Carole G. Clarkson: adv bd

Jennifer M. Clarkson: adv bd

Charlotte Giannini: exec dir

APPLICATION INFORMATION

Initial Approach: Send a brief letter of inquiry. Include a description of organization, amount requested, purpose of funds sought, recently audited financial statement, and proof of tax-exempt status. There are no deadlines.

GRANTS ANALYSIS

Total Grants: $177,750

Number of Grants: 18

Highest Grant: $62,500

Typical Range: $100 to $55,000

Disclosure Period: 1993

Note: Recent grants are derived from a 1993 Form 990.

RECENT GRANTS

Library
500	New Canaan Library, New Canaan, CT

General
55,000	New York Zoological Society Wildlife Conservation Society, Bronx, NY — for permanent housing for and research on Maribou storks
16,000	Horizons, New Canaan, CT — fund study to provide summer program for disadvantaged students
5,000	Family and Children's Aid, New Canaan, CT — capital fund for acquisition of office building
5,000	Greenwich Academy, New Canaan, CT
5,000	Interfaith Services, New Canaan, CT — form study group to review gaps in community's elderly care services

First Tennessee Bank

Parent Company: First Tennessee National Corp.
Parent Employees: 4,563
Headquarters: Memphis, TN
SIC Major Group: National Commercial Banks

CONTACT
Carol C. Coletta
Community Investment Representative
First Tennessee Bank
41 Union Ave.
Memphis, TN 38103
(901) 528-0800

FINANCIAL SUMMARY

Recent Giving: $1,100,000 (1991 approx.); $900,000 (1990); $900,000 (1989)

Fiscal Note: Company gives directly.

CONTRIBUTIONS SUMMARY

Typical Recipients: • *Arts & Humanities:* Arts Associations & Councils, Arts Centers, Arts Festivals, Arts Funds, Arts Institutes, Community Arts, Dance, Ethnic & Folk Arts, Historic Preservation, Libraries, Museums/Galleries, Music, Opera, Performing Arts, Public Broadcasting, Theater, Visual Arts • *Civic & Public Affairs:* Business/Free Enterprise, Civil Rights, Economic Development, Professional & Trade Associations, Public Policy, Urban & Community Affairs, Zoos/Aquariums • *Education:* Colleges & Universities, Economic Education, Elementary Education (Private), Faculty Development, Preschool Education, Public Education (Precollege) • *Environment:* General • *Health:* Hospitals • *Social Services:* Community Service Organizations, United Funds/United Ways, Volunteer Services, Youth Organizations

Grant Types: capital, challenge, general support, professorship, and project

Nonmonetary Support: $5,000 (1990); $10,000 (1989); $15,000 (1988)

Nonmonetary Support Types: donated equipment, donated products, in-kind services, loaned employees, loaned executives, and workplace solicitation

Note: Value of nonmonetary support is not available. For information on noncash requests and employee volunteer programs, contact Sue Jacks, corporate communications, at the above address. For other nonmonetary giving contacts, see "Other Things To Know."

Geographic Distribution: in Tennessee, near operating locations only

Operating Locations: TN (Chattanooga, Cookeville, Dandridge, Dyersburg, Franklin, Gallatin, Greenville, Jackson, Johnson City, Kingsport, Knoxville, Maryville, Memphis, Morristown, Murfreesboro, Nashville)

CORP. OFFICERS
John C. Kelley, Jr.: *ED* Memphis St Univ 1967 *CURR EMPL* exec vp, group mgr: First TN Natl Corp Memphis Banking Group *CORP AFFIL* exec vp: First TN Bank NA Natl Assn

K. Nerator Raff: *CURR EMPL* pres: First TN Bank

GIVING OFFICERS

Carol C. Coletta: *CURR EMPL* commun investment rep: First TN Bank

APPLICATION INFORMATION

Initial Approach: *Initial Contact:* brief letter of inquiry to determine interest; proposal only after review by First Tennessee Bank results in invitation to apply *Include Information On:* (after interest has been shown by First Tennessee Bank) a proposal that includes: name, address, telephone number and contact person of organization; brief description of the organization's history, accomplishments, and goals; objectives of program to be funded; amount sought in relation to total need; expected project outcomes; proposed evaluation method; geographic area and number of people served; current operating budget, expected project costs, and most recently audited financial statement; other funding sources, including government, individuals, foundations, corporations, and united funds; list of officers, board of directors, and other principals of the organization; involvement of volunteers in the organization; and proof of tax-exempt status *Deadlines:* submit proposal by the October prior to the year for which funding is requested *Note:* The program is decentralized; apply to Memphis office for proposals with a statewide or Memphis area focus; apply to local bank president for proposals of a local or regional focus.

Restrictions on Giving: Grants are not made to individuals; charities sponsored solely by a single civic organization; charities that redistribute funds to other organizations, except recognized united funds and arts funds; member agencies of the United Way or united arts funds; bank "clearinghouse" organizations; religious, veterans, social, athletic, or fraternal organizations; political organizations or other groups promoting a specific ideological point of view; trips or tours; operating budget deficits; multiyear commitments of four years or more; endowments; tickets to fund-raising benefits; goodwill advertising; or member agencies of united funds.

OTHER THINGS TO KNOW

For information on sponsorships and marketing promotion, contact Terry Lee, Vice President, Corporate Communications, c/o First Tennessee Bank, Box 84, Memphis, TN 38101, (901) 523-4380.

HCA Foundation

CONTACT
Kenneth L. Roberts
President and Executive Director
HCA Foundation
One Park Plz.
PO Box 550
Nashville, TN 37202-0550
(615) 320-2165

FINANCIAL SUMMARY
Recent Giving: $4,500,000 (1995 est.);
$3,300,000 (1994 approx.); $2,377,351
(1993)

Assets: $55,434,212 (1990); $22,649,548
(1988)

EIN: 62-1134070

CONTRIBUTIONS SUMMARY
Donor(s): The HCA Foundation was established in 1982 as a corporate foundation, sponsored by Hospital Corporation of America.

Typical Recipients: • *Arts & Humanities:* Arts Appreciation, Arts Associations & Councils, Arts Centers, Arts Funds, Arts Institutes, Dance, Historic Preservation, Libraries, Museums/Galleries, Music, Opera, Performing Arts, Public Broadcasting, Theater, Visual Arts • *Civic & Public Affairs:* Business/Free Enterprise, Civil Rights, Economic Development, Economic Policy, Employment/Job Training, Housing, Law & Justice, Nonprofit Management, Public Policy, Rural Affairs, Safety, Urban & Community Affairs, Women's Affairs, Zoos/Aquariums • *Education:* Arts/Humanities Education, Business Education, Colleges & Universities, Community & Junior Colleges, Economic Education, Education Associations, Education Funds, Health & Physical Education, Literacy, Medical Education, Minority Education, Preschool Education, Public Education (Precollege), Student Aid • *Environment:* General • *Health:* Health Policy/Cost Containment, Health Organizations, Medical Training, Mental Health, Nursing Services, Public Health • *Religion:* Religious Organizations, Religious Welfare • *Science:* Science Exhibits & Fairs • *Social Services:* Child Welfare, Community Centers, Community Service Organizations, Delinquency & Criminal Rehabilitation, Domestic Violence, Family Planning, Family Services, Food/Clothing Distribution, Homes, People with Disabilities, Recreation & Athletics, Senior Services, Shelters/Homelessness, Substance Abuse, United Funds/United Ways, Volunteer Services, Youth Organizations

Grant Types: capital, general support, and project

Geographic Distribution: restricted to Nashville, TN organizations

GIVING OFFICERS
Peter F. Bird, Jr.: sr program off, secy

Jack Oliver Bovender, Jr.: dir *B* Winston-Salem NC 1945 *ED* Duke Univ AB 1967;
Duke Univ MHA 1969 *CURR EMPL* sr vp: Hosp Corp Am *CORP AFFIL* dir: Quorum *NONPR AFFIL* fellow: Am Coll Healthcare Execs; mem: Duke Univ Gen Alumni Bd, Duke Univ Hosp Health Admin, Leadership Nashville; mem editorial bd: Health Admin Press, Journal Health Admin Ed *CLUB AFFIL* Rotary

Robert C. Crosby: dir *CORP AFFIL* pres, ceo, dir: AM Transitional Hosps

Helen K. Cummings: dir

Frank F. Drowota III: dir *B* Williamsburg KY 1938 *ED* Vanderbilt Univ BA 1960; Vanderbilt Univ JD 1965 *NONPR AFFIL* chief justice: TN Supreme Ct

Thomas Fearn Frist, Jr.: chmn *B* Nashville TN 1938 *ED* Vanderbilt Univ BS 1961; Washington Univ MD 1966 *CURR EMPL* chmn, dir: Columbia/HCA Healthcare Corp

Carolyn Gaines: adm asst

Amelia Green: program assoc

Charles J. Kane: dir *CURR EMPL* chmn exec comm: Third Natl Corp

Ralph Clayton McWhorter: dir *B* Chattanooga TN 1933 *ED* Univ TN 1951-1952; Samford Univ BS 1955 *CURR EMPL* chmn, pres, ceo: HealthTrust Inc

Kenneth Lewis Roberts: pres, exec dir *B* Dungannon VA 1932 *ED* Vanderbilt Univ BA 1954; Vanderbilt Univ LLB 1959 *CURR EMPL* chmn mgmt devel ctr: First Am Corp *CORP AFFIL* dir: Central Natl Corp *NONPR AFFIL* dir: Leadership Nashville; mem: Am Bar Assn, Nashville Bar Assn, Nashville Chamber Commerce, TN Bar Assn; mem exec bd: Boy Scouts Am Middle TN Counc; trust: Vanderbilt Univ *CLUB AFFIL* Belle Meade CC, Cumberland, Ponte Vedra FL Inn & Club

Mary Ellen Vanderwilt: program off

APPLICATION INFORMATION
Initial Approach:

Send a letter of inquiry or call the foundation.

The initial inquiry should include an annual report of the applicant organization, a record accomplishments, objectives of program to be funded and who will benefit, amount sought from foundation in relation to total need, how foundation funds will be used, proposed method of evaluating program's success, copy of IRS determination letter; foundation may also request copy of Form 990, budget, list of board members and their affiliations, list of current sources of support and amounts contributed, and list of other funding sources being approached for support.

Proposals are accepted and reviewed throughout the year. Decisions on proposals are generally made within one month of submission, except for those scheduled for review at quarterly board meetings. All proposals are acknowledged promptly.

Among the issues considered during the evaluation are the organization's history of success, including financial statements reflecting an ability to manage funds well; the program objectives and its intended beneficiaries; whether the program treats the causes of the problem or its effects; duplication of effort of other groups; the organization's efforts to collaborate with others; how the organization proposes to measure the results of its effort; what plans the organization has for future funding. Foundation staff review proposals and conducts personal interviews or site visits, as necesssary. Requests for more than $1,000 require review and approval by the board of directors.

Restrictions on Giving: For legal reasons, the foundation does not support individuals or their projects, private foundations, political activities, advertising or sponsorships. As a matter of policy, the foundation does not ordinarily support organizations outside the Nashville area; operating expenses of individual United Way member agencies; schools below the college level; colleges and universities outside the Nashville area; disease-specific organizations seeking support for national projects and programs; biomedical or clinical research; hospitals; newsletters, magazines, or books; trips or tours; projects or programs of religious, fraternal, athletic or veterans groups when the primary beneficiaries of such undertakings would be their own members; endowments; social events, telethons, or similar fundraising activities.

OTHER THINGS TO KNOW
In 1993, when HCA merged with Columbia Healthcare to become Columbia/HCA, the foundation retained its status as a private, independent foundation.

The HCA Foundation has discontinued its hospital grants program and is limiting its grantmaking to the greater Nashville area.

The foundation expects an annual report from recipients once a grant is made. Demonstration of accountability is an important factor in considering future funding.

PUBLICATIONS
HCA Foundation Newsletter

GRANTS ANALYSIS
Total Grants: $2,377,351*

Number of Grants: 127*

Highest Grant: $196,055

Average Grant: $18,719*

Typical Range: $1,000 to $30,000

Disclosure Period: 1993

Note: Total grants, number of grants, and average grant figures exclude 71 matching gifts of less than $5,000 each. Recent grants are derived from a partial 1994 grants list.

RECENT GRANTS

General

50,000	Boy Scouts of America/Middle Tennessee Council, Nashville, TN — additional support for $7.8 million capital, endowment, and operating campaign, to help match a challenge grant from the Kresge foundation
50,000	Martha O'Bryan Center, Nashville, TN — support for

50,000	a $2 million capital and endowment campaign McNeilly Center for Children, Nashville, TN — support for a $500,000 capital campaign to rebuild the building serving school-age children
50,000	Tennessee State University Foundation, Nashville, TN — funding to retain a director for the alumni scholarship fund campaign
50,000	YMCA of Nashville and Middle Tennessee, Nashville, TN — additional support for the Outdoor Family Center at the East Nashville YMCA

Massengill-DeFriece Foundation

CONTACT
Frank W. DeFriece, Jr.
Vice President
Massengill-DeFriece Fdn.
Holston Plaza, Ste. 208
516 Holston Ave.
Bristol, TN 37620
(615) 764-3833

FINANCIAL SUMMARY
Recent Giving: $188,400 (1991); $172,850 (1990); $160,580 (1989)

Assets: $4,425,311 (1991); $3,911,294 (1990); $4,067,628 (1989)

EIN: 62-6044873

CONTRIBUTIONS SUMMARY
Donor(s): the late Frank W. DeFriece, the late Pauline M. DeFriece, Frank W. De-Friece, Jr., Josephine D. Wilson

Typical Recipients: • *Arts & Humanities:* Historic Preservation, Libraries, Museums/Galleries • *Civic & Public Affairs:* Municipalities/Towns • *Education:* Colleges & Universities, Health & Physical Education, Literacy • *Environment:* General • *Health:* Medical Rehabilitation, Mental Health • *Social Services:* Child Welfare, Community Service Organizations, Counseling, United Funds/United Ways, Youth Organizations

Grant Types: capital, emergency, endowment, general support, multiyear/continuing support, operating expenses, professorship, and project

Geographic Distribution: focus on the Bristol, TN, and Bristol, VA, areas

GIVING OFFICERS
Frank W. DeFriece, Jr.: vp

Mark W. DeFriece: dir

Paul E. DeFriece: dir

C. Richard Hagerstrom, Jr.: dir

Albert S. Kelly, Jr.: pres

John C. Paty, Jr.: secy, treas

Josephine D. Wilson: vp

APPLICATION INFORMATION
Initial Approach: Send brief letter of inquiry and full proposal. There are no deadlines.

Restrictions on Giving: Does not support individuals or provide loans.

GRANTS ANALYSIS
Total Grants: $188,400

Number of Grants: 18

Highest Grant: $32,000

Typical Range: $2,000 to $10,000

Disclosure Period: 1991

Note: Recent grants are derived from a 1991 Form 990.

RECENT GRANTS
General
32,000	Virginia Intermont College, Richmond, VA
30,000	Bristol Regional Counseling Center, Bristol, TN
10,000	Appalachian Girl Scout Council, Bristol, TN
10,000	Children's Advocacy Center of Sullivan County, Bristol, TN
5,000	Bristol Regional Rehabilitation Center, Bristol, TN

Potter Foundation, Justin and Valere

CONTACT
Justin P. Wilson
Chairman and Trustee
Justin and Valere Potter Foundation
c/o Waller, Lansden, Dortch and Davis
511 Union St., Ste. 2100
Nashville, TN 37219
(615) 244-6380
Note: Another contact is Lois Squires, trust officer, NationsBank, One NationsBank Plaza M-7, Nashville, TN 37239-1697, (615) 749-3336.

FINANCIAL SUMMARY
Recent Giving: $1,490,000 (1993); $977,500 (1991); $1,177,000 (1990)

Assets: $27,028,075 (1993); $25,898,867 (1991); $21,563,402 (1990)

EIN: 62-6033081

CONTRIBUTIONS SUMMARY
Donor(s): The Justin and Valere Potter Foundation was established in Tennessee in 1951 by the late Justin Potter and his wife, Valere Blair Potter. Mr. Potter, a financier and industrialist, founded the Nashville Coal Company and was chairman of the Virginia-Carolina Chemical Corporation. He also served as president of the Chemical Securities Company, chairman of the Cherokee Insurance Company, and director of Commerce Union Bank. The foundation holds a significant portion of Mobil Oil Corporation stock.

Typical Recipients: • *Arts & Humanities:* Historic Preservation, Libraries, Museums/Galleries, Music • *Education:* Colleges & Universities, Medical Education, Student Aid • *Religion:* Religious Welfare • *Social Services:* Family Services, Youth Organizations

Grant Types: capital, general support, operating expenses, and scholarship

Geographic Distribution: focus on metropolitan Nashville, TN

GIVING OFFICERS
Albert L. Menefee, Jr.: trust *B* 1927 *CURR EMPL* chmn bd, dir: Menefee Crushed Stone Co Inc

David K. Wilson: trust

Justin Potter Wilson: chmn, trust *B* Oakland CA 1945 *ED* Univ Florence 1964; Stanford Univ AB 1967; Vanderbilt Univ JD 1970; NY Univ LLM 1974 *CURR EMPL* ptnr: Waller Lansden Dortch & Davis *NONPR AFFIL* chmn comm visitors: Blair Sch Music; dir, treas: Nashville Tree Fdn; trust: Cumberland Heights Fdn, Fund Am Studies, Intl Exchange Counc, Robert A Taft Inst Govt; trust, mem exec comm: Meharry Med Coll

APPLICATION INFORMATION
Initial Approach:

Applicants should send a letter to the foundation.

The letter should include a description of the organization, with proof of tax-exempt status.

There are no specific deadlines for submitting proposals. Applications may be submitted at any time.

Notification is sent within two months of receipt of proposal.

Restrictions on Giving: No grants are given to individuals.

OTHER THINGS TO KNOW
NationsBank is the corporate trustee for the foundation.

GRANTS ANALYSIS
Total Grants: $977,500

Number of Grants: 29

Highest Grant: $245,000

Average Grant: $26,161*

Typical Range: $10,000 to $50,000

Disclosure Period: 1991

Note: The average grant figure excludes the highest grant. Recent grants are derived from a 1991 Form 990.

RECENT GRANTS
General
245,000	Vanderbilt University School of Medicine, Nashville, TN — for Justin Potter Merit Scholarship
100,000	Dominican Campus
35,000	David Lipscomb University, Nashville, TN
35,000	YCAP (YMCA), McKendree, TN

30,000   Meharry Medical Center,
          Nashville, TN

Provident Life & Accident Insurance Company of America

Revenue: $2.76 billion
Employees: 5,000
Headquarters: Chattanooga, TN
SIC Major Group: Life Insurance and Accident
& Health Insurance

CONTACT
Jeffrey G. McCall
Assistant to the President
Provident Life & Accident Insurance Company
of America
1 Fountain Sq.
Chattanooga, TN 37402
(615) 755-1947

FINANCIAL SUMMARY
Recent Giving: $875,000 (1995 est.);
$856,000 (1994 approx.); $1,191,000 (1993)

Fiscal Note: Company gives directly.
Above figures exclude nonmonetary support.

CONTRIBUTIONS SUMMARY
Typical Recipients: • *Arts & Humanities:*
Arts Associations & Councils, Arts Festivals, Libraries, Museums/Galleries, Music, Performing Arts, Visual Arts • *Civic & Public Affairs:* Civil Rights, Economic Development, Housing, Urban & Community Affairs • *Education:* Colleges & Universities, Community & Junior Colleges, Economic Education, Health & Physical Education, Private Education (Precollege), Public Education (Precollege), Science/Mathematics Education • *Environment:* General • *Social Services:* Community Service Organizations, Food/Clothing Distribution, Shelters/Homelessness, Substance Abuse, United Funds/United Ways, Youth Organizations

Grant Types: capital, employee matching gifts, and operating expenses

Note: Employee matching gifts are made for education only. Employee matching gift ratio: 1 to 1.

Nonmonetary Support: $20,000 (1994)

Nonmonetary Support Types: donated equipment, in-kind services, loaned executives, and workplace solicitation

Note: Contact for nonmonetary support is Jeffrey G. McCall, assistant to the president.

Geographic Distribution: headquarters and operating locations

Operating Locations: TN (Chattanooga)

Note: The company operates approximately 130 offices in all 50 states, the District of Columbia, and four Canadian provinces for its sales and service forces.

CORP. OFFICERS
J. Harold Chandler: *B* 1949 *CURR EMPL* ceo, pres, dir: Provident Life & Accident Ins Co Am

Thomas R. Watjen: *CURR EMPL* exec vp, cfo: Provident Life & Accident Ins Co Am

Thomas A.H. White: *CURR EMPL* vp corp affs: Provident Life & Accident Ins Co

APPLICATION INFORMATION
Initial Approach: *Initial Contact:* brief letter of inquiry *Include Information On:* description of the organization, amount requested, purpose of funds sought, audited financial statement, and proof of tax-exempt status *Deadlines:* apply by early fall for the next year

Restrictions on Giving: Does not support individuals or operating funds for colleges/universities.

GRANTS ANALYSIS
Total Grants: $876,000*

Disclosure Period: 1994

Note: Total grants figure is approximate.

Sedgwick James Inc.

Employees: 175
Parent Company: Sedgwick Group Inc.
Headquarters: Memphis, TN
SIC Major Group: Insurance Agents, Brokers
& Service

CONTACT
Jamie Anderson
Matching Gifts Program
Sedgwick James Inc.
5350 Poplar Ave.
Memphis, TN 38119
(901) 761-1550
Note: Barbara Durson may also be used as an additional contact name.

FINANCIAL SUMMARY
Fiscal Note: Annual Giving Range: less than $100,000

CONTRIBUTIONS SUMMARY
Support goes to local education, human service, arts, and civic organizations. Company also sponsors Community Service Awards for volunteer activity. Company operates a matching gift program for employees and their spouses.

Typical Recipients: • *Arts & Humanities:* Arts Appreciation, Arts Associations & Councils, Arts Centers, Arts Festivals, Arts Funds, Arts Institutes, Community Arts, Dance, Ethnic & Folk Arts, Historic Preservation, Libraries, Literary Arts, Museums/Galleries, Music, Opera, Performing Arts, Public Broadcasting, Theater, Visual Arts • *Civic & Public Affairs:* Safety, Zoos/Aquariums • *Education:* Agricultural Education, Arts/Humanities Education, Business Education, Colleges & Universities, Community & Junior Colleges, Continuing Education, Economic Education, Education Associations, Education Funds, Elementary Education (Private), Engineering/Technological Education, Faculty Development, Health & Physical Education, International Exchange, International Studies, Journalism/Media Education, Legal Education, Lit-

eracy, Medical Education, Minority Education, Preschool Education, Private Education (Precollege), Public Education (Precollege), Science/Mathematics Education, Social Sciences Education, Special Education, Student Aid • *Environment:* General • *Science:* Observatories & Planetariums, Scientific Organizations • *Social Services:* General

Grant Types: employee matching gifts

Geographic Distribution: primarily in TN

Operating Locations: TN (Memphis)

CORP. OFFICERS
Donald K. Morford: *CURR EMPL* pres, dir: Sedgwick James

Quill O'Healy: *CURR EMPL* chmn, ceo, dir: Sedgwick James

James B. Wiertelak: *CURR EMPL* sr vp, cfo, dir: Sedgwick James

GIVING OFFICERS
Gannie Harris: *CURR EMPL* matching gifts coordinator: Sedgwick James

APPLICATION INFORMATION
Initial Approach: Send brief letter of inquiry, including a description of the organization, amount requested, purpose of funds sought, recently audited financial statements, and proof of tax-exempt status. Deadline is December 15, and all requests after the deadline will be considered the following year.

Restrictions on Giving: Does not support individuals, religious organizations for sectarian purposes (however programs sponsored by a religious organization may be eligible), fraternal organizations, veteran's organizations, unions, or political or lobbying groups.

Stokely, Jr. Foundation, William B.

CONTACT
William B. Stokely, III
President
William B. Stokely, Jr. Fdn.
620 Campbell Sta. Rd., Ste. 27
Knoxville, TN 37922
(615) 966-4878

FINANCIAL SUMMARY
Recent Giving: $489,249 (1993); $466,943 (1991); $410,504 (1990)

Assets: $9,837,660 (1993); $9,120,682 (1991); $7,873,714 (1990)

EIN: 35-6016402

CONTRIBUTIONS SUMMARY
Donor(s): the late William B. Stokely, Jr

Typical Recipients: • *Arts & Humanities:* Arts Festivals, Community Arts, History & Archaeology, Libraries, Museums/Galleries, Music • *Civic & Public Affairs:* Women's Affairs • *Education:* Arts/Humanities Education, Business Education, Colleges & Universities, Elementary Education (Public), General, Private Education (Precollege), Student Aid • *Environment:* General, Resource Conservation • *Health:* Cancer, Children's Health/Hospitals, Clinics/Medical Centers, Geriatric Health, Health Organizations, Hospitals, Medical Rehabilitation, Medical Research, Mental Health, Preventive Medicine/Wellness Organizations, Single-Disease Health Associations • *Religion:* Churches, Missionary Activities (Domestic), Religious Organizations, Religious Welfare • *Social Services:* Child Welfare, Community Service Organizations, Family Services, Recreation & Athletics, Scouts, Shelters/Homelessness, United Funds/United Ways, Youth Organizations

Grant Types: general support

Geographic Distribution: focus on eastern TN

GIVING OFFICERS
Stacy S. Byerly: dir

Kay H. Stokely: exec vp, dir

William B. Stokely III: pres, dir

William B. Stokely IV: dir

Andrea A. White-Randall: vp, secy, treas

APPLICATION INFORMATION
Initial Approach: Send letter of inquiry and full proposal. Include a description of organization, amount requested, purpose of funds sought, recently audited financial statement, and proof of tax-exempt status. Submit proposal preferably in the fall. Board meets in February, May, August, and November.

Restrictions on Giving: Does not support individuals.

GRANTS ANALYSIS
Total Grants: $489,249

Number of Grants: 104

Highest Grant: $66,000

Typical Range: $100 to $50,000

Disclosure Period: 1993

Note: Recent grants are derived from a 1993 Form 990.

RECENT GRANTS
Library
25,000	Stokely Memorial Library, Newport, TN
5,000	Tellico Plains Library, Tellico Plains, TN

General
66,000	Carson-Newman College, Franklin, IN
50,000	Berry College, Rome, GA — Bonner Foundation scholarship challenge
50,000	Webb School, Knoxville, TN
22,000	Carson-Newman College, Franklin, IN
20,000	Boy Scouts of America Smoky Mountain Council, Knoxville, TN

Thompson Charitable Foundation

CONTACT
Monica Luke
Administrative Manager
Thompson Charitable Foundation
PO Box 10516
Knoxville, TN 37939-0516
(615) 588-0491

FINANCIAL SUMMARY
Recent Giving: $1,945,000 (fiscal 1995 est.); $1,944,000 (fiscal 1994 approx.); $1,943,485 (fiscal 1993)

Assets: $22,906,000 (fiscal 1995 est.); $22,906,000 (fiscal 1994 approx.); $22,906,226 (fiscal 1993)

Gifts Received: $4,353,795 (fiscal 1993); $2,000,000 (fiscal 1992); $4,350,000 (fiscal 1990)

Fiscal Note: In fiscal 1993, contributions were received from the estate of B. R. Thompson, Sr.

EIN: 58-1754763

CONTRIBUTIONS SUMMARY
Donor(s): The Thompson Charitable Foundation Foundation was established in 1987 by the estate of B. Ray Thompson, Sr.

Typical Recipients: • *Arts & Humanities:* Libraries, Music • *Civic & Public Affairs:* Housing, Philanthropic Organizations • *Education:* Colleges & Universities, Community & Junior Colleges, Elementary Education (Public), Religious Education • *Health:* Cancer, Children's Health/Hospitals, Clinics/Medical Centers, Geriatric Health, Hospitals, Nursing Services, Prenatal Health Issues • *Religion:* General, Religious Welfare • *Social Services:* Homes, YMCA/YWCA/YMHA/YWHA

Grant Types: capital, department, and general support

Geographic Distribution: focus on Knox, Anderson, Scott, and Blount Counties in TN; Bell, Clay, Laurel, and Leslie Counties in KY; and Buchanan and Tazewell Counties in VA

GIVING OFFICERS
Carl Ensor, Jr.: dir

B. Ray Thompson, Jr.: dir

Jesse J. Thompson: dir

Merle Wolfe: pres, dir *CURR EMPL* pres, dir: Sun Coal Co

Lindsay Young: dir *PHIL AFFIL* dir: Frank and Virginia Rogers Foundation; trust: Lucille S. Thompson Family Fund

APPLICATION INFORMATION
Initial Approach:

The foundation reports no specific application guidelines. Send a brief two-page letter of inquiry.

Information should include statement of purpose, amount requested, and proof of tax-exempt status.

Deadlines are March 31, June 30, September 30, and December 31.

Restrictions on Giving: The foundation does not support endowments or operating deficits.

GRANTS ANALYSIS
Total Grants: $1,943,485

Number of Grants: 20

Highest Grant: $536,875

Average Grant: $97,174

Typical Range: $1,800 to $200,000

Disclosure Period: fiscal year ending June 30, 1993

Note: Recent grants are derived from a fiscal 1993 Form 990.

RECENT GRANTS
Library
1,800	Manchester Christian Academy, Manchester, KY — library books and playground equipment

General
536,875	Oneida Special School District, Oneida, TN — completion of high school, gym, middle school, and cafeteria
200,000	Children's Hospital, Knoxville, TN — general support
200,000	Southwest Virginia Community College, Richlands, VA — new building construction
125,000	Knoxville College, Knoxville, TN — renovation of dormitories
118,000	Cumberland Valley District Health Department, Manchester, KY — 4-wheel drive vehicle, supplement home care program for the elderly, cholesterol machine, and re-establishment of acute ambulatory care services in the Clay County Health Department

Toms Foundation

CONTACT
William C. Wilson
Trustee
Toms Fdn.
PO Box 2466
Knoxville, TN 37901
(615) 544-3000

FINANCIAL SUMMARY
Recent Giving: $11,725 (fiscal 1994); $11,400 (fiscal 1990); $94,969 (fiscal 1989)

Assets: $3,566,523 (fiscal 1994); $3,250,368 (fiscal 1990); $3,138,716 (fiscal 1989)

EIN: 62-6037668

CONTRIBUTIONS SUMMARY
Donor(s): the late W. P. Toms

Typical Recipients: • *Arts & Humanities:* Arts Associations & Councils, Community Arts, Libraries, Museums/Galleries, Opera • *Civic & Public Affairs:* Zoos/Aquariums • *Education:* Colleges & Universities, Legal Education, Private Education (Precollege) • *Environment:* General • *Health:* Health Organizations, Medical Research, Single-Disease Health Associations • *Religion:* Religious Organizations • *Social Services:* Community Service Organizations, Food/Clothing Distribution, United Funds/United Ways, Youth Organizations

Grant Types: capital, emergency, research, and seed money

Geographic Distribution: focus on eastern TN

GIVING OFFICERS
Ronald L. Grimm: trust

Eleanor C. Krug: trust

Mary Mayne Perry: trust

Dorothy B. Wilson: trust

William C. Wilson: trust

APPLICATION INFORMATION
Initial Approach: Send letter of inquiry followed by proposal. Submit proposal preferably in June. Deadline is June 30. Board meets in August. Decisions are made one month after annual meeting.

Restrictions on Giving: Does not support individuals.

PUBLICATIONS
Annual Report

GRANTS ANALYSIS
Total Grants: $11,725

Number of Grants: 11

Highest Grant: $4,000

Typical Range: $200 to $2,000

Disclosure Period: fiscal year ending June 30, 1994

Note: Recent grants are derived from a fiscal 1994 Form 990.

RECENT GRANTS

Library
575	Belmont University, Nashville, TN

General
4,000	University of Tennessee Law School, Knoxville, TN
2,000	Ijams Nature Center, Knoxville, TN
1,500	Florence Crittenton Agency, Knoxville, TN
750	Knoxville Zoological Gardens, Knoxville, TN
500	Kingwood School

Tonya Memorial Foundation

CONTACT
Maurice H. Martin
President
Tonya Memorial Fdn.
c/o American National Bank and Trust Co.
American National Bank Bldg.
736 Market St.
Chattanooga, TN 37402
Note: Additional addresses for application information : James Hitching and Whitney Durand, 1033 Volunteer Bldg., Chattanooga, TN, 37402.

FINANCIAL SUMMARY
Recent Giving: $5,435,152 (1993); $3,008,152 (1992); $3,623,939 (1991)

Assets: $679,186 (1993); $5,987,636 (1992); $8,943,988 (1991)

EIN: 62-6042269

CONTRIBUTIONS SUMMARY
Donor(s): the late Burkett Miller

Typical Recipients: • *Arts & Humanities:* Libraries, Performing Arts, Public Broadcasting • *Civic & Public Affairs:* Botanical Gardens/Parks, Business/Free Enterprise, Community Foundations, Economic Development, Municipalities/Towns, Urban & Community Affairs, Zoos/Aquariums • *Education:* Colleges & Universities, Private Education (Precollege), Public Education (Precollege) • *Environment:* General • *Social Services:* Community Centers, Community Service Organizations, Homes, United Funds/United Ways, Youth Organizations

Grant Types: capital and multiyear/continuing support

Geographic Distribution: focus on Chattanooga, TN

GIVING OFFICERS
H. Whitney Durand: secy, trust

James R. Hedges III: vp, asst secy, trust

Harry James Hitching: chmn, trust *B* New York NY 1909 *ED* Columbia Univ AB 1929; Columbia Univ LLB 1931; Columbia Univ JD 1969 *CURR EMPL* ptnr: Miller & Martin *CORP AFFIL* dir: Krystal Co; div coun: Vulcan Materials Co; gen coun: Skyland Intl Corp *NONPR AFFIL* chmn adv bd: Chattanooga Salavation Army, Salvation Army Chattanooga; dir: Chattanooga Commun Fdn, Chattanooga Ophthalmological Fdn; mem: Am Bar Assn, Benwood Fdn, Chattanooga Bar Assn, Chattanooga Bar Fdn, Chattanooga Chamber Commerce, Estate Planning Counc Chattanooga, GA Bar Assn, Miller Park Bd, Newcomen Soc North Am, TN Bar Assn

Maurice H. Martin: pres, treas, trust

APPLICATION INFORMATION
Initial Approach: Include a description of organization, amount requested, purpose of funds sought, recently audited financial statement, and proof of tax-exempt status. Send one copy to each of the four trustees. Deadlines are January 10, March 10, May

10, July 10, September 10, and November 10.

Restrictions on Giving: Limited to the Chattanooga, TN area.

GRANTS ANALYSIS
Total Grants: $5,435,152

Number of Grants: 12

Highest Grant: $2,782,206

Typical Range: 5,883 to $600,000

Disclosure Period: 1993

Note: Recent grants are derived from a 1993 Form 990.

RECENT GRANTS

Library
500,000	Baylor School Hedges Library, Chattanooga, TN

General
2,782,206	RiverCity Company, Chattanooga, TN — for expenses relating to design and construction of Vistors Center
600,000	McCallie School, Chattanooga, TN — capital campaign
417,000	Girls Preparatory School, Chattanooga, TN — endowment
66,000	Enterprise Fund, Chattanooga, TN — operating fund
28,140	RiverCity Company, Chattanooga, TN — for Miller Plaza Fund

TEXAS

Abell-Hanger Foundation

CONTACT
David. L. Smith
Executive Director
Abell-Hanger Foundation
PO Box 430
Midland, TX 79702
(915) 684-6655

FINANCIAL SUMMARY
Recent Giving: $5,000,000 (fiscal 1995 est.); $4,425,177 (fiscal 1994); $5,079,276 (fiscal 1993)

Assets: $95,000,000 (fiscal 1995 est.); $104,759,687 (fiscal 1994); $106,727,104 (fiscal 1993)

Gifts Received: $2,174,812 (fiscal 1991); $256,979 (fiscal 1990); $42,581,031 (fiscal 1989)

Fiscal Note: In fiscal 1990, the foundation received $256,979 from the Gladys H. Abell Irrevocable Trust and $2,174,812 in fiscal 1991.

EIN: 75-6020781

CONTRIBUTIONS SUMMARY

Donor(s): The foundation was established in Texas in 1954 by George T. Abell and his wife, Gladys Hanger Abell. Mr. Abell achieved success as an independent oil operator in the fields of west Texas. He served on the local school board, and was involved with fund raising for the Boy Scouts of America, for which he was awarded the highest recognition, the Silver Beaver Award.

Typical Recipients: • *Arts & Humanities:* Arts Associations & Councils, Dance, Historic Preservation, History & Archaeology, Libraries, Museums/Galleries, Music, Theater • *Civic & Public Affairs:* Botanical Gardens/Parks, Business/Free Enterprise, Community Foundations, Employment/Job Training, Hispanic Affairs, Housing, Law & Justice, Municipalities/Towns, Philanthropic Organizations, Professional & Trade Associations, Public Policy, Safety • *Education:* Agricultural Education, Colleges & Universities, Community & Junior Colleges, Education Associations, Faculty Development, Literacy, Medical Education, Minority Education, Science/Mathematics Education, Special Education, Student Aid • *Environment:* General • *Health:* AIDS/HIV, Alzheimers Disease, Cancer, Emergency/Ambulance Services, Health Funds, Health Organizations, Hospices, Hospitals, Medical Research, Medical Training, Multiple Sclerosis, Nursing Services, Public Health, Single-Disease Health Associations • *International:* Health Care/Hospitals, Missionary/Religious Activities • *Religion:* Ministries, Religious Welfare, Seminaries • *Science:* Scientific Organizations • *Social Services:* At-Risk Youth, Child Abuse, Child Welfare, Community Service Organizations, Counseling, Crime Prevention, Day Care, Delinquency & Criminal Rehabilitation, Domestic Violence, Family Planning, Family Services, Food/Clothing Distribution, Homes, People with Disabilities, Recreation & Athletics, Senior Services, Shelters/Homelessness, Substance Abuse, United Funds/United Ways, Veterans, Youth Organizations

Grant Types: capital, challenge, general support, and seed money

Geographic Distribution: primarily Texas

GIVING OFFICERS

John P. Butler: hon trust *B* Mt Calm TX 1901 *CURR EMPL* sr chmn: First Natl Bank Midland

Arlen L. Edgar: trust

Jerome M. Fullinwider: trust

Robert M. Leibrock: pres, trust

David L. Smith: exec dir

James I. Trott: vp, asst secy

Lester Van Pelt, Jr.: secy-treas, trust

John F. Younger: trust

APPLICATION INFORMATION
Initial Approach:

If applicant has never received funding from the Abell-Hanger Foundation, initial contact should be by letter requesting a "Pre-Proposal Questionnaire." Upon return of the questionnaire, the trustees will review the request to determine whether it warrants a complete proposal. A full application form will then be sent to the applicant.

Application should be submitted on the original forms supplied by the foundation. These forms should include the "Grant Affidavit," "Institutional Profile," "Grant Request Summary," "Current Year Operating Budget" and "Current Fiscal Year Budget Comparison," "Staff Salaries and Benefits," and "Contributions Analysis." The applicant will also be asked to supply the organization's latest audited financial statement.

Applications should be received on or before August 31, November 15, February 28, and May 31. Applicants are encouraged to submit their application well in advance of the deadline.

Trustee meetings are held in September, December, March, and June. Applicants will be notified within a week of the trustee meeting.

Restrictions on Giving: Only 501(c)(3) organizations need apply. The foundation does not make grants to private foundations. The foundation does not fund loans, grants, scholarships, or fellowships for individual students. Block scholarship grants are made only to higher education institutions in Texas. Sole sponsorship of programs rarely is undertaken.

PUBLICATIONS
Annual report

GRANTS ANALYSIS
Total Grants: $4,425,177

Number of Grants: 123

Highest Grant: $282,609

Average Grant: $35,977

Typical Range: $20,000 to $50,000

Disclosure Period: fiscal year ending June 30, 1994

Note: Recent grants are derived from a fiscal 1994 grants list.

RECENT GRANTS

Library

250,000	Permian Basin Petroleum Museum, Library, and Hall of Fame, Midland, TX — challenge grant for the permanent endowment
175,000	Permian Basin Petroleum Museum, Library, and Hall of Fame, Midland, TX
25,000	Nita Stewart Haley Memorial Library, Midland, TX

General

282,609	United Way of Midland, Midland, TX — matching grant for the 1994 campaign
250,000	Midland College, Midland, TX — for the Midland County Scholarship Program
200,000	Midland College, Midland, TX — for the Chaparral Circle Fund
120,000	Midland Memorial Foundation Auxiliary Nursing Education Fund, Midland, TX — for

	nursing scholarships and stipends administered by the auxiliary
100,000	Austin Presbyterian Theological Seminary, Austin, TX — construction of a community center

Alcon Laboratories, Inc. / Alcon Foundation

Sales: $929.0 million
Employees: 5,316
Parent Company: Nestle S.A.
Headquarters: Ft. Worth, TX
SIC Major Group: Pharmaceutical Preparations, Surgical & Medical Instruments, and Ophthalmic Goods

CONTACT
Mary Dulle
Director, Professional Relations
Alcon Laboratories, Inc.
6201 S Fwy.
Ft. Worth, TX 76134
(817) 293-0450
Note: An alternative contact is Mr. J. A. Walters, who is the foundation's co-chairman.

FINANCIAL SUMMARY
Recent Giving: $400,000 (1995 est.); $396,450 (1994); $462,426 (1993)

Assets: $24,137 (1993); $26,705 (1992); $12,485 (1991)

Gifts Received: $460,000 (1993); $434,000 (1992); $430,000 (1991)

Fiscal Note: Figures include foundation grants only. Company does not release figures for direct giving. Above figures exclude nonmonetary support. The foundation received all donations from Alcon Laboratories, Inc.

EIN: 75-6034736

CONTRIBUTIONS SUMMARY
Typical Recipients: • *Arts & Humanities:* Arts Associations & Councils, Libraries, Music, Opera, Public Broadcasting, Theater • *Civic & Public Affairs:* African American Affairs, Business/Free Enterprise, Clubs, General • *Education:* Colleges & Universities, Community & Junior Colleges, Medical Education, Minority Education, Private Education (Precollege), Public Education (Precollege), Science/Mathematics Education, Secondary Education (Private), Student Aid • *Health:* Children's Health/Hospitals, Clinics/Medical Centers, Eyes/Blindness, Health Funds, Hospitals, Medical Research • *International:* Health Care/Hospitals • *Religion:* Religious Welfare • *Science:* Science Museums • *Social Services:* Child Welfare, Community Centers, Community Service Organizations, Counseling, Family Services, Food/Clothing Distribution, People with Disabilities, Shelters/Homelessness, Youth Organizations

Grant Types: conference/seminar and research

Nonmonetary Support Types: donated equipment and donated products

Note: Nonmonetary support is donated exclusively to vision care specialists doing medical mission eye care. Support is supplied by the company. Company does not release figures for nonmonetary support. Contact Winona Mueller, Administration, Medical Missions Coordinator for information.

Geographic Distribution: nationally, with emphasis on Ft. Worth, TX

Operating Locations: TX (Ft. Worth)

CORP. OFFICERS
C. Allen Baker: *CURR EMPL* exec vp: Alcon Laboratories Inc

Robert Raynor Montgomery: *B* Sydney Australia 1943 *ED* St Patricks Coll Australia 1961 *CURR EMPL* cfo, exec vp: Alcon Laboratories Inc *CORP AFFIL* dir: Dermatological Products TX, Ryder Intl; vchmn, exec vp fin: Alcon Puerto Rico; vchmn, vp fin: Alcon Surgical

Dilip N. Raval: *ED* Univ Bombay BS 1953; Univ Bombay MS 1953; Univ OR PhD 1962 *CURR EMPL* exec vp res & devel: Alcon Laboratories Inc

Edgar H. Schollmaier: *B* 1933 *ED* Harvard Univ MBA 1958 *CURR EMPL* chmn, pres, ceo, dir: Alcon Laboratories Inc *CORP AFFIL* pres, ceo: Alcon Puerto Rico; pres, ceo, dir: Alcon Surgical

Timothy R. G. Sear: *B* 1937 *ED* Manchester Coll 1962 *CURR EMPL* exec vp, dir: Alcon Laboratories Inc

Richard Hampton Sisson: *B* Roanoke VA 1932 *ED* Roanoke Coll BA 1955; Harvard Univ Advanced Mgmt Program 1973 *CURR EMPL* exec vp, dir: Alcon Laboratories Inc *CORP AFFIL* chmn, exec vp, dir: Alcon Puerto Rico

GIVING OFFICERS
C. Allen Baker: trust *CURR EMPL* exec vp: Alcon Laboratories Inc (see above)

C. H. Beasley: trust

Mary Dulle: co-chmn *CURR EMPL* dir, professional rels: Alcon Laboratories Inc

J. Hiddeman: trust

L. Liguori: trust

R. Nelson: trust

Richard Hampton Sisson: trust *CURR EMPL* exec vp, dir: Alcon Laboratories Inc (see above)

John Alexander Walters: co-chmn *B* Philadelphia PA 1938 *ED* Wagner Coll BA 1960 *CURR EMPL* corp vp human resources: Alcon Laboratories Inc

APPLICATION INFORMATION
Initial Approach: *Initial Contact:* a letter or proposal *Include Information On:* a description of the organization, amount requested, purpose of the grant, a recently audited financial statement including list of other major contributors, and proof of tax-exempt status *Deadlines:* none; decisions are announced bimonthly

OTHER THINGS TO KNOW
Alcon limits contributions to education and research institutions within Alcon's areas of specialization, for example ophthalmology, optometry, and vision care. Arts, civic and public affairs, and social services are limited to headquarters area.

GRANTS ANALYSIS
Total Grants: $396,450
Number of Grants: 230
Highest Grant: $27,000
Average Grant: $1,724
Typical Range: $250 to $1,000
Disclosure Period: 1994

Note: Recent grants are derived from a 1993 Form 990.

RECENT GRANTS
General
27,000	Junior Achievement of Tarrant County, Ft. Worth, TX
25,000	Association for Research in Vision and Ophthalmology, Bethesda, MD
25,000	Association of University Professors in Ophthalmology, San Francisco, CA
25,000	Foundation for Advanced Education in the Sciences (NEI), Bethesda, MD
18,000	Illinois Masonic Medical Center, Chicago, IL

AMR Corp. / AMR/American Airlines Foundation

Revenue: $16.13 billion
Employees: 118,900
Headquarters: Dallas/Ft. Worth, TX
SIC Major Group: Holding Companies Nec and Air Transportation—Scheduled

CONTACT
Kathy Andersen
Administrator Corporate Contributions
AMR/American Airlines Fdn.
PO Box 619616
Mail Drop 5575
DFW Airport, TX 75261-9616
(817) 967-3545
Note: Foundation asks that facsimiles be limited to one page plus transmittal sheet. The company's World Wide Web address is http://www.amrcorp.com

FINANCIAL SUMMARY
Recent Giving: $710,463 (1994 approx.); $619,257 (1993); $849,825 (1992)

Assets: $785,512 (1993); $428,543 (1992); $1,278,015 (1991)

Gifts Received: $1,174,155 (1993); $1,113,840 (1992)

Fiscal Note: Above figures are for the foundation only. Company's Sales Department provides in-kind services to nonprofits. Contact local Sales Promotion Manager for information. Direct giving is not handled by the foundation, and it is not included in the above figures. In 1993, the foundation received gifts from American Airlines Inc. and Flagship and Chicago Charities, both of which are unincorporated associations of American Airlines employees.

EIN: 76-2086656

CONTRIBUTIONS SUMMARY
Typical Recipients: • *Arts & Humanities:* Arts Associations & Councils, Community Arts, Historic Preservation, History & Archaeology, Libraries, Music, Opera, Performing Arts • *Civic & Public Affairs:* African American Affairs, Botanical Gardens/Parks, Business/Free Enterprise, Civil Rights, Philanthropic Organizations, Professional & Trade Associations, Public Policy, Urban & Community Affairs, Women's Affairs • *Education:* Arts/Humanities Education, Business Education, Colleges & Universities, Minority Education, Science/Mathematics Education, Student Aid • *Health:* Children's Health/Hospitals, Clinics/Medical Centers, Health Funds, Hospitals, Public Health, Single-Disease Health Associations • *International:* International Relations • *Religion:* Jewish Causes, Religious Welfare • *Social Services:* Child Welfare, Community Service Organizations, Family Services, United Funds/United Ways, Volunteer Services, Youth Organizations

Grant Types: project

Nonmonetary Support: $1,000,000 (1992)

Nonmonetary Support Types: donated products

Note: Sales Department provides in-kind services for nonprofits. Company also donates travel vouchers to organizations. Contact Ms. Kathy Andersen for further information. Above figures include nonmonetary support.

Geographic Distribution: nationwide and international

Operating Locations: CA

CORP. OFFICERS
Robert Woodward Baker: *B* Bronxville NY 1944 *ED* Trinity Coll BA 1966; Univ PA Wharton Sch MBA 1968 *CURR EMPL* exec vp oper: AMR Corp *CORP AFFIL* chmn: AMR Eagle Inc; exec vp: Am Airlines Inc; vchmn: Simmons Airlines Inc

Donald J. Carty: *B* 1946 *ED* Queene Univ Kingston BA 1968; Harvard Univ MBA 1971 *CURR EMPL* exec vp fin & planning, cfo: AMR Corp *CORP AFFIL* chmn: AMR Training Consult Group; exec vp: Am Airlines Inc

Robert Lloyd Crandall: *B* Westerly RI 1935 *ED* Coll William & Mary 1953-1955; Univ RI BS 1957; Univ PA Wharton Sch MBA 1960 *CURR EMPL* chmn, pres, ceo: AMR Corp *CORP AFFIL* chmn, pres, ceo: Am Airlines Inc; dir: AMR Eagle Inc, Halliburton Co, Republic Bank Dallas, Simmons Airlines Inc

Anne H. McNamara: *B* Shanghai People's Republic of China 1947 *ED* Vassar Coll AB 1969; Cornell Univ JD 1973 *CURR EMPL* sr vp, admin gen couns: AMR Corp *CORP AFFIL* dir: LG&E Energy Corp, Louisville Gas & Electric Co; sr vp, gen couns: Am Airlines Inc

GIVING OFFICERS
Kathy Andersen: admin corp contributions

Donald J. Carty: treas, vp *CURR EMPL* exec vp fin & planning, cfo: AMR Corp (see above)

Timothy J. Doke: secy, mgr

APPLICATION INFORMATION
Initial Approach: *Initial Contact:* brief letter or proposal *Include Information On:* purpose of organization, intended use of funds, proof of tax-exempt status *Deadlines:* none *Note:* Foundation requests that organizations contact foundation administrator only.

GRANTS ANALYSIS
Total Grants: $619,257

Number of Grants: 75

Highest Grant: $175,000

Average Grant: $8,257

Typical Range: $100 to $30,000

Disclosure Period: 1993

Note: Recent grants are derived from a 1993 Form 990.

RECENT GRANTS
Library

5,000	Broward Public Library Foundation, Ft. Lauderdale, FL
5,000	Friends of Miami-Dade Public Library, Miami, FL

General

175,000	United Way Dallas/Ft. Worth, Dallas, TX
108,000	United Way, Tulsa, OK
50,000	United Way, Miami, FL
50,000	University Medical Center, Dallas, TX — fifth year of a five-year commitment
30,000	Community Trust Fund of VL/SFV, Van Nuys, CA

Anderson Foundation, M. D.

CONTACT
Elizabeth Calvert
Secretary and Treasurer
M. D. Anderson Foundation
c/o Texas Commerce Bank
PO Box 2558
Houston, TX 77252-8037
Note: The foundation does not list a phone number.

FINANCIAL SUMMARY
Recent Giving: $3,000,000 (1995 est.); $2,927,000 (1994 approx.); $4,462,820 (1993)

Assets: $90,000,000 (1995 est.); $89,324,945 (1994 approx.); $93,164,605 (1993)

Gifts Received: $18,050 (1992); $16,300 (1991); $3,848 (1990)

EIN: 74-6035669

CONTRIBUTIONS SUMMARY
Donor(s): The foundation was established in 1936 to institutionalize the philanthropy of Monroe D. Anderson , a founder of Anderson, Clayton & Co., Houston cotton merchants. Mr. Anderson, who died in 1939, intended the foundation to continue to reflect his interests after his death, although he gave the trustees wide latitude in the choice of funding recipients.

Typical Recipients: • *Arts & Humanities:* Ballet, Libraries, Museums/Galleries, Music, Opera, Performing Arts • *Civic & Public Affairs:* Community Foundations, Economic Development, Employment/Job Training, Legal Aid • *Education:* Colleges & Universities, Legal Education, Literacy, Medical Education, Minority Education, Private Education (Precollege), Special Education • *Health:* Children's Health/Hospitals, Clinics/Medical Centers, Emergency/Ambulance Services, Eyes/Blindness, Health Organizations, Hospices, Hospitals, Medical Rehabilitation, Medical Research, Nursing Services, Research/Studies Institutes, Single-Disease Health Associations, Transplant Networks/Donor Banks • *Religion:* Jewish Causes • *Science:* Science Museums • *Social Services:* Child Welfare, Community Service Organizations, People with Disabilities, Senior Services, Shelters/Homelessness, Youth Organizations

Grant Types: capital, general support, project, and research

Geographic Distribution: primarily Houston area and Harris County, TX

GIVING OFFICERS
Elizabeth Calvert: treas, secy

Uriel E. Dutton: trust *B* Hamilton TX 1930 *ED* Howard Payne Univ 1946-1948; Baylor Univ LLB 1951 *CURR EMPL* atty: Fulbright & Jaworski *NONPR AFFIL* mem: Am Bar Assn, Am Bar Fdn, Houston Bar Assn, Phi Delta Phi, TX Bar Assn, TX Bar Fdn

Gibson Gayle, Jr.: pres, trust *B* Waco TX 1926 *ED* Baylor Univ LLB 1950; Baylor Univ AB *CURR EMPL* atty, sr ptnr: Fulbright & Jaworski *CORP AFFIL* dir: Daniel Indus, MBank, MCorp *NONPR AFFIL* bd govs: Leon Jaworski Fdn, TX Med Ctr; fellow: Am Bar Assn, TX Bar Assn; mem: Houston Bar Assn, Houston Chamber Commerce, Intl Bar Assn

Charles W. Hall: trust *B* Dallas TX 1930 *CURR EMPL* sr ptnr, atty: Fulbright & Jaworski

John T. Trotter: vp, trust *PHIL AFFIL* trust: Vivian L. Smith Foundation; vp, trust: J. M. West Texas Corporation Foundation

APPLICATION INFORMATION
Initial Approach:

Applicants should send a brief letter describing the proposed project, along with an original and four copies of the proposal. If applying for a matching grant, indicate other sources of funding.

With the cover letter, include the amount needed and proof of tax-exempt status. If the project falls within the foundation's

scope of interest, further information may be requested.

Board meetings are held on the third Tuesday of each month. Applications should be received a month prior to the meeting at which consideration is desired.

The foundation reports that it respond to all proposals by letter detailing whether the application has been approved or denied.

GRANTS ANALYSIS
Total Grants: $4,462,820

Number of Grants: 125

Highest Grant: $1,100,000

Average Grant: $27,120*

Typical Range: $5,000 to $50,000

Disclosure Period: 1993

Note: The average grant figure excludes the largest grant of $1,100,000. Recent grants are derived from a 1992 Form 990.

RECENT GRANTS
Library

100,000	University of Houston, Houston, TX — M.D. Anderson Library
20,000	Houston Public Library, Houston, TX

General

245,000	Texas Medical Center, TX
150,000	University of Houston Law Center, Houston, TX
120,000	Episcopal High School, Bellaire, TX
100,000	San Jose Clinic, San Jose, CA
100,000	Texas Children's Hospital, Houston, TX

Baker Hughes Inc.

Sales: $2.7 billion
Employees: 19,600
Headquarters: Houston, TX
SIC Major Group: Business Services, Holding & Other Investment Offices, Industrial Machinery & Equipment, and Oil & Gas Extraction

CONTACT
Ike Kerridge
Vice President
Baker Hughes Inc.
PO Box 4740
Houston, TX 77210
(713) 439-8600

CONTRIBUTIONS SUMMARY
Typical Recipients: • *Arts & Humanities:* Historic Preservation, Libraries, Museums/Galleries, Performing Arts • *Education:* Engineering/Technological Education, Science/Mathematics Education • *Health:* Medical Research

Grant Types: matching

Geographic Distribution: primarily TX

Operating Locations: CA (Sacramento, San Jose), LA (Bossier City), MA (South Walpole), MN (St. Paul), MO (St. Louis),

OK (Claremore), TX (Austin, Grand Prairie, Houston), UT (Salt Lake City)

CORP. OFFICERS
James D. Woods: *B* Falmouth KY 1931 *ED* Long Beach City Coll AA 1958; CA St Univ Fullerton BA 1967 *CURR EMPL* chmn, pres, ceo, dir: Baker Hughes *CORP AFFIL* dir: Baker Intl Corp

APPLICATION INFORMATION
Initial Approach: Send brief letter of inquiry, including a description of the organization, amount requested, purpose of funds sought, recently audited financial statements, and proof of tax-exempt status. There are no deadlines.

Restrictions on Giving: Does not support individuals, religious organizations for sectarian purposes, or political or lobbying groups.

Bank One, Texas-Houston Office

Employees: 1,660
Parent Company: Bank One, Texas
Assets: $13.91 billion
Headquarters: Houston, TX
SIC Major Group: Depository Institutions

CONTACT
Randy A. Graham
Regional Director of Human Resources
Bank One, Texas-Houston Office
910 Travis
3rd Floor
Houston, TX 77002
(713) 751-6604
Note: An alternate phone number is
   (713)751-2287.

FINANCIAL SUMMARY
Recent Giving: $330,000 (1995 est.); $323,000 (1994 approx.); $305,000 (1993)

Fiscal Note: Company gives directly.

CONTRIBUTIONS SUMMARY
Typical Recipients: • *Arts & Humanities:* Arts Associations & Councils, Ethnic & Folk Arts, General, Libraries, Museums/Galleries, Performing Arts, Public Broadcasting • *Civic & Public Affairs:* Business/Free Enterprise, Civil Rights, Economic Development, General, Housing, Law & Justice, Municipalities/Towns, Urban & Community Affairs • *Education:* Colleges & Universities, Continuing Education, Elementary Education (Private), General, Private Education (Precollege), Public Education (Precollege), Student Aid • *Environment:* General • *Health:* General, Health Organizations, Hospitals, Medical Research • *Social Services:* Community Service Organizations, General, Substance Abuse, United Funds/United Ways, Youth Organizations

Grant Types: employee matching gifts and general support

Nonmonetary Support Types: donated equipment and in-kind services

Geographic Distribution: primarily in Houston, TX

Operating Locations: TX (Houston)

CORP. OFFICERS
Gary Parker: *CURR EMPL* cfo: Bank One TX Houston *CORP AFFIL* vp: Commercial Natl Bank Beeville

David L. Stith: *CURR EMPL* chmn, ceo: Bank One TX Houston

GIVING OFFICERS
Randy A. Graham: *CURR EMPL* regional dir human resources: Bank One TX Houston

APPLICATION INFORMATION
Initial Approach: *Initial Contact:* written proposal *Include Information On:* brief summary of organization, its activities and mission; current executive staff and board of directors; statement of the specific amount requested and purpose of the funds; copy of IRS 501(c)(3) statement; audited financial statements; and level of United Way funding and application of those funds *Deadlines:* none

Restrictions on Giving: Requests are not approved to support partisan political organizations, to fraternal organizations, to individuals, to hospital or other patient care institution operating funds, to any customer or supplier directly for general operating purposes, or for community services outside Houston's operating area.

Company only supports private, nonprofit, and tax-exempt organizations with certified 501(c)(3) status.

OTHER THINGS TO KNOW
Bank One's other regional offices have budgets for corporate giving.

PUBLICATIONS
Community relations and contributions policies and guidelines

GRANTS ANALYSIS
Total Grants: $323,000

Typical Range: $1,000 to $2,500

Disclosure Period: 1994

Beal Foundation

CONTACT
Spencer E. Beal
Trustee
Beal Fdn.
104 S Pecos
Midland, TX 79702-0270
(915) 682-3753

FINANCIAL SUMMARY
Recent Giving: $434,000 (1993); $494,000 (1991); $377,000 (1990)

Assets: $3,239,231 (1993); $2,707,124 (1991); $2,827,072 (1990)

EIN: 75-6034480

CONTRIBUTIONS SUMMARY
Donor(s): Carlton Beal, W.R. Davis

Typical Recipients: • *Arts & Humanities:* Libraries, Museums/Galleries, Music • *Civic & Public Affairs:* Hispanic Affairs, Public Policy • *Education:* Colleges & Universities, Community & Junior Colleges, Private Education (Precollege), Special Education, Student Aid • *Health:* Cancer, Children's Health/Hospitals, Hospices, Hospitals, Medical Research, Single-Disease Health Associations • *Religion:* Religious Organizations, Religious Welfare • *Social Services:* Big Brother/Big Sister, Child Welfare, Community Service Organizations, Domestic Violence, Family Services, Food/Clothing Distribution, People with Disabilities, United Funds/United Ways, YMCA/YWCA/YMHA/YWHA, Youth Organizations

Grant Types: general support

Geographic Distribution: focus on the Midland, TX, area

GIVING OFFICERS
Barry A. Beal: trust

Carlton E. Beal: don, chmn, trust *B* Los Angeles CA 1916 *ED* MA Inst Tech MS; Stanford Univ *CURR EMPL* co-fdr: BTA Oil Producers

Carlton E. Beal, Jr.: trust

Keleen H. Beal: vchmn

Kelly Beal: trust

Spencer E. Beal: trust

Larry Bell: trust

Robert J. Cowen: trust

Karlene Beal Garber: trust

Bill J. Hill: secy, treas

Jane B. Ramsland: trust

Paul Rea: trust

Pomeroy Smith: trust

Ray K. Smith: trust

APPLICATION INFORMATION
Initial Approach: Application form required. Deadline is one month before meetings for first-time applicants; two weeks for repeat applicants. Board meets on April 1 and November 1.

GRANTS ANALYSIS
Total Grants: $434,000

Number of Grants: 44

Highest Grant: $80,000

Typical Range: $1,000 to $50,000

Disclosure Period: 1993

Note: Recent grants are derived from a 1993 Form 990.

RECENT GRANTS

Library

7,000	Midland County Public Library, Midland, TX

General

80,000	United Way, Midland, TX
50,000	Midland College, Midland, TX
15,000	Midland Association for Retarded Citizens, Midland, TX
15,000	Trinity School of Midland, Midland, TX

15,000	Trinity School of Midland, Midland, TX

Bertha Foundation

CONTACT
Douglas A. Stroud
Vice President
Bertha Fdn.
PO Box 1110
Graham, TX 76450
(817) 549-1400

FINANCIAL SUMMARY
Recent Giving: $1,221,434 (1993); $121,864 (1992); $193,454 (1991)

Assets: $3,643,924 (1993); $3,511,602 (1992); $3,748,205 (1991)

Gifts Received: $1,082,273 (1993); $91,600 (1992); $861,600 (1991)

Fiscal Note: In 1992, contributions were received from City of Graham, TX ($200,000), E. Bruce Street ($315,000), M. Boyd Street ($380,000), and Virginia O. Street ($50,000); eight other donors made contributions of less than $30,000 each.

EIN: 75-6050023

CONTRIBUTIONS SUMMARY
Donor(s): E. Bruce Street, M. Boyd Street Foundation

Typical Recipients: • *Arts & Humanities:* Arts Associations & Councils, Arts Festivals, Libraries, Music • *Civic & Public Affairs:* Botanical Gardens/Parks, Municipalities/Towns • *Education:* Business-School Partnerships, Colleges & Universities, Education Funds, Literacy, Medical Education, Public Education (Precollege), Student Aid • *Health:* Health Organizations, Hospitals, Preventive Medicine/Wellness Organizations • *Religion:* Religious Organizations • *Science:* Science Exhibits & Fairs • *Social Services:* Family Services, Substance Abuse, Youth Organizations

Grant Types: general support, operating expenses, and scholarship

Geographic Distribution: focus on Graham, TX

GIVING OFFICERS
S. Estess: dir

J. R. Montgomery: secy, dir

Alice Ann Street: pres, dir

E. Bruce Street: dir

M. B. Street, Jr.: dir

M. Boyd Street: dir

Douglas A. Stroud: vp, dir

APPLICATION INFORMATION
Initial Approach: Send a brief letter of inquiry. Include a description of organization, amount requested, purpose of funds sought, recently audited financial statement, and proof of tax-exempt status. There are no deadlines.

GRANTS ANALYSIS
Total Grants: $1,221,434

Number of Grants: 10

Highest Grant: $1,193,487

Typical Range: $300 to $10,712

Disclosure Period: 1993

Note: Recent grants are derived from a 1993 Form 990.

RECENT GRANTS

Library
1,193,487	Graham Public Library, Graham, TX — building construction

General
10,712	University of Texas Austin, Austin, TX — computers
6,685	Graham Independent School District, Graham, TX — computers and conferences
5,000	Rotary Club of Graham, Graham, TX — scholarship fund
2,450	City of Graham, Graham, TX — trees for the park
1,850	Graham General Hospital, Graham, TX — health fair

Brackenridge Foundation, George W.

CONTACT
Gilbert M. Denman, Jr.
Trustee
George W. Brackenridge Foundation
711 Navarro St., Ste. 535
San Antonio, TX 78205
(210) 224-1011

FINANCIAL SUMMARY
Recent Giving: $763,423 (1993); $837,003 (1992); $715,526 (1991)

Assets: $16,273,341 (1993); $15,662,779 (1992); $15,966,515 (1991)

EIN: 74-6034977

CONTRIBUTIONS SUMMARY
Donor(s): The foundation was established in 1920 by the late George W. Brackenridge

Typical Recipients: • *Arts & Humanities:* Arts Institutes, Arts Outreach, Ballet, Ethnic & Folk Arts, Libraries, Museums/Galleries, Music, Public Broadcasting • *Civic & Public Affairs:* Community Foundations, Nonprofit Management, Parades/Festivals, Philanthropic Organizations, Zoos/Aquariums • *Education:* Colleges & Universities, Elementary Education (Private), Engineering/Technological Education, Faculty Development, Gifted & Talented Programs, Health & Physical Education, Medical Education, Private Education (Precollege), Public Education (Precollege), Science/Mathematics Education, Student Aid • *Health:* Clinics/Medical Centers, Medical Training • *Social Services:* YMCA/YWCA/YMHA/YWHA, Youth Organizations

Grant Types: endowment, project, research, and scholarship

Geographic Distribution: limited to Texas

GIVING OFFICERS
Gilbert M. Denman, Jr.: trust *B* San Antonio TX 1921 *ED* Univ TX BA 1940; Univ TX LLB 1942 *CURR EMPL* atty: Denman Franklin & Denman *PHIL AFFIL* trust: Ewing Halsell Foundation, Sarah Campbell Blaffer Foundation

Leroy G. Denman, Jr.: trust *B* San Antonio TX 1918 *ED* Univ TX BA 1939; Univ TX LLB 1939 *CURR EMPL* atty: Denman Franklin & Denman *PHIL AFFIL* trust: Caesar Kleberg Foundation for Wildlife Conservation, Ewing Halsell Foundation; secy: Sarah Campbell Blaffer Foundation

John Moore: trust

APPLICATION INFORMATION
Initial Approach:

The foundation requests that the application be made in writing on the organization's letterhead and signed by a member of its board of directors or an officer of the organization.

The application should contain specific information related to the desired use of the grant, a copy of the organization's charter and by-laws, and a copy of the organization's exemption letter from the IRS, including the most recent financial statement.

Proposals are accepted throughout the year.

The board meets in March, June, September, and December.

Restrictions on Giving: The organization must be located in Texas and must be an accredited education organization, or the grant must support one or more accredited educational organizations. The foundation does not support individuals; provide general support, continuing support, seed money, or matching gifts; or fund emergency funds, operating budgets, annual campaigns, deficit financing, or land acquisition.

GRANTS ANALYSIS
Total Grants: $763,423

Number of Grants: 42

Highest Grant: $100,000

Average Grant: $18,177

Typical Range: $1,000 to $20,000

Disclosure Period: 1993

Note: Recent grants are derived from a 1993 Form 990.

RECENT GRANTS

General
100,000	Judson Montessori, San Antonio, TX — purchase of land
62,895	Trinity University, San Antonio, TX — spring '93 affirmative action
59,773	Trinity University, San Antonio, TX — affirmation action
52,000	Texas Military Academy, San Antonio, TX — scholarship, affirmative action

36,000   Trinity University, San
          Antonio, TX — scholarship

Bridwell Foundation, J. S.

CONTACT
Clifford G. Tinsley
Vice President and Treasurer
J. S. Bridwell Foundation
807 8th St., Ste. 500
Wichita Falls, TX 76301-3381
(817) 322-4436

FINANCIAL SUMMARY
Recent Giving: $179,800 (1993); $131,223
(1992); $838,300 (1991)

Assets: $34,287,507 (1993); $32,346,246
(1992); $30,434,852 (1991)

Fiscal Note: Decrease in giving caused by
the fulfillment of the foundation's financial
commitment for the renovation of the Bridwell Library at Southern Methodist University.

EIN: 75-6032988

CONTRIBUTIONS SUMMARY
Donor(s): The J. S. Bridwell Foundation
was founded in 1949 with funds provided by
J. S. Bridwell of Wichita Falls, TX. Mr.
Bridwell owned the Bridwell Oil Company
and a large cattle ranch near Wichita Falls.
Mr. Bridwell left half of his estate to the
foundation when he died in 1966.

Typical Recipients: • *Arts & Humanities:*
Arts Centers, Libraries, Museums/Galleries,
Music • *Civic & Public Affairs:* Municipali-
ties/Towns, Public Policy, Rural Affairs,
Safety, Women's Affairs • *Education:* Agri-
cultural Education, Colleges & Universities,
Private Education (Precollege), Public Edu-
cation (Precollege), Special Education
• *Health:* Cancer, Children's Health/Hospi-
tals, Emergency/Ambulance Services, Heart,
Hospices, Medical Rehabilitation, Medical
Research, Single-Disease Health Associa-
tions • *Religion:* Missionary Activities (Do-
mestic), Religious Welfare • *Social
Services:* At-Risk Youth, Big Brother/Big
Sister, Child Welfare, Family Services,
Food/Clothing Distribution, People with Dis-
abilities, Recreation & Athletics, Scouts,
Senior Services, Substance Abuse, United
Funds/United Ways,
YMCA/YWCA/YMHA/YWHA, Youth Or-
ganizations

Grant Types: capital, endowment, and operating expenses

Geographic Distribution: limited to Texas

GIVING OFFICERS
Ralph S. Bridwell: dir

Mac W. Cannedy, Jr.: dir

Garrett Oliver: dir, secy

Paul Schoppa, Jr.: dir

Herbert B. Story: pres *PHIL AFFIL* dir:
Joe and Lois Perkins Foundation; vp, secy,
dir: Bryant Edwards Foundation

Clifford G. Tinsley: vp, treas

APPLICATION INFORMATION
Initial Approach:
Send a brief letter describing the project and
the applicant's organization, along with the
name of the contact person for the proposal.

The foundation will request additional information if necessary.

Proposals may be submitted at any time.

Proposals are reviewed and evaluated periodically throughout the year by the foundation's officers.

Restrictions on Giving: The foundation
does not support individuals and stresses
that it only makes grants to organizationas
and projects in Texas.

GRANTS ANALYSIS
Total Grants: $179,800

Number of Grants: 49

Highest Grant: $100,000

Average Grant: $3,669

Typical Range: $200 to $2,500

Disclosure Period: 1993

Note: Recent grants are derived from a 1993
Form 990.

RECENT GRANTS

General
100,000	Harmony Family Services, Abilene, TX — boys residential treatment center
12,500	United Way of Greater Wichita Falls, Wichita Falls, TX — operating budget
10,000	University of Kansas, Lawrence, KS — McGregor Herbarium
5,000	American Red Cross, Wichita Falls, TX — operating budget
5,000	Sears Methodist Centers, Abilene, TX — alzheimer care program

Brown Foundation, M. K.

CONTACT
Bill W. Waters
Chairman
M. K. Brown Fdn.
PO Box 662
Pampa, TX 79066-0662
(806) 669-6851

FINANCIAL SUMMARY
Recent Giving: $298,960 (1993); $175,039
(1992); $117,860 (1991)

Assets: $3,927,221 (1993); $3,984,320
(1992); $3,881,661 (1991)

EIN: 75-6034058

CONTRIBUTIONS SUMMARY
Donor(s): the late M. K. Brown

Typical Recipients: • *Arts & Humanities:*
Ballet, Dance, Historic Preservation, Libraries, Museums/Galleries, Music • *Civic &
Public Affairs:* Economic Development, Mu-
nicipalities/Towns, Urban & Community Affairs • *Education:* Colleges & Universities,

Public Education (Precollege) • *Environ-
ment:* General • *Health:* Cancer, Prenatal
Health Issues, Single-Disease Health Asso-
ciations • *Religion:* Churches, Religious
Welfare • *Social Services:* Camps, Child
Welfare, Community Service Organizations,
Day Care, Food/Clothing Distribution, Peo-
ple with Disabilities, Recreation & Athlet-
ics, Scouts, Senior Services, Substance
Abuse, United Funds/United Ways, Youth
Organizations

Grant Types: general support

Geographic Distribution: limited to the
Panhandle area of TX, with emphasis on
Pampa and Gray County

GIVING OFFICERS
David E. Holt: secy, trust

Alice T. Smith: vchmn

Bill W. Waters: chmn

Sandra Waters: trust

APPLICATION INFORMATION
Initial Approach: Send cover letter and full
proposal. Include a description of organization, amount requested, purpose of funds
sought, recently audited financial statement,
and proof of tax-exempt status. Deadlines
are July 1 and December 1.

GRANTS ANALYSIS
Total Grants: $298,960

Number of Grants: 29

Highest Grant: $85,000

Typical Range: $500 to $39,300

Disclosure Period: 1993

Note: Recent grants are derived from a 1993
Form 990.

RECENT GRANTS

General
31,000	Boy Scouts of America Golden Spread Council
15,000	Community Day Care Center, Moberly, MO
15,000	Texas Plains Girl Scouts, TX
13,160	Pampa United Way, Pampa, TX
10,000	Gray County Association for the Retarded, Pampa, TX

Burkitt Foundation

CONTACT
Cornelius O. Ryan
President
Burkitt Fdn.
5847 San Felipe, Ste. 4290
Houston, TX 77057
(713) 780-7638

FINANCIAL SUMMARY
Recent Giving: $151,445 (fiscal 1993);
$192,400 (fiscal 1992); $211,600 (fiscal
1991)

Assets: $9,450,144 (fiscal 1993);
$9,288,116 (fiscal 1992); $9,209,002 (fiscal
1991)

EIN: 74-6053270

8

8

CONTRIBUTIONS SUMMARY
Donor(s): the late Elizabeth B. Crane

Typical Recipients: • *Arts & Humanities:* Ethnic & Folk Arts, Libraries • *Civic & Public Affairs:* Clubs, Hispanic Affairs, Nonprofit Management, Philanthropic Organizations, Professional & Trade Associations, Women's Affairs, Zoos/Aquariums • *Education:* Colleges & Universities, International Exchange, Leadership Training, Private Education (Precollege), Religious Education, Secondary Education (Private), Special Education, Student Aid • *Health:* Heart, Outpatient Health Care • *International:* Health Care/Hospitals, International Affairs, International Environmental Issues, International Organizations, Missionary/Religious Activities • *Religion:* Churches, Dioceses, Missionary Activities (Domestic), Religious Organizations, Religious Welfare • *Social Services:* Community Service Organizations, Family Planning, Shelters/Homelessness, United Funds/United Ways, Volunteer Services, Youth Organizations

Grant Types: capital, conference/seminar, endowment, fellowship, general support, multiyear/continuing support, operating expenses, professorship, project, research, scholarship, and seed money

Geographic Distribution: focus on the southwestern US, with emphasis on TX, NM, AZ, and LA

GIVING OFFICERS
Rev. John E. McCarthy: trust

James A. McClain: asst secy, asst treas

Carl E. Ryan: trust

Cornelius O'Brien Ryan: pres, trust *B* Abilene TX 1917 *ED* Rice Univ BA 1937; Southern Methodist Univ LLB 1940 *CURR EMPL* atty: Kelley & Ryan *NONPR AFFIL* dir, treas: Am Irish Fdn; mem: Am Bar Assn, Am Judicature Soc, Houston Bar Assn

Gerald F. Ryan: mem

Joseph W. Ryan: vp, secy, treas, trust

John F. Webre: trust

APPLICATION INFORMATION
Initial Approach: Prospective applicants should write to the foundation for a copy of their application guidelines. Applications should be sumbitted by August 15 for the fall meeting or by February 15 for the spring meeting. Grants are made only to organizations that are tax-exempt under IRS Code 501(c)(3); no grants are made to individuals.

Restrictions on Giving: Does not support individuals.

PUBLICATIONS
Annual Report

GRANTS ANALYSIS
Total Grants: $151,445

Number of Grants: 45

Highest Grant: $10,000

Typical Range: $700 to $10,000

Disclosure Period: fiscal year ending September 30, 1993

Note: Recent grants are derived from a fiscal 1993 Form 990.

RECENT GRANTS
General

10,000	Rice University Department of Religious Studies, Houston, TX
10,000	St. Thomas High School, Houston, TX — payment of construction debt
7,500	St. Joseph Academy, Brownsville, TX — building renovation and expansion
6,000	Phi Beta Kappa Alumni Association, Houston, TX — scholarship funds
5,000	Cathedral High School, El Paso, TX — building renovations and expansion

Burnett-Tandy Foundation

Former Foundation Name: Anne Burnett and Charles Tandy Foundation

CONTACT
Thomas F. Beech
Executive Vice President
The Burnett-Tandy Foundation
801 Cherry St., Ste. 1400
Ft. Worth, TX 76102
(817) 877-3344
Note: The foundation was formerly named the Anne Burnett and Charles Tandy Foundation.

FINANCIAL SUMMARY
Recent Giving: $11,600,000 (1995 est.); $11,600,000 (1994 approx.); $10,611,238 (1993)

Assets: $218,000,000 (1995 est.); $218,418,490 (1994 approx.); $228,258,159 (1993)

EIN: 75-1638517

CONTRIBUTIONS SUMMARY
Donor(s): The foundation was established in 1978 by Anne Burnett Tandy in memory of her husband, Charles D. Tandy (d. 1978). Mr. Tandy bought Radio Shack in 1963 and built it from a debt-ridden chain of nine electronics stores to a national chain with over 7,000 outlets.

Typical Recipients: • *Arts & Humanities:* Arts Associations & Councils, Arts Institutes, Arts Outreach, Ballet, Libraries, Museums/Galleries, Music, Opera, Performing Arts, Visual Arts • *Civic & Public Affairs:* Botanical Gardens/Parks, Community Foundations, Economic Development, Employment/Job Training, Hispanic Affairs, Housing, Municipalities/Towns, Parades/Festivals, Public Policy, Urban & Community Affairs, Women's Affairs, Zoos/Aquariums • *Education:* After-school/Enrichment Programs, Colleges & Universities, Education Funds, Education Reform, Leadership Training, Medical Education, Minority Education, Private Education (Precollege), Public Education (Precollege) • *Health:* AIDS/HIV, Alzheimers Disease, Clinics/Medical Centers, Health Policy/Cost Containment, Hospitals, Mental Health, Single-Disease Health Associations • *Religion:* Religious Welfare • *Science:* Science Museums • *Social Services:* At-Risk Youth, Big Brother/Big Sister, Child Welfare, Crime Prevention, Emergency Relief, Family Planning, Family Services, Food/Clothing Distribution, People with Disabilities, Recreation & Athletics, Scouts, Shelters/Homelessness, Substance Abuse, United Funds/United Ways, YMCA/YWCA/YMHA/YWHA, Youth Organizations

Grant Types: capital, challenge, endowment, general support, project, and seed money

Geographic Distribution: primarily Texas, with an emphasis on the Ft. Worth metropolitan area

GIVING OFFICERS
Thomas Foster Beech: exec vp *B* St Paul MN 1939 *NONPR AFFIL* pres: SW Fdns

Benjamin J. Fortson: vp, trust, treas

Edward R. Hudson, Jr.: vp, trust, secy

Anne Burnett Windfohr Marion: pres, trust *B* 1939 *ED* Briarcliff Jr Coll; Univ Geneva; Univ TX

John Louis Marion: trust *B* New York NY 1933 *ED* Fordham Univ BS 1956; Columbia Univ 1960-1961 *CURR EMPL* chmn, dir: Sothebys Inc *CORP AFFIL* dir: Intl Fdn Art Research, Sothebys Holdings Inc *NONPR AFFIL* chmn fine arts comm: Am Cancer Soc New York City; dir: Intl Fdn Art Res; mem: Appraisers Assn Am *CLUB AFFIL* Eldorado CC, Lotos, Shady Oaks CC, Vintage

Anne W. Phillips: adv trust

APPLICATION INFORMATION
Initial Approach:

Applicants should write a succinct letter of inquiry describing the organization, the specific program to be considered, the amount requested, and a budget summary.

A detailed application form will be sent if the program fits within the foundation's guidelines and priorities.

There are no application deadlines.

Grant review meetings normally are held in February, June, and November.

Restrictions on Giving: Funding is limited to organizations with 501(c)(3) status. Individual scholarships are not given. The foundation will not fund religious organizations for sectarian purposes.

PUBLICATIONS
Annual report

GRANTS ANALYSIS
Total Grants: $10,611,238

Number of Grants: 89

Highest Grant: $5,000,000

Average Grant: $119,227

Typical Range: $20,000 to $50,000 and $100,000 to $300,000

Disclosure Period: 1993

Note: Recent grants are derived from a 1993 annual report.

RECENT GRANTS

Library

500,000	Frick Collection, New York, NY — endowment of the Frick Library

General

500,000	Central Park Conservancy, New York, NY — capital campaign
500,000	Southwestern Exposition and Livestock Show, Ft. Worth, TX — capital campaign
400,000	Ft. Worth Zoological Association, Ft. Worth, TX — capital and renovation campaign
400,000	Tarrant County Hospital District, Ft. Worth, TX — community health centers in the Stop Six and Diamond Hill neighborhoods
300,000	Boys and Girls Clubs of Greater Ft. Worth, Ft. Worth, TX — capital campaign/East Side facility

Cain Foundation, Effie and Wofford

CONTACT
Harvey L. Walker
Executive Director, Secretary, and Treasurer
Effie and Wofford Cain Foundation
4131 Spicewood Springs Rd., Ste. A-1
Austin, TX 78759
(512) 346-7490

FINANCIAL SUMMARY
Recent Giving: $2,600,000 (fiscal 1994 est.); $2,458,987 (fiscal 1993); $2,104,900 (fiscal 1992)

Assets: $66,000,000 (fiscal 1994 est.); $63,993,277 (fiscal 1993); $56,037,358 (fiscal 1992)

Gifts Received: $600,000 (fiscal 1994 est.); $2,161,266 (fiscal 1993); $595,860 (fiscal 1992)

Fiscal Note: In fiscal 1991, 1992, and 1993, the foundation received gifts from Effie Marie Cain, president of the foundation.

EIN: 75-6030774

CONTRIBUTIONS SUMMARY
Donor(s): The foundation was incorporated in Texas in 1952. Effie Marie Cain and the late Wofford R. Cain were the principal donors.

Typical Recipients: • *Arts & Humanities:* Arts Centers, Arts Outreach, Libraries, Public Broadcasting • *Civic & Public Affairs:* Employment/Job Training, Municipalities/Towns, Nonprofit Management • *Education:* Colleges & Universities, Engineering/Technological Education, Legal Education, Medical Education, Minority Education, Private Education (Precollege), Student Aid • *Environment:* Wildlife Protection • *Health:* Alzheimers Disease, Arthritis,

Cancer, Children's Health/Hospitals, Clinics/Medical Centers, Emergency/Ambulance Services, Heart, Hospitals, Medical Research, Medical Training, Single-Disease Health Associations • *Religion:* Churches, Jewish Causes, Missionary Activities (Domestic), Religious Organizations, Religious Welfare • *Social Services:* Camps, Child Welfare, Community Centers, Domestic Violence, Emergency Relief, People with Disabilities, Recreation & Athletics, Scouts, Substance Abuse, United Funds/United Ways, Youth Organizations

Grant Types: capital, endowment, operating expenses, and project

Geographic Distribution: Texas

GIVING OFFICERS
Effie Marie Cain: pres, dir

James B. Cain: vp, dir *ED* Univ TX BBA; Univ TX LLB *NONPR AFFIL* adv trust: Schreiner Coll; dir: TX Research League; mem: Am Bar Assn, Travis County Bar Assn, TX Bar Assn, TX Philosophical Soc, Univ TX Ex-Students Assn; Mem chancellor counc: Univ TX *CLUB AFFIL* mem: Longhorn, Masons, W Austin Optomistists; pres, secy, trust: Headliners *PHIL AFFIL* vp, secy: Ginger Murchison Foundation

John C. Cain: dir

F. Wofford Denius: dir

Franklin Wofford Denius: exec vp, dir *B* Athens TX 1925 *ED* Univ TX BBA; Univ TX LLB *CURR EMPL* atty: Frank W Denius Law Offices *CORP AFFIL* chmn emeritus, dir: Southern Union Co; dir: TX Commerce Bank-Austin; first vp: Un Fund *NONPR AF-FIL* adv trust: Schreiner Coll; dir: TX Research League; mem: Am Bar Assn, Travis County Bar Assn, TX Bar Assn, TX Philosophical Soc, Univ TX Ex-Students Assn; mem chancellors counc: Univ TX *CLUB AF-FIL* mem: Longhorn, Masons, W Austin Optomistists; pres, secy, trust: Headliners

Charmaine D. McGill: dir

Joyce Reynolds: asst secy

Harvey L. Walker: exec dir, secy, treas

APPLICATION INFORMATION
Initial Approach:

Organizations should contact the foundation for an application form.

Applicants must provide current contact information, a description of the program, and the amount requested. Applicants also must enclose a copy of 501(c)(3) tax-exempt status letter; description of the organizational structure, purpose, history, and programs; copy of latest Form 990; copy of most recent internal financial statements; and a list of expected contributions with amounts.

Completed applications must be returned within two months after receiving the application form. The deadline for receiving applications is the last day of August.

Complete applications are summarized periodically for review. If a director expresses interest in an application, it is placed on the agenda for the next directors' meeting. Although the foundation directors meet several times a year, grants generally are allocated

by the end of July or earlier. The foundation discourages contact with the directors.

Restrictions on Giving: Grants are not made to individuals, and are seldom made to organizations outside Texas.

OTHER THINGS TO KNOW
In addition to its grant making activities, the foundation also provides direct technical assistance to charitable organizations.

GRANTS ANALYSIS
Total Grants: $2,458,987

Number of Grants: 90

Highest Grant: $300,000

Average Grant: $27,322

Typical Range: $1,000 to $50,000

Disclosure Period: fiscal year ending October 31, 1993

Note: Recent grants are derived from a fiscal 1993 Form 990.

RECENT GRANTS

General

300,000	University of Texas Southwestern Medical Center, Dallas, TX — endowed Alzheimers disease research chair and center
250,000	Baylor College of Medicine, Houston, TX — endowed research chair in cardiology
250,000	University of Texas Austin, Austin, TX — regents chair in LBJ School of Public Affairs
80,000	Justin Paul Foundation, Round Rock, TX — developmental disabilities and other programs
75,000	Southwestern University, Georgetown, TX — endowed scholarships

Cain Foundation, Gordon and Mary

CONTACT
James D. Weaver
President
The Gordon and Mary Cain Foundation
Eight Greenway Plz., Ste. 702
Houston, TX 77046
(713) 960-9283

FINANCIAL SUMMARY
Recent Giving: $1,277,350 (1992); $1,222,450 (1991); $1,142,250 (1990)

Assets: $26,697,135 (1992); $26,801,141 (1991); $25,582,237 (1990)

Gifts Received: $25,000 (1990)

Fiscal Note: In 1990, contributions were received from William Camp.

EIN: 76-0251558

CONTRIBUTIONS SUMMARY

Donor(s): The foundation was established in 1988 by Gordon A. Cain and Mary H. Cain.

Typical Recipients: • *Arts & Humanities:* Arts Outreach, Ballet, Dance, Libraries, Museums/Galleries, Music, Public Broadcasting, Theater • *Civic & Public Affairs:* Botanical Gardens/Parks, Economic Policy, Housing, Law & Justice, Philanthropic Organizations, Public Policy, Urban & Community Affairs, Zoos/Aquariums • *Education:* Business Education, Business-School Partnerships, Colleges & Universities, Education Funds, Education Reform, Minority Education, Private Education (Precollege), Science/Mathematics Education • *Environment:* General, Wildlife Protection • *Health:* AIDS/HIV, Cancer, Children's Health/Hospitals, Eyes/Blindness, Hospices, Hospitals, Medical Rehabilitation, Medical Research, Single-Disease Health Associations • *International:* International Organizations • *Religion:* Churches, Jewish Causes, Religious Welfare • *Science:* Science Museums • *Social Services:* Child Welfare, Community Centers, Community Service Organizations, Day Care, Family Planning, Homes, Recreation & Athletics, Substance Abuse, United Funds/United Ways, Youth Organizations

Grant Types: capital, general support, multiyear/continuing support, operating expenses, research, and scholarship

Geographic Distribution: national, with a focus on Houston, TX

GIVING OFFICERS

Gordon Arbuthnot Cain: trust, dir *B* Baton Rouge LA 1912 *ED* LA St Univ BS 1933 *CURR EMPL* chmn, dir: Sterling Chem *CORP AFFIL* chmn: Sterling Group; chmn, dir: Ultrair; dir: Arcadian Corp

Mary H. Cain: trust

Margaret W. Oehmig: trust *PHIL AFFIL* pres: Oehmig Foundation

William C. Oehmig: secy, treas, cfo *PHIL AFFIL* ceo: Oehmig Foundation

James D. Weaver: pres, coo *B* 1918 *CURR EMPL* chmn bd, dir: Weaver Trucking Inc

Sharyn A. Weaver: trust

APPLICATION INFORMATION

Initial Approach:

The foundation has no application forms. Written requests should be mailed directly to the foundation.

Written proposals should include a statement of purpose of the organization; the organization's budget with a balance sheet, fund balance, distribution of funds, audited statement, and number of employees; the latest copy of the organization's IRS 501(c)(3) tax-exempt status letter; a list of current projects for which funding is sought with total amounts needed for each project; the total amount requested, with a breakdown of proposed expenses, including salaries, construction, and operating expenses; and a proposed method of evaluating the impact of success of project. If the proposal is for seed money for an area of new interest in the community, it should state the reasons this

area has not been funded in the past and the reasons why the applying organization can make a difference in this area. Proposals also should include information on the sustainability of proposed programs.

Proposals should be received two weeks prior to a board meeting.

The board meets twice a year, usually in May or June, and in November or December. Applicants should contact the foundation to determine the date of the next board meeting.

Restrictions on Giving: The foundation does not make grants to individuals.

GRANTS ANALYSIS

Total Grants: $1,277,350

Number of Grants: 123

Highest Grant: $250,000

Average Grant: $10,385

Typical Range: $1,000 to $25,000

Disclosure Period: 1992

Note: Recent grants are derived from a 1992 grants list.

RECENT GRANTS

General

250,000	Texas Children's Hospital, Houston, TX — building fund
100,000	Good Samaritan Foundation, Houston, TX — annual grant
50,000	Cato Institute, Washington, DC — general operations
50,000	Houston Museum of Natural Science, Houston, TX — general operations
50,000	Lees-McRae College, Banner Elk, NC — math program

Carter Foundation, Amon G.

CONTACT

Bob J. Crow
Executive Director
Amon G. Carter Foundation
500 W Seventh St., Ste. 1212
PO Box 1036
Ft. Worth, TX 76101
(817) 332-2783

FINANCIAL SUMMARY

Recent Giving: $10,500,000 (1995 est.); $10,500,000 (1994 approx.); $10,500,000 (1993 approx.)

Assets: $210,000,000 (1995 est.); $210,000,000 (1994 approx.); $205,000,000 (1993 approx.)

EIN: 75-6000331

CONTRIBUTIONS SUMMARY

Donor(s): The Amon G. Carter Foundation was established in 1945 by Amon G. Carter, publisher of the *Ft. Worth Star Telegram* and founder of Carter Publications. Ruth Carter Stevenson, the donor's daughter and the only living member of the Carter family, is president of the foundation. The Carter

family's interests in art are reflected in the Amon Carter Museum, which specializes in western and early American art.

Typical Recipients: • *Arts & Humanities:* Arts Associations & Councils, Community Arts, Ethnic & Folk Arts, Film & Video, Historic Preservation, Libraries, Museums/Galleries, Music, Public Broadcasting, Theater • *Civic & Public Affairs:* Botanical Gardens/Parks, Community Foundations, Housing, Law & Justice, Safety, Urban & Community Affairs, Women's Affairs, Zoos/Aquariums • *Education:* Arts/Humanities Education, Colleges & Universities, Community & Junior Colleges, Economic Education, Education Associations, Elementary Education (Private), Engineering/Technological Education, General, Medical Education, Minority Education, Private Education (Precollege), Public Education (Precollege), Science/Mathematics Education, Special Education • *Environment:* General • *Health:* Children's Health/Hospitals, Emergency/Ambulance Services, Health Policy/Cost Containment, Health Organizations, Hospitals, Medical Rehabilitation, Medical Research, Mental Health, Nursing Services, Public Health, Research/Studies Institutes, Single-Disease Health Associations • *International:* International Affairs • *Religion:* Religious Organizations • *Science:* Science Exhibits & Fairs • *Social Services:* At-Risk Youth, Child Welfare, Community Service Organizations, Day Care, Delinquency & Criminal Rehabilitation, Family Planning, Family Services, Food/Clothing Distribution, Homes, People with Disabilities, Recreation & Athletics, Senior Services, Shelters/Homelessness, Substance Abuse, United Funds/United Ways, Volunteer Services, Youth Organizations

Grant Types: capital, challenge, general support, project, and seed money

Geographic Distribution: primarily Ft. Worth/Tarrant County, TX, area

GIVING OFFICERS

Robert William Brown, MD: vp, dir *B* Seattle WA 1924 *ED* Tulane Univ MD 1950 *CURR EMPL* pres: Am Baseball League *NONPR AFFIL* mem: Am Med Assn

J.H. Connelly: trust *PHIL AFFIL* trust: J. W. and Eula Carter Scholarship Fund in Memory of Newt Bryson

Bob J. Crow: exec dir *ED* TX Christian Univ

W. Patrick Harris: asst secy-treas *ED* LA St Univ *NONPR AFFIL* pres: Amon Carter Mus Western Art

J. Lee Johnson IV: dir

Mark L. Johnson: dir *PHIL AFFIL* dir: Amon G. Carter Star Telegram Employees Fund

Ruth Carter Stevenson: pres, dir *B* Ft Worth TX 1925 *ED* Sarah Lawrence Coll BA 1945 *NONPR AFFIL* chmn: Amon Carter Mus Western Art; dir: Natl Gallery Art, Natl Trust Historic Preservation; trust: Madeira Sch *CLUB AFFIL* Chevy Chase CC, Colony, Downtown, Links, Metropolitan, Sulgrave

APPLICATION INFORMATION
Initial Approach:

Applicants should contact the foundation by letter.

Letters of request should include proof of the organization's tax-exempt status and the purpose of the requested grant. The foundation may require additional information at a later date.

There are no deadlines for funding requests.

All grants must be approved by the four-member board of directors, which meets three times a year.

Restrictions on Giving: No grants are made to individuals or for loans. Applying organizations usually must qualify for exemption under Section 501(c)(3) of the Internal Revenue Code. Special consideration is required if an applying organization is not exempt as a private foundation under Section 509(a) of the Code. Grants outside the Ft. Worth area are initiated only by the staff and board of directors.

PUBLICATIONS
Policy and guidelines statement

GRANTS ANALYSIS
Total Grants: $9,543,058

Number of Grants: 161

Highest Grant: $4,624,975

Average Grant: $30,738*

Typical Range: $10,000 to $100,000

Disclosure Period: 1992

Note: The average grant figure excludes a $4,624,975 grant. Recent grants are derived from a 1992 grants list.

RECENT GRANTS
Library
75,000	Southwest Adventist College, Keene, TX — library program

General
500,000	Scott and White Hospital, Temple, TX — equipment purchase
350,000	Tarrant County Housing Partnership, Ft. Worth, TX — special program
250,000	University of Texas Galveston Medical Branch, Galveston, TX — special program
200,000	University of Texas Austin School of Architecture, Austin, TX — chair endowment
150,000	Lake County Christian Foundation, Ft. Worth, TX — building program

Clayton Fund

CONTACT
William Askey
Secretary and Treasurer
Clayton Fund
c/o Texas Commerce Bank
PO Box 2558
Houston, TX 77252-8037
(713) 216-3447

FINANCIAL SUMMARY
Recent Giving: $1,500,000 (1995 est.); $1,500,000 (1994 est.); $1,000,000 (1993)

Assets: $30,600,000 (1995 est.); $29,852,417 (1994); $25,000,000 (1993)

Gifts Received: $28,000 (1987); $28,000 (1985)

Fiscal Note: In 1987, the fund received a contribution of $28,000 from the OCF Foundation in New York City.

EIN: 76-0285764

CONTRIBUTIONS SUMMARY
Donor(s): The Clayton Fund was established in Texas as a trust in 1952 through donations by the late William L. Clayton and his late wife, Susan V. Clayton . William L. Clayton, founder of the insurance and food processing company, Anderson, Clayton and Company, was also active in the federal government, including his service as Assistant Secretary of State. He was also vice president of the Export-Import Bank, and wrote extensively on international trade, economics, and foreign affairs. The William L. Clayton Center for International Economic Affairs at the Fletcher School of Law and Diplomacy of Tufts University is named after him.

Typical Recipients: • *Arts & Humanities:* Libraries • *Civic & Public Affairs:* Public Policy, Rural Affairs • *Education:* Colleges & Universities, Medical Education, Private Education (Precollege), Special Education • *Health:* Health Organizations, Single-Disease Health Associations • *Social Services:* People with Disabilities, Shelters/Homelessness

Grant Types: fellowship, general support, professorship, and scholarship

Geographic Distribution: primarily Texas, with emphasis on Houston; limited support elsewhere

GIVING OFFICERS
William Askey: treas, secy

William C. Baker: trust *PHIL AFFIL* trust: Clayton Baker Trust

William L. Garwood, Jr.: vp *PHIL AFFIL* vp, trust: Patrick Henry Foundation

Burdine C. Johnson: pres *PHIL AFFIL* trust: Burdine Johnson Foundation

APPLICATION INFORMATION
Initial Approach:

A brief proposal and description of the organization and project should be sent along with a preliminary letter. There is no standard application form. There is, however, an application form for those seeking scholarship funds.

A summary concerning the applicant, details of the project, total amount required for the project, amount requested from the Clayton fund, other sources of funds which have been contacted for funding of the project with a statement of results of such contacts, and a balance sheet and income statement of the organization. The preceding items should be sent in quintuplicate accompanied by a copy of the determination letter issued to the applicant by the I.R.S. The determination letter must state that the organization is exempt from federal income taxation.

The board of trustees reviews applications as they are received. There are no deadlines for general funding.

OTHER THINGS TO KNOW
Scholarship recipients may attend any accredited college or university in the United States and select any course of study. The scholarship recipient who maintains satisfactory progress toward a degree may retain the scholarship for the normal four-year college attendance or until the program is discontinued. The program provides grants only for a full school year, except when the student graduates at the end of the first semester. Scholarships commence only at the beginning of a regular school year.

GRANTS ANALYSIS
Total Grants: $138,600

Number of Grants: 16

Highest Grant: $30,000

Average Grant: $8,663

Typical Range: $1,000 to $30,000

Disclosure Period: 1989

Note: Recent grants are derived from a 1989 grants list.

RECENT GRANTS
Library
1,800	Houston Public Library, Houston, TX

General
30,000	Population Crisis Committee, Washington, DC
25,000	American Farmland Trust, Washington, DC
20,000	Friends of Ronald McDonald House, Austin, TX
10,000	Center for Battered Women, Austin, TX — Shelter Fund
10,000	Houston School for Deaf Children, Houston, TX

Clements Foundation

CONTACT
Shirley Warren
Secretary
Clements Fdn.
1901 N Akard St.
Dallas, TX 75201
(214) 720-0377

FINANCIAL SUMMARY
Recent Giving: $209,750 (1993); $100,816 (1992); $356,356 (1991)

Assets: $4,269,534 (1993); $4,789,046 (1992); $5,009,443 (1991)

Gifts Received: $255,000 (1993)

Fiscal Note: In 1993, contributions were received from William P. Clements, Jr.

EIN: 75-6065076

CONTRIBUTIONS SUMMARY

Typical Recipients: • *Arts & Humanities:* Arts Outreach, Historic Preservation, History & Archaeology, Libraries, Museums/Galleries • *Civic & Public Affairs:* Botanical Gardens/Parks, Clubs, General, Parades/Festivals, Urban & Community Affairs, Zoos/Aquariums • *Education:* Colleges & Universities, Education Funds, Private Education (Precollege), Secondary Education (Private) • *Health:* Arthritis • *Religion:* Churches • *Science:* Science Museums • *Social Services:* Child Welfare, Community Service Organizations, Scouts, United Funds/United Ways, Youth Organizations

Grant Types: general support and scholarship

Geographic Distribution: focus on the Dallas, TX, area

GIVING OFFICERS

B. Gill Clements: vp *PHIL AFFIL* vp, trust: Pauline Allen Gill Foundation

William P. Clements: pres *B* Dallas TX 1917 *ED* Southern Methodist Univ DHL 1974 *CORP AFFIL* chmn: SEDCO; dir: Gen Motors Corp, Interfirst Corp *NONPR AFFIL* mem: Am Assn Oil Well Drilling Contractors, Intl Assn Drilling Contractors, Southern Methodist Univ, Southwestern Med Sch; mem natl exec bd: Boy Scouts Am

Nancy Clements Seay: vp *PHIL AFFIL* vp, trust: Pauline Allen Gill Foundation

Shirley Warren: secy

APPLICATION INFORMATION

Initial Approach: Send a brief letter of inquiry. Include a description of organization, amount requested, purpose of funds sought, recently audited financial statement, and proof of tax-exempt status. There are no deadlines.

GRANTS ANALYSIS

Total Grants: $209,750

Number of Grants: 14

Highest Grant: $61,000

Typical Range: $200 to $50,000

Disclosure Period: 1993

Note: Recent grants are derived from a 1993 Form 990.

RECENT GRANTS

General

61,000	Southern Methodist University, Dallas, TX	
50,000	Dallas Museum of Natural History Association, Dallas, TX	
15,000	St. Michael's Church, Dallas, TX	
10,000	Hockaday School, Dallas, TX	
10,000	United Way, Dallas, TX	

Contran Corporation / Simmons Foundation, Inc., Harold

Revenue: $1.14 billion
Employees: 10,000
Headquarters: Dallas, TX
SIC Major Group: Holding Companies Nec, Crude Petroleum & Natural Gas, Beet Sugar, and Sawmills & Planing Mills—General

CONTACT

Lisa K. Simmons
President
Harold Simmons Foundation, Inc.
5430 LBJ Fwy., Ste. 1700
Dallas, TX 75240-2697
(214) 233-2134

FINANCIAL SUMMARY

Recent Giving: $1,000,000 (1995 est.); $1,000,000 (1994 approx.); $895,852 (1993)

Assets: $1,854 (1993); $27,385 (1992); $13,219 (1991)

Gifts Received: $860,600 (1993); $4,695,000 (1992)

Fiscal Note: Figures reflect foundation giving only. Contran gives a small, undisclosed amount of direct support. Contributions to U.S.-based nonprofit organizations are included in the above figures. In 1993, contributions were received from Contran Corporation.

EIN: 75-2222091

CONTRIBUTIONS SUMMARY

Typical Recipients: • *Arts & Humanities:* Dance, Historic Preservation, Libraries, Museums/Galleries, Music, Public Broadcasting, Theater • *Civic & Public Affairs:* Economic Development, Housing, Philanthropic Organizations, Professional & Trade Associations, Zoos/Aquariums • *Education:* Colleges & Universities, Education Reform, Faculty Development, General, Literacy, Medical Education, Private Education (Precollege), Public Education (Precollege) • *Health:* Cancer, Children's Health/Hospitals, Clinics/Medical Centers, Health Organizations, Kidney, Medical Research, Nursing Services, Prenatal Health Issues, Public Health, Transplant Networks/Donor Banks • *International:* International Development • *Religion:* Churches, Religious Welfare • *Social Services:* Child Welfare, Counseling, Domestic Violence, Family Services, Shelters/Homelessness, Substance Abuse, United Funds/United Ways, Volunteer Services, Youth Organizations

Grant Types: capital, challenge, employee matching gifts, operating expenses, and project

Note: Employee matching gift ratio: 1 to 1.

Geographic Distribution: only in the Dallas, TX, area

Operating Locations: TX (Dallas)

Note: Also operates worldwide

CORP. OFFICERS

Eugene Karl Anderson: *B* Omaha NE 1935 *ED* Wayne St Univ 1958; Univ NE 1962 *CURR EMPL* vp: Contran Corp

Glenn Reuben Simmons: *B* Golden TX 1928 *ED* E TX St Univ BS 1950; TX Christian Univ *CURR EMPL* vchmn: Contran Corp *CORP AFFIL* chmn, ceo, dir: Keystone Consolidated Indus; dir: Am Iron & Steel Inst, LLC Corp; vchmn: Valhi Inc

Harold Clark Simmons: *B* Alba TX 1931 *ED* Univ TX BA 1952; Univ TX MA *CURR EMPL* chmn, ceo, dir: Amalgamated Sugar Co *CORP AFFIL* chmn: Natl City Bancorp; chmn, ceo: Contran Corp; chmn, ceo, dir: Valhi Inc; dir: LLC Corp, Natl City Lines, NL Indus Inc, TIME-DC, Transtar Airlines Corp *NONPR AFFIL* mem: Phi Beta Kappa

Michael Alan Snetzer: *B* Denver CO 1940 *ED* Univ AR BS 1963; Southern Methodist Univ MBA 1969 *CURR EMPL* pres, dir: Valhi Inc *CORP AFFIL* chmn: Medite Corp; chmn, ceo, dir: Medford Corp; dir: Amalgamated Sugar Co, Baroid Corp, NL Indus Inc, Tremont Corp; pres, dir: Contran Corp *CLUB AFFIL* Bent Tree CC, Univ

Steven L. Watson: *CURR EMPL* vp, secy: Contran Corp

GIVING OFFICERS

Eugene Karl Anderson: treas *CURR EMPL* vp: Contran Corp (see above)

John Mark Hollingsworth: asst secy *B* Dallas TX 1951 *ED* Rhodes Coll BA 1973; Southern Methodist Univ JD 1977 *CURR EMPL* gen corp couns: Valhi Inc

Harold Clark Simmons: chmn, dir *CURR EMPL* chmn, ceo, dir: Amalgamated Sugar Co (see above)

Lisa K. Simmons: pres

Steven L. Watson: vp, secy, dir *CURR EMPL* vp, secy: Contran Corp (see above)

APPLICATION INFORMATION

Initial Approach: *Initial Contact:* proposal *Include Information On:* brief history of organization and its purpose; explanation of proposed project, funds requested; list of foundation's directors, including professional affiliations; description of staff; description of use of volunteers; list of major donors; copy of organization's tax determination letter from IRS; financial information; most recent audited statement or form 990; current year's budget for organization and project; fundraising costs *Deadlines:* none

Restrictions on Giving: Foundation does not support individuals, endowments, deficit financing, or organizations that discriminate on the basis of race, religion, or sex. Multiyear grants are limited in number.

GRANTS ANALYSIS

Total Grants: $876,097*

Number of Grants: 136*

Highest Grant: $100,000

Average Grant: $6,442*

Typical Range: $1,000 to $20,000

Disclosure Period: 1993

Note: Above figures exclude 80 matching gifts totaling $19,755. Recent grants are derived from a 1993 Form 990.

RECENT GRANTS

General
100,000	Marrow Foundation, Arlington, VA — three-year pledge to promote expansion of national registry of bone marrow donors
50,000	Crystal Charity Ball, Dallas, TX
34,000	Stanford University Medical Center, Stanford, CA — renovation of a laboratory
33,000	Greenhill School, Dallas, TX — faculty support
25,000	CARE, Dallas, TX — small business enterprise development projects in Peru, Guatemala, and Costa Rica

Cooper Industries, Inc. / Cooper Industries Foundation

Revenue: $6.25 billion
Employees: 49,500
Headquarters: Houston, TX
SIC Major Group: Transformers Except Electronic, Nonferrous Wiredrawing & Insulating, Hand & Edge Tools Nec, and Industrial Valves

CONTACT
Virginia Weiler
Assistant Secretary
Cooper Industries Foundation
PO Box 4446
Houston, TX 77002
(713) 739-5400
Note: Subsidiaries have separate contact persons; call the foundation office for information.

FINANCIAL SUMMARY
Recent Giving: $4,300,000 (1995 est.); $2,529,917 (1994); $4,800,000 (1993)
Assets: $131,333 (1993); $1,300,000 (1991); $466,978 (1990)
Fiscal Note: Total giving figures include both foundation and direct giving. Direct contributions by the company amount to approximately $523,000 annually, in grants of less than $1,000 each. Above figures include nonmonetary support.
EIN: 31-6060698

CONTRIBUTIONS SUMMARY
Typical Recipients: • *Arts & Humanities:* Arts Associations & Councils, Arts Funds, Dance, Historic Preservation, Libraries, Museums/Galleries, Music, Opera, Performing Arts, Public Broadcasting, Theater • *Civic & Public Affairs:* Business/Free Enterprise, Economic Development, Economic Policy, Law & Justice, Public Policy, Safety, Urban & Community Affairs, Women's Affairs,

Zoos/Aquariums • *Education:* Business Education, Colleges & Universities, Community & Junior Colleges, Economic Education, Education Associations, Education Funds, Engineering/Technological Education, Medical Education, Science/Mathematics Education, Secondary Education (Public), Student Aid • *Environment:* General • *Health:* Cancer, Emergency/Ambulance Services, Health Funds, Health Organizations, Heart, Hospices, Hospitals, Mental Health, Single-Disease Health Associations • *Science:* Science Museums, Scientific Centers & Institutes • *Social Services:* Animal Protection, Child Welfare, Community Centers, Community Service Organizations, Emergency Relief, Food/Clothing Distribution, People with Disabilities, Recreation & Athletics, Senior Services, United Funds/United Ways, YMCA/YWCA/YMHA/YWHA, Youth Organizations

Grant Types: capital, challenge, employee matching gifts, general support, project, and seed money

Note: Employee matching gift ratio: 1 to 1 and 2 to 1 for volunteer services.

Nonmonetary Support: $50,000 (1993); $76,000 (1991); $20,000 (1990)

Nonmonetary Support Types: donated equipment and donated products

Note: Requests for nonmonetary support should be addressed to Virginia Weiler (see above). The company also sponsors a volunteer program, Private Sector Initiatives, for housing improvement.

Geographic Distribution: locations where company maintains facilities

Operating Locations: AL (Boaz, Cullman, Eufaula, Huntsville), AR (Clinton, Dumas, Pine Bluff), CA (Cerritos, Irvine, Redding, Torrence), CT (Beacon Falls, Windsor), GA (Americus, Ellaville, Preston), IA (Burlington, Ottumwa), IL (Chicago, Elk Grove Village, Forest View, Macomb, Melrose Park, Quincy, Sycamore), IN (Michigan City, Middlebury, Richmond), KY (Elizabethtown, Monticello, Tompkinsville), LA (Berwick, Patterson, Ville Platte), MA (Brighton), ME (Brunswick, Madison), MI (Brighton, Sturgis), MO (Berkely, Chesterfield, Ellisville, La Grange, Sedalia, St. Louis), MS (Greenville, Lumberton, Vicksburg), NC (Apex, Black Mountain, Franklin, Goldsboro, LaGrange, Monroe, Raleigh), NJ (Newark, Parsippany), NY (Buffalo, Cortland, Orlean, Syracuse), OH (Cambridge, Cincinnati, Dayton, Hicksville, Hilliard, Mt. Vernon, Springfield, Toledo, Zanesville), OK (Oklahoma City), PA (Boyertown, Cannonsburg, Coraopolis, East Stroudsburg, Easton, Grove City, Pittsburgh, Shamokin, Weatherly, York), SC (Cheraw, Columbia, Duncan, Greenville, Greenwood, Lexington, Liberty, Orangeburg, Sumter), TN (Covington, Memphis, Sevierville, Sparta), TX (Amarillo, Ft. Worth, Houston, Missouri City, Nacogdoches, Richmond, Tyler, Waco), VA (Charlottesville, Earlysville, Hampton, Roanoke), VT (Essex Junction), WA (Tacoma), WI (Franksville, Pewaukee, South Milwaukee, Waukesha)

CORP. OFFICERS
Thomas Wood Campbell: *B* Monticello AR 1930 *ED* Univ MO BA 1953; Fairfield Univ 1972 *CURR EMPL* vp pub aff: Cooper Indus Inc *NONPR AFFIL* chmn pub aff counc: Machinery & Allied Products Inst; mem: Pub Rels Soc Am

Robert Cizik: *B* Scranton PA 1931 *ED* Univ CT BS 1953; Harvard Univ MBA 1958 *CURR EMPL* chmn, ceo, dir: Cooper Indus Inc *CORP AFFIL* Air Products & Chem Inc, Panhandle Eastern Corp; dir: Harris Corp, Temple-Inland Inc *NONPR AFFIL* co-chmn: Wortham Theater Fdn; dir: Assn Harvard Univ, Central Houston, Greater Houston Partnership, Natl Bus Comm Arts, TX Bus Ed Coalition, TX Res League; mem: Bus Roundtable, Electrical Mfrs Club, Houston Bus Comm Arts, Natl Assn Mfrs, TX Strategic Econ Policy Comm; mem exec comm, dir: Machinery Allied Products Inst; mem natl adv counc: TX Heart Inst; trust: Houston Grand Opera, Un Way TX Gulf Coast; trust, mem res & policy comm: Comm Econ Devel *CLUB AFFIL* Electronics Mfrs, Forum, Houston Ctr, Ramada, River Oaks CC

Dewain Kingsley Cross: *B* Watertown NY 1937 *ED* Clarkson Univ BBA 1961; Harvard Univ AMP 1978 *CURR EMPL* sr vp fin: Cooper Indus Inc *CORP AFFIL* dir: Aviall Inc, Wyman-Gordon Co *NONPR AFFIL* mem: Am Inst CPAs, NY Soc CPAs; mem fin counc: Machinery Allied Products Inst *CLUB AFFIL* Houston

GIVING OFFICERS
Thomas Wood Campbell: pres, trust *CURR EMPL* vp pub aff: Cooper Indus Inc (see above)

Robert Cizik: chmn, trust *CURR EMPL* chmn, ceo, dir: Cooper Indus Inc (see above)

Dewain Kingsley Cross: treas, trust *CURR EMPL* sr vp fin: Cooper Indus Inc (see above)

Pat Meinecke: secy

Virginia Weiler: asst secy

APPLICATION INFORMATION
Initial Approach: *Initial Contact:* brief letter or proposal *Include Information On:* description of the organization, amount requested, purpose for which funds are sought, recently audited financial statement, and proof of tax-exempt status *Deadlines:* none

Restrictions on Giving: The following types of organizations normally are not eligible for grants: religious organizations (especially for sectarian purposes), national health and welfare organizations (except through a local united fund drive), fraternal or veterans' organizations (unless projects benefit a wide spectrum of community life), goodwill advertising, political candidates or organizations, labor organizations, and lobbying organizations. The company also does not support endowment funds or individuals.

GRANTS ANALYSIS
Total Grants: $2,529,917
Number of Grants: 525
Highest Grant: $100,000

Average Grant: $4,819

Typical Range: $1,000 to $20,000

Disclosure Period: 1994

Note: Recent grants are derived from a 1994 Grants List.

RECENT GRANTS

General
100,000	Ohio University College of Engineering and Technology, Athens, OH
35,950	National Merit Scholarship Corporation, Evanston, IL
34,716	United Way of Elk Grove, Elk Grove, IL
32,215	United Way of Central New York, Syracuse, NY
32,000	Onondaga Community College, Syracuse, NY

Cullen Foundation

CONTACT
Alan M. Stewart
Executive Director
Cullen Foundation
PO Box 1600
Houston, TX 77251
(713) 651-8600

FINANCIAL SUMMARY
Recent Giving: $11,000,000 (1995 est.); $17,500,000 (1994 approx.); $17,143,740 (1993)

Assets: $185,000,000 (1995 est.); $186,500,000 (1994 approx.); $187,264,157 (1993)

EIN: 74-6048769

CONTRIBUTIONS SUMMARY
Donor(s): The Cullen Foundation was established in 1947 by Hugh Roy Cullen, a Houston oilman. The original grant funding the foundation was in the form of oil properties. The donor's daughter and grandsons serve on the board of trustees.

Typical Recipients: • *Arts & Humanities:* Ballet, Dance, Film & Video, History & Archaeology, Libraries, Museums/Galleries, Music, Opera, Public Broadcasting, Theater • *Civic & Public Affairs:* Botanical Gardens/Parks, General, Legal Aid, Municipalities/Towns, Philanthropic Organizations, Safety, Zoos/Aquariums • *Education:* Colleges & Universities, Education Reform, Medical Education, Private Education (Precollege), Public Education (Precollege), Science/Mathematics Education, Secondary Education (Private), Special Education, Student Aid • *Health:* Cancer, Children's Health/Hospitals, Clinics/Medical Centers, Heart, Hospices, Hospitals, Medical Rehabilitation, Medical Research • *Religion:* Religious Welfare • *Science:* Science Museums • *Social Services:* At-Risk Youth, Family Planning, Food/Clothing Distribution, Scouts, Shelters/Homelessness, United Funds/United Ways, Youth Organizations

Grant Types: capital, department, endowment, general support, professorship, and project

Geographic Distribution: Texas, primarily Houston

GIVING OFFICERS
Isaac Arnold, Jr.: secy-treas, trust *CORP AFFIL* chmn, dir: Quintana Petroleum Corp; dir: Comtex Scientific Corp, Cullen Ctr Bank & Trust

Bert L. Campbell: trust *B* Tyler TX 1939 *ED* Univ TX BA 1961; Univ TX JD 1970 *CURR EMPL* ptnr: Vinson & Elkins *CORP AFFIL* secy: QMC Holding Co

Roy Henry Cullen: vp, dir *B* 1929

William H. Drushel, Jr.: trust *CURR EMPL* ptnr: Vinson & Elkins *CORP AFFIL* vp, secy: Quintana Petroleum Corp

Wilhelmina Cullen Robertson: pres, trust *B* 1923 *ED* Sweet Briar Coll

Alan M. Stewart: exec dir

APPLICATION INFORMATION
Initial Approach:

Initial contact should be a letter briefly describing the project. A complete application should not be submitted until the foundation's interest in the project has been ascertained. The foundation also may be contacted by telephone for this purpose.

A complete application should include a brief description of the grant requested, with the following information: amount of the grant; purpose of the grant, including the total funds needed for the project; existence of a challenge grant, including the name of grantor; all other grants received or anticipated for the project; source or sources of funds available for the project apart from grants; and timing of the grant requested, including installment payments if desired. Applications also should include a description of the recipient organization listing the purpose, scope of operations, history, affiliations, trustees or directors, officers, and managers; and principal contributors and supporters, including the dollar amounts of the support and major grants received. Financial information should include an income and expense statement, balance sheet for the latest year, and the coming year's budget. All applicants also must include proof of tax-exempt status. Applications for grants to be used for building construction or purchase of property also should include an architectural rendering or drawing of the facilities to be built or a photograph of the property to be acquired, a description of the property, and a cost estimate.

There are no deadlines for submitting requests.

The board of trustees meets four to seven times a year. Applications will be considered at the first meeting after the completed application is received.

Restrictions on Giving: Grants are restricted to Texas-based organizations for programs in Texas, primarily in the Houston area. No grants are made to political or lobbying groups, religious organizations for sectarian purposes, other foundations, operating foundations, or to individuals.

PUBLICATIONS
Checklist of information for grant requests

GRANTS ANALYSIS
Total Grants: $17,143,740

Number of Grants: 45

Highest Grant: $6,000,000

Average Grant: $253,267*

Typical Range: $50,000 to $400,000

Disclosure Period: 1993

Note: Average grant figure excludes the highest grant of $6,000,000. Recent grants are derived from a 1993 Form 990.

RECENT GRANTS

Library
166,667	River Oaks Baptist School, Houston, TX — new library and media center

General
6,000,000	University of Houston System, Houston, TX — Lillie and Roy Cullen Endowment
3,108,407	City of Houston Parks and Recreation Department, Houston, TX — development of Cullen Park
600,000	Texas Children's Hospital, Houston, TX — defray cost of construction
580,000	Baylor College of Medicine, Houston, TX — endowment for molecular genetics
400,000	University of St. Thomas, Houston, TX — defray cost of science building construction

Davidson Family Charitable Foundation

CONTACT
Steve Davidson
Vice Chairman
Davidson Family Charitable Foundation
310 W Texas, Ste. 709
Midland, TX 79701
(915) 687-0995

FINANCIAL SUMMARY
Recent Giving: $750,000 (fiscal 1994 est.); $936,000 (fiscal 1993); $691,075 (fiscal 1992)

Assets: $20,000,000 (fiscal 1994 est.); $22,387,907 (fiscal 1993); $21,410,291 (fiscal 1992)

Gifts Received: $8,250 (fiscal 1989); $4,000 (fiscal 1988); $42,625 (fiscal 1987)

Fiscal Note: In fiscal 1989, the foundation received a contribution from the Frances M. Davidson Estate.

EIN: 23-7440630

CONTRIBUTIONS SUMMARY

Donor(s): The foundation was established in 1961, with the late C. J. Davidson and members of the Davidson family as donors.

Typical Recipients: • *Arts & Humanities:* Arts Associations & Councils, Arts Festivals, Libraries, Museums/Galleries, Music, Theater • *Civic & Public Affairs:* Hispanic Affairs, Municipalities/Towns • *Education:* Business Education, Colleges & Universities, Literacy, Public Education (Precollege), Special Education, Student Aid • *Health:* Cancer, Diabetes, Eyes/Blindness, Hospices, Hospitals, Single-Disease Health Associations • *Religion:* Ministries, Religious Welfare • *Social Services:* Big Brother/Big Sister, Child Welfare, Community Centers, Community Service Organizations, Day Care, Emergency Relief, Food/Clothing Distribution, Homes, People with Disabilities, Recreation & Athletics, Scouts, Senior Services, Sexual Abuse, Shelters/Homelessness, Substance Abuse, United Funds/United Ways, YMCA/YWCA/YMHA/YWHA, Youth Organizations

Grant Types: capital and operating expenses

Geographic Distribution: primarily west Texas

GIVING OFFICERS
H. W. Davidson: chmn

Steve Davidson: vchmn

APPLICATION INFORMATION
Initial Approach:

Letters of application should be addressed to H. W. Davidson.

Requests for funding should include financial statements, a list of current aid being received, proof of tax-exempt status, and other general information.

Letters of request should be submitted four weeks prior to each board meeting.

The board meets in June and December of each year to consider proposals.

OTHER THINGS TO KNOW
Bank One of Fort Worth serves as the corporate trustee for the foundation.

GRANTS ANALYSIS
Total Grants: $936,000

Number of Grants: 69

Highest Grant: $50,000

Average Grant: $13,565

Typical Range: $5,000 to $25,000

Disclosure Period: fiscal year ending June 30, 1993

Note: Recent grants are derived from a fiscal 1993 Form 990.

RECENT GRANTS

Library
25,000	Friends of the Midland Public Library, Midland, TX — for Children and Youth Department fixtures
5,000	Nita Stewart Haley Memorial Library/aka Haley Library, Midland, TX — for general operating support

General
50,000	Bynum School Development Disabilities Center, Midland, TX — for general operating support
50,000	Texas Tech University Foundation, Lubbock, TX — for Davidson Foundation Fund for Excellence
47,500	United Way of Midland, Midland, TX
42,500	United Way of Metropolitan Tarrant County, Ft. Worth, TX
40,000	Midland Cerebral Palsy Treatment Center, Midland, TX — for general operating support

Diamond Shamrock Inc.

Revenue: $2.62 billion
Employees: 6,000
Headquarters: San Antonio, TX
SIC Major Group: Petroleum Refining, Grocery Stores, and Gasoline Service Stations

CONTACT
Kathy Hughes
Manager, Public Relations
Diamond Shamrock Inc.
PO Box 696000
San Antonio, TX 78269
(210) 641-6800
Note: For a recorded message on application procedures, call 210-641-8780.

FINANCIAL SUMMARY
Fiscal Note: Annual Giving Range: $250,000 to $500,000

CONTRIBUTIONS SUMMARY
Typical Recipients: • *Arts & Humanities:* General, Libraries • *Civic & Public Affairs:* Economic Development, General • *Education:* Business Education, General • *Health:* Emergency/Ambulance Services, General • *Social Services:* Community Centers, General

Grant Types: matching and scholarship

Nonmonetary Support Types: donated equipment, donated products, loaned executives, and workplace solicitation

Geographic Distribution: headquarters and operating locations

Operating Locations: TX (Amarillo, Houston, Mont Belvieu, San Antonio, Sunray, Three Rivers)

CORP. OFFICERS
Robert Sheldon Beadle: *B* Orange NJ 1949 *ED* Cornell Univ 1971; Cornell Univ 1976 *CURR EMPL* vp, dir: Diamond Shamrock Inc

Timothy Jon Fretthold: *B* Berea OH 1949 *ED* Yale Univ BA 1971; Case Western Reserve Univ JD 1975 *CURR EMPL* sr vp, gen couns, dir: Diamond Shamrock Inc *CORP AFFIL* sr vp, gen couns: Diamond Shamrock Refining & Mktg Co; vp, dir: Petroleum/Chem Environmental Svcs *NONPR AFFIL* mem: Am Bar Assn, Am Soc Corp Secys, Dallas Bar Assn, OH Bar Assn, TX Bar Assn, Yale Univ Alumni Assn

Roger Roy Hemminghaus: *B* St Louis MO 1936 *ED* Purdue Univ 1954-1956; Auburn Univ BS 1958 *CURR EMPL* chmn, pres, ceo: Diamond Shamrock Inc *CORP AFFIL* ceo, pres, dir: Sigmor Corp; dir: InterFirst Bank NA, SW Pub Svc Co; pres, ceo, dir: Autotronic Sys Inc; pres, dir: Diamond Shamrock Refining & Mktg Co, Diamond Shamrock Stas *NONPR AFFIL* dir: Natl Petroleum Counc; mem: Am Chem Soc, Am Inst Chem Engrs, Am Petroleum Inst, Kappa Alpha, Naval Archt & Marine Engrs, Phi Kappa Phi, Phi Lambda Upsilon, San Antonio Chamber Commerce, Tau Beta Pi *CLUB AFFIL* Fair Oaks CC, Petroleum, Plz

GIVING OFFICERS
Robert Sheldon Beadle: mem contributions comm *CURR EMPL* vp, dir: Diamond Shamrock Inc (see above)

Timothy Jon Fretthold: mem contributions comm *CURR EMPL* sr vp, gen couns, dir: Diamond Shamrock Inc (see above)

Kathy Hughes: mem contributions comm *CURR EMPL* mgr pub rels: Diamond Shamrock Inc

Gary E. Johnson: mem contributions comm *B* Canton OH 1935 *ED* Kent St Univ 1960 *CURR EMPL* vp, contr, dir: Diamond Shamrock Inc *CORP AFFIL* vp, dir: Sigmos Pipeline Co *NONPR AFFIL* mem: Fin Execs Inst

Ed Prater: mem contributions comm *B* E St Louis IL 1938 *ED* TX Tech Univ 1962 *CURR EMPL* sr vp, dir: Diamond Shamrock Inc *CORP AFFIL* sr vp, group exec: Diamond Shamrock Refining & Mktg Co

APPLICATION INFORMATION
Initial Approach: *Initial Contact:* written request *Include Information On:* name and purpose of organization, amount requested, description of project funded, and financial background *Deadlines:* none *Note:* Organizations applying for the employee recommendation grant should send a written proposal with the employee's recommendation. Recommendation grants are made during March, June, September, and December.

Restrictions on Giving: The company does not support individuals, religious organizations for sectarian purposes, political or lobbying groups, ticket mailings, or telephone solicitation fund-raising activities.

Only organizations exempt under 501(c)(3) of the IRS code are eligible for funding.

PUBLICATIONS
Corporate Contributions Policy Guidelines

GRANTS ANALYSIS
Typical Range: $1,000 to $2,500

Dishman Charitable Foundation Trust, H. E. and Kate

CONTACT
Pam Parish
Trust Officer
H. E. and Kate Dishman Charitable Fdn Trust
c/o Texas Commerce Bank
PO Box 2751
Beaumont, TX 77704
(409) 838-0234

FINANCIAL SUMMARY
Recent Giving: $114,433 (1993); $221,140 (1992); $299,460 (1991)

Assets: $2,428,570 (1993); $2,708,202 (1992); $2,693,225 (1991)

Gifts Received: $502,019 (1989); $1,000,764 (1987)

EIN: 76-6024806

CONTRIBUTIONS SUMMARY
Donor(s): Dishman Foundation, the late H. E. Dishman, Kate Dishman Foundation

Typical Recipients: • _Arts & Humanities:_ Arts Associations & Councils, Libraries, Museums/Galleries • _Civic & Public Affairs:_ African American Affairs, Nonprofit Management, Philanthropic Organizations • _Education:_ Colleges & Universities, Public Education (Precollege) • _Health:_ Hospitals, Medical Research, Single-Disease Health Associations • _Religion:_ Religious Organizations, Religious Welfare • _Social Services:_ Child Welfare, Community Service Organizations, Family Services, Food/Clothing Distribution, Homes, Scouts, Shelters/Homelessness, Substance Abuse, United Funds/United Ways, Volunteer Services

Grant Types: general support

Geographic Distribution: focus on Georgetown, TX

GIVING OFFICERS
First City, Texas-Beaumont: trust

APPLICATION INFORMATION
Initial Approach: Application form required. Deadline is November 30.

Restrictions on Giving: Limited to Jefferson County, TX.

PUBLICATIONS
Application Guidelines

GRANTS ANALYSIS
Total Grants: $114,433
Number of Grants: 10
Highest Grant: $50,000
Typical Range: $500 to $10,000
Disclosure Period: 1993

Note: Recent grants are derived from a 1993 Form 990.

RECENT GRANTS
General

50,000	Salvation Army Beaumont Corps, Beaumont, TX	
15,833	HOW Center, Beaumont, TX — contribution for center repairs	
10,000	Beaumont Public Schools Foundation, Beaumont, TX — contribution to Start Up Foundation	
10,000	Some Other Place, Beaumont, TX — grant for the Back to School Clothing Program	
7,667	HOW Center, Beaumont, TX	

Dodge Jones Foundation

CONTACT
Lawrence Gill
Grants Administrator
Dodge Jones Foundation
PO Box 176
Abilene, TX 79604
(915) 673-6429

FINANCIAL SUMMARY
Recent Giving: $3,000,000 (1995 est.); $3,600,000 (1994); $2,478,305 (1993)

Assets: $45,479,265 (1995 est.); $45,479,265 (1994); $45,479,265 (1993 est.)

EIN: 75-6006386

CONTRIBUTIONS SUMMARY
Donor(s): The foundation was established in 1954 by the late Ruth Leggett Jones .

Typical Recipients: • _Arts & Humanities:_ Arts Associations & Councils, Historic Preservation, Libraries, Museums/Galleries, Theater • _Civic & Public Affairs:_ Botanical Gardens/Parks, Business/Free Enterprise, Chambers of Commerce, Economic Development, Employment/Job Training, Housing, Municipalities/Towns, Nonprofit Management, Public Policy, Safety • _Education:_ Colleges & Universities, Education Funds, Elementary Education (Private), Faculty Development, Medical Education, Private Education (Precollege), Public Education (Precollege), Special Education, Student Aid • _Health:_ AIDS/HIV, Alzheimers Disease, Clinics/Medical Centers, Emergency/Ambulance Services, Health Organizations, Hospices, Hospitals, Medical Rehabilitation • _Religion:_ Religious Welfare • _Science:_ Scientific Organizations • _Social Services:_ Camps, Community Service Organizations, Day Care, Family Services, Food/Clothing Distribution, People with Disabilities, United Funds/United Ways, Youth Organizations

Grant Types: general support

Geographic Distribution: principally Texas

GIVING OFFICERS
Eugene M. Allen: secy, treas
Joseph E. Canon: exec vp, dir
Lawrence Gill: grants admin, vp, dir
Melvin W. Holt: vp, dir

John A. Matthews, Jr.: dir
Joseph B. Matthews: dir
Julia Jones Matthews: pres, dir
Kade L. Matthews: dir
Julia Matthews Wilkinson: dir

APPLICATION INFORMATION
Initial Approach:

The foundation reports that applicants should submit a letter of request describing the purpose for the proposed funding.

There are no deadlines for submitting proposals.

Restrictions on Giving: The foundation does not make grants to individuals, or to organizations on behalf of individuals.

GRANTS ANALYSIS
Total Grants: $2,478,305
Number of Grants: 92
Highest Grant: $477,897
Average Grant: $26,938
Typical Range: $1,000 to $10,000 and $25,000 to $100,000
Disclosure Period: 1993

Note: Recent grants are derived from a 1992 Form 990.

RECENT GRANTS

Library

7,500	Anson Public Library, Anson, TX — to promote the Cowboy Christmas Ball, which showcases cowboy heritage	

General

420,022	Ben Richey Boys Ranch, Abilene, TX — to forgive the loan given to construct new cottages	
250,000	West Texas Rehabilitation Center, Abilene, TX — to expand and renovate facilities and replace equipment	
200,000	Abilene Christian University, Abilene, TX — to help fund renovation of educational facilities	
125,000	Texas Tech University, Lubbock, TX — to fund the presidential endowed scholarship program	
118,722	City of Abilene, Abilene, TX — to fund Redbud Park development costs	

Doss Foundation, M. S.

CONTACT
Joe K. McGill
President
M. S. Doss Foundation
PO Box 1677
Seminole, TX 79360-1677
(915) 758-2770

FINANCIAL SUMMARY

Recent Giving: $1,750,000 (1995 est.); $1,750,000 (1994 approx.); $1,740,254 (1993)

Assets: $40,000,000 (1995 est.); $40,000,000 (1994 approx.); $38,511,727 (1993)

Gifts Received: $8,100 (1993)

EIN: 75-1945227

CONTRIBUTIONS SUMMARY

Donor(s): The foundation was established in 1959 by the late M. S. Doss and the late Meek Lane Doss .

Typical Recipients: • *Arts & Humanities:* Historic Preservation, Libraries • *Civic & Public Affairs:* Botanical Gardens/Parks, Municipalities/Towns • *Education:* Agricultural Education, Private Education (Precollege), Public Education (Precollege), Student Aid • *Health:* Diabetes, Hospices • *Religion:* Religious Welfare • *Social Services:* Camps, Child Abuse, Child Welfare, Community Centers, Community Service Organizations, Day Care, Delinquency & Criminal Rehabilitation, Family Services, Food/Clothing Distribution, Homes, People with Disabilities, Recreation & Athletics, Youth Organizations

Grant Types: capital

Geographic Distribution: focus on eastern New Mexico and west Texas

GIVING OFFICERS

Joe K. McGill: chmn, pres, trust

Rebecca Narvarte: asst treas, trust

Stuart Robertson: treas, trust

James W. Satterwhite: exec dir, secy

Richard Spraberry: vp, trust

Billie Thompson: secy, trust

APPLICATION INFORMATION

Initial Approach:

The foundation reports that organizations submitting a proposal for the first time should send a brief letter of inquiry. Organizations applying for grants for a second time should send a grant application packet.

There are no specific deadlines.

2The foundation prefers to support charitable youth organizations.

GRANTS ANALYSIS

Total Grants: $1,740,254

Number of Grants: 33

Highest Grant: $550,133

Average Grant: $52,735

Typical Range: $500 to $55,000

Disclosure Period: 1993

Note: Recent grants are derived from a 1993 Form 990.

RECENT GRANTS

General

550,133	M.S. Doss Youth Center, Seminole, TX — endowment, operations equipment
500,000	Midland Presbyterian Home, Midland, TX — building construction
135,000	Children's Home, Amarillo, TX — building renovation
75,000	South Plains Food Bank, Lubbock, TX — equipment
73,313	Buckner Baptist Benevolence, Lubbock, TX — dorm renovations

---

Dresser Industries, Inc. / Dresser Foundation, Inc.

Revenue: $5.33 billion
Employees: 27,400
Headquarters: Dallas, TX
SIC Major Group: Oil & Gas Field Machinery, Oil & Gas Exploration Services, Water, Sewer & Utility Lines, and Industrial Valves

CONTACT

Libby McClarren
Contact
Dresser Foundation, Inc.
PO Box 718
Dallas, TX 75221
(214) 740-6741

FINANCIAL SUMMARY

Recent Giving: $1,051,424 (fiscal 1993); $1,900,000 (fiscal 1992); $1,883,457 (fiscal 1991)

Assets: $7,600,267 (fiscal 1993); $7,548,432 (fiscal 1992); $10,000,000 (fiscal 1989)

Fiscal Note: Above figures include foundation and direct contributions by the company. Direct giving is usually less than $100,000 annually. Above figures exclude nonmonetary support.

EIN: 23-7309548

CONTRIBUTIONS SUMMARY

Typical Recipients: • *Arts & Humanities:* Arts Associations & Councils, Arts Centers, Arts Festivals, Arts Funds, Dance, Historic Preservation, Libraries, Museums/Galleries, Music, Opera, Performing Arts, Public Broadcasting, Theater • *Civic & Public Affairs:* Business/Free Enterprise, Civil Rights, Economic Policy, Employment/Job Training, General, Law & Justice, Professional & Trade Associations, Public Policy, Safety, Urban & Community Affairs, Women's Affairs, Zoos/Aquariums • *Education:* Business-School Partnerships, Colleges & Universities, Economic Education, Education Funds, Education Reform, Engineering/Technological Education, International Studies, Medical Education, Minority Education, Science/Mathematics Education, Student Aid • *Health:* Clinics/Medical Centers, Emergency/Ambulance Services, Health Organizations, Heart, Hospices, Hospitals, Medical Research, Mental Health, Nursing Services, Single-Disease Health Associations • *International:* International Peace & Security Issues, International Relations • *Religion:* Religious Organizations, Religious Welfare • *Science:* Science Muse-

ums, Scientific Centers & Institutes, Scientific Organizations • *Social Services:* Animal Protection, Child Welfare, Community Centers, Community Service Organizations, Family Planning, Family Services, People with Disabilities, Senior Services, Shelters/Homelessness, Substance Abuse, United Funds/United Ways, Youth Organizations

Grant Types: capital, department, employee matching gifts, general support, operating expenses, project, and research

Geographic Distribution: in operating communities

Operating Locations: CA (Huntington Park, Montebello), CO (Colorado Springs), CT (Stratford), IN (Connersville), KY (Berea), LA (Alexandria), MA (Avon, Canton), MD (Salisbury), MI, MN (Minneapolis), NJ (Liberty Corner), NY (Olean, Painted Post, Wellsville), OH (Columbus, Galion, Marion, Sidney), OK (Broken Arrow), PA (Bradford, Pittsburgh), SC (Greenville), TX (Austin, Dallas, Houston, Longview), WI (Waukesha)

CORP. OFFICERS

William Edward Bradford: *B* Dallas TX 1935 *ED* Centenary Coll BS 1958 *CURR EMPL* pres, coo, dir: Dresser Indus Inc *CORP AFFIL* pres: Baroid Corp, Wheatley TXT Corp; pres, coo: Dresser Rand Corning; pres, dir: Baroid Corp; vp: TK Valve & Mfg *NONPR AFFIL* mem: Am Assn Advancement Sci, Am Assn Petroleum Geologists, Assn Oilwell Drilling Contractors, Intl Petroleum Assn, Natl Ocean Indus Assn, Petroleum Equipment Suppliers Assn, Soc Petroleum Engrs, TX Mid-Continent Oil & Gas Assn *CLUB AFFIL* Champions GC, Heritage, Houston, Petroleum, Raveneaux CC, Univ

Grace Anna Jones: *CURR EMPL* dir pub aff: Dresser Indus Inc

Rebecca Robinson Morris: *B* McKinney TX 1945 *ED* Southern Methodist Univ BBA 1974; Southern Methodist Univ JD 1978 *CURR EMPL* secy, vp, corp couns: Dresser Indus Inc *CORP AFFIL* vp: Baroid Corp; vp, secy: TK Valve & Mfg *NONPR AFFIL* dir: Plano Futures Fdn; dir, mem: Am Soc Corp Secys; mem: Am Bar Assn, Am Inst Aeronautics & Astronautics, Am Inst CPAs, Dallas Bar Assn, TX Bar Assn, TX Soc CPAs; mem (corp & securities law comm): Am Corp Couns Assn

John Joseph Murphy: *B* Olean NY 1931 *ED* Rochester Inst Tech AAS 1952; Southern Methodist Univ MBA 1981 *CURR EMPL* chmn, ceo: Dresser Indus Inc *CORP AFFIL* chmn: Baroid Corp; dir: Kerr-McGee Corp, Nationsbank Corp, PepsiCo *NONPR AFFIL* chmn: Citizens Democracy Corp; dir: US-Russia Bus Counc; mem: Bus Counc, Bus Roundtable; trust: Southern Methodist Univ, St Bonaventure Univ

Bill Dean St. John: *B* Wewoka OK 1931 *ED* Southern Methodist Univ BBA 1952 *CURR EMPL* vchmn, cfo: Dresser Indus Inc *CORP AFFIL* vchmn: Baroid Corp, Baroid Corp, Wheatley TXT Corp *NONPR AFFIL* mem: Am Inst CPAs, Conf Bd, Mfrs Alliance Productivity & Innovation; mem fin counc: Machinery Allied Products Inst

GIVING OFFICERS
Libby McClarren: contact

John Joseph Murphy: chmn *CURR EMPL* chmn, ceo: Dresser Indus Inc (see above)

APPLICATION INFORMATION
Initial Approach: *Initial Contact:* full proposal *Include Information On:* outline of what organization seeks to accomplish, funding needed, overall outreach of activity, 501(c)(3) tax-exemption letter, other supporting materials *Deadlines:* none

Restrictions on Giving: Foundation does not support individuals or endowments and does not provide in-kind support or loans.

GRANTS ANALYSIS
Total Grants: $772,315*

Number of Grants: 127*

Highest Grant: $100,000

Average Grant: $6,081*

Typical Range: $1,000 to $10,000

Disclosure Period: fiscal year ending October 31, 1994

Note: Total grants figure represents foundation giving only. Number of grants and average grant figures exclude $138,225 in matching gifts and $140,884 in scholarships. Recent grants are derived from a fiscal 1993 Form 990.

RECENT GRANTS
General

100,000	St. Bonaventure University, St. Bonaventure, NY
57,250	United Way Waukesha, Waukesha, WI
50,000	United Way Metro Dallas, Dallas, TX
33,000	United Way Lower Eastern Shore, Salisbury, MD
31,000	United Way Bradford Area, Brainerd, MN

Dunagan Foundation

CONTACT
J. Conrad Dunagan
President
Dunagan Fdn.
PO Box 387
Monahans, TX 79796
(915) 943-2571

FINANCIAL SUMMARY
Recent Giving: $151,070 (1993); $175,100 (1992); $165,550 (1991)

Assets: $2,689,901 (1993); $2,615,832 (1992); $2,523,530 (1991)

Gifts Received: $109,725 (1993); $111,250 (1992); $86,125 (1991)

Fiscal Note: In 1992, major contributions were received from Deanna Dunagan ($5,000), J. Conrad and Kathlyn C. Dunagan ($92,000), John Charles Dunagan ($5,000), and Dr. Clay Dunagan ($6,725); two other donors made contributions of less than $1,000.

EIN: 75-1561848

CONTRIBUTIONS SUMMARY
Donor(s): J. Conrad Dunagan, Kathlyn C. Dunagan, John C. Dunagan

Typical Recipients: • *Arts & Humanities:* Arts Centers, Historic Preservation, Libraries, Museums/Galleries, Theater • *Civic & Public Affairs:* Employment/Job Training, General, Housing • *Education:* Business Education, Colleges & Universities, Education Funds, Legal Education, Private Education (Precollege), Student Aid • *Environment:* General, Wildlife Protection • *Health:* AIDS/HIV, Health Funds, Hospitals, Hospitals (University Affiliated), Public Health, Research/Studies Institutes, Single-Disease Health Associations • *International:* Health Care/Hospitals, International Peace & Security Issues • *Religion:* Dioceses, Religious Organizations, Religious Welfare • *Science:* Science Museums, Scientific Centers & Institutes • *Social Services:* Child Welfare, Community Service Organizations, Counseling, Family Planning, Family Services, Scouts, United Funds/United Ways, Veterans, Youth Organizations

Grant Types: professorship, project, and scholarship

Geographic Distribution: focus on TX

GIVING OFFICERS
J. Conrad Dunagan: pres

John C. Dunagan: secy, treas

Kathlyn C. Dunagan: vp

APPLICATION INFORMATION
Initial Approach: Send a brief letter of inquiry. Include a description of organization, amount requested, purpose of funds sought, recently audited financial statement, and proof of tax-exempt status. There are no deadlines.

GRANTS ANALYSIS
Total Grants: $151,070

Number of Grants: 34

Highest Grant: $57,000

Typical Range: $500 to $15,000

Disclosure Period: 1993

Note: Recent grants are derived from a 1993 Form 990.

RECENT GRANTS
General

57,000	Permian Honor Scholarship, Odessa, TX
15,000	Green Farms Academy, Greens Farm, CT
10,000	Population Committee International, New York, NY
5,200	Opportunity Workshop, Monahans, TX
5,000	Boy Scouts of America Buffalo Trail Council, Midland, TX

Duncan Foundation, Lillian H. and C. W.

CONTACT
Ellen Tipton
Trustee
Lillian H. and C. W. Duncan Fdn.
c/o Texas Commerce Bank Trust Dept.
PO Box 2558
Houston, TX 77252-8037
(713) 216-4412

FINANCIAL SUMMARY
Recent Giving: $277,750 (fiscal 1993); $260,253 (fiscal 1990); $317,056 (fiscal 1989)

Assets: $4,763,754 (fiscal 1993); $4,119,900 (fiscal 1990); $4,345,196 (fiscal 1989)

EIN: 74-6064215

CONTRIBUTIONS SUMMARY
Donor(s): the late C. W. Duncan

Typical Recipients: • *Arts & Humanities:* Ballet, Ethnic & Folk Arts, General, Historic Preservation, Libraries, Museums/Galleries, Music, Performing Arts, Theater • *Civic & Public Affairs:* Hispanic Affairs, Housing, Public Policy • *Education:* Arts/Humanities Education, Business Education, Colleges & Universities, Education Reform, Medical Education, Public Education (Precollege), School Volunteerism, Special Education • *Environment:* Resource Conservation • *Health:* Children's Health/Hospitals, Clinics/Medical Centers, Heart, Hospices, Hospitals, Hospitals (University Affiliated), Long-Term Care, Medical Research, Prenatal Health Issues • *International:* International Affairs • *Religion:* Churches, Ministries, Religious Organizations • *Science:* Science Museums • *Social Services:* Child Welfare, Community Service Organizations, People with Disabilities, Recreation & Athletics, United Funds/United Ways, Volunteer Services, YMCA/YWCA/YMHA/YWHA, Youth Organizations

Grant Types: general support

Geographic Distribution: focus on TX

GIVING OFFICERS
Mary Anne Duncan Dingus: dir *PHIL AFFIL* dir: Early Foundation

Anne S. Duncan: dir *PHIL AFFIL* dir: Early Foundation

Brenda Duncan: dir *PHIL AFFIL* dir: Early Foundation

C. W. Duncan III: vp, dir *PHIL AFFIL* vp, dir: Early Foundation

Charles W. Duncan, Jr.: pres, dir *B* Houston TX 1926 *ED* Rice Univ BSCheE 1947; Univ TX 1948-1949 *CORP AFFIL* dir: Am Express Co, Chem Banking Corp, Coca-Cola Co, Panhandle Eastern Corp, TX Commerce BancShares, Un Tech Corp *NONPR AFFIL* chmn bd trusts: Rice Univ; mem: Counc Foreign Rels, Sigma Alpha Epsilon, Sigma Iota Epsilon; trust: Brookings Inst *CLUB AFFIL*

Allegro, Houston CC, River Oaks CC *PHIL AFFIL* vchmn, dir: Robert A. Welch Foundation; chmn, dir: Early Foundation

John H. Duncan, Jr.: dir *PHIL AFFIL* dir: Early Foundation

John H. Duncan, Sr.: chmn, dir *B* Houston TX 1928 *ED* Univ TX BBA 1949 *CURR EMPL* ptnr: Duncan Cook & Co *CORP AF-FIL* dir: Enron Corp, King Ranch Inc, Mosher Inc, Proler Intl Corp, TX Commerce Bancshares *NONPR AFFIL* mem: Sigma Alpha Epsilon *CLUB AFFIL* Houston CC, River Oaks CC *PHIL AFFIL* pres, dir: Early Foundation

John H. Duncan, Jr.: dir

Robert J. Faust: secy, treas *PHIL AFFIL* treas, secy, dir: Early Foundation

Jeaneane Duncan Marsh: dir *PHIL AFFIL* dir: Early Foundation

APPLICATION INFORMATION
Initial Approach: The foundation requests applications be made in writing. There are no deadlines.

Restrictions on Giving: Considerations to applicants from IRC Section 501 (c)(3) organizations.

GRANTS ANALYSIS
Total Grants: $277,750

Number of Grants: 45

Highest Grant: $31,000

Typical Range: $500 to $25,000

Disclosure Period: fiscal year ending September 30, 1993

Note: Recent grants are derived from a fiscal 1993 Form 990.

RECENT GRANTS
Library
5,000	Houston Public Library, Houston, TX — support Library Enhancement Campaign

General
25,000	Rice University, Houston, TX — support the Shepherd School of Music
25,000	YMCA, Houston, TX
20,000	Communities in Schools, Houston, TX
20,000	United Way of Texas Gulf Coast, Houston, TX — to support membership in Alexis de Taqueville Society
16,000	Aspen Foundation, Aspen, CO

Early Foundation

CONTACT
Inez Winston
Early Fdn.
6319 Mimosa Ln.
Dallas, TX 75230
(214) 373-7114

FINANCIAL SUMMARY
Recent Giving: $266,869 (fiscal 1992); $101,375 (fiscal 1990); $89,550 (fiscal 1989)

Assets: $4,716,098 (fiscal 1992); $2,286,393 (fiscal 1990); $2,048,421 (fiscal 1989)

EIN: 75-6011853

CONTRIBUTIONS SUMMARY
Typical Recipients: • *Arts & Humanities:* Ballet, Libraries, Museums/Galleries, Music, Opera, Performing Arts • *Civic & Public Affairs:* Parades/Festivals, Public Policy, Urban & Community Affairs, Zoos/Aquariums • *Education:* Arts/Humanities Education, Business Education, Colleges & Universities, Community & Junior Colleges, Religious Education, Special Education, Student Aid • *Environment:* General • *Health:* Children's Health/Hospitals, Eyes/Blindness, Health Organizations, Heart, Hospices, Medical Research, Prenatal Health Issues, Single-Disease Health Associations • *International:* International Relations • *Religion:* Churches, Ministries, Religious Organizations • *Social Services:* Child Welfare, Community Service Organizations, Delinquency & Criminal Rehabilitation, Homes, Substance Abuse, United Funds/United Ways, Volunteer Services, Youth Organizations

Grant Types: general support

Geographic Distribution: focus on TX

GIVING OFFICERS
Mary Anne Duncan Dingus: dir *PHIL AFFIL* dir: Lillian H. and C. W. Duncan Foundation

Anne S. Duncan: dir *PHIL AFFIL* dir: Lillian H. and C. W. Duncan Foundation

Brenda Duncan: dir *PHIL AFFIL* dir: Lillian H. and C. W. Duncan Foundation

C. W. Duncan III: vp, dir *PHIL AFFIL* vp, dir: Lillian H. and C. W. Duncan Foundation

Charles W. Duncan, Jr.: chmn, dir *B* Houston TX 1926 *ED* Rice Univ BSCheE 1947; Univ TX 1948-1949 *CORP AFFIL* dir: Am Express Co, Chem Banking Corp, Coca-Cola Co, Panhandle Eastern Corp, TX Commerce BancShares, Un Tech Corp *NONPR AFFIL* chmn bd trusts: Rice Univ; mem: Counc Foreign Rels, Sigma Alpha Epsilon, Sigma Iota Epsilon; trust: Brookings Inst *CLUB AFFIL* Allegro, Houston CC, River Oaks CC *PHIL AFFIL* vchmn, dir: Robert A. Welch Foundation; pres, dir: Lillian H. and C. W. Duncan Foundation

John H. Duncan, Jr.: dir *PHIL AFFIL* dir: Lillian H. and C. W. Duncan Foundation

John H. Duncan, Sr.: pres, dir *B* Houston TX 1928 *ED* Univ TX BBA 1949 *CURR EMPL* ptnr: Duncan Cook & Co *CORP AF-FIL* dir: Enron Corp, King Ranch Inc, Mosher Inc, Proler Intl Corp, TX Commerce Bancshares *NONPR AFFIL* mem: Sigma Alpha Epsilon *CLUB AFFIL* Houston CC, River Oaks CC *PHIL AFFIL* chmn, dir: Lillian H. and C. W. Duncan Foundation

Robert J. Faust: treas, secy, dir *PHIL AFFIL* secy, treas: Lillian H. and C. W. Duncan Foundation

Jeaneane Duncan Marsh: dir *PHIL AFFIL* dir: Lillian H. and C. W. Duncan Foundation

APPLICATION INFORMATION
Initial Approach: Send brief letter describing program. There are no deadlines.

Restrictions on Giving: Does not support individuals.

GRANTS ANALYSIS
Total Grants: $266,869

Number of Grants: 44

Highest Grant: $30,000

Typical Range: $500 to $10,000

Disclosure Period: fiscal year ending September 30, 1992

Note: Recent grants are derived from a fiscal 1992 Form 990.

RECENT GRANTS
Library
5,000	Friends of Midland Public Library, Midland, TX — furnishings for new addition
5,000	Houston Public Library, Houston, TX — support Library Enhancement Campaign

General
30,000	DePelchin Children's Center, Houston, TX — to aid children/families in need
25,000	Brookings Institution, Washington, DC — public policy issues
25,000	Brookwood Community Volunteers, Brookshire, TX — streets of Sante Fe Underwriter Pledge and new men's hom
25,000	YMCA, Houston, TX — to support Second Century Development Programs
20,000	Houston Leadership Circle, Houston, TX — to support on-going programs

Elkins, Jr. Foundation, Margaret and James A.

CONTACT
James A. Elkins, Jr.
President
Margaret and James A. Elkins, Jr. Fdn.
1001 Fannin, Ste. 1166
Houston, TX 77002
(713) 658-6878

FINANCIAL SUMMARY
Recent Giving: $220,500 (fiscal 1993); $203,000 (fiscal 1992); $183,000 (fiscal 1991)

Assets: $4,673,395 (fiscal 1993); $4,468,150 (fiscal 1992); $4,380,036 (fiscal 1991)

EIN: 74-6051746

CONTRIBUTIONS SUMMARY
Typical Recipients: • *Arts & Humanities:* Community Arts, Dance, Libraries, Literary Arts, Museums/Galleries, Public Broadcast-

ing, Theater • *Civic & Public Affairs:* Municipalities/Towns, Safety • *Education:* Arts/Humanities Education, Colleges & Universities, International Studies, Medical Education, Private Education (Precollege), Secondary Education (Private) • *Environment:* General • *Health:* Cancer, Hospices, Hospitals • *International:* Health Care/Hospitals • *Religion:* Churches, Religious Organizations, Religious Welfare • *Social Services:* Animal Protection, Community Service Organizations, Day Care, Family Planning, Homes, Substance Abuse, United Funds/United Ways

Grant Types: general support

Geographic Distribution: focus on Houston, TX

GIVING OFFICERS

James A. Elkins, Jr.: pres *B* Galveston TX 1919 *ED* Princeton Univ BA *CORP AFFIL* dir: Am Gen Cos, First City Bancorp TX, Freeport McMoRan *NONPR AFFIL* dir: Houston Grand Opera; trust: Baylor Univ Coll Med, TX Childrens Hosp *PHIL AFFIL* trust: J. A. and Isabel M. Elkins Foundation; vp: Henderson-Wessendorf Foundation; trust: Lulu Bryan Ramboud Charitable Trust

James Anderson Elkins III: treas *PHIL AFFIL* trust: J. A. and Isabel M. Elkins Foundation

APPLICATION INFORMATION

Initial Approach: Send brief letter of inquiry describing program or project. There are no deadlines.

GRANTS ANALYSIS

Total Grants: $220,500

Number of Grants: 8

Highest Grant: $100,000

Typical Range: $500 to $50,000

Disclosure Period: fiscal year ending October 31, 1993

Note: Recent grants are derived from a fiscal 1993 Form 990.

RECENT GRANTS

General

100,000	M.D. Anderson Cancer Center, Houston, TX	
50,000	Episcopal High School, Bellaire, TX	
25,000	University of St. Thomas, Houston, TX	
20,000	Project Orbis, Houston, TX	
10,000	Briarwood School, Houston, TX	

Enron Corp. / Enron Foundation

Revenue: $8.98 billion
Employees: 7,800
Headquarters: Houston, TX

SIC Major Group: Petroleum Bulk Stations & Terminals, Crude Petroleum & Natural Gas, Plastics Materials & Resins, and Industrial Organic Chemicals Nec

CONTACT

Rebecca King
Contributions Representative
Enron Foundation
PO Box 1188
Houston, TX 77251-1188
(713) 853-5400
Note: An alternative contact is A. Hardie Davis, Director, Community Affairs.

FINANCIAL SUMMARY

Recent Giving: $4,400,000 (1993 approx.); $4,400,000 (1992 approx.); $4,400,000 (1991 approx.)

Assets: $8,000,000 (1991 approx.); $10,508,952 (1990); $9,538,739 (1989)

Fiscal Note: Company gives directly and through foundation. Above figures exclude nonmonetary support.

EIN: 74-2124032

CONTRIBUTIONS SUMMARY

Typical Recipients: • *Arts & Humanities:* Arts Festivals, Arts Funds, Dance, Ethnic & Folk Arts, Historic Preservation, Libraries, Museums/Galleries, Music, Opera, Performing Arts, Public Broadcasting • *Civic & Public Affairs:* Business/Free Enterprise, Economic Development, Public Policy, Urban & Community Affairs, Women's Affairs, Zoos/Aquariums • *Education:* Business Education, Colleges & Universities, Economic Education, Education Associations, Education Funds, Elementary Education (Private), Engineering/Technological Education, Medical Education, Minority Education, Private Education (Precollege), Public Education (Precollege), Science/Mathematics Education • *Environment:* General • *Health:* Geriatric Health, Health Organizations, Hospitals, Medical Research, Mental Health, Nursing Services, Public Health, Single-Disease Health Associations • *Social Services:* Animal Protection, Child Welfare, Community Service Organizations, Delinquency & Criminal Rehabilitation, Emergency Relief, Food/Clothing Distribution, Homes, Senior Services, Shelters/Homelessness, United Funds/United Ways, Volunteer Services, Youth Organizations

Grant Types: employee matching gifts, general support, operating expenses, project, and research

Nonmonetary Support Types: loaned executives and workplace solicitation

Note: Estimated value of nonmonetary support is $100,000 to $500,000. Nonmonetary support is provided by both the company and foundation.

Geographic Distribution: in headquarters and operating locations only

Operating Locations: KS, LA, ND, NM, OH (Dublin), TX (Houston, Midland), WY

GIVING OFFICERS

Joseph H. Allen: trust

Ronald J. Burns: trust *B* 1952 *ED* Univ NE BS 1974 *CURR EMPL* co-chmn: Enron Gas Svcs Corp *CORP AFFIL* chmn: Houston Pipeline Co, Transwestern Pipeline Co; pres, dir: Enron Pipeline Co

A. Hardie Davis: dir commun aff

Richard Dan Kinder: dir *B* Cape Girardeau MO 1944 *ED* Univ MO BA 1966; Univ MO JD 1968 *CURR EMPL* pres, coo, dir: Enron Corp *CORP AFFIL* dir: BJ Svcs Corp, Enron Liquids Pipeline Co, Enron Oil & Gas Co, FL Gas Transmission Co *NONPR AFFIL* dir: Interstate Natural Gas Assn Am, Mus Fine Arts, Soc Performing Arts; mem: Am Bar Assn, Houston Bar Assn, MO Bar Assn *CLUB AFFIL* Houston Racquet

Rebecca King: contributions rep

Elizabeth J. Labanowski: trust *CURR EMPL* couns, dir: Enson Property Co

Peggy Beard Menchaca: trust *B* San Angelo TX 1938 *ED* Alvin Commun Coll *CURR EMPL* vp, secy; Transwestern Pipeline Co *CORP AFFIL* secy: Enron Liquids Pipeline Co; secy, dir: NGP Pipeline Co; vp, dir: Enron LA Energy Co Inc; vp, secy, dir: Enron Helium Co Inc *NONPR AFFIL* dir: Houston Downtown Mgmt Corp; mem: Supreme Ct TX Task Force Gender Bias, TX Bar Assn; pres: Am Soc Corp Secys *CLUB AFFIL* Inwood Forest GC

William C. Moore: trust

Edmund Peter Segner III: trust *B* Dallas TX 1953 *ED* Rice Univ BSCE 1976; Univ Houston MA 1980 *CURR EMPL* exec vp: Enron Corp *NONPR AFFIL* chmn: Commun Ptnrs; dir: Alley Theatre, Boy Scouts Am Sam Houston Area Counc Nature Conservancy, Greater Houston Partnership Ed Excellence, Rice Univ Fund Counc, Zoological Soc; mem: Am Inst CPAs, Houston Soc Fin Analysts, Petroleum Investors Rels Assn *CLUB AFFIL* Brae Burn CC, Briar, Coronado, Houston City

R. Leon Ullrich: trust

APPLICATION INFORMATION

Initial Approach: *Initial Contact:* formal letter, not more than three pages *Include Information On:* purpose of organization, how requested funds will be used, names and affiliations of board members, explanation of activities for which funding is sought, evidence of need for project, rationale for amount requested, anticipated benefits, population served, detailed budget (including financial analysis of proposed project and independent audit), names and qualifications of those carrying out activity, plans for evaluation and reporting of results, proof of tax-exempt status *Deadlines:* none; apply before October 1 to be considered for following year's budget

Restrictions on Giving: Foundation will not typically award grants to fraternal organizations; political activities or lobbying groups; organizations outside the United States or its territories; direct aid to individuals or student scholarships; goodwill advertising; endowment funds; projects of religious denominations or sects other than institutions of higher learning with religious affiliations; tickets or tables for benefit purposes;

individual or group travel; sports team sponsorships or athletic scholarships.

GRANTS ANALYSIS
Total Grants: $4,400,000*

Typical Range: $5,000 to $10,000

Disclosure Period: 1993

Note: Total grants figure includes matching gifts and direct giving and is an approximate.

Exxon Corporation / Exxon Education Foundation

Revenue: $101.45 billion
Employees: 91,000
Headquarters: Irving, TX
SIC Major Group: Crude Petroleum & Natural Gas and Petroleum Refining

CONTACT
Edward F. Ahnert
Manager, Contributions
Exxon Corp.
225 E John W. Carpenter Fwy., Rm. 1429
Irving, TX 75062-2298
(214) 444-1000
Note: Edward F. Ahnert is also executive director of the Exxon Education Foundation.

FINANCIAL SUMMARY
Recent Giving: $40,000,000 (1995 est.); $53,759,042 (1994); $53,759,439 (1993)

Assets: $32,763,000 (1990); $25,946,000 (1989); $42,621,000 (1988)

Fiscal Note: Above figures include $19,427,367 in gifts paid by the Exxon Education Foundation in 1994. In 1994, direct giving by the company and its divisions and affiliates totaled $22,204,540 to organizations in the U.S. and $12,127,135 to organizations outside the U.S. Figure for 1994 is corporate U.S. giving only.

EIN: 13-6082357

CONTRIBUTIONS SUMMARY
Typical Recipients: • *Arts & Humanities:* Arts Associations & Councils, Arts Centers, Arts Festivals, Arts Institutes, Community Arts, Dance, Ethnic & Folk Arts, Historic Preservation, Libraries, Museums/Galleries, Music, Opera, Performing Arts, Public Broadcasting, Theater • *Civic & Public Affairs:* African American Affairs, Botanical Gardens/Parks, Community Foundations, Economic Development, Economic Policy, Employment/Job Training, Hispanic Affairs, Housing, Law & Justice, Minority Business, Nonprofit Management, Professional & Trade Associations, Public Policy, Safety, Urban & Community Affairs, Women's Affairs, Zoos/Aquariums • *Education:* Business Education, Business-School Partnerships, Colleges & Universities, Economic Education, Education Associations, Education Funds, Education Reform, Engineering/Technological Education, Faculty

Development, General, Medical Education, Minority Education, Public Education (Precollege), Science/Mathematics Education, Secondary Education (Public), Special Education • *Environment:* Energy, General, Resource Conservation, Wildlife Protection • *Health:* Cancer, Clinics/Medical Centers, Emergency/Ambulance Services, Health Organizations, Hospitals, Medical Rehabilitation, Medical Research, Medical Training, Nursing Services, Public Health • *International:* Health Care/Hospitals, International Affairs, International Environmental Issues, International Peace & Security Issues, International Relations • *Science:* Science Museums, Scientific Centers & Institutes, Scientific Labs, Scientific Research • *Social Services:* Child Welfare, Community Service Organizations, Day Care, Delinquency & Criminal Rehabilitation, Family Services, Scouts, Shelters/Homelessness, Substance Abuse, United Funds/United Ways, Volunteer Services, YMCA/YWCA/YMHA/YWHA, Youth Organizations

Grant Types: award, conference/seminar, department, emergency, employee matching gifts, fellowship, general support, matching, multiyear/continuing support, project, and research

Note: Employee matching gift ratio: 3 to 1 for up to $5,000 in gifts per individual per year to colleges and universities and to certain consortia of minority colleges and universities, from the Exxon Education Foundation. Employee matching gift ratio: 1 to 1 for up to $1,000 in gifts per individual per year to the arts, museums, and historical preservation organizations, from the Exxon Corporation.

Geographic Distribution: nationally and internationally

Operating Locations: AK (Anchorage), CA (Benicia, Thousand Oaks), GA (Columbus), LA (Baton Rouge, New Orleans), MT (Billings), NC (Greensboro), NJ (Florham Park), TX (Baytown, Dallas, Houston, Midland), WY (Gillette)

CORP. OFFICERS
Lee R. Raymond: *B* Watertown SD 1938 *ED* Univ WI BSChE 1960; Univ MN PhD 1963 *CURR EMPL* chmn, ceo: Exxon Corp *CORP AFFIL* dir: JP Morgan & Co, Morgan Guaranty Trust Co; sr vp, dir: Esso Intl-Am *NONPR AFFIL* bd govs: Dallas Symphony Assn; dir: Am Petroleum Inst, Counc Aid Ed, Dallas Citizens Counc, German Am Chamber Commerce, Natl Action Counc Minorities Engg, New Am Schs Devel Corp, Project Shelter PRO-AM, Un Negro Coll Fund, Un Way Tri-St, Univ TX Southwestern Med Ctr; mem: Am Counc Germany, British N Am Comm, Counc Foreign Rels, Dallas Partnership, Trilateral Commn, TX Festival Comm, Univ WI Fdn; mem bd visitors: Southern Methodist Univ Cox Sch Bus; ptnr emeritus: New York City Partnership; trust: WI Alumni Res Fdn, WI Res Fdn; visiting comm: Univ WI Dept Chem Engg

GIVING OFFICERS
Edward F. Ahnert: pres *CURR EMPL* mgr contributions: Exxon Corp

Anthony W. Atkiss: chmn, trust

APPLICATION INFORMATION
Initial Approach: *Initial Contact:* five copies of proposal outline, not exceeding five pages *Include Information On:* contact person, list of members of board of directors and other key individuals, project goals and needs addressed, amount requested, project description, project evaluation criteria, detailed budget (including other funding sources), project duration, how project differs from and expands upon related work in field, and list of current public and private contributors and level of support *Deadlines:* none *Note:* Exxon Education Foundation programs are not open to application.

Restrictions on Giving: Exxon Corporation does not provide funds for religious or political purposes or to individuals. Generally excluded are contributions to endowments, organizations formed to combat a single disease, and operating support to agencies funded by the United Way.

PUBLICATIONS
Dimensions 94: A Report on Exxon's 1994 Contributions in the Public Interest, Including the Exxon Education Foundation Report

GRANTS ANALYSIS
Total Grants: $53,759,042*

Highest Grant: $1,631,000

Typical Range: $5,000 to $25,000

Disclosure Period: 1994

Note: Total grants include $34,331,675 in corporate direct gifts and $19,427,367 in grants by the Exxon Education Foundation. Recent grants are derived from a 1994 annual report and includes grants made by the foundation and the corporation.

RECENT GRANTS
General

1,631,000	United Way Campaign of the Texas Gulf Coast, Houston, TX
1,200,000	United Negro College Fund, New York, NY —organizational support grant
879,974	Volunteer Involvement Fund Employee/Annuitant Volunteer Involvement Program
833,333	New American Schools Development Corporation, Arlington, VA —in general support of its efforts to create a new generation of American schools
625,000	Tri-State United Way Campaign (Connecticut, New Jersey, and New York), Tri-State, NY

Fair Foundation, R. W.

CONTACT
Wilton H. Fair
President
R. W. Fair Foundation
PO Box 689
Tyler, TX 75710
(214) 592-3811

FINANCIAL SUMMARY
Recent Giving: $1,250,000 (1994); $1,316,108 (1993); $1,300,000 (1992 approx.)

Assets: $13,824,003 (1993); $15,417,136 (1991); $14,517,580 (1990)

EIN: 75-6015270

CONTRIBUTIONS SUMMARY
Donor(s): R. W. Fair and Mattie Allen Fair donated funds to establish the R. W. Fair Foundation as a trust in 1936. The foundation was incorporated in 1960, after the death of Mattie Fair. The majority of income derives from the Fair Oil Company. Two sons, Wilton and James, are now in charge of the foundation.

Typical Recipients: • *Arts & Humanities:* Historic Preservation, Libraries, Museums/Galleries, Public Broadcasting • *Civic & Public Affairs:* Economic Development, General, Municipalities/Towns • *Education:* Colleges & Universities, Community & Junior Colleges, Minority Education, Private Education (Precollege) • *Health:* Cancer, Clinics/Medical Centers • *Religion:* Churches, Ministries, Religious Organizations, Religious Welfare • *Science:* Scientific Centers & Institutes • *Social Services:* Family Services, Food/Clothing Distribution, United Funds/United Ways, YMCA/YWCA/YMHA/YWHA, Youth Organizations

Grant Types: general support

Geographic Distribution: Texas, with emphasis on Tyler, TX

GIVING OFFICERS
Sam Raymond Bright: vp, dir *B* Tyler TX 1936 *ED* Univ TX Austin 1959; Harvard Univ Grad Sch Bus Admin 1963 *CURR EMPL* pres: Bright Res Assoc *CORP AFFIL* ptnr: Bright Investments Ltd; vp, treas, dir: Fair Oil Co *NONPR AFFIL* mem: Am Petroleum Inst, Inst Chartered Fin Analysts, Natl Assn Petroleum Investment Analysts

James W. Fair: sr vp, dir, don son *B* 1924 *CURR EMPL* pres, dir: Fair Oil Co

Wilton H. Fair: pres, dir, don son *B* 1920 *CURR EMPL* vp, dir: Fair Oil Co *CORP AFFIL* ptnr: Fair Oil Ltd

Will A. Knight: dir

B. B. Palmore: dir

Richard L. Ray: dir *CURR EMPL* vp, dir: Fair Oil Co

APPLICATION INFORMATION
Initial Approach:

The foundation prefers an initial letter of inquiry before a proposal is submitted.

An official application is required for complete proposals. Applicants should include a brief description of the organization and project to be funded, IRS tax-exempt determination letter, amount needed for the project, amount going toward administrative needs, and a list of other sources of support.

Applications should be submitted before quarterly board meetings on the first of March, June, September, and December.

Prospective grantees should expect a three-month decision-making period.

Restrictions on Giving: No grants are given to individuals.

GRANTS ANALYSIS
Total Grants: $1,316,108

Number of Grants: 131

Highest Grant: $133,000

Average Grant: $10,047

Typical Range: $1,000 to $20,000

Disclosure Period: 1993

Note: Recent grants are derived from a 1993 Form 990.

RECENT GRANTS

General

133,000	Tyler Economics Development Council, Tyler, TX
117,600	Baylor University, Waco, TX
105,000	Tyler Metropolitan YMCA, Tyler, TX
60,250	University of Texas M.D. Anderson Cancer Center, Houston, TX
55,000	First Baptist Church, Tyler, TX

Farish Fund, William Stamps

CONTACT
William Stamps Farish
President
William Stamps Farish Fund
1000 Memorial Dr., Ste. 920
Houston, TX 77024
(713) 757-7300

FINANCIAL SUMMARY
Recent Giving: $4,721,740 (fiscal 1993); $4,383,617 (fiscal 1992); $4,180,000 (fiscal 1991)

Assets: $98,561,967 (fiscal 1993); $94,157,203 (fiscal 1992); $90,766,926 (fiscal 1991)

Gifts Received: $1,718,412 (fiscal 1986)

EIN: 74-6043019

CONTRIBUTIONS SUMMARY
Donor(s): Mrs. Libbie Rice Farish, wife of William Stamps Farish, established the William Stamps Farish Fund in 1951 in Texas. Mr. Farish was one of the Humble Oil Company organizers. The fund receives contributions from various family trusts.

Typical Recipients: • *Arts & Humanities:* Arts Centers, Arts Outreach, Dance, Libraries, Museums/Galleries, Music, Performing Arts, Public Broadcasting • *Civic & Public Affairs:* Botanical Gardens/Parks, Business/Free Enterprise, Urban & Community Affairs • *Education:* Arts/Humanities Education, Business Education, Colleges & Universities, Education Associations, Education Funds, General, Medical Education, Minority Education, Private Education (Precollege), Religious Education, Science/Mathematics Education, Secondary Education (Private), Special Education, Student Aid • *Environment:* General • *Health:* Cancer, Clinics/Medical Centers, Emergency/Ambulance Services, Eyes/Blindness, Health Organizations, Hospices, Medical Research, Single-Disease Health Associations • *Religion:* Churches, Religious Organizations, Religious Welfare • *Science:* Science Museums, Scientific Research • *Social Services:* Animal Protection, Child Abuse, Child Welfare, Community Service Organizations, Family Planning, Family Services, Food/Clothing Distribution, People with Disabilities, Recreation & Athletics, Scouts, Substance Abuse, Volunteer Services, Youth Organizations

Grant Types: project, research, and scholarship

Geographic Distribution: near headquarters only

GIVING OFFICERS
Laura Chadwick: trust

Cornelia Corbett: trust

William Stamps Farish: pres *B* Houston TX 1939 *ED* Univ VA *CURR EMPL* owner, pres: WS Farish & Co *CORP AFFIL* adv dir: Pogo Producing Co; chmn: Churchill Downs; dir: Keeneland Assn, KY Derby Mus Corp; owner, pres: Lands End Farm *NONPR AFFIL* adv bd govs: Rice Univ; fdr: Houston Polo Assn *CLUB AFFIL* Jockey

Martha Farish Gerry: vp, trust

Caroline P. Rotan: secy

Terry W. Ward: treas

APPLICATION INFORMATION
Initial Approach:

Applicants should send a copy of a full proposal to the fund.

A complete proposal must include proof of tax-exempt status; brief history of the organization; description of the proposed project and a concise statement of the necessity for such a project; copy of a detailed financial statement; and an explanation of the proposed use of funds, detailed project budget, other potential sources of funding, and specific amount requested.

The board meets annually.

Restrictions on Giving: No grants are given to individuals, endowments or ongoing operating expenses.

PUBLICATIONS
Application guidelines

GRANTS ANALYSIS
Total Grants: $4,721,740

Number of Grants: 105

Highest Grant: $300,000

Average Grant: $44,970

Typical Range: $10,000 to $50,000

Disclosure Period: fiscal year ending June 30, 1993

Note: Recent grants are derived from a fiscal 1993 Form 990.

RECENT GRANTS

Library
30,000   River Oaks Baptist School, Houston, TX — books for new library

General
300,000   Independent Day School, Tampa, FL — expansion
250,000   South Kent School Corporation, South Kent, CT — annual giving
236,000   Episcopal High School, Bellaire, TX — land purchase, retirement, and language enrichment program
200,000   Columbia Presbyterian Medical Center Fund, New York, NY — capital campaign for expansion
200,000   Family Service Association of Nassau County, Hempstead, NY — family programs

Favrot Fund

CONTACT
Julie Richardson
Trustee
Favrot Fund
1770 Saint James, No. 510
Houston, TX 77056
(713) 622-1442

FINANCIAL SUMMARY
Recent Giving: $650,580 (1993); $549,000 (1992); $547,002 (1991)

Assets: $12,437,880 (1993); $13,162,295 (1992); $13,443,245 (1991)

EIN: 74-6045648

CONTRIBUTIONS SUMMARY
Donor(s): the late Laurence H. Favrot, Johanna A. Favrot, George B. Strong

Typical Recipients: • *Arts & Humanities:* Arts Associations & Councils, Arts Centers, Arts Outreach, Ballet, Film & Video, Historic Preservation, History & Archaeology, Libraries, Museums/Galleries, Music, Theater, Visual Arts • *Civic & Public Affairs:* Botanical Gardens/Parks, Urban & Community Affairs, Women's Affairs, Zoos/Aquariums • *Education:* Afterschool/Enrichment Programs, Colleges & Universities, Education Funds, International Exchange, Minority Education, Preschool Education, Private Education (Precollege), Public Education (Precollege), Science/Mathematics Education, Student Aid • *Environment:* Air/Water Quality, General, Resource Conservation, Wildlife Protection • *Health:* Cancer, Heart, Hospitals, Medical Research, Single-Disease Health Associations • *International:* Health Care/Hospitals, International Development

• *Religion:* Social/Policy Issues • *Science:* Science Museums • *Social Services:* At-Risk Youth, Child Abuse, Child Welfare, Domestic Violence, Family Planning, Family Services, People with Disabilities, Recreation & Athletics, Shelters/Homelessness, United Funds/United Ways, YMCA/YWCA/YMHA/YWHA, Youth Organizations

Grant Types: capital, general support, operating expenses, and research

Geographic Distribution: focus on TX, CA, NY, and Washington, DC

GIVING OFFICERS
Celestine Favrot Arndt: trust
Johanna A. Favrot: trust
Laurence de Kanter Favrot: trust
Leo Mortimer Favrot: trust
Romelia Favrot: trust
Marcia Favrot-Anderson: trust
Lenoir M. Josey: mgr, trust
Jeannette Favrot Peterson: trust
Julie Richardson: trust

APPLICATION INFORMATION
Initial Approach: The foundation has no formal grant application procedure or application form. Send brief letter of inquiry and full proposal. There are no deadlines.

GRANTS ANALYSIS
Total Grants: $650,580
Number of Grants: 45
Highest Grant: $50,000
Typical Range: $1,000 to $50,000
Disclosure Period: 1993

Note: Recent grants are derived from a 1993 Form 990.

RECENT GRANTS
Library
5,000   Alice and Hamilton Fish Library, Garrison, NY — to maintain high-quality video collection

General
50,000   Sharp Hospital Foundation, San Diego, CA — to develop a preventive educational and rehabilitation building and develop an endowment for cardiovascular program, second of five-year $250,000 pledge
40,000   Natural Resources Defense Council, New York, NY — for urban environmental issues in New York City
40,000   Population Communications International, New York, NY — support programs in Asia
37,000   Bastian School, Houston, TX — salary for person to work in the Quiet Room
30,000   Court Appointed Special Advocates, Houston, TX — to provide a bilingual supervisor of volunteers

Fikes Foundation, Leland

CONTACT
Nancy Solana
Vice President and Secretary
Leland Fikes Foundation
3050 Lincoln Plz.
500 N Akard, Ste. 3060
Dallas, TX 75201
(214) 754-0144

FINANCIAL SUMMARY
Recent Giving: $2,645,520 (1993); $3,090,202 (1992); $3,974,094 (1991)

Assets: $52,699,462 (1993); $50,460,000 (1992); $48,817,190 (1991)

Gifts Received: $182,000 (1993); $91,000 (1990); $91,499 (1989)

Fiscal Note: In 1989, the McIvey Charitable Trust No. 1 contributed $91,499 to the foundation. In 1990, the McIvey Charitable Trust donated $91,000. In 1993, contributions were received from the McIvey Charitable Trust.

EIN: 75-6035984

CONTRIBUTIONS SUMMARY
Donor(s): The Fikes Foundation was established in 1952 by Leland Fikes, a Texas oil producer and philanthropist. Mr. Fikes was also involved in many other business interests, including real estate. Family members are active in the foundation.

Typical Recipients: • *Arts & Humanities:* Ethnic & Folk Arts, Historic Preservation, Libraries, Museums/Galleries, Music, Theater • *Civic & Public Affairs:* Housing, Nonprofit Management, Public Policy, Urban & Community Affairs, Women's Affairs, Zoos/Aquariums • *Education:* Colleges & Universities, Education Funds, Elementary Education (Private), Literacy, Medical Education, Preschool Education, Private Education (Precollege), Public Education (Precollege), Science/Mathematics Education • *Environment:* General, Wildlife Protection • *Health:* AIDS/HIV, Cancer, Children's Health/Hospitals, Eyes/Blindness, Health Organizations, Heart, Hospitals, Medical Research, Mental Health, Nursing Services, Public Health, Trauma Treatment • *International:* Health Care/Hospitals, Human Rights, International Development, International Environmental Issues, Missionary/Religious Activities • *Religion:* Churches, Jewish Causes, Religious Welfare • *Science:* Observatories & Planetariums, Science Exhibits & Fairs, Science Museums, Scientific Organizations • *Social Services:* Camps, Child Welfare, Community Service Organizations, Domestic Violence, Family Planning, Family Services, Food/Clothing Distribution, Homes, People with Disabilities, Senior Services, Shelters/Homelessness, Substance Abuse, United Funds/United Ways, Volunteer Services, YMCA/YWCA/YMHA/YWHA, Youth Organizations

Grant Types: capital, endowment, general support, multiyear/continuing support, operating expenses, project, research, and seed money

Geographic Distribution: primarily in Dallas, TX

GIVING OFFICERS
Amy L. Fikes: vp, trust

Catherine W. Fikes: chwm, trust

Lee Fikes: pres, treas, trust

Nancy Solana: vp, secy

APPLICATION INFORMATION
Initial Approach:

Applicants should submit concise and complete written proposals.

The foundation does not have an application form. Proposals should contain a cover letter on organization letterhead (signed by the chief executive officer) describing the project, amount requested, and date by which funds are needed; copy of IRS tax-exempt status letter; names and affiliations of the board directors or trustees; and a brief history of the organization's work and purpose. Applicants should also include a specific description of the program or project, copy of total budget for current and preceding year, budget information pertaining to the project, information on key personnel, contact person, other funding sources, and plans for evaluating the program or project.

Applications may be submitted throughout the year.

After the board of trustees has received an application, it may request a meeting or additional information.

Restrictions on Giving: The foundation does not make grants to individuals.

PUBLICATIONS
Application guidelines

GRANTS ANALYSIS
Total Grants: $2,645,520

Number of Grants: 107

Highest Grant: $250,000

Average Grant: $24,724

Typical Range: $10,000 to $50,000

Disclosure Period: 1993

Note: Recent grants are derived from a 1993 Form 990.

RECENT GRANTS
General

250,000	St. Mark's School of Texas, Dallas, TX — phase III of a building campaign
250,000	St. Michael and All Angels Church, Dallas, TX
120,000	University of Texas Southwestern Medical Center, Dallas, TX — molecular cardiology research
100,000	Children's Medical Center, Dallas, TX — expansion and renovation
100,000	Fund for Excellence in Education in the Dallas

Independent School District, Dallas, TX — school performance improvement award fund

---

Fish Foundation, Ray C.

CONTACT
Barbara F. Daniel
President
Ray C. Fish Foundation
2001 Kirby Dr., Ste. 1005
Houston, TX 77019
(713) 522-0741

FINANCIAL SUMMARY
Recent Giving: $970,918 (fiscal 1993); $917,800 (fiscal 1992); $908,750 (fiscal 1991)

Assets: $23,896,800 (fiscal 1993); $22,443,597 (fiscal 1992); $21,021,856 (fiscal 1991)

Gifts Received: $60,004 (fiscal 1993); $74,930 (fiscal 1992); $74,857 (fiscal 1991)

Fiscal Note: The foundation has received contributions from the Ray C. and Martha G. Fish Trust in Houston, TX.

EIN: 74-6043047

CONTRIBUTIONS SUMMARY
Donor(s): The late Raymond Clinton Fish established the foundation in Texas in 1957, five years before his death. Mr. Fish was board chairman of the Fish Engineering Corporation and president and director of numerous gas pipeline and petrochemical firms. He helped create the Transcontinental Gas Pipeline System (Transco), the Pacific Northwest Pipeline System, and the Texas-Illinois Pipeline Company. His wife, Mirtha Galvez Fish, chaired the foundation prior to her death in 1967. A large portion of their estates went to benefit the foundation.

Typical Recipients: • *Arts & Humanities:* Dance, Ethnic & Folk Arts, Historic Preservation, Libraries, Museums/Galleries, Music, Performing Arts, Public Broadcasting, Theater • *Civic & Public Affairs:* Botanical Gardens/Parks, Clubs, General, Hispanic Affairs, Parades/Festivals, Public Policy, Urban & Community Affairs, Zoos/Aquariums • *Education:* Business Education, Colleges & Universities, Education Reform, Faculty Development, General, Literacy, Minority Education, Private Education (Precollege), Secondary Education (Private), Special Education, Student Aid • *Environment:* General, Resource Conservation • *Health:* Cancer, Clinics/Medical Centers, Emergency/Ambulance Services, Health Organizations, Heart, Hospitals, Medical Rehabilitation, Medical Research, Single-Disease Health Associations • *Religion:* Churches, Ministries, Religious Organizations, Religious Welfare • *Science:* Science Museums • *Social Services:* At-Risk Youth, Child Welfare, Community Service Organizations, Counseling, Emergency Relief, Family Planning, Food/Clothing Distribution, Homes, People

with Disabilities, Senior Services, Volunteer Services, Youth Organizations

Grant Types: capital, general support, operating expenses, research, and scholarship

Geographic Distribution: Texas, primarily the metropolitan Houston area, Kerrville, and Galveston.

GIVING OFFICERS
Robert J. Cruikshank: vp, asst secy, trust

Barbara Fish Daniel: pres, trust

Christopher J. Daniel: treas, trust

James L. Daniel, Jr.: vp, trust

Paula Hooton: secy

APPLICATION INFORMATION
Initial Approach:

Applications should be submitted in writing.

Complete information on applications may be obtained by calling the foundation office.

There are no deadlines.

The foundation will review the proposal and respond as quickly as possible. The board of trustees may request an interview and supplementary information.

PUBLICATIONS
Information brochure

GRANTS ANALYSIS
Total Grants: $970,918

Number of Grants: 128

Highest Grant: $55,000

Average Grant: $7,585

Typical Range: $1,000 to $15,000

Disclosure Period: fiscal year ending June 30, 1993

Note: Recent grants are derived from a fiscal 1993 Form 990.

RECENT GRANTS

Library

55,000	Schreiner College, Kerrville, TX — Weir building renovation/library
50,000	George Bush Presidential Library, College Station, TX — capital campaign

General

50,000	Foundation for the Retarded, Houston, TX — building campaign
50,000	Stehlin Foundation for Cancer Research, Houston, TX — cancer research
30,000	Houston Arboretum and Nature Center, Houston, TX — capital campaign
25,150	Nature Conservancy of Texas, San Antonio, TX — conservation program
25,000	Austin College, Sherman, TX — recruitment program for Hispanic students

Fondren Foundation

CONTACT
Melanie Boone Scioneaux
Assistant Secretary/Treasurer
Fondren Foundation
c/o Texas Commerce Bank
PO Box 2558
Houston, TX 77252-8037
(713) 236-4403

FINANCIAL SUMMARY
Recent Giving: $5,192,900 (fiscal 1993);
$4,871,600 (fiscal 1992); $5,028,483 (fiscal 1991)

Assets: $109,997,441 (fiscal 1993);
$105,170,800 (fiscal 1992); $103,763,724 (fiscal 1991)

Gifts Received: $58,508 (fiscal 1989)

Fiscal Note: The foundation received
$58,508 from the Ella F. Fondren 1982 Trust f/b/o David M. Underwood in fiscal 1989.

EIN: 74-6042565

CONTRIBUTIONS SUMMARY
Donor(s): Walter William Fondren , a Houston oilman, philanthropist, and founder of Humble Oil and Refining Co., established the Fondren Foundation in Texas in 1948.

Mrs. Walter Fondren administered his estate following his death and became the principal contributor to the foundation.

Typical Recipients: • *Arts & Humanities:* Art History, Arts Outreach, Dance, Historic Preservation, History & Archaeology, Libraries, Museums/Galleries, Music, Theater • *Civic & Public Affairs:* Botanical Gardens/Parks, Economic Development, Employment/Job Training, General, Housing, Philanthropic Organizations, Public Policy, Urban & Community Affairs • *Education:* Business Education, Colleges & Universities, Engineering/Technological Education, General, Leadership Training, Medical Education, Private Education (Precollege), Public Education (Precollege), Religious Education, Science/Mathematics Education, Secondary Education (Private), Special Education, Student Aid • *Environment:* General, Wildlife Protection • *Health:* AIDS/HIV, Cancer, Children's Health/Hospitals, Clinics/Medical Centers, Emergency/Ambulance Services, Hospices, Hospitals, Medical Rehabilitation, Medical Research, Mental Health, Prenatal Health Issues, Research/Studies Institutes, Single-Disease Health Associations • *International:* International Relations • *Religion:* Churches, Religious Welfare • *Science:* Science Museums • *Social Services:* At-Risk Youth, Child Welfare, Community Service Organizations, Family Services, Scouts, Substance Abuse, Volunteer Services, Youth Organizations

Grant Types: capital, endowment, general support, project, and research

Geographic Distribution: Texas, particularly Houston

GIVING OFFICERS
Doris Fondren Allday: bd gov

R. Edwin Allday: bd gov

Ellanor Allday Beard: mem bd govs

Melanie Boone Scioneaux: asst secy/treas

Celia Whitfield Crank: mem bd govs

Bentley B. Fondren: bd gov

Robert E. Fondren: bd gov *B* 1962 *CURR EMPL* vp, dir: Trend Devel *CORP AFFIL* off: CNO Devel, Companeros Devel Co, Lake Colony Four, Plantation Devel Corp

Walter W. Fondren III: bd gov

Walter W. Fondren IV: secy, treas

Marie Fondren Hall: mem bd govs

Frances Fondren Hanson: mem bd govs

Ann Gordon Trammell: bd gov

Catherine Fondren Underwood: vchmn

David M. Underwood: mem bd govs *B* 1937 *ED* Yale Univ 1959 *CURR EMPL* pres, dir: Feliciana Corp *PHIL AFFIL* vp, dir: Damon Wells Foundation

David M. Underwood, Jr: bd gov

Lynda Knapp Underwood: bd gov *B* 1937 *CURR EMPL* vp, dir: Feliciana Corp

Sue Trammell Whitfield: bd gov

Susan T. Whitfield: chmn

W. Trammell Whitfield: mem bd govs

William F. Whitfield, Jr.: mem bd govs

William F. Whitfield, Sr.: bd gov

APPLICATION INFORMATION
Initial Approach:

Applicants should send one copy of a concise proposal.

Proposals should include a brief narrative history of the organization's purpose and work, specific description of the proposed program or project for which funds are requested, amount requested from the foundation as well as total amount needed, date by which funds are needed, proof of tax-exempt status, and a list of trustees or directors and principal staff.

GRANTS ANALYSIS
Total Grants: $5,192,900

Number of Grants: 74

Highest Grant: $380,000

Average Grant: $70,174

Typical Range: $10,000 to $100,000

Disclosure Period: fiscal year ending October 31, 1993

Note: Recent grants are derived from a fiscal 1993 Form 990.

RECENT GRANTS

Library

380,000	Southern Methodist University, Dallas, TX — library renovation

General

340,000	Baylor College of Medicine Vascular Biology Laboratory, Houston, TX
280,000	Texas Medical Center, Houston, TX — acquisition of properties

250,000	Episcopal High School, Bellaire, TX — debt retirement
208,500	St. John the Divine Episcopal Church, Houston, TX — capital campaign
200,000	Jordan School, Crockett, TX — memorial endowment fund

Frost National Bank / The Charitable Foundation of Frost National Bank

Sales: $145.61 million
Employees: 1,700
Headquarters: San Antonio, TX
SIC Major Group: National Commercial Banks and Nonresidential Building Operators

CONTACT
Melissa J. Adams
Donations Coordinator
Frost National Bank
PO Box 1600
San Antonio, TX 78296
(210) 220-4353

FINANCIAL SUMMARY
Fiscal Note: Company gives directly. Annual Giving Range: $250,000 to $500,000

CONTRIBUTIONS SUMMARY
Typical Recipients: • *Arts & Humanities:* Arts Appreciation, Arts Associations & Councils, Arts Festivals, Arts Funds, Arts Institutes, Community Arts, Ethnic & Folk Arts, Historic Preservation, Libraries, Museums/Galleries, Music, Performing Arts, Public Broadcasting, Theater • *Civic & Public Affairs:* Business/Free Enterprise, Economic Development, Employment/Job Training, Professional & Trade Associations, Zoos/Aquariums • *Education:* Agricultural Education, Arts/Humanities Education, Business Education, Colleges & Universities, Education Funds, Engineering/Technological Education, Faculty Development, Health & Physical Education, International Exchange, Literacy, Medical Education, Preschool Education, Private Education (Precollege), Public Education (Precollege), Science/Mathematics Education • *Environment:* General • *Health:* Hospices, Hospitals, Medical Rehabilitation, Medical Research, Mental Health, Public Health, Single-Disease Health Associations • *International:* International Relations • *Religion:* Churches, Religious Organizations • *Science:* Scientific Organizations • *Social Services:* Child Welfare, Community Centers, Community Service Organizations, Counseling, Delinquency & Criminal Rehabilitation, Domestic Violence, Emergency Relief, Family Services, Food/Clothing Distribution, People with Disabilities, Recreation & Athletics, Senior Services, Substance Abuse, Volunteer Services, Youth Organizations

Grant Types: capital, general support, matching, and multiyear/continuing support

Nonmonetary Support Types: donated equipment, donated products, in-kind services, loaned employees, and loaned executives

Note: Value of nonmonetary support is unavailable.

Geographic Distribution: in headquarters and operating communities

Operating Locations: TX (Austin, Corpus Christi, Houston, McAllen, San Antonio)

CORP. OFFICERS

Tom C. Frost: *B* San Antonio TX 1927 *ED* Washington & Lee Univ BS 1950; Austin Univ LLD *CURR EMPL* chmn, ceo: Cullen/Frost Bankers Inc *CORP AFFIL* adv dir: Elsinore Cattle Co; dir: Cullen Ctr Bank & Trust Co, Cullen/Frost Bank Dallas NA, Fed Reserve Bank Dallas, SBC Commun Inc, Southwestern Bell Corp *NONPR AFFIL* chmn devel: Univ TX San Antonio; dir: San Antonio Econ Devel Fdn; hon trust: SW TX Methodist Hosp; mem: Assn Reserve City Bankers, Philosophy Soc TX, San Antonio Clearinghouse Assn, TX Assn Bank Holding Cos, TX Bankers Assn; mem devel bd: Univ TX Health Sci Ctr; trust: Austin Coll, McNay Art Inst, San Antonio Med Fdn, SW Res Inst, TX Res & Tech Fdn; trust emeritus: Washington & Lee Univ

Robert S. McClane: *B* Kenedy TX 1939 *ED* Trinity Univ 1961 *CURR EMPL* pres, dir: Cullen/Frost Bankers Inc *CORP AFFIL* dir: Cullen/Frost Life Ins Co, Daltex Gen Agency, Frost Natl Bank, Main Plaza Corp *NONPR AFFIL* dir: Plaza Club San Antonio; mem: Am Bankers Assn, Assn Bank Holding Cos, Greater San Antonio Chamber Commerce, San Antonio German Club, Trinity Univ Alumni Assn; trust: Trinity Univ

GIVING OFFICERS

Melissa J. Adams: *CURR EMPL* donations coordinator: Frost Natl Bank

APPLICATION INFORMATION

Initial Approach: *Initial Contact:* brief letter of inquiry *Include Information On:* description of the organization, amount requested, purpose of funds sought, recently audited financial statements, proof of tax-exempt status, deadline for project approval, and signature of authorization by organization's highest ranking officer *Deadlines:* at least three weeks before funds are needed

GRANTS ANALYSIS

Typical Range: $1,000 to $2,500

Gulf Coast Medical Foundation

CONTACT

Gulf Coast Medical Fdn.
PO Box 30
Wharton, TX 77488
(409) 532-0904

FINANCIAL SUMMARY

Recent Giving: $622,680 (fiscal 1994)

Assets: $13,889,104 (fiscal 1994)

EIN: 74-1285242

CONTRIBUTIONS SUMMARY

Typical Recipients: • *Arts & Humanities:* Libraries, Museums/Galleries, Theater • *Civic & Public Affairs:* Municipalities/Towns, Parades/Festivals, Urban & Community Affairs • *Education:* Community & Junior Colleges, Literacy, Medical Education, Public Education (Precollege), Student Aid • *Health:* Cancer, Children's Health/Hospitals, Clinics/Medical Centers, Emergency/Ambulance Services, Mental Health, Nutrition • *Religion:* Churches, Ministries • *Science:* Scientific Centers & Institutes • *Social Services:* Crime Prevention, Day Care

Grant Types: general support

Geographic Distribution: focus on TX

GIVING OFFICERS

Laurance Hearne Armour, Jr.: dir *B* Chicago IL 1923 *ED* Princeton Univ AA 1945; Northwestern Univ 1947-1948 *NONPR AFFIL* hon trust: Northwestern Meml Hosp; mem natl bd govs: Inst Living *CLUB AFFIL* Casino, Chicago, Chicago YC, New York YC, Onwentsia, Shoreacres *PHIL AFFIL* pres: Gulf Coast Medical Foundation

R. B. Caraway: dir

Charles Davis, Jr.: treas

Charles F. Drees: dir

Kent Hill: pres

Bert Huebner: dir

Dee McElroy: exec vp

Sylvan Miori: dir

Irving Moore, Jr.: secy *B* Wharton City TX 1912 *ED* Univ TX LLB *PHIL AFFIL* pres, trust: M. G. and Lillie A. Johnson Foundation

Jack Moore: vp

Max Rotholz: dir

Clive Runnells: dir

Clive Runnells III: dir

David Stovall: dir

Guy F. Stovall III: dir

C. E. Woodson, MD: exec vp

APPLICATION INFORMATION

Initial Approach: Send a brief letter of inquiry. Include a description of organization, amount requested, purpose of funds sought, recently audited financial statement, and proof of tax-exempt status.

GRANTS ANALYSIS

Total Grants: $622,680

Number of Grants: 39

Highest Grant: $50,000

Typical Range: $390 to $50,000

Disclosure Period: fiscal year ending May 31, 1994

Note: Recent grants are derived from a fiscal 1994 Form 990.

RECENT GRANTS

Library

25,000	Bay City Library Association, Bay City, TX — for library relocation	

General

50,000	Bay City Day Care, Bay City, TX — for home renovation	
50,000	Northside Health Center, Wharton, TX	
50,000	Wharton County Junior College, Wharton, TX — for medical education programs	
50,000	Wharton County Junior College, Wharton, TX — for new construction	
35,000	City of El Campo, El Campo, TX — for a new ambulance	

Hachar Charitable Trust, D. D.

CONTACT

Adrienne Trevino
Administrator
D. D. Hachar Charitable Trust
PO Box 59
Laredo, TX 78042
(512) 723-1151

Note: Adrienne Trevino's extension is 442.

FINANCIAL SUMMARY

Recent Giving: $1,172,279 (fiscal 1994); $943,793 (fiscal 1993); $727,752 (fiscal 1992)

Assets: $9,995,579 (fiscal 1994); $8,711,221 (fiscal 1993); $8,603,044 (fiscal 1992)

EIN: 74-2093680

CONTRIBUTIONS SUMMARY

Typical Recipients: • *Arts & Humanities:* Libraries, Music, Performing Arts • *Civic & Public Affairs:* Zoos/Aquariums • *Education:* Business Education, Community & Junior Colleges, Medical Education, Preschool Education, Private Education (Precollege), Public Education (Precollege) • *Health:* Cancer, Children's Health/Hospitals, Emergency/Ambulance Services, Health Organizations, Kidney, Nursing Services, Single-Disease Health Associations • *Social Services:* Animal Protection, Child Welfare, Food/Clothing Distribution, Recreation & Athletics, Scouts, United Funds/United Ways, Youth Organizations

Grant Types: general support, loan, and scholarship

Geographic Distribution: limited to Laredo and Webb County, TX

GIVING OFFICERS

The Laredo National Bank: trust

Joaquin G. Cigarroa: trust

John Keck: trust

Dennis Nixon: trust

Rogelio G. Rios: trust

Roque Vela: trust

APPLICATION INFORMATION

Initial Approach: Application form required for student loans. Deadline is last Friday in April and October.

PUBLICATIONS

Annual Report, Informational Brochure, Application Guidelines. Provides scholarships and student loans for higher education.

GRANTS ANALYSIS

Total Grants: $1,172,279

Number of Grants: 12

Highest Grant: $250,000

Typical Range: $3,000 to $90,000

Disclosure Period: fiscal year ending April 30, 1994

Note: Recent grants are derived from a fiscal 1994 Form 990. Number of grants and typical range do not include scholarships to individuals.

RECENT GRANTS

General

250,000	Laredo Independent School District, Laredo, TX
90,000	Boys and Girls Clubs of Laredo, Laredo, TX
83,333	Texas State Aquarium, Corpus Christi, TX
56,430	United Day School, Laredo, TX
41,667	Texas State Aquarium, Corpus Christi, TX

Halff Foundation, G. A. C.

CONTACT

Thomas F. Bibb
Vice President
G. A. C. Halff Fdn.
745 E Mulberry, Ste. 400
San Antonio, TX 78212
(210) 735-3300

FINANCIAL SUMMARY

Recent Giving: $255,000 (fiscal 1994); $280,000 (fiscal 1993); $257,000 (fiscal 1992)

Assets: $6,707,425 (fiscal 1994); $6,508,670 (fiscal 1993); $6,391,584 (fiscal 1992)

EIN: 74-6042432

CONTRIBUTIONS SUMMARY

Donor(s): the late G. A. C. Halff

Typical Recipients: • *Arts & Humanities:* Arts Institutes, Ethnic & Folk Arts, Libraries, Museums/Galleries, Music, Public Broadcasting • *Civic & Public Affairs:* General • *Education:* Colleges & Universities, Education Funds, Private Education (Precollege) • *Health:* Cancer, Eyes/Blindness, Health Organizations, Hospices, Hospitals, Medical Rehabilitation, Medical Research, Single-Disease Health Associations • *Religion:* Religious Welfare • *Social Services:* Camps, Child Welfare, Community Centers, Community Service Organizations, Counseling, Family Planning, Food/Clothing Distribution, People with Disabilities, Substance Abuse, United Funds/United Ways, Youth Organizations

Grant Types: general support and research

Geographic Distribution: focus on San Antonio, TX

GIVING OFFICERS

Roland R. Arnold: trust

Thomas F. Bibb: vp, treas, trust

Catherine H. Edson: trust

Thomas H. Edson: trust

Hugh Halff, Jr.: pres *B* 1936 *NONPR AFFIL* mem: Charity Ball Assn, McNay Friends Gallery Counc, Order Alamo *CLUB AFFIL* Argyle, Club Giraud, San Antonio CC, San Antonio German

Marie M. Halff: trust

Catherine H. Luhn: trust

APPLICATION INFORMATION

Initial Approach: Send brief letter of inquiry describing program or project. Deadline is May 15.

Restrictions on Giving: Does not support individuals. Limited to state of Texas.

GRANTS ANALYSIS

Total Grants: $255,000

Number of Grants: 34

Highest Grant: $25,000

Typical Range: $3,000 to $10,000

Disclosure Period: fiscal year ending February 28, 1994

Note: Recent grants are derived from a fiscal 1994 Form 990.

RECENT GRANTS

Library

8,000	San Antonio Public Library, San Antonio, TX

General

30,000	Cancer Therapy and Research, San Antonio, TX
25,000	United Way, San Antonio, TX
10,000	Big Brothers and Big Sisters, San Antonio, TX
10,000	Community Guidance Center, San Antonio, TX
10,000	Good Samaritan Center, San Antonio, TX

Hallberg Foundation, E. L. and R. F.

CONTACT

E. L. and R. F. Hallberg Fdn.
2705 S Cooper St., Ste. 300
Arlington, TX 76015
(817) 844-4457

FINANCIAL SUMMARY

Recent Giving: $140,600 (fiscal 1993); $151,000 (fiscal 1992); $192,000 (fiscal 1990)

Assets: $3,259,721 (fiscal 1993); $3,134,822 (fiscal 1992); $2,681,669 (fiscal 1990)

EIN: 75-6356892

CONTRIBUTIONS SUMMARY

Typical Recipients: • *Arts & Humanities:* Ballet, Libraries, Music, Theater • *Civic & Public Affairs:* General, Hispanic Affairs, Housing, Philanthropic Organizations, Safety • *Education:* Colleges & Universities, Engineering/Technological Education, Environmental Education, School Volunteerism, Secondary Education (Public), Student Aid • *Health:* Alzheimers Disease • *International:* International Organizations • *Religion:* Churches, Religious Welfare, Synagogues/Temples • *Social Services:* Child Welfare, Community Service Organizations, Food/Clothing Distribution, People with Disabilities, Recreation & Athletics, Shelters/Homelessness

Grant Types: general support

Geographic Distribution: focus on TX

GIVING OFFICERS

Bank One: trust

Virginia Winkler: trust

APPLICATION INFORMATION

Initial Approach: The foundation reports no specific application guidelines. Send a brief letter of inquiry, including statement of purpose, amount requested, and proof of tax-exempt status.

GRANTS ANALYSIS

Total Grants: $140,600

Number of Grants: 35

Highest Grant: $18,000

Typical Range: $400 to $10,000

Disclosure Period: fiscal year ending September 30, 1993

Note: Recent grants are derived from a fiscal 1993 Form 990.

RECENT GRANTS

Library

3,875	Friends of Mansfield Public Library, Mansfield, TX — towards purchase of additional books for library

General

18,000	Lubbock Area Foundation, Lubbock, TX
10,000	First Baptist Church, El Paso, TX
10,000	University of Texas Austin, Austin, TX — to further education of students in civil engineering
7,500	First United Methodist Church, Lubbock, TX
6,000	Christian Church Foundation, Indianapolis, IN — to establish permanent fund

Halsell Foundation, Ewing

CONTACT
Gilbert M. Denman, Jr.
Trustee
Ewing Halsell Foundation
711 Navarro, Ste. 537
San Antonio, TX 78205
(210) 223-2640

FINANCIAL SUMMARY
Recent Giving: $1,987,857 (fiscal 1993); $1,998,759 (fiscal 1992); $1,680,472 (fiscal 1991)

Assets: $41,555,682 (fiscal 1993); $45,427,841 (fiscal 1992); $44,308,515 (fiscal 1991)

EIN: 74-6063016

CONTRIBUTIONS SUMMARY
Donor(s): The foundation's donors were Ewing Halsell , who died in 1965, and his sister-in-law, Grace Fortner Rider , who died in 1971. Mr. Halsell was a cattle rancher whose interests centered in Texas, Oklahoma, and Kansas.

Typical Recipients: • *Arts & Humanities:* Arts Associations & Councils, Arts Centers, Arts Festivals, Dance, Ethnic & Folk Arts, Libraries, Literary Arts, Museums/Galleries, Music, Opera, Public Broadcasting • *Civic & Public Affairs:* General, Nonprofit Management, Philanthropic Organizations, Urban & Community Affairs, Zoos/Aquariums • *Education:* Colleges & Universities, Education Reform, General, Private Education (Precollege), Science/Mathematics Education • *Environment:* Resource Conservation, Watershed, Wildlife Protection • *Health:* Geriatric Health, Single-Disease Health Associations • *International:* International Organizations • *Religion:* Churches, Religious Welfare • *Social Services:* Child Welfare, Community Service Organizations, Domestic Violence, Family Planning, Family Services, People with Disabilities, Scouts, Shelters/Homelessness, Substance Abuse, United Funds/United Ways

Grant Types: capital, project, research, and scholarship

Geographic Distribution: Texas, primarily the San Antonio area

GIVING OFFICERS
Helen Campbell: secy, treas, trust

Jean Deacy: trust

Gilbert M. Denman, Jr.: trust *B* San Antonio TX 1921 *ED* Univ TX BA 1940; Univ TX LLB 1942 *CURR EMPL* atty: Denman Franklin & Denman *PHIL AFFIL* trust: George W. Brackenridge Foundation, Sarah Campbell Blaffer Foundation

Leroy G. Denman, Jr.: trust *B* San Antonio TX 1918 *ED* Univ TX BA 1939; Univ TX LLB 1939 *CURR EMPL* atty: Denman Franklin & Denman *PHIL AFFIL* trust: Caesar Kleberg Foundation for Wildlife Conservation, George W. Brackenridge Foundation; secy: Sarah Campbell Blaffer Foundation

Hugh A. Fitzsimmons, Jr.: trust

APPLICATION INFORMATION
Initial Approach:

Applicants should submit a letter and a short summary of the proposed project.

Proposals should include the history and purposes of the organization, proposed use of funds, anticipated results of expenditures, and explanation of financial need (including other sources of funds, if any, to be used for the project). Also include a copy of the IRS tax exemption letter. Applications should be signed or approved in writing by the chief executive of the applicant organization.

There are no deadlines for submitting proposals.

The foundation's trustees meet three to four times a year. Applicants will be notified in writing of receipt of application. Interviews are conducted only at the foundation's initiative.

Restrictions on Giving: The foundation discourages proposals for general support, deficit reduction, or continuing or additional support for current or previous programs. Grants are not made to individuals.

OTHER THINGS TO KNOW
Grant commitments may cover several years. Matching funding is encouraged. The foundation trustees also initiate grants, and may make challenge grants to stimulate other financial participation.

PUBLICATIONS
Application guidelines

GRANTS ANALYSIS
Total Grants: $1,987,857

Number of Grants: 66

Highest Grant: $421,000

Average Grant: $30,119

Typical Range: $5,000 to $50,000

Disclosure Period: fiscal year ending June 30, 1993

Note: Recent grants are derived from a fiscal 1993 Form 990.

RECENT GRANTS

Library

421,000	Our Lady of the Lake University, San Antonio, TX — automation of library and capital campaign
250,000	San Antonio Public Library Foundation, San Antonio, TX — acquisition of major art piece for permanent exhibition at new library
18,500	Redeemer Episcopal School, Ealge Pass, TX — library automation equipment and books

General

195,000	Trinity University, San Antonio, TX — curriculum reform project Hawthorne elementary
80,000	Judson Montessori School, San Antonio, TX — acquisition of land for new campus
52,500	Youth Alternatives, San Antonio, TX — renovate emergency shelter and acquire new security system
50,000	Family Service Association, San Antonio, TX — to establish volunteer database program
30,000	Planned Parenthood of San Antonio, San Antonio, TX — expansion of community education programs

Hamman Foundation, George and Mary Josephine

CONTACT
Stephen I. Gelsey
Administrator
George and Mary Josephine Hamman Foundation
910 Travis St., No. 1990
Houston, TX 77002-5816
(713) 658-8345

FINANCIAL SUMMARY
Recent Giving: $1,058,000 (fiscal 1994); $945,800 (fiscal 1993); $901,805 (fiscal 1992)

Assets: $29,000,000 (fiscal 1994 est.); $29,550,120 (fiscal 1993); $28,366,273 (fiscal 1992)

EIN: 74-6061447

CONTRIBUTIONS SUMMARY
Donor(s): The foundation was incorporated in 1954 by George Hamman and the late Mary Josephine Hamman .

Typical Recipients: • *Arts & Humanities:* Ballet, Dance, Libraries, Museums/Galleries, Music, Performing Arts, Theater • *Civic & Public Affairs:* Botanical Gardens/Parks, Economic Development, General, Hispanic Affairs, Housing, Urban & Community Affairs, Zoos/Aquariums • *Education:* Colleges & Universities, Education Reform, General, Health & Physical Education, Literacy, Minority Education, Private Education (Precollege), Religious Education, Special Education, Student Aid • *Environment:* General • *Health:* Cancer, Clinics/Medical Centers, Eyes/Blindness, Health Organizations, Heart, Hospices, Hospitals, Medical Rehabilitation, Medical Research, Mental Health, Single-Disease Health Associations • *Religion:* Churches, Religious Organizations • *Social Services:* Child Welfare, Community Centers, Community Service Organizations, Family Planning, Family Services, Food/Clothing Distribution, Homes, Shelters/Homelessness, Youth Organizations

Grant Types: capital, matching, research, and scholarship

Geographic Distribution: limited to Texas, primarily the Houston area

GIVING OFFICERS
Stephen I. Gelsey: admin

Henry R. Hamman: secy, dir *B* 1937 *ED*
Univ TX BS 1959; Univ TX MA 1961
CURR EMPL pres, ceo, dir: Hamman Oil &
Refining Co

Charles D. Milby, Jr.: dir

Charles D. Milby, Sr.: pres, dir

Ann H. Shepherd: dir

APPLICATION INFORMATION
Initial Approach:

The foundation requests applications be
made in writing. Applications for scholarships should be obtained from the foundation.

Grant applications should include an IRS
tax-exemption letter and budget information. Scholarship applicants should attach
the following to the completed application
form: a financial qualification statement,
high school transcript, proof of SAT or ACT
results, recent photo, and a complete copy of
the parents' or student's latest federal income tax return.

There is no deadline for submitting grant applications. The deadline for submitting
scholarship applications is February 28.

Restrictions on Giving: The foundation
does not support post-graduate education or
individuals.

PUBLICATIONS
Application guidelines

GRANTS ANALYSIS
Total Grants: $945,800

Number of Grants: 116*

Highest Grant: $100,000

Average Grant: $6,084*

Typical Range: $1,000 to $10,000

Disclosure Period: fiscal year ending April
30, 1993

Note: Number of grants and average grant
figures exclude scholarships totaling
$240,000. Recent grants are derived from a
fiscal 1993 Form 990.

RECENT GRANTS

Library
5,000	Houston Public Library, Houston, TX — community funds

General
30,000	Neuhaus Education Center, Houston, TX — community funds
20,000	Planned Parenthood of Houston, Houston, TX — community funds
17,000	American Heart Association, Houston, TX — medical treatment
15,000	Christ Church Cathedral, Houston, TX — churches and affiliated organizations
15,000	Stehlin Foundation, Houston, TX — medical treatment

Hammer Foundation, Armand

CONTACT
Michael A. Hammer
Chairman
Armand Hammer Foundation
3500 Oaklawn Ave., Ste. 640
Dallas, TX 75219
(214) 559-6193

FINANCIAL SUMMARY
Recent Giving: $396,770 (1992); $241,455
(1991); $25,326,857 (1990)

Assets: $9,057,134 (1992); $8,303,486
(1991); $330,805 (1990)

Gifts Received: $1,748,800 (1992);
$9,140,789 (1991); $1,390,000 (1990)

Fiscal Note: In 1989, the foundation received $1,555,000 from Armand Hammer
and in 1990, the foundation received
$1,390,000 from Armand Hammer.

EIN: 23-7010813

CONTRIBUTIONS SUMMARY
Donor(s): The Armand Hammer Foundation
was established in California in 1968 by Dr.
Armand Hammer , former chairman and
chief executive officer of Occidental Petroleum Corporation. Dr. Hammer was a noted
art collector and philanthropist. Known donations include $6 million to the Armand
Hammer United World College of the American West, which he founded in 1982; $5 mil-
lion each to Columbia University and the
Salk Institute; and numerous gifts and art-
work to the Corcoran Gallery of Art. Dr.
Hammer died in 1990.

Typical Recipients: • *Arts & Humanities:*
Arts Associations & Councils, Arts Centers,
Historic Preservation, Libraries, Muse-
ums/Galleries, Music, Theater • *Civic &
Public Affairs:* Clubs, General, Parades/Fes-
tivals, Public Policy • *Education:* Business
Education, Colleges & Universities, Gen-
eral, Medical Education, Private Education
(Precollege), Public Education (Precollege),
Student Aid, Vocational & Technical Educa-
tion • *Health:* Cancer, Children's
Health/Hospitals, Clinics/Medical Centers,
Emergency/Ambulance Services, Health Organizations, Hospices, Hospitals, Medical
Research, Medical Training, Multiple Sclerosis, Single-Disease Health Associations • *International:* Foreign Educational
Institutions, International Organizations, International Peace & Security Issues, Mission-
ary/Religious Activities • *Religion:*
Churches, Jewish Causes, Ministries, Religious Organizations, Religious Welfare • *Science:* Scientific Centers & Institutes • *Social
Services:* Community Service Organizations, Crime Prevention, Day Care, Family
Services, People with Disabilities, Recreation & Athletics, Scouts,
YMCA/YWCA/YMHA/YWHA, Youth Organizations

Grant Types: capital, general support, mul-
tiyear/continuing support, project, and research

Geographic Distribution: broad geographic
distribution

GIVING OFFICERS
Dru Hammer: dir

Michael A. Hammer: chmn, ceo

APPLICATION INFORMATION
Initial Contact: Applicants should send a
letter to the foundation.

Include Information On: Applications
need not be submitted in any particular
form. Send a letter stating the reason for the
grant, and give brief background material.

Deadlines: There are no deadlines for requests.

Review Process: Applications are reviewed
by the contact person, who then presents applications that fall within foundation's priorities to the directors for a final decision.

Note: No grants are given to individuals.

GRANTS ANALYSIS
Total Grants: $396,770

Number of Grants: 57

Highest Grant: $175,000

Average Grant: $6,961

Typical Range: $500 to $10,000

Disclosure Period: 1992

Note: Recent grants are derived from a 1992
Form 990.

RECENT GRANTS

General
175,000	Armand Hammer United World College, Los Angeles, CA
75,000	International Foundation
13,700	Crystal Charity Ball, Dallas, TX
10,000	Columbia Business School, New York, NY
10,000	First United Pentecost Church

Hawn Foundation

CONTACT
William R. Hawn
President
Hawn Foundation
5956 Sherry Ln., Ste. 1210
Dallas, TX 75225
(214) 265-8435

FINANCIAL SUMMARY
Recent Giving: $971,750 (fiscal 1993);
$929,820 (fiscal 1992); $862,250 (fiscal
1991)

Assets: $25,176,110 (fiscal 1993);
$23,704,210 (fiscal 1992); $22,279,648 (fiscal 1991)

EIN: 75-6036761

CONTRIBUTIONS SUMMARY
Donor(s): The foundation was incorporated
in 1962 by the late Mildred Hawn .

Typical Recipients: • *Arts & Humanities:*
Arts Associations & Councils, Community

Arts, Dance, Historic Preservation, Libraries, Museums/Galleries, Music, Opera, Performing Arts, Theater • *Civic & Public Affairs:* Professional & Trade Associations • *Education:* Colleges & Universities, Literacy, Minority Education, Private Education (Precollege), Religious Education, Secondary Education (Private), Special Education, Student Aid • *Health:* Arthritis, Children's Health/Hospitals, Clinics/Medical Centers, Diabetes, Eyes/Blindness, Health Funds, Health Organizations, Heart, Hospitals, Long-Term Care, Medical Rehabilitation, Medical Research, Multiple Sclerosis, Nursing Services, Single-Disease Health Associations • *International:* Health Care/Hospitals • *Religion:* Churches, Religious Welfare • *Social Services:* Animal Protection, Child Abuse, Community Centers, Counseling, Emergency Relief, Family Services, People with Disabilities, Substance Abuse, United Funds/United Ways, YMCA/YWCA/YMHA/YWHA, Youth Organizations

Grant Types: general support and research

Geographic Distribution: focus on Texas, with emphasis on Dallas

GIVING OFFICERS
Ed Copley: dir

C. F. Hawn: dir

Jim J. Hawn: dir

Joe Verne Hawn, Jr.: secy, treas, dir

W. A. Hawn, Jr.: dir

William Russell Hawn: pres, dir

William Russell Hawn, Jr.: dir

Irby N. Taylor: dir

APPLICATION INFORMATION
Initial Approach:

The foundation has no formal grant application procedure or application form.

Written proposals should state the goals of the project and the type of contribution requested.

The foundation has no deadline for submitting proposals.

GRANTS ANALYSIS
Total Grants: $971,750

Number of Grants: 50

Highest Grant: $100,000

Average Grant: $19,435

Typical Range: $1,000 to $20,000

Disclosure Period: fiscal year ending August 31, 1993

Note: Recent grants are derived from a fiscal 1993 Form 990.

RECENT GRANTS
Library

100,000	Southern Methodist University, Dallas, TX — arts library fund
1,000	Christian Education for the Blind, Ft. Worth, TX — library services for visually impaired

General

100,000	Highland Park Presbyterian Church, Dallas, TX
100,000	Texas Scottish Rite Hospital, Dallas, TX — medical assistance
76,000	Juvenile Diabetes Foundation, Dallas, TX — medical research
75,000	Scripps Clinic and Research Foundation, La Jolla, CA — medical research
50,000	Presbyterian Healthcare Foundation, Dallas, TX — arthritis research

Henry Foundation, Patrick

CONTACT
Diane Post
Trust Officer
Patrick Henry Fdn.
c/o NationsBank Texas Trust Div.
PO Box 908
Austin, TX 78781
(512) 397-2574

FINANCIAL SUMMARY
Recent Giving: $100,000 (fiscal 1994); $159,400 (fiscal 1993); $143,300 (fiscal 1992)

Assets: $2,596,737 (fiscal 1994); $2,692,950 (fiscal 1993); $2,525,968 (fiscal 1992)

EIN: 74-2418070

CONTRIBUTIONS SUMMARY
Donor(s): Ellen Clayton Garwood

Typical Recipients: • *Arts & Humanities:* Libraries, Performing Arts, Theater • *Civic & Public Affairs:* Civil Rights, General, Legal Aid, Public Policy, Urban & Community Affairs, Women's Affairs • *Education:* Colleges & Universities, Private Education (Precollege), Social Sciences Education • *International:* International Peace & Security Issues, International Relations • *Religion:* Religious Organizations • *Social Services:* Counseling, Domestic Violence, Family Services, United Funds/United Ways, Youth Organizations

Grant Types: general support

Geographic Distribution: national, with focus on TX

GIVING OFFICERS
William L. Garwood, Jr.: vp, trust *PHIL AFFIL* vp: Clayton Fund

Susan Garwood Knapp: trust *PHIL AFFIL* trust: Susan Vaughan Foundation

Lew Little: treas

Mary Garwood Yancy: pres

APPLICATION INFORMATION
Initial Approach: Application form required. There are no deadlines.

GRANTS ANALYSIS
Total Grants: $100,000

Number of Grants: 1

Highest Grant: $100,000

Disclosure Period: fiscal year ending April 30, 1994

Note: Recent grants are derived from a fiscal 1994 Form 990.

RECENT GRANTS
General

100,000	Hoover Institution of War, Revolution, and Peace, Stanford, CA — for educational purposes

Herzstein Charitable Foundation, Albert and Ethel

CONTACT
Albert H. Herzstein
Manager
Albert and Ethel Herzstein Charitable Foundation
6131 Westview
Houston, TX 77055
(713) 681-7868

FINANCIAL SUMMARY
Recent Giving: $1,393,630 (1993); $1,415,020 (1992); $1,318,994 (1991)

Assets: $29,870,453 (1993); $29,445,698 (1992); $28,661,494 (1991)

EIN: 74-6070484

CONTRIBUTIONS SUMMARY
Donor(s): The foundation was established in 1965 by the Herzstein family.

Typical Recipients: • *Arts & Humanities:* Arts Associations & Councils, Arts Festivals, Arts Funds, Ballet, History & Archaeology, Libraries, Museums/Galleries • *Civic & Public Affairs:* Chambers of Commerce, Clubs, Economic Development, General, Hispanic Affairs, Municipalities/Towns, Parades/Festivals, Urban & Community Affairs, Zoos/Aquariums • *Education:* Colleges & Universities, Education Reform, General, Medical Education, Private Education (Precollege), Secondary Education (Public), Special Education • *Health:* Cancer, Children's Health/Hospitals, Clinics/Medical Centers, Diabetes, Emergency/Ambulance Services, Eyes/Blindness, Health Organizations, Heart, Hospitals, Multiple Sclerosis, Prenatal Health Issues • *International:* International Organizations, Missionary/Religious Activities • *Religion:* Churches, Jewish Causes, Ministries, Religious Organizations, Religious Welfare, Social/Policy Issues, Synagogues/Temples • *Science:* Science Museums • *Social Services:* Child Welfare, Community Service Organizations, Food/Clothing Distribution, People with Disabilities, Scouts, Substance Abuse, United Funds/United Ways, YMCA/YWCA/YMHA/YWHA, Youth Organizations

Grant Types: general support

Geographic Distribution: focus on Texas

GIVING OFFICERS
Albert H. Herzstein: mgr, trust

APPLICATION INFORMATION
Initial Approach:

Applicants should send a brief letter of inquiry.

The letter should include the amount requested and describe in detail how the funds will be used.

There are no deadlines for submitting proposals.

GRANTS ANALYSIS
Total Grants: $1,393,630

Number of Grants: 81

Highest Grant: $500,000

Average Grant: $11,170*

Typical Range: $50 to $500 and $1,000 to $15,000

Disclosure Period: 1993

Note: Average grant figure excludes the highest grant of $500,000. Recent grants are derived from a 1993 Form 990.

RECENT GRANTS

Library

1,000	Friench Simpson Library, Halletsville, TX — cultural	

General

500,000	Search, Houston, TX
450,783	First United Methodist Church, Fulshear, TX
100,000	Baylor College Medicine, Houston, TX — research
50,000	American Society for Technion, New York, NY
50,000	Technion-Israel Institute, Haifa, Israel — research

Hillcrest Foundation

CONTACT
Daniel J. Kelly
Trust Officer
Hillcrest Foundation
c/o NationsBank Texas
PO Box 830241
Dallas, TX 75283
(214) 508-1965

FINANCIAL SUMMARY
Recent Giving: $6,500,000 (fiscal 1995 est.); $3,849,095 (fiscal 1994); $3,510,544 (fiscal 1993)

Assets: $105,000,000 (fiscal 1995 est.); $89,000,000 (fiscal 1994 approx.); $93,336,540 (fiscal 1993)

EIN: 75-6007565

CONTRIBUTIONS SUMMARY
Donor(s): The late Mrs. W. W. Caruth, Sr., (also known as Earle Clark Caruth) established the Hillcrest Foundation in 1959. The Caruth family, by the 1900s, had amassed some 30,000 acres of land in what is now

North Dallas. The late W. W. Caruth, Jr., a former trustee of the Hillcrest Foundation, developed family land over the past four decades. He is succeeded by his widow, Mabel P. Caruth. Additionally, NationsBank and individuals named by the donor serve as trustees.

Typical Recipients: • *Arts & Humanities:* Arts Outreach, Historic Preservation, Libraries, Museums/Galleries • *Civic & Public Affairs:* Employment/Job Training, Housing, Nonprofit Management, Urban & Community Affairs • *Education:* Business Education, Colleges & Universities, General, Legal Education, Literacy, Private Education (Precollege), Public Education (Precollege), School Volunteerism, Science/Mathematics Education, Special Education • *Health:* Arthritis, Children's Health/Hospitals, Clinics/Medical Centers, Emergency/Ambulance Services, Heart, Hospitals, Long-Term Care, Medical Research, Mental Health, Nursing Services, Outpatient Health Care, Respiratory, Single-Disease Health Associations • *Religion:* Churches, Religious Welfare, Seminaries • *Social Services:* Child Welfare, Community Centers, Community Service Organizations, Counseling, Day Care, Delinquency & Criminal Rehabilitation, Domestic Violence, Emergency Relief, Family Services, Food/Clothing Distribution, Homes, People with Disabilities, Recreation & Athletics, Senior Services, Shelters/Homelessness, Substance Abuse, Youth Organizations

Grant Types: capital and project

Geographic Distribution: Texas, emphasis on Dallas

GIVING OFFICERS
D. Harold Byrd, Jr.: trust

Mrs. Mabel P. Caruth: trust, don dtr-in-law *B* 1914

Daniel J. Kelly: trust off *PHIL AFFIL* trust off: Roy and Christine Sturgis Charitable and Educational Trust

Harry A. Shuford: trust

Charles Porter Storey: trust *B* Austin TX 1922 *ED* Univ TX BA 1947; Univ TX LLB 1948; Southern Methodist Univ LLM 1952 *CORP AFFIL* dir: Storey Armstrong Steger & Martin Professional Corp; secy, dir: Hargrove Electric Co *NONPR AFFIL* fellow: Am Bar Fdn, Am Coll Trial Lawyers, TX Bar Fdn; mem: Am Bar Assn, Dallas Bar Assn, Philosophers Soc TX, TX Bar Assn *CLUB AFFIL* Crescent, Dallas CC, Idlewild

APPLICATION INFORMATION
Initial Approach:

A formal application form, provided by the foundation, must be submitted. A copy of the full proposal is requested.

The proposal should include a brief history, purpose of proposal, use of funds, other contributors, budget information, copy of IRS tax exemption letter, and a statement that the organization is not a private foundation.

Application deadlines are March 31, August 31, and November 30.

All applications are considered as long as they pertain to the purposes of the foundation. The trustees meet in January, May, and October.

Restrictions on Giving: The foundation does not fund individuals, propaganda, political campaigns, groups influencing legislation, or religious organizations. No loans are distributed.

OTHER THINGS TO KNOW
NationsBank Texas is listed as the corporate trustee of the foundation.

GRANTS ANALYSIS
Total Grants: $3,849,095

Number of Grants: 173

Highest Grant: $125,000

Average Grant: $22,249

Typical Range: $10,000 to $30,000

Disclosure Period: fiscal year ending May 31, 1994

Note: Recent grants are derived from a fiscal 1993 Form 990.

RECENT GRANTS

Library

125,000	Southern Methodist University, Dallas, TX — for Underwood Law Library renovation
35,000	Brackett Independent School District, Brackettsville, TX — school library furniture and equipment, one PLATO Site license, computer education literacy, and GED for students and adults
30,000	Weise Memorial Academy, Richardson, TX — upgrade library materials, learning materials for disabled, purchase computers, science lab equipment, and physical education equipment

General

150,000	University of Texas Dallas, Richardson, TX — commitment for endowed chair of applied ethics
100,000	Baylor University Medical Center, Dallas, TX — for Baylor Pediatric Center for Restorative Care
100,000	United Cerebral Palsy of Metropolitan Dallas, Dallas, TX — campaign for new treatment facility
75,000	Munger Place United Methodist Church, Dallas, TX — purchase elevator for building and programs for needy adults and children
60,000	Buckner Baptist Benevolences, Dallas, TX — help build Ledbetter Community Center at Buckner Retirement Village

Hobby Foundation

CONTACT
Peggy C. Buchanan
Treasurer
Hobby Foundation
2131 San Felipe
Houston, TX 77019-5620
(713) 521-1163

FINANCIAL SUMMARY
Recent Giving: $1,416,125 (1993); $1,416,125 (1992); $1,107,348 (1991)

Assets: $28,760,501 (1993); $30,091,838 (1991); $23,316,526 (1990)

Gifts Received: $100,000 (1993); $100,918 (1991); $460,900 (1990)

Fiscal Note: In 1993, contributions were received from Mrs. Oveta Culp Hobby.

EIN: 74-6026606

CONTRIBUTIONS SUMMARY
Donor(s): The foundation was incorporated in 1945 by Oveta Culp Hobby, the late W. P. Hobby , and the Houston Post Co.

Typical Recipients: • *Arts & Humanities:* Historic Preservation, Libraries, Literary Arts, Museums/Galleries, Music, Opera, Theater • *Civic & Public Affairs:* General, Housing, Municipalities/Towns, Parades/Festivals, Philanthropic Organizations, Women's Affairs • *Education:* Colleges & Universities, General, Minority Education, Private Education (Precollege), Social Sciences Education • *Environment:* Wildlife Protection • *Health:* AIDS/HIV, Alzheimers Disease, Cancer, Children's Health/Hospitals, Emergency/Ambulance Services, Eyes/Blindness, Health Funds, Health Organizations, Heart, Hospitals, Mental Health, Single-Disease Health Associations • *Religion:* Churches, Religious Organizations, Religious Welfare • *Science:* Science Museums, Scientific Organizations • *Social Services:* Animal Protection, Child Welfare, Emergency Relief, Family Planning, Food/Clothing Distribution, People with Disabilities, Scouts, Shelters/Homelessness, United Funds/United Ways, YMCA/YWCA/YMHA/YWHA, Youth Organizations

Grant Types: general support

Geographic Distribution: focus on Texas, with an emphasis on Houston

GIVING OFFICERS
Laura H. Beckworth: trust

Peggy Carr Buchanan: treas *B* Newton MS 1925 *ED* Millsaps Coll BA 1947

Jessica Hobby Catto: trust *B* 1935 *ED* Barnard Coll *CURR EMPL* vchmn: H&C Communs *NONPR AFFIL* dir: Environmental Defense Fund *PHIL AFFIL* don, pres: Catto Foundation

Pamela L. George: dir

Diana P. Hobby: trust

William Pettus Hobby, Jr.: vp, trust *B* Houston TX 1932 *ED* Rice Univ BA 1953 *CURR EMPL* chmn, ceo: H&C Communs

CORP AFFIL dir: Southwest Airlines Co *NONPR AFFIL* dir: TX Hunter & Jumper Assn; mem: Jefferson Davis Assn, Houston Chamber Commerce, Houston Symphony Soc *PHIL AFFIL* dir: Catto Foundation

Audrey Horn: secy

APPLICATION INFORMATION
Initial Approach:

The foundation has no formal grant application procedure or application form.

The foundation has no deadline for submitting proposals.

PUBLICATIONS
Application guidelines

GRANTS ANALYSIS
Total Grants: $1,416,125

Number of Grants: 151

Highest Grant: $200,500

Average Grant: $9,378

Typical Range: $500 to $10,000

Disclosure Period: 1993

Note: Recent grants are derived from a 1993 Form 990.

RECENT GRANTS

Library

7,500	Houston Public Library, Houston, TX	

General

200,000	United Negro College Fund - educational, New York, NY
126,000	St. John's School, Houston, TX
125,000	Kinkaid School, Houston, TX — educational
125,000	St. Andrews Episcopal School, Austin, TX
50,050	M.D. Anderson Cancer Center, Houston, TX

Houston Endowment

CONTACT
H. Joe Nelson III
President
Houston Endowment
600 Travis, Ste. 6400
Houston, TX 77002-3007
(713) 238-8120

FINANCIAL SUMMARY
Recent Giving: $36,000,000 (1994 est.); $42,519,673 (1993); $19,821,376 (1992)

Assets: $825,000,000 (1994); $873,302,388 (1993); $827,714,968 (1992)

EIN: 74-6013920

CONTRIBUTIONS SUMMARY
Donor(s): The Houston Endowment was established in 1937 by the late Mr. and Mrs. Jesse H. Jones . Mr. Jones was a Houston financier, owner-publisher of the *Houston Chronicle*, and a builder and real estate developer. In addition to his local leadership in civic affairs, Mr. Jones was nationally prominent as head of the Reconstruction Finance Corporation during the Depression, and Secretary of Commerce from 1940 to 1945.

Typical Recipients: • *Arts & Humanities:* Arts Associations & Councils, Arts Outreach, Ballet, Historic Preservation, History & Archaeology, Libraries, Literary Arts, Museums/Galleries, Music, Opera, Performing Arts, Theater • *Civic & Public Affairs:* African American Affairs, Asian American Affairs, Botanical Gardens/Parks, Employment/Job Training, Hispanic Affairs, Municipalities/Towns, Professional & Trade Associations, Public Policy, Safety, Urban & Community Affairs, Women's Affairs, Zoos/Aquariums • *Education:* Afterschool/Enrichment Programs, Arts/Humanities Education, Business Education, Colleges & Universities, Economic Education, Education Associations, Education Reform, Elementary Education (Public), Engineering/Technological Education, Environmental Education, Faculty Development, Health & Physical Education, Legal Education, Literacy, Medical Education, Minority Education, Preschool Education, Private Education (Precollege), Public Education (Precollege), Religious Education, Science/Mathematics Education, Secondary Education (Private), Special Education, Student Aid • *Environment:* General, Resource Conservation • *Health:* AIDS/HIV, Cancer, Children's Health/Hospitals, Clinics/Medical Centers, Emergency/Ambulance Services, Geriatric Health, Health Policy/Cost Containment, Health Organizations, Heart, Hospices, Hospitals, Medical Training, Mental Health, Research/Studies Institutes, Single-Disease Health Associations, Transplant Networks/Donor Banks • *Religion:* Churches, Jewish Causes, Ministries, Religious Organizations, Religious Welfare • *Science:* Science Museums • *Social Services:* Animal Protection, At-Risk Youth, Child Welfare, Community Centers, Community Service Organizations, Counseling, Crime Prevention, Day Care, Domestic Violence, Family Planning, Homes, People with Disabilities, Recreation & Athletics, Scouts, Shelters/Homelessness, Substance Abuse, United Funds/United Ways, Volunteer Services, YMCA/YWCA/YMHA/YWHA, Youth Organizations

Grant Types: capital, fellowship, general support, operating expenses, professorship, project, and scholarship

Geographic Distribution: Texas, primarily the Houston area

GIVING OFFICERS
Audrey Jones Beck: dir *PHIL AFFIL* dir: Houston Endowment

Jack S. Blanton: chmn, dir *B* Shreveport LA 1927 *ED* Univ TX BA 1947; Univ TX LLB 1950 *CURR EMPL* ceo, pres, dir: Eddy Refining Co *CORP AFFIL* dir: Ashland Oil, Baker Hughes, Burlington Northern, Pogo Producing Co, Southwestern Bell Corp, TX Commerce Bancshares, TX Commerce Bank *NONPR AFFIL* mem: Delta Kappa Epsilon, Houston Chamber Commerce, Sam Houston Meml Assn, Mid-Continent Oil & Gas Assn, Natl Petroleum Counc, Natl Tennis Assn,

Phi Alpha Delta, Phi Delta Phi, Sons Republic TX, TX Independent Oil Producers & Refiners, Univ TX Ex-Students Assn, US Lawn Tennis Assn *CLUB AFFIL* Eldorado CC, Houston, River Oaks CC

Milton Carroll: dir *CURR EMPL* chmn, pres, ceo: Instrument Products Inc

Sheryl Lightfoot Johns: vp, treas *B* Pasadena TX 1956 *ED* Univ Houston BS 1986

Harold Metts: dir

Jo Murphy: dir

David Nelson: vp, grant dir

H. Joe Nelson III: pres, dir

Melissa Jones Stevens: dir

Philip G. Warner: dir

Rosie Zamora-Cope: dir

APPLICATION INFORMATION
Initial Approach:

An application for a grant should be presented in written form. A specific application form is not required.

Applications should contain a cover letter signed by the president or executive officer of the organization, general information about the oganization, including its purpose and goals, a brief history, and the programs offered.

Grant requests should include a description of the people who will benefit from the proposal; need or problem to be addressed; specific program objectives, with a chronology of proposed activities and projected dates for implementation and conclusion; detailed revenue and expense budget for the program; amount of funding requested and proposed funding schedule; other anticipated sources of support; how the program will continue after endowment funding ceases; proposed method for measuring and reporting the program's effectiveness; and information about the specific people responsible for administering the proposed program.

All applications must include a copy of the latest IRS tax-exempt determination letter; signed statement that no change has occurred in exempt status, purpose, or method of operation subsequent to IRS ruling; most recent financial statements; complete copy of most recent IRS Form 990; and the name and telephone number of the person to contact for additional information.

Applications are accepted any time.

The review and decision process typically takes three to six months. An applicant will be notified if additional information is requested, or an interview or site visit is planned. All applicants are notified in writing of the action taken by the directors on their requests.

Restrictions on Giving: The endowment does not make loans of any type and does not support individuals. Recipients of the endowment's scholarship programs are chosen through Houston area high schools or through the colleges or universities at which scholarship programs are sponsored.

GRANTS ANALYSIS
Total Grants: $42,519,673

Number of Grants: 464

Highest Grant: $3,000,000

Average Grant: $91,637

Typical Range: $10,000 to $100,000 and $200,000 to $1,000,000

Disclosure Period: 1993

Note: Recent grants are derived from a 1993 Form 990.

RECENT GRANTS

Library

3,000,000	Baylor University, Waco, TX — toward construction of the Jesse H. Jones library
750,000	Stella Link Redevelopment Association, Houston, TX — toward acquisition of a site for construction of a new public library in the educational/recreational service corridor being developed in the Stella Link area of Houston

General

2,000,000	Gulf Coast Regional Blood Center, Houston, TX — toward building expansion
2,000,000	Texas Children's Hospital, Houston, TX — toward the Building for Children Campaign to expand hospital facilities
1,333,334	University of Houston, Houston, TX — establishment of the Jesse H. Jones Business Leadership Development Program
1,000,000	Episcopal High School, Bellaire, TX — toward the school's property acquisition program
1,000,000	Rice University, Houston, TX — establishment of the J. Howard Creekmore Endowment for the Jesse H. Jones Graduate School of Administration

Houston Industries Incorporated

Revenue: $4.0 billion
Employees: 11,350
Headquarters: Houston, TX
SIC Major Group: Holding Companies Nec, Cable & Other Pay Television Services, Electric Services, and Electrical Apparatus & Equipment

CONTACT
Robert Gibbs
Director, Community Relations
Houston Industries Incorporated
PO Box 4567
Houston, TX 77210
(713) 629-3239

FINANCIAL SUMMARY
Fiscal Note: Company does not release contributions totals.

CONTRIBUTIONS SUMMARY
Typical Recipients: • *Arts & Humanities:* Arts Associations & Councils, Arts Funds, Community Arts, Dance, Ethnic & Folk Arts, Historic Preservation, Libraries, Museums/Galleries, Music, Performing Arts, Public Broadcasting, Theater • *Civic & Public Affairs:* Business/Free Enterprise, Economic Development, Law & Justice, Municipalities/Towns, Professional & Trade Associations, Public Policy, Safety, Urban & Community Affairs, Women's Affairs, Zoos/Aquariums • *Education:* Colleges & Universities, Community & Junior Colleges, Economic Education, Literacy, Minority Education • *Environment:* General • *Health:* Health Organizations, Hospitals, Medical Research, Mental Health, Single-Disease Health Associations • *Science:* Scientific Organizations • *Social Services:* Child Welfare, Community Centers, Community Service Organizations, Delinquency & Criminal Rehabilitation, Family Services, People with Disabilities, Refugee Assistance, Senior Services, Substance Abuse, United Funds/United Ways, Volunteer Services, Youth Organizations

Grant Types: capital, general support, research, and seed money

Nonmonetary Support: $246,472 (1987)

Nonmonetary Support Types: donated equipment, in-kind services, loaned employees, and loaned executives

Note: Value of nonmonetary support is unavailable.

Geographic Distribution: near headquarters and operating locations

Operating Locations: TX (Houston)

CORP. OFFICERS
Don D. Jordan: *B* Corpus Christi TX 1932 *ED* Univ TX BBA 1954; S TX Coll Law JD 1969 *CURR EMPL* chmn, ceo, dir: Houston Lighting & Power Co *CORP AFFIL* chmn, ceo: Houston Indus Inc, KBL Cable Inc, KBL CBL Sys SW, KBL COM; dir: BJ Svcs Co, Hughes Tool Co, TX Commerce Bancshares Inc, TX Med Ctr *NONPR AFFIL* dir: TX Heart Inst

Donald D. Sykora: *B* Stamford TX 1930 *ED* Univ Houston BBA 1957; South TX Coll Law JD 1969 *CURR EMPL* pres, coo, dir: Houston Indus Inc *CORP AFFIL* dir: Pool Energy Svcs Co, Powell Indus Inc, Primary Fuels Inc, TransTexas Gas Corp, Utility Fuels Inc; pres, coo: Houston Lighting & Power Co *NONPR AFFIL* chmn exec adv bd customer svc & mktg comm: Edison Electric Inst; chmn exec comm: Electrification Counc; dir: Salvation Army Houston; mem: Houston Chamber Commerce, TX Bar Assn *CLUB AFFIL* Houston

GIVING OFFICERS
Robert Gibbs: *CURR EMPL* dir commun rels: Houston Indus Inc

APPLICATION INFORMATION

Initial Approach: *Initial Contact:* letter and proposal *Include Information On:* description of the organization, amount requested and purpose, recently audited financial statement, proof of tax-exempt status, list of officers and directors, and list of past contributors *Deadlines:* by July for following year's budget

Restrictions on Giving: Does not support dinners or special events, fraternal organizations, individuals, political or lobbying groups, or religious organizations for sectarian purposes.

Huthsteiner Fine Arts Trust

CONTACT

Terry Crenshaw
Vice President and Charitable Services Officer
Huthsteiner Fine Arts Trust
c/o Texas Commerce Bank-El Paso
PO Drawer 140
El Paso, TX 79980
(915) 546-6515

FINANCIAL SUMMARY

Recent Giving: $74,000 (fiscal 1994); $66,000 (fiscal 1993); $76,100 (fiscal 1992)

Assets: $1,989,998 (fiscal 1994); $2,044,817 (fiscal 1993); $1,915,803 (fiscal 1992)

EIN: 74-6308412

CONTRIBUTIONS SUMMARY

Donor(s): Robert and Pauline Huthsteiner Trust

Typical Recipients: • *Arts & Humanities:* Arts Associations & Councils, Arts Funds, Ballet, Community Arts, Dance, Libraries, Literary Arts, Museums/Galleries, Music, Performing Arts, Public Broadcasting, Theater • *Civic & Public Affairs:* Professional & Trade Associations • *Education:* Colleges & Universities • *Health:* Clinics/Medical Centers, Health Organizations, Hospitals • *Religion:* Churches, Religious Welfare • *Social Services:* Youth Organizations

Grant Types: emergency, endowment, general support, multiyear/continuing support, and operating expenses

Geographic Distribution: focus on west TX

GIVING OFFICERS

Texas Commerce Bank NA: trust

APPLICATION INFORMATION

Initial Approach: Send a brief letter of inquiry. Include a description of organization, amount requested, purpose of funds sought, recently audited financial statement, and proof of tax-exempt status. There are no deadlines.

GRANTS ANALYSIS

Total Grants: $74,000

Number of Grants: 18

Highest Grant: $29,000

Typical Range: $1,000 to $12,500

Disclosure Period: fiscal year ending July 31, 1994

Note: Recent grants are derived from a fiscal 1994 Form 990.

RECENT GRANTS

General

7,500	University of Texas El Paso, El Paso, TX — to support music department	
2,000	Baptist Spanish Publishing House, El Paso, TX — for equipment	
1,500	Lincoln County Medical, Ridoso, NM	

Hygeia Dairy Co. / Hygeia Foundation

Sales: $40.0 million
Employees: 395
Parent Company: Cohyco
Headquarters: Harlingen, TX
SIC Major Group: Food & Kindred Products

CONTACT

Lee Richards
Chairman of Board
Hygeia Dairy Co.
720 South F St.
Harlingen, TX 78550
(210) 423-2050

FINANCIAL SUMMARY

Recent Giving: $100,976 (fiscal 1993); $99,924 (fiscal 1992)

Assets: $756,801 (fiscal 1993); $733,501 (fiscal 1992)

Gifts Received: $55,000 (fiscal 1992)

EIN: 74-6047054

CONTRIBUTIONS SUMMARY

Typical Recipients: • *Arts & Humanities:* Libraries, Museums/Galleries, Music, Public Broadcasting • *Civic & Public Affairs:* Clubs, Economic Development, Housing, Municipalities/Towns, Rural Affairs, Zoos/Aquariums • *Education:* Colleges & Universities, Engineering/Technological Education, General, Minority Education, Preschool Education, Private Education (Precollege), Public Education (Precollege), Student Aid • *Environment:* Research • *Health:* Cancer, Children's Health/Hospitals, Clinics/Medical Centers • *Religion:* Churches, Social/Policy Issues • *Science:* Scientific Research • *Social Services:* Community Service Organizations, Food/Clothing Distribution, People with Disabilities, Scouts, Substance Abuse, United Funds/United Ways, Youth Organizations

Grant Types: capital and general support

Geographic Distribution: focus on TX

CORP. OFFICERS

H. Lee Richards: *CURR EMPL* chmn: Hygeia Dairy Co

Donald R. Smith: *CURR EMPL* pres: Hygeia Dairy Co

GIVING OFFICERS

Noble C. Kidd: trust

James D. Pure, Jr.: trust

H. Lee Richards: trust *CURR EMPL* chmn: Hygeia Dairy Co (see above)

APPLICATION INFORMATION

Initial Approach: Send a brief letter of inquiry. Include a description of organization, amount requested, purpose of funds sought, recently audited financial statement, and proof of tax-exempt status. There are no deadlines.

GRANTS ANALYSIS

Total Grants: $100,976

Number of Grants: 120

Highest Grant: $5,200

Typical Range: $100 to $1,000

Disclosure Period: fiscal year ending March 31, 1993

Note: Recent grants are derived from a fiscal 1993 Form 990.

RECENT GRANTS

Library

1,000	Harlingen Public Library, Harlingen, TX — for building purposes	

General

5,200	University of Texas Pan America, Edinburg, TX — for educational purposes	
5,000	Rio Grande Radiation Treatment/Cancer Foundation, El Paso, TX — for building purposes	
5,000	Texas State Aquarium, Austin, TX — for building purposes	
4,000	Marine Military Academy, Harlingen, TX — for building purposes	
3,200	United Way of Coastal Bend, Coastal Bend, TX	

Johnson Foundation, Burdine

CONTACT

Robert C. Giberson
Trustee
Burdine Johnson Foundation
760 Southpark One Bldg.
1701 Directors Blvd.
Austin, TX 78744-1066
(512) 441-1588

FINANCIAL SUMMARY

Recent Giving: $760,000 (1994 est.); $1,011,170 (1993); $760,156 (1992 approx.)

Assets: $19,000,000 (1995 est.); $19,000,000 (1994 approx.); $18,422,841 (1993)

EIN: 74-6036669

CONTRIBUTIONS SUMMARY

Donor(s): The foundation was established in 1960 by Burdine C. Johnson and J. M. Johnson.

Typical Recipients: • *Arts & Humanities:* Libraries, Museums/Galleries, Performing Arts, Theater • *Civic & Public Affairs:* Municipalities/Towns, Women's Affairs, Zoos/Aquariums • *Education:* Colleges & Universities, Literacy, Medical Education, Private Education (Precollege), Public Education (Precollege) • *Environment:* General • *Health:* Cancer, Medical Research, Single-Disease Health Associations • *International:* Health Care/Hospitals • *Religion:* Churches, Religious Welfare • *Social Services:* Domestic Violence, Family Planning, Family Services, Food/Clothing Distribution, Recreation & Athletics, Senior Services, Sexual Abuse

Grant Types: general support

Geographic Distribution: focus on Texas

GIVING OFFICERS

Robert C. Giberson: trust

Burdine C. Johnson: trust *PHIL AFFIL* pres: Clayton Fund

William T. Johnson: trust

APPLICATION INFORMATION
Initial Approach:

The foundation has no formal grant application procedure or application form.

Applicants must submit full details about the applying organization and the use of the proposed grant. The foundation also requests applicants attach a copy of the IRS ruling or determination letter.

The foundation has no deadline for submitting proposals.

Restrictions on Giving: Grants made by the foundation are limited to religious, charitable, scientific, literary, or educational purposes.

GRANTS ANALYSIS
Total Grants: $1,011,170

Number of Grants: 20

Highest Grant: $438,200

Average Grant: $4,969*

Typical Range: $1,000 to $5,000

Disclosure Period: 1993

Note: Average grant excludes three grants totaling $926,700. Recent grants are derived from a 1993 Form 990.

RECENT GRANTS

Library

15,000	City of Kyle Community Library, Kyle, TX
1,000	Friends of Public Library of Buda, Buda, TX

General

438,200	St. Stephen's Episcopal School, Austin, TX — building and operating funds
288,500	Hays Consolidated Independent School District, Kyle, TX — Kodaly music program, playgrounds, and landscaping
22,500	Planned Parenthood of Austin, Austin, TX — computer software and operating funds
15,000	Hays Youth Athletic Association, Buda, TX — septic system
5,000	Berea College, Berea, KY — nursing professorship

Johnson Foundation, M. G. and Lillie A.

CONTACT
Robert Halepeska
Executive Vice President
M. G. and Lillie A. Johnson Foundation
PO Drawer 2269
Victoria, TX 77902
(512) 575-7970

FINANCIAL SUMMARY
Recent Giving: $1,600,000 (fiscal 1995 est.); $1,585,031 (fiscal 1994); $1,667,715 (fiscal 1993)

Assets: $33,500,000 (fiscal 1995 est.); $32,746,449 (fiscal 1994); $31,781,498 (fiscal 1993)

Gifts Received: $1,200,000 (fiscal 1995 est.); $600,000 (fiscal 1994); $10,117,698 (fiscal 1991)

EIN: 74-6076961

CONTRIBUTIONS SUMMARY
Donor(s): The foundation was established in 1958, with contributions from M. G. Johnson and Lillie A. Johnson.

Typical Recipients: • *Arts & Humanities:* Libraries, Museums/Galleries • *Civic & Public Affairs:* Botanical Gardens/Parks, Municipalities/Towns, Parades/Festivals, Safety • *Education:* Colleges & Universities, Community & Junior Colleges, Continuing Education, Science/Mathematics Education, Student Aid, Vocational & Technical Education • *Health:* Clinics/Medical Centers, Emergency/Ambulance Services, Hospices, Hospitals, Nursing Services, Transplant Networks/Donor Banks • *Religion:* Religious Organizations, Religious Welfare • *Social Services:* Child Welfare, Community Centers, Community Service Organizations, Day Care, Domestic Violence, Emergency Relief, Food/Clothing Distribution, Homes, People with Disabilities, Recreation & Athletics, Senior Services, Substance Abuse, Youth Organizations

Grant Types: capital, challenge, project, and scholarship

Geographic Distribution: primary emhasis on the state of Texas; priority is given to organizations in the Gulf Coast area located between San Patricio and Wharton counties

GIVING OFFICERS
M. H. Brock: trust

Robert Halepeska: exec vp

Dick Koop: trust

Rev. M. H. Lehnhart: secy, trust

Irving Moore, Jr.: pres, trust *B* Wharton City TX 1912 *ED* Univ TX LLB *PHIL AFFIL* secy: Gulf Coast Medical Foundation

Jack R. Morrison: vp, trust

M. Munson Smith: trust, asst secy *CURR EMPL* secy, treas, dir: Texas Concrete Co

APPLICATION INFORMATION
Initial Approach:

Submit one copy of a detailed proposal.

Applications should include an institutional profile of the applying organization including name, address, phone number and contact person; purpose and history of the organization; classified statement of receipts and disbursements for the past three years; and a list of grants for the previous three years. Applicants must also provide proof of tax exemption under IRS section 501(c)(3); a copy of notice of private foundation status from the IRS; and an IRS examination report (if any). The applicant should also specify the amount of funds requested, intended use of funds, and a time frame for the project.

The board of trustees usually meets in March, July, and October. Proposals should be received no later than one month prior to a meeting for consideration.

Applicants whose proposals are not approved will be informed only if the proposal conforms to the foundation's stated criteria.

Restrictions on Giving: Grants are seldom provided for operational expenses. The foundation does not fund national charities, fellowship programs, or organizations outside its geographic area of interest.

PUBLICATIONS
Application guidelines

GRANTS ANALYSIS
Total Grants: $1,585,031

Number of Grants: 34

Highest Grant: $160,000

Average Grant: $46,619

Typical Range: $10,000 to $100,000

Disclosure Period: fiscal year ending November 30, 1994

Note: Recent grants are derived from a fiscal 1993 Form 990.

RECENT GRANTS

Library

29,500	Beautify Hallettsville, Hallettsville, TX — to purchase furniture and fixtures for public library

General

153,000	Community Food Bank, Victoria, TX — to construct new building
150,000	Concordia Lutheran College, Austin, TX — additional funds for the reconstruction of the Science Building, Beto Hall
150,000	Victoria College, Victoria, TX — for renovation of science building

| 100,000 | Concordia Lutheran College, Austin, TX — provide additional funds for the renovation and expansion of the Science Building, Beto Hall |
| 100,000 | Victoria College, Victoria, TX — for the endowed scholarship program previously created by the foundation |

Jones Foundation, Helen

CONTACT
Louise Arnold
President, Executive Secretary
Helen Jones Fdn.
4603 92nd St.
Lubbock, TX 79424
(806) 794-8078

FINANCIAL SUMMARY
Recent Giving: $509,168 (1993); $392,111 (1991); $385,165 (1990)
Assets: $12,514,141 (1993); $12,015,366 (1991); $11,371,277 (1990)
EIN: 75-1977748

CONTRIBUTIONS SUMMARY
Donor(s): Helen DeVitt Jones

Typical Recipients: • *Arts & Humanities:* Arts Centers, Ballet, Ethnic & Folk Arts, Historic Preservation, Libraries, Museums/Galleries, Music, Public Broadcasting, Theater • *Civic & Public Affairs:* Housing • *Education:* Arts/Humanities Education, Colleges & Universities, Education Reform, Preschool Education, Science/Mathematics Education, Student Aid • *Health:* Hospitals • *International:* International Relations • *Religion:* Churches • *Science:* Scientific Centers & Institutes, Scientific Organizations • *Social Services:* Child Welfare, Community Service Organizations, Homes, People with Disabilities, Scouts, Shelters/Homelessness, YMCA/YWCA/YMHA/YWHA, Youth Organizations

Grant Types: operating expenses and scholarship

Geographic Distribution: focus on KS and TX

GIVING OFFICERS
Louise Wilson Arnold: pres, exec secy, dir
Robert Neff Arnold: vp, secy, dir
Helen Devitt Jones: dir
L. Edwin Smith: treas, dir

APPLICATION INFORMATION
Initial Approach: Include a description of organization, amount requested, purpose of funds sought, recently audited financial statement, and proof of tax-exempt status. There are no deadlines.

Restrictions on Giving: Does not support individuals.

GRANTS ANALYSIS
Total Grants: $509,168

Number of Grants: 38
Highest Grant: $65,000
Typical Range: $3,000 to $50,000
Disclosure Period: 1993
Note: Recent grants are derived from a 1993 Form 990.

RECENT GRANTS
General
45,000	North Carolina State University, Raleigh, NC — education fund education project
26,500	Texas Tech University Southwest Collection, Lubbock, TX — book research
25,000	Science Spectrum, Lubbock, TX — grant
25,000	South Plains Council 694 Boys Scouts of America, Lubbock, TX — renovation of camp
25,000	Texas Tech University College of Education, Lubbock, TX — center for excellence

Jonsson Foundation

CONTACT
Margaret J. Rogers
Vice President, Assistant Secretary
Jonsson Fdn.
5600 W Lovers Ln., Ste. 323
Dallas, TX 75209
(214) 350-4626

FINANCIAL SUMMARY
Recent Giving: $258,166 (1992); $136,500 (1991); $199,000 (1990)
Assets: $4,229,723 (1992); $4,366,619 (1991); $3,984,098 (1990)
EIN: 75-6012565

CONTRIBUTIONS SUMMARY
Donor(s): J. E. Jonsson, the late Margaret E. Jonsson

Typical Recipients: • *Arts & Humanities:* Arts Associations & Councils, Arts Centers, Libraries, Museums/Galleries, Music • *Civic & Public Affairs:* General, Legal Aid, Municipalities/Towns, Zoos/Aquariums • *Education:* Business Education, Colleges & Universities, Community & Junior Colleges, Education Associations, Education Funds, Literacy, Private Education (Precollege), Public Education (Precollege), Religious Education • *Health:* Cancer, Children's Health/Hospitals, Clinics/Medical Centers, Health Organizations, Hospitals, Single-Disease Health Associations • *Science:* Science Museums, Scientific Centers & Institutes • *Social Services:* Child Welfare, Community Centers, Community Service Organizations, Family Planning, Food/Clothing Distribution, Youth Organizations

Grant Types: capital and general support

Geographic Distribution: focus on the Dallas, TX, area

GIVING OFFICERS
Kenneth A. Jonsson: pres, treas, trust
Philip R. Jonsson: vp, treas, trust
Margaret J. Rogers: vp, asst secy, trust

APPLICATION INFORMATION
Initial Approach: Send a brief letter of inquiry. Include a description of organization, amount requested, purpose of funds sought, recently audited financial statement, and proof of tax-exempt status. There are no deadlines.

PUBLICATIONS
Application Guidelines

GRANTS ANALYSIS
Total Grants: $258,166
Number of Grants: 21
Highest Grant: $66,700
Typical Range: $1,000 to $25,000
Disclosure Period: 1992
Note: Recent grants are derived from a 1992 Form 990.

RECENT GRANTS
Library
| 12,500 | University of Arkansas Little Rock, Little Rock, AR — special endowment fund and materials for library of college of science and engineering technology |

General
66,700	National Academy of Sciences, Washington, DC — endowment for operation of study center
50,000	Winston School, Dallas, TX — "Operation Clean Slate" program
25,000	Southern Methodist University, Dallas, TX — endowment
20,000	California Institute Cancer Research at University of California Los Angeles, Los Angeles, CA — construction-outpatient service center
10,000	Dallas Museum of Natural History, Dallas, TX

Kayser Foundation

CONTACT
Henry O. Weaver
President
Kayser Fdn.
Texas Commerce Bank Bldg.
712 Main St., Ste. 1810
Houston, TX 77002
(713) 222-7234

FINANCIAL SUMMARY
Recent Giving: $155,635 (1993); $148,950 (1992); $140,200 (1991)

Assets: $4,089,412 (1993); $3,809,996 (1992); $3,677,680 (1991)

EIN: 74-6050591

CONTRIBUTIONS SUMMARY

Donor(s): Paul Kayser, Mrs. Paul Kayser

Typical Recipients: • *Arts & Humanities:* Ballet, Libraries, Museums/Galleries, Music • *Civic & Public Affairs:* Employment/Job Training, Law & Justice, Safety • *Education:* Colleges & Universities, Legal Education, Medical Education, Private Education (Precollege), Public Education (Precollege), Student Aid • *Environment:* Forestry, General, Wildlife Protection • *Health:* Arthritis, Cancer, Children's Health/Hospitals, Clinics/Medical Centers, Diabetes, Emergency/Ambulance Services, Eyes/Blindness, Health Organizations, Hospices, Hospitals, Medical Rehabilitation, Medical Research, Multiple Sclerosis, Prenatal Health Issues, Public Health, Single-Disease Health Associations • *Religion:* Jewish Causes, Religious Organizations, Religious Welfare, Social/Policy Issues • *Social Services:* Animal Protection, At-Risk Youth, Child Abuse, Child Welfare, Community Service Organizations, Crime Prevention, Emergency Relief, Family Planning, Family Services, Food/Clothing Distribution, Homes, People with Disabilities, Scouts, Shelters/Homelessness, Substance Abuse, United Funds/United Ways, Youth Organizations

Grant Types: general support and research

Geographic Distribution: focus on TX

GIVING OFFICERS

Robert Bruce La Boon: vp *B* St. Louis MO 1941 *ED* TX Christian Univ BSC 1963; Southern Methodist Univ LLB 1965 *CURR EMPL* ptnr: Liddell Sapp Zivley Hill & LaBoon *CORP AFFIL* dir: Big Three Indus, Gamma Biological, TX Commerce Bankshares, TX Med Ctr Bd *NONPR AFFIL* adv dir: Retina Res Fdn; dir: Greater Houston Ptnr & Commun Schs Houston, Houston Intl Festival, TX Inst Rehabilitation Res Intl Ctr Arbitration; fellow: Am Coll Probate Couns, TX Bar Fdn; mem: Am Bar Assn, Am Law Inst, Houston Bar Assn, TX Assn Bank Couns; mem bd visitors: Univ Cancer Ctr MD Anderson Cancer Ctr; trust: Kayser Fdn, TX Christian Univ

Charles Sapp: vp

Henry O. Weaver: trust, pres

APPLICATION INFORMATION

Initial Approach: Include a description of organization, amount requested, purpose of funds sought, recently audited financial statement, and proof of tax-exempt status. There are no deadlines.

Restrictions on Giving: Does not support individuals.

GRANTS ANALYSIS

Total Grants: $155,635

Number of Grants: 86

Highest Grant: $70,000

Typical Range: $100 to $20,000

Disclosure Period: 1993

Note: Recent grants are derived from a 1993 Form 990.

RECENT GRANTS

Library
1,500	Houston Public Library, Houston, TX — help to add up-to-date quality material

General
70,000	Retina Research Foundation, Houston, TX — help with the International Award of Merit in Retina Research
20,000	M.D. Anderson Hospital, Houston, TX — help with more technologically sophisticated facilities
5,000	Baylor University Waco, Waco, TX — contribution to scholarship fund
3,500	Scenic Houston, Houston, TX — help in new forestery for parks in Houston
3,000	Texas Institute for Rehabilitation and Research, Houston, TX — help purchase needed exercise equipment for new outpatient therapy center

Kempner Fund, Harris and Eliza

CONTACT

Elaine Perachio
Executive Director
Harris and Eliza Kempner Fund
PO Box 119
Galveston, TX 77553-0119
(409) 765-6671

FINANCIAL SUMMARY

Recent Giving: $1,334,331 (1994); $1,510,000 (1993 approx.); $1,093,837 (1992)

Assets: $33,249,022 (1993); $30,138,645 (1992); $28,092,568 (1991)

Gifts Received: $55,000 (1993); $78,100 (1990); $69,394 (1989)

Fiscal Note: In 1990, the fund received $78,100 from three donors including a $75,000 gift from the Imperial Holly Sugar Company.

EIN: 74-6042458

CONTRIBUTIONS SUMMARY

Donor(s): The Kempner family established the "Galveston Fund" in 1946 with an initial donation of $38,500. In 1950 the name was changed to the Harris and Eliza Kempner Fund to honor the family's first American generation and founder of the family's business interests.

Harris Kempner, a Jewish refugee from Poland, served in the Confederate Army and shortly after the war he started a general mercantile business in Galveston, TX. The following generations developed extensive

interests in banking, farming, ranching, cotton, and sugar refining. In the early 1900s, the family bought a bank, which today is known as the United States National Bank in Galveston. The bank is a subsidiary of Cullen/Frost Bankers located in San Antonio, TX. Harris L. Kempner, Jr., and Isaac Herbert Kempner III, both serve on the boards of directors of Cullen/Frost and the Imperial Holly Corporation, which contributed $75,000 to the foundation in 1990. Isaac H. Kempner III, also serves as the chairman of the Imperial Holly Corporation.

Typical Recipients: • *Arts & Humanities:* Arts Associations & Councils, Arts Centers, Historic Preservation, History & Archaeology, Libraries, Museums/Galleries, Music, Public Broadcasting • *Civic & Public Affairs:* Civil Rights, Employment/Job Training, Municipalities/Towns, Public Policy • *Education:* Colleges & Universities, Engineering/Technological Education, Medical Education, Public Education (Precollege) • *Environment:* General, Resource Conservation • *Health:* Adolescent Health Issues, AIDS/HIV, Alzheimers Disease, Emergency/Ambulance Services, Health Organizations, Heart, Research/Studies Institutes, Single-Disease Health Associations • *International:* Health Care/Hospitals, International Development, International Relations, International Relief Efforts • *Religion:* Religious Welfare, Synagogues/Temples • *Social Services:* Child Welfare, Community Service Organizations, Crime Prevention, Domestic Violence, Family Planning, People with Disabilities, Scouts, Special Olympics, Substance Abuse, Youth Organizations

Grant Types: capital, endowment, matching, multiyear/continuing support, operating expenses, project, research, and seed money

Geographic Distribution: focus on Galveston, TX

GIVING OFFICERS

Arthur Malcolm Alpert: trust

Jack Thornton Currie: trust

Ann Oppenheimer Hamilton: vchwm, trust

Hetta Ellen Towler Kempner: trust

Robert Lee Kempner Lynch: secy, treas

Elaine Perachio: exec dir

Barbara Weston Sasser: trust

Lyda Ann Quinn Thomas: chmn

Leonora Kempner Thompson: chmn emeritus

Peter K. Thompson, MD: trust

Harris Kempner Weston: trust *B* Cincinnati OH 1918 *ED* Harvard Univ AB 1940; Harvard Univ Law Sch LLB 1946 *CURR EMPL* atty: Dinsmore & Shohl *CORP AFFIL* dir: Imperial Holly Corp *NONPR AFFIL* chmn: Contemporary Arts Ctr, Harvard Univ Law Sch Fund, Jewish Welfare Fund Cincinnati; mem: Am Bar Assn, Cincinnati Bar Assn, OH Bar Assn; pres: Harvard Univ Law Sch Assn, Jewish Fed Cincinnati; trust: Jewish Hosp; vchmn: Natl Conf Christians & Jews Southwestern OH; vp: Jewish Fed Counc *CLUB AFFIL* Harvard, University

APPLICATION INFORMATION
Initial Approach:

Applicants should send a grant proposal to the fund.

The proposal should include a brief cover letter signed by the executive director and the board chairman stating the need and the amount requested. The proposal should also provide information concerning the organization including the name and telephone number of a contact person; names of present officers and board members; statement of purpose and brief history; statement of previous Kempner Fund support, if any; financial statements that are audited, if possible, for the most recent fiscal year; operating budget (revenue and expenses) for year for which funds are sought; and copy of IRS determination letter to document tax-exempt status. The proposal should also provide project information including objectives and potential benefits; timetable; budget (revenue and expenses); sources and amounts being solicited and/or received or pledged; future funding plans, if the project is new and continuing; and evaluation plan of progress and/or results of project.

Deadlines are March 15, June 15, and October 15.

Proposals are reviewed three times a year at trustee meetings in April, July, and December. Requests of a national/international nature related to the areas of education, environment, population control and Third World development will be reviewed at the April meeting and must be submitted by December 1 of the previous year.

Restrictions on Giving: The Kempner Fund does not participate in fund-raising benefits, respond to direct-mail solicitations, or make grants to individuals.

PUBLICATIONS
Biennial report includes application guidelines

GRANTS ANALYSIS
Total Grants: $1,334,331

Number of Grants: 177

Highest Grant: $50,000

Average Grant: $7,539

Typical Range: $2,500 to $10,000

Disclosure Period: 1994

Note: Recent grants are derived from a 1994 grants list.

RECENT GRANTS

General

50,000	Temple B'nai Israel, Galveston, TX
20,000	Boys and Girls Club of Galveston, Galveston, TX
20,000	City of Galveston Police Department, Galveston, TX
15,000	City of Galveston Police Department, Galveston, TX
10,000	Ashoka, Arlington, VA

Kilroy Foundation, William S. and Lora Jean

CONTACT
William S. Kilroy
Trustee
William S. and Lora Jean Kilroy Fdn.
1021 Main St., Ste. 1900
Houston, TX 77002-6662
(713) 651-0101

FINANCIAL SUMMARY
Recent Giving: $267,103 (1993); $260,450 (1991); $76,125 (1989)

Assets: $5,503,729 (1993); $5,964,780 (1991); $3,629,088 (1989)

Gifts Received: $1,776,241 (1991)

Fiscal Note: In 1991, contributions were received from W.S. and L.J. Kilroy.

EIN: 76-0169904

CONTRIBUTIONS SUMMARY
Donor(s): William S. Kilroy, Lora Jean Kilroy

Typical Recipients: • *Arts & Humanities:* Community Arts, Dance, Historic Preservation, Libraries, Museums/Galleries • *Civic & Public Affairs:* Municipalities/Towns, Urban & Community Affairs • *Education:* Colleges & Universities, Private Education (Precollege) • *Religion:* Religious Organizations, Religious Welfare • *Social Services:* Community Service Organizations, Family Services, United Funds/United Ways, Youth Organizations

Grant Types: multiyear/continuing support and operating expenses

GIVING OFFICERS
William S. Kilroy: trust

APPLICATION INFORMATION
Initial Approach: Include a description of organization, amount requested, purpose of funds sought, recently audited financial statement, and proof of tax-exempt status. There are no deadlines.

GRANTS ANALYSIS
Total Grants: $267,103

Typical Range: $1,000 to $5,000

Disclosure Period: 1993

Note: Recent grants are derived from a 1991 Form 990. No grants list was provided for 1993.

RECENT GRANTS

Library

33,300	University School Library, Shaker Heights, OH

General

50,000	Bayou Bend Capital Campaign, Houston, TX
50,000	Kinkaid School, Houston, TX — computer purchase
25,000	Kinkaid School, Houston, TX — computer purchase
25,000	Yale University, New Haven, CT

10,000	Fellowship of Christian Athletes, Houston, TX

Kimberly-Clark Corp. / Kimberly-Clark Foundation

Revenue: $7.36 billion
Employees: 42,131
Headquarters: Dallas, TX
SIC Major Group: Sanitary Paper Products and Paper Mills

CONTACT
Colleen B. Berman
Vice President
Kimberly-Clark Foundation
PO Box 619100
Dallas, TX 75261-9100
(214) 830-1200

FINANCIAL SUMMARY
Recent Giving: $6,200,000 (1994); $5,600,000 (1993); $4,700,000 (1992)

Assets: $161,915 (1992); $538,781 (1991); $5,283,900 (1989)

Gifts Received: $2,207,007 (1992)

Fiscal Note: Figures include both foundation and direct giving. For information on receiving direct corporate funds, contact the local plant manager. Above figures exclude nonmonetary support.

EIN: 39-6044304

CONTRIBUTIONS SUMMARY
Typical Recipients: • *Arts & Humanities:* Arts Appreciation, Arts Associations & Councils, Arts Centers, Arts Funds, Community Arts, Dance, Historic Preservation, History & Archaeology, Libraries, Museums/Galleries, Music, Opera, Performing Arts, Public Broadcasting, Theater • *Civic & Public Affairs:* African American Affairs, Business/Free Enterprise, Civil Rights, Economic Policy, Municipalities/Towns, Philanthropic Organizations, Public Policy, Safety, Urban & Community Affairs, Zoos/Aquariums • *Education:* Arts/Humanities Education, Business Education, Colleges & Universities, Community & Junior Colleges, Economic Education, Education Associations, Education Funds, Engineering/Technological Education, Literacy, Medical Education, Minority Education, Science/Mathematics Education, Student Aid • *Environment:* General, Resource Conservation • *Health:* Cancer, Emergency/Ambulance Services, Geriatric Health, Hospitals, Medical Research, Multiple Sclerosis, Nursing Services, Single-Disease Health Associations • *International:* International Relations • *Social Services:* Child Welfare, Community Centers, Community Service Organizations, Counseling, Delinquency & Criminal Rehabilitation, Domestic Violence, Family Services, Food/Clothing Distribution, People with Disabilities, Senior Services, Shelters/Homelessness, Substance Abuse, United Funds/United Ways, Volunteer Services, Youth Organizations

Grant Types: capital, general support, operating expenses, and project

Note: Employee matching gift ratio: 1 to 1.

Nonmonetary Support Types: donated products

Note: The company provides nonmonetary support in the form donated products for disaster relief only. The estimated dollar value for this support is not available. For more information contact the local plant manager.

Geographic Distribution: in areas where the company maintains facilities; limited number of contributions to national organizations

Operating Locations: AL (Ashville, Coosa Pines, Goodwater, Nixburg, Roanoke, Westover), AR (Conway), AZ (Tucson), CA (Fullerton, Hendersonville), CT (New Milford), GA (Atlanta, La Grange, Roswell), MA (Lee), MI (Munising), MS (Corinth), NC (Balfour, Lexington), NE, NJ (Spotswood), NY (Ancram), OK (Tulsa), SC (Beech Island), TN (Knoxville, Loudon, Memphis), TX (Dallas, Paris, Waco), UT (Ogden), WI (Appleton, Milwaukee, Neenah, Whiting)

CORP. OFFICERS
Wayne R. Sanders: *B* Chicago IL 1947 *ED* IL Inst Tech BCE 1969; Marquette Univ MBA 1972 *CURR EMPL* chmn, ceo, dir: Kimberly-Clark Corp

GIVING OFFICERS
Tina S. Barry: pres, dir

Colleen B. Berman: vp

Donald Martin Crook: secy *B* Wichita KS 1947 *ED* Univ KS 1970; Univ Chicago Law Sch 1973 *CURR EMPL* vp, secy: Kimberly-Clark Corp *NONPR AFFIL* mem: Am Bar Assn, Dallas Bar Assn, Phi Beta Kappa

W. Anthony Gamron: treas, dir *B* Seymour IN 1948 *ED* IN St Univ BS 1971; IN Univ MBA 1976 *CURR EMPL* vp, treas: Kimberly-Clark Corp *CORP AFFIL* treas: Avent Inc; treas, dir: Kimberly-Clark Aviation Inc *NONPR AFFIL* dir: Sr Citizens Greater Dallas; mem: Fin Execs Inst

Brendan M. O'Neill: dir

APPLICATION INFORMATION
Initial Approach: *Initial Contact:* proposal *Include Information On:* amount requested, purpose, proof of tax-exempt 501(c)(3) status *Deadlines:* none (proposals reviewed as received)

Restrictions on Giving: The foundation does not make grants to sports or athletic activities; dinners or special events; individuals; fraternal organizations; state or secondary schools (except through matching gifts); religious organizations; goodwill advertising; member agencies of united funds; or political parties or candidates.

OTHER THINGS TO KNOW
Kimberly-Clark Corp. annually budgets 1% of average pre-tax domestic income of preceding three years for charitable contributions, which may be given directly to qualified recipients or to the Kimberly-Clark Foundation for distribution. Since 1952, the foundation has served as the prin-

cipal means through which the corporation supports tax-exempt charitable organizations.

GRANTS ANALYSIS
Total Grants: $2,367,450

Number of Grants: 42

Highest Grant: $400,000

Average Grant: $56,368

Typical Range: $500 to $50,000

Disclosure Period: 1992

Note: Figures represent foundation giving only. Total grants includes $590,000 in 1991 contributions that were paid in 1992. Recent grants are derived from a 1993 partial grants list.

RECENT GRANTS

Knox, Sr., and Pearl Wallis Knox Charitable Foundation, Robert W.

CONTACT
Carl Schumacher
Vice President
Robert W. Knox, Sr., and Pearl Wallis Knox Charitable Fdn.
Nation's Bank of Texas, N.A.
PO Box 298502
Houston, TX 77298-0502
(713) 787-4551

FINANCIAL SUMMARY
Recent Giving: $176,209 (fiscal 1992); $171,388 (fiscal 1991); $149,552 (fiscal 1990)

Assets: $3,886,790 (fiscal 1992); $3,915,976 (fiscal 1991); $3,357,003 (fiscal 1990)

EIN: 74-6064974

CONTRIBUTIONS SUMMARY
Donor(s): Robert W. Knox, Jr.

Typical Recipients: • *Arts & Humanities:* Arts Centers, Community Arts, Ethnic & Folk Arts, Historic Preservation, History & Archaeology, Libraries, Museums/Galleries, Music, Opera, Theater • *Civic & Public Affairs:* Asian American Affairs, Botanical Gardens/Parks, Clubs, General, Law & Justice, Municipalities/Towns, Parades/Festivals, Urban & Community Affairs, Women's Affairs, Zoos/Aquariums • *Education:* Colleges & Universities, Minority Education, Private Education (Precollege) • *Health:* Clinics/Medical Centers, Emergency/Ambulance Services, Mental Health, Prenatal Health Issues • *International:* International Relations • *Religion:* Churches, Ministries, Religious Organizations, Religious Welfare • *Science:* Science Museums • *Social Services:* Child Welfare, Community Service Organizations, Food/Clothing Distribution, People with Disabilities, Shelters/Homelessness, Substance Abuse, United Funds/United Ways, Volunteer Services, Youth Organizations

Grant Types: general support

Geographic Distribution: focus on Houston, TX

GIVING OFFICERS
Nations Bank of Texas, N.A.: trust

APPLICATION INFORMATION
Initial Approach: Send brief letter of inquiry describing program or project. There are no deadlines.

GRANTS ANALYSIS
Total Grants: $176,209

Number of Grants: 45

Highest Grant: $11,547

Typical Range: $1,000 to $5,000

Disclosure Period: fiscal year ending August 31, 1992

Note: Recent grants are derived from a fiscal 1992 Form 990.

RECENT GRANTS
Library
5,000	Rosenberg Library, Galveston, TX	

General
11,547	Goodwill Industries, Houston, TX	
10,500	United Way of the Texas Gulf Coast, Houston, TX	
10,000	Houston Foundation, Houston, TX	
5,000	Austin College, Sherman, TX	
5,000	Bayou Bend Capital Campaign	

Koehler Foundation, Marcia and Otto

CONTACT
Mary Ann Rybacki
Vice President
Marcia and Otto Koehler Fdn.
c/o NationsBank of Texas
PO Box 121
San Antonio, TX 78291
(210) 270-5405

FINANCIAL SUMMARY
Recent Giving: $246,750 (fiscal 1993); $270,130 (fiscal 1991); $320,925 (fiscal 1990)

Assets: $7,242,692 (fiscal 1993); $7,090,481 (fiscal 1991); $6,832,874 (fiscal 1990)

EIN: 74-2131195

CONTRIBUTIONS SUMMARY
Donor(s): the late Marcia Koehler

Typical Recipients: • *Arts & Humanities:* Arts Associations & Councils, Arts Centers, Arts Institutes, Community Arts, Ethnic & Folk Arts, Libraries, Museums/Galleries, Music, Public Broadcasting, Theater • *Civic & Public Affairs:* Botanical Gardens/Parks, Municipalities/Towns, Zoos/Aquariums • *Education:* Arts/Humanities Education, Business Education, Colleges & Universities,

Community & Junior Colleges, Private Education (Precollege), Public Education (Precollege) • *Health:* Geriatric Health, Health Organizations, Hospitals, Hospitals (University Affiliated), Medical Research • *Religion:* Religious Welfare • *Social Services:* Big Brother/Big Sister, Child Welfare, Community Centers, Community Service Organizations, Family Services, Homes, Senior Services, Substance Abuse, YMCA/YWCA/YMHA/YWHA, Youth Organizations

Grant Types: capital, operating expenses, and research

Geographic Distribution: focus on San Antonio, TX

GIVING OFFICERS
NationsBank TX: trust

APPLICATION INFORMATION
Initial Approach: Application form required. There are no deadlines.

Restrictions on Giving: Does not support individuals.

GRANTS ANALYSIS
Total Grants: $246,750

Number of Grants: 28

Highest Grant: $25,000

Typical Range: $2,000 to $18,000

Disclosure Period: fiscal year ending July 31, 1993

Note: Recent grants are derived from a fiscal 1993 Form 990.

RECENT GRANTS

General

25,000	Friends of Milam Park, San Antonio, TX — operation
15,000	Southwest Foundation, San Antonio, TX — operation
12,500	Alamo Community College District, San Antonio, TX — operation
12,000	Catholic Family and Children, San Antonio, TX — operation
10,000	Alpha Home, San Antonio, TX — operation

LBJ Family Foundation

CONTACT
Luci B. Johnson
Trustee
LBJ Family Fdn.
8309 N IH-35
Austin, TX 78753
(512) 832-4001

FINANCIAL SUMMARY
Recent Giving: $212,728 (1992); $185,417 (1990); $196,153 (1989)

Assets: $3,170,921 (1992); $2,363,973 (1990); $3,061,706 (1989)

EIN: 74-6045768

CONTRIBUTIONS SUMMARY
Donor(s): the late Lyndon B. Johnson, Mrs. Lyndon B. Johnson, Texas Broadcasting Corp.

Typical Recipients: • *Arts & Humanities:* Historic Preservation, History & Archaeology, Libraries, Museums/Galleries, Music • *Civic & Public Affairs:* Business/Free Enterprise, Economic Development, General, Philanthropic Organizations, Public Policy, Safety, Urban & Community Affairs, Women's Affairs, Zoos/Aquariums • *Education:* Colleges & Universities, Education Funds, General, International Studies, Legal Education, Literacy, Minority Education, Private Education (Precollege), Public Education (Precollege), Social Sciences Education, Student Aid • *Environment:* General • *Health:* Cancer, Diabetes, Hospitals, Prenatal Health Issues, Research/Studies Institutes • *International:* International Organizations, International Relations • *Religion:* Churches, Religious Organizations, Religious Welfare • *Social Services:* Child Welfare, Community Service Organizations, Food/Clothing Distribution, Homes, People with Disabilities, Recreation & Athletics, Shelters/Homelessness, United Funds/United Ways, Youth Organizations

Grant Types: general support, multi-year/continuing support, project, and scholarship

Geographic Distribution: focus on Austin, TX

GIVING OFFICERS
John M. Barr: mgr

Claudia Lady Bird Taylor Johnson: trust *B* Karnack TX 1912 *ED* Univ TX Austin BA 1933; Univ TX Austin BJ 1934 *CORP AFFIL* dir: Coin Acceptors; secy: Tallasi Land & Devel Corp *NONPR AFFIL* fdr, co-chwm: Natl Wildflower Res Ctr; hon chwm: Town Lake Beautification Project; life mem: Univ TX Ex-Student Assn; mem: Am Conservation Assn; mem adv counc: Natl Pks Historic Sites Bldgs & Monuments; trust: Jackson Hole Preserve, Natl Geographic Soc *PHIL AFFIL* trust: Jackson Hole Preserve

Luci Baines Johnson: trust *CURR EMPL* co-owner: LBJ Co *NONPR AFFIL* mem: Daughters Charity Natl Health Sys, Natl Wildflower Res Ctr; mem, dir: Covenant House

Lynda Bird Johnson Robb: trust *B* Washington DC 1944 *ED* Univ TX BA 1966 *CURR EMPL* co-owner: LBJ Co *NONPR AFFIL* dir: Ford Theatre, Reading Is Fundamental; mem: Natl Commn Prevent Infant Mortality, Natl Wildflower Res Ctr, VA St Counc Infant Mortality, Zeta Tau Alpha; mem adv bd: Commn Presidential Debates *PHIL AFFIL* dir: National Home Library Foundation

APPLICATION INFORMATION
Initial Approach: The foundation has no formal grant application procedure or application form. There are no deadlines.

GRANTS ANALYSIS
Total Grants: $212,728

Number of Grants: 89

Highest Grant: $6,500

Typical Range: $250 to $5,000

Disclosure Period: 1992

Note: Recent grants are derived from a 1992 Form 990.

RECENT GRANTS

Library

5,000	LBJ Museum and Library, Austin, TX
5,000	Sam Rayburn Library
1,000	Richard Nixion Library

General

6,500	University of Texas, Austin, TX
6,000	Lyndon B. Johnson School, Austin, TX
5,000	Catholic Home Study Institute
5,000	Daughters of Charity — Seton
5,000	Mayo Clinic, Rochester, MN

Management Compensation Group/Dulworth Inc.

Revenue: $4.0 million
Employees: 25
Headquarters: Houston, TX
SIC Major Group: Engineering & Management Services

CONTACT
Laura Lenhart
Operations Manager
Management Compensation Group/Dulworth Inc.
811 Rusk Ave. Ste. 1200
Houston, TX 77002
(713) 222-8383

FINANCIAL SUMMARY
Recent Giving: $12,000 (1994)

Fiscal Note: Annual Giving Range: less than $100,000

CONTRIBUTIONS SUMMARY
Company allocates 40% of contributions to the arts; 25% to health and human service organizations; 25% to civic organizations; and 10% to education.

Typical Recipients: • *Arts & Humanities:* Arts Appreciation, Arts Associations & Councils, Arts Centers, Arts Funds, Arts Institutes, Ballet, Community Arts, General, Libraries, Museums/Galleries, Music, Performing Arts, Public Broadcasting, Theater, Visual Arts • *Civic & Public Affairs:* Business/Free Enterprise, Civil Rights, Ethnic Organizations, General, Inner-City Development, Philanthropic Organizations, Professional & Trade Associations • *Education:* Arts/Humanities Education, Business Education, Colleges & Universities, General • *Health:* Cancer, General, Geriatric Health, Multiple Sclerosis • *Religion:* Jewish Causes • *Social Services:* Animal Protection, At-Risk Youth, Camps, Family Planning, General, United Funds/United Ways, Youth Organizations

Grant Types: award, employee matching gifts, and multiyear/continuing support

Nonmonetary Support Types: donated equipment

Geographic Distribution: only in headquarters area

Operating Locations: TX (Houston, Houston)

CORP. OFFICERS
James Phillips: *CURR EMPL* pres, ceo: Mgmt Compensation Group/Dulworth

APPLICATION INFORMATION
Initial Approach: Contributions budget is modest. Inquiries may be forwarded in the form of a brief letter. Include a description of organization, purpose of funds sought, and proof of tax-exempt status.

Restrictions on Giving: Does not support political or lobbying groups, fraternal or social organizations, or organizations outside operating areas.

GRANTS ANALYSIS
Typical Range: $10 to $1,000

Note: Recent grants are derived from a grants list provided by company in 1995.

RECENT GRANTS

General
American Red Cross, Houston, TX
Cal Farley's Boys Ranch, Richardson, TX
Houston Jewish Geriatric Foundation, Houston, TX
National Conference of Christian and Jews, Houston, TX
Rice University, Houston, TX

Mayer Foundation, James and Eva

CONTACT
Gene V. Owen
Trustee
James and Eva Mayer Foundation
PO Box 328
Plainview, TX 79073-0328
(806) 296-6304

FINANCIAL SUMMARY
Recent Giving: $58,728 (1993); $251,500 (1992); $203,500 (1991)

Assets: $4,042,444 (1993); $3,815,346 (1992); $3,928,248 (1991)

EIN: 75-6360908

CONTRIBUTIONS SUMMARY
Donor(s): the donor was the late Eva H. Mayer

Typical Recipients: • *Arts & Humanities:* Community Arts, Libraries, Music • *Education:* Colleges & Universities, Legal Education, Literacy, Science/Mathematics Education, Secondary Education (Public) • *Health:* Cancer, Health Organizations, Hospices, Hospitals, Public Health, Single-Disease Health Associations • *Religion:* Religious Welfare • *Social Services:* Child Welfare, Day Care, United Funds/United Ways, Youth Organizations

Grant Types: department, general support, matching, project, and scholarship

Geographic Distribution: IL and TX

GIVING OFFICERS
Paul Lyle: trust
Gene V. Owen: trust

APPLICATION INFORMATION
Initial Approach: Send a brief letter of inquiry. Include a description of organization, amount requested, purpose of funds sought, recently audited financial statement, and proof of tax-exempt status. There are no deadlines.

GRANTS ANALYSIS
Total Grants: $58,728

Number of Grants: 4

Highest Grant: $20,000

Typical Range: $5,000 to $19,384

Disclosure Period: 1993

Note: Recent grants are derived from a 1993 Form 990.

RECENT GRANTS

Library
14,344 — Friends of Unger Memorial Library, Plainview, TX — purchase hardware, software and furniture to be used in library

General
20,000 — Faith in Sharing House, Plainview, TX — purchase building for office space and storage
19,384 — Wee Care Child Care Center, Plainview, TX — purchase 1994 van, 15 passenger to transport children
5,000 — American Cancer Society Hale County Unit, Plainview, TX — assist in the underwriting of the Hale County Cotton Baron's Ball

---

Mayor Foundation, Oliver Dewey

CONTACT
Phil McKinzie
Governor
Oliver Dewey Mayor Fdn.
c/o Aliance Trust Co. N.A.
PO Box 1088
Sherman, TX 75091-1088
(214) 868-0800

FINANCIAL SUMMARY
Recent Giving: $467,573 (fiscal 1994); $604,919 (fiscal 1992); $400,121 (fiscal 1991)

Assets: $10,034,525 (fiscal 1994); $9,862,492 (fiscal 1992); $9,780,675 (fiscal 1991)

EIN: 75-1864630

CONTRIBUTIONS SUMMARY
Donor(s): the late Oliver Dewey Mayor

Typical Recipients: • *Arts & Humanities:* Community Arts, Historic Preservation, Libraries, Museums/Galleries, Performing Arts, Theater • *Civic & Public Affairs:* General, Municipalities/Towns, Parades/Festivals, Safety • *Education:* Colleges & Universities, Community & Junior Colleges, Literacy, Medical Education, Public Education (Precollege), Science/Mathematics Education, Student Aid • *Health:* Hospitals, Medical Rehabilitation, Nursing Services, Nutrition, Transplant Networks/Donor Banks • *Religion:* Religious Welfare • *Social Services:* Community Centers, Community Service Organizations, Crime Prevention, Recreation & Athletics, Senior Services, United Funds/United Ways, Youth Organizations

Grant Types: general support

Geographic Distribution: limited to Grayson County, TX, and Mayes County, OK

GIVING OFFICERS
Samuel W. Graber: gov *PHIL AFFIL* trust: Martin W. and Betty J. Halsell Foundation
Tony J. Lyons: gov
Philip S. L. McKinzie: gov

APPLICATION INFORMATION
Initial Approach: Send cover letter and full proposal. Include a description of organization, amount requested, purpose of funds sought, recently audited financial statement, and proof of tax-exempt status. There are no deadlines.

Restrictions on Giving: Does not support individuals.

PUBLICATIONS
Application Guidelines

GRANTS ANALYSIS
Total Grants: $467,573

Number of Grants: 63

Highest Grant: $60,000

Typical Range: $500 to $54,943

Disclosure Period: fiscal year ending June 30, 1994

Note: Recent grants are derived from a fiscal 1994 Form 990.

RECENT GRANTS

General
60,000 — Senior Citizens of Pryor, Pryor, OK — senior citizen center
54,943 — Boys Club, Sherman, TX — computers and operating support
50,000 — Consortium for Community Development Education, Brooklyn, NY — public school research
40,000 — Denison Industrial Foundation — Reed Tool acquisition and move of subsidiary of Garner Denver of Virginia

30,000	Grand Valley Hospital — lifeline units/personal call buttons

Mays Foundation

CONTACT
Troy M. Mays
Trustee
Mays Foundation
914 South Tyler St.
Amarillo, TX 79101
(806) 376-5417

FINANCIAL SUMMARY
Recent Giving: $129,617 (fiscal 1993); $132,950 (fiscal 1992); $82,137 (fiscal 1990)

Assets: $4,459,639 (fiscal 1993); $2,830,686 (fiscal 1992); $1,914,216 (fiscal 1990)

Gifts Received: $1,212,593 (fiscal 1993)

EIN: 75-1213346

CONTRIBUTIONS SUMMARY
Donor(s): W. A. Mays

Typical Recipients: • *Arts & Humanities:* Libraries • *Education:* Colleges & Universities, General, Private Education (Precollege) • *Religion:* Bible Study/Translation, Churches • *Social Services:* Community Centers, Community Service Organizations

Grant Types: general support

Geographic Distribution: focus on TX and AR

GIVING OFFICERS
Karra Mays Hill: trust

Armon Mays: trust

Troy M. Mays: trust

APPLICATION INFORMATION
Initial Approach: The foundation requests applications be made in writing. There are no deadlines.

GRANTS ANALYSIS
Total Grants: $129,617

Number of Grants: 62

Highest Grant: $26,000

Typical Range: $100 to $3,000

Disclosure Period: fiscal year ending July 31, 1993

Note: Recent grants are derived from a fiscal 1993 Form 990.

RECENT GRANTS
Library

5,000	Friends of the Library Newton Company, Jasper, AR
3,600	Searcy County Library, Marshall, AR

General

26,000	Hawaii Baptist Academy, Honolulu, HI
25,800	Baylor University, Waco, TX
6,300	First Baptist Church, Amarillo, TX

5,000	Friendship Services Center, Russelville, AR
4,000	Amarillo Community Center, Amarillo, TX

McDermott Foundation, Eugene

CONTACT
Eugene McDermott
President
Eugene McDermott Foundation
3808 Euclid Ave.
Dallas, TX 75205
(214) 521-2924
Note: Patty Brown, assistant secretary, is another contact for the foundation.

FINANCIAL SUMMARY
Recent Giving: $2,000,000 (fiscal 1994 est.); $2,525,000 (fiscal 1993); $2,000,800 (fiscal 1991)

Assets: $58,408,166 (fiscal 1993); $39,654,499 (fiscal 1991); $36,156,642 (fiscal 1990)

EIN: 23-7237919

CONTRIBUTIONS SUMMARY
Donor(s): The Eugene McDermott Foundation was founded by Eugene McDermott , a geophysicist and a founder of Texas Instruments. Mr. McDermott died in 1973.

Typical Recipients: • *Arts & Humanities:* Arts Associations & Councils, Arts Festivals, Arts Outreach, Ethnic & Folk Arts, Historic Preservation, History & Archaeology, Libraries, Museums/Galleries, Music, Opera, Theater • *Civic & Public Affairs:* Botanical Gardens/Parks, Economic Development, Municipalities/Towns, Philanthropic Organizations, Professional & Trade Associations, Zoos/Aquariums • *Education:* Arts/Humanities Education, Colleges & Universities, Engineering/Technological Education, General, Health & Physical Education, Medical Education, Private Education (Precollege), Public Education (Precollege), Student Aid • *Environment:* Resource Conservation • *Health:* Cancer, Clinics/Medical Centers, Hospitals, Hospitals (University Affiliated) • *Religion:* Churches • *Science:* Science Museums, Scientific Centers & Institutes • *Social Services:* Domestic Violence, Food/Clothing Distribution, People with Disabilities, Recreation & Athletics, Shelters/Homelessness, Substance Abuse, United Funds/United Ways, Youth Organizations

Grant Types: capital, challenge, endowment, general support, operating expenses, project, research, and scholarship

Geographic Distribution: predominantly Dallas, TX, with some national giving

GIVING OFFICERS
Patricia Brown: asst secy *PHIL AFFIL* secy, trust: Biological Humanics Foundation

Mary McDermott Cook: secy, treas, trust *PHIL AFFIL* pres, trust: Biological Humanics Foundation

Charles Cullum: vp, trust *B* Dallas TX 1916 *ED* Southern Methodist Univ BS 1936; TX Coll LLD 1982 *CURR EMPL* chmn exec comm, dir: Cullum Cos

Mrs. Eugene McDermott: pres, trust

Zin Prothro: trust

C. J. Thomsen: trust

APPLICATION INFORMATION
Initial Approach:

The foundation has no set application form or guidelines. Applicants should send a letter of inquiry and submit one copy of a proposal.

There are no deadlines for applications. The board of trustees meets quarterly.

The foundation will acknowledge letters of inquiry and provide applicants with an initial assessment of the likelihood of its consideration for a grant. The applicant will be notified approximately three months after the application is received.

Restrictions on Giving: The foundation does not make grants to individuals.

GRANTS ANALYSIS
Total Grants: $2,525,000

Number of Grants: 72

Highest Grant: $500,000

Average Grant: $35,069

Typical Range: $5,000 to $50,000

Disclosure Period: fiscal year ending August 31, 1993

Note: Recent grants are derived from a fiscal 1993 Form 990.

RECENT GRANTS
Library

150,000	State Preservation Board, Austin, TX — for capital fund for restoration of Legislative Library

General

500,000	University of Texas Southwestern Medical Center, Dallas, TX — to upgrade Margaret Milam McDermott Chair in Anesthesiology
250,000	University of Texas Southwestern Medical Foundation, Dallas, TX — endowment of Margaret Milam McDermott Chair in Anesthesiology
150,000	M.D. Anderson Cancer Center, Houston, TX — capital improvement campaign
50,000	Dallas Zoological Society, Dallas, TX — for the design of new animal hospital
25,000	Callas City Plan, Dallas, TX — for developing long-term capital improvements plan for Dallas

McQueen Foundation, Adeline and George

CONTACT
Robert Lansford
Trust Officer
Adeline and George McQueen Fdn.
c/o Bank One of Texas, N.A.
PO Box 2050
Fort Worth, TX 76113
(817) 884-4448

FINANCIAL SUMMARY
Recent Giving: $457,000 (fiscal 1994)
Assets: $8,685,517 (fiscal 1994)
EIN: 75-6014459

CONTRIBUTIONS SUMMARY
Typical Recipients: • *Arts & Humanities:* Ballet, Libraries • *Civic & Public Affairs:* Clubs, Community Foundations, Economic Development, General, Urban & Community Affairs, Women's Affairs, Zoos/Aquariums • *Education:* Afterschool/Enrichment Programs, Business Education, Medical Education, Private Education (Precollege), Religious Education, Special Education • *Health:* Health Organizations, Hospitals, Single-Disease Health Associations • *Religion:* Religious Organizations, Religious Welfare, Seminaries • *Social Services:* Counseling, Food/Clothing Distribution, YMCA/YWCA/YMHA/YWHA, Youth Organizations

Grant Types: general support
Geographic Distribution: focus on TX

GIVING OFFICERS
Bank One TX NA: trust

APPLICATION INFORMATION
Initial Approach: Send a brief letter of inquiry. Include a description of organization, amount requested, purpose of funds sought, recently audited financial statement, and proof of tax-exempt status. There are no deadlines.

GRANTS ANALYSIS
Total Grants: $457,000
Number of Grants: 43
Highest Grant: $50,000
Typical Range: $3,000 to $30,000
Disclosure Period: fiscal year ending June 30, 1994
Note: Recent grants are derived from a fiscal 1994 Form 990.

RECENT GRANTS

Library
10,000	Ft. Worth Library, Ft. Worth, TX

General
30,000	Ft. Worth Zoological Society, Ft. Worth, TX
25,000	Community Enrichment Center, Ft. Worth, TX
25,000	Health Care Foundation, Ft. Worth, TX
25,000	Jewel Charity Ball, Ft. Worth, TX
25,000	Texas College of Osteopathic Medicine, Ft. Worth, TX

Meadows Foundation

CONTACT
Meadows Foundation
3003 Swiss Ave.
Wilson Historic District
Dallas, TX 75204-6090
(214) 826-9431
Note: The foundation does not list a specific contact person.

FINANCIAL SUMMARY
Recent Giving: $12,244,044 (1993); $17,435,827 (1992); $16,732,561 (1991)
Assets: $600,000,000 (1994 approx.); $614,416,989 (1993); $579,334,150 (1992)
Gifts Received: $3,433,769 (1987)
Fiscal Note: Above figure for gifts received in 1987 is comprised of cash, furniture, and common stock from the estate of A. H. Meadows.
EIN: 75-6015322

CONTRIBUTIONS SUMMARY
Donor(s): The Meadows Foundation was incorporated in 1948 by the late Algur Hurtle Meadows and his first wife, the late Virginia Meadows . Mr. Meadows helped found the General American Oil Company of Texas in 1936 and diversified its corporate empire into mortgage banking, insurance, real estate, and crude oil and gas development. Mr. Meadows was named chairman of General American Oil in 1950, and most of the foundation's original assets were securities of the company. The company was purchased by Phillips Petroleum in 1983 and dissolved as a corporate entity.

Mr. Meadows was interested in art, and over the years donated millions of dollars to Southern Methodist University for the Meadows Museum (developed as a memorial to his first wife), for art acquisitions, the museum's endowment, and for Southern Methodist University's School of Arts. Until his death in 1978, Mr. Meadows was the foundation's president.

Typical Recipients: • *Arts & Humanities:* Arts Associations & Councils, Arts Centers, Arts Funds, Arts Institutes, Arts Outreach, Ballet, Community Arts, Dance, Ethnic & Folk Arts, Historic Preservation, History & Archaeology, Libraries, Museums/Galleries, Music, Opera, Performing Arts, Public Broadcasting, Theater, Visual Arts • *Civic & Public Affairs:* Asian American Affairs, Botanical Gardens/Parks, Business/Free Enterprise, Economic Development, Employment/Job Training, Hispanic Affairs, Housing, Law & Justice, Municipalities/Towns, Nonprofit Management, Parades/Festivals, Safety, Urban & Community Affairs, Zoos/Aquariums • *Education:* Afterschool/Enrichment Programs, Arts/Humanities Education, Colleges & Universities, Community & Junior Colleges, Continuing Education, Education Reform, Elementary Education (Private), Faculty Development, Health & Physical Education, Literacy, Medical Education, Minority Education, Preschool Education, Private Education (Precollege), Public Education (Precollege), Science/Mathematics Education, Secondary Education (Private), Student Aid, Vocational & Technical Education • *Environment:* Forestry, General, Research, Resource Conservation • *Health:* AIDS/HIV, Alzheimers Disease, Cancer, Children's Health/Hospitals, Clinics/Medical Centers, Emergency/Ambulance Services, Eyes/Blindness, Geriatric Health, Health Policy/Cost Containment, Health Organizations, Heart, Home-Care Services, Hospices, Hospitals, Long-Term Care, Medical Training, Mental Health, Outpatient Health Care, Preventive Medicine/Wellness Organizations, Speech & Hearing, Transplant Networks/Donor Banks • *Religion:* Churches, Ministries, Religious Welfare • *Science:* Science Museums, Scientific Centers & Institutes • *Social Services:* Animal Protection, At-Risk Youth, Camps, Child Welfare, Community Centers, Community Service Organizations, Counseling, Day Care, Delinquency & Criminal Rehabilitation, Domestic Violence, Emergency Relief, Family Services, Food/Clothing Distribution, Homes, People with Disabilities, Refugee Assistance, Senior Services, Shelters/Homelessness, Substance Abuse, United Funds/United Ways, Volunteer Services, YMCA/YWCA/YMHA/YWHA, Youth Organizations

Grant Types: capital, challenge, general support, operating expenses, and project
Geographic Distribution: Texas only

GIVING OFFICERS
Evelyn Meadows Acton: trust, dir emeritus

John W. Broadfoot: dir

Vela Meadows Broadfoot: dir emeritus

J. W. Bullion: trust, dir *B* 1914 *CURR EMPL* atty: Thompson & Knight *CORP AFFIL* secy: Toreador Royalty Corp

Eudine Meadows Cheney: trust, dir emeritus

Judy B. Culbertson: vp, trust

Bruce H. Esterline: vp grants

Linda Evans: vp, trust, dir

John A. Hammack: trust, dir

Anne P. Herrscher: asst vp program admin

Emily J. Jones: asst vp, asst secy

Sally R. Lancaster, PhD: trust, dir *NONPR AFFIL* regent: E TX St Univ

P. Mike McCulbugh: dir

Curtis W. Meadows, Jr.: pres, ceo, trust, dir *B* 1938

Robert A. Meadows: chmn, trust, vp, dir

Harvey K. Mitchell: trust, dir

Nancy J. Nelson: asst secy

G. Tom Rhodus: vp, secy, special couns

Evy Kay Ritzen: vp, dir

Eloise Meadows Rouse: vp, dir *NONPR AFFIL* secy: Natl Wildflower Res Ctr

Robert E. Weiss: vp admin
Dorothy Clarke Wilson: dir *B* Gardiner ME 1904
Robert E. Wise: cfo, vp, treas

APPLICATION INFORMATION
Initial Approach:
Applicants should submit a proposal describing the project and organization for which funds are sought.

The proposal should include, in order: a brief history of the organization's purpose and work; a description of program; the specific request of the Meadows Foundation including desired payment date; a list of others asked to support the project, with amounts and responses to date; a project income/expense budget; methods of project evaluation; a listing of organization's officers and directors, with information on profession, gender, and ethnicity; information on the number of times per year the board meets and information on attendance figures; names and qualifications of staff; the organization's current financial statement; the most recently audited financial statement (or the latest Form 990 for a young organizations); and a copy of all documents from the IRS pertaining to tax-exempt status. Only one unbound proposal copy should be submitted. The foundation only considers one request from the same organization witin a twelve month period.

There are no application deadlines. The full board meets two or three times a year, with interim officers' meetings each month.

A concise and brief proposal will speed the foundation's processing of a grant application. All requests are reviewed as soon as possible after their receipt. The foundation will try to respond without delay. The time required to process a proposal is generally 90 to 120 days.

Restrictions on Giving: The foundation's charter prohibits donations to charities outside of the state of Texas. Also, the foundation generally does not favor contributions for church or seminary construction projects, annual fund-raising drives, or media projects in initial planning stages. Because of restrictions imposed by federal tax laws, the foundation cannot give or lend money to individuals. The foundation also reports that endowment gifts are rare.

OTHER THINGS TO KNOW
The foundation finds special value in a proposal in which one or more of the following conditions are present: support of the foundation could be vital or catalytic to the project's success; synergistic or networking opportunities are present which could multiply the impact of a grant; potential exists for project impact lasting beyond grant peroid; a innovative and creative proposal, which increases earned income or reduces expenses; economies of operation would be obtained through the sharing of resources by serveral agencies or populations; the proposal reflects a well-planned approach to a problem solution; the activity to be funded could promote better human relationships and sense of community; and the program would enhance the capabilities of families and/or foster traditional family values.

The foundation maintains a twenty-two acre nonprofit agency campus with over twenty-five tenant agencies and a conference center where seminars, workshops, conferences, and proposal writing assistance are available.

PUBLICATIONS
Annual report

GRANTS ANALYSIS
Total Grants: $12,244,044
Number of Grants: 275
Highest Grant: $1,250,000
Average Grant: $44,524
Typical Range: $25,000 to $250,000
Disclosure Period: 1993

Note: Recent grants are derived from a 1993 Form 990.

RECENT GRANTS
Library
95,000   Bay City Library Association, Bay City, TX — to furnish and equip a new library

General
1,250,000   South Plains Food Bank, Lubbock, TX — final funding for innovative surplus food drying and distribution operation
1,000,000   Presbyterian Healthcare Foundation, Dallas, TX — toward redesign and expansion of the hospital's Emergency Department
500,000   Cancer Therapy and Research Foundation of South Texas, San Antonio, TX — toward constructing and equipping of a patient treatment/clinical research building
500,000   City of Angelo, Texas, Angelo, TX — toward construction and landscaping of the Plaza to serve as a site for a farmers' market and community festivals as part of a comprehensive effort to revitalize the Historic City Center
300,000   Buckner Baptist Benevolence, Lubbock, TX — toward construction of a new Activity Center for elderly residents of Buckner Retirement Home and youth from Buckner Children's Home

Meyer Family Foundation, Paul J.

CONTACT
Paul J. Meyer, Sr.
President
Paul J. Meyer Family Fdn.
PO Box 7411
Waco, TX 76714-7411
(817) 776-0034

FINANCIAL SUMMARY
Recent Giving: $1,226,976 (1993); $1,831,210 (1992); $1,163,590 (1991)
Assets: $3,502,364 (1993); $2,883,606 (1992); $1,334,670 (1991)
Gifts Received: $1,630,197 (1993); $3,298,642 (1992); $1,781,435 (1991)
Fiscal Note: In 1993, contributions were received from Japale, Ltd. ($878,362), Paul J. Meyer ($692,693), and Larry Meyer ($33,982); two other grants of less than $17,000 each were also received.
EIN: 74-2357421

CONTRIBUTIONS SUMMARY
Donor(s): Paul J. Meyer and Alice Jane Meyer

Typical Recipients: • *Arts & Humanities:* History & Archaeology, Libraries, Museums/Galleries • *Civic & Public Affairs:* Clubs, General, Housing, Public Policy, Urban & Community Affairs • *Education:* Colleges & Universities, General, Private Education (Precollege), Public Education (Precollege), Religious Education, Secondary Education (Private), Student Aid • *Health:* Arthritis, Cancer, Eyes/Blindness, Heart, Prenatal Health Issues • *International:* International Peace & Security Issues, Missionary/Religious Activities • *Religion:* Churches, Ministries, Missionary Activities (Domestic), Religious Organizations, Religious Welfare, Social/Policy Issues • *Social Services:* Child Welfare, Community Service Organizations, Family Services, Scouts, United Funds/United Ways, Youth Organizations

Grant Types: general support
Geographic Distribution: focus on TX

GIVING OFFICERS
Joe E. Baxter: secy, treas, dir
Dr. William M. Hinson: dir *PHIL AFFIL* vp: Passport to Success Foundation
Alice Jane Meyer: vp, dir
Paul J. Meyer, Sr.: pres, dir *PHIL AFFIL* chmn: Passport to Success Foundation
William A. Meyer: vp, dir

APPLICATION INFORMATION
Initial Approach: Submit a typed statement with a description of need and purpose. There are no deadlines.

GRANTS ANALYSIS
Total Grants: $1,226,976
Number of Grants: 34
Highest Grant: 427,000

Typical Range: $100 to $125,010

Disclosure Period: 1993

Note: Recent grants are derived from a 1993 Form 990.

RECENT GRANTS

Library

250	Waco McLennan County Library Foundation, Waco, TX

General

427,000	First Baptist Church, Waco, TX
125,010	HOT Council Boy Scouts, Waco, TX
101,561	Boys and Girls Club of Waco, Waco, TX
50,112	Jefferson National Life Insurance Fund — for the benefit of Haggai Institute, Boy Scouts, and Boys and Girls Club of Waco
37,000	LaRue Learning Center, Waco, TX

Mitchell Energy & Development Corp.

Revenue: $952.8 million
Employees: 2,900
Headquarters: The Woodlands, TX
SIC Major Group: Crude Petroleum & Natural Gas, Natural Gas Liquids, Natural Gas Transmission, and Subdividers & Developers Nec

CONTACT

Debra McCoy
Secretary to the Chairman
Mitchell Energy & Development Corp.
PO Box 4000
The Woodlands, TX 77387
(713) 377-5500

FINANCIAL SUMMARY

Fiscal Note: Company gives directly. Annual Giving Range: $500,000 to $1 million.

CONTRIBUTIONS SUMMARY

Typical Recipients: • *Arts & Humanities:* Historic Preservation, Libraries, Museums/Galleries, Opera, Performing Arts • *Civic & Public Affairs:* Business/Free Enterprise, Professional & Trade Associations • *Education:* Colleges & Universities, Continuing Education, Literacy, Science/Mathematics Education • *Health:* Hospices, Medical Research, Mental Health • *Science:* Science Exhibits & Fairs, Scientific Organizations • *Social Services:* Community Service Organizations, United Funds/United Ways, Youth Organizations

Grant Types: capital, endowment, matching, research, and scholarship

Nonmonetary Support Types: donated equipment, in-kind services, and loaned employees

Geographic Distribution: operating locations

Operating Locations: NM, OK, TX (Bridgeport, Houston, Mineral Wells, The Woodlands)

CORP. OFFICERS

George Phydias Mitchell: *B* Galveston TX 1919 *ED* TX A&M Univ BS 1940 *CURR EMPL* co-fdr, chmn, ceo, dir: Mitchell Energy & Devel Corp *CORP AFFIL* chmn, dir: Liquid Energy Corp, Southwestern Gas Pipeline Inc, Woodlands Corp; chmn, pres, ceo, dir: Mitchell Energy Corp, MND Energy Corp; dir: MCorp, George Mitchell & Assocs; partner: Fort Crockett Hotel Ltd; pres, dir: Eighteen Seventy Strand Corp *PHIL AFFIL* off: Cynthia and George Mitchell Foundation, Cynthia & George Mitchell Foundation

Philip S. Smith: *B* Chewalla TN 1936 *ED* MS St Univ BS 1957 *CURR EMPL* sr vp: Mitchell Energy & Devel Corp

GIVING OFFICERS

Minnie Adams: *CURR EMPL* vp: Mitchell Energy & Devel Corp

Debra McCoy: *CURR EMPL* secy to chmn: Mitchell Energy & Devel Corp

APPLICATION INFORMATION

Initial Approach: *Initial Contact:* brief letter of inquiry *Include Information On:* description of the organization, amount requested, purpose of funds sought, audited financial statement (including budget), list of contributors, project goals, and proof of tax-exempt status *Deadlines:* none

Restrictions on Giving: Does not support individuals, religious organizations for sectarian purposes, or political or lobbying groups.

GRANTS ANALYSIS

Typical Range: $1,000 to $2,500

Munson Foundation Trust, W. B.

Former Foundation Name: W. B. Munson Foundation

CONTACT

Wayne Cabaniss
Board of Govenors
W. B. Munson Fdn Trust
231 W Main St.
Denison, TX 75020
(817) 884-4000

FINANCIAL SUMMARY

Recent Giving: $378,757 (1993); $336,912 (1991); $280,224 (1990)

Assets: $6,150,746 (1993); $6,125,803 (1991); $5,594,041 (1990)

EIN: 75-6015068

CONTRIBUTIONS SUMMARY

Typical Recipients: • *Arts & Humanities:* Community Arts, Historic Preservation, Libraries, Museums/Galleries, Music, Performing Arts • *Civic & Public Affairs:* Community Foundations • *Education:* Colleges & Universities, Literacy, Public Education (Precollege), Science/Mathematics Education • *Health:* Clinics/Medical Centers, Diabetes, Emergency/Ambulance Services, Health Organizations, Hospitals • *International:* International Organizations • *Social Services:* At-Risk Youth, Community Centers, Shelters/Homelessness, United Funds/United Ways, Volunteer Services, Youth Organizations

Grant Types: capital, endowment, operating expenses, and scholarship

Geographic Distribution: limited to Grayson County, TX

GIVING OFFICERS

Bank One: trust

Wayne Cabaniss: gov

David M. Munson: gov

Peter Munson: gov

APPLICATION INFORMATION

Initial Approach: Send brief letter of inquiry describing program or project. Include a description of organization, amount requested, purpose of funds sought, recently audited financial statement, and proof of tax-exempt status. There are no deadlines.

GRANTS ANALYSIS

Total Grants: $378,757

Number of Grants: 25

Highest Grant: $125,000

Typical Range: $1,500 to $60,000

Disclosure Period: 1993

Note: Recent grants are derived from a 1993 Form 990. Number of grants and typical range do not include scholarships to individuals.

RECENT GRANTS

Library

45,626	Denison Public Library, Denison, TX — for heating and air conditioning project
7,900	Friends of the Sherman Public Library, Sherman, TX
1,500	Denison Public Library Endowment Fund, Denison, TX

General

125,000	Texoma Medical Center, Denison, TX — for cardiac catherization laboratory
60,000	Denison Community Foundation, Denison, TX — for Eisenhower birthplace capital improvement
30,890	Grayson Adult Literacy Team Advisory Council, Sherman, TX — for read to win project
24,948	Grayson Adult Literacy Team, Sherman, TX
24,948	Grayson Adult Literacy Team, Sherman, TX — for children's one-on-one reading program

Norman Foundation, Summers A.

CONTACT
Evelyn Underhill
Trustee
Summers A. Norman Foundation
218 S Main
Jacksonville, TX 75766
(903) 586-4291

FINANCIAL SUMMARY
Recent Giving: $383,324 (1993); $476,484 (1992); $581,188 (1991)
Assets: $2,043,011 (1993); $2,368,561 (1992); $2,892,387 (1991)
EIN: 75-2249004

CONTRIBUTIONS SUMMARY
Typical Recipients: • *Arts & Humanities:* Libraries, Museums/Galleries, Music, Theater • *Civic & Public Affairs:* Botanical Gardens/Parks, Clubs, Municipalities/Towns, Safety • *Education:* Colleges & Universities, Literacy, Public Education (Precollege), Student Aid • *Health:* Hospitals, Medical Research • *Religion:* Churches, Dioceses, Religious Welfare, Seminaries • *Social Services:* Animal Protection, Counseling, Crime Prevention, Food/Clothing Distribution, Recreation & Athletics, Scouts, United Funds/United Ways, Youth Organizations

Grant Types: general support

Geographic Distribution: focus on TX

GIVING OFFICERS
Crawford Godfrey: trust
Jimmy Staton: trust
Gordon Thrall: trust
Evelyn Underhill: trust

APPLICATION INFORMATION
Initial Approach: Send a brief letter of inquiry and a full proposal. Include a description of organization, amount requested, purpose of funds sought, recently audited financial statement, and proof of tax-exempt status. There are no deadlines.

GRANTS ANALYSIS
Total Grants: $383,324
Number of Grants: 25
Highest Grant: $75,000
Typical Range: $500 to $62,750
Disclosure Period: 1993

Note: Recent grants are derived from a 1993 Form 990.

RECENT GRANTS
Library
5,000	City of Frankston, Frankston, TX — for library
2,000	City of Bullard, Bullard, TX — for library

General
75,000	First Presbyterian Church, Jacksonville, TX — for monetary contribution
75,000	Nan Travis Hospital, Jacksonville, TX — for monetary contribution
62,750	Jacksonville Rodeo Association, Jacksonville, TX — for monetary contribution
38,784	Rusk Independent School District, Rusk, TX — for computers
25,000	Cherokee County Crisis Center, Jacksonville, TX — for monetary contribution

O'Connor Foundation, Kathryn

CONTACT
Dennis O'Connor
President
Kathryn O'Connor Fdn.
One O'Connor Plaza, Ste. 1100
Victoria, TX 77901
(512) 578-6271

FINANCIAL SUMMARY
Recent Giving: $360,120 (1991); $431,548 (1990); $369,181 (1989)
Assets: $6,258,972 (1991); $5,933,541 (1990); $5,587,122 (1989)
EIN: 74-6039415

CONTRIBUTIONS SUMMARY
Donor(s): the late Kathryn S. O'Connor, Tom O'Connor, Jr., and Dennis O'Connor

Typical Recipients: • *Arts & Humanities:* Libraries • *Civic & Public Affairs:* Municipalities/Towns • *Education:* Medical Education, Private Education (Precollege), Religious Education • *Health:* Hospices • *Religion:* Churches, Religious Organizations • *Social Services:* Community Service Organizations

Grant Types: capital, emergency, endowment, general support, multiyear/continuing support, operating expenses, professorship, and seed money

Geographic Distribution: limited to southern TX, especially Victoria and Refugio counties and the surrounding area

GIVING OFFICERS
Mary O'Connor Braman: treas *B* Victoria TX 1910 *ED* Incarnate Word Coll
Dennis O'Connor: pres *B* Victoria TX 1907 *ED* Univ TX BA 1928 *CURR EMPL* sr dir emeritus: Victoria Bankshares *PHIL AFFIL* pres: Dorothy O'Connor Foundation
Thomas O'Connor, Jr.: vp *B* Victoria TX 1915 *ED* Victoria Jr Coll *CURR EMPL* sr chmn, dir: Victoria Bankshares
Venable B. Proctor: secy

APPLICATION INFORMATION
Initial Approach: Send brief letter of inquiry describing program or project. There are no deadlines.

Restrictions on Giving: Does not support individuals.

GRANTS ANALYSIS
Total Grants: $360,120
Number of Grants: 16
Highest Grant: $100,000
Typical Range: $5,000 to $25,000
Disclosure Period: 1991

Note: Recent grants are derived from a 1991 Form 990.

RECENT GRANTS
General
100,000	Diocese of Victoria, Victoria, TX
50,000	Hospice of South Texas, TX
50,000	St. Joseph High School, Victoria, TX
45,870	St. Dennis Church, Refugio, TX
25,000	Nazareth Academy, Victoria, TX

O'Quinn Foundation, John M. and Nancy C.

CONTACT
John M. O'Quinn
President
John M. and Nancy C. O'Quinn Foundation
440 Louisiana
Houston, TX 77002
(713) 223-1000

FINANCIAL SUMMARY
Recent Giving: $3,623,276 (1993); $226,849 (1992); $52,500 (1990)
Assets: $307,265 (1993); $3,967,191 (1992); $4,104,126 (1990)
Gifts Received: $1,800,000 (1990)
EIN: 76-0206844

CONTRIBUTIONS SUMMARY
Typical Recipients: • *Arts & Humanities:* Libraries, Museums/Galleries, Opera, Public Broadcasting, Theater • *Civic & Public Affairs:* African American Affairs, Clubs, General, Law & Justice, Legal Aid, Municipalities/Towns, Public Policy, Safety, Urban & Community Affairs • *Education:* Colleges & Universities, Continuing Education, Education Funds, Elementary Education (Public), General, Legal Education, Medical Education, Private Education (Precollege), Public Education (Precollege), School Volunteerism, Secondary Education (Private), Student Aid • *Environment:* General, Resource Conservation • *Health:* AIDS/HIV, Cancer, Children's Health/Hospitals, Clinics/Medical Centers, Diabetes, Health Organizations, Heart, Hospitals, Multiple Sclerosis, Respiratory, Single-Disease Health Associations • *International:* International Relief Efforts • *Religion:* Churches, Religious Welfare • *Social Services:* Child Welfare, Community Service Organizations,

Family Planning, Food/Clothing Distribution, People with Disabilities, Substance Abuse, Youth Organizations

Grant Types: general support

Geographic Distribution: focus on TX

GIVING OFFICERS
Robert A. Higley: secy, treas

John M. O'Quinn: pres *B* 1941 *ED* Univ Houston BS 1965; Univ Houston JD 1967; Rice Univ *CURR EMPL* ptnr: OQuinn Kerensky & McAninch *NONPR AFFIL* mem: St Bar TX

Chris B. Parsons: vp

APPLICATION INFORMATION
Initial Approach: The foundation has no formal grant application procedure or application form. There are no deadlines.

GRANTS ANALYSIS
Total Grants: $3,623,276

Number of Grants: 40

Highest Grant: $1,700,000

Typical Range: $100 to $500,000

Disclosure Period: 1993

Note: Recent grants are derived from a 1993 Form 990.

RECENT GRANTS

General

1,700,000	University of Houston Law Foundation, Houston, TX — for general support
1,162,000	University of Houston Law Foundation, Houston, TX — for general support
500,000	University of Houston, Houston, TX — for general support
25,000	Be An Angel Fund, Houston, TX — for general support
25,000	Save Our Schools, Houston, TX — for general support

Overlake Foundation

CONTACT
Donald J. Malouf
Vice President
Overlake Fdn.
700 Preston Commons W.
8117 Preston Rd.
Dallas, TX 75225
(214) 750-0722

FINANCIAL SUMMARY
Recent Giving: $216,684 (fiscal 1993); $206,422 (fiscal 1992); $204,300 (fiscal 1991)

Assets: $4,571,206 (fiscal 1993); $4,471,619 (fiscal 1992); $3,961,156 (fiscal 1991)

EIN: 75-1793068

CONTRIBUTIONS SUMMARY
Donor(s): Mary Alice Fitzpatrick

Typical Recipients: • *Arts & Humanities:* Historic Preservation, History & Archaeol-

ogy, Libraries, Museums/Galleries, Music, Public Broadcasting, Theater • *Civic & Public Affairs:* Clubs, Community Foundations, General, Nonprofit Management, Parades/Festivals, Professional & Trade Associations, Women's Affairs, Zoos/Aquariums • *Education:* Agricultural Education, Arts/Humanities Education, Colleges & Universities, Education Funds, Medical Education, Secondary Education (Private), Student Aid • *Health:* Cancer, Children's Health/Hospitals, Emergency/Ambulance Services, Health Funds, Hospices, Hospitals, Medical Rehabilitation, Medical Research, Single-Disease Health Associations • *Religion:* Churches, Religious Organizations, Religious Welfare • *Science:* Scientific Labs • *Social Services:* Animal Protection, At-Risk Youth, Camps, Child Welfare, Community Service Organizations, Counseling, Domestic Violence, Sexual Abuse, Shelters/Homelessness, Substance Abuse, Youth Organizations

Grant Types: general support

Geographic Distribution: focus on TX

GIVING OFFICERS
Michael Scott Anderson: dir

Steven C. Anderson: dir

Rayford L. Keller: pres, dir *PHIL AFFIL* secy, treas: South Texas Charitable Foundation

Thomas L. Keller: vp, treas

Donald J. Malouf: vp, secy, dir

APPLICATION INFORMATION
Initial Approach: The foundation has no formal grant application procedure or application form.

GRANTS ANALYSIS
Total Grants: $216,684

Number of Grants: 37

Highest Grant: $30,000

Typical Range: $1,000 to $10,000

Disclosure Period: fiscal year ending November 30, 1993

Note: Recent grants are derived from a fiscal 1993 Form 990.

RECENT GRANTS

Library

1,000	Degolyer Library, Dallas, TX

General

30,000	Texas Agricultural Experiment Station, College Station, TX
20,000	Our Lady of Victory Cathedral, Victoria, TX
16,000	Palmer Drug Abuse Program, Victoria, TX
10,400	Hope of South Texas, Victoria, TX
10,000	American Social Health Association, Research Triangle Park, NC

Owsley Foundation, Alvin and Lucy

CONTACT
Alvin Owsley, Jr.
Trustee
Alvin and Lucy Owsley Fdn.
3000 One Shell Plz.
Houston, TX 77002
(713) 229-1234

FINANCIAL SUMMARY
Recent Giving: $158,799 (1993); $194,555 (1991); $144,737 (1990)

Assets: $4,474,381 (1993); $5,058,184 (1991); $3,722,396 (1990)

EIN: 75-6047221

CONTRIBUTIONS SUMMARY
Donor(s): the late Alvin M. Owsley, Lucy B. Owsley

Typical Recipients: • *Arts & Humanities:* Ballet, Community Arts, Dance, Historic Preservation, Libraries, Museums/Galleries, Music, Opera, Theater • *Civic & Public Affairs:* Clubs, General, Municipalities/Towns, Urban & Community Affairs • *Education:* Colleges & Universities, Medical Education, Private Education (Precollege), Public Education (Precollege) • *Environment:* General • *Health:* Cancer, Children's Health/Hospitals, Clinics/Medical Centers, Hospitals, Medical Research, Mental Health, Single-Disease Health Associations • *Religion:* Churches, Missionary Activities (Domestic), Religious Welfare • *Science:* Science Museums, Scientific Centers & Institutes • *Social Services:* Animal Protection, Child Welfare, Community Service Organizations, Family Planning, Family Services, Volunteer Services, Youth Organizations

Grant Types: capital, emergency, general support, multiyear/continuing support, operating expenses, scholarship, and seed money

Geographic Distribution: limited to TX

GIVING OFFICERS
Wendy Garrett: trust

Alvin Mansfield Owsley, Jr.: mgr, trust *B* Dallas TX 1926 *ED* Princeton Univ AB 1949; Univ TX JD, LLB 1952 *CURR EMPL* chmn: Ball Corp *NONPR AFFIL* fellow: Am Coll Trial Lawyers, Houston Bar Assn Fdn; mem: Am Bar Assn, Houston Bar Assn, Phi Delta Phi, Soc Mayflower Descendants, TX Bar Assn; mem bd visitors: M D Anderson Cancer Ctr *CLUB AFFIL* Houston CC, Leland CC, Tejas

David Thomas Owsley: trust *B* Dallas TX 1929 *ED* Harvard Univ AB 1951; NY Univ MFA 1964

APPLICATION INFORMATION
Initial Approach: Send brief letter of inquiry and full proposal. Board meets in March, June, September, and December. Decisions are made within two months.

Restrictions on Giving: Does not support individuals or provide loans.

GRANTS ANALYSIS
Total Grants: $158,799

Number of Grants: 58

Highest Grant: $29,989

Typical Range: $500 to $22,000

Disclosure Period: 1993

Note: Recent grants are derived from a 1993 Form 990.

RECENT GRANTS
General

22,000	St. John's School, Houston, TX — public educational
11,880	Planned Parenthood Houston, Houston, TX — public civic
10,000	Child Advocates, Houston, TX — public civic
10,000	University of Texas Cancer Foundation, Houston, TX — public scientific
6,500	Earth Promise, Glen Rose, TX — public civic

Panhandle Eastern Corporation

Revenue: $4.58 billion
Employees: 5,000
Headquarters: Houston, TX
SIC Major Group: Holding Companies Nec, Bituminous Coal & Lignite—Surface, Bituminous Coal—Underground, and Natural Gas Liquids

CONTACT
Marla Bernard
Manager, Community Relations
Panhandle Eastern Corporation
5400 Westheimer Ct.
Houston, TX 77056-5310
(713) 627-4078

FINANCIAL SUMMARY
Recent Giving: $2,400,000 (1995 est.); $2,200,000 (1994 approx.); $2,200,000 (1993)

Fiscal Note: All contributions are made directly by the company and its subsidiaries. Above figures exclude nonmonetary support.

CONTRIBUTIONS SUMMARY
Typical Recipients: • *Arts & Humanities:* Arts Associations & Councils, Arts Centers, Libraries, Museums/Galleries, Music, Opera, Performing Arts • *Civic & Public Affairs:* Economic Policy, Employment/Job Training, Urban & Community Affairs, Zoos/Aquariums • *Education:* Business Education, Colleges & Universities, Economic Education, Education Funds, Elementary Education (Private), Engineering/Technological Education, Minority Education, Private Education (Precollege), Public Education (Precollege), Science/Mathematics Education • *Health:* Hospitals, Medical Research • *Social Services:* Child Welfare, Community Service Organizations, Recreation & Athletics, Senior Services, Shelters/Homelessness, Substance Abuse, United Funds/United Ways, Volunteer Services

Grant Types: capital, employee matching gifts, endowment, fellowship, general support, professorship, and research

Note: Company matches dollar-for-dollar employee gifts to education, arts and culture, hospitals, and health-related research.

Nonmonetary Support: $150,000 (1992); $60,000 (1990); $978,358 (1987)

Nonmonetary Support Types: donated equipment, in-kind services, loaned employees, and loaned executives

Geographic Distribution: primarily in Houston metropolitan area

Operating Locations: AR, CT, DC, IL, IN, KY, LA, MA (Boston), MS, NJ (Hanover, Lambertville), NY (New York), OH, RI, TN, TX (Houston)

CORP. OFFICERS
Paul M. Anderson: *B* 1945 *ED* Univ WA BSME 1967; Stanford Univ Grad Sch Bus Admin MBA 1969 *CURR EMPL* ceo, dir: Panhandle Eastern Corp *CORP AFFIL* dir: Centana Energy Corp, Pan Svc Co, Panhandle Eastern Pipe Line Co, Source Cogeneration Co Inc, Trunkline Gas Co, TX Eastern Transmission Corp

James W. Hart, Jr.: *CURR EMPL* vp pub aff: Panhandle Eastern Corp

Dennis Ralph Hendrix: *B* Selmer TN 1940 *ED* Univ TN BS 1962; GA St Univ MBA 1967 *CURR EMPL* chmn, pres, ceo: Panhandle Eastern Corp *CORP AFFIL* dir: TX Commerce Bancshares Inc *NONPR AFFIL* chmn: Harris County Childrens Protective Svcs Fund; dir: Am Gas Assn, Am Petroleum Inst, Counc Higher Ed, DePelchin Childrens Ctr, Greater Houston Partnership, Jr Achievement, Mus Fine Arts, Natl Assn Mfrs, Natl Ocean Indus Assn, TX Med Ctr, Un Way TX Gulf Coast, Univ TN Devel Counc, Welch Fdn; mem: GA St Univ Bus Sch Adv Bd, Interstate Natural Gas Assn Am, Natl Petroleum Counc, TX Dept Corrections; trust: Brescia Coll *CLUB AFFIL* Burning Tree, Castle Pines GC, Eldorado CC, Forum, Houston Ctr, Ramada, River Oaks CC

GIVING OFFICERS
Marla Barnard: *CURR EMPL* mgr commun rels: Panhandle Eastern Corp

APPLICATION INFORMATION
Initial Approach: *Initial Contact:* brief letter or proposal *Include Information On:* organization's goals and purpose, project and purpose for which funds are being requested, proposed budget for the project, any benefits the company will receive as a contributor, a list of board of directors, a financial statement and/or annual report, a list of other organizations contributing, and any other pertinent or helpful information *Deadlines:* October 1

OTHER THINGS TO KNOW
Texas Eastern Corporation and its giving program were acquired by Panhandle Eastern Corporation in 1989. Texas Eastern is now a subsidiary of Panhandle Eastern.

GRANTS ANALYSIS
Total Grants: $2,355,629*

Typical Range: $1,000 to $10,000

Disclosure Period: 1992

Note: Total grants figure includes $300,000 in employee matching gifts and $150,000 donated from individual field locations.

Pennzoil Co.

Revenue: $2.56 billion
Employees: 11,694
Headquarters: Houston, TX
SIC Major Group: Petroleum Refining, Crude Petroleum & Natural Gas, Chemical & Fertilizer Mining Nec, and Patent Owners & Lessors

CONTACT
Barb Tambakakis
Coordinator, Contributions
Pennzoil Co.
PO Box 2967
Houston, TX 77252
(713) 546-8590

FINANCIAL SUMMARY
Recent Giving: $2,750,000 (1995 est.); $3,000,000 (1994 approx.); $3,000,000 (1992 approx.)

Fiscal Note: Company gives directly.

CONTRIBUTIONS SUMMARY
Typical Recipients: • *Arts & Humanities:* Arts Associations & Councils, Arts Centers, Arts Festivals, Community Arts, Dance, Historic Preservation, Libraries, Museums/Galleries, Music, Opera, Performing Arts, Public Broadcasting, Theater • *Civic & Public Affairs:* Public Policy, Safety, Urban & Community Affairs, Zoos/Aquariums • *Education:* Business Education, Colleges & Universities, Engineering/Technological Education, Science/Mathematics Education, Student Aid • *Health:* Emergency/Ambulance Services, Health Organizations, Hospices, Hospitals, Medical Rehabilitation, Medical Research, Single-Disease Health Associations • *Social Services:* Child Welfare, Community Service Organizations, Delinquency & Criminal Rehabilitation, Emergency Relief, People with Disabilities, Shelters/Homelessness, Substance Abuse, United Funds/United Ways, Youth Organizations

Grant Types: employee matching gifts, general support, and research

Note: Employee matching gift ratio: 3 to 1, for gifts to education. Employee matching gift ratio: 1 to 1, for gifts to cultural and health organizations.

Geographic Distribution: primary consideration given at local level to communities in which company has plants, warehouses, or refineries; rarely gives to national or international organizations

Operating Locations: LA (Shreveport), PA (Bradford, Butler, Oil City, Pittsburgh), TX (Houston)

CORP. OFFICERS
Robert G. Harper: *CURR EMPL* vp pub aff: Pennzoil Co

James Leonard Pate: *B* Mt Sterling IL 1935 *ED* Monmouth Coll BA 1963; Univ IN MBA 1967 *CURR EMPL* chmn, pres, ceo: Pennzoil Co *CORP AFFIL* dir: Heritage Merchandising Co Inc, Jiffy Lube Intl Inc; pres, ceo, dir: Pennzoil Products Co; pres, dir: Richland Devel Corp *NONPR AFFIL* bd govs: Rice Univ; dir: Am Petroleum Inst, Natl Petroleum Counc; fellow: Royal Econ Soc; mem: Am Econ Assn, Natl Assn Bus Econ, Pi Gamma Mu, Senate Monmouth Coll, Soc Social Political Sci

James W. Shaddix: *B* Lubbock TX 1946 *ED* Univ TX 1968; Univ TX Law Sch 1971 *CURR EMPL* gen couns: Pennzoil Co *CORP AFFIL* vp, dir: Richland Devel Corp

GIVING OFFICERS

David P. Alderson II: mem contributions comm *B* Wilmington DE 1949 *ED* Dartmouth Coll BA 1972; Univ PA Wharton Sch MBA 1978 *CURR EMPL* group vp fin, treas: Pennzoil Co *CORP AFFIL* treas: Heritage Merchandising Co Inc; treas, dir: Jiffy-Lube Intl Inc, Richland Devel Corp, Vermejo Park Corp; vp, treas: Atlas Processing Co; vp, treas, dir: Pennzoil Products Co

Thomas Hamilton: mem contributions comm *B* 1943 *CURR EMPL* group vp oil & gas: Pennzoil Co

Terry Hemeyer: *B* Cleveland OH 1938 *ED* OH St Univ BS 1960; Univ Denver MA 1969; Rice Univ 1981; Stanford Univ 1985 *CURR EMPL* group vp admin: Pennzoil Co *CORP AFFIL* vp, dir: Vermejo Park Corp *NONPR AFFIL* assoc chmn: Am Cancer Soc S TX; dir: KUHT-TV; life mem: Retired Offs Assn; mem: Disabled Vets Assn

Mark A. Malinski: mem contributions comm *B* Chicago IL 1955 *ED* Northern AZ Univ 1977 *CURR EMPL* group vp, contr: Pennzoil Co *CORP AFFIL* contr, dir: Richland Devel Corp; pres, dir: Strategic Info Svcs Co

James W. Shaddix: mem contributions comm *CURR EMPL* gen couns: Pennzoil Co (see above)

Barb Tambakakis: *CURR EMPL* contributions coordinator: Pennzoil Co

Richard A. Valentine: *CURR EMPL* group vp motor oil & automotive products: Pennzoil Co

APPLICATION INFORMATION

Initial Approach: *Initial Contact:* brief letter; no telephone inquiries will be accepted *Include Information On:* description of the organization, amount requested, purpose for which funds are sought, recently audited financial statement, copy of 501(c)(3) statement *Deadlines:* before Fall, when budget is completed; proposals received after the budgeting process are not likely to be considered until the following year

Restrictions on Giving: Company generally does not support strictly sectarian or denomi-

national religious activities, secondary schools, veterans or fraternal organizations, individual testimonial dinners, donations that are not tax-deductible, charitable advertising, or donations of products.

GRANTS ANALYSIS

Total Grants: $3,000,000*

Disclosure Period: 1994

Note: Total grants figure is an approximation.

Peterson Foundation, Hal and Charlie

CONTACT
John Mosty
Secretary-Treasurer
Hal and Charlie Peterson Fdn.
741 Water St., Ste. 210
Kerrville, TX 78028
(210) 896-2262

FINANCIAL SUMMARY

Recent Giving: $1,162,051 (1993)

Assets: $41,607,135 (1993)

Gifts Received: $161,902 (1993)

Fiscal Note: In 1993, substantial contributors were the Ralph Fawcett Estate and the Gladys Fawcett Estate.

EIN: 74-1109626

CONTRIBUTIONS SUMMARY

Typical Recipients: • *Arts & Humanities:* Arts Associations & Councils, General, Historic Preservation, History & Archaeology, Libraries • *Civic & Public Affairs:* Clubs, Housing, Safety • *Education:* Agricultural Education, Colleges & Universities, Preschool Education, Public Education (Precollege) • *Environment:* General, Resource Conservation • *Health:* Cancer, Emergency/Ambulance Services, Hospitals • *Religion:* Religious Welfare • *Social Services:* At-Risk Youth, Community Service Organizations, Day Care, Recreation & Athletics, Scouts, Senior Services, United Funds/United Ways, YMCA/YWCA/YMHA/YWHA, Youth Organizations

Grant Types: general support

Geographic Distribution: focus on TX

GIVING OFFICERS
W. H. Cowden, Jr.: vp

Charles H. Johnston: dir

Nowlin McBryde: dir

John Mosty: secy, treas

Scott Parker: pres

C. D. Peterson: dir

James Stehling: dir

APPLICATION INFORMATION

Initial Approach: Send a brief letter of inquiry. Include a description of organization, amount requested, purpose of funds sought, recently audited financial statement, and proof of tax-exempt status.

GRANTS ANALYSIS

Total Grants: $1,162,051

Number of Grants: 37

Highest Grant: $311,760

Typical Range: $1,000 to $166,177

Disclosure Period: 1993

Note: Recent grants are derived from a 1993 Form 990. Number of grants and typical range do not include a refund of $76,000 and a matching grant of $33,000.

RECENT GRANTS
Library

7,656	Real County, Leakey, TX — assist library in establishing a branch in Camp Wood
5,000	Kerrville Independent School District, Kerrville, TX — replacement of water-damaged books at Starkey Elementary School Library

General

311,760	City of Kerrville, Kerrville, TX — fund purchase of four ambulances for fire department's newly established Emergency Medical Services Unit
166,177	Kerrville Independent School District, Kerrville, TX — funding of various programs for each of the district's schools
135,000	Schreiner College, Kerrville, TX — funding of nursing program and Senior Vice President's position
76,500	Tivy Athletic Booster Club, Kerrville, TX — funding for construction of new bleachers at Tivy High School Baseball Field
51,500	Hill Country Crisis Council, Kerrville, TX — funds to the children's program, construction of counseling house, and shelter repair

---

Pineywoods Foundation

CONTACT
Bob Bowman
Secretary, Trustee
Pineywoods Fdn.
515 S First St.
Lufkin, TX 75901
(409) 634-7444

FINANCIAL SUMMARY

Recent Giving: $40,816 (1993); $171,008 (1992); $95,737 (1991)

Assets: $2,157,456 (1992); $2,108,813 (1991); $1,942,387 (1990)

Gifts Received: $89,944 (1992)

EIN: 75-1922533

CONTRIBUTIONS SUMMARY

Donor(s): The Southland Foundation

Typical Recipients: • *Arts & Humanities:* Community Arts, History & Archaeology, Libraries, Museums/Galleries, Theater • *Civic & Public Affairs:* African American Affairs, Economic Development, Employment/Job Training, General, Law & Justice, Municipalities/Towns, Urban & Community Affairs • *Education:* Colleges & Universities, Education Associations, Minority Education, Public Education (Precollege), Student Aid • *Environment:* General • *Health:* Cancer, Health Organizations, Hospices, Hospitals • *Social Services:* Community Service Organizations, Family Services, Senior Services, Substance Abuse, United Funds/United Ways, Youth Organizations

Grant Types: capital, general support, project, and seed money

Geographic Distribution: focus on TX

GIVING OFFICERS

John Firth Anderson: chmn, trust *B* Saginaw MI 1928 *ED* MI St Univ BA 1949; Univ IL MS 1950 *CURR EMPL* exec presbyter: Presbytery de Cristo *NONPR AFFIL* charter mem: Freedom Read Fdn; mem: Am Library Assn, AZ Assn County Librarians, AZ China Counc, AZ Library Assn, Beta Phi Mu, CA Library Assn, Southwestern Library Assn, World Alliance Reformed Churches *CLUB AFFIL* mem: Beta Phi Mu

Bob Bowman: secy, trust

George Henderson: treas, trust *B* Hurtsboro AL 1932 *ED* Wayne St Univ BA 1957; Wayne St Univ MA 1959; Wayne St Univ PhD 1965 *NONPR AFFIL* mem: Am Assn Higher Ed, Am Assn Univ Profs, Am Sociological Assn, Assn Black Sociologists, Assn Supervision Curriculum Devel, Delta Tau Kappa, Golden Key, Inter-Univ Seminar Armed Forces Soc, Intl Soc Law Enforcement Criminal Justice Instructors, Kappa Alpha Psi, Natl Assn Human Rights Workers, Omicron Delta Kappa, Phi Kappa Phi; prof sociology: Univ OK

APPLICATION INFORMATION

Initial Approach: Send a brief letter of inquiry. Include a description of organization, amount requested, purpose of funds sought, recently audited financial statement, and proof of tax-exempt status. There are no deadlines.

PUBLICATIONS
Application Guidelines

GRANTS ANALYSIS
Total Grants: $40,816
Number of Grants: 11
Highest Grant: $10,000
Typical Range: $1,200 to $6,400
Disclosure Period: 1993

Note: Recent grants are derived from a 1993 Form 990.

RECENT GRANTS

Library

3,500	Newton County Library, Newton, TX — for general operations

General

10,000	Anglina County Illegal Dumping, Lufkin, TX — for general operations
6,400	City of Lufkin, Lufkin, TX — for general operations
5,000	Shelby Foundation, Center, TX — for general operations
3,029	Lufkin Independent School District, Lufkin, TX — for general operations
2,000	Deep East Texas Development, Lufkin, TX — for general operations

---

Piper Foundation, Minnie Stevens

CONTACT
Michael J. Balint
Executive Director
Minnie Stevens Piper Foundation
GPM South Tower, Ste. 200
800 NW Loop 410
San Antonio, TX 78216-5699
(210) 525-8494

FINANCIAL SUMMARY

Recent Giving: $267,650 (1993); $254,704 (1992); $257,594 (1990)

Assets: $21,284,305 (1993); $21,062,886 (1992); $19,706,366 (1990)

Gifts Received: $62,815 (1993); $10,000 (1992)

Fiscal Note: In 1993, the foundation received a gift from Save Our Schools in Austin, TX.

EIN: 74-1292695

CONTRIBUTIONS SUMMARY

Donor(s): The foundation was incorporated in 1950 by the late Randall G. Piper and the late Minnie Stevens Piper .

Typical Recipients: • *Arts & Humanities:* Arts Centers, Arts Festivals, Arts Funds, Arts Institutes, Community Arts, Historic

Preservation, Libraries, Museums/Galleries, Music, Opera, Performing Arts, Public Broadcasting, Theater • *Civic & Public Affairs:* Hispanic Affairs, Law & Justice, Nonprofit Management, Philanthropic Organizations, Professional & Trade Associations • *Education:* Arts/Humanities Education, Colleges & Universities, Community & Junior Colleges, Education Funds, Engineering/Technological Education, Faculty Development, International Studies, Legal Education, Literacy, Minority Education, Private Education (Precollege), Public Education (Precollege), Religious Education, Secondary Education (Private), Student Aid • *Health:* Health Organizations, Medical Research, Mental Health • *Religion:* Churches • *Science:* Science Exhibits & Fairs • *Social Services:* Crime Prevention, People with Disabilities, Substance Abuse, United Funds/United Ways, Youth Organizations

Grant Types: fellowship and scholarship

Geographic Distribution: focus on Texas

GIVING OFFICERS

Michael J. Balint: exec dir, secy

Leatrice F. Cleveland: vp

Martin R. Harris: treas

Carlos Otero: asst dir, asst secy-treas

Frank Slavik: dir

J. Burleson Smith: dir

Bruce Thomas: dir

John H. Wilson II: pres *B* 1927 *ED* CO Sch Mines 1944-1949 *CURR EMPL* pres, dir: Piper Petroleum Co *CORP AFFIL* prin: Wilson Exploration Co

APPLICATION INFORMATION
Initial Approach:

The foundation has no formal grant application procedure or application form.

Applications should be submitted by February 1 and July 1.

The board meets twice annually.

Restrictions on Giving: Grants are made to organizations having a nonprofit status as stated by the IRS. The foundation reports no grants are given to organizations which discriminate on the grounds of race, color, creed, or sex, or to building or endowment funds.

PUBLICATIONS

Application guidelines, program policy statement, newsletter, and occasional reports

GRANTS ANALYSIS
Total Grants: $267,650
Number of Grants: 26*
Highest Grant: $10,000*
Average Grant: $2,308*
Typical Range: $500 to $2,500
Disclosure Period: 1993

Note: Number of grants, average grant, and highest grant figures exclude $25,000 awarded to individuals for the Piper Professors Program and $182,650 awarded to individuals for the Piper Scholars Program. Recent grants are derived from a 1993 Form 990 and do not include grants made to individuals in above programs.

RECENT GRANTS

Library

2,500	Oil Information Library of Ft. Worth, Ft. Worth, TX
2,500	San Antonio Public Library Foundation, San Antonio, TX

General

2,500	Archdiocese of San Antonio Pilot Program for Deaf Children, San Antonio, TX — pilot project mainstreaming deaf students into high schools
2,500	College of St. Thomas More, Ft. Worth, TX
2,500	First Presbyterian Church, San Antonio, TX — pipe organ competition
2,500	Our Lady of Refuge School, Eagle Pass, TX — for purchase of educational books
2,500	Our Lady of the Lake University, San Antonio, TX — for doctoral program in psychology

---

Potts and Sibley Foundation

CONTACT
Robert W. Bechtel
Director and Manager
Potts and Sibley Fdn.
PO Box 8907
Midland, TX 79708
(915) 686-8636

FINANCIAL SUMMARY
Recent Giving: $70,590 (fiscal 1994); $57,000 (fiscal 1993); $67,000 (fiscal 1992)

Assets: $2,901,760 (fiscal 1994); $2,771,008 (fiscal 1993); $2,435,384 (fiscal 1992)

EIN: 75-6081070

CONTRIBUTIONS SUMMARY
Donor(s): Effie Potts Sibley Irrevocable Trust

Typical Recipients: • *Arts & Humanities:* Arts Institutes, Community Arts, Libraries, Museums/Galleries, Music • *Civic & Public Affairs:* Zoos/Aquariums • *Education:* Colleges & Universities, Community & Junior Colleges, Engineering/Technological Education, Private Education (Precollege), Science/Mathematics Education, Social Sciences Education • *Environment:* General, Resource Conservation • *Health:* Eyes/Blindness, Hospices, Hospitals, Medical Re-

search, Mental Health • *International:* International Environmental Issues • *Religion:* Churches, Religious Welfare • *Science:* Scientific Research

Grant Types: general support

Geographic Distribution: focus on TX

GIVING OFFICERS
Robert W. Bechtel: dir, mgr

Maurice Randolph Bullock: co-trust, dir *B* Colorado City TX 1913 *ED* Univ TX LLB 1936 *NONPR AFFIL* fellow: Am Bar Fdn, Am Coll Trust Estate Counc, TX Bar Fdn; mem: Am Bar Assn, Am Judicature Soc, Ft Stockton Historical Soc, Midland County Bar Assn, Pecos County Chamber Commerce, Permian Basin Petroleum Mus, Lib & Hall of Fame, Trans-Pecos Bar Assn, TX Bar Assn, TX Trial Lawyers Assn, West TX Chamber Commerce; mem exec comm: TX Law Enforcement Fdn; mem, hon trust: Southwestern Legal Fdn

D. J. Sibley: dir

APPLICATION INFORMATION
Initial Approach: Application form required. There are no deadlines.

GRANTS ANALYSIS
Total Grants: $70,590

Number of Grants: 30

Highest Grant: $5,000

Typical Range: $90 to $5,000

Disclosure Period: fiscal year ending July 31, 1994

Note: Recent grants are derived from a fiscal 1994 Form 990.

RECENT GRANTS

Library

2,000	Recording Library for the Blind, Midland, TX

General

5,000	Alpine Montessori School, Alpine, TX
5,000	University of Texas, Austin, TX — for Cecil lectures
4,000	Sibley Environmental Learning Center, Midland, TX
3,000	First United Methodist Church, Ft. Stockton, TX
3,000	Southern Methodist University School of Archaeology, Dallas, TX

Prairie Foundation

CONTACT
Benjamin L. Blake
Grants Committee Chairman
Prairie Fdn.
303 W Wall, Ste. 1901
Midland, TX 79701
(915) 683-1777

FINANCIAL SUMMARY
Recent Giving: $87,250 (1993); $173,866 (1992); $163,200 (1991)

Assets: $2,117,043 (1993); $2,021,175 (1992); $2,091,123 (1991)

EIN: 75-6012458

CONTRIBUTIONS SUMMARY
Donor(s): David Fasken Special Trust

Typical Recipients: • *Arts & Humanities:* Community Arts, Libraries, Opera, Theater • *Civic & Public Affairs:* Botanical Gardens/Parks, Clubs, Hispanic Affairs, Public Policy, Zoos/Aquariums • *Education:* General, Literacy, Private Education (Precollege) • *Environment:* Air/Water Quality, General • *Health:* Health Organizations, Hospitals, Medical Rehabilitation • *Religion:* Churches, Religious Organizations, Religious Welfare • *Science:* Scientific Labs • *Social Services:* Animal Protection, At-Risk Youth, Community Service Organizations, Domestic Violence, Homes, People with Disabilities, Scouts, Senior Services, Substance Abuse, United Funds/United Ways, Veterans, Youth Organizations

Grant Types: general support

Geographic Distribution: focus on the San Francisco, CA, area

GIVING OFFICERS
Louis A. Bartha: secy, treas
Benjamin L. Blake: dir
Norbert J. Dickman: dir
Robert T. Dickson: vp, dir
Barbara T. Fasken: dir, pres

APPLICATION INFORMATION
Initial Approach: The foundation has no formal grant application procedure or application form. There are no deadlines.

GRANTS ANALYSIS
Total Grants: $87,250

Number of Grants: 18

Highest Grant: $25,000

Typical Range: $500 to $10,000

Disclosure Period: 1993

Note: Recent grants are derived from a 1993 Form 990.

RECENT GRANTS

General

25,000	United Way of Midland, Midland, TX
10,000	Midland Memorial Foundation, Midland, TX
7,500	High Sky Children's Ranch, Midland, TX
5,000	Boy Scouts of America, San Rafael, CA
5,000	Boy Scouts of America, Midland, TX

Priddy Foundation

CONTACT

Berneice Leath
Secretary, Treasurer
Priddy Fdn.
807 8th St., Ste. 600
Wichita Falls, TX 76301
(817) 723-2127

FINANCIAL SUMMARY

Recent Giving: $321,814 (fiscal 1993); $300,000 (fiscal 1992); $282,100 (fiscal 1991)

Assets: $7,239,476 (fiscal 1993); $6,747,199 (fiscal 1992); $6,325,193 (fiscal 1991)

Gifts Received: $316,662 (fiscal 1993); $7,500 (fiscal 1991); $735,738 (fiscal 1989)

Fiscal Note: In fiscal 1993, contributions were received from Mr. and Mrs. Robert T. Priddy.

EIN: 75-6029882

CONTRIBUTIONS SUMMARY

Donor(s): the late Ashley H. Priddy, Robert T. Priddy, the late Swannanoa H. Priddy, the late Walter M. Priddy

Typical Recipients: • *Arts & Humanities:* Arts Centers, Community Arts, Historic Preservation, Libraries, Museums/Galleries, Music • *Civic & Public Affairs:* Community Foundations, Housing, Urban & Community Affairs • *Education:* Private Education (Precollege), Student Aid • *Health:* Health Organizations, Hospitals, Medical Rehabilitation • *Religion:* Churches, Ministries • *Social Services:* Big Brother/Big Sister, Child Welfare, Community Service Organizations, Counseling, Food/Clothing Distribution, People with Disabilities, Senior Services, Shelters/Homelessness, United Funds/United Ways, Volunteer Services, YMCA/YWCA/YMHA/YWHA, Youth Organizations

Grant Types: operating expenses and project

Geographic Distribution: focus on northern TX, with emphasis on Wichita Falls

GIVING OFFICERS

Jay A. Cantrell: dir

John Raymond Clymer, Jr.: dir

Mary Jo Dudley: asst secy treas, dir

Charles B. Kreutz: dir

Berneice R. Leath: secy, treas, dir

Leslie Priddy Moffitt: dir

James Montgomery: dir

Betsy Priddy: adv dir

Charles Horne Priddy: vp, dir *B* Wichita Falls KS 1937 *ED* Univ TX 1946; Harvard Univ 1948 *CURR EMPL* chmn: Magnatex Corp

Hervey Amsler Priddy: dir

Randy Priddy: adv dir

Robert T. Priddy: pres, dir

Ruby N. Priddy: dir

Louis J. Rodriguez: dir

APPLICATION INFORMATION

Initial Approach: Request application from foundation. Deadlines are April 1 and September 15. Board meets in May and November.

Restrictions on Giving: Does not support individuals.

PUBLICATIONS

Program policy statement, Application Guidelines

GRANTS ANALYSIS

Total Grants: $321,814

Number of Grants: 24

Highest Grant: $182,500

Typical Range: $2,000 to $22,500

Disclosure Period: fiscal year ending November 30, 1993

Note: Recent grants are derived from a fiscal 1993 Form 990.

RECENT GRANTS
Library

8,500	Friends of Charlotte County Library, Charlotte Court House, VA

General

182,500	Communities Foundation of Texas, Dallas, TX
22,500	Midwestern State University, Wichita Falls, TX — scholarships
10,000	Camp Fire Council of North Texas, Wichita Falls, TX
10,000	Senior Citizens Service of North Texas, Wichita Falls, TX
10,000	Trinity Ministry to the Poor, Dallas, TX

Rachal Foundation, Ed

CONTACT

Curtis D. Robert
President
Ed Rachal Fdn.
104 E Rice
Falfurrias, TX 78355
(512) 325-3422

FINANCIAL SUMMARY

Recent Giving: $2,288,595 (1993); $625,210 (1992); $670,200 (1990)

Assets: $19,307,615 (1993); $20,354,579 (1992); $12,040,550 (1990)

EIN: 74-1116595

CONTRIBUTIONS SUMMARY

Typical Recipients: • *Arts & Humanities:* Libraries • *Civic & Public Affairs:* Parades/Festivals, Safety • *Education:* Colleges & Universities, Education Funds, Engineering/Technological Education, Public Education (Precollege) • *Health:* Cancer, Emergency/Ambulance Services, Medical Research, Single-Disease Health Associations • *Religion:* Churches • *Social Services:* Emergency Relief, Recreation & Athletics, Substance Abuse

Grant Types: general support

Geographic Distribution: focus on TX

GIVING OFFICERS

John R. Blocker: asst vp

Curtis D. Robert: pres

Robert L. Walker: asst vp *PHIL AFFIL* pres: Turf Paradise Foundation

Marianne R. Warner: vp

APPLICATION INFORMATION

Initial Approach: Send brief letter of inquiry describing program or project. There are no deadlines.

GRANTS ANALYSIS

Total Grants: $2,288,595

Number of Grants: 16

Highest Grant: $900,000

Typical Range: $500 to $775,000

Disclosure Period: 1993

Note: Recent grants are derived from a 1993 Form 990.

RECENT GRANTS

General

900,000	Texas A&I University Foundation, Kingsville, TX
775,000	Texas A&M University Development Foundation, College Station, TX
200,000	Brooks County Independent School District, Falfurrias, TX
160,000	New Covenant Church, Falfurrias, TX
50,000	Muscular Dystrophy Association, Weslaco, TX

Rockwell Fund

CONTACT
Martha Vogt
Program Officer
Rockwell Fund
1360 Post Oak Blvd., Ste. 780
Houston, TX 77056
(713) 629-9022

FINANCIAL SUMMARY
Recent Giving: $3,100,000 (1995 est.); $3,042,250 (1994 approx.); $2,932,800 (1993)

Assets: $69,000,000 (1995 est.); $67,000,000 (1994 approx.); $68,632,926 (1993)

EIN: 74-6040258

CONTRIBUTIONS SUMMARY
Donor(s): The fund was established in 1931, with members of the James M. Rockwell family, Rockwell Brothers & Company, and Rockwell Lumber Company as donors.

Typical Recipients: • *Arts & Humanities:* Arts Associations & Councils, Arts Outreach, Dance, Historic Preservation, History & Archaeology, Libraries, Museums/Galleries, Music, Opera, Performing Arts, Public Broadcasting, Theater • *Civic & Public Affairs:* Botanical Gardens/Parks, Economic Development, Employment/Job Training, Zoos/Aquariums • *Education:* Colleges & Universities, Community & Junior Colleges, Education Reform, Elementary Education (Private), Environmental Education, Faculty Development, General, Legal Education, Literacy, Preschool Education, Private Education (Precollege), Religious Education, Secondary Education (Private), Special Education, Student Aid • *Environment:* General • *Health:* Cancer, Children's Health/Hospitals, Clinics/Medical Centers, Emergency/Ambulance Services, Eyes/Blindness, Health Organizations, Hospices, Hospitals, Medical Rehabilitation, Medical Research, Mental Health, Nursing Services, Prenatal Health Issues, Single-Disease Health Associations • *Religion:* Churches, Ministries, Religious Organizations, Religious Welfare • *Science:* Science Exhibits & Fairs, Science Museums • *Social Services:* Animal Protection, At-Risk Youth, Child Welfare, Community Centers, Community Service Organizations, Counseling, Day Care, Delinquency & Criminal Rehabilitation, Emergency Relief, Family Planning, Family Services, Food/Clothing Distribution, Homes, People with Disabilities, Scouts, Senior Services, Shelters/Homelessness, Substance Abuse, United Funds/United Ways, Volunteer Services, YMCA/YWCA/YMHA/YWHA, Youth Organizations

Grant Types: capital, operating expenses, and project

Geographic Distribution: Texas, primarily the Houston area; limited giving out of Houston area

GIVING OFFICERS
R. Terry Bell: pres, trust

Bennie Green: treas, trust

Mary Jo Loyd: corp secy, trust

Helen N. Sterling: vp, trust

Martha Vogt: trust

APPLICATION INFORMATION
Initial Approach:

Applicants should contact the fund to request a copy of its application data sheet and guidelines.

Applications should include the name, address, and telephone number of the organization; name of contact person; number of years organization has been in continuous operation; brief statement regarding the project; current operating budget; audited financial statement for previous year which includes fund-raising expenses and sources of income; list of board members; amount requested; whether grant will be used exclusively for public purposes; and a copy of the organization's IRS determination letter of tax-exempt status.

One month prior to each quarterly trustee meeting.

PUBLICATIONS
Application data sheet, guidelines

GRANTS ANALYSIS
Total Grants: $2,932,800

Number of Grants: 197

Highest Grant: $50,000

Average Grant: $14,887

Typical Range: $10,000 to $25,000

Disclosure Period: 1993

Note: Recent grants are derived from a 1993 grants list.

RECENT GRANTS

Library

25,000	University of Houston University Park, Houston, TX — library collections	

General

50,000	American National Red Cross, Houston, TX — disaster relief services	
50,000	Houston-Galveston Area Food Bank, Houston, TX	
50,000	South Texas College of Law, Houston, TX — capital fund drive	
50,000	St. Lukes Methodist Church Foundation, Houston, TX — capital campaign	
50,000	Texas Tech University Foundation, Lubbock, TX — Rockwell Fund professorship in plan and soil science and professorship in merchandising, environmental design and consumer economics	

SBC Communications Inc. / SBC Communications Foundation

Revenue: $10.69 billion
Employees: 58,400
Headquarters: San Antonio, TX
SIC Major Group: Holding Companies Nec and Telephone Communications Except Radiotelephone

CONTACT
Rudy Reyna
Executive Director
SBC Communications Foundation
175 E Houston, Ste. 200
San Antonio, TX 78205
(210) 351-2210

FINANCIAL SUMMARY
Recent Giving: $20,200,000 (1995 est.); $19,300,000 (1994 approx.); $17,675,000 (1993 approx.)

Assets: $47,000,000 (1993); $39,011,627 (1992); $34,300,000 (1991)

Gifts Received: $14,000,000 (1992)

Fiscal Note: Figures represent foundation giving only. In 1992, contributions were recieved from SBC Communications Inc. and its subsidiaries.

EIN: 43-1353948

CONTRIBUTIONS SUMMARY
Typical Recipients: • *Arts & Humanities:* Arts Appreciation, Arts Associations & Councils, Arts Centers, Arts Festivals, Arts Funds, Arts Institutes, Community Arts, Dance, Ethnic & Folk Arts, Historic Preservation, History & Archaeology, Libraries, Museums/Galleries, Music, Opera, Performing Arts, Public Broadcasting, Theater • *Civic & Public Affairs:* African American Affairs, Community Foundations, Economic Development, Employment/Job Training, Ethnic Organizations, General, Hispanic Affairs, Municipalities/Towns, Public Policy, Urban & Community Affairs, Zoos/Aquariums • *Education:* Arts/Humanities Education, Business Education, Colleges & Universities, Education Associations, Education Funds, Engineering/Technological Education, Faculty Development, Literacy, Medical Education, Minority Education, Public Education (Precollege), Science/Mathematics Education • *Health:* Cancer, Emergency/Ambulance Services, Hospitals, Mental Health • *Religion:* Religious Welfare • *Science:* Scientific Centers & Institutes • *Social Services:* Child Welfare, Community Centers, Community Service Organizations, Family Services, People with Disabilities, Senior Services, Shelters/Homelessness, United Funds/United Ways, Volunteer Services, Youth Organizations

Grant Types: employee matching gifts and project

Note: Employee matching gift ratio: 1 to 1 to higher education and cultural institutions. The foundation's Volunteer Involvement

Program provides grants to organizations where employees volunteer their time.

Geographic Distribution: nationally, with emphasis on corporate operating locations

Operating Locations: AR, KS, MO, OK, TX

CORP. OFFICERS
James R. Adams: *B* Jefferson TX 1939 *ED* TX A&M Univ BA 1961; Univ TX MBA 1965 *CURR EMPL* group pres: SBC Commun Inc

Donald E. Kiernan, Sr.: *ED* Boston Coll BS 1962; FL St Univ MBA 1970 *CURR EMPL* vp, cfo, treas: SBC Commun Inc

Edward E. Whitacre, Jr.: *B* Ennis TX 1941 *ED* TX Tech Univ BS 1964 *CURR EMPL* chmn, ceo: SBC Commun Inc *CORP AFFIL* dir: Anheuser-Busch Cos Inc, Burlington Northern Inc, Emerson Electric Co, May Dept Stores Co *NONPR AFFIL* bd regents: TX Tech Univ & Health Sci; mem exec bd natl counc & southern region: Boy Scouts Am

GIVING OFFICERS
James R. Adams: dir *CURR EMPL* group pres: SBC Commun Inc (see above)

Royce S. Caldwell: dir *ED* Abilene Christian Univ BBA 1961 *CURR EMPL* pres, ceo: Southwestern Bell Corp

Cassandra Colvin Carr: dir *B* Champaign IL 1944 *ED* Vanderbilt Univ BA 1966; Univ TX MA 1973 *CURR EMPL* sr vp human resources: SBC Commun Inc *CORP AFFIL* dir: Destec Energy Inc *NONPR AFFIL* commr: St Louis Regional Conv Sports Complex Authority; dir: Arch Funds Inc, Conf Bd, Fdn Womens Resources, TX Telephone Assn; mem: Fin Execs Inst, Natl Assn Corp Treas *CLUB AFFIL* Forest Hills CC, St Louis

Robert A. Dickemper: chmn *B* 1943 *ED* Southeast MO St Univ BS 1965 *CURR EMPL* sr vp corp commun: SBC Commun Inc *NONPR AFFIL* chmn: Southeast MO Univ Fdn

William E. Dreyer: dir *B* 1937 *ED* William Jewell Coll BA 1960 *CURR EMPL* sr exec vp external aff: SBC Commun Inc

James D. Ellis: dir *B* 1943 *ED* Univ IA BBA 1965; Univ MO JD 1968 *CURR EMPL* sr exec vp, gen coun: SBC Commun Inc

Charles E. Foster: dir *B* 1936 *ED* Univ OK BSME 1961; WA Univ 1967 *CURR EMPL* group pres: SBC Commun Inc

Donald E. Kiernan, Sr.: dir *CURR EMPL* vp, cfo, treas: SBC Commun Inc (see above)

Harold E. Rainbolt: vp, secy *B* Norman OK 1929 *ED* Univ OK 1951; Univ OK 1957 *CURR EMPL* chmn: BancFirst Corp *CORP AFFIL* dir: First Natl Bank, Trend Venture Corp; owner: Trencor

Rudy Reyna: exec dir

Roger W. Wohlert: vp, treas

APPLICATION INFORMATION
Initial Approach: *Initial Contact:* grant requests of a local or statewide nature should be sent to local subsidiary or division; requests of a regional or national nature should be addressed directly to the Founda-

tion's executive director *Include Information On:* proof of tax-exempt status; brief statement of history and accomplishments; statement of current objectives, including problem being addressed, program budget and amount sought; linkage of project's goals to the Foundation's priorities; timetable for implementation and description of expected results; details of fund-raising plans, including sources, amounts, and commitments; plans for sustaining activities after conclusion of foundation support; annual report or budget for organization, showing all income sources and expenditures; list of board members; list of accrediting agencies *Deadlines:* none; however, organizations are asked not to submit a proposal more than once in a 12-month period

Restrictions on Giving: Foundation does not support private foundations or organizations without tax-exempt status; organizations that practice discrimination by race, color, creed, sex, age, or national origin; hospital operating funds or capital funds; organizations supported by the United Way; individuals; political activities or organizations; religious organizations; fraternal, veterans, or labor groups when serving only their membership; or special occasion goodwill advertising and ticket or dinner purchases.

OTHER THINGS TO KNOW
Foundation states a preference for organizations that operate in corporate operating locations and in communities where a significant number of employees live; project-oriented proposals rather than requests for grants to underwrite operating or capital budgets; projects that promote citizen participation and voluntarism; projects that generate public awareness and offer opportunities to leverage contributions; projects that address human needs and whose services are provided directly rather than through intermediary organizations; and projects that develop leadership skills.

PUBLICATIONS
Contributions guidelines

GRANTS ANALYSIS
Total Grants: $17,675,000*

Number of Grants: 1,300*

Highest Grant: $500,000

Average Grant: $12,500*

Typical Range: $1,000 to $10,000

Disclosure Period: 1993

Note: Total giving includes matching gifts and contributions from the Volunteer Involvement Program. Number of grants is approximate. Average grant figure was supplied by the foundation. Recent grants are derived from a 1992 Form 990.

RECENT GRANTS
General

567,000	United Way of Texas, Houston, TX
240,000	St. Louis Science Center, St. Louis, MO
216,500	United Way of Greater, St. Louis, MO
216,500	United Way of Greater, St. Louis, MO
216,500	United Way of Greater, St. Louis, MO

Scott Foundation, William E.

CONTACT
Robert W. Decker
President
William E. Scott Fdn.
City Ctr. Two
301 Commerce St., Ste. 2400
Ft. Worth, TX 76102
(817) 336-0361

FINANCIAL SUMMARY
Recent Giving: $643,924 (fiscal 1994); $540,500 (fiscal 1993); $463,200 (fiscal 1992)

Assets: $13,075,361 (fiscal 1994); $13,188,749 (fiscal 1993); $12,628,621 (fiscal 1992)

EIN: 75-6024661

CONTRIBUTIONS SUMMARY
Donor(s): the late William E. Scott

Typical Recipients: • *Arts & Humanities:* Arts Associations & Councils, Arts Festivals, Ballet, Community Arts, Dance, Historic Preservation, Libraries, Museums/Galleries, Music, Opera, Public Broadcasting, Theater • *Civic & Public Affairs:* Clubs, Community Foundations, Nonprofit Management, Professional & Trade Associations, Safety, Zoos/Aquariums • *Education:* Colleges & Universities, Community & Junior Colleges, General, Medical Education, Private Education (Precollege), Public Education (Precollege) • *Health:* Children's Health/Hospitals, Emergency/Ambulance Services, Health Organizations, Medical Research, Prenatal Health Issues, Research/Studies Institutes, Respiratory, Single-Disease Health Associations • *International:* Foreign Arts Organizations • *Religion:* Churches, Social/Policy Issues • *Science:* Science Museums • *Social Services:* Child Welfare, Community Centers, Community Service Organizations, Delinquency & Criminal Rehabilitation, Domestic Violence, Homes, Scouts, Substance Abuse, United Funds/United Ways, Volunteer Services, YMCA/YWCA/YMHA/YWHA, Youth Organizations

Grant Types: capital, general support, and project

Geographic Distribution: limited to TX, with emphasis on the Fort Worth-Tarrant County area, and in LA, OK, and NM

GIVING OFFICERS
Robert W. Decker: pres, treas, dir

Raymond B. Kelly III: vp, secy, dir

APPLICATION INFORMATION
Initial Approach: The foundation requests applications be made in writing. There are no deadlines.

Restrictions on Giving: Limited to Texas, Louisiana, Oklahoma, or New Mexico.

PUBLICATIONS
Application Guidelines

GRANTS ANALYSIS
Total Grants: $643,924

Number of Grants: 39

Highest Grant: $150,000

Typical Range: $1,000 to $75,000

Disclosure Period: fiscal year ending May 31, 1994

Note: Recent grants are derived from a fiscal 1994 Form 990.

RECENT GRANTS

General

150,000	Ft. Worth Zoological Association, Ft. Worth, TX — for charitable purposes	
75,000	James L. West Presbyterian Special Care Center, Ft. Worth, TX — for charitable purposes	
50,000	Child Study Center, Ft. Worth, TX — for educational purposes	
40,000	Country Day School of Arlington, Arlington, TX — for charitable purposes	
25,000	Friends of Children, Ft. Worth, TX — for charitable purposes	

Scurlock Foundation

CONTACT
L. L. Blanton
President
Scurlock Fdn.
700 Louisiana, Ste. 3920
Houston, TX 77002
(713) 236-1500

FINANCIAL SUMMARY
Recent Giving: $538,454 (1993); $604,720 (1992); $545,166 (1991)

Assets: $11,794,830 (1993); $9,017,001 (1992); $8,873,597 (1991)

Gifts Received: $2,609,777 (1993); $105,968 (1992); $62,708 (1991)

Fiscal Note: In fiscal 1993, contributions were received from Scurlock Oil Company ($12,551), Lee E. Loeffler ($100,000), and Loeffler Estate ($2,497,226).

EIN: 74-1488953

CONTRIBUTIONS SUMMARY
Donor(s): the late E. C. Scurlock, Scurlock Oil Co., the late D. E. Farnsworth, the late W. C. Scurlock, I. S. Blanton

Typical Recipients: • *Arts & Humanities:* Arts Associations & Councils, Arts Outreach, Dance, Historic Preservation, Libraries, Museums/Galleries, Opera, Performing Arts • *Civic & Public Affairs:* Botanical Gardens/Parks, Clubs, Urban & Community Affairs, Women's Affairs, Zoos/Aquariums • *Education:* Arts/Humanities Education,

Colleges & Universities, Engineering/Technological Education, General, Health & Physical Education, Medical Education, Private Education (Precollege), Secondary Education (Private), Secondary Education (Public), Special Education, Student Aid • *Environment:* General, Wildlife Protection • *Health:* Cancer, Children's Health/Hospitals, Clinics/Medical Centers, Diabetes, Eyes/Blindness, Hospices, Hospitals, Medical Research, Mental Health, Single-Disease Health Associations • *Religion:* Churches, Jewish Causes, Ministries, Religious Organizations, Religious Welfare • *Social Services:* Child Welfare, Community Service Organizations, Crime Prevention, Day Care, Delinquency & Criminal Rehabilitation, Emergency Relief, People with Disabilities, United Funds/United Ways, Volunteer Services, Youth Organizations

Grant Types: capital, emergency, endowment, general support, and research

Geographic Distribution: focus on TX

GIVING OFFICERS
Eddy S. Blanton: vp, dir

Jack S. Blanton, Jr.: vp, dir *B* Houston TX 1953 *ED* Univ TX 1975 *CURR EMPL* chmn: Nicklos Drilling Co *CORP AFFIL* chmn: Nicklos Drilling Co

Laura L. Blanton: pres, dir

Kenneth Fisher: secy, treas, dir *B* Tacoma WA 1944 *ED* Univ OR BS 1968; Univ OR BFA 1969; Univ OR MFA 1971 *NONPR AFFIL* mem: Portland Art Assn

Elizabeth B. Wareing: vp, dir

APPLICATION INFORMATION
Initial Approach: Include a description of organization, amount requested, purpose of funds sought, recently audited financial statement, and proof of tax-exempt status. There are no deadlines.

Restrictions on Giving: Does not support individuals or provide loans.

GRANTS ANALYSIS
Total Grants: $538,454

Number of Grants: 136

Highest Grant: $50,000

Typical Range: $100 to $41,375

Disclosure Period: 1993

Note: Recent grants are derived from a 1993 Form 990.

RECENT GRANTS

Library

6,500	Texas University General Libraries, Austin, TX	

General

50,000	Texas Children's Hospital, Houston, TX	
41,375	Lon Morris College	
35,000	Episcopal High School, Houston, TX	
21,666	M.D. Anderson Cancer Center, Houston, TX	
20,000	Hurricane Allen St. Lucia Foundation, Houston, TX	

Semmes Foundation

CONTACT
Thomas R. Semmes
President
Semmes Fdn.
800 Navarro, Ste. 210
San Antonio, TX 78205
(512) 225-0807

FINANCIAL SUMMARY
Recent Giving: $422,025 (1993); $383,868 (1991); $380,851 (1990)

Assets: $9,634,447 (1993); $9,447,390 (1991); $8,419,661 (1990)

EIN: 74-6062264

CONTRIBUTIONS SUMMARY
Donor(s): the late Douglas R. Semmes

Typical Recipients: • *Arts & Humanities:* Arts Centers, Arts Festivals, Ethnic & Folk Arts, Libraries, Museums/Galleries, Public Broadcasting • *Civic & Public Affairs:* Community Foundations, Nonprofit Management, Philanthropic Organizations • *Education:* Colleges & Universities, Private Education (Precollege), Public Education (Precollege) • *Health:* Cancer, Children's Health/Hospitals, Heart • *Religion:* Churches, Social/Policy Issues • *Science:* Scientific Centers & Institutes • *Social Services:* Community Service Organizations, Day Care, Family Planning, Family Services, People with Disabilities, United Funds/United Ways, YMCA/YWCA/YMHA/YWHA, Youth Organizations

Grant Types: capital, conference/seminar, emergency, general support, multiyear/continuing support, operating expenses, professorship, project, research, and seed money

Geographic Distribution: focus on the San Antonio, TX, area

GIVING OFFICERS
Carol Duffell: secy, treas

John R. Hannah: dir

Lucian L. Morrison, Jr.: dir

D. R. Semmes, Jr.: dir

Julia Yates Semmes: dir

Thomas R. Semmes: pres

APPLICATION INFORMATION
Initial Approach: Include a description of organization, amount requested, purpose of funds sought, recently audited financial statement, and proof of tax-exempt status. There are no deadlines.

Restrictions on Giving: Does not support individuals or provide loans.

GRANTS ANALYSIS
Total Grants: $422,025

Number of Grants: 20

Highest Grant: $200,000

Typical Range: $250 to $100,000

Disclosure Period: 1993

Note: Recent grants are derived from a 1993 Form 990.

RECENT GRANTS

Library

20,000	San Antonio Public Library Foundation, San Antonio, TX — towards construction library
3,000	Funding Information Center, San Antonio, TX — library support
2,000	Texas State Library, Austin, TX — support for Blind Programs

General

200,000	University of Alabama, Tuscaloosa, AL — toward construction of Collections Building
100,000	Cancer Therapy and Research Center, San Antonio, TX — capital campaign
20,000	United Way of San Antonio, San Antonio, TX — general support
5,000	Bexar County Community Corrections Department, San Antonio, TX — equipment purchase
5,000	Chinquapin School, Highlands, TX — general support

Shell Oil Company / Shell Oil Company Foundation

Revenue: $21.09 billion
Employees: 22,212
Parent Company: Royal Dutch/Shell Group of Companies
Headquarters: Houston, TX
SIC Major Group: Crude Petroleum & Natural Gas, Industrial Inorganic Chemicals Nec, Synthetic Rubber, and Agricultural Chemicals Nec

CONTACT
J. N. Doherty
Senior Vice President
Shell Oil Company Foundation
2 Shell Plz.
Box 2099
Houston, TX 77252
(713) 241-4512

FINANCIAL SUMMARY
Recent Giving: $19,400,000 (fiscal 1995 est.); $17,700,000 (fiscal 1994 approx.); $24,811,367 (fiscal 1993)

Assets: $48,317,126 (fiscal 1993); $7,048,255 (fiscal 1992); $7,563,736 (fiscal 1991)

Gifts Received: $42,517,892 (fiscal 1993)

Fiscal Note: Company gives directly and through the foundation. In 1993, foundation contributions totaled $20,511,367; direct giving totaled $4,300,000. Employee matching gifts to educational institutions are included in foundation giving figure; in 1993, matching gifts totaled $2,879,427. Above figures exclude nonmonetary support. In 1993, the foundation received gifts from the Shell Oil Company and its subsidiaries.
EIN: 13-6066583

CONTRIBUTIONS SUMMARY
Typical Recipients: • *Arts & Humanities:* Arts Festivals, Ballet, Dance, Historic Preservation, Libraries, Museums/Galleries, Music, Opera, Performing Arts, Theater • *Civic & Public Affairs:* Business/Free Enterprise, Civil Rights, Economic Development, Economic Policy, Housing, Law & Justice, Public Policy, Safety, Urban & Community Affairs, Women's Affairs, Zoos/Aquariums • *Education:* Business Education, Colleges & Universities, Economic Education, Education Associations, Education Reform, Elementary Education (Private), Engineering/Technological Education, Faculty Development, International Studies, Journalism/Media Education, Legal Education, Medical Education, Minority Education, Private Education (Precollege), Public Education (Precollege), Science/Mathematics Education, Student Aid • *Environment:* General • *Health:* Children's Health/Hospitals, Clinics/Medical Centers, Health Funds, Health Organizations, Heart, Hospices, Hospitals, Medical Rehabilitation, Medical Research, Mental Health, Single-Disease Health Associations • *International:* International Peace & Security Issues, International Relations • *Religion:* Religious Welfare • *Science:* Science Exhibits & Fairs, Scientific Organizations • *Social Services:* Child Welfare, Community Centers, Community Service Organizations, Delinquency & Criminal Rehabilitation, Emergency Relief, Family Services, Food/Clothing Distribution, People with Disabilities, Senior Services, Shelters/Homelessness, Substance Abuse, United Funds/United Ways, Volunteer Services, Youth Organizations

Grant Types: capital, department, employee matching gifts, general support, operating expenses, project, and research

Note: Capital and project grants not made in the area of education. Matching gifts are for degree-granting educational institutions only.

Nonmonetary Support Types: loaned employees and loaned executives

Note: Value of nonmonetary support is not available. For details on company's nonmonetary giving, contact Manager, Corporate Relations.

Geographic Distribution: nationally, with emphasis on communities where Shell employees are located

Operating Locations: AK (Anchorage), AL, CA (Anaheim, Bakersfield, Huntington Beach, Los Angeles, Martinez, San Francisco), DC, FL (Ft. Lauderdale, Tampa), IL (Chicago, Oak Brook, Wood River), IN (Indianapolis), LA (Baton Rouge, Geismar, New Orleans, Norco), MA (Boston, Fall River), MD (Baltimore), MI (Detroit, Gaylord, Kalkaska, Manistee, Traverse City), MO (St. Louis), NJ (Newark, Sewaren), NM (Hobbs), NY (New York), OH (Belpre, Cleveland, Columbus, Dayton, Marietta), TX (Dallas, Houston, Midland, Odessa), WA (Anacortes, Mount Vernon, Seattle), WV (Parkersburg)

Note: Also operates internationally.

CORP. OFFICERS
Philip Joseph Carroll: *B* New Orleans LA 1937 *ED* Loyola Univ BS 1958; Tulane Univ MS 1961 *CURR EMPL* pres, ceo, dir: Shell Oil Co *NONPR AFFIL* adv counc: Tulane Univ Ctr Bioenvironmental Res; bd regents: Univ Houston; dir: Am Counc Capital Formation, Am Petroleum Inst, TX Med Ctr, Western States Petroleum Assn; mem: Gov Bus Counc Conf Bd, Natl Action Counc Minorities Engg; mem bd visitors: Univ IA Coll Bus Admin; mem conf bd: Counc Chief Admin Offs; trust: Comm Econ Devel, Fdn Bus Politics Econs, Harris County Childrens Protective Svcs Fund, Keystone Ctr *CLUB AFFIL* Tchefuncta CC, 25 Year

GIVING OFFICERS
Bruce E. Bernard: dir *B* 1946 *ED* LA St Univ BS *CURR EMPL* vp: Shell Oil Co *CORP AFFIL* principal: Smackover-Shell Ltd Partnership

J. N. Doherty: sr vp, mem exec comm, dir

Michael Howard Grasley: mem exec comm, dir *B* Barberton OH 1937 *ED* OH Univ 1958; Univ FL PhD 1963; Univ KY MS *CURR EMPL* pres: Shell Oil Co Chem Co div *NONPR AFFIL* dir: Chem Mfrs Assn; mem: Soc Chem Indus

H. R. Hutchins: secy

S. Allen Lackey: dir *B* Jackson MS 1942 *ED* Univ MS BBA 1963; Univ MS JD 1968 *CURR EMPL* vp, gen couns: Shell Oil Co

B. W. Levan: vp, dir *B* St Louis IL 1941 *ED* Southern IL Univ 1964; Univ IL 1966 *CURR EMPL* vp human resources: Shell Oil Co

James McClay Morgan: mem exec comm, dir *B* Burgettstown PA 1947 *ED* PA St Univ BS 1969; Case Western Reserve Univ MBA 1974 *CURR EMPL* pres: Shell Oil Co Shell Oil Products Div

Jere Paul Parrish: pres, chmn exec comm, dir *B* Lovington NM 1941 *ED* Univ TX BS 1965 *CURR EMPL* vp corp aff: Shell Oil Co

Fred M. Rabbe: sr admin rep *B* 1928 *CURR EMPL* owner: Rabbe Oil Co

Steven Charles Stryker: dir *B* Omaha NE 1944 *ED* Univ IA BS 1967; Northwestern Univ Grad Sch Bus Admin 1969-1970; Univ IA JD 1969; DePaul Univ 1971 *CURR EMPL* vp, gen tax couns: Shell Oil Co *CORP AFFIL* vp taxes: Shell Petroleum Inc *NONPR AFFIL* mem: Am Bar Assn, Am Inst CPAs, Am Petroleum Inst, IA Bar Assn, IA Soc CPAs, IL Soc CPAs, Tax Execs Inst, TX Bar Assn

P. G. Turberville: vp, dir *B* 1951 *ED* Aberdeen Univ MA 1972 *CURR EMPL* vp fin: Shell Oil Co

APPLICATION INFORMATION
Initial Approach: *Initial Contact:* brief letter *Include Information On:* description of structure, purpose, history, and program of organization; summary of need and use for support; detailed financial data on organization (independent audit, budget, sources of income, breakdown of expenditures by pro-

gram, administration, and fund raising); copies of forms 501(c)(3), 509(a), and 990; list of donors and level of support *Deadlines:* none; contributions are planned in advance for each calendar year

Restrictions on Giving: Foundation prefers not to contribute to capital campaigns of national organizations; endowment or development funds; special requests from colleges and universities or state or area college fundraising associations; or hospital operating expenses.

Does not support individuals, dinners or special events, fraternal organizations, goodwill advertising, political or lobbying groups, or religious organizations for sectarian purposes.

OTHER THINGS TO KNOW

Companies participating in the Shell Oil Co. Foundation include Shell Oil Co., Shell Offshore, Inc., Shell Pipe Line Corp., Shell Western E&P, Inc., Pecten Chemicals, Inc., Pecten International Co., and Pecten Middle East Services Co.

Individual employee contributions of up to $500 to colleges, universities, and private secondary schools are matched on a two-for-one basis. Amounts contributed in excess of $500 up to the maximum $2,500 limit will be matched on a dollar-for-dollar basis. Minimum gift matched is $25.

PUBLICATIONS

Pattern for Giving

GRANTS ANALYSIS

Total Grants: $17,631,940

Number of Grants: 1,002

Highest Grant: $2,100,000

Average Grant: $17,597

Typical Range: $500 to $50,000

Disclosure Period: fiscal year ending March 15, 1994

Note: Analysis is based on foundation giving only. Total grants, number of grants, and average grant exclude employee matching gifts totaling $2,879,427. Recent grants are derived from a fiscal 1993 Form 990.

RECENT GRANTS

General

2,100,000	United Way Texas Gulf Coast, Houston, TX
819,181	National Merit Scholarship Corporation, Evanston, IL
474,950	Inroads, Pittsburgh, PA
400,000	Baylor College of Medicine, Houston, TX
350,000	National Association of Secondary School Principals, Reston, VA

Smith Charitable Foundation, Clara Blackford Smith and W. Aubrey

CONTACT
Jane Ayres
Trust Officer
Clara Blackford Smith and W. Aubrey Smith
  Charitable Foundation
c/o NationsBank
300 W Main St.
Denison, TX 75020
(903) 465-2131

FINANCIAL SUMMARY
Recent Giving: $1,000,000 (fiscal 1995 est.); $927,000 (fiscal 1994 approx.); $927,008 (fiscal 1993)

Assets: $14,100,000 (fiscal 1995 est.); $14,100,000 (fiscal 1994 approx.); $14,009,935 (fiscal 1993)

EIN: 75-6314114

CONTRIBUTIONS SUMMARY
Donor(s): The foundation was established in 1985 by the late Clara Blackford Smith .

Typical Recipients: • *Arts & Humanities:* Historic Preservation, Libraries, Museums/Galleries • *Civic & Public Affairs:* Municipalities/Towns • *Education:* Colleges & Universities, Community & Junior Colleges, Medical Education, Public Education (Precollege) • *Health:* Health Funds, Hospitals, Medical Research, Nursing Services • *Religion:* Churches • *Social Services:* Child Welfare, Recreation & Athletics, United Funds/United Ways, Youth Organizations

Grant Types: capital and general support

Geographic Distribution: focus on Denison, TX

GIVING OFFICERS
Jane Ayres: chmn, trust off

Wayne E. Delaney: dir adv

Donald Harper: dir

Jack Lilley: dir

Robby Roberts: secy

H. W. Totten, Jr.: dir

APPLICATION INFORMATION
Initial Approach:

The foundation requests applicants contact the foundation for a formal application form.

The foundation has no deadline for submitting proposals.

The officers meet in January, April, July, and November each year to consider requests for funds.

GRANTS ANALYSIS
Total Grants: $1,006,572

Number of Grants: 28

Highest Grant: $400,000

Average Grant: $22,466*

Typical Range: $2,000 to $25,000

Disclosure Period: fiscal year ending June 30, 1992

Note: Average grant figure excludes the highest grant of $400,000. Recent grants are derived from a fiscal 1992 grants list.

RECENT GRANTS
General

400,000	Texoma Medical Center, Denison, TX — ICU
250,000	Texoma Medical Foundation, Denison, TX — fund drive
62,265	Grayson County College, Denison, TX — lab learning center
58,000	M.D. Anderson Cancer Center, Houston, TX
53,500	Grayson County Rehabilitation Center, Sherman, TX — computer network

Steinhagen Benevolent Trust, B. A. and Elinor

CONTACT
B. A. and Elinor Steinhagen Benevolent Trust
c/o Texas Commerce Bank
PO Box 2751
Beaumont, TX 77704
(409) 838-0234

FINANCIAL SUMMARY
Recent Giving: $167,250 (fiscal 1994); $315,659 (fiscal 1992); $151,000 (fiscal 1991)

Assets: $4,189,684 (fiscal 1994); $4,166,453 (fiscal 1992); $3,954,505 (fiscal 1991)

EIN: 74-6039544

CONTRIBUTIONS SUMMARY
Donor(s): the late B.A. Steinhagen, the late Elinor Steinhagen

Typical Recipients: • *Arts & Humanities:* Arts Associations & Councils, Community Arts, Historic Preservation, History & Archaeology, Libraries, Museums/Galleries • *Civic & Public Affairs:* Botanical Gardens/Parks, Community Foundations, Hispanic Affairs, Housing • *Education:* Business Education, Private Education (Precollege), Science/Mathematics Education • *Health:* Geriatric Health, Medical Research, Mental Health, Single-Disease Health Associations • *Religion:* Ministries, Religious Welfare • *Science:* Science Museums • *Social Services:* At-Risk Youth, Child Welfare, Community Service Organizations, Day Care, Food/Clothing Distribution, Senior Services, Sexual Abuse, Shelters/Homelessness, United Funds/United Ways, Youth Organizations

Grant Types: capital, endowment, research, and seed money

Geographic Distribution: limited to Jefferson County, TX

GIVING OFFICERS
TX Commerce Bank: trust

APPLICATION INFORMATION
Initial Approach: Application form required. Deadline is May 31.

Restrictions on Giving: Limited to Jefferson County, TX.

PUBLICATIONS
Application Guidelines

GRANTS ANALYSIS
Total Grants: $167,250

Number of Grants: 12

Highest Grant: $50,000

Typical Range: $5,000 to $30,000

Disclosure Period: fiscal year ending August 31, 1994

Note: Recent grants are derived from a fiscal 1994 Form 990.

RECENT GRANTS

General
50,000	Salvation Army, Beaumont, TX — building construction
30,000	Boys Harbor, Beaumont, TX
15,000	Habitat for Humanity, Beaumont, TX
11,000	Some Other Place, Beaumont, TX
10,607	Family Life Ministry, Beaumont, TX

Stemmons Foundation

CONTACT
Ann C. Carlisle
Secretary-Treasurer, Fdn. Mgr.
Stemmons Fdn.
PO Box 568047
Dallas, TX 75356-8047
(214) 630-6374

FINANCIAL SUMMARY
Recent Giving: $206,700 (1993); $206,961 (1991); $328,099 (1990)

Assets: $3,711,146 (1993); $3,602,258 (1991); $3,544,601 (1990)

EIN: 75-6039966

CONTRIBUTIONS SUMMARY
Typical Recipients: • *Arts & Humanities:* Arts Outreach, Community Arts, Dance, Historic Preservation, Libraries, Music, Opera, Public Broadcasting, Theater • *Civic & Public Affairs:* General • *Education:* Arts/Humanities Education, Colleges & Universities, Education Funds, General, Private Education (Precollege), Public Education (Precollege) • *Health:* Alzheimers Disease, Emergency/Ambulance Services, Hospitals, Medical Research, Nursing Services, Single-Disease Health Associations • *Religion:* Churches, Ministries, Religious Welfare • *Social Services:* Animal Protection, Community Centers, Community Service Organizations, Family Services, People with Disabilities,

YMCA/YWCA/YMHA/YWHA, Youth Organizations

Grant Types: general support and scholarship

Geographic Distribution: focus on Dallas, TX

GIVING OFFICERS
Ann C. Carlisle: secy, treas

Ann M. Roberts: vp

Allison S. Simon: pres

Heinz K. Simon: vp

Jean H. Stemmons: vp

John M. Stemmons, Sr.: vp

Ruth T. Stemmons: vp

APPLICATION INFORMATION
Initial Approach: Include a description of organization, amount requested, purpose of funds sought, recently audited financial statement, and proof of tax-exempt status. There are no deadlines.

GRANTS ANALYSIS
Total Grants: $206,700

Number of Grants: 39

Highest Grant: $50,000

Typical Range: $2,500 to $10,000

Disclosure Period: 1993

Note: Recent grants are derived from a 1993 Form 990.

RECENT GRANTS

Library
2,500	Friends of Dallas Public Library, Dallas, TX — education

General
50,000	Episcopal School of Dallas, Dallas, TX — education
10,000	Society for the Prevention of Cruelty to Animals of Texas, Dallas, TX — community
10,000	Turtle Creek Manor, Dallas, TX — community
10,000	YMCA of Metropolitan Dallas, Dallas, TX — community
7,500	Son Scape Ministries, Pagosa Springs, CO — religious

Sturgis Charitable and Educational Trust, Roy and Christine

CONTACT
Daniel J. Kelly
Trust Officer
Roy and Christine Sturgis Charitable and Educational Trust
c/o Nations Bank
P.O.Box 830241
Dallas, TX 75283
(214) 508-1965

FINANCIAL SUMMARY
Recent Giving: $2,200,000 (fiscal 1994); $1,898,000 (fiscal 1993); $1,891,000 (fiscal 1992)

Assets: $44,000,000 (fiscal 1994); $38,000,000 (fiscal 1993 est.); $37,994,358 (fiscal 1992)

Gifts Received: $317,755 (fiscal 1988); $3,888,507 (fiscal 1986)

Fiscal Note: The trust has received contributions from the estate of Christine Sturgis which is now closed.

EIN: 75-6331832

CONTRIBUTIONS SUMMARY
Donor(s): The trust was established in 1981 from the estate of Christine Sturgis . There is a Roy and Christine Sturgis Charitable and Educational Trust in Arkansas, as well as a Roy and Christine Sturgis Foundation, also in Arkansas.

Typical Recipients: • *Arts & Humanities:* Dance, Ethnic & Folk Arts, Libraries, Museums/Galleries, Music, Performing Arts • *Civic & Public Affairs:* Botanical Gardens/Parks, Housing, Legal Aid, Nonprofit Management, Urban & Community Affairs, Zoos/Aquariums • *Education:* Colleges & Universities, Elementary Education (Public), Literacy, Medical Education, Private Education (Precollege), Public Education (Precollege), Secondary Education (Public) • *Environment:* General • *Health:* Cancer, Children's Health/Hospitals, Clinics/Medical Centers, Diabetes, Health Organizations, Nursing Services, Single-Disease Health Associations • *Religion:* Ministries, Missionary Activities (Domestic), Religious Organizations, Religious Welfare • *Social Services:* At-Risk Youth, Child Welfare, Community Centers, Domestic Violence, Family Services, Food/Clothing Distribution, Substance Abuse, Volunteer Services, Youth Organizations

Grant Types: capital, project, and research

Geographic Distribution: primarily Arkansas and Texas

GIVING OFFICERS
Daniel J. Kelly: trust off *PHIL AFFIL* trust off: Hillcrest Foundation

APPLICATION INFORMATION
Initial Approach:

Potential applicants must request an application form by mail.

Application form should be filled out completely. Information that should be included with application is a copy of IRS 501(c)(3) letter; brief history of organization, its purpose and the people it serves; a one page budget outline; list of board members; and a previous audited financial statement.

Proposals must be postmarked by December 31.

Grant decision meetings are held in late April. Receipients must wait one year after final payment to reapply.

Restrictions on Giving: The trust does not fund individuals, scholarship for individuals, seminars, loans, or political organizations.

OTHER THINGS TO KNOW
Nations Bank of Texas serves as corporate trustee for the trust.

Trustees consider grant requests which do not exceed $200,000. Funding for amounts above $200,000 will be considered on very limited basis.

Charitable organizations which received a one payment grant must skip a year before applying for a new grant. Organizations which receive multiyear support cannot apply again while receiving payments and must skip a year from the date last payment is received.

The foundation designates 65% of funds for the state of Arkansas and 35% for the state of Texas and other areas.

PUBLICATIONS
Application form

GRANTS ANALYSIS
Total Grants: $1,898,000

Number of Grants: 49

Highest Grant: $575,000

Average Grant: $38,735

Typical Range: $5,000 to $75,000

Disclosure Period: fiscal year ending September 30, 1993

Note: Recent grants are derived from a fiscal 1992 Form 990.

RECENT GRANTS

Library
15,000	Central Arkansas Library System, Little Rock, AR

General
575,000	University of Arkansas-Fayetteville, Fayetteville, AR
200,000	YMCA of Metropolitan Dallas, Dallas, TX
100,000	Centers for Youth and Families, Little Rock, AR
65,000	Kingsland Public Schools, Kingsland, AR
60,000	SCAN New York Volunteer Parent Aides Association, Little Rock, AR

Sumners Foundation, Hatton W.

CONTACT
Hugh C. Akin
Executive Director
Hatton W. Sumners Foundation
325 N St. Paul St., Ste. 3210
Dallas, TX 75201-3817
(214) 220-2128

FINANCIAL SUMMARY
Recent Giving: $1,448,902 (1994); $1,706,396 (1993); $1,440,187 (1992)

Assets: $36,816,738 (1994 approx.); $35,475,184 (1993); $38,452,871 (1992)

Gifts Received: $3,000 (1994 approx.); $5,850 (1992); $5,150 (1991)

Fiscal Note: In 1992, $1,000 gifts to the foundation were made by — Steven R. Brook, San Antonio, TX; Philip J. Pfeiffer, Sr., San Antonio, TX; and Theodore G. Baroody, Houston, TX.

EIN: 75-6003490

CONTRIBUTIONS SUMMARY
Donor(s): The foundation was established in 1949 by the late Hatton W. Sumners for the teaching and science of self-government. Born near Fayetteville, TN, in 1875, Hatton Sumners had a deep conviction for the laws and principles behind the system of democratic self-government. He started his career in the office of the Dallas City Attorney, and he was admitted to the bar at the age of twenty-two. He later served two terms as Dallas County District Attorney. Sumners served as a U.S. Senator from Texas for 34 years before his retirement in 1947. Upon his death in 1962, Sumners bequested the majority of his estate to the foundation to aid in the continuation of his work and ideas. Hatton W. Sumners never married.

Typical Recipients: • *Arts & Humanities:* Libraries, Public Broadcasting • *Civic & Public Affairs:* Community Foundations, Native American Affairs, Nonprofit Management, Public Policy • *Education:* Colleges & Universities, Engineering/Technological Education, Journalism/Media Education, Legal Education, Minority Education, Religious Education, Secondary Education (Public), Social Sciences Education, Student Aid • *Health:* Medical Research, Medical Training, Mental Health • *Religion:* Religious Organizations • *Social Services:* Child Welfare, Community Service Organizations, Counseling, Delinquency & Criminal Rehabilitation, Family Services, Substance Abuse, YMCA/YWCA/YMHA/YWHA, Youth Organizations

Grant Types: conference/seminar, endowment, general support, research, and scholarship

Geographic Distribution: focus on Texas and Oklahoma

GIVING OFFICERS
Hugh C. Akin: exec dir

Gordon Russell Carpenter: trust *B* Denton TX 1920 *ED* N TX St Univ BS 1940; Georgetown Univ Law Sch 1941-1942; Southern Methodist Univ LLB 1948 *CURR EMPL* vp, sr fin planning off: InterFirst Bank Dallas *NONPR AFFIL* chmn: N TX St Univ Ed Fdn; exec secy: Southwestern Legal Fdn; fellow: TX Bar Fdn; mem: Am Bar Assn, Dallas Bar Assn, Delta Theta Phi; trust, secy, treas: Dallas Bar Fdn

Alfred P. Murrah, Jr.: vchmn, trust

William C. Pannell: secy, trust

James Cleo Thompson, Jr.: chmn, trust

Thomas Slater Walker: treas, trust

APPLICATION INFORMATION
Initial Approach:

Grant applications must be in writing but need not be formal.

Letters of application should include the full name of the organization and the date when it was founded; a brief narrative of the primary purpose and work of the organization; a list of trustees or directors and the principal administrative officer; evidence of the organization's tax-exempt status; a brief description of the specific program for which funds are requested, together with an expression of how this conforms to the foundation's purpose; a budget, or proposed budget, for the project or program; the grant amount requested; and date the funds are needed. Brief and concise applications are preferred. If any of the requested information is contained within an annual report or another document, simply refer to the document and enclose a copy.

Proposals must be received by August 1 to be considered by the trustees in October.

Applicants will be acknowledged as promptly as possible once the funding decisions are made.

Restrictions on Giving: The foundation does not make loans, grants-in-aid, scholarships, or fellowships directly to individuals. Grants for such purposes are made to selected schools, colleges, and universities, and each school administers the grant funds. The foundation is non-political and non-partisan; its funds are not to be used for political or propagandistic purposes.

GRANTS ANALYSIS
Total Grants: $1,448,902

Number of Grants: 44

Highest Grant: $395,554

Average Grant: $24,496*

Typical Range: $5,000 to $50,000

Disclosure Period: 1994

Note: Average grant figure excludes highest grant of $395,554. Recent grants are derived from a 1993 annual report.

RECENT GRANTS

Library
25,000	Oklahoma City University School of Law, Oklahoma City, OK — library fund
25,000	Schreiner College, Kerrville, TX — library acquisitions
10,000	Happy Hill Farm Academy, Granbury, TX — library acquisitions
5,500	Austin College, Sherman, TX — political science library acquisition

General
308,396	Law Focused Education, Austin, TX — teacher training institutes
300,000	Texas Wesleyan University, Ft. Worth, TX — Sumners scholarship endowment
108,000	National Center for Policy Analysis, Dallas, TX — Hatton W. Sumners distinguished lecture series
100,000	Children's Village, Tyler, TX — endowed scholarship fund

100,000   Oklahoma City University School of Law, Oklahoma City, OK — building fund

Swalm Foundation

CONTACT
Jo Beth Camp Swalm
President
Swalm Foundation
8707 Katy Fwy., Ste. 300
Houston, TX 77024
(713) 464-1321

FINANCIAL SUMMARY
Recent Giving: $1,586,692 (fiscal 1993); $187,400 (fiscal 1991); $1,125,466 (fiscal 1990)

Assets: $51,915,915 (fiscal 1993); $30,023,624 (fiscal 1991); $19,604,112 (fiscal 1990)

Gifts Received: $7,500,000 (fiscal 1993); $7,650,000 (fiscal 1991); $7,578,032 (fiscal 1990)

Fiscal Note: In 1991, contributions were received from Dave Swalm ($2,500,000), Texas Olefins Company ($2,000,000), Texas Petrochemicals Corporation ($2,500,000), and Clark Swalm ($650,000). In fiscal 1993, gifts were received from Dave Swalm, Texas Petrochemicals, and Texas Olefins Company.

EIN: 74-2073420

CONTRIBUTIONS SUMMARY
Donor(s): The foundation was established in 1980 by Dave C. Swalm, Ron Woliver, and Texas Olefins Co.

Typical Recipients: • *Arts & Humanities:* Libraries, Museums/Galleries • *Civic & Public Affairs:* Botanical Gardens/Parks, Municipalities/Towns, Safety, Urban & Community Affairs • *Education:* Colleges & Universities, Elementary Education (Private), Private Education (Precollege), Public Education (Precollege), Special Education, Student Aid • *Health:* Clinics/Medical Centers, Emergency/Ambulance Services, Hospices, Hospitals, Mental Health • *Religion:* Churches, Religious Organizations • *Social Services:* Child Welfare, Community Centers, Community Service Organizations, Family Services, Food/Clothing Distribution, People with Disabilities, Recreation & Athletics, Shelters/Homelessness, Substance Abuse, United Funds/United Ways, Youth Organizations

Grant Types: capital, emergency, endowment, general support, matching, operating expenses, and scholarship

Geographic Distribution: focus on Texas

GIVING OFFICERS
Mark C. Mendelovitz: secy, trust

Dave C. Swalm: vp, trust

Jo Beth Camp Swalm: pres, trust

APPLICATION INFORMATION
Initial Approach:

The foundation requests applications be made in writing.

The foundation has no deadline for submitting proposals.

Restrictions on Giving: The foundation only makes grants to charitable organizations.

PUBLICATIONS
Informational brochure including application guidelines

GRANTS ANALYSIS
Total Grants: $1,586,692

Number of Grants: 73

Highest Grant: $77,850

Average Grant: $21,736

Typical Range: $5,000 to $30,000

Disclosure Period: fiscal year ending November 30, 1993

Note: Recent grants are derived from a fiscal 1993 Form 990.

RECENT GRANTS
General

77,850   Wesley Community Center, Houston, TX — for the Community Center east of downtown Houston to continue to provide services to the underprivileged; and support of a capital campaign to renovate the present facility, and to build a new activities/multi-prupose building

72,993   Julia C. Hester House, Houston, TX — for support to complete a capital campaign to build a new building to house Juila C. hester House in the Fifth Ward Area; and provide expenses to teach entreprenurial skills to cildren to prevent juvenile delinquency

70,300   Child Care Services and Resource Center, Jackson, MS — for roof repairs and purchase of substructure materials for the Habitat for Humans Project; match emergency assistance funds to help indigent with basic needs; expenses of a federal/state funds-assisted day care program

60,000   Northwest Assistance Ministries, Houston, TX — for the Family Violence Program to continue services for victims of domestic abuse in Northwest Harris County; and funding to complete a capital campaign for the ministry's service center facility

60,000   Young People in Action Ministry, Jackson, MS — for operating expenses to

provide tutoring and counseling of disadvantaged youths and training and counseling for ex-offenders

Temple Foundation, T. L. L.

CONTACT
Phillip M. Leach
Executive Director
T. L. L. Temple Foundation
109 Temple Blvd.
Lufkin, TX 75901
(409) 639-5197

FINANCIAL SUMMARY
Recent Giving: $12,250,000 (fiscal 1995 est.); $13,100,000 (fiscal 1994); $12,681,972 (fiscal 1993)

Assets: $280,000,000 (fiscal 1995 est.); $277,000,000 (fiscal 1994); $277,099,599 (fiscal 1993)

Gifts Received: 100,000 (fiscal 1995 est.); $100,000 (fiscal 1994); $100,000 (fiscal 1993)

Fiscal Note: In fiscal 1990, the foundation received a contribution of $100,000 from the estate of Katherine S. Temple.

EIN: 75-6037406

CONTRIBUTIONS SUMMARY
Donor(s): In 1894, Thomas Lewis Latane Temple started a sawmill and began acquiring timberland in eastern Texas. Arthur Temple, one of his sons, eventually served as president of Temple Industries. He was later succeeded by his son, Arthur Temple, Jr.

By 1973, the Temples owned 50% of Temple Industries stock. That same year, they merged their company into Time, Inc., and in return, the Temple family received 15% of Time stock, worth over $60 million. In 1984, Time spun off Temple-Inland, a holding company of which Arthur Temple, Jr., is chairman.

The T. L. L. Temple Foundation was established in 1962 with donations from the late Georgia T. Munz and the late Katherine S. Temple .

Typical Recipients: • *Arts & Humanities:* Arts Associations & Councils, Historic Preservation, History & Archaeology, Libraries, Museums/Galleries, Music, Opera, Performing Arts, Theater • *Civic & Public Affairs:* Chambers of Commerce, Clubs, Employment/Job Training, General, Housing, Municipalities/Towns, Native American Affairs, Safety, Urban & Community Affairs • *Education:* Agricultural Education, Business Education, Colleges & Universities, Elementary Education (Private), Elementary Education (Public), Engineering/Technological Education, Medical Education, Minority Education, Private Education (Precollege), Public Education (Precollege), Science/Mathematics Education, Special Education, Student Aid • *Environment:* General, Resource Conservation • *Health:* Alzheimers Disease, Cancer, Children's Health/Hospitals, Clinics/Medical Centers, Emergency/Ambulance Services, Eyes/Blindness, Health Organizations, Hospices, Hospitals, Hospitals (University Affiliated), Kidney, Medical Rehabilitation, Medical Research, Mental Health, Transplant Networks/Donor Banks • *Religion:* Churches, Religious Organizations, Religious Welfare, Synagogues/Temples • *Social Services:* Animal Protection, Camps, Community Service Organizations, Counseling, Day Care, Delinquency & Criminal Rehabilitation, Domestic Violence, Family Planning, Family Services, Food/Clothing Distribution, People with Disabilities, Recreation & Athletics, Senior Services, Shelters/Homelessness, Special Olympics, Substance Abuse, United Funds/United Ways, Volunteer Services, Youth Organizations

Grant Types: capital, general support, project, and scholarship

Geographic Distribution: primarily to the East Texas Pine Timber Belt area

GIVING OFFICERS
Ward R. Burke: trust

Phillip M. Leach: exec dir, trust

Arthur Temple III: trust *B* 1942 *CURR EMPL* chmn, ceo: Exeter Investment Co *CORP AFFIL* chmn: First Bank & Trust E TX; dir: Temple-Inland Inc; dir, off: Demco Mfg Co *PHIL AFFIL* dir: Temple-Inland Foundation

Arthur Temple, Jr.: trust *B* Texarkana AR 1920 *ED* Univ TX 1937-1938; Williams Coll *CORP AFFIL* chmn: Exeter Investment Co, Lufkin Pineland St Bank; chmn bd: T&T Corp; dir: AMCA Intl Ltd, Austin Crest Hotel, Contractors Supplies, Great Am Restaurant Ins Co, Henley Mfg Corp, Lumbermans Investment Corp, Signal Cos, Sunbelt Ins Co, Temple-Eastex, Temple-Inland Fin Svcs, Temple-Inland Properties; dir, chmn emeritus: Temple-Inland; exec vp, dir: Temple-White Co; mem exec comm, dir: Republic Bank Corp; pres bd regents, dir: TX Southeastern RR; pres, dir: John E Gray Inst; ptnr: Dallas Cowboys *NONPR AFFIL* dir: Lumberman Merchants Assn, Natl Forest Products Assn, Natl Park Fdn, Southern Forest Products Assn, St Michael Hosp Fdn; trust: Am Forest Products Assn *CLUB AFFIL* Crown Colony CC

W. Temple Webber: trust

M. F. Zeagler: asst exec dir, contr

APPLICATION INFORMATION
Initial Approach:

Prospective applicants should send a written request to the foundation.

Applicants should furnish the following information: name, address, phone number, charter, articles of incorporation, constitution and by-laws; copy of exemption letters; names and addresses of officers and directors; brief, factual resume of the operations of the applicant; and an explanation of the request, with evidence of need.

Applicants should detail the services to be rendered and explain the benefits to members of the public. They should also include copies of present and prior year budgets and financial statements reflecting sources and amounts of receipts and disbursements, and an audit for the prior year, if available.

There are no application deadlines. The foundation board meets as case load demands.

Restrictions on Giving: The foundation gives only to governmental units, exempt under the Internal Revenue Code, or to nonprofit, charitable organizations having exempt status under Section 501(c)(3) of the Internal Revenue Code evidencing that it is such an organization and is not classified as a "Private Foundation."

No grants are made to churches, religious organizations, or other entities for the propagation of religious faith and/or practices. Grants are also not made to individuals for scholarships, research, or other purposes.

GRANTS ANALYSIS
Total Grants: $13,100,000

Number of Grants: 144

Highest Grant: $4,500,000

Average Grant: $90,972

Typical Range: $15,000 to $75,000

Disclosure Period: fiscal year ending November 30, 1994

Note: Recent grants are derived from a fiscal 1993 Form 990.

RECENT GRANTS

Library
242,600	T.L.L. Temple Memorial Library, Diboll, TX — support archives budget
68,700	Slocum Independent School District, Slocum, TX — construct school library

General
1,250,000	Diboll Independent School District, Diboll, TX — computer technology implementation
1,000,000	St. Michael's Hospital Foundation, Texarkana, AR — capital campaign
1,000,000	University of Texas Health Science Center at Houston, Houston, TX — Institute of Molecular Medicine
1,000,000	University of Texas M.D. Anderson Cancer Center, Houston, TX — capital campaign
651,900	Deep East Texas Regional MH-HR Services, Lufkin, TX — residential facilities for mentally ill

Temple-Inland Inc. / Temple-Inland Foundation

Revenue: $2.93 billion
Employees: 13,000
Headquarters: Diboll, TX
SIC Major Group: Holding Companies Nec, Sawmills & Planing Mills—General, Pulp Mills, and Paper Mills

CONTACT
James R. Wash
Secretary & Treasurer
Temple-Inland Foundation
303 S Temple Dr.
PO Box N
Diboll, TX 75941
(409) 829-1314

FINANCIAL SUMMARY
Recent Giving: $3,200,000 (fiscal 1995 est.); $3,131,646 (fiscal 1994); $3,288,556 (fiscal 1993)

Assets: $9,093,074 (fiscal 1994); $11,793,274 (fiscal 1993); $14,508,325 (fiscal 1992)

Fiscal Note: Company gives through foundation only. A subsidiary, Inland Container Corp., sponsors its own independent foundation.

EIN: 75-1977109

CONTRIBUTIONS SUMMARY
Typical Recipients: • *Arts & Humanities:* Ethnic & Folk Arts, Libraries, Museums/Galleries, Theater • *Civic & Public Affairs:* African American Affairs, Clubs, Community Foundations, Employment/Job Training, Housing, Law & Justice, Municipalities/Towns, Public Policy, Safety, Urban & Community Affairs • *Education:* Business Education, Colleges & Universities, Elementary Education (Private), Engineering/Technological Education, General, Private Education (Precollege), Public Education (Precollege), Religious Education, Secondary Education (Private), Secondary Education (Public), Vocational & Technical Education • *Environment:* Forestry, Wildlife Protection • *Health:* Children's Health/Hospitals, Clinics/Medical Centers, Health Organizations, Hospices, Hospitals • *Religion:* Religious Organizations, Religious Welfare • *Social Services:* Camps, Child Welfare, People with Disabilities, Substance Abuse, United Funds/United Ways, YMCA/YWCA/YMHA/YWHA, Youth Organizations

Grant Types: employee matching gifts, general support, and scholarship

Geographic Distribution: primarily near company headquarters

Operating Locations: AL (Monroeville), AR (Ft. Smith, West Memphis), CA (Bell, El Cajon, El Centro, Los Angeles, Newark, Ontario, Sacramento, Santa Fe Springs, Tracy), CO (Denver, Wheat Ridge), FL (Orlando), GA (Macon, Rome, Thomson), IL (Chicago), IN (Crawfordsville, Evansville, Indianapolis, Newport), KS (Garden City, Kansas City), KY (Louisville, Maysville),

LA (DeQuincy, Minden, Monroe), MO (St. Louis), MS (Hattiesburg), NJ (Edison, Spotswood), OH (Carlisle, Middletown), OK (Fletcher), PA (Biglerville, Erie, Hazleton), PR (Vega Alta), SC (Lexington, Rock Hill), TN (Elizabethton, New Johnsonville), TX (Austin, Dallas, Diboll, Edinburg, Evadale, Houston, Irving, Killeen, Orange, Temple), VA (Petersburg)

CORP. OFFICERS

Clifford J. Grum: *B* Davenport IA 1934 *ED* Austin Coll BA 1956; Univ PA Wharton Sch MBA 1958 *CURR EMPL* chmn, pres, ceo, dir: Temple-Inland Inc *CORP AFFIL* chmn, ceo, pres, dir: Temple-Inland Forest Products Corp; chmn, dir: Temple Assocs; dir: Cooper Indus Inc, Inland Container Corp, Premark Intl Inc *NONPR AFFIL* dir: TX Chamber Commerce; trust: Austin Coll, Meml Med Ctr E TX

GIVING OFFICERS

Glenn A. Chancellor: dir *B* Nacogdoches TX 1937 *ED* Stephen F Austin St Univ 1959 *CURR EMPL* vp forest group: Temple-Inland Inc *CORP AFFIL* dir: Sabine River & Northern Railroad; group vp: Temple-Inland Forest Products Corp *NONPR AFFIL* chmn: Am Pulpwood Assn

Clifford J. Grum: dir *CURR EMPL* chmn, pres, ceo, dir: Temple-Inland Inc (see above)

Kenneth M. Jastrow II: dir *B* 1947 *ED* Univ TX BA; Univ TX MBA *CURR EMPL* cfo: Temple-Inland Inc *CORP AFFIL* chmn: Sunbelt Ins Co; chmn, ceo: Temple-Inland Mortgage Corp; pres, coo, dir: Temple-Inland Fin Svcs Inc

Robert Grant Luttrell: pres, dir *B* Eagletown OK 1937 *ED* Univ TX BBA 1960; Southern Methodist Univ MBA 1981 *CURR EMPL* vp admin, dir: Temple-Inland Forest Products Corp *CORP AFFIL* pres, ceo, dir: Universal Electric Construction Co; pres, dir: Topaz Oil Co Inc; treas, dir: Big Tin Barn Inc

Harold C. Maxwell: dir *B* 1940 *ED* TX A&M Univ 1963 *CURR EMPL* group vp: Temple-Inland Inc *CORP AFFIL* group vp, dir: Temple-Inland Forest Products Corp; pres, dir: Big Tin Barn Inc

Evonne Nerren: vp

Arthur Temple III: dir *B* 1942 *CURR EMPL* chmn, ceo: Exeter Investment Co *CORP AFFIL* chmn: First Bank & Trust E TX; dir: Temple-Inland Inc; dir, off: Demco Mfg Co *PHIL AFFIL* trust: T. L. L. Temple Foundation

M. Richard Warner: vp, dir *B* Lufkin TX 1951 *ED* Baylor Univ 1974 *CURR EMPL* vp, secy, gen couns: Temple-Inland Inc *CORP AFFIL* corp secy, dir: Inland Orange Inc; dir: Temple-Inland Forest Products Corp; vp: Temple-Inland Fin Svcs Inc; vp, corp secy: Guaranty Holdings Inc I; vp, corp secy, dir: Inland Container Corp, Inland Rome Inc, Temple-Inland Realty Inc

James R. Wash: secy, treas *B* TX 1930 *ED* Sam Houston St Univ 1951 *CURR EMPL* secy: Temple-Inland Forest Products Corp *CORP AFFIL* asst secy: Temple-Inland Inc; asst treas: Big Tin Barn Inc; asst vp, asst

secy: Temple-Inland Fin Svcs Inc; secy, dir: Topaz Oil Co Inc

APPLICATION INFORMATION

Initial Approach: *Initial Contact:* brief letter *Include Information On:* description of the organization; amount requested; purpose for which funds are sought; recently audited financial statements; proof of tax-exempt status *Deadlines:* none

Restrictions on Giving: Does not provide support to individuals; fraternal or veterans organizations; political or lobbying groups; or religious organizations.

GRANTS ANALYSIS

Total Grants: $3,131,646

Number of Grants: 1,620*

Highest Grant: $256,312

Average Grant: $1,933*

Typical Range: $1,000 to $20,000

Disclosure Period: fiscal year ending June 30, 1994

Note: The number of grants and average grant figures are approximate. Recent grants are derived from a fiscal 1994 Form 990.

RECENT GRANTS

Library

24,430	T.L.L. Temple Memorial Library, Diboll, TX
10,100	Kurth Memorial Library, Lufkin, TX
10,000	J.R. Huffman Public Library, Hemphill, TX

General

256,312	Texas A&M University, College Station, TX
79,705	University of Texas Austin, Austin, TX
70,000	Jasper Memorial Hospital, Jasper, TX
62,053	City of Diboll, Diboll, TX
60,000	Habitat for Humanity, Dallas, TX

Tenneco Inc.

Revenue: $13.22 billion
Employees: 75,000
Headquarters: Houston, TX
SIC Major Group: Holding Companies Nec

CONTACT

Jo Ann Swinney
Director, Community Affairs
Tenneco Inc.
PO Box 2511
Houston, TX 77252
(713) 757-3930
Note: Jo Ann Swinney handles Houston area and national activities; all other requests are handled by the contributions coordinator at the divisional company operating most prominently in the geographhic area.

FINANCIAL SUMMARY

Recent Giving: $6,316,987 (1995 est.); $5,426,361 (1994); $5,655,696 (1993)

Assets: $350,000 (1995 est.); $415,000 (1994 approx.); $400,000 (1992)

Fiscal Note: Company gives directly. Above figures include international subsidiary giving. Above figures exclude nonmonetary support.

CONTRIBUTIONS SUMMARY

Typical Recipients: • *Arts & Humanities:* Arts Associations & Councils, Arts Centers, Arts Festivals, Arts Funds, Community Arts, Dance, Historic Preservation, Libraries, Museums/Galleries, Music, Opera, Performing Arts, Public Broadcasting, Theater, Visual Arts • *Civic & Public Affairs:* Business/Free Enterprise, Employment/Job Training, Housing, Law & Justice, Professional & Trade Associations, Public Policy, Safety, Urban & Community Affairs, Women's Affairs, Zoos/Aquariums • *Education:* Business Education, Colleges & Universities, Community & Junior Colleges, Economic Education, Education Associations, Education Funds, Engineering/Technological Education, Faculty Development, Literacy, Minority Education, Public Education (Precollege), Science/Mathematics Education, Student Aid • *Environment:* General • *Health:* Emergency/Ambulance Services, Health Organizations, Hospices, Hospitals, Medical Research, Mental Health, Nutrition, Single-Disease Health Associations • *Science:* Science Exhibits & Fairs • *Social Services:* Animal Protection, Community Centers, Community Service Organizations, Delinquency & Criminal Rehabilitation, Emergency Relief, Food/Clothing Distribution, People with Disabilities, Senior Services, Shelters/Homelessness, Substance Abuse, United Funds/United Ways, Volunteer Services, Youth Organizations

Grant Types: capital, employee matching gifts, endowment, fellowship, general support, and multiyear/continuing support

Note: Employee matching gift ratio: 1 to 1.

Nonmonetary Support: $200,000 (1994); $400,000 (1993); $350,000 (1992)

Nonmonetary Support Types: donated equipment, donated products, in-kind services, and loaned executives

Note: The contact person for nonmonetary support is Jo Ann Swinney.

Geographic Distribution: near operating locations; limited nationally

Operating Locations: CT (Hartford), GA (Cartersville), IL (Chicago, Deerfield, Evanston, Lincolnshire, Wheeling), IN (Blufton), KS (Wichita), LA (Lafayette, Westwego), MI (Monroe), NC (Arden), ND (Fargo, Valley City), NJ (Norwood, Old Tappon, Orange), OH (Perry), OK (Pryor), PA (Pittsburgh, Springfield), TN (Counce, Greeneville, Knoxville, Nashville), TX (Houston), VA (Charlottesville, Newport News), WA (Brookfield), WI (Racine, Wausau)

CORP. OFFICERS

Arthur H. House: *CURR EMPL* sr vp corp aff: Tenneco Inc

Dana George Mead: *B* Cresco IA 1936 *ED* US Military Acad BS 1957; MA Inst Tech

PhD 1967 *CURR EMPL* chmn, ceo: Tenneco Inc *CORP AFFIL* chmn: Case Corp, Tenneco InterAmerica Inc; dir: Alco Standard Corp, Baker Hughes Inc, Cummins Engine Co Inc, Natl Westminster Bancorp, Natl Westminster Bank USA *NONPR AFFIL* dir: Natl Assn Mfrs; mem: Am Soc Corp Execs, Counc Foreign Rels, Pres Comm White House Fellowships, W Point Soc, White House Fellows Assn & Fdn; trust: Assn Grads W Point *CLUB AFFIL* Houston Racquet, Houstonian, Metro, Univ

Ethel Samuels: *CURR EMPL* contributions coordinator: Tenneco Inc

GIVING OFFICERS

Ethel Samuels: *CURR EMPL* contributions coordinator: Tenneco Inc (see above)

Jo Ann Swinney: *CURR EMPL* dir commun aff: Tenneco Inc

APPLICATION INFORMATION

Initial Approach: *Initial Contact:* brief letter or proposal on organization's letterhead to contributions coordinator at divisional company operating most prominently in the geographic area; for Houston area and national activities, send brief letter or proposal to Jo Ann Swinney *Include Information On:* description of the organization, amount requested, purpose for which funds are sought, proof of tax-exempt status, financial report, board of directors, and budget for project *Deadlines:* August 15

Restrictions on Giving: Company does not give to political or lobbying groups; religious organizations; or individuals

OTHER THINGS TO KNOW

Each operating location administers its own contributions program. Together these local programs account for around 50% of overall Tenneco giving.

Tenneco has considered reactivating the Tenneco Foundation for educational/scholarship purposes.

GRANTS ANALYSIS

Total Grants: $5,426,361

Typical Range: $1,000 to $10,000

Disclosure Period: 1994

Note: Recent grants are derived from a 1992 grants list.

RECENT GRANTS

General
250,000   Houston Host Committee Fund, Houston, TX — for construction cost inside the Astrodome for GOP national convention

Texas Commerce Bank-Houston, N.A. / Texas Commerce Bank Foundation, Inc.

Employees: 9,500
Parent Company: Texas Commerce Bancshares, Inc. (subs. Chemical Banking Corporation)
Headquarters: Houston, TX
SIC Major Group: State Commercial Banks

CONTACT
Belinda Griffin
Secretary, Manager, Community Relations
Texas Commerce Bank-Houston, N.A.
PO Box 2558
Houston, TX 77252-8050
(713) 216-4004

FINANCIAL SUMMARY
Recent Giving: $1,500,000 (1995 est.); $1,500,000 (1994 approx.); $1,247,636 (1993)

Assets: $1,500,000 (1995 est.); $1,500,000 (1994 approx.); $647,230 (1993)

Gifts Received: $1,168,731 (1993); $1,176,000 (1992); $1,023,781 (1991)

Fiscal Note: Total includes contributions by subsidiaries. Company gives primarily through the foundation, and reports that the budget for direct giving programs is $40,000. Above figures exclude nonmonetary support. In 1993, the foundation received $1,168,731 from Texas Commerce Bank.

EIN: 74-6036696

CONTRIBUTIONS SUMMARY
Typical Recipients: • *Arts & Humanities:* Arts Associations & Councils, Arts Centers, Arts Funds, Ballet, Community Arts, Historic Preservation, Libraries, Museums/Galleries, Music, Opera, Performing Arts, Public Broadcasting, Theater • *Civic & Public Affairs:* African American Affairs, Botanical Gardens/Parks, Economic Development, Economic Policy, Employment/Job Training, General, Housing, Municipalities/Towns, Nonprofit Management, Women's Affairs, Zoos/Aquariums • *Education:* Business Education, Colleges & Universities, Education Funds, Literacy, Medical Education, Minority Education • *Environment:* Resource Conservation • *Health:* Cancer, Children's Health/Hospitals, Clinics/Medical Centers, Diabetes, Health Organizations, Heart, Hospices, Hospitals, Medical Research, Medical Training, Mental Health, Prenatal Health Issues, Single-Disease Health Associations • *Religion:* Jewish Causes, Ministries • *Science:* Science Exhibits & Fairs • *Social Services:* Child Welfare, Community Service Organizations, Delinquency & Criminal Rehabilitation, Family Planning, Food/Clothing Distribution, Homes, People with Disabilities, Recreation & Athletics, Senior Services, Shelters/Homelessness, Substance Abuse, United Funds/United Ways, Volunteer Services, Youth Organizations

Grant Types: capital, employee matching gifts, general support, professorship, and project
Note: General Support for non-United Way agencies only.

Nonmonetary Support Types: donated equipment, in-kind services, loaned employees, and workplace solicitation
Note: Value of noncash support is unavailable and is not included in figures above. Please contact Belinda Griffin, VP, Manager of Community Relations.

Geographic Distribution: limited to Houston, TX

Operating Locations: TX (Houston)

CORP. OFFICERS
Alan R. Buckwalter III: *B* 1947 *ED* Fairleigh Dickinson Univ 1970 *CURR EMPL* vchmn, dir: TX Commerce Bank NA *CORP AFFIL* vchmn, dir: TX Commerce Bancshares Inc

Walter Buckwalter: *CURR EMPL* vchmn: TX Commerce Bank Houston

Belinda Griffin: *CURR EMPL* mgr commun rels: TX Commerce Bank NA

Beverly H. McCaskill: *CURR EMPL* secy: TX Commerce Bank NA

Marc J. Shapiro: *B* Houston TX 1947 *ED* Harvard Univ 1969; Stanford Univ 1971 *CURR EMPL* chmn, pres, ceo: TX Commerce Bank Houston *PHIL AFFIL* trust: Pauline Sterne Wolff Memorial Foundation

GIVING OFFICERS
Alan R. Buckwalter III: pres *CURR EMPL* vchmn, dir: TX Commerce Bank NA (see above)

Belinda Griffin: secy *CURR EMPL* mgr commun rels: TX Commerce Bank NA (see above)

Beverly H. McCaskill: vp, treas *CURR EMPL* secy: TX Commerce Bank NA (see above)

Edward N. Robinson: dir *B* Savannah GA 1945 *ED* Univ MI 1967; NY Univ 1974 *CURR EMPL* exec vp: TX Commerce Bancshares Inc

Marc J. Shapiro: trust *CURR EMPL* chmn, pres, ceo: TX Commerce Bank Houston *PHIL AFFIL* trust: Pauline Sterne Wolff Memorial Foundation (see above)

Larry Shyrock: dir

APPLICATION INFORMATION
Initial Approach: *Initial Contact:* proposal *Include Information On:* description of the organization, budget, amount requested, purpose for which funds are sought, recently audited financial statement, copy of 501(c)(3) letter of tax-exempt status, list of board members, and recent contributions *Deadlines:* by the 15th of each month

Restrictions on Giving: Grants are not made to support political or lobbying groups, or individuals.

GRANTS ANALYSIS
Total Grants: $1,500,000

Average Grant: $250

Typical Range: $100 to $5,000

Disclosure Period: 1995

Note: Recent grants are derived from a 1993 Form 990.

RECENT GRANTS

General

452,770	United Way of the Texas Gulf Coast, Houston, TX
100,000	New Foundations, Houston, TX
22,000	University of Houston, Houston, TX
15,000	Depelchin Children's Center, Houston, TX
15,000	Houston Housing Partnership, Houston, TX

Tobin Foundation

CONTACT

Arnold Swartz
President
Tobin Fdn.
PO Box 2101
San Antonio, TX 78297
(210) 223-6203

FINANCIAL SUMMARY

Recent Giving: $231,900 (1993); $749,570 (1992); $387,415 (1991)

Assets: $20,913,570 (1993); $3,308,242 (1992); $2,986,710 (1991)

Gifts Received: $17,075,514 (1993); $1,003,053 (1992); $600,000 (1991)

Fiscal Note: In 1993, contributions were received from the estate of Margaret Batts Tobin.

EIN: 74-6035718

CONTRIBUTIONS SUMMARY

Donor(s): the late Edgar G. Tobin, Margaret Batts Tobin

Typical Recipients: • *Arts & Humanities:* Arts Centers, Arts Institutes, Community Arts, Ethnic & Folk Arts, Libraries, Museums/Galleries, Music, Opera, Performing Arts, Public Broadcasting • *Civic & Public Affairs:* Community Foundations, Nonprofit Management, Parades/Festivals, Urban & Community Affairs, Women's Affairs • *Education:* Health & Physical Education • *Environment:* Wildlife Protection • *Health:* Medical Research, Single-Disease Health Associations • *Religion:* Churches, Religious Welfare • *Science:* Scientific Centers & Institutes • *Social Services:* Community Centers, Community Service Organizations, People with Disabilities, United Funds/United Ways, Youth Organizations

Grant Types: general support

Geographic Distribution: limited to TX

GIVING OFFICERS

J. Bruce Bugg: secy

John R. Harrison: vp, treas

Arnold Swartz: pres, trust

Robert Lynn Batts Tobin: ceo *B* San Antonio TX 1934 *ED* Univ TX 1951-1952 *CURR EMPL* chmn: Tobin Res Inc *CORP AFFIL*

ceo, secy, treas: Tobin Surveys Inc *NONPR AFFIL* dir: Childrens Hosp Fdn, Fine Arts Fdn, Our Lady Lake Coll, Worden Sch Soc Work; mem: Kappa Alpha; mem bd managing dirs: Metro Opera Co NY; pres: Natl Opera Inst; trust: Mus Modern Art *CLUB AFFIL* Argyle, German, Grolier, San Antonio, San Antonio CC

APPLICATION INFORMATION

Initial Approach: Send a brief letter of inquiry. Include a description of organization, amount requested, purpose of funds sought, recently audited financial statement, and proof of tax-exempt status. There are no deadlines.

GRANTS ANALYSIS

Total Grants: $231,900

Number of Grants: 17

Highest Grant: $100,000

Typical Range: $100 to $50,000

Disclosure Period: 1993

Note: Recent grants are derived from a 1993 Form 990.

RECENT GRANTS

General

25,000	Cathedral of St. John the Divine, San Antonio, TX
25,000	United Way, San Antonio, TX
2,500	University of Texas Health Science Center, San Antonio, TX
2,000	Battle of Flowers Association, San Antonio, TX
1,000	Festival Institute at Round Top, Round Top, TX

Transco Energy Co.

Revenue: $2.81 billion
Parent Employees: 4,345
Headquarters: Houston, TX
SIC Major Group: Holding Companies Nec, Bituminous Coal & Lignite—Surface, Bituminous Coal—Underground, and Crude Petroleum & Natural Gas

CONTACT

Grace Hughes
Manager, Community Affairs
Transco Energy Co.
2800 Post Oak Blvd.
Houston, TX 77056
(713) 439-2348

FINANCIAL SUMMARY

Recent Giving: $1,050,000 (1995 est.); $1,120,000 (1994 approx.); $1,050,000 (1993 approx.)

Fiscal Note: Company gives directly. Above figures exclude nonmonetary support.

CONTRIBUTIONS SUMMARY

Typical Recipients: • *Arts & Humanities:* Arts Centers, Community Arts, Dance, Ethnic & Folk Arts, Libraries, Museums/Galleries, Music, Opera, Performing Arts, Public Broadcasting, Theater, Visual Arts • *Civic & Public Affairs:* Business/Free Enterprise,

Economic Development, Economic Policy, Employment/Job Training, Housing, Law & Justice, Public Policy, Urban & Community Affairs, Women's Affairs, Zoos/Aquariums • *Education:* Arts/Humanities Education, Business Education, Colleges & Universities, Community & Junior Colleges, Economic Education, Elementary Education (Private), Engineering/Technological Education, Literacy, Minority Education, Preschool Education, Public Education (Precollege), Science/Mathematics Education • *Environment:* General • *Health:* Hospices, Medical Research, Mental Health • *Science:* Science Exhibits & Fairs • *Social Services:* Child Welfare, Community Service Organizations, Delinquency & Criminal Rehabilitation, Domestic Violence, People with Disabilities, Recreation & Athletics, Substance Abuse, United Funds/United Ways, Youth Organizations

Grant Types: capital, employee matching gifts, general support, project, and scholarship

Nonmonetary Support Types: loaned employees and workplace solicitation

Note: Estimated value of nonmonetary support is not available. Company reports that workplace solicitation is for the United Way only.

Geographic Distribution: near headquarters and operating locations only

Operating Locations: AL, GA, LA, MD, MS, NC, NJ, NY (New York), PA, SC, TX (Houston), VA

Note: Above represents major operating locations; company operates in the Gulf Coast and Atlantic Seaboard areas of the United States.

CORP. OFFICERS

John P. Des Barres: *CURR EMPL* chmn, pres, ceo: Transco Energy Co

GIVING OFFICERS

Grace Hughes: *CURR EMPL* mgr commun aff: Transco Energy Co

APPLICATION INFORMATION

Initial Approach: *Initial Contact:* telephone call, brief letter, or proposal *Include Information On:* general purpose of organization and the population it serves; name of contact person and executive director; purpose for which organization is seeking funds; need for program; amount requested; number of Transco employees involved; names of directors and trustees, including affiliations; notation if organization is a United Way member; most recent financial statement; proposed annual budget; sources of funds, including government funding; identity and amounts of major donors; and copy of IRS 501 (c)(3) determination letter *Deadlines:* before December for next year's funding

Restrictions on Giving: Company does not purchase benefit tickets; contribute to advertising space in souvenir books, programs, or benefit performances; offer loans or financial aid to individuals; or make grants to fraternal, political, veterans, or religious organizations, or to member agencies of united funds.

Also does not fund school sports activities or organizations in foreign countries.

OTHER THINGS TO KNOW

No contribution is automatically renewable; company tries to rotate support in many categories among as many recipients as possible. Company suggests brief progress reports outlining use of contributions at 6-month intervals.

Company reports that it funds approximately 10 percent of all requests received.

PUBLICATIONS

Guidelines

GRANTS ANALYSIS

Total Grants: $899,678

Number of Grants: 190

Highest Grant: $20,000*

Average Grant: $4,735

Typical Range: $1,000 to $5,000

Disclosure Period: 1992

Note: Figures for average grants and highest grant are approximate.

Trull Foundation

CONTACT

Colleen Claybourn
Executive Director
Trull Foundation
404 Fourth St.
Palacios, TX 77465
(512) 972-5241

FINANCIAL SUMMARY

Recent Giving: $900,000 (1995 est.); $900,000 (1994 approx.); $851,540 (1993)

Assets: $17,750,000 (1995 est.); $18,750,000 (1994 approx.); $18,500,000 (1993 approx.)

Gifts Received: $9,126 (1987)

Fiscal Note: In 1987, the foundation received a gift of stock in Aberdeen 68.7 Ltd. from Rick Reese.

EIN: 23-7423943

CONTRIBUTIONS SUMMARY

Donor(s): The B. W. Trull Foundation was established in 1948 by B. W. Trull and Florence M. Trull for religious, charitable, and educational purposes. Trustees were Robert B. Trull, Harry H. Sisson, and Ralph P. Newsom. By the terms of its indenture, the original foundation expired in 1973. In 1967, the Trull family (Florence M. Trull and her four children) established a new foundation to receive the assets of the old foundation and to run until its assets were expended. The Trull family's fortune stems from farming, land management, and investments.

Typical Recipients: • *Arts & Humanities:* Ethnic & Folk Arts, Historic Preservation, History & Archaeology, Libraries, Museums/Galleries, Music, Opera, Performing Arts, Public Broadcasting, Theater, Visual Arts • *Civic & Public Affairs:* Economic Development, Employment/Job Training, Hispanic Affairs, Housing, Law & Justice, Legal Aid, Nonprofit Management, Women's Affairs • *Education:* Arts/Humanities Education, Colleges & Universities, Community & Junior Colleges, Medical Education, Minority Education, Private Education (Precollege), Public Education (Precollege), Religious Education, Student Aid • *Environment:* General • *Health:* AIDS/HIV, Cancer, Mental Health, Nutrition, Preventive Medicine/Wellness Organizations • *International:* Health Care/Hospitals, International Development, International Peace & Security Issues, International Relief Efforts, Missionary/Religious Activities • *Religion:* Bible Study/Translation, Churches, Ministries, Missionary Activities (Domestic), Religious Organizations, Religious Welfare, Seminaries • *Science:* Observatories & Planetariums • *Social Services:* Child Welfare, Community Centers, Community Service Organizations, Counseling, Day Care, Delinquency & Criminal Rehabilitation, Domestic Violence, Emergency Relief, Family Planning, Family Services, Homes, Refugee Assistance, Senior Services, Shelters/Homelessness, Substance Abuse, United Funds/United Ways, Youth Organizations

Grant Types: multiyear/continuing support, operating expenses, project, and scholarship

Geographic Distribution: primarily Texas area, but no geographic restrictions

GIVING OFFICERS

Garland M. Brooking: fdr

Gladys Trull Brooking: fdr

Colleen Claybourn: exec dir, secy, treas, trust, mem contributions comm

Jean Trull Herlin: fdr, mem contributions comm, trust

J. Fred Huitt: vchmn bd trusts, mem investment comm

Rose C. Lancaster: trust, mem contributions comm

B. B. Shiflett: fdr

Laura Trull Shiflett: fdr

Robert B. Trull: fdr, chmn bd trusts, mem investment comm

APPLICATION INFORMATION

Initial Approach:

Applicant should contact foundation in order to receive the proposal fact sheet and grant proposal guidelines.

Applicant's should submit the following in duplicate: cover letter (2 page max.), the proposal fact sheet, current agency operating budget (one page), project budget (one page), and IRS information.

Applications may be submitted at any time.

The Contributions Committee meets throughout the year and will respond to proposal within three months.

Restrictions on Giving: The foundation reports that it usually will not make long term commitments; make grants for buildings, endowments, or research; repeat grants in the same project longer than three years; fund operational expenses except during initial years; or make grants to individuals.

OTHER THINGS TO KNOW

The foundation supports established organizations to develop new programs, assists in proposal writing to work in coordination with other foundations, and conducts seminars/workshops.

The foundation expects periodic progress reports during the funding period.

PUBLICATIONS

Biennial report

GRANTS ANALYSIS

Total Grants: $851,540

Number of Grants: 269

Highest Grant: $50,000

Average Grant: $3,166

Typical Range: $3,000 to $6,000

Disclosure Period: 1993

Note: Recent grants are derived from a 1993 grants list.

RECENT GRANTS

Library

15,000	Bay City Library Association, Bay City, TX — expansion and modernization

General

50,000	Austin College, Sherman, TX — Clinica Promesa project/Mexico
20,000	World Neighbors, Oklahoma City, OK — reproductive health activities
15,000	Friends of Elder Citizens, Palacios, TX — nutrition program
12,000	Palacios Independent School District, Palacios, TX — scholarship fund
10,000	Manos De Cristo, Austin, TX — pastoral care director position

Turner Charitable Foundation

CONTACT

Eyvonne Moser
Assistant Secretary and Assistant Treasurer
Turner Charitable Foundation
811 Rusk, Ste. 205
Houston, TX 77002
(713) 237-1117

FINANCIAL SUMMARY

Recent Giving: $807,000 (fiscal 1995 est.); $812,267 (fiscal 1994); $806,000 (fiscal 1993)

Assets: $20,000,000 (fiscal 1995 est.); $21,693,000 (fiscal 1994); $18,900,000 (fiscal 1993)

EIN: 74-1460482

CONTRIBUTIONS SUMMARY

Donor(s): The foundation was incorporated in 1956 by the late Isla Carroll Turner and the late P. E. Turner .

Typical Recipients: • *Arts & Humanities:* Arts Associations & Councils, Ballet, Dance, General, Historic Preservation, Libraries, Museums/Galleries, Music, Opera, Performing Arts, Public Broadcasting, Theater • *Civic & Public Affairs:* Botanical Gardens/Parks, Clubs, Economic Development, Philanthropic Organizations, Urban & Community Affairs, Zoos/Aquariums • *Education:* Agricultural Education, Colleges & Universities, Environmental Education, Literacy, Medical Education, Preschool Education, Private Education (Precollege), Secondary Education (Private), Special Education, Student Aid • *Health:* Cancer, Children's Health/Hospitals, Clinics/Medical Centers, Emergency/Ambulance Services, Eyes/Blindness, Hospices, Hospitals, Medical Research, Mental Health, Single-Disease Health Associations • *International:* Missionary/Religious Activities • *Religion:* Churches, Religious Organizations, Religious Welfare, Social/Policy Issues • *Science:* Science Museums • *Social Services:* At-Risk Youth, Child Welfare, Community Centers, Community Service Organizations, Family Planning, Food/Clothing Distribution, Homes, People with Disabilities, Recreation & Athletics, Substance Abuse, YMCA/YWCA/YMHA/YWHA, Youth Organizations

Grant Types: capital, conference/seminar, emergency, endowment, fellowship, general support, matching, multiyear/continuing support, operating expenses, professorship, project, research, scholarship, and seed money

Geographic Distribution: restricted to Texas

GIVING OFFICERS

Thomas Eugene Berry: asst secy *B* San Antonio TX 1923 *ED* Southwestern Univ BBA 1944; Univ TX 1949; Univ TX LLB 1951 *CORP AFFIL* vp: Goodrich Oper Co *NONPR AFFIL* bd dir: Student Aid Fdn; fellow: Am Coll Tax Couns, Am Coll Trust & Estate Couns; mem: Am Bar Assn, Houston Bar Assn, NG Assn TX, TX Academy Probate & Trust Lawyers; trust: MB Flake Home Old Ladies, R H and E F Goodrich Fdn, Home Center Youth & Family Svcs, Isla Carroll Turner Friendship Trust

Chaille W. Hawkins: trust, asst secy

Christiana R. McConn: trust, asst secy

Eyvonne Moser: asst secy, asst treas

Isla C. Reckling: treas, asst secy

James S. Reckling: trust, asst secy

Stephen C. Reckling: asst secy, trust

T. R. Reckling III: pres, trust

Thomas R. Reckling IV: trust, asst secy

Clyde J. Verheyden: secy, trust

Bert F. Winston, Jr.: vp, trust *PHIL AFFIL* trust: Rienzi Foundation

Blake Winston: asst secy, trust

APPLICATION INFORMATION

Initial Approach:

The foundation requests applications be made in writing.

The application must include a copy of IRS code section 501(c)(3) exemption letter.

The deadline for submitting applications is March 1.

The board meets on the first Tuesday in April.

Restrictions on Giving: The foundation makes grants only to public charities. The foundation does not make grants to individuals.

GRANTS ANALYSIS

Total Grants: $812,267

Number of Grants: 69

Highest Grant: $166,667

Average Grant: $11,772

Typical Range: $1,000 to $15,000

Disclosure Period: fiscal year ending February 28, 1994

Note: Recent grants are derived from a fiscal 1994 grants list.

RECENT GRANTS

Library
15,000	Schreiner College, Kerrville, TX — library challenge

General
75,000	St. Peter Episcopal Church, Houston, TX — building expansion fund
50,000	Fay School, Southborough, MA — building fund challenge
50,000	Houston Parks Board, Houston, TX — Memorial Golf Course restoration
28,000	Good Samaritan Foundation, Houston, TX — nursing scholarships
25,000	Houston Baptist University, Houston, TX — seminar room in McNair Center

Vaughn, Jr. Foundation Fund, James M.

CONTACT

James M. Vaughn, Jr.
President
James M. Vaughn, Jr. Fdn Fund
2235 Brentwood
Houston, TX 77019

FINANCIAL SUMMARY

Recent Giving: $126,497 (1992); $58,500 (1990); $122,535 (1988)

Assets: $2,279,152 (1992); $2,564,725 (1990); $2,812,325 (1988)

EIN: 23-7166546

CONTRIBUTIONS SUMMARY

Typical Recipients: • *Arts & Humanities:* Arts Centers, Libraries, Museums/Galleries • *Civic & Public Affairs:* General • *Educa-*

tion: Colleges & Universities • *Health:* Mental Health • *Religion:* Churches

Grant Types: fellowship and research

GIVING OFFICERS

James M. Vaughn, Jr.: pres, dir *PHIL AFFIL* dir: Vaughn Foundation

Sally Vaughn: vp

Jon Werner: secy, treas

APPLICATION INFORMATION

Initial Approach: Send resume and cover letter. There are no deadlines.

GRANTS ANALYSIS

Total Grants: $126,497

Number of Grants: 11

Highest Grant: $40,000

Typical Range: $1,000 to $10,000

Disclosure Period: 1992

Note: Recent grants are derived from a 1992 Form 990.

RECENT GRANTS

General
40,000	OSU Foundation, Corvallis, OR
21,625	William Patrick Watson Center
10,000	Foundation Endowment, Alexandria, VA
3,272	Bernard Fund
2,500	Palmer Memorial, W. Union, IA

Walsh Foundation

CONTACT

F. Howard Walsh, Sr.
President
Walsh Fdn.
500 W 7th St., Ste. 1007
Ft. Worth, TX 76102
(817) 335-3741

FINANCIAL SUMMARY

Recent Giving: $26,880 (1993); $116,845 (1992); $331,725 (1991)

Assets: $2,332,337 (1993); $1,999,824 (1992); $1,819,508 (1991)

Gifts Received: $296,551 (1993); $233,061 (1992); $217,164 (1991)

Fiscal Note: In 1993, contributions were received from Wm. F. Bonnell, Jr., Ellen King Walsh, Michael Clinton Porter ($35,051 each), Allison Karen Walsh, Laura Elisabeth Bonnel ($23,268 each), Jonathan Richard Bonnell, Tara Winston Walsh ($22,557 each), and Holland Fleming Walsh ($21,235); seven other grants of $12,400 or less each were received.

EIN: 75-6021726

CONTRIBUTIONS SUMMARY

Donor(s): Mary D. Walsh, F. Howard Walsh, Sr.

Typical Recipients: • *Arts & Humanities:* Arts Associations & Councils, Arts Centers, Arts Institutes, Ballet, Community Arts, Dance, Historic Preservation, History & Archaeology, Libraries, Museums/Galleries,

Music, Opera, Performing Arts, Public Broadcasting, Theater • *Civic & Public Affairs:* Clubs, Housing, Parades/Festivals, Urban & Community Affairs, Women's Affairs, Zoos/Aquariums • *Education:* Colleges & Universities, Education Funds, Minority Education, Private Education (Precollege), Secondary Education (Public) • *Health:* AIDS/HIV, Alzheimers Disease, Arthritis, Cancer, Children's Health/Hospitals, Health Organizations, Hospitals, Mental Health, Research/Studies Institutes • *International:* Foreign Arts Organizations • *Religion:* Churches, Religious Organizations, Religious Welfare • *Science:* Science Museums • *Social Services:* Big-Brother/Big Sister, Child Welfare, Community Service Organizations, Counseling, Domestic Violence, Food/Clothing Distribution, People with Disabilities, Recreation & Athletics, Scouts, United Funds/United Ways, Youth Organizations

Grant Types: general support, multiyear/continuing support, operating expenses, and project

Geographic Distribution: focus on Ft. Worth, TX

GIVING OFFICERS
G. Malcolm Louden: secy, treas, dir *B* 1945 *ED* TX Christian Univ BBA 1969 *CURR EMPL* vp, dir: Walsh & Watts Inc *CORP AFFIL* exec vp, dir: F. Howard Walsh Jr Oper Co *PHIL AFFIL* treas, secy, gen mgr: Fleming Foundation

F. Howard Walsh, Sr.: pres, don *B* Waco TX 1913 *ED* TX Christian Univ BBA 1933 *CURR EMPL* pres, dir: Walsh & Watts Inc *NONPR AFFIL* dir, guarantor, hon bd mem: Ft Worth Arts Counc; guarantor: Ft Worth Ballet, Ft Worth Opera, Ft Worth Theatre, Schola Cantorum, TX Boys Choir; hon trust: TX Christian Univ; mem: Am Intl Charolais Assn, Independent Petroleum Assn Am, N TX Oil & Gas Assn, TX Christian Univ Ex-Lettermans Assn, TX Independent Producers & Royalty Owners, TX Mid-Continent Oil & Gas Assn, W Central TX Oil & Gas Assn *CLUB AFFIL* Breakfast, Century II, City, Colonial CC, Colorado Springs CC, Fort Worth, Frog, Garden of Gods, Petroleum, Ridglea CC, River Crest CC, Shady Oaks CC, Steeplechase *PHIL AFFIL* vp: Fleming Foundation

F. Howard Walsh, Jr.: asst secy, asst treas *B* 1941 *ED* TX Christian Univ BBA 1963 *CURR EMPL* pres, dir: F Howard Walsh Jr Oper Co *PHIL AFFIL* trust: Fleming Foundation

Mary D. Fleming Walsh: vp *B* Whitewright TX 1913 *ED* Southern Methodist Univ BA 1934 *CORP AFFIL* ptnr: Walsh Co *NONPR AFFIL* charter mem: Lloyd Shaw Fdn; co-fdr: Am Field Svc Ft Worth; guarantor: Ft Worth Opera, Ft Worth Theatre, Schola Cantorum, TX Boys Choir; guarantor, mem: Ft Worth Arts Counc, Ft Worth Ballet; hon dir: Van Cliburn Intl Piano Competition; life mem: YWCA; mem: Am Assn Univ Women, Am Guild Organists, Big Bros Tarrant Co, Chi Omega, Child Study Ctr, Childrens Hosp Womens Bd, Colorado Springs Fine Art Ctr, Ft Worth Art Assn, Ft

Worth Boys Club, Ft Worth Childrens Hosp, Ft Worth Pan Hellenic, Girls Svc League, Goodwill Indus Auxiliary, Jewel Charity Ball, Natl Assn Cowbelles, Opera Guild, Round Table, Tarrant County Auxiliary Edna Gladney Home, TX Christian Univ Fine Arts Fdn Guild, TX League Composers *PHIL AFFIL* pres, trust: Fleming Foundation *CLUB AFFIL* Colonial CC, Colorado Springs CC, Garden of Gods, Ridglea CC, Shady Oaks CC, TCU Womens, Womens

APPLICATION INFORMATION
Initial Approach: The foundation requests applications be made in writing. Include a description of organization, amount requested, purpose of funds sought, recently audited financial statement, and proof of tax-exempt status. There are no deadlines.

GRANTS ANALYSIS
Total Grants: $26,880

Number of Grants: 34

Highest Grant: $10,000

Typical Range: $50 to $5,000

Disclosure Period: 1993

Note: Recent grants are derived from a 1993 Form 990.

RECENT GRANTS

General

10,000	Broadway Baptist Church, Ft. Worth, TX
2,000	Chi Omega Community Charities, Ft. Worth, TX
1,100	Mental Health Association, Ft. Worth, TX
1,000	Food Bank of Greater Tarrant County, Ft. Worth, TX
500	American Cancer Society, Ft. Worth, TX

Weaver Foundation, Gil and Dody

CONTACT
Debbie L. Cain
Manager
Gil and Dody Weaver Fdn.
500 W Seventh St., Ste. 1714
Ft. Worth, TX 76102
(817) 877-1712

FINANCIAL SUMMARY
Recent Giving: $235,000 (fiscal 1993); $230,000 (fiscal 1992); $230,000 (fiscal 1991)

Assets: $4,125,746 (fiscal 1993); $4,039,679 (fiscal 1992); $3,936,872 (fiscal 1991)

EIN: 75-1729449

CONTRIBUTIONS SUMMARY
Donor(s): Galbraith Weaver

Typical Recipients: • *Arts & Humanities:* Libraries • *Civic & Public Affairs:* Economic Development, General, Women's Affairs, Zoos/Aquariums • *Education:* Colleges & Universities, Medical Education,

Private Education (Precollege), Special Education • *Health:* Alzheimers Disease, Cancer, Children's Health/Hospitals, Diabetes, Health Organizations, Hospitals, Long-Term Care, Mental Health, Research/Studies Institutes • *Religion:* Churches, Ministries, Religious Organizations, Religious Welfare, Social/Policy Issues • *Science:* Science Museums • *Social Services:* Big Brother/Big Sister, Child Welfare, Community Centers, Community Service Organizations, Counseling, Crime Prevention, Family Planning, Family Services, Food/Clothing Distribution, People with Disabilities, Scouts, Senior Services, Shelters/Homelessness, Substance Abuse, United Funds/United Ways, YMCA/YWCA/YMHA/YWHA, Youth Organizations

Grant Types: multiyear/continuing support, operating expenses, project, and research

Geographic Distribution: focus on TX

GIVING OFFICERS
Debbie L. Cain: mgr

Galbraith M. Weaver: trust

Eudora J. Weaver: trust

William R. Weaver, MD: trust

APPLICATION INFORMATION
Initial Approach: The foundation requests applications be made in writing. Deadline is July 31.

Restrictions on Giving: Gives only in TX, OK, LA, NM, KS, PA, and WV. No grants to the arts, building or construction entities, scholarships, or annuities.

GRANTS ANALYSIS
Total Grants: $235,000

Number of Grants: 49

Highest Grant: $15,000

Typical Range: $20 to $15,000

Disclosure Period: fiscal year ending September 30, 1993

Note: Recent grants are derived from a fiscal 1993 Form 990.

RECENT GRANTS

Library

500	Friends of Mansfield Public Library, Mansfield, TX — purchase of children's books

General

15,000	Food Bank of Greater Tarrant County, Ft. Worth, TX — memorial donation
15,000	Meals on Wheels, Ft. Worth, TX
15,000	YWCA, Ft. Worth, TX — special needs daycare program
11,000	Child Study Center, Ft. Worth, TX
11,000	St. John's Episcopal Church, Ft. Worth, TX

White Trust, G. R.

CONTACT
Joe T. Lenamon
Officer
G. R. White Trust
c/o Team Bank
PO Box 2050
Ft. Worth, TX 76113
(817) 884-4162

FINANCIAL SUMMARY
Recent Giving: $302,546 (fiscal 1993); $370,018 (fiscal 1992); $360,522 (fiscal 1991)

Assets: $6,372,483 (fiscal 1993); $6,277,835 (fiscal 1992); $6,391,308 (fiscal 1991)

EIN: 75-6094930

CONTRIBUTIONS SUMMARY
Donor(s): G.R. White

Typical Recipients: • *Arts & Humanities:* Libraries • *Civic & Public Affairs:* Municipalities/Towns, Safety • *Education:* Agricultural Education, Colleges & Universities, Continuing Education, Engineering/Technological Education, Legal Education, Religious Education, Student Aid • *Health:* Hospitals, Medical Rehabilitation • *Religion:* Churches, Religious Organizations • *Social Services:* Child Welfare, People with Disabilities, United Funds/United Ways, Youth Organizations

Grant Types: capital, general support, and scholarship

Geographic Distribution: limited to TX

GIVING OFFICERS
TeamBank: trust

APPLICATION INFORMATION
Initial Approach: Include a description of organization, amount requested, purpose of funds sought, recently audited financial statement, and proof of tax-exempt status. Deadline is September 1.

Restrictions on Giving: Limited to Texas.

GRANTS ANALYSIS
Total Grants: $302,546

Highest Grant: $75,000

Typical Range: $1,000 to $10,000

Disclosure Period: fiscal year ending September 30, 1993

Note: Recent grants are derived from a fiscal 1993 Form 990.

RECENT GRANTS
Library
165   F.M. Buck Richards Memorial Library, Brady, TX — purchase of equipment and improvements

General
75,000   University of Texas Law School Foundation, Austin, TX — final commitment installment for addition to

White & Wulff professorships to upgrade to chairs
53,399   Texas A&M University Student Loan Fund, College Station, TX — distribution of pro rata share of income for 1992 tax year
50,000   Texas A&M Development Foundation, College Station, TX — improvements to G. Rollie White Center of Animal Science
25,000   Texas and Southwestern Cattle Raisers Foundation, Fort Worth, TX — museum acquisitions
10,000   Baptist General Convention of Texas, Dallas, TX — for work with young men and retirees

Wilder Foundation

CONTACT
Rita Wilder
President
Wilder Fdn.
24 Greenway Plaza, Ste. 1212
Houston, TX 77046
(713) 850-8787

FINANCIAL SUMMARY
Recent Giving: $97,575 (1993); $106,206 (1991); $97,681 (1990)

Assets: $2,628,216 (1993); $2,652,191 (1991); $2,655,909 (1990)

EIN: 74-6049547

CONTRIBUTIONS SUMMARY
Donor(s): the late Candace Mossler, Jacques Mossler

Typical Recipients: • *Arts & Humanities:* Arts Associations & Councils, Community Arts, Dance, Historic Preservation, Libraries, Museums/Galleries, Music, Opera, Public Broadcasting • *Civic & Public Affairs:* Economic Development, General • *Education:* Colleges & Universities, Private Education (Precollege), Religious Education • *Environment:* General • *Health:* Cancer, Health Organizations, Hospitals, Prenatal Health Issues • *International:* International Environmental Issues • *Social Services:* Community Service Organizations, People with Disabilities

Grant Types: capital, endowment, general support, research, and scholarship

Geographic Distribution: focus on FL

GIVING OFFICERS
Gary Wilder: vp

Rita Wilder: pres *PHIL AFFIL* secy: Jeffrey and Rita Wilder Foundation

APPLICATION INFORMATION
Initial Approach: Send brief letter describing program. Include a description of organization, amount requested, purpose of funds sought, recently audited financial statement,

and proof of tax-exempt status. There are no deadlines.

Restrictions on Giving: Does not support individuals.

GRANTS ANALYSIS
Total Grants: $97,575

Number of Grants: 18

Highest Grant: $63,000

Typical Range: $100 to $10,000

Disclosure Period: 1993

Note: Recent grants are derived from a 1993 Form 990.

RECENT GRANTS
Library
2,000   Key Biscayne Library Garden Beautification, Key Biscayne, FL

General
63,000   Kinkaid School, Houston, TX
10,000   University of Miami, Miami, FL
5,000   M.D. Anderson Cancer Center, Houston, TX
4,500   Parish School, Houston, TX
4,500   Save Venice, New York, NY

Willard Helping Fund, Cecilia Young

CONTACT
Nancy May
Trust Officer
Cecilia Young Willard Helping Fund
c/o Broadway National Bank, Trust Div.
1177 N.E. Loop 410
San Antonio, TX 78209
(210) 283-6700

FINANCIAL SUMMARY
Recent Giving: $225,091 (fiscal 1994); $215,745 (fiscal 1993); $203,900 (fiscal 1991)

Assets: $4,494,860 (fiscal 1994); $4,637,292 (fiscal 1993); $4,203,727 (fiscal 1991)

Gifts Received: $24,021 (fiscal 1991); $150,000 (fiscal 1989); $2,004,571 (fiscal 1988)

EIN: 74-6350893

CONTRIBUTIONS SUMMARY
Donor(s): Celia Young Willard Trust

Typical Recipients: • *Arts & Humanities:* Arts Associations & Councils, Arts Institutes, Community Arts, Libraries, Museums/Galleries, Music, Public Broadcasting • *Civic & Public Affairs:* General, Hispanic Affairs, Municipalities/Towns, Rural Affairs, Safety • *Education:* Colleges & Universities, Legal Education, Private Education (Precollege) • *Environment:* General, Resource Conservation, Wildlife Protection • *Health:* AIDS/HIV, Cancer, Eyes/Blindness, Heart, Hospices, Hospitals, Prenatal Health Issues • *Religion:* Churches, Religious Organizations, Religious Welfare • *So-*

cial Services: Child Welfare, Community Service Organizations, Homes, People with Disabilities, Youth Organizations

Grant Types: operating expenses

Geographic Distribution: focus on NC

GIVING OFFICERS
Broadway National Bank: trust

APPLICATION INFORMATION
Initial Approach: Send a brief letter of inquiry. Include a description of organization, amount requested, purpose of funds sought, recently audited financial statement, and proof of tax-exempt status. Deadline is June 1.

GRANTS ANALYSIS
Total Grants: $225,091

Number of Grants: 48

Highest Grant: $40,309

Typical Range: $375 to $24,184

Disclosure Period: fiscal year ending May 31, 1994

Note: Recent grants are derived from a fiscal 1994 Form 990.

RECENT GRANTS

General

40,309	First Presbyterian Church, Hickory, NC
24,184	Crossnore School, Crossnore, NC
24,184	Grandfather Home for Children, Banner Elk, NC
24,184	Lees-McRae College, Banner Elk, NC
10,000	Johns Hopkins Cancer Center, Baltimore, MD — building fund

Wise Foundation and Charitable Trust, Watson W.

CONTACT
Will Knight
Trustee
Watson W. Wise Foundation and Charitable Trust
110 N College, Ste. 1002
Tyler, TX 75702
(903) 531-9615

FINANCIAL SUMMARY
Recent Giving: $325,000 (1993); $250,500 (1992); $0 (1991)

Assets: $8,068,853 (1993); $5,564,872 (1992); $4,398,780 (1991)

Gifts Received: $1,667,109 (1993); $881,116 (1992); $3,018,253 (1991)

Fiscal Note: In 1993, contributions were received from Watson W. Wise Estate.

EIN: 75-6064539

CONTRIBUTIONS SUMMARY
Donor(s): the donor is the estate of Watson W. Wise

Typical Recipients: • *Arts & Humanities:* Libraries • *Civic & Public Affairs:* Community Foundations, Urban & Community Affairs • *Education:* Agricultural Education, Colleges & Universities, Engineering/Technological Education, General, Literacy, Private Education (Precollege), Public Education (Precollege) • *Health:* Clinics/Medical Centers, Health Organizations, Hospices • *Religion:* Churches • *Science:* Science Museums, Scientific Centers & Institutes • *Social Services:* Community Service Organizations, Day Care, Food/Clothing Distribution, People with Disabilities, Youth Organizations

Grant Types: general support

Geographic Distribution: focus on Tyler, TX

GIVING OFFICERS
Calvin N. Clyde, Jr.: trust

Herman A. Engel: trust

Will Knight: trust

Emma F. Wise: trust

APPLICATION INFORMATION
Initial Approach: The foundation reports that there is no specific application form. There are no deadlines.

GRANTS ANALYSIS
Total Grants: $325,000

Number of Grants: 43

Highest Grant: $35,000

Typical Range: $2,500 to $25,000

Disclosure Period: 1993

Note: Recent grants are derived from a 1993 Form 990.

RECENT GRANTS

Library

5,000	Cameron Jarvis Library, Troup, TX — educational

General

35,000	Tyler Junior College, Tyler, TX — education
35,000	University of Texas Health Center, Tyler, TX — medical
25,000	Louisiana State University, Baton Rouge, LA — education
25,000	Tyler Junior College, Tyler, TX — education
10,000	All Saints School, Tyler, TX — educational

Wright Foundation, Lola

CONTACT
Patrick H. O'Donnell, Jr.
President
Lola Wright Fdn.
c/o Texas Commerce Bank
PO Box 550
Austin, TX 78789-0001
(512) 479-2628

FINANCIAL SUMMARY
Recent Giving: $779,590 (1993); $876,585 (1991); $935,643 (1990)

Assets: $12,299,364 (1993); $11,671,486 (1991); $8,812,301 (1990)

EIN: 74-6054717

CONTRIBUTIONS SUMMARY
Donor(s): the late Miss Johnie E. Wright

Typical Recipients: • *Arts & Humanities:* Ballet, Community Arts, Libraries, Museums/Galleries, Music, Performing Arts • *Civic & Public Affairs:* Housing, Urban & Community Affairs, Women's Affairs • *Education:* Arts/Humanities Education, Colleges & Universities, Literacy • *Environment:* General • *Health:* AIDS/HIV, Hospices, Hospitals, Mental Health, Research/Studies Institutes • *Religion:* Churches • *Social Services:* At-Risk Youth, Child Welfare, Community Centers, Community Service Organizations, Counseling, Domestic Violence, Emergency Relief, Family Planning, Family Services, Food/Clothing Distribution, Homes, People with Disabilities, Scouts, Senior Services, Shelters/Homelessness, Youth Organizations

Grant Types: capital, endowment, multiyear/continuing support, project, and research

Geographic Distribution: limited to TX

GIVING OFFICERS
Texas Commerce Bank: trust

Wilford Flowers: dir

Linda H. Guerrero: dir

William Hilgers: vp, dir

James Meyers: dir

Patrick H. O'Donnell: pres, dir

Carole Rylander: dir

APPLICATION INFORMATION
Initial Approach: Request application packet. Deadlines are April 1 and October 1.

Restrictions on Giving: Does not support individuals.

PUBLICATIONS
Application Guidelines, Annual Report

GRANTS ANALYSIS
Total Grants: $779,590

Number of Grants: 12

Highest Grant: $37,880

Typical Range: $1,500 to $25,000

Disclosure Period: 1993

Note: Recent grants are derived from a 1993 Form 990.

RECENT GRANTS

General

37,880	Ceden Family Resource Center, Austin, TX — Volunteer Program
31,200	Believe in Me Project, Austin, TX — training and operating funds
30,000	Goodwill Industries of Central Texas, Austin, TX — fire sprinkler system

28,375	Center for Battered Women, Austin, TX — van and stove
25,000	Child and Family Service, Austin, TX — computer system

Zachry Co., H.B. / Zachry Foundation

Revenue: $500.0 million
Employees: 7,000
Headquarters: San Antonio, TX
SIC Major Group: Heavy Construction Except Building Construction

CONTACT
Pam O'Connor
Executive Director
Zachry Foundation
310 S St. Mary's, Ste. 2500
San Antonio, TX 78205
(210) 554-4663

FINANCIAL SUMMARY
Recent Giving: $598,265 (1993); $591,731 (1992); $402,995 (1991)

Assets: $7,757,246 (1993); $7,780,173 (1992); $7,118,852 (1991)

Gifts Received: $702,000 (1992); $4,561,968 (1989); $1,090,000 (1988)

Fiscal Note: In 1992, major contributions were received from H. B. Zachry Company.

EIN: 74-1485544

CONTRIBUTIONS SUMMARY
Typical Recipients: • *Arts & Humanities:* General, Libraries, Museums/Galleries, Music, Performing Arts • *Civic & Public Affairs:* Botanical Gardens/Parks, General, Philanthropic Organizations • *Education:* Afterschool/Enrichment Programs, Arts/Humanities Education, Business Education, Business-School Partnerships, Colleges & Universities, Community & Junior Colleges, Continuing Education, Faculty Development, General, Literacy, Vocational & Technical Education • *Health:* Clinics/Medical Centers, General, Hospitals, Hospitals (University Affiliated), Medical Research • *International:* International Affairs, International Relations • *Religion:* Jewish Causes, Religious Welfare • *Science:* General, Observatories & Planetariums, Science Museums, Scientific Centers & Institutes, Scientific Research • *Social Services:* At-Risk Youth, Camps, Child Welfare, Community Centers, Community Service Organizations, Delinquency & Criminal Rehabilitation, Domestic Violence, Family Services, General, People with Disabilities, Senior Services, United Funds/United Ways, Youth Organizations

Grant Types: capital, challenge, emergency, multiyear/continuing support, and research

Geographic Distribution: limited to TX, with emphasis on San Antonio

CORP. OFFICERS
Charles E. Ebrom: *CURR EMPL* exec vp, dir: Zachry (HB) Co *CORP AFFIL* exec vp, dir: Zachry (HB) Co

Murray L. Johnston, Jr.: *B* Lake Charles LA 1940 *ED* Austin Coll 1962; Univ TX 1965 *CURR EMPL* vp, secy, gen coun, dir: Zachry (HB) Co *NONPR AFFIL* mem: Am Bar Assn, Am Judicature Soc, Intl Assn Defense Counc

H. B. Zachry, Jr.: *B* Laredo TX 1933 *ED* TX A&M Univ BS 1954; Harvard Univ Sch Bus Admin *CURR EMPL* chmn, dir: HB Zachry Co *CORP AFFIL* chmn, pres, dir: Capitol Aggregates; dir: Southwest Res Inst

GIVING OFFICERS
Charles E. Ebrom: trust *CURR EMPL* exec vp, dir: Zachry (HB) Co (see above)

Murray L. Johnston, Jr.: trust *CURR EMPL* vp, secy, gen coun, dir: Zachry (HB) Co (see above)

Pamela O'Connor: exec dir

H. B. Zachry, Jr.: trust *CURR EMPL* chmn, dir: HB Zachry Co (see above)

J. P. Zachry: pres, trust

Mollie S. Zachry: trust

APPLICATION INFORMATION
Restrictions on Giving: Does not support individuals, religious organizations for sectarian purposes, or organizations outside operating areas.

GRANTS ANALYSIS
Total Grants: $598,265

Number of Grants: 34

Highest Grant: $100,000

Typical Range: $1,500 to $80,000

Disclosure Period: 1993

Note: Recent grants are derived from a 1993 Form 990.

RECENT GRANTS

Library
50,000	San Antonio Public Library Foundation, San Antonio, TX — education
50,000	San Antonio Public Library Foundation, San Antonio, TX — general funding

General
100,000	Texas A&M University Engineering Fund, College Station, TX
100,000	Texas Research and Technology Foundation, San Antonio, TX — development fund
100,000	United Way of San Antonio and Bexar County, San Antonio, TX — general funding
75,000	UTSA Engineering and Bioscience, San Antonio, TX — education
40,000	Cancer Therapy and Research Foundation of South Texas, San Antonio, TX — general funding

UTAH

Kennecott Corporation

Sales: $1.0 billion
Employees: 3,500
Headquarters: Salt Lake City, UT
SIC Major Group: Copper Ores, Lead & Zinc Ores, Abrasive Products, and Nonclay Refractories

CONTACT
Drew Cherrington
Public Relations Specialist
Kennecott Corporation
PO Box 11248
Salt Lake City, UT 84147
(801) 322-7232

FINANCIAL SUMMARY
Recent Giving: $1,000,000 (1995 est.); $1,500,000 (1994 approx.); $500,000 (1992 approx.)

Fiscal Note: Company gives directly.

CONTRIBUTIONS SUMMARY
Typical Recipients: • *Arts & Humanities:* Arts Appreciation, Arts Associations & Councils, Arts Centers, Arts Festivals, Community Arts, Dance, Ethnic & Folk Arts, Film & Video, Historic Preservation, Libraries, Museums/Galleries, Music, Opera, Performing Arts, Public Broadcasting, Theater, Visual Arts • *Civic & Public Affairs:* Civil Rights, Economic Development, Employment/Job Training, Housing, Law & Justice, Legal Aid, Professional & Trade Associations, Safety, Women's Affairs, Zoos/Aquariums • *Education:* Business Education, Colleges & Universities, Community & Junior Colleges, Economic Education, Elementary Education (Private), Engineering/Technological Education, General, Minority Education, Private Education (Precollege), Public Education (Precollege), Science/Mathematics Education, Special Education • *Environment:* General • *Health:* General, Geriatric Health, Hospices, Hospitals, Mental Health, Public Health • *Science:* General, Observatories & Planetariums, Science Exhibits & Fairs, Scientific Organizations • *Social Services:* Animal Protection, Child Welfare, Community Centers, Counseling, Delinquency & Criminal Rehabilitation, Domestic Violence, Family Planning, Family Services, General, People with Disabilities, Recreation & Athletics, Senior Services, Shelters/Homelessness, Substance Abuse, United Funds/United Ways, Youth Organizations

Grant Types: employee matching gifts, multiyear/continuing support, and scholarship

Note: Employee matching gift ratio: 1 to 1.

Nonmonetary Support Types: donated equipment and in-kind services

Note: The visitor center charges a nominal fee and these proceeds are reviewed quarterly and distributed. The company provides nonmonetary support but the monetary amount is not available. Contact Drew Cherrington for more information.

Geographic Distribution: headquarters and operating locations

Operating Locations: AK, MT, NV (Fallon), SC (Columbia), UT (Salt Lake City), WI (Ladysmith), WY

CORP. OFFICERS
Bob E. Cooper: *B* 1951 *CURR EMPL* pres, ceo: Kennecott Corp *CORP AFFIL* ceo: Greens Creek Joint Venture; pres, dir: Kennecott Rawhide Mining Co, Kennecott Ridgeway Mining Co

GIVING OFFICERS
Drew Cherrington: *CURR EMPL* pub rels specialist: Kennecott Corp

APPLICATION INFORMATION
Initial Approach: *Initial Contact:* brief letter of inquiry and full proposal *Include Information On:* description of the organization, statement of need, amount requested, purpose of funds sought, audited financial statement, and proof of tax-exempt status *Deadlines:* none, preferably by January 1

Restrictions on Giving: Does not support individuals.

GRANTS ANALYSIS
Total Grants: $1,500,000*

Typical Range: $1,000 to $2,500

Disclosure Period: 1994

Note: Total grants figure is an approximation.

Novell Inc.

Sales: $2.0 billion
Employees: 8,000
Headquarters: Provo, UT
SIC Major Group: Business Services and Industrial Machinery & Equipment

CONTACT
Linda Linfield
Senior Manager, Community Relations
Novell Inc.
1555 N Technology Way, K-152
Orem, UT 84057
800-321-5906

CONTRIBUTIONS SUMMARY
Company allocates 40% of contributions to health and human services; 20% to education; and 10% each to environmental, sports, arts, and civic organizations. Novell also has sponsored projects with the World Wildlife Fund, the Columbus Center, SMART Utah Initiative, and the San Jose Education Network.

Volunteerism: Employee volunteerism is promted through an internal electronic newsletter.

Typical Recipients: • *Arts & Humanities:* Arts Associations & Councils, Arts Centers, Arts Festivals, Arts Outreach, Ballet, Community Arts, Dance, Ethnic & Folk Arts,

General, Libraries, Museums/Galleries, Music, Opera, Performing Arts, Theater • *Civic & Public Affairs:* Business/Free Enterprise, Community Foundations, General, Philanthropic Organizations, Professional & Trade Associations • *Education:* Business Education, Faculty Development, General, Science/Mathematics Education, Vocational & Technical Education • *Environment:* Wildlife Protection • *Health:* Arthritis, Cancer, Diabetes, General, Home-Care Services, Nursing Services • *Science:* General, Observatories & Planetariums, Science Museums, Scientific Centers & Institutes, Scientific Organizations • *Social Services:* Community Centers, Community Service Organizations, Food/Clothing Distribution, General, Homes, People with Disabilities, Shelters/Homelessness, United Funds/United Ways, Volunteer Services

Grant Types: award, multiyear/continuing support, and project

Nonmonetary Support Types: donated products

Geographic Distribution: principally near operating locations and to national organizations

Operating Locations: UT (Provo)

CORP. OFFICERS
Robert Frankenberg: *CURR EMPL* chmn, pres, ceo, dir: Novell

James R. Tolonen: *CURR EMPL* sr vp, cfo: Novell

APPLICATION INFORMATION
Initial Approach: Send a full proposal. Include a description of organization, amount requested, purpose of funds sought, recently audited financial statement, and proof of tax-exempt status. The company's fiscal year ends October 31. Applications for support were being accepted as of November 1, 1995.

Restrictions on Giving: Does not support individuals, religious organizations for sectarian purposes, political or lobbying groups, or organizations outside operating areas.

OTHER THINGS TO KNOW
Grant making suspended until 1995.

GRANTS ANALYSIS
Typical Range: $1,000 to $2,500

Note: Annual Giving Range: $500,000 to $1,000,000

RECENT GRANTS

General
Computerworld Smithsonian Innovation Network, Washington, DC
Highway One, Washington, DC
Junior Achievement, Salt Lake City, UT
San Jose Education Network, San Jose, CA
Second Harvest Food Bank, San Jose, CA

Swanson Family Foundation, Dr. W.C.

CONTACT
Lew Costley
Trustee and Manager
Dr. W. C. Swanson Family Foundation
1104 Country Hills
Suite 411
Ogden, UT 84401
(801) 399-5837

FINANCIAL SUMMARY
Recent Giving: $1,600,000 (1995 est.); $2,000,000 (1994); $1,195,284 (1993)

Assets: $28,000,000 (1994); $32,188,873 (1993); $25,666,172 (1992)

EIN: 94-2478549

CONTRIBUTIONS SUMMARY
Donor(s): The foundation was established in 1978, by the late Dr. W. C. Swanson .

Typical Recipients: • *Arts & Humanities:* Arts Centers, Ballet, Film & Video, Historic Preservation, History & Archaeology, Libraries, Music, Opera, Public Broadcasting • *Civic & Public Affairs:* General, Municipalities/Towns, Philanthropic Organizations, Public Policy, Urban & Community Affairs • *Education:* Colleges & Universities, Private Education (Precollege), Public Education (Precollege) • *Environment:* General • *Health:* Cancer, Children's Health/Hospitals, Hospices, Hospitals • *Religion:* Churches, Religious Organizations, Religious Welfare • *Science:* Scientific Centers & Institutes • *Social Services:* Animal Protection, Child Welfare, Community Service Organizations, Domestic Violence, Family Services, People with Disabilities, Senior Services, Youth Organizations

Grant Types: general support, operating expenses, and scholarship

Geographic Distribution: giving primarily in Utah, with primary emphasis on Weber County, then northern Utah

GIVING OFFICERS
Lew Costley: trust

Harry L. Gibbons: exec comm

W. Charles Swanson: mgr

APPLICATION INFORMATION
Initial Approach:

Submit one copy of a written proposal. Proposal should be a maximum of five pages. There are no deadlines. Board meetings are held in May and November. Final notification is given in six to nine months.

Include a copy of requesting organization's IRS 501(c)(3) tax-exemption letter, as well as a copy of the organization's annual report and financial statement.

Note: At press time, the foundation had not yet prepared written application procedures. These will be available after January 1, 1995. Contact the foundation for more information.

Restrictions on Giving: Does not provide grants to individuals. No support given for studies in the areas of abortion, reproductive physiology, contraceptive technology, or sexually transmitted diseases.

PUBLICATIONS
Multi-year report (including application guidelines), informational brochure

GRANTS ANALYSIS
Total Grants: $1,195,284

Number of Grants: 75

Highest Grant: $195,000

Average Grant: $15,937

Typical Range: $1,000 to $25,000

Disclosure Period: 1993

Note: Recent grants are derived from a 1993 Form 990.

RECENT GRANTS

General

195,000	Ogden City School, Ogden, UT — building funds
100,000	Ogden City Downtown Civic Center, Ogden, UT — building funds
39,500	Avatar, Inc., Ogden, UT — operating funds
35,000	Weber County School Foundation, Ogden, UT — to purchase equipment
32,000	Ogden River Parkway, Ogden, UT — building funds

VERMONT

Central Vermont Public Service Corp.

Revenue: $277.15 million
Employees: 755
Headquarters: Rutland, VT
SIC Major Group: Electric, Gas & Sanitary Services and Real Estate

CONTACT
Charles F. Satterfield
Manager, Community Relations, Governmental Affairs
Central Vermont Public Service Corp.
PO Box 39
Montpelier, VT 05601-0039
(802) 773-2711

FINANCIAL SUMMARY
Recent Giving: $202,332 (1994)

Fiscal Note: Annual Giving Range: $100,000 to $250,000

CONTRIBUTIONS SUMMARY
Support goes to local education, human services, arts, and civic organizations.

Typical Recipients: • *Arts & Humanities:* Community Arts, Libraries, Museums/Galleries, Music, Public Broadcasting • *Civic & Public Affairs:* Economic Development, Nonprofit Management • *Education:* Colleges & Universities • *Environment:* General • *Health:* Mental Health • *Science:* Science Exhibits & Fairs • *Social Services:* Community Service Organizations

Grant Types: emergency, endowment, general support, and multiyear/continuing support

Geographic Distribution: primarily VT

Operating Locations: VT (Bennington, Brattleboro, Brattleboro, Manchester, Middleburg, Montpelier, Randolph, Rutland, Rutland, Springfield, St. Albans, St. Johnsburg, Woodstock)

CORP. OFFICERS
F. Ray Keyser, Jr.: *B* Chelsea VT 1927 *ED* Boston Univ Law Sch 1952; Tufts Univ *CURR EMPL* chmn, dir: Central Vermont Pub Svc Corp *CORP AFFIL* chmn: Keyser Crowley & Meub PC, Proctor Bank Co, Un VT Bancorp; dir: Central VT Railway, Grand Trunk Corp, Keystone Custodian Funds, S-K-I Ltd, Union Mutual Fire Ins Co, VT Electric Power Co, VT Yankee Nuclear Power Co *NONPR AFFIL* dir: Associate Indus VT; mem: Am Bar Assn

Thomas C. Webb: *B* Guthrie Center IA 1934 *ED* Univ MN 1957 *CURR EMPL* pres, ceo, dir: Central VT Pub Svc Corp *CORP AFFIL* chmn: VT Yankee Nuclear Power Co; dir: CT Yankee Atomic, ME Yankee Atomic, Un VT Bancorp, VT Electric Power Co; pres, ceo, dir: CT Valley Electric Co *NONPR AFFIL* dir: Edison Electric Inst

Robert H. Young: *CURR EMPL* exec vp, coo: Central Vermont Public Svc Corp

APPLICATION INFORMATION
Initial Approach: Send brief letter of inquiry, including a description of the organization, amount requested, and purpose of funds sought. Deadline for January 1 Fiscal year is August 15th.

Restrictions on Giving: Does not support individuals, religious organizations for sectarian purposes, political or lobbying groups, or organizations outside operating areas.

GRANTS ANALYSIS
Typical Range: $1,000 to $2,500

Proctor Trust, Mortimer R.

CONTACT
Mortimer R. Proctor Trust
c/o Green Mountain Bank Trust Dept.
80 W St.
Rutland, VT 05701
(802) 775-2525

FINANCIAL SUMMARY
Recent Giving: $153,110 (1993); $157,823 (1992); $201,968 (1991)

Assets: $2,890,954 (1993); $2,839,795 (1992); $2,797,987 (1991)

EIN: 03-6020099

CONTRIBUTIONS SUMMARY
Typical Recipients: • *Arts & Humanities:* Libraries, Music • *Civic & Public Affairs:* Housing, Municipalities/Towns, Safety, Urban & Community Affairs • *Education:* Business Education, Elementary Education (Private), Elementary Education (Public), International Studies, Private Education (Precollege), Public Education (Precollege), Religious Education • *Religion:* Churches, Religious Organizations • *Social Services:* Child Welfare, Community Service Organizations, Crime Prevention, Food/Clothing Distribution, Recreation & Athletics, Scouts, Youth Organizations

Grant Types: emergency, operating expenses, and project

Geographic Distribution: limited to Proctor, VT

GIVING OFFICERS
Green Mountain Bank: trust

APPLICATION INFORMATION
Initial Approach: The foundation requests applications be made in writing. There are no deadlines.

PUBLICATIONS
Annual Report

GRANTS ANALYSIS
Total Grants: $153,110

Number of Grants: 16

Highest Grant: $30,000

Typical Range: $1,500 to $11,000

Disclosure Period: 1993

Note: Recent grants are derived from a 1993 Form 990.

RECENT GRANTS

Library

3,000	Proctor Free Library, Proctor, VT — book budget

General

30,000	Town of Proctor, Proctor, VT — fire department, purchase of new pumper
28,639	Town of Proctor, Proctor, VT — maintenance of Taranovich field, youth league, pool operations, and skating rink
27,950	Proctor School District, Proctor, VT
18,000	Union Church of Proctor, Proctor, VT — restoration of pipe organ
10,875	St. Paul Lutheran Church, Gloucester, MA — church siding, windows, wash bowl, and piping

Scott Foundation, Walter

CONTACT
Thorpe A. Nickerson
President
Walter Scott Fdn.
PO Box 1161
Wilmington, VT 05363
(802) 464-5016

FINANCIAL SUMMARY
Recent Giving: $220,000 (fiscal 1992);
$218,900 (fiscal 1991); $199,500 (fiscal
1990)

Assets: $4,780,144 (fiscal 1992);
$4,853,296 (fiscal 1991); $4,813,341 (fiscal
1990)

EIN: 13-5681161

CONTRIBUTIONS SUMMARY
Typical Recipients: • *Arts & Humanities:*
Libraries • *Civic & Public Affairs:* General,
Professional & Trade Associations • *Educa-
tion:* Colleges & Universities, Legal Educa-
tion, Medical Education, Special Education
• *Environment:* General • *Health:* Children's
Health/Hospitals, Emergency/Ambulance
Services, Eyes/Blindness, Health Funds,
Health Organizations, Hospices, Hospitals,
Medical Research • *Religion:* Churches • *So-
cial Services:* Child Welfare, Emergency Re-
lief, People with Disabilities, Recreation &
Athletics, Youth Organizations

Grant Types: capital, endowment, multi-
year/continuing support, operating expenses,
research, and seed money

Geographic Distribution: focus on the
New York, NY, metropolitan area and lower
CT

GIVING OFFICERS
Dr. Norman A. Hill: dir

Brett R. Nickerson: dir

Glendon A. Nickerson: dir

Jocelyn A. Nickerson: vp, exec dir

Lisa B. Nickerson: dir

Thorpe A. Nickerson: pres, secy, treas, dir

APPLICATION INFORMATION
Initial Approach: Send brief letter describing program. There are no deadlines.

GRANTS ANALYSIS
Total Grants: $220,000

Number of Grants: 33

Highest Grant: $36,000

Typical Range: $3,000 to $10,000

Disclosure Period: fiscal year ending September 30, 1992

Note: Recent grants are derived from a fiscal 1992 Form 990.

RECENT GRANTS

Library
400	Foundation Center, New York, NY — general support	

General
36,000	Helen Hayes Hospital, Albany, NY — continuation of doctoral program and general support	
32,700	Breckenridge Outdoor Education Center, Breckenridge, CO	
30,000	Clarke School for the Deaf, Northampton, MA — general support for handicapped deaf children	
10,000	AGMA Emergency Relief Fund, New York, NY	
10,000	Deafness Research Foundation, New York, NY — general support	

Windham Foundation

CONTACT
Stephan A. Morse
President
Windham Foundation
Grafton, VT 05146
(802) 843-2211

FINANCIAL SUMMARY
Recent Giving: $230,000 (fiscal 1995 est.);
$311,733 (fiscal 1994); $328,268 (fiscal
1993)

Assets: $36,115,350 (fiscal 1994);
$37,367,259 (fiscal 1993); $37,959,453 (fiscal 1992)

Gifts Received: $30,000 (fiscal 1995);
$40,000 (fiscal 1994); $40,300 (fiscal 1993)

Fiscal Note: The foundation received contributions from the Bunbury Co. and the estate
of Dean Mathey.

EIN: 13-6142024

CONTRIBUTIONS SUMMARY
Donor(s): The Windham Foundation receives donations from the Bunbury Company, which was incorporated in New York
by the late Dean Mathey. Stephan A. Morse,
the foundation's president and CEO is a
member of Bunbury's board of directors.

Typical Recipients: • *Arts & Humanities:*
Arts Associations & Councils, Film &
Video, Historic Preservation, History & Ar-
chaeology, Libraries, Museums/Galleries,
Music, Theater • *Civic & Public Affairs:*
Clubs, Economic Development, General,
Housing, Municipalities/Towns, Safety,
Women's Affairs • *Education:* After-
school/Enrichment Programs, Colleges &
Universities, General, Literacy, Preschool
Education, Private Education (Precollege),
Science/Mathematics Education, Secondary
Education (Public), Student Aid • *Environ-
ment:* Protection • *Health:* Arthritis, Cancer,
Diabetes, Emergency/Ambulance Services,
General, Health Organizations, Hospitals,
Kidney, Prenatal Health Issues, Trauma
Treatment • *Religion:* Religious Welfare
• *Science:* Observatories & Planetariums
• *Social Services:* Community Centers, Com-
munity Service Organizations, Day Care, Do-
mestic Violence, Family Planning, Family
Services, Recreation & Athletics, Youth Or-
ganizations

Grant Types: general support, operating expenses, project, and scholarship

Geographic Distribution: limited to Vermont, in particular to Windham County

GIVING OFFICERS
Charles B. Atwater: vp, secy *CORP AFFIL*
treas, secy: Grafton Village Cheese Co
PHIL AFFIL dir: Bunbury Company

James Richard Cogan: chmn *B* Jersey City
NJ 1928 *ED* Yale Univ BA 1950; Columbia
Univ LLB 1953 *CURR EMPL* ptnr: Walter
Conston Alexander & Green PC *CORP AF-
FIL* chmn bd: Grafton Village Cheese Co;
pres, dir: S Forest Co *NONPR AFFIL* dir:
Aging Am, Am Friends Plantin-Moretus
Mus, Corp Relief Widows & Children Cler-
gymen, Village Nursing Home NY; mem:
Am Bar Assn, Am Coll Probate Couns, Assn
Bar City New York, NY County Lawyers
Assn; trust: Charlotte Palmer Phillips Fdn
CLUB AFFIL mem: Salmagundi Artists,
Yale *PHIL AFFIL* treas, dir: Bunbury Com-
pany

Samuel Waldron Lambert III: vp, trust *B*
New York NY 1938 *CURR EMPL* mng ptnr:
Drinker Biddle & Reath *CORP AFFIL* dir:
Chem Bank NJ, Peterson Guides *NONPR AF-
FIL* dir: Curtis W McGraw Fdn; mem: Am
Bar Assn, NJ Bar Assn, Princeton Bar Assn
PHIL AFFIL pres, trust: Bunbury Company;
secy, treas, trust: Curtis W. McGraw Founda-
tion; trust: Winslow Foundation

Stephan A. Morse: pres, ceo *B* 1947 *CORP
AFFIL* pres, admin, dir: Grafton Village
Cheese Co *PHIL AFFIL* dir: Bunbury Com-
pany

Arthur Schubert: assoc dir

Edward Joseph Toohey: trust *B* Jersey City
NJ 1930 *ED* Yale Univ BA 1953 *CURR
EMPL* first vp: Merrill Lynch Pierce Fenner
& Smith *CORP AFFIL* dir: New York City
Ballet *NONPR AFFIL* dir: New York City
Ballet; vchmn: Peddie Sch *CLUB AFFIL* Ca-
noe Brook CC, Georgetown, Sky, Univ,
Yale *PHIL AFFIL* vp, dir: Bunbury Company

William Bigelow Wright: vp, treas, trust *B*
Rutland VT 1924 *ED* Princeton Univ AB
CURR EMPL chmn: Marble Fin Corp *CORP
AFFIL* chmn: Marble Bank *NONPR AFFIL*
first vp, treas, dir: 10th Mountain Div Assn
NE Chap; pres: Princeton Alumni Assn VT;
trust, treas: Green Mountain Coll; vp, treas,
dir: Windham Fdn *CLUB AFFIL* Ivy, Princeton *PHIL AFFIL* dir: Bunbury Company

APPLICATION INFORMATION
Initial Approach:

Before submitting a grant request, organization's must first review the foundation's
guidelines. Requests for a grant application
and guidelines (including an annual report
and application cover sheet) can be obtained
either by phone or by mail. Requests for applications should be addressed to Lora Graham. A grant request consists of the

following: a complete cover sheet, a cover letter, a project narrative explaining the need for assistance and relative financial data. Other necessary materials include an IRS 501(c)(3) letter of tax free determination, most recent audit or latest available balance sheet and income statement, and a budget for the project.

The grant application deadlines for all materials are: December 16, 1994; March 17, 1995; June 16, 1995; September 15, 1995. Grants must arrive at the foundation's offices before 4:30 pm. Grants received after the deadline will be included in the following grant cycle.

Organizations requesting grants will be notified by mail of the board's decision approximately six weeks after the deadline.

Restrictions on Giving: Scholarship grants are limited to Windham county residents. Aside from restoration and preservation, grants are primarily confined to the following areas: arts, education, social services, and health. Grants are given only to tax-exempt organizations in Vermont.

GRANTS ANALYSIS
Total Grants: $311,733

Number of Grants: 99*

Highest Grant: $25,000

Average Grant: $1,651*

Typical Range: $1,000 to $5,000

Disclosure Period: fiscal year ending October 31, 1994

Note: Number of grants and average grant exclude $148,283 in individual scholarships. Recent grants are derived from a fiscal 1994 Form 990.

RECENT GRANTS

Library

1,500	Visiting Nurse Association, Maternal Child Health Division, Colchester, VT — parent education library project
1,000	Cavendish Fletcher Community Library, Proctorsville, VT — program funding
1,000	St. Johnsbury Athenaeum, St. Johnsbury, VT

General

25,000	Town of Grafton, Grafton, VT — Village Bridge repair
20,000	Grafton Church, Grafton, VT — building renovations
10,000	Stratton Mountain School, Stratton Mountain, VT — scholarship fund
5,000	US Olympic Committee, Vermont State Committee, Burlington, VT — olympic program funding
3,000	East School, Springfield, VT — community publishing center

VIRGINIA

Beazley Foundation/Frederick Foundation

CONTACT
Lawrence W. I'Anson, Jr.
President and Executive Director
Beazley Foundation/Frederick Foundation
3720 Brighton St.
Portsmouth, VA 23707
(804) 393-1605

FINANCIAL SUMMARY
Recent Giving: $1,800,000 (1994 est.);
$1,827,447 (1993); $886,232 (1992)

Assets: $48,000,000 (1994 est.);
$47,797,630 (1993); $21,760,781 (1992)

Fiscal Note: Figures for 1992 or earlier are for the Beazley Foundation only.

EIN: 54-0550100

CONTRIBUTIONS SUMMARY
Donor(s): The Beazley Foundation was founded in December 1948 with funds provided by the late Fred W. Beazley , his wife Marie C. Beazley, and son Fred W. Beazley, Jr., all of Portsmouth, VA. A sister foundation, Foundation Boys Academy was founded by Mr. Beazley in 1956. In 1986, the charter of Foundation Boys Academy was amended, the name changed to Frederick Foundation and its purpose changed to fund charitable and religious, in addition to educational endeavors. However, in 1993, the Frederick Foundation merged into the Beazley Foundation and now follows its program interests.

The main goal of the chief benefactor of the foundations, Mr. Beazley, was to provide what was not otherwise available to the citizens of Portsmouth, primarily to the youth. He was interested in a quality secondary education for deserving youngsters, as well as recreational facilities for the children of the city. He established the City Dental Clinic in cooperation with the city of Portsmouth to provide dental care to those who could not afford it. Affordable rental housing was also one of his most satisfying accomplishments.

Typical Recipients: • *Arts & Humanities:* Libraries • *Civic & Public Affairs:* African American Affairs, Economic Development, Housing, Municipalities/Towns, Nonprofit Management, Professional & Trade Associations • *Education:* Afterschool/Enrichment Programs, Colleges & Universities, Education Funds, Legal Education, Medical Education, Minority Education, Public Education (Precollege), Student Aid • *Health:* Cancer, Children's Health/Hospitals, Clinics/Medical Centers, Emergency/Ambulance Services, Geriatric Health, Health Organizations, Hospitals, Single-Disease Health Associations • *Religion:* Churches, Religious Welfare • *Social Services:* At-Risk Youth,

Camps, Child Welfare, Community Centers, Community Service Organizations, Crime Prevention, Day Care, Domestic Violence, Emergency Relief, Food/Clothing Distribution, Homes, People with Disabilities, Recreation & Athletics, Shelters/Homelessness, Substance Abuse, United Funds/United Ways, Youth Organizations

Grant Types: capital, emergency, endowment, general support, operating expenses, project, research, and scholarship

Geographic Distribution: primarily Portsmouth, VA, and the South Hampton Roads area

GIVING OFFICERS
Richard S. Bray: trust

Jeannette C. Bridgeman: treas, asst secy

Leroy T. Canoles, Jr.: trust *B* 1925 *ED* Univ VA Law Sch 1951 *CURR EMPL* pres, dir: Kaufman and Canoles PC

Mills E. Godwin, Jr.: trust *PHIL AFFIL* dir: Camp Foundation

Lawrence W. I'Anson, Jr.: pres, exec dir

John T. Kavanaugh: vp, trust

W. Ashton Lewis: secy, trust

Oriana M. McKinnon: trust *CURR EMPL* sec, dir: The Chrysler Museum

Joseph J. Quadros, Jr.: vp, trust

P. Ward Robinett, Jr.: trust

APPLICATION INFORMATION
Initial Approach:

Applicants are encouraged to write to request grant application guidelines.

Requests should include: description of the need to be addressed; amount requested and how the need will be met; specific list of those served by the project; names and qualifications of staff working on the project; budget for the project and other potential sources of support; evaluation plan for the project; deadline for requested funds; and details of how the project will be supported after the requested grant expires. Additional information should include a brief background of the organization; list of board members; the most recently audited financial statement; copy of the current operating budget; evidence of tax-exempt status; evidence of accreditation or licensing; any interest shown by a foundation trustee and/or any contact made with a trustee about the project; and, if a school, the annual cost to attend and a description of the financial aid program.

The cover letter of the proposal must be signed by an authorized officer, with an address and telephone number included.

Proposals may be submitted at any time, but they should be submitted by December 15th for January board meeting; by March 15th for April meeting; by June 15th for July meeting; and September 15th for October meeting. Otherwise, the request will be presented at the next meeting.

The board will contact the applicant if there are any questions regarding the proposal.

Restrictions on Giving: The foundation makes some gifts to organizations outside Virginia, however, its major thrust is support within Virginia, with a preference for Tidewater, VA, and the city of Portsmouth.

Restrictions on Giving: The foundation does not fund individuals, conferences, symposia, publications or media projects, environmental protection projects, or programs relating to the arts and humanities.

OTHER THINGS TO KNOW
The Foundation operates the Beazley Senior Center in Portsmouth, VA.

PUBLICATIONS
Application guidelines, foundation policy, and annual report

GRANTS ANALYSIS
Total Grants: $1,827,447

Number of Grants: 86

Highest Grant: $186,791

Average Grant: $21,249

Typical Range: $5,000 to $200,000

Disclosure Period: 1993

Note: Recent grants are derived from a 1993 Form 990 for the Beazley Foundation.

RECENT GRANTS

Library

25,000	Norfolk Academy, Norfolk, VA — new library project
800	Portsmouth Public Library, Portsmouth, VA — forum

General

186,791	City of Department of Public Health, Portsmouth, VA — city dental clinic
85,000	Medical College of Hampton Roads, Norfolk, VA — geriatric evaluation clinic in Portsmouth
85,000	William and Mary College of Marshall-Wythe School of Law, Williamsburg, VA — Panson law scholar program
79,167	Portsmouth Public Schools, Portsmouth, VA — planetarium
78,000	Portsmouth Public Schools, Portsmouth, VA — scholarship

Bell Atlantic Corp. / Bell Atlantic Foundation

Revenue: $13.79 billion
Employees: 71,400
Headquarters: Philadelphia, PA
SIC Major Group: Holding Companies Nec and Telephone Communications Except Radiotelephone

CONTACT
Denise Bailey
Director
Bell Atlantic Foundation
1310 N Court House Rd., 10th Fl.
Arlington, VA 22201
(703) 974-8845

Note: Ms. Bailey is the contact for national and regional programs, which are handled by the foundation. State, local, or community programs and projects are handled by Bell Atlantic operating companies or subsidiaries. Local groups should submit requests for support to the closest operating company. The company's World Wide Web address is http://www.bell-atl.com

FINANCIAL SUMMARY
Recent Giving: $13,031,339 (1994); $12,475,385 (1993); $14,899,830 (1992)

Assets: $10,369,841 (1994); $11,862,152 (1993); $9,904,298 (1992)

Fiscal Note: Figures represent combined foundation giving and direct giving by the corporation, its subsidiaries, and its enterprise companies. In 1994, foundation donated $1,575,803. See "Other Things You Should Know" for a list of contributing subsidiaries.

EIN: 23-2502809

CONTRIBUTIONS SUMMARY
Typical Recipients: • *Arts & Humanities:* Libraries, Music, Public Broadcasting, Theater • *Civic & Public Affairs:* African American Affairs • *Education:* Colleges & Universities, Education Reform, Engineering/Technological Education, Literacy, Minority Education, Public Education (Precollege), Science/Mathematics Education • *Science:* Scientific Organizations

Grant Types: employee matching gifts

Note: Employee matching gift ratio: 1 to 1, for support to education.

Nonmonetary Support Types: donated equipment and loaned executives

Note: Figures for nonmonetary support are unavailable and are not included in above totals. Equipment is donated through nonregulated companies only.

Geographic Distribution: principally in operating locations and to national organizations

Operating Locations: DC, DE (Wilmington), MD (Baltimore), NJ (Newark), PA (Philadelphia), VA (Arlington, Richmond), WV (Charleston)

CORP. OFFICERS
Raymond W. Smith: *B* Pittsburgh PA 1937 *ED* Carnegie-Mellon Univ BS 1959; Univ Pittsburgh MBA 1967 *CURR EMPL* chmn, ceo, dir: Bell Atlantic Corp *CORP AFFIL* dir: CoreStates Fin Corp, USAir Group *NONPR AFFIL* dir: Univ PA Sch Engg & Applied Sci; mem: Bus Roundtable, Lib Congress James Madison Natl Counc; mem natl adv bd: Pvt Sector Counc; trust: Univ Pittsburgh

GIVING OFFICERS
Denise Bailey: dir *CURR EMPL* dir contributions programs: Bell Atlantic Corp

James G. Cullen: pres *B* 1942 *ED* Rutgers Univ BA 1964; MA Inst Tech *CURR EMPL* pres: Bell Atlantic Corp

APPLICATION INFORMATION
Initial Approach: *Initial Contact:* letter *Include Information On:* description and his-

tory of organization and statement of primary objective; amount requested; project budget; description, purpose, and objective of project and anticipated results; activities and time frame; population served; names of other funders; current audited financial statement; list of staff, consultants, and board of directors; proof of tax-exempt status *Deadlines:* none *Note:* Foundation does not respond to telephone or mass solicitations.

Restrictions on Giving: Foundation does not make grants to individuals, private foundations, or "flow-through" organizations whose primary purpose is grant making to other recipient organizations; sports programs or fund-raising events that involve ticket sales or advertising; hospitals, medical clinics, or medical research; endowment funds or capital campaigns; religious organizations for sectarian purposes or that serve only one religious group; veterans groups or labor organizations that serve only their own membership; political groups or candidates; single-issue health organizations; individual primary and secondary schools or school districts; local organizations eligible for support from Bell Atlantic subsidiaries; or organizations tied to cause-related marketing. Foundation also does not provide loans.

OTHER THINGS TO KNOW
Foundation support is restricted to national and regional organizations that develop and implement programs affecting constituencies in the Bell Atlantic service areas and organizations described in section 501(c)(3) or section 170(c)(1) of the Internal Revenue code.

Contributing subsidiaries include New Jersey Bell, Bell of Pennsylvania, Bell Atlantic-Delaware, Bell Atlantic-Maryland, C & P of Virginia, C & P of West Virginia, and C & P Telephone (DC). Amount given through each is relative to the size of the subsidiary.

GRANTS ANALYSIS
Total Grants: $939,500

Number of Grants: 55

Highest Grant: $100,000

Average Grant: $17,082

Typical Range: $5,000 to $30,000

Disclosure Period: 1994

Note: Above information represents foundation giving only and excludes $636,303 in matching gifts to education. Recent grants are derived from a 1992 Form 990.

RECENT GRANTS

Library

96,341	American Library Association, Chicago, IL
10,000	Prince George's County Memorial Library System, Hyattsville, MD
8,500	Wissahickon Valley Public Library, Philadelphia, PA
6,000	Barnegat Branch of Ocean County Library, Barnegat, NJ

General

419,000	American Association for the Advancement of Sciences, New York, NY

50,000	International Geographical Congress, Bethesda, MD
30,000	NAACP, Baltimore, MD
20,000	Stevens Institute of Technology, Hoboken, NJ
10,000	Center for Excellence in Education, McLean, VA

Bryant Foundation

CONTACT
Arthur H. Bryant II
President and Treasurer
The Bryant Foundation
PO Box 2929
Winchester, VA 22604
(703) 662-3800

FINANCIAL SUMMARY
Recent Giving: $1,739,568 (1992);
$828,250 (1991); $1,219,300 (1990)
Assets: $29,483,873 (1992); $25,639,761
(1991); $5,394,159 (1988)
EIN: 54-6032840

CONTRIBUTIONS SUMMARY
Donor(s): The foundation was established in 1949 by the late J. C. Herbert Bryant .

Typical Recipients: • *Arts & Humanities:*
Arts Centers, Historic Preservation, History & Archaeology, Libraries, Museums/Galleries • *Civic & Public Affairs:* Municipalities/Towns, Urban & Community Affairs, Zoos/Aquariums • *Education:* Colleges & Universities, Education Funds, Legal Education, Private Education (Precollege), Religious Education, Secondary Education (Private) • *Environment:* General • *Health:* Cancer, Emergency/Ambulance Services, Health Organizations, Hospitals, Medical Research, Respiratory, Single-Disease Health Associations • *Religion:* Churches, Religious Organizations, Religious Welfare • *Science:* Science Museums • *Social Services:* Animal Protection, Child Welfare, Community Centers, Community Service Organizations, Day Care, General, Recreation & Athletics, Youth Organizations

Grant Types: general support

Geographic Distribution: focus on Virginia

GIVING OFFICERS
Arthur Herbert Bryant II: pres, treas *B* Washington DC 1942 *ED* Lees McRae Coll 1960-1962; Miami Dade Coll 1962-1963 *CURR EMPL* chmn, ceo, dir: O'Sullivan Corp *CORP AFFIL* chmn, dir: O'Sullivan Plastics Corp, Regalite Plastics Corp; dir: Gen Paving Corp; gen ptnr: Herbert Bryant Assocs *NONPR AFFIL* mem: Shenandoah Valley Mfrs Assn, VA Mfrs Assn *CLUB AFFIL* Belle Haven CC, Gulf Stream Bath & Tennis, Gulf Stream GC, Loudoun GC & CC, Middleburg Tennis, Winchester CC

Howard W. Smith, Jr.: secy

APPLICATION INFORMATION
Initial Approach:
The foundation has no formal grant procedure or grant application form.

The foundation has no deadline for submitting proposals.

Restrictions on Giving: The foundation reports that grants are made only to nonprofit, charitable organizations. The foundation does not make grants to individuals.

GRANTS ANALYSIS
Total Grants: $1,739,568

Number of Grants: 70

Highest Grant: $1,194,743

Average Grant: $7,896*

Typical Range: $1,000 to $15,000

Disclosure Period: 1992

Note: Average grant figure excludes the highest grant of $1,194,743. Recent grants are derived from a 1992 grants list.

RECENT GRANTS

Library

30,000	Alexandria Library, Alexandria, VA — community welfare
5,000	Athenaeum, Philadelphia, PA — community welfare

General

1,194,743	Owens Foundation — 100,000 shares of O'Sullivan Corp. Stock
75,000	Christ Church Endowment — community welfare
75,000	Virginia College Fund, Richmond, VA — education fund
50,000	Hampden-Sydney College Endowment, Hampden-Sydney, VA — education fund
50,000	Shenandoah University, Winchester, VA — education fund

Cabell Foundation, Robert G. Cabell III and Maude Morgan

CONTACT
John B. Werner
Executive Director
Robert G. Cabell III & Maude Morgan Cabell
Foundation
PO Box 85678
Richmond, VA 23285
(804) 780-2050

FINANCIAL SUMMARY
Recent Giving: $1,385,000 (1993);
$1,420,000 (1992); $1,190,000 (1991)

Assets: $28,716,236 (1993); $27,741,580
(1992); $26,360,006 (1991)

EIN: 54-6039157

CONTRIBUTIONS SUMMARY
Donor(s): The foundation was incorporated in 1957 by the late Robert G. Cabell III and the late Maude Morgan Cabell .

Typical Recipients: • *Arts & Humanities:*
Arts Associations & Councils, Historic Preservation, History & Archaeology, Libraries, Museums/Galleries, Music, Theater • *Civic & Public Affairs:* Economic Development, Municipalities/Towns, Philanthropic Organizations, Zoos/Aquariums • *Education:* Colleges & Universities, Faculty Development, Literacy, Science/Mathematics Education • *Environment:* Air/Water Quality, Forestry, General • *Health:* Children's Health/Hospitals, Clinics/Medical Centers, Diabetes, Emergency/Ambulance Services, Health Organizations • *Religion:* Churches, Religious Organizations, Religious Welfare, Seminaries • *Social Services:* Animal Protection, Child Welfare, Community Service Organizations, Family Planning, Family Services, Food/Clothing Distribution, People with Disabilities, Recreation & Athletics, Senior Services, Shelters/Homelessness, United Funds/United Ways, Youth Organizations

Grant Types: capital and project

Geographic Distribution: Virginia, with a preference for Richmond area

GIVING OFFICERS
Joseph L. Antrim III: dir *CURR EMPL* exec vp, dir: Davenport & Co of Virginia

J. Read Branch: pres, dir

J. Read Branch, Jr.: dir

Patteson Branch, Jr.: dir

Charles Cabell: dir

Robert G. Cabell: vp

Royal E. Cabell, Jr.: secy, dir *PHIL AFFIL* secy, trust: William R., John G., and Emma Scott Foundation

Edmund A. Rennolds, Jr.: dir

John K. B. Rennolds: dir

John B. Werner: exec dir *B* St Marys PA 1931 *ED* Univ VA postgrad 1953-1955; Randolph-Macon Coll BA; Rutgers Univ postgrad *CURR EMPL* sr exec vp: Sovran Fin Corp *NONPR AFFIL* mem: Comptroller Currencys Natl Adv Comm, Poplar Forest Fdn, Robert Morris Assocs, VA Chamber Commerce; trust, mem fin comm: Randolph-Macon Coll *CLUB AFFIL* Commonwealth

APPLICATION INFORMATION
Initial Approach:

The foundation has no formal grant procedure or grant application form.

Applicants should submit written proposals, including an explanation of the intended use of the grant.

Proposals should be submitted by April 1 and October 1.

Restrictions on Giving: The foundation does not support individuals, endowment funds, operating budgets, or research programs.

GRANTS ANALYSIS
Total Grants: $1,385,000

Number of Grants: 26

Highest Grant: $125,000

Average Grant: $53,269

Typical Range: $25,000 to $100,000

Disclosure Period: 1993

Note: Recent grants are derived from a 1993 Form 990.

RECENT GRANTS

Library
20,000	Friends of the West Point Library, W. Point, VA — renovation of museum

General
125,000	Richmond Renaissance, Richmond, VA — 7th Street fountain
100,000	Diabetes Institution Foundation, Virginia Beach, VA — renovation of foundation building
100,000	Randolph-Macon College, Ashland, VA — faculty development
100,000	Randolph-Macon Women's College, Lynchburg, VA — renovation of Martin science building
100,000	Sweet Briar College, Sweet Briar, VA — faculty development

---

Cable & Wireless Holdings, Inc.

Revenue: $650.0 million
Employees: 2,200
Headquarters: Vienna, VA
SIC Major Group: Communications

CONTACT
Margaret Krull
Human Resources Director
Cable & Wireless of North America, Inc.
8219 Leesburg Pike
Vienna, VA 22182
(703) 790-5300

CONTRIBUTIONS SUMMARY
The company's donations are directed toward those local or national programs whose activities will have the most direct and immediate impact on its employee base. Consequently, local organizations or local chapters of national organizations are favored.

Typical Recipients: • *Arts & Humanities:* Arts Associations & Councils, Community Arts, Libraries, Music, Performing Arts • *Civic & Public Affairs:* Urban & Community Affairs • *Education:* Education Associations, Elementary Education (Private) • *Health:* Hospitals, Medical Research, Single-Disease Health Associations • *Social Services:* Child Welfare, Community Centers, Community Service Organizations, United Funds/United Ways, Youth Organizations

Grant Types: general support

Geographic Distribution: principally near operating locations and to national organizations

Operating Locations: NY, TX, VA (Vienna)

CORP. OFFICERS
Gabe Battista: *CURR EMPL* pres: Cable & Wireless Holdings
Scott Yancy: *CURR EMPL* cfo: Cable & Wireless Holdings

GIVING OFFICERS
Margaret Krull: chmn contributions comm *CURR EMPL* dir human resources: Cable & Wireless Communs

APPLICATION INFORMATION
Initial Approach: Initial contact may be made at any time by letter, including a description of the organization, amount requested, and purpose for which funds are sought.

Campbell Foundation, Ruth and Henry

CONTACT
Donald D. Koonce
Trust Officer
Ruth and Henry Campbell Fdn.
c/o Nationsbank of Virginia
PO Box 26903
Richmond, VA 23261
(804) 788-2573

FINANCIAL SUMMARY
Recent Giving: $315,600 (1993); $553,950 (1992); $541,020 (1991)

Assets: $11,063,747 (1993); $10,739,873 (1992); $10,896,354 (1991)

Gifts Received: $3,500 (1992); $17,931 (1990)

Fiscal Note: In fiscal 1992, contributions were received from the Ruth and Henry Campbell Foundation.

EIN: 54-6031023

CONTRIBUTIONS SUMMARY
Typical Recipients: • *Arts & Humanities:* Arts Associations & Councils, Arts Funds, Historic Preservation, History & Archaeology, Libraries, Museums/Galleries, Opera, Theater • *Civic & Public Affairs:* Clubs, General, Municipalities/Towns, Parades/Festivals, Public Policy, Urban & Community Affairs • *Education:* Agricultural Education, Colleges & Universities, Community & Junior Colleges, Education Funds, Private Education (Precollege), Public Education (Precollege), Student Aid • *Environment:* General • *Health:* Children's Health/Hospitals, Health Organizations, Heart, Home-Care Services, Hospices, Hospitals, Nursing Services • *Religion:* Churches, Dioceses, Religious Welfare, Seminaries • *Science:* Science Museums, Scientific Centers & Institutes • *Social Services:* Child Welfare, Community Service Organizations, Homes, People with Disabilities, Recreation & Athletics, Volunteer Services, YMCA/YWCA/YMHA/YWHA, Youth Organizations

Grant Types: general support

Geographic Distribution: focus on VA

GIVING OFFICERS
Nationsbank of VA, NA: trust

John M. Camp, Jr.: dir *PHIL AFFIL* dir, trust: Camp Younts Foundation; treas, dir: Camp Foundation; dir: Ruth Camp McDougall Charitable Trust

Paul D. Camp III: dir *PHIL AFFIL* dir: Ruth Camp McDougall Charitable Trust

Paul Camp Marks: dir *PHIL AFFIL* dir: Ruth Camp McDougall Charitable Trust

Harry W. Walker III: dir

Paul C. Walker: dir *PHIL AFFIL* dir, trust: Camp Younts Foundation; dir: Camp Foundation, Ruth Camp McDougall Charitable Trust

APPLICATION INFORMATION
Initial Approach: Send brief letter of inquiry describing program or project. Include a description of organization, amount requested, purpose of funds sought, recently audited financial statement, and proof of tax-exempt status. There are no deadlines.

Restrictions on Giving: Limited to applicants in the commonwealth of Virginia.

GRANTS ANALYSIS
Total Grants: $315,600
Number of Grants: 52
Highest Grant: $43,500
Typical Range: $1,000 to $37,100
Disclosure Period: 1993

Note: Recent grants are derived from a 1993 Form 990.

RECENT GRANTS

Library
2,000	Wadsworth Athenaeum, Hartford, CT

General
43,500	Southeast 4-H Educational Center, Wakefield, VA
37,100	Southampton County, Courtland, VA
30,000	Virginia Foundation for Independent Colleges, Richmond, VA
12,000	United Congregational Church, Bridgeport, CT
10,000	St. Edward's School, Vero Beach, FL

Carter Foundation, Beirne

CONTACT
J. Samuel Gillespie, Jr.
Advisor
Beirne Carter Foundation
PO Box 26903
Richmond, VA 23261
(804) 788-2964

FINANCIAL SUMMARY
Recent Giving: $866,335 (1993); $823,200 (1992); $474,415 (1991)

Assets: $18,422,053 (1993); $18,992,048 (1992); $17,846,152 (1991)

Gifts Received: $4,245 (1991); $17,838,615 (1990)

Fiscal Note: In 1991, contributions were received from the estate of Beirne Carter.

EIN: 54-1397827

CONTRIBUTIONS SUMMARY
Donor(s): The foundation was established in 1986 by the late Beirne B. Carter.

Typical Recipients: • *Arts & Humanities:* Arts Associations & Councils, Arts Centers, Ballet, Historic Preservation, History & Archaeology, Libraries, Museums/Galleries, Music, Opera, Theater • *Civic & Public Affairs:* Botanical Gardens/Parks, General, Housing, Legal Aid, Nonprofit Management, Philanthropic Organizations, Urban & Community Affairs • *Education:* Agricultural Education, Business Education, Colleges & Universities, Community & Junior Colleges, Education Funds, Medical Education, Private Education (Precollege) • *Environment:* Air/Water Quality, General, Resource Conservation • *Health:* AIDS/HIV • *Religion:* Churches, Religious Welfare, Seminaries • *Science:* Science Museums • *Social Services:* Big Brother/Big Sister, Child Welfare, Community Service Organizations, Domestic Violence, Family Planning, Family Services, General, Homes, People with Disabilities, Shelters/Homelessness, Youth Organizations

Grant Types: general support

Geographic Distribution: focus on Virginia

GIVING OFFICERS
Dr. J. Samuel Gillespie, Jr.: adv *PHIL AFFIL* dir: Thomas F. and Kate Miller Jeffress Memorial Trust; trust: Elizabeth G. Jeffress Memorial Trust

Mary Ross Carter Hutcheson: pres

Talfourd H. Kemper: secy, treas *CURR EMPL* partner: Woods Rogers & Hazlegrove

Mary T. Bryan Perkins: vp

APPLICATION INFORMATION
Initial Approach:

The foundation requests applications be made in writing and be submitted in quadruplicate.

Include a brief description of the organization, its history, and its purpose; a concise description of the project or activity proposed, including the specific purpose for which the grant is requested, the benefits to be provided, and the needs to be met; the names and affiliations of the organization's trustees, directors, advisors, and principal staff; and evidence that the organization is exempt from federal income tax under section 501(c)(3) and is not classified as a private foundation or private operating foundation, and a certification that the organization's status is unchanged. The foundation also requests that applicants include financial statements for the current and two prior years showing the major sources of organizational support and endowment; a detailed financial plan that includes the total cost, the specific amount requested, the amount raised to date, plans for procuring the remainder, other funding sources, and

provisions for contingencies and ongoing support; a brief biographical sketch of the person who will conduct or supervise the proposed program; plans for evaluation of the project's results and for sustaining the project after grant funds expire; and a cover letter from an official of the organization stating that the organization has formally approved the proposed program.

The deadlines are March 1 and September 1.

The board meets in April and October.

Restrictions on Giving: The foundation does not make grants to individuals. In general, grants are not made to endowment funds or for on-going general operating expenses or existing deficits.

OTHER THINGS TO KNOW
Funding requests that are not of a recurring nature are given preference.

PUBLICATIONS
Informational brochure including application guidelines

GRANTS ANALYSIS
Total Grants: $866,335

Number of Grants: 48

Highest Grant: $250,000

Average Grant: $18,049

Typical Range: $1,000 to $25,000

Disclosure Period: 1993

Note: Recent grants are derived from a 1993 Form 990.

RECENT GRANTS
Library
5,000   Lancaster County Public Library, Kilmarnock, VA

General
250,000   River Foundation, Roanoke, VA
100,000   Maymont Foundation, Richmond, VA
50,000   University of Virginia Darden School, Charlottesville, VA
38,200   Medical College of Virginia, Richmond, VA
36,114   Planned Parenthood of the Blue Ridge, Roanoke, VA

Central Fidelity Banks, Inc. / Central Fidelity Banks Inc. Foundation

Employees: 3,300
Headquarters: Richmond, VA
SIC Major Group: Holding & Other Investment Offices and National Commercial Banks

CONTACT
Charles Tysinger
Foundation Manager
Central Fidelity Banks, Inc.
PO Box 27602
Richmond, VA 23261
(804) 697-7038

FINANCIAL SUMMARY
Recent Giving: $1,500,000 (1995 est.); $1,300,000 (1994 approx.); $1,220,713 (1993)

Assets: $78,000 (1993); $95,810 (1992); $366,325 (1991)

Gifts Received: $1,200,000 (1993); $601,300 (1992)

Fiscal Note: Giving is through the foundation only. Company reports that public relations department also makes limited gifts. Above figures exclude nonmonetary support. The foundation receives contributions from Central Fidelity National Bank.

EIN: 54-6173939

CONTRIBUTIONS SUMMARY
Typical Recipients: • *Arts & Humanities:* Arts Associations & Councils, Historic Preservation, Libraries, Museums/Galleries, Music, Performing Arts, Public Broadcasting • *Civic & Public Affairs:* Economic Development, General • *Education:* Business Education, Colleges & Universities, Education Funds, Public Education (Precollege), Student Aid • *Health:* Cancer, Clinics/Medical Centers, Health Organizations, Hospitals, Single-Disease Health Associations • *Social Services:* Child Welfare, Community Service Organizations, Family Services, Homes, Senior Services, Shelters/Homelessness, United Funds/United Ways, Youth Organizations

Grant Types: capital, endowment, and scholarship

Note: Scholarships are only awarded to schools and universities, not individuals.

Nonmonetary Support: $200,000 (1994); $10,000 (1992)

Nonmonetary Support Types: donated equipment and loaned executives

Note: The company provides nonmonetary support.

Geographic Distribution: in locations served by their facilities

Operating Locations: VA (Richmond)

CORP. OFFICERS
Lewis Nelson Miller, Jr.: B 1944 *ED* Washington & Lee Univ BA 1966 *CURR EMPL* pres: Central Fidelity Banks Inc

GIVING OFFICERS
Lewis Nelson Miller, Jr.: dir *CURR EMPL* pres: Central Fidelity Banks Inc (see above)

Charles W. Tysinger: fdn mgr *CURR EMPL* corp exec off, treas: Central Fidelity Banks Inc

APPLICATION INFORMATION
Initial Approach: *Initial Contact:* letter *Deadlines:* none

Restrictions on Giving: Foundation does not consider requests from organizations located outside market areas.

GRANTS ANALYSIS
Total Grants: $1,220,713

Number of Grants: 398

Highest Grant: $76,875

Average Grant: $3,067

Typical Range: $500 to $5,000

Disclosure Period: 1993

Note: Recent grants are derived from a 1993 Form 990.

RECENT GRANTS

Library

6,000 Amherst County Main Library, Amherst, VA

General

322,342 Central Fidelity Bank Special Education Initiatives, Richmond, VA

76,875 United Way Greater Richmond, Richmond, VA

40,000 United Way Central Virginia, Lynchburg, VA

35,300 United Way South Hampton Roads, Norfolk, VA

30,000 Forward Hampton Roads, Norfolk, VA

Chesapeake Corp. / Chesapeake Corporate Foundation

Sales: $885.0 million
Employees: 5,062
Headquarters: Richmond, VA
SIC Major Group: Paperboard Mills, Hardwood Veneer & Plywood, Paper Mills, and Corrugated & Solid Fiber Boxes

CONTACT

Alvah H. Eubank, Jr.
Secretary-Treasurer
Chesapeake Corp. Foundation
PO Box 2350
Richmond, VA 23218-2350
(804) 697-1000

FINANCIAL SUMMARY

Recent Giving: $490,000 (1995 est.); $495,000 (1994 approx.); $552,324 (1993)

Assets: $752,881 (1993); $976,144 (1992); $1,200,177 (1991)

Gifts Received: $292,500 (1993); $380,000 (1992); $670,000 (1990)

Fiscal Note: Figures reflect foundation contributions only. Company also gives directly through marketing or public affairs departments within each operating group. Contributions received from The Chesapeake Corporation.

EIN: 54-0605823

CONTRIBUTIONS SUMMARY

Typical Recipients: • *Arts & Humanities:* Arts Associations & Councils, Community Arts, Historic Preservation, History & Archaeology, Libraries, Museums/Galleries, Music, Theater • *Civic & Public Affairs:* Economic Development, Municipalities/Towns, Nonprofit Management, Philanthropic Organizations, Professional & Trade Associations, Safety • *Education:* Agricultural Education, Colleges & Universities, Community & Junior Colleges, Education Associations, Education Funds, Engineer-

ing/Technological Education, Minority Education, Private Education (Precollege), Public Education (Precollege), Science/Mathematics Education, Student Aid • *Environment:* Air/Water Quality, General • *Health:* Emergency/Ambulance Services, Hospitals, Mental Health • *International:* International Relief Efforts • *Science:* Scientific Centers & Institutes • *Social Services:* Community Service Organizations, Family Services, Homes, United Funds/United Ways, Youth Organizations

Grant Types: capital, employee matching gifts, and scholarship

Geographic Distribution: primarily in areas where company employees live and work

Operating Locations: IA (West Des Moines), IN (Richmond, St. Anthony), KY (Louisville), MD (Baltimore, Pocomoke City, Princess Anne), NC (Elizabeth City, Greensboro, Rural Hall, Winston-Salem), NJ (Pennsauken), NY (Binghamton, Buffalo, Le Roy, North Tonawanda, Scotia), OH (Madison, Sandusky), PA (Scranton), VA (Keysville, Milford, Norfolk, Richmond, Roanoke, West Point, Williamsburgh), WI (Appleton, Menasha, Neenah)

CORP. OFFICERS

Christopher R. Burgess: *CURR EMPL* contr: Chesapeake Corp

John Paul Causey, Jr.: *B* Takoma Park MD 1943 *ED* Davidson Coll AB 1965; Univ Richmond TC Williams Sch Law JD 1968 *CURR EMPL* vp, secy, gen couns: Chesapeake Corp *CORP AFFIL* dir: Citizens & Farmers Bank *NONPR AFFIL* mem: Am Corp Couns Assn, Am Soc Corp Secys

Paul Alton Dresser, Jr.: *B* Corsicana TX 1942 *ED* TX A&M Univ BA 1964; Harvard Univ MBA 1970 *CURR EMPL* coo, exec vp, dir: Chesapeake Corp *CORP AFFIL* dir: Crestar Bank *NONPR AFFIL* chmn: James City County Sch Bd Selection Commn; dir: Coll William & Mary Sch Bus Admin; mem: Am Paper Inst, VA Bus Higher Ed Counc; mem bd gov: Natl Counc Air & Stream Improvement *CLUB AFFIL* Focus, Forum

Joseph Carter Fox: *B* Petersburg VA 1939 *ED* Washington & Lee Univ BS 1961; Univ VA MBA 1963 *CURR EMPL* ceo, dir, chmn: Chesapeake Corp *CORP AFFIL* dir: Crestar Fin Corp *NONPR AFFIL* dir: Am Forest & Paper Assn, YMCA Richmond; pres: NC St Pulp & Paper Fdn *CLUB AFFIL* Commonwealth, W Point CC

Andrew J. Kohut: *CURR EMPL* vp fin, cfo: Chesapeake Corp

Louis K. Matherne: *B* Brownsville TN 1951 *ED* Univ VA 1973; Univ PA 1978 *CURR EMPL* treas: Chesapeake Corp

GIVING OFFICERS

James E. Asmuth: trust

O. D. Dennis: trust

Alvah H. Eubank, Jr.: secy, treas *B* Richmond VA 1926 *ED* VA Polytech Inst & St Univ BA 1949

T. G. Harris: trust

Sture Gordon Olsson: trust *B* Richmond VA 1920 *ED* Univ VA BS 1942 *CURR EMPL* chmn: Chesapeake Corp *CORP AFFIL* dir: Citizens & Farmers Bank *PHIL AFFIL* pres, trust: Elis Olsson Memorial Foundation

W. T. Robinson: trust

APPLICATION INFORMATION

Initial Approach: *Initial Contact:* address inquiries and applications to foundation secretary *Include Information On:* purpose of request and results sought; budget for project and organization's total budget; personnel involved in project; members of governing body; amounts requested from other funding sources; evidence of tax-exempt status; statement that application has been reviewed and approved by organization's governing body *Deadlines:* none; foundation trustees meet in January, May, and October; meeting dates available upon request

Restrictions on Giving: Foundation does not support individuals, organizations which are not tax-exempt under IRS standards, athletic organizations or events, or organizations outside the foundation's geographical or philosophical areas of responsibility.

OTHER THINGS TO KNOW

After organization has received grant, the foundation requires an accounting of the distribution of funds and recent financial statements.

Foundation reviews all specific requests for funds but does not respond to routine fundraising appeals.

GRANTS ANALYSIS

Total Grants: $552,324

Number of Grants: 113

Highest Grant: $92,500

Average Grant: $4,888

Typical Range: $1,000 to $10,000

Disclosure Period: 1993

Note: Fiscal information reflects foundation contributions only. Recent grants are derived from a 1993 Form 990.

RECENT GRANTS

Library

15,000 West Point Public Library, West Point, VA

7,000 Ells Olsson Memorial Library Fund, West Point, VA

General

92,500 University of Virginia, Charlottesville, VA

78,600 College Scholarship Service, Princeton, NJ — scholarships

22,500 Virginia Foundation for Independent Colleges, Richmond, VA

21,500 United Way Neenah-Menasha, Neenah, WI

12,000 Parent Child Development Center, West Point, VA

Cole Trust, Quincy

CONTACT
Judith M. McCoy
Trust Officer
Quincy Cole Trust
c/o NationsBank of VA
PO Box 26903
Richmond, VA 23261
(804) 788-2067

FINANCIAL SUMMARY
Recent Giving: $286,126 (fiscal 1994);
$325,345 (fiscal 1991); $296,037 (fiscal 1990)

Assets: $8,919,400 (fiscal 1994);
$6,501,280 (fiscal 1991); $6,146,668 (fiscal 1990)

EIN: 54-6086247

CONTRIBUTIONS SUMMARY
Donor(s): the late Quincy Cole

Typical Recipients: • *Arts & Humanities:* Ballet, Community Arts, Dance, Historic Preservation, History & Archaeology, Libraries, Museums/Galleries, Music • *Civic & Public Affairs:* General, Municipalities/Towns, Public Policy • *Education:* Colleges & Universities, Private Education (Precollege), Public Education (Precollege) • *International:* Foreign Arts Organizations • *Religion:* Churches • *Social Services:* Community Service Organizations, Homes, Recreation & Athletics, Shelters/Homelessness, United Funds/United Ways, Youth Organizations

Grant Types: general support

Geographic Distribution: limited to the Richmond, VA, metropolitan area

GIVING OFFICERS
Nationsbank VA NA: trust

APPLICATION INFORMATION
Initial Approach: Send brief letter of inquiry describing program. Deadline is April 20.

GRANTS ANALYSIS
Total Grants: $286,126

Number of Grants: 13

Highest Grant: $54,126

Typical Range: $4,000 to $36,000

Disclosure Period: fiscal year ending June 30, 1994

Note: Recent grants are derived from a fiscal 1994 Form 990.

RECENT GRANTS

Library
36,000   Virginia State Library and Archives, Richmond, VA — fund processing and housing of Charles Gilette's correspondence

General
54,126   Windsor House, Richmond, VA — upkeep and maintenance of real estate

25,000   Council for America's First Freedom, Richmond, VA — monument to the Virginia Statute for Religious Freedom
25,000   Henricus Foundation, Richmond, VA
25,000   New Community School, Richmond, VA — multipurpose activity center
25,000   University of Richmond, Richmond, VA — construction of the arts center complex

---

Ethyl Corp

Sales: $1.03 billion
Employees: 1,800
Headquarters: Richmond, VA
SIC Major Group: Industrial Organic Chemicals Nec and Chemicals & Allied Products Nec

---

CONTACT
A. Prescott Rowe
External Affairs
Ethyl Corp.
330 S 4th St.
Richmond, VA 23219
(804) 788-5413

FINANCIAL SUMMARY
Recent Giving: $1,200,000 (1994 approx.);
$2,400,000 (1993 approx.); $2,600,000 (1992)

Fiscal Note: All contributions are made directly by the company. Above figures exclude nonmonetary support.

CONTRIBUTIONS SUMMARY
Typical Recipients: • *Arts & Humanities:* Arts Associations & Councils, Arts Centers, Arts Funds, Community Arts, Historic Preservation, Libraries, Museums/Galleries, Music, Opera, Performing Arts, Public Broadcasting • *Civic & Public Affairs:* Business/Free Enterprise, Economic Development, Urban & Community Affairs • *Education:* Colleges & Universities, Economic Education, Science/Mathematics Education • *Environment:* General • *Health:* Emergency/Ambulance Services, Health Organizations, Hospitals • *Science:* Observatories & Planetariums, Science Exhibits & Fairs, Scientific Centers & Institutes, Scientific Organizations • *Social Services:* Community Service Organizations, Shelters/Homelessness, United Funds/United Ways, Youth Organizations

Grant Types: capital, challenge, employee matching gifts, endowment, general support, professorship, and scholarship

Note: Employee matching gift ratio: 1 to 1.

Nonmonetary Support Types: donated equipment and loaned employees

Note: Value of nonmonetary support is not available.

Geographic Distribution: in headquarters and operating locations only

Operating Locations: AR (Magnolia), IL (Elk Grove Village, Sauget), LA (Baton Rouge), MO (St. Louis), MS (Natchez), SC (Orangeburg), TX (Deer Park, Houston), VA (Lynchburg, Richmond)

Note: Also operates in Austria, France, Japan, Singapore, and Germany.

CORP. OFFICERS
Bruce Cobb Gottwald: *B* Richmond VA 1933 *ED* VA Military Inst BS 1954; Univ VA *CURR EMPL* chmn, ceo, dir: Ethyl Corp *CORP AFFIL* dir: CSX Corp, Dominion Resources Inc, First Colony Corp, James River Corp VA, Tredegar Indus *NONPR AFFIL* bd govs: VA Counc Econ Ed; dir: Natl Assn Mfrs; mem: Chem Mfrs Assn; trust: VA Military Inst *PHIL AFFIL* secy, treas: Gottwald Foundation

Floyd D. Gottwald, Jr.: *B* Richmond VA 1922 *ED* VA Military Inst BS 1943; Univ Richmond MS 1951 *CURR EMPL* vchmn: Ethyl Corp *CORP AFFIL* dir: Tredegar Indus *NONPR AFFIL* dir: Am Petroleum Inst, Natl Petroleum Counc; trust: VA Military Inst *CLUB AFFIL* Alfalfa, CC VA, Commonwealth *PHIL AFFIL* trust: Herndon Foundation; pres: Gottwald Foundation

Thomas E. Gottwald: *B* 1962 *ED* Harvard Univ MBA 1984; VA Military Inst BS *CURR EMPL* pres, coo, dir: Ethyl Corp *CORP AFFIL* pres, dir: Ethyl Petroleum Additives Inc

William M. Gottwald, MD: *B* Richmond VA 1948 *ED* Tulane Univ MD; Univ Richmond MBA; Washington & Lee Univ BS *CURR EMPL* sr vp, dir: Ethyl Corp *CORP AFFIL* chmn, dir: Whitby Pharmaceuticals; chmn, pres, dir: Whitby Inc, Whitby Res

GIVING OFFICERS
Bruce Cobb Gottwald: mem contributions mgmt comm *CURR EMPL* chmn, ceo, dir: Ethyl Corp *PHIL AFFIL* secy, treas: Gottwald Foundation (see above)

Floyd D. Gottwald, Jr.: mem contributions mgmt comm *CURR EMPL* vchmn: Ethyl Corp *PHIL AFFIL* trust: Herndon Foundation; pres: Gottwald Foundation (see above)

A. Prescott Rowe: mem contributions mgmt comm *B* Fredericksburg VA 1938 *ED* Washington & Lee Univ 1960 *CURR EMPL* vp external aff: Ethyl Corp *CORP AFFIL* chmn: Central VA Telecommun Corp *NONPR AFFIL* chmn: Central VA ETV Corp

Charles B. Walker: mem contributions mgmt comm *B* Richmond VA 1939 *ED* Univ Richmond 1961 *CURR EMPL* vchmn, treas, cfo, dir: Ethyl Corp *CORP AFFIL* vchmn, cfo: Albermarle Corp; vp: Ethyl Petroleum Additives Inc *NONPR AFFIL* mem: Natl Assn Mfrs; trust: Nations Fund Trust/Nations Fund Inc

APPLICATION INFORMATION
Initial Approach: *Initial Contact:* brief letter or proposal to A. Prescott Rowe, vice president of external affairs, or to appropriate contact at nearest field location *Include Information On:* statement of purpose; brief description of nature and scope of activities; current financial condition (balance sheet); list of board members and staff manager;

copy of IRS determination letter; rationale for why company is appropriate donor *Deadlines:* before September 1; contributions management committee makes grant decisions based on recommendations of vice president, external affairs

Restrictions on Giving: Contributions are not made to religious organizations for religious purposes, individuals in support of a personal project for profit, fraternal groups, local organizations in communities where company does not have significant operations, or in response to telephone or mass mail solicitations.

The corporation does not directly support political contributions. However, limited contributions are made through Ethyl Corporation Political Action Committee, which consists of funds contributed by Ethyl employees.

OTHER THINGS TO KNOW
Company annually budgets a limited amount to support charitable organizations with small advertisements in printed programs aimed at raising funds.

GRANTS ANALYSIS
Total Grants: $1,200,000*

Typical Range: $1,000 to $5,000

Disclosure Period: 1994

Note: Total grants figure is approximate.

Goodman & Co. / Dalis Foundation

Sales: $8.2 million
Employees: 120
Headquarters: Norfolk, VA

CONTACT
Joan D. Martone
President
Goodman & Co.
PO Box 3247
Norfolk, VA 23514
(804) 624-5100

FINANCIAL SUMMARY
Recent Giving: $103,972 (fiscal 1993); $241,200 (fiscal 1992); $215,000 (fiscal 1991)

Assets: $5,401,778 (fiscal 1993); $5,450,410 (fiscal 1992); $4,937,116 (fiscal 1991)

EIN: 54-6046229

CONTRIBUTIONS SUMMARY
Typical Recipients: • *Arts & Humanities:* Libraries, Museums/Galleries, Music • *Civic & Public Affairs:* Municipalities/Towns, Urban & Community Affairs, Zoos/Aquariums • *Health:* Hospitals, Medical Research, Single-Disease Health Associations • *Social Services:* Community Service Organizations, Senior Services

Grant Types: general support and research

Geographic Distribution: focus on Norfolk, VA

CORP. OFFICERS
Joan Dalis Martone: *CURR EMPL* pres: Goodman & Co

GIVING OFFICERS
Joan Dalis Martone: pres, treas *CURR EMPL* pres: Goodman & Co (see above)

APPLICATION INFORMATION
Initial Approach: Send brief letter of inquiry describing program or project. There are no deadlines.

GRANTS ANALYSIS
Total Grants: $103,972

Number of Grants: 2

Highest Grant: $100,300

Disclosure Period: fiscal year ending May 31, 1993

Note: Recent grants are derived from a fiscal 1993 Form 990.

RECENT GRANTS

General
3,672   Candii House, Norfolk, VA

James River Corp. of Virginia / James River Corp. Foundation

Revenue: $5.41 billion
Employees: 35,000
Headquarters: Richmond, VA
SIC Major Group: Sanitary Paper Products, Paper Mills, Sanitary Food Containers, and Folding Paperboard Boxes

CONTACT
Carol A. Akin
Executive Administrator, Community Affairs and Corporate Contributions
James River Corp. of Virginia
PO Box 2218
Richmond, VA 23217
(804) 649-4406
Note: Ms. Akin is the contact for Virginia only; requests from other areas should be directed to the nearest James River Corp. facility. For information about company's matching gifts to education program, write or call Secretary, Corporate Contributions, at the address and telephone number above. For more information, see "Other Things You Should Know." The company's World Wide Web address is http://www.jriver.com

FINANCIAL SUMMARY
Recent Giving: $1,200,000 (1995 est.); $1,200,000 (1994 approx.); $1,500,000 (1993 approx.)

Fiscal Note: Company gives directly. The company's Marketing Department makes direct contributions for event sponsorships. The company is starting a foundation and anticipates its establishment in the fall of 1995.

CONTRIBUTIONS SUMMARY
Typical Recipients: • *Arts & Humanities:* Arts Associations & Councils, Arts Centers, Arts Funds, Community Arts, Libraries, Museums/Galleries, Performing Arts, Public

Broadcasting, Theater, Visual Arts • *Civic & Public Affairs:* Business/Free Enterprise, Economic Development, Employment/Job Training, Housing, Professional & Trade Associations, Safety • *Education:* Colleges & Universities, Economic Education • *Environment:* General • *Health:* Emergency/Ambulance Services • *Social Services:* Delinquency & Criminal Rehabilitation, Shelters/Homelessness, Substance Abuse, United Funds/United Ways, Volunteer Services, Youth Organizations

Grant Types: capital, employee matching gifts, endowment, general support, multi-year/continuing support, and project

Note: Employee matching gift ratio: 1 to 1. Matching gifts are for education and eligible employees only.

Geographic Distribution: communities where company employees live and work

Operating Locations: AL (Pennington), AR (Fort Smith), CA (Antioch, Corte Madera, Fullerton, Garden Grove, Oakland, Rancho Dominguez, San Leandro), CT (Norwalk), DE (New Castle, Newark), IL (Bedford Park, West Chicago), IN (Greensburg, Kendallville), KY (Bowling Green, Lexington), LA (Shreveport, St. Francisville), MA (Adams, Leominster), ME (Old Town), MI (Kalamazoo, Parchment, Port Huron, Ypsilanti), MO (Hazelwood, St. Louis), MS (Meridian, Rolling Fork), NH (Berlin, Groveton), NJ (Metuchen, Milford), NY (Carthage, Gouveneur), OH (Cincinnati, Dayton, Minerva, Perrysburg), OR (Clatskanie, Halsey, Portland), PA (Chambersburg, Easton, Lionville, Southampton), SC (Darlington), TN (Gordonsville, Jackson), TX (Orange), VA (Richmond, Williamsburg), WA (Camas, Redmond, Sunnyside, Vancouver), WI (Ashland, Green Bay, Neenah, Wausau)

CORP. OFFICERS
Thomas Norman Bush: *B* Lancaster County VA 1947 *ED* VA Polytech Inst & St Univ BS 1970; Univ Richmond JD 1977 *CURR EMPL* vp, tax couns, dir: James River Paper Co *NONPR AFFIL* dir: Tax Execs Inst; mem: Am Bar Assn, Am Inst CPAs, Civitans, VA Mfg Assn, VA Soc CPAs; mem, mem tax comm: Am Forest & Paper Assn

Richard Elder: *CURR EMPL* vp commun: James River Corp VA

Daniel J. Girvan: *CURR EMPL* sr vp human resources: James River Corp VA

John M. Nevin: *B* 1935 *ED* Princeton Univ BS 1957 *CURR EMPL* sr vp strategic svcs: James River Corp VA

Robert C. Williams: *B* OH 1930 *ED* Univ Cincinnati BSME 1953; Xavier Univ MBA 1957 *CURR EMPL* chmn, pres, ceo, co-fdr: James River Corp VA *CORP AFFIL* dir: NationsBank NA

GIVING OFFICERS
Thomas Norman Bush: vp *CURR EMPL* vp, tax couns, dir: James River Paper Co (see above)

Clifford Armstrong Cutchins III: vp, secy, treas *B* Southampton County VA 1923

ED VA Polytech Inst & St Univ BS 1947; Rutgers Univ Stonier Grad Sch Banking 1953 *CURR EMPL* chmn, dir: Shenandoah Life Ins Co *CORP AFFIL* dir: Capital Corp, Commerce Corp, Franklin Equipment Co, Mid-Atlantic Exchange, Pulaski Furniture Corp, Sentra Health Sys, Shenandoah Life Ins Co, VA Natl Bldg Corp, Vaughan Corp *NONPR AFFIL* bd visitors: VA Polytech Inst; dir: Assn Bank Holding Cos, Assn Reserve City Bankers, Natl Maritime Ctr Fdn, Tidewater Scholarship Fdn, VA Recreational Facilities Authority; trust: VA Fdn Independent Colls *PHIL AFFIL* dir: Camp Foundation

Richard C. Erickson: vp

Daniel J. Girvan: vp *CURR EMPL* sr vp human resources: James River Corp VA (see above)

John M. Nevin: pres *CURR EMPL* sr vp strategic svcs: James River Corp VA (see above)

Robert C. Williams: vp *CURR EMPL* chmn, pres, ceo, co-fdr: James River Corp VA (see above)

APPLICATION INFORMATION

Initial Approach: *Initial Contact:* brief letter or proposal; no phone calls *Include Information On:* name, address, and telephone number of organization; contact person and title; amount of money or types of services requested; description of the organization or proposed project; brief statement citing the project's relevance to company, its employees, and local community; description of the organization's experience and ability to complete project; method of testing success of project; proof of tax-exempt status; audited financial statement; constituency supported; budget, salaries, and benefits of staff; and organizational structure *Deadlines:* by August 1 for funding in following year

Restrictions on Giving: Company does not make grants to individuals; organizations without tax-exempt status; political organizations; religious, veterans, or fraternal organizations; journal advertisement, entertainment, or the purchase of tickets; organizations supported by the United Way; organizations not located within a company community; telephone or mass-mail solicitations; or organizations not approved by the Better Business Bureau.

OTHER THINGS TO KNOW

The company is currently planning to establish a foundation. Officers and Directors of the foundation are listed above. Additional information regarding the foundation will not be available until fall of 1995. Contact Carol Akin for further details at that time.

For information regarding contributions to international organizations by the company's foreign subsidiaries, contact Ron Singer, Chief Executive Officer of the JA/MONT N.V. division at the company's headquarters in Richmond, VA.

For information about the James River Scholars Program, write or call James Rivers Scholars Director, Human Resources Development Office, at the address listed under "Contact," or at (804)649-4436.

An alternative source of funding may be accessed by contacting Barbara Lanier, Manager, Recruitment at (804)343-4935. In 1991, the company gave approximately $146,000 through this contact.

Contributions are considered one-time gifts, although some multiyear commitments are made in order to distribute payments evenly over several years.

Succeeding grants to the same organization generally are not considered until two years after the payment of the previous grant.

Pledges should compare favorably with other companies in the community as to total amount of employees, total payroll, or other measures of company's local obligation.

GRANTS ANALYSIS
Total Grants: $1,200,000*

Typical Range: $500 to $5,000

Disclosure Period: 1994

Note: Total grants figure is approximate. Recent grants are derived from a partial 1992 grants list.

RECENT GRANTS

General
Hurricane Andrew Relief Efforts, FL — donation of more than six million food service items

---

Mars Foundation

CONTACT
Robert C. Cargo
Secretary
Mars Foundation
6885 Elm St.
Mc Lean, VA 22101
(703) 821-4900

FINANCIAL SUMMARY
Recent Giving: $704,500 (1993); $770,500 (1992); $819,000 (1991)

Assets: $5,399,732 (1993); $4,973,199 (1992); $4,898,035 (1991)

Gifts Received: $600,000 (1993); $600,000 (1992); $602,406 (1991)

Fiscal Note: In 1993, the foundation received $600,000 from Mars, Inc. In 1992, the foundation received $600,000 from Mars, Inc., and in 1991 the foundation received $602,406 from Mars, Inc.; $1,830 from Buffalo News, NY; and $576 in student loan repayments.

EIN: 54-6037592

CONTRIBUTIONS SUMMARY
Donor(s): The Mars Foundation was established in 1956 by Forrest Edward Mars. Mr. Mars built his parents' candy company into Mars, Inc., the largest confectioner in the world. Mr. Mars retired from the company in 1973. The foundation is run by his daughter, Jaqueline Mars Vogel. His sons, John and Forrest, Jr., are on the board of directors. The foundation was organized to provide educational assistance to individuals

and to assist in the improvement of living, social, and working conditions through support to various charitable, educational, and scientific/medical groups.

Typical Recipients: • *Arts & Humanities:* Arts Centers, Arts Outreach, Dance, Historic Preservation, History & Archaeology, Libraries, Museums/Galleries, Music, Opera, Performing Arts, Theater • *Civic & Public Affairs:* Zoos/Aquariums • *Education:* Business Education, Colleges & Universities, Education Funds, Elementary Education (Private), Faculty Development, Medical Education, Minority Education, Private Education (Precollege), Student Aid • *Environment:* Air/Water Quality, General, Resource Conservation, Wildlife Protection • *Health:* Cancer, Children's Health/Hospitals, Health Funds, Hospices, Medical Research, Nursing Services, Single-Disease Health Associations • *International:* International Environmental Issues • *Religion:* Churches, Religious Welfare • *Science:* Scientific Centers & Institutes • *Social Services:* Animal Protection, Child Welfare, Community Centers, Counseling, Emergency Relief, Family Planning, Food/Clothing Distribution, People with Disabilities, Recreation & Athletics, Senior Services, Shelters/Homelessness, Substance Abuse, Volunteer Services, Youth Organizations

Grant Types: capital, general support, project, and research

Geographic Distribution: national

GIVING OFFICERS
Robert C. Cargo: secy

Rita Langsam Davis: asst secy

Forrest Edward Mars, Jr.: vp *B* Oak Park IL 1931 *ED* Yale Univ BS 1953; Univ VA *CURR EMPL* co-pres, ceo, dir: Mars

John Franklyn Mars: vp *B* London England 1935 *ED* Yale Univ BS 1957 *CURR EMPL* co-pres, dir: Mars

Jacqueline Mars Vogel: pres *B* 1940 *ED* Bryn Mawr Coll 1961 *CURR EMPL* vp: Mars

APPLICATION INFORMATION
Initial Approach:

Proposals should be in the form of a letter. There is no formal program policy or application procedure.

Letters of application should include details of history and purpose of organization seeking funding, its goals, description of project for which funding is sought, specific amount requested, and copy of IRS letter confirming tax-exempt status.

The board meets in June and December. Applications must be received at least six weeks prior to either board meeting.

All grant proposals are reviewed on an individual basis.

GRANTS ANALYSIS
Total Grants: $704,500

Number of Grants: 136

Highest Grant: $100,000

Average Grant: $5,180

Typical Range: $2,000 to $10,000

Disclosure Period: 1993

Note: Recent grants are derived from a 1993 Form 990.

RECENT GRANTS

Library

10,000	Langley School, McLean, VA — for learning center/library	

General

100,000	Wheaton College, Norton, MA — NEH Challenge Program
30,000	Virginia Foundation for Independent Colleges, Lynchburg, PA — capital campaign and scholarships
25,000	Ethel Walker School, Simsbury, CT — to the general endowment fund
15,000	Salvation Army, Washington, DC — for shelter
15,000	Virginia Foundation for Independent Colleges, Lynchburg, VA

Mobil Oil Corp. / Mobil Foundation

Revenue: $59.62 billion
Employees: 10,000
Parent Company: Mobil Corporation
Headquarters: Fairfax, VA
SIC Major Group: Crude Petroleum & Natural Gas, Petroleum Refining, and Petroleum Products Nec

CONTACT

Richard G. Mund
Secretary & Executive Director
Mobil Foundation
3225 Gallows Rd.
Fairfax, VA 22037-0001
(703) 846-3381
Note: For matching gifts information, contact Tobi Allen, Matching Gift Coordinator, at above address, (703) 846-3385. The company's World Wide Web address is http://www.mobil.com

FINANCIAL SUMMARY

Recent Giving: $11,750,000 (1995 est.); $11,750,000 (1994 approx.); $11,197,888 (1993)

Assets: $8,480,778 (1993); $10,246,252 (1990); $15,288,987 (1989)

Gifts Received: $15,992,851 (1993)

Fiscal Note: Figures for 1994 include approximately $9,000,000 in foundation giving and about $2,750,000 in matching gifts. Figures for 1993 represent foundation giving, totaling $8,942,958, and matching gifts, totaling about $2,254,930. The foundation did not make any direct contributions in 1993. Above figures exclude nonmonetary support.

EIN: 13-6177075

CONTRIBUTIONS SUMMARY

Typical Recipients: • *Arts & Humanities:* Arts Associations & Councils, Arts Centers, Arts Festivals, Arts Funds, Arts Institutes, Community Arts, Dance, Ethnic & Folk Arts, Historic Preservation, Libraries, Literary Arts, Museums/Galleries, Music, Opera, Performing Arts, Public Broadcasting, Theater • *Civic & Public Affairs:* Business/Free Enterprise, Economic Development, Employment/Job Training, Housing, Law & Justice, Legal Aid, Municipalities/Towns, Nonprofit Management, Professional & Trade Associations, Public Policy, Safety, Urban & Community Affairs, Women's Affairs, Zoos/Aquariums • *Education:* Agricultural Education, Arts/Humanities Education, Business Education, Colleges & Universities, Continuing Education, Economic Education, Education Associations, Education Funds, Engineering/Technological Education, International Exchange, International Studies, Legal Education, Literacy, Medical Education, Minority Education, Public Education (Precollege), Science/Mathematics Education, Special Education, Student Aid • *Environment:* General • *Health:* Emergency/Ambulance Services, Geriatric Health, Health Funds, Health Organizations, Hospices, Hospitals, Medical Rehabilitation, Medical Research, Nursing Services • *International:* Health Care/Hospitals, International Peace & Security Issues, International Relations • *Religion:* Religious Welfare • *Science:* Science Exhibits & Fairs, Scientific Centers & Institutes, Scientific Organizations • *Social Services:* Child Welfare, Community Centers, Community Service Organizations, Counseling, Delinquency & Criminal Rehabilitation, Domestic Violence, Emergency Relief, Family Services, Food/Clothing Distribution, Homes, People with Disabilities, Recreation & Athletics, Refugee Assistance, Senior Services, Shelters/Homelessness, Substance Abuse, United Funds/United Ways, Volunteer Services, Youth Organizations

Grant Types: capital, department, employee matching gifts, general support, project, research, and scholarship

Geographic Distribution: primarily in communities where company has operations; some emphasis on corporate headquarters

Operating Locations: AZ, CA (Bakersfield, Santa Ana, Torrance, Woodland), CO (Denver), CT (Stamford), IL (Joliet), LA (New Orleans), MA (Holyoke), NJ (Edison, Paulsboro, Princeton), NY (New York, Pittsford), TX (Austin, Beaumont, Dallas, Houston, Midland, Temple), VA (Fairfax, Reston, Richmond), WA (Ferndale), WY (Gillette)

CORP. OFFICERS

Lucio A. Noto: *B* 1939 *CURR EMPL* chmn, pres, ceo, coo: Mobil Corp *CORP AFFIL* chmn, ceo, coo, pres: Mobil Oil Corp

GIVING OFFICERS

George Broadhead: dir *CURR EMPL* treas, dir: Mobil Petroleum Co Inc *CORP AFFIL* treas, contr, dir: Mobil Intl Petroleum Corp

Anthony Cavaliere: treas *CURR EMPL* asst treas, dir: Mobil Oil Indonesia Inc

Robert A. Dobies: dir *B* 1943 *CURR EMPL* treas, dir: Mobil Petrochemicals Intl Ltd

Ellen Z. McCloy: pres

Richard Gordon Mund: secy, exec dir *B* Baltimore MD 1942 *ED* Johns Hopkins Univ 1960-1963; IL Wesleyan Univ BS 1965; Univ Denver MA 1967; Univ Denver PhD 1970 *NONPR AFFIL* mem: Kappa Alpha Order, Kappa Delta Pi, Phi Delta Kappa; mem contributions counc: Conf Bd; trust: Fairfax County Pub Sch Ed Fund, Huntington Art Gallery

Barbara A. Patocka: dir *CURR EMPL* vp, dir: Mobil Oil Indonesia Inc

Richard Stock: contr

Jerome F. Trautschold, Jr.: dir

John James Wise: dir *B* Cambridge MA 1932 *ED* Tufts Univ BS 1953; MA Inst Tech PhD 1966 *CURR EMPL* vp res: Mobil Res & Devel Corp *NONPR AFFIL* mem: Am Inst Chem Engrs, Indus Res Inst, Natl Acad Engg, Sigma Xi, World Petroleum Congress

APPLICATION INFORMATION

Initial Approach: *Initial Contact:* proposal (local, community-based organizations should contact Mobil manager in their area) *Include Information On:* description of the organization and its goals, amount requested and specific purpose, other sources of funding, budget and audited financial statement, other pertinent supporting data (such as annual report, if available), copy of IRS determination letter showing proof of 501(c)(3) status *Deadlines:* none

Restrictions on Giving: Grants are not made to individuals; religious organizations; veterans or military organizations; fraternal organizations; benefits such as charity dinners and special performances; endowments or chairs; athletic events; goodwill advertising; or local or national organizations concerned with specific diseases.

GRANTS ANALYSIS

Total Grants: $8,942,958

Number of Grants: 726

Highest Grant: $300,000

Average Grant: $12,318

Typical Range: $1,000 to $25,000

Disclosure Period: 1993

Note: Figures are for foundation only and exclude $2,254,930 in employee matching gifts. Recent grants are derived from a 1993 Form 990.

RECENT GRANTS

General

300,000	Greater Washington Educational Telecommunications Association, Washington, DC
275,000	United Way National Capital Area, Vienna, VA
250,000	City of Dallas, Dallas, TX
226,000	United Way Metro Dallas, Dallas, TX
206,833	National Merit Scholarship Corporation, Evanston, IL

Morgan and Samuel Tate Morgan, Jr. Foundation, Marietta McNeil

CONTACT
Judith M. McCoy
Trust Officer
Marietta McNeil Morgan and Samuel Tate
  Morgan, Jr. Fdn.
c/o NationsBank of Virginia
PO Box 26903
Richmond, VA 23261
(804) 788-2052

FINANCIAL SUMMARY
Recent Giving: $478,500 (fiscal 1994);
$510,000 (fiscal 1992); $579,300 (fiscal
1991)

Assets: $14,144,399 (fiscal 1994);
$13,559,380 (fiscal 1992); $12,587,598 (fiscal 1991)

Gifts Received: $1,389 (fiscal 1994)

Fiscal Note: In fiscal 1994, contributions
were received from S.T. Morgan Trust .

EIN: 54-6069447

CONTRIBUTIONS SUMMARY
Donor(s): the late Marietta McNeill Morgan
and the late Samuel T. Morgan, Jr.

Typical Recipients: • *Arts & Humanities:*
Arts Centers, Community Arts, Dance, Historic Preservation, Libraries • *Civic & Public Affairs:* General, Housing, Urban &
Community Affairs, Zoos/Aquariums • *Education:* Colleges & Universities, Education
Funds, Private Education (Precollege), Public Education (Precollege), Secondary Education (Private) • *Health:* AIDS/HIV,
Children's Health/Hospitals, Clinics/Medical Centers, Emergency/Ambulance Services, Hospitals • *Religion:* Religious
Welfare • *Social Services:* Camps, Community Service Organizations, Family Services,
Food/Clothing Distribution, Recreation &
Athletics, United Funds/United Ways,
YMCA/YWCA/YMHA/YWHA, Youth Organizations

Grant Types: capital

Geographic Distribution: limited to VA

GIVING OFFICERS
NationsBank of Virginia: trust

Elizabeth D. Seaman: consult *PHIL AFFIL*
consult: George and Effie Seay Memorial
Trust

APPLICATION INFORMATION
Initial Approach: The foundation reports
that applicants should submit a proposal
which includes a concise description of the
project, detailed project budget and schedule, description of the organization, current
balance sheet and operating statement, list
of qualifications of project personnel, names
and affiliations of organization's trustees or
directors, and proof of tax-exempt status. A
statement from the chief administrator of the
organization must also be provided, indicating approval of the grant request and assurance that the grant will be spent within one

year of its receipt. Applications may be submitted any time, however, proposals must be
received by May 1, for the June meeting of
the trust committee, and by November 1, for
the December meeting. The foundation
strongly encourages matching or challenge
grants.
Restrictions on Giving: Does not support
individuals.

PUBLICATIONS
Informational Brochure (including Application Guidelines)

GRANTS ANALYSIS
Total Grants: $478,500

Number of Grants: 31

Highest Grant: $50,000

Typical Range: $3,500 to $50,000

Disclosure Period: fiscal year ending June
30, 1994

Note: Recent grants are derived from a fiscal 1994 Form 990.

RECENT GRANTS
Library
50,000   Friends of Richmond Public
         Library, Richmond, VA

General
50,000   St. Paul's University,
         Lawrenceville, VA
30,000   Westminster Canterbury:
         Virginia Beach, Virginia
         Beach, VA
25,000   Richmond Better Housing
         Coalition, Richmond, VA
25,000   Salvation Army, Waynesboro,
         VA
25,000   Washington and Lee
         University, Lexington, VA

Norfolk Shipbuilding & Drydock Corp. / Norfolk Shipbuilding and Drydock Corp. Charitable Trust

Sales: $247.5 million
Employees: 3,000
Headquarters: Norfolk, VA
SIC Major Group: Transportation Equipment

CONTACT
Norfolk Shipbuilding & Drydock Corp.
  Charitable Trust
c/o NationsBank of Virginia, N.A.
PO Box 26903
Norfolk, VA 23261
(804) 788-2067

FINANCIAL SUMMARY
Recent Giving: $112,550 (1993); $140,350
(1992); $191,250 (1991)

Assets: $624,459 (1993); $635,819 (1992);
$543,059 (1991)

Gifts Received: $200,144 (1992); $100,297
(1991); $105,000 (1990)

Fiscal Note: In 1992, major contributions
were received from Norfolk Shipbuilding &
Drydock Corp. ($200,000).
EIN: 54-6036745

CONTRIBUTIONS SUMMARY
Typical Recipients: • *Arts & Humanities:*
Arts Associations & Councils, Arts Centers,
General, Historic Preservation, History & Archaeology, Libraries, Museums/Galleries,
Music, Opera, Public Broadcasting • *Civic & Public Affairs:* African American Affairs,
Business/Free Enterprise, General, Professional & Trade Associations, Urban & Community Affairs, Zoos/Aquariums
• *Education:* Business Education, Colleges
& Universities, Community & Junior Colleges, Economic Education, Education Associations, Education Funds, Medical
Education, Minority Education • *Health:*
Children's Health/Hospitals, Emergency/Ambulance Services, General, Health Organizations, Hospitals • *Science:* Science Exhibits
& Fairs, Scientific Centers & Institutes, Scientific Organizations • *Social Services:*
Child Welfare, Community Service Organizations, Emergency Relief, General, United
Funds/United Ways

Grant Types: capital, general support, and
multiyear/continuing support

Geographic Distribution: in headquarters
and operating communities

Operating Locations: VA (Norfolk)

CORP. OFFICERS
John L. Roper III: B Norfolk VA 1927 *ED*
Univ VA BSME 1949; MA Inst Tech BS
1951 *CURR EMPL* pres, ceo, dir: Norfolk
Shipbuilding & Drydock Corp *NONPR AFFIL* dir: Am Bur Shipping, Cruise Intl, Flagship Group Ltd, John L. Roper Corp; dir;
mem: Shipbuilders Counc Am; pres, dir:
Londsale Bldg Corp, Marepcon Corp Intl

John L. Roper IV: *CURR EMPL* exec vp,
coo, secy, dir: Norfolk Shipbuilding & Drydock Corp

GIVING OFFICERS
NationsBank of Virginia, NA: trust

APPLICATION INFORMATION
Initial Approach: Send a brief letter of inquiry. There are no deadlines.

OTHER THINGS TO KNOW
Company reported in June 1994 that contributions had been suspended due to corporate
downsizing.

GRANTS ANALYSIS
Total Grants: $112,550

Number of Grants: 14

Highest Grant: $20,000

Typical Range: $2,000 to $16,550

Disclosure Period: 1993

Note: Recent grants are derived from a 1993
Form 990.

RECENT GRANTS
General
20,000   National Maritime Center
         Foundation, Norfolk, VA

10,000	Urban League of Hampton Roads, Norfolk, VA
10,000	Virginia Wesleyan College, Norfolk, VA
8,000	Medical College of Hampton Roads Foundation, Norfolk, VA
5,000	Old Dominion University Educational Foundation, Norfolk, VA

North Shore Foundation

CONTACT
Toy O. Savage, Jr.
Secretary and Treasurer
North Shore Fdn.
Nationsbank Center
Norfolk, VA 23510
(804) 640-1414

FINANCIAL SUMMARY
Recent Giving: $582,900 (fiscal 1993); $643,014 (fiscal 1992); $569,596 (fiscal 1991)

Assets: $1,062 (fiscal 1993); $51,695 (fiscal 1992); $217,548 (fiscal 1991)

Gifts Received: $534,806 (fiscal 1993); $480,583 (fiscal 1992); $768,473 (fiscal 1991)

EIN: 52-1296293

CONTRIBUTIONS SUMMARY
Donor(s): Constance S. duPont Darden

Typical Recipients: • *Arts & Humanities:* Arts Centers, Arts Funds, History & Archaeology, Libraries, Museums/Galleries, Music, Opera, Performing Arts, Public Broadcasting • *Civic & Public Affairs:* Civil Rights, General, Housing • *Education:* Colleges & Universities, Education Funds, Minority Education, Private Education (Precollege) • *Environment:* General • *Health:* Health Funds, Medical Research • *International:* Health Care/Hospitals, Human Rights, International Development, International Organizations, International Relations, International Relief Efforts, Missionary/Religious Activities • *Religion:* Churches, Dioceses, Missionary Activities (Domestic), Religious Organizations, Religious Welfare • *Social Services:* Animal Protection, Community Service Organizations, Day Care, Family Planning, Family Services, Homes, Senior Services, United Funds/United Ways, Youth Organizations

Grant Types: general support

Geographic Distribution: focus on VA

GIVING OFFICERS
Constance S. Du Pont Darden: dir *B* 1904

Joshua P. Darden, Jr.: pres, dir

Toy D. Savage, Jr.: secy, treas, dir *PHIL AFFIL* dir: Camp Foundation

APPLICATION INFORMATION
Initial Approach: Send brief letter of inquiry describing program or project. There are no deadlines.

GRANTS ANALYSIS
Total Grants: $582,900

Number of Grants: 43

Highest Grant: $75,000

Typical Range: $1,000 to $20,000

Disclosure Period: fiscal year ending April 30, 1993

Note: Recent grants are derived from a fiscal 1993 Form 990.

RECENT GRANTS
Library

5,000	Ruth Camp Campbell Memorial Library, Franklin, VA

General

70,000	Virginia Foundation for Independent Colleges, Richmond, VA
53,000	Heathwood Hall Episcopal School, Columbia, SC
30,000	Diocese of Southern Virginia-Episcopal, Norfolk, VA
29,000	Church of the Good Shepherd, Norfolk, VA
27,500	Planned Parenthood of Southeastern Virginia, Norfolk, VA

Old Dominion Box Co. / Old Dominion Box Co. Foundation

Sales: $57.5 million
Employees: 600
Headquarters: Lynchburg, VA
SIC Major Group: Paper & Allied Products

CONTACT
Frank H. Buhler
Chairman
Old Dominion Box Co.
PO Box 680
Lynchburg, VA 24505
(804) 929-6701

FINANCIAL SUMMARY
Recent Giving: $53,048 (fiscal 1992); $55,578 (fiscal 1991); $66,125 (fiscal 1990)

Assets: $409,340 (fiscal 1992); $423,317 (fiscal 1991); $429,603 (fiscal 1990)

Gifts Received: $100 (fiscal 1992)

Fiscal Note: In 1992, contributions were received from Old Dominion Box Co.

EIN: 54-6036792

CONTRIBUTIONS SUMMARY
Typical Recipients: • *Arts & Humanities:* Arts Centers, Historic Preservation, Libraries • *Civic & Public Affairs:* General, Safety, Women's Affairs • *Education:* Arts/Humanities Education, Business Education, Colleges & Universities, Community & Junior Colleges, Education Associations, Education Funds • *Health:* Health Organizations, Heart, Single-Disease Health Associations • *Religion:* Churches, Jewish Causes,

Social/Policy Issues • *Social Services:* Community Service Organizations, Food/Clothing Distribution, Recreation & Athletics, United Funds/United Ways, Youth Organizations

Grant Types: general support

Geographic Distribution: focus on VA

Operating Locations: VA (Lynchburg)

CORP. OFFICERS
Frank H. Buhler: *B* Arlington VA 1926 *ED* Miami Univ 1950 *CURR EMPL* chmn, dir: Old Dominion Box Co

GIVING OFFICERS
Frank H. Buhler: chmn, pres, dir *CURR EMPL* chmn, dir: Old Dominion Box Co (see above)

M. O. Buhler: vp

R. Lewis Frances: secy,treas, dir *CURR EMPL* vp, cfo: Old Dominion Box Co

APPLICATION INFORMATION
Initial Approach: Send brief letter describing program. There are no deadlines.

GRANTS ANALYSIS
Total Grants: $53,048

Number of Grants: 26

Highest Grant: $20,000

Typical Range: $100 to $1,000

Disclosure Period: fiscal year ending November 30, 1992

Note: Recent grants are derived from a fiscal 1992 Form 990.

RECENT GRANTS
Library

5,000	Amherst County Public Library, Amherst, VA

General

20,000	Lynchburg College, Lynchburg, VA
10,000	Randolph-Macon Woman's College Indoor Riding Arena Fund, Lynchburg, VA
3,333	Westminster-Canterbury, Lynchburg, VA
2,500	United Way of Jefferson County, Charleston, WV
2,500	Virginia School of the Arts, Lynchburg, VA

Olsson Memorial Foundation, Elis

CONTACT
Elis Olsson Memorial Foundation
PO Box 311
West Point, VA 23181
(804) 843-5354
Note: The foundation does not list a specific contact person.

FINANCIAL SUMMARY
Recent Giving: $700,000 (1995 est.); $701,240 (1994); $705,000 (1993)

Assets: $15,200,000 (1995 est.); $15,200,000 (1994 approx.); $15,543,526 (1993)

Gifts Received: $733,417 (1989); $520,287 (1988)

EIN: 54-6062436

CONTRIBUTIONS SUMMARY
Donor(s): The foundation was established in 1966 by the late Inga Olsson Nylander and the late Signe Maria Olsson .

Typical Recipients: • *Arts & Humanities:* Arts Appreciation, Arts Associations & Councils, Arts Centers, Arts Festivals, Arts Institutes, Historic Preservation, History & Archaeology, Libraries, Museums/Galleries, Performing Arts, Theater • *Civic & Public Affairs:* Employment/Job Training, General, Municipalities/Towns, Philanthropic Organizations, Safety, Urban & Community Affairs, Zoos/Aquariums • *Education:* Arts/Humanities Education, Colleges & Universities, Education Funds, Elementary Education (Private), Engineering/Technological Education, General, Legal Education, Literacy, Medical Education, Minority Education, Private Education (Precollege), Religious Education, Secondary Education (Private), Secondary Education (Public), Vocational & Technical Education • *Environment:* Air/Water Quality, General, Resource Conservation, Wildlife Protection • *Health:* Cancer, Children's Health/Hospitals, Clinics/Medical Centers, Emergency/Ambulance Services, Health Organizations, Hospitals, Long-Term Care, Medical Rehabilitation, Medical Research, Respiratory, Single-Disease Health Associations • *Religion:* Churches, Ministries, Religious Organizations, Seminaries • *Science:* Scientific Centers & Institutes • *Social Services:* Camps, Child Welfare, Community Service Organizations, Family Services, Food/Clothing Distribution, Homes, People with Disabilities, Shelters/Homelessness, Youth Organizations

Grant Types: fellowship, general support, and professorship

Geographic Distribution: focus on Virginia

GIVING OFFICERS
Dennis Irl Belcher: treas, trust *B* Wheeling WV 1951 *ED* Coll William & Mary BA 1973; Univ Richmond JD 1976 *CURR EMPL* ptnr: McGuire Woods Battle & Boothe *NONPR AFFIL* mem: Am Bar Assn, VA Bar Assn *CLUB AFFIL* Bull Bear, CC Virginia

Thelma L. Downey: asst secy, asst treas

Shirley G. Olsson: vp, treas, trust

Sture Gordon Olsson: pres, trust *B* Richmond VA 1920 *ED* Univ VA BS 1942 *CURR EMPL* chmn: Chesapeake Corp *CORP AFFIL* dir: Citizens & Farmers Bank *PHIL AFFIL* trust: Chesapeake Corporate Foundation

APPLICATION INFORMATION
Initial Approach:

The foundation requests applications be made in writing.

Applications should be in written form and a copy of the organization's tax determination

letter should be attached to the proposal. The foundation notes that the applicant's charitable purpose should be clearly stated. There are no deadlines.

Restrictions on Giving: The foundation does not make grants to individuals.

GRANTS ANALYSIS
Total Grants: $705,000

Number of Grants: 120

Highest Grant: $100,000

Average Grant: $5,875

Typical Range: $500 to $10,000

Disclosure Period: 1993

Note: Recent grants are derived from a 1993 Form 990.

RECENT GRANTS

Library

12,500	Middlesex County Public Library, Urbana, VA
3,500	Lancaster County Public Library, Kilmarnock, VA

General

100,000	Episcopal High School, Alexandria, VA
75,000	University of Virginia Alumni Association, Charlottesville, VA
50,000	Episcopal Theological Seminary, Alexandria, VA
50,000	Episcopal Theological Seminary, Alexandria, VA
25,000	University of Virginia School of Engineering and Applied Science, Charlottesville, VA

Richardson Benevolent Foundation, C. E.

CONTACT
Betty S. King
Secretary
C. E. Richardson Benevolent Fdn.
74 W Main St., Rm. 211
PO Box 1120
Pulaski, VA 24301
(703) 980-6628

FINANCIAL SUMMARY
Recent Giving: $103,250 (fiscal 1994); $136,720 (fiscal 1991); $128,845 (fiscal 1990)

Assets: $3,289,182 (fiscal 1993); $2,696,403 (fiscal 1991); $2,965,867 (fiscal 1990)

EIN: 51-0227549

CONTRIBUTIONS SUMMARY
Typical Recipients: • *Arts & Humanities:* Arts Centers, History & Archaeology, Libraries, Museums/Galleries • *Civic & Public Affairs:* General, Municipalities/Towns, Safety, Women's Affairs • *Education:* Agricultural Education, Colleges & Universities, Community & Junior Colleges, Education Funds, General, Religious Education, Science/Mathematics Education, Secondary

Education (Public), Student Aid • *Health:* Cancer, Children's Health/Hospitals, Emergency/Ambulance Services, Hospices • *Religion:* Churches, Religious Welfare • *Social Services:* Animal Protection, Big Brother/Big Sister, Community Service Organizations, Family Services, Food/Clothing Distribution, Recreation & Athletics, Scouts, Senior Services, Special Olympics, United Funds/United Ways, YMCA/YWCA/YMHA/YWHA, Youth Organizations

Grant Types: general support

Geographic Distribution: limited to 30 miles north and south of Interstate 81 from Lexington to Abingdon, VA

GIVING OFFICERS
Betty S. King: secy

James D. Miller: trust

Annie S. Muire: trust

James C. Turk: trust *B* Roanoke VA 1923 *ED* Roanoke Coll AB 1949; Washington & Lee Univ LLB 1952 *CORP AFFIL* chief judge: US District Court; dir: 1st & Merchants Natl Bank Rafford *NONPR AFFIL* mem: Omnicron Delta Kappa, Order Coif, Phi Beta Kappa; trust: Rafford Commun Hosp

APPLICATION INFORMATION
Initial Approach: Application form required. Deadline is September 15.

Restrictions on Giving: Does not support individuals.

PUBLICATIONS
Application Guidelines

GRANTS ANALYSIS
Total Grants: $103,250

Number of Grants: 37

Highest Grant: $20,000

Typical Range: $500 to $10,000

Disclosure Period: fiscal year ending May 31, 1994

Note: Recent grants are derived from a fiscal 1994 Form 990.

RECENT GRANTS

Library

5,000	Virginia Foundation for Independent Colleges, Richmond, VA — strengthening library services on fifteen member colleges' campuses

General

20,000	Ferrum College, Ferrum, VA — partial financing of two-story addition to Garber Hall science building
10,000	Bluefield State College, Bluefield, VA — renovation of enrollment management suite
6,000	Radford University Foundation, Radford, VA — student scholarship assistance
5,000	Hensel Eckman YMCA, Pulaski, VA — pool therapy and disability swim

5,000   programs and for
membership scholarships
New River Community
College Educational
Foundation, Dublin, VA —
partial financing of
equipment for mathematics
and computer information
system departments

Shenandoah Life Insurance Co.

Premiums: $173.96 million
Employees: 212
Headquarters: Roanoke, VA
SIC Major Group: Insurance Carriers

CONTACT
Betty Lafon
Administrative Assistant to the President
Shenandoah Life Insurance Co.
PO Box 12847
Roanoke, VA 24029
(703) 985-4400
Note: Telephone extension is ext. 203.

FINANCIAL SUMMARY
Recent Giving: $105,000 (1993); $108,392
(1992); $87,440 (1991)

Fiscal Note: Figures do not include public
relations donations.

CONTRIBUTIONS SUMMARY
Typical Recipients: • *Arts & Humanities:*
Arts Appreciation, Arts Associations &
Councils, Arts Centers, Dance, Ethnic &
Folk Arts, Historic Preservation, Libraries,
Literary Arts, Museums/Galleries, Music,
Opera, Performing Arts, Public Broadcast-
ing, Theater, Visual Arts • *Civic & Public
Affairs:* Civil Rights, Economic Develop-
ment, Economic Policy, Employment/Job
Training, Professional & Trade Associa-
tions, Safety, Urban & Community Affairs,
Zoos/Aquariums • *Education:* Business Edu-
cation, Colleges & Universities, Community
& Junior Colleges, Economic Education,
Education Associations, Education Funds,
Faculty Development, Health & Physical
Education, Medical Education, Minority
Education, Special Education, Student Aid
• *Environment:* General • *Health:* Emer-
gency/Ambulance Services, Health Pol-
icy/Cost Containment, Health Funds, Health
Organizations, Medical Research, Medical
Training, Mental Health, Single-Disease
Health Associations • *Science:* Observato-
ries & Planetariums, Science Exhibits &
Fairs • *Social Services:* Community Service
Organizations, Counseling, Emergency Re-
lief, Food/Clothing Distribution, Recreation
& Athletics, Shelters/Homelessness, United
Funds/United Ways, Youth Organizations

Grant Types: capital, emergency, employee
matching gifts, general support, operating
expenses, project, and scholarship

Nonmonetary Support Types: donated
equipment, in-kind services, loaned employees, loaned executives, and workplace solicitation

Geographic Distribution: primarily VA

Operating Locations: VA (Roanoke)

CORP. OFFICERS
Robert W. Clark: *CURR EMPL* pres, ceo:
Shenandoah Life Ins Co

Clifford Armstrong Cutchins III: *B*
Southampton County VA 1923 *ED* VA
Polytech Inst & St Univ BS 1947; Rutgers
Univ Stonier Grad Sch Banking 1953 *CURR
EMPL* chmn, dir: Shenandoah Life Ins Co
CORP AFFIL dir: Capital Corp, Commerce
Corp, Franklin Equipment Co, Mid-Atlantic
Exchange, Pulaski Furniture Corp, Sentra
Health Sys, Shenandoah Life Ins Co, VA
Natl Bldg Corp, Vaughan Corp *NONPR AF-
FIL* bd visitors: VA Polytech Inst; dir: Assn
Bank Holding Cos, Assn Reserve City Bank-
ers, Natl Maritime Ctr Fdn, Tidewater Schol-
arship Fdn, VA Recreational Facilities
Authority; trust: VA Fdn Independent Colls
PHIL AFFIL dir: Camp Foundation; vp,
secy, treas: James River Corp. Foundation

Pearl H. Gearhart: *CURR EMPL* vp-
admin: Shenandoah Life Ins Co

James E. Harshaw: *CURR EMPL* vp-
group: Shenandoah Life Ins Co

Edward Machado: *CURR EMPL* vp, cfo:
Shenandoah Life Ins Co

APPLICATION INFORMATION
Initial Approach: Send full proposal including a description of the organization,
amount requested, the purpose of the funds
sought, and proof of tax exempt status. All
requests must be in writing. There are no
deadlines.

Restrictions on Giving: Does not support
individuals, religious organizations for sectarian purposes, entertainment groups, war
veterans organizations, advertising, athletic
events such as golf or tennis tournaments,
fund-raising endeavors of United Way agencies, or political or lobbying groups.

PUBLICATIONS
Contributions Policy

GRANTS ANALYSIS
Note: Company reports that grant size varies.

RECENT GRANTS

Library
Roanoke College Library, Salem, VA

General
American Red Cross, Roanoke, VA
Foundation for Roanoke Valley, Roanoke, VA
Jefferson Center Foundation, Roanoke, VA
Julian Stanley Wise Foundation, Roanoke, VA
River Foundation, Roanoke, VA

Thalhimer and Family Foundation, Charles G.

CONTACT
Charles G. Thalhimer,, Sr.
President and Director
Charles G. Thalhimer and Family Fdn.
600 E Main St.
Richmond, VA 23219
(804) 648-0103

FINANCIAL SUMMARY
Recent Giving: $149,368 (fiscal 1993);
$177,976 (fiscal 1992); $176,875 (fiscal
1990)

Assets: $2,249,476 (fiscal 1993);
$2,175,854 (fiscal 1992); $2,064,055 (fiscal
1990)

Gifts Received: $20,000 (fiscal 1992)

Fiscal Note: In fiscal 1992, contributions
were received from Charles G. Thalhimer,
Jr. ($10,000) and Harry R. Thalhimer
($10,000).

EIN: 54-6047108

CONTRIBUTIONS SUMMARY
Donor(s): members of the Thalhimer family

Typical Recipients: • *Arts & Humanities:*
Arts Associations & Councils, Arts Insti-
tutes, Ballet, Community Arts, Ethnic &
Folk Arts, Historic Preservation, History &
Archaeology, Libraries, Museums/Galleries,
Music, Public Broadcasting, Theater • *Civic
& Public Affairs:* General, Municipali-
ties/Towns • *Education:* Colleges & Univer-
sities, Community & Junior Colleges,
Medical Education, Private Education (Prec-
ollege) • *Environment:* Forestry, General •
Health: Cancer, Emergency/Ambulance
Services, Hospitals, Medical Research, Sin-
gle-Disease Health Associations, Trauma
Treatment • *Religion:* Jewish Causes, Relig-
ious Organizations, Religious Welfare, Syna-
gogues/Temples • *Science:* Scientific
Centers & Institutes • *Social Services:* Child
Welfare, Community Service Organizations,
Family Services, Food/Clothing Distribu-
tion, Homes, People with Disabilities,
United Funds/United Ways, Youth Organiza-
tions

Grant Types: general support

Geographic Distribution: focus on VA

GIVING OFFICERS
Ellen T. Holland: asst secy, asst treas

Charles G. Thalhimer, Jr.: vp, secy

Charles G. Thalhimer, Sr.: pres, dir

Harry R. Thalhimer: vp, treas

Rhoda R. Thalhimer: exec vp, dir

William B. Thalhimer, Jr.: vp *B* Richmond
VA 1914 *CORP AFFIL* dir: Fidelity Bankers
Life Ins Co *PHIL AFFIL* vp, dir: William B.
Thalhimer, Jr. and Family Foundation; pres,
dir, don: Thalhimer Brothers Foundation
CLUB AFFIL Bull & Bear, Commonwealth,
Jefferson, Lakeside

APPLICATION INFORMATION
Initial Approach: Send brief letter describing program. There are no deadlines.

GRANTS ANALYSIS
Total Grants: $149,368

Number of Grants: 47

Highest Grant: $65,000

Typical Range: $50 to $15,300

Disclosure Period: fiscal year ending October 31, 1993

Note: Recent grants are derived from a fiscal 1993 Form 990.

RECENT GRANTS

General

65,000	Collegiate Schools, Richmond, VA
15,300	Jewish Community Federation, Richmond, VA
13,500	United Way Services, Richmond, VA
11,848	Maymount Foundation, Richmond, VA — aviary and small animal habitat
10,100	Boys and Girls Clubs of Richmond, Richmond, VA

Treakle Foundation, J. Edwin

CONTACT
John Warren Cooke
President, Treasurer
J. Edwin Treakle Fdn.
PO Box 1157
Gloucester, VA 23061
(804) 693-0881

FINANCIAL SUMMARY
Recent Giving: $190,000 (fiscal 1994); $172,400 (fiscal 1992); $166,000 (fiscal 1991)

Assets: $4,874,050 (fiscal 1994); $4,852,529 (fiscal 1992); $4,369,639 (fiscal 1991)

Gifts Received: $100,000 (fiscal 1992)

Fiscal Note: In 1992, contributions were received from the estate of James B. Martin.

EIN: 54-6051620

CONTRIBUTIONS SUMMARY
Donor(s): the late J. Edwin Treakle

Typical Recipients: • *Arts & Humanities:* Historic Preservation, History & Archaeology, Libraries, Music • *Civic & Public Affairs:* Housing, Safety, Urban & Community Affairs • *Education:* Colleges & Universities, Community & Junior Colleges, Literacy, Private Education (Precollege) • *Environment:* General, Resource Conservation • *Health:* Cancer, Emergency/Ambulance Services, Medical Research, Nursing Services, Single-Disease Health Associations • *Religion:* Churches • *Social Services:* Animal Protection, Community Service Organizations, Scouts, Youth Organizations

Grant Types: capital, general support, multiyear/continuing support, research, and scholarship

Geographic Distribution: focus on VA

GIVING OFFICERS
John Warren Cooke: pres, treas

Harry E. Dunn: vp, dir

Cynthia B. Horsley: asst secy, grant admin

J. Kirkland Jarvis: secy, dir

Nancy Powell: asst treas

APPLICATION INFORMATION
Initial Approach: Application form required. Deadlines are between January 1 and April 30.

Restrictions on Giving: Does not support individuals.

GRANTS ANALYSIS
Total Grants: $190,000

Number of Grants: 46

Highest Grant: $22,800

Typical Range: $300 to $5,000

Disclosure Period: fiscal year ending April 30, 1994

Note: Recent grants are derived from a fiscal 1994 Form 990.

RECENT GRANTS

Library

13,600	Gloucester Library Endowment, Gloucester, VA
13,600	Mathews Memorial Library, Mathews, VA

General

22,800	Gloucester Volunteer Fire Company and Rescue Squad, Gloucester, VA
11,400	Abingdon Volunteer Fire Company, Bene, VA
11,400	Abingdon Volunteer Rescue Squad, Gloucester Point, VA
11,400	Mathews Volunteer Fire Department, Mathews, VA
10,200	Animal Care Society, Mathews, VA

Truland Foundation

CONTACT
Robert W. Truland
Trustee
Truland Fdn.
3330 Washington Blvd.
Arlington, VA 22201
(703) 516-2600

FINANCIAL SUMMARY
Recent Giving: $139,090 (fiscal 1994); $117,177 (fiscal 1993); $112,347 (fiscal 1992)

Assets: $2,552,302 (fiscal 1994); $2,533,653 (fiscal 1993); $2,526,830 (fiscal 1992)

Gifts Received: $100,000 (fiscal 1994)

Fiscal Note: In fiscal 1994, contributions were received from the Truland Systems Corp.

EIN: 54-6037172

CONTRIBUTIONS SUMMARY
Donor(s): Truland of Florida, Inc., and members of the Truland family

Typical Recipients: • *Arts & Humanities:* Arts Associations & Councils, Arts Centers, Ballet, Community Arts, Dance, Libraries, Literary Arts, Museums/Galleries, Music, Performing Arts, Public Broadcasting • *Civic & Public Affairs:* Clubs, General, Housing, Philanthropic Organizations, Professional & Trade Associations, Urban & Community Affairs, Zoos/Aquariums • *Education:* Colleges & Universities, Education Funds, Minority Education, Private Education (Precollege), Secondary Education (Private) • *Environment:* General, Resource Conservation, Wildlife Protection • *Health:* Alzheimers Disease, Cancer, Children's Health/Hospitals, Emergency/Ambulance Services, Health Organizations, Heart, Hospitals, Medical Research, Single-Disease Health Associations, Speech & Hearing • *International:* Human Rights • *Religion:* Churches, Jewish Causes, Ministries, Religious Organizations, Religious Welfare • *Social Services:* Community Service Organizations, Food/Clothing Distribution, People with Disabilities, Recreation & Athletics, Scouts, Shelters/Homelessness, United Funds/United Ways, Youth Organizations

Grant Types: general support

Geographic Distribution: focus on VA

GIVING OFFICERS
Alice O. Truland: trust

Robert W. Truland: trust *CURR EMPL* pres: Truland Sys Corp

Walter R. Truland: trust

APPLICATION INFORMATION
Initial Approach: The foundation requests applications be made in writing. Include a description of organization, amount requested, purpose of funds sought, recently audited financial statement, and proof of tax-exempt status. There are no deadlines.

GRANTS ANALYSIS
Total Grants: $139,090

Number of Grants: 67

Highest Grant: $30,000

Typical Range: $100 to $26,370

Disclosure Period: fiscal year ending March 31, 1994

Note: Recent grants are derived from a fiscal 1994 Form 990.

RECENT GRANTS

General

30,000	Chelonia Institute, Arlington, VA
26,370	Marymount University, Arlington, VA
16,180	Barnesville School, Barnesville, MD

| 10,000 | Samaritan Inns, Washington, DC |
| 5,125 | St. Anselm's Abbey, Washington, DC |

Virginia Environmental Endowment

CONTACT
Gerald P. McCarthy
Executive Director
Virginia Environmental Endowment
PO Box 790
Richmond, VA 23206-0790
(804) 644-5000

FINANCIAL SUMMARY
Recent Giving: $900,000 (fiscal 1995 est.); $772,588 (fiscal 1994); $897,087 (fiscal 1993)

Assets: $17,900,000 (fiscal 1995 est.); $17,822,241 (fiscal 1994); $17,723,613 (fiscal 1993)

Gifts Received: $50,000 (fiscal 1992)

Fiscal Note: In fiscal 1992, the endowment received settlement funds from IR International, Inc., and from Hauni Richmond, Inc.

CONTRIBUTIONS SUMMARY
Donor(s): The Virginia Environmental Endowment was created in 1977 with an $8 million contribution paid by Allied Chemical Corporation as part of a federal court agreement for polluting the James River. The endowment has since received large settlement funds paid by the FMC Corporation, Bethlehem Steel Corporation, Wheeling-Pittsburgh Steel Corporation, IR International, Inc., and Hauni Richmond, Inc., after each was cited for environmental violations.

Typical Recipients: • *Arts & Humanities:* Libraries • *Civic & Public Affairs:* Municipalities/Towns • *Education:* Education Reform, Engineering/Technological Education • *Environment:* Air/Water Quality, General, Resource Conservation

Grant Types: challenge, general support, and project

Geographic Distribution: in Virginia; limited funding in the Chesapeake Bay and the Kanawha and Ohio River Valleys

GIVING OFFICERS
Jeannie P. Baliles: vp, dir

Dixon M. Butler: sr vp, dir

Paul U. Elbling: dir

Virginia R. Holton: pres

Patricia Kluge: dir

Gerald Patrick McCarthy: exec dir, secy *B* New York NY 1943 *ED* Manhattan Coll BEE 1965; Univ WA MS 1967 *NONPR AF-FIL* mem: VA Conservation & Recreation Fdn; visiting prof environmental studies: Duke Univ

Alson H. Smith, Jr.: dir

Byron Lee Yost: treas, dir *B* Roanoke County VA 1939 *ED* VA Polytech Inst

1961; Rutgers Univ 1972 *CURR EMPL* pres: First Union Natl Bank VA

APPLICATION INFORMATION
Initial Approach:

Applicants should request application guidelines.

The full proposal should include a cover letter detailing the applicant, project title and schedule, the grant request and matching funds. It must also include the project description (five pages maximum), that states the need for and goals of the project and how it will be accomplished; a description of the organization, names and qualifications of major project personnel, a governing board members list, and a copy of the IRS tax-exempt ruling, if applicable. Additional information required is a line-item budget showing total costs, amount and allocation of grant funds, and sources and amounts of matching funds. Also include a plan for both evaluating project results and continuing project activities. Four copies of the complete proposal, signed by the organization's chairman or chief executive officer, must be submitted.

Proposals must be received on or before one of the following deadlines: January 15, September 15, or May 15 for the Virginia Program and the Virginia Mini-Grant Program, and May 15 for the Kanawha and Ohio River Valleys Program and the Martins Ferry-Ohio River Program.

The endowment does not review preliminary proposals. The board of directors meets three times per year.

Restrictions on Giving: Grants are made to nonprofit, tax-exempt organizations and governmental agencies. Typically, matching funds are required and challenge grants may be offered. Grant funds are not considered for overhead, indirect costs, building renovation or construction, endowments, lawsuits or individuals. Proposals outside of geographic limitations are not reviewed.

OTHER THINGS TO KNOW
Grantees are required to submit periodic progress reports and lists of expenditures as well as final evaluation reports.

PUBLICATIONS
Annual report and application guidelines

GRANTS ANALYSIS
Total Grants: $772,588

Number of Grants: 54*

Highest Grant: $80,000

Average Grant: $14,307

Typical Range: $1,000 to $5,000 and $10,000 to $30,000

Disclosure Period: fiscal year ending March 31, 1994

Note: Out of 54 total grants, 29 were given by the Virginia Program, 19 by the Virginia Mini-Grants Program, five by the Kanawha and Ohio River Valleys Program, and one by the Martins Ferry-Ohio River Program. Recent grants are derived from a fiscal 1994 partial grants list.

RECENT GRANTS
Library
| 1,000 | Foundation Center, New York, NY — philanthropic center |

General
50,000	Chesapeake Bay Foundation, Annapolis, MD — partial support for Phase III of "Managing Growth to Conserve Natural and Cultural Resources in the Lower Rappahannock River Valley"
50,000	West Virginia Rivers Coalition, Buckhannon, WV — to support the Coalition's development of West Virginia's first comprehensive strategic plan for river protection
40,000	Management Institute for Environment and Business, Washington, DC — two-year pilot program in Environmental Management Education at the University of Virginia (Darden School)
34,000	Martins Ferry City Schools, Martins Ferry, OH — renewed support of Project Ohio River Education in Martins Ferry City Schools to increase knowledge and awareness of the Ohio River environment
32,500	National Committee for the New River, Jefferson, NC — establishment of a Greeway Plan along the New River corridor in Giles County, Virginia

Virginia Power Co.

Sales: $11.52 billion
Employees: 11,861
Parent Company: Dominion Resources
Headquarters: Richmond, VA
SIC Major Group: Electric Services

CONTACT
Kathryn M. Fessler
Contributions Administrator
Virginia Power Co.
PO Box 26666
Richmond, VA 23261
(804) 771-4417

FINANCIAL SUMMARY
Recent Giving: $1,500,000 (1994 est.); $1,246,000 (1993 approx.); $1,615,000 (1992 approx.)

Fiscal Note: All contributions are made directly by the company. Figures for 1994 include matching gifts. All other figures exclude nonmonetary support.

CONTRIBUTIONS SUMMARY
Typical Recipients: • *Arts & Humanities:* Arts Associations & Councils, Arts Centers,

Arts Festivals, Community Arts, Dance, Libraries, Literary Arts, Museums/Galleries, Music, Opera, Performing Arts, Public Broadcasting, Theater, Visual Arts • *Civic & Public Affairs:* Employment/Job Training, Housing, Safety, Urban & Community Affairs, Women's Affairs • *Education:* Colleges & Universities, Education Funds, Engineering/Technological Education • *Environment:* General • *Health:* Emergency/Ambulance Services, Health Organizations, Hospices, Hospitals, Mental Health • *Social Services:* Child Welfare, Food/Clothing Distribution, Homes, People with Disabilities, Senior Services, Shelters/Homelessness, Substance Abuse

Grant Types: capital, employee matching gifts, general support, project, and seed money

Note: Employee matching gift ratio: 0.5 to 1.

Nonmonetary Support: $245,000 (1993); $325,500 (1991); $152,000 (1989)

Nonmonetary Support Types: donated equipment, donated products, in-kind services, and loaned employees

Geographic Distribution: organizations serving areas where company does business

Operating Locations: NC (Roanoke Rapids), VA (Alexandria, Charlottesville, Fairfax, Norfolk, Richmond), WV (Mount Storm)

CORP. OFFICERS

James Thomas Rhodes: *B* Lincolnton NC 1941 *ED* NC St Univ BS 1963; Catholic Univ Am MS 1968; Purdue Univ PhD 1972 *CURR EMPL* pres, ceo, dir: VA Power Co *CORP AFFIL* dir: Dominion Resources Inc, NationsBank VA

GIVING OFFICERS

Thomas Edward Capps: *B* Wilmington NC 1935 *ED* Univ NC AB 1958; Univ NC JD 1965 *CURR EMPL* chmn, ceo: Dominion Resources Inc *CORP AFFIL* chmn: Dominion Energy Inc, Dominion Lands Inc, VA Electric & Power Co; dir: Bassett Furniture Indus Inc, Bassett Furniture Indus NC, NationsBank Corp *NONPR AFFIL* mem: Am Bar Assn, Bd Bar Overseers, FL Bar Assn, MA Bar Assn, NC Bar Assn; trust: Univ NC Chapel Hill

Kathryn M. Fessler: *CURR EMPL* contributions admin: Virginia Power Co

Robert F. Hill: mem contributions comm *B* Chincoteague VA 1936 *ED* Old Dominion Univ BBA 1963; George Washington Univ MS 1965 *CURR EMPL* sr vp: VA Electric & Power Co

James Thomas Rhodes: mem contributions comm *CURR EMPL* pres, ceo, dir: VA Power Co (see above)

Eva S. Teig: *CURR EMPL* mem contributions comm: VA Power Co

APPLICATION INFORMATION

Initial Approach: *Initial Contact:* letter or proposal to Kathryn Fessler, contributions administrator, for organizations serving broad areas where company does business; local organizations should apply to nearest division office of Virginia Power Co. or to North Carolina Power Co. *Include Information On:* organization's purpose and goals, most recent financial statement, proof of tax-exempt status, amount of grant requested and overall goal for contributions, and purpose of grant *Deadlines:* none

Restrictions on Giving: The company does not contribute to individuals; churches or religious organizations; national health and welfare agencies; political campaigns; landmark restoration; primary or secondary schools; individual Boy or Girl Scout troops, unless not supported by the United Way; fraternal organizations; veterans' groups; groups which are United Way supported, unless for capital contributions; goodwill advertising; or organizations to which the company has awarded capital funding until two years have elapsed since final payment.

OTHER THINGS TO KNOW

Local community organizations should apply to nearest company offices. Their addresses and phone numbers are listed in Virginia Power Company's Corporate Giving Program brochure, available upon request from the contributions administrator.

GRANTS ANALYSIS

Total Grants: $1,246,000

Number of Grants: 875

Highest Grant: $110,000

Average Grant: $1,424

Typical Range: $1,000 to $5,000

Disclosure Period: 1993

Note: Figures exclude matching gifts.

Washington Forrest Foundation

CONTACT

Lindsey D. Peete
Executive Director
Washington Forrest Fdn.
2300 S 9th St.
Arlington, VA 22204
(703) 920-2200

FINANCIAL SUMMARY

Recent Giving: $292,540 (fiscal 1994); $306,829 (fiscal 1993); $303,357 (fiscal 1992)

Assets: $8,402,376 (fiscal 1994); $8,186,137 (fiscal 1993); $7,930,148 (fiscal 1992)

Gifts Received: $457,000 (fiscal 1992)

Fiscal Note: In 1992, contributions were received from the Virginia Smith Charitable Foundation.

EIN: 23-7002944

CONTRIBUTIONS SUMMARY

Donor(s): the late Benjamin M. Smith

Typical Recipients: • *Arts & Humanities:* Arts Associations & Councils, Community Arts, Dance, Libraries, Music, Opera, Performing Arts, Public Broadcasting, Theater • *Civic & Public Affairs:* Community Foundations, Economic Development, General, Housing, Philanthropic Organizations, Professional & Trade Associations, Public Policy, Urban & Community Affairs • *Education:* Colleges & Universities, Education Funds, Elementary Education (Public), Literacy, Medical Education, Private Education (Precollege), Public Education (Precollege), Religious Education, Secondary Education (Public), Student Aid • *Health:* AIDS/HIV, Arthritis, Cancer, Children's Health/Hospitals, Clinics/Medical Centers, Emergency/Ambulance Services, Health Organizations, Home-Care Services, Hospices, Mental Health, Research/Studies Institutes, Respiratory • *Religion:* Churches, Religious Organizations, Religious Welfare • *Social Services:* Child Abuse, Child Welfare, Community Service Organizations, Delinquency & Criminal Rehabilitation, Domestic Violence, Family Planning, Family Services, Food/Clothing Distribution, Recreation & Athletics, Scouts, Shelters/Homelessness, Substance Abuse, United Funds/United Ways, Youth Organizations

Grant Types: capital, emergency, general support, multiyear/continuing support, operating expenses, scholarship, and seed money

Geographic Distribution: focus on northern VA

GIVING OFFICERS

Leslie S. Ariail: secy, trust

Deborah G. Lucckese: vp, trust

Lindsey D. Peete: exec dir

Margaret S. Peete: pres, trust

APPLICATION INFORMATION

Initial Approach: Applicants must complete the foundation's application forms, which are available from the executive director. Applications are considered by the foundation board four times annually. Deadlines vary from year to yaer.

Restrictions on Giving: Limited to Northern Virginia.

PUBLICATIONS

Program policy statement

GRANTS ANALYSIS

Total Grants: $292,540

Number of Grants: 78

Highest Grant: $20,284

Typical Range: $250 to $16,000

Disclosure Period: fiscal year ending June 30, 1994

Note: Recent grants are derived from a fiscal 1994 Form 990.

RECENT GRANTS

Library
400   Arlington Public Schools Patrick Henry Elementary, Arlington, VA — Parent Resource Library

General
20,284   Arlington Public Schools Transitional First Grade Program, Arlington, VA — restricted purpose for paying

	the salary of a part-time teacher for the At-Risk first-grade language arts class
16,000	Arlington United Methodist Church, Arlington, VA — restricted purpose in support of asbestos removal
15,000	Arlington Community Foundation, Arlington, VA — restricted purpose in support of a neighborhood tutoring program
15,000	Christchurch School, Christchurch, VA — restricted support for the construction of a field house in honor of Edward M. Smith
10,000	Antietam Elementary School, Woodbrige, VA — restricted purpose in support of the Accelerated Reader program

Wheat First Butcher Singer, Inc. / Wheat, First Securities/Butcher & Singer Foundation

Former Foundation Name: Wheat Foundation
Sales: $204.0 million
Employees: 1,100
Parent Company: WFS Financial Corp.
Headquarters: Richmond, VA
SIC Major Group: Security Brokers & Dealers and Investors Nec

CONTACT
William V. Daniel
Vice President and Treasurer
Wheat, First Securities/Butcher and Singer Foundation
PO Box 1357
Richmond, VA 23211
(804) 649-2311

FINANCIAL SUMMARY
Recent Giving: $751,134 (fiscal 1994); $605,204 (fiscal 1993); $626,008 (fiscal 1992)

Assets: $2,643,386 (fiscal 1994); $1,926,650 (fiscal 1993); $1,227,870 (fiscal 1992)

Gifts Received: $1,593,960 (fiscal 1994); $1,283,042 (fiscal 1993); $700,000 (fiscal 1992)

Fiscal Note: Contributes through foundation only. Above figures exclude nonmonetary support. Contributions were received from Wheat, First Securities, Inc.

EIN: 54-6047119

CONTRIBUTIONS SUMMARY
Typical Recipients: • *Arts & Humanities:* Arts Funds, Ethnic & Folk Arts, Historic Preservation, History & Archaeology, Libraries, Museums/Galleries, Music, Performing Arts, Theater • *Civic & Public Affairs:* Business/Free Enterprise, Economic Development, Housing, Municipalities/Towns • *Education:* Colleges & Universities, Community & Junior Colleges, Education Associations, Education Funds, Legal Education, Medical Education, Private Education (Precollege) • *Environment:* Air/Water Quality • *Health:* Children's Health/Hospitals, Emergency/Ambulance Services, Eyes/Blindness, Health Organizations, Hospitals, Medical Research, Single-Disease Health Associations • *Religion:* Jewish Causes • *Science:* Science Museums • *Social Services:* Child Welfare, Community Centers, Community Service Organizations, People with Disabilities, United Funds/United Ways, Youth Organizations

Grant Types: capital, employee matching gifts, and general support

Geographic Distribution: in headquarters and operating communities

Operating Locations: VA (Richmond)

CORP. OFFICERS
William Verner Daniel: *B* Philadelphia PA 1928 *ED* Univ VA 1950 *CURR EMPL* mng dir: Wheat First Butcher Singer *CORP AFFIL* dir: Fidelity Bankers Life Ins Co

John Lee McElroy, Jr.: *B* Richmond VA 1931 *ED* Univ VA Bachelors 1953; Univ VA 1964 *CURR EMPL* chmn, ceo, dir: Wheat First Securities *CORP AFFIL* dir: Piper Jaffray & Hopwood; vchmn, ceo, dir: WFS Fin Corp *NONPR AFFIL* dir: Central Richmond Assn, Childrens Home Soc, Church Sch Diocese VA, St Catherines Sch, St Timothys Sch, Vestry St Pauls Church; pres: VA Historical Soc; trust: St Pauls Episcopal Church Home

Marshall B. Wishnack: *CURR EMPL* pres, dir: Wheat First Securities *CORP AFFIL* pres, ceo, dir: WFS Fin Corp

GIVING OFFICERS
William Verner Daniel: vp, treas, dir *CURR EMPL* mng dir: Wheat First Butcher Singer (see above)

Sharon L. Hobart: asst secy

Howard T. Macrae, Jr.: secy

John Lee McElroy, Jr.: pres, dir *CURR EMPL* chmn, ceo, dir: Wheat First Securities (see above)

James C. Wheat, Jr.: dir

Marshall B. Wishnack: dir *CURR EMPL* pres, dir: Wheat First Securities (see above)

APPLICATION INFORMATION
Initial Approach: *Initial Contact:* letter of inquiry *Include Information On:* Include a description of organization, amount requested, purpose of funds sought, recently audited financial statement, and proof of tax-exempt status. *Deadlines:* none

Restrictions on Giving: Does not support individuals, religious organizations for sectarian purposes, political or lobbying groups, or organizations outside operating areas.

GRANTS ANALYSIS
Total Grants: $643,587

Number of Grants: 236

Highest Grant: $20,000

Average Grant: $2,727

Typical Range: $50 to $1,000 and $2,500 to $10,000

Disclosure Period: fiscal year ending March 31, 1994

Note: Above figures do not include $107,547 in matching contributions. Recent grants are derived from a fiscal 1994 Form 990.

RECENT GRANTS

General

20,000	Catholic Schools Foundation, Boston, MA
20,000	College of William and Mary, Williamsburg, VA
20,000	Hampden-Sydney College, Hampden-Sydney, VA
20,000	James Madison University, Harrisonburg, VA
20,000	United Way Services, Cleveland, OH

WASHINGTON

Aldus Corp.

Sales: $206.78 million
Employees: 952
Parent Company: Adobe Systems Incorporated
Headquarters: Seattle, WA
SIC Major Group: Business Services

CONTACT
Louisa Ragucci
Public Affairs
Aldus Corp.
411 First Ave. S
Seattle, WA 98104
(206) 622-5500

CONTRIBUTIONS SUMMARY
Provides software programs to select nonprofit organizations, including those that have medical, human service, environmental, and cultural missions.

Volunteerism: The company plans 12 to 14 volunteer activities each year. In addition, each month it sends out an e-mail message to all employees regarding individual volunteer opportunities.

Typical Recipients: • *Arts & Humanities:* Arts Appreciation, Arts Centers, Arts Funds, Arts Outreach, Ballet, Community Arts, Dance, General, Libraries, Literary Arts, Museums/Galleries, Music, Performing Arts, Public Broadcasting, Theater, Visual Arts • *Civic & Public Affairs:* Botanical Gardens/Parks, Community Foundations, Employment/Job Training, Ethnic Organizations, General, Housing, Inner-City Development, Native American Affairs, Nonprofit Management, Women's Affairs, Zoos/Aquariums • *Education:* After-school/Enrichment Programs, Arts/Humanities Education, Business Education, Business-School Partnerships, Faculty Development, General, Literacy, Minority Education, Preschool Education • *Environment:* Air/Water Quality, Resource Conservation, Wildlife Protection • *Health:* Adolescent Health Issues, AIDS/HIV, Alzheimers Disease, Arthritis, Cancer, Children's Health/Hospitals, Diabetes, Eyes/Blindness, General, Heart, Hospices • *Science:* General, Science Exhibits & Fairs, Science Museums, Scientific Research • *Social Services:* Animal Protection, At-Risk Youth, Child Welfare, Community Centers, Counseling, Delinquency & Criminal Rehabilitation, Domestic Violence, Family Services, Food/Clothing Distribution, General, People with Disabilities, Recreation & Athletics, Sexual Abuse, Shelters/Homelessness, United Funds/United Ways, Volunteer Services, Youth Organizations

Grant Types: award, capital, emergency, general support, operating expenses, and project

Nonmonetary Support Types: donated products, in-kind services, and loaned employees

Geographic Distribution: only in headquarters area

Operating Locations: WA (Seattle)

CORP. OFFICERS
Chuck Geschke: *CURR EMPL* pres: Aldus Corp

John Warnock: *CURR EMPL* ceo: Aldus Corp

APPLICATION INFORMATION
Initial Approach: Send a full proposal. Include a description of organization, amount requested, purpose of funds sought, recently audited financial statement, and proof of tax-exempt status.

Restrictions on Giving: Does not support individuals, religious organizations for sectarian purposes, political or lobbying groups, organizations outside operating areas, or organizations which discriminate against any kind of person.

GRANTS ANALYSIS
Typical Range: $1,000 to $2,500

Bishop Foundation, E. K. and Lillian F.

CONTACT
Tom Nevers
Grant Manager
E.K. and Lillian F. Bishop Foundation
c/o Seafirst Bank Charitable Dept.
PO Box 24565, CSC-23
Seattle, WA 98124
(206) 358-0806

FINANCIAL SUMMARY
Recent Giving: $905,000 (fiscal 1995 est.); $915,190 (fiscal 1994 approx.); $905,496 (fiscal 1993)

Assets: $19,000,000 (fiscal 1995 est.); $19,000,000 (fiscal 1994 approx.); $19,272,855 (fiscal 1993)
EIN: 91-6116724

CONTRIBUTIONS SUMMARY
Donor(s): The foundation was established in 1971 by the late E. K. Bishop and the late Lillian F. Bishop .

Typical Recipients: • *Arts & Humanities:* Arts Centers, Ballet, Community Arts, Dance, History & Archaeology, Libraries, Museums/Galleries, Music, Performing Arts, Theater • *Civic & Public Affairs:* Asian American Affairs, Clubs, Economic Development, General, Inner-City Development, Municipalities/Towns, Parades/Festivals, Philanthropic Organizations, Urban & Community Affairs, Women's Affairs, Zoos/Aquariums • *Education:* Agricultural Education, Arts/Humanities Education, Colleges & Universities, Education Funds, Elementary Education (Private), Elementary Education (Public), Private Education (Precollege), Public Education (Precollege), Special Education • *Health:* Children's Health/Hospitals, Clinics/Medical Centers, Health Funds, Hospitals, Medical Research, Nursing Services, Single-Disease Health Associations • *Religion:* Churches, Dioceses, Religious Welfare • *Science:* Science Museums • *Social Services:* Big Brother/Big Sister, Child Welfare, Community Centers, Community Service Organizations, Family Planning, Family Services, Recreation & Athletics, Shelters/Homelessness, Substance Abuse, United Funds/United Ways, Volunteer Services, YMCA/YWCA/YMHA/YWHA, Youth Organizations

Grant Types: capital, general support, matching, project, and seed money

Geographic Distribution: focus on Washington State

GIVING OFFICERS
Isabelle Lamb: dir *B* 1922 *ED* Charleton Univ Canada 1947 *CURR EMPL* pres-treas, dir: Enterprises Intl *CORP AFFIL* dir: Independent Coll WA, US Bank WA; secy, dir: Ovalstrapping Inc; treas, dir: EII Ltd/Limitee

James Mason: dir

Tom Nevers: grant mgr

Janet T. Skadon: dir

APPLICATION INFORMATION
Initial Approach:

Applicants seeking grants should write to the foundation for a brochure and an application.

PUBLICATIONS
Program policy statement and informational brochure including application guidelines

GRANTS ANALYSIS
Total Grants: $905,496

Number of Grants: 159*

Highest Grant: $55,000

Average Grant: $4,835*

Typical Range: $1,000 to $15,000

Disclosure Period: fiscal year ending April 30, 1993

Note: Average grant and number of grants figures exclude 80 scholarships totaling $136,833. Recent grants are derived from a fiscal 1993 Form 990.

RECENT GRANTS
Library

10,000	Seattle Public Library Foundation, Seattle, WA

General

55,000	Hoquiam Kiwanis Club, WA
37,598	Grays Harbor Schools, Aberdeen, WA
25,000	Children's Hospital Foundation, Seattle, WA
20,000	Lincoln Elementary School, WA
20,000	Wishkah Valley School, WA

Boeing Co., The

Revenue: $21.92 billion
Employees: 123,000
Headquarters: Seattle, WA
SIC Major Group: Aircraft, Communications Equipment Nec, Electronic Components Nec, and Magnetic & Optical Recording Media

CONTACT
Christine G. Jones
Corporate Manager M/S 11-83
Boeing Co.
PO Box 3707
Seattle, WA 98124
(206) 655-0803
Note: The company's World Wide Web address is http://www.boeing.com

FINANCIAL SUMMARY
Recent Giving: $34,400,000 (1995 est.); $33,400,000 (1994 approx.); $32,405,929 (1993)

Fiscal Note: Total giving figures include direct contributions by the company and its subsidiaries. Above figures include nonmonetary support.

EIN: 91-6056738

CONTRIBUTIONS SUMMARY
Typical Recipients: • *Arts & Humanities:* Arts Centers, Arts Funds, Dance, Ethnic & Folk Arts, Libraries, Museums/Galleries, Music, Opera, Performing Arts, Theater • *Civic & Public Affairs:* Economic Development, Housing, Zoos/Aquariums • *Education:* Business Education, Colleges & Universities, Community & Junior Colleges, Continuing Education, Economic Education, Education Funds, Elementary Education (Private), Engineering/Technological Education, Faculty Development, Literacy, Minority Education, Preschool Education, Private Education (Precollege), Public Education (Precollege), Science/Mathematics Education, Special Education, Student Aid • *Environment:* General • *Health:* Hospices, Mental Health • *Social Services:* Child Welfare, Community Centers, Community Service Or-

ganizations, Delinquency & Criminal Rehabilitation, Domestic Violence, Food/Clothing Distribution, Homes, People with Disabilities, Senior Services, Shelters/Homelessness, Substance Abuse, United Funds/United Ways, Volunteer Services, Youth Organizations

Grant Types: capital, challenge, employee matching gifts, professorship, scholarship, and seed money

Note: Employee matching gift ratio: 1 to 1 for current employees. Employee matching gift ratio: 0.50 to 1 for retirees.

Nonmonetary Support: $7,300,000 (1994); $6,300,000 (1993); $6,000,000 (1992)

Nonmonetary Support Types: donated equipment, in-kind services, loaned employees, and loaned executives

Geographic Distribution: near operating locations where Boeing employees work and reside, primarily Philadelphia, PA; Wichita, KS; and Seattle, WA (contributions near small operations primarily go to United Way)

Operating Locations: AL (Huntsville), CA (Sunnyvale), GA (Macon), KS (Wichita), MT (Glasgow), OR (Boardman, Portland), PA (Philadelphia), TN (Oak Ridge), TX (Corinth, Irving), VA (Arlington, Vienna), WA (Auburn, Bellevue, Everett, Kent, Renton, Seattle, Spokane)

CORP. OFFICERS

Lawrence William Clarkson: *B* Grove City PA 1938 *ED* DePauw Univ BA 1960; Univ FL JD 1962 *CURR EMPL* sr vp planning & intl devel: Boeing Co *NONPR AFFIL* chmn: Counc Foreign Rels, Natl Bur Asia Res, US PECC; chmn, trust: Interlochen Ctr Arts; chmn trusts: Seattle Opera; dir: Natl Assn Mfrs, Partnership Improved Air Travel; overseer: Dartmouth Coll Amos Tuck Sch Bus Admin; pres: Japan-Am Soc, WA St China Rels Comm; trust: DePauw Univ *CLUB AFFIL* Metro Opera, NY YC, Seattle YC; gov: Wings

Frank Anderson Shrontz: *B* Boise ID 1931 *ED* George Washington Univ 1953; Univ ID LLB 1954; Harvard Univ MBA 1958; Stanford Univ 1969-1970 *CURR EMPL* chmn, ceo, dir: Boeing Co *CORP AFFIL* dir: Boise Cascade Corp, Citicorp, MN Mining & Mfg Co; pres: Commercial Airplane Co Boeing Div *NONPR AFFIL* mem: Beta Theta Pi, Bus Counc, Bus Roundtable, Phi Alpha Delta; mem citizen regent bd: Smithsonian Inst *CLUB AFFIL* Columbia Tower, Overlake Golf & CC

GIVING OFFICERS

Richard Raymond Albrecht: *B* Storm Lake IA 1932 *ED* Univ IA BA 1958; Univ IA JD 1961 *CURR EMPL* exec vp: Boeing Co *NONPR AFFIL* mem: Am Bar Assn, Am Judicature Soc, Omicron Delta Kappa, Order Coif, Phi Delta Phi, Seattle-King County Bar Assn, Sigma Nu, WA St Bar Assn; mem bd regents: WA St Univ *CLUB AFFIL* Rainier Seattle

Douglas Paul Beighle: *B* Deer Lodge MT 1932 *ED* Univ MT BS Bus 1954; Univ MT JD 1958; Harvard Univ LLM 1960 *CURR EMPL* sr vp: Boeing Co *CORP AFFIL* dir:

Puget Sound Power Light Co, WA Mutual Savings Bank; exec dir: US W Commun *NONPR AFFIL* dir: Jr Achievement Greater Puget Sound, Odyssey Maritime Mus, Odyssey Maritime Mus, Pacific Sci Ctr; mem: Am Bar Assn, Greater Seattle Chamber Commerce, Greater Seattle Chamber Commerce, MT Bar Assn, Natl Assn Mfrs, Seattle-King County Bar Assn, WA St Bar Assn; natl dir: Jr Achievement; trust: Mansfield Fdn, Univ MT Fdn *CLUB AFFIL* Rainier Seattle, Seattle YC

Harold Carr: *B* Kansas City KS 1921 *ED* TX A&M Univ BS 1943; Am Univ 1944-1946 *CURR EMPL* vp pub rels: Boeing Co *CORP AFFIL* chmn: Carr & Assocs; dir: Cayman Mile Ltd, Cayman Water Co, First Natl Bank Bryan, Governors Sound Ltd, Metro Airlines *NONPR AFFIL* mem: Am Econ Assn, Am Mgmt Assn, Beta Gamma Sigma, Intl Inst Effective Commun, Natl Aeronautics Assn, Natl Trust Historic Preservation, Pine Beach Peninsula Assoc, TX A&M Former Students Assn, World Bus Counc; mem bd nominations: Natl Aviation Hall Fame; mem chancellor's century counc: TX A&M Univ; mem exec adv counc: Natl Register Prominent Ams & Intl Notables; trust: TX A&M Res Fdn *CLUB AFFIL* Aero, Briarcrest CC, Gull Lake YC, Minneapolis, Natl Aviation, Racquet, Stearman Alumnus, Twelfth Man Fdn, TX A&M Century, Wings

Lawrence William Clarkson: vp *CURR EMPL* sr vp planning & intl devel: Boeing Co (see above)

Boyd Eugene Givan: *B* 1936 *ED* MA Inst Tech BS 1957; Univ WA MBA 1959 *CURR EMPL* sr vp, cfo: Boeing Co

Christine G. Jones: *CURR EMPL* corp mgr commun & ed rels: Boeing Co

Lawrence McKean: *CURR EMPL* corp vp: Boeing Co

APPLICATION INFORMATION

Initial Approach: *Initial Contact:* call to discuss proposal or write a brief letter describing your organization's needs *Include Information On:* description of the organization; history of service; statement of purpose and organizational objectives; definition of project describing community need, goals for project, specific activities, timeline, and plan for measuring results; itemized budget; list of committed financial supporters; plans for multiyear funding, if appropriate; evidence of nonprofit status; most recent audited financial statements; and list of board of directors, officers, and their affiliations *Deadlines:* none

Restrictions on Giving: No support given to individuals, political candidates, fraternal organizations, goodwill advertising, or religious organizations.

Company does not support hospitals or medical research organizations.

OTHER THINGS TO KNOW

The company reported that in 1994 Boeing and its employees contributed more than $60.4 million to support a wide range of community projects. Corporate gifts totaled $33.4 milion including cash and nonmone-

tary support. Boeing employees and retirees donated $27 million through the Boeing Employees Good Neighbor Fund and the company's matching gift program.

PUBLICATIONS
Corporate Citizenship Report

GRANTS ANALYSIS
Total Grants: $33,400,000*

Highest Grant: $3,000,000*

Typical Range: $5,000 to $10,000 and $20,000 to $30,000

Disclosure Period: 1994

Note: Number of grants and average grant figures unavailable. Total grants figure does not include $27,000,000 of employee and retiree gifts and $7,300,000 of in-kind services, equipment and supplies. In total, Boeing contributed $60,400,000 in 1994. Recent grants are derived from a 1994 annual report.

Cheney Foundation, Ben B.

CONTACT
William O. Rieke, MD
Executive Director
Ben B. Cheney Foundation
1201 Pacific Ave. South
Ste. 1600
Tacoma, WA 98402
(206) 572-2442

FINANCIAL SUMMARY
Recent Giving: $2,700,000 (1995 est.); $2,782,500 (1994); $2,475,900 (1993)

Assets: $60,000,000 (1995 est.); $60,000,000 (1994 est.); $62,933,184 (1993)

Gifts Received: $25,735,833 (1991); $1,238,663 (1989); $1,205,717 (1988)

Fiscal Note: The combined assets of the Ben B. Cheney Foundation and the Ben B.Cheney Trust totaled $56,940,660 in 1989. In 1989, the foundation received a gift of $1,238,663 from the Trust for the Ben B. Cheney Foundation. In 1991, the foundation received the remaining funds from the Ben B. Cheney Trust totaling $25,735,833.

EIN: 91-6053760

CONTRIBUTIONS SUMMARY
Donor(s): The foundation was established in 1955 by the late Ben B. Cheney , who died in 1971, and Marian Cheney Olrogg , who died in 1975. Mr. Cheney founded the Cheney Lumber Company in 1936, and remained in the industry until his death. In 1975, the foundation began active grant making and offices were established in Tacoma, WA.

Typical Recipients: • *Arts & Humanities:* Arts Associations & Councils, Arts Centers, Dance, Historic Preservation, Libraries, Museums/Galleries, Music, Opera, Performing Arts, Public Broadcasting, Theater • *Civic & Public Affairs:* Community Foundations, Housing, Parades/Festivals, Philanthropic Organizations, Urban & Community Affairs,

Zoos/Aquariums • *Education:* Colleges & Universities, Community & Junior Colleges, Education Reform, Private Education (Precollege), Special Education, Student Aid • *Environment:* General, Wildlife Protection • *Health:* Cancer, Children's Health/Hospitals, Clinics/Medical Centers, Emergency/Ambulance Services, Hospitals, Medical Training, Mental Health, Single-Disease Health Associations • *Science:* Science Museums, Scientific Centers & Institutes • *Social Services:* Child Welfare, Community Centers, Community Service Organizations, Counseling, Food/Clothing Distribution, People with Disabilities, Recreation & Athletics, Senior Services, Shelters/Homelessness, United Funds/United Ways, Volunteer Services, Youth Organizations

Grant Types: capital, general support, and project

Geographic Distribution: southwest Washington, southern Oregon, and northern California

GIVING OFFICERS
Bradbury B. Cheney: secy, dir

Piper Cheney: dir

R. Gene Grant: pres, dir

John F. Hansler: treas, dir

Elgin E. Olrogg: vp, dir

William Oliver Rieke, MD: exec dir *B* Odessa WA 1931 *ED* Pacific Lutheran Unic BA 1953; Univ WA MD 1958 *NONPR AFFIL* affil prof biological structure: Univ WA Sch Medicine; fellow: Am Coll Physicians; mem: Alpha Kappa Psi, Am Assn Advancement Science, Am Assn Anatomists, Am Soc Cell Biology, Beta Gamma Sigma, Natl Assn Independent Colls Univs, Sigma Xi

Kenneth I. Ristine: program off

APPLICATION INFORMATION
Initial Approach:

Applicants should mail a query letter to the executive director.

Query letters should provide a short history and the mission of the applicant and summarize the proposal to be considered. This summary should include the nature of the need(s) to be addressed, the goal of the project, and the amount and purpose of funds requested of the foundation, and the total project budget.

Query letters are accepted at any time. The agenda items for board meetings are set six to eight weeks in advance of meetings. Board meetings are held in April, June, September, and December.

The foundation considers requests on the basis of priorities and funds available. Queries go to a review committee, and if the committee deems a proposal to be of interest to the foundation, a staff contact and application form will follow. The foundation responds to all serious inquiries.

Restrictions on Giving: The foundation does not contribute to programs where government funding is available, to operating budgets, research, loans, endowments, religious organizations for sectarian purposes, to

the preparation or publication of videos, or to individuals.

OTHER THINGS TO KNOW
The foundation awards grants primarily in Southwest Washington, Tacoma-Pierce County, Southern Oregon-particularly around Medford, and the seven northernmost counties of California where the Cheney Lumber Company was active.

PUBLICATIONS
Application guidelines, informational brochure

GRANTS ANALYSIS
Total Grants: $2,475,900

Number of Grants: 167

Highest Grant: $100,000

Average Grant: $14,826

Typical Range: $2,500 to $5,000 and $10,000 to $25,000

Disclosure Period: 1993

Note: Recent grants are derived from a 1992 Form 990.

RECENT GRANTS
Library
25,000 Heritage College, Toppenish, WA — build library and learning center

General
1,250,000 Greater Tacoma Community Foundation, Tacoma, WA — Ben B. Cheney Foundation Advised Fund
250,000 Tacoma General Hospital, Tacoma, WA — establish endowment fund for oncology nurses' training
100,000 Children's Home Society of Washington, Seattle, WA — establish Families First program in Pierce County
100,000 Mary Bridge Children's Hospital and Health Center, Tacoma, WA — increase number of beds
100,000 Pierce County Alliance, Tacoma, WA — renovate old funeral home for future home of the alliance

Forest Foundation

CONTACT
Frank D. Underwood
Executive Director
Forest Foundation
820 A St., Ste. 345
Tacoma, WA 98402
(206) 627-1634

FINANCIAL SUMMARY
Recent Giving: $784,400 (fiscal 1992); $956,195 (fiscal 1991); $977,628 (fiscal 1990)

Assets: $22,223,332 (fiscal 1992); $21,228,046 (fiscal 1991); $18,972,795 (fiscal 1990)

Gifts Received: $250,000 (fiscal 1990)

Fiscal Note: In fiscal 1990, contributions were received from the 1975 Trust of CDW.

EIN: 91-6020514

CONTRIBUTIONS SUMMARY
Donor(s): The foundation was incorporated in 1962 by C. Davis Weyerhaeuser and William T. Weyerhaeuser.

Typical Recipients: • *Arts & Humanities:* Arts Associations & Councils, Dance, Historic Preservation, Libraries, Museums/Galleries, Music, Opera, Performing Arts, Theater • *Civic & Public Affairs:* Civil Rights, Community Foundations, General, Municipalities/Towns, Parades/Festivals, Philanthropic Organizations, Public Policy, Urban & Community Affairs, Women's Affairs • *Education:* Colleges & Universities, Community & Junior Colleges, Continuing Education, Economic Education, Health & Physical Education, Public Education (Precollege), Religious Education, Secondary Education (Private), Special Education • *Environment:* General • *Health:* Cancer, Clinics/Medical Centers, Health Funds, Health Organizations, Medical Research, Single-Disease Health Associations • *Religion:* Churches, Ministries, Religious Organizations, Religious Welfare • *Science:* Scientific Centers & Institutes • *Social Services:* Camps, Child Welfare, Community Centers, Community Service Organizations, Counseling, Domestic Violence, Family Planning, Family Services, Food/Clothing Distribution, Homes, People with Disabilities, Recreation & Athletics, Youth Organizations

Grant Types: capital, operating expenses, and project

Geographic Distribution: Southwest Washington with a focus on Pierce County

GIVING OFFICERS
Linda P. BeMiller: dir *PHIL AFFIL* program dir: Sequoia Foundation; program off: New Horizon Foundation

James R. Hanson: dir *PHIL AFFIL* secy, dir: Stewardship Foundation; mem: Sequoia Foundation

Nicholas C. Spika: secy *PHIL AFFIL* secy: Sequoia Foundation

Frank D. Underwood: exec dir *PHIL AFFIL* exec dir, mem: Sequoia Foundation; pres, treas, dir: New Horizon Foundation

Annette Thayer Black Weyerhaeuser: vp, dir, mem *PHIL AFFIL* dir, mem: Sequoia Foundation; vp, treas, dir: Stewardship Foundation

Charles Davis Weyerhaeuser: dir, mem *B* St Paul MN *ED* Yale Univ BA 1933 *CORP AFFIL* dir: Weyerhaeuser Timber Co *NONPR AFFIL* chmn: YMCA Campaign; trust: Fuller Theological Seminary, InterVarsity Christian Fellowship, Moody Bible Inst, Whitworth Coll, Young Life; vchmn: Natl Alliance Businessmen *PHIL AFFIL* don, pres, treas, dir: Stewardship Foundation; don: Sequoia Foundation

Gail T. Weyerhaeuser: pres, treas, dir *PHIL AFFIL* vp, dir, mem: Sequoia Foundation

William Toycen Weyerhaeuser: dir *B* Tacoma WA 1943 *ED* Stanford Univ 1966; Fuller Grad Sch Psychology PhD 1975 *CURR EMPL* owner, chmn: Yelm Telephone Co *CORP AFFIL* dir: Potlatch Corp *NONPR AFFIL* mem: Am Psychological Assn; vchmn: Univ Puget Sound *PHIL AFFIL* pres, treas, dir, mem: Sequoia Foundation; trust: Weyerhaeuser Family Foundation; dir: Stewardship Foundation

APPLICATION INFORMATION
Initial Approach:

Applications may be submitted in one of two ways: submit two copies of a typewritten summary letter addressed to Frank D. Underwood, or submit five copies of a complete application.

Applicants who submit a typewritten summary letter should include a concise statement of the proposed project, a description of the organization, a project budget, the amount requested, and an IRS ruling regarding the applicant's tax-exempt status.

Applicants submitting a complete application should include a letter describing the project and the amount requested. Grant requests should also include the following information on the organization: legal name, address, and telephone number; the name of the chief adminstrative officer and a statement that the officer will take full responsibility for the proper fiscal management, accounting, and submission of reports applying to the grant; a statement that the grant will not be used to propagandize or influence elections or legislation; a description of the organization and the qualifications of the organizations in the area for which funds are requested; a list of the organization's board of directors and their affiliations; audited financial statements for the most recent year; the current operating budget; a copy of the most recent ruling by the IRS that the organization is tax-exempt under section 501(c)(3).

The following information regarding project data should also be included in the formal application: a description of the project and why it is important to undertake, descriptions of the people or organizations expected to benefit from the project and the ways in which they would benefit, substantiation of need and comments on other attempts to address the need, a plan and timetable of action, a method for assessing the project's effectiveness, and the qualifications of the people involved in the project and the amount of time each person will spend on the project.

Each of the program areas has specific deadlines. The Community Improvement program, April 15 and December 15; Culture and the Arts program, February 15 and August 15; the Education program, August 15 and December 15; the Environment program, April 15 and August 15; and the Social Services program, February 15, June 15, and October 15.

The foundation meets six times a year. Decisions on complete proposals in each of the program areas are made at least twice annually. Action will be taken on proposals between 45 and 75 days from the deadline.

Restrictions on Giving: The foundation only makes grants to tax-exempt charitable organizations, and does not support religious organizations, endowment funds, research, scholarships, fellowships, films, or publications. No grants are made to individuals or for loans.

PUBLICATIONS
Program policy statement and application guidelines

GRANTS ANALYSIS
Total Grants: $784,400

Number of Grants: 66

Highest Grant: $100,000

Average Grant: $11,885

Typical Range: $5,000 to $25,000

Disclosure Period: fiscal year ending October 31, 1992

Note: Recent grants are derived from a fiscal 1992 grants list.

RECENT GRANTS

General

100,000	Fred Hutchinson Cancer Research Center, Dayton, OH — capital needs	
100,000	Greater Tacoma Community Foundation, Tacoma, WA — capital needs	
75,000	Northwest Trek Foundation, Eatonville, WA — capital needs	
34,000	Multicare Medical Center, Tacoma, WA — capital needs	
30,000	Franciscan Foundation for Health Care, Tacoma, WA — capital needs	

Foster Foundation

CONTACT
Jill Goodsell
Administrator
Foster Foundation
1201 Third Ave., Ste. 2101
Seattle, WA 98101
(206) 624-5200

FINANCIAL SUMMARY
Recent Giving: $1,239,500 (1992); $1,200,000 (1991); $914,625 (1990)

Assets: $21,170,534 (1992); $20,271,333 (1991); $17,978,546 (1990)

Gifts Received: $13,235,691 (1990)

Fiscal Note: In 1990, contributions were received from Evelyn W. Foster.

EIN: 91-1265474

CONTRIBUTIONS SUMMARY
Donor(s): The foundation was established in 1984 by Evelyn W. Foster.

Typical Recipients: • *Arts & Humanities:* Libraries, Museums/Galleries, Music, Opera, Performing Arts • *Civic & Public Affairs:* Housing, Public Policy, Urban & Community Affairs • *Education:* Colleges & Universities, Literacy, Private Education (Precollege) • *Environment:* General, Resource Conservation • *Health:* AIDS/HIV, Cancer, Children's Health/Hospitals, Clinics/Medical Centers, Emergency/Ambulance Services, Health Organizations, Hospitals, Nursing Services, Public Health • *Religion:* Churches, Missionary Activities (Domestic), Religious Organizations, Religious Welfare • *Science:* Scientific Centers & Institutes • *Social Services:* Child Welfare, Community Centers, Community Service Organizations, Emergency Relief, Family Planning, Family Services, Food/Clothing Distribution, Homes, Senior Services, Shelters/Homelessness, United Funds/United Ways, Youth Organizations

Grant Types: capital, matching, project, research, scholarship, and seed money

Geographic Distribution: focus on Seattle, WA

GIVING OFFICERS
Evelyn W. Foster: dir

Michael G. Foster: dir *CURR EMPL* ceo, dir: Foster Pausell & Baker Inc

Thomas B. Foster: dir *B* 1916 *CURR EMPL* chmn: CA Newell Co *CORP AFFIL* gen ptnr: Tile Distributors

Jill Goodsell: admin, dir *CURR EMPL* treas, dir: Foster Paulsell & Baker, Inc.

APPLICATION INFORMATION
Initial Approach:

Inquiries for funding should be described briefly in letter form. If the inquiry is deemed appropriate, a formal application will be requested.

Inquiries should include a brief description of the project and its intended purpose. Formal applications must contain the name and address of the organization, proof of tax-exempt status, a list of officers and directors, a brief history of the program and its acomplishments, and financial reports including a budget for the current year. The formal application must also include a project plan defining the need and the methods for achieving the objectives and for evaluating the results, and a detailed budget for the project.

The foundation has no deadline for submitting proposals.

Applicants should allow three months before a decision from the board is made.

Restrictions on Giving: Grants will be awarded to organizations for one year only. Grants to individuals will be made as scholarships. The foundation does not support endowment funds, fundraising activities, loans, or unrestricted operating funds.

GRANTS ANALYSIS
Total Grants: $1,239,500

Number of Grants: 50

Highest Grant: $500,000

Average Grant: $24,790

Typical Range: $5,000 to $50,000

Disclosure Period: 1992

Note: Recent grants are derived from a 1992 Form 990.

RECENT GRANTS

Library
15,000	Seattle Public Library, Seattle, WA

General
500,000	University of Washington, Seattle, WA
85,000	Childhaven, Seattle, WA
50,000	Overlake School, Seattle, WA
40,000	United Way of King County, Seattle, WA
35,000	Children's Hospital and Medical Center, Seattle, WA

Glaser Foundation

CONTACT
R. Thomas Olson
President
Glaser Fdn.
PO Box 6548
Bellevue, WA 98008-0548
(206) 881-2485

FINANCIAL SUMMARY
Recent Giving: $315,077 (fiscal 1993); $310,450 (fiscal 1992); $271,000 (fiscal 1990)

Assets: $7,560,059 (fiscal 1993); $7,263,754 (fiscal 1992); $6,117,357 (fiscal 1990)

EIN: 91-6028694

CONTRIBUTIONS SUMMARY
Donor(s): the late Paul F. Glaser

Typical Recipients: • *Arts & Humanities:* Arts Associations & Councils, Arts Centers, Community Arts, Ethnic & Folk Arts, Libraries, Music, Performing Arts, Theater • *Civic & Public Affairs:* African American Affairs, Housing, Professional & Trade Associations, Urban & Community Affairs, Women's Affairs, Zoos/Aquariums • *Education:* Colleges & Universities, Elementary Education (Private), General, Preschool Education, Private Education (Precollege), Public Education (Precollege), Social Sciences Education, Special Education • *Health:* AIDS/HIV, Cancer, Children's Health/Hospitals, Clinics/Medical Centers, Health Funds, Health Organizations, Hospices, Hospitals, Mental Health, Single-Disease Health Associations, Speech & Hearing • *Religion:* Missionary Activities (Domestic), Religious Welfare • *Science:* Scientific Centers & Institutes • *Social Services:* At-Risk Youth, Camps, Child Welfare, Community Centers, Community Service Organizations, Counseling, Day Care, Domestic Violence, Family Planning, Family Services, Food/Clothing Distribution, Homes, People with Disabilities, Recreation & Athletics, Senior Services, Shelters/Homelessness, Substance Abuse, United Funds/United Ways, Youth Organizations

Grant Types: project and seed money

Geographic Distribution: focus on the Puget Sound, WA, area

GIVING OFFICERS
R. N. Brandenburg: vp, dir

R. William Carlstrom: treas

R. Thomas Olson: pres, dir

Janet L. Politeo: secy, dir

Walt Smith: bd mem

APPLICATION INFORMATION
Initial Approach: Application form required. There are no deadlines.

Restrictions on Giving: Does not support individuals or provide loans.

PUBLICATIONS
Application Guidelines

GRANTS ANALYSIS
Total Grants: $315,077

Number of Grants: 68

Highest Grant: $25,000

Typical Range: $250 to $20,000

Disclosure Period: fiscal year ending November 30, 1993

Note: Recent grants are derived from a fiscal 1993 Form 990.

RECENT GRANTS
Library
10,000	Washington Library for the Blind and Physically Handicapped, Seattle, WA — social services radio reader
5,000	Seattle Public Library Foundation, Seattle, WA — social services teen health education

General
25,000	Olympia Childcare Center, Olympia, WA — social services low-income daycare center
20,000	Snohomish Valley Seniors, Carnation, WA — social services elderly
15,000	Catholic Community Services, Seattle, WA — social services women's shelters
10,000	First Place, Seattle, WA — social services homelessness
10,000	Snohomish County Youth Foundation, Edmonds, VA — social services teen philanthropy

Leuthold Foundation

CONTACT
John H. Leuthold
President
Leuthold Fdn.
1006 US Bank Bldg.
Spokane, WA 99201
(509) 624-3944

FINANCIAL SUMMARY
Recent Giving: $346,271 (fiscal 1994); $356,082 (fiscal 1993); $350,275 (fiscal 1992)

Assets: $7,005,923 (fiscal 1994); $7,193,134 (fiscal 1993); $7,242,644 (fiscal 1992)

Gifts Received: $700 (fiscal 1991)

EIN: 91-6028589

CONTRIBUTIONS SUMMARY
Donor(s): members of the Leuthold family

Typical Recipients: • *Arts & Humanities:* Arts Associations & Councils, Arts Festivals, Community Arts, Libraries, Music, Opera, Public Broadcasting, Theater • *Civic & Public Affairs:* Botanical Gardens/Parks, Economic Development, General, Housing, Legal Aid, Urban & Community Affairs, Women's Affairs • *Education:* Arts/Humanities Education, Business Education, Colleges & Universities, Community & Junior Colleges, Engineering/Technological Education, Medical Education, Preschool Education, Private Education (Precollege), Religious Education, Special Education • *Health:* Cancer, Clinics/Medical Centers, Emergency/Ambulance Services, Health Organizations, Home-Care Services, Hospitals, Medical Rehabilitation, Medical Research, Nursing Services, Single-Disease Health Associations • *Religion:* Churches, Dioceses, Ministries, Religious Organizations, Religious Welfare • *Social Services:* Camps, Child Abuse, Child Welfare, Community Centers, Community Service Organizations, Day Care, Domestic Violence, Family Planning, Family Services, Food/Clothing Distribution, People with Disabilities, Scouts, YMCA/YWCA/YMHA/YWHA, Youth Organizations

Grant Types: capital, endowment, general support, multiyear/continuing support, operating expenses, and scholarship

Geographic Distribution: limited to Spokane County, WA

GIVING OFFICERS
O. M. Kimmel, Jr.: secy, treas, trust

Betty B. Leuthold: vp, trust

John H. Leuthold: pres, trust

Allan H. Toole: asst secy, treas, trust *B* Spokane WA 1920 *ED* Gonzaga Univ LLB 1948 *CURR EMPL* couns: Witherspoon Kelly Davenport & Tool *NONPR AFFIL* fellow: Am Coll Trust Estate Counc; mem: Am Bar Assn, Spokane County Bar Assn, WA Bar Assn; trust: Leuthold Fdn, Wasmer Fdn *PHIL AFFIL* trust: Wasmer Foundation

APPLICATION INFORMATION
Initial Approach: Send letter requesting application form. Deadlines are May 15 and November 15.

Restrictions on Giving: Limited to Spokane County, WA.

PUBLICATIONS
Application Guidelines

GRANTS ANALYSIS
Total Grants: $346,271

Number of Grants: 74

Highest Grant: $44,912

Typical Range: $10000 to $20,000

Disclosure Period: fiscal year ending June 30, 1994

Note: Recent grants are derived from a fiscal 1994 Form 990.

RECENT GRANTS

General

44,912	St. George's School, Spokane, WA — class room edition Wall St. Journal general use and computer aquisition program
20,000	Spokane Food Bank, Spokane, WA — building campaign/general use
19,000	Cathedral of St. John, Spokane, WA — Bishop and Dean's Discretionary Fund operating budget
15,000	Children's Ark, Spokane, WA — purchase and renovation of Foster Care Home
10,000	Episcopal Diocese of Spokane, Spokane, WA — refurbishment of expansion of Camp Cross

Murdock Charitable Trust, M. J.

CONTACT
Ford A. Anderson II
Executive Director
M. J. Murdock Charitable Trust
PO Box 1618
Vancouver, WA 98668
(360) 694-8415
Note: An alternative phone number is (503) 285-4086.

FINANCIAL SUMMARY
Recent Giving: $16,764,325 (1993); $15,565,140 (1992); $14,177,550 (1991)

Assets: $285,541,345 (1993); $263,699,731 (1992); $256,359,883 (1991)

EIN: 23-7456468

CONTRIBUTIONS SUMMARY
Donor(s): M. J. (Jack) Murdock was born in Portland, OR, in 1917. Upon completion of high school, he opened a shop for the sale and service of radio and electrical appliances. In 1937, he began an association with Howard Vollum which culminated in the founding of Tektronix. He served as secretary-treasurer until 1960 when he was elected chairman of the board. Mr. Murdock died in 1971. The trust was established by the terms of his will.

Typical Recipients: • *Arts & Humanities:* Arts Festivals, Ballet, History & Archaeology, Libraries, Museums/Galleries, Music, Opera, Theater • *Civic & Public Affairs:* Economic Development, Housing, Legal Aid, Native American Affairs, Philanthropic Organizations, Professional & Trade Associations, Public Policy, Rural Affairs, Zoos/Aquariums • *Education:* After-school/Enrichment Programs, Arts/Humanities Education, Colleges & Universities, Education Reform, Engineering/Technological Education, Environmental Education, Faculty Development, Medical Education, Private Education (Precollege), Religious Education, Science/Mathematics Education, Special Education • *Environment:* General, Resource Conservation, Wildlife Protection • *Health:* Cancer, Children's Health/Hospitals, Clinics/Medical Centers, Health Policy/Cost Containment, Medical Rehabilitation, Medical Research, Preventive Medicine/Wellness Organizations • *International:* International Peace & Security Issues, International Relief Efforts • *Religion:* Bible Study/Translation, Ministries, Religious Welfare, Seminaries • *Science:* Scientific Centers & Institutes • *Social Services:* Child Welfare, Community Centers, Community Service Organizations, Family Services, People with Disabilities, United Funds/United Ways, Youth Organizations

Grant Types: capital, challenge, project, research, and seed money

Geographic Distribution: regional, with emphasis on the Pacific Northwest, including Alaska, Idaho, Montana, Oregon, and Washington

GIVING OFFICERS
Colleen Allbee: secy grants program

Ford A. Anderson II: exec dir

James B. Castles: trust *B* Missoula MT 1915 *ED* Univ MT LLB 1938

Walter P. Dyke: trust

Lynwood W. Swanson: trust

Neal O. Thorpe: sr program off

APPLICATION INFORMATION
Initial Approach:

If the proposal represents a major priority of the overall organization, an applicant should request a copy of the "Grant Application Packet," which gives details on preparing a grant application. A potential applicant may find it helpful to send a brief letter of inquiry summarizing the main elements of the proposal in order to determine whether a formal application would be within the trust's interests.

The trust now has an application form which is contained in the grant application packet. Proposals should be written and presented in a concise manner. Tables, charts, and appendices may be used. Elaborate and bulky bindings should be avoided.

There are no specific deadlines. Review of proposals may take two to six months.

Restrictions on Giving: The foundation does not consider grants to individuals; for loans; for political purposes; to institutions which discriminate on the basis of race, ethnic origin, sex, creed, or religion; to sectarian or religious organizations whose principal activity is for the benefit of their own members; or for projects requiring a financial obligation over a period of several years. Member agencies of the United Way of Columbia-Willamette and organizations outside the United States also are excluded from consideration.

In addition, the foundation will not consider funding requests for endowment; debt retirement; continuation of programs previously financed by external sources; general fund drives or annual charitable appeals; and requests from organizations whose priorities do not match the foundation's major priorities. Requests from organizations and projects normally financed by tax funds are not favored.

PUBLICATIONS
Grant application packet, annual report

GRANTS ANALYSIS
Total Grants: $16,764,325

Number of Grants: 141

Highest Grant: $2,000,000

Average Grant: $118,896

Typical Range: $25,000 to $200,000

Disclosure Period: 1993

Note: Recent grants are derived from a 1993 Form 990.

RECENT GRANTS

Library

500,000	Gonzaga University, Spokane, WA — instructional media services center in new library
500,000	Heritage College, Toppenish, WA — library and learning center
394,500	Marylhurst Education Center, Marylhurst, OR — Shoen Library Automation
67,500	Northern Montana College, Havre, MT — library automation project

General

2,000,000	Oregon Graduate Institute of Science and Technology, Portland, OR — new chemical and biological sciences/environmental science and engineering building
1,000,000	Pacific University, Forest Grove, OR — new science center
850,000	Western Evangelical Seminary, Valley Forge, PA — New Directions in Theological Education
720,000	University of Washington, Seattle, WA — instrumentation for the Center for Bimolecular Structure
700,000	Fred Hutchinson Cancer Research Center, Seattle, WA — core equipment for structural biology program

Nesholm Family Foundation

CONTACT
Rod Johnson
Vice President
Nesholm Family Fdn.
PO Box 3586
Seattle, WA 98124
(206) 358-3388

FINANCIAL SUMMARY
Recent Giving: $599,605 (1993); $535,119 (1992); $470,815 (1990)

Assets: $14,654,694 (1993); $13,636,831 (1992); $11,599,424 (1990)

EIN: 94-3055422

CONTRIBUTIONS SUMMARY
Donor(s): the late Elmer J. Nesholm

Typical Recipients: • *Arts & Humanities:* Arts Centers, Arts Funds, Ballet, Community Arts, Ethnic & Folk Arts, Libraries, Museums/Galleries, Music, Opera, Performing Arts, Public Broadcasting, Theater • *Civic & Public Affairs:* Civil Rights, Economic Development, Housing, Municipalities/Towns, Native American Affairs, Public Policy, Urban & Community Affairs, Women's Affairs, Zoos/Aquariums • *Education:* Colleges & Universities, Education Reform, Literacy, Private Education (Precollege), Public Education (Precollege), Science/Mathematics Education, Special Education • *Health:* Adolescent Health Issues, AIDS/HIV, Alzheimers Disease, Children's Health/Hospitals, Clinics/Medical Centers, Emergency/Ambulance Services, Health Organizations, Hospices, Long-Term Care, Mental Health, Prenatal Health Issues • *Religion:* Religious Welfare • *Social Services:* At-Risk Youth, Child Welfare, Community Service Organizations, Day Care, Domestic Violence, Emergency Relief, Family Services, Homes, Refugee Assistance, Senior Services, Substance Abuse, United Funds/United Ways, Youth Organizations

Grant Types: project

Geographic Distribution: limited to Seattle, WA

GIVING OFFICERS
Seattle First National Bank: trust

Joseph M. Gaffney: dir

Edgar K. Marcuse, MD: dir

John F. Nesholm: dir

Laurel Nesholm: exec dir

Laurel Nesholm: exec dir (see above)

APPLICATION INFORMATION
Initial Approach: Send a brief letter of inquiry. Include a description of organization, amount requested, purpose of funds sought, recently audited financial statement, and proof of tax-exempt status. Send five copies. Deadlines is the seventh day of each month, excluding July and August.

PUBLICATIONS
Application Guidelines

GRANTS ANALYSIS
Total Grants: $599,605

Number of Grants: 62

Highest Grant: $50,000

Typical Range: $1,000 to $50,000

Disclosure Period: 1993

Note: Recent grants are derived from a 1993 Form 990.

RECENT GRANTS

Library
15,000	Seattle Public Library Foundation, Seattle, WA	

General
50,000	Seattle Commons, Seattle, WA — operating support	
50,000	Seattle Commons, Seattle, WA — operating support	
25,000	Powerful Schools, King County, WA — educational projects	
20,000	United Indians of All Tribes, Seattle, WA — Daybreak Star Magazine	
15,727	Youth Investment, Seattle, WA — High School Jobs Project/Summer School Incentives	

Petrie Trust, Lorene M.

CONTACT
Doug McIntyre
Vice President and Manager
Lorene M. Petrie Trust
c/o Security Pacific Bank Washington, Tax Services Dept.
PO Box 136
Yakima, WA 98907
(509) 575-6720

FINANCIAL SUMMARY
Recent Giving: $107,556 (fiscal 1992); $372,733 (fiscal 1991); $156,612 (fiscal 1990)

Assets: $2,416,360 (fiscal 1992); $2,220,405 (fiscal 1991); $2,408,921 (fiscal 1990)

EIN: 91-6256555

CONTRIBUTIONS SUMMARY
Donor(s): the late Lorene Petrie

Typical Recipients: • *Arts & Humanities:* Arts Associations & Councils, Community Arts, Libraries, Museums/Galleries, Public Broadcasting, Theater • *Civic & Public Affairs:* Municipalities/Towns • *Education:* Colleges & Universities • *Environment:* General • *Health:* Hospitals

Grant Types: general support

Geographic Distribution: limited to Yakima and Kittitas counties, WA

GIVING OFFICERS
Security Pacific Bank, Washington: trust

APPLICATION INFORMATION
Initial Approach: Send brief letter describing program. There are no deadlines.

GRANTS ANALYSIS
Total Grants: $107,556

Number of Grants: 7

Highest Grant: $100,000

Typical Range: $7,508 to $50,000

Disclosure Period: fiscal year ending July 31, 1992

Note: Recent grants are derived from a fiscal 1992 Form 990.

RECENT GRANTS

General
100,000	St. Elizabeth Medical Center, WA	
50,000	Heritage College, Toppenish, WA	
22,225	Children's Activity Museum, Ellensburg, WA	
15,000	Central Washington University, Ellensburg, WA	
3,000	Cowiche Canyon Conservancy, Yakima, WA	

SAFECO Corp.

Revenue: $3.55 billion
Employees: 8,424
Headquarters: Seattle, WA
SIC Major Group: Holding Companies Nec, Miscellaneous Business Credit Institutions, Security Brokers & Dealers, and Life Insurance

CONTACT
Jill Ryan
Chairman, Contributions Committee
SAFECO Corp.
SAFECO Plz.
Seattle, WA 98185
(206) 545-5015
Note: The company's World Wide Web address is
http://www.tricon.net/Comm/safeco

FINANCIAL SUMMARY
Recent Giving: $6,500,000 (1994 approx.); $5,874,000 (1993 approx.); $5,591,000 (1992 approx.)

Fiscal Note: Company gives directly. Above figures exclude nonmonetary support.

CONTRIBUTIONS SUMMARY
Typical Recipients: • *Arts & Humanities:* Arts Funds, Community Arts, Dance, Historic Preservation, Libraries, Museums/Galleries, Opera, Performing Arts, Public Broadcasting, Visual Arts • *Civic & Public Affairs:* Economic Development, Employment/Job Training, Housing, Nonprofit Management, Public Policy, Safety, Urban & Community Affairs, Zoos/Aquariums • *Education:* Arts/Humanities Education, Business Education, Colleges & Universities, Continuing Education, Economic Education, Education Associations, Elementary Education (Private), Literacy, Minority Education, Pri-

vate Education (Precollege), Public Education (Precollege) • *Environment:* General • *Health:* Health Policy/Cost Containment, Health Organizations, Mental Health, Nutrition, Public Health, Single-Disease Health Associations • *Social Services:* Community Service Organizations, Day Care, Delinquency & Criminal Rehabilitation, Emergency Relief, People with Disabilities, Senior Services, Shelters/Homelessness, Substance Abuse, United Funds/United Ways, Volunteer Services, Youth Organizations

Grant Types: capital, challenge, employee matching gifts, general support, and operating expenses

Note: Company matches employee gifts to local organizations and the United Way.

Nonmonetary Support Types: donated equipment and in-kind services

Note: Value of nonmonetary support is not available.

Geographic Distribution: near corporate operating locations in the United States

Operating Locations: CA (Fountain Valley, Los Angeles, Pleasanton), CO (Lakewood), FL (Maitland), GA (Stone Mountain), IL (Chicago), MO (Sunset Hills), OH (Cincinnati), OR (Lake Oswego), TN (Nashville), TX (Dallas), VA (Richmond), WA (Redmond, Seattle, Spokane)

CORP. OFFICERS
Boh A. Dickey: *B* Helena MT 1944 *ED* Univ MT 1966 *CURR EMPL* exec vp, cfo, dir: SAFECO Corp *CORP AFFIL* chmn: SAFECO Mutual Funds; exec vp: Gen Am Corp; exec vp, dir: SAFECO Credit Co Inc, SAFECO Ins Co Am, SAFECO Ins Co IL

Roger Harry Eigsti: *B* Vancouver WA 1942 *ED* Linfield Coll BS 1964 *CURR EMPL* chmn, pres, ceo, dir: SAFECO Corp *CORP AFFIL* chmn: Gen Ins Co Am, SAFECO Life Ins Co; dir: Employee Benefit Claims WI, First Natl Ins Co Am, Gen Am Corp TX, GSL Corp, SAFECO Natl Ins Co, SAFECO Natl Life Ins, SAFECO Properties Inc, SAFECO Surplus Lines Ins Co, WI Pension & Group Svc; pres, ceo: Gen Am Corp *CLUB AFFIL* Mercer Island CC

GIVING OFFICERS
Robert C. Alexander: mem contributions comm *CURR EMPL* vp Seattle branch: SAFECO Ins Cos

Boh A. Dickey: mem (contributions comm) *CURR EMPL* exec vp, cfo, dir: SAFECO Corp (see above)

Roger Harry Eigsti: mem (contributions comm) *CURR EMPL* chmn, pres, ceo, dir: SAFECO Corp (see above)

Mary Frawley: mem contributions comm *CURR EMPL* asst dir claims: SAFECO Ins Cos

Gordon C. Hamilton: mem contributions comm *CURR EMPL* vp pub rels: SAFECO Ins Cos

Jill Ryan: chmn contributions comm *CURR EMPL* community rels mgr, asst vp: SAFECO Ins Cos

Richard E. Zunker: mem contributions comm *B* 1938 *ED* Univ WI BS 1964 *CURR*

EMPL pres, dir: SAFECO Life Ins Co
CORP AFFIL dir: Gen Ins Co Am

APPLICATION INFORMATION
Initial Approach: *Initial Contact:* brief letter or proposal, no more than two pages in length, to SAFECO headquarters in Seattle or to branch office nearest the proposed project location *Include Information On:* description of the organization; amount requested; assessment of need; purpose for which funds are sought; project's scope; geographical area and people served; evaluation plans and methods; audited financial statement for the last two years; overall budget of organization, including income and expenses for last two years and year in which contribution is sought; donor's list for past 12 months; list of board of directors and their affiliations; proof of tax-exempt status *Deadlines:* none

Restrictions on Giving: As a general rule, SAFECO does not make contributions to individuals; projects or programs operating outside the United States; national programs, endowment funds, or unrestricted operating funds for agencies that receive United Way or similar umbrella support from organizations already supported by SAFECO; religious or political groups or projects; general fundraising events; goodwill advertising; loans and investments; or fraternal organizations.

OTHER THINGS TO KNOW
Company sets aside approximately two percent of pretax income annually for contributions programs.

Company will consider requests from communities where significant numbers of SAFECO employees live and work.

Contributions are given for one year with no implied renewals.

Company may require recipients to provide an audited financial statement at year's end and periodic reports on the project.

GRANTS ANALYSIS
Total Grants: $4,708,000

Number of Grants: 839*

Average Grant: $5,611*

Disclosure Period: 1991

Note: Total grants, number of grants and average grants figures exclude approximately 1,700 matching grants valued at about $196,456. Recent grants are derived from a partial 1994 grants list.

RECENT GRANTS

General

$100,000   Intercollegiate Center for Nursing Education — pilot phase of a project aimed at increasing the recruitment and retention of Native American students at ICNE nursing programs, to eventually improve health care for Native Americans

Seafirst Corporation / Seafirst Foundation

Employees: 7,200
Parent Company: BankAmerica Corp.
Headquarters: Seattle, WA
SIC Major Group: Bank Holding Companies and National Commercial Banks

CONTACT
Nadine Troyer
President, Trustee
Seafirst Foundation
PO Box 34661
Seattle, WA 98124-1661
(206) 358-3443

FINANCIAL SUMMARY
Recent Giving: $1,940,006 (1995 est.); $1,400,000 (1994 approx.); $1,399,721 (1993)

Assets: $391,132 (1993); $1,377,441 (1991); $1,400,000 (1989)

Gifts Received: $1,400,000 (1993)

Fiscal Note: Above figures exclude nonmonetary support.

EIN: 91-1094720

CONTRIBUTIONS SUMMARY
Typical Recipients: • *Arts & Humanities:* Arts Associations & Councils, Arts Centers, Ballet, Community Arts, Dance, General, History & Archaeology, Libraries, Museums/Galleries, Music, Opera, Performing Arts, Theater • *Civic & Public Affairs:* Business/Free Enterprise, Economic Development, Economic Policy, Employment/Job Training, Housing, Public Policy, Urban & Community Affairs, Zoos/Aquariums • *Education:* Business Education, Colleges & Universities, Community & Junior Colleges, Economic Education, Elementary Education (Public), General, Literacy, Minority Education, Secondary Education (Public), Special Education, Student Aid • *Health:* AIDS/HIV, Cancer, Children's Health/Hospitals, Emergency/Ambulance Services, Health Organizations, Heart, Hospitals • *Religion:* Dioceses, Jewish Causes, Religious Welfare • *Science:* Science Museums, Scientific Centers & Institutes • *Social Services:* Child Welfare, Community Service Organizations, Day Care, Family Services, People with Disabilities, United Funds/United Ways, YMCA/YWCA/YMHA/YWHA, Youth Organizations

Grant Types: challenge, employee matching gifts, general support, project, and seed money

Note: Company matches employee gifts up to $5,000 annually per employee.

Nonmonetary Support: $1,308,050 (1993); $222,105 (1986)

Nonmonetary Support Types: donated equipment, in-kind services, and loaned executives

Note: Contact Vicki Foege, Community Relations, for information.

Geographic Distribution: primarily in Washington

Operating Locations: WA (Seattle)
Note: Operates 300 branches in the state of Washington.

CORP. OFFICERS
Mitchell Baker: *CURR EMPL* sr vp, mgr pub aff: Seafirst Corp

Joan L. Enticknap: *B* 1950 *ED* Univ WA BA 1973; Univ WA MBA 1978 *CURR EMPL* exec vp, cfo: Seafirst Corp

W. Thomas Porter, Jr.: *B* Corning NY 1934 *ED* Rutgers Univ BS 1954; Univ WA MBA 1959; Columbia Univ PhD 1964 *CURR EMPL* exec vp: Seafirst Corp *NONPR AFFIL* mem: Am Inst CPAs; trust: VA Mason Med Fdn *CLUB AFFIL* Sand Point CC, WA Athletic

John V. Rindlaub: *B* 1944 *ED* Bucknell Univ BA 1965 *CURR EMPL* chmn, ceo: Seafirst Corp

Stanley D. Savage: *B* 1945 *ED* Univ WA BA 1967; Univ Southern CA MBA 1972 *CURR EMPL* vchmn: Seafirst Corp

Earl N. Schulman: *B* 1943 *ED* Univ WA BA 1965 *CURR EMPL* vchmn: Seafirst Corp *CORP AFFIL* vchmn: Seattle First Natl Bank

GIVING OFFICERS
John R. Arbini: trust

Mitchell Baker: trust *CURR EMPL* sr vp, mgr pub aff: Seafirst Corp (see above)

Richard J. Collette: trust *B* 1947 *ED* OR St Univ 1969 *CURR EMPL* sr vp: Seafirst Bank

Joan L. Enticknap: trust *CURR EMPL* exec vp, cfo: Seafirst Corp (see above)

Harold H. Greene: trust *B* 1943 *ED* Cornell Univ 1966; Univ OR MBA 1969 *CURR EMPL* exec vp: Seafirst Corp

Marie Gum: trust

Becki Johnson: trust

W. Thomas Porter, Jr.: vchmn, trust *CURR EMPL* exec vp: Seafirst Corp (see above)

Nadine Troyer: pres, trust

Peter Warner: trust

Wally Webster: trust

APPLICATION INFORMATION
Initial Approach: *Initial Contact:* request application (letter no longer than two pages) *Include Information On:* specific amount of request; how funds will be used; purpose and objectives of organization; geographical area and population served; names and qualifications of persons who will administer funds; proposed timetable for project; potential benefit to Seafirst; list of Seafirst employees involved in organization; most recent financial statement; list of current officers and directors; project budget; most recent financial statement; list of other funding sources; and proof of tax-exempt status *Deadlines:* none, but requests received after October 1 may be carried over to January

Restrictions on Giving: Funding is generally restricted to the state of Washington.

Foundation generally does not support research; endowments, memorials, or operating deficits; travel expenses; political issues; individuals; fraternal organizations;

production of video tapes, films, or publications; hospital operating funds and the maintenance of medical facilities; single-disease organizations; primary or secondary schools; parent-teacher associations; discriminatory organizations; national organizations, including national conventions held locally or scholarships other than Seafirst scholarship programs. Does not support churches or other religious organizations for purposes of religious advocacy.

OTHER THINGS TO KNOW
Priority given to special project support; less emphasis on capital campaigns.

PUBLICATIONS
Seafirst Contributions, Guidelines for Giving

GRANTS ANALYSIS
Total Grants: $1,940,006
Number of Grants: 400
Highest Grant: $650,100
Average Grant: $4,850
Typical Range: $1,000 to $20,000
Disclosure Period: 1995

Note: Fiscal information for foundation only. Recent grants are derived from a 1995 grants list.

RECENT GRANTS
General

650,100	United Way of Washington State, Seattle, WA — for human services
250,000	University of Washington, Seattle, WA — for Campaign for Washington; payment on a multiyear pledge
75,000	Seafirst Scholarships — for education
52,500	Washington State Housing Finance Commission, WA — for community reinvestment support
50,000	Seattle Commons, Seattle, WA — for community development; payment on a multiyear pledge totaling 100,000

Sequoia Foundation

CONTACT
Frank D. Underwood
Executive Director
Sequoia Foundation
820 A St., Ste. 345
Tacoma, WA 98402
(206) 627-1634

FINANCIAL SUMMARY
Recent Giving: $2,210,833 (fiscal 1993); $1,994,179 (fiscal 1992); $3,816,949 (fiscal 1991)

Assets: $24,349,327 (fiscal 1993); $20,765,306 (fiscal 1992); $18,766,633 (fiscal 1991)

Gifts Received: $2,355,000 (fiscal 1993); $2,480,000 (fiscal 1992); $2,410,000 (fiscal 1991)

Fiscal Note: The foundation receives contributions from both the 1973 and 1975 Irrevocable Trusts of C. Davis Weyerhaeuser. In fiscal 1992, the foundation also received $20,000 from William T. Weyerhaeuser, president, treasurer, and director of the foundation.

EIN: 91-1178052

CONTRIBUTIONS SUMMARY
Donor(s): The foundation was established in 1982 by C. Davis Weyerhaeuser, a son of the late Frederick Edward Weyerhaeuser, who was a president of Weyerhaeuser Timber Company. Born in Tacoma, WA, in 1902, and educated at Yale University, C. Davis Weyerhaeuser served as an executive with Weyerhaeuser for twenty-five years.

Typical Recipients: • *Arts & Humanities:* History & Archaeology, Libraries, Museums/Galleries, Theater • *Civic & Public Affairs:* Community Foundations, General, Parades/Festivals, Philanthropic Organizations, Public Policy, Zoos/Aquariums • *Education:* Business Education, Colleges & Universities, Legal Education, Private Education (Precollege), Religious Education, Secondary Education (Private), Social Sciences Education • *Environment:* Air/Water Quality, Forestry, General, Resource Conservation, Wildlife Protection • *Health:* Health Organizations, Hospitals, Medical Rehabilitation, Mental Health • *International:* Health Care/Hospitals, International Development, International Environmental Issues, International Relations • *Religion:* Ministries, Religious Welfare • *Social Services:* Child Welfare, Crime Prevention, Family Planning, Food/Clothing Distribution, Recreation & Athletics, Scouts, United Funds/United Ways, Youth Organizations

Grant Types: capital, general support, and project

Geographic Distribution: national with emphasis on the western and northwestern United States, especially Tacoma and Seattle, WA

GIVING OFFICERS
Linda P. BeMiller: program dir *PHIL AFFIL* program off: New Horizon Foundation; dir: Forest Foundation

Walter John Driscoll: don *B* St Paul MN 1929 *ED* Yale Univ BS 1951 *CURR EMPL* pres, dir: Rock Island Corp *CORP AFFIL* chmn, dir: Dietzgen Corp, First Natl Bank Palm Beach; dir: Comshare, Gould Inc, MIP Properties, Northern States Power Co, St Paul Cos, Weyerhaeuser Co *NONPR AFFIL* chmn: Minneapolis Art Inst *PHIL AFFIL* don, pres, dir: Driscoll Foundation; don: Weyerhaeuser Family Foundation; dir, trust: Northwest Area Foundation

James R. Hanson: mem *PHIL AFFIL* secy, dir: Stewardship Foundation; dir: Forest Foundation

Nicholas C. Spika: secy *PHIL AFFIL* secy: Forest Foundation

Frank D. Underwood: exec dir, mem *PHIL AFFIL* exec dir: Forest Foundation; pres, treas, dir: New Horizon Foundation

Annette Thayer Black Weyerhaeuser: dir, mem *PHIL AFFIL* vp, dir, mem: Forest Foundation; vp, treas, dir: Stewardship Foundation

Charles Davis Weyerhaeuser: don *B* St Paul MN *ED* Yale Univ BA 1933 *CORP AFFIL* dir: Weyerhaeuser Timber Co *NONPR AFFIL* chmn: YMCA Campaign; trust: Fuller Theological Seminary, Inter-Varsity Christian Fellowship, Moody Bible Inst, Whitworth Coll, Young Life; vchmn: Natl Alliance Businessmen *PHIL AFFIL* don, pres, treas, dir: Stewardship Foundation; dir, mem: Forest Foundation

Frederick Theodore Weyerhaeuser: don *B* Duluth MN 1931 *CURR EMPL* chmn, treas: Clearwater Mgmt Co *PHIL AFFIL* trust: Charles and Ellora Alliss Educational Foundation; don: Weyerhaeuser Family Foundation; chmn, dir: St. Paul Foundation

Gail T. Weyerhaeuser: vp, dir, mem *PHIL AFFIL* pres, treas, dir: Forest Foundation

William Toycen Weyerhaeuser: pres, treas, dir, mem *B* Tacoma WA 1943 *ED* Stanford Univ 1966; Fuller Grad Sch Psychology PhD 1975 *CURR EMPL* owner, chmn: Yelm Telephone Co *CORP AFFIL* dir: Potlatch Corp *NONPR AFFIL* mem: Am Psychological Assn; vchmn: Univ Puget Sound *PHIL AFFIL* trust: Weyerhaeuser Family Foundation; dir: Forest Foundation, Stewardship Foundation

APPLICATION INFORMATION
Initial Approach:

Applicants may contact the foundation by submitting two copies of a typewritten summary letter, or by submitting two copies of a complete application.

A summary letter should include a statement of the project with objectives, description of the organization, project budget, amount requested, and proof of IRS tax-exempt status.

Grant seekers submitting a full proposal should include a summary letter; legal name, address, and telephone number of the organization; a list of names and affiliations of the organization's board of directors and chief administrative officer; complete financial statements for the organization's most recent fiscal year and current operating budget; description of the project and objectives; description of beneficiaries of the project; substantiation of the extent of need for these benefits; project timetable; method and criteria for assessing the project's effectiveness; qualifications of key personnel; detailed expense budget; list of other possible sources of support; and, if appropriate, an explanation of how the project is to be continued after the funding period ends. The full proposal must also include copies of the most recent IRS 501(c)(3) and 509(a) status determination letters and a statement by the chief administrative officer claiming that he will take full responsibility for proper fiscal

management and accounting for any grant received, that he will file timely reports, and that no part of the grant will be used to propagandize or to influence elections or legislation.

Requests for funding are accepted throughout the year.

The foundation staff will review requests to determine if the project falls within current guidelines. In the case of an applicant submitting a summary letter, the staff will seek additional detailed information. Action on proposals ordinarily occurs between 60 and 90 days from the date a complete grant request is received. The foundation may request an interview or site visit before making a final decision.

Restrictions on Giving: The foundation gives a high priority to organizations that seek other sources of funding and that receive little or no support from public tax funds. The foundation generally will not provide funding for annual appeals; debt retirement; individuals; scholarships or fellowships; endowments; film production or the publication of books, periodicals, or monographs; local organizations; private foundations or operating foundations; propaganda; conferences, seminars, or travel of individuals or groups; or for voter registration programs.

OTHER THINGS TO KNOW
The Sequoia Foundation was the donor of the New Horizon Foundation, established in 1984.

GRANTS ANALYSIS
Total Grants: $2,210,833

Number of Grants: 44

Highest Grant: $1,280,000

Average Grant: $50,246

Typical Range: $5,000 to $55,000

Disclosure Period: fiscal year ending August 31, 1993

Note: Recent grants are derived from a fiscal 1993 Form 990.

RECENT GRANTS

Library

1,500	Foundation Center, New York, NY

General

1,280,000	New Horizon Foundation, Seattle, WA
305,000	University of Puget Sound, Tacoma, WA — capital needs
50,000	Catholic Community Services, Tacoma, WA — capital needs
46,000	World Wildlife Fund, Washington, DC
37,500	Food Research and Action Center, Washington, DC

Simpson Investment Company / Matlock Foundation

Sales: $970.0 million
Employees: 8,400
Parent Company: Kamilche Company
Headquarters: Seattle, WA
SIC Major Group: Holding Companies Nec

CONTACT
Lin Smith
Public Affairs Assistant
Matlock Foundation
1201 3rd Ave.
Seattle, WA 98101
(206) 292-5000

FINANCIAL SUMMARY
Recent Giving: $1,000,000 (1995 est.); $907,725 (1994); $618,784 (1993)

Assets: $1,320 (1993); $13,642 (1992); $188,860 (1989)

Gifts Received: $670,000 (1993)

Fiscal Note: Figures above are for foundation only. An estimated $200,000 in contributions is budgeted for direct corporate giving in 1995. Contact Maureen Frisch, vice president of public affairs, for direct corporate support. In 1993, contributions were received from Simpson Investment Company and its subsidiaries. Above figures include nonmonetary support.

EIN: 91-6029303

CONTRIBUTIONS SUMMARY
Typical Recipients: • *Arts & Humanities:* Arts Associations & Councils, Arts Institutes, Historic Preservation, Libraries, Museums/Galleries, Music, Opera, Performing Arts, Theater • *Civic & Public Affairs:* Economic Development, Municipalities/Towns, Zoos/Aquariums • *Education:* Business Education, Colleges & Universities, Community & Junior Colleges, Continuing Education, Economic Education, Private Education (Precollege), Public Education (Precollege), Science/Mathematics Education • *Environment:* General • *Health:* Emergency/Ambulance Services, Hospices, Hospitals, Nursing Services • *Religion:* Churches • *Science:* Science Exhibits & Fairs • *Social Services:* Child Welfare, Community Centers, Community Service Organizations, Food/Clothing Distribution, Senior Services, United Funds/United Ways, Youth Organizations

Grant Types: capital, emergency, employee matching gifts, endowment, general support, matching, and multiyear/continuing support

Note: Employee matching gift ratio: 1 to 1.

Nonmonetary Support: $1,000,000 (1994); $75,000 (1993); $75,000 (1992)

Nonmonetary Support Types: donated products

Note: Contact Maureen Frisch, vice president of public affairs or Lin Smith, public affairs assistant, for more information.

Geographic Distribution: Washington, Oregon, California, Michigan, Pennsylvania, Texas, Vermont, Iowa, New York

Operating Locations: CA (San Francisco), IA, MI (Plainwell, Vicksburg), NY (Warwick), OR (Eugene, Portland, West Linn), PA, TX, VT, WA (Seattle, Shelton, Tacoma)

Note: Operating locations reflect only major facilities; company also operates in various cities and towns in the above states.

CORP. OFFICERS

Maureen Frisch: *CURR EMPL* vp pub aff: Simpson Investment Co

Furman Colin Moseley: *B* Spartanburg SC 1934 *ED* Elon Coll BA 1956 *CURR EMPL* pres, dir: Simpson Investment Co *CORP AFFIL* chmn, dir: Simpson Paper Co, Simpson Plainwell Paper Co; dir: Eaton Corp, Owens Corning Fiberglas Corp

William Garrard Reed, Jr.: *B* 1940 *ED* Harvard Univ Sch Bus Admin MBA 1969; Duke Univ *CURR EMPL* chmn, dir: Simpson Investment Co *CORP AFFIL* chmn, dir: Simpson Timber Co; dir: Microsoft Corp, SAFECO Corp, Seafirst Corp, Seattle First Natl Bank, Simpson Paper Co, Simpson Plainwell Paper Co, WA Mutual Savings Bank

J. Thurston Roach: *B* Little Rock AR 1941 *ED* Vanderbilt Univ BA 1963; Stanford Univ MBA 1969 *CURR EMPL* sr vp, secy, cfo: Simpson Investment Co *CORP AFFIL* sr vp fin & securities: Simpson Paper Co; vp, cfo, dir: Simpson Plainwell Paper Co

GIVING OFFICERS

John J. Fannon: dir *B* 1934 *CURR EMPL* pres, dir: Simpson Paper Co

Maureen Frisch: pres, dir *CURR EMPL* vp pub aff: Simpson Investment Co (see above)

Thomas R. Ingham, Jr.: dir *B* 1941 *CURR EMPL* pres, dir: Simpson Timber Co *CORP AFFIL* pres, dir: Commencement Bay Mill Co; secy, treas, dir: Olympia Oyster Co

Furman Colin Moseley: dir *CURR EMPL* pres, dir: Simpson Investment Co (see above)

Susan R. Moseley: dir

Colleen Musgrave: secy

E. H. Reed: dir *CORP AFFIL* dir: Simpson Investment Co

William Garrard Reed, Jr.: dir *CURR EMPL* chmn, dir: Simpson Investment Co (see above)

J. Thurston Roach: treas, dir *CURR EMPL* sr vp, secy, cfo: Simpson Investment Co (see above)

Lin Smith: pub aff asst

APPLICATION INFORMATION

Initial Approach: *Initial Contact:* letter or telephone call requesting grant application *Deadlines:* one month before the board meetings (usually in March, July, and November)

Restrictions on Giving: Does not support individuals or provide funds for endowments or loans.

OTHER THINGS TO KNOW

Foundation is sponsored by Simpson Investment Company and its subsidiaries, which include Simpson Paper Company, Simpson Timber Company, and Pacific Western Extruded Plastics Company.

GRANTS ANALYSIS

Total Grants: $907,725

Number of Grants: 435

Highest Grant: $76,226

Average Grant: $2,087

Typical Range: $100 to $15,000

Disclosure Period: 1994

Note: Recent grants are derived from a 1993 grants list.

RECENT GRANTS

General

76,226	United Way of King County, Seattle, WA — operating
41,000	United Funds of Humboldt County, Eureka, CA — operating
26,900	United Way of Pierce County, Tacoma, WA — operating
21,000	United Good Neighbors of Mason County, Shelton, WA — operating
20,000	Fred Hutchinson Cancer Research Center Foundation, Seattle, WA — capital

U.S. Bank of Washington

Employees: 3,500
Parent Company: U.S. Bancorp
Headquarters: Seattle, WA
SIC Major Group: Depository Institutions

CONTACT

Molly W. Reed
Vice President, Manager, Community Relations
U.S. Bank of Washington
PO Box 720, WWH658
Seattle, WA 98111-0720
(206) 344-2360
Note: The company's main line is (206) 344-4683.

FINANCIAL SUMMARY

Recent Giving: $1,400,000 (1994); $1,400,000 (1993)

CONTRIBUTIONS SUMMARY

Company reports that 50% of contributions support health and human services; 28%, education; 18%, arts and humanities; and 4% to civic and public affairs.

Volunteerism: Company promotes employee volunteerism through an electronic bulletin board, which reports on team participation in local fund raising events and board memberships.

Typical Recipients: • *Arts & Humanities:* Arts Associations & Councils, Arts Centers, Arts Festivals, Arts Funds, Arts Outreach, Ballet, Community Arts, Dance, Ethnic & Folk Arts, General, Historic Preservation, Libraries, Museums/Galleries, Music, Opera, Performing Arts, Theater, Visual Arts • *Civic & Public Affairs:* African American Affairs, Asian American Affairs, Business/Free Enterprise, Chambers of Commerce, Civil Rights, Economic Development, Employment/Job Training, Ethnic Organizations, Gay/Lesbian Issues, General, Hispanic Affairs, Housing, Inner-City Development, Native American Affairs, Professional & Trade Associations, Public Policy, Urban & Community Affairs, Women's Affairs, Zoos/Aquariums • *Education:* Afterschool/Enrichment Programs, Business Education, Business-School Partnerships, Colleges & Universities, Economic Education, Education Reform, General, Literacy, Minority Education, Preschool Education, Special Education • *Health:* Adolescent Health Issues, AIDS/HIV, Cancer, Children's Health/Hospitals, General, Hospices, Mental Health, Prenatal Health Issues • *Science:* Science Museums • *Social Services:* At-Risk Youth, Camps, Child Welfare, Community Centers, Community Service Organizations, Counseling, Day Care, Domestic Violence, Emergency Relief, Family Services, Food/Clothing Distribution, General, Homes, People with Disabilities, Refugee Assistance, Senior Services, Sexual Abuse, Shelters/Homelessness, Substance Abuse, United Funds/United Ways, Volunteer Services, YMCA/YWCA/YMHA/YWHA, Youth Organizations

Grant Types: capital, emergency, employee matching gifts, general support, multi-year/continuing support, operating expenses, project, scholarship, and seed money

Nonmonetary Support Types: donated equipment, loaned employees, loaned executives, and workplace solicitation

Geographic Distribution: headquarters and operating locations throughout Washington state

Operating Locations: WA (Seattle)

CORP. OFFICERS

Phyllis J. Campbell: *CURR EMPL* pres, ceo: US Bank WA

APPLICATION INFORMATION

Initial Approach: Call local branches or corporate headquarters for information.

Restrictions on Giving: Does not support The foundation does not make grants to individuals., religious organizations for sectarian purposes, political or lobbying groups, travel expenses, or organizations outside operating areas.

GRANTS ANALYSIS

Typical Range: $1,000 to $2,500

Note: Recent grants are derived from a grants list provided by company in 1995.

RECENT GRANTS

General
Center for Ethical Leadership, Seattle, WA
Local Initiatives Support Corporation, Seattle, WA
Powerful Schools, Seattle, WA
Sean Humphrey House, Bellingham, WA
Spokane Food Bank, Spokane, WA

Washington Mutual Savings Bank / Washington Mutual Savings Bank Foundation

Assets: $15.8 billion
Employees: 4,858
Headquarters: Seattle, WA
SIC Major Group: Savings Institutions Except Federal

CONTACT
Tim Otani
Program Administration
Washington Mutual Savings Bank Fdn.
1201 Third Ave., 12th floor
Seattle, WA 98101
(206) 461-4663

FINANCIAL SUMMARY
Recent Giving: $1,500,000 (1995 est.); $1,400,000 (1994 approx.); $1,070,238 (1993)

Assets: $1,652,135 (1992); $1,349,640 (1991); $1,137,340 (1990)

Gifts Received: $750,000 (1992)

Fiscal Note: Giving figures reflect foundation contributions only. Above figures exclude nonmonetary support.

EIN: 91-1070920

CONTRIBUTIONS SUMMARY
Typical Recipients: • *Arts & Humanities:* Arts Associations & Councils, Arts Centers, Community Arts, Ethnic & Folk Arts, Libraries, Performing Arts, Theater • *Civic & Public Affairs:* Asian American Affairs, Economic Development, Employment/Job Training, General, Hispanic Affairs, Housing, Native American Affairs, Urban & Community Affairs, Women's Affairs
• *Education:* Business Education, Colleges & Universities, Community & Junior Colleges, Economic Education, Education Funds, Education Reform, Elementary Education (Public), Faculty Development, General, Leadership Training, Literacy, Minority Education, Preschool Education, Public Education (Precollege), Science/Mathematics Education, Special Education • *Environment:* Resource Conservation • *Health:* AIDS/HIV, Cancer, Children's Health/Hospitals, Clinics/Medical Centers, Emergency/Ambulance Services, Long-Term Care • *Religion:* Churches, Ministries, Religious Welfare • *Social Services:* Camps, Child Welfare, Community Centers, Community Service Organizations, Domestic Violence, Family Services, Food/Clothing Distribution, Scouts, Senior Services, United Funds/United Ways, Volunteer Services, YMCA/YWCA/YMHA/YWHA, Youth Organizations

Grant Types: employee matching gifts and general support

Note: Employee matching gift ratio: 1 to 1.

Nonmonetary Support: $30,000 (1994); $52,000 (1990)

Nonmonetary Support Types: donated equipment

Note: Company provides nonmonetary support. Contact is Mary Klco, coordinator, civic relations.

Geographic Distribution: primarily Washington state, western Oregon, and other company operating areas

Operating Locations: ID, OR, WA

CORP. OFFICERS
Kerry Kent Killinger: *B* Des Moines IA 1949 *ED* Univ IA BBA 1970; Univ IA MBA 1971 *CURR EMPL* chmn, pres, ceo: WA Mutual Savings Bank *CORP AFFIL* pres: WA Mutual Fin Inc; pres, dir: WM Fin Inc *NONPR AFFIL* dir: Downtown Seattle Assn, Leadership Tomorrow, Savings Commun Bankers Am, Seattle Repertory Theatre, WA Roundtable, WA Savings League; mem: Life Mgmt Inst, Seattle Chamber Commerce, Soc Fin Analysts; mem adv counc: Fed Reserve Bd *CLUB AFFIL* Rotary

GIVING OFFICERS
Tim Otani: program admin

APPLICATION INFORMATION
Initial Approach: *Initial Contact:* by letter or phone to request application form *Include Information On:* completed grant application form along with any other fundraising efforts, most recent financial statement, a copy of IRS letter of nonprofit status, a copy of audited financial statements *Deadlines:* Submit by January 1, to be notified by March 15; by April 1, to be notified by June 15; by July 1, to be notified by September 15; or by October 1, to be notified by December 15. Applications are reviewed at quarterly meetings.

Restrictions on Giving: Does not support individuals; organizations without tax-exempt status; organizations which discriminate based on race, color, religion, creed, age, sex, national origin, or any reason; political organizations or groups that influence legislation; veterans organizations; labor organizations; or religious-oriented projects.

Does not provide funds, other than for capital campaigns, to organizations that already receive support from the United Way.

Accepts one application per organization per calendar year. Generally does not fund an organization for more than three successive years.

Foundation does not accept requests that are not made on application form.

OTHER THINGS TO KNOW
The foundation receives its funds from the financial services companies of the Washington Mutual Financial Group (WMFG), including: Washington Mutual Savings Bank; Benefit Service Corp.; Composite Research & Management Co.; Murphey Favre, Inc.; Mutual Travel, Inc.; Washington Mutual, a Federal Savings Bank; Washington Mutual Insurance Services; and WM Life Insurance Co.

GRANTS ANALYSIS
Total Grants: $1,070,238

Number of Grants: 133

Average Grant: $8,047

Typical Range: $1,000 to $10,000

Disclosure Period: 1993

Note: Recent grants are derived from a 1993 Annual Report

RECENT GRANTS

General
American Association of University Women Wenatchee, Wenatchee, WA — for education
Asian Counseling and Referral Service, Seattle, WA — for community reinvestment
Bainbridge Youth Services, Bainbridge Island, WA — for health and human services
Beaverton Education Foundation, Beaverton, OR — for education
Boyer Children's Clinic — for health and human services

Washington Water Power Co.

Revenue: $640.6 million
Employees: 1,438
Headquarters: Spokane, WA
SIC Major Group: Electric & Other Services Combined

CONTACT
Debbie Simock
Community Relations Coordinator
Washington Water Power Co.
E 1411 Mission Ave.
Spokane, WA 99202
(509) 482-8031

FINANCIAL SUMMARY
Recent Giving: $525,000 (1994 approx.); $500,000 (1993 approx.); $500,000 (1992 approx.)

Fiscal Note: Company gives directly. Above figures exclude nonmonetary support.

CONTRIBUTIONS SUMMARY
Typical Recipients: • *Arts & Humanities:* General, Libraries, Museums/Galleries, Performing Arts, Public Broadcasting, Theater • *Civic & Public Affairs:* General, Safety, Women's Affairs • *Education:* Colleges & Universities, Community & Junior Colleges, Economic Education, Elementary Education (Private), Engineering/Technological Education, Faculty Development, Minority Education, Public Education (Precollege) • *Environment:* General • *Social Services:* Community Service Organizations, Senior Services, United Funds/United Ways, Youth Organizations

Grant Types: project

Nonmonetary Support Types: donated equipment and in-kind services

Note: Value of nonmonetary support is unavailable.

Geographic Distribution: eastern Washington and northern Idaho service area only

Operating Locations: ID (Bonners Ferry, Coer d'Alene, Kellogg, Lewiston, Moscow, Orofino, Post Falls, Sandpoint), OR (Ashland, Grants Pass, Klamath Falls, La Grande, Medford, Roseburg), WA (Clark-

ston, Colfax, Colville, Othello, Pullman,
Spokane)

CORP. OFFICERS

Paul Anthony Redmond: *B* Lakeview OR
1937 *ED* Gonzaga Univ BSEE 1965 *CURR
EMPL* chmn, pres, ceo: WA Water Power
Co *CORP AFFIL* chmn: NW Telecom, Pen-
tzer Corp, Pentzer Devel Corp, Pentzer Fin
Svcs, Pentzer Jefferson Corp, Pentzer Sun-
rise Corp; dir: Devel Assocs Inc, Hecla Min-
ing Co, Itron Inc, Limestone Co Inc,
Security Pacific Bank WA, Spokane Indus
Park Inc, WA Water Power Co, Water
Power Improvement Co

GIVING OFFICERS

Debbie Simock: *CURR EMPL* commun rels
coordinator: WA Water Power Co

APPLICATION INFORMATION

Initial Approach: *Initial Contact:* requests
must be submitted in writing *Include Information On:* a brief summary of the organization including date of establishment, history,
mission statement, and objectives; copy of
IRS letter designating the organization's
501(c)(3) status; current financial statement;
list of board of directors and key staff; a
brief overview of the program/project for
which funding is requested including purpose, targeted population, evaluation strategies, anticipated results, budget, other
organizations providing support, and timeline; and current or past WWP involvement,
if any, in the organization or program, including employee volunteers, board members, etc. *Deadlines:* none *Note:* Applicants
outside Spokane are encouraged to submit requests to regional offices. Contact headquarters for further information.

Restrictions on Giving: Generally does not
contribute to individuals, team or extra-curricular school events, tournament fund raisers, trips or tours, churches or other
religious organizations, organizations that
discriminate for any reason, endowments or
foundations, or hospital or patient care institution operating funds.

OTHER THINGS TO KNOW

Priority is given to requests that demonstrate partnerships and cooperative efforts
between organizations and agencies and
which directly benefit people within areas
where company conducts business.

PUBLICATIONS

Contributions guidelines

GRANTS ANALYSIS

Total Grants: $525,000*

Typical Range: $500 to $1,000

Disclosure Period: 1994

Note: Total grants figure is approximate.

RECENT GRANTS

General
Cannon Hill Children's Services, Spokane, WA
Civic Theater, Spokane, WA

Welch Testamentary Trust, George T.

CONTACT

Holly T. Howard
Assistant Vice President
George T. Welch Testamentary Trust
c/o Baker Boyer National Bank
PO Box 1796
Walla Walla, WA 99362
(509) 525-2000

FINANCIAL SUMMARY

Recent Giving: $104,011 (fiscal 1993);
$153,454 (fiscal 1992); $184,983 (fiscal
1991)

Assets: $3,565,048 (fiscal 1993);
$3,432,993 (fiscal 1992); $3,230,013 (fiscal
1991)

Gifts Received: $1,000 (fiscal 1993);
$3,000 (fiscal 1991)

Fiscal Note: In fiscal 1993, contributions
were received from Dennis K.L. Kinc.

EIN: 91-6024318

CONTRIBUTIONS SUMMARY

Typical Recipients: • *Arts & Humanities:*
Arts Centers, Community Arts, Dance, His-
toric Preservation, Libraries, Museums/Gal-
leries • *Education:* Colleges & Universities,
Community & Junior Colleges, Literacy
• *Social Services:* Animal Protection, Child
Welfare, Community Service Organizations,
Day Care, Family Planning, Food/Clothing
Distribution, Homes, Recreation & Athlet-
ics, Shelters/Homelessness

Grant Types: project and scholarship

Geographic Distribution: limited to Walla
Walla County, WA

GIVING OFFICERS

Baker Boyer National Bank: trust

APPLICATION INFORMATION

Initial Approach: Send letter stating academic plans and financial resources. Deadline for medical is February 20, May 20,
August 20, and November 20; for academic
is May 1; and for community requests is
July 31.

OTHER THINGS TO KNOW

Provides medical assistance and scholarships to individuals.

PUBLICATIONS

Application Guidelines

GRANTS ANALYSIS

Total Grants: $104,011

Number of Grants: 4

Highest Grant: $3,288

Typical Range: $656 to $3,288

Disclosure Period: fiscal year ending September 30, 1993

Note: Recent grants are derived from a fiscal 1993 Form 990. Number of grants and
typical range do not include grants to individuals.

RECENT GRANTS

General
| 1,625 | Project Read, Atlanta, GA |
| 656 | Blue Mountain Humane Society, Walla Walla, WA |

Weyerhaeuser Co. / Weyerhaeuser Company Foundation

Revenue: $10.39 billion
Employees: 39,022
Headquarters: Tacoma, WA
SIC Major Group: Sawmills & Planing
Mills—General, Logging, Millwork, and
Hardwood Veneer & Plywood

CONTACT

Elizabeth A. Crossman
Vice Presidnet
Weyerhaeuser Co. Fdn.
CH1F 31
Tacoma, WA 98477
(206) 924-3159

FINANCIAL SUMMARY

Recent Giving: $5,633,000 (1995 est.);
$5,462,000 (1994 approx.); $5,142,028
(1993)

Assets: $14,356,780 (1993); $9,207,547
(1992); $6,558,515 (1991)

Gifts Received: $13,150,932 (1993)

Fiscal Note: Above figures are for foundation contributions only. Local subsidiaries
and operations also give directly. In 1993,
this support was estimated at
$6,000,000.Above figures include nonmone-
tary support. Because these contribution programs are highly decentralized, detailed
information is not available. Foundation receives contributions from Weyerhaeuser
Company.

EIN: 91-6024225

CONTRIBUTIONS SUMMARY

Typical Recipients: • *Arts & Humanities:*
Arts Associations & Councils, Arts Funds,
Community Arts, Dance, Historic Preserva-
tion, Libraries, Museums/Galleries, Music,
Opera, Public Broadcasting, Theater • *Civic
& Public Affairs:* Business/Free Enterprise,
Economic Development, Employment/Job
Training, Housing, Municipalities/Towns,
Rural Affairs, Safety, Urban & Community
Affairs, Zoos/Aquariums • *Education:* Busi-
ness Education, Colleges & Universities,
Community & Junior Colleges, Economic
Education, Education Associations, Educa-
tion Funds, Elementary Education (Private),
Engineering/Technological Education, Mi-
nority Education, Private Education (Precol-
lege), Public Education (Precollege),
Science/Mathematics Education • *Environ-
ment:* General • *Health:* Hospices, Hospitals
• *Social Services:* Child Welfare, Community Centers, Community Service Organizations, Family Services,
Shelters/Homelessness, Substance Abuse,
United Funds/United Ways, Volunteer Services, Youth Organizations

Grant Types: capital, employee matching gifts, general support, project, and research

Note: Employee matching gift ratio: 1 to 1.

Nonmonetary Support: $4,700,000 (1993)

Nonmonetary Support Types: in-kind services and loaned executives

Note: Nonmonetary support is contributed directly through the company. Elizabeth Crossman, vice president, is the contact for nonmonetary support and may be reached at the above address.

Geographic Distribution: nationally and in Canada, with emphasis on communities, particularly remote communities, in which company has significant numbers of employees

Operating Locations: AL, AR (Hot Springs), CA (Alameda, Altadena, Anaheim, Belmont, City of Commerce, Colton, Emeryville, La Puente, Los Angeles, Modesto, Oceanside, Pleasanton, Rohnert Park, Salinas, San Francisco, San Jose, Santa Paula, West Sacramento), FL (Miami, Tampa), GA, HI (Honolulu), IA (Cedar Rapids, Waterloo), IL (Belleville, Elgin, Itasca, Rockford), KY (Franklin), MD (Dorsey, Millersville), ME (Westbrooke), MI (Warren), MN (Albert Lea, Austin, White Bear), MO (Clayton, St. Joseph, St. Louis), MS (Columbus, Jackson), NC (Charlotte, Durham, Greensboro, New Bern, Plymouth), NJ (Barrington, Closter, Marlton, Teaneck), OH (Columbus, Mount Vernon), OK (Oklahoma City, Valliant, Wright City), OR (Beaverton, Eugene, Klamath Falls, North Bend, Portland, Springfield), PA (Valley Forge), TX (Amarillo, Dallas, Grand Prairie, Houston, McAllen), VA (Lynchburg, Richmond), WA (Bellevue, Centralia, Chehalis, Cosmopolis, Everett, Federal Way, Kent, Longview, Olympia, Seattle, Tacoma, Union Gap, Vancouver), WI (Manitowoc, Rothschild)

Note: Also operates in Tokyo, Japan and Beijing, China.

CORP. OFFICERS

John W. Creighton, Jr.: *B* Pittsburgh PA 1932 *ED* OH St Univ BS 1954; OH St Univ JD 1957; Univ Miami MBA 1966 *CURR EMPL* pres, ceo, dir: Weyerhaeuser Co *CORP AFFIL* chmn: Fed Home Loan Bank Seattle; dir: Am Paper Inst, MIP Properties Inc, Mortgage Investments Plus Inc, Portland Gen Corp, Puget Sound Bancorp, Quality Food Ctrs, WA Energy Co; pres: Weyerhaeuser Intl, Weyerhaeuser Real Estate Co; pres, dir: Weyerhaeuser Fin Svcs *NONPR AFFIL* dir: Natl Corp Housing Partnerships; dir, chief Seattle Coun: Boy Scouts Am, Un Way King County; trust: Univ Puget Sound

Elizabeth A. Crossman: *CURR EMPL* vp corp contributions: Weyerhaeuser Co

Steven Richard Hill: *B* Oakland CA 1947 *ED* Univ CA Berkeley BS 1969; Univ CA Los Angeles MBA 1971 *CURR EMPL* sr vp human resources: Weyerhaeuser Co

Norman E. Johnson: *B* 1933 *ED* Harvard Univ Advanced Mgmt Program; OR St Univ MS; Univ CA Berkeley PhD *CURR EMPL* sr vp tech: Weyerhaeuser Co

C. Stephen Lewis: *B* 1944 *CURR EMPL* pres, dir: Weyerhaeuser Real Estate Co *CORP AFFIL* pres, dir: Babcock Co Inc

Richard K. Long: *CURR EMPL* vp corp commun: Weyerhaeuser Co

Sandy D. McDade: *B* 1952 *ED* Whitman Coll 1974; Univ Puget Sound 1979 *CURR EMPL* secy, sr legal couns: Weyerhaeuser Co *CORP AFFIL* secy: Weyerhaeuser Intl; secy, dir: Weyerhaeuser Fin Svcs, Weyerhaeuser Real Estate Co *NONPR AFFIL* mem: Am Soc Corp Secys

Kenneth J. Stancato: *ED* CO Univ BS 1960 *CURR EMPL* vp, contr: Weyerhaeuser Co

George Hunt Weyerhaeuser: *B* Seattle WA 1926 *ED* Yale Univ BS 1949 *CURR EMPL* chmn: Weyerhaeuser Co *CORP AFFIL* chmn: Weyerhaeuser Export; dir: Boeing Co, Chevron Corp, Fed Reserve Bank San Francisco, SAFECO Corp, Weyerhaeuser Real Estate Co; pres: Day Island Marina; pres, dir: Weyerhaeuser Intl, Weyerhaeuser SA *NONPR AFFIL* mem: Bus Counc; mem adv bd: Bus Roundtable, Univ WA Sch Bus Admin, WA St Bus Roundtable; trust: RAND Corp *PHIL AFFIL* don: Weyerhaeuser Family Foundation

GIVING OFFICERS

Charles W. Bingham: chmn, trust *B* Myrtle Point OR 1933 *ED* Harvard Univ BA 1955; Harvard Univ LLB 1960 *CURR EMPL* exec vp: Weyerhaeuser Co *CORP AFFIL* dir: Puget Sound Power & Light Co *NONPR AFFIL* mem bd govs: Natl Forest Products Assn

Mary L. Cabral: asst contr

William R. Corbin: trust

John W. Creighton, Jr.: trust *CURR EMPL* pres, ceo, dir: Weyerhaeuser Co (see above)

Elizabeth A. Crossman: vp *CURR EMPL* vp corp contributions: Weyerhaeuser Co (see above)

Steven Richard Hill: trust *CURR EMPL* sr vp human resources: Weyerhaeuser Co (see above)

Mack L. Hogans: pres, trust *B* Abbeville AL 1949 *ED* Univ MI 1971; Univ WA 1976 *CURR EMPL* vp govt aff: Weyerhaeuser Co

Norman E. Johnson: trust *CURR EMPL* sr vp tech: Weyerhaeuser Co (see above)

C. Stephen Lewis: trust *CURR EMPL* pres, dir: Weyerhaeuser Real Estate Co (see above)

Sandy D. McDade: asst secy legal aff *CURR EMPL* secy, sr legal couns: Weyerhaeuser Co (see above)

William Howarth Meadowcroft: trust *ED* Harvard Univ MBA 1954; Univ Puget Sound *CURR EMPL* asst to chmn: Weyerhaeuser Co *NONPR AFFIL* bd mem: Mus Flight; mem: Leukemia Soc Am, VA Mason Med Fdn, WA St Games Fdn; trust: Takoma Art Mus; trust, vchmn: Univ Puget Sound *CLUB AFFIL* Rainier, Tacoma, Washington Athletic Ctr *PHIL AFFIL* trust: Weyerhaeuser Family Foundation

Susan M. Mersereau: trust *B* Portland OR 1946 *ED* Scripps Coll BA 1968; Univ Chicago MA 1971; Antioch Coll MA 1990 *CURR EMPL* vp, gen mgr: Weyerhaeuser

Info Sys *NONPR AFFIL* mem commun group: Soc Info Sys

Kenneth J. Stancato: contr *CURR EMPL* vp, contr: Weyerhaeuser Co (see above)

William Charles Stivers: treas, trust *B* Modesto CA 1938 *ED* Stanford Univ BA 1960; Univ Southern CA MBA 1963; Harvard Univ Sch Bus Admin 1977 *CURR EMPL* sr vp, cfo: Weyerhaeuser Co *CORP AFFIL* dir: First Interstate Bank WA, GNA Corp, Great Northern Ins Annuity Co, Protection Mutual Ins Co, Republic Fed Savings & Loan; exec vp: Weyerhaeuser Intl; mem natl adv bd: Chem Bank; pres, dir: S&S Land & Cattle Co; vp fin, dir: Weyerhaeuser Real Estate Co *NONPR AFFIL* dir: Univ WA Ctr Study Banking Fin Markets; mem: Am Forest & Paper Assn, Fin Execs Inst; mem fin comm: Am Paper Inst; trust, chmn: St Francis Commun Hosp

Linda L. Terrien: asst treas

Karen L. Veitenhans: secy

George Hunt Weyerhaeuser: trust *CURR EMPL* chmn: Weyerhaeuser Co *PHIL AFFIL* don: Weyerhaeuser Family Foundation (see above)

Robert B. Wilson: trust

APPLICATION INFORMATION

Initial Approach: *Initial Contact:* brief letter or proposal *Include Information On:* description of project and sponsoring organization; statement of why project is consistent with foundation guidelines; project cost, sources of funding, and amount requested; evidence of tax-exempt status *Deadlines:* none; requests received after September may not be considered until budgets are established for the following year *Note:* If further consideration is warranted, may ask for additional information or formal proposal; personal meetings or site visits are normally arranged only for projects that have passed initial letter of inquiry.

Restrictions on Giving: Does not support religious, sacramental, or theological functions; political campaigns; individuals; or direct grants to organizations already receiving foundation funds through an umbrella organization. Does not make grants for less than $1,000.

Discourages applications seeking to cover operating deficits; for services that the public sector should reasonably be expected to provide; to purchase tables at fund-raising benefits; to establish endowments or to memorialize individuals; for research or conferences on topics outside the forest products industry; for hospital building of equipment campaigns that will result in significantly higher costs to health-care users; for services outside locales in which Weyerhaeuser has an operating facility or a significant number or employees; for general administrative expenses (with prior approval, direct costs for reasonable levels of institutional support services may be included in the project's budget); or for amounts that are clearly unrealistic given the foundation's total annual budget (foundation follows accounting practices that require it to charge the full amount of a pledge against its current annual budget).

Grants will be made only to private, nonprofit, tax-exempt organizations with certified 501(c)(3) status, and to public entities qualifying under Section 170(c) of the Internal Revenue Code.

The foundation will not consider requests that do not meet its program and geographic criterion. If organizations are unsure about the presence of a Weyerhaeuser facility in their community, write or call the foundation for confirmation before submitting a grant request.

OTHER THINGS TO KNOW
Foundation makes cash grants only, with a $1,000 minimum. Normally, support is committed for one year at a time. Grants are given to eligible organizations primarily for special projects, with funding of general operations limited to a very small number of high-priority organizations.

Organizations receiving grants must practice equal opportunity.

Grants may be made to umbrella organizations or combined campaigns. Level of foundation support to such causes is influenced by the degree to which the organization rigorously reviews its annual priorities and allocations among member agencies; improves the efficiency of members' operations; provides leadership in responding to new needs; and evaluates the outcomes and impact of its members' activities.

Tends to make fewer but larger grants in order to concentrate sufficient resources to produce significant outcomes.

Foundation relies on advice of local review committees who represent company's regional operations. These volunteers establish local philanthropic priorities, review requests, recommend decisions, serve as grant monitors, and often assist with specific projects.

PUBLICATIONS
Biennial report and current guidelines, grant application, volunteer employee pamphlet

GRANTS ANALYSIS
Total Grants: $5,142,028

Number of Grants: 698

Highest Grant: $176,029

Average Grant: $5,000*

Typical Range: $1,000 to $10,000

Disclosure Period: 1993

Note: Average grant figure provided by the company. Recent grants are derived from a 1993 Form 990.

RECENT GRANTS
General

176,029	National Merit Scholarship Corporation, Evanston, IL
145,000	United Way of Pierce County, Tacoma, WA
125,265	Citizens Scholarship Foundation of America, St. Peter, MN
120,000	United Way of King County, Seattle, WA

100,000	Columbus Municipal School District, Columbus, OH

Wyman Youth Trust

CONTACT
Wyman Youth Trust
304 Pioneer Bldg., 600 First Ave.
Seattle, WA 98104
(206) 682-2255

FINANCIAL SUMMARY
Recent Giving: $242,657 (1993); $201,780 (1992); $203,936 (1991)

Assets: $4,057,683 (1993); $3,702,370 (1992); $3,485,639 (1991)

EIN: 91-6031590

CONTRIBUTIONS SUMMARY
Donor(s): members of the Wyman family

Typical Recipients: • *Arts & Humanities:* Arts Associations & Councils, Arts Centers, Ballet, Community Arts, Dance, Ethnic & Folk Arts, Historic Preservation, History & Archaeology, Libraries, Museums/Galleries, Music, Opera, Performing Arts, Theater • *Civic & Public Affairs:* Business/Free Enterprise, General, Parades/Festivals • *Education:* Arts/Humanities Education, Business Education, Colleges & Universities, Education Reform, Elementary Education (Private), General, Private Education (Precollege), Social Sciences Education, Student Aid • *Environment:* Protection • *Health:* AIDS/HIV, Children's Health/Hospitals, Clinics/Medical Centers, Hospitals • *Religion:* Churches, Ministries, Religious Organizations • *Social Services:* Child Welfare, Community Service Organizations, Counseling, Recreation & Athletics, United Funds/United Ways, Volunteer Services, Youth Organizations

Grant Types: general support

Geographic Distribution: limited to King County, WA, and York County, NE

GIVING OFFICERS
Ann M. Wyman: trust

David C. Wyman: trust

Deehan M. Wyman: trust

APPLICATION INFORMATION
Initial Approach: Send a brief letter of inquiry. Include a description of organization, amount requested, purpose of funds sought, recently audited financial statement, and proof of tax-exempt status.

Restrictions on Giving: Limited to King, Pierce, and Snohomish Counties in WA; and York, Custer, and Lancaster Counties in NE.

PUBLICATIONS
Application Guidelines

GRANTS ANALYSIS
Total Grants: $242,657

Number of Grants: 174

Highest Grant: $20,000

Typical Range: $100 to $10,000

Disclosure Period: 1993

Note: Recent grants are derived from a 1993 Form 990.

RECENT GRANTS
General

20,000	Overlake Hospital Foundation, Bellevue, WA
10,000	United Way
8,600	Lakeside School, Seattle, WA
7,500	Overlake School, Seattle, WA
6,000	Lakeside School, Seattle, WA — Ned Skinner Fund

WEST VIRGINIA

Bowen Foundation, Ethel N.

CONTACT
Ethel N. Bowen Fdn.
c/o First National Bank of Bluefield
500 Federal St.
Bluefield, WV 24701
(304) 325-8181

FINANCIAL SUMMARY
Recent Giving: $370,340 (1993); $433,174 (1992); $395,670 (1991)

Assets: $7,187,409 (1993); $6,855,757 (1992); $6,992,886 (1991)

EIN: 23-7010740

CONTRIBUTIONS SUMMARY
Donor(s): the late Ethel N. Bowen

Typical Recipients: • *Arts & Humanities:* Arts Associations & Councils, Arts Centers, Film & Video, Historic Preservation, History & Archaeology, Libraries, Music • *Civic & Public Affairs:* Business/Free Enterprise, Clubs, General, Municipalities/Towns • *Education:* Colleges & Universities, Elementary Education (Private), Elementary Education (Public), General, International Studies, Private Education (Precollege), Public Education (Precollege), Science/Mathematics Education, Secondary Education (Private), Secondary Education (Public), Student Aid • *Health:* Cancer, Emergency/Ambulance Services • *Religion:* Bible Study/Translation, Churches, Religious Organizations, Religious Welfare • *Social Services:* Community Centers, Counseling, General, Recreation & Athletics, Scouts, Shelters/Homelessness, United Funds/United Ways, Youth Organizations

Grant Types: general support and scholarship

Geographic Distribution: limited to southern WV and southwestern VA

GIVING OFFICERS
First National Bank of Bluefield: trust

Henry Bowen: dir

Virginia M. Bowen: dir

L. R. Coulling: dir *CORP AFFIL* dir: First Natl Bank Bluefield

Basil L. Jackson: dir *B* Portsmouth VA 1924 *ED* VA Polytech Inst 1950; Univ WI 1961 *CURR EMPL* chmn: First Natl Bank Bluefield *CORP AFFIL* chmn: Pocahontas Bankshares Corp; dir: Bluefield Area Devel Corp, Flat Top Ins Agency

B. K. Satterfield: dir *CURR EMPL* exec vp, trust off, dir: First Natl Bank Bluefield

Richard W. Wilkinson: secy, treas *B* Welch WV 1932 *ED* Univ VA 1955-1962; Univ VA JD 1962 *CURR EMPL* pres, ceo, dir: First Natl Bank Bluefield *CORP AFFIL* chmn, trust off: First Century Bank; pres, dir: Bank Oceana, Pocahontas Bankshares *PHIL AFFIL* pres: Hugh I. Shott, Jr. Foundation

APPLICATION INFORMATION
Initial Approach: The foundation has no formal grant application procedure or application form. Students must submit transcripts. Deadline is prior to beginning of academic year.

OTHER THINGS TO KNOW
Provides scholarships for higher education to residents of southern WV and southwestern VA.

GRANTS ANALYSIS
Total Grants: $370,340

Number of Grants: 53

Highest Grant: $10,000

Typical Range: $150 to $10,000

Disclosure Period: 1993

Note: Recent grants are derived from a 1993 Form 990. Number of grants and typical range do not include scholarships to individuals.

RECENT GRANTS

Library
5,000	Craft Memorial Library, Craft, WV

General
10,000	City of Bluefield, Bluefield, WV — Bowen Field
10,000	Virginia Student Aid, Charlottesville, VA
5,000	Bluefield Junior High School, Bluefield, WV
5,000	Elizabeth Bowen Jones Memorial UM Church, WV
5,000	Salvation Army, Bluefield, WV

Clay Foundation

CONTACT
Charles M. Avampato
President
Clay Foundation
1426 Kanawha Blvd., E
Charleston, WV 25301
(304) 344-8656

FINANCIAL SUMMARY
Recent Giving: $811,865 (fiscal 1993); $1,227,541 (fiscal 1992); $4,347,178 (fiscal 1991)

Assets: $43,045,094 (fiscal 1993); $38,675,788 (fiscal 1992); $35,582,987 (fiscal 1991)

Gifts Received: $660,489 (fiscal 1992); $1,066 (fiscal 1990)

Fiscal Note: In 1992, contributions were received from Lyell B. Clay.

EIN: 55-0670193

CONTRIBUTIONS SUMMARY
Donor(s): The foundation was established in 1987 by Lyell B. Clay, the chairman of the foundation, and Buckner Clay, also chairman of the foundation. Lyell B. Clay is the chairman of the board of Clay Communications, Inc.

Typical Recipients: • *Arts & Humanities:* Arts Centers, Arts Funds, History & Archaeology, Libraries, Museums/Galleries, Music, Opera, Public Broadcasting, Theater • *Civic & Public Affairs:* Botanical Gardens/Parks, Chambers of Commerce, Community Foundations, Economic Development, Housing, Nonprofit Management, Philanthropic Organizations, Professional & Trade Associations, Public Policy • *Education:* Business-School Partnerships, Colleges & Universities, Health & Physical Education, Medical Education, Private Education (Precollege), Public Education (Precollege), Student Aid • *Health:* Health Policy/Cost Containment, Health Organizations, Hospices, Hospitals, Mental Health, Preventive Medicine/Wellness Organizations • *Religion:* Churches, Religious Organizations, Religious Welfare • *Science:* Science Museums • *Social Services:* At-Risk Youth, Child Welfare, Community Service Organizations, Counseling, Family Services, Food/Clothing Distribution, Homes, People with Disabilities, Shelters/Homelessness, United Funds/United Ways, Volunteer Services, YMCA/YWCA/YMHA/YWHA, Youth Organizations

Grant Types: capital, challenge, general support, and scholarship

Geographic Distribution: primarily West Virginia, with emphasis on Kanawha Valley

GIVING OFFICERS
Charles M. Avampato: pres

James Knight Brown: secy *B* Rainelle WV 1929 *ED* WV Univ BS 1951; WV Univ LLB 1956 *CURR EMPL* ptnr: Jackson & Kelly *CORP AFFIL* dir: One Valley Bancorp WV *NONPR AFFIL* fellow: Am Bar Fdn; mem: Am Bar Assn, Order of Coif, Phi Beta Kappa

Buckner W. Clay: chmn

Hamilton G. Clay: vp

Lyell Buffington Clay: chmn *B* Baltimore MD 1923 *ED* Williams Coll 1944; Univ VA 1948 *PHIL AFFIL* chmn: Lyell B and Patricia K Clay Foundation Inc

Whitney Clay Diller: treas

Louis Sweetland Southworth II: asst secy-treas *B* Huntington WV 1943 *ED* Marshall Univ AB 1965; WV Univ JD 1968; NY Univ

LLM 1970 *CURR EMPL* atty: Jackson & Kelly *NONPR AFFIL* dir: CAMC Fdn; fellow: Am Coll Tax Couns; trust: Kanawha Valley Fdn, Univ Charleston *CLUB AFFIL* Edgewood CC, Rotary *PHIL AFFIL* dir: Lyell B and Patricia K Clay Foundation Inc

APPLICATION INFORMATION
Initial Approach:

The foundation reports that applicants should submit, in triplicate, a letter of inquiry (two to three pages) that briefly describes the proposed project.

Letters should include the name, address, and phone number of the organization; contact's name; descriptive title of project; amount of funds requested; timetable for use of funds; outline of objectives, specific goals, and target population; methods which will be used to accomplish these goals; other sources of funding for the project; and plans for evaluation of the project (if applicable). Attachments should include information about the sponsoring organization, names and brief statements of qualification for individuals who will be involved in the project, most recently audited financial statement, and tax-exempt identification.

There are no set deadlines for letters of inquiry.

All grant requests are first reviewed to determine if the request falls within the current program interest of the foundation. Only those requests that clearly fall outside the foundation's priorities are declined on the first review.

In reviewing grant applications, the foundation gives careful consideration to: the potential impact of the request and the number of people who will benefit; the degree to which the applicant works with, or complements, the services of other community organizations; the organization's fiscal responsibility and management qualifications; the possibility of the use of its grants as seed money for matching funds from other sources; the ability of the program to obtain necessary additional funding to implement the project; the commitment of the organization's board of directors; the imaginative and experimental quality of the proposed project; the extent of local volunteer involvement and support for the project; and the ability of the organization to provide ongoing funding after the term of the grant.

The foundation may request additional information and, in some cases, may arrange for the applicant to meet with the staff for further discussion. A project site visit may be scheduled, and the advice of outside consultants may be sought.

Final approval of each major grant is the responsibility of the board of directors. Certain other grants that require a smaller amount of support may be authorized by the president of the foundation. All grants are suject to the same review and monitoring criteria.

Applicants should allow the foundation 60 working days to review a request. If the foundation's priorities and resources permit consideration of the request, a detailed proposal may be requested. The board of directors meets four times a year, generally in January, April, July, and October.

Restrictions on Giving: In general, the foundation does not fund ongoing normal operations, debt retirement or operational deficits, national fundraising campaigns, endowment or scholarship funds, religious organizations for religious purposes, or conduit organizations. The foundation may not award grants to individuals, designate funds for legislation, or support activities that seek to influence the legislative process.

GRANTS ANALYSIS
Total Grants: $811,865
Number of Grants: 32
Highest Grant: $100,000
Average Grant: $25,371
Typical Range: $5,000 to $50,000
Disclosure Period: fiscal year ending October 31, 1993
Note: Recent grants are derived from a fiscal 1993 Form 990.

RECENT GRANTS
General

100,000	University of Charleston, Charleston, WV — scholarship fund
82,000	United Way, Charleston, WV — new building construction
66,924	YWCA, Charleston, WV — building maintenance grant
65,000	West Virginia University Foundation Program, Morgantown, WV — preventicare project
50,000	BIDCO Foundation, Charleston, WV — economic development programs

Daywood Foundation

CONTACT
William W. Booker
Secretary-Treasurer
Daywood Fdn.
Bank One, Ste. 1500
Charleston, WV 25301
(304) 345-8900

FINANCIAL SUMMARY
Recent Giving: $425,200 (1993); $344,500 (1992); $435,500 (1991)
Assets: $11,620,516 (1993); $11,587,321 (1992); $11,238,600 (1991)
EIN: 55-6018107

CONTRIBUTIONS SUMMARY
Donor(s): the late Ruth Woods Dayton

Typical Recipients: • *Arts & Humanities:* Arts Centers, Arts Funds, Community Arts, Film & Video, History & Archaeology, Libraries, Music, Theater • *Civic & Public Affairs:* Economic Development, General, Housing, Urban & Community Affairs • *Education:* Colleges & Universities, Education Funds, Education Reform, Faculty Develop-

ment, General, Minority Education, Private Education (Precollege), Public Education (Precollege), Religious Education, Science/Mathematics Education, Student Aid • *Environment:* General • *Health:* Emergency/Ambulance Services, Health Organizations, Hospices • *Religion:* Religious Organizations, Religious Welfare • *Social Services:* At-Risk Youth, Camps, Child Welfare, Community Service Organizations, Domestic Violence, Emergency Relief, Family Services, Food/Clothing Distribution, Homes, People with Disabilities, Recreation & Athletics, Scouts, Senior Services, Shelters/Homelessness, United Funds/United Ways, YMCA/YWCA/YMHA/YWHA, Youth Organizations

Grant Types: capital, emergency, general support, and seed money

Geographic Distribution: limited to Barbour, Charleston, Greenbrier, Kanawha, and Lewisburg counties, WV

GIVING OFFICERS
William W. Booker: secy, treas, dir

Richard Edmond Ford: vp, dir *B* Ronceverte WV 1927 *ED* WV Univ BS 1951; WV Univ LLB 1954 *CURR EMPL* ptnr: Hayne Ford & Rowe *CORP AFFIL* dir: First Natl Bank Ronceverte, Greenbrier Cable Corp, WV Power Co *NONPR AFFIL* dir: Faculty Merit Fdn, WV Univ Fdn; fellow: Am Bar Fdn, Am Judicature Soc; mem: Am Bar Assn, Am Coll Real Estate Lawyers, Greenbrier County Bar Assn, Natl Conf Commrs Uniform St Laws, Order of Vandalia, Phi Beta Kappa, Phi Delta Phi, Sigma Chi, WV Bar Assn, WV Law Sch Assn, WV Univ Alumni Assn; mem adv bd: Greenbrier Community Coll Ctr; mem exec bd: Boy Scouts Am, Buckskin Counc; vp, dir: Daywood Fdn *CLUB AFFIL* KT, Lewisburg Elks, Masons, Shriners

John Oscar Kizer: asst secy, treas, dir *B* Wheeling WV 1913 *ED* WV Univ AB 1934; WV Univ LLB 1936 *CURR EMPL* ptnr: Kay Casto Chaney Love & Wise *NONPR AFFIL* dir, past pres: Childrens Mus Charleston; mem: Am Bar Assn, WV Bar Assn, WV St Bar, Delta Tau Delta *CLUB AFFIL* Berry Hills CC

L. Newton Thomas, Jr.: pres, dir *PHIL AFFIL* trust: Bernard H. and Blanche E. Jacobson Foundation

APPLICATION INFORMATION
Initial Approach: Send a brief letter of inquiry. Include a description of organization, amount requested, purpose of funds sought, recently audited financial statement, and proof of tax-exempt status. There are no deadlines.

Restrictions on Giving: Limited to West Virginia.

PUBLICATIONS
Application Guidelines

GRANTS ANALYSIS
Total Grants: $425,200
Number of Grants: 57
Highest Grant: $48,000
Typical Range: $1,000 to $30,000

Disclosure Period: 1993
Note: Recent grants are derived from a 1993 Form 990.

RECENT GRANTS
Library

10,000	Ohio-West Virginia YMCA, Charleston, WV — Camp Horseshoe library
5,000	Greenbrier County Library, Lewisburg, WV

General

48,000	United Way of Kenawha Valley, Charleston, WV
32,500	Davis and Elkins College, Elkins, WV — scholarship program
30,000	West Virginia Wesleyan College, Buckhannon, WV — scholarships
25,000	West Virginia Wesleyan College, Buckhannon, WV — capital campaign
17,000	University of Charleston, Charleston, WV — scholarship program

Fenton Foundation

CONTACT
Frank M. Fenton
Treasurer
Fenton Fdn.
310 W Fourth St.
Williamstown, WV 26187
(304) 375-7943

FINANCIAL SUMMARY
Recent Giving: $160,123 (1993); $142,087 (1992); $113,697 (1990)
Assets: $2,098,241 (1993); $2,038,982 (1992); $1,773,944 (1990)
Gifts Received: $33,654 (1993); $22,241 (1992); $25,179 (1990)
Fiscal Note: In 1993, contributions were received from Fenton Gift Shops Inc.
EIN: 55-6017260

CONTRIBUTIONS SUMMARY
Typical Recipients: • *Arts & Humanities:* Arts Associations & Councils, Arts Centers, Film & Video, Libraries, Music • *Civic & Public Affairs:* Clubs, Community Foundations, General, Municipalities/Towns • *Education:* Arts/Humanities Education, Business-School Partnerships, Colleges & Universities, Education Funds, Education Reform, Elementary Education (Public), General, International Exchange, Medical Education, Private Education (Precollege), Public Education (Precollege), Secondary Education (Public) • *Health:* Children's Health/Hospitals, Health Organizations, Hospices, Hospitals, Research/Studies Institutes, Single-Disease Health Associations • *Religion:* Churches, Religious Organizations, Religious Welfare • *Social Services:* Child Welfare, Community Service Organizations,

Homes, Recreation & Athletics, Scouts, Substance Abuse, United Funds/United Ways

Grant Types: general support

Geographic Distribution: focus on Wood County, WV, and Washington County, OH

GIVING OFFICERS
Elinor P. Fenton: dir, secy

Frank M. Fenton: dir, treas

Thomas K. Fenton: dir, vp

Wilmer C. Fenton: dir, pres

APPLICATION INFORMATION
Initial Approach: Send brief letter describing program. There are no deadlines.

Restrictions on Giving: Does not support individuals. Limited to Wood County, WV, and Washington County, OH.

GRANTS ANALYSIS
Total Grants: $160,123

Number of Grants: 76

Highest Grant: $28,000

Typical Range: $25 to $27,500

Disclosure Period: 1993

Note: Recent grants are derived from a 1993 Form 990.

RECENT GRANTS

General
28,000	Marietta College, Marietta, OH
27,500	Wood County Senior Citizens, Williamstown, WV
10,000	City of Williamstown, Williamstown, WV
10,000	Marietta College, Marietta, OH
10,000	Marietta Memorial Hospital, Marietta, OH

Jacobson Foundation, Bernard H. and Blanche E.

CONTACT
John L. Ray

Trustee

Bernard H. and Blanche E. Jacobson Fdn.

1210 One Valley Sq.

Charleston, WV 25301

(304) 342-1141

FINANCIAL SUMMARY
Recent Giving: $402,571 (1993); $232,850 (1992); $324,860 (1991)

Assets: $6,708,111 (1993); $6,845,168 (1992); $6,793,125 (1991)

Gifts Received: $56,153 (1991); $81,066 (1990); $2,222,992 (1989)

Fiscal Note: In 1991, contributions were received from the Bernard H. Jacobson Marital Trust.

EIN: 55-6014902

CONTRIBUTIONS SUMMARY
Donor(s): Bernard H. Jacobson, Blanche E. Jacobson

Typical Recipients: • *Arts & Humanities:* Community Arts, Film & Video, Historic Preservation, History & Archaeology, Li-

braries, Museums/Galleries, Music, Public Broadcasting • *Civic & Public Affairs:* Chambers of Commerce, Economic Development, General, Housing, Philanthropic Organizations, Professional & Trade Associations, Urban & Community Affairs, Women's Affairs • *Education:* Arts/Humanities Education, Business Education, Colleges & Universities, Education Funds, Education Reform, Minority Education, Public Education (Precollege), Science/Mathematics Education, Secondary Education (Private) • *Environment:* General • *Health:* Clinics/Medical Centers, Emergency/Ambulance Services, Health Organizations, Mental Health • *International:* International Affairs • *Religion:* Jewish Causes, Religious Organizations, Religious Welfare • *Science:* Scientific Centers & Institutes, Scientific Research • *Social Services:* At-Risk Youth, Child Welfare, Community Service Organizations, Counseling, Food/Clothing Distribution, Homes, Recreation & Athletics, Shelters/Homelessness, United Funds/United Ways, Volunteer Services, YMCA/YWCA/YMHA/YWHA, Youth Organizations

Grant Types: general support

Geographic Distribution: focus on WV, particularly Kanawha Valley and Charleston

GIVING OFFICERS
One Valley Bank, N.A.: trust

Charles W. Loeb: trust

John L. Ray: trust

L. N. Thomas, Jr.: trust

L. Newton Thomas, Jr.: trust *PHIL AFFIL* pres, dir: Daywood Foundation

APPLICATION INFORMATION
Initial Approach: The foundation has no formal grant application procedure or application form. There are no deadlines.

GRANTS ANALYSIS
Total Grants: $402,571

Number of Grants: 53

Highest Grant: $56,800

Typical Range: $900 to $55,000

Disclosure Period: 1993

Note: Recent grants are derived from a 1993 Form 990.

RECENT GRANTS

Library
4,550	Kanawha County Public Library, Charleston, WV

General
56,800	United Way of Kanawha Valley, Charleston, WV
55,000	Greater Kanawha Valley Foundation, Charleston, WV
27,500	Daymark, Charleston, WV
20,000	University of Charleston, Charleston, WV
16,932	Women's Health Center, Charleston, WV

Shott, Jr. Foundation, Hugh I.

CONTACT
Richard W. Wilkinson

President

Hugh I. Shott, Jr., Foundation

c/o First Century Bank, NA

500 Federal St.

Bluefield, WV 24701

(304) 325-8181

FINANCIAL SUMMARY
Recent Giving: $960,000 (1995 est.); $960,000 (1994 approx.); $780,014 (1993)

Assets: $24,500,000 (1995 est.); $24,500,000 (1994 approx.); $24,685,633 (1993)

Gifts Received: $13,017,748 (1990); $910,362 (1989)

Fiscal Note: In 1990, contributions were received from the estate of Jane Shott.

EIN: 55-0650833

CONTRIBUTIONS SUMMARY
Donor(s): The foundation was established in 1985 by the late Hugh I. Shott, Jr. .

Typical Recipients: • *Arts & Humanities:* Arts Appreciation, Arts Associations & Councils, Arts Funds, Community Arts, Film & Video, Libraries, Museums/Galleries • *Civic & Public Affairs:* Business/Free Enterprise, Economic Development, Municipalities/Towns, Philanthropic Organizations, Urban & Community Affairs, Women's Affairs • *Education:* Colleges & Universities, Community & Junior Colleges, Private Education (Precollege), Public Education (Precollege) • *Environment:* Sanitary Systems • *Religion:* Religious Welfare • *Social Services:* Community Centers, Community Service Organizations, People with Disabilities

Grant Types: capital, general support, and matching

Geographic Distribution: focus on Bluefield County, WV

GIVING OFFICERS
Scott Shott: vp *B* Bluefield WV 1926 *ED* WV Univ 1950; Washington & Lee Univ JD 1951 *CURR EMPL* secy, dir: Paper Supply Co *CORP AFFIL* chmn: Bluefield Regional Med Ctr Fdn; dir: Bluefield Gas Co, First Natl Bank Bluefield; vchmn: Bluefield Health Sys

Richard W. Wilkinson: pres *B* Welch WV 1932 *ED* Univ VA 1955-1962; Univ VA JD 1962 *CURR EMPL* pres, ceo, dir: First Natl Bank Bluefield *CORP AFFIL* chmn, trust off: First Century Bank; pres, dir: Bank Oceana, Pocahontas Bankshares *PHIL AFFIL* secy, treas: Ethel N. Bowen Foundation

APPLICATION INFORMATION
Initial Approach:

The foundation requests applications be made in writing.

The foundation has no deadline for submitting proposals.

The board meets every other month.

OTHER THINGS TO KNOW

First National Bank of Bluefield is the foundation's corporate trustee.

GRANTS ANALYSIS

Total Grants: $780,014

Number of Grants: 13

Highest Grant: $255,763

Average Grant: $60,001

Typical Range: $5,000 to $100,000

Disclosure Period: 1993

Note: Recent grants are derived from a 1993 Form 990.

RECENT GRANTS

Library

10,000	McDowell County Public Library, Welch, WV

General

255,763	Bluefield State College Foundation, Bluefield, WV — soccer field
100,000	Mountain Mission School, Grundy, VA
100,000	West Virginia University Foundation, Morgantown, WV — educational
75,000	Salvation Army, Princeton, WV — renovation project
63,751	Sanitary Board of Bluefield, Bluefield, WV — Cumberland road project

Teubert Charitable Trust, James H. and Alice

CONTACT

Jimelle Bowen
Executive Director
James H. and Alice Teubert Charitable Trust
PO Box 2131
Huntington, WV 25701
(304) 525-6337

FINANCIAL SUMMARY

Recent Giving: $529,236 (fiscal 1992); $606,944 (fiscal 1990); $409,100 (fiscal 1989)

Assets: $14,323,946 (fiscal 1992); $13,339,992 (fiscal 1990); $11,385,577 (fiscal 1989)

EIN: 55-6101813

CONTRIBUTIONS SUMMARY

Typical Recipients: • *Arts & Humanities:* Libraries • *Education:* Colleges & Universities, Public Education (Precollege), Special Education • *Health:* Hospitals • *Social Services:* People with Disabilities, Recreation & Athletics, Youth Organizations

Grant Types: general support

Geographic Distribution: focus on Cabell and Wayne Counties, WV

GIVING OFFICERS

Jimelle Bowen: exec dir

APPLICATION INFORMATION

Initial Approach: Send letter requesting application form. Deadlines are October 1 and March 1. Board meets in April and November.

GRANTS ANALYSIS

Total Grants: $529,236

Number of Grants: 12

Highest Grant: $338,819

Typical Range: $5,000 to $20,000

Disclosure Period: fiscal year ending September 30, 1992

Note: Recent grants are derived from a fiscal 1992 Form 990.

RECENT GRANTS

General

338,819	Cabell Wayne Association of Blind, Huntington, WV
59,283	West Virginia Lions Sight Conservation Foundation, Huntington, WV
40,668	Marshall University Research, Huntington, WV
40,000	Blind Ambition, Huntington, WV
34,492	Cabell County Public Schools, Huntington, WV

WISCONSIN

Andres Charitable Trust, Frank G.

CONTACT

David Myer
Trustee
Frank G. Andres Charitable Trust
c/o First Bank of Tomah
PO Box 753
Tomah, WI 54660
(608) 372-2131

FINANCIAL SUMMARY

Recent Giving: $119,752 (fiscal 1994); $123,270 (fiscal 1991); $109,460 (fiscal 1989)

Assets: $2,245,845 (fiscal 1994); $2,152,481 (fiscal 1991); $2,037,898 (fiscal 1989)

EIN: 51-0172405

CONTRIBUTIONS SUMMARY

Typical Recipients: • *Arts & Humanities:* Libraries • *Civic & Public Affairs:* Municipalities/Towns, Urban & Community Affairs • *Education:* Education Funds, Public Education (Precollege) • *Environment:* General • *Health:* Hospitals • *Social Services:* Child Welfare, Community Service Organizations, Youth Organizations

Grant Types: general support

Geographic Distribution: focus on Tomah, WI

GIVING OFFICERS

R. W. Ahlstrom: trust

Jay Charmichael: trust

Donald Kortbein: trust

David Myer: trust

Roxana O'Connor: trust, secy

Raymond Paulis: trust

APPLICATION INFORMATION

Initial Approach: Application form required. Deadline is May 15.

GRANTS ANALYSIS

Total Grants: $119,752

Typical Range: $1,000 to $8,000

Disclosure Period: fiscal year ending June 30, 1994

Note: Recent grants are derived from a fiscal 1991 Form 990. No grants list was provided for fiscal 1994.

RECENT GRANTS

Library

7,890	Tomah Public Library, Tomah, WI — on-line computer catalog

General

30,000	Tomah Memorial Hospital, Tomah, WI
15,800	Tomah Area Ambulance, Tomah, WI — rescue equipment and protective gear
13,570	Monroe County Crime Stoppers, Tomah, WI — education training
12,536	Tomah Police Department, Tomah, WI — Drug Abuse Resistance Education
9,000	Tomah Area School District, Tomah, WI — landscaping ball fields

Appleton Papers Inc.

Sales: $900.0 million
Employees: 3,600
Parent Company: Arjo Wiggins Appleton plc
Headquarters: Appleton, WI
SIC Major Group: Paper Mills and Coated & Laminated Paper Nec

CONTACT

Dennis N. Hultgren
Director, Environmental & Public Affairs
Appleton Papers Inc.
825 E Wisconsin Ave., PO Box 359
Appleton, WI 54911
(414) 734-9841

FINANCIAL SUMMARY

Recent Giving: $600,000 (1995 est.); $600,000 (1994 approx.); $500,000 (1993)

Fiscal Note: Company gives directly. Above figures include nonmonetary support.

CONTRIBUTIONS SUMMARY

Typical Recipients: • *Arts & Humanities:* Arts Associations & Councils, Libraries, Museums/Galleries, Music, Performing Arts, Visual Arts • *Civic & Public Affairs:* Business/Free Enterprise • *Education:* Colleges & Universities, Economic Education, Engineering/Technological Education, Faculty Development, Minority Education, Science/Mathematics Education, Student Aid • *Environment:* General • *Health:* Single-Disease Health Associations • *Social Services:* Child Welfare, Community Service Organizations, Counseling, Domestic Violence, Emergency Relief, Food/Clothing Distribution, People with Disabilities, Recreation & Athletics, Senior Services, Shelters/Homelessness, Substance Abuse, United Funds/United Ways, Youth Organizations

Grant Types: award, employee matching gifts, project, and scholarship

Note: Employee matching gift ratio: 1 to 1, only for education.

Nonmonetary Support: $25,000 (1993); $20,000 (1992)

Nonmonetary Support Types: donated equipment and donated products

Note: Bill Van Den Brandt, staff public relations representative, is the contact.

Geographic Distribution: principally near operating locations in Appleton, WI; Dayton, OH; and Harrisburg and Roaring Spring, PA

Operating Locations: OH (Dayton), PA (Harrisburg, Roaring Spring), WI (Appleton)

CORP. OFFICERS

Dale H. Schumaker: *B* Red Wing MN 1933 *ED* Univ WI BS 1955 *CURR EMPL* ceo, dir: Appleton Papers

GIVING OFFICERS

Dennis N. Hultgren: *B* Milwaukee WI 1946 *ED* Univ WI 1969; Univ WI 1973 *CURR EMPL* dir environmental & pub aff: Appleton Papers *CORP AFFIL* dir: Norwest Bank

APPLICATION INFORMATION

Initial Approach: *Initial Contact:* brief letter of inquiry and proposal *Include Information On:* a description of the organization, amount requested, purpose for which funds are sought, a recently audited financial statement, proof of tax-exempt status, number of people benefiting from the project, and extent of Appleton employees' involvement *Deadlines:* August or September for funding the following year

Restrictions on Giving: The company does not consider funding for the following: dinners or special events, goodwill advertising, member agencies of united funds, individuals, hospitals, fraternal organizations, political or lobbying groups, religious organizations for sectarian purposes, or groups whose agendas differ from the goals of the company.

GRANTS ANALYSIS

Total Grants: $600,000*

Typical Range: $5,000 to $10,000

Disclosure Period: 1994

Note: Total grants figure is an approximate. Recent grants are derived from a 1993 partial grants list.

RECENT GRANTS

General

20,000	St. Josephs Food Pantry
10,000	Salvation Army
5,000	Boy Scouts
5,000	Girl Scouts

Banc One Wisconsin Corp. / Banc One Wisconsin Foundation

Employees: 3,000
Parent Company: Banc One Corp.
Assets: $79.9 billion
Headquarters: Milwaukee, WI
SIC Major Group: Bank Holding Companies and National Commercial Banks

---

CONTACT

Frances G. Smyth
Secretary
Banc One Wisconsin Corp.
111 E Wisconsin Ave.
Milwaukee, WI 53201
(414) 765-3000
Note: Wisconsin organizations outside Milwaukee may contact their local branch office.

FINANCIAL SUMMARY

Recent Giving: $950,000 (1995 est.); $940,000 (1993 approx.); $938,196 (1991)

Assets: $513,905 (1991)

Fiscal Note: All contributions are made through the foundation. Above figures exclude nonmonetary support.

CONTRIBUTIONS SUMMARY

Typical Recipients: • *Arts & Humanities:* Arts Associations & Councils, Arts Funds, Historic Preservation, Libraries, Music, Theater • *Civic & Public Affairs:* Economic Development, Professional & Trade Associations, Urban & Community Affairs, Zoos/Aquariums • *Education:* Business Education, Colleges & Universities, Education Funds, Public Education (Precollege) • *Health:* Hospitals, Single-Disease Health Associations • *Social Services:* Community Centers, Delinquency & Criminal Rehabilitation, Food/Clothing Distribution, People with Disabilities, Recreation & Athletics, United Funds/United Ways, Youth Organizations

Grant Types: capital, employee matching gifts, and general support

Nonmonetary Support: $279,000 (1989)

Nonmonetary Support Types: cause-related marketing & promotion, donated equipment, in-kind services, loaned employees, loaned executives, and workplace solicitation

Geographic Distribution: near headquarters and operating locations only

Operating Locations: WI (Antigo, Appleton, Beaver Dam, Campbellsport, Elkhorn, Green Bay, Janesville, Madison, Mequon, Milwaukee, Monroe, Neenah, Oshkosh, Racine, Stevens Point, Waukesha, West Bend)

CORP. OFFICERS

Frederick Landis Cullen: *B* Cleveland OH 1947 *ED* Denison Univ BA 1970; IN Univ MBA 1972 *CURR EMPL* cfo: Banc One WI Corp *CORP AFFIL* dir: Bank One Milwaukee

Jon Robert Schumacher: *B* Milwaukee WI 1937 *ED* Valparaiso Univ 1959 *CURR EMPL* exec vp: Banc One WI Corp

GIVING OFFICERS

Frederick Landis Cullen: pres, dir *CURR EMPL* cfo: Banc One WI Corp (see above)

Michael P. Johnson: vp, dir

Timothy L. King: treas *CURR EMPL* vp: Banc One WI Corp

David Jon Kundert: vp, dir *B* Monroe WI 1942 *ED* Luther Coll 1964; Valparaiso Univ 1967 *NONPR AFFIL* mem: Am Bar Assn

James C. Lavelle: vp, dir *B* Evanston IL 1938 *ED* Univ IL BS 1961; Univ Chicago MBA 1965 *CURR EMPL* sr vp: Banc One Corp *NONPR AFFIL* pres: Milwaukee Un Performing Arts Fund; trust: Milwaukee Boys Club

Thomas C. Martin: vp, dir

Susanne A. Schilke: asst treas

Jon Robert Schumacher: vp, dir *CURR EMPL* exec vp: Banc One WI Corp (see above)

Frances G. Smyth: secy

William C. Werner: vp, dir *CURR EMPL* exec vp: Banc One WI Corp *CORP AFFIL* pres, ceo, dir: Bank One WI Trust Co

APPLICATION INFORMATION

Initial Approach: *Initial Contact:* brief letter or proposal *Include Information On:* description of the organization, amount requested, purpose for which funds are sought, and proof of tax-exempt status *Deadlines:* none

Restrictions on Giving: Does not support churches or political or lobbying groups, or provide scholarships.

OTHER THINGS TO KNOW

The foundation makes grants primarily to Milwaukee-area organizations. Other grants are approved by local banks and paid through the foundation.

GRANTS ANALYSIS

Total Grants: $940,000

Typical Range: $500 to $3,000

Disclosure Period: 1993

Note: Total grants figure is approximate. Recent grants are derived from a 1991 Form 990.

RECENT GRANTS

Library

2,000	Friends of the Ludlow Memorial Library

General

48,600	United Way
16,176	United Way
15,000	United Way of Dane County, Madison, WI
11,000	United Way of North Rock County
10,500	United Way, Dane County, Madison, WI

Banta Corp. / Banta Co. Foundation

Sales: $691.24 million
Employees: 4,100
Headquarters: Menasha, WI
SIC Major Group: Business Services, Motion Pictures, and Printing & Publishing

CONTACT
Gerald Henseler
Executive Vice President, Chief Financial Officer
Banta Corp.
225 Main St., Box 8003
Menasha, WI 54952-8003
(414) 722-7777

FINANCIAL SUMMARY
Recent Giving: $294,208 (1993); $207,978 (1990); $266,123 (1989)

Assets: $216,361 (1993); $3,621 (1990); $1,642 (1989)

Gifts Received: $500,667 (1993); $210,000 (1990); $265,000 (1989)

Fiscal Note: Contributions in 1993 were received from the Banta Corp.

EIN: 39-6050779

CONTRIBUTIONS SUMMARY
Typical Recipients: • *Arts & Humanities:* Arts Centers, History & Archaeology, Libraries, Museums/Galleries, Music • *Civic & Public Affairs:* Botanical Gardens/Parks, Business/Free Enterprise, Economic Development, General, Urban & Community Affairs • *Education:* Colleges & Universities, Education Funds, Engineering/Technological Education, General, Medical Education, Minority Education, Preschool Education, Student Aid • *Health:* Cancer, Children's Health/Hospitals, Heart, Hospitals • *Religion:* Religious Organizations, Religious Welfare • *Social Services:* Community Service Organizations, Counseling, Domestic Violence, Food/Clothing Distribution, People with Disabilities, Recreation & Athletics, United Funds/United Ways, YMCA/YWCA/YMHA/YWHA, Youth Organizations

Grant Types: general support

Geographic Distribution: focus on WI

Operating Locations: CA (San Francisco), MN (Long Prairie), MO (North Kansas City), NC (Charlotte, Mountain Home), WI (Menasha, Menasha, Milwaukee, Neenah, Rhinelander)

Note: List includes division locations

CORP. OFFICERS
Donald D. Belcher: *CURR EMPL* chmn, pres, ceo: Banta Co

GIVING OFFICERS
Calvin W. Aurand, Jr.: pres *CURR EMPL* chmn, pres, ceo, dir: Banta Corp

Dean E. Bergstrom: vp, secy, treas

Gerald A. Henseler: vp, dir *B* Hilbert WI 1940 *ED* Univ WI Madison BS 1962 *CURR EMPL* sr vp, treas, dir: Banta Corp *CORP AFFIL* dir: First Natl Bank Me Natl Academy Science *NONPR AFFIL* mem: Am Inst CPAs, Fin Execs Inst, Fox Cities Chamber Commerce; pres Y Commun Ctr Neenah

Margaret Banta Humleker: vp, dir

APPLICATION INFORMATION
Initial Approach: Send a brief letter of inquiry. Include a description of organization, amount requested, purpose of funds sought, recently audited financial statement, and proof of tax-exempt status. Deadline is November 1.

GRANTS ANALYSIS
Total Grants: $294,208
Number of Grants: 102
Highest Grant: $15,000
Typical Range: $100 to $1,000
Disclosure Period: 1993

Note: Recent grants are derived from a 1993 Form 990.

RECENT GRANTS

General

15,000	YMCA of Neenah-Menasha, Neenah, WI
10,000	Children's Hospital Foundation, Denver, CO
10,000	Lawrence University, Appleton, WI
10,000	Long Prairie Hockey Association
10,000	St. Joseph Food Program

Birnschein Foundation, Alvin and Marion

CONTACT
Peter C. Haensel
President
Alvin and Marion Birnschein Fdn.
111 E Wisconsin Ave.
Milwaukee, WI 53202
(414) 276-3400

FINANCIAL SUMMARY
Recent Giving: $191,700 (1993); $165,100 (1990); $160,600 (1989)

Assets: $3,424,015 (1993); $2,501,650 (1990); $2,800,298 (1989)

Gifts Received: $500 (1990)

EIN: 39-6126798

CONTRIBUTIONS SUMMARY
Typical Recipients: • *Arts & Humanities:* Arts Associations & Councils, Community Arts, Dance, Libraries, Opera, Performing Arts, Theater • *Civic & Public Affairs:* General, Hispanic Affairs, Law & Justice, Public Policy • *Education:* Colleges & Universities, Engineering/Technological Education • *Environment:* Wildlife Protection • *Health:* AIDS/HIV, Children's Health/Hospitals, Health Organizations, Hospitals, Long-Term Care • *Religion:* Churches, Religious Organizations, Religious Welfare • *Social Services:* Community Centers, Community Service Organizations, Domestic Violence, Food/Clothing Distribution, Homes, People with Disabilities, Senior Services, Shelters/Homelessness, United Funds/United Ways, Volunteer Services, Youth Organizations

Grant Types: general support

Geographic Distribution: focus on Milwaukee, WI

GIVING OFFICERS
Peter C. Haensel: pres, dir *PHIL AFFIL* secy: Glenn and Gertrude Humphrey Foundation; pres, dir: Schoenleber Foundation

Janet M. Moehnen: secy, dir

Loraine E. Schuffler: dir *PHIL AFFIL* pres, dir: Glenn and Gertrude Humphrey Foundation

APPLICATION INFORMATION
Initial Approach: Request application form. Deadline is August 31.

GRANTS ANALYSIS
Total Grants: $191,700
Number of Grants: 30
Highest Grant: $20,000
Typical Range: $1,000 to $15,000
Disclosure Period: 1993

Note: Recent grants are derived from a 1993 Form 990.

RECENT GRANTS

Library

10,000	Milwaukee Public Library Foundation, Milwaukee, WI — for restricted use

General

20,000	Sunrise Nursing Home for the Blind, Milwaukee, WI — for restricted use
15,000	Boys and Girls Club of Greater Milwaukee, Milwaukee, WI — for restricted use
15,000	Lutheran Counseling and Family Services, Wauwatosa, WI — for unrestricted use
10,000	Children's Hospital, Milwaukee, WI — for restricted use
10,000	Concordia University, Mequon, WI — for restricted use

Blue Cross & Blue Shield United of Wisconsin / Blue Cross & Blue Shield United of Wisconsin Foundation

Assets: $924.11 million
Employees: 1,526
Headquarters: Milwaukee, WI
SIC Major Group: Insurance Carriers

CONTACT
Tom Luljaky
Director, Corporate Communications
Blue Cross & Blue Shield United of Wisconsin
401 W Michigan
Milwaukee, WI 53203
(414) 226-5756

FINANCIAL SUMMARY
Recent Giving: $235,000 (1992); $180,171 (1990)

Assets: $47,059 (1992); $22,987 (1990)

Gifts Received: $275,000 (1992); $180,000 (1990)

Fiscal Note: In 1992, contributions were received from Blue Cross & Blue Shield United of Wisconsin ($75,000), Compcare Health Services Insurance Corp. ($100,000), United Wisconsin Insurance Co. ($70,000), and United Wisconsin Life Insurance Co. ($30,000).

EIN: 39-1514703

CONTRIBUTIONS SUMMARY
Typical Recipients: • *Arts & Humanities:* Arts Festivals, Community Arts, Libraries, Museums/Galleries, Opera, Performing Arts, Public Broadcasting, Theater • *Civic & Public Affairs:* African American Affairs, Business/Free Enterprise, Economic Development, Parades/Festivals, Public Policy • *Education:* Business Education, Colleges & Universities, Continuing Education, Education Funds, Education Reform, Faculty Development, Literacy, Student Aid • *Environment:* General • *Health:* Alzheimers Disease, Clinics/Medical Centers, Eyes/Blindness, Health Organizations, Mental Health, Prenatal Health Issues, Respiratory, Single-Disease Health Associations • *Social Services:* Community Centers, Family Services, Recreation & Athletics, Substance Abuse, United Funds/United Ways, Volunteer Services, Youth Organizations

Grant Types: general support, operating expenses, and scholarship

Geographic Distribution: limited to WI

CORP. OFFICERS
Thomas R. Hefty: *B* 1947 *ED* Univ WI BA 1968; Johns Hopkins Univ MA 1969; Univ WI Law Sch JD 1973 *CURR EMPL* chmn, pres, ceo: Blue Cross & Blue Shield Un WI *CORP AFFIL* chmn: Compcare Health Svcs Ins Corp, Un WI Ins Co, Un WI Life Ins; chmn, pres: Take Control, Un WI Proservices, Un WI Svcs

Essie Whitelaw: *CURR EMPL* pres, coo: Blue Cross & Blue Shield Un WI

GIVING OFFICERS
Mark Granoff: vp

Thomas R. Hefty: chmn, pres *CURR EMPL* chmn, pres, ceo: Blue Cross & Blue Shield Un WI (see above)

Tom Luljak: exec dir

Jeff Nohl: vp

Mary Traver: vp

Essie Whitelaw: vp *CURR EMPL* pres, coo: Blue Cross & Blue Shield Un WI (see above)

APPLICATION INFORMATION
Initial Approach: The foundation has no formal grant application procedure or application form. There are no deadlines.

Restrictions on Giving: Contribuions support nonprofit, charitable organizations with proof of 501(c)(3) status. Emphasis is on health and wellness activities, as well as other activities that add to the quality of life. Foundation will not contribute to providers or capital building projects.

GRANTS ANALYSIS
Total Grants: $235,000

Number of Grants: 117

Highest Grant: $21,200

Typical Range: $100 to $5,000

Disclosure Period: 1992

Note: Recent grants are derived from a 1992 grants list.

RECENT GRANTS
Library

1,500	Portage County Library Fund, Stevens Point, WI

General

21,200	American Lung Association, Brookfield, WI — Don't Start campaign and Waiting Game table
16,980	United Way of Greater Milwaukee, Milwaukee, WI
16,980	United Way of Greater Milwaukee, Milwaukee, WI
16,980	United Way of Greater Milwaukee, Milwaukee, WI
7,500	University of Wisconsin Foundation, Madison, WI — scholarships

Brillion Iron Works / Brillion Foundation

Sales: $100.0 million
Employees: 1,032
Parent Company: Truck Components, Inc.
Headquarters: Brillion, WI
SIC Major Group: Fabricated Metal Products, Industrial Machinery & Equipment, and Primary Metal Industries

CONTACT
Harold J. Wolf
Secretary and Treasurer
Brillion Foundation
200 Pk. Ave.
Brillion, WI 54110
(414) 756-2121

FINANCIAL SUMMARY
Recent Giving: $55,715 (fiscal 1994); $70,000 (fiscal 1993); $86,684 (fiscal 1992)

Assets: $447,532 (fiscal 1994); $437,318 (fiscal 1992); $425,989 (fiscal 1991)

Gifts Received: $50,000 (fiscal 1994); $50,000 (fiscal 1992); $100,000 (fiscal 1991)

EIN: 39-6043916

CONTRIBUTIONS SUMMARY
Typical Recipients: • *Arts & Humanities:* Historic Preservation, Libraries, Music, Public Broadcasting • *Civic & Public Affairs:* General, Municipalities/Towns, Urban & Community Affairs • *Education:* Agricultural Education, Colleges & Universities, Economic Education, General, Journalism/Media Education • *Environment:* General • *Health:* Cancer, Children's Health/Hospitals, Health Organizations, Single-Disease Health Associations • *International:* International Peace & Security Issues • *Religion:* Churches, Religious Organizations, Religious Welfare • *Social Services:* Community Service Organizations, People with Disabilities, Recreation & Athletics, Scouts, Substance Abuse, Youth Organizations

Grant Types: capital, challenge, general support, operating expenses, and scholarship

Geographic Distribution: focus on Brillion, WI

Operating Locations: WI (Brillion)

CORP. OFFICERS
J. David McClain: *CURR EMPL* pres: Brillion Iron Works

GIVING OFFICERS
Richard Larson: pres, dir

Carl Miller: dir

Lowell O. Reese: vp, dir *PHIL AFFIL* dir: R. D. and Linda Peters Foundation

Lin Wittmann: dir

Harold J. Wolf: secy, treas, dir

APPLICATION INFORMATION
Initial Approach: Send brief letter including a description of the organization, amount requested, purpose of funds sought, audited financial statement, and proof of tax-exempt status. There are no deadlines.

OTHER THINGS TO KNOW
Provides support for churches, public broadcasting, community services, and restricted scholarships.

GRANTS ANALYSIS
Total Grants: $55,715

Number of Grants: 26

Highest Grant: $10,400

Typical Range: $125 to $5,000

Disclosure Period: fiscal year ending June 30, 1994

Note: Recent grants are derived from a fiscal 1994 Form 990.

RECENT GRANTS
General

10,400	City of Brillion, Brillion, WI — swimming pool

5,000	Faith United Methodist Church, Brillion, WI
5,000	Peace United Church of Christ, Brillion, WI
5,000	St. Bartholomew Lutheran Church, Brillion, WI
5,000	St. Mary's Catholic Church, Brillion, WI

Bucyrus-Erie Company / Bucyrus-Erie Foundation

Sales: $240.0 million
Employees: 925
Parent Company: B-E Holding, Inc.
Headquarters: South Milwaukee, WI
SIC Major Group: Mining Machinery and Oil & Gas Field Machinery

CONTACT
Dennis L. Strawderman
Manager & Secretary
Bucyrus-Erie Foundation
PO Box 500
South Milwaukee, WI 53172-0500
(414) 768-5005

FINANCIAL SUMMARY
Recent Giving: $712,000 (1995 est.); $716,412 (1994 approx.); $831,481 (1993)

Assets: $11,253,138 (1989)

Fiscal Note: All giving is through the foundation.

EIN: 39-6075537

CONTRIBUTIONS SUMMARY
Typical Recipients: • *Arts & Humanities:* Arts Associations & Councils, Arts Funds, Dance, Historic Preservation, Libraries, Museums/Galleries, Music, Opera, Public Broadcasting, Theater • *Civic & Public Affairs:* Business/Free Enterprise, Economic Development, Housing, Municipalities/Towns, Professional & Trade Associations, Safety, Urban & Community Affairs, Zoos/Aquariums • *Education:* Business Education, Colleges & Universities, Economic Education, Education Funds, Elementary Education (Private), Engineering/Technological Education, Literacy, Medical Education, Minority Education, Private Education (Precollege), Public Education (Precollege), Religious Education, Science/Mathematics Education, Student Aid • *Health:* Health Organizations, Hospitals, Medical Rehabilitation, Medical Research, Single-Disease Health Associations • *Social Services:* Community Service Organizations, Day Care, Domestic Violence, Family Services, Food/Clothing Distribution, Homes, People with Disabilities, Recreation & Athletics, Senior Services, Shelters/Homelessness, United Funds/United Ways, Youth Organizations

Grant Types: capital, employee matching gifts, general support, and project

Note: Foundation matches employee gifts to education, health and social service, and the arts.

Geographic Distribution: primarily Milwaukee, WI, and communities where company has business operations or subsidiaries
Operating Locations: CA (City of Industry), ND (Jamestown), WI (Milwaukee)

CORP. OFFICERS
Phillip W. Mork: *B* Milwaukee WI 1939 *ED* Univ WI 1962; Univ WI 1963 *CURR EMPL* pres, dir: Bucyrus-Erie Co *CORP AFFIL* dir: S Milwaukee Savings Bank *NONPR AFFIL* dir: Trinity Meml Hosp

Dennis L. Strawderman: *CURR EMPL* dir pub aff, asst secy, commercial atty: Bucyrus-Erie Co

Norbert J. Verville: *CURR EMPL* vp, treas, cfo, dir: Bucyrus-Erie Co

William Bergford Winter: *B* La Crosse WI 1928 *ED* Univ WI 1951 *CURR EMPL* chmn, ceo: Bucyrus-Erie Co *CORP AFFIL* chmn: Ruston-Bucyrus Ltd; dir: First Savings Assn WI, WI Gas Co, WICOR Inc *NONPR AFFIL* mem exec bd: YMCA Metro Milwaukee *CLUB AFFIL* Milwaukee CC, Univ, Western Racquet

GIVING OFFICERS
Patrick William Cotter: dir *PHIL AFFIL* secy, dir: Stackner Family Foundation; vp, treas, dir: Ralph Evinrude Foundation

Donald E. Porter: dir

Brenton H. Rupple: dir *B* Waukeesha WI 1924 *ED* Univ WI 1948 *CURR EMPL* chmn, dir: Robert W Baird & Co

Dennis L. Strawderman: mgr, secy, dir *CURR EMPL* dir pub aff, asst secy, commercial atty: Bucyrus-Erie Co (see above)

Norbert J. Verville: treas *CURR EMPL* vp, treas, cfo, dir: Bucyrus-Erie Co (see above)

Charles Weigell: dir

William Bergford Winter: chmn, pres, dir *CURR EMPL* chmn, ceo: Bucyrus-Erie Co (see above)

APPLICATION INFORMATION
Initial Approach: *Initial Contact:* brief proposal in outline form on organization's letterhead *Include Information On:* description of the organization; amount requested; purpose for which funds are sought; size and characteristics of target population; recently audited financial statement; most recent IRS Form-990; proof of tax-exempt status under IRS code 501(c)(3) *Deadlines:* none *Note:* Above lists only the basic information required by the foundation; complete list is lengthy. Contact foundation for complete guidelines.

Restrictions on Giving: Does not give to individuals, purchase tickets or tables at dinners or other functions, or purchase goodwill advertising.

Generally does not make more than one grant per fiscal year to any one organization.

Company does not make contributions of equipment or supplies.

PUBLICATIONS
Application guidelines

GRANTS ANALYSIS
Total Grants: $716,412

Typical Range: $100 to $10,000
Disclosure Period: 1994
Note: Recent grants are derived from a 1992 Form 990.

RECENT GRANTS
General
94,874	United Way of Greater Milwaukee, Milwaukee, WI
50,240	Trinity Memorial Hospital, Cudahy, WI
26,000	South Milwaukee Police Department, S. Milwaukee, WI — D.A.R.E. Program
25,050	Children's Outing Association, Milwaukee, WI
24,183	Milwaukee School of Engineering, Milwaukee, WI

Christensen Charitable and Religious Foundation, L. C.

CONTACT
Stephen J. Smith
Secretary
L. C. Christensen Charitable and Religious Fdn.
c/o Tompson and Coated, Ltd.
PO Box 516
Racine, WI 53401
(414) 632-7541
Note: Another contact person is Harold K. Christensen, Jr., 403 Spruce St., Abbotsford, WI, 54405.

FINANCIAL SUMMARY
Recent Giving: $111,820 (1992); $95,400 (1990); $89,338 (1989)

Assets: $3,431,370 (1992); $2,184,195 (1990); $2,129,655 (1989)

EIN: 39-6096022

CONTRIBUTIONS SUMMARY
Donor(s): the late Harold K. Christensen, Sr.

Typical Recipients: • *Arts & Humanities:* Arts Associations & Councils, Community Arts, Historic Preservation, Libraries, Music, Performing Arts • *Civic & Public Affairs:* Housing, Municipalities/Towns, Safety, Urban & Community Affairs, Zoos/Aquariums • *Education:* Colleges & Universities, Education Funds, Literacy, Private Education (Precollege), Public Education (Precollege), Secondary Education (Private), Secondary Education (Public) • *Environment:* General • *Health:* Children's Health/Hospitals, Health Organizations • *Religion:* Churches, Religious Welfare • *Social Services:* Camps, Child Welfare, Community Service Organizations, Family Services, Homes, People with Disabilities, Recreation & Athletics, Senior Services, Youth Organizations

Grant Types: general support

Geographic Distribution: focus on Racine, WI

GIVING OFFICERS
Harold K. Christensen, Jr.: pres

John E. Erskine, Jr.: dir

Russel I. Kortendick, Sr.: vp

Dennis E. Schelling: dir

Stephen J. Smith: secy

John F. Thompson: treas

APPLICATION INFORMATION
Initial Approach: The foundation requests applications be made in writing. There are no deadlines.

GRANTS ANALYSIS
Total Grants: $111,820

Number of Grants: 39

Highest Grant: $22,500

Typical Range: $500 to $8,000

Disclosure Period: 1992

Note: Recent grants are derived from a 1992 Form 990.

RECENT GRANTS

Library

945	City of Abbotsford Library, Abbottsford, WI — Clements Encyclopedia of World Governments

General

22,500	Racine County Zoo, Racine, WI
20,000	Lincoln Lutheran Community Care Center, Racine, WI — restore center
8,000	Abbotsford High School, Abbotsford, WI — POP program
7,500	Kick in for Kids, Racine, WI — Racine Soccer Association
5,000	Racine Habitat for Humanity, Racine, WI — challenge grant

Consolidated Papers, Inc. / Consolidated Papers Foundation, Inc.

Sales: $947.34 million
Employees: 4,946
Headquarters: Wisconsin Rapids, WI
SIC Major Group: Paper Mills, Pulp Mills, Paperboard Mills, and Corrugated & Solid Fiber Boxes

CONTACT
Susan Feith
Vice President and Executive Director
Consolidated Papers Foundation, Inc.
PO Box 3
Wisconsin Rapids, WI 54495-0003
(715) 424-3004

FINANCIAL SUMMARY
Recent Giving: $1,485,000 (1995 est.); $1,485,000 (1994 approx.); $1,066,032 (1993)

Assets: $35,409,263 (1993); $31,582,000 (1992); $28,620,000 (1991)

Gifts Received: $1,268,030 (1993); $1,536,984 (1992)

Fiscal Note: Above figures are for the foundation only. Company also makes limited gifts directly from corporate funds which are not included in the figures listed above. In 1993, the foundation received $750,000 from Consolidated Papers, $468,530 from Emily Baldwin Trust, $24,250 from Ruth B. Barker, and $25,250 from Sally M. Hands.

EIN: 39-6040071

CONTRIBUTIONS SUMMARY
Typical Recipients: • *Arts & Humanities:* Arts Associations & Councils, Arts Institutes, Community Arts, Historic Preservation, History & Archaeology, Libraries, Museums/Galleries, Music, Performing Arts, Public Broadcasting, Theater • *Civic & Public Affairs:* Economic Development, Municipalities/Towns, Public Policy, Safety, Zoos/Aquariums • *Education:* Arts/Humanities Education, Business Education, Colleges & Universities, Economic Education, Education Funds, Engineering/Technological Education, General, Literacy, Medical Education, Minority Education, Science/Mathematics Education, Secondary Education (Private), Student Aid • *Health:* Health Organizations, Hospices, Hospitals, Trauma Treatment • *Science:* Scientific Centers & Institutes • *Social Services:* Animal Protection, Community Service Organizations, Family Planning, People with Disabilities, Recreation & Athletics, United Funds/United Ways, Youth Organizations

Grant Types: capital, employee matching gifts, endowment, general support, project, and scholarship

Note: Employee matching gift ratio: 1 to 1.

Geographic Distribution: primarily near headquarters and operating locations in central Wisconsin

Operating Locations: IL (Chicago), NY (New York), WI (Adams, Biron, Rhinelander, Stevens Point, Whiting, Wisconsin Rapids)

CORP. OFFICERS
Patrick Francis Brennan: *B* New York NY 1931 *ED* Fordham Univ 1957; Harvard Univ Advanced Mgmt Program 1983 *CURR EMPL* pres, ceo, coo, dir: Consolidated Papers Inc *CORP AFFIL* dir: Betz Labs Inc, Consolidated Water Power Co, Mead Realty, Northland Cranberries Inc *NONPR AFFIL* dir paper science & engg: Univ MN Coll Natural Resources; mem: Am Forest & Paper Assn, Am Paper Inst *CLUB AFFIL* Bulls Eye CC, Rotary

Susan Feith: *CURR EMPL* dir pub aff: Consolidated Papers Inc

James R. Kolinski: *B* 1939 *ED* Univ WI Stevens Point BS 1961 *CURR EMPL* vp: Consolidated Papers Inc

George Wilson Mead II: *B* Milwaukee WI 1927 *ED* Yale Univ BS 1950; Inst Paper Chem MS 1952 *CURR EMPL* chmn, dir: Consolidated Papers Inc *CORP AFFIL* chmn: Firstar Bank Wisconsin Rapids; dir: Firstar Corp, Newaygo Timber Co Ltd, Snap-On Tools Inc; pres, dir: Consolidated Water Power Co; vchmn, dir: Natl Counc *NONPR AFFIL* dir: Consolidated Civic Fdn, Natl Counc Air Stream Improvement; mem: Am

Paper Inst, Tech Assn Pulp & Paper Indus; trust: Inst Paper Chem, Lawrence Univ *CLUB AFFIL* Chicago, Elks, Milwaukee Athletic, Rotary

GIVING OFFICERS
Patrick Francis Brennan: dir *CURR EMPL* pres, ceo, coo, dir: Consolidated Papers Inc (see above)

Susan Feith: vp, exec dir, dir *CURR EMPL* dir pub aff: Consolidated Papers Inc (see above)

Richard John Kenney: dir *B* Evanston IL 1941 *ED* Loras Coll BA 1963; IN Univ MBA 1965 *CURR EMPL* vp fin: Consolidated Papers Inc *CORP AFFIL* vp: Walker Parking Consult/Engrs

James R. Kolinski: dir *CURR EMPL* vp: Consolidated Papers Inc (see above)

David Krommenacker: dir

Carl R. Lemke: secy *ED* Univ WI BBA 1965 *CURR EMPL* asst secy: Consolidated Papers Inc *CORP AFFIL* secy, asst treas: Hotel Mead Corp

J. Richard Matsch: treas

Emily B. McKay: dir

George Wilson Mead II: pres, dir *CURR EMPL* chmn, dir: Consolidated Papers Inc (see above)

APPLICATION INFORMATION
Initial Approach: *Initial Contact:* brief letter or proposal *Include Information On:* description of the organization, amount requested, purpose for which funds are sought, recently audited financial statement, and proof of IRS nonprofit status *Deadlines:* end of March for June meeting; end of September for fall meetings

Restrictions on Giving: There are no restrictions or limitations on grants. However, educational institions and charities geographically close to corporate installations of Consolidated Papers, Inc. have been favored in the past.

GRANTS ANALYSIS
Total Grants: $1,066,032

Number of Grants: 129

Highest Grant: $131,580

Average Grant: $8,264

Typical Range: $1000 to $15,000

Disclosure Period: 1993

Note: Recent grants are derived from a 1993 Form 990.

RECENT GRANTS

Library

20,000	Stevens Point Library, Stevens Point, WI — capital
5,000	Pittsville Community Library, Pittsville, WI — capital

General

131,580	United Way South Wood County, Wisconsin Rapids, WI
75,745	National Merit Scholarship Corporation, Evanston, IL — scholarships
52,000	Wisconsin Foundation of Independent Colleges,

	Milwaukee, WI —
	scholarships
40,000	Assumption High School, Wisconsin Rapids, WI
37,400	Marquette University, Milwaukee, WI

Cremer Foundation

CONTACT
James A. Berkenstadt
Administrator
Cremer Fdn.
PO Box 1
Madison, WI 53701
(608) 837-5166

FINANCIAL SUMMARY
Recent Giving: $155,200 (1993); $98,968 (1992); $101,650 (1991)

Assets: $2,516,025 (1993); $2,470,856 (1992); $2,387,782 (1991)

Gifts Received: $63,000 (1989); $245,000 (1988)

EIN: 39-6086822

CONTRIBUTIONS SUMMARY
Typical Recipients: • *Arts & Humanities:* Arts Festivals, Libraries • *Civic & Public Affairs:* Housing, Urban & Community Affairs • *Education:* Colleges & Universities, Elementary Education (Public), Literacy, Medical Education, Special Education, Student Aid • *Health:* Arthritis, Children's Health/Hospitals, Geriatric Health, Health Organizations, Mental Health, Nursing Services • *Religion:* Religious Welfare • *Social Services:* At-Risk Youth, Child Welfare, Community Centers, Community Service Organizations, Family Planning, Family Services, Food/Clothing Distribution, Homes, People with Disabilities, Scouts, Senior Services, United Funds/United Ways, YMCA/YWCA/YMHA/YWHA, Youth Organizations

Grant Types: general support, scholarship, and seed money

Geographic Distribution: limited to the Madison and Baraboo, WI, area

GIVING OFFICERS
James A. Berkenstadt: admin, dir

Holly L. Cremer: treas, dir

Helen A. George: secy

Frederick W. Haberman: vp, dir *PHIL AFFIL* dir: R. D. and Linda Peters Foundation

H. B. Klotzbach: dir

James T. Skyes: pres

Robert R. Stroud: dir

APPLICATION INFORMATION
Initial Approach: The foundation requests applications be made in writing. There are no deadlines.

Restrictions on Giving: Limited to Madison, WI.

PUBLICATIONS
Application Guidelines

GRANTS ANALYSIS
Total Grants: $155,200

Number of Grants: 25

Highest Grant: $25,000

Typical Range: $500 to $20,000

Disclosure Period: 1993

Note: Recent grants are derived from a 1993 Form 990.

RECENT GRANTS
Library
| 2,200 | Deerfield Public Library, Deerfield, WI — for funding for a handicap accessible entrance |

General
25,000	Colonial Club Group Home, Sun Prairie, WI — for assistance for elderly residents
20,000	Southern Wisconsin Foodbank, Madison, WI — for funding to expand foodbank facility
15,000	University of Wisconsin Foundation, Madison, WI — for funding for epidemiologist at University of Wisconsin Medical School
11,000	Madison Literacy Council, Madison, WI — for training and pairing volunteer tutors with students in need of literacy assistance
10,000	Briarpatch, Madison, WI — for crisis intervention and run-away program

---

DEC International, Inc. / DEC International-Albrecht Foundation

Sales: $100.0 million
Employees: 750
Headquarters: Madison, WI
SIC Major Group: Food & Kindred Products, Holding & Other Investment Offices, and Industrial Machinery & Equipment

CONTACT
Eli Durst
Office Manager
DEC International, Inc.
PO Box 8050
Madison, WI 53708
(608) 222-3484
Note: Contact's extension number is 203.

FINANCIAL SUMMARY
Recent Giving: $46,440 (1994); $37,970 (1993); $35,000 (1992 approx.)

Assets: $1,416 (1990); $309 (1989)

Gifts Received: $36,500 (1990); $25,500 (1989)

EIN: 39-6075225

CONTRIBUTIONS SUMMARY
Typical Recipients: • *Arts & Humanities:* Arts Centers, Community Arts, General, Libraries, Performing Arts • *Civic & Public Affairs:* Economic Development, General, Zoos/Aquariums • *Education:* Agricultural Education, Business Education, Economic Education, General • *Environment:* General • *Health:* General, Health Organizations, Hospitals • *Social Services:* Animal Protection, Community Centers, General, Senior Services, United Funds/United Ways, Volunteer Services, Youth Organizations

Grant Types: general support

Geographic Distribution: focus on Dane County, WI

Operating Locations: WI (Lodi, Madison, Stanley)

CORP. OFFICERS
H. Moe: *CURR EMPL* pres, dir: DEC Intl

GIVING OFFICERS
Randal A. Albrecht: secy, dir

Eli Durst: treas

APPLICATION INFORMATION
Initial Approach: Send a brief letter of inquiry. Include a description of organization, amount requested, purpose of funds sought, and proof of tax-exempt status. There are no deadlines.

Restrictions on Giving: Does not support individuals, religious organizations for sectarian purposes, political or lobbying groups, or organizations outside operating areas.

GRANTS ANALYSIS
Total Grants: $37,970

Typical Range: $100 to $500

Disclosure Period: 1993

First Financial Bank FSB / First Financial Foundation

Sales: $334.41 million
Employees: 1,409
Parent Company: First Financial Corp
Headquarters: Stevens Point, WI
SIC Major Group: Depository Institutions

CONTACT
Judy Buchanan
Assistant Secretary
First Financial Bank FSB
1305 Main St.
Stevens Point, WI 54481
(715) 341-0400

FINANCIAL SUMMARY
Recent Giving: $104,064 (1992); $82,119 (1990)

Assets: $569,142 (1992); $315,411 (1990)

Gifts Received: $240,000 (1992); $144,000 (1990)

Fiscal Note: In 1992, contributions were received from First Financial Bank, F.S.B.

EIN: 39-1277461

CONTRIBUTIONS SUMMARY

Typical Recipients: • *Arts & Humanities:* Libraries, Museums/Galleries, Music, Performing Arts, Public Broadcasting • *Civic & Public Affairs:* Chambers of Commerce, Clubs, Economic Development, General, Housing, Municipalities/Towns • *Education:* Agricultural Education, Colleges & Universities, Economic Education, Student Aid • *Environment:* General • *Health:* AIDS/HIV, Children's Health/Hospitals, Clinics/Medical Centers, Health Funds, Hospitals, Medical Research • *Religion:* Religious Organizations • *Social Services:* Community Centers, Community Service Organizations, People with Disabilities, Recreation & Athletics, United Funds/United Ways, Youth Organizations

Grant Types: capital, employee matching gifts, and general support

Geographic Distribution: giving limited to areas of business in WI and IL

Operating Locations: WI (Stevens Point)

CORP. OFFICERS

Robert S. Gaiswinkler: *CURR EMPL* chmn, dir: First Fin Bank FSB

Tom Newschaffer: *CURR EMPL* exec vp, cfo: First Fin Bank FSB

John C. Seramur: *B* 1943 *CURR EMPL* pres, ceo, dir: First Fin Bank FSB

GIVING OFFICERS

David W. Drought: treas

Robert S. Gaiswinkler: dir *CURR EMPL* chmn, dir: First Fin Bank FSB (see above)

G. M. Haferbecker: dir

Richard N. Hunter: dir

Robert M. Salinger: secy *B* Milwaukee WI 1950 *ED* Univ WI BA 1972; Univ WI JD 1976 *CORP AFFIL* chmn: First Fin Political Action comm; exec vp: First Fin Bank; gen couns,secy: First Fin Corp *NONPR AFFIL* mem: Am Bar Assn, Corp Couns Assn, WI Bar Assn *CLUB AFFIL* Order Coif, Rotary, Stevens Point CC,

John C. Seramur: dir *CURR EMPL* pres, ceo, dir: First Fin Bank FSB (see above)

Ralph R. Staven: pres, mgr

David H. Waite: chmn

APPLICATION INFORMATION

Initial Approach: Application form required. Deadline is October 31.

Restrictions on Giving: The foundation does not make grants to individuals.

GRANTS ANALYSIS

Total Grants: $104,064

Number of Grants: 86

Highest Grant: $20,983

Typical Range: $500 to $5,000

Disclosure Period: 1992

Note: Recent grants are derived from a 1992 Form 990.

RECENT GRANTS

Library
5,000	Stevens Point Public Library, Stevens Point, WI	
2,500	Whitewater Public Library, Whitewater, WI — building fund	
500	Twin Lakes Library, Twin Lakes, WI	

General
20,983	United Way, Portage County, WI	
6,773	United Way, Greater St. Louis, IL	
5,284	United Way, Milwaukee, WI	
5,164	United Way, Branches, WI	
5,000	Lawton Medical Research Foundation, Marshfield, WI	

Firstar Bank Milwaukee, N.A. / Firstar Milwaukee Foundation

Former Foundation Name: First Wisconsin Foundation
Sales: $5.3 billion
Employees: 2,967
Parent Company: Firstar Corp.
Headquarters: Milwaukee, WI
SIC Major Group: National Commercial Banks

CONTACT

Dennis Fredrickson
Secretary-Treasurer
Firstar Milwaukee Foundation
777 E Wisconsin Ave.
Milwaukee, WI 53202
(414) 765-4579

FINANCIAL SUMMARY

Recent Giving: $1,500,000 (1995 est.); $1,518,000 (1994 approx.); $1,425,000 (1993 approx.)

Assets: $6,016,000 (1995); $6,016,000 (1994); $5,542,000 (1993)

Gifts Received: $950,000 (1992)

Fiscal Note: The company makes contributions through the foundation. The Public Affairs department also makes contributions with a budget of $20,000 annually. Anne Curley, vice president, is the contact for departmental support. Above figures exclude nonmonetary support. In 1992, gifts were received from Firstar Bank Milwaukee, N.A.

EIN: 39-6042050

CONTRIBUTIONS SUMMARY

Typical Recipients: • *Arts & Humanities:* Arts Centers, Arts Institutes, Ballet, Dance, Historic Preservation, Libraries, Museums/Galleries, Music, Opera, Performing Arts, Theater • *Civic & Public Affairs:* Business/Free Enterprise, Civil Rights, Economic Development, Employment/Job Training, Hispanic Affairs, Parades/Festivals, Urban & Community Affairs, Women's Affairs, Zoos/Aquariums • *Education:* Business Education, Colleges & Universities, Economic Education, Engineering/Technological Education, Literacy, Medical Education, Minority Education, Secondary Education (Public), Student Aid • *Health:* Children's Health/Hospitals, Clinics/Medical Centers, Heart, Hospitals, Nursing Services, Single-Disease Health Associations, Transplant Networks/Donor Banks • *Religion:* Jewish Causes, Religious Welfare • *Social Services:* Child Welfare, Community Centers, Community Service Organizations, Delinquency & Criminal Rehabilitation, Family Services, People with Disabilities, Recreation & Athletics, Senior Services, Shelters/Homelessness, Substance Abuse, United Funds/United Ways, Volunteer Services, Youth Organizations

Grant Types: capital, general support, multiyear/continuing support, and operating expenses

Nonmonetary Support Types: donated products, loaned employees, and loaned executives

Note: Value of nonmonetary support is unavailable. Contact for nonmonetary support is Anne Curley, vice president.

Geographic Distribution: Wisconsin, with emphasis on Milwaukee

Operating Locations: AZ (Phoenix), FL (West Palm Beach), IA (Ames, Burlington, Cedar Falls, Cedar Rapids, Council Bluffs, Davenport, Des Moines, Mt Pleasant, Ottumwa, Red Oak, Sioux City), IL (Bolingbrook, Glen Ellyn, Naperville, Northbrook, Park Forest), MN (Bloomington, Brogan, Hugo, Minneapolis, New Brighton, Roseville, St. Anthony, St. Louis Park, Stillwater), WI (Brookfield, Cedarburg, Eau Claire, Eldorado, Fond du Lac, Grantsburg, Green Bay, Greenfield, Madison, Manitowoc, Mayfair, Menasha, Mequon, Milwaukee, Minocqua, Oshkosh, Portage, Princeton, Racine, Rice Lake, Sheboygan, Two Rivers, Waukesha, Waunahee, Wausau, Wisconsin Rapids)

CORP. OFFICERS

John A. Becker: *B* Kenosha WI 1942 *ED* Marquette Univ 1963; Marquette Univ 1965 *CURR EMPL* pres, coo, dir: Firstar Corp *CORP AFFIL* dir: Giddings & Lewis Corp *NONPR AFFIL* chmn: Milwaukee Econ Devel Corp; mem: Greater Madison Chamber Commerce; mem fin comm: WI Bankers Assn; trust: Edgewood Coll, Marquette Univ *CLUB AFFIL* Madison, Maple Bluff CC

Arnold Curley: *CURR EMPL* vp pub aff: Firstar Bank Milwaukee NA

Roger Leon Fitzsimonds: *B* Milwaukee WI 1938 *ED* Univ WI Milwaukee BBA 1960; Univ WI Milwaukee MBA 1971 *CURR EMPL* chmn, ceo, dir: Firstar Corp *CORP AFFIL* dir: First WI Natl Bank Milwaukee, First WI Trust Co *NONPR AFFIL* bd dirs: Milwaukee Boys & Girls Clubs; bd dirs, mem exec comm: Assn Bank Holding Cos; chmn adv counc: Univ WI Sch Bus; chmn bd dirs: Columbia Health Sys, Greater Milwaukee Comm; dir: Competitive WI Inc, Metro Milwaukee Assn Commerce; mem: Am Bankers Assn, Assn Reserve City Bankers, Bus Roundtable, WI Assn Mfrs & Commerce *CLUB AFFIL* Milwaukee, Milwaukee CC

GIVING OFFICERS

Chris Michael Bauer: pres *B* Milwaukee WI 1948 *ED* Univ WI BBA 1970; Marquette Univ MBA 1976 *CURR EMPL* chmn, ceo:

Firstar Bank Milwaukee NA *NONPR AFFIL* dir: Bankers Roundtable, Jr Achievement, Milwaukee Pub Lib Fdn, Milwaukee World Festival Inc, Next Door Fdn, St Lukes Med Ctr, Un Way Greater Milwaukee, Univ WI Milwaukee Fdn; mem: Univ WI Bus Alumni Assn *CLUB AFFIL* Milwaukee CC, Univ, Westmoor CC

Ned W. Bechtold: dir

John A. Becker: vchmn *CURR EMPL* pres, coo, dir: Firstar Corp (see above)

Ann L. Curley: asst secy, asst treas *B* Oak Park IL 1953 *ED* Northwestern Univ 1975; Marquette Univ 1988 *CURR EMPL* vp pub aff: Firstar Corp

Roger Leon Fitzsimonds: chmn *CURR EMPL* chmn, ceo, dir: Firstar Corp (see above)

Dennis Fredrickson: secy-treas

John H. Hendee, Jr.: dir *B* Milwaukee WI 1926 *ED* Williams Coll BA 1949; Univ WI MBA 1956 *CORP AFFIL* dir: Firstar Corp

Sheldon B. Lubar: dir *B* Milwaukee WI 1929 *ED* Univ WI BA 1951; Univ WI LLB 1953 *CURR EMPL* chmn, pres, ceo, coo, dir: Christiana Cos *CORP AFFIL* chmn: Lubar & Co; dir: Briggs & Stratton Corp, Firstar Corp, MA Mutual Life Ins Co, MGIC Investment Corp, Milwaukee Ins Group, Schwitzer Inc *PHIL AFFIL* vp, secy, dir: Lubar Family Foundation

Robert Joseph O'Toole: dir *B* Chicago IL 1941 *ED* Loyola Univ BS 1961 *CURR EMPL* pres, ceo, chmn: AO Smith Corp *CORP AFFIL* dir: AgriStor Credit Corp, First WI Natl Bank, Metalsa SA, Protection Mutual Ins Co, Protection Mutual Ins Co, Smith Fiberglass Products Inc, AO Smith Harvestore Products Inc *NONPR AFFIL* dir: Metro Milwaukee Assn Commerce; mem: Bus Roundtable, Competitive WI Inc, Greater Milwaukee Comm, Mfrs Alliance Productivity & Innovation; mem exec comm: TEC XIV, WI Mgrs & Commerce Assn *CLUB AFFIL* Milwaukee CC, Univ *PHIL AFFIL* vp: A.O. Smith Foundation, Inc.

William H. Risch: vp *B* Stevens Point WI 1938 *ED* Univ WI BBA 1959; Univ WI MBA 1971 *CURR EMPL* chmn, ceo: Firstar Corp

APPLICATION INFORMATION

Initial Approach: *Initial Contact:* brief letter or proposal *Include Information On:* description of the organization; amount requested; purpose for which funds are sought; recently audited financial statement; proof of tax-exempt status; budget for both project and organization; names of officers and directors; history of achievement; description of program activities and goals; other pertinent material *Deadlines:* none

Restrictions on Giving: Foundation does not make grants to individuals and does not match grants or make loans. Rarely supports endowments or research.

GRANTS ANALYSIS

Total Grants: $1,518,000

Number of Grants: 160

Highest Grant: $328,000

Average Grant: $9,500

Typical Range: $500 to $5,000

Disclosure Period: 1994

Note: Above figures provided by the Company. Recent grants are derived from a 1992 Form 990.

RECENT GRANTS

Library

7,000	Milwaukee Public Library, Milwaukee, WI — computer equipment

General

292,500	United Way of Greater Milwaukee, Milwaukee, WI — 1991 pledge
100,000	New Hope Project, Milwaukee, WI — operating programs
43,000	University of Wisconsin Foundation at Madison, Madison, WI — capital campaign
40,000	Columbia Hospital, Milwaukee, WI — capital campaign
35,000	Froedtert Memorial Lutheran Hospital, Milwaukee, WI — capital campaign

---

Fleming Cos. Food Distribution Center / Godfrey Foundation

Sales: $560.0 million
Employees: 4,500
Parent Company: Fleming Cos., Inc.
Headquarters: Waukesha, WI
SIC Major Group: Agricultural Production— Crops, Agricultural Production— Livestock, Food & Kindred Products, and Food Stores

CONTACT

Ronald Lusic
President
Fleming Companies Food Distribution Center
1200 W Sunset Dr.
Waukesha, WI 53186-6597
(414) 542-9311

FINANCIAL SUMMARY

Recent Giving: $88,588 (1991); $55,688 (1990); $64,102 (1989)

Assets: $517,954 (1991); $474,607 (1990); $423,293 (1989)

Gifts Received: $100,000 (1991); $75,000 (1990); $85,000 (1989)

EIN: 23-7423938

CONTRIBUTIONS SUMMARY

Typical Recipients: • *Arts & Humanities:* Arts Festivals, Arts Institutes, Historic Preservation, History & Archaeology, Libraries, Museums/Galleries, Opera, Performing Arts • *Civic & Public Affairs:* African American Affairs, Clubs, Economic Development, General, Municipalities/Towns, Parades/Festivals, Professional & Trade Associations, Urban & Community Affairs • *Education:* Business Education, Colleges & Universities, Private Education (Precollege), Secondary Education (Private) • *Environment:* General • *Health:* Arthritis, Health Organizations, Hospitals, Prenatal Health Issues, Single-Disease Health Associations, Transplant Networks/Donor Banks • *Religion:* Ministries, Religious Organizations, Religious Welfare • *Social Services:* Child Welfare, Community Service Organizations, Family Services, Senior Services, United Funds/United Ways

Geographic Distribution: central VA

Operating Locations: WI (Marshfield, Palmyra, Waukesha, Waukesha, West Allis)

CORP. OFFICERS

Ronald Lusic: *CURR EMPL* pres: Fleming Cos Food Distr Ctr

GIVING OFFICERS

James H. DeWees: pres, dir

Allen C. Gehrke: dir *B* Milwaukee WI 1934 *CURR EMPL* sr vp corp devel: Godfrey Co *NONPR AFFIL* mem: Food Mktg Inst, WI Food Dealers Assn

Michael J. George: vp, dir *B* Milwaukee WI 1947 *ED* Marquette Univ 1969

Rodger G. Scott: dir

APPLICATION INFORMATION

Initial Approach: Send a brief letter of inquiry and a full proposal. Include amount requested, purpose of funds sought, and a description of organization. Deadline in August 31.

GRANTS ANALYSIS

Total Grants: $88,588

Number of Grants: 59

Highest Grant: $50,000

Typical Range: $250 to $2,500

Disclosure Period: 1991

Note: Recent grants are derived from a 1991 Form 990.

RECENT GRANTS

Library

1,000	Whitewater Public Library, Whitewater, WI

General

50,000	University of Virginia, Charlottesville, VA
25,000	Blue Ridge School, Dyke, VA
25,000	Corporation for Jefferson's Poplar Forest, Forest, VA
25,000	St. Christopher's School, Richmond, VA
25,000	Virginia Union University, Richmond, VA

Janesville Foundation

CONTACT
Alan W. Dunwiddie, Jr.
President
Janesville Fdn.
PO Box 8123
Janesville, WI 53547-8123
(608) 752-1032

FINANCIAL SUMMARY
Recent Giving: $534,139 (1992); $466,630 (1989)

Assets: $8,494,961 (1992); $8,223,512 (1989)

Gifts Received: $6,145 (1992)

Fiscal Note: In 1992, major contributions were received from G.S. Parker High S chool (Macke Fund) ($3,528) and Richard F. Schwarer ($2,000).

EIN: 39-6034645

CONTRIBUTIONS SUMMARY
Donor(s): Merchants and Savings Bank, The Parker Pen Co., and others.

Typical Recipients: • *Arts & Humanities:* Historic Preservation, History & Archaeology, Libraries, Music • *Civic & Public Affairs:* General, Housing, Municipalities/Towns, Nonprofit Management, Parades/Festivals, Professional & Trade Associations • *Education:* Colleges & Universities, International Studies, Private Education (Precollege), Public Education (Precollege), Student Aid • *Health:* Emergency/Ambulance Services, Health Organizations • *Religion:* Religious Welfare • *Social Services:* Community Service Organizations, United Funds/United Ways, Youth Organizations

Grant Types: capital, conference/seminar, multiyear/continuing support, project, scholarship, and seed money

Geographic Distribution: limited to Janesville, WI; scholarships limited to Janesville, WI, high school students.

GIVING OFFICERS
Roger E. Axtell: vp

Alfred Peter Diotte: vp, dir *B* Newport NH 1925 *ED* Marquette Univ BS 1950; Univ WI JD 1953; Univ WI MBA 1979 *CURR EMPL* pres: DOTT Assocs Ltd *CORP AFFIL* dir: Valley Bancorp, Valley Bank *NONPR AFFIL* mem: Am Bar Assn, Rock County Bar Assn, WI Bar Assn

Alan W. Dunwiddie, Jr.: pres, exec dir

Rowland J. McClellan: dir

George S. Parker: chmn, dir *B* Janesville WI 1925 *ED* Brown Univ BA 1951; Univ MI MA 1952 *CORP AFFIL* pres: Caxambas Assocs FL *NONPR AFFIL* fellow: Lake Forest Academy; trust emeritus: Beloit Coll, Brown Univ

Phyllis Saevre: secy, treas

APPLICATION INFORMATION
Initial Approach: Send a brief letter of inquiry. Deadlines are January 15, April 15, July 15, and October 15.

Restrictions on Giving: Limited to Janesville, WI, area.

PUBLICATIONS
Informational Brochure (including Application Guidelines)

GRANTS ANALYSIS
Total Grants: $534,139

Number of Grants: 52

Highest Grant: $100,000

Typical Range: $100 to $10,000

Disclosure Period: 1992

Note: Recent grants are derived from a 1992 Form 990.

RECENT GRANTS
Library

1,000	Foundation Center, New York, NY

General

100,000	United Way of Northern Rock County, Madison, WI
100,000	United Way of Northern Rock County, Madison, WI
40,000	Marquette University, Milwaukee, WI
40,000	Marquette University, Milwaukee, WI
30,000	Forward Foundation, WI

Johnson Controls Inc. / Johnson Controls Foundation

Revenue: $6.87 billion
Employees: 56,000
Headquarters: Milwaukee, WI
SIC Major Group: Environmental Controls, Public Building & Related Furniture, Unsupported Plastics Film & Sheet, and Plastics Bottles

---

CONTACT
Valerie Adisek
Administrative Secretary
Johnson Controls Fdn.
5757 N Green Bay Ave.
Box 591
Milwaukee, WI 53201-0591
(414) 228-2296

FINANCIAL SUMMARY
Recent Giving: $3,650,000 (1995 est.); $3,765,000 (1994 approx.); $3,841,827 (1993)

Assets: $20,586,841 (1993); $18,058,677 (1991); $16,679,236 (1990)

Fiscal Note: Figures above are for foundation only; company provides some direct giving through local branches. Above figures exclude nonmonetary support.

EIN: 39-6036639

CONTRIBUTIONS SUMMARY
Typical Recipients: • *Arts & Humanities:* Arts Associations & Councils, Arts Centers, Arts Festivals, Arts Funds, Arts Institutes, Dance, Historic Preservation, Libraries, Museums/Galleries, Music, Opera, Performing Arts, Public Broadcasting • *Civic & Public Affairs:* Business/Free Enterprise, Civil Rights, Economic Development, Housing, Nonprofit Management, Professional & Trade Associations, Urban & Community Affairs, Women's Affairs, Zoos/Aquariums • *Education:* Agricultural Education, Business Education, Colleges & Universities, Community & Junior Colleges, Continuing Education, Economic Education, Education Associations, Education Funds, Elementary Education (Private), Engineering/Technological Education, General, Literacy, Medical Education, Minority Education, Science/Mathematics Education, Student Aid • *Environment:* General • *Health:* Children's Health/Hospitals, Clinics/Medical Centers, Health Organizations, Hospitals, Public Health, Single-Disease Health Associations, Transplant Networks/Donor Banks • *International:* International Relations • *Religion:* Religious Welfare • *Science:* Scientific Centers & Institutes • *Social Services:* Child Welfare, Community Centers, Community Service Organizations, Counseling, Family Services, Food/Clothing Distribution, People with Disabilities, Recreation & Athletics, Senior Services, Substance Abuse, United Funds/United Ways, Youth Organizations

Grant Types: capital, emergency, employee matching gifts, general support, and multiyear/continuing support

Nonmonetary Support Types: in-kind services

Note: Nonmonetary support is provided directly by the company. No estimate is available for the value of this support.

Geographic Distribution: in Wisconsin and nationally

Operating Locations: AL (Tuscaloosa), AR (Texarkana), CA (City of Industry, Fullerton, Livermore, Los Angeles, Milpitas, Modesta, Stockton), CO (Denver), DE (Middletown, New Castle), FL (Cape Canaveral, Orlando, Tampa), GA (Atlanta, Cumming), IL (Geneva, Itasca, Sycamore), IN (Franklin, Goshen, Greencastle, Ossian, Vincennes), KS (Lexena), KY (Bardstown, Cadiz, Florence, Georgetown, Glasgow, Harrodsburg, Lexington, Louisville, Maysville, Nicholasville), LA (Shreveport), MA (East Longmeadow), MD (Belcamp, North East), MI (Ann Arbor, Lapeer, Madison Heights, Manchester, Mt. Clemens, Novi, Owosso, Plymouth, Saline, Sault Ste. Marie, Whitmore Lake, Williamston), MO (Jefferson City, St. Joseph), NC (Winston-Salem), NH (Merrimack), NJ (Edison, Pine Brook, Somerville), NY (Middletown), OH (Columbus, Greenfield, Strongsville, Toledo, Warren), OK (Poteau), OR (Canby), PA (Erie, Pittsburgh), SC (Columbia, Oconee), TN (Athens, Lewisburg, Lexington, Linden, Murfreesboro, Pulaski), TX (Carrollton, Dallas, Ft. Worth, Garland, New Braunfels), VT

(Bennington), WA (Tacoma), WI (Milwaukee, Watertown)

Note: Also has 130 branch offices of systems and services divisions in all 50 states. Operates internationally in Canada, England, Germany, Italy, Japan, Mexico, and the Netherlands.

CORP. OFFICERS

James Henry Keyes: *B* LaCrosse WI 1940 *ED* Marquette Univ BS 1962; Northwestern Univ MBA 1963 *CURR EMPL* chmn, pres, ceo, dir: Johnson Controls Inc *CORP AFFIL* dir: Baird Capital Devel Fund, First WI Trust Co, LSI Logic Corp, Universal Foods Corp *NONPR AFFIL* active: Milwaukee Symphony Orchestra; mem: Am Inst CPAs, Fin Execs Inst, Machinery & Allied Products Inst, WI Soc CPAs

GIVING OFFICERS

Valerie Adisek: admin secy

Fred L. Brengel: dir *B* Hicksville NY 1923 *ED* FL Inst Tech BSME 1944 *CORP AFFIL* dir: First WI Corp, Harley-Davidson Inc, Heil Co, WI Bell

James Henry Keyes: adv *CURR EMPL* chmn, pres, ceo, dir: Johnson Controls Inc (see above)

R. Douglas Ziegler: adv *B* Milwaukee WI 1927 *ED* Northwestern Univ 1949 *CURR EMPL* chmn: Ziegler Co *CORP AFFIL* chmn: Ziegler Asset Mgmt Co; dir: Applied Power, Johnson Controls Inc, Maxicare Health Plans Inc, Prin Preservation Portfolios, Ziegler Fin Corp, Ziegler Leasing Corp, Ziegler Securities, Ziegler Thrift Trading *PHIL AFFIL* vp, secy, treas, dir: Ziegler Foundation

APPLICATION INFORMATION

Initial Approach: *Initial Contact:* one- or two-page letter on organization letterhead *Include Information On:* proof of tax-exempt status; description of the organization's structure, purpose, history, and programs and a list of current officers and governing board members, including their outside affiliations; summary of need for support and its intended use; geographic area served; current income and expense budget and copy of most recent audited financial statement; statement of other funding sources; copy of 501 (c)(3) status letter *Deadlines:* none *Note:* In preliminary stage, personal visits, phone calls to the foundation, and video tapes are discouraged.

Restrictions on Giving: Foundation does not support individuals; private foundations or endowment funds; political or lobbying groups; goodwill advertising; fraternal, veterans, or labor groups; or organizations based or located outside the United States. Additionally, generally does not support precollege educational institutions; individual medical or academic research; sectarian institutions whose services are limited to members of any one religious group or whose funds are used primarily for religious purposes; industrial groups or industrial trade associations; testimonials, fund-raising events, tickets to benefits, or shows; advertising; or travel, tours, seminars, conferences, or publications.

Company does not donate equipment, products, or labor.

GRANTS ANALYSIS

Total Grants: $3,841,827

Number of Grants: 1,290

Highest Grant: $151,451

Average Grant: $2,525*

Typical Range: $500 to $5,000

Disclosure Period: 1993

Note: Average grant figure excludes five grants totaling $596,389. Recent grants are derived from a 1993 Form 990.

RECENT GRANTS

General

151,451	Washtenaw United Way, Ann Arbor, MI
119,310	United Way of Greater Milwaukee, Milwaukee, WI
112,814	United Way of Greater Milwaukee, Milwaukee, WI
112,814	United Way of Greater Milwaukee, Milwaukee, WI
100,000	Pave, Milwaukee, WI

Johnson & Son, S.C. / Johnson's Wax Fund

Sales: $2.59 billion
Employees: 13,800
Headquarters: Racine, WI
SIC Major Group: Polishes & Sanitation Goods, Soap & Other Detergents, Toilet Preparations, and Agricultural Chemicals Nec

---

CONTACT

Reva Holmes
Vice President & Secretary
The Johnson's Wax Fund
1525 Howe St., Mail Sta. 809
Racine, WI 53403
(414) 631-2826

FINANCIAL SUMMARY

Recent Giving: $3,000,000 (fiscal 1995 est.); $2,598,318 (fiscal 1994 approx.); $1,625,776 (fiscal 1993)

Assets: $4,966,446 (fiscal 1992); $1,553,051 (fiscal 1991); $2,180,164 (fiscal 1989)

Fiscal Note: Giving figures are for fund only. Company also administers an informal corporate donations program that supports the Johnson Foundation, a private operating foundation, and provides direct corporate support totaling $500,000 to $1 million annually. Above figures exclude nonmonetary support.

EIN: 39-6052089

CONTRIBUTIONS SUMMARY

Typical Recipients: • *Arts & Humanities:* Arts Associations & Councils, Arts Centers, Arts Funds, Community Arts, Ethnic & Folk Arts, Historic Preservation, Libraries, Museums/Galleries, Music, Performing Arts, Public Broadcasting, Theater • *Civic & Public Affairs:* Business/Free Enterprise, Civil

Rights, Economic Development, Employment/Job Training, Housing, Law & Justice, Municipalities/Towns, Professional & Trade Associations, Public Policy, Safety, Urban & Community Affairs, Zoos/Aquariums • *Education:* Arts/Humanities Education, Business Education, Colleges & Universities, Economic Education, Education Funds, International Exchange, Medical Education, Minority Education, Private Education (Precollege), Public Education (Precollege), Science/Mathematics Education, Secondary Education (Private), Special Education, Student Aid • *Environment:* Air/Water Quality, General, Resource Conservation • *Health:* Children's Health/Hospitals, Clinics/Medical Centers, Health Organizations, Hospitals, Medical Research, Medical Training, Nutrition, Single-Disease Health Associations • *International:* International Relations • *Religion:* Religious Welfare • *Social Services:* Animal Protection, Child Welfare, Community Service Organizations, Delinquency & Criminal Rehabilitation, Emergency Relief, Family Services, Homes, Recreation & Athletics, Scouts, United Funds/United Ways, YMCA/YWCA/YMHA/YWHA, Youth Organizations

Grant Types: employee matching gifts, fellowship, general support, project, scholarship, and seed money

Geographic Distribution: nationally, but primarily in Wisconsin and the Midwest

Operating Locations: CA, FL (Miami), GA (Ft. Valley), MA, MN, MO, NY, TN, TX (San Antonio), WI (Racine)

CORP. OFFICERS

James F. DiMarco: *B* 1935 *ED* Univ MN BS 1959; Univ MN MA 1964 *CURR EMPL* sr vp: SC Johnson & Son Inc

William Douglas George, Jr.: *B* Chicago IL 1932 *ED* DePauw Univ BA 1954; Harvard Univ MBA 1959 *CURR EMPL* pres, ceo, dir: SC Johnson & Son Inc *CORP AFFIL* dir: Arvin Indus Inc, Moorman Mfg Co, Ralcorp Holdings Inc

Rogers Grothans: *ED* Earlham Coll 1959; Purdue Univ 1962 *CURR EMPL* vp: SC Johnson & Son Inc

Samuel Curtis Johnson: *B* Racine WI 1928 *ED* Cornell Univ BA 1950; Harvard Univ MBA 1952 *CURR EMPL* chmn, dir: SC Johnson & Son Inc *CORP AFFIL* chmn: Heritage WI Corp, Johnson Heritage Bancorp, Johnson Intl Bancorp, Johnson Worldwide Assocs; dir: John Deere & Co, H J Heinz Co, Mobil Corp *NONPR AFFIL* bd regents: Smithsonian Assocs; mem adv counc: Cornell Univ Johnson Grad Sch Mgmt; trust emeritus: Cornell Univ *PHIL AFFIL* chmn: Johnson Foundation, Johnson Foundation Trust *CLUB AFFIL* Am, Cornell, Racine CC, Univ

GIVING OFFICERS

William Douglas George, Jr.: vchmn *CURR EMPL* pres, ceo, dir: SC Johnson & Son Inc (see above)

Rogers Grothans: trust *CURR EMPL* vp: SC Johnson & Son Inc (see above)

Sue A. Helland: trust

Reva A. Holmes: vp, secy, trust

Samuel Curtis Johnson: chmn, pres, trust
CURR EMPL chmn, dir: SC Johnson & Son
Inc (see above)

Donald M. Milestone: trust

Julie A. Ringo: asst secy

John M. Schroeder: treas

APPLICATION INFORMATION
Initial Approach: *Initial Contact:* brief letter or proposal *Include Information On:* statement of purpose and brief history of organization, description of the overall program, explanation regarding specific request for support, itemized annual and project budgets, list of corporate and foundation donors, proof of tax-exempt status *Deadlines:* funding cycle deadlines are March 1, July 1, and November 1

Restrictions on Giving: The fund does not support individuals; social, athletic, veterans, labor, or fraternal organizations; or churches. A program may be considered if it is not restricted to organization members and is available to the community as a whole. The fund also does not support political actions or lobbying efforts; national health fund drives or national health organizations; or salary or wage support. Fund does not make individual grants to United Way agencies for operating expenses, but will consider major capital requests.

The Johnson Foundation, Inc., an entirely separate institution, operates the Wingspread Conference Center and also receives contributions from S.C. Johnson & Son, Inc. Therefore, the fund generally does not support conferences, workshops, or seminars.

OTHER THINGS TO KNOW
Foundation encourages phone calls to get detailed information before applying for grants.

The fund should not be the sole funding source for an organization or its program, but may be sole source for a specific program. Fund considers only one request per organization during a one-year period. Generally, only one major grant is made in a given fiscal year, and most grants are for a one-year period only.

Preference is given to agencies and programs in the communities in which company employees live and work and to organizations and projects not primarily or normally financed by public tax funds. Grants outside the United States are rare.

Corporation contributes at least 5% of pretax profit to nonprofit organizations.

If seed money is the purpose of the contribution, specific plans for future operating expenses and funding for projects must be provided.

Most grants shall be made to private institutions and organizations receiving no tax support; contributions to tax-supported organizations shall not be automatically excluded, but must be for projects in which the fund has a specific interest.

PUBLICATIONS
Social Responsibility Report of SC Johnson Wax and The Johnson's Wax Fund, Inc., contributions policy and guidelines pamphlet

GRANTS ANALYSIS
Total Grants: $2,598,318

Number of Grants: 91

Highest Grant: $379,338

Average Grant: $28,553

Typical Range: $1,000 to $30,000

Disclosure Period: fiscal year ending June 30, 1994

Note: Fiscal information for fund only. Recent grants are derived from a fiscal 1994 annual report.

RECENT GRANTS

General

379,338	Sons and Daughters Scholarship Program — for scholarships and fellowships
100,000	Boy Scouts of America Southeastern Wisconsin Council, WI — for social, cultural, and community concerns
100,000	Racine Zoological Society, Racine, WI — for medical, health, and environmental protection
60,000	Racine Area Soccer Association, Racine, WI — for social, cultural, and community concerns
50,000	Medical College of Wisconsin, Milwaukee, WI — for medical, health, and environmental protection

Lunda Charitable Trust

CONTACT
Carl Holmquist
Trustee
Lunda Charitable Trust
620 Gebhardt Rd.
Black River Falls, WI 54615-9152
(715) 284-9491

FINANCIAL SUMMARY
Recent Giving: $42,883 (1992); $4,300 (1990)

Assets: $2,304,985 (1992); $438,621 (1990)

Gifts Received: $690,812 (1992); $300,000 (1990)

Fiscal Note: In 1992, contributions were received from Milton Lunda.

EIN: 39-6491037

CONTRIBUTIONS SUMMARY
Typical Recipients: • *Arts & Humanities:* Libraries • *Civic & Public Affairs:* General, Safety • *Health:* Hospitals, Long-Term Care • *Religion:* Religious Welfare • *Social Services:* Community Service Organizations, Day Care, People with Disabilities, Recreation & Athletics

Grant Types: general support

GIVING OFFICERS
Carl Holmquist: trust

Larry Lunda: trust

Lydia Lunda: trust

Milton Lunda: trust

Marlee Slifka: trust

APPLICATION INFORMATION
Initial Approach: The foundation reports no specific application guidelines. Send a brief letter of inquiry, including statement of purpose, amount requested, and proof of tax-exempt status.

GRANTS ANALYSIS
Total Grants: $42,883

Number of Grants: 15

Highest Grant: $18,600

Typical Range: $500 to $4,400

Disclosure Period: 1992

Note: Recent grants are derived from a 1992 Form 990.

RECENT GRANTS

Library

2,000	Black River Public Library, Black River Falls, WI

General

18,600	Black River Falls Fire Department, Black River Falls, WI — rescue truck
4,400	River Front, Black River Falls, WI — transportation vehicle
3,200	City Parks and Recreation Department, Black River Falls, WI — handicap accessible picnic table backstops
3,050	Black River Youth Hockey, Black River Falls, WI — bleachers
2,016	Black River Falls Memorial Hospital, Black River Falls, WI — patient entertainment equipment

Madison Gas & Electric Co. / Madison Gas & Electric Foundation

Revenue: $244.0 million
Employees: 721
Headquarters: Madison, WI
SIC Major Group: Electric, Gas & Sanitary Services

CONTACT
James Boll
Assistant Vice President, Law & Corporate Communications
Madison Gas & Electric Co.
PO Box 1231
Madison, WI 53701-1231
(608) 252-7923

FINANCIAL SUMMARY

Recent Giving: $174,169 (1993); $164,883 (1992); $159,264 (1990)

Assets: $4,148,427 (1993); $3,903,905 (1992); $2,514,433 (1990)

Gifts Received: $57,514 (1993); $135,940 (1992); $1,050,257 (1990)

Fiscal Note: In 1993, contributions were received from Edward R. Felber Estate ($1,014) and Madison Gas & Electric Co. ($56,500).

EIN: 39-6098118

CONTRIBUTIONS SUMMARY

Typical Recipients: • *Arts & Humanities:* Arts Associations & Councils, Arts Centers, Community Arts, History & Archaeology, Libraries, Museums/Galleries, Music, Public Broadcasting, Theater • *Civic & Public Affairs:* African American Affairs, Botanical Gardens/Parks, Business/Free Enterprise, Chambers of Commerce, Clubs, Economic Development, General, Safety, Women's Affairs, Zoos/Aquariums • *Education:* Business-School Partnerships, Colleges & Universities, Education Funds, Elementary Education (Public), Minority Education, Preschool Education, Public Education (Precollege), Secondary Education (Public), Student Aid • *Environment:* General • *Health:* AIDS/HIV, Health Organizations, Heart, Hospitals, Medical Research, Single-Disease Health Associations • *Religion:* Religious Organizations, Religious Welfare • *Social Services:* Child Welfare, Community Centers, Community Service Organizations, Domestic Violence, Family Services, Food/Clothing Distribution, Homes, People with Disabilities, Recreation & Athletics, Scouts, Senior Services, United Funds/United Ways, Veterans, YMCA/YWCA/YMHA/YWHA, Youth Organizations

Grant Types: general support and research

Geographic Distribution: focus on WI

Operating Locations: WI (Madison)

CORP. OFFICERS

David C. Mebane: *B* Toledo OH 1933 *ED* AZ St Univ 1957; Univ WI 1960 *CURR EMPL* chmn, pres, ceo, dir: Madison Gas & Electric Co

GIVING OFFICERS

Robert E. Domek: asst secy, dir

Donald J. Helfrecht: chmn, dir

Joseph T. Krzos: treas, dir

David C. Mebane: vp, dir *CURR EMPL* chmn, pres, ceo, dir: Madison Gas & Electric Co (see above)

Richard H. Thies: asst treas

Frank C. Vondrasek, Jr.: pres, dir *B* Omaha NE 1928 *ED* IA St Coll BSEE 1949; Creighton Univ MBA 1965

Carol A. Wiskowski: secy, dir

Gary J. Wolter: vp, dir

APPLICATION INFORMATION

Initial Approach: Send brief letter requesting application form. There are no deadlines.

Restrictions on Giving: Organization must be located within Madison Gas & Electric Co.'s service territory in order to be considered

GRANTS ANALYSIS

Total Grants: $174,169

Number of Grants: 74

Highest Grant: $75,755

Typical Range: $50 to $55,000

Disclosure Period: 1993

Note: Recent grants are derived from a 1993 Form 990.

RECENT GRANTS

Library

2,500	Lodi City Library, Lodi City, WI
1,000	Mazomanie Depot Library, Mazomanie Depot, WI

General

75,755	University of Wisconsin Foundation, Madison, WI
55,000	United Way of Dane County, Madison, WI — for multiple charities
5,000	Edgewood College, Madison, WI
5,000	YMCA, Madison, WI
3,000	Tenney Nursery and Parent Center, Madison, WI

Marquette Electronics, Inc. / Marquette Electronics Foundation

Sales: $250.2 million
Employees: 1,356
Headquarters: Milwaukee, WI
SIC Major Group: Electromedical Equipment

CONTACT

Bill Browne
Manager
Marquette Electronics Foundation
8200 W Tower Ave.
Milwaukee, WI 53223
(414) 355-5000
Note: The company's World Wide Web address is http://www.mei.com

FINANCIAL SUMMARY

Recent Giving: $700,000 (1995 est.); $700,000 (1994 approx.); $500,000 (1993 approx.)

Assets: $320,259 (1991)

Gifts Received: $387,541 (1991)

Fiscal Note: Contributes through foundation only. In fiscal 1991, contributions were received from Marquette Electronics, Inc.

CONTRIBUTIONS SUMMARY

Typical Recipients: • *Arts & Humanities:* Arts Associations & Councils, Arts Festivals, Community Arts, Dance, Historic Preservation, Libraries, Literary Arts, Museums/Galleries, Music, Opera, Public Broadcasting, Theater • *Civic & Public Affairs:* Municipalities/Towns, Zoos/Aquariums • *Education:* Arts/Humanities Education, Engineering/Technological Education, Literacy, Medical Education, Private Education (Precollege), Student Aid • *Health:* Medical Research, Nursing Services, Single-Disease Health Associations • *Social Services:* Child Welfare, Community Centers, Recreation & Athletics, United Funds/United Ways

Grant Types: general support

Geographic Distribution: focus on Milwaukee, WI

Operating Locations: CT (Wallingford), FL (Jupiter), WI (Milwaukee)

CORP. OFFICERS

Michael J. Cudahy: *CURR EMPL* pres, dir: Marquette Electronics Inc

Mary M. Kabacinski: *CURR EMPL* vp, treas: Marquette Electronics Inc

Frederick George Luber: *B* Milwaukee WI 1925 *ED* Purdue Univ 1950 *CURR EMPL* chmn: Super Steel Products Corp *CORP AFFIL* dir: Interstate Drop Forge, Marquette Electronics Inc, Milwaukee Resistor; pres, dir: W Capital; ptnr, dir: Marquette Capital; trust: Northwestern Mutual Life Ins Co

GIVING OFFICERS

B. K. Allen: trust

William D. Browne: mgr

Michael J. Cudahy: trust *CURR EMPL* pres, dir: Marquette Electronics Inc (see above)

Mary M. Kabacinski: treas *CURR EMPL* vp, treas: Marquette Electronics Inc (see above)

Frederick George Luber: trust *CURR EMPL* chmn: Super Steel Products Corp (see above)

M. S. Newman: trust *CORP AFFIL* dir: Marquette Electronics Inc

APPLICATION INFORMATION

Initial Approach: *Initial Contact:* brief letter *Include Information On:* specific amount requested and minimum necessary materials *Deadlines:* none

GRANTS ANALYSIS

Total Grants: $700,000*

Typical Range: $500 to $6,000

Disclosure Period: 1994

Note: Total grants figure is approximate. Recent grants are derived from a 1990 grants list.

RECENT GRANTS

Library

1,000	Milwaukee Public Library, Milwaukee, WI

General

29,250	Zoological Society of Milwaukee County, Milwaukee, WI
25,901	UPAF, Milwaukee, WI
25,000	Rx for Reading in Wisconsin, Milwaukee, WI
20,000	United Way, Milwaukee, WI
10,000	Marquette University, Milwaukee, WI

Mautz Paint Co. / Mautz Paint Foundation

Employees: 250
Headquarters: Madison, WI
SIC Major Group: Chemicals & Allied Products

CONTACT
Bernhard F. Mautz, Jr.
Chairman
Mautz Paint Co.
939 E Washington Ave.
Madison, WI 53703
(608) 255-1661

FINANCIAL SUMMARY
Recent Giving: $69,568 (fiscal 1993); $73,954 (fiscal 1991); $70,776 (fiscal 1989)

Assets: $588,873 (fiscal 1993); $660,504 (fiscal 1991); $686,326 (fiscal 1989)

EIN: 39-6040508

CONTRIBUTIONS SUMMARY
Typical Recipients: • *Arts & Humanities:* Arts Centers, General, History & Archaeology, Libraries, Museums/Galleries, Music, Opera, Performing Arts, Public Broadcasting, Theater • *Civic & Public Affairs:* Clubs, Employment/Job Training, General, Housing, Women's Affairs, Zoos/Aquariums • *Education:* Agricultural Education, Colleges & Universities, General, Literacy, Preschool Education, Private Education (Precollege), Public Education (Precollege), Religious Education, Secondary Education (Public), Student Aid • *Environment:* Wildlife Protection • *Health:* Children's Health/Hospitals, Heart • *Religion:* Churches • *Social Services:* Animal Protection, Big Brother/Big Sister, General, Homes, Scouts, United Funds/United Ways, Veterans, Volunteer Services, Youth Organizations

Grant Types: professorship

Geographic Distribution: giving primarily in WI and MN

Operating Locations: WI (Madison)

CORP. OFFICERS
Robert J. Gurske: *CURR EMPL* pres: Mautz Paint Co

Bernhard F. Mautz, Jr.: *CURR EMPL* chmn: Mautz Paint Co

GIVING OFFICERS
Nathan Brand: dir

Robert J. Gurske: dir *CURR EMPL* pres: Mautz Paint Co (see above)

Ken Kimport: dir

Bernhard F. Mautz, Jr.: dir *CURR EMPL* chmn: Mautz Paint Co (see above)

Louise U. Mautz: dir

APPLICATION INFORMATION
Initial Approach: Send a full proposal. Include a description of organization, purpose of funds sought, and proof of tax-exempt status. There are no deadlines. Company will not respond to phone calls. Only organizations chosen favorably will be notified. A decision is made usually within two weeks.

Restrictions on Giving: Does not support individuals, religious organizations for sectarian purposes, political or lobbying groups, or organizations outside operating areas.

OTHER THINGS TO KNOW
Awards grants only to areas where company-owned stores are located.

GRANTS ANALYSIS
Total Grants: $69,568

Number of Grants: 66

Highest Grant: $5,000

Typical Range: $25 to $5,000

Disclosure Period: fiscal year ending November 30, 1993

Note: Recent grants are derived from a fiscal 1993 Form 990.

RECENT GRANTS

Library

100	Portage Library Building Fund, Portage, WI — for government programs	

General

9,000	Project Home, Philadelphia, PA — for help for disadvantaged	
5,000	Leelanau Schools, Leelanau, WI — for youth welfare	
5,000	United Way of Dane County, Madison, WI — for help for disadvantaged	
4,400	University of Wisconsin Foundation, Madison, WI — for youth welfare	
3,000	Grace Episcopal Church, Sterling, IL — for churches	

Mielke Family Foundation

CONTACT
Paul Groth
Vice President
Mielke Family Fdn.
10 Sunnyslope Ct.
Appleton, WI 54914
(414) 734-3416

FINANCIAL SUMMARY
Recent Giving: $255,587 (1993); $221,064 (1992); $195,105 (1989)

Assets: $5,945,806 (1993); $5,727,890 (1992); $4,787,015 (1989)

EIN: 39-6074258

CONTRIBUTIONS SUMMARY
Typical Recipients: • *Arts & Humanities:* Ballet, Community Arts, Libraries, Museums/Galleries, Public Broadcasting • *Civic & Public Affairs:* Community Foundations • *Education:* Arts/Humanities Education, Colleges & Universities, General, Public Education (Precollege), Student Aid • *Environment:* General • *Health:* Hospitals • *Social Services:* Community Centers, People with Disabilities, Recreation & Athletics

Grant Types: general support

Geographic Distribution: limited to the Appleton and Shawano, WI, areas

GIVING OFFICERS
Harold C. Adams: dir

Paul H. Groth: vp, dir

Phillip Keller: vp, dir

Dr. John E. Mielke: dir

Marion Nemetz: dir

Warren F. Parsons: secy, treas, dir *B* St Louis MO 1910 *ED* DePauw Univ 1962; IN Univ 1966 *CURR EMPL* pres, ceo: Boldt (Oscar J) Construction Co *CORP AFFIL* pres, ceo: Boldt (Oscar J) Construction Co

Jeffrey Riester: pres, dir

APPLICATION INFORMATION
Initial Approach: Send letter describing program. Include a description of organization, amount requested, purpose of funds sought, recently audited financial statement, and proof of tax-exempt status. Deadlines are April 15 and October 15.

GRANTS ANALYSIS
Total Grants: $255,587

Number of Grants: 17

Highest Grant: $76,500

Typical Range: $2,000 to $57,364

Disclosure Period: 1993

Note: Recent grants are derived from a 1993 Form 990.

RECENT GRANTS

Library

20,000	Appleton Public Library Foundation, Appleton, WI — for educational purposes	

General

76,500	Lawrence University, Appleton, WI — for educational purposes	
57,364	Community Foundation for the Fox Valley Region, WI — for support of arts and education	
22,000	Shawano/Gresham School District, Shawano, WI — for educational purposes	
10,500	Appleton Area School District, Appleton, WI — for educational purposes	
8,000	Shawano Community Hospital, Shawano, WI — for health service	

Mosinee Paper Corp. / Mosinee Paper Corp. Foundation

Revenue: $266.7 million
Employees: 1,300
Headquarters: Mosinee, WI
SIC Major Group: Paper & Allied Products

CONTACT
Theresa Legner
Manager, Pension & Savings
Mosinee Paper Corp.
1244 Kronenwetter Dr.
Mosinee, WI 54455-9099
(715) 693-4470

FINANCIAL SUMMARY
Recent Giving: $127,417 (1994); $130,974 (1993); $93,971 (1992)
Assets: $3,247 (1993); $11,469 (1992); $74,821 (1989)
Gifts Received: $123,000 (1993); $45,000 (1992); $55,000 (1989)
Fiscal Note: In 1993, contributions were received from the Mosinee Paper Corp.
EIN: 39-6074298

CONTRIBUTIONS SUMMARY
Typical Recipients: • *Arts & Humanities:* Arts Associations & Councils, Arts Festivals, Community Arts, General, Historic Preservation, History & Archaeology, Libraries, Museums/Galleries, Performing Arts, Theater, Visual Arts • *Civic & Public Affairs:* Botanical Gardens/Parks, Business/Free Enterprise, Chambers of Commerce, Community Foundations, Economic Development, General, Municipalities/Towns, Philanthropic Organizations, Professional & Trade Associations, Public Policy • *Education:* Business Education, Colleges & Universities, Education Funds, General, Public Education (Precollege), Science/Mathematics Education • *Environment:* General, Resource Conservation, Wildlife Protection • *Health:* AIDS/HIV, Cancer, Children's Health/Hospitals, Emergency/Ambulance Services, General, Hospitals, Single-Disease Health Associations • *Social Services:* Camps, Community Service Organizations, Family Services, General, People with Disabilities, Recreation & Athletics, Scouts, Special Olympics, United Funds/United Ways, Volunteer Services, YMCA/YWCA/YMHA/YWHA, Youth Organizations

Grant Types: capital, general support, and scholarship

Nonmonetary Support Types: donated products

Geographic Distribution: in headquarters and operating communities

Operating Locations: KY (Harrodsburg), MS (Jackson), OH (Middletown), WI (Columbus, Mosinee)

CORP. OFFICERS
Theresa M. Legner: *CURR EMPL* mgr pension & savings: Mosinee Paper Corp

Daniel R. Olvey: *CURR EMPL* pres, dir: Mosinee Paper Corp

GIVING OFFICERS
Walter Alexander: dir

Richard Jacobus: dir

Theresa M. Legner: asst secy *CURR EMPL* mgr pension & savings: Mosinee Paper Corp (see above)

Daniel R. Olvey: pres, dir *CURR EMPL* pres, dir: Mosinee Paper Corp (see above)

San Watterson Orr, Jr.: vp, dir *B* Madison WI 1941 *ED* Univ WI 1963; Univ WI JD 1966 *CURR EMPL* chmn, ceo, dir: Wausau Paper Mills Co *CORP AFFIL* chmn: Mosinee Paper Corp; dir: Marshall & Ilsley Corp, MDU Resources Group Inc *PHIL AFFIL* dir: Wausau Paper Mills Foundation; trust: John and Alice Forester Charitable Trust; vp, dir: Aytchmonde Woodson Foundation

Gary P. Peterson: secy, asst treas *CURR EMPL* secy: Mosinee Paper Corp *PHIL AFFIL* treas: IASD Health Care Foundation

Richard L. Radt: treas, dir *B* Chicago IL 1932 *ED* Univ IL 1956

APPLICATION INFORMATION
Initial Approach: Company provides scholarships to graduating seniors of the local high school. Applications should be addressed to the Principal of the Mosinee High School, 1000 High St., Mosinee, WI 54455, (715) 693-3200. For general requests, send a brief letter of inquiry and a full proposal. Include a description of organization, amount requested, purpose of funds sought, and proof of tax-exempt status. There are no deadlines.

Restrictions on Giving: Does not support individuals, religious organizations for sectarian purposes, political or lobbying groups, or organizations outside operating areas.

GRANTS ANALYSIS
Total Grants: $130,974

Number of Grants: 45

Highest Grant: $29,000

Typical Range: $50 to $12,000

Disclosure Period: 1993

Note: Recent grants are derived from a 1993 Form 990.

RECENT GRANTS

Library
5,000	Marathon County Public Library, Wausau, WI	

General
29,000	United Way of Marathon County, Wausau, WI	
12,000	Middletown Area United Way, Middletown, OH	
10,526	McDevco, Wausau, WI	
10,200	Wausau Area Community Foundation, Wausau, WI	
10,000	Wausau YMCA Foundation, Wausau, WI	

Peters Foundation, R. D. and Linda

CONTACT
Richard Hugo
Assistant Treasurer and Assistant Secretary
R. D. and Linda Peters Fdn.
c/o Bank One Wisconsin Trust Co., N.A.
PO Box 1308
Milwaukee, WI 53202
(414) 765-2800

FINANCIAL SUMMARY
Recent Giving: $250,800 (1993); $278,400 (1991); $381,924 (1990)
Assets: $5,322,377 (1993); $5,180,289 (1991); $5,068,758 (1990)
EIN: 39-6097994

CONTRIBUTIONS SUMMARY
Donor(s): the late R. D. Peters

Typical Recipients: • *Arts & Humanities:* Libraries • *Civic & Public Affairs:* Municipalities/Towns • *Education:* Colleges & Universities, Medical Education, Public Education (Precollege), Science/Mathematics Education, Secondary Education (Public), Student Aid • *Environment:* General • *International:* International Environmental Issues • *Religion:* Churches, Religious Organizations, Religious Welfare • *Social Services:* Homes, People with Disabilities, Senior Services, YMCA/YWCA/YMHA/YWHA

Grant Types: general support, research, and scholarship

Geographic Distribution: focus on the Brillion, WI, area

GIVING OFFICERS
Bank One Wisconsin Trust Co.: trust

John P. Botsch: dir

Frederick W. Haberman: dir *PHIL AFFIL* vp, dir: Cremer Foundation

Richard Hugo: asst secy, asst treas

Lowell O. Reese: dir *PHIL AFFIL* vp, dir: Brillion Foundation

Harold Wolf: dir

Edmond C. Young: dir

APPLICATION INFORMATION
Initial Approach: Send cover letter and full proposal. Include a description of organization, amount requested, purpose of funds sought, recently audited financial statement, and proof of tax-exempt status. There are no deadlines. Board meets quarterly.

GRANTS ANALYSIS
Total Grants: $250,800

Number of Grants: 15

Highest Grant: $80,000

Typical Range: $500 to $62,500

Disclosure Period: 1993

Note: Recent grants are derived from a 1993 Form 990.

RECENT GRANTS

Library
3,000   Brillion Public Library Trust, Brillion, WI — for general support

General
80,000   Brillion High School Scholarship Fund, Brillion, WI — for scholarships
62,500   Medical College of Wisconsin, Milwaukee, WI — for endowment for prevention of eye disease
36,000   Northland College, Ashland, WI — for classroom and parking area construction
25,000   YMCA, Milwaukee, WI — for grounds improvements
15,000   St. Mary's Catholic Church, Brillion, WI — for religious purposes

Phillips Family Foundation, L. E.

CONTACT
Eileen Phillips Cohen
Director
L. E. Phillips Family Foundation
c/o National Presto Industries
3925 N Hastings Way
Eau Claire, WI 54703
(715) 839-2139

FINANCIAL SUMMARY
Recent Giving: $2,500,428 (fiscal 1994); $2,166,573 (fiscal 1992); $1,987,391 (fiscal 1991)

Assets: $47,104,201 (fiscal 1994); $52,771,528 (fiscal 1992); $47,054,224 (fiscal 1991)

Gifts Received: $127,201 (fiscal 1993); $127,201 (fiscal 1992); $127,201 (fiscal 1991)

Fiscal Note: In fiscal 1993, contributions were received from Edith Phillips 1983 Charitable Trust.

EIN: 39-6046126

CONTRIBUTIONS SUMMARY
Donor(s): Lewis E. Phillips established the L. E. Phillips Charities in Wisconsin in 1943. The foundation's name recently was changed to the L. E. Phillips Family Foundation. Mr. Phillips was president and director of the manufacturing business of Ed Phillips and Sons Company. He was head of National Presto Industries, formerly named the National Pressure Cooker Company, for over 25 years. The foundation is administered primarily by members of the Phillips family, including Lewis E. Phillip's son-in-law, Melvin Samuel Cohen, who is the current chairman of National Presto Industries.

Typical Recipients: • *Arts & Humanities:* Libraries • *Civic & Public Affairs:* Philan-thropic Organizations, Public Policy, Safety • *Education:* Colleges & Universities • *Health:* Hospitals • *Religion:* Synagogues/Temples • *Social Services:* Recreation & Athletics, United Funds/United Ways, Youth Organizations

Grant Types: capital, general support, operating expenses, research, and scholarship

Geographic Distribution: primarily northwestern Wisconsin, with emphasis on Eau Claire and Chippewa counties

GIVING OFFICERS
James F. Bartl: secy, dir *B* St Paul MN 1940 *ED* St Thomas Univ 1962; Marquette Univ JD 1965 *CURR EMPL* secy, couns, dir industrial rels: Natl Presto Indus *NONPR AFFIL* mem: Am Soc Corp Secys

Eileen Phillips Cohen: dir *PHIL AFFIL* trust: The Presto Foundation

Maryjo Rose Cohen: vp, treas, dir *B* Eau Claire WI 1952 *ED* Univ MI 1973; Univ MI JD 1976 *CURR EMPL* pres, ceo, coo, cfo, dir: Natl Presto Indus Inc *CORP AFFIL* secy, asst treas, dir: Natl Holding Investment Co; secy, treas, dir: Canton Sales & Storage Co, Century Leasing & Liquidating Inc, Natl Defense Corp, Presto Export Ltd, Presto Mfg Co; vp, dir: Natl Automatic Pipeline Oper Inc, Natl Pipeline Co; vp, secy, treas, dir: Jackson Sales & Storage Co *PHIL AFFIL* vp, treas, trust: The Presto Foundation

Melvin Samuel Cohen: pres, dir *B* Minneapolis MN 1918 *ED* Univ MN BS 1939; Univ MN JD 1941 *CURR EMPL* chmn: Natl Presto Indus Inc *CORP AFFIL* chmn, pres: Presto Mfg Co; chmn, pres, dir: Natl Presto Indus Export Corp, Presto Intl Ltd; pres: Canton Sales & Storage Co, Century Leasing & Liquidating Inc, Natl Defense Corp, Natl Holding Investment Co, Presto Export Ltd; pres, dir: Jackson Sales Storage Co; vp, dir: Natl Automatic Pipeline Oper Inc, Natl Pipeline Co *PHIL AFFIL* chmn, pres, trust: The Presto Foundation

Allen D. Hanson: asst secy, asst treas *B* 1936 *PHIL AFFIL* vchmn: Harvest States Foundation

Edith Phillips: vp, dir

APPLICATION INFORMATION
Initial Approach:

The foundation has no formal application requirements or procedures. Applicants should send a letter of inquiry.

The letter should describe the organization and project for which funds are sought, and include a budget.

There are no application deadlines, although the foundation prefers to receive inquiries before the end of the fiscal year.

Restrictions on Giving: The foundation does not make grants to individuals.

GRANTS ANALYSIS
Total Grants: $2,166,573

Number of Grants: 70

Highest Grant: $1,935,000
Average Grant: $3,356*
Typical Range: $500 to $15,000
Disclosure Period: fiscal year ending February 29, 1992

Note: The average grant figure excludes one grant of $1,935,000. Recent grants are derived from a fiscal 1992 Form 990.

RECENT GRANTS
Library
24,260   L. E. Phillips Memorial Public Library, Eau Claire, WI — building remodeling

General
1,935,000   Melvin S. Cohen Trust F/B/O, Eau Claire, WI — trust principal for the benefit of Minneapolis Federation for Jewish Service
32,500   University of Wisconsin Eau Claire Foundation, Eau Claire, WI — visiting professorship
20,000   L. E. Phillips Boy Scout Camp Trust, Eau Claire, WI — trust capital for benefit of boy scout camp
17,500   University of Wisconsin Eau Claire Foundation, Eau Claire, WI — internship program
15,000   United Way of Eau Claire, Eau Claire, WI — operating funds

Rennebohm Foundation, Oscar

CONTACT
Steven F. Skolaski
President
Oscar Rennebohm Foundation
PO Box 5187
Madison, WI 53719
(608) 274-5991

FINANCIAL SUMMARY
Recent Giving: $1,608,500 (1992); $1,431,380 (1991); $1,264,400 (1990)

Assets: $33,651,631 (1992); $31,950,288 (1991); $24,755,202 (1990)

Gifts Received: $20,691 (1991)

EIN: 39-6039252

CONTRIBUTIONS SUMMARY
Donor(s): The foundation was incorporated in 1949 by the late Oscar Rennebohm .

Typical Recipients: • *Arts & Humanities:* Arts Centers, Historic Preservation, Libraries, Museums/Galleries, Music • *Civic & Public Affairs:* Botanical Gardens/Parks, Housing, Municipalities/Towns, Public Policy, Zoos/Aquariums • *Education:* Colleges & Universities, Education Funds, Public Education (Precollege) • *Health:* Health Organizations, Hospitals, Medical Rehabilitation, Mental Health, Prenatal Health Issues • *Religion:* Religious Welfare • *Social Services:* Child Welfare, Community Service Organizations, Family Services, Food/Clothing Distribution, People with Disabilities, Recreation & Athletics, Senior Services, Shelters/Homelessness, United Funds/United Ways, Volunteer Services, Youth Organizations

Grant Types: capital, general support, and research

Geographic Distribution: limited to Madison, WI

GIVING OFFICERS

Patrick E. Coyle: dir

Frederick W. Jensen: dir

Dennis G. Maki: dir *B* River Falls WI 1940 *ED* Univ WI BS; Univ WI MS; Univ WI MD

Robert B. Rennebohm: dir

Steven F. Skolaski: pres, treas, dir *B* 1945 *CURR EMPL* pres, dir: Mastergraphics Inc

Leona A. Sonderegger: secy, dir

William H. Young: vp, dir

Lenor B. Zeeh: asst secy, dir

APPLICATION INFORMATION
Initial Approach:

The foundation has no formal grant application procedure or application form.

The foundation has no deadline for submitting proposals.

Restrictions on Giving: The foundation makes grants to charitable, educational, scientific, or religious organizations.

GRANTS ANALYSIS
Total Grants: $1,608,500

Number of Grants: 16

Highest Grant: $918,500

Average Grant: $46,000*

Typical Range: $10,000 to $100,000

Disclosure Period: 1992

Note: Average grant figure excludes the highest grant of $918,500. Recent grants are derived from a 1991 grants list.

RECENT GRANTS

Library
25,000	Library for Wisconsin Artists, Beloit, WI — equipment

General
855,630	University of Wisconsin Foundation, Madison, WI — education
200,000	Salvation Army, Madison, WI — care for needy
100,000	Edgewood College, Madison, WI — education
65,000	Meriter Foundation, Madison, WI — neonatal care
30,000	Child Development, Madison, WI — equipment

Ross Memorial Foundation, Will

CONTACT
Maryann Labahn
Vice President and Treasurer
Will Ross Memorial Fdn.
Bank One Wisconsin Trust
111 E Wisconsin Ave.
Milwaukee, WI 53201
(414) 765-2800

FINANCIAL SUMMARY
Recent Giving: $354,550 (1993); $380,950 (1992); $340,700 (1990)

Assets: $3,227,448 (1993); $3,414,474 (1992); $3,302,444 (1990)

Gifts Received: $11,618 (1990); $706,354 (1989)

EIN: 39-6044673

CONTRIBUTIONS SUMMARY
Typical Recipients: • *Arts & Humanities:* Arts Centers, Arts Institutes, Community Arts, Libraries, Literary Arts, Museums/Galleries, Music, Opera, Performing Arts, Theater • *Civic & Public Affairs:* Botanical Gardens/Parks, Economic Development, General, Hispanic Affairs, Housing, Municipalities/Towns, Urban & Community Affairs • *Education:* Arts/Humanities Education, Colleges & Universities, Health & Physical Education, Literacy, Medical Education, Private Education (Precollege), Public Education (Precollege), Secondary Education (Public) • *Environment:* General • *Health:* AIDS/HIV, Children's Health/Hospitals, Clinics/Medical Centers, Eyes/Blindness, Health Organizations, Hospitals, Mental Health, Nursing Services, Respiratory, Transplant Networks/Donor Banks • *International:* International Environmental Issues • *Religion:* Religious Organizations, Religious Welfare • *Science:* Scientific Centers & Institutes • *Social Services:* At-Risk Youth, Community Centers, Community Service Organizations, Family Planning, Food/Clothing Distribution, Homes, People with Disabilities, Shelters/Homelessness, United Funds/United Ways, Youth Organizations

Grant Types: general support

Geographic Distribution: focus on Milwaukee, WI

GIVING OFFICERS
John D. Bryson, Jr.: pres, dir

David L. Kinnamon: secy, dir

Maryann W. Labahn: vp, treas, dir

Richard R. Teschner: dir *B* Milwaukee WI 1908 *ED* Univ WI BA 1931; Univ WI LLB 1934 *NONPR AFFIL* mem: Am Bar Assn, Greater Milwaukee Comm, Milwaukee Bar Assn, Phi Delta Phi, Pi Kappa Alpha, WI Bar Assn; pres: Will Ross Meml Fdn

APPLICATION INFORMATION
Initial Approach: The foundation has no formal grant application procedure or application form. There are no deadlines.

GRANTS ANALYSIS
Total Grants: $354,550

Number of Grants: 48

Highest Grant: $75,000

Typical Range: $200 to $65,000

Disclosure Period: 1993

Note: Recent grants are derived from a 1993 Form 990.

RECENT GRANTS

Library
1,000	Milwaukee Public Library, Milwaukee, WI

General
75,000	United Way, Milwaukee, WI
25,000	Alverno College, Milwaukee, WI
25,000	Planned Parenthood Association, Milwaukee, WI
20,000	Medical College of Wisconsin, Milwaukee, WI
16,500	Second Harvestors of Wisconsin, Milwaukee, WI

Schoenleber Foundation

CONTACT
Peter C. Haensel
President
Schoenleber Fdn.
111 E Wisconsin Ave., Ste. 1800
Milwaukee, WI 53202
(414) 276-3400

FINANCIAL SUMMARY
Recent Giving: $316,550 (1993); $264,350 (1991); $262,649 (1990)

Assets: $5,772,784 (1993); $5,169,242 (1991); $4,322,690 (1990)

Gifts Received: $500 (1991); $800 (1990); $1,200,000 (1989)

Fiscal Note: In 1991, contributions were received from Arnold Investment Counse l, Inc.

EIN: 39-1049364

CONTRIBUTIONS SUMMARY
Donor(s): the late Marie and Louise Schoenleber

Typical Recipients: • *Arts & Humanities:* Arts Institutes, Community Arts, Historic Preservation, History & Archaeology, Libraries, Museums/Galleries, Music, Theater • *Civic & Public Affairs:* Business/Free Enterprise, General, Hispanic Affairs, Housing, Public Policy • *Education:* Colleges & Universities, Engineering/Technological Education, Literacy, Private Education (Precollege), Student Aid • *Health:* Children's Health/Hospitals, Hospitals, Long-Term Care • *International:* International Affairs • *Religion:* Churches, Religious Welfare • *Social Services:* Counseling, Family Planning, Family Services, People with Disabilities, Recreation & Athletics, Youth Organizations

Grant Types: general support and scholarship

Geographic Distribution: focus on the greater Milwaukee, WI, area

GIVING OFFICERS

Frank W. Bastian: secy, dir

Peter C. Haensel: pres, dir *PHIL AFFIL* secy: Glenn and Gertrude Humphrey Foundation; pres, dir: Alvin and Marion Birnschein Foundation

Walter Schorrak: dir

APPLICATION INFORMATION

Initial Approach: Request application form. Deadline is September 30.

GRANTS ANALYSIS

Total Grants: $316,550

Number of Grants: 26

Highest Grant: $50,000

Typical Range: $2,000 to $25,000

Disclosure Period: 1993

Note: Recent grants are derived from a 1993 Form 990.

RECENT GRANTS

Library

15,000	Milwaukee Public Library, Milwaukee, WI

General

50,000	University of Wisconsin Foundation, Madison, WI
20,000	First United Methodist Church of Whitewater — renovations
15,000	Boys and Girls Club, Everett, PA
15,000	Children's Hospital, Pittsburgh, MI
15,000	Congress for a Working America

Schroeder Foundation, Walter

CONTACT

William T. Gaus
Vice President and Treasurer
Walter Schroeder Foundation
1000 N Water St.
13th Fl.
Milwaukee, WI 53202
(414) 287-7177

FINANCIAL SUMMARY

Recent Giving: $665,500 (fiscal 1995 est.); $665,500 (fiscal 1994 approx.); $665,654 (fiscal 1993)

Assets: $8,300,000 (fiscal 1995 est.); $8,300,000 (fiscal 1994 approx.); $8,250,816 (fiscal 1993)

EIN: 39-6065789

CONTRIBUTIONS SUMMARY

Donor(s): Walter Schroeder established the foundation in 1963. Mr. Schroeder was president of Chris Schroeder and Son Company, a general insurance, real estate, and mortgage loan company in Milwaukee. He was also president of several hotel companies, and was a member of numerous hotel and restaurant associations. The foundation is principally funded from Mr. Schroeder's trust.

Typical Recipients: • *Arts & Humanities:* Arts Centers, Arts Festivals, Arts Funds, Arts Institutes, History & Archaeology, Libraries, Museums/Galleries, Music, Opera, Performing Arts, Theater • *Civic & Public Affairs:* Business/Free Enterprise, Zoos/Aquariums • *Education:* Arts/Humanities Education, Business Education, Colleges & Universities, Education Funds, General, Medical Education, Private Education (Precollege), Public Education (Precollege), Secondary Education (Private) • *Environment:* General, Wildlife Protection • *Health:* Cancer, Children's Health/Hospitals, Emergency/Ambulance Services, Eyes/Blindness, Health Organizations, Hospitals, Medical Research, Nursing Services, Single-Disease Health Associations • *International:* International Environmental Issues • *Religion:* Religious Organizations, Religious Welfare • *Science:* Scientific Organizations • *Social Services:* Animal Protection, Child Welfare, Community Centers, Community Service Organizations, Counseling, Family Services, Homes, People with Disabilities, Recreation & Athletics, Senior Services, United Funds/United Ways, Volunteer Services, Youth Organizations

Grant Types: capital, general support, project, and research

Geographic Distribution: focus on Milwaukee County, WI

GIVING OFFICERS

William Thomas Gaus: vp, treas, dir *B* Berlin Germany 1928 *ED* Marquette Univ 1951; Marquette Univ JD 1954 *CURR EMPL* sr vp, chief trust off: Marshall & Ilsley Trust Co *PHIL AFFIL* treas: Steve J. Miller Foundation

Robert M. Hoffer: dir *B* Muncie IN 1921 *ED* Ball St Univ BS 1948; Univ MI MBA 1949

Ruthmarie Lawrenz: dir

John A. Puelicher: pres, dir *B* Milwaukee WI 1920 *ED* Univ WI BA 1943; Harvard Univ Grad Sch Bus Admin *CORP AFFIL* dir: WR Grace & Co Inc, Great Northern Nekoosa Corp, M&I Capital Markets Group, M&I Data Svcs Inc, Marshall & Ilsley Bank, Modine Mfg Co, Mosinee Paper Corp, Sentry Ins Co, Sundstrand Corp *NONPR AFFIL* trust emeritus: Marquette Univ *PHIL AFFIL* pres, dir: Marshall and Ilsley Foundation, Inc., Puelicher Foundation

Marjorie Vallier: secy, dir

APPLICATION INFORMATION

Initial Contact: Applicants should send a letter to the foundation.

Include Information On: There is no formal policy for applications. A letter outlining the nature of the proposed grant is recommended.

Deadlines: Proposals should be submitted before meetings in May and October.

Review Process: Final notification on decisions varies.

Restrictions on Giving: Grants are made only to charitable organizations and agencies operating in Milwaukee County. Grants are not made to individuals.

GRANTS ANALYSIS

Total Grants: $665,654

Number of Grants: 89

Highest Grant: $50,000

Average Grant: $7,479

Typical Range: $500 to $10,000

Disclosure Period: fiscal year ending June 30, 1993

Note: Recent grants are derived from a fiscal 1993 Form 990.

RECENT GRANTS

Library

6,000	Milwaukee Public Library, Milwaukee, WI — education

General

50,000	Cardinal Stritch College, Milwaukee, WI — education
50,000	Children's Hospital of Wisconsin, Milwaukee, WI — health care
50,000	Columbia Hospital, Milwaukee, WI — health care
50,000	Riveredge Nature Center, Newburg, WI — natural resources
50,000	United Lutheran Homes for the Aging, Milwaukee, WI — social services

Sentry Insurance A Mutual Company / Sentry Foundation Inc.

Premiums: $810.49 million
Employees: 4,550
Headquarters: Stevens Point, WI
SIC Major Group: Life Insurance

CONTACT

Debbie Berkholtz
Administrative Assistant
Sentry Insurance A Mutual Company
1800 N Point Dr.
Stevens Point, WI 54481
(715) 346-6000

FINANCIAL SUMMARY

Recent Giving: $465,000 (1994); $456,069 (1993); $294,186 (1991)

Assets: $2,007 (1993); $18,329 (1991); $23,954 (1990)

Gifts Received: $456,612 (1993); $289,000 (1991); $305,000 (1990)

Fiscal Note: Contributes through foundation only. In 1993, contributions were received from Sentry Insurance, A Mutual Company.

EIN: 39-1037370

CONTRIBUTIONS SUMMARY

Typical Recipients: • *Arts & Humanities:* Community Arts, Libraries, Music, Public Broadcasting • *Civic & Public Affairs:* Business/Free Enterprise, General • *Education:* Business Education, Colleges & Universities, Education Funds, Engineering/Technological Education, Gifted & Talented Programs, Private Education (Precollege), Religious Education, Secondary Education (Public), Student Aid • *Health:* Health Organizations, Hospitals, Medical Research • *Religion:* Religious Organizations • *Social Services:* Animal Protection, Community Service Organizations, People with Disabilities, Recreation & Athletics, Scouts, Special Olympics, United Funds/United Ways, Veterans, Youth Organizations

Grant Types: general support

Geographic Distribution: nationally

Operating Locations: WI (Stevens Point)

CORP. OFFICERS

Larry Coleman Ballard: *B* Des Moines IA 1935 *ED* Drake Univ BS 1957 *CURR EMPL* chmn, pres, ceo: Sentry Ins Co *CORP AFFIL* chmn: Dairyland Ins, Middlesex Ins Co, Patriot Gen Ins Co, Sentry Aviation Svcs, Sentry Investors Life Ins Co, Sentry Svcs; chmn, ceo: Sentry Life Ins; dir: Century Commun Corp, Competitive WI, M&I First Natl Bank, Sentry Equity Svcs, Sentry Investment Mgmt *NONPR AFFIL* fellow: Soc Actuaries; mem: Am Acad Actuaries; trust: Am Inst Property Liability Underwriters, Ins Inst Am

GIVING OFFICERS

Debbie Berkholtz: admin asst

William R. Beversdorf: vp

Bernard C. Hlavac: dir

Alfred C. Noel: pres, dir *CURR EMPL* vp: Sentry Ins A Mutual Co

Carroll George Smith: dir

APPLICATION INFORMATION

Initial Approach: *Initial Contact:* brief letter *Include Information On:* description of program and amount of contribution sought *Deadlines:* none

GRANTS ANALYSIS

Total Grants: $465,069

Number of Grants: 230

Highest Grant: $103,500

Average Grant: $2,022

Typical Range: $100 to $7,000

Disclosure Period: 1993

Note: Recent grants are derived from a 1993 grants list.

RECENT GRANTS

Library
20,000	Portage County Library Foundation

General
103,500	United Way of Portage County, Ravenna, OH
55,000	University of Wisconsin Stevens Point Foundation,

	Stevens Point, WI — for scholarship program
44,052	SPACS — for matching gift
25,000	Wisconsin Foundation for Independent Colleges, Milwaukee, WI
12,370	University of Wisconsin Stevens Point, Madison, WI — for matching gift

---

Smith Corp., A.O. / Smith Foundation, Inc., A.O.

Sales: $1.19 billion
Employees: 10,800
Headquarters: Milwaukee, WI
SIC Major Group: Motor Vehicle Parts & Accessories, Plastics Products Nec, Fabricated Plate Work—Boiler Shops, and Farm Machinery & Equipment

---

CONTACT

Edward J. O'Connor
Secretary
A.O. Smith Foundation
11270 W Park Pl.
Milwaukee, WI 53223
(414) 359-4100

FINANCIAL SUMMARY

Recent Giving: $700,000 (fiscal 1994 approx.); $600,000 (fiscal 1993 approx.); $630,822 (fiscal 1991)

Assets: $116,659 (fiscal 1991); $788,300 (fiscal 1990); $14,766 (fiscal 1989)

Fiscal Note: Company gives primarily through the foundation. Above figures exclude nonmonetary support.

EIN: 39-6076724

CONTRIBUTIONS SUMMARY

Typical Recipients: • *Arts & Humanities:* Arts Funds, Dance, Historic Preservation, Libraries, Museums/Galleries, Music, Performing Arts • *Civic & Public Affairs:* Business/Free Enterprise, Civil Rights, Economic Development, Nonprofit Management, Safety, Urban & Community Affairs • *Education:* Business Education, Colleges & Universities, Community & Junior Colleges, Economic Education, Education Funds, Engineering/Technological Education, Literacy, Medical Education, Minority Education, Student Aid • *Environment:* General • *Health:* Emergency/Ambulance Services, Hospitals, Medical Rehabilitation, Mental Health, Public Health • *Social Services:* Child Welfare, Community Centers, Community Service Organizations, Family Services, Homes, People with Disabilities, Recreation & Athletics, Senior Services, Shelters/Homelessness, Substance Abuse, United Funds/United Ways, Youth Organizations

Grant Types: capital, employee matching gifts, general support, operating expenses, project, and scholarship

Note: Company matches employee gifts up to $1,000.

Nonmonetary Support Types: donated equipment, donated products, in-kind services, loaned employees, and loaned executives

Note: Estimated value of noncash support is unavailable.

Geographic Distribution: primarily in communities where company has manufacturing facilities

Operating Locations: AR (Little Rock), CA (Irvine), FL (Williston), IL (Chicago, DeKalb, Granite City), KS (Wichita), KY (Bowling Green, Florence, Mount Sterling), MD (Belcamp), MI (Farmington Hills), NC (Mebane), OH (Bellevue, Tipp City, Upper Sandusky), SC (McBee), TN (Milan), TX (El Paso, Irving), WA (Seattle), WI (Milwaukee)

Note: Also operates in Bermuda, Canada, Ireland, Mexico, and the Netherlands.

CORP. OFFICERS

Robert Joseph O'Toole: *B* Chicago IL 1941 *ED* Loyola Univ BS 1961 *CURR EMPL* pres, ceo, chmn: AO Smith Corp *CORP AFFIL* dir: AgriStor Credit Corp, First WI Natl Bank, Metalsa SA, Protection Mutual Ins Co, Protection Mutual Ins Co, Smith Fiberglass Products Inc, AO Smith Harvestore Products Inc *NONPR AFFIL* dir: Metro Milwaukee Assn Commerce; mem: Bus Roundtable, Competitive WI Inc, Greater Milwaukee Comm, Mfrs Alliance Productivity & Innovation; mem exec comm: TEC XIV, WI Mgrs & Commerce Assn *CLUB AFFIL* Milwaukee CC, Univ *PHIL AFFIL* dir: Firstar Milwaukee Foundation

GIVING OFFICERS

Edward J. O'Connor: secy, dir *B* St Louis MO *ED* St Louis Univ 1962 *CURR EMPL* vp human resources & pub aff: AO Smith Corp

Robert Joseph O'Toole: vp *CURR EMPL* pres, ceo, chmn: AO Smith Corp *PHIL AFFIL* dir: Firstar Milwaukee Foundation (see above)

Thomas R. Ryan: treas *B* Detroit MI 1947 *ED* Wayne St Univ BSBA 1969 *CURR EMPL* vp, treas, contr: AO Smith Corp *CORP AFFIL* asst treas, asst secy: Smith Investment Co; treas, dir: Agristor Credit Corp; treas, real estate mgr: Smith Fiberglass Products Inc *NONPR AFFIL* bd dirs: Greater Milwaukee Healthcare Network; mem: Fin Execs Inst, Natl Assn Accts

Arthur O. Smith: pres *B* 1930 *CURR EMPL* chmn: Arthur Smith Indus *CORP AFFIL* chmn, ceo: Smith Investment Co; dir: AO Smith Corp; vchmn: Berlin Indus Inc

APPLICATION INFORMATION

Initial Approach: *Initial Contact:* letter or proposal on organization's letterhead *Include Information On:* name, location, and description of the organization; proof of tax-exempt status; geographic area served; explanation of activity for which support is sought; amount requested; description of benefits to be achieved and who will receive them; budget; other sources of income; plans for reporting results *Deadlines:* by March 30 to be considered for following year's budget; requests reviewed in order received

Note: Also forward any printed materials describing organization that may lend support to application.

Restrictions on Giving: Foundation does not make contributions to politically active organizations seeking to influence legislation.

OTHER THINGS TO KNOW
A.O. Smith Corp. employees are encouraged to take an active part in civic affairs.

GRANTS ANALYSIS
Total Grants: $630,822

Number of Grants: 107

Highest Grant: $210,000

Average Grant: $5,896

Typical Range: $500 to $10,000

Disclosure Period: fiscal year ending June 30, 1991

Note: Recent grants are derived from a fiscal 1991 Form 990.

RECENT GRANTS

Library

5,000	Milwaukee Public Library, Milwaukee, WI — to aid in the purchase of books and materials for the new Center Street Library

General

210,000	United Way of Greater Milwaukee, Milwaukee, WI
32,500	Zoological Society of Milwaukee County, Milwaukee, WI — to maintain membership with the Platypus Society
20,000	Children's Hospital of Wisconsin, Milwaukee, WI — to aid in the purchase of an Echocardiograph Machine
20,000	Medical College of Wisconsin, Milwaukee, WI — in support of medical education, teaching and research
16,000	Sinai Samaritan Medical Center, Milwaukee, WI — in support of the Commitment for Tomorrow program

WICOR, Inc. / WICOR Foundation

Revenue: $849.53 million
Employees: 3,222
Headquarters: Milwaukee, WI
SIC Major Group: Holding Companies Nec, Crude Petroleum & Natural Gas, Process Control Instruments, and Natural Gas Distribution

CONTACT
Carolyn Simpson
Foundation Coordinator
WICOR Foundation
626 E Wisconsin Ave.
Milwaukee, WI 53202
(414) 291-6565

FINANCIAL SUMMARY
Recent Giving: $600,000 (1994 est.); $600,000 (1993); $584,177 (1992)

Assets: $332,504 (1992); $429,018 (1990); $354,078 (1989)

Gifts Received: $539,209 (1992); $684,890 (1990); $687,194 (1989)

Fiscal Note: Contributes through foundation only. Above figures exclude nonmonetary support. Contributions were received from the Wisconsin Gas Company and Sta-Rite Industries.

EIN: 39-1522073

CONTRIBUTIONS SUMMARY
Typical Recipients: • *Arts & Humanities:* Arts Institutes, Libraries, Museums/Galleries, Music, Opera, Performing Arts • *Civic & Public Affairs:* Botanical Gardens/Parks, Employment/Job Training, Hispanic Affairs, Housing, Nonprofit Management, Urban & Community Affairs, Women's Affairs, Zoos/Aquariums • *Education:* Business Education, Colleges & Universities, Economic Education, Education Reform, Elementary Education (Private), Engineering/Technological Education, General, Literacy, Medical Education, Minority Education, Private Education (Precollege), Public Education (Precollege), Student Aid • *Environment:* General • *Health:* Clinics/Medical Centers, Emergency/Ambulance Services, General, Health Policy/Cost Containment, Hospitals, Transplant Networks/Donor Banks • *Religion:* Religious Organizations, Religious Welfare • *Social Services:* Child Welfare, Community Centers, Domestic Violence, General, People with Disabilities, Recreation & Athletics, Substance Abuse, United Funds/United Ways, Youth Organizations

Grant Types: capital and general support

Nonmonetary Support: $106,000 (1993)

Nonmonetary Support Types: donated equipment and loaned executives

Note: The company reports that they donate used furniture to nonprofits.

Geographic Distribution: giving largely limited to WICOR plant locations and service territory

Operating Locations: CA (Oxnard), NE, WI (Delavan, Milwaukee, Racine)

CORP. OFFICERS
James Charles Donnelly: *B* Boston MA 1945 *ED* Northeastern Univ BS 1969; Northeastern Univ MBA 1974; Suffolk Univ JD 1978 *CURR EMPL* vp, treas: WICOR Inc *NONPR AFFIL* mem: Am Gas Assn, Fin Execs Inst, New England Gas Assn

George E. Wardeberg: *CURR EMPL* pres, ceo, dir: WICOR Inc

Joseph P. Wenzler: *B* Fond du Lac WI 1942 *ED* Marquette Univ BS 1964; Univ WI MBA 1983 *CURR EMPL* cfo, dir: WICOR Inc

GIVING OFFICERS
James Charles Donnelly: vp, dir *CURR EMPL* vp, treas: WICOR Inc (see above)

Thomas F. Schrader: vp, dir *B* Indianapolis IN 1950 *ED* Princeton Univ BS 1972; Princeton Univ MS 1978 *CURR EMPL* pres, ceo, dir: WI Gas Co *CORP AFFIL* dir: First WI Trust Co, Milwaukee Mgmt Support Org, Portal Indus, Sta-Rite Indus Inc, Wexco DE, WI Utilities Assn; vp, dir: WICOR Inc *NONPR AFFIL* dir: Goodwill Indus; head: New Hope Project

Carolyn Simpson: coordinator

George E. Wardeberg: dir *CURR EMPL* pres, ceo, dir: WICOR Inc (see above)

Joseph P. Wenzler: secy, treas *CURR EMPL* cfo, dir: WICOR Inc (see above)

APPLICATION INFORMATION
Initial Approach: *Initial Contact:* written proposal *Include Information On:* legal name, address, and telephone number of organization; name of representative who can be contacted by telephone; statement of purpose and a brief history of organization, including past projects; description of overall program, including any collaboration with other nonprofit organizations; an explanation regarding specific request for support; most recent audited financial statement; itemized annual and project budget with projected revenues and expenses; list of funding sources contacted and funds received; copy of tax-exempt letter; list of current board of directors; description of unique facets of request and what differentiates it from other projects of the same nature; and a description of how results will be measured *Deadlines:* there are four deadlines a year: January 31, April 30, July 31, and October 31

Restrictions on Giving: Does not support individuals, religious organizations for sectarian purposes, political or lobbying groups, or organizations outside operating areas.

PUBLICATIONS
Fact sheet

GRANTS ANALYSIS
Total Grants: $584,177

Number of Grants: 180

Highest Grant: $40,000

Average Grant: $3,245

Typical Range: $500 to $5,000

Disclosure Period: 1992

Note: Recent grants are derived from a 1992 Form 990.

RECENT GRANTS

General

34,500	United Way of Greater Milwaukee, Milwaukee, WI
34,500	United Way of Greater Milwaukee, Milwaukee, WI
34,500	United Way of Greater Milwaukee, Milwaukee, WI
34,500	United Way of Greater Milwaukee, Milwaukee, WI
25,000	Marquette University, Milwaukee, WI

Wisconsin Power & Light Co. / Wisconsin Power & Light Foundation, Inc.

Sales: $645.5 million
Employees: 2,661
Parent Company: WPL Holdings, Inc.
Headquarters: Madison, WI
SIC Major Group: Electric Services, Natural Gas Distribution, and Water Supply

CONTACT
Jo Ann Healy
Vice President
Wisconsin Power & Light Foundation, Inc.
PO Box 192
Madison, WI 53701
(608) 252-5545

FINANCIAL SUMMARY
Recent Giving: $931,292 (1994); $1,006,693 (1993); $991,571 (1992)

Assets: $7,688,089 (1993); $7,947,849 (1992); $6,887,141 (1991)

Gifts Received: $400,000 (1993)

Fiscal Note: Above figures do not include company direct giving of approximately $250,000 annually to local social services agencies for a community fuel fund. Company gives primarily through the foundation. Above figures exclude nonmonetary support. In 1993, foundation received contributions from Wisconsin Power & Light Company.

EIN: 39-1444065

CONTRIBUTIONS SUMMARY
Typical Recipients: • *Arts & Humanities:* Arts Festivals, Community Arts, Historic Preservation, History & Archaeology, Libraries, Music, Performing Arts, Public Broadcasting, Theater • *Civic & Public Affairs:* African American Affairs, Botanical Gardens/Parks, Business/Free Enterprise, Community Foundations, Economic Development, Economic Policy, Employment/Job Training, General, Municipalities/Towns, Safety, Urban & Community Affairs • *Education:* Business Education, Colleges & Universities, Education Funds, General, Preschool Education, Student Aid, Vocational & Technical Education • *Environment:* General • *Health:* Cancer, Children's Health/Hospitals, Emergency/Ambulance Services, Health Organizations, Hospitals, Nursing Services, Single-Disease Health Associations • *Social Services:* Child Welfare, Community Centers, Community Service Organizations, Emergency Relief, Family Services, Food/Clothing Distribution, General, People with Disabilities, Shelters/Homelessness, United Funds/United Ways, YMCA/YWCA/YMHA/YWHA, Youth Organizations

Grant Types: capital, employee matching gifts, and general support

Note: Employee matching gift ratio: 1 to 1.

Nonmonetary Support: $23,200 (1992); $40,000 (1990); $55,000 (1989)

Nonmonetary Support Types: donated equipment, loaned employees, and loaned executives

Geographic Distribution: principally near headquarters and service areas (Central and South-Central WI)

Operating Locations: WI (Madison, South & Central regions)

CORP. OFFICERS
Anthony J. Amato: *B* Madison WI 1951 *CURR EMPL* sr vp: WI Power & Light Co

Erroll Brown Davis, Jr.: *B* Pittsburgh PA 1944 *ED* Carnegie-Mellon Univ 1965; Univ Chicago MBA 1967 *CURR EMPL* pres, ceo: WI Power & Light Co *CORP AFFIL* dir: Amoco Corp, WPL Sentry Ins; pres, dir: WPL Holdings *NONPR AFFIL* bd regents: Univ WI; commnr: Madison Police & Fire Commn; dir: Am Gas Assn, Competitive WI Inc, Higher Ed AIDS Bd, Un Way Dane County, WI Assn Mfrs & Commerce, WI Utilities Assn; mem: Am Assn Blacks Energy, Selective Svc Bd

GIVING OFFICERS
Joanne Acomb: dir

Anthony J. Amato: pres, dir *CURR EMPL* sr vp: WI Power & Light Co (see above)

Linda Brei: vp

Jo Ann Healy: vp

Bill Howliski: dir

Carol Kreager: dir

Jules Nicolet: dir

APPLICATION INFORMATION
Initial Approach: *Initial Contact:* brief letter or proposal *Include Information On:* name and history of organization, overview of proposed project, purpose for which funds are sought, proof of tax-exempt status, audited financial statement *Deadlines:* by July 15 for funding the next year

GRANTS ANALYSIS
Total Grants: $1,006,693

Number of Grants: 1,200*

Highest Grant: $70,500

Average Grant: $839*

Typical Range: $250 to $1,000

Disclosure Period: 1993

Note: Number of grants and average grant figures are approximations. Recent grants are derived from a 1993 Form 990.

RECENT GRANTS

General

70,500	United Way of Dane County, Madison, WI — 1992 campaign	
57,000	Madison Urban League, Madison, WI	
39,000	Madison Urban League, Madison, WI	
30,000	Citizens Scholars — WP&L scholars	
21,500	Board of Regents	

Wisconsin Public Service Corp. / Wisconsin Public Service Foundation, Inc.

Revenue: $680.63 million
Employees: 2,603
Headquarters: Green Bay, WI
SIC Major Group: Electric Services and Natural Gas Distribution

CONTACT
Daniel A. Bollom
President & Chief Executive Officer
Wisconsin Public Service Foundation, Inc.
700 North Adams St.
PO Box 19001
Green Bay, WI 54307-9001
(414) 433-1464

FINANCIAL SUMMARY
Recent Giving: $913,677 (1994); $779,311 (1993); $481,506 (1992)

Assets: $12,256,449 (1994); $12,256,000 (1993); $10,227,000 (1992)

Gifts Received: $775,000 (1993); $200,000 (1990)

Fiscal Note: The company reports that other departments also make contributions directly from corporate funds. The budget for this funding is $66,800 and is not included in the above figures. The contacts for direct support are the seven Wisconsin Public Service Corp. division managers. Above figures exclude nonmonetary support.

EIN: 39-6075016

CONTRIBUTIONS SUMMARY
Typical Recipients: • *Arts & Humanities:* Arts Festivals, General, Libraries, Museums/Galleries, Performing Arts • *Civic & Public Affairs:* General, Zoos/Aquariums • *Education:* Agricultural Education, Business Education, Colleges & Universities, Engineering/Technological Education • *Health:* Hospitals • *Social Services:* Community Centers, Senior Services, Substance Abuse, United Funds/United Ways, Youth Organizations

Grant Types: capital, emergency, general support, and scholarship

Nonmonetary Support Types: donated equipment and loaned employees

Note: Estimated value of nonmonetary support is not available. Employee matching gift ratio: $1 to every $2 donated by employees.

Geographic Distribution: northeast Wisconsin and parts of northern Michigan

Operating Locations: WI (Green Bay)

CORP. OFFICERS
Daniel Arthur Bollom: *B* Oshkosh WI 1936 *ED* Univ WI 1958 *CURR EMPL* pres, ceo, dir: WI Pub Svc Corp *CORP AFFIL* dir: Prime Fed Bank *NONPR AFFIL* mem: WI Soc CPAs

GIVING OFFICERS
D. P. Bittner: treas *CURR EMPL* sr vp cust svc: WI Pub Svc Corp

Daniel Arthur Bollom: pres *CURR EMPL* pres, ceo, dir: WI Pub Svc Corp (see above)

Patrick D. Schrickel: mem bd *CURR EMPL* sr vp fin & corp svcs: WI Pub Svc Corp

APPLICATION INFORMATION

Initial Approach: *Initial Contact:* brief letter requesting a formal application *Include Information On:* organization name, explanation of organization, funds desired, and reason for request *Deadlines:* none

Restrictions on Giving: Foundation only supports 501(c)(3) organizations.

OTHER THINGS TO KNOW

Company reports that its funding through 1995 is committed.

GRANTS ANALYSIS

Total Grants: $779,311

Number of Grants: 204

Highest Grant: $72,000

Average Grant: $3,820

Typical Range: $500 to $1,500

Disclosure Period: 1993

Note: Figures exclude $66,800 in departmental giving. Recent grants are derived from a 1993 Form 990.

RECENT GRANTS

Library

5,000	Marathon County Public Library Foundation, Wausau, WI — capital funds
5,000	Waupaca Public Library Foundation, Wausau, WI
3,000	Portage County Public Library Foundation, Wausau, WI — capital funds

General

72,000	United Way of Brown County, Green Bay, WI
40,000	St. Vincent Hospital, Green Bay, WI — capital funds
40,000	University of Wisconsin, Green Bay, WI — capital funds
30,000	Cerebral Palsy Association, Green Bay, WI — capital funds
30,000	Salvation Army, Green Bay, WI — capital funds

Young Foundation, Irvin L.

CONTACT

Fern D. Young
President and Treasurer
Irvin L. Young Fdn.
Rt. 1, Box 239
Palmyra, WI 53156
(414) 495-2485

FINANCIAL SUMMARY

Recent Giving: $578,849 (1993); $1,977,260 (1992); $1,110,623 (1990)

Assets: $5,448,932 (1993); $4,562,225 (1992); $7,840,191 (1990)

EIN: 39-6077858

CONTRIBUTIONS SUMMARY

Donor(s): the late Irvin L. Young

Typical Recipients: • *Arts & Humanities:* Libraries • *Education:* Colleges & Universities, Public Education (Precollege), Religious Education • *Health:* Hospitals, Respiratory • *International:* Health Care/Hospitals, International Environmental Issues, International Peace & Security Issues, International Relations, International Relief Efforts, Missionary/Religious Activities • *Religion:* Bible Study/Translation, Churches, Missionary Activities (Domestic), Religious Organizations, Religious Welfare • *Social Services:* Child Welfare, Community Service Organizations, Food/Clothing Distribution, Shelters/Homelessness, Youth Organizations

Grant Types: capital, general support, operating expenses, and scholarship

Geographic Distribution: national, with focus on CA and WI

GIVING OFFICERS

Dr. L. Arden Almquist: dir

David S. Fisher: dir

Mary Longbrake: vp, dir

Robert W. Reninger: secy, dir

Mitchell J. Simon: dir

David A. Voetman: dir

Fern D. Young: pres, treas, dir

APPLICATION INFORMATION

Initial Approach: Send brief letter of inquiry and full proposal. Include a description of organization, amount requested, purpose of funds sought, recently audited financial statement, and proof of tax-exempt status. There are no deadlines.

GRANTS ANALYSIS

Total Grants: $578,849

Number of Grants: 33

Highest Grant: $90,000

Typical Range: $500 to $75,000

Disclosure Period: 1993

Note: Recent grants are derived from a 1993 Form 990.

RECENT GRANTS

General

90,000	Mission Aviation Fellowship, Redlands, CA
75,000	Evangelical Covenant Church — staff housing
50,000	Mission Aviation Fellowship, Redlands, CA — for damage to gas turbine engine section
31,675	Christian Missions in Many Lands — building funds
28,000	World Gospel Missions, Tenwek Hospital — oxygen concentrator

WYOMING

Sargent Foundation, Newell B.

CONTACT

Newell B. Sargent
Trustee
Newell B. Sargent Fdn.
821 Pulliam Ave.
Worland, WY 82401
(307) 577-1712

FINANCIAL SUMMARY

Recent Giving: $171,480 (fiscal 1993); $183,918 (fiscal 1992); $37,430 (fiscal 1991)

Assets: $5,483,750 (fiscal 1993); $4,976,705 (fiscal 1992); $4,016,114 (fiscal 1991)

Gifts Received: $500,000 (fiscal 1993); $800,000 (fiscal 1992); $400,000 (fiscal 1991)

Fiscal Note: In fiscal 1993, contributions were received from Newell B. Sargent.

EIN: 83-0271536

CONTRIBUTIONS SUMMARY

Donor(s): Newell B. Sargent

Typical Recipients: • *Arts & Humanities:* Arts Festivals, Community Arts, Dance, History & Archaeology, Libraries, Museums/Galleries, Music, Theater • *Civic & Public Affairs:* Business/Free Enterprise, Chambers of Commerce, Clubs, Community Foundations, Economic Development, Employment/Job Training, Law & Justice, Municipalities/Towns, Urban & Community Affairs, Women's Affairs • *Education:* Colleges & Universities, Community & Junior Colleges, Literacy, Student Aid • *Environment:* General • *Health:* Alzheimers Disease, Cancer, Children's Health/Hospitals, Emergency/Ambulance Services, Eyes/Blindness, Heart, Hospitals • *Religion:* Churches, Religious Organizations, Religious Welfare • *Social Services:* Animal Protection, Community Service Organizations, Emergency Relief, Food/Clothing Distribution, Homes, People with Disabilities, Scouts, Senior Services, Veterans, Youth Organizations

Grant Types: general support and scholarship

Geographic Distribution: focus on WY, with emphasis on Worland

GIVING OFFICERS

Douglas W. Morrison: trust

Newell B. Sargent: trust

Charles W. Smith: trust

APPLICATION INFORMATION

Initial Approach: Send brief letter describing program. Include a description of organization, amount requested, purpose of funds sought, recently audited financial statement, and proof of tax-exempt status. There are no deadlines.

GRANTS ANALYSIS

Total Grants: $171,480

Number of Grants: 42

Highest Grant: $115,000

Typical Range: $200 to $12,000

Disclosure Period: fiscal year ending October 31, 1993

Note: Recent grants are derived from a fiscal 1993 Form 990.

RECENT GRANTS

General

5,000	Primary Children's Medical Center, Salt Lake City, UT
5,000	Shriners Hospital for Crippled Children, Tampa, FL
4,500	Montana Rescue, Billings, MT
3,000	New Horizons Care Center, Lovell, WY — Alzheimers wing
2,500	Boys and Girls Club of Central Wyoming, Casper, WY — building fund

Indexes

Index to Corporations and Foundations by Headquarters

Please refer to the Master Index to Corporations and Foundations for profile page numbers.

Alabama

Birmingham
Alabama Gas Corp.
Alabama Power Co.
BE&K Inc.
Daniel Foundation of Alabama
Ebsco Industries, Inc.
Linn-Henley Charitable Trust
Sonat Inc.
Vulcan Materials Co.

Brewton
McMillan Foundation, D. W.

Decatur
Tennessee Valley Printing Co.

Mobile
Bedsole Foundation, J. L.
Smith, Jr. Foundation, M. W.

Montgomery
Blount, Inc.

Sylacauga
Comer Foundation

Tallassee
Blount Educational and
   Charitable Foundation,
   Mildred Weedon

Arizona

Phoenix
Phelps Dodge Corporation

Prescott
Morris Foundation, Margaret T.

Tucson
Mulcahy Foundation
Spalding Foundation, Eliot

Arkansas

Bentonville
Wal-Mart Stores, Inc.

De Queen
De Queen General Hospital
   Foundation

El Dorado
Murphy Foundation

Little Rock
Arkansas Power & Light Co.
Ottenheimer Brothers
   Foundation
Riggs Benevolent Fund

Malvern
Sturgis Charitable and
   Educational Trust, Roy and
   Christine

Springdale
Jones Foundation, Harvey and
   Bernice

California

Arcadia
Berger Foundation, H. N. and
   Frances C.

Bakersfield
Arkelian Foundation, Ben H.
   and Gladys
West Foundation, Harry and
   Ethel

Belmont
Taube Family Foundation

Beverly Hills
Ahmanson Foundation
Bettingen Corporation, Burton
   G.
Hanover Foundation
Pickford Foundation, Mary
Stein Foundation, Jules and
   Doris

Burbank
Thornton Foundation, Flora L.

Cameron Park
Ghidotti Foundation

Carmel
McMahan Foundation,
   Catherine L. and Robert O.

Claremont
Hafif Family Foundation

Commerce
Strauss Foundation, Leon

Costa Mesa
Argyros Foundation

Cupertino
Apple Computer, Inc.

Cypress
Mitsubishi Motor Sales of
   America, Inc.

Davis
Haigh-Scatena Foundation

El Segundo
Mattel, Inc.

Glendale
Baskin-Robbins USA Co.
Nestle USA Inc.

Indian Wells
Philibosian Foundation,
   Stephen

Inglewood
Imperial Bancorp

La Jolla
Copley Press, Inc.
Dr. Seuss Foundation

La Quinta
Murphey Foundation, Lluella
   Morey

Long Beach
McDonnell Douglas
   Corp.-West

Los Altos
Packard Foundation, David
   and Lucile

Los Angeles
Amado Foundation, Maurice
Boswell Foundation, James G.
Chartwell Foundation
Darling Foundation, Hugh and
   Hazel
Durfee Foundation
Goldwyn Foundation, Samuel
Haynes Foundation, John
   Randolph and Dora
Hoag Family Foundation,
   George
Jones Foundation, Fletcher
Knudsen Foundation, Tom and
   Valley
Leavey Foundation, Thomas
   and Dorothy
Munger Foundation, Alfred C.
Parsons Foundation, Ralph M.
Parvin Foundation, Albert
Salvatori Foundation, Henry
Seaver Charitable Trust,
   Richard C.
Seaver Institute
Stauffer Foundation, John and
   Beverly
Taper Foundation, Mark
Thornton Foundation
Times Mirror Company, The
Union Bank
Unocal Corp.
Van Nuys Foundation, I. N.
   and Susanna H.
Weingart Foundation
Whitecap Foundation

Menlo Park
Hewlett Foundation, William
   and Flora

Modesto
Bright Family Foundation

Newport Beach
Pacific Mutual Life Insurance
   Co.
Steele Foundation, Harry and
   Grace

North Hollywood
Lund Foundation

Novato
Fireman's Fund Insurance Co.

Oakland
American President
   Companies, Ltd.
Clorox Co.
Hedco Foundation
Skaggs Foundation, L. J. and
   Mary C.

Orinda
Y and H Soda Foundation

Palo Alto
Hancock Foundation, Luke B.
Hewlett-Packard Co.

Pasadena
Essick Foundation

Garland Foundation, John
Jewett and H. Chandler
Golden West Foundation
Hoover, Jr. Foundation,
   Margaret W. and Herbert
Howe and Mitchell B. Howe
   Foundation, Lucille Horton
Peppers Foundation, Ann
Stans Foundation
Stauffer Charitable Trust, John

Redding
McConnell Foundation
Sierra Pacific Industries

Rosemead
Southern California Edison Co.

Sacramento
Teichert & Son, A.

San Diego
Jacobs Family Foundation
Johnson Charitable
   Educational Trust, James
   Hervey
Ryan Foundation, David
   Claude
San Diego Gas & Electric

San Francisco
BankAmerica Corp.
Bechtel, Jr. Foundation, S. D.
Bothin Foundation
Brenner Foundation, Mervyn
Campini Foundation, Frank A.
Chevron Corporation
Columbia Foundation
Cowell Foundation, S. H.
Crocker Trust, Mary A.
Fleishhacker Foundation
Gamble Foundation
Gap, Inc., The
Gellert Foundation, Carl
Gellert Foundation, Celia Berta
Gilmore Foundation, William
   G.
Haas, Jr. Fund, Evelyn and
   Walter
Heller Charitable Foundation,
   Clarence E.
Irvine Foundation, James
Irwin Charity Foundation,
   William G.
Jewett Foundation, George
   Frederick
Komes Foundation
Koret Foundation
Lurie Foundation, Louis R.
Lux Foundation, Miranda
Magowan Family Foundation
Margoes Foundation
McBean Charitable Trust,
   Alletta Morris
Meyer Fund, Milton and
   Sophie
Odell Fund, Robert Stewart
Odell and Helen Pfeiffer
Osher Foundation, Bernard
Pacific Telesis Group
Rosenberg Foundation
Rosenberg, Jr. Family
   Foundation, Louise and
   Claude
Saroyan Foundation, William
Schwab & Co., Inc., Charles
Smith Trust, May and Stanley
Sumitomo Bank of California
TransAmerica Corporation
   Trust Funds
USL Capital Corporation
Witter Foundation, Dean

San Jose
Fujitsu America, Inc.

San Leandro
Specialty Manufacturing Co.

San Marino
Scott Foundation, Virginia
   Steele

San Mateo
Friedman Family Foundation

San Rafael
Bay Area Foods

Santa Monica
Getty Trust, J. Paul
Norton Family Foundation,
   Peter

Sierra Madre
Jameson Foundation, J. W. and
   Ida M.

St. Helena
LEF Foundation

Universal City
MCA Inc.

Valley Center
Muller Foundation

Walnut Creek
Long Foundation, J.M.

West Covina
Femino Foundation

Colorado

Aurora
Weckbaugh Foundation,
   Eleanore Mullen

Brush
Joslin-Needham Family
   Foundation
Petteys Memorial Foundation,
   Jack

Colorado Springs
El Pomar Foundation
Muchnic Foundation
Stone Trust, H. Chase

Denver
Boettcher Foundation
Comprecare Foundation
Coors Foundation, Adolph
Duncan Trust, John G.
Gates Foundation
Hewit Family Foundation
JFM Foundation
Johnson Foundation, Helen K.
   and Arthur E.
Morrison Charitable Trust,
   Pauline A. and George R.
Mullen Foundation, J. K.
Norgren Foundation, Carl A.
O'Fallon Trust, Martin J. and
   Mary Anne
Schuller International
Security Life of Denver
   Insurance Co.
Taylor Foundation, Ruth and
   Vernon

Englewood

Fishback Foundation Trust,
Harmes C.
Great-West Life Assurance Co.
Pittsburg Midway Coal Mining
Co.
Rabb Foundation, Harry W.
US WEST, Inc.

Grand Junction

Bacon Foundation, E. L. and
Oma

Greeley

Monfort Family Foundation

Holyoke

Heginbotham Trust, Will E.

Lakewood

KN Energy, Inc.

Wray

Kitzmiller/Bales Trust

Connecticut

Botsford

Huisking Foundation

Farmington

Heublein Inc.

Greenwich

Chesebrough-Pond's USA Co.
Fairchild Foundation, Sherman
Moore Foundation, Edward S.
Mosbacher, Jr. Foundation,
Emil
Oaklawn Foundation
Smart Family Foundation
Young Foundation, Robert R.

Hartford

Aetna Life & Casualty Co.
Bissell Foundation, J. Walton
Connecticut Mutual Life
Insurance Company
ITT Hartford Insurance Group,
Inc.
Shawmut National Corp.

Kensington

Vance Charitable Foundation,
Robert C.

Manchester

Lydall, Inc.
Price Foundation, Lucien B.
and Katherine E.

New Britain

Stanley Works

New Canann

Chadwick Fund, Dorothy
Jordan

New Haven

Southern New England
Telephone Company

New London

Palmer Fund, Frank Loomis

New Milford

Harcourt Foundation, Ellen
Knowles
NewMil Bancorp

Norwalk

Culpeper Memorial
Foundation, Daphne Seybolt
Dell Foundation, Hazel
Perkin-Elmer Corp.
Vanderbilt Trust, R. T.

Old Greenwich

American Brands, Inc.

Old Lyme

MacCurdy Salisbury
Educational Foundation

Shelton

Tetley, Inc.

Simsbury

Ensign-Bickford Industries

Southport

Kreitler Foundation
Larsen Fund
Wheeler Foundation, Wilmot

Stamford

Champion International
Corporation
Crane Co.
Culpeper Foundation, Charles
E.
Day Foundation, Nancy Sayles
Olin Corp.
Thomson Information
Publishing Group

Waterbury

Matthies Foundation, Katharine
Moore Charitable Foundation,
Marjorie
Stanley Charitable Foundation,
A.W.

West Hartford

Auerbach Foundation,
Beatrice Fox
Hoffman Foundation,
Maximilian E. and Marion O.
Kohn-Joseloff Foundation
Koopman Fund
Schiro Fund
Valentine Foundation, Lawson
Wiremold Co.

Westport

Newman's Own, Inc.

Windsor Locks

Dexter Corporation

Woodstock

Crabtree & Evelyn

Delaware

Claymont

Lovett Foundation

Greenville

Borkee Hagley Foundation
Glencoe Foundation

Wilmington

Caspersen Foundation for Aid
to Health and Education, O.
W.
Crestlea Foundation
Crystal Trust
du Pont de Nemours & Co., E.
I.
Fair Play Foundation
Good Samaritan
ICI Americas Inc.
Kent-Lucas Foundation
Kutz Foundation, Milton and
Hattie
Laffey-McHugh Foundation
Longwood Foundation
Marmot Foundation
Mohasco Corp.
Vale Foundation, Ruby R.
Welfare Foundation
Wilmington Trust Co.

District of Columbia

Washington

Appleby Trust, Scott B. and
Annie P.
Bloedorn Foundation, Walter
A.
Cafritz Foundation, Morris and
Gwendolyn
Covington and Burling
Folger Fund
Freed Foundation
Giant Food Inc.
Graham Fund, Philip L.
Higginson Trust, Corina
Kiplinger Foundation
Koch Charitable Foundation,
Charles G.
Lea Foundation, Helen Sperry
Marpat Foundation
Marriott Foundation, J. Willard
MCI Communications Corp.
Potomac Electric Power Co.
Public Welfare Foundation
Strong Foundation, Hattie M.

Florida

Arcadia

Morgan Foundation, Louie R.
and Gertrude

Boca Raton

Beveridge Foundation, Frank
Stanley

Delray Beach

Lattner Foundation, Forrest C.

Ft. Lauderdale

Peterson Charitable
Foundation, Folke H.

Holiday

Speer Foundation, Roy M.

Hollywood

Einstein Fund, Albert E. and
Birdie W.

Jacksonville

Adams Foundation, Arthur F.
and Alice E.
Davis Foundations, Arthur
Vining
duPont Foundation, Alfred I.
Kirbo Charitable Trust,
Thomas M. and Irene B.

Jupiter

Whitehead Charitable
Foundation

Longwood

Chatlos Foundation

Miami

Burdines Inc.
Kelly Tractor Co.
Knight Foundation, John S.
and James L.
Wertheim Foundation, Dr.
Herbert A.

Moore Haven

Wiggins Memorial Trust, J. J.

Naples

MacLeod Stewardship
Foundation
Royal Foundation, May
Mitchell

New Smyrna Beach

Landegger Charitable
Foundation

Palm Beach

Breyer Foundation
Chastain Charitable
Foundation, Robert Lee and
Thomas M.

Pensacola

Gulf Power Co.

Sarasota

Beattie Foundation Trust,
Cordelia Lee
Selby and Marie Selby
Foundation, William G.

Tallahassee

Frueauff Foundation, Charles
A.

Venice

Catlin Charitable Trust,
Kathleen K.

Vero Beach

Wahlstrom Foundation

West Palm Beach

Howell Foundation of Florida

Georgia

Albany

Haley Foundation, W. B.

Atlanta

Arnold Fund
English Memorial Fund,
Florence C. and H. L.
Evans Foundation, Lettie Pate
Fuqua Foundation, J. B.
Georgia-Pacific Corporation
Georgia Power Co.
Harland Charitable
Foundation, John and
Wilhelmina D.
Jewell Memorial Foundation,
Daniel Ashley and Irene
Houston
Life Insurance Co. of Georgia
Marshall Foundation, Mattie H.
Marshall Trust in Memory of
Sanders McDaniel, Harriet
McDaniel
McCarty Foundation, John and
Margaret
Trust Company Bank
Winter Construction Co.
Woolley Foundation, Vasser

Columbus

Schwob Foundation, Simon

La Grange

Callaway Foundation

Macon

Porter Testamentary Trust,
James Hyde

Norcross

Alumax Inc.

Hawaii

Honolulu

Amfac/JMB Hawaii Inc.
Atherton Family Foundation
Baldwin Memorial
Foundation, Fred
Cooke Foundation
First Hawaiian, Inc.

Frear Eleemosynary Trust,
Mary D. and Walter F.
McInerny Foundation

Kailua

Castle Foundation, Harold K.
L.

Idaho

Boise

Albertson's Inc.
Boise Cascade Corporation
Morrison Knudsen Corporation
Ore-Ida Foods, Inc.
West One Bancorp

Caldwell

Whittenberger Foundation,
Claude R. and Ethel B.

Idaho Falls

CHC Foundation
Daugherty Foundation

Ketchum

Helms Foundation

Sun Valley

Whiting Foundation,
Macauley and Helen Dow

Illinois

Abbott Park

Abbott Laboratories

Cairo

Hastings Charitable
Foundation, Oris B.

Centralia

Centralia Foundation

Chicago

Akzo America
Akzo Chemicals Inc.
American National Bank &
Trust Co. of Chicago
Amoco Corporation
AON Corporation
Blair and Co., William
Blum Foundation, Harry and
Maribel G.
Blum-Kovler Foundation
Boothroyd Foundation,
Charles H. and Bertha L.
Brach Foundation, Helen
Butz Foundation
Caestecker Foundation,
Charles and Marie
Chicago Sun-Times, Inc.
CNA Financial
Corporation/CNA Insurance
Companies
Commonwealth Edison Co.
Crown Memorial, Arie and Ida
Demos Foundation, N.
Donnelley Foundation,
Gaylord and Dorothy
Donnelly & Sons Co., R.R.
Encyclopaedia Britannica, Inc.
First Chicago Corp.
Fry Foundation, Lloyd A.
GATX Corp.
Graham Foundation for
Advanced Studies in the
Fine Arts
Hartmarx Corporation
Heller Financial, Inc.
Hermann Foundation, Grover
Kelly Foundation, T. Lloyd
Kern Foundation Trust
Lederer Foundation, Francis L.
Lehmann Foundation, Otto W.
MacArthur Foundation, John
D. and Catherine T.

McCormick Foundation, Chauncey and Marion Deering
Norton Memorial Corporation, Geraldi
Offield Family Foundation
Payne Foundation, Frank E. and Seba B.
Peoples Energy Corp.
Pick, Jr. Fund, Albert
Playboy Enterprises, Inc.
Prince Trust, Abbie Norman
R. F. Foundation
Rand McNally & Co.
Regenstein Foundation
Retirement Research Foundation
Sara Lee Corp.
Scholl Foundation, Dr.
United Airlines, Inc.
USG Corporation

Decatur

Andreas Foundation
Archer-Daniels-Midland Co.

Des Plaines

Blowitz-Ridgeway Foundation

Elgin

CR Industries

Elmhurst

Duchossois Industries Inc.

Evanston

Packaging Corporation of America

Geneseo

Geneseo Foundation

Glenview

Illinois Tool Works, Inc.

Godfrey

Monticello College Foundation

Herrin

Harrison Foundation, Fred G.

Itasca

Ringier-America

Lake Forest

Brunswick Corp.

Long Grove

Kemper National Insurance Cos.

Mattoon

Illinois Consolidated Telephone Co.

Moline

Deere & Co.

Monmouth

Mellinger Educational Foundation, Edward Arthur

Naperville

Nalco Chemical Co.

Niles

Cuneo Foundation

Oak Brook

CBI Industries, Inc.
Russell Charitable Foundation, Tom

Palatine

Square D Co.

Riverwoods

Commerce Clearing House, Incorporated
CT Corp. System

Rock Island

Geifman Family Foundation

Rockford

AMCORE Bank, N.A. Rockford
CLARCOR Inc.

Roscoe

Beloit Foundation

Schaumburg

Santa Fe Pacific Corporation

Skokie

Rice Foundation

Sterling

Dillon Foundation

Waukegan

Outboard Marine Corp.

Indiana

Auburn

Rieke Corp.

Columbus

Cummins Engine Co.

Evansville

American General Finance Corp.
Kuehn Foundation
Old National Bank in Evansville

Ft. Wayne

Cole Foundation, Olive B.
Fort Wayne National Bank
Journal-Gazette Co.
Zollner Foundation

Indianapolis

American United Life Insurance Co.
Ayres Foundation, Inc.
CINergy
Clowes Fund
Glick Foundation, Eugene and Marilyn
Griffith Foundation, W. C.
Hook Drugs
Inland Container Corp.
NBD Indiana, Inc.
Plumsock Fund

Jasper

Habig Foundation, Arnold F.

Kendallville

Dekko Foundation

Mishawaka

National Steel Corp.

Muncie

Ball Brothers Foundation
Ball Foundation, George and Frances

South Bend

First Source Corp.
Leighton-Oare Foundation
Oliver Memorial Trust Foundation
South Bend Tribune

Valparaiso

Anderson Foundation, John W.

Vevay

Vevay-Switzerland County Foundation

Winchester

Winchester Foundation

Iowa

Audubon

Audubon State Bank

Cedar Rapids

Gazette Co.
Guaranty Bank & Trust Co.
IES Industries, Inc.

Center Lake

Owen Industries, Inc.

Davenport

Adler Foundation Trust, Philip D. and Henrietta B.
Bechtel Charitable Remainder Uni-Trust, Marie H.
Bechtel Testamentary Charitable Trust, H. R.
Iowa-Illinois Gas & Electric Co.
Lee Enterprises

Des Moines

Cowles Foundation, Gardner and Florence Call
Mid-Iowa Health Foundation
Ruan Foundation Trust, John

Forest City

Winnebago Industries, Inc.

Ft. Madison

Sheaffer Inc.

Keosauqua

Van Buren Foundation

Mason City

Kinney-Lindstrom Foundation
Lee Endowment Foundation

Muscatine

Carver Charitable Trust, Roy J.

Newton

Maytag Family Foundation, Fred

Pella

Kuyper Foundation, Peter H. and E. Lucille
Pella Corporation

Rock Rapids

Forster Charitable Trust, James W. and Ella B.

Waterloo

McElroy Trust, R. J.

Waverly

Century Companies of America

Kansas

Atchison

Exchange National Bank

Garden City

Williams Charitable Trust, Mary Jo

Goodland

First National Bank

Hutchinson

Davis Foundation, James A. and Juliet L.

Junction City

Central National Bank

Liberal

Baughman Foundation

McPherson

Mingenback Foundation, Julia J.

Newton

Schowalter Foundation

Paola

Baehr Foundation, Louis W. and Dolpha

Wichita

Beech Aircraft Corp.
DeVore Foundation

Kentucky

Bowling Green

Houchens Foundation, Ervin G.

Grayson

Commercial Bank

Louisville

Brown & Williamson Tobacco Corp.
Gheens Foundation
Humana, Inc.
Norton Foundation Inc.
Providian Corporation
Thomas Foundation, Joan and Lee
Thomas Industries

Owensboro

Yeager Charitable Trust, Lester E.

Louisiana

Alexandria

Coughlin-Saunders Foundation

New Orleans

Babcock & Wilcox Co.
Freeport-McMoRan Inc.
German Protestant Orphan Asylum Association

Shreveport

Southwestern Electric Power Co.

Maine

Augusta

Central Maine Power Co.

Bangor

Webber Oil Co.

Bath

Davenport Trust Fund

Fryeburg

Mulford Trust, Clarence E.

Portland

Gannett Publishing Co., Guy

Maryland

Baltimore

AEGON USA Inc.
Blaustein Foundation, Louis and Henrietta
Campbell Foundation
France Foundation, Jacob and Annita
Goldseker Foundation of Maryland, Morris
Hecht-Levi Foundation
Leidy Foundation, John J.
Lockhart Vaughan Foundation
Meyerhoff Fund, Joseph
Middendorf Foundation
Mulford Foundation, Vincent
Price Associates, T. Rowe
Unger Foundation, Aber D.
Warfield Memorial Fund, Anna Emory

Bethesda

Martin Marietta Corp.

Columbia

Rouse Co.

Easton

Widgeon Foundation

Hunt Valley

PHH Corporation

Landover

Crown Books
Dart Group Corp.
Hechinger Co.

Linthicum

M.E. Foundation

Potomac

Smith Foundation, Gordon V. and Helen C.

Sparks

McCormick & Co. Inc.

St. Michaels

Knapp Foundation

Takoma Park

Merck Family Fund

Massachusetts

Boston

Babson Foundation, Paul and Edith
Balfour Foundation, L. G.
Bank of Boston Corp.
Beaucourt Foundation
Boston Edison Co.
Cabot Corp.
Cabot Family Charitable Trust
Friendship Fund
Germeshausen Foundation, Kenneth J.
Gillette Co.
Globe Newspaper Co.
Goldberg Family Foundation
Henderson Foundation, George B.
John Hancock Mutual Life Insurance Co.
Johnson Fund, Edward C.
Ladd Charitable Corporation, Helen and George
Peabody Charitable Fund, Amelia
Phillips Foundation, Ellis L.
Pierce Charitable Trust, Harold Whitworth
Prouty Foundation, Olive Higgins
Rabb Charitable Foundation, Sidney and Esther

Reisman Charitable Trust, George C. and Evelyn R.
Saltonstall Charitable Foundation, Richard
Sawyer Charitable Foundation
Thompson Trust, Thomas
Tupancy-Harris Foundation of 1986
Wallace Foundation, George R.
Weber Charities Corp., Frederick E.
Winthrop Trust, Clara B.

Burlington

Dexter Charitable Fund, Eugene A.
Heydt Fund, Nan and Matilda

Cambridge

Little, Inc., Arthur D.
Polaroid Corp.
Rowland Foundation

Chestnut Hill

Harcourt General, Inc.

Concord

GenRad
Hershey Foundation, Barry J.

East Longmeadow

Davis Foundation, Irene E. and George A.

Fairhaven

Acushnet Co.

Fitchburg

Safety Fund National Bank

Groton

New England Business Service

Hopedale

Hopedale Foundation

Hyannis

Kelley and Elza Kelley Foundation, Edward Bangs

Lawrence

Rogers Family Foundation

Leominster

Ansin Private Foundation, Ronald M.

Longmeadow

Blake Foundation, S. P.

Lowell

M/A-COM, Inc.

Maynard

Digital Equipment Corp.

Methuen

Russell Trust, Josephine G.
Stearns Trust, Artemas W.

Needham

Dewing Foundation, Frances R.

Newburyport

Arakelian Foundation, Mary Alice

North Andover

Childs Charitable Foundation, Roberta M.
Stevens Foundation, Abbot and Dorothy H.

Norwood

Bird Corp.

Southbridge

American Optical Corp.

Springfield

Massachusetts Mutual Life Insurance Co.

Stockbridge

Housatonic Curtain Co.

Tewksbury

Demoulas Supermarkets Inc.

Waltham

Thermo Electron Corp.

Wareham

Stone Charitable Foundation

Waverley

Linnell Foundation

Wellesley Hills

Rubin Family Fund, Cele H. and William B.

Weston

Levy Foundation, June Rockwell

Worcester

Bank of Boston
Fletcher Foundation
Harrington Foundation, Francis A. and Jacquelyn H.
McEvoy Foundation, Mildred H.
Memorial Foundation for the Blind
Morgan Construction Co.
Norton Co.
Rice Charitable Foundation, Albert W.

Michigan

Alpena

Besser Foundation

Ann Arbor

Towsley Foundation, Harry A. and Margaret D.

Battle Creek

Miller Foundation

Bay City

Kantzler Foundation

Benton Harbor

Whirlpool Corporation

Birmingham

Vollbrecht Foundation, Frederick A.

Bloomfield Hills

Mardigian Foundation
Taubman Foundation, A. Alfred

Dearborn

Ford Motor Co.

Detroit

American Natural Resources Company
Comerica Incorporated
DeRoy Foundation, Helen L.
DeRoy Testamentary Foundation
Detroit Edison Co.
Federal-Mogul Corporation
Ford Fund, William and Martha
Ford II Fund, Henry
General Motors Corp.

Herrick Foundation
Hudson-Webber Foundation
Scherer Foundation, Karla
Skillman Foundation
Tecumseh Products Co.
Whitney Fund, David M.
Wilson Fund, Matilda R.

Dundee

Holnam

Farmington Hills

Douglas & Lomason Company

Flint

Merkley Charitable Trust
Mott Foundation, Charles Stewart
Mott Fund, Ruth
Whiting Foundation

Grand Haven

Westerman Foundation, Samuel L.

Grand Rapids

Grand Rapids Label Co.
Seidman Family Foundation
Wege Foundation

Highland Park

Chrysler Corp.

Jackson

Consumers Power Co.

Kalamazoo

Delano Foundation, Mignon Sherwood
Fabri-Kal Corp.
Interkal, Inc.
Todd Co., A.M.
Upjohn Foundation, Harold and Grace
Vicksburg Foundation

Lansing

Abrams Foundation, Talbert and Leota

Midland

Dow Corning Corp.
Dow Foundation, Herbert H. and Grace A.

Monroe

La-Z-Boy Chair Co.

Muskegon

SPX Corp.

Saginaw

Boutell Memorial Fund
Eddy Family Memorial Fund, C. K.
Mills Fund, Frances Goll
Wickes Foundation, Harvey Randall
Wickson-Link Memorial Foundation

Saline

R&B Machine Tool Co.

Southfield

Borman's Inc.
Ratner Foundation, Milton M.

St. Clair Shores

Fruehauf Foundation

St. Joseph

Tiscornia Foundation
Upton Foundation, Frederick S.

Suttons Bay

Bauervic Foundation, Charles M.

Troy

Kmart Corporation
Kresge Foundation

Zeeland

Batts Foundation

Minnesota

Bayport

Andersen Corp.
Andersen Foundation
Mahadh Foundation

Grand Rapids

Blandin Foundation

Mankato

Hickory Tech Corp.

Minneapolis

Allianz Life Insurance Co. of North America
Bemis Company, Inc.
Cargill Inc.
Carolyn Foundation
Cowles Media Co.
Donaldson Company, Inc.
General Mills, Inc.
Jostens, Inc.
Marbrook Foundation
Medtronic, Inc.
Northern States Power Co. (Minnesota)
Norwest Corporation
Phillips Family Foundation, Jay and Rose
Piper Jaffray Companies Inc.
Sundet Foundation

Minnetonka

Bell Foundation, James F.

Owatonna

Federated Mutual Insurance Co.

St. Paul

Bigelow Foundation, F. R.
Bremer Foundation, Otto
Bush Foundation
Davis Foundation, Edwin W. and Catherine M.
Griggs and Mary Griggs Burke Foundation, Mary Livingston
Hallett Charitable Trust, E. W.
Hallett Charitable Trust, Jessie F.
Mardag Foundation
Minnesota Mining & Mfg. Co.
Saint Paul Companies, Inc.
Tozer Foundation
Weyerhaeuser Memorial Foundation, Charles A.

Thief River Falls

Hartz Foundation

Mississippi

Jackson

Feild Co-Operative Association

Meridian

Hardin Foundation, Phil

Natchez

Armstrong Foundation

Missouri

Birch Tree

Shaw Foundation, Arch W.

Chesterfield

Pott Foundation, Herman T. and Phenie R.

Clayton

Pettus Crowe Foundation
Stupp Foundation, Norman J.

Fenton

Maritz Inc.

Hazelwood

ACF Industries, Inc.

Kansas City

Block, H&R
Commerce Bancshares, Inc.
Kansas City Southern Industries
Kemper Foundation, William T.
McGee Foundation
Miller-Mellor Association
Oppenstein Brothers Foundation
Smith Foundation, Ralph L.

Mexico

Green Foundation, Allen P. and Josephine B.

Rockport

Morgan Charitable Residual Trust, W. and E.

St. Louis

Anheuser-Busch Companies, Inc.
Boatmen's Bancshares, Inc.
Gaylord Foundation, Clifford Willard
General American Life Insurance Co.
Jordan Charitable Foundation, Mary Ranken Jordan and Ettie A.
Lichtenstein Foundation, David B.
May Department Stores Company, The
Messing Family Charitable Foundation
Olin Foundation, Spencer T. and Ann W.
Pulitzer Publishing Co.
Ralston Purina Co.
Sunnen Foundation
Swift Co. Inc., John S.
Union Electric Co.
Van Evera Foundation, Dewitt

Montana

Butte

Montana Power Co.

Nebraska

Aurora

Farr Trust, Frank M. and Alice M.

Dakota City

IBP, Inc.

Grand Island

Reynolds Foundation, Edgar

Lincoln
Ameritas Life Insurance Corp.

Omaha
Kiewit Foundation, Peter
Norwest Bank Nebraska, N.A.
Pamida, Inc.

Scottsbluff
Quivey-Bay State Foundation

Valley
Valmont Industries, Inc.

Nevada

Las Vegas
PriMerit Bank

Reno
Cord Foundation, E. L.
Hawkins Foundation, Robert Z.
May Foundation, Wilbur
Sierra Pacific Resources
Wiegand Foundation, E. L.

New Hampshire

Bennington
Monadnock Paper Mills

Concord
Bean Foundation, Norwin S.
and Elizabeth N.
Smith Charitable Foundation,
Lou and Lutza

Hampton
Dingman Foundation, Michael
D.

Keene
Kingsbury Corp.
Putnam Foundation

Lebanon
Mascoma Savings Bank

Manchester
Cogswell Benevolent Trust
Hunt Foundation, Samuel P.

Merrimack
Unitrode Corp.

Rye Beach
Fuller Foundation

New Jersey

Bernardsville
Jockey Hollow Foundation

Cedar Grove
Martini Foundation, Nicholas

Chatham Township
Hyde and Watson Foundation

Cherry Hill
Subaru of America Inc.

Collingswood
Maneely Fund

Englewood Cliffs
CPC International Inc.
Holzer Memorial Foundation,
Richard H.
Lipton, Thomas J.

Gladstone
Brady Foundation

Jersey City
National Westminster Bank
New Jersey

Madison
Schering-Plough Corp.

Millburn
Jaydor Corp.
Read Foundation, Charles L.

Montclair
Schumann Fund for New
Jersey
Turrell Fund

Moorestown
Snyder Foundation, Harold B.
and Dorothy A.

Morristown
AlliedSignal Inc.
Dodge Foundation, Geraldine
R.
Kirby Foundation, F. M.
Sandy Hill Foundation
Simon Foundation, William E.
and Carol G.
Sullivan Foundation, Algernon
Sydney

New Brunswick
Fund for New Jersey

New Vernon
Klipstein Foundation, Ernest
Christian

Newark
Prudential Insurance Co. of
America, The
Public Service Electric & Gas
Co.
Seton Leather Co.
Van Houten Memorial Fund

Nutley
Hoffmann-La Roche Inc.

Paramus
Lazarus Charitable Trust,
Helen and Charles

Parsippany
Nabisco Foods Group

Princeton
Bunbury Company
Cape Branch Foundation
Church & Dwight Co., Inc.
Dow Jones & Company, Inc.
High Foundation
Newcombe Foundation,
Charlotte W.
Rhone-Poulenc Inc.

Ridgewood
Schenck Fund, L. P.

Roseland
Barker Foundation, J.M.R.

Rumson
Huber Foundation

Shrewsbury
Beck Foundation, Elsie E. and
Joseph W.

Somerville
South Branch Foundation

Summit
Darby Foundation

Wall
New Jersey Natural Gas Co.

Warren
Schwartz Foundation, Arnold
A.

Wayne
International Foundation
Union Camp Corporation

Whitehouse Station
Merck & Co.

New Mexico

Albuquerque
Public Service Co. of New
Mexico

Hobbs
Maddox Foundation, J. F.

Santa Fe
McCune Charitable
Foundation, Marshall and
Perrine D.

New York

Armonk
International Business
Machines Corp.
MBIA Inc.

Auburn
Emerson Foundation, Inc.,
Fred L.
Everett Charitable Trust
French Foundation, D.E.

Bayside
Vogler Foundation, Laura B.

Binghamton
Hoyt Foundation, Stewart W.
and Willma C.

Bronx
Dodge Foundation, Cleveland
H.
Wilson Foundation, H. W.

Brooklyn
Parshelsky Foundation, Moses
L.

Buffalo
Burchfield Foundation,
Charles E.
Cornell Trust, Peter C.
Cummings Foundation, James
H.
Delaware North Co., Inc.
Julia R. and Estelle L.
Foundation
Rich Products Corporation
Wendt Foundation, Margaret L.
Western New York Foundation

Canajoharie
Arkell Hall Foundation

Carmel
Weinstein Foundation, J.

Cayuga
Allyn Foundation

Cold Spring Harbor
Kennedy Foundation, Ethel

Corning
Corning Incorporated

East Rochester
Schmitt Foundation, Kilian J.
and Caroline F.

Elizabethtown
Crary Foundation, Bruce L.

Elmira
Anderson Foundation

Garden City
Brooks Foundation, Gladys

Geneva
Delavan Foundation, Nelson B.

Gloversville
City National Bank and Trust
Co.

Greene
Raymond Corp.

Hammondsport
Mercury Aircraft

Hicksville
Long Island Lighting Co.

Hobart
O'Connor Foundation, A.
Lindsay and Olive B.

Hudson Falls
Hill Foundation, Sandy

Ithaca
Park Foundation

Jamestown
Carnahan-Jackson Foundation
Gebbie Foundation
Hultquist Foundation
Lenna Foundation, Reginald
A. and Elizabeth S.

Kingston
Klock and Lucia Klock
Kingston Foundation, Jay E.

Lake Placid
Lake Placid Education
Foundation

Lake Success
Canon U.S.A., Inc.

Long Island City
Fife Foundation, Elias and
Bertha
Mathis-Pfohl Foundation

Mamaroneck
Nias Foundation, Henry

Millbrook
Millbrook Tribute Garden

Mt. Kisco
Icahn Foundation, Carl C.

New York
Achelis Foundation
Air France
AKC Fund
Alavi Foundation of New York
Alexander Foundation, Joseph
Allen Brothers Foundation
Altman Foundation
Altschul Foundation
AMETEK, Inc.
Arnhold Foundation

ASDA Foundation
Astor Foundation, Vincent
AT&T Corp.
Atran Foundation
Avery Arts Foundation, Milton
and Sally
Avon Products, Inc.
Badgeley Residuary Charitable
Trust, Rose M.
Baker Trust, George F.
Baldwin Foundation, David
M. and Barbara
Bank of New York Company,
Inc.
Bankers Trust Company
Barth Foundation, Theodore H.
Bay Foundation
Benenson Foundation, Frances
and Benjamin
Benetton Services Corp.
Bingham Second Betterment
Fund, William
Bobst Foundation, Elmer and
Mamdouha
Bodman Foundation
Booth Ferris Foundation
Bowne Foundation, Robert
Bristol-Myers Squibb
Company
Burden Foundation, Florence
V.
Calder Foundation, Louis
Carnegie Corporation of New
York
CBS, Inc.
Charina Foundation
Chase Manhattan Bank, N.A.
Chazen Foundation
Cheatham Foundation, Owen
Christian Dior New York, Inc.
CIBC Wood Gundy
Citibank
Claiborne and Art Ortenberg
Foundation, Liz
Clark Foundation
Coleman Foundation, George
E.
Coltec Industries, Inc.
Continental Corp.
Cooperman Foundation, Leon
and Toby
Cosmair, Inc.
Cowles Charitable Trust
CS First Boston Corporation
Culver Foundation, Constans
Daily News
Dana Charitable Trust, Eleanor
Naylor
Dana Foundation, Charles A.
Diamond Foundation, Aaron
Dillon Dunwalke Trust,
Clarence and Anne
Donner Foundation, William H.
Dreyfus Foundation, Jean and
Louis
Dula Educational and
Charitable Foundation,
Caleb C. and Julia W.
Dun & Bradstreet Corp.
Edmonds Foundation, Dean S.
Erpf Fund, Armand G.
Ettinger Foundation
Evans Foundation, T. M.
Feil Foundation, Louis and
Gertrude
Fink Foundation
Forbes Inc.
Ford Foundation
Freeman Charitable Trust,
Samuel
Frese Foundation, Arnold D.
Fribourg Foundation
Fuld Health Trust, Helene
Gilman Foundation, Howard
Givenchy Corp.
Glanville Family Foundation
Goldie-Anna Charitable Trust
Goldsmith Foundation, Horace
W.
Goodstein Family Foundation,
David
Gordon/Rousmaniere/Roberts
Fund
Gould Foundation, The
Florence

Greenwall Foundation
Greve Foundation, William and Mary
Griffis Foundation
Guardian Life Insurance Company of America
Guggenheim Foundation, Harry Frank
Guttman Foundation, Stella and Charles
Hagedorn Fund
Handy and Harman Foundation
Hanson Industries North America
HarperCollins Publishers Inc.
Harriman Foundation, Gladys and Roland
Harriman Foundation, Mary W.
Hartford Foundation, John A.
Hatch Charitable Trust, Margaret Milliken
Hauser Foundation
Hazen Foundation, Edward W.
Hearst Foundation, William Randolph
Hebrew Technical Institute
Heckscher Foundation for Children
Hillman Family Foundation, Alex
Homeland Foundation
Hopkins Foundation, Josephine Lawrence
Hugoton Foundation
Ittleson Foundation
JM Foundation
Johnson Charitable Trust, Keith Wold
Johnson Foundation, Willard T. C.
Johnson & Higgins
Jurzykowski Foundation, Alfred
Kaplan Fund, J. M.
Kaplun Foundation, Morris J. and Betty
Kaufmann Foundation, Henry
Kaye, Scholer, Fierman, Hays & Handler
Klosk Fund, Louis and Rose
Kornfeld Foundation, Emily Davie and Joseph S.
Kress Foundation, Samuel H.
Lang Foundation, Eugene M.
Lasdon Foundation
Lasdon Foundation, William and Mildred
Lauder Foundation
Lemberg Foundation
Liberman Foundation, Bertha and Isaac
Link, Jr. Foundation, George
Littauer Foundation, Lucius N.
Liz Claiborne, Inc.
Loews Corporation
Lowenstein Foundation, Leon
Lurcy Charitable and Educational Trust, Georges
Macy & Co., Inc., R.H.
Mailman Foundation
Mandeville Foundation
Markle Foundation, John and Mary R.
Marsh & McLennan Companies, Inc.
McGraw-Hill, Inc.
Mellon Foundation, Andrew W.
Memton Fund
Merrill Lynch & Co., Inc.
Metropolitan Life Insurance Co.
Miller Fund, Kathryn and Gilbert
Mitsubishi International Corp.
Mnuchin Foundation
Monell Foundation, Ambrose
Morgan & Company, J.P.
Morgan Stanley & Co., Inc.
Morris Foundation, William T.
Moses Fund, Henry and Lucy
Neuberger Foundation, Roy R. and Marie S.
New-Land Foundation
New York Life Insurance Co.
New York Mercantile Exchange

New York Stock Exchange, Inc.
New York Times Company
Noble Foundation, Edward John
Normandie Foundation
NYNEX Corporation
Ohrstrom Foundation
Olin Foundation, F. W.
Osborn Charitable Trust, Edward B.
Osceola Foundation
Overbrook Foundation
PaineWebber
Paley Foundation, William S.
Palisades Educational Foundation
Penguin Books USA, Inc.
Pfizer, Inc.
Pforzheimer Foundation, Carl and Lily
Phipps Foundation, Howard
Piankova Foundation, Tatiana
Porter Foundation, Mrs. Cheever
Price Foundation, Louis and Harold
Prospect Hill Foundation
Prudential Securities, Inc.
Reed Foundation
Reicher Foundation, Anne and Harry J.
Republic NY Corp.
Reynolds Foundation, Christopher
Richardson Charitable Trust, Anne S.
RJR Nabisco Inc.
Robinson Fund, Maurice R.
Rockefeller Fund, David
Rohatyn Foundation, Felix and Elizabeth
Rose Foundation, Billy
Rosen Foundation, Joseph
Rubin Foundation, Samuel
Rubinstein Foundation, Helena
Rudin Foundation
Salomon Inc.
Salomon Foundation, Richard and Edna
Sasco Foundation
Scherman Foundation
Schiff Foundation, Dorothy
Schlumberger Ltd.
Schwartz Fund for Education and Health Research, Arnold and Marie
Seagram & Sons, Inc., Joseph E.
Shubert Foundation
Slifka Foundation, Joseph and Sylvia
Sloan Foundation, Alfred P.
Smeal Foundation, Mary Jean and Frank P.
Solow Foundation
Sprague Educational and Charitable Foundation, Seth
Starr Foundation
Steele-Reese Foundation
Steinbach Fund, Ruth and Milton
Sulzberger Foundation
Swiss Bank Corp.
Taconic Foundation
Teagle Foundation
The New Yorker Magazine, Inc.
Thompson Co., J. Walter
Thorne Foundation
Titus Foundation, Roy and Niuta
Travelers Inc.
Tuch Foundation, Michael
Unilever United States, Inc.
Uris Brothers Foundation
van Ameringen Foundation
Vetlesen Foundation, G. Unger
Wallace-Reader's Digest Fund, DeWitt
Wallace-Reader's Digest Fund, Lila
Warner Fund, Albert and Bessie
Weezie Foundation
Weil, Gotshal and Manges Foundation

WestLB New York Branch
Westvaco Corporation
Wiley & Sons, Inc., John
Winston Foundation, Norman and Rosita
Witco Corp.
Zenkel Foundation
Zlinkoff Fund for Medical Research and Education, Sergei S.

North Tarrytown

Vernon Fund, Miles Hodsdon

North Tonawanda

Joy Family Foundation

Oneida

Chapman Charitable Corporation, Howard and Bess

Oneonta

Hulbert Foundation, Nila B.
Warren and Beatrice W. Blanding Foundation, Riley J. and Lillian N.

Orangeburg

Hino Diesel Trucks (U.S.A.)

Orchard Park

Palisano Foundation, Vincent and Harriet

Pittsford

Seneca Foods Corp.

Poughkeepsie

Central Hudson Gas & Electric Corp.
McCann Foundation

Pound Ridge

Blum Foundation, Edna F.

Pulaski

Snow Foundation, John Ben

Purchase

International Paper Co.
McGonagle Foundation, Dextra Baldwin

Rochester

Curtice-Burns Foods, Inc.
Davenport-Hatch Foundation
Eastman Kodak Company
Gleason Foundation
Jones Foundation, Daisy Marquis
Taylor Foundation, Fred and Harriett
Woodward Fund

Rye

Fischbach Foundation

Scarsdale

Marx Foundation, Virginia and Leonard

Stamford

Robinson-Broadhurst Foundation

Syracuse

Gifford Charitable Corporation, Rosamond
Mather Fund, Richard
Snow Memorial Trust, John Ben

Troy

Howard and Bush Foundation

Utica

Utica National Insurance Group

White Plains

Dreyfus Foundation, Max and Victoria
Mailman Family Foundation, A. L.
Texaco Inc.

Yonkers

Carvel Foundation, Thomas and Agnes

North Carolina

Asheboro

Acme-McCrary Corp./Sapona Manufacturing Co.

Asheville

Janirve Foundation

Charlotte

Dalton Foundation, Harry L.
Duke Endowment
Duke Power Co.
First Union Corp.
First Union National Bank of Florida
Giles Foundation, Edward C.
National Gypsum Co.
Royal Group, Inc.
Van Every Foundation, Philip L.

Eden

Fieldcrest Cannon Inc.
Miller Brewing Company/North Carolina

Elkin

Chatham Manufacturing Co.

Greensboro

Blue Bell, Inc.
Burlington Industries, Inc.
Connemara Fund
Hillsdale Fund
Sternberger Foundation, Tannenbaum

Henderson

Rose's Stores, Inc.

Hendersonville

Rixson Foundation, Oscar C.

Kinston

Harvey Foundation, Felix

Raleigh

Martin Marietta Materials

Research Triangle Park

Reichhold Chemicals, Inc.

Shelby

Dover Foundation

Thomasville

Finch Foundation, Doak
Thomasville Furniture Industries

Wadesboro

Moore & Sons, B.C.

Wilson

Glenn Foundation, Carrie C. and Lena V.

Winston-Salem

Ferebee Endowment, Percy O.

Finch Foundation, Thomas Austin
Hanes Foundation, John W. and Anna H.
Ottley Trust-Watertown, Marion W.
Sara Lee Hosiery, Inc.
Wachovia Bank of North Carolina, N.A.

North Dakota

Grand Forks

Myra Foundation

Ohio

Akron

Calhoun Charitable Trust, Kenneth
Firestone, Jr. Foundation, Harvey
Gallagher Family Foundation, Lewis P.
GAR Foundation
Goodrich Co., The B.F.
McFawn Trust No. 2, Lois Sisler
Morgan Foundation, Burton D.
Musson Charitable Foundation, R. C. and Katharine M.

Ashtabula

Ashtabula Foundation

Beachwood

Eaton Foundation, Cyrus

Bryan

Markey Charitable Fund, John C.

Canton

Flowers Charitable Trust, Albert W. and Edith V.
Hoover Fund-Trust, W. Henry
Timken Foundation of Canton

Cincinnati

Dater Foundation, Charles H.
Frisch's Restaurants Inc.
Griswold Foundation, John C.
Jarson-Stanley and Mickey Kaplan Foundation, Isaac and Esther
Scripps Co., E.W.
Slemp Foundation

Cleveland

Andrews Foundation
Bingham Foundation, William
BP America Inc.
Centerior Energy Corp.
Eaton Corporation
Firman Fund
Frohring Foundation, Paul and Maxine
Frohring Foundation, William O. and Gertrude Lewis
Humphrey Fund, George M. and Pamela S.
Mather and William Gwinn Mather Fund, Elizabeth Ring
Mather Charitable Trust, S. Livingston
McDonald & Company Securities, Inc.
Parker Hannifin Corp.
Premier Industrial Corp.
Reinberger Foundation
Second Foundation
Smith Foundation, Kelvin and Eleanor
South Waite Foundation

Columbus

Barry Corp., R. G.

Battelle Memorial Institute
Borden, Inc.
Columbus Dispatch Printing Co.
Ross Laboratories
Wildermuth Foundation, E. F.

Dayton
Amcast Industrial Corp.
Kettering Fund
Mead Corporation, The
Tait Foundation, Frank M.

Eastlake
Gould Electronics Inc.

Fairlawn
GenCorp Inc.

Loudonville
Young Foundation, Hugo H. and Mabel B.

Maumee
Andersons, The
Seaway Food Town, Inc.

Newark
Evans Foundation, Thomas J.

North Canton
Deuble Foundation, George H.
Hoover Foundation

Norwalk
Schlink Foundation, Albert G. and Olive H.

Piqua
French Oil Mill Machinery Co.

Sandusky
Sandusky International Inc.

Shaker Heights
Ingalls Foundation, Louise H. and David S.

Solon
Lennon Foundation, Fred A.

Toledo
Cayuga Foundation
Ritter Charitable Trust, George W. and Mary F.

Van Wert
Van Wert County Foundation

Warren
Freedom Forge Corp.
Wean Foundation, Raymond John

Westlake
Scott Fetzer Co.

Worthington
Worthington Foods

Youngstown
Bank One, Youngstown, NA
Crandall Memorial Foundation, J. Ford
Kilcawley Fund, William H.
Pollock Company Foundation, William B.

Oklahoma

Ardmore
Goddard Foundation, Charles B.
Merrick Foundation

Noble Foundation, Samuel Roberts

Bartlesville
Lyon Foundation

Blackwell
Beatty Trust, Cordelia Lunceford

Duncan
McCasland Foundation

Lawton
McMahon Foundation

McAlester
Puterbaugh Foundation

Norman
Sarkeys Foundation

Oklahoma City
American Fidelity Corporation
Kerr Foundation
Kirkpatrick Foundation
OG&E Electric Services
Share Trust, Charles Morton

Tulsa
Broadhurst Foundation
Collins Foundation, George and Jennie
Collins, Jr. Foundation, George Fulton
Harmon Foundation, Pearl M. and Julia J.
Helmerich Foundation
Oxy USA Inc.
Reynolds Foundation, Donald W.
Williams Companies, The
Zarrow Foundation, Anne and Henry

Oregon

Eugene
Hunt Charitable Trust, C. Giles

Klamath Falls
JELD-WEN, Inc.

Lake Oswego
OCRI Foundation

Medford
Carpenter Foundation

Portland
Collins Foundation
Collins Medical Trust
First Interstate Bank of Oregon
Jackson Foundation
Louisiana-Pacific Corp.
Meyer Memorial Trust
Northwest Natural Gas Co.
Tucker Charitable Trust, Rose E.
Wheeler Foundation

Roseburg
Fohs Foundation
Roseburg Forest Products Co.

Salem
Pioneer Trust Bank, NA
Siltec Corp.

Pennsylvania

Allentown
Air Products and Chemicals, Inc.

Baker Foundation, Dexter F. and Dorothy H.
Holt Family Foundation
Lebovitz Fund
Lehigh Portland Cement Co.
Trexler Trust, Harry C.

Bethlehem
Bethlehem Steel Corp.
Union Pacific Corp.

Bradford
Forest Oil Corp.

Bristol
Grundy Foundation

Broomall
Kavanagh Foundation, T. James

Bryn Mawr
Bryn Mawr Trust Co.
McLean Contributionship

Butler
Spang & Co.

Camp Hill
Harsco Corp.
Kunkel Foundation, John Crain

Carlisle
Giant Food Stores

Chambersburg
Wood Foundation of Chambersburg, PA

Cleona
Lebanon Mutual Insurance Co.

Coatesville
Huston Charitable Trust, Stewart

Cogan Station
Plankenhorn Foundation, Harry

Conshohocken
Quaker Chemical Corp.

Doylestown
Warwick Foundation

DuBois
Mengle Foundation, Glenn and Ruth

East Greenville
Knoll Group

Easton
Binney & Smith Inc.

Ephrata
GSM Industrial

Farrell
Sharon Steel Corp.

Forty Fort
Sordoni Foundation

Freeport
Freeport Brick Co.

Gulph Mills
Henkel Corp.

Hanover
Sheppard Foundation, Lawrence B.

Harrisburg
AMP Incorporated
Kline Foundation, Josiah W. and Bessie H.
McCormick Trust, Anne
Stabler Foundation, Donald B. and Dorothy L.

Hazleton
Reidler Foundation

Hershey
Hershey Foods Corp.

Irvine
National Forge Co.

Johnstown
Glosser Foundation, David A.

Kulpsville
Clemens Markets Corp.

Lancaster
Hamilton Bank
Steinman Foundation, James Hale
Steinman Foundation, John Frederick

Latrobe
McFeely-Rogers Foundation
McKenna Foundation, Katherine Mabis
McKenna Foundation, Philip M.

Lewisburg
Sheary for Charity, Edna M.

Limerick
Teleflex Inc.

McKeesport
Crawford Estate, E. R.
Murphy Co. Foundation, G.C.

Mechanicsburg
Wells Foundation, Franklin H. and Ruth L.

Mount Holly Springs
Pennsylvania Dutch Co.

New Castle
Hoyt Foundation

Norristown
Arcadia Foundation

Oakmont
Edgewater Steel Corp.

Oil City
Eccles Foundation, Ralph M. and Ella M.
Justus Trust, Edith C.
Phillips Charitable Trust, Dr. and Mrs. Arthur William

Philadelphia
Bard Foundation, Robert
Berwind Corporation
Binswanger Cos.
Carpenter Foundation, E. Rhodes and Leona B.
Cassett Foundation, Louis N.
CIGNA Corporation
Elf Atochem North America, Inc.
First Fidelity Bank
Groome Beatty Trust, Helen D.
Independence Foundation
Kardon Foundation, Samuel and Rebecca
Levitt Foundation
McShain Charities, John

Mutual Assurance Co.
PECO Energy Company
Penn Foundation, William
Pew Charitable Trusts
Rohm & Haas Co.
Smith Memorial Fund, Ethel Sergeant Clark
SmithKline Beecham Corp.

Pittsburgh
Allegheny Foundation
Allegheny Ludlum Corp.
Aluminum Co. of America
Aristech Chemical Corp.
Armco Inc.
Benedum Foundation, Claude Worthington
Buhl Foundation
Clapp Charitable and Educational Trust, George H.
Consolidated Natural Gas Co.
Eden Hall Foundation
Fair Oaks Foundation, Inc.
Foster Charitable Trust
Giant Eagle, Inc.
Heinz Company, H. J.
Heinz Endowment, Howard
Heinz Endowment, Vira I.
Heinz Trust, Drue
Hillman Foundation
Hopwood Charitable Trust, John M.
Hulme Charitable Foundation, Milton G.
Hunt Foundation
Hunt Foundation, Roy A.
Jennings Foundation, Mary Hillman
Jewish Healthcare Foundation of Pittsburgh
Laurel Foundation
Love Foundation, George H. and Margaret McClintic
McCune Charitable Trust, John R.
Mellon Family Foundation, R. K.
Mellon Foundation, Richard King
Miller Charitable Foundation, Howard E. and Nell E.
Mine Safety Appliances Co.
Neville Chemical Co.
Patterson Charitable Fund, W. I.
Peters Foundation, Charles F.
Pitt-Des Moines Inc.
Pittsburgh Child Guidance Foundation
PNC Bank, N.A.
PPG Industries, Inc.
Rockwell International Corporation
Scaife Family Foundation
Speyer Foundation, Alexander C. and Tillie S.
Staunton Farm Foundation
Trees Charitable Trust, Edith L.
USX Corporation
Waters Charitable Trust, Robert S.
Williams Charitable Trust, John C.

Plymouth Meeting
Douty Foundation

Pottsville
Snayberger Memorial Foundation, Harry E. and Florence W.

Reading
Carpenter Technology Corp.

Rydal
Gershman Foundation, Joel

St. Davids
Ames Charitable Trust, Harriett
Annenberg Foundation

St. Marys
Stackpole-Hall Foundation

Uniontown
Eberly Foundation
Integra Bank of Uniontown

Warren
Betts Industries

Washington
Coen Family Foundation, Charles S. and Mary
Dynamet, Inc.

Wayne
Strawbridge Foundation of Pennsylvania II, Margaret Dorrance

West Conshohocken
Connelly Foundation
Huston Foundation

West Point
Merck & Co. Human Health Division

Williamsport
LamCo. Communications

Willow Grove
Asplundh Foundation

Wyndmoor
Barra Foundation

Wynnewood
Superior Tube Co.

Wyomissing
Wyomissing Foundation

York
Dentsply International Inc.

Rhode Island

Cranston
Cranston Print Works Company

Johnston
Allendale Insurance Co.

Pawtucket
Hasbro Inc.
Hassenfeld Foundation

Providence
Champlin Foundations
Citizens Bank of Rhode Island
Clarke Trust, John
Dimeo Construction Co.
Fleet Financial Group, Inc.
Jaffe Foundation
Providence Gas Co.
Providence Journal Company
Textron, Inc.

Westerly
Kimball Foundation, Horace A. Kimball and S. Ella

South Carolina

Columbia
Colonial Life & Accident Insurance Co.
Fuller Foundation, C. G.
Symmes Foundation, F. W.

Graniteville
Gregg-Graniteville Foundation

Greenville
Bowater Incorporated

Greenwood
Self Foundation

Kershaw
Stevens Foundation, John T.

Lancaster
Close Foundation
Springs Foundation

Myrtle Beach
Chapin Foundation of Myrtle Beach, South Carolina

Tennessee

Bristol
Massengill-DeFriece Foundation

Chattanooga
Benwood Foundation
Provident Life & Accident Insurance Company of America
Tonya Memorial Foundation

Knoxville
Stokely, Jr. Foundation, William B.
Thompson Charitable Foundation
Toms Foundation

Memphis
Clarkson Foundation, Jeniam
First Tennessee Bank
Sedgwick James Inc.

Murfreesboro
Christy-Houston Foundation

Nashville
Ansley Foundation, Dantzler Bond
Bridgestone/Firestone, Inc.
HCA Foundation
Potter Foundation, Justin and Valere

Texas

Abilene
Dodge Jones Foundation

Amarillo
Mays Foundation

Arlington
Hallberg Foundation, E. L. and R. F.

Austin
Cain Foundation, Effie and Wofford
Henry Foundation, Patrick
Johnson Foundation, Burdine
LBJ Family Foundation
Wright Foundation, Lola

Beaumont
Dishman Charitable Foundation Trust, H. E. and Kate
Steinhagen Benevolent Trust, B. A. and Elinor

Dallas
Clements Foundation
Contran Corporation
Dresser Industries, Inc.
Early Foundation

Fikes Foundation, Leland
Hammer Foundation, Armand
Hawn Foundation
Hillcrest Foundation
Jonsson Foundation
Kimberly-Clark Corp.
McDermott Foundation, Eugene
Meadows Foundation
Overlake Foundation
Stemmons Foundation
Sturgis Charitable and Educational Trust, Roy and Christine
Sumners Foundation, Hatton W.

Denison
Munson Foundation Trust, W. B.
Smith Charitable Foundation, Clara Blackford Smith and W. Aubrey

DFW Airport
AMR Corp.

Diboll
Temple-Inland Inc.

El Paso
Huthsteiner Fine Arts Trust

Falfurrias
Rachal Foundation, Ed

Ft. Worth
Alcon Laboratories, Inc.
Burnett-Tandy Foundation
Carter Foundation, Amon G.
McQueen Foundation, Adeline and George
Scott Foundation, William E.
Walsh Foundation
Weaver Foundation, Gil and Dody
White Trust, G. R.

Galveston
Kempner Fund, Harris and Eliza

Graham
Bertha Foundation

Harlingen
Hygeia Dairy Co.

Houston
Anderson Foundation, M. D.
Baker Hughes Inc.
Bank One, Texas-Houston Office
Burkitt Foundation
Cain Foundation, Gordon and Mary
Clayton Fund
Cooper Industries, Inc.
Cullen Foundation
Duncan Foundation, Lillian H. and C. W.
Elkins, Jr. Foundation, Margaret and James A.
Enron Corp.
Farish Fund, William Stamps Favrot Fund
Fish Foundation, Ray C.
Fondren Foundation
Hamman Foundation, George and Mary Josephine
Herzstein Charitable Foundation, Albert and Ethel
Hobby Foundation
Houston Endowment
Houston Industries Incorporated
Kayser Foundation
Kilroy Foundation, William S. and Lora Jean

Knox, Sr., and Pearl Wallis Knox Charitable Foundation, Robert W.
Management Compensation Group/Dulworth Inc.
O'Quinn Foundation, John M. and Nancy C.
Owsley Foundation, Alvin and Lucy
Panhandle Eastern Corporation
Pennzoil Co.
Rockwell Fund
Scurlock Foundation
Shell Oil Company
Swalm Foundation
Tenneco Inc.
Texas Commerce Bank-Houston, N.A.
Transco Energy Co.
Turner Charitable Foundation
Vaughn, Jr. Foundation Fund, James M.
Wilder Foundation

Irving
Exxon Corporation

Jacksonville
Norman Foundation, Summers A.

Kerrville
Peterson Foundation, Hal and Charlie

Laredo
Hachar Charitable Trust, D. D.

Lubbock
Jones Foundation, Helen

Lufkin
Pineywoods Foundation
Temple Foundation, T. L. L.

Midland
Abell-Hanger Foundation
Beal Foundation
Davidson Family Charitable Foundation
Potts and Sibley Foundation
Prairie Foundation

Monahans
Dunagan Foundation

Palacios
Trull Foundation

Pampa
Brown Foundation, M. K.

Plainview
Mayer Foundation, James and Eva

San Antonio
Brackenridge Foundation, George W.
Diamond Shamrock Inc.
Frost National Bank
Halff Foundation, G. A. C.
Halsell Foundation, Ewing
Koehler Foundation, Marcia and Otto
Piper Foundation, Minnie Stevens
SBC Communications Inc.
Semmes Foundation
Tobin Foundation
Willard Helping Fund, Cecilia Young
Zachry Co., H.B.

Seminole
Doss Foundation, M. S.

Sherman
Mayor Foundation, Oliver Dewey

The Woodlands
Mitchell Energy & Development Corp.

Tyler
Fair Foundation, R. W.
Wise Foundation and Charitable Trust, Watson W.

Victoria
Johnson Foundation, M. G. and Lillie A.
O'Connor Foundation, Kathryn

Waco
Meyer Family Foundation, Paul J.

Wharton
Gulf Coast Medical Foundation

Wichita Falls
Bridwell Foundation, J. S.
Priddy Foundation

Utah

Ogden
Swanson Family Foundation, Dr. W.C.

Orem
Novell Inc.

Salt Lake City
Kennecott Corporation

Vermont

Grafton
Windham Foundation

Montpelier
Central Vermont Public Service Corp.

Rutland
Proctor Trust, Mortimer R.

Wilmington
Scott Foundation, Walter

Virginia

Arlington
Bell Atlantic Corp.
Truland Foundation
Washington Forrest Foundation

Fairfax
Mobil Oil Corp.

Gloucester
Treakle Foundation, J. Edwin

Lynchburg
Old Dominion Box Co.

Mc Lean
Mars Foundation

Norfolk
Goodman & Co.
Norfolk Shipbuilding & Drydock Corp.
North Shore Foundation

Portsmouth

Beazley Foundation/Frederick Foundation

Pulaski

Richardson Benevolent Foundation, C. E.

Richmond

Cabell Foundation, Robert G.
Cabell III and Maude Morgan
Campbell Foundation, Ruth and Henry
Carter Foundation, Beirne
Central Fidelity Banks, Inc.
Chesapeake Corp.
Cole Trust, Quincy
Ethyl Corp
James River Corp. of Virginia
Morgan and Samuel Tate Morgan, Jr. Foundation, Marietta McNeil
Thalhimer and Family Foundation, Charles G.
Virginia Environmental Endowment
Virginia Power Co.
Wheat First Butcher Singer, Inc.

Roanoke

Shenandoah Life Insurance Co.

Vienna

Cable & Wireless Holdings, Inc.

West Point

Olsson Memorial Foundation, Elis

Winchester

Bryant Foundation

Washington

Bellevue

Glaser Foundation

Seattle

Aldus Corp.
Bishop Foundation, E. K. and Lillian F.
Boeing Co., The
Foster Foundation
Nesholm Family Foundation
SAFECO Corp.
Seafirst Corporation
Simpson Investment Company
U.S. Bank of Washington
Washington Mutual Savings Bank
Wyman Youth Trust

Spokane

Leuthold Foundation
Washington Water Power Co.

Tacoma

Cheney Foundation, Ben B.
Forest Foundation
Sequoia Foundation
Weyerhaeuser Co.

Vancouver

Murdock Charitable Trust, M. J.

Walla Walla

Welch Testamentary Trust, George T.

Yakima

Petrie Trust, Lorene M.

West Virginia

Bluefield

Bowen Foundation, Ethel N.
Shott, Jr. Foundation, Hugh I.

Charleston

Clay Foundation
Daywood Foundation
Jacobson Foundation, Bernard H. and Blanche E.

Huntington

Teubert Charitable Trust, James H. and Alice

Williamstown

Fenton Foundation

Wisconsin

Appleton

Appleton Papers Inc.
Mielke Family Foundation

Black River Falls

Lunda Charitable Trust

Brillion

Brillion Iron Works

Eau Claire

Phillips Family Foundation, L. E.

Green Bay

Wisconsin Public Service Corp.

Janesville

Janesville Foundation

Madison

Cremer Foundation
DEC International, Inc.
Madison Gas & Electric Co.
Mautz Paint Co.
Rennebohm Foundation, Oscar
Wisconsin Power & Light Co.

Menasha

Banta Corp.

Milwaukee

Banc One Wisconsin Corp.
Birnschein Foundation, Alvin and Marion
Blue Cross & Blue Shield United of Wisconsin
Firstar Bank Milwaukee, N.A.
Johnson Controls Inc.
Marquette Electronics, Inc.
Peters Foundation, R. D. and Linda
Ross Memorial Foundation, Will
Schoenleber Foundation
Schroeder Foundation, Walter
Smith Corp., A.O.
WICOR, Inc.

Mosinee

Mosinee Paper Corp.

Palmyra

Young Foundation, Irvin L.

Racine

Christensen Charitable and Religious Foundation, L. C.
Johnson & Son, S.C.

South Milwaukee

Bucyrus-Erie Company

Stevens Point

First Financial Bank FSB
Sentry Insurance A Mutual Company

Tomah

Andres Charitable Trust, Frank G.

Waukesha

Fleming Cos. Food Distribution Center

Wisconsin Rapids

Consolidated Papers, Inc.

Wyoming

Worland

Sargent Foundation, Newell B.

Index to Corporations by Operating Location

Please refer to the Master Index to Corporations and Foundations for profile page numbers.

Alabama

Air Products and Chemicals, Inc.
Akzo America
Alabama Gas Corp.
Alabama Power Co.
AlliedSignal Inc.
Alumax Inc.
Aluminum Co. of America
American Brands, Inc.
Amoco Corporation
Archer-Daniels-Midland Co.
Armco Inc.
Bank of Boston Corp.
BE&K Inc.
Blount, Inc.
Boeing Co., The
Boise Cascade Corporation
Borden, Inc.
Bowater Incorporated
Brunswick Corp.
CBI Industries, Inc.
Champion International Corporation
Chevron Corporation
Chrysler Corp.
CLARCOR Inc.
Cooper Industries, Inc.
Dexter Corporation
du Pont de Nemours & Co., E. I.
Dun & Bradstreet Corp.
Eaton Corporation
Ebsco Industries, Inc.
Elf Atochem North America, Inc.
Fieldcrest Cannon Inc.
GenCorp Inc.
General Mills, Inc.
General Motors Corp.
Georgia-Pacific Corporation
Hanson Industries North America
Harsco Corp.
Hartmarx Corporation
Humana, Inc.
Inland Container Corp.
International Paper Co.
James River Corp. of Virginia
Johnson Controls Inc.
Johnson & Higgins
Kimberly-Clark Corp.
Lehigh Portland Cement Co.
Louisiana-Pacific Corp.
McDonald & Company Securities, Inc.
McDonnell Douglas Corp.-West
Mead Corporation, The
Minnesota Mining & Mfg. Co.
Montana Power Co.
New York Times Company
Norton Co.
Olin Corp.
Parker Hannifin Corp.
Pittsburg Midway Coal Mining Co.
Sara Lee Corp.
Scripps Co., E.W.
Shell Oil Company
Sonat Inc.
Square D Co.
Temple-Inland Inc.
Tennessee Valley Printing Co.
Textron, Inc.
Transco Energy Co.
Union Camp Corporation
USG Corporation
USX Corporation
Vulcan Materials Co.
Wal-Mart Stores, Inc.
Weyerhaeuser Co.
Witco Corp.

Alaska

AON Corporation
BP America Inc.
Chevron Corporation
Exxon Corporation
Johnson & Higgins
Kennecott Corporation
Louisiana-Pacific Corp.
Minnesota Mining & Mfg. Co.
Norton Co.
Sara Lee Hosiery, Inc.
Shell Oil Company
Unocal Corp.

Arizona

Abbott Laboratories
Air Products and Chemicals, Inc.
Albertson's Inc.
AlliedSignal Inc.
Alumax Inc.
Aluminum Co. of America
AMP Incorporated
Armco Inc.
Bank of Boston Corp.
Boise Cascade Corporation
Borden, Inc.
Brunswick Corp.
Chase Manhattan Bank, N.A.
Chevron Corporation
Cowles Media Co.
Crane Co.
Donnelley & Sons Co., R.R.
Dow Jones & Company, Inc.
Federated Mutual Insurance Co.
Firstar Bank Milwaukee, N.A.
GenCorp Inc.
General Mills, Inc.
General Motors Corp.
Georgia-Pacific Corporation
Goodrich Co., The B.F.
Gould Electronics Inc.
Hanson Industries North America
Henkel Corp.
Humana, Inc.
ICI Americas Inc.
International Business Machines Corp.
ITT Hartford Insurance Group, Inc.
JELD-WEN, Inc.
Johnson & Higgins
Jostens, Inc.
Kimberly-Clark Corp.
Lee Enterprises
Loews Corporation
Mattel, Inc.
McDonnell Douglas Corp.-West
Mead Corporation, The
Medtronic, Inc.
Minnesota Mining & Mfg. Co.
Mobil Oil Corp.
Morrison Knudsen Corporation
New England Business Service
Norwest Corporation
Olin Corp.
Parker Hannifin Corp.
Phelps Dodge Corporation
Piper Jaffray Companies Inc.
Prudential Insurance Co. of America, The
Pulitzer Publishing Co.
Ringier-America
Santa Fe Pacific Corporation
Sara Lee Corp.
Schuller International
Schwab & Co., Inc., Charles
Scripps Co., E.W.
Southern California Edison Co.

Stanley Works
Times Mirror Company, The
US WEST, Inc.
Wal-Mart Stores, Inc.

Arkansas

AEGON USA Inc.
Air Products and Chemicals, Inc.
Albertson's Inc.
Alumax Inc.
Aluminum Co. of America
Amcast Industrial Corp.
Anheuser-Busch Companies, Inc.
Archer-Daniels-Midland Co.
Arkansas Power & Light Co.
Bemis Company, Inc.
Boatmen's Bancshares, Inc.
Boise Cascade Corporation
Bridgestone/Firestone, Inc.
Brunswick Corp.
Burlington Industries, Inc.
Coltec Industries, Inc.
Cooper Industries, Inc.
CPC International Inc.
Douglas & Lomason Company
du Pont de Nemours & Co., E. I.
Ethyl Corp
GenCorp Inc.
General Mills, Inc.
Georgia-Pacific Corporation
Hartmarx Corporation
Heinz Company, H. J.
Illinois Tool Works, Inc.
Inland Container Corp.
International Paper Co.
James River Corp. of Virginia
Johnson Controls Inc.
Kimberly-Clark Corp.
La-Z-Boy Chair Co.
Mead Corporation, The
Minnesota Mining & Mfg. Co.
New York Times Company
OG&E Electric Services
Panhandle Eastern Corporation
Phelps Dodge Corporation
PPG Industries, Inc.
Prudential Insurance Co. of America, The
Ringier-America
Rouse Co.
Sara Lee Corp.
SBC Communications Inc.
Schering-Plough Corp.
Smith Corp., A.O.
Southwestern Electric Power Co.
Temple-Inland Inc.
Union Camp Corporation
Union Pacific Corp.
Wal-Mart Stores, Inc.
Weyerhaeuser Co.
Whirlpool Corporation

California

Abbott Laboratories
AEGON USA Inc.
Air France
Air Products and Chemicals, Inc.
Akzo America
Albertson's Inc.
AlliedSignal Inc.
Alumax Inc.
Aluminum Co. of America
Amcast Industrial Corp.
American President Companies, Ltd.
AMETEK, Inc.
AMP Incorporated

AMR Corp.
Anheuser-Busch Companies, Inc.
AON Corporation
Apple Computer, Inc.
Archer-Daniels-Midland Co.
AT&T Corp.
Avon Products, Inc.
Baker Hughes Inc.
Bank of Boston Corp.
Bank of New York Company, Inc.
BankAmerica Corp.
Bankers Trust Company
Banta Corp.
Baskin-Robbins USA Co.
Bay Area Foods
Bemis Company, Inc.
Bird Corp.
Blount, Inc.
Boeing Co., The
Boise Cascade Corporation
Borden, Inc.
Brunswick Corp.
Bucyrus-Erie Company
Carpenter Technology Corp.
CBI Industries, Inc.
CBS, Inc.
Chase Manhattan Bank, N.A.
Chesebrough-Pond's USA Co.
Chevron Corporation
Chrysler Corp.
CIBC Wood Gundy
Citibank
CLARCOR Inc.
Clorox Co.
Coltec Industries, Inc.
Comerica Incorporated
Commerce Clearing House, Incorporated
Continental Corp.
Cooper Industries, Inc.
Copley Press, Inc.
Corning Incorporated
CPC International Inc.
Crane Co.
Daily News
Dexter Corporation
Digital Equipment Corp.
Donaldson Company, Inc.
Donnelley & Sons Co., R.R.
Dow Jones & Company, Inc.
Dresser Industries, Inc.
du Pont de Nemours & Co., E. I.
Dun & Bradstreet Corp.
Eaton Corporation
Elf Atochem North America, Inc.
Exxon Corporation
Fieldcrest Cannon Inc.
Fireman's Fund Insurance Co.
Fleet Financial Group, Inc.
Fujitsu America, Inc.
Gap, Inc., The
GATX Corp.
GenCorp Inc.
General Mills, Inc.
General Motors Corp.
Georgia-Pacific Corporation
Giant Food Inc.
Gillette Co.
Goodrich Co., The B.F.
Hanson Industries North America
Harcourt General, Inc.
HarperCollins Publishers Inc.
Harsco Corp.
Heinz Company, H. J.
Heller Financial, Inc.
Hershey Foods Corp.
Heublein Inc.
Hewlett-Packard Co.
Hickory Tech Corp.
Illinois Tool Works, Inc.
Imperial Bancorp

Inland Container Corp.
International Business Machines Corp.
International Paper Co.
ITT Hartford Insurance Group, Inc.
James River Corp. of Virginia
Johnson Controls Inc.
Johnson & Higgins
Johnson & Son, S.C.
Jostens, Inc.
Kemper National Insurance Cos.
Kimberly-Clark Corp.
La-Z-Boy Chair Co.
Lee Enterprises
Lipton, Thomas J.
Little, Inc., Arthur D.
Loews Corporation
Louisiana-Pacific Corp.
M/A-COM, Inc.
Macy & Co., Inc., R.H.
Maritz Inc.
Mattel, Inc.
May Department Stores Company, The
MCA Inc.
McCormick & Co. Inc.
McDonald & Company Securities, Inc.
McDonnell Douglas Corp.-West
McGraw-Hill, Inc.
MCI Communications Corp.
Mead Corporation, The
Medtronic, Inc.
Merck & Co.
Minnesota Mining & Mfg. Co.
Mitsubishi Motor Sales of America, Inc.
Mobil Oil Corp.
Morgan & Company, J.P.
Morgan Stanley & Co., Inc.
Morrison Knudsen Corporation
Nalco Chemical Co.
Nestle USA Inc.
New York Times Company
Norton Co.
Norwest Corporation
Olin Corp.
Pacific Mutual Life Insurance Co.
Pacific Telesis Group
Parker Hannifin Corp.
Perkin-Elmer Corp.
Phelps Dodge Corporation
PHH Corporation
Piper Jaffray Companies Inc.
Playboy Enterprises, Inc.
Polaroid Corp.
Providian Corporation
Prudential Insurance Co. of America, The
Quaker Chemical Corp.
Ralston Purina Co.
Republic NY Corp.
Rich Products Corporation
Ringier-America
RJR Nabisco Inc.
Rockwell International Corporation
Rohm & Haas Co.
Roseburg Forest Products Co.
Rouse Co.
SAFECO Corp.
Salomon Inc.
San Diego Gas & Electric
Santa Fe Pacific Corporation
Sara Lee Corp.
Sara Lee Hosiery, Inc.
Schering-Plough Corp.
Schlumberger Ltd.
Schuller International
Schwab & Co., Inc., Charles
Scripps Co., E.W.

Seagram & Sons, Inc., Joseph E.
Shell Oil Company
Sierra Pacific Industries
Simpson Investment Company
Smith Corp., A.O.
Southern California Edison Co.
Specialty Manufacturing Co.
Square D Co.
Stanley Works
Sumitomo Bank of California
Swiss Bank Corp.
Teichert & Son, A.
Teleflex Inc.
Temple-Inland Inc.
Texaco Inc.
Textron, Inc.
Thompson Co., J. Walter
Times Mirror Company, The
TransAmerica Corporation
Unilever United States, Inc.
Union Bank
Union Camp Corporation
Union Pacific Corp.
United Airlines, Inc.
Unitrode Corp.
Unocal Corp.
USG Corporation
USL Capital Corporation
Wal-Mart Stores, Inc.
Westvaco Corporation
Weyerhaeuser Co.
WICOR, Inc.
Witco Corp.

Colorado

Air Products and Chemicals, Inc.
Akzo America
Albertson's Inc.
Alumax Inc.
Aluminum Co. of America
American Natural Resources Company
Amoco Corporation
Anheuser-Busch Companies, Inc.
Apple Computer, Inc.
Archer-Daniels-Midland Co.
Armco Inc.
AT&T Corp.
Boise Cascade Corporation
Borden, Inc.
Chevron Corporation
Chrysler Corp.
Citibank
Curtice-Burns Foods, Inc.
Digital Equipment Corp.
Donnelley & Sons Co., R.R.
Dow Jones & Company, Inc.
Dresser Industries, Inc.
du Pont de Nemours & Co., E. I.
Eastman Kodak Company
Forest Oil Corp.
GenCorp Inc.
General Mills, Inc.
Georgia-Pacific Corporation
Great-West Life Assurance Co.
Hewlett-Packard Co.
Illinois Tool Works, Inc.
Inland Container Corp.
International Business Machines Corp.
ITT Hartford Insurance Group, Inc.
Johnson Controls Inc.
Johnson & Higgins
Kemper National Insurance Cos.
KN Energy, Inc.
Loews Corporation
Louisiana-Pacific Corp.
Martin Marietta Corp.
Martin Marietta Materials
May Department Stores Company, The
McDonnell Douglas Corp.-West
McGraw-Hill, Inc.
MCI Communications Corp.
Mead Corporation, The
Medtronic, Inc.

Minnesota Mining & Mfg. Co.
Mobil Oil Corp.
Montana Power Co.
Norwest Corporation
Oxy USA Inc.
Parker Hannifin Corp.
Pfizer, Inc.
PHH Corporation
Piper Jaffray Companies Inc.
Pittsburg Midway Coal Mining Co.
Ralston Purina Co.
Rouse Co.
Royal Group, Inc.
SAFECO Corp.
Saint Paul Companies, Inc.
Santa Fe Pacific Corporation
Schuller International
Schwab & Co., Inc., Charles
Scripps Co., E.W.
Security Life of Denver Insurance Co.
Temple-Inland Inc.
Texaco Inc.
Times Mirror Company, The
Union Camp Corporation
Union Pacific Corp.
US WEST, Inc.
Valmont Industries, Inc.
Wal-Mart Stores, Inc.

Connecticut

Aetna Life & Casualty Co.
Air Products and Chemicals, Inc.
Allegheny Ludlum Corp.
AlliedSignal Inc.
Aluminum Co. of America
American Brands, Inc.
AMETEK, Inc.
AMP Incorporated
Armco Inc.
Bank of Boston Corp.
Bank of New York Company, Inc.
Bankers Trust Company
Baskin-Robbins USA Co.
Boise Cascade Corporation
Bristol-Myers Squibb Company
Brunswick Corp.
Champion International Corporation
Chase Manhattan Bank, N.A.
Chesebrough-Pond's USA Co.
Chrysler Corp.
CIGNA Corporation
Citibank
Coltec Industries, Inc.
Connecticut Mutual Life Insurance Company
Cooper Industries, Inc.
Cowles Media Co.
Crabtree & Evelyn
Crane Co.
Dexter Corporation
Donnelley & Sons Co., R.R.
Dow Corning Corp.
Dow Jones & Company, Inc.
Dresser Industries, Inc.
du Pont de Nemours & Co., E. I.
Dun & Bradstreet Corp.
Eaton Corporation
Ensign-Bickford Industries
Fleet Financial Group, Inc.
Forbes Inc.
General Mills, Inc.
Georgia-Pacific Corporation
Harsco Corp.
Heinz Company, H. J.
Hershey Foods Corp.
Heublein Inc.
Illinois Tool Works, Inc.
International Business Machines Corp.
ITT Hartford Insurance Group, Inc.
James River Corp. of Virginia
Johnson & Higgins
Kimberly-Clark Corp.
Lydall, Inc.
Marquette Electronics, Inc.

May Department Stores Company, The
Merck & Co.
Minnesota Mining & Mfg. Co.
Mobil Oil Corp.
New York Life Insurance Co.
New York Times Company
Newman's Own, Inc.
NewMil Bancorp
Norton Co.
Olin Corp.
Panhandle Eastern Corporation
Perkin-Elmer Corp.
Pfizer, Inc.
Phelps Dodge Corporation
PHH Corporation
Ralston Purina Co.
Rhone-Poulenc Inc.
Rohm & Haas Co.
Rouse Co.
Royal Group, Inc.
Saint Paul Companies, Inc.
Salomon Inc.
Sara Lee Corp.
Schlumberger Ltd.
Shawmut National Corp.
Southern New England Telephone Company
Stanley Works
Teleflex Inc.
Tenneco Inc.
Tetley, Inc.
Textron, Inc.
Thomson Information Publishing Group
Times Mirror Company, The
Unilever United States, Inc.
Union Camp Corporation
Wal-Mart Stores, Inc.
Westvaco Corporation
Wiremold Co.
Witco Corp.

Delaware

Air Products and Chemicals, Inc.
Akzo America
Akzo Chemicals Inc.
AMETEK, Inc.
AMP Incorporated
Avon Products, Inc.
Bank of Boston Corp.
Bank of New York Company, Inc.
Bankers Trust Company
Bell Atlantic Corp.
Blount, Inc.
Cabot Corp.
CBI Industries, Inc.
Chase Manhattan Bank, N.A.
Chrysler Corp.
Citibank
Dentsply International Inc.
Dexter Corporation
du Pont de Nemours & Co., E. I.
Duke Power Co.
General Mills, Inc.
Georgia-Pacific Corporation
Hechinger Co.
Hewlett-Packard Co.
ICI Americas Inc.
James River Corp. of Virginia
Johnson Controls Inc.
Johnson & Higgins
Merck & Co.
Mohasco Corp.
Morgan & Company, J.P.
New York Life Insurance Co.
Quaker Chemical Corp.
Saint Paul Companies, Inc.
Sara Lee Corp.
Travelers Inc.
Wal-Mart Stores, Inc.
Westvaco Corporation
Wilmington Trust Co.

District of Columbia

Air France

AlliedSignal Inc.
Armco Inc.
AT&T Corp.
Bell Atlantic Corp.
CBS, Inc.
Chevron Corporation
Citibank
Commerce Clearing House, Incorporated
Covington and Burling
Digital Equipment Corp.
Dun & Bradstreet Corp.
First Union Corp.
GenCorp Inc.
Giant Food Inc.
Harcourt General, Inc.
Hechinger Co.
Humana, Inc.
International Business Machines Corp.
ITT Hartford Insurance Group, Inc.
Johnson & Higgins
Little, Inc., Arthur D.
Loews Corporation
May Department Stores Company, The
McDonnell Douglas Corp.-West
McGraw-Hill, Inc.
MCI Communications Corp.
Minnesota Mining & Mfg. Co.
Olin Corp.
Panhandle Eastern Corporation
Potomac Electric Power Co.
Prudential Insurance Co. of America, The
RJR Nabisco Inc.
Rouse Co.
Scripps Co., E.W.
Security Life of Denver Insurance Co.
Shell Oil Company
Times Mirror Company, The
United Airlines, Inc.

Florida

AEGON USA Inc.
Air France
Air Products and Chemicals, Inc.
Albertson's Inc.
AlliedSignal Inc.
Alumax Inc.
Aluminum Co. of America
AMETEK, Inc.
AMP Incorporated
Anheuser-Busch Companies, Inc.
Archer-Daniels-Midland Co.
Armco Inc.
AT&T Corp.
Bank of Boston Corp.
Bank of New York Company, Inc.
BankAmerica Corp.
Bankers Trust Company
Boise Cascade Corporation
Borden, Inc.
Brunswick Corp.
Burdines Inc.
CBS, Inc.
Champion International Corporation
Chase Manhattan Bank, N.A.
Chevron Corporation
Chrysler Corp.
Citibank
Clorox Co.
CNA Financial Corporation/CNA Insurance Companies
Comerica Incorporated
Continental Corp.
Crane Co.
Donnelley & Sons Co., R.R.
Dow Jones & Company, Inc.
du Pont de Nemours & Co., E. I.
Dun & Bradstreet Corp.
Eaton Corporation
First Union Corp.

First Union National Bank of Florida
Firstar Bank Milwaukee, N.A.
Fleet Financial Group, Inc.
GATX Corp.
General Mills, Inc.
General Motors Corp.
Georgia-Pacific Corporation
Goodrich Co., The B.F.
Gulf Power Co.
Hanson Industries North America
Harcourt General, Inc.
Harsco Corp.
Heinz Company, H. J.
Humana, Inc.
ICI Americas Inc.
Inland Container Corp.
International Business Machines Corp.
International Paper Co.
ITT Hartford Insurance Group, Inc.
Johnson Controls Inc.
Johnson & Higgins
Johnson & Son, S.C.
Kelly Tractor Co.
Lehigh Portland Cement Co.
Lipton, Thomas J.
Louisiana-Pacific Corp.
Marquette Electronics, Inc.
Martin Marietta Corp.
Martin Marietta Materials
McDonnell Douglas Corp.-West
Mead Corporation, The
Merck & Co.
Minnesota Mining & Mfg. Co.
Mitsubishi Motor Sales of America, Inc.
Morgan & Company, J.P.
Morrison Knudsen Corporation
New York Times Company
Norwest Corporation
Olin Corp.
Outboard Marine Corp.
Parker Hannifin Corp.
Phelps Dodge Corporation
Prudential Insurance Co. of America, The
Republic NY Corp.
Rouse Co.
Royal Group, Inc.
SAFECO Corp.
Saint Paul Companies, Inc.
Sara Lee Corp.
Schering-Plough Corp.
Schwab & Co., Inc., Charles
Scripps Co., E.W.
Seagram & Sons, Inc., Joseph E.
Shawmut National Corp.
Shell Oil Company
Smith Corp., A.O.
Square D Co.
Stanley Works
Swiss Bank Corp.
Teleflex Inc.
Temple-Inland Inc.
Tetley, Inc.
Texaco Inc.
Textron, Inc.
Unilever United States, Inc.
Union Camp Corporation
USG Corporation
Wal-Mart Stores, Inc.
Westvaco Corporation
Weyerhaeuser Co.
Witco Corp.

Georgia

AEGON USA Inc.
Air Products and Chemicals, Inc.
Akzo America
Alumax Inc.
Aluminum Co. of America
Amoco Corporation
AMP Incorporated
Anheuser-Busch Companies, Inc.
Archer-Daniels-Midland Co.
Armco Inc.

AT&T Corp.
Avon Products, Inc.
Boeing Co., The
Boise Cascade Corporation
Borden, Inc.
Brown & Williamson Tobacco
Corp.
Brunswick Corp.
Burlington Industries, Inc.
Cabot Corp.
CBI Industries, Inc.
Champion International
Corporation
Chevron Corporation
Chrysler Corp.
CIBC Wood Gundy
Citibank
CLARCOR Inc.
Clorox Co.
Cooper Industries, Inc.
Curtice-Burns Foods, Inc.
Deere & Co.
Digital Equipment Corp.
Douglas & Lomason Company
Dow Jones & Company, Inc.
du Pont de Nemours & Co.,
E. I.
Dun & Bradstreet Corp.
Eaton Corporation
Elf Atochem North America,
Inc.
Exxon Corporation
Federated Mutual Insurance
Co.
Fieldcrest Cannon Inc.
Fireman's Fund Insurance Co.
First Union Corp.
Fleet Financial Group, Inc.
GATX Corp.
GenCorp Inc.
General American Life
Insurance Co.
General Mills, Inc.
General Motors Corp.
Georgia-Pacific Corporation
Georgia Power Co.
Givenchy Corp.
Harsco Corp.
Hartmarx Corporation
Heller Financial, Inc.
Hewlett-Packard Co.
Inland Container Corp.
International Business
Machines Corp.
ITT Hartford Insurance Group,
Inc.
Johnson Controls Inc.
Johnson & Higgins
Johnson & Son, S.C.
Jostens, Inc.
Kimberly-Clark Corp.
Life Insurance Co. of Georgia
Louisiana-Pacific Corp.
Macy & Co., Inc., R.H.
McCormick & Co. Inc.
McDonald & Company
Securities, Inc.
McDonnell Douglas
Corp.-West
McGraw-Hill, Inc.
MCI Communications Corp.
Mead Corporation, The
Merck & Co.
Minnesota Mining & Mfg. Co.
Mohasco Corp.
Nalco Chemical Co.
New York Life Insurance Co.
New York Times Company
Norton Co.
Norwest Corporation
Olin Corp.
Outboard Marine Corp.
Parker Hannifin Corp.
Phelps Dodge Corporation
Playboy Enterprises, Inc.
Polaroid Corp.
Prudential Insurance Co. of
America, The
Quaker Chemical Corp.
Rich Products Corporation
Rouse Co.
Royal Group, Inc.
SAFECO Corp.
Salomon Inc.
Sara Lee Corp.

Schering-Plough Corp.
Schlumberger Ltd.
Schuller International
Scripps Co., E.W.
Security Life of Denver
Insurance Co.
Sonat Inc.
SPX Corp.
Stanley Works
Swiss Bank Corp.
Temple-Inland Inc.
Tenneco Inc.
Tetley, Inc.
Textron, Inc.
Thompson Co., J. Walter
Transco Energy Co.
Travelers Inc.
Trust Company Bank
Unilever United States, Inc.
Union Camp Corporation
USG Corporation
USX Corporation
Vulcan Materials Co.
Wal-Mart Stores, Inc.
Westvaco Corporation
Weyerhaeuser Co.
Winter Construction Co.

Hawaii

Amfac/JMB Hawaii Inc.
AON Corporation
Armco Inc.
Boise Cascade Corporation
Chevron Corporation
Fireman's Fund Insurance Co.
First Hawaiian, Inc.
General Mills, Inc.
Johnson & Higgins
Lee Enterprises
Mead Corporation, The
Minnesota Mining & Mfg. Co.
Morrison Knudsen Corporation
Saint Paul Companies, Inc.
United Airlines, Inc.
Wal-Mart Stores, Inc.
Weyerhaeuser Co.

Idaho

Albertson's Inc.
Alumax Inc.
Anheuser-Busch Companies,
Inc.
Blount, Inc.
Boise Cascade Corporation
General Mills, Inc.
Heinz Company, H. J.
Hewlett-Packard Co.
Johnson & Higgins
Louisiana-Pacific Corp.
Mead Corporation, The
Morrison Knudsen Corporation
Ore-Ida Foods, Inc.
Piper Jaffray Companies Inc.
Saint Paul Companies, Inc.
Union Pacific Corp.
US WEST, Inc.
Wal-Mart Stores, Inc.
Washington Mutual Savings
Bank
Washington Water Power Co.
West One Bancorp

Illinois

Abbott Laboratories
AEGON USA Inc.
Aetna Life & Casualty Co.
Air France
Air Products and Chemicals,
Inc.
Akzo America
Akzo Chemicals Inc.
Allegheny Ludlum Corp.
AlliedSignal Inc.
Alumax Inc.
Aluminum Co. of America
AMCORE Bank, N.A.
Rockford
American Brands, Inc.

American National Bank &
Trust Co. of Chicago
AMETEK, Inc.
Amoco Corporation
Andersons, The
Anheuser-Busch Companies,
Inc.
AON Corporation
Archer-Daniels-Midland Co.
Armco Inc.
AT&T Corp.
Avon Products, Inc.
BankAmerica Corp.
Bankers Trust Company
Bemis Company, Inc.
Blair and Co., William
Blount, Inc.
Boatmen's Bancshares, Inc.
Boise Cascade Corporation
Borden, Inc.
Bowater Incorporated
Bridgestone/Firestone, Inc.
Brunswick Corp.
Cabot Corp.
CBI Industries, Inc.
CBS, Inc.
Chase Manhattan Bank, N.A.
Chesebrough-Pond's USA Co.
Chicago Sun-Times, Inc.
Chrysler Corp.
CIBC Wood Gundy
Citibank
CLARCOR Inc.
Clorox Co.
CNA Financial
Corporation/CNA Insurance
Companies
Coltec Industries, Inc.
Comerica Incorporated
Commerce Clearing House,
Incorporated
Commonwealth Edison Co.
Consolidated Papers, Inc.
Continental Corp.
Cooper Industries, Inc.
Copley Press, Inc.
Corning Incorporated
CPC International Inc.
CR Industries
Crane Co.
Curtice-Burns Foods, Inc.
Deere & Co.
Dexter Corporation
Digital Equipment Corp.
Donaldson Company, Inc.
Donnelley & Sons Co., R.R.
Douglas & Lomason Company
Dow Jones & Company, Inc.
du Pont de Nemours & Co.,
E. I.
Duchossois Industries Inc.
Dun & Bradstreet Corp.
Eastman Kodak Company
Eaton Corporation
Elf Atochem North America,
Inc.
Encyclopaedia Britannica, Inc.
Ethyl Corp
Fireman's Fund Insurance Co.
First Chicago Corp.
Firstar Bank Milwaukee, N.A.
GATX Corp.
General Mills, Inc.
General Motors Corp.
Georgia-Pacific Corporation
Gillette Co.
Goodrich Co., The B.F.
Harcourt General, Inc.
HarperCollins Publishers Inc.
Harsco Corp.
Hartmarx Corporation
Heller Financial, Inc.
Henkel Corp.
Hewlett-Packard Co.
Hook Drugs
Humana, Inc.
ICI Americas Inc.
Illinois Consolidated
Telephone Co.
Illinois Tool Works, Inc.
Inland Container Corp.
International Business
Machines Corp.
International Paper Co.

Iowa-Illinois Gas & Electric
Co.
ITT Hartford Insurance Group,
Inc.
James River Corp. of Virginia
Johnson Controls Inc.
Johnson & Higgins
Jostens, Inc.
Kemper National Insurance
Cos.
Lee Enterprises
Loews Corporation
Maritz Inc.
Mattel, Inc.
MCA Inc.
McCormick & Co. Inc.
McDonald & Company
Securities, Inc.
McGraw-Hill, Inc.
MCI Communications Corp.
Mead Corporation, The
Minnesota Mining & Mfg. Co.
Mitsubishi Motor Sales of
America, Inc.
Mobil Oil Corp.
Morgan & Company, J.P.
Morgan Stanley & Co., Inc.
Morrison Knudsen Corporation
Nalco Chemical Co.
New York Times Company
Norton Co.
Norwest Corporation
Olin Corp.
Outboard Marine Corp.
Packaging Corporation of
America
Pamida, Inc.
Panhandle Eastern Corporation
Parker Hannifin Corp.
Peoples Energy Corp.
PHH Corporation
Playboy Enterprises, Inc.
Polaroid Corp.
Premier Industrial Corp.
Prudential Insurance Co. of
America, The
Prudential Securities, Inc.
Rand McNally & Co.
Ringier-America
Rockwell International
Corporation
Rohm & Haas Co.
Rouse Co.
Royal Group, Inc.
SAFECO Corp.
Saint Paul Companies, Inc.
Salomon Inc.
Santa Fe Pacific Corporation
Sara Lee Corp.
Sara Lee Hosiery, Inc.
Schering-Plough Corp.
Schuller International
Seagram & Sons, Inc., Joseph
E.
Shell Oil Company
Smith Corp., A.O.
SPX Corp.
Square D Co.
Swift Co. Inc., John S.
Swiss Bank Corp.
Temple-Inland Inc.
Tenneco Inc.
Textron, Inc.
Thompson Co., J. Walter
Times Mirror Company, The
TransAmerica Corporation
Union Camp Corporation
Union Electric Co.
Union Pacific Corp.
United Airlines, Inc.
USG Corporation
USX Corporation
Valmont Industries, Inc.
Vulcan Materials Co.
Wal-Mart Stores, Inc.
Westvaco Corporation
Weyerhaeuser Co.
Witco Corp.

Indiana

Air Products and Chemicals,
Inc.
Allegheny Ludlum Corp.

AlliedSignal Inc.
Alumax Inc.
Aluminum Co. of America
Amcast Industrial Corp.
American Brands, Inc.
American General Finance
Corp.
American United Life
Insurance Co.
Amoco Corporation
Andersons, The
AON Corporation
Archer-Daniels-Midland Co.
Armco Inc.
Bemis Company, Inc.
Bethlehem Steel Corp.
Blount, Inc.
Boise Cascade Corporation
Borden, Inc.
Bridgestone/Firestone, Inc.
Bristol-Myers Squibb
Company
Brunswick Corp.
Cabot Corp.
Chesapeake Corp.
Chrysler Corp.
CINergy
CLARCOR Inc.
Coltec Industries, Inc.
Cooper Industries, Inc.
CPC International Inc.
CR Industries
Cummins Engine Co.
Curtice-Burns Foods, Inc.
Dexter Corporation
Donaldson Company, Inc.
Donnelley & Sons Co., R.R.
Dow Corning Corp.
Dresser Industries, Inc.
du Pont de Nemours & Co.,
E. I.
Eaton Corporation
Federal-Mogul Corporation
First Source Corp.
Fort Wayne National Bank
Frisch's Restaurants Inc.
GATX Corp.
GenCorp Inc.
General Mills, Inc.
General Motors Corp.
Georgia-Pacific Corporation
Goodrich Co., The B.F.
Hanson Industries North
America
Harsco Corp.
Hartmarx Corporation
Hook Drugs
Inland Container Corp.
ITT Hartford Insurance Group,
Inc.
James River Corp. of Virginia
Johnson Controls Inc.
Journal-Gazette Co.
Lehigh Portland Cement Co.
May Department Stores
Company, The
McCormick & Co. Inc.
McDonald & Company
Securities, Inc.
McGraw-Hill, Inc.
Mead Corporation, The
Minnesota Mining & Mfg. Co.
National Steel Corp.
NBD Indiana, Inc.
Norwest Corporation
Old National Bank in
Evansville
Outboard Marine Corp.
Panhandle Eastern Corporation
Parker Hannifin Corp.
Pfizer, Inc.
Phelps Dodge Corporation
Premier Industrial Corp.
Prudential Insurance Co. of
America, The
Pulitzer Publishing Co.
Rieke Corp.
Saint Paul Companies, Inc.
Sara Lee Corp.
Schuller International
Schwab & Co., Inc., Charles
Scripps Co., E.W.
Seagram & Sons, Inc., Joseph
E.

Security Life of Denver
 Insurance Co.
Shell Oil Company
South Bend Tribune
SPX Corp.
Square D Co.
Stanley Works
Temple-Inland Inc.
Tenneco Inc.
Textron, Inc.
Unilever United States, Inc.
Union Camp Corporation
USG Corporation
USX Corporation
Valmont Industries, Inc.
Vulcan Materials Co.
Wal-Mart Stores, Inc.
Westvaco Corporation
Whirlpool Corporation
Witco Corp.

Iowa

AEGON USA Inc.
Aluminum Co. of America
American Brands, Inc.
Archer-Daniels-Midland Co.
Armco Inc.
Audubon State Bank
Blount, Inc.
Boatmen's Bancshares, Inc.
Bridgestone/Firestone, Inc.
Century Companies of America
Chesapeake Corp.
Coltec Industries, Inc.
Cooper Industries, Inc.
Cummins Engine Co.
Curtice-Burns Foods, Inc.
Deere & Co.
Donaldson Company, Inc.
Donnelley & Sons Co., R.R.
Douglas & Lomason Company
Dow Jones & Company, Inc.
du Pont de Nemours & Co.,
 E. I.
Dun & Bradstreet Corp.
Eaton Corporation
Fireman's Fund Insurance Co.
Firstar Bank Milwaukee, N.A.
Gazette Co.
General Mills, Inc.
Georgia-Pacific Corporation
Gillette Co.
Guaranty Bank & Trust Co.
Harsco Corp.
Heinz Company, H. J.
Hickory Tech Corp.
IES Industries, Inc.
Iowa-Illinois Gas & Electric
 Co.
JELD-WEN, Inc.
Kemper National Insurance
 Cos.
Lee Enterprises
Lehigh Portland Cement Co.
Lipton, Thomas J.
MCI Communications Corp.
Minnesota Mining & Mfg. Co.
Norwest Corporation
Olin Corp.
Owen Industries, Inc.
Pamida, Inc.
Pella Corporation
Piper Jaffray Companies Inc.
Ralston Purina Co.
Rouse Co.
Sara Lee Corp.
Sheaffer Inc.
Simpson Investment Company
Square D Co.
Union Camp Corporation
US WEST, Inc.
USG Corporation
Vulcan Materials Co.
Wal-Mart Stores, Inc.
Weyerhaeuser Co.
Winnebago Industries, Inc.
Witco Corp.

Kansas

Air Products and Chemicals,
 Inc.
Albertson's Inc.
AlliedSignal Inc.
Alumax Inc.
Archer-Daniels-Midland Co.
Armco Inc.
Beech Aircraft Corp.
Bemis Company, Inc.
Binney & Smith Inc.
Block, H&R
Blount, Inc.
Boatmen's Bancshares, Inc.
Boeing Co., The
Boise Cascade Corporation
Borden, Inc.
Central National Bank
Clorox Co.
CR Industries
Deere & Co.
du Pont de Nemours & Co.,
 E. I.
Eastman Kodak Company
Eaton Corporation
Enron Corp.
Exchange National Bank
First National Bank
General Mills, Inc.
Georgia-Pacific Corporation
Heinz Company, H. J.
Humana, Inc.
Inland Container Corp.
ITT Hartford Insurance Group,
 Inc.
Johnson Controls Inc.
Jostens, Inc.
Louisiana-Pacific Corp.
Macy & Co., Inc., R.H.
Maritz Inc.
May Department Stores
 Company, The
Merck & Co.
Norwest Corporation
Olin Corp.
Pamida, Inc.
Parker Hannifin Corp.
Phelps Dodge Corporation
Piper Jaffray Companies Inc.
PPG Industries, Inc.
Ringier-America
Royal Group, Inc.
Saint Paul Companies, Inc.
Santa Fe Pacific Corporation
Sara Lee Corp.
SBC Communications Inc.
Schuller International
Smith Corp., A.O.
Stanley Works
Temple-Inland Inc.
Tenneco Inc.
Texaco Inc.
Union Pacific Corp.
Vulcan Materials Co.
Wal-Mart Stores, Inc.
Williams Companies, The
Witco Corp.

Kentucky

Air Products and Chemicals,
 Inc.
Akzo America
Alumax Inc.
American Brands, Inc.
AMETEK, Inc.
Archer-Daniels-Midland Co.
Aristech Chemical Corp.
Armco Inc.
Bemis Company, Inc.
Berwind Corporation
Bird Corp.
Boise Cascade Corporation
Borden, Inc.
Brown & Williamson Tobacco
 Corp.
Brunswick Corp.
Chesapeake Corp.
Chevron Corporation
CINergy
CLARCOR Inc.
Clorox Co.

Coltec Industries, Inc.
Commercial Bank
Cooper Industries, Inc.
Corning Incorporated
Donaldson Company, Inc.
Donnelley & Sons Co., R.R.
Dow Corning Corp.
Dow Jones & Company, Inc.
Dresser Industries, Inc.
du Pont de Nemours & Co.,
 E. I.
Eaton Corporation
Elf Atochem North America,
 Inc.
Frisch's Restaurants Inc.
General Mills, Inc.
General Motors Corp.
Goodrich Co., The B.F.
Harsco Corp.
Hartmarx Corporation
Hershey Foods Corp.
Hook Drugs
Humana, Inc.
Inland Container Corp.
International Business
 Machines Corp.
James River Corp. of Virginia
Johnson Controls Inc.
Johnson & Higgins
Mattel, Inc.
Mead Corporation, The
Minnesota Mining & Mfg. Co.
Mosinee Paper Corp.
New York Times Company
Olin Corp.
Panhandle Eastern Corporation
Parker Hannifin Corp.
Phelps Dodge Corporation
Providian Corporation
Pulitzer Publishing Co.
Ralston Purina Co.
Rohm & Haas Co.
Rouse Co.
Sara Lee Corp.
Scripps Co., E.W.
Seagram & Sons, Inc., Joseph
 E.
Smith Corp., A.O.
SPX Corp.
Square D Co.
Temple-Inland Inc.
Thomas Industries
Union Camp Corporation
Vulcan Materials Co.
Wal-Mart Stores, Inc.
Westvaco Corporation
Weyerhaeuser Co.

Louisiana

Air Products and Chemicals,
 Inc.
Albertson's Inc.
AlliedSignal Inc.
Aluminum Co. of America
Amoco Corporation
Anheuser-Busch Companies,
 Inc.
Archer-Daniels-Midland Co.
Armco Inc.
Babcock & Wilcox Co.
Baker Hughes Inc.
Bank of Boston Corp.
Bird Corp.
Boise Cascade Corporation
Borden, Inc.
BP America Inc.
Bridgestone/Firestone, Inc.
Brunswick Corp.
Cabot Corp.
CBI Industries, Inc.
Chevron Corporation
Consolidated Natural Gas Co.
Cooper Industries, Inc.
Dresser Industries, Inc.
du Pont de Nemours & Co.,
 E. I.
Enron Corp.
Ethyl Corp
Exxon Corporation
Fireman's Fund Insurance Co.
Freeport-McMoRan Inc.
GATX Corp.
General Mills, Inc.

Georgia-Pacific Corporation
Harsco Corp.
Inland Container Corp.
International Paper Co.
ITT Hartford Insurance Group,
 Inc.
James River Corp. of Virginia
Johnson Controls Inc.
Johnson & Higgins
Kansas City Southern
 Industries
Loews Corporation
Louisiana-Pacific Corp.
Martin Marietta Corp.
Martin Marietta Materials
Mobil Oil Corp.
Nalco Chemical Co.
New York Times Company
Olin Corp.
Panhandle Eastern Corporation
Pennzoil Co.
Phelps Dodge Corporation
PPG Industries, Inc.
Prudential Insurance Co. of
 America, The
Pulitzer Publishing Co.
Rouse Co.
Saint Paul Companies, Inc.
Sara Lee Corp.
Shell Oil Company
Sonat Inc.
Southwestern Electric Power
 Co.
Temple-Inland Inc.
Tenneco Inc.
Texaco Inc.
Textron, Inc.
Transco Energy Co.
Union Camp Corporation
Union Pacific Corp.
Unocal Corp.
USG Corporation
Vulcan Materials Co.
Wal-Mart Stores, Inc.
Westvaco Corporation
Williams Companies, The
Witco Corp.

Maine

Armco Inc.
Bank of Boston Corp.
Bankers Trust Company
Boise Cascade Corporation
Borden, Inc.
Bowater Incorporated
Carpenter Technology Corp.
Central Maine Power Co.
Champion International
 Corporation
Cooper Industries, Inc.
Fleet Financial Group, Inc.
Gannett Publishing Co., Guy
General Mills, Inc.
Georgia-Pacific Corporation
International Paper Co.
James River Corp. of Virginia
Johnson & Higgins
Louisiana-Pacific Corp.
New York Times Company
Parker Hannifin Corp.
Royal Group, Inc.
Schuller International
Union Camp Corporation
Wal-Mart Stores, Inc.
Webber Oil Co.
Weyerhaeuser Co.

Maryland

AEGON USA Inc.
AlliedSignal Inc.
Alumax Inc.
Aluminum Co. of America
Armco Inc.
Bell Atlantic Corp.
Berwind Corporation
Bethlehem Steel Corp.
Boise Cascade Corporation
Borden, Inc.
Brunswick Corp.
Chase Manhattan Bank, N.A.

Chesapeake Corp.
Chevron Corporation
Citibank
Clorox Co.
CPC International Inc.
Crown Books
Dart Group Corp.
Dexter Corporation
Dow Jones & Company, Inc.
Dresser Industries, Inc.
Dun & Bradstreet Corp.
First Union Corp.
General Mills, Inc.
General Motors Corp.
Giant Food Inc.
Giant Food Stores
Gould Electronics Inc.
Hanson Industries North
 America
Harsco Corp.
Hartmarx Corporation
Hechinger Co.
Hewlett-Packard Co.
International Business
 Machines Corp.
ITT Hartford Insurance Group,
 Inc.
Johnson Controls Inc.
Johnson & Higgins
Lehigh Portland Cement Co.
Loews Corporation
M/A-COM, Inc.
Martin Marietta Corp.
Martin Marietta Materials
May Department Stores
 Company, The
McCormick & Co. Inc.
McDonnell Douglas
 Corp.-West
Mine Safety Appliances Co.
Minnesota Mining & Mfg. Co.
Morrison Knudsen Corporation
Norwest Corporation
PaineWebber
PHH Corporation
Potomac Electric Power Co.
Price Associates, T. Rowe
Rouse Co.
Royal Group, Inc.
Scripps Co., E.W.
Seagram & Sons, Inc., Joseph
 E.
Shell Oil Company
Smith Corp., A.O.
Times Mirror Company, The
Transco Energy Co.
Travelers Inc.
Unilever United States, Inc.
USG Corporation
Wal-Mart Stores, Inc.
Westvaco Corporation
Weyerhaeuser Co.

Massachusetts

Abbott Laboratories
Acushnet Co.
Air France
Alumax Inc.
American Brands, Inc.
American Natural Resources
 Company
American Optical Corp.
AMETEK, Inc.
AMP Incorporated
Anheuser-Busch Companies,
 Inc.
AON Corporation
Armco Inc.
AT&T Corp.
Baker Hughes Inc.
Bank of Boston
Bank of Boston Corp.
Bemis Company, Inc.
Berwind Corporation
Bird Corp.
Blount, Inc.
Boise Cascade Corporation
Borden, Inc.
Boston Edison Co.
Cabot Corp.
CBS, Inc.
Chrysler Corp.
Citibank

The Big Book of Library Grant Money

Nebraska

Albertson's Inc.
Ameritas Life Insurance Corp.
Archer-Daniels-Midland Co.
Armco Inc.
Bemis Company, Inc.
Blount, Inc.
Borden, Inc.
Brunswick Corp.
City National Bank and Trust Co.
CLARCOR Inc.
Curtice-Burns Foods, Inc.
Donnelley & Sons Co., R.R.
Douglas & Lomason Company
Dun & Bradstreet Corp.
Eaton Corporation
General Mills, Inc.
Heinz Company, H. J.
Hershey Foods Corp.
IBP, Inc.
Inland Container Corp.
ITT Hartford Insurance Group, Inc.
Jostens, Inc.
Kimberly-Clark Corp.
KN Energy, Inc.
Lee Enterprises
Minnesota Mining & Mfg. Co.
Norwest Bank Nebraska, N.A.
Norwest Corporation
Pamida, Inc.
Piper Jaffray Companies Inc.
Prudential Insurance Co. of America, The
Pulitzer Publishing Co.
Saint Paul Companies, Inc.
Schering-Plough Corp.
Square D Co.
Union Pacific Corp.
US WEST, Inc.
Valmont Industries, Inc.
Wal-Mart Stores, Inc.
WICOR, Inc.
Witco Corp.

Nevada

Albertson's Inc.
Bemis Company, Inc.
Boise Cascade Corporation
Chevron Corporation
Citibank
Clorox Co.
Deere & Co.
Donnelley & Sons Co., R.R.
General Mills, Inc.
Humana, Inc.
ITT Hartford Insurance Group, Inc.
Johnson & Higgins
Kennecott Corporation
Louisiana-Pacific Corp.
Mead Corporation, The
Pacific Telesis Group
PriMerit Bank
Sara Lee Corp.
Sara Lee Hosiery, Inc.
Sierra Pacific Resources
Union Pacific Corp.
USG Corporation
Wal-Mart Stores, Inc.
Witco Corp.

New Hampshire

Anheuser-Busch Companies, Inc.
Armco Inc.
Crabtree & Evelyn
Dexter Corporation
Digital Equipment Corp.
Dow Jones & Company, Inc.
Fleet Financial Group, Inc.
GenCorp Inc.
General Mills, Inc.
Hewlett-Packard Co.
ITT Hartford Insurance Group, Inc.
James River Corp. of Virginia
Johnson Controls Inc.

Kingsbury Corp.
Lydall, Inc.
Mascoma Savings Bank
McGraw-Hill, Inc.
Merck & Co.
Monadnock Paper Mills
New England Business Service
Norton Co.
Royal Group, Inc.
Security Life of Denver Insurance Co.
Stanley Works
Teleflex Inc.
Textron, Inc.
Unitrode Corp.
Wal-Mart Stores, Inc.

New Jersey

AEGON USA Inc.
Aetna Life & Casualty Co.
Air Products and Chemicals, Inc.
Akzo America
Akzo Chemicals Inc.
AlliedSignal Inc.
Alumax Inc.
AMP Incorporated
Anheuser-Busch Companies, Inc.
AON Corporation
Armco Inc.
AT&T Corp.
Bank of New York Company, Inc.
Bankers Trust Company
Baskin-Robbins USA Co.
Bell Atlantic Corp.
Bemis Company, Inc.
Berwind Corporation
Boise Cascade Corporation
Borden, Inc.
Bristol-Myers Squibb Company
Chesapeake Corp.
Chrysler Corp.
Church & Dwight Co., Inc.
Citibank
Clorox Co.
Coltec Industries, Inc.
Commerce Clearing House, Incorporated
Continental Corp.
Cooper Industries, Inc.
Corning Incorporated
Cosmair, Inc.
CPC International Inc.
Curtice-Burns Foods, Inc.
Dexter Corporation
Dow Jones & Company, Inc.
Dresser Industries, Inc.
du Pont de Nemours & Co., E. I.
Dun & Bradstreet Corp.
Eastman Kodak Company
Eaton Corporation
Exxon Corporation
Federal-Mogul Corporation
Fireman's Fund Insurance Co.
GATX Corp.
GenCorp Inc.
General Mills, Inc.
Georgia-Pacific Corporation
Goodrich Co., The B.F.
Hanson Industries North America
Harsco Corp.
Hasbro Inc.
Hechinger Co.
Heinz Company, H. J.
Henkel Corp.
Hewlett-Packard Co.
Hoffmann-La Roche Inc.
ICI Americas Inc.
Illinois Tool Works, Inc.
Inland Container Corp.
International Business Machines Corp.
ITT Hartford Insurance Group, Inc.
James River Corp. of Virginia
Jaydor Corp.
Johnson Controls Inc.
Johnson & Higgins

Kimberly-Clark Corp.
Lipton, Thomas J.
Liz Claiborne, Inc.
Macy & Co., Inc., R.H.
Martin Marietta Corp.
MCA Inc.
McCormick & Co. Inc.
McGraw-Hill, Inc.
MCI Communications Corp.
Merck & Co.
Minnesota Mining & Mfg. Co.
Mitsubishi Motor Sales of America, Inc.
Mobil Oil Corp.
Nabisco Foods Group
Nalco Chemical Co.
National Westminster Bank New Jersey
New Jersey Natural Gas Co.
New York Life Insurance Co.
New York Times Company
Norton Co.
Norwest Corporation
Olin Corp.
Panhandle Eastern Corporation
PECO Energy Company
Pfizer, Inc.
Phelps Dodge Corporation
PHH Corporation
Polaroid Corp.
Prudential Insurance Co. of America, The
Prudential Securities, Inc.
Public Service Electric & Gas Co.
Rhone-Poulenc Inc.
Rich Products Corporation
RJR Nabisco Inc.
Rouse Co.
Royal Group, Inc.
Saint Paul Companies, Inc.
Sara Lee Corp.
Schering-Plough Corp.
Schuller International
Seton Leather Co.
Shell Oil Company
Subaru of America Inc.
Temple-Inland Inc.
Tenneco Inc.
Tetley, Inc.
Transco Energy Co.
Unilever United States, Inc.
Union Camp Corporation
USG Corporation
Wal-Mart Stores, Inc.
Weyerhaeuser Co.
Witco Corp.

New Mexico

Albertson's Inc.
Boatmen's Bancshares, Inc.
Chevron Corporation
Citibank
Digital Equipment Corp.
du Pont de Nemours & Co., E. I.
Enron Corp.
GenCorp Inc.
General Mills, Inc.
Hershey Foods Corp.
Lee Enterprises
Mitchell Energy & Development Corp.
Phelps Dodge Corporation
Pittsburg Midway Coal Mining Co.
Public Service Co. of New Mexico
Pulitzer Publishing Co.
Santa Fe Pacific Corporation
Sara Lee Corp.
Sara Lee Hosiery, Inc.
Scripps Co., E.W.
Shell Oil Company
US WEST, Inc.
Wal-Mart Stores, Inc.

New York

Air France

Air Products and Chemicals, Inc.
Akzo America
Allegheny Ludlum Corp.
Alumax Inc.
Aluminum Co. of America
American Brands, Inc.
American Natural Resources Company
AMETEK, Inc.
Anheuser-Busch Companies, Inc.
AON Corporation
Archer-Daniels-Midland Co.
Armco Inc.
AT&T Corp.
Avon Products, Inc.
Bank of New York Company, Inc.
BankAmerica Corp.
Bankers Trust Company
Baskin-Robbins USA Co.
Benetton Services Corp.
Berwind Corporation
Bethlehem Steel Corp.
Boise Cascade Corporation
Borden, Inc.
BP America Inc.
Bristol-Myers Squibb Company
Burlington Industries, Inc.
Cable & Wireless Holdings, Inc.
Canon U.S.A., Inc.
CBS, Inc.
Central Hudson Gas & Electric Corp.
Champion International Corporation
Chase Manhattan Bank, N.A.
Chesapeake Corp.
Christian Dior New York, Inc.
Chrysler Corp.
CIBC Wood Gundy
Citibank
Coltec Industries, Inc.
Commerce Clearing House, Incorporated
Consolidated Papers, Inc.
Continental Corp.
Cooper Industries, Inc.
Corning Incorporated
Cosmair, Inc.
Crane Co.
Cranston Print Works Company
CS First Boston Corporation
CT Corp. System
Cummins Engine Co.
Curtice-Burns Foods, Inc.
Daily News
Delaware North Co., Inc.
Dexter Corporation
Donnelley & Sons Co., R.R.
Dow Jones & Company, Inc.
Dresser Industries, Inc.
du Pont de Nemours & Co., E. I.
Dun & Bradstreet Corp.
Eastman Kodak Company
Eaton Corporation
Elf Atochem North America, Inc.
Fieldcrest Cannon Inc.
First Chicago Corp.
Fleet Financial Group, Inc.
Forbes Inc.
GATX Corp.
GenCorp Inc.
General Mills, Inc.
General Motors Corp.
Georgia-Pacific Corporation
Givenchy Corp.
Guardian Life Insurance Company of America
Hanson Industries North America
Harcourt General, Inc.
HarperCollins Publishers Inc.
Harsco Corp.
Hartmarx Corporation
Hasbro Inc.
Hechinger Co.
Heinz Company, H. J.
Heller Financial, Inc.

Hershey Foods Corp.
Hino Diesel Trucks (U.S.A.)
Illinois Tool Works, Inc.
International Business Machines Corp.
International Paper Co.
ITT Hartford Insurance Group, Inc.
James River Corp. of Virginia
Johnson Controls Inc.
Johnson & Higgins
Johnson & Son, S.C.
Jostens, Inc.
Kaye, Scholer, Fierman, Hays & Handler
Kimberly-Clark Corp.
Lehigh Portland Cement Co.
Lipton, Thomas J.
Little, Inc., Arthur D.
Liz Claiborne, Inc.
Loews Corporation
Long Island Lighting Co.
Lydall, Inc.
Macy & Co., Inc., R.H.
Maritz Inc.
Marsh & McLennan Companies, Inc.
Martin Marietta Corp.
Mattel, Inc.
May Department Stores Company, The
MBIA Inc.
MCA Inc.
McCormick & Co. Inc.
McGraw-Hill, Inc.
MCI Communications Corp.
Medtronic, Inc.
Mercury Aircraft
Merrill Lynch & Co., Inc.
Metropolitan Life Insurance Co.
Minnesota Mining & Mfg. Co.
Mitsubishi International Corp.
Mobil Oil Corp.
Morgan & Company, J.P.
Morgan Stanley & Co., Inc.
Morrison Knudsen Corporation
New York Life Insurance Co.
New York Mercantile Exchange
New York Stock Exchange, Inc.
New York Times Company
The New Yorker Magazine, Inc.
Norton Co.
Norwest Corporation
NYNEX Corporation
Olin Corp.
PaineWebber
Panhandle Eastern Corporation
Parker Hannifin Corp.
Penguin Books USA, Inc.
Perkin-Elmer Corp.
Pfizer, Inc.
Phelps Dodge Corporation
Playboy Enterprises, Inc.
Premier Industrial Corp.
Prudential Insurance Co. of America, The
Prudential Securities, Inc.
Ralston Purina Co.
Raymond Corp.
Republic NY Corp.
Rich Products Corporation
RJR Nabisco Inc.
Rouse Co.
Royal Group, Inc.
Saint Paul Companies, Inc.
Salomon Inc.
Sara Lee Corp.
Schering-Plough Corp.
Schlumberger Ltd.
Scripps Co., E.W.
Seagram & Sons, Inc., Joseph E.
Seneca Foods Corp.
Shawmut National Corp.
Shell Oil Company
Simpson Investment Company
Swiss Bank Corp.
Tetley, Inc.
Texaco Inc.
Textron, Inc.
Thompson Co., J. Walter
Times Mirror Company, The
TransAmerica Corporation
Transco Energy Co.

Travelers Inc.
Unilever United States, Inc.
USG Corporation
Utica National Insurance Group
Wal-Mart Stores, Inc.
WestLB New York Branch
Westvaco Corporation
Wiley & Sons, Inc., John
Witco Corp.

North Carolina

Abbott Laboratories
Acme-McCrary Corp./Sapona Manufacturing Co.
Air Products and Chemicals, Inc.
Akzo America
Akzo Chemicals Inc.
AlliedSignal Inc.
Alumax Inc.
Aluminum Co. of America
American Brands, Inc.
AMETEK, Inc.
AMP Incorporated
Anheuser-Busch Companies, Inc.
Archer-Daniels-Midland Co.
Armco Inc.
Bank of Boston Corp.
Banta Corp.
Benetton Services Corp.
Blount, Inc.
Blue Bell, Inc.
Boise Cascade Corporation
Borden, Inc.
Bridgestone/Firestone, Inc.
Bristol-Myers Squibb Company
Brown & Williamson Tobacco Corp.
Brunswick Corp.
Burlington Industries, Inc.
Champion International Corporation
Chatham Manufacturing Co.
Chesapeake Corp.
Chesebrough-Pond's USA Co.
Clorox Co.
Coltec Industries, Inc.
Cooper Industries, Inc.
Corning Incorporated
CPC International Inc.
CR Industries
Crane Co.
Cranston Print Works Company
Cummins Engine Co.
Dexter Corporation
Donnelley & Sons Co., R.R.
Dow Corning Corp.
Dow Jones & Company, Inc.
du Pont de Nemours & Co., E. I.
Duke Power Co.
Eaton Corporation
Exxon Corporation
Fieldcrest Cannon Inc.
First Union Corp.
General Mills, Inc.
Georgia-Pacific Corporation
Harsco Corp.
Hartmarx Corporation
Heinz Company, H. J.
Henkel Corp.
Hoffmann-La Roche Inc.
International Business Machines Corp.
ITT Hartford Insurance Group, Inc.
JELD-WEN, Inc.
Johnson Controls Inc.
Johnson & Higgins
Jostens, Inc.
Kimberly-Clark Corp.
La-Z-Boy Chair Co.
Loews Corporation
Louisiana-Pacific Corp.
Lydall, Inc.
Martin Marietta Materials
MCI Communications Corp.
Mead Corporation, The
Miller Brewing Company/North Carolina

Minnesota Mining & Mfg. Co.
Mohasco Corp.
Moore & Sons, B.C.
National Gypsum Co.
New York Times Company
Norton Co.
Outboard Marine Corp.
Phelps Dodge Corporation
PHH Corporation
Providian Corporation
Prudential Insurance Co. of America, The
Pulitzer Publishing Co.
Reichhold Chemicals, Inc.
Republic NY Corp.
Rhone-Poulenc Inc.
Ringier-America
RJR Nabisco Inc.
Rohm & Haas Co.
Rose's Stores, Inc.
Rouse Co.
Royal Group, Inc.
Sara Lee Corp.
Sara Lee Hosiery, Inc.
Schuller International
Smith Corp., A.O.
Square D Co.
Stanley Works
Tenneco Inc.
Textron, Inc.
Thomasville Furniture Industries
Transco Energy Co.
Union Camp Corporation
Unitrode Corp.
USG Corporation
Virginia Power Co.
Vulcan Materials Co.
Wachovia Bank of North Carolina, N.A.
Wal-Mart Stores, Inc.
Westvaco Corporation
Weyerhaeuser Co.

North Dakota

Archer-Daniels-Midland Co.
Armco Inc.
Bucyrus-Erie Company
Enron Corp.
General Mills, Inc.
Lee Enterprises
Minnesota Mining & Mfg. Co.
Northern States Power Co. (Minnesota)
Norwest Corporation
Pamida, Inc.
Piper Jaffray Companies Inc.
Saint Paul Companies, Inc.
Sara Lee Corp.
Tenneco Inc.
US WEST, Inc.
Wal-Mart Stores, Inc.

Ohio

Abbott Laboratories
Air Products and Chemicals, Inc.
Akzo America
AlliedSignal Inc.
Alumax Inc.
Aluminum Co. of America
Amcast Industrial Corp.
American Brands, Inc.
AMETEK, Inc.
Andersons, The
Anheuser-Busch Companies, Inc.
AON Corporation
Appleton Papers Inc.
Archer-Daniels-Midland Co.
Aristech Chemical Corp.
Armco Inc.
AT&T Corp.
Avon Products, Inc.
Bank One, Youngstown, NA
Barry Corp., R. G.
Battelle Memorial Institute
Bemis Company, Inc.
Bethlehem Steel Corp.
Block, H&R

Boise Cascade Corporation
Borden, Inc.
BP America Inc.
Brunswick Corp.
Centerior Energy Corp.
Champion International Corporation
Chesapeake Corp.
Chevron Corporation
Chrysler Corp.
CINergy
CLARCOR Inc.
Clorox Co.
Columbus Dispatch Printing Co.
Consolidated Natural Gas Co.
Continental Corp.
Cooper Industries, Inc.
Corning Incorporated
Crane Co.
Cummins Engine Co.
Curtice-Burns Foods, Inc.
Dentsply International Inc.
Dexter Corporation
Donnelley & Sons Co., R.R.
Dow Jones & Company, Inc.
Dresser Industries, Inc.
du Pont de Nemours & Co., E. I.
Eaton Corporation
Elf Atochem North America, Inc.
Enron Corp.
Federal-Mogul Corporation
Fireman's Fund Insurance Co.
Freedom Forge Corp.
French Oil Mill Machinery Co.
Frisch's Restaurants Inc.
GATX Corp.
GenCorp Inc.
General Mills, Inc.
General Motors Corp.
Georgia-Pacific Corporation
Goodrich Co., The B.F.
Gould Electronics Inc.
Harsco Corp.
Hasbro Inc.
Hechinger Co.
Heinz Company, H. J.
Hook Drugs
Humana, Inc.
Illinois Tool Works, Inc.
Inland Container Corp.
International Paper Co.
ITT Hartford Insurance Group, Inc.
James River Corp. of Virginia
JELD-WEN, Inc.
Johnson Controls Inc.
Johnson & Higgins
Kemper National Insurance Cos.
Louisiana-Pacific Corp.
May Department Stores Company, The
McDonald & Company Securities, Inc.
McGraw-Hill, Inc.
Mead Corporation, The
Minnesota Mining & Mfg. Co.
Morrison Knudsen Corporation
Mosinee Paper Corp.
Norton Co.
Norwest Corporation
Panhandle Eastern Corporation
Parker Hannifin Corp.
Phelps Dodge Corporation
PPG Industries, Inc.
Premier Industrial Corp.
Prudential Insurance Co. of America, The
Ralston Purina Co.
Rich Products Corporation
Rockwell International Corporation
Ross Laboratories
Rouse Co.
Royal Group, Inc.
SAFECO Corp.
Saint Paul Companies, Inc.
Sandusky International Inc.
Sara Lee Corp.
Schuller International
Scott Fetzer Co.
Scripps Co., E.W.

Seagram & Sons, Inc., Joseph E.
Seaway Food Town, Inc.
Shell Oil Company
Smith Corp., A.O.
SPX Corp.
Square D Co.
Stanley Works
Teleflex Inc.
Temple-Inland Inc.
Tenneco Inc.
Textron, Inc.
Union Camp Corporation
USG Corporation
USX Corporation
Wal-Mart Stores, Inc.
Westvaco Corporation
Weyerhaeuser Co.
Whirlpool Corporation
Witco Corp.
Worthington Foods

Oklahoma

Air Products and Chemicals, Inc.
Akzo America
Albertson's Inc.
Allegheny Ludlum Corp.
AlliedSignal Inc.
American Fidelity Corporation
Anheuser-Busch Companies, Inc.
AON Corporation
Archer-Daniels-Midland Co.
Armco Inc.
Baker Hughes Inc.
Blount, Inc.
Boatmen's Bancshares, Inc.
Bridgestone/Firestone, Inc.
Brunswick Corp.
Cabot Corp.
CBI Industries, Inc.
Chevron Corporation
Chrysler Corp.
Coltec Industries, Inc.
Cooper Industries, Inc.
CR Industries
Dresser Industries, Inc.
du Pont de Nemours & Co., E. I.
Eaton Corporation
Elf Atochem North America, Inc.
General Mills, Inc.
Georgia-Pacific Corporation
Hanson Industries North America
Harsco Corp.
Heinz Company, H. J.
ITT Hartford Insurance Group, Inc.
Johnson Controls Inc.
Johnson & Higgins
Kimberly-Clark Corp.
Louisiana-Pacific Corp.
McDonnell Douglas Corp.-West
Mead Corporation, The
Merck & Co.
Minnesota Mining & Mfg. Co.
Mitchell Energy & Development Corp.
Norwest Corporation
OG&E Electric Services
Oxy USA Inc.
Prudential Insurance Co. of America, The
Quaker Chemical Corp.
Santa Fe Pacific Corporation
SBC Communications Inc.
Scripps Co., E.W.
Temple-Inland Inc.
Tenneco Inc.
Texaco Inc.
Union Pacific Corp.
USG Corporation
Valmont Industries, Inc.
Wal-Mart Stores, Inc.
Weyerhaeuser Co.
Williams Companies, The
Witco Corp.

Oregon

Air Products and Chemicals, Inc.
Albertson's Inc.
Alumax Inc.
Aluminum Co. of America
AMP Incorporated
AON Corporation
Archer-Daniels-Midland Co.
Armco Inc.
Bankers Trust Company
Berwind Corporation
Bird Corp.
Blount, Inc.
Boeing Co., The
Boise Cascade Corporation
Borden, Inc.
Chevron Corporation
Chrysler Corp.
Citibank
Clorox Co.
Curtice-Burns Foods, Inc.
Donnelley & Sons Co., R.R.
Dow Jones & Company, Inc.
Eaton Corporation
Elf Atochem North America, Inc.
First Interstate Bank of Oregon
GATX Corp.
General Mills, Inc.
Georgia-Pacific Corporation
Heinz Company, H. J.
Hewlett-Packard Co.
International Paper Co.
James River Corp. of Virginia
JELD-WEN, Inc.
Johnson Controls Inc.
Johnson & Higgins
Lee Enterprises
Louisiana-Pacific Corp.
May Department Stores Company, The
Mead Corporation, The
Minnesota Mining & Mfg. Co.
Northwest Natural Gas Co.
Ore-Ida Foods, Inc.
Parker Hannifin Corp.
Pioneer Trust Bank, NA
Piper Jaffray Companies Inc.
Rhone-Poulenc Inc.
Roseburg Forest Products Co.
SAFECO Corp.
Saint Paul Companies, Inc.
Sara Lee Corp.
Schlumberger Ltd.
Siltec Corp.
Simpson Investment Company
Stanley Works
Union Pacific Corp.
US WEST, Inc.
Wal-Mart Stores, Inc.
Washington Mutual Savings Bank
Washington Water Power Co.
West One Bancorp
Weyerhaeuser Co.
Witco Corp.

Pennsylvania

AEGON USA Inc.
Air France
Air Products and Chemicals, Inc.
Akzo America
Akzo Chemicals Inc.
Allegheny Ludlum Corp.
AlliedSignal Inc.
Alumax Inc.
Aluminum Co. of America
American Brands, Inc.
American Natural Resources Company
AMETEK, Inc.
AMP Incorporated
Anheuser-Busch Companies, Inc.
AON Corporation
Appleton Papers Inc.
Archer-Daniels-Midland Co.
Aristech Chemical Corp.
Armco Inc.

Chrysler Corp.
CIBC Wood Gundy
Citibank
CLARCOR Inc.
Clorox Co.
Coltec Industries, Inc.
Comerica Incorporated
Contran Corporation
Cooper Industries, Inc.
Curtice-Burns Foods, Inc.
Dexter Corporation
Diamond Shamrock Inc.
Donnelley & Sons Co., R.R.
Douglas & Lomason Company
Dow Jones & Company, Inc.
Dresser Industries, Inc.
du Pont de Nemours & Co.,
  E. I.
Dun & Bradstreet Corp.
Eaton Corporation
Elf Atochem North America,
  Inc.
Enron Corp.
Ethyl Corp
Exxon Corporation
Fieldcrest Cannon Inc.
Fireman's Fund Insurance Co.
Frost National Bank
GATX Corp.
General Mills, Inc.
General Motors Corp.
Georgia-Pacific Corporation
Goodrich Co., The B.F.
Hanson Industries North
  America
Harcourt General, Inc.
Harsco Corp.
Hasbro Inc.
Heinz Company, H. J.
Heller Financial, Inc.
Hickory Tech Corp.
Houston Industries
  Incorporated
Humana, Inc.
Hygeia Dairy Co.
Illinois Tool Works, Inc.
Inland Container Corp.
International Business
  Machines Corp.
International Paper Co.
ITT Hartford Insurance Group,
  Inc.
James River Corp. of Virginia
Johnson Controls Inc.
Johnson & Higgins
Johnson & Son, S.C.
Jostens, Inc.
Kimberly-Clark Corp.
Lehigh Portland Cement Co.
Little, Inc., Arthur D.
Loews Corporation
Louisiana-Pacific Corp.
Management Compensation
  Group/Dulworth Inc.
Maritz Inc.
Mattel, Inc.
May Department Stores
  Company, The
McCormick & Co. Inc.
McDonnell Douglas
  Corp.-West
MCI Communications Corp.
Mead Corporation, The
Medtronic, Inc.
Minnesota Mining & Mfg. Co.
Mitchell Energy &
  Development Corp.
Mitsubishi Motor Sales of
  America, Inc.
Mobil Oil Corp.
Montana Power Co.
Morgan & Company, J.P.
Morrison Knudsen Corporation
Nalco Chemical Co.
New York Life Insurance Co.
Norton Co.
Norwest Corporation
Olin Corp.
Oxy USA Inc.
PaineWebber
Panhandle Eastern Corporation
Pennzoil Co.
Phelps Dodge Corporation
PHH Corporation
Potomac Electric Power Co.

Prudential Insurance Co. of
  America, The
Quaker Chemical Corp.
Rhone-Poulenc Inc.
Rockwell International
  Corporation
Rohm & Haas Co.
Rouse Co.
Royal Group, Inc.
SAFECO Corp.
Saint Paul Companies, Inc.
Salomon Inc.
Santa Fe Pacific Corporation
Sara Lee Corp.
SBC Communications Inc.
Schering-Plough Corp.
Schlumberger Ltd.
Schuller International
Scripps Co., E.W.
Shell Oil Company
Simpson Investment Company
Smith Corp., A.O.
Sonat Inc.
Southwestern Electric Power
  Co.
Square D Co.
Stanley Works
Swiss Bank Corp.
Teleflex Inc.
Temple-Inland Inc.
Tenneco Inc.
Texaco Inc.
Texas Commerce
  Bank-Houston, N.A.
Textron, Inc.
Times Mirror Company, The
TransAmerica Corporation
Transco Energy Co.
Travelers Inc.
Union Camp Corporation
Union Pacific Corp.
Unocal Corp.
USG Corporation
USX Corporation
Valmont Industries, Inc.
Vulcan Materials Co.
Wal-Mart Stores, Inc.
Westvaco Corporation
Weyerhaeuser Co.
Witco Corp.
Zachry Co., H.B.

Utah

Abbott Laboratories
Air Products and Chemicals,
  Inc.
Albertson's Inc.
AlliedSignal Inc.
Aluminum Co. of America
Armco Inc.
Baker Hughes Inc.
Boise Cascade Corporation
Borden, Inc.
Chevron Corporation
Donnelley & Sons Co., R.R.
Eaton Corporation
GATX Corp.
General Mills, Inc.
Georgia-Pacific Corporation
Harsco Corp.
Johnson & Higgins
Jostens, Inc.
Kennecott Corporation
Kimberly-Clark Corp.
La-Z-Boy Chair Co.
McDonald & Company
  Securities, Inc.
McDonnell Douglas
  Corp.-West
Mead Corporation, The
Minnesota Mining & Mfg. Co.
Norwest Corporation
Novell Inc.
Parker Hannifin Corp.
Piper Jaffray Companies Inc.
Royal Group, Inc.
Teleflex Inc.
Union Pacific Corp.
US WEST, Inc.
USG Corporation
Valmont Industries, Inc.
West One Bancorp
Williams Companies, The

Vermont

Armco Inc.
Bank of Boston Corp.
Central Vermont Public
  Service Corp.
Cooper Industries, Inc.
Donnelley & Sons Co., R.R.
General Mills, Inc.
Georgia-Pacific Corporation
Hasbro Inc.
International Business
  Machines Corp.
Johnson Controls Inc.
Martin Marietta Corp.
Olin Corp.
Simpson Investment Company
Stanley Works
Textron, Inc.

Virgin Islands

American General Finance
  Corp.
Raymond Corp.

Virginia

Abbott Laboratories
AlliedSignal Inc.
Alumax Inc.
Aluminum Co. of America
American Brands, Inc.
American Natural Resources
  Company
Amoco Corp.
AMP Incorporated
Anheuser-Busch Companies,
  Inc.
AON Corporation
Archer-Daniels-Midland Co.
Armco Inc.
Bay Area Foods
Bell Atlantic Corp.
Boeing Co., The
Borden, Inc.
Bridgestone/Firestone, Inc.
Brunswick Corp.
Burlington Industries, Inc.
Cable & Wireless Holdings,
  Inc.
Central Fidelity Banks, Inc.
Chesapeake Corp.
Chrysler Corp.
Citibank
Consolidated Natural Gas Co.
Cooper Industries, Inc.
Corning Incorporated
Donnelley & Sons Co., R.R.
Dow Jones & Company, Inc.
du Pont de Nemours & Co.,
  E. I.
Ethyl Corp
Federal-Mogul Corporation
Fieldcrest Cannon Inc.
First Union Corp.
General Mills, Inc.
Georgia-Pacific Corporation
Giant Food Inc.
Giant Food Stores
Goodman & Co.
Hechinger Co.
Heinz Company, H. J.
Hershey Foods Corp.
Illinois Tool Works, Inc.
Inland Container Corp.
International Business
  Machines Corp.
ITT Hartford Insurance Group,
  Inc.
James River Corp. of Virginia
Johnson & Higgins
Lipton, Thomas J.
Loews Corporation
Louisiana-Pacific Corp.
Lydall, Inc.
May Department Stores
  Company, The
McCormick & Co. Inc.
McDonald & Company
  Securities, Inc.
Mead Corporation, The

Minnesota Mining & Mfg. Co.
Mobil Oil Corp.
Mohasco Corp.
Norfolk Shipbuilding &
  Drydock Corp.
Old Dominion Box Co.
PHH Corporation
Prudential Insurance Co. of
  America, The
Rouse Co.
SAFECO Corp.
Sara Lee Corp.
Sara Lee Hosiery, Inc.
Schuller International
Scripps Co., E.W.
Shenandoah Life Insurance Co.
Stanley Works
Temple-Inland Inc.
Tenneco Inc.
Thomasville Furniture
  Industries
Transco Energy Co.
Union Camp Corporation
USG Corporation
Virginia Power Co.
Vulcan Materials Co.
Wal-Mart Stores, Inc.
Westvaco Corporation
Weyerhaeuser Co.
Wheat First Butcher Singer,
  Inc.

Washington

Albertson's Inc.
Aldus Corp.
Alumax Inc.
Aluminum Co. of America
AMETEK, Inc.
Archer-Daniels-Midland Co.
Armco Inc.
BankAmerica Corp.
Battelle Memorial Institute
Bemis Company, Inc.
Boeing Co., The
Boise Cascade Corporation
Borden, Inc.
BP America Inc.
Bristol-Myers Squibb
  Company
Brunswick Corp.
Champion International
  Corporation
Chevron Corporation
Citibank
Cooper Industries, Inc.
CPC International Inc.
Curtice-Burns Foods, Inc.
Donnelley & Sons Co., R.R.
Dow Jones & Company, Inc.
Elf Atochem North America,
  Inc.
GATX Corp.
General Mills, Inc.
Georgia-Pacific Corporation
Goodrich Co., The B.F.
Guardian Life Insurance
  Company of America
Hanson Industries North
  America
Hasbro Inc.
Heinz Company, H. J.
Hewlett-Packard Co.
ITT Hartford Insurance Group,
  Inc.
Johnson Controls Inc.
Johnson & Higgins
Louisiana-Pacific Corp.
McGraw-Hill, Inc.
Mead Corporation, The
Minnesota Mining & Mfg. Co.
Mobil Oil Corp.
Montana Power Co.
Olin Corp.
Piper Jaffray Companies Inc.
Prudential Insurance Co. of
  America, The
Rhone-Poulenc Inc.
Rouse Co.
Royal Group, Inc.
SAFECO Corp.
Saint Paul Companies, Inc.

Sara Lee Corp.
Scripps Co., E.W.
Seafirst Corporation
Shell Oil Company
Simpson Investment Company
Smith Corp., A.O.
Tenneco Inc.
Union Pacific Corp.
United Airlines, Inc.
U.S. Bank of Washington
US WEST, Inc.
USG Corporation
Wal-Mart Stores, Inc.
Washington Mutual Savings
  Bank
Washington Water Power Co.
West One Bancorp
Weyerhaeuser Co.
Witco Corp.

West Virginia

American Natural Resources
  Company
Aristech Chemical Corp.
Armco Inc.
Bell Atlantic Corp.
Berwind Corporation
Bethlehem Steel Corp.
Borden, Inc.
Cabot Corp.
Clorox Co.
Consolidated Natural Gas Co.
Corning Incorporated
du Pont de Nemours & Co.,
  E. I.
General Mills, Inc.
Georgia-Pacific Corporation
Giant Food Stores
Goodrich Co., The B.F.
Hanson Industries North
  America
Harsco Corp.
Heinz Company, H. J.
Lee Enterprises
Minnesota Mining & Mfg. Co.
Olin Corp.
Phelps Dodge Corporation
PPG Industries, Inc.
Schuller International
Scripps Co., E.W.
Shell Oil Company
USX Corporation
Virginia Power Co.
Wal-Mart Stores, Inc.
Westvaco Corporation

Wisconsin

Akzo America
Alumax Inc.
Amcast Industrial Corp.
American Brands, Inc.
AMETEK, Inc.
Andersen Corp.
Anheuser-Busch Companies,
  Inc.
AON Corporation
Appleton Papers Inc.
Archer-Daniels-Midland Co.
Armco Inc.
Banc One Wisconsin Corp.
Banta Corp.
Bemis Company, Inc.
Blount, Inc.
Blue Cross & Blue Shield
  United of Wisconsin
Boise Cascade Corporation
Borden, Inc.
Brillion Iron Works
Brunswick Corp.
Bucyrus-Erie Company
CBS, Inc.
Chesapeake Corp.
Chrysler Corp.
Coltec Industries, Inc.
Consolidated Papers, Inc.
Cooper Industries, Inc.
Corning Incorporated
CPC International Inc.
DEC International, Inc.
Deere & Co.

Donaldson Company, Inc.
Dresser Industries, Inc.
Dun & Bradstreet Corp.
Eaton Corporation
Fireman's Fund Insurance Co.
First Financial Bank FSB
Firstar Bank Milwaukee, N.A.
Fleet Financial Group, Inc.
Fleming Cos. Food
  Distribution Center
GenCorp Inc.
General Mills, Inc.
General Motors Corp.
Georgia-Pacific Corporation
Gillette Co.
Guardian Life Insurance
  Company of America
Heinz Company, H. J.
Illinois Tool Works, Inc.
Inland Container Corp.

International Paper Co.
James River Corp. of Virginia
Johnson Controls Inc.
Johnson & Son, S.C.
Kemper National Insurance
  Cos.
Kennecott Corporation
Kimberly-Clark Corp.
Lee Enterprises
Louisiana-Pacific Corp.
Madison Gas & Electric Co.
Marquette Electronics, Inc.
Mautz Paint Co.
McDonald & Company
  Securities, Inc.
Mead Corporation, The
Minnesota Mining & Mfg. Co.
Mosinee Paper Corp.
New England Business Service
Norwest Corporation

Olin Corp.
Ore-Ida Foods, Inc.
Outboard Marine Corp.
Pamida, Inc.
Parker Hannifin Corp.
Piper Jaffray Companies Inc.
PPG Industries, Inc.
Ringier-America
RJR Nabisco Inc.
Rockwell International
  Corporation
Rouse Co.
Saint Paul Companies, Inc.
Sara Lee Corp.
Sentry Insurance A Mutual
  Company
Smith Corp., A.O.
Square D Co.
Tenneco Inc.
Textron, Inc.

Union Camp Corporation
USG Corporation
Vulcan Materials Co.
Wal-Mart Stores, Inc.
Weyerhaeuser Co.
WICOR, Inc.
Wisconsin Power & Light Co.
Wisconsin Public Service Corp.
Witco Corp.

Wyoming

Albertson's Inc.
Archer-Daniels-Midland Co.
Armco Inc.
Chevron Corporation
Chrysler Corp.
Eaton Corporation
Enron Corp.

Exxon Corporation
General Mills, Inc.
Georgia-Pacific Corporation
Kennecott Corporation
KN Energy, Inc.
Louisiana-Pacific Corp.
Mobil Oil Corp.
Montana Power Co.
Norwest Corporation
Pamida, Inc.
Piper Jaffray Companies Inc.
Pittsburg Midway Coal Mining
  Co.
Prudential Insurance Co. of
  America, The
US WEST, Inc.
Wal-Mart Stores, Inc.
Williams Companies, The

Index to Officers and Directors

Please refer to the Master Index to Corporations and Foundations for profile page numbers.

Bacheller, Glenn, pres: Baskin-Robbins USA Co.

Bachman, Dale, trust: Cooke Foundation

Bachman, Laura, asst secy: Fairchild Foundation, Sherman

Bachner, Robert L., asst secy, dir: Uris Brothers Foundation; dir: Wishnick Foundation, Robert I.

Bacigalupi, Jean, pres, dir: Haigh-Scatena Foundation

Bacon, Herbert L., pres: Bacon Foundation, E. L. and Oma

Bacon, Laura M., treas: Bacon Foundation, E. L. and Oma

Bacon, Robert L., secy: Femino Foundation

Bacot, John Carter, chmn, ceo: Bank of New York Company, Inc.

Bader, William Banks, secy, treas, trust: Kress Foundation, Samuel H.

Badman, Benjamin, Jr., exec vp, dir: Sordoni Foundation

Baer, Marion C., secy: Altman Foundation

Bahrt, Fred R., pres, dir: Gellert Foundation, Carl; dir, vchmn: Gellert Foundation, Celia Berta

Bailey, Anita Lamb, chmn, dir: OCRI Foundation

Bailey, David R., dir: Ensign-Bickford Foundation

Bailey, Denise, dir: Bell Atlantic Corp.; dir: Bell Atlantic Foundation

Bailey, Gregory J., mgr: Jostens Foundation Inc., The

Bailey, Hoyt Q., pres: Dover Foundation

Bailey, Irving Widmer, II, chmn: Providian Corporation

Bailey, Keith E., chmn, pres, ceo, dir: Williams Companies, The; pres, dir: Williams Companies Foundation, The

Bailey, Ruth, secy: Sunnen Foundation

Baiocchi, Ramona D., asst secy: Regenstein Foundation

Baird, Dugald Euan, chmn, ceo: Schlumberger Ltd.

Baird, Joni, vp, fund admin: Schuller Fund

Baird, Patrick S., cfo, sr vp: AEGON USA Inc.

Baker, Ann Cassidy, chmn: Broadhurst Foundation

Baker, Anthony K., trust: Baker Trust, George F.

Baker, Benjamin M., III, dir: Lockhart Vaughan Foundation

Baker, C. Allen, exec vp: Alcon Laboratories, Inc.; trust: Alcon Foundation

Baker, Dennis J., vp, dir: Norton Co. Foundation

Baker, Dexter Farrington, trust: Trexler Trust, Harry C.

Baker, George F., III, trust: Baker Trust, George F.

Baker, James E., treas: Gannett Foundation, Guy P.

Baker, Kane K., trust: Baker Trust, George F.

Baker, Laurin M., dir pub aff: Outboard Marine Corp.; secy, dir: OMC Foundation

Baker, Leslie Mayo, Jr., pres, ceo, dir: Wachovia Bank of North Carolina, N.A.; dir: Wachovia Foundation, Inc.

Baker, Mitchell, sr vp, mgr pub aff: Seafirst Corporation; trust: Seafirst Foundation

Baker, Norman D., Jr., dir: Allendale Insurance Foundation; trust: Kimball Foundation, Horace A. Kimball and S. Ella

Baker, Paula W., vp: IBM International Foundation

Baker, Richard Eugene, vp, cfo, dir: MCA Inc.; vp, treas, cfo: MCA Foundation, Ltd.

Baker, Richard M., secy: Imperial Bank Foundation

Baker, Richard W., trust: Speer Foundation, Roy M.

Baker, Robbie L., trust: Kantzler Foundation

Baker, Robert Woodward, exec vp oper: AMR Corp.

Baker, Roger William Weatherburn, secy corp responsibility & pub aff comm: American Brands, Inc.

Baker, William, group vp, cao: HarperCollins Publishers Inc.

Baker, William C., trust: Clayton Fund

Baker, William Oliver, trust: Fund for New Jersey; dir: Guggenheim Foundation, Harry Frank

Bakken, Douglas Adair, exec dir: Ball Brothers Foundation

Bakkensen, Ralph V. G., asst secy: M/A-COM Foundation

Balderston, Frederick E., dir: Osher Foundation, Bernard

Baldwin, Barbara, vp, trust: Baldwin Foundation, David M. and Barbara

Baldwin, Bennet M., trust: Baldwin Memorial Foundation, Fred

Baldwin, David M., trust, pres: Baldwin Foundation, David M. and Barbara

Baldwin, John C., trust: Baldwin Memorial Foundation, Fred; dir: Castle Foundation, Harold K. L.

Baldwin, Robert Hayes Burns, chmn, trust: Dodge Foundation, Geraldine R.

Balich, Nicholas S., vp: Phelps Dodge Corporation

Baliles, Jeannie P., vp, dir: Virginia Environmental Endowment

Balint, Michael J., exec dir, secy: Piper Foundation, Minnie Stevens

Balkas, Denise M., dir: Hoyt Foundation, Stewart W. and Willma C.

Ball, Anne F., trust: Firestone, Jr. Foundation, Harvey

Ball, Braden, pres, dir: duPont Foundation, Alfred I.

Ball, Edmund Ferdinand, chmn, dir: Ball Brothers Foundation

Ball, Frank E., vp, dir: Ball Brothers Foundation

Ball, James Herington, sr vp, asst secy, gen couns: Nestle USA Inc.; dir: Nestle USA Foundation

Ballantine, Dewey, trust: Adams Foundation, Arthur F. and Alice E.

Ballantine, Elizabeth, trust: Cowles Foundation, Gardner and Florence Call

Ballantine, Morley Cowles, don granddaughter, trust: Cowles Foundation, Gardner and Florence Call

Ballard, Larry Coleman, chmn, pres, ceo: Sentry Insurance A Mutual Company

Ballengee, Jerry Hunter, exec vp, dir: Union Camp Corporation

Balog, James, dir: Donner Foundation, William H.

Balter, William H., Esq., admin: Peters Foundation, Charles F.

Bancroft, Bettina, mem adv comm: Dow Jones Foundation

Bancroft, James Ramsey, vp: Witter Foundation, Dean

Banner, Stephen Edward, trust: Bronfman Foundation, Samuel

Barad, Jill EliKann, pres, coo, dir: Mattel, Inc.; dir: Mattel Foundation

Bardes, Judith L., exec dir, trust: Douty Foundation

Bardige, Betty S., trust: Mailman Family Foundation, A. L.

Bardusch, William E., Jr., pres, trust: Sullivan Foundation, Algernon Sydney

Barfield-Johnson, Becky, trust: CS First Boston Foundation Trust

Barker, Ann S., dir: Barker Foundation, J.M.R.

Barker, Edwin F., vp, cfo: Winnebago Industries, Inc.

Barker, Elizabeth S., vp, dir: Barker Foundation, J.M.R.

Barker, James R., vp, dir: Barker Foundation, J.M.R.

Barker, Judith, pres, dir: Unocal Foundation; pres: Borden Foundation, Inc.

Barker, Robert R., pres, dir: Barker Foundation, J.M.R.

Barker, William Benjamin, dir: Barker Foundation, J.M.R.

Barker, William P., trust: McFeely-Rogers Foundation

Barksdale, Robert M., trust: Besser Foundation

Barletta, Robert, treas: Prospect Hill Foundation

Barlow, Robert C., pres: Crestlea Foundation; asst secy: Longwood Foundation; asst secy: Welfare Foundation

Barmore, Beryl A., asst vp: Wilmington Trust Co.; trust: Wilmington Trust Co. Foundation

Barnard, Marla, mgr commun rels: Panhandle Eastern Corporation

Barnes, Celici K., vp: Medtronic, Inc.

Barnes, Frances M., III, trust: Gaylord Foundation, Clifford Willard

Barnes, W. Michael, sr vp fin & planning, cfo: Rockwell International Corporation; mem trust comm: Rockwell International Corporation Trust

Barnes, Wallace W., chmn: Aetna Foundation

Barnette, Curtis Handley, chmn, ceo, dir: Bethlehem Steel Corp.

Barney, Austin D., dir: Ensign-Bickford Foundation

Barnhardt, C. C., Jr., secy: Fieldcrest Cannon Foundation

Barnhart, Lorraine, exec dir: Freed Foundation; asst secy, exec dir, trust: Huber Foundation

Barpal, Isaac Ruben, dir: AlliedSignal Foundation Inc.

Barr, John M., mgr: LBJ Family Foundation

Barre, Steven C., asst secy: Hanson White Foundation

Barrett, Allen M., Jr., vp, corp commun: McCormick & Co. Inc.

Barrett, M. Patricia, vp corp commun: Union Electric Co.

Barron, M.P., dir: Audubon State Bank Charitable Foundation

Barroso, Carmen, dir (population program): MacArthur Foundation, John D. and Catherine T.

Barry, Elizabeth J., trust: Jewell Memorial Foundation, Daniel Ashley and Irene Houston

Barry, Elizabeth T., dir: Gazette Foundation

Barry, Tina S., pres, dir: Kimberly-Clark Foundation

Barsky, Barbara, secy, treas, dir: PNM Foundation

Bartelt, Sarah Caswell, dir: Beveridge Foundation, Frank Stanley

Barter, John William, III, dir: AlliedSignal Foundation Inc.

Bartha, Louis A., secy, treas: Prairie Foundation

Bartl, James F., secy, dir: Phillips Family Foundation, L. E.

Bartleson, Leslie E. S., dir: Stauffer Foundation, John and Beverly

Bartlett, Buzz, dir pub & commun rels: Martin Marietta Corp.

Bartlett, Pamela, dir: Ensign-Bickford Foundation

Bartlett, Richard M., dir: Lebanon Mutual Foundation

Barton, C. Ann, treas: Jewell Memorial Foundation, Daniel Ashley and Irene Houston

Barton, Gerard, vp: WestLB New York Branch

Barton, James F., chmn: Raymond Foundation

Barton, Robert M., dir: Berger Foundation, H. N. and Frances C.

Barton, Willis H., Jr., vp: New Milford Savings Bank Foundation

Barwick, Kent L., dir: Clark Foundation

Bashara, George N., Jr., chmn contributions comm: Federal-Mogul Corp. Charitable Trust Fund

Bass, Robert P., Jr., dir: Bird Corp. Charitable Foundation

Bastian, Frank W., secy, dir: Schoenleber Foundation

Bate, David S., vp, trust: International Foundation

Bates, James C., vp, cfo: ACF Industries, Inc.

Batson, R. Neal, trust: Woolley Foundation, Vasser

Battey, Charles W., chmn, dir: KN Energy, Inc.; pres, dir: KN Energy Foundation

Battista, Gabe, pres: Cable & Wireless Holdings, Inc.

Battram, Richard L., vchmn: May Department Stores Company, The

Batts, James L., dir: Batts Foundation

Batts, John H., pres, dir: Batts Foundation

Batts, John T., dir: Batts Foundation

Batts, Michael A., dir: Batts Foundation

Batts, Robert H., dir: Batts Foundation

Batts, Warren Leighton, pres: Batts Foundation

Bauder, Lillian, trust: Skillman Foundation

Bauer, Chris Michael, pres: Firstar Milwaukee Foundation

Bauer, Douglas F., secy, treas: Bowne Foundation, Robert

Bauernfeind, George G., vp (taxes): Humana Foundation

Bauman, Steve, secy: Ottenheimer Brothers Foundation

Baumgardner, Anita A., secy, trust: Copley Foundation, James S.

Baumgarner, John C., Jr., sr vp corp devel plan: Williams Companies, The; dir: Williams Companies Foundation, The

Baumgartner, Howard E., trust: Schowalter Foundation

Bautz, Sheila M., asst treas: Taconic Foundation

Baxter, Barbara J., vp, trust: Andrews Foundation

Baxter, Joe E., secy, treas, dir: Meyer Family Foundation, Paul J.

Baxter, Laura S., asst secy, treas, trust: Andrews Foundation

Bay, Frederick, chmn, dir: Bay Foundation

Bay, Mogens C., pres, ceo: Valmont Industries, Inc.

Bay-Hansen, Christopher, dir: Bay Foundation

Bayard, Jane, vp, dir: Uris Brothers Foundation

Bazany, LeRoy Francis, trust: Bemis Company Foundation

Beach, Richard F., admin: Kettering Fund; trust: Tait Foundation, Frank M.

Beadle, Robert Sheldon, vp, dir: Diamond Shamrock Inc.

Beal, Barry A., trust: Beal Foundation

Beal, Carlton E., don, chmn, trust: Beal Foundation

Beal, Carlton E., Jr., trust: Beal Foundation

Beal, Keleen H., vchmn: Beal Foundation

Beal, Kelly, trust: Beal Foundation

Beal, Spencer E., trust: Beal Foundation

Beale, Deborah B., dir: Osceola Foundation

Beale, Susan M., dir: Detroit Edison Foundation

Beall, Carolyn C., asst treas: Campbell Foundation

Beall, Donald Ray, chmn, ceo: Rockwell International Corporation; mem trust comm: Rockwell International Corporation Trust

Bean, Barbara, pub trust: Carpenter Foundation

Bean, Ralph J., Jr., trust: Benedum Foundation, Claude Worthington; trust: Consolidated Natural Gas System Foundation

Bean, Roy H., trust: Ashtabula Foundation

Beard, D. Paul, sr vp, contr: PNC Bank, N.A.; treas, secy distr comm: PNC Bank Foundation

Beard, Ellanor Allday, mem bd govs: Fondren Foundation

Beardsley, George B., trust: Gates Foundation

Beardsley, James M., trust: Palisano Foundation, Vincent and Harriet

Beasley, C. H., trust: Alcon Foundation

Bird, David, dir: Bird Corp. Charitable Foundation

Bird, Peter F., Jr., sr program off, secy: HCA Foundation

Birk, Joe, asst to gen couns & vp: Union Electric Co.

Bischoff, Robert A., vp: Martin Marietta Philanthropic Trust

Bishop, Donald F., II, pres, mem adv comm: O'Connor Foundation, A. Lindsay and Olive B.

Bishop, Leslie R., secy, dir: Russell Charitable Foundation, Tom

Bishop, Robert L., secy, mem adv comm: O'Connor Foundation, A. Lindsay and Olive B.

Bishop, Robert L., II, chmn, mem adv comm: O'Connor Foundation, A. Lindsay and Olive B.

Bishop, Timothy R., treas: Collins Foundation

Bissetta, Bruno George, first vp: Prudential Securities, Inc.; vp, treas: Prudential Securities Foundation

Bissonette, Paul A., vp, dir: Daily News Foundation

Bittner, D. P., treas: Wisconsin Public Service Foundation, Inc.

Bittner, R. Richard, trust, dir: Bechtel Charitable Remainder Uni-Trust, Marie H.; trust: Bechtel Testamentary Charitable Trust, H. R.

Bjornson, Donald R., MD, mem: CHC Foundation

Bjornson, Edith C., program off: Markle Foundation, John and Mary R.

Black, Creed Carter, pres, ceo, trust: Knight Foundation, John S. and James L.

Black, Gary E., exec vp, dir: Fireman's Fund Insurance Co.; pres, dir: Fireman's Fund Foundation

Black, Kent March, exec vp, coo: Rockwell International Corporation

Black, Lennox K., chmn, ceo, dir: Teleflex Inc.; pres: Teleflex Foundation

Black, Thomas F., III, pres, trust: Kimball Foundation, Horace A. Kimball and S. Ella

Blackwell, Angela Glover, dir: Irvine Foundation, James

Blackwell, Anna Delby, trust: Cooke Foundation

Blair, Ian D., trust: Todd Co. Foundation, A.M.

Blair, Pat, pub trust: Carpenter Foundation

Blake, Benjamin L., dir: Prairie Foundation

Blake, Bensen P., trust: Blake Foundation, S. P.

Blake, Lucy, trust: Crocker Trust, Mary A.

Blake, Stewart P., trust: Blake Foundation, S. P.

Blaney, Carolyn E., trust: Eberly Foundation

Blank, David M., treas: Centerior Energy Foundation

Blank, Robert, secy: BT Foundation

Blanke, Gail, sr vp pub aff: Avon Products, Inc.; vp: Avon Products Foundation, Inc.

Blankley, Walter Elwood, chmn, dir: AMETEK, Inc.; pres, dir: AMETEK Foundation

Blanton, Eddy S., vp, dir: Scurlock Foundation

Blanton, Jack S., chmn, dir: Houston Endowment

Blanton, Jack S., Jr., vp, dir: Scurlock Foundation

Blanton, Laura L., pres, dir: Scurlock Foundation

Blass, Noland, Jr., bd dir: Ottenheimer Brothers Foundation

Blattman, H. Eugene, pres, ceo, coo: McCormick & Co. Inc.

Blaxter, H. Vaughan, III, secy, dir: Hillman Foundation

Bleck, Max Emil, dir: Beech Aircraft Foundation

Bloch, Henry Wollman, chmn: Block, H&R; chmn: Block Foundation, H&R

Bloch, Mary, mem disbursement comm: Oppenstein Brothers Foundation

Bloch, Robert L., secy, program off: Block Foundation, H&R

Bloch, Thomas Morton, ceo, pres, dir: Block, H&R

Block, Ellen, secy: Hassenfeld Foundation

Block, Leonard Nathan, vp, dir: Kaufmann Foundation, Henry

Blocker, John R., asst vp: Rachal Foundation, Ed

Bloedorn, John H., Jr., dir: Bloedorn Foundation, Walter A.

Blohm, Donald E., admin: La-Z-Boy Foundation

Bloodworth, Carolyn A., asst secy: Consumers Power Foundation

Bloom, Aimee Simon, dir: Simon Foundation, William E. and Carol G.

Bloom, Cliffton E., trust: Mulcahy Foundation

Blossom, C. Bingham, trust, chmn investment comm treas: Bingham Foundation, William

Blossom, C. Perry, trust: Bingham Foundation, William

Blossom, Dudley S., trust: Bingham Foundation, William

Blossom, Laurel, trust: Bingham Foundation, William

Blossom, Robin Dunn, trust: Bingham Foundation, William

Blount, Winton Malcolm, Jr., chmn, dir: Blount, Inc.; dir: Blount Foundation

Bluemle, Lewis William, Jr., vp fin, trust: Connelly Foundation

Blum, Michael S., chmn, pres, ceo: Heller Financial, Inc.

Blum, Richard C., dir: Koret Foundation

Boardman, Harold Frederick, Jr., trust: Hoffmann-La Roche Foundation

Bobrow, Irving S., vp, asst treas: Rosen Foundation, Joseph

Bobst, Mamdouha S., pres, treas, dir: Bobst Foundation, Elmer and Mamdouha

Bocko, Miranda Fuller, trust: Fuller Foundation

Bockway, Jerome, trust: Ashtabula Foundation

Boddie, J. Herbert, trust: Blount Educational and Charitable Foundation, Mildred Weedon

Bodeen, Kay, admin: Marriott Foundation, J. Willard

Bodine, Jean, trust: McLean Contributionship

Bodman, Samuel Wright, III, chmn, pres, ceo, dir: Cabot Corp.; pres, dir: Cabot Corp. Foundation

Boedeker, Lucy, off mgr: Bechtel Charitable Remainder Uni-Trust, Marie H.

Boekenheide, Russell W., sr vp: Union Camp Corporation; trust: Union Camp Charitable Trust

Boesel, Stephen W., vp: Price Associates Foundation, T. Rowe

Boesen, James M., treas, dir: Dillon Foundation

Boettcher, Mrs. Charles, II, trust: Boettcher Foundation

Boettiger, John R., dir: Reynolds Foundation, Christopher

Bogert, H. Lawrence, vp, dir: JM Foundation

Bogert, Jeremiah Milbank, dir: JM Foundation

Bohn, Karen M., pres: Piper Jaffray Companies Foundation

Bohne, P. W., vp, dir: German Protestant Orphan Asylum Association

Boice, John E., Jr., secy, treas, dir: Bloedorn Foundation, Walter A.

Boitano, Caroline O., pres, exec dir: BankAmerica Foundation

Boklund, Thomas B., trust: Gilmore Foundation, William G.

Bolliger, Ralph, vp, dir: Collins Foundation

Bolling, Robert H., Jr., pres, trust: Welfare Foundation

Bollman, Brooks, III, trust: Mott Fund, Ruth

Bollom, Daniel Arthur, pres, ceo, dir: Wisconsin Public Service Corp.; pres: Wisconsin Public Service Foundation, Inc.

Bolt, John F., secy: Landegger Charitable Foundation

Boman, Gerald A., pres: Winnebago Industries Foundation

Boman, Keith, trust: Reynolds Foundation, Donald W.

Bommer, William Russell, trust: Acushnet Foundation

Bond, Arthur D., III, dir: Green Foundation, Allen P. and Josephine B.

Bond, Christopher Samuel, dir: Green Foundation, Allen P. and Josephine B.

Bond, Marcus J., MD, vchmn: Comprecare Foundation

Bond, Sara K., vp, asst secy, trust: Hoover, Jr. Foundation, Margaret W. and Herbert

Boney, Sion A., admin vp, secy, treas, trust: Hillsdale Fund

Bonner, Henry M., dir: Lake Placid Education Foundation

Bonney, John Dennis, vchmn, dir: Chevron Corporation

Booker, William W., secy, treas, dir: Daywood Foundation

Boone Scioneaux, Melanie, asst secy/treas: Fondren Foundation

Boorstin, Daniel J., dir: Cafritz Foundation, Morris and Gwendolyn

Booth, Beatrice Crosby, trust: Carolyn Foundation

Booth, Chesley Peter Washburn, sr vp devel: Corning Incorporated; trust: Corning Incorporated Foundation

Borek, JoAnne, exec dir: Peabody Charitable Fund, Amelia

Boren, Molly, secy, treas, trust: Sarkeys Foundation

Borman, Gilbert, secy, treas, dir: Borman Fund, The

Borman, Marlene, vp, dir: Borman Fund, The

Borman, Paul, chmn: Borman's Inc.; pres, dir: Borman Fund, The

Born, Allen, chmn, ceo: Alumax Inc.

Borneo, Rudolph John, pres: Macy & Co., Inc., R.H.

Borton, Karl, trust: Wildermuth Foundation, E. F.

Borzymowski, Frank P., secy: Goldseker Foundation of Maryland, Morris

Bosacker, Lyle T., trust: Hickory Tech Corp. Foundation

Boschulte, Alfred F., mem contributions comm: NYNEX Corporate Philanthropy and Foundation

Boskin, Michael J., dir: Koret Foundation

Boss, W. Andrew, pres, dir: Boss Foundation, William

Bossidy, Lawrence Arthur, chmn, ceo, dir: AlliedSignal Inc.; chmn, dir: AlliedSignal Foundation Inc.

Boswell, James G., II, pres, trust: Boswell Foundation, James G.

Boswell, Robert S., pres: Forest Oil Corp.

Boswell, Rosalind M., secy-treas, trust: Boswell Foundation, James G.

Boswell, William D., dir: Kline Foundation, Josiah W. and Bessie H.

Botsch, John P., dir: Peters Foundation, R. D. and Linda

Bottomley, John T., exec dir, trust: Fuller Foundation

Bottomley, Lydia Fuller, trust: Fuller Foundation

Bottomley, Stephen D., trust: Fuller Foundation

Boudreau, Donald L., vp, trust: Chase Manhattan Foundation

Boulay, Toni, staff assoc matching gifts: Southern New England Telephone Company

Bouldin, Granville S. R., dir: Christy-Houston Foundation

Boulette, E. Thomas, trust: Boston Edison Foundation

Boulos, Marta, commun aff specialist: Binney & Smith Inc.

Boulware, C. Diane, dir: Sunnen Foundation

Bouma, Mary, trust: Ghidotti Foundation

Boumann, Robert L., asst secy: KN Energy Foundation

Bourgois, Nicole, mem adv comm: Dow Jones Foundation

Bovender, Jack Oliver, Jr., dir: HCA Foundation

Bowden, Travis J., pres, ceo, dir: Gulf Power Co.

Bowden, William, trust: CS First Boston Foundation Trust

Bowdoin, William R., Jr., group vp: Trust Company

Bank; secy: Trust Co. of Georgia Foundation

Bowen, Henry, dir: Bowen Foundation, Ethel N.

Bowen, Jimelle, exec dir: Teubert Charitable Trust, James H. and Alice

Bowen, Virginia M., dir: Bowen Foundation, Ethel N.

Bowen, William Gordon, PhD, trust: Merck Co. Foundation; pres, trust: Mellon Foundation, Andrew W.; trust: Wallace-Reader's Digest Fund, DeWitt; trust: Wallace-Reader's Digest Fund, Lila

Bowes, Donald C., dir: Howard and Bush Foundation

Bowles, Beatrice, secy, treas: Lux Foundation, Miranda

Bowles, Crandall Close, vp, treas, dir: Close Foundation; dir: Springs Foundation

Bowles, Margaret C., secy: Clowes Fund

Bowman, Bob, secy, trust: Pineywoods Foundation

Bowman, Charles H., pres, ceo: BP America Inc.

Bowman, Harold, chmn, pres, ceo: Outboard Marine Corp.

Bowman, Jocelyn, dir: Kelley and Elza Kelley Foundation, Edward Bangs

Boxx, Linda McKenna, secy, dir: McKenna Foundation, Katherine Mabis

Boxx, T. William, treas: McKenna Foundation, Katherine Mabis; secy, treas, off: McKenna Foundation, Philip M.

Boyan, William L., pres, coo, dir: John Hancock Mutual Life Insurance Co.

Boyce, Doreen E., pres, exec dir: Buhl Foundation

Boyd, F.J., pres, dir: Audubon State Bank Charitable Foundation

Boyd, Willard Lee, trust: Carver Charitable Trust, Roy J.

Boyer, David S., pres: Teleflex Inc.

Boyer, Joyce, pres: Einstein Fund, Albert E. and Birdie W.

Boyer, Ray, dir (communs): MacArthur Foundation, John D. and Catherine T.

Boyer, Robert L., dir: Georgia Power Foundation

Boylan, Elizabeth J., vp: Maneely Fund

Boyle, Dennis, dir: Vicksburg Foundation

Boyle, Judy, corp contributions comm: AUL Foundation Inc.

Boyle, Richard James, vchmn, dir: Chase Manhattan Bank, N.A.; trust: Chase Manhattan Foundation

Bozzone, Robert P., pres, ceo, dir: Allegheny Ludlum Corp.; trust: Allegheny Ludlum Foundation

Bracken, Frank A., pres, dir: Ball Foundation, George and Frances

Bracken, Rosemary B., dir emeritus: Ball Foundation, George and Frances

Bracken, William M., dir: Ball Brothers Foundation

Brademas, John, chmn: Texaco Foundation

Braden, Katherine F., vp, treas: Castle Foundation, Harold K. L.

Bradford, Martina, trust: AT&T Foundation

Bradford, William Edward, pres, coo, dir: Dresser Industries, Inc.

Bradley, Darby, secy, trust: Friendship Fund

Bradley, James, dir: Close Foundation; dir: Springs Foundation

Bradley, Jane C., trust: Cabot Family Charitable Trust

Bradley, William O., trust: Cord Foundation, E. L.

Brady, James C., Jr., pres, treas, trust: Brady Foundation

Brady, Katherine D., trust: Darby Foundation

Brady, Nicholas Frederick, trust: Brady Foundation; trust: Darby Foundation

Braga, Mary A., trust: Bodman Foundation

Braga, Mary B., trust: Achelis Foundation

Braman, Mary O'Connor, treas: O'Connor Foundation, Kathryn

Bramble, Forrest F., Jr., vp, trust: Middendorf Foundation

Brame, Scott O., dir: Coughlin-Saunders Foundation

Bramley, Christopher W., chmn, ceo: Safety Fund National Bank; pres, dir: Safety Fund Foundation

Branch, J. Read, pres, dir: Cabell Foundation, Robert G. Cabell III and Maude Morgan

Branch, J. Read, Jr., dir: Cabell Foundation, Robert G. Cabell III and Maude Morgan

Branch, Joseph P., trust: Wiggins Memorial Trust, J. J.

Branch, Patteson, Jr., trust: Cabell Foundation, Robert G. Cabell III and Maude Morgan

Brand, Elizabeth D., secy: Dalton Foundation, Harry L.

Brand, Nathan, dir: Mautz Paint Foundation

Brandenburg, R. N., vp, dir: Glaser Foundation

Brant, Terri, asst exec secy: Raymond Foundation

Branum, Frances Daniel, dir: Daniel Foundation of Alabama

Braun, Hugo E., Jr., vp, secy, trust: Wickes Foundation, Harvey Randall

Brauntuch, Jack, special couns, trust: JM Foundation

Bray, Richard S., trust: Beazley Foundation/Frederick Foundation

Brechbiel, Stephen G., corp communications mgr: Reichhold Chemicals, Inc.

Brecher, Kenneth S., pres, dir: Penn Foundation, William

Breen, Marion I., vp, dir: Starr Foundation

Breene, William E., trust: Phillips Charitable Trust, Dr. and Mrs. Arthur William

Bregar, H. H., secy, dir: Blum Foundation, Harry and Maribel G.; secy: Blum-Kovler Foundation

Brei, Linda, vp: Wisconsin Power & Light Foundation, Inc.

Bremer, Richard H., chmn exec comm, ceo, pres, dir: Southwestern Electric Power Co.

Brengel, Fred L., dir: Johnson Controls Foundation

Brennan, Leo Joseph, Jr., vp, exec dir: Ford Motor Co. Fund

Brennan, Michael J., cfo, treas: Binswanger Cos.

Brennan, Patrick Francis, pres, ceo, coo, dir: Consolidated Papers, Inc.; dir: Consolidated Papers Foundation, Inc.

Brennan, Virginia S., trust: Self Foundation

Brenner, Charles S., dir: Guttman Foundation, Stella and Charles

Brenner, Edgar H., vp, dir: Guttman Foundation, Stella and Charles

Brenner, Paul R., trust: Calder Foundation, Louis

Bresko, Andrew G., trust: Crandall Memorial Foundation, J. Ford

Bressler, Alfred M., vp, treas, dir: Moses Fund, Henry and Lucy

Brewer, Cornelia B., asst secy: Georgia-Pacific Foundation

Brewer, Sebert, Jr., chmn, trust: Benwood Foundation

Brewer, William C., dir: Crabtree & Evelyn Foundation

Breyer, Henry W., III, dir, pres: Breyer Foundation

Breyer, Henry W., IV, treas: Breyer Foundation

Breyer, Joanne, secy, trust: Breyer Foundation

Brian, Pierre Leonce, vp engg, dir: Air Products and Chemicals, Inc.; trust: Air Products Foundation

Brickner, Bulfour, secy: Reicher Foundation, Anne and Harry J.

Brickson, Richard Alan, asst secy: May Stores Foundation

Bridenbaugh, Peter Reese, exec vp, chief tech off: Aluminum Co. of America; dir: Alcoa Foundation

Bridgeman, Jeannette C., treas, asst secy: Beazley Foundation/Frederick Foundation

Bridges, Kenneth, trust: McMahon Foundation

Bridwell, Ralph S., dir: Bridwell Foundation, J. S.

Briggs, Eleanor, dir: Griggs and Mary Griggs Burke Foundation, Mary Livingston

Briggs, Graham D., dir: General Motors Foundation

Briggs, Robert W., co-trust: GAR Foundation

Brigham, Margaret Hoover, vp, secy, trust: Hoover, Jr. Foundation, Margaret W. and Herbert

Bright, Calvin E., pres: Bright Family Foundation

Bright, Lyn, secy, treas: Bright Family Foundation

Bright, Marjorie, vp: Bright Family Foundation

Bright, Sam Raymond, vp, dir: Fair Foundation, R. W.

Bright, Stanley J., chmn, pres, ceo: Iowa-Illinois Gas & Electric Co.

Brill, Arthur W., secy, dir: Whitehead Charitable Foundation

Brinberg, Simeon, dir: Wishnick Foundation, Robert I.

Brinch, Peter, dir pub rels: PHH Corporation

Brinegar, Claude Stout, vchmn, exec vp, dir: Unocal

Corp.; dir: Unocal Foundation

Bring, Robert L., trust: Towsley Foundation, Harry A. and Margaret D.

Brink, William P., exec vp fin, contr, cfo: Square D Co.; treas, dir: Square D Foundation

Brinkman, Robert J., dir: Davenport-Hatch Foundation

Brinn, Mildred Cunningham, pres, treas, dir: Piankova Foundation, Tatiana

Bristol, Barbara F., vp: Fruehauf Foundation

Britton, Dennis A., trust: Chicago Sun-Times Charity Trust

Broadfoot, John W., dir: Meadows Foundation

Broadfoot, Vela Meadows, dir emeritus: Meadows Foundation

Broadhead, George, dir: Mobil Foundation

Broadus, Thomas H., Jr., vp: Price Associates Foundation, T. Rowe

Brock, Harry Blackwell, Jr., pres, dir: Daniel Foundation of Alabama

Brock, M. H., trust: Johnson Foundation, M. G. and Lillie A.

Brodhead, William McNulty, chmn, trust: Skillman Foundation

Broidy, Steven D., dir: Weingart Foundation

Bronfman, Charles R., trust: Bronfman Foundation, Samuel

Bronfman, Edgar Miles, chmn: Seagram & Sons, Inc., Joseph E.; chmn, trust: Bronfman Foundation, Samuel

Bronfman, Edgar Miles, Jr., pres, ceo, dir: Seagram & Sons, Inc., Joseph E.; trust: Bronfman Foundation, Samuel

Bronfman, Samuel, II, pres, trust: Bronfman Foundation, Samuel

Brook, Peter A., dir: NEBS Foundation

Brookes, Nick, chmn, ceo: Brown & Williamson Tobacco Corp.

Brooking, Garland M., fdr: Trull Foundation

Brooking, Gladys Trull, fdr: Trull Foundation

Brooklier, John, vp mktg: Heller Financial, Inc.

Brooks, C. A., asst secy: Texaco Foundation

Brooks, Carroll H., trust: Self Foundation

Brooks, Conley, Jr., trust: Marbrook Foundation

Brooks, Frank J., trust: Kavanagh Foundation, T. James

Brooks, Jim, pres: Life Insurance Co. of Georgia

Brooks, Markell, trust: Marbrook Foundation

Broome, Burton Edward, vp, contr: TransAmerica Corporation; vp, treas: TransAmerica Foundation

Browder, Carol J., trust: Jewell Memorial Foundation, Daniel Ashley and Irene Houston

Brower, Sam R., secy, treas: Owen Foundation

Brown, Ann Noble, trust: Noble Foundation, Samuel Roberts

Brown, Arthur W., Jr., vp, dir: Pick, Jr. Fund, Albert

Brown, Barbara J., pres, dir: Abrams Foundation, Talbert and Leota

Brown, Bruce E., pres: Boothroyd Foundation, Charles H. and Bertha L.

Brown, Craig C., dir: Abrams Foundation, Talbert and Leota

Brown, David, mgr external rels: McDonnell Douglas Corp.-West

Brown, David Lloyd, dir: Phillips Foundation, Ellis L.

Brown, David N., dir: Covington and Burling Foundation

Brown, David R., MD, trust: Noble Foundation, Samuel Roberts

Brown, Evelina, treas: Vevay-Switzerland County Foundation

Brown, Forrest C., MD, trust: Lattner Foundation, Forrest C.

Brown, Frances Carroll, vp, treas, dir: M.E. Foundation

Brown, Fred E., dir: Lake Placid Education Foundation

Brown, Graham M., Jr., treas: Polaroid Foundation

Brown, Harold, PhD, chmn: Mattel Foundation

Brown, Hillary, dir: Scherman Foundation

Brown, James Knight, secy: Clay Foundation

Brown, Jerry M., dir: Amoco Foundation

Brown, Jo Ann Fitzpatrick, vp: Housatonic Curtain Co.; dir: High Meadow Foundation

Brown, JoBeth Goode, trust: Anheuser-Busch Companies, Inc.

Brown, Larry G., sr vp, secy, gen couns: AEGON USA Inc.

Brown, Lindsay W., treas: Corning Incorporated Foundation

Brown, Lorne J., vp: Golden West Foundation

Brown, Louise Ingalls, pres, trust: Ingalls Foundation, Louise H. and David S.

Brown, Marvin, pres: Penguin Books USA, Inc.

Brown, Michael, ceo, pres: Thomson Information Publishing Group

Brown, Michele Courton, dir corp contributions: Bank of Boston Corp.; dir: Bank of Boston Corp. Charitable Foundation

Brown, N. A., trust: Firman Fund

Brown, Nancy Juckett, trust: Hill Foundation, Sandy

Brown, Patricia, asst secy: McDermott Foundation, Eugene

Brown, Patricia A., secy, treas, exec dir, dir: Bettingen Corporation, Burton G.

Brown, Prudence, trust: Levitt Foundation

Brown, Robert S., dir: Hewit Family Foundation

Brown, Robert William, MD, vp, dir: Carter Foundation, Amon G.

Brown, Stephen Lee, chmn, ceo, dir: John Hancock Mutual Life Insurance Co.

Brown, Timothy Charles, pres, ceo, dir: Thomas Industries; pres: Thomas Foundation

Brown, Willard W., treas: Ingalls Foundation, Louise H. and David S.

Browne, Rodney M., dir: Porter Testamentary Trust, James Hyde

Browne, William D., mgr: Marquette Electronics Foundation

Brownlee, R. Jean, trust: McLean Contributionship

Brownlie, Edward Carter, asst secy, asst treas: duPont Foundation, Alfred I.

Brozyna, Jeffry H., trust: Lehigh Portland Cement Charitable Trust

Bruce, Carl, adv: Harrison Foundation, Fred G.

Bruce, Julia Harrison, adv: Harrison Foundation, Fred G.

Bruggen, Richard J., dir: Adair-Exchange Bank Foundation

Bruhn, Lynn R., asst secy: JM Foundation

Brumback, D. L., Jr., trust: Van Wert County Foundation

Brumm, James E., pres: Mitsubishi International Corp. Foundation

Bruns, Carl H., trust emeritus: Davis Foundations, Arthur Vining

Brusati, Peter J., secy, dir: Gellert Foundation, Carl; secy, mgr, dir: Gellert Foundation, Celia Berta

Bryan, John H., chmn, ceo, dir: Sara Lee Corp.; dir: Sara Lee Foundation

Bryant, Arthur Herbert, II, pres, treas: Bryant Foundation

Bryant, Hugh F., dir: Glenn Foundation, Carrie C. and Lena V.

Bryant, Magalen Ohrstrom, trust: Ohrstrom Foundation

Bryant, Oscar Sims, Jr., secy, trust: Gheens Foundation

Bryant, Paul M., vp human resources: Dresser Industries, Inc.

Bryson, John D., Jr., pres, dir: Ross Memorial Foundation, Will

Bryson, John E., chmn, ceo: Southern California Edison Co.

Bubb, Harry Geiple, chmn emeritus, dir: Pacific Mutual Life Insurance Co.; dir: Pacific Mutual Charitable Foundation

Bucci, Mary Ellen, program off: Culpeper Foundation, Charles E.

Buchanan, John, pres, ceo, dir: Integra Bank of Uniontown

Buchanan, Peggy Carr, treas: Hobby Foundation

Buchanan, Ruth Hale, trust: Dow Foundation, Herbert H. and Grace A.

Buchanan, Valda M., secy, trust: Merrick Foundation

Buchanan, William Hobart, Jr., asst secy: Dun & Bradstreet Corp. Foundation, Inc.

Buck, James E., secy: New York Stock Exchange Foundation, Inc.

Buckler, Robert J., dir: Detroit Edison Foundation

Buckler, Sheldon A., trust: Polaroid Foundation

Buckmaster, Raleigh D., chmn, dir: McElroy Trust, R. J.

Buckwalter, Alan R., III, vchmn, dir: Texas Commerce Bank-Houston,

N.A.; pres: Texas Commerce Bank Foundation, Inc.

Buckwalter, John M., trust: Steinman Foundation, James Hale; trust: Steinman Foundation, John Frederick

Buckwalter, Walter, vchmn: Texas Commerce Bank-Houston, N.A.

Budd, MacDonald, dir: Cheatham Foundation, Owen

Budge, William W., dir: Bothin Foundation

Budzik, Ronald F., exec dir, vp: Mead Corp. Foundation

Buechel, Kathleen W., vp: Alcoa Foundation

Buechner, Thomas Scharman, trust: Corning Incorporated Foundation

Buffett, Howard G., vp, asst to pres: Archer-Daniels-Midland Foundation

Bugg, J. Bruce, secy: Tobin Foundation

Bughman, Harry R., secy, mgr, dir: Kline Foundation, Josiah W. and Bessie H.

Bugliarello, George, MD, dir: Greenwall Foundation

Buhler, Frank H., chmn, dir: Old Dominion Box Co.; chmn, pres, dir: Old Dominion Box Co. Foundation

Buhler, M. O., vp: Old Dominion Box Co. Foundation

Buhr, James D., trust: Redies Foundation, Edward F.

Buhrmaster, Robert C., pres, ceo, dir: Jostens, Inc.

Buhsmer, John Henry, pres, secy, trust: McLean Contributionship

Buice, William T., III, co-trust: Steele-Reese Foundation

Bullard, Robert L., trust: Bigelow Foundation, F. R.; trust: Blandin Foundation

Buller, Allan R., chmn, treas, dir: Worthington Foods; trust: Worthington Foods Foundation

Bullion, J. W., trust, dir: Meadows Foundation

Bullock, A. Stanley, Jr., dir: Davis Foundations, Arthur Vining

Bullock, Herbert E., dir: New Milford Savings Bank Foundation

Bullock, Maurice Randolph, co-trust, dir: Potts and Sibley Foundation

Bult, John A., chmn: PaineWebber

Bumsted, William J., dir: Lake Placid Education Foundation

Bundschuh, George August William, pres, dir: New York Life Insurance Co.; dir: New York Life Foundation

Bundy, Charles Alan, pres, dir: Close Foundation; pres, dir: Springs Foundation

Bundy, Mary Lothrop, chwm, trust: Hazen Foundation, Edward W.

Bunting, Josiah, III, dir: Guggenheim Foundation, Harry Frank

Burchfield, Albert H., III, pres, dir: Staunton Farm Foundation

Burchfield, C. Arthur, pres, dir: Burchfield Foundation, Charles E.

Burchfield, Violet P., dir: Burchfield Foundation, Charles E.

Burden, Carter, dir, mem exec comm: Burden Foundation, Florence V.

Burden, Edward P. H., dir, co-chair: Burden Foundation, Florence V.

Burden, Floebelle F., dir: Burden Foundation, Florence V.

Burden, Jean Prussing, dir: Burden Foundation, Florence V.

Burden, Margaret L., dir, don daughter: Burden Foundation, Florence V.

Burden, Norah M., dir: Burden Foundation, Florence V.

Burden, Ordway Partridge, vp, dir: Burden Foundation, Florence V.

Burden, S. Carter, III, dir: Burden Foundation, Florence V.

Burden, Susan L., secy, treas, dir: Burden Foundation, Florence V.

Burden, Wendy, dir: Burden Foundation, Florence V.

Burden, William A. M., IV, dir: Burden Foundation, Florence V.

Burdeno, Kenneth, dir, commun fund: McDonnell Douglas Corp.-West

Burdge, Jeffrey John, dir: Kline Foundation, Josiah W. and Bessie H.

Burenga, Kenneth L., pres, coo, dir: Dow Jones & Company, Inc.

Burford, A. L., Jr., vp, dir: Peppers Foundation, Ann

Burgan, Kathleen R., secy, treas: Alcoa Foundation

Burger, Warren Earl, dir: Cafritz Foundation, Morris and Gwendolyn

Burgess, Christopher R., contr: Chesapeake Corp.

Burgess, J. Phillip, vp, dir corp commun: Republic NY Corp.

Burkart, Walter M., chmn, dir: Kingsbury Corp.

Burke, John S., pres, trust: Altman Foundation

Burke, Kathleen J., exec vp personnel rels off: BankAmerica Corp.; trust: BankAmerica Foundation

Burke, Mary Livingston Griggs, pres, dir: Griggs and Mary Griggs Burke Foundation, Mary Livingston

Burke, Michael, exec vp, dir: Christian Dior New York, Inc.

Burke, Moira E., contr, secy: Heublein Foundation, Inc.

Burke, Thomas C., vp, trust: Altman Foundation

Burke, Walter, pres, treas, dir: Fairchild Foundation, Sherman

Burke, Walter F., III, dir: Fairchild Foundation, Sherman

Burke, Ward R., trust: Temple Foundation, T. L. L.

Burkholder, Robert E., secy, treas: Gooding Group Foundation

Burleigh, William Robert, mem: Scripps Howard Foundation

Burlingame, John Hunter, mem: Scripps Howard Foundation

Burnand, Alphonse A., III, secy: Steele Foundation, Harry and Grace

Burnand, Audrey Steele, pres: Steele Foundation, Harry and Grace

Burnett, James F., vp, trust: Fair Play Foundation

Burnett, Nancy Packard, trust: Packard Foundation, David and Lucile

Burnett, Rebecca, adv: Delano Foundation, Mignon Sherwood

Burnett, Stephanie, dir, treas: Memorial Foundation for the Blind

Burnette, Ty W., awards adv comm: Ferebee Endowment, Percy O.

Burnham, Daniel Patrick, dir: AlliedSignal Foundation Inc.

Burnham, Duane Lee, chmn, ceo, dir: Abbott Laboratories; dir: Abbott Laboratories Fund

Burns, Rex, secy, treas: Mid-Iowa Health Foundation

Burns, Ronald J., trust: Enron Foundation

Burns, Ruthelen Griffith, adv: Griffith Foundation, W. C.

Burns, Valerie, secy: Henderson Foundation, George B.

Burr, Robert B., Jr., secy, dir: Mellon Family Foundation, R. K.; asst treas: Mellon Foundation, Richard King

Burrell, Richard L., vp fin: Barry Corp., R. G.; treas: Barry Foundation

Burrill, W. Gregory, trust: Hopedale Foundation

Burrow, Harold, chmn: American Natural Resources Company

Burrows, Sunny Harvey, asst secy: Harvey Foundation, Felix

Burrus, Clark D., vp, dir: First National Bank of Chicago Foundation

Burton, Rae R., mem screening comm: PPG Industries Foundation

Bury, Anita, asst secy: Regenstein Foundation

Busby, Gail, secy: Daily News Foundation

Busch, August Adolphus, III, chmn, pres, dir: Anheuser-Busch Companies, Inc.

Busch, Lawrence S., asst treas: Mellon Family Foundation, R. K.

Bush, Thomas Norman, vp, tax couns, dir: James River Corp. of Virginia; vp: James River Corp. Foundation

Bushyeager, Peter, program off health & human svcs: Prudential Foundation

Butler, Carol H., pres, trust: Humphrey Fund, George M. and Pamela S.

Butler, Dixon M., sr vp, dir: Virginia Environmental Endowment

Butler, Henry King, dir: Christy-Houston Foundation

Butler, John G., vp, trust: Humphrey Fund, George M. and Pamela S.

Butler, John P., hon trust: Abell-Hanger Foundation

Butler, William E., chmn, ceo: Eaton Corporation

Butterfield, Reeder, vp: Osher Foundation, Bernard

Butters, Gerald J., trust: AT&T Foundation

Butz, Barbara T., dir: Butz Foundation

Butz, Elvira M., vp, trust: Butz Foundation

Butz, Theodore H., pres, dir: Butz Foundation

Butz, Thompson H., treas, trust: Butz Foundation

Buxton, Charles I., II, chmn, ceo: Federated Mutual Insurance Co.; pres: Federated Insurance Foundation

Byerly, Stacy S., dir: Stokely, Jr. Foundation, William B.

Byers, Karen D., dir fin oper: Markle Foundation, John and Mary R.

Byers, R. A., trust: Pitt-Des Moines Inc. Charitable Trust

Byers, Raymond Lester, Jr., mgr contributions programs: Ford Motor Co.

Byland, Peter, chmn: Holnam

Byrd, Ann, dir: Kirkpatrick Foundation

Byrd, D. Harold, Jr., trust: Hillcrest Foundation

Byrd, Edward R., cfo: Pacific Mutual Charitable Foundation

Byrd, Richard Hays, treas: Borden Foundation, Inc.

Byrne, Arthur P., chmn, pres, dir: Wiremold Co.; treas: Wiremold Foundation

Byrne, Brendan T., dir: Carvel Foundation, Thomas and Agnes

Byrne, Patricia, grants mgr: Travelers Foundation

Byrns, Priscilla U., trust: Upton Foundation, Frederick S.

C

Caamano, Rafael F., trust: Homeland Foundation

Cabaniss, Wayne, gov: Munson Foundation Trust, W. B.

Cabell, Charles, dir: Cabell Foundation, Robert G. Cabell III and Maude Morgan

Cabell, Robert G., vp: Cabell Foundation, Robert G. Cabell III and Maude Morgan

Cabell, Royal E., Jr., secy, dir: Cabell Foundation, Robert G. Cabell III and Maude Morgan

Cabonet, Frank V., trust: Heinz Endowment, Howard

Cabot, Carroll, dir: Cabot Corp. Foundation

Cabot, John Godfrey Lowell, trust: Cabot Family Charitable Trust

Cabot, Louis Wellington, trust: Cabot Family Charitable Trust

Cabot, Maryellen, dir: Cabot Corp. Foundation

Cabral, Mary L., asst contr: Weyerhaeuser Company Foundation

Caestecker, Thomas E., trust: Caestecker Foundation, Charles and Marie

Cafritz, Calvin, chmn, pres, ceo, treas: Cafritz Foundation, Morris and Gwendolyn

Cagigas, Donald, chmn, ceo, dir: Bank One, Youngstown, NA

Cagle, Ronald E., MD, trust: McMahon Foundation

Cahill, George Francis, Jr., chmn: Greenwall Foundation

Cahill, John, sr vp, cfo: CBI Industries, Inc.

Cahill, Robert V., vp: Chartwell Foundation

Cahners-Kaplan, Helene R., trust: Rabb Charitable Foundation, Sidney and Esther

Caimi, Gina, secy: Erpf Fund, Armand G.

Cain, Alan F., dir: MPCo/Entech Foundation

Cain, Debbie L., mgr: Weaver Foundation, Gil and Dody

Cain, Effie Marie, pres, dir: Cain Foundation, Effie and Wofford

Cain, Gordon Arbuthnot, trust, dir: Cain Foundation, Gordon and Mary

Cain, James B., vp, dir: Cain Foundation, Effie and Wofford

Cain, John C., dir: Cain Foundation, Effie and Wofford

Cain, Mary H., trust: Cain Foundation, Gordon and Mary

Caine, Raymond William, Jr., vp corp commun: Textron, Inc.

Calabresi, Guido, trust: Carolyn Foundation

Calder, Frederick C., vp: Lake Placid Education Foundation

Calder, Peter D., trust: Calder Foundation, Louis

Caldwell, Royce S., dir: SBC Communications Foundation

Calhoun, Essie L., pres: Eastman Kodak Charitable Trust

Calhoun, Nancy H., asst secy, trust: Gifford Charitable Corporation, Rosamond

Calise, Nicholas James, vp, assoc gen couns, secy: Goodrich Co., The B.F.; secy: Goodrich Foundation, Inc., B.F.

Call, Richard W., MD, pres, ceo, dir: Seaver Institute

Call, Robert V., Jr., chmn, trust: Curtice-Burns/Pro-Fac Foundation

Callahan, F. J., secy: Lennon Foundation, Fred A.

Callaway, Mark Clayton, trust: Callaway Foundation

Calligaris, Alfred E., dir: Utica National Group Foundation

Calnan, Philippa, dir pub affairs: Getty Trust, J. Paul

Calvert, Elizabeth, treas, secy: Anderson Foundation, M. D.

Cambell, Colin G., dir: Rockefeller Fund, David

Cameris, Chris, sr vp corp aff: National Westminster Bank New Jersey

Cames, Edwina, commun svc admin: Colonial Life & Accident Insurance Co.

Camp, John M., Jr., dir: Campbell Foundation, Ruth and Henry

Camp, Paul D., III, dir: Campbell Foundation, Ruth and Henry

Campanaro, Leonard A., treas: Harsco Corp. Fund

Campbell, Bert L., trust: Cullen Foundation

Campbell, Bruce S., III, trust, secy: Campbell Foundation

Campbell, Bruce S., Jr., trust, vp: Campbell Foundation

Campbell, Carol, exec dir: Argyros Foundation

Campbell, Colin Goetze, dir: Culpeper Foundation, Charles E.

Campbell, Douglas, exec vp, trust: Erpf Fund, Armand G.

Collins, Dennis Arthur, pres: Irvine Foundation, James

Collins, Donald A., trust: Scaife Family Foundation

Collins, Douglas, trust: Dillon Dunwalke Trust, Clarence and Anne

Collins, Duane E., pres, ceo, dir: Parker Hannifin Corp.; vp, trust: Parker Hannifin Foundation

Collins, Frances, trust: Dillon Dunwalke Trust, Clarence and Anne

Collins, Fulton, chmn: Collins, Jr. Foundation, George Fulton

Collins, James, mem adv comm: Pott Foundation, Herman T. and Phenie R.

Collins, John P., Jr., trust: Smith Trust, May and Stanley

Collins, Maribeth Wilson, pres, dir: Collins Foundation; trust: Collins Medical Trust

Collins, Michael E., trust: Williams Charitable Trust, Mary Jo

Collins, Paul John, vchmn: Citibank

Collins, Phyllis Dillon, trust: Dillon Dunwalke Trust, Clarence and Anne

Collins, Richard B., ceo, pres, dir: Bank of Boston; trust: Mechanics Bank Foundation

Collins, Robert R., dir: Green Foundation, Allen P. and Josephine B.

Collins, Roger B., trust: Collins Foundation, George and Jennie

Collins, Truman W., Jr., trust: Collins Medical Trust

Collins, William Edward, trust: Clapp Charitable and Educational Trust, George H.

Collision, Arthur, trust: Blowitz-Ridgeway Foundation

Colman, John Charles, trust: Premier Industrial Foundation

Colopy, Hugh, trust, mem distribution comm: GAR Foundation

Colquhoun, Ross K., pres, ceo, dir: Raymond Corp.

Colson, Charles Wendell, vp, dir: M.E. Foundation

Colton, Sterling Don, mgr: Marriott Foundation, J. Willard

Columbo, John, trust: Providence Journal Charitable Foundation

Colvard, Karen, program off: Guggenheim Foundation, Harry Frank

Colver, Dave O., trust: Heginbotham Trust, Will E.

Colwell, W. Paul, pres, dir: Peppers Foundation, Ann

Comai, Barbara L., treas, trust: Miller Foundation

Combs, W. G., vp, treas, trust: Long Foundation, J.M.

Comer, James Pierpont, trust, mem nominating comm: Carnegie Corporation of New York

Comer, Richard J., trust: Comer Foundation

Compton, Ronald E., chmn, pres, ceo: Aetna Life & Casualty Co.; pres, dir: Aetna Foundation

Comstock, Henry W., dir: Beaucourt Foundation

Comstock, Robert L., Jr., trust, mem exec comm: Blandin Foundation

Conant, Colleen Christner, trust: Scripps Howard Foundation

Conant, John A., secy: Harland Charitable Foundation, John and Wilhelmina D.

Conant, Miriam Harland, pres: Harland Charitable Foundation, John and Wilhelmina D.

Condon, James Edward, treas: Hartmarx Charitable Foundation

Conely, James, awards adv comm: Ferebee Endowment, Percy O.

Congdon, Elizabeth C., trust: Memorial Foundation for the Blind

Conklin, Charles, secy adv comm: Blue Bell Foundation

Conklin, Donald Ransford, exec vp: Schering-Plough Corp.; trust: Schering-Plough Foundation

Conley, Kathleen R., secy, dir: Mahadh Foundation

Conley, Renae, gen mgr corp commun: CINergy

Conn, James P., trust: Odell Fund, Robert Stewart Odell and Helen Pfeiffer

Connable, Genevieve, secy, trust: Wildermuth Foundation, E. F.

Connally, Ruth, trust: Winchester Foundation

Connars, David, ceo, dir: Sheaffer Inc.

Connelly, Christine C., trust, don daughter: Connelly Foundation

Connelly, Daniele, trust: Connelly Foundation

Connelly, J.H., trust: Carter Foundation, Amon G.

Connelly, Martha L., chmn, trust: Lattner Foundation, Forrest C.

Connelly, Thomas S., trust, don son: Connelly Foundation

Conner, Robert P., treas, dir: Barker Foundation, J.M.R.

Connolly, Arthur Gould, Jr., treas, dir: Laffey-McHugh Foundation

Connolly, Arthur Gould, Sr., pres: Laffey-McHugh Foundation

Connolly, David I., vp, treas: Albertson's Inc.

Connolly, Eugene B., chmn, ceo: USG Corporation

Connolly, John J., dir corp rels: Boston Edison Co.; dir: Boston Edison Foundation

Connor, James Richard, exec dir: Kemper Foundation, James S.

Connor, James W., pres: Lyon Foundation

Connors, Martin F., treas, dir: Safety Fund Foundation

Conomikes, John G., vp, dir: Hearst Foundation, William Randolph

Conrad, Carol, secy: Castle Foundation, Harold K. L.

Conrad, Gene R., Upjohn Foundation, Harold and Grace

Conrad, William C., exec secy: Stackpole-Hall Foundation

Conti, Elaine, trust: PaineWebber Foundation

Convisser, Theodora S., trust: Boston Edison Foundation

Conway, Jill Cathryn Ker, trust: Knight Foundation, John S. and James L.; dir: Kresge Foundation

Conway, John P., vp, secy, dir: Dillon Foundation

Cook, Charles W., secy, trust: Sullivan Foundation, Algernon Sydney

Cook, Jane Bancroft, chmn adv comm: Dow Jones Foundation

Cook, John Rowland, trust: Harcourt General, Inc.

Cook, Mary McDermott, secy, treas, trust: McDermott Foundation, Eugene

Cook, Phyllis, dir: Rosenberg Foundation

Cook, Thomas P., secy, trust: Phillips Family Foundation, Jay and Rose

Cook, Wallace Lawrence, dir, chmn investment comm: Dana Foundation, Charles A.

Cooke, Geoffrey B., exec dir, mem contributions comm: NYNEX Corporate Philanthropy and Foundation

Cooke, John Warren, pres, treas: Treakle Foundation, J. Edwin

Cooke, Joseph P., Jr., secy, treas, trust: Baldwin Memorial Foundation, Fred

Cooke, Richard A., Jr., vp, trust: Cooke Foundation

Cooke, Samuel A., pres, trust: Cooke Foundation

Cookson, John S., trust: Kingsbury Fund

Coolidge, E. David, III, mng ptnr, ceo: Blair and Co., William; vp: Blair and Co. Foundation, William

Coolidge, Nancy, bd mem: Henderson Foundation, George B.

Coolidge, Thomas R., trust: Astor Foundation, Vincent

Coombs, John W., trust: Davenport Trust Fund

Cooper, Adrian R. T., trust: CS First Boston Foundation Trust

Cooper, Barry, trust: Klosk Fund, Louis and Rose

Cooper, Bob E., pres, ceo: Kennecott Corporation

Cooper, Cameron, dir: Seaver Institute

Cooper, Lance E., cfo, vp fin: Iowa-Illinois Gas & Electric Co.

Cooper, Nathan, trust: Klosk Fund, Louis and Rose

Cooper, Robert, dir: Bird Corp. Charitable Foundation

Cooper, Rose Mary, secy, treas: Fohs Foundation

Cooperman, Leon, trust: Cooperman Foundation, Leon and Toby

Cooperman, Michael S., trust: Cooperman Foundation, Leon and Toby

Cooperman, Toby F., trust: Cooperman Foundation, Leon and Toby

Cooperman, Wayne M., trust: Cooperman Foundation, Leon and Toby

Coors, Ambassador Holland, dir: Coors Foundation, Adolph

Coors, Jeffrey H., treas: Coors Foundation, Adolph

Coors, Peter Hanson, vp, trust: Coors Foundation, Adolph

Coors, William K., pres: Coors Foundation, Adolph

Copeland, Gerret van Sweringen, trust: Longwood Foundation

Copes, Ronald A., second vp: Massachusetts Mutual Life Insurance Co.

Copley, David C., pres, dir: Copley Press, Inc.; pres, trust: Copley Foundation, James S.

Copley, Ed, dir: Hawn Foundation

Copley, Helen K., chmn, ceo, dir: Copley Press, Inc.; chmn, trust: Copley Foundation, James S.

Copp, Eugenie T., trust: Carolyn Foundation

Coppinger, John J., Jr., asst comptr: Texaco Foundation

Corbally, John Edward, dir: MacArthur Foundation, John D. and Catherine T.

Corbally, Richard V., secy, dir: McCann Foundation

Corbett, Cornelia, trust: Farish Fund, William Stamps

Corbin, Hunter W., vp, dir: Hyde and Watson Foundation

Corbin, Lee Harrison, dir, asst secy, asst treas: Hopkins Foundation, Josephine Lawrence

Corbin, William R., trust: Weyerhaeuser Company Foundation

Corcoran, Walter G., vp bd dirs, mem investment comm: Dana Foundation, Charles A.

Corcoran, William G., trust: Clarke Trust, John

Corcoran, William J., treas: Harriman Foundation, Gladys and Roland; treas: Harriman Foundation, Mary W.

Cordes, James F., pres, ceo, dir: American Natural Resources Company; pres, dir: ANR Foundation, Inc.

Corken, Milton C., trust: Higginson Trust, Corina

Corley, Margaret, mgr: Dewing Foundation, Frances R.

Corley, Mary Jo Ratner, pres, trust: Ratner Foundation, Milton M.

Cornelius, Iris H., trust: Bigelow Foundation, F. R.

Cornell, S. Douglas, trust: Cornell Trust, Peter C.

Cornwall, John W., trust: Fund for New Jersey

Cornwall, Joseph C., chmn, treas, trust: Fund for New Jersey

Cornwell, Diane, admin dir: Haynes Foundation, John Randolph and Dora

Correll, Alston Dayton "Pete", Jr., chmn, pres, ceo: Georgia-Pacific Corporation; trust: Georgia-Pacific Foundation

Corrigan, Ann G., trust: Goddard Foundation, Charles B.

Corry, Charles Albert, chmn, ceo, dir: USX Corporation; chmn, trust: USX Foundation

Corson, Madeline G., dir: Gannett Foundation, Guy P.

Cortese, Arline Snyder, trust: Snyder Foundation, Harold B. and Dorothy A.

Corti, Mario A., sr vp, chief admin off: Nestle USA Inc.; vp, dir: Nestle USA Foundation

Cortner, Nancy, trust: Sullivan Foundation, Algernon Sydney

Corwin, Laura J., secy: New York Times Co. Foundation

Cory, William F., trust: Carver Charitable Trust, Roy J.

Corzo, Miguel Angel, dir (Getty Conservation Inst): Getty Trust, J. Paul

Costello, James P., dir: French Foundation, D.E.

Costello, John J., dir pub aff: Commonwealth Edison Co.

Costley, Gary Edward, trust: Miller Foundation

Costley, Lew, trust: Swanson Family Foundation, Dr. W.C.

Cota-Robles, Eugene H., vchmn, trust, nominating comm: Carnegie Corporation of New York

Cotsen, Lloyd Edward, trust: Ahmanson Foundation

Cotter, Patrick William, dir: Bucyrus-Erie Foundation

Cottle, John I., III, secy: Blount Educational and Charitable Foundation, Mildred Weedon

Cottrell, G. Walton, sr vp, cfo: Carpenter Technology Corp.

Coughenour, Katherine N., trust: Quaker Chemical Foundation

Coughlan, Gary Patrick, cfo, sr vp fin: Abbott Laboratories; dir: Abbott Laboratories Fund

Coughlin, Barring, asst secy, trust: Eaton Foundation, Cyrus

Coughlin, Thomas Martin, mem: Wal-Mart Foundation

Coulling, L. R., dir: Bowen Foundation, Ethel N.

Couper, Richard Watrous, dir: Pforzheimer Foundation, Carl and Lily

Couric, Charles M., mem contributions comm: Clorox Co.

Covington, Joe S., MD, dir: Hardin Foundation, Phil

Covitt, Regina, asst treas: Bettingen Corporation, Burton G.

Cowan, Fairman C., trust: Mechanics Bank Foundation

Cowan, John C., Jr., trust: Burlington Industries Foundation

Cowan, Rory J., exec vp, info tech: Donnelley & Sons Co., R.R.

Cowden, W. H., Jr., vp: Peterson Foundation, Hal and Charlie

Cowen, Robert J., trust: Beal Foundation

Cowles, Charles, trust: Cowles Charitable Trust

Cowles, Gardner, III, pres, trust: Cowles Charitable Trust

Cowles, Jan Streate, trust: Cowles Charitable Trust

Cowles, John, III, chmn: Cowles Media Co.; dir: Cowles Media Foundation

Cox, C. Richard, sr program off: Penn Foundation, William

Cox, Clint V., trust: Broadhurst Foundation

Cox, Daniel T., exec vp: AON Corporation

Cox, David Carson, pres, ceo, dir: Cowles Media Co.; vp, dir: Cowles Media Foundation

Cox, Donald M., chmn, dir: Teagle Foundation

Cox, Douglas Lynn, sr vp fin, cfo: Elf Atochem North America, Inc.; trust: Elf Atochem North America Foundation

Cox, Russell N., trust: Linnell Foundation

Coyle, Patrick E., dir: Rennebohm Foundation, Oscar

Fidelity Corporation Founders Fund

Devereux, N. Paul, vp, dir: Nestle USA Foundation

Devine, Mildred E., vp, admin: Palmer Fund, Frank Loomis

DeVita, M. Christine, pres, dir: Wallace-Reader's Digest Fund, DeWitt; pres, dir: Wallace-Reader's Digest Fund, Lila

DeVito, Mathias Joseph, chmn, ceo: Rouse Co.

DeVore, Richard A., pres, secy: DeVore Foundation

DeVore, William O., vp, treas: DeVore Foundation

Devries, Robert K., mem admin comm: Nabisco Foundation Trust

DeWees, James H., pres, dir: Godfrey Foundation

Dewey, Francis H., III, trust: Mechanics Bank Foundation

Dewey, Robert F., pres, trust: Gifford Charitable Corporation, Rosamond

DeWind, Adrian W., dir: Diamond Foundation, Aaron

Dewing, Merlin E., dir: Bush Foundation

DeWoody, Beth Rudin, vp, dir: Rudin Foundation

Dexel, Albert, asst secy, asst treas: Tiscornia Foundation

Di San Faustino, Genevieve Bothin Lyman, pres, dir, don granddaughter: Bothin Foundation

Dial, Benton W., pres, dir: Rosenberg Foundation

Diamond, Irene, pres, dir: Diamond Foundation, Aaron

Dibert, Dan, trust: Saroyan Foundation, William

DiBuono, Anthony Joseph, exec vp, secy, chief legal off: Coltec Industries, Inc.; vp, secy, dir: Coltec Industries Charitable Foundation, Inc.

Dickason, Richard R., vp, dir: Adair-Exchange Bank Foundation

Dickemper, Robert A., chmn: SBC Communications Foundation

Dickes, Don D., secy, treas, trust: Timken Foundation of Canton

Dickey, Boh A., exec vp, cfo, dir: SAFECO Corp.

Dickinson, Karen, asst corp secy: Guardian Life Insurance Company of America

Dickman, Norbert J., dir: Prairie Foundation

Dickoff, Gil, treas: Crane Co.; treas: Crane Foundation

Dickson, Margaret C., vp, treas: Harland Charitable Foundation, John and Wilhelmina D.

Dickson, Robert J., cfo, vp fin: Dynamet, Inc.

Dickson, Robert T., vp, dir: Prairie Foundation

Dickson, W. W., dir: Glenn Foundation, Carrie C. and Lena V.

Dicovitsky, Gary, chmn fdn comm: International Foundation

Diebel, William C., secy, dir: Demos Foundation, N.

Diederich, John Leroy, dir: Alcoa Foundation

Diekman, Susan, exec dir: Telesis Foundation

Dietrich, G. Phillip, adv: Delano Foundation, Mignon Sherwood

Dietrich, Loreine C., chmn, trust: Collins Foundation,

George and Jennie; treas: Collins, Jr. Foundation, George Fulton

Dietz, Carolyn Emmerson, treas: Sierra Pacific Foundation

Dietz, Vida, admin: Sierra Pacific Resources Charitable Foundation

Dik, Carolyn, trust: Memorial Foundation for the Blind

DiLeo, Victor, trust: Schwartz Foundation, Arnold A.

DiLeonardi, Robert N., admin: Blowitz-Ridgeway Foundation

Diller, Whitney Clay, treas: Clay Foundation

Dillon, C. Douglas, trust: Dillon Dunwalke Trust, Clarence and Anne

Dillon, Margo, asst secy, dir: Dillon Foundation

Dillon, Peter W., pres, dir: Dillon Foundation

Dillon, Victoria, trust: M/A-COM Foundation

DiMarco, James F., sr vp: Johnson & Son, S.C.

Dimeo, Bradford S., vp, dir: Dimeo Construction Co.

Dimeo, Thomas P., chmn, pres, dir: Dimeo Construction Co.

Dimon, James R., pres, cfo, coo, dir: Travelers Inc.; trust: Travelers Foundation

Dingell, Deborah I., pres: General Motors Foundation

Dingledy, Thomas, secy, dir: Hook Drug Foundation

Dingman, Elizabeth T., vp: Dingman Foundation, Michael D.

Dingman, Michael David, pres: Dingman Foundation, Michael D.; trust: Hartford Foundation, John A.

Dingus, Mary Anne Duncan, dir: Duncan Foundation, Lillian H. and C. W.; dir: Early Foundation

Dinkins, David N., dir: Diamond Foundation, Aaron

Dinome, Anthony J., secy, treas: Benenson Foundation, Frances and Benjamin

Dinse, Ann G., trust: Turrell Fund

Dionne, Joseph Lewis, chmn, ceo: McGraw-Hill, Inc.

Diotte, Alfred Peter, vp, dir: Janesville Foundation

Dircher, Dick, trust: National Gypsum Foundation, Inc.

Disher, J. William, mem bd admns: Van Every Foundation, Philip L.

Disney, Lillian B., pres: Lund Foundation

Dixon, Marcus K., trust: Dentsply International Foundation

Dixon, Michelle, commun rels coordinator: American General Finance Corp.

Dixon, Paul E., secy: Handy and Harman Foundation

Dixon, Thomas F., dir: Harriman Foundation, Gladys and Roland

Dmitrieff, Alexander, dir: Griffis Foundation

Doan, Herbert Dow, secy: Dow Foundation, Herbert H. and Grace A.

Doar, Gael, dir contributions & commun support program: Champion International Corporation

Dobbs, Harold S., trust: Meyer Fund, Milton and Sophie

Dobbs, W. L., dir: Porter Testamentary Trust, James Hyde

Doberstein, Stephen C., exec dir: Crystal Trust

Dobies, Robert A., dir: Mobil Foundation

Dobrowolski, John, treas: Fabri-Kal Foundation

Dobson, Douglas R., trust: Stackpole-Hall Foundation

Dockson, Robert Ray, first vp, trust: Haynes Foundation, John Randolph and Dora

Dodge, Cleveland Earl, Jr., pres, chmn exec comm, mem fin comm, dir: Dodge Foundation, Cleveland H.

Dodge, David S., mem exec comm, dir: Dodge Foundation, Cleveland H.

Dodge, James H., chmn, ceo, pres, dir: Providence Gas Co.

Dods, Walter Arthur, Jr., chmn, ceo: First Hawaiian, Inc.; pres, dir: First Hawaiian Foundation

Dodson, Sheila, treas: Goldseker Foundation of Maryland, Morris

Doermann, Humphrey, pres: Bush Foundation

Doerr, Henry, trust: Blandin Foundation

Doggett, W. B., dir communs & commun rels: BP America Inc.

Doherty, J. N., sr vp, mem exec comm, dir: Shell Oil Company Foundation

Doherty, Leonard Edward, mem adv comm, admin off: Dow Jones Foundation

Dohrmann, Fred G., pres, ceo, dir: Winnebago Industries, Inc.

Doke, Timothy J., secy, mgr: AMR/American Airlines Foundation

Dolan, James F., secy, treas, dir, adv: Weezie Foundation; trust: Heinz Trust, Drue

Dolan, Joseph S., exec dir, secy: Achelis Foundation; exec dir, secy: Bodman Foundation

Dolan, Myles, trust, vp: Rabb Foundation, Harry W.

Dolden, Roger, sr vp fin, cfo: Cosmair, Inc.

Dolohanty, Shane, cfo: Sheaffer Inc.

Domek, Robert E., asst secy, dir: Madison Gas & Electric Foundation

Domke, Doreta, dir: McConnell Foundation

Donahoe, Patricia P., program dir: Homeland Foundation

Donahoe, Tom, mgr corp contributions: USL Capital Corporation

Donahue, Donald Jordan, dir: Greenwall Foundation

Donahue, Frank R., Jr., secy, dir: Barra Foundation

Donahue, Jeffrey H., sr vp, cfo: Rouse Co.

Donahue, Norman E., II, trust: Bard Foundation, Robert

Donaldson, Don, vp, asst secy: Lyon Foundation

Donaldson, F. A. Sandy, trust: Hudson-Webber Foundation

Donavan, Thomas J., trust: Bean Foundation, Norwin S. and Elizabeth N.

Donches, Steven G., vp pub aff: Bethlehem Steel Corp.; pres: Bethlehem Steel Foundation

Donnelley, Dorothy R., vp: Donnelley Foundation, Gaylord and Dorothy

Donnelley, Elliott R., vp, dir: Donnelley Foundation, Gaylord and Dorothy

Donnelley, James R., vchmn, chmn contributions comm: Donnelley & Sons Co., R.R.; vp, treas, trust: Griswold Foundation, John C.

Donnelley, Strachan, chmn, dir: Donnelley Foundation, Gaylord and Dorothy

Donnelley-Morton, Laura, vp, dir: Donnelley Foundation, Gaylord and Dorothy

Donnelly, James Charles, vp, treas: WICOR, Inc.; vp, dir: WICOR Foundation

Donnelly, John L., treas, dir: Gazette Foundation

Donner, Alexander, dir: Donner Foundation, William H.

Donner, Frederick H., vp, dir: Independence Foundation

Donner, Robert, Jr., vp, asst treas: Donner Foundation, William H.

Donner, Timothy E., dir: Donner Foundation, William H.

Donoghue, Norman E., II, trust: Bard Foundation, Robert

Donohue, Elise R., dir: Weyerhaeuser Memorial Foundation, Charles A.

Donovan, Anne Fuller, trust: Fuller Foundation

Donovan, Pat, dir: Norwest Foundation

Dooner, Marie E., secy: Maneely Fund

Dopson, Arnold B., chmn: Blount Educational and Charitable Foundation, Mildred Weedon

Dora, James E., dir: AUL Foundation Inc.

Doran, Gary, vp policy & admin: AT&T Foundation

Dorety, J. C., trust: Finch Foundation, Doak

Dorn, David F., trust: Glendorn Foundation

Dorn, Frederick M., trust: Glendorn Foundation

Dorn, John C., trust: Glendorn Foundation

Dorn, William L., chmn, ceo, dir: Forest Oil Corp.

Dornsife, David H., vp, dir: Hedco Foundation

Dornsife, Ester M., pres, dir: Hedco Foundation

Dornsife, Harold W., cfo, dir: Hedco Foundation

Dorothy, James A., dir: Van Buren Foundation

Dorr, Donald, dir: Sheppard Foundation, Lawrence B.

Dorrenbacher, Carol James, sr vp: McDonnell Douglas Corp.-West

Dorsey, James R., dir corp aff: Citizens Bank of Rhode Island; trust: Citizens Charitable Foundation

Dorskind, Albert A., vp, cfo, dir: Parsons Foundation, Ralph M.

Doss, Lawrence Paul, dir: ANR Foundation, Inc.; trust: Hudson-Webber Foundation

Doss, Marion K., dir: Fieldcrest Cannon Foundation

Dossa, Alfred, pres: Y and H Soda Foundation

Doucette, James Willard, vp, treas: Humana Foundation

Dougherty, Ada M., asst secy: Hyde and Watson Foundation

Doughty, H. C., Jr., secy: Borden Foundation, Inc.

Douglas, Walter E., trust: Skillman Foundation

Douglas, William Allan, pres, exec dir: Boettcher Foundation

Douglass, Robert Royal, trust: Chase Manhattan Foundation

Douthat, Anne S., mgr: Smith Foundation, Ralph L.

Dover, Vera M., secy: Butz Foundation

Dow, Herbert H., pres: Dow Foundation, Herbert H. and Grace A.

Dow, Michael Lloyd, treas: Dow Foundation, Herbert H. and Grace A.

Dow, Michael Lorence, assoc: Dow Foundation, Herbert H. and Grace A.

Dowd, Hector G., secy: Frese Foundation, Arnold D.

Dowhan, Kerry, secy: Taube Family Foundation

Downer, Edwin E., dir: Hardin Foundation, Phil

Downes, Laurence M., pres, ceo: New Jersey Natural Gas Co.; treas: New Jersey Resources Foundation

Downey, Thelma L., asst secy, asst treas: Olsson Memorial Foundation, Elis

Doyle, Alice P., trust: Valentine Foundation, Lawson

Doyle, Allen, trust: Valentine Foundation, Lawson

Doyle, Donald W., trust: Gheens Foundation

Doyle, Patricia, grants admin: Morgan Stanley Foundation

Doyle, Robert A., dir: AMCORE Foundation, Inc.

Doyle, Valentine, trust: Valentine Foundation, Lawson

Drake, Carl Bigelow, Jr., chmn, trust: Bigelow Foundation, F. R.

Drake, Philip M., vp, secy, treas, dir: Culpeper Foundation, Charles E.

Draper, Cecil Vanoy, pres: Schuller Fund

Drasner, Fred, pres, ceo, dir: Daily News

Draughon, K. Robert, vp: Fuqua Foundation, J. B.

Dray, James R., dir: Schmitt Foundation, Kilian J. and Caroline F.

Drees, Charles F., dir: Gulf Coast Medical Foundation

Drees, Donna, dir: Mid-Iowa Health Foundation

Dreiling, Daniel D., Jr., vp: Freeport-McMoRan Inc.

Dresser, Joyce G., trust: Arkell Hall Foundation

Dresser, Paul Alton, Jr., coo, exec vp, dir: Chesapeake Corp.

Drew, Helen Hall, trust: Stackpole-Hall Foundation

Drexel, Noreen, trust: McBean Charitable Trust, Alletta Morris

Drexler, Millard S., pres, dir: Gap, Inc., The; trust: Gap Foundation

Dreyer, William E., dir: SBC Communications Foundation

Driscoll, Leo C., vp human resources: Cranston Print Works Company; trust: Cranston Foundation

Driscoll, Walter John, don: Sequoia Foundation

Dristal, Kathy, vp: John Hancock Mutual Life Insurance Co.

Drossman, Mitchell A., asst secy: Kaufmann Foundation, Henry

Drost, Jill, trust: Eberly Foundation

Drought, David W., treas: First Financial Foundation

Drowota, Frank F., III, dir: HCA Foundation

Druckenmiller, Bruce, trust: Plankenhorn Foundation, Harry

Drummer, Marina, exec dir: LEF Foundation

Drummond, Burke W., dir: French Foundation, D.E.

Drumwright, Elenita M., dir: Memton Fund

Drury, W. Roger, sr vp: Humana Foundation

Drushel, William H., Jr., trust: Cullen Foundation

Drymalski, Raymond Hibner, treas: Offield Family Foundation

Du Bain, Myron, chmn, dir: Irvine Foundation, James

du Pont, Edward Bradford, vp, trust: Longwood Foundation; treas, trust: Welfare Foundation

du Pont, Irenee, Jr., trust: Crystal Trust

du Pont, Lammot Joseph, trust: Marmot Foundation

du Pont, Miren de Amezola, trust: Marmot Foundation

du Pont, Pierre Samuel, IV, trust: Longwood Foundation

du Pont, Willis Harrington, pres, trust: Marmot Foundation

Dubiel, Robert, trust: Acushnet Foundation

Dubin, Seth, dir: Hebrew Technical Institute

Dubler, Robert, trust: Young Foundation, Hugo H. and Mabel B.

DuBois, Jennifer Land, trust, don daughter: Rowland Foundation

DuBois, Philip, vp, trust: Rowland Foundation

DuBose, Suzanne A., vp, programs: NYNEX Corporate Philanthropy and Foundation

DuBose, Vivian Noble, trust: Noble Foundation, Samuel Roberts

Dubow, Isabella B., dir: Marpat Foundation

Duchossois, Dayle Paige, dir: Duchossois Foundation

Duchossois, R. Bruce, dir: Duchossois Foundation

Duchossois, Richard Louis, chmn, ceo, dir: Duchossois Industries Inc.; secy: Duchossois Foundation

Dudley, Mary Jo, asst secy treas, dir: Priddy Foundation

Dudte, James, pres, trust: Young Foundation, Hugo H. and Mabel B.

Duff, James George, chmn, ceo, dir: USL Capital Corporation

Duffell, Carol, secy, treas: Semmes Foundation

Duffy, Bernard J., Jr., mem: McGee Foundation

Duffy, Edward W., dir: Utica National Group Foundation

Duffy, John J., Esq., dir, trust: Badgeley Residuary Charitable Trust, Rose M.

Duffy, Stephen M., pres: CBI Foundation

Duffy, Vivien Stiles, exec dir: Rohatyn Foundation, Felix and Elizabeth

Duhaime, William, pub trust: Carpenter Foundation

Duke, Anthony Drexel, trust: Achelis Foundation; trust: Bodman Foundation

Duke, David Allen, vchmn tech, dir: Corning Incorporated; trust: Corning Incorporated Foundation

Duke, Jennifer Johnson, dir: South Branch Foundation

Duke, Lani Lattin, dir (Getty Ctr Ed Arts): Getty Trust, J. Paul

Duke, Robin Chandler, trust: Packard Foundation, David and Lucile

Duker, Brack, cfo, secy: Whitecap Foundation

Duker, Elizabeth, pres: Whitecap Foundation

Dulaney, Jane Norton, pres, dir: Norton Foundation Inc.

Dulaney, Robert W., vp, dir: Norton Foundation Inc.

Dulany, Peggy, dir: Rockefeller Fund, David

Dulin, Susan W., vp: Boswell Foundation, James G.

Dulle, Mary, co-chmn: Alcon Foundation

Dumas, Betty A., philanthropy & govt rels coordinator: Nestle USA Foundation

DuMont, Vera, asst to dir: Dodge Foundation, Geraldine R.

Dunagan, J. Conrad, pres: Dunagan Foundation

Dunagan, John C., secy, treas: Dunagan Foundation

Dunagan, Kathlyn C., vp: Dunagan Foundation

Dunbar, C. Wendell, treas, trust: Towsley Foundation, Harry A. and Margaret D.

Dunbar, Leslie W., trust: Mott Fund, Ruth

Duncan, Anne S., dir: Duncan Foundation, Lillian H. and C. W.; dir: Early Foundation

Duncan, Brenda, dir: Duncan Foundation, Lillian H. and C. W.; dir: Early Foundation

Duncan, C. W., III, vp, dir: Duncan Foundation, Lillian H. and C. W.; vp, dir: Early Foundation

Duncan, Charles W., Jr., pres, dir: Duncan Foundation, Lillian H. and C. W.; chmn, dir: Early Foundation

Duncan, John H., Jr., dir: Duncan Foundation, Lillian H. and C. W.; dir: Early Foundation

Duncan, John H., Sr., chmn, dir: Duncan Foundation, Lillian H. and C. W.; pres, dir: Early Foundation

Duncan, Robert D., exec vp: PPG Industries, Inc.; chmn, dir: PPG Industries Foundation

Dunckel, Jeanette M., secy, dir: Haigh-Scatena Foundation

Dunford, Betty P., vp, trust: Cooke Foundation

Dunkerton, Donald, dir: Rixson Foundation, Oscar C.

Dunkerton, Nathan R., vp, secy, dir: Rixson Foundation, Oscar C.

Dunleavy, Francis J., dir: Bird Corp. Charitable Foundation

Dunlop, John T., trust: Bird Corp. Charitable Foundation

Dunlop, Joy S., secy, dir: Dell Foundation, Hazel

Dunlop, Robert Galbraith, dir: Pew Charitable Trusts

Dunn, Edward K., Jr., treas, trust: Warfield Memorial Fund, Anna Emory

Dunn, Frank H., Jr., dir: First Union Foundation

Dunn, Harry E., vp, dir: Treakle Foundation, J. Edwin

Dunn, James J., vchmn, dir: Forbes Inc.

Dunn, Lisa, corp rels mgr: Mitsubishi Motor Sales of America, Inc.

Dunn, Peter M., Esq., secy, gen coun: Chapman Charitable Corporation, Howard and Bess

Dunnigan, Joseph J., vp, trust: Upjohn Foundation, Harold and Grace

Dunnington, Walter Grey, Jr., trust: Sullivan Foundation, Algernon Sydney; trust: Sprague Educational and Charitable Foundation, Seth

Dunwiddie, Alan W., Jr., pres, exec dir: Janesville Foundation

Dunwoody, Atwood, trust: Davis Foundations, Arthur Vining

Dunworth, Gerald J., treas: Palisades Educational Foundation

DuPont, Elizabeth Lee, vp: Good Samaritan

Duquette, Ernest A., trust: American Optical Foundation

Durand, H. Whitney, secy, trust: Tonya Memorial Foundation

Durgin, Diane, asst secy: Georgia-Pacific Foundation

Durham, Earl, trust: Hazen Foundation, Edward W.

Durkin, Sean, cfo: Winter Construction Co.

Durrett, William E., chmn: American Fidelity Corporation; pres: American Fidelity Corporation Founders Fund

Durst, Eli, treas: DEC International-Albrecht Foundation

Dutton, Uriel E., trust: Anderson Foundation, M. D.

Dwek, Cyril S., vchmn: Republic NY Corp.

Dye, James, secy: Y and H Soda Foundation

Dye, Sherman, mem, trust: South Waite Foundation

Dyer, Sara R., trust: Reinberger Foundation

Dyke, Walter P., trust: Murdock Charitable Trust, M. J.

Dykes, Martha M., dir: Marshall Foundation, Mattie H.

Dyson, E. Charles, mem adv comm: Janirve Foundation

E

Eagan, Murray, trust: Trees Charitable Trust, Edith L.

Earley, Anthony Francis, Jr., pres, coo, dir: Detroit Edison Co.

Early, Patrick Joseph, vchmn, dir: Amoco Corporation

Early, William Bernard, sr vp, asst secy, dir: JELD-WEN, Inc.; trust: JELD-WEN Foundation

Easterly, Clark, trust: City National Bank Foundation

Eastham, Thomas, vp, western dir: Hearst Foundation, William Randolph

Easton, Kenneth, trust: McMahon Foundation

Eastwood, M. Jacqueline, chmn health comm: Medtronic Foundation

Eaton, George H., comptr: Texaco Foundation

Eaton, Mary Stephens, vp, trust: Eaton Foundation, Cyrus

Eaton, Robert James, chmn, ceo: Chrysler Corp.

Eber, Andrew, vp, dir: Haigh-Scatena Foundation

Eberly, Paul O., trust: Eberly Foundation

Eberly, Robert E., Jr., trust: Eberly Foundation

Eberly, Robert E., Sr., pres, treas: Eberly Foundation

Ebrahimi, Alireza, secy: Alavi Foundation of New York

Ebrom, Charles E., exec vp, dir: Zachry Co., H.B.; trust: Zachry Foundation

Eddy, Jane Lee, exec dir, secy, trust: Taconic Foundation

Edelman, Marian Wright, dir: Aetna Foundation; dir: Diamond Foundation, Aaron

Edelman, Murray Richard, vchmn: Centerior Energy Foundation

Edelman, Peter, dir: Public Welfare Foundation

Edelman, Richard J., asst secy: Nias Foundation, Henry

Edelman, Stanley, MD, chmn: Nias Foundation, Henry

Edelstein, Lester, pres, secy: Glosser Foundation, David A.

Edey, Helen W., dir: Scherman Foundation

Edgar, Arlen L., trust: Abell-Hanger Foundation

Edgar, Robert V., dir: Memton Fund

Edmonds, Campbell S., agent: Slemp Foundation

Edmonds, Dean S., III, trust: Edmonds Foundation, Dean S.

Edmonds, George P., trust: Fair Play Foundation

Edmonds, Mary Virginia, trust: Slemp Foundation

Edmunds, Marie M., asst secy, asst treas: Comer Foundation

Edmunds, R. Larry, secy, treas: Comer Foundation

Edmundson, Kathryn L., pres: CBS Foundation

Edson, Catherine H., trust: Halff Foundation, G. A. C.

Edson, Thomas H., trust: Halff Foundation, G. A. C.

Edwards, Charles C., Jr., trust: Cowles Foundation, Gardner and Florence Call

Edwards, David L., mem dispensing comm: McCune Charitable Trust, John R.

Edwards, Earnest Jonathan, dir: Alcoa Foundation

Edwards, Frank G., trust: Puterbaugh Foundation

Edwards, James Burrows, dir: Donnelley Foundation, Gaylord and Dorothy; dir: Guggenheim Foundation, Harry Frank

Edwards, James K., trust: Levy Foundation, June Rockwell

Edwards, James M., mem: McCune Charitable Foundation, Marshall and Perrine D.; mem dispensing comm: McCune Charitable Trust, John R.

Edwards, John H., mem dispensing comm: McCune Charitable Trust, John R.

Edwards, Michael M., mem dispensing comm: McCune Charitable Trust, John R.

Efroymson, Daniel R., mem commun concerns comm: NBD Indiana, Inc.

Egan, Michael, sr vp, cfo: Aristech Chemical Corp.

Egan, Thomas P., Jr., off: Valmont Foundation

Ege, Hans A., vp, dir: Bay Foundation

Eggum, John, secy, treas, dir: Regenstein Foundation

Ehrlich, Delia F., dir: Fleishhacker Foundation

Ehrlich, Jodi, dir: Fleishhacker Foundation

Ehrlich, John Stephen, Jr., dir: Fleishhacker Foundation

Eichenbaum, E. C., chmn: Ottenheimer Brothers Foundation

Eichman, Thelma L., dir: Strong Foundation, Hattie M.

Eielson, Rodney S., pres: Culpeper Memorial Foundation, Daphne Seybolt

Eigner, Michael, pres, dir: Daily News Foundation

Eigsti, Roger Harry, chmn, pres, ceo, dir: SAFECO Corp.

Eilert, Norman E., sr vp, cfo: Teichert & Son, A.

Eiseman, Constance, exec dir, secy: Prospect Hill Foundation

Eisenberg, Richard, vp: Read Foundation, Charles L.

Eisenberg, Saul, treas: Read Foundation, Charles L.

Eisenhardt, Dianne L., asst treas, asst secy: Gebbie Foundation

Eisenhardt, Elizabeth Haas, don daughter, trust: Haas, Jr. Fund, Evelyn and Walter

Eitel, Karl E., chmn exec comm, trust: El Pomar Foundation

Eklund, Dariel Ann, vp: Norton Memorial Corporation, Geraldi

Eklund, Roger P., pres, treas: Norton Memorial Corporation, Geraldi

Eklund, Sally S., secy: Norton Memorial Corporation, Geraldi

Ekman, Richard, secy: Mellon Foundation, Andrew W.

Elam, Ed, trust: Christy-Houston Foundation

Elam, Lloyd Charles, MD, trust: Merck Co. Foundation; trust: Sloan Foundation, Alfred P.

Elbel, Christine, exec dir: Fleishhacker Foundation

Elbert, P. O., chmn, dir: Pitt-Des Moines Inc.; trust: Pitt-Des Moines Inc. Charitable Trust

Elbling, Paul U., dir: Virginia Environmental Endowment

Elder, Richard, vp commun: James River Corp. of Virginia

Eletz, Bonnie, vp: Lasdon Foundation, William and Mildred

F

Fazzano, Mary Louise, dir: Hasbro Charitable Trust Inc.

Fearon, Greer J., exec secy: Boswell Foundation, James G.

Fearon, Janet A., exec dir, trust: Newcombe Foundation, Charlotte W.

Fearon, Robert H., Jr., vp: Chapman Charitable Corporation, Howard and Bess

Federal, Joseph L., dir: Price Foundation, Lucien B. and Katherine E.

Feese, Phillis, trust: Plankenhorn Foundation, Harry

Fegan, Ann B., pres: Reidler Foundation

Fegan, Howard D., dir: Reidler Foundation

Fehlman, Bruce, mgr: Geneseo Foundation

Feidner, Robert J., fin off: Jewish Healthcare Foundation of Pittsburgh

Feil, Gertrude, pres, dir: Feil Foundation, Louis and Gertrude

Feil, Jeffrey, vp, dir: Feil Foundation, Louis and Gertrude

Feil, Louis, secy, treas, dir: Feil Foundation, Louis and Gertrude

Feinblatt, Eugene M., pres, treas: Unger Foundation, Aber D.

Feinblatt, John, dir: Unger Foundation, Aber D.

Feinblatt, Marjorie W., dir: Unger Foundation, Aber D.

Feinstein, Karen Wolk, PhD, pres: Jewish Healthcare Foundation of Pittsburgh

Feith, Susan, dir pub aff: Consolidated Papers, Inc.; vp, exec dir, dir: Consolidated Papers Foundation, Inc.

Feitler, Joan, dir, mem: Smart Family Foundation

Feitler, Robert, chmn: Smart Family Foundation

Fejes, Frank S., dir: Hugoton Foundation

Feldberg, Charles, mem contributions comm: CPC International Inc.

Feldhouse, Lynn Alexandra, mgr, secy: Chrysler Corporation Fund

Feldstein, Lewis M., treas, trust: Hazen Foundation, Edward W.

Fella, Leon, dir: Schmitt Foundation, Kilian J. and Caroline F.

Fella, Robert H., pres: Schmitt Foundation, Kilian J. and Caroline F.

Feller, Nancy P., assoc gen counc, dir legal svcs: Ford Foundation

Felman, Roberta, trust: Graham Foundation for Advanced Studies in the Fine Arts

Femino, James J., pres: Femino Foundation

Femino, Sue, vp: Femino Foundation

Fenton, Elinor P., dir, secy: Fenton Foundation

Fenton, Frank M., dir, treas: Fenton Foundation

Fenton, Thomas K., dir, vp: Fenton Foundation

Fenton, Wilmer C., dir, pres: Fenton Foundation

Fenwick, Roberta, admin: Wean Foundation, Raymond John

Ferguson, C. David, pres, ceo, dir: Gould Electronics Inc.

Ferguson, David, dir: Hyde and Watson Foundation

Ferguson, James M., III, contact: Trees Charitable Trust, Edith L.

Ferguson, Sanford B., pres: Scaife Family Foundation

Ferguson, William Charles, chmn, ceo: NYNEX Corporation

Fergusson, Frances Daly, trust: Ford Foundation

Ferland, E. James, chmn, pres, ceo: Public Service Electric & Gas Co.

Fernandes, Alvin C., Jr., vp, secy, dir: Ayres Foundation, Inc.

Fernandez, Rolando E., asst treas: Magowan Family Foundation

Ferranti, Anthony L., comptr: Pforzheimer Foundation, Carl and Lily

Ferrara, Arthur Vincent, chmn, ceo, pres: Guardian Life Insurance Company of America

Fery, John Bruce, chmn, ceo, dir, coo: Boise Cascade Corporation

Fessler, Kathryn M., contributions admin: Virginia Power Co.

Fetzer, Carol J., fdn admin, secy, trust: Carolyn Foundation

Field, Lyman, Esq., trust: Kress Foundation, Samuel H.

Fielding, Craig, dir: Glenn Foundation, Carrie C. and Lena V.

Fields, Bill, mem: Wal-Mart Foundation

Fields, Kenneth H., asst treas: Steinbach Fund, Ruth and Milton

Fields, Laura Kemper, mem disbursement comm: Oppenstein Brothers Foundation

Fields, Marvin G., sr vp, coo, dir: Frisch's Restaurants Inc.

Fields, Michael D., vp, treas: Commerce Bancshares Foundation

Fierce, Hughlyn F., trust: Chase Manhattan Foundation

Fies, Larry R., treas, corp secy: Irvine Foundation, James

Fife, Arlene R., dir: Fife Foundation, Elias and Bertha

Fife, Bernard, pres, dir: Fife Foundation, Elias and Bertha

Fikes, Amy L., vp, trust: Fikes Foundation, Leland

Fikes, Catherine W., chwm, trust: Fikes Foundation, Leland

Fikes, Lee, pres, treas, trust: Fikes Foundation, Leland

Filippell, Mark, trust: McDonald & Company Securities Foundation

Fillo, Stephen W., dir: Markle Foundation, John and Mary R.

Finberg, Barbara Denning, exec vp, program chmn (special projects): Carnegie Corporation of New York

Finch, David, chmn: Finch Foundation, Thomas Austin

Finch, Helen, trust: Finch Foundation, Doak

Finch, John L., trust: Finch Foundation, Thomas Austin

Finch, Richard J., trust: Finch Foundation, Doak

Finch, Sumner, trust: Finch Foundation, Thomas Austin

Findlay, Robert W., trust: Morrison Charitable Trust, Pauline A. and George R.

Findley, Barry B., trust: Sturgis Charitable and Educational Trust, Roy and Christine

Fink, Eleanor, dir art history info program: Getty Trust, J. Paul

Fink, John E., dir: Leighton-Oare Foundation

Fink, Richard M., vp, dir: Koch Charitable Foundation, Charles G.

Finkbeiner, James V., pres, trust: Wickes Foundation, Harvey Randall

Finkelstein, Bernard, trust: Altman Foundation

Finkle, Leon, trust: City National Bank Foundation

Finlay, John David, Jr., trust: McMillan Foundation, D. W.

Finley, Louis M., Jr., comm mem: Smith, Jr. Foundation, M. W.

Finley, Warren, trust: Argyros Foundation

Finn, Richard Henry, pres, ceo, dir: TransAmerica Corporation; dir: TransAmerica Foundation

Finnell, Lisa J., asst secy: Prudential Securities Foundation

Finneran, Laurey, trust: LEF Foundation

Finney, Graham Stanley, dir: Penn Foundation, William

Finney, Jon, vchmn: Van Buren Foundation

Finney, Redmond C. S., dir: France Foundation, Jacob and Annita

Finora, Joseph, asst treas: Thorne Foundation, Oakleigh L.

Fiola, Janet S., chmn, mem ed comm: Medtronic Foundation

Fiorani, R. P., vp, dir: Square D Foundation

Firestine, Larry, mem scholarship selection comm: Ritter Charitable Trust, George W. and Mary F.

Firman, Pamela, pres: Firman Fund

Firman, Royal, trust: Firman Fund

Firth, Edmee de Montmollin, exec dir: Dreyfus Foundation, Jean and Louis

Firth, Nicholas L. D., pres: Dreyfus Foundation, Jean and Louis

Fischbach, Jerome, pres: Fischbach Foundation

Fischer, Diane, corp secy, dir: Atran Foundation

Fischer, Donald, dir: Cole Foundation, Olive B.

Fischer, Richard Lawrence, dir: Alcoa Foundation

Fischer, William J., Jr., trust: Hagedorn Fund

Fish, Eugene C., dir: Reidler Foundation

Fish, Lawrence K., chmn, ceo: Citizens Bank of Rhode Island; trust: Citizens Charitable Foundation

Fishbein, Donna Jaffe, trust: Jaffe Foundation

Fishbein, Peter M., trust: Kaye Foundation

Fisher, Allan Herbert, Jr., secy, trust: Leidy Foundation, John J.

Fisher, Bernard, dir: Uris Brothers Foundation

Fisher, Blake O., Jr., exec vp, cfo, dir: IES Industries, Inc.

Fisher, Bruce C., trust: Friendship Fund

Fisher, David S., dir: Young Foundation, Irvin L.

Fisher, Donald George, fdr, chmn, ceo: Gap, Inc., The; pres: Gap Foundation

Fisher, Doris F., treas: Gap Foundation

Fisher, Ellen Kingman, program off: Gates Foundation

Fisher, Francis M., Jr., vp: Gulf Power Co.; chmn: Gulf Power Foundation

Fisher, George Myles Cordell, chmn, pres, ceo: Eastman Kodak Company

Fisher, John Wesley, pres, dir: Ball Brothers Foundation

Fisher, Kenneth, secy, treas, dir: Scurlock Foundation

Fisher, Max M., trust: Taubman Foundation, A. Alfred

Fisher, Orville Earl, Jr., sr vp, gen couns, secy: Jostens, Inc.; treas, mem contributions comm: Jostens Foundation Inc., The

Fisher, Richard B., chmn, mng dir: Morgan Stanley & Co., Inc.

Fisher, Robert J., exec vp, coo: Gap, Inc., The; vp: Gap Foundation

Fishman, Fred N., trust: Kaye Foundation

Fishman, Joseph L., vp, dir: Moses Fund, Henry and Lucy

Fishman, Steven S., pres, dir: Pamida, Inc.

Fisk, Mary A., dir: Harriman Foundation, Mary W.

Fiske, Guy W., dir: Bird Corp. Charitable Foundation

Fitch, Gale, contact: Dula Educational and Charitable Foundation, Caleb C. and Julia W.

Fitz, William R., asst secy: Rockwell International Corporation Trust

Fitzgerald, Dennis M., vp, secy, dir: Vernon Fund, Miles Hodsdon

Fitzgerald, J. T., vp: Price Foundation, Lucien B. and Katherine E.

Fitzgerald, John A., vp, trust: Merrill Lynch & Co. Foundation Inc.

Fitzgibbons, James M., chmn, ceo: Fieldcrest Cannon Inc.

Fitzpatrick, Henry B., trust: McShain Charities, John

Fitzpatrick, Jane P., chmn, treas: High Meadow Foundation

Fitzpatrick, John H., vchmn, chmn plan and fin comm: Housatonic Curtain Co.; pres: High Meadow Foundation

Fitzpatrick, Nancy, secy, dir: Thompson Co. Fund, J. Walter

Fitzpatrick, Nancy F., dir: Friendship Fund

Fitzsimmons, Hugh A., Jr., trust: Halsell Foundation, Ewing

Fitzsimonds, Roger Leon, chmn, ceo, dir: Firstar Bank Milwaukee, N.A.; chmn: Firstar Milwaukee Foundation

Fix, Duard, trust: Kitzmiller/Bales Trust

Fix, James H., asst comptr: USX Foundation

Fjellman, Carl Gustaf, trust: Turrell Fund

Flanagan, Craig H., dir: Stauffer Foundation, John and Beverly

Flanagan, David T., pres, ceo, dir: Central Maine Power Co.

Flanagan, Edward P., secy: Price Foundation, Lucien B. and Katherine E.

Flanagin, Neil, dir: Scholl Foundation, Dr.

Flanders, Grame L., trust: Acushnet Foundation

Flaville, Victoria K., vp, secy: Connelly Foundation

Fleischman, Charles D., vp, treas: Nias Foundation, Henry

Fleisher, David Lee, cfo, sr exec vp: Maritz Inc.

Fleishhacker, David, pres, dir: Fleishhacker Foundation

Fleishhacker, Mortimer, III, treas, dir: Fleishhacker Foundation

Fleishman, Ernest B., trust: Robinson Fund, Maurice R.

Fleishman, Joel L., dir: Centralia Foundation

Fleishman, Joel Lawrence, dir: Markle Foundation, John and Mary R.

Fleming, David D., pres, trust: Mellinger Educational Foundation, Edward Arthur

Fleming, Richard Harrison, cfo, vp: USG Corporation; treas, trust: USG Foundation

Fleming-McGrath, Lucy, trust: Homeland Foundation

Fletcher, Allen W., chmn, trust: Fletcher Foundation

Fletcher, Mary F., trust: Fletcher Foundation

Fletcher, Nina M., trust: Fletcher Foundation

Fletcher, Patricia A., trust: Fletcher Foundation

Fletcher, Warner S., treas, trust: Fletcher Foundation

Flettrich, Albert J., dir: German Protestant Orphan Asylum Association

Flippin, Doreen D., exec asst: Davis Foundations, Arthur Vining

Flom, Douglas, cfo: Burdines Inc.

Flood, Al, chmn, ceo: CIBC Wood Gundy

Flores, Rosemary, dir: Sierra Pacific Resources Charitable Foundation

Flournoy, Houston Irvine, vp: Jones Foundation, Fletcher

Flower, Walter C., III, dir: German Protestant Orphan Asylum Association

Flowers, Thomas J., pres, dir: Hultquist Foundation

Flowers, Wilford, dir: Wright Foundation, Lola

Flynn, James T., coo: Long Island Lighting Co.

Flynn, Thomas G., vp: Bechtel, Jr. Foundation, S. D.

Foege, William H., M.D., dir: MacArthur Foundation, John D. and Catherine T.

Foley, Cheryl M., vp, secy, gen couns: CINergy; secy: CINergy Foundation

Foley, Patricia, asst secy: Inland Container Corp.; secy, treas, dir: Inland Container Corp. Foundation

Folger, John Dulin, trust: Folger Fund

Folger, Kathrine Dulin, pres, treas: Folger Fund

Folger, Lee Merritt, vp, secy: Folger Fund

Fondren, Bentley B., bd gov: Fondren Foundation

Fondren, Robert E., bd gov: Fondren Foundation
Fondren, Walter W., III, bd gov: Fondren Foundation
Fondren, Walter W., IV, secy, treas: Fondren Foundation
Fonseca, Caio, trust: Kaplan Fund, J. M.
Fonseca, Elizabeth K., vp, trust: Kaplan Fund, J. M.
Fonseca, Isabel, trust: Kaplan Fund, J. M.
Fonseca, Quina, trust: Kaplan Fund, J. M.
Fontaine, John C. "Jack", chmn, trust: Kress Foundation, Samuel H.
Fonteyne, Herman J., pres, ceo, dir: Ensign-Bickford Industries
Foote, Marion, vp, dir: First National Bank of Chicago Foundation
Foote, Susan Green, dir: Green Foundation, Allen P. and Josephine B.
Forbes, Christopher, vchmn, corp secy, dir: Forbes Inc.; vp: Forbes Foundation
Forbes, Dorothy L., vp, exec dir: Cabot Corp. Foundation
Forbes, Malcolm Stevenson, Jr., pres: Forbes Inc.; pres: Forbes Foundation
Ford, Alfred B., trust: Ford Motor Co. Fund
Ford, David S., vp, dir: Chase Manhattan Foundation
Ford, Edsel B., II, pres, trust, mem: Ford II Fund, Henry
Ford, Frank L., Jr., cfo, secy, treas: Arkelian Foundation, Ben H. and Gladys
Ford, Joanne C., pres, dir: Nalco Foundation
Ford, Kenneth W., chmn: Roseburg Forest Products Co.
Ford, Martha F., trust, mem: Ford Fund, William and Martha; trust: Firestone, Jr. Foundation, Harvey
Ford, Richard Edmond, vp, dir: Daywood Foundation
Ford, Thomas Patrick, trust: Cord Foundation, E. L.
Ford, Virginia, trust: Curtice-Burns/Pro-Fac Foundation
Ford, William Clay, pres, trust, mem: Ford Fund, William and Martha
Forest, Ruth, secy to admin vp: Hillsdale Fund
Forkner, Joanne S., vp, trust: Jockey Hollow Foundation
Formica, Mark J., pres: Citizens Bank of Rhode Island; trust: Citizens Charitable Foundation
Forrester, Margretta, co-trust: Van Evera Foundation, Dewitt
Forster, Peter Hans, vp, trust: Tait Foundation, Frank M.
Fortson, Benjamin J., vp, trust, treas: Burnett-Tandy Foundation
Foskett, Nettie, adm: Prospect Hill Foundation
Foss, John H., vp, treas, cfo, dir: Tecumseh Products Co.
Foster, Charles E., dir: SBC Communications Foundation
Foster, Evelyn W., dir: Foster Foundation
Foster, Howard K., dir: Staunton Farm Foundation
Foster, J. R., trust: Foster Charitable Trust
Foster, Jay L., trust: Foster Charitable Trust
Foster, Joe C., Jr., secy, dir: Abrams Foundation, Talbert and Leota

Foster, L. B., II, trust: Foster Charitable Trust
Foster, Michael G., dir: Foster Foundation
Foster, Stephen A., exec vp: Dana Foundation, Charles A.
Foster, Thomas B., dir: Foster Foundation
Foster, Tom, trust: Chicago Sun-Times Charity Trust
Foulke, Walter L., trust: Mutual Assurance Co. Charitable Trust
Foulkrod, Fred A., vp: Plankenhorn Foundation, Harry
Fountaine, George J., dir: Guggenheim Foundation, Harry Frank
Fowler, Anderson, trust: Brady Foundation
Fowler, Dolores C., dir (El Pomar Center): El Pomar Foundation
Fowler, Robert E., Jr., trust: Schuller Fund
Fowler, Robert F., III, trust: Arnold Fund
Fox, Bill, pres VA Gas: Consolidated Natural Gas Co.
Fox, Jerry D., secy, treas, dir: Journal-Gazette Foundation, Inc.
Fox, Joseph Carter, ceo, dir, chmn: Chesapeake Corp.
Fox, Lawrence E., vp, dir: First National Bank of Chicago Foundation
Fox, Mary Ann, secy: Koch Charitable Foundation, Charles G.
Fox, W.A., trust: Consolidated Natural Gas Co.
Foxworthy, James C., vp human resources: Inland Container Corp.; vp, dir: Inland Container Corp. Foundation
Foy, Douglas J., treas, asst secy, dir: Ball Brothers Foundation; treas, asst secy: Ball Foundation, George and Frances
Frahm, Donald Robert, chmn, ceo, dir: ITT Hartford Insurance Group, Inc.; pres, dir: ITT Hartford Insurance Group Foundation
France, Beatrice Murdock, dir: Ensign-Bickford Foundation
France, Phyllis B., dir: Bush Foundation
Frances, R. Lewis, secy,treas, dir: Old Dominion Box Co. Foundation
Franceschelli, Anthony D., treas, dir: Emerson Foundation, Inc., Fred L.
Francis, Carol Feather, vp, trust: Baughman Foundation
Francis, Frank, trust: Ghidotti Foundation
Francis, Kenneth A., exec vp, chmn giving program: McDonnell Douglas Corp.-West
Francis, Philip H., vp, dir: Square D Foundation
Frank, Anthony Melchior, trust: Saroyan Foundation, William
Frank, John V., pres, trust: Morgan Foundation, Burton D.
Frank, Michael J., comptr, vp: City National Bank and Trust Co.
Frank, Seth E., trust: Lurcy Charitable and Educational Trust, Georges
Frank, Stanley J., Jr., vp, trust: Dater Foundation, Charles H.

Frank, Stephen E., pres, coo: Southern California Edison Co.
Frankenberg, Robert, chmn, pres, ceo, dir: Novell Inc.
Frankenhoff, Mary Ann, dir: Stauffer Foundation, John and Beverly
Franklin, Carl M., co-trust: Stauffer Charitable Trust, John
Franklin, H. Allen, pres: Georgia Power Co.
Franklin, John Hope, trust: Duke Endowment
Franks, Myron B., vp, dir: Gebbie Foundation
Fraser, Howard H., pres: Gallagher Family Foundation, Lewis P.
Fraser, Kenneth William, Jr., treas, dir: Fieldcrest Cannon Foundation
Frastaci, Barbara A., asst treas: Centerior Energy Foundation
Frater, Janice, trust: First Interstate Bank of Oregon Charitable Foundation
Frawley, Mary, mem contributions comm: SAFECO Corp.
Frazier, Arlene, dir: Lichtenstein Foundation, David B.
Frazier, Wayne, dir: Lichtenstein Foundation, David B.
Frecon, Leslie M., sr vp, corp fin: General Mills, Inc.; trust: General Mills Foundation
Frederick, Catherine H., trust: Harmon Foundation, Pearl M. and Julia J.
Frederick, David C., dir: Staunton Farm Foundation
Fredrickson, Dennis, secy-treas: Firstar Milwaukee Foundation
Freed, Elizabeth Ann, pres, trust: Freed Foundation
Freeman, David Forgan, treas: Scherman Foundation
Freeman, Houghton, dir: Starr Foundation
Freeman, Jim, vp, corp commun: American United Life Insurance Co.
Freeman, Kenneth W., pres, coo: Corning Incorporated; trust: Corning Incorporated Foundation
Frehner, Walter G., pres, gen mgr: Swiss Bank Corp.
Frehse, Robert M., Jr., vp, exec dir: Hearst Foundation, William Randolph
Frelinghuysen, George L. K., asst treas, dir: Pforzheimer Foundation, Carl and Lily
Frelinghuysen, Peter, trust: Achelis Foundation; trust: Bodman Foundation
French, Daniel P., Jr., pres, ceo, dir: French Oil Mill Machinery Co.
French, James H., hon dir: Dana Foundation, Charles A.
Frenchman, Gerald, vp: Fribourg Foundation
Frese, Ines, chmn, trust: Frese Foundation, Arnold D.
Fressola, Peter, commun dir: Benetton Services Corp.
Fretthold, Timothy Jon, sr vp, gen couns, dir: Diamond Shamrock Inc.
Frey, Eugene U., trust: Bigelow Foundation, F. R.
Fribourg, Mary Ann, mem, dir: Fribourg Foundation
Fribourg, Michel, pres, mem, dir: Fribourg Foundation

Frick, L. Frank, asst secy: Oxy USA Charitable Foundation
Friede, Barbara, secy, operating dir: Fireman's Fund Foundation
Friedewald, William Thomas, MD, dir: Metropolitan Life Foundation
Friedlaender, Helmut N., dir: AMETEK Foundation
Friedland, Laurie, dir: Winston Foundation, Norman and Rosita
Friedlander, W. John, dir: Lake Placid Education Foundation
Friedman, Bob, treas: Friedman Family Foundation
Friedman, David, secy: Friedman Family Foundation
Friedman, Ellie, vp: Friedman Family Foundation
Friedman, Judith E., asst secy: Mitsubishi International Corp. Foundation
Friedman, Milton, dir: Glosser Foundation, David A.
Friedman, Phyllis K., pres: Friedman Family Foundation
Friedman, Robert F., vp, dir: Rosenberg Foundation
Friedman, Robert S., secy, treas: Rubinstein Foundation, Helena
Friedman, Sidney O., trust: Lurcy Charitable and Educational Trust, Georges
Friedman, William K., vp corp aff: Seagram & Sons, Inc., Joseph E.; trust: Bronfman Foundation, Samuel
Friend, Eugene L., vchmn, dir: Koret Foundation
Friend, Robert, dir: Osher Foundation, Bernard
Friiedman, David G., asst secy: Fribourg Foundation
Frisch, Maureen, vp pub aff: Simpson Investment Company; pres, dir: Matlock Foundation
Frist, Thomas Fearn, Jr., chmn: HCA Foundation
Fritsche, William F., Jr., trust: Consolidated Natural Gas System Foundation
Fritz, Ron, chmn, corp contributions comm: AUL Foundation Inc.
Fritz, Sandra, adv: Cayuga Foundation
Fritz, William J., treas: Moore & Sons Foundation, B.C.
Froelicher, F. Charles, trust: Gates Foundation
Frohlich, William O., vp: Dun & Bradstreet Corp. Foundation, Inc.
Frohring, Glenn H., chmn, trust: Frohring Foundation, William O. and Gertrude Lewis
Frohring, Lloyd W., treas, trust: Frohring Foundation, William O. and Gertrude Lewis
Frohring, Paul Robert, pres, trust: Frohring Foundation, Paul and Maxine
Fronek, David T., exec vp, dir commun rels: NBD Indiana, Inc.
Frost, Camilla Chandler, dir: Irvine Foundation, James
Frost, Herbert G., Jr., dir: Jones Foundation, Harvey and Bernice

Frost, Joan M., trust: Dillon Dunwalke Trust, Clarence and Anne
Frost, Tom C., chmn, ceo: Frost National Bank
Frost, William Lee, pres, treas, dir: Littauer Foundation, Lucius N.
Frueauff, David, exec dir, secy: Frueauff Foundation, Charles A.
Frueauff, Sue M., trust: Frueauff Foundation, Charles A.
Frueauff-Cochran, Anna Kay, trust: Frueauff Foundation, Charles A.
Fruehauf, Harvey C., Jr., pres, dir: Fruehauf Foundation; trust: Wiegand Foundation, E. L.
Fry, John D., trust: SharonSteel Foundation
Fry, Lloyd A., III, dir: Fry Foundation, Lloyd A.
Fryling, Victor J., dir: Consumers Power Foundation
Fujiki, Y., chmn, ceo, dir: Subaru of America Inc.
Fukunaga, Mark H., alternate mem distr comm: McInerny Foundation
Fuller, Carl W., trust: Blount Educational and Charitable Foundation, Mildred Weedon
Fuller, Harry Laurance, chmn, pres, ceo, dir: Amoco Corporation
Fuller, Kathryn Scott, trust: Ford Foundation
Fuller, Peter, trust: Fuller Foundation
Fuller, Peter, Jr., trust: Fuller Foundation
Fullinwider, Jerome M., trust: Abell-Hanger Foundation
Fulstone, Suellen, vp, legal counsel: May Foundation, Wilbur
Fulton, V. Neil, asst secy: Gilmore Foundation, William G.
Funaro, Patricia P., program admin: USX Foundation
Funderburk, Charles B., trust: Blount Educational and Charitable Foundation, Mildred Weedon
Fuqua, Dorothy C., secy: Fuqua Foundation, J. B.
Fuqua, J. Rex, treas: Fuqua Foundation, J. B.
Fuqua, John Brooks, pres: Fuqua Foundation, J. B.
Furek, Robert M., dir: Connecticut Mutual Life Foundation Inc.; pres, ceo, dir: Heublein Inc.; chmn, dir: Heublein Foundation, Inc.
Furlong, James P., dir civic aff: Gillette Charitable & Educational Foundation
Furman, James Merle, dir: MacArthur Foundation, John D. and Catherine T.
Furr, Anthony Lloyd, vp: Wachovia Foundation, Inc.
Futo, Kyle, vp: Monfort Family Foundation

G

Gabelli, Mario Joseph, trust: Wiegand Foundation, E. L.
Gaberman, Barry D., dep vp: Ford Foundation
Gable, Robert L., chmn, pres, ceo, dir: Unitrode Corp.
Gabriel, Nicholas M., treas, comptr, dir fin svcs: Ford Foundation

Gaffney, Joseph M., dir: Nesholm Family Foundation

Gagnier, Charles E., pres, ceo, dir: AMCORE Bank, N.A. Rockford; dir: AMCORE Foundation, Inc.

Gaines, Alexander P., trust: Woolley Foundation, Vasser

Gaines, Carolyn, adm asst: HCA Foundation

Gainey, W. W., Jr., treas: Dover Foundation

Gaiser, Mary Jewett, don, trust: Jewett Foundation, George Frederick

Gaiswinkler, Robert S., chmn, dir: First Financial Bank FSB; dir: First Financial Foundation

Gaiter, William S., trust: Mutual Assurance Co. Charitable Trust

Gaither, James C., dir: Irvine Foundation, James

Galbraith, William A., Jr., trust: Clapp Charitable and Educational Trust, George H.

Gale, Benjamin, trust: Bingham Foundation, William

Gale, Thomas H., trust: Bingham Foundation, William

Gale, Thomas V., trust: Bingham Foundation, William

Gale-Holweger, Mary E., vp, trust: Bingham Foundation, William

Gallagher, J. Peter, trust: Hillsdale Fund

Gallagher, Margaret W., trust: Hillsdale Fund

Gallagher, Patrick S., exec dir: Paley Foundation, William S.

Gallagher, Terence Joseph, vp corp gov, asst secy: Pfizer, Inc.; secy, dir: Pfizer Foundation

Galler, Ida E., secy: Starr Foundation

Galligan, Richard P., secy, dir: Lee Foundation

Galliker, Franz, chmn: Swiss Bank Corp.

Galloway-May, Diane L., asst secy: Ford Foundation

Gallup, John G., dir: Beveridge Foundation, Frank Stanley

Gambill, Malcolm W., pres, trust: Harsco Corp. Fund

Gamble, George F., vp, secy ,treas: Gamble Foundation

Gamble, Launce E., pres: Gamble Foundation

Gamble, Mary S., vp: Gamble Foundation

Gambrel, Amy H., trust: Crandall Memorial Foundation, J. Ford

Games, Robert W., exec secy: Van Wert County Foundation

Gammill, Lee Morgan, Jr., exec vp, dir: New York Life Insurance Co.; dir: New York Life Foundation

Gamron, W. Anthony, treas, dir: Kimberly-Clark Foundation

Gancer, Donald C., vp: Boothroyd Foundation, Charles H. and Bertha L.

Ganci, Paul J., pres, coo, dir: Central Hudson Gas & Electric Corp.

Gandolfo, Joseph C., dir: Mattel Foundation

Gannett, John H., dir: Gannett Foundation, Guy P.

Gannett, William B., trust: Hopedale Foundation

Gannon, R. P., pres, dir: Montana Power Co.; dir: MPCo/Entech Foundation

Garber, John Paul, joint chmn N Am: WestLB New York Branch

Garber, Karlene Beal, trust: Beal Foundation

Garberding, Larry Gailbert, cfo, exec vp: Detroit Edison Co.; dir: Detroit Edison Foundation

Gardella, Raymond, vp, dir: Daily News Foundation

Gardner, David Pierpont, trust: Getty Trust, J. Paul; pres: Hewlett Foundation, William and Flora

Gardner, James Richard, vp corp investor rels: Pfizer, Inc.; vp: Pfizer Foundation

Gardner, R. M., vp: Einstein Fund, Albert E. and Birdie W.

Gardner, Robert R., sr vp finance, treas: Allendale Insurance Foundation

Gardner, Roger L., pres, trust: Jones Foundation, Daisy Marquis

Gardner, William L., Jr., vp, dir: McCann Foundation

Gareau, Joseph H., dir: ITT Hartford Insurance Group Foundation

Garlotte, Helen, trust: Winchester Foundation

Garner, William S., Jr., secy, dir: KN Energy Foundation

Garnier, Jean-Pierre, exec vp: SmithKline Beecham Corp.

Garrett, J. Richard, treas: ITT Hartford Insurance Group Foundation

Garrett, Margaret Dodge, dir emerita: Dodge Foundation, Cleveland H.

Garrett, Robert, chmn fin comm, dir: Dodge Foundation, Cleveland H.

Garrett, Wendy, trust: Owsley Foundation, Alvin and Lucy

Garrison, Milton, dir: Lebanon Mutual Foundation

Garrity, Norman E., exec vp: Corning Incorporated; trust: Corning Incorporated Foundation

Garst, Mary, dir: Audubon State Bank Charitable Foundation

Garst, Stephen, dir: Audubon State Bank Charitable Foundation

Gartland, John J., Jr., pres, dir: McCann Foundation

Gartland, Michael G., asst secy, dir: McCann Foundation

Gartland, Robert F., trust: Morgan Stanley Foundation

Garvey, Nancy, treas: AlliedSignal Foundation Inc.

Garwood, William L., Jr., vp: Clayton Fund; vp, trust: Henry Foundation, Patrick

Gassaway, James M., trust: Grundy Foundation

Gassman, Robert S., treas, dir: Guttman Foundation, Stella and Charles

Gast, Aaron E., trust: Newcombe Foundation, Charlotte W.

Gates, Charles Cassius, Jr., pres, trust, don son: Gates Foundation

Gates, Peter P. M., secy: Astor Foundation, Vincent

Gates, Van E., chmn: First Source Corp. Foundation

Gath, Marie, asst secy: Stans Foundation

Gaus, William Thomas, vp, treas, dir: Schroeder Foundation, Walter

Gayle, Gibson, Jr., pres, trust: Anderson Foundation, M. D.

Gearhart, Pearl H., vp-admin: Shenandoah Life Insurance Co.

Geary, Bruce, trust: Centralia Foundation

Gebhard, Elizabeth R., dir: Demos Foundation, N.

Gehrke, Allen C., dir: Godfrey Foundation

Geifman, Geraldine, secy, dir: Geifman Family Foundation

Geifman, Morris M., pres, dir: Geifman Family Foundation

Geifman, Stephen, vp, treas, dir: Geifman Family Foundation

Geifman, Terri, asst treas, dir: Geifman Family Foundation

Geisel, Audrey, pres, asst secy: Dr. Seuss Foundation

Gelb, Arthur, pres, dir: New York Times Co. Foundation

Gelb, Richard Lee, chmn: Bristol-Myers Squibb Company; chmn, dir: Bristol-Myers Squibb Foundation Inc.; dir: New York Times Co. Foundation

Gelder, John William, vp, secy, trust: Herrick Foundation

Gell-Mann, Murray, dir: MacArthur Foundation, John D. and Catherine T.

Gellert, Celia B., dir: Gellert Foundation, Carl; dir: Gellert Foundation, Celia Berta

Gellhorn, Alfred, MD, dir: Diamond Foundation, Aaron

Gelsey, Stephen I., admin: Hamman Foundation, George and Mary Josephine

Gelston, Steven, contributions off: Chase Manhattan Bank, N.A.

Gemmill, Helen H., trust: Warwick Foundation

Gemmill, William K., secy: Warwick Foundation

Generett, Mona N., trust: Pittsburgh Child Guidance Foundation

Genin, Roland, vchmn, dir: Schlumberger Ltd.

Gentry, John R., pres: Brenner Foundation, Mervyn

George, Helen A., secy: Cremer Foundation

George, Margaret E., trust: Eberly Foundation

George, Michael J., vp, dir: Godfrey Foundation

George, Pamela L., dir: Hobby Foundation

George, Paul, vp, dir: United Airlines Foundation

George, William Douglas, Jr., pres, ceo, dir: Johnson & Son, S.C.; vchmn: Johnson's Wax Fund

George, William Wallace, pres: Medtronic, Inc.

Georges, John A., chmn, ceo: International Paper Co.; dir: International Paper Co. Foundation

Georgius, John R., pres, dir: First Union Corp.; dir: First Union Foundation

Geramian, Mohammad, pres: Alavi Foundation of New York

Gerard, Jamie K., secy: Newman's Own Foundation

Gerber, Peter H., dir (ed program): MacArthur

Foundation, John D. and Catherine T.

Gerber, Terry, dir: First Source Corp. Foundation

Gerdes, John, dir: Lebanon Mutual Foundation

Gerhart, Jack S., trust: Steinman Foundation, James Hale; trust: Steinman Foundation, John Frederick

Gerken, Walter Bland, dir: Irvine Foundation, James; chmn exec comm, dir: Pacific Mutual Life Insurance Co.; dir: Pacific Mutual Charitable Foundation

Gerlicher, Andrew, sr vp, mgr bank rel: First Interstate Bank of Oregon; trust: First Interstate Bank of Oregon Charitable Foundation

Gerlinger, Charles D., clerk: Cabot Corp. Foundation

Germeshausen, Paline S., trust: Germeshausen Foundation, Kenneth J.

Gerry, Elbridge Thomas, pres, dir: Harriman Foundation, Gladys and Roland; dir: Harriman Foundation, Mary W.

Gerry, Elbridge Thomas, Jr., dir: Harriman Foundation, Gladys and Roland

Gerry, Martha Farish, vp, trust: Farish Fund, William Stamps

Gershman, Joel, pres: Gershman Foundation, Joel

Gerstein, David, trust: Price Foundation, Louis and Harold

Gerstley-Hofheimer, Carol, trust: Cassett Foundation, Louis N.

Gerstner, Louis Vincent, Jr., chmn, ceo: International Business Machines Corp.; dir: New York Times Co. Foundation

Gerstung, Sandra L., pres: Hecht-Levi Foundation

Geschke, Chuck, pres: Aldus Corp.

Gessula, Benjamin, treas: Uris Brothers Foundation

Getty, Gordon Peter, trust: Getty Trust, J. Paul

Getz, Barbara J., sr program off: Kresge Foundation

Getz, Dennis A., secy, trust: Steinman Foundation, James Hale; secy, trust: Steinman Foundation, John Frederick

Geurin, Bob, asst secy-treas: Noble Foundation, Samuel Roberts

Gherlein, Gerald Lee, mem contributions comm: Eaton Charitable Fund

Ghisalbert, Adele F., dir: Harcourt Foundation, Ellen Knowles

Gianas, Peter T., dir, secy, trust: Spalding Foundation, Eliot

Giannini, Charlotte, exec dir: Clarkson Foundation, Jeniam

Giaramita, Phillip S., chmn gifts & grants comm: Martin Marietta Corp. Foundation

Giarusso, Cathy, trust: Cranston Foundation

Giavono, Joseph A., dir: Safety Fund Foundation

Gibbons, Harry L., exec comm: Swanson Family Foundation, Dr. W.C.

Gibbons, John Joseph, vp, trust: Fund for New Jersey

Gibbons, Miles J., Jr., exec dir: Wells Foundation, Franklin H. and Ruth L.

Gibbs, J. Ronald, trust: Smith Trust, May and Stanley

Gibbs, Robert, dir commun rels: Houston Industries Incorporated

Gibby, Jon S., vp: Unocal Foundation

Giberson, Robert C., trust: Johnson Foundation, Burdine

Gibson, Charles Colmery, trust: Knight Foundation, John S. and James L.

Gibson, D. Bruce, dir: Guaranty Bank and Trust Co. Charitable Trust

Gibson, Edgar A., mem scholarship selection comm: Ritter Charitable Trust, George W. and Mary F.

Gibson, Kay, trust: Morgan Charitable Residual Trust, W. and E.

Gibson, Thomas Joseph, treas: Gates Foundation

Gibson, Tom, trust: Subaru of America Foundation

Gibson, William Shepard, vp, secy: Continental Corp. Foundation

Gicking, Robert K., vp: Reidler Foundation

Gifford, Charles Kilvert, pres, dir: Bank of Boston Corp.; trust: Bank of Boston Corp. Charitable Foundation

Gifford, Russell R., trust: Consolidated Natural Gas System Foundation

Gifford, Samuel L., II, vp commun: Delaware North Co., Inc.

Gigray, Margaret, treas: Whittenberger Foundation, Claude R. and Ethel B.

Gilbert, James M., trust: Rixson Foundation, Oscar C.

Gilbert, Louisa, dir: Moore Foundation, Edward S.

Gilbert, Marion Moore, vp, dir: Moore Foundation, Edward S.

Gilbert, S. Parker, trust, mem: Sloan Foundation, Alfred P.

Gilbertson, Laura C. Hitchcock, dir: Bingham Foundation, William

Giles, Lucille P., pres: Giles Foundation, Edward C.

Gill, Barbara E., vp: Dana Foundation, Charles A.

Gill, Juliann, admin: Dun & Bradstreet Corp. Foundation, Inc.

Gill, Lawrence, grants admin, vp, dir: Dodge Jones Foundation

Gillen, James Robert, sr vp, gen couns: Prudential Insurance Co. of America, The; trust: Prudential Foundation

Gillespie, Ann, trust: Little Foundation, Arthur D.

Gillespie, George Joseph, III, dir: Paley Foundation, William S.

Gillespie, J. Samuel, Jr., adv: Carter Foundation, Beirne

Gillespie, Tyrone W., grant comm: Royal Foundation, May Mitchell

Gillies, Linda, dir, trust: Astor Foundation, Vincent

Gillig, Edward C., pres: Myra Foundation

Gillstrom, Mary, asst secy: Andersen Foundation

Gilman, E. Atwill, trust: Boettcher Foundation

Gilman, Howard L., pres, dir: Gilman Foundation, Howard

Gilman, Sylvia P., dir: Gilman Foundation, Howard

Gilmartin, Raymond V., chmn, pres, ceo: Merck & Co.

Gimon, Eleanor H., dir: Hewlett Foundation, William and Flora

Ginnis, Sandra, dir: Ensign-Bickford Foundation

Ginsberg, Ernest, vchmn, dir: Republic NY Corp.

Gioia, Lucy, off adm: Dreyfus Foundation, Max and Victoria

Giordano, Joseph, trust: Rixson Foundation, Oscar C.

Girvan, Daniel J., sr vp human resources: James River Corp. of Virginia; vp: James River Corp. Foundation

Gische, Samuel R., fin dir, contr: Hartford Foundation, John A.

Gisel, William George, pres, dir: Cummings Foundation, James H.

Giuggio, John Peter, vchmn, dir: Globe Newspaper Co.

Givan, Boyd Eugene, sr vp, cfo: Boeing Co., The

Given, Davis, trust: Davis Foundations, Arthur Vining

Glade, Fred M., Jr., chmn, dir: Reynolds Foundation, Edgar

Gladfelter, Millard E., trust emeritus: Newcombe Foundation, Charlotte W.

Glancy, Alfred Robinson, III, trust: Hudson-Webber Foundation

Glanville, Charles D., dir: Glanville Family Foundation

Glanville, John, vp, dir: Glanville Family Foundation

Glanville, Nancy H., pres, dir: Glanville Family Foundation

Glanville, Robert E., dir: Glanville Family Foundation

Glanville, Thomas, vp, dir: Glanville Family Foundation

Glaser, Robert Joy, MD, trust: Packard Foundation, David and Lucile

Glass, David Dayne, pres, ceo, dir: Wal-Mart Stores, Inc.; trust: Wal-Mart Foundation

Glass, Ron, pres: Bay Area Foods

Glasser, James Jay, chmn, pres, ceo: GATX Corp.

Glassmoyer, Thomas Parvin, trust: Newcombe Foundation, Charlotte W.

Glaudel, Robert H., trust: M/A-COM Foundation

Glazer, Patricia, trust: Bronfman Foundation, Samuel

Gleason, James S., pres, dir: Gleason Foundation

Gleason, Janis F., dir: Gleason Foundation

Gleaves, James L., asst treas: American General Finance Foundation

Glennon, John, treas: Taube Family Foundation

Glick, Darwin, dir: Lebanon Mutual Foundation

Glick, Eugene B., pres: Glick Foundation, Eugene and Marilyn

Glick, Marilyn K., secy, treas: Glick Foundation, Eugene and Marilyn

Glickstein, Linda S., trust: Schiro Fund

Gloyd, Lawrence Eugene, chmn, pres, ceo, dir: CLARCOR Inc.; trust: CLARCOR Foundation

Glusac, M. M., trust: Chrysler Corporation Fund

Glynn, Gary Allen, vp (investments): USX Foundation

Goberville, Gary J., trust: GenCorp Foundation, Inc.

Goddard, Samuel P., Jr., dir, vp, trust: Spalding Foundation, Eliot

Goddard, William R., trust: Goddard Foundation, Charles B.; trust: Noble Foundation, Samuel Roberts

Goddard, William R., Jr., trust: Goddard Foundation, Charles B.; trust: Merrick Foundation

Godfrey, Crawford, trust: Norman Foundation, Summers A.

Godfrey, William K., vp, mem exec comm, dir: Lipton, Thomas J.; trust: Lipton Foundation, Thomas J.

Godwin, Mills E., Jr., trust: Beazley Foundation/Frederick Foundation

Goett, Edward G., dir: Laffey-McHugh Foundation

Goettler, Ralph H., trust: Allegheny Foundation

Gogins, Kenneth L., mgr corp commun: Peoples Energy Corp.

Goizueta, Roberto Crispulo, trust: Evans Foundation, Lettie Pate

Gold, Peter Stephen, trust: Akzo America Foundation

Goldberg, Avram Jacob, trust: Goldberg Family Foundation

Goldberg, Carol Rabb, trust: Goldberg Family Foundation; trust: Rabb Charitable Foundation, Sidney and Esther

Goldberg, Edward Jay, vp consumer aff: Macy & Co., Inc., R.H.

Golden, Gail, secy, asst treas, dir: ACF Foundation; secy, treas: Icahn Foundation, Carl C.

Golden, William Theodore, treas, dir: Kaufmann Foundation, Henry

Goldman, Guido, dir: ASDA Foundation

Goldseker, Sheldon, chmn, trust: Goldseker Foundation of Maryland, Morris

Goldseker, Simon, vchmn, trust: Goldseker Foundation of Maryland, Morris

Goldsmith, Deborah L., vp: Zlinkoff Fund for Medical Research and Education, Sergei S.

Goldstein, Bruce, dir: Haigh-Scatena Foundation

Goldstein, Lester, dir: Glosser Foundation, David A.

Goldstein, Richard A., pres, ceo, dir: Unilever United States, Inc.

Goldstein, Robert, MD, vp: Zlinkoff Fund for Medical Research and Education, Sergei S.

Goldwyn, Anthony, trust: Goldwyn Foundation, Samuel

Goldwyn, Francis, trust: Goldwyn Foundation, Samuel

Goldwyn, John, trust: Goldwyn Foundation, Samuel

Goldwyn, Peggy E., vp, trust: Goldwyn Foundation, Samuel

Goldwyn, Samuel John, Jr., pres: Goldwyn Foundation, Samuel

Golem, Dennis, trust: McDonald & Company Securities Foundation

Golloway, Zoe Cole, asst exec dir: Frueauff Foundation, Charles A.

Gomer, Adelaide P., dir: Park Foundation

Gomory, Ralph Edward, pres, trust, mem exec & investment comms: Sloan Foundation, Alfred P.

Gonring, Matthew P., vp, trust: USG Foundation

Gonthier, Laurie G., dir: New Milford Savings Bank Foundation

Good, Robert Alan, MD, trust: Dana Charitable Trust, Eleanor Naylor

Gooden, Andrea, program mgr ed grants: Apple Computer, Inc.

Gooding, John S., chmn, dir: GSM Industrial; pres: Gooding Group Foundation

Goodman, Charles B., vp, dir: Crown Memorial, Arie and Ida

Goodman, Harold S., trust: Messing Family Charitable Foundation

Goodman, Helen, sr vp: ITT Hartford Insurance Group, Inc.

Goodrich, Enid, vchmn: Winchester Foundation

Goodrich, Gillian C., trust: Comer Foundation

Goodrich, T. Michael, pres, ceo, dir: BE&K Inc.; trust: BE&K Foundation

Goodsell, Jill, admin, dir: Foster Foundation

Goodstein, Robert, pres: Goodstein Family Foundation, David

Goodwin, David P., trust: Cogswell Benevolent Trust

Goodwin, Jeanne, secy: Goodstein Family Foundation, David

Goodwin, Neva R., pres, dir: Rockefeller Fund, David

Goodwin, V. John, pres, ceo: National Steel Corp.

Goodyear, Patricia O., secy: Price Associates Foundation, T. Rowe

Googe, W.J., III, vp: Southwestern Electric Power Co.

Goolsby, John L., trust: Reynolds Foundation, Donald W.

Gordon, Charles O., trust: Thomasville Furniture Industries Foundation

Gordon, Ellen R., pres, dir: Rubin Family Fund, Cele H. and William B.

Gordon, Jonathan R., trust: Mailman Family Foundation, A. L.

Gordon, Joseph K., trust: McLean Contributionship

Gordon, Lois, dir: Fleishhacker Foundation

Gordon, Melvin Jay, vp, dir: Rubin Family Fund, Cele H. and William B.

Gore, Ruth T., dir: Chapin Foundation of Myrtle Beach, South Carolina

Goren, Vri, dir: Porter Testamentary Trust, James Hyde

Gorham, David A., sr vp, treas: New York Times Co. Foundation

Gorham, John, mem distribution comm, mem investigating comm: Champlin Foundations

Goriup, Mary A., mgr: Hedco Foundation

Gorman, Joseph M., secy: General American Charitable Foundation

Gorman, Michael R., exec dir: Irwin Charity Foundation, William G.

Gormley, Dennis James, chmn, ceo, dir: Federal-Mogul Corporation; mem contributions comm: Federal-Mogul Corp. Charitable Trust Fund

Gormley, Patrick A., vp: Bacon Foundation, E. L. and Oma

Gorski, Walter Joseph, sr vp, gen couns, asst secy: Connecticut Mutual Life Insurance Company; vp, dir: Connecticut Mutual Life Foundation

Gosnell, M. Ann, asst secy: Corning Incorporated Foundation

Gother, Ronald E., asst secy: Lund Foundation

Gottlieb, Meyer, treas, dir: Goldwyn Foundation, Samuel

Gottlieb, Richard, ceo, pres: Lee Enterprises

Gottwald, Bruce Cobb, chmn, ceo, dir: Ethyl Corp

Gottwald, Floyd D., Jr., vchmn: Ethyl Corp

Gottwald, Thomas E., pres, coo, dir: Ethyl Corp

Gottwald, William M., MD, sr vp, dir: Ethyl Corp

Goudy, Grace Collins, fdr, vp, dir: Collins Foundation

Gould, Brian, contr, treas: Interkal, Inc.

Gould, Edward P., chmn: English Memorial Fund, Florence C. and H. L.; chmn: Trust Company Bank

Gould, John T., Jr., dir corp aff: Unilever United States, Inc.; vp: Unilever Foundation

Gould, Laurence K., Jr., dir: Stauffer Foundation, John and Beverly

Gould, Paul A., vp: Allen Brothers Foundation

Graber, Samuel W., gov: Mayor Foundation, Oliver Dewey

Grabowski, Gary G., exec dir, treas, dir: Beloit Foundation

Grace, Philip M., treas: MacArthur Foundation, John D. and Catherine T.

Graddick, Mirian M., trust: AT&T Foundation

Grado, John, Jr., trust: Wallace Foundation, George R.

Graf, Alan B., trust: Akzo America Foundation

Grafe, Tim, trust: Donaldson Foundation

Graham, Carolyn C., treas, trust: Carolyn Foundation

Graham, Donald Edward, trust: Graham Fund, Philip L.

Graham, George E., Jr., dir: Asplundh Foundation

Graham, Julie, dir: Overbrook Foundation

Graham, Katharine Meyer, trust, don: Graham Fund, Philip L.

Graham, Michelle C., dir: Overbrook Foundation

Graham, Randy A., regional dir human resources: Bank One, Texas-Houston Office

Graham, Robert C., Jr., dir: Overbrook Foundation

Granger, Jack, dir: Morrison Knudsen Corporation Foundation

Granger, John C., trust: Blount Educational and Charitable Foundation, Mildred Weedon

Grano, Joseph J., Jr., pres: PaineWebber

Granoff, Mark, vp: Blue Cross & Blue Shield United of Wisconsin Foundation

Granoien, Linda J., corp contributions consult, mem exec contributions comm: Northern States Power Co. (Minnesota)

Grant, Frederic R., trust: Irwin Charity Foundation, William G.

Grant, H. Raymond, treas: Hopedale Foundation

Grant, Madeline H., trust: Mulford Foundation, Vincent

Grant, Munro J., trust, pres: Pittsburgh Child Guidance Foundation

Grant, R. Gene, pres, dir: Cheney Foundation, Ben B.

Grant, William West, III, trust: Gates Foundation

Grasley, Michael Howard, mem exec comm, dir: Shell Oil Company Foundation

Grasmere, Robert H., pres, trust: Turrell Fund

Grassilli, Robert J., treas, dir: Gellert Foundation, Carl; dir: Gellert Foundation, Celia Berta

Grasso, Richard A., chmn, ceo: New York Stock Exchange, Inc.

Graves, Earl Gilbert, dir: Aetna Foundation

Gray, Charles Agustus, vp tech: Cabot Corp.; dir: Cabot Corp. Foundation

Gray, Charles M., dir: Demos Foundation, N.

Gray, Hanna Holborn, PhD, dir: Cummins Engine Foundation; trust: Mellon Foundation, Andrew W.

Gray, James, pres: Burdines Inc.

Gray, Josef E., pres: Seafirst Corporation

Graybill, Charles S., MD, chmn, trust: McMahon Foundation

Graziadio, George L., Jr., chmn, pres, ceo, dir: Imperial Bancorp; dir: Imperial Bank Foundation

Green, Amelia, program assoc: HCA Foundation

Green, Bennie, treas, trust: Rockwell Fund

Green, Don C., dir: Mid-Iowa Health Foundation

Green, Ellen Z., MD, first vchmn, dir: Bush Foundation

Green, Friday Ann, trust: Taylor Foundation, Ruth and Vernon

Greenbaum, Maurice C., secy, dir: Mandeville Foundation

Greenberg, Barbara Reynolds, exec dir: Burden Foundation, Florence V.

Greenberg, Maurice Raymond, chmn bd, dir: Starr Foundation

Greene, Harold H., trust: Seafirst Foundation

Greene, Marion E., pres: LEF Foundation

Greene, Richard L., dir: Koret Foundation

Greenewalt, David, adv trust, don grandson: Crystal Trust

Hessinger, Carl John William, trust: Trexler Trust, Harry C.

Hessler, Curtis Alan, exec vp: Times Mirror Company, The; dir: Times Mirror Foundation

Hester, James McNaughton, pres, dir: Guggenheim Foundation, Harry Frank

Heston, W. Craig, chmn, ceo, dir: Utica National Insurance Group; pres, dir: Utica National Group Foundation

Heuchling, Theodore Paul, trust: Little Foundation, Arthur D.

Heuschele, Richard P., MD, trust: Wickes Foundation, Harvey Randall

Hewit, Betty R., vp, dir: Hewit Family Foundation

Hewit, William D., pres, treas, dir: Hewit Family Foundation

Hewit, William E., vp, dir: Hewit Family Foundation

Hewlett, Walter B., chmn: Hewlett Foundation, William and Flora

Hewlett, William Redington, chmn emeritus: Hewlett Foundation, William and Flora

Heyns, Roger William, dir: Hewlett Foundation, William and Flora; vchmn, dir: Irvine Foundation, James

Hiatt, Howard H., MD, dir: Diamond Foundation, Aaron

Hibberd, William F., secy: Harriman Foundation, Gladys and Roland; secy: Harriman Foundation, Mary W.

Hiddeman, J., trust: Alcon Foundation

Hield, James S., secy contributions comm: Cargill Inc.; exec dir: Cargill Foundation

Higbee, David M., secy: Williams Companies, The; secy, treas: Williams Companies Foundation, The

Higginbotham, A. Leon, Jr., dir: New York Times Co. Foundation

Higgins, Eunice O., secy, trust: Olin Foundation, Spencer T. and Ann W.

Higgins, Gloria J., dir: JFM Foundation

Higgins, John Joseph, trust: Boston Edison Foundation

Higgins, Michael R., treas: Amcast Industrial Corp.

Higgins, Ralph P., treas, trust: Eaton Foundation, Cyrus

Higgins, Robert J., vchmn: Fleet Financial Group, Inc.

Higgins, Walter M., chmn, pres, ceo, dir: Sierra Pacific Resources

Higgins, William Waugh, trust: Olin Foundation, Spencer T. and Ann W.

High, Calvin G., trust: High Foundation

High, Joseph C., dir: Cummins Engine Foundation

Higie, David G., exec dir: Aristech Foundation

Higie, William F., secy, mgr: Glendorn Foundation

Higley, Robert A., secy, treas: O'Quinn Foundation, John M. and Nancy C.

Higurashi, Takeshi, vp, trust: Subaru of America Foundation

Hilbert, Robert, secy, treas, vp (admin), trust: El Pomar Foundation

Hildahl, Joanne C., vp (grants program): Wiegand Foundation, E. L.

Hildebrandt, A. Thomas, dir: Davenport-Hatch Foundation

Hildebrandt, Austin E., pres, dir: Davenport-Hatch Foundation

Hildebrandt, Elizabeth H., dir: Davenport-Hatch Foundation

Hildreth, Gary R., vp, gen couns, secy: Armco Inc.; asst secy: Armco Foundation

Hilgers, William, vp, dir: Wright Foundation, Lola

Hilinski, Chester C., vp, trust, gen counc: Connelly Foundation

Hill, Bill J., secy, treas: Beal Foundation

Hill, Caroline N., trust: Steinman Foundation, James Hale

Hill, Charlotte Bishop, vchwm, mem adv comm: O'Connor Foundation, A. Lindsay and Olive B.

Hill, George, dir: Burchfield Foundation, Charles E.

Hill, James, sr vp, corp aff: SmithKline Beecham Corp.; dir: SmithKline Beecham Foundation

Hill, Karra Mays, trust: Mays Foundation

Hill, Kent, pres: Gulf Coast Medical Foundation

Hill, Luther Lyons, Jr., secy, trust: Cowles Foundation, Gardner and Florence Call

Hill, Norman A., dir: Scott Foundation, Walter

Hill, Robert F., mem contributions comm: Virginia Power Co.

Hill, Sally B., vp, dir: Burchfield Foundation, Charles E.

Hill, Steven Richard, sr vp human resources: Weyerhaeuser Co.; trust: Weyerhaeuser Company Foundation

Hillard, Robert Glen, ceo, dir: Security Life of Denver Insurance Co.

Hillman, Alex, dir: Hillman Family Foundation, Alex

Hillman, Elsie H., dir: Hillman Foundation

Hillman, Henry Lea, chmn, dir, don son: Hillman Foundation

Hillman, Rita K., pres, dir: Hillman Family Foundation, Alex

Hills, Lee, chmn, trust: Knight Foundation, John S. and James L.

Hillson, David R., exec dir, secy: Robinson-Broadhurst Foundation

Hillyard, Gerald R., Jr., secy, trust: Johnson Foundation, Helen K. and Arthur E.

Himmelman, Bonnie, exec vp, dir: Fairchild Foundation, Sherman

Hinderliter, Harry E., chief admin off, corp secy, chief counc: PriMerit Bank

Hing, Bill Ong, dir: Rosenberg Foundation

Hinson, William M., dir: Meyer Family Foundation, Paul J.

Hinton, Michael R., pres, coo, dir: Old National Bank in Evansville

Hirsch, Bruce A., exec dir: Heller Charitable Foundation, Clarence E.

Hirsch, Philip J., vp, treas, dir: Miller Fund, Kathryn and Gilbert

Hirschfeld, A. Barry, trust: Boettcher Foundation

Hirschfield, Ira S., pres, trust: Haas, Jr. Fund, Evelyn and Walter

Hirschhorn, David, vp, trust: Blaustein Foundation, Louis and Henrietta

Hirschman, Frank Frederick, asst vp fin, asst secy: Inland Container Corp.; pres, dir: Inland Container Corp. Foundation

Hirsh, Philip J., dir: Kaufmann Foundation, Henry

Hiser, Harold Russell, Jr., trust: Schering-Plough Foundation

Hitching, Harry James, chmn, trust: Tonya Memorial Foundation

Hitchner, Ruth, asst secy: Sordoni Foundation

Hladky, J. F., Jr., dir: Gazette Foundation

Hladky, Joseph F., III, ed, publ: Gazette Co.; pres, dir: Gazette Foundation

Hlavac, Bernard C., dir: Sentry Foundation Inc.

Hoag, George Grant, II, pres, dir: Hoag Family Foundation, George

Hoag, John Arthur, vp, dir: First Hawaiian Foundation

Hoag, Patricia H., vp, dir: Hoag Family Foundation, George

Hobart, Sharon L., asst secy: Wheat, First Securities/Butcher & Singer Foundation

Hobbs, F. Worth, pres, dir: Alcoa Foundation

Hobby, Diana P., trust: Hobby Foundation

Hobby, William Pettus, Jr., vp, trust: Hobby Foundation

Hobson, Henry W., secy, trust: Griswold Foundation, John C.

Hockaday, Irvine O., Jr., trust: Continental Corp. Foundation

Hodder, William Alan, chmn, pres, ceo: Donaldson Company, Inc.

Hodge, Katherine K., treas: Kreitler Foundation

Hodge, Lynn W., trust: Self Foundation

Hodges, Gene R., dir: Georgia Power Foundation

Hodges, John E., Jr., trust: Gulf Power Foundation

Hodgson, Thomas Richard, pres, coo, dir: Abbott Laboratories

Hodjat, Mehdi, dir: Alavi Foundation of New York

Hodnett, Byron E., chmn, ceo: First Union National Bank of Florida

Hoekzema, Barbara, secy, treas: Vicksburg Foundation

Hoenemeyer, Frank Joseph, chmn, trust: Turrell Fund

Hoester, Robert G. H., trust: Gaylord Foundation, Clifford Willard

Hoey, James J., sr vp, cfo: Douglas & Lomason Company

Hoffer, Robert M., dir: Schroeder Foundation, Walter

Hoffman, Carter O., vp, treas: Price Associates Foundation, T. Rowe

Hoffman, Karen A., secy: Ahmanson Foundation

Hoffman, Ronald R., dir: Alcoa Foundation

Hofland, Brian F., PhD, vp, program off: Retirement Research Foundation

Hogan, Alan D., vp: Prudential Securities Foundation

Hogan, Dan, dir: Kirkpatrick Foundation

Hogan, John E., exec vp: Cole Foundation, Olive B.

Hogans, Mack L., pres, trust: Weyerhaeuser Company Foundation

Hogen, Charles R, Jr., exec vp: Merck Co. Foundation

Hogg, Christopher Anthony, trust: Ford Foundation

Hoglund, William Elis, trust: General Motors Foundation; chmn bd trusts: Skillman Foundation

Hogue, Elaine L., assoc admin: Castle Foundation, Harold K. L.

Hohn, Harry George, Jr., chmn, ceo, dir: New York Life Insurance Co.; chmn, dir: New York Life Foundation

Hohn, James Samonte, contact: Van Houten Memorial Fund

Hoke, Michael N., Jr., trust: McMillan Foundation, D. W.

Holbrook, John H., trust: Wiggins Memorial Trust, J. J.

Holder, J. R., trust: Share Trust, Charles Morton

Holder, Vickie L., off admin: Thomasville Furniture Industries; admin comm: Thomasville Furniture Industries Foundation

Holderness, Craig J., asst treas: Nalco Foundation

Holdrege, James H., trust: Hickory Tech Corp. Foundation

Holdren, John Paul, dir: MacArthur Foundation, John D. and Catherine T.

Holland, Ellen T., asst secy, asst treas: Thalhimer and Family Foundation, Charles G.

Holland, G. Edison, Jr., trust: Gulf Power Foundation

Holland, Hudson, Jr., secy, trust: Hudson-Webber Foundation

Holland, John G., trust: Hastings Charitable Foundation, Oris B.

Holland, Linda, dir commun rels: Royal Group, Inc.; contact: Royal Insurance Foundation

Hollett, Byron P., dir: Clowes Fund

Holliman, Vonda, treas: Koch Charitable Foundation, Charles G.

Hollingsworth, John Mark, asst secy: Simmons Foundation, Inc., Harold

Hollingsworth, Susan Hunt, trust: Hunt Foundation; trust: Hunt Foundation, Roy A.

Hollis, Meredith H., dir: Mandeville Foundation

Holloran, Thomas Edward, chmn bd: Bush Foundation

Holloway, Alan, treas, cfo: Y and H Soda Foundation

Holm, Richard T., asst treas: Davis Foundation, Edwin W. and Catherine M.

Holman, David W., corp trust rep: Kern Foundation Trust

Holman, John W., Jr., dir: Barker Foundation, J.M.R.;

Holman, Virginia, trust: Haley Foundation, W. B.

Holmes, Edward A., grants chmn, trust: International Foundation

Holmes, John S., Jr., dir: Christy-Houston Foundation

Holmes, Reva A., vp, secy, trust: Johnson's Wax Fund

Holmquist, Carl, trust: Lunda Charitable Trust

Holt, David E., secy, trust: Brown Foundation, M. K.

Holt, June W., trust: Holt Family Foundation

Holt, Leon C., Jr., trust: Holt Family Foundation

Holt, Melvin W., vp, dir: Dodge Jones Foundation

Holt, Richard W., Jr., trust: Holt Family Foundation

Holt, Timothy Arthur, vp portfolio mgmt: Aetna Life & Casualty Co.; treas, investment mgr: Aetna Foundation

Holton, Virginia R., pres: Virginia Environmental Endowment

Holtz, Doris, dir: Knudsen Foundation, Tom and Valley

Holtzberg, Celia, treas: New York Life Foundation

Holzer, Erich, secy, treas: Holzer Memorial Foundation, Richard H.

Holzer, Eva, vp: Holzer Memorial Foundation, Richard H.

Holzer, Vivian, pres: Holzer Memorial Foundation, Richard H.

Hom, Gloria, dir: Haigh-Scatena Foundation

Homberger, Rosmarie E., secy: Greenwall Foundation

Honda, Yoshio, pres: Fujitsu America, Inc.

Hood, Leroy Edward, dir: Seaver Institute

Hook, Clifford, cfo: Kaye, Scholer, Fierman, Hays & Handler

Hook, Harold Swanson, Sr., mem: American General Finance Foundation

Hoolihan, James, trust: Blandin Foundation

Hoolihan, Thomas J., secy: Unilever Foundation

Hooser, Karen R., trust: Reinberger Foundation

Hooton, Paula, secy: Fish Foundation, Ray C.

Hoover, Herbert, III, pres, trust: Hoover, Jr. Foundation, Margaret W. and Herbert

Hoover, Lawrence Richard, chmn, trust: Hoover Foundation

Hoover, Rose, secy: Fair Oaks Foundation, Inc.

Hoover, Thomas H., trust: Hoover Foundation

Hopiak, George A., secy-treas: Cowell Foundation, S. H.

Hopkins, Maureen A., secy, adm: Barker Foundation, J.M.R.

Hopkinson, Sealy H., trust: Middendorf Foundation

Hopwood, William T., trust: Hopwood Charitable Trust, John M.

Horan, John J., trust: Merck Co. Foundation

Horn, Audrey, secy: Hobby Foundation

Horn, Charles G., pres, coo: Fieldcrest Cannon Inc.; pres,

I

Ireland, James D., III, pres: Mather and William Gwinn Mather Fund, Elizabeth Ring

Irwin, John N., III, first vp, trust: Achelis Foundation; first vp, trust: Bodman Foundation

Irwin, Robert James Armstrong, treas, dir: Cummings Foundation, James H.

Isakower, Gloria, vp: Kaplun Foundation, Morris J. and Betty

Ishirashi, Nancy, mem bd: Telesis Foundation

Ishkenian, Mark, pub aff: Central Maine Power Co.

Isom, Ralph, mem: CHC Foundation

Ittleson, Henry Anthony, chmn, pres, dir: Ittleson Foundation

Ittleson, Marianne S., dir: Ittleson Foundation

Ivey, Ray N., vp, exec dir: Consolidated Natural Gas System Foundation

J

Jacangelo, Nicholas, treas: Baldwin Foundation, David M. and Barbara

Jackson, Alexander, treas, asst secy, dir: Moore Foundation, Edward S.

Jackson, Basil L., dir: Bowen Foundation, Ethel N.

Jackson, Edgar R., vp, dir: Parsons Foundation, Ralph M.

Jackson, Frederick H., dir: La-Z-Boy Foundation

Jackson, Graham, vp pub rels: Nalco Chemical Co.

Jackson, Herrick, trust: Connemara Fund

Jackson, Ira A., trust: Bank of Boston Corp. Charitable Foundation

Jackson, J. W., trust: Blowitz-Ridgeway Foundation

Jackson, John N., trust: Bigelow Foundation, F. R.

Jackson, Robert W., trust: Connemara Fund

Jackson, W. R., trust: Pitt-Des Moines Inc. Charitable Trust

Jacob, John Edward, trust: Continental Corp. Foundation

Jacobs, Bernard B., pres: Shubert Foundation

Jacobs, Jere A., pres, dir: Telesis Foundation

Jacobs, Jeremy Maurice, chmn, dir: Delaware North Co., Inc.

Jacobs, Jeremy Maurice, Jr., sr exec vp: Delaware North Co., Inc.

Jacobs, Joseph J., pres, ceo, cfo: Jacobs Family Foundation

Jacobs, Linda E., vp for programs: Culpeper Foundation, Charles E.

Jacobs, Linda K., vp: Jacobs Family Foundation

Jacobs, Louis M., sr exec vp: Delaware North Co., Inc.

Jacobs, Margaret E., vp: Jacobs Family Foundation

Jacobs, Violet J., secy: Jacobs Family Foundation

Jacobson, Lyle G., trust: Hickory Tech Corp. Foundation

Jacobson, Malcolm, trust: Cassett Foundation, Louis N.

Jacobson, Sibyl C., pres, ceo, dir: Metropolitan Life Foundation

Jacobus, Richard, dir: Mosinee Paper Corp. Foundation

Jacoby, A. James, chmn: New York Stock Exchange Foundation, Inc.

Jaffe, Edwin A., chmn: Jaffe Foundation

Jaffe, Lola, vchmn: Jaffe Foundation

Jaffe, Mary Hewlett, dir: Hewlett Foundation, William and Flora

Jaffe, Robert, trust: Jaffe Foundation

Jaffe, Ruth, trust: Kantzler Foundation

Jagow, Elmer, trust: Frohring Foundation, Paul and Maxine

Jalkut, Thomas P., trust: Prouty Foundation, Olive Higgins

Jallow, Raymond, dir: Seaver Institute

James, Diana L., secy, treas: Reidler Foundation

James, Edie, treas: Sonat Foundation

James, J. Hatcher, III, vp: Armstrong Foundation

James, Jean Butz, dir: Butz Foundation

James, John H., vp, treas: Armstrong Foundation

James, Owen, coo, dir: Sheaffer Inc.

James, Ronald E., dir: Butz Foundation

Jamison, Zean, Jr., exec dir: Van Every Foundation, Philip L.

Jammal, Eleanor A., vp, trust: Ashtabula Foundation

Janney, Mary Draper, dir: Strong Foundation, Hattie M.

Jannotta, Edgar D., pres: Blair and Co. Foundation, William

Jansen, Wolfgang, co-chmn: Sharon Steel Corp.

Jantz, Sue Ann, trust: Schowalter Foundation

Jao, C. S. Daisy, tax adv: Boston Edison Foundation

Jarc, Frank Robert, exec vp fin: Donnelley & Sons Co., R.R.

Jarcho, Fredrica, program off: Greenwall Foundation

Jarvis, J. Kirkland, secy, dir: Treakle Foundation, J. Edwin

Jaskol, Leonard R., chmn, pres, ceo, dir: Lydall, Inc.

Jastrow, Kenneth W., II, trust: Temple-Inland Foundation

Javitch, Jonathan, dir: Lebovitz Fund

Jelley, Philip M., secy, fdn mgr, mem bd dirs: Skaggs Foundation, L. J. and Mary C.

Jenifer, Franklyn Green, trust: Texaco Foundation

Jenkins, Paul R., pres, trust: Benedum Foundation, Claude Worthington

Jenkins, William, vp human resources: Henkel Corp.

Jenks, John T., trust: Kirbo Charitable Trust, Thomas M. and Irene B.

Jenks, R. Murray, pres, trust: Kirbo Charitable Trust, Thomas M. and Irene B.

Jennings, Christina W., dir: Jennings Foundation, Mary Hillman

Jennings, Evan D., pres: Jennings Foundation, Mary Hillman

Jennings, Louis C., dir: Christy-Houston Foundation

Jenrette, Richard Hampton, trust: Duke Endowment

Jensen, A. C., trust: Hallett Charitable Trust, Jessie F.

Jensen, Frederick W., dir: Rennebohm Foundation, Oscar

Jensen, Kathryn L., vp: Blandin Foundation

Jenson, Thor, chmn, trust: Kinney-Lindstrom Foundation

Jepsen, Sarah, exec dir: AT&T Foundation

Jernstedt, Dorothy, secy, dir: Hedco Foundation

Jerwers, James R., dir: American General Finance Foundation

Jeschke, Thomas, dir: Mid-Iowa Health Foundation

Jess, Mary Jo, vchwn, mem exec comm: Blandin Foundation

Jessup, John B., secy: Thorne Foundation

Jewell, D. Ashley, V, secy, trust: Jewell Memorial Foundation, Daniel Ashley and Irene Houston

Jewell, E. Dunbar, trust: Jewell Memorial Foundation, Daniel Ashley and Irene Houston

Jewell, George Hiram, dir: Schlumberger Foundation

Jewell, Robert, vp commun: Goodrich Co., The B.F.

Jewell, William H., trust, chmn: Jewell Memorial Foundation, Daniel Ashley and Irene Houston

Jewett, George F., Jr., chmn: Jewett Foundation, George Frederick

Jewett, Lucille Winifred McIntyre, trust: Jewett Foundation, George Frederick

Jinks, Larry, chmn journalism adv comm: Knight Foundation, John S. and James L.

Jobe, Warren Yancey, exec vp, cfo, treas, dir: Georgia Power Co.; pres, dir: Georgia Power Foundation

Jochum, Richard A., off: IBP Foundation, Inc., The

Joffe, Harvey G., cfo, dir: Parvin Foundation, Albert

John, Victor B., trust: Fuller Foundation, C. G.

Johns, Sheryl Lightfoot, vp, treas: Houston Endowment

Johns, William M., trust: Goddard Foundation, Charles B.

Johnson, Abigail P., trust: Johnson Fund, Edward C.

Johnson, Becki, trust: Seafirst Foundation

Johnson, Berkley D., trust: Chadwick Fund, Dorothy Jordan

Johnson, Bruce R., vp: Wahlstrom Foundation

Johnson, Bruce W., pres, dir: Premier Industrial Corp.

Johnson, Burdine C., pres: Clayton Fund; trust: Johnson Foundation, Burdine

Johnson, C. E., trust: Share Trust, Charles Morton

Johnson, Carmella J., contributions mgr: Clorox Co.

Johnson, Carol R., chmn: Henderson Foundation, George B.

Johnson, Cecily M., vp, trust: Western New York Foundation

Johnson, Charlotte, trust: Bremer Foundation, Otto

Johnson, Christopher W., trust: Johnson Charitable Trust, Keith Wold

Johnson, Cindy, grants admin: Bristol-Myers Squibb Foundation Inc.

Johnson, Claudia Lady Bird Taylor, trust: LBJ Family Foundation

Johnson, Dale A., chmn, ceo, dir: SPX Corp.; trust: SPX Foundation

Johnson, David L., treas: Larsen Fund

Johnson, Dennis R., asst treas: Santa Fe Pacific Foundation

Johnson, Don R., dir: First Union Foundation

Johnson, Donald E., Jr., pres, trust: Whiting Foundation

Johnson, Edward Crosby, III, trust: Johnson Fund, Edward C.

Johnson, Edward Crosby, IV, trust: Johnson Fund, Edward C.

Johnson, Edward Eric, sr vp: Times Mirror Company, The; dir: Times Mirror Foundation

Johnson, Elizabeth L., trust: Johnson Fund, Edward C.

Johnson, Elizabeth Ross, trust: Johnson Charitable Trust, Keith Wold

Johnson, Esther U., trust: South Branch Foundation

Johnson, Frank M., trust: Wickes Foundation, Harvey Randall

Johnson, Gary E., mem contributions comm: Diamond Shamrock Inc.

Johnson, Glenn, trust: Acushnet Foundation

Johnson, Gretchen W., dir, trust: Cape Branch Foundation

Johnson, Hilda, vp: Myra Foundation

Johnson, Howard Wesley, commission trust, chmn exec comm, mem investment comm: Sloan Foundation, Alfred P.

Johnson, Ivan, chmn, dir: Mid-Iowa Health Foundation

Johnson, J. Lee, IV, dir: Carter Foundation, Amon G.

Johnson, J. M. Hamlin, trust: Stackpole-Hall Foundation

Johnson, James A., trust, mem fin & admin comm: Carnegie Corporation of New York

Johnson, James Lawrence, dir: Cape Branch Foundation; trust: South Branch Foundation

Johnson, Jerry Ray, pres, bd mem, dir: Gregg-Graniteville Foundation

Johnson, Joan L., secy: Wiremold Foundation

Johnson, Ken, program off: Chevron Corporation

Johnson, Lael Frederic, dir: Abbott Laboratories Fund

Johnson, Larry, pres: Guaranty Bank & Trust Co.

Johnson, Luci Baines, trust: LBJ Family Foundation

Johnson, Margaret P., vp: BT Foundation

Johnson, Mark L., dir: Carter Foundation, Amon G.

Johnson, Michael P., vp, dir: Banc One Wisconsin Foundation

Johnson, Norman E., trust: CLARCOR Foundation; sr vp tech: Weyerhaeuser Co.; trust: Weyerhaeuser Company Foundation

Johnson, Peter Lawson, dir: Donner Foundation, William H.

Johnson, Raymond, mgr: Geneseo Foundation

Johnson, Robert Wood, IV, trust, prin mgr: Johnson Charitable Trust, Keith Wold; pres, dir: Johnson Foundation, Willard T. C.

Johnson, Roland H., exec dir: Grundy Foundation

Johnson, Samuel Curtis, chmn, dir: Johnson & Son, S.C.; chmn, pres, trust: Johnson's Wax Fund

Johnson, William L., vp: ANR Foundation, Inc.

Johnson, William T., trust: Johnson Foundation, Burdine

Johnson, Wyatt Thomas, Jr., trust: Knight Foundation, John S. and James L.; secy, treas, trust: Mellinger Educational Foundation, Edward Arthur

Johnston, Charles H., dir: Peterson Foundation, Hal and Charlie

Johnston, Harry A., II, trust: Chastain Charitable Foundation, Robert Lee and Thomas M.

Johnston, James W., dir: La-Z-Boy Foundation

Johnston, M. James, pres, dir: Fort Wayne National Bank

Johnston, Martha, secy, treas: De Queen General Hospital Foundation

Johnston, Murray L., Jr., vp, secy, gen coun, dir: Zachry Co., H.B.; trust: Zachry Foundation

Johnston, William R., dir: New York Stock Exchange Foundation, Inc.

Johnstone, John William, Jr., chmn, ceo: Olin Corp.; trust: Olin Corporation Charitable Trust

Jolley, C., asst treas: Oxy USA Charitable Foundation

Jones, Bernard B., II, chmn, dir: Feild Co-Operative Association

Jones, Bernard Bryan, III, 1st vp, dir: Feild Co-Operative Association

Jones, Bernice, chmn: Jones Foundation, Harvey and Bernice

Jones, Charles, M.D., dir: De Queen General Hospital Foundation

Jones, Chris, co-pres: Thompson Co., J. Walter

Jones, Christine G., corp mgr commun & ed rels: Boeing Co., The

Jones, Clayton M., sr vp govt oper & intl: Rockwell International Corporation

Jones, D. Michael, pres: West One Bancorp

Jones, D. Whitman, dir: Whittenberger Foundation, Claude R. and Ethel B.

Jones, David Allen, co-fdr, chmn, ceo, dir: Humana, Inc.; chmn, ceo, dir: Humana Foundation

Jones, Edward L., vp commun rels & pub aff: Morgan & Company, J.P.; dir: Arcadia Foundation

Jones, Emily S., asst vp, asst secy: Meadows Foundation

Jones, Farrell, pres, trust: Levitt Foundation

Jones, Grace Anna, dir pub aff: Dresser Industries, Inc.

Jones, Helen Devitt, dir: Jones Foundation, Helen

Jones, Jack, vp: Winter Construction Co.

Jones, John Earl, chmn, ceo, pres: CBI Industries, Inc.

Jones, John L., sr vp human resources: Jostens, Inc.

Jones, Joseph Wayne, chmn, trust: Evans Foundation, Lettie Pate

Jones, Judith H., asst secy: Aetna Foundation

Jones, Leonade Diane, asst treas: Graham Fund, Philip L.

Jones, Lewis B., vp, contr: USX Foundation

Jones, Mary Duke Trent, trust: Duke Endowment

Jones, O. D., trust: Long Foundation, J.M.

Jones, Rebecca S., dir charitable contributions: Southern California Edison Co.

Jones, Robert T., trust: Anderson Foundation

Jones, Susan, grants admin: Cooke Foundation

Jonsson, Kenneth A., pres, treas, trust: Jonsson Foundation

Jonsson, Philip R., vp, treas, trust: Jonsson Foundation

Joralemon, Jane G., vp, trust: Anderson Foundation

Jordan, Don D., chmn, ceo, dir: Houston Industries Incorporated

Jordan, Leria L., vp: Sonat Foundation

Jordan, Richard E., vp, dir: Kline Foundation, Josiah W. and Bessie H.; dir: Stabler Foundation, Donald B. and Dorothy L.

Jordan, Vernon Eulion, Jr., trust: Ford Foundation

Jordan, William B., III, dir: Scholl Foundation, Dr.

Joseph, Burton, chmn, dir: Playboy Foundation

Josey, Lenoir M., mgr, trust: Favrot Fund

Joslyn, Robert B., trust: Fruehauf Foundation

Joy, Joan H., trust: Joy Family Foundation

Joy, Paul W., trust, don: Joy Family Foundation

Joy, Stephen T., trust: Joy Family Foundation

Joy Reinhold, Paula, trust: Joy Family Foundation

Joy Sullivan, Marsha, trust: Joy Family Foundation

Joyce, Bernard F., vp, secy, dir: Link, Jr. Foundation, George

Joyroe, Jane, vp, trust: Sarkeys Foundation

Juetten, George H., vp, mem contribution comm: Dresser Industries, Inc.

Jurzykowski, M. Christine, secy, treas, trust: Jurzykowski Foundation, Alfred

Jurzykowski, Yolande, exec vp, trust: Jurzykowski Foundation, Alfred

Justice, Larry, dir: Porter Testamentary Trust, James Hyde

K

Kabacinski, Mary M., vp, treas: Marquette Electronics, Inc.; treas: Marquette Electronics Foundation

Kabbani, Raja, dir: Bobst Foundation, Elmer and Mamdouha

Kacher, Phyllis Okada, dir mktg: Amfac/JMB Hawaii Inc.

Kaemmer, Arthur W., M.D., vp: Mahadh Foundation

Kaemmer, Martha H., vp: Mahadh Foundation

Kahle, Shann, vp corp aff: Kmart Corporation

Kahn, Joan F., trust: Freed Foundation

Kahn, Michael, pres, dir: Reynolds Foundation, Christopher

Kahn, Richard D., asst secy, dir: Barker Foundation, J.M.R.

Kai, Gary K., dir: First Hawaiian Foundation

Kaiser, Ferdinand C., vp, secy, trust: Arkell Hall Foundation

Kaku, Ryuzaburo, chmn: Canon U.S.A., Inc.

Kalb, Bettie A., vp, trust: Wildermuth Foundation, E. F.

Kalis, David B., vp commun: International Business Machines Corp.; dir: RJR Nabisco Foundation

Kalish, Katherine M., dir: Porter Testamentary Trust, James Hyde

Kalisman, Gayle T., pres: Taubman Foundation, A. Alfred

Kallok, Michael John, dir, chmn (ed comm): Medtronic Foundation

Kaltenbacher, Philip D., trust: Seton Co. Foundation

Kamen, Harry Paul, chmn, ceo: Metropolitan Life Insurance Co.

Kametches, Chris L., sr vp: Fieldcrest Cannon Inc.; vp, dir: Fieldcrest Cannon Foundation

Kamimura, Jiro, chmn, ceo: Aristech Chemical Corp.; trust: Aristech Foundation

Kamimura, Tetsuo, chmn bd: Mitsubishi International Corp. Foundation

Kamprath, Stanley, vp, exec dir: Johnson Foundation, Helen K. and Arthur E.

Kane, Alice Theresa, exec vp, gen couns, secy: New York Life Insurance Co.; dir: New York Life Foundation

Kane, Charles J., dir: HCA Foundation

Kane, John F., treas: Lyon Foundation

Kangisser, Dianne, vp, exec dir, trust: Bowne Foundation, Robert

Kann, Peter Robert, chmn, ceo, publ, dir: Dow Jones & Company, Inc.; mem adv comm: Dow Jones Foundation

Kanne, Frank J., Jr., trust: Helms Foundation

Kaplan, Burton B., dir: Pick, Jr. Fund, Albert

Kaplan, Helene Lois, trust: Getty Trust, J. Paul; dir, mem fin & admin comm: Carnegie Corporation of New York

Kaplan, Louis L., exec vp: Meyerhoff Fund, Joseph

Kaplan, Martin S., trust: Germeshausen Foundation, Kenneth J.

Kaplan, Mary E., vp, trust: Kaplan Fund, J. M.

Kaplan, Myran J., trust: Jarson-Stanley and Mickey

Kaplan Foundation, Isaac and Esther

Kaplan, Renee, dir: Amado Foundation, Maurice

Kaplan, Richard D., co-chmn, trust: Kaplan Fund, J. M.

Kaplan, Richard J., dir grants mgmt, res and information: MacArthur Foundation, John D. and Catherine T.

Kaplan, Stanley Meisel, trust: Jarson-Stanley and Mickey Kaplan Foundation, Isaac and Esther

Kapnick, Joanne, dir pub aff: Andersons, The

Karaba, Frank Andrew, trust: Caestecker Foundation, Charles and Marie

Karageorge, Gus, intl communs specialist: Rhone-Poulenc Inc.

Kardon, Emanuel S., pres, trust: Kardon Foundation, Samuel and Rebecca

Karpen, John, vp human resources: Illinois Tool Works, Inc.; dir: Illinois Tool Works Foundation

Karr, Howard Henry, treas, dir: First Hawaiian Foundation

Karter, Elias M., mem gov comm: Mead Corp. Foundation

Kassel, Sylvia, dir: Schwartz Fund for Education and Health Research, Arnold and Marie

Katchadourian, Herant, MD, dir: Hewlett Foundation, William and Flora

Katigan, Carrie McCune, mem dispensing comm: McCune Charitable Trust, John R.

Katke, Harleen, admin, trust: First Interstate Bank of Oregon Charitable Foundation

Kaufman, Charles B., secy: Wahlstrom Foundation

Kaufman, Frank Albert, dir: Hecht-Levi Foundation

Kaufman, Frank Joseph, vp, dir: McGraw-Hill Foundation

Kaufman, Jacob B., trust, pres: Rabb Foundation, Harry W.

Kaufman, James, secy: Neuberger Foundation, Roy R. and Marie S.

Kaufman, Ron, dir: Osher Foundation, Bernard

Kaufmann, Barbara W., dir: Minnesota Mining & Mfg. Co.

Kavanagh, Thomas E., trust: Kavanagh Foundation, T. James

Kavanaugh, John T., vp, trust: Beazley Foundation/Frederick Foundation

Kay, Herma Hill, dir: Rosenberg Foundation

Kayajan, John M., dir: Kelley and Elza Kelley Foundation, Edward Bangs

Kayser, Kraig H., pres, ceo: Seneca Foods Corp.; pres, ceo, dir: Seneca Foods Foundation

Kaze, Barbara, program off: Weingart Foundation

Kean, Thomas H., trust: Carnegie Corporation of New York

Kearney, R. Wynn, Jr., trust: Hickory Tech Corp. Foundation

Kearns, David Todd, trust: Ford Foundation

Kearns, Joseph James, vp, treas: Getty Trust, J. Paul

Keast, Colleen D., exec dir: Whirlpool Foundation

Keating, Kevin, treas: Pfizer Foundation

Keating, Veronica T., treas, dir: Public Welfare Foundation

Keatts, Harry, dir: Osceola Foundation

Keck, John, trust: Hachar Charitable Trust, D. D.

Kedrowski, Leonard W., asst treas, dir: Andersen Foundation

Kee, Mrs. John L., Jr., trust: Davis Foundations, Arthur Vining

Kee, William G., trust: Davis Foundations, Arthur Vining

Keedy, Phil, pres: Rieke Corp.

Keefe, Pamela B., trust: Humphrey Fund, George M. and Pamela S.

Keegan, John P., secy: Beck Foundation, Elsie E. and Joseph W.

Keeler, John M., dir: Hoyt Foundation, Stewart W. and Willma C.

Keenan, Julie A., exec dir: Schumann Fund for New Jersey

Keeney, Edmund Ludlow, MD, med adv: Copley Foundation, James S.

Keesee, Christian Kirkpatrick, vp, dir: Kirkpatrick Foundation

Kegerreis, Robert James, trust: Tait Foundation, Frank M.

Kehrl, Howard H., trust: Sloan Foundation, Alfred P.

Keil, Jeffrey Craig, pres, dir: Republic NY Corp.

Keiser, Ann T., mgr fin admin: Davis Foundation, Irene E. and George A.

Keith, Garnett Lee, Jr., vchmn: Prudential Insurance Co. of America, The

Keith, Robert Drake, pres, dir: Arkansas Power & Light Co.

Kelleher, Paul F., trust: Thermo Electron Foundation

Keller, Phillip, vp, dir: Mielke Family Foundation

Keller, Rayford L., pres, dir: Overlake Foundation

Keller, Thomas L., vp, treas: Overlake Foundation

Kelley, Donald E., trust: Rieke Corp. Foundation

Kelley, Gaynor N., chmn, ceo, dir: Perkin-Elmer Corp.

Kelley, John C., Jr., exec vp, group mgr: First Tennessee Bank

Kelley, Ruth B., dir: Kelley and Elza Kelley Foundation, Edward Bangs

Kelling, Gilbert V., Jr., secy: Gallagher Family Foundation, Lewis P.

Kellstrom, Donna, vp, exec asst to ceo: Comerica Incorporated

Kelly, Albert S., Jr., pres: Massengill-DeFriece Foundation

Kelly, Arthur L., dir: Kelly Foundation, T. Lloyd

Kelly, Daniel J., trust off: Hillcrest Foundation; trust off: Sturgis Charitable and Educational Trust, Roy and Christine

Kelly, Edward J., chmn bd, trust: Retirement Research Foundation

Kelly, Eileen I., dir: Kelly Foundation

Kelly, James Patrick, Jr., trust: Pittsburgh Child Guidance Foundation

Kelly, John J., treas, dir: Hook Drug Foundation

Kelly, Joy, dir: Kelly Foundation

Kelly, L. Patrick, pres: Kelly Tractor Co.; dir: Kelly Foundation

Kelly, Loyd G., chmn, dir: Kelly Tractor Co.; vp, dir: Kelly Foundation

Kelly, Marjorie H., dir: Kelly Foundation

Kelly, Nancy J., comptr: Culpeper Foundation, Charles E.

Kelly, Nick, dir: Kelly Foundation

Kelly, Paul Edward, Jr., dir: Superior-Pacific Fund, Inc.

Kelly, Raymond B., III, vp, secy, dir: Scott Foundation, William F.

Kelly, Robert W., pres, dir: Kelly Foundation

Kelly, Robert W., Jr., dir: Kelly Foundation

Kelson, Richard B., dir: Alcoa Foundation

Kemper, David Woods, II, chmn, pres, ceo, dir: Commerce Bancshares, Inc.

Kemper, James Scott, Jr., hon chmn: Kemper Foundation, James S.

Kemper, Talfourd H., secy, treas: Carter Foundation, Beirne

Kempner, Carl L., treas, trust: Erpf Fund, Armand G.

Kempner, Hetta Ellen Towler, trust: Kempner Fund, Harris and Eliza

Kenan, Frank H., trust emeritus: Duke Endowment

Kenan, Thomas Stephen, III, trust: Duke Endowment

Kendrick, William J., vp pub aff: Air Products and Chemicals, Inc.; chmn: Air Products Foundation

Kennan, Christopher J., dir: Rockefeller Fund, David

Kennedy, Bruce C., trust: Van Wert County Foundation

Kennedy, George D., trust: Kemper Foundation, James S.

Kennedy, Jack E., dir: Hewit Family Foundation

Kennedy, Jean, trust: Mascoma Savings Bank Foundation

Kennedy, Nancy C., trust: Yeager Charitable Trust, Lester E.

Kennedy, Parker S., trust: Jones Foundation, Fletcher

Kennedy, Theodore C., chmn, dir: BE&K Inc.; trust: BE&K Foundation

Kenney, Richard John, dir: Consolidated Papers Foundation, Inc.

Kenny, John J., secy, treas, trust: Loews Foundation

Kent, Wendel, mem admin comm: Selby and Marie Selby Foundation, William G.

Kenyon, Alfred K., pres, coo: Kemper National Insurance Cos.

Kenyon, Robert W., mem distribution comm: Champlin Foundations

Keough, J. David, asst treas: Texaco Foundation

Kerlin, Gilbert, secy, mem exec & fin comms, dir: Dodge Foundation, Cleveland H.

Kota, Leslie, mgr commun aff: Kmart Corporation

Kotthaus, Kim M., secy: Beloit Foundation

Kovacevich, Richard M., pres, ceo: Norwest Corporation; dir: Norwest Foundation

Kovats, Ann Mize, dir: Muchnic Foundation

Koven, Joan F., secy, treas, dir: Marpat Foundation

Kovler, Everett, pres: Blum-Kovler Foundation

Kovler, H. Jonathan, pres, dir: Blum Foundation, Harry and Maribel G.; treas: Blum-Kovler Foundation

Kovler, Peter, dir: Blum Foundation, Harry and Maribel G.; asst secy: Blum-Kovler Foundation

Kowert, Marie F., asst secy: Steele Foundation, Harry and Grace

Kozlowski, J. A., asst secy: Chrysler Corporation Fund

Kraft, John F., Jr., vp, trust: Laurel Foundation

Krain, Leon J., treas: General Motors Foundation

Kramarsky, Sarah-Ann, secy: Schiff Foundation, Dorothy

Kramer, Irwin H., vp: Allen Brothers Foundation

Kramer, Joel Roy, pres: Cowles Media Co.; dir: Cowles Media Foundation

Kramer, Lawrence I., Jr., exec dir: Lux Foundation, Miranda

Krames, Michael, chmn exec comm: Kaye, Scholer, Fierman, Hays & Handler

Krannich, Beverly Turner, vp, secy: Sonat Inc.; pres: Sonat Foundation

Krantzer, Robert, treas: Glosser Foundation, David A.

Krasne, Hale S., trust: Steinman Foundation, James Hale

Kraus, John P., trust: Anderson Foundation

Krause, Jeffrey M., contact: General Motors Foundation

Krause, Jim L., asst treas: Mott Foundation, Charles Stewart

Kravis, Henry R., dir: RJR Nabisco Foundation

Kreager, Carol, dir: Wisconsin Power & Light Foundation, Inc.

Krebs, Robert Duncan, chmn, pres, ceo: Santa Fe Pacific Corporation

Kreider, Esther S., dir, fdr daughter: Sunnen Foundation

Kreindler, Peter Michael, sr vp, gen couns: AlliedSignal Inc.; pres, dir: AlliedSignal Foundation Inc.

Kreitler, Hobart C., pres: Kreitler Foundation

Kreitler, James S., dir: Kreitler Foundation

Kreitler, John M., dir: Kreitler Foundation

Kreitler, Karen R., dir: Kreitler Foundation

Kreitler, Sally S., secy: Kreitler Foundation

Kreitler, Thomas, vp: Kreitler Foundation

Kreps, Juanita Morris, trust: Duke Endowment

Kresge, Bruce Anderson, vp, trust: Kresge Foundation

Kresky, Edward M., dir: Greenwall Foundation

Kress, Eleanor D., admin, vp: Badgeley Residuary Charitable Trust, Rose M.

Kresse, Robert J., secy, trust: Wendt Foundation, Margaret L.

Kressley, Larry, exec dir: Public Welfare Foundation

Kretschmar, Lanie, coordinator: Dexter Corp. Foundation

Kreutz, Charles B., dir: Priddy Foundation

Krinsky, Josephine B., trust: Parshelsky Foundation, Moses L.

Krinsky, Robert Daniel, trust: Parshelsky Foundation, Moses L.

Krivsky, William A., dir: Bird Corp. Charitable Foundation

Kroes, Leo P., cfo: Chesebrough-Pond's USA Co.

Kroll, Paula M., pres, dir: Crabtree & Evelyn Foundation

Krommenacker, David, dir: Consolidated Papers Foundation, Inc.

Krone, Bruce A., secy, trust: Dater Foundation, Charles H.

Krone, Paul W., pres, trust: Dater Foundation, Charles H.

Kruch, Elinor, trust: Heckscher Foundation for Children

Krueger, Harvey M., trust: Barry Foundation

Krug, Eleanor C., trust: Toms Foundation

Kruidenier, Elizabeth Stuart, trust: Cowles Foundation, Gardner and Florence Call

Krukowski, Francis V., pres: Price Foundation, Lucien B. and Katherine E.

Krull, Margaret, chmn contributions comm: Cable & Wireless Holdings, Inc.

Krzos, Joseph T., secy, dir: Madison Gas & Electric Foundation

Kucharski, Robert Joseph, vp, secy: IES Industries, Inc.; secy, treas: IES Industries Charitable Foundation

Kuehn, Henry, trust: Graham Foundation for Advanced Studies in the Fine Arts

Kuehn, Ronald L., Jr., chmn, pres, ceo, dir: Sonat Inc.

Kuhn, Jim, dir: Berger Foundation, H. N. and Frances C.

Kuhrtz, Steve, mem contributions comm: GATX Corp.

Kulp, Jill Clemens, trust: Clemens Foundation

Kump, Marsha A., exec dir: Whiting Foundation

Kunce, Marquita L., asst treas: Olin Foundation, Spencer T. and Ann W.

Kundert, David Jon, vp, dir: Banc One Wisconsin Foundation

Kunisch, Robert Dietrich, chmn, pres, ceo: PHH Corporation; chmn, dir: PHH Foundation, Inc.

Kunkel, W. Minster, trust: Kunkel Foundation, John Crain

Kuntz, Jean M., trust: Harmon Foundation, Pearl M. and Julia J.

Kuntzman, Ronald G., trust: Hoffmann-La Roche Foundation

Kunz, Daniel J., dir: Morrison Knudsen Corporation Foundation

Kunzman, Edward D., pres: Schwartz Foundation, Arnold A.

Kunzman, Steven, secy, treas: Schwartz Foundation, Arnold A.

Kupferberg, Max, dir: Vogler Foundation, Laura B.

Kuprionis, M. Denise, secy: Scripps Howard Foundation

Kurczewski, Walter W., vp, secy, gen couns: Square D Co.; pres, dir: Square D Foundation

Kurtz, Melvin H., vp, dir, secy, gen couns: Chesebrough-Pond's USA Co.; secy, dir: Chesebrough Foundation

Kurtz, Samuel B., dir: Lebanon Mutual Foundation

Kurtz, Samuel G., chmn, dir: Lebanon Mutual Insurance Co.; dir: Lebanon Mutual Foundation

Kurzman, H. Michael, vp, dir: Lurie Foundation, Louis R.

Kurzman, Jayne M., couns: Fuld Health Trust, Helene

Kusche, William R., dir: Rixson Foundation, Oscar C.

Kushen, Allan Stanford, pres: Schering-Plough Foundation

Kushen, Ivan, treas: Goodstein Family Foundation, David

Kushen, Marilyn, vp, dir: Goodstein Family Foundation, David

Kushlan, Paula Frohring, trust: Frohring Foundation, Paul and Maxine

Kuth, Dean, vp: LEF Foundation

Kuth, Lyda Ebert, secy, cfo: LEF Foundation

L

La Boon, Robert Bruce, vp: Kayser Foundation

Labahn, Maryann W., vp, treas, dir: Ross Memorial Foundation, Will

Labanowski, Elizabeth J., trust: Enron Foundation

Labaree, Frances L., dir: Overbrook Foundation

Labaree, Robert, dir: Overbrook Foundation

Labin, Emanuel, vp: Benenson Foundation, Frances and Benjamin

Labosky, Bonnie, dir, mem health comm: Medtronic Foundation

Labrato, Ronnie R., secy: Gulf Power Foundation

Labrecque, Thomas Goulet, chmn, ceo, dir: Chase Manhattan Bank, N.A.; pres: Chase Manhattan Foundation

Labutka, Carolyn E., dir: AON Foundation

Lackey, John, trust: Centralia Foundation

Lackey, S. Allen, dir: Shell Oil Company Foundation

Lackland, David, trust: Schwartz Foundation, Arnold A.

Lacy, Benjamin H., treas, dir: NEBS Foundation

Ladd, Edward, trust: Forster Charitable Trust, James W. and Ella B.

Ladd, George E., III, dir: Ladd Charitable Corporation, Helen and George

Ladd, Lincoln F., dir: Ladd Charitable Corporation, Helen and George

Ladd, Robert M., dir: Ladd Charitable Corporation, Helen and George

Ladds, Herbert P., Jr., dir: Utica National Group Foundation

Ladehoff, Leo William, chmn, ceo, dir: Amcast Industrial Corp.; pres, trust: Amcast Industrial Foundation

Ladish, John H., trust: Armco Foundation

Lafferty, Frederick W., exec dir: France Foundation, Jacob and Annita

Lafollette, Patricia A., pub aff asst: Brown & Williamson Tobacco Corp.

LaFond, Laura J. Van Evera, co-trust: Van Evera Foundation, Dewitt

LaFreniere, Norma B., secy distribution comm: Champlin Foundations

Lagomasino, Maria Elena, trust: Chase Manhattan Foundation

Laird, Melvin Robert, dir: Wallace-Reader's Digest Fund, DeWitt; dir: Wallace-Reader's Digest Fund, Lila

Laird, Walter J., Jr., dir: Glencoe Foundation

Laitman, Nanette L., secy, treas: Lasdon Foundation, William and Mildred

Lake, Carolyn, admin: Cranston Print Works Company; admin: Cranston Foundation

Lake, Timothy, trust: Wyomissing Foundation

Lamade, Howard, dir: LamCo. Foundation

Lamade, J. Robert, dir: LamCo. Foundation

Lamade, James S., dir: LamCo. Foundation

LaMantia, Charles Robert, pres, ceo, dir: Little, Inc., Arthur D.

Lamb, Dorothy, dir: OCRI Foundation

Lamb, F. Gilbert, treas, dir: OCRI Foundation

Lamb, Frank, dir: OCRI Foundation

Lamb, Helen, secy, dir: OCRI Foundation

Lamb, Isabelle, dir: Bishop Foundation, E. K. and Lillian F.

Lamb, Joseph P., secy: Mohasco Foundation

Lamb, Maryann, dir: OCRI Foundation

Lamb, Paula L., vchmn, dir: OCRI Foundation

Lamb, Peter, dir: OCRI Foundation

Lambe, James F., sr vp human resources: Nalco Chemical Co.; dir: Nalco Foundation

Lamberg, Harold, pres: Reicher Foundation, Anne and Harry J.

Lambert, Samuel Waldron, III, pres, trust: Bunbury Company; vp, trust: Windham Foundation

Lambert, Sandra L., trust: Thermo Electron Foundation

Lamblin, Wendell, chmn: Centralia Foundation

Lancaster, Robert Charles, sr vp, cfo: Bowater Incorporated

Lancaster, Rose C., trust, mem contributions comm: Trull Foundation

Lancaster, Ruth, treas: Mingenback Foundation, Julia J.

Lancaster, Sally R., PhD, trust, dir: Meadows Foundation

Land, Edwin Herbert, don, pres, trust: Rowland Foundation

Land, Helen Maislen, vp, treas, trust: Rowland Foundation

Land, Lillie S., secy, dir: duPont Foundation, Alfred I.

Landegger, Carl Clement, treas, dir: Landegger Charitable Foundation

Landegger, George Francis, pres, dir: Landegger Charitable Foundation

Landers, Joseph L., Jr., asst secy: Rand McNally Foundation

Landes, Robert Nathan, vp, dir: McGraw-Hill Foundation

Landes, Stephanie, trust: Philibosian Foundation, Stephen

Landesman, Rocco, trust: Ettinger Foundation

Landin, Thomas Milton, vp: Norton Co. Foundation

Landman, Carole, trust: Heckscher Foundation for Children

Landon, Gardner F., dir: Lake Placid Education Foundation

Landry, Edward A., trust: Thornton Foundation, Flora L.

Landry, Lawrence L., vp, cfo: MacArthur Foundation, John D. and Catherine T.

Lane, Joan F., dir: Irvine Foundation, James

Lane, Nancy Wolfe, vp: Wolfe Associates, Inc.

Lane, R. W., mem gov comm: Mead Corp. Foundation

Lane, Richard, pres: Merck & Co. Human Health Division

Lang, David, trust: Lang Foundation, Eugene M.

Lang, Eugene Michael, don, trust: Lang Foundation, Eugene M.

Lang, Jane, trust: Lang Foundation, Eugene M.

Lang, Margaret A., vp, dir: Overbrook Foundation

Lang, Robert Todd, chmn, dir: Weil, Gotshal and Manges Foundation

Lang, Stephen, trust: Lang Foundation, Eugene M.

Lang, Theresa, trust: Lang Foundation, Eugene M.

Langdon, George Dorland, Jr., dir: Kresge Foundation

Lange, Beverly J., contact: Anderson Foundation

Langenberg, Donald Newton, trust: Sloan Foundation, Alfred P.

Langfitt, Thomas W., MD, dir: Pew Charitable Trusts

Langford, J. Beverly, treas, trust: Ratner Foundation, Milton M.

Langford, Thomas A., trust: Duke Endowment

Langner, Jay B., trust: Mailman Family Foundation, A. L.

Langstaff, Carol, dir: Guggenheim Foundation, Harry Frank

Lanigan, Joanne, trust: Blowitz-Ridgeway Foundation

Lansing, John S., exec dir: Lake Placid Education Foundation

Larance, Charles L., vp corp rels: General American Life Insurance Co.; pres: General American Charitable Foundation

Larkin, Frank Y., vchmn, dir: Noble Foundation, Edward John

Larkin, June Noble, chmn, pres, dir: Noble Foundation, Edward John

LaRocca, Robert J., vp: Independence Foundation

LaRoche, Elaine, trust: Morgan Stanley Foundation

Larry, Richard M., dir: McKenna Foundation, Philip M.

Larsen, Christopher, vp, dir: Larsen Fund

Larsen, Jonathan Zerbe, secy, dir: Larsen Fund

Larsen, Marianne, mgr contribution programs: International Paper Co. Foundation

Larsen, Robert R., pres, dir: Larsen Fund

Larson, Carl E., vp: Julia R. and Estelle L. Foundation

Larson, Jennifer, trust: Saroyan Foundation, William

Larson, Marie, secy, dir: Offield Family Foundation

Larson, Richard, pres, dir: Brillion Foundation

LaRue, Mary, chp contributions comm: Berwind Corporation

Lary, Jacqueline A., trust: Mascoma Savings Bank Foundation

Lasdon, Gene S., vp, dir: Lasdon Foundation

Lasdon, Jeffrey S., vp, dir: Lasdon Foundation

Lasdon, Mildred D., vp, dir: Lasdon Foundation; pres: Lasdon Foundation, William and Mildred

Lashley, Eleanor H., dir: Huston Foundation

Laske, A. C., Jr., treas, dir: Morris Foundation, William T.

Lasker, Joan, vp corp pub rels: Cosmair, Inc.

Lassalle, Nancy Norman, vp, secy: Normandie Foundation

Lathan, Roger D., dir: Schmitt Foundation, Kilian J. and Caroline F.

Lathem, Edward, dir: Dr. Seuss Foundation

Latiolais, Rene Louis, pres, coo, dir: Freeport-McMoRan Inc.

Latzer, Richard Neal, vp, dir: TransAmerica Foundation

Laube, F. H., III, pres: Freeport Brick Co.; chmn: Freeport Brick Co. Charitable Trust

Laube, Harry R., asst secy, asst treas: Freeport Brick Co. Charitable Trust

Laubenstein, John R., asst secy: Amoco Foundation

Lauck, Joseph, dir: Lebanon Mutual Foundation

Lauder, Estee, pres: Lauder Foundation

Lauder, Leonard Alan, secy-treas: Lauder Foundation

Lauder, Ronald Stephen, vp: Lauder Foundation

Lauderbach, C. Ward, dir: Wickson-Link Memorial Foundation

Lauer, Robert L., sr vp: Sara Lee Corp.; pres, dir: Sara Lee Foundation

Laughlin, Alexander Mellon, trust: Hartford Foundation, John A.

Lauren, Charles B., trust: Hagedorn Fund

Laurie, Marilyn, sr vp pub rels & employee commun: AT&T Corp.; chmn, trust: AT&T Foundation

Lautenbach, Terry Robert, trust: Air Products Foundation

Lavelle, James C., vp, dir: Banc One Wisconsin Foundation

Lavergne, Rosa N., trust: Bowne Foundation, Robert

Lavis, Stella Amado, pres, dir: Amado Foundation, Maurice

Lavis, Victor R., dir: Amado Foundation, Maurice

LaVoie, Ray, dir, mem health comm: Medtronic Foundation

Law, D. Brian, dir: Kantzler Foundation

Lawin, Bruce A., pres: Specialty Manufacturing Co.; treas: Boss Foundation, William

Lawrence, Anne, dir: Gap Foundation

Lawrence, Anne I., trust: Ingalls Foundation, Louise H. and David S.

Lawrence, Barbara Childs, pres: AKC Fund

Lawrence, J. Vinton, dir: AKC Fund

Lawrence, Pauline W., trust: Meyer Memorial Trust

Lawrence, Richard Wesley, Jr., pres, trust: Crary Foundation, Bruce L.

Lawrence, Robert Ashton, trust: Saltonstall Charitable Foundation, Richard

Lawrence, Sull, secy, dir: Pickford Foundation, Mary

Lawrence, Warren, dir: Vicksburg Foundation

Lawrenz, Ruthmarie, dir: Schroeder Foundation, Walter

Laws, Don P., mem adv comm: Blue Bell Foundation

Lawson-Johnston, Peter Orman, chmn, dir: Guggenheim Foundation, Harry Frank

Lawton, Barbara P., trust: Gaylord Foundation, Clifford Willard

Laybourne, Everett Broadstone, vp, dir: Parsons Foundation, Ralph M.

Layman, Sandy, trust: Blandin Foundation

Lazarof, Janice Anne, vp, treas, dir: Taper Foundation, Mark

Lazarus, Charles, trust: Lazarus Charitable Trust, Helen and Charles

Lazarus, Leonard, secy: Solow Foundation

Le Buhn, Robert, pres, trust: Dodge Foundation, Geraldine R.

Le Feber, Marilyn Stein, assoc vp: Retirement Research Foundation

Le Grand, Clay, trust: Carver Charitable Trust, Roy J.

Lea, Anna, dir, vp: Lea Foundation, Helen Sperry

Lea, Helena, dir, vp: Lea Foundation, Helen Sperry

Lea, R. Brooke, II, dir, vp: Lea Foundation, Helen Sperry

Lea, Sperry, dir, pres, treas: Lea Foundation, Helen Sperry

Leach, Phillip M., exec dir, trust: Temple Foundation, T. L. L.

Leahy, Richard, trust: Peabody Charitable Fund, Amelia

Leahy, Robert D., vp corp rels: Bowater Incorporated

Leath, Berneice R., secy, treas, dir: Priddy Foundation

Leatherdale, Douglas West, chmn, pres, ceo: Saint Paul Companies, Inc.

Leavey, Dorothy E., don, trust: Leavey Foundation, Thomas and Dorothy

Leavey, Joseph James, trust: Leavey Foundation, Thomas and Dorothy

LeBeau, Bernard G., dir: Imperial Bank Foundation

Lebedoff, Randy Miller, asst secy: Cowles Media Co.; secy, dir: Cowles Media Foundation

LeBlanc, Michael, trust: Polaroid Foundation

LeBoeuf, Raymond W., vp, dir: PPG Industries Foundation

Lebovitz, Clara H., pres: Lebovitz Fund

Lebovitz, Herbert C., treas: Lebovitz Fund

Lebovitz, James, dir: Lebovitz Fund

Lederer, Adrienne, vp, dir: Lederer Foundation, Francis L.

Lederer, Francis L., II, pres, treas, dir: Lederer Foundation, Francis L.

Ledgett, Ronald A., sr vp power delivery: Boston Edison Co.; trust: Boston Edison Foundation

Lee, Dwight E., vp, dir: Barker Foundation, J.M.R.

Lee, Greg, sr vp, human resources: Saint Paul Companies, Inc.

Lee, Homer W., treas, trust: Wildermuth Foundation, E. F.

Lee, Joe R., vchmn, ceo of Darden: General Mills, Inc.; trust: General Mills Foundation

Lee, Robert E., sr vp, coo: Hanson Industries North America; vp, treas: Hanson White Foundation

Lee, Robert W., trust: Wildermuth Foundation, E. F.

Legner, Theresa M., mgr pension & savings: Mosinee Paper Corp.; asst secy: Mosinee Paper Corp. Foundation

Lehman, Edward, trust: Boettcher Foundation

Lehman, Jackson R., chmn, ceo, dir: Fort Wayne National Bank

Lehnhart, Rev. M. H., secy, trust: Johnson Foundation, M. G. and Lillie A.

Lehr, Ronald L., trust: Johnson Foundation, Helen K. and Arthur E.

Lehr, William N., Jr., sr vp, secy, assoc gen couns: Hershey Foods Corp.

Lehrkind, Carl, III, dir: MPCo/Entech Foundation

Leiberman, Patricia S., trust: Mailman Family Foundation, A. L.

Leibrock, Robert M., pres, trust: Abell-Hanger Foundation

Leick, Frederick W., pres, ceo: Seneca Foods Corp.

Leighton, Judd C., secy, treas, dir: Leighton-Oare Foundation

Leighton, Mary Morris, pres, dir: Leighton-Oare Foundation

Leininger, Joan E., dir commun programs: Georgia-Pacific Foundation

Leitch, Daniel, III, pres, ceo, dir: American General Finance Corp.; chmn, ceo, pres: American General Finance Foundation

Leman, Eugene D., dir: IBP Foundation, Inc., The

LeMieux, Linda J., trust: Whiting Foundation

Lemke, Carl R., secy: Consolidated Papers Foundation, Inc.

Lemole, Daniel A., asst secy: Continental Corp. Foundation

Lemon, Clinton, trust: Fuller Foundation, C. G.

Lemons, Wishard, trust: Broadhurst Foundation

Lenczuk, Kimberly Duchossois, pres: Duchossois Foundation

Lenhart, Carole S., treas: Beveridge Foundation, Frank Stanley

Lenkowsky, Leslie, PhD, trust: Achelis Foundation; trust: Bodman Foundation

Lenna, Elizabeth S., dir: Lenna Foundation, Reginald A. and Elizabeth S.

Lenna, Reginald A., dir: Lenna Foundation, Reginald A. and Elizabeth S.

Lennartz, Ann F., vp, dir: Kuyper Foundation, Peter H. and E. Lucille

Lennon, A. P., vp: Lennon Foundation, Fred A.

Lennon, Fred A., pres: Lennon Foundation, Fred A.

Lentz, Hover T., vchmn, trust: Boettcher Foundation

Lentz, Kevin, coo: Century Companies of America

Leonard, J. Wayne, group vp, cfo: CINergy; dir: CINergy Foundation

Leonard, Kathryn, treas: Bauervic Foundation, Charles M.

Leonard, Patricia A., pres, secy: Bauervic Foundation, Charles M.

Leonard, Theodore J., dir: Bauervic Foundation, Charles M.

Leonard, Timothy J., dir: Bauervic Foundation, Charles M.

Leongomez, Carol W., secy, trust: Chatlos Foundation

Lepak, Robert R., trust: Davis Foundation, Irene E. and George A.

Lerchen, Edward H., trust: Kresge Foundation

Lerner, Irwin, chmn, dir: Hoffmann-La Roche Inc.; trust: Hoffmann-La Roche Foundation

Leschley, Jan, chmn: SmithKline Beecham Corp.

Leser, Lawrence Arthur, chmn, ceo: Scripps Co., E.W.; mem: Scripps Howard Foundation

Lesilinski, Dean A., exec dir: Gifford Charitable Corporation, Rosamond

Lesley, J. Kenneth, vp personnel & pub rels: Burlington Industries, Inc.; trust: Burlington Industries Foundation

Leslie, Gaylord E., trust: Van Wert County Foundation

Leslie, Marc C., legal couns: Fleet Charitable Trust

Leslie, Mary, exec dir: Telesis Foundation

Lethbridge, Caryl A., asst secy: Hyde and Watson Foundation

Leube, Helmut, trust: Lehigh Portland Cement Charitable Trust

Leuthold, Betty B., vp, trust: Leuthold Foundation

Leuthold, John H., pres, trust: Leuthold Foundation

Levan, B. W., vp, dir: Shell Oil Company Foundation

Levavy, Zvi, pres: Kaplun Foundation, Morris J. and Betty

Levering, Walter B., chmn, dir: Oaklawn Foundation

Levett, Edith, secy emerita: Greenwall Foundation

Levi, Alexander H., vp, dir: Hecht-Levi Foundation

Levi, Arlo Dane, dir: Minnesota Mining & Mfg. Co.

Levi, Richard H., vp, treas, dir: Hecht-Levi Foundation

Levi, Robert Henry, vp, dir: Hecht-Levi Foundation

Levi, Ryda H., vp, dir: Hecht-Levi Foundation

Levi, Virginia, assoc dir: Premier Industrial Foundation

Levin, Gail C., sr program off: Annenberg Foundation

Levin, Jack I., trust: Phillips Family Foundation, Jay and Rose

Levin, John, trust: Phillips Family Foundation, Jay and Rose

Levin, John P., Jr., dir: Rosenberg, Jr. Family Foundation, Louise and Claude

Levin, Suzan, trust: Phillips Family Foundation, Jay and Rose

Levine, Arnold, dir: Kaufmann Foundation, Henry

Levinson, Beatrice, secy: Fischbach Foundation

Levinson, Donald M., dir: CIGNA Corporation

Levinson, Julius, asst treas: Coltec Industries Charitable Foundation, Inc.

Levitan, David M., vp: Fink Foundation

Levitt, Arthur, Jr., emeritus: Winston Foundation, Norman and Rosita

Levy, David B., treas, dir: Rudin Foundation

Levy, Ellen White, dir: Memton Fund

Levy, Gaston Raymond, exec vp: Gillette Co.

Levy, Reynold, trust: AT&T Foundation

Levy, Susan M., secy, contributions comm: Donnelley & Sons Co., R.R.

Lewin, John, dir: Rudin Foundation

Lewis, Andrew Lindsay, Jr., chmn: Union Pacific Foundation

Lewis, C. Stephen, pres, dir: Weyerhaeuser Co.; trust: Weyerhaeuser Company Foundation

Lewis, Craig, treas, trust: Middendorf Foundation

Murphy, John Davis, chmn emeritus, dir: Wiremold Co.; pres: Wiremold Foundation

Murphy, John Joseph, chmn, ceo: Dresser Industries, Inc.; chmn: Dresser Foundation, Inc.

Murphy, Johnie W., pres, dir: Murphy Foundation

Murphy, Judith, vp, ceo: Y and H Soda Foundation

Murphy, Mark M., secy, exec dir: Fund for New Jersey

Murphy, Michael Emmett, vchmn, cfo, chief admin off: Sara Lee Corp.; dir: Sara Lee Foundation

Murphy, Robert H., vchmn emeritus, dir: Wiremold Co.; vp: Wiremold Foundation

Murphy, William J., mem adv comm: O'Connor Foundation, A. Lindsay and Olive B.

Murrah, Alfred P., Jr., vchmn, trust: Sumners Foundation, Hatton W.

Murray, Archibald R., dir: Scherman Foundation

Murray, Dennis J., dir: McCann Foundation

Murray, Diana T., dir: Markle Foundation, John and Mary R.

Murray, J. Terrance, treas, dir: Demos Foundation, N.

Murray, J. Terrence, chmn, pres, ceo: Fleet Financial Group, Inc.; mem: Fleet Charitable Trust

Murray, James E., vp: Humana Foundation

Murray, Lawrence D., Jr., trust: Mercury Aircraft Foundation

Murray, Malcolm T., Jr., dir: First Union Foundation

Murray, Robert G., exec vp: First Interstate Bank of Oregon; trust: First Interstate Bank of Oregon Charitable Foundation

Murray, William E., trust: Freeman Charitable Trust, Samuel

Murrell, Kathryn A., dir: Fireman's Fund Foundation

Murrin, Regis, trust: Pittsburgh Child Guidance Foundation

Murtagh, Robert J., trust: Booth Ferris Foundation

Murtaugh, James, program dir: Claiborne and Art Ortenberg Foundation, Liz

Musen, Ken, asst secy: ASDA Foundation

Musgrave, Colleen, secy: Matlock Foundation

Musson, Irvin J., III, trust: Musson Charitable Foundation, R. C. and Katharine M.

Musson, Irvin J., Jr., trust: Musson Charitable Foundation, R. C. and Katharine M.

Mustain, Phyllis S., dir: Burchfield Foundation, Charles E.

Mustain, Robert D., trust, secy: Burchfield Foundation, Charles E.

Mycek, Ernest S., pres, coo, dir: Cargill Inc.

Myer, David, trust: Andres Charitable Trust, Frank G.

Myers, Barbara C., mgr: Union Pacific Foundation

Myers, Charles F., Jr., trust: Duke Endowment

Myers, Emilie W., trust: Wood Foundation of Chambersburg, PA

Myers, Gertrude, trust: Share Trust, Charles Morton

Myers, Lynn H., chmn: Howe and Mitchell B. Howe Foundation, Lucille Horton

Myers, Marilyn B., dir, asst secy: Kirkpatrick Foundation

Myers, Michele Tolela, dir: Fairchild Foundation, Sherman

Myers, Roy A., exec vp, dir: Curtice-Burns Foods, Inc.

Myers, Stanley T., pres, ceo: Siltec Corp.

Myrum, Stan, chmn communs comm: Medtronic Foundation

N

Nabers, Hugh C., Jr., trust: Comer Foundation

Nackerud, Norman, ceo, pres: City National Bank and Trust Co.

Nagel, Robert D., treas: Wallace-Reader's Digest Fund, DeWitt; treas: Wallace-Reader's Digest Fund, Lila

Nagin, Lawrence M., dir: United Airlines Foundation

Nagle, James, trust: Graham Foundation for Advanced Studies in the Fine Arts

Nagy, Julia Ann, treas: Huber Foundation

Naidoff, Stephanie, dir: Penn Foundation, William

Najarian, Richard, trust: Raymond Foundation

Nalbach, Kay C., pres: Hartmarx Charitable Foundation

Nania, Anthony J., chmn, ceo: NewMil Bancorp; pres, dir: New Milford Savings Bank Foundation

Napolitan, Tony, univ grants mgr: Hewlett-Packard Co.

Nardi, Nicholas J., secy, treas: Culpeper Memorial Foundation, Daphne Seybolt

Narvarte, Rebecca, asst treas, trust: Doss Foundation, M. S.

Nasby, David Asher, vp, dir commun aff: General Mills, Inc.; vp: General Mills Foundation

Naschke, Arlene M., trust: Messing Family Charitable Foundation

Nash, Lucia S., vp, trust: Smith Foundation, Kelvin and Eleanor

Natele, Joseph P., chmn, dir: Comprecare Foundation

Nathan, Robert R., dir: Public Welfare Foundation

Nation, Robert F., trust: Harsco Corp. Fund; pres, dir: Kline Foundation, Josiah W. and Bessie H.

Naughton, John Patrick, MD, dir: Cummings Foundation, James H.

Nayak, P. Ranganath, sr vp: Little, Inc., Arthur D.; trust: Little Foundation, Arthur D.

Naylor, Phyllis, dir corp comm: Amcast Industrial Corp.; asst secy: Amcast Industrial Foundation

Nedley, Robert E., dir: duPont Foundation, Alfred I.

Neeleman, Stanley D., trust: Johnson Foundation, Helen K. and Arthur E.

Neely, Grant F., treas, trust: McFeely-Rogers Foundation

Neely, Walter Emerson, vp: Humana Foundation

Neese, Alonzo A., Jr., dir: Beloit Foundation

Neese, Elbert Haven, pres, dir: Beloit Foundation

Neese-Malik, Laura, dir: Beloit Foundation

Neff, Peter J., pres, ceo, coo, dir: Rhone-Poulenc Inc.

Negri, Richard F., secy, treas, dir: Comprecare Foundation

Nehman, Simone, secy, treas: Schwob Foundation, Simon

Neill, Arthur K., exec vp, dir: Montana Power Co.; dir: MPCo/Entech Foundation

Neilson, Phillippe Crowe, vp, asst treas: Pettus Crowe Foundation

Neimann, Diane B., exec dir: Bell Foundation, James F.

Neish, Francis E., Jr., trust: Crawford Estate, E. R.

Neisser, Edward, dir: Pick, Jr. Fund, Albert

Neithercut, Mark E., program off: Kresge Foundation

Nelb, Jeffrey J., treas, dir: Ensign-Bickford Foundation

Nelson, Charles E., dir: Kirkpatrick Foundation

Nelson, Daniel Raymond, chmn, ceo, dir: West One Bancorp

Nelson, David, vp, grant dir: Houston Endowment

Nelson, Fredric C., dir: Cowell Foundation, S. H.

Nelson, Glen David, MD, vchmn, dir: Medtronic, Inc.

Nelson, H. Joe, III, pres, dir: Houston Endowment

Nelson, Joyce, treas: International Paper Co. Foundation

Nelson, Kirk N., pres, coo: Federated Mutual Insurance Co.; vp: Federated Insurance Foundation

Nelson, Leonard B., dir: McConnell Foundation

Nelson, Nancy J., asst secy: Meadows Foundation

Nelson, R., trust: Alcon Foundation

Nelson, Steve, pub aff off: Sumitomo Bank of California

Nelson, Thomas P., sr vp, contr: General Mills, Inc.; trust: General Mills Foundation

Nelson, Wilbur, Jr., trust: Clarke Trust, John

Nelson, William D., dir: AMCORE Foundation, Inc.

Nelson, William F., Jr., trust: Wickes Foundation, Harvey Randall

Nemetz, Marion, dir: Mielke Family Foundation

Neri, Tom, trust: Chicago Sun-Times Charity Trust

Nern, Christopher C., vp, gen couns: Detroit Edison Co.; dir: Detroit Edison Foundation

Nerren, Evonne, vp: Temple-Inland Foundation

Nesholm, John F., dir: Nesholm Family Foundation

Nesholm, Laurel, exec dir: Nesholm Family Foundation

Nessier, Stephen, trust: Witter Foundation, Dean

Netzer, Leon, vchmn: Jewish Healthcare Foundation of Pittsburgh

Neuberger, James A., vp, dir: Neuberger Foundation, Roy R. and Marie S.

Neuberger, Marie S., vp, dir: Neuberger Foundation, Roy R. and Marie S.

Neuberger, Roy R., pres, treas, dir: Neuberger

Foundation, Roy R. and Marie S.

Neuberger, Roy S., vp, dir: Neuberger Foundation, Roy R. and Marie S.

Nevers, Tom, grant mgr: Bishop Foundation, E. K. and Lillian F.

Neville, James Morton, mem bd control: Ralston Purina Trust Fund

Neville, Thomas N., trust: Odell Fund, Robert Stewart Odell and Helen Pfeiffer

Nevin, John M., sr vp strategic svcs: James River Corp. of Virginia; pres: James River Corp. Foundation

Nevius, Blake Reynolds, dir: Scott Foundation, Virginia Steele

Newburger, May W., trust: Levitt Foundation

Newcomb, David R., dir: Utica National Group Foundation

Newcombe, Margaret P., trust: Knapp Foundation

Newcomer, Arthur S., secy, trust: Markey Charitable Fund, John C.

Newell, David, sr vp pub aff: First Fidelity Bank

Newhouse, Victoria, trust: Kress Foundation, Samuel H.

Newkirk, Judith A., vp, asst treas: Durfee Foundation

Newkirk, Michael A., treas: Durfee Foundation

Newman, David, trust: Arnold Fund

Newman, Gordon Harold, sr vp, secy, gen couns: Sara Lee Corp.; vp, secy: Sara Lee Foundation

Newman, Louise K., trust: Smith Charitable Foundation, Lou and Lutza

Newman, M. S., trust: Marquette Electronics Foundation

Newman, Paul L., pres: Newman's Own, Inc.; pres, dir, don: Newman's Own Foundation

Newschaffer, Tom, exec vp, cfo: First Financial Bank FSB

Newton, Charles, pres, dir: Scott Foundation, Virginia Steele

Ney, Dr. Lillian V., dir: Gebbie Foundation

Ney, Edward N., dir: Mattel Foundation

Neys, Alan, dir: Campini Foundation, Frank A.

Neys, Patricia, secy, treas: Campini Foundation, Frank A.

Ng, Henry, secy, dir: Kaplan Fund, J. M.

Nichols, Dan, trust: Centralia Foundation

Nichols, James R., trust: Babson Foundation, Paul and Edith; trust: Pierce Charitable Trust, Harold Whitworth

Nichols, John Doane, chmn, ceo: Illinois Tool Works, Inc.; trust: Illinois Tool Works Foundation

Nichols, Kate Cowles, trust: Cowles Charitable Trust

Nichols, Kenwood C., vchmn, dir: Champion International Corporation

Nichols, Marguerite S., MD, trust: Achelis Foundation; trust: Bodman Foundation

Nichols, William Ford, Jr., treas: Hewlett Foundation, William and Flora

Nickelson, Donald Eugene, trust: Jones Foundation, Fletcher

Nickerson, Brett R., dir: Scott Foundation, Walter

Nickerson, E. Carlton, dir: Kelley and Elza Kelley Foundation, Edward Bangs

Nickerson, Frank L., dir: Kelley and Elza Kelley Foundation, Edward Bangs

Nickerson, Glendon A., dir: Scott Foundation, Walter

Nickerson, Jocelyn A., vp, exec dir: Scott Foundation, Walter

Nickerson, Joshua A., Jr., dir: Kelley and Elza Kelley Foundation, Edward Bangs

Nickerson, Lisa B., dir: Scott Foundation, Walter

Nickerson, Lucille M., couns, corp secy: Aetna Life & Casualty Co.; secy: Aetna Foundation

Nickerson, Thorpe A., pres, secy, treas, dir: Scott Foundation, Walter

Nicolet, Jules, dir: Wisconsin Power & Light Foundation, Inc.

Niehaus, James R., pres, dir: Oxy USA Inc.; pres, trust: Oxy USA Charitable Foundation

Nielsen, Richard A., pres, coo, dir: Johnson & Higgins

Niemeyer, Ken, admin: Bedsole Foundation, J. L.

Niffenegger, Joyce U., trust: Hoover Foundation

Niles, Clayton E., dir, treas: Spalding Foundation, Eliot

Nimick, Francis B., Jr., chmn bd dir: Buhl Foundation

Nisen, Charles M., trust: Payne Foundation, Frank E. and Seba B.

Nixon, Dennis, trust: Hachar Charitable Trust, D. D.

Noble, Edward E., trust: Noble Foundation, Samuel Roberts

Noble, Mary Jane, trust: Noble Foundation, Samuel Roberts

Noble, Rusty, trust: Noble Foundation, Samuel Roberts

Noddle, Allen, pres, dir: Giant Food Stores

Noecker, Marshal R., pres, ceo: LamCo. Communications

Noel, Alfred C., pres, dir: Sentry Foundation Inc.

Nogales, Luis Guerrero, trust: Ford Foundation

Nogawa, K., cfo: Fujitsu America, Inc.

Nohl, Jeff, vp: Blue Cross & Blue Shield United of Wisconsin Foundation

Nolan, Arthur A., Jr., pres, dir: Rice Foundation

Nolan, Patricia, vp, treas, dir: Rice Foundation

Nolan, Peter, vp, dir, secy: Rice Foundation

Noonan, James W., secy, trust: Levy Foundation, June Rockwell

Nordberg, Linda C., mgr: Thermo Electron Foundation

Norden, William B., Esq., secy, counc, dir: Olin Foundation, F. W.

Nordlof, Richard, dir: AMCORE Foundation, Inc.

Norgren, Donald K., trust: Norgren Foundation, Carl A.

Norgren, Leigh H., pres, treas, trust: Norgren Foundation, Carl A.

Norman, Andrew E., pres, treas: Normandie Foundation

Page, David A., dir: Kresge Foundation

Page, David Keith, dir: Kresge Foundation

Page, Pilar M., vp: PHH Foundation, Inc.

Page, Robert A., vp, cfo: Packaging Corporation of America

Page, Thomas Alexander, chmn, pres, ceo: San Diego Gas & Electric

Paight, Audrey S., treas, asst secy, dir: Oaklawn Foundation

Paine, Andrew J., Jr., vchmn: NBD Indiana, Inc.

Paine, Peter S., adv trust: Astor Foundation, Vincent

Paine, Walter C., dir: Phillips Foundation, Ellis L.

Painter, Alan S., vp, exec dir: AlliedSignal Foundation Inc.

Pakula, Randall H., dir: Utica National Group Foundation

Palazzo, Anthony J., vp textile oper: Cranston Print Works Company; trust: Cranston Foundation

Palenchar, David J., vp (programs): El Pomar Foundation

Paley, Kate C., dir: Paley Foundation, William S.

Paley, William Cushing, vp, dir: Paley Foundation, William S.

Palisano, Charles J., trust: Palisano Foundation, Vincent and Harriet

Palisano, Joseph S., trust: Palisano Foundation, Vincent and Harriet

Pallotti, Marianne Marguerite, vp, corp secy: Hewlett Foundation, William and Flora

Palmer, Joseph Beveridge, dir: Beveridge Foundation, Frank Stanley

Palmer, L. Guy, II, mem bd dirs, mem investment comm: Dana Foundation, Charles A.

Palmer, Patricia S., grants admin: Larsen Fund

Palmer, Robert B., pres, ceo, dir, chmn: Digital Equipment Corp.

Palmieri, Peter C., vchmn, chief credit off: First Fidelity Bank

Palmore, B. B., dir: Fair Foundation, R. W.

Palumbo, Lillian, trust: Snyder Foundation, Harold B. and Dorothy A.

Pampusch, Anita M., dir: Bush Foundation

Panaritis, Andrea, exec dir: Reynolds Foundation, Christopher

Panazzi, Donna M., exec dir, secy: Laurel Foundation

Pancetti, John A., chmn, ceo, pres: Republic NY Corp.

Panettiere, John Michael, pres, ceo: Blount, Inc.; dir: Blount Foundation

Pang, Gerald M., dir: First Hawaiian Foundation

Pannell, William C., secy, trust: Sumners Foundation, Hatton W.

Papale, Victor J., trust: Pittsburgh Child Guidance Foundation

Papo, Michael A., exec dir, ceo: Koret Foundation

Pappert, E. T., trust: Chrysler Corporation Fund

Paquet, Joseph F., trust: Collins Medical Trust

Paquette, Joseph F., Jr., chmn, ceo: PECO Energy Company

Parham, Joseph G., Jr., vp human resources: Polaroid Corp.; trust: Polaroid Foundation

Park, Dorothy D., pres, dir: Park Foundation

Park, James C., trust: Besser Foundation

Parker, Bertram B., dir: Gebbie Foundation

Parker, Charles A., vp: Continental Corp. Foundation

Parker, Ellen, vp: Zlinkoff Fund for Medical Research and Education, Sergei S.

Parker, Gary, cfo: Bank One, Texas-Houston Office

Parker, George Edward, III, trust, vp, secy: Whitney Fund, David M.

Parker, George S., chmn, dir: Janesville Foundation

Parker, Geraldine M., dir: Gebbie Foundation

Parker, Maclyn T., secy, dir: Cole Foundation, Olive B.

Parker, Patrick Streeter, chmn: Parker Hannifin Corp.; pres, trust: Parker Hannifin Foundation

Parker, Ronald C., cfo: Roseburg Forest Products Co.; treas: Ford Family Foundation

Parker, Scott, pres: Peterson Foundation, Hal and Charlie

Parker, William I., secy, dir: Gebbie Foundation

Parks, Carol S., exec dir, trust: Sawyer Charitable Foundation

Parks, Floyd L., secy, treas: Upjohn Foundation, Harold and Grace

Parks, Martin A., trust: Robinson-Broadhurst Foundation

Parmelee, David W., trust: Howard and Bush Foundation

Parris, John, chmn, awards adv comm: Ferebee Endowment, Percy O.

Parrish, Jere Paul, pres, chmn exec comm, dir: Shell Oil Company Foundation

Parrott, John C., Jr., dir: Audubon State Bank Charitable Foundation

Parry, Gwyn, dir: Hoag Family Foundation, George

Parsons, Chris B., vp: O'Quinn Foundation, John M. and Nancy C.

Parsons, Earl B., Jr., trust: Gulf Power Foundation

Parsons, Myers B., dir: Christy-Houston Foundation

Parsons, Robert W., Jr., pres, prin off, dir: Hyde and Watson Foundation

Parsons, Roger B., vp, secy, dir: Hyde and Watson Foundation

Parsons, Warren F., secy, treas, dir: Mielke Family Foundation

Parvin, Phyllis, pres, dir: Parvin Foundation, Albert

Parvin, Stanley, dir: Parvin Foundation, Albert

Pasqual, Leandro, dir: Harcourt Foundation, Ellen Knowles

Pasternak, Ed, asst treas: General Motors Foundation

Pastin, Max, pres, trust: Blowitz-Ridgeway Foundation

Pate, James Leonard, chmn, pres, ceo: Pennzoil Co.

Patel, Homi Burjor, pres, coo, dir: Hartmarx Corporation

Patino, Douglas Xavier, trust: Mott Foundation, Charles Stewart

Patocka, Barbara A., dir: Mobil Foundation

Paton, Leland B., pres capital markets, dir, mem exec comm: Prudential Securities, Inc.

Patram, Bruce, secy, treas: Acme-McCrary and Sapona Foundation

Patrick, Charles F., secy, vp fin: Copley Press, Inc.; treas, trust: Copley Foundation, James S.

Patterson, David R., asst to pres, trust: Wildermuth Foundation, E. F.

Patterson, David T., trust: Wildermuth Foundation, E. F.

Patterson, E. H., vchmn, trust: Reynolds Foundation, Donald W.

Patterson, James R., trust: Collins Medical Trust

Patterson, Marvin Breckinridge, pres, dir: Marpat Foundation

Patterson, Melissa, trust: Mott Fund, Ruth

Patterson, Richard, pres: Interkal, Inc.

Patton, Henry, dir: Porter Testamentary Trust, James Hyde

Patton, Pat, trust: Donaldson Foundation

Patton, Shirley, pub trust: Carpenter Foundation

Paty, John C., Jr., secy, treas: Massengill-DeFriece Foundation

Paul, Alice, exec dir, secy: Uris Brothers Foundation

Paul, Douglas L., trust: CS First Boston Foundation Trust

Paul, James Robert, chmn, ceo: American Natural Resources Company; chmn, dir: ANR Foundation, Inc.

Paul, Robert Arthur, vp, trust: Fair Oaks Foundation, Inc.; treas: Jewish Healthcare Foundation of Pittsburgh

Paulam, Joseph, Jr., trust: Polaroid Foundation

Pauley, Robert L., dir, chmn: Gellert Foundation, Celia Berta

Paulis, Raymond, trust: Andres Charitable Trust, Frank G.

Pauly, Robert L., vp, dir: Gellert Foundation, Carl

Paumgarten, Nicholas Biddle, mem: Scripps Howard Foundation

Pavlicek, Michele D., asst secy: Wickes Foundation, Harvey Randall

Pawley, Dennis K., exec vp mfg: Chrysler Corp.; trust: Chrysler Corporation Fund

Payawal, Claire, mgr: Bristol-Myers Squibb Foundation Inc.

Payne, Delbert S., mgr corp social investment: Rohm & Haas Co.

Payton, Sylvia, secy: Boston Globe Foundation

Peacock, John E. D., pres, dir: Ayres Foundation, Inc.

Pear, Henry E., treas, trust: Leidy Foundation, John J.

Pearce, William R., pres: Cargill Foundation

Pearl, Mary, dir: Claiborne and Art Ortenberg Foundation, Liz

Pearlstine, Jules, asst secy: Clemens Foundation

Pearson, John Edgar, vp, dir: Cargill Foundation

Pearson, Maida S., chmn: Smith, Jr. Foundation, M. W.

Pearson, Stanley C., dir: Vogler Foundation, Laura B.

Peck, Arthur John, Jr., secy: Corning Incorporated Foundation

Peckham, Eugene E., mem adv comm: O'Connor Foundation, A. Lindsay and Olive B.

Peckham, Judith C., exec dir: Hoyt Foundation, Stewart W. and Willma C.

Pederson, Jerrold P., vp, cfo, dir: Montana Power Co.; dir: MPCo/Entech Foundation

Pedley, J. Douglas, pres, dir: French Foundation, D.E.

Peel, Michael A., sr vp: General Mills, Inc.; trust: General Mills Foundation

Peeler, Butch, trust: Vicksburg Foundation

Peeler, Stuart Thorne, trust: Getty Trust, J. Paul

Peete, Lindsey D., exec dir: Washington Forrest Foundation

Peete, Margaret S., pres, trust: Washington Forrest Foundation

Peipers, David H., trust: Dillon Dunwalke Trust, Clarence and Anne

Pell, Nuala, trust: Hartford Foundation, John A.

Pelletier, Edith, trust: Ottley Trust-Watertown, Marion W.

Pendergast, Edward G., trust: Bigelow Foundation, F. R.

Pendergraft, Ross, vchmn, trust: Reynolds Foundation, Donald W.

Pendexter, Harold E., Jr., sr vp admin, chief admin off: USG Corporation; pres, dir: USG Foundation

Pendleton, William J., dir corp aff: Carpenter Technology Corp.

Penglase, Frank Dennis, vp, treas: McGraw-Hill Foundation

Penick, Edward M., bd dir: Ottenheimer Brothers Foundation

Penn, Kevin, secy: ASDA Foundation

Penn, Milton L., pres, dir: Kelley and Elza Kelley Foundation, Edward Bangs

Penner, Betty J., asst secy: Johnson Foundation, Helen K. and Arthur E.

Pennoyer, Russell Parsons, second vp, trust: Achelis Foundation; second vp: Bodman Foundation

Penny, George L., trust: Knapp Foundation

Penny, Roger Pratt, pres, coo, dir: Bethlehem Steel Corp.

Penny, Sylvia V., trust: Knapp Foundation

Pepin, E. Lyle, secy: Centerior Energy Foundation

Pepper, Jane G., trust: Mutual Assurance Co. Charitable Trust

Perabo, Fred H., secy bd control: Ralston Purina Trust Fund

Perachio, Elaine, exec dir: Kempner Fund, Harris and Eliza

Perata, Bobbie, cfo, dir: Specialty Manufacturing Co.

Percio, Janis T., asst secy: Centerior Energy Foundation

Percy, Steven W., pres, ceo: BP America Inc.

Perenchio, Andrew Jerrold, pres: Chartwell Foundation

Perenchio, John, vp: Chartwell Foundation

Peretz, Anne Labouisse, dir: Clark Foundation

Perkins, Arnold, dir: Haigh-Scatena Foundation

Perkins, Donald S., dir: AON Foundation

Perkins, Homer G., dir: Beveridge Foundation, Frank Stanley

Perkins, John, trust: Higginson Trust, Corina

Perkins, Mary T. Bryan, vp: Carter Foundation, Beirne

Perkins, Richard S., adv trust: Astor Foundation, Vincent

Perkins, Robert E., admin agent: Beattie Foundation Trust, Cordelia Lee; exec dir: Selby and Marie Selby Foundation, William G.

Perkins, Tanga C., admin corp contributions: Eaton Charitable Fund

Perlman, Julian S., dir: Winston Foundation, Norman and Rosita

Perpich, Joseph George, MD, dir: Greenwall Foundation

Perrella, Frank E., trust: City National Bank Foundation

Perry, Carrolle, trust: Douty Foundation

Perry, Marilyn, pres, trust: Kress Foundation, Samuel H.

Perry, Martha J., mng dir: McCune Charitable Trust, John R.

Perry, Mary Mayne, trust: Toms Foundation

Person, Meredith S., trust: Finch Foundation, Thomas Austin

Persons, Oscar N., trust: Woolley Foundation, Vasser

Pertzik, Marvin J., secy, treas, dir: Griggs and Mary Griggs Burke Foundation, Mary Livingston

Peschka, Thomas Alan, secy, dir: Commerce Bancshares Foundation

Pestillo, Peter John, exec vp corp rels: Ford Motor Co.; trust: Ford Motor Co. Fund

Peters, Alton E., dir: Porter Foundation, Mrs. Cheever

Peters, Bruce, vp fin: ICI Americas Inc.

Peters, Charles E., Jr, trust: Boston Edison Foundation

Peters, Jeanette, cfo: Rose's Stores, Inc.

Peters, Ronald G., exec secy: Oxy USA Inc.; exec secy: Oxy USA Charitable Foundation

Petersen, Raymond Joseph, vp, dir: Hearst Foundation, William Randolph

Peterson, C. D., dir: Peterson Foundation, Hal and Charlie

Peterson, David W., trust: Lehmann Foundation, Otto W.

Peterson, Dwight A., treas, dir: Minnesota Mining & Mfg. Co.

Peterson, Edward M., mgr corp responsibility: Commonwealth Edison Co.

Peterson, Gary P., secy, asst treas: Mosinee Paper Corp. Foundation

Peterson, J. Charles, admin: Peters Foundation, Charles F.

Peterson, Jeannette Favrot, trust: Favrot Fund

Peterson, Lucille S., trust: Lehmann Foundation, Otto W.

Peterson, Neal L., secy, dir: Margoes Foundation

Peterson, Richard J., trust: Lehmann Foundation, Otto W.

Peterson, Robert L., chmn, pres, ceo: IBP, Inc.

Peterson, Thomas E., vchmn: BankAmerica Corp.; trust: BankAmerica Foundation

Petit-Moore, Jane, dir: Beloit Foundation

Petkus, Donald Allen, sr vp: Commonwealth Edison Co.

Petteys, Robert, trust: Joslin-Needham Family Foundation

Petteys, Robert A., trust: Petteys Memorial Foundation, Jack

Pettis, Shirley Neil, trust: Kemper Foundation, James S.

Pettker, John D., secy: Jones Foundation, Fletcher

Petts, John A., pres, ceo, dir: National Westminster Bank New Jersey

Pew, J. Howard, II, dir: Pew Charitable Trusts

Pew, Joseph N., IV, MD, dir: Pew Charitable Trusts

Pew, Richard F., dir: Pew Charitable Trusts

Pew, Robert Anderson, dir: Pew Charitable Trusts

Peyrelongue, Guy, pres, ceo, dir: Cosmair, Inc.

Pfenninger, Elizabeth M., adv: Cayuga Foundation

Pflugradt, Jane, secy: GenRad Foundation

Pfohl, James M., pres: Mathis-Pfohl Foundation

Pforzheimer, Carl Howard, III, pres, treas, dir: Pforzheimer Foundation, Carl and Lily

Pforzheimer, Carl Howard, Jr., hon chmn, dir: Pforzheimer Foundation, Carl and Lily

Pforzheimer, Carol K., dir: Pforzheimer Foundation, Carl and Lily

Pforzheimer, Gary M., dir: Pforzheimer Foundation, Carl and Lily

Phelps, Don C., mng trust: Puterbaugh Foundation

Phelps, W. H., trust: McCasland Foundation

Phibbs, Joan F., secy, treas, admin: Gregg-Graniteville Foundation

Philipps, Carole, trust: Scripps Howard Foundation

Phillips, Anne W., adv trust: Burnett-Tandy Foundation

Phillips, Blaine T., pres, trust: Fair Play Foundation

Phillips, Daniel Anthony, vp, treas, dir: Weber Charities Corp., Frederick E.

Phillips, Derwyn Fraser, vchmn N Atlantic: Gillette Co.

Phillips, Edith, vp, dir: Phillips Family Foundation, L. E.

Phillips, Ellis L., III, pres, dir, mem: Phillips Foundation, Ellis L.

Phillips, Ellis L., Jr., vp, dir, mem: Phillips Foundation, Ellis L.

Phillips, James, pres, ceo: Management Compensation Group/Dulworth Inc.

Phillips, Jeanne, trust: Phillips Family Foundation, Jay and Rose

Phillips, Morton B., don, co-chmn: Phillips Family Foundation, Jay and Rose

Phillips, Pauline, trust: Phillips Family Foundation, Jay and Rose

Phillips, Richard B., vp: Crane Foundation

Phillips, Rose, don, co-chmn: Phillips Family Foundation, Jay and Rose

Phillips, T. Ward, dir: Mid-Iowa Health Foundation

Phillipson, Phillip N., trust: Wildermuth Foundation, E. F.

Phin, Sydney N., dir human resources: Union Camp Corporation; trust: Union Camp Charitable Trust

Phipps, Mary Stone, trust: Achelis Foundation; trust: Bodman Foundation

Piacentini, Carmella V., admin: Olin Corporation Charitable Trust

Piasecki, Vivian O'Gara Weyerhaeuser, trust: Mutual Assurance Co. Charitable Trust

Piatuff, Mary, dir: Neuberger Foundation, Roy R. and Marie S.

Piazza, John, pres: Sara Lee Hosiery, Inc.

Picard, William, dir: Hedco Foundation

Picher, Helen Davis, program off: Penn Foundation, William

Pichon, John N., pres: Cole Foundation, Olive B.

Pick, Albert, III, vp, dir: Pick, Jr. Fund, Albert

Pickard, Mary, commun aff off: Saint Paul Companies, Inc.

Pidherny, Dennis N., asst treas: Dun & Bradstreet Corp. Foundation, Inc.

Piedra, L. J., trust: Chrysler Corporation Fund

Piel, Barbara W., dir: Woodward Fund

Pierce, A. Kenneth, Jr., vp, secy, treas: Wolfe Associates, Inc.

Pierpont, Wilbur K., trust: Redies Foundation, Edward F.

Pierrepont, John, trust: Astor Foundation, Vincent

Pierson, Edward M., gen mgr: Eden Hall Foundation

Pierson, Robert, vp: Leidy Foundation, John J.

Pierson, W. Michel, vp, trust: Leidy Foundation, John J.

Pierson, Wayne G., treas, contr: Meyer Memorial Trust

Pifer, Alan Jay Parrish, dir: Guggenheim Foundation, Harry Frank

Pildner, Henry, Jr., trust: Steinman Foundation, John Frederick

Pillsbury, Marnie, exec dir: Rockefeller Fund, David

Pincus, Lionel I., dir: Ittleson Foundation

Pine, William C., vp, exec dir: Collins Foundation

Pinkard, Anne M., pres: France Foundation, Jacob and Annita

Pinkard, Robert M., secy/treas, dir: France Foundation, Jacob and Annita

Pinkard, Walter D., Jr., vp, dir: France Foundation, Jacob and Annita

Piper, Addison Lewis, chmn, ceo, dir: Piper Jaffray Companies Inc.

Piper, William H., trust, mem investment comm: Mott Foundation, Charles Stewart

Pirayandeh, Mohammad, dir: Alavi Foundation of New York

Pisano, Jane G., chmn comm research & grants, trust: Haynes Foundation, John Randolph and Dora

Piskor, Frank P., dir: Noble Foundation, Edward John

Pitluk, Marvin, trust: Blowitz-Ridgeway Foundation

Pitte, Brenda S., dir: Cummins Engine Foundation

Pittinger, Vernon T., dir: France Foundation, Jacob and Annita

Pitts, C. L., secy: Callaway Foundation

Pitts, James D., vp urban aff: Peoples Energy Corp.

Platt, Lewis Emmett, chmn, pres, ceo, dir: Hewlett-Packard Co.

Player, Willa B., trust: Mott Foundation, Charles Stewart

Plourde, Robert J., vp, asst treas, trust: Hoover, Jr. Foundation, Margaret W. and Herbert

Plung, Donald, trust: Giant Eagle Foundation

Plunkett, Michael Stewart, treas, dir: Deere Foundation, John

Poff, W. Herbert, III, trust: Plankenhorn Foundation, Harry

Poissant, Gerald R., asst treas: Taubman Foundation, A. Alfred

Polakovic, Michael, trust: Weckbaugh Foundation, Eleanore Mullen

Polakovic, Teresa, secy, trust: Weckbaugh Foundation, Eleanore Mullen

Polis, Nancy E., mgr: General Motors Foundation

Politeo, Janet L., secy, dir: Glaser Foundation

Polk, Eugene P., trust: Morris Foundation, Margaret T.; dir: Charina Foundation

Pollard, David R., exec vp: Fireman's Fund Insurance Co.; dir: Fireman's Fund Foundation

Pollock, Davis E., pres: Van Buren Foundation

Pollock, John Phleger, pres: Jones Foundation, Fletcher

Pollock, Thomas, vchmn: MCA Inc.

Pomeroy, Gay M., trust: Mather Fund, Richard

Pontz, Curtis M., asst secy: Norton Co. Foundation

Pope, John Charles, pres, coo: United Airlines, Inc.; dir: United Airlines Foundation

Pope, Norwood W., dir: First Hawaiian Foundation

Porges, Carol Leigh Simon, dir: Simon Foundation, William E. and Carol G.

Portenoy, Norman S., vp, dir: Dreyfus Foundation, Max and Victoria

Portenoy, Winifred Riggs, pres, dir: Dreyfus Foundation, Max and Victoria

Porter, Donald E., dir: Bucyrus-Erie Foundation

Porter, Irwin W., chmn: Giant Eagle, Inc.; trust: Giant Eagle Foundation

Porter, John Wilson A., trust, chmn audit comm: Mott Foundation, Charles Stewart

Porter, Mark M., vp, dir: Hardin Foundation, Phil

Porter, Milton, trust: Foster Charitable Trust

Porter, Sue, trust: Scripps Howard Foundation

Porter, Victor B., dir: Cole Foundation, Olive B.

Porter, W. Thomas, Jr., exec vp: Seafirst Corporation; vchmn, trust: Seafirst Foundation

Portera, Vito S., vchmn: Republic NY Corp.

Poses, Frederick M., dir: AlliedSignal Foundation Inc.

Posner, Roy Edward, sr vp, cfo: Loews Corporation; trust: Loews Foundation

Poston, Met R., chmn adv comm: Janirve Foundation

Poteat-Flores, Jennifer, trust: Towsley Foundation, Harry A. and Margaret D.

Pottruck, David S., pres, ceo, dir: Schwab & Co., Inc., Charles

Powell, Cornelius Patrick, pres: Air Products Foundation

Powell, George Everett, Jr., vchmn: Kuehn Foundation

Powell, Joseph B., Jr., trust: Haley Foundation, W. B.; dir: Lockhart Vaughan Foundation

Powell, Mary C., chmn: Kuehn Foundation

Powell, Myrtis H., dir: Public Welfare Foundation

Powell, Nancy, asst treas: Treakle Foundation, J. Edwin

Powell, Nicholas K., secy: Kuehn Foundation

Powell, Peter E., trust: Kuehn Foundation

Powell, Richard K., trust: Kuehn Foundation

Powell, Susan Baker, dir: Lockhart Vaughan Foundation

Powers, Edward, fdn mng, trust: Acushnet Foundation

Powers, John A., chmn, dir: Heublein Inc.

Powers, John P., trust: Ettinger Foundation

Powers, June M., pres, dir: Dell Foundation, Hazel

Powers, Suzanne L., dir: New Milford Savings Bank Foundation

Pramberg, John H., Jr., pres, dir: Arakelian Foundation, Mary Alice

Prancan, Jane, exec dir: US WEST Foundation

Prater, Ed, mem contributions comm: Diamond Shamrock Inc.

Pratt, G. Gerald, trust: Meyer Memorial Trust

Pratt, Harold I., trust: Pierce Charitable Trust, Harold Whitworth

Pray, Donald E., exec dir: Reynolds Foundation, Donald W.

Prendergast, G. Joseph, exec vp: Wachovia Bank of North Carolina, N.A.; dir: Wachovia Foundation, Inc.

Prendergast, Larry, trust: Turrell Fund

Press, Frank D., trust, mem exec comm: Sloan Foundation, Alfred P.

Preston, James Edward, chmn, ceo: Avon Products, Inc.; vp, dir: Avon Products Foundation, Inc.

Preston, James M., dir: AKC Fund

Preston, James Y., secy: Giles Foundation, Edward C.

Preston, Jenny Childs, dir: AKC Fund

Preston, Lewis Thompson, trust, chmn audit comm: Sloan Foundation, Alfred P.

Price, Charles, pres, trust: Chicago Sun-Times Charity Trust

Price, Charles H., vp, dir: Hultquist Foundation

Price, Clement A., trust: Fund for New Jersey

Price, Donald, dir: Whittenberger Foundation, Claude R. and Ethel B.

Price, Donna S., coordinator gifts and grants: Martin Marietta Corp. Foundation

Price, Gordon A., McDonald & Company Securities, Inc.; treas: McDonald & Company Securities Foundation

Price, Harold, chmn, treas, trust: Price Foundation, Louis and Harold

Price, Pauline, vp, secy, trust: Price Foundation, Louis and Harold

Price, Samuel P., dir: Lenna Foundation, Reginald A. and Elizabeth S.

Price, Sol, dir: Weingart Foundation

Priddy, Betsy, adv dir: Priddy Foundation

Priddy, Charles Horne, vp, dir: Priddy Foundation

Priddy, Hervey Amsler, dir: Priddy Foundation

Priddy, Randy, adv dir: Priddy Foundation

Priddy, Robert T., pres, dir: Priddy Foundation

Priddy, Ruby N., dir: Priddy Foundation

Prime, Meredith, trust: Crary Foundation, Bruce L.

Primis, Lance Roy, pres, coo: New York Times Company

Prina, Barbara A., secy: Dingman Foundation, Michael D.

Prince, Charles O., III, sr vp, sec, gen couns: Travelers Inc.; sec, trust: Travelers Foundation

Prince, Frederick Henry, trust: Prince Trust, Abbie Norman

Prince, William Wood, trust: Prince Trust, Abbie Norman

Printz, Albert, trust: Flowers Charitable Trust, Albert W. and Edith V.

Pritzlaff, John C., trust: Olin Foundation, Spencer T. and Ann W.

Procknow, Donald E., trust: Prudential Foundation

Proctor, Venable B., secy: O'Connor Foundation, Kathryn

Prokay, Robert, vp, cfo: National Gypsum Co.

Prosser, Max W., vp, secy, treas: Santa Fe Pacific Foundation

Prothro, Zin, trust: McDermott Foundation, Eugene

Prouty, Lewis J., treas: Prouty Foundation, Olive Higgins

Prouty, Richard, trust, pres: Prouty Foundation, Olive Higgins

Pruis, John J., dir: Ball Brothers Foundation; exec vp, dir: Ball Foundation, George and Frances

Puckett, Marlene, chmn: Morrison Knudsen Corporation Foundation

Puelicher, John A., pres, dir: Schroeder Foundation, Walter

Pugh, Lawrence R., chmn, dir: Blue Bell, Inc.

Pugh, Linda, asst secy: Winchester Foundation

Pulitzer, Joseph, IV, dir: Pulitzer Publishing Co. Foundation

Pulitzer, Michael Edgar, chmn, ceo: Pulitzer Publishing Co.; chmn, pres, ceo: Pulitzer Publishing Co. Foundation

Pullen, Dave, vp: Schuller Fund

Pulliam, Larry, vp, treas, cfo: Noble Foundation, Samuel Roberts

Purcell, Patrick E., treas, trust: O'Fallon Trust, Martin J. and Mary Anne

Pure, James D., Jr., trust: Hygeia Foundation

Purmort, Paul W., Jr., trust: Van Wert County Foundation

Purser, Charles A., secy: Oxy USA Inc.; secy: Oxy USA Charitable Foundation

Purvis, Sarah Banda, mgr, secy: Consolidated Natural Gas System Foundation

Puryear, Mary, program off culture & the arts: Prudential Foundation

Putnam, David F., trust: Putnam Foundation

Putnam, James A., trust: Putnam Foundation

Putnam, Rosamond P., trust: Putnam Foundation

Pyka, William, MD, trust: Jurzykowski Foundation, Alfred

Pyle, Edwin T., dir: Mingenback Foundation, Julia J.

Pytte, Agnar, dir: Fairchild Foundation, Sherman

Q

Quadros, Joseph J., Jr., vp, trust: Beazley Foundation/Frederick Foundation

Quammen, David, dir: Claiborne and Art Ortenberg Foundation, Liz

Quern, Arthur Foster, corp secy: AON Foundation

Quigley, Philip J., chmn, ceo, pres: Pacific Telesis Group; chmn: Telesis Foundation

Quill, Leonard W., chmn, pres, ceo, dir: Wilmington Trust Co.

Quinlan, Bernard V., dir corp & commun aff: ANR Foundation, Inc.

Quinn, James W., asst secy: Allen Brothers Foundation

Quinn, Jane Bryant, program dir: Wallace-Reader's Digest Fund, DeWitt

Quinn, Mary S., mgr: Sawyer Charitable Foundation

R

Rabbe, Fred M., sr admin rep: Shell Oil Company Foundation

Rabin, Paul I., asst treas: AON Foundation

Rabinowitch, Victor, sr vp: MacArthur Foundation, John D. and Catherine T.

Raclin, Ernestine, dir: First Source Corp. Foundation

Raclin, Ernestine Morris, chmn, dir: First Source Corp.; dir: First Source Corp. Foundation

Radcliffe, R. Stephen, sr vp, chief actuary: American United Life Insurance Co.

Radt, Richard L., dir, trust: Mosinee Paper Corp. Foundation

Raff, K. Nerator, pres: First Tennessee Bank

Rahill, Richard E., trust: Corning Incorporated Foundation

Rainbolt, Harold E., vp, secy: SBC Communications Foundation

Raines, Osborne L., Jr., dir: Fieldcrest Cannon Foundation

Rainger, Charles W., pres, dir: Sandusky International Inc.; trust: Sandusky International Foundation

Rains, Sharon, secy: Adair-Exchange Bank Foundation

Raiser, Herbert A., pres, dir: Hebrew Technical Institute

Ramel, Ruth, admin: Hancock Foundation, Luke B.

Ramich, James M., trust: Corning Incorporated Foundation

Ramm, Richard W., pres, treas: Pamida Foundation

Ramsey, David, dir: Trust Funds

Ramsland, Jane B., trust: Beal Foundation

Randall, Edward Vincent, Jr., sr exec vp: PNC Bank, N.A.; chmn distribution comm: PNC Bank Foundation

Randall, James A., dir, bd mem: Gregg-Graniteville Foundation

Randall, James R., pres, dir: Archer-Daniels-Midland Co.

Randall, Sandra Fleishhacker, dir: Fleishhacker Foundation

Randle, Kathryn A., vchmn bd, trust: Chatlos Foundation

Randolph, Jackson H., chmn, ceo: CINergy

Randolph, Jennings, emeritus trust: Benedum Foundation, Claude Worthington

Randolph, Susan R., secy, treas: Benwood Foundation

Rankin, Susan T., secy, treas, exec dir: Tait Foundation, Frank M.

Rankin, William J., chmn: Whittenberger Foundation, Claude R. and Ethel B.

Ranney, George A., Jr., dir: MacArthur Foundation, John D. and Catherine T.

Ranney, Phillip A., secy, treas, dir: Second Foundation; counc, trust: Young Foundation, Hugo H. and Mabel B.

Rapaport, Bernard R., secy, treas: Lowenstein Foundation, Leon

Rappaport, Daniel, chmn, dir: New York Mercantile Exchange

Rappleye, Richard Kent, vp, secy, treas: Mott Foundation, Charles Stewart

Rash, Janet, grants mgr: US WEST Foundation

Rasmus, Robert N., dir: Brunswick Foundation

Raspe, Phillip A., asst secy, asst treas: Paley Foundation, William S.

Rassas, George, dir: Cuneo Foundation

Rath, Frank E., chmn, dir: Spang & Co.

Rath, Frank E., Jr., pres, dir: Spang & Co.; trust: Spang and Co. Charitable Trust

Rath, Robert A., vchmn, dir: Spang & Co.

Rathgeber, Susan, dir, trust: Stanley Charitable Foundation, A.W.

Ratliff, Floyd, dir: Guggenheim Foundation, Harry Frank

Rauch, John G., Jr., secy, treas: Plumsock Fund

Rauch, William T., asst treas: Plumsock Fund

Rauchenberger, Louis J., Jr., treas: CBS Foundation

Rautenberg, Ellen L., program dir: Diamond Foundation, Aaron

Rautio, Trudy A., dir: Jostens Foundation Inc., The

Raval, Dilip N., exec vp res & devel: Alcon Laboratories, Inc.

Rawlins, Charles O., treas, asst secy: Georgia Power Foundation

Ray, Gilbert T., trust: Haynes Foundation, John Randolph and Dora

Ray, John L., trust: Jacobson Foundation, Bernard H. and Blanche E.

Ray, Richard L., dir: Fair Foundation, R. W.

Rayfield, Allan Laverne, pres, ceo, dir: M/A-COM, Inc.

Raymond, George G., Jr., chmn, dir: Raymond Corp.; trust: Raymond Foundation

Raymond, Jean C., trust: Raymond Foundation

Raymond, Lee R., chmn, ceo: Exxon Corporation

Raymond, Michael, secy, treas: Worthy Causes Foundation

Raymond, Stephen S., vchmn: Raymond Foundation

Raymond III, George G., exec secy: Raymond Foundation

Rea, Paul, trust: Beal Foundation

Rea, William H., vchmn: Buhl Foundation; trust: Heinz Endowment, Howard; trust: Heinz Endowment, Vira I.; trust: Heinz Trust, Drue

Read, Michael, dir pub aff: Albertson's Inc.

Read, William B., dir human resources: Henkel Corp.

Real, William, vp, dir: PNM Foundation

Reale, Lisa Cleri, asst secy: Times Mirror Foundation

Reardon, Edward J., secy, mem, dir: McGee Foundation

Reaves, Gregory, mgr pub affs: Merck & Co. Human Health Division

Reavis, Lincoln, trust: Smith Foundation, Kelvin and Eleanor

Recchia, Richard D., coo, exec vp: Mitsubishi Motor Sales of America, Inc.

Reckling, Isla C., treas, asst secy: Turner Charitable Foundation

Reckling, James S., trust, asst secy: Turner Charitable Foundation

Reckling, Stephen C., asst secy, trust: Turner Charitable Foundation

Reckling, T. R., III, pres, trust: Turner Charitable Foundation

Reckling, Thomas R., IV, trust, asst secy: Turner Charitable Foundation

Records, George J., dir: Kirkpatrick Foundation

Redden, Virgil F., trust: Blount Educational and Charitable Foundation, Mildred Weedon

Redies, Robert D., chmn, dir: R&B Machine Tool Co.; trust: Redies Foundation, Edward F.

Redlinger, Donald J., dir: AlliedSignal Foundation Inc.

Redman, Manville, vchmn: McMahon Foundation

Redmond, Charles Robert, pres, ceo, dir: Times Mirror Foundation

Redmond, Paul Anthony, chmn, pres, ceo: Washington Water Power Co.

Redpath, Frederick L., treas, trust: Sullivan Foundation, Algernon Sydney

Reed, Cordell, sr vp: Commonwealth Edison Co.

Reed, Donald B., pres, dir: NYNEX Corporate Philanthropy and Foundation

Reed, E. H., dir: Matlock Foundation

Reed, James M., vchmn, cfo: Union Camp Corporation; trust: Union Camp Charitable Trust

Reed, John Shepard, chmn, ceo: Citibank

Reed, Samuel L., dir: Ball Foundation, George and Frances

Reed, Vincent Emory, trust: Graham Fund, Philip L.; dir: Strong Foundation, Hattie M.

Reed, William Garrard, Jr., chmn, dir: Simpson Investment Company; dir: Matlock Foundation

Reese, J. Gilbert, pres, trust: Evans Foundation, Thomas J.

Reese, Lowell O., vp, dir: Brillion Foundation; dir: Peters Foundation, R. D. and Linda

Reese, Terry W., asst treas: Vulcan Materials Company Foundation

Reeves, Charles B., Jr., pres, trust: Warfield Memorial Fund, Anna Emory

Reeves, J. Paul, vp, bd mem, dir: Gregg-Graniteville Foundation

Reeves, Woodie, vp: Vevay-Switzerland County Foundation

Regenstein, Joseph, Jr., pres, dir: Regenstein Foundation

Reichman, Vivian C., secy, treas, trust: Altschul Foundation

Reicker, Steven, trust: Towsley Foundation, Harry A. and Margaret D.

Reid, Charles M., secy, treas, dir: Sternberger Foundation, Tannenbaum

Reid, Fergus, III, treas, trust: Astor Foundation, Vincent

Reid, James, exec vp, gen mng oper, dir: Lipton, Thomas J.; exec vp: Lipton Foundation, Thomas J.

Reid, John A., trust: Slemp Foundation

Reid, Robert J., exec vp: Maddox Foundation, J. F.

Reidler, Carl J., dir: Reidler Foundation

Reidler, Paul G., pres emeritus: Reidler Foundation

Reilly, Donald C., pres, ceo: Superior Tube Co.

Reilly, Edward, grants coordinator: Rice Foundation

Reilly, Marie Ford, trust: Pittsburgh Child Guidance Foundation

Reilly, Richard R., cultural & the arts adv: Copley Foundation, James S.

Rein, Catherine Amelia, exec vp admin svcs: Metropolitan Life Insurance Co.; dir: Metropolitan Life Foundation

Reinberger, Robert N., co-dir, trust: Reinberger Foundation

Reinberger, William C., co-dir, trust: Reinberger Foundation

Reince, Jean M., mgr commun rels: Church & Dwight Co., Inc.

Reinhart, M. H., dir: Carpenter Foundation, E. Rhodes and Leona B.

Reising, Richard P., secy, vp, gen, couns: Archer-Daniels-Midland Co.; secy: Archer-Daniels-Midland Foundation

Reisler, Raymond F., exec dir: Taper Foundation, Mark

Reisman, Evelyn R., trust: Reisman Charitable Trust, George C. and Evelyn R.

Reisman, Howard, trust: Reisman Charitable Trust, George C. and Evelyn R.

Reisman, Robert, trust: Reisman Charitable Trust, George C. and Evelyn R.

Reiss, Bernard, dir: Lichtenstein Foundation, David B.

Reiss, Craig K., MD, dir: Lichtenstein Foundation, David B.

Reiss, Vicki, exec dir: Shubert Foundation

Reitz, Carl F., secy, trust: Besser Foundation

Renfrew, Alan M., vp, asst secy: Dingman Foundation, Michael D.

Reninger, Robert W., secy, dir: Young Foundation, Irvin L.

Rennebohm, Robert B., dir: Rennebohm Foundation, Oscar

Rennie, Robert, trust: Sarkeys Foundation

Rennolds, Edmund A., Jr., dir: Cabell Foundation, Robert G. Cabell III and Maude Morgan

Rennolds, John K. B., dir: Cabell Foundation, Robert G. Cabell III and Maude Morgan

Reno, Larry, vp: CS First Boston Foundation Trust

Renyi, Thomas A., pres, dir: Bank of New York Company, Inc.

Reusche, Robert F., dir: Demos Foundation, N.

Reusing, Vincent P., dir: Metropolitan Life Foundation

Reuss, John F., trust: American National Bank & Trust Co. of Chicago Foundation

Reuter, Carol Joan, corp vp: New York Life Insurance

Co.; pres: New York Life Foundation

Reveley, W. Taylor, III, trust: Mellon Foundation, Andrew W.

Rex, John, exec vp, cfo: American Fidelity Corporation; treas: American Fidelity Corporation Founders Fund

Reyna, Rudy, exec dir: SBC Communications Foundation

Reynolds, Frances, secy, treas, dir: Reynolds Foundation, Edgar

Reynolds, Joyce, asst secy: Cain Foundation, Effie and Wofford

Reynolds, P. R., trust: Bissell Foundation, J. Walton

Reynolds, Sigrid S., dir: Strong Foundation, Hattie M.

Reynolds, Thomas A., Jr., trust: Hartford Foundation, John A.

Rhatigan, Joseph, vp: Republic NY Corp.

Rhees, Carol A., secy: Lea Foundation, Helen Sperry

Rhein, Timothy J., pres, dir: American President Companies, Ltd.; sr vp, dir: American President Companies Foundation

Rhinehart, M. K., vp, treas: Schuller Fund

Rhoads, Jay R., Jr., pres, dir: NEBS Foundation

Rhoads, Katheryn V., dir: Hermann Foundation, Grover

Rhoads, Paul Kelly, pres, dir: Hermann Foundation, Grover

Rhoads, R. Carl, trust: Clemens Foundation

Rhoads, Richard H., chmn, dir: New England Business Service

Rhodes, Frank Harold Trevor, trust: Mellon Foundation, Andrew W.

Rhodes, J.W. Skip, Jr., mgr corp contributions dir: Chevron Corporation

Rhodes, James Thomas, pres, ceo, dir: Virginia Power Co.

Rhodes, William Reginald, vchmn: Citibank

Rhodus, G. Tom, vp, secy, special couns: Meadows Foundation

Rice, Charles M., vp: CHC Foundation

Rice, Condoleezza, trust: Carnegie Corporation of New York

Rice, Henry F., trust: Baldwin Memorial Foundation, Fred

Rice, J. Elisabeth, trust: Peabody Charitable Fund, Amelia

Rice, Lois Dickson, dir: Guggenheim Foundation, Harry Frank

Rice, Mary H., vp: Mahadh Foundation

Rice, Patricia E., trust: Peabody Charitable Fund, Amelia

Rice, Shelia, program off: Oppenstein Brothers Foundation

Rich, David A., secy, dir: Rich Products Corporation; exec dir: Rich Family Foundation

Rich, Janet W., vp, dir: Rich Products Corporation; asst secy: Rich Family Foundation

Rich, Leonard, trust: Williams Charitable Trust, Mary Jo

Rich, Marsha E., trust: Russell Trust, Josephine G.; trust: Stearns Trust, Artemas W.

Rich, Robert E., Jr., pres, dir: Rich Products Corporation; secy: Rich Family Foundation

Rich, Robert E., Sr., fdr, chmn, dir: Rich Products Corporation; pres, treas: Rich Family Foundation

Rich, William, III, vp: Harriman Foundation, Gladys and Roland; vp: Harriman Foundation, Mary W.

Rich, Zan McKenna, dir: McKenna Foundation, Katherine Mabis

Richards, E. D., mem bd control: Ralston Purina Trust Fund

Richards, H. Lee, chmn: Hygeia Dairy Co.; trust: Hygeia Foundation

Richards, Mariana Silliman, trust: Borkee Hagley Foundation

Richards, Robert J., trust: Linnell Foundation

Richardson, Beatrix W., trust, don: Hillsdale Fund

Richardson, Dean Eugene, trust: Taubman Foundation, A. Alfred

Richardson, Eudora L., trust: Hillsdale Fund

Richardson, Julie, trust: Favrot Fund

Richardson, Lunsford, Jr., pres, trust: Hillsdale Fund

Richardson, Sarah Beinecke, dir: Prospect Hill Foundation

Richardson, William Chase, PhD, dir: Pew Charitable Trusts

Richelson, Raymond C., group vp Memory Tech: Minnesota Mining & Mfg. Co.; dir: 3M Foundation

Richie, Leroy C., vp, gen couns, auto legal aff: Chrysler Corp.; trust: Chrysler Corporation Fund

Richman, Martin Franklin, secy: Pforzheimer Foundation, Carl and Lily

Richmond, Charles P., trust: Arakelian Foundation, Mary Alice

Richmond, John L., asst treas: USX Foundation

Richter, James, vp, dir: Hook Drug Foundation

Richter, Linda, asst treas: CBS Foundation

Rickman, Ronald L., vp, dir: Lee Foundation

Ridder, Kathleen C., trust: Bigelow Foundation, F. R.

Ridgley, Robert Louis, pres, ceo, dir: Northwest Natural Gas Co.

Ridgway, Ronald H., sr vp fin, dir: Pulitzer Publishing Co.; secy, treas, dir: Pulitzer Publishing Co. Foundation

Ridings, Dorothy Sattes, trust: Ford Foundation

Riecker, John E., secy: Towsley Foundation, Harry A. and Margaret D.

Riecker, John T., assoc: Dow Foundation, Herbert H. and Grace A.

Riecker, Margaret Ann, vp, trust, don granddaughter: Dow Foundation, Herbert H. and Grace A.; pres, trust: Towsley Foundation, Harry A. and Margaret D.

Rieger, Kathryn K., vp, dir: Kohn-Joseloff Foundation

Rieke, Glenn T., trust: Rieke Corp. Foundation

Rieke, Mahlon E., trust: Rieke Corp. Foundation

Rieke, William Oliver, MD, exec dir: Cheney Foundation, Ben B.

Riester, Jeffrey, pres, dir: Mielke Family Foundation

Rifkind, Richard, dir: Winston Foundation, Norman and Rosita

Rifkind, Simon Hirsh, dir emeritus: Winston Foundation, Norman and Rosita

Riggs, John A., III, trust: Riggs Benevolent Fund

Riggs, Judson T., dir: Teichert Foundation

Riggs, Louis V., pres, ceo: Teichert & Son, A.

Riker, Bernard, adv: Delano Foundation, Mignon Sherwood

Riley, Becky, trust: Sierra Pacific Foundation

Riley, C. Ronald, dir: Royal Insurance Foundation

Riley, Christopher J., trust: Connelly Foundation

Riley, Emily C., exec vp, trust, don daughter: Connelly Foundation

Riley, J. J., dir: Fieldcrest Cannon Foundation

Riley, John, trust: Raymond Foundation

Riley, Michael J., treas, dir: Lee Foundation

Riley, Rebecca, dir (community initiatives program), vp (Chicago aff): MacArthur Foundation, John D. and Catherine T.

Riley, Thomas A., trust: Connelly Foundation

Rimel, Rebecca Webster, pres, dir: Pew Charitable Trusts

Rincker, William, secy, treas, dir: Hoyt Foundation, Stewart W. and Willma C.

Rindlaub, John V., chmn, ceo: Seafirst Corporation

Ring, Lucy A., dir: Murphy Foundation

Ringo, Julie A., asst secy: Johnson's Wax Fund

Rintamaki, John M., secy: Ford Motor Co.; secy: Ford Motor Co. Fund

Rios, Rogelio G., trust: Hachar Charitable Trust, D. D.

Risch, William H., vp: Firstar Milwaukee Foundation

Riser, Mary M., secy: Smith, Jr. Foundation, M. W.

Rishel, Jane, pres, treas, dir: Donnelley Foundation, Gaylord and Dorothy

Risinger, James A., chmn, ceo: Old National Bank in Evansville

Rissinger, Roland, pres, dir: Lebanon Mutual Insurance Co.

Ristine, Kenneth I., program off: Cheney Foundation, Ben B.

Ritchey, S. Donley, treas, dir: Rosenberg Foundation

Ritchie, Jane Olds, vp, trust: Irwin Charity Foundation, William G.

Ritchin, Hyman B., dir: Hebrew Technical Institute

Ritzen, Evy Kay, vp, trust: Meadows Foundation

Rizley, Robert, secy-treas: Sarkeys Foundation

Roach, J. Thurston, sr vp, secy, cfo: Simpson Investment Company; treas, dir: Matlock Foundation

Roach, Michele C., asst secy, asst treas, trust: Chatlos Foundation

Roath, S. D., trust: Long Foundation, J.M.

Robb, Lynda Bird Johnson, trust: LBJ Family Foundation

Robbins, Donald M., asst secy: Hasbro Charitable Trust Inc.

Robert, Curtis D., pres: Rachal Foundation, Ed

Roberts, Ann M., vp: Stemmons Foundation

Roberts, Clarence Lewis, Jr., treas: Unilever Foundation

Roberts, Edith M., dir: Mullen Foundation, J. K.

Roberts, Frank H., trust: Packard Foundation, David and Lucile; asst secy, trust: Witter Foundation, Dean

Roberts, George Rosenberg, ptnr: RJR Nabisco Inc.

Roberts, John Joseph, dir: Starr Foundation

Roberts, Kenneth Lewis, pres, exec dir: HCA Foundation

Roberts, Mary G., trust: Gordon/Rousmaniere/Roberts Fund

Roberts, Robby, secy: Smith Charitable Foundation, Clara Blackford Smith and W. Aubrey

Roberts, Thomas H., III, vp, dir: R. F. Foundation

Roberts, Thomas Humphrey, Jr., treas, dir: R. F. Foundation

Robertson, Felix W., dir: Stauffer Foundation, John and Beverly

Robertson, Jim, vp, dir mktg: First Union National Bank of Florida

Robertson, Oran B., trust: Meyer Memorial Trust

Robertson, Stuart, treas, trust: Doss Foundation, M. S.

Robertson, Wilhelmina Cullen, pres, trust: Cullen Foundation

Robinett, P. Ward, Jr., trust: Beazley Foundation/Frederick Foundation

Robinson, Barbara, secy/treas: Staunton Farm Foundation

Robinson, Edward Joseph, pres, coo, dir: Avon Products, Inc.

Robinson, Edward N., dir: Texas Commerce Bank Foundation, Inc.

Robinson, Elizabeth H., dir, pres, treas: Widgeon Foundation

Robinson, Gary, vp: Scripps Co., E.W.; trust: Scripps Howard Foundation

Robinson, Jean A., treas: Buhl Foundation

Robinson, Joseph R., chmn, trust: Mott Fund, Ruth

Robinson, Kathleen M., trust: Smith Charitable Foundation, Lou and Lutza

Robinson, Michael J., treas, dir: Illinois Tool Works Foundation

Robinson, Michael J., III, vp, trust: Lovett Foundation

Robinson, Ray M., trust: AT&T Foundation

Robinson, Richard, dir, vp: Widgeon Foundation

Robinson, Russell M., II, trust: Duke Endowment

Robinson, Stanley D., trust: Kaye Foundation

Robinson, W. T., trust: Chesapeake Corporate Foundation

Robinson, W.R., mem mgmt comm: CBI Foundation

Robinson, Walter G., dir: Kelley and Elza Kelley Foundation, Edward Bangs

Robinson, Winnie M., trust: Robinson-Broadhurst Foundation

Robson, Hannah Davis, mng dir: Williams Companies Foundation, The

Roby, Carolyn H., asst secy, asst treas, program mgr: Norwest Foundation

Roche, George A., mng dir, cfo, vp: Price Associates, T. Rowe

Rockefeller, Frederic Lincoln, chmn: Cranston Print Works Company; trust: Cranston Foundation

Rockefeller, Mary French, dir: Bobst Foundation, Elmer and Mamdouha

Rockwell, D. M., secy, trust: Bissell Foundation, J. Walton

Rodenbough, Dean, dir corp aff: Binney & Smith Inc.

Rodewig, John Stuart, mem corp contributions comm: Eaton Charitable Fund

Rodgers, James R., trust: Beattie Foundation Trust, Cordelia Lee; trust: Beatty Trust, Cordelia Lunceford

Rodgers, William W., trust: Beattie Foundation Trust, Cordelia Lee; trust: Beatty Trust, Cordelia Lunceford

Rodman, Michael, mem commun concerns comm: NBD Indiana, Inc.

Rodriguez, Louis J., dir: Priddy Foundation

Rodriguez, Lynne, treas: ASDA Foundation

Rodriguez, Mike, mem bd: Telesis Foundation

Roe, Benson Bertheau, MD, pres: Lux Foundation, Miranda

Roe, John H., pres, ceo, dir: Bemis Company, Inc.

Roe, Lynne, trust: Donaldson Foundation

Roedel, Paul Robert, pres, trust: Wyomissing Foundation

Roepe, Thomas, trust: Homeland Foundation

Roesch, John R., dir: Hook Drug Foundation

Rogan, Donna, secy to pres: Akzo America

Roge, Paul E., secy: Abbott Laboratories Fund

Rogers, Bernard William, trust: Kemper Foundation, James S.

Rogers, Catherine, dir, trust: Stanley Charitable Foundation, A.W.

Rogers, Charles B., treas, dir: Pickford Foundation, Mary

Rogers, Christopher W., trust: Stevens Foundation, Abbot and Dorothy H.

Rogers, Fred McFeely, pres: McFeely-Rogers Foundation

Rogers, Irving E., III, trust: Rogers Family Foundation

Rogers, Irving E., Jr., trust: Rogers Family Foundation

Rogers, James B., trust: McFeely-Rogers Foundation

Rogers, James E., Jr., vp: CINergy; chmn: CINergy Foundation

Rogers, Margaret J., vp, asst secy, trust: Jonsson Foundation

Rogers, Nancy, mem grantmaking comm: Liz Claiborne Foundation

Rogers, Richard J., asst secy: Duchossois Foundation

Shugrue, Margaret, asst vp, dir (pub rels): Norwest Bank Nebraska, N.A.

Shulman, Lloyd J., vp, dir: Weinstein Foundation, J.

Shulman, Max L., pres, dir: Weinstein Foundation, J.

Shulman, Sylvia W., vp, dir: Weinstein Foundation, J.

Shumaker, John W., dir, trust: Stanley Charitable Foundation, A.W.

Shuman, Stanley S., dir: Markle Foundation, John and Mary R.

Shumway, Forrest Nelson, dir: Irvine Foundation, James

Shust, Robert B., trust: Patterson Charitable Fund, W. I.

Shuster, George Whitcomb, pres, ceo, dir: Cranston Print Works Company; trust: Cranston Foundation

Shyrock, Larry, dir: Texas Commerce Bank Foundation, Inc.

Sibley, D. J., dir: Potts and Sibley Foundation

Sibley, James Malcolm, trust: Evans Foundation, Lettie Pate; trust: Harland Charitable Foundation, John and Wilhelmina D.

Siciliano, Rocco Carmine, trust: Getty Trust, J. Paul

Sidamon-Eristoff, Anne Phipps, trust: Phipps Foundation, Howard

Sidford, Holly, program dir: Wallace-Reader's Digest Fund, Lila

Sieben, Todd W., mgr: Geneseo Foundation

Sieckman, Walter, co-chmn, ceo: Sharon Steel Corp.

Siegel, Bernard L., trust: Kutz Foundation, Milton and Hattie

Siegfried, Ellen J., trust: Jewell Memorial Foundation, Daniel Ashley and Irene Houston

Siegle, Helen, admin: Lipton Foundation, Thomas J.

Sierk, James E., dir: AlliedSignal Foundation Inc.

Sigler, Andrew Clark, chmn, ceo, dir: Champion International Corporation

Signom, Lola, trust: AT&T Foundation

Signorile, A. J., treas, trust: Dana Charitable Trust, Eleanor Naylor

Sikkema, Karen Ann, dir: Unocal Foundation

Silas, Cecil Jesse, dir: Wallace-Reader's Digest Fund, DeWitt; dir: Wallace-Reader's Digest Fund, Lila

Silberman, Sidney, trust: Kaye Foundation

Silbersack, Donna C., asst secy, treas: France Foundation, Jacob and Annita

Silbert, Bernard, dir: Parvin Foundation, Albert

Silbert, Steven, dir: Parvin Foundation, Albert

Silk, Susan Clark, exec dir: Columbia Foundation

Silliman, Henry Harper, trust: Borkee Hagley Foundation

Silliman, Henry Harper, Jr., pres: Borkee Hagley Foundation; treas, trust: Longwood Foundation

Silliman, John E., vp: Borkee Hagley Foundation

Silliman, Perry, secy-treas: Murphy Foundation

Silliman, Robert M., vp, treas: Borkee Hagley Foundation

Sills, Barbara A., dir commun rels: Battelle Memorial Institute

Sills, John, dir: Rudin Foundation

Sills, Nathaniel L., secy, treas, dir: Fife Foundation, Elias and Bertha

Sills, Ruth, dir: Fife Foundation, Elias and Bertha

Silvati, John D., vp, trust: Dater Foundation, Charles H.

Silver, Julius, secy: Rowland Foundation

Silver, Leanor H., trust, secy: Lovett Foundation

Silver, Robert C., trust: Linnell Foundation

Silverman, Arnold P., pres, coo: Winter Construction Co.

Silverman, Barry S., chmn, dir: Jaydor Corp.; trust: Jaydor Foundation, The

Silverman, Fred, mgr commun aff: Apple Computer, Inc.

Silverman, Jeffrey, trust: Jaydor Foundation, The

Silverman, Michael D., pres, dir: Jaydor Corp.; trust: Jaydor Foundation, The

Silverman, Robert L., chmn, ceo: Winter Construction Co.

Silverman, Sandra, exec dir, asst secy: Scherman Foundation

Simmons, Adele Smith, pres: MacArthur Foundation, John D. and Catherine T.

Simmons, Glenn Reuben, vchmn: Contran Corporation

Simmons, Hardwick, pres, ceo, dir: Prudential Securities, Inc.

Simmons, Harold Clark, chmn, ceo, dir: Contran Corporation; chmn, dir: Simmons Foundation, Inc., Harold

Simmons, Hildy J., mng dir commun rels & pub aff: Morgan & Company, J.P.

Simmons, Lisa K., pres: Simmons Foundation, Inc., Harold

Simmons, Sue, contributions coordinator: Giant Food Stores

Simock, Debbie, commun rels coordinator: Washington Water Power Co.

Simon, Allison S., pres: Stemmons Foundation

Simon, Carol G., pres, dir: Simon Foundation, William E. and Carol G.

Simon, Heinz K., vp: Stemmons Foundation

Simon, J. Peter, vp, secy, dir: Simon Foundation, William E. and Carol G.

Simon, Johanna K., dir: Simon Foundation, William E. and Carol G.

Simon, John Gerald, pres, treas, trust: Taconic Foundation

Simon, Julie A., dir: Simon Foundation, William E. and Carol G.

Simon, Mitchell J., dir: Young Foundation, Irvin L.

Simon, Paul, trust: Strauss Foundation, Leon

Simon, R. Matthew, dir: Brach Foundation, Helen

Simon, Ralph, trust: Strauss Foundation, Leon

Simon, Raymond F., pres, dir: Brach Foundation, Helen

Simon, William, trust: Strauss Foundation, Leon

Simon, William Edward, chmn, dir: Simon Foundation, William E. and Carol G.

Simone, Virginia, secy: Dun & Bradstreet Corp. Foundation, Inc.

Simonet, John Thomas, dir: Tozer Foundation

Simons, John Farr, dir: Marpat Foundation

Simonson, Anne Larsen, vp, dir: Larsen Fund

Simpkins, Jacqueline DeNeuflize, trust: Sprague Educational and Charitable Foundation, Seth

Simpson, Carolyn, coordinator: WICOR Foundation

Simpson, James A., dir, trust: Stanley Charitable Foundation, A.W.

Simpson, Phyllis T., asst secy: Duke Power Co. Foundation

Sims, Philip Stuart, vchmn, treas: Premier Industrial Corp.

Sinclair, John P., dir: Glencoe Foundation

Single, Richard Wayne, Sr., vp, secy, gen couns, dir: McCormick & Co. Inc.

Sinon, Frank A., secy, trust: Stabler Foundation, Donald B. and Dorothy L.

Sinrod, Allison R., trust: McMillan Foundation, D. W.

Sipp, Donald C., treas: Allegheny Foundation

Sircy, Melissa Smith, trust: Slemp Foundation

Sirota, Wilbert H., secy, dir: Hecht-Levi Foundation

Sisco, Jean Head, trust: Higginson Trust, Corina

Sisley, Christine, secy, exec dir: Parsons Foundation, Ralph M.

Sissel, Mary R., dir: Ball Foundation, George and Frances

Sisson, Richard Hampton, exec vp, dir: Alcon Laboratories, Inc.; trust: Alcon Foundation

Sitnick, Irving, secy, dir: Moses Fund, Henry and Lucy

Sivertsen, Robert J., vp, dir: Weyerhaeuser Memorial Foundation, Charles A.

Sizemore, Mary, admin asst: Davis Foundations, Arthur Vining

Skadon, Janet T., dir: Bishop Foundation, E. K. and Lillian F.

Skaggs, Mary C., pres, mem bd dirs: Skaggs Foundation, L. J. and Mary C.

Skarbek, Cynthia, dir: Smith Foundation, Gordon V. and Helen C.

Skelly, Thomas Francis, off: Gillette Charitable & Educational Foundation

Skilling, Raymond Inwood, exec vp, chief couns, dir: AON Corporation; dir: AON Foundation

Skinner, Samuel Knox, pres, dir: Commonwealth Edison Co.

Sklar, David A., cfo: Imperial Bank Foundation

Sklenar, Herbert Anthony, chmn, ceo: Vulcan Materials Co.; chmn, trust: Vulcan Materials Company Foundation

Skolaski, Steven F., pres, treas, dir: Rennebohm Foundation, Oscar

Skrzypczak, Casimir S., mem contributions comm:

NYNEX Corporate Philanthropy and Foundation

Skule, John, vp: Bristol-Myers Squibb Company

Skyes, James T., pres: Cremer Foundation

Slaten, Paul Edward, treas, dir: Sunnen Foundation

Slaughter, James C., ceo, dir: Goldsmith Foundation, Horace W.

Slaughter, Ken, cfo: Gazette Co.; dir, vp: Gazette Foundation

Slaughter, Thomas R., dir: Goldsmith Foundation, Horace W.

Slaughter, William A., dir: Goldsmith Foundation, Horace W.

Slavik, Frank, dir: Piper Foundation, Minnie Stevens

Slaymaker, Eugene W., pres, trust: Baughman Foundation

Slesin, Louis E., dir: Rubinstein Foundation, Helena; vp: Titus Foundation, Roy and Niuta

Slesin, Suzzanne, dir: Rubinstein Foundation, Helena; vp: Titus Foundation, Roy and Niuta

Slifka, Alan B., treas: Slifka Foundation, Joseph and Sylvia

Slifka, Barbara S., secy, trust: Slifka Foundation, Joseph and Sylvia

Slifka, Marlee, trust: Lunda Charitable Trust

Slifka, Sylvia, vp: Slifka Foundation, Joseph and Sylvia

Sliwinski, Robert A., asst treas: Centerior Energy Foundation

Slizewski, Bea, dir corp communs: Curtice-Burns Foods, Inc.

Sloan, Albert Frazier, mem bd admins: Van Every Foundation, Philip L.

Sloan, Sue, secy: PPG Industries Foundation

Sloane, Howard Grant, trust: Heckscher Foundation for Children

Sloane, Virginia, pres, trust: Heckscher Foundation for Children

Sloss, Deborah, secy: Fleishhacker Foundation

Sloss, Laurie, secy: Fleishhacker Foundation

Sloss, Leon, vp, dir: Fleishhacker Foundation

Sly, Helen S., pres, dir, fdr daughter: Sunnen Foundation

Smadbeck, Arthur J., trust: Heckscher Foundation for Children

Smadbeck, Mina, trust: Heckscher Foundation for Children

Smadbeck, Paul, trust: Heckscher Foundation for Children

Smale, John Gray, chmn: General Motors Corp.

Smart, Louis Edwin, Jr., trust: Continental Corp. Foundation

Smart, Mary, secy: Smart Family Foundation

Smart, Raymond, pres: Smart Family Foundation

Smeal, Frank P., trust: Smeal Foundation, Mary Jean and Frank P.

Smeal, Mary Jean, trust: Smeal Foundation, Mary Jean and Frank P.

Smith, Alexander John Court, chmn: Marsh & McLennan Companies, Inc.

Smith, Alice T., vchmn: Brown Foundation, M. K.

Smith, Alson H., Jr., dir: Virginia Environmental Endowment

Smith, Arthur O., pres: Smith Foundation, Inc., A.O.

Smith, Betty, dir, commun fund: McDonnell Douglas Corp.-West

Smith, Bruce G., dir: Smith Foundation, Gordon V. and Helen C.

Smith, C. A., contr: Chrysler Corporation Fund

Smith, Carroll George, dir: Sentry Foundation Inc.

Smith, Charles W., trust: Sargent Foundation, Newell B.

Smith, Cherida C., vp, trust: Collins Foundation

Smith, Claibourne D., vp tech & professional devel: du Pont de Nemours & Co., E. I.

Smith, Clyde M., cfo: BE&K Inc.; trust: BE&K Foundation

Smith, Crosby R., trust: Dillon Dunwalke Trust, Clarence and Anne

Smith, Dale E., dir (FL real estate): MacArthur Foundation, John D. and Catherine T.

Smith, David A., dir: Kline Foundation, Josiah W. and Bessie H.

Smith, David L., exec dir: Abell-Hanger Foundation

Smith, David S., exec vp, dir: Crane Foundation

Smith, David S., Jr., dir: Noble Foundation, Edward John

Smith, Derek, exec vp: Penguin Books USA, Inc.

Smith, Diane M., vp, dir: First National Bank of Chicago Foundation

Smith, Donald R., pres: Hygeia Dairy Co.

Smith, Douglas I., dir: Smith Foundation, Gordon V. and Helen C.

Smith, E. Berry, secy, treas: Schurz Communications Foundation

Smith, Edward A., vchmn, dir: Block Foundation, H&R

Smith, Elizabeth, mgr: Smith Foundation, Ralph L.

Smith, Elizabeth Patience, vp investor rels & shareholder svcs: Texaco Inc.; dir: Texaco Foundation

Smith, Fred Wesley, chmn: Reynolds Foundation, Donald W.

Smith, Gary M., vp, secy, gen coun, dir: American General Finance Foundation

Smith, George A., vp: MCA Foundation, Ltd.

Smith, Gordon H., chmn, dir: Demos Foundation, N.

Smith, Gordon Victor, dir: Smith Foundation, Gordon V. and Helen C.

Smith, Harold Byron, Jr., chmn exec comm, dir: Illinois Tool Works, Inc.; chmn, pres, dir: Illinois Tool Works Foundation

Smith, Helen C., dir: Smith Foundation, Gordon V. and Helen C.

Smith, Howard W., Jr., secy: Bryant Foundation

Smith, Hulett C., emeritus trust: Benedum Foundation, Claude Worthington

Smith, J. Burleson, dir: Piper Foundation, Minnie Stevens

Smith, James, trust: Slemp Foundation

Smith, James S., pres, treas: Frese Foundation, Arnold D.

Smith, Jean M., vchmn commun concerns comm: NBD Indiana, Inc.

Smith, John Francis, Jr., trust: General Motors Foundation

Smith, John M., trust: Gheens Foundation

Smith, L. Edwin, treas, dir: Jones Foundation, Helen

Smith, Leonard W., pres, secy, trust: Skillman Foundation

Smith, Lewis W., trust: Morgan Foundation, Louie R. and Gertrude

Smith, Lin, pub aff asst: Matlock Foundation

Smith, Lunsford Richardson, dir: Hillsdale Fund

Smith, M. Munson, trust, asst secy: Johnson Foundation, M. G. and Lillie A.

Smith, Margaret T., chmn: Kresge Foundation

Smith, Melinda Hoag, dir: Hoag Family Foundation, George

Smith, Molly R., trust: Hillsdale Fund

Smith, Nancey E., trust: Slemp Foundation

Smith, Nancy, treas: Levy Foundation, June Rockwell

Smith, Noble, exec dir: Noble Foundation, Edward John

Smith, Norvel, dir: Rosenberg Foundation

Smith, Orville D., trust: McMahon Foundation

Smith, Paul E., trust: City National Bank Foundation

Smith, Philip S., sr vp: Mitchell Energy & Development Corp.

Smith, Pomeroy, trust: Beal Foundation

Smith, Ralph L., Jr., mgr: Smith Foundation, Ralph L.

Smith, Ray K., trust: Beal Foundation

Smith, Raymond W., chmn, ceo, dir: Bell Atlantic Corp.

Smith, Richard Alan, chmn, dir: Harcourt General, Inc.

Smith, Richard G., III, trust: Hillsdale Fund

Smith, Richard L., vp: Sierra Pacific Foundation

Smith, Robert A., trust: Harcourt General Charitable Foundation

Smith, Roger B., trust: Sloan Foundation, Alfred P.

Smith, S. Garry, secy, treas, fdn mgr: Daniel Foundation of Alabama

Smith, Stanton Kinnie, Jr., vchmn: Consumers Power Co.; dir: Consumers Power Foundation

Smith, Stephen Byron, dir: Illinois Tool Works Foundation

Smith, Stephen J., secy: Christensen Charitable and Religious Foundation, L. C.

Smith, Steven James, exec vp: Continental Corp. Foundation

Smith, Thelma G., pres, dir: Second Foundation

Smith, Tom, pres: Woolley Foundation, Vasser

Smith, W. Read, asst secy: RJR Nabisco Foundation

Smith, Walt, bd mem: Glaser Foundation

Smith, Wayne Thomas, pres, coo, dir: Humana, Inc.; pres, dir: Humana Foundation

Smith, Wendy L., pres, dir: Brunswick Foundation

Smith, William A., vp: Sonat Foundation

Smith, William C., pres, dir: Ameritas Charitable Foundation

Smith, William M., III, trust: Prouty Foundation, Olive Higgins

Smith, William N., pres, dir: City National Bank and Trust Co.; pres, dir: City National Bank Foundation

Smith-Ganey, Anne L., asst vp: Freeman Charitable Trust, Samuel; asst vp, contact: Sprague Educational and Charitable Foundation, Seth

Smitson, Robert M., dir: Ball Foundation, George and Frances

Smyth, Frances G., secy: Banc One Wisconsin Foundation

Smyth, Maureen H., vp (programs): Mott Foundation, Charles Stewart

Smythe, John W., exec dir, treas: Jones Foundation, Fletcher

Sneag, Lawrence, treas: Ittleson Foundation

Snetzer, Michael Alan, pres, dir: Contran Corporation

Snider, Richard C., secy, dir: Rudin Foundation

Snodgrass, John F., trust: Noble Foundation, Samuel Roberts

Snow, David H., vp, treas: Snow Foundation, John Ben

Snow, Vernon F., dir: Snow Foundation, John Ben; trust: Snow Memorial Trust, John Ben

Snyder, Arlene J., grants off admin: Fuld Health Trust, Helene

Snyder, Audrey, exec dir, trust: Snyder Foundation, Harold B. and Dorothy A.

Snyder, Frank Ronald, II, trust: Lehigh Portland Cement Charitable Trust

Snyder, Leonard N., trust: Grundy Foundation

Snyder, Mary Ann, dir: High Meadow Foundation

Snyder, Nancy T., trust: Whirlpool Foundation

Snyder, Phyllis Johnson, trust: Snyder Foundation, Harold B. and Dorothy A.

Socol, Howard, chmn, ceo: Burdines Inc.

Socolofsky, Robert D., vp fin & admin: Maddox Foundation, J. F.

Soda, Rosemary, vp: Y and H Soda Foundation

Soderberg, Elsa A., dir: Allyn Foundation

Soderberg, Peter, dir: Allyn Foundation

Soderberg, Robert C., dir: Allyn Foundation

Soderquist, Donald G., vchmn, coo, dir: Wal-Mart Stores, Inc.; trust: Wal-Mart Foundation

Sohn, Edward, trust: Fohs Foundation

Sohn, Frances F., chmn: Fohs Foundation

Sohn, Fred, vchmn: Fohs Foundation

Sohn, Howard, trust: Fohs Foundation

Sohn, Ruth, trust: Fohs Foundation

Solana, Nancy, vp, secy: Fikes Foundation, Leland

Solano, Patrick, dir: Sordoni Foundation

Sollins, Karen R., pres, dir: Scherman Foundation

Solnit, Albert Jay, dir: New-Land Foundation

Solomon, Peter J., dir: Littauer Foundation, Lucius N.

Solomon, Richard, dir: Graham Foundation for Advanced Studies in the Fine Arts

Solow, Robert Metron, trust: Sloan Foundation, Alfred P.

Solow, Sheldon Henry, don, pres: Solow Foundation

Solso, Theodore Mathew, dir: Cummins Engine Foundation

Sommer, Barbara, grants program mgr: Calder Foundation, Louis

Sommer, C. S., mem bd control: Ralston Purina Trust Fund

Somnolet, Michel, coo, exec vp, dir: Cosmair, Inc.

Sonderegger, Leona A., secy, dir: Rennebohm Foundation, Oscar

Sonne, Christian R., trust: Mulford Foundation, Vincent

Sontag, Howard V., secy, treas: Glanville Family Foundation

Sordoni, Andrew John, III, pres: Sordoni Foundation

Sordoni, Stephen, asst treas: Sordoni Foundation

Sordoni, Susan F., dir: Sordoni Foundation

Sorkin, Cathy, vp: Lasdon Foundation, William and Mildred

Sosland, Estelle G., mem disbursement comm: Oppenstein Brothers Foundation

Sosland, Morton Irvin, dir: Block Foundation, H&R

Soublet, Richard C., mem contributions comm: Clorox Co.

Soulliere, Anne-Marie, dir: Johnson Fund, Edward C.

Souris, Theodore, asst secy, trust: Scherer Foundation, Karla

Soussand, Philippe, trcas, admin vp fin: Christian Dior New York, Inc.

Southworth, Louis Sweetland, II, asst secy-treas: Clay Foundation

Souyoultzis, M. J., trust: Long Foundation, J.M.

Sovern, Michael Ira, vp: Shubert Foundation

Spaeth, Edmund Benjamin, Jr., dir: Penn Foundation, William

Spaeth, Karl Henry, chmn, trust: Quaker Chemical Foundation

Spalding, Charles C., vp, trust: Cooke Foundation

Spalding, Hughes, Jr., vchmn, trust: Evans Foundation, Lettie Pate

Spalding, Philip F., vp: Lux Foundation, Miranda

Spanier, David B., pres, dir: McGonagle Foundation, Dextra Baldwin

Spanier, Helen G., vp, secy, treas, dir: McGonagle Foundation, Dextra Baldwin

Spanier, Maury L., chmn, dir: McGonagle Foundation, Dextra Baldwin

Spaniolo, James D., vp, chief program off: Knight Foundation, John S. and James L.

Sparling, Alfred H., Jr., trust: Hopedale Foundation

Speakman, Linda, secy-treas: Dekko Foundation

Speedie, David C., III, program chmn preventing deadly conflict: Carnegie Corporation of New York

Speer, Harlan, dir: Reynolds Foundation, Edgar

Speer, Katie, trust: Sturgis Charitable and Educational Trust, Roy and Christine

Spencer, George S., off, dir: IBP Foundation, Inc., The

Spencer, William R., dir: Wachovia Foundation, Inc.

Spendiff, James, pres: Freedom Forge Corp.

Speyer, Alexander C., Jr., mgr: Speyer Foundation, Alexander C. and Tillie S.

Speyer, Darthea, trust: Speyer Foundation, Alexander C. and Tillie S.

Spiegel, John W., mem: Trust Co. of Georgia Foundation

Spika, Nicholas C., secy: Forest Foundation; secy: Sequoia Foundation

Spindiff, James, trust: Freedom Forge Foundation

Spindler, George S., sr vp, gen coun exec off: Amoco Corporation; pres, dir: Amoco Foundation

Spindler, Michael H., pres, ceo, dir: Apple Computer, Inc.

Spink, William, asst secy: Schuller Fund

Spiro, William, dir: Hillman Family Foundation, Alex

Spraberry, Richard, vp, trust: Doss Foundation, M. S.

Sprehe, William, trust: Centralia Foundation

Springsted, Osmon R., trust: Hallett Charitable Trust, E. W.

Springsted, Osmond R., trust: Hallett Charitable Trust, Jessie F.

St. Clair, David Willard, sr vp law & admin: Lipton, Thomas J.; vp, secy: Lipton Foundation, Thomas J.

St. Jacques, Robert H., chmn, pres, ceo, dir: Life Insurance Co. of Georgia

St. John, Bill Dean, vchmn, cfo: Dresser Industries, Inc.

St. John, Howard C., vchmn, dir: Central Hudson Gas & Electric Corp.

St. Thomas, James W., trust: City National Bank Foundation

Staab, Thomas Robert, vp fin, cfo: Fieldcrest Cannon Inc.; asst treas: Fieldcrest Cannon Foundation

Staaterman, Robyn, pres: CT Corp. System

Staats, Elmer Boyd, trust: Kerr Foundation

Stabler, Andrew, chmn, dir: LamCo. Foundation

Stabler, Mrs. W. Laird, Jr., secy, trust: Welfare Foundation

Stack, Edward William, vp, dir: Clark Foundation

Stack, Richard L., trust: Darling Foundation, Hugh and Hazel

Stackpole, Harrison Clinton, chmn, trust: Stackpole-Hall Foundation

Stackpole, R. Dauer, trust: Stackpole-Hall Foundation

Stadler, Martin F., trust: Hoffmann-La Roche Foundation

Stainback, Thomas N., dir: Lake Placid Education Foundation

Stalder, Ruedi, cfo, mem exec bd: CS First Boston Corporation; trust: CS First Boston Foundation Trust

Staley, Walter G., Jr., trust: Green Foundation, Allen P. and Josephine B.

Staley, Warren R., vp, dir: Cargill Inc.

Stallmen, Richard, pres, dir: Specialty Manufacturing Co.

Stamas, Stephen, vchmn, dir: Greenwall Foundation

Stancato, Kenneth J., vp, contr: Weyerhaeuser Co.; contr: Weyerhaeuser Company Foundation

Stanfill, Dennis Carothers, dir: Weingart Foundation

Stanford, Henry King, trust: Knight Foundation, John S. and James L.

Staniar, Burton B., chmn, ceo, dir: Knoll Group

Stanley, Brian C., off: Valmont Foundation

Stanley, Edmund Allport, Jr., pres, chmn, trust: Bowne Foundation, Robert

Stanley, Jennifer, vp, trust: Bowne Foundation, Robert

Stanley, Talcott, vp, trust: Stanley Charitable Foundation, A.W.

Stanley, Walter G., secy, treas: Green Foundation, Allen P. and Josephine B.

Stans, Maurice H., chmn, treas, dir: Stans Foundation

Stans, Steven H., pres, dir: Stans Foundation

Stans, Theodore M., vp, dir: Stans Foundation

Stapleton, Katharine H., trust: Fishback Foundation Trust, Harmes C.

Stark, Donald B., treas: Ahmanson Foundation

Stark, K. R., trust: Kunkel Foundation, John Crain

Stark, Nathan Julius, trust: Allegheny Foundation

Starkins, Clifford E., dir: Porter Foundation, Mrs. Cheever

Starr, Edward, III, trust: Mutual Assurance Co. Charitable Trust

Starr, Frederick B., pres, ceo, dir: Thomasville Furniture Industries; chmn: Thomasville Furniture Industries Foundation

Starr, Karen, sr program off: Bremer Foundation, Otto

Starrett, Cam, exec vp human resources & corp rels: Nestle USA Inc.; dir: Nestle USA Foundation

Staten, Marcea Bland, mem communs comm: Medtronic Foundation

Staton, Jimmy, trust: Norman Foundation, Summers A.

Staton, Robert Emmett, chmn: Colonial Life & Accident Insurance Co.

Staven, Ralph R., pres, mgr: First Financial Foundation

Stecher, Patsy Palmer, dir: Beveridge Foundation, Frank Stanley

Stecko, Paul T., ceo, pres: Packaging Corporation of America

Steel, Arthur J., trust: Warner Fund, Albert and Bessie

Steel, Kitty, trust: Warner Fund, Albert and Bessie

Steel, Lewis M., trust: Warner Fund, Albert and Bessie

Steel, Ruth M., trust: Warner Fund, Albert and Bessie

Steele, Elizabeth R., trust: Steele Foundation, Harry and Grace

Steele, Richard, treas: Steele Foundation, Harry and Grace

Steere, William Campbell, Jr., chmn, pres, ceo: Pfizer, Inc.

Steffens, Marian I., secy: Robinson Fund, Maurice R.

Steffes, Don C., pres: Mingenback Foundation, Julia J.

Stegall, Ruth, asst secy: Taper Foundation, Mark

Stegemeier, Richard Joseph, chmn, ceo: Unocal Corp.; dir: Unocal Foundation

Stehling, James, dir: Peterson Foundation, Hal and Charlie

Stein, Jean, vp, dir: Stein Foundation, Jules and Doris

Stein, Joyce P., trust: Philibosian Foundation, Stephen

Stein, Kenneth L., trust: Goldie-Anna Charitable Trust

Steinbright, Marilyn L., don, pres: Arcadia Foundation

Steiner, L., trust: Bissell Foundation, J. Walton

Steinman, Beverly R., vchmn, trust: Steinman Foundation, James Hale

Steinman, Jeffrey, dir: Rudin Foundation

Steinman, Lewis, dir: Rudin Foundation

Steinschneider, Jean M., dir: Huisking Foundation

Steinweg, Bernard, mem, dir: Fribourg Foundation

Steiss, Albert J., pres, dir: Trust Funds

Stemen, Milton E., pres, dir: R&B Machine Tool Co.; trust: Redies Foundation, Edward F.

Stemmons, Jean H., vp: Stemmons Foundation

Stemmons, John M., Sr., vp: Stemmons Foundation

Stemmons, Ruth T., vp: Stemmons Foundation

Stempel, Ernest Edward, dir: Starr Foundation

Stender, Bruce W., chmn, mem exec comm: Blandin Foundation

Stepanian, Ira, chmn, ceo: Bank of Boston Corp.; trust: Bank of Boston Corp. Charitable Foundation

Stepanian, Tania W., chmn: Crocker Trust, Mary A.

Stephan, Edmund Anton, chmn, dir: Fry Foundation, Lloyd A.

Stephanoff, Katherine, trust: Trexler Trust, Harry C.

Stephans, Joan R., trust: Dynamet Foundation

Stephans, Peter N., pres, dir: Dynamet, Inc.; pres, trust: Dynamet Foundation

Stephans, William W. T., vp, treas: Scott Fetzer Foundation

Stephens, Elton Bryson, fdr, chmn, pres: Ebsco Industries, Inc.

Stephens, Georgina Y., treas: Cowles Media Co.; dir: Cowles Media Foundation

Stephens, James T., chmn exec comm, pres, ceo, dir: Ebsco Industries, Inc.

Stephens, Louis Cornelius, Jr., vchmn, trust: Duke Endowment

Stephens, Richard T., pres, dir: Delaware North Co., Inc.

Stephens, William Thomas, chmn, pres, ceo, dir: Schuller International; trust: Schuller Fund

Stephenson, Ann, secy: Feild Co-Operative Association

Sterling, Helen N., vp, trust: Rockwell Fund

Sterling, Mary K., secy: Phelps Dodge Foundation

Sterling, Sonja J., secy: Deere Foundation, John

Stern, Jean L., trust: Blum Foundation, Edna F.

Stern, Robert A., trust: Blum Foundation, Edna F.

Stern, William, vp: Atran Foundation

Stevens, Gratia, program off: Reynolds Foundation, Christopher

Stevens, Lorne G., dir: La-Z-Boy Foundation

Stevens, Melissa Jones, dir: Houston Endowment

Stevens, Robert L., pres, dir: Bryn Mawr Trust Co.

Stevens, Rowland, trust: Chapman Charitable Corporation, Howard and Bess

Stevenson, Ruth Carter, pres, dir: Carter Foundation, Amon G.

Stewart, Alan M., exec dir: Cullen Foundation

Stewart, Donald M., dir: New York Times Co. Foundation

Stewart, Elizabeth T., dir: Glenn Foundation, Carrie C. and Lena V.

Stewart, James Gathings, dir: CIGNA Corporation

Stewart, John, dir: Glenn Foundation, Carrie C. and Lena V.

Stewart, Vivien, program chmn (education & development of youth): Carnegie Corporation of New York

Stiles, Meredith N., Jr., vp, asst treas, secy, dir: Hopkins Foundation, Josephine Lawrence

Stimson, Bruce, cfo: Teichert Foundation

Stimson, Rebecca, exec dir: Crown Memorial, Arie and Ida

Stinnette, Joe L., Jr., pres, ceo, dir: Fireman's Fund Insurance Co.; dir: Fireman's Fund Foundation

Stinson, George A., emeritus trust: Benedum Foundation, Claude Worthington

Stiritz, William Paul, chmn, ceo, pres, dir: Ralston Purina Co.

Stirn, Cara S., vp, trust: Smith Foundation, Kelvin and Eleanor

Stith, David L., chmn, ceo: Bank One, Texas-Houston Office

Stivers, William Charles, treas, trust: Weyerhaeuser Company Foundation

Stock, Richard, contr: Mobil Foundation

Stockly, Doris Silliman, trust: Borkee Hagley Foundation

Stoel, Thomas B., secy: Collins Foundation; trust: Tucker Charitable Trust, Rose E.

Stokely, Kay H., exec vp, dir: Stokely, Jr. Foundation, William B.

Stokely, William B., III, pres, dir: Stokely, Jr. Foundation, William B.

Stokely, William B., IV, dir: Stokely, Jr. Foundation, William B.

Stokes, Jerome W. D., dir: Public Welfare Foundation

Stokes, Samuel N., dir: Marpat Foundation

Stokes, Thomas C., exec dir, secy: Gates Foundation

Stone, David Kendal, dir: Smart Family Foundation

Stone, Deborah A., treas, trust: Stone Charitable Foundation

Stone, Richard, dir: Daily News Foundation

Stone, Robert A., admin: Peters Foundation, Charles F.

Stone, Roger D., dir: Erpf Fund, Armand G.

Stone, Stephen A., pres, trust: Stone Charitable Foundation

Stone, Sue Smart, mem: Smart Family Foundation

Stonecutter, Harrison C., chmn, ceo, pres, dir: McDonnell Douglas Corp.-West

Stoner, Richard B., Jr., vchmn: Cummins Engine Foundation

Stookey, John Hoyt, dir: Clark Foundation

Stopher, Joseph E., pres, trust: Gheens Foundation

Storey, Charles Porter, trust: Hillcrest Foundation

Storey, Will Miller, exec vp, cfo, treas, dir: American President Companies, Ltd.; exec vp, cfo: American President Companies Foundation; trust: Schuller Fund

Story, Herbert B., pres: Bridwell Foundation, J. S.

Stotsenberg, Edward G., pres, ceo, dir: Pickford Foundation, Mary

Stottlemyer, Charles E., chmn, mem admin comm: Selby and Marie Selby Foundation, William G.

Stoughton, W. Vickery, dir: SmithKline Beecham Foundation

Stout, Jean C., treas, dir: Hugoton Foundation

Stout, Joan K., pres, mng dir: Hugoton Foundation

Stout, Joan M., secy, dir: Hugoton Foundation

Stout, John K., dir: Hugoton Foundation

Stout, Ray E., III, vp, dir: Hugoton Foundation

Stout, William J., dir: Ayres Foundation, Inc.

Stovall, David, dir: Gulf Coast Medical Foundation

Stovall, Guy F., III, dir: Gulf Coast Medical Foundation

Stover, Matthew J., chmn contributions comm: NYNEX Corporate Philanthropy and Foundation

Stowe, David H., Jr., pres, coo, dir: Deere & Co.; dir: Deere Foundation, John

Stowe, Nonni, vp corp aff: Life Insurance Co. of Georgia

Straine, James J., treas: Prudential Foundation

Strait, Rex, first vp: Van Buren Foundation

Straitor, George A., asst treas: Ford Fund, William and Martha

Stranahan, Julie, trust: Fruehauf Foundation

Straughn, Edward L., pres: Freeport Brick Co.

Straus, Roger W., dir: Guggenheim Foundation, Harry Frank

Strauss, Sam B., Jr., bd dir: Ottenheimer Brothers Foundation

Strawderman, Dennis L., dir pub aff, asst secy, commercial atty: Bucyrus-Erie Company; mgr, secy, dir: Bucyrus-Erie Foundation

Strawn, Kathryn, admin off: Mead Corp. Foundation

Strecker, A. M., vp, dir: Oklahoma Gas & Electric Co. Foundation

Streep, Mary B. Simon, dir: Simon Foundation, William E. and Carol G.

Street, Alice Ann, pres, dir: Bertha Foundation

Street, E. Bruce, dir: Bertha Foundation

Street, M. B., Jr., dir: Bertha Foundation

Street, M. Boyd, dir: Bertha Foundation

Stribling, Jera G., exec vp: Alabama Power Foundation

Strickland, Robert, trust: English Memorial Fund, Florence C. and H. L.

Strobel, Pamela, vp, gen couns: Commonwealth Edison Co.

Strong, C. Peter, dir: Strong Foundation, Hattie M.

Strong, George V., Jr., dir, secy: Widgeon Foundation

Strong, Henry, chmn, pres, off: Strong Foundation, Hattie M.

Strong, Henry L., vp, off: Strong Foundation, Hattie M.

Strong, Mary S., trust: Fund for New Jersey

Strope, L. E., trust: Wiggins Memorial Trust, J. J.

Strother, Jack W., Sr., chmn: Commercial Bank; trust: Commercial Bank Foundation

Stroud, Douglas A., vp, dir: Bertha Foundation

Stroud, Robert R., dir: Cremer Foundation

Stroup, Paul, mem bd adms: Van Every Foundation, Philip L.

Stroup, Stanley Stephenson, gen couns, exec vp: Norwest Corporation

Strudwick, Lewis C., trust: Warfield Memorial Fund, Anna Emory

Strumpf, Linda B., vp, chief investment off: Ford Foundation

Stryker, Steven Charles, dir: Shell Oil Company Foundation

Strzelczyk, Frank A., secy, treas: Blaustein Foundation, Louis and Henrietta

Stuart, James G., dir: Glenn Foundation, Carrie C. and Lena V.

Stuart, Susan W., dir: Seneca Foods Foundation

Stubblefield, Joel R., trust: Reynolds Foundation, Donald W.

Stubbs, Mary, corp commun: Morgan Stanley & Co., Inc.

Stubing, William C., pres, dir: Greenwall Foundation

Stuebe, Patricia D., asst vp: Bank of New York Company, Inc.

Stuebgen, William J., treas: American President Companies Foundation

Stuecker, Phillip J., vp, cfo: Thomas Industries; cfo, vp, secy: Thomas Foundation

Stumler, David J., asst secy: Thomas Foundation

Stupski, Lawrence J., vchmn: Schwab & Co., Inc., Charles

Sturgeon, Barry M., trust: Davenport Trust Fund

Sturmer, Ellen, commun cordinator: Security Life of Denver Insurance Co.

Suarez, Rocio, exec dir: Baker Trust, George F.

Subramaniam, Shivan Sivaswamy, pres, ceo, dir: Allendale Insurance Co.; dir: Allendale Insurance Foundation

Sudderth, Robert J., Jr., vp, trust: Benwood Foundation

Sullivan, Barbara D., Esq, trust: Robinson Fund, Maurice R.

Sullivan, D. Harold, trust: Demoulas Foundation

Sullivan, Dennis W., exec vp, coo, dir: Parker Hannifin Corp.

Sullivan, Elizabeth C., grants coordinator: Kresge Foundation

Sullivan, G. Craig, chmn, pres, ceo: Clorox Co.; trust: Clorox Company Foundation

Sullivan, James Norman, vchmn, dir: Chevron Corporation

Sullivan, K. F., mem screening comm: PPG Industries Foundation

Sullivan, Kerry H., trust off, dir grant making: Balfour Foundation, L. G.

Sullivan, Margaret B., secy: Teagle Foundation

Sullivan, Richard J., pres, trust: Fund for New Jersey

Sullivan, T. Dennis, vp fin: Mellon Foundation, Andrew W.

Sullivan, Thomas John, vp, dir: McGraw-Hill Foundation

Sullivan, Tracie L., grants mgr: Markle Foundation, John and Mary R.

Sullivan, Virginia M., secy, treas, trust: Mott Fund, Ruth

Sullivan, William J., treas: Connecticut Mutual Life Foundation; trust: Dell Foundation, Hazel

Sultana, Joan, asst secy, asst treas: DeRoy Testamentary Foundation

Sulzberger, Arthur Ochs, Jr., publ: New York Times Company

Sulzberger, Arthur Ochs, Sr., vp, sec, treas, dir: Sulzberger Foundation

Sulzberger, Judith P., dir: New York Times Co. Foundation; vp, dir: Sulzberger Foundation

Sumegi, Lois, admin: Goodrich Foundation, Inc., B.F.

Summerall, Robert, Jr., dir: Morgan Foundation, Louie R. and Gertrude

Summers, Anita Arrow, dir: Penn Foundation, William

Summers, William B., Jr., pres, ceo, dir: McDonald & Company Securities, Inc.; trust: McDonald & Company Securities Foundation

Sump, Carl H., dir, secy: Plankenhorn Foundation, Harry

Sunada, Chris, grants mgr: Atherton Family Foundation

Sundet, Leland N., pres, dir: Sundet Foundation

Sundet, Louise C., vp, dir: Sundet Foundation

Sundet, Scott A., secy, treas, dir: Sundet Foundation

Surdam, Robert McCellan, treas, trust: Wilson Fund, Matilda R.

Surrey, Mary P., secy, treas, dir: Dreyfus Foundation, Max and Victoria

Sutphen, Harry D., treas: Retirement Research Foundation

Sutton, Donald C., trust: Van Wert County Foundation

Sutton, Thomas C., chmn, ceo, dir: Pacific Mutual Life Insurance Co.; chmn: Pacific Mutual Charitable Foundation

Suwinski, Jan H., trust: Corning Incorporated Foundation

Suwyn, Mark A., exec vp, forest & special products: International Paper Co.; dir: International Paper Co. Foundation

Swain, Kristin A., pres: Corning Incorporated Foundation

Swalm, Dave C., vp, trust: Swalm Foundation

Swalm, Jo Beth Camp, pres, trust: Swalm Foundation

Swaminathan, Monkombu S., trust: Ford Foundation

Swaney, Robert E., Jr., vp, chief investment off: Mott Foundation, Charles Stewart

Swaney, Thomas E., secy, dir: R. F. Foundation

Swanson, Earl C., trust: Bayport Foundation; dir: Andersen Foundation; trust: Tozer Foundation

Swanson, Lynwood W., trust: Murdock Charitable Trust, M. J.

Swanson, Thomas A., sr vp, gen couns, secy: Fireman's Fund Insurance Co.; dir: Fireman's Fund Foundation

Swanson, W. Charles, mgr: Swanson Family Foundation, Dr. W.C.

Swantak, Judy L., vp, secy: Union Pacific Corp.; pres, secy, trust: Union Pacific Foundation

Swartz, Arnold, pres, trust: Tobin Foundation

Swasey, Hope Halsey, trust: Fuller Foundation

Sweeney, Thomas Joseph, Jr., vp, treas: Dreyfus Foundation, Jean and Louis

Sweet, Adele Hall, pres: Schiff Foundation, Dorothy

Sweeterman, John W., trust: Graham Fund, Philip L.

Swift, Bryan, pres: Swift Co. Inc., John S.

Swift, Hampden M., trust: Swift Co. Inc. Charitable Trust, John S.

Swift, Sara Taylor, trust, don daughter: Taylor Foundation, Ruth and Vernon

Swinney, Jo Ann, dir commun aff: Tenneco Inc.

Sykes, James W., Jr., dir: Greve Foundation, William and Mary

Sykora, Donald D., pres, coo, dir: Houston Industries Incorporated

Synder, Abram M., dir, treas: Plankenhorn Foundation, Harry

Syrmis, Pamela, vp, dir: Ittleson Foundation

Syrmis, Victor, MD, dir: Ittleson Foundation

Szabo, Raymond, secy, trust: Eaton Foundation, Cyrus

Szilagyi, Elaine A., secy, trust: Frohring Foundation, William O. and Gertrude Lewis

T

Taber, George H., chmn, trust: Mellon Family Foundation, R. K.; vp, dir, trust: Mellon Foundation, Richard King

Taboni, Viola G., treas, asst secy, trust: Dynamet Foundation

Tafoya, Linda S., exec dir, secy: Coors Foundation, Adolph

Tail, Norbert, trust: McKenna Foundation, Philip M.

Tait, Peter B., trust: Lehigh Portland Cement Charitable Trust

Takeda, Kent M., trust: AT&T Foundation

Takeuchi, Tohei, pres, ceo: Mitsubishi Motor Sales of America, Inc.

Talbot, Deborah L., trust: Chase Manhattan Foundation

Talbot, Samuel S., trust: Fuller Foundation

Taleff, Lynne, dir: Hardin Foundation, Phil

Tallent, Charles J., trust: Arkell Hall Foundation

Talley, Chris L., chmn: Winchester Foundation

Tambakakis, Barb, contributions coordinator: Pennzoil Co.

Tannenbaum, Jeanne L., dir: Sternberger Foundation, Tannenbaum

Tannenbaum, Leah Louise B., chmn: Sternberger Foundation, Tannenbaum

Tannenbaum, Nancy B., dir: Sternberger Foundation, Tannenbaum

Tannenbaum, Sigmund, dir: Sternberger Foundation, Tannenbaum

Tannenbaum, Susan M., dir: Sternberger Foundation, Tannenbaum

Tanner, Henry J., fin adv: Scott Foundation, Virginia Steele

Tanner, Robin C., treas, dir loans: Strong Foundation, Hattie M.

Tanquist, Dwight, vp: Hartz Foundation

Taper, Barry H., vp, secy, dir: Taper Foundation, Mark

Tarasovich, Barbara, treas: Chesebrough Foundation

Tarica, Regina A., treas, dir: Amado Foundation, Maurice

Tarica, Samuel R., asst secy: Amado Foundation, Maurice

Tarnow, Robert L., dir: Utica National Group Foundation

Tata, Ratan Naval, trust: Ford Foundation

Tate, Warren E., treas: Gulf Power Foundation

Taube, Thaddeus N., pres, dir: Koret Foundation; pres, dir: Taube Family Foundation

Taubman, A. Alfred, chmn, treas, trust: Taubman Foundation, A. Alfred

Taubman, Robert S., trust: Taubman Foundation, A. Alfred

Taubman, William S., trust: Taubman Foundation, A. Alfred

Taveras, Barbara, exec dir: Hazen Foundation, Edward W.

Taylor, Alfred Hendricks, Jr., chmn, trust: Kresge Foundation

Taylor, Alice, dir, pres: Memorial Foundation for the Blind

Taylor, Barbara O., trust: Olin Foundation, Spencer T. and Ann W.

Taylor, Benjamin B., dir: Boston Globe Foundation

Taylor, Bernard J., II, trust: Wilmington Trust Co. Foundation

Taylor, Betsy, exec dir: Merck Family Fund

Taylor, David H., vp, dir: Davenport-Hatch Foundation

Taylor, Douglas F., dir: Davenport-Hatch Foundation

Taylor, F. Morgan, trust: Olin Foundation, Spencer T. and Ann W.

Taylor, Hart, dir: Davenport-Hatch Foundation

Taylor, Irby N., dir: Hawn Foundation

Taylor, John R., exec vp: Merck Co. Foundation

Taylor, Lynn, mng dir: Koch Charitable Foundation, Charles G.

Taylor, Margaret C., trust: Dula Educational and Charitable Foundation, Caleb C. and Julia W.

Taylor, Martha, secy: Howe and Mitchell B. Howe Foundation, Lucille Horton

Taylor, S. Martin, pres, dir: Detroit Edison Foundation

Taylor, Steven W., trust: Puterbaugh Foundation

Taylor, Teddy O., trust: Blount Educational and Charitable Foundation, Mildred Weedon

Taylor, Terrence J., treas: Nalco Foundation

Taylor, Vernon F., Jr., trust, don: Taylor Foundation, Ruth and Vernon

Taylor, W. Ed, pres network svc: Donnelley & Sons Co., R.R.

Taylor, William Osgood, chmn, ceo, dir: Globe Newspaper Co.; pres, dir: Boston Globe Foundation

Taylor, Wilson H., chmn, ceo: CIGNA Corporation

Tebinka, Constance M., treas: Klipstein Foundation, Ernest Christian

Teichert, Frederick A., exec dir: Teichert Foundation

Teichert, Melita M., dir: Teichert Foundation

Teig, Eva S., mem contributions comm: Virginia Power Co.

Temple, Arthur, III, trust: Temple Foundation, T. L. L.; dir: Temple-Inland Foundation

Temple, Arthur, Jr., trust: Temple Foundation, T. L. L.

Templer, Charles E., vp: Commerce Bancshares Foundation

Templin, Gary, dir: Haigh-Scatena Foundation

Tengi, Frank R., treas: Starr Foundation

Tenney, Daniel Gleason, Jr., secy, dir: JM Foundation

Tenniman, Nicholas G., IV, vp newspaper oper: Pulitzer Publishing Co.; dir: Pulitzer Publishing Co. Foundation

Tenny, Barron M., vp, secy, gen couns: Ford Foundation

Teplow, Theodore Herzl, secy, trust: Stone Charitable Foundation

Tepperman, Marvin T., vp: Brenner Foundation, Mervyn

Termondt, M. James, pres, treas, dir: Fry Foundation, Lloyd A.

Terracciano, Anthony Patrick, chmn, pres, ceo: First Fidelity Bank

Terrien, Linda L., asst treas: Weyerhaeuser Company Foundation

Terry, Richard Edward, chmn, ceo, dir: Peoples Energy Corp.

Teschner, Richard R., dir: Ross Memorial Foundation, Will

Tessler, C., secy: Long Foundation, J.M.

Testa, Richard J., pres, treas, dir: Beaucourt Foundation

Thaler, Manley H., pres: Howell Foundation of Florida

Thalheimer, Louis B., vp, trust: Blaustein Foundation, Louis and Henrietta

Thalhimer, Charles G., Jr., vp, secy: Thalhimer and Family Foundation, Charles G.

Thalhimer, Charles G., Sr., pres, dir: Thalhimer and Family Foundation, Charles G.

Thalhimer, Harry R., vp, treas: Thalhimer and Family Foundation, Charles G.

Thalhimer, Rhoda R., exec vp, dir: Thalhimer and Family Foundation, Charles G.

Thalhimer, William B., Jr., vp: Thalhimer and Family Foundation, Charles G.

Tharin, Judson, program off: Davis Foundations, Arthur Vining

Thatcher, Elizabeth N., trust: Schenck Fund, L. P.

Theisen, Edwin Mathew, pres, coo, dir: Northern States Power Co. (Minnesota)

Thelen, Cindy, coordinator: General Mills Foundation

Thelen, Max, Jr., vp: Cowell Foundation, S. H.

Theobald, Jon A., trust: Bigelow Foundation, F. R.; dir: Tozer Foundation

Theobald, Thomas Charles, dir: MacArthur Foundation, John D. and Catherine T.

Theobold, Veronica R., fdn specialist: Jostens Foundation Inc., The

Theriot, Charles H., mem adv comm: Weezie Foundation

Thiele, Randy, trust: Donaldson Foundation

Thies, Richard H., asst treas: Madison Gas & Electric Foundation

Thomas, Bruce, dir: Piper Foundation, Minnie Stevens

Thomas, Franklin Augustine, dir: CBS Foundation

Thomas, Gladys R., vp: Starr Foundation

Thomas, Glenn E., dir: Thomas Foundation, Joan and Lee

Thomas, Gregory N., secy: Blair and Co. Foundation, William

Thomas, Jane R., vchmn, trust: Skillman Foundation

Thomas, Joan E., dir: Thomas Foundation, Joan and Lee

Thomas, L. N., Jr., trust: Jacobson Foundation, Bernard H. and Blanche E.

Thomas, L. Newton, Jr., pres, dir: Daywood Foundation; trust: Jacobson Foundation, Bernard H. and Blanche E.

Thomas, Lawrason D., vchmn, dir: Amoco Corporation

Thomas, Lee B., dir: Thomas Foundation, Joan and Lee

Thomas, Lyda Ann Quinn, chmn: Kempner Fund, Harris and Eliza

Thomas, Nancy, natl contributions mgr: Hewlett-Packard Co.

Thomas, Richard Lee, chmn, ceo: First Chicago Corp.; vp: First National Bank of Chicago Foundation

Thomasson, Dan King, trust: Scripps Howard Foundation

Thompson, Alyce, secy: Ottley Trust-Watertown, Marion W.

Thompson, B. Ray, Jr., dir: Thompson Charitable Foundation

Thompson, Billie, secy, trust: Doss Foundation, M. S.

Thompson, E. Edward, trust: Ottley Trust-Watertown, Marion W.

Thompson, Elizabeth H., trust: Upjohn Foundation, Harold and Grace

Thompson, Gary, trust: Wachovia Foundation, Inc.

Thompson, Gene, trust: Jones Foundation, Harvey and Bernice

Thompson, George C., treas, dir: Phillips Foundation, Ellis L.

Thompson, Harry A., II, mgr: Heinz Trust, Drue

Thompson, James Cleo, Jr., chmn, trust: Sumners Foundation, Hatton W.

Thompson, Jesse J., trust: Thompson Charitable Foundation

Thompson, John D., treas: Dexter Corp. Foundation

Thompson, John F., treas: Christensen Charitable and Religious Foundation, L. C.

Thompson, Leonora Kempner, chmn emeritus: Kempner Fund, Harris and Eliza

Thompson, Lori, secy: National Gypsum Foundation, Inc.

Thompson, Marcia T., dir: Scherman Foundation

Thompson, Margaret E., MD, trust: Towsley Foundation, Harry A. and Margaret D.

Thompson, Mark E., asst treas: Amoco Foundation

Thompson, Mary M., vp, dir: Muller Foundation

Thompson, Mona, trust: Coen Family Foundation, Charles S. and Mary

Thompson, Peter K., MD, trust: Kempner Fund, Harris and Eliza

Thompson, R. Patrick, pres, dir: New York Mercantile Exchange

Thompson, Roger K., trust: Van Wert County Foundation

Thomsen, C. J., trust: McDermott Foundation, Eugene

Walsh, Frank E., III, vp: Sandy Hill Foundation

Walsh, Frank E., Jr., vp: Sandy Hill Foundation

Walsh, Jeffrey R., vp, asst treas, secy: Sandy Hill Foundation

Walsh, John, Jr., dir (J Paul Getty Museum): Getty Trust, J. Paul

Walsh, John N., III, trust: Western New York Foundation

Walsh, John N., Jr., dir: Cummings Foundation, James H.

Walsh, Joseph, pres: Sandy Hill Foundation

Walsh, Mary D., treas: Sandy Hill Foundation

Walsh, Mary D. Fleming, vp: Walsh Foundation

Walsh, Mason, Jr., trust: Mellon Family Foundation, R. K.; trust: Mellon Foundation, Richard King

Walsh, Meghan, vp: Sandy Hill Foundation

Walsh, Michael J., treas: Norton Co.; treas, dir: Norton Co. Foundation

Walsh, Patrick, trust: Merrill Lynch & Co. Foundation Inc.

Walter, Henry G., Jr., dir: Monell Foundation, Ambrose; dir: van Ameringen Foundation; dir: Vetlesen Foundation, G. Unger

Walter, John Robert, chmn, ceo: Donnelley & Sons Co., R.R.

Walters, John Alexander, co-chmn: Alcon Foundation

Walters, Mary, head of pub rels: Thorne Foundation, Oakleigh L.

Walters, Sumner J., trust: Van Wert County Foundation

Walton, James Mellon, chmn: Heinz Endowment, Vira I.; trust: Scaife Family Foundation

Walton, Jon David, trust: Allegheny Ludlum Foundation

Walton, Joseph C., trust: Scaife Family Foundation

Walton, Richard E., secy, dir: Heublein Foundation, Inc.

Walton, S. Robson, chmn, dir: Wal-Mart Stores, Inc.; mem: Wal-Mart Foundation

Waltz, Walter, contr: Sheaffer Inc.

Wamhoff, Richard M., pres: Ore-Ida Foods, Inc.

Ward, James J., vp, secy, dir: Trust Funds

Ward, Jon, group pres: Donnelley & Sons Co., R.R.

Ward, Mabel B., exec dir: Bedsole Foundation, J. L.

Ward, Robert F., dir: Hardin Foundation, Phil

Ward, T. Bestor, III, mem distribution comm: Bedsole Foundation, J. L.

Ward, Terry W., treas: Farish Fund, William Stamps

Wardeberg, George E., pres, ceo, dir: WICOR, Inc.; dir: WICOR Foundation

Wardley, George P., III, secy: Utica National Group Foundation

Wareing, Elizabeth B., vp, dir: Scurlock Foundation

Wargo, Bruce W., trust: Anderson Foundation, John W.

Wark, Robert R., dir: Scott Foundation, Virginia Steele

Warner, Donald T., chmn, dir: Public Welfare Foundation

Warner, Douglas Alexander, III, chmn, pres, ceo: Morgan & Company, J.P.

Warner, Glen W., trust: Ashtabula Foundation

Warner, M. Richard, vp, dir: Temple-Inland Foundation

Warner, Marianne R., vp: Rachal Foundation, Ed

Warner, Peter, trust: Seafirst Foundation

Warner, Philip G., dir: Houston Endowment

Warner, Steve, trust: Hoyt Foundation

Warner, Theodore Kugler, Jr., pres, dir: Independence Foundation

Warnock, John, ceo: Aldus Corp.

Warrell, Lincoln A., chmn, ceo, dir: Pennsylvania Dutch Co.; secy, mgr: Pennsylvania Dutch Co. Foundation

Warren, Arthur M., sr vp, cfo: MBIA Inc.

Warren, Harriet H., dir: Kornfeld Foundation, Emily Davie and Joseph S.

Warren, Ingrid R., mem exec comm, dir: Dodge Foundation, Cleveland H.

Warren, Peter F., Jr., trust: Martin Marietta Corp. Foundation

Warren, Rupert, pres, dir: Julia R. and Estelle L. Foundation

Warren, Shirley, secy: Clements Foundation

Warren, William Michael, Jr., pres, coo, dir: Alabama Gas Corp.

Warsh, Herman E., trust: Mott Fund, Ruth

Wash, James R., secy, treas: Temple-Inland Foundation

Washburn, Frank, vp: Pamida Foundation

Washburn, Monica Winsor, dir: Donner Foundation, William H.

Washburn, Wilcomb Edward, dir: Donner Foundation, William H.

Washington, Don, mgr commun & investor rels: Babcock & Wilcox Co.

Wasserlein, John Henry, pres, dir: Boise Cascade Corporation

Wasserman, Bronna, mem contributions: GATX Corp.

Wasserman, Lew Robert, chmn emeritus, mem exec comm: MCA Inc.; chmn: Stein Foundation, Jules and Doris

Watanabe, Anita, secy: Cooke Foundation

Waterbury, James B., trust: McElroy Trust, R. J.

Waters, Bill W., chmn: Brown Foundation, M. K.

Waters, James R., mem: Central Charities Foundation

Waters, Sandra, trust: Brown Foundation, M. K.

Watjen, Thomas R., exec vp, cfo: Provident Life & Accident Insurance Company of America

Watkins, Randall A., contr, asst treas: Regenstein Foundation

Watkins, Ruth Ann, trust: Retirement Research Foundation

Watrous, Helen, secy: Joslin-Needham Family Foundation

Watrous, Helen C., dir: Petteys Memorial Foundation, Jack

Watson, Jane W., asst secy, asst treas: Ingalls Foundation, Louise H. and David S.

Watson, Michael B., asst secy: Mellon Family Foundation, R. K.; secy: Mellon Foundation, Richard King

Watson, Solomon Brown, IV, vp: New York Times Co. Foundation

Watson, Steven L., vp, secy: Contran Corporation; vp, secy, dir: Simmons Foundation, Inc., Harold

Watson, Stuart, secy: Haley Foundation, W. B.

Watts, Elise Phillips, dir: Phillips Foundation, Ellis L.

Waxlax, Lorne R., exec vp diversified oper: Gillette Co.

Wean, Gordon B., mem bd adms: Wean Foundation, Raymond John

Wean, Raymond John, III, vchmn bd adms: Wean Foundation, Raymond John

Wean, Raymond John, Jr., don, chmn bd adms: Wean Foundation, Raymond John

Weary, Robert K., mem: Central Charities Foundation

Weatherstone, Dennis, trust: Merck Co. Foundation

Weaver, Connie, contributions admin: Boise Cascade Corporation

Weaver, Eudora J., trust: Weaver Foundation, Gil and Dody

Weaver, Henry O., trust, pres: Kayser Foundation

Weaver, James D., pres, coo: Cain Foundation, Gordon and Mary

Weaver, James R., secy: Kent-Lucas Foundation

Weaver, John F., dir: La-Z-Boy Foundation

Weaver, Patricia A., admin, commus & commun rels: Carpenter Technology Corp.

Weaver, Sharyn A., trust: Cain Foundation, Gordon and Mary

Weaver, Sterling L., chmn, dir: Gleason Foundation

Weaver, Thomas C., trust: Acushnet Foundation

Weaver, Warren W., vchmn: Commerce Bancshares, Inc.; pres, dir: Commerce Bancshares Foundation

Weaver, William R., MD, trust: Weaver Foundation, Gil and Dody

Webb, Lewis, Jr., vp, dir: Berger Foundation, H. N. and Frances C.

Webb, Thomas C., pres, ceo, dir: Central Vermont Public Service Corp.

Webber, W. Temple, trust: Temple-Inland Foundation, T. L. L.

Webre, John F., trust: Burkitt Foundation

Webster, Cindy, trust: Firman Fund

Webster, Wally, trust: Seafirst Foundation

Wechsler, Irving A., treas: Jennings Foundation, Mary Hillman

Weckenbaugh, Anne H., dir: Mullen Foundation, J. K.

Weckbaugh, J. Kernan, pres, dir: Mullen Foundation, J. K.

Weckbaugh, John K., vp, dir: Mullen Foundation, J. K.

Weckbaugh, Walter S., treas, dir: Mullen Foundation, J. K.

Weese, Benjamin Horace, pres, trust: Graham

Foundation for Advanced Studies in the Fine Arts

Wege, Peter M., pres: Wege Foundation

Wege, Peter M., II, vp: Wege Foundation

Wegner, Arthur E., dir: Dexter Corp. Foundation; chmn: Beech Aircraft Corp.; pres: Beech Aircraft Foundation

Weidlein, Mary Rea, dir: Dodge Foundation, Cleveland H.

Weigell, Charles, dir: Bucyrus-Erie Foundation

Weiksner, George B., dir: Markle Foundation, John and Mary R.

Weil, Andrew L., secy: Jennings Foundation, Mary Hillman

Weil, Deborah Holt, trust: Holt Family Foundation

Weiler, Harold J., pres: Acme-McCrary and Sapona Foundation

Weiler, Virginia, asst secy: Cooper Industries Foundation

Weill, Sanford I., chmn, ceo: Travelers Inc.; chmn bd of trust: Travelers Foundation

Weinberger, Caspar Willard, chmn, dir: Forbes Inc.

Weiner, Leonard H., vp, trust: DeRoy Foundation, Helen L.; pres, trust: DeRoy Testamentary Foundation

Weiner, Walter Herman, chmn, ceo: Republic NY Corp.

Weins, Leo M., pres, treas, dir: Wilson Foundation, H. W.

Weintraub, Robert M., vp, dir: Alexander Foundation, Joseph

Weinzapfel, Jonathan, mgr pub rels: Old National Bank in Evansville

Weisbruch, Craig, trust: National Gypsum Foundation, Inc.

Weisenfluh, Laura, contact: Davenport-Hatch Foundation

Weisglass, Celeste C., pres, dir: Cheatham Foundation, Owen

Weisglass, Stephen S., vp, treas, dir: Cheatham Foundation, Owen

Weiss, Catherine, trust: Huber Foundation

Weiss, Cathy M., program off: Penn Foundation, William

Weiss, Cora, pres: Rubin Foundation, Samuel

Weiss, Daniel, dir: Rubin Foundation, Samuel

Weiss, Judy, vp: Rubin Foundation, Samuel

Weiss, Peter, treas: Rubin Foundation, Samuel

Weiss, Robert E., vp admin: Meadows Foundation

Weiss, Tamara, dir: Rubin Foundation, Samuel

Weissman, Robert Evan, pres, ceo, dir: Dun & Bradstreet Corp.; trust: Dun & Bradstreet Corp. Foundation, Inc.

Weizenbaum, Norman, trust: Giant Eagle Foundation

Welch, Don E., trust: Winchester Foundation

Welch, Martin E., III, sr vp, cfo: Federal-Mogul Corporation

Welch, William J., vp, dir: Kornfeld Foundation, Emily Davie and Joseph S.

Welder, Paul E., trust: Self Foundation

Welker, Norris J., trust: Puterbaugh Foundation

Weller, Jane, secy: Morgan Foundation, Louie R. and Gertrude

Weller, Joseph M., pres, coo, dir: Nestle USA Inc.; pres, dir: Nestle USA Foundation

Weller, Lucy I., vp, trust: Mather and William Gwinn Mather Fund, Elizabeth Ring

Welling, Eleanor, trust: Symmes Foundation, F. W.

Wells, A. E., trust: Wiggins Memorial Trust, J. J.

Wells, W. David, mem adv comm: Jordan Charitable Foundation, Mary Ranken Jordan and Ettie A.

Welton, Robert Breen, vp, asst contr: Beech Aircraft Corp.; secy-treas: Beech Aircraft Foundation

Welty, John Rider, secy: Carpenter Technology Corp. Foundation

Wendel, Larry L., vp: Van Wert County Foundation

Wendlandt, Gary Edward, exec vp, chief investment off: Massachusetts Mutual Life Insurance Co.

Wendt, Nancy, trust: JELD-WEN Foundation

Wendt, Richard L., fdr, chmn: JELD-WEN, Inc.; trust: JELD-WEN Foundation

Wendt, Roderick C., pres, dir: JELD-WEN, Inc.

Wenrich, Jay H., secy: Steinman Foundation, John Frederick

Wentling, Thomas L., Jr., dir: Staunton Farm Foundation

Wenzler, Joseph P., cfo, dir: WICOR, Inc.; secy, treas: WICOR Foundation

Weppler, Lawrence, vp, dir: Fribourg Foundation

Werbel, Robert H., secy: Allen Brothers Foundation

Werderman, Del V., treas: Hoag Family Foundation, George

Werner, John B., exec dir: Cabell Foundation, Robert G. Cabell III and Maude Morgan

Werner, Jon, secy, treas: Vaughn, Jr. Foundation Fund, James M.

Werner, Sally Roush, mem distribution comm: GAR Foundation

Werner, Vanda N., secy: Norgren Foundation, Carl A.

Werner, William C., vp, dir: Banc One Wisconsin Foundation

Wertenberger, Maurice R., vp: Batts Foundation

Wertheim, Herbert A., pres, dir: Wertheim Foundation, Dr. Herbert A.

Wertheim, Nicole J., secy, dir: Wertheim Foundation, Dr. Herbert A.

Wertheimer, Thomas, vp, dir: MCA Foundation, Ltd.

Wertz, Ronald W., pres: Hillman Foundation

Wescoe, William Clarke, MD, trust emer: Kress Foundation, Samuel H.

West, Millard Farrar, Jr., trust: Giant Food Foundation

West, Ronald D., exec dir, secy, dir: Emerson Foundation, Inc., Fred L.; dir: French Foundation, D.E.

West, Sandra, asst secy: BT Foundation

Willis, Dudley H., trust: Saltonstall Charitable Foundation, Richard

Willis, Lois Cross, dir: Moore Foundation, Edward S.

Willis, Sally S., trust: Saltonstall Charitable Foundation, Richard

Willner, Robin, dir corp social policy and programs: International Business Machines Corp.

Wills, Kenneth, dir: Feild Co-Operative Association

Wills, Rosemary C., asst secy, asst treas: duPont Foundation, Alfred I.

Willson, George C., III, pres: Green Foundation, Allen P. and Josephine B.

Wilsey, Alfred S., Sr., dir: Osher Foundation, Bernard

Wilson, Beth, dir pub aff: Pella Corporation

Wilson, Blenda Jacqueline, trust: Getty Trust, J. Paul

Wilson, Cleo F., exec dir: Playboy Foundation

Wilson, David K., trust: Potter Foundation, Justin and Valere

Wilson, Donald Malcolm, trust: Schumann Fund for New Jersey

Wilson, Dorothy B., trust: Toms Foundation

Wilson, Dorothy Clarke, dir: Meadows Foundation

Wilson, Douglas A., alternate mem distr comm: GAR Foundation

Wilson, Faye, secy: Gilmore Foundation, William G.

Wilson, Frank S., dir: Ensign-Bickford Foundation

Wilson, G. Dale, trust: Van Wert County Foundation

Wilson, Harry, trust: Haley Foundation, W. B.

Wilson, Howard O., treas, dir: Peppers Foundation, Ann

Wilson, J. Richard, pres, trust: Besser Foundation

Wilson, Jack, dir: Porter Testamentary Trust, James Hyde

Wilson, James Lawrence, chmn, ceo: Rohm & Haas Co.

Wilson, Janice J., area pres, dir: First Interstate Bank of Oregon; trust: First Interstate Bank of Oregon Charitable Foundation

Wilson, Jess C., Jr., vp: Jones Foundation, Fletcher

Wilson, John H., II, pres: Piper Foundation, Minnie Stevens

Wilson, John Hill Tucker, trust: Morgan Stanley Foundation

Wilson, Josephine D., vp: Massengill-DeFriece Foundation

Wilson, Justin Potter, chmn, trust: Potter Foundation, Justin and Valere

Wilson, Kirke P., exec dir, secy: Rosenberg Foundation

Wilson, L. M., asst secy: Lumpkin Foundation

Wilson, Lee Anne, trust: Sarkeys Foundation

Wilson, Malcolm, dir: Carvel Foundation, Thomas and Agnes; dir: Clark Foundation

Wilson, Robert Albert, pres: Pfizer Foundation

Wilson, Robert B., trust: Weyerhaeuser Company Foundation

Wilson, Robert L., vp, secy, treas: Lund Foundation

Wilson, Roderick T., pres, ceo: Amfac/JMB Hawaii Inc.

Wilson, Rodney M., treas: Mahadh Foundation

Wilson, Sam, dir corp commun: Iowa-Illinois Gas & Electric Co.

Wilson, Sandra C., vp admin, dir: International Paper Co. Foundation

Wilson, William C., trust: Toms Foundation

Wilson, William L., trust: Yeager Charitable Trust, Lester E.

Winchester, David P., dir: Rice Foundation

Winding, Charles A., trust, vp: Anderson Foundation

Windle, Timothy J., asst secy: American President Companies Foundation

Windsor, Rev. Robert G., dir: Coors Foundation, Adolph

Winget, C. Nelson, treas: Beck Foundation, Elsie E. and Joseph W.

Winham, C., dir pub aff: Burlington Industries, Inc.

Winiger, Leonard J., asst treas, asst contr: American General Finance Corporation

Winkhaus, Hans-Dietrich, chmn, dir: Henkel Corp.

Winkler, Virginia, trust: Hallberg Foundation, E. L. and R. F.

Winship, William B., trust: Bingham Second Betterment Fund, William

Winsor, Curtin, III, dir: Donner Foundation, William H.

Winsor, Curtin, Jr., secy, dir: Donner Foundation, William H.

Winston, Bert F., Jr., vp, trust: Turner Charitable Foundation

Winston, Blake, asst secy, trust: Turner Charitable Foundation

Winston, Samuel, trust: Blowitz-Ridgeway Foundation

Winter, William Bergford, chmn, ceo: Bucyrus-Erie Company; chmn, pres, dir: Bucyrus-Erie Foundation

Winters, Robert Cushing, chmn, dir: Prudential Securities, Inc.

Wise, Emma F., trust: Wise Foundation and Charitable Trust, Watson W.

Wise, John James, dir: Mobil Foundation

Wise, Robert E., cfo, vp, treas: Meadows Foundation

Wise, Robert Edward, MD, trust: Dana Charitable Trust, Eleanor Naylor

Wiseman, Ronald D., treas: Thomas Foundation

Wishnack, Marshall B., pres, dir: Wheat First Butcher Singer, Inc.; dir: Wheat, First Securities/Butcher & Singer Foundation

Wishnick, Lisa, dir: Wishnick Foundation, Robert I.

Wishnick, William, pres, dir: Wishnick Foundation, Robert I.

Wiskowski, Carol A., secy, dir: Madison Gas & Electric Foundation

Wisnom, David, Jr., pres: Lux Foundation, Miranda

Wisnosky, Karen, secy: Brady Foundation

Wister, Diana S., pres: Strawbridge Foundation of Pennsylvania II, Margaret Dorrance

Witham, Louise F., trust: Webber Oil Foundation

Witherspoon, Douglas C., dir: Scholl Foundation, Dr.

Witherspoon, Jere Wathen, exec dir: Duke Endowment

Withum, Lawrence A., Jr., trust: Coen Family Foundation, Charles S. and Mary

Witter, Dean, III, pres, dir: Witter Foundation, Dean

Witter, Malcolm G., trust: Witter Foundation, Dean

Witter, William D., secy, treas: Witter Foundation, Dean

Wittmann, Lin, dir: Brillion Foundation

Wohlert, Roger W., vp, treas: SBC Communications Foundation

Wohlstetter, Charles, pres, dir: Rose Foundation, Billy

Wojtak, Barry, treas: Abbott Laboratories Fund

Wolcott, Arthur S., chmn, dir: Seneca Foods Foundation

Wolf, Daniel A., vp: Plumsock Fund

Wolf, Harold, dir: Peters Foundation, R. D. and Linda

Wolf, Harold J., secy, treas, dir: Brillion Foundation

Wolf, John W., Sr., dir: Kaufmann Foundation, Henry

Wolf, Lee J., trust: Raymond Foundation

Wolf, Lester K., trust: Patterson Charitable Fund, W. I.

Wolf, Richard Lloyd, vp, dir: Julia R. and Estelle L. Foundation

Wolf, Robert, pres: New-Land Foundation

Wolf, Stephanie R., exec dir: Cowell Foundation, S. H.

Wolf, Stephen M., chmn, ceo, pres: United Airlines, Inc.; pres, dir: United Airlines Foundation

Wolfe, James F., trust: Gaylord Foundation, Clifford Willard

Wolfe, Joan M., vp, asst secy: Mailman Foundation

Wolfe, John F., pub, pres, ceo, dir: Columbus Dispatch Printing Co.; pres: Wolfe Associates, Inc.

Wolfe, Judson, vp, trust: Mailman Foundation

Wolfe, Kenneth L., chmn, ceo: Hershey Foods Corp.

Wolfe, Laurence A., vp (admin): Weingart Foundation

Wolfe, Merle, pres, dir: Thompson Charitable Foundation

Wolfe, William C., Jr., vp: Wolfe Associates, Inc.

Wolfensperger, Diana Potter, trust: Lux Foundation, Miranda

Wolff, Byron L., vp: Pamida Foundation

Wolff, Herbert E., secy, dir: First Hawaiian Foundation

Wolff, Jesse D., treas, dir: Weil, Gotshal and Manges Foundation

Wolff, Rosalie S., vp: Solow Foundation

Wollen, Carolyn S., trust: Bingham Second Betterment Fund, William

Wolman, J. Martin, vp, treas: Lee Endowment Foundation

Wolman, Paul C., III, dir: Unger Foundation, Aber D.

Woloshyn, Sonyia, trust, treas: Turrell Fund

Wolter, Gary J., vp, dir: Madison Gas & Electric Foundation

Womack, Christopher C., dir: Alabama Power Foundation

Woner, Bruce J., mem: Central Charities Foundation

Woo, William Franklin, dir: Pulitzer Publishing Co. Foundation

Wood, Anthony C., exec dir: Ittleson Foundation

Wood, Barbara M. J., dir: Rice Foundation

Wood, Charles O., III, trust: Wood Foundation of Chambersburg, PA

Wood, Clyde H., pres: Alabama Power Foundation

Wood, David S., trust: Wood Foundation of Chambersburg, PA

Wood, Dick, mem contributions comm: GATX Corp.

Wood, Edward Jenner, mem: Trust Co. of Georgia Foundation

Wood, James F., dir: McMahon Foundation

Wood, Kate D., dir: Hyde and Watson Foundation

Wood, Miriam M., trust: Wood Foundation of Chambersburg, PA

Wood, Robert A., dir: Green Foundation, Allen P. and Josephine B.

Wood, Susannah C. L., dir: AKC Fund

Wood, Sylvia Upton, secy, trust: Upton Foundation, Frederick S.

Wood, William Philler, trust: Grundy Foundation

Woodruff, Fred M., Jr., trust: Miller Foundation

Woods, David F., clerk, dir: Beveridge Foundation, Frank Stanley

Woods, Elizabeth J., asst secy: Fruehauf Foundation

Woods, James D., chmn, pres, ceo, dir: Baker Hughes Inc.

Woodson, C. E., MD, exec vp: Gulf Coast Medical Foundation

Woodward, Joanne Gignilliat, dir: Newman's Own Foundation

Woodward, Reid T., dir: Woodward Fund

Woodward, Stephen S., dir: Woodward Fund

Woodward, William S., dir: Woodward Fund

Woolard, Edgar Smith, Jr., chmn, ceo, dir: du Pont de Nemours & Co., E. I.

Woollcott, James, mem adv comm: Janirve Foundation

Workman, Maurice C., trust: Moore & Sons Foundation, B.C.

Worls, G. Randolph, trust: Benedum Foundation, Claude Worthington

Worthington, John Rice, sr vp, gen couns, dir: MCI Communications Corp.; dir: MCI Foundation

Wortman, Judy, trust: Kutz Foundation, Milton and Hattie

Wright, Arnold W., Jr., exec dir: CIGNA Foundation

Wright, Barbara, secy, trust: Packard Foundation, David and Lucile

Wright, Charles E., trust: Arkell Hall Foundation

Wright, Donald Franklin, sr vp: Times Mirror Company,

The; dir: Times Mirror Foundation

Wright, Hasbrouck S., exec trust: Kunkel Foundation, John Crain

Wright, J., trust: Cranston Foundation

Wright, James, dir: Fairchild Foundation, Sherman

Wright, Patricia Donovan, exec dir, secy: Amoco Foundation

Wright, Roger Ellerton, pres: Consolidated Natural Gas Co.; pres: Consolidated Natural Gas System Foundation

Wright, Rose Bauervic, vp: Bauervic Foundation, Charles M.

Wright, Samuel H., secy: PHH Foundation, Inc.

Wright, Thomas H., Jr., dir: Lowenstein Foundation, Leon

Wright, Wesley, mem: Wal-Mart Foundation

Wright, William Bigelow, dir: Bunbury Company; vp, treas, trust: Windham Foundation

Wright, William L., vp, dir: Hultquist Foundation

Wright, William R., trust: Davis Foundations, Arthur Vining

Wriston, Kathryn Dineen, trust: Hartford Foundation, John A.

Wroughton, Philip L., vchmn, dir: Marsh & McLennan Companies, Inc.

Wulf, Jerold W., pres, dir: Andersen Corp.

Wulff, Dr. Harald P., pres, ceo, dir: Henkel Corp.

Wyckoff, E. Lisk, Jr., pres, treas, trust: Homeland Foundation

Wyland, Susan T., trust: Towsley Foundation, Harry A. and Margaret D.

Wyman, Ann M., trust: Wyman Youth Trust

Wyman, David C., trust: Wyman Youth Trust

Wyman, Deehan M., trust: Wyman Youth Trust

Wynia, Ann, dir: Bush Foundation

Wynkoop, Roger D., exec vp: ACF Industries, Inc.

Wynne, Richard B., mem adv comm: Janirve Foundation

Wyse, Alden M., secy, treas, dir: Kelly Foundation

Wyse, J. Christopher, mgr commun: Whirlpool Foundation

Wyszomierski, Jack L., treas: Schering-Plough Foundation

Y

Yablon, Leonard Harold, secy-treas: Forbes Foundation

Yaconetti, Dianne Mary, vp admin, corp secy: Brunswick Corp.; vp, dir: Brunswick Foundation

Yamaguchi, Tamotsu, chmn: Union Bank

Yamashiro-Omi, Dianne, program off: Gap Foundation

Yancy, Mary Garwood, pres: Henry Foundation, Patrick

Yancy, Scott, cfo: Cable & Wireless Holdings, Inc.

Yannarell, Robert W., secy, treas: AMETEK Foundation

Index to Corporations and Foundations by Recipient Type

Please refer to the Master Index to Corporations and Foundations for profile page numbers.

Arts & Humanities

Art History

Chicago Sun-Times, Inc.
Christian Dior New York, Inc.
CT Corp. System
Federated Mutual Insurance Co.
Fondren Foundation
LamCo. Communications
Lauder Foundation
McGonagle Foundation, Dextra Baldwin
Millbrook Tribute Garden
Morris Foundation, Margaret T.
Woodward Fund

Arts Appreciation

Ahmanson Foundation
Albertson's Inc.
Aldus Corp.
American Natural Resources Company
Amfac/JMB Hawaii Inc.
Annenberg Foundation
Armco Inc.
Baker Trust, George F.
Bank of New York Company, Inc.
BankAmerica Corp.
Bemis Company, Inc.
Bingham Foundation, William
Binney & Smith Inc.
Blair and Co., William
Blandin Foundation
Block, H&R
Cabot Corp.
Centerior Energy Corp.
Century Companies of America
Chase Manhattan Bank, N.A.
Chicago Sun-Times, Inc.
Christian Dior New York, Inc.
Citibank
Clorox Co.
Cole Foundation, Olive B.
Colonial Life & Accident Insurance Co.
Cowles Charitable Trust
Cummins Engine Co.
Diamond Foundation, Aaron
Dimeo Construction Co.
Dodge Foundation, Geraldine R.
Dreyfus Foundation, Max and Victoria
du Pont de Nemours & Co., E. I.
Federated Mutual Insurance Co.
First Fidelity Bank
First Interstate Bank of Oregon
Fleishhacker Foundation
Freeport-McMoRan Inc.
Frost National Bank
Fry Foundation, Lloyd A.
Gilman Foundation, Howard
HCA Foundation
Hechinger Co.
John Hancock Mutual Life Insurance Co.
Johnson & Higgins
Journal-Gazette Co.
Kennecott Corporation
Kimberly-Clark Corp.
Kingsbury Corp.
LamCo. Communications
Levitt Foundation
Management Compensation Group/Dulworth Inc.
McEvoy Foundation, Mildred H.

Miller Brewing Company/North Carolina
The New Yorker Magazine, Inc.
Northwest Natural Gas Co.
Norton Co.
Olsson Memorial Foundation, Elis
Owen Industries, Inc.
Pacific Telesis Group
Pittsburg Midway Coal Mining Co.
Providence Gas Co.
Providence Journal Company
Pulitzer Publishing Co.
Rohm & Haas Co.
Roseburg Forest Products Co.
Rosenberg, Jr. Family Foundation, Louise and Claude
Royal Group, Inc.
Sara Lee Hosiery, Inc.
SBC Communications Inc.
Seaway Food Town, Inc.
Security Life of Denver Insurance Co.
Sedgwick James Inc.
Shenandoah Life Insurance Co.
Shott, Jr. Foundation, Hugh I.
Steinman Foundation, John Frederick
Textron, Inc.
Trust Company Bank
Vevay-Switzerland County Foundation
Wallace-Reader's Digest Fund, Lila
Wertheim Foundation, Dr. Herbert A.
Winter Construction Co.

Arts Associations & Councils

Abell-Hanger Foundation
Acushnet Co.
Aetna Life & Casualty Co.
Alabama Gas Corp.
Alabama Power Co.
Alcon Laboratories, Inc.
AlliedSignal Inc.
Altman Foundation
Alumax Inc.
Aluminum Co. of America
AMCORE Bank, N.A. Rockford
American Fidelity Corporation
American General Finance Corp.
American National Bank & Trust Co. of Chicago
American Natural Resources Company
American President Companies, Ltd.
American United Life Insurance Co.
Ameritas Life Insurance Corp.
Ames Charitable Trust, Harriett
Amfac/JMB Hawaii Inc.
AMP Incorporated
AMR Corp.
Andersons, The
Anheuser-Busch Companies, Inc.
Annenberg Foundation
AON Corporation
Appleton Papers Inc.
Arcadia Foundation
Archer-Daniels-Midland Co.
Argyros Foundation
Aristech Chemical Corp.
Arkansas Power & Light Co.
Armco Inc.
Armstrong Foundation
Astor Foundation, Vincent

AT&T Corp.
Auerbach Foundation, Beatrice Fox
Avery Arts Foundation, Milton and Sally
Avon Products, Inc.
Baker Foundation, Dexter F. and Dorothy H.
Ball Brothers Foundation
Ball Foundation, George and Frances
Banc One Wisconsin Corp.
Bank of Boston Corp.
Bank of New York Company, Inc.
Bank One, Texas-Houston Office
BankAmerica Corp.
Barra Foundation
Battelle Memorial Institute
Baughman Foundation
Bay Foundation
Bean Foundation, Norwin S. and Elizabeth N.
BE&K Inc.
Beattie Foundation Trust, Cordelia Lee
Bedsole Foundation, J. L.
Beech Aircraft Corp.
Bemis Company, Inc.
Benenson Foundation, Frances and Benjamin
Benwood Foundation
Berger Foundation, H. N. and Frances C.
Bertha Foundation
Besser Foundation
Bethlehem Steel Corp.
Betts Industries
Beveridge Foundation, Frank Stanley
Bingham Foundation, William
Bingham Second Betterment Fund, William
Binney & Smith Inc.
Binswanger Cos.
Birnschein Foundation, Alvin and Marion
Blandin Foundation
Block, H&R
Blount Educational and Charitable Foundation, Mildred Weedon
Blount, Inc.
Blue Bell, Inc.
Boatmen's Bancshares, Inc.
Borden, Inc.
Borman's Inc.
Bothin Foundation
Bowater Incorporated
Bowen Foundation, Ethel N.
Bowne Foundation, Robert
BP America Inc.
Brady Foundation
Breyer Foundation
Bridgestone/Firestone, Inc.
Bristol-Myers Squibb Company
Brown & Williamson Tobacco Corp.
Bryn Mawr Trust Co.
Bucyrus-Erie Company
Burdines Inc.
Burlington Industries, Inc.
Burnett-Tandy Foundation
Bush Foundation
Butz Foundation
Cabell Foundation, Robert G. Cabell III and Maude Morgan
Cable & Wireless Holdings, Inc.
Cabot Corp.
Cafritz Foundation, Morris and Gwendolyn
Callaway Foundation

Campbell Foundation, Ruth and Henry
Cape Branch Foundation
Carolyn Foundation
Carpenter Foundation
Carpenter Foundation, E. Rhodes and Leona B.
Carpenter Technology Corp.
Carter Foundation, Amon G.
Carter Foundation, Beirne
Caspersen Foundation for Aid to Health and Education, O. W.
CBI Industries, Inc.
Centerior Energy Corp.
Central Fidelity Banks, Inc.
Central Hudson Gas & Electric Corp.
Central Maine Power Co.
Centralia Foundation
Chadwick Fund, Dorothy Jordan
Chapman Charitable Corporation, Howard and Bess
Chase Manhattan Bank, N.A.
Chatham Manufacturing Co.
Chazen Foundation
CHC Foundation
Cheney Foundation, Ben B.
Chesapeake Corp.
Chevron Corporation
Chicago Sun-Times, Inc.
Christensen Charitable and Religious Foundation, L. C.
Christian Dior New York, Inc.
Chrysler Corp.
CIGNA Corporation
Citibank
CLARCOR Inc.
Clarkson Foundation, Jeniam
Clorox Co.
Clowes Fund
Collins Foundation
Colonial Life & Accident Insurance Co.
Columbia Foundation
Columbus Dispatch Printing Co.
Comer Foundation
Commerce Bancshares, Inc.
Commerce Clearing House, Incorporated
Connecticut Mutual Life Insurance Company
Consolidated Papers, Inc.
Continental Corp.
Cooke Foundation
Cooper Industries, Inc.
Coors Foundation, Adolph
Cord Foundation, E. L.
Corning Incorporated
Coughlin-Saunders Foundation
Cowles Charitable Trust
Cowles Media Co.
CPC International Inc.
CR Industries
Crandall Memorial Foundation, J. Ford
Crane Co.
Crown Books
CS First Boston Corporation
Cummins Engine Co.
Curtice-Burns Foods, Inc.
Daily News
Daniel Foundation of Alabama
Daugherty Foundation
Davidson Family Charitable Foundation
Davis Foundation, Edwin W. and Catherine M.
Davis Foundation, Irene E. and George A.
Davis Foundation, James A. and Juliet L.
Delaware North Co., Inc.

Demoulas Supermarkets Inc.
DeRoy Foundation, Helen L.
Detroit Edison Co.
DeVore Foundation
Dewing Foundation, Frances R.
Dexter Charitable Fund, Eugene A.
Dexter Corporation
Dimeo Construction Co.
Dishman Charitable Foundation Trust, H. E. and Kate
Dodge Foundation, Cleveland H.
Dodge Foundation, Geraldine R.
Dodge Jones Foundation
Donnelley Foundation, Gaylord and Dorothy
Douglas & Lomason Company
Douty Foundation
Dow Corning Corp.
Dresser Industries, Inc.
Dreyfus Foundation, Jean and Louis
Dreyfus Foundation, Max and Victoria
du Pont de Nemours & Co., E. I.
Duchossois Industries Inc.
Duke Power Co.
Dun & Bradstreet Corp.
Eastman Kodak Company
Eaton Corporation
Eaton Foundation, Cyrus
El Pomar Foundation
Emerson Foundation, Inc., Fred L.
Ensign-Bickford Industries
Erpf Fund, Armand G.
Ethyl Corp
Ettinger Foundation
Everett Charitable Trust
Exchange National Bank
Exxon Corporation
Favrot Fund
Federal-Mogul Corporation
Federated Mutual Insurance Co.
Fenton Foundation
Ferebee Endowment, Percy O.
Fieldcrest Cannon Inc.
Finch Foundation, Doak
Finch Foundation, Thomas Austin
First Fidelity Bank
First Interstate Bank of Oregon
First Tennessee Bank
First Union Corp.
First Union National Bank of Florida
Fleishhacker Foundation
Folger Fund
Forbes Inc.
Ford Foundation
Ford Motor Co.
Forest Foundation
Fort Wayne National Bank
Foster Charitable Trust
Freedom Forge Corp.
Freeman Charitable Trust, Samuel
Freeport-McMoRan Inc.
Frese Foundation, Arnold D.
Fribourg Foundation
Frisch's Restaurants Inc.
Frost National Bank
Gannett Publishing Co., Guy
GATX Corp.
Gazette Co.
General Mills, Inc.
General Motors Corp.
Geneseo Foundation
GenRad
Georgia-Pacific Corporation
Georgia Power Co.
Getty Trust, J. Paul

Giant Food Stores
Gilmore Foundation, William G.
Glaser Foundation
Glick Foundation, Eugene and Marilyn
Globe Newspaper Co.
Goldie-Anna Charitable Trust
Goldsmith Foundation, Horace W.
Goldwyn Foundation, Samuel
Graham Foundation for Advanced Studies in the Fine Arts
Grand Rapids Label Co.
Great-West Life Assurance Co.
Greenwall Foundation
Gregg-Graniteville Foundation
Greve Foundation, William and Mary
Griffis Foundation
Griffith Foundation, W. C.
Griggs and Mary Griggs Burke Foundation, Mary Livingston
Groome Beatty Trust, Helen D.
Gulf Power Co.
Habig Foundation, Arnold F.
Halsell Foundation, Ewing
Hamilton Bank
Hammer Foundation, Armand
Harcourt General, Inc.
Hardin Foundation, Phil
Harmon Foundation, Pearl M. and Julia J.
Harsco Corp.
Hartford Foundation, John A.
Hawn Foundation
HCA Foundation
Hechinger Co.
Heginbotham Trust, Will E.
Heinz Company, H. J.
Heinz Endowment, Howard
Heinz Endowment, Vira I.
Heinz Trust, Drue
Henderson Foundation, George B.
Hershey Foods Corp.
Herzstein Charitable Foundation, Albert and Ethel
Heublein Inc.
Hewlett Foundation, William and Flora
Higginson Trust, Corina
Hill Foundation, Sandy
Hillman Family Foundation, Alex
Hillsdale Fund
Hoffman Foundation, Maximilian E. and Marion O.
Holnam
Holzer Memorial Foundation, Richard H.
Hook Drugs
Hopedale Foundation
Houchens Foundation, Ervin G.
Houston Endowment
Houston Industries Incorporated
Howard and Bush Foundation
Hoyt Foundation, Stewart W. and Willma C.
Hudson-Webber Foundation
Hultquist Foundation
Humana, Inc.
Humphrey Fund, George M. and Pamela S.
Hunt Charitable Trust, C. Giles
Hunt Foundation, Samuel P.
Huthsteiner Fine Arts Trust
Icahn Foundation, Carl C.
ICI Americas Inc.
IES Industries, Inc.
Illinois Tool Works, Inc.
Inland Container Corp.
Interkal, Inc.
International Business Machines Corp.
International Paper Co.
ITT Hartford Insurance Group, Inc.
Ittleson Foundation
Jackson Foundation
James River Corp. of Virginia
Janirve Foundation

Jarson-Stanley and Mickey Kaplan Foundation, Isaac and Esther
JELD-WEN, Inc.
Jockey Hollow Foundation
John Hancock Mutual Life Insurance Co.
Johnson Controls Inc.
Johnson Fund, Edward C.
Johnson & Higgins
Johnson & Son, S.C.
Jonsson Foundation
Jordan Charitable Foundation, Mary Ranken Jordan and Ettie A.
Jostens, Inc.
Journal-Gazette Co.
Justus Trust, Edith C.
Kansas City Southern Industries
Kantzler Foundation
Kardon Foundation, Samuel and Rebecca
Kemper Foundation, William T.
Kempner Fund, Harris and Eliza
Kennecott Corporation
Kent-Lucas Foundation
Kiewit Foundation, Peter
Kimberly-Clark Corp.
Kingsbury Corp.
Kinney-Lindstrom Foundation
Kiplinger Foundation
Kirby Foundation, F. M.
Kirkpatrick Foundation
Kline Foundation, Josiah W. and Bessie H.
Klipstein Foundation, Ernest Christian
KN Energy, Inc.
Knight Foundation, John S. and James L.
Koch Charitable Foundation, Charles G.
Koehler Foundation, Marcia and Otto
Kohn-Joseloff Foundation
Kress Foundation, Samuel H.
Kunkel Foundation, John Crain
Kuyper Foundation, Peter H. and E. Lucille
Lasdon Foundation, William and Mildred
Lauder Foundation
Laurel Foundation
Leavey Foundation, Thomas and Dorothy
Lebovitz Fund
LEF Foundation
Leighton-Oare Foundation
Lemberg Foundation
Leuthold Foundation
Life Insurance Co. of Georgia
Link, Jr. Foundation, George
Lipton, Thomas J.
Little, Inc., Arthur D.
Liz Claiborne, Inc.
Loews Corporation
Long Island Lighting Co.
Lurcy Charitable and Educational Trust, Georges
Lydall, Inc.
MacArthur Foundation, John D. and Catherine T.
Macy & Co., Inc., R.H.
Madison Gas & Electric Co.
Magowan Family Foundation
Management Compensation Group/Dulworth Inc.
Mandeville Foundation
Mardigian Foundation
Maritz Inc.
Markey Charitable Fund, John C.
Marmot Foundation
Marpat Foundation
Marquette Electronics, Inc.
Marriott Foundation, J. Willard
Marsh & McLennan Companies, Inc.
Marshall Trust in Memory of Sanders McDaniel, Harriet McDaniel
Martin Marietta Corp.

Mather Charitable Trust, S. Livingston
Mather Fund, Richard
Mather and William Gwinn Mather Fund, Elizabeth Ring
May Department Stores Company, The
MBIA Inc.
MCA Inc.
McBean Charitable Trust, Alletta Morris
McCasland Foundation
McCormick Trust, Anne
McCune Charitable Foundation, Marshall and Perrine D.
McCune Charitable Trust, John R.
McDermott Foundation, Eugene
McDonald & Company Securities, Inc.
McDonnell Douglas Corp.-West
McEvoy Foundation, Mildred H.
McFawn Trust No. 2, Lois Sisler
McGonagle Foundation, Dextra Baldwin
McLean Contributionship
McShain Charities, John
Mead Corporation, The
Meadows Foundation
Mellon Foundation, Andrew W.
Mercury Aircraft
Merrick Foundation
Messing Family Charitable Foundation
Metropolitan Life Insurance Co.
Millbrook Tribute Garden
Miller Brewing Company/North Carolina
Miller Charitable Foundation, Howard E. and Nell E.
Miller Foundation
Miller Fund, Kathryn and Gilbert
Miller-Mellor Association
Mingenback Foundation, Julia J.
Mnuchin Foundation
Mobil Oil Corp.
Mohasco Corp.
Monadnock Paper Mills
Moore Charitable Foundation, Marjorie
Moore & Sons, B.C.
Morgan & Company, J.P.
Morris Foundation, Margaret T.
Mosinee Paper Corp.
Mott Fund, Ruth
Muchnic Foundation
National Gypsum Co.
National Westminster Bank New Jersey
NBD Indiana, Inc.
Neuberger Foundation, Roy R. and Marie S.
New York Life Insurance Co.
New York Stock Exchange, Inc.
The New Yorker Magazine, Inc.
NewMil Bancorp
Noble Foundation, Edward John
Norfolk Shipbuilding & Drydock Corp.
Northwest Natural Gas Co.
Norton Co.
Norton Family Foundation, Peter
Norwest Bank Nebraska, N.A.
Novell Inc.
O'Connor Foundation, A. Lindsay and Olive B.
OCRI Foundation
Offield Family Foundation
Old National Bank in Evansville
Olin Corp.
Olin Foundation, Spencer T. and Ann W.
Oliver Memorial Trust Foundation

Olsson Memorial Foundation, Elis
Overbrook Foundation
Owen Industries, Inc.
Packard Foundation, David and Lucile
PaineWebber
Paley Foundation, William S.
Palisades Educational Foundation
Panhandle Eastern Corporation
Park Foundation
Parshelsky Foundation, Moses L.
Penn Foundation, William
Pennzoil Co.
Peoples Energy Corp.
Peterson Foundation, Hal and Charlie
Petrie Trust, Lorene M.
Petteys Memorial Foundation, Jack
Pfizer, Inc.
Pforzheimer Foundation, Carl and Lily
Phillips Family Foundation, Jay and Rose
Phillips Foundation, Ellis L.
Piankova Foundation, Tatiana
Pick, Jr. Fund, Albert
Pioneer Trust Bank, NA
Pittsburg Midway Coal Mining Co.
Plumsock Fund
PNC Bank, N.A.
Polaroid Corp.
Porter Foundation, Mrs. Cheever
Porter Testamentary Trust, James Hyde
Potomac Electric Power Co.
PPG Industries, Inc.
Premier Industrial Corp.
Price Foundation, Louis and Harold
Providence Gas Co.
Providence Journal Company
Provident Life & Accident Insurance Company of America
Providian Corporation
Prudential Insurance Co. of America, The
Pulitzer Publishing Co.
Puterbaugh Foundation
Putnam Foundation
Ralston Purina Co.
Raymond Corp.
Reed Foundation
Reinberger Foundation
Reynolds Foundation, Donald W.
Rice Charitable Foundation, Albert W.
Rice Foundation
Rich Products Corporation
RJR Nabisco Inc.
Robinson Fund, Maurice R.
Rockwell Fund
Rockwell International Corporation
Rohatyn Foundation, Felix and Elizabeth
Rohm & Haas Co.
Rose Foundation, Billy
Roseburg Forest Products Co.
Ross Laboratories
Rouse Co.
Rowland Foundation
Royal Group, Inc.
Rubin Foundation, Samuel
Rudin Foundation
Saint Paul Companies, Inc.
Salomon Foundation, Richard and Edna
Sandusky International Inc.
Santa Fe Pacific Corporation
Sara Lee Corp.
Sara Lee Hosiery, Inc.
Sarkeys Foundation
SBC Communications Inc.
Schering-Plough Corp.
Schiff Foundation, Dorothy
Schuller International
Schwab & Co., Inc., Charles

Schwartz Fund for Education and Health Research, Arnold and Marie
Scott Fetzer Co.
Scott Foundation, Virginia Steele
Scott Foundation, William E.
Scurlock Foundation
Seafirst Corporation
Seaver Institute
Seaway Food Town, Inc.
Security Life of Denver Insurance Co.
Sedgwick James Inc.
Seidman Family Foundation
Selby and Marie Selby Foundation, William G.
Seneca Foods Corp.
Shawmut National Corp.
Sheaffer Inc.
Shenandoah Life Insurance Co.
Shott, Jr. Foundation, Hugh I.
Shubert Foundation
Sierra Pacific Industries
Simon Foundation, William E. and Carol G.
Simpson Investment Company
Skaggs Foundation, L. J. and Mary C.
Skillman Foundation
Slifka Foundation, Joseph and Sylvia
Sloan Foundation, Alfred P.
Smith Charitable Foundation, Lou and Lutza
Smith Foundation, Kelvin and Eleanor
Snayberger Memorial Foundation, Harry E. and Florence W.
Snow Foundation, John Ben
Snow Memorial Trust, John Ben
Solow Foundation
Sonat Inc.
South Waite Foundation
Southern California Edison Co.
Southern New England Telephone Company
Southwestern Electric Power Co.
Speyer Foundation, Alexander C. and Tillie S.
Springs Foundation
Square D Co.
Stackpole-Hall Foundation
Stanley Works
Starr Foundation
Stauffer Foundation, John and Beverly
Steinhagen Benevolent Trust, B. A. and Elinor
Steinman Foundation, James Hale
Steinman Foundation, John Frederick
Sternberger Foundation, Tannenbaum
Stevens Foundation, John T.
Strauss Foundation, Leon
Strawbridge Foundation of Pennsylvania II, Margaret Dorrance
Subaru of America Inc.
Sulzberger Foundation
Tait Foundation, Frank M.
Taylor Foundation, Ruth and Vernon
Teleflex Inc.
Temple Foundation, T. L. L.
Tenneco Inc.
Texaco Inc.
Texas Commerce Bank-Houston, N.A.
Textron, Inc.
Thalhimer and Family Foundation, Charles G.
Thomas Industries
Thomasville Furniture Industries
Times Mirror Company, The
Tiscornia Foundation
Titus Foundation, Roy and Niuta
Todd Co., A.M.

Toms Foundation
Towsley Foundation, Harry A. and Margaret D.
Travelers Inc.
Trexler Trust, Harry C.
Truland Foundation
Trust Company Bank
Tupancy-Harris Foundation of 1986
Turner Charitable Foundation
Union Camp Corporation
Union Electric Co.
Union Pacific Corp.
United Airlines, Inc.
U.S. Bank of Washington
Uris Brothers Foundation
US WEST, Inc.
USL Capital Corporation
USX Corporation
Valentine Foundation, Lawson
Valmont Industries, Inc.
van Ameringen Foundation
Van Every Foundation, Philip L.
Virginia Power Co.
Vulcan Materials Co.
Wachovia Bank of North Carolina, N.A.
Wallace-Reader's Digest Fund, Lila
Walsh Foundation
Washington Forrest Foundation
Washington Mutual Savings Bank
Wean Foundation, Raymond John
Wells Foundation, Franklin H. and Ruth L.
Wendt Foundation, Margaret L.
Wertheim Foundation, Dr. Herbert A.
Western New York Foundation
Weyerhaeuser Co.
Whirlpool Corporation
Whiting Foundation
Whitney Fund, David M.
Whittenberger Foundation, Claude R. and Ethel B.
Wickson-Link Memorial Foundation
Wilder Foundation
Willard Helping Fund, Cecilia Young
Williams Companies, The
Wilson Foundation, H. W.
Wilson Fund, Matilda R.
Winchester Foundation
Windham Foundation
Winnebago Industries, Inc.
Winter Construction Co.
Wiremold Co.
Wood Foundation of Chambersburg, PA
Wyman Youth Trust
Yeager Charitable Trust, Lester E.
Zarrow Foundation, Anne and Henry

Arts Centers

Adler Foundation Trust, Philip D. and Henrietta B.
Ahmanson Foundation
Alabama Power Co.
Albertson's Inc.
Aldus Corp.
Alexander Foundation, Joseph
Allegheny Ludlum Corp.
Allendale Insurance Co.
AlliedSignal Inc.
Alumax Inc.
Aluminum Co. of America
Amcast Industrial Corp.
American Brands, Inc.
American National Bank & Trust Co. of Chicago
American Natural Resources Company
American United Life Insurance Co.
Ames Charitable Trust, Harriett
AMETEK, Inc.
Amfac/JMB Hawaii Inc.

Amoco Corporation
Andersen Corp.
Andersen Foundation
Andersons, The
Andrews Foundation
Anheuser-Busch Companies, Inc.
Annenberg Foundation
Archer-Daniels-Midland Co.
Argyros Foundation
Aristech Chemical Corp.
Arkansas Power & Light Co.
Arkell Hall Foundation
Armco Inc.
Astor Foundation, Vincent
AT&T Corp.
Atherton Family Foundation
Auerbach Foundation, Beatrice Fox
Avery Arts Foundation, Milton and Sally
Avon Products, Inc.
Babcock & Wilcox Co.
Baehr Foundation, Louis W. and Dolpha
Baldwin Memorial Foundation, Fred
Bank of New York Company, Inc.
Bank One, Youngstown, NA
BankAmerica Corp.
Banta Corp.
Barra Foundation
Barry Corp., R. G.
Batts Foundation
Bauervic Foundation, Charles M.
Bay Foundation
Bean Foundation, Norwin S. and Elizabeth N.
Bedsole Foundation, J. L.
Bemis Company, Inc.
Benenson Foundation, Frances and Benjamin
Bingham Foundation, William
Binney & Smith Inc.
Bishop Foundation, E. K. and Lillian F.
Blair and Co., William
Blake Foundation, S. P.
Blandin Foundation
Block, H&R
Blount, Inc.
Blum Foundation, Harry and Maribel G.
Blum-Kovler Foundation
Boeing Co., The
Boettcher Foundation
Borden, Inc.
Borman's Inc.
Boswell Foundation, James G.
Bowater Incorporated
Bowen Foundation, Ethel N.
BP America Inc.
Brach Foundation, Helen
Breyer Foundation
Bridwell Foundation, J. S.
Bristol-Myers Squibb Company
Broadhurst Foundation
Bryant Foundation
Bryn Mawr Trust Co.
Burchfield Foundation, Charles E.
Burden Foundation, Florence V.
Burdines Inc.
Bush Foundation
Cabot Corp.
Cafritz Foundation, Morris and Gwendolyn
Cain Foundation, Effie and Wofford
Campbell Foundation
Canon U.S.A., Inc.
Carpenter Foundation, E. Rhodes and Leona B.
Carter Foundation, Beirne
Cassett Foundation, Louis N.
Castle Foundation, Harold K. L.
CBI Industries, Inc.
Centerior Energy Corp.
Chadwick Fund, Dorothy Jordan

Charina Foundation
Chase Manhattan Bank, N.A.
Chastain Charitable Foundation, Robert Lee and Thomas M.
Chazen Foundation
Cheney Foundation, Ben B.
Chesebrough-Pond's USA Co.
Chevron Corporation
Chicago Sun-Times, Inc.
Christian Dior New York, Inc.
Chrysler Corp.
Citibank
Citizens Bank of Rhode Island
Claiborne and Art Ortenberg Foundation, Liz
Clay Foundation
Clorox Co.
Colonial Life & Accident Insurance Co.
Coltec Industries, Inc.
Columbia Foundation
Commerce Clearing House, Incorporated
Consolidated Natural Gas Co.
Continental Corp.
Cooke Foundation
Coors Foundation, Adolph
Copley Press, Inc.
Cord Foundation, E. L.
Cowles Charitable Trust
Cowles Foundation, Gardner and Florence Call
Cowles Media Co.
CPC International Inc.
CR Industries
Crane Co.
Crary Foundation, Bruce L.
Crestlea Foundation
CS First Boston Corporation
Culpeper Foundation, Charles E.
Culpeper Memorial Foundation, Daphne Seybolt
Culver Foundation, Constans
Curtice-Burns Foods, Inc.
Daily News
Dana Charitable Trust, Eleanor Naylor
Dart Group Corp.
Davis Foundations, Arthur Vining
Day Foundation, Nancy Sayles
Daywood Foundation
DEC International, Inc.
Deere & Co.
Delaware North Co., Inc.
Demoulas Supermarkets Inc.
DeRoy Foundation, Helen L.
DeRoy Testamentary Foundation
Detroit Edison Co.
Deuble Foundation, George H.
DeVore Foundation
Dewing Foundation, Frances R.
Dimeo Construction Co.
Dodge Foundation, Geraldine R.
Donaldson Company, Inc.
Donnelley Foundation, Gaylord and Dorothy
Donner Foundation, William H.
Douty Foundation
Dow Corning Corp.
Dow Foundation, Herbert H. and Grace A.
Dresser Industries, Inc.
Dreyfus Foundation, Jean and Louis
du Pont de Nemours & Co., E. I.
Duke Power Co.
Dun & Bradstreet Corp.
Dunagan Foundation
Duncan Trust, John G.
Eaton Corporation
Eaton Foundation, Cyrus
Eden Hall Foundation
El Pomar Foundation
Elf Atochem North America, Inc.
Emerson Foundation, Inc., Fred L.
English Memorial Fund, Florence C. and H. L.

Erpf Fund, Armand G.
Ethyl Corp
Evans Foundation, Lettie Pate
Everett Charitable Trust
Exxon Corporation
Fair Oaks Foundation, Inc.
Fair Play Foundation
Fairchild Foundation, Sherman
Farish Fund, William Stamps
Favrot Fund
Federal-Mogul Corporation
Federated Mutual Insurance Co.
Feil Foundation, Louis and Gertrude
Femino Foundation
Fenton Foundation
Fireman's Fund Insurance Co.
First Fidelity Bank
First Hawaiian, Inc.
First Interstate Bank of Oregon
First Source Corp.
First Tennessee Bank
First Union Corp.
Firstar Bank Milwaukee, N.A.
Fishback Foundation Trust, Harmes C.
Fleet Financial Group, Inc.
Fleishhacker Foundation
Flowers Charitable Trust, Albert W. and Edith V.
Folger Fund
Forbes Inc.
Ford Foundation
Ford Fund, William and Martha
Ford Motor Co.
Freeport-McMoRan Inc.
French Foundation, D.E.
French Oil Mill Machinery Co.
Fribourg Foundation
Fry Foundation, Lloyd A.
Fuqua Foundation, J. B.
GAR Foundation
Gates Foundation
General Mills, Inc.
General Motors Corp.
Georgia-Pacific Corporation
Georgia Power Co.
Gershman Foundation, Joel
Gheens Foundation
Giant Eagle, Inc.
Giant Food Inc.
Gillette Co.
Gilmore Foundation, William G.
Glaser Foundation
Glosser Foundation, David A.
Goldberg Family Foundation
Goldsmith Foundation, Horace W.
Goodrich Co., The B.F.
Gould Foundation, The Florence
Graham Foundation for Advanced Studies in the Fine Arts
Great-West Life Assurance Co.
Griffis Foundation
Griggs and Mary Griggs Burke Foundation, Mary Livingston
Groome Beatty Trust, Helen D.
Guardian Life Insurance Company of America
Halsell Foundation, Ewing
Hamilton Bank
Hammer Foundation, Armand
Handy and Harman Foundation
Harrington Foundation, Francis A. and Jacquelyn H.
Harrison Foundation, Fred G.
Harsco Corp.
Hasbro Inc.
HCA Foundation
Hearst Foundation, William Randolph
Hechinger Co.
Heckscher Foundation for Children
Heinz Company, H. J.
Heinz Endowment, Vira I.
Henderson Foundation, George B.
Henkel Corp.
Hewlett-Packard Co.
Higginson Trust, Corina

High Foundation
Hillman Foundation
Hillsdale Fund
Hoffman Foundation, Maximilian E. and Marion O.
Holzer Memorial Foundation, Richard H.
Hoover Foundation
Hoover Fund-Trust, W. Henry
Hopkins Foundation, Josephine Lawrence
Hopwood Charitable Trust, John M.
Howard and Bush Foundation
Howe and Mitchell B. Howe Foundation, Lucille Horton
Howell Foundation of Florida
Hoyt Foundation, Stewart W. and Willma C.
Hudson-Webber Foundation
Humana, Inc.
Hunt Foundation, Roy A.
Hunt Foundation, Samuel P.
Independence Foundation
Ingalls Foundation, Louise H. and David S.
Inland Container Corp.
Interkal, Inc.
International Business Machines Corp.
International Paper Co.
ITT Hartford Insurance Group, Inc.
Ittleson Foundation
Jaffe Foundation
James River Corp. of Virginia
Janirve Foundation
Jarson-Stanley and Mickey Kaplan Foundation, Isaac and Esther
Jewett Foundation, George Frederick
JFM Foundation
John Hancock Mutual Life Insurance Co.
Johnson Controls Inc.
Johnson & Higgins
Johnson & Son, S.C.
Jones Foundation, Harvey and Bernice
Jones Foundation, Helen
Jonsson Foundation
Jostens, Inc.
Kansas City Southern Industries
Kaufmann Foundation, Henry
Kelley and Elza Kelley Foundation, Edward Bangs
Kempner Fund, Harris and Eliza
Kennecott Corporation
Kennedy Foundation, Ethel
Kerr Foundation
Kettering Fund
Kilcawley Fund, William H.
Kimberly-Clark Corp.
Kingsbury Corp.
Kiplinger Foundation
Kirbo Charitable Trust, Thomas M. and Irene B.
Kirkpatrick Foundation
KN Energy, Inc.
Knoll Group
Knox, Sr., and Pearl Wallis Knox Charitable Foundation, Robert W.
Knudsen Foundation, Tom and Valley
Koehler Foundation, Marcia and Otto
Koret Foundation
Kresge Foundation
Kuyper Foundation, Peter H. and E. Lucille
La-Z-Boy Chair Co.
Landegger Charitable Foundation
Lauder Foundation
Lebovitz Fund
LEF Foundation
Lemberg Foundation
Lennon Foundation, Fred A.
Life Insurance Co. of Georgia
Link, Jr. Foundation, George
Lipton, Thomas J.

Liz Claiborne, Inc.
Long Island Lighting Co.
Longwood Foundation
Lund Foundation
Lurie Foundation, Louis R.
Lydall, Inc.
MacArthur Foundation, John D. and Catherine T.
Macy & Co., Inc., R.H.
Madison Gas & Electric Co.
Mahadh Foundation
Mailman Family Foundation, A. L.
Mailman Foundation
Management Compensation Group/Dulworth Inc.
Markey Charitable Fund, John C.
Marmot Foundation
Mars Foundation
Marsh & McLennan Companies, Inc.
Marshall Trust in Memory of Sanders McDaniel, Harriet McDaniel
Martin Marietta Corp.
Martin Marietta Materials
Mather Charitable Trust, S. Livingston
Mautz Paint Co.
May Department Stores Company, The
Maytag Family Foundation, Fred
MCA Inc.
McCasland Foundation
McDonald & Company Securities, Inc.
McElroy Trust, R. J.
McGraw-Hill, Inc.
MCI Communications Corp.
McKenna Foundation, Philip M.
McMahan Foundation, Catherine L. and Robert O.
Mead Corporation, The
Meadows Foundation
Medtronic, Inc.
Mellon Foundation, Richard King
Merck & Co.
Merrill Lynch & Co., Inc.
Metropolitan Life Insurance Co.
Meyer Memorial Trust
Middendorf Foundation
Miller Fund, Kathryn and Gilbert
Mine Safety Appliances Co.
Mobil Oil Corp.
Monadnock Paper Mills
Monticello College Foundation
Moore & Sons, B.C.
Morgan Construction Co.
Morgan and Samuel Tate Morgan, Jr. Foundation, Marietta McNeil
Morris Foundation, Margaret T.
Morris Foundation, William T.
Morrison Knudsen Corporation
Mott Fund, Ruth
Muller Foundation
Murphy Foundation
National Westminster Bank New Jersey
Nesholm Family Foundation
Nestle USA Inc.
Neuberger Foundation, Roy R. and Marie S.
New York Life Insurance Co.
New York Stock Exchange, Inc.
New York Times Company
The New Yorker Magazine, Inc.
Noble Foundation, Edward John
Noble Foundation, Samuel Roberts
Norfolk Shipbuilding & Drydock Corp.
Normandie Foundation
North Shore Foundation
Northern States Power Co. (Minnesota)
Northwest Natural Gas Co.
Norton Co.

Norton Foundation Inc.
Norton Memorial Corporation, Geraldi
Novell Inc.
O'Connor Foundation, A. Lindsay and Olive B.
Offield Family Foundation
Ohrstrom Foundation
Old Dominion Box Co.
Olin Corp.
Olsson Memorial Foundation, Elis
Osborn Charitable Trust, Edward B.
Overbrook Foundation
Pacific Mutual Life Insurance Co.
PaineWebber
Palmer Fund, Frank Loomis
Panhandle Eastern Corporation
Parker Hannifin Corp.
Parsons Foundation, Ralph M.
Penn Foundation, William
Pennzoil Co.
Peppers Foundation, Ann
Pfizer, Inc.
Pforzheimer Foundation, Carl and Lily
Phillips Family Foundation, Jay and Rose
Piper Foundation, Minnie Stevens
Piper Jaffray Companies Inc.
Pitt-Des Moines Inc.
Pittsburg Midway Coal Mining Co.
Pittsburgh Child Guidance Foundation
Plumsock Fund
PNC Bank, N.A.
Polaroid Corp.
Porter Foundation, Mrs. Cheever
Potomac Electric Power Co.
Premier Industrial Corp.
Priddy Foundation
Prouty Foundation, Olive Higgins
Providence Journal Company
Providian Corporation
Prudential Insurance Co. of America, The
Public Service Co. of New Mexico
Public Service Electric & Gas Co.
Quaker Chemical Corp.
Quivey-Bay State Foundation
Ralston Purina Co.
Reed Foundation
Reinberger Foundation
Rennebohm Foundation, Oscar
Reynolds Foundation, Donald W.
Rice Charitable Foundation, Albert W.
Rich Products Corporation
Richardson Benevolent Foundation, C. E.
Riggs Benevolent Fund
RJR Nabisco Inc.
Robinson-Broadhurst Foundation
Robinson Fund, Maurice R.
Rockwell International Corporation
Rohatyn Foundation, Felix and Elizabeth
Rose Foundation, Billy
Roseburg Forest Products Co.
Rosenberg, Jr. Family Foundation, Louise and Claude
Ross Memorial Foundation, Will
Rouse Co.
Rowland Foundation
Royal Group, Inc.
Rubin Foundation, Samuel
Saint Paul Companies, Inc.
Salomon Foundation, Richard and Edna
San Diego Gas & Electric
Santa Fe Pacific Corporation
Sara Lee Corp.

Sawyer Charitable Foundation
SBC Communications Inc.
Schenck Fund, L. P.
Scherer Foundation, Karla
Schering-Plough Corp.
Schlumberger Ltd.
Schroeder Foundation, Walter
Schuller International
Scott Fetzer Co.
Scott Foundation, Virginia Steele
Seafirst Corporation
Seagram & Sons, Inc., Joseph E.
Seaver Charitable Trust, Richard C.
Seaway Food Town, Inc.
Security Life of Denver Insurance Co.
Sedgwick James Inc.
Semmes Foundation
Shawmut National Corp.
Sheaffer Inc.
Shenandoah Life Insurance Co.
Sierra Pacific Resources
Skaggs Foundation, L. J. and Mary C.
Skillman Foundation
Smith Charitable Foundation, Lou and Lutza
Smith Foundation, Gordon V. and Helen C.
Smith Foundation, Kelvin and Eleanor
Smith Memorial Fund, Ethel Sergeant Clark
Snow Memorial Trust, John Ben
Solow Foundation
Sonat Inc.
South Bend Tribune
South Branch Foundation
Southern California Edison Co.
Specialty Manufacturing Co.
Speyer Foundation, Alexander C. and Tillie S.
SPX Corp.
Square D Co.
Starr Foundation
Steele Foundation, Harry and Grace
Sternberger Foundation, Tannenbaum
Stevens Foundation, John T.
Stone Trust, H. Chase
Strauss Foundation, Leon
Stupp Foundation, Norman J.
Sturgis Charitable and Educational Trust, Roy and Christine
Subaru of America Inc.
Swanson Family Foundation, Dr. W.C.
Swift Co. Inc., John S.
Swiss Bank Corp.
Symmes Foundation, F. W.
Tait Foundation, Frank M.
Taylor Foundation, Ruth and Vernon
Teleflex Inc.
Tenneco Inc.
Tetley, Inc.
Texas Commerce Bank-Houston, N.A.
Textron, Inc.
Thermo Electron Corp.
Thomas Foundation, Joan and Lee
Thompson Co., J. Walter
Thompson Trust, Thomas
Thornton Foundation
Times Mirror Company, The
Timken Foundation of Canton
Tiscornia Foundation
Tobin Foundation
Tozer Foundation
Transco Energy Co.
Travelers Inc.
Truland Foundation
Trust Company Bank
Unger Foundation, Aber D.
Unilever United States, Inc.
Union Bank
Union Electric Co.
U.S. Bank of Washington

Unitrode Corp.
Unocal Corp.
Upton Foundation, Frederick S.
Uris Brothers Foundation
USX Corporation
Van Wert County Foundation
Vaughn, Jr. Foundation Fund, James M.
Virginia Power Co.
Vulcan Materials Co.
Wachovia Bank of North Carolina, N.A.
Wahlstrom Foundation
Wallace-Reader's Digest Fund, Lila
Walsh Foundation
Warwick Foundation
Washington Mutual Savings Bank
Waters Charitable Trust, Robert S.
Wean Foundation, Raymond John
Wege Foundation
Weil, Gotshal and Manges Foundation
Weingart Foundation
Welch Testamentary Trust, George T.
Welfare Foundation
Wendt Foundation, Margaret L.
Westerman Foundation, Samuel L.
Westvaco Corporation
Weyerhaeuser Memorial Foundation, Charles A.
Whirlpool Corporation
Whiting Foundation
Whitney Fund, David M.
Widgeon Foundation
Williams Companies, The
Wilson Fund, Matilda R.
Winnebago Industries, Inc.
Winston Foundation, Norman and Rosita
Winter Construction Co.
Witco Corp.
Woodward Fund
Woolley Foundation, Vasser
Wyman Youth Trust

Arts Festivals

Air Products and Chemicals, Inc.
Alabama Gas Corp.
Alabama Power Co.
Allegheny Ludlum Corp.
Alumax Inc.
Aluminum Co. of America
Ames Charitable Trust, Harriett
Andreas Foundation
AON Corporation
Archer-Daniels-Midland Co.
Armco Inc.
AT&T Corp.
Avon Products, Inc.
Baker Foundation, Dexter F. and Dorothy H.
Ball Foundation, George and Frances
Bank One, Youngstown, NA
BankAmerica Corp.
Bean Foundation, Norwin S. and Elizabeth N.
BE&K Inc.
Beattie Foundation Trust, Cordelia Lee
Bedsole Foundation, J. L.
Benedum Foundation, Claude Worthington
Berger Foundation, H. N. and Frances C.
Bertha Foundation
Bethlehem Steel Corp.
Binney & Smith Inc.
Block, H&R
Blount, Inc.
Blue Bell, Inc.
Blue Cross & Blue Shield United of Wisconsin
Blum-Kovler Foundation
Bryn Mawr Trust Co.
Butz Foundation

Carpenter Foundation
Carpenter Technology Corp.
Centerior Energy Corp.
Central Maine Power Co.
Chase Manhattan Bank, N.A.
Chastain Charitable Foundation, Robert Lee and Thomas M.
Chevron Corporation
Chicago Sun-Times, Inc.
Christian Dior New York, Inc.
CIGNA Corporation
Citibank
Clorox Co.
Collins Foundation
Colonial Life & Accident Insurance Co.
Commerce Clearing House, Incorporated
Consolidated Natural Gas Co.
Cowles Media Co.
CPC International Inc.
Cremer Foundation
Cummins Engine Co.
Dana Charitable Trust, Eleanor Naylor
Daniel Foundation of Alabama
Davidson Family Charitable Foundation
Delano Foundation, Mignon Sherwood
Delaware North Co., Inc.
Dell Foundation, Hazel
Dimeo Construction Co.
Dodge Foundation, Geraldine R.
Donnelley Foundation, Gaylord and Dorothy
Dow Corning Corp.
Dresser Industries, Inc.
Dreyfus Foundation, Max and Victoria
du Pont de Nemours & Co., E. I.
Duke Power Co.
Eaton Corporation
Eaton Foundation, Cyrus
Emerson Foundation, Inc., Fred L.
English Memorial Fund, Florence C. and H. L.
Enron Corp.
Exxon Corporation
Fair Oaks Foundation, Inc.
Fair Play Foundation
Federal-Mogul Corporation
Federated Mutual Insurance Co.
Fieldcrest Cannon Inc.
First Interstate Bank of Oregon
First Tennessee Bank
First Union Corp.
Fleishhacker Foundation
Fleming Cos. Food Distribution Center
Ford Motor Co.
Forest Oil Corp.
Foster Charitable Trust
Frear Eleemosynary Trust, Mary D. and Walter F.
Freeport-McMoRan Inc.
French Oil Mill Machinery Co.
Fribourg Foundation
Friedman Family Foundation
Frost National Bank
GAR Foundation
General Motors Corp.
Georgia-Pacific Corporation
Georgia Power Co.
Globe Newspaper Co.
Goldsmith Foundation, Horace W.
Grand Rapids Label Co.
Halsell Foundation, Ewing
Hartmarx Corporation
Hechinger Co.
Heinz Company, H. J.
Heinz Endowment, Howard
Herzstein Charitable Foundation, Albert and Ethel
Hillsdale Fund
Hoag Family Foundation, George
Holnam
Humana, Inc.

Hunt Foundation, Roy A.
Inland Container Corp.
International Paper Co.
Jackson Foundation
JELD-WEN, Inc.
Jewett Foundation, George Frederick
Johnson Controls Inc.
Johnson & Higgins
Kansas City Southern Industries
Kaplan Fund, J. M.
Kemper National Insurance Cos.
Kennecott Corporation
Kerr Foundation
Kettering Fund
Kingsbury Corp.
Kinney-Lindstrom Foundation
Kirby Foundation, F. M.
Knoll Group
Leighton-Oare Foundation
Leuthold Foundation
Lipton, Thomas J.
Long Island Lighting Co.
Lyon Foundation
MacArthur Foundation, John D. and Catherine T.
Macy & Co., Inc., R.H.
Marquette Electronics, Inc.
Martin Marietta Corp.
McDermott Foundation, Eugene
McDonald & Company Securities, Inc.
McDonnell Douglas Corp.-West
Mead Corporation, The
Meyer Memorial Trust
Miller Brewing Company/North Carolina
Miller Charitable Foundation, Howard E. and Nell E.
Mine Safety Appliances Co.
Mobil Oil Corp.
Morris Foundation, Margaret T.
Morrison Knudsen Corporation
Mosinee Paper Corp.
Mott Fund, Ruth
Murdock Charitable Trust, M. J.
National Westminster Bank New Jersey
New York Times Company
The New Yorker Magazine, Inc.
Noble Foundation, Edward John
Northwest Natural Gas Co.
Norton Foundation Inc.
Norton Memorial Corporation, Geraldi
Norwest Bank Nebraska, N.A.
Novell Inc.
Odell Fund, Robert Stewart Odell and Helen Pfeiffer
Olsson Memorial Foundation, Elis
Osher Foundation, Bernard
Overbrook Foundation
Pacific Mutual Life Insurance Co.
Palmer Fund, Frank Loomis
Penguin Books USA, Inc.
Penn Foundation, William
Pennzoil Co.
Pew Charitable Trusts
Phillips Foundation, Ellis L.
Pick, Jr. Fund, Albert
Piper Foundation, Minnie Stevens
Piper Jaffray Companies Inc.
Pittsburg Midway Coal Mining Co.
PNC Bank, N.A.
Porter Testamentary Trust, James Hyde
PPG Industries, Inc.
Price Associates, T. Rowe
Providence Gas Co.
Provident Life & Accident Insurance Company of America
Reed Foundation
Reinberger Foundation
Robinson Fund, Maurice R.

Rockwell International Corporation
Rogers Family Foundation
Rohm & Haas Co.
Rose Foundation, Billy
Rose's Stores, Inc.
Rubinstein Foundation, Helena
San Diego Gas & Electric
Sara Lee Corp.
Sargent Foundation, Newell B.
SBC Communications Inc.
Schering-Plough Corp.
Schroeder Foundation, Walter
Schwartz Fund for Education and Health Research, Arnold and Marie
Scott Foundation, William E.
Seaway Food Town, Inc.
Security Life of Denver Insurance Co.
Sedgwick James Inc.
Semmes Foundation
Shell Oil Company
Siltec Corp.
Skaggs Foundation, L. J. and Mary C.
Smart Family Foundation
Sonat Inc.
South Bend Tribune
Southwestern Electric Power Co.
Speyer Foundation, Alexander C. and Tillie S.
Square D Co.
Starr Foundation
Steinman Foundation, John Frederick
Sternberger Foundation, Tannenbaum
Stokely, Jr. Foundation, William B.
Taubman Foundation, A. Alfred
Taylor Foundation, Ruth and Vernon
Tenneco Inc.
Texaco Inc.
Trexler Trust, Harry C.
Trust Company Bank
Tuch Foundation, Michael
Tucker Charitable Trust, Rose E.
Union Camp Corporation
Union Electric Co.
U.S. Bank of Washington
Unitrode Corp.
Upton Foundation, Frederick S.
USL Capital Corporation
USX Corporation
Virginia Power Co.
Vulcan Materials Co.
Wachovia Bank of North Carolina, N.A.
Wal-Mart Stores, Inc.
Wallace-Reader's Digest Fund, Lila
Wean Foundation, Raymond John
Wheeler Foundation
Winnebago Industries, Inc.
Winter Construction Co.
Wisconsin Power & Light Co.
Wisconsin Public Service Corp.
Witco Corp.
Wood Foundation of Chambersburg, PA

Arts Funds

Ahmanson Foundation
Air Products and Chemicals, Inc.
Aldus Corp.
Allendale Insurance Co.
Alumax Inc.
Aluminum Co. of America
Amcast Industrial Corp.
American Fidelity Corporation
American National Bank & Trust Co. of Chicago
Amfac/JMB Hawaii Inc.
AMP Incorporated
Andersen Foundation
Anheuser-Busch Companies, Inc.

Annenberg Foundation
Arakelian Foundation, Mary Alice
Archer-Daniels-Midland Co.
Armco Inc.
Arnhold Foundation
Atherton Family Foundation
Avery Arts Foundation, Milton and Sally
Avon Products, Inc.
Ball Brothers Foundation
Ball Foundation, George and Frances
Banc One Wisconsin Corp.
Bank One, Youngstown, NA
BankAmerica Corp.
Barra Foundation
Barry Corp., R. G.
Baughman Foundation
BE&K Inc.
Benedum Foundation, Claude Worthington
Benwood Foundation
Beveridge Foundation, Frank Stanley
Bingham Foundation, William
Binney & Smith Inc.
Blaustein Foundation, Louis and Henrietta
Block, H&R
Blue Bell, Inc.
Blum Foundation, Harry and Maribel G.
Blum-Kovler Foundation
Boatmen's Bancshares, Inc.
Boeing Co., The
Booth Ferris Foundation
Bristol-Myers Squibb Company
Brunswick Corp.
Bryn Mawr Trust Co.
Bucyrus-Erie Company
Burdines Inc.
Burlington Industries, Inc.
Cabot Corp.
Cabot Family Charitable Trust
Campbell Foundation, Ruth and Henry
Carolyn Foundation
Carpenter Foundation, E. Rhodes and Leona B.
Central Hudson Gas & Electric Corp.
Chartwell Foundation
Chase Manhattan Bank, N.A.
Chastain Charitable Foundation, Robert Lee and Thomas M.
Chazen Foundation
Cheatham Foundation, Owen
Chevron Corporation
Christian Dior New York, Inc.
Citibank
Citizens Bank of Rhode Island
Claiborne and Art Ortenberg Foundation, Liz
Clay Foundation
Columbia Foundation
Columbus Dispatch Printing Co.
Connecticut Mutual Life Insurance Company
Consumers Power Co.
Continental Corp.
Cooper Industries, Inc.
Cowles Charitable Trust
Cowles Media Co.
CPC International Inc.
Crestlea Foundation
Crown Books
CS First Boston Corporation
Cummins Engine Co.
Daily News
Davis Foundation, Irene E. and George A.
Daywood Foundation
Delano Foundation, Mignon Sherwood
Dentsply International Inc.
DeRoy Foundation, Helen L.
Deuble Foundation, George H.
Dr. Seuss Foundation
Donaldson Company, Inc.
Dresser Industries, Inc.

du Pont de Nemours & Co., E. I.
Duke Power Co.
Dula Educational and Charitable Foundation, Caleb C. and Julia W.
Eastman Kodak Company
Eaton Corporation
Enron Corp.
Ethyl Corp
Evans Foundation, Lettie Pate
Federal-Mogul Corporation
Federated Mutual Insurance Co.
First Interstate Bank of Oregon
First Tennessee Bank
First Union Corp.
First Union National Bank of Florida
Forbes Inc.
Ford Fund, William and Martha
Foster Charitable Trust
Frear Eleemosynary Trust, Mary D. and Walter F.
Freeport-McMoRan Inc.
Frisch's Restaurants Inc.
Frost National Bank
Fruehauf Foundation
Gates Foundation
Gebbie Foundation
General American Life Insurance Co.
General Motors Corp.
Georgia Power Co.
Getty Trust, J. Paul
Gilman Foundation, Howard
Globe Newspaper Co.
Goldsmith Foundation, Horace W.
Gould Electronics Inc.
Greenwall Foundation
Griggs and Mary Griggs Burke Foundation, Mary Livingston
Hamilton Bank
Hazen Foundation, Edward W.
HCA Foundation
Hecht-Levi Foundation
Heinz Endowment, Vira I.
Heinz Trust, Drue
Herzstein Charitable Foundation, Albert and Ethel
Hewlett-Packard Co.
Hillman Family Foundation, Alex
Hoover Foundation
Hoover Fund-Trust, W. Henry
Houchens Foundation, Ervin G.
Houston Industries Incorporated
Hoyt Foundation, Stewart W. and Willma C.
Hultquist Foundation
Humana, Inc.
Hunt Foundation
Huthsteiner Fine Arts Trust
Inland Container Corp.
International Business Machines Corp.
International Foundation
International Paper Co.
ITT Hartford Insurance Group, Inc.
James River Corp. of Virginia
Jarson-Stanley and Mickey Kaplan Foundation, Isaac and Esther
JFM Foundation
Johnson Controls Inc.
Johnson & Higgins
Johnson & Son, S.C.
Jordan Charitable Foundation, Mary Ranken Jordan and Ettie A.
Journal-Gazette Co.
Kansas City Southern Industries
Kerr Foundation
Kettering Fund
Kiewit Foundation, Peter
Kimberly-Clark Corp.
Kingsbury Corp.
Klipstein Foundation, Ernest Christian
Knight Foundation, John S. and James L.

Kress Foundation, Samuel H.
Kunkel Foundation, John Crain
Laffey-McHugh Foundation
Laurel Foundation
LEF Foundation
Lehigh Portland Cement Co.
Lenna Foundation, Reginald A. and Elizabeth S.
Levitt Foundation
Lichtenstein Foundation, David B.
Long Island Lighting Co.
Longwood Foundation
Lydall, Inc.
Macy & Co., Inc., R.H.
Mailman Foundation
Management Compensation Group/Dulworth Inc.
Maritz Inc.
Marmot Foundation
Martin Marietta Corp.
Marx Foundation, Virginia and Leonard
May Department Stores Company, The
MCA Inc.
McCasland Foundation
Meadows Foundation
Mellon Family Foundation, R. K.
Mengle Foundation, Glenn and Ruth
Merck Family Fund
Merrick Foundation
Miller Brewing Company/North Carolina
Mobil Oil Corp.
Monadnock Paper Mills
Monell Foundation, Ambrose
Montana Power Co.
Morgan & Company, J.P.
Morris Foundation, Margaret T.
Muchnic Foundation
Nabisco Foods Group
Nalco Chemical Co.
Nesholm Family Foundation
The New Yorker Magazine, Inc.
Noble Foundation, Edward John
North Shore Foundation
Northern States Power Co. (Minnesota)
Northwest Natural Gas Co.
Norton Co.
Norton Foundation Inc.
Norwest Bank Nebraska, N.A.
Norwest Corporation
OG&E Electric Services
Olin Foundation, Spencer T. and Ann W.
Oppenstein Brothers Foundation
Ore-Ida Foods, Inc.
Pacific Mutual Life Insurance Co.
Packard Foundation, David and Lucile
Pamida, Inc.
PECO Energy Company
Penn Foundation, William
Pew Charitable Trusts
Pfizer, Inc.
Phelps Dodge Corporation
Philibosian Foundation, Stephen
Phillips Foundation, Ellis L.
Piper Foundation, Minnie Stevens
Polaroid Corp.
Price Associates, T. Rowe
Prince Trust, Abbie Norman
Providian Corporation
Prudential Insurance Co. of America, The
Public Service Electric & Gas Co.
Pulitzer Publishing Co.
Quaker Chemical Corp.
Reed Foundation
Reichhold Chemicals, Inc.
Rice Foundation
Robinson Fund, Maurice R.
Rockwell International Corporation

Rohatyn Foundation, Felix and
Elizabeth
Rohm & Haas Co.
Rose Foundation, Billy
Rouse Co.
Rubin Family Fund, Cele H.
and William B.
Rubin Foundation, Samuel
SAFECO Corp.
Saint Paul Companies, Inc.
San Diego Gas & Electric
Sandy Hill Foundation
Santa Fe Pacific Corporation
Sara Lee Hosiery, Inc.
SBC Communications Inc.
Schroeder Foundation, Walter
Seaver Institute
Sedgwick James Inc.
Shawmut National Corp.
Shott, Jr. Foundation, Hugh I.
Sierra Pacific Resources
Simon Foundation, William E.
and Carol G.
Smith Corp., A.O.
Specialty Manufacturing Co.
Sprague Educational and
Charitable Foundation, Seth
Square D Co.
Starr Foundation
Stein Foundation, Jules and
Doris
Stone Charitable Foundation
Sulzberger Foundation
Swiss Bank Corp.
Teleflex Inc.
Tenneco Inc.
Texaco Inc.
Texas Commerce
Bank-Houston, N.A.
Textron, Inc.
Towsley Foundation, Harry A.
and Margaret D.
Tozer Foundation
Trust Company Bank
Union Bank
Union Camp Corporation
Union Electric Co.
Union Pacific Corp.
U.S. Bank of Washington
Upton Foundation, Frederick S.
Utica National Insurance
Group
Vicksburg Foundation
Vulcan Materials Co.
Wachovia Bank of North
Carolina, N.A.
Wallace-Reader's Digest Fund,
Lila
Warner Fund, Albert and
Bessie
Wean Foundation, Raymond
John
Welfare Foundation
Weyerhaeuser Co.
Wheat First Butcher Singer,
Inc.
Whirlpool Corporation
Whitney Fund, David M.
Winter Construction Co.
Woodward Fund

Arts Institutes

Abbott Laboratories
Ahmanson Foundation
Alexander Foundation, Joseph
Allendale Insurance Co.
AlliedSignal Inc.
Aluminum Co. of America
Amcast Industrial Corp.
American Fidelity Corporation
American National Bank &
Trust Co. of Chicago
American Natural Resources
Company
Amfac/JMB Hawaii Inc.
Amoco Corporation
Andersen Corp.
Andersen Foundation
AON Corporation
Archer-Daniels-Midland Co.
Aristech Chemical Corp.
Armco Inc.

Avery Arts Foundation, Milton
and Sally
Avon Products, Inc.
Ayres Foundation, Inc.
Bank of Boston Corp.
Bank One, Youngstown, NA
BankAmerica Corp.
Barra Foundation
Barry Corp., R. G.
Bean Foundation, Norwin S.
and Elizabeth N.
Bell Foundation, James F.
Benenson Foundation, Frances
and Benjamin
Berwind Corporation
Binney & Smith Inc.
Blair and Co., William
Blandin Foundation
Block, H&R
Blount, Inc.
Blum-Kovler Foundation
Booth Ferris Foundation
Boothroyd Foundation,
Charles H. and Bertha L.
Borden, Inc.
Borman's Inc.
Boston Edison Co.
BP America Inc.
Brach Foundation, Helen
Brackenridge Foundation,
George W.
Bridgestone/Firestone, Inc.
Bristol-Myers Squibb
Company
Brunswick Corp.
Bryn Mawr Trust Co.
Burchfield Foundation,
Charles E.
Burnett-Tandy Foundation
Cabot Corp.
Cafritz Foundation, Morris and
Gwendolyn
Cargill Inc.
Carpenter Technology Corp.
Cassett Foundation, Louis N.
CBI Industries, Inc.
Centerior Energy Corp.
Central Maine Power Co.
Chartwell Foundation
Chastain Charitable
Foundation, Robert Lee and
Thomas M.
Cheatham Foundation, Owen
Chesebrough-Pond's USA Co.
Chicago Sun-Times, Inc.
Christian Dior New York, Inc.
Chrysler Corp.
Citibank
Citizens Bank of Rhode Island
CNA Financial
Corporation/CNA Insurance
Companies
Colonial Life & Accident
Insurance Co.
Columbia Foundation
Columbus Dispatch Printing
Co.
Comerica Incorporated
Commerce Clearing House,
Incorporated
Commonwealth Edison Co.
Connelly Foundation
Consolidated Natural Gas Co.
Consolidated Papers, Inc.
Consumers Power Co.
Continental Corp.
Cowles Charitable Trust
Cowles Media Co.
CS First Boston Corporation
CT Corp. System
Delavan Foundation, Nelson B.
Delaware North Co., Inc.
DeRoy Foundation, Helen L.
DeRoy Testamentary
Foundation
Dewing Foundation, Frances R.
Donaldson Company, Inc.
Donnelley & Sons Co., R.R.
Douglas & Lomason Company
Dow Corning Corp.
Dreyfus Foundation, Jean and
Louis
du Pont de Nemours & Co., E.
I.
Duchossois Industries Inc.

Dynamet, Inc.
Eaton Foundation, Cyrus
Emerson Foundation, Inc.,
Fred L.
Erpf Fund, Armand G.
Essick Foundation
Exxon Corporation
Fair Play Foundation
Fairchild Foundation, Sherman
Federal-Mogul Corporation
Federated Mutual Insurance
Co.
Fireman's Fund Insurance Co.
First Fidelity Bank
First Interstate Bank of Oregon
First Tennessee Bank
First Union Corp.
Firstar Bank Milwaukee, N.A.
Fleming Cos. Food
Distribution Center
Ford Fund, William and Martha
Ford II Fund, Henry
Ford Motor Co.
France Foundation, Jacob and
Annita
Freeport-McMoRan Inc.
Frohring Foundation, William
O. and Gertrude Lewis
Frost National Bank
Fruehauf Foundation
Fry Foundation, Lloyd A.
GAR Foundation
GATX Corp.
GenCorp Inc.
General Mills, Inc.
General Motors Corp.
Georgia Power Co.
Gershman Foundation, Joel
Getty Trust, J. Paul
Giant Eagle, Inc.
Goldsmith Foundation, Horace
W.
Graham Foundation for
Advanced Studies in the
Fine Arts
Greve Foundation, William
and Mary
Halff Foundation, G. A. C.
Hanes Foundation, John W.
and Anna H.
Hardin Foundation, Phil
Hartmarx Corporation
Hauser Foundation
HCA Foundation
Hecht-Levi Foundation
Heckscher Foundation for
Children
Heinz Endowment, Howard
Hoover Foundation
Hoover Fund-Trust, W. Henry
Hoyt Foundation
Hudson-Webber Foundation
Hunt Foundation, Samuel P.
Huston Foundation
Illinois Consolidated
Telephone Co.
Illinois Tool Works, Inc.
Independence Foundation
Ingalls Foundation, Louise H.
and David S.
International Business
Machines Corp.
Irvine Foundation, James
Jackson Foundation
Jewett Foundation, George
Frederick
John Hancock Mutual Life
Insurance Co.
Johnson Controls Inc.
Johnson & Higgins
Jones Foundation, Fletcher
Jostens, Inc.
Julia R. and Estelle L.
Foundation
Kansas City Southern
Industries
Kelly Foundation, T. Lloyd
Kemper Foundation, William T.
Kerr Foundation
Kettering Fund
Kilcawley Fund, William H.
Kiplinger Foundation
Kirkpatrick Foundation
Kmart Corporation

Knight Foundation, John S.
and James L.
Knoll Group
Koehler Foundation, Marcia
and Otto
Kresge Foundation
Kress Foundation, Samuel H.
Larsen Fund
Lederer Foundation, Francis L.
Lehmann Foundation, Otto W.
Leidy Foundation, John J.
Lund Foundation
Lydall, Inc.
MacArthur Foundation, John
D. and Catherine T.
Macy & Co., Inc., R.H.
Mailman Foundation
Management Compensation
Group/Dulworth Inc.
Marbrook Foundation
Mardigian Foundation
Maritz Inc.
Marsh & McLennan
Companies, Inc.
Mather Charitable Trust, S.
Livingston
Mather and William Gwinn
Mather Fund, Elizabeth Ring
Mattel, Inc.
MCA Inc.
McCasland Foundation
McCormick Foundation,
Chauncey and Marion
Deering
McMahon Foundation
Mead Corporation, The
Meadows Foundation
Medtronic, Inc.
Mellon Family Foundation, R.
K.
Mellon Foundation, Richard
King
Merkley Charitable Trust
Merrick Foundation
Metropolitan Life Insurance
Co.
Middendorf Foundation
Minnesota Mining & Mfg. Co.
Mobil Oil Corp.
Morgan Construction Co.
Morgan Stanley & Co., Inc.
Morris Foundation, Margaret T.
Musson Charitable
Foundation, R. C. and
Katharine M.
Nalco Chemical Co.
National Gypsum Co.
New-Land Foundation
New York Times Company
The New Yorker Magazine, Inc.
Nias Foundation, Henry
Northern States Power Co.
(Minnesota)
Northwest Natural Gas Co.
Norton Family Foundation,
Peter
Norton Memorial Corporation,
Geraldi
O'Connor Foundation, A.
Lindsay and Olive B.
OG&E Electric Services
Olin Corp.
Olsson Memorial Foundation,
Elis
Osher Foundation, Bernard
Outboard Marine Corp.
Overbrook Foundation
Parker Hannifin Corp.
Parshelsky Foundation, Moses
L.
Parsons Foundation, Ralph M.
Penn Foundation, William
Peoples Energy Corp.
Pforzheimer Foundation, Carl
and Lily
Philibosian Foundation,
Stephen
Piankova Foundation, Tatiana
Pick, Jr. Fund, Albert
Piper Foundation, Minnie
Stevens
Piper Jaffray Companies Inc.
Pollock Company Foundation,
William B.

Porter Testamentary Trust,
James Hyde
Potts and Sibley Foundation
Premier Industrial Corp.
Price Associates, T. Rowe
Providian Corporation
Prudential Insurance Co. of
America, The
Pulitzer Publishing Co.
Rand McNally & Co.
Regenstein Foundation
Reinberger Foundation
Rice Foundation
Rich Products Corporation
Robinson Fund, Maurice R.
Rockwell International
Corporation
Rohm & Haas Co.
Rose Foundation, Billy
Rosen Foundation, Joseph
Ross Memorial Foundation,
Will
Saint Paul Companies, Inc.
Salomon Foundation, Richard
and Edna
San Diego Gas & Electric
Santa Fe Pacific Corporation
Sara Lee Corp.
Sarkeys Foundation
SBC Communications Inc.
Scherer Foundation, Karla
Schoenleber Foundation
Schroeder Foundation, Walter
Schwartz Fund for Education
and Health Research, Arnold
and Marie
Scott Foundation, Virginia
Steele
Seaver Charitable Trust,
Richard C.
Seaver Institute
Sedgwick James Inc.
Share Trust, Charles Morton
Sharon Steel Corp.
Shawmut National Corp.
Simpson Investment Company
Skillman Foundation
Southern California Edison Co.
Specialty Manufacturing Co.
Speyer Foundation, Alexander
C. and Tillie S.
Sprague Educational and
Charitable Foundation, Seth
Square D Co.
Starr Foundation
Steele Foundation, Harry and
Grace
Stein Foundation, Jules and
Doris
Sundet Foundation
Swift Co. Inc., John S.
Tait Foundation, Frank M.
Taylor Foundation, Ruth and
Vernon
Teleflex Inc.
Textron, Inc.
Thalhimer and Family
Foundation, Charles G.
Thorne Foundation
Timken Foundation of Canton
Tobin Foundation
Todd Co., A.M.
Towsley Foundation, Harry A.
and Margaret D.
Tucker Charitable Trust, Rose
E.
Unger Foundation, Aber D.
Unilever United States, Inc.
Union Bank
Union Electric Co.
United Airlines, Inc.
Unocal Corp.
Upton Foundation, Frederick S.
USG Corporation
Van Wert County Foundation
Vulcan Materials Co.
Wallace-Reader's Digest Fund,
Lila
Walsh Foundation
Wean Foundation, Raymond
John
Weingart Foundation
Westerman Foundation,
Samuel L.
Whirlpool Corporation

Whiting Foundation
Whitney Fund, David M.
WICOR, Inc.
Willard Helping Fund, Cecilia
Young
Williams Companies, The
Wilmington Trust Co.
Wilson Fund, Matilda R.
Wyomissing Foundation
Zarrow Foundation, Anne and
Henry

Arts Outreach

Ahmanson Foundation
Aldus Corp.
Altman Foundation
Amado Foundation, Maurice
Arnhold Foundation
Astor Foundation, Vincent
Ball Brothers Foundation
Bean Foundation, Norwin S.
and Elizabeth N.
Benedum Foundation, Claude
Worthington
Berger Foundation, H. N. and
Frances C.
Blandin Foundation
Block, H&R
Boston Edison Co.
Brackenridge Foundation,
George W.
Bristol-Myers Squibb
Company
Buhl Foundation
Burnett-Tandy Foundation
Cabot Corp.
Cafritz Foundation, Morris and
Gwendolyn
Cain Foundation, Effie and
Wofford
Cain Foundation, Gordon and
Mary
Calder Foundation, Louis
Campbell Foundation
Carolyn Foundation
Carver Charitable Trust, Roy J.
Chadwick Fund, Dorothy
Jordan
Chicago Sun-Times, Inc.
Christian Dior New York, Inc.
Clements Foundation
Clorox Co.
Clowes Fund
Cole Foundation, Olive B.
Connelly Foundation
Cornell Trust, Peter C.
Corning Incorporated
Culpeper Foundation, Charles
E.
Daily News
Davis Foundation, Edwin W.
and Catherine M.
Dekko Foundation
DeRoy Foundation, Helen L.
DeRoy Testamentary
Foundation
Dewing Foundation, Frances R.
Dr. Seuss Foundation
Dodge Foundation, Cleveland
H.
Dodge Foundation, Geraldine
R.
Donner Foundation, William H.
Dreyfus Foundation, Jean and
Louis
Dreyfus Foundation, Max and
Victoria
Duchossois Industries Inc.
Duncan Trust, John G.
Eberly Foundation
Eden Hall Foundation
Farish Fund, William Stamps
Favrot Fund
Federated Mutual Insurance
Co.
Fireman's Fund Insurance Co.
Fleishhacker Foundation
Fondren Foundation
Freed Foundation
Fribourg Foundation
GATX Corp.
Gellert Foundation, Celia Berta

General American Life
Insurance Co.
Graham Fund, Philip L.
Greenwall Foundation
Greve Foundation, William
and Mary
Griggs and Mary Griggs Burke
Foundation, Mary Livingston
Grundy Foundation
Harland Charitable
Foundation, John and
Wilhelmina D.
Hazen Foundation, Edward W.
Hechinger Co.
Hecht-Levi Foundation
Heckscher Foundation for
Children
Heinz Company, H. J.
Heinz Endowment, Vira I.
Heller Charitable Foundation,
Clarence E.
Hickory Tech Corp.
Hillcrest Foundation
Houston Endowment
Hoyt Foundation, Stewart W.
and Willma C.
Integra Bank of Uniontown
Irvine Foundation, James
Ittleson Foundation
Jewett Foundation, George
Frederick
JFM Foundation
Jones Foundation, Daisy
Marquis
Jurzykowski Foundation,
Alfred
Kansas City Southern
Industries
Kardon Foundation, Samuel
and Rebecca
Kaufmann Foundation, Henry
Kuehn Foundation
Laurel Foundation
Littauer Foundation, Lucius N.
Little, Inc., Arthur D.
Marpat Foundation
Mars Foundation
McDermott Foundation,
Eugene
McElroy Trust, R. J.
McFawn Trust No. 2, Lois
Sisler
MCI Communications Corp.
Meadows Foundation
Meyer Memorial Trust
Miller Brewing
Company/North Carolina
Monadnock Paper Mills
Morgan & Company, J.P.
Morris Foundation, Margaret T.
Nestle USA Inc.
New-Land Foundation
New York Times Company
Nias Foundation, Henry
Noble Foundation, Edward
John
Novell Inc.
NYNEX Corporation
Palmer Fund, Frank Loomis
Parsons Foundation, Ralph M.
Penguin Books USA, Inc.
Pew Charitable Trusts
Polaroid Corp.
Porter Testamentary Trust,
James Hyde
PriMerit Bank
Quaker Chemical Corp.
Rockwell Fund
Rose Foundation, Billy
Rosenberg, Jr. Family
Foundation, Louise and
Claude
Rubinstein Foundation, Helena
Saint Paul Companies, Inc.
Schuller International
Scurlock Foundation
Seidman Family Foundation
Slemp Foundation
Smith Foundation, Kelvin and
Eleanor
Smith Trust, May and Stanley
Snow Memorial Trust, John
Ben
Stemmons Foundation
Stone Trust, H. Chase

Strong Foundation, Hattie M.
Stupp Foundation, Norman J.
Subaru of America Inc.
Taper Foundation, Mark
Travelers Inc.
U.S. Bank of Washington
USL Capital Corporation
van Ameringen Foundation
Vogler Foundation, Laura B.
Wallace-Reader's Digest Fund,
Lila
Weingart Foundation
Wendt Foundation, Margaret L.
Whittenberger Foundation,
Claude R. and Ethel B.
Woolley Foundation, Vasser

Ballet

Achelis Foundation
AKC Fund
Alabama Gas Corp.
Aldus Corp.
Aluminum Co. of America
American Fidelity Corporation
American President
Companies, Ltd.
AMETEK, Inc.
Anderson Foundation, M. D.
Andrews Foundation
Arcadia Foundation
Argyros Foundation
Aristech Chemical Corp.
Arnhold Foundation
Baker Foundation, Dexter F.
and Dorothy H.
Baker Trust, George F.
Bank One, Youngstown, NA
BankAmerica Corp.
Barry Corp., R. G.
Barth Foundation, Theodore H.
Beattie Foundation Trust,
Cordelia Lee
Bedsole Foundation, J. L.
Beech Aircraft Corp.
Benedum Foundation, Claude
Worthington
Benwood Foundation
Bingham Foundation, William
Bishop Foundation, E. K. and
Lillian F.
Block, H&R
Blount, Inc.
Booth Ferris Foundation
Borden, Inc.
Boston Edison Co.
Brackenridge Foundation,
George W.
Brady Foundation
Brown Foundation, M. K.
Bunbury Company
Burden Foundation, Florence
V.
Burnett-Tandy Foundation
Cafritz Foundation, Morris and
Gwendolyn
Cain Foundation, Gordon and
Mary
Calhoun Charitable Trust,
Kenneth
Carpenter Foundation, E.
Rhodes and Leona B.
Carter Foundation, Beirne
Cheatham Foundation, Owen
Chevron Corporation
Chicago Sun-Times, Inc.
Christian Dior New York, Inc.
CINergy
Clark Foundation
Clorox Co.
Clowes Fund
Cole Foundation, Olive B.
Columbia Foundation
Columbus Dispatch Printing
Co.
Comer Foundation
Consolidated Natural Gas Co.
Coughlin-Saunders Foundation
Cowell Foundation, S. H.
Crane Co.
Crown Books
Cullen Foundation
Culpeper Foundation, Charles
E.

Dana Charitable Trust, Eleanor
Naylor
Demoulas Supermarkets Inc.
Deuble Foundation, George H.
Diamond Foundation, Aaron
Dillon Dunwalke Trust,
Clarence and Anne
Dreyfus Foundation, Max and
Victoria
Duchossois Industries Inc.
Duncan Foundation, Lillian H.
and C. W.
Early Foundation
Eaton Corporation
Elf Atochem North America,
Inc.
English Memorial Fund,
Florence C. and H. L.
Erpf Fund, Armand G.
Fair Oaks Foundation, Inc.
Favrot Fund
Fireman's Fund Insurance Co.
First Interstate Bank of Oregon
Firstar Bank Milwaukee, N.A.
Fleishhacker Foundation
Flowers Charitable Trust,
Albert W. and Edith V.
Foster Charitable Trust
Freeman Charitable Trust,
Samuel
Freeport-McMoRan Inc.
Gamble Foundation
GAR Foundation
Giant Eagle, Inc.
Giant Food Inc.
Gilman Foundation, Howard
Givenchy Corp.
Globe Newspaper Co.
Goldsmith Foundation, Horace
W.
Gould Electronics Inc.
Graham Fund, Philip L.
Grand Rapids Label Co.
Greenwall Foundation
Gregg-Graniteville Foundation
Greve Foundation, William
and Mary
Griggs and Mary Griggs Burke
Foundation, Mary Livingston
Haas, Jr. Fund, Evelyn and
Walter
Hallberg Foundation, E. L. and
R. F.
Hamman Foundation, George
and Mary Josephine
Harcourt General, Inc.
Harland Charitable
Foundation, John and
Wilhelmina D.
Harriman Foundation, Gladys
and Roland
Harriman Foundation, Mary W.
Hearst Foundation, William
Randolph
Hechinger Co.
Hecht-Levi Foundation
Heinz Company, H. J.
Heinz Endowment, Howard
Heinz Endowment, Vira I.
Heinz Trust, Drue
Helmerich Foundation
Hershey Foundation, Barry J.
Herzstein Charitable
Foundation, Albert and Ethel
Hewlett Foundation, William
and Flora
Higginson Trust, Corina
Hook Drugs
Hoover Foundation
Hopwood Charitable Trust,
John M.
Houston Endowment
Hulme Charitable Foundation,
Milton G.
Huthsteiner Fine Arts Trust
Icahn Foundation, Carl C.
Independence Foundation
Integra Bank of Uniontown
Irvine Foundation, James
Irwin Charity Foundation,
William G.
Jackson Foundation
Jarson-Stanley and Mickey
Kaplan Foundation, Isaac
and Esther

Jones Foundation, Helen
Kansas City Southern
Industries
Kavanagh Foundation, T.
James
Kayser Foundation
Kerr Foundation
Kiplinger Foundation
Kirkpatrick Foundation
Koret Foundation
Kresge Foundation
Kuehn Foundation
Kunkel Foundation, John Crain
Lasdon Foundation
Lasdon Foundation, William
and Mildred
Lauder Foundation
Lea Foundation, Helen Sperry
Lurie Foundation, Louis R.
Lydall, Inc.
M/A-COM, Inc.
Magowan Family Foundation
Management Compensation
Group/Dulworth Inc.
Maneely Fund
Marshall Trust in Memory of
Sanders McDaniel, Harriet
McDaniel
Martin Marietta Corp.
Mathis-Pfohl Foundation
Mattel, Inc.
May Department Stores
Company, The
Maytag Family Foundation,
Fred
McDonald & Company
Securities, Inc.
McFawn Trust No. 2, Lois
Sisler
McQueen Foundation, Adeline
and George
Meadows Foundation
Mellon Foundation, Richard
King
Memton Fund
Metropolitan Life Insurance
Co.
Meyer Memorial Trust
Mielke Family Foundation
Miller Fund, Kathryn and
Gilbert
Monell Foundation, Ambrose
Monticello College Foundation
Morgan & Company, J.P.
Morgan Foundation, Burton D.
Morgan Stanley & Co., Inc.
Morris Foundation, Margaret T.
Morris Foundation, William T.
Moses Fund, Henry and Lucy
Mulford Foundation, Vincent
Murdock Charitable Trust, M.
J.
Musson Charitable
Foundation, R. C. and
Katharine M.
National Gypsum Co.
Nesholm Family Foundation
New York Times Company
Nias Foundation, Henry
Novell Inc.
Osborn Charitable Trust,
Edward B.
Osher Foundation, Bernard
Owsley Foundation, Alvin and
Lucy
Packard Foundation, David
and Lucile
Parker Hannifin Corp.
Peabody Charitable Fund,
Amelia
Penn Foundation, William
Pennsylvania Dutch Co.
Philibosian Foundation,
Stephen
Piankova Foundation, Tatiana
Polaroid Corp.
Porter Foundation, Mrs.
Cheever
Prince Trust, Abbie Norman
Prospect Hill Foundation
Providence Journal Company
Reinberger Foundation
Rohatyn Foundation, Felix and
Elizabeth
Rose Foundation, Billy

Rosenberg, Jr. Family Foundation, Louise and Claude
Ross Laboratories
Rubin Family Fund, Cele H. and William B.
Rubinstein Foundation, Helena
Salomon Inc.
Sarkeys Foundation
Scherman Foundation
Schiro Fund
Schlumberger Ltd.
Schuller International
Schwartz Fund for Education and Health Research, Arnold and Marie
Scott Foundation, William E.
Seafirst Corporation
Shell Oil Company
Shubert Foundation
Smart Family Foundation
SmithKline Beecham Corp.
Spang & Co.
Sprague Educational and Charitable Foundation, Seth
Stein Foundation, Jules and Doris
Stevens Foundation, Abbot and Dorothy H.
Subaru of America Inc.
Swanson Family Foundation, Dr. W.C.
Taube Family Foundation
Taylor Foundation, Ruth and Vernon
Teleflex Inc.
Texaco Inc.
Texas Commerce Bank-Houston, N.A.
Thalhimer and Family Foundation, Charles G.
Thermo Electron Corp.
Thompson Co., J. Walter
Travelers Inc.
Truland Foundation
Turner Charitable Foundation
Union Pacific Corp.
United Airlines, Inc.
U.S. Bank of Washington
USL Capital Corporation
USX Corporation
Valmont Industries, Inc.
Wahlstrom Foundation
Walsh Foundation
Wendt Foundation, Margaret L.
Wertheim Foundation, Dr. Herbert A.
Whirlpool Corporation
Whiting Foundation, Macauley and Helen Dow
Whittenberger Foundation, Claude R. and Ethel B.
Wiegand Foundation, E. L.
Wildermuth Foundation, E. F.
Wiley & Sons, Inc., John
Wiremold Co.
Witco Corp.
Wright Foundation, Lola
Wyman Youth Trust
Wyomissing Foundation
Young Foundation, Robert R.
Zarrow Foundation, Anne and Henry

Community Arts

Abbott Laboratories
Acushnet Co.
Adler Foundation Trust, Philip D. and Henrietta B.
AEGON USA Inc.
Air Products and Chemicals, Inc.
Akzo America
Alabama Gas Corp.
Alabama Power Co.
Albertson's Inc.
Aldus Corp.
AlliedSignal Inc.
Altschul Foundation
Alumax Inc.
Aluminum Co. of America
American Brands, Inc.

American National Bank & Trust Co. of Chicago
American Natural Resources Company
Ames Charitable Trust, Harriett
Amfac/JMB Hawaii Inc.
AMR Corp.
Anderson Foundation
Andrews Foundation
Anheuser-Busch Companies, Inc.
Ansin Private Foundation, Ronald M.
Apple Computer, Inc.
Appleby Trust, Scott B. and Annie P.
Arakelian Foundation, Mary Alice
Arkansas Power & Light Co.
Armstrong Foundation
Arnold Fund
Atherton Family Foundation
Avery Arts Foundation, Milton and Sally
Avon Products, Inc.
Baker Foundation, Dexter F. and Dorothy H.
Baldwin Memorial Foundation, Fred
Bank of Boston
Bank of Boston Corp.
Bank One, Youngstown, NA
BankAmerica Corp.
Barker Foundation, J.M.R.
Barra Foundation
Barry Corp., R. G.
Battelle Memorial Institute
Bean Foundation, Norwin S. and Elizabeth N.
Beattie Foundation Trust, Cordelia Lee
Bethlehem Steel Corp.
Binney & Smith Inc.
Birnschein Foundation, Alvin and Marion
Bishop Foundation, E. K. and Lillian F.
Blaustein Foundation, Louis and Henrietta
Block, H&R
Blount Educational and Charitable Foundation, Mildred Weedon
Blue Bell, Inc.
Blue Cross & Blue Shield United of Wisconsin
Boatmen's Bancshares, Inc.
Boise Cascade Corporation
Borden, Inc.
Borman's Inc.
Boutell Memorial Fund
Bowater Incorporated
BP America Inc.
Brach Foundation, Helen
Bridgestone/Firestone, Inc.
Brunswick Corp.
Bryn Mawr Trust Co.
Burdines Inc.
Butz Foundation
Cable & Wireless Holdings, Inc.
Cabot Corp.
Cafritz Foundation, Morris and Gwendolyn
Callaway Foundation
Campbell Foundation
Carolyn Foundation
Carpenter Foundation, E. Rhodes and Leona B.
Carpenter Technology Corp.
Carter Foundation, Amon G.
Cassett Foundation, Louis N.
Castle Foundation, Harold K. L.
Cayuga Foundation
Central Maine Power Co.
Central Vermont Public Service Corp.
Century Companies of America
Chase Manhattan Bank, N.A.
Chastain Charitable Foundation, Robert Lee and Thomas M.
Chazen Foundation
Cheatham Foundation, Owen

Chesapeake Corp.
Chevron Corporation
Chicago Sun-Times, Inc.
Christensen Charitable and Religious Foundation, L. C.
Christian Dior New York, Inc.
Church & Dwight Co., Inc.
CINergy
Clorox Co.
Cogswell Benevolent Trust
Cole Trust, Quincy
Collins Foundation, George and Jennie
Collins, Jr. Foundation, George Fulton
Colonial Life & Accident Insurance Co.
Columbia Foundation
Commerce Bancshares, Inc.
Commerce Clearing House, Incorporated
Commonwealth Edison Co.
Connecticut Mutual Life Insurance Company
Consolidated Papers, Inc.
Continental Corp.
Corning Incorporated
Cowles Charitable Trust
Cowles Media Co.
CPC International Inc.
Crandall Memorial Foundation, J. Ford
Crocker Trust, Mary A.
Crown Memorial, Arie and Ida
Culver Foundation, Constans
Cummins Engine Co.
Curtice-Burns Foods, Inc.
Daily News
Dalton Foundation, Harry L.
Davis Foundation, James A. and Juliet L.
Day Foundation, Nancy Sayles
Daywood Foundation
DEC International, Inc.
Deere & Co.
Delano Foundation, Mignon Sherwood
Delaware North Co., Inc.
DeRoy Foundation, Helen L.
Deuble Foundation, George H.
Dewing Foundation, Frances R.
Dexter Charitable Fund, Eugene A.
Digital Equipment Corp.
Dimeo Construction Co.
Dodge Foundation, Geraldine R.
Donaldson Company, Inc.
Dow Corning Corp.
Dreyfus Foundation, Max and Victoria
du Pont de Nemours & Co., E. I.
Duchossois Industries Inc.
Duke Power Co.
Durfee Foundation
Eaton Corporation
Eaton Foundation, Cyrus
Edgewater Steel Corp.
El Pomar Foundation
Elkins, Jr. Foundation, Margaret and James A.
Erpf Fund, Armand G.
Ethyl Corp
Exxon Corporation
Fair Oaks Foundation, Inc.
Federal-Mogul Corporation
Federated Mutual Insurance Co.
Feild Co-Operative Association
Fireman's Fund Insurance Co.
First Chicago Corp.
First Fidelity Bank
First Interstate Bank of Oregon
First Tennessee Bank
First Union Corp.
Fishback Foundation Trust, Harmes C.
Fleet Financial Group, Inc.
Fleishhacker Foundation
Fletcher Foundation
Ford Motor Co.
Frear Eleemosynary Trust, Mary D. and Walter F.
Freeport-McMoRan Inc.

French Oil Mill Machinery Co.
Fribourg Foundation
Friedman Family Foundation
Frost National Bank
GAR Foundation
GATX Corp.
Gaylord Foundation, Clifford Willard
Geifman Family Foundation
Gellert Foundation, Carl
General American Life Insurance Co.
Geneseo Foundation
GenRad
Georgia Power Co.
Gershman Foundation, Joel
Giant Eagle, Inc.
Giant Food Inc.
Glaser Foundation
Glick Foundation, Eugene and Marilyn
Glosser Foundation, David A.
Goldberg Family Foundation
Goldsmith Foundation, Horace W.
Goodrich Co., The B.F.
Gould Electronics Inc.
Great-West Life Assurance Co.
Griffith Foundation, W. C.
Groome Beatty Trust, Helen D.
Guaranty Bank & Trust Co.
Guardian Life Insurance Company of America
Haley Foundation, W. B.
Handy and Harman Foundation
Hanes Foundation, John W. and Anna H.
Harsco Corp.
Hawn Foundation
Heinz Endowment, Vira I.
Heinz Trust, Drue
Higginson Trust, Corina
High Foundation
Hillman Family Foundation, Alex
Holzer Memorial Foundation, Richard H.
Hopkins Foundation, Josephine Lawrence
Houston Industries Incorporated
Hoyt Foundation
Hoyt Foundation, Stewart W. and Willma C.
Hulme Charitable Foundation, Milton G.
Humana, Inc.
Hunt Charitable Trust, C. Giles
Hunt Foundation
Hunt Foundation, Samuel P.
Huthsteiner Fine Arts Trust
Icahn Foundation, Carl C.
ICI Americas Inc.
Interkal, Inc.
International Business Machines Corp.
Iowa-Illinois Gas & Electric Co.
ITT Hartford Insurance Group, Inc.
Jacobson Foundation, Bernard H. and Blanche E.
James River Corp. of Virginia
Jameson Foundation, J. W. and Ida M.
Jarson-Stanley and Mickey Kaplan Foundation, Isaac and Esther
JFM Foundation
John Hancock Mutual Life Insurance Co.
Johnson & Higgins
Johnson & Son, S.C.
Kansas City Southern Industries
Kantzler Foundation
Kelley and Elza Kelley Foundation, Edward Bangs
Kennecott Corporation
Kettering Fund
Kilroy Foundation, William S. and Lora Jean
Kimberly-Clark Corp.
Kingsbury Corp.
Kirby Foundation, F. M.

Klipstein Foundation, Ernest Christian
Knox, Sr., and Pearl Wallis Knox Charitable Foundation, Robert W.
Koehler Foundation, Marcia and Otto
Komes Foundation
Koopman Fund
Kuehn Foundation
Kunkel Foundation, John Crain
La-Z-Boy Chair Co.
Ladd Charitable Corporation, Helen and George
LamCo. Communications
Laurel Foundation
Lazarus Charitable Trust, Helen and Charles
Lebovitz Fund
Lee Endowment Foundation
Leidy Foundation, John J.
Lemberg Foundation
Lennon Foundation, Fred A.
Leuthold Foundation
Linn-Henley Charitable Trust
Liz Claiborne, Inc.
Long Island Lighting Co.
Love Foundation, George H. and Margaret McClintic
Lurie Foundation, Louis R.
Lydall, Inc.
Lyon Foundation
MacArthur Foundation, John D. and Catherine T.
MacCurdy Salisbury Educational Foundation
Macy & Co., Inc., R.H.
Madison Gas & Electric Co.
Magowan Family Foundation
Management Compensation Group/Dulworth Inc.
Mandeville Foundation
Marbrook Foundation
Maritz Inc.
Markey Charitable Fund, John C.
Marquette Electronics, Inc.
Martin Marietta Materials
Mather Fund, Richard
Mather and William Gwinn Mather Fund, Elizabeth Ring
Mathis-Pfohl Foundation
May Department Stores Company, The
Mayer Foundation, James and Eva
Mayor Foundation, Oliver Dewey
McDonald & Company Securities, Inc.
McDonnell Douglas Corp.-West
McFawn Trust No. 2, Lois Sisler
McGonagle Foundation, Dextra Baldwin
McInerny Foundation
McMahon Foundation
Mead Corporation, The
Meadows Foundation
Mellon Foundation, Richard King
Memton Fund
Merck & Co. Human Health Division
Mielke Family Foundation
Miller Brewing Company/North Carolina
Miller Charitable Foundation, Howard E. and Nell E.
Miller Fund, Kathryn and Gilbert
Miller-Mellor Association
Mingenback Foundation, Julia J.
Mitsubishi International Corp.
Mitsubishi Motor Sales of America, Inc.
Mnuchin Foundation
Mobil Oil Corp.
Monadnock Paper Mills
Morgan Construction Co.
Morgan and Samuel Tate Morgan, Jr. Foundation, Marietta McNeil

Morrison Knudsen Corporation
Mosinee Paper Corp.
Mott Fund, Ruth
Mulcahy Foundation
Mulford Foundation, Vincent
Munson Foundation Trust, W. B.
Myra Foundation
Nabisco Foods Group
Nalco Chemical Co.
National Gypsum Co.
National Westminster Bank New Jersey
Nesholm Family Foundation
New England Business Service
New York Mercantile Exchange
New York Stock Exchange, Inc.
New York Times Company
The New Yorker Magazine, Inc.
Newman's Own, Inc.
Nias Foundation, Henry
Normandie Foundation
Northern States Power Co. (Minnesota)
Northwest Natural Gas Co.
Norton Co.
Norton Foundation Inc.
Norwest Bank Nebraska, N.A.
Novell Inc.
Oaklawn Foundation
OCRI Foundation
O'Fallon Trust, Martin J. and Mary Anne
Old National Bank in Evansville
Olin Corp.
Oliver Memorial Trust Foundation
Owen Industries, Inc.
Owsley Foundation, Alvin and Lucy
Oxy USA Inc.
Pacific Telesis Group
Packaging Corporation of America
Packard Foundation, David and Lucile
Penguin Books USA, Inc.
Penn Foundation, William
Pennzoil Co.
Perkin-Elmer Corp.
Petrie Trust, Lorene M.
Pforzheimer Foundation, Carl and Lily
Phelps Dodge Corporation
PHH Corporation
Phillips Foundation, Ellis L.
Piankova Foundation, Tatiana
Pineywoods Foundation
Piper Foundation, Minnie Stevens
Pitt-Des Moines Inc.
Pittsburg Midway Coal Mining Co.
Playboy Enterprises, Inc.
PNC Bank, N.A.
Polaroid Corp.
Pollock Company Foundation, William B.
Potts and Sibley Foundation
PPG Industries, Inc.
Prairie Foundation
Price Associates, T. Rowe
Priddy Foundation
Providian Corporation
Prudential Insurance Co. of America, The
Putnam Foundation
Quaker Chemical Corp.
Rabb Foundation, Harry W.
Reed Foundation
Reynolds Foundation, Donald W.
Rice Charitable Foundation, Albert W.
RJR Nabisco Inc.
Robinson Fund, Maurice R.
Rockwell International Corporation
Rogers Family Foundation
Rohatyn Foundation, Felix and Elizabeth
Rohm & Haas Co.
Rosen Foundation, Joseph

Rose's Stores, Inc.
Ross Laboratories
Ross Memorial Foundation, Will
Rouse Co.
Royal Group, Inc.
Ruan Foundation Trust, John
Rubin Foundation, Samuel
SAFECO Corp.
Saint Paul Companies, Inc.
San Diego Gas & Electric
Sandusky International Inc.
Santa Fe Pacific Corporation
Sara Lee Corp.
Sara Lee Hosiery, Inc.
Sargent Foundation, Newell B.
SBC Communications Inc.
Schenck Fund, L. P.
Schering-Plough Corp.
Schoenleber Foundation
Schuller International
Schwab & Co., Inc., Charles
Schwob Foundation, Simon
Scott Fetzer Co.
Scott Foundation, Virginia Steele
Scott Foundation, William E.
Seafirst Corporation
Seaway Food Town, Inc.
Security Life of Denver Insurance Co.
Sedgwick James Inc.
Seidman Family Foundation
Sentry Insurance A Mutual Company
Sharon Steel Corp.
Shawmut National Corp.
Sheaffer Inc.
Shott, Jr. Foundation, Hugh I.
Sierra Pacific Resources
Slemp Foundation
Smith, Jr. Foundation, M. W.
Smith Memorial Fund, Ethel Sergeant Clark
Solow Foundation
Sordoni Foundation
South Branch Foundation
Southern California Edison Co.
Southwestern Electric Power Co.
Speyer Foundation, Alexander C. and Tillie S.
Springs Foundation
Stanley Charitable Foundation, A.W.
Stanley Works
Steinhagen Benevolent Trust, B. A. and Elinor
Steinman Foundation, James Hale
Steinman Foundation, John Frederick
Stemmons Foundation
Sternberger Foundation, Tannenbaum
Stokely, Jr. Foundation, William B.
Strawbridge Foundation of Pennsylvania II, Margaret Dorrance
Sumitomo Bank of California
Superior Tube Co.
Tait Foundation, Frank M.
Taper Foundation, Mark
Taylor Foundation, Ruth and Vernon
Teleflex Inc.
Tenneco Inc.
Tetley, Inc.
Texaco Inc.
Textron, Inc.
Texas Commerce Bank-Houston, N.A.
Thalhimer and Family Foundation, Charles G.
Thomasville Furniture Industries
Thompson Trust, Thomas
Titus Foundation, Roy and Niuta
Tobin Foundation
Todd Co., A.M.
Toms Foundation
Transco Energy Co.
Travelers Inc.

Truland Foundation
Trust Company Bank
Tuch Foundation, Michael
Unger Foundation, Aber D.
Union Camp Corporation
U.S. Bank of Washington
Unitrode Corp.
Unocal Corp.
Vance Charitable Foundation, Robert C.
Virginia Power Co.
Vulcan Materials Co.
Wachovia Bank of North Carolina, N.A.
Wahlstrom Foundation
Wal-Mart Stores, Inc.
Wallace-Reader's Digest Fund, Lila
Walsh Foundation
Washington Forrest Foundation
Washington Mutual Savings Bank
Waters Charitable Trust, Robert S.
Wege Foundation
Welch Testamentary Trust, George T.
Wells Foundation, Franklin H. and Ruth L.
Wertheim Foundation, Dr. Herbert A.
West One Bancorp
Western New York Foundation
Weyerhaeuser Co.
Weyerhaeuser Memorial Foundation, Charles A.
Wheeler Foundation, Wilmot
Whirlpool Corporation
Whitney Fund, David M.
Whittenberger Foundation, Claude R. and Ethel B.
Wilder Foundation
Willard Helping Fund, Cecilia Young
Wilmington Trust Co.
Winchester Foundation
Winnebago Industries, Inc.
Winter Construction Co.
Winthrop Trust, Clara B.
Wisconsin Power & Light Co.
Woolley Foundation, Vasser
Wright Foundation, Lola
Wyman Youth Trust
Young Foundation, Hugo H. and Mabel B.
Zarrow Foundation, Anne and Henry

Dance

Abbott Laboratories
Abell-Hanger Foundation
Achelis Foundation
Adams Foundation, Arthur F. and Alice E.
AEGON USA Inc.
Air France
Air Products and Chemicals, Inc.
Alabama Gas Corp.
Alabama Power Co.
Aldus Corp.
Allegheny Ludlum Corp.
AlliedSignal Inc.
Alumax Inc.
Aluminum Co. of America
AMCORE Bank, N.A. Rockford
American General Finance Corp.
American National Bank & Trust Co. of Chicago
American President Companies, Ltd.
Ameritas Life Insurance Corp.
AMETEK, Inc.
Amfac/JMB Hawaii Inc.
AON Corporation
Aristech Chemical Corp.
Arkansas Power & Light Co.
AT&T Corp.
Atherton Family Foundation
Avery Arts Foundation, Milton and Sally

Baker Foundation, Dexter F. and Dorothy H.
Baldwin Foundation, David M. and Barbara
Baldwin Memorial Foundation, Fred
Barry Corp., R. G.
Barth Foundation, Theodore H.
Battelle Memorial Institute
Beattie Foundation Trust, Cordelia Lee
Bell Foundation, James F.
Benedum Foundation, Claude Worthington
Benetton Services Corp.
Beveridge Foundation, Frank Stanley
Bingham Foundation, William
Binney & Smith Inc.
Birnschein Foundation, Alvin and Marion
Bishop Foundation, E. K. and Lillian F.
Bissell Foundation, J. Walton
Blair and Co., William
Block, H&R
Blount, Inc.
Blum-Kovler Foundation
Boatmen's Bancshares, Inc.
Bodman Foundation
Boeing Co., The
Boise Cascade Corporation
Borden, Inc.
Borman's, Inc.
Boston Edison Co.
BP America Inc.
Brach Foundation, Helen
Brady Foundation
Bridgestone/Firestone, Inc.
Brown Foundation, M. K.
Brown & Williamson Tobacco Corp.
Brunswick Corp.
Bucyrus-Erie Company
Bunbury Company
Burden Foundation, Florence V.
Burdines Inc.
Cabot Corp.
Cafritz Foundation, Morris and Gwendolyn
Cain Foundation, Gordon and Mary
Carolyn Foundation
Carpenter Foundation, E. Rhodes and Leona B.
CBI Industries, Inc.
CBS, Inc.
Centerior Energy Corp.
Central Maine Power Co.
Chase Manhattan Bank, N.A.
Chastain Charitable Foundation, Robert Lee and Thomas M.
Cheatham Foundation, Owen
Cheney Foundation, Ben B.
Chevron Corporation
Chicago Sun-Times, Inc.
Christian Dior New York, Inc.
Citibank
CLARCOR Inc.
Clorox Co.
Clowes Fund
CNA Financial Corporation/CNA Insurance Companies
Cole Foundation, Olive B.
Cole Trust, Quincy
Collins Foundation
Colonial Life & Accident Insurance Co.
Columbia Foundation
Columbus Dispatch Printing Co.
Commonwealth Edison Co.
Consolidated Natural Gas Co.
Continental Corp.
Contran Corporation
Cooper Industries, Inc.
Cooperman Foundation, Leon and Toby
Copley Press, Inc.
Cord Foundation, E. L.
Cosmair, Inc.
Cowles Charitable Trust

Cowles Media Co.
CPC International Inc.
CS First Boston Corporation
Cullen Foundation
Culpeper Foundation, Charles E.
Cummins Engine Co.
Dana Charitable Trust, Eleanor Naylor
Day Foundation, Nancy Sayles
Demoulas Supermarkets Inc.
Dewing Foundation, Frances R.
Dexter Corporation
Diamond Foundation, Aaron
Digital Equipment Corp.
Dodge Foundation, Geraldine R.
Donaldson Company, Inc.
Douty Foundation
Dow Corning Corp.
Dresser Industries, Inc.
Dreyfus Foundation, Max and Victoria
du Pont de Nemours & Co., E. I.
Duchossois Industries Inc.
Duke Power Co.
Eaton Corporation
Eaton Foundation, Cyrus
Eddy Family Memorial Fund, C. K.
Elf Atochem North America, Inc.
Elkins, Jr. Foundation, Margaret and James A.
Emerson Foundation, Inc., Fred L.
Encyclopaedia Britannica, Inc.
English Memorial Fund, Florence C. and H. L.
Enron Corp.
Erpf Fund, Armand G.
Exxon Corporation
Farish Fund, William Stamps
Feild Co-Operative Association
Fireman's Fund Insurance Co.
First Chicago Corp.
First Fidelity Bank
First Interstate Bank of Oregon
First Tennessee Bank
First Union Corp.
Firstar Bank Milwaukee, N.A.
Fischbach Foundation
Fish Foundation, Ray C.
Fleet Financial Group, Inc.
Fleishhacker Foundation
Fondren Foundation
Forbes Inc.
Ford Foundation
Forest Foundation
Forest Oil Corp.
Frear Eleemosynary Trust, Mary D. and Walter F.
Freeman Charitable Trust, Samuel
Freeport-McMoRan Inc.
Frisch's Restaurants Inc.
Fry Foundation, Lloyd A.
Gates Foundation
GATX Corp.
GenCorp Inc.
General American Life Insurance Co.
General Mills, Inc.
General Motors Corp.
Georgia-Pacific Corporation
Georgia Power Co.
Giant Eagle, Inc.
Giant Food Inc.
Gillette Co.
Gilman Foundation, Howard
Globe Newspaper Co.
Goldsmith Foundation, Horace W.
Goldwyn Foundation, Samuel
Goodrich Co., The B.F.
Gould Foundation, The Florence
Graham Fund, Philip L.
Great-West Life Assurance Co.
Greenwall Foundation
Gregg-Graniteville Foundation
Griffis Foundation
Griggs and Mary Griggs Burke Foundation, Mary Livingston

Guttman Foundation, Stella
and Charles
Halsell Foundation, Ewing
Hamman Foundation, George
and Mary Josephine
Harsco Corp.
Hawn Foundation
HCA Foundation
Hechinger Co.
Hecht-Levi Foundation
Heckscher Foundation for
Children
Heinz Company, H. J.
Heinz Endowment, Howard
Heinz Endowment, Vira I.
Heinz Trust, Drue
Henkel Corp.
Hewlett Foundation, William
and Flora
Higginson Trust, Corina
Hillman Family Foundation,
Alex
Hillsdale Fund
Holzer Memorial Foundation,
Richard H.
Homeland Foundation
Hook Drugs
Hopwood Charitable Trust,
John M.
Houston Industries
Incorporated
Howard and Bush Foundation
Hoyt Foundation
Humana, Inc.
Hunt Foundation
Hunt Foundation, Roy A.
Huston Charitable Trust,
Stewart
Huthsteiner Fine Arts Trust
Illinois Tool Works, Inc.
Integra Bank of Uniontown
International Business
Machines Corp.
International Paper Co.
Irwin Charity Foundation,
William G.
ITT Hartford Insurance Group,
Inc.
Jackson Foundation
Jaffe Foundation
Jarson-Stanley and Mickey
Kaplan Foundation, Isaac
and Esther
Jewett Foundation, George
Frederick
JFM Foundation
John Hancock Mutual Life
Insurance Co.
Johnson Controls Inc.
Johnson & Higgins
Jones Foundation, Daisy
Marquis
Jordan Charitable Foundation,
Mary Ranken Jordan and
Ettie A.
Kansas City Southern
Industries
Kennecott Corporation
Kilroy Foundation, William S.
and Lora Jean
Kimberly-Clark Corp.
Kingsbury Corp.
Kirkpatrick Foundation
Knight Foundation, John S.
and James L.
Koopman Fund
Lauder Foundation
Laurel Foundation
Lazarus Charitable Trust,
Helen and Charles
Lea Foundation, Helen Sperry
LEF Foundation
Leighton-Oare Foundation
Lemberg Foundation
Life Insurance Co. of Georgia
Lipton, Thomas J.
Loews Corporation
MacArthur Foundation, John
D. and Catherine T.
Macy & Co., Inc., R.H.
Magowan Family Foundation
Mailman Foundation
Mardigian Foundation
Maritz Inc.
Marquette Electronics, Inc.

Mars Foundation
Marsh & McLennan
Companies, Inc.
Marshall Trust in Memory of
Sanders McDaniel, Harriet
McDaniel
Martin Marietta Corp.
Martini Foundation, Nicholas
May Foundation, Wilbur
Maytag Family Foundation,
Fred
MCA Inc.
McCormick Trust, Anne
McDonnell Douglas
Corp.-West
McFawn Trust No. 2, Lois
Sisler
McInerny Foundation
McLean Contributionship
Mead Corporation, The
Meadows Foundation
Mellon Foundation, Andrew W.
Mellon Foundation, Richard
King
Memton Fund
Messing Family Charitable
Foundation
Metropolitan Life Insurance
Co.
Meyer Memorial Trust
Middendorf Foundation
Miller Brewing
Company/North Carolina
Mine Safety Appliances Co.
Mitsubishi Motor Sales of
America, Inc.
Mnuchin Foundation
Mobil Oil Corp.
Monticello College Foundation
Morgan & Company, J.P.
Morgan Foundation, Burton D.
Morgan and Samuel Tate
Morgan, Jr. Foundation,
Marietta McNeil
Morgan Stanley & Co., Inc.
Morris Foundation, Margaret T.
Morris Foundation, William T.
Moses Fund, Henry and Lucy
Mott Fund, Ruth
Myra Foundation
Nabisco Foods Group
Nalco Chemical Co.
National Gypsum Co.
National Steel Corp.
National Westminster Bank
New Jersey
NBD Indiana, Inc.
Neuberger Foundation, Roy R.
and Marie S.
New York Times Company
The New Yorker Magazine, Inc.
Northwest Natural Gas Co.
Norton Co.
Norton Family Foundation,
Peter
Norwest Bank Nebraska, N.A.
Novell Inc.
Old National Bank in
Evansville
Olin Corp.
Ore-Ida Foods, Inc.
Osborn Charitable Trust,
Edward B.
Osher Foundation, Bernard
Overbrook Foundation
Owsley Foundation, Alvin and
Lucy
Pacific Mutual Life Insurance
Co.
Pacific Telesis Group
Packard Foundation, David
and Lucile
Paley Foundation, William S.
Parshelsky Foundation, Moses
L.
PECO Energy Company
Penn Foundation, William
Pennzoil Co.
Peoples Energy Corp.
Pew Charitable Trusts
Pfizer, Inc.
Pforzheimer Foundation, Carl
and Lily
Piankova Foundation, Tatiana
Pick, Jr. Fund, Albert

Plumsock Fund
Polaroid Corp.
Potomac Electric Power Co.
PPG Industries, Inc.
Premier Industrial Corp.
Prince Trust, Abbie Norman
Pulitzer Publishing Co.
Putnam Foundation
Read Foundation, Charles L.
Republic NY Corp.
Rhone-Poulenc Inc.
RJR Nabisco Inc.
Rockwell Fund
Rockwell International
Corporation
Rohatyn Foundation, Felix and
Elizabeth
Rohm & Haas Co.
Rose Foundation, Billy
Rosenberg, Jr. Family
Foundation, Louise and
Claude
Rouse Co.
Royal Group, Inc.
Rubinstein Foundation, Helena
Rudin Foundation
SAFECO Corp.
Saint Paul Companies, Inc.
Saltonstall Charitable
Foundation, Richard
San Diego Gas & Electric
Santa Fe Pacific Corporation
Sara Lee Corp.
Sargent Foundation, Newell B.
Sarkeys Foundation
SBC Communications Inc.
Schering-Plough Corp.
Scherman Foundation
Schiro Fund
Schlumberger Ltd.
Schwartz Fund for Education
and Health Research, Arnold
and Marie
Scott Foundation, William E.
Scurlock Foundation
Seafirst Corporation
Seaver Charitable Trust,
Richard C.
Security Life of Denver
Insurance Co.
Sedgwick James Inc.
Shawmut National Corp.
Sheaffer Inc.
Shell Oil Company
Shenandoah Life Insurance Co.
Shubert Foundation
Simon Foundation, William E.
and Carol G.
Smith Corp., A.O.
Smith, Jr. Foundation, M. W.
Smith Trust, May and Stanley
South Branch Foundation
Southern California Edison Co.
Southern New England
Telephone Company
Sprague Educational and
Charitable Foundation, Seth
Square D Co.
Stanley Works
Starr Foundation
Stauffer Foundation, John and
Beverly
Stein Foundation, Jules and
Doris
Stemmons Foundation
Stevens Foundation, Abbot
and Dorothy H.
Sturgis Charitable and
Educational Trust, Roy and
Christine
Subaru of America Inc.
Swiss Bank Corp.
Tait Foundation, Frank M.
Taylor Foundation, Ruth and
Vernon
Teleflex Inc.
Tenneco Inc.
Tetley, Inc.
Texaco Inc.
Textron, Inc.
Thermo Electron Corp.
Thompson Co., J. Walter
Times Mirror Company, The
Titus Foundation, Roy and
Niuta

Transco Energy Co.
Travelers Inc.
Trexler Trust, Harry C.
Truland Foundation
Trust Company Bank
Tucker Charitable Trust, Rose
E.
Turner Charitable Foundation
Union Bank
Union Electric Co.
Union Pacific Corp.
United Airlines, Inc.
U.S. Bank of Washington
Unocal Corp.
Upton Foundation, Frederick S.
USL Capital Corporation
USX Corporation
Valentine Foundation, Lawson
Virginia Power Co.
Vulcan Materials Co.
Wachovia Bank of North
Carolina, N.A.
Wahlstrom Foundation
Wal-Mart Stores, Inc.
Wallace Foundation, George R.
Wallace-Reader's Digest Fund,
Lila
Walsh Foundation
Warner Fund, Albert and
Bessie
Washington Forrest Foundation
Wean Foundation, Raymond
John
Weil, Gotshal and Manges
Foundation
Welch Testamentary Trust,
George T.
Wendt Foundation, Margaret L.
Wertheim Foundation, Dr.
Herbert A.
West One Bancorp
Weyerhaeuser Co.
Wheeler Foundation, Wilmot
Whirlpool Corporation
Whitecap Foundation
Whiting Foundation,
Macauley and Helen Dow
Whittenberger Foundation,
Claude R. and Ethel B.
Wilder Foundation
Wildermuth Foundation, E. F.
Wiley & Sons, Inc., John
Williams Companies, The
Winston Foundation, Norman
and Rosita
Winter Construction Co.
Witco Corp.
Wyman Youth Trust
Zenkel Foundation

Ethnic & Folk Arts

Ahmanson Foundation
Alumax Inc.
Amado Foundation, Maurice
AMETEK, Inc.
Amoco Corporation
Archer-Daniels-Midland Co.
Avon Products, Inc.
Bank of Boston Corp.
Bank One, Texas-Houston
Office
Bank One, Youngstown, NA
BankAmerica Corp.
Barra Foundation
Barry Corp., R. G.
Baughman Foundation
Benenson Foundation, Frances
and Benjamin
Block, H&R
Boeing Co., The
Borman's Inc.
Brackenridge Foundation,
George W.
Brown & Williamson Tobacco
Corp.
Burkitt Foundation
Bush Foundation
Cabot Corp.
Carolyn Foundation
Carter Foundation, Amon G.
CBS, Inc.
Central Maine Power Co.
Chase Manhattan Bank, N.A.

Chazen Foundation
Chicago Sun-Times, Inc.
Childs Charitable Foundation,
Roberta M.
Christian Dior New York, Inc.
Citibank
Clorox Co.
Colonial Life & Accident
Insurance Co.
Columbia Foundation
Commonwealth Edison Co.
Continental Corp.
Cosmair, Inc.
Cowell Foundation, S. H.
Cowles Media Co.
CPC International Inc.
Cranston Print Works Company
Dr. Seuss Foundation
du Pont de Nemours & Co., E.
I.
Duchossois Industries Inc.
Duke Power Co.
Duncan Foundation, Lillian H.
and C. W.
Eberly Foundation
Enron Corp.
Essick Foundation
Exxon Corporation
Fikes Foundation, Leland
Fireman's Fund Insurance Co.
First Chicago Corp.
First Fidelity Bank
First Tennessee Bank
First Union Corp.
Fish Foundation, Ray C.
Fleet Financial Group, Inc.
Fleishhacker Foundation
Forbes Inc.
Ford Foundation
Foster Charitable Trust
Freeport-McMoRan Inc.
Frost National Bank
Fry Foundation, Lloyd A.
GATX Corp.
Gazette Co.
Georgia Power Co.
Gershman Foundation, Joel
Getty Trust, J. Paul
Gilman Foundation, Howard
Glaser Foundation
Globe Newspaper Co.
Graham Foundation for
Advanced Studies in the
Fine Arts
Graham Fund, Philip L.
Grand Rapids Label Co.
Greenwall Foundation
Griffith Foundation, W. C.
Grundy Foundation
Guaranty Bank & Trust Co.
Guggenheim Foundation,
Harry Frank
Halff Foundation, G. A. C.
Halsell Foundation, Ewing
HarperCollins Publishers Inc.
Hartford Foundation, John A.
Heckscher Foundation for
Children
Heinz Endowment, Vira I.
Higginson Trust, Corina
Houston Industries
Incorporated
International Business
Machines Corp.
Jockey Hollow Foundation
John Hancock Mutual Life
Insurance Co.
Johnson Fund, Edward C.
Johnson & Higgins
Johnson & Son, S.C.
Jones Foundation, Helen
Jordan Charitable Foundation,
Mary Ranken Jordan and
Ettie A.
Jostens, Inc.
Jurzykowski Foundation,
Alfred
Kansas City Southern
Industries
Kennecott Corporation
Kingsbury Corp.
Kirkpatrick Foundation
Knight Foundation, John S.
and James L.

Knox, Sr., and Pearl Wallis Knox Charitable Foundation, Robert W.
Koehler Foundation, Marcia and Otto
Komes Foundation
Koret Foundation
Laurel Foundation
LEF Foundation
Life Insurance Co. of Georgia
Link, Jr. Foundation, George
Littauer Foundation, Lucius N.
Long Island Lighting Co.
Lurie Foundation, Louis R.
MacArthur Foundation, John D. and Catherine T.
Mandeville Foundation
Mardigian Foundation
Maritz Inc.
Marpat Foundation
May Department Stores Company, The
McCasland Foundation
McDermott Foundation, Eugene
McDonald & Company Securities, Inc.
McEvoy Foundation, Mildred H.
Meadows Foundation
Metropolitan Life Insurance Co.
Meyer Memorial Trust
Miller Brewing Company/North Carolina
Miller Charitable Foundation, Howard E. and Nell E.
Minnesota Mining & Mfg. Co.
Mitsubishi International Corp.
Mitsubishi Motor Sales of America, Inc.
Mnuchin Foundation
Mobil Oil Corp.
Mott Fund, Ruth
National Westminster Bank New Jersey
Nesholm Family Foundation
Neuberger Foundation, Roy R. and Marie S.
New York Times Company
The New Yorker Magazine, Inc.
Noble Foundation, Samuel Roberts
Northern States Power Co. (Minnesota)
Northwest Natural Gas Co.
Norton Co.
Norton Family Foundation, Peter
Norton Foundation Inc.
Novell Inc.
OG&E Electric Services
Osher Foundation, Bernard
Pacific Mutual Life Insurance Co.
Pacific Telesis Group
Parsons Foundation, Ralph M.
PECO Energy Company
Penn Foundation, William
Peoples Energy Corp.
Pew Charitable Trusts
Playboy Enterprises, Inc.
Plumsock Fund
Porter Testamentary Trust, James Hyde
Public Service Co. of New Mexico
Putnam Foundation
Rogers Family Foundation
Rohm & Haas Co.
Rose Foundation, Billy
Rosenberg, Jr. Family Foundation, Louise and Claude
Rouse Co.
Royal Group, Inc.
Saint Paul Companies, Inc.
Salomon Foundation, Richard and Edna
San Diego Gas & Electric
Sara Lee Corp.
SBC Communications Inc.
Schlumberger Ltd.

Schwartz Fund for Education and Health Research, Arnold and Marie
Seaway Food Town, Inc.
Security Life of Denver Insurance Co.
Sedgwick James Inc.
Semmes Foundation
Shawmut National Corp.
Shenandoah Life Insurance Co.
Smith Foundation, Ralph L.
Smith Trust, May and Stanley
Snow Memorial Trust, John Ben
Solow Foundation
Southern California Edison Co.
Speyer Foundation, Alexander C. and Tillie S.
Sprague Educational and Charitable Foundation, Seth
Starr Foundation
Stevens Foundation, Abbot and Dorothy H.
Sturgis Charitable and Educational Trust, Roy and Christine
Swiss Bank Corp.
Teleflex Inc.
Temple-Inland Inc.
Thalhimer and Family Foundation, Charles G.
Thornton Foundation, Flora L.
Times Mirror Company, The
Tobin Foundation
Transco Energy Co.
Trull Foundation
Trust Company Bank
Tupancy-Harris Foundation of 1986
Union Bank
Union Camp Corporation
United Airlines, Inc.
U.S. Bank of Washington
USL Capital Corporation
Vulcan Materials Co.
Wallace-Reader's Digest Fund, Lila
Washington Mutual Savings Bank
Wheat First Butcher Singer, Inc.
Whirlpool Corporation
Winter Construction Co.
Wyman Youth Trust

Film & Video

Ames Charitable Trust, Harriett
Bay Foundation
Benedum Foundation, Claude Worthington
Benenson Foundation, Frances and Benjamin
Binney & Smith Inc.
Blount, Inc.
Booth Ferris Foundation
Bowen Foundation, Ethel N.
Cabot Family Charitable Trust
Carter Foundation, Amon G.
Charina Foundation
Chartwell Foundation
Chevron Corporation
Christian Dior New York, Inc.
Clorox Co.
Coltec Industries, Inc.
Columbia Foundation
Cooke Foundation
Crocker Trust, Mary A.
CT Corp. System
Cullen Foundation
Davis Foundations, Arthur Vining
Daywood Foundation
Donner Foundation, William H.
Evans Foundation, Lettie Pate
Favrot Fund
Fenton Foundation
Fleishhacker Foundation
Ford Foundation
Friendship Fund
General Mills, Inc.
Gilman Foundation, Howard
Goldsmith Foundation, Horace W.

Graham Foundation for Advanced Studies in the Fine Arts
Harland Charitable Foundation, John and Wilhelmina D.
Harriman Foundation, Mary W.
Heinz Endowment, Howard
Hillman Family Foundation, Alex
Hillsdale Fund
Hunt Foundation
Independence Foundation
Irvine Foundation, James
Ittleson Foundation
Jacobson Foundation, Bernard H. and Blanche E.
Johnson Fund, Edward C.
Kansas City Southern Industries
Kaplan Fund, J. M.
Kennecott Corporation
Lasdon Foundation, William and Mildred
Laurel Foundation
LEF Foundation
Markle Foundation, John and Mary R.
MCA Inc.
McCarty Foundation, John and Margaret
MCI Communications Corp.
Mnuchin Foundation
New York Times Company
Nias Foundation, Henry
Offield Family Foundation
Osher Foundation, Bernard
Parvin Foundation, Albert
Pettus Crowe Foundation
Pforzheimer Foundation, Carl and Lily
Phillips Foundation, Ellis L.
Providian Corporation
Reed Foundation
Retirement Research Foundation
Rose Foundation, Billy
Rubin Foundation, Samuel
Salomon Foundation, Richard and Edna
Sara Lee Hosiery, Inc.
Selby and Marie Selby Foundation, William G.
Shott, Jr. Foundation, Hugh I.
Stevens Foundation, Abbot and Dorothy H.
Swanson Family Foundation, Dr. W.C.
Tait Foundation, Frank M.
Thorne Foundation
Titus Foundation, Roy and Niuta
Tucker Charitable Trust, Rose E.
Whitney Fund, David M.
Windham Foundation
Zenkel Foundation

General

Abbott Laboratories
Acme-McCrary Corp./Sapona Manufacturing Co.
Aetna Life & Casualty Co.
Ahmanson Foundation
Akzo America
Alabama Gas Corp.
Aldus Corp.
Amcast Industrial Corp.
AMCORE Bank, N.A. Rockford
Andrews Foundation
Ansin Private Foundation, Ronald M.
Aristech Chemical Corp.
Avery Arts Foundation, Milton and Sally
Baldwin Memorial Foundation, Fred
Bank of Boston Corp.
Bank One, Texas-Houston Office
Bank One, Youngstown, NA
Barry Corp., R. G.

Bay Foundation
Benenson Foundation, Frances and Benjamin
Benwood Foundation
Berwind Corporation
Bingham Second Betterment Fund, William
Binswanger Cos.
Blair and Co., William
Bowne Foundation, Robert
Bryn Mawr Trust Co.
Buhl Foundation
Bush Foundation
Campbell Foundation
Central Maine Power Co.
Chadwick Fund, Dorothy Jordan
Chicago Sun-Times, Inc.
Christian Dior New York, Inc.
CINergy
Commerce Clearing House, Incorporated
Consumers Power Co.
Cooke Foundation
Cooperman Foundation, Leon and Toby
Copley Press, Inc.
Cosmair, Inc.
Coughlin-Saunders Foundation
Cowles Charitable Trust
Crawford Estate, E. R.
CT Corp. System
Dana Charitable Trust, Eleanor Naylor
DEC International, Inc.
Demoulas Supermarkets Inc.
Dentsply International Inc.
Dewing Foundation, Frances R.
Diamond Shamrock Inc.
Douglas & Lomason Company
Duchossois Industries Inc.
Duncan Foundation, Lillian H. and C. W.
Ebsco Industries, Inc.
Encyclopaedia Britannica, Inc.
Evans Foundation, T. M.
Fabri-Kal Corp.
Fair Play Foundation
Federated Mutual Insurance Co.
First Union National Bank of Florida
French Oil Mill Machinery Co.
Frese Foundation, Arnold D.
Fribourg Foundation
Gellert Foundation, Celia Berta
General Mills, Inc.
GenRad
Gilmore Foundation, William G.
Gleason Foundation
Glick Foundation, Eugene and Marilyn
Goldwyn Foundation, Samuel
Goodstein Family Foundation, David
Gould Electronics Inc.
Gould Foundation, The Florence
Graham Foundation for Advanced Studies in the Fine Arts
Grand Rapids Label Co.
Greenwall Foundation
Greve Foundation, William and Mary
Handy and Harman Foundation
Harcourt General, Inc.
Harmon Foundation, Pearl M. and Julia J.
Hartmarx Corporation
Hatch Charitable Trust, Margaret Milliken
Hickory Tech Corp.
Holnam
Housatonic Curtain Co.
Howard and Bush Foundation
Hudson-Webber Foundation
Independence Foundation
Integra Bank of Uniontown
Irvine Foundation, James
Jaydor Corp.
JM Foundation
Johnson Fund, Edward C.

Jones Foundation, Daisy Marquis
Jones Foundation, Fletcher
Jostens, Inc.
Kansas City Southern Industries
Kaye, Scholer, Fierman, Hays & Handler
KN Energy, Inc.
Knoll Group
Kreitler Foundation
LamCo. Communications
Lee Enterprises
LEF Foundation
Lichtenstein Foundation, David B.
Lydall, Inc.
Maddox Foundation, J. F.
Management Compensation Group/Dulworth Inc.
Mandeville Foundation
Marmot Foundation
Martin Marietta Materials
Mascoma Savings Bank
Massachusetts Mutual Life Insurance Co.
Mather Charitable Trust, S. Livingston
Mather Fund, Richard
Mautz Paint Co.
MBIA Inc.
McCasland Foundation
McFawn Trust No. 2, Lois Sisler
Merkley Charitable Trust
Miller Brewing Company/North Carolina
Mitsubishi Motor Sales of America, Inc.
Mosinee Paper Corp.
Mott Fund, Ruth
National Forge Co.
Neuberger Foundation, Roy R. and Marie S.
New Jersey Natural Gas Co.
New York Mercantile Exchange
The New Yorker Magazine, Inc.
Norfolk Shipbuilding & Drydock Corp.
Northwest Natural Gas Co.
Norton Family Foundation, Peter
Novell Inc.
Old National Bank in Evansville
Olin Foundation, Spencer T. and Ann W.
Ore-Ida Foods, Inc.
Osceola Foundation
Osher Foundation, Bernard
Packaging Corporation of America
Palisades Educational Foundation
Pamida, Inc.
Peterson Foundation, Hal and Charlie
PHH Corporation
Pioneer Trust Bank, NA
Pitt-Des Moines Inc.
Pittsburg Midway Coal Mining Co.
PriMerit Bank
Prince Trust, Abbie Norman
Providence Gas Co.
Reed Foundation
Rose Foundation, Billy
Rose's Stores, Inc.
Ross Laboratories
Royal Group, Inc.
Sandusky International Inc.
Schering-Plough Corp.
Schuller International
Seafirst Corporation
Seaver Charitable Trust, Richard C.
Seaver Institute
Security Life of Denver Insurance Co.
Seneca Foods Corp.
Shubert Foundation
Sierra Pacific Resources
Siltec Corp.
Speyer Foundation, Alexander C. and Tillie S.

International Business Machines Corp.
International Paper Co.
Jackson Foundation
Jacobson Foundation, Bernard H. and Blanche E.
Janesville Foundation
Jarson-Stanley and Mickey Kaplan Foundation, Isaac and Esther
Jewett Foundation, George Frederick
Jockey Hollow Foundation
John Hancock Mutual Life Insurance Co.
Johnson Controls Inc.
Johnson Fund, Edward C.
Johnson & Higgins
Johnson & Son, S.C.
Jones Foundation, Helen
Jordan Charitable Foundation, Mary Ranken Jordan and Ettie A.
Joy Family Foundation
Kansas City Southern Industries
Kantzler Foundation
Kaplan Fund, J. M.
Kelley and Elza Kelley Foundation, Edward Bangs
Kelly Foundation, T. Lloyd
Kempner Fund, Harris and Eliza
Kennecott Corporation
Kent-Lucas Foundation
Kettering Fund
Kiewit Foundation, Peter
Kilroy Foundation, William S. and Lora Jean
Kimberly-Clark Corp.
Kingsbury Corp.
Kinney-Lindstrom Foundation
Kiplinger Foundation
Kirkpatrick Foundation
Kline Foundation, Josiah W. and Bessie H.
KN Energy, Inc.
Knapp Foundation
Knight Foundation, John S. and James L.
Knox, Sr., and Pearl Wallis Knox Charitable Foundation, Robert W.
Komes Foundation
Koopman Fund
Kresge Foundation
Kress Foundation, Samuel H.
Kuyper Foundation, Peter H. and E. Lucille
La-Z-Boy Chair Co.
Landegger Charitable Foundation
Lauder Foundation
Laurel Foundation
LBJ Family Foundation
Lea Foundation, Helen Sperry
Lebanon Mutual Insurance Co.
Lederer Foundation, Francis L.
Lee Enterprises
Lehigh Portland Cement Co.
Lemberg Foundation
Lennon Foundation, Fred A.
Life Insurance Co. of Georgia
Linn-Henley Charitable Trust
Lipton, Thomas J.
Littauer Foundation, Lucius N.
Loews Corporation
Long Island Lighting Co.
Longwood Foundation
Lovett Foundation
Lydall, Inc.
Lyon Foundation
MacArthur Foundation, John D. and Catherine T.
Macy & Co., Inc., R.H.
Magowan Family Foundation
Mahadh Foundation
Mandeville Foundation
Mardag Foundation
Maritz Inc.
Markle Foundation, John and Mary R.
Marmot Foundation
Marpat Foundation
Marquette Electronics, Inc.

Marriott Foundation, J. Willard
Mars Foundation
Marsh & McLennan Companies, Inc.
Marshall Foundation, Mattie H.
Marshall Trust in Memory of Sanders McDaniel, Harriet McDaniel
Martin Marietta Corp.
Marx Foundation, Virginia and Leonard
Massengill-DeFriece Foundation
Mather Charitable Trust, S. Livingston
Mather and William Gwinn Mather Fund, Elizabeth Ring
Mathis-Pfohl Foundation
May Department Stores Company, The
Mayor Foundation, Oliver Dewey
Maytag Family Foundation, Fred
MBIA Inc.
MCA Inc.
McBean Charitable Trust, Alletta Morris
McCann Foundation
McCarty Foundation, John and Margaret
McCasland Foundation
McConnell Foundation
McCormick & Co. Inc.
McDermott Foundation, Eugene
McDonald & Company Securities, Inc.
McDonnell Douglas Corp.-West
McElroy Trust, R. J.
McEvoy Foundation, Mildred H.
McFawn Trust No. 2, Lois Sisler
McInerny Foundation
McKenna Foundation, Katherine Mabis
McLean Contributionship
McMahon Foundation
Mead Corporation, The
Meadows Foundation
Mellon Foundation, Andrew W.
Mellon Foundation, Richard King
Merrick Foundation
Metropolitan Life Insurance Co.
Meyer Memorial Trust
Middendorf Foundation
Miller Brewing Company/North Carolina
Minnesota Mining & Mfg. Co.
Mitchell Energy & Development Corp.
Mobil Oil Corp.
Montana Power Co.
Moore Foundation, Edward S.
Morgan Construction Co.
Morgan Foundation, Burton D.
Morgan and Samuel Tate Morgan, Jr. Foundation, Marietta McNeil
Morgan Stanley & Co., Inc.
Morris Foundation, Margaret T.
Morris Foundation, William T.
Morrison Charitable Trust, Pauline A. and George R.
Mosinee Paper Corp.
Mott Fund, Ruth
Mulford Trust, Clarence E.
Munson Foundation Trust, W. B.
Murphey Foundation, Lluella Morey
Murphy Foundation
Myra Foundation
Nalco Chemical Co.
National Gypsum Co.
National Steel Corp.
National Westminster Bank New Jersey
NBD Indiana, Inc.
Neuberger Foundation, Roy R. and Marie S.

New York Life Insurance Co.
New York Times Company
The New Yorker Magazine, Inc.
NewMil Bancorp
Noble Foundation, Edward John
Noble Foundation, Samuel Roberts
Norfolk Shipbuilding & Drydock Corp.
Norgren Foundation, Carl A.
Northwest Natural Gas Co.
Norton Co.
Norton Memorial Corporation, Geraldi
O'Connor Foundation, A. Lindsay and Olive B.
O'Fallon Trust, Martin J. and Mary Anne
OG&E Electric Services
Old Dominion Box Co.
Old National Bank in Evansville
Olin Corp.
Olin Foundation, Spencer T. and Ann W.
Oliver Memorial Trust Foundation
Olsson Memorial Foundation, Elis
Osceola Foundation
Overbrook Foundation
Overlake Foundation
Owsley Foundation, Alvin and Lucy
Packard Foundation, David and Lucile
Palmer Fund, Frank Loomis
Parker Hannifin Corp.
Parsons Foundation, Ralph M.
Patterson Charitable Fund, W. I.
Payne Foundation, Frank E. and Seba B.
Peabody Charitable Fund, Amelia
Pella Corporation
Penn Foundation, William
Pennzoil Co.
Peoples Energy Corp.
Peterson Foundation, Hal and Charlie
Pew Charitable Trusts
Pfizer, Inc.
Pforzheimer Foundation, Carl and Lily
Phillips Family Foundation, Jay and Rose
Phillips Foundation, Ellis L.
Phipps Foundation, Howard
Pickford Foundation, Mary
Piper Foundation, Minnie Stevens
Pitt-Des Moines Inc.
Plumsock Fund
PNC Bank, N.A.
Pollock Company Foundation, William B.
Porter Testamentary Trust, James Hyde
Potomac Electric Power Co.
Pott Foundation, Herman T. and Phenie R.
Potter Foundation, Justin and Valere
PPG Industries, Inc.
Premier Industrial Corp.
Price Associates, T. Rowe
Priddy Foundation
PriMerit Bank
Prince Trust, Abbie Norman
Prospect Hill Foundation
Providence Journal Company
Providian Corporation
Prudential Insurance Co. of America, The
Public Service Electric & Gas Co.
Pulitzer Publishing Co.
Putnam Foundation
Quaker Chemical Corp.
Quivey-Bay State Foundation
Ralston Purina Co.
Raymond Corp.
Read Foundation, Charles L.

Reed Foundation
Regenstein Foundation
Reicher Foundation, Anne and Harry J.
Reinberger Foundation
Rennebohm Foundation, Oscar
Rice Charitable Foundation, Albert W.
Rice Foundation
Rich Products Corporation
Richardson Charitable Trust, Anne S.
Rieke Corp.
RJR Nabisco Inc.
Rockefeller Fund, David
Rockwell Fund
Rockwell International Corporation
Rogers Family Foundation
Rohm & Haas Co.
Rose Foundation, Billy
Rowland Foundation
Royal Group, Inc.
Ruan Foundation Trust, John
Rubin Family Fund, Cele H. and William B.
Russell Charitable Foundation, Tom
SAFECO Corp.
Salomon Inc.
Salvatori Foundation, Henry
San Diego Gas & Electric
Santa Fe Pacific Corporation
Sara Lee Corp.
Sara Lee Hosiery, Inc.
Sasco Foundation
Sawyer Charitable Foundation
Scaife Family Foundation
Schering-Plough Corp.
Schlumberger Ltd.
Schoenleber Foundation
Schuller International
Schwartz Fund for Education and Health Research, Arnold and Marie
Scott Foundation, William E.
Scurlock Foundation
Seaver Charitable Trust, Richard C.
Security Life of Denver Insurance Co.
Sedgwick James Inc.
Self Foundation
Shaw Foundation, Arch W.
Shawmut National Corp.
Sheaffer Inc.
Shell Oil Company
Shenandoah Life Insurance Co.
Siltec Corp.
Simon Foundation, William E. and Carol G.
Simpson Investment Company
Skaggs Foundation, L. J. and Mary C.
Smeal Foundation, Mary Jean and Frank P.
Smith Charitable Foundation, Clara Blackford Smith and W. Aubrey
Smith Charitable Foundation, Lou and Lutza
Smith Corp., A.O.
Smith Foundation, Kelvin and Eleanor
Smith, Jr. Foundation, M. W.
Smith Memorial Fund, Ethel Sergeant Clark
Snow Foundation, John Ben
Snow Memorial Trust, John Ben
Sonat Inc.
South Bend Tribune
South Branch Foundation
South Waite Foundation
Southern California Edison Co.
Southwestern Electric Power Co.
Sprague Educational and Charitable Foundation, Seth
Stackpole-Hall Foundation
Stanley Charitable Foundation, A.W.
Stans Foundation
Starr Foundation

Stauffer Foundation, John and Beverly
Steele-Reese Foundation
Steinhagen Benevolent Trust, B. A. and Elinor
Steinman Foundation, James Hale
Stemmons Foundation
Sternberger Foundation, Tannenbaum
Stevens Foundation, Abbot and Dorothy H.
Stone Charitable Foundation
Strawbridge Foundation of Pennsylvania II, Margaret Dorrance
Stupp Foundation, Norman J.
Sulzberger Foundation
Sunnen Foundation
Swanson Family Foundation, Dr. W.C.
Swiss Bank Corp.
Symmes Foundation, F. W.
Tait Foundation, Frank M.
Taubman Foundation, A. Alfred
Taylor Foundation, Ruth and Vernon
Teleflex Inc.
Temple Foundation, T. L. L.
Tenneco Inc.
Tetley, Inc.
Texas Commerce Bank-Houston, N.A.
Textron, Inc.
Thalhimer and Family Foundation, Charles G.
Thompson Trust, Thomas
Thorne Foundation
Times Mirror Company, The
Timken Foundation of Canton
Todd Co., A.M.
TransAmerica Corporation
Treakle Foundation, J. Edwin
Trexler Trust, Harry C.
Trull Foundation
Trust Company Bank
Tupancy-Harris Foundation of 1986
Turner Charitable Foundation
Union Bank
Union Camp Corporation
Union Electric Co.
Union Pacific Corp.
U.S. Bank of Washington
Unocal Corp.
Upton Foundation, Frederick S.
US WEST, Inc.
USG Corporation
USX Corporation
Utica National Insurance Group
Van Every Foundation, Philip L.
Van Nuys Foundation, I. N. and Susanna H.
Van Wert County Foundation
Vanderbilt Trust, R. T.
Vulcan Materials Co.
Wachovia Bank of North Carolina, N.A.
Wal-Mart Stores, Inc.
Wallace Foundation, George R.
Walsh Foundation
Warwick Foundation
Waters Charitable Trust, Robert S.
Wean Foundation, Raymond John
Welch Testamentary Trust, George T.
Wendt Foundation, Margaret L.
Western New York Foundation
Westvaco Corporation
Weyerhaeuser Co.
Wheat First Butcher Singer, Inc.
Wheeler Foundation
Whirlpool Corporation
Wickes Foundation, Harvey Randall
Wickson-Link Memorial Foundation
Wilder Foundation
Williams Charitable Trust, John C.

Williams Companies, The
Wilson Foundation, H. W.
Windham Foundation
Winston Foundation, Norman
and Rosita
Winter Construction Co.
Winthrop Trust, Clara B.
Wiremold Co.
Wisconsin Power & Light Co.
Witter Foundation, Dean
Woolley Foundation, Vasser
Wyman Youth Trust
Wyomissing Foundation
Zarrow Foundation, Anne and
Henry

History &
Archaeology

Abell-Hanger Foundation
Acushnet Co.
Aetna Life & Casualty Co.
AKC Fund
Alexander Foundation, Joseph
Allegheny Foundation
Altman Foundation
Aluminum Co. of America
American Fidelity Corporation
American National Bank &
Trust Co. of Chicago
Ames Charitable Trust, Harriett
AMR Corp.
Anderson Foundation
Andersons, The
Ansin Private Foundation,
Ronald M.
Arcadia Foundation
Argyros Foundation
Arkelian Foundation, Ben H.
and Gladys
Armco Inc.
Armstrong Foundation
Ashtabula Foundation
Asplundh Foundation
Astor Foundation, Vincent
Atherton Family Foundation
Auerbach Foundation,
Beatrice Fox
Babson Foundation, Paul and
Edith
Baker Foundation, Dexter F.
and Dorothy H.
Baker Trust, George F.
Baldwin Memorial
Foundation, Fred
Ball Brothers Foundation
Ball Foundation, George and
Frances
Banta Corp.
Bard Foundation, Robert
Barra Foundation
Bauervic Foundation, Charles
M.
Baughman Foundation
Bay Foundation
Bean Foundation, Norwin S.
and Elizabeth N.
BE&K Inc.
Bechtel, Jr. Foundation, S. D.
Bedsole Foundation, J. L.
Bell Foundation, James F.
Benedum Foundation, Claude
Worthington
Bethlehem Steel Corp.
Bingham Second Betterment
Fund, William
Bishop Foundation, E. K. and
Lillian F.
Blandin Foundation
Bloedorn Foundation, Walter
A.
Bobst Foundation, Elmer and
Mamdouha
Boettcher Foundation
Borkee Hagley Foundation
Boswell Foundation, James G.
Bowen Foundation, Ethel N.
Bowne Foundation, Robert
Breyer Foundation
Bryant Foundation
Buhl Foundation
Bunbury Company

Burchfield Foundation,
Charles E.
Cabell Foundation, Robert G.
Cabell III and Maude
Morgan
Cabot Family Charitable Trust
Caestecker Foundation,
Charles and Marie
Cafritz Foundation, Morris and
Gwendolyn
Calhoun Charitable Trust,
Kenneth
Callaway Foundation
Campbell Foundation
Campbell Foundation, Ruth
and Henry
Carpenter Foundation
Carpenter Technology Corp.
Carter Foundation, Beirne
Carver Charitable Trust, Roy J.
Castle Foundation, Harold K.
L.
CBS, Inc.
Champlin Foundations
Charina Foundation
Chatham Manufacturing Co.
CHC Foundation
Chesapeake Corp.
Chesebrough-Pond's USA Co.
Christian Dior New York, Inc.
CIGNA Corporation
CINergy
Clapp Charitable and
Educational Trust, George H.
CLARCOR Inc.
Clarkson Foundation, Jeniam
Clay Foundation
Clements Foundation
Close Foundation
Clowes Fund
Cogswell Benevolent Trust
Cole Trust, Quincy
Coleman Foundation, George
E.
Collins Foundation
Columbus Dispatch Printing
Co.
Commerce Bancshares, Inc.
Commerce Clearing House,
Incorporated
Connecticut Mutual Life
Insurance Company
Connelly Foundation
Consolidated Papers, Inc.
Consumers Power Co.
Cooke Foundation
Cord Foundation, E. L.
Cornell Trust, Peter C.
Cowles Charitable Trust
Cranston Print Works Company
Crary Foundation, Bruce L.
Crawford Estate, E. R.
Crestlea Foundation
Crown Books
Crystal Trust
Cullen Foundation
Culpeper Memorial
Foundation, Daphne Seybolt
Culver Foundation, Constans
Cummings Foundation, James
H.
Dana Foundation, Charles A.
Darling Foundation, Hugh and
Hazel
Dater Foundation, Charles H.
Davenport-Hatch Foundation
Davis Foundation, Edwin W.
and Catherine M.
Davis Foundation, Irene E. and
George A.
Davis Foundation, James A.
and Juliet L.
Davis Foundations, Arthur
Vining
Day Foundation, Nancy Sayles
Daywood Foundation
Dekko Foundation
Delano Foundation, Mignon
Sherwood
Demoulas Supermarkets Inc.
Dentsply International Inc.
DeRoy Foundation, Helen L.
Deuble Foundation, George H.
Dexter Charitable Fund,
Eugene A.

Diamond Foundation, Aaron
Dillon Foundation
Dingman Foundation, Michael
D.
Dodge Foundation, Cleveland
H.
Dodge Foundation, Geraldine
R.
Donnelley Foundation,
Gaylord and Dorothy
Dow Jones & Company, Inc.
Dula Educational and
Charitable Foundation,
Caleb C. and Julia W.
Duncan Trust, John G.
duPont Foundation, Alfred I.
Durfee Foundation
Dynamet, Inc.
Eaton Foundation, Cyrus
Eberly Foundation
Eddy Family Memorial Fund,
C. K.
Edmonds Foundation, Dean S.
El Pomar Foundation
Emerson Foundation, Inc.,
Fred L.
English Memorial Fund,
Florence C. and H. L.
Ensign-Bickford Industries
Evans Foundation, T. M.
Fair Oaks Foundation, Inc.
Fair Play Foundation
Farr Trust, Frank M. and Alice
M.
Favrot Fund
Federated Mutual Insurance
Co.
Femino Foundation
Fife Foundation, Elias and
Bertha
Firestone, Jr. Foundation,
Harvey
Firman Fund
First Hawaiian, Inc.
First Interstate Bank of Oregon
First Source Corp.
Fishback Foundation Trust,
Harmes C.
Fleming Cos. Food
Distribution Center
Fletcher Foundation
Flowers Charitable Trust,
Albert W. and Edith V.
Fondren Foundation
Forbes Inc.
Ford Fund, William and Martha
Ford II Fund, Henry
Forster Charitable Trust, James
W. and Ella B.
France Foundation, Jacob and
Annita
Freeport-McMoRan Inc.
Fribourg Foundation
Frohring Foundation, Paul and
Maxine
Frohring Foundation, William
O. and Gertrude Lewis
Frueauff Foundation, Charles
A.
Fruehauf Foundation
Fuller Foundation, C. G.
Gannett Publishing Co., Guy
GAR Foundation
Gates Foundation
Gaylord Foundation, Clifford
Willard
Gazette Co.
Gebbie Foundation
Gellert Foundation, Celia Berta
General Mills, Inc.
Gershman Foundation, Joel
Getty Trust, J. Paul
Gheens Foundation
Giant Eagle, Inc.
Glosser Foundation, David A.
Goodrich Co., The B.F.
Goodstein Family Foundation,
David
Graham Foundation for
Advanced Studies in the
Fine Arts
Greenwall Foundation
Griffith Foundation, W. C.
Groome Beatty Trust, Helen D.
Grundy Foundation

Guggenheim Foundation,
Harry Frank
Gulf Power Co.
Habig Foundation, Arnold F.
Haley Foundation, W. B.
Hanson Industries North
America
Harcourt Foundation, Ellen
Knowles
Harcourt General, Inc.
Hardin Foundation, Phil
Harmon Foundation, Pearl M.
and Julia J.
Harriman Foundation, Gladys
and Roland
Harriman Foundation, Mary W.
Harrington Foundation,
Francis A. and Jacquelyn H.
Hartmarx Corporation
Hastings Charitable
Foundation, Oris B.
Haynes Foundation, John
Randolph and Dora
Heckscher Foundation for
Children
Heinz Company, H. J.
Heinz Endowment, Howard
Heinz Endowment, Vira I.
Heller Charitable Foundation,
Clarence E.
Helmerich Foundation
Henderson Foundation,
George B.
Herrick Foundation
Herzstein Charitable
Foundation, Albert and Ethel
Hewlett-Packard Co.
Higginson Trust, Corina
Hill Foundation, Sandy
Hillman Foundation
Hillsdale Fund
Hoover Foundation
Houchens Foundation, Ervin G.
Housatonic Curtain Co.
Houston Endowment
Howard and Bush Foundation
Hudson-Webber Foundation
Hulme Charitable Foundation,
Milton G.
Humana, Inc.
Humphrey Fund, George M.
and Pamela S.
Hunt Charitable Trust, C. Giles
Hunt Foundation
Hunt Foundation, Roy A.
Hunt Foundation, Samuel P.
Hyde and Watson Foundation
Icahn Foundation, Carl C.
Independence Foundation
Ingalls Foundation, Louise H.
and David S.
Integra Bank of Uniontown
Jackson Foundation
Jacobson Foundation, Bernard
H. and Blanche E.
Janesville Foundation
Janirve Foundation
Jennings Foundation, Mary
Hillman
JFM Foundation
Jockey Hollow Foundation
Johnson Foundation, Helen K.
and Arthur E.
Johnson Fund, Edward C.
Jones Foundation, Fletcher
Jordan Charitable Foundation,
Mary Ranken Jordan and
Ettie A.
Journal-Gazette Co.
Julia R. and Estelle L.
Foundation
Justus Trust, Edith C.
Kansas City Southern
Industries
Kaplan Fund, J. M.
Kelley and Elza Kelley
Foundation, Edward Bangs
Kelly Foundation, T. Lloyd
Kelly Tractor Co.
Kempner Fund, Harris and
Eliza
Kent-Lucas Foundation
Kettering Fund
Kiewit Foundation, Peter
Kilcawley Fund, William H.

Kimberly-Clark Corp.
Kingsbury Corp.
Kinney-Lindstrom Foundation
Kiplinger Foundation
Kirby Foundation, F. M.
Kitzmiller/Bales Trust
Kline Foundation, Josiah W.
and Bessie H.
KN Energy, Inc.
Knapp Foundation
Knight Foundation, John S.
and James L.
Knox, Sr., and Pearl Wallis
Knox Charitable
Foundation, Robert W.
Knudsen Foundation, Tom and
Valley
Kohn-Joseloff Foundation
Koopman Fund
Kreitler Foundation
Kresge Foundation
Kress Foundation, Samuel H.
Kunkel Foundation, John Crain
Ladd Charitable Corporation,
Helen and George
Larsen Fund
Laurel Foundation
Lazarus Charitable Trust,
Helen and Charles
LBJ Family Foundation
Leavey Foundation, Thomas
and Dorothy
Lederer Foundation, Francis L.
Lee Enterprises
Lehmann Foundation, Otto W.
Leighton-Oare Foundation
Levitt Foundation
Littauer Foundation, Lucius N.
Lovett Foundation
Lowenstein Foundation, Leon
MacArthur Foundation, John
D. and Catherine T.
Madison Gas & Electric Co.
Magowan Family Foundation
Mahadh Foundation
Mandeville Foundation
Maneely Fund
Marbrook Foundation
Markey Charitable Fund, John
C.
Marpat Foundation
Mars Foundation
Marshall Foundation, Mattie H.
Marshall Trust in Memory of
Sanders McDaniel, Harriet
McDaniel
Martini Foundation, Nicholas
Marx Foundation, Virginia and
Leonard
Mather Charitable Trust, S.
Livingston
Mather and William Gwinn
Mather Fund, Elizabeth Ring
Mathis-Pfohl Foundation
Matthies Foundation, Katharine
Mautz Paint Co.
Maytag Family Foundation,
Fred
McCann Foundation
McCasland Foundation
McConnell Foundation
McCormick Trust, Anne
McCune Charitable Trust,
John R.
McDermott Foundation,
Eugene
McEvoy Foundation, Mildred
H.
McFawn Trust No. 2, Lois
Sisler
McGonagle Foundation,
Dextra Baldwin
McInerny Foundation
McMahan Foundation,
Catherine L. and Robert O.
McMahon Foundation
Meadows Foundation
Mellon Family Foundation, R.
K.
Mellon Foundation, Richard
King
Merck Family Fund
Merrick Foundation
Merrill Lynch & Co., Inc.

Meyer Family Foundation, Paul J.
Meyer Memorial Trust
Miller Foundation
Miller-Mellor Association
Mills Fund, Frances Goll
Monadnock Paper Mills
Montana Power Co.
Moore Charitable Foundation, Marjorie
Moore Foundation, Edward S.
Morgan Charitable Residual Trust, W. and E.
Morgan & Company, J.P.
Morgan Construction Co.
Morgan Foundation, Burton D.
Morris Foundation, Margaret T.
Morris Foundation, William T.
Mosbacher, Jr. Foundation, Emil
Mosinee Paper Corp.
Mott Fund, Ruth
Muchnic Foundation
Mulford Foundation, Vincent
Mulford Trust, Clarence E.
Murdock Charitable Trust, M. J.
Murphey Foundation, Lluella Morey
Murphy Co. Foundation, G.C.
Murphy Foundation
Musson Charitable Foundation, R. C. and Katharine M.
Mutual Assurance Co.
Nestle USA Inc.
New York Times Company
NewMil Bancorp
Noble Foundation, Edward John
Noble Foundation, Samuel Roberts
Norfolk Shipbuilding & Drydock Corp.
Normandie Foundation
North Shore Foundation
Northern States Power Co. (Minnesota)
Norton Memorial Corporation, Geraldi
O'Connor Foundation, A. Lindsay and Olive B.
OCRI Foundation
Odell Fund, Robert Stewart Odell and Helen Pfeiffer
Offield Family Foundation
OG&E Electric Services
Old National Bank in Evansville
Olin Foundation, Spencer T. and Ann W.
Oliver Memorial Trust Foundation
Olsson Memorial Foundation, Elis
Osceola Foundation
Osher Foundation, Bernard
Ottenheimer Brothers Foundation
Overbrook Foundation
Overlake Foundation
Packard Foundation, David and Lucile
Palmer Fund, Frank Loomis
Parsons Foundation, Ralph M.
Payne Foundation, Frank E. and Seba B.
Pella Corporation
Pennsylvania Dutch Co.
Peppers Foundation, Ann
Peterson Foundation, Hal and Charlie
Pew Charitable Trusts
Pfizer, Inc.
PHH Corporation
Phillips Foundation, Ellis L.
Pineywoods Foundation
Pioneer Trust Bank, NA
Plumsock Fund
PNC Bank, N.A.
Pollock Company Foundation, William B.
Porter Testamentary Trust, James Hyde
Premier Industrial Corp.

Price Associates, T. Rowe
Prouty Foundation, Olive Higgins
Public Service Co. of New Mexico
Puterbaugh Foundation
Putnam Foundation
Quivey-Bay State Foundation
Rabb Charitable Foundation, Sidney and Esther
Rand McNally & Co.
Raymond Corp.
Read Foundation, Charles L.
Regenstein Foundation
Reidler Foundation
Reinberger Foundation
Rice Charitable Foundation, Albert W.
Rice Foundation
Rich Products Corporation
Richardson Benevolent Foundation, C. E.
Rieke Corp.
Robinson-Broadhurst Foundation
Robinson Fund, Maurice R.
Rockefeller Fund, David
Rockwell Fund
Rockwell International Corporation
Rogers Family Foundation
Rohatyn Foundation, Felix and Elizabeth
Rowland Foundation
Russell Trust, Josephine G.
Saint Paul Companies, Inc.
Salvatori Foundation, Henry
Sandy Hill Foundation
Sargent Foundation, Newell B.
Sarkeys Foundation
Sasco Foundation
SBC Communications Inc.
Scherer Foundation, Karla
Schiff Foundation, Dorothy
Schoenleber Foundation
Scholl Foundation, Dr.
Schowalter Foundation
Schroeder Foundation, Walter
Schwartz Fund for Education and Health Research, Arnold and Marie
Scripps Co., E.W.
Seafirst Corporation
Seidman Family Foundation
Sequoia Foundation
Shaw Foundation, Arch W.
Shawmut National Corp.
Sheppard Foundation, Lawrence B.
Skaggs Foundation, L. J. and Mary C.
Skillman Foundation
Smart Family Foundation
Smith Charitable Foundation, Lou and Lutza
Smith, Jr. Foundation, M. W.
SmithKline Beecham Corp.
Snow Memorial Trust, John Ben
Snyder Foundation, Harold B. and Dorothy A.
South Bend Tribune
South Waite Foundation
Specialty Manufacturing Co.
Sprague Educational and Charitable Foundation, Seth
Stackpole-Hall Foundation
Stans Foundation
Starr Foundation
Stauffer Foundation, John and Beverly
Stearns Trust, Artemas W.
Steele-Reese Foundation
Steinhagen Benevolent Trust, B. A. and Elinor
Steinman Foundation, James Hale
Steinman Foundation, John Frederick
Stevens Foundation, Abbot and Dorothy H.
Stevens Foundation, John T.
Stokely, Jr. Foundation, William B.

Strawbridge Foundation of Pennsylvania II, Margaret Dorrance
Stupp Foundation, Norman J.
Subaru of America Inc.
Sulzberger Foundation
Sunnen Foundation
Superior Tube Co.
Swanson Family Foundation, Dr. W.C.
Swift Co. Inc., John S.
Taubman Foundation, A. Alfred
Tecumseh Products Co.
Teleflex Inc.
Temple Foundation, T. L. L.
Texaco Inc.
Thalhimer and Family Foundation, Charles G.
Thomas Industries
Thorne Foundation
Thornton Foundation, Flora L.
Timken Foundation of Canton
Tiscornia Foundation
Titus Foundation, Roy and Niuta
Todd Co., A.M.
Tozer Foundation
Travelers Inc.
Treakle Foundation, J. Edwin
Trexler Trust, Harry C.
Trull Foundation
Tucker Charitable Trust, Rose E.
Tupancy-Harris Foundation of 1986
Upton Foundation, Frederick S.
USX Corporation
Valentine Foundation, Lawson
Van Buren Foundation
Van Wert County Foundation
Vanderbilt Trust, R. T.
Vernon Fund, Miles Hodson
Vevay-Switzerland County Foundation
Wahlstrom Foundation
Wallace Foundation, George R.
Wallace-Reader's Digest Fund, Lila
Walsh Foundation
Warwick Foundation
Waters Charitable Trust, Robert S.
Weil, Gotshal and Manges Foundation
Welfare Foundation
Wells Foundation, Franklin H. and Ruth L.
West Foundation, Harry and Ethel
Westerman Foundation, Samuel L.
Wheat First Butcher Singer, Inc.
Wheeler Foundation
Wheeler Foundation, Wilmot
Whirlpool Corporation
Whittenberger Foundation, Claude R. and Ethel B.
Wickes Foundation, Harvey Randall
Wickson-Link Memorial Foundation
Widgeon Foundation
Wildermuth Foundation, E. F.
Wilson Foundation, H. W.
Wilson Fund, Matilda R.
Windham Foundation
Winnebago Industries, Inc.
Winthrop Trust, Clara B.
Wisconsin Power & Light Co.
Witter Foundation, Dean
Wood Foundation of Chambersburg, PA
Woodward Fund
Woolley Foundation, Vasser
Worthington Foods
Wyman Youth Trust
Wyomissing Foundation
Young Foundation, Robert R.
Zarrow Foundation, Anne and Henry
Zollner Foundation

Libraries

Abbott Laboratories
Abell-Hanger Foundation
Abrams Foundation, Talbert and Leota
ACF Industries, Inc.
Achelis Foundation
Acme-McCrary Corp./Sapona Manufacturing Co.
Acushnet Co.
Adams Foundation, Arthur F. and Alice E.
Adler Foundation Trust, Philip D. and Henrietta B.
AEGON USA Inc.
Aetna Life & Casualty Co.
Ahmanson Foundation
Air France
Air Products and Chemicals, Inc.
AKC Fund
Akzo America
Akzo Chemicals Inc.
Alabama Gas Corp.
Alabama Power Co.
Alavi Foundation of New York
Albertson's Inc.
Alcon Laboratories, Inc.
Aldus Corp.
Alexander Foundation, Joseph
Allegheny Foundation
Allegheny Ludlum Corp.
Allen Brothers Foundation
Allendale Insurance Co.
Allianz Life Insurance Co. of North America
AlliedSignal Inc.
Allyn Foundation
Altman Foundation
Altschul Foundation
Alumax Inc.
Aluminum Co. of America
Amado Foundation, Maurice
Amcast Industrial Corp.
AMCORE Bank, N.A. Rockford
American Brands, Inc.
American Fidelity Corporation
American General Finance Corp.
American National Bank & Trust Co. of Chicago
American Natural Resources Company
American Optical Corp.
American President Companies, Ltd.
American United Life Insurance Co.
Ameritas Life Insurance Corp.
Ames Charitable Trust, Harriett
AMETEK, Inc.
Amfac/JMB Hawaii Inc.
Amoco Corporation
AMP Incorporated
AMR Corp.
Andersen Corp.
Andersen Foundation
Anderson Foundation
Anderson Foundation, John W.
Anderson Foundation, M. D.
Andersons, The
Andreas Foundation
Andres Charitable Trust, Frank G.
Andrews Foundation
Anheuser-Busch Companies, Inc.
Ansin Private Foundation, Ronald M.
Ansley Foundation, Dantzler Bond
AON Corporation
Appleby Trust, Scott B. and Annie P.
Appleton Papers Inc.
Arakelian Foundation, Mary Alice
Arcadia Foundation
Archer-Daniels-Midland Co.
Argyros Foundation
Aristech Chemical Corp.

Arkansas Power & Light Co.
Arkelian Foundation, Ben H. and Gladys
Arkell Hall Foundation
Armco Inc.
Armstrong Foundation
Arnhold Foundation
Arnold Fund
ASDA Foundation
Ashtabula Foundation
Asplundh Foundation
Astor Foundation, Vincent
Atherton Family Foundation
Atran Foundation
Audubon State Bank
Auerbach Foundation, Beatrice Fox
Avery Arts Foundation, Milton and Sally
Avon Products, Inc.
Ayres Foundation, Inc.
Babcock & Wilcox Co.
Babson Foundation, Paul and Edith
Bacon Foundation, E. L. and Oma
Badgeley Residuary Charitable Trust, Rose M.
Baehr Foundation, Louis W. and Dolpha
Baker Foundation, Dexter F. and Dorothy H.
Baker Hughes Inc.
Baker Trust, George F.
Baldwin Foundation, David M. and Barbara
Baldwin Memorial Foundation, Fred
Balfour Foundation, L. G.
Ball Brothers Foundation
Ball Foundation, George and Frances
Banc One Wisconsin Corp.
Bank of Boston
Bank of Boston Corp.
Bank of New York Company, Inc.
Bank One, Texas-Houston Office
Bank One, Youngstown, NA
BankAmerica Corp.
Bankers Trust Company
Banta Corp.
Bard Foundation, Robert
Barker Foundation, J.M.R.
Barra Foundation
Barry Corp., R. G.
Barth Foundation, Theodore H.
Baskin-Robbins USA Co.
Battelle Memorial Institute
Batts Foundation
Bauervic Foundation, Charles M.
Baughman Foundation
Bay Area Foods
Bay Foundation
Beal Foundation
Bean Foundation, Norwin S. and Elizabeth N.
BE&K Inc.
Beattie Foundation Trust, Cordelia Lee
Beatty Trust, Cordelia Lunceford
Beaucourt Foundation
Beazley Foundation/Frederick Foundation
Bechtel Charitable Remainder Uni-Trust, Marie H.
Bechtel, Jr. Foundation, S. D.
Bechtel Testamentary Charitable Trust, H. R.
Beck Foundation, Elsie E. and Joseph W.
Bedsole Foundation, J. L.
Beech Aircraft Corp.
Bell Atlantic Corp.
Bell Foundation, James F.
Beloit Foundation
Bemis Company, Inc.
Benedum Foundation, Claude Worthington
Benenson Foundation, Frances and Benjamin
Benetton Services Corp.

Benwood Foundation
Berger Foundation, H. N. and Frances C.
Bertha Foundation
Berwind Corporation
Besser Foundation
Bethlehem Steel Corp.
Bettingen Corporation, Burton G.
Betts Industries
Beveridge Foundation, Frank Stanley
Bigelow Foundation, F. R.
Bingham Foundation, William
Bingham Second Betterment Fund, William
Binney & Smith Inc.
Binswanger Cos.
Bird Corp.
Birnschein Foundation, Alvin and Marion
Bishop Foundation, E. K. and Lillian F.
Bissell Foundation, J. Walton
Blair and Co., William
Blake Foundation, S. P.
Blandin Foundation
Blaustein Foundation, Louis and Henrietta
Block, H&R
Bloedorn Foundation, Walter A.
Blount Educational and Charitable Foundation, Mildred Weedon
Blount, Inc.
Blowitz-Ridgeway Foundation
Blue Bell, Inc.
Blue Cross & Blue Shield United of Wisconsin
Blum Foundation, Edna F.
Blum Foundation, Harry and Maribel G.
Blum-Kovler Foundation
Boatmen's Bancshares, Inc.
Bobst Foundation, Elmer and Mamdouha
Bodman Foundation
Boeing Co., The
Boettcher Foundation
Boise Cascade Corporation
Booth Ferris Foundation
Boothroyd Foundation, Charles H. and Bertha L.
Borden, Inc.
Borkee Hagley Foundation
Borman's Inc.
Boston Edison Co.
Boswell Foundation, James G.
Bothin Foundation
Boutell Memorial Fund
Bowater Incorporated
Bowen Foundation, Ethel N.
Bowne Foundation, Robert
BP America Inc.
Brach Foundation, Helen
Brackenridge Foundation, George W.
Brady Foundation
Bremer Foundation, Otto
Brenner Foundation, Mervyn
Breyer Foundation
Bridgestone/Firestone, Inc.
Bridwell Foundation, J. S.
Bright Family Foundation
Brillion Iron Works
Bristol-Myers Squibb Company
Broadhurst Foundation
Brooks Foundation, Gladys
Brown Foundation, M. K.
Brown & Williamson Tobacco Corp.
Brunswick Corp.
Bryant Foundation
Bryn Mawr Trust Co.
Bucyrus-Erie Company
Buhl Foundation
Bunbury Company
Burchfield Foundation, Charles E.
Burden Foundation, Florence V.
Burdines Inc.
Burkitt Foundation

Burlington Industries, Inc.
Burnett-Tandy Foundation
Bush Foundation
Butz Foundation
Cabell Foundation, Robert G. Cabell III and Maude Morgan
Cable & Wireless Holdings, Inc.
Cabot Corp.
Cabot Family Charitable Trust
Caestecker Foundation, Charles and Marie
Cafritz Foundation, Morris and Gwendolyn
Cain Foundation, Effie and Wofford
Cain Foundation, Gordon and Mary
Calder Foundation, Louis
Calhoun Charitable Trust, Kenneth
Callaway Foundation
Campbell Foundation
Campbell Foundation, Ruth and Henry
Campini Foundation, Frank A.
Canon U.S.A., Inc.
Cape Branch Foundation
Cargill Inc.
Carnahan-Jackson Foundation
Carnegie Corporation of New York
Carolyn Foundation
Carpenter Foundation
Carpenter Foundation, E. Rhodes and Leona B.
Carpenter Technology Corp.
Carter Foundation, Amon G.
Carter Foundation, Beirne
Carvel Foundation, Thomas and Agnes
Carver Charitable Trust, Roy J.
Caspersen Foundation for Aid to Health and Education, O. W.
Cassett Foundation, Louis N.
Castle Foundation, Harold K. L.
Catlin Charitable Trust, Kathleen K.
Cayuga Foundation
CBI Industries, Inc.
CBS, Inc.
Centerior Energy Corp.
Central Fidelity Banks, Inc.
Central Hudson Gas & Electric Corp.
Central Maine Power Co.
Central National Bank
Central Vermont Public Service Corp.
Centralia Foundation
Century Companies of America
Chadwick Fund, Dorothy Jordan
Champion International Corporation
Champlin Foundations
Chapin Foundation of Myrtle Beach, South Carolina
Chapman Charitable Corporation, Howard and Bess
Charina Foundation
Chartwell Foundation
Chase Manhattan Bank, N.A.
Chastain Charitable Foundation, Robert Lee and Thomas M.
Chatham Manufacturing Co.
Chatlos Foundation
Chazen Foundation
CHC Foundation
Cheatham Foundation, Owen
Cheney Foundation, Ben B.
Chesapeake Corp.
Chesebrough-Pond's USA Co.
Chevron Corporation
Chicago Sun-Times, Inc.
Childs Charitable Foundation, Roberta M.
Christensen Charitable and Religious Foundation, L. C.
Christian Dior New York, Inc.

Christy-Houston Foundation
Chrysler Corp.
Church & Dwight Co., Inc.
CIBC Wood Gundy
CIGNA Corporation
CINergy
Citibank
Citizens Bank of Rhode Island
City National Bank and Trust Co.
Claiborne and Art Ortenberg Foundation, Liz
Clapp Charitable and Educational Trust, George H.
CLARCOR Inc.
Clark Foundation
Clarke Trust, John
Clarkson Foundation, Jeniam
Clay Foundation
Clayton Fund
Clemens Markets Corp.
Clements Foundation
Clorox Co.
Close Foundation
Clowes Fund
CNA Financial Corporation/CNA Insurance Companies
Coen Family Foundation, Charles S. and Mary
Cogswell Benevolent Trust
Cole Foundation, Olive B.
Cole Trust, Quincy
Coleman Foundation, George E.
Collins Foundation
Collins Foundation, George and Jennie
Collins, Jr. Foundation, George Fulton
Collins Medical Trust
Colonial Life & Accident Insurance Co.
Coltec Industries, Inc.
Columbia Foundation
Columbus Dispatch Printing Co.
Comer Foundation
Comerica Incorporated
Commerce Bancshares, Inc.
Commerce Clearing House, Incorporated
Commercial Bank
Commonwealth Edison Co.
Comprecare Foundation
Connecticut Mutual Life Insurance Company
Connelly Foundation
Connemara Fund
Consolidated Natural Gas Co.
Consolidated Papers, Inc.
Consumers Power Co.
Continental Corp.
Contran Corporation
Cooke Foundation
Cooper Industries, Inc.
Cooperman Foundation, Leon and Toby
Coors Foundation, Adolph
Copley Press, Inc.
Cord Foundation, E. L.
Cornell Trust, Peter C.
Corning Incorporated
Cosmair, Inc.
Coughlin-Saunders Foundation
Covington and Burling
Cowell Foundation, S. H.
Cowles Charitable Trust
Cowles Foundation, Gardner and Florence Call
Cowles Media Co.
CPC International Inc.
CR Industries
Crabtree & Evelyn
Crandall Memorial Foundation, J. Ford
Crane Co.
Cranston Print Works Company
Crary Foundation, Bruce L.
Crawford Estate, E. R.
Cremer Foundation
Creslea Foundation
Crocker Trust, Mary A.
Crown Books
Crown Memorial, Arie and Ida

Crystal Trust
CS First Boston Corporation
CT Corp. System
Cullen Foundation
Culpeper Foundation, Charles E.
Culpeper Memorial Foundation, Daphne Seybolt
Culver Foundation, Constans
Cummings Foundation, James H.
Cummins Engine Co.
Cuneo Foundation
Curtice-Burns Foods, Inc.
Daily News
Dalton Foundation, Harry L.
Dana Charitable Trust, Eleanor Naylor
Dana Foundation, Charles A.
Daniel Foundation of Alabama
Darby Foundation
Darling Foundation, Hugh and Hazel
Dart Group Corp.
Dater Foundation, Charles H.
Daugherty Foundation
Davenport-Hatch Foundation
Davenport Trust Fund
Davidson Family Charitable Foundation
Davis Foundation, Edwin W. and Catherine M.
Davis Foundation, Irene E. and George A.
Davis Foundation, James A. and Juliet L.
Davis Foundations, Arthur Vining
Day Foundation, Nancy Sayles
Daywood Foundation
De Queen General Hospital Foundation
DEC International, Inc.
Deere & Co.
Dekko Foundation
Delano Foundation, Mignon Sherwood
Delavan Foundation, Nelson B.
Delaware North Co., Inc.
Dell Foundation, Hazel
Demos Foundation, N.
Demoulas Supermarkets Inc.
Dentsply International Inc.
DeRoy Foundation, Helen L.
DeRoy Testamentary Foundation
Detroit Edison Co.
Deuble Foundation, George H.
DeVore Foundation
Dewing Foundation, Frances R.
Dexter Charitable Fund, Eugene A.
Dexter Corporation
Diamond Foundation, Aaron
Diamond Shamrock Inc.
Digital Equipment Corp.
Dillon Dunwalke Trust, Clarence and Anne
Dillon Foundation
Dimeo Construction Co.
Dingman Foundation, Michael D.
Dishman Charitable Foundation Trust, H. E. and Kate
Dr. Seuss Foundation
Dodge Foundation, Cleveland H.
Dodge Foundation, Geraldine R.
Dodge Jones Foundation
Donaldson Company, Inc.
Donnelley Foundation, Gaylord and Dorothy
Donnelley & Sons Co., R.R.
Donner Foundation, William H.
Doss Foundation, M. S.
Douglas & Lomason Company
Douty Foundation
Dover Foundation
Dow Corning Corp.
Dow Foundation, Herbert H. and Grace A.
Dow Jones & Company, Inc.
Dresser Industries, Inc.

Dreyfus Foundation, Jean and Louis
Dreyfus Foundation, Max and Victoria
du Pont de Nemours & Co., E. I.
Duchossois Industries Inc.
Duke Endowment
Duke Power Co.
Dula Educational and Charitable Foundation, Caleb C. and Julia W.
Dun & Bradstreet Corp.
Dunagan Foundation
Duncan Foundation, Lillian H. and C. W.
Duncan Trust, John G.
duPont Foundation, Alfred I.
Durfee Foundation
Dynamet, Inc.
Early Foundation
Eastman Kodak Company
Eaton Corporation
Eaton Foundation, Cyrus
Eberly Foundation
Ebsco Industries, Inc.
Eccles Foundation, Ralph M. and Ella M.
Eddy Family Memorial Fund, C. K.
Eden Hall Foundation
Edgewater Steel Corp.
Edmonds Foundation, Dean S.
Einstein Fund, Albert E. and Birdie W.
El Pomar Foundation
Elf Atochem North America, Inc.
Elkins, Jr. Foundation, Margaret and James A.
Emerson Foundation, Inc., Fred L.
Encyclopaedia Britannica, Inc.
English Memorial Fund, Florence C. and H. L.
Enron Corp.
Ensign-Bickford Industries
Erpf Fund, Armand G.
Essick Foundation
Ethyl Corp
Ettinger Foundation
Evans Foundation, Lettie Pate
Evans Foundation, T. M.
Evans Foundation, Thomas J.
Everett Charitable Trust
Exchange National Bank
Exxon Corporation
Fabri-Kal Corp.
Fair Foundation, R. W.
Fair Oaks Foundation, Inc.
Fair Play Foundation
Fairchild Foundation, Sherman
Farish Fund, William Stamps
Farr Trust, Frank M. and Alice M.
Favrot Fund
Federal-Mogul Corporation
Federated Mutual Insurance Co.
Feil Foundation, Louis and Gertrude
Feild Co-Operative Association
Femino Foundation
Fenton Foundation
Ferebee Endowment, Percy O.
Fieldcrest Cannon Inc.
Fife Foundation, Elias and Bertha
Fikes Foundation, Leland
Finch Foundation, Doak
Finch Foundation, Thomas Austin
Fink Foundation
Fireman's Fund Insurance Co.
Firestone, Jr. Foundation, Harvey
Firman Fund
First Chicago Corp.
First Fidelity Bank
First Financial Bank FSB
First Hawaiian, Inc.
First Interstate Bank of Oregon
First National Bank
First Source Corp.
First Tennessee Bank

First Union Corp.
First Union National Bank of Florida
Firstar Bank Milwaukee, N.A.
Fischbach Foundation
Fish Foundation, Ray C.
Fishback Foundation Trust, Harmes C.
Fleet Financial Group, Inc.
Fleishhacker Foundation
Fleming Cos. Food Distribution Center
Fletcher Foundation
Flowers Charitable Trust, Albert W. and Edith V.
Fohs Foundation
Folger Fund
Fondren Foundation
Forbes Inc.
Ford Foundation
Ford Fund, William and Martha
Ford II Fund, Henry
Ford Motor Co.
Forest Foundation
Forest Oil Corp.
Forster Charitable Trust, James W. and Ella B.
Fort Wayne National Bank
Foster Charitable Trust
Foster Foundation
France Foundation, Jacob and Annita
Frear Eleemosynary Trust, Mary D. and Walter F.
Freed Foundation
Freedom Forge Corp.
Freeman Charitable Trust, Samuel
Freeport Brick Co.
Freeport-McMoRan Inc.
French Foundation, D.E.
French Oil Mill Machinery Co.
Frese Foundation, Arnold D.
Fribourg Foundation
Friedman Family Foundation
Friendship Fund
Frisch's Restaurants Inc.
Frohring Foundation, Paul and Maxine
Frohring Foundation, William O. and Gertrude Lewis
Frost National Bank
Frueauff Foundation, Charles A.
Fruehauf Foundation
Fry Foundation, Lloyd A.
Fujitsu America, Inc.
Fuld Health Trust, Helene
Fuller Foundation
Fuller Foundation, C. G.
Fund for New Jersey
Fuqua Foundation, J. B.
Gallagher Family Foundation, Lewis P.
Gamble Foundation
Gannett Publishing Co., Guy
Gap, Inc., The
GAR Foundation
Garland Foundation, John Jewett and H. Chandler
Gates Foundation
GATX Corp.
Gaylord Foundation, Clifford Willard
Gazette Co.
Gebbie Foundation
Geifman Family Foundation
Gellert Foundation, Carl
Gellert Foundation, Celia Berta
GenCorp Inc.
General American Life Insurance Co.
General Mills, Inc.
General Motors Corp.
Geneseo Foundation
GenRad
Georgia-Pacific Corporation
Georgia Power Co.
German Protestant Orphan Asylum Association
Germeshausen Foundation, Kenneth J.
Gershman Foundation, Joel
Getty Trust, J. Paul
Gheens Foundation

Ghidotti Foundation
Giant Eagle, Inc.
Giant Food Inc.
Giant Food Stores
Gifford Charitable Corporation, Rosamond
Giles Foundation, Edward C.
Gillette Co.
Gilman Foundation, Howard
Gilmore Foundation, William G.
Givenchy Corp.
Glanville Family Foundation
Glaser Foundation
Gleason Foundation
Glencoe Foundation
Glenn Foundation, Carrie C. and Lena V.
Glick Foundation, Eugene and Marilyn
Globe Newspaper Co.
Glosser Foundation, David A.
Goddard Foundation, Charles B.
Goldberg Family Foundation
Golden West Foundation
Goldie-Anna Charitable Trust
Goldseker Foundation of Maryland, Morris
Goldsmith Foundation, Horace W.
Goldwyn Foundation, Samuel
Good Samaritan
Goodman & Co.
Goodrich Co., The B.F.
Goodstein Family Foundation, David
Gordon/Rousmaniere/Roberts Fund
Gould Electronics Inc.
Gould Foundation, The Florence
Graham Foundation for Advanced Studies in the Fine Arts
Graham Fund, Philip L.
Grand Rapids Label Co.
Great-West Life Assurance Co.
Green Foundation, Allen P. and Josephine B.
Greenwall Foundation
Gregg-Graniteville Foundation
Greve Foundation, William and Mary
Griffis Foundation
Griffith Foundation, W. C.
Griggs and Mary Griggs Burke Foundation, Mary Livingston
Griswold Foundation, John C.
Groome Beatty Trust, Helen D.
Grundy Foundation
GSM Industrial
Guaranty Bank & Trust Co.
Guardian Life Insurance Company of America
Guggenheim Foundation, Harry Frank
Gulf Coast Medical Foundation
Gulf Power Co.
Guttman Foundation, Stella and Charles
Haas, Jr. Fund, Evelyn and Walter
Habig Foundation, Arnold F.
Hachar Charitable Trust, D. D.
Hafif Family Foundation
Hagedorn Fund
Haigh-Scatena Foundation
Haley Foundation, W. B.
Halff Foundation, G. A. C.
Hallberg Foundation, E. L. and R. F.
Hallett Charitable Trust, E. W.
Hallett Charitable Trust, Jessie F.
Halsell Foundation, Ewing
Hamilton Bank
Hamman Foundation, George and Mary Josephine
Hammer Foundation, Armand
Hancock Foundation, Luke B.
Handy and Harman Foundation
Hanes Foundation, John W. and Anna H.
Hanover Foundation

Hanson Industries North America
Harcourt Foundation, Ellen Knowles
Harcourt General, Inc.
Hardin Foundation, Phil
Harland Charitable Foundation, John and Wilhelmina D.
Harmon Foundation, Pearl M. and Julia J.
HarperCollins Publishers Inc.
Harriman Foundation, Gladys and Roland
Harriman Foundation, Mary W.
Harrington Foundation, Francis A. and Jacquelyn H.
Harrison Foundation, Fred G.
Harsco Corp.
Hartford Foundation, John A.
Hartmarx Corporation
Hartz Foundation
Harvey Foundation, Felix
Hasbro Inc.
Hassenfeld Foundation
Hastings Charitable Foundation, Oris B.
Hatch Charitable Trust, Margaret Milliken
Hauser Foundation
Hawkins Foundation, Robert Z.
Hawn Foundation
Haynes Foundation, John Randolph and Dora
Hazen Foundation, Edward W.
HCA Foundation
Hearst Foundation, William Randolph
Hebrew Technical Institute
Hechinger Co.
Hecht-Levi Foundation
Heckscher Foundation for Children
Hedco Foundation
Heginbotham Trust, Will E.
Heinz Company, H. J.
Heinz Endowment, Howard
Heinz Endowment, Vira I.
Heinz Trust, Drue
Heller Charitable Foundation, Clarence E.
Heller Financial, Inc.
Helmerich Foundation
Helms Foundation
Henderson Foundation, George B.
Henkel Corp.
Henry Foundation, Patrick
Hermann Foundation, Grover
Herrick Foundation
Hershey Foods Corp.
Hershey Foundation, Barry J.
Herzstein Charitable Foundation, Albert and Ethel
Heublein Inc.
Hewit Family Foundation
Hewlett Foundation, William and Flora
Heydt Fund, Nan and Matilda
Hickory Tech Corp.
Higginson Trust, Corina
High Foundation
Hill Foundation, Sandy
Hillcrest Foundation
Hillman Family Foundation, Alex
Hillman Foundation
Hillsdale Fund
Hino Diesel Trucks (U.S.A.)
Hoag Family Foundation, George
Hobby Foundation
Hoffman Foundation, Maximilian E. and Marion O.
Hoffmann-La Roche Inc.
Holnam
Holt Family Foundation
Holzer Memorial Foundation, Richard H.
Homeland Foundation
Hook Drugs
Hoover Foundation
Hoover Fund-Trust, W. Henry
Hoover, Jr. Foundation, Margaret W. and Herbert

Hopedale Foundation
Hopkins Foundation, Josephine Lawrence
Hopwood Charitable Trust, John M.
Houchens Foundation, Ervin G.
Housatonic Curtain Co.
Houston Endowment
Houston Industries Incorporated
Howard and Bush Foundation
Howe and Mitchell B. Howe Foundation, Lucille Horton
Howell Foundation of Florida
Hoyt Foundation
Hoyt Foundation, Stewart W. and Willma C.
Huber Foundation
Hudson-Webber Foundation
Hugoton Foundation
Huisking Foundation
Hulbert Foundation, Nila B.
Hulme Charitable Foundation, Milton G.
Hultquist Foundation
Humana, Inc.
Humphrey Fund, George M. and Pamela S.
Hunt Charitable Trust, C. Giles
Hunt Foundation
Hunt Foundation, Roy A.
Hunt Foundation, Samuel P.
Huston Charitable Trust, Stewart
Huston Foundation
Huthsteiner Fine Arts Trust
Hyde and Watson Foundation
Hygeia Dairy Co.
IBP, Inc.
Icahn Foundation, Carl C.
ICI Americas Inc.
IES Industries, Inc.
Illinois Consolidated Telephone Co.
Illinois Tool Works, Inc.
Imperial Bancorp
Independence Foundation
Ingalls Foundation, Louise H. and David S.
Inland Container Corp.
Integra Bank of Uniontown
Interkal, Inc.
International Business Machines Corp.
International Foundation
International Paper Co.
Iowa-Illinois Gas & Electric Co.
Irvine Foundation, James
Irwin Charity Foundation, William G.
ITT Hartford Insurance Group, Inc.
Ittleson Foundation
Jackson Foundation
Jacobs Family Foundation
Jacobson Foundation, Bernard H. and Blanche E.
Jaffe Foundation
James River Corp. of Virginia
Jameson Foundation, J. W. and Ida M.
Janesville Foundation
Janirve Foundation
Jarson-Stanley and Mickey Kaplan Foundation, Isaac and Esther
Jaydor Corp.
JELD-WEN, Inc.
Jennings Foundation, Mary Hillman
Jewell Memorial Foundation, Daniel Ashley and Irene Houston
Jewett Foundation, George Frederick
Jewish Healthcare Foundation of Pittsburgh
JFM Foundation
JM Foundation
Jockey Hollow Foundation
John Hancock Mutual Life Insurance Co.

Johnson Charitable Educational Trust, James Hervey
Johnson Charitable Trust, Keith Wold
Johnson Controls Inc.
Johnson Foundation, Burdine
Johnson Foundation, Helen K. and Arthur E.
Johnson Foundation, M. G. and Lillie A.
Johnson Foundation, Willard T. C.
Johnson Fund, Edward C.
Johnson & Higgins
Johnson & Son, S.C.
Jones Foundation, Daisy Marquis
Jones Foundation, Fletcher
Jones Foundation, Harvey and Bernice
Jones Foundation, Helen
Jonsson Foundation
Jordan Charitable Foundation, Mary Ranken Jordan and Ettie A.
Joslin-Needham Family Foundation
Jostens, Inc.
Journal-Gazette Co.
Joy Family Foundation
Julia R. and Estelle L. Foundation
Jurzykowski Foundation, Alfred
Justus Trust, Edith C.
Kansas City Southern Industries
Kantzler Foundation
Kaplan Fund, J. M.
Kaplun Foundation, Morris J. and Betty
Kardon Foundation, Samuel and Rebecca
Kaufmann Foundation, Henry
Kavanagh Foundation, T. James
Kaye, Scholer, Fierman, Hays & Handler
Kayser Foundation
Kelley and Elza Kelley Foundation, Edward Bangs
Kelly Foundation, T. Lloyd
Kelly Tractor Co.
Kemper Foundation, William T.
Kemper National Insurance Cos.
Kempner Fund, Harris and Eliza
Kennecott Corporation
Kennedy Foundation, Ethel
Kent-Lucas Foundation
Kern Foundation Trust
Kerr Foundation
Kettering Fund
Kiewit Foundation, Peter
Kilcawley Fund, William H.
Kilroy Foundation, William S. and Lora Jean
Kimball Foundation, Horace A. Kimball and S. Ella
Kimberly-Clark Corp.
Kingsbury Corp.
Kinney-Lindstrom Foundation
Kiplinger Foundation
Kirbo Charitable Trust, Thomas M. and Irene B.
Kirby Foundation, F. M.
Kirkpatrick Foundation
Kitzmiller/Bales Trust
Kline Foundation, Josiah W. and Bessie H.
Klipstein Foundation, Ernest Christian
Klock and Lucia Klock Kingston Foundation, Jay E.
Klosk Fund, Louis and Rose
Kmart Corporation
KN Energy, Inc.
Knapp Foundation
Knight Foundation, John S. and James L.
Knoll Group

Knox, Sr., and Pearl Wallis Knox Charitable Foundation, Robert W.
Knudsen Foundation, Tom and Valley
Koch Charitable Foundation, Charles G.
Koehler Foundation, Marcia and Otto
Kohn-Joseloff Foundation
Komes Foundation
Koopman Fund
Koret Foundation
Kornfeld Foundation, Emily Davie and Joseph S.
Kreitler Foundation
Kresge Foundation
Kress Foundation, Samuel H.
Kuehn Foundation
Kunkel Foundation, John Crain
Kutz Foundation, Milton and Hattie
Kuyper Foundation, Peter H. and E. Lucille
La-Z-Boy Chair Co.
Ladd Charitable Corporation, Helen and George
Laffey-McHugh Foundation
Lake Placid Education Foundation
LamCo. Communications
Landegger Charitable Foundation
Lang Foundation, Eugene M.
Larsen Fund
Lasdon Foundation
Lasdon Foundation, William and Mildred
Lattner Foundation, Forrest C.
Lauder Foundation
Laurel Foundation
Lazarus Charitable Trust, Helen and Charles
LBJ Family Foundation
Lea Foundation, Helen Sperry
Leavey Foundation, Thomas and Dorothy
Lebanon Mutual Insurance Co.
Lebovitz Fund
Lederer Foundation, Francis L.
Lee Endowment Foundation
Lee Enterprises
LEF Foundation
Lehigh Portland Cement Co.
Lehmann Foundation, Otto W.
Leidy Foundation, John J.
Leighton-Oare Foundation
Lemberg Foundation
Lenna Foundation, Reginald A. and Elizabeth S.
Lennon Foundation, Fred A.
Leuthold Foundation
Levitt Foundation
Levy Foundation, June Rockwell
Liberman Foundation, Bertha and Isaac
Lichtenstein Foundation, David B.
Life Insurance Co. of Georgia
Link, Jr. Foundation, George
Linn-Henley Charitable Trust
Linnell Foundation
Lipton, Thomas J.
Littauer Foundation, Lucius N.
Little, Inc., Arthur D.
Liz Claiborne, Inc.
Lockhart Vaughan Foundation
Loews Corporation
Long Foundation, J.M.
Long Island Lighting Co.
Longwood Foundation
Louisiana-Pacific Corp.
Love Foundation, George H. and Margaret McClintic
Lovett Foundation
Lowenstein Foundation, Leon
Lund Foundation
Lunda Charitable Trust
Lurcy Charitable and Educational Trust, Georges
Lurie Foundation, Louis R.
Lux Foundation, Miranda
Lydall, Inc.
Lyon Foundation

M/A-COM, Inc.
MacArthur Foundation, John D. and Catherine T.
MacCurdy Salisbury Educational Foundation
MacLeod Stewardship Foundation
Macy & Co., Inc., R.H.
Maddox Foundation, J. F.
Madison Gas & Electric Co.
Magowan Family Foundation
Mahadh Foundation
Mailman Family Foundation, A. L.
Mailman Foundation
Management Compensation Group/Dulworth Inc.
Mandeville Foundation
Maneely Fund
Marbrook Foundation
Mardag Foundation
Mardigian Foundation
Margoes Foundation
Maritz Inc.
Markey Charitable Fund, John C.
Markle Foundation, John and Mary R.
Marmot Foundation
Marpat Foundation
Marquette Electronics, Inc.
Marriott Foundation, J. Willard
Mars Foundation
Marsh & McLennan Companies, Inc.
Marshall Foundation, Mattie H.
Marshall Trust in Memory of Sanders McDaniel, Harriet McDaniel
Martin Marietta Corp.
Martin Marietta Materials
Martini Foundation, Nicholas
Marx Foundation, Virginia and Leonard
Mascoma Savings Bank
Massachusetts Mutual Life Insurance Co.
Massengill-DeFriece Foundation
Mather Charitable Trust, S. Livingston
Mather Fund, Richard
Mather and William Gwinn Mather Fund, Elizabeth Ring
Mathis-Pfohl Foundation
Mattel, Inc.
Matthies Foundation, Katharine
Mautz Paint Co.
May Department Stores Company, The
May Foundation, Wilbur
Mayer Foundation, James and Eva
Mayor Foundation, Oliver Dewey
Mays Foundation
Maytag Family Foundation, Fred
MBIA Inc.
MCA Inc.
McBean Charitable Trust, Alletta Morris
McCann Foundation
McCarty Foundation, John and Margaret
McCasland Foundation
McConnell Foundation
McCormick & Co. Inc.
McCormick Foundation, Chauncey and Marion Deering
McCormick Trust, Anne
McCune Charitable Foundation, Marshall and Perrine D.
McCune Charitable Trust, John R.
McDermott Foundation, Eugene
McDonald & Company Securities, Inc.
McDonnell Douglas Corp.-West
McElroy Trust, R. J.

McEvoy Foundation, Mildred H.
McFawn Trust No. 2, Lois Sisler
McFeely-Rogers Foundation
McGee Foundation
McGonagle Foundation, Dextra Baldwin
McGraw-Hill, Inc.
McInerny Foundation
McKenna Foundation, Katherine Mabis
McKenna Foundation, Philip M.
McLean Contributionship
McMahan Foundation, Catherine L. and Robert O.
McMahon Foundation
McMillan Foundation, D. W.
McQueen Foundation, Adeline and George
McShain Charities, John
M.E. Foundation
Mead Corporation, The
Meadows Foundation
Medtronic, Inc.
Mellinger Educational Foundation, Edward Arthur
Mellon Family Foundation, R. K.
Mellon Foundation, Andrew W.
Mellon Foundation, Richard King
Memorial Foundation for the Blind
Memton Fund
Mengle Foundation, Glenn and Ruth
Merck & Co.
Merck & Co. Human Health Division
Merck Family Fund
Mercury Aircraft
Merkley Charitable Trust
Merrick Foundation
Merrill Lynch & Co., Inc.
Messing Family Charitable Foundation
Metropolitan Life Insurance Co.
Meyer Family Foundation, Paul J.
Meyer Fund, Milton and Sophie
Meyer Memorial Trust
Meyerhoff Fund, Joseph
Mid-Iowa Health Foundation
Middendorf Foundation
Mielke Family Foundation
Millbrook Tribute Garden
Miller Brewing Company/North Carolina
Miller Charitable Foundation, Howard E. and Nell E.
Miller Foundation
Miller Fund, Kathryn and Gilbert
Miller-Mellor Association
Mills Fund, Frances Goll
Mine Safety Appliances Co.
Mingenback Foundation, Julia J.
Minnesota Mining & Mfg. Co.
Mitchell Energy & Development Corp.
Mitsubishi International Corp.
Mitsubishi Motor Sales of America, Inc.
Mnuchin Foundation
Mobil Oil Corp.
Mohasco Corp.
Monadnock Paper Mills
Monell Foundation, Ambrose
Monfort Family Foundation
Montana Power Co.
Monticello College Foundation
Moore Charitable Foundation, Marjorie
Moore Foundation, Edward S.
Moore & Sons, B.C.
Morgan Charitable Residual Trust, W. and E.
Morgan & Company, J.P.
Morgan Construction Co.
Morgan Foundation, Burton D.

Morgan Foundation, Louie R. and Gertrude
Morgan and Samuel Tate Morgan, Jr. Foundation, Marietta McNeil
Morgan Stanley & Co., Inc.
Morris Foundation, Margaret T.
Morris Foundation, William T.
Morrison Charitable Trust, Pauline A. and George R.
Morrison Knudsen Corporation
Mosbacher, Jr. Foundation, Emil
Moses Fund, Henry and Lucy
Mosinee Paper Corp.
Mott Foundation, Charles Stewart
Mott Fund, Ruth
Muchnic Foundation
Mulcahy Foundation
Mulford Foundation, Vincent
Mulford Trust, Clarence E.
Mullen Foundation, J. K.
Muller Foundation
Munger Foundation, Alfred C.
Munson Foundation Trust, W. B.
Murdock Charitable Trust, M. J.
Murphey Foundation, Lluella Morey
Murphy Co. Foundation, G.C.
Murphy Foundation
Musson Charitable Foundation, R. C. and Katharine M.
Mutual Assurance Co.
Myra Foundation
Nabisco Foods Group
Nalco Chemical Co.
National Forge Co.
National Gypsum Co.
National Steel Corp.
National Westminster Bank New Jersey
NBD Indiana, Inc.
Nesholm Family Foundation
Nestle USA Inc.
Neuberger Foundation, Roy R. and Marie S.
Neville Chemical Co.
New England Business Service
New Jersey Natural Gas Co.
New-Land Foundation
New York Life Insurance Co.
New York Mercantile Exchange
New York Stock Exchange, Inc.
New York Times Company
The New Yorker Magazine, Inc.
Newcombe Foundation, Charlotte W.
Newman's Own, Inc.
NewMil Bancorp
Nias Foundation, Henry
Noble Foundation, Edward John
Noble Foundation, Samuel Roberts
Norfolk Shipbuilding & Drydock Corp.
Norgren Foundation, Carl A.
Norman Foundation, Summers A.
Normandie Foundation
North Shore Foundation
Northern States Power Co. (Minnesota)
Northwest Natural Gas Co.
Norton Co.
Norton Family Foundation, Peter
Norton Foundation Inc.
Norton Memorial Corporation, Geraldi
Norwest Bank Nebraska, N.A.
Norwest Corporation
Novell Inc.
Oaklawn Foundation
O'Connor Foundation, A. Lindsay and Olive B.
O'Connor Foundation, Kathryn
OCRI Foundation
Odell Fund, Robert Stewart Odell and Helen Pfeiffer

O'Fallon Trust, Martin J. and Mary Anne
Offield Family Foundation
OG&E Electric Services
Ohrstrom Foundation
Old Dominion Box Co.
Old National Bank in Evansville
Olin Corp.
Olin Foundation, F. W.
Olin Foundation, Spencer T. and Ann W.
Oliver Memorial Trust Foundation
Olsson Memorial Foundation, Elis
Oppenstein Brothers Foundation
O'Quinn Foundation, John M. and Nancy C.
Ore-Ida Foods, Inc.
Osborn Charitable Trust, Edward B.
Osceola Foundation
Osher Foundation, Bernard
Ottenheimer Brothers Foundation
Ottley Trust-Watertown, Marion W.
Outboard Marine Corp.
Overbrook Foundation
Overlake Foundation
Owen Industries, Inc.
Owsley Foundation, Alvin and Lucy
Oxy USA Inc.
Pacific Mutual Life Insurance Co.
Pacific Telesis Group
Packaging Corporation of America
Packard Foundation, David and Lucile
PaineWebber
Paley Foundation, William S.
Palisades Educational Foundation
Palisano Foundation, Vincent and Harriet
Palmer Fund, Frank Loomis
Pamida, Inc.
Panhandle Eastern Corporation
Park Foundation
Parker Hannifin Corp.
Parshelsky Foundation, Moses L.
Parsons Foundation, Ralph M.
Parvin Foundation, Albert
Patterson Charitable Fund, W. I.
Payne Foundation, Frank E. and Seba B.
Peabody Charitable Fund, Amelia
PECO Energy Company
Pella Corporation
Penguin Books USA, Inc.
Penn Foundation, William
Pennsylvania Dutch Co.
Pennzoil Co.
Peoples Energy Corp.
Peppers Foundation, Ann
Perkin-Elmer Corp.
Peters Foundation, Charles F.
Peters Foundation, R. D. and Linda
Peterson Charitable Foundation, Folke H.
Peterson Foundation, Hal and Charlie
Petrie Trust, Lorene M.
Petteys Memorial Foundation, Jack
Pettus Crowe Foundation
Pew Charitable Trusts
Pfizer, Inc.
Pforzheimer Foundation, Carl and Lily
Phelps Dodge Corporation
PHH Corporation
Philibosian Foundation, Stephen
Phillips Charitable Trust, Dr. and Mrs. Arthur William

Phillips Family Foundation, Jay and Rose
Phillips Family Foundation, L. E.
Phillips Foundation, Ellis L.
Phipps Foundation, Howard
Piankova Foundation, Tatiana
Pick, Jr. Fund, Albert
Pickford Foundation, Mary
Pierce Charitable Trust, Harold Whitworth
Pineywoods Foundation
Pioneer Trust Bank, NA
Piper Foundation, Minnie Stevens
Piper Jaffray Companies Inc.
Pitt-Des Moines Inc.
Pittsburg Midway Coal Mining Co.
Pittsburgh Child Guidance Foundation
Plankenhorn Foundation, Harry
Playboy Enterprises, Inc.
Plumsock Fund
PNC Bank, N.A.
Polaroid Corp.
Pollock Company Foundation, William B.
Porter Foundation, Mrs. Cheever
Porter Testamentary Trust, James Hyde
Potomac Electric Power Co.
Pott Foundation, Herman T. and Phenie R.
Potter Foundation, Justin and Valere
Potts and Sibley Foundation
PPG Industries, Inc.
Prairie Foundation
Premier Industrial Corp.
Price Associates, T. Rowe
Price Foundation, Louis and Harold
Price Foundation, Lucien B. and Katherine E.
Priddy Foundation
PriMerit Bank
Prince Trust, Abbie Norman
Proctor Trust, Mortimer R.
Prospect Hill Foundation
Prouty Foundation, Olive Higgins
Providence Gas Co.
Providence Journal Company
Provident Life & Accident Insurance Company of America
Providian Corporation
Prudential Insurance Co. of America, The
Prudential Securities, Inc.
Public Service Co. of New Mexico
Public Service Electric & Gas Co.
Public Welfare Foundation
Pulitzer Publishing Co.
Puterbaugh Foundation
Putnam Foundation
Quaker Chemical Corp.
Quivey-Bay State Foundation
R. F. Foundation
Rabb Charitable Foundation, Sidney and Esther
Rabb Foundation, Harry W.
Rachal Foundation, Ed
Ralston Purina Co.
Rand McNally & Co.
R&B Machine Tool Co.
Ratner Foundation, Milton M.
Raymond Corp.
Read Foundation, Charles L.
Reed Foundation
Regenstein Foundation
Reicher Foundation, Anne and Harry J.
Reichhold Chemicals, Inc.
Reidler Foundation
Reinberger Foundation
Reisman Charitable Trust, George C. and Evelyn R.
Rennebohm Foundation, Oscar
Republic NY Corp.

Retirement Research Foundation
Reynolds Foundation, Christopher
Reynolds Foundation, Donald W.
Reynolds Foundation, Edgar
Rhone-Poulenc Inc.
Rice Charitable Foundation, Albert W.
Rice Foundation
Rich Products Corporation
Richardson Benevolent Foundation, C. E.
Richardson Charitable Trust, Anne S.
Rieke Corp.
Riggs Benevolent Fund
Ringier-America
Ritter Charitable Trust, George W. and Mary F.
Rixson Foundation, Oscar C.
RJR Nabisco Inc.
Robinson-Broadhurst Foundation
Robinson Fund, Maurice R.
Rockefeller Fund, David
Rockwell Fund
Rockwell International Corporation
Rogers Family Foundation
Rohatyn Foundation, Felix and Elizabeth
Rohm & Haas Co.
Rose Foundation, Billy
Roseburg Forest Products Co.
Rosen Foundation, Joseph
Rosenberg Foundation
Rosenberg, Jr. Family Foundation, Louise and Claude
Rose's Stores, Inc.
Ross Laboratories
Ross Memorial Foundation, Will
Rouse Co.
Rowland Foundation
Royal Foundation, May Mitchell
Royal Group, Inc.
Ruan Foundation Trust, John
Rubin Family Fund, Cele H. and William B.
Rubin Foundation, Samuel
Rubinstein Foundation, Helena
Rudin Foundation
Russell Charitable Foundation, Tom
Russell Trust, Josephine G.
Ryan Foundation, David Claude
SAFECO Corp.
Safety Fund National Bank
Saint Paul Companies, Inc.
Salomon Foundation, Richard and Edna
Salomon Inc.
Saltonstall Charitable Foundation, Richard
Salvatori Foundation, Henry
San Diego Gas & Electric
Sandusky International Inc.
Sandy Hill Foundation
Santa Fe Pacific Corporation
Sara Lee Corp.
Sara Lee Hosiery, Inc.
Sargent Foundation, Newell B.
Sarkeys Foundation
Saroyan Foundation, William
Sasco Foundation
Sawyer Charitable Foundation
SBC Communications Inc.
Scaife Family Foundation
Schenck Fund, L. P.
Scherer Foundation, Karla
Schering-Plough Corp.
Scherman Foundation
Schiff Foundation, Dorothy
Schiro Fund
Schlink Foundation, Albert G. and Olive H.
Schlumberger Ltd.
Schmitt Foundation, Kilian J. and Caroline F.
Schoenleber Foundation

Scholl Foundation, Dr.
Schowalter Foundation
Schroeder Foundation, Walter
Schuller International
Schumann Fund for New Jersey
Schwab & Co., Inc., Charles
Schwartz Foundation, Arnold A.
Schwartz Fund for Education and Health Research, Arnold and Marie
Schwob Foundation, Simon
Scott Fetzer Co.
Scott Foundation, Virginia Steele
Scott Foundation, Walter
Scott Foundation, William E.
Scripps Co., E.W.
Scurlock Foundation
Seafirst Corporation
Seagram & Sons, Inc., Joseph E.
Seaver Charitable Trust, Richard C.
Seaver Institute
Seaway Food Town, Inc.
Second Foundation
Security Life of Denver Insurance Co.
Sedgwick James Inc.
Seidman Family Foundation
Selby and Marie Selby Foundation, William G.
Self Foundation
Semmes Foundation
Seneca Foods Corp.
Sentry Insurance A Mutual Company
Sequoia Foundation
Seton Leather Co.
Share Trust, Charles Morton
Sharon Steel Corp.
Shaw Foundation, Arch W.
Shawmut National Corp.
Sheaffer Inc.
Sheary for Charity, Edna M.
Shell Oil Company
Shenandoah Life Insurance Co.
Sheppard Foundation, Lawrence B.
Shott, Jr. Foundation, Hugh I.
Shubert Foundation
Sierra Pacific Industries
Sierra Pacific Resources
Siltec Corp.
Simon Foundation, William E. and Carol G.
Simpson Investment Company
Skaggs Foundation, L. J. and Mary C.
Skillman Foundation
Slemp Foundation
Slifka Foundation, Joseph and Sylvia
Sloan Foundation, Alfred P.
Smart Family Foundation
Smeal Foundation, Mary Jean and Frank P.
Smith Charitable Foundation, Clara Blackford Smith and W. Aubrey
Smith Charitable Foundation, Lou and Lutza
Smith Corp., A.O.
Smith Foundation, Gordon V. and Helen C.
Smith Foundation, Kelvin and Eleanor
Smith Foundation, Ralph L.
Smith, Jr. Foundation, M. W.
Smith Memorial Fund, Ethel Sergeant Clark
Smith Trust, May and Stanley
SmithKline Beecham Corp.
Snayberger Memorial Foundation, Harry E. and Florence W.
Snow Foundation, John Ben
Snow Memorial Trust, John Ben
Snyder Foundation, Harold B. and Dorothy A.
Solow Foundation
Sonat Inc.

Sordoni Foundation
South Bend Tribune
South Branch Foundation
South Waite Foundation
Southern California Edison Co.
Southern New England Telephone Company
Southwestern Electric Power Co.
Spalding Foundation, Eliot
Spang & Co.
Specialty Manufacturing Co.
Speer Foundation, Roy M.
Speyer Foundation, Alexander C. and Tillie S.
Sprague Educational and Charitable Foundation, Seth
Springs Foundation
SPX Corp.
Square D Co.
Stabler Foundation, Donald B. and Dorothy L.
Stackpole-Hall Foundation
Stanley Charitable Foundation, A.W.
Stanley Works
Stans Foundation
Starr Foundation
Stauffer Charitable Trust, John
Stauffer Foundation, John and Beverly
Staunton Farm Foundation
Stearns Trust, Artemas W.
Steele Foundation, Harry and Grace
Steele-Reese Foundation
Stein Foundation, Jules and Doris
Steinbach Fund, Ruth and Milton
Steinhagen Benevolent Trust, B. A. and Elinor
Steinman Foundation, James Hale
Steinman Foundation, John Frederick
Stemmons Foundation
Sternberger Foundation, Tannenbaum
Stevens Foundation, Abbot and Dorothy H.
Stevens Foundation, John T.
Stokely, Jr. Foundation, William B.
Stone Charitable Foundation
Stone Trust, H. Chase
Strauss Foundation, Leon
Strawbridge Foundation of Pennsylvania II, Margaret Dorrance
Strong Foundation, Hattie M.
Stupp Foundation, Norman J.
Sturgis Charitable and Educational Trust, Roy and Christine
Sturgis Charitable and Educational Trust, Roy and Christine
Subaru of America Inc.
Sullivan Foundation, Algernon Sydney
Sulzberger Foundation
Sumitomo Bank of California
Sumners Foundation, Hatton W.
Sundet Foundation
Sunnen Foundation
Superior Tube Co.
Swalm Foundation
Swanson Family Foundation, Dr. W.C.
Swift Co. Inc., John S.
Swiss Bank Corp.
Symmes Foundation, F. W.
Taconic Foundation
Tait Foundation, Frank M.
Taper Foundation, Mark
Taube Family Foundation
Taubman Foundation, A. Alfred
Taylor Foundation, Fred and Harriett
Taylor Foundation, Ruth and Vernon
Teagle Foundation
Tecumseh Products Co.

Teichert & Son, A.
Teleflex Inc.
Temple Foundation, T. L. L.
Temple-Inland Inc.
Tenneco Inc.
Tennessee Valley Printing Co.
Tetley, Inc.
Teubert Charitable Trust, James H. and Alice
Texaco Inc.
Texas Commerce Bank-Houston, N.A.
Textron, Inc.
Thalhimer and Family Foundation, Charles G.
Thermo Electron Corp.
Thomas Foundation, Joan and Lee
Thomas Industries
Thomasville Furniture Industries
Thompson Charitable Foundation
Thompson Co., J. Walter
Thompson Trust, Thomas
Thomson Information Publishing Group
Thorne Foundation
Thornton Foundation
Thornton Foundation, Flora L.
Times Mirror Company, The
Timken Foundation of Canton
Tiscornia Foundation
Titus Foundation, Roy and Niuta
Tobin Foundation
Todd Co., A.M.
Toms Foundation
Tonya Memorial Foundation
Towsley Foundation, Harry A. and Margaret D.
Tozer Foundation
TransAmerica Corporation
Transco Energy Co.
Travelers Inc.
Treakle Foundation, J. Edwin
Trees Charitable Trust, Edith L.
Trexler Trust, Harry C.
Truland Foundation
Trull Foundation
Trust Company Bank
Trust Funds
Tuch Foundation, Michael
Tucker Charitable Trust, Rose E.
Tupancy-Harris Foundation of 1986
Turner Charitable Foundation
Turrell Fund
Unger Foundation, Aber D.
Unilever United States, Inc.
Union Bank
Union Camp Corporation
Union Electric Co.
Union Pacific Corp.
United Airlines, Inc.
U.S. Bank of Washington
Unitrode Corp.
Unocal Corp.
Upjohn Foundation, Harold and Grace
Upton Foundation, Frederick S.
Uris Brothers Foundation
USG Corporation
USL Capital Corporation
USX Corp.
Utica National Insurance Group
Vale Foundation, Ruby R.
Valentine Foundation, Lawson
Valmont Industries, Inc.
van Ameringen Foundation
Van Buren Foundation
Van Evera Foundation, Dewitt
Van Every Foundation, Philip L.
Van Houten Memorial Fund
Van Nuys Foundation, I. N. and Susanna H.
Van Wert County Foundation
Vance Charitable Foundation, Robert C.
Vanderbilt Trust, R. T.
Vaughn, Jr. Foundation Fund, James M.

Vernon Fund, Miles Hodsdon
Vetlesen Foundation, G. Unger
Vevay-Switzerland County Foundation
Vicksburg Foundation
Virginia Environmental Endowment
Virginia Power Co.
Vogler Foundation, Laura B.
Vollbrecht Foundation, Frederick A.
Vulcan Materials Co.
Wachovia Bank of North Carolina, N.A.
Wahlstrom Foundation
Wal-Mart Stores, Inc.
Wallace Foundation, George R.
Wallace-Reader's Digest Fund, DeWitt
Wallace-Reader's Digest Fund, Lila
Walsh Foundation
Warfield Memorial Fund, Anna Emory
Warner Fund, Albert and Bessie
Warren and Beatrice W. Blanding Foundation, Riley J. and Lillian N.
Warwick Foundation
Washington Forrest Foundation
Washington Mutual Savings Bank
Washington Water Power Co.
Waters Charitable Trust, Robert S.
Wean Foundation, Raymond John
Weaver Foundation, Gil and Dody
Webber Oil Co.
Weber Charities Corp., Frederick E.
Weckbaugh Foundation, Eleanore Mullen
Weezie Foundation
Wege Foundation
Weil, Gotshal and Manges Foundation
Weingart Foundation
Weinstein Foundation, J.
Welch Testamentary Trust, George T.
Welfare Foundation
Wells Foundation, Franklin H. and Ruth L.
Wendt Foundation, Margaret L.
Wertheim Foundation, Dr. Herbert A.
West Foundation, Harry and Ethel
West One Bancorp
Westerman Foundation, Samuel F.
Western New York Foundation
WestLB New York Branch
Westvaco Corporation
Weyerhaeuser Co.
Weyerhaeuser Memorial Foundation, Charles A.
Wheat First Butcher Singer, Inc.
Wheeler Foundation
Wheeler Foundation, Wilmot
Whirlpool Corporation
White Trust, G. R.
Whitecap Foundation
Whitehead Charitable Foundation
Whiting Foundation
Whiting Foundation, Macauley and Helen Dow
Whitney Fund, David M.
Whittenberger Foundation, Claude R. and Ethel B.
Wickes Foundation, Harvey Randall
Wickson-Link Memorial Foundation
WICOR, Inc.
Widgeon Foundation
Wiegand Foundation, E. L.
Wiggins Memorial Trust, J. J.
Wilder Foundation
Wildermuth Foundation, E. F.

Wiley & Sons, Inc., John
Willard Helping Fund, Cecilia Young
Williams Charitable Trust, John C.
Williams Charitable Trust, Mary Jo
Williams Companies, The
Wilmington Trust Co.
Wilson Foundation, H. W.
Wilson Fund, Matilda R.
Winchester Foundation
Windham Foundation
Winnebago Industries, Inc.
Winston Foundation, Norman and Rosita
Winter Construction Co.
Winthrop Trust, Clara B.
Wiremold Co.
Wisconsin Power & Light Co.
Wisconsin Public Service Corp.
Wise Foundation and Charitable Trust, Watson W.
Witco Corp.
Witter Foundation, Dean
Wood Foundation of Chambersburg, PA
Woodward Fund
Woolley Foundation, Vasser
Worthington Foods
Wright Foundation, Lola
Wyman Youth Trust
Wyomissing Foundation
Y and H Soda Foundation
Yeager Charitable Trust, Lester E.
Young Foundation, Hugo H. and Mabel B.
Young Foundation, Irvin L.
Young Foundation, Robert R.
Zachry Co., H.B.
Zarrow Foundation, Anne and Henry
Zenkel Foundation
Zlinkoff Fund for Medical Research and Education, Sergei S.
Zollner Foundation

Literary Arts

Ahmanson Foundation
Aldus Corp.
Aluminum Co. of America
AMCORE Bank, N.A. Rockford
Avery Arts Foundation, Milton and Sally
Bank of New York Company, Inc.
Bankers Trust Company
Barker Foundation, J.M.R.
Barth Foundation, Theodore H.
Bay Foundation
Bingham Foundation, William
Binney & Smith Inc.
Blandin Foundation
Block, H&R
Blount, Inc.
Booth Ferris Foundation
Borman's Inc.
Cabot Corp.
Cafritz Foundation, Morris and Gwendolyn
Carpenter Foundation
Central Maine Power Co.
Central National Bank
Chadwick Fund, Dorothy Jordan
Chase Manhattan Bank, N.A.
Chicago Sun-Times, Inc.
Christian Dior New York, Inc.
Clorox Co.
CNA Financial Corporation/CNA Insurance Companies
Columbus Dispatch Printing Co.
Cosmair, Inc.
Crawford Estate, E. R.
Crown Books
Dart Group Corp.
Dewing Foundation, Frances R.

Dexter Charitable Fund, Eugene A.
Dodge Foundation, Geraldine R.
Donnelley Foundation, Gaylord and Dorothy
Donnelley & Sons Co., R.R.
Douty Foundation
Dreyfus Foundation, Jean and Louis
Dreyfus Foundation, Max and Victoria
du Pont de Nemours & Co., E. I.
Duchossois Industries Inc.
Elkins, Jr. Foundation, Margaret and James A.
Ettinger Foundation
Evans Foundation, T. M.
Federated Mutual Insurance Co.
Feild Co-Operative Association
First Fidelity Bank
First Union Corp.
Fleishhacker Foundation
Forbes Inc.
General Mills, Inc.
Gleason Foundation
Graham Foundation for Advanced Studies in the Fine Arts
Greve Foundation, William and Mary
Halsell Foundation, Ewing
Harcourt Foundation, Ellen Knowles
Hardin Foundation, Phil
HarperCollins Publishers Inc.
Hechinger Co.
Heinz Company, H. J.
Heinz Trust, Drue
Hill Foundation, Sandy
Hillsdale Fund
Hobby Foundation
Hopkins Foundation, Josephine Lawrence
Houston Endowment
Huthsteiner Fine Arts Trust
ITT Hartford Insurance Group, Inc.
Johnson & Higgins
Jones Foundation, Daisy Marquis
Jordan Charitable Foundation, Mary Ranken Jordan and Ettie A.
Kansas City Southern Industries
Kaplan Fund, J. M.
Kaplun Foundation, Morris J. and Betty
Kelley and Elza Kelley Foundation, Edward Bangs
Kohn-Joseloff Foundation
Laurel Foundation
Littauer Foundation, Lucius N.
Long Island Lighting Co.
Lurie Foundation, Louis R.
Lydall, Inc.
Macy & Co., Inc., R.H.
Magowan Family Foundation
Marpat Foundation
Marquette Electronics, Inc.
MCA Co.
McCune Charitable Foundation, Marshall and Perrine D.
Mellon Foundation, Andrew W.
Mobil Oil Corp.
Monadnock Paper Mills
New York Times Company
The New Yorker Magazine, Inc.
Norton Co.
OCRI Foundation
Packard Foundation, David and Lucile
Payne Foundation, Frank E. and Seba B.
Penn Foundation, William
Pforzheimer Foundation, Carl and Lily
Plumsock Fund
PNC Bank, N.A.
PPG Industries, Inc.
Prince Trust, Abbie Norman

Puterbaugh Foundation
Reed Foundation
Robinson Fund, Maurice R.
Rosenberg, Jr. Family Foundation, Louise and Claude
Ross Memorial Foundation, Will
Rouse Co.
Rubin Foundation, Samuel
Saint Paul Companies, Inc.
Sara Lee Hosiery, Inc.
Scherman Foundation
Schlumberger Ltd.
Schowalter Foundation
Schuller International
Scripps Co., E.W.
Sedgwick James Inc.
Security Life of Denver Insurance Co.
Shenandoah Life Insurance Co.
Snow Foundation, John Ben
Sprague Educational and Charitable Foundation, Seth
Stauffer Foundation, John and Beverly
Steele-Reese Foundation
Stein Foundation, Jules and Doris
Steinman Foundation, John Frederick
Sulzberger Foundation
Teleflex Inc.
TransAmerica Corporation
Truland Foundation
Union Camp Corporation
Virginia Power Co.
Vulcan Materials Co.
Wallace-Reader's Digest Fund, Lila
Wean Foundation, Raymond John
Wege Foundation
Wendt Foundation, Margaret L.
Whirlpool Corporation
Whittenberger Foundation, Claude R. and Ethel B.
Winter Construction Co.

Museums/Galleries

Abbott Laboratories
Abell-Hanger Foundation
ACF Industries, Inc.
Achelis Foundation
Acushnet Co.
Adams Foundation, Arthur F. and Alice E.
Adler Foundation Trust, Philip D. and Henrietta B.
AEGON USA Inc.
Ahmanson Foundation
Air France
Air Products and Chemicals, Inc.
Akzo Chemicals Inc.
Alabama Gas Corp.
Aldus Corp.
Alexander Foundation, Joseph
Allegheny Foundation
Allegheny Ludlum Corp.
Allen Brothers Foundation
Allendale Insurance Co.
Allianz Life Insurance Co. of North America
AlliedSignal Inc.
Allyn Foundation
Altman Foundation
Alumax Inc.
Aluminum Co. of America
Amado Foundation, Maurice
AMCORE Bank, N.A. Rockford
American Brands, Inc.
American Fidelity Corporation
American General Finance Corp.
American National Bank & Trust Co. of Chicago
American Natural Resources Company
American President Companies, Ltd.

American United Life Insurance Co.
Ames Charitable Trust, Harriett
AMETEK, Inc.
Amfac/JMB Hawaii Inc.
Amoco Corporation
AMP Incorporated
Andersen Corp.
Anderson Foundation
Anderson Foundation, M. D.
Andersons, The
Andrews Foundation
Anheuser-Busch Companies, Inc.
Annenberg Foundation
Ansin Private Foundation, Ronald M.
Ansley Foundation, Dantzler Bond
AON Corporation
Apple Computer, Inc.
Appleby Trust, Scott B. and Annie P.
Appleton Papers Inc.
Arakelian Foundation, Mary Alice
Arcadia Foundation
Archer-Daniels-Midland Co.
Argyros Foundation
Aristech Chemical Corp.
Arkansas Power & Light Co.
Arkelian Foundation, Ben H. and Gladys
Arkell Hall Foundation
Armco Inc.
Arnhold Foundation
Asplundh Foundation
Astor Foundation, Vincent
AT&T Corp.
Atherton Family Foundation
Atran Foundation
Audubon State Bank
Auerbach Foundation, Beatrice Fox
Avery Arts Foundation, Milton and Sally
Avon Products, Inc.
Ayres Foundation, Inc.
Babcock & Wilcox Co.
Babson Foundation, Paul and Edith
Baker Foundation, Dexter F. and Dorothy H.
Baker Hughes Inc.
Baker Trust, George F.
Baldwin Memorial Foundation, Fred
Ball Brothers Foundation
Ball Foundation, George and Frances
Bank of Boston Corp.
Bank of New York Company, Inc.
Bank One, Texas-Houston Office
Bank One, Youngstown, NA
BankAmerica Corp.
Bankers Trust Company
Banta Corp.
Barker Foundation, J.M.R.
Barra Foundation
Barry Corp., R. G.
Barth Foundation, Theodore H.
Battelle Memorial Institute
Batts Foundation
Bauervic Foundation, Charles M.
Baughman Foundation
Bay Foundation
Beal Foundation
Bean Foundation, Norwin S. and Elizabeth N.
BE&K Inc.
Beattie Foundation Trust, Cordelia Lee
Bechtel, Jr. Foundation, S. D.
Bechtel Testamentary Charitable Trust, H. R.
Bedsole Foundation, J. L.
Beech Aircraft Corp.
Bell Foundation, James F.
Beloit Foundation
Bemis Company, Inc.
Benedum Foundation, Claude Worthington

Benenson Foundation, Frances and Benjamin
Benetton Services Corp.
Benwood Foundation
Berger Foundation, H. N. and Frances C.
Berwind Corporation
Besser Foundation
Bethlehem Steel Corp.
Beveridge Foundation, Frank Stanley
Bigelow Foundation, F. R.
Bingham Foundation, William
Bingham Second Betterment Fund, William
Binney & Smith Inc.
Binswanger Cos.
Bird Corp.
Bishop Foundation, E. K. and Lillian F.
Blake Foundation, S. P.
Blandin Foundation
Blaustein Foundation, Louis and Henrietta
Block, H&R
Blount Educational and Charitable Foundation, Mildred Weedon
Blount, Inc.
Blue Bell, Inc.
Blue Cross & Blue Shield United of Wisconsin
Blum Foundation, Edna F.
Blum Foundation, Harry and Maribel G.
Blum-Kovler Foundation
Boatmen's Bancshares, Inc.
Bobst Foundation, Elmer and Mamdouha
Bodman Foundation
Boeing Co., The
Boettcher Foundation
Boise Cascade Corporation
Booth Ferris Foundation
Borden, Inc.
Borman's Inc.
Boston Edison Co.
Bothin Foundation
Bowne Foundation, Robert
BP America Inc.
Brach Foundation, Helen
Brackenridge Foundation, George W.
Brady Foundation
Breyer Foundation
Bridgestone/Firestone, Inc.
Bridwell Foundation, J. S.
Bright Family Foundation
Bristol-Myers Squibb Company
Broadhurst Foundation
Brooks Foundation, Gladys
Brown Foundation, M. K.
Brown & Williamson Tobacco Corp.
Brunswick Corp.
Bryant Foundation
Bryn Mawr Trust Co.
Bucyrus-Erie Company
Buhl Foundation
Bunbury Company
Burchfield Foundation, Charles E.
Burdines Inc.
Burlington Industries, Inc.
Burnett-Tandy Foundation
Cabell Foundation, Robert G.
Cabell III and Maude Morgan
Cabot Corp.
Cafritz Foundation, Morris and Gwendolyn
Cain Foundation, Gordon and Mary
Calhoun Charitable Trust, Kenneth
Callaway Foundation
Campbell Foundation
Campbell Foundation, Ruth Blount and Henry
Campini Foundation, Frank A.
Canon U.S.A., Inc.
Cape Branch Foundation
Cargill Inc.
Carolyn Foundation

Carpenter Foundation
Carpenter Foundation, E. Rhodes and Leona B.
Carpenter Technology Corp.
Carter Foundation, Amon G.
Carter Foundation, Beirne
Carvel Foundation, Thomas and Agnes
Carver Charitable Trust, Roy J.
Castle Foundation, Harold K. L.
CBI Industries, Inc.
CBS, Inc.
Centerior Energy Corp.
Central Fidelity Banks, Inc.
Central Maine Power Co.
Central Vermont Public Service Corp.
Century Companies of America
Chadwick Fund, Dorothy Jordan
Champion International Corporation
Champlin Foundations
Charina Foundation
Chartwell Foundation
Chase Manhattan Bank, N.A.
Chazen Foundation
Cheatham Foundation, Owen
Cheney Foundation, Ben B.
Chesapeake Corp.
Chesebrough-Pond's USA Co.
Chevron Corporation
Chicago Sun-Times, Inc.
Christian Dior New York, Inc.
Chrysler Corp.
Church & Dwight Co., Inc.
CIGNA Corporation
CINergy
Citibank
Citizens Bank of Rhode Island
Claiborne and Art Ortenberg Foundation, Liz
Clapp Charitable and Educational Trust, George H.
CLARCOR Inc.
Clark Foundation
Clarkson Foundation, Jeniam
Clay Foundation
Clements Foundation
Clorox Co.
Clowes Fund
CNA Financial Corporation/CNA Insurance Companies
Cogswell Benevolent Trust
Cole Foundation, Olive B.
Cole Trust, Quincy
Coleman Foundation, George E.
Collins Foundation
Collins Foundation, George and Jennie
Collins, Jr. Foundation, George Fulton
Colonial Life & Accident Insurance Co.
Columbia Foundation
Columbus Dispatch Printing Co.
Comer Foundation
Commerce Bancshares, Inc.
Commerce Clearing House, Incorporated
Commonwealth Edison Co.
Connecticut Mutual Life Insurance Company
Connemara Fund
Consolidated Natural Gas Co.
Consolidated Papers, Inc.
Consumers Power Co.
Continental Corp.
Contran Corporation
Cooke Foundation
Cooper Industries, Inc.
Coors Foundation, Adolph
Copley Press, Inc.
Cord Foundation, E. L.
Corning Incorporated
Cosmair, Inc.
Coughlin-Saunders Foundation
Cowell Foundation, S. H.
Cowles Charitable Trust
Cowles Foundation, Gardner and Florence Call

Cowles Media Co.
CPC International Inc.
CR Industries
Crane Co.
Crestlea Foundation
Crown Memorial, Arie and Ida
Crystal Trust
CS First Boston Corporation
CT Corp. System
Cullen Foundation
Culpeper Foundation, Charles E.
Culpeper Memorial Foundation, Daphne Seybolt
Culver Foundation, Constans
Cummins Engine Co.
Curtice-Burns Foods, Inc.
Daily News
Dana Foundation, Charles A.
Daniel Foundation of Alabama
Darby Foundation
Dart Group Corp.
Dater Foundation, Charles H.
Davenport-Hatch Foundation
Davidson Family Charitable Foundation
Davis Foundation, Edwin W. and Catherine M.
Davis Foundation, Irene E. and George A.
Davis Foundation, James A. and Juliet L.
Day Foundation, Nancy Sayles
Deere & Co.
Dekko Foundation
Delaware North Co., Inc.
Demoulas Supermarkets Inc.
Dentsply International Inc.
DeRoy Foundation, Helen L.
DeRoy Testamentary Foundation
Detroit Edison Co.
Dewing Foundation, Frances R.
Dexter Corporation
Diamond Foundation, Aaron
Digital Equipment Corp.
Dimeo Construction Co.
Dingman Foundation, Michael D.
Dishman Charitable Foundation Trust, H. E. and Kate
Dr. Seuss Foundation
Dodge Foundation, Cleveland H.
Dodge Foundation, Geraldine R.
Dodge Jones Foundation
Donaldson Company, Inc.
Donnelley Foundation, Gaylord and Dorothy
Donnelley & Sons Co., R.R.
Donner Foundation, William H.
Douglas & Lomason Company
Douty Foundation
Dow Corning Corp.
Dow Jones & Company, Inc.
Dresser Industries, Inc.
Dreyfus Foundation, Jean and Louis
Dreyfus Foundation, Max and Victoria
du Pont de Nemours & Co., E. I.
Duchossois Industries Inc.
Duke Power Co.
Dula Educational and Charitable Foundation, Caleb C. and Julia W.
Dun & Bradstreet Corp.
Dunagan Foundation
Duncan Foundation, Lillian H. and C. W.
duPont Foundation, Alfred I.
Durfee Foundation
Dynamet, Inc.
Early Foundation
Eastman Kodak Company
Eaton Corporation
Eaton Foundation, Cyrus
Eberly Foundation
Edgewater Steel Corp.
Edmonds Foundation, Dean S.
El Pomar Foundation

Elf Atochem North America, Inc.
Elkins, Jr. Foundation, Margaret and James A.
Emerson Foundation, Inc., Fred L.
Encyclopaedia Britannica, Inc.
English Memorial Fund, Florence C. and H. L.
Enron Corp.
Ensign-Bickford Industries
Erpf Fund, Armand G.
Essick Foundation
Ethyl Corp
Evans Foundation, Lettie Pate
Evans Foundation, T. M.
Evans Foundation, Thomas J.
Exchange National Bank
Exxon Corporation
Fair Foundation, R. W.
Fair Oaks Foundation, Inc.
Fair Play Foundation
Fairchild Foundation, Sherman
Farish Fund, William Stamps
Favrot Fund
Federal-Mogul Corporation
Federated Mutual Insurance Co.
Fieldcrest Cannon Inc.
Fife Foundation, Elias and Bertha
Fikes Foundation, Leland
Fink Foundation
Fireman's Fund Insurance Co.
Firman Fund
First Chicago Corp.
First Fidelity Bank
First Financial Bank FSB
First Hawaiian, Inc.
First Interstate Bank of Oregon
First Source Corp.
First Tennessee Bank
First Union Corp.
First Union National Bank of Florida
Firstar Bank Milwaukee, N.A.
Fischbach Foundation
Fish Foundation, Ray C.
Fishback Foundation Trust, Harmes C.
Fleet Financial Group, Inc.
Fleishhacker Foundation
Fleming Cos. Food Distribution Center
Fletcher Foundation
Flowers Charitable Trust, Albert W. and Edith V.
Folger Fund
Fondren Foundation
Forbes Inc.
Ford Motor Co.
Forest Foundation
Forest Oil Corp.
Foster Charitable Trust
Foster Foundation
France Foundation, Jacob and Annita
Frear Eleemosynary Trust, Mary D. and Walter F.
Freed Foundation
Freeman Charitable Trust, Samuel
Freeport-McMoRan Inc.
French Foundation, D.E.
Frese Foundation, Arnold D.
Fribourg Foundation
Friedman Family Foundation
Friendship Fund
Frisch's Restaurants Inc.
Frohring Foundation, Paul and Maxine
Frohring Foundation, William O. and Gertrude Lewis
Frost National Bank
Fry Foundation, Lloyd A.
Fujitsu America, Inc.
Fuqua Foundation, J. B.
Gamble Foundation
Gannett Publishing Co., Guy
GAR Foundation
Gates Foundation
GATX Corp.
Gaylord Foundation, Clifford Willard
Gazette Co.

Geifman Family Foundation
Gellert Foundation, Celia Berta
GenCorp Inc.
General Mills, Inc.
General Motors Corp.
Georgia-Pacific Corporation
Georgia Power Co.
German Protestant Orphan Asylum Association
Germeshausen Foundation, Kenneth J.
Gershman Foundation, Joel
Getty Trust, J. Paul
Gheens Foundation
Giant Eagle, Inc.
Giant Food Inc.
Gifford Charitable Corporation, Rosamond
Gillette Co.
Gilman Foundation, Howard
Gilmore Foundation, William G.
Givenchy Corp.
Glanville Family Foundation
Gleason Foundation
Glencoe Foundation
Glick Foundation, Eugene and Marilyn
Globe Newspaper Co.
Glosser Foundation, David A.
Goddard Foundation, Charles B.
Goldberg Family Foundation
Golden West Foundation
Goldsmith Foundation, Horace W.
Goldwyn Foundation, Samuel
Goodman & Co.
Goodrich Co., The B.F.
Goodstein Family Foundation, David
Gordon/Rousmaniere/Roberts Fund
Gould Electronics Inc.
Gould Foundation, The Florence
Graham Foundation for Advanced Studies in the Fine Arts
Graham Fund, Philip L.
Grand Rapids Label Co.
Great-West Life Assurance Co.
Green Foundation, Allen P. and Josephine B.
Greenwall Foundation
Gregg-Graniteville Foundation
Griffis Foundation
Griffith Foundation, W. C.
Griggs and Mary Griggs Burke Foundation, Mary Livingston
Groome Beatty Trust, Helen D.
Grundy Foundation
GSM Industrial
Guardian Life Insurance Company of America
Guggenheim Foundation, Harry Frank
Gulf Coast Medical Foundation
Gulf Power Co.
Guttman Foundation, Stella and Charles
Haas, Jr. Fund, Evelyn and Walter
Habig Foundation, Arnold F.
Hafif Family Foundation
Haley Foundation, W. B.
Halff Foundation, G. A. C.
Halsell Foundation, Ewing
Hamilton Bank
Hamman Foundation, George and Mary Josephine
Hammer Foundation, Armand
Hancock Foundation, Luke B.
Handy and Harman Foundation
Hanes Foundation, John W. and Anna H.
Hanover Foundation
Harcourt General, Inc.
Hardin Foundation, Phil
Harland Charitable Foundation, John and Wilhelmina D.
Harmon Foundation, Pearl M. and Julia J.

Harriman Foundation, Gladys and Roland
Harriman Foundation, Mary W.
Harrington Foundation, Francis A. and Jacquelyn H.
Harsco Corp.
Hartmarx Corporation
Hassenfeld Foundation
Hauser Foundation
Hawn Foundation
Haynes Foundation, John Randolph and Dora
HCA Foundation
Hearst Foundation, William Randolph
Hechinger Co.
Hecht-Levi Foundation
Heckscher Foundation for Children
Hedco Foundation
Heginbotham Trust, Will E.
Heinz Company, H. J.
Heinz Endowment, Howard
Heinz Endowment, Vira I.
Heinz Trust, Drue
Helmerich Foundation
Helms Foundation
Henkel Corp.
Hershey Foods Corp.
Herzstein Charitable Foundation, Albert and Ethel
Heublein Inc.
Hewit Family Foundation
Hewlett-Packard Co.
Higginson Trust, Corina
Hill Foundation, Sandy
Hillcrest Foundation
Hillman Family Foundation, Alex
Hillman Foundation
Hillsdale Fund
Hoag Family Foundation, George
Hobby Foundation
Holt Family Foundation
Holzer Memorial Foundation, Richard H.
Homeland Foundation
Hook Drugs
Hoover Fund-Trust, W. Henry
Hopedale Foundation
Hopwood Charitable Trust, John M.
Housatonic Curtain Co.
Houston Endowment
Houston Industries Incorporated
Hudson-Webber Foundation
Hulme Charitable Foundation, Milton G.
Humana, Inc.
Humphrey Fund, George M. and Pamela S.
Hunt Foundation
Hunt Foundation, Roy A.
Hunt Foundation, Samuel P.
Huston Charitable Trust, Stewart
Huston Foundation
Huthsteiner Fine Arts Trust
Hyde and Watson Foundation
Hygeia Dairy Co.
Icahn Foundation, Carl C.
ICI Americas Inc.
Illinois Tool Works, Inc.
Independence Foundation
Ingalls Foundation, Louise H. and David S.
Inland Container Corp.
Integra Bank of Uniontown
International Business Machines Corp.
International Paper Co.
Irvine Foundation, James
Irwin Charity Foundation, William G.
ITT Hartford Insurance Group, Inc.
Ittleson Foundation
Jackson Foundation
Jacobs Family Foundation
Jacobson Foundation, Bernard H. and Blanche E.
Jaffe Foundation
James River Corp. of Virginia

Jameson Foundation, J. W. and Ida M.
Janirve Foundation
Jarson-Stanley and Mickey Kaplan Foundation, Isaac and Esther
Jaydor Corp.
JELD-WEN, Inc.
Jewett Foundation, George Frederick
JFM Foundation
Jockey Hollow Foundation
John Hancock Mutual Life Insurance Co.
Johnson Charitable Educational Trust, James Hervey
Johnson Controls Inc.
Johnson Foundation, Burdine
Johnson Foundation, Helen K. and Arthur E.
Johnson Foundation, M. G. and Lillie A.
Johnson Fund, Edward C.
Johnson & Higgins
Johnson & Son, S.C.
Jones Foundation, Fletcher
Jones Foundation, Helen
Jonsson Foundation
Jordan Charitable Foundation, Mary Ranken Jordan and Ettie A.
Jostens, Inc.
Journal-Gazette Co.
Jurzykowski Foundation, Alfred
Justus Trust, Edith C.
Kansas City Southern Industries
Kaplan Fund, J. M.
Kardon Foundation, Samuel and Rebecca
Kaufmann Foundation, Henry
Kayser Foundation
Kelley and Elza Kelley Foundation, Edward Bangs
Kelly Tractor Co.
Kemper Foundation, William T.
Kemper National Insurance Cos.
Kempner Fund, Harris and Eliza
Kennecott Corporation
Kennedy Foundation, Ethel
Kent-Lucas Foundation
Kern Foundation Trust
Kerr Foundation
Kettering Fund
Kiewit Foundation, Peter
Kilroy Foundation, William S. and Lora Jean
Kimberly-Clark Corp.
Kingsbury Corp.
Kinney-Lindstrom Foundation
Kiplinger Foundation
Kirby Foundation, F. M.
Kirkpatrick Foundation
Kitzmiller/Bales Trust
Kline Foundation, Josiah W. and Bessie H.
Klipstein Foundation, Ernest Christian
Kmart Corporation
KN Energy, Inc.
Knapp Foundation
Knight Foundation, John S. and James L.
Knoll Group
Knox, Sr., and Pearl Wallis Knox Charitable Foundation, Robert W.
Knudsen Foundation, Tom and Valley
Koehler Foundation, Marcia and Otto
Kohn-Joseloff Foundation
Komes Foundation
Koopman Fund
Koret Foundation
Kreitler Foundation
Kresge Foundation
Kress Foundation, Samuel H.
Kuehn Foundation
Kunkel Foundation, John Crain

Kuyper Foundation, Peter H. and E. Lucille
La-Z-Boy Chair Co.
Laffey-McHugh Foundation
LamCo. Communications
Lang Foundation, Eugene M.
Larsen Fund
Lasdon Foundation, William and Mildred
Lattner Foundation, Forrest C.
Lauder Foundation
Laurel Foundation
Lazarus Charitable Trust, Helen and Charles
LBJ Family Foundation
Lea Foundation, Helen Sperry
Lebovitz Fund
Lederer Foundation, Francis L.
Lee Endowment Foundation
Lee Enterprises
LEF Foundation
Leighton-Oare Foundation
Lemberg Foundation
Lennon Foundation, Fred A.
Levitt Foundation
Levy Foundation, June Rockwell
Liberman Foundation, Bertha and Isaac
Life Insurance Co. of Georgia
Link, Jr. Foundation, George
Linn-Henley Charitable Trust
Linnell Foundation
Lipton, Thomas J.
Littauer Foundation, Lucius N.
Little, Inc., Arthur D.
Liz Claiborne, Inc.
Loews Corporation
Long Foundation, J.M.
Long Island Lighting Co.
Longwood Foundation
Louisiana-Pacific Corp.
Lovett Foundation
Lowenstein Foundation, Leon
Lurcy Charitable and Educational Trust, Georges
Lurie Foundation, Louis R.
Lydall, Inc.
Lyon Foundation
M/A-COM, Inc.
MacArthur Foundation, John D. and Catherine T.
MacCurdy Salisbury Educational Foundation
Macy & Co., Inc., R.H.
Maddox Foundation, J. F.
Madison Gas & Electric Co.
Magowan Family Foundation
Mailman Family Foundation, A. L.
Mailman Foundation
Management Compensation Group/Dulworth Inc.
Mandeville Foundation
Maneely Fund
Marbrook Foundation
Mardag Foundation
Maritz Inc.
Markey Charitable Fund, John C.
Marmot Foundation
Marpat Foundation
Marquette Electronics, Inc.
Marriott Foundation, J. Willard
Mars Foundation
Marsh & McLennan Companies, Inc.
Marshall Trust in Memory of Sanders McDaniel, Harriet McDaniel
Martin Marietta Corp.
Martin Marietta Materials
Marx Foundation, Virginia and Leonard
Massachusetts Mutual Life Insurance Co.
Massengill-DeFriece Foundation
Mather Charitable Trust, S. Livingston
Mather Fund, Richard
Mather and William Gwinn Mather Fund, Elizabeth Ring
Mathis-Pfohl Foundation
Mautz Paint Co.

May Department Stores Company, The
Mayor Foundation, Oliver Dewey
Maytag Family Foundation, Fred
MBIA Inc.
MCA Inc.
McBean Charitable Trust, Alletta Morris
McCasland Foundation
McConnell Foundation
McCormick & Co. Inc.
McCormick Trust, Anne
McCune Charitable Foundation, Marshall and Perrine D.
McDermott Foundation, Eugene
McDonald & Company Securities, Inc.
McDonnell Douglas Corp.-West
McElroy Trust, R. J.
McEvoy Foundation, Mildred H.
McFawn Trust No. 2, Lois Sisler
McFeely-Rogers Foundation
McGee Foundation
McGonagle Foundation, Dextra Baldwin
McGraw-Hill, Inc.
MCI Communications Corp.
McInerny Foundation
McKenna Foundation, Katherine Mabis
McKenna Foundation, Philip M.
McLean Contributionship
McMahon Foundation
McShain Charities, John
Mead Corporation, The
Meadows Foundation
Medtronic, Inc.
Mellon Family Foundation, R. K.
Mellon Foundation, Andrew W.
Mellon Foundation, Richard King
Memton Fund
Mengle Foundation, Glenn and Ruth
Merck & Co.
Merck & Co. Human Health Division
Merck Family Fund
Mercury Aircraft
Merrill Lynch & Co., Inc.
Metropolitan Life Insurance Co.
Meyer Family Foundation, Paul J.
Meyer Fund, Milton and Sophie
Meyer Memorial Trust
Middendorf Foundation
Mielke Family Foundation
Miller Brewing Company/North Carolina
Miller-Mellor Association
Mills Fund, Frances Goll
Mine Safety Appliances Co.
Mingenback Foundation, Julia J.
Minnesota Mining & Mfg. Co.
Mitchell Energy & Development Corp.
Mitsubishi International Corp.
Mnuchin Foundation
Mobil Oil Corp.
Monadnock Paper Mills
Monell Foundation, Ambrose
Montana Power Co.
Monticello College Foundation
Moore Charitable Foundation, Marjorie
Moore Foundation, Edward S.
Morgan & Company, J.P.
Morgan Construction Co.
Morgan Foundation, Burton D.
Morgan Stanley & Co., Inc.
Morris Foundation, Margaret T.
Morris Foundation, William T.

Morrison Charitable Trust, Pauline A. and George R.
Morrison Knudsen Corporation
Mosbacher, Jr. Foundation, Emil
Moses Fund, Henry and Lucy
Mosinee Paper Corp.
Mott Fund, Ruth
Muchnic Foundation
Mulcahy Foundation
Mulford Foundation, Vincent
Mullen Foundation, J. K.
Munger Foundation, Alfred C.
Munson Foundation Trust, W. B.
Murdock Charitable Trust, M. J.
Murphy Foundation
Mutual Assurance Co.
Nabisco Foods Group
Nalco Chemical Co.
National Gypsum Co.
National Steel Corp.
National Westminster Bank New Jersey
NBD Indiana, Inc.
Nesholm Family Foundation
Nestle USA Inc.
Neuberger Foundation, Roy R. and Marie S.
New-Land Foundation
New York Life Insurance Co.
New York Mercantile Exchange
New York Stock Exchange, Inc.
New York Times Company
The New Yorker Magazine, Inc.
Newman's Own, Inc.
Nias Foundation, Henry
Noble Foundation, Edward John
Noble Foundation, Samuel Roberts
Norfolk Shipbuilding & Drydock Corp.
Norgren Foundation, Carl A.
Norman Foundation, Summers A.
Normandie Foundation
North Shore Foundation
Northern States Power Co. (Minnesota)
Northwest Natural Gas Co.
Norton Co.
Norton Family Foundation, Peter
Norton Foundation Inc.
Norton Memorial Corporation, Geraldi
Norwest Corporation
Novell Inc.
O'Connor Foundation, A. Lindsay and Olive B.
OCRI Foundation
Odell Fund, Robert Stewart Odell and Helen Pfeiffer
O'Fallon Trust, Martin J. and Mary Anne
Offield Family Foundation
OG&E Electric Services
Ohrstrom Foundation
Old National Bank in Evansville
Olin Corp.
Olin Foundation, Spencer T. and Ann W.
Oliver Memorial Trust Foundation
Olsson Memorial Foundation, Elis
Oppenstein Brothers Foundation
O'Quinn Foundation, John M. and Nancy C.
Ore-Ida Foods, Inc.
Osborn Charitable Trust, Edward B.
Osceola Foundation
Osher Foundation, Bernard
Outboard Marine Corp.
Overbrook Foundation
Overlake Foundation
Owen Industries, Inc.
Owsley Foundation, Alvin and Lucy
Oxy USA Inc.

Pacific Mutual Life Insurance Co.
Pacific Telesis Group
Packaging Corporation of America
Packard Foundation, David and Lucile
PaineWebber
Paley Foundation, William S.
Palmer Fund, Frank Loomis
Pamida, Inc.
Panhandle Eastern Corporation
Park Foundation
Parker Hannifin Corp.
Parshelsky Foundation, Moses L.
Parsons Foundation, Ralph M.
Payne Foundation, Frank E. and Seba B.
Peabody Charitable Fund, Amelia
Pella Corporation
Penn Foundation, William
Pennzoil Co.
Peoples Energy Corp.
Peppers Foundation, Ann
Perkin-Elmer Corp.
Petrie Trust, Lorene M.
Petteys Memorial Foundation, Jack
Pew Charitable Trusts
Pfizer, Inc.
Pforzheimer Foundation, Carl and Lily
Phelps Dodge Corporation
PHH Corporation
Philbosian Foundation, Stephen
Phillips Charitable Trust, Dr. and Mrs. Arthur William
Phillips Family Foundation, Jay and Rose
Phillips Foundation, Ellis L.
Phipps Foundation, Howard
Piankova Foundation, Tatiana
Pick, Jr. Fund, Albert
Pickford Foundation, Mary
Pierce Charitable Trust, Harold Whitworth
Pineywoods Foundation
Pioneer Trust Bank, NA
Piper Foundation, Minnie Stevens
Piper Jaffray Companies Inc.
Pitt-Des Moines Inc.
Pittsburg Midway Coal Mining Co.
Plumsock Fund
PNC Bank, N.A.
Polaroid Corp.
Porter Foundation, Mrs. Cheever
Porter Testamentary Trust, James Hyde
Potomac Electric Power Co.
Pott Foundation, Herman T. and Phenie R.
Potter Foundation, Justin and Valere
Potts and Sibley Foundation
PPG Industries, Inc.
Premier Industrial Corp.
Price Associates, T. Rowe
Priddy Foundation
PriMerit Bank
Prince Trust, Abbie Norman
Prospect Hill Foundation
Prouty Foundation, Olive Higgins
Providence Gas Co.
Providence Journal Company
Provident Life & Accident Insurance Company of America
Providian Corporation
Prudential Insurance Co. of America, The
Prudential Securities, Inc.
Public Service Co. of New Mexico
Public Service Electric & Gas Co.
Pulitzer Publishing Co.
Putnam Foundation
Quaker Chemical Corp.

Rabb Charitable Foundation, Sidney and Esther
Rabb Foundation, Harry W.
Ralston Purina Co.
Reed Foundation
Regenstein Foundation
Reicher Foundation, Anne and Harry J.
Reichhold Chemicals, Inc.
Reinberger Foundation
Reisman Charitable Trust, George C. and Evelyn R.
Rennebohm Foundation, Oscar
Republic NY Corp.
Reynolds Foundation, Donald W.
Reynolds Foundation, Edgar
Rhone-Poulenc Inc.
Rice Charitable Foundation, Albert W.
Rice Foundation
Rich Products Corporation
Richardson Benevolent Foundation, C. E.
Richardson Charitable Trust, Anne S.
Rieke Corp.
Riggs Benevolent Fund
Ringier-America
Ritter Charitable Trust, George W. and Mary F.
RJR Nabisco Inc.
Robinson-Broadhurst Foundation
Robinson Fund, Maurice R.
Rockefeller Fund, David
Rockwell Fund
Rockwell International Corporation
Rogers Family Foundation
Rohatyn Foundation, Felix and Elizabeth
Rohm & Haas Co.
Rose Foundation, Billy
Rosen Foundation, Joseph
Rosenberg, Jr. Family Foundation, Louise and Claude
Ross Laboratories
Ross Memorial Foundation, Will
Rouse Co.
Rowland Foundation
Royal Group, Inc.
Rubin Foundation, Samuel
Rubinstein Foundation, Helena
Rudin Foundation
Russell Trust, Josephine G.
Ryan Foundation, David Claude
SAFECO Corp.
Safety Fund National Bank
Saint Paul Companies, Inc.
Salomon Foundation, Richard and Edna
Salomon Inc.
Saltonstall Charitable Foundation, Richard
San Diego Gas & Electric
Sandusky International Inc.
Santa Fe Pacific Corporation
Sara Lee Corp.
Sara Lee Hosiery, Inc.
Sargent Foundation, Newell B.
Sarkeys Foundation
Sawyer Charitable Foundation
SBC Communications Inc.
Schenck Fund, L. P.
Scherer Foundation, Karla
Schering-Plough Corp.
Scherman Foundation
Schiff Foundation, Dorothy
Schlumberger Ltd.
Schoenleber Foundation
Scholl Foundation, Dr.
Schroeder Foundation, Walter
Schuller International
Schwab & Co., Inc., Charles
Schwartz Fund for Education and Health Research, Arnold and Marie
Schwob Foundation, Simon
Scott Foundation, Virginia Steele
Scott Foundation, William E.

Scurlock Foundation
Seafirst Corporation
Seagram & Sons, Inc., Joseph E.
Seaver Charitable Trust, Richard C.
Seaver Institute
Seaway Food Town, Inc.
Second Foundation
Security Life of Denver Insurance Co.
Sedgwick James Inc.
Seidman Family Foundation
Selby and Marie Selby Foundation, William G.
Self Foundation
Semmes Foundation
Seneca Foods Corp.
Sequoia Foundation
Share Trust, Charles Morton
Shaw Foundation, Arch W.
Shawmut National Corp.
Sheaffer Inc.
Sheary for Charity, Edna M.
Shell Oil Company
Shenandoah Life Insurance Co.
Sheppard Foundation, Lawrence B.
Shott, Jr. Foundation, Hugh I.
Sierra Pacific Industries
Sierra Pacific Resources
Siltec Corp.
Simon Foundation, William E. and Carol G.
Simpson Investment Company
Skaggs Foundation, L. J. and Mary C.
Slemp Foundation
Slifka Foundation, Joseph and Sylvia
Sloan Foundation, Alfred P.
Smart Family Foundation
Smeal Foundation, Mary Jean and Frank P.
Smith Charitable Foundation, Clara Blackford Smith and W. Aubrey
Smith Corp., A.O.
Smith Foundation, Kelvin and Eleanor
Smith, Jr. Foundation, M. W.
SmithKline Beecham Corp.
Snow Foundation, John Ben
Snow Memorial Trust, John Ben
Solow Foundation
Sonat Inc.
Sordoni Foundation
South Bend Tribune
South Waite Foundation
Southern California Edison Co.
Specialty Manufacturing Co.
Speyer Foundation, Alexander C. and Tillie S.
Sprague Educational and Charitable Foundation, Seth
SPX Corp.
Square D Co.
Stanley Charitable Foundation, A.W.
Stanley Works
Stans Foundation
Starr Foundation
Stauffer Foundation, John and Beverly
Steele Foundation, Harry and Grace
Stein Foundation, Jules and Doris
Steinbach Fund, Ruth and Milton
Steinhagen Benevolent Trust, B. A. and Elinor
Steinman Foundation, James Hale
Steinman Foundation, John Frederick
Stevens Foundation, Abbot and Dorothy H.
Stokely, Jr. Foundation, William B.
Stone Charitable Foundation
Stone Trust, H. Chase

Strawbridge Foundation of Pennsylvania II, Margaret Dorrance
Stupp Foundation, Norman J.
Sturgis Charitable and Educational Trust, Roy and Christine
Sulzberger Foundation
Sumitomo Bank of California
Sundet Foundation
Swalm Foundation
Swift Co. Inc., John S.
Swiss Bank Corp.
Tait Foundation, Frank M.
Taube Family Foundation
Taylor Foundation, Fred and Harriett
Taylor Foundation, Ruth and Vernon
Tecumseh Products Co.
Teichert & Son, A.
Teleflex Inc.
Temple Foundation, T. L. L.
Temple-Inland Inc.
Tenneco Inc.
Tetley, Inc.
Texaco Inc.
Texas Commerce Bank-Houston, N.A.
Textron, Inc.
Thalhimer and Family Foundation, Charles G.
Thermo Electron Corp.
Thomas Industries
Thomasville Furniture Industries
Thompson Co., J. Walter
Thorne Foundation
Thornton Foundation
Thornton Foundation, Flora L.
Times Mirror Company, The
Timken Foundation of Canton
Tiscornia Foundation
Titus Foundation, Roy and Niuta
Tobin Foundation
Toms Foundation
Towsley Foundation, Harry A. and Margaret D.
TransAmerica Corporation
Transco Energy Co.
Travelers Inc.
Trexler Trust, Harry C.
Truland Foundation
Trull Foundation
Trust Company Bank
Trust Funds
Tuch Foundation, Michael
Tucker Charitable Trust, Rose E.
Turner Charitable Foundation
Unilever United States, Inc.
Union Bank
Union Camp Corporation
Union Electric Co.
Union Pacific Corp.
United Airlines, Inc.
U.S. Bank of Washington
Unitrode Corp.
Unocal Corp.
Upton Foundation, Frederick S.
US WEST, Inc.
USG Corporation
USL Capital Corporation
USX Corporation
Utica National Insurance Group
Valmont Industries, Inc.
van Ameringen Foundation
Van Every Foundation, Philip L.
Van Nuys Foundation, I. N. and Susanna H.
Van Wert County Foundation
Vance Charitable Foundation, Robert C.
Vanderbilt Trust, R. T.
Vaughn, Jr. Foundation Fund, James M.
Virginia Power Co.
Vogler Foundation, Laura B.
Vulcan Materials Co.
Wachovia Bank of North Carolina, N.A.
Wahlstrom Foundation

Wal-Mart Stores, Inc.
Wallace Foundation, George R.
Wallace-Reader's Digest Fund, Lila
Walsh Foundation
Warner Fund, Albert and Bessie
Warwick Foundation
Washington Water Power Co.
Waters Charitable Trust, Robert S.
Wean Foundation, Raymond John
Webber Oil Co.
Wege Foundation
Weil, Gotshal and Manges Foundation
Weingart Foundation
Weinstein Foundation, J.
Welch Testamentary Trust, George T.
Welfare Foundation
Wells Foundation, Franklin H. and Ruth L.
Wendt Foundation, Margaret L.
West Foundation, Harry and Ethel
West One Bancorp
WestLB New York Branch
Westvaco Corporation
Weyerhaeuser Co.
Wheat First Butcher Singer, Inc.
Wheeler Foundation
Wheeler Foundation, Wilmot
Whitehead Charitable Foundation
Whiting Foundation
Whittenberger Foundation, Claude R. and Ethel B.
Wickes Foundation, Harvey Randall
Wickson-Link Memorial Foundation
WICOR, Inc.
Widgeon Foundation
Wiegand Foundation, E. L.
Wilder Foundation
Wiley & Sons, Inc., John
Willard Helping Fund, Cecilia Young
Williams Companies, The
Wilmington Trust Co.
Wilson Foundation, H. W.
Wilson Fund, Matilda R.
Windham Foundation
Winnebago Industries, Inc.
Winston Foundation, Norman and Rosita
Winter Construction Co.
Winthrop Trust, Clara B.
Wiremold Co.
Wisconsin Public Service Corp.
Witco Corp.
Witter Foundation, Dean
Wood Foundation of Chambersburg, PA
Woodward Fund
Woolley Foundation, Vasser
Wright Foundation, Lola
Wyman Youth Trust
Wyomissing Foundation
Y and H Soda Foundation
Yeager Charitable Trust, Lester E.
Young Foundation, Robert R.
Zachry Co., H.B.
Zarrow Foundation, Anne and Henry
Zenkel Foundation
Zollner Foundation

Music

Abbott Laboratories
Abell-Hanger Foundation
Achelis Foundation
Acme-McCrary Corp./Sapona Manufacturing Co.
Acushnet Co.
Adams Foundation, Arthur F. and Alice E.

Adler Foundation Trust, Philip D. and Henrietta B.
AEGON USA Inc.
Ahmanson Foundation
Air France
Air Products and Chemicals, Inc.
AKC Fund
Akzo America
Akzo Chemicals Inc.
Alabama Gas Corp.
Alabama Power Co.
Albertson's Inc.
Alcon Laboratories, Inc.
Aldus Corp.
Allegheny Foundation
Allegheny Ludlum Corp.
Allendale Insurance Co.
Allianz Life Insurance Co. of North America
AlliedSignal Inc.
Allyn Foundation
Altschul Foundation
Alumax Inc.
Aluminum Co. of America
Amado Foundation, Maurice
AMCORE Bank, N.A. Rockford
American Brands, Inc.
American Fidelity Corporation
American General Finance Corp.
American National Bank & Trust Co. of Chicago
American Natural Resources Company
American President Companies, Ltd.
American United Life Insurance Co.
Ameritas Life Insurance Corp.
Ames Charitable Trust, Harriett
AMETEK, Inc.
Amfac/JMB Hawaii Inc.
AMP Incorporated
AMR Corp.
Andersen Corp.
Andersen Foundation
Anderson Foundation
Anderson Foundation, M. D.
Andersons, The
Andreas Foundation
Andrews Foundation
Anheuser-Busch Companies, Inc.
Annenberg Foundation
Ansin Private Foundation, Ronald M.
Ansley Foundation, Dantzler Bond
AON Corporation
Apple Computer, Inc.
Appleby Trust, Scott B. and Annie P.
Appleton Papers Inc.
Arcadia Foundation
Archer-Daniels-Midland Co.
Argyros Foundation
Aristech Chemical Corp.
Arkansas Power & Light Co.
Arkelian Foundation, Ben H. and Gladys
Armco Inc.
Arnhold Foundation
Arnold Fund
Asplundh Foundation
AT&T Corp.
Atherton Family Foundation
Audubon State Bank
Auerbach Foundation, Beatrice Fox
Avery Arts Foundation, Milton and Sally
Avon Products, Inc.
Ayres Foundation, Inc.
Babcock & Wilcox Co.
Babson Foundation, Paul and Edith
Badgeley Residuary Charitable Trust, Rose M.
Baker Foundation, Dexter F. and Dorothy H.
Baker Trust, George F.
Baldwin Memorial Foundation, Fred

Ball Foundation, George and Frances
Banc One Wisconsin Corp.
Bank of Boston Corp.
Bank of New York Company, Inc.
Bank One, Youngstown, NA
BankAmerica Corp.
Banta Corp.
Barker Foundation, J.M.R.
Barry Corp., R. G.
Barth Foundation, Theodore H.
Battelle Memorial Institute
Batts Foundation
Bauervic Foundation, Charles M.
Beal Foundation
Bean Foundation, Norwin S. and Elizabeth N.
Beattie Foundation Trust, Cordelia Lee
Beatty Trust, Cordelia Lunceford
Bechtel, Jr. Foundation, S. D.
Beech Aircraft Corp.
Bell Atlantic Corp.
Bell Foundation, James F.
Beloit Foundation
Bemis Company, Inc.
Benedum Foundation, Claude Worthington
Benwood Foundation
Berger Foundation, H. N. and Frances C.
Bertha Foundation
Berwind Corporation
Bethlehem Steel Corp.
Bettingen Corporation, Burton G.
Betts Industries
Beveridge Foundation, Frank Stanley
Bigelow Foundation, F. R.
Binney & Smith Inc.
Binswanger Cos.
Bishop Foundation, E. K. and Lillian F.
Bissell Foundation, J. Walton
Blake Foundation, S. P.
Blandin Foundation
Blaustein Foundation, Louis and Henrietta
Block, H&R
Bloedorn Foundation, Walter A.
Blount, Inc.
Blue Bell, Inc.
Blum Foundation, Edna F.
Blum-Kovler Foundation
Boatmen's Bancshares, Inc.
Bobst Foundation, Elmer and Mamdouha
Bodman Foundation
Boeing Co., The
Boettcher Foundation
Boise Cascade Corporation
Booth Ferris Foundation
Borden, Inc.
Borman's Inc.
Boston Edison Co.
Boswell Foundation, James G.
Bothin Foundation
Boutell Memorial Fund
Bowater Incorporated
Bowen Foundation, Ethel N.
BP America Inc.
Brach Foundation, Helen
Brackenridge Foundation, George W.
Brady Foundation
Bremer Foundation, Otto
Brenner Foundation, Mervyn
Breyer Foundation
Bridgestone/Firestone, Inc.
Bridwell Foundation, J. S.
Brillion Iron Works
Bristol-Myers Squibb Company
Brown Foundation, M. K.
Brunswick Corp.
Bryn Mawr Trust Co.
Bucyrus-Erie Company
Buhl Foundation
Bunbury Company

Burchfield Foundation, Charles E.
Burdines Inc.
Burnett-Tandy Foundation
Bush Foundation
Butz Foundation
Cabell Foundation, Robert G. Cabell III and Maude Morgan
Cable & Wireless Holdings, Inc.
Cabot Corp.
Cabot Family Charitable Trust
Cafritz Foundation, Morris and Gwendolyn
Cain Foundation, Gordon and Mary
Calhoun Charitable Trust, Kenneth
Callaway Foundation
Campbell Foundation
Campini Foundation, Frank A.
Cargill Inc.
Carolyn Foundation
Carpenter Foundation
Carpenter Foundation, E. Rhodes and Leona B.
Carpenter Technology Corp.
Carter Foundation, Amon G.
Carter Foundation, Beirne
Cassett Foundation, Louis N.
Castle Foundation, Harold K. L.
CBI Industries, Inc.
Centerior Energy Corp.
Central Fidelity Banks, Inc.
Central Maine Power Co.
Central Vermont Public Service Corp.
Chadwick Fund, Dorothy Jordan
Charina Foundation
Chartwell Foundation
Chase Manhattan Bank, N.A.
Chastain Charitable Foundation, Robert Lee and Thomas M.
Chazen Foundation
Cheatham Foundation, Owen
Cheney Foundation, Ben B.
Chesapeake Corp.
Chesebrough-Pond's USA Co.
Chevron Corporation
Chicago Sun-Times, Inc.
Christensen Charitable and Religious Foundation, L. C.
Christian Dior New York, Inc.
Christy-Houston Foundation
Chrysler Corp.
Church & Dwight Co., Inc.
CIGNA Corporation
CINergy
Citibank
CLARCOR Inc.
Clark Foundation
Clarke Trust, John
Clarkson Foundation, Jeniam
Clay Foundation
Clorox Co.
Clowes Fund
CNA Financial Corporation/CNA Insurance Companies
Coen Family Foundation, Charles S. and Mary
Cogswell Benevolent Trust
Cole Foundation, Olive B.
Cole Trust, Quincy
Coleman Foundation, George E.
Collins Foundation
Colonial Life & Accident Insurance Co.
Columbia Foundation
Columbus Dispatch Printing Co.
Comer Foundation
Comerica Incorporated
Commerce Bancshares, Inc.
Commerce Clearing House, Incorporated
Connelly Foundation
Consolidated Natural Gas Co.
Consolidated Papers, Inc.
Consumers Power Co.

Continental Corp.
Contran Corporation
Cooke Foundation
Cooper Industries, Inc.
Coors Foundation, Adolph
Copley Press, Inc.
Cord Foundation, E. L.
Cornell Trust, Peter C.
Corning Incorporated
Cosmair, Inc.
Coughlin-Saunders Foundation
Cowles Charitable Trust
Cowles Foundation, Gardner and Florence Call
Cowles Media Co.
CPC International Inc.
CR Industries
Crandall Memorial Foundation, J. Ford
Crane Co.
Crawford Estate, E. R.
Crestlea Foundation
Crown Books
Crown Memorial, Arie and Ida Crystal Trust
CS First Boston Corporation
Cullen Foundation
Culpeper Foundation, Charles E.
Culpeper Memorial Foundation, Daphne Seybolt
Culver Foundation, Constans
Cummings Foundation, James H.
Cummins Engine Co.
Cuneo Foundation
Curtice-Burns Foods, Inc.
Daily News
Dalton Foundation, Harry L.
Dana Charitable Trust, Eleanor Naylor
Dana Foundation, Charles A.
Daniel Foundation of Alabama
Davenport-Hatch Foundation
Davidson Family Charitable Foundation
Davis Foundation, Edwin W. and Catherine M.
Davis Foundation, James A. and Juliet L.
Day Foundation, Nancy Sayles
Daywood Foundation
Deere & Co.
Delavan Foundation, Nelson B.
Delaware North Co., Inc.
Demoulas Supermarkets Inc.
DeRoy Foundation, Helen L.
DeRoy Testamentary Foundation
Detroit Edison Co.
Deuble Foundation, George H.
DeVore Foundation
Dewing Foundation, Frances R.
Dexter Charitable Fund, Eugene A.
Dexter Corporation
Diamond Foundation, Aaron
Dillon Dunwalke Trust, Clarence and Anne
Dillon Foundation
Dimeo Construction Co.
Dingman Foundation, Michael D.
Dr. Seuss Foundation
Dodge Foundation, Geraldine R.
Donaldson Company, Inc.
Douglas & Lomason Company
Dow Corning Corp.
Dow Jones & Company, Inc.
Dresser Industries, Inc.
Dreyfus Foundation, Jean and Louis
Dreyfus Foundation, Max and Victoria
du Pont de Nemours & Co., E. I.
Duchossois Industries Inc.
Duke Power Co.
Dula Educational and Charitable Foundation, Caleb C. and Julia W.
Duncan Foundation, Lillian H. and C. W.
Duncan Trust, John G.

duPont Foundation, Alfred I.
Dynamet, Inc.
Early Foundation
Eastman Kodak Company
Eaton Corporation
Eaton Foundation, Cyrus
Eberly Foundation
Eddy Family Memorial Fund, C. K.
Eden Hall Foundation
Edgewater Steel Corp.
Edmonds Foundation, Dean S.
El Pomar Foundation
Elf Atochem North America, Inc.
Emerson Foundation, Inc., Fred L.
Encyclopaedia Britannica, Inc.
Enron Corp.
Ensign-Bickford Industries
Erpf Fund, Armand G.
Ethyl Corp
Ettinger Foundation
Everett Charitable Trust
Exxon Corporation
Fair Oaks Foundation, Inc.
Fair Play Foundation
Farish Fund, William Stamps
Farr Trust, Frank M. and Alice M.
Favrot Fund
Federal-Mogul Corporation
Federated Mutual Insurance Co.
Feild Co-Operative Association
Femino Foundation
Fenton Foundation
Fieldcrest Cannon Inc.
Fikes Foundation, Leland
Fink Foundation
Fireman's Fund Insurance Co.
Firestone, Jr. Foundation, Harvey
Firman Fund
First Chicago Corp.
First Fidelity Bank
First Financial Bank FSB
First Hawaiian, Inc.
First Interstate Bank of Oregon
First Source Corp.
First Tennessee Bank
First Union Corp.
Firstar Bank Milwaukee, N.A.
Fischbach Foundation
Fish Foundation, Ray C.
Fishback Foundation Trust, Harmes C.
Fleet Financial Group, Inc.
Fleishhacker Foundation
Fletcher Foundation
Flowers Charitable Trust, Albert W. and Edith V.
Folger Fund
Fondren Foundation
Forbes Inc.
Ford Foundation
Ford Fund, William and Martha
Ford Motor Co.
Forest Foundation
Forest Oil Corp.
Foster Charitable Trust
Foster Foundation
France Foundation, Jacob and Annita
Frear Eleemosynary Trust, Mary D. and Walter F.
Freedom Forge Corp.
Freeman Charitable Trust, Samuel
Freeport-McMoRan Inc.
Frese Foundation, Arnold D.
Fribourg Foundation
Friedman Family Foundation
Friendship Fund
Frisch's Restaurants Inc.
Frohring Foundation, William O. and Gertrude Lewis
Frost National Bank
Fruehauf Foundation
Fry Foundation, Lloyd A.
Fuller Foundation
Fuqua Foundation, J. B.
Gannett Publishing Co., Guy
Gap, Inc., The
GAR Foundation

Gates Foundation
GATX Corp.
Gazette Co.
Gebbie Foundation
Gellert Foundation, Carl
General American Life Insurance Co.
General Mills, Inc.
General Motors Corp.
GenRad
Georgia-Pacific Corporation
Georgia Power Co.
Germeshausen Foundation, Kenneth J.
Gershman Foundation, Joel
Ghidotti Foundation
Giant Eagle, Inc.
Giant Food Inc.
Gillette Co.
Gilman Foundation, Howard
Gilmore Foundation, William G.
Glaser Foundation
Gleason Foundation
Glencoe Foundation
Glick Foundation, Eugene and Marilyn
Globe Newspaper Co.
Glosser Foundation, David A.
Goldberg Family Foundation
Golden West Foundation
Goldie-Anna Charitable Trust
Goldsmith Foundation, Horace W.
Goodman & Co.
Goodrich Co., The B.F.
Gordon/Rousmaniere/Roberts Fund
Gould Electronics Inc.
Gould Foundation, The Florence
Graham Fund, Philip L.
Great-West Life Assurance Co.
Greenwall Foundation
Gregg-Graniteville Foundation
Greve Foundation, William and Mary
Griffis Foundation
Griffith Foundation, W. C.
Griggs and Mary Griggs Burke Foundation, Mary Livingston
Groome Beatty Trust, Helen D.
Grundy Foundation
Guaranty Bank & Trust Co.
Guardian Life Insurance Company of America
Guttman Foundation, Stella and Charles
Haas, Jr. Fund, Evelyn and Walter
Habig Foundation, Arnold F.
Hachar Charitable Trust, D. D.
Hafif Family Foundation
Haley Foundation, W. B.
Halff Foundation, G. A. C.
Hallberg Foundation, E. L. and R. F.
Halsell Foundation, Ewing
Hamilton Bank
Hamman Foundation, George and Mary Josephine
Hammer Foundation, Armand
Hancock Foundation, Luke B.
Hanes Foundation, John W. and Anna H.
Hanover Foundation
Harcourt Foundation, Ellen Knowles
Harcourt General, Inc.
Harmon Foundation, Pearl M. and Julia J.
Harriman Foundation, Mary W.
Harrington Foundation, Francis A. and Jacquelyn H.
Harsco Corp.
Hartmarx Corporation
Harvey Foundation, Felix
Hasbro Inc.
Hauser Foundation
Hawkins Foundation, Robert Z.
Hawn Foundation
Hazen Foundation, Edward W.
HCA Foundation
Hearst Foundation, William Randolph

Hechinger Co.
Hecht-Levi Foundation
Heckscher Foundation for Children
Heinz Company, H. J.
Heinz Endowment, Howard
Heinz Endowment, Vira I.
Heinz Trust, Drue
Heller Charitable Foundation, Clarence E.
Heller Financial, Inc.
Helms Foundation
Henkel Corp.
Hermann Foundation, Grover
Herrick Foundation
Hershey Foundation, Barry J.
Hewlett Foundation, William and Flora
Hewlett-Packard Co.
Hickory Tech Corp.
Higginson Trust, Corina
High Foundation
Hill Foundation, Sandy
Hillman Family Foundation, Alex
Hillsdale Fund
Hoag Family Foundation, George
Hobby Foundation
Hoffman Foundation, Maximilian E. and Marion O.
Holnam
Holzer Memorial Foundation, Richard H.
Homeland Foundation
Hook Drugs
Hoover Foundation
Hopedale Foundation
Hopkins Foundation, Josephine Lawrence
Hopwood Charitable Trust, John M.
Housatonic Curtain Co.
Houston Endowment
Houston Industries Incorporated
Howard and Bush Foundation
Howe and Mitchell B. Howe Foundation, Lucille Horton
Howell Foundation of Florida
Hoyt Foundation, Stewart W. and Willma C.
Hudson-Webber Foundation
Hugoton Foundation
Hulbert Foundation, Nila B.
Hulme Charitable Foundation, Milton G.
Hultquist Foundation
Humana, Inc.
Humphrey Fund, George M. and Pamela S.
Hunt Foundation
Hunt Foundation, Roy A.
Hunt Foundation, Samuel P.
Huston Charitable Trust, Stewart
Huston Foundation
Huthsteiner Fine Arts Trust
Hyde and Watson Foundation
Hygeia Dairy Co.
Icahn Foundation, Carl C.
ICI Americas Inc.
IES Industries, Inc.
Illinois Consolidated Telephone Co.
Illinois Tool Works, Inc.
Imperial Bancorp
Independence Foundation
Ingalls Foundation, Louise H. and David S.
Inland Container Corp.
Integra Bank of Uniontown
Interkal, Inc.
International Business Machines Corp.
International Paper Co.
Iowa-Illinois Gas & Electric Co.
Irvine Foundation, James
Irwin Charity Foundation, William G.
ITT Hartford Insurance Group, Inc.
Jackson Foundation

Jacobson Foundation, Bernard H. and Blanche E.
Jaffe Foundation
Jameson Foundation, J. W. and Ida M.
Janesville Foundation
Janirve Foundation
Jarson-Stanley and Mickey Kaplan Foundation, Isaac and Esther
Jaydor Corp.
Jewett Foundation, George Frederick
JFM Foundation
Jockey Hollow Foundation
John Hancock Mutual Life Insurance Co.
Johnson Controls Inc.
Johnson Foundation, Helen K. and Arthur E.
Johnson Fund, Edward C.
Johnson & Higgins
Johnson & Son, S.C.
Jones Foundation, Daisy Marquis
Jones Foundation, Fletcher
Jones Foundation, Helen
Jonsson Foundation
Jordan Charitable Foundation, Mary Ranken Jordan and Ettie A.
Jostens, Inc.
Journal-Gazette Co.
Joy Family Foundation
Julia R. and Estelle L. Foundation
Jurzykowski Foundation, Alfred
Kansas City Southern Industries
Kardon Foundation, Samuel and Rebecca
Kavanagh Foundation, T. James
Kayser Foundation
Kelley and Elza Kelley Foundation, Edward Bangs
Kemper Foundation, William T.
Kemper National Insurance Cos.
Kempner Fund, Harris and Eliza
Kennecott Corporation
Kettering Fund
Kiewit Foundation, Peter
Kilcawley Fund, William H.
Kimberly-Clark Corp.
Kingsbury Corp.
Kinney-Lindstrom Foundation
Kiplinger Foundation
Kirbo Charitable Trust, Thomas M. and Irene B.
Kirkpatrick Foundation
Kline Foundation, Josiah W. and Bessie H.
Klipstein Foundation, Ernest Christian
Klock and Lucia Klock Kingston Foundation, Jay E.
Klosk Fund, Louis and Rose
Kmart Corporation
KN Energy, Inc.
Knight Foundation, John S. and James L.
Knox, Sr., and Pearl Wallis Knox Charitable Foundation, Robert W.
Knudsen Foundation, Tom and Valley
Koehler Foundation, Marcia and Otto
Kohn-Joseloff Foundation
Komes Foundation
Koopman Fund
Kresge Foundation
Kuehn Foundation
La-Z-Boy Chair Co.
Ladd Charitable Corporation, Helen and George
Lang Foundation, Eugene M.
Larsen Fund
Lasdon Foundation
Lasdon Foundation, William and Mildred
Lauder Foundation

Laurel Foundation
Lazarus Charitable Trust, Helen and Charles
LBJ Family Foundation
Lea Foundation, Helen Sperry
Leavey Foundation, Thomas and Dorothy
Lebovitz Fund
Lederer Foundation, Francis L.
Lee Endowment Foundation
LEF Foundation
Lehigh Portland Cement Co.
Lehmann Foundation, Otto W.
Leidy Foundation, John J.
Leighton-Oare Foundation
Lemberg Foundation
Lenna Foundation, Reginald A. and Elizabeth S.
Leuthold Foundation
Levitt Foundation
Levy Foundation, June Rockwell
Life Insurance Co. of Georgia
Linnell Foundation
Lipton, Thomas J.
Littauer Foundation, Lucius N.
Little, Inc., Arthur D.
Liz Claiborne, Inc.
Loews Corporation
Long Island Lighting Co.
Longwood Foundation
Louisiana-Pacific Corp.
Love Foundation, George H. and Margaret McClintic
Lovett Foundation
Lund Foundation
Lurie Foundation, Louis R.
Lux Foundation, Miranda
Lydall, Inc.
Lyon Foundation
M/A-COM, Inc.
MacArthur Foundation, John D. and Catherine T.
MacCurdy Salisbury Educational Foundation
Macy & Co., Inc., R.H.
Maddox Foundation, J. F.
Madison Gas & Electric Co.
Magowan Family Foundation
Mahadh Foundation
Management Compensation Group/Dulworth Inc.
Mandeville Foundation
Maneely Fund
Marbrook Foundation
Mardigian Foundation
Maritz Inc.
Markey Charitable Fund, John C.
Marpat Foundation
Marquette Electronics, Inc.
Marriott Foundation, J. Willard
Mars Foundation
Marsh & McLennan Companies, Inc.
Martin Marietta Corp.
Martin Marietta Materials
Marx Foundation, Virginia and Leonard
Massachusetts Mutual Life Insurance Co.
Mather Charitable Trust, S. Livingston
Mather Fund, Richard
Mather and William Gwinn Mather Fund, Elizabeth Ring
Mathis-Pfohl Foundation
Mattel, Inc.
Matthies Foundation, Katharine
Mautz Paint Co.
May Department Stores Company, The
Mayer Foundation, James and Eva
Maytag Family Foundation, Fred
MCA Inc.
McCann Foundation
McCasland Foundation
McConnell Foundation
McCormick & Co. Inc.
McCormick Foundation, Chauncey and Marion Deering
McCormick Trust, Anne

McDermott Foundation, Eugene
McDonald & Company Securities, Inc.
McDonnell Douglas Corp.-West
McElroy Trust, R. J.
McEvoy Foundation, Mildred H.
McFawn Trust No. 2, Lois Sisler
McFeely-Rogers Foundation
McGonagle Foundation, Dextra Baldwin
MCI Communications Corp.
McInerny Foundation
McKenna Foundation, Katherine Mabis
McLean Contributionship
McMahan Foundation, Catherine L. and Robert O.
McMahon Foundation
M.E. Foundation
Mead Corporation, The
Meadows Foundation
Medtronic, Inc.
Mellon Family Foundation, R. K.
Mellon Foundation, Andrew W.
Mellon Foundation, Richard King
Memton Fund
Merck & Co.
Merck Family Fund
Merrill Lynch & Co., Inc.
Metropolitan Life Insurance Co.
Meyer Memorial Trust
Meyerhoff Fund, Joseph
Middendorf Foundation
Miller Brewing Company/North Carolina
Miller Charitable Foundation, Howard E. and Nell E.
Miller Fund, Kathryn and Gilbert
Miller-Mellor Association
Mine Safety Appliances Co.
Minnesota Mining & Mfg. Co.
Mitsubishi Motor Sales of America, Inc.
Mnuchin Foundation
Mobil Oil Corp.
Monadnock Paper Mills
Monell Foundation, Ambrose
Monfort Family Foundation
Montana Power Co.
Monticello College Foundation
Moore Foundation, Edward S.
Morgan & Company, J.P.
Morgan Construction Co.
Morgan Foundation, Burton D.
Morris Foundation, William T.
Morrison Knudsen Corporation
Moses Fund, Henry and Lucy
Mott Fund, Ruth
Mulford Foundation, Vincent
Mulford Trust, Clarence E.
Mullen Foundation, J. K.
Muller Foundation
Munger Foundation, Alfred C.
Munson Foundation Trust, W. B.
Murdock Charitable Trust, M. J.
Murphey Foundation, Lluella Morey
Murphy Co. Foundation, G.C.
Murphy Foundation
Musson Charitable Foundation, R. C. and Katharine M.
Mutual Assurance Co.
Myra Foundation
Nalco Chemical Co.
National Forge Co.
National Gypsum Co.
National Steel Corp.
National Westminster Bank New Jersey
NBD Indiana, Inc.
Nesholm Family Foundation
Nestle USA Inc.
Neuberger Foundation, Roy R. and Marie S.

New England Business Service
New-Land Foundation
New York Life Insurance Co.
New York Stock Exchange, Inc.
New York Times Company
The New Yorker Magazine, Inc.
NewMil Bancorp
Nias Foundation, Henry
Noble Foundation, Edward John
Norfolk Shipbuilding & Drydock Corp.
Norgren Foundation, Carl A.
Norman Foundation, Summers A.
North Shore Foundation
Northern States Power Co. (Minnesota)
Northwest Natural Gas Co.
Norton Co.
Norton Memorial Corporation, Geraldi
Norwest Bank Nebraska, N.A.
Norwest Corporation
Novell Inc.
Oaklawn Foundation
O'Connor Foundation, A. Lindsay and Olive B.
OCRI Foundation
Odell Fund, Robert Stewart Odell and Helen Pfeiffer
O'Fallon Trust, Martin J. and Mary Anne
Offield Family Foundation
OG&E Electric Services
Old National Bank in Evansville
Olin Corp.
Olin Foundation, Spencer T. and Ann W.
Oliver Memorial Trust Foundation
Oppenstein Brothers Foundation
Ore-Ida Foods, Inc.
Osborn Charitable Trust, Edward B.
Osher Foundation, Bernard
Ottley Trust-Watertown, Marion W.
Overbrook Foundation
Overlake Foundation
Owen Industries, Inc.
Owsley Foundation, Alvin and Lucy
Oxy USA Inc.
Pacific Mutual Life Insurance Co.
Pacific Telesis Group
Packard Foundation, David and Lucile
PaineWebber
Palisades Educational Foundation
Palmer Fund, Frank Loomis
Panhandle Eastern Corporation
Parker Hannifin Corp.
Parshelsky Foundation, Moses L.
Parsons Foundation, Ralph M.
Parvin Foundation, Albert
Patterson Charitable Fund, W. I.
Peabody Charitable Fund, Amelia
PECO Energy Company
Pella Corporation
Penn Foundation, William
Pennzoil Co.
Peppers Foundation, Ann
Peters Foundation, Charles F.
Pew Charitable Trusts
Pfizer, Inc.
Pforzheimer Foundation, Carl and Lily
Phelps Dodge Corporation
PHH Corporation
Philibosian Foundation, Stephen
Phillips Family Foundation, Jay and Rose
Phillips Foundation, Ellis L.
Phipps Foundation, Howard
Piankova Foundation, Tatiana
Pick, Jr. Fund, Albert

Pickford Foundation, Mary
Pierce Charitable Trust, Harold Whitworth
Piper Foundation, Minnie Stevens
Piper Jaffray Companies Inc.
Pittsburg Midway Coal Mining Co.
PNC Bank, N.A.
Polaroid Corp.
Pollock Company Foundation, William B.
Porter Testamentary Trust, James Hyde
Potomac Electric Power Co.
Potter Foundation, Justin and Valere
Potts and Sibley Foundation
PPG Industries, Inc.
Premier Industrial Corp.
Price Associates, T. Rowe
Priddy Foundation
Prince Trust, Abbie Norman
Proctor Trust, Mortimer R.
Prospect Hill Foundation
Prouty Foundation, Olive Higgins
Providence Gas Co.
Providence Journal Company
Provident Life & Accident Insurance Company of America
Providian Corporation
Prudential Insurance Co. of America, The
Prudential Securities, Inc.
Public Service Co. of New Mexico
Pulitzer Publishing Co.
Putnam Foundation
Quaker Chemical Corp.
Quivey-Bay State Foundation
Rabb Charitable Foundation, Sidney and Esther
Rabb Foundation, Harry W.
Ralston Purina Co.
Rand McNally & Co.
Ratner Foundation, Milton M.
Read Foundation, Charles L.
Reed Foundation
Regenstein Foundation
Reichhold Chemicals, Inc.
Reidler Foundation
Reinberger Foundation
Reisman Charitable Trust, George C. and Evelyn R.
Rennebohm Foundation, Oscar
Republic NY Corp.
Reynolds Foundation, Donald W.
Rhone-Poulenc Inc.
Rice Charitable Foundation, Albert W.
Rich Products Corporation
Richardson Charitable Trust, Anne S.
Riggs Benevolent Fund
RJR Nabisco Inc.
Robinson-Broadhurst Foundation
Robinson Fund, Maurice R.
Rockefeller Fund, David
Rockwell Fund
Rockwell International Corporation
Rogers Family Foundation
Rohatyn Foundation, Felix and Elizabeth
Rohm & Haas Co.
Rose Foundation, Billy
Roseburg Forest Products Co.
Rosenberg, Jr. Family Foundation, Louise and Claude
Ross Memorial Foundation, Will
Rouse Co.
Rowland Foundation
Royal Group, Inc.
Ruan Foundation Trust, John
Rubin Family Fund, Cele H. and William B.
Rubinstein Foundation, Helena
Rudin Foundation
Safety Fund National Bank

Saint Paul Companies, Inc.
Salomon Inc.
Saltonstall Charitable Foundation, Richard
San Diego Gas & Electric
Sandusky International Inc.
Santa Fe Pacific Corporation
Sara Lee Corp.
Sara Lee Hosiery, Inc.
Sargent Foundation, Newell B.
Sarkeys Foundation
Sasco Foundation
SBC Communications Inc.
Schenck Fund, L. P.
Scherer Foundation, Karla
Schering-Plough Corp.
Scherman Foundation
Schiro Fund
Schoenleber Foundation
Scholl Foundation, Dr.
Schowalter Foundation
Schroeder Foundation, Walter
Schwab & Co., Inc., Charles
Schwartz Fund for Education and Health Research, Arnold and Marie
Schwob Foundation, Simon
Scott Fetzer Co.
Scott Foundation, Virginia Steele
Scott Foundation, William E.
Seafirst Corporation
Seaver Charitable Trust, Richard C.
Seaver Institute
Security Life of Denver Insurance Co.
Sedgwick James Inc.
Seneca Foods Corp.
Sentry Insurance A Mutual Company
Seton Leather Co.
Share Trust, Charles Morton
Sharon Steel Corp.
Shawmut National Corp.
Sheaffer Inc.
Sheary for Charity, Edna M.
Shell Oil Company
Shenandoah Life Insurance Co.
Shubert Foundation
Sierra Pacific Industries
Sierra Pacific Resources
Siltec Corp.
Simon Foundation, William E. and Carol G.
Simpson Investment Company
Skaggs Foundation, L. J. and Mary C.
Skillman Foundation
Slemp Foundation
Slifka Foundation, Joseph and Sylvia
Smart Family Foundation
Smith Charitable Foundation, Lou and Lutza
Smith Corp., A.O.
Smith Foundation, Gordon V. and Helen C.
Smith Foundation, Kelvin and Eleanor
Smith Foundation, Ralph L.
Smith Memorial Fund, Ethel Sergeant Clark
Smith Trust, May and Stanley
SmithKline Beecham Corp.
Snayberger Memorial Foundation, Harry E. and Florence W.
Solow Foundation
Sonat Inc.
Sordoni Foundation
South Bend Tribune
South Branch Foundation
South Waite Foundation
Southern California Edison Co.
Southern New England Telephone Company
Spang & Co.
Specialty Manufacturing Co.
Sprague Educational and Charitable Foundation, Seth
SPX Corp.
Square D Co.
Stabler Foundation, Donald B. and Dorothy L.

Stackpole-Hall Foundation
Stanley Charitable Foundation, A.W.
Stanley Works
Stans Foundation
Starr Foundation
Stauffer Foundation, John and Beverly
Steele Foundation, Harry and Grace
Stein Foundation, Jules and Doris
Steinman Foundation, James Hale
Steinman Foundation, John Frederick
Stemmons Foundation
Sternberger Foundation, Tannenbaum
Stevens Foundation, Abbot and Dorothy H.
Stokely, Jr. Foundation, William B.
Stone Charitable Foundation
Stone Fund, H. Chase
Strauss Foundation, Leon
Strawbridge Foundation of Pennsylvania II, Margaret Dorrance
Stupp Foundation, Norman J.
Sturgis Charitable and Educational Trust, Roy and Christine
Subaru of America Inc.
Sulzberger Foundation
Sumitomo Bank of California
Sundet Foundation
Superior Tube Co.
Swanson Family Foundation, Dr. W.C.
Swiss Bank Corp.
Tait Foundation, Frank M.
Taube Family Foundation
Teichert & Son, A.
Teleflex Inc.
Temple Foundation, T. L. L.
Tenneco Inc.
Tetley, Inc.
Texaco Inc.
Texas Commerce Bank-Houston, N.A.
Textron, Inc.
Thalhimer and Family Foundation, Charles G.
Thermo Electron Corp.
Thomas Foundation, Joan and Lee
Thomas Industries
Thomasville Furniture Industries
Thompson Charitable Foundation
Thompson Co., J. Walter
Thompson Trust, Thomas
Thornton Foundation
Thornton Foundation, Flora L.
Times Mirror Company, The
Tiscornia Foundation
Tobin Foundation
Todd Co., A.M.
Towsley Foundation, Harry A. and Margaret D.
Tozer Foundation
TransAmerica Corporation
Transco Energy Co.
Travelers Inc.
Treakle Foundation, J. Edwin
Trexler Trust, Harry C.
Truland Foundation
Trull Foundation
Trust Company Bank
Trust Funds
Tuch Foundation, Michael
Tucker Charitable Trust, Rose E.
Tupancy-Harris Foundation of 1986
Turner Charitable Foundation
Turrell Fund
Unger Foundation, Aber D.
Unilever United States, Inc.
Union Bank
Union Camp Corporation
Union Electric Co.
Union Pacific Corp.

United Airlines, Inc.
U.S. Bank of Washington
Unitrode Corp.
Unocal Corp.
Upjohn Foundation, Harold and Grace
Upton Foundation, Frederick S.
Uris Brothers Foundation
US WEST, Inc.
USL Capital Corporation
USX Corporation
Valmont Industries, Inc.
Van Buren Foundation
Van Wert County Foundation
Vance Charitable Foundation, Robert C.
Vernon Fund, Miles Hodsdon
Vevay-Switzerland County Foundation
Virginia Power Co.
Vollbrecht Foundation, Frederick A.
Vulcan Materials Co.
Wahlstrom Foundation
Wal-Mart Stores, Inc.
Wallace Foundation, George R.
Wallace-Reader's Digest Fund, Lila
Walsh Foundation
Warren and Beatrice W. Blanding Foundation, Riley J. and Lillian N.
Warwick Foundation
Washington Forrest Foundation
Waters Charitable Trust, Robert S.
Wean Foundation, Raymond John
Webber Oil Co.
Weckbaugh Foundation, Eleanore Mullen
Wege Foundation
Wells Foundation, Franklin H. and Ruth L.
Wendt Foundation, Margaret L.
West Foundation, Harry and Ethel
West One Bancorp
Westerman Foundation, Samuel L.
Western New York Foundation
WestLB New York Branch
Weyerhaeuser Co.
Weyerhaeuser Memorial Foundation, Charles A.
Wheat First Butcher Singer, Inc.
Wheeler Foundation
Wheeler Foundation, Wilmot
Whirlpool Corporation
Whiting Foundation
Whiting Foundation, Macauley and Helen Dow
Whitney Fund, David M.
Whittenberger Foundation, Claude R. and Ethel B.
Wickes Foundation, Harvey Randall
Wickson-Link Memorial Foundation
WICOR, Inc.
Wiegand Foundation, E. L.
Wilder Foundation
Wildermuth Foundation, E. F.
Willard Helping Fund, Cecilia Young
Williams Charitable Trust, John C.
Williams Charitable Trust, Mary Jo
Williams Companies, The
Wilmington Trust Co.
Wilson Fund, Matilda R.
Winchester Foundation
Windham Foundation
Winston Foundation, Norman and Rosita
Winter Construction Co.
Winthrop Trust, Clara B.
Wiremold Co.
Wisconsin Power & Light Co.
Witco Corp.
Wood Foundation of Chambersburg, PA
Woodward Fund

Woolley Foundation, Vasser
Wright Foundation, Lola
Wyman Youth Trust
Wyomissing Foundation
Y and H Soda Foundation
Yeager Charitable Trust,
Lester E.
Young Foundation, Hugo H.
and Mabel B.
Young Foundation, Robert R.
Zachry Co., H.B.

Opera

Abbott Laboratories
Achelis Foundation
Adams Foundation, Arthur F.
and Alice E.
Air Products and Chemicals,
Inc.
Akzo America
Alabama Gas Corp.
Albertson's Inc.
Alcon Laboratories, Inc.
Allegheny Foundation
Allegheny Ludlum Corp.
AlliedSignal Inc.
Alumax Inc.
Aluminum Co. of America
American Brands, Inc.
American National Bank &
Trust Co. of Chicago
American Natural Resources
Company
American United Life
Insurance Co.
Amfac/JMB Hawaii Inc.
AMR Corp.
Andersen Foundation
Anderson Foundation
Anderson Foundation, M. D.
Andersons, The
Annenberg Foundation
AON Corporation
Archer-Daniels-Midland Co.
Argyros Foundation
Aristech Chemical Corp.
Arkansas Power & Light Co.
Arkelian Foundation, Ben H.
and Gladys
Armco Inc.
Arnhold Foundation
Astor Foundation, Vincent
AT&T Corp.
Atherton Family Foundation
Avon Products, Inc.
Babson Foundation, Paul and
Edith
Badgeley Residuary Charitable
Trust, Rose M.
Baker Foundation, Dexter F.
and Dorothy H.
Bank of New York Company,
Inc.
Bank One, Youngstown, NA
BankAmerica Corp.
Bankers Trust Company
Barry Corp., R. G.
Barth Foundation, Theodore H.
Battelle Memorial Institute
Batts Foundation
BE&K Inc.
Beattie Foundation Trust,
Cordelia Lee
Bechtel, Jr. Foundation, S. D.
Bedsole Foundation, J. L.
Bell Foundation, James F.
Bemis Company, Inc.
Benedum Foundation, Claude
Worthington
Benenson Foundation, Frances
and Benjamin
Benwood Foundation
Binney & Smith Inc.
Birnschein Foundation, Alvin
and Marion
Blair and Co., William
Blandin Foundation
Block, H&R
Blount, Inc.
Blue Cross & Blue Shield
United of Wisconsin
Blum-Kovler Foundation

Bobst Foundation, Elmer and
Mamdouha
Bodman Foundation
Boeing Co., The
Boettcher Foundation
Boise Cascade Corporation
Boothroyd Foundation,
Charles H. and Bertha L.
Borden, Inc.
BP America Inc.
Breyer Foundation
Bristol-Myers Squibb
Company
Broadhurst Foundation
Bryn Mawr Trust Co.
Bucyrus-Erie Company
Burdines Inc.
Burnett-Tandy Foundation
Bush Foundation
Cabot Corp.
Cafritz Foundation, Morris and
Gwendolyn
Campbell Foundation
Campbell Foundation, Ruth
and Henry
Campini Foundation, Frank A.
Cargill Inc.
Carpenter Foundation
Carpenter Foundation, E.
Rhodes and Leona B.
Carter Foundation, Beirne
CBI Industries, Inc.
Centerior Energy Corp.
Central National Bank
Chartwell Foundation
Chase Manhattan Bank, N.A.
Chastain Charitable
Foundation, Robert Lee and
Thomas M.
Chazen Foundation
Cheatham Foundation, Owen
Cheney Foundation, Ben B.
Chesebrough-Pond's USA Co.
Chevron Corporation
Chicago Sun-Times, Inc.
Christian Dior New York, Inc.
Chrysler Corp.
CIGNA Corporation
CINergy
Citibank
Clark Foundation
Clay Foundation
Clorox Co.
Clowes Fund
CNA Financial
Corporation/CNA Insurance
Companies
Cole Foundation, Olive B.
Collins Foundation
Colonial Life & Accident
Insurance Co.
Columbia Foundation
Columbus Dispatch Printing
Co.
Comerica Incorporated
Commerce Bancshares, Inc.
Commerce Clearing House,
Incorporated
Commonwealth Edison Co.
Connelly Foundation
Consolidated Natural Gas Co.
Consumers Power Co.
Cooke Foundation
Cooper Industries, Inc.
Copley Press, Inc.
Cord Foundation, E. L.
Cosmair, Inc.
Cowles Charitable Trust
Cowles Foundation, Gardner
and Florence Call
Cowles Media Co.
Crown Books
Crown Memorial, Arie and Ida
Crystal Trust
CS First Boston Corporation
Cullen Foundation
Culpeper Foundation, Charles
E.
Culver Foundation, Constans
Dana Charitable Trust, Eleanor
Naylor
Daniel Foundation of Alabama
Dart Group Corp.
Dater Foundation, Charles H.

Davis Foundation, Edwin W.
and Catherine M.
Day Foundation, Nancy Sayles
Deere & Co.
Delaware North Co., Inc.
Demoulas Supermarkets Inc.
DeRoy Testamentary
Foundation
Detroit Edison Co.
Dewing Foundation, Frances R.
Dexter Corporation
Diamond Foundation, Aaron
Dillon Foundation
Dimeo Construction Co.
Dr. Seuss Foundation
Dodge Foundation, Geraldine
R.
Donaldson Company, Inc.
Douglas & Lomason Company
Dresser Industries, Inc.
Dreyfus Foundation, Jean and
Louis
Dreyfus Foundation, Max and
Victoria
du Pont de Nemours & Co., E.
I.
Duchossois Industries Inc.
Duke Power Co.
Dula Educational and
Charitable Foundation,
Caleb C. and Julia W.
Dynamet, Inc.
Early Foundation
Eaton Corporation
Eaton Foundation, Cyrus
Eberly Foundation
Edgewater Steel Corp.
Edmonds Foundation, Dean S.
Einstein Fund, Albert E. and
Birdie W.
El Pomar Foundation
Elf Atochem North America,
Inc.
Encyclopaedia Britannica, Inc.
Enron Corp.
Erpf Fund, Armand G.
Ethyl Corp
Evans Foundation, T. M.
Exxon Corporation
Fair Oaks Foundation, Inc.
Federal-Mogul Corporation
Feild Co-Operative Association
Fireman's Fund Insurance Co.
Firman Fund
First Chicago Corp.
First Fidelity Bank
First Interstate Bank of Oregon
First Tennessee Bank
First Union Corp.
Firstar Bank Milwaukee, N.A.
Fischbach Foundation
Fishback Foundation Trust,
Harmes C.
Fleming Cos. Food
Distribution Center
Fohs Foundation
Folger Fund
Forbes Inc.
Ford Motor Co.
Forest Foundation
Forest Oil Corp.
Foster Charitable Trust
Foster Foundation
France Foundation, Jacob and
Annita
Frear Eleemosynary Trust,
Mary D. and Walter F.
Freeman Charitable Trust,
Samuel
Freeport-McMoRan Inc.
Fribourg Foundation
Friendship Fund
Frohring Foundation, Paul and
Maxine
Frohring Foundation, William
O. and Gertrude Lewis
Fry Foundation, Lloyd A.
Gamble Foundation
Gannett Publishing Co., Guy
GAR Foundation
Gates Foundation
GATX Corp.
Gebbie Foundation
General American Life
Insurance Co.

General Mills, Inc.
General Motors Corp.
Georgia-Pacific Corporation
Gheens Foundation
Giant Eagle, Inc.
Giant Food Inc.
Gilman Foundation, Howard
Gilmore Foundation, William
G.
Givenchy Corp.
Glick Foundation, Eugene and
Marilyn
Goldsmith Foundation, Horace
W.
Goodrich Co., The B.F.
Graham Fund, Philip L.
Grand Rapids Label Co.
Greenwall Foundation
Gregg-Graniteville Foundation
Griffith Foundation, W. C.
Griggs and Mary Griggs Burke
Foundation, Mary Livingston
GSM Industrial
Guardian Life Insurance
Company of America
Haas, Jr. Fund, Evelyn and
Walter
Haley Foundation, W. B.
Halsell Foundation, Ewing
Hamilton Bank
Harmon Foundation, Pearl M.
and Julia J.
Harsco Corp.
Hartmarx Corporation
Hauser Foundation
Hawn Foundation
HCA Foundation
Hearst Foundation, William
Randolph
Hechinger Co.
Hecht-Levi Foundation
Heckscher Foundation for
Children
Heinz Company, H. J.
Heinz Endowment, Howard
Heinz Endowment, Vira I.
Helmerich Foundation
Hewlett Foundation, William
and Flora
Heydt Fund, Nan and Matilda
Hillman Foundation
Hillsdale Fund
Hobby Foundation
Holzer Memorial Foundation,
Richard H.
Homeland Foundation
Hopwood Charitable Trust,
John M.
Housatonic Curtain Co.
Houston Endowment
Hoyt Foundation, Stewart W.
and Willma C.
Hudson-Webber Foundation
Hulme Charitable Foundation,
Milton G.
Humphrey Fund, George M.
and Pamela S.
Hunt Foundation
Hunt Foundation, Samuel P.
Hyde and Watson Foundation
Icahn Foundation, Carl C.
ICI Americas Inc.
Illinois Tool Works, Inc.
Independence Foundation
Integra Bank of Uniontown
International Business
Machines Corp.
International Paper Co.
Irvine Foundation, James
Irwin Charity Foundation,
William G.
ITT Hartford Insurance Group,
Inc.
Ittleson Foundation
Jackson Foundation
Jaffe Foundation
Jarson-Stanley and Mickey
Kaplan Foundation, Isaac
and Esther
Jennings Foundation, Mary
Hillman
JFM Foundation
John Hancock Mutual Life
Insurance Co.
Johnson Controls Inc.

Johnson Foundation, Helen K.
and Arthur E.
Johnson Foundation, Willard
T. C.
Johnson & Higgins
Jones Foundation, Fletcher
Jordan Charitable Foundation,
Mary Ranken Jordan and
Ettie A.
Jostens, Inc.
Justus Trust, Edith C.
Kansas City Southern
Industries
Kardon Foundation, Samuel
and Rebecca
Kavanagh Foundation, T.
James
Kelly Foundation, T. Lloyd
Kemper Foundation, William T.
Kemper National Insurance
Cos.
Kennecott Corporation
Kiewit Foundation, Peter
Kimberly-Clark Corp.
Kingsbury Corp.
Kirby Foundation, F. M.
Kirkpatrick Foundation
Kline Foundation, Josiah W.
and Bessie H.
Klipstein Foundation, Ernest
Christian
Klosk Fund, Louis and Rose
Kmart Corporation
Knight Foundation, John S.
and James L.
Knox, Sr., and Pearl Wallis
Knox Charitable
Foundation, Robert W.
Kohn-Joseloff Foundation
Kuyper Foundation, Peter H.
and E. Lucille
Lang Foundation, Eugene M.
Lasdon Foundation
Lasdon Foundation, William
and Mildred
Laurel Foundation
Lebovitz Fund
Lederer Foundation, Francis L.
Lehmann Foundation, Otto W.
Leidy Foundation, John J.
Leighton-Oare Foundation
Lemberg Foundation
Leuthold Foundation
Levitt Foundation
Liz Claiborne, Inc.
Long Island Lighting Co.
Lurcy Charitable and
Educational Trust, Georges
Lurie Foundation, Louis R.
Lydall, Inc.
MacArthur Foundation, John
D. and Catherine T.
Macy & Co., Inc., R.H.
Magoon Family Foundation
Mahadh Foundation
Mailman Foundation
Maneely Fund
Maritz Inc.
Markey Charitable Fund, John
C.
Marquette Electronics, Inc.
Mars Foundation
Marsh & McLennan
Companies, Inc.
Martin Marietta Corp.
Mascoma Savings Bank
Mather Charitable Trust, S.
Livingston
Mather Fund, Richard
Mather and William Gwinn
Mather Fund, Elizabeth Ring
Mathis-Pfohl Foundation
Mautz Paint Co.
Maytag Family Foundation,
Fred
McCormick Trust, Anne
McCune Charitable
Foundation, Marshall and
Perrine D.
McDermott Foundation,
Eugene
McDonald & Company
Securities, Inc.

McDonnell Douglas Corp.-West
McGonagle Foundation, Dextra Baldwin
McInerny Foundation
Meadows Foundation
Medtronic, Inc.
Mellon Foundation, Andrew W.
Mellon Foundation, Richard King
Metropolitan Life Insurance Co.
Meyer Memorial Trust
Middendorf Foundation
Miller Charitable Foundation, Howard E. and Nell E.
Miller Fund, Kathryn and Gilbert
Mine Safety Appliances Co.
Minnesota Mining & Mfg. Co.
Mitchell Energy & Development Corp.
Mnuchin Foundation
Mobil Oil Corp.
Monell Foundation, Ambrose
Moore Foundation, Edward S.
Morgan & Company, J.P.
Morris Foundation, Margaret T.
Morris Foundation, William T.
Moses Fund, Henry and Lucy
Mulcahy Foundation
Mulford Foundation, Vincent
Murdock Charitable Trust, M. J.
Mutual Assurance Co.
Nalco Chemical Co.
National Gypsum Co.
NBD Indiana, Inc.
Nesholm Family Foundation
New York Times Company
The New Yorker Magazine, Inc.
Nias Foundation, Henry
Noble Foundation, Edward John
Norfolk Shipbuilding & Drydock Corp.
Norgren Foundation, Carl A.
North Shore Foundation
Northern States Power Co. (Minnesota)
Northwest Natural Gas Co.
Norton Co.
Norton Memorial Corporation, Geraldi
Norwest Corporation
Novell Inc.
Oaklawn Foundation
Olin Corp.
Oppenstein Brothers Foundation
O'Quinn Foundation, John M. and Nancy C.
Osborn Charitable Trust, Edward B.
Osher Foundation, Bernard
Overbrook Foundation
Owsley Foundation, Alvin and Lucy
Oxy USA Inc.
Pacific Mutual Life Insurance Co.
Pacific Telesis Group
Packard Foundation, David and Lucile
Palmer Fund, Frank Loomis
Panhandle Eastern Corporation
Parker Hannifin Corp.
Patterson Charitable Fund, W. I.
PECO Energy Company
Pella Corporation
Penn Foundation, William
Pennzoil Co.
Peoples Energy Corp.
Pew Charitable Trusts
Pfizer, Inc.
Pforzheimer Foundation, Carl and Lily
Phelps Dodge Corporation
PHH Corporation
Philibosian Foundation, Stephen
Phillips Foundation, Ellis L.
Piankova Foundation, Tatiana
Pick, Jr. Fund, Albert

Piper Foundation, Minnie Stevens
Piper Jaffray Companies Inc.
Pitt-Des Moines Inc.
PNC Bank, N.A.
Polaroid Corp.
Porter Foundation, Mrs. Cheever
Porter Testamentary Trust, James Hyde
Potomac Electric Power Co.
Pott Foundation, Herman T. and Phenie R.
PPG Industries, Inc.
Prairie Foundation
Premier Industrial Corp.
Price Associates, T. Rowe
Prince Trust, Abbie Norman
Providence Gas Co.
Providian Corporation
Prudential Insurance Co. of America, The
Pulitzer Publishing Co.
Quaker Chemical Corp.
Rabb Foundation, Harry W.
Regenstein Foundation
Reinberger Foundation
Republic NY Corp.
Richardson Charitable Trust, Anne S.
Rockwell Fund
Rockwell International Corporation
Rohatyn Foundation, Felix and Elizabeth
Rohm & Haas Co.
Rose Foundation, Billy
Rosen Foundation, Joseph
Rosenberg, Jr. Family Foundation, Louise and Claude
Ross Laboratories
Ross Memorial Foundation, Will
Rouse Co.
Royal Group, Inc.
SAFECO Corp.
Salomon Inc.
San Diego Gas & Electric
Santa Fe Pacific Corporation
Sara Lee Corp.
Sarkeys Foundation
SBC Communications Inc.
Scherman Foundation
Schiro Fund
Schlumberger Ltd.
Scholl Foundation, Dr.
Schroeder Foundation, Walter
Schwab & Co., Inc., Charles
Schwartz Fund for Education and Health Research, Arnold and Marie
Schwob Foundation, Simon
Scott Foundation, William E.
Scurlock Foundation
Seafirst Corporation
Seaver Charitable Trust, Richard C.
Seaway Food Town, Inc.
Security Life of Denver Insurance Co.
Sedgwick James Inc.
Self Foundation
Sharon Steel Corp.
Shawmut National Corp.
Shell Oil Company
Shenandoah Life Insurance Co.
Shubert Foundation
Sierra Pacific Resources
Simpson Investment Company
Skaggs Foundation, L. J. and Mary C.
Skillman Foundation
Smart Family Foundation
Smith Foundation, Kelvin and Eleanor
SmithKline Beecham Corp.
Sonat Inc.
Southern California Edison Co.
Spang & Co.
Specialty Manufacturing Co.
Sprague Educational and Charitable Foundation, Seth
Square D Co.

Stanley Charitable Foundation, A.W.
Stanley Works
Starr Foundation
Stauffer Foundation, John and Beverly
Steele Foundation, Harry and Grace
Stein Foundation, Jules and Doris
Steinman Foundation, James Hale
Steinman Foundation, John Frederick
Stemmons Foundation
Stevens Foundation, Abbot and Dorothy H.
Stone Trust, H. Chase
Sulzberger Foundation
Superior Tube Co.
Swanson Family Foundation, Dr. W.C.
Tait Foundation, Frank M.
Taylor Foundation, Ruth and Vernon
Teichert & Son, A.
Teleflex Inc.
Temple Foundation, T. L. L.
Tenneco Inc.
Texaco Inc.
Texas Commerce Bank-Houston, N.A.
Textron, Inc.
Thompson Co., J. Walter
Thornton Foundation, Flora L.
Tobin Foundation
Toms Foundation
Tozer Foundation
TransAmerica Corporation
Transco Energy Co.
Travelers Inc.
Trexler Trust, Harry C.
Trull Foundation
Trust Company Bank
Trust Funds
Tuch Foundation, Michael
Tucker Charitable Trust, Rose E.
Turner Charitable Foundation
Union Bank
Union Pacific Corp.
United Airlines, Inc.
U.S. Bank of Washington
Unocal Corp.
Uris Brothers Foundation
US WEST, Inc.
USG Corporation
USL Capital Corporation
USX Corporation
Valentine Foundation, Lawson
Virginia Power Co.
Vulcan Materials Co.
Wachovia Bank of North Carolina, N.A.
Wallace-Reader's Digest Fund, Lila
Walsh Foundation
Warwick Foundation
Washington Forrest Foundation
Wean Foundation, Raymond John
Webber Oil Co.
Weckbaugh Foundation, Eleanore Mullen
Wells Foundation, Franklin H. and Ruth L.
Wendt Foundation, Margaret L.
West One Bancorp
Westerman Foundation, Samuel L.
Weyerhaeuser Co.
Wheeler Foundation
Wheeler Foundation, Wilmot
Whirlpool Corporation
Whitney Fund, David M.
WICOR, Inc.
Wilder Foundation
Wiley & Sons, Inc., John
Williams Companies, The
Wilmington Trust Co.
Wilson Fund, Matilda R.
Winston Foundation, Norman and Rosita
Winter Construction Co.
Witco Corp.

Wyman Youth Trust
Zarrow Foundation, Anne and Henry

Performing Arts

Abbott Laboratories
Ahmanson Foundation
Air France
Air Products and Chemicals, Inc.
Alabama Gas Corp.
Alabama Power Co.
Albertson's Inc.
Aldus Corp.
Alexander Foundation, Joseph
Allendale Insurance Co.
AlliedSignal Inc.
Alumax Inc.
Aluminum Co. of America
Amcast Industrial Corp.
AMCORE Bank, N.A. Rockford
American Brands, Inc.
American Natural Resources Company
American President Companies, Ltd.
American United Life Insurance Co.
Ames Charitable Trust, Harriett
Amfac/JMB Hawaii Inc.
Amoco Corporation
AMR Corp.
Andersen Foundation
Anderson Foundation
Anderson Foundation, M. D.
Andrews Foundation
Anheuser-Busch Companies, Inc.
Ansin Private Foundation, Ronald M.
AON Corporation
Apple Computer, Inc.
Appleton Papers Inc.
Archer-Daniels-Midland Co.
Argyros Foundation
Arkansas Power & Light Co.
Armco Inc.
AT&T Corp.
Atherton Family Foundation
Auerbach Foundation, Beatrice Fox
Avon Products, Inc.
Babson Foundation, Paul and Edith
Badgeley Residuary Charitable Trust, Rose M.
Baker Foundation, Dexter F. and Dorothy H.
Baker Hughes Inc.
Baker Trust, George F.
Baldwin Foundation, David M. and Barbara
Baldwin Memorial Foundation, Fred
Bank of Boston Corp.
Bank of New York Company, Inc.
Bank One, Texas-Houston Office
Bank One, Youngstown, NA
BankAmerica Corp.
Bankers Trust Company
Barker Foundation, J.M.R.
Barra Foundation
Barry Corp., R. G.
Barth Foundation, Theodore H.
Battelle Memorial Institute
Batts Foundation
Bean Foundation, Norwin S. and Elizabeth N.
Beattie Foundation Trust, Cordelia Lee
Bedsole Foundation, J. L.
Bell Foundation, James F.
Bemis Company, Inc.
Benedum Foundation, Claude Worthington
Benenson Foundation, Frances and Benjamin
Benetton Services Corp.
Benwood Foundation
Berwind Corporation

Bethlehem Steel Corp.
Beveridge Foundation, Frank Stanley
Bigelow Foundation, F. R.
Binney & Smith Inc.
Birnschein Foundation, Alvin and Marion
Bishop Foundation, E. K. and Lillian F.
Bissell Foundation, J. Walton
Blair and Co., William
Blake Foundation, S. P.
Blandin Foundation
Block, H&R
Blount, Inc.
Blue Cross & Blue Shield United of Wisconsin
Blum-Kovler Foundation
Boatmen's Bancshares, Inc.
Bobst Foundation, Elmer and Mamdouha
Bodman Foundation
Boeing Co., The
Boettcher Foundation
Boise Cascade Corporation
Borden, Inc.
Borman's Inc.
Boston Edison Co.
Bowater Incorporated
BP America Inc.
Brenner Foundation, Mervyn
Breyer Foundation
Bristol-Myers Squibb Company
Brunswick Corp.
Bryn Mawr Trust Co.
Buhl Foundation
Burden Foundation, Florence V.
Burdines Inc.
Burnett-Tandy Foundation
Bush Foundation
Butz Foundation
Cable & Wireless Holdings, Inc.
Cabot Corp.
Cafritz Foundation, Morris and Gwendolyn
Calhoun Charitable Trust, Kenneth
Callaway Foundation
Campbell Foundation
Canon U.S.A., Inc.
Carpenter Foundation
Carpenter Foundation, E. Rhodes and Leona B.
Carpenter Technology Corp.
Cassett Foundation, Louis N.
CBI Industries, Inc.
CBS, Inc.
Centerior Energy Corp.
Central Fidelity Banks, Inc.
Central Hudson Gas & Electric Corp.
Central Maine Power Co.
Chadwick Fund, Dorothy Jordan
Charina Foundation
Chase Manhattan Bank, N.A.
Chastain Charitable Foundation, Robert Lee and Thomas M.
Chazen Foundation
Cheney Foundation, Ben B.
Chesebrough-Pond's USA Co.
Chevron Corporation
Chicago Sun-Times, Inc.
Christensen Charitable and Religious Foundation, L. C.
Christian Dior New York, Inc.
Chrysler Corp.
CINergy
Citibank
Clark Foundation
Clarkson Foundation, Jeniam
Clorox Co.
Close Foundation
Clowes Fund
CNA Financial Corporation/CNA Insurance Companies
Colonial Life & Accident Insurance Co.
Coltec Industries, Inc.

Columbus Dispatch Printing Co.
Commerce Clearing House, Incorporated
Commonwealth Edison Co.
Connecticut Mutual Life Insurance Company
Connelly Foundation
Consolidated Papers, Inc.
Continental Corp.
Cooke Foundation
Cooper Industries, Inc.
Coors Foundation, Adolph
Copley Press, Inc.
Cord Foundation, E. L.
Corning Incorporated
Cosmair, Inc.
Coughlin-Saunders Foundation
Cowell Foundation, S. H.
Cowles Charitable Trust
Cowles Foundation, Gardner and Florence Call
Cowles Media Co.
CPC International Inc.
CR Industries
Crane Co.
Crown Memorial, Arie and Ida
CS First Boston Corporation
CT Corp. System
Culpeper Foundation, Charles E.
Culver Foundation, Constans
Cummins Engine Co.
Curtice-Burns Foods, Inc.
Daily News
Dalton Foundation, Harry L.
Dana Charitable Trust, Eleanor Naylor
Dana Foundation, Charles A.
Darby Foundation
Dart Group Corp.
Dater Foundation, Charles H.
Day Foundation, Nancy Sayles
DEC International, Inc.
Delavan Foundation, Nelson B.
Delaware North Co., Inc.
Dentsply International Inc.
DeRoy Foundation, Helen L.
DeRoy Testamentary Foundation
Detroit Edison Co.
Deuble Foundation, George H.
Dewing Foundation, Frances R.
Dexter Charitable Fund, Eugene A.
Diamond Foundation, Aaron
Digital Equipment Corp.
Dimeo Construction Co.
Dr. Seuss Foundation
Dodge Foundation, Cleveland H.
Dodge Foundation, Geraldine R.
Donaldson Company, Inc.
Donnelley & Sons Co., R.R.
Douty Foundation
Dow Corning Corp.
Dresser Industries, Inc.
Dreyfus Foundation, Max and Victoria
du Pont de Nemours & Co., E. I.
Duchossois Industries Inc.
Duke Power Co.
Dun & Bradstreet Corp.
Duncan Foundation, Lillian H. and C. W.
Duncan Trust, John G.
Dynamet, Inc.
Early Foundation
Eastman Kodak Company
Eaton Corporation
Eaton Foundation, Cyrus
Eddy Family Memorial Fund, C. K.
Edmonds Foundation, Dean S.
Einstein Fund, Albert E. and Birdie W.
Elf Atochem North America, Inc.
Emerson Foundation, Inc., Fred L.
Encyclopaedia Britannica, Inc.
Enron Corp.
Ensign-Bickford Industries

Ethyl Corp
Evans Foundation, Lettie Pate
Everett Charitable Trust
Exxon Corporation
Fairchild Foundation, Sherman
Farish Fund, William Stamps
Federal-Mogul Corporation
Federated Mutual Insurance Co.
Femino Foundation
Fireman's Fund Insurance Co.
First Chicago Corp.
First Fidelity Bank
First Financial Bank FSB
First Interstate Bank of Oregon
First Tennessee Bank
First Union Corp.
First Union National Bank of Florida
Firstar Bank Milwaukee, N.A.
Fish Foundation, Ray C.
Fishback Foundation Trust, Harmes C.
Fleet Financial Group, Inc.
Fleishhacker Foundation
Fleming Cos. Food Distribution Center
Folger Fund
Ford Foundation
Ford Fund, William and Martha
Ford II Fund, Henry
Ford Motor Co.
Forest Foundation
Forest Oil Corp.
Foster Foundation
Freedom Forge Corp.
Freeman Charitable Trust, Samuel
Freeport-McMoRan Inc.
Frese Foundation, Arnold D.
Fribourg Foundation
Friendship Fund
Frisch's Restaurants Inc.
Frohring Foundation, William O. and Gertrude Lewis
Frost National Bank
Fry Foundation, Lloyd A.
Fuller Foundation
Gannett Publishing Co., Guy
GAR Foundation
Gates Foundation
GATX Corp.
Gaylord Foundation, Clifford Willard
Gazette Co.
Gebbie Foundation
GenCorp Inc.
General American Life Insurance Co.
General Mills, Inc.
General Motors Corp.
GenRad
Georgia Power Co.
Giant Eagle, Inc.
Giant Food Inc.
Gifford Charitable Corporation, Rosamond
Gilman Foundation, Howard
Givenchy Corp.
Glaser Foundation
Globe Newspaper Co.
Glosser Foundation, David A.
Goddard Foundation, Charles B.
Goldberg Family Foundation
Goldsmith Foundation, Horace W.
Goodrich Co., The B.F.
Gould Electronics Inc.
Gould Foundation, The Florence
Graham Foundation for Advanced Studies in the Fine Arts
Graham Fund, Philip L.
Grand Rapids Label Co.
Great-West Life Assurance Co.
Green Foundation, Allen P. and Josephine B.
Greenwall Foundation
Gregg-Graniteville Foundation
Griffith Foundation, W. C.
Guardian Life Insurance Company of America

Haas, Jr. Fund, Evelyn and Walter
Hachar Charitable Trust, D. D.
Hafif Family Foundation
Hamilton Bank
Hamman Foundation, George and Mary Josephine
Hanes Foundation, John W. and Anna H.
Harcourt Foundation, Ellen Knowles
Harcourt General, Inc.
Harland Charitable Foundation, John and Wilhelmina D.
Harriman Foundation, Mary W.
Harrington Foundation, Francis A. and Jacquelyn H.
Harsco Corp.
Hartmarx Corporation
Hasbro Inc.
Hawn Foundation
HCA Foundation
Hearst Foundation, William Randolph
Hechinger Co.
Hecht-Levi Foundation
Heckscher Foundation for Children
Heinz Company, H. J.
Heinz Endowment, Howard
Heinz Endowment, Vira I.
Henry Foundation, Patrick
Herrick Foundation
Hewlett Foundation, William and Flora
Hickory Tech Corp.
Higginson Trust, Corina
High Foundation
Hill Foundation, Sandy
Hillman Family Foundation, Alex
Hillsdale Fund
Hoag Family Foundation, George
Holnam
Holzer Memorial Foundation, Richard H.
Hopkins Foundation, Josephine Lawrence
Housatonic Curtain Co.
Houston Endowment
Houston Industries Incorporated
Howard and Bush Foundation
Hoyt Foundation
Hoyt Foundation, Stewart W. and Willma C.
Hudson-Webber Foundation
Hugoton Foundation
Hulme Charitable Foundation, Milton G.
Humana, Inc.
Hunt Foundation
Hunt Foundation, Samuel P.
Huston Foundation
Huthsteiner Fine Arts Trust
Hyde and Watson Foundation
Icahn Foundation, Carl C.
ICI Americas Inc.
Illinois Tool Works, Inc.
Inland Container Corp.
Integra Bank of Uniontown
Interkal, Inc.
International Business Machines Corp.
Irvine Foundation, James
Irwin Charity Foundation, William G.
ITT Hartford Insurance Group, Inc.
Jackson Foundation
James River Corp. of Virginia
Jaydor Corp.
Jewett Foundation, George Frederick
John Hancock Mutual Life Insurance Co.
Johnson Controls Inc.
Johnson Foundation, Burdine
Johnson & Higgins
Johnson & Son, S.C.
Jones Foundation, Fletcher

Jordan Charitable Foundation, Mary Ranken Jordan and Ettie A.
Jostens, Inc.
Journal-Gazette Co.
Jurzykowski Foundation, Alfred
Kansas City Southern Industries
Kavanagh Foundation, T. James
Kelley and Elza Kelley Foundation, Edward Bangs
Kennecott Corporation
Kettering Fund
Kiewit Foundation, Peter
Kilcawley Fund, William H.
Kimball Foundation, Horace A. Kimball and S. Ella
Kimberly-Clark Corp.
Kingsbury Corp.
Kinney-Lindstrom Foundation
Kiplinger Foundation
Kirbo Charitable Trust, Thomas M. and Irene B.
Kirby Foundation, F. M.
Kirkpatrick Foundation
Kline Foundation, Josiah W. and Bessie H.
Klock and Lucia Klock Kingston Foundation, Jay E.
Kmart Corporation
KN Energy, Inc.
Knight Foundation, John S. and James L.
Knoll Group
Kohn-Joseloff Foundation
Koret Foundation
Kreitler Foundation
Kresge Foundation
Kuehn Foundation
Ladd Charitable Corporation, Helen and George
Lang Foundation, Eugene M.
Larsen Fund
Lasdon Foundation, William and Mildred
Lattner Foundation, Forrest C.
Lea Foundation, Helen Sperry
Leavey Foundation, Thomas and Dorothy
Lebanon Mutual Insurance Co.
Lee Endowment Foundation
LEF Foundation
Lehigh Portland Cement Co.
Lemberg Foundation
Lipton, Thomas J.
Little, Inc., Arthur D.
Loews Corporation
Long Island Lighting Co.
Louisiana-Pacific Corp.
Lowenstein Foundation, Leon
Lux Foundation, Miranda
Lydall, Inc.
M/A-COM, Inc.
MacArthur Foundation, John D. and Catherine T.
Macy & Co., Inc., R.H.
Magowan Family Foundation
Mahadh Foundation
Mailman Family Foundation, A. L.
Mailman Foundation
Management Compensation Group/Dulworth Inc.
Maritz Inc.
Marriott Foundation, J. Willard
Mars Foundation
Marsh & McLennan Companies, Inc.
Martin Marietta Corp.
Mather Charitable Trust, S. Livingston
Mattel, Inc.
Mautz Paint Co.
May Department Stores Company, The
Mayer Foundation, Oliver Dewey
Maytag Family Foundation, Fred
MBIA Inc.
MCA Inc.
McCann Foundation

McDonald & Company Securities, Inc.
McDonnell Douglas Corp.-West
McElroy Trust, R. J.
McEvoy Foundation, Mildred H.
McFawn Trust No. 2, Lois Sisler
McGonagle Foundation, Dextra Baldwin
McGraw-Hill, Inc.
MCI Communications Corp.
McInerny Foundation
McLean Contributionship
Mead Corporation, The
Meadows Foundation
Medtronic, Inc.
Mellon Foundation, Andrew W.
Mellon Foundation, Richard King
Memton Fund
Merck & Co.
Merck & Co. Human Health Division
Merrick Foundation
Merrill Lynch & Co., Inc.
Metropolitan Life Insurance Co.
Meyer Memorial Trust
Miller Brewing Company/North Carolina
Miller Fund, Kathryn and Gilbert
Miller-Mellor Association
Mine Safety Appliances Co.
Minnesota Mining & Mfg. Co.
Mitchell Energy & Development Corp.
Mitsubishi International Corp.
Mitsubishi Motor Sales of America, Inc.
Mnuchin Foundation
Mobil Oil Corp.
Monadnock Paper Mills
Monell Foundation, Ambrose
Monfort Family Foundation
Moore & Sons, B.C.
Morgan & Company, J.P.
Morgan Construction Co.
Morgan Stanley & Co., Inc.
Morrison Knudsen Corporation
Moses Fund, Henry and Lucy
Mosinee Paper Corp.
Mott Fund, Ruth
Muchnic Foundation
Mulford Foundation, Vincent
Muller Foundation
Munson Foundation Trust, W. B.
Murphy Foundation
Myra Foundation
Nabisco Foods Group
Nalco Chemical Co.
National Forge Co.
National Gypsum Co.
National Westminster Bank New Jersey
NBD Indiana, Inc.
Nesholm Family Foundation
Nestle USA Inc.
Neuberger Foundation, Roy R. and Marie S.
New England Business Service
New York Life Insurance Co.
New York Stock Exchange, Inc.
New York Times Company
The New Yorker Magazine, Inc.
NewMil Bancorp
Nias Foundation, Henry
Noble Foundation, Edward John
Noble Foundation, Samuel Roberts
Normandie Foundation
North Shore Foundation
Northern States Power Co. (Minnesota)
Northwest Natural Gas Co.
Norton Co.
Norwest Bank Nebraska, N.A.
Novell Inc.
NYNEX Corporation
Odell Fund, Robert Stewart Odell and Helen Pfeiffer

Old National Bank in
 Evansville
Olin Corp.
Olsson Memorial Foundation,
 Elis
Ore-Ida Foods, Inc.
Osborn Charitable Trust,
 Edward B.
Osceola Foundation
Osher Foundation, Bernard
Outboard Marine Corp.
Owen Industries, Inc.
Pacific Mutual Life Insurance
 Co.
Pacific Telesis Group
Packard Foundation, David
 and Lucile
Panhandle Eastern Corporation
Parker Hannifin Corp.
Parshelsky Foundation, Moses
 L.
Pella Corporation
Penn Foundation, William
Pennzoil Co.
Peoples Energy Corp.
Perkin-Elmer Corp.
Pew Charitable Trusts
Pfizer, Inc.
Pforzheimer Foundation, Carl
 and Lily
PHH Corporation
Piankova Foundation, Tatiana
Piper Foundation, Minnie
 Stevens
Piper Jaffray Companies Inc.
PNC Bank, N.A.
Polaroid Corp.
Potomac Electric Power Co.
PPG Industries, Inc.
Premier Industrial Corp.
Prince Trust, Abbie Norman
Prouty Foundation, Olive
 Higgins
Providence Gas Co.
Providence Journal Company
Provident Life & Accident
 Insurance Company of
 America
Providian Corporation
Prudential Insurance Co. of
 America, The
Prudential Securities, Inc.
Public Service Electric & Gas
 Co.
Quaker Chemical Corp.
Rabb Foundation, Harry W.
Ralston Purina Co.
Read Foundation, Charles L.
Reed Foundation
Reichhold Chemicals, Inc.
Reinberger Foundation
Republic NY Corp.
Rhone-Poulenc Inc.
Rice Charitable Foundation,
 Albert W.
Rice Foundation
Rich Products Corporation
Richardson Charitable Trust,
 Anne S.
RJR Nabisco Inc.
Rockwell Fund
Rockwell International
 Corporation
Rohm & Haas Co.
Rose Foundation, Billy
Roseburg Forest Products Co.
Rosen Foundation, Joseph
Rosenberg, Jr. Family
 Foundation, Louise and
 Claude
Ross Memorial Foundation,
 Will
Rouse Co.
Royal Group, Inc.
Rubin Foundation, Samuel
Rubinstein Foundation, Helena
Rudin Foundation
SAFECO Corp.
Saint Paul Companies, Inc.
Salomon Foundation, Richard
 and Edna
Salomon Inc.
San Diego Gas & Electric
Sandusky International Inc.
Santa Fe Pacific Corporation

Sara Lee Corp.
Sara Lee Hosiery, Inc.
Sarkeys Foundation
Sawyer Charitable Foundation
SBC Communications Inc.
Schering-Plough Corp.
Scherman Foundation
Schroeder Foundation, Walter
Schuller International
Schwab & Co., Inc., Charles
Schwartz Fund for Education
 and Health Research, Arnold
 and Marie
Scott Fetzer Co.
Scott Foundation, Virginia
 Steele
Scurlock Foundation
Seafirst Corporation
Seaver Charitable Trust,
 Richard C.
Seaway Food Town, Inc.
Security Life of Denver
 Insurance Co.
Sedgwick James Inc.
Seidman Family Foundation
Selby and Marie Selby
 Foundation, William G.
Seneca Foods Corp.
Sharon Steel Corp.
Shawmut National Corp.
Sheaffer Inc.
Shell Oil Company
Shenandoah Life Insurance Co.
Shubert Foundation
Simpson Investment Company
Skaggs Foundation, L. J. and
 Mary C.
Skillman Foundation
Slifka Foundation, Joseph and
 Sylvia
Smart Family Foundation
Smeal Foundation, Mary Jean
 and Frank P.
Smith Corp., A.O.
Smith Foundation, Gordon V.
 and Helen C.
Smith Foundation, Kelvin and
 Eleanor
Solow Foundation
Sonat Inc.
South Bend Tribune
Southern California Edison Co.
Southern New England
 Telephone Company
Sprague Educational and
 Charitable Foundation, Seth
SPX Corp.
Stanley Charitable Foundation,
 A.W.
Stanley Works
Starr Foundation
Stauffer Foundation, John and
 Beverly
Steele Foundation, Harry and
 Grace
Stein Foundation, Jules and
 Doris
Stevens Foundation, Abbot
 and Dorothy H.
Stevens Foundation, John T.
Stone Trust, H. Chase
Strawbridge Foundation of
 Pennsylvania II, Margaret
 Dorrance
Strong Foundation, Hattie M.
Sturgis Charitable and
 Educational Trust, Roy and
 Christine
Swiss Bank Corp.
Symmes Foundation, F. W.
Tait Foundation, Frank M.
Taylor Foundation, Ruth and
 Vernon
Teleflex Inc.
Temple Foundation, T. L. L.
Tenneco Inc.
Tetley, Inc.
Texaco Inc.
Textron, Inc.
Texas Commerce
 Bank-Houston, N.A.
Thermo Electron Corp.
Thomasville Furniture
 Industries
Thompson Co., J. Walter

Thorne Foundation
Times Mirror Company, The
Titus Foundation, Roy and
 Niuta
Tobin Foundation
Todd Co., A.M.
Tonya Memorial Foundation
TransAmerica Corporation
Transco Energy Co.
Travelers Inc.
Trexler Trust, Harry C.
Truland Foundation
Trull Foundation
Trust Company Bank
Turner Charitable Foundation
Unilever United States, Inc.
Union Bank
Union Electric Co.
Union Pacific Corp.
U.S. Bank of Washington
Unitrode Corp.
Unocal Corp.
Uris Brothers Foundation
USL Capital Corporation
USX Corporation
Utica National Insurance
 Group
Valentine Foundation, Lawson
Van Wert County Foundation
Vanderbilt Trust, R. T.
Virginia Power Co.
Vulcan Materials Co.
Wachovia Bank of North
 Carolina, N.A.
Wahlstrom Foundation
Wallace-Reader's Digest Fund,
 Lila
Walsh Foundation
Washington Forrest Foundation
Washington Mutual Savings
 Bank
Washington Water Power Co.
Weber Charities Corp.,
 Frederick E.
Weckbaugh Foundation,
 Eleanore Mullen
Weil, Gotshal and Manges
 Foundation
West One Bancorp
Westerman Foundation,
 Samuel L.
Western New York Foundation
Westvaco Corporation
Weyerhaeuser Memorial
 Foundation, Charles A.
Wheat First Butcher Singer,
 Inc.
Whirlpool Corporation
WICOR, Inc.
Wiegand Foundation, E. L.
Wiley & Sons, Inc., John
Williams Companies, The
Wilmington Trust Co.
Wilson Fund, Matilda R.
Winter Construction Co.
Wiremold Co.
Wisconsin Power & Light Co.
Wisconsin Public Service Corp.
Witco Corp.
Wright Foundation, Lola
Wyman Youth Trust
Young Foundation, Robert R.
Zachry Co., H.B.

Public Broadcasting

Abbott Laboratories
Acushnet Co.
AEGON USA Inc.
Ahmanson Foundation
Air France
Air Products and Chemicals,
 Inc.
AKC Fund
Akzo America
Akzo Chemicals Inc.
Alabama Gas Corp.
Alavi Foundation of New York
Albertson's Inc.
Alcon Laboratories, Inc.
Aldus Corp.
Alexander Foundation, Joseph
Allegheny Ludlum Corp.
Allendale Insurance Co.

AlliedSignal Inc.
Allyn Foundation
Alumax Inc.
Aluminum Co. of America
American Brands, Inc.
American General Finance
 Corp.
American National Bank &
 Trust Co. of Chicago
American Natural Resources
 Company
American United Life
 Insurance Co.
Ameritas Life Insurance Corp.
Amfac/JMB Hawaii Inc.
AMP Incorporated
Andersen Corp.
Andersen Foundation
Anderson Foundation
Anderson Foundation, John W.
Andersons, The
Annenberg Foundation
AON Corporation
Arakelian Foundation, Mary
 Alice
Arcadia Foundation
Archer-Daniels-Midland Co.
Aristech Chemical Corp.
Arkelian Foundation, Ben H.
 and Gladys
Armco Inc.
Astor Foundation, Vincent
Atherton Family Foundation
Atran Foundation
Audubon State Bank
Auerbach Foundation,
 Beatrice Fox
Avery Arts Foundation, Milton
 and Sally
Avon Products, Inc.
Babson Foundation, Paul and
 Edith
Bacon Foundation, E. L. and
 Oma
Baker Foundation, Dexter F.
 and Dorothy H.
Baldwin Foundation, David
 M. and Barbara
Baldwin Memorial
 Foundation, Fred
Ball Brothers Foundation
Ball Foundation, George and
 Frances
Bank of Boston Corp.
Bank of New York Company,
 Inc.
Bank One, Texas-Houston
 Office
BankAmerica Corp.
Barker Foundation, J.M.R.
Barra Foundation
Barry Corp., R. G.
Barth Foundation, Theodore H.
Battelle Memorial Institute
Baughman Foundation
Bay Foundation
BE&K Inc.
Bechtel Testamentary
 Charitable Trust, H. R.
Bedsole Foundation, J. L.
Beech Aircraft Corp.
Bell Atlantic Corp.
Bell Foundation, James F.
Benenson Foundation, Frances
 and Benjamin
Berwind Corporation
Bethlehem Steel Corp.
Bettingen Corporation, Burton
 G.
Beveridge Foundation, Frank
 Stanley
Bigelow Foundation, F. R.
Bingham Foundation, William
Binney & Smith Inc.
Bird Corp.
Blake Foundation, S. P.
Blandin Foundation
Bloedorn Foundation, Walter
 A.
Blount, Inc.
Blue Cross & Blue Shield
 United of Wisconsin
Blum-Kovler Foundation
Bobst Foundation, Elmer and
 Mamdouha

Boettcher Foundation
Booth Ferris Foundation
Boswell Foundation, James G.
Bothin Foundation
Bowater Incorporated
BP America Inc.
Brackenridge Foundation,
 George W.
Brady Foundation
Bremer Foundation, Otto
Brenner Foundation, Mervyn
Breyer Foundation
Bridgestone/Firestone, Inc.
Bright Family Foundation
Brillion Iron Works
Bristol-Myers Squibb
 Company
Brown & Williamson Tobacco
 Corp.
Bucyrus-Erie Company
Bunbury Company
Burden Foundation, Florence
 V.
Burdines Inc.
Bush Foundation
Cabot Family Charitable Trust
Cafritz Foundation, Morris and
 Gwendolyn
Cain Foundation, Effie and
 Wofford
Cain Foundation, Gordon and
 Mary
Calder Foundation, Louis
Calhoun Charitable Trust,
 Kenneth
Campini Foundation, Frank A.
Canon U.S.A., Inc.
Carnegie Corporation of New
 York
Carolyn Foundation
Carpenter Foundation
Carpenter Foundation, E.
 Rhodes and Leona B.
Carter Foundation, Amon G.
Carvel Foundation, Thomas
 and Agnes
Cassett Foundation, Louis N.
Castle Foundation, Harold K.
 L.
Cayuga Foundation
Central Fidelity Banks, Inc.
Central Maine Power Co.
Central Vermont Public
 Service Corp.
Century Companies of America
Chadwick Fund, Dorothy
 Jordan
Chase Manhattan Bank, N.A.
Chastain Charitable
 Foundation, Robert Lee and
 Thomas M.
Chatham Manufacturing Co.
Chazen Foundation
Cheatham Foundation, Owen
Cheney Foundation, Ben B.
Chesebrough-Pond's USA Co.
Chevron Corporation
Chicago Sun-Times, Inc.
Childs Charitable Foundation,
 Roberta M.
Christian Dior New York, Inc.
Chrysler Corp.
Church & Dwight Co., Inc.
CIGNA Corporation
CINergy
Citibank
Claiborne and Art Ortenberg
 Foundation, Liz
Clapp Charitable and
 Educational Trust, George H.
Clark Foundation
Clay Foundation
Clorox Co.
Close Foundation
Clowes Fund
Cogswell Benevolent Trust
Collins Foundation
Columbia Foundation
Comerica Incorporated
Commerce Bancshares, Inc.
Commerce Clearing House,
 Incorporated
Commonwealth Edison Co.

Neuberger Foundation, Roy R. and Marie S.
New York Life Insurance Co.
New York Stock Exchange, Inc.
New York Times Company
The New Yorker Magazine, Inc.
Newman's Own, Inc.
Nias Foundation, Henry
Norfolk Shipbuilding & Drydock Corp.
Normandie Foundation
North Shore Foundation
Northern States Power Co. (Minnesota)
Northwest Natural Gas Co.
Norton Co.
Norton Family Foundation, Peter
Norton Foundation Inc.
Norton Memorial Corporation, Geraldi
Norwest Corporation
NYNEX Corporation
Oaklawn Foundation
OCRI Foundation
Offield Family Foundation
Olin Corp.
O'Quinn Foundation, John M. and Nancy C.
Ore-Ida Foods, Inc.
Osher Foundation, Bernard
Outboard Marine Corp.
Overbrook Foundation
Overlake Foundation
Pacific Mutual Life Insurance Co.
Packaging Corporation of America
Palisano Foundation, Vincent and Harriet
Parsons Foundation, Ralph M.
Patterson Charitable Fund, W. I.
Payne Foundation, Frank E. and Seba B.
Pella Corporation
Penn Foundation, William
Pennsylvania Dutch Co.
Pennzoil Co.
Peoples Energy Corp.
Peppers Foundation, Ann
Perkin-Elmer Corp.
Petrie Trust, Lorene M.
Petteys Memorial Foundation, Jack
Pew Charitable Trusts
Pfizer, Inc.
Pforzheimer Foundation, Carl and Lily
Phelps Dodge Corporation
Phillips Family Foundation, Jay and Rose
Phillips Foundation, Ellis L.
Pick, Jr. Fund, Albert
Pickford Foundation, Mary
Pierce Charitable Trust, Harold Whitworth
Pioneer Trust Bank, NA
Piper Foundation, Minnie Stevens
Pitt-Des Moines Inc.
Pittsburg Midway Coal Mining Co.
Playboy Enterprises, Inc.
PNC Bank, N.A.
Potomac Electric Power Co.
PPG Industries, Inc.
Premier Industrial Corp.
Price Associates, T. Rowe
Prouty Foundation, Olive Higgins
Providence Journal Company
Providian Corporation
Prudential Insurance Co. of America, The
Public Service Co. of New Mexico
Public Service Electric & Gas Co.
Pulitzer Publishing Co.
Puterbaugh Foundation
Putnam Foundation
Rabb Charitable Foundation, Sidney and Esther
Rabb Foundation, Harry W.

Ralston Purina Co.
Raymond Corp.
Regenstein Foundation
Reidler Foundation
Reinberger Foundation
Reisman Charitable Trust, George C. and Evelyn R.
Republic NY Corp.
Rice Charitable Foundation, Albert W.
Rice Foundation
Rich Products Corporation
Richardson Charitable Trust, Anne S.
RJR Nabisco Inc.
Robinson-Broadhurst Foundation
Rockefeller Fund, David
Rockwell Fund
Rockwell International Corporation
Rohatyn Foundation, Felix and Elizabeth
Rohm & Haas Co.
Rose Foundation, Billy
Rosen Foundation, Joseph
Rosenberg, Jr. Family Foundation, Louise and Claude
Rouse Co.
Rowland Foundation
Royal Group, Inc.
Rubin Foundation, Samuel
Rubinstein Foundation, Helena
Ryan Foundation, David Claude
SAFECO Corp.
Saint Paul Companies, Inc.
Salomon Foundation, Richard and Edna
Salomon Inc.
Saltonstall Charitable Foundation, Richard
Salvatori Foundation, Henry
Sara Lee Hosiery, Inc.
Sasco Corporation
SBC Communications Inc.
Scaife Family Foundation
Scherman Foundation
Schiff Foundation, Dorothy
Schiro Fund
Schlumberger Ltd.
Schmitt Foundation, Kilian J. and Caroline F.
Scholl Foundation, Dr.
Schumann Fund for New Jersey
Schwab & Co., Inc., Charles
Schwartz Fund for Education and Health Research, Arnold and Marie
Schwob Foundation, Simon
Scott Fetzer Co.
Scott Foundation, William E.
Seagram & Sons, Inc., Joseph E.
Seaway Food Town, Inc.
Security Life of Denver Insurance Co.
Sedgwick James Inc.
Seidman Family Foundation
Semmes Foundation
Seneca Foods Corp.
Sentry Insurance A Mutual Company
Seton Company
Sharon Steel Corp.
Shawmut National Corp.
Shenandoah Life Insurance Co.
Sierra Pacific Industries
Sierra Pacific Resources
Skillman Foundation
Slifka Foundation, Joseph and Sylvia
Sloan Foundation, Alfred P.
Smith Charitable Foundation, Lou and Lutza
Smith Foundation, Gordon V. and Helen C.
Smith Foundation, Kelvin and Eleanor
Smith Foundation, Ralph L.
Snow Memorial Trust, John Ben
Sonat Inc.

Sordoni Foundation
South Bend Tribune
South Branch Foundation
South Waite Foundation
Southern California Edison Co.
Southwestern Electric Power Co.
Spang & Co.
Specialty Manufacturing Co.
Sprague Educational and Charitable Foundation, Seth
SPX Corp.
Square D Co.
Stabler Foundation, Donald B. and Dorothy L.
Stanley Charitable Foundation, A.W.
Stanley Works
Starr Foundation
Steele Foundation, Harry and Grace
Stein Foundation, Jules and Doris
Stemmons Foundation
Stevens Foundation, Abbot and Dorothy H.
Stone Charitable Foundation
Strauss Foundation, Leon
Strawbridge Foundation of Pennsylvania II, Margaret Dorrance
Strong Foundation, Hattie M.
Stupp Foundation, Norman J.
Sulzberger Foundation
Sumners Foundation, Hatton W.
Sundet Foundation
Superior Tube Co.
Swanson Family Foundation, Dr. W.C.
Swift Co. Inc., John S.
Tait Foundation, Frank M.
Taube Family Foundation
Taylor Foundation, Ruth and Vernon
Tecumseh Products Co.
Teichert & Son, A.
Tenneco Inc.
Tetley, Inc.
Texas Commerce Bank-Houston, N.A.
Textron, Inc.
Thalhimer and Family Foundation, Charles G.
Thermo Electron Corp.
Thorne Foundation
Thornton Foundation
Thornton Foundation, Flora L.
Times Mirror Company, The
Tobin Foundation
Tonya Memorial Foundation
Tozer Foundation
TransAmerica Corporation
Transco Energy Co.
Truland Foundation
Trull Foundation
Trust Company Bank
Tucker Charitable Trust, Rose E.
Tupancy-Harris Foundation of 1986
Turner Charitable Foundation
Unilever United States, Inc.
Union Bank
Union Camp Corporation
Union Pacific Corp.
Uris Brothers Foundation
US WEST, Inc.
USG Corporation
USL Capital Corporation
USX Corporation
Utica National Insurance Group
Valentine Foundation, Lawson
Valmont Industries, Inc.
van Ameringen Foundation
Van Evera Foundation, Dewitt
Vernon Fund, Miles Hodsdon
Virginia Power Co.
Vulcan Materials Co.
Wachovia Bank of North Carolina, N.A.
Wal-Mart Stores, Inc.
Wallace Foundation, George R.
Walsh Foundation

Warner Fund, Albert and Bessie
Warwick Foundation
Washington Forrest Foundation
Washington Water Power Co.
Wean Foundation, Raymond John
Weckbaugh Foundation, Eleanore Mullen
Wege Foundation
Weil, Gotshal and Manges Foundation
Weingart Foundation
Welfare Foundation
Wendt Foundation, Margaret L.
Wertheim Foundation, Dr. Herbert A.
West Foundation, Harry and Ethel
West One Bancorp
Western New York Foundation
Weyerhaeuser Co.
Weyerhaeuser Memorial Foundation, Charles A.
Wheeler Foundation, Wilmot
Whirlpool Corporation
Whiting Foundation, Macauley and Helen Dow
Whitney Fund, David M.
Whittenberger Foundation, Claude R. and Ethel B.
Wiegand Foundation, E. L.
Wilder Foundation
Wildermuth Foundation, E. F.
Wiley & Sons, Inc., John
Willard Helping Fund, Cecilia Young
Wilmington Trust Co.
Wilson Foundation, H. W.
Wilson Fund, Matilda R.
Winnebago Industries, Inc.
Winthrop Trust, Clara B.
Wiremold Co.
Wisconsin Power & Light Co.
Wyomissing Foundation
Zenkel Foundation
Zollner Foundation

Theater

Abbott Laboratories
Abell-Hanger Foundation
Achelis Foundation
Acushnet Co.
Adams Foundation, Arthur F. and Alice E.
Adler Foundation Trust, Philip D. and Henrietta B.
Ahmanson Foundation
Air France
Air Products and Chemicals, Inc.
Alabama Gas Corp.
Alabama Power Co.
Alcon Laboratories, Inc.
Aldus Corp.
Allegheny Ludlum Corp.
Allendale Insurance Co.
AlliedSignal Inc.
Allyn Foundation
Alumax Inc.
Aluminum Co. of America
AMCORE Bank, N.A. Rockford
American Brands, Inc.
American Fidelity Corporation
American General Finance Corp.
American National Bank & Trust Co. of Chicago
American Natural Resources Company
American President Companies, Ltd.
American United Life Insurance Co.
Ameritas Life Insurance Corp.
Ames Charitable Trust, Harriett
Amfac/JMB Hawaii Inc.
AMP Incorporated
Andersen Corp.
Andersen Foundation
Andreas Foundation
Andrews Foundation

Annenberg Foundation
Ansin Private Foundation, Ronald M.
AON Corporation
Apple Computer, Inc.
Appleby Trust, Scott B. and Annie P.
Arcadia Foundation
Archer-Daniels-Midland Co.
Armco Inc.
Astor Foundation, Vincent
AT&T Corp.
Atherton Family Foundation
Auerbach Foundation, Beatrice Fox
Avon Products, Inc.
Ayres Foundation, Inc.
Babson Foundation, Paul and Edith
Baker Foundation, Dexter F. and Dorothy H.
Baldwin Foundation, David M. and Barbara
Baldwin Memorial Foundation, Fred
Ball Brothers Foundation
Banc One Wisconsin Corp.
Bank of Boston Corp.
Bank One, Youngstown, NA
BankAmerica Corp.
Barra Foundation
Barry Corp., R. G.
Battelle Memorial Institute
Bay Foundation
Bean Foundation, Norwin S. and Elizabeth N.
Beattie Foundation Trust, Cordelia Lee
Bedsole Foundation, J. L.
Beech Aircraft Corp.
Bell Atlantic Corp.
Bell Foundation, James F.
Beloit Foundation
Bemis Company, Inc.
Benedum Foundation, Claude Worthington
Benenson Foundation, Frances and Benjamin
Benwood Foundation
Berwind Corporation
Bethlehem Steel Corp.
Bigelow Foundation, F. R.
Bingham Foundation, William
Binney & Smith Inc.
Birnschein Foundation, Alvin and Marion
Bishop Foundation, E. K. and Lillian F.
Blair and Co., William
Blandin Foundation
Block, H&R
Blount, Inc.
Blue Cross & Blue Shield United of Wisconsin
Blum Foundation, Edna F.
Blum-Kovler Foundation
Boeing Co., The
Boise Cascade Corporation
Booth Ferris Foundation
Borden, Inc.
Borman's Inc.
Bothin Foundation
BP America Inc.
Brenner Foundation, Mervyn
Breyer Foundation
Bridgestone/Firestone, Inc.
Bristol-Myers Squibb Company
Bryn Mawr Trust Co.
Bucyrus-Erie Company
Bunbury Company
Burden Foundation, Florence V.
Burdines Inc.
Bush Foundation
Cabell Foundation, Robert G. Cabell III and Maude Morgan
Cabot Corp.
Cabot Family Charitable Trust
Cafritz Foundation, Morris and Gwendolyn
Cain Foundation, Gordon and Mary

MCA Inc.
McCasland Foundation
McConnell Foundation
McCormick & Co. Inc.
McDermott Foundation, Eugene
McDonald & Company Securities, Inc.
McDonnell Douglas Corp.-West
McElroy Trust, R. J.
McFawn Trust No. 2, Lois Sisler
McFeely-Rogers Foundation
McInerny Foundation
McKenna Foundation, Philip M.
McMahan Foundation, Catherine L. and Robert O.
Mead Corporation, The
Meadows Foundation
Medtronic, Inc.
Mellon Foundation, Andrew W.
Mellon Foundation, Richard King
Memton Fund
Merck & Co.
Merck Family Fund
Merkley Charitable Trust
Merrill Lynch & Co., Inc.
Metropolitan Life Insurance Co.
Meyer Memorial Trust
Miller Brewing Company/North Carolina
Miller Charitable Foundation, Howard E. and Nell E.
Miller Fund, Kathryn and Gilbert
Miller-Mellor Association
Mine Safety Appliances Co.
Mitsubishi International Corp.
Mnuchin Foundation
Mobil Oil Corp.
Monfort Family Foundation
Moore & Sons, B.C.
Morgan & Company, J.P.
Morgan Construction Co.
Morris Foundation, Margaret T.
Mosinee Paper Corp.
Mott Fund, Ruth
Murdock Charitable Trust, M. J.
Musson Charitable Foundation, R. C. and Katharine M.
Mutual Assurance Co.
Myra Foundation
Nabisco Foods Group
National Forge Co.
National Gypsum Co.
National Steel Corp.
National Westminster Bank New Jersey
NBD Indiana, Inc.
Nesholm Family Foundation
Nestle USA Inc.
New York Stock Exchange, Inc.
New York Times Company
The New Yorker Magazine, Inc.
Newman's Own, Inc.
Norman Foundation, Summers A.
Northern States Power Co. (Minnesota)
Northwest Natural Gas Co.
Norton Co.
Norton Foundation Inc.
Norton Memorial Corporation, Geraldi
Norwest Bank Nebraska, N.A.
Norwest Corporation
Novell Inc.
O'Connor Foundation, A. Lindsay and Olive B.
OCRI Foundation
O'Fallon Trust, Martin J. and Mary Anne
OG&E Electric Services
Old National Bank in Evansville
Olin Corp.
Olsson Memorial Foundation, Elis

Oppenstein Brothers Foundation
O'Quinn Foundation, John M. and Nancy C.
Osceola Foundation
Osher Foundation, Bernard
Overbrook Foundation
Overlake Foundation
Owen Industries, Inc.
Owsley Foundation, Alvin and Lucy
Oxy USA Inc.
Pacific Mutual Life Insurance Co.
Pacific Telesis Group
Packard Foundation, David and Lucile
PaineWebber
Palmer Fund, Frank Loomis
Parker Hannifin Corp.
Parsons Foundation, Ralph M.
Payne Foundation, Frank E. and Seba B.
Peabody Charitable Fund, Amelia
Pella Corporation
Penn Foundation, William
Pennzoil Co.
Peoples Energy Corp.
Petrie Trust, Lorene M.
Pew Charitable Trusts
Pfizer, Inc.
Pforzheimer Foundation, Carl and Lily
Phelps Dodge Corporation
PHH Corporation
Philibosian Foundation, Stephen
Phillips Family Foundation, Jay and Rose
Phillips Foundation, Ellis L.
Piankova Foundation, Tatiana
Pick, Jr. Fund, Albert
Pickford Foundation, Mary
Pineywoods Foundation
Pioneer Trust Bank, NA
Piper Foundation, Minnie Stevens
Piper Jaffray Companies Inc.
Plumsock Fund
PNC Bank, N.A.
Polaroid Corp.
Porter Foundation, Mrs. Cheever
Porter Testamentary Trust, James Hyde
Potomac Electric Power Co.
Prairie Foundation
Premier Industrial Corp.
Price Associates, T. Rowe
Prince Trust, Abbie Norman
Prospect Hill Foundation
Providence Journal Company
Providian Corporation
Prudential Securities, Inc.
Public Service Electric & Gas Co.
Pulitzer Publishing Co.
Putnam Foundation
R&B Machine Tool Co.
Read Foundation, Charles L.
Reed Foundation
Reinberger Foundation
Republic NY Corp.
Reynolds Foundation, Donald W.
Rice Charitable Foundation, Albert W.
Riggs Benevolent Fund
Rockwell Fund
Rockwell International Corporation
Rogers Family Foundation
Rohatyn Foundation, Felix and Elizabeth
Rohm & Haas Co.
Rose Foundation, Billy
Roseburg Forest Products Co.
Rosen Foundation, Joseph
Rosenberg, Jr. Family Foundation, Louise and Claude
Ross Laboratories
Ross Memorial Foundation, Will

Rouse Co.
Royal Group, Inc.
Rubin Foundation, Samuel
Rubinstein Foundation, Helena
Rudin Foundation
Saint Paul Companies, Inc.
Salomon Inc.
San Diego Gas & Electric
Sandusky International Inc.
Santa Fe Pacific Corporation
Sara Lee Corp.
Sargent Foundation, Newell B.
Sarkeys Foundation
SBC Communications Inc.
Schenck Fund, L. P.
Scherer Foundation, Karla
Schering-Plough Corp.
Scherman Foundation
Schlumberger Ltd.
Schoenleber Foundation
Schroeder Foundation, Walter
Schuller International
Scott Fetzer Co.
Scott Foundation, William E.
Scripps Co., E.W.
Seafirst Corporation
Seaver Charitable Trust, Richard C.
Seaway Food Town, Inc.
Security Life of Denver Insurance Co.
Sedgwick James Inc.
Selby and Marie Selby Foundation, William G.
Self Foundation
Sequoia Foundation
Sharon Steel Corp.
Shawmut National Corp.
Sheaffer Inc.
Shell Oil Company
Shenandoah Life Insurance Co.
Shubert Foundation
Sierra Pacific Resources
Simpson Investment Company
Skaggs Foundation, L. J. and Mary C.
Skillman Foundation
Slemp Foundation
Smart Family Foundation
Smeal Foundation, Mary Jean and Frank P.
Smith Foundation, Kelvin and Eleanor
Smith Foundation, Ralph L.
SmithKline Beecham Corp.
Snow Memorial Trust, John Ben
Solow Foundation
Sonat Inc.
Sordoni Foundation
Southern California Edison Co.
Southern New England Telephone Company
Southwestern Electric Power Co.
Spang & Co.
Specialty Manufacturing Co.
Sprague Educational and Charitable Foundation, Seth
SPX Corp.
Square D Co.
Stanley Works
Starr Foundation
Stauffer Foundation, John and Beverly
Steele Foundation, Harry and Grace
Stein Foundation, Jules and Doris
Stemmons Foundation
Sternberger Foundation, Tannenbaum
Stevens Foundation, Abbot and Dorothy H.
Strong Foundation, Hattie M.
Sturgis Charitable and Educational Trust, Roy and Christine
Subaru of America Inc.
Sulzberger Foundation
Superior Tube Co.
Swiss Bank Corp.
Symmes Foundation, F. W.
Tait Foundation, Frank M.
Teichert & Son, A.

Teleflex Inc.
Temple Foundation, T. L. L.
Temple-Inland Inc.
Tenneco Inc.
Tennessee Valley Printing Co.
Texas Commerce Bank-Houston, N.A.
Textron, Inc.
Thalhimer and Family Foundation, Charles G.
Thomasville Furniture Industries
Thompson Co., J. Walter
Thorne Foundation
Thornton Foundation, Flora L.
Times Mirror Company, The
Timken Foundation of Canton
Titus Foundation, Roy and Niuta
Towsley Foundation, Harry A. and Margaret D.
Transco Energy Co.
Travelers Inc.
Trexler Trust, Harry C.
Trull Foundation
Trust Company Bank
Tuch Foundation, Michael
Tucker Charitable Trust, Rose E.
Tupancy-Harris Foundation of 1986
Turner Charitable Foundation
Unger Foundation, Aber D.
Unilever United States, Inc.
Union Bank
Union Electric Co.
Union Pacific Corp.
U.S. Bank of Washington
Unitrode Corp.
Unocal Corp.
US WEST, Inc.
USG Corporation
USL Capital Corporation
USX Corporation
Valentine Foundation, Lawson
Valmont Industries, Inc.
Van Evera Foundation, Dewitt
Van Wert County Foundation
Vevay-Switzerland County Foundation
Virginia Power Co.
Vulcan Materials Co.
Wahlstrom Foundation
Wal-Mart Stores, Inc.
Wallace-Reader's Digest Fund, Lila
Walsh Foundation
Warner Fund, Albert and Bessie
Washington Forrest Foundation
Washington Mutual Savings Bank
Washington Water Power Co.
Wean Foundation, Raymond John
Webber Oil Co.
Wege Foundation
Wells Foundation, Franklin H. and Ruth L.
Wendt Foundation, Margaret L.
Wertheim Foundation, Dr. Herbert A.
West One Bancorp
Westerman Foundation, Samuel L.
Western New York Foundation
Westvaco Corporation
Weyerhaeuser Co.
Wheat First Butcher Singer, Inc.
Wheeler Foundation
Whirlpool Corporation
Whiting Foundation
Whittenberger Foundation, Claude R. and Ethel B.
Wiley & Sons, Inc., John
Williams Companies, The
Wilmington Trust Co.
Wilson Fund, Matilda R.
Windham Foundation
Winston Foundation, Norman and Rosita
Winter Construction Co.
Winthrop Trust, Clara B.
Wisconsin Power & Light Co.

Witco Corp.
Wood Foundation of Chambersburg, PA
Woolley Foundation, Vasser
Wyman Youth Trust
Wyomissing Foundation
Zenkel Foundation

Visual Arts

Ahmanson Foundation
Alabama Power Co.
Aldus Corp.
Aluminum Co. of America
American National Bank & Trust Co. of Chicago
American Natural Resources Company
American United Life Insurance Co.
Ames Charitable Trust, Harriett
Appleton Papers Inc.
AT&T Corp.
Avery Arts Foundation, Milton and Sally
Baldwin Memorial Foundation, Fred
Bank of Boston Corp.
Barth Foundation, Theodore H.
Bedsole Foundation, J. L.
Bemis Company, Inc.
Bethlehem Steel Corp.
Bingham Foundation, William
Binney & Smith Inc.
Block, H&R
Blount, Inc.
Burdines Inc.
Burnett-Tandy Foundation
Bush Foundation
Central Maine Power Co.
Champion International Corporation
Chase Manhattan Bank, N.A.
Chicago Sun-Times, Inc.
Christian Dior New York, Inc.
Clorox Co.
Colonial Life & Accident Insurance Co.
Columbia Foundation
Continental Corp.
Corning Incorporated
Cosmair, Inc.
Cowles Charitable Trust
Cowles Media Co.
Daily News
Dodge Foundation, Geraldine R.
Dow Corning Corp.
Dreyfus Foundation, Max and Victoria
du Pont de Nemours & Co., E. I.
Duchossois Industries Inc.
Eaton Corporation
Encyclopaedia Britannica, Inc.
Evans Foundation, Thomas J.
Favrot Fund
Federated Mutual Insurance Co.
Fireman's Fund Insurance Co.
First Tennessee Bank
First Union Corp.
Fleet Financial Group, Inc.
Gates Foundation
GATX Corp.
General Motors Corp.
Getty Trust, J. Paul
Globe Newspaper Co.
Goldsmith Foundation, Horace W.
Goldwyn Foundation, Samuel
Goodrich Co., The B.F.
Gould Foundation, The Florence
Graham Foundation for Advanced Studies in the Fine Arts
Graham Fund, Philip L.
Grand Rapids Label Co.
Greenwall Foundation
Griggs and Mary Griggs Burke Foundation, Mary Livingston
Hardin Foundation, Phil
Hauser Foundation

HCA Foundation
Hechinger Co.
Heinz Trust, Drue
Heublein Inc.
Hillman Family Foundation, Alex
Hyde and Watson Foundation
International Business Machines Corp.
James River Corp. of Virginia
Jaydor Corp.
Johnson & Higgins
Jones Foundation, Daisy Marquis
Kansas City Southern Industries
Kennecott Corporation
Kingsbury Corp.
Lemberg Foundation
Long Island Lighting Co.
MacArthur Foundation, John D. and Catherine T.
Macy & Co., Inc., R.H.
Management Compensation Group/Dulworth Inc.
Maritz Inc.
May Foundation, Wilbur
McDonald & Company Securities, Inc.
Meadows Foundation
Medtronic, Inc.
Meyer Memorial Trust
Miller Brewing Company/North Carolina
Morgan & Company, J.P.
Morgan Stanley & Co., Inc.
Morrison Charitable Trust, Pauline A. and George R.
Mosinee Paper Corp.
Mott Fund, Ruth
The New Yorker Magazine, Inc.
Northwest Natural Gas Co.
Norton Co.
Norton Foundation Inc.
Norwest Bank Nebraska, N.A.
Olin Corp.
Pacific Telesis Group
Penn Foundation, William
Pew Charitable Trusts
Pforzheimer Foundation, Carl and Lily
Piankova Foundation, Tatiana
Pioneer Trust Bank, NA
Polaroid Corp.
Providence Gas Co.
Provident Life & Accident Insurance Company of America
Pulitzer Publishing Co.
Rohatyn Foundation, Felix and Elizabeth
Rose Foundation, Billy
Rouse Co.
Royal Group, Inc.
Rubinstein Foundation, Helena
SAFECO Corp.
Salomon Inc.
San Diego Gas & Electric
Sara Lee Corp.
Sara Lee Hosiery, Inc.
Scherman Foundation
Schuller International
Seaway Food Town, Inc.
Security Life of Denver Insurance Co.
Sedgwick James Inc.
Shawmut National Corp.
Shenandoah Life Insurance Co.
Smith Trust, May and Stanley
Tait Foundation, Frank M.
Tenneco Inc.
Transco Energy Co.
Travelers Inc.
Trull Foundation
Union Camp Corporation
Union Electric Co.
U.S. Bank of Washington
Unitrode Corp.
Upton Foundation, Frederick S.
Vale Foundation, Ruby R.
Virginia Power Co.
Vulcan Materials Co.
Wallace-Reader's Digest Fund, Lila
West One Bancorp

Whirlpool Corporation
Winchester Foundation
Winston Foundation, Norman and Rosita
Winter Construction Co.
Witco Corp.
Zenkel Foundation

Civic & Public Affairs

African American Affairs

Aetna Life & Casualty Co.
Alavi Foundation of New York
Alcon Laboratories, Inc.
AlliedSignal Inc.
Allyn Foundation
Aluminum Co. of America
American National Bank & Trust Co. of Chicago
American President Companies, Ltd.
Amoco Corporation
AMR Corp.
Astor Foundation, Vincent
AT&T Corp.
Atran Foundation
Avery Arts Foundation, Milton and Sally
Bank One, Youngstown, NA
Beazley Foundation/Frederick Foundation
Bell Atlantic Corp.
Bethlehem Steel Corp.
Blue Cross & Blue Shield United of Wisconsin
Blum-Kovler Foundation
Boettcher Foundation
Borden, Inc.
Bremer Foundation, Otto
Bristol-Myers Squibb Company
Bryn Mawr Trust Co.
Cabot Corp.
Carnegie Corporation of New York
Carpenter Technology Corp.
Chartwell Foundation
Chesebrough-Pond's USA Co.
Chevron Corporation
Chicago Sun-Times, Inc.
Citizens Bank of Rhode Island
Clarke Trust, John
Clorox Co.
Columbus Dispatch Printing Co.
Commerce Bancshares, Inc.
Connecticut Mutual Life Insurance Company
Continental Corp.
Cornell Trust, Peter C.
Cowles Charitable Trust
CS First Boston Corporation
Deuble Foundation, George H.
Dexter Charitable Fund, Eugene A.
Dishman Charitable Foundation Trust, H. E. and Kate
Donner Foundation, William H.
Dun & Bradstreet Corp.
Eastman Kodak Company
Eaton Foundation, Cyrus
Eddy Family Memorial Fund, C. K.
Edgewater Steel Corp.
Evans Foundation, Lettie Pate
Exxon Corporation
Fair Oaks Foundation, Inc.
Federal-Mogul Corporation
Fleming Cos. Food Distribution Center
Flowers Charitable Trust, Albert W. and Edith V.
Ford Foundation
Ford Motor Co.
Freeport-McMoRan Inc.
Friedman Family Foundation

General Motors Corp.
German Protestant Orphan Asylum Association
Gheens Foundation
Giant Eagle, Inc.
Giant Food Inc.
Glaser Foundation
Gleason Foundation
Glick Foundation, Eugene and Marilyn
Goldseker Foundation of Maryland, Morris
Gould Electronics Inc.
Gulf Power Co.
Harcourt General, Inc.
Harsco Corp.
Hartmarx Corporation
Hasbro Inc.
Hazen Foundation, Edward W.
Hechinger Co.
Heinz Company, H. J.
Heinz Endowment, Vira I.
Hoover Foundation
Houston Endowment
Howard and Bush Foundation
Huber Foundation
ITT Hartford Insurance Group, Inc.
Jacobs Family Foundation
Jaffe Foundation
Jarson-Stanley and Mickey Kaplan Foundation, Isaac and Esther
Jewish Healthcare Foundation of Pittsburgh
JM Foundation
Jockey Hollow Foundation
Johnson Foundation, Willard T. C.
Jones Foundation, Daisy Marquis
Kansas City Southern Industries
Kimberly-Clark Corp.
Kresge Foundation
Ladd Charitable Corporation, Helen and George
LEF Foundation
Levitt Foundation
Levy Foundation, June Rockwell
Loews Corporation
M/A-COM, Inc.
MacArthur Foundation, John D. and Catherine T.
Madison Gas & Electric Co.
Martin Marietta Corp.
Mattel, Inc.
May Department Stores Company, The
MCA Inc.
McDonald & Company Securities, Inc.
McFeely-Rogers Foundation
MCI Communications Corp.
Medtronic, Inc.
Merrick Foundation
Merrill Lynch & Co., Inc.
Metropolitan Life Insurance Co.
Miller Brewing Company/North Carolina
Mills Fund, Frances Goll
Mitsubishi Motor Sales of America, Inc.
Morgan & Company, J.P.
Moses Fund, Henry and Lucy
Mott Foundation, Charles Stewart
Mott Fund, Ruth
Neuberger Foundation, Roy R. and Marie S.
New Jersey Natural Gas Co.
New-Land Foundation
New York Life Insurance Co.
Norfolk Shipbuilding & Drydock Corp.
Norton Foundation Inc.
Old National Bank in Evansville
Olin Foundation, Spencer T. and Ann W.
O'Quinn Foundation, John M. and Nancy C.
PHH Corporation

Pineywoods Foundation
Pitt-Des Moines Inc.
PNC Bank, N.A.
Premier Industrial Corp.
Providence Journal Company
Public Service Co. of New Mexico
Public Welfare Foundation
Rockwell International Corporation
Rowland Foundation
Ruan Foundation Trust, John
Saint Paul Companies, Inc.
Sawyer Charitable Foundation
SBC Communications Inc.
Scherman Foundation
Scripps Co., E.W.
Seagram & Sons, Inc., Joseph E.
Shawmut National Corp.
Sierra Pacific Resources
Solow Foundation
Stanley Works
Sternberger Foundation, Tannenbaum
Stone Charitable Foundation
Stupp Foundation, Norman J.
Taconic Foundation
Tait Foundation, Frank M.
Taubman Foundation, A. Alfred
Temple-Inland Inc.
Texaco Inc.
Texas Commerce Bank-Houston, N.A.
Thompson Co., J. Walter
Times Mirror Company, The
Unilever United States, Inc.
Union Bank
Union Electric Co.
United Airlines, Inc.
U.S. Bank of Washington
Unocal Corp.
Wachovia Bank of North Carolina, N.A.
Weil, Gotshal and Manges Foundation
Wiremold Co.
Wisconsin Power & Light Co.
Zenkel Foundation

Asian American Affairs

Bank One, Youngstown, NA
BankAmerica Corp.
Bishop Foundation, E. K. and Lillian F.
Bodman Foundation
Booth Ferris Foundation
Bothin Foundation
Bremer Foundation, Otto
Carnegie Corporation of New York
Carolyn Foundation
Carver Charitable Trust, Roy J.
CBS, Inc.
Chase Manhattan Bank, N.A.
Clorox Co.
Columbia Foundation
Cooke Foundation
Cowell Foundation, S. H.
Davis Foundation, Edwin W. and Catherine M.
Douty Foundation
First Hawaiian, Inc.
Friedman Family Foundation
General Mills, Inc.
Haas, Jr. Fund, Evelyn and Walter
Hazen Foundation, Edward W.
Houston Endowment
Humana, Inc.
Irvine Foundation, James
Kansas City Southern Industries
Kirkpatrick Foundation
Knox, Sr., and Pearl Wallis Knox Charitable Foundation, Robert W.
Lux Foundation, Miranda
McDonald & Company Securities, Inc.
Meadows Foundation

Meyer Memorial Trust
Mitsubishi Motor Sales of America, Inc.
Nestle USA Inc.
New York Life Insurance Co.
Pick, Jr. Fund, Albert
Retirement Research Foundation
Reynolds Foundation, Christopher
Rosenberg Foundation
Russell Trust, Josephine G.
Saint Paul Companies, Inc.
Sarkeys Foundation
Taconic Foundation
Teleflex Inc.
Times Mirror Company, The
Union Bank
U.S. Bank of Washington
USL Capital Corporation
Washington Mutual Savings Bank
Whitecap Foundation

Botanical Gardens/Parks

Abell-Hanger Foundation
Achelis Foundation
Ahmanson Foundation
Aldus Corp.
Allegheny Foundation
Altman Foundation
Aluminum Co. of America
AMCORE Bank, N.A. Rockford
American General Finance Corp.
AMR Corp.
Arkell Hall Foundation
Arnhold Foundation
Asplundh Foundation
Astor Foundation, Vincent
Atherton Family Foundation
Atran Foundation
Audubon State Bank
Auerbach Foundation, Beatrice Fox
Ayres Foundation, Inc.
Baldwin Foundation, David M. and Barbara
Ball Brothers Foundation
Ball Foundation, George and Frances
Bank of Boston
BankAmerica Corp.
Banta Corp.
Barra Foundation
Barth Foundation, Theodore H.
Bay Foundation
Bechtel, Jr. Foundation, S. D.
Bedsole Foundation, J. L.
Beech Aircraft Corp.
Bell Foundation, James F.
Berger Foundation, H. N. and Frances C.
Bertha Foundation
Bethlehem Steel Corp.
Binswanger Cos.
Blandin Foundation
Blue Bell, Inc.
Bobst Foundation, Elmer and Mamdouha
Bodman Foundation
Boettcher Foundation
Booth Ferris Foundation
Bremer Foundation, Otto
Breyer Foundation
Bristol-Myers Squibb Company
Bryn Mawr Trust Co.
Burnett-Tandy Foundation
Butz Foundation
Cain Foundation, Gordon and Mary
Callaway Foundation
Carolyn Foundation
Carpenter Foundation
Carpenter Foundation, E. Rhodes and Leona B.
Carter Foundation, Amon G.
Carter Foundation, Beirne

Castle Foundation, Harold K. L.
Chadwick Fund, Dorothy Jordan
Charina Foundation
Chase Manhattan Bank, N.A.
Chastain Charitable Foundation, Robert Lee and Thomas M.
CINergy
Claiborne and Art Ortenberg Foundation, Liz
CLARCOR Inc.
Clay Foundation
Clements Foundation
Cogswell Benevolent Trust
Cole Foundation, Olive B.
Commerce Bancshares, Inc.
Cooke Foundation
Cord Foundation, E. L.
Coughlin-Saunders Foundation
Cowles Charitable Trust
Crandall Memorial Foundation, J. Ford
Crane Co.
Crocker Trust, Mary A.
CS First Boston Corporation
CT Corp. System
Cullen Foundation
Culpeper Foundation, Charles E.
Culver Foundation, Constans
Cummins Engine Co.
Daily News
Darby Foundation
Davis Foundation, Edwin W. and Catherine M.
Dekko Foundation
Dentsply International Inc.
Dillon Foundation
Dodge Foundation, Cleveland H.
Dodge Jones Foundation
Donnelley Foundation, Gaylord and Dorothy
Doss Foundation, M. S.
Douty Foundation
Dow Foundation, Herbert H. and Grace A.
Dula Educational and Charitable Foundation, Caleb C. and Julia W.
Eastman Kodak Company
Eaton Foundation, Cyrus
Eberly Foundation
Erpf Fund, Armand G.
Evans Foundation, T. M.
Evans Foundation, Thomas J.
Exxon Corporation
Fair Oaks Foundation, Inc.
Fair Play Foundation
Farish Fund, William Stamps
Farr Trust, Frank M. and Alice M.
Favrot Fund
Federated Mutual Insurance Co.
Femino Foundation
Firman Fund
Fish Foundation, Ray C.
Fishback Foundation Trust, Harmes C.
Folger Fund
Fondren Foundation
Ford Motor Co.
Fort Wayne National Bank
Frear Eleemosynary Trust, Mary D. and Walter F.
Freeport Brick Co.
Freeport-McMoRan Inc.
Fribourg Foundation
Frohring Foundation, Paul and Maxine
Frohring Foundation, William O. and Gertrude Lewis
Fuqua Foundation, J. B.
GAR Foundation
Gates Foundation
Gaylord Foundation, Clifford Willard
Geneseo Foundation
Gershman Foundation, Joel
Gleason Foundation
Goldsmith Foundation, Horace W.

Grand Rapids Label Co.
Green Foundation, Allen P. and Josephine B.
Greenwall Foundation
Greve Foundation, William and Mary
Griffis Foundation
Griffith Foundation, W. C.
Griggs and Mary Griggs Burke Foundation, Mary Livingston
Hagedorn Fund
Hamman Foundation, George and Mary Josephine
Handy and Harman Foundation
Harcourt Foundation, Ellen Knowles
Harland Charitable Foundation, John and Wilhelmina D.
Harmon Foundation, Pearl M. and Julia J.
Harriman Foundation, Mary W.
Harrington Foundation, Francis A. and Jacquelyn H.
Hartz Foundation
Harvey Foundation, Felix
Heckscher Foundation for Children
Helmerich Foundation
Henderson Foundation, George B.
Heydt Fund, Nan and Matilda
Hickory Tech Corp.
Hill Foundation, Sandy
Hillsdale Fund
Hopedale Foundation
Houston Endowment
Howard and Bush Foundation
Hugoton Foundation
Huisking Foundation
Humphrey Fund, George M. and Pamela S.
Hunt Charitable Trust, C. Giles
Hunt Foundation
Hyde and Watson Foundation
Independence Foundation
Integra Bank of Uniontown
Jameson Foundation, J. W. and Ida M.
Jaydor Corp.
JELD-WEN, Inc.
Johnson Foundation, M. G. and Lillie A.
Johnson Fund, Edward C.
Jones Foundation, Daisy Marquis
Jones Foundation, Fletcher
Jordan Charitable Foundation, Mary Ranken Jordan and Ettie A.
Journal-Gazette Co.
Justus Trust, Edith C.
Kansas City Southern Industries
Kantzler Foundation
Kaplan Fund, J. M.
Kavanagh Foundation, T. James
Kelly Tractor Co.
Kemper Foundation, William T.
Kettering Fund
Kiewit Foundation, Peter
Kline Foundation, Josiah W. and Bessie H.
Knight Foundation, John S. and James L.
Knox, Sr., and Pearl Wallis Knox Charitable Foundation, Robert W.
Koehler Foundation, Marcia and Otto
Kohn-Joseloff Foundation
Kresge Foundation
Kuehn Foundation
Kunkel Foundation, John Crain
Laffey-McHugh Foundation
Lang Foundation, Eugene M.
Lauder Foundation
Lemberg Foundation
Leuthold Foundation
Littauer Foundation, Lucius N.
Lockhart Vaughan Foundation
Loews Corporation
Long Foundation, J.M.
Longwood Foundation

Louisiana-Pacific Corp.
Lurie Foundation, Louis R.
Maddox Foundation, J. F.
Madison Gas & Electric Co.
Magowan Family Foundation
Mailman Foundation
Maneely Fund
Marpat Foundation
Marshall Trust in Memory of Sanders McDaniel, Harriet McDaniel
Martin Marietta Materials
Mather Charitable Trust, S. Livingston
Mather and William Gwinn Mather Fund, Elizabeth Ring
McCasland Foundation
McConnell Foundation
McCormick Trust, Anne
McDermott Foundation, Eugene
McEvoy Foundation, Mildred H.
McGonagle Foundation, Dextra Baldwin
McInerny Foundation
McLean Contributionship
McMahon Foundation
Meadows Foundation
Mellon Family Foundation, R. K.
Mellon Foundation, Andrew W.
Memton Fund
Merck & Co.
Merrill Lynch & Co., Inc.
Meyer Memorial Trust
Middendorf Foundation
Monell Foundation, Ambrose
Moore & Sons, B.C.
Morgan Charitable Residual Trust, W. and E.
Morgan & Company, J.P.
Morgan Foundation, Burton D.
Morris Foundation, William T.
Morrison Charitable Trust, Pauline A. and George R.
Mosbacher, Jr. Foundation, Emil
Moses Fund, Henry and Lucy
Mosinee Paper Corp.
Munger Foundation, Alfred C.
Nestle USA Inc.
New-Land Foundation
New York Times Company
Noble Foundation, Edward John
Noble Foundation, Samuel Roberts
Norman Foundation, Summers A.
Northern States Power Co. (Minnesota)
O'Connor Foundation, A. Lindsay and Olive B.
O'Fallon Trust, Martin J. and Mary Anne
Offield Family Foundation
Olin Foundation, Spencer T. and Ann W.
Oliver Memorial Trust Foundation
Osborn Charitable Trust, Edward B.
Overbrook Foundation
Owen Industries, Inc.
Pacific Mutual Life Insurance Co.
Packard Foundation, David and Lucile
Pamida, Inc.
Parsons Foundation, Ralph M.
Peabody Charitable Fund, Amelia
Pella Corporation
Penn Foundation, William
Pfizer, Inc.
Phipps Foundation, Howard
Pierce Charitable Trust, Harold Whitworth
Pitt-Des Moines Inc.
Pittsburg Midway Coal Mining Co.
Pittsburgh Child Guidance Foundation

Porter Foundation, Mrs. Cheever
PPG Industries, Inc.
Prairie Foundation
Prospect Hill Foundation
Prudential Insurance Co. of America, The
Puterbaugh Foundation
Putnam Foundation
Reinberger Foundation
Rennebohm Foundation, Oscar
Reynolds Foundation, Edgar
Rice Foundation
Richardson Charitable Trust, Anne S.
Rixson Foundation, Oscar C.
RJR Nabisco Inc.
Robinson-Broadhurst Foundation
Rockwell Fund
Rohatyn Foundation, Felix and Elizabeth
Rose Foundation, Billy
Roseburg Forest Products Co.
Rosen Foundation, Joseph
Ross Memorial Foundation, Will
Ruan Foundation Trust, John
Rubin Foundation, Samuel
Rudin Foundation
Salomon Foundation, Richard and Edna
Saltonstall Charitable Foundation, Richard
Sasco Foundation
Scaife Family Foundation
Scherman Foundation
Schlumberger Ltd.
Schuller International
Schwartz Fund for Education and Health Research, Arnold and Marie
Scott Foundation, Virginia Steele
Scurlock Foundation
Seaver Charitable Trust, Richard C.
Seidman Family Foundation
Sharon Steel Corp.
Shaw Foundation, Arch W.
Skaggs Foundation, L. J. and Mary C.
Slifka Foundation, Joseph and Sylvia
Smith Foundation, Kelvin and Eleanor
Solow Foundation
South Bend Tribune
South Waite Foundation
Spalding Foundation, Eliot
Speyer Foundation, Alexander C. and Tillie S.
Sprague Educational and Charitable Foundation, Seth
Springs Foundation
Starr Foundation
Steinhagen Benevolent Trust, B. A. and Elinor
Steinman Foundation, James Hale
Strawbridge Foundation of Pennsylvania II, Margaret Dorrance
Stupp Foundation, Norman J.
Sturgis Charitable and Educational Trust, Roy and Christine
Sulzberger Foundation
Superior Tube Co.
Swalm Foundation
Tait Foundation, Frank M.
Teleflex Inc.
Texaco Inc.
Texas Commerce Bank-Houston, N.A.
Thomas Industries
Thorne Foundation
Todd Co., A.M.
Tonya Memorial Foundation
Travelers Inc.
Trexler Trust, Harry C.
Tucker Charitable Trust, Rose E.
Turner Charitable Foundation
Unilever United States, Inc.

Union Bank
Union Electric Co.
Upjohn Foundation, Harold and Grace
Uris Brothers Foundation
Valentine Foundation, Lawson
Valmont Industries, Inc.
Van Wert County Foundation
Wallace-Reader's Digest Fund, Lila
Warwick Foundation
Wege Foundation
Weil, Gotshal and Manges Foundation
Wertheim Foundation, Dr. Herbert A.
Westerman Foundation, Samuel L.
Western New York Foundation
Wheeler Foundation
Whirlpool Corporation
Whittenberger Foundation, Claude R. and Ethel B.
Wickes Foundation, Harvey Randall
WICOR, Inc.
Wiley & Sons, Inc., John
Wilson Foundation, H. W.
Wisconsin Power & Light Co.
Witter Foundation, Dean
Yeager Charitable Trust, Lester E.
Zachry Co., H.B.

Business/Free Enterprise

Abell-Hanger Foundation
Air Products and Chemicals, Inc.
Alabama Power Co.
Alcon Laboratories, Inc.
Allegheny Foundation
Allegheny Ludlum Corp.
Alumax Inc.
Aluminum Co. of America
AMCORE Bank, N.A. Rockford
American Natural Resources Company
American United Life Insurance Co.
Amfac/JMB Hawaii Inc.
Amoco Corporation
AMP Incorporated
AMR Corp.
Andersen Corp.
Andreas Foundation
AON Corporation
Appleton Papers Inc.
Archer-Daniels-Midland Co.
Arkansas Power & Light Co.
Armco Inc.
Armstrong Foundation
Audubon State Bank
Avon Products, Inc.
Babcock & Wilcox Co.
Bank of Boston Corp.
Bank of New York Company, Inc.
Bank One, Texas-Houston Office
Bank One, Youngstown, NA
BankAmerica Corp.
Banta Corp.
Barry Corp., R. G.
Battelle Memorial Institute
Bay Area Foods
BE&K Inc.
Bemis Company, Inc.
Bethlehem Steel Corp.
Bettingen Corporation, Burton G.
Betts Industries
Binney & Smith Inc.
Binswanger Cos.
Bird Corp.
Block, H&R
Blue Cross & Blue Shield United of Wisconsin
Blum-Kovler Foundation
Boatmen's Bancshares, Inc.
Boise Cascade Corporation

Borden, Inc.
Boswell Foundation, James G.
Bowen Foundation, Ethel N.
Bridgestone/Firestone, Inc.
Bristol-Myers Squibb Company
Brown & Williamson Tobacco Corp.
Bryn Mawr Trust Co.
Bucyrus-Erie Company
Buhl Foundation
Burlington Industries, Inc.
Cabot Corp.
Callaway Foundation
Centerior Energy Corp.
Chase Manhattan Bank, N.A.
Chesebrough-Pond's USA Co.
Chevron Corporation
Citibank
CNA Financial Corporation/CNA Insurance Companies
Colonial Life & Accident Insurance Co.
Coltec Industries, Inc.
Columbus Dispatch Printing Co.
Comerica Incorporated
Connecticut Mutual Life Insurance Company
Consolidated Natural Gas Co.
Continental Corp.
Cooke Foundation
Cooper Industries, Inc.
Coors Foundation, Adolph
CPC International Inc.
CR Industries
Crane Co.
Crestlea Foundation
CS First Boston Corporation
Curtice-Burns Foods, Inc.
Davis Foundation, Edwin W. and Catherine M.
Delaware North Co., Inc.
Detroit Edison Co.
Dexter Charitable Fund, Eugene A.
Dodge Jones Foundation
Donner Foundation, William H.
Douglas & Lomason Company
Dresser Industries, Inc.
du Pont de Nemours & Co., E. I.
Duke Power Co.
Dun & Bradstreet Corp.
Eastman Kodak Company
Eaton Corporation
Eddy Family Memorial Fund, C. K.
English Memorial Fund, Florence C. and H. L.
Enron Corp.
Ethyl Corp
Exchange National Bank
Farish Fund, William Stamps
Federal-Mogul Corporation
Federated Mutual Insurance Co.
First Fidelity Bank
First Interstate Bank of Oregon
First Source Corp.
First Tennessee Bank
First Union Corp.
Firstar Bank Milwaukee, N.A.
Ford Foundation
Ford Motor Co.
Forest Oil Corp.
Freeman Charitable Trust, Samuel
Freeport-McMoRan Inc.
Frost National Bank
GAR Foundation
Gates Foundation
GenCorp Inc.
General Mills, Inc.
General Motors Corp.
Georgia-Pacific Corporation
Giant Food Stores
Goodrich Co., The B.F.
Gould Electronics Inc.
Guardian Life Insurance Company of America
Gulf Power Co.
Handy and Harman Foundation
Harrison Foundation, Fred G.

Harsco Corp.
Hartmarx Corporation
Hawkins Foundation, Robert Z.
HCA Foundation
Hechinger Co.
Heinz Company, H. J.
Heinz Endowment, Vira I.
Heller Financial, Inc.
Henkel Corp.
Hershey Foods Corp.
Hickory Tech Corp.
Hook Drugs
Houston Industries Incorporated
Howard and Bush Foundation
Hoyt Foundation
Hudson-Webber Foundation
Hulme Charitable Foundation, Milton G.
Humana, Inc.
ICI Americas Inc.
Illinois Tool Works, Inc.
Inland Container Corp.
International Foundation
ITT Hartford Insurance Group, Inc.
Jacobs Family Foundation
James River Corp. of Virginia
Jaydor Corp.
JELD-WEN, Inc.
JM Foundation
John Hancock Mutual Life Insurance Co.
Johnson Controls Inc.
Johnson Foundation, Willard T. C.
Johnson & Higgins
Johnson & Son, S.C.
Kansas City Southern Industries
Kimberly-Clark Corp.
Koch Charitable Foundation, Charles G.
Laurel Foundation
LBJ Family Foundation
Life Insurance Co. of Georgia
Linn-Henley Charitable Trust
Lipton, Thomas J.
Lux Foundation, Miranda
MacArthur Foundation, John D. and Catherine T.
Macy & Co., Inc., R.H.
Madison Gas & Electric Co.
Management Compensation Group/Dulworth Inc.
Mardag Foundation
Maritz Inc.
Marsh & McLennan Companies, Inc.
Marshall Trust in Memory of Sanders McDaniel, Harriet McDaniel
Martin Marietta Corp.
Mattel, Inc.
MCA Inc.
McCasland Foundation
McCormick & Co. Inc.
McCune Charitable Foundation, Marshall and Perrine D.
McCune Charitable Trust, John R.
McDonald & Company Securities, Inc.
McDonnell Douglas Corp.-West
McFawn Trust No. 2, Lois Sisler
MCI Communications Corp.
McKenna Foundation, Philip M.
McLean Contributionship
Mead Corporation, The
Meadows Foundation
Mellon Foundation, Richard King
Memton Fund
Merck & Co. Human Health Division
Merrill Lynch & Co., Inc.
Metropolitan Life Insurance Co.
Miller Brewing Company/North Carolina

Mitchell Energy & Development Corp.
Mobil Oil Corp.
Morgan & Company, J.P.
Morrison Knudsen Corporation
Mosinee Paper Corp.
Mott Foundation, Charles Stewart
Nabisco Foods Group
Nalco Chemical Co.
National Steel Corp.
National Westminster Bank New Jersey
Nestle USA Inc.
New York Life Insurance Co.
Noble Foundation, Samuel Roberts
Norfolk Shipbuilding & Drydock Corp.
Norton Co.
Novell Inc.
NYNEX Corporation
Ohrstrom Foundation
Old National Bank in Evansville
Olin Corp.
Outboard Marine Corp.
Park Foundation
Pew Charitable Trusts
Pfizer, Inc.
Phelps Dodge Corporation
Pitt-Des Moines Inc.
PNC Bank, N.A.
Pollock Company Foundation, William B.
Potomac Electric Power Co.
PPG Industries, Inc.
Prudential Insurance Co. of America, The
Prudential Securities, Inc.
Public Service Co. of New Mexico
Public Welfare Foundation
Pulitzer Publishing Co.
Putnam Foundation
Ralston Purina Co.
Raymond Corp.
Reynolds Foundation, Donald W.
RJR Nabisco Inc.
Rockwell International Corporation
Rohm & Haas Co.
Rosenberg Foundation
Rose's Stores, Inc.
Royal Group, Inc.
Rubin Foundation, Samuel
Rudin Foundation
Saint Paul Companies, Inc.
Salomon Foundation, Richard and Edna
Sandusky International Inc.
Sara Lee Hosiery, Inc.
Sargent Foundation, Newell B.
Scherer Foundation, Karla
Schoenleber Foundation
Schroeder Foundation, Walter
Seafirst Corporation
Seagram & Sons, Inc., Joseph E.
Sentry Insurance A Mutual Company
Sharon Steel Corp.
Shawmut National Corp.
Shell Oil Company
Shott, Jr. Foundation, Hugh I.
Sierra Pacific Industries
Sierra Pacific Resources
Simon Foundation, William E. and Carol G.
Sloan Foundation, Alfred P.
Smith Corp., A.O.
Sonat Inc.
Southern California Edison Co.
Sprague Educational and Charitable Foundation, Seth
Square D Co.
Stanley Works
Taube Family Foundation
Teleflex Inc.
Tenneco Inc.
Texaco Inc.
Textron, Inc.
Thermo Electron Corp.
Thompson Co., J. Walter

Timken Foundation of Canton
Tonya Memorial Foundation
Tozer Foundation
Transco Energy Co.
Travelers Inc.
Trust Company Bank
Unilever United States, Inc.
Union Camp Corporation
Union Pacific Corp.
United Airlines, Inc.
U.S. Bank of Washington
Unocal Corp.
US WEST, Inc.
USL Capital Corporation
USX Corporation
Valmont Industries, Inc.
Van Every Foundation, Philip L.
Vollbrecht Foundation, Frederick A.
Vulcan Materials Co.
Wachovia Bank of North Carolina, N.A.
Wal-Mart Stores, Inc.
Weil, Gotshal and Manges Foundation
West Foundation, Harry and Ethel
Western New York Foundation
Westvaco Corporation
Weyerhaeuser Co.
Wheat First Butcher Singer, Inc.
Whirlpool Corporation
Whitehead Charitable Foundation
Wickes Foundation, Harvey Randall
Williams Companies, The
Wisconsin Power & Light Co.
Wyman Youth Trust

Chambers of Commerce

Acme-McCrary Corp./Sapona Manufacturing Co.
Aetna Life & Casualty Co.
Alabama Gas Corp.
Allegheny Ludlum Corp.
AlliedSignal Inc.
Altschul Foundation
Amcast Industrial Corp.
AMCORE Bank, N.A. Rockford
American National Bank & Trust Co. of Chicago
Armco Inc.
Batts Foundation
Baughman Foundation
BE&K Inc.
Benwood Foundation
Bingham Second Betterment Fund, William
Bryn Mawr Trust Co.
Carpenter Technology Corp.
CIBC Wood Gundy
CIGNA Corporation
CINergy
Clay Foundation
Cole Foundation, Olive B.
Columbus Dispatch Printing Co.
Connecticut Mutual Life Insurance Company
Crawford Estate, E. R.
Dentsply International Inc.
Dodge Jones Foundation
Donner Foundation, William H.
Duchossois Industries Inc.
Duke Power Co.
Eberly Foundation
Edgewater Steel Corp.
Elf Atochem North America, Inc.
Federated Mutual Insurance Co.
First Financial Bank FSB
Folger Fund
France Foundation, Jacob and Annita
French Oil Mill Machinery Co.
Gazette Co.

Giant Food Inc.
Gulf Power Co.
Harrison Foundation, Fred G.
Herzstein Charitable Foundation, Albert and Ethel
Hickory Tech Corp.
Hill Foundation, Sandy
Holnam
Hudson-Webber Foundation
Ittleson Foundation
Jacobson Foundation, Bernard H. and Blanche E.
JELD-WEN, Inc.
Kansas City Southern Industries
Kemper Foundation, William T.
KN Energy, Inc.
Knoll Group
LamCo. Communications
Lydall, Inc.
Madison Gas & Electric Co.
Martin Marietta Materials
Mead Corporation, The
Merrick Foundation
Miller Brewing Company/North Carolina
Mitsubishi Motor Sales of America, Inc.
Moore Charitable Foundation, Marjorie
Mosinee Paper Corp.
Murphy Co. Foundation, G.C.
NewMil Bancorp
Pella Corporation
Pittsburg Midway Coal Mining Co.
Raymond Corp.
Rieke Corp.
RJR Nabisco Inc.
Rockwell International Corporation
Rose's Stores, Inc.
Ross Foundation
Ruan Foundation Trust, John
Russell Trust, Josephine G.
Safety Fund National Bank
Saint Paul Companies, Inc.
Sargent Foundation, Newell B.
Seneca Foods Corp.
Southwestern Electric Power Co.
Stanley Charitable Foundation, A.W.
Stearns Trust, Artemas W.
Tait Foundation, Frank M.
Temple Foundation, T. L. L.
Times Mirror Company, The
Timken Foundation of Canton
Union Bank
U.S. Bank of Washington
Unitrode Corp.
Wilson Fund, Matilda R.
Wood Foundation of Chambersburg, PA

Civil Rights

Acme-McCrary Corp./Sapona Manufacturing Co.
Acushnet Co.
Ahmanson Foundation
Air Products and Chemicals, Inc.
Alabama Gas Corp.
Aluminum Co. of America
American Brands, Inc.
Amfac/JMB Hawaii Inc.
AMP Incorporated
AMR Corp.
Andersen Corp.
Andreas Foundation
Anheuser-Busch Companies, Inc.
Ansin Private Foundation, Ronald M.
AON Corporation
Archer-Daniels-Midland Co.
Aristech Chemical Corp.
Arkansas Power & Light Co.
Armco Inc.
AT&T Corp.
Auerbach Foundation, Beatrice Fox
Avon Products, Inc.

O'Quinn Foundation, John M. and Nancy C.
Overlake Foundation
Owsley Foundation, Alvin and Lucy
Pamida, Inc.
Pella Corporation
Penn Foundation, William
Peters Foundation, Charles F.
Peterson Foundation, Hal and Charlie
Pew Charitable Trusts
Pittsburg Midway Coal Mining Co.
Pollock Company Foundation, William B.
Porter Testamentary Trust, James Hyde
Prairie Foundation
Puterbaugh Foundation
Quivey-Bay State Foundation
Raymond Corp.
Regenstein Foundation
Reynolds Foundation, Donald W.
Rice Charitable Foundation, Albert W.
Richardson Charitable Trust, Anne S.
Ritter Charitable Trust, George W. and Mary F.
Rose's Stores, Inc.
Ruan Foundation Trust, John
Saint Paul Companies, Inc.
Saltonstall Charitable Foundation, Richard
Sargent Foundation, Newell B.
Schiff Foundation, Dorothy
Schmitt Foundation, Kilian J. and Caroline F.
Schuller International
Schwartz Foundation, Arnold A.
Schwartz Fund for Education and Health Research, Arnold and Marie
Scott Fetzer Co.
Scott Foundation, William E.
Scurlock Foundation
Seaver Charitable Trust, Richard C.
Seneca Foods Corp.
Seton Leather Co.
Share Trust, Charles Morton
Sharon Steel Corp.
Sierra Pacific Industries
Sierra Pacific Resources
Slemp Foundation
Smith Foundation, Gordon V. and Helen C.
Sonat Inc.
Southwestern Electric Power Co.
Specialty Manufacturing Co.
Springs Foundation
SPX Corp.
Stabler Foundation, Donald B. and Dorothy L.
Stauffer Foundation, John and Beverly
Stevens Foundation, John T.
Strawbridge Foundation of Pennsylvania II, Margaret Dorrance
Sulzberger Foundation
Sundet Foundation
Sunnen Foundation
Taylor Foundation, Fred and Harriett
Temple Foundation, T. L. L.
Temple-Inland Inc.
Thomas Industries
Truland Foundation
Tucker Charitable Trust, Rose E.
Turner Charitable Foundation
Valmont Industries, Inc.
Vevay-Switzerland County Foundation
Vollbrecht Foundation, Frederick A.
Wallace Foundation, George R.
Walsh Foundation
Warwick Foundation

Wean Foundation, Raymond John
Wertheim Foundation, Dr. Herbert A.
West Foundation, Harry and Ethel
Wheeler Foundation
Wheeler Foundation, Wilmot
Whirlpool Corporation
Whitney Fund, David M.
Windham Foundation
Winnebago Industries, Inc.
Witco Corp.
Y and H Soda Foundation
Yeager Charitable Trust, Lester E.
Young Foundation, Robert R.
Zollner Foundation

Community Foundations

Abbott Laboratories
Abell-Hanger Foundation
Alabama Gas Corp.
Aldus Corp.
Allendale Insurance Co.
Allyn Foundation
Amcast Industrial Corp.
American Fidelity Corporation
American President Companies, Ltd.
Amoco Corporation
Anderson Foundation
Anderson Foundation, M. D.
Ansin Private Foundation, Ronald M.
Arnold Fund
Atherton Family Foundation
Ayres Foundation, Inc.
Baldwin Foundation, David M. and Barbara
Ball Brothers Foundation
Ball Foundation, George and Frances
Bank One, Youngstown, NA
BankAmerica Corp.
Barra Foundation
Barry Corp., R. G.
Barth Foundation, Theodore H.
Beloit Foundation
Benwood Foundation
Besser Foundation
Bethlehem Steel Corp.
Bingham Second Betterment Fund, William
Binney & Smith Inc.
Blandin Foundation
Blaustein Foundation, Louis and Henrietta
Blount, Inc.
Bobst Foundation, Elmer and Mamdouha
Borden, Inc.
Boswell Foundation, James G.
Boutell Memorial Fund
Brackenridge Foundation, George W.
Bremer Foundation, Otto
Breyer Foundation
Brunswick Corp.
Bryn Mawr Trust Co.
Bunbury Company
Burnett-Tandy Foundation
Carter Foundation, Amon G.
Centralia Foundation
Champion International Corporation
Charina Foundation
Cheney Foundation, Ben B.
Chicago Sun-Times, Inc.
CINergy
Clay Foundation
Clorox Co.
Cole Foundation, Olive B.
Columbus Dispatch Printing Co.
Commerce Bancshares, Inc.
Consumers Power Co.
Corning Incorporated
Cowell Foundation, S. H.
Curtice-Burns Foods, Inc.
Daugherty Foundation

Davis Foundation, Irene E. and George A.
Deere & Co.
Dekko Foundation
Dexter Charitable Fund, Eugene A.
Dillon Dunwalke Trust, Clarence and Anne
Dillon Foundation
Dr. Seuss Foundation
Donnelley Foundation, Gaylord and Dorothy
Douty Foundation
Dow Corning Corp.
Dow Foundation, Herbert H. and Grace A.
Dreyfus Foundation, Max and Victoria
Evans Foundation, Lettie Pate
Exxon Corporation
Federated Mutual Insurance Co.
Fenton Foundation
Fife Foundation, Elias and Bertha
Finch Foundation, Thomas Austin
Firestone, Jr. Foundation, Harvey
First Interstate Bank of Oregon
First Source Corp.
Ford Foundation
Ford Motor Co.
Forest Foundation
France Foundation, Jacob and Annita
French Oil Mill Machinery Co.
Friendship Fund
Fund for New Jersey
GAR Foundation
Gebbie Foundation
General Motors Corp.
Geneseo Foundation
Glanville Family Foundation
Glosser Foundation, David A.
Goldseker Foundation of Maryland, Morris
Good Samaritan
Haas, Jr. Fund, Evelyn and Walter
Hafif Family Foundation
Haigh-Scatena Foundation
Handy and Harman Foundation
Hardin Foundation, Phil
Harland Charitable Foundation, John and Wilhelmina D.
Harrington Foundation, Francis A. and Jacquelyn H.
Hazen Foundation, Edward W.
Hecht-Levi Foundation
Heinz Company, H. J.
Heinz Endowment, Howard
Heinz Endowment, Vira I.
Herrick Foundation
Hershey Foods Corp.
Hewlett Foundation, William and Flora
Hickory Tech Corp.
Higginson Trust, Corina
Hoffmann-La Roche Inc.
Holnam
Hudson-Webber Foundation
Humana, Inc.
Icahn Foundation, Carl C.
Irvine Foundation, James
Jaydor Corp.
Jewett Foundation, George Frederick
JFM Foundation
Jones Foundation, Fletcher
Kansas City Southern Industries
Kantzler Foundation
Kirkpatrick Foundation
KN Energy, Inc.
Knight Foundation, John S. and James L.
Koret Foundation
Kreitler Foundation
Kresge Foundation
Kutz Foundation, Milton and Hattie
Kuyper Foundation, Peter H. and E. Lucille

La-Z-Boy Chair Co.
LamCo. Communications
Lee Enterprises
Leighton-Oare Foundation
Lenna Foundation, Reginald A. and Elizabeth S.
Lockhart Vaughan Foundation
MacLeod Stewardship Foundation
Mailman Family Foundation, A. L.
Mardigian Foundation
Marmot Foundation
Mather Fund, Richard
Mather and William Gwinn Mather Fund, Elizabeth Ring
Mattel, Inc.
McCann Foundation
McCune Charitable Foundation, Marshall and Perrine D.
McDonald & Company Securities, Inc.
McEvoy Foundation, Mildred H.
McInerny Foundation
McMahan Foundation, Catherine L. and Robert O.
McQueen Foundation, Adeline and George
Mead Corporation, The
Merrill Lynch & Co., Inc.
Middendorf Foundation
Mielke Family Foundation
Miller-Mellor Association
Monfort Family Foundation
Mosinee Paper Corp.
Mott Foundation, Charles Stewart
Munson Foundation Trust, W. B.
Murphey Foundation, Lluella Morey
New York Mercantile Exchange
Newcombe Foundation, Charlotte W.
Norton Co.
Norton Family Foundation, Peter
Norton Foundation Inc.
Novell Inc.
Offield Family Foundation
OG&E Electric Services
Old National Bank in Evansville
Oppenstein Brothers Foundation
Overbrook Foundation
Overlake Foundation
Packard Foundation, David and Lucile
PaineWebber
Pamida, Inc.
Penguin Books USA, Inc.
Pforzheimer Foundation, Carl and Lily
Piper Jaffray Companies Inc.
Polaroid Corp.
Premier Industrial Corp.
Priddy Foundation
Prouty Foundation, Olive Higgins
Providence Journal Company
Public Service Co. of New Mexico
R. F. Foundation
Rand McNally & Co.
Reed Foundation
Reinberger Foundation
Reynolds Foundation, Edgar
Rogers Family Foundation
Rosenberg, Jr. Family Foundation, Louise and Claude
Rose's Stores, Inc.
Rubin Foundation, Samuel
Russell Trust, Josephine G.
Sandy Hill Foundation
Sargent Foundation, Newell B.
Sarkeys Foundation
SBC Communications Inc.
Schering-Plough Corp.
Schumann Fund for New Jersey
Scott Foundation, William E.

Second Foundation
Selby and Marie Selby Foundation, William G.
Semmes Foundation
Sequoia Foundation
Siltec Corp.
Sloan Foundation, Alfred P.
Smith Foundation, Ralph L.
Snow Memorial Trust, John Ben
Snyder Foundation, Harold B. and Dorothy A.
South Bend Tribune
Southwestern Electric Power Co.
Stanley Works
Stearns Trust, Artemas W.
Steele Foundation, Harry and Grace
Steele-Reese Foundation
Steinhagen Benevolent Trust, B. A. and Elinor
Strawbridge Foundation of Pennsylvania II, Margaret Dorrance
Sumners Foundation, Hatton W.
Tait Foundation, Frank M.
Taube Family Foundation
Tecumseh Products Co.
Temple-Inland Inc.
Thorne Foundation
Tobin Foundation
Tonya Memorial Foundation
Union Bank
Unitrode Corp.
USX Corporation
Wallace Foundation, George R.
Washington Forrest Foundation
Weingart Foundation
Wells Foundation, Franklin H. and Ruth L.
Westerman Foundation, Samuel L.
Wheeler Foundation
Whiting Foundation
Whitney Fund, David M.
Whittenberger Foundation, Claude R. and Ethel B.
Wickes Foundation, Harvey Randall
Wickson-Link Memorial Foundation
Wisconsin Power & Light Co.
Wise Foundation and Charitable Trust, Watson W.
Wood Foundation of Chambersburg, PA
Young Foundation, Hugo H. and Mabel B.
Zollner Foundation

Economic Development

Abbott Laboratories
Achelis Foundation
Aetna Life & Casualty Co.
Air Products and Chemicals, Inc.
AKC Fund
Akzo America
Akzo Chemicals Inc.
Allegheny Foundation
Allegheny Ludlum Corp.
Allianz Life Insurance Co. of North America
AlliedSignal Inc.
Allyn Foundation
Altman Foundation
Alumax Inc.
Aluminum Co. of America
Amcast Industrial Corp.
AMCORE Bank, N.A. Rockford
American Brands, Inc.
American Fidelity Corporation
American General Finance Corp.
American National Bank & Trust Co. of Chicago
American Natural Resources Company

Economic Policy

Employment/Job Training

Bell Foundation, James F.
Beloit Foundation
Bemis Company, Inc.
Benedum Foundation, Claude Worthington
Bethlehem Steel Corp.
Bigelow Foundation, F. R.
Bingham Second Betterment Fund, William
Blandin Foundation
Block, H&R
Blue Bell, Inc.
Blum Foundation, Harry and Maribel G.
Boatmen's Bancshares, Inc.
Bodman Foundation
Booth Ferris Foundation
Borkee Hagley Foundation
Boston Edison Co.
Bothin Foundation
Boutell Memorial Fund
Bowne Foundation, Robert
Brach Foundation, Helen
Bremer Foundation, Otto
Bridgestone/Firestone, Inc.
Bristol-Myers Squibb Company
Brown & Williamson Tobacco Corp.
Buhl Foundation
Burden Foundation, Florence V.
Burlington Industries, Inc.
Burnett-Tandy Foundation
Bush Foundation
Cabot Corp.
Cafritz Foundation, Morris and Gwendolyn
Cain Foundation, Effie and Wofford
Callaway Foundation
Cargill Inc.
Carolyn Foundation
Carpenter Foundation
Castle Foundation, Harold K. L.
Centerior Energy Corp.
Central Maine Power Co.
Champlin Foundations
Chase Manhattan Bank, N.A.
CHC Foundation
Chesebrough-Pond's USA Co.
Chevron Corporation
Chicago Sun-Times, Inc.
CIBC Wood Gundy
Citibank
Clapp Charitable and Educational Trust, George H.
Clark Foundation
Clorox Co.
Clowes Fund
CNA Financial Corporation/CNA Insurance Companies
Cole Foundation, Olive B.
Colonial Life & Accident Insurance Co.
Columbia Foundation
Columbus Dispatch Printing Co.
Commerce Clearing House, Incorporated
Connecticut Mutual Life Insurance Company
Cooke Foundation
Coors Foundation, Adolph
Corning Incorporated
Cowell Foundation, S. H.
Cowles Charitable Trust
Cowles Media Co.
CPC International Inc.
Crocker Trust, Mary A.
Crown Memorial, Arie and Ida
Crystal Trust
Cummings Foundation, James H.
Cummins Engine Co.
Curtice-Burns Foods, Inc.
Dart Group Corp.
Daugherty Foundation
Davenport-Hatch Foundation
Davis Foundation, James A. and Juliet L.
Dexter Charitable Fund, Eugene A.

Digital Equipment Corp.
Dodge Foundation, Cleveland H.
Dodge Jones Foundation
Donaldson Company, Inc.
Donnelley & Sons Co., R.R.
Donner Foundation, William H.
Douty Foundation
Dresser Industries, Inc.
Dreyfus Foundation, Max and Victoria
du Pont de Nemours & Co., E. I.
Dunagan Foundation
Duncan Trust, John G.
Dynamet, Inc.
Eastman Kodak Company
Eaton Corporation
Eddy Family Memorial Fund, C. K.
Elf Atochem North America, Inc.
English Memorial Fund, Florence C. and H. L.
Ensign-Bickford Industries
Evans Foundation, T. M.
Exxon Corporation
Federal-Mogul Corporation
Federated Mutual Insurance Co.
Ferebee Endowment, Percy O.
Fieldcrest Cannon Inc.
Fife Foundation, Elias and Bertha
Fireman's Fund Insurance Co.
Firman Fund
First Fidelity Bank
First Interstate Bank of Oregon
First Union Corp.
Firstar Bank Milwaukee, N.A.
Fondren Foundation
Ford Foundation
Ford Motor Co.
Freed Foundation
Freeport-McMoRan Inc.
French Foundation, D.E.
French Oil Mill Machinery Co.
Friedman Family Foundation
Frohring Foundation, Paul and Maxine
Frost National Bank
Frueauff Foundation, Charles A.
Fry Foundation, Lloyd A.
GAR Foundation
Gates Foundation
GATX Corp.
GenCorp Inc.
General American Life Insurance Co.
General Mills, Inc.
General Motors Corp.
Georgia Power Co.
German Protestant Orphan Asylum Association
Giant Food Inc.
Gillette Co.
Gilman Foundation, Howard
Gleason Foundation
Glenn Foundation, Carrie C. and Lena V.
Glick Foundation, Eugene and Marilyn
Globe Newspaper Co.
Goldseker Foundation of Maryland, Morris
Goodrich Co., The B.F.
Gould Electronics Inc.
Graham Fund, Philip L.
Griggs and Mary Griggs Burke Foundation, Mary Livingston
GSM Industrial
Guttman Foundation, Stella and Charles
Haas, Jr. Fund, Evelyn and Walter
Haigh-Scatena Foundation
Hancock Foundation, Luke B.
Handy and Harman Foundation
Hanson Industries North America
Harcourt Foundation, Ellen Knowles

Harland Charitable Foundation, John and Wilhelmina D.
Harmon Foundation, Pearl M. and Julia J.
Harriman Foundation, Gladys and Roland
Harsco Corp.
Hartz Foundation
Hazen Foundation, Edward W.
HCA Foundation
Hearst Foundation, William Randolph
Hechinger Co.
Heinz Company, H. J.
Heinz Endowment, Howard
Heinz Endowment, Vira I.
Heller Charitable Foundation, Clarence E.
Hershey Foods Corp.
Hewlett Foundation, William and Flora
Higginson Trust, Corina
Hillcrest Foundation
Hillman Foundation
Hoffman Foundation, Maximilian E. and Marion O.
Housatonic Curtain Co.
Houston Endowment
Hudson-Webber Foundation
Humphrey Fund, George M. and Pamela S.
Hyde and Watson Foundation
IBP, Inc.
ICI Americas Inc.
Illinois Tool Works, Inc.
Ingalls Foundation, Louise H. and David S.
Integra Bank of Uniontown
International Business Machines Corp.
International Foundation
ITT Hartford Insurance Group, Inc.
Jacobs Family Foundation
James River Corp. of Virginia
JM Foundation
John Hancock Mutual Life Insurance Co.
Johnson Foundation, Helen K. and Arthur E.
Johnson & Son, S.C.
Jones Foundation, Harvey and Bernice
Jostens, Inc.
Journal-Gazette Co.
Jurzykowski Foundation, Alfred
Justus Trust, Edith C.
Kaplan Fund, J. M.
Kayser Foundation
Kemper Foundation, William T.
Kempner Fund, Harris and Eliza
Kennecott Corporation
Kennedy Foundation, Ethel
Kent-Lucas Foundation
Kettering Fund
Kiewit Foundation, Peter
Kinney-Lindstrom Foundation
Kiplinger Foundation
Kline Foundation, Josiah W. and Bessie H.
Knight Foundation, John S. and James L.
Ladd Charitable Corporation, Helen and George
Laffey-McHugh Foundation
Lattner Foundation, Forrest C.
Lee Enterprises
Lehmann Foundation, Otto W.
Life Insurance Co. of Georgia
Little, Inc., Arthur D.
Liz Claiborne, Inc.
Lockhart Vaughan Foundation
Long Island Lighting Co.
Longwood Foundation
Lurie Foundation, Louis R.
Lux Foundation, Miranda
Macy & Co., Inc., R.H.
Mardag Foundation
Margoes Foundation
Maritz Inc.
Marmot Foundation
Marpat Foundation

Mather Charitable Trust, S. Livingston
Mautz Paint Co.
May Department Stores Company, The
MBIA Inc.
MCA Inc.
McCann Foundation
McCune Charitable Trust, John R.
McDonald & Company Securities, Inc.
McElroy Trust, R. J.
McFawn Trust No. 2, Lois Sisler
MCI Communications Corp.
McInerny Foundation
McLean Contributionship
Meadows Foundation
Medtronic, Inc.
Mellon Foundation, Richard King
Merrill Lynch & Co., Inc.
Metropolitan Life Insurance Co.
Meyer Memorial Trust
Mid-Iowa Health Foundation
Middendorf Foundation
Miller Brewing Company/North Carolina
Minnesota Mining & Mfg. Co.
Mitsubishi International Corp.
Mobil Oil Corp.
Monell Foundation, Ambrose
Morgan & Company, J.P.
Morgan Stanley & Co., Inc.
Mott Foundation, Charles Stewart
Murphey Foundation, Lluella Morey
Musson Charitable Foundation, R. C. and Katharine M.
Mutual Assurance Co.
Nalco Chemical Co.
National Steel Corp.
National Westminster Bank New Jersey
Nestle USA Inc.
New England Business Service
New York Life Insurance Co.
New York Mercantile Exchange
New York Times Company
Northern States Power Co. (Minnesota)
Norton Co.
NYNEX Corporation
Olsson Memorial Foundation, Elis
Overbrook Foundation
Pacific Mutual Life Insurance Co.
Packard Foundation, David and Lucile
Panhandle Eastern Corporation
Parker Hannifin Corp.
Parsons Foundation, Ralph M.
Patterson Charitable Fund, W. I.
Penn Foundation, William
Pennsylvania Dutch Co.
Peoples Energy Corp.
Perkin-Elmer Corp.
Pew Charitable Trusts
Pfizer, Inc.
Phillips Foundation, Ellis L.
Pick, Jr. Fund, Albert
Pierce Charitable Trust, Harold Whitworth
Pineywoods Foundation
Piper Jaffray Companies Inc.
PNC Bank, N.A.
Potomac Electric Power Co.
PPG Industries, Inc.
Premier Industrial Corp.
PriMerit Bank
Prudential Insurance Co. of America, The
Public Service Co. of New Mexico
Public Service Electric & Gas Co.
Public Welfare Foundation
Pulitzer Publishing Co.
Quaker Chemical Corp.

Rabb Foundation, Harry W.
Ralston Purina Co.
Raymond Corp.
Read Foundation, Charles L.
Republic NY Corp.
Retirement Research Foundation
Riggs Benevolent Fund
Robinson Fund, Maurice R.
Rockwell Fund
Rockwell International Corporation
Rohm & Haas Co.
Roseburg Forest Products Co.
Rose's Stores, Inc.
Rouse Co.
Rowland Foundation
Rubin Foundation, Samuel
Rubinstein Foundation, Helena
SAFECO Corp.
Saint Paul Companies, Inc.
Salomon Inc.
San Diego Gas & Electric
Sandy Hill Foundation
Santa Fe Pacific Corporation
Sara Lee Corp.
Sargent Foundation, Newell B.
Sarkeys Foundation
Sawyer Charitable Foundation
SBC Communications Inc.
Scherman Foundation
Scholl Foundation, Dr.
Schwab & Co., Inc., Charles
Schwartz Foundation, Arnold A.
Seafirst Corporation
Shawmut National Corp.
Sheaffer Co.
Shenandoah Life Insurance Co.
Skillman Foundation
Smith Charitable Foundation, Lou and Lutza
Smith Foundation, Kelvin and Eleanor
Snyder Foundation, Harold B. and Dorothy A.
Sonat Inc.
Sprague Educational and Charitable Foundation, Seth
Springs Foundation
Stackpole-Hall Foundation
Stanley Charitable Foundation, A.W.
Stanley Works
Starr Foundation
Steele-Reese Foundation
Stein Foundation, Jules and Doris
Steinman Foundation, John Frederick
Strong Foundation, Hattie M.
Sumitomo Bank of California
Taconic Foundation
Tait Foundation, Frank M.
Taubman Foundation, A. Alfred
Temple Foundation, T. L. L.
Temple-Inland Inc.
Tenneco Inc.
Texaco Inc.
Texas Commerce Bank-Houston, N.A.
Textron, Inc.
Thermo Electron Corp.
Times Mirror Company, The
Transco Energy Co.
Travelers Inc.
Trees Charitable Trust, Edith L.
Trull Foundation
Trust Company Bank
Trust Funds
Turrell Fund
Unger Foundation, Aber D.
Unilever United States, Inc.
Union Camp Corporation
United Airlines, Inc.
U.S. Bank of Washington
Unocal Corp.
Uris Brothers Foundation
US WEST, Inc.
USL Capital Corporation
USX Corporation
Virginia Power Co.
Vogler Foundation, Laura B.
Wallace-Reader's Digest Fund, DeWitt

Warren and Beatrice W.
  Blanding Foundation, Riley
  J. and Lillian N.
Washington Mutual Savings
  Bank
Wean Foundation, Raymond
  John
Weber Charities Corp.,
  Frederick E.
Weckbaugh Foundation,
  Eleanore Mullen
Wege Foundation
Welfare Foundation
Wells Foundation, Franklin H.
  and Ruth L.
Wendt Foundation, Margaret L.
Westvaco Corporation
Weyerhaeuser Co.
Whirlpool Corporation
Wickes Foundation, Harvey
  Randall
Wickson-Link Memorial
  Foundation
WICOR, Inc.
Wilmington Trust Co.
Wiremold Co.
Wisconsin Power & Light Co.
Wood Foundation of
  Chambersburg, PA
Woolley Foundation, Vasser

Environmental Affairs (General)

Bryn Mawr Trust Co.

Ethnic Organizations

Achelis Foundation
Alavi Foundation of New York
Aldus Corp.
Allyn Foundation
Bank One, Youngstown, NA
Bobst Foundation, Elmer and
  Mamdouha
Borden, Inc.
CBS, Inc.
Chicago Sun-Times, Inc.
Claiborne and Art Ortenberg
  Foundation, Liz
Cogswell Benevolent Trust
Crocker Trust, Mary A.
Dexter Charitable Fund,
  Eugene A.
Diamond Foundation, Aaron
Erpf Fund, Armand G.
Fribourg Foundation
Friedman Family Foundation
Gellert Foundation, Celia Berta
General Motors Corp.
Hamilton Bank
Harland Charitable
  Foundation, John and
  Wilhelmina D.
Heinz Trust, Drue
High Foundation
Hillsdale Fund
Housatonic Curtain Co.
Jurzykowski Foundation,
  Alfred
Kansas City Southern
  Industries
Kennedy Foundation, Ethel
Lauder Foundation
Lea Foundation, Helen Sperry
Management Compensation
  Group/Dulworth Inc.
Mardigian Foundation
McDonald & Company
  Securities, Inc.
Meyer Memorial Trust
Miller Brewing
  Company/North Carolina
Mitsubishi Motor Sales of
  America, Inc.
Mutual Assurance Co.
Philibosian Foundation,
  Stephen
Polaroid Corp.
Saroyan Foundation, William
SBC Communications Inc.

Seaver Institute
Sprague Educational and
  Charitable Foundation, Seth
Starr Foundation
Steinman Foundation, James
  Hale
Thompson Co., J. Walter
U.S. Bank of Washington
Weber Charities Corp.,
  Frederick E.
Weckbaugh Foundation,
  Eleanore Mullen

First Amendment Issues

Binney & Smith Inc.
Columbia Foundation
Coors Foundation, Adolph
Cowles Media Co.
Diamond Foundation, Aaron
Donnelley Foundation,
  Gaylord and Dorothy
Dow Jones & Company, Inc.
Dula Educational and
  Charitable Foundation,
  Caleb C. and Julia W.
Eaton Foundation, Cyrus
Encyclopaedia Britannica, Inc.
Ford Foundation
General Motors Corp.
Graham Fund, Philip L.
HarperCollins Publishers Inc.
McGraw-Hill, Inc.
New York Times Company
The New Yorker Magazine, Inc.
Overbrook Foundation
Pew Charitable Trusts
Playboy Enterprises, Inc.
Price Foundation, Louis and
  Harold
Pulitzer Publishing Co.
Reynolds Foundation, Donald
  W.
Scripps Co., E.W.
Simon Foundation, William E.
  and Carol G.
Sunnen Foundation
Thomas Foundation, Joan and
  Lee
Times Mirror Company, The
Whirlpool Corporation
Wiley & Sons, Inc., John

Gay/Lesbian Issues

Columbia Foundation
Eaton Foundation, Cyrus
Givenchy Corp.
Hazen Foundation, Edward W.
Ittleson Foundation
Kresge Foundation
Miller Brewing
  Company/North Carolina
Pettus Crowe Foundation
Smith Foundation, Ralph L.
Stein Foundation, Jules and
  Doris
U.S. Bank of Washington

General

Abbott Laboratories
Achelis Foundation
Acme-McCrary Corp./Sapona
  Manufacturing Co.
Adler Foundation Trust, Philip
  D. and Henrietta B.
Ahmanson Foundation
AKC Fund
Alabama Gas Corp.
Alavi Foundation of New York
Alcon Laboratories, Inc.
Aldus Corp.
Allegheny Foundation
Allegheny Ludlum Corp.
AlliedSignal Inc.
Altschul Foundation
Amado Foundation, Maurice
Amcast Industrial Corp.

AMCORE Bank, N.A.
  Rockford
American Fidelity Corporation
American General Finance
  Corp.
American National Bank &
  Trust Co. of Chicago
American Optical Corp.
Ameritas Life Insurance Corp.
Ames Charitable Trust, Harriett
Andreas Foundation
Andrews Foundation
Ansin Private Foundation,
  Ronald M.
Ansley Foundation, Dantzler
  Bond
Appleby Trust, Scott B. and
  Annie P.
Argyros Foundation
Aristech Chemical Corp.
Armco Inc.
Arnhold Foundation
ASDA Foundation
Asplundh Foundation
Astor Foundation, Vincent
Atherton Family Foundation
Audubon State Bank
Auerbach Foundation,
  Beatrice Fox
Avery Arts Foundation, Milton
  and Sally
Ayres Foundation, Inc.
Babson Foundation, Paul and
  Edith
Baldwin Foundation, David
  M. and Barbara
Baldwin Memorial
  Foundation, Fred
Ball Foundation, George and
  Frances
Bank One, Texas-Houston
  Office
Bank One, Youngstown, NA
Bankers Trust Company
Banta Corp.
Bard Foundation, Robert
Barker Foundation, J.M.R.
Barra Foundation
Barry Corp., R. G.
Batts Foundation
Baughman Foundation
Bay Foundation
Bean Foundation, Norwin S.
  and Elizabeth N.
BE&K Inc.
Beck Foundation, Elsie E. and
  Joseph W.
Bedsole Foundation, J. L.
Beech Aircraft Corp.
Bell Foundation, James F.
Benenson Foundation, Frances
  and Benjamin
Berwind Corporation
Besser Foundation
Bethlehem Steel Corp.
Betts Industries
Bingham Second Betterment
  Fund, William
Binney & Smith Inc.
Binswanger Cos.
Bird Corp.
Birnschein Foundation, Alvin
  and Marion
Bishop Foundation, E. K. and
  Lillian F.
Blair and Co., William
Blake Foundation, S. P.
Blount Educational and
  Charitable Foundation,
  Mildred Weedon
Bobst Foundation, Elmer and
  Mamdouha
Booth Ferris Foundation
Boothroyd Foundation,
  Charles H. and Bertha L.
Borkee Hagley Foundation
Borman's Inc.
Bowen Foundation, Ethel N.
Bowne Foundation, Robert
Brady Foundation
Breyer Foundation
Bridgestone/Firestone, Inc.
Bright Family Foundation
Brillion Iron Works

Bristol-Myers Squibb
  Company
Brooks Foundation, Gladys
Bryn Mawr Trust Co.
Burchfield Foundation,
  Charles E.
Burden Foundation, Florence
  V.
Bush Foundation
Campbell Foundation
Campbell Foundation, Ruth
  and Henry
Campini Foundation, Frank A.
Carolyn Foundation
Carpenter Foundation
Carpenter Foundation, E.
  Rhodes and Leona B.
Carter Foundation, Beirne
Carver Charitable Trust, Roy J.
Cassett Foundation, Louis N.
Cayuga Foundation
Central Fidelity Banks, Inc.
Centralia Foundation
Chadwick Fund, Dorothy
  Jordan
Chapman Charitable
  Corporation, Howard and
  Bess
Charina Foundation
Chartwell Foundation
Chase Manhattan Bank, N.A.
Chatham Manufacturing Co.
Chazen Foundation
CHC Foundation
Chesebrough-Pond's USA Co.
Chicago Sun-Times, Inc.
Childs Charitable Foundation,
  Roberta M.
CIBC Wood Gundy
CINergy
Citizens Bank of Rhode Island
Claiborne and Art Ortenberg
  Foundation, Liz
Clapp Charitable and
  Educational Trust, George H.
CLARCOR Inc.
Clarke Trust, John
Clarkson Foundation, Jeniam
Clements Foundation
Clorox Co.
Close Foundation
CNA Financial
  Corporation/CNA Insurance
  Companies
Coen Family Foundation,
  Charles S. and Mary
Cole Foundation, Olive B.
Cole Trust, Quincy
Coleman Foundation, George
  E.
Columbus Dispatch Printing
  Co.
Comer Foundation
Commerce Bancshares, Inc.
Commerce Clearing House,
  Incorporated
Comprecare Foundation
Consumers Power Co.
Cooke Foundation
Cooperman Foundation, Leon
  and Toby
Copley Press, Inc.
Cord Foundation, E. L.
Cosmair, Inc.
Coughlin-Saunders Foundation
Covington and Burling
Cowell Foundation, S. H.
Cowles Charitable Trust
Crabtree & Evelyn
Crawford Estate, E. R.
Crestlea Foundation
Crown Books
Crystal Trust
CS First Boston Corporation
Cullen Foundation
Culver Foundation, Constans
Cummings Foundation, James
  H.
Curtice-Burns Foods, Inc.
Daily News
Davenport Trust Fund
Davis Foundation, James A.
  and Juliet L.
Day Foundation, Nancy Sayles
Daywood Foundation

DEC International, Inc.
Delano Foundation, Mignon
  Sherwood
Demos Foundation, N.
Dentsply International Inc.
DeRoy Foundation, Helen L.
DeRoy Testamentary
  Foundation
Dewing Foundation, Frances R.
Dexter Charitable Fund,
  Eugene A.
Diamond Shamrock Inc.
Dillon Dunwalke Trust,
  Clarence and Anne
Dr. Seuss Foundation
Dodge Foundation, Cleveland
  H.
Donnelley Foundation,
  Gaylord and Dorothy
Donner Foundation, William H.
Douglas & Lomason Company
Douty Foundation
Dow Jones & Company, Inc.
Dresser Industries, Inc.
Dreyfus Foundation, Jean and
  Louis
Dula Educational and
  Charitable Foundation,
  Caleb C. and Julia W.
Dunagan Foundation
Duncan Trust, John G.
Eastman Kodak Company
Eaton Foundation, Cyrus
Eberly Foundation
Ebsco Industries, Inc.
Eden Hall Foundation
Edgewater Steel Corp.
Edmonds Foundation, Dean S.
Emerson Foundation, Inc.,
  Fred L.
Encyclopaedia Britannica, Inc.
English Memorial Fund,
  Florence C. and H. L.
Ensign-Bickford Industries
Erpf Fund, Armand G.
Ettinger Foundation
Evans Foundation, T. M.
Evans Foundation, Thomas J.
Exchange National Bank
Fabri-Kal Corp.
Fair Foundation, R. W.
Fair Oaks Foundation, Inc.
Fair Play Foundation
Federated Mutual Insurance
  Co.
Feil Foundation, Louis and
  Gertrude
Femino Foundation
Fenton Foundation
Fife Foundation, Elias and
  Bertha
Finch Foundation, Doak
Fireman's Fund Insurance Co.
Firestone, Jr. Foundation,
  Harvey
Firman Fund
First Financial Bank FSB
First Source Corp.
First Union National Bank of
  Florida
Fish Foundation, Ray C.
Fishback Foundation Trust,
  Harmes C.
Fleishhacker Foundation
Fleming Cos. Food
  Distribution Center
Fletcher Foundation
Flowers Charitable Trust,
  Albert W. and Edith V.
Fondren Foundation
Ford Fund, William and Martha
Forest Foundation
Forest Oil Corp.
Frear Eleemosynary Trust,
  Mary D. and Walter F.
Freed Foundation
French Foundation, D.E.
French Oil Mill Machinery Co.
Frese Foundation, Arnold D.
Fribourg Foundation
Friedman Family Foundation
Friendship Fund
Frohring Foundation, William
  O. and Gertrude Lewis
Fruehauf Foundation

Fuller Foundation
Fuqua Foundation, J. B.
Gamble Foundation
Gannett Publishing Co., Guy
Gaylord Foundation, Clifford
  Willard
Gazette Co.
Geifman Family Foundation
GenCorp Inc.
General American Life
  Insurance Co.
General Mills, Inc.
General Motors Corp.
GenRad
German Protestant Orphan
  Asylum Association
Gershman Foundation, Joel
Gheens Foundation
Giant Eagle, Inc.
Giles Foundation, Edward C.
Gilman Foundation, Howard
Gilmore Foundation, William
  G.
Glanville Family Foundation
Gleason Foundation
Glick Foundation, Eugene and
  Marilyn
Goddard Foundation, Charles
  B.
Goldie-Anna Charitable Trust
Goldsmith Foundation, Horace
  W.
Goldwyn Foundation, Samuel
Gould Electronics Inc.
Gould Foundation, The
  Florence
Grand Rapids Label Co.
Greenwall Foundation
Gregg-Graniteville Foundation
Griffis Foundation
Griffith Foundation, W. C.
Griswold Foundation, John C.
Groome Beatty Trust, Helen D.
GSM Industrial
Guaranty Bank & Trust Co.
Haas, Jr. Fund, Evelyn and
  Walter
Habig Foundation, Arnold F.
Hafif Family Foundation
Haigh-Scatena Foundation
Halff Foundation, G. A. C.
Hallberg Foundation, E. L. and
  R. F.
Halsell Foundation, Ewing
Hamman Foundation, George
  and Mary Josephine
Hammer Foundation, Armand
Handy and Harman Foundation
Harcourt Foundation, Ellen
  Knowles
Harland Charitable
  Foundation, John and
  Wilhelmina D.
Harmon Foundation, Pearl M.
  and Julia J.
Harriman Foundation, Gladys
  and Roland
Harrison Foundation, Fred G.
Harvey Foundation, Felix
Hassenfeld Foundation
Hauser Foundation
Hazen Foundation, Edward W.
Hecht-Levi Foundation
Heckscher Foundation for
  Children
Hedco Foundation
Heinz Company, H. J.
Heinz Endowment, Howard
Heinz Endowment, Vira I.
Heinz Trust, Drue
Helms Foundation
Henry Foundation, Patrick
Hershey Foods Corp.
Herzstein Charitable
  Foundation, Albert and Ethel
Heydt Fund, Nan and Matilda
Hickory Tech Corp.
Higginson Trust, Corina
Hill Foundation, Sandy
Hillman Family Foundation,
  Alex
Hillman Foundation
Hoag Family Foundation,
  George
Hobby Foundation

Holnam
Holzer Memorial Foundation,
  Richard H.
Homeland Foundation
Hook Drugs
Hoover Foundation
Hoover Fund-Trust, W. Henry
Hoover, Jr. Foundation,
  Margaret W. and Herbert
Hopkins Foundation,
  Josephine Lawrence
Housatonic Curtain Co.
Howard and Bush Foundation
Howe and Mitchell B. Howe
  Foundation, Lucille Horton
Hoyt Foundation
Hoyt Foundation, Stewart W.
  and Willma C.
Huber Foundation
Hulme Charitable Foundation,
  Milton G.
Humana, Inc.
Humphrey Fund, George M.
  and Pamela S.
Hunt Charitable Trust, C. Giles
Hunt Foundation
Hyde and Watson Foundation
IBP, Inc.
Illinois Consolidated
  Telephone Co.
Independence Foundation
Integra Bank of Uniontown
International Paper Co.
ITT Hartford Insurance Group,
  Inc.
Ittleson Foundation
Jacobs Family Foundation
Jacobson Foundation, Bernard
  H. and Blanche E.
Jaffe Foundation
Jameson Foundation, J. W. and
  Ida M.
Janesville Foundation
Janirve Foundation
Jarson-Stanley and Mickey
  Kaplan Foundation, Isaac
  and Esther
Jaydor Corp.
Jennings Foundation, Mary
  Hillman
Jewish Healthcare Foundation
  of Pittsburgh
JFM Foundation
JM Foundation
Jockey Hollow Foundation
Johnson Foundation, Helen K.
  and Arthur E.
Johnson Fund, Edward C.
Jones Foundation, Daisy
  Marquis
Jones Foundation, Fletcher
Jonsson Foundation
Jordan Charitable Foundation,
  Mary Ranken Jordan and
  Ettie A.
Joy Family Foundation
Justus Trust, Edith C.
Kansas City Southern
  Industries
Kantzler Foundation
Kaplun Foundation, Morris J.
  and Betty
Kardon Foundation, Samuel
  and Rebecca
Kaye, Scholer, Fierman, Hays
  & Handler
Kelly Tractor Co.
Kemper Foundation, William T.
Kennedy Foundation, Ethel
Kent-Lucas Foundation
Kilcawley Fund, William H.
Kimball Foundation, Horace
  A. Kimball and S. Ella
Kingsbury Corp.
Kiplinger Foundation
Kirkpatrick Foundation
Klosk Fund, Louis and Rose
KN Energy, Inc.
Knapp Foundation
Knoll Group
Knox, Sr., and Pearl Wallis
  Knox Charitable
  Foundation, Robert W.
Koch Charitable Foundation,
  Charles G.

Kohn-Joseloff Foundation
Komes Foundation
Koopman Fund
Kreitler Foundation
Kress Foundation, Samuel H.
Kuehn Foundation
Kuyper Foundation, Peter H.
  and E. Lucille
Ladd Charitable Corporation,
  Helen and George
Laffey-McHugh Foundation
LamCo. Communications
Landegger Charitable
  Foundation
Larsen Fund
Lasdon Foundation, William
  and Mildred
Lauder Foundation
Laurel Foundation
Lazarus Charitable Trust,
  Helen and Charles
LBJ Family Foundation
Lea Foundation, Helen Sperry
Leavey Foundation, Thomas
  and Dorothy
Lebanon Mutual Insurance Co.
Lebovitz Fund
Lee Endowment Foundation
LEF Foundation
Lehigh Portland Cement Co.
Lemberg Foundation
Lennon Foundation, Fred A.
Leuthold Foundation
Levitt Foundation
Levy Foundation, June
  Rockwell
Lichtenstein Foundation,
  David B.
Louisiana-Pacific Corp.
Love Foundation, George H.
  and Margaret McClintic
Lovett Foundation
Lowenstein Foundation, Leon
Lunda Charitable Trust
Lydall, Inc.
M/A-COM, Inc.
MacLeod Stewardship
  Foundation
Madison Gas & Electric Co.
Magowan Family Foundation
Mahadh Foundation
Mailman Foundation
Management Compensation
  Group/Dulworth Inc.
Mandeville Foundation
Maneely Fund
Mardigian Foundation
Margoes Foundation
Markey Charitable Fund, John
  C.
Markle Foundation, John and
  Mary R.
Marmot Foundation
Martin Marietta Corp.
Martin Marietta Materials
Martini Foundation, Nicholas
Marx Foundation, Virginia and
  Leonard
Mascoma Savings Bank
Massachusetts Mutual Life
  Insurance Co.
Mathis-Pfohl Foundation
Mattel, Inc.
Matthies Foundation, Katharine
Mautz Paint Co.
May Department Stores
  Company, The
Mayer Foundation, Oliver
  Dewey
Maytag Family Foundation,
  Fred
MBIA Inc.
MCA Inc.
McBean Charitable Trust,
  Alletta Morris
McCasland Foundation
McCormick Trust, Anne
McCune Charitable
  Foundation, Marshall and
  Perrine D.
McDonald & Company
  Securities, Inc.
McEvoy Foundation, Mildred
  H.

McFawn Trust No. 2, Lois
  Sisler
McFeely-Rogers Foundation
McGee Foundation
McGonagle Foundation,
  Dextra Baldwin
MCI Communications Corp.
McInerny Foundation
McLean Contributionship
McMahon Foundation
McMillan Foundation, D. W.
McQueen Foundation, Adeline
  and George
M.E. Foundation
Mellon Foundation, Richard
  King
Mengle Foundation, Glenn and
  Ruth
Merck & Co.
Merrick Foundation
Merrill Lynch & Co., Inc.
Meyer Family Foundation,
  Paul J.
Meyer Fund, Milton and
  Sophie
Meyerhoff Fund, Joseph
Mid-Iowa Health Foundation
Millbrook Tribute Garden
Miller Brewing
  Company/North Carolina
Miller Charitable Foundation,
  Howard E. and Nell E.
Miller-Mellor Association
Mitsubishi Motor Sales of
  America, Inc.
Mnuchin Foundation
Mohasco Corp.
Monadnock Paper Mills
Monfort Family Foundation
Montana Power Co.
Moore Charitable Foundation,
  Marjorie
Moore & Sons, B.C.
Morgan Charitable Residual
  Trust, W. and E.
Morgan Construction Co.
Morgan Foundation, Burton D.
Morgan and Samuel Tate
  Morgan, Jr. Foundation,
  Marietta McNeil
Mosbacher, Jr. Foundation,
  Emil
Mosinee Paper Corp.
Munger Foundation, Alfred C.
Murphey Foundation, Lluella
  Morey
Musson Charitable
  Foundation, R. C. and
  Katharine M.
Mutual Assurance Co.
Nabisco Foods Group
National Forge Co.
National Gypsum Co.
Neuberger Foundation, Roy R.
  and Marie S.
New Jersey Natural Gas Co.
New-Land Foundation
New York Mercantile Exchange
The New Yorker Magazine, Inc.
NewMil Bancorp
Nias Foundation, Henry
Norfolk Shipbuilding &
  Drydock Corp.
Norgren Foundation, Carl A.
Normandie Foundation
North Shore Foundation
Northwest Natural Gas Co.
Norton Family Foundation,
  Peter
Norton Foundation Inc.
Novell Inc.
OCRI Foundation
O'Fallon Trust, Martin J. and
  Mary Anne
Offield Family Foundation
Old Dominion Box Co.
Old National Bank in
  Evansville
Olin Foundation, Spencer T.
  and Ann W.
Oliver Memorial Trust
  Foundation
Olsson Memorial Foundation,
  Elis

Oppenstein Brothers
  Foundation
O'Quinn Foundation, John M.
  and Nancy C.
Ore-Ida Foods, Inc.
Osborn Charitable Trust,
  Edward B.
Ottenheimer Brothers
  Foundation
Overbrook Foundation
Overlake Foundation
Owen Industries, Inc.
Owsley Foundation, Alvin and
  Lucy
Packaging Corporation of
  America
PaineWebber
Palisano Foundation, Vincent
  and Harriet
Palmer Fund, Frank Loomis
Pamida, Inc.
Park Foundation
Parker Hannifin Corp.
Parshelsky Foundation, Moses
  L.
Parvin Foundation, Albert
Payne Foundation, Frank E.
  and Seba B.
Peabody Charitable Fund,
  Amelia
Penguin Books USA, Inc.
Petteys Memorial Foundation,
  Jack
Pettus Crowe Foundation
PHH Corporation
Philibosian Foundation,
  Stephen
Piankova Foundation, Tatiana
Pick, Jr. Fund, Albert
Pierce Charitable Trust, Harold
  Whitworth
Pineywoods Foundation
Pioneer Trust Bank, NA
Piper Jaffray Companies Inc.
Pitt-Des Moines Inc.
Pittsburg Midway Coal Mining
  Co.
Plankenhorn Foundation, Harry
Plumsock Fund
PNC Bank, N.A.
Pollock Company Foundation,
  William B.
Porter Foundation, Mrs.
  Cheever
Porter Testamentary Trust,
  James Hyde
Premier Industrial Corp.
Price Foundation, Lucien B.
  and Katherine E.
PriMerit Bank
Prince Trust, Abbie Norman
Prouty Foundation, Olive
  Higgins
Providence Gas Co.
Providence Journal Company
Providian Corporation
Public Service Co. of New
  Mexico
Putnam Foundation
R. F. Foundation
Rabb Foundation, Harry W.
Rand McNally & Co.
R&B Machine Tool Co.
Ratner Foundation, Milton M.
Raymond Corp.
Read Foundation, Charles L.
Reidler Foundation
Reisman Charitable Trust,
  George C. and Evelyn R.
Retirement Research
  Foundation
Reynolds Foundation,
  Christopher
Richardson Benevolent
  Foundation, C. E.
Riggs Benevolent Fund
Ritter Charitable Trust, George
  W. and Mary F.
Rixson Foundation, Oscar C.
RJR Nabisco Inc.
Robinson-Broadhurst
  Foundation
Robinson Fund, Maurice R.
Rogers Family Foundation

Rohatyn Foundation, Felix and Elizabeth
Rose Foundation, Billy
Roseburg Forest Products Co.
Rosen Foundation, Joseph
Rosenberg, Jr. Family Foundation, Louise and Claude
Rose's Stores, Inc.
Ross Laboratories
Ross Memorial Foundation, Will
Rouse Co.
Rowland Foundation
Royal Group, Inc.
Ruan Foundation Trust, John
Rubin Family Fund, Cele H. and William B.
Rubin Foundation, Samuel
Rudin Foundation
Russell Trust, Josephine G.
Ryan Foundation, David Claude
Safety Fund National Bank
Saint Paul Companies, Inc.
Salomon Foundation, Richard and Edna
Saltonstall Charitable Foundation, Richard
Salvatori Foundation, Henry
Sandusky International Inc.
Sandy Hill Foundation
Sara Lee Hosiery, Inc.
Sarkeys Foundation
Saroyan Foundation, William
Sasco Foundation
Sawyer Charitable Foundation
SBC Communications Inc.
Scherer Foundation, Karla
Schiff Foundation, Dorothy
Schiro Fund
Schlink Foundation, Albert G. and Olive H.
Schoenleber Foundation
Schuller International
Schwartz Foundation, Arnold A.
Schwartz Fund for Education and Health Research, Arnold and Marie
Scott Fetzer Co.
Scott Foundation, Walter
Seaver Charitable Trust, Richard C.
Seaver Institute
Second Foundation
Security Life of Denver Insurance Co.
Seidman Family Foundation
Seneca Foods Corp.
Sentry Insurance A Mutual Company
Sequoia Foundation
Seton Leather Co.
Share Trust, Charles Morton
Sharon Steel Corp.
Sheary for Charity, Edna M.
Sheppard Foundation, Lawrence B.
Sierra Pacific Industries
Sierra Pacific Resources
Siltec Corp.
Simon Foundation, William E. and Carol G.
Slifka Foundation, Joseph and Sylvia
Smeal Foundation, Mary Jean and Frank P.
Smith Foundation, Ralph L.
Snow Memorial Trust, John Ben
Snyder Foundation, Harold B. and Dorothy A.
Solow Foundation
Sonat Inc.
Sordoni Foundation
South Waite Foundation
Spalding Foundation, Eliot
Spang & Co.
Speyer Foundation, Alexander C. and Tillie S.
Sprague Educational and Charitable Foundation, Seth
SPX Corp.

Stabler Foundation, Donald B. and Dorothy L.
Stanley Charitable Foundation, A.W.
Stanley Works
Stans Foundation
Stauffer Foundation, John and Beverly
Stearns Trust, Artemas W.
Steinman Foundation, James Hale
Steinman Foundation, John Frederick
Stemmons Foundation
Sternberger Foundation, Tannenbaum
Stone Charitable Foundation
Strauss Foundation, Leon
Strawbridge Foundation of Pennsylvania II, Margaret Dorrance
Sulzberger Foundation
Sundet Foundation
Sunnen Foundation
Swanson Family Foundation, Dr. W.C.
Taube Family Foundation
Taubman Foundation, A. Alfred
Taylor Foundation, Fred and Harriet
Taylor Foundation, Ruth and Vernon
Teichert & Son, A.
Teleflex Inc.
Temple Foundation, T. L. L.
Texas Commerce Bank-Houston, N.A.
Thalhimer and Family Foundation, Charles G.
Thermo Electron Corp.
Thomas Foundation, Joan and Lee
Thomas Industries
Thomasville Furniture Industries
Thompson Co., J. Walter
Thompson Trust, Thomas
Thorne Foundation
Thornton Foundation
Thornton Foundation, Flora L.
Times Mirror Company, The
Tiscornia Foundation
Titus Foundation, Roy and Niuta
Todd Co., A.M.
TransAmerica Corporation
Trees Charitable Trust, Edith L.
Truland Foundation
Tucker Charitable Trust, Rose E.
Tupancy-Harris Foundation of 1986
Unger Foundation, Aber D.
Union Bank
Union Camp Corporation
U.S. Bank of Washington
Unitrode Corp.
USX Corporation
Utica National Insurance Group
Valentine Foundation, Lawson
Vance Charitable Foundation, Robert C.
Vanderbilt Trust, R. T.
Vaughn, Jr. Foundation Fund, James M.
Vetlesen Foundation, G. Unger
Vicksburg Foundation
Vollbrecht Foundation, Frederick A.
Wachovia Bank of North Carolina, N.A.
Wallace Foundation, George R.
Warner Fund, Albert and Bessie
Warren and Beatrice W. Blanding Foundation, Riley J. and Lillian N.
Washington Forrest Foundation
Washington Mutual Savings Bank
Washington Water Power Co.
Waters Charitable Trust, Robert S.

Weaver Foundation, Gil and Dody
Webber Oil Co.
Weber Charities Corp., Frederick E.
Weckbaugh Foundation, Eleanore Mullen
Weezie Foundation
Weinstein Foundation, J.
Welfare Foundation
Wells Foundation, Franklin H. and Ruth L.
Wertheim Foundation, Dr. Herbert A.
West Foundation, Harry and Ethel
West One Bancorp
Westerman Foundation, Samuel L.
Wheeler Foundation
Wheeler Foundation, Wilmot
Whirlpool Corporation
Whitecap Foundation
Whitehead Charitable Foundation
Whiting Foundation
Wickson-Link Memorial Foundation
Widgeon Foundation
Wilder Foundation
Wildermuth Foundation, E. F.
Willard Helping Fund, Cecilia Young
Williams Charitable Trust, John C.
Wilson Fund, Matilda R.
Windham Foundation
Winnebago Industries, Inc.
Winthrop Trust, Clara B.
Wiremold Co.
Wisconsin Power & Light Co.
Wisconsin Public Service Corp.
Witco Corp.
Witter Foundation, Dean
Wood Foundation of Chambersburg, PA
Woodward Fund
Wyman Youth Trust
Y and H Soda Foundation
Zachry Co., H.B.
Zarrow Foundation, Anne and Henry
Zenkel Foundation
Zollner Foundation

Hispanic Affairs

Abbott Laboratories
Abell-Hanger Foundation
Acme-McCrary Corp./Sapona Manufacturing Co.
Aetna Life & Casualty Co.
Ahmanson Foundation
Amoco Corporation
Andreas Foundation
Anheuser-Busch Companies, Inc.
Argyros Foundation
AT&T Corp.
Auerbach Foundation, Beatrice Fox
Babson Foundation, Paul and Edith
Bank One, Youngstown, NA
BankAmerica Corp.
Barra Foundation
Beal Foundation
Bethlehem Steel Corp.
Binney & Smith Inc.
Birnschein Foundation, Alvin and Marion
Borden, Inc.
Bothin Foundation
Bowne Foundation, Robert
Brach Foundation, Helen
Bunbury Company
Burkitt Foundation
Burnett-Tandy Foundation
Carnegie Corporation of New York
Carpenter Foundation
Carver Charitable Trust, Roy J.
CBS, Inc.
Chartwell Foundation

Chazen Foundation
Chevron Corporation
Chicago Sun-Times, Inc.
CIGNA Corporation
CLARCOR Inc.
Clorox Co.
Columbia Foundation
Comprecare Foundation
Cord Foundation, E. L.
Crane Co.
Daily News
Davidson Family Charitable Foundation
Dentsply International Inc.
Dewing Foundation, Frances R.
Dexter Charitable Fund, Eugene A.
Douty Foundation
Dow Jones & Company, Inc.
Dreyfus Foundation, Jean and Louis
Duncan Foundation, Lillian H. and C. W.
Durfee Foundation
El Pomar Foundation
Exxon Corporation
Femino Foundation
First Union Corp.
Firstar Bank Milwaukee, N.A.
Fish Foundation, Ray C.
Fletcher Foundation
Ford Foundation
Friedman Family Foundation
Fund for New Jersey
General Motors Corp.
Gilmore Foundation, William G.
Globe Newspaper Co.
Graham Fund, Philip L.
GSM Industrial
Haas, Jr. Fund, Evelyn and Walter
Hafif Family Foundation
Hallberg Foundation, E. L. and R. F.
Hamman Foundation, George and Mary Josephine
Harcourt General, Inc.
Harmon Foundation, Pearl M. and Julia J.
Haynes Foundation, John Randolph and Dora
Hazen Foundation, Edward W.
Hearst Foundation, William Randolph
Heckscher Foundation for Children
Herzstein Charitable Foundation, Albert and Ethel
Heydt Fund, Nan and Matilda
Hill Foundation, Sandy
Houston Endowment
Hudson-Webber Foundation
Humana, Inc.
Hyde and Watson Foundation
Irvine Foundation, James
ITT Hartford Insurance Group, Inc.
Jackson Foundation
Jaydor Corp.
JFM Foundation
Johnson Foundation, Helen K. and Arthur E.
Journal-Gazette Co.
Kansas City Southern Industries
Kaplan Fund, J. M.
Kelly Tractor Co.
Kettering Fund
Koopman Fund
Levy Foundation, June Rockwell
Lurie Foundation, Louis R.
Lux Foundation, Miranda
MacArthur Foundation, John D. and Catherine T.
Maddox Foundation, J. F.
Magowan Family Foundation
Mailman Family Foundation, A. L.
Margoes Foundation
Martini Foundation, Nicholas
McCune Charitable Foundation, Marshall and Perrine D.

McDonald & Company Securities, Inc.
McGee Foundation
Meadows Foundation
Medtronic, Inc.
Mellon Foundation, Andrew W.
Merck & Co.
Meyer Memorial Trust
Miller Brewing Company/North Carolina
Mitsubishi Motor Sales of America, Inc.
Monfort Family Foundation
Morgan & Company, J.P.
Morgan Foundation, Louie R. and Gertrude
Morgan Stanley & Co., Inc.
Mosbacher, Jr. Foundation, Emil
Mott Foundation, Charles Stewart
Mott Fund, Ruth
Mulcahy Foundation
New-Land Foundation
Northern States Power Co. (Minnesota)
Norton Co.
OCRI Foundation
Old National Bank in Evansville
Oppenstein Brothers Foundation
Pacific Mutual Life Insurance Co.
Palmer Fund, Frank Loomis
Parsons Foundation, Ralph M.
Penn Foundation, William
Philibosian Foundation, Stephen
Pick, Jr. Fund, Albert
Pierce Charitable Trust, Harold Whitworth
Piper Foundation, Minnie Stevens
Plumsock Fund
Prairie Foundation
Prudential Insurance Co. of America, The
Public Service Co. of New Mexico
Putnam Foundation
Reynolds Foundation, Donald W.
Rockwell International Corporation
Rosenberg Foundation
Ross Memorial Foundation, Will
Rubin Family Fund, Cele H. and William B.
Russell Trust, Josephine G.
Saint Paul Companies, Inc.
SBC Communications Inc.
Schering-Plough Corp.
Scherman Foundation
Schoenleber Foundation
Schumann Fund for New Jersey
Seaver Charitable Trust, Richard C.
Selby and Marie Selby Foundation, William G.
Skillman Foundation
Smith Foundation, Ralph L.
Stauffer Foundation, John and Beverly
Stearns Trust, Artemas W.
Steinhagen Benevolent Trust, B. A. and Elinor
Strong Foundation, Hattie M.
Taubman Foundation, A. Alfred
Times Mirror Company, The
Trexler Trust, Harry C.
Trull Foundation
Turrell Fund
U.S. Bank of Washington
Unocal Corp.
Wallace-Reader's Digest Fund, DeWitt
Washington Mutual Savings Bank
Weber Charities Corp., Frederick E.
Wege Foundation

Pacific Mutual Life Insurance Co.
Pacific Telesis Group
Packard Foundation, David and Lucile
Palmer Fund, Frank Loomis
Parsons Foundation, Ralph M.
Peabody Charitable Fund, Amelia
PECO Energy Company
Pella Corporation
Penn Foundation, William
Peoples Energy Corp.
Peppers Foundation, Ann
Perkin-Elmer Corp.
Peterson Foundation, Hal and Charlie
Pew Charitable Trusts
Pfizer, Inc.
Phillips Family Foundation, Jay and Rose
Phillips Foundation, Ellis L.
Piper Jaffray Companies Inc.
Pittsburgh Child Guidance Foundation
Plankenhorn Foundation, Harry
PNC Bank, N.A.
Polaroid Corp.
Porter Testamentary Trust, James Hyde
PPG Industries, Inc.
Price Foundation, Louis and Harold
Priddy Foundation
Prince Trust, Abbie Norman
Proctor Trust, Mortimer R.
Providence Gas Co.
Providence Journal Company
Provident Life & Accident Insurance Company of America
Providian Corporation
Prudential Securities, Inc.
Public Service Electric & Gas Co.
Public Welfare Foundation
Putnam Foundation
Read Foundation, Charles L.
Reicher Foundation, Anne and Harry J.
Reisman Charitable Trust, George C. and Evelyn R.
Rennebohm Foundation, Oscar
Republic NY Corp.
Retirement Research Foundation
Rockefeller Fund, David
Rockwell International Corporation
Rogers Family Foundation
Rohm & Haas Co.
Rosenberg Foundation
Ross Memorial Foundation, Will
Rouse Co.
Royal Group, Inc.
Rubin Foundation, Samuel
Rubinstein Foundation, Helena
Russell Trust, Josephine G.
SAFECO Corp.
Safety Fund National Bank
Saint Paul Companies, Inc.
Salomon Foundation, Richard and Edna
Sandusky International Inc.
Sara Lee Corp.
Sarkeys Foundation
Scaife Family Foundation
Scherman Foundation
Schoenleber Foundation
Schowalter Foundation
Schuller International
Schumann Fund for New Jersey
Schwartz Foundation, Arnold A.
Schwartz Fund for Education and Health Research, Arnold and Marie
Seafirst Corporation
Selby and Marie Selby Foundation, William G.
Seneca Foods Corp.
Shawmut National Corp.
Shell Oil Company

Simon Foundation, William E. and Carol G.
Skillman Foundation
Smith Charitable Foundation, Lou and Lutza
Smith Foundation, Ralph L.
Smith Memorial Fund, Ethel Sergeant Clark
Smith Trust, May and Stanley
Snow Foundation, John Ben
Snyder Foundation, Harold B. and Dorothy A.
Southern California Edison Co.
Springs Foundation
SPX Corp.
Stanley Charitable Foundation, A.W.
Stanley Works
Stans Foundation
Stearns Trust, Artemas W.
Steinhagen Benevolent Trust, B. A. and Elinor
Sternberger Foundation, Tannenbaum
Stevens Foundation, Abbot and Dorothy H.
Sturgis Charitable and Educational Trust, Roy and Christine
Sumitomo Bank of California
Sunnen Foundation
Taconic Foundation
Tait Foundation, Frank M.
Tecumseh Products Co.
Teichert & Son, A.
Temple Foundation, T. L. L.
Temple-Inland Inc.
Tenneco Inc.
Texaco Inc.
Texas Commerce Bank-Houston, N.A.
Thomas Foundation, Joan and Lee
Thomas Industries
Thomasville Furniture Industries
Thompson Charitable Foundation
Times Mirror Company, The
Timken Foundation of Canton
Todd Co., A.M.
Towsley Foundation, Harry A. and Margaret D.
Transco Energy Co.
Travelers Inc.
Treakle Foundation, J. Edwin
Trexler Trust, Harry C.
Truland Foundation
Trull Foundation
Trust Company Bank
Trust Funds
Tucker Charitable Trust, Rose E.
Turrell Fund
Unger Foundation, Aber D.
Union Bank
Union Electric Co.
U.S. Bank of Washington
Unocal Corp.
Upjohn Foundation, Harold and Grace
Uris Brothers Foundation
USL Capital Corporation
van Ameringen Foundation
Van Every Foundation, Philip L.
Van Wert County Foundation
Virginia Power Co.
Wahlstrom Foundation
Walsh Foundation
Washington Forrest Foundation
Washington Mutual Savings Bank
Weber Charities Corp., Frederick E.
Weckbaugh Foundation, Eleanore Mullen
Wells Foundation, Franklin H. and Ruth L.
Wendt Foundation, Margaret L.
West One Bancorp
Westerman Foundation, Samuel L.
Weyerhaeuser Co.

Wheat First Butcher Singer, Inc.
Whirlpool Corporation
Whittenberger Foundation, Claude R. and Ethel B.
Wickes Foundation, Harvey Randall
Wickson-Link Memorial Foundation
WICOR, Inc.
Williams Charitable Trust, John C.
Williams Charitable Trust, Mary Jo
Williams Companies, The
Wilmington Trust Co.
Windham Foundation
Wiremold Co.
Wood Foundation of Chambersburg, PA
Woodward Fund
Woolley Foundation, Vasser
Wright Foundation, Lola
Wyomissing Foundation
Yeager Charitable Trust, Lester E.
Zenkel Foundation

Inner-City Development

Alabama Gas Corp.
Aldus Corp.
Amcast Industrial Corp.
Bank One, Youngstown, NA
Bishop Foundation, E. K. and Lillian F.
Brach Foundation, Helen
Bryn Mawr Trust Co.
Chicago Sun-Times, Inc.
CIBC Wood Gundy
Handy and Harman Foundation
Kansas City Southern Industries
LamCo. Communications
Management Compensation Group/Dulworth Inc.
McDonald & Company Securities, Inc.
New York Mercantile Exchange
Old National Bank in Evansville
Puterbaugh Foundation
Ross Laboratories
Schuller International
U.S. Bank of Washington

Law & Justice

Abbott Laboratories
Abell-Hanger Foundation
Acushnet Co.
Aetna Life & Casualty Co.
Ahmanson Foundation
Akzo America
Alabama Gas Corp.
Allegheny Ludlum Corp.
Allendale Insurance Co.
AlliedSignal Inc.
Altschul Foundation
Aluminum Co. of America
American National Bank & Trust Co. of Chicago
Amoco Corporation
Anderson Foundation, John W.
Andrews Foundation
Anheuser-Busch Companies, Inc.
Ansley Foundation, Dantzler Bond
AON Corporation
Archer-Daniels-Midland Co.
Armco Inc.
Atran Foundation
Avon Products, Inc.
Bank One, Texas-Houston Office
Baughman Foundation
Beck Foundation, Elsie E. and Joseph W.
Beech Aircraft Corp.
Bethlehem Steel Corp.

Bettingen Corporation, Burton G.
Bingham Second Betterment Fund, William
Birnschein Foundation, Alvin and Marion
Blair and Co., William
Block, H&R
Borden, Inc.
Boswell Foundation, James G.
Bridgestone/Firestone, Inc.
Bristol-Myers Squibb Company
Brown & Williamson Tobacco Corp.
Burchfield Foundation, Charles E.
Burden Foundation, Florence V.
Burlington Industries, Inc.
Cabot Corp.
Cain Foundation, Gordon and Mary
Calhoun Charitable Trust, Kenneth
Carnegie Corporation of New York
Carter Foundation, Amon G.
Centerior Energy Corp.
Chase Manhattan Bank, N.A.
Chevron Corporation
Childs Charitable Foundation, Roberta M.
Clorox Co.
Clowes Fund
CNA Financial Corporation/CNA Insurance Companies
Colonial Life & Accident Insurance Co.
Columbia Foundation
Columbus Dispatch Printing Co.
Commerce Clearing House, Incorporated
Comprecare Foundation
Connecticut Mutual Life Insurance Company
Continental Corp.
Cooper Industries, Inc.
Coors Foundation, Adolph
Cord Foundation, E. L.
Covington and Burling
CPC International Inc.
CR Industries
Crane Co.
Crestlea Foundation
Culpeper Foundation, Charles E.
Cuneo Foundation
Dekko Foundation
Douty Foundation
Dresser Industries, Inc.
Dreyfus Foundation, Max and Victoria
du Pont de Nemours & Co., E. I.
Dun & Bradstreet Corp.
Eaton Corporation
Elf Atochem North America, Inc.
Exxon Corporation
Federal-Mogul Corporation
Federated Mutual Insurance Co.
Fieldcrest Cannon Inc.
First Chicago Corp.
First Fidelity Bank
First Hawaiian, Inc.
Fletcher Foundation
Ford Foundation
Ford Motor Co.
Frear Eleemosynary Trust, Mary D. and Walter F.
Freeport Brick Co.
Friedman Family Foundation
Fruehauf Foundation
Fry Foundation, Lloyd A.
Fund for New Jersey
General Mills, Inc.
General Motors Corp.
Georgia-Pacific Corporation
Giant Eagle, Inc.
Giant Food Inc.
Giant Food Stores

Gillette Co.
Goddard Foundation, Charles B.
Goldseker Foundation of Maryland, Morris
Goldsmith Foundation, Horace W.
Goldwyn Foundation, Samuel
Good Samaritan
Goodrich Co., The B.F.
Gould Foundation, The Florence
Greenwall Foundation
Guardian Life Insurance Company of America
Haas, Jr. Fund, Evelyn and Walter
Hafif Family Foundation
Handy and Harman Foundation
Hanover Foundation
Harland Charitable Foundation, John and Wilhelmina D.
Harsco Corp.
Hartmarx Corporation
Hartz Foundation
Haynes Foundation, John Randolph and Dora
Hazen Foundation, Edward W.
HCA Foundation
Hechinger Co.
Heginbotham Trust, Will E.
Heinz Company, H. J.
Henkel Corp.
Hewlett-Packard Co.
Higginson Trust, Corina
Hoag Family Foundation, George
Hoffman Foundation, Maximilian E. and Marion O.
Homeland Foundation
Houston Industries Incorporated
Howard and Bush Foundation
Howe and Mitchell B. Howe Foundation, Lucille Horton
Hudson-Webber Foundation
Huston Foundation
Illinois Tool Works, Inc.
Independence Foundation
Irvine Foundation, James
Irwin Charity Foundation, William G.
ITT Hartford Insurance Group, Inc.
Ittleson Foundation
Janirve Foundation
JM Foundation
John Hancock Mutual Life Insurance Co.
Johnson & Higgins
Johnson & Son, S.C.
Jones Foundation, Daisy Marquis
Jones Foundation, Fletcher
Joy Family Foundation
Kaye, Scholer, Fierman, Hays & Handler
Kayser Foundation
Kemper Foundation, William T.
Kennecott Corporation
Kettering Fund
Knox, Sr., and Pearl Wallis Knox Charitable Foundation, Robert W.
Komes Foundation
Lang Foundation, Eugene M.
Lennon Foundation, Fred A.
Link, Jr. Foundation, George
Linnell Foundation
Lipton, Thomas J.
Lurie Foundation, Louis R.
MacArthur Foundation, John D. and Catherine T.
Macy & Co., Inc., R.H.
Mailman Family Foundation, A. L.
Marpat Foundation
May Foundation, Wilbur
Maytag Family Foundation, Fred
MCA Inc.
McCann Foundation
McCarty Foundation, John and Margaret

Auerbach Foundation,
Beatrice Fox
Ayres Foundation, Inc.
Babson Foundation, Paul and
Edith
Bacon Foundation, E. L. and
Oma
Ball Brothers Foundation
Bank of Boston Corp.
Bank One, Texas-Houston
Office
Batts Foundation
Baughman Foundation
Bay Area Foods
Bay Foundation
Bean Foundation, Norwin S.
and Elizabeth N.
BE&K Inc.
Beattie Foundation Trust,
Cordelia Lee
Beatty Trust, Cordelia
Lunceford
Beazley Foundation/Frederick
Foundation
Bechtel Charitable Remainder
Uni-Trust, Marie H.
Bedsole Foundation, J. L.
Benenson Foundation, Frances
and Benjamin
Berger Foundation, H. N. and
Frances C.
Bertha Foundation
Bethlehem Steel Corp.
Betts Industries
Bigelow Foundation, F. R.
Bingham Second Betterment
Fund, William
Bishop Foundation, E. K. and
Lillian F.
Blandin Foundation
Bloedorn Foundation, Walter
A.
Blount Educational and
Charitable Foundation,
Mildred Weedon
Blount, Inc.
Blue Bell, Inc.
Booth Ferris Foundation
Boothroyd Foundation,
Charles H. and Bertha L.
Borden, Inc.
Boston Edison Co.
Boswell Foundation, James G.
Boutell Memorial Fund
Bowen Foundation, Ethel N.
Bowne Foundation, Robert
Brady Foundation
Bridwell Foundation, J. S.
Brillion Iron Works
Brown Foundation, M. K.
Bryant Foundation
Bryn Mawr Trust Co.
Bucyrus-Erie Company
Burnett-Tandy Foundation
Cabell Foundation, Robert G.
Cabell III and Maude
Morgan
Cabot Corp.
Cain Foundation, Effie and
Wofford
Callaway Foundation
Campbell Foundation, Ruth
and Henry
Canon U.S.A., Inc.
Carnahan-Jackson Foundation
Carpenter Foundation
Cayuga Foundation
Centralia Foundation
Champlin Foundations
Chase Manhattan Bank, N.A.
Chatham Manufacturing Co.
CHC Foundation
Chesapeake Corp.
Chesebrough-Pond's USA Co.
Christensen Charitable and
Religious Foundation, L. C.
CIBC Wood Gundy
City National Bank and Trust
Co.
Clarke Trust, John
Clorox Co.
Cole Foundation, Olive B.
Cole Trust, Quincy
Coleman Foundation, George
E.

Columbia Foundation
Columbus Dispatch Printing
Co.
Comer Foundation
Commerce Bancshares, Inc.
Consolidated Natural Gas Co.
Consolidated Papers, Inc.
Continental Corp.
Cornell Trust, Peter C.
Corning Incorporated
CPC International Inc.
Crabtree & Evelyn
Crocker Trust, Mary A.
Crown Memorial, Arie and Ida
CS First Boston Corporation
Cullen Foundation
Cummings Foundation, James
H.
Cummins Engine Co.
Daily News
Dana Foundation, Charles A.
Davenport Trust Fund
Davidson Family Charitable
Foundation
Deere & Co.
Dekko Foundation
Delano Foundation, Mignon
Sherwood
Dell Foundation, Hazel
Demoulas Supermarkets Inc.
DeRoy Foundation, Helen L.
DeRoy Testamentary
Foundation
Deuble Foundation, George H.
DeVore Foundation
Dexter Charitable Fund,
Eugene A.
Dillon Foundation
Dimeo Construction Co.
Dodge Jones Foundation
Doss Foundation, M. S.
Dow Corning Corp.
Dow Foundation, Herbert H.
and Grace A.
Dreyfus Foundation, Jean and
Louis
Dreyfus Foundation, Max and
Victoria
du Pont de Nemours & Co., E.
I.
Duke Power Co.
Dun & Bradstreet Corp.
Eaton Corporation
Eaton Foundation, Cyrus
Eberly Foundation
Eccles Foundation, Ralph M.
and Ella M.
Eddy Family Memorial Fund,
C. K.
Edgewater Steel Corp.
Einstein Fund, Albert E. and
Birdie W.
El Pomar Foundation
Elkins, Jr. Foundation,
Margaret and James A.
Emerson Foundation, Inc.,
Fred L.
English Memorial Fund,
Florence C. and H. L.
Ensign-Bickford Industries
Evans Foundation, Thomas J.
Exchange National Bank
Fair Foundation, R. W.
Farr Trust, Frank M. and Alice
M.
Feild Co-Operative Association
Fenton Foundation
Ferebee Endowment, Percy O.
Finch Foundation, Doak
Finch Foundation, Thomas
Austin
Firman Fund
First Financial Bank FSB
First Interstate Bank of Oregon
First Source Corp.
First Union Corp.
Fleishhacker Foundation
Fleming Cos. Food
Distribution Center
Fletcher Foundation
Flowers Charitable Trust,
Albert W. and Edith V.
Ford Foundation
Ford Fund, William and Martha
Ford II Fund, Henry

Forest Foundation
Freedom Forge Corp.
Freeman Charitable Trust,
Samuel
Freeport Brick Co.
Freeport-McMoRan Inc.
Frohring Foundation, Paul and
Maxine
Fund for New Jersey
Gannett Publishing Co., Guy
GAR Foundation
Gates Foundation
Gaylord Foundation, Clifford
Willard
Gebbie Foundation
Gellert Foundation, Carl
GenCorp Inc.
General American Life
Insurance Co.
General Mills, Inc.
General Motors Corp.
Geneseo Foundation
Georgia-Pacific Corporation
Getty Trust, J. Paul
Giant Eagle, Inc.
Giant Food Stores
Gifford Charitable
Corporation, Rosamond
Gilman Foundation, Howard
Goodman & Co.
Graham Foundation for
Advanced Studies in the
Fine Arts
Graham Fund, Philip L.
Griffis Foundation
Griffith Foundation, W. C.
Grundy Foundation
Gulf Coast Medical Foundation
Hallett Charitable Trust, E. W.
Hallett Charitable Trust, Jessie
F.
Hancock Foundation, Luke B.
Hanes Foundation, John W.
and Anna H.
Harmon Foundation, Pearl M.
and Julia J.
Harrington Foundation,
Francis A. and Jacquelyn H.
Harrison Foundation, Fred G.
Hasbro Inc.
Hastings Charitable
Foundation, Oris B.
Hechinger Co.
Heginbotham Trust, Will E.
Heinz Endowment, Howard
Heinz Endowment, Vira I.
Henderson Foundation,
George B.
Henkel Corp.
Herrick Foundation
Herzstein Charitable
Foundation, Albert and Ethel
Hillsdale Fund
Hobby Foundation
Hoover Foundation
Hopedale Foundation
Houston Endowment
Houston Industries
Incorporated
Howard and Bush Foundation
Howe and Mitchell B. Howe
Foundation, Lucille Horton
Hoyt Foundation, Stewart W.
and Willma C.
Hudson-Webber Foundation
Hunt Charitable Trust, C. Giles
Huston Foundation
Hygeia Dairy Co.
Icahn Foundation, Carl C.
Integra Bank of Uniontown
International Paper Co.
Janesville Foundation
Jaydor Corp.
Johnson Foundation, Burdine
Johnson Foundation, M. G.
and Lillie A.
Johnson & Son, S.C.
Jones Foundation, Daisy
Marquis
Jonsson Foundation
Joslin-Needham Family
Foundation
Journal-Gazette Co.
Justus Trust, Edith C.

Kansas City Southern
Industries
Kantzler Foundation
Kaufmann Foundation, Henry
Kempner Fund, Harris and
Eliza
Kent-Lucas Foundation
Kettering Fund
Kiewit Foundation, Peter
Kilcawley Fund, William H.
Kilroy Foundation, William S.
and Lora Jean
Kimball Foundation, Horace
A. Kimball and S. Ella
Kimberly-Clark Corp.
Kinney-Lindstrom Foundation
Kirbo Charitable Trust,
Thomas M. and Irene B.
Kirkpatrick Foundation
Kitzmiller/Bales Trust
KN Energy, Inc.
Knapp Foundation
Knight Foundation, John S.
and James L.
Knox, Sr., and Pearl Wallis
Knox Charitable
Foundation, Robert W.
Knudsen Foundation, Tom and
Valley
Koehler Foundation, Marcia
and Otto
Kuehn Foundation
Kunkel Foundation, John Crain
La-Z-Boy Chair Co.
Ladd Charitable Corporation,
Helen and George
Lazarus Charitable Trust,
Helen and Charles
Lebovitz Fund
Lee Endowment Foundation
Lennon Foundation, Fred A.
Levy Foundation, June
Rockwell
Lichtenstein Foundation,
David B.
Loews Corporation
Lyon Foundation
MacCurdy Salisbury
Educational Foundation
Maritz Inc.
Marquette Electronics, Inc.
Martin Marietta Corp.
Massengill-DeFriece
Foundation
Mather Fund, Richard
May Foundation, Wilbur
Mayor Foundation, Oliver
Dewey
MBIA Inc.
McCann Foundation
McCarty Foundation, John and
Margaret
McCasland Foundation
McConnell Foundation
McCormick Trust, Anne
McCune Charitable
Foundation, Marshall and
Perrine D.
McDermott Foundation,
Eugene
McElroy Trust, R. J.
McFeely-Rogers Foundation
McGonagle Foundation,
Dextra Baldwin
McKenna Foundation,
Katherine Mabis
McMahon Foundation
McMillan Foundation, D. W.
Mead Corporation, The
Meadows Foundation
Mengle Foundation, Glenn and
Ruth
Merck Family Fund
Meyer Memorial Trust
Millbrook Tribute Garden
Miller Brewing
Company/North Carolina
Miller Charitable Foundation,
Howard E. and Nell E.
Miller Foundation
Miller-Mellor Association
Mnuchin Foundation
Mobil Oil Corp.
Mohasco Corp.
Monfort Family Foundation

Moore Charitable Foundation,
Marjorie
Morgan Charitable Residual
Trust, W. and E.
Morgan & Company, J.P.
Morgan Foundation, Burton D.
Morgan Foundation, Louie R.
and Gertrude
Morris Foundation, Margaret T.
Mosinee Paper Corp.
Muchnic Foundation
Mulford Trust, Clarence E.
Murphy Co. Foundation, G.C.
Musson Charitable
Foundation, R. C. and
Katharine M.
Mutual Assurance Co.
Nesholm Family Foundation
New York Stock Exchange, Inc.
Noble Foundation, Samuel
Roberts
Norman Foundation, Summers
A.
Northern States Power Co.
(Minnesota)
Norton Co.
O'Connor Foundation, A.
Lindsay and Olive B.
O'Connor Foundation, Kathryn
OG&E Electric Services
Ohrstrom Foundation
Old National Bank in
Evansville
Olsson Memorial Foundation,
Elis
O'Quinn Foundation, John M.
and Nancy C.
Owsley Foundation, Alvin and
Lucy
Pacific Mutual Life Insurance
Co.
Packaging Corporation of
America
Packard Foundation, David
and Lucile
PaineWebber
Palmer Fund, Frank Loomis
Parker Hannifin Corp.
Payne Foundation, Frank E.
and Seba B.
Pella Corporation
Peters Foundation, R. D. and
Linda
Petrie Trust, Lorene M.
Petteys Memorial Foundation,
Jack
Pfizer, Inc.
PHH Corporation
Pierce Charitable Trust, Harold
Whitworth
Pineywoods Foundation
Pioneer Trust Bank, NA
Porter Foundation, Mrs.
Cheever
Potomac Electric Power Co.
PPG Industries, Inc.
Proctor Trust, Mortimer R.
Providence Journal Company
Prudential Insurance Co. of
America, The
Puterbaugh Foundation
Putnam Foundation
R&B Machine Tool Co.
Ratner Foundation, Milton M.
Raymond Corp.
Reicher Foundation, Anne and
Harry J.
Rennebohm Foundation, Oscar
Reynolds Foundation, Donald
W.
Richardson Benevolent
Foundation, C. E.
Rieke Corp.
Riggs Benevolent Fund
Robinson-Broadhurst
Foundation
Rockefeller Fund, David
Rohatyn Foundation, Felix and
Elizabeth
Roseburg Forest Products Co.
Rosenberg, Jr. Family
Foundation, Louise and
Claude
Ross Memorial Foundation,
Will

Sturgis Charitable and
Educational Trust, Roy and
Christine
Subaru of America Inc.
Sumners Foundation, Hatton
W.
Tait Foundation, Frank M.
Tecumseh Products Co.
Teichert & Son, A.
Texas Commerce
Bank-Houston, N.A.
Times Mirror Company, The
Tobin Foundation
Tozer Foundation
TransAmerica Corporation
Trull Foundation
Trust Company Bank
Trust Funds
Unilever United States, Inc.
Union Bank
Unocal Corp.
US WEST, Inc.
Wallace-Reader's Digest Fund,
DeWitt
Warner Fund, Albert and
Bessie
Welfare Foundation
Westvaco Corporation
Weyerhaeuser Memorial
Foundation, Charles A.
Whirlpool Corporation
Whitecap Foundation
Whittenberger Foundation,
Claude R. and Ethel B.
WICOR, Inc.
Wilson Foundation, H. W.
Witter Foundation, Dean
Woodward Fund

Parades/Festivals

Ahmanson Foundation
AMCORE Bank, N.A.
Rockford
American General Finance
Corp.
American National Bank &
Trust Co. of Chicago
American Natural Resources
Company
American President
Companies, Ltd.
Ameritas Life Insurance Corp.
Andrews Foundation
Arnhold Foundation
Bank One, Youngstown, NA
Benwood Foundation
Bishop Foundation, E. K. and
Lillian F.
Blount, Inc.
Blue Cross & Blue Shield
United of Wisconsin
Boettcher Foundation
Borden, Inc.
Borman's Inc.
Boutell Memorial Fund
Brackenridge Foundation,
George W.
Bryn Mawr Trust Co.
Burnett-Tandy Foundation
Campbell Foundation
Campbell Foundation, Ruth
and Henry
Carpenter Foundation
Carpenter Technology Corp.
Chatham Manufacturing Co.
Cheney Foundation, Ben B.
Clements Foundation
Cole Foundation, Olive B.
Commerce Bancshares, Inc.
Consumers Power Co.
Cooke Foundation
Coors Foundation, Adolph
Crane Co.
Deere & Co.
Dell Foundation, Hazel
Demoulas Supermarkets Inc.
DeRoy Testamentary
Foundation
Deuble Foundation, George H.
Dreyfus Foundation, Max and
Victoria
Early Foundation

Emerson Foundation, Inc.,
Fred L.
Ensign-Bickford Industries
Fair Oaks Foundation, Inc.
Federated Mutual Insurance
Co.
Fireman's Fund Insurance Co.
First Source Corp.
Firstar Bank Milwaukee, N.A.
Fish Foundation, Ray C.
Fleishhacker Foundation
Fleming Cos. Food
Distribution Center
Ford Fund, William and Martha
Forest Foundation
Forster Charitable Trust, James
W. and Ella B.
Fort Wayne National Bank
Friedman Family Foundation
Gates Foundation
General American Life
Insurance Co.
Goddard Foundation, Charles
B.
Goldseker Foundation of
Maryland, Morris
Grand Rapids Label Co.
Griffith Foundation, W. C.
Gulf Coast Medical Foundation
Hafif Family Foundation
Hammer Foundation, Armand
Harcourt Foundation, Ellen
Knowles
Harmon Foundation, Pearl M.
and Julia J.
Hartz Foundation
Heinz Endowment, Vira I.
Herzstein Charitable
Foundation, Albert and Ethel
Hickory Tech Corp.
High Foundation
Hill Foundation, Sandy
Hobby Foundation
Holnam
Hopwood Charitable Trust,
John M.
Housatonic Curtain Co.
Hoyt Foundation
Hudson-Webber Foundation
Janesville Foundation
Jaydor Corp.
Jennings Foundation, Mary
Hillman
JFM Foundation
Johnson Foundation, M. G.
and Lillie A.
Johnson Foundation, Willard
T. C.
Journal-Gazette Co.
Kansas City Southern
Industries
Kiewit Foundation, Peter
Kingsbury Corp.
Kinney-Lindstrom Foundation
Knoll Group
Knox, Sr., and Pearl Wallis
Knox Charitable
Foundation, Robert W.
Kuehn Foundation
Lee Endowment Foundation
Longwood Foundation
Lyon Foundation
Markey Charitable Fund, John
C.
Martin Marietta Corp.
Mayor Foundation, Oliver
Dewey
McConnell Foundation
McInerny Foundation
McMahan Foundation,
Catherine L. and Robert O.
Meadows Foundation
Miller Brewing
Company/North Carolina
Mills Fund, Frances Goll
Mitsubishi Motor Sales of
America, Inc.
Monfort Family Foundation
Morgan Charitable Residual
Trust, W. and E.
NewMil Bancorp
Northern States Power Co.
(Minnesota)
Norton Co.

Norton Family Foundation,
Peter
Odell Fund, Robert Stewart
Odell and Helen Pfeiffer
Old National Bank in
Evansville
Oliver Memorial Trust
Foundation
Osher Foundation, Bernard
Overlake Foundation
Pamida, Inc.
Parker Hannifin Corp.
Parvin Foundation, Albert
Pittsburg Midway Coal Mining
Co.
PNC Bank, N.A.
Providence Journal Company
Rabb Charitable Foundation,
Sidney and Esther
Rachal Foundation, Ed
Raymond Corp.
Rockefeller Fund, David
Roseburg Forest Products Co.
Rose's Stores, Inc.
Rudin Foundation
Salvatori Foundation, Henry
Scaife Family Foundation
Schwartz Fund for Education
and Health Research, Arnold
and Marie
Scott Fetzer Co.
Seneca Foods Corp.
Sequoia Foundation
Share Trust, Charles Morton
Sierra Pacific Industries
Sierra Pacific Resources
Skillman Foundation
Smith Trust, May and Stanley
South Bend Tribune
Southwestern Electric Power
Co.
SPX Corp.
Stans Foundation
Steinman Foundation, James
Hale
Steinman Foundation, John
Frederick
Sternberger Foundation,
Tannenbaum
Times Mirror Company, The
Timken Foundation of Canton
Tobin Foundation
Todd Co., A.M.
Tozer Foundation
Travelers Inc.
Unitrode Corp.
USL Capital Corporation
Valmont Industries, Inc.
Van Wert County Foundation
Walsh Foundation
Whiting Foundation
Winnebago Industries, Inc.
Wyman Youth Trust
Wyomissing Foundation

Philanthropic Organizations

Abell-Hanger Foundation
Acushnet Co.
Adams Foundation, Arthur F.
and Alice E.
Ahmanson Foundation
Akzo America
Alabama Gas Corp.
Alexander Foundation, Joseph
Allendale Insurance Co.
Aluminum Co. of America
Amado Foundation, Maurice
AMCORE Bank, N.A.
Rockford
American National Bank &
Trust Co. of Chicago
Ames Charitable Trust, Harriett
AMR Corp.
Anderson Foundation, John W.
Annenberg Foundation
AON Corporation
Arcadia Foundation
Argyros Foundation
Arkell Hall Foundation
Atran Foundation

Auerbach Foundation,
Beatrice Fox
Babcock & Wilcox Co.
Baker Trust, George F.
Ball Brothers Foundation
Ball Foundation, George and
Frances
Barker Foundation, J.M.R.
Barra Foundation
Baughman Foundation
Bean Foundation, Norwin S.
and Elizabeth N.
Bechtel Charitable Remainder
Uni-Trust, Marie H.
Bechtel, Jr. Foundation, S. D.
Beech Aircraft Corp.
Bethlehem Steel Corp.
Bettingen Corporation, Burton
G.
Beveridge Foundation, Frank
Stanley
Bingham Second Betterment
Fund, William
Binney & Smith Inc.
Bishop Foundation, E. K. and
Lillian F.
Blair and Co., William
Blake Foundation, S. P.
Bloedorn Foundation, Walter
A.
Blount, Inc.
Blum-Kovler Foundation
Bobst Foundation, Elmer and
Mamdouha
Bodman Foundation
Borden, Inc.
Borman's Inc.
Boston Edison Co.
Boswell Foundation, James G.
Bowne Foundation, Robert
Brach Foundation, Helen
Brackenridge Foundation,
George W.
Brady Foundation
Buhl Foundation
Bunbury Company
Burkitt Foundation
Cabell Foundation, Robert G.
Cabell III and Maude
Morgan
Cabot Family Charitable Trust
Cain Foundation, Gordon and
Mary
Carnegie Corporation of New
York
Carpenter Foundation, E.
Rhodes and Leona B.
Carter Foundation, Beirne
Central Hudson Gas & Electric
Corp.
Century Companies of America
Champlin Foundations
Charina Foundation
Chase Manhattan Bank, N.A.
Cheney Foundation, Ben B.
Chesapeake Corp.
Childs Charitable Foundation,
Roberta M.
Citizens Bank of Rhode Island
Claiborne and Art Ortenberg
Foundation, Liz
Clay Foundation
Close Foundation
Clowes Fund
Cole Foundation, Olive B.
Coleman Foundation, George
E.
Colonial Life & Accident
Insurance Co.
Coltec Industries, Inc.
Columbia Foundation
Columbus Dispatch Printing
Co.
Consumers Power Co.
Contran Corporation
Cosmair, Inc.
Crawford Estate, E. R.
Crocker Trust, Mary A.
Crown Books
Cullen Foundation
Davis Foundation, Edwin W.
and Catherine M.
Dekko Foundation
Demoulas Supermarkets Inc.

Dexter Charitable Fund,
Eugene A.
Dishman Charitable
Foundation Trust, H. E. and
Kate
Dodge Foundation, Cleveland
H.
Dow Foundation, Herbert H.
and Grace A.
Dreyfus Foundation, Max and
Victoria
du Pont de Nemours & Co., E.
I.
Duchossois Industries Inc.
Durfee Foundation
Dynamet, Inc.
Eden Hall Foundation
Edmonds Foundation, Dean S.
Essick Foundation
Fair Play Foundation
Federated Mutual Insurance
Co.
Feil Foundation, Louis and
Gertrude
Fireman's Fund Insurance Co.
First Union Corp.
Fondren Foundation
Ford Foundation
Forest Foundation
Forest Oil Corp.
Foster Charitable Trust
France Foundation, Jacob and
Annita
Freeman Charitable Trust,
Samuel
Frisch's Restaurants Inc.
Fruehauf Foundation
Fuller Foundation
Fund for New Jersey
Fuqua Foundation, J. B.
Gannett Publishing Co., Guy
Gazette Co.
General American Life
Insurance Co.
Georgia Power Co.
Gheens Foundation
Giant Eagle, Inc.
Giles Foundation, Edward C.
Globe Newspaper Co.
Goldberg Family Foundation
Goldie-Anna Charitable Trust
Goldseker Foundation of
Maryland, Morris
Gould Foundation, The
Florence
Griffis Foundation
Griggs and Mary Griggs Burke
Foundation, Mary Livingston
Haas, Jr. Fund, Evelyn and
Walter
Habig Foundation, Arnold F.
Haigh-Scatena Foundation
Hallberg Foundation, E. L. and
R. F.
Halsell Foundation, Ewing
Hanson Industries North
America
Harcourt General, Inc.
Harland Charitable
Foundation, John and
Wilhelmina D.
Harsco Corp.
Hartford Foundation, John A.
Hassenfeld Foundation
Hazen Foundation, Edward W.
Hecht-Levi Foundation
Heckscher Foundation for
Children
Heinz Endowment, Howard
Heinz Endowment, Vira I.
Heinz Trust, Drue
Helms Foundation
Higginson Trust, Corina
Hobby Foundation
Hoffmann-La Roche Inc.
Hoover Foundation
Hoover, Jr. Foundation,
Margaret W. and Herbert
Hoyt Foundation, Stewart W.
and Willma C.
Huber Foundation
Hulbert Foundation, Nila B.
Humana, Inc.
Humphrey Fund, George M.
and Pamela S.

IBP, Inc.
Illinois Tool Works, Inc.
Irvine Foundation, James
ITT Hartford Insurance Group, Inc.
Ittleson Foundation
Jacobson Foundation, Bernard H. and Blanche E.
James River Corp. of Virginia
Janesville Foundation
Jaydor Corp.
JM Foundation
John Hancock Mutual Life Insurance Co.
Johnson Controls Inc.
Johnson & Higgins
Johnson & Son, S.C.
Kaye, Scholer, Fierman, Hays & Handler
Kennecott Corporation
Kerr Foundation
Kettering Fund
Kiplinger Foundation
Kirby Foundation, F. M.
Kline Foundation, Josiah W. and Bessie H.
Knight Foundation, John S. and James L.
Kresge Foundation
Kress Foundation, Samuel H.
Kuehn Foundation
Larsen Fund
Lauder Foundation
Laurel Foundation
Leavey Foundation, Thomas and Dorothy
Lee Enterprises
Lennon Foundation, Fred A.
Life Insurance Co. of Georgia
Linnell Foundation
Little, Inc., Arthur D.
Loews Corporation
Long Island Lighting Co.
Lurie Foundation, Louis R.
MacArthur Foundation, John D. and Catherine T.
Macy & Co., Inc., R.H.
Maddox Foundation, J. F.
Mahadh Foundation
Mailman Family Foundation, A. L.
Mailman Foundation
Management Compensation Group/Dulworth Inc.
Markle Foundation, John and Mary R.
Marmot Foundation
Marpat Foundation
Marriott Foundation, J. Willard
Martin Marietta Corp.
Mather and William Gwinn Mather Fund, Elizabeth Ring
MCA Inc.
McCann Foundation
McCormick & Co. Inc.
McDermott Foundation, Eugene
McDonald & Company Securities, Inc.
McFawn Trust No. 2, Lois Sisler
McFeely-Rogers Foundation
MCI Communications Corp.
McMahon Foundation
Mellon Family Foundation, R. K.
Mellon Foundation, Richard King
Memton Fund
Mengle Foundation, Glenn and Ruth
Merck & Co.
Metropolitan Life Insurance Co.
Middendorf Foundation
Miller Charitable Foundation, Howard E. and Nell E.
Mine Safety Appliances Co.
Mitchell Energy & Development Corp.
Mitsubishi Motor Sales of America, Inc.
Mobil Oil Corp.
Monfort Family Foundation
Montana Power Co.

Morgan Foundation, Burton D.
Morrison Knudsen Corporation
Mosinee Paper Corp.
Mott Foundation, Charles Stewart
Murdock Charitable Trust, M. J.
Nabisco Foods Group
National Westminster Bank New Jersey
New-Land Foundation
New York Life Insurance Co.
New York Times Company
Noble Foundation, Samuel Roberts
Norfolk Shipbuilding & Drydock Corp.
Northwest Natural Gas Co.
Norton Co.
Novell Inc.
O'Connor Foundation, A. Lindsay and Olive B.
Old National Bank in Evansville
Olin Foundation, Spencer T. and Ann W.
Oppenstein Brothers Foundation
Ore-Ida Foods, Inc.
Overbrook Foundation
Overlake Foundation
Packard Foundation, David and Lucile
Paley Foundation, William S.
Palmer Fund, Frank Loomis
Parsons Foundation, Ralph M.
Penn Foundation, William
Peoples Energy Corp.
Pfizer, Inc.
Pforzheimer Foundation, Carl and Lily
PHH Corporation
Piper Foundation, Minnie Stevens
Pittsburg Midway Coal Mining Co.
PNC Bank, N.A.
Premier Industrial Corp.
Price Associates, T. Rowe
Providence Journal Company
Prudential Insurance Co. of America, The
Public Service Electric & Gas Co.
Pulitzer Publishing Co.
Putnam Foundation
Ralston Purina Co.
Read Foundation, Charles L.
Reed Foundation
Regenstein Foundation
Reinberger Foundation
Retirement Research Foundation
Reynolds Foundation, Donald W.
Rich Products Corporation
RJR Nabisco Inc.
Robinson Fund, Maurice R.
Rockwell International Corporation
Rosenberg Foundation
Rose's Stores, Inc.
Salomon Foundation, Richard and Edna
Salvatori Foundation, Henry
San Diego Gas & Electric
Schering-Plough Corp.
Scherman Foundation
Schiff Foundation, Dorothy
Schlumberger Ltd.
Scholl Foundation, Dr.
Scott Foundation, Walter
Scott Foundation, William E.
Scripps Co., E.W.
Self Foundation
Seneca Foods Corp.
Sharon Steel Corp.
Shenandoah Life Insurance Co.
Sierra Pacific Resources
Simon Foundation, William E. and Carol G.
Skillman Foundation
Sloan Foundation, Alfred P.
Smart Family Foundation
SmithKline Beecham Corp.

Snow Foundation, John Ben
Snow Memorial Trust, John Ben
Snyder Foundation, Harold B. and Dorothy A.
Solow Foundation
Sonat Inc.
Southern California Edison Co.
Sprague Educational and Charitable Foundation, Seth
SPX Corp.
Stackpole-Hall Foundation
Staunton Farm Foundation
Stein Foundation, Jules and Doris
Strong Foundation, Hattie M.
Sulzberger Foundation
Superior Tube Co.
Tait Foundation, Frank M.
Teleflex Inc.
Tenneco Inc.
Textron, Inc.
Thermo Electron Corp.
Thompson Co., J. Walter
Times Mirror Company, The
Tozer Foundation
Truland Foundation
Unilever United States, Inc.
Union Camp Corporation
Union Pacific Corp.
U.S. Bank of Washington
Unitrode Corp.
Unocal Corp.
USX Corporation
Valmont Industries, Inc.
Vetlesen Foundation, G. Unger
Wachovia Bank of North Carolina, N.A.
Wahlstrom Foundation
Wal-Mart Stores, Inc.
Wallace-Reader's Digest Fund, DeWitt
Wallace-Reader's Digest Fund, Lila
Warwick Foundation
Washington Forrest Foundation
Wean Foundation, Raymond John
Weckbaugh Foundation, Eleanore Mullen
WestLB New York Branch
Westvaco Corporation
Whirlpool Corporation
Whitecap Foundation
Wiggins Memorial Trust, J. J.
Williams Charitable Trust, Mary Jo
Williams Companies, The
Wilmington Trust Co.
Wilson Fund, Matilda R.
Winchester Foundation
Young Foundation, Hugo H. and Mabel B.
Zollner Foundation

Public Policy

Abbott Laboratories
Abell-Hanger Foundation
Achelis Foundation
Acushnet Co.
Ahmanson Foundation
Air Products and Chemicals, Inc.
Akzo America
Alabama Gas Corp.
Allegheny Foundation
Allendale Insurance Co.
AlliedSignal Inc.
Allyn Foundation
Altschul Foundation
Alumax Inc.
Aluminum Co. of America
Amcast Industrial Corp.
AMCORE Bank, N.A. Rockford
American Natural Resources Company
Ames Charitable Trust, Harriett
Amoco Corporation
AMR Corp.
Andersen Corp.
Andersen Foundation
Andersons, The

Andreas Foundation
Anheuser-Busch Companies, Inc.
Annenberg Foundation
Ansin Private Foundation, Ronald M.
AON Corporation
Archer-Daniels-Midland Co.
Argyros Foundation
Armco Inc.
Armstrong Foundation
AT&T Corp.
Atherton Family Foundation
Atran Foundation
Auerbach Foundation, Beatrice Fox
Avon Products, Inc.
Babson Foundation, Paul and Edith
Baker Trust, George F.
Ball Brothers Foundation
Bank of Boston Corp.
BankAmerica Corp.
Bankers Trust Company
Barker Foundation, J.M.R.
Bauervic Foundation, Charles M.
Beal Foundation
BE&K Inc.
Beech Aircraft Corp.
Bemis Company, Inc.
Benedum Foundation, Claude Worthington
Berger Foundation, H. N. and Frances C.
Bethlehem Steel Corp.
Bettingen Corporation, Burton G.
Betts Industries
Bingham Second Betterment Fund, William
Bird Corp.
Birnschein Foundation, Alvin and Marion
Blake Foundation, S. P.
Block, H&R
Blount, Inc.
Blue Bell, Inc.
Blue Cross & Blue Shield United of Wisconsin
Blum-Kovler Foundation
Bodman Foundation
Boise Cascade Corporation
Borden, Inc.
Borman's Inc.
Bowne Foundation, Robert
BP America Inc.
Brach Foundation, Helen
Bridgestone/Firestone, Inc.
Bridwell Foundation, J. S.
Bristol-Myers Squibb Company
Brown & Williamson Tobacco Corp.
Burden Foundation, Florence V.
Burnett-Tandy Foundation
Cabot Corp.
Cabot Family Charitable Trust
Cain Foundation, Gordon and Mary
Campbell Foundation, Ruth and Henry
Carnegie Corporation of New York
Carolyn Foundation
Carpenter Technology Corp.
Cassett Foundation, Louis N.
Castle Foundation, Harold K. L.
Cayuga Foundation
Centerior Energy Corp.
Central Maine Power Co.
Chartwell Foundation
Chase Manhattan Bank, N.A.
Chazen Foundation
Chevron Corporation
Chicago Sun-Times, Inc.
Chrysler Corp.
CIGNA Corporation
Citibank
Clay Foundation
Clayton Fund
Close Foundation
Clowes Fund

CNA Financial Corporation/CNA Insurance Companies
Cole Trust, Quincy
Coleman Foundation, George E.
Columbia Foundation
Commerce Clearing House, Incorporated
Connecticut Mutual Life Insurance Company
Connelly Foundation
Consolidated Natural Gas Co.
Consolidated Papers, Inc.
Consumers Power Co.
Continental Corp.
Cooke Foundation
Cooper Industries, Inc.
Cooperman Foundation, Leon and Toby
Coors Foundation, Adolph
Copley Press, Inc.
Corning Incorporated
Covington and Burling
Cowell Foundation, S. H.
CPC International Inc.
CR Industries
Crane Co.
Crestlea Foundation
Crown Memorial, Arie and Ida
CS First Boston Corporation
Culver Foundation, Constans
Cummins Engine Co.
Daily News
Dana Foundation, Charles A.
Darby Foundation
Davis Foundation, Edwin W. and Catherine M.
Davis Foundation, Irene E. and George A.
Dekko Foundation
Delavan Foundation, Nelson B.
DeRoy Foundation, Helen L.
Diamond Foundation, Aaron
Dillon Dunwalke Trust, Clarence and Anne
Dingman Foundation, Michael D.
Dr. Seuss Foundation
Dodge Foundation, Cleveland H.
Dodge Foundation, Geraldine R.
Dodge Jones Foundation
Donnelley Foundation, Gaylord and Dorothy
Donnelley & Sons Co., R.R.
Donner Foundation, William H.
Douglas & Lomason Company
Dresser Industries, Inc.
Dreyfus Foundation, Jean and Louis
du Pont de Nemours & Co., E. I.
Duchossois Industries Inc.
Duke Power Co.
Dula Educational and Charitable Foundation, Caleb C. and Julia W.
Dun & Bradstreet Corp.
Duncan Foundation, Lillian H. and C. W.
duPont Foundation, Alfred I.
Early Foundation
Eastman Kodak Company
Eaton Corporation
Eaton Foundation, Cyrus
Eberly Foundation
Einstein Fund, Albert E. and Birdie W.
Elf Atochem North America, Inc.
English Memorial Fund, Florence C. and H. L.
Enron Corp.
Ensign-Bickford Industries
Exxon Corporation
Federal-Mogul Corporation
Fife Foundation, Elias and Bertha
Fikes Foundation, Leland
First Tennessee Bank
Fish Foundation, Ray C.
Folger Fund
Fondren Foundation

Rural Affairs

First Interstate Bank of Oregon
Ford Foundation
Freeport-McMoRan Inc.
Fund for New Jersey
General Motors Corp.
Georgia Power Co.
Gregg-Graniteville Foundation
Greve Foundation, William
    and Mary
Gulf Power Co.
Harrington Foundation,
    Francis A. and Jacquelyn H.
Hazen Foundation, Edward W.
HCA Foundation
Heinz Company, H. J.
Heller Charitable Foundation,
    Clarence E.
Hygeia Dairy Co.
IBP, Inc.
Independence Foundation
Irvine Foundation, James
Journal-Gazette Co.
Kaplan Fund, J. M.
Kettering Fund
KN Energy, Inc.
Kreitler Foundation
Laurel Foundation
Mardag Foundation
McCormick Foundation,
    Chauncey and Marion
    Deering
McElroy Trust, R. J.
McMahan Foundation,
    Catherine L. and Robert O.
Mellon Foundation, Richard
    King
Meyer Memorial Trust
Miller Brewing
    Company/North Carolina
Morgan & Company, J.P.
Mott Foundation, Charles
    Stewart
Mott Fund, Ruth
Murdock Charitable Trust, M.
    J.
Nabisco Foods Group
Noble Foundation, Samuel
    Roberts
Norton Co.
Pew Charitable Trusts
Plumsock Fund
Public Welfare Foundation
Raymond Corp.
Read Foundation, Charles L.
Rice Charitable Foundation,
    Albert W.
RJR Nabisco Inc.
Rosenberg Foundation
Rose's Stores, Inc.
Saltonstall Charitable
    Foundation, Richard
Sierra Pacific Industries
Square D Co.
Starr Foundation
Steele-Reese Foundation
Trust Funds
Valentine Foundation, Lawson
West Foundation, Harry and
    Ethel
Weyerhaeuser Co.
Willard Helping Fund, Cecilia
    Young
Williams Companies, The
Winnebago Industries, Inc.
Young Foundation, Hugo H.
    and Mabel B.

Safety

Abbott Laboratories
Abell-Hanger Foundation
Ahmanson Foundation
Air Products and Chemicals,
    Inc.
Akzo America
Akzo Chemicals Inc.
Alavi Foundation of New York
AlliedSignal Inc.
Allyn Foundation
Altman Foundation
Aluminum Co. of America
Amado Foundation, Maurice
Amcast Industrial Corp.

AMCORE Bank, N.A.
    Rockford
AMETEK, Inc.
Amfac/JMB Hawaii Inc.
AMP Incorporated
Andersen Corp.
AON Corporation
Appleby Trust, Scott B. and
    Annie P.
Arcadia Foundation
Archer-Daniels-Midland Co.
Argyros Foundation
Arkansas Power & Light Co.
Armco Inc.
Asplundh Foundation
Atherton Family Foundation
Baker Foundation, Dexter F.
    and Dorothy H.
Baker Trust, George F.
Baldwin Foundation, David
    M. and Barbara
Ball Foundation, George and
    Frances
Bauervic Foundation, Charles
    M.
Baughman Foundation
Bay Area Foods
Beatty Trust, Cordelia
    Lunceford
Beech Aircraft Corp.
Bemis Company, Inc.
Berger Foundation, H. N. and
    Frances C.
Besser Foundation
Bethlehem Steel Corp.
Betts Industries
Bird Corp.
Blair and Co., William
Blandin Foundation
Blaustein Foundation, Louis
    and Henrietta
Block, H&R
Blount, Inc.
Boston Edison Co.
Boutell Memorial Fund
Brady Foundation
Breyer Foundation
Bridwell Foundation, J. S.
Bristol-Myers Squibb
    Company
Bucyrus-Erie Company
Burchfield Foundation,
    Charles E.
Burlington Industries, Inc.
Cabot Corp.
Carpenter Technology Corp.
Carter Foundation, Amon G.
CBS, Inc.
Central Maine Power Co.
Central National Bank
Century Companies of America
Champlin Foundations
Chase Manhattan Bank, N.A.
Chatlos Foundation
CHC Foundation
Chesapeake Corp.
Chevron Corporation
Christensen Charitable and
    Religious Foundation, L. C.
Chrysler Corp.
CIGNA Corporation
City National Bank and Trust
    Co.
Clapp Charitable and
    Educational Trust, George H.
Clemens Markets Corp.
Clorox Co.
CNA Financial
    Corporation/CNA Insurance
    Companies
Cole Foundation, Olive B.
Colonial Life & Accident
    Insurance Co.
Columbus Dispatch Printing
    Co.
Consolidated Papers, Inc.
Continental Corp.
Cooper Industries, Inc.
Cornell Trust, Peter C.
CPC International Inc.
Crane Co.
Cranston Print Works Company
Cullen Foundation
Curtice-Burns Foods, Inc.
Darby Foundation

Davis Foundation, Edwin W.
    and Catherine M.
Dekko Foundation
Dell Foundation, Hazel
Demoulas Supermarkets Inc.
Dentsply International Inc.
DeRoy Foundation, Helen L.
Detroit Edison Co.
Dillon Foundation
Dimeo Construction Co.
Dingman Foundation, Michael
    D.
Dodge Jones Foundation
Douglas & Lomason Company
Douty Foundation
Dow Foundation, Herbert H.
    and Grace A.
Dresser Industries, Inc.
Dreyfus Foundation, Max and
    Victoria
du Pont de Nemours & Co., E.
    I.
Duchossois Industries Inc.
Duke Power Co.
Eaton Corporation
Eberly Foundation
Eccles Foundation, Ralph M.
    and Ella M.
Eddy Family Memorial Fund,
    C. K.
Edgewater Steel Corp.
Edmonds Foundation, Dean S.
Elf Atochem North America,
    Inc.
Elkins, Jr. Foundation,
    Margaret and James A.
Emerson Foundation, Inc.,
    Fred L.
Ensign-Bickford Industries
Exxon Corporation
Fair Oaks Foundation, Inc.
Farr Trust, Frank M. and Alice
    M.
Federal-Mogul Corporation
Federated Mutual Insurance
    Co.
Fieldcrest Cannon Inc.
First Interstate Bank of Oregon
First Union Corp.
Fleet Financial Group, Inc.
Forbes Inc.
Ford Motor Co.
Forster Charitable Trust, James
    W. and Ella B.
Freeman Charitable Trust,
    Samuel
Freeport Brick Co.
Freeport-McMoRan Inc.
Friendship Fund
Frohring Foundation, William
    O. and Gertrude Lewis
Fruehauf Foundation
Gazette Co.
General Motors Corp.
Giant Food Stores
Givenchy Corp.
Goddard Foundation, Charles
    B.
Goldwyn Foundation, Samuel
Gould Electronics Inc.
Gregg-Graniteville Foundation
Griffith Foundation, W. C.
GSM Industrial
Guardian Life Insurance
    Company of America
Guggenheim Foundation,
    Harry Frank
Gulf Power Co.
Habig Foundation, Arnold F.
Hallberg Foundation, E. L. and
    R. F.
Handy and Harman Foundation
Harsco Corp.
Hartmarx Corporation
Harvey Foundation, Felix
Hazen Foundation, Edward W.
HCA Foundation
Hearst Foundation, William
    Randolph
Hechinger Co.
Heginbotham Trust, Will E.
Heinz Company, H. J.
Henkel Corp.
Herrick Foundation
Heydt Fund, Nan and Matilda

Hillsdale Fund
Hoffman Foundation,
    Maximilian E. and Marion O.
Holnam
Hook Drugs
Hoover Foundation
Houchens Foundation, Ervin G.
Houston Endowment
Houston Industries
    Incorporated
Howard and Bush Foundation
Hunt Charitable Trust, C. Giles
Hyde and Watson Foundation
IBP, Inc.
Integra Bank of Uniontown
ITT Hartford Insurance Group,
    Inc.
Ittleson Foundation
James River Corp. of Virginia
Jameson Foundation, J. W. and
    Ida M.
JELD-WEN, Inc.
JM Foundation
Jockey Hollow Foundation
Johnson Foundation, M. G.
    and Lillie A.
Johnson & Higgins
Johnson & Son, S.C.
Jones Foundation, Daisy
    Marquis
Joslin-Needham Family
    Foundation
Justus Trust, Edith C.
Kansas City Southern
    Industries
Kavanagh Foundation, T.
    James
Kayser Foundation
Kennecott Corporation
Kent-Lucas Foundation
Kerr Foundation
Kiewit Foundation, Peter
Kimball Foundation, Horace
    A. Kimball and S. Ella
Kimberly-Clark Corp.
Kingsbury Corp.
Kiplinger Foundation
Kitzmiller/Bales Trust
Kline Foundation, Josiah W.
    and Bessie H.
Klipstein Foundation, Ernest
    Christian
Klock and Lucia Klock
    Kingston Foundation, Jay E.
Kmart Corporation
Knapp Foundation
Koopman Fund
La-Z-Boy Chair Co.
LBJ Family Foundation
Lebovitz Fund
Leighton-Oare Foundation
Lennon Foundation, Fred A.
Life Insurance Co. of Georgia
Link, Jr. Foundation, George
Lipton, Thomas J.
Loews Corporation
Long Island Lighting Co.
Lunda Charitable Trust
Lyon Foundation
M/A-COM, Inc.
Macy & Co., Inc., R.H.
Madison Gas & Electric Co.
Mandeville Foundation
Maneely Fund
Markey Charitable Fund, John
    C.
Marpat Foundation
Martin Marietta Corp.
May Department Stores
    Company, The
Mayor Foundation, Oliver
    Dewey
McCann Foundation
McConnell Foundation
McMahon Foundation
Meadows Foundation
Mellon Family Foundation, R.
    K.
Merck & Co.
Merck & Co. Human Health
    Division
Mercury Aircraft
Metropolitan Life Insurance
    Co.
Meyer Memorial Trust

Miller Brewing
    Company/North Carolina
Miller-Mellor Association
Mine Safety Appliances Co.
Minnesota Mining & Mfg. Co.
Mitsubishi Motor Sales of
    America, Inc.
Mobil Oil Corp.
Moore Charitable Foundation,
    Marjorie
Moore & Sons, B.C.
Morgan Charitable Residual
    Trust, W. and E.
Morrison Knudsen Corporation
Mutual Assurance Co.
National Steel Corp.
National Westminster Bank
    New Jersey
New Jersey Natural Gas Co.
New York Stock Exchange, Inc.
New York Times Company
NewMil Bancorp
Norman Foundation, Summers
    A.
Northern States Power Co.
    (Minnesota)
Norton Co.
O'Connor Foundation, A.
    Lindsay and Olive B.
Odell Fund, Robert Stewart
    Odell and Helen Pfeiffer
Old Dominion Box Co.
Old National Bank in
    Evansville
Olsson Memorial Foundation,
    Elis
O'Quinn Foundation, John M.
    and Nancy C.
Overbrook Foundation
Pacific Mutual Life Insurance
    Co.
Palmer Fund, Frank Loomis
Pamida, Inc.
Parker Hannifin Corp.
Parsons Foundation, Ralph M.
Pennzoil Co.
Peterson Foundation, Hal and
    Charlie
Petteys Memorial Foundation,
    Jack
Pfizer, Inc.
Phelps Dodge Corporation
PHH Corporation
Phillips Family Foundation, L.
    E.
PNC Bank, N.A.
Polaroid Corp.
PPG Industries, Inc.
Premier Industrial Corp.
Proctor Trust, Mortimer R.
Providian Corporation
Prudential Insurance Co. of
    America, The
Public Service Electric & Gas
    Co.
Public Welfare Foundation
Rachal Foundation, Ed
Raymond Corp.
Read Foundation, Charles L.
Rice Foundation
Richardson Benevolent
    Foundation, C. E.
Robinson-Broadhurst
    Foundation
Rockefeller Fund, David
Rockwell International
    Corporation
Roseburg Forest Products Co.
Rose's Stores, Inc.
Royal Group, Inc.
Rubin Foundation, Samuel
SAFECO Corp.
San Diego Gas & Electric
Scaife Family Foundation
Schwartz Fund for Education
    and Health Research, Arnold
    and Marie
Scott Foundation, William E.
Seaver Charitable Trust,
    Richard C.
Sedgwick James Inc.
Self Foundation
Seneca Foods Corp.
Seton Leather Co.
Share Trust, Charles Morton

Shell Oil Company
Shenandoah Life Insurance Co.
Sierra Pacific Industries
Sierra Pacific Resources
Simon Foundation, William E. and Carol G.
Slemp Foundation
Smeal Foundation, Mary Jean and Frank P.
Smith Charitable Foundation, Lou and Lutza
Smith Corp., A.O.
Smith Foundation, Gordon V. and Helen C.
Snayberger Memorial Foundation, Harry E. and Florence W.
Snow Memorial Trust, John Ben
Southern California Edison Co.
Spang & Co.
Springs Foundation
Square D Co.
Stanley Charitable Foundation, A.W.
Stevens Foundation, Abbot and Dorothy H.
Stevens Foundation, John T.
Stone Trust, H. Chase
Strauss Foundation, Leon
Strawbridge Foundation of Pennsylvania II, Margaret Dorrance
Subaru of America Inc.
Sulzberger Foundation
Sunnen Foundation
Swalm Foundation
Taylor Foundation, Fred and Harriett
Tecumseh Products Co.
Teichert & Son, A.
Temple Foundation, T. L. L.
Temple-Inland Inc.
Tenneco Inc.
Tetley, Inc.
Texaco Inc.
Textron, Inc.
Thompson Co., J. Walter
Thompson Trust, Thomas
Treakle Foundation, J. Edwin
Trust Company Bank
Unilever United States, Inc.
Union Camp Corporation
Union Electric Co.
United Airlines, Inc.
Unitrode Corp.
Unocal Corp.
Upjohn Foundation, Harold and Grace
Van Buren Foundation
Van Every Foundation, Philip L.
Van Wert County Foundation
Vevay-Switzerland County Foundation
Vicksburg Foundation
Virginia Power Co.
Wal-Mart Stores, Inc.
Washington Water Power Co.
Wean Foundation, Raymond John
Weckbaugh Foundation, Eleanore Mullen
Weinstein Foundation, J.
West Foundation, Harry and Ethel
Westvaco Corporation
Weyerhaeuser Co.
Whirlpool Corporation
White Trust, G. R.
Whiting Foundation
Wickes Foundation, Harvey Randall
Widgeon Foundation
Wiggins Memorial Trust, J. J.
Willard Helping Fund, Cecilia Young
Williams Companies, The
Windham Foundation
Winnebago Industries, Inc.
Winter Construction Co.
Wisconsin Power & Light Co.
Witco Corp.
Wood Foundation of Chambersburg, PA

Young Foundation, Hugo H. and Mabel B.
Young Foundation, Robert R.

Urban & Community Affairs

Abbott Laboratories
Achelis Foundation
Acushnet Co.
Ahmanson Foundation
Air Products and Chemicals, Inc.
AKC Fund
Alabama Gas Corp.
Alabama Power Co.
Alexander Foundation, Joseph
Allegheny Foundation
Allegheny Ludlum Corp.
Allendale Insurance Co.
Allianz Life Insurance Co. of North America
AlliedSignal Inc.
Altman Foundation
Aluminum Co. of America
Amcast Industrial Corp.
AMCORE Bank, N.A. Rockford
American Brands, Inc.
American Fidelity Corporation
American General Finance Corp.
American National Bank & Trust Co. of Chicago
American Natural Resources Company
American President Companies, Ltd.
American United Life Insurance Co.
AMETEK, Inc.
Amfac/JMB Hawaii Inc.
Amoco Corporation
AMP Incorporated
AMR Corp.
Andersen Corp.
Andersen Foundation
Anderson Foundation
Andersons, The
Andres Charitable Trust, Frank G.
Andrews Foundation
Anheuser-Busch Companies, Inc.
Ansin Private Foundation, Ronald M.
AON Corporation
Arcadia Foundation
Archer-Daniels-Midland Co.
Aristech Chemical Corp.
Arkansas Power & Light Co.
Arkell Hall Foundation
Armco Inc.
Arnold Fund
ASDA Foundation
Ashtabula Foundation
Astor Foundation, Vincent
AT&T Corp.
Atherton Family Foundation
Audubon State Bank
Auerbach Foundation, Beatrice Fox
Avery Arts Foundation, Milton and Sally
Avon Products, Inc.
Babson Foundation, Paul and Edith
Bacon Foundation, E. L. and Oma
Baehr Foundation, Louis W. and Dolpha
Baker Trust, George F.
Baldwin Foundation, David M. and Barbara
Baldwin Memorial Foundation, Fred
Ball Brothers Foundation
Banc One Wisconsin Corp.
Bank of Boston Corp.
Bank One, Texas-Houston Office
Bank One, Youngstown, NA
BankAmerica Corp.

Bankers Trust Company
Banta Corp.
Bard Foundation, Robert
Barker Foundation, J.M.R.
Barra Foundation
Barry Corp., R. G.
Barth Foundation, Theodore H.
Baughman Foundation
Bay Area Foods
Bean Foundation, Norwin S. and Elizabeth N.
BE&K Inc.
Bedsole Foundation, J. L.
Bell Foundation, James F.
Bemis Company, Inc.
Benedum Foundation, Claude Worthington
Benenson Foundation, Frances and Benjamin
Bethlehem Steel Corp.
Betts Industries
Beveridge Foundation, Frank Stanley
Bingham Second Betterment Fund, William
Binswanger Cos.
Bishop Foundation, E. K. and Lillian F.
Blandin Foundation
Blaustein Foundation, Louis and Henrietta
Block, H&R
Bloedorn Foundation, Walter A.
Blount Educational and Charitable Foundation, Mildred Weedon
Blount, Inc.
Blue Bell, Inc.
Blum Foundation, Edna F.
Blum-Kovler Foundation
Boatmen's Bancshares, Inc.
Bodman Foundation
Booth Ferris Foundation
Borden, Inc.
Borkee Hagley Foundation
Borman's Inc.
Boston Edison Co.
Boswell Foundation, James G.
Bothin Foundation
Boutell Memorial Fund
Bowater Incorporated
Bowne Foundation, Robert
BP America Inc.
Brach Foundation, Helen
Brady Foundation
Breyer Foundation
Bridgestone/Firestone, Inc.
Brillion Iron Works
Bristol-Myers Squibb Company
Brown Foundation, M. K.
Brown & Williamson Tobacco Corp.
Brunswick Corp.
Bryant Foundation
Bucyrus-Erie Company
Buhl Foundation
Burden Foundation, Florence V.
Burlington Industries, Inc.
Burnett-Tandy Foundation
Bush Foundation
Cable & Wireless Holdings, Inc.
Cafritz Foundation, Morris and Gwendolyn
Cain Foundation, Gordon and Mary
Calder Foundation, Louis
Callaway Foundation
Campbell Foundation
Campbell Foundation, Ruth and Henry
Campini Foundation, Frank A.
Canon U.S.A., Inc.
Carnegie Corporation of New York
Carolyn Foundation
Carpenter Foundation
Carter Foundation, Amon G.
Carter Foundation, Beirne
Carver Charitable Trust, Roy J.
Catlin Charitable Trust, Kathleen K.

Cayuga Foundation
CBS, Inc.
Centerior Energy Corp.
Central Maine Power Co.
Century Companies of America
Chadwick Fund, Dorothy Jordan
Champion International Corporation
Champlin Foundations
Charina Foundation
Chase Manhattan Bank, N.A.
Chastain Charitable Foundation, Robert Lee and Thomas M.
Chazen Foundation
Cheney Foundation, Ben B.
Chesebrough-Pond's USA Co.
Chevron Corporation
Chicago Sun-Times, Inc.
Childs Charitable Foundation, Roberta M.
Christensen Charitable and Religious Foundation, L. C.
Chrysler Corp.
Church & Dwight Co., Inc.
CIBC Wood Gundy
CIGNA Corporation
CINergy
Citibank
Citizens Bank of Rhode Island
City National Bank and Trust Co.
Claiborne and Art Ortenberg Foundation, Liz
Clark Foundation
Clarke Trust, John
Clements Foundation
Clorox Co.
Clowes Fund
CNA Financial Corporation/CNA Insurance Companies
Cogswell Benevolent Trust
Cole Foundation, Olive B.
Coleman Foundation, George E.
Collins Foundation
Columbia Foundation
Comer Foundation
Comerica Incorporated
Commerce Bancshares, Inc.
Commerce Clearing House, Incorporated
Commonwealth Edison Co.
Comprecare Foundation
Connecticut Mutual Life Insurance Company
Connelly Foundation
Consolidated Natural Gas Co.
Consumers Power Co.
Continental Corp.
Cooke Foundation
Cooper Industries, Inc.
Copley Press, Inc.
Cornell Trust, Peter C.
Corning Incorporated
Cosmair, Inc.
Cowell Foundation, S. H.
Cowles Charitable Trust
Cowles Foundation, Gardner and Florence Call
Cowles Media Co.
CPC International Inc.
CR Industries
Crane Co.
Crary Foundation, Bruce L.
Cremer Foundation
Crestlea Foundation
Crocker Trust, Mary A.
Crystal Trust
CS First Boston Corporation
Culver Foundation, Constans
Cummings Foundation, James H.
Cummins Engine Co.
Curtice-Burns Foods, Inc.
Daniel Foundation of Alabama
Davenport-Hatch Foundation
Davenport Trust Fund
Daywood Foundation
De Queen General Hospital Foundation
Deere & Co.
Dekko Foundation

Delano Foundation, Mignon Sherwood
Delaware North Co., Inc.
Demoulas Supermarkets Inc.
DeRoy Testamentary Foundation
Deuble Foundation, George H.
Dewing Foundation, Frances R.
Dexter Charitable Fund, Eugene A.
Dexter Corporation
Diamond Foundation, Aaron
Digital Equipment Corp.
Dillon Foundation
Dodge Foundation, Cleveland H.
Dodge Foundation, Geraldine R.
Donnelley Foundation, Gaylord and Dorothy
Donnelley & Sons Co., R.R.
Donner Foundation, William H.
Douglas & Lomason Company
Douty Foundation
Dow Corning Corp.
Dow Foundation, Herbert H. and Grace A.
Dow Jones & Company, Inc.
Dresser Industries, Inc.
Dreyfus Foundation, Jean and Louis
Dreyfus Foundation, Max and Victoria
du Pont de Nemours & Co., E. I.
Duchossois Industries Inc.
Duke Power Co.
Dula Educational and Charitable Foundation, Caleb C. and Julia W.
Dun & Bradstreet Corp.
Duncan Trust, John G.
Durfee Foundation
Dynamet, Inc.
Early Foundation
Eastman Kodak Company
Eaton Corporation
Eaton Foundation, Cyrus
Eberly Foundation
Eden Hall Foundation
Edgewater Steel Corp.
El Pomar Foundation
Elf Atochem North America, Inc.
Enron Corp.
Ensign-Bickford Industries
Ethyl Corp
Evans Foundation, T. M.
Exchange National Bank
Exxon Corporation
Fabri-Kal Corp.
Fair Oaks Foundation, Inc.
Farish Fund, William Stamps
Farr Trust, Frank M. and Alice M.
Favrot Fund
Federal-Mogul Corporation
Ferebee Endowment, Percy O.
Fife Foundation, Elias and Bertha
Fikes Foundation, Leland
First Chicago Corp.
First Fidelity Bank
First Hawaiian, Inc.
First Interstate Bank of Oregon
First Source Corp.
First Tennessee Bank
First Union Corp.
Firstar Bank Milwaukee, N.A.
Fischbach Foundation
Fish Foundation, Ray C.
Fleet Financial Group, Inc.
Fleishhacker Foundation
Fleming Cos. Food Distribution Center
Fletcher Foundation
Fondren Foundation
Forbes Inc.
Ford Foundation
Ford Fund, William and Martha
Ford II Fund, Henry
Ford Motor Co.
Forest Foundation
Foster Foundation
Freedom Forge Corp.

Freeman Charitable Trust, Samuel
Freeport Brick Co.
Freeport-McMoRan Inc.
Friedman Family Foundation
Friendship Fund
Frisch's Restaurants Inc.
Fruehauf Foundation
Fry Foundation, Lloyd A.
Fund for New Jersey
Fuqua Foundation, J. B.
Gamble Foundation
Gannett Publishing Co., Guy
GAR Foundation
Gates Foundation
GATX Corp.
Gebbie Foundation
Geifman Family Foundation
GenCorp Inc.
General American Life Insurance Co.
General Mills, Inc.
General Motors Corp.
Geneseo Foundation
Georgia-Pacific Corporation
Gershman Foundation, Joel
Giant Eagle, Inc.
Giant Food Inc.
Giant Food Stores
Gifford Charitable Corporation, Rosamond
Gillette Co.
Gilman Foundation, Howard
Glaser Foundation
Gleason Foundation
Globe Newspaper Co.
Goddard Foundation, Charles B.
Goldseker Foundation of Maryland, Morris
Goldwyn Foundation, Samuel
Good Samaritan
Goodman & Co.
Goodrich Co., The B.F.
Gould Electronics Inc.
Graham Foundation for Advanced Studies in the Fine Arts
Graham Fund, Philip L.
Gregg-Graniteville Foundation
Greve Foundation, William and Mary
Griffith Foundation, W. C.
Griggs and Mary Griggs Burke Foundation, Mary Livingston
Grundy Foundation
Guaranty Bank & Trust Co.
Guardian Life Insurance Company of America
Gulf Coast Medical Foundation
Gulf Power Co.
Guttman Foundation, Stella and Charles
Haas, Jr. Fund, Evelyn and Walter
Habig Foundation, Arnold F.
Hafif Family Foundation
Haigh-Scatena Foundation
Hallett Charitable Trust, E. W.
Hamilton Bank
Hamman Foundation, George and Mary Josephine
Hancock Foundation, Luke B.
Handy and Harman Foundation
Hanover Foundation
Hanson Industries North America
Harcourt General, Inc.
Hardin Foundation, Phil
Harland Charitable Foundation, John and Wilhelmina D.
Harmon Foundation, Pearl M. and Julia J.
Harriman Foundation, Gladys and Roland
Harrington Foundation, Francis A. and Jacquelyn H.
Harsco Corp.
Hartmarx Corporation
Hartz Foundation
Hastings Charitable Foundation, Oris B.
Hauser Foundation

Haynes Foundation, John Randolph and Dora
Hazen Foundation, Edward W.
HCA Foundation
Hechinger Co.
Hecht-Levi Foundation
Heckscher Foundation for Children
Heginbotham Trust, Will E.
Heinz Company, H. J.
Heinz Endowment, Howard
Heinz Endowment, Vira I.
Heinz Trust, Drue
Henderson Foundation, George B.
Henry Foundation, Patrick
Herzstein Charitable Foundation, Albert and Ethel
Heublein Inc.
Hewlett Foundation, William and Flora
Heydt Fund, Nan and Matilda
Hickory Tech Corp.
Hill Foundation, Sandy
Hillcrest Foundation
Hillman Family Foundation, Alex
Hillman Foundation
Hoffman Foundation, Maximilian E. and Marion O.
Holnam
Hoover Foundation
Hoover Fund-Trust, W. Henry
Hopwood Charitable Trust, John M.
Houston Endowment
Houston Industries Incorporated
Howard and Bush Foundation
Hoyt Foundation
Hoyt Foundation, Stewart W. and Willma C.
Huber Foundation
Hudson-Webber Foundation
Hultquist Foundation
Humana, Inc.
Hunt Charitable Trust, C. Giles
Hunt Foundation
Hunt Foundation, Roy A.
Hunt Foundation, Samuel P.
Huston Charitable Trust, Stewart
IBP, Inc.
Illinois Tool Works, Inc.
Independence Foundation
Ingalls Foundation, Louise H. and David S.
Inland Container Corp.
International Business Machines Corp.
Iowa-Illinois Gas & Electric Co.
Irvine Foundation, James
Irwin Charity Foundation, William G.
ITT Hartford Insurance Group, Inc.
Ittleson Foundation
Jackson Foundation
Jacobson Foundation, Bernard H. and Blanche E.
Jaffe Foundation
Janirve Foundation
Jarson-Stanley and Mickey Kaplan Foundation, Isaac and Esther
Jaydor Corp.
JELD-WEN, Inc.
Jennings Foundation, Mary Hillman
JFM Foundation
JM Foundation
Jockey Hollow Foundation
John Hancock Mutual Life Insurance Co.
Johnson Controls Inc.
Johnson Foundation, Helen K. and Arthur E.
Johnson & Higgins
Johnson & Son, S.C.
Jones Foundation, Daisy Marquis
Joslin-Needham Family Foundation
Journal-Gazette Co.

Justus Trust, Edith C.
Kansas City Southern Industries
Kantzler Foundation
Kaufmann Foundation, Henry
Kelley and Elza Kelley Foundation, Edward Bangs
Kemper Foundation, William T.
Kerr Foundation
Kettering Fund
Kiewit Foundation, Peter
Kilcawley Fund, William H.
Kilroy Foundation, William S. and Lora Jean
Kimberly-Clark Corp.
Kingsbury Corp.
Kiplinger Foundation
Kirby Foundation, F. M.
Kirkpatrick Foundation
Kitzmiller/Bales Trust
Klipstein Foundation, Ernest Christian
Klock and Lucia Klock Kingston Foundation, Jay E.
Kmart Corporation
KN Energy, Inc.
Knapp Foundation
Knox, Sr., and Pearl Wallis Knox Charitable Foundation, Robert W.
Komes Foundation
Koopman Fund
Kreitler Foundation
Kress Foundation, Samuel H.
Kuehn Foundation
Ladd Charitable Corporation, Helen and George
Laffey-McHugh Foundation
LamCo. Communications
Landegger Charitable Foundation
Lang Foundation, Eugene M.
Laurel Foundation
Lazarus Charitable Trust, Helen and Charles
LBJ Family Foundation
Lederer Foundation, Francis L.
LEF Foundation
Lehigh Portland Cement Co.
Leidy Foundation, John J.
Lenna Foundation, Reginald A. and Elizabeth S.
Lennon Foundation, Fred A.
Leuthold Foundation
Levitt Foundation
Levy Foundation, June Rockwell
Lipton, Thomas J.
Little, Inc., Arthur D.
Liz Claiborne, Inc.
Lockhart Vaughan Foundation
Loews Corporation
Long Island Lighting Co.
Longwood Foundation
Louisiana-Pacific Corp.
Love Foundation, George H. and Margaret McClintic
Lovett Foundation
Lurie Foundation, Louis R. and Marie S.
Lydall, Inc.
M/A-COM, Inc.
MacArthur Foundation, John D. and Catherine T.
Macy & Co., Inc., R.H.
Mailman Family Foundation, A. L.
Mailman Foundation
Marbrook Foundation
Mardag Foundation
Markey Charitable Fund, John C.
Marmot Foundation
Marshall Trust in Memory of Sanders McDaniel, Harriet McDaniel
Martin Marietta Corp.
Martin Marietta Materials
Mather Charitable Trust, S. Livingston
Mather and William Gwinn Mather Fund, Elizabeth Ring
Matthies Foundation, Katharine
May Department Stores Company, The
MCA Inc.

McConnell Foundation
McCormick & Co. Inc.
McCune Charitable Trust, John R.
McDonald & Company Securities, Inc.
McElroy Trust, R. J.
McFawn Trust No. 2, Lois Sisler
McGee Foundation
MCI Communications Corp.
McLean Contributionship
McMillan Foundation, D. W.
McQueen Foundation, Adeline and George
Mead Corporation, The
Meadows Foundation
Medtronic, Inc.
Mellon Family Foundation, R. K.
Mellon Foundation, Richard King
Mengle Foundation, Glenn and Ruth
Merck & Co.
Merck Family Fund
Mercury Aircraft
Merkley Charitable Trust
Merrick Foundation
Messing Family Charitable Foundation
Metropolitan Life Insurance Co.
Meyer Family Foundation, Paul J.
Meyer Memorial Trust
Meyerhoff Fund, Joseph
Miller Foundation
Miller-Mellor Association
Mine Safety Appliances Co.
Minnesota Mining & Mfg. Co.
Mitsubishi International Corp.
Mobil Oil Corp.
Mohasco Corp.
Monadnock Paper Mills
Moore & Sons, B.C.
Morgan & Company, J.P.
Morgan Construction Co.
Morgan and Samuel Tate Morgan, Jr. Foundation, Marietta McNeil
Morris Foundation, Margaret T.
Morris Foundation, William T.
Morrison Knudsen Corporation
Moses Fund, Henry and Lucy
Mott Foundation, Charles Stewart
Mott Fund, Ruth
Mulford Foundation, Vincent
Mulford Trust, Clarence E.
Murphy Co. Foundation, G.C.
Mutual Assurance Co.
Nalco Chemical Co.
National Westminster Bank New Jersey
Nesholm Family Foundation
Nestle USA Inc.
Neuberger Foundation, Roy R. and Marie S.
New Jersey Natural Gas Co.
New-Land Foundation
New York Life Insurance Co.
New York Stock Exchange, Inc.
New York Times Company
NewMil Bancorp
Nias Foundation, Henry
Noble Foundation, Edward John
Noble Foundation, Samuel Roberts
Norfolk Shipbuilding & Drydock Corp.
Northern States Power Co. (Minnesota)
Northwest Natural Gas Co.
Norton Co.
Norton Foundation Inc.
Norwest Corporation
NYNEX Corporation
OCRI Foundation
Odell Fund, Robert Stewart Odell and Helen Pfeiffer
OG&E Electric Services
Ohrstrom Foundation

Old National Bank in Evansville
Olsson Memorial Foundation, Elis
O'Quinn Foundation, John M. and Nancy C.
Osceola Foundation
Osher Foundation, Bernard
Overbrook Foundation
Owsley Foundation, Alvin and Lucy
Pacific Mutual Life Insurance Co.
Pacific Telesis Group
Palmer Fund, Frank Loomis
Pamida, Inc.
Panhandle Eastern Corporation
Parker Hannifin Corp.
Parsons Foundation, Ralph M.
PECO Energy Company
Pella Corporation
Penguin Books USA, Inc.
Penn Foundation, William
Pennzoil Co.
Peoples Energy Corp.
Perkin-Elmer Corp.
Petteys Memorial Foundation, Jack
Pettus Crowe Foundation
Pew Charitable Trusts
Pfizer, Inc.
Pforzheimer Foundation, Carl and Lily
Phelps Dodge Corporation
PHH Corporation
Phillips Charitable Trust, Dr. and Mrs. Arthur William
Phillips Family Foundation, Jay and Rose
Phillips Foundation, Ellis L.
Piankova Foundation, Tatiana
Pick, Jr. Fund, Albert
Pineywoods Foundation
Pioneer Trust Bank, NA
Piper Jaffray Companies Inc.
Pitt-Des Moines Inc.
Pittsburg Midway Coal Mining Co.
Pittsburgh Child Guidance Foundation
Plankenhorn Foundation, Harry
Plumsock Fund
PNC Bank, N.A.
Polaroid Corp.
Porter Foundation, Mrs. Cheever
Potomac Electric Power Co.
PPG Industries, Inc.
Premier Industrial Corp.
Price Associates, T. Rowe
Priddy Foundation
PriMerit Bank
Prince Trust, Abbie Norman
Proctor Trust, Mortimer R.
Prouty Foundation, Olive Higgins
Providence Gas Co.
Provident Life & Accident Insurance Company of America
Providian Corporation
Prudential Insurance Co. of America, The
Public Service Electric & Gas Co.
Public Welfare Foundation
Puterbaugh Foundation
Putnam Foundation
Quaker Chemical Corp.
Quivey-Bay State Foundation
Ralston Purina Co.
Rand McNally & Co.
Raymond Corp.
Reed Foundation
Retirement Research Foundation
Reynolds Foundation, Donald W.
Rich Products Corporation
Rieke Corp.
Riggs Benevolent Fund
RJR Nabisco Inc.
Robinson-Broadhurst Foundation
Rockefeller Fund, David

Zoos/Aquariums

Colonial Life & Accident Insurance Co.
Columbus Dispatch Printing Co.
Commerce Bancshares, Inc.
Commerce Clearing House, Incorporated
Commonwealth Edison Co.
Connemara Fund
Consolidated Natural Gas Co.
Consolidated Papers, Inc.
Consumers Power Co.
Continental Corp.
Contran Corporation
Cooke Foundation
Cooper Industries, Inc.
Coors Foundation, Adolph
Copley Press, Inc.
Cornell Trust, Peter C.
Cowles Charitable Trust
Cowles Media Co.
CPC International Inc.
CR Industries
Crestlea Foundation
Crown Memorial, Arie and Ida
CT Corp. System
Cullen Foundation
Culpeper Foundation, Charles E.
Culver Foundation, Constans
Daily News
Dalton Foundation, Harry L.
Dana Foundation, Charles A.
Darby Foundation
Dart Group Corp.
Dater Foundation, Charles H.
Davis Foundation, Edwin W. and Catherine M.
Davis Foundation, Irene E. and George A.
Davis Foundation, James A. and Juliet L.
DEC International, Inc.
Delaware North Co., Inc.
DeRoy Foundation, Helen L.
Detroit Edison Co.
DeVore Foundation
Dexter Charitable Fund, Eugene A.
Dillon Foundation
Dimeo Construction Co.
Dingman Foundation, Michael D.
Dr. Seuss Foundation
Dodge Foundation, Cleveland H.
Donaldson Company, Inc.
Donnelley & Sons Co., R.R.
Douglas & Lomason Company
Dow Corning Corp.
Dow Foundation, Herbert H. and Grace A.
Dresser Industries, Inc.
Dreyfus Foundation, Max and Victoria
du Pont de Nemours & Co., E. I.
Duchossois Industries Inc.
Duke Power Co.
Dula Educational and Charitable Foundation, Caleb C. and Julia W.
Dynamet, Inc.
Early Foundation
Eden Hall Foundation
Einstein Fund, Albert E. and Birdie W.
El Pomar Foundation
Elf Atochem North America, Inc.
English Memorial Fund, Florence C. and H. L.
Enron Corp.
Erpf Fund, Armand G.
Essick Foundation
Evans Foundation, Lettie Pate
Evans Foundation, T. M.
Exxon Corporation
Fair Oaks Foundation, Inc.
Fair Play Foundation
Favrot Fund
Federal-Mogul Corporation
Federated Mutual Insurance Co.
Fieldcrest Cannon Inc.

Fikes Foundation, Leland
Fireman's Fund Insurance Co.
First Chicago Corp.
First Fidelity Bank
First Tennessee Bank
First Union Corp.
Firstar Bank Milwaukee, N.A.
Fish Foundation, Ray C.
Fishback Foundation Trust, Harmes C.
Fleet Financial Group, Inc.
Forbes Inc.
Ford Fund, William and Martha
Forest Oil Corp.
Fort Wayne National Bank
France Foundation, Jacob and Annita
Freed Foundation
Freeport Brick Co.
Freeport-McMoRan Inc.
Frisch's Restaurants Inc.
Frohring Foundation, Paul and Maxine
Frost National Bank
Fry Foundation, Lloyd A.
Fuqua Foundation, J. B.
GAR Foundation
Gates Foundation
GATX Corp.
GenCorp Inc.
General American Life Insurance Co.
General Mills, Inc.
General Motors Corp.
Geneseo Foundation
GenRad
Georgia-Pacific Corporation
Georgia Power Co.
Giant Eagle, Inc.
Giant Food Inc.
Gillette Co.
Gilmore Foundation, William G.
Glaser Foundation
Glick Foundation, Eugene and Marilyn
Goddard Foundation, Charles B.
Goldsmith Foundation, Horace W.
Goodman & Co.
Grand Rapids Label Co.
Greve Foundation, William and Mary
Griffis Foundation
Griffith Foundation, W. C.
Griggs and Mary Griggs Burke Foundation, Mary Livingston
Guardian Life Insurance Company of America
Hachar Charitable Trust, D. D.
Halsell Foundation, Ewing
Hamman Foundation, George and Mary Josephine
Handy and Harman Foundation
Hanes Foundation, John W. and Anna H.
Harcourt General, Inc.
Harrison Foundation, Fred G.
Hartmarx Corporation
Hasbro Inc.
Hatch Charitable Trust, Margaret Milliken
Hazen Foundation, Edward W.
HCA Foundation
Hechinger Co.
Hecht-Levi Foundation
Heckscher Foundation for Children
Heinz Company, H. J.
Heinz Endowment, Howard
Heinz Endowment, Vira I.
Heinz Trust, Drue
Helmerich Foundation
Henderson Foundation, George B.
Henkel Corp.
Herrick Foundation
Herzstein Charitable Foundation, Albert and Ethel
Hewit Family Foundation
Hillman Foundation
Hoffmann-La Roche Inc.
Hook Drugs
Hopedale Foundation

Hopkins Foundation, Josephine Lawrence
Hopwood Charitable Trust, John M.
Houston Endowment
Houston Industries Incorporated
Hoyt Foundation
Hoyt Foundation, Stewart W. and Willma C.
Hudson-Webber Foundation
Humana, Inc.
Hunt Foundation, Roy A.
Hygeia Dairy Co.
IBP, Inc.
Illinois Tool Works, Inc.
Inland Container Corp.
International Business Machines Corp.
International Paper Co.
Jackson Foundation
Jameson Foundation, J. W. and Ida M.
Jennings Foundation, Mary Hillman
Johnson Charitable Trust, Keith Wold
Johnson Controls Inc.
Johnson Foundation, Burdine
Johnson Foundation, Helen K. and Arthur E.
Johnson & Higgins
Johnson & Son, S.C.
Jonsson Foundation
Jordan Charitable Foundation, Mary Ranken Jordan and Ettie A.
Journal-Gazette Co.
Joy Family Foundation
Julia R. and Estelle L. Foundation
Jurzykowski Foundation, Alfred
Kansas City Southern Industries
Kelly Tractor Co.
Kemper Foundation, William T.
Kennecott Corporation
Kettering Fund
Kiewit Foundation, Peter
Kimberly-Clark Corp.
Kirkpatrick Foundation
Kmart Corporation
Knapp Foundation
Knight Foundation, John S. and James L.
Knox, Sr., and Pearl Wallis Knox Charitable Foundation, Robert W.
Koehler Foundation, Marcia and Otto
Koopman Fund
Koret Foundation
Kresge Foundation
Kuehn Foundation
Kunkel Foundation, John Crain
Ladd Charitable Corporation, Helen and George
Laffey-McHugh Foundation
Lattner Foundation, Forrest C.
Lauder Foundation
Laurel Foundation
LBJ Family Foundation
Lee Enterprises
Lehigh Portland Cement Co.
Lehmann Foundation, Otto W.
Lennon Foundation, Fred A.
Levy Foundation, June Rockwell
Life Insurance Co. of Georgia
Linn-Henley Charitable Trust
Lipton, Thomas J.
Little, Inc., Arthur D.
Liz Claiborne, Inc.
Loews Corporation
Long Island Lighting Co.
Longwood Foundation
Louisiana-Pacific Corp.
Lovett Foundation
Lowenstein Foundation, Leon
Lurie Foundation, Louis R.
MacArthur Foundation, John D. and Catherine T.
Macy & Co., Inc., R.H.
Madison Gas & Electric Co.

Magowan Family Foundation
Mailman Family Foundation, A. L.
Mailman Foundation
Mardigian Foundation
Maritz Inc.
Marmot Foundation
Marquette Electronics, Inc.
Mars Foundation
Marsh & McLennan Companies, Inc.
Marshall Trust in Memory of Sanders McDaniel, Harriet McDaniel
Martin Marietta Corp.
Martin Marietta Materials
Mather and William Gwinn Mather Fund, Elizabeth Ring
Mathis-Pfohl Foundation
Mautz Paint Co.
May Department Stores Company, The
McCann Foundation
McCormick Foundation, Chauncey and Marion Deering
McDermott Foundation, Eugene
McDonald & Company Securities, Inc.
McDonnell Douglas Corp.-West
McFawn Trust No. 2, Lois Sisler
McFeely-Rogers Foundation
McGonagle Foundation, Dextra Baldwin
McLean Contributionship
McMahan Foundation, Catherine L. and Robert O.
McQueen Foundation, Adeline and George
Meadows Foundation
Medtronic, Inc.
Mellon Family Foundation, R. K.
Mellon Foundation, Andrew W.
Mellon Foundation, Richard King
Memton Fund
Merck & Co. Human Health Division
Merrill Lynch & Co., Inc.
Messing Family Charitable Foundation
Metropolitan Life Insurance Co.
Meyer Memorial Trust
Middendorf Foundation
Miller Foundation
Mine Safety Appliances Co.
Mobil Oil Corp.
Morgan & Company, J.P.
Morgan Construction Co.
Morgan Foundation, Burton D.
Morgan and Samuel Tate Morgan, Jr. Foundation, Marietta McNeil
Morgan Stanley & Co., Inc.
Morris Foundation, Margaret T.
Morris Foundation, William T.
Morrison Charitable Trust, Pauline A. and George R.
Morrison Knudsen Corporation
Moses Fund, Henry and Lucy
Mott Fund, Ruth
Mullen Foundation, J. K.
Murdock Charitable Trust, M. J.
Musson Charitable Foundation, R. C. and Katharine M.
Mutual Assurance Co.
Nalco Chemical Co.
National Gypsum Co.
National Steel Corp.
NBD Indiana, Inc.
Nesholm Family Foundation
Nestle USA Inc.
Neuberger Foundation, Roy R. and Marie S.
New England Business Service
New York Life Insurance Co.
The New Yorker Magazine, Inc.

Noble Foundation, Edward John
Norfolk Shipbuilding & Drydock Corp.
Norgren Foundation, Carl A.
Northern States Power Co. (Minnesota)
Northwest Natural Gas Co.
Norton Co.
Norton Memorial Corporation, Geraldi
Norwest Bank Nebraska, N.A.
Oaklawn Foundation
O'Connor Foundation, A. Lindsay and Olive B.
Odell Fund, Robert Stewart
Odell and Helen Pfeiffer
O'Fallon Trust, Martin J. and Mary Anne
OG&E Electric Services
Ohrstrom Foundation
Old National Bank in Evansville
Olin Foundation, Spencer T. and Ann W.
Oliver Memorial Trust Foundation
Olsson Memorial Foundation, Elis
Oppenstein Brothers Foundation
Ore-Ida Foods, Inc.
Osborn Charitable Trust, Edward B.
Outboard Marine Corp.
Overbrook Foundation
Overlake Foundation
Owen Industries, Inc.
Oxy USA Inc.
Pacific Mutual Life Insurance Co.
Packard Foundation, David and Lucile
Paley Foundation, William S.
Palmer Fund, Frank Loomis
Panhandle Eastern Corporation
Parker Hannifin Corp.
Peabody Charitable Fund, Amelia
Penn Foundation, William
Pennzoil Co.
Peoples Energy Corp.
Perkin-Elmer Corp.
Pfizer, Inc.
PHH Corporation
Phipps Foundation, Howard
Pierce Charitable Trust, Harold Whitworth
PNC Bank, N.A.
Porter Foundation, Mrs. Cheever
Pott Foundation, Herman T. and Phenie R.
Potts and Sibley Foundation
Prairie Foundation
Premier Industrial Corp.
Price Associates, T. Rowe
Prospect Hill Foundation
Providian Corporation
Prudential Securities, Inc.
Quaker Chemical Corp.
Quivey-Bay State Foundation
Rand McNally & Co.
Raymond Corp.
Regenstein Foundation
Reidler Foundation
Reinberger Foundation
Rennebohm Foundation, Oscar
Republic NY Corp.
Rice Foundation
Rich Products Corporation
Rockwell Fund
Rockwell International Corporation
Rohm & Haas Co.
Rosen Foundation, Joseph
Rosenberg, Jr. Family Foundation, Louise and Claude
Ross Laboratories
Rouse Co.
Rudin Foundation
Ryan Foundation, David Claude
SAFECO Corp.

Salomon Inc.
Saltonstall Charitable
  Foundation, Richard
San Diego Gas & Electric
Sara Lee Corp.
Sarkeys Foundation
Sasco Foundation
SBC Communications Inc.
Schering-Plough Corp.
Scherman Foundation
Scholl Foundation, Dr.
Schroeder Foundation, Walter
Schuller International
Schwab & Co., Inc., Charles
Schwartz Fund for Education
  and Health Research, Arnold
  and Marie
Scott Foundation, William E.
Scurlock Foundation
Seafirst Corporation
Seaver Institute
Seaway Food Town, Inc.
Security Life of Denver
  Insurance Co.
Sedgwick James Inc.
Seneca Foods Corp.
Sequoia Foundation
Shaw Foundation, Arch W.
Shawmut National Corp.
Shell Oil Company
Shenandoah Life Insurance Co.
Simpson Investment Company
Smith, Jr. Foundation, M. W.
SmithKline Beecham Corp.
Sonat Inc.
South Branch Foundation
Southern California Edison Co.
Sprague Educational and
  Charitable Foundation, Seth
Starr Foundation
Stauffer Foundation, John and
  Beverly
Steele Foundation, Harry and
  Grace
Stein Foundation, Jules and
  Doris
Strawbridge Foundation of
  Pennsylvania II, Margaret
  Dorrance
Stupp Foundation, Norman J.
Sturgis Charitable and
  Educational Trust, Roy and
  Christine
Sulzberger Foundation
Swift Co. Inc., John S.
Swiss Bank Corp.
Taube Family Foundation
Taylor Foundation, Ruth and
  Vernon
Teichert & Son, A.
Teleflex Inc.
Tenneco Inc.
Texaco Inc.
Texas Commerce
  Bank-Houston, N.A.
Textron, Inc.
Thorne Foundation
Times Mirror Company, The
Todd Co., A.M.
Toms Foundation
Tonya Memorial Foundation
TransAmerica Corporation
Transco Energy Co.
Truland Foundation
Trust Company Bank
Tuch Foundation, Michael
Tucker Charitable Trust, Rose
  E.
Turner Charitable Foundation
Unilever United States, Inc.
Union Camp Corporation
United Airlines, Inc.
U.S. Bank of Washington
Uris Brothers Foundation
USG Corporation
USL Capital Corporation
Van Every Foundation, Philip
  L.
Vanderbilt Trust, R. T.
Vetlesen Foundation, G. Unger
Vulcan Materials Co.
Wachovia Bank of North
  Carolina, N.A.
Wal-Mart Stores, Inc.

Wallace-Reader's Digest Fund,
  Lila
Walsh Foundation
Warwick Foundation
Wean Foundation, Raymond
  John
Weaver Foundation, Gil and
  Dody
Wege Foundation
Welfare Foundation
Wendt Foundation, Margaret L.
Wertheim Foundation, Dr.
  Herbert A.
West One Bancorp
Western New York Foundation
Westvaco Corporation
Weyerhaeuser Co.
Weyerhaeuser Memorial
  Foundation, Charles A.
Whiting Foundation,
  Macauley and Helen Dow
Whitney Fund, David M.
Wickes Foundation, Harvey
  Randall
Wickson-Link Memorial
  Foundation
WICOR, Inc.
Widgeon Foundation
Wiley & Sons, Inc., John
Williams Companies, The
Wilmington Trust Co.
Wilson Foundation, H. W.
Wilson Fund, Matilda R.
Winter Construction Co.
Winthrop Trust, Clara B.
Wisconsin Public Service Corp.
Witter Foundation, Dean
Woodward Fund
Wyomissing Foundation
Yeager Charitable Trust,
  Lester E.
Zollner Foundation

Education

Afterschool/Enrichment Programs

Achelis Foundation
Aetna Life & Casualty Co.
Aldus Corp.
Astor Foundation, Vincent
Atherton Family Foundation
BankAmerica Corp.
Beazley Foundation/Frederick
  Foundation
Binney & Smith Inc.
Boston Edison Co.
Brach Foundation, Helen
Burnett-Tandy Foundation
Calder Foundation, Louis
Carnegie Corporation of New
  York
Carolyn Foundation
Carpenter Foundation
Chicago Sun-Times, Inc.
Clark Foundation
Columbia Foundation
Davis Foundation, James A.
  and Juliet L.
Dewing Foundation, Frances R.
Dreyfus Foundation, Jean and
  Louis
duPont Foundation, Alfred I.
Favrot Fund
Federated Mutual Insurance
  Co.
First Interstate Bank of Oregon
French Oil Mill Machinery Co.
GATX Corp.
Gilmore Foundation, William
  G.
Globe Newspaper Co.
Goodrich Co., The B.F.
Haas, Jr. Fund, Evelyn and
  Walter
Hafif Family Foundation
Hancock Foundation, Luke B.
Houston Endowment
Imperial Bancorp
Integra Bank of Uniontown

Janirve Foundation
Kansas City Southern
  Industries
Kreitler Foundation
Lux Foundation, Miranda
Margoes Foundation
Mather Charitable Trust, S.
  Livingston
McQueen Foundation, Adeline
  and George
Meadows Foundation
Mellon Foundation, Richard
  King
Meyer Memorial Trust
Mid-Iowa Health Foundation
Miller Brewing
  Company/North Carolina
Mitsubishi Motor Sales of
  America, Inc.
Murdock Charitable Trust, M.
  J.
New York Mercantile Exchange
Northern States Power Co.
  (Minnesota)
Odell Fund, Robert Stewart
  Odell and Helen Pfeiffer
Old National Bank in
  Evansville
Olin Foundation, Spencer T.
  and Ann W.
Packard Foundation, David
  and Lucile
Palmer Fund, Frank Loomis
Penguin Books USA, Inc.
Pittsburgh Child Guidance
  Foundation
PriMerit Bank
Rosenberg, Jr. Family
  Foundation, Louise and
  Claude
Schumann Fund for New
  Jersey
Siltec Corp.
Starr Foundation
Staunton Farm Foundation
Steinman Foundation, James
  Hale
Strong Foundation, Hattie M.
Subaru of America Inc.
Timken Foundation of Canton
Travelers Inc.
Turrell Fund
U.S. Bank of Washington
Unitrode Corp.
Van Wert County Foundation
Vogler Foundation, Laura B.
Weckbaugh Foundation,
  Eleanore Mullen
Whirlpool Corporation
Windham Foundation
Zachry Co., H.B.

Agricultural Education

Abell-Hanger Foundation
Aluminum Co. of America
American General Finance
  Corp.
American Natural Resources
  Company
Amfac/JMB Hawaii Inc.
Andersons, The
Anheuser-Busch Companies,
  Inc.
Archer-Daniels-Midland Co.
Audubon State Bank
Auerbach Foundation,
  Beatrice Fox
BankAmerica Corp.
Baughman Foundation
Beatty Trust, Cordelia
  Lunceford
Beech Aircraft Corp.
Beloit Foundation
Bingham Second Betterment
  Fund, William
Bishop Foundation, E. K. and
  Lillian F.
Blue Bell, Inc.
Boswell Foundation, James G.
Bremer Foundation, Otto
Bridgestone/Firestone, Inc.

Bridwell Foundation, J. S.
Brillion Iron Works
Campbell Foundation, Ruth
  and Henry
Carter Foundation, Beirne
Central National Bank
Chesapeake Corp.
Chevron Corporation
Church & Dwight Co., Inc.
Colonial Life & Accident
  Insurance Co.
Commerce Bancshares, Inc.
Consumers Power Co.
Curtice-Burns Foods, Inc.
DEC International, Inc.
Deere & Co.
Delano Foundation, Mignon
  Sherwood
Demos Foundation, N.
DeRoy Foundation, Helen L.
DeRoy Testamentary
  Foundation
Donaldson Company, Inc.
Doss Foundation, M. S.
Dreyfus Foundation, Max and
  Victoria
du Pont de Nemours & Co., E.
  I.
Duke Power Co.
Dula Educational and
  Charitable Foundation,
  Caleb C. and Julia W.
duPont Foundation, Alfred I.
Exchange National Bank
Fair Play Foundation
Farr Trust, Frank M. and Alice
  M.
Federated Mutual Insurance
  Co.
First Financial Bank FSB
First Interstate Bank of Oregon
First Union Corp.
Fohs Foundation
Ford Foundation
Ford Motor Co.
Freedom Forge Corp.
Freeport-McMoRan Inc.
Frost National Bank
Gamble Foundation
Gazette Co.
General Mills, Inc.
General Motors Corp.
Georgia Power Co.
Gheens Foundation
Ghidotti Foundation
Green Foundation, Allen P.
  and Josephine B.
Gulf Power Co.
Habig Foundation, Arnold F.
Harcourt Foundation, Ellen
  Knowles
Heinz Company, H. J.
Hillsdale Fund
Holnam
Hook Drugs
Hunt Charitable Trust, C. Giles
Hunt Foundation, Roy A.
IBP, Inc.
IES Industries, Inc.
International Foundation
International Paper Co.
ITT Hartford Insurance Group,
  Inc.
Johnson Controls Inc.
Joslin-Needham Family
  Foundation
Justus Trust, Edith C.
Kansas City Southern
  Industries
Koopman Fund
Leavey Foundation, Thomas
  and Dorothy
Mautz Paint Co.
May Foundation, Wilbur
McLean Contributionship
Mellon Foundation, Richard
  King
Mid-Iowa Health Foundation
Miller Brewing
  Company/North Carolina
Mobil Oil Corp.
Monadnock Paper Mills
Monfort Family Foundation
Nestle USA Inc.

Noble Foundation, Samuel
  Roberts
Norgren Foundation, Carl A.
Norwest Bank Nebraska, N.A.
O'Connor Foundation, A.
  Lindsay and Olive B.
Ohrstrom Foundation
Ore-Ida Foods, Inc.
Overlake Foundation
Pamida, Inc.
Pennsylvania Dutch Co.
Peterson Foundation, Hal and
  Charlie
Pick, Jr. Fund, Albert
Plankenhorn Foundation, Harry
Prouty Foundation, Olive
  Higgins
Richardson Benevolent
  Foundation, C. E.
Riggs Benevolent Fund
RJR Nabisco Inc.
Rohm & Haas Co.
Ruan Foundation Trust, John
Saltonstall Charitable
  Foundation, Richard
Santa Fe Pacific Corporation
Sarkeys Foundation
Schuller International
Sedgwick James Inc.
Selby and Marie Selby
  Foundation, William G.
Seneca Foods Corp.
Sierra Pacific Resources
Skillman Foundation
Slemp Foundation
Smith Charitable Foundation,
  Lou and Lutza
Strawbridge Foundation of
  Pennsylvania II, Margaret
  Dorrance
Temple Foundation, T. L. L.
Todd Co., A.M.
Turner Charitable Foundation
Unilever United States, Inc.
Union Camp Corporation
Union Pacific Corp.
Unocal Corp.
Valmont Industries, Inc.
Van Buren Foundation
Van Wert County Foundation
Wachovia Bank of North
  Carolina, N.A.
Wal-Mart Stores, Inc.
Warwick Foundation
Weezie Foundation
West One Bancorp
White Trust, G. R.
Wisconsin Public Service Corp.
Wise Foundation and
  Charitable Trust, Watson W.

Arts/Humanities Education

Achelis Foundation
Ahmanson Foundation
Air Products and Chemicals,
  Inc.
Aldus Corp.
AlliedSignal Inc.
Altman Foundation
Aluminum Co. of America
American Brands, Inc.
American Natural Resources
  Company
Ames Charitable Trust, Harriett
AMR Corp.
Andersen Corp.
Andreas Foundation
Anheuser-Busch Companies,
  Inc.
Annenberg Foundation
AON Corporation
Arcadia Foundation
Arnhold Foundation
Atherton Family Foundation
Avery Arts Foundation, Milton
  and Sally
Avon Products, Inc.
Baker Foundation, Dexter F.
  and Dorothy H.
Baldwin Memorial
  Foundation, Fred

Bank One, Youngstown, NA
Barra Foundation
Barth Foundation, Theodore H.
Bauervic Foundation, Charles M.
Bay Foundation
Bean Foundation, Norwin S. and Elizabeth N.
BE&K Inc.
Bell Foundation, James F.
Berger Foundation, H. N. and Frances C.
Bethlehem Steel Corp.
Bingham Foundation, William
Bingham Second Betterment Fund, William
Binney & Smith Inc.
Binswanger Cos.
Bishop Foundation, E. K. and Lillian F.
Blandin Foundation
Block, H&R
Blount, Inc.
Blum-Kovler Foundation
Bodman Foundation
Booth Ferris Foundation
Bowne Foundation, Robert
BP America Inc.
Brach Foundation, Helen
Brady Foundation
Breyer Foundation
Bryn Mawr Trust Co.
Buhl Foundation
Burdines Inc.
Cafritz Foundation, Morris and Gwendolyn
Calder Foundation, Louis
Callaway Foundation
Campbell Foundation
Cape Branch Foundation
Carpenter Foundation, E. Rhodes and Leona B.
Carpenter Technology Corp.
Carter Foundation, Amon G.
Carver Charitable Trust, Roy J.
Cassett Foundation, Louis N.
Castle Foundation, Harold K. L.
CBI Industries, Inc.
Centerior Energy Corp.
Central Maine Power Co.
Chadwick Fund, Dorothy Jordan
Champlin Foundations
Chazen Foundation
Chesebrough-Pond's USA Co.
Chevron Corporation
Chicago Sun-Times, Inc.
Church & Dwight Co., Inc.
CIGNA Corporation
Citibank
Clark Foundation
Clorox Co.
Close Foundation
Clowes Fund
CNA Financial Corporation/CNA Insurance Companies
Cogswell Benevolent Trust
Colonial Life & Accident Insurance Co.
Commerce Bancshares, Inc.
Commerce Clearing House, Incorporated
Connecticut Mutual Life Insurance Company
Connelly Foundation
Consolidated Papers, Inc.
Continental Corp.
Cooke Foundation
Coors Foundation, Adolph
Cornell Trust, Peter C.
Cowles Charitable Trust
Cowles Media Co.
Crane Co.
Cranston Print Works Company
Crestlea Foundation
Crown Books
Culpeper Memorial Foundation, Daphne Seybolt
Culver Foundation, Constans
Cummins Engine Co.
Dana Charitable Trust, Eleanor Naylor
Dana Foundation, Charles A.

Daniel Foundation of Alabama
Dart Group Corp.
Davenport Trust Fund
Davis Foundations, Arthur Vining
Dekko Foundation
Dentsply International Inc.
DeRoy Foundation, Helen L.
DeRoy Testamentary Foundation
Dexter Charitable Fund, Eugene A.
Diamond Foundation, Aaron
Dimeo Construction Co.
Dodge Foundation, Cleveland H.
Dodge Foundation, Geraldine R.
Douty Foundation
Dreyfus Foundation, Jean and Louis
Dreyfus Foundation, Max and Victoria
Duchossois Industries Inc.
Duke Endowment
Duke Power Co.
Duncan Foundation, Lillian H. and C. W.
Early Foundation
Eaton Foundation, Cyrus
Elf Atochem North America, Inc.
Elkins, Jr. Foundation, Margaret and James A.
Erpf Fund, Armand G.
Fairchild Foundation, Sherman
Farish Fund, William Stamps
Federated Mutual Insurance Co.
Fenton Foundation
Firestone, Jr. Foundation, Harvey
First Fidelity Bank
First Hawaiian, Inc.
First Source Corp.
First Union Corp.
Fischbach Foundation
Fleet Financial Group, Inc.
Fleishhacker Foundation
Folger Fund
Ford Foundation
France Foundation, Jacob and Annita
Frear Eleemosynary Trust, Mary D. and Walter F.
Freeman Charitable Trust, Samuel
French Oil Mill Machinery Co.
Fribourg Foundation
Frisch's Restaurants Inc.
Frohring Foundation, William O. and Gertrude Lewis
Frost National Bank
Fry Foundation, Lloyd A.
Fund for New Jersey
Gamble Foundation
GAR Foundation
Gates Foundation
GATX Corp.
Gellert Foundation, Carl
General Mills, Inc.
General Motors Corp.
Georgia Power Co.
German Protestant Orphan Asylum Association
Gershman Foundation, Joel
Getty Trust, J. Paul
Giant Food Inc.
Gifford Charitable Corporation, Rosamond
Gilman Foundation, Howard
Goldsmith Foundation, Horace W.
Goldwyn Foundation, Samuel
Gordon/Rousmaniere/Roberts Fund
Gould Foundation, The Florence
Graham Foundation for Advanced Studies in the Fine Arts
Graham Fund, Philip L.
Grand Rapids Label Co.
Greenwall Foundation

Greve Foundation, William and Mary
Griggs and Mary Griggs Burke Foundation, Mary Livingston
Guardian Life Insurance Company of America
Habig Foundation, Arnold F.
Hancock Foundation, Luke B.
Handy and Harman Foundation
Hanes Foundation, John W. and Anna H.
Harcourt Foundation, Ellen Knowles
Hardin Foundation, Phil
Harsco Corp.
HCA Foundation
Hearst Foundation, William Randolph
Hebrew Technical Institute
Hechinger Co.
Hecht-Levi Foundation
Heckscher Foundation for Children
Heinz Company, H. J.
Heinz Endowment, Vira I.
Heller Charitable Foundation, Clarence E.
Herrick Foundation
Higginson Trust, Corina
High Foundation
Hillman Family Foundation, Alex
Hillman Foundation
Hillsdale Fund
Housatonic Curtain Co.
Houston Endowment
Howard and Bush Foundation
Hoyt Foundation, Stewart W. and Willma C.
Hudson-Webber Foundation
Huston Charitable Trust, Stewart
Hyde and Watson Foundation
Icahn Foundation, Carl C.
Independence Foundation
Ingalls Foundation, Louise H. and David S.
Integra Bank of Uniontown
Ittleson Foundation
Jacobs Family Foundation
Jacobson Foundation, Bernard H. and Blanche E.
Jaffe Foundation
JFM Foundation
JM Foundation
Johnson & Higgins
Johnson & Son, S.C.
Jones Foundation, Daisy Marquis
Jones Foundation, Helen
Kansas City Southern Industries
Kaplun Foundation, Morris J. and Betty
Kardon Foundation, Samuel and Rebecca
Kaufmann Foundation, Henry
Kelley and Elza Kelley Foundation, Edward Bangs
Kemper Foundation, William T.
Kemper National Insurance Cos.
Kent-Lucas Foundation
Kern Foundation Trust
Kimberly-Clark Corp.
Kingsbury Corp.
Kiplinger Foundation
Knight Foundation, John S. and James L.
Koehler Foundation, Marcia and Otto
Komes Foundation
Kreitler Foundation
Kresge Foundation
Kress Foundation, Samuel H.
Lang Foundation, Eugene M.
Lasdon Foundation, William and Mildred
Lauder Foundation
Leavey Foundation, Thomas and Dorothy
Leighton-Oare Foundation
Lemberg Foundation
Leuthold Foundation
Levitt Foundation

Levy Foundation, June Rockwell
Link, Jr. Foundation, George
Liz Claiborne, Inc.
Loews Corporation
Lovett Foundation
Maddox Foundation, J. F.
Management Compensation Group/Dulworth Inc.
Maneely Fund
Marpat Foundation
Marquette Electronics, Inc.
Mather Charitable Trust, S. Livingston
Mathis-Pfohl Foundation
MCA Inc.
McCasland Foundation
McCune Charitable Trust, John R.
McDermott Foundation, Eugene
McElroy Trust, R. J.
McInerny Foundation
McShain Charities, John
Mead Corporation, The
Meadows Foundation
Mellon Foundation, Andrew W.
Mellon Foundation, Richard King
Metropolitan Life Insurance Co.
Meyer Memorial Trust
Middendorf Foundation
Mielke Family Foundation
Miller Brewing Company/North Carolina
Mobil Oil Corp.
Monell Foundation, Ambrose
Morgan & Company, J.P.
Morgan Stanley & Co., Inc.
Morris Foundation, Margaret T.
Morris Foundation, William T.
Morrison Knudsen Corporation
Moses Fund, Henry and Lucy
Mulcahy Foundation
Murdock Charitable Trust, M. J.
Murphy Foundation
Musson Charitable Foundation, R. C. and Katharine M.
Mutual Assurance Co.
Neuberger Foundation, Roy R. and Marie S.
New York Life Insurance Co.
The New Yorker Magazine, Inc.
NewMil Bancorp
Noble Foundation, Edward John
Norton Co.
Norton Family Foundation, Peter
OCRI Foundation
Old Dominion Box Co.
Olsson Memorial Foundation, Elis
Osceola Foundation
Osher Foundation, Bernard
Overbrook Foundation
Overlake Foundation
Pacific Telesis Group
Packaging Corporation of America
Packard Foundation, David and Lucile
Palisades Educational Foundation
Palmer Fund, Frank Loomis
Parsons Foundation, Ralph M.
Payne Foundation, Frank E. and Seba B.
Penn Foundation, William
Pew Charitable Trusts
Pforzheimer Foundation, Carl and Lily
Philibosian Foundation, Stephen
Phillips Foundation, Ellis L.
Piankova Foundation, Tatiana
Pick, Jr. Fund, Albert
Piper Foundation, Minnie Stevens
Plumsock Fund
Polaroid Corp.

Porter Testamentary Trust, James Hyde
Price Associates, T. Rowe
Providence Journal Company
Prudential Insurance Co. of America, The
Putnam Foundation
Rabb Charitable Foundation, Sidney and Esther
Ralston Purina Co.
Reed Foundation
Reinberger Foundation
Rice Foundation
Richardson Charitable Trust, Anne S.
RJR Nabisco Inc.
Robinson Fund, Maurice R.
Rohm & Haas Co.
Rose Foundation, Billy
Rosen Foundation, Joseph
Rosenberg, Jr. Family Foundation, Louise and Claude
Ross Memorial Foundation, Will
Rouse Co.
Rowland Foundation
Rubin Foundation, Samuel
Rubinstein Foundation, Helena
Rudin Foundation
SAFECO Corp.
Salomon Inc.
San Diego Gas & Electric
Sandy Hill Foundation
Sara Lee Corp.
Sarkeys Foundation
SBC Communications Inc.
Scherer Foundation, Karla
Schering-Plough Corp.
Scherman Foundation
Schlumberger Ltd.
Scholl Foundation, Dr.
Schroeder Foundation, Walter
Schwartz Fund for Education and Health Research, Arnold and Marie
Schwob Foundation, Simon
Scott Foundation, Virginia Steele
Scurlock Foundation
Seaver Charitable Trust, Richard C.
Seaver Institute
Security Life of Denver Insurance Co.
Sedgwick James Inc.
Selby and Marie Selby Foundation, William G.
Self Foundation
Shaw Foundation, Arch W.
Shawmut National Corp.
Shubert Foundation
Simon Foundation, William E. and Carol G.
Slemp Foundation
Sloan Foundation, Alfred P.
Smart Family Foundation
Smith Foundation, Kelvin and Eleanor
Snow Memorial Trust, John Ben
Solow Foundation
Sonat Inc.
South Branch Foundation
Specialty Manufacturing Co.
Speyer Foundation, Alexander C. and Tillie S.
Sprague Educational and Charitable Foundation, Seth
Springs Foundation
Square D Co.
Starr Foundation
Steinman Foundation, James Hale
Steinman Foundation, John Frederick
Stemmons Foundation
Stevens Foundation, Abbot and Dorothy H.
Stokely, Jr. Foundation, William B.
Strawbridge Foundation of Pennsylvania II, Margaret Dorrance

Taylor Foundation, Ruth and
Vernon
Teagle Foundation
Tecumseh Products Co.
Textron, Inc.
Thompson Co., J. Walter
Thornton Foundation, Flora L.
Times Mirror Company, The
Titus Foundation, Roy and
Niuta
Transco Energy Co.
Travelers Inc.
Trexler Trust, Harry C.
Trull Foundation
Trust Company Bank
Tuch Foundation, Michael
Tucker Charitable Trust, Rose
E.
Turrell Fund
Unger Foundation, Aber D.
Union Bank
United Airlines, Inc.
Unocal Corp.
Upton Foundation, Frederick S.
Uris Brothers Foundation
USL Capital Corporation
USX Corporation
Valentine Foundation, Lawson
Van Buren Foundation
Van Wert County Foundation
Wallace-Reader's Digest Fund,
Lila
Warwick Foundation
Wean Foundation, Raymond
John
Weber Charities Corp.,
Frederick E.
Weezie Foundation
Wege Foundation
Weil, Gotshal and Manges
Foundation
Weingart Foundation
Wendt Foundation, Margaret L.
Wertheim Foundation, Dr.
Herbert A.
West One Bancorp
Wheeler Foundation
Whirlpool Corporation
Whiting Foundation
Whittenberger Foundation,
Claude R. and Ethel B.
Wiegand Foundation, E. L.
Wildermuth Foundation, E. F.
Wiley & Sons, Inc., John
Williams Charitable Trust,
Mary Jo
Wilson Fund, Matilda R.
Winter Construction Co.
Woolley Foundation, Vasser
Wright Foundation, Lola
Wyman Youth Trust
Wyomissing Foundation
Y and H Soda Foundation
Zachry Co., H.B.

Business Education

Abbott Laboratories
Abrams Foundation, Talbert
and Leota
ACF Industries, Inc.
Acushnet Co.
Aetna Life & Casualty Co.
Ahmanson Foundation
Air Products and Chemicals,
Inc.
Albertson's Inc.
Aldus Corp.
Allegheny Ludlum Corp.
Allendale Insurance Co.
AlliedSignal Inc.
Alumax Inc.
Aluminum Co. of America
AMCORE Bank, N.A.
Rockford
American Brands, Inc.
American Fidelity Corporation
American General Finance
Corp.
American Natural Resources
Company
Ameritas Life Insurance Corp.
Amfac/JMB Hawaii Inc.
Amoco Corporation

AMR Corp.
Andersons, The
Anheuser-Busch Companies,
Inc.
Archer-Daniels-Midland Co.
Argyros Foundation
Aristech Chemical Corp.
Armco Inc.
Armstrong Foundation
AT&T Corp.
Avon Products, Inc.
Babcock & Wilcox Co.
Baker Trust, George F.
Ball Brothers Foundation
Ball Foundation, George and
Frances
Banc One Wisconsin Corp.
Bank of Boston
Bank of Boston Corp.
Bank One, Youngstown, NA
BankAmerica Corp.
Bankers Trust Company
Battelle Memorial Institute
Batts Foundation
BE&K Inc.
Beaucourt Foundation
Beck Foundation, Elsie E. and
Joseph W.
Beech Aircraft Corp.
Benwood Foundation
Berwind Corporation
Bethlehem Steel Corp.
Betts Industries
Binney & Smith Inc.
Bird Corp.
Blake Foundation, S. P.
Block, H&R
Blount Educational and
Charitable Foundation,
Mildred Weedon
Blount, Inc.
Blue Bell, Inc.
Blue Cross & Blue Shield
United of Wisconsin
Blum-Kovler Foundation
Boatmen's Bancshares, Inc.
Boeing Co., The
Boettcher Foundation
Boise Cascade Corporation
Booth Ferris Foundation
Borden, Inc.
Bowater Incorporated
Bridgestone/Firestone, Inc.
Bristol-Myers Squibb
Company
Brooks Foundation, Gladys
Brunswick Corp.
Bucyrus-Erie Company
Buhl Foundation
Burdines Inc.
Burlington Industries, Inc.
Cabot Corp.
Cain Foundation, Gordon and
Mary
Carpenter Technology Corp.
Carter Foundation, Beirne
CBI Industries, Inc.
Central Fidelity Banks, Inc.
Central Maine Power Co.
Charina Foundation
Chase Manhattan Bank, N.A.
Chazen Foundation
Chevron Corporation
Chrysler Corp.
Church & Dwight Co., Inc.
CIBC Wood Gundy
CIGNA Corporation
Citibank
Citizens Bank of Rhode Island
CLARCOR Inc.
Clorox Co.
Close Foundation
CNA Financial
Corporation/CNA Insurance
Companies
Cole Foundation, Olive B.
Colonial Life & Accident
Insurance Co.
Columbia Foundation
Columbus Dispatch Printing
Co.
Commerce Bancshares, Inc.
Connecticut Mutual Life
Insurance Company
Consolidated Natural Gas Co.

Consolidated Papers, Inc.
Consumers Power Co.
Continental Corp.
Cooper Industries, Inc.
Cooperman Foundation, Leon
and Toby
Coors Foundation, Adolph
Cord Foundation, E. L.
Corning Incorporated
Cowles Media Co.
CPC International Inc.
CR Industries
Crane Co.
Crawford Estate, E. R.
CS First Boston Corporation
Cummins Engine Co.
Curtice-Burns Foods, Inc.
Daniel Foundation of Alabama
Darling Foundation, Hugh and
Hazel
Dater Foundation, Charles H.
Davenport-Hatch Foundation
Davidson Family Charitable
Foundation
Davis Foundation, Irene E. and
George A.
DEC International, Inc.
Deere & Co.
Delaware North Co., Inc.
Demoulas Supermarkets Inc.
Dentsply International Inc.
DeRoy Testamentary
Foundation
Detroit Edison Co.
Deuble Foundation, George H.
Diamond Shamrock Inc.
Dimeo Construction Co.
Dingman Foundation, Michael
D.
Donaldson Company, Inc.
Donner Foundation, William H.
Douglas & Lomason Company
du Pont de Nemours & Co., E.
I.
Duchossois Industries Inc.
Duke Power Co.
Dun & Bradstreet Corp.
Dunagan Foundation
Duncan Foundation, Lillian H.
and C. W.
Early Foundation
Eastman Kodak Company
Eaton Corporation
Eddy Family Memorial Fund,
C. K.
Eden Hall Foundation
Edgewater Steel Corp.
Edmonds Foundation, Dean S.
Einstein Fund, Albert E. and
Birdie W.
El Pomar Foundation
Elf Atochem North America,
Inc.
Emerson Foundation, Inc.,
Fred L.
Encyclopaedia Britannica, Inc.
Enron Corp.
Evans Foundation, Lettie Pate
Exchange National Bank
Exxon Corporation
Fabri-Kal Corp.
Fair Oaks Foundation, Inc.
Farish Fund, William Stamps
Federal-Mogul Corporation
Federated Mutual Insurance
Co.
Fieldcrest Cannon Inc.
Fireman's Fund Insurance Co.
First Chicago Corp.
First Fidelity Bank
First Hawaiian, Inc.
First Interstate Bank of Oregon
First Source Corp.
First Union Corp.
Firstar Bank Milwaukee, N.A.
Fish Foundation, Ray C.
Fleming Cos. Food
Distribution Center
Fondren Foundation
Ford Motor Co.
Fort Wayne National Bank
Frear Eleemosynary Trust,
Mary D. and Walter F.
Freedom Forge Corp.
Freeport-McMoRan Inc.

Frost National Bank
Frueauff Foundation, Charles
A.
Fruehauf Foundation
Fuqua Foundation, J. B.
GAR Foundation
Gates Foundation
Gazette Co.
GenCorp Inc.
General American Life
Insurance Co.
General Mills, Inc.
General Motors Corp.
Georgia-Pacific Corporation
Georgia Power Co.
Gheens Foundation
Giant Eagle, Inc.
Gifford Charitable
Corporation, Rosamond
Gillette Co.
Gleason Foundation
Goldberg Family Foundation
Goldsmith Foundation, Horace
W.
Goodrich Co., The B.F.
Gould Electronics Inc.
Graham Fund, Philip L.
Great-West Life Assurance Co.
Gregg-Graniteville Foundation
Griffith Foundation, W. C.
GSM Industrial
Guaranty Bank & Trust Co.
Guardian Life Insurance
Company of America
Gulf Power Co.
Haas, Jr. Fund, Evelyn and
Walter
Hachar Charitable Trust, D. D.
Hamilton Bank
Hammer Foundation, Armand
Handy and Harman Foundation
Harcourt General, Inc.
Harsco Corp.
Hartmarx Corporation
Harvey Foundation, Felix
Hasbro Inc.
Hawkins Foundation, Robert Z.
Haynes Foundation, John
Randolph and Dora
HCA Foundation
Hearst Foundation, William
Randolph
Hechinger Co.
Hecht-Levi Foundation
Heinz Company, H. J.
Heinz Endowment, Howard
Herrick Foundation
Hewlett-Packard Co.
Hickory Tech Corp.
Hillcrest Foundation
Hillman Foundation
Holnam
Holzer Memorial Foundation,
Richard H.
Hook Drugs
Hoover Foundation
Houchens Foundation, Ervin G.
Houston Endowment
Howe and Mitchell B. Howe
Foundation, Lucille Horton
Hudson-Webber Foundation
Hugoton Foundation
Humana, Inc.
IBP, Inc.
Illinois Tool Works, Inc.
Imperial Bancorp
Interkal, Inc.
International Paper Co.
ITT Hartford Insurance Group,
Inc.
Jacobson Foundation, Bernard
H. and Blanche E.
Jaydor Corp.
JM Foundation
John Hancock Mutual Life
Insurance Co.
Johnson Controls Inc.
Johnson & Higgins
Johnson & Son, S.C.
Jones Foundation, Fletcher
Jonsson Foundation
Jostens, Inc.
Journal-Gazette Co.
Joy Family Foundation

Kansas City Southern
Industries
Kemper National Insurance
Cos.
Kennecott Corporation
Kilcawley Fund, William H.
Kimberly-Clark Corp.
Kingsbury Corp.
Kirby Foundation, F. M.
Klock and Lucia Klock
Kingston Foundation, Jay E.
Koehler Foundation, Marcia
and Otto
Kreitler Foundation
Kresge Foundation
Kuehn Foundation
LamCo. Communications
Lehigh Portland Cement Co.
Leuthold Foundation
Life Insurance Co. of Georgia
Lipton, Thomas J.
Little, Inc., Arthur D.
Long Foundation, J.M.
Long Island Lighting Co.
Louisiana-Pacific Corp.
Lowenstein Foundation, Leon
Lux Foundation, Miranda
Lydall, Inc.
MacArthur Foundation, John
D. and Catherine T.
MacLeod Stewardship
Foundation
Macy & Co., Inc., R.H.
Management Compensation
Group/Dulworth Inc.
Maneely Fund
Margoes Foundation
Marriott Foundation, J. Willard
Mars Foundation
Marsh & McLennan
Companies, Inc.
Martin Marietta Corp.
Mattel, Inc.
May Department Stores
Company, The
MBIA Inc.
MCA Inc.
McCasland Foundation
McCormick & Co. Inc.
McDonald & Company
Securities, Inc.
McFawn Trust No. 2, Lois
Sisler
McGee Foundation
MCI Communications Corp.
McKenna Foundation, Philip
M.
McQueen Foundation, Adeline
and George
Mellon Foundation, Richard
King
Merck & Co.
Merrill Lynch & Co., Inc.
Metropolitan Life Insurance
Co.
Miller Foundation
Mine Safety Appliances Co.
Mitsubishi International Corp.
Mitsubishi Motor Sales of
America, Inc.
Mobil Oil Corp.
Moore Foundation, Edward S.
Morgan & Company, J.P.
Morgan Foundation, Burton D.
Morgan Stanley & Co., Inc.
Mosinee Paper Corp.
Murphy Co. Foundation, G.C.
Mutual Assurance Co.
Nabisco Foods Group
Nalco Chemical Co.
National Gypsum Co.
National Westminster Bank
New Jersey
New York Life Insurance Co.
New York Stock Exchange, Inc.
Noble Foundation, Samuel
Roberts
Norfolk Shipbuilding &
Drydock Corp.
Northern States Power Co.
(Minnesota)
Northwest Natural Gas Co.
Norton Co.
Novell Inc.
NYNEX Corporation

Business-School Partnerships

Colleges & Universities

Bird Corp.
Birnschein Foundation, Alvin and Marion
Bishop Foundation, E. K. and Lillian F.
Bissell Foundation, J. Walton
Blake Foundation, S. P.
Blandin Foundation
Blaustein Foundation, Louis and Henrietta
Block, H&R
Bloedorn Foundation, Walter A.
Blount Educational and Charitable Foundation, Mildred Weedon
Blount, Inc.
Blue Bell, Inc.
Blue Cross & Blue Shield United of Wisconsin
Blum Foundation, Harry and Maribel G.
Blum-Kovler Foundation
Boatmen's Bancshares, Inc.
Bobst Foundation, Elmer and Mamdouha
Bodman Foundation
Boeing Co., The
Boettcher Foundation
Boise Cascade Corporation
Booth Ferris Foundation
Boothroyd Foundation, Charles H. and Bertha L.
Borden, Inc.
Borman's Inc.
Boston Edison Co.
Boswell Foundation, James G.
Boutell Memorial Fund
Bowater Incorporated
Bowen Foundation, Ethel N.
Bowne Foundation, Robert
BP America Inc.
Brach Foundation, Helen
Brackenridge Foundation, George W.
Bremer Foundation, Otto
Brenner Foundation, Mervyn
Breyer Foundation
Bridgestone/Firestone, Inc.
Bridwell Foundation, J. S.
Bright Family Foundation
Brillion Iron Works
Bristol-Myers Squibb Company
Broadhurst Foundation
Brooks Foundation, Gladys
Brown Foundation, M. K.
Brown & Williamson Tobacco Corp.
Brunswick Corp.
Bryant Foundation
Bryn Mawr Trust Co.
Bucyrus-Erie Company
Buhl Foundation
Bunbury Company
Burchfield Foundation, Charles E.
Burden Foundation, Florence V.
Burdines Inc.
Burkitt Foundation
Burlington Industries, Inc.
Burnett-Tandy Foundation
Bush Foundation
Butz Foundation
Cabell Foundation, Robert G. Cabell III and Maude Morgan
Cabot Corp.
Cabot Family Charitable Trust
Caestecker Foundation, Charles and Marie
Cafritz Foundation, Morris and Gwendolyn
Cain Foundation, Effie and Wofford
Cain Foundation, Gordon and Mary
Calder Foundation, Louis
Calhoun Charitable Trust, Kenneth
Callaway Foundation
Campbell Foundation
Campbell Foundation, Ruth and Henry

Campini Foundation, Frank A.
Canon U.S.A., Inc.
Cape Branch Foundation
Cargill Inc.
Carnahan-Jackson Foundation
Carnegie Corporation of New York
Carolyn Foundation
Carpenter Foundation
Carpenter Foundation, E. Rhodes and Leona B.
Carpenter Technology Corp.
Carter Foundation, Amon G.
Carter Foundation, Beirne
Carvel Foundation, Thomas and Agnes
Carver Charitable Trust, Roy J.
Caspersen Foundation for Aid to Health and Education, O. W.
Cassett Foundation, Louis N.
Castle Foundation, Harold K. L.
Cayuga Foundation
CBI Industries, Inc.
CBS, Inc.
Centerior Energy Corp.
Central Fidelity Banks, Inc.
Central Hudson Gas & Electric Corp.
Central Maine Power Co.
Central National Bank
Central Vermont Public Service Corp.
Century Companies of America
Chadwick Fund, Dorothy Jordan
Champion International Corporation
Champlin Foundations
Chapman Charitable Corporation, Howard and Bess
Charina Foundation
Chartwell Foundation
Chase Manhattan Bank, N.A.
Chastain Charitable Foundation, Robert Lee and Thomas M.
Chatlos Foundation
Chazen Foundation
Cheatham Foundation, Owen
Cheney Foundation, Ben B.
Chesapeake Corp.
Chesebrough-Pond's USA Co.
Chevron Corporation
Childs Charitable Foundation, Roberta M.
Christensen Charitable and Religious Foundation, L. C.
Christian Dior New York, Inc.
Christy-Houston Foundation
Chrysler Corp.
Church & Dwight Co., Inc.
CIGNA Corporation
CINergy
Citibank
Citizens Bank of Rhode Island
Claiborne and Art Ortenberg Foundation, Liz
Clapp Charitable and Educational Trust, George H.
CLARCOR Inc.
Clark Foundation
Clarke Trust, John
Clay Foundation
Clayton Fund
Clemens Markets Corp.
Clements Foundation
Clorox Co.
Close Foundation
Clowes Fund
Coen Family Foundation, Charles S. and Mary
Cogswell Benevolent Trust
Cole Foundation, Olive B.
Cole Trust, Quincy
Coleman Foundation, George E.
Collins Foundation
Collins Foundation, George and Jennie
Collins, Jr. Foundation, George Fulton

Colonial Life & Accident Insurance Co.
Coltec Industries, Inc.
Columbia Foundation
Columbus Dispatch Printing Co.
Comer Foundation
Comerica Incorporated
Commerce Bancshares, Inc.
Commerce Clearing House, Incorporated
Commercial Bank
Commonwealth Edison Co.
Connecticut Mutual Life Insurance Company
Connelly Foundation
Connemara Fund
Consolidated Natural Gas Co.
Consolidated Papers, Inc.
Consumers Power Co.
Continental Corp.
Contran Corporation
Cooke Foundation
Cooper Industries, Inc.
Cooperman Foundation, Leon and Toby
Coors Foundation, Adolph
Copley Press, Inc.
Cord Foundation, E. L.
Cornell Trust, Peter C.
Corning Incorporated
Coughlin-Saunders Foundation
Covington and Burling
Cowell Foundation, S. H.
Cowles Charitable Trust
Cowles Foundation, Gardner and Florence Call
Cowles Media Co.
CPC International Inc.
CR Industries
Crandall Memorial Foundation, J. Ford
Crane Co.
Cranston Print Works Company
Crawford Estate, E. R.
Cremer Foundation
Crestlea Foundation
Crocker Trust, Mary A.
Crown Books
Crown Memorial, Arie and Ida
Crystal Trust
CS First Boston Corporation
CT Corp. System
Cullen Foundation
Culpeper Foundation, Charles E.
Culpeper Memorial Foundation, Daphne Seybolt
Culver Foundation, Constans
Cummings Foundation, James H.
Cummins Engine Co.
Cuneo Foundation
Curtice-Burns Foods, Inc.
Daily News
Dalton Foundation, Harry L.
Dana Charitable Trust, Eleanor Naylor
Dana Foundation, Charles A.
Daniel Foundation of Alabama
Darby Foundation
Darling Foundation, Hugh and Hazel
Dart Group Corp.
Daugherty Foundation
Davenport-Hatch Foundation
Davenport Trust Fund
Davidson Family Charitable Foundation
Davis Foundation, Edwin W. and Catherine M.
Davis Foundation, Irene E. and George A.
Davis Foundation, James A. and Juliet L.
Davis Foundations, Arthur Vining
Day Foundation, Nancy Sayles
Daywood Foundation
Deere & Co.
Dekko Foundation
Delavan Foundation, Nelson B.
Delaware North Co., Inc.
Dell Foundation, Hazel
Demos Foundation, N.

Demoulas Supermarkets Inc.
Dentsply International Inc.
DeRoy Foundation, Helen L.
DeRoy Testamentary Foundation
Detroit Edison Co.
Deuble Foundation, George H.
DeVore Foundation
Dewing Foundation, Frances R.
Dexter Charitable Fund, Eugene A.
Dexter Corporation
Diamond Foundation, Aaron
Digital Equipment Corp.
Dillon Dunwalke Trust, Clarence and Anne
Dillon Foundation
Dimeo Construction Co.
Dingman Foundation, Michael D.
Dishman Charitable Foundation Trust, H. E. and Kate
Dr. Seuss Foundation
Dodge Foundation, Cleveland H.
Dodge Foundation, Geraldine R.
Dodge Jones Foundation
Donaldson Company, Inc.
Donnelley Foundation, Gaylord and Dorothy
Donnelley & Sons Co., R.R.
Donner Foundation, William H.
Douglas & Lomason Company
Douty Foundation
Dover Foundation
Dow Corning Corp.
Dow Foundation, Herbert H. and Grace A.
Dow Jones & Company, Inc.
Dresser Industries, Inc.
Dreyfus Foundation, Jean and Louis
Dreyfus Foundation, Max and Victoria
du Pont de Nemours & Co., E. I.
Duchossois Industries Inc.
Duke Endowment
Duke Power Co.
Dula Educational and Charitable Foundation, Caleb C. and Julia W.
Dun & Bradstreet Corp.
Dunagan Foundation
Duncan Foundation, Lillian H. and C. W.
Duncan Trust, John G.
duPont Foundation, Alfred I.
Durfee Foundation
Dynamet, Inc.
Early Foundation
Eastman Kodak Company
Eaton Corporation
Eaton Foundation, Cyrus
Eberly Foundation
Eccles Foundation, Ralph M. and Ella M.
Eddy Family Memorial Fund, C. K.
Eden Hall Foundation
Edmonds Foundation, Dean S.
Einstein Fund, Albert E. and Birdie W.
El Pomar Foundation
Elf Atochem North America, Inc.
Elkins, Jr. Foundation, Margaret and James A.
Emerson Foundation, Inc., Fred L.
English Memorial Fund, Florence C. and H. L.
Enron Corp.
Ensign-Bickford Industries
Erpf Fund, Armand G.
Essick Foundation
Ethyl Corp
Ettinger Foundation
Evans Foundation, Lettie Pate
Evans Foundation, T. M.
Evans Foundation, Thomas J.
Everett Charitable Trust
Exchange National Bank

Exxon Corporation
Fabri-Kal Corp.
Fair Foundation, R. W.
Fair Oaks Foundation, Inc.
Fair Play Foundation
Fairchild Foundation, Sherman
Farish Fund, William Stamps
Favrot Fund
Federal-Mogul Corporation
Federated Mutual Insurance Co.
Feil Foundation, Louis and Gertrude
Femino Foundation
Fenton Foundation
Fieldcrest Cannon Inc.
Fife Foundation, Elias and Bertha
Fikes Foundation, Leland
Finch Foundation, Thomas Austin
Fink Foundation
Fireman's Fund Insurance Co.
Firestone, Jr. Foundation, Harvey
Firman Fund
First Chicago Corp.
First Fidelity Bank
First Financial Bank FSB
First Hawaiian, Inc.
First Interstate Bank of Oregon
First National Bank
First Source Corp.
First Tennessee Bank
First Union Corp.
First Union National Bank of Florida
Firstar Bank Milwaukee, N.A.
Fischbach Foundation
Fish Foundation, Ray C.
Fishback Foundation Trust, Harmes C.
Fleet Financial Group, Inc.
Fleishhacker Foundation
Fleming Cos. Food Distribution Center
Fletcher Foundation
Flowers Charitable Trust, Albert W. and Edith V.
Fohs Foundation
Fondren Foundation
Forbes Inc.
Ford Foundation
Ford Fund, William and Martha
Ford II Fund, Henry
Ford Motor Co.
Forest Foundation
Forest Oil Corp.
Foster Charitable Trust
Foster Foundation
France Foundation, Jacob and Annita
Frear Eleemosynary Trust, Mary D. and Walter F.
Freedom Forge Corp.
Freeman Charitable Trust, Samuel
Freeport-McMoRan Inc.
French Oil Mill Machinery Co.
Frese Foundation, Arnold D.
Fribourg Foundation
Friedman Family Foundation
Friendship Fund
Frisch's Restaurants Inc.
Frohring Foundation, Paul and Maxine
Frohring Foundation, William O. and Gertrude Lewis
Frost National Bank
Frueauff Foundation, Charles A.
Fruehauf Foundation
Fry Foundation, Lloyd A.
Fujitsu America, Inc.
Fuld Health Trust, Helene
Fuller Foundation, C. G.
Fund for New Jersey
Fuqua Foundation, J. B.
Gallagher Family Foundation, Lewis P.
Gannett Publishing Co., Guy
GAR Foundation
Garland Foundation, John Jewett and H. Chandler
Gates Foundation

GATX Corp.
Gaylord Foundation, Clifford Willard
Gazette Co.
Gebbie Foundation
Geifman Family Foundation
Gellert Foundation, Carl
Gellert Foundation, Celia Berta
GenCorp Inc.
General American Life Insurance Co.
General Mills, Inc.
General Motors Corp.
GenRad
Georgia-Pacific Corporation
Georgia Power Co.
German Protestant Orphan Asylum Association
Gershman Foundation, Joel
Getty Trust, J. Paul
Gheens Foundation
Giant Eagle, Inc.
Giant Food Inc.
Giant Food Stores
Gifford Charitable Corporation, Rosamond
Gillette Co.
Gilman Foundation, Howard
Gilmore Foundation, William G.
Givenchy Corp.
Glanville Family Foundation
Glaser Foundation
Gleason Foundation
Glenn Foundation, Carrie C. and Lena V.
Glick Foundation, Eugene and Marilyn
Globe Newspaper Co.
Goddard Foundation, Charles B.
Goldberg Family Foundation
Golden West Foundation
Goldie-Anna Charitable Trust
Goldseker Foundation of Maryland, Morris
Goldsmith Foundation, Horace W.
Goldwyn Foundation, Samuel
Good Samaritan
Goodrich Co., The B.F.
Goodstein Family Foundation, David
Gordon/Rousmaniere/Roberts Fund
Gould Electronics Inc.
Gould Foundation, The Florence
Graham Foundation for Advanced Studies in the Fine Arts
Graham Fund, Philip L.
Grand Rapids Label Co.
Great-West Life Assurance Co.
Green Foundation, Allen P. and Josephine B.
Greenwall Foundation
Gregg-Graniteville Foundation
Greve Foundation, William and Mary
Griffis Foundation
Griffith Foundation, W. C.
Griggs and Mary Griggs Burke Foundation, Mary Livingston
Griswold Foundation, John C.
Groome Beatty Trust, Helen D.
GSM Industrial
Guaranty Bank & Trust Co.
Guardian Life Insurance Company of America
Guggenheim Foundation, Harry Frank
Gulf Power Co.
Guttman Foundation, Stella and Charles
Haas, Jr. Fund, Evelyn and Walter
Habig Foundation, Arnold F.
Hafif Family Foundation
Hagedorn Fund
Haigh-Scatena Foundation
Haley Foundation, W. B.
Halff Foundation, G. A. C.
Hallberg Foundation, E. L. and R. F.

Hallett Charitable Trust, E. W.
Hallett Charitable Trust, Jessie F.
Halsell Foundation, Ewing
Hamilton Bank
Hamman Foundation, George and Mary Josephine
Hammer Foundation, Armand
Hancock Foundation, Luke B.
Handy and Harman Foundation
Hanes Foundation, John W. and Anna H.
Hanover Foundation
Hanson Industries North America
Harcourt Foundation, Ellen Knowles
Harcourt General, Inc.
Hardin Foundation, Phil
Harland Charitable Foundation, John and Wilhelmina D.
Harriman Foundation, Gladys and Roland
Harriman Foundation, Mary W.
Harrington Foundation, Francis A. and Jacquelyn H.
Harsco Corp.
Hartford Foundation, John A.
Hartmarx Corporation
Harvey Foundation, Felix
Hasbro Inc.
Hassenfeld Foundation
Hatch Charitable Trust, Margaret Milliken
Hawkins Foundation, Robert Z.
Hawn Foundation
Haynes Foundation, John Randolph and Dora
HCA Foundation
Hearst Foundation, William Randolph
Hebrew Technical Institute
Hechinger Co.
Hecht-Levi Foundation
Heckscher Foundation for Children
Hedco Foundation
Heinz Company, H. J.
Heinz Endowment, Howard
Heinz Endowment, Vira I.
Heinz Trust, Drue
Heller Charitable Foundation, Clarence E.
Heller Financial, Inc.
Helmerich Foundation
Helms Foundation
Henderson Foundation, George B.
Henkel Corp.
Henry Foundation, Patrick
Hermann Foundation, Grover
Herrick Foundation
Hershey Foods Corp.
Herzstein Charitable Foundation, Albert and Ethel
Heublein Inc.
Hewlett Foundation, William and Flora
Hewlett-Packard Co.
Heydt Fund, Nan and Matilda
Hickory Tech Corp.
High Foundation
Hill Foundation, Sandy
Hillcrest Foundation
Hillman Family Foundation, Alex
Hillman Foundation
Hillsdale Fund
Hoag Family Foundation, George
Hobby Foundation
Hoffman Foundation, Maximilian E. and Marion O.
Hoffmann-La Roche Inc.
Holnam
Holt Family Foundation
Holzer Memorial Foundation, Richard H.
Homeland Foundation
Hook Drugs
Hoover Foundation
Hoover Fund-Trust, W. Henry
Hoover, Jr. Foundation, Margaret W. and Herbert

Hopedale Foundation
Hopkins Foundation, Josephine Lawrence
Hopwood Charitable Trust, John M.
Houchens Foundation, Ervin G.
Houston Endowment
Houston Industries Incorporated
Howard and Bush Foundation
Howe and Mitchell B. Howe Foundation, Lucille Horton
Howell Foundation of Florida
Hoyt Foundation
Huber Foundation
Hudson-Webber Foundation
Hugoton Foundation
Huisking Foundation
Hulbert Foundation, Nila B.
Hulme Charitable Foundation, Milton G.
Hultquist Foundation
Humana, Inc.
Humphrey Fund, George M. and Pamela S.
Hunt Foundation
Hunt Foundation, Roy A.
Hunt Foundation, Samuel P.
Huston Charitable Trust, Stewart
Huston Foundation
Huthsteiner Fine Arts Trust
Hyde and Watson Foundation
Hygeia Dairy Co.
Icahn Foundation, Carl C.
ICI Americas Inc.
IES Industries, Inc.
Illinois Consolidated Telephone Co.
Illinois Tool Works, Inc.
Imperial Bancorp
Independence Foundation
Ingalls Foundation, Louise H. and David S.
Inland Container Corp.
Integra Bank of Uniontown
Interkal, Inc.
International Business Machines Corp.
International Foundation
International Paper Co.
Irvine Foundation, James
Irwin Charity Foundation, William G.
ITT Hartford Insurance Group, Inc.
Ittleson Foundation
Jackson Foundation
Jacobs Family Foundation
Jacobson Foundation, Bernard H. and Blanche E.
Jaffe Foundation
James River Corp. of Virginia
Jameson Foundation, J. W. and Ida M.
Janesville Foundation
Janirve Foundation
Jarson-Stanley and Mickey Kaplan Foundation, Isaac and Esther
Jaydor Corp.
JELD-WEN, Inc.
Jennings Foundation, Mary Hillman
Jewell Memorial Foundation, Daniel Ashley and Irene Houston
Jewett Foundation, George Frederick
JFM Foundation
Jockey Hollow Foundation
Johnson Charitable Trust, Keith Wold
Johnson Controls Inc.
Johnson Foundation, Burdine
Johnson Foundation, Helen K. and Arthur E.
Johnson Foundation, M. G. and Lillie A.
Johnson Fund, Edward C.
Johnson & Higgins
Johnson & Son, S.C.
Jones Foundation, Daisy Marquis
Jones Foundation, Fletcher

Jones Foundation, Harvey and Bernice
Jones Foundation, Helen
Jonsson Foundation
Jordan Charitable Foundation, Mary Ranken Jordan and Ettie A.
Journal-Gazette Co.
Joy Family Foundation
Julia R. and Estelle L. Foundation
Jurzykowski Foundation, Alfred
Kansas City Southern Industries
Kantzler Foundation
Kaplun Foundation, Morris J. and Betty
Kardon Foundation, Samuel and Rebecca
Kaufmann Foundation, Henry
Kavanagh Foundation, T. James
Kayser Foundation
Kelley and Elza Kelley Foundation, Edward Bangs
Kelly Foundation, T. Lloyd
Kelly Tractor Co.
Kemper Foundation, William T.
Kemper National Insurance Cos.
Kempner Fund, Harris and Eliza
Kennecott Corporation
Kennedy Foundation, Ethel
Kent-Lucas Foundation
Kern Foundation Trust
Kerr Foundation
Kettering Fund
Kiewit Foundation, Peter
Kilcawley Fund, William H.
Kilroy Foundation, William S. and Lora Jean
Kimball Foundation, Horace A. Kimball and S. Ella
Kimberly-Clark Corp.
Kingsbury Corp.
Kinney-Lindstrom Foundation
Kiplinger Foundation
Kirbo Charitable Trust, Thomas M. and Irene B.
Kirby Foundation, F. M.
Kirkpatrick Foundation
Kline Foundation, Josiah W. and Bessie H.
Klipstein Foundation, Ernest Christian
Klosk Fund, Louis and Rose
Kmart Corporation
KN Energy, Inc.
Knapp Foundation
Knight Foundation, John S. and James L.
Knox, Sr., and Pearl Wallis Knox Charitable Foundation, Robert W.
Knudsen Foundation, Tom and Valley
Koch Charitable Foundation, Charles G.
Koehler Foundation, Marcia and Otto
Kohn-Joseloff Foundation
Komes Foundation
Koopman Fund
Koret Foundation
Kornfeld Foundation, Emily Davie and Joseph S.
Kreitler Foundation
Kresge Foundation
Kress Foundation, Samuel H.
Kuehn Foundation
Kunkel Foundation, John Crain
Kutz Foundation, Milton and Hattie
Kuyper Foundation, Peter H. and E. Lucille
La-Z-Boy Chair Co.
Ladd Charitable Corporation, Helen and George
Laffey-McHugh Foundation
LamCo. Communications
Landegger Charitable Foundation
Lang Foundation, Eugene M.

Larsen Fund
Lasdon Foundation
Lasdon Foundation, William and Mildred
Lauder Foundation
Laurel Foundation
Lazarus Charitable Trust, Helen and Charles
LBJ Family Foundation
Lea Foundation, Helen Sperry
Leavey Foundation, Thomas and Dorothy
Lebanon Mutual Insurance Co.
Lebovitz Fund
Lederer Foundation, Francis L.
Lee Endowment Foundation
Lee Enterprises
Lehigh Portland Cement Co.
Lehmann Foundation, Otto W.
Leidy Foundation, John J.
Leighton-Oare Foundation
Lemberg Foundation
Lenna Foundation, Reginald A. and Elizabeth S.
Lennon Foundation, Fred A.
Leuthold Foundation
Levitt Foundation
Levy Foundation, June Rockwell
Liberman Foundation, Bertha and Isaac
Lichtenstein Foundation, David B.
Life Insurance Co. of Georgia
Link, Jr. Foundation, George
Linn-Henley Charitable Trust
Linnell Foundation
Lipton, Thomas J.
Littauer Foundation, Lucius N.
Little, Inc., Arthur D.
Liz Claiborne, Inc.
Lockhart Vaughan Foundation
Loews Corporation
Long Foundation, J.M.
Long Island Lighting Co.
Longwood Foundation
Louisiana-Pacific Corp.
Love Foundation, George H. and Margaret McClintic
Lovett Foundation
Lowenstein Foundation, Leon
Lurcy Charitable and Educational Trust, Georges
Lurie Foundation, Louis R.
Lux Foundation, Miranda
Lydall, Inc.
M/A-COM, Inc.
MacArthur Foundation, John D. and Catherine T.
Macy & Co., Inc., R.H.
Maddox Foundation, J. F.
Madison Gas & Electric Co.
Magowan Family Foundation
Mahadh Foundation
Mailman Family Foundation, A. L.
Mailman Foundation
Management Compensation Group/Dulworth Inc.
Mandeville Foundation
Maneely Fund
Marbrook Foundation
Mardag Foundation
Mardigian Foundation
Margoes Foundation
Maritz Inc.
Markey Charitable Fund, John C.
Markle Foundation, John and Mary R.
Marmot Foundation
Marpat Foundation
Marriott Foundation, J. Willard
Mars Foundation
Marshall Foundation, Mattie H.
Marshall Trust in Memory of Sanders McDaniel, Harriet McDaniel
Martin Marietta Corp.
Martin Marietta Materials
Martini Foundation, Nicholas
Marx Foundation, Virginia and Leonard
Mascoma Savings Bank

Massachusetts Mutual Life Insurance Co.
Massengill-DeFriece Foundation
Mather Charitable Trust, S. Livingston
Mather Fund, Richard
Mather and William Gwinn
Mather Fund, Elizabeth Ring
Mathis-Pfohl Foundation
Mattel, Inc.
Mautz Paint Co.
May Department Stores Company, The
May Foundation, Wilbur
Mayer Foundation, James and Eva
Mayor Foundation, Oliver Dewey
Mays Foundation
Maytag Family Foundation, Fred
MBIA Inc.
MCA Inc.
McCann Foundation
McCarty Foundation, John and Margaret
McCasland Foundation
McConnell Foundation
McCormick & Co. Inc.
McCormick Foundation, Chauncey and Marion Deering
McCormick Trust, Anne
McCune Charitable Foundation, Marshall and Perrine D.
McCune Charitable Trust, John R.
McDermott Foundation, Eugene
McDonald & Company Securities, Inc.
McElroy Trust, R. J.
McEvoy Foundation, Mildred H.
McFawn Trust No. 2, Lois Sisler
McFeely-Rogers Foundation
McGee Foundation
McGonagle Foundation, Dextra Baldwin
MCI Communications Corp.
McInerny Foundation
McKenna Foundation, Katherine Mabis
McKenna Foundation, Philip M.
McLean Contributionship
McMahan Foundation, Catherine L. and Robert O.
McMahon Foundation
McShain Charities, John
M.E. Foundation
Mead Corporation, The
Meadows Foundation
Medtronic, Inc.
Mellon Family Foundation, R. K.
Mellon Foundation, Andrew W.
Mellon Foundation, Richard King
Memorial Foundation for the Blind
Memton Fund
Mengle Foundation, Glenn and Ruth
Merck & Co.
Merck & Co. Human Health Division
Mercury Aircraft
Merrick Foundation
Merrill Lynch & Co., Inc.
Messing Family Charitable Foundation
Metropolitan Life Insurance Co.
Meyer Family Foundation, Paul J.
Meyer Fund, Milton and Sophie
Meyer Memorial Trust
Meyerhoff Fund, Joseph
Mid-Iowa Health Foundation
Middendorf Foundation

Mielke Family Foundation
Millbrook Tribute Garden
Miller Brewing Company/North Carolina
Miller Charitable Foundation, Howard E. and Nell E.
Miller Foundation
Miller Fund, Kathryn and Gilbert
Miller-Mellor Association
Mills Fund, Frances Goll
Mine Safety Appliances Co.
Mingenback Foundation, Julia J.
Minnesota Mining & Mfg. Co.
Mitchell Energy & Development Corp.
Mitsubishi Motor Sales of America, Inc.
Mnuchin Foundation
Mobil Oil Corp.
Mohasco Corp.
Monell Foundation, Ambrose
Monfort Family Foundation
Montana Power Co.
Monticello College Foundation
Moore Foundation, Edward S.
Moore & Sons, B.C.
Morgan & Company, J.P.
Morgan Construction Co.
Morgan Foundation, Burton D.
Morgan and Samuel Tate Morgan, Jr. Foundation, Marietta McNeil
Morgan Stanley & Co., Inc.
Morris Foundation, Margaret T.
Morris Foundation, William T.
Morrison Knudsen Corporation
Mosbacher, Jr. Foundation, Emil
Moses Fund, Henry and Lucy
Mosinee Paper Corp.
Mott Foundation, Charles Stewart
Mott Fund, Ruth
Muchnic Foundation
Mulcahy Foundation
Mulford Foundation, Vincent
Mulford Trust, Clarence E.
Mullen Foundation, J. K.
Muller Foundation
Munger Foundation, Alfred C.
Munson Foundation Trust, W. B.
Murdock Charitable Trust, M. J.
Murphey Foundation, Lluella Morey
Murphy Co. Foundation, G.C.
Murphy Foundation
Musson Charitable Foundation, R. C. and Katharine M.
Mutual Assurance Co.
Myra Foundation
Nabisco Foods Group
Nalco Chemical Co.
National Forge Co.
National Gypsum Co.
National Steel Corp.
National Westminster Bank New Jersey
NBD Indiana, Inc.
Nesholm Family Foundation
Nestle USA Inc.
Neuberger Foundation, Roy R. and Marie S.
New England Business Service
New Jersey Natural Gas Co.
New-Land Foundation
New York Life Insurance Co.
New York Stock Exchange, Inc.
New York Times Company
The New Yorker Magazine, Inc.
Newcombe Foundation, Charlotte W.
Nias Foundation, Henry
Noble Foundation, Edward John
Noble Foundation, Samuel Roberts
Norfolk Shipbuilding & Drydock Corp.
Norgren Foundation, Carl A.

Norman Foundation, Summers A.
Normandie Foundation
North Shore Foundation
Northern States Power Co. (Minnesota)
Northwest Natural Gas Co.
Norton Co.
Norton Family Foundation, Peter
Norton Foundation Inc.
Norton Memorial Corporation, Geraldi
Norwest Bank Nebraska, N.A.
Norwest Corporation
NYNEX Corporation
Oaklawn Foundation
OCRI Foundation
Odell Fund, Robert Stewart Odell and Helen Pfeiffer
Offield Family Foundation
OG&E Electric Services
Ohrstrom Foundation
Old Dominion Box Co.
Old National Bank in Evansville
Olin Corp.
Olin Foundation, F. W.
Olin Foundation, Spencer T. and Ann W.
Oliver Memorial Trust Foundation
Olsson Memorial Foundation, Elis
Oppenstein Brothers Foundation
O'Quinn Foundation, John M. and Nancy C.
Ore-Ida Foods, Inc.
Osborn Charitable Trust, Edward B.
Osceola Foundation
Osher Foundation, Bernard
Ottley Trust-Watertown, Marion W.
Outboard Marine Corp.
Overbrook Foundation
Overlake Foundation
Owen Industries, Inc.
Owsley Foundation, Alvin and Lucy
Oxy USA Inc.
Pacific Mutual Life Insurance Co.
Pacific Telesis Group
Packaging Corporation of America
Packard Foundation, David and Lucile
PaineWebber
Paley Foundation, William S.
Palisades Educational Foundation
Palisano Foundation, Vincent and Harriet
Palmer Fund, Frank Loomis
Pamida, Inc.
Panhandle Eastern Corporation
Park Foundation
Parker Hannifin Corp.
Parshelsky Foundation, Moses L.
Parsons Foundation, Ralph M.
Parvin Foundation, Albert
Patterson Charitable Fund, W. I.
Payne Foundation, Frank E. and Seba B.
Peabody Charitable Fund, Amelia
PECO Energy Company
Pella Corporation
Penn Foundation, William
Pennsylvania Dutch Co.
Pennzoil Co.
Peoples Energy Corp.
Peppers Foundation, Ann
Perkin-Elmer Corp.
Peters Foundation, Charles F.
Peters Foundation, R. D. and Linda
Peterson Charitable Foundation, Folke H.
Peterson Foundation, Hal and Charlie

Petrie Trust, Lorene M.
Petteys Memorial Foundation, Jack
Pettus Crowe Foundation
Pew Charitable Trusts
Pfizer, Inc.
Pforzheimer Foundation, Carl and Lily
Phelps Dodge Corporation
PHH Corporation
Philibosian Foundation, Stephen
Phillips Charitable Trust, Dr. and Mrs. Arthur William
Phillips Family Foundation, Jay and Rose
Phillips Family Foundation, L. E.
Phillips Foundation, Ellis L.
Phipps Foundation, Howard
Pick, Jr. Fund, Albert
Pickford Foundation, Mary
Pierce Charitable Trust, Harold Whitworth
Pineywoods Foundation
Piper Foundation, Minnie Stevens
Piper Jaffray Companies Inc.
Pitt-Des Moines Inc.
Pittsburg Midway Coal Mining Co.
Plumsock Fund
PNC Bank, N.A.
Polaroid Corp.
Pollock Company Foundation, William B.
Porter Foundation, Mrs. Cheever
Porter Testamentary Trust, James Hyde
Potomac Electric Power Co.
Pott Foundation, Herman T. and Phenie R.
Potter Foundation, Justin and Valere
Potts and Sibley Foundation
PPG Industries, Inc.
Premier Industrial Corp.
Price Associates, T. Rowe
Price Foundation, Louis and Harold
Price Foundation, Lucien B. and Katherine E.
PriMerit Bank
Prince Trust, Abbie Norman
Prospect Hill Foundation
Prouty Foundation, Olive Higgins
Providence Gas Co.
Providence Journal Company
Provident Life & Accident Insurance Company of America
Providian Corporation
Prudential Insurance Co. of America, The
Prudential Securities, Inc.
Public Service Co. of New Mexico
Public Service Electric & Gas Co.
Public Welfare Foundation
Pulitzer Publishing Co.
Puterbaugh Foundation
Putnam Foundation
Quaker Chemical Corp.
Quivey-Bay State Foundation
R. F. Foundation
Rabb Charitable Foundation, Sidney and Esther
Rabb Foundation, Harry W.
Rachal Foundation, Ed
Ralston Purina Co.
Rand McNally & Co.
Ratner Foundation, Milton M.
Raymond Corp.
Read Foundation, Charles L.
Reed Foundation
Regenstein Foundation
Reicher Foundation, Anne and Harry J.
Reichhold Chemicals, Inc.
Reidler Foundation
Reinberger Foundation

Reisman Charitable Trust, George C. and Evelyn R.
Rennebohm Foundation, Oscar
Republic NY Corp.
Retirement Research Foundation
Reynolds Foundation, Christopher
Reynolds Foundation, Donald W.
Reynolds Foundation, Edgar
Rice Foundation
Rich Products Corporation
Richardson Benevolent Foundation, C. E.
Richardson Charitable Trust, Anne S.
Riggs Benevolent Fund
Ringier-America
Ritter Charitable Trust, George W. and Mary F.
Rixson Foundation, Oscar C.
RJR Nabisco Inc.
Robinson Fund, Maurice R.
Rockefeller Fund, David
Rockwell Fund
Rockwell International Corporation
Rogers Family Foundation
Rohatyn Foundation, Felix and Elizabeth
Rohm & Haas Co.
Rose Foundation, Billy
Roseburg Forest Products Co.
Rosen Foundation, Joseph
Rosenberg, Jr. Family Foundation, Louise and Claude
Rose's Stores, Inc.
Ross Laboratories
Ross Memorial Foundation, Will
Rouse Co.
Rowland Foundation
Royal Foundation, May Mitchell
Royal Group, Inc.
Ruan Foundation Trust, John
Rubin Family Fund, Cele H. and William B.
Rubin Foundation, Samuel
Rubinstein Foundation, Helena
Rudin Foundation
Russell Charitable Foundation, Tom
Russell Trust, Josephine G.
Ryan Foundation, David Claude
SAFECO Corp.
Safety Fund National Bank
Saint Paul Companies, Inc.
Salomon Foundation, Richard and Edna
Salvatori Foundation, Henry
San Diego Gas & Electric
Sandusky International Inc.
Sandy Hill Foundation
Santa Fe Pacific Corporation
Sara Lee Corp.
Sargent Foundation, Newell B.
Sarkeys Foundation
Sasco Foundation
SBC Communications Inc.
Scaife Family Foundation
Scherer Foundation, Karla
Schering-Plough Corp.
Scherman Foundation
Schiff Foundation, Dorothy
Schiro Fund
Schlink Foundation, Albert G. and Olive H.
Schlumberger Ltd.
Schmitt Foundation, Kilian J. and Caroline F.
Schoenleber Foundation
Scholl Foundation, Dr.
Schowalter Foundation
Schroeder Foundation, Walter
Schuller International
Schumann Fund for New Jersey
Schwartz Foundation, Arnold A.

Community & Junior Colleges

Cummings Foundation, James H.
Cummins Engine Co.
Curtice-Burns Foods, Inc.
Davenport-Hatch Foundation
Davis Foundation, James A. and Juliet L.
Deere & Co.
Delaware North Co., Inc.
DeRoy Foundation, Helen L.
DeRoy Testamentary Foundation
Detroit Edison Co.
Dexter Corporation
Dillon Foundation
Dimeo Construction Co.
Donaldson Company, Inc.
Douglas & Lomason Company
Dow Corning Corp.
du Pont de Nemours & Co., E. I.
duPont Foundation, Alfred I.
Durfee Foundation
Early Foundation
Eastman Kodak Company
Eaton Corporation
Eaton Foundation, Cyrus
Einstein Fund, Albert E. and Birdie W.
Elf Atochem North America, Inc.
Emerson Foundation, Inc., Fred L.
Everett Charitable Trust
Exchange National Bank
Fair Foundation, R. W.
Fieldcrest Cannon Inc.
Finch Foundation, Doak
Finch Foundation, Thomas Austin
Fink Foundation
Fireman's Fund Insurance Co.
First Fidelity Bank
First Interstate Bank of Oregon
First Union Corp.
Fleet Financial Group, Inc.
Ford Foundation
Ford II Fund, Henry
Forest Foundation
Freeport-McMoRan Inc.
French Foundation, D.E.
French Oil Mill Machinery Co.
Fuld Health Trust, Helene
Gannett Publishing Co., Guy Gazette Inc.
Gebbie Foundation
GenCorp Inc.
General Mills, Inc.
General Motors Corp.
Georgia Power Co.
Giant Food Inc.
Gleason Foundation
Good Samaritan
Goodrich Co., The B.F.
Gould Electronics Inc.
Gregg-Graniteville Foundation
Grundy Foundation
Guardian Life Insurance Company of America
Gulf Coast Medical Foundation
Gulf Power Co.
Hachar Charitable Trust, D. D.
Hagedorn Fund
Hamilton Bank
Hardin Foundation, Phil
Harrington Foundation, Francis A. and Jacquelyn H.
Harsco Corp.
Hartmarx Corporation
Hartz Foundation
Harvey Foundation, Felix
Hawkins Foundation, Robert Z.
HCA Foundation
Hechinger Co.
Heinz Company, H. J.
Heinz Endowment, Vira I.
Herrick Foundation
Hershey Foods Corp.
Hickory Tech Corp.
Hillman Foundation
Hillsdale Fund
Holnam
Hopwood Charitable Trust, John M.

Houston Industries Incorporated
Howe and Mitchell B. Howe Foundation, Lucille Horton
Hultquist Foundation
Hunt Charitable Trust, C. Giles
Hunt Foundation
ICI Americas Inc.
IES Industries, Inc.
Illinois Tool Works, Inc.
International Business Machines Corp.
ITT Hartford Insurance Group, Inc.
Jackson Foundation
Jaffe Foundation
Jameson Foundation, J. W. and Ida M.
Janirve Foundation
JELD-WEN, Inc.
Jennings Foundation, Mary Hillman
Johnson Controls Inc.
Johnson Foundation, M. G. and Lillie A.
Johnson & Higgins
Jones Foundation, Daisy Marquis
Jonsson Foundation
Joy Family Foundation
Kansas City Southern Industries
Kelley and Elza Kelley Foundation, Edward Bangs
Kemper National Insurance Cos.
Kennecott Corporation
Kimberly-Clark Corp.
Kingsbury Corp.
Kiplinger Foundation
Kline Foundation, Josiah W. and Bessie H.
Klock and Lucia Klock Kingston Foundation, Jay E.
Koehler Foundation, Marcia and Otto
Kreitler Foundation
Kuehn Foundation
La-Z-Boy Chair Co.
Landegger Charitable Foundation
Lattner Foundation, Forrest C.
Lee Endowment Foundation
Lehigh Portland Cement Co.
Leuthold Foundation
Link, Jr. Foundation, George
Lipton, Thomas J.
Long Island Lighting Co.
Lydall, Inc.
Macy & Co., Inc., R.H.
Mahadh Foundation
Maritz Inc.
Martin Marietta Corp.
Martin Marietta Materials
Marx Foundation, Virginia and Leonard
Massachusetts Mutual Life Insurance Co.
Mayor Foundation, Oliver Dewey
MCA Inc.
McCann Foundation
McCasland Foundation
McCormick Trust, Anne
McCune Charitable Foundation, Marshall and Perrine D.
McElroy Trust, R. J.
McEvoy Foundation, Mildred H.
Mead Corporation, The
Meadows Foundation
Medtronic, Inc.
Mellon Foundation, Richard King
Merck & Co.
Metropolitan Life Insurance Co.
Meyer Memorial Trust
Mid-Iowa Health Foundation
Miller Brewing Company/North Carolina
Mine Safety Appliances Co.
Mitsubishi Motor Sales of America, Inc.

Mohasco Corp.
Monfort Family Foundation
Montana Power Co.
Monticello College Foundation
Mulcahy Foundation
National Gypsum Co.
National Westminster Bank New Jersey
Nestle USA Inc.
New England Business Service
New Jersey Natural Gas Co.
New York Life Insurance Co.
New York Times Company
Newcombe Foundation, Charlotte W.
Norfolk Shipbuilding & Drydock Corp.
Northern States Power Co. (Minnesota)
Norton Co.
Norwest Bank Nebraska, N.A.
Norwest Corporation
O'Connor Foundation, A. Lindsay and Olive B.
OCRI Foundation
OG&E Electric Services
Old Dominion Box Co.
Olin Corp.
Olin Foundation, Spencer T. and Ann W.
Oppenstein Brothers Foundation
Outboard Marine Corp.
Oxy USA Inc.
Pacific Telesis Group
Palisades Educational Foundation
Parker Hannifin Corp.
PECO Energy Company
Pella Corporation
Penn Foundation, William
Peoples Energy Corp.
Perkin-Elmer Corp.
Petteys Memorial Foundation, Jack
Pfizer, Inc.
Pforzheimer Foundation, Carl and Lily
Phelps Dodge Corporation
Piper Foundation, Minnie Stevens
Pittsburg Midway Coal Mining Co.
PNC Bank, N.A.
Polaroid Corp.
Potts and Sibley Foundation
PriMerit Bank
Providence Gas Co.
Provident Life & Accident Insurance Company of America
Providian Corporation
Prudential Insurance Co. of America, The
Public Service Electric & Gas Co.
R&B Machine Tool Co.
Retirement Research Foundation
Reynolds Foundation, Edgar
Rice Charitable Foundation, Albert W.
Richardson Benevolent Foundation, C. E.
Robinson-Broadhurst Foundation
Rockwell Fund
Rockwell International Corporation
Rohm & Haas Co.
Roseburg Forest Products Co.
Rouse Co.
Saint Paul Companies, Inc.
Sara Lee Hosiery, Inc.
Sargent Foundation, Newell B.
Sawyer Charitable Foundation
Schuller International
Scott Foundation, William E.
Seafirst Corporation
Sedgwick James Inc.
Selby and Marie Selby Foundation, William G.
Seneca Foods Corp.
Shawmut National Corp.
Shenandoah Life Insurance Co.

Shott, Jr. Foundation, Hugh I.
Sierra Pacific Resources
Simon Foundation, William E. and Carol G.
Simpson Investment Company
Slemp Foundation
Sloan Foundation, Alfred P.
Smith Charitable Foundation, Clara Blackford Smith and W. Aubrey
Smith Corp., A.O.
Snow Memorial Trust, John Ben
Southern New England Telephone Company
Southwestern Electric Power Co.
Spalding Foundation, Eliot
Sprague Educational and Charitable Foundation, Seth
SPX Corp.
Square D Co.
Stabler Foundation, Donald B. and Dorothy L.
Sternberger Foundation, Tannenbaum
Stevens Foundation, Abbot and Dorothy H.
Strauss Foundation, Leon
Strong Foundation, Hattie M.
Stupp Foundation, Norman J.
Teagle Foundation
Tenneco Inc.
Tennessee Valley Printing Co.
Texaco Inc.
Textron, Inc.
Thalhimer and Family Foundation, Charles G.
Thermo Electron Corp.
Thomas Industries
Thomasville Furniture Industries
Thompson Charitable Foundation
Timken Foundation of Canton
Towsley Foundation, Harry A. and Margaret D.
Transco Energy Co.
Treakle Foundation, J. Edwin
Trexler Trust, Harry C.
Trull Foundation
Tupancy-Harris Foundation of 1986
Union Camp Corporation
Union Electric Co.
Union Pacific Corp.
Unitrode Corp.
Upjohn Foundation, Harold and Grace
USX Corporation
Valmont Industries, Inc.
Vevay-Switzerland County Foundation
Vollbrecht Foundation, Frederick A.
Wachovia Bank of North Carolina, N.A.
Wallace Foundation, George R.
Wallace-Reader's Digest Fund, DeWitt
Warwick Foundation
Washington Mutual Savings Bank
Washington Water Power Co.
Weezie Foundation
Wege Foundation
Welch Testamentary Trust, George T.
Wells Foundation, Franklin H. and Ruth L.
Westvaco Corporation
Weyerhaeuser Co.
Wheat First Butcher Singer, Inc.
Whirlpool Corporation
Wiggins Memorial Trust, J. J.
Wiley & Sons, Inc., John
Williams Charitable Trust, Mary Jo
Williams Companies, The
Wilson Foundation, H. W.
Wyomissing Foundation
Yeager Charitable Trust, Lester E.
Zachry Co., H.B.

Continuing Education

Abbott Laboratories
AlliedSignal Inc.
American Brands, Inc.
American President Companies, Ltd.
Anderson Foundation, John W.
Anheuser-Busch Companies, Inc.
Bank One, Texas-Houston Office
Bauervic Foundation, Charles M.
Benwood Foundation
Binney & Smith Inc.
Block, H&R
Blue Cross & Blue Shield United of Wisconsin
Boeing Co., The
Borden, Inc.
Bowater Incorporated
Bremer Foundation, Otto
Central Maine Power Co.
Citibank
Clorox Co.
Cornell Trust, Peter C.
CS First Boston Corporation
Dimeo Construction Co.
Duncan Trust, John G.
duPont Foundation, Alfred I.
Federated Mutual Insurance Co.
Fireman's Fund Insurance Co.
First Interstate Bank of Oregon
First Union Corp.
First Union National Bank of Florida
Fishback Foundation Trust, Harmes C.
Ford Foundation
Forest Foundation
Freed Foundation
Gates Foundation
Gellert Foundation, Celia Berta
General Mills, Inc.
General Motors Corp.
Gilmore Foundation, William G.
Gould Foundation, The Florence
Haigh-Scatena Foundation
Harcourt General, Inc.
Heinz Company, H. J.
Holnam
Hook Drugs
Humana, Inc.
Huston Charitable Trust, Stewart
JFM Foundation
John Hancock Mutual Life Insurance Co.
Johnson Controls Inc.
Johnson Foundation, M. G. and Lillie A.
Johnson & Higgins
Jones Foundation, Fletcher
Journal-Gazette Co.
Kansas City Southern Industries
Kingsbury Corp.
Koret Foundation
Lehigh Portland Cement Co.
Little, Inc., Arthur D.
Long Island Lighting Co.
Lydall, Inc.
Macy & Co., Inc., R.H.
Mailman Family Foundation, A. L.
May Department Stores Company, The
McCann Foundation
McKenna Foundation, Philip M.
Meadows Foundation
Mellon Foundation, Andrew W.
Meyer Fund, Milton and Sophie
Meyer Memorial Trust
Mitchell Energy & Development Corp.
Mobil Oil Corp.

Newcombe Foundation, Charlotte W.
Noble Foundation, Samuel Roberts
OCRI Foundation
Olin Foundation, Spencer T. and Ann W.
O'Quinn Foundation, John M. and Nancy C.
Osher Foundation, Bernard
Perkin-Elmer Corp.
Polaroid Corp.
PriMerit Bank
Prouty Foundation, Olive Higgins
Providian Corporation
Prudential Insurance Co. of America, The
Ratner Foundation, Milton M.
Retirement Research Foundation
Rich Products Corporation
Rockwell International Corporation
Rosenberg, Jr. Family Foundation, Louise and Claude
Rose's Stores, Inc.
Royal Group, Inc.
Rubin Family Fund, Cele H. and William B.
SAFECO Corp.
Santa Fe Pacific Corporation
Sedgwick James Inc.
Shawmut National Corp.
Simpson Investment Company
Sonat Inc.
Sunnen Foundation
Tucker Charitable Trust, Rose E.
Union Camp Corporation
Unitrode Corp.
Unocal Corp.
Wal-Mart Stores, Inc.
Wean Foundation, Raymond John
Weckbaugh Foundation, Eleanore Mullen
Westvaco Corporation
White Trust, G. R.
Wiley & Sons, Inc., John
Winter Construction Co.
Zachry Co., H.B.

Economic Education

Acushnet Co.
Air Products and Chemicals, Inc.
Akzo America
Akzo Chemicals Inc.
Albertson's Inc.
Allegheny Foundation
Allegheny Ludlum Corp.
Allianz Life Insurance Co. of North America
Alumax Inc.
Aluminum Co. of America
AMCORE Bank, N.A. Rockford
American Brands, Inc.
American United Life Insurance Co.
Ameritas Life Insurance Corp.
Amfac/JMB Hawaii Inc.
Andersen Corp.
Appleton Papers Inc.
Archer-Daniels-Midland Co.
Arkansas Power & Light Co.
Armco Inc.
Armstrong Foundation
Avon Products, Inc.
Ball Brothers Foundation
Ball Foundation, George and Frances
Bank One, Youngstown, NA
BankAmerica Corp.
Barra Foundation
Battelle Memorial Institute
Baughman Foundation
BE&K Inc.
Bechtel, Jr. Foundation, S. D.
Bedsole Foundation, J. L.
Beech Aircraft Corp.

Bethlehem Steel Corp.
Betts Industries
Binney & Smith Inc.
Blair and Co., William
Block, H&R
Blount, Inc.
Blum-Kovler Foundation
Boatmen's Bancshares, Inc.
Boeing Co., The
Boettcher Foundation
Boise Cascade Corporation
Bowater Incorporated
Bridgestone/Firestone, Inc.
Brillion Iron Works
Bucyrus-Erie Company
Cabot Corp.
Callaway Foundation
Cargill Inc.
Carpenter Technology Corp.
Carter Foundation, Amon G.
Castle Foundation, Harold K. L.
Centerior Energy Corp.
Central Maine Power Co.
Central National Bank
Chase Manhattan Bank, N.A.
Chesebrough-Pond's USA Co.
Chevron Corporation
Chrysler Corp.
Citibank
Citizens Bank of Rhode Island
CLARCOR Inc.
Clorox Co.
CNA Financial Corporation/CNA Insurance Companies
Colonial Life & Accident Insurance Co.
Columbus Dispatch Printing Co.
Comer Foundation
Connecticut Mutual Life Insurance Company
Consolidated Natural Gas Co.
Consolidated Papers, Inc.
Consumers Power Co.
Continental Corp.
Cooper Industries, Inc.
Coors Foundation, Adolph
Cowles Media Co.
CPC International Inc.
CR Industries
Crane Co.
CS First Boston Corporation
DEC International, Inc.
Deere & Co.
Delaware North Co., Inc.
Detroit Edison Co.
Dillon Foundation
Dimeo Construction Co.
Donaldson Company, Inc.
Dresser Industries, Inc.
du Pont de Nemours & Co., E. I.
Duke Power Co.
Eaton Corporation
El Pomar Foundation
Elf Atochem North America, Inc.
English Memorial Fund, Florence C. and H. L.
Enron Corp.
Ethyl Corp
Exxon Corporation
Federal-Mogul Corporation
Federated Mutual Insurance Co.
First Chicago Corp.
First Fidelity Bank
First Financial Bank FSB
First Hawaiian, Inc.
First Interstate Bank of Oregon
First Source Corp.
First Tennessee Bank
First Union Corp.
Firstar Bank Milwaukee, N.A.
Fleet Financial Group, Inc.
Ford Foundation
Ford Motor Co.
Forest Foundation
France Foundation, Jacob and Annita
Frear Eleemosynary Trust, Mary D. and Walter F.
Freeport-McMoRan Inc.

Frisch's Restaurants Inc.
Gates Foundation
General American Life Insurance Co.
General Mills, Inc.
General Motors Corp.
Georgia-Pacific Corporation
Georgia Power Co.
Gheens Foundation
Goodrich Co., The B.F.
Great-West Life Assurance Co.
Gregg-Graniteville Foundation
Guardian Life Insurance Company of America
Handy and Harman Foundation
Harsco Corp.
Hartmarx Corporation
Hasbro Inc.
HCA Foundation
Hechinger Co.
Heinz Company, H. J.
Hershey Foods Corp.
Hickory Tech Corp.
Hoover Foundation
Houston Endowment
Houston Industries Incorporated
Illinois Tool Works, Inc.
Integra Bank of Uniontown
International Paper Co.
James River Corp. of Virginia
Jewett Foundation, George Frederick
John Hancock Mutual Life Insurance Co.
Johnson Controls Inc.
Johnson Foundation, Helen K. and Arthur E.
Johnson & Higgins
Johnson & Son, S.C.
Jostens, Inc.
Kansas City Southern Industries
Kemper National Insurance Cos.
Kennecott Corporation
Kimberly-Clark Corp.
LamCo. Communications
Lehigh Portland Cement Co.
Lennon Foundation, Fred A.
Life Insurance Co. of Georgia
Lipton, Thomas J.
Lydall, Inc.
Macy & Co., Inc., R.H.
Marbrook Foundation
Maritz Inc.
Marshall Trust in Memory of Sanders McDaniel, Harriet McDaniel
Martin Marietta Corp.
Mattel, Inc.
McCormick & Co. Inc.
McDonald & Company Securities, Inc.
McElroy Trust, R. J.
MCI Communications Corp.
McInerny Foundation
McKenna Foundation, Philip M.
Mead Corporation, The
Mellon Foundation, Andrew W.
Mellon Foundation, Richard King
Merck & Co.
Merrill Lynch & Co., Inc.
Metropolitan Life Insurance Co.
Mine Safety Appliances Co.
Mitsubishi International Corp.
Mobil Oil Corp.
Monfort Family Foundation
Moore Foundation, Edward S.
Nalco Chemical Co.
National Westminster Bank New Jersey
NBD Indiana, Inc.
New York Stock Exchange, Inc.
Noble Foundation, Samuel Roberts
Norfolk Shipbuilding & Drydock Corp.
Norton Co.
Norton Foundation Inc.
NYNEX Corporation
OG&E Electric Services

Olin Foundation, Spencer T. and Ann W.
Oppenstein Brothers Foundation
Pacific Mutual Life Insurance Co.
Pacific Telesis Group
Packaging Corporation of America
Panhandle Eastern Corporation
Parsons Foundation, Ralph M.
Perkin-Elmer Corp.
Pfizer, Inc.
Phelps Dodge Corporation
PHH Corporation
Piper Jaffray Companies Inc.
PPG Industries, Inc.
Providence Gas Co.
Provident Life & Accident Insurance Company of America
Providian Corporation
Prudential Insurance Co. of America, The
Puterbaugh Foundation
Rand McNally & Co.
Reichhold Chemicals, Inc.
Rockwell International Corporation
Rohm & Haas Co.
Rose's Stores, Inc.
SAFECO Corp.
Salomon Inc.
San Diego Gas & Electric
Santa Fe Pacific Corporation
Scaife Family Foundation
Schlumberger Ltd.
Schwab & Co., Inc., Charles
Scott Fetzer Co.
Seafirst Corporation
Security Life of Denver Insurance Co.
Sedgwick James Inc.
Selby and Marie Selby Foundation, William G.
Shawmut National Corp.
Shell Oil Company
Shenandoah Life Insurance Co.
Simpson Investment Company
Sloan Foundation, Alfred P.
Smith Corp., A.O.
Snow Memorial Trust, John Ben
Sonat Inc.
Southern California Edison Co.
Square D Co.
Stanley Works
Starr Foundation
Sunnen Foundation
Tenneco Inc.
Textron, Inc.
Thermo Electron Corp.
Thomas Industries
Tozer Foundation
TransAmerica Corporation
Transco Energy Co.
Travelers Inc.
Trexler Trust, Harry C.
Trust Company Bank
Unilever United States, Inc.
Union Bank
Union Camp Corporation
Union Electric Co.
Union Pacific Corp.
U.S. Bank of Washington
Unitrode Corp.
Unocal Corp.
US WEST, Inc.
USX Corporation
Valmont Industries, Inc.
Vulcan Materials Co.
Wachovia Bank of North Carolina, N.A.
Wal-Mart Stores, Inc.
Washington Mutual Savings Bank
Washington Water Power Co.
Weyerhaeuser Co.
Wheeler Foundation, Wilmot
Whirlpool Corporation
Whiting Foundation, Macauley and Helen Dow
Whittenberger Foundation, Claude R. and Ethel B.
WICOR, Inc.

Williams Companies, The
Winchester Foundation

Education Associations

Abbott Laboratories
Abell-Hanger Foundation
Adams Foundation, Arthur F. and Alice E.
Aetna Life & Casualty Co.
Ahmanson Foundation
Air Products and Chemicals, Inc.
Akzo America
Allegheny Foundation
Allegheny Ludlum Corp.
Aluminum Co. of America
American Brands, Inc.
American Natural Resources Company
American President Companies, Ltd.
AMETEK, Inc.
AMP Incorporated
Andersen Corp.
Anderson Foundation, John W.
Andersons, The
Annenberg Foundation
Archer-Daniels-Midland Co.
Arkansas Power & Light Co.
Armco Inc.
AT&T Corp.
Atherton Family Foundation
Balfour Foundation, L. G.
Bank of New York Company, Inc.
Barra Foundation
Barry Corp., R. G.
Bedsole Foundation, J. L.
Benwood Foundation
Beveridge Foundation, Frank Stanley
Bigelow Foundation, F. R.
Bingham Foundation, William
Binney & Smith Inc.
Bird Corp.
Blount, Inc.
Blue Bell, Inc.
Blum-Kovler Foundation
Borden, Inc.
Brach Foundation, Helen
Brown & Williamson Tobacco Corp.
Brunswick Corp.
Buhl Foundation
Burlington Industries, Inc.
Cable & Wireless Holdings, Inc.
Cafritz Foundation, Morris and Gwendolyn
Callaway Foundation
Carnegie Corporation of New York
Carolyn Foundation
Carpenter Technology Corp.
Carter Foundation, Amon G.
CBI Industries, Inc.
CBS, Inc.
Centerior Energy Corp.
Central Maine Power Co.
Chase Manhattan Bank, N.A.
Chesapeake Corp.
Chesebrough-Pond's USA Co.
Chevron Corporation
Christian Dior New York, Inc.
Chrysler Corp.
Citibank
Citizens Bank of Rhode Island
Clorox Co.
Clowes Fund
Cole Foundation, Olive B.
Columbus Dispatch Printing Co.
Commerce Clearing House, Incorporated
Connecticut Mutual Life Insurance Company
Connelly Foundation
Cooper Industries, Inc.
Coors Foundation, Adolph
Cowell Foundation, S. H.
Cowles Media Co.

CPC International Inc.
Davis Foundation, Irene E. and George A.
Detroit Edison Co.
Diamond Foundation, Aaron
Dillon Foundation
Dodge Foundation, Geraldine R.
Donnelley & Sons Co., R.R.
Donner Foundation, William H.
Douglas & Lomason Company
Dow Foundation, Herbert H. and Grace A.
Dow Jones & Company, Inc.
Dreyfus Foundation, Max and Victoria
du Pont de Nemours & Co., E. I.
Duke Power Co.
Dun & Bradstreet Corp.
Eaton Corporation
Eden Hall Foundation
Enron Corp.
Exxon Corporation
Farish Fund, William Stamps
Federal-Mogul Corporation
Federated Mutual Insurance Co.
First Chicago Corp.
First Source Corp.
Forbes Inc.
Ford Foundation
Ford II Fund, Henry
Ford Motor Co.
Freeman Charitable Trust, Samuel
Freeport-McMoRan Inc.
Fry Foundation, Lloyd A.
Fund for New Jersey
Fuqua Foundation, J. B.
GAR Foundation
Gates Foundation
General American Life Insurance Co.
General Mills, Inc.
General Motors Corp.
Georgia-Pacific Corporation
Georgia Power Co.
Gheens Foundation
Goodrich Co., The B.F.
Grand Rapids Label Co.
Greenwall Foundation
Gulf Power Co.
Guttman Foundation, Stella and Charles
Hamilton Bank
Hancock Foundation, Luke B.
Harcourt General, Inc.
Hardin Foundation, Phil
Harriman Foundation, Mary W.
Harsco Corp.
Hassenfeld Foundation
HCA Foundation
Hechinger Co.
Heckscher Foundation for Children
Heinz Company, H. J.
Heinz Endowment, Howard
Heinz Endowment, Vira I.
Herrick Foundation
Hoag Family Foundation, George
Homeland Foundation
Houston Endowment
Hoyt Foundation, Stewart W. and Willma C.
Humana, Inc.
Imperial Bancorp
Inland Container Corp.
International Business Machines Corp.
Irvine Foundation, James
Ittleson Foundation
Janirve Foundation
JFM Foundation
JM Foundation
Johnson Controls Inc.
Johnson & Higgins
Jonsson Foundation
Jostens, Inc.
Journal-Gazette Co.
Kaufmann Foundation, Henry
Kettering Fund
Kimberly-Clark Corp.
Kirby Foundation, F. M.

Laffey-McHugh Foundation
Laurel Foundation
Leavey Foundation, Thomas and Dorothy
Lebanon Mutual Insurance Co.
Life Insurance Co. of Georgia
Lipton, Thomas J.
Lurie Foundation, Louis R.
Mandeville Foundation
Marriott Foundation, J. Willard
May Department Stores Company, The
MCA Inc.
McCasland Foundation
McGraw-Hill, Inc.
MCI Communications Corp.
McKenna Foundation, Katherine Mabis
Mead Corporation, The
Mellon Foundation, Andrew W.
Mellon Foundation, Richard King
Merck & Co.
Merrick Foundation
Mine Safety Appliances Co.
Minnesota Mining & Mfg. Co.
Mitsubishi International Corp.
Mobil Oil Corp.
Monell Foundation, Ambrose
Morris Foundation, Margaret T.
Moses Fund, Henry and Lucy
Mott Foundation, Charles Stewart
Nalco Chemical Co.
National Westminster Bank New Jersey
New-Land Foundation
New York Life Insurance Co.
The New Yorker Magazine, Inc.
Noble Foundation, Edward John
Norfolk Shipbuilding & Drydock Corp.
Norton Co.
Old Dominion Box Co.
Olin Foundation, Spencer T. and Ann W.
Oliver Memorial Trust Foundation
Overbrook Foundation
Packard Foundation, David and Lucile
PaineWebber
Palisades Educational Foundation
Parsons Foundation, Ralph M.
Payne Foundation, Frank E. and Seba B.
Peabody Charitable Fund, Amelia
Pennsylvania Dutch Co.
Perkin-Elmer Corp.
Pew Charitable Trusts
Pfizer, Inc.
Pforzheimer Foundation, Carl and Lily
Phelps Dodge Corporation
Phillips Charitable Trust, Dr. and Mrs. Arthur William
Phillips Family Foundation, Jay and Rose
Pick, Jr. Fund, Albert
Pierce Charitable Trust, Harold Whitworth
Pineywoods Foundation
Pitt-Des Moines Inc.
PNC Bank, N.A.
Pollock Company Foundation, William B.
Potomac Electric Power Co.
PPG Industries, Inc.
Premier Industrial Corp.
PriMerit Bank
Prouty Foundation, Olive Higgins
Providian Corporation
Prudential Insurance Co. of America, The
Prudential Securities, Inc.
Rand McNally & Co.
Raymond Corp.
Reynolds Foundation, Donald W.
Ringier-America

Rockwell International Corporation
Rohm & Haas Co.
Rose Foundation, Billy
Ross Laboratories
Rubin Foundation, Samuel
SAFECO Corp.
Sandy Hill Foundation
Santa Fe Pacific Corporation
SBC Communications Inc.
Scherer Foundation, Karla
Schering-Plough Corp.
Scherman Foundation
Schlumberger Ltd.
Scholl Foundation, Dr.
Schumann Fund for New Jersey
Scott Fetzer Co.
Sedgwick James Inc.
Shawmut National Corp.
Shell Oil Company
Shenandoah Life Insurance Co.
Simon Foundation, William E. and Carol G.
Sloan Foundation, Alfred P.
Solow Foundation
Sonat Inc.
Southern New England Telephone Company
Sprague Educational and Charitable Foundation, Seth
Stackpole-Hall Foundation
Starr Foundation
Steele-Reese Foundation
Steinman Foundation, James Hale
Stone Charitable Foundation
Taconic Foundation
Taube Family Foundation
Taubman Foundation, A. Alfred
Teagle Foundation
Tenneco Inc.
Texaco Inc.
Textron, Inc.
Todd Co., A.M.
TransAmerica Corporation
Turrell Fund
Unilever United States, Inc.
Union Camp Corporation
Unocal Corp.
Upjohn Foundation, Harold and Grace
USX Corporation
Van Every Foundation, Philip L.
Wal-Mart Stores, Inc.
Wallace-Reader's Digest Fund, DeWitt
Wean Foundation, Raymond John
Weezie Foundation
Westvaco Corporation
Weyerhaeuser Co.
Wheat First Butcher Singer, Inc.
Whirlpool Corporation
Wiley & Sons, Inc., John
Williams Companies, The
Wilson Fund, Matilda R.
Winthrop Trust, Clara B.
Yeager Charitable Trust, Lester E.

Education Funds

Achelis Foundation
Acushnet Co.
Aetna Life & Casualty Co.
Ahmanson Foundation
Air Products and Chemicals, Inc.
Alexander Foundation, Joseph
Allegheny Foundation
Allegheny Ludlum Corp.
Allianz Life Insurance Co. of North America
AlliedSignal Inc.
Allyn Foundation
Aluminum Co. of America
Amado Foundation, Maurice
American General Finance Corp.
American National Bank & Trust Co. of Chicago

American Optical Corp.
American President Companies, Ltd.
AMETEK, Inc.
Amfac/JMB Hawaii Inc.
Andersen Corp.
Andersen Foundation
Anderson Foundation, John W.
Andersons, The
Andres Charitable Trust, Frank G.
Anheuser-Busch Companies, Inc.
Annenberg Foundation
AON Corporation
Archer-Daniels-Midland Co.
Argyros Foundation
Aristech Chemical Corp.
Arkansas Power & Light Co.
Armco Inc.
Armstrong Foundation
AT&T Corp.
Atherton Family Foundation
Auerbach Foundation, Beatrice Fox
Avon Products, Inc.
Ayres Foundation, Inc.
Balfour Foundation, L. G.
Ball Brothers Foundation
Ball Foundation, George and Frances
Banc One Wisconsin Corp.
BankAmerica Corp.
Banta Corp.
Batts Foundation
Baughman Foundation
Beazley Foundation/Frederick Foundation
Bedsole Foundation, J. L.
Beech Aircraft Corp.
Bemis Company, Inc.
Benedum Foundation, Claude Worthington
Benwood Foundation
Berger Foundation, H. N. and Frances C.
Bertha Foundation
Betts Industries
Beveridge Foundation, Frank Stanley
Bigelow Foundation, F. R.
Bingham Second Betterment Fund, William
Binney & Smith Inc.
Bird Corp.
Bishop Foundation, E. K. and Lillian F.
Blake Foundation, S. P.
Block, H&R
Blount, Inc.
Blue Cross & Blue Shield United of Wisconsin
Blum-Kovler Foundation
Boeing Co., The
Booth Ferris Foundation
Borden, Inc.
Brach Foundation, Helen
Bridgestone/Firestone, Inc.
Bristol-Myers Squibb Company
Bryant Foundation
Bucyrus-Erie Company
Buhl Foundation
Burchfield Foundation, Charles E.
Burdines Foundation
Burlington Industries, Inc.
Burnett-Tandy Foundation
Cabot Corp.
Cafritz Foundation, Morris and Gwendolyn
Cain Foundation, Gordon and Mary
Callaway Foundation
Campbell Foundation
Campbell Foundation, Ruth and Henry
Carpenter Foundation
Carpenter Foundation, E. Rhodes and Leona B.
Carpenter Technology Corp.
Carter Foundation, Beirne
Carver Charitable Trust, Roy J.
CBS, Inc.

Central Fidelity Banks, Inc.
Central Maine Power Co.
Chapman Charitable Corporation, Howard and Bess
Chase Manhattan Bank, N.A.
CHC Foundation
Chesapeake Corp.
Chesebrough-Pond's USA Co.
Chevron Corporation
Christensen Charitable and Religious Foundation, L. C.
Citibank
Citizens Bank of Rhode Island
Clapp Charitable and Educational Trust, George H.
Clark Foundation
Clarke Trust, John
Clements Foundation
Clorox Co.
Cole Foundation, Olive B.
Coleman Foundation, George E.
Collins Foundation
Collins Foundation, George and Jennie
Collins Medical Trust
Coltec Industries, Inc.
Columbus Dispatch Printing Co.
Comer Foundation
Commerce Clearing House, Incorporated
Consolidated Natural Gas Co.
Consolidated Papers, Inc.
Continental Corp.
Cooke Foundation
Cooper Industries, Inc.
Coors Foundation, Adolph
Copley Press, Inc.
Cornell Trust, Peter C.
Cowles Media Co.
Crane Co.
Crocker Trust, Mary A.
CS First Boston Corporation
Cummins Engine Co.
Curtice-Burns Foods, Inc.
Daily News
Daniel Foundation of Alabama
Darling Foundation, Hugh and Hazel
Davis Foundation, James A. and Juliet L.
Daywood Foundation
Demoulas Supermarkets Inc.
Detroit Edison Co.
Deuble Foundation, George H.
Dillon Foundation
Dr. Seuss Foundation
Dodge Jones Foundation
Donaldson Company, Inc.
Douty Foundation
Dresser Industries, Inc.
du Pont de Nemours & Co., E. I.
Duchossois Industries Inc.
Duke Power Co.
Dun & Bradstreet Corp.
Dunagan Foundation
duPont Foundation, Alfred I.
Eastman Kodak Company
Eaton Corporation
Eccles Foundation, Ralph M. and Ella M.
Eden Hall Foundation
Einstein Fund, Albert E. and Birdie W.
Enron Corp.
Essick Foundation
Ettinger Foundation
Exchange National Bank
Exxon Corporation
Fair Oaks Foundation, Inc.
Fair Play Foundation
Farish Fund, William Stamps
Favrot Fund
Federal-Mogul Corporation
Federated Mutual Insurance Co.
Feil Foundation, Louis and Gertrude
Fenton Foundation
Fieldcrest Cannon Inc.
Fikes Foundation, Leland
First Chicago Corp.

First Hawaiian, Inc.
First Interstate Bank of Oregon
First Union Corp.
Fleet Financial Group, Inc.
Fletcher Foundation
Fohs Foundation
Ford Foundation
Fort Wayne National Bank
France Foundation, Jacob and Annita
Freed Foundation
Freedom Forge Corp.
Frohring Foundation, William O. and Gertrude Lewis
Frost National Bank
Frueauff Foundation, Charles A.
Fry Foundation, Lloyd A.
GAR Foundation
Gebbie Foundation
GenCorp Inc.
General American Life Insurance Co.
General Mills, Inc.
General Motors Corp.
Georgia-Pacific Corporation
Georgia Power Co.
Giant Eagle, Inc.
Giant Food Inc.
Gillette Co.
Gilmore Foundation, William G.
Glick Foundation, Eugene and Marilyn
Glosser Foundation, David A.
Goddard Foundation, Charles B.
Goldberg Family Foundation
Goldseker Foundation of Maryland, Morris
Goldsmith Foundation, Horace W.
Goldwyn Foundation, Samuel
Good Samaritan
Goodrich Co., The B.F.
Grand Rapids Label Co.
Greenwall Foundation
Gregg-Graniteville Foundation
Griffith Foundation, W. C.
Grundy Foundation
Guaranty Bank & Trust Co.
Guardian Life Insurance Company of America
Gulf Power Co.
Guttman Foundation, Stella and Charles
Haas, Jr. Fund, Evelyn and Walter
Halff Foundation, G. A. C.
Hallett Charitable Trust, E. W.
Hancock Foundation, Luke B.
Handy and Harman Foundation
Hanover Foundation
Hanson Industries North America
Harcourt General, Inc.
Hardin Foundation, Phil
Harland Charitable Foundation, John and Wilhelmina D.
Harsco Corp.
Hartmarx Corporation
Hartz Foundation
Harvey Foundation, Felix
Hasbro Inc.
Hatch Charitable Trust, Margaret Milliken
Hazen Foundation, Edward W.
HCA Foundation
Hecht-Levi Foundation
Heinz Company, H. J.
Heinz Endowment, Howard
Heinz Endowment, Vira I.
Henderson Foundation, George H.
Hermann Foundation, Grover
Hershey Foundation, Barry J.
Hewit Family Foundation
Hickory Tech Corp.
High Foundation
Hill Foundation, Sandy
Hoffman Foundation, Maximilian E. and Marion O.
Hoffmann-La Roche Inc.
Homeland Foundation

Hook Drugs
Hoover Foundation
Hoover, Jr. Foundation, Margaret W. and Herbert
Hopedale Foundation
Houchens Foundation, Ervin G.
Huisking Foundation
Hultquist Foundation
Humana, Inc.
IES Industries, Inc.
Illinois Tool Works, Inc.
ITT Hartford Insurance Group, Inc.
Jacobson Foundation, Bernard H. and Blanche E.
Jarson-Stanley and Mickey Kaplan Foundation, Isaac and Esther
Jennings Foundation, Mary Hillman
Jockey Hollow Foundation
John Hancock Mutual Life Insurance Co.
Johnson Controls Inc.
Johnson Foundation, Willard T. C.
Johnson & Higgins
Johnson & Son, S.C.
Jones Foundation, Fletcher
Jonsson Foundation
Jostens, Inc.
Journal-Gazette Co.
Jurzykowski Foundation, Alfred
Kansas City Southern Industries
Kaplun Foundation, Morris J. and Betty
Kennedy Foundation, Ethel
Kettering Fund
Kilcawley Fund, William H.
Kimberly-Clark Corp.
Kingsbury Corp.
Kiplinger Foundation
Kirby Foundation, F. M.
Kreitler Foundation
La-Z-Boy Chair Co.
Laffey-McHugh Foundation
Lang Foundation, Eugene M.
Laurel Foundation
LBJ Family Foundation
Leavey Foundation, Thomas and Dorothy
Lederer Foundation, Francis L.
Lee Enterprises
Lehigh Portland Cement Co.
Lemberg Foundation
Lennon Foundation, Fred A.
Link, Jr. Foundation, George
Lipton, Thomas J.
Littauer Foundation, Lucius N.
Little, Inc., Arthur D.
Liz Claiborne, Inc.
Long Foundation, J.M.
Lund Foundation
Lurie Foundation, Louis R.
Lux Foundation, Miranda
M/A-COM, Inc.
Macy & Co., Inc., R.H.
Madison Gas & Electric Co.
Mahadh Foundation
Maneely Fund
Mars Foundation
Martin Marietta Corp.
Martin Marietta Materials
Massachusetts Mutual Life Insurance Co.
Mather Charitable Trust, S. Livingston
Mathis-Pfohl Foundation
Mattel, Inc.
May Department Stores Company, The
MCA Inc.
McCann Foundation
McCasland Foundation
McConnell Foundation
McCormick Foundation, Chauncey and Marion Deering
McCormick Trust, Anne
McCune Charitable Trust, John R.
McElroy Trust, R. J.
McFeely-Rogers Foundation

McGee Foundation
MCI Communications Corp.
McKenna Foundation, Philip M.
McLean Contributionship
McShain Charities, John
Mead Corporation, The
Mellon Family Foundation, R. K.
Mellon Foundation, Richard King
Mengle Foundation, Glenn and Ruth
Merck & Co.
Meyerhoff Fund, Joseph
Middendorf Foundation
Miller Charitable Foundation, Howard E. and Nell E.
Miller Foundation
Mine Safety Appliances Co.
Minnesota Mining & Mfg. Co.
Mobil Oil Corp.
Moore & Sons, B.C.
Morgan Construction Co.
Morgan and Samuel Tate Morgan, Jr. Foundation, Marietta McNeil
Morris Foundation, William T.
Morrison Knudsen Corporation
Mosinee Paper Corp.
Mulford Foundation, Vincent
Musson Charitable Foundation, R. C. and Katharine M.
Nabisco Foods Group
National Forge Co.
New England Business Service
New Jersey Natural Gas Co.
New-Land Foundation
New York Life Insurance Co.
The New Yorker Magazine, Inc.
Newcombe Foundation, Charlotte W.
Noble Foundation, Samuel Roberts
Norfolk Shipbuilding & Drydock Corp.
Normandie Foundation
North Shore Foundation
Norton Co.
Norton Foundation Inc.
Norton Memorial Corporation, Geraldi
Norwest Bank Nebraska, N.A.
Norwest Corporation
Oaklawn Foundation
O'Connor Foundation, A. Lindsay and Olive B.
Odell Fund, Robert Stewart Odell and Helen Pfeiffer
Offield Family Foundation
Ohrstrom Foundation
Old Dominion Box Co.
Old National Bank in Evansville
Oliver Memorial Trust Foundation
Olsson Memorial Foundation, Elis
Oppenstein Brothers Foundation
O'Quinn Foundation, John M. and Nancy C.
Overbrook Foundation
Overlake Foundation
Oxy USA Inc.
Pacific Mutual Life Insurance Co.
Palisades Educational Foundation
Panhandle Eastern Corporation
Park Foundation
Parker Hannifin Corp.
Parsons Foundation, Ralph M.
Parvin Foundation, Albert
Patterson Charitable Fund, W. I.
Payne Foundation, Frank E. and Seba B.
PECO Energy Company
Pella Corporation
Pennsylvania Dutch Co.
Peppers Foundation, Ann
Perkin-Elmer Corp.
Pfizer, Inc.

Phelps Dodge Corporation
PHH Corporation
Phillips Charitable Trust, Dr. and Mrs. Arthur William
Phillips Family Foundation, Jay and Rose
Pierce Charitable Trust, Harold Whitworth
Piper Foundation, Minnie Stevens
Pitt-Des Moines Inc.
Pittsburg Midway Coal Mining Co.
PNC Bank, N.A.
Pollock Company Foundation, William B.
Potomac Electric Power Co.
Pott Foundation, Herman T. and Phenie R.
PPG Industries, Inc.
Premier Industrial Corp.
Price Associates, T. Rowe
Providence Journal Company
Providian Corporation
Prudential Insurance Co. of America, The
Public Service Co. of New Mexico
Pulitzer Publishing Co.
Putnam Foundation
Quivey-Bay State Foundation
Rachal Foundation, Ed
Ralston Purina Co.
Ratner Foundation, Milton M.
Raymond Corp.
Read Foundation, Charles L.
Reicher Foundation, Anne and Harry J.
Reidler Foundation
Reinberger Foundation
Rennebohm Foundation, Oscar
Reynolds Foundation, Donald W.
Reynolds Foundation, Edgar
Rice Foundation
Richardson Benevolent Foundation, C. E.
Riggs Benevolent Fund
Robinson Fund, Maurice R.
Rockwell International Corporation
Rohatyn Foundation, Felix and Elizabeth
Rohm & Haas Co.
Roseburg Forest Products Co.
Rosenberg, Jr. Family Foundation, Louise and Claude
Ross Laboratories
Royal Group, Inc.
Rubin Family Fund, Cele H. and William B.
Rubin Foundation, Samuel
Salomon Foundation, Richard and Edna
Salvatori Foundation, Henry
San Diego Gas & Electric
Sandusky International Inc.
Sandy Hill Foundation
Sara Lee Hosiery, Inc.
SBC Communications Inc.
Scaife Family Foundation
Schering-Plough Corp.
Schroeder Foundation, Walter
Scott Fetzer Co.
Security Life of Denver Insurance Co.
Sedgwick James Inc.
Self Foundation
Sentry Insurance A Mutual Company
Seton Leather Co.
Share Trust, Charles Morton
Shenandoah Life Insurance Co.
Siltec Corp.
Simon Foundation, William E. and Carol G.
Skillman Foundation
Smith Corp., A.O.
Snow Memorial Trust, John Ben
Sonat Inc.
Sordoni Foundation
South Bend Tribune

Speyer Foundation, Alexander C. and Tillie S.
Sprague Educational and Charitable Foundation, Seth
Springs Foundation
SPX Corp.
Square D Co.
Stabler Foundation, Donald B. and Dorothy L.
Stein Foundation, Jules and Doris
Stemmons Foundation
Sternberger Foundation, Tannenbaum
Stevens Foundation, Abbot and Dorothy H.
Strong Foundation, Hattie M.
Sulzberger Foundation
Superior Tube Co.
Taconic Foundation
Tait Foundation, Frank M.
Taylor Foundation, Fred and Harriett
Taylor Foundation, Ruth and Vernon
Tenneco Inc.
Texaco Inc.
Texas Commerce Bank-Houston, N.A.
Textron, Inc.
Thomas Industries
Thomasville Furniture Industries
Thompson Co., J. Walter
Thornton Foundation, Flora L.
Times Mirror Company, The
Timken Foundation of Canton
Tiscornia Foundation
TransAmerica Corporation
Travelers Inc.
Truland Foundation
Trust Company Bank
Tucker Charitable Trust, Rose E.
Turrell Fund
Union Bank
Union Camp Corporation
Union Electric Co.
Union Pacific Corp.
Unitrode Corp.
Unocal Corp.
Upton Foundation, Frederick S.
US WEST, Inc.
USL Capital Corporation
Valmont Industries, Inc.
Van Every Foundation, Philip L.
Vetlesen Foundation, G. Unger
Vicksburg Foundation
Virginia Power Co.
Vulcan Materials Co.
Wachovia Bank of North Carolina, N.A.
Wal-Mart Stores, Inc.
Wallace-Reader's Digest Fund, DeWitt
Walsh Foundation
Washington Forrest Foundation
Washington Mutual Savings Bank
Waters Charitable Trust, Robert S.
Wean Foundation, Raymond John
Weckbaugh Foundation, Eleanore Mullen
Wege Foundation
Wells Foundation, Franklin H. and Ruth L.
Westvaco Corporation
Weyerhaeuser Co.
Wheat First Butcher Singer, Inc.
Wheeler Foundation
Whirlpool Corporation
Whiting Foundation
Whiting Foundation, Macauley and Helen Dow
Whittenberger Foundation, Claude R. and Ethel B.
Wickes Foundation, Harvey Randall
Wiley & Sons, Inc., John
Williams Charitable Trust, Mary Jo

Williams Companies, The
Winchester Foundation
Wiremold Co.
Wisconsin Power & Light Co.
Wood Foundation of
Chambersburg, PA
Worthington Foods
Yeager Charitable Trust,
Lester E.

Education Reform

Aetna Life & Casualty Co.
Ahmanson Foundation
Air Products and Chemicals,
Inc.
Allegheny Foundation
AlliedSignal Inc.
Aluminum Co. of America
American Natural Resources
Company
Anheuser-Busch Companies,
Inc.
Annenberg Foundation
Armstrong Foundation
AT&T Corp.
Atran Foundation
BankAmerica Corp.
Barth Foundation, Theodore H.
Bay Foundation
Bean Foundation, Norwin S.
and Elizabeth N.
BE&K Inc.
Bell Atlantic Corp.
Benedum Foundation, Claude
Worthington
Benwood Foundation
Bingham Second Betterment
Fund, William
Blandin Foundation
Block, H&R
Blount, Inc.
Blue Cross & Blue Shield
United of Wisconsin
Bodman Foundation
Booth Ferris Foundation
Bristol-Myers Squibb
Company
Burden Foundation, Florence
V.
Burlington Industries, Inc.
Burnett-Tandy Foundation
Cain Foundation, Gordon and
Mary
Calhoun Charitable Trust,
Kenneth
Callaway Foundation
Carnegie Corporation of New
York
Carolyn Foundation
Chadwick Fund, Dorothy
Jordan
Chase Manhattan Bank, N.A.
Cheney Foundation, Ben B.
Chevron Corporation
CIGNA Corporation
CINergy
Clapp Charitable and
Educational Trust, George H.
Clark Foundation
Comer Foundation
Connecticut Mutual Life
Insurance Company
Contran Corporation
Coors Foundation, Adolph
Cornell Trust, Peter C.
Corning Incorporated
Crane Co.
Crocker Trust, Mary A.
CS First Boston Corporation
Cullen Foundation
Dana Foundation, Charles A.
Dart Group Corp.
Day Foundation, Nancy Sayles
Daywood Foundation
Deuble Foundation, George H.
Dewing Foundation, Frances R.
Diamond Foundation, Aaron
Dr. Seuss Foundation
Dodge Foundation, Cleveland
H.
Dodge Foundation, Geraldine
R.
Donner Foundation, William H.

Dresser Industries, Inc.
Duchossois Industries Inc.
Duncan Foundation, Lillian H.
and C. W.
Dynamet, Inc.
Eastman Kodak Company
Eaton Corporation
Elf Atochem North America,
Inc.
English Memorial Fund,
Florence C. and H. L.
Evans Foundation, Lettie Pate
Evans Foundation, Thomas J.
Exxon Corporation
Fenton Foundation
Fish Foundation, Ray C.
Fleishhacker Foundation
Folger Fund
Forbes Inc.
Ford Foundation
Ford Motor Co.
France Foundation, Jacob and
Annita
Freeport-McMoRan Inc.
Fry Foundation, Lloyd A.
Fuld Health Trust, Helene
Fund for New Jersey
GAR Foundation
GATX Corp.
Gebbie Foundation
GenCorp Inc.
General Mills, Inc.
General Motors Corp.
Geneseo Foundation
Gheens Foundation
Globe Newspaper Co.
Goddard Foundation, Charles
B.
Goldsmith Foundation, Horace
W.
Gould Electronics Inc.
Greenwall Foundation
Griffith Foundation, W. C.
Halsell Foundation, Ewing
Hamman Foundation, George
and Mary Josephine
Hanover Foundation
Hanson Industries North
America
Harcourt General, Inc.
Hardin Foundation, Phil
Hazen Foundation, Edward W.
Heinz Endowment, Howard
Heinz Endowment, Vira I.
Heinz Trust, Drue
Helmerich Foundation
Herzstein Charitable
Foundation, Albert and Ethel
Hewlett Foundation, William
and Flora
Hillman Foundation
Hoover Foundation
Hoover Fund-Trust, W. Henry
Houston Endowment
Humana, Inc.
Integra Bank of Uniontown
Ittleson Foundation
Jacobs Family Foundation
Jacobson Foundation, Bernard
H. and Blanche E.
Janirve Foundation
JELD-WEN, Inc.
Jennings Foundation, Mary
Hillman
JFM Foundation
JM Foundation
Jones Foundation, Helen
Jostens, Inc.
Kaufmann Foundation, Henry
Kornfeld Foundation, Emily
Davie and Joseph S.
Leidy Foundation, John J.
Loews Corporation
Lowenstein Foundation, Leon
Lurie Foundation, Louis R.
MacArthur Foundation, John
D. and Catherine T.
Maddox Foundation, J. F.
Mailman Family Foundation,
A. L.
Marriott Foundation, J. Willard
Marshall Trust in Memory of
Sanders McDaniel, Harriet
McDaniel
Martin Marietta Corp.

Mather Charitable Trust, S.
Livingston
Mathis-Pfohl Foundation
May Department Stores
Company, The
MCA Inc.
McCasland Foundation
McDonald & Company
Securities, Inc.
McGee Foundation
McInerny Foundation
McLean Contributionship
Meadows Foundation
Mellon Family Foundation, R.
K.
Mellon Foundation, Andrew W.
Mellon Foundation, Richard
King
Merrick Foundation
Merrill Lynch & Co., Inc.
Metropolitan Life Insurance
Co.
Meyer Memorial Trust
Meyerhoff Fund, Joseph
Mohasco Corp.
Mott Foundation, Charles
Stewart
Murdock Charitable Trust, M.
J.
Murphey Foundation, Lluella
Morey
Musson Charitable
Foundation, R. C. and
Katharine M.
Nesholm Family Foundation
New-Land Foundation
Northern States Power Co.
(Minnesota)
Norton Co.
Oaklawn Foundation
O'Connor Foundation, A.
Lindsay and Olive B.
Olin Foundation, Spencer T.
and Ann W.
PaineWebber
Palmer Fund, Frank Loomis
Parker Hannifin Corp.
Parsons Foundation, Ralph M.
Peppers Foundation, Ann
Pfizer, Inc.
Piper Jaffray Companies Inc.
Pittsburg Midway Coal Mining
Co.
Prudential Insurance Co. of
America, The
Public Service Co. of New
Mexico
Rabb Foundation, Harry W.
RJR Nabisco Inc.
Robinson Fund, Maurice R.
Rockwell Fund
Rockwell International
Corporation
Rohatyn Foundation, Felix and
Elizabeth
Rose Foundation, Billy
Rubin Foundation, Samuel
Rubinstein Foundation, Helena
Saint Paul Companies, Inc.
Sandy Hill Foundation
Sarkeys Foundation
Scaife Family Foundation
Scherman Foundation
Schumann Fund for New
Jersey
Seaver Charitable Trust,
Richard C.
Seaver Institute
Shawmut National Corp.
Shell Oil Company
Skillman Foundation
Solow Foundation
Speyer Foundation, Alexander
C. and Tillie S.
Starr Foundation
Steele-Reese Foundation
Strong Foundation, Hattie M.
Subaru of America Inc.
Superior Tube Co.
Tait Foundation, Frank M.
Thompson Co., J. Walter
Thornton Foundation
Times Mirror Company, The
Timken Foundation of Canton
Todd Co., A.M.

Towsley Foundation, Harry A.
and Margaret D.
Travelers Inc.
Turrell Fund
Unger Foundation, Aber D.
Union Bank
Union Electric Co.
U.S. Bank of Washington
Unocal Corp.
Upjohn Foundation, Harold
and Grace
Vicksburg Foundation
Virginia Environmental
Endowment
Wallace-Reader's Digest Fund,
DeWitt
Washington Mutual Savings
Bank
Weingart Foundation
Wendt Foundation, Margaret L.
Whirlpool Corporation
Whittenberger Foundation,
Claude R. and Ethel B.
WICOR, Inc.
Winchester Foundation
Wyman Youth Trust
Wyomissing Foundation

Elementary Education (Private)

Achelis Foundation
Ahmanson Foundation
Alabama Power Co.
Albertson's Inc.
Allendale Insurance Co.
Altman Foundation
Aluminum Co. of America
American Brands, Inc.
AMETEK, Inc.
Andersen Corp.
Andersen Foundation
Andreas Foundation
AON Corporation
Apple Computer, Inc.
Atherton Family Foundation
Babcock & Wilcox Co.
Bank of New York Company,
Inc.
Bank One, Texas-Houston
Office
BankAmerica Corp.
Battelle Memorial Institute
Benenson Foundation, Frances
and Benjamin
Benwood Foundation
Binney & Smith Inc.
Bishop Foundation, E. K. and
Lillian F.
Blair and Co., William
Bodman Foundation
Boeing Co., The
Boettcher Foundation
Bowen Foundation, Ethel N.
Brackenridge Foundation,
George W.
Bucyrus-Erie Company
Buhl Foundation
Cable & Wireless Holdings,
Inc.
Cabot Corp.
Calder Foundation, Louis
Canon U.S.A., Inc.
Carolyn Foundation
Carpenter Foundation, E.
Rhodes and Leona B.
Carpenter Technology Corp.
Carter Foundation, Amon G.
Carver Charitable Trust, Roy J.
Castle Foundation, Harold K.
L.
Central Maine Power Co.
Chase Manhattan Bank, N.A.
Chevron Corporation
CIGNA Corporation
CINergy
Citibank
Claiborne and Art Ortenberg
Foundation, Liz
Clark Foundation
Clorox Co.
Close Foundation

Commerce Clearing House,
Incorporated
Connecticut Mutual Life
Insurance Company
Connelly Foundation
Consolidated Natural Gas Co.
Cowell Foundation, S. H.
Cowles Media Co.
Cummins Engine Co.
Dana Foundation, Charles A.
Davenport-Hatch Foundation
Delaware North Co., Inc.
Digital Equipment Corp.
Dodge Foundation, Geraldine
R.
Dodge Jones Foundation
Duchossois Industries Inc.
Duke Power Co.
Duncan Trust, John G.
Encyclopaedia Britannica, Inc.
Enron Corp.
Federal-Mogul Corporation
Fieldcrest Cannon Inc.
Fikes Foundation, Leland
First Tennessee Bank
First Union National Bank of
Florida
Freeport-McMoRan Inc.
Fry Foundation, Lloyd A.
Gallagher Family Foundation,
Lewis P.
GAR Foundation
GenCorp Inc.
General Motors Corp.
Georgia Power Co.
Gheens Foundation
Ghidotti Foundation
Giant Eagle, Inc.
Glaser Foundation
Globe Newspaper Co.
Goddard Foundation, Charles
B.
Gregg-Graniteville Foundation
Gulf Power Co.
Hardin Foundation, Phil
Harmon Foundation, Pearl M.
and Julia J.
Heckscher Foundation for
Children
Heinz Endowment, Howard
Heinz Trust, Drue
Heller Financial, Inc.
Herrick Foundation
Hewlett-Packard Co.
Hillsdale Fund
Hopedale Foundation
Humana, Inc.
International Paper Co.
Ittleson Foundation
JFM Foundation
Johnson Controls Inc.
Johnson Foundation, Helen K.
and Arthur E.
Johnson & Higgins
Kennecott Corporation
Kirby Foundation, F. M.
Leidy Foundation, John J.
Long Island Lighting Co.
Lowenstein Foundation, Leon
Mardag Foundation
Maritz Inc.
Mars Foundation
Marsh & McLennan
Companies, Inc.
Mattel, Inc.
MBIA Inc.
McElroy Trust, R. J.
McInerny Foundation
Meadows Foundation
Medtronic, Inc.
Mellon Foundation, Richard
King
Merck & Co. Human Health
Division
Meyer Memorial Trust
Miller Brewing
Company/North Carolina
Moore Foundation, Edward S.
Murphy Foundation
Nabisco Foods Group
National Westminster Bank
New Jersey
The New Yorker Magazine, Inc.
Northwest Natural Gas Co.
Norwest Bank Nebraska, N.A.

O'Connor Foundation, A. Lindsay and Olive B.
Ohrstrom Foundation
Old National Bank in Evansville
Olsson Memorial Foundation, Elis
Ore-Ida Foods, Inc.
Osceola Foundation
Pacific Telesis Group
Packaging Corporation of America
Packard Foundation, David and Lucile
Panhandle Eastern Corporation
Parsons Foundation, Ralph M.
Penn Foundation, William
Peoples Energy Corp.
Pew Charitable Trusts
Pfizer, Inc.
Piper Jaffray Companies Inc.
Pittsburgh Child Guidance Foundation
Polaroid Corp.
Price Associates, T. Rowe
Proctor Trust, Mortimer R.
Providian Corporation
Prudential Insurance Co. of America, The
Public Service Electric & Gas Co.
RJR Nabisco Inc.
Rockwell Fund
Rohatyn Foundation, Felix and Elizabeth
Roseburg Forest Products Co.
Royal Group, Inc.
SAFECO Corp.
Salomon Inc.
San Diego Gas & Electric
Sandusky International Inc.
Sara Lee Hosiery, Inc.
Scholl Foundation, Dr.
Schumann Fund for New Jersey
Seaver Charitable Trust, Richard C.
Seaway Food Town, Inc.
Security Life of Denver Insurance Co.
Sedgwick James Inc.
Shell Oil Company
Smart Family Foundation
Snow Foundation, John Ben
Stanley Works
Sullivan Foundation, Algernon Sydney
Sulzberger Foundation
Swalm Foundation
Temple Foundation, T. L. L.
Temple-Inland Inc.
TransAmerica Corporation
Transco Energy Co.
Turrell Fund
Unilever United States, Inc.
Union Camp Corporation
Union Electric Co.
Van Buren Foundation
Vulcan Materials Co.
Wachovia Bank of North Carolina, N.A.
Wal-Mart Stores, Inc.
Washington Water Power Co.
Weingart Foundation
West One Bancorp
Western New York Foundation
Westvaco Corporation
Weyerhaeuser Co.
Weyerhaeuser Memorial Foundation, Charles A.
Whirlpool Corporation
WICOR, Inc.
Wiegand Foundation, E. L.
Wiggins Memorial Trust, J. J.
Wiley & Sons, Inc., John
Williams Companies, The
Wilson Fund, Matilda R.
Wyman Youth Trust

Elementary Education (Public)

Ahmanson Foundation

Alabama Gas Corp.
AlliedSignal Inc.
Bank One, Youngstown, NA
Bay Foundation
Bingham Foundation, William
Bishop Foundation, E. K. and Lillian F.
Blandin Foundation
Bodman Foundation
Bowen Foundation, Ethel N.
Burlington Industries, Inc.
Carnegie Corporation of New York
Carvel Foundation, Thomas and Agnes
Catlin Charitable Trust, Kathleen K.
Cayuga Foundation
Clark Foundation
Clowes Fund
Consolidated Natural Gas Co.
Cord Foundation, E. L.
Cowell Foundation, S. H.
Cremer Foundation
Dekko Foundation
Delano Foundation, Mignon Sherwood
Dodge Foundation, Cleveland H.
Dodge Foundation, Geraldine R.
Donner Foundation, William H.
Douty Foundation
Eberly Foundation
Evans Foundation, Thomas J.
Federated Mutual Insurance Co.
Fenton Foundation
Freeport-McMoRan Inc.
French Foundation, D.E.
General Mills, Inc.
Goldsmith Foundation, Horace W.
Grand Rapids Label Co.
Gregg-Graniteville Foundation
Gulf Power Co.
Guttman Foundation, Stella and Charles
Hancock Foundation, Luke B.
Harmon Foundation, Pearl M. and Julia J.
Harriman Foundation, Gladys and Roland
Heinz Endowment, Howard
Helmerich Foundation
Hewlett-Packard Co.
Heydt Fund, Nan and Matilda
Hopedale Foundation
Houston Endowment
Howard and Bush Foundation
JELD-WEN, Inc.
Jennings Foundation, Mary Hillman
Kansas City Southern Industries
Kaplan Fund, J. M.
Kavanagh Foundation, T. James
Kelly Tractor Co.
Knight Foundation, John S. and James L.
La-Z-Boy Chair Co.
Lehigh Portland Cement Co.
Lockhart Vaughan Foundation
Madison Gas & Electric Co.
Markey Charitable Fund, John C.
Martin Marietta Materials
Mattel, Inc.
McCune Charitable Trust, John R.
McDonald & Company Securities, Inc.
Mellon Foundation, Richard King
Meyer Memorial Trust
Miller Fund, Kathryn and Gilbert
Mitsubishi Motor Sales of America, Inc.
Monfort Family Foundation
Moore Foundation, Edward S.
Morgan Foundation, Burton D.
New York Mercantile Exchange

Northern States Power Co. (Minnesota)
O'Quinn Foundation, John M. and Nancy C.
Pamida, Inc.
Pfizer, Inc.
Pittsburg Midway Coal Mining Co.
PriMerit Bank
Prince Trust, Abbie Norman
Proctor Trust, Mortimer R.
Prudential Insurance Co. of America, The
RJR Nabisco Inc.
Roseburg Forest Products Co.
Rosenberg, Jr. Family Foundation, Louise and Claude
Salvatori Foundation, Henry
Scaife Family Foundation
Schumann Fund for New Jersey
Seafirst Corporation
Siltec Corp.
Springs Foundation
Stanley Works
Stevens Foundation, John T.
Stokely, Jr. Foundation, William B.
Strong Foundation, Hattie M.
Sturgis Charitable and Educational Trust, Roy and Christine
Subaru of America Inc.
Teichert & Son, A.
Temple Foundation, T. L. L.
Thompson Charitable Foundation
Trust Funds
Unitrode Corp.
Washington Forrest Foundation
Washington Mutual Savings Bank
Whitecap Foundation
Whittenberger Foundation, Claude R. and Ethel B.
Wiley & Sons, Inc., John
Wood Foundation of Chambersburg, PA

Engineering/Techno-logical Education

Abbott Laboratories
Abrams Foundation, Talbert and Leota
ACF Industries, Inc.
Acushnet Co.
Ahmanson Foundation
Air Products and Chemicals, Inc.
Alabama Power Co.
Allegheny Ludlum Corp.
AlliedSignal Inc.
Alumax Inc.
Aluminum Co. of America
American National Bank & Trust Co. of Chicago
American Natural Resources Company
American Optical Corp.
AMETEK, Inc.
Amoco Corporation
AMP Incorporated
Andersen Corp.
Anheuser-Busch Companies, Inc.
Appleton Papers Inc.
Aristech Chemical Corp.
Arkansas Power & Light Co.
Arkell Hall Foundation
Armco Inc.
Arnold Fund
AT&T Corp.
Ayres Foundation, Inc.
Babcock & Wilcox Co.
Baker Foundation, Dexter F. and Dorothy H.
Baker Hughes Inc.
Baker Trust, George F.
Bank of Boston
Bank of Boston Corp.
BankAmerica Corp.

Banta Corp.
Barker Foundation, J.M.R.
Battelle Memorial Institute
Bay Foundation
BE&K Inc.
Bechtel, Jr. Foundation, S. D.
Bell Atlantic Corp.
Berger Foundation, H. N. and Frances C.
Bethlehem Steel Corp.
Betts Industries
Birnschein Foundation, Alvin and Marion
Blandin Foundation
Blount, Inc.
Boeing Co., The
Boettcher Foundation
Boise Cascade Corporation
Booth Ferris Foundation
Borden, Inc.
Boston Edison Co.
Boswell Foundation, James G.
Bowater Incorporated
BP America Inc.
Brackenridge Foundation, George W.
Bridgestone/Firestone, Inc.
Brunswick Corp.
Bucyrus-Erie Company
Bush Foundation
Cabot Corp.
Caestecker Foundation, Charles and Marie
Cain Foundation, Effie and Wofford
Carter Foundation, Amon G.
CBI Industries, Inc.
CBS, Inc.
Central Maine Power Co.
Champion International Corporation
Chase Manhattan Bank, N.A.
Chesapeake Corp.
Chesebrough-Pond's USA Co.
Chevron Corporation
Chrysler Corp.
Clarke Trust, John
Cole Foundation, Olive B.
Coltec Industries, Inc.
Comer Foundation
Connelly Foundation
Consolidated Natural Gas Co.
Consolidated Papers, Inc.
Consumers Power Co.
Cooper Industries, Inc.
Coors Foundation, Adolph
Cord Foundation, E. L.
Corning Incorporated
Cowles Media Co.
CR Industries
CS First Boston Corporation
Cummins Engine Co.
Dana Foundation, Charles A.
Daniel Foundation of Alabama
Davenport-Hatch Foundation
Davenport Trust Fund
Deere & Co.
Dekko Foundation
DeRoy Foundation, Helen L.
DeRoy Testamentary Foundation
Detroit Edison Co.
Diamond Foundation, Aaron
Digital Equipment Corp.
Dodge Foundation, Geraldine R.
Donaldson Company, Inc.
Douglas & Lomason Company
Dow Corning Corp.
Dresser Industries, Inc.
Dreyfus Foundation, Max and Victoria
du Pont de Nemours & Co., E. I.
Duchossois Industries Inc.
Duke Endowment
Duke Power Co.
Dynamet, Inc.
Eastman Kodak Company
Eaton Corporation
Eddy Family Memorial Fund, C. K.
Edmonds Foundation, Dean S.
English Memorial Fund, Florence C. and H. L.

Enron Corp.
Essick Foundation
Exxon Corporation
Fairchild Foundation, Sherman
Federal-Mogul Corporation
First Source Corp.
Firstar Bank Milwaukee, N.A.
Fischbach Foundation
Fondren Foundation
Ford Motor Co.
Fort Wayne National Bank
Freeport-McMoRan Inc.
Frost National Bank
Frueauff Foundation, Charles A.
Fuld Health Trust, Helene
Fuller Foundation
Gates Foundation
GenCorp Inc.
General Mills, Inc.
General Motors Corp.
GenRad
Georgia Power Co.
Germeshausen Foundation, Kenneth J.
Glanville Family Foundation
Gleason Foundation
Good Samaritan
Goodrich Co., The B.F.
Gould Electronics Inc.
Gould Foundation, The Florence
Graham Foundation for Advanced Studies in the Fine Arts
Greenwall Foundation
Greve Foundation, William and Mary
Gulf Power Co.
Habig Foundation, Arnold F.
Hallberg Foundation, E. L. and R. F.
Handy and Harman Foundation
Harcourt General, Inc.
Harriman Foundation, Gladys and Roland
Hartmarx Corporation
Hawkins Foundation, Robert Z.
Hearst Foundation, William Randolph
Hechinger Co.
Heinz Endowment, Vira I.
Hermann Foundation, Grover
Hershey Foods Corp.
Hewlett-Packard Co.
Hickory Tech Corp.
Hoover Fund-Trust, W. Henry
Houston Endowment
Huisking Foundation
Hyde and Watson Foundation
Hygeia Dairy Co.
Illinois Tool Works, Inc.
International Business Machines Corp.
International Paper Co.
Irvine Foundation, James
Jarson-Stanley and Mickey Kaplan Foundation, Isaac and Esther
JELD-WEN, Inc.
Jewell Memorial Foundation, Daniel Ashley and Irene Houston
Johnson Controls Inc.
Johnson & Higgins
Jones Foundation, Fletcher
Kemper National Insurance Cos.
Kempner Fund, Harris and Eliza
Kennecott Corporation
Kettering Fund
Kimberly-Clark Corp.
Kingsbury Corp.
Kiplinger Foundation
Klipstein Foundation, Ernest Christian
KN Energy, Inc.
Knapp Foundation
Knudsen Foundation, Tom and Valley
Koopman Fund
Kresge Foundation
Lebovitz Fund
Lehigh Portland Cement Co.

Lehmann Foundation, Otto W.
Leuthold Foundation
Levy Foundation, June Rockwell
Littauer Foundation, Lucius N.
Little, Inc., Arthur D.
Long Island Lighting Co.
M/A-COM, Inc.
Markey Charitable Fund, John C.
Marquette Electronics, Inc.
Marshall Trust in Memory of Sanders McDaniel, Harriet McDaniel
Martin Marietta Corp.
Martin Marietta Materials
Mattel, Inc.
May Department Stores Company, The
McDermott Foundation, Eugene
McEvoy Foundation, Mildred H.
Mead Corporation, The
Medtronic, Inc.
Mellon Foundation, Andrew W.
Merck & Co.
Miller Brewing Company/North Carolina
Mills Fund, Frances Goll
Mine Safety Appliances Co.
Minnesota Mining & Mfg. Co.
Mobil Oil Corp.
Montana Power Co.
Monticello College Foundation
Morgan Construction Co.
Morgan Stanley & Co., Inc.
Mott Foundation, Charles Stewart
Muchnic Foundation
Mulford Foundation, Vincent
Munger Foundation, Alfred C.
Murdock Charitable Trust, M. J.
Murphey Foundation, Lluella Morey
Mutual Assurance Co.
Nalco Chemical Co.
National Westminster Bank New Jersey
New-Land Foundation
New York Times Company
Norton Co.
NYNEX Corporation
Olin Corp.
Olsson Memorial Foundation, Elis
Outboard Marine Corp.
Pacific Telesis Group
Packaging Corporation of America
Packard Foundation, David and Lucile
Palmer Fund, Frank Loomis
Panhandle Eastern Corporation
Parker Hannifin Corp.
Parsons Foundation, Ralph M.
Peabody Charitable Fund, Amelia
Penn Foundation, William
Pennsylvania Dutch Co.
Pennzoil Co.
Peppers Foundation, Ann
Pfizer, Inc.
Phillips Foundation, Ellis L.
Piper Foundation, Minnie Stevens
Pittsburg Midway Coal Mining Co.
Plumsock Fund
Polaroid Corp.
Potts and Sibley Foundation
PPG Industries, Inc.
Prouty Foundation, Olive Higgins
Public Service Co. of New Mexico
Public Service Electric & Gas Co.
Putnam Foundation
Quivey-Bay State Foundation
Rachal Foundation, Ed
Rice Charitable Foundation, Albert W.
Riggs Benevolent Fund

RJR Nabisco Inc.
Rockwell International Corporation
Rohm & Haas Co.
Rubin Family Fund, Cele H. and William B.
San Diego Gas & Electric
Santa Fe Pacific Corporation
Sarkeys Foundation
SBC Communications Inc.
Scherer Foundation, Karla
Schering-Plough Corp.
Schiff Foundation, Dorothy
Schlumberger Ltd.
Schmitt Foundation, Kilian J. and Caroline F.
Schoenleber Foundation
Scholl Foundation, Dr.
Scripps Co., E.W.
Scurlock Foundation
Seaver Institute
Sedgwick James Inc.
Sentry Insurance A Mutual Company
Shawmut National Corp.
Shell Oil Company
Sloan Foundation, Alfred P.
Smith Corp., A.O.
Sonat Inc.
Southern California Edison Co.
Southern New England Telephone Company
Square D Co.
Stanley Works
Stans Foundation
Stein Foundation, Jules and Doris
Sumners Foundation, Hatton W.
Teagle Foundation
Temple Foundation, T. L. L.
Temple-Inland Inc.
Tenneco Inc.
Texaco Inc.
Textron, Inc.
Thermo Electron Corp.
Thompson Co., J. Walter
Times Mirror Company, The
Transco Energy Co.
Unilever United States, Inc.
Union Bank
Union Camp Corporation
Union Electric Co.
Union Pacific Corp.
Unitrode Corp.
Unocal Corp.
US WEST, Inc.
USX Corporation
Valmont Industries, Inc.
Van Evera Foundation, Dewitt
Van Nuys Foundation, I. N. and Susanna H.
Virginia Environmental Endowment
Virginia Power Co.
Vulcan Materials Co.
Wahlstrom Foundation
Wallace Foundation, George R.
Washington Water Power Co.
Weingart Foundation
Weyerhaeuser Co.
Whirlpool Corporation
White Trust, G. R.
WICOR, Inc.
Wisconsin Public Service Corp.
Wise Foundation and Charitable Trust, Watson W.
Witco Corp.
Zollner Foundation

Environmental Education

BankAmerica Corp.
Bay Foundation
Bingham Foundation, William
Borkee Hagley Foundation
Castle Foundation, Harold K. L.
Culpeper Foundation, Charles E.
Dodge Foundation, Geraldine R.

Dreyfus Foundation, Max and Victoria
Gebbie Foundation
Hallberg Foundation, E. L. and R. F.
Hanson Industries North America
Hewlett Foundation, William and Flora
Houston Endowment
Hunt Foundation, Samuel P.
Ittleson Foundation
Longwood Foundation
Marpat Foundation
McCann Foundation
Mellon Foundation, Andrew W.
Mellon Foundation, Richard King
Merck Family Fund
Meyer Memorial Trust
Millbrook Tribute Garden
Mulcahy Foundation
Murdock Charitable Trust, M. J.
Noble Foundation, Edward John
Norgren Foundation, Carl A.
Phillips Foundation, Ellis L.
Rockwell Fund
Schumann Fund for New Jersey
Scripps Co., E.W.
Shaw Foundation, Arch W.
Turner Charitable Foundation
Wege Foundation

Faculty Development

Abell-Hanger Foundation
Alabama Gas Corp.
Aldus Corp.
AlliedSignal Inc.
Aluminum Co. of America
American Fidelity Corporation
American Natural Resources Company
AON Corporation
Appleton Papers Inc.
Archer-Daniels-Midland Co.
AT&T Corp.
Atherton Family Foundation
Ball Foundation, George and Frances
Battelle Memorial Institute
Bean Foundation, Norwin S. and Elizabeth N.
Benedum Foundation, Claude Worthington
Bettingen Corporation, Burton G.
Bingham Foundation, William
Bingham Second Betterment Fund, William
Blandin Foundation
Blue Cross & Blue Shield United of Wisconsin
Boeing Co., The
Booth Ferris Foundation
Brackenridge Foundation, George W.
Burlington Industries, Inc.
Bush Foundation
Cabell Foundation, Robert G. Cabell III and Maude Morgan
Cabot Corp.
Carpenter Foundation
Carpenter Technology Corp.
CBS, Inc.
Central Maine Power Co.
Chase Manhattan Bank, N.A.
Chevron Corporation
CIGNA Corporation
CINergy
Connelly Foundation
Contran Corporation
Corning Incorporated
Cowles Charitable Trust
Cowles Media Co.
CPC International Inc.
Dana Foundation, Charles A.
Daywood Foundation

Dekko Foundation
DeRoy Testamentary Foundation
Diamond Foundation, Aaron
Dodge Foundation, Geraldine R.
Dodge Jones Foundation
Donaldson Company, Inc.
du Pont de Nemours & Co., E. I.
Duchossois Industries Inc.
Duke Endowment
Exxon Corporation
Fairchild Foundation, Sherman
Fife Foundation, Elias and Bertha
Fink Foundation
First Tennessee Bank
First Union Corp.
Fish Foundation, Ray C.
Ford Foundation
Frear Eleemosynary Trust, Mary D. and Walter F.
Frost National Bank
Frueauff Foundation, Charles A.
Fry Foundation, Lloyd A.
GAR Foundation
GATX Corp.
General Mills, Inc.
General Motors Corp.
Georgia Power Co.
Giant Eagle, Inc.
Good Samaritan
Griffith Foundation, W. C.
Hardin Foundation, Phil
Harriman Foundation, Mary W.
Haynes Foundation, John Randolph and Dora
Hearst Foundation, William Randolph
Heinz Endowment, Howard
Heinz Endowment, Vira I.
Hermann Foundation, Grover
Herrick Foundation
Hewlett Foundation, William and Flora
Hickory Tech Corp.
Hillman Foundation
Houston Endowment
Independence Foundation
International Business Machines Corp.
Irvine Foundation, James
Ittleson Foundation
Johnson & Higgins
Joy Family Foundation
Jurzykowski Foundation, Alfred
Kemper National Insurance Cos.
Kerr Foundation
Kiewit Foundation, Peter
Knight Foundation, John S. and James L.
Kresge Foundation
Long Island Lighting Co.
Mandeville Foundation
Mars Foundation
Mather Charitable Trust, S. Livingston
Matthies Foundation, Katharine
McElroy Trust, R. J.
McInerny Foundation
Meadows Foundation
Medtronic, Inc.
Mellon Foundation, Andrew W.
Merck & Co.
Meyer Memorial Trust
Morgan & Company, J.P.
Murdock Charitable Trust, M. J.
National Forge Co.
National Westminster Bank New Jersey
Noble Foundation, Edward John
Noble Foundation, Samuel Roberts
Norton Co.
Novell Inc.
Pacific Telesis Group
Perkin-Elmer Corp.
Pew Charitable Trusts
Pfizer, Inc.

Piper Foundation, Minnie Stevens
PPG Industries, Inc.
Prince Trust, Abbie Norman
Prudential Insurance Co. of America, The
Public Service Co. of New Mexico
Republic NY Corp.
RJR Nabisco Inc.
Robinson Fund, Maurice R.
Rockwell Fund
Rockwell International Corporation
Rohm & Haas Co.
Rose's Stores, Inc.
Saint Paul Companies, Inc.
Salvatori Foundation, Henry
SBC Communications Inc.
Schering-Plough Corp.
Schiro Fund
Schlumberger Ltd.
Scholl Foundation, Dr.
Schumann Fund for New Jersey
Sedgwick James Inc.
Shell Oil Company
Shenandoah Life Insurance Co.
Sloan Foundation, Alfred P.
Smith Foundation, Ralph L.
Snow Memorial Trust, John Ben
Southern California Edison Co.
Steele Foundation, Harry and Grace
Subaru of America Inc.
Teagle Foundation
Tenneco Inc.
Towsley Foundation, Harry A. and Margaret D.
Trust Funds
Union Camp Corporation
Union Pacific Corp.
Unocal Corp.
Uris Brothers Foundation
Wallace-Reader's Digest Fund, DeWitt
Washington Mutual Savings Bank
Washington Water Power Co.
Wean Foundation, Raymond John
Weingart Foundation
Wendt Foundation, Margaret L.
Whittenberger Foundation, Claude R. and Ethel B.
Widgeon Foundation
Zachry Co., H.B.

General

Acme-McCrary Corp./Sapona Manufacturing Co.
Acushnet Co.
Aetna Life & Casualty Co.
Ahmanson Foundation
Air Products and Chemicals, Inc.
Akzo America
Alabama Gas Corp.
Aldus Corp.
Allegheny Foundation
Allendale Insurance Co.
AlliedSignal Inc.
Altman Foundation
Aluminum Co. of America
Amcast Industrial Corp.
AMCORE Bank, N.A. Rockford
Andersen Corp.
Andersen Foundation
Andreas Foundation
Anheuser-Busch Companies, Inc.
Annenberg Foundation
Archer-Daniels-Midland Co.
Aristech Chemical Corp.
Arkelian Foundation, Ben H. and Gladys
Armco Inc.
Armstrong Foundation
Ayres Foundation, Inc.
Babson Foundation, Paul and Edith

1185

Baehr Foundation, Louis W. and Dolpha
Baker Foundation, Dexter F. and Dorothy H.
Baldwin Foundation, David M. and Barbara
Bank One, Texas-Houston Office
Bank One, Youngstown, NA
BankAmerica Corp.
Banta Corp.
Barry Corp., R. G.
Barth Foundation, Theodore H.
Baskin-Robbins USA Co.
Bauervic Foundation, Charles M.
BE&K Inc.
Beck Foundation, Elsie E. and Joseph W.
Beech Aircraft Corp.
Benedum Foundation, Claude Worthington
Berwind Corporation
Bingham Foundation, William
Bingham Second Betterment Fund, William
Binney & Smith Inc.
Blair and Co., William
Blandin Foundation
Block, H&R
Bodman Foundation
Booth Ferris Foundation
Borden, Inc.
Bowen Foundation, Ethel N.
Bowne Foundation, Robert
Brillion Iron Works
Bryn Mawr Trust Co.
Burden Foundation, Florence V.
Burlington Industries, Inc.
Bush Foundation
Butz Foundation
Cabot Corp.
Calhoun Charitable Trust, Kenneth
Carnegie Corporation of New York
Carolyn Foundation
Carter Foundation, Amon G.
Carver Charitable Trust, Roy J.
Caspersen Foundation for Aid to Health and Education, O. W.
Castle Foundation, Harold K. L.
CBS, Inc.
Chapman Charitable Corporation, Howard and Bess
Chase Manhattan Bank, N.A.
Chazen Foundation
Chesebrough-Pond's USA Co.
Chevron Corporation
Chicago Sun-Times, Inc.
Christian Dior New York, Inc.
CIGNA Corporation
CINergy
Clark Foundation
Clarke Trust, John
Clorox Co.
CNA Financial Corporation/CNA Insurance Companies
Cole Foundation, Olive B.
Coleman Foundation, George E.
Columbus Dispatch Printing Co.
Comer Foundation
Consolidated Papers, Inc.
Contran Corporation
Cooperman Foundation, Leon and Toby
Coors Foundation, Adolph
Cosmair, Inc.
Coughlin-Saunders Foundation
Covington and Burling
Cowell Foundation, S. H.
Crane Co.
Crawford Estate, E. R.
Crocker Trust, Mary A.
Crown Memorial, Arie and Ida
CT Corp. System
Culpeper Foundation, Charles E.

Culver Foundation, Constans
Cummings Foundation, James H.
Dana Foundation, Charles A.
Darby Foundation
Dart Group Corp.
Davenport Trust Fund
Davis Foundation, Edwin W. and Catherine M.
Davis Foundation, Irene E. and George A.
Day Foundation, Nancy Sayles
Daywood Foundation
DEC International, Inc.
Deere & Co.
Demoulas Supermarkets Inc.
Dentsply International Inc.
DeRoy Testamentary Foundation
Dewing Foundation, Frances R.
Dexter Charitable Fund, Eugene A.
Diamond Shamrock Inc.
Dodge Foundation, Cleveland H.
Donnelley Foundation, Gaylord and Dorothy
Donner Foundation, William H.
Douglas & Lomason Company
Dreyfus Foundation, Jean and Louis
Dreyfus Foundation, Max and Victoria
Duke Power Co.
Eastman Kodak Company
Eaton Foundation, Cyrus
Ebsco Industries, Inc.
Elf Atochem North America, Inc.
Encyclopaedia Britannica, Inc.
Erpf Fund, Armand G.
Ettinger Foundation
Evans Foundation, Lettie Pate
Exxon Corporation
Fabri-Kal Corp.
Fairchild Foundation, Sherman
Farish Fund, William Stamps
Federated Mutual Insurance Co.
Feild Co-Operative Association
Fenton Foundation
Firman Fund
First National Bank
First Source Corp.
First Union National Bank of Florida
Fischbach Foundation
Fish Foundation, Ray C.
Fondren Foundation
Ford Foundation
Ford Fund, William and Martha
Ford Motor Co.
France Foundation, Jacob and Annita
Freeport-McMoRan Inc.
French Oil Mill Machinery Co.
Friendship Fund
Frohring Foundation, Paul and Maxine
Frueauff Foundation, Charles A.
Fry Foundation, Lloyd A.
Gamble Foundation
GAR Foundation
Gates Foundation
Gaylord Foundation, Clifford Willard
Gellert Foundation, Celia Berta
GenCorp Inc.
General Mills, Inc.
General Motors Corp.
GenRad
Georgia-Pacific Corporation
Gheens Foundation
Gilmore Foundation, William G.
Glaser Foundation
Globe Newspaper Co.
Goldseker Foundation of Maryland, Morris
Goldsmith Foundation, Horace W.
Goldwyn Foundation, Samuel
Gould Electronics Inc.
Grand Rapids Label Co.

Greenwall Foundation
Gregg-Graniteville Foundation
Griswold Foundation, John C.
Guggenheim Foundation, Harry Frank
Gulf Power Co.
Hafif Family Foundation
Haigh-Scatena Foundation
Halsell Foundation, Ewing
Hamman Foundation, George and Mary Josephine
Hammer Foundation, Armand
Hancock Foundation, Luke B.
Handy and Harman Foundation
Hanson Industries North America
Harcourt Foundation, Ellen Knowles
Harcourt General, Inc.
Hardin Foundation, Phil
Harland Charitable Foundation, John and Wilhelmina D.
Harmon Foundation, Pearl M. and Julia J.
HarperCollins Publishers Inc.
Harriman Foundation, Mary W.
Harrison Foundation, Fred G.
Harsco Corp.
Hasbro Inc.
Haynes Foundation, John Randolph and Dora
Hazen Foundation, Edward W.
Heinz Company, H. J.
Helms Foundation
Hermann Foundation, Grover
Herzstein Charitable Foundation, Albert and Ethel
Hewit Family Foundation
Hewlett Foundation, William and Flora
Hewlett-Packard Co.
Heydt Fund, Nan and Matilda
Hickory Tech Corp.
Hillcrest Foundation
Hoag Family Foundation, George
Hobby Foundation
Holnam
Homeland Foundation
Hoover Foundation
Huisking Foundation
Hunt Foundation
Hygeia Dairy Co.
IBP, Inc.
Icahn Foundation, Carl C.
Independence Foundation
Integra Bank of Uniontown
International Paper Co.
Iowa-Illinois Gas & Electric Co.
Irvine Foundation, James
Jackson Foundation
Jameson Foundation, J. W. and Ida M.
Jaydor Corp.
JELD-WEN, Inc.
JFM Foundation
Johnson Charitable Educational Trust, James Hervey
Johnson Controls Inc.
Johnson Foundation, Helen K. and Arthur E.
Jones Foundation, Daisy Marquis
Jones Foundation, Fletcher
Jostens, Inc.
Joy Family Foundation
Justus Trust, Edith C.
Kansas City Southern Industries
Kaplun Foundation, Morris J. and Betty
Kaye, Scholer, Fierman, Hays & Handler
Kemper Foundation, William T.
Kemper National Insurance Cos.
Kennecott Corporation
Kettering Fund
Kingsbury Corp.
Kirkpatrick Foundation
Kitzmiller/Bales Trust

Kline Foundation, Josiah W. and Bessie H.
KN Energy, Inc.
Knight Foundation, John S. and James L.
Knoll Group
Kornfeld Foundation, Emily Davie and Joseph S.
Kreitler Foundation
Kuehn Foundation
LamCo. Communications
Larsen Fund
Laurel Foundation
LBJ Family Foundation
Lehigh Portland Cement Co.
Lenna Foundation, Reginald A. and Elizabeth S.
Lennon Foundation, Fred A.
Lockhart Vaughan Foundation
Loews Corporation
Longwood Foundation
Lydall, Inc.
Mailman Family Foundation, A. L.
Management Compensation Group/Dulworth Inc.
Maneely Fund
Margoes Foundation
Marmot Foundation
Marshall Trust in Memory of Sanders McDaniel, Harriet McDaniel
Martin Marietta Corp.
Martin Marietta Materials
Mascoma Savings Bank
Mattel, Inc.
Matthies Foundation, Katharine
Mautz Paint Co.
Mays Foundation
Maytag Family Foundation, Fred
MBIA Inc.
McCarty Foundation, John and Margaret
McCasland Foundation
McCune Charitable Foundation, Marshall and Perrine D.
McDermott Foundation, Eugene
McDonald & Company Securities, Inc.
McElroy Trust, R. J.
McFawn Trust No. 2, Lois Sisler
McGee Foundation
McMahan Foundation, Catherine L. and Robert O.
McMillan Foundation, D. W.
McShain Charities, John
Mellon Foundation, Andrew W.
Merck & Co.
Merck Family Fund
Meyer Family Foundation, Paul J.
Mielke Family Foundation
Miller Brewing Company/North Carolina
Mitsubishi Motor Sales of America, Inc.
Morgan Foundation, Burton D.
Morris Foundation, Margaret T.
Mosinee Paper Corp.
Mulcahy Foundation
Murphey Foundation, Lluella Morey
Musson Charitable Foundation, R. C. and Katharine M.
Nabisco Foods Group
National Forge Co.
Nestle USA Inc.
New Jersey Natural Gas Co.
New York Mercantile Exchange
The New Yorker Magazine, Inc.
Noble Foundation, Samuel Roberts
Northwest Natural Gas Co.
Norton Foundation Inc.
Novell Inc.
OCRI Foundation
Offield Family Foundation
Old National Bank in Evansville

Olsson Memorial Foundation, Elis
Oppenstein Brothers Foundation
O'Quinn Foundation, John M. and Nancy C.
Ore-Ida Foods, Inc.
Pacific Mutual Life Insurance Co.
Packaging Corporation of America
Packard Foundation, David and Lucile
Palisano Foundation, Vincent and Harriet
Pamida, Inc.
Park Foundation
PECO Energy Company
Penguin Books USA, Inc.
Pennsylvania Dutch Co.
Peppers Foundation, Ann
Pew Charitable Trusts
Pforzheimer Foundation, Carl and Lily
PHH Corporation
Phillips Family Foundation, Jay and Rose
Pierce Charitable Trust, Harold Whitworth
Pioneer Trust Bank, NA
Pitt-Des Moines Inc.
Pittsburg Midway Coal Mining Co.
Plumsock Fund
PNC Bank, N.A.
Prairie Foundation
PriMerit Bank
Providence Gas Co.
Providian Corporation
Prudential Insurance Co. of America, The
Public Service Co. of New Mexico
Putnam Foundation
Quivey-Bay State Foundation
Raymond Corp.
Regenstein Foundation
Reicher Foundation, Anne and Harry J.
Richardson Benevolent Foundation, C. E.
RJR Nabisco Inc.
Robinson-Broadhurst Foundation
Rockwell Fund
Rockwell International Corporation
Rogers Family Foundation
Rose Foundation, Billy
Roseburg Forest Products Co.
Rosenberg, Jr. Family Foundation, Louise and Claude
Rose's Stores, Inc.
Ross Laboratories
Royal Group, Inc.
Rubin Family Fund, Cele H. and William B.
Russell Trust, Josephine G.
Ryan Foundation, David Claude
Salvatori Foundation, Henry
Sandusky International Inc.
Sara Lee Hosiery, Inc.
Sarkeys Foundation
Scherer Foundation, Karla
Scherman Foundation
Schroeder Foundation, Walter
Schumann Fund for New Jersey
Scott Fetzer Co.
Scott Foundation, William E.
Scurlock Foundation
Seafirst Corporation
Seaver Charitable Trust, Richard C.
Security Life of Denver Insurance Co.
Seneca Foods Corp.
Seton Leather Co.
Sierra Pacific Industries
Sierra Pacific Resources
Siltec Corp.
Slemp Foundation
Sloan Foundation, Alfred P.

The Big Book of Library Grant Money

Smart Family Foundation
Smith Charitable Foundation, Lou and Lutza
Snow Memorial Trust, John Ben
Solow Foundation
Southern California Edison Co.
Southwestern Electric Power Co.
Speyer Foundation, Alexander C. and Tillie S.
SPX Corp.
Stackpole-Hall Foundation
Stanley Charitable Foundation, A.W.
Stans Foundation
Steinman Foundation, John Frederick
Stemmons Foundation
Stevens Foundation, Abbot and Dorothy H.
Stokely, Jr. Foundation, William B.
Strong Foundation, Hattie M.
Sulzberger Foundation
Sundet Foundation
Tait Foundation, Frank M.
Taubman Foundation, A. Alfred
Teichert & Son, A.
Temple-Inland Inc.
Texaco Inc.
Thermo Electron Corp.
Thomas Foundation, Joan and Lee
Thompson Co., J. Walter
Thornton Foundation
Times Mirror Company, The
Tozer Foundation
Travelers Inc.
Trust Funds
Turrell Fund
Unger Foundation, Aber D.
Union Electric Co.
U.S. Bank of Washington
Unitrode Corp.
Upton Foundation, Frederick S.
Van Wert County Foundation
Vance Charitable Foundation, Robert C.
Vernon Fund, Miles Hodsdon
Vevay-Switzerland County Foundation
Vicksburg Foundation
Wahlstrom Foundation
Wallace-Reader's Digest Fund, DeWitt
Washington Mutual Savings Bank
Waters Charitable Trust, Robert S.
Webber Oil Co.
Weber Charities Corp., Frederick E.
Weezie Foundation
Wege Foundation
Welfare Foundation
Wertheim Foundation, Dr. Herbert A.
West Foundation, Harry and Ethel
West One Bancorp
Wheeler Foundation
Whirlpool Corporation
Whitecap Foundation
WICOR, Inc.
Wiley & Sons, Inc., John
Wilson Fund, Matilda R.
Windham Foundation
Winnebago Industries, Inc.
Wiremold Co.
Wisconsin Power & Light Co.
Wise Foundation and Charitable Trust, Watson W.
Wood Foundation of Chambersburg, PA
Wyman Youth Trust
Zachry Co., H.B.

Gifted & Talented Programs

Alexander Foundation, Joseph
Anderson Foundation

BE&K Inc.
Beloit Foundation
Bingham Foundation, William
Brackenridge Foundation, George W.
Crawford Estate, E. R.
Dodge Foundation, Geraldine R.
Durfee Foundation
General Mills, Inc.
Hardin Foundation, Phil
Higginson Trust, Corina
Hoag Family Foundation, George
Holzer Memorial Foundation, Richard H.
Jostens, Inc.
Martini Foundation, Nicholas
McElroy Trust, R. J.
McInerny Foundation
McMahon Foundation
Mellon Foundation, Richard King
Piper Jaffray Companies Inc.
Schwartz Foundation, Arnold A.
Sentry Insurance A Mutual Company
Steele Foundation, Harry and Grace
Westerman Foundation, Samuel L.
Whiting Foundation
Whittenberger Foundation, Claude R. and Ethel B.

Health & Physical Education

Abbott Laboratories
AlliedSignal Inc.
AMCORE Bank, N.A. Rockford
American National Bank & Trust Co. of Chicago
Ameritas Life Insurance Corp.
Anheuser-Busch Companies, Inc.
AON Corporation
Archer-Daniels-Midland Co.
Barra Foundation
Bemis Company, Inc.
Bingham Second Betterment Fund, William
Brackenridge Foundation, George W.
Cabot Corp.
Cabot Family Charitable Trust
Carnegie Corporation of New York
Chase Manhattan Bank, N.A.
Chrysler Corp.
Clay Foundation
Collins Medical Trust
Coors Foundation, Adolph
Crestlea Foundation
Dentsply International Inc.
Diamond Foundation, Aaron
Dula Educational and Charitable Foundation, Caleb C. and Julia W.
Eastman Kodak Company
Federated Mutual Insurance Co.
First Interstate Bank of Oregon
Ford Motor Co.
Forest Foundation
Foster Charitable Trust
France Foundation, Jacob and Annita
Frost National Bank
General Motors Corp.
Georgia Power Co.
Goldsmith Foundation, Horace W.
Gregg-Graniteville Foundation
Guttman Foundation, Stella and Charles
Hamman Foundation, George and Mary Josephine
Harcourt General, Inc.
HCA Foundation
Heinz Company, H. J.

Hermann Foundation, Grover
Herrick Foundation
Hillsdale Fund
Houston Endowment
Hoyt Foundation, Stewart W. and Willma C.
ITT Hartford Insurance Group, Inc.
Johnson & Higgins
Jones Foundation, Daisy Marquis
Lipton, Thomas J.
Long Foundation, J.M.
Lurie Foundation, Louis R.
MacArthur Foundation, John D. and Catherine T.
Massengill-DeFriece Foundation
McDermott Foundation, Eugene
Meadows Foundation
Medtronic, Inc.
Merck & Co.
Metropolitan Life Insurance Co.
Mid-Iowa Health Foundation
Monell Foundation, Ambrose
Morgan Foundation, Burton D.
Morris Foundation, Margaret T.
New York Life Insurance Co.
New York Stock Exchange, Inc.
Noble Foundation, Edward John
Noble Foundation, Samuel Roberts
Norton Co.
O'Connor Foundation, A. Lindsay and Olive B.
Pacific Mutual Life Insurance Co.
Phelps Dodge Corporation
Providence Gas Co.
Provident Life & Accident Insurance Company of America
Prudential Insurance Co. of America, The
Ross Memorial Foundation, Will
Rubin Foundation, Samuel
San Diego Gas & Electric
Santa Fe Pacific Corporation
Schering-Plough Corp.
Schwartz Fund for Education and Health Research, Arnold and Marie
Scurlock Foundation
Security Life of Denver Insurance Co.
Sedgwick James Inc.
Shawmut National Corp.
Shenandoah Life Insurance Co.
South Waite Foundation
Southwestern Electric Power Co.
Starr Foundation
Strong Foundation, Hattie M.
Thermo Electron Corp.
Tobin Foundation
Tucker Charitable Trust, Rose E.
Unger Foundation, Aber D.
Worthington Foods

International Exchange

Acushnet Co.
Akzo America
AlliedSignal Inc.
Aluminum Co. of America
American Optical Corp.
American President Companies, Ltd.
Anheuser-Busch Companies, Inc.
Arkell Hall Foundation
AT&T Corp.
Audubon State Bank
Ball Brothers Foundation
BankAmerica Corp.
Bingham Foundation, William
Bunbury Company

Burkitt Foundation
Cabot Corp.
Callaway Foundation
Citibank
Colonial Life & Accident Insurance Co.
CPC International Inc.
Culpeper Foundation, Charles E.
Cummins Engine Co.
Day Foundation, Nancy Sayles
DeRoy Testamentary Foundation
Dodge Foundation, Cleveland H.
Dodge Foundation, Geraldine R.
du Pont de Nemours & Co., E. I.
Favrot Fund
Federated Mutual Insurance Co.
Fenton Foundation
First Fidelity Bank
Freeman Charitable Trust, Samuel
Friedman Family Foundation
Frost National Bank
Fry Foundation, Lloyd A.
General Mills, Inc.
General Motors Corp.
Getty Trust, J. Paul
Gould Foundation, The Florence
Hanson Industries North America
Heinz Company, H. J.
Hoffman Foundation, Maximilian E. and Marion O.
Hunt Foundation, Roy A.
Interkal, Inc.
Johnson & Son, S.C.
Jurzykowski Foundation, Alfred
Kent-Lucas Foundation
Kiplinger Foundation
Kirby Foundation, F. M.
Leavey Foundation, Thomas and Dorothy
Lurcy Charitable and Educational Trust, Georges
MacArthur Foundation, John D. and Catherine T.
Marpat Foundation
McElroy Trust, R. J.
M.E. Foundation
Merck & Co.
Meyer Memorial Trust
Mitsubishi International Corp.
Mitsubishi Motor Sales of America, Inc.
Mobil Oil Corp.
Mott Foundation, Charles Stewart
Mutual Assurance Co.
National Westminster Bank New Jersey
Overbrook Foundation
Pew Charitable Trusts
Pfizer, Inc.
Phelps Dodge Corporation
Pulitzer Publishing Co.
Reed Foundation
Reynolds Foundation, Christopher
RJR Nabisco Inc.
Sara Lee Corp.
Sedgwick James Inc.
Sloan Foundation, Alfred P.
Starr Foundation
Subaru of America Inc.
Thompson Co., J. Walter
Thompson Trust, Thomas
Trust Company Bank
Unocal Corp.
Westerman Foundation, Samuel L.
Winnebago Industries, Inc.
Woodward Fund
Zlinkoff Fund for Medical Research and Education, Sergei S.

International Studies

Air France
AKC Fund
Alumax Inc.
Aluminum Co. of America
American President Companies, Ltd.
Annenberg Foundation
Archer-Daniels-Midland Co.
ASDA Foundation
Atran Foundation
Baker Trust, George F.
BankAmerica Corp.
Beaucourt Foundation
Bechtel, Jr. Foundation, S. D.
Bingham Foundation, William
Blum-Kovler Foundation
Bowen Foundation, Ethel N.
Bridgestone/Firestone, Inc.
Cabot Corp.
Cabot Family Charitable Trust
Cafritz Foundation, Morris and Gwendolyn
Campini Foundation, Frank A.
Carnegie Corporation of New York
Carpenter Foundation, E. Rhodes and Leona B.
Chase Manhattan Bank, N.A.
Chevron Corporation
Christian Dior New York, Inc.
Citibank
Cole Foundation, Olive B.
Coleman Foundation, George E.
Colonial Life & Accident Insurance Co.
Columbia Foundation
CPC International Inc.
Culpeper Foundation, Charles E.
Davis Foundation, Irene E. and George A.
Davis Foundations, Arthur Vining
Dekko Foundation
Dodge Foundation, Cleveland H.
Dodge Foundation, Geraldine R.
Donner Foundation, William H.
Dresser Industries, Inc.
du Pont de Nemours & Co., E. I.
Duke Endowment
Durfee Foundation
Eaton Foundation, Cyrus
Elkins, Jr. Foundation, Margaret and James A.
Erpf Fund, Armand G.
Ettinger Foundation
First Hawaiian, Inc.
Fishback Foundation Trust, Harmes C.
Ford Foundation
Fribourg Foundation
Fuqua Foundation, J. B.
General Mills, Inc.
General Motors Corp.
Gould Foundation, The Florence
Griffith Foundation, W. C.
Griggs and Mary Griggs Burke Foundation, Mary Livingston
Guggenheim Foundation, Harry Frank
Hardin Foundation, Phil
Harland Charitable Foundation, John and Wilhelmina D.
Harriman Foundation, Mary W.
Hauser Foundation
Haynes Foundation, John Randolph and Dora
Heinz Company, H. J.
Heinz Endowment, Howard
Hewlett Foundation, William and Flora
Hickory Tech Corp.
Hunt Foundation, Samuel P.
Hyde and Watson Foundation
Independence Foundation

Toms Foundation
Trust Company Bank
Union Camp Corporation
Unocal Corp.
Uris Brothers Foundation
Vale Foundation, Ruby R.
Warner Fund, Albert and Bessie
Warwick Foundation
Wean Foundation, Raymond John
Weil, Gotshal and Manges Foundation
Wheat First Butcher Singer, Inc.
White Trust, G. R.
Wiegand Foundation, E. L.
Wiley & Sons, Inc., John
Willard Helping Fund, Cecilia Young
Winston Foundation, Norman and Rosita
Woolley Foundation, Vasser

Literacy

Abell-Hanger Foundation
Achelis Foundation
Ahmanson Foundation
Air Products and Chemicals, Inc.
Alabama Gas Corp.
Alabama Power Co.
Aldus Corp.
Alexander Foundation, Joseph
Allegheny Foundation
Allendale Insurance Co.
AlliedSignal Inc.
Allyn Foundation
Altman Foundation
Alumax Inc.
Aluminum Co. of America
AMCORE Bank, N.A. Rockford
American Brands, Inc.
American General Finance Corp.
AMETEK, Inc.
AMP Incorporated
Anderson Foundation
Anderson Foundation, M. D.
Andersons, The
Anheuser-Busch Companies, Inc.
Annenberg Foundation
Arcadia Foundation
Armco Inc.
Astor Foundation, Vincent
Auerbach Foundation, Beatrice Fox
Avon Products, Inc.
Ball Brothers Foundation
Bank of Boston Corp.
Bank One, Youngstown, NA
Battelle Memorial Institute
BE&K Inc.
Beatty Trust, Cordelia Lunceford
Beech Aircraft Corp.
Bell Atlantic Corp.
Benedum Foundation, Claude Worthington
Bertha Foundation
Bethlehem Steel Corp.
Bigelow Foundation, F. R.
Bingham Second Betterment Fund, William
Binney & Smith Inc.
Blair and Co., William
Blaustein Foundation, Louis and Henrietta
Block, H&R
Blount, Inc.
Blue Cross & Blue Shield United of Wisconsin
Boeing Co., The
Boettcher Foundation
Boise Cascade Corporation
Borden, Inc.
Bowne Foundation, Robert
Bremer Foundation, Otto
Brunswick Corp.
Bucyrus-Erie Company
Buhl Foundation

Burden Foundation, Florence V.
Cabell Foundation, Robert G. Cabell III and Maude Morgan
Calder Foundation, Louis
Callaway Foundation
Carnegie Corporation of New York
Carolyn Foundation
Castle Foundation, Harold K. L.
Central Maine Power Co.
Champion International Corporation
Chartwell Foundation
Chase Manhattan Bank, N.A.
Chevron Corporation
Chicago Sun-Times, Inc.
Christensen Charitable and Religious Foundation, L. C.
CIGNA Corporation
CINergy
Citibank
City National Bank and Trust Co.
Clorox Co.
Clowes Fund
CNA Financial Corporation/CNA Insurance Companies
Coen Family Foundation, Charles S. and Mary
Cole Foundation, Olive B.
Columbus Dispatch Printing Co.
Comer Foundation
Commerce Bancshares, Inc.
Commerce Clearing House, Incorporated
Connecticut Mutual Life Insurance Company
Connelly Foundation
Consolidated Natural Gas Co.
Consolidated Papers, Inc.
Contran Corporation
Coors Foundation, Adolph
Copley Press, Inc.
Cornell Trust, Peter C.
Coughlin-Saunders Foundation
Cowell Foundation, S. H.
Cowles Charitable Trust
Cowles Media Co.
CPC International Inc.
Crane Co.
Crawford Estate, E. R.
Cremer Foundation
Crocker Trust, Mary A.
Crown Books
Crown Memorial, Arie and Ida
Curtice-Burns Foods, Inc.
Davenport-Hatch Foundation
Davidson Family Charitable Foundation
Dekko Foundation
DeRoy Foundation, Helen L.
Detroit Edison Co.
Dewing Foundation, Frances R.
Diamond Foundation, Aaron
Digital Equipment Corp.
Dr. Seuss Foundation
Donaldson Company, Inc.
Donnelley & Sons Co., R.R.
Donner Foundation, William H.
Dreyfus Foundation, Jean and Louis
du Pont de Nemours & Co., E. I.
Duke Power Co.
Dun & Bradstreet Corp.
Edgewater Steel Corp.
Encyclopaedia Britannica, Inc.
Ettinger Foundation
Evans Foundation, Lettie Pate
Federated Mutual Insurance Co.
Fikes Foundation, Leland
First Fidelity Bank
First Hawaiian, Inc.
First Union Corp.
First Union National Bank of Florida
Firstar Bank Milwaukee, N.A.
Fish Foundation, Ray C.
Fleet Financial Group, Inc.

Ford Foundation
Forest Oil Corp.
Foster Foundation
France Foundation, Jacob and Annita
Frear Eleemosynary Trust, Mary D. and Walter F.
Freed Foundation
Freeport-McMoRan Inc.
Frost National Bank
Fry Foundation, Lloyd A.
Gates Foundation
GATX Corp.
Gebbie Foundation
GenCorp Inc.
General Mills, Inc.
General Motors Corp.
Georgia-Pacific Corporation
Georgia Power Co.
Gheens Foundation
Ghidotti Foundation
Giant Food Stores
Gifford Charitable Corporation, Rosamond
Gilman Foundation, Howard
Glenn Foundation, Carrie C. and Lena V.
Globe Newspaper Co.
Goddard Foundation, Charles B.
Goldseker Foundation of Maryland, Morris
Grand Rapids Label Co.
Griggs and Mary Griggs Burke Foundation, Mary Livingston
Guardian Life Insurance Company of America
Gulf Coast Medical Foundation
Gulf Power Co.
Hamman Foundation, George and Mary Josephine
Hancock Foundation, Luke B.
Hardin Foundation, Phil
Harland Charitable Foundation, John and Wilhelmina D.
HarperCollins Publishers Inc.
Hasbro Inc.
Hawn Foundation
HCA Foundation
Hearst Foundation, William Randolph
Heinz Company, H. J.
Heinz Endowment, Howard
Heinz Trust, Drue
Heller Financial, Inc.
Hermann Foundation, Grover
Hershey Foods Corp.
Heublein Inc.
Hewlett Foundation, William and Flora
Higginson Trust, Corina
Hill Foundation, Sandy
Hillcrest Foundation
Hillsdale Fund
Hoag Family Foundation, George
Hoffman Foundation, Maximilian E. and Marion O.
Hopwood Charitable Trust, John M.
Houchens Foundation, Ervin G.
Houston Endowment
Houston Industries Incorporated
Howard and Bush Foundation
Hoyt Foundation, Stewart W. and Wilma C.
Hunt Charitable Trust, C. Giles
Huston Charitable Trust, Stewart
Huston Foundation
ICI Americas Inc.
Illinois Tool Works, Inc.
International Business Machines Corp.
International Paper Co.
ITT Hartford Insurance Group, Inc.
Janirve Foundation
Jarson-Stanley and Mickey Kaplan Foundation, Isaac and Esther

Jewell Memorial Foundation, Daniel Ashley and Irene Houston
Johnson Controls Inc.
Johnson Foundation, Burdine
Johnson & Higgins
Jones Foundation, Daisy Marquis
Jonsson Foundation
Journal-Gazette Co.
Joy Family Foundation
Jurzykowski Foundation, Alfred
Kansas City Southern Industries
Kaplun Foundation, Morris J. and Betty
Kaufmann Foundation, Henry
Kerr Foundation
Kettering Fund
Kiewit Foundation, Peter
Kimberly-Clark Corp.
Kiplinger Foundation
Kirkpatrick Foundation
Kline Foundation, Josiah W. and Bessie H.
Klock and Lucia Klock Kingston Foundation, Jay E.
Kmart Corporation
Knight Foundation, John S. and James L.
Komes Foundation
Lake Placid Education Foundation
Lattner Foundation, Forrest C.
Lauder Foundation
Laurel Foundation
LBJ Family Foundation
Lehigh Portland Cement Co.
Leidy Foundation, John J.
Lemberg Foundation
Life Insurance Co. of Georgia
Lipton, Thomas J.
Long Island Lighting Co.
Longwood Foundation
Louisiana-Pacific Corp.
Lux Foundation, Miranda
Lydall, Inc.
MacArthur Foundation, John D. and Catherine T.
Mardag Foundation
Maritz Inc.
Marquette Electronics, Inc.
Marshall Trust in Memory of Sanders McDaniel, Harriet McDaniel
Massengill-DeFriece Foundation
Mather Fund, Richard
Mattel, Inc.
Matthies Foundation, Katharine
Mautz Paint Co.
May Department Stores Company, The
Mayer Foundation, James and Eva
Mayor Foundation, Oliver Dewey
MCA Inc.
McCasland Foundation
McConnell Foundation
McDonald & Company Securities, Inc.
McFawn Trust No. 2, Lois Sisler
McFeely-Rogers Foundation
McInerny Foundation
McKenna Foundation, Katherine Mabis
McLean Contributionship
Mead Corporation, The
Meadows Foundation
Mellon Foundation, Andrew W.
Mellon Foundation, Richard King
Memton Fund
Merck Family Fund
Merrill Lynch & Co., Inc.
Metropolitan Life Insurance Co.
Meyerhoff Fund, Joseph
Millbrook Tribute Garden
Miller Brewing Company/North Carolina

Miller Charitable Foundation, Howard E. and Nell E.
Mitchell Energy & Development Corp.
Mobil Oil Corp.
Monfort Family Foundation
Moore Charitable Foundation, Marjorie
Morgan & Company, J.P.
Moses Fund, Henry and Lucy
Mulford Trust, Clarence E.
Munson Foundation Trust, W. B.
Murphy Foundation
Nalco Chemical Co.
National Gypsum Co.
National Westminster Bank New Jersey
Nesholm Family Foundation
Nestle USA Inc.
New-Land Foundation
New York Life Insurance Co.
New York Times Company
The New Yorker Magazine, Inc.
Newman's Own, Inc.
Norman Foundation, Summers A.
Norton Co.
OCRI Foundation
Olin Corp.
Olsson Memorial Foundation, Elis
Ore-Ida Foods, Inc.
Ottenheimer Brothers Foundation
Overbrook Foundation
Pacific Telesis Group
Paley Foundation, William S.
Palmer Fund, Frank Loomis
Parsons Foundation, Ralph M.
Payne Foundation, Frank E. and Seba B.
Peoples Energy Corp.
Peppers Foundation, Ann
Perkin-Elmer Corp.
Pew Charitable Trusts
Pfizer, Inc.
Pforzheimer Foundation, Carl and Lily
PHH Corporation
Pick, Jr. Fund, Albert
Piper Foundation, Minnie Stevens
Pittsburgh Child Guidance Foundation
PNC Bank, N.A.
Polaroid Corp.
Potomac Electric Power Co.
Prairie Foundation
Price Associates, T. Rowe
Providence Journal Company
Providian Corporation
Prudential Insurance Co. of America, The
Prudential Securities, Inc.
Puterbaugh Foundation
Raymond Corp.
Retirement Research Foundation
Reynolds Foundation, Donald W.
Riggs Benevolent Fund
Rockwell Fund
Rockwell International Corporation
Rohatyn Foundation, Felix and Elizabeth
Rohm & Haas Co.
Rose's Stores, Inc.
Ross Memorial Foundation, Will
Royal Group, Inc.
Rubinstein Foundation, Helena
SAFECO Corp.
Saint Paul Companies, Inc.
Salomon Foundation, Richard and Edna
Salomon Inc.
San Diego Gas & Electric
Sara Lee Corp.
Sara Lee Hosiery, Inc.
Sargent Foundation, Newell B.
Sarkeys Foundation
SBC Communications Inc.
Scaife Family Foundation

Morris Foundation, Margaret T.
Morris Foundation, William T.
Mosbacher, Jr. Foundation, Emil
Moses Fund, Henry and Lucy
Mulcahy Foundation
Munger Foundation, Alfred C.
Murdock Charitable Trust, M. J.
Murphy Foundation
Nabisco Foods Group
Nalco Chemical Co.
New-Land Foundation
New York Life Insurance Co.
New York Mercantile Exchange
New York Stock Exchange, Inc.
The New Yorker Magazine, Inc.
Nias Foundation, Henry
Noble Foundation, Edward John
Norfolk Shipbuilding & Drydock Corp.
Norton Family Foundation, Peter
NYNEX Corporation
Oaklawn Foundation
O'Connor Foundation, A. Lindsay and Olive B.
O'Connor Foundation, Kathryn
Offield Family Foundation
Olsson Memorial Foundation, Elis
O'Quinn Foundation, John M. and Nancy C.
Osher Foundation, Bernard
Overlake Foundation
Owsley Foundation, Alvin and Lucy
Pacific Mutual Life Insurance Co.
Packard Foundation, David and Lucile
Paley Foundation, William S.
Palisades Educational Foundation
Peters Foundation, R. D. and Linda
Pew Charitable Trusts
Pfizer, Inc.
Phelps Dodge Corporation
Phillips Family Foundation, Jay and Rose
Piankova Foundation, Tatiana
Polaroid Corp.
Porter Foundation, Mrs. Cheever
Porter Testamentary Trust, James Hyde
Potter Foundation, Justin and Valere
Prudential Insurance Co. of America, The
Pulitzer Publishing Co.
Ralston Purina Co.
Ratner Foundation, Milton M.
Reed Foundation
Regenstein Foundation
Reinberger Foundation
Rice Foundation
RJR Nabisco Inc.
Rosen Foundation, Joseph
Ross Memorial Foundation, Will
Rowland Foundation
Royal Foundation, May Mitchell
Rubin Family Fund, Cele H. and William B.
Rubinstein Foundation, Helena
Ryan Foundation, David Claude
Saltonstall Charitable Foundation, Richard
San Diego Gas & Electric
Santa Fe Pacific Corporation
Sarkeys Foundation
SBC Communications Inc.
Scaife Family Foundation
Schering-Plough Corp.
Schiff Foundation, Dorothy
Schlumberger Ltd.
Scholl Foundation, Dr.
Schroeder Foundation, Walter

Schwartz Fund for Education and Health Research, Arnold and Marie
Scott Foundation, Walter
Scott Foundation, William E.
Scurlock Foundation
Sedgwick James Inc.
Seton Leather Co.
Shaw Foundation, Arch W.
Shell Oil Company
Shenandoah Life Insurance Co.
Slifka Foundation, Joseph and Sylvia
Smith Charitable Foundation, Clara Blackford Smith and W. Aubrey
Smith Corp., A.O.
SmithKline Beecham Corp.
Snow Memorial Trust, John Ben
Solow Foundation
Sonat Inc.
Spang & Co.
Sprague Educational and Charitable Foundation, Seth
Springs Foundation
Stabler Foundation, Donald B. and Dorothy L.
Stackpole-Hall Foundation
Starr Foundation
Staunton Farm Foundation
Steinbach Fund, Ruth and Milton
Stevens Foundation, John T.
Stupp Foundation, Norman J.
Sturgis Charitable and Educational Trust, Roy and Christine
Sulzberger Foundation
Sunnen Foundation
Swift Co. Inc., John S.
Taubman Foundation, A. Alfred
Teagle Foundation
Temple Foundation, T. L. L.
Texaco Inc.
Texas Commerce Bank-Houston, N.A.
Textron, Inc.
Thalhimer and Family Foundation, Charles G.
Towsley Foundation, Harry A. and Margaret D.
Travelers Inc.
Trull Foundation
Trust Company Bank
Turner Charitable Foundation
Turrell Fund
Union Camp Corporation
Unocal Corp.
Uris Brothers Foundation
Van Houten Memorial Fund
Vernon Fund, Miles Hodsdon
Vetlesen Foundation, G. Unger
Wal-Mart Stores, Inc.
Washington Forrest Foundation
Waters Charitable Trust, Robert S.
Wean Foundation, Raymond John
Weaver Foundation, Gil and Dody
Weezie Foundation
Weingart Foundation
Weinstein Foundation, J.
Wells Foundation, Franklin H. and Ruth L.
Wertheim Foundation, Dr. Herbert A.
Westvaco Corporation
Wheat First Butcher Singer, Inc.
Whirlpool Corporation
Whitehead Charitable Foundation
Whiting Foundation
WICOR, Inc.
Widgeon Foundation
Wiegand Foundation, E. L.
Wildermuth Foundation, E. F.
Wiley & Sons, Inc., John
Winston Foundation, Norman and Rosita
Witco Corp.
Worthington Foods
Zenkel Foundation

Zlinkoff Fund for Medical Research and Education, Sergei S.

Minority Education

Abbott Laboratories
Abell-Hanger Foundation
Achelis Foundation
Acushnet Co.
Aetna Life & Casualty Co.
Ahmanson Foundation
Air Products and Chemicals, Inc.
AKC Fund
Akzo America
Akzo Chemicals Inc.
Alabama Power Co.
Albertson's Inc.
Alcon Laboratories, Inc.
Aldus Corp.
Allegheny Ludlum Corp.
Allendale Insurance Co.
AlliedSignal Inc.
Allyn Foundation
Altman Foundation
Alumax Inc.
Aluminum Co. of America
AMCORE Bank, N.A. Rockford
American Brands, Inc.
American National Bank & Trust Co. of Chicago
American Natural Resources Company
American President Companies, Ltd.
American United Life Insurance Co.
Ameritas Life Insurance Corp.
Amoco Corporation
AMP Incorporated
AMR Corp.
Andersen Corp.
Andersen Foundation
Anderson Foundation, John W.
Anderson Foundation, M. D.
Andersons, The
Andrews Foundation
Anheuser-Busch Companies, Inc.
Annenberg Foundation
Apple Computer, Inc.
Appleby Trust, Scott B. and Annie P.
Appleton Papers Inc.
Archer-Daniels-Midland Co.
Arkansas Power & Light Co.
Arkell Hall Foundation
Armco Inc.
AT&T Corp.
Atran Foundation
Avon Products, Inc.
Babson Foundation, Paul and Edith
Baehr Foundation, Louis W. and Dolpha
Balfour Foundation, L. G.
Ball Foundation, George and Frances
Bank of New York Company, Inc.
Bank One, Youngstown, NA
BankAmerica Corp.
Bankers Trust Company
Banta Corp.
Barker Foundation, J.M.R.
Barra Foundation
Battelle Memorial Institute
BE&K Inc.
Beazley Foundation/Frederick Foundation
Bell Atlantic Corp.
Bemis Company, Inc.
Benenson Foundation, Frances and Benjamin
Berwind Corporation
Besser Foundation
Bethlehem Steel Corp.
Bettingen Corporation, Burton G.
Bigelow Foundation, F. R.
Blandin Foundation
Block, H&R

Blount, Inc.
Blum-Kovler Foundation
Bodman Foundation
Boeing Co., The
Boise Cascade Corporation
Borden, Inc.
Borman's Inc.
Boston Edison Co.
Bowater Incorporated
BP America Inc.
Brach Foundation, Helen
Bremer Foundation, Otto
Bridgestone/Firestone, Inc.
Bristol-Myers Squibb Company
Brown & Williamson Tobacco Corp.
Brunswick Corp.
Bucyrus-Erie Company
Buhl Foundation
Burlington Industries, Inc.
Burnett-Tandy Foundation
Bush Foundation
Cabot Corp.
Cain Foundation, Effie and Wofford
Cain Foundation, Gordon and Mary
Calder Foundation, Louis
Calhoun Charitable Trust, Kenneth
Campbell Foundation
Carnegie Corporation of New York
Carpenter Technology Corp.
Carter Foundation, Amon G.
Cayuga Foundation
CBS, Inc.
Centerior Energy Corp.
Central Maine Power Co.
Champion International Corporation
Charina Foundation
Chase Manhattan Bank, N.A.
Chesapeake Corp.
Chesebrough-Pond's USA Co.
Chevron Corporation
Chicago Sun-Times, Inc.
Childs Charitable Foundation, Roberta M.
Chrysler Corp.
Citibank
Clapp Charitable and Educational Trust, George H.
Clark Foundation
Clorox Co.
Clowes Fund
CNA Financial Corporation/CNA Insurance Companies
Coen Family Foundation, Charles S. and Mary
Cogswell Benevolent Trust
Comerica Incorporated
Commerce Clearing House, Incorporated
Connecticut Mutual Life Insurance Company
Consolidated Natural Gas Co.
Consolidated Papers, Inc.
Continental Corp.
Coors Foundation, Adolph
Cornell Trust, Peter C.
Corning Incorporated
Cowles Charitable Trust
Cowles Media Co.
CPC International Inc.
Cranston Print Works Company
Crocker Trust, Mary A.
Crown Books
CS First Boston Corporation
Culver Foundation, Constans
Cummings Foundation, James H.
Cummins Engine Co.
Curtice-Burns Foods, Inc.
Dana Foundation, Charles A.
Davis Foundation, Edwin W. and Catherine M.
Davis Foundation, Irene E. and George A.
Daywood Foundation
Deere & Co.
Dekko Foundation
Delaware North Co., Inc.

Dentsply International Inc.
DeRoy Testamentary Foundation
Detroit Edison Co.
Dexter Charitable Fund, Eugene A.
Dexter Corporation
Diamond Foundation, Aaron
Digital Equipment Corp.
Dodge Foundation, Cleveland H.
Dodge Foundation, Geraldine R.
Donaldson Company, Inc.
Douglas & Lomason Company
Douty Foundation
Dow Corning Corp.
Dow Jones & Company, Inc.
Dresser Industries, Inc.
Dreyfus Foundation, Max and Victoria
du Pont de Nemours & Co., E. I.
Duchossois Industries Inc.
Duke Endowment
Duke Power Co.
Dun & Bradstreet Corp.
Duncan Trust, John G.
Durfee Foundation
Eastman Kodak Company
Eaton Corporation
Eden Hall Foundation
El Pomar Foundation
Elf Atochem North America, Inc.
Enron Corp.
Ettinger Foundation
Evans Foundation, Lettie Pate
Exxon Corporation
Fair Foundation, R. W.
Fair Oaks Foundation, Inc.
Farish Fund, William Stamps
Favrot Fund
Federal-Mogul Corporation
Fink Foundation
First Chicago Corp.
First Fidelity Bank
First Interstate Bank of Oregon
First Union Corp.
Firstar Bank Milwaukee, N.A.
Fischbach Foundation
Fish Foundation, Ray C.
Fleet Financial Group, Inc.
Fleishhacker Foundation
Fohs Foundation
Folger Fund
Forbes Fund
Ford Foundation
Ford Fund, William and Martha
Ford II Fund, Henry
Ford Motor Co.
Fort Wayne National Bank
Freeman Charitable Trust, Samuel
Freeport-McMoRan Inc.
Frohring Foundation, Paul and Maxine
Frueauff Foundation, Charles A.
Fry Foundation, Lloyd A.
Fujitsu America, Inc.
Gap, Inc., The
GAR Foundation
GATX Corp.
Gebbie Foundation
GenCorp Inc.
General American Life Insurance Co.
General Mills, Inc.
General Motors Corp.
Georgia-Pacific Corporation
Georgia Power Co.
Getty Trust, J. Paul
Giant Eagle, Inc.
Giant Food Inc.
Giant Food Stores
Gleason Foundation
Goldberg Family Foundation
Goldie-Anna Charitable Trust
Good Samaritan
Goodrich Co., The B.F.
Graham Fund, Philip L.
Grand Rapids Label Co.
Great-West Life Assurance Co.
Greenwall Foundation

First Union Corp.
Frear Eleemosynary Trust, Mary D. and Walter F.
Freeport-McMoRan Inc.
Frohring Foundation, William O. and Gertrude Lewis
Frost National Bank
Fry Foundation, Lloyd A.
GATX Corp.
General Mills, Inc.
Glaser Foundation
Globe Newspaper Co.
Glosser Foundation, David A.
Goldseker Foundation of Maryland, Morris
Graham Fund, Philip L.
Greve Foundation, William and Mary
Grundy Foundation
Hachar Charitable Trust, D. D.
Hancock Foundation, Luke B.
Hardin Foundation, Phil
HCA Foundation
Heckscher Foundation for Children
Heginbotham Trust, Will E.
Houston Endowment
Hoyt Foundation, Stewart W. and Willma C.
Humana, Inc.
Hygeia Dairy Co.
Jackson Foundation
JELD-WEN, Inc.
Johnson & Higgins
Jones Foundation, Daisy Marquis
Jones Foundation, Helen
Kansas City Southern Industries
Kiewit Foundation, Peter
Koret Foundation
Lee Endowment Foundation
Lehigh Portland Cement Co.
Leuthold Foundation
Liz Claiborne, Inc.
Longwood Foundation
Madison Gas & Electric Co.
Mailman Family Foundation, A. L.
Mandeville Foundation
Maneely Fund
Mardag Foundation
Maritz Inc.
Marmot Foundation
Martini Foundation, Nicholas
Mautz Paint Co.
McCune Charitable Foundation, Marshall and Perrine D.
McElroy Trust, R. J.
McGonagle Foundation, Dextra Baldwin
McInerny Foundation
Meadows Foundation
Meyer Memorial Trust
Miller Foundation
Murphey Foundation, Lluella Morey
The New Yorker Magazine, Inc.
Northern States Power Co. (Minnesota)
Norton Co.
Norton Family Foundation, Peter
NYNEX Corporation
Odell Fund, Robert Stewart Odell and Helen Pfeiffer
Ore-Ida Foods, Inc.
Pacific Telesis Group
Parsons Foundation, Ralph M.
Pella Corporation
Penn Foundation, William
Peterson Foundation, Hal and Charlie
PHH Corporation
Polaroid Corp.
Price Foundation, Lucien B. and Katherine E.
Prince Trust, Abbie Norman
Providian Corporation
Prudential Insurance Co. of America, The
Regenstein Foundation
RJR Nabisco Inc.
Rockwell Fund

Rohm & Haas Co.
Roseburg Forest Products Co.
Royal Group, Inc.
Rubin Family Fund, Cele H. and William B.
Rubinstein Foundation, Helena
San Diego Gas & Electric
Sara Lee Hosiery, Inc.
Scherer Foundation, Karla
Schumann Fund for New Jersey
Sedgwick James Inc.
Selby and Marie Selby Foundation, William G.
Skillman Foundation
Snow Foundation, John Ben
Snyder Foundation, Harold B. and Dorothy A.
Taylor Foundation, Ruth and Vernon
Tecumseh Products Co.
Thomas Foundation, Joan and Lee
Towsley Foundation, Harry A. and Margaret D.
Transco Energy Co.
Travelers Inc.
Trees Charitable Trust, Edith L.
Tucker Charitable Trust, Rose E.
Turner Charitable Foundation
Turrell Fund
Union Camp Corporation
U.S. Bank of Washington
Uris Brothers Foundation
Utica National Insurance Group
Van Buren Foundation
Wal-Mart Stores, Inc.
Wallace-Reader's Digest Fund, DeWitt
Washington Mutual Savings Bank
Weingart Foundation
Wheeler Foundation, Wilmot
Wiley & Sons, Inc., John
Williams Charitable Trust, Mary Jo
Windham Foundation
Wisconsin Power & Light Co.
Witco Corp.
Woodward Fund

Private Education (Precollege)

ACF Industries, Inc.
Achelis Foundation
Adams Foundation, Arthur F. and Alice E.
AEGON USA Inc.
Ahmanson Foundation
AKC Fund
Alavi Foundation of New York
Alcon Laboratories, Inc.
Alexander Foundation, Joseph
Allegheny Foundation
Allen Brothers Foundation
Allendale Insurance Co.
AlliedSignal Inc.
Allyn Foundation
Altman Foundation
Aluminum Co. of America
Amado Foundation, Maurice
AMCORE Bank, N.A. Rockford
American Brands, Inc.
American Fidelity Corporation
American General Finance Corp.
American National Bank & Trust Co. of Chicago
American Optical Corp.
American President Companies, Ltd.
Ameritas Life Insurance Corp.
Ames Charitable Trust, Harriett
AMETEK, Inc.
Amfac/JMB Hawaii Inc.
AMP Incorporated
Andersen Corp.
Andersen Foundation
Anderson Foundation, John W.

Anderson Foundation, M. D.
Andersons, The
Andreas Foundation
Andrews Foundation
Anheuser-Busch Companies, Inc.
Annenberg Foundation
Ansin Private Foundation, Ronald M.
Ansley Foundation, Dantzler Bond
Appleby Trust, Scott B. and Annie P.
Arcadia Foundation
Archer-Daniels-Midland Co.
Arkelian Foundation, Ben H. and Gladys
Armstrong Foundation
Arnhold Foundation
Arnold Fund
Asplundh Foundation
Atherton Family Foundation
Auerbach Foundation, Beatrice Fox
Avery Arts Foundation, Milton and Sally
Ayres Foundation, Inc.
Babson Foundation, Paul and Edith
Baehr Foundation, Louis W. and Dolpha
Baker Trust, George F.
Baldwin Foundation, David M. and Barbara
Baldwin Memorial Foundation, Fred
Ball Brothers Foundation
Bank of New York Company, Inc.
Bank One, Texas-Houston Office
Bard Foundation, Robert
Barker Foundation, J.M.R.
Barra Foundation
Batts Foundation
Bauervic Foundation, Charles M.
Baughman Foundation
Bay Foundation
Beal Foundation
Bean Foundation, Norwin S. and Elizabeth N.
BE&K Inc.
Beattie Foundation Trust, Cordelia Lee
Beatty Trust, Cordelia Lunceford
Bechtel Charitable Remainder Uni-Trust, Marie H.
Bechtel, Jr. Foundation, S. D.
Beck Foundation, Elsie E. and Joseph W.
Bedsole Foundation, J. L.
Bell Foundation, James F.
Beloit Foundation
Bemis Company, Inc.
Benedum Foundation, Claude Worthington
Benenson Foundation, Frances and Benjamin
Benetton Services Corp.
Benwood Foundation
Bethlehem Steel Corp.
Bettingen Corporation, Burton G.
Beveridge Foundation, Frank Stanley
Bingham Foundation, William
Bingham Second Betterment Fund, William
Binney & Smith Inc.
Binswanger Cos.
Bird Corp.
Bishop Foundation, E. K. and Lillian F.
Blake Foundation, S. P.
Blaustein Foundation, Louis and Henrietta
Block, H&R
Bloedorn Foundation, Walter A.
Blount, Inc.
Blue Bell, Inc.
Blum Foundation, Edna F.
Blum-Kovler Foundation

Bodman Foundation
Boeing Co., The
Boettcher Foundation
Booth Ferris Foundation
Borden, Inc.
Borkee Hagley Foundation
Borman's Inc.
Boston Edison Co.
Boswell Foundation, James G.
Bowen Foundation, Ethel N.
Brach Foundation, Helen
Brackenridge Foundation, George W.
Brady Foundation
Bremer Foundation, Otto
Brenner Foundation, Mervyn
Breyer Foundation
Bridwell Foundation, J. S.
Bright Family Foundation
Bristol-Myers Squibb Company
Broadhurst Foundation
Bryant Foundation
Bucyrus-Erie Company
Buhl Foundation
Bunbury Company
Burchfield Foundation, Charles E.
Burden Foundation, Florence V.
Burdines Inc.
Burkitt Foundation
Burlington Industries, Inc.
Burnett-Tandy Foundation
Butz Foundation
Cabot Corp.
Cabot Family Charitable Trust
Cafritz Foundation, Morris and Gwendolyn
Cain Foundation, Effie and Wofford
Cain Foundation, Gordon and Mary
Calder Foundation, Louis
Calhoun Charitable Trust, Kenneth
Campbell Foundation
Campbell Foundation, Ruth and Henry
Campini Foundation, Frank A.
Cape Branch Foundation
Carolyn Foundation
Carter Foundation, Amon G.
Carter Foundation, Beirne
Caspersen Foundation for Aid to Health and Education, O. W.
Castle Foundation, Harold K. L.
Cayuga Foundation
CBS, Inc.
Centerior Energy Corp.
Central National Bank
Chadwick Fund, Dorothy Jordan
Champlin Foundations
Charina Foundation
Chartwell Foundation
Chase Manhattan Bank, N.A.
Chazen Foundation
Cheatham Foundation, Owen
Cheney Foundation, Ben B.
Chesapeake Corp.
Chesebrough-Pond's USA Co.
Childs Charitable Foundation, Roberta M.
Christensen Charitable and Religious Foundation, L. C.
CIGNA Corporation
Citibank
Citizens Bank of Rhode Island
Claiborne and Art Ortenberg Foundation, Liz
Clapp Charitable and Educational Trust, George H.
CLARCOR Inc.
Clark Foundation
Clarke Trust, John
Clarkson Foundation, Jeniam
Clay Foundation
Clayton Fund
Clements Foundation
Clorox Co.
Close Foundation
Clowes Fund

CNA Financial Corporation/CNA Insurance Companies
Coen Family Foundation, Charles S. and Mary
Cogswell Benevolent Trust
Cole Foundation, Olive B.
Cole Trust, Quincy
Coleman Foundation, George E.
Collins Foundation
Collins, Jr. Foundation, George Fulton
Colonial Life & Accident Insurance Co.
Columbia Foundation
Columbus Dispatch Printing Co.
Commerce Bancshares, Inc.
Commerce Clearing House, Incorporated
Connecticut Mutual Life Insurance Company
Connelly Foundation
Connemara Fund
Contran Corporation
Cooke Foundation
Coors Foundation, Adolph
Copley Press, Inc.
Cord Foundation, E. L.
Cornell Trust, Peter C.
Coughlin-Saunders Foundation
Cowles Charitable Trust
Cowles Foundation, Gardner and Florence Call
Cowles Media Co.
CPC International Inc.
Crandall Memorial Foundation, J. Ford
Crane Co.
Crestlea Foundation
Crocker Trust, Mary A.
Crown Books
Crown Memorial, Arie and Ida
Crystal Trust
CS First Boston Corporation
Cullen Foundation
Culpeper Memorial Foundation, Daphne Seybolt
Culver Foundation, Constans
Cummings Foundation, James H.
Cummins Engine Co.
Cuneo Foundation
Daily News
Dalton Foundation, Harry L.
Dana Charitable Trust, Eleanor Naylor
Dana Foundation, Charles A.
Daniel Foundation of Alabama
Darby Foundation
Dart Group Corp.
Dater Foundation, Charles H.
Davenport-Hatch Foundation
Davis Foundation, Edwin W. and Catherine M.
Davis Foundation, Irene E. and George A.
Day Foundation, Nancy Sayles
Daywood Foundation
Deere & Co.
Dekko Foundation
Delaware North Co., Inc.
Dell Foundation, Hazel
DeRoy Foundation, Helen L.
DeRoy Testamentary Foundation
Detroit Edison Co.
Deuble Foundation, George H.
DeVore Foundation
Dewing Foundation, Frances R.
Dillon Dunwalke Trust, Clarence and Anne
Dillon Foundation
Dingman Foundation, Michael D.
Dodge Foundation, Cleveland H.
Dodge Foundation, Geraldine R.
Dodge Jones Foundation
Donaldson Company, Inc.
Donnelley Foundation, Gaylord and Dorothy

Winthrop Trust, Clara B.
Wise Foundation and
 Charitable Trust, Watson W.
Witco Corp.
Wood Foundation of
 Chambersburg, PA
Woodward Fund
Woolley Foundation, Vasser
Worthington Foods
Wyman Youth Trust
Y and H Soda Foundation
Yeager Charitable Trust,
 Lester E.
Young Foundation, Hugo H.
 and Mabel B.
Young Foundation, Robert R.
Zarrow Foundation, Anne and
 Henry

Public Education (Precollege)

Acushnet Co.
Adler Foundation Trust, Philip
 D. and Henrietta B.
AEGON USA Inc.
Aetna Life & Casualty Co.
Ahmanson Foundation
Akzo Chemicals Inc.
Alabama Power Co.
Alcon Laboratories, Inc.
Allegheny Foundation
Allendale Insurance Co.
AlliedSignal Inc.
Allyn Foundation
Aluminum Co. of America
AMCORE Bank, N.A.
 Rockford
American Brands, Inc.
American Fidelity Corporation
American General Finance
 Corp.
American Natural Resources
 Company
American Optical Corp.
American President
 Companies, Ltd.
Amfac/JMB Hawaii Inc.
Amoco Corporation
AMP Incorporated
Andersen Corp.
Andersen Foundation
Andres Charitable Trust, Frank
 G.
Andrews Foundation
Annenberg Foundation
AON Corporation
Apple Computer, Inc.
Arkansas Power & Light Co.
Arkelian Foundation, Ben H.
 and Gladys
Arkell Hall Foundation
Arnold Fund
Ashtabula Foundation
Astor Foundation, Vincent
AT&T Corp.
Babcock & Wilcox Co.
Babson Foundation, Paul and
 Edith
Baehr Foundation, Louis W.
 and Dolpha
Balfour Foundation, L. G.
Ball Brothers Foundation
Ball Foundation, George and
 Frances
Banc One Wisconsin Corp.
Bank of Boston Corp.
Bank One, Texas-Houston
 Office
Bankers Trust Company
Bard Foundation, Robert
Barker Foundation, J.M.R.
Battelle Memorial Institute
Batts Foundation
Baughman Foundation
Bay Area Foods
Bay Foundation
Beattie Foundation Trust,
 Cordelia Lee
Beatty Trust, Cordelia
 Lunceford
Beazley Foundation/Frederick
 Foundation

Beck Foundation, Elsie E. and
 Joseph W.
Bedsole Foundation, J. L.
Bell Atlantic Corp.
Bemis Company, Inc.
Benetton Services Corp.
Benwood Foundation
Berger Foundation, H. N. and
 Frances C.
Bertha Foundation
Besser Foundation
Bethlehem Steel Corp.
Betts Industries
Bingham Foundation, William
Binney & Smith Inc.
Bird Corp.
Bishop Foundation, E. K. and
 Lillian F.
Bissell Foundation, J. Walton
Blandin Foundation
Block, H&R
Blount Educational and
 Charitable Foundation,
 Mildred Weedon
Blount, Inc.
Blue Bell, Inc.
Bodman Foundation
Boeing Co., The
Borden, Inc.
Boswell Foundation, James G.
Boutell Memorial Fund
Bowen Foundation, Ethel N.
BP America Inc.
Brach Foundation, Helen
Brackenridge Foundation,
 George W.
Brenner Foundation, Mervyn
Bridgestone/Firestone, Inc.
Bridwell Foundation, J. S.
Brown Foundation, M. K.
Bucyrus-Erie Company
Buhl Foundation
Burden Foundation, Florence
 V.
Burdines Inc.
Burlington Industries, Inc.
Burnett-Tandy Foundation
Bush Foundation
Cabot Corp.
Cafritz Foundation, Morris and
 Gwendolyn
Calder Foundation, Louis
Campbell Foundation, Ruth
 and Henry
Carnahan-Jackson Foundation
Carnegie Corporation of New
 York
Carolyn Foundation
Carpenter Foundation, E.
 Rhodes and Leona B.
Carter Foundation, Amon G.
Carver Charitable Trust, Roy J.
Catlin Charitable Trust,
 Kathleen K.
Cayuga Foundation
Central Fidelity Banks, Inc.
Central Maine Power Co.
Champion International
 Corporation
Champlin Foundations
Chartwell Foundation
Chase Manhattan Bank, N.A.
CHC Foundation
Chesapeake Corp.
Chevron Corporation
Christensen Charitable and
 Religious Foundation, L. C.
CIGNA Corporation
CINergy
Citibank
Clapp Charitable and
 Educational Trust, George H.
Clark Foundation
Clay Foundation
Clorox Co.
Close Foundation
CNA Financial
 Corporation/CNA Insurance
 Companies
Cole Foundation, Olive B.
Cole Trust, Quincy
Colonial Life & Accident
 Insurance Co.
Columbus Dispatch Printing
 Co.

Comer Foundation
Comerica Incorporated
Commerce Bancshares, Inc.
Commercial Bank
Connecticut Mutual Life
 Insurance Company
Connelly Foundation
Consolidated Natural Gas Co.
Consumers Power Co.
Contran Corporation
Cooke Foundation
Cord Foundation, E. L.
Corning Incorporated
Cowell Foundation, S. H.
Cowles Media Co.
CPC International Inc.
Crane Co.
Crocker Trust, Mary A.
CS First Boston Corporation
Cullen Foundation
Cummins Engine Co.
Cuneo Foundation
Dana Foundation, Charles A.
Daniel Foundation of Alabama
Daugherty Foundation
Davenport Trust Fund
Davidson Family Charitable
 Foundation
Davis Foundation, Irene E. and
 George A.
Davis Foundations, Arthur
 Vining
Daywood Foundation
Deere & Co.
Dekko Foundation
Delano Foundation, Mignon
 Sherwood
Dentsply International Inc.
DeRoy Testamentary
 Foundation
Detroit Edison Co.
Dewing Foundation, Frances R.
Dexter Charitable Fund,
 Eugene A.
Dexter Corporation
Diamond Foundation, Aaron
Dillon Foundation
Dishman Charitable
 Foundation Trust, H. E. and
 Kate
Dodge Foundation, Cleveland
 H.
Dodge Foundation, Geraldine
 R.
Dodge Jones Foundation
Donaldson Company, Inc.
Doss Foundation, M. S.
Douty Foundation
Dow Foundation, Herbert H.
 and Grace A.
Dreyfus Foundation, Max and
 Victoria
du Pont de Nemours & Co., E.
 I.
Duchossois Industries Inc.
Duke Power Co.
Duncan Foundation, Lillian H.
 and C. W.
Eastman Kodak Company
Eaton Corporation
Eberly Foundation
Eccles Foundation, Ralph M.
 and Ella M.
Eddy Family Memorial Fund,
 C. K.
El Pomar Foundation
Enron Corp.
Ettinger Foundation
Evans Foundation, Lettie Pate
Evans Foundation, Thomas J.
Exxon Corporation
Favrot Fund
Federal-Mogul Corporation
Fenton Foundation
Fieldcrest Cannon Inc.
Fikes Foundation, Leland
Finch Foundation, Doak
Finch Foundation, Thomas
 Austin
Fink Foundation
Fireman's Fund Insurance Co.
First Hawaiian, Inc.
First Tennessee Bank
First Union Corp.

First Union National Bank of
 Florida
Fleet Financial Group, Inc.
Fleishhacker Foundation
Flowers Charitable Trust,
 Albert W. and Edith V.
Fondren Foundation
Forbes Inc.
Ford Foundation
Ford Motor Co.
Forest Foundation
Freeman Charitable Trust,
 Samuel
Freeport-McMoRan Inc.
Frese Foundation, Arnold D.
Friedman Family Foundation
Friendship Fund
Frost National Bank
Fry Foundation, Lloyd A.
Fund for New Jersey
Gallagher Family Foundation,
 Lewis P.
Gannett Publishing Co., Guy
Gap, Inc., The
GAR Foundation
Garland Foundation, John
 Jewett and H. Chandler
Gates Foundation
Gebbie Foundation
Gellert Foundation, Celia Berta
GenCorp Inc.
General American Life
 Insurance Co.
General Mills, Inc.
General Motors Corp.
Geneseo Foundation
GenRad
Georgia Power Co.
German Protestant Orphan
 Asylum Association
Gheens Foundation
Ghidotti Foundation
Gifford Charitable
 Corporation, Rosamond
Gilmore Foundation, William
 G.
Glaser Foundation
Glenn Foundation, Carrie C.
 and Lena V.
Glick Foundation, Eugene and
 Marilyn
Globe Newspaper Co.
Glosser Foundation, David A.
Goddard Foundation, Charles
 B.
Good Samaritan
Graham Fund, Philip L.
Greenwall Foundation
Gregg-Graniteville Foundation
Groome Beatty Trust, Helen D.
Grundy Foundation
Guaranty Bank & Trust Co.
Gulf Coast Medical Foundation
Gulf Power Co.
Guttman Foundation, Stella
 and Charles
Hachar Charitable Trust, D. D.
Haigh-Scatena Foundation
Hallett Charitable Trust, E. W.
Hammer Foundation, Armand
Hancock Foundation, Luke B.
Handy and Harman Foundation
Hanson Industries North
 America
Harcourt General, Inc.
Hardin Foundation, Phil
Harland Charitable
 Foundation, John and
 Wilhelmina D.
Harmon Foundation, Pearl M.
 and Julia J.
Harriman Foundation, Gladys
 and Roland
Harriman Foundation, Mary W.
Harrison Foundation, Fred G.
Harsco Corp.
Hartmarx Corporation
Hawkins Foundation, Robert Z.
Hazen Foundation, Edward W.
HCA Foundation
Hechinger Co.
Heckscher Foundation for
 Children
Heginbotham Trust, Will E.
Heinz Company, H. J.

Heinz Endowment, Howard
Heinz Endowment, Vira I.
Heller Charitable Foundation,
 Clarence E.
Heller Financial, Inc.
Herrick Foundation
Hewlett-Packard Co.
Hickory Tech Corp.
Hill Foundation, Sandy
Hillcrest Foundation
Hillsdale Fund
Hoag Family Foundation,
 George
Hoover Foundation
Hopwood Charitable Trust,
 John M.
Houston Endowment
Howard and Bush Foundation
Howe and Mitchell B. Howe
 Foundation, Lucille Horton
Hudson-Webber Foundation
Hulbert Foundation, Nila B.
Humana, Inc.
Hunt Charitable Trust, C. Giles
Huston Charitable Trust,
 Stewart
Hyde and Watson Foundation
Hygeia Dairy Co.
IBP, Inc.
IES Industries, Inc.
Inland Container Corp.
International Business
 Machines Corp.
International Paper Co.
ITT Hartford Insurance Group,
 Inc.
Jackson Foundation
Jacobson Foundation, Bernard
 H. and Blanche E.
Jameson Foundation, J. W. and
 Ida M.
Janesville Foundation
Jarson-Stanley and Mickey
 Kaplan Foundation, Isaac
 and Esther
Jennings Foundation, Mary
 Hillman
Jewell Memorial Foundation,
 Daniel Ashley and Irene
 Houston
Jewish Healthcare Foundation
 of Pittsburgh
JFM Foundation
Johnson Foundation, Burdine
Johnson Foundation, Helen K.
 and Arthur E.
Johnson & Higgins
Johnson & Son, S.C.
Jonsson Foundation
Joslin-Needham Family
 Foundation
Jostens, Inc.
Journal-Gazette Co.
Kansas City Southern
 Industries
Kantzler Foundation
Kaufmann Foundation, Henry
Kayser Foundation
Kempner Fund, Harris and
 Eliza
Kennecott Corporation
Kern Foundation Trust
Kerr Foundation
Kiewit Foundation, Peter
Kiplinger Foundation
Kirbo Charitable Trust,
 Thomas M. and Irene B.
Kirkpatrick Foundation
Kitzmiller/Bales Trust
Klipstein Foundation, Ernest
 Christian
Knapp Foundation
Knight Foundation, John S.
 and James L.
Knudsen Foundation, Tom and
 Valley
Koehler Foundation, Marcia
 and Otto
Kohn-Joseloff Foundation
Koret Foundation
Kuyper Foundation, Peter H.
 and E. Lucille
La-Z-Boy Chair Co.
Laffey-McHugh Foundation
Lang Foundation, Eugene M.

Fohs Foundation
Fondren Foundation
Forest Foundation
French Oil Mill Machinery Co.
Fruehauf Foundation
Gellert Foundation, Carl
Gellert Foundation, Celia Berta
General Mills, Inc.
Gheens Foundation
Giant Eagle, Inc.
Gillette Co.
Gilmore Foundation, William G.
Glanville Family Foundation
Gleason Foundation
Glosser Foundation, David A.
Guttman Foundation, Stella and Charles
Habig Foundation, Arnold F.
Hafif Family Foundation
Hagedorn Fund
Hallett Charitable Trust, E. W.
Hallett Charitable Trust, Jessie F.
Hamilton Bank
Hamman Foundation, George and Mary Josephine
Hanes Foundation, John W. and Anna H.
Hardin Foundation, Phil
Harland Charitable Foundation, John and Wilhelmina D.
Harriman Foundation, Mary W.
Harsco Corp.
Hawn Foundation
Hearst Foundation, William Randolph
Hechinger Co.
Hecht-Levi Foundation
Heinz Company, H. J.
Heinz Endowment, Vira I.
Helmerich Foundation
Helms Foundation
Herrick Foundation
Hershey Foods Corp.
Hickory Tech Corp.
High Foundation
Hillman Foundation
Hillsdale Fund
Homeland Foundation
Houston Endowment
Huston Charitable Trust, Stewart
Huston Foundation
Hyde and Watson Foundation
International Foundation
ITT Hartford Insurance Group, Inc.
Jameson Foundation, J. W. and Ida M.
Jewett Foundation, George Frederick
Jones Foundation, Harvey and Bernice
Jonsson Foundation
Kaplun Foundation, Morris J. and Betty
Kavanagh Foundation, T. James
Kelly Tractor Co.
Kent-Lucas Foundation
Kirby Foundation, F. M.
Kline Foundation, Josiah W. and Bessie H.
Knapp Foundation
Komes Foundation
Koret Foundation
Kuyper Foundation, Peter H. and E. Lucille
La-Z-Boy Chair Co.
Landegger Charitable Foundation
Leavey Foundation, Thomas and Dorothy
Lemberg Foundation
Lennon Foundation, Fred A.
Leuthold Foundation
Link, Jr. Foundation, George
Littauer Foundation, Lucius N.
Love Foundation, George H. and Margaret McClintic
M/A-COM, Inc.
Mahadh Foundation
Maneely Fund

Marshall Foundation, Mattie H.
Marshall Trust in Memory of Sanders McDaniel, Harriet McDaniel
Mautz Paint Co.
McCarty Foundation, John and Margaret
McCasland Foundation
McCune Charitable Trust, John R.
McGee Foundation
McKenna Foundation, Philip M.
McQueen Foundation, Adeline and George
McShain Charities, John
M.E. Foundation
Meyer Family Foundation, Paul J.
Meyerhoff Fund, Joseph
Moore Foundation, Edward S.
Moore & Sons, B.C.
Morgan Charitable Residual Trust, W. and E.
Morgan Foundation, Burton D.
Mulcahy Foundation
Mulford Foundation, Vincent
Mullen Foundation, J. K.
Murdock Charitable Trust, M. J.
Musson Charitable Foundation, R. C. and Katharine M.
New York Life Insurance Co.
Norwest Bank Nebraska, N.A.
O'Connor Foundation, Kathryn
Ohrstrom Foundation
Old National Bank in Evansville
Oliver Memorial Trust Foundation
Olsson Memorial Foundation, Elis
Palisano Foundation, Vincent and Harriet
Parshelsky Foundation, Moses L.
Payne Foundation, Frank E. and Seba B.
Pew Charitable Trusts
PHH Corporation
Phillips Family Foundation, Jay and Rose
Phillips Foundation, Ellis L.
Piper Foundation, Minnie Stevens
Price Foundation, Louis and Harold
Price Foundation, Lucien B. and Katherine E.
Proctor Trust, Mortimer R.
Prudential Insurance Co. of America, The
Quivey-Bay State Foundation
Ratner Foundation, Milton M.
Read Foundation, Charles L.
Reicher Foundation, Anne and Harry J.
Republic NY Corp.
Richardson Benevolent Foundation, C. E.
Rixson Foundation, Oscar C.
Rockwell Fund
Roseburg Forest Products Co.
Salvatori Foundation, Henry
Schowalter Foundation
Seagram & Sons, Inc., Joseph E.
Seaver Charitable Trust, Richard C.
Sentry Insurance A Mutual Company
Sequoia Foundation
Sierra Pacific Resources
Simon Foundation, William E. and Carol G.
Smith Foundation, Gordon V. and Helen C.
Snyder Foundation, Harold B. and Dorothy A.
Solow Foundation
Sonat Inc.
Speer Foundation, Roy M.
Sprague Educational and Charitable Foundation, Seth

Starr Foundation
Stearns Trust, Artemas W.
Steinman Foundation, John Frederick
Sumners Foundation, Hatton W.
Taube Family Foundation
Taylor Foundation, Ruth and Vernon
Teagle Foundation
Temple-Inland Inc.
Thermo Electron Corp.
Thompson Charitable Foundation
Trull Foundation
Trust Company Bank
Trust Funds
Union Camp Corporation
Upton Foundation, Frederick S.
Wal-Mart Stores, Inc.
Wallace Foundation, George R.
Warren and Beatrice W. Blanding Foundation, Riley J. and Lillian N.
Warwick Foundation
Washington Forrest Foundation
Wean Foundation, Raymond John
Weezie Foundation
Westvaco Corporation
White Trust, G. R.
Whiting Foundation
Whitney Fund, David M.
Wiegand Foundation, E. L.
Wilder Foundation
Young Foundation, Irvin L.

School Volunteerism

Barker Foundation, J.M.R.
Bean Foundation, Norwin S. and Elizabeth N.
Benedum Foundation, Claude Worthington
Bodman Foundation
Bush Foundation
City National Bank and Trust Co.
Clorox Co.
Connelly Foundation
Davis Foundation, Irene E. and George A.
Deuble Foundation, George H.
Dexter Charitable Fund, Eugene A.
Dodge Foundation, Cleveland H.
Duncan Foundation, Lillian H. and C. W.
Eccles Foundation, Ralph M. and Ella M.
Feild Co-Operative Association
Fife Foundation, Elias and Bertha
Fleishhacker Foundation
Goldsmith Foundation, Horace W.
Haas, Jr. Fund, Evelyn and Walter
Hallberg Foundation, E. L. and R. F.
Harriman Foundation, Mary W.
Hazen Foundation, Edward W.
Heinz Endowment, Vira I.
Heller Charitable Foundation, Clarence E.
Hillcrest Foundation
Jacobs Family Foundation
Lea Foundation, Helen Sperry
Littauer Foundation, Lucius N.
Meyer Memorial Trust
Moses Fund, Henry and Lucy
Noble Foundation, Edward John
O'Quinn Foundation, John M. and Nancy C.
Packard Foundation, David and Lucile
Pamida, Inc.
Read Foundation, Charles L.
Rosenberg, Jr. Family Foundation, Louise and Claude
Scherman Foundation

Schiff Foundation, Dorothy
Sulzberger Foundation
Taconic Foundation
Taube Family Foundation
Tuch Foundation, Michael
Vetlesen Foundation, G. Unger
Woodward Fund

Science/Mathematics Education

Abbott Laboratories
Abell-Hanger Foundation
Acushnet Co.
Aetna Life & Casualty Co.
Ahmanson Foundation
Air Products and Chemicals, Inc.
Akzo America
Alabama Gas Corp.
Alabama Power Co.
Alcon Laboratories, Inc.
Alexander Foundation, Joseph
Allegheny Foundation
Allegheny Ludlum Corp.
AlliedSignal Inc.
Aluminum Co. of America
Amado Foundation, Maurice
American Fidelity Corporation
American National Bank & Trust Co. of Chicago
American Natural Resources Company
American Optical Corp.
Ameritas Life Insurance Corp.
AMETEK, Inc.
Amfac/JMB Hawaii Inc.
Amoco Corporation
AMP Incorporated
AMR Corp.
Andersen Corp.
Anheuser-Busch Companies, Inc.
Annenberg Foundation
AON Corporation
Appleton Papers Inc.
Archer-Daniels-Midland Co.
Aristech Chemical Corp.
Arkansas Power & Light Co.
Arkell Hall Foundation
Armco Inc.
Astor Foundation, Vincent
AT&T Corp.
Baker Hughes Inc.
Ball Brothers Foundation
BankAmerica Corp.
Bankers Trust Company
Barra Foundation
Barth Foundation, Theodore H.
Battelle Memorial Institute
Batts Foundation
Bauervic Foundation, Charles M.
Baughman Foundation
Bay Foundation
Bean Foundation, Norwin S. and Elizabeth N.
BE&K Inc.
Bechtel, Jr. Foundation, S. D.
Bedsole Foundation, J. L.
Beech Aircraft Corp.
Bell Atlantic Corp.
Beloit Foundation
Benedum Foundation, Claude Worthington
Berger Foundation, H. N. and Frances C.
Besser Foundation
Bethlehem Steel Corp.
Blandin Foundation
Block, H&R
Blount, Inc.
Blum-Kovler Foundation
Bodman Foundation
Boeing Co., The
Boettcher Foundation
Booth Ferris Foundation
Borden, Inc.
Borman's Inc.
Boston Edison Co.
Boswell Foundation, James G.
Bothin Foundation
Bowen Foundation, Ethel N.

Bowne Foundation, Robert
BP America Inc.
Brackenridge Foundation, George W.
Bridgestone/Firestone, Inc.
Brown & Williamson Tobacco Corp.
Brunswick Corp.
Bucyrus-Erie Company
Buhl Foundation
Burlington Industries, Inc.
Bush Foundation
Cabell Foundation, Robert G. Cabell III and Maude Morgan
Cabot Corp.
Cabot Family Charitable Trust
Caestecker Foundation, Charles and Marie
Cafritz Foundation, Morris and Gwendolyn
Cain Foundation, Gordon and Mary
Carnegie Corporation of New York
Carolyn Foundation
Carpenter Technology Corp.
Carter Foundation, Amon G.
Carver Charitable Trust, Roy J.
Central Hudson Gas & Electric Corp.
Central Maine Power Co.
Chase Manhattan Bank, N.A.
Chesapeake Corp.
Chevron Corporation
Chrysler Corp.
Citibank
Claiborne and Art Ortenberg Foundation, Liz
Clorox Co.
Close Foundation
Cogswell Benevolent Trust
Cole Foundation, Olive B.
Collins Foundation
Connelly Foundation
Consolidated Natural Gas Co.
Consolidated Papers, Inc.
Consumers Power Co.
Cooper Industries, Inc.
Coors Foundation, Adolph
Cord Foundation, E. L.
Corning Incorporated
Coughlin-Saunders Foundation
CPC International Inc.
Cranston Print Works Company
Crocker Trust, Mary A.
Cullen Foundation
Cummins Engine Co.
Dana Foundation, Charles A.
Daniel Foundation of Alabama
Darling Foundation, Hugh and Hazel
Davenport-Hatch Foundation
Davis Foundations, Arthur Vining
Daywood Foundation
Deere & Co.
Dekko Foundation
DeRoy Testamentary Foundation
Detroit Edison Co.
Digital Equipment Corp.
Dillon Foundation
Dodge Foundation, Cleveland H.
Dodge Foundation, Geraldine R.
Donaldson Company, Inc.
Dow Corning Corp.
Dow Foundation, Herbert H. and Grace A.
Dresser Industries, Inc.
Dreyfus Foundation, Max and Victoria
du Pont de Nemours & Co., E. I.
Duke Endowment
Duke Power Co.
Duncan Trust, John G.
duPont Foundation, Alfred I.
Durfee Foundation
Eastman Kodak Company
Eaton Corporation
Eberly Foundation

Secondary Education (Private)

Social Sciences Education

Special Education

New York Times Company
The New Yorker Magazine, Inc.
Noble Foundation, Edward John
Norton Foundation Inc.
Oaklawn Foundation
Old National Bank in Evansville
Olin Foundation, Spencer T. and Ann W.
Oppenstein Brothers Foundation
Ottley Trust-Watertown, Marion W.
Packaging Corporation of America
Palisano Foundation, Vincent and Harriet
Parsons Foundation, Ralph M.
Peabody Charitable Fund, Amelia
Peppers Foundation, Ann
Pick, Jr. Fund, Albert
Polaroid Corp.
Providian Corporation
Prudential Insurance Co. of America, The
Quaker Chemical Corp.
Rich Products Corporation
Rieke Corp.
RJR Nabisco Inc.
Rockwell Fund
Rockwell International Corporation
Rohatyn Foundation, Felix and Elizabeth
Rohm & Haas Co.
Rowland Foundation
Salomon Foundation, Richard and Edna
Santa Fe Pacific Corporation
Sarkeys Foundation
Sawyer Charitable Foundation
Scaife Family Foundation
Schlumberger Ltd.
Scholl Foundation, Dr.
Schumann Fund for New Jersey
Schwartz Foundation, Arnold A.
Scott Foundation, Walter
Scurlock Foundation
Seafirst Corporation
Sedgwick James Inc.
Seidman Family Foundation
Shenandoah Life Insurance Co.
Siltec Corp.
Simon Foundation, William E. and Carol G.
Smith Foundation, Kelvin and Eleanor
Smith Trust, May and Stanley
Southern California Edison Co.
Spang & Co.
Sprague Educational and Charitable Foundation, Seth
Stanley Charitable Foundation, A.W.
Starr Foundation
Steele Foundation, Harry and Grace
Steinbach Fund, Ruth and Milton
Stevens Foundation, Abbot and Dorothy H.
Strong Foundation, Hattie M.
Stupp Foundation, Norman J.
Subaru of America Inc.
Sunnen Foundation
Swalm Foundation
Temple Foundation, T. L. L.
Teubert Charitable Trust, James H. and Alice
Texaco Inc.
Todd Co., A.M.
TransAmerica Corporation
Trees Charitable Trust, Edith L.
Trexler Trust, Harry C.
Trust Company Bank
Turner Charitable Foundation
Turrell Fund
Union Camp Corporation
Union Pacific Corp.
U.S. Bank of Washington
Unitrode Corp.

Uris Brothers Foundation
van Ameringen Foundation
Van Houten Memorial Fund
Vance Charitable Foundation, Robert C.
Vulcan Materials Co.
Wal-Mart Stores, Inc.
Warwick Foundation
Washington Mutual Savings Bank
Weaver Foundation, Gil and Dody
Wege Foundation
Weingart Foundation
Weinstein Foundation, J.
Welfare Foundation
Wendt Foundation, Margaret L.
Westerman Foundation, Samuel L.
Whiting Foundation
Wyomissing Foundation

Student Aid

Abbott Laboratories
Abell-Hanger Foundation
ACF Industries, Inc.
Achelis Foundation
Acushnet Co.
Adams Foundation, Arthur F. and Alice E.
Aetna Life & Casualty Co.
Ahmanson Foundation
Akzo Chemicals Inc.
Alcon Laboratories, Inc.
Alexander Foundation, Joseph
Allegheny Foundation
Allegheny Ludlum Corp.
Allendale Insurance Co.
AlliedSignal Inc.
Allyn Foundation
Altman Foundation
Aluminum Co. of America
American General Finance Corp.
American Natural Resources Company
American Optical Corp.
AMETEK, Inc.
Amfac/JMB Hawaii Inc.
Amoco Corporation
AMR Corp.
Andersen Corp.
Anderson Foundation, John W.
Andreas Foundation
Andrews Foundation
AON Corporation
Appleton Papers Inc.
Archer-Daniels-Midland Co.
Argyros Foundation
Aristech Chemical Corp.
Arkansas Power & Light Co.
Arkell Hall Foundation
Armco Inc.
Arnold Fund
Astor Foundation, Vincent
AT&T Corp.
Atherton Family Foundation
Audubon State Bank
Auerbach Foundation, Beatrice Fox
Avon Products, Inc.
Babson Foundation, Paul and Edith
Baker Foundation, Dexter F. and Dorothy H.
Baker Trust, George F.
Baldwin Foundation, David M. and Barbara
Balfour Foundation, L. G.
Bank One, Texas-Houston Office
BankAmerica Corp.
Banta Corp.
Baughman Foundation
Beal Foundation
Beattie Foundation Trust, Cordelia Lee
Beazley Foundation/Frederick Foundation
Bechtel, Jr. Foundation, S. D.
Beck Foundation, Elsie E. and Joseph W.
Beech Aircraft Corp.

Bell Foundation, James F.
Beloit Foundation
Bemis Company, Inc.
Benenson Foundation, Frances and Benjamin
Berger Foundation, H. N. and Frances C.
Bertha Foundation
Besser Foundation
Bingham Foundation, William
Binney & Smith Inc.
Bird Corp.
Blake Foundation, S. P.
Blandin Foundation
Blaustein Foundation, Louis and Henrietta
Blount, Inc.
Blue Bell, Inc.
Blue Cross & Blue Shield United of Wisconsin
Blum-Kovler Foundation
Bodman Foundation
Boeing Co., The
Boettcher Foundation
Borden, Inc.
Boswell Foundation, James G.
Bowen Foundation, Ethel N.
Brach Foundation, Helen
Brackenridge Foundation, George W.
Bridgestone/Firestone, Inc.
Bristol-Myers Squibb Company
Broadhurst Foundation
Brunswick Corp.
Bucyrus-Erie Company
Burchfield Foundation, Charles E.
Burden Foundation, Florence V.
Burkitt Foundation
Cabot Corp.
Caestecker Foundation, Charles and Marie
Cafritz Foundation, Morris and Gwendolyn
Cain Foundation, Effie and Wofford
Calder Foundation, Louis
Campbell Foundation
Campbell Foundation, Ruth and Henry
Campini Foundation, Frank A.
Cape Branch Foundation
Cargill Inc.
Carpenter Foundation
Carpenter Technology Corp.
Carver Charitable Trust, Roy J.
CBS, Inc.
Central Fidelity Banks, Inc.
Central Maine Power Co.
Chapman Charitable Corporation, Howard and Bess
Charina Foundation
Chase Manhattan Bank, N.A.
Chatham Manufacturing Corp.
Chatlos Foundation
Cheney Foundation, Ben B.
Chesapeake Corp.
Chesebrough-Pond's USA Co.
Chevron Corporation
Christy-Houston Foundation
CIGNA Corporation
CINergy
Citizens Bank of Rhode Island
Clark Foundation
Clay Foundation
Clemens Markets Corp.
Clorox Co.
Cogswell Benevolent Trust
Cole Foundation, Olive B.
Collins Foundation
Colonial Life & Accident Insurance Co.
Columbus Dispatch Printing Co.
Comer Foundation
Commercial Bank
Connecticut Mutual Life Insurance Company
Connelly Foundation
Consolidated Papers, Inc.
Continental Corp.

Cooper Industries, Inc.
Copley Press, Inc.
Cord Foundation, E. L.
Corning Incorporated
Coughlin-Saunders Foundation
CPC International Inc.
Crandall Memorial Foundation, J. Ford
Crane Co.
Cranston Print Works Company
Crawford Estate, E. R.
Cremer Foundation
Crestlea Foundation
Cullen Foundation
Culpeper Foundation, Charles E.
Culpeper Memorial Foundation, Daphne Seybolt
Culver Foundation, Constans
Cummings Foundation, James H.
Curtice-Burns Foods, Inc.
Dana Foundation, Charles A.
Darby Foundation
Darling Foundation, Hugh and Hazel
Dart Group Corp.
Dater Foundation, Charles H.
Davenport Trust Fund
Davidson Family Charitable Foundation
Davis Foundation, Edwin W. and Catherine M.
Davis Foundation, James A. and Juliet L.
Daywood Foundation
De Queen General Hospital Foundation
Dekko Foundation
Demoulas Supermarkets Inc.
DeRoy Foundation, Helen L.
DeRoy Testamentary Foundation
Detroit Edison Co.
Deuble Foundation, George H.
Diamond Foundation, Aaron
Dillon Dunwalke Trust, Clarence and Anne
Dodge Foundation, Cleveland H.
Dodge Jones Foundation
Donaldson Company, Inc.
Doss Foundation, M. S.
Dow Jones & Company, Inc.
Dresser Industries, Inc.
Dreyfus Foundation, Max and Victoria
du Pont de Nemours & Co., E. I.
Duchossois Industries Inc.
Duke Endowment
Duke Power Co.
Dun & Bradstreet Corp.
Dunagan Foundation
duPont Foundation, Alfred I.
Early Foundation
Eastman Kodak Company
Eaton Corporation
Eaton Foundation, Cyrus
Eddy Family Memorial Fund, C. K.
Eden Hall Foundation
Edmonds Foundation, Dean S.
El Pomar Foundation
Emerson Foundation, Inc., Fred L.
Ensign-Bickford Industries
Evans Foundation, Lettie Pate
Evans Foundation, Thomas J.
Fairchild Foundation, Sherman
Farish Fund, William Stamps
Farr Trust, Frank M. and Alice M.
Favrot Fund
Federal-Mogul Corporation
Feil Foundation, Louis and Gertrude
Femino Foundation
Ferebee Endowment, Percy O.
Fieldcrest Cannon Inc.
Firman Fund
First Financial Bank FSB
First Hawaiian, Inc.
First Interstate Bank of Oregon
First Source Corp.

Firstar Bank Milwaukee, N.A.
Fish Foundation, Ray C.
Fleet Financial Group, Inc.
Fleishhacker Foundation
Flowers Charitable Trust, Albert W. and Edith V.
Fohs Foundation
Folger Fund
Fondren Foundation
Forbes Inc.
Ford Fund, William and Martha
Forster Charitable Trust, James W. and Ella B.
France Foundation, Jacob and Annita
Frear Eleemosynary Trust, Mary D. and Walter F.
Freeport Brick Co.
Freeport-McMoRan Inc.
French Foundation, D.E.
Friendship Fund
Frohring Foundation, William O. and Gertrude Lewis
Frueauff Foundation, Charles A.
Fry Foundation, Lloyd A.
Gallagher Family Foundation, Lewis P.
Gamble Foundation
Gannett Publishing Co., Guy
GAR Foundation
Gates Foundation
GATX Corp.
Gazette Co.
Gebbie Foundation
Geifman Family Foundation
Gellert Foundation, Carl
Gellert Foundation, Celia Berta
GenCorp Inc.
General American Life Insurance Co.
General Mills, Inc.
General Motors Corp.
Georgia-Pacific Corporation
Giant Eagle, Inc.
Giant Food Inc.
Giant Food Stores
Gleason Foundation
Globe Newspaper Co.
Glosser Foundation, David A.
Goldie-Anna Charitable Trust
Goldseker Foundation of Maryland, Morris
Goldwyn Foundation, Samuel
Good Samaritan
Goodrich Co., The B.F.
Great-West Life Assurance Co.
Green Foundation, Allen P. and Josephine B.
Griffith Foundation, W. C.
Griggs and Mary Griggs Burke Foundation, Mary Livingston
Grundy Foundation
GSM Industrial
Gulf Coast Medical Foundation
Gulf Power Co.
Guttman Foundation, Stella and Charles
Habig Foundation, Arnold F.
Hagedorn Fund
Haigh-Scatena Foundation
Hallberg Foundation, E. L. and R. F.
Hallett Charitable Trust, E. W.
Hamilton Bank
Hamman Foundation, George and Mary Josephine
Hammer Foundation, Armand
Hancock Foundation, Luke B.
Hanover Foundation
Hanson Industries North America
Harcourt Foundation, Ellen Knowles
Hardin Foundation, Phil
Harriman Foundation, Gladys and Roland
Harrington Foundation, Francis A. and Jacquelyn H.
Harsco Corp.
Hartmarx Corporation
Hatch Charitable Trust, Margaret Milliken
Hawn Foundation

Haynes Foundation, John Randolph and Dora
HCA Foundation
Hearst Foundation, William Randolph
Hechinger Co.
Heckscher Foundation for Children
Heinz Company, H. J.
Heinz Endowment, Howard
Heinz Endowment, Vira I.
Heller Charitable Foundation, Clarence E.
Hermann Foundation, Grover
Herrick Foundation
Hewlett Foundation, William and Flora
Hickory Tech Corp.
High Foundation
Hill Foundation, Sandy
Hillman Foundation
Hillsdale Fund
Hoffman Foundation, Maximilian E. and Marion O.
Holzer Memorial Foundation, Richard H.
Homeland Foundation
Hook Drugs
Hoover Foundation
Hopwood Charitable Trust, John M.
Houchens Foundation, Ervin G.
Houston Endowment
Howe and Mitchell B. Howe Foundation, Lucille Horton
Hoyt Foundation
Hoyt Foundation, Stewart W. and Willma C.
Hugoton Foundation
Huisking Foundation
Hulme Charitable Foundation, Milton G.
Humana, Inc.
Humphrey Fund, George M. and Pamela S.
Huston Charitable Trust, Stewart
Huston Foundation
Hygeia Dairy Co.
Illinois Tool Works, Inc.
Independence Foundation
Irvine Foundation, James
ITT Hartford Insurance Group, Inc.
Jackson Foundation
Jacobs Family Foundation
Janesville Foundation
Jarson-Stanley and Mickey Kaplan Foundation, Isaac and Esther
Jaydor Corp.
Jewell Memorial Foundation, Daniel Ashley and Irene Houston
Jockey Hollow Foundation
Johnson Controls Inc.
Johnson Foundation, Helen K. and Arthur E.
Johnson Foundation, M. G. and Lillie A.
Johnson & Higgins
Johnson & Son, S.C.
Jones Foundation, Fletcher
Jones Foundation, Helen
Journal-Gazette Co.
Jurzykowski Foundation, Alfred
Kavanagh Foundation, T. James
Kayser Foundation
Kelley and Elza Kelley Foundation, Edward Bangs
Kelly Tractor Co.
Kemper National Insurance Cos.
Kennedy Foundation, Ethel
Kent-Lucas Foundation
Kiewit Foundation, Peter
Kimberly-Clark Corp.
Kingsbury Corp.
Kinney-Lindstrom Foundation
Kirby Foundation, F. M.
Klock and Lucia Klock Kingston Foundation, Jay E.

Knight Foundation, John S. and James L.
Knudsen Foundation, Tom and Valley
Koopman Fund
Koret Foundation
Kreitler Foundation
Kutz Foundation, Milton and Hattie
Laffey-McHugh Foundation
Landegger Charitable Foundation
Lang Foundation, Eugene M.
Laurel Foundation
LBJ Family Foundation
Leavey Foundation, Thomas and Dorothy
Lebovitz Fund
Lehigh Portland Cement Co.
Lehmann Foundation, Otto W.
Leidy Foundation, John J.
Lemberg Foundation
Lennon Foundation, Fred A.
Lichtenstein Foundation, David B.
Link, Jr. Foundation, George
Linnell Foundation
Little, Inc., Arthur D.
Loews Corporation
Longwood Foundation
Louisiana-Pacific Corp.
Lowenstein Foundation, Leon
Lurie Foundation, Louis R.
Lux Foundation, Miranda
M/A-COM, Inc.
Madison Gas & Electric Co.
Mailman Foundation
Mandeville Foundation
Maneely Fund
Margoes Foundation
Markey Charitable Fund, John C.
Marquette Electronics, Inc.
Marriott Foundation, J. Willard
Mars Foundation
Martin Marietta Materials
Mascoma Savings Bank
Mather Charitable Trust, S. Livingston
Mather and William Gwinn Mather Fund, Elizabeth Ring
Mattel, Inc.
Mautz Paint Co.
May Department Stores Company, The
Mayor Foundation, Oliver Dewey
Maytag Family Foundation, Fred
MCA Inc.
McCann Foundation
McCarty Foundation, John and Margaret
McCasland Foundation
McConnell Foundation
McCormick & Co. Inc.
McDermott Foundation, Eugene
McDonald & Company Securities, Inc.
McDonnell Douglas Corp.-West
McElroy Trust, R. J.
McEvoy Foundation, Mildred H.
McFeely-Rogers Foundation
McGee Foundation
McGraw-Hill, Inc.
MCI Communications Corp.
McInerny Foundation
McKenna Foundation, Philip M.
McMahon Foundation
McMillan Foundation, D. W.
McShain Charities, John
Meadows Foundation
Mellon Family Foundation, R. K.
Mellon Foundation, Richard King
Memton Fund
Mengle Foundation, Glenn and Ruth
Merrick Foundation
Merrill Lynch & Co., Inc.

Messing Family Charitable Foundation
Metropolitan Life Insurance Co.
Meyer Family Foundation, Paul J.
Meyerhoff Fund, Joseph
Mielke Family Foundation
Millbrook Tribute Garden
Miller Foundation
Mills Fund, Frances Goll
Mobil Oil Corp.
Mohasco Corp.
Monfort Family Foundation
Montana Power Co.
Monticello College Foundation
Morgan Charitable Residual Trust, W. and E.
Morgan & Company, J.P.
Morgan Construction Co.
Morgan Foundation, Burton D.
Morris Foundation, Margaret T.
Morrison Knudsen Corporation
Moses Fund, Henry and Lucy
Muchnic Foundation
Mulcahy Foundation
Murphey Foundation, Lluella Morey
Murphy Foundation
Mutual Assurance Co.
Nabisco Foods Group
National Westminster Bank New Jersey
Nestle USA Inc.
New York Stock Exchange, Inc.
New York Times Company
Newcombe Foundation, Charlotte W.
NewMil Bancorp
Noble Foundation, Samuel Roberts
Norman Foundation, Summers A.
Northern States Power Co. (Minnesota)
Norton Co.
Norton Memorial Corporation, Geraldi
O'Connor Foundation, A. Lindsay and Olive B.
Odell Fund, Robert Stewart Odell and Helen Pfeiffer
O'Fallon Trust, Martin J. and Mary Anne
Offield Family Foundation
Old National Bank in Evansville
Olin Foundation, Spencer T. and Ann W.
Oliver Memorial Trust Foundation
O'Quinn Foundation, John M. and Nancy C.
Overlake Foundation
Pacific Mutual Life Insurance Co.
Pacific Telesis Group
Packard Foundation, David and Lucile
PaineWebber
Palisades Educational Foundation
Palisano Foundation, Vincent and Harriet
Palmer Fund, Frank Loomis
Pamida, Inc.
Parker Hannifin Corp.
Parsons Foundation, Ralph M.
Payne Foundation, Frank E. and Seba B.
Pella Corporation
Pennsylvania Dutch Co.
Pennzoil Co.
Peppers Foundation, Ann
Peters Foundation, R. D. and Linda
Petteys Memorial Foundation, Jack
Pfizer, Inc.
Phelps Dodge Corporation
PHH Corporation
Phillips Charitable Trust, Dr. and Mrs. Arthur William
Phillips Family Foundation, Jay and Rose

Pierce Charitable Trust, Harold Whitworth
Pineywoods Foundation
Piper Foundation, Minnie Stevens
Piper Jaffray Companies Inc.
Polaroid Corp.
Potomac Electric Power Co.
Potter Foundation, Justin and Valere
PPG Industries, Inc.
Premier Industrial Corp.
Price Associates, T. Rowe
Price Foundation, Lucien B. and Katherine E.
Priddy Foundation
Prospect Hill Foundation
Prudential Insurance Co. of America, The
Public Service Co. of New Mexico
Pulitzer Publishing Co.
Putnam Foundation
Quaker Chemical Corp.
Quivey-Bay State Foundation
R&B Machine Tool Co.
Read Foundation, Charles L.
Reidler Foundation
Reynolds Foundation, Christopher
Reynolds Foundation, Donald W.
Rich Products Corporation
Richardson Benevolent Foundation, C. E.
Riggs Benevolent Fund
Ritter Charitable Trust, George W. and Mary F.
RJR Nabisco Inc.
Robinson-Broadhurst Foundation
Rockwell Fund
Rockwell International Corporation
Rogers Family Foundation
Rohatyn Foundation, Felix and Elizabeth
Rohm & Haas Co.
Rosenberg, Jr. Family Foundation, Louise and Claude
Rouse Co.
Rowland Foundation
Royal Foundation, May Mitchell
Rubinstein Foundation, Helena
Saint Paul Companies, Inc.
Salvatori Foundation, Henry
Sandusky International Inc.
Sandy Hill Foundation
Santa Fe Pacific Corporation
Sargent Foundation, Newell B.
Sarkeys Foundation
Scaife Family Foundation
Scherer Foundation, Karla
Schering-Plough Corp.
Schiro Fund
Schlumberger Ltd.
Schmitt Foundation, Kilian J. and Caroline F.
Schoenleber Foundation
Scholl Foundation, Dr.
Schowalter Foundation
Scripps, E.W.
Scurlock Foundation
Seafirst Corporation
Seagram & Sons, Inc., Joseph E.
Sedgwick James Inc.
Seidman Family Foundation
Selby and Marie Selby Foundation, William G.
Seneca Foods Corp.
Sentry Insurance A Mutual Company
Shawmut National Corp.
Shell Oil Company
Shenandoah Life Insurance Co.
Sierra Pacific Industries
Simon Foundation, William E. and Carol G.
Skillman Foundation
Slemp Foundation
Slifka Foundation, Joseph and Sylvia

Smeal Foundation, Mary Jean and Frank P.
Smith Charitable Foundation, Lou and Lutza
Smith Corp., A.O.
Smith Foundation, Kelvin and Eleanor
Smith Trust, May and Stanley
SmithKline Beecham Corp.
Snow Foundation, John Ben
Snow Memorial Trust, John Ben
Solow Foundation
South Waite Foundation
Spalding Foundation, Eliot
Sprague Educational and Charitable Foundation, Seth
Springs Foundation
Square D Co.
Stabler Foundation, Donald B. and Dorothy L.
Starr Foundation
Stauffer Charitable Trust, John
Steele Foundation, Harry and Grace
Steele-Reese Foundation
Stein Foundation, Jules and Doris
Steinman Foundation, James Hale
Sternberger Foundation, Tannenbaum
Stokely, Jr. Foundation, William B.
Strauss Foundation, Leon
Strawbridge Foundation of Pennsylvania II, Margaret Dorrance
Sulzberger Foundation
Sumners Foundation, Hatton W.
Sundet Foundation
Superior Tube Co.
Swalm Foundation
Taylor Foundation, Ruth and Vernon
Teagle Foundation
Tecumseh Products Co.
Temple Foundation, T. L. L.
Tenneco Inc.
Texaco Inc.
Textron, Inc.
Thomas Foundation, Joan and Lee
Thomasville Furniture Industries
Thompson Co., J. Walter
Thompson Trust, Thomas
Thornton Foundation, Flora L.
Times Mirror Company, The
Timken Foundation of Canton
Tiscornia Foundation
Towsley Foundation, Harry A. and Margaret D.
Trexler Trust, Harry C.
Trull Foundation
Trust Funds
Tucker Charitable Trust, Rose E.
Turner Charitable Foundation
Turrell Fund
Unger Foundation, Aber D.
Unilever United States, Inc.
Union Camp Corporation
Union Electric Co.
Union Pacific Corp.
United Airlines, Inc.
Unocal Corp.
Upton Foundation, Frederick S.
Valmont Industries, Inc.
Van Nuys Foundation, I. N. and Susanna H.
Vernon Fund, Miles Hodsdon
Vetlesen Foundation, G. Unger
Vicksburg Foundation
Vollbrecht Foundation, Frederick A.
Wahlstrom Foundation
Wal-Mart Stores, Inc.
Wallace-Reader's Digest Fund, DeWitt
Warwick Foundation
Washington Forrest Foundation
Wean Foundation, Raymond John

Weber Charities Corp., Frederick E.
Weezie Foundation
Weingart Foundation
Welfare Foundation
Wendt Foundation, Margaret L.
Wertheim Foundation, Dr. Herbert A.
Westerman Foundation, Samuel L.
Western New York Foundation
Wheeler Foundation, Wilmot
Whirlpool Corporation
White Trust, G. R.
Whittenberger Foundation, Claude R. and Ethel B.
Wickes Foundation, Harvey Randall
WICOR, Inc.
Wiggins Memorial Trust, J. J.
Wilson Foundation, H. W.
Winchester Foundation
Windham Foundation
Winnebago Industries, Inc.
Wiremold Co.
Wisconsin Power & Light Co.
Witco Corp.
Worthington Foods
Wyman Youth Trust
Young Foundation, Hugo H. and Mabel B.
Young Foundation, Robert R.
Zarrow Foundation, Anne and Henry
Zenkel Foundation

Vocational & Technical Education

ACF Industries, Inc.
Ahmanson Foundation
AMETEK, Inc.
Annenberg Foundation
Ansin Private Foundation, Ronald M.
Ball Foundation, George and Frances
Blaustein Foundation, Louis and Henrietta
Booth Ferris Foundation
Bowne Foundation, Robert
Buhl Foundation
Callaway Foundation
Carpenter Technology Corp.
Champlin Foundations
Clark Foundation
Close Foundation
Comer Foundation
Connelly Foundation
Crestlea Foundation
Dekko Foundation
Dreyfus Foundation, Max and Victoria
Federated Mutual Insurance Co.
Green Foundation, Allen P. and Josephine B.
Gregg-Graniteville Foundation
GSM Industrial
Habig Foundation, Arnold F.
Hammer Foundation, Armand
Hartz Foundation
Heinz Endowment, Howard
Hickory Tech Corp.
Hook Drugs
Howe and Mitchell B. Howe Foundation, Lucille Horton
Johnson Foundation, M. G. and Lillie A.
Jones Foundation, Fletcher
Jordan Charitable Foundation, Mary Ranken Jordan and Ettie A.
Kingsbury Corp.
Lehigh Portland Cement Co.
Lichtenstein Foundation, David B.
Martini Foundation, Nicholas
McMahon Foundation
McShain Charities, John
Meadows Foundation
Mitsubishi Motor Sales of America, Inc.

Moore & Sons, B.C.
Morgan & Company, J.P.
Novell Inc.
Olin Foundation, Spencer T. and Ann W.
Olsson Memorial Foundation, Elis
Peppers Foundation, Ann
Pierce Charitable Trust, Harold Whitworth
Piper Jaffray Companies Inc.
Quaker Chemical Corp.
Schwob Foundation, Simon
Scripps Co., E.W.
Self Foundation
Skillman Foundation
Sordoni Foundation
Stupp Foundation, Norman J.
Sturgis Charitable and Educational Trust, Roy and Christine
Temple-Inland Inc.
Unitrode Corp.
Wallace-Reader's Digest Fund, DeWitt
Webber Oil Co.
Weingart Foundation
Whirlpool Corporation
Winchester Foundation
Wisconsin Power & Light Co.
Zachry Co., H.B.
Zollner Foundation

Environment

Air/Water Quality

Achelis Foundation
Ahmanson Foundation
Air Products and Chemicals, Inc.
Alavi Foundation of New York
Aldus Corp.
Allegheny Foundation
Amoco Corporation
Andersen Foundation
Ansin Private Foundation, Ronald M.
Baker Trust, George F.
Bank of Boston
Barth Foundation, Theodore H.
Bechtel, Jr. Foundation, S. D.
Benedum Foundation, Claude Worthington
Benwood Foundation
Bethlehem Steel Corp.
Bingham Foundation, William
Bingham Second Betterment Fund, William
Bird Corp.
Blandin Foundation
Blaustein Foundation, Louis and Henrietta
Bodman Foundation
Booth Ferris Foundation
Brady Foundation
Bristol-Myers Squibb Company
Bryn Mawr Trust Co.
Bunbury Company
Burden Foundation, Florence V.
Cabell Foundation, Robert G. Cabell III and Maude Morgan
Cafritz Foundation, Morris and Gwendolyn
Cape Branch Foundation
Carolyn Foundation
Carpenter Technology Corp.
Carter Foundation, Beirne
Castle Foundation, Harold K. L.
Charina Foundation
Chazen Foundation
Chesapeake Corp.
Claiborne and Art Ortenberg Foundation, Liz
Clark Foundation
Collins Foundation
Columbia Foundation

Commerce Clearing House, Incorporated
Cooke Foundation
Crestlea Foundation
Crocker Trust, Mary A.
Crown Memorial, Arie and Ida
CS First Boston Corporation
DeRoy Testamentary Foundation
DeVore Foundation
Dodge Foundation, Cleveland H.
Dodge Foundation, Geraldine R.
Emerson Foundation, Inc., Fred L.
Fair Play Foundation
Favrot Fund
Fischbach Foundation
Ford Foundation
France Foundation, Jacob and Annita
Freed Foundation
Frese Foundation, Arnold D.
Frisch's Restaurants Inc.
Fund for New Jersey
Gebbie Foundation
Georgia-Pacific Corporation
Gheens Foundation
Goldie-Anna Charitable Trust
Grand Rapids Label Co.
Guttman Foundation, Stella and Charles
Harriman Foundation, Gladys and Roland
Hasbro Inc.
Hazen Foundation, Edward W.
Heinz Trust, Drue
Helms Foundation
Hoffman Foundation, Maximilian E. and Marion O.
Hopkins Foundation, Josephine Lawrence
Hoyt Foundation, Stewart W. and Willma C.
Hyde and Watson Foundation
Irvine Foundation, James
Ittleson Foundation
Janirve Foundation
Jarson-Stanley and Mickey Kaplan Foundation, Isaac and Esther
Jaydor Corp.
Jewish Healthcare Foundation of Pittsburgh
Johnson Foundation, Helen K. and Arthur E.
Johnson & Son, S.C.
Kaplan Fund, J. M.
Kelley and Elza Kelley Foundation, Edward Bangs
Kennedy Foundation, Ethel
Kingsbury Corp.
Kirby Foundation, F. M.
Klipstein Foundation, Ernest Christian
Knight Foundation, John S. and James L.
Knoll Group
Kresge Foundation
LamCo. Communications
Larsen Fund
Lasdon Foundation
Lattner Foundation, Forrest C.
Levy Foundation, June Rockwell
Lydall, Inc.
MacArthur Foundation, John D. and Catherine T.
Magowan Family Foundation
Mandeville Foundation
Marbrook Foundation
Marpat Foundation
Mars Foundation
Martin Marietta Materials
Mascoma Savings Bank
Mather and William Gwinn Mather Fund, Elizabeth Ring
Mathis-Pfohl Foundation
McLean Contributionship
Mellon Foundation, Richard King
Mengle Foundation, Glenn and Ruth
Merck Family Fund

Meyer Memorial Trust
Moore Foundation, Edward S.
Morgan & Company, J.P.
Morgan Stanley & Co., Inc.
Morris Foundation, William T.
New England Business Service
New-Land Foundation
New York Times Company
Normandie Foundation
Norton Family Foundation, Peter
Offield Family Foundation
Olsson Memorial Foundation, Elis
Packard Foundation, David and Lucile
Pick, Jr. Fund, Albert
Pittsburg Midway Coal Mining Co.
Porter Foundation, Mrs. Cheever
Prairie Foundation
Prospect Hill Foundation
Public Welfare Foundation
Putnam Foundation
Roseburg Forest Products Co.
Rubin Foundation, Samuel
Salomon Foundation, Richard and Edna
Saltonstall Charitable Foundation, Richard
Sawyer Charitable Foundation
Schumann Fund for New Jersey
Selby and Marie Selby Foundation, William G.
Sequoia Foundation
Seton Leather Co.
Slifka Foundation, Joseph and Sylvia
Solow Foundation
Speyer Foundation, Alexander C. and Tillie S.
Steinman Foundation, John Frederick
Sullivan Foundation, Algernon Sydney
Teichert & Son, A.
Teleflex Inc.
Titus Foundation, Roy and Niuta
Tuch Foundation, Michael
Union Camp Corporation
Valentine Foundation, Lawson
Vanderbilt Trust, R. T.
Virginia Environmental Endowment
Warner Fund, Albert and Bessie
Waters Charitable Trust, Robert S.
Wendt Foundation, Margaret L.
Westerman Foundation, Samuel L.
Wheat First Butcher Singer, Inc.
Witter Foundation, Dean
Wyomissing Foundation

Energy

Dodge Foundation, Geraldine R.
Exxon Corporation
Hoffman Foundation, Maximilian E. and Marion O.
MacArthur Foundation, John D. and Catherine T.
Mascoma Savings Bank
New-Land Foundation
Pew Charitable Trusts
Pittsburg Midway Coal Mining Co.
Tucker Charitable Trust, Rose E.

Forestry

Auerbach Foundation, Beatrice Fox
Blandin Foundation

Cabell Foundation, Robert G. Cabell III and Maude Morgan
Carolyn Foundation
Chazen Foundation
Claiborne and Art Ortenberg Foundation, Liz
Columbia Foundation
Crocker Trust, Mary A.
Heinz Endowment, Vira I.
Hoover Foundation
Kayser Foundation
McConnell Foundation
McMahan Foundation, Catherine L. and Robert O.
Meadows Foundation
Merck Family Fund
Mott Fund, Ruth
Pew Charitable Trusts
Sequoia Foundation
Temple-Inland Inc.
Thalhimer and Family Foundation, Charles G.
Valentine Foundation, Lawson
Wheeler Foundation

General

Abbott Laboratories
Abell-Hanger Foundation
Acushnet Co.
Ahmanson Foundation
Air Products and Chemicals, Inc.
AKC Fund
Akzo America
Alabama Gas Corp.
Alabama Power Co.
Allegheny Foundation
Allendale Insurance Co.
AlliedSignal Inc.
Aluminum Co. of America
American Brands, Inc.
American Natural Resources Company
American President Companies, Ltd.
Ameritas Life Insurance Corp.
AMETEK, Inc.
Amfac/JMB Hawaii Inc.
Amoco Corporation
AMP Incorporated
Andersen Corp.
Andersons, The
Andreas Foundation
Andres Charitable Trust, Frank G.
Anheuser-Busch Companies, Inc.
Annenberg Foundation
Ansin Private Foundation, Ronald M.
AON Corporation
Apple Computer, Inc.
Appleton Papers Inc.
Arcadia Foundation
Archer-Daniels-Midland Co.
Aristech Chemical Corp.
Arkansas Power & Light Co.
Armco Inc.
Armstrong Foundation
Arnhold Foundation
Astor Foundation, Vincent
AT&T Corp.
Atherton Family Foundation
Atran Foundation
Auerbach Foundation, Beatrice Fox
Avon Products, Inc.
Babcock & Wilcox Co.
Babson Foundation, Paul and Edith
Baker Trust, George F.
Baldwin Foundation, David M. and Barbara
Baldwin Memorial Foundation, Fred
Ball Brothers Foundation
Ball Foundation, George and Frances
Bank of New York Company, Inc.
Bank One, Texas-Houston Office

Bank One, Youngstown, NA
Bankers Trust Company
Barker Foundation, J.M.R.
Barra Foundation
Barth Foundation, Theodore H.
Batts Foundation
Bay Foundation
Bean Foundation, Norwin S. and Elizabeth N.
Beattie Foundation Trust, Cordelia Lee
Bechtel Charitable Remainder Uni-Trust, Marie H.
Bechtel, Jr. Foundation, S. D.
Bedsole Foundation, J. L.
Beech Aircraft Corp.
Bell Foundation, James F.
Bemis Company, Inc.
Benedum Foundation, Claude Worthington
Benwood Foundation
Berger Foundation, H. N. and Frances C.
Berwind Corporation
Bethlehem Steel Corp.
Beveridge Foundation, Frank Stanley
Bigelow Foundation, F. R.
Bingham Foundation, William
Bingham Second Betterment Fund, William
Binney & Smith Inc.
Bird Corp.
Blandin Foundation
Blaustein Foundation, Louis and Henrietta
Blount, Inc.
Blue Cross & Blue Shield United of Wisconsin
Blum-Kovler Foundation
Bodman Foundation
Boeing Co., The
Boettcher Foundation
Boise Cascade Corporation
Booth Ferris Foundation
Borden, Inc.
Borkee Hagley Foundation
Borman's Inc.
Boswell Foundation, James G.
Bowater Incorporated
BP America Inc.
Brach Foundation, Helen
Brady Foundation
Breyer Foundation
Bridgestone/Firestone, Inc.
Brillion Iron Works
Bristol-Myers Squibb Company
Brown Foundation, M. K.
Brown & Williamson Tobacco Corp.
Brunswick Corp.
Bryant Foundation
Bunbury Company
Burdines Inc.
Bush Foundation
Cabell Foundation, Robert G. Cabell III and Maude Morgan
Cabot Corp.
Cabot Family Charitable Trust
Cafritz Foundation, Morris and Gwendolyn
Cain Foundation, Gordon and Mary
Callaway Foundation
Campbell Foundation
Campbell Foundation, Ruth and Henry
Campini Foundation, Frank A.
Cape Branch Foundation
Cargill Inc.
Carnahan-Jackson Foundation
Carnegie Corporation of New York
Carolyn Foundation
Carpenter Foundation, E. Rhodes and Leona B.
Carpenter Technology Corp.
Carter Foundation, Amon G.
Carter Foundation, Beirne
Carver Charitable Trust, Roy J.
Castle Foundation, Harold K. L.
Cayuga Foundation

Centerior Energy Corp.
Central Maine Power Co.
Central Vermont Public Service Corp.
Chadwick Fund, Dorothy Jordan
Champion International Corporation
Champlin Foundations
Charina Foundation
Chartwell Foundation
Chase Manhattan Bank, N.A.
Chastain Charitable Foundation, Robert Lee and Thomas M.
CHC Foundation
Cheatham Foundation, Owen
Cheney Foundation, Ben B.
Chesapeake Corp.
Chesebrough-Pond's USA Co.
Chevron Corporation
Childs Charitable Foundation, Roberta M.
Christensen Charitable and Religious Foundation, L. C.
Church & Dwight Co., Inc.
CINergy
Citibank
Claiborne and Art Ortenberg Foundation, Liz
Clapp Charitable and Educational Trust, George H.
Clark Foundation
Clorox Co.
Close Foundation
Cogswell Benevolent Trust
Cole Foundation, Olive B.
Coleman Foundation, George E.
Collins Foundation
Colonial Life & Accident Insurance Co.
Columbia Foundation
Comer Foundation
Commerce Clearing House, Incorporated
Connecticut Mutual Life Insurance Company
Connelly Foundation
Connemara Fund
Consolidated Natural Gas Co.
Consumers Power Co.
Continental Corp.
Cooke Foundation
Cooper Industries, Inc.
Coors Foundation, Adolph
Corning Incorporated
Covington and Burling
Cowell Foundation, S. H.
Cowles Charitable Trust
CPC International Inc.
Crane Co.
Crary Foundation, Bruce L.
Crestlea Foundation
Crocker Trust, Mary A.
Crystal Trust
Culver Foundation, Constans
Cummins Engine Co.
Curtice-Burns Foods, Inc.
Dalton Foundation, Harry L.
Dana Foundation, Charles A.
Daniel Foundation of Alabama
Darby Foundation
Daugherty Foundation
Davis Foundation, Edwin W. and Catherine M.
Davis Foundation, James A. and Juliet L.
Day Foundation, Nancy Sayles
Daywood Foundation
DEC International, Inc.
Deere & Co.
Delavan Foundation, Nelson B.
Delaware North Co., Inc.
Demoulas Supermarkets Inc.
DeRoy Testamentary Foundation
Dewing Foundation, Frances R.
Dexter Charitable Fund, Eugene A.
Dexter Corporation
Digital Equipment Corp.
Dillon Dunwalke Trust, Clarence and Anne
Dillon Foundation

Dingman Foundation, Michael D.
Dodge Foundation, Cleveland H.
Dodge Foundation, Geraldine R.
Donaldson Company, Inc.
Donnelley Foundation, Gaylord and Dorothy
Donner Foundation, William H.
Douty Foundation
Dow Corning Corp.
Dreyfus Foundation, Max and Victoria
du Pont de Nemours & Co., E. I.
Duchossois Industries Inc.
Duke Power Co.
Dula Educational and Charitable Foundation, Caleb C. and Julia W.
Dunagan Foundation
duPont Foundation, Alfred I.
Durfee Foundation
Early Foundation
Eastman Kodak Company
Eaton Corporation
Eberly Foundation
El Pomar Foundation
Elf Atochem North America, Inc.
Elkins, Jr. Foundation, Margaret and James A.
English Memorial Fund, Florence C. and H. L.
Enron Corp.
Ensign-Bickford Industries
Erpf Fund, Armand G.
Ethyl Corp
Ettinger Foundation
Evans Foundation, T. M.
Evans Foundation, Thomas J.
Exxon Corporation
Fabri-Kal Corp.
Fair Play Foundation
Farish Fund, William Stamps
Favrot Fund
Federated Mutual Insurance Co.
Fieldcrest Cannon Inc.
Fikes Foundation, Leland
Fireman's Fund Insurance Co.
Firman Fund
First Chicago Corp.
First Financial Bank FSB
First Hawaiian, Inc.
First Interstate Bank of Oregon
First Tennessee Bank
First Union Corp.
First Union National Bank of Florida
Fish Foundation, Ray C.
Fishback Foundation Trust, Harmes C.
Fleishhacker Foundation
Fleming Cos. Food Distribution Center
Fletcher Foundation
Fohs Foundation
Fondren Foundation
Forbes Inc.
Ford Foundation
Ford Fund, William and Martha
Ford Motor Co.
Forest Foundation
Foster Foundation
France Foundation, Jacob and Annita
Frear Eleemosynary Trust, Mary D. and Walter F.
Freed Foundation
Freedom Forge Corp.
Freeport-McMoRan Inc.
Frese Foundation, Arnold D.
Friedman Family Foundation
Friendship Fund
Frohring Foundation, William O. and Gertrude Lewis
Frost National Bank
Fry Foundation, Lloyd A.
Fuller Foundation
Fund for New Jersey
Fuqua Foundation, J. B.
Gap, Inc., The

Garland Foundation, John Jewett and H. Chandler
Gates Foundation
Gazette Co.
Gebbie Foundation
GenCorp Inc.
General Mills, Inc.
General Motors Corp.
Georgia-Pacific Corporation
Getty Trust, J. Paul
Giant Eagle, Inc.
Giant Food Stores
Gilman Foundation, Howard
Glanville Family Foundation
Goldberg Family Foundation
Goldsmith Foundation, Horace W.
Goldwyn Foundation, Samuel
Good Samaritan
Gordon/Rousmaniere/Roberts Fund
Gould Foundation, The Florence
Graham Foundation for Advanced Studies in the Fine Arts
Green Foundation, Allen P. and Josephine B.
Greve Foundation, William and Mary
Griffith Foundation, W. C.
Griggs and Mary Griggs Burke Foundation, Mary Livingston
Griswold Foundation, John C.
Groome Beatty Trust, Helen D.
Grundy Foundation
Guaranty Bank & Trust Co.
Guggenheim Foundation, Harry Frank
Gulf Power Co.
Guttman Foundation, Stella and Charles
Hamilton Bank
Hamman Foundation, George and Mary Josephine
Hanes Foundation, John W. and Anna H.
Hanover Foundation
Harcourt Foundation, Ellen Knowles
Harriman Foundation, Gladys and Roland
Harriman Foundation, Mary W.
Harrington Foundation, Francis A. and Jacquelyn H.
Harrison Foundation, Fred G.
Hartz Foundation
Hauser Foundation
Haynes Foundation, John Randolph and Dora
Hazen Foundation, Edward W.
HCA Foundation
Hebrew Technical Institute
Hechinger Co.
Heckscher Foundation for Children
Heinz Company, H. J.
Heinz Endowment, Howard
Heinz Endowment, Vira I.
Heinz Trust, Drue
Heller Charitable Foundation, Clarence E.
Helmerich Foundation
Helms Foundation
Henderson Foundation, George B.
Hermann Foundation, Grover
Hewlett Foundation, William and Flora
Hewlett-Packard Co.
Heydt Fund, Nan and Matilda
Hickory Tech Corp.
Higginson Trust, Corina
Hill Foundation, Sandy
Hillsdale Fund
Hoffman Foundation, Maximilian E. and Marion O.
Hoffmann-La Roche Inc.
Holnam
Hopkins Foundation, Josephine Lawrence
Hopwood Charitable Trust, John M.
Houchens Foundation, Ervin G.
Housatonic Curtain Co.

Houston Endowment
Houston Industries Incorporated
Huber Foundation
Hudson-Webber Foundation
Humana, Inc.
Humphrey Fund, George M. and Pamela S.
Hunt Foundation
Hunt Foundation, Roy A.
Huston Foundation
Hyde and Watson Foundation
Icahn Foundation, Carl C.
ICI Americas Inc.
IES Industries, Inc.
Imperial Bancorp
Ingalls Foundation, Louise H. and David S.
Inland Container Corp.
International Business Machines Corp.
International Foundation
International Paper Co.
Irvine Foundation, James
ITT Hartford Insurance Group, Inc.
Ittleson Foundation
Jackson Foundation
Jacobson Foundation, Bernard H. and Blanche E.
Jaffe Foundation
James River Corp. of Virginia
Janirve Foundation
JELD-WEN, Inc.
Jewell Memorial Foundation, Daniel Ashley and Irene Houston
Jewett Foundation, George Frederick
Jockey Hollow Foundation
John Hancock Mutual Life Insurance Co.
Johnson Controls Inc.
Johnson Foundation, Burdine
Johnson Foundation, Helen K. and Arthur E.
Johnson & Higgins
Johnson & Son, S.C.
Jurzykowski Foundation, Alfred
Justus Trust, Edith C.
Kansas City Southern Industries
Kantzler Foundation
Kaplan Fund, J. M.
Kaufmann Foundation, Henry
Kayser Foundation
Kelley and Elza Kelley Foundation, Edward Bangs
Kelly Tractor Co.
Kempner Fund, Harris and Eliza
Kennecott Corporation
Kennedy Foundation, Ethel
Kent-Lucas Foundation
Kerr Foundation
Kettering Fund
Kiewit Foundation, Peter
Kimball Foundation, Horace A. Kimball and S. Ella
Kimberly-Clark Corp.
Kingsbury Corp.
Kinney-Lindstrom Foundation
Kiplinger Foundation
Kirbo Charitable Trust, Thomas M. and Irene B.
Kirby Foundation, F. M.
Klipstein Foundation, Ernest Christian
KN Energy, Inc.
Knapp Foundation
Knudsen Foundation, Tom and Valley
Kohn-Joseloff Foundation
Komes Foundation
Kreitler Foundation
Kresge Foundation
Kuehn Foundation
Ladd Charitable Corporation, Helen and George
Larsen Fund
Lattner Foundation, Forrest C.
Lauder Foundation
Laurel Foundation

Mott Fund, Ruth
Windham Foundation
Wyman Youth Trust

Research

Columbia Foundation
Cord Foundation, E. L.
Heinz Endowment, Vira I.
Heller Charitable Foundation, Clarence E.
Hygeia Dairy Co.
Meadows Foundation
Mellon Foundation, Andrew W.

Resource Conservation

Achelis Foundation
Acme-McCrary Corp./Sapona Manufacturing Co.
Ahmanson Foundation
Air Products and Chemicals, Inc.
AKC Fund
Aldus Corp.
Allegheny Foundation
Allen Brothers Foundation
Aluminum Co. of America
American Fidelity Corporation
AMETEK, Inc.
Amoco Corporation
Anderson Foundation
Annenberg Foundation
Ansin Private Foundation, Ronald M.
Appleby Trust, Scott B. and Annie P.
Argyros Foundation
Aristech Chemical Corp.
Armstrong Foundation
Astor Foundation, Vincent
Atherton Family Foundation
Auerbach Foundation, Beatrice Fox
Ayres Foundation, Inc.
Baker Foundation, Dexter F. and Dorothy H.
Baker Trust, George F.
Baldwin Memorial Foundation, Fred
Ball Brothers Foundation
Ball Foundation, George and Frances
Barker Foundation, J.M.R.
Barra Foundation
Barth Foundation, Theodore H.
Batts Foundation
Bay Foundation
Bean Foundation, Norwin S. and Elizabeth N.
Bechtel, Jr. Foundation, S. D.
Beech Aircraft Corp.
Bell Foundation, James F.
Benedum Foundation, Claude Worthington
Benwood Foundation
Bettingen Corporation, Burton G.
Bingham Foundation, William
Bingham Second Betterment Fund, William
Blandin Foundation
Blaustein Foundation, Louis and Henrietta
Bobst Foundation, Elmer and Mamdouha
Bodman Foundation
Boettcher Foundation
Boothroyd Foundation, Charles H. and Bertha L.
Bothin Foundation
Brady Foundation
Breyer Foundation
Bryn Mawr Trust Co.
Bush Foundation
Cape Branch Foundation
Carolyn Foundation
Carpenter Foundation
Carpenter Technology Corp.
Carter Foundation, Beirne

Caspersen Foundation for Aid to Health and Education, O. W.
Cassett Foundation, Louis N.
Champlin Foundations
Childs Charitable Foundation, Roberta M.
CINergy
Claiborne and Art Ortenberg Foundation, Liz
Clapp Charitable and Educational Trust, George H.
Clorox Co.
Coen Family Foundation, Charles S. and Mary
Cogswell Benevolent Trust
Cole Foundation, Olive B.
Coleman Foundation, George E.
Collins Foundation
Columbia Foundation
Commerce Clearing House, Incorporated
Consolidated Natural Gas Co.
Cooke Foundation
Cowell Foundation, S. H.
Crestlea Foundation
Crocker Trust, Mary A.
Crystal Trust
CT Corp. System
Curtice-Burns Foods, Inc.
Daily News
Darby Foundation
Davis Foundation, Edwin W. and Catherine M.
Davis Foundations, Arthur Vining
Day Foundation, Nancy Sayles
Dewing Foundation, Frances R.
Dillon Dunwalke Trust, Clarence and Anne
Dodge Foundation, Geraldine R.
Donnelley Foundation, Gaylord and Dorothy
Dula Educational and Charitable Foundation, Caleb C. and Julia W.
Duncan Foundation, Lillian H. and C. W.
Eaton Foundation, Cyrus
English Memorial Fund, Florence C. and H. L.
Erpf Fund, Armand G.
Exxon Corporation
Fair Play Foundation
Favrot Fund
First Hawaiian, Inc.
Fish Foundation, Ray C.
Fletcher Foundation
Ford Foundation
Foster Foundation
Freed Foundation
Freedom Forge Corp.
Freeman Charitable Trust, Samuel
Freeport-McMoRan Inc.
Fribourg Foundation
Fruehauf Foundation
Fund for New Jersey
Fuqua Foundation, J. B.
Gannett Publishing Co., Guy
Gates Foundation
Gebbie Foundation
Gheens Foundation
Giant Eagle, Inc.
Gilmore Foundation, William G.
Goldwyn Foundation, Samuel
Good Samaritan
Grand Rapids Label Co.
Griffith Foundation, W. C.
Griggs and Mary Griggs Burke Foundation, Mary Livingston
Grundy Foundation
Haas, Jr. Fund, Evelyn and Walter
Habig Foundation, Arnold F.
Hagedorn Fund
Halsell Foundation, Ewing
Hancock Foundation, Luke B.
Hanover Foundation
Harcourt Foundation, Ellen Knowles
Hardin Foundation, Phil

Harland Charitable Foundation, John and Wilhelmina D.
Harriman Foundation, Gladys and Roland
Harrington Foundation, Francis A. and Jacquelyn H.
Hazen Foundation, Edward W.
Hebrew Technical Institute
Hecht-Levi Foundation
Heinz Endowment, Vira I.
Heller Charitable Foundation, Clarence E.
Henderson Foundation, George B.
Hershey Foods Corp.
Hewlett Foundation, William and Flora
Heydt Fund, Nan and Matilda
Higginson Trust, Corina
Hillsdale Fund
Hoffman Foundation, Maximilian E. and Marion O.
Holt Family Foundation
Hoover Fund-Trust, W. Henry
Hopkins Foundation, Josephine Lawrence
Hopwood Charitable Trust, John M.
Housatonic Curtain Co.
Houston Endowment
Hugoton Foundation
Huisking Foundation
Hulme Charitable Foundation, Milton G.
Humphrey Fund, George M. and Pamela S.
Hunt Foundation
Hunt Foundation, Samuel P.
Hyde and Watson Foundation
Imperial Bancorp
Ingalls Foundation, Louise H. and David S.
International Foundation
Irvine Foundation, James
Ittleson Foundation
Jackson Foundation
Janirve Foundation
Jewett Foundation, George Frederick
Jockey Hollow Foundation
Johnson Foundation, Helen K. and Arthur E.
Johnson Fund, Edward C.
Johnson & Son, S.C.
Journal-Gazette Co.
Jurzykowski Foundation, Alfred
Kansas City Southern Industries
Kaplan Fund, J. M.
Kelley and Elza Kelley Foundation, Edward Bangs
Kempner Fund, Harris and Eliza
Kennedy Foundation, Ethel
Kent-Lucas Foundation
Kiewit Foundation, Peter
Kimball Foundation, Horace A. Kimball and S. Ella
Kimberly-Clark Corp.
Kinney-Lindstrom Foundation
Kirby Foundation, F. M.
Klipstein Foundation, Ernest Christian
Knapp Foundation
Knoll Group
Koret Foundation
Kresge Foundation
Kuyper Foundation, Peter H. and E. Lucille
Ladd Charitable Corporation, Helen and George
Laffey-McHugh Foundation
Larsen Fund
Laurel Foundation
Lazarus Charitable Trust, Helen and Charles
Lee Enterprises
Levy Foundation, June Rockwell
Lockhart Vaughan Foundation
Long Foundation, J.M.
Lux Foundation, Miranda
Lydall, Inc.

MacArthur Foundation, John D. and Catherine T.
Mahadh Foundation
Mandeville Foundation
Marbrook Foundation
Marmot Foundation
Marpat Foundation
Mars Foundation
Martin Marietta Materials
Mather Charitable Trust, S. Livingston
Mather and William Gwinn Mather Fund, Elizabeth Ring
Matthies Foundation, Katharine
Maytag Family Foundation, Fred
McCann Foundation
McCune Charitable Trust, John R.
McDermott Foundation, Eugene
McElroy Trust, R. J.
McLean Contributionship
Meadows Foundation
Mellon Family Foundation, R. K.
Mellon Foundation, Andrew W.
Mellon Foundation, Richard King
Memton Fund
Mengle Foundation, Glenn and Ruth
Merck & Co.
Merck Family Fund
Meyer Memorial Trust
Millbrook Tribute Garden
Miller Brewing Company/North Carolina
Monadnock Paper Mills
Moore & Sons, B.C.
Morgan Construction Co.
Morris Foundation, Margaret T.
Morris Foundation, William T.
Mosinee Paper Corp.
Mott Foundation, Charles Stewart
Mott Fund, Ruth
Muchnic Foundation
Murdock Charitable Trust, M. J.
Nestle USA Inc.
Neuberger Foundation, Roy R. and Marie S.
New-Land Foundation
Noble Foundation, Edward John
Normandie Foundation
Norton Foundation Inc.
O'Connor Foundation, A. Lindsay and Olive B.
OCRI Foundation
Offield Family Foundation
Old National Bank in Evansville
Olin Foundation, Spencer T. and Ann W.
Olsson Memorial Foundation, Elis
O'Quinn Foundation, John M. and Nancy C.
Osceola Foundation
Osher Foundation, Bernard
Overbrook Foundation
Peabody Charitable Fund, Amelia
Penn Foundation, William
Peterson Foundation, Hal and Charlie
Pettus Crowe Foundation
Pew Charitable Trusts
Pfizer, Inc.
Phipps Foundation, Howard
Pick, Jr. Fund, Albert
Pioneer Trust Bank, NA
Piper Jaffray Companies Inc.
Pitt-Des Moines Inc.
Pittsburg Midway Coal Mining Co.
Plumsock Fund
Potts and Sibley Foundation
Price Associates, T. Rowe
Prospect Hill Foundation
Prouty Foundation, Olive Higgins
Providence Journal Company

Public Welfare Foundation
Putnam Foundation
Reicher Foundation, Anne and Harry J.
Reidler Foundation
Rice Charitable Foundation, Albert W.
Rice Foundation
Richardson Charitable Trust, Anne S.
Rockefeller Fund, David
Rowland Foundation
Rubin Family Fund, Cele H. and William B.
Safety Fund National Bank
Saltonstall Charitable Foundation, Richard
Sarkeys Foundation
Sasco Foundation
Scherman Foundation
Schiff Foundation, Dorothy
Schiro Fund
Schlumberger Ltd.
Schumann Fund for New Jersey
Seaver Institute
Second Foundation
Sequoia Foundation
Seton Leather Co.
Shaw Foundation, Arch W.
Simon Foundation, William E. and Carol G.
Skaggs Foundation, L. J. and Mary C.
Slifka Foundation, Joseph and Sylvia
Smart Family Foundation
Smith Foundation, Ralph L.
Snow Memorial Trust, John Ben
Sonat Inc.
South Waite Foundation
Speyer Foundation, Alexander C. and Tillie S.
Sprague Educational and Charitable Foundation, Seth
Stanley Works
Steele-Reese Foundation
Stein Foundation, Jules and Doris
Stevens Foundation, Abbot and Dorothy H.
Stevens Foundation, John T.
Stokely, Jr. Foundation, William B.
Strawbridge Foundation of Pennsylvania II, Margaret Dorrance
Subaru of America Inc.
Sulzberger Foundation
Superior Tube Co.
Taubman Foundation, A. Alfred
Taylor Foundation, Ruth and Vernon
Teichert & Son, A.
Temple Foundation, T. L. L.
Texas Commerce Bank-Houston, N.A.
Thermo Electron Corp.
Thompson Co., J. Walter
Thorne Foundation
Travelers Inc.
Treakle Foundation, J. Edwin
Trexler Trust, Harry C.
Truland Foundation
Tucker Charitable Trust, Rose E.
Tupancy-Harris Foundation of 1986
Union Camp Corporation
United Airlines, Inc.
Unocal Corp.
Valentine Foundation, Lawson
Van Buren Foundation
Van Wert County Foundation
Vanderbilt Trust, R. T.
Vetlesen Foundation, G. Unger
Virginia Environmental Endowment
Wallace Foundation, George R.
Warner Fund, Albert and Bessie
Warwick Foundation
Washington Mutual Savings Bank

Waters Charitable Trust,
Robert S.
Wege Foundation
Welfare Foundation
Whiting Foundation
Whiting Foundation,
Macauley and Helen Dow
Whittenberger Foundation,
Claude R. and Ethel B.
Wiley & Sons, Inc., John
Willard Helping Fund, Cecilia
Young
Williams Charitable Trust,
Mary Jo
Wilson Foundation, H. W.
Winnebago Industries, Inc.
Winthrop Trust, Clara B.
Witter Foundation, Dean
Woodward Fund
Woolley Foundation, Vasser
Wyomissing Foundation
Young Foundation, Robert R.
Zenkel Foundation

Sanitary Systems

Shott, Jr. Foundation, Hugh I.

Watershed

Ansin Private Foundation,
Ronald M.
Bingham Foundation, William
Brady Foundation
Cape Branch Foundation
Carolyn Foundation
Dewing Foundation, Frances R.
Fund for New Jersey
Gebbie Foundation
Graham Fund, Philip L.
Halsell Foundation, Ewing
Hartz Foundation
Heinz Endowment, Vira I.
Klipstein Foundation, Ernest
Christian
Marpat Foundation
Meyer Memorial Trust
Morgan Construction Co.
New England Business Service
Offield Family Foundation
Read Foundation, Charles L.
Rogers Family Foundation
Saltonstall Charitable
Foundation, Richard
Stevens Foundation, Abbot
and Dorothy H.
Welfare Foundation

Wildlife Protection

Acme-McCrary Corp./Sapona
Manufacturing Co.
Ahmanson Foundation
AKC Fund
Aldus Corp.
Ames Charitable Trust, Harriett
Annenberg Foundation
Arcadia Foundation
Arnold Fund
Astor Foundation, Vincent
Baker Trust, George F.
Barker Foundation, J.M.R.
Bay Foundation
Bell Foundation, James F.
Bingham Foundation, William
Bingham Second Betterment
Fund, William
Binney & Smith Inc.
Birnschein Foundation, Alvin
and Marion
Blaustein Foundation, Louis
and Henrietta
Blount, Inc.
Bodman Foundation
Bothin Foundation
Brady Foundation
Breyer Foundation
Cain Foundation, Effie and
Wofford
Cain Foundation, Gordon and
Mary
Carolyn Foundation

Catlin Charitable Trust,
Kathleen K.
Cayuga Foundation
Chase Manhattan Bank, N.A.
CHC Foundation
Cheney Foundation, Ben B.
Claiborne and Art Ortenberg
Foundation, Liz
Clark Foundation
Clarkson Foundation, Jeniam
Clorox Co.
Clowes Fund
Coleman Foundation, George
E.
Commerce Clearing House,
Incorporated
Cooke Foundation
Crocker Trust, Mary A.
CT Corp. System
Daniel Foundation of Alabama
Davis Foundation, Edwin W.
and Catherine M.
Dewing Foundation, Frances R.
Dillon Dunwalke Trust,
Clarence and Anne
Dodge Foundation, Cleveland
H.
Dodge Foundation, Geraldine
R.
Donnelley Foundation,
Gaylord and Dorothy
Dreyfus Foundation, Max and
Victoria
Dula Educational and
Charitable Foundation,
Caleb C. and Julia W.
Dunagan Foundation
Erpf Fund, Armand G.
Exxon Corporation
Fair Play Foundation
Favrot Fund
Fikes Foundation, Leland
Firman Fund
Fondren Foundation
Forbes Inc.
Freed Foundation
Freedom Forge Corp.
Freeport-McMoRan Inc.
Gamble Foundation
GAR Foundation
Gheens Foundation
Gilmore Foundation, William
G.
Goddard Foundation, Charles
B.
Grand Rapids Label Co.
Griswold Foundation, John C.
Gulf Power Co.
Halsell Foundation, Ewing
Harriman Foundation, Mary W.
Harrington Foundation,
Francis A. and Jacquelyn H.
Heinz Endowment, Vira I.
Hill Foundation, Sandy
Hoag Family Foundation,
George
Hobby Foundation
Hoffmann-La Roche Inc.
Holnam
Holt Family Foundation
Hoover, Jr. Foundation,
Margaret W. and Herbert
Humphrey Fund, George M.
and Pamela S.
Hunt Charitable Trust, C. Giles
Hunt Foundation
Independence Foundation
Ingalls Foundation, Louise H.
and David S.
Ittleson Foundation
JELD-WEN, Inc.
Kansas City Southern
Industries
Kayser Foundation
Kelley and Elza Kelley
Foundation, Edward Bangs
Knapp Foundation
Knoll Group
Kresge Foundation
Larsen Fund
Laurel Foundation
Lebovitz Fund
Linnell Foundation
Long Foundation, J.M.

MacArthur Foundation, John
D. and Catherine T.
Magowan Family Foundation
Mahadh Foundation
Mailman Foundation
Markey Charitable Fund, John
C.
Mars Foundation
Martin Marietta Materials
Matthies Foundation, Katharine
Mautz Paint Co.
McCasland Foundation
McConnell Foundation
McDonald & Company
Securities, Inc.
McElroy Trust, R. J.
McLean Contributionship
McMahon Foundation
Mellon Family Foundation, R.
K.
Mellon Foundation, Richard
King
Middendorf Foundation
Millbrook Tribute Garden
Miller Brewing
Company/North Carolina
Miller-Mellor Association
Monadnock Paper Mills
Morgan Stanley & Co., Inc.
Morrison Charitable Trust,
Pauline A. and George R.
Mosinee Paper Corp.
Murdock Charitable Trust, M.
J.
New-Land Foundation
New York Times Company
Noble Foundation, Edward
John
Northern States Power Co.
(Minnesota)
Novell Inc.
OCRI Foundation
Offield Family Foundation
Olsson Memorial Foundation,
Elis
Packard Foundation, David
and Lucile
Phillips Foundation, Ellis L.
Phipps Foundation, Howard
Pierce Charitable Trust, Harold
Whitworth
Pittsburg Midway Coal Mining
Co.
Porter Foundation, Mrs.
Cheever
Prospect Hill Foundation
Reidler Foundation
Rosen Foundation, Joseph
Rosenberg, Jr. Family
Foundation, Louise and
Claude
Ross Laboratories
Ruan Foundation Trust, John
Rubin Family Fund, Cele H.
and William B.
Schiro Fund
Schroeder Foundation, Walter
Schwartz Foundation, Arnold
A.
Scurlock Foundation
Seaver Institute
Seneca Foods Corp.
Sequoia Foundation
Sierra Pacific Industries
Skaggs Foundation, L. J. and
Mary C.
South Waite Foundation
Sulzberger Foundation
Taylor Foundation, Ruth and
Vernon
Temple-Inland Inc.
Thornton Foundation
Tobin Foundation
Truland Foundation
Union Pacific Corp.
Valmont Industries, Inc.
Vanderbilt Trust, R. T.
Vetlesen Foundation, G. Unger
Waters Charitable Trust,
Robert S.
Wells Foundation, Franklin H.
and Ruth L.
Wendt Foundation, Margaret L.
Whitecap Foundation

Whittenberger Foundation,
Claude R. and Ethel B.
Widgeon Foundation
Wiley & Sons, Inc., John
Willard Helping Fund, Cecilia
Young
Witter Foundation, Dean
Woodward Fund
Wyomissing Foundation
Y and H Soda Foundation
Young Foundation, Robert R.
Zenkel Foundation

Health

Adolescent Health Issues

Ahmanson Foundation
Aldus Corp.
Baskin-Robbins USA Co.
Cafritz Foundation, Morris and
Gwendolyn
Carnegie Corporation of New
York
Deuble Foundation, George H.
Donner Foundation, William H.
Douty Foundation
Duke Endowment
Federated Mutual Insurance
Co.
Givenchy Corp.
Hewlett Foundation, William
and Flora
Hoffman Foundation,
Maximilian E. and Marion O.
Janirve Foundation
Jewish Healthcare Foundation
of Pittsburgh
Jones Foundation, Daisy
Marquis
Kansas City Southern
Industries
Kempner Fund, Harris and
Eliza
Knoll Group
Kornfeld Foundation, Emily
Davie and Joseph S.
Lasdon Foundation
Little, Inc., Arthur D.
Medtronic, Inc.
Nesholm Family Foundation
Old National Bank in
Evansville
Pew Charitable Trusts
Pfizer, Inc.
PriMerit Bank
Public Welfare Foundation
Roseburg Forest Products Co.
Saint Paul Companies, Inc.
U.S. Bank of Washington
Unitrode Corp.
Worthington Foods

AIDS/HIV

Abell-Hanger Foundation
Achelis Foundation
Ahmanson Foundation
Akzo America
Alabama Gas Corp.
Aldus Corp.
Alexander Foundation, Joseph
Altman Foundation
Altschul Foundation
Aluminum Co. of America
Amcast Industrial Corp.
American President
Companies, Ltd.
Ameritas Life Insurance Corp.
Ansin Private Foundation,
Ronald M.
AON Corporation
Argyros Foundation
Asplundh Foundation
Auerbach Foundation,
Beatrice Fox
Baldwin Foundation, David
M. and Barbara

Baldwin Memorial
Foundation, Fred
Ball Brothers Foundation
Bank of Boston Corp.
Bean Foundation, Norwin S.
and Elizabeth N.
BE&K Inc.
Benenson Foundation, Frances
and Benjamin
Berger Foundation, H. N. and
Frances C.
Birnschein Foundation, Alvin
and Marion
Blowitz-Ridgeway Foundation
Bobst Foundation, Elmer and
Mamdouha
Boettcher Foundation
Borden, Inc.
Borman's Inc.
Boston Edison Co.
Brach Foundation, Helen
Bremer Foundation, Otto
Bristol-Myers Squibb
Company
Bunbury Company
Burden Foundation, Florence
V.
Burlington Industries, Inc.
Burnett-Tandy Foundation
Bush Foundation
Butz Foundation
Cafritz Foundation, Morris and
Gwendolyn
Cain Foundation, Gordon and
Mary
Calder Foundation, Louis
Campbell Foundation
Campini Foundation, Frank A.
Cape Branch Foundation
Carpenter Technology Corp.
Carter Foundation, Beirne
Chartwell Foundation
Chatlos Foundation
Chazen Foundation
Chevron Corporation
Chicago Sun-Times, Inc.
Christian Dior New York, Inc.
Cogswell Benevolent Trust
Cole Foundation, Olive B.
Columbia Foundation
Connecticut Mutual Life
Insurance Company
Connelly Foundation
Cooke Foundation
Cooperman Foundation, Leon
and Toby
Copley Press, Inc.
Cowell Foundation, S. H.
Cowles Charitable Trust
Crown Books
Dana Charitable Trust, Eleanor
Naylor
Dana Foundation, Charles A.
Dart Group Corp.
Davis Foundation, Edwin W.
and Catherine M.
Dentsply International Inc.
Dexter Charitable Fund,
Eugene A.
Diamond Foundation, Aaron
Dodge Jones Foundation
Douty Foundation
Dreyfus Foundation, Jean and
Louis
Duchossois Industries Inc.
Duke Endowment
Dun & Bradstreet Corp.
Dunagan Foundation
Federated Mutual Insurance
Co.
Femino Foundation
Fikes Foundation, Leland
First Financial Bank FSB
Fishback Foundation Trust,
Harmes C.
Fleet Financial Group, Inc.
Fondren Foundation
Forbes Inc.
Ford Foundation
Foster Charitable Trust
Foster Foundation
Freed Foundation
Freeman Charitable Trust,
Samuel
Friedman Family Foundation

Fry Foundation, Lloyd A.
Fuller Foundation
Fund for New Jersey
GATX Corp.
Gellert Foundation, Celia Berta
General American Life
  Insurance Co.
Gershman Foundation, Joel
Giant Eagle, Inc.
Gilman Foundation, Howard
Glaser Foundation
Globe Newspaper Co.
Goldsmith Foundation, Horace
  W.
Goldwyn Foundation, Samuel
Graham Fund, Philip L.
Griffith Foundation, W. C.
Guttman Foundation, Stella
  and Charles
Hagedorn Fund
Hanson Industries North
  America
Harriman Foundation, Mary W.
Hauser Foundation
Hazen Foundation, Edward W.
Heinz Company, H. J.
Heinz Trust, Drue
Heller Charitable Foundation,
  Clarence E.
Hill Foundation, Sandy
Hillsdale Fund
Hobby Foundation
Houston Endowment
Howard and Bush Foundation
Humphrey Fund, George M.
  and Pamela S.
Hunt Foundation
Huston Charitable Trust,
  Stewart
Imperial Bancorp
Irvine Foundation, James
Ittleson Foundation
Jarson-Stanley and Mickey
  Kaplan Foundation, Isaac
  and Esther
Jewish Healthcare Foundation
  of Pittsburgh
Johnson Foundation, Helen K.
  and Arthur E.
Johnson Foundation, Willard
  T. C.
Jones Foundation, Daisy
  Marquis
Journal-Gazette Co.
Kansas City Southern
  Industries
Kaplan Fund, J. M.
Kaufmann Foundation, Henry
Kempner Fund, Harris and
  Eliza
Kiewit Foundation, Peter
Kilcawley Fund, William H.
Kirby Foundation, F. M.
Klipstein Foundation, Ernest
  Christian
Knoll Group
Koopman Fund
Kresge Foundation
Lattner Foundation, Forrest C.
Lazarus Charitable Trust,
  Helen and Charles
Lederer Foundation, Francis L.
Little, Inc., Arthur D.
Liz Claiborne, Inc.
Loews Corporation
M/A-COM, Inc.
Madison Gas & Electric Co.
Mailman Foundation
Mather Charitable Trust, S.
  Livingston
Mattel, Inc.
May Department Stores
  Company, The
McCune Charitable
  Foundation, Marshall and
  Perrine D.
McFawn Trust No. 2, Lois
  Sisler
McInerny Foundation
Meadows Foundation
Mellon Foundation, Richard
  King
Memton Fund
Merrill Lynch & Co., Inc.

Metropolitan Life Insurance
  Co.
Meyer Memorial Trust
Mid-Iowa Health Foundation
Miller Brewing
  Company/North Carolina
Mnuchin Foundation
Monell Foundation, Ambrose
Monfort Family Foundation
Moore Charitable Foundation,
  Marjorie
Morgan and Samuel Tate
  Morgan, Jr. Foundation,
  Marietta McNeil
Morgan Stanley & Co., Inc.
Morris Foundation, Margaret T.
Mosinee Paper Corp.
Mott Foundation, Charles
  Stewart
Nesholm Family Foundation
New York Life Insurance Co.
Northern States Power Co.
  (Minnesota)
Norton Co.
Oppenstein Brothers
  Foundation
O'Quinn Foundation, John M.
  and Nancy C.
Osher Foundation, Bernard
Overbrook Foundation
Pacific Mutual Life Insurance
  Co.
PaineWebber
Palmer Fund, Frank Loomis
Parsons Foundation, Ralph M.
Payne Foundation, Frank E.
  and Seba B.
Pella Corporation
Pettus Crowe Foundation
Pew Charitable Trusts
Pick, Jr. Fund, Albert
Polaroid Corp.
Premier Industrial Corp.
Prince Trust, Abbie Norman
Prudential Insurance Co. of
  America, The
Public Welfare Foundation
Rabb Foundation, Harry W.
Reicher Foundation, Anne and
  Harry J.
Rosen Foundation, Joseph
Ross Laboratories
Ross Memorial Foundation,
  Will
Rubinstein Foundation, Helena
Saint Paul Companies, Inc.
Salomon Foundation, Richard
  and Edna
Sandy Hill Foundation
Sarkeys Foundation
Sawyer Charitable Foundation
Scherman Foundation
Schiff Foundation, Dorothy
Schiro Fund
Schuller International
Seafirst Corporation
Shawmut National Corp.
Slifka Foundation, Joseph and
  Sylvia
Smith Foundation, Ralph L.
Smith Trust, May and Stanley
Starr Foundation
Staunton Farm Foundation
Steele-Reese Foundation
Stupp Foundation, Norman J.
Subaru of America Inc.
Sulzberger Foundation
Taubman Foundation, A. Alfred
Thermo Electron Corp.
Titus Foundation, Roy and
  Niuta
Towsley Foundation, Harry A.
  and Margaret D.
Travelers Inc.
Trull Foundation
Tuch Foundation, Michael
Tupancy-Harris Foundation of
  1986
Turrell Fund
Unger Foundation, Aber D.
U.S. Bank of Washington
USL Capital Corporation
van Ameringen Foundation
Vanderbilt Trust, R. T.
Vogler Foundation, Laura B.

Wahlstrom Foundation
Walsh Foundation
Washington Forrest Foundation
Washington Mutual Savings
  Bank
Weber Charities Corp.,
  Frederick E.
Weil, Gotshal and Manges
  Foundation
Wendt Foundation, Margaret L.
Whiting Foundation
Wiley & Sons, Inc., John
Willard Helping Fund, Cecilia
  Young
Wiremold Co.
Wright Foundation, Lola
Wyman Youth Trust
Wyomissing Foundation
Y and H Soda Foundation
Zenkel Foundation

Alzheimers Disease

Abell-Hanger Foundation
Ahmanson Foundation
Aldus Corp.
Allyn Foundation
Altschul Foundation
Amcast Industrial Corp.
American General Finance
  Corp.
American National Bank &
  Trust Co. of Chicago
Ames Charitable Trust, Harriett
AON Corporation
ASDA Foundation
Ashtabula Foundation
Baldwin Foundation, David
  M. and Barbara
Bank One, Youngstown, NA
Baskin-Robbins USA Co.
Bauervic Foundation, Charles
  M.
Berger Foundation, H. N. and
  Frances C.
Blue Cross & Blue Shield
  United of Wisconsin
Boothroyd Foundation,
  Charles H. and Bertha L.
Borman's Inc.
Boston Edison Co.
Brady Foundation
Burden Foundation, Florence
  V.
Burnett-Tandy Foundation
Cain Foundation, Effie and
  Wofford
Callaway Foundation
Chadwick Fund, Dorothy
  Jordan
Chartwell Foundation
Chicago Sun-Times, Inc.
Collins Foundation
Collins Foundation, George
  and Jennie
Connelly Foundation
Consumers Power Co.
Cornell Trust, Peter C.
Crown Memorial, Arie and Ida
Cuneo Foundation
Dodge Jones Foundation
Dreyfus Foundation, Jean and
  Louis
Duke Endowment
duPont Foundation, Alfred I.
El Pomar Foundation
Farr Trust, Frank M. and Alice
  M.
Femino Foundation
Frisch's Restaurants Inc.
Frohring Foundation, William
  O. and Gertrude Lewis
GAR Foundation
Geifman Family Foundation
Gellert Foundation, Carl
General American Life
  Insurance Co.
General Motors Corp.
Gifford Charitable
  Corporation, Rosamond
Grand Rapids Label Co.
Guaranty Bank & Trust Co.
Guttman Foundation, Stella
  and Charles

Haas, Jr. Fund, Evelyn and
  Walter
Hallberg Foundation, E. L. and
  R. F.
Hanson Industries North
  America
Hillsdale Fund
Hobby Foundation
Hook Drugs
Hoyt Foundation, Stewart W.
  and Willma C.
Hugoton Foundation
Hunt Foundation, Roy A.
Icahn Foundation, Carl C.
Imperial Bancorp
Jackson Foundation
Jennings Foundation, Mary
  Hillman
Jewish Healthcare Foundation
  of Pittsburgh
Johnson Foundation, Helen K.
  and Arthur E.
Johnson Fund, Edward C.
Jones Foundation, Daisy
  Marquis
Kansas City Southern
  Industries
Kardon Foundation, Samuel
  and Rebecca
Kelley and Elza Kelley
  Foundation, Edward Bangs
Kempner Fund, Harris and
  Eliza
Kirby Foundation, F. M.
Kline Foundation, Josiah W.
  and Bessie H.
LamCo. Communications
Lattner Foundation, Forrest C.
Lederer Foundation, Francis L.
Lehmann Foundation, Otto W.
Lovett Foundation
Lydall, Inc.
Mardigian Foundation
Markey Charitable Fund, John
  C.
McCarty Foundation, John and
  Margaret
McCasland Foundation
McMahan Foundation,
  Catherine L. and Robert O.
Meadows Foundation
Meyer Memorial Trust
Miller Fund, Kathryn and
  Gilbert
Monell Foundation, Ambrose
Nesholm Family Foundation
Olin Foundation, Spencer T.
  and Ann W.
Parsons Foundation, Ralph M.
Parvin Foundation, Albert
Philibosian Foundation,
  Stephen
Prince Trust, Abbie Norman
Prouty Foundation, Olive
  Higgins
Reinberger Foundation
Reisman Charitable Trust,
  George C. and Evelyn R.
Ross Laboratories
Salomon Foundation, Richard
  and Edna
Saltonstall Charitable
  Foundation, Richard
Sargent Foundation, Newell B.
Sarkeys Foundation
Schlumberger Ltd.
Shaw Foundation, Arch W.
Stemmons Foundation
Sternberger Foundation,
  Tannenbaum
Stupp Foundation, Norman J.
Temple Foundation, T. L. L.
Truland Foundation
Tucker Charitable Trust, Rose
  E.
Union Pacific Corp.
United Airlines, Inc.
Walsh Foundation
Weaver Foundation, Gil and
  Dody
Wendt Foundation, Margaret L.
Westerman Foundation,
  Samuel L.
Widgeon Foundation
Worthington Foods

Arthritis

Alabama Gas Corp.
Alavi Foundation of New York
Aldus Corp.
American Fidelity Corporation
American General Finance
  Corp.
Arcadia Foundation
Arkelian Foundation, Ben H.
  and Gladys
Bank One, Youngstown, NA
Blount, Inc.
Breyer Foundation
Bryn Mawr Trust Co.
Cain Foundation, Effie and
  Wofford
Catlin Charitable Trust,
  Kathleen K.
Chatlos Foundation
Chazen Foundation
Clarkson Foundation, Jeniam
Clements Foundation
Commerce Clearing House,
  Incorporated
Cremer Foundation
duPont Foundation, Alfred I.
Eden Hall Foundation
El Pomar Foundation
Ettinger Foundation
Fair Play Foundation
Fleming Cos. Food
  Distribution Center
Fuqua Foundation, J. B.
Gamble Foundation
Gellert Foundation, Carl
Gould Electronics Inc.
Hagedorn Fund
Handy and Harman Foundation
Hawn Foundation
Hillcrest Foundation
Jostens, Inc.
Kansas City Southern
  Industries
Kayser Foundation
Kennedy Foundation, Ethel
Kirby Foundation, F. M.
Knoll Group
Ladd Charitable Corporation,
  Helen and George
Lydall, Inc.
M/A-COM, Inc.
McCormick Trust, Anne
McFawn Trust No. 2, Lois
  Sisler
MCI Communications Corp.
Meyer Family Foundation,
  Paul J.
Mid-Iowa Health Foundation
Monell Foundation, Ambrose
Monfort Family Foundation
Morris Foundation, William T.
Muchnic Foundation
Novell Inc.
Olin Foundation, Spencer T.
  and Ann W.
Patterson Charitable Fund, W.
  I.
Rabb Foundation, Harry W.
Reisman Charitable Trust,
  George C. and Evelyn R.
Rice Foundation
Schwob Foundation, Simon
Scott Fetzer Co.
Smith Trust, May and Stanley
Sturgis Charitable and
  Educational Trust, Roy and
  Christine
Taube Family Foundation
Taubman Foundation, A. Alfred
Thomas Industries
Thornton Foundation, Flora L.
Unger Foundation, Aber D.
Unocal Corp.
Valmont Industries, Inc.
Walsh Foundation
Washington Forrest Foundation
West Foundation, Harry and
  Ethel
Westerman Foundation,
  Samuel L.
Windham Foundation
Young Foundation, Robert R.

Cancer

Abell-Hanger Foundation
Achelis Foundation
Ahmanson Foundation
Air Products and Chemicals, Inc.
Alabama Gas Corp.
Alavi Foundation of New York
Aldus Corp.
Alexander Foundation, Joseph
Allegheny Foundation
Allen Brothers Foundation
AlliedSignal Inc.
Allyn Foundation
Altman Foundation
Altschul Foundation
Aluminum Co. of America
Amcast Industrial Corp.
AMCORE Bank, N.A. Rockford
American General Finance Corp.
American National Bank & Trust Co. of Chicago
Ames Charitable Trust, Harriett
AMETEK, Inc.
AMP Incorporated
Andersen Foundation
Anderson Foundation, John W.
Andreas Foundation
Annenberg Foundation
Ansley Foundation, Dantzler Bond
Appleby Trust, Scott B. and Annie P.
Archer-Daniels-Midland Co.
Argyros Foundation
Arkelian Foundation, Ben H. and Gladys
Arkell Hall Foundation
ASDA Foundation
Asplundh Foundation
Ayres Foundation, Inc.
Baldwin Foundation, David M. and Barbara
Bank One, Youngstown, NA
Banta Corp.
Beal Foundation
Bean Foundation, Norwin S. and Elizabeth N.
Beazley Foundation/Frederick Foundation
Bechtel, Jr. Foundation, S. D.
Beech Aircraft Corp.
Benenson Foundation, Frances and Benjamin
Berger Foundation, H. N. and Frances C.
Bingham Second Betterment Fund, William
Binswanger Cos.
Blaustein Foundation, Louis and Henrietta
Block, H&R
Blowitz-Ridgeway Foundation
Blue Bell, Inc.
Bobst Foundation, Elmer and Mamdouha
Bodman Foundation
Borden, Inc.
Borman's Inc.
Boston Edison Co.
Bowen Foundation, Ethel N.
Brady Foundation
Breyer Foundation
Bridwell Foundation, J. S.
Brillion Iron Works
Bristol-Myers Squibb Company
Brown Foundation, M. K.
Bryant Foundation
Bryn Mawr Trust Co.
Cabot Corp.
Cain Foundation, Effie and Wofford
Cain Foundation, Gordon and Mary
Callaway Foundation
Campini Foundation, Frank A.
Carpenter Technology Corp.
Catlin Charitable Trust, Kathleen K.
Cayuga Foundation

Central Fidelity Banks, Inc.
Charina Foundation
Chartwell Foundation
Chastain Charitable Foundation, Robert Lee and Thomas M.
Chatlos Foundation
Chazen Foundation
Cheney Foundation, Ben B.
Chesebrough-Pond's USA Co.
Christian Dior New York, Inc.
City National Bank and Trust Co.
Clapp Charitable and Educational Trust, George H.
Clark Foundation
Cole Foundation, Olive B.
Columbus Dispatch Printing Co.
Commerce Bancshares, Inc.
Commerce Clearing House, Incorporated
Connelly Foundation
Contran Corporation
Cooper Industries, Inc.
Cooperman Foundation, Leon and Toby
Cowles Charitable Trust
Crabtree & Evelyn
Crane Co.
Crawford Estate, E. R.
Crestlea Foundation
Crown Books
Crystal Trust
CS First Boston Corporation
Cullen Foundation
Culpeper Foundation, Charles E.
Culpeper Memorial Foundation, Daphne Seybolt
Cummings Foundation, James H.
Cuneo Foundation
Dana Charitable Trust, Eleanor Naylor
Dana Foundation, Charles A.
Daniel Foundation of Alabama
Dart Group Corp.
Dater Foundation, Charles H.
Davenport-Hatch Foundation
Davidson Family Charitable Foundation
Davis Foundation, Edwin W. and Catherine M.
Demoulas Supermarkets Inc.
Dentsply International Inc.
DeRoy Testamentary Foundation
DeVore Foundation
Dillon Foundation
Dr. Seuss Foundation
Dreyfus Foundation, Jean and Louis
Dreyfus Foundation, Max and Victoria
Duchossois Industries Inc.
Duke Endowment
Dula Educational and Charitable Foundation, Caleb C. and Julia W.
Dun & Bradstreet Corp.
Duncan Trust, John G.
Dynamet, Inc.
Eaton Corporation
Eden Hall Foundation
Einstein Fund, Albert E. and Birdie W.
El Pomar Foundation
Elkins, Jr. Foundation, Margaret and James A.
Emerson Foundation, Inc., Fred L.
English Memorial Fund, Florence C. and H. L.
Ensign-Bickford Industries
Evans Foundation, T. M.
Exchange National Bank
Exxon Corporation
Fair Foundation, R. W.
Fair Oaks Foundation, Inc.
Fairchild Foundation, Sherman
Farish Fund, William Stamps
Favrot Fund
Federal-Mogul Corporation

Federated Mutual Insurance Co.
Femino Foundation
Fieldcrest Cannon Inc.
Fife Foundation, Elias and Bertha
Fikes Foundation, Leland
Fischbach Foundation
Fish Foundation, Ray C.
Fishback Foundation Trust, Harmes C.
Fleet Financial Group, Inc.
Fletcher Foundation
Folger Fund
Fondren Foundation
Forbes Inc
Forest Foundation
Foster Foundation
Freedom Forge Corp.
Freeman Charitable Trust, Samuel
Freeport-McMoRan Inc.
French Oil Mill Machinery Co.
Frese Foundation, Arnold D.
Fribourg Foundation
Frisch's Restaurants Inc.
Frohring Foundation, William O. and Gertrude Lewis
Fruehauf Foundation
Fuller Foundation
Fuller Foundation, C. G.
GATX Corp.
Gazette Co.
Geifman Family Foundation
General Mills, Inc.
General Motors Corp.
Geneseo Foundation
Gershman Foundation, Joel
Gheens Foundation
Giant Eagle, Inc.
Giant Food Inc.
Gilmore Foundation, William G.
Givenchy Corp.
Glanville Family Foundation
Glaser Foundation
Glick Foundation, Eugene and Marilyn
Goldsmith Foundation, Horace W.
Goldwyn Foundation, Samuel
Gould Electronics Inc.
Grand Rapids Label Co.
Gregg-Graniteville Foundation
Griffis Foundation
Griffith Foundation, W. C.
Griswold Foundation, John C.
Grundy Foundation
GSM Industrial
Gulf Coast Medical Foundation
Gulf Power Co.
Guttman Foundation, Stella and Charles
Hachar Charitable Trust, D. D.
Hagedorn Fund
Haley Foundation, W. B.
Halff Foundation, G. A. C.
Hamman Foundation, George and Mary Josephine
Hammer Foundation, Armand
Handy and Harman Foundation
Hanover Foundation
Hanson Industries North America
Harriman Foundation, Gladys and Roland
Harriman Foundation, Mary W.
Harrington Foundation, Francis A. and Jacquelyn H.
Hartmarx Corporation
Hatch Charitable Trust, Margaret Milliken
Hearst Foundation, William Randolph
Hechinger Co.
Heckscher Foundation for Children
Heinz Endowment, Vira I.
Heinz Trust, Drue
Herzstein Charitable Foundation, Albert and Ethel
Hill Foundation, Sandy
Hillman Foundation
Hillsdale Fund

Hoag Family Foundation, George
Hobby Foundation
Holzer Memorial Foundation, Richard H.
Homeland Foundation
Hoover Fund-Trust, W. Henry
Hoover, Jr. Foundation, Margaret W. and Herbert
Hopwood Charitable Trust, John M.
Houston Endowment
Hoyt Foundation
Hudson-Webber Foundation
Hugoton Foundation
Hunt Foundation
Hyde and Watson Foundation
Hygeia Dairy Co.
Icahn Foundation, Carl C.
Integra Bank of Uniontown
Irwin Charity Foundation, William G.
Ittleson Foundation
Jarson-Stanley and Mickey Kaplan Foundation, Isaac and Esther
Jaydor Corp.
Jennings Foundation, Mary Hillman
Jewett Foundation, George Frederick
Jewish Healthcare Foundation of Pittsburgh
JM Foundation
Johnson Foundation, Burdine
Johnson Foundation, Helen K. and Arthur E.
Johnson Fund, Edward C.
Jonsson Foundation
Jostens, Inc.
Jurzykowski Foundation, Alfred
Kansas City Southern Industries
Kardon Foundation, Samuel and Rebecca
Kaufmann Foundation, Henry
Kayser Foundation
Kelly Tractor Co.
Kemper Foundation, William T.
Kennedy Foundation, Ethel
Kimberly-Clark Corp.
Kingsbury Corp.
Kinney-Lindstrom Foundation
Kirby Foundation, F. M.
Kline Foundation, Josiah W. and Bessie H.
Klock and Lucia Klock Kingston Foundation, Jay E.
Knapp Foundation
Knight Foundation, John S. and James L.
Knoll Group
Kohn-Joseloff Foundation
Komes Foundation
Kresge Foundation
Kunkel Foundation, John Crain
Laffey-McHugh Foundation
LamCo. Communications
Lasdon Foundation
Lasdon Foundation, William and Mildred
Lattner Foundation, Forrest C.
Lauder Foundation
Lazarus Charitable Trust, Helen and Charles
LBJ Family Foundation
Lehigh Portland Cement Co.
Lehmann Foundation, Otto W.
Lennon Foundation, Fred A.
Leuthold Foundation
Levy Foundation, June Rockwell
Lichtenstein Foundation, David B.
Liz Claiborne, Inc.
Lockhart Vaughan Foundation
Loews Corporation
Lovett Foundation
Lowenstein Foundation, Leon
Lydall, Inc.
M/A-COM, Inc.
Maddox Foundation, J. F.
Mailman Family Foundation, A. L.

Management Compensation Group/Dulworth Inc.
Mandeville Foundation
Marbrook Foundation
Markey Charitable Fund, John C.
Mars Foundation
Martin Marietta Corp.
Martini Foundation, Nicholas
Mascoma Savings Bank
Mather and William Gwinn Mather Fund, Elizabeth Ring
Mattel, Inc.
May Department Stores Company, The
Mayer Foundation, James and Eva
Maytag Family Foundation, Fred
MCA Inc.
McCormick Trust, Anne
McDermott Foundation, Eugene
McEvoy Foundation, Mildred H.
McFawn Trust No. 2, Lois Sisler
McGee Foundation
McGonagle Foundation, Dextra Baldwin
MCI Communications Corp.
McInerny Foundation
McMillan Foundation, D. W.
Meadows Foundation
Medtronic, Inc.
Mellon Foundation, Richard King
Merck & Co.
Mercury Aircraft
Merrill Lynch & Co., Inc.
Meyer Family Foundation, Paul J.
Meyer Fund, Milton and Sophie
Meyer Memorial Trust
Mid-Iowa Health Foundation
Middendorf Foundation
Miller Fund, Kathryn and Gilbert
Monell Foundation, Ambrose
Monfort Family Foundation
Montana Power Co.
Morgan & Company, J.P.
Morgan Stanley & Co., Inc.
Morris Foundation, Margaret T.
Morris Foundation, William T.
Mosbacher, Jr. Foundation, Emil
Moses Fund, Henry and Lucy
Mosinee Paper Corp.
Muchnic Foundation
Murdock Charitable Trust, M. J.
Murphey Foundation, Lluella Morey
Murphy Co. Foundation, G.C.
Musson Charitable Foundation, R. C. and Katharine M.
New Jersey Natural Gas Co.
New York Stock Exchange, Inc.
Noble Foundation, Edward John
Noble Foundation, Samuel Roberts
Norgren Foundation, Carl A.
Northern States Power Co. (Minnesota)
Norton Co.
Norton Memorial Corporation, Geraldi
Novell Inc.
Olsson Memorial Foundation, Elis
O'Quinn Foundation, John M. and Nancy C.
Osborn Charitable Trust, Edward B.
Ottley Trust-Watertown, Marion W.
Overlake Foundation
Owsley Foundation, Alvin and Lucy
PaineWebber

Palisades Educational Foundation
Park Foundation
Parshelsky Foundation, Moses L.
Parsons Foundation, Ralph M.
Parvin Foundation, Albert
Patterson Charitable Fund, W. I.
Peppers Foundation, Ann
Peterson Foundation, Hal and Charlie
Pew Charitable Trusts
Philibosian Foundation, Stephen
Phillips Charitable Trust, Dr. and Mrs. Arthur William
Piankova Foundation, Tatiana
Pineywoods Foundation
Piper Jaffray Companies Inc.
Plankenhorn Foundation, Harry
PNC Bank, N.A.
Porter Foundation, Mrs. Cheever
Quivey-Bay State Foundation
Rabb Foundation, Harry W.
Rachal Foundation, Ed
Reicher Foundation, Anne and Harry J.
Reidler Foundation
Reinberger Foundation
Reisman Charitable Trust, George C. and Evelyn R.
Rice Foundation
Richardson Benevolent Foundation, C. E.
Richardson Charitable Trust, Anne S.
Rockwell Fund
Rockwell International Corporation
Rohatyn Foundation, Felix and Elizabeth
Rose Foundation, Billy
Roseburg Forest Products Co.
Rosen Foundation, Joseph
Rosenberg, Jr. Family Foundation, Louise and Claude
Ross Laboratories
Rowland Foundation
Rubin Family Fund, Cele H. and William B.
Rubinstein Foundation, Helena
Saint Paul Companies, Inc.
Salomon Foundation, Richard and Edna
Sandusky International Inc.
Sandy Hill Foundation
Sargent Foundation, Newell B.
Sasco Foundation
Sawyer Charitable Foundation
SBC Communications Inc.
Schenck Fund, L. P.
Scherer Foundation, Karla
Schering-Plough Corp.
Schiff Foundation, Dorothy
Schiro Fund
Schlink Foundation, Albert G. and Olive H.
Scholl Foundation, Dr.
Schroeder Foundation, Walter
Schuller International
Schwartz Foundation, Arnold A.
Schwartz Fund for Education and Health Research, Arnold and Marie
Schwob Foundation, Simon
Scurlock Foundation
Seafirst Corporation
Seaver Charitable Trust, Richard C.
Semmes Foundation
Seneca Foods Corp.
Seton Leather Co.
Sheary for Charity, Edna M.
Sheppard Foundation, Lawrence B.
Sierra Pacific Industries
Simon Foundation, William E. and Carol G.
Slifka Foundation, Joseph and Sylvia

Smith Foundation, Gordon V. and Helen C.
Smith Foundation, Ralph L.
SmithKline Beecham Corp.
Snow Memorial Trust, John Ben
Southwestern Electric Power Co.
Springs Foundation
Stanley Works
Starr Foundation
Stauffer Charitable Trust, John
Stauffer Foundation, John and Beverly
Steele Foundation, Harry and Grace
Stein Foundation, Jules and Doris
Steinman Foundation, James Hale
Stokely, Jr. Foundation, William B.
Stone Trust, H. Chase
Strauss Foundation, Leon
Strawbridge Foundation of Pennsylvania II, Margaret Dorrance
Stupp Foundation, Norman J.
Sturgis Charitable and Educational Trust, Roy and Christine
Subaru of America Inc.
Sullivan Foundation, Algernon Sydney
Superior Tube Co.
Swanson Family Foundation, Dr. W.C.
Taube Family Foundation
Taubman Foundation, A. Alfred
Taylor Foundation, Fred and Harriett
Taylor Foundation, Ruth and Vernon
Temple Foundation, T. L. L.
Texas Commerce Bank-Houston, N.A.
Thalhimer and Family Foundation, Charles G.
Thompson Charitable Foundation
Thompson Co., J. Walter
Thorne Foundation
Thornton Foundation
Thornton Foundation, Flora L.
Times Mirror Company, The
Towsley Foundation, Harry A. and Margaret D.
TransAmerica Corporation
Travelers Inc.
Treakle Foundation, J. Edwin
Truland Foundation
Trull Foundation
Turner Charitable Foundation
Union Pacific Corp.
United Airlines, Inc.
U.S. Bank of Washington
Valentine Foundation, Lawson van Ameringen Foundation
Van Houten Memorial Fund
Vanderbilt Trust, R. T.
Vernon Fund, Miles Hodsdon
Vollbrecht Foundation, Frederick A.
Wahlstrom Foundation
Walsh Foundation
Washington Forrest Foundation
Washington Mutual Savings Bank
Weaver Foundation, Gil and Dody
Weingart Foundation
Weinstein Foundation, J.
Wells Foundation, Franklin H. and Ruth L.
Wheeler Foundation
Whiting Foundation
Widgeon Foundation
Wiegand Foundation, E. L.
Wilder Foundation
Willard Helping Fund, Cecilia Young
Windham Foundation
Winnebago Industries, Inc.
Wisconsin Power & Light Co.
Witco Corp.

Wood Foundation of Chambersburg, PA
Y and H Soda Foundation
Young Foundation, Hugo H. and Mabel B.
Young Foundation, Robert R.
Zarrow Foundation, Anne and Henry
Zenkel Foundation

Children's Health/Hospitals

Abbott Laboratories
ACF Industries, Inc.
Achelis Foundation
Acushnet Co.
Aetna Life & Casualty Co.
Ahmanson Foundation
Alabama Gas Corp.
Alavi Foundation of New York
Alcon Laboratories, Inc.
Aldus Corp.
Alexander Foundation, Joseph
Allegheny Ludlum Corp.
AlliedSignal Inc.
Allyn Foundation
Altman Foundation
Aluminum Co. of America
Amcast Industrial Corp.
American General Finance Corp.
American Optical Corp.
American President Companies, Ltd.
Amoco Corporation
AMP Incorporated
AMR Corp.
Andersen Foundation
Anderson Foundation, John W.
Anderson Foundation, M. D.
Anheuser-Busch Companies, Inc.
Ansin Private Foundation, Ronald M.
Ansley Foundation, Dantzler Bond
AON Corporation
Appleby Trust, Scott B. and Annie P.
Arkell Hall Foundation
AT&T Corp.
Auerbach Foundation, Beatrice Fox
Baker Trust, George F.
Ball Foundation, George and Frances
Bank of Boston
Bank One, Youngstown, NA
BankAmerica Corp.
Banta Corp.
Barra Foundation
Baskin-Robbins USA Co.
Beal Foundation
Bean Foundation, Norwin S. and Elizabeth N.
BE&K Inc.
Beazley Foundation/Frederick Foundation
Benedum Foundation, Claude Worthington
Benenson Foundation, Frances and Benjamin
Berger Foundation, H. N. and Frances C.
Bettingen Corporation, Burton G.
Binney & Smith Inc.
Birnschein Foundation, Alvin and Marion
Bishop Foundation, E. K. and Lillian F.
Blake Foundation, S. P.
Block, H&R
Bloedorn Foundation, Walter A.
Blowitz-Ridgeway Foundation
Blue Bell, Inc.
Blum-Kovler Foundation
Boettcher Foundation
Booth Ferris Foundation
Borman's Inc.
Brach Foundation, Helen

Breyer Foundation
Bridgestone/Firestone, Inc.
Bridwell Foundation, J. S.
Brillion Iron Works
Bristol-Myers Squibb Company
Brooks Foundation, Gladys
Brunswick Corp.
Bryn Mawr Trust Co.
Bush Foundation
Cabell Foundation, Robert G. Cabell III and Maude Morgan
Cafritz Foundation, Morris and Gwendolyn
Cain Foundation, Effie and Wofford
Cain Foundation, Gordon and Mary
Calder Foundation, Louis
Calhoun Charitable Trust, Kenneth
Campbell Foundation
Campbell Foundation, Ruth and Henry
Carnegie Corporation of New York
Carolyn Foundation
Carter Foundation, Amon G.
Carvel Foundation, Thomas and Agnes
Cassett Foundation, Louis N.
Centralia Foundation
Chartwell Foundation
Chase Manhattan Bank, N.A.
Cheney Foundation, Ben B.
Childs Charitable Foundation, Roberta M.
Christensen Charitable and Religious Foundation, L. C.
CINergy
Clapp Charitable and Educational Trust, George H.
Clarkson Foundation, Jeniam
Clemens Markets Corp.
Clorox Co.
Coen Family Foundation, Charles S. and Mary
Cogswell Benevolent Trust
Columbus Dispatch Printing Co.
Comer Foundation
Commerce Bancshares, Inc.
Connecticut Mutual Life Insurance Company
Connelly Foundation
Consumers Power Co.
Contran Corporation
Cooperman Foundation, Leon and Toby
Cord Foundation, E. L.
Cornell Trust, Peter C.
Crawford Estate, E. R.
Cremer Foundation
Crown Books
Crown Memorial, Arie and Ida
CS First Boston Corporation
Cullen Foundation
Cummings Foundation, James H.
Cuneo Foundation
Curtice-Burns Foods, Inc.
Dana Charitable Trust, Eleanor Naylor
Dart Group Corp.
Dater Foundation, Charles H.
Daugherty Foundation
Davis Foundation, Edwin W. and Catherine M.
Davis Foundation, Irene E. and George A.
Davis Foundations, Arthur Vining
Dell Foundation, Hazel
Demos Foundation, N.
Demoulas Supermarkets Inc.
Dentsply International Inc.
DeRoy Testamentary Foundation
Deuble Foundation, George H.
Diamond Foundation, Aaron
Dillon Foundation
Dr. Seuss Foundation
Douty Foundation

Dow Foundation, Herbert H. and Grace A.
Duchossois Industries Inc.
Duke Endowment
Dula Educational and Charitable Foundation, Caleb C. and Julia W.
Duncan Foundation, Lillian H. and C. W.
Duncan Trust, John G.
duPont Foundation, Alfred I.
Early Foundation
Eaton Foundation, Cyrus
Eddy Family Memorial Fund, C. K.
Eden Hall Foundation
Edgewater Steel Corp.
Edmonds Foundation, Dean S.
Ensign-Bickford Industries
Essick Foundation
Fair Oaks Foundation, Inc.
Federal-Mogul Corp.
Federated Mutual Insurance Co.
Fenton Foundation
Fife Foundation, Elias and Bertha
Fikes Foundation, Leland
Firman Fund
First Financial Bank FSB
First National Bank
First Union Corp.
Firstar Bank Milwaukee, N.A.
Fleet Financial Group, Inc.
Fletcher Foundation
Flowers Charitable Trust, Albert W. and Edith V.
Fondren Foundation
Ford Fund, William and Martha
Ford II Fund, Henry
Foster Foundation
Freedom Forge Corp.
Freeport-McMoRan Inc.
Fribourg Foundation
Frueauff Foundation, Charles A.
Fruehauf Foundation
Fuqua Foundation, J. B.
GAR Foundation
Gazette Co.
Gebbie Foundation
Gellert Foundation, Celia Berta
GenCorp Inc.
Georgia-Pacific Corporation
German Protestant Orphan Asylum Association
Gheens Foundation
Giant Eagle, Inc.
Gilmore Foundation, William G.
Glaser Foundation
Globe Newspaper Co.
Goldberg Family Foundation
Goldwyn Foundation, Samuel
Gould Electronics Inc.
Graham Fund, Philip L.
Grand Rapids Label Co.
Green Foundation, Allen P. and Josephine B.
Griswold Foundation, John C.
Grundy Foundation
GSM Industrial
Gulf Coast Medical Foundation
Hachar Charitable Trust, D. D.
Hamilton Bank
Hammer Foundation, Armand
Hancock Foundation, Luke B.
Handy and Harman Foundation
Hanover Foundation
Hanson Industries North America
Harcourt General, Inc.
Harland Charitable Foundation, John and Wilhelmina D.
Harriman Foundation, Mary W.
Harsco Corp.
Hassenfeld Foundation
Hawkins Foundation, Robert Z.
Hawn Foundation
Hearst Foundation, William Randolph
Hechinger Co.
Heckscher Foundation for Children

Blowitz-Ridgeway Foundation
Blue Cross & Blue Shield United of Wisconsin
Blum Foundation, Harry and Maribel G.
Blum-Kovler Foundation
Bobst Foundation, Elmer and Mamdouha
Bodman Foundation
Boettcher Foundation
Boston Edison Co.
Brach Foundation, Helen
Brackenridge Foundation, George W.
Brady Foundation
Bremer Foundation, Otto
Bright Family Foundation
Bryn Mawr Trust Co.
Bunbury Company
Burchfield Foundation, Charles E.
Burden Foundation, Florence V.
Burnett-Tandy Foundation
Bush Foundation
Cabell Foundation, Robert G. Cabell III and Maude Morgan
Cabot Family Charitable Trust
Caestecker Foundation, Charles and Marie
Cain Foundation, Effie and Wofford
Callaway Foundation
Campbell Foundation
Campini Foundation, Frank A.
Carnegie Corporation of New York
Carolyn Foundation
Carvel Foundation, Thomas and Agnes
Cassett Foundation, Louis N.
Castle Foundation, Harold K. L.
Cayuga Foundation
Central Fidelity Banks, Inc.
Chadwick Fund, Dorothy Jordan
Champlin Foundations
Chatlos Foundation
Cheatham Foundation, Owen
Cheney Foundation, Ben B.
Chesebrough-Pond's USA Co.
Childs Charitable Foundation, Roberta M.
Clorox Co.
Coen Family Foundation, Charles S. and Mary
Comer Foundation
Connecticut Mutual Life Insurance Company
Connelly Foundation
Consolidated Natural Gas Co.
Contran Corporation
Cooperman Foundation, Leon and Toby
Coors Foundation, Adolph
Cornell Trust, Peter C.
Covington and Burling
Cowell Foundation, S. H.
Cowles Charitable Trust
Crandall Memorial Foundation, J. Ford
Crestlea Foundation
Crown Memorial, Arie and Ida
CS First Boston Corporation
Cullen Foundation
Culpeper Foundation, Charles E.
Culpeper Memorial Foundation, Daphne Seybolt
Cummings Foundation, James H.
Curtice-Burns Foods, Inc.
Dana Charitable Trust, Eleanor Naylor
Dana Foundation, Charles A.
Daniel Foundation of Alabama
Darby Foundation
Daugherty Foundation
Davenport-Hatch Foundation
Davenport Trust Fund
Davis Foundation, Edwin W. and Catherine M.

Davis Foundation, Irene E. and George A.
Delano Foundation, Mignon Sherwood
Dell Foundation, Hazel
Dexter Charitable Fund, Eugene A.
Dillon Foundation
Dingman Foundation, Michael D.
Dr. Seuss Foundation
Dodge Jones Foundation
Donner Foundation, William H.
Dow Foundation, Herbert H. and Grace A.
Dow Jones & Company, Inc.
Dresser Industries, Inc.
Dreyfus Foundation, Jean and Louis
Duchossois Industries Inc.
Duke Endowment
Duncan Foundation, Lillian H. and C. W.
Dynamet, Inc.
Eastman Kodak Company
Eaton Foundation, Cyrus
Eberly Foundation
Eccles Foundation, Ralph M. and Ella M.
Eddy Family Memorial Fund, C. K.
Eden Hall Foundation
El Pomar Foundation
Essick Foundation
Evans Foundation, T. M.
Exxon Corporation
Fair Foundation, R. W.
Farish Fund, William Stamps
Federal-Mogul Corporation
Federated Mutual Insurance Co.
Feil Foundation, Louis and Gertrude
Femino Foundation
First Financial Bank FSB
First Hawaiian, Inc.
First Interstate Bank of Oregon
Firstar Bank Milwaukee, N.A.
Fischbach Foundation
Fish Foundation, Ray C.
Fleet Financial Group, Inc.
Fletcher Foundation
Fondren Foundation
Forbes Inc.
Forest Foundation
Forest Oil Corp.
Foster Charitable Trust
Foster Foundation
Freed Foundation
Freeman Charitable Trust, Samuel
Freeport-McMoRan Inc.
Frese Foundation, Arnold D.
Friedman Family Foundation
Friendship Fund
Frueauff Foundation, Charles A.
Fruehauf Foundation
Fry Foundation, Lloyd A.
Fuld Health Trust, Helene
Fuqua Foundation, J. B.
Gamble Foundation
Gannett Publishing Co., Guy
GATX Corp.
Gellert Foundation, Carl
Gellert Foundation, Celia Berta
Gilman Foundation, Howard
Gilmore Foundation, William G.
Glaser Foundation
Globe Newspaper Co.
Goddard Foundation, Charles B.
Goldsmith Foundation, Horace W.
Goldwyn Foundation, Samuel
Gould Electronics Inc.
Gould Foundation, The Florence
Graham Fund, Philip L.
Greenwall Foundation
Gulf Coast Medical Foundation
Gulf Power Co.
Haas, Jr. Fund, Evelyn and Walter

Hafif Family Foundation
Hagedorn Fund
Hallett Charitable Trust, E. W.
Hamman Foundation, George and Mary Josephine
Hammer Foundation, Armand
Handy and Harman Foundation
Harcourt General, Inc.
Harland Charitable Foundation, John and Wilhelmina D.
Harriman Foundation, Gladys and Roland
Hartford Foundation, John A.
Hartmarx Corporation
Hasbro Inc.
Hatch Charitable Trust, Margaret Milliken
Hawn Foundation
Heckscher Foundation for Children
Heinz Endowment, Howard
Helmerich Foundation
Helms Foundation
Henderson Foundation, George B.
Hershey Foods Corp.
Herzstein Charitable Foundation, Albert and Ethel
Higginson Trust, Corina
Hill Foundation, Sandy
Hillcrest Foundation
Hoag Family Foundation, George
Hook Drugs
Hopedale Foundation
Houston Endowment
Huber Foundation
Hugoton Foundation
Humana, Inc.
Hunt Charitable Trust, C. Giles
Hunt Foundation
Huston Foundation
Huthsteiner Fine Arts Trust
Hyde and Watson Foundation
Hygeia Dairy Co.
Illinois Consolidated Telephone Co.
Imperial Bancorp
Independence Foundation
International Foundation
International Paper Co.
Irvine Foundation, James
Irwin Charity Foundation, William G.
ITT Hartford Insurance Group, Inc.
Jacobs Family Foundation
Jacobson Foundation, Bernard H. and Blanche E.
Janirve Foundation
Jewish Healthcare Foundation of Pittsburgh
JM Foundation
Jockey Hollow Foundation
Johnson Controls Inc.
Johnson Foundation, Helen K. and Arthur E.
Johnson Foundation, M. G. and Lillie A.
Johnson & Son, S.C.
Jones Foundation, Daisy Marquis
Jones Foundation, Fletcher
Jonsson Foundation
Jurzykowski Foundation, Alfred
Kansas City Southern Industries
Kayser Foundation
Kemper Foundation, William T.
Kent-Lucas Foundation
Kerr Foundation
Kettering Fund
Kingsbury Corp.
Kirkpatrick Foundation
Kline Foundation, Josiah W. and Bessie H.
Klipstein Foundation, Ernest Christian
Klosk Fund, Louis and Rose
Knox, Sr., and Pearl Wallis Knox Charitable Foundation, Robert W.

Knudsen Foundation, Tom and Valley
Komes Foundation
Koopman Fund
Kornfeld Foundation, Emily Davie and Joseph S.
Kresge Foundation
Landegger Charitable Foundation
Lang Foundation, Eugene M.
Lasdon Foundation
Lasdon Foundation, William and Mildred
Lattner Foundation, Forrest C.
Lauder Foundation
Lazarus Charitable Trust, Helen and Charles
Leavey Foundation, Thomas and Dorothy
Lederer Foundation, Francis L.
Lee Enterprises
Lemberg Endowment
Lennon Foundation, Fred A.
Leuthold Foundation
Link, Jr. Foundation, George
Liz Claiborne, Inc.
Longwood Foundation
Lowenstein Foundation, Leon
Lund Foundation
Lurie Foundation, Louis R.
Lux Foundation, Miranda
Mahadh Foundation
Mailman Family Foundation, A. L.
Mailman Foundation
Mandeville Foundation
Markey Charitable Fund, John C.
Marmot Foundation
Marshall Foundation, Mattie H.
Martin Marietta Materials
Mather Charitable Trust, S. Livingston
Mattel, Inc.
Maytag Family Foundation, Fred
MCA Inc.
McCasland Foundation
McConnell Foundation
McCormick Trust, Anne
McCune Charitable Foundation, Marshall and Perrine D.
McCune Charitable Trust, John R.
McDermott Foundation, Eugene
McEvoy Foundation, Mildred H.
McGee Foundation
McGonagle Foundation, Dextra Baldwin
McInerny Foundation
McMahan Foundation, Catherine L. and Robert O.
McShain Charities, John
Meadows Foundation
Mellon Foundation, Richard King
Memton Fund
Mengle Foundation, Glenn and Ruth
Merck & Co.
Merrick Foundation
Merrill Lynch & Co., Inc.
Meyer Fund, Milton and Sophie
Meyer Memorial Trust
Mid-Iowa Health Foundation
Middendorf Foundation
Monfort Family Foundation
Montana Power Co.
Morgan & Company, J.P.
Morgan Construction Co.
Morgan and Samuel Tate Morgan, Jr. Foundation, Marietta McNeil
Morris Foundation, Margaret T.
Morris Foundation, William T.
Mosbacher, Jr. Foundation, Emil
Moses Fund, Henry and Lucy
Munson Foundation Trust, W. B.

Murdock Charitable Trust, M. J.
Murphey Foundation, Lluella Morey
Nesholm Family Foundation
Nestle USA Inc.
New Jersey Natural Gas Co.
New-Land Foundation
Nias Foundation, Henry
Norgren Foundation, Carl A.
Northern States Power Co. (Minnesota)
Norton Co.
Norton Family Foundation, Peter
OCRI Foundation
Odell Fund, Robert Stewart Odell and Helen Pfeiffer
Offield Family Foundation
OG&E Electric Services
Old National Bank in Evansville
Olin Foundation, Spencer T. and Ann W.
Olsson Memorial Foundation, Elis
Oppenstein Brothers Foundation
O'Quinn Foundation, John M. and Nancy C.
Owsley Foundation, Alvin and Lucy
Packard Foundation, David and Lucile
Palisades Educational Foundation
Parshelsky Foundation, Moses L.
Parsons Foundation, Ralph M.
Payne Foundation, Frank E. and Seba B.
Peabody Charitable Fund, Amelia
Peppers Foundation, Ann
Petteys Memorial Foundation, Jack
Pforzheimer Foundation, Carl and Lily
PHH Corporation
Phillips Family Foundation, Jay and Rose
Phillips Foundation, Ellis L.
Pick, Jr. Fund, Albert
Pittsburg Midway Coal Mining Co.
Porter Foundation, Mrs. Cheever
PPG Industries, Inc.
Prince Trust, Abbie Norman
Prouty Foundation, Olive Higgins
Prudential Insurance Co. of America, The
Public Welfare Foundation
Puterbaugh Foundation
Putnam Foundation
Quivey-Bay State Foundation
R. F. Foundation
R&B Machine Tool Co.
Ratner Foundation, Milton M.
Reicher Foundation, Anne and Harry J.
Reidler Foundation
Reinberger Foundation
Retirement Research Foundation
Reynolds Foundation, Edgar
Rice Charitable Foundation, Albert W.
Rice Foundation
Robinson-Broadhurst Foundation
Rockwell Fund
Rogers Family Foundation
Roseburg Forest Products Co.
Rosen Foundation, Joseph
Rosenberg, Jr. Family Foundation, Louise and Claude
Ross Memorial Foundation, Will
Rouse Co.
Royal Foundation, May Mitchell
Rudin Foundation

Saint Paul Companies, Inc.
Saltonstall Charitable Foundation, Richard
Sandy Hill Foundation
Scherer Foundation, Karla
Schering-Plough Corp.
Schwartz Foundation, Arnold A.
Schwob Foundation, Simon
Scurlock Foundation
Self Foundation
Share Trust, Charles Morton
Shaw Foundation, Arch W.
Shawmut National Corp.
Shell Oil Company
Shubert Foundation
Simon Foundation, William E. and Carol G.
Slemp Foundation
Slifka Foundation, Joseph and Sylvia
Smeal Foundation, Mary Jean and Frank P.
Smith Foundation, Kelvin and Eleanor
Solow Foundation
Sonat Inc.
South Waite Foundation
Southwestern Electric Power Co.
Springs Foundation
Stabler Foundation, Donald B. and Dorothy L.
Stauffer Charitable Trust, John
Stearns Trust, Artemas W.
Steele-Reese Foundation
Steinbach Fund, Ruth and Milton
Steinman Foundation, James Hale
Steinman Foundation, John Frederick
Stevens Foundation, Abbot and Dorothy H.
Stokely, Jr. Foundation, William B.
Stone Charitable Foundation
Strauss Foundation, Leon
Sturgis Charitable and Educational Trust, Roy and Christine
Sulzberger Foundation
Superior Tube Co.
Swalm Foundation
Symmes Foundation, F. W.
Taper Foundation, Mark
Taubman Foundation, A. Alfred
Temple Foundation, T. L. L.
Temple-Inland Inc.
Texas Commerce Bank-Houston, N.A.
Thompson Charitable Foundation
Thorne Foundation
Thornton Foundation
Tiscornia Foundation
Tozer Foundation
TransAmerica Corporation
Travelers Inc.
Tucker Charitable Trust, Rose E.
Tupancy-Harris Foundation of 1986
Turner Charitable Foundation
Turrell Fund
Union Camp Corporation
Union Pacific Corp.
Unocal Corp.
Upjohn Foundation, Harold and Grace
USL Capital Corporation
van Ameringen Foundation
Van Houten Memorial Fund
Vernon Fund, Miles Hodsdon
Washington Forrest Foundation
Washington Mutual Savings Bank
Weezie Foundation
Weingart Foundation
Wheeler Foundation
Whirlpool Corporation
Whiting Foundation
Whiting Foundation, Macauley and Helen Dow

Wickes Foundation, Harvey Randall
WICOR, Inc.
Wiegand Foundation, E. L.
Williams Charitable Trust, John C.
Wilmington Trust Co.
Wise Foundation and Charitable Trust, Watson W.
Witco Corp.
Wyman Youth Trust
Young Foundation, Hugo H. and Mabel B.
Young Foundation, Robert R.
Zachry Co., H.B.
Zarrow Foundation, Anne and Henry
Zlinkoff Fund for Medical Research and Education, Sergei S.

Diabetes

Alabama Gas Corp.
Aldus Corp.
Alexander Foundation, Joseph
AlliedSignal Inc.
American General Finance Corp.
American National Bank & Trust Co. of Chicago
Ames Charitable Trust, Harriett
Arcadia Foundation
Baker Trust, George F.
Baldwin Foundation, David M. and Barbara
Baldwin Memorial Foundation, Fred
Barry Corp., R. G.
Baskin-Robbins USA Co.
Baughman Foundation
Benenson Foundation, Frances and Benjamin
Bingham Foundation, William
Bingham Second Betterment Fund, William
Blum Foundation, Harry and Maribel G.
Blum-Kovler Foundation
Breyer Foundation
Bristol-Myers Squibb Company
Cabell Foundation, Robert G. Cabell III and Maude Morgan
Cassett Foundation, Louis N.
Chartwell Foundation
Clowes Fund
Cord Foundation, E. L.
Crawford Estate, E. R.
Crown Books
Crown Memorial, Arie and Ida
Dana Charitable Trust, Eleanor Naylor
Davidson Family Charitable Foundation
Demoulas Supermarkets Inc.
Dentsply International Inc.
Doss Foundation, M. S.
Duke Endowment
Dula Educational and Charitable Foundation, Caleb C. and Julia W.
Dynamet, Inc.
Edmonds Foundation, Dean S.
Firman Fund
Fischbach Foundation
Fishback Foundation Trust, Harmes C.
General American Life Insurance Co.
Gheens Foundation
Givenchy Corp.
Glick Foundation, Eugene and Marilyn
Goodstein Family Foundation, David
Gould Electronics Inc.
Green Foundation, Allen P. and Josephine B.
Greenwall Foundation
Guttman Foundation, Stella and Charles
Hagedorn Fund

Handy and Harman Foundation
Hanson Industries North America
Harcourt General, Inc.
Harriman Foundation, Gladys and Roland
Hawn Foundation
Herzstein Charitable Foundation, Albert and Ethel
Hook Drugs
Hoover, Jr. Foundation, Margaret W. and Herbert
Icahn Foundation, Carl C.
Jarson-Stanley and Mickey Kaplan Foundation, Isaac and Esther
Jaydor Corp.
Jewett Foundation, George Frederick
Johnson Foundation, Willard T. C.
Jordan Charitable Foundation, Mary Ranken Jordan and Ettie A.
Kansas City Southern Industries
Kayser Foundation
Knoll Group
Kreitler Foundation
La-Z-Boy Chair Co.
LamCo. Communications
Lazarus Charitable Trust, Helen and Charles
LBJ Family Foundation
Lennon Foundation, Fred A.
Lichtenstein Foundation, David B.
Loews Corporation
Marmot Foundation
Mattel, Inc.
McLean Contributionship
Merrick Foundation
Mid-Iowa Health Foundation
Monadnock Paper Mills
Montana Power Co.
Munson Foundation Trust, W. B.
Musson Charitable Foundation, R. C. and Katharine M.
Noble Foundation, Samuel Roberts
Norton Memorial Corporation, Geraldi
Novell Inc.
OCRI Foundation
O'Quinn Foundation, John M. and Nancy C.
Osborn Charitable Trust, Edward B.
Osher Foundation, Bernard
PaineWebber
Park Foundation
Philibosian Foundation, Stephen
Polaroid Corp.
Prouty Foundation, Olive Higgins
Rabb Foundation, Harry W.
Retirement Research Foundation
Rosenberg, Jr. Family Foundation, Louise and Claude
Royal Foundation, May Mitchell
Rubin Family Fund, Cele H. and William B.
Schlink Foundation, Albert G. and Olive H.
Schumann Fund for New Jersey
Scurlock Foundation
Seneca Foods Corp.
Share Trust, Charles Morton
Shaw Foundation, Arch W.
Sierra Pacific Resources
Skaggs Foundation, L. J. and Mary C.
Smith Foundation, Gordon V. and Helen C.
Stein Foundation, Jules and Doris

Sturgis Charitable and Educational Trust, Roy and Christine
Taubman Foundation, A. Alfred
Texaco Inc.
Texas Commerce Bank-Houston, N.A.
Thompson Co., J. Walter
Times Mirror Company, The
Titus Foundation, Roy and Niuta
Todd Co., A.M.
Vernon Fund, Miles Hodsdon
Vollbrecht Foundation, Frederick A.
Weaver Foundation, Gil and Dody
Widgeon Foundation
Wiegand Foundation, E. L.
Windham Foundation
Young Foundation, Robert R.

Emergency/Ambulance Services

Abbott Laboratories
Abell-Hanger Foundation
ACF Industries, Inc.
Achelis Foundation
Adler Foundation Trust, Philip D. and Henrietta B.
Aetna Life & Casualty Co.
Ahmanson Foundation
Air Products and Chemicals, Inc.
Akzo America
Albertson's Inc.
Alexander Foundation, Joseph
Allendale Insurance Co.
Allyn Foundation
Altschul Foundation
Aluminum Co. of America
AMCORE Bank, N.A. Rockford
American Brands, Inc.
American General Finance Corp.
American Natural Resources Company
Amfac/JMB Hawaii Inc.
Amoco Corporation
AMP Incorporated
Andersen Corp.
Andersen Foundation
Anderson Foundation, John W.
Anderson Foundation, M. D.
Andersons, The
Andreas Foundation
Andrews Foundation
Annenberg Foundation
AON Corporation
Appleby Trust, Scott B. and Annie P.
Arcadia Foundation
Aristech Chemical Corp.
Arkelian Foundation, Ben H. and Gladys
Arkell Hall Foundation
Armco Inc.
Armstrong Foundation
Arnhold Foundation
Asplundh Foundation
AT&T Corp.
Atran Foundation
Audubon State Bank
Auerbach Foundation, Beatrice Fox
Avon Products, Inc.
Baker Trust, George F.
Baldwin Foundation, David M. and Barbara
BankAmerica Corp.
Bard Foundation, Robert
Barra Foundation
Batts Foundation
Baughman Foundation
BE&K Inc.
Beazley Foundation/Frederick Foundation
Bemis Company, Inc.
Benedum Foundation, Claude Worthington

Benenson Foundation, Frances and Benjamin
Berger Foundation, H. N. and Frances C.
Bethlehem Steel Corp.
Bettingen Corporation, Burton G.
Betts Industries
Binney & Smith Inc.
Bird Corp.
Blandin Foundation
Blaustein Foundation, Louis and Henrietta
Bloedorn Foundation, Walter A.
Blount Educational and Charitable Foundation, Mildred Weedon
Blum Foundation, Edna F.
Bodman Foundation
Boettcher Foundation
Boise Cascade Corporation
Booth Ferris Foundation
Borkee Hagley Foundation
Borman's Inc.
Boston Edison Co.
Bowen Foundation, Ethel N.
Brady Foundation
Bremer Foundation, Otto
Breyer Foundation
Bridwell Foundation, J. S.
Bristol-Myers Squibb Company
Brunswick Corp.
Bryant Foundation
Bryn Mawr Trust Co.
Bunbury Company
Cabell Foundation, Robert G. Cabell III and Maude Morgan
Cafritz Foundation, Morris and Gwendolyn
Cain Foundation, Effie and Wofford
Calhoun Charitable Trust, Kenneth
Callaway Foundation
Carpenter Foundation, E. Rhodes and Leona B.
Carpenter Technology Corp.
Carter Foundation, Amon G.
Carvel Foundation, Thomas and Agnes
Caspersen Foundation for Aid to Health and Education, O. W.
Central Maine Power Co.
Centralia Foundation
Century Companies of America
Champlin Foundations
Chastain Charitable Foundation, Robert Lee and Thomas M.
Chatham Manufacturing Co.
Chatlos Foundation
Chazen Foundation
CHC Foundation
Cheney Foundation, Ben B.
Chesapeake Corp.
Chesebrough-Pond's USA Co.
Chevron Corporation
Church & Dwight Co., Inc.
Citibank
Citizens Bank of Rhode Island
City National Bank and Trust Co.
Clapp Charitable and Educational Trust, George H.
Clark Foundation
Clorox Co.
Close Foundation
Cogswell Benevolent Trust
Cole Foundation, Olive B.
Collins Foundation
Collins, Jr. Foundation, George Fulton
Colonial Life & Accident Insurance Co.
Columbus Dispatch Printing Co.
Commerce Bancshares, Inc.
Connelly Foundation
Consolidated Natural Gas Co.
Continental Corp.
Cooper Industries, Inc.

Cord Foundation, E. L.
Cornell Trust, Peter C.
Corning Incorporated
Coughlin-Saunders Foundation
Cowles Charitable Trust
Crane Co.
Crary Foundation, Bruce L.
Crown Books
CS First Boston Corporation
Culpeper Foundation, Charles E.
Culver Foundation, Constans
Curtice-Burns Foods, Inc.
Darby Foundation
Davenport-Hatch Foundation
Davis Foundation, Edwin W. and Catherine M.
Davis Foundation, Irene E. and George A.
Davis Foundation, James A. and Juliet L.
Daywood Foundation
Deere & Co.
Delavan Foundation, Nelson B.
Dell Foundation, Hazel
DeRoy Foundation, Helen L.
Deuble Foundation, George H.
Diamond Shamrock Inc.
Dillon Dunwalke Trust, Clarence and Anne
Dillon Foundation
Dingman Foundation, Michael D.
Dodge Foundation, Cleveland H.
Dodge Jones Foundation
Dow Foundation, Herbert H. and Grace A.
Dresser Industries, Inc.
Dreyfus Foundation, Max and Victoria
du Pont de Nemours & Co., E. I.
Duke Endowment
Duke Power Co.
Dula Educational and Charitable Foundation, Caleb C. and Julia W.
Dun & Bradstreet Corp.
duPont Foundation, Alfred I.
Dynamet, Inc.
Eastman Kodak Company
Eden Hall Foundation
El Pomar Foundation
Elf Atochem North America, Inc.
Emerson Foundation, Inc., Fred L.
English Memorial Fund, Florence C. and H. L.
Essick Foundation
Ethyl Corp
Exxon Corporation
Fair Oaks Foundation, Inc.
Farish Fund, William Stamps
Fieldcrest Cannon Inc.
Fife Foundation, Elias and Bertha
Firman Fund
First Hawaiian, Inc.
First Union Corp.
Fischbach Foundation
Fish Foundation, Ray C.
Flowers Charitable Trust, Albert W. and Edith V.
Folger Fund
Fondren Foundation
Forbes Inc.
Ford Fund, William and Martha
Ford II Fund, Henry
Ford Motor Co.
Foster Foundation
Freed Foundation
Freeport Brick Co.
Freeport-McMoRan Inc.
Gamble Foundation
Gannett Publishing Co., Guy
GAR Foundation
Geifman Family Foundation
General American Life Insurance Co.
General Mills, Inc.
General Motors Corp.
Georgia-Pacific Corporation
Giant Eagle, Inc.

Gifford Charitable Corporation, Rosamond
Gilmore Foundation, William G.
Glick Foundation, Eugene and Marilyn
Goodrich Co., The B.F.
Goodstein Family Foundation, David
Gould Electronics Inc.
Griffis Foundation
Griffith Foundation, W. C.
GSM Industrial
Guaranty Bank & Trust Co.
Gulf Coast Medical Foundation
Gulf Power Co.
Habig Foundation, Arnold F.
Hachar Charitable Trust, D. D.
Hafif Family Foundation
Hagedorn Fund
Hamilton Bank
Hammer Foundation, Armand
Hancock Foundation, Luke B.
Harland Charitable Foundation, John and Wilhelmina D.
Harriman Foundation, Gladys and Roland
Harriman Foundation, Mary W.
Harsco Corp.
Hartz Foundation
Hastings Charitable Foundation, Oris B.
Hechinger Co.
Heckscher Foundation for Children
Heginbotham Trust, Will E.
Herzstein Charitable Foundation, Albert and Ethel
Hewlett-Packard Co.
Hill Foundation, Sandy
Hillcrest Foundation
Hillman Family Foundation, Alex
Hoag Family Foundation, George
Hobby Foundation
Hoffman Foundation, Maximilian E. and Marion O.
Hook Drugs
Hoover Fund-Trust, W. Henry
Hoover, Jr. Foundation, Margaret W. and Herbert
Hopkins Foundation, Josephine Lawrence
Hopwood Charitable Trust, John M.
Houston Endowment
Howell Foundation of Florida
Hoyt Foundation
Hoyt Foundation, Stewart W. and Willma C.
Hugoton Foundation
Huisking Foundation
Hulme Charitable Foundation, Milton G.
Humana, Inc.
Humphrey Fund, George M. and Pamela S.
Hunt Charitable Trust, C. Giles
Huston Foundation
Hyde and Watson Foundation
Illinois Consolidated Telephone Co.
Independence Foundation
Integra Bank of Uniontown
International Foundation
International Paper Co.
Jackson Foundation
Jacobson Foundation, Bernard H. and Blanche E.
James River Corp. of Virginia
Jameson Foundation, J. W. and Ida M.
Janesville Foundation
Jarson-Stanley and Mickey Kaplan Foundation, Isaac and Esther
Jaydor Corp.
JELD-WEN, Inc.
Jewell Memorial Foundation, Daniel Ashley and Irene Houston
Jockey Hollow Foundation

Johnson Foundation, M. G. and Lillie A.
Johnson Foundation, Willard T. C.
Johnson Fund, Edward C.
Johnson & Higgins
Jones Foundation, Daisy Marquis
Jordan Charitable Foundation, Mary Ranken Jordan and Ettie A.
Joslin-Needham Family Foundation
Journal-Gazette Co.
Julia R. and Estelle L. Foundation
Kavanagh Foundation, T. James
Kayser Foundation
Kelly Tractor Co.
Kempner Fund, Harris and Eliza
Kent-Lucas Foundation
Kettering Fund
Kiewit Foundation, Peter
Kimberly-Clark Corp.
Kinney-Lindstrom Foundation
Kiplinger Foundation
Kirby Foundation, F. M.
Kirkpatrick Foundation
Kitzmiller/Bales Trust
Kline Foundation, Josiah W. and Bessie H.
Klipstein Foundation, Ernest Christian
Knapp Foundation
Knight Foundation, John S. and James L.
Knoll Group
Knox, Sr., and Pearl Wallis Knox Charitable Foundation, Robert W.
Knudsen Foundation, Tom and Valley
Kohn-Joseloff Foundation
Komes Foundation
Koopman Fund
Koret Foundation
Kresge Foundation
Kuehn Foundation
La-Z-Boy Chair Co.
Laurel Foundation
Lazarus Charitable Trust, Helen and Charles
Lee Endowment Foundation
Lee Enterprises
Lehigh Portland Cement Co.
Lehmann Foundation, Otto W.
Leidy Foundation, John J.
Lenna Foundation, Reginald A. and Elizabeth S.
Leuthold Foundation
Levy Foundation, June Rockwell
Lockhart Vaughan Foundation
Loews Corporation
Longwood Foundation
Louisiana-Pacific Corp.
Lovett Foundation
Lowenstein Foundation, Leon
Lund Foundation
Lurie Foundation, Louis R.
Lyon Foundation
Macy & Co., Inc., R.H.
Maddox Foundation, J. F.
Magowan Family Foundation
Mahadh Foundation
Mandeville Foundation
Maneely Fund
Markey Charitable Fund, John C.
Marmot Foundation
Martin Marietta Corp.
Martini Foundation, Nicholas
Mascoma Savings Bank
Mather Charitable Trust, S. Livingston
Matthies Foundation, Katharine
MCA Inc.
McCasland Foundation
McCormick Trust, Anne
McDonald & Company Securities, Inc.
McEvoy Foundation, Mildred H.

McFawn Trust No. 2, Lois Sisler
McFeely-Rogers Foundation
McGonagle Foundation, Dextra Baldwin
MCI Communications Corp.
McInerny Foundation
McMillan Foundation, D. W.
Mead Corporation, The
Meadows Foundation
Medtronic, Inc.
Mellon Family Foundation, R. K.
Mellon Foundation, Richard King
Merck & Co.
Mercury Aircraft
Merrick Foundation
Merrill Lynch & Co., Inc.
Mid-Iowa Health Foundation
Miller Brewing Company/North Carolina
Miller Charitable Foundation, Howard E. and Nell E.
Miller-Mellon Association
Mills Fund, Frances Goll
Mobil Oil Corp.
Mohasco Corp.
Monell Foundation, Ambrose
Moore Charitable Foundation, Marjorie
Moore & Sons, B.C.
Morgan Charitable Residual Trust, W. and E.
Morgan & Company, J.P.
Morgan Construction Co.
Morgan Foundation, Burton D.
Morgan and Samuel Tate Morgan, Jr. Foundation, Marietta McNeil
Morris Foundation, Margaret T.
Morrison Knudsen Corporation
Mosinee Paper Corp.
Mulford Foundation, Vincent
Munson Foundation Trust, W. B.
Murphey Foundation, Lluella Morey
Nalco Chemical Co.
National Gypsum Co.
Nesholm Family Foundation
Nestle USA Inc.
New Jersey Natural Gas Co.
New York Life Insurance Co.
The New Yorker Magazine, Inc.
NewMil Bancorp
Noble Foundation, Samuel Roberts
Norfolk Shipbuilding & Drydock Corp.
Norton Co.
Norton Family Foundation, Peter
OCRI Foundation
Offield Family Foundation
OG&E Electric Services
Old National Bank in Evansville
Olin Corp.
Olin Foundation, Spencer T. and Ann W.
Olsson Memorial Foundation, Elis
Oppenstein Brothers Foundation
Overbrook Foundation
Overlake Foundation
Pacific Mutual Life Insurance Co.
Packaging Corporation of America
PaineWebber
Palmer Fund, Frank Loomis
Pamida, Inc.
Parker Hannifin Corp.
Parvin Foundation, Albert
Payne Foundation, Frank E. and Seba B.
Pella Corporation
Pennzoil Co.
Peppers Foundation, Ann
Peterson Foundation, Hal and Charlie
Petteys Memorial Foundation, Jack

Pew Charitable Trusts
Pfizer, Inc.
Pforzheimer Foundation, Carl and Lily
PHH Corporation
Pick, Jr. Fund, Albert
Pioneer Trust Bank, NA
Pittsburg Midway Coal Mining Co.
Plankenhorn Foundation, Harry
Pollock Company Foundation, William B.
Porter Testamentary Trust, James Hyde
Prospect Hill Foundation
Providence Journal Company
Prudential Insurance Co. of America, The
Public Service Electric & Gas Co.
Puterbaugh Foundation
Putnam Foundation
Quivey-Bay State Foundation
Rachal Foundation, Ed
R&B Machine Tool Co.
Raymond Corp.
Read Foundation, Charles L.
Reidler Foundation
Reisman Charitable Trust, George C. and Evelyn R.
Retirement Research Foundation
Reynolds Foundation, Donald W.
Richardson Benevolent Foundation, C. E.
Robinson-Broadhurst Foundation
Rockwell Fund
Rockwell International Corporation
Rogers Family Foundation
Rohatyn Foundation, Felix and Elizabeth
Rohm & Haas Co.
Roseburg Forest Products Co.
Royal Foundation, May Mitchell
Royal Group, Inc.
Ruan Foundation Trust, John
Ryan Foundation, David Claude
Sara Lee Hosiery, Inc.
Sargent Foundation, Newell B.
Sasco Foundation
Sawyer Charitable Foundation
SBC Communications Inc.
Schenck Fund, L. P.
Schiro Fund
Schowalter Foundation
Schroeder Foundation, Walter
Schuller International
Schwartz Foundation, Arnold A.
Schwartz Fund for Education and Health Research, Arnold and Marie
Schwob Foundation, Simon
Scott Foundation, Walter
Scott Foundation, William E.
Seafirst Corporation
Seidman Family Foundation
Selby and Marie Selby Foundation, William G.
Seneca Foods Corp.
Shaw Foundation, Arch W.
Shawmut National Corp.
Sheary for Charity, Edna M.
Shenandoah Life Insurance Co.
Sheppard Foundation, Lawrence B.
Simpson Investment Company
Slemp Foundation
Smeal Foundation, Mary Jean and Frank P.
Smith Corp., A.O.
Smith Foundation, Gordon V. and Helen C.
SmithKline Beecham Corp.
Specialty Manufacturing Co.
Speyer Foundation, Alexander C. and Tillie S.
Sprague Educational and Charitable Foundation, Seth

Springs Foundation
SPX Corp.
Square D Co.
Stackpole-Hall Foundation
Stanley Works
Starr Foundation
Steinman Foundation, James
  Hale
Stemmons Foundation
Stevens Foundation, John T.
Strawbridge Foundation of
  Pennsylvania II, Margaret
  Dorrance
Stupp Foundation, Norman J.
Subaru of America Inc.
Sunnen Foundation
Swalm Foundation
Taper Foundation, Mark
Taylor Foundation, Fred and
  Harriett
Taylor Foundation, Ruth and
  Vernon
Teleflex Inc.
Temple Foundation, T. L. L.
Tenneco Inc.
Texaco Inc.
Thalhimer and Family
  Foundation, Charles G.
Thermo Electron Corp.
Thomas Industries
Thorne Foundation
Thornton Foundation
Times Mirror Company, The
Timken Foundation of Canton
Treakle Foundation, J. Edwin
Truland Foundation
Trust Funds
Tucker Charitable Trust, Rose
  E.
Turner Charitable Foundation
Union Bank
Union Camp Corporation
Union Electric Co.
Union Pacific Corp.
Unocal Corp.
Uris Brothers Foundation
Utica National Insurance
  Group
Van Buren Foundation
Vanderbilt Trust, R. T.
Vernon Fund, Miles Hodsdon
Vevay-Switzerland County
  Foundation
Virginia Power Co.
Vogler Foundation, Laura B.
Vollbrecht Foundation,
  Frederick A.
Wachovia Bank of North
  Carolina, N.A.
Wahlstrom Foundation
Wal-Mart Stores, Inc.
Warwick Foundation
Washington Forrest Foundation
Washington Mutual Savings
  Bank
Wege Foundation
Weil, Gotshal and Manges
  Foundation
Weingart Foundation
Wendt Foundation, Margaret L.
West One Bancorp
Wheat First Butcher Singer,
  Inc.
Wheeler Foundation
Wheeler Foundation, Wilmot
Whiting Foundation
Whitney Fund, David M.
Wickson-Link Memorial
  Foundation
WICOR, Inc.
Widgeon Foundation
Wildermuth Foundation, E. F.
Williams Charitable Trust,
  John C.
Wilson Fund, Matilda R.
Windham Foundation
Winnebago Industries, Inc.
Wisconsin Power & Light Co.
Witco Corp.
Woodward Fund
Wyomissing Foundation
Yeager Charitable Trust,
  Lester E.
Young Foundation, Robert R.

Eyes/Blindness

Ahmanson Foundation
Alabama Gas Corp.
Alcon Laboratories, Inc.
Aldus Corp.
Alexander Foundation, Joseph
Altschul Foundation
American National Bank &
  Trust Co. of Chicago
Ames Charitable Trust, Harriett
Anderson Foundation, M. D.
Baldwin Foundation, David
  M. and Barbara
Bedsole Foundation, J. L.
Blue Cross & Blue Shield
  United of Wisconsin
Bodman Foundation
Booth Ferris Foundation
Borden, Inc.
Borman's Inc.
Broadhurst Foundation
Cain Foundation, Gordon and
  Mary
Campbell Foundation
Chartwell Foundation
Chase Manhattan Bank, N.A.
Chatlos Foundation
Chazen Foundation
Clapp Charitable and
  Educational Trust, George H.
Cogswell Benevolent Trust
Daniel Foundation of Alabama
Darby Foundation
Davidson Family Charitable
  Foundation
Davis Foundation, Edwin W.
  and Catherine M.
Delano Foundation, Mignon
  Sherwood
DeRoy Testamentary
  Foundation
Dingman Foundation, Michael
  D.
Douglas & Lomason Company
Dynamet, Inc.
Early Foundation
Emerson Foundation, Inc.,
  Fred L.
Essick Foundation
Farish Fund, William Stamps
Fife Foundation, Elias and
  Bertha
Fikes Foundation, Leland
Firman Fund
Fischbach Foundation
Ford II Fund, Henry
Foster Charitable Trust
Freeman Charitable Trust,
  Samuel
Frohring Foundation, William
  O. and Gertrude Lewis
Fuqua Foundation, J. B.
Gheens Foundation
Glanville Family Foundation
Grand Rapids Label Co.
Hagedorn Fund
Halff Foundation, G. A. C.
Hallett Charitable Trust, Jessie
  F.
Hamman Foundation, George
  and Mary Josephine
Handy and Harman Foundation
Hanson Industries North
  America
Hawn Foundation
Heinz Trust, Drue
Helmerich Foundation
Herzstein Charitable
  Foundation, Albert and Ethel
Hobby Foundation
Hook Drugs
Hoover, Jr. Foundation,
  Margaret W. and Herbert
Humphrey Fund, George M.
  and Pamela S.
Huston Foundation
Hyde and Watson Foundation
Ingalls Foundation, Louise H.
  and David S.
Integra Bank of Uniontown
Jaydor Corp.
Johnson Fund, Edward C.
Jostens, Inc.

Kansas City Southern
  Industries
Kayser Foundation
Kelley and Elza Kelley
  Foundation, Edward Bangs
Kemper Foundation, William T.
Kirby Foundation, F. M.
Kresge Foundation
LamCo. Communications
Lasdon Foundation
Lattner Foundation, Forrest C.
Lauder Foundation
Lehmann Foundation, Otto W.
Lennon Foundation, Fred A.
Liz Claiborne, Inc.
Lowenstein Foundation, Leon
Lydall, Inc.
Marmot Foundation
Marriott Foundation, J. Willard
McFawn Trust No. 2, Lois
  Sisler
Meadows Foundation
Meyer Family Foundation,
  Paul J.
Middendorf Foundation
Mnuchin Foundation
Monell Foundation, Ambrose
Munger Foundation, Alfred C.
Odell Fund, Robert Stewart
  Odell and Helen Pfeiffer
Park Foundation
Parvin Foundation, Albert
Pioneer Trust Bank, NA
Pittsburg Midway Coal Mining
  Co.
Potts and Sibley Foundation
Premier Industrial Corp.
Raymond Corp.
Read Foundation, Charles L.
Rockwell Fund
Rohatyn Foundation, Felix and
  Elizabeth
Rosenberg, Jr. Family
  Foundation, Louise and
  Claude
Ross Memorial Foundation,
  Will
Rowland Foundation
Royal Foundation, May
  Mitchell
Sargent Foundation, Newell B.
Scaife Family Foundation
Schlink Foundation, Albert G.
  and Olive H.
Schlumberger Ltd.
Scholl Foundation, Dr.
Schroeder Foundation, Walter
Schwartz Foundation, Arnold
  A.
Scott Foundation, Walter
Scurlock Foundation
Seaver Charitable Trust,
  Richard C.
Seaver Institute
Slifka Foundation, Joseph and
  Sylvia
Smart Family Foundation
Smith Foundation, Kelvin and
  Eleanor
Smith Trust, May and Stanley
Sonat Inc.
Stans Foundation
Steinman Foundation, James
  Hale
Stupp Foundation, Norman J.
Superior Tube Co.
Temple Foundation, T. L. L.
Times Mirror Company, The
Titus Foundation, Roy and
  Niuta
Turner Charitable Foundation
Weckbaugh Foundation,
  Eleanore Mullen
Weinstein Foundation, J.
Wertheim Foundation, Dr.
  Herbert A.
Wheat First Butcher Singer,
  Inc.
Willard Helping Fund, Cecilia
  Young
Wilson Foundation, H. W.
Wilson Fund, Matilda R.
Winnebago Industries, Inc.

General

Acme-McCrary Corp./Sapona
  Manufacturing Co.
Alabama Gas Corp.
Aldus Corp.
Amcast Industrial Corp.
AMCORE Bank, N.A.
  Rockford
Bank One, Texas-Houston
  Office
Bank One, Youngstown, NA
Barry Corp., R. G.
Berwind Corporation
Binney & Smith Inc.
Blair and Co., William
Bryn Mawr Trust Co.
CBS, Inc.
Central Maine Power Co.
Christian Dior New York, Inc.
CIBC Wood Gundy
CINergy
CNA Financial
  Corporation/CNA Insurance
  Companies
Columbus Dispatch Printing
  Co.
Cosmair, Inc.
DEC International, Inc.
Dentsply International Inc.
Diamond Shamrock Inc.
Douglas & Lomason Company
Ebsco Industries, Inc.
Encyclopaedia Britannica, Inc.
Fabri-Kal Corp.
Federated Mutual Insurance
  Co.
First Union National Bank of
  Florida
French Oil Mill Machinery Co.
GenRad
Givenchy Corp.
Gould Electronics Inc.
Grand Rapids Label Co.
Handy and Harman Foundation
Holnam
Integra Bank of Uniontown
Jaydor Corp.
Kansas City Southern
  Industries
Kaye, Scholer, Fierman, Hays
  & Handler
Kennecott Corporation
KN Energy, Inc.
Knoll Group
LamCo. Communications
Lehigh Portland Cement Co.
Lydall, Inc.
Management Compensation
  Group/Dulworth Inc.
Maritz Inc.
Martin Marietta Materials
Mascoma Savings Bank
MBIA Inc.
McDonald & Company
  Securities, Inc.
Miller Brewing
  Company/North Carolina
Mitsubishi Motor Sales of
  America, Inc.
Mosinee Paper Corp.
National Forge Co.
New Jersey Natural Gas Co.
New York Mercantile Exchange
The New Yorker Magazine, Inc.
Norfolk Shipbuilding &
  Drydock Corp.
Northwest Natural Gas Co.
Novell Inc.
Old National Bank in
  Evansville
Packaging Corporation of
  America
Pamida, Inc.
Penguin Books USA, Inc.
PHH Corporation
Pioneer Trust Bank, NA
Pitt-Des Moines Inc.
Pittsburg Midway Coal Mining
  Co.
PriMerit Bank
Providence Gas Co.
Providian Corporation
Roseburg Forest Products Co.

Rose's Stores, Inc.
Ross Laboratories
Royal Group, Inc.
Sandusky International Inc.
Sara Lee Hosiery, Inc.
Security Life of Denver
  Insurance Co.
Seneca Foods Corp.
Southwestern Electric Power
  Co.
SPX Corp.
Times Mirror Company, The
U.S. Bank of Washington
Unitrode Corp.
Webber Oil Co.
West One Bancorp
WICOR, Inc.
Windham Foundation
Wiremold Co.
Zachry Co., H.B.

Geriatric Health

Abbott Laboratories
Albertson's Inc.
Alexander Foundation, Joseph
AlliedSignal Inc.
Altman Foundation
Aluminum Co. of America
Atherton Family Foundation
Atran Foundation
Battelle Memorial Institute
Beazley Foundation/Frederick
  Foundation
Bethlehem Steel Corp.
Beveridge Foundation, Frank
  Stanley
Block, H&R
Borkee Hagley Foundation
Borman's Inc.
Brach Foundation, Helen
Bremer Foundation, Otto
Bryn Mawr Trust Co.
Burden Foundation, Florence
  V.
Cafritz Foundation, Morris and
  Gwendolyn
Central Maine Power Co.
Chase Manhattan Bank, N.A.
Chatham Manufacturing Co.
Clemens Markets Corp.
Clorox Co.
Colonial Life & Accident
  Insurance Co.
Comprecare Foundation
Connelly Foundation
Cremer Foundation
Crestlea Foundation
Cummings Foundation, James
  H.
Curtice-Burns Foods, Inc.
Dana Foundation, Charles A.
Dart Group Corp.
Dentsply International Inc.
Dillon Dunwalke Trust,
  Clarence and Anne
Donner Foundation, William H.
Dreyfus Foundation, Jean and
  Louis
du Pont de Nemours & Co., E.
  I.
Duke Endowment
Enron Corp.
Federated Mutual Insurance
  Co.
Feil Foundation, Louis and
  Gertrude
First Fidelity Bank
First Union Corp.
Fribourg Foundation
Frohring Foundation, William
  O. and Gertrude Lewis
Fry Foundation, Lloyd A.
GATX Corp.
General Mills, Inc.
GenRad
Georgia Power Co.
Gershman Foundation, Joel
Gheens Foundation
Giant Eagle, Inc.
Goldberg Family Foundation
Goldsmith Foundation, Horace
  W.
Goodrich Co., The B.F.

Gregg-Graniteville Foundation
Habig Foundation, Arnold F.
Halsell Foundation, Ewing
Harriman Foundation, Gladys and Roland
Hartford Foundation, John A.
Hasbro Inc.
Hearst Foundation, William Randolph
Hechinger Co.
Heinz Endowment, Vira I.
Higginson Trust, Corina
Hoffman Foundation, Maximilian E. and Marion O.
Hopkins Foundation, Josephine Lawrence
Houston Endowment
Hugoton Foundation
Hulme Charitable Foundation, Milton G.
ICI Americas Inc.
Imperial Bancorp
Irwin Charity Foundation, William G.
ITT Hartford Insurance Group, Inc.
Ittleson Foundation
Janirve Foundation
Jewish Healthcare Foundation of Pittsburgh
JM Foundation
Johnson & Higgins
Jones Foundation, Daisy Marquis
Kansas City Southern Industries
Kennecott Corporation
Kimberly-Clark Corp.
Kirby Foundation, F. M.
Klosk Fund, Louis and Rose
Koehler Foundation, Marcia and Otto
Koret Foundation
Laffey-McHugh Foundation
Lasdon Foundation
Lee Enterprises
Leighton-Oare Foundation
Levy Foundation, June Rockwell
Littauer Foundation, Lucius N.
Long Island Lighting Co.
Lurie Foundation, Louis R.
Lyon Foundation
MacArthur Foundation, John D. and Catherine T.
Management Compensation Group/Dulworth Inc.
Mardag Foundation
Marshall Trust in Memory of Sanders McDaniel, Harriet McDaniel
MBIA Inc.
McGee Foundation
McLean Contributionship
Meadows Foundation
Medtronic, Inc.
Mellon Foundation, Richard King
Merck & Co.
Merkley Charitable Trust
Merrill Lynch & Co., Inc.
Meyer Memorial Trust
Mid-Iowa Health Foundation
Middendorf Foundation
Minnesota Mining & Mfg. Co.
Mobil Oil Corp.
Monell Foundation, Ambrose
Morgan & Company, J.P.
New York Life Insurance Co.
The New Yorker Magazine, Inc.
Nias Foundation, Henry
Norton Co.
Pacific Mutual Life Insurance Co.
Pamida, Inc.
Parshelsky Foundation, Moses L.
Parvin Foundation, Albert
Penn Foundation, William
Petteys Memorial Foundation, Jack
Pew Charitable Trusts
Pfizer, Inc.
Providian Corporation

Prudential Insurance Co. of America, The
Public Welfare Foundation
Reicher Foundation, Anne and Harry J.
Retirement Research Foundation
Rice Foundation
Rieke Corp.
Rohm & Haas Co.
Royal Group, Inc.
Rubinstein Foundation, Helena
San Diego Gas & Electric
Schwob Foundation, Simon
Seaway Food Town, Inc.
Slifka Foundation, Joseph and Sylvia
Smeal Foundation, Mary Jean and Frank P.
Snow Memorial Trust, John Ben
Southern California Edison Co.
Sprague Educational and Charitable Foundation, Seth
Starr Foundation
Steinhagen Benevolent Trust, B. A. and Elinor
Stokely, Jr. Foundation, William B.
Taper Foundation, Mark
Thompson Charitable Foundation
Trust Company Bank
Trust Funds
Union Camp Corporation
van Ameringen Foundation
Van Houten Memorial Fund
Wal-Mart Stores, Inc.
Weber Charities Corp., Frederick E.
Whitehead Charitable Foundation
Whiting Foundation
Wickson-Link Memorial Foundation

Health Policy/Cost Containment

Aluminum Co. of America
American Natural Resources Company
Anheuser-Busch Companies, Inc.
Battelle Memorial Institute
Bemis Company, Inc.
Bethlehem Steel Corp.
Burnett-Tandy Foundation
Carnegie Corporation of New York
Carter Foundation, Amon G.
Chase Manhattan Bank, N.A.
Chevron Corporation
Citibank
Clay Foundation
Collins Medical Trust
Colonial Life & Accident Insurance Co.
Connecticut Mutual Life Insurance Company
CPC International Inc.
Culpeper Foundation, Charles E.
du Pont de Nemours & Co., E. I.
Duke Endowment
Duke Power Co.
Eaton Corporation
Federated Mutual Insurance Co.
Ford Motor Co.
Friedman Family Foundation
Fry Foundation, Lloyd A.
Gallagher Family Foundation, Lewis P.
Gates Foundation
Gellert Foundation, Celia Berta
General Mills, Inc.
Goddard Foundation, Charles B.
Great-West Life Assurance Co.
Guardian Life Insurance Company of America

Hagedorn Fund
Hardin Foundation, Phil
Hartford Foundation, John A.
Haynes Foundation, John Randolph and Dora
HCA Foundation
Heinz Endowment, Howard
Heinz Endowment, Vira I.
Hewlett Foundation, William and Flora
Houston Endowment
International Business Machines Corp.
Irvine Foundation, James
ITT Hartford Insurance Group, Inc.
Jewish Healthcare Foundation of Pittsburgh
JM Foundation
John Hancock Mutual Life Insurance Co.
Johnson & Higgins
Life Insurance Co. of Georgia
Lydall, Inc.
Meadows Foundation
Medtronic, Inc.
Mellon Foundation, Richard King
Merck & Co.
Merck & Co. Human Health Division
Metropolitan Life Insurance Co.
Meyer Memorial Trust
Miller Brewing Company/North Carolina
Minnesota Mining & Mfg. Co.
Morgan & Company, J.P.
Morris Foundation, Margaret T.
Mott Fund, Ruth
Murdock Charitable Trust, M. J.
Nalco Chemical Co.
The New Yorker Magazine, Inc.
Noble Foundation, Samuel Roberts
Norton Co.
NYNEX Corporation
Pacific Mutual Life Insurance Co.
Packard Foundation, David and Lucile
Pew Charitable Trusts
PPG Industries, Inc.
Prince Trust, Abbie Norman
Prudential Insurance Co. of America, The
Ralston Purina Co.
Retirement Research Foundation
Rockwell International Corporation
Rohm & Haas Co.
SAFECO Corp.
Security Life of Denver Insurance Co.
Sheaffer Inc.
Shenandoah Life Insurance Co.
Sonat Inc.
Sunnen Foundation
Textron, Inc.
West One Bancorp
WICOR, Inc.

Health Funds

Abell-Hanger Foundation
ACF Industries, Inc.
Achelis Foundation
Acushnet Co.
Alcon Laboratories, Inc.
Altman Foundation
Aluminum Co. of America
American National Bank & Trust Co. of Chicago
Ames Charitable Trust, Harriett
AMETEK, Inc.
AMR Corp.
Annenberg Foundation
AON Corporation
Arkelian Foundation, Ben H. and Gladys
Arkell Hall Foundation
Armco Inc.

Atherton Family Foundation
Auerbach Foundation, Beatrice Fox
Avon Products, Inc.
Baker Foundation, Dexter F. and Dorothy H.
Barker Foundation, J.M.R.
Barry Corp., R. G.
Barth Foundation, Theodore H.
Batts Foundation
Bemis Company, Inc.
Bingham Second Betterment Fund, William
Bishop Foundation, E. K. and Lillian F.
Block, H&R
Blum-Kovler Foundation
Bodman Foundation
Boothroyd Foundation, Charles H. and Bertha L.
Brach Foundation, Helen
Brady Foundation
Carpenter Technology Corp.
Chevron Corporation
Church & Dwight Co., Inc.
Clark Foundation
Clorox Co.
Clowes Fund
Collins Foundation
Collins, Jr. Foundation, George Fulton
Coltec Industries, Inc.
Columbia Foundation
Columbus Dispatch Printing Co.
Commerce Clearing House, Incorporated
Connecticut Mutual Life Insurance Company
Continental Corp.
Cooper Industries, Inc.
CPC International Inc.
Davis Foundation, Edwin W. and Catherine M.
Detroit Edison Co.
Deuble Foundation, George H.
Dexter Corporation
Dimeo Construction Co.
Donaldson Company, Inc.
Dover Foundation
Dreyfus Foundation, Jean and Louis
Duchossois Industries Inc.
Dunagan Foundation
Eaton Corporation
Eden Hall Foundation
Federal-Mogul Corporation
First Financial Bank FSB
First Interstate Bank of Oregon
First Source Corp.
First Union Corp.
Forest Foundation
GAR Foundation
Georgia-Pacific Corporation
Giant Food Stores
Glaser Foundation
Goldwyn Foundation, Samuel
Guggenheim Foundation, Harry Frank
Gulf Power Co.
Hanes Foundation, John W. and Anna H.
Harcourt General, Inc.
Hartford Foundation, John A.
Hawn Foundation
Hearst Foundation, William Randolph
Hechinger Co.
Herrick Foundation
Heublein Inc.
Heydt Fund, Nan and Matilda
Hobby Foundation
Hoover Foundation
International Foundation
Jackson Foundation
Jewish Healthcare Foundation of Pittsburgh
Jockey Hollow Foundation
Kirby Foundation, F. M.
Lattner Foundation, Forrest C.
Lauder Foundation
Laurel Foundation
Leavey Foundation, Thomas and Dorothy
Leighton-Oare Foundation

Levy Foundation, June Rockwell
Link, Jr. Foundation, George
Lipton, Thomas J.
Long Foundation, J.M.
Lurie Foundation, Louis R.
Macy & Co., Inc., R.H.
Mahadh Foundation
Mars Foundation
May Department Stores Company, The
McCune Charitable Trust, John R.
Mellon Family Foundation, R. K.
Metropolitan Life Insurance Co.
Mine Safety Appliances Co.
Mobil Oil Corp.
Morris Foundation, William T.
National Westminster Bank New Jersey
The New Yorker Magazine, Inc.
Newman's Own, Inc.
NewMil Bancorp
North Shore Foundation
Offield Family Foundation
Overlake Foundation
Pamida, Inc.
Parker Hannifin Corp.
Parshelsky Foundation, Moses L.
Phelps Dodge Corporation
Phillips Foundation, Ellis L.
Reynolds Foundation, Donald W.
Robinson-Broadhurst Foundation
Royal Group, Inc.
Scaife Family Foundation
Scott Fetzer Co.
Scott Foundation, Walter
Second Foundation
Sharon Steel Corp.
Shawmut National Corp.
Shell Oil Company
Shenandoah Life Insurance Co.
Simon Foundation, William E. and Carol G.
Smith Charitable Foundation, Clara Blackford Smith and W. Aubrey
SmithKline Beecham Corp.
Snow Memorial Trust, John Ben
Sonat Inc.
Sprague Educational and Charitable Foundation, Seth
Square D Co.
Staunton Farm Foundation
Stone Charitable Foundation
Tait Foundation, Frank M.
Taylor Foundation, Ruth and Vernon
Thomas Industries
Thompson Trust, Thomas
Tiscornia Foundation
TransAmerica Corporation
Tucker Charitable Trust, Rose E.
Union Camp Corporation
Wachovia Bank of North Carolina, N.A.
Wal-Mart Stores, Inc.
Wendt Foundation, Margaret L.
Westvaco Corporation
Wheeler Foundation
Wickes Foundation, Harvey Randall
Williams Companies, The
Wilmington Trust Co.

Health Organizations

Abbott Laboratories
Abell-Hanger Foundation
Achelis Foundation
Acushnet Co.
Aetna Life & Casualty Co.
Ahmanson Foundation
Air Products and Chemicals, Inc.

AKC Fund
Akzo America
Akzo Chemicals Inc.
Alabama Power Co.
Alexander Foundation, Joseph
Allendale Insurance Co.
Allianz Life Insurance Co. of
  North America
AlliedSignal Inc.
Altman Foundation
Altschul Foundation
Alumax Inc.
Aluminum Co. of America
Amado Foundation, Maurice
Amcast Industrial Corp.
AMCORE Bank, N.A.
  Rockford
American Brands, Inc.
American Natural Resources
  Company
American Optical Corp.
American United Life
  Insurance Co.
Ames Charitable Trust, Harriett
AMETEK, Inc.
AMP Incorporated
Andersen Corp.
Andersen Foundation
Anderson Foundation, John W.
Anderson Foundation, M. D.
Andrews Foundation
Anheuser-Busch Companies,
  Inc.
Annenberg Foundation
Ansley Foundation, Dantzler
  Bond
Appleby Trust, Scott B. and
  Annie P.
Arcadia Foundation
Archer-Daniels-Midland Co.
Arkansas Power & Light Co.
Armco Inc.
Asplundh Foundation
Atherton Family Foundation
Avon Products, Inc.
Ayres Foundation, Inc.
Badgeley Residuary Charitable
  Trust, Rose M.
Baehr Foundation, Louis W.
  and Dolpha
Baldwin Foundation, David
  M. and Barbara
Ball Foundation, George and
  Frances
Bank of Boston
Bank of Boston Corp.
Bank of New York Company,
  Inc.
Bank One, Texas-Houston
  Office
Bank One, Youngstown, NA
BankAmerica Corp.
Barra Foundation
Barry Corp., R. G.
Barth Foundation, Theodore H.
Batts Foundation
Bauervic Foundation, Charles
  M.
Baughman Foundation
Bean Foundation, Norwin S.
  and Elizabeth N.
Beazley Foundation/Frederick
  Foundation
Bedsole Foundation, J. L.
Benedum Foundation, Claude
  Worthington
Benenson Foundation, Frances
  and Benjamin
Benwood Foundation
Bertha Foundation
Besser Foundation
Bethlehem Steel Corp.
Bettingen Corporation, Burton
  G.
Betts Industries
Beveridge Foundation, Frank
  Stanley
Bingham Second Betterment
  Fund, William
Bird Corp.
Birnschein Foundation, Alvin
  and Marion
Bissell Foundation, J. Walton
Blandin Foundation

Blaustein Foundation, Louis
  and Henrietta
Block, H&R
Blount, Inc.
Blowitz-Ridgeway Foundation
Blue Cross & Blue Shield
  United of Wisconsin
Boatmen's Bancshares, Inc.
Bobst Foundation, Elmer and
  Mamdouha
Bodman Foundation
Booth Ferris Foundation
Boothroyd Foundation,
  Charles H. and Bertha L.
Borman's Inc.
Boston Edison Co.
Boswell Foundation, James G.
Bothin Foundation
Bowater Incorporated
BP America Inc.
Brach Foundation, Helen
Brady Foundation
Bremer Foundation, Otto
Breyer Foundation
Bridgestone/Firestone, Inc.
Bright Family Foundation
Brillion Iron Works
Bristol-Myers Squibb
  Company
Brunswick Corp.
Bryant Foundation
Bucyrus-Erie Company
Burden Foundation, Florence
  V.
Burlington Industries, Inc.
Bush Foundation
Cabell Foundation, Robert G.
  Cabell III and Maude
  Morgan
Cabot Corp.
Cabot Family Charitable Trust
Cafritz Foundation, Morris and
  Gwendolyn
Calhoun Charitable Trust,
  Kenneth
Callaway Foundation
Campbell Foundation, Ruth
  and Henry
Canon U.S.A., Inc.
Carnegie Corporation of New
  York
Carolyn Foundation
Carpenter Foundation, E.
  Rhodes and Leona B.
Carpenter Technology Corp.
Carter Foundation, Amon G.
Caspersen Foundation for Aid
  to Health and Education, O.
  W.
Castle Foundation, Harold K.
  L.
Cayuga Foundation
CBI Industries, Inc.
Centerior Energy Corp.
Central Fidelity Banks, Inc.
Central Maine Power Co.
Century Companies of America
Champlin Foundations
Chase Manhattan Bank, N.A.
Chatlos Foundation
CHC Foundation
Chesebrough-Pond's USA Co.
Chevron Corporation
Christensen Charitable and
  Religious Foundation, L. C.
Christy-Houston Foundation
Church & Dwight Co., Inc.
CIGNA Corporation
Citibank
Citizens Bank of Rhode Island
Claiborne and Art Ortenberg
  Foundation, Liz
Clapp Charitable and
  Educational Trust, George H.
CLARCOR Inc.
Clarke Trust, John
Clay Foundation
Clayton Fund
Clorox Co.
Clowes Fund
CNA Financial
  Corporation/CNA Insurance
  Companies
Cole Foundation, Olive B.
Collins Foundation

Collins, Jr. Foundation,
  George Fulton
Collins Medical Trust
Coltec Industries, Inc.
Commerce Bancshares, Inc.
Commonwealth Edison Co.
Comprecare Foundation
Connecticut Mutual Life
  Insurance Company
Connelly Foundation
Consolidated Natural Gas Co.
Consolidated Papers, Inc.
Continental Corp.
Contran Corporation
Cooke Foundation
Cooper Industries, Inc.
Coors Foundation, Adolph
Cornell Trust, Peter C.
Coughlin-Saunders Foundation
Cowles Charitable Trust
CPC International Inc.
Crane Co.
Crawford Estate, E. R.
Cremer Foundation
Crestlea Foundation
Crystal Trust
Culpeper Memorial
  Foundation, Daphne Seybolt
Cummings Foundation, James
  H.
Curtice-Burns Foods, Inc.
Dana Foundation, Charles A.
Daniel Foundation of Alabama
Davenport-Hatch Foundation
Davenport Trust Fund
Davis Foundation, Edwin W.
  and Catherine M.
Davis Foundations, Arthur
  Vining
Day Foundation, Nancy Sayles
Daywood Foundation
DEC International, Inc.
Deere & Co.
Delavan Foundation, Nelson B.
Dell Foundation, Hazel
Demoulas Supermarkets Inc.
Dentsply International Inc.
DeRoy Testamentary
  Foundation
Dewing Foundation, Frances R.
Dexter Charitable Fund,
  Eugene A.
Dexter Corporation
Diamond Foundation, Aaron
Digital Equipment Corp.
Dillon Foundation
Dimeo Construction Co.
Dingman Foundation, Michael
  D.
Dodge Foundation, Cleveland
  H.
Dodge Jones Foundation
Douty Foundation
Dresser Industries, Inc.
du Pont de Nemours & Co., E.
  I.
Duke Endowment
Duke Power Co.
Dula Educational and
  Charitable Foundation,
  Caleb C. and Julia W.
Dun & Bradstreet Corp.
Duncan Trust, John G.
duPont Foundation, Alfred I.
Durfee Foundation
Dynamet, Inc.
Early Foundation
Eastman Kodak Company
Eaton Corporation
Eden Hall Foundation
Einstein Fund, Albert E. and
  Birdie W.
El Pomar Foundation
Emerson Foundation, Inc.,
  Fred L.
Encyclopaedia Britannica, Inc.
English Memorial Fund,
  Florence C. and H. L.
Enron Corp.
Ensign-Bickford Industries
Essick Foundation
Ethyl Corp
Exxon Corporation
Farish Fund, William Stamps

Farr Trust, Frank M. and Alice
  M.
Federal-Mogul Corporation
Federated Mutual Insurance
  Co.
Femino Foundation
Fenton Foundation
Fieldcrest Cannon Inc.
Fife Foundation, Elias and
  Bertha
Fikes Foundation, Leland
Fink Foundation
Firestone, Jr. Foundation,
  Harvey
First Interstate Bank of Oregon
First National Bank
First Source Corp.
First Union Corp.
First Union National Bank of
  Florida
Fish Foundation, Ray C.
Fleming Cos. Food
  Distribution Center
Fohs Foundation
Folger Fund
Forbes Inc.
Ford Foundation
Ford Fund, William and Martha
Ford II Fund, Henry
Ford Motor Co.
Forest Foundation
Foster Foundation
Freeport Brick Co.
Freeport-McMoRan Inc.
Fribourg Foundation
Friedman Family Foundation
Friendship Fund
Frisch's Restaurants Inc.
Frueauff Foundation, Charles
  A.
Fry Foundation, Lloyd A.
Fuld Health Trust, Helene
Fund for New Jersey
Gannett Publishing Co., Guy
GATX Corp.
Gaylord Foundation, Clifford
  Willard
Gazette Co.
Gellert Foundation, Carl
Gellert Foundation, Celia Berta
General Mills, Inc.
General Motors Corp.
GenRad
Georgia-Pacific Corporation
Georgia Power Co.
German Protestant Orphan
  Asylum Association
Giant Eagle, Inc.
Giant Food Stores
Gifford Charitable
  Corporation, Rosamond
Giles Foundation, Edward C.
Gillette Co.
Gilman Foundation, Howard
Glaser Foundation
Glenn Foundation, Carrie C.
  and Lena V.
Glick Foundation, Eugene and
  Marilyn
Globe Newspaper Co.
Goddard Foundation, Charles
  B.
Goodrich Co., The B.F.
Gould Electronics Inc.
Graham Fund, Philip L.
Greenwall Foundation
Gregg-Graniteville Foundation
Griffith Foundation, W. C.
Guaranty Bank & Trust Co.
Gulf Power Co.
Haas, Jr. Fund, Evelyn and
  Walter
Hachar Charitable Trust, D. D.
Hafif Family Foundation
Hagedorn Fund
Halff Foundation, G. A. C.
Hallett Charitable Trust, Jessie
  F.
Hamman Foundation, George
  and Mary Josephine
Hammer Foundation, Armand
Hancock Foundation, Luke B.
Handy and Harman Foundation

Harland Charitable
  Foundation, John and
  Wilhelmina D.
Harriman Foundation, Gladys
  and Roland
Harsco Corp.
Hartford Foundation, John A.
Hartmarx Corporation
Harvey Foundation, Felix
Hastings Charitable
  Foundation, Oris B.
Hawn Foundation
HCA Foundation
Hearst Foundation, William
  Randolph
Hechinger Co.
Hecht-Levi Foundation
Heckscher Foundation for
  Children
Heinz Company, H. J.
Helmerich Foundation
Helms Foundation
Henderson Foundation,
  George B.
Hermann Foundation, Grover
Herrick Foundation
Hershey Foundation, Barry J.
Herzstein Charitable
  Foundation, Albert and Ethel
Heublein Inc.
Hewit Family Foundation
Hillman Foundation
Hillsdale Fund
Hobby Foundation
Hoffman Foundation,
  Maximilian E. and Marion O.
Hoffmann-La Roche Inc.
Holzer Memorial Foundation,
  Richard H.
Hook Drugs
Hoover Foundation
Hopkins Foundation,
  Josephine Lawrence
Hopwood Charitable Trust,
  John M.
Houston Endowment
Houston Industries
  Incorporated
Howard and Bush Foundation
Howe and Mitchell B. Howe
  Foundation, Lucille Horton
Hoyt Foundation, Stewart W.
  and Willma C.
Huber Foundation
Hudson-Webber Foundation
Hugoton Foundation
Hunt Charitable Trust, C. Giles
Hunt Foundation
Huston Foundation
Huthsteiner Fine Arts Trust
Hyde and Watson Foundation
IBP, Inc.
Icahn Foundation, Carl C.
Illinois Consolidated
  Telephone Co.
Imperial Bancorp
Independence Foundation
Ingalls Foundation, Louise H.
  and David S.
Inland Container Corp.
International Business
  Machines Corp.
International Paper Co.
Irvine Foundation, James
Irwin Charity Foundation,
  William G.
ITT Hartford Insurance Group,
  Inc.
Ittleson Foundation
Jackson Foundation
Jacobson Foundation, Bernard
  H. and Blanche E.
Jaffe Foundation
Janesville Foundation
Janirve Foundation
Jarson-Stanley and Mickey
  Kaplan Foundation, Isaac
  and Esther
Jaydor Corp.
JELD-WEN, Inc.
Jennings Foundation, Mary
  Hillman
Jewish Healthcare Foundation
  of Pittsburgh
JM Foundation

Jockey Hollow Foundation
Johnson Charitable
   Educational Trust, James
   Hervey
Johnson Charitable Trust,
   Keith Wold
Johnson Controls Inc.
Johnson Foundation, Helen K.
   and Arthur E.
Johnson & Higgins
Johnson & Son, S.C.
Jones Foundation, Daisy
   Marquis
Jones Foundation, Fletcher
Jonsson Foundation
Joslin-Needham Family
   Foundation
Journal-Gazette Co.
Jurzykowski Foundation,
   Alfred
Justus Trust, Edith C.
Kansas City Southern
   Industries
Kantzler Foundation
Kaplun Foundation, Morris J.
   and Betty
Kavanagh Foundation, T.
   James
Kayser Foundation
Kelly Tractor Co.
Kemper Foundation, William T.
Kempner Fund, Harris and
   Eliza
Kennedy Foundation, Ethel
Kettering Fund
Kiewit Foundation, Peter
Kilcawley Fund, William H.
Kimball Foundation, Horace
   A. Kimball and S. Ella
Kingsbury Corp.
Kiplinger Foundation
Kline Foundation, Josiah W.
   and Bessie H.
Klipstein Foundation, Ernest
   Christian
Klock and Lucia Klock
   Kingston Foundation, Jay E.
Koehler Foundation, Marcia
   and Otto
Komes Foundation
Koopman Fund
Kresge Foundation
Kunkel Foundation, John Crain
Kuyper Foundation, Peter H.
   and E. Lucille
Lang Foundation, Eugene M.
Larsen Fund
Lazarus Charitable Trust,
   Helen and Charles
Leavey Foundation, Thomas
   and Dorothy
Lebovitz Fund
Lederer Foundation, Francis L.
Lee Endowment Foundation
Lehigh Portland Cement Co.
Lehmann Foundation, Otto W.
Leidy Foundation, John J.
Lemberg Foundation
Leuthold Foundation
Levy Foundation, June
   Rockwell
Lichtenstein Foundation,
   David B.
Life Insurance Co. of Georgia
Link, Jr. Foundation, George
Lipton, Thomas J.
Littauer Foundation, Lucius N.
Lockhart Vaughan Foundation
Longwood Foundation
Louisiana-Pacific Corp.
Lowenstein Foundation, Leon
Lurie Foundation, Louis R.
Lydall, Inc.
Lyon Foundation
M/A-COM, Inc.
MacArthur Foundation, John
   D. and Catherine T.
MacLeod Stewardship
   Foundation
Macy & Co., Inc., R.H.
Madison Gas & Electric Co.
Magowan Family Foundation
Mailman Family Foundation,
   A. L.
Maneely Fund

Mardag Foundation
Marpat Foundation
Marriott Foundation, J. Willard
Martini Foundation, Nicholas
Mather Charitable Trust, S.
   Livingston
Mather and William Gwinn
   Mather Fund, Elizabeth Ring
Mathis-Pfohl Foundation
Matthies Foundation, Katharine
May Department Stores
   Company, The
May Foundation, Wilbur
Mayer Foundation, James and
   Eva
Maytag Family Foundation,
   Fred
MBIA Inc.
McCarty Foundation, John and
   Margaret
McCasland Foundation
McCormick & Co. Inc.
McCormick Foundation,
   Chauncey and Marion
   Deering
McCune Charitable Trust,
   John R.
McDonnell Douglas
   Corp.-West
McFeely-Rogers Foundation
McGee Foundation
McGraw-Hill, Inc.
MCI Communications Corp.
McInerny Foundation
McMillan Foundation, D. W.
McQueen Foundation, Adeline
   and George
McShain Charities, John
Meadows Foundation
Medtronic, Inc.
Mellon Foundation, Richard
   King
Memorial Foundation for the
   Blind
Merck & Co.
Mercury Aircraft
Merrill Lynch & Co., Inc.
Metropolitan Life Insurance
   Co.
Meyer Memorial Trust
Mid-Iowa Health Foundation
Middendorf Foundation
Miller-Mellor Association
Mine Safety Appliances Co.
Minnesota Mining & Mfg. Co.
Mobil Oil Corp.
Montana Power Co.
Moore Charitable Foundation,
   Marjorie
Moore Foundation, Edward S.
Morgan & Company, J.P.
Morris Foundation, Margaret T.
Morrison Knudsen Corporation
Mosbacher, Jr. Foundation,
   Emil
Moses Fund, Henry and Lucy
Mott Fund, Ruth
Mulford Trust, Clarence E.
Munson Foundation Trust, W.
   B.
Murphey Foundation, Lluella
   Morey
Murphy Co. Foundation, G.C.
Musson Charitable
   Foundation, R. C. and
   Katharine M.
Mutual Assurance Co.
Nabisco Foods Group
Nalco Chemical Co.
National Forge Co.
National Gypsum Co.
National Steel Corp.
Nesholm Family Foundation
Neuberger Foundation, Roy R.
   and Marie S.
New Jersey Natural Gas Co.
New York Life Insurance Co.
The New Yorker Magazine, Inc.
Nias Foundation, Henry
Noble Foundation, Edward
   John
Noble Foundation, Samuel
   Roberts
Norfolk Shipbuilding &
   Drydock Corp.

Northern States Power Co.
   (Minnesota)
Northwest Natural Gas Co.
Norton Co.
Norton Memorial Corporation,
   Geraldi
Norwest Bank Nebraska, N.A.
OCRI Foundation
Odell Fund, Robert Stewart
   Odell and Helen Pfeiffer
Offield Family Foundation
OG&E Electric Services
Old Dominion Box Co.
Old National Bank in
   Evansville
Olin Corp.
Olsson Memorial Foundation,
   Elis
Oppenstein Brothers
   Foundation
O'Quinn Foundation, John M.
   and Nancy C.
Osher Foundation, Bernard
Ottley Trust-Watertown,
   Marion W.
Overbrook Foundation
Owen Industries, Inc.
Pacific Mutual Life Insurance
   Co.
Packard Foundation, David
   and Lucile
Palmer Fund, Frank Loomis
Parker Hannifin Corp.
Parsons Foundation, Ralph M.
Parvin Foundation, Albert
Penn Foundation, William
Pennzoil Co.
Peoples Energy Corp.
Peppers Foundation, Ann
Perkin-Elmer Corp.
Petteys Memorial Foundation,
   Jack
Pettus Crowe Foundation
Pew Charitable Trusts
Pfizer, Inc.
Phelps Dodge Corporation
PHH Corporation
Philibosian Foundation,
   Stephen
Phillips Charitable Trust, Dr.
   and Mrs. Arthur William
Phillips Family Foundation,
   Jay and Rose
Piankova Foundation, Tatiana
Pick, Jr. Fund, Albert
Pierce Charitable Trust, Harold
   Whitworth
Pineywoods Foundation
Pioneer Trust Bank, NA
Piper Foundation, Minnie
   Stevens
PNC Bank, N.A.
Pollock Company Foundation,
   William B.
Potomac Electric Power Co.
Pott Foundation, Herman T.
   and Phenie R.
PPG Industries, Inc.
Prairie Foundation
Premier Industrial Corp.
Price Associates, T. Rowe
Priddy Foundation
Prince Trust, Abbie Norman
Prouty Foundation, Olive
   Higgins
Providence Journal Company
Prudential Insurance Co. of
   America, The
Prudential Securities, Inc.
Public Service Co. of New
   Mexico
Public Welfare Foundation
Puterbaugh Foundation
Putnam Foundation
Quaker Chemical Corp.
Quivey-Bay State Foundation
R. F. Foundation
R&B Machine Tool Co.
Ratner Foundation, Milton M.
Raymond Corp.
Read Foundation, Charles L.
Reicher Foundation, Anne and
   Harry J.
Reichhold Chemicals, Inc.
Reinberger Foundation

Reisman Charitable Trust,
   George C. and Evelyn R.
Rennebohm Foundation, Oscar
Retirement Research
   Foundation
Reynolds Foundation, Donald
   W.
Rice Foundation
Rich Products Corporation
Rieke Corp.
Robinson-Broadhurst
   Foundation
Rockwell Fund
Rockwell International
   Corporation
Rohm & Haas Co.
Rose Foundation, Billy
Roseburg Forest Products Co.
Rosenberg, Jr. Family
   Foundation, Louise and
   Claude
Rose's Stores, Inc.
Ross Laboratories
Ross Memorial Foundation,
   Will
Rowland Foundation
Royal Foundation, May
   Mitchell
Royal Group, Inc.
Ruan Foundation Trust, John
Rubin Family Fund, Cele H.
   and William B.
Rubinstein Foundation, Helena
Rudin Foundation
SAFECO Corp.
Salomon Foundation, Richard
   and Edna
San Diego Gas & Electric
Sandy Hill Foundation
Sara Lee Corp.
Sara Lee Hosiery, Inc.
Sarkeys Foundation
Sawyer Charitable Foundation
Scaife Family Foundation
Scherer Foundation, Karla
Scherman Foundation
Scholl Foundation, Dr.
Schroeder Foundation, Walter
Schuller International
Schwartz Foundation, Arnold
   A.
Schwartz Fund for Education
   and Health Research, Arnold
   and Marie
Scott Fetzer Co.
Scott Foundation, Walter
Scott Foundation, William E.
Seafirst Corporation
Seaway Food Town, Inc.
Security Life of Denver
   Insurance Co.
Seneca Foods Corp.
Sentry Insurance A Mutual
   Company
Sequoia Foundation
Shawmut National Corp.
Sheaffer Inc.
Sheary for Charity, Edna M.
Shell Oil Company
Shenandoah Life Insurance Co.
Sheppard Foundation,
   Lawrence B.
Sierra Pacific Industries
Simon Foundation, William E.
   and Carol G.
Skillman Foundation
Smart Family Foundation
Smeal Foundation, Mary Jean
   and Frank P.
Smith Foundation, Gordon V.
   and Helen C.
Smith Foundation, Kelvin and
   Eleanor
Smith Memorial Fund, Ethel
   Sergeant Clark
Smith Trust, May and Stanley
SmithKline Beecham Corp.
Snow Foundation, John Ben
Snyder Foundation, Harold B.
   and Dorothy A.
Sonat Inc.
Sordoni Foundation
South Waite Foundation
Southern California Edison Co.

Sprague Educational and
   Charitable Foundation, Seth
Springs Foundation
SPX Corp.
Starr Foundation
Stauffer Charitable Trust, John
Stauffer Foundation, John and
   Beverly
Staunton Farm Foundation
Stearns Trust, Artemas W.
Stein Foundation, Jules and
   Doris
Stevens Foundation, John T.
Stokely, Jr. Foundation,
   William B.
Stone Charitable Foundation
Stone Trust, H. Chase
Strauss Foundation, Leon
Stupp Foundation, Norman J.
Sturgis Charitable and
   Educational Trust, Roy and
   Christine
Sumitomo Bank of California
Sundet Foundation
Sunnen Foundation
Tait Foundation, Frank M.
Taper Foundation, Mark
Taubman Foundation, A. Alfred
Taylor Foundation, Fred and
   Harriett
Taylor Foundation, Ruth and
   Vernon
Temple Foundation, T. L. L.
Temple-Inland Inc.
Tenneco Inc.
Texas Commerce
   Bank-Houston, N.A.
Textron, Inc.
Thorne Foundation
Tiscornia Foundation
Titus Foundation, Roy and
   Niuta
Todd Co., A.M.
Toms Foundation
Travelers Inc.
Trees Charitable Trust, Edith L.
Truland Foundation
Trust Company Bank
Tucker Charitable Trust, Rose
   E.
Unger Foundation, Aber D.
Unilever United States, Inc.
Union Camp Corporation
Union Electric Co.
Union Pacific Corp.
Unocal Corp.
Upton Foundation, Frederick S.
USG Corporation
USX Corporation
Utica National Insurance
   Group
Van Buren Foundation
Vernon Fund, Miles Hodsdon
Virginia Power Co.
Vollbrecht Foundation,
   Frederick A.
Vulcan Materials Co.
Wachovia Bank of North
   Carolina, N.A.
Wahlstrom Foundation
Wal-Mart Stores, Inc.
Walsh Foundation
Washington Forrest Foundation
Wean Foundation, Raymond
   John
Weaver Foundation, Gil and
   Dody
Weber Charities Corp.,
   Frederick E.
Wege Foundation
Weingart Foundation
Weinstein Foundation, J.
Welfare Foundation
Wells Foundation, Franklin H.
   and Ruth L.
Wendt Foundation, Margaret L.
Western New York Foundation
Westvaco Corporation
Wheat First Butcher Singer,
   Inc.
Wheeler Foundation
Whirlpool Corporation
Whitehead Charitable
   Foundation

Wickes Foundation, Harvey
Randall
Wilder Foundation
Wildermuth Foundation, E. F.
Williams Companies, The
Wilmington Trust Co.
Windham Foundation
Winnebago Industries, Inc.
Wisconsin Power & Light Co.
Wise Foundation and
Charitable Trust, Watson W.
Woodward Fund
Y and H Soda Foundation
Young Foundation, Hugo H.
and Mabel B.
Zlinkoff Fund for Medical
Research and Education,
Sergei S.
Zollner Foundation

Heart

Abbott Laboratories
Ahmanson Foundation
Air Products and Chemicals,
Inc.
Akzo America
Alabama Gas Corp.
Alavi Foundation of New York
Aldus Corp.
Allianz Life Insurance Co. of
North America
AlliedSignal Inc.
Amcast Industrial Corp.
American Fidelity Corporation
American General Finance
Corp.
Andersen Foundation
Andreas Foundation
Andrews Foundation
Anheuser-Busch Companies,
Inc.
Arkell Hall Foundation
Ashtabula Foundation
Audubon State Bank
Auerbach Foundation,
Beatrice Fox
Baldwin Foundation, David
M. and Barbara
Ball Brothers Foundation
Bank One, Youngstown, NA
Banta Corp.
Baskin-Robbins USA Co.
Berger Foundation, H. N. and
Frances C.
Bobst Foundation, Elmer and
Mamdouha
Breyer Foundation
Bridwell Foundation, J. S.
Bristol-Myers Squibb
Company
Bryn Mawr Trust Co.
Burkitt Foundation
Cabot Corp.
Cain Foundation, Effie and
Wofford
Calder Foundation, Louis
Calhoun Charitable Trust,
Kenneth
Callaway Foundation
Campbell Foundation, Ruth
and Henry
Carpenter Technology Corp.
City National Bank and Trust
Co.
Columbus Dispatch Printing
Co.
Connelly Foundation
Cooke Foundation
Cooper Industries, Inc.
Crown Books
Cullen Foundation
Culpeper Memorial
Foundation, Daphne Seybolt
Cummings Foundation, James
H.
Cuneo Foundation
Curtice-Burns Foods, Inc.
Dentsply International Inc.
Deuble Foundation, George H.
Dresser Industries, Inc.
Duke Endowment
Duncan Foundation, Lillian H.
and C. W.

Early Foundation
Eberly Foundation
Einstein Fund, Albert E. and
Birdie W.
Favrot Fund
Federated Mutual Insurance
Co.
Fieldcrest Cannon Inc.
Fikes Foundation, Leland
Fireman's Fund Insurance Co.
First Interstate Bank of Oregon
Firstar Bank Milwaukee, N.A.
Fish Foundation, Ray C.
Ford Fund, William and Martha
French Oil Mill Machinery Co.
Frisch's Restaurants Inc.
Gebbie Foundation
Geifman Family Foundation
Gellert Foundation, Celia Berta
Gershman Foundation, Joel
Giant Food Inc.
Gifford Charitable
Corporation, Rosamond
Glosser Foundation, David A.
Goldsmith Foundation, Horace
W.
Gould Electronics Inc.
Griggs and Mary Griggs Burke
Foundation, Mary Livingston
GSM Industrial
Hagedorn Fund
Haley Foundation, W. B.
Hamman Foundation, George
and Mary Josephine
Handy and Harman Foundation
Hanover Foundation
Hawn Foundation
Herzstein Charitable
Foundation, Albert and Ethel
Hill Foundation, Sandy
Hillcrest Foundation
Hoag Family Foundation,
George
Hobby Foundation
Hoffman Foundation,
Maximilian E. and Marion O.
Hoover Fund-Trust, W. Henry
Houston Endowment
Hoyt Foundation
Hoyt Foundation, Stewart W.
and Willma C.
Hugoton Foundation
Humana, Inc.
Integra Bank of Uniontown
Jaydor Corp.
JM Foundation
Kansas City Southern
Industries
Kardon Foundation, Samuel
and Rebecca
Kempner Fund, Harris and
Eliza
Kingsbury Corp.
Kirby Foundation, F. M.
Kline Foundation, Josiah W.
and Bessie H.
Klock and Lucia Klock
Kingston Foundation, Jay E.
Komes Foundation
Lauder Foundation
Lehigh Portland Cement Co.
Lennon Foundation, Fred A.
Lichtenstein Foundation,
David B.
Link, Jr. Foundation, George
Louisiana-Pacific Corp.
Lovett Foundation
Lydall, Inc.
Madison Gas & Electric Co.
Magowan Family Foundation
Mandeville Foundation
Mardigian Foundation
Margoes Foundation
Markey Charitable Fund, John
C.
Marmot Foundation
Martini Foundation, Nicholas
Mautz Paint Co.
May Department Stores
Company, The
McCormick Trust, Anne
McMahan Foundation,
Catherine L. and Robert O.
McMillan Foundation, D. W.
Meadows Foundation

Merck & Co.
Meyer Family Foundation,
Paul J.
OG&E Electric Services
Old Dominion Box Co.
Oppenstein Brothers
Foundation
O'Quinn Foundation, John M.
and Nancy C.
Parvin Foundation, Albert
Peabody Charitable Fund,
Amelia
Phillips Charitable Trust, Dr.
and Mrs. Arthur William
Plankenhorn Foundation, Harry
Ratner Foundation, Milton M.
Reisman Charitable Trust,
George C. and Evelyn R.
Richardson Charitable Trust,
Anne S.
Rowland Foundation
Rubin Family Fund, Cele H.
and William B.
Sandusky International Inc.
Sargent Foundation, Newell B.
Scholl Foundation, Dr.
Schwob Foundation, Simon
Seafirst Corporation
Self Foundation
Semmes Foundation
Seneca Foods Corp.
Shell Oil Company
Sierra Pacific Resources
Slifka Foundation, Joseph and
Sylvia
Smith Foundation, Gordon V.
and Helen C.
Solow Foundation
Southwestern Electric Power
Co.
Stabler Foundation, Donald B.
and Dorothy L.
Steele-Reese Foundation
Steinman Foundation, James
Hale
Sundet Foundation
Superior Tube Co.
Taylor Foundation, Fred and
Harriett
Teichert & Son, A.
Texas Commerce
Bank-Houston, N.A.
Truland Foundation
United Airlines, Inc.
Uris Brothers Foundation
Vanderbilt Trust, R. T.
Vollbrecht Foundation,
Frederick A.
Weckbaugh Foundation,
Eleanore Mullen
Westerman Foundation,
Samuel L.
Widgeon Foundation
Wiegand Foundation, E. L.
Wildermuth Foundation, E. F.
Willard Helping Fund, Cecilia
Young
Winnebago Industries, Inc.
Wood Foundation of
Chambersburg, PA
Worthington Foods
Young Foundation, Robert R.

Home-Care Services

Ayres Foundation, Inc.
Barra Foundation
Bingham Second Betterment
Fund, William
Blowitz-Ridgeway Foundation
Blum Foundation, Edna F.
Bryn Mawr Trust Co.
Campbell Foundation, Ruth
and Henry
Childs Charitable Foundation,
Roberta M.
Cole Foundation, Olive B.
Crabtree & Evelyn
Diamond Foundation, Aaron
Duke Endowment
Federated Mutual Insurance
Co.
Feil Foundation, Louis and
Gertrude

GenRad
Ghidotti Foundation
Graham Fund, Philip L.
Groome Beatty Trust, Helen D.
Handy and Harman Foundation
Heinz Company, H. J.
Hoyt Foundation, Stewart W.
and Willma C.
Integra Bank of Uniontown
Jewish Healthcare Foundation
of Pittsburgh
Kansas City Southern
Industries
Kilcawley Fund, William H.
Kreitler Foundation
Leuthold Foundation
Marpat Foundation
McGee Foundation
Meadows Foundation
Merck Family Fund
Mid-Iowa Health Foundation
Morgan Stanley & Co., Inc.
Mott Foundation, Charles
Stewart
NewMil Bancorp
Novell Inc.
Old National Bank in
Evansville
Ottley Trust-Watertown,
Marion W.
Pew Charitable Trusts
Pollock Company Foundation,
William B.
Reisman Charitable Trust,
George C. and Evelyn R.
Retirement Research
Foundation
Rogers Family Foundation
Schmitt Foundation, Kilian J.
and Caroline F.
Self Foundation
Smith Trust, May and Stanley
Stevens Foundation, Abbot
and Dorothy H.
Unitrode Corp.
Vogler Foundation, Laura B.
Washington Forrest Foundation

Hospices

Abbott Laboratories
Abell-Hanger Foundation
Alabama Gas Corp.
Aldus Corp.
Allendale Insurance Co.
Alumax Inc.
Aluminum Co. of America
Amcast Industrial Corp.
AMCORE Bank, N.A.
Rockford
American General Finance
Corp.
American National Bank &
Trust Co. of Chicago
American Natural Resources
Company
Amfac/JMB Hawaii Inc.
AMP Incorporated
Andersen Foundation
Anderson Foundation, John W.
Anderson Foundation, M. D.
Appleby Trust, Scott B. and
Annie P.
Arcadia Foundation
Aristech Chemical Corp.
Armco Inc.
Atherton Family Foundation
Auerbach Foundation,
Beatrice Fox
Avon Products, Inc.
Baldwin Foundation, David
M. and Barbara
Baldwin Memorial
Foundation, Fred
Bank One, Youngstown, NA
Barra Foundation
Barth Foundation, Theodore H.
Beal Foundation
Beech Aircraft Corp.
Berger Foundation, H. N. and
Frances C.
Besser Foundation
Betts Industries

Beveridge Foundation, Frank
Stanley
Blandin Foundation
Block, H&R
Bloedorn Foundation, Walter
A.
Blowitz-Ridgeway Foundation
Blue Bell, Inc.
Blum-Kovler Foundation
Bobst Foundation, Elmer and
Mamdouha
Bodman Foundation
Boeing Co., The
Boettcher Foundation
Borkee Hagley Foundation
Borman's Inc.
Boston Edison Co.
Brach Foundation, Helen
Bremer Foundation, Otto
Breyer Foundation
Bridwell Foundation, J. S.
Brunswick Corp.
Bryn Mawr Trust Co.
Burden Foundation, Florence
V.
Cafritz Foundation, Morris and
Gwendolyn
Cain Foundation, Gordon and
Mary
Campbell Foundation, Ruth
and Henry
Campini Foundation, Frank A.
Carpenter Foundation, E.
Rhodes and Leona B.
Catlin Charitable Trust,
Kathleen K.
CBI Industries, Inc.
Central Hudson Gas & Electric
Corp.
Central Maine Power Co.
Central National Bank
Century Companies of America
Champlin Foundations
Cheatham Foundation, Owen
Chevron Corporation
Christy-Houston Foundation
Citibank
City National Bank and Trust
Co.
Clay Foundation
Clorox Co.
Coen Family Foundation,
Charles S. and Mary
Collins Foundation
Collins Medical Trust
Colonial Life & Accident
Insurance Co.
Coltec Industries, Inc.
Columbia Foundation
Comer Foundation
Connelly Foundation
Consolidated Papers, Inc.
Cooke Foundation
Cooper Industries, Inc.
Copley Press, Inc.
Cornell Trust, Peter C.
Crabtree & Evelyn
Crary Foundation, Bruce L.
Crestlea Foundation
Crystal Trust
CT Corp. System
Cullen Foundation
Culpeper Memorial
Foundation, Daphne Seybolt
Cummings Foundation, James
H.
Cummins Engine Co.
Cuneo Foundation
Curtice-Burns Foods, Inc.
Daniel Foundation of Alabama
Davenport-Hatch Foundation
Davidson Family Charitable
Foundation
Davis Foundation, James A.
and Juliet L.
Davis Foundations, Arthur
Vining
Day Foundation, Nancy Sayles
Daywood Foundation
Delano Foundation, Mignon
Sherwood
Dentsply International Inc.
DeRoy Testamentary
Foundation

Hospitals

Geneseo Foundation
GenRad
Georgia-Pacific Corporation
Georgia Power Co.
German Protestant Orphan Asylum Association
Gershman Foundation, Joel
Ghidotti Foundation
Giant Eagle, Inc.
Giant Food Inc.
Giant Food Stores
Gifford Charitable Corporation, Rosamond
Gillette Co.
Gilman Foundation, Howard
Gilmore Foundation, William G.
Glaser Foundation
Glencoe Foundation
Glick Foundation, Eugene and Marilyn
Globe Newspaper Co.
Goddard Foundation, Charles B.
Goldberg Family Foundation
Golden West Foundation
Goldie-Anna Charitable Trust
Goldsmith Foundation, Horace W.
Goldwyn Foundation, Samuel
Good Samaritan
Goodman & Co.
Goodrich Co., The B.F.
Goodstein Family Foundation, David
Gordon/Rousmaniere/Roberts Fund
Gould Electronics Inc.
Great-West Life Assurance Co.
Greenwall Foundation
Gregg-Graniteville Foundation
Griffis Foundation
Griffith Foundation, W. C.
Griswold Foundation, John C.
Groome Beatty Trust, Helen D.
Grundy Foundation
GSM Industrial
Gulf Power Co.
Guttman Foundation, Stella and Charles
Haas, Jr. Fund, Evelyn and Walter
Habig Foundation, Arnold F.
Hagedorn Fund
Haley Foundation, W. B.
Halff Foundation, G. A. C.
Hallett Charitable Trust, E. W.
Hamilton Bank
Hamman Foundation, George and Mary Josephine
Hammer Foundation, Armand
Handy and Harman Foundation
Hanes Foundation, John W. and Anna H.
Hanson Industries North America
Harcourt Foundation, Ellen Knowles
Harcourt General, Inc.
Harland Charitable Foundation, John and Wilhelmina D.
Harriman Foundation, Gladys and Roland
Harriman Foundation, Mary W.
Harsco Corp.
Hartford Foundation, John A.
Hartmarx Corporation
Hasbro Inc.
Hatch Charitable Trust, Margaret Milliken
Hawn Foundation
Hearst Foundation, William Randolph
Hechinger Co.
Heckscher Foundation for Children
Hedco Foundation
Heginbotham Trust, Will E.
Heinz Company, H. J.
Heinz Endowment, Howard
Heinz Endowment, Vira I.
Heinz Trust, Drue
Helms Foundation
Henkel Corp.

Hermann Foundation, Grover
Herrick Foundation
Hershey Foods Corp.
Herzstein Charitable Foundation, Albert and Ethel
Heublein Inc.
Hewit Family Foundation
Hewlett-Packard Co.
Heydt Fund, Nan and Matilda
Hickory Tech Corp.
High Foundation
Hill Foundation, Sandy
Hillcrest Foundation
Hillman Family Foundation, Alex
Hillsdale Fund
Hoag Family Foundation, George
Hobby Foundation
Hoffman Foundation, Maximilian E. and Marion O.
Hoffmann-La Roche Inc.
Holzer Memorial Foundation, Richard H.
Homeland Foundation
Hook Drugs
Hoover Foundation
Hoover, Jr. Foundation, Margaret W. and Herbert
Hopedale Foundation
Hopkins Foundation, Josephine Lawrence
Hopwood Charitable Trust, John M.
Housatonic Curtain Co.
Houston Endowment
Houston Industries Incorporated
Howard and Bush Foundation
Howe and Mitchell B. Howe Foundation, Lucille Horton
Howell Foundation of Florida
Hoyt Foundation, Stewart W. and Willma C.
Huber Foundation
Hudson-Webber Foundation
Hugoton Foundation
Huisking Foundation
Hulbert Foundation, Nila B.
Hulme Charitable Foundation, Milton G.
Hultquist Foundation
Humana, Inc.
Humphrey Fund, George M. and Pamela S.
Hunt Charitable Trust, C. Giles
Hunt Foundation
Hunt Foundation, Roy A.
Hunt Foundation, Samuel P.
Huston Foundation
Huthsteiner Fine Arts Trust
Hyde and Watson Foundation
IBP, Inc.
Icahn Foundation, Carl C.
ICI Americas Inc.
IES Industries, Inc.
Illinois Consolidated Telephone Co.
Illinois Tool Works, Inc.
Imperial Bancorp
Ingalls Foundation, Louise H. and David S.
Inland Container Corp.
Integra Bank of Uniontown
International Business Machines Corp.
International Foundation
International Paper Co.
Irvine Foundation, James
Irwin Charity Foundation, William G.
ITT Hartford Insurance Group, Inc.
Ittleson Foundation
Jackson Foundation
Jacobs Family Foundation
Jaffe Foundation
Jameson Foundation, J. W. and Ida M.
Janirve Foundation
Jarson-Stanley and Mickey Kaplan Foundation, Isaac and Esther
Jaydor Corp.
JELD-WEN, Inc.

Jennings Foundation, Mary Hillman
Jewell Memorial Foundation, Daniel Ashley and Irene Houston
Jewett Foundation, George Frederick
Jewish Healthcare Foundation of Pittsburgh
JM Foundation
Jockey Hollow Foundation
John Hancock Mutual Life Insurance Co.
Johnson Controls Inc.
Johnson Foundation, Helen K. and Arthur E.
Johnson Foundation, M. G. and Lillie A.
Johnson Foundation, Willard T. C.
Johnson Fund, Edward C.
Johnson & Higgins
Johnson & Son, S.C.
Jones Foundation, Daisy Marquis
Jones Foundation, Fletcher
Jones Foundation, Helen
Jonsson Foundation
Jordan Charitable Foundation, Mary Ranken Jordan and Ettie A.
Joslin-Needham Family Foundation
Journal-Gazette Co.
Joy Family Foundation
Julia R. and Estelle L. Foundation
Jurzykowski Foundation, Alfred
Kansas City Southern Industries
Kantzler Foundation
Kaplun Foundation, Morris J. and Betty
Kardon Foundation, Samuel and Rebecca
Kaufmann Foundation, Henry
Kayser Foundation
Kelley and Elza Kelley Foundation, Edward Bangs
Kelly Foundation, T. Lloyd
Kelly Tractor Co.
Kemper Foundation, William T.
Kennecott Corporation
Kennedy Foundation, Ethel
Kent-Lucas Foundation
Kettering Fund
Kiewit Foundation, Peter
Kimberly-Clark Corp.
Kiplinger Foundation
Kirbo Charitable Trust, Thomas M. and Irene B.
Kirby Foundation, F. M.
Kirkpatrick Foundation
Kitzmiller/Bales Trust
Kline Foundation, Josiah W. and Bessie H.
Klipstein Foundation, Ernest Christian
Klock and Lucia Klock Kingston Foundation, Jay E.
Klosk Fund, Louis and Rose
KN Energy, Inc.
Knapp Foundation
Knight Foundation, John S. and James L.
Koehler Foundation, Marcia and Otto
Kohn-Joseloff Foundation
Komes Foundation
Koopman Fund
Kreitler Foundation
Kresge Foundation
Kuehn Foundation
Kuyper Foundation, Peter H. and E. Lucille
La-Z-Boy Chair Co.
Ladd Charitable Corporation, Helen and George
Laffey-McHugh Foundation
Landegger Charitable Foundation
Lang Foundation, Eugene M.
Larsen Fund
Lasdon Foundation

Lasdon Foundation, William and Mildred
Lattner Foundation, Forrest C.
Lauder Foundation
Laurel Foundation
Lazarus Charitable Trust, Helen and Charles
LBJ Family Foundation
Leavey Foundation, Thomas and Dorothy
Lebanon Mutual Insurance Co.
Lebovitz Fund
Lee Endowment Foundation
Lee Enterprises
Lehigh Portland Cement Co.
Lehmann Foundation, Otto W.
Leidy Foundation, John J.
Lemberg Foundation
Lennon Foundation, Fred A.
Leuthold Foundation
Levy Foundation, June Rockwell
Liberman Foundation, Bertha and Isaac
Lichtenstein Foundation, David B.
Link, Jr. Foundation, George
Linn-Henley Charitable Trust
Linnell Foundation
Lipton, Thomas J.
Littauer Foundation, Lucius N.
Little, Inc., Arthur D.
Liz Claiborne, Inc.
Loews Corporation
Long Foundation, J.M.
Longwood Foundation
Louisiana-Pacific Corp.
Love Foundation, George H. and Margaret McClintic
Lovett Foundation
Lowenstein Foundation, Leon
Lund Foundation
Lunda Charitable Trust
Lurie Foundation, Louis R.
Lydall, Inc.
M/A-COM, Inc.
Macy & Co., Inc., R.H.
Madison Gas & Electric Co.
Magowan Family Foundation
Mahadh Foundation
Mailman Foundation
Maneely Fund
Marbrook Foundation
Mardag Foundation
Margoes Foundation
Maritz Inc.
Markey Charitable Fund, John C.
Marmot Foundation
Marpat Foundation
Marriott Foundation, J. Willard
Marshall Foundation, Mattie H.
Marshall Trust in Memory of Sanders McDaniel, Harriet McDaniel
Martin Marietta Corp.
Martin Marietta Materials
Martini Foundation, Nicholas
Mather and William Gwinn Mather Fund, Elizabeth Ring
Mathis-Pfohl Foundation
Matthies Foundation, Katharine
May Department Stores Company, The
May Foundation, Wilbur
Mayer Foundation, James and Eva
Mayor Foundation, Oliver Dewey
Maytag Family Foundation, Fred
MCA Inc.
McCann Foundation
McCarty Foundation, John and Margaret
McCasland Foundation
McCormick Trust, Anne
McCune Charitable Foundation, Marshall and Perrine D.
McCune Charitable Trust, John R.
McDermott Foundation, Eugene

McDonald & Company Securities, Inc.
McDonnell Douglas Corp.-West
McEvoy Foundation, Mildred H.
McFawn Trust No. 2, Lois Sisler
McFeely-Rogers Foundation
McGee Foundation
McGonagle Foundation, Dextra Baldwin
MCI Communications Corp.
McInerny Foundation
McKenna Foundation, Katherine Mabis
McKenna Foundation, Philip M.
McLean Contributionship
McMillan Foundation, D. W.
McQueen Foundation, Adeline and George
McShain Charities, John
Meadows Foundation
Mellon Family Foundation, R. K.
Mellon Foundation, Richard King
Memorial Foundation for the Blind
Memton Fund
Mengle Foundation, Glenn and Ruth
Merck & Co.
Merck & Co. Human Health Division
Merck Family Fund
Mercury Aircraft
Merrick Foundation
Merrill Lynch & Co., Inc.
Messing Family Charitable Foundation
Metropolitan Life Insurance Co.
Meyer Memorial Trust
Meyerhoff Fund, Joseph
Mid-Iowa Health Foundation
Middendorf Foundation
Mielke Family Foundation
Millbrook Tribute Garden
Miller Charitable Foundation, Howard E. and Nell E.
Miller Fund, Kathryn and Gilbert
Miller-Mellor Association
Mine Safety Appliances Co.
Mingenback Foundation, Julia J.
Minnesota Mining & Mfg. Co.
Mnuchin Foundation
Mobil Oil Corp.
Mohasco Corp.
Monadnock Paper Mills
Monell Foundation, Ambrose
Montana Power Co.
Moore Charitable Foundation, Marjorie
Moore Foundation, Edward S.
Moore & Sons, B.C.
Morgan Charitable Residual Trust, W. and E.
Morgan & Company, J.P.
Morgan Foundation, Louie R. and Gertrude
Morgan and Samuel Tate Morgan, Jr. Foundation, Marietta McNeil
Morgan Stanley & Co., Inc.
Morris Foundation, Margaret T.
Morris Foundation, William T.
Mosbacher, Jr. Foundation, Emil
Moses Fund, Henry and Lucy
Mosinee Paper Corp.
Mott Fund, Ruth
Mulford Foundation, Vincent
Mulford Trust, Clarence E.
Mullen Foundation, J. K.
Muller Foundation
Munger Foundation, Alfred C.
Munson Foundation Trust, W. B.
Murphey Foundation, Lluella Morey
Murphy Co. Foundation, G.C.

Musson Charitable Foundation, R. C. and Katharine M.
Mutual Assurance Co.
Nabisco Foods Group
Nalco Chemical Co.
National Forge Co.
National Gypsum Co.
National Westminster Bank New Jersey
NBD Indiana, Inc.
Nestle USA Inc.
Neuberger Foundation, Roy R. and Marie S.
New England Business Service
New Jersey Natural Gas Co.
New-Land Foundation
New York Life Insurance Co.
New York Stock Exchange, Inc.
The New Yorker Magazine, Inc.
Newman's Own, Inc.
NewMil Bancorp
Nias Foundation, Henry
Noble Foundation, Edward John
Noble Foundation, Samuel Roberts
Norfolk Shipbuilding & Drydock Corp.
Norgren Foundation, Carl A.
Norman Foundation, Summers A.
Normandie Foundation
Northern States Power Co. (Minnesota)
Northwest Natural Gas Co.
Norton Co.
Norton Memorial Corporation, Geraldi
Oaklawn Foundation
O'Connor Foundation, A. Lindsay and Olive B.
OCRI Foundation
Odell Fund, Robert Stewart Odell and Helen Pfeiffer
Offield Family Foundation
OG&E Electric Services
Ohrstrom Foundation
Old National Bank in Evansville
Olin Corp.
Olin Foundation, Spencer T. and Ann W.
Oliver Memorial Trust Foundation
Olsson Memorial Foundation, Elis
Oppenstein Brothers Foundation
O'Quinn Foundation, John M. and Nancy C.
Ore-Ida Foods, Inc.
Osborn Charitable Trust, Edward B.
Osceola Foundation
Ottley Trust-Watertown, Marion W.
Outboard Marine Corp.
Overbrook Foundation
Overlake Foundation
Owen Industries, Inc.
Owsley Foundation, Alvin and Lucy
Oxy USA Inc.
Pacific Mutual Life Insurance Co.
Packaging Corporation of America
Packard Foundation, David and Lucile
PaineWebber
Paley Foundation, William S.
Palisades Educational Foundation
Palmer Fund, Frank Loomis
Pamida, Inc.
Panhandle Eastern Corporation
Park Foundation
Parker Hannifin Corp.
Parshelsky Foundation, Moses L.
Parsons Foundation, Ralph M.
Parvin Foundation, Albert
Patterson Charitable Fund, W. I.

Payne Foundation, Frank E. and Seba B.
Peabody Charitable Fund, Amelia
PECO Energy Company
Pella Corporation
Pennsylvania Dutch Co.
Pennzoil Co.
Peoples Energy Corp.
Perkin-Elmer Corp.
Peters Foundation, Charles F.
Peterson Foundation, Hal and Charlie
Petrie Trust, Lorene M.
Petteys Memorial Foundation, Jack
Pfizer, Inc.
Pforzheimer Foundation, Carl and Lily
Phelps Dodge Corporation
PHH Corporation
Philibosian Foundation, Stephen
Phillips Charitable Trust, Dr. and Mrs. Arthur William
Phillips Family Foundation, Jay and Rose
Phillips Family Foundation, L. E.
Piankova Foundation, Tatiana
Pick, Jr. Fund, Albert
Pickford Foundation, Mary
Pierce Charitable Trust, Harold Whitworth
Pineywoods Foundation
Pioneer Trust Bank, NA
Pitt-Des Moines Inc.
Pittsburg Midway Coal Mining Co.
Plankenhorn Foundation, Harry
Plumsock Fund
PNC Bank, N.A.
Polaroid Corp.
Pollock Company Foundation, William B.
Porter Foundation, Mrs. Cheever
Potomac Electric Power Co.
Pott Foundation, Herman T. and Phenie R.
Potts and Sibley Foundation
PPG Industries, Inc.
Prairie Foundation
Premier Industrial Corp.
Price Associates, T. Rowe
Price Foundation, Louis and Harold
Price Foundation, Lucien B. and Katherine E.
Priddy Foundation
Prince Trust, Abbie Norman
Prospect Hill Foundation
Prouty Foundation, Olive Higgins
Providence Journal Company
Prudential Insurance Co. of America, The
Prudential Securities, Inc.
Public Service Co. of New Mexico
Public Service Electric & Gas Co.
Public Welfare Foundation
Pulitzer Publishing Co.
Puterbaugh Foundation
Putnam Foundation
Quaker Chemical Corp.
R. F. Foundation
Rabb Charitable Foundation, Sidney and Esther
Ralston Purina Co.
R&B Machine Tool Co.
Ratner Foundation, Milton M.
Raymond Corp.
Read Foundation, Charles L.
Regenstein Foundation
Reicher Foundation, Anne and Harry J.
Reichhold Chemicals, Inc.
Reidler Foundation
Reinberger Foundation
Reisman Charitable Trust, George C. and Evelyn R.
Rennebohm Foundation, Oscar

Retirement Research Foundation
Reynolds Foundation, Donald W.
Reynolds Foundation, Edgar
Rhone-Poulenc Inc.
Rice Foundation
Rich Products Corporation
Richardson Charitable Trust, Anne S.
Rieke Corp.
Riggs Benevolent Fund
Ringier-America
Ritter Charitable Trust, George W. and Mary F.
RJR Nabisco Inc.
Robinson Fund, Maurice R.
Rockefeller Fund, David
Rockwell Fund
Rockwell International Corporation
Rogers Family Foundation
Rohatyn Foundation, Felix and Elizabeth
Rohm & Haas Co.
Rose Foundation, Billy
Rosen Foundation, Joseph
Rosenberg, Jr. Family Foundation, Louise and Claude
Ross Laboratories
Ross Memorial Foundation, Will
Rouse Co.
Rowland Foundation
Royal Foundation, May Mitchell
Royal Group, Inc.
Rubin Family Fund, Cele H. and William B.
Rubin Foundation, Samuel
Rubinstein Foundation, Helena
Rudin Foundation
Russell Trust, Josephine G.
Safety Fund National Bank
Salomon Foundation, Richard and Edna
Salomon Inc.
Saltonstall Charitable Foundation, Richard
San Diego Gas & Electric
Sandy Hill Foundation
Sara Lee Hosiery, Inc.
Sargent Foundation, Newell B.
Sarkeys Foundation
Sasco Foundation
Sawyer Charitable Foundation
SBC Communications Inc.
Scaife Family Foundation
Schenck Fund, L. P.
Scherer Foundation, Karla
Schering-Plough Corp.
Schiff Foundation, Dorothy
Schiro Fund
Schlink Foundation, Albert G. and Olive H.
Schlumberger Ltd.
Schoenleber Foundation
Scholl Foundation, Dr.
Schroeder Foundation, Walter
Schwartz Foundation, Arnold A.
Schwartz Fund for Education and Health Research, Arnold and Marie
Schwob Foundation, Simon
Scott Fetzer Co.
Scott Foundation, Walter
Scurlock Foundation
Seafirst Corporation
Seaver Charitable Trust, Richard C.
Seaver Institute
Seaway Food Town, Inc.
Second Foundation
Seidman Family Foundation
Self Foundation
Seneca Foods Corp.
Sentry Insurance A Mutual Company
Sequoia Foundation
Seton Leather Co.
Share Trust, Charles Morton
Sharon Steel Corp.
Shaw Foundation, Arch W.

Shawmut National Corp.
Sheaffer Inc.
Sheary for Charity, Edna M.
Shell Oil Company
Sheppard Foundation, Lawrence B.
Sierra Pacific Resources
Simon Foundation, William E. and Carol G.
Simpson Investment Company
Slifka Foundation, Joseph and Sylvia
Smart Family Foundation
Smeal Foundation, Mary Jean and Frank P.
Smith Charitable Foundation, Clara Blackford Smith and W. Aubrey
Smith Charitable Foundation, Lou and Lutza
Smith Corp., A.O.
Smith Foundation, Gordon V. and Helen C.
Snow Foundation, John Ben
Snow Memorial Trust, John Ben
Snyder Foundation, Harold B. and Dorothy A.
Solow Foundation
Sonat Inc.
Sordoni Foundation
South Waite Foundation
Southern California Edison Co.
Southern New England Telephone Company
Southwestern Electric Power Co.
Spang & Co.
Speer Foundation, Roy M.
Sprague Educational and Charitable Foundation, Seth
Springs Foundation
SPX Corp.
Square D Co.
Stabler Foundation, Donald B. and Dorothy L.
Stackpole-Hall Foundation
Stanley Charitable Foundation, A.W.
Stanley Works
Stans Foundation
Starr Foundation
Stauffer Charitable Trust, John
Stauffer Foundation, John and Beverly
Staunton Farm Foundation
Stearns Trust, Artemas W.
Steele Foundation, Harry and Grace
Steele-Reese Foundation
Steinbach Fund, Ruth and Milton
Steinman Foundation, James Hale
Steinman Foundation, John Frederick
Stemmons Foundation
Stevens Foundation, Abbot and Dorothy H.
Stevens Foundation, John T.
Stokely, Jr. Foundation, William B.
Stone Charitable Foundation
Strauss Foundation, Leon
Strawbridge Foundation of Pennsylvania II, Margaret Dorrance
Stupp Foundation, Norman J.
Sturgis Charitable and Educational Trust, Roy and Christine
Sullivan Foundation, Algernon Sydney
Sulzberger Foundation
Superior Tube Co.
Swalm Foundation
Swanson Family Foundation, Dr. W.C.
Swift Co. Inc., John S.
Swiss Bank Corp.
Symmes Foundation, F. W.
Taube Family Foundation
Taubman Foundation, A. Alfred
Taylor Foundation, Fred and Harriett

Taylor Foundation, Ruth and Vernon
Teagle Foundation
Tecumseh Products Co.
Teleflex Inc.
Temple Foundation, T. L. L.
Temple-Inland Inc.
Tenneco Inc.
Tennessee Valley Printing Co.
Tetley, Inc.
Teubert Charitable Trust, James H. and Alice
Texaco Inc.
Texas Commerce Bank-Houston, N.A.
Textron, Inc.
Thalhimer and Family Foundation, Charles G.
Thermo Electron Corp.
Thomas Industries
Thomasville Furniture Industries
Thompson Charitable Foundation
Thompson Trust, Thomas
Thorne Foundation
Thornton Foundation
Thornton Foundation, Flora L.
Timken Foundation of Canton
Towsley Foundation, Harry A. and Margaret D.
Tozer Foundation
TransAmerica Corporation
Travelers Inc.
Truland Foundation
Trust Company Bank
Trust Funds
Tucker Charitable Trust, Rose E.
Tupancy-Harris Foundation of 1986
Turner Charitable Foundation
Unger Foundation, Aber D.
Unilever United States, Inc.
Union Bank
Union Camp Corporation
Union Pacific Corp.
United Airlines, Inc.
Unitrode Corp.
Unocal Corp.
Upjohn Foundation, Harold and Grace
Upton Foundation, Frederick S.
USG Corporation
Utica National Insurance Group
Valmont Industries, Inc.
van Ameringen Foundation
Van Buren Foundation
Van Every Foundation, Philip L.
Van Houten Memorial Fund
Van Nuys Foundation, I. N. and Susanna H.
Van Wert County Foundation
Vance Charitable Foundation, Robert C.
Vanderbilt Trust, R. T.
Vernon Fund, Miles Hodsdon
Virginia Power Co.
Vollbrecht Foundation, Frederick A.
Wachovia Bank of North Carolina, N.A.
Wahlstrom Foundation
Wal-Mart Stores, Inc.
Wallace Foundation, George R.
Walsh Foundation
Warfield Memorial Fund, Anna Emory
Warner Fund, Albert and Bessie
Warren and Beatrice W. Blanding Foundation, Riley J. and Lillian N.
Warwick Foundation
Waters Charitable Trust, Robert S.
Wean Foundation, Raymond John
Weaver Foundation, Gil and Dody
Webber Oil Co.
Weber Charities Corp., Frederick E.

Weckbaugh Foundation, Eleanore Mullen
Weezie Foundation
Wege Foundation
Weingart Foundation
Weinstein Foundation, J.
Wells Foundation, Franklin H. and Ruth L.
Wendt Foundation, Margaret L.
Wertheim Foundation, Dr. Herbert A.
West Foundation, Harry and Ethel
West One Bancorp
Westerman Foundation, Samuel L.
Western New York Foundation
Westvaco Corporation
Weyerhaeuser Co.
Wheat First Butcher Singer, Inc.
Wheeler Foundation
Whirlpool Corporation
White Trust, G. R.
Whiting Foundation
Whiting Foundation, Macauley and Helen Dow
Whitney Fund, David M.
Wickes Foundation, Harvey Randall
Wickson-Link Memorial Foundation
WICOR, Inc.
Wiegand Foundation, E. L.
Wilder Foundation
Wildermuth Foundation, E. F.
Willard Helping Fund, Cecilia Young
Williams Charitable Trust, John C.
Williams Companies, The
Wilmington Trust Co.
Wilson Foundation, H. W.
Wilson Fund, Matilda R.
Windham Foundation
Winnebago Industries, Inc.
Winston Foundation, Norman and Rosita
Winthrop Trust, Clara B.
Wiremold Co.
Wisconsin Power & Light Co.
Wisconsin Public Service Corp.
Witco Corp.
Wood Foundation of Chambersburg, PA
Woodward Fund
Woolley Foundation, Vasser
Wright Foundation, Lola
Wyman Youth Trust
Wyomissing Foundation
Yeager Charitable Trust, Lester E.
Young Foundation, Hugo H. and Mabel B.
Young Foundation, Irvin L.
Young Foundation, Robert R.
Zachry Co., H.B.
Zarrow Foundation, Anne and Henry
Zenkel Foundation
Zlinkoff Fund for Medical Research and Education, Sergei S.
Zollner Foundation

Hospitals (University Affiliated)

Allyn Foundation
Astor Foundation, Vincent
Baldwin Foundation, David M. and Barbara
Bloedorn Foundation, Walter A.
Clowes Fund
Corning Incorporated
Dreyfus Foundation, Max and Victoria
Duke Endowment
Dunagan Foundation
Duncan Foundation, Lillian H. and C. W.

Einstein Fund, Albert E. and Birdie W.
Feil Foundation, Louis and Gertrude
Femino Foundation
Fife Foundation, Elias and Bertha
General American Life Insurance Co.
Gilman Foundation, Howard
Goldsmith Foundation, Horace W.
Gregg-Graniteville Foundation
Handy and Harman Foundation
Hanover Foundation
Hardin Foundation, Phil
Hoffman Foundation, Maximilian E. and Marion O.
Hopedale Foundation
Humphrey Fund, George M. and Pamela S.
Jewish Healthcare Foundation of Pittsburgh
Kansas City Southern Industries
Koehler Foundation, Marcia and Otto
Koret Foundation
Kornfeld Foundation, Emily Davie and Joseph S.
Lemberg Foundation
Levitt Foundation
Lovett Foundation
Marriott Foundation, J. Willard
McDermott Foundation, Eugene
McGonagle Foundation, Dextra Baldwin
Munger Foundation, Alfred C.
Ross Laboratories
Schwartz Fund for Education and Health Research, Arnold and Marie
Second Foundation
Spang & Co.
Temple Foundation, T. L. L.
Thorne Foundation
Travelers Inc.
Van Houten Memorial Fund
Weinstein Foundation, J.
Zachry Co., H.B.

Kidney

Abbott Laboratories
Alabama Gas Corp.
Andersen Corp.
Andersen Foundation
Bank One, Youngstown, NA
Bothin Foundation
Clark Foundation
Contran Corporation
Crown Books
Davenport-Hatch Foundation
Dynamet, Inc.
Einstein Fund, Albert E. and Birdie W.
Ford Motor Co.
Freedom Forge Corp.
Gazette Co.
Giant Eagle, Inc.
Gifford Charitable Corporation, Rosamond
Hachar Charitable Trust, D. D.
Hopwood Charitable Trust, John M.
Howe and Mitchell B. Howe Foundation, Lucille Horton
Jarson-Stanley and Mickey Kaplan Foundation, Isaac and Esther
Jewish Healthcare Foundation of Pittsburgh
Klosk Fund, Louis and Rose
Murphey Foundation, Lluella Morey
Peppers Foundation, Ann
Quivey-Bay State Foundation
Raymond Corp.
Ruan Foundation Trust, John
Rubin Family Fund, Cele H. and William B.
Schmitt Foundation, Kilian J. and Caroline F.

Smeal Foundation, Mary Jean and Frank P.
Spang & Co.
Temple Foundation, T. L. L.
Thornton Foundation, Flora L.
Valmont Industries, Inc.
Vanderbilt Trust, R. T.
Vollbrecht Foundation, Frederick A.
Windham Foundation

Long-Term Care

Ahmanson Foundation
Allyn Foundation
Altschul Foundation
AMCORE Bank, N.A. Rockford
Anderson Foundation
Arkell Hall Foundation
Atran Foundation
Ayres Foundation, Inc.
Batts Foundation
Bauervic Foundation, Charles M.
Bingham Second Betterment Fund, William
Birnschein Foundation, Alvin and Marion
Bloedorn Foundation, Walter A.
Blowitz-Ridgeway Foundation
Boettcher Foundation
Borkee Hagley Foundation
Bryn Mawr Trust Co.
Burden Foundation, Florence V.
Carpenter Foundation
Cayuga Foundation
Clapp Charitable and Educational Trust, George H.
Cogswell Benevolent Trust
Columbus Dispatch Printing Co.
Connelly Foundation
Cornell Trust, Peter C.
Crestlea Foundation
Daily News
Davenport-Hatch Foundation
Demoulas Supermarkets Inc.
Duke Endowment
Duncan Foundation, Lillian H. and C. W.
Federated Mutual Insurance Co.
Ferebee Endowment, Percy O.
Fink Foundation
French Foundation, D.E.
Frohring Foundation, Paul and Maxine
Gellert Foundation, Carl
Groome Beatty Trust, Helen D.
Grundy Foundation
Haas, Jr. Fund, Evelyn and Walter
Habig Foundation, Arnold F.
Harland Charitable Foundation, John and Wilhelmina D.
Hartford Foundation, John A.
Hawkins Foundation, Robert Z.
Hawn Foundation
Hillcrest Foundation
Hillman Foundation
Hopwood Charitable Trust, John M.
Huisking Foundation
Humphrey Fund, George M. and Pamela S.
Ingalls Foundation, Louise H. and David S.
Jewish Healthcare Foundation of Pittsburgh
Joslin-Needham Family Foundation
Julia R. and Estelle L. Foundation
Kansas City Southern Industries
Kaufmann Foundation, Henry
Kavanagh Foundation, T. James
Kimball Foundation, Horace A. Kimball and S. Ella

Koret Foundation
Longwood Foundation
Lunda Charitable Trust
Maneely Fund
McLean Contributionship
McShain Charities, John
Meadows Foundation
Mellon Foundation, Richard King
Memton Fund
Mengle Foundation, Glenn and Ruth
Merck Family Fund
Meyer Memorial Trust
Musson Charitable Foundation, R. C. and Katharine M.
National Forge Co.
Nesholm Family Foundation
Nias Foundation, Henry
Olsson Memorial Foundation, Elis
Packard Foundation, David and Lucile
Parsons Foundation, Ralph M.
Phillips Family Foundation, Jay and Rose
Phipps Foundation, Howard
Pick, Jr. Fund, Albert
PNC Bank, N.A.
PPG Industries, Inc.
R&B Machine Tool Co.
Read Foundation, Charles L.
Retirement Research Foundation
Rudin Foundation
Schering-Plough Corp.
Schoenleber Foundation
Smith Charitable Foundation, Lou and Lutza
SmithKline Beecham Corp.
Superior Tube Co.
Taubman Foundation, A. Alfred
Trexler Trust, Harry C.
Utica National Insurance Group
Van Nuys Foundation, I. N. and Susanna H.
Vernon Fund, Miles Hodsdon
Vogler Foundation, Laura B.
Washington Mutual Savings Bank
Weaver Foundation, Gil and Dody
Wiegand Foundation, E. L.
Wood Foundation of Chambersburg, PA

Medical Rehabilitation

Abbott Laboratories
Achelis Foundation
Acushnet Co.
Adams Foundation, Arthur F. and Alice E.
Alabama Gas Corp.
Albertson's Inc.
Alexander Foundation, Joseph
Allegheny Ludlum Corp.
AlliedSignal Inc.
Altschul Foundation
Aluminum Co. of America
American General Finance Corp.
American National Bank & Trust Co. of Chicago
American Natural Resources Company
AMETEK, Inc.
Amfac/JMB Hawaii Inc.
Anderson Foundation, M. D.
AON Corporation
Armco Inc.
Atherton Family Foundation
Avon Products, Inc.
Baker Foundation, Dexter F. and Dorothy H.
Baker Trust, George F.
Baldwin Memorial Foundation, Fred
Ball Foundation, George and Frances

Barra Foundation
Bay Foundation
Beech Aircraft Corp.
Besser Foundation
Block, H&R
Blowitz-Ridgeway Foundation
Blum-Kovler Foundation
Bodman Foundation
Bothin Foundation
Bridwell Foundation, J. S.
Bristol-Myers Squibb Company
Bucyrus-Erie Company
Bush Foundation
Cafritz Foundation, Morris and Gwendolyn
Cain Foundation, Gordon and Mary
Callaway Foundation
Carpenter Foundation, E. Rhodes and Leona B.
Carter Foundation, Amon G.
Castle Foundation, Harold K. L.
CBI Industries, Inc.
Central Maine Power Co.
Century Companies of America
Champlin Foundations
Chase Manhattan Bank, N.A.
Chevron Corporation
Childs Charitable Foundation, Roberta M.
Citizens Bank of Rhode Island
Clapp Charitable and Educational Trust, George H.
Comer Foundation
Connelly Foundation
Coors Foundation, Adolph
Cullen Foundation
Curtice-Burns Foods, Inc.
Daugherty Foundation
Davenport-Hatch Foundation
Davis Foundation, Edwin W. and Catherine M.
Dell Foundation, Hazel
Demoulas Supermarkets Inc.
DeRoy Testamentary Foundation
Digital Equipment Corp.
Dodge Jones Foundation
Donnelley Foundation, Gaylord and Dorothy
Dreyfus Foundation, Max and Victoria
du Pont de Nemours & Co., E. I.
Duke Endowment
Duncan Trust, John G.
Dynamet, Inc.
Eastman Kodak Company
Eden Hall Foundation
Edgewater Steel Corp.
Einstein Fund, Albert E. and Birdie W.
El Pomar Foundation
Elf Atochem North America, Inc.
Emerson Foundation, Inc., Fred L.
English Memorial Fund, Florence C. and H. L.
Exxon Corporation
Federated Mutual Insurance Co.
Firman Fund
First Interstate Bank of Oregon
First Union Corp.
Fischbach Foundation
Fish Foundation, Ray C.
Fishback Foundation Trust, Harmes C.
Folger Fund
Fondren Foundation
Ford II Fund, Henry
Foster Charitable Trust
Frear Eleemosynary Trust, Mary D. and Walter F.
French Foundation, D.E.
French Oil Mill Machinery Co.
Frost National Bank
GATX Corp.
Gellert Foundation, Carl
General American Life Insurance Co.
General Mills, Inc.

General Motors Corp.
Georgia-Pacific Corporation
Georgia Power Co.
German Protestant Orphan Asylum Association
Gheens Foundation
Giant Eagle, Inc.
Gillette Co.
Goddard Foundation, Charles B.
Goldberg Family Foundation
Goldsmith Foundation, Horace W.
Gregg-Graniteville Foundation
Griffith Foundation, W. C.
Hafif Family Foundation
Hagedorn Fund
Halff Foundation, G. A. C.
Hallett Charitable Trust, E. W.
Hamman Foundation, George and Mary Josephine
Hardin Foundation, Phil
Hartford Foundation, John A.
Hawn Foundation
Hearst Foundation, William Randolph
Hechinger Co.
Heckscher Foundation for Children
Heinz Company, H. J.
Heinz Endowment, Howard
Heinz Trust, Drue
Hermann Foundation, Grover
Hillman Foundation
Hoffman Foundation, Maximilian E. and Marion O.
Holzer Memorial Foundation, Richard H.
Hook Drugs
Hopwood Charitable Trust, John M.
Howard and Bush Foundation
Hulme Charitable Foundation, Milton G.
Humphrey Fund, George M. and Pamela S.
Hunt Foundation
Hunt Foundation, Roy A.
Hunt Foundation, Samuel P.
Huston Charitable Trust, Stewart
Huston Foundation
Hyde and Watson Foundation
Illinois Consolidated Telephone Co.
Illinois Tool Works, Inc.
Independence Foundation
Ingalls Foundation, Louise H. and David S.
International Foundation
Irwin Charity Foundation, William G.
ITT Hartford Insurance Group, Inc.
Jarson-Stanley and Mickey Kaplan Foundation, Isaac and Esther
Jaydor Corp.
Jennings Foundation, Mary Hillman
JM Foundation
Johnson & Higgins
Jones Foundation, Daisy Marquis
Kansas City Southern Industries
Kardon Foundation, Samuel and Rebecca
Kayser Foundation
Kelley and Elza Kelley Foundation, Edward Bangs
Kemper National Insurance Cos.
Kirby Foundation, F. M.
Kitzmiller/Bales Trust
Knoll Group
Koopman Fund
Kreitler Foundation
Kresge Foundation
Kuehn Foundation
Lang Foundation, Eugene M.
Lehmann Foundation, Otto W.
Leuthold Foundation
Lipton, Thomas J.
Lydall, Inc.

Lyon Foundation
Macy & Co., Inc., R.H.
Massengill-DeFriece Foundation
May Foundation, Wilbur
Mayor Foundation, Oliver Dewey
Maytag Family Foundation, Fred
McDonnell Douglas Corp.-West
McGee Foundation
McInerny Foundation
McLean Contributionship
McMillan Foundation, D. W.
Memton Fund
Meyer Memorial Trust
Mine Safety Appliances Co.
Mobil Oil Corp.
Monell Foundation, Ambrose
Monfort Family Foundation
Morgan Stanley & Co., Inc.
Morris Foundation, William T.
Morrison Knudsen Corporation
Mosbacher, Jr. Foundation, Emil
Mulford Foundation, Vincent
Murdock Charitable Trust, M. J.
Nalco Chemical Co.
New York Life Insurance Co.
The New Yorker Magazine, Inc.
Nias Foundation, Henry
Noble Foundation, Samuel Roberts
Norgren Foundation, Carl A.
Northwest Natural Gas Co.
Norton Co.
Norton Memorial Corporation, Geraldi
Old National Bank in Evansville
Olin Corp.
Olsson Memorial Foundation, Elis
Oppenstein Brothers Foundation
Overlake Foundation
Oxy USA Inc.
Park Foundation
Pennzoil Co.
Perkin-Elmer Corp.
Petteys Memorial Foundation, Jack
Pfizer, Inc.
Piper Jaffray Companies Inc.
Pittsburg Midway Coal Mining Co.
PNC Bank, N.A.
PPG Industries, Inc.
Prairie Foundation
Price Foundation, Louis and Harold
Price Foundation, Lucien B. and Katherine E.
Priddy Foundation
Prince Trust, Abbie Norman
Prudential Insurance Co. of America, The
Rabb Charitable Foundation, Sidney and Esther
Regenstein Foundation
Reisman Charitable Trust, George C. and Evelyn R.
Rennebohm Foundation, Oscar
Rice Foundation
Rockwell Fund
Rockwell International Corporation
Rogers Family Foundation
Rohm & Haas Co.
Rose Foundation, Billy
Rowland Foundation
Rubin Family Fund, Cele H. and William B.
Rubinstein Foundation, Helena
Santa Fe Pacific Corporation
Sarkeys Foundation
Scaife Family Foundation
Schlink Foundation, Albert G. and Olive H.
Seneca Foods Corp.
Sequoia Foundation
Seton Leather Co.
Shaw Foundation, Arch W.

Shawmut National Corp.
Shell Oil Company
Smith Corp., A.O.
South Waite Foundation
Sprague Educational and Charitable Foundation, Seth
Stauffer Charitable Trust, John
Staunton Farm Foundation
Stein Foundation, Jules and Doris
Stokely, Jr. Foundation, William B.
Stone Charitable Foundation
Strawbridge Foundation of Pennsylvania II, Margaret Dorrance
Strong Foundation, Hattie M.
Subaru of America Inc.
Sundet Foundation
Taylor Foundation, Ruth and Vernon
Tecumseh Products Co.
Temple Foundation, T. L. L.
Texaco Inc.
Thomas Industries
Thorne Foundation
Towsley Foundation, Harry A. and Margaret D.
Trexler Trust, Harry C.
Trust Company Bank
Union Bank
Union Camp Corporation
Union Pacific Corp.
Unocal Corp.
USX Corporation
Valmont Industries, Inc.
Van Houten Memorial Fund
Wal-Mart Stores, Inc.
Wean Foundation, Raymond John
Westvaco Corporation
White Trust, G. R.
Wickes Foundation, Harvey Randall
Woodward Fund
Wyomissing Foundation
Zarrow Foundation, Anne and Henry

Medical Research

Abbott Laboratories
Abell-Hanger Foundation
Abrams Foundation, Talbert and Leota
Ahmanson Foundation
Air France
AKC Fund
Akzo Chemicals Inc.
Alcon Laboratories, Inc.
Alexander Foundation, Joseph
Allen Brothers Foundation
Allendale Insurance Co.
AlliedSignal Inc.
Allyn Foundation
Altschul Foundation
Alumax Inc.
Aluminum Co. of America
Amado Foundation, Maurice
American Brands, Inc.
American National Bank & Trust Co. of Chicago
American Natural Resources Company
American United Life Insurance Co.
Ameritas Life Insurance Corp.
Ames Charitable Trust, Harriett
AMETEK, Inc.
Andersen Corp.
Andersen Foundation
Anderson Foundation, M. D.
Andersons, The
Andreas Foundation
Anheuser-Busch Companies, Inc.
Annenberg Foundation
Ansley Foundation, Dantzler Bond
AON Corporation
Argyros Foundation
Arkell Hall Foundation
Atherton Family Foundation
Atran Foundation

Avon Products, Inc.
Babcock & Wilcox Co.
Badgeley Residuary Charitable Trust, Rose M.
Baker Hughes Inc.
Baker Trust, George F.
Baldwin Foundation, David M. and Barbara
Ball Foundation, George and Frances
Bank of Boston
Bank One, Texas-Houston Office
Barra Foundation
Barry Corp., R. G.
Battelle Memorial Institute
Bauervic Foundation, Charles M.
Beal Foundation
BE&K Inc.
Bechtel, Jr. Foundation, S. D.
Benetton Services Corp.
Berger Foundation, H. N. and Frances C.
Bettingen Corporation, Burton G.
Binswanger Cos.
Bishop Foundation, E. K. and Lillian F.
Blair and Co., William
Blandin Foundation
Blaustein Foundation, Louis and Henrietta
Blowitz-Ridgeway Foundation
Blue Bell, Inc.
Blum Foundation, Harry and Maribel G.
Blum-Kovler Foundation
Bodman Foundation
Boothroyd Foundation, Charles H. and Bertha L.
Borden, Inc.
Boswell Foundation, James G.
Brady Foundation
Breyer Foundation
Bridgestone/Firestone, Inc.
Bridwell Foundation, J. S.
Bristol-Myers Squibb Company
Broadhurst Foundation
Brooks Foundation, Gladys
Bryant Foundation
Bucyrus-Erie Company
Bunbury Company
Burchfield Foundation, Charles E.
Butz Foundation
Cable & Wireless Holdings, Inc.
Cain Foundation, Effie and Wofford
Cain Foundation, Gordon and Mary
Campini Foundation, Frank A.
Canon U.S.A., Inc.
Carnegie Corporation of New York
Carter Foundation, Amon G.
Carvel Foundation, Thomas and Agnes
Cassett Foundation, Louis N.
CBI Industries, Inc.
Charina Foundation
Chartwell Foundation
Chatlos Foundation
Chazen Foundation
Cheatham Foundation, Owen
Childs Charitable Foundation, Roberta M.
Church & Dwight Co., Inc.
Citibank
Citizens Bank of Rhode Island
Clapp Charitable and Educational Trust, George H.
Clemens Markets Corp.
Clowes Fund
Coen Family Foundation, Charles S. and Mary
Collins Medical Trust
Colonial Life & Accident Insurance Co.
Coltec Industries, Inc.
Columbia Foundation
Comer Foundation
Continental Corp.

Contran Corporation
Coors Foundation, Adolph
Cosmair, Inc.
Cowles Charitable Trust
CPC International Inc.
Crane Co.
Crawford Estate, E. R.
CS First Boston Corporation
Cullen Foundation
Culpeper Foundation, Charles E.
Culpeper Memorial Foundation, Daphne Seybolt
Cummings Foundation, James H.
Cuneo Foundation
Daily News
Dana Charitable Trust, Eleanor Naylor
Dana Foundation, Charles A.
Daniel Foundation of Alabama
Darby Foundation
Dart Group Corp.
Davenport-Hatch Foundation
Davis Foundation, Edwin W. and Catherine M.
Delaware North Co., Inc.
Demoulas Supermarkets Inc.
Dentsply International Inc.
DeRoy Foundation, Helen L.
DeRoy Testamentary Foundation
Deuble Foundation, George H.
DeVore Foundation
Diamond Foundation, Aaron
Digital Equipment Corp.
Dillon Foundation
Dingman Foundation, Michael D.
Dishman Charitable Foundation Trust, H. E. and Kate
Dodge Foundation, Geraldine R.
Donnelley Foundation, Gaylord and Dorothy
Douglas & Lomason Company
Dresser Industries, Inc.
Dreyfus Foundation, Max and Victoria
du Pont de Nemours & Co., E. I.
Duchossois Industries Inc.
Duke Endowment
Duncan Foundation, Lillian H. and C. W.
Duncan Trust, John G.
Dynamet, Inc.
Early Foundation
Eaton Foundation, Cyrus
El Pomar Foundation
Elf Atochem North America, Inc.
Emerson Foundation, Inc., Fred L.
English Memorial Fund, Florence C. and H. L.
Enron Corp.
Essick Foundation
Ettinger Foundation
Evans Foundation, T. M.
Exxon Corporation
Fair Play Foundation
Fairchild Foundation, Sherman
Farish Fund, William Stamps
Favrot Fund
Federal-Mogul Corporation
Federated Mutual Insurance Co.
Feil Foundation, Louis and Gertrude
Feild Co-Operative Association
Femino Foundation
Fife Foundation, Elias and Bertha
Fikes Foundation, Leland
First Financial Bank FSB
First Interstate Bank of Oregon
Fischbach Foundation
Fish Foundation, Ray C.
Fishback Foundation Trust, Harmes C.
Fleet Financial Group, Inc.
Fondren Foundation
Forbes Inc.

Ford Foundation
Ford Fund, William and Martha
Ford II Fund, Henry
Forest Foundation
Forest Oil Corp.
Foster Charitable Trust
Frear Eleemosynary Trust, Mary D. and Walter F.
Freedom Forge Corp.
Freeport Brick Co.
Freeport-McMoRan Inc.
Fribourg Foundation
Friedman Family Foundation
Frohring Foundation, William O. and Gertrude Lewis
Frost National Bank
Fruehauf Foundation
Fuller Foundation, C. G.
Fuqua Foundation, J. B.
Gannett Publishing Co., Guy Gap, Inc., The
Gaylord Foundation, Clifford Willard
Gebbie Foundation
Gellert Foundation, Carl
Gellert Foundation, Celia Berta
General American Life Insurance Co.
General Mills, Inc.
Georgia-Pacific Corporation
Georgia Power Co.
Giant Eagle, Inc.
Giant Food Stores
Gifford Charitable Corporation, Rosamond
Gillette Co.
Gilmore Foundation, William G.
Glanville Family Foundation
Glick Foundation, Eugene and Marilyn
Globe Newspaper Co.
Goddard Foundation, Charles B.
Goldberg Family Foundation
Goldie-Anna Charitable Trust
Goldsmith Foundation, Horace W.
Goodman & Co.
Goodstein Family Foundation, David
Gould Electronics Inc.
Grand Rapids Label Co.
Great-West Life Assurance Co.
Greenwall Foundation
Griffis Foundation
Griffith Foundation, W. C.
Griggs and Mary Griggs Burke Foundation, Mary Livingston
Guardian Life Insurance Company of America
Guggenheim Foundation, Harry Frank
Guttman Foundation, Stella and Charles
Haley Foundation, W. B.
Halff Foundation, G. A. C.
Hamilton Bank
Hamman Foundation, George and Mary Josephine
Hammer Foundation, Armand
Hanson Industries North America
Harcourt General, Inc.
Hardin Foundation, Phil
Harriman Foundation, Gladys and Roland
Harsco Corp.
Hartford Foundation, John A.
Hartz Foundation
Hawn Foundation
Hazen Foundation, Edward W.
Hearst Foundation, William Randolph
Heckscher Foundation for Children
Hedco Foundation
Heinz Company, H. J.
Heinz Endowment, Howard
Heinz Endowment, Vira I.
Heinz Trust, Drue
Heller Charitable Foundation, Clarence E.
Hillcrest Foundation

Hoag Family Foundation, George
Hoffmann-La Roche Inc.
Holzer Memorial Foundation, Richard H.
Hoover, Jr. Foundation, Margaret W. and Herbert
Hopkins Foundation, Josephine Lawrence
Houston Industries Incorporated
Howe and Mitchell B. Howe Foundation, Lucille Horton
Hugoton Foundation
Huisking Foundation
Humana, Inc.
Humphrey Fund, George M. and Pamela S.
Hunt Foundation
Hunt Foundation, Samuel P.
Hyde and Watson Foundation
Icahn Foundation, Carl C.
ICI Americas Inc.
Illinois Tool Works, Inc.
Imperial Bancorp
Independence Foundation
Irwin Charity Foundation, William G.
ITT Hartford Insurance Group, Inc.
Jackson Foundation
Jacobs Family Foundation
Jaffe Foundation
Jameson Foundation, J. W. and Ida M.
Jarson-Stanley and Mickey Kaplan Foundation, Isaac and Esther
Jennings Foundation, Mary Hillman
Jewish Healthcare Foundation of Pittsburgh
JM Foundation
Jockey Hollow Foundation
John Hancock Mutual Life Insurance Co.
Johnson Foundation, Burdine
Johnson Foundation, Helen K. and Arthur E.
Johnson Fund, Edward C.
Johnson & Higgins
Johnson & Son, S.C.
Julia R. and Estelle L. Foundation
Kaplun Foundation, Morris J. and Betty
Kardon Foundation, Samuel and Rebecca
Kavanagh Foundation, T. James
Kayser Foundation
Kelley and Elza Kelley Foundation, Edward Bangs
Kelly Foundation, T. Lloyd
Kemper Foundation, William T.
Kennedy Foundation, Ethel
Kent-Lucas Foundation
Kimball Foundation, Horace A. Kimball and S. Ella
Kimberly-Clark Corp.
Kirkpatrick Foundation
Kline Foundation, Josiah W. and Bessie H.
Klipstein Foundation, Ernest Christian
Klock and Lucia Klock Kingston Foundation, Jay E.
Klosk Fund, Louis and Rose
Koehler Foundation, Marcia and Otto
Kohn-Joseloff Foundation
Komes Foundation
Koopman Fund
Kresge Foundation
LamCo. Communications
Lasdon Foundation
Lattner Foundation, Forrest C.
Lauder Foundation
Laurel Foundation
Lazarus Charitable Trust, Helen and Charles
Lebovitz Fund
Lederer Foundation, Francis L.
Lehmann Foundation, Otto W.
Leidy Foundation, John J.

Lemberg Foundation
Lennon Foundation, Fred A.
Leuthold Foundation
Levy Foundation, June Rockwell
Lichtenstein Foundation, David B.
Life Insurance Co. of Georgia
Link, Jr. Foundation, George
Linn-Henley Charitable Trust
Linnell Foundation
Lipton, Thomas J.
Little, Inc., Arthur D.
Loews Corporation
Love Foundation, George H. and Margaret McClintic
Lovett Foundation
Lowenstein Foundation, Leon
Lurie Foundation, Louis R.
Lydall, Inc.
MacArthur Foundation, John D. and Catherine T.
Macy & Co., Inc., R.H.
Madison Gas & Electric Co.
Magowan Family Foundation
Mailman Foundation
Mandeville Foundation
Maneely Fund
Margoes Foundation
Marquette Electronics, Inc.
Mars Foundation
Marshall Foundation, Mattie H.
Martin Marietta Corp.
Massachusetts Mutual Life Insurance Co.
Mather and William Gwinn Mather Fund, Elizabeth Ring
May Foundation, Wilbur
MBIA Inc.
MCA Inc.
McCasland Foundation
McCormick & Co. Inc.
McCormick Foundation, Chauncey and Marion Deering
McCormick Trust, Anne
McCune Charitable Trust, John R.
McDonald & Company Securities, Inc.
McDonnell Douglas Corp.-West
McEvoy Foundation, Mildred H.
McFawn Trust No. 2, Lois Sisler
McGonagle Foundation, Dextra Baldwin
McLean Contributionship
Mellon Family Foundation, R. K.
Mellon Foundation, Richard King
Merck & Co.
Merrick Foundation
Merrill Lynch & Co., Inc.
Messing Family Charitable Foundation
Metropolitan Life Insurance Co.
Meyer Fund, Milton and Sophie
Meyer Memorial Trust
Mitchell Energy & Development Corp.
Mitsubishi International Corp.
Mnuchin Foundation
Mobil Oil Corp.
Monell Foundation, Ambrose
Moore Charitable Foundation, Marjorie
Moore Foundation, Edward S.
Morgan Construction Co.
Morris Foundation, Margaret T.
Morris Foundation, William T.
Mosbacher, Jr. Foundation, Emil
Moses Fund, Henry and Lucy
Mott Fund, Ruth
Muller Foundation
Munger Foundation, Alfred C.
Murdock Charitable Trust, M. J.
Murphey Foundation, Lluella Morey

National Gypsum Co.
National Westminster Bank New Jersey
Neuberger Foundation, Roy R. and Marie S.
New-Land Foundation
New York Life Insurance Co.
The New Yorker Magazine, Inc.
Noble Foundation, Edward John
Noble Foundation, Samuel Roberts
Norgren Foundation, Carl A.
Norman Foundation, Summers A.
North Shore Foundation
Norton Co.
Norton Memorial Corporation, Geraldi
Odell Fund, Robert Stewart Odell and Helen Pfeiffer
Offield Family Foundation
Ohrstrom Foundation
Olsson Memorial Foundation, Elis
Osborn Charitable Trust, Edward B.
Overbrook Foundation
Overlake Foundation
Owsley Foundation, Alvin and Lucy
Pacific Mutual Life Insurance Co.
PaineWebber
Palisades Educational Foundation
Panhandle Eastern Corporation
Parker Hannifin Corp.
Parshelsky Foundation, Moses L.
Parsons Foundation, Ralph M.
Parvin Foundation, Albert
Patterson Charitable Fund, W. I.
Pennzoil Co.
Peppers Foundation, Ann
Perkin-Elmer Corp.
Pfizer, Inc.
PHH Corporation
Phillips Family Foundation, Jay and Rose
Piankova Foundation, Tatiana
Pickford Foundation, Mary
Pierce Charitable Trust, Harold Whitworth
Piper Foundation, Minnie Stevens
Pittsburgh Child Guidance Foundation
Playboy Enterprises, Inc.
Potomac Electric Power Co.
Pott Foundation, Herman T. and Phenie R.
Potts and Sibley Foundation
Price Foundation, Louis and Harold
Prouty Foundation, Olive Higgins
Providian Corporation
Puterbaugh Foundation
Quaker Chemical Corp.
Rachal Foundation, Ed
Ralston Purina Co.
Ratner Foundation, Milton M.
Read Foundation, Charles L.
Reed Foundation
Reicher Foundation, Anne and Harry J.
Reinberger Foundation
Reisman Charitable Trust, George C. and Evelyn R.
Retirement Research Foundation
RJR Nabisco Inc.
Rockwell Fund
Rogers Family Foundation
Rohatyn Foundation, Felix and Elizabeth
Rohm & Haas Co.
Rose Foundation, Billy
Rosen Foundation, Joseph
Rosenberg, Jr. Family Foundation, Louise and Claude
Ross Laboratories

Rowland Foundation
Royal Foundation, May Mitchell
Rubin Foundation, Samuel
Rubinstein Foundation, Helena
Rudin Foundation
Russell Charitable Foundation, Tom
Russell Trust, Josephine G.
Salomon Foundation, Richard and Edna
Salomon Inc.
San Diego Gas & Electric
Sandy Hill Foundation
Sasco Foundation
Sawyer Charitable Foundation
Scaife Family Foundation
Scherer Foundation, Karla
Schering-Plough Corp.
Schiff Foundation, Dorothy
Schiro Fund
Schlink Foundation, Albert G. and Olive H.
Schlumberger Ltd.
Scholl Foundation, Dr.
Schroeder Foundation, Walter
Schwartz Fund for Education and Health Research, Arnold and Marie
Schwob Foundation, Simon
Scott Fetzer Co.
Scott Foundation, Walter
Scott Foundation, William E.
Scurlock Foundation
Seagram & Sons, Inc., Joseph E.
Seaver Charitable Trust, Richard C.
Seaver Institute
Security Life of Denver Insurance Co.
Selby and Marie Selby Foundation, William G.
Sentry Insurance A Mutual Company
Share Trust, Charles Morton
Sharon Steel Corp.
Shell Oil Company
Shenandoah Life Insurance Co.
Sheppard Foundation, Lawrence B.
Sierra Pacific Industries
Slifka Foundation, Joseph and Sylvia
Smart Family Foundation
Smith Charitable Foundation, Clara Blackford Smith and W. Aubrey
Smith Trust, May and Stanley
Snow Memorial Trust, John Ben
Sordoni Foundation
South Waite Foundation
Southwestern Electric Power Co.
Spang & Co.
Sprague Educational and Charitable Foundation, Seth
Square D Co.
Stanley Charitable Foundation, A.W.
Stanley Works
Stans Foundation
Starr Foundation
Stauffer Foundation, John and Beverly
Stein Foundation, Jules and Doris
Steinbach Fund, Ruth and Milton
Steinhagen Benevolent Trust, B. A. and Elinor
Steinman Foundation, James Hale
Steinman Foundation, John Frederick
Stemmons Foundation
Stokely, Jr. Foundation, William B.
Stone Trust, H. Chase
Strauss Foundation, Leon
Strawbridge Foundation of Pennsylvania II, Margaret Dorrance
Stupp Foundation, Norman J.

Sulzberger Foundation
Sumners Foundation, Hatton W.
Swift Co. Inc., John S.
Taper Foundation, Mark
Taube Family Foundation
Taubman Foundation, A. Alfred
Taylor Foundation, Fred and Harriett
Taylor Foundation, Ruth and Vernon
Temple Foundation, T. L. L.
Tenneco Inc.
Tetley, Inc.
Texaco Inc.
Texas Commerce Bank-Houston, N.A.
Thalhimer and Family Foundation, Charles G.
Thomasville Furniture Industries
Thompson Co., J. Walter
Thorne Foundation
Thornton Foundation, Flora L.
Tobin Foundation
Toms Foundation
Towsley Foundation, Harry A. and Margaret D.
Transco Energy Co.
Treakle Foundation, J. Edwin
Truland Foundation
Turner Charitable Foundation
Union Bank
Union Camp Corporation
Unocal Corp.
USG Corporation
Utica National Insurance Group
Valentine Foundation, Lawson
Van Every Foundation, Philip L.
Van Houten Memorial Fund
Vance Charitable Foundation, Robert C.
Vanderbilt Foundation, R. T.
Vernon Fund, Miles Hodsdon
Vollbrecht Foundation, Frederick A.
Wal-Mart Stores, Inc.
Weber Charities Corp., Frederick E.
Weil, Gotshal and Manges Foundation
Weingart Foundation
Wells Foundation, Franklin H. and Ruth L.
Wendt Foundation, Margaret L.
Wertheim Foundation, Dr. Herbert A.
West Foundation, Harry and Ethel
Westerman Foundation, Samuel L.
Westvaco Corporation
Wheat First Butcher Singer, Inc.
Whitehead Charitable Foundation
Whiting Foundation
Wiegand Foundation, E. L.
Winston Foundation, Norman and Rosita
Woodward Fund
Young Foundation, Robert R.
Zachry Co., H.B.
Zarrow Foundation, Anne and Henry
Zenkel Foundation

Medical Training

Abbott Laboratories
Abell-Hanger Foundation
Achelis Foundation
Aluminum Co. of America
American United Life Insurance Co.
Armco Inc.
Atherton Family Foundation
Brackenridge Foundation, George W.
Bristol-Myers Squibb Company
Bush Foundation

Cain Foundation, Effie and Wofford
Centerior Energy Corp.
Cheney Foundation, Ben B.
Clark Foundation
Colonial Life & Accident Insurance Co.
Coltec Industries, Inc.
Comer Foundation
Cummings Foundation, James H.
Dana Foundation, Charles A.
Dreyfus Foundation, Jean and Louis
du Pont de Nemours & Co., E. I.
Exxon Corporation
General Motors Corp.
Hammer Foundation, Armand
Handy and Harman Foundation
Hartford Foundation, John A.
HCA Foundation
Hearst Foundation, William Randolph
Hoffmann-La Roche Inc.
Houston Endowment
International Foundation
Johnson & Higgins
Johnson & Son, S.C.
Lipton, Thomas J.
Macy & Co., Inc., R.H.
McElroy Trust, R. J.
MCI Communications Corp.
Meadows Foundation
Mellon Family Foundation, R. K.
Mellon Foundation, Richard King
Merck & Co.
Metropolitan Life Insurance Co.
Meyer Memorial Trust
New York Life Insurance Co.
The New Yorker Magazine, Inc.
Noble Foundation, Edward John
Pacific Mutual Life Insurance Co.
Phelps Dodge Corporation
Prudential Insurance Co. of America, The
Rubinstein Foundation, Helena
Santa Fe Pacific Corporation
Schering-Plough Corp.
Shawmut National Corp.
Shenandoah Life Insurance Co.
Sprague Educational and Charitable Foundation, Seth
Starr Foundation
Sumners Foundation, Hatton W.
Texaco Inc.
Texas Commerce Bank-Houston, N.A.
Trust Company Bank
Union Camp Corporation
Unocal Corp.

Mental Health

Achelis Foundation
Ahmanson Foundation
AKC Fund
Akzo Chemicals Inc.
Alabama Gas Corp.
Alabama Power Co.
Albertson's Inc.
Alexander Foundation, Joseph
Allegheny Ludlum Corp.
Allendale Insurance Co.
Aluminum Co. of America
AMCORE Bank, N.A. Rockford
American General Finance Corp.
American United Life Insurance Co.
AMETEK, Inc.
Andersen Foundation
Anderson Foundation, John W.
Andersons, The
Ansley Foundation, Dantzler Bond
Atherton Family Foundation

Avon Products, Inc.
Bacon Foundation, E. L. and Oma
Baehr Foundation, Louis W. and Dolpha
Baldwin Foundation, David M. and Barbara
Bank One, Youngstown, NA
Bean Foundation, Norwin S. and Elizabeth N.
BE&K Inc.
Benwood Foundation
Besser Foundation
Beveridge Foundation, Frank Stanley
Block, H&R
Blount, Inc.
Blowitz-Ridgeway Foundation
Blue Cross & Blue Shield United of Wisconsin
Blum-Kovler Foundation
Boeing Co., The
Boettcher Foundation
Boothroyd Foundation, Charles H. and Bertha L.
Borden, Inc.
Borman's Inc.
Bothin Foundation
Brady Foundation
Bremer Foundation, Otto
Brunswick Corp.
Burnett-Tandy Foundation
Bush Foundation
Cabot Family Charitable Trust
Cafritz Foundation, Morris and Gwendolyn
Carnegie Corporation of New York
Carter Foundation, Amon G.
Centerior Energy Corp.
Central Hudson Gas & Electric Corp.
Central Maine Power Co.
Central Vermont Public Service Corp.
Chastain Charitable Foundation, Robert Lee and Thomas M.
Cheatham Foundation, Owen
Cheney Foundation, Ben B.
Chesapeake Corp.
Chevron Corporation
Church & Dwight Co., Inc.
CINergy
CLARCOR Inc.
Clay Foundation
Clemens Markets Corp.
Clorox Co.
Close Foundation
Cogswell Benevolent Trust
Colonial Life & Accident Insurance Co.
Comerica Incorporated
Comprecare Foundation
Cooke Foundation
Cooper Industries, Inc.
Copley Press, Inc.
Cowles Charitable Trust
CPC International Inc.
Crane Co.
Crary Foundation, Bruce L.
Cremer Foundation
Crown Memorial, Arie and Ida
CS First Boston Corporation
Cummins Engine Co.
Curtice-Burns Foods, Inc.
Dana Foundation, Charles A.
Daniel Foundation of Alabama
Davis Foundation, Edwin W. and Catherine M.
Davis Foundation, James A. and Juliet L.
Davis Foundations, Arthur Vining
DeRoy Testamentary Foundation
Detroit Edison Co.
Dexter Charitable Fund, Eugene A.
Dexter Corporation
Digital Equipment Corp.
Dimeo Construction Co.
Donaldson Company, Inc.
Donnelley & Sons Co., R.R.
Donner Foundation, William H.

Douglas & Lomason Company
Dover Foundation
Dresser Industries, Inc.
Dreyfus Foundation, Jean and Louis
Dreyfus Foundation, Max and Victoria
du Pont de Nemours & Co., E. I.
Duchossois Industries Inc.
Duke Power Co.
Dun & Bradstreet Corp.
Eastman Kodak Company
Eden Hall Foundation
El Pomar Foundation
Enron Corp.
Evans Foundation, T. M.
Exchange National Bank
Femino Foundation
Fikes Foundation, Leland
First Interstate Bank of Oregon
First Union Corp.
Fondren Foundation
Forbes Inc.
Freed Foundation
Freeport-McMoRan Inc.
Frost National Bank
Fruehauf Foundation
Fry Foundation, Lloyd A.
GAR Foundation
GATX Corp.
Gellert Foundation, Carl
Gellert Foundation, Celia Berta
GenCorp Inc.
General Mills, Inc.
General Motors Corp.
GenRad
Georgia Power Co.
Gheens Foundation
Giant Food Inc.
Giant Food Stores
Gifford Charitable Corporation, Rosamond
Gillette Co.
Glaser Foundation
Glencoe Foundation
Glick Foundation, Eugene and Marilyn
Globe Newspaper Co.
Goldseker Foundation of Maryland, Morris
Graham Fund, Philip L.
Great-West Life Assurance Co.
Green Foundation, Allen P. and Josephine B.
Gregg-Graniteville Foundation
Griffith Foundation, W. C.
Gulf Coast Medical Foundation
Hagedorn Fund
Hamilton Bank
Hamman Foundation, George and Mary Josephine
Hanover Foundation
Harland Charitable Foundation, John and Wilhelmina D.
Harmon Foundation, Pearl M. and Julia J.
Harriman Foundation, Mary W.
Harsco Corp.
Hazen Foundation, Edward W.
HCA Foundation
Hechinger Co.
Hecht-Levi Foundation
Heckscher Foundation for Children
Heinz Endowment, Howard
Heinz Endowment, Vira I.
Heller Financial, Inc.
Hermann Foundation, Grover
Heydt Fund, Nan and Matilda
Hillcrest Foundation
Hobby Foundation
Hoffmann-La Roche Inc.
Houston Endowment
Houston Industries Incorporated
Hoyt Foundation, Stewart W. and Willma C.
Hugoton Foundation
Humana, Inc.
Hunt Foundation
Hunt Foundation, Roy A.
Huston Charitable Trust, Stewart

Icahn Foundation, Carl C.
ICI Americas Inc.
Illinois Tool Works, Inc.
International Business Machines Corp.
Ittleson Foundation
Jackson Foundation
Jacobson Foundation, Bernard H. and Blanche E.
Jarson-Stanley and Mickey Kaplan Foundation, Isaac and Esther
Jaydor Corp.
Jewish Healthcare Foundation of Pittsburgh
Johnson & Higgins
Jones Foundation, Daisy Marquis
Journal-Gazette Co.
Kaufmann Foundation, Henry
Kennecott Corporation
Kiplinger Foundation
Klock and Lucia Klock Kingston Foundation, Jay E.
Knox, Sr., and Pearl Wallis Knox Charitable Foundation, Robert W.
Komes Foundation
Kunkel Foundation, John Crain
Lang Foundation, Eugene M.
Lasdon Foundation
Lattner Foundation, Forrest C.
Lazarus Charitable Trust, Helen and Charles
Levitt Foundation
Lichtenstein Foundation, David B.
Life Insurance Co. of Georgia
Link, Jr. Foundation, George
Lipton, Thomas J.
Little, Inc., Arthur D.
Lockhart Vaughan Foundation
Lurie Foundation, Louis R.
Lydall, Inc.
Lyon Foundation
MacArthur Foundation, John D. and Catherine T.
Macy & Co., Inc., R.H.
Magowan Family Foundation
Mahadh Foundation
Mailman Family Foundation, A. L.
Mailman Foundation
Mardag Foundation
Margoes Foundation
Maritz Inc.
Martini Foundation, Nicholas
Marx Foundation, Virginia and Leonard
Massengill-DeFriece Foundation
Mather Charitable Trust, S. Livingston
Mathis-Pfohl Foundation
Maytag Family Foundation, Fred
MCA Inc.
McCarty Foundation, John and Margaret
McCune Charitable Trust, John R.
McDonald & Company Securities, Inc.
McDonnell Douglas Corp.-West
McFawn Trust No. 2, Lois Sisler
McGonagle Foundation, Dextra Baldwin
McInerny Foundation
McMillan Foundation, D. W.
Meadows Foundation
Mellon Foundation, Richard King
Merrick Foundation
Meyer Memorial Trust
Mid-Iowa Health Foundation
Middendorf Foundation
Mine Safety Appliances Co.
Minnesota Mining & Mfg. Co.
Mitchell Energy & Development Corp.
Monell Foundation, Ambrose
Moore Charitable Foundation, Marjorie

Moore Foundation, Edward S.
Morgan Foundation, Burton D.
Mullen Foundation, J. K.
Murphey Foundation, Lluella Morey
Murphy Co. Foundation, G.C.
Nalco Chemical Co.
National Westminster Bank New Jersey
Nesholm Family Foundation
New-Land Foundation
New York Life Insurance Co.
The New Yorker Magazine, Inc.
NewMil Bancorp
Noble Foundation, Samuel Roberts
Northern States Power Co. (Minnesota)
Northwest Natural Gas Co.
Norton Co.
Norton Family Foundation, Peter
Norton Memorial Corporation, Geraldi
Norwest Bank Nebraska, N.A.
O'Fallon Trust, Martin J. and Mary Anne
Olin Corp.
Oppenstein Brothers Foundation
Osher Foundation, Bernard
Ottley Trust-Watertown, Marion W.
Owsley Foundation, Alvin and Lucy
Oxy USA Inc.
Pacific Mutual Life Insurance Co.
Palmer Fund, Frank Loomis
Parker Hannifin Corp.
Parsons Foundation, Ralph M.
Peppers Foundation, Ann
Perkin-Elmer Corp.
Pettus Crowe Foundation
Pfizer, Inc.
Piper Foundation, Minnie Stevens
Pittsburgh Child Guidance Foundation
Plankenhorn Foundation, Harry
Polaroid Corp.
Pott Foundation, Herman T. and Phenie R.
Potts and Sibley Foundation
PPG Industries, Inc.
Price Foundation, Louis and Harold
Prudential Insurance Co. of America, The
Prudential Securities, Inc.
Public Welfare Foundation
Pulitzer Publishing Co.
Read Foundation, Charles L.
Rennebohm Foundation, Oscar
Retirement Research Foundation
Rice Foundation
Rockwell Fund
Rockwell International Corporation
Rohm & Haas Co.
Roseburg Forest Products Co.
Ross Memorial Foundation, Will
SAFECO Corp.
San Diego Gas & Electric
Santa Fe Pacific Corporation
SBC Communications Inc.
Scaife Family Foundation
Schenck Fund, L. P.
Scherer Foundation, Karla
Schwartz Foundation, Arnold A.
Scurlock Foundation
Selby and Marie Selby Foundation, William G.
Sequoia Foundation
Seton Leather Co.
Shawmut National Corp.
Sheaffer Inc.
Shell Oil Company
Shenandoah Life Insurance Co.
Sierra Pacific Resources
Skillman Foundation

Smeal Foundation, Mary Jean and Frank P.
Smith Charitable Foundation, Lou and Lutza
Smith Corp., A.O.
Smith Trust, May and Stanley
Sprague Educational and Charitable Foundation, Seth
Springs Foundation
Square D Co.
Stackpole-Hall Foundation
Stanley Charitable Foundation, A.W.
Stans Foundation
Staunton Farm Foundation
Steinhagen Benevolent Trust, B. A. and Elinor
Steinman Foundation, John Frederick
Sternberger Foundation, Tannenbaum
Stokely, Jr. Foundation, William B.
Strauss Foundation, Leon
Sumners Foundation, Hatton W.
Swalm Foundation
Temple Foundation, T. L. L.
Tenneco Inc.
Tetley, Inc.
Texas Commerce Bank-Houston, N.A.
Thompson Trust, Thomas
TransAmerica Corporation
Transco Energy Co.
Trees Charitable Trust, Edith L.
Trull Foundation
Trust Company Bank
Trust Funds
Tucker Charitable Trust, Rose E.
Turner Charitable Foundation
Unger Foundation, Aber D.
Union Camp Corporation
Union Pacific Corp.
U.S. Bank of Washington
Unocal Corp.
USG Corporation
USX Corporation
Utica National Insurance Group
van Ameringen Foundation
Van Houten Memorial Fund
Vance Charitable Foundation, Robert C.
Vaughn, Jr. Foundation Fund, James M.
Vernon Fund, Miles Hodsdon
Virginia Power Co.
Vulcan Materials Co.
Wal-Mart Stores, Inc.
Walsh Foundation
Warner Fund, Albert and Bessie
Washington Forrest Foundation
Wean Foundation, Raymond John
Weaver Foundation, Gil and Dody
Weber Charities Corp., Frederick E.
Weezie Foundation
Wells Foundation, Franklin H. and Ruth L.
Wendt Foundation, Margaret L.
Whitecap Foundation
Wiley & Sons, Inc., John
Wood Foundation of Chambersburg, PA
Wright Foundation, Lola
Young Foundation, Robert R.
Zarrow Foundation, Anne and Henry

Multiple Sclerosis

Abell-Hanger Foundation
Air Products and Chemicals, Inc.
Alabama Gas Corp.
Alavi Foundation of New York
AlliedSignal Inc.
Altschul Foundation

American President Companies, Ltd.
Ames Charitable Trust, Harriett
Anderson Foundation
Arkelian Foundation, Ben H. and Gladys
Bank One, Youngstown, NA
BE&K Inc.
Beech Aircraft Corp.
Bingham Foundation, William
Blaustein Foundation, Louis and Henrietta
Borman's Inc.
Burlington Industries, Inc.
Butz Foundation
Catlin Charitable Trust, Kathleen K.
Chartwell Foundation
Clapp Charitable and Educational Trust, George H.
Crawford Estate, E. R.
Crown Books
Dater Foundation, Charles H.
Davenport-Hatch Foundation
Eaton Foundation, Cyrus
Einstein Fund, Albert E. and Birdie W.
Fife Foundation, Elias and Bertha
Freedom Forge Corp.
GAR Foundation
Glosser Foundation, David A.
Hammer Foundation, Armand
Hanson Industries North America
Hawn Foundation
Herzstein Charitable Foundation, Albert and Ethel
Hickory Tech Corp.
Hoover Foundation
Hoover, Jr. Foundation, Margaret W. and Herbert
Hopwood Charitable Trust, John M.
Huisking Foundation
Humphrey Fund, George M. and Pamela S.
Icahn Foundation, Carl C.
Jaydor Corp.
Kayser Foundation
Kimberly-Clark Corp.
Kline Foundation, Josiah W. and Bessie H.
Klosk Fund, Louis and Rose
Knoll Group
Lazarus Charitable Trust, Helen and Charles
Lederer Foundation, Francis L.
Leighton-Oare Foundation
Loews Corporation
Lydall, Inc.
Management Compensation Group/Dulworth Inc.
Martin Marietta Materials
Mattel, Inc.
May Department Stores Company, The
MCA Inc.
McCormick Trust, Anne
McCune Charitable Trust, John R.
McDonald & Company Securities, Inc.
Monfort Family Foundation
Musson Charitable Foundation, R. C. and Katharine M.
O'Quinn Foundation, John M. and Nancy C.
PHH Corporation
Phillips Family Foundation, Jay and Rose
Piper Jaffray Companies Inc.
Plankenhorn Foundation, Harry
Rabb Foundation, Harry W.
Reidler Foundation
Rich Products Corporation
Rosenberg, Jr. Family Foundation, Louise and Claude
Schwartz Foundation, Arnold A.
Seneca Foods Corp.
Seton Leather Co.

Simon Foundation, William E. and Carol G.
Smith Foundation, Gordon V. and Helen C.
Solow Foundation
Steinman Foundation, James Hale
Taube Family Foundation
Thornton Foundation, Flora L.
Van Houten Memorial Fund
Whiting Foundation
Young Foundation, Robert R.

Nursing Services

Abbott Laboratories
Abell-Hanger Foundation
Achelis Foundation
Aetna Life & Casualty Co.
Ahmanson Foundation
Alexander Foundation, Joseph
Allegheny Ludlum Corp.
Allendale Insurance Co.
AlliedSignal Inc.
Altschul Foundation
AMCORE Bank, N.A. Rockford
American United Life Insurance Co.
Anderson Foundation
Anderson Foundation, John W.
Anderson Foundation, M. D.
Arcadia Foundation
Armco Inc.
Arnhold Foundation
Atherton Family Foundation
Auerbach Foundation, Beatrice Fox
Ayres Foundation, Inc.
Bank of New York Company, Inc.
Bard Foundation, Robert
Barth Foundation, Theodore H.
Battelle Memorial Institute
Bean Foundation, Norwin S. and Elizabeth N.
Benedum Foundation, Claude Worthington
Berger Foundation, H. N. and Frances C.
Bethlehem Steel Corp.
Bishop Foundation, E. K. and Lillian F.
Blandin Foundation
Boothroyd Foundation, Charles H. and Bertha L.
Boston Edison Co.
Brach Foundation, Helen
Bremer Foundation, Otto
Brunswick Corp.
Bryn Mawr Trust Co.
Cafritz Foundation, Morris and Gwendolyn
Calhoun Charitable Trust, Kenneth
Campbell Foundation, Ruth and Henry
Carolyn Foundation
Carpenter Foundation
Carpenter Foundation, E. Rhodes and Leona B.
Carter Foundation, Amon G.
Champlin Foundations
Chatlos Foundation
Clapp Charitable and Educational Trust, George H.
CLARCOR Inc.
Clarke Trust, John
Collins Medical Trust
Colonial Life & Accident Insurance Co.
Comer Foundation
Commerce Clearing House, Incorporated
Comprecare Foundation
Connelly Foundation
Contran Corporation
Cornell Trust, Peter C.
Cosmair, Inc.
CPC International Inc.
Cremer Foundation
Curtice-Burns Foods, Inc.
Davenport-Hatch Foundation

Davis Foundation, Edwin W. and Catherine M.
Davis Foundation, Irene E. and George A.
DeRoy Foundation, Helen L.
Dexter Corporation
Dodge Foundation, Cleveland H.
Douty Foundation
Dresser Industries, Inc.
Dreyfus Foundation, Jean and Louis
Duke Endowment
Dula Educational and Charitable Foundation, Caleb C. and Julia W.
duPont Foundation, Alfred I.
Eddy Family Memorial Fund, C. K.
Eden Hall Foundation
El Pomar Foundation
Enron Corp.
Evans Foundation, Lettie Pate
Exxon Corporation
Fikes Foundation, Leland
Firestone, Jr. Foundation, Harvey
Firman Fund
Firstar Bank Milwaukee, N.A.
Forbes Inc.
Ford Fund, William and Martha
Foster Foundation
Frohring Foundation, Paul and Maxine
Fruehauf Foundation
Fry Foundation, Lloyd A.
Fuld Health Trust, Helene
Fuqua Foundation, J. B.
GAR Foundation
Gebbie Foundation
Gillette Co.
Goldsmith Foundation, Horace W.
Groome Beatty Trust, Helen D.
GSM Industrial
Haas, Jr. Fund, Evelyn and Walter
Hachar Charitable Trust, D. D.
Hamilton Bank
Handy and Harman Foundation
Harcourt Foundation, Ellen Knowles
Hawn Foundation
HCA Foundation
Hechinger Co.
Heckscher Foundation for Children
Heinz Endowment, Howard
Hermann Foundation, Grover
Heydt Fund, Nan and Matilda
Hillcrest Foundation
Hillman Family Foundation, Alex
Hoffman Foundation, Maximilian E. and Marion O.
Hook Drugs
Hopedale Foundation
Hopwood Charitable Trust, John M.
Hugoton Foundation
Hulme Charitable Foundation, Milton G.
Humana, Inc.
Humphrey Fund, George M. and Pamela S.
Hunt Foundation, Samuel P.
ICI Americas Inc.
Illinois Consolidated Telephone Co.
Illinois Tool Works, Inc.
Independence Foundation
Ingalls Foundation, Louise H. and David S.
Jaffe Foundation
Jockey Hollow Foundation
Johnson Charitable Trust, Keith Wold
Johnson Foundation, Helen K. and Arthur E.
Johnson Foundation, M. G. and Lillie A.
Johnson & Higgins
Jones Foundation, Daisy Marquis
Jones Foundation, Fletcher

Justus Trust, Edith C.
Kansas City Southern Industries
Kemper Foundation, William T.
Kent-Lucas Foundation
Kettering Fund
Kimberly-Clark Corp.
Kiplinger Foundation
Kirbo Charitable Trust, Thomas M. and Irene B.
Kirby Foundation, F. M.
Kohn-Joseloff Foundation
Koopman Fund
Kresge Foundation
Kuehn Foundation
Lasdon Foundation, William and Mildred
Leavey Foundation, Thomas and Dorothy
Lehmann Foundation, Otto W.
Lennon Foundation, Fred A.
Leuthold Foundation
Levy Foundation, June Rockwell
Lovett Foundation
Lowenstein Foundation, Leon
Lydall, Inc.
Mailman Foundation
Markey Charitable Fund, John C.
Marpat Foundation
Marquette Electronics, Inc.
Mars Foundation
Mather and William Gwinn Mather Fund, Elizabeth Ring
Mayor Foundation, Oliver Dewey
McBean Charitable Trust, Alletta Morris
McCarty Foundation, John and Margaret
McDonald & Company Securities, Inc.
McFawn Trust No. 2, Lois Sisler
Medtronic, Inc.
Memton Fund
Mengle Foundation, Glenn and Ruth
Metropolitan Life Insurance Co.
Meyer Memorial Trust
Mid-Iowa Health Foundation
Miller Foundation
Miller-Mellor Association
Mobil Oil Corp.
Moore Charitable Foundation, Marjorie
Moses Fund, Henry and Lucy
Musson Charitable Foundation, R. C. and Katharine M.
Neuberger Foundation, Roy R. and Marie S.
New York Life Insurance Co.
The New Yorker Magazine, Inc.
Northern States Power Co. (Minnesota)
Norton Co.
Novell Inc.
Oaklawn Foundation
Olin Foundation, Spencer T. and Ann W.
Osborn Charitable Trust, Edward B.
Overbrook Foundation
Packaging Corporation of America
Packard Foundation, David and Lucile
Palmer Fund, Frank Loomis
Payne Foundation, Frank E. and Seba B.
Peabody Charitable Fund, Amelia
Perkin-Elmer Corp.
Pforzheimer Foundation, Carl and Lily
Phillips Charitable Trust, Dr. and Mrs. Arthur William
Polaroid Corp.
PPG Industries, Inc.
Premier Industrial Corp.
Puterbaugh Foundation
Quaker Chemical Corp.

Ralston Purina Co.
R&B Machine Tool Co.
Regenstein Foundation
Reicher Foundation, Anne and Harry J.
Reidler Foundation
Reisman Charitable Trust, George C. and Evelyn R.
Retirement Research Foundation
Riggs Benevolent Fund
Rockefeller Fund, David
Rockwell Fund
Rohm & Haas Co.
Rose Foundation, Billy
Ross Memorial Foundation, Will
Rubinstein Foundation, Helena
Russell Trust, Josephine G.
Salomon Foundation, Richard and Edna
Sasco Foundation
Schroeder Foundation, Walter
Sheppard Foundation, Lawrence B.
Simon Foundation, William E. and Carol G.
Simpson Investment Company
Skillman Foundation
Smith Charitable Foundation, Clara Blackford Smith and W. Aubrey
Smith Charitable Foundation, Lou and Lutza
Smith Foundation, Kelvin and Eleanor
Southern California Edison Co.
Sprague Educational and Charitable Foundation, Seth
Stackpole-Hall Foundation
Starr Foundation
Stemmons Foundation
Stevens Foundation, Abbot and Dorothy H.
Sturgis Charitable and Educational Trust, Roy and Christine
Sullivan Foundation, Algernon Sydney
Thomas Foundation, Joan and Lee
Thompson Charitable Foundation
Titus Foundation, Roy and Niuta
Towsley Foundation, Harry A. and Margaret D.
Treakle Foundation, J. Edwin
Trexler Trust, Harry C.
Trust Company Bank
Union Camp Corporation
Upjohn Foundation, Harold and Grace
Vernon Fund, Miles Hodsdon
Vicksburg Foundation
Vogler Foundation, Laura B.
Wahlstrom Foundation
Wean Foundation, Raymond John
Weingart Foundation
Wendt Foundation, Margaret L.
Wickson-Link Memorial Foundation
Winnebago Industries, Inc.
Winthrop Trust, Clara B.
Wisconsin Power & Light Co.
Wyomissing Foundation

Nutrition

Abbott Laboratories
Air Products and Chemicals, Inc.
AMCORE Bank, N.A. Rockford
Baldwin Memorial Foundation, Fred
Battelle Memorial Institute
Benedum Foundation, Claude Worthington
Bethlehem Steel Corp.
Brach Foundation, Helen
Bristol-Myers Squibb Company

Carvel Foundation, Thomas and Agnes
Cassett Foundation, Louis N.
Central Maine Power Co.
Dimeo Construction Co.
Duke Endowment
Duke Power Co.
Federated Mutual Insurance Co.
Ferebee Endowment, Percy O.
Ford Foundation
Freed Foundation
GATX Corp.
Gellert Foundation, Celia Berta
General Mills, Inc.
Globe Newspaper Co.
Gulf Coast Medical Foundation
Hafif Family Foundation
Hechinger Co.
Heinz Company, H. J.
Heinz Endowment, Howard
Hershey Foods Corp.
Hoffman Foundation, Maximilian E. and Marion O.
International Foundation
Jewish Healthcare Foundation of Pittsburgh
John Hancock Mutual Life Insurance Co.
Johnson & Higgins
Johnson & Son, S.C.
Jones Foundation, Daisy Marquis
Kiewit Foundation, Peter
Lipton, Thomas J.
Loews Corporation
Long Island Lighting Co.
Lydall, Inc.
Lyon Foundation
Mayor Foundation, Oliver Dewey
McCormick & Co. Inc.
Metropolitan Life Insurance Co.
Miller Brewing Company/North Carolina
Mott Fund, Ruth
Nabisco Foods Group
The New Yorker Magazine, Inc.
Norton Co.
Ore-Ida Foods, Inc.
Pacific Mutual Life Insurance Co.
Packard Foundation, David and Lucile
Perkin-Elmer Corp.
Pew Charitable Trusts
Pollock Company Foundation, William B.
Quaker Chemical Corp.
Ross Laboratories
SAFECO Corp.
Seaway Food Town, Inc.
Shawmut National Corp.
Sierra Pacific Industries
Sternberger Foundation, Tannenbaum
Tenneco Inc.
Trull Foundation
Valmont Industries, Inc.
Wal-Mart Stores, Inc.
Worthington Foods

Outpatient Health Care

Achelis Foundation
Altman Foundation
Blandin Foundation
Burkitt Foundation
Clark Foundation
Connelly Foundation
Diamond Foundation, Aaron
Duke Endowment
Gazette Co.
Hillcrest Foundation
Hillman Foundation
Jones Foundation, Daisy Marquis
Kline Foundation, Josiah W. and Bessie H.
Kresge Foundation
Larsen Fund

Meadows Foundation
Parker Hannifin Corp.
Schwob Foundation, Simon
Stauffer Charitable Trust, John
Steele Foundation, Harry and Grace
Weingart Foundation
Zlinkoff Fund for Medical Research and Education, Sergei S.

Prenatal Health Issues

Aetna Life & Casualty Co.
Ahmanson Foundation
AKC Fund
Aluminum Co. of America
American General Finance Corp.
Arakelian Foundation, Mary Alice
Ashtabula Foundation
Auerbach Foundation, Beatrice Fox
Baldwin Foundation, David M. and Barbara
BankAmerica Corp.
Bean Foundation, Norwin S. and Elizabeth N.
Bechtel, Jr. Foundation, S. D.
Beloit Foundation
Blue Cross & Blue Shield United of Wisconsin
Borden, Inc.
Brady Foundation
Brown Foundation, M. K.
Brunswick Corp.
Bryn Mawr Trust Co.
Butz Foundation
Carnegie Corporation of New York
Chartwell Foundation
Chazen Foundation
CIGNA Corporation
CINergy
Clorox Co.
Cogswell Benevolent Trust
Connecticut Mutual Life Insurance Company
Connelly Foundation
Contran Corporation
Cooperman Foundation, Leon and Toby
Culpeper Memorial Foundation, Daphne Seybolt
Dart Group Corp.
DeRoy Foundation, Helen L.
Dillon Dunwalke Trust, Clarence and Anne
Dr. Seuss Foundation
Donner Foundation, William H.
Douty Foundation
Duke Endowment
Duncan Foundation, Lillian H. and C. W.
Early Foundation
Eccles Foundation, Ralph M. and Ella M.
Essick Foundation
Federated Mutual Insurance Co.
Fife Foundation, Elias and Bertha
Fleming Cos. Food Distribution Center
Fondren Foundation
Freedom Forge Corp.
Freeport-McMoRan Inc.
Frese Foundation, Arnold D.
Friendship Fund
Fry Foundation, Lloyd A.
Gebbie Foundation
Geifman Family Foundation
Giant Eagle, Inc.
Goldie-Anna Charitable Trust
Gulf Power Co.
Hafif Family Foundation
Harcourt General, Inc.
Harmon Foundation, Pearl M. and Julia J.
Hasbro Inc.

Hearst Foundation, William Randolph
Heginbotham Trust, Will E.
Heinz Endowment, Howard
Herzstein Charitable Foundation, Albert and Ethel
Higginson Trust, Corina
Housatonic Curtain Co.
Hunt Charitable Trust, C. Giles
Hyde and Watson Foundation
Irvine Foundation, James
ITT Hartford Insurance Group, Inc.
Jarson-Stanley and Mickey Kaplan Foundation, Isaac and Esther
Jaydor Corp.
Jewish Healthcare Foundation of Pittsburgh
JM Foundation
Jostens, Inc.
Kaplun Foundation, Morris J. and Betty
Kaufmann Foundation, Henry
Kayser Foundation
Kelly Foundation, T. Lloyd
Knight Foundation, John S. and James L.
Knoll Group
Knox, Sr., and Pearl Wallis Knox Charitable Foundation, Robert W.
Kreitler Foundation
LBJ Family Foundation
Leavey Foundation, Thomas and Dorothy
Lederer Foundation, Francis L.
Levitt Foundation
Liberman Foundation, Bertha and Isaac
Liz Claiborne, Inc.
Mailman Family Foundation, A. L.
Marriott Foundation, J. Willard
McCune Charitable Trust, John R.
McGee Foundation
McGonagle Foundation, Dextra Baldwin
McInerny Foundation
Meyer Family Foundation, Paul J.
Meyer Memorial Trust
Middendorf Foundation
Miller-Mellor Association
Monfort Family Foundation
Muchnic Foundation
Musson Charitable Foundation, R. C. and Katharine M.
Nesholm Family Foundation
New Jersey Natural Gas Co.
Norton Memorial Corporation, Geraldi
Packard Foundation, David and Lucile
Palisades Educational Foundation
Parsons Foundation, Ralph M.
Parvin Foundation, Albert
Penn Foundation, William
Pew Charitable Trusts
Phillips Foundation, Ellis L.
Pittsburg Midway Coal Mining Co.
Pittsburgh Child Guidance Foundation
Porter Foundation, Mrs. Cheever
Public Welfare Foundation
Quivey-Bay State Foundation
Regenstein Foundation
Rennebohm Foundation, Oscar
Rich Products Corporation
Rockefeller Fund, David
Rockwell Fund
Roseburg Forest Products Co.
Ross Laboratories
Rouse Co.
Ruan Foundation Trust, John
Rubin Family Fund, Cele H. and William B.
Rubinstein Foundation, Helena
Scaife Family Foundation
Scherer Foundation, Karla

Schiff Foundation, Dorothy
Schumann Fund for New Jersey
Scott Fetzer Co.
Scott Foundation, William E.
Seneca Foods Corp.
Shaw Foundation, Arch W.
Smeal Foundation, Mary Jean and Frank P.
Smith Charitable Foundation, Lou and Lutza
Smith Foundation, Gordon V. and Helen C.
Springs Foundation
Stabler Foundation, Donald B. and Dorothy L.
Stevens Foundation, John T.
Strawbridge Foundation of Pennsylvania II, Margaret Dorrance
Texas Commerce Bank-Houston, N.A.
Thompson Charitable Foundation
Thornton Foundation, Flora L.
Tiscornia Foundation
Todd Co., A.M.
Travelers Inc.
Tupancy-Harris Foundation of 1986
Union Pacific Corp.
U.S. Bank of Washington
USL Capital Corporation
Van Houten Memorial Fund
Weil, Gotshal and Manges Foundation
Weingart Foundation
Welfare Foundation
Whitehead Charitable Foundation
Wilder Foundation
Willard Helping Fund, Cecilia Young
Windham Foundation

Preventive Medicine/Wellness Organizations

Argyros Foundation
Ball Brothers Foundation
Bank One, Youngstown, NA
Beech Aircraft Corp.
Benedum Foundation, Claude Worthington
Bertha Foundation
Bettingen Corporation, Burton G.
Bingham Second Betterment Fund, William
Bryn Mawr Trust Co.
Campini Foundation, Frank A.
Clay Foundation
Columbia Foundation
Connelly Foundation
Duke Endowment
Federated Mutual Insurance Co.
Ferebee Endowment, Percy O.
Fireman's Fund Insurance Co.
Hafif Family Foundation
Heckscher Foundation for Children
Hillsdale Fund
Hoag Family Foundation, George
Imperial Bancorp
Independence Foundation
Jacobs Family Foundation
Jameson Foundation, J. W. and Ida M.
Janirve Foundation
Jarson-Stanley and Mickey Kaplan Foundation, Isaac and Esther
Johnson Fund, Edward C.
Kelley and Elza Kelley Foundation, Edward Bangs
Kresge Foundation
LamCo. Communications
Lichtenstein Foundation, David B.
Long Foundation, J.M.

MacArthur Foundation, John D. and Catherine T.
Markey Charitable Fund, John C.
Meadows Foundation
Merck Family Fund
Middendorf Foundation
Miller-Mellor Association
Murdock Charitable Trust, M. J.
Murphey Foundation, Lluella Morey
Nestle USA Inc.
Olin Foundation, Spencer T. and Ann W.
Pick, Jr. Fund, Albert
Plankenhorn Foundation, Harry
Schiro Fund
Stokely, Jr. Foundation, William B.
Travelers Inc.
Trull Foundation
Upjohn Foundation, Harold and Grace
USL Capital Corporation
van Ameringen Foundation

Public Health

Abbott Laboratories
Abell-Hanger Foundation
Adams Foundation, Arthur F. and Alice E.
Albertson's Inc.
AMCORE Bank, N.A. Rockford
American Brands, Inc.
American Natural Resources Company
AMR Corp.
Anheuser-Busch Companies, Inc.
Armco Inc.
Auerbach Foundation, Beatrice Fox
Babson Foundation, Paul and Edith
Bedsole Foundation, J. L.
Benedum Foundation, Claude Worthington
Bethlehem Steel Corp.
Block, H&R
Brach Foundation, Helen
Breyer Foundation
Carnegie Corporation of New York
Carter Foundation, Amon G.
Central Maine Power Co.
Chase Manhattan Bank, N.A.
Chevron Corporation
Colonial Life & Accident Insurance Co.
Connecticut Mutual Life Insurance Company
Contran Corporation
Cowell Foundation, S. H.
Cummins Engine Co.
Curtice-Burns Foods, Inc.
Dunagan Foundation
duPont Foundation, Alfred I.
Enron Corp.
Exxon Corporation
Federated Mutual Insurance Co.
Feild Co-Operative Association
Femino Foundation
Fikes Foundation, Leland
Ford Foundation
Foster Foundation
Friedman Family Foundation
Frost National Bank
Fry Foundation, Lloyd A.
Gallagher Family Foundation, Lewis P.
General Motors Corp.
Goldsmith Foundation, Horace W.
Greenwall Foundation
Guttman Foundation, Stella and Charles
HCA Foundation
Hechinger Co.
Hillsdale Fund

Howe and Mitchell B. Howe Foundation, Lucille Horton
Hudson-Webber Foundation
Irvine Foundation, James
ITT Hartford Insurance Group, Inc.
Ittleson Foundation
Jackson Foundation
Jewish Healthcare Foundation of Pittsburgh
JM Foundation
John Hancock Mutual Life Insurance Co.
Johnson Controls Inc.
Johnson & Higgins
Kayser Foundation
Kennecott Corporation
Kimball Foundation, Horace A. Kimball and S. Ella
Kiplinger Foundation
Kline Foundation, Josiah W. and Bessie H.
Lee Endowment Foundation
Leidy Foundation, John J.
Lennon Foundation, Fred A.
Lydall, Inc.
Macy & Co., Inc., R.H.
Markey Charitable Fund, John C.
Mayer Foundation, James and Eva
McCune Charitable Trust, John R.
McLean Contributionship
Medtronic, Inc.
Merck & Co. Human Health Division
Meyer Memorial Trust
Mid-Iowa Health Foundation
National Forge Co.
The New Yorker Magazine, Inc.
Norton Co.
Norwest Bank Nebraska, N.A.
Pacific Mutual Life Insurance Co.
Packard Foundation, David and Lucile
Penn Foundation, William
Perkin-Elmer Corp.
Pew Charitable Trusts
Pick, Jr. Fund, Albert
Polaroid Corp.
Premier Industrial Corp.
Public Welfare Foundation
R. F. Foundation
Rockefeller Fund, David
Rohm & Haas Co.
Rose's Stores, Inc.
Royal Foundation, May Mitchell
Rubin Family Fund, Cele H. and William B.
Rubinstein Foundation, Helena
SAFECO Corp.
Sara Lee Hosiery, Inc.
Schering-Plough Corp.
Scott Fetzer Co.
Security Life of Denver Insurance Co.
Shawmut National Corp.
Simon Foundation, William E. and Carol G.
Skillman Foundation
Smith Corp., A.O.
Snow Foundation, John Ben
Texaco Inc.
Towsley Foundation, Harry A. and Margaret D.
Wal-Mart Stores, Inc.
Webber Oil Co.

Research/Studies Institutes

Ahmanson Foundation
Ameritas Life Insurance Corp.
Ames Charitable Trust, Harriett
Andersen Foundation
Anderson Foundation, John W.
Anderson Foundation, M. D.
Annenberg Foundation
Auerbach Foundation, Beatrice Fox

Baldwin Foundation, David M. and Barbara
Barth Foundation, Theodore H.
Bettingen Corporation, Burton G.
Booth Ferris Foundation
Calder Foundation, Louis
Carter Foundation, Amon G.
CBS, Inc.
Chartwell Foundation
Cogswell Benevolent Trust
Connelly Foundation
Crandall Memorial Foundation, J. Ford
Crocker Trust, Mary A.
Crown Books
Daniel Foundation of Alabama
Darby Foundation
Davis Foundation, Edwin W. and Catherine M.
Davis Foundations, Arthur Vining
Dexter Charitable Fund, Eugene A.
Dillon Foundation
Dr. Seuss Foundation
Duchossois Industries Inc.
Dunagan Foundation
Essick Foundation
Femino Foundation
Fenton Foundation
First Union Corp.
Fleet Financial Group, Inc.
Fondren Foundation
Foster Charitable Trust
Frohring Foundation, William O. and Gertrude Lewis
Gebbie Foundation
Geifman Family Foundation
Goldsmith Foundation, Horace W.
Goldwyn Foundation, Samuel
Gregg-Graniteville Foundation
Habig Foundation, Arnold F.
Hartford Foundation, John A.
Hartz Foundation
Hasbro Inc.
Hauser Foundation
Helms Foundation
Hewlett Foundation, William and Flora
Hillman Foundation
Houston Endowment
Howe and Mitchell B. Howe Foundation, Lucille Horton
Imperial Bancorp
Irwin Charity Foundation, William G.
Ittleson Foundation
Jameson Foundation, J. W. and Ida M.
Jones Foundation, Fletcher
Journal-Gazette Co.
Kelley and Elza Kelley Foundation, Edward Bangs
Kempner Fund, Harris and Eliza
Kilcawley Fund, William H.
Klipstein Foundation, Ernest Christian
Knudsen Foundation, Tom and Valley
Kresge Foundation
Lattner Foundation, Forrest C.
LBJ Family Foundation
Leighton-Oare Foundation
Mailman Family Foundation, A. L.
Mailman Foundation
Margoes Foundation
Marmot Foundation
Marx Foundation, Virginia and Leonard
McCune Charitable Trust, John R.
McGonagle Foundation, Dextra Baldwin
McKenna Foundation, Philip M.
Merck & Co.
Monell Foundation, Ambrose
Moore & Sons, B.C.
Mott Foundation, Charles Stewart
Muchnic Foundation

New-Land Foundation
Noble Foundation, Samuel Roberts
Norton Memorial Corporation, Geraldi
Phillips Family Foundation, Jay and Rose
Reed Foundation
Rosenberg, Jr. Family Foundation, Louise and Claude
Schlink Foundation, Albert G. and Olive H.
Scholl Foundation, Dr.
Scott Foundation, William E.
Seaver Charitable Trust, Richard C.
Sheary for Charity, Edna M.
Smart Family Foundation
Stans Foundation
Strauss Foundation, Leon
Taylor Foundation, Ruth and Vernon
Thorne Foundation
Thornton Foundation
Walsh Foundation
Washington Forrest Foundation
Weaver Foundation, Gil and Dody
Weinstein Foundation, J.
Williams Charitable Trust, John C.
Wright Foundation, Lola
Zarrow Foundation, Anne and Henry

Respiratory

Alabama Gas Corp.
Ansley Foundation, Dantzler Bond
Blue Cross & Blue Shield United of Wisconsin
Broadhurst Foundation
Bryant Foundation
Burchfield Foundation, Charles E.
City National Bank and Trust Co.
Cummings Foundation, James H.
Demoulas Supermarkets Inc.
DeRoy Foundation, Helen L.
Donnelley Foundation, Gaylord and Dorothy
Duke Endowment
Fishback Foundation Trust, Harmes C.
French Oil Mill Machinery Co.
Gellert Foundation, Celia Berta
Grundy Foundation
Hartmarx Corporation
Hillcrest Foundation
Hoover Foundation
Hoover Fund-Trust, W. Henry
Kirby Foundation, F. M.
Knoll Group
Lovett Foundation
Mercury Aircraft
Merkley Charitable Trust
Mid-Iowa Health Foundation
Morris Foundation, William T.
Old National Bank in Evansville
Olsson Memorial Foundation, Elis
O'Quinn Foundation, John M. and Nancy C.
Parshelsky Foundation, Moses L.
PHH Corporation
Plankenhorn Foundation, Harry
Quivey-Bay State Foundation
Raymond Corp.
Ross Memorial Foundation, Will
Salomon Foundation, Richard and Edna
Sawyer Charitable Foundation
Schuller International
Schwob Foundation, Simon
Scott Foundation, William E.
Sierra Pacific Resources
Skillman Foundation

Smith Foundation, Gordon V. and Helen C.
Sullivan Foundation, Algernon Sydney
Thorne Foundation
Times Mirror Company, The
Van Houten Memorial Fund
Vollbrecht Foundation, Frederick A.
Wachovia Bank of North Carolina, N.A.
Washington Forrest Foundation
Westerman Foundation, Samuel L.
Wildermuth Foundation, E. F.
Young Foundation, Irvin L.

Single-Disease Health Associations

Abbott Laboratories
Abell-Hanger Foundation
Abrams Foundation, Talbert and Leota
AEGON USA Inc.
Ahmanson Foundation
Air France
Air Products and Chemicals, Inc.
AKC Fund
Akzo America
Akzo Chemicals Inc.
Alabama Gas Corp.
Alabama Power Co.
Alavi Foundation of New York
Alexander Foundation, Joseph
Allegheny Ludlum Corp.
Allendale Insurance Co.
AlliedSignal Inc.
Allyn Foundation
Altschul Foundation
Alumax Inc.
Aluminum Co. of America
AMCORE Bank, N.A. Rockford
American Brands, Inc.
American Fidelity Corporation
American General Finance Corp.
American National Bank & Trust Co. of Chicago
American Natural Resources Company
American President Companies, Ltd.
American United Life Insurance Co.
Ames Charitable Trust, Harriett
Amfac/JMB Hawaii Inc.
Amoco Corporation
AMP Incorporated
AMR Corp.
Andersen Corp.
Andersen Foundation
Anderson Foundation, John W.
Anderson Foundation, M. D.
Andersons, The
Andreas Foundation
Anheuser-Busch Companies, Inc.
Ansin Private Foundation, Ronald M.
Ansley Foundation, Dantzler Bond
AON Corporation
Apple Computer, Inc.
Appleton Papers Inc.
Argyros Foundation
Aristech Chemical Corp.
Arkansas Power & Light Co.
Arkelian Foundation, Ben H. and Gladys
Arkell Hall Foundation
Armco Inc.
Auerbach Foundation, Beatrice Fox
Avon Products, Inc.
Ayres Foundation, Inc.
Badgeley Residuary Charitable Trust, Rose M.
Baldwin Foundation, David M. and Barbara
Banc One Wisconsin Corp.

Bank of New York Company, Inc.
Barra Foundation
Barry Corp., R. G.
Barth Foundation, Theodore H.
Battelle Memorial Institute
Baughman Foundation
Bay Foundation
Beal Foundation
Beattie Foundation Trust, Cordelia Lee
Beazley Foundation/Frederick Foundation
Bechtel, Jr. Foundation, S. D.
Bedsole Foundation, J. L.
Beech Aircraft Corp.
Bemis Company, Inc.
Benenson Foundation, Frances and Benjamin
Benetton Services Corp.
Berger Foundation, H. N. and Frances C.
Bettingen Corporation, Burton G.
Beveridge Foundation, Frank Stanley
Bigelow Foundation, F. R.
Binswanger Cos.
Bird Corp.
Bishop Foundation, E. K. and Lillian F.
Blair and Co., William
Blount, Inc.
Blowitz-Ridgeway Foundation
Blue Bell, Inc.
Blue Cross & Blue Shield United of Wisconsin
Blum Foundation, Harry and Maribel G.
Blum-Kovler Foundation
Bobst Foundation, Elmer and Mamdouha
Boothroyd Foundation, Charles H. and Bertha L.
Borden, Inc.
Borman's Inc.
Boston Edison Co.
Brady Foundation
Bridgestone/Firestone, Inc.
Bridwell Foundation, J. S.
Bright Family Foundation
Brillion Iron Works
Broadhurst Foundation
Brooks Foundation, Gladys
Brown Foundation, M. K.
Brunswick Corp.
Bryant Foundation
Bucyrus-Erie Company
Burchfield Foundation, Charles E.
Burden Foundation, Florence V.
Burlington Industries, Inc.
Burnett-Tandy Foundation
Cable & Wireless Holdings, Inc.
Cafritz Foundation, Morris and Gwendolyn
Cain Foundation, Effie and Wofford
Cain Foundation, Gordon and Mary
Callaway Foundation
Campini Foundation, Frank A.
Carpenter Foundation, E. Rhodes and Leona B.
Carter Foundation, Amon G.
Carvel Foundation, Thomas and Agnes
Caspersen Foundation for Aid to Health and Education, O. W.
Cassett Foundation, Louis N.
Castle Foundation, Harold K. L.
Catlin Charitable Trust, Kathleen K.
CBI Industries, Inc.
Central Fidelity Banks, Inc.
Central Maine Power Co.
Charina Foundation
Chartwell Foundation
Cheatham Foundation, Owen
Cheney Foundation, Ben B.
Chevron Corporation

Childs Charitable Foundation, Roberta M.
Christian Dior New York, Inc.
Citibank
Citizens Bank of Rhode Island
Claiborne and Art Ortenberg Foundation, Liz
Clapp Charitable and Educational Trust, George H.
Clayton Fund
Clorox Co.
Coen Family Foundation, Charles S. and Mary
Collins Medical Trust
Colonial Life & Accident Insurance Co.
Columbus Dispatch Printing Co.
Comerica Incorporated
Commerce Clearing House, Incorporated
Commonwealth Edison Co.
Comprecare Foundation
Connecticut Mutual Life Insurance Company
Connemara Fund
Continental Corp.
Cooke Foundation
Cooper Industries, Inc.
Cooperman Foundation, Leon and Toby
Cord Foundation, E. L.
Cornell Trust, Peter C.
Cosmair, Inc.
Cowles Charitable Trust
CPC International Inc.
Crawford Estate, E. R.
Crestlea Foundation
Crown Memorial, Arie and Ida
Crystal Trust
CS First Boston Corporation
Culpeper Memorial Foundation, Daphne Seybolt
Cuneo Foundation
Curtice-Burns Foods, Inc.
Daniel Foundation of Alabama
Darby Foundation
Dart Group Corp.
Davenport-Hatch Foundation
Davidson Family Charitable Foundation
Davis Foundation, Edwin W. and Catherine M.
Davis Foundation, Irene E. and George A.
Davis Foundation, James A. and Juliet L.
Delaware North Co., Inc.
Demoulas Supermarkets Inc.
Dentsply International Inc.
DeRoy Foundation, Helen L.
Detroit Edison Co.
Deuble Foundation, George H.
DeVore Foundation
Dexter Corporation
Dillon Foundation
Dimeo Construction Co.
Dingman Foundation, Michael D.
Dishman Charitable Foundation Trust, H. E. and Kate
Donnelley Foundation, Gaylord and Dorothy
Douglas & Lomason Company
Dresser Industries, Inc.
Dreyfus Foundation, Max and Victoria
du Pont de Nemours & Co., E. I.
Duchossois Industries Inc.
Duke Power Co.
Dula Educational and Charitable Foundation, Caleb C. and Julia W.
Dun & Bradstreet Corp.
Dunagan Foundation
Duncan Trust, John G.
duPont Foundation, Alfred I.
Dynamet, Inc.
Early Foundation
Eaton Corporation
Eaton Foundation, Cyrus
Eden Hall Foundation

Einstein Fund, Albert E. and Birdie W.
Emerson Foundation, Inc., Fred L.
English Memorial Fund, Florence C. and H. L.
Enron Corp.
Essick Foundation
Ettinger Foundation
Evans Foundation, T. M.
Fair Play Foundation
Farish Fund, William Stamps
Favrot Fund
Federal-Mogul Corporation
Federated Mutual Insurance Co.
Feil Foundation, Louis and Gertrude
Feild Co-Operative Association
Fenton Foundation
Fife Foundation, Elias and Bertha
First Union Corp.
Firstar Bank Milwaukee, N.A.
Fischbach Foundation
Fish Foundation, Ray C.
Fleming Cos. Food Distribution Center
Fohs Foundation
Folger Fund
Fondren Foundation
Forbes Inc.
Forest Foundation
Foster Charitable Trust
Freedom Forge Corp.
Freeman Charitable Trust, Samuel
Freeport Brick Co.
Fribourg Foundation
Friedman Family Foundation
Frohring Foundation, William O. and Gertrude Lewis
Frost National Bank
Fruehauf Foundation
Fry Foundation, Lloyd A.
Fujitsu America, Inc.
Fuller Foundation, C. G.
Fuqua Foundation, J. B.
Gap, Inc., The
Garland Foundation, John Jewett and H. Chandler
GATX Corp.
Geifman Family Foundation
General American Life Insurance Co.
General Motors Corp.
Geneseo Foundation
GenRad
Georgia-Pacific Corporation
Georgia Power Co.
German Protestant Orphan Asylum Association
Gershman Foundation, Joel
Gheens Foundation
Giant Eagle, Inc.
Giant Food Inc.
Giant Food Stores
Gifford Charitable Corporation, Rosamond
Gillette Co.
Gilman Foundation, Howard
Gilmore Foundation, William G.
Givenchy Corp.
Glaser Foundation
Glenn Foundation, Carrie C. and Lena V.
Glick Foundation, Eugene and Marilyn
Glosser Foundation, David A.
Goddard Foundation, Charles B.
Goldberg Family Foundation
Goldsmith Foundation, Horace W.
Goodman & Co.
Gordon/Rousmaniere/Roberts Fund
Gould Electronics Inc.
Gregg-Graniteville Foundation
Griffis Foundation
Griffith Foundation, W. C.
Guaranty Bank & Trust Co.
Guardian Life Insurance Company of America

Gulf Power Co.
Guttman Foundation, Stella and Charles
Hachar Charitable Trust, D. D.
Hafif Family Foundation
Haley Foundation, W. B.
Halff Foundation, G. A. C.
Halsell Foundation, Ewing
Hamilton Bank
Hamman Foundation, George and Mary Josephine
Hammer Foundation, Armand
Hanes Foundation, John W. and Anna H.
Hanson Industries North America
Harland Charitable Foundation, John and Wilhelmina D.
Harsco Corp.
Hartmarx Corporation
Harvey Foundation, Felix
Hawn Foundation
Hazen Foundation, Edward W.
Hechinger Co.
Heckscher Foundation for Children
Hedco Foundation
Heinz Company, H. J.
Heinz Endowment, Vira I.
Heinz Trust, Drue
Hermann Foundation, Grover
Herrick Foundation
Hillcrest Foundation
Hillman Foundation
Hoag Family Foundation, George
Hobby Foundation
Hook Drugs
Hoover, Jr. Foundation, Margaret W. and Herbert
Hopwood Charitable Trust, John M.
Houchens Foundation, Ervin G.
Houston Endowment
Houston Industries Incorporated
Howe and Mitchell B. Howe Foundation, Lucille Horton
Hugoton Foundation
Huisking Foundation
Hulme Charitable Foundation, Milton G.
Humana, Inc.
Humphrey Fund, George M. and Pamela S.
Hunt Foundation
Hunt Foundation, Roy A.
Hunt Foundation, Samuel P.
Hyde and Watson Foundation
Icahn Foundation, Carl C.
ICI Americas Inc.
IES Industries, Inc.
Imperial Bancorp
Ingalls Foundation, Louise H. and David S.
Inland Container Corp.
International Business Machines Corp.
International Foundation
Irwin Charity Foundation, William G.
Ittleson Foundation
Jaffe Foundation
Jarson-Stanley and Mickey Kaplan Foundation, Isaac and Esther
Jaydor Corp.
John Hancock Mutual Life Insurance Co.
Johnson Controls Inc.
Johnson Foundation, Burdine
Johnson Foundation, Helen K. and Arthur E.
Johnson & Higgins
Johnson & Son, S. C.
Jonsson Foundation
Journal-Gazette Co.
Kansas City Southern Industries
Kaplun Foundation, Morris J. and Betty
Kaufmann Foundation, Henry
Kavanagh Foundation, T. James

Speech & Hearing

Zenkel Foundation

Transplant Networks/Donor Banks

Alexander Foundation, Joseph
AlliedSignal Inc.
Altschul Foundation
Anderson Foundation, M. D.
Barth Foundation, Theodore H.
Besser Foundation
Blum Foundation, Harry and Maribel G.
Burden Foundation, Florence V.
Callaway Foundation
Carvel Foundation, Thomas and Agnes
Champlin Foundations
Chase Manhattan Bank, N.A.
Connelly Foundation
Contran Corporation
Crane Co.
CS First Boston Corporation
Dana Charitable Trust, Eleanor Naylor
Firstar Bank Milwaukee, N.A.
Fishback Foundation Trust, Harmes C.
Fleming Cos. Food Distribution Center
Fribourg Foundation
Gulf Power Co.
Hancock Foundation, Luke B.
Hanson Industries North America
Hearst Foundation, William Randolph
Heckscher Foundation for Children
Hook Drugs
Hoover, Jr. Foundation, Margaret W. and Herbert
Houston Endowment
Hudson-Webber Foundation
Hugoton Foundation
Ingalls Foundation, Louise H. and David S.
Jewish Healthcare Foundation of Pittsburgh
Johnson Controls Inc.
Johnson Foundation, M. G. and Lillie A.
Lehigh Portland Cement Co.
Mahadh Foundation
Mayor Foundation, Oliver Dewey
McLean Contributionship
Meadows Foundation
Merrill Lynch & Co., Inc.
Metropolitan Life Insurance Co.
Morgan & Company, J.P.
Noble Foundation, Samuel Roberts
Offield Family Foundation
PaineWebber
Payne Foundation, Frank E. and Seba B.
Pella Corporation
Pfizer, Inc.
Ross Memorial Foundation, Will
Royal Foundation, May Mitchell
Sawyer Charitable Foundation
Schering-Plough Corp.
Starr Foundation
Steele-Reese Foundation
Temple Foundation, T. L. L.
Texaco Inc.
Titus Foundation, Roy and Niuta
Weil, Gotshal and Manges Foundation
Westerman Foundation, Samuel L.
WICOR, Inc.

Trauma Treatment

Alexander Foundation, Joseph
Ames Charitable Trust, Harriett
Armco Inc.
Chatlos Foundation
Childs Charitable Foundation, Roberta M.
Collins Foundation
Consolidated Papers, Inc.
DeRoy Testamentary Foundation
Fikes Foundation, Leland
France Foundation, Jacob and Annita
Hanover Foundation
Harvey Foundation, Felix
Hickory Tech Corp.
Jockey Hollow Foundation
Jostens, Inc.
Marmot Foundation
McGee Foundation
Medtronic, Inc.
Mid-Iowa Health Foundation
Noble Foundation, Edward John
Offield Family Foundation
Parsons Foundation, Ralph M.
Sawyer Charitable Foundation
Skillman Foundation
Subaru of America Inc.
Thalhimer and Family Foundation, Charles G.
Unilever United States, Inc.
USX Corporation
Vernon Fund, Miles Hodson
Whiting Foundation
Windham Foundation

International

Foreign Arts Organizations

Ahmanson Foundation
Alexander Foundation, Joseph
Aluminum Co. of America
Amado Foundation, Maurice
Avery Arts Foundation, Milton and Sally
Babson Foundation, Paul and Edith
Bank of Boston
Barth Foundation, Theodore H.
Benenson Foundation, Frances and Benjamin
Boswell Foundation, James G.
Chartwell Foundation
Chazen Foundation
Cole Trust, Quincy
Crown Books
Dr. Seuss Foundation
Eastman Kodak Company
Feild Co-Operative Association
Fink Foundation
Fischbach Foundation
Fletcher Foundation
Ford Foundation
Ford Fund, William and Martha
Fribourg Foundation
Frohring Foundation, William O. and Gertrude Lewis
Getty Trust, J. Paul
Gilman Foundation, Howard
Givenchy Corp.
Glencoe Foundation
Glick Foundation, Eugene and Marilyn
Goldsmith Foundation, Horace W.
Gould Foundation, The Florence
Graham Foundation for Advanced Studies in the Fine Arts
Hanover Foundation
Harrington Foundation, Francis A. and Jacquelyn H.
Hazen Foundation, Edward W.
Heinz Trust, Drue

Hewlett-Packard Co.
Hillman Family Foundation, Alex
Homeland Foundation
Hunt Foundation
International Foundation
Jaffe Foundation
Jarson-Stanley and Mickey Kaplan Foundation, Isaac and Esther
Jurzykowski Foundation, Alfred
Kress Foundation, Samuel H.
Kuehn Foundation
Lauder Foundation
Lemberg Foundation
Littauer Foundation, Lucius N.
Mailman Foundation
Marpat Foundation
Mather Charitable Trust, S. Livingston
McEvoy Foundation, Mildred H.
Mellon Foundation, Andrew W.
Memton Fund
Metropolitan Life Insurance Co.
Meyerhoff Fund, Joseph
Mnuchin Foundation
Morgan & Company, J.P.
Morgan Construction Co.
Morris Foundation, Margaret T.
New York Times Company
Norton Family Foundation, Peter
Paley Foundation, William S.
Park Foundation
Parvin Foundation, Albert
Pew Charitable Trusts
Pfizer, Inc.
Pforzheimer Foundation, Carl and Lily
Piankova Foundation, Tatiana
Reicher Foundation, Anne and Harry J.
Reynolds Foundation, Christopher
Rohatyn Foundation, Felix and Elizabeth
Rose Foundation, Billy
Rosen Foundation, Joseph
Rubinstein Foundation, Helena
Scholl Foundation, Dr.
Scott Foundation, William E.
Skaggs Foundation, L. J. and Mary C.
Slifka Foundation, Joseph and Sylvia
Solow Foundation
Starr Foundation
Times Mirror Company, The
Timken Foundation of Canton
Titus Foundation, Roy and Niuta
Vetlesen Foundation, G. Unger
Vicksburg Foundation
Walsh Foundation
Weinstein Foundation, J.
Wendt Foundation, Margaret L.
Wilson Fund, Matilda R.
Zarrow Foundation, Anne and Henry
Zenkel Foundation

Foreign Educational Institutions

Aetna Life & Casualty Co.
Ahmanson Foundation
Alavi Foundation of New York
Alexander Foundation, Joseph
Allen Brothers Foundation
Altschul Foundation
Aluminum Co. of America
Amado Foundation, Maurice
Amoco Corporation
Annenberg Foundation
Avery Arts Foundation, Milton and Sally
Benenson Foundation, Frances and Benjamin
Blake Foundation, S. P.
Blum-Kovler Foundation

Bobst Foundation, Elmer and Mamdouha
Borman's Inc.
Boswell Foundation, James G.
Breyer Foundation
Bristol-Myers Squibb Company
Cabot Family Charitable Trust
Carnegie Corporation of New York
Carpenter Technology Corp.
Chartwell Foundation
Chase Manhattan Bank, N.A.
Cheatham Foundation, Owen
Chevron Corporation
Citibank
Columbia Foundation
Connelly Foundation
Continental Corp.
Covington and Burling
Cowles Charitable Trust
Crown Books
Crown Memorial, Arie and Ida
Cummins Engine Co.
Darby Foundation
Demos Foundation, N.
Digital Equipment Corp.
Dingman Foundation, Michael D.
Dodge Foundation, Cleveland H.
Donnelley Foundation, Gaylord and Dorothy
Donner Foundation, William H.
Dreyfus Foundation, Jean and Louis
du Pont de Nemours & Co., E. I.
duPont Foundation, Alfred I.
Durfee Foundation
Eaton Foundation, Cyrus
Edmonds Foundation, Dean S.
Erpf Foundation, Armand G.
Fink Foundation
First Hawaiian, Inc.
Fohs Foundation
Forbes Inc.
Ford Foundation
Foster Charitable Trust
Fribourg Foundation
Frohring Foundation, Paul and Maxine
Fuld Health Trust, Helene
Gamble Foundation
Getty Trust, J. Paul
Gillette Co.
Givenchy Corp.
Gleason Foundation
Glencoe Foundation
Goldsmith Foundation, Horace W.
Good Samaritan
Gould Foundation, The Florence
Graham Foundation for Advanced Studies in the Fine Arts
Guggenheim Foundation, Harry Frank
Hammer Foundation, Armand
Hanson Industries North America
Harriman Foundation, Gladys and Roland
Hauser Foundation
Heinz Company, H. J.
Heinz Trust, Drue
Hewlett Foundation, William and Flora
Hewlett-Packard Co.
Humana, Inc.
Hunt Foundation
Ingalls Foundation, Louise H. and David S.
International Business Machines Corp.
International Foundation
Jaydor Corp.
Jewett Foundation, George Frederick
Kaplun Foundation, Morris J. and Betty
Knoll Group
Koret Foundation
Kresge Foundation

Kress Foundation, Samuel H.
Lasdon Foundation
Leavey Foundation, Thomas and Dorothy
Littauer Foundation, Lucius N.
Lurcy Charitable and Educational Trust, Georges
MacArthur Foundation, John D. and Catherine T.
MacLeod Stewardship Foundation
Mandeville Foundation
Marpat Foundation
McCasland Foundation
McGonagle Foundation, Dextra Baldwin
Mellon Foundation, Andrew W.
Merck & Co.
Merrill Lynch & Co., Inc.
Metropolitan Life Insurance Co.
Meyer Fund, Milton and Sophie
Meyerhoff Fund, Joseph
Morgan & Company, J.P.
Mosbacher, Jr. Foundation, Emil
Moses Fund, Henry and Lucy
Mott Foundation, Charles Stewart
New York Times Company
Newman's Own, Inc.
Olin Corp.
Packard Foundation, David and Lucile
Paley Foundation, William S.
Parvin Foundation, Albert
Pennsylvania Dutch Co.
Pew Charitable Trusts
Pfizer, Inc.
Philibosian Foundation, Stephen
Piankova Foundation, Tatiana
Plumsock Fund
Reed Foundation
Reynolds Foundation, Christopher
Rixson Foundation, Oscar C.
Rosenberg, Jr. Family Foundation, Louise and Claude
Schiro Fund
Schlumberger Ltd.
Scholl Foundation, Dr.
Schwartz Fund for Education and Health Research, Arnold and Marie
Scott Fetzer Co.
Seagram & Sons, Inc., Joseph E.
Skaggs Foundation, L. J. and Mary C.
Smith Foundation, Ralph L.
Smith Trust, May and Stanley
SmithKline Beecham Corp.
Starr Foundation
Stone Charitable Foundation
Sulzberger Foundation
Taube Family Foundation
Taylor Foundation, Ruth and Vernon
Texaco Inc.
Thorne Foundation
Timken Foundation of Canton
Van Evera Foundation, Dewitt
Weinstein Foundation, J.
Westerman Foundation, Samuel L.
Whirlpool Corporation
Widgeon Foundation
Wilson Foundation, H. W.

General

Alabama Gas Corp.
Cabot Corp.
CIBC Wood Gundy
Marpat Foundation
Mitsubishi Motor Sales of America, Inc.
Pitt-Des Moines Inc.

Health Care/Hospitals

Abbott Laboratories
Abell-Hanger Foundation
Adams Foundation, Arthur F. and Alice E.
Aetna Life & Casualty Co.
Ahmanson Foundation
Alavi Foundation of New York
Alcon Laboratories, Inc.
Alexander Foundation, Joseph
Allegheny Foundation
Aluminum Co. of America
American Brands, Inc.
Amoco Corporation
Archer-Daniels-Midland Co.
Arkelian Foundation, Ben H. and Gladys
Asplundh Foundation
Besser Foundation
Blum-Kovler Foundation
Bobst Foundation, Elmer and Mamdouha
Burkitt Foundation
Cabot Corp.
Cabot Family Charitable Trust
Carnegie Corporation of New York
Carolyn Foundation
Chase Manhattan Bank, N.A.
Chatlos Foundation
Chevron Corporation
Citibank
Claiborne and Art Ortenberg Foundation, Liz
Coen Family Foundation, Charles S. and Mary
Connelly Foundation
Cooperman Foundation, Leon and Toby
Cowell Foundation, S. H.
Crane Co.
Crocker Trust, Mary A.
CS First Boston Corporation
Cummings Foundation, James H.
Dana Charitable Trust, Eleanor Naylor
Davis Foundation, Irene E. and George A.
Dingman Foundation, Michael D.
Dodge Foundation, Geraldine R.
Dreyfus Foundation, Jean and Louis
du Pont de Nemours & Co., E. I.
Dunagan Foundation
duPont Foundation, Alfred I.
Eastman Kodak Company
Eaton Foundation, Cyrus
Elkins, Jr. Foundation, Margaret and James A.
Ettinger Foundation
Exxon Corporation
Favrot Fund
Fikes Foundation, Leland
Fink Foundation
Fischbach Foundation
Ford Foundation
Fruehauf Foundation
Fry Foundation, Lloyd A.
Fuld Health Trust, Helene
Geifman Family Foundation
Gilman Foundation, Howard
Goldsmith Foundation, Horace W.
Gould Foundation, The Florence
Hagedorn Fund
Hawn Foundation
Heinz Company, H. J.
Hermann Foundation, Grover
Hewlett Foundation, William and Flora
Hewlett-Packard Co.
Higginson Trust, Corina
Hillman Family Foundation, Alex
Hoffmann-La Roche Inc.
Homeland Foundation
Hoover Fund-Trust, W. Henry

Huber Foundation
International Business Machines Corp.
International Foundation
Jarson-Stanley and Mickey Kaplan Foundation, Isaac and Esther
Jewett Foundation, George Frederick
Jewish Healthcare Foundation of Pittsburgh
Johnson Foundation, Burdine
Johnson Fund, Edward C.
Jurzykowski Foundation, Alfred
Kempner Fund, Harris and Eliza
Kennedy Foundation, Ethel
Kirby Foundation, F. M.
Knoll Group
Kreitler Foundation
Kresge Foundation
LamCo. Communications
Laurel Foundation
Leavey Foundation, Thomas and Dorothy
Link, Jr. Foundation, George
Littauer Foundation, Lucius N.
MacArthur Foundation, John D. and Catherine T.
Mahadh Foundation
Mailman Family Foundation, A. L.
Mailman Foundation
Markey Charitable Fund, John C.
Marpat Foundation
Maytag Family Foundation, Fred
Medtronic, Inc.
Mellon Foundation, Andrew W.
Memton Fund
Merck & Co.
Meyer Fund, Milton and Sophie
Miller Brewing Company/North Carolina
Mobil Oil Corp.
Monell Foundation, Ambrose
Morris Foundation, Margaret T.
Mosbacher, Jr. Foundation, Emil
Muchnic Foundation
Munger Foundation, Alfred C.
New-Land Foundation
The New Yorker Magazine, Inc.
Newman's Own, Inc.
Noble Foundation, Edward John
North Shore Foundation
Overbrook Foundation
Packard Foundation, David and Lucile
Parsons Foundation, Ralph M.
Patterson Charitable Fund, W. I.
Peppers Foundation, Ann
Pew Charitable Trusts
Pfizer, Inc.
Phelps Dodge Corporation
Phillips Family Foundation, Jay and Rose
Plumsock Fund
Price Foundation, Lucien B. and Katherine E.
Prospect Hill Foundation
Public Welfare Foundation
Quivey-Bay State Foundation
Reisman Charitable Trust, George C. and Evelyn R.
Reynolds Foundation, Christopher
Rubinstein Foundation, Helena
Ryan Foundation, David Claude
Sasco Foundation
Sawyer Charitable Foundation
Scherman Foundation
Schiro Fund
Scholl Foundation, Dr.
Schowalter Foundation
Seidman Family Foundation
Sequoia Foundation

Skaggs Foundation, L. J. and Mary C.
Skillman Foundation
Sloan Foundation, Alfred P.
Smith Foundation, Ralph L.
Speyer Foundation, Alexander C. and Tillie S.
Starr Foundation
Stauffer Charitable Trust, John
Steele Foundation, Harry and Grace
Taconic Foundation
Taylor Foundation, Fred and Harriett
Texaco Inc.
Timken Foundation of Canton
Trull Foundation
Unger Foundation, Aber D.
Vanderbilt Trust, R. T.
Weber Charities Corp., Frederick E.
Whirlpool Corporation
Whiting Foundation
Wilson Foundation, H. W.
Young Foundation, Irvin L.

Human Rights

Ames Charitable Trust, Harriett
Atran Foundation
Baker Trust, George F.
Baldwin Foundation, David M. and Barbara
Bothin Foundation
Breyer Foundation
Cabot Family Charitable Trust
Carnegie Corporation of New York
Cayuga Foundation
Covington and Burling
Davis Foundation, Edwin W. and Catherine M.
Diamond Foundation, Aaron
Dr. Seuss Foundation
Donner Foundation, William H.
Everett Charitable Trust
Fikes Foundation, Leland
Ford Foundation
Ford Fund, William and Martha
Frese Foundation, Arnold D.
Friedman Family Foundation
Gilman Foundation, Howard
Globe Newspaper Co.
Griffis Foundation
Hauser Foundation
Hazen Foundation, Edward W.
Homeland Foundation
Jaffe Foundation
Jurzykowski Foundation, Alfred
Kaplan Fund, J. M.
Kennedy Foundation, Ethel
Knight Foundation, John S. and James L.
Kornfeld Foundation, Emily Davie and Joseph S.
Lazarus Charitable Trust, Helen and Charles
Loews Corporation
MacArthur Foundation, John D. and Catherine T.
Mailman Foundation
Morgan & Company, J.P.
Mott Fund, Ruth
New-Land Foundation
Normandie Foundation
North Shore Foundation
Odell Fund, Robert Stewart Odell and Helen Pfeiffer
Overbrook Foundation
Pettus Crowe Foundation
Pew Charitable Trusts
Pierce Charitable Trust, Harold Whitworth
Polaroid Corp.
Reicher Foundation, Anne and Harry J.
Rohatyn Foundation, Felix and Elizabeth
Rosen Foundation, Joseph
Rosenberg Foundation
Rosenberg, Jr. Family Foundation, Louise and Claude

Ruan Foundation Trust, John
Salomon Foundation, Richard and Edna
Scherman Foundation
Schiro Fund
Schuller International
Schwartz Fund for Education and Health Research, Arnold and Marie
Smart Family Foundation
Stein Foundation, Jules and Doris
Truland Foundation
Unger Foundation, Aber D.
Valentine Foundation, Lawson
Weil, Gotshal and Manges Foundation
Wiley & Sons, Inc., John
Woodward Fund

International Affairs

AlliedSignal Inc.
Amoco Corporation
Annenberg Foundation
AON Corporation
Archer-Daniels-Midland Co.
Argyros Foundation
Arnhold Foundation
Atherton Family Foundation
Auerbach Foundation, Beatrice Fox
Barry Corp., R. G.
Binswanger Cos.
Blum-Kovler Foundation
Bodman Foundation
Borman's Inc.
Breyer Foundation
Burkitt Foundation
Burlington Industries, Inc.
Carnegie Corporation of New York
Carter Foundation, Amon G.
CBS, Inc.
Chase Manhattan Bank, N.A.
Chevron Corporation
Clorox Co.
Crown Memorial, Arie and Ida
Culpeper Foundation, Charles E.
Dana Charitable Trust, Eleanor Naylor
Davis Foundation, Irene E. and George A.
Dexter Charitable Fund, Eugene A.
Dodge Foundation, Cleveland H.
Donner Foundation, William H.
Duncan Foundation, Lillian H. and C. W.
Dynamet, Inc.
Exxon Corporation
Forbes Inc.
Ford Foundation
France Foundation, Jacob and Annita
Freeport-McMoRan Inc.
Friendship Fund
Fuqua Foundation, J. B.
GenCorp Inc.
General Motors Corp.
Gershman Foundation, Joel
Gilman Foundation, Howard
Greve Foundation, William and Mary
Haas, Jr. Fund, Evelyn and Walter
Haley Foundation, W. B.
Handy and Harman Foundation
Harriman Foundation, Mary W.
Hasbro Inc.
Hatch Charitable Trust, Margaret Milliken
Hauser Foundation
Hazen Foundation, Edward W.
Heinz Company, H. J.
Heinz Endowment, Vira I.
Hewlett Foundation, William and Flora
Jacobs Family Foundation
Jacobson Foundation, Bernard H. and Blanche E.

Jurzykowski Foundation, Alfred
Kardon Foundation, Samuel and Rebecca
Kaufmann Foundation, Henry
Kirby Foundation, F. M.
Koopman Fund
Kuehn Foundation
Ladd Charitable Corporation, Helen and George
Landegger Charitable Foundation
Larsen Fund
Lea Foundation, Helen Sperry
Levy Foundation, June Rockwell
MacArthur Foundation, John D. and Catherine T.
Mardigian Foundation
Marpat Foundation
Mather Charitable Trust, S. Livingston
McShain Charities, John
Mellon Foundation, Andrew W.
Merck & Co.
Montana Power Co.
Morgan & Company, J.P.
Mott Fund, Ruth
Musson Charitable Foundation, R. C. and Katharine M.
Mutual Assurance Co.
Noble Foundation, Samuel Roberts
OCRI Foundation
OG&E Electric Services
Peppers Foundation, Ann
Pew Charitable Trusts
Pforzheimer Foundation, Carl and Lily
Premier Industrial Corp.
Providence Journal Company
Reynolds Foundation, Christopher
Robinson Fund, Maurice R.
Rockwell International Corporation
Rubin Foundation, Samuel
Rubinstein Foundation, Helena
Saint Paul Companies, Inc.
Salvatori Foundation, Henry
Schoenleber Foundation
Scholl Foundation, Dr.
Simon Foundation, William E. and Carol G.
Sloan Foundation, Alfred P.
Smith Foundation, Kelvin and Eleanor
Stans Foundation
Starr Foundation
Stearns Trust, Artemas W.
Subaru of America Inc.
Superior Tube Co.
Teleflex Inc.
Texaco Inc.
Thornton Foundation
Thornton Foundation, Flora L.
Times Mirror Company, The
Tucker Charitable Trust, Rose E.
Union Bank
Unocal Corp.
van Ameringen Foundation
Weber Charities Corp., Frederick E.
Weil, Gotshal and Manges Foundation
Western New York Foundation
Wiegand Foundation, E. L.
Wilson Foundation, H. W.
Wyomissing Foundation
Zachry Co., H.B.

International Development

Aetna Life & Casualty Co.
Archer-Daniels-Midland Co.
Avon Products, Inc.
Blaustein Foundation, Louis and Henrietta
Cabot Corp.

Carnegie Corporation of New York
Chase Manhattan Bank, N.A.
Chatlos Foundation
Clorox Co.
Columbia Foundation
Contran Corporation
Coors Foundation, Adolph
Covington and Burling
Culver Foundation, Constans
Dana Charitable Trust, Eleanor Naylor
Day Foundation, Nancy Sayles
Dodge Foundation, Geraldine R.
Donner Foundation, William H.
Erpf Fund, Armand G.
Favrot Fund
Fikes Foundation, Leland
Fohs Foundation
Ford Foundation
Ford Motor Co.
Friedman Family Foundation
Gilman Foundation, Howard
Glanville Family Foundation
Hatch Charitable Trust, Margaret Milliken
Hauser Foundation
Heinz Company, H. J.
Hewlett Foundation, William and Flora
Hoffman Foundation, Maximilian E. and Marion O.
Hoover, Jr. Foundation, Margaret W. and Herbert
Hunt Foundation
International Foundation
Jacobs Family Foundation
Jones Foundation, Fletcher
Jurzykowski Foundation, Alfred
Kempner Fund, Harris and Eliza
Kettering Fund
Laurel Foundation
MacArthur Foundation, John D. and Catherine T.
Marriott Foundation, J. Willard
Mattel, Inc.
M.E. Foundation
Mellon Foundation, Andrew W.
Morgan & Company, J.P.
Morris Foundation, Margaret T.
Mott Foundation, Charles Stewart
Mott Fund, Ruth
National Forge Co.
New-Land Foundation
North Shore Foundation
PaineWebber
Pew Charitable Trusts
Pfizer, Inc.
Price Foundation, Louis and Harold
Public Welfare Foundation
R. F. Foundation
Reicher Foundation, Anne and Harry J.
Reidler Foundation
Reynolds Foundation, Christopher
Rubin Foundation, Samuel
Scherman Foundation
Sequoia Foundation
Solow Foundation
Stanley Works
Starr Foundation
Sundet Foundation
Texaco Inc.
Thermo Electron Corp.
Trull Foundation
Unger Foundation, Aber D.
Valentine Foundation, Lawson
Wheeler Foundation, Wilmot
Woodward Fund

International Environmental Issues

Ahmanson Foundation
Aluminum Co. of America

Ames Charitable Trust, Harriett
Annenberg Foundation
Ansin Private Foundation, Ronald M.
Asplundh Foundation
Barker Foundation, J.M.R.
Bay Foundation
Bell Foundation, James F.
Bingham Foundation, William
Bright Family Foundation
Burkitt Foundation
Carolyn Foundation
Castle Foundation, Harold K. L.
Chadwick Fund, Dorothy Jordan
Chastain Charitable Foundation, Robert Lee and Thomas M.
Claiborne and Art Ortenberg Foundation, Liz
Clapp Charitable and Educational Trust, George H.
Coleman Foundation, George E.
Columbia Foundation
Cooperman Foundation, Leon and Toby
Cowell Foundation, S. H.
Crabtree & Evelyn
Day Foundation, Nancy Sayles
Donnelley Foundation, Gaylord and Dorothy
Donner Foundation, William H.
Eastman Kodak Company
Erpf Fund, Armand G.
Ettinger Foundation
Exxon Corporation
Fair Play Foundation
Fikes Foundation, Leland
Ford Foundation
Getty Trust, J. Paul
Glencoe Foundation
Hazen Foundation, Edward W.
Heinz Trust, Drue
Higginson Trust, Corina
Icahn Foundation, Carl C.
International Foundation
Ittleson Foundation
Jewett Foundation, George Frederick
Johnson Foundation, Helen K. and Arthur E.
Jurzykowski Foundation, Alfred
Kinney-Lindstrom Foundation
Koret Foundation
Kresge Foundation
Laurel Foundation
Louisiana-Pacific Corp.
MacArthur Foundation, John D. and Catherine T.
Mahadh Foundation
Mailman Foundation
Mars Foundation
McLean Con ibutionship
Mellon Foundation, Andrew W.
Mellon Foundation, Richard King
Merck Family Fund
Mott Foundation, Charles Stewart
Mott Fund, Ruth
Noble Foundation, Edward John
Normandie Foundation
Overbrook Foundation
Packard Foundation, David and Lucile
Peters Foundation, R. D. and Linda
Pew Charitable Trusts
Potts and Sibley Foundation
Prospect Hill Foundation
Public Welfare Foundation
Reynolds Foundation, Christopher
Roseburg Forest Products Co.
Rosenberg, Jr. Family Foundation, Louise and Claude
Ross Memorial Foundation, Will
Rubin Foundation, Samuel

Scherman Foundation
Schroeder Foundation, Walter
Sequoia Foundation
South Waite Foundation
Stans Foundation
Sulzberger Foundation
Thomas Foundation, Joan and Lee
Valentine Foundation, Lawson
Wege Foundation
Wheeler Foundation
Wilder Foundation
Young Foundation, Irvin L.

International Organizations

Aetna Life & Casualty Co.
Aluminum Co. of America
Ames Charitable Trust, Harriett
Amoco Corporation
Annenberg Foundation
Ansin Private Foundation, Ronald M.
ASDA Foundation
Binswanger Cos.
Bobst Foundation, Elmer and Mamdouha
Borman's Inc.
Bristol-Myers Squibb Company
Burkitt Foundation
Cain Foundation, Gordon and Mary
Carnegie Corporation of New York
Cayuga Foundation
Cheatham Foundation, Owen
Commerce Clearing House, Incorporated
Copley Press, Inc.
Cowell Foundation, S. H.
Demos Foundation, N.
Digital Equipment Corp.
Dillon Foundation
Dr. Seuss Foundation
Dodge Foundation, Cleveland H.
Donner Foundation, William H.
Dow Jones & Company, Inc.
Dreyfus Foundation, Jean and Louis
Duncan Trust, John G.
Erpf Fund, Armand G.
Fabri-Kal Corp.
Feil Foundation, Louis and Gertrude
Fleishhacker Foundation
Ford Foundation
Fribourg Foundation
Friedman Family Foundation
Friendship Fund
Fruehauf Foundation
Giant Eagle, Inc.
Glencoe Foundation
Goldberg Family Foundation
Goldsmith Foundation, Horace W.
Gould Foundation, The Florence
Graham Fund, Philip L.
Hafif Family Foundation
Hallberg Foundation, E. L. and R. F.
Halsell Foundation, Ewing
Hammer Foundation, Armand
Hanson Industries North America
Hauser Foundation
Heinz Company, H. J.
Heinz Endowment, Vira I.
Heinz Trust, Drue
Heller Charitable Foundation, Clarence E.
Hermann Foundation, Grover
Hershey Foundation, Barry J.
Herzstein Charitable Foundation, Albert and Ethel
Hewlett-Packard Co.
Hoffman Foundation, Maximilian E. and Marion O.
Hunt Foundation
International Foundation

Johnson Charitable Educational Trust, James Hervey
Johnson Fund, Edward C.
Jurzykowski Foundation, Alfred
Kaufmann Foundation, Henry
Kelley and Elza Kelley Foundation, Edward Bangs
Klipstein Foundation, Ernest Christian
Knight Foundation, John S. and James L.
Koch Charitable Foundation, Charles G.
Komes Foundation
Koret Foundation
Kress Foundation, Samuel H.
Kuehn Foundation
LBJ Family Foundation
Lea Foundation, Helen Sperry
Levy Foundation, June Rockwell
Link, Jr. Foundation, George
Littauer Foundation, Lucius N.
MacArthur Foundation, John D. and Catherine T.
Mandeville Foundation
Margoes Foundation
Markle Foundation, John and Mary R.
Marpat Foundation
Mather Charitable Trust, S. Livingston
Mather Fund, Richard
McCarty Foundation, John and Margaret
McGonagle Foundation, Dextra Baldwin
M.E. Foundation
Mead Foundation, The
Mellon Family Foundation, R. K.
Metropolitan Life Insurance Co.
Middendorf Foundation
Mosbacher, Jr. Foundation, Emil
Mott Foundation, Charles Stewart
Munson Foundation Trust, W. B.
New-Land Foundation
Newman's Own, Inc.
Noble Foundation, Samuel Roberts
Normandie Foundation
Norton Co.
Odell Fund, Robert Stewart Odell and Helen Pfeiffer
Osher Foundation, Bernard
Overbrook Foundation
Pennsylvania Dutch Co.
Pew Charitable Trusts
Piankova Foundation, Tatiana
Plumsock Fund
Rabb Foundation, Harry W.
Reynolds Foundation, Christopher
Richardson Charitable Trust, Anne S.
Rixson Foundation, Oscar C.
Rohatyn Foundation, Felix and Elizabeth
Rosen Foundation, Joseph
Rubin Foundation, Samuel
Russell Trust, Josephine G.
Ryan Foundation, David Claude
Scherman Foundation
Schmitt Foundation, Kilian J. and Caroline F.
Scholl Foundation, Dr.
Seagram & Sons, Inc., Joseph E.
Simon Foundation, William E. and Carol G.
Sloan Foundation, Alfred P.
Smeal Foundation, Mary Jean and Frank P.
Smith Foundation, Gordon V. and Helen C.
Smith Trust, May and Stanley

Solow Foundation
South Waite Foundation
Starr Foundation
Stauffer Foundation, John and Beverly
Sulzberger Foundation
Sundet Foundation
Taube Family Foundation
Taylor Foundation, Ruth and Vernon
Teleflex Inc.
Thermo Electron Corp.
Times Mirror Company, The
Timken Foundation of Canton
Turrell Fund
Unocal Corp.
Valentine Foundation, Lawson
Vetlesen Foundation, G. Unger
Wendt Foundation, Margaret L.
Western New York Foundation
Whirlpool Corporation
Wilson Foundation, H. W.
Winthrop Trust, Clara B.

International Peace & Security Issues

Ahmanson Foundation
Air Products and Chemicals, Inc.
Alavi Foundation of New York
Alexander Foundation, Joseph
Aluminum Co. of America
American Brands, Inc.
Ansin Private Foundation, Ronald M.
Archer-Daniels-Midland Co.
Atran Foundation
Bay Foundation
Blum-Kovler Foundation
Booth Ferris Foundation
Brillion Iron Works
Cabot Family Charitable Trust
Carnegie Corporation of New York
CBS, Inc.
Chadwick Fund, Dorothy Jordan
Chase Manhattan Bank, N.A.
Chastain Charitable Foundation, Robert Lee and Thomas M.
Chatlos Foundation
Chevron Corporation
Citibank
Claiborne and Art Ortenberg Foundation, Liz
Coleman Foundation, George E.
Columbia Foundation
Coors Foundation, Adolph
CPC International Inc.
Crane Co.
Cummins Engine Co. tr
Dater Foundation, Charles H.
Davenport-Hatch Foundation
Davis Foundation, Edwin W. and Catherine M.
Day Foundation, Nancy Sayles
Delaware North Co., Inc.
Demos Foundation, N.
Dimeo Construction Co.
Dodge Foundation, Cleveland H.
Donner Foundation, William H.
Dresser Industries, Inc.
du Pont de Nemours & Co., E. I.
Duke Power Co.
Dunagan Foundation
Eaton Foundation, Cyrus
English Memorial Fund, Florence C. and H. L.
Erpf Fund, Armand G.
Exxon Corporation
Fairchild Foundation, Sherman
Federal-Mogul Corporation
Fohs Foundation
Forbes Inc.
Ford Foundation
Frese Foundation, Arnold D.
Fribourg Foundation

AON Corporation
Archer-Daniels-Midland Co.
Armco Inc.
ASDA Foundation
Astor Foundation, Vincent
AT&T Corp.
Auerbach Foundation,
Beatrice Fox
Baehr Foundation, Louis W.
and Dolpha
Baldwin Memorial
Foundation, Fred
BankAmerica Corp.
Bankers Trust Company
Barker Foundation, J.M.R.
Barra Foundation
Benenson Foundation, Frances
and Benjamin
Binney & Smith Inc.
Block, H&R
Blum-Kovler Foundation
Borden, Inc.
Bristol-Myers Squibb
Company
Cabot Corp.
Carnegie Corporation of New
York
Cayuga Foundation
Chase Manhattan Bank, N.A.
Chazen Foundation
Chevron Corporation
Citibank
Coleman Foundation, George
E.
Columbia Foundation
Columbus Dispatch Printing
Co.
Consumers Power Co.
Continental Corp.
CPC International Inc.
CS First Boston Corporation
Cummins Engine Co.
Davis Foundation, Edwin W.
and Catherine M.
Delaware North Co., Inc.
Dewing Foundation, Frances R.
Dillon Dunwalke Trust,
Clarence and Anne
Dodge Foundation, Cleveland
H.
Donner Foundation, William H.
Dow Jones & Company, Inc.
Dresser Industries, Inc.
du Pont de Nemours & Co., E.
I.
Duke Power Co.
Dynamet, Inc.
Early Foundation
Eaton Corporation
Erpf Fund, Armand G.
Ettinger Foundation
Exxon Corporation
Ferebee Endowment, Percy O.
First Fidelity Bank
Fohs Foundation
Fondren Foundation
Forbes Inc.
Ford Foundation
Ford Motor Co.
Freeman Charitable Trust,
Samuel
Fribourg Foundation
Friedman Family Foundation
Frost National Bank
Fry Foundation, Lloyd A.
Fuqua Foundation, J. B.
Gallagher Family Foundation,
Lewis P.
General Motors Corp.
Goldsmith Foundation, Horace
W.
Gordon/Rousmaniere/Roberts
Fund
Gould Foundation, The
Florence
Graham Fund, Philip L.
Greve Foundation, William
and Mary
Griggs and Mary Griggs Burke
Foundation, Mary Livingston
Guttman Foundation, Stella
and Charles
Haley Foundation, W. B.
Hancock Foundation, Luke B.
Harriman Foundation, Mary W.

Hassenfeld Foundation
Hauser Foundation
Hazen Foundation, Edward W.
Hechinger Co.
Hedco Foundation
Heinz Company, H. J.
Heinz Trust, Drue
Henkel Corp.
Henry Foundation, Patrick
Hermann Foundation, Grover
Hewlett Foundation, William
and Flora
Hewlett-Packard Co.
Hoffmann-La Roche Inc.
Hoover Fund-Trust, W. Henry
Hunt Foundation
Hunt Foundation, Roy A.
Independence Foundation
Jacobs Family Foundation
Jewett Foundation, George
Frederick
Johnson Controls Inc.
Johnson & Son, S.C.
Jones Foundation, Helen
Jordan Charitable Foundation,
Mary Ranken Jordan and
Ettie A.
Jurzykowski Foundation,
Alfred
Kaplun Foundation, Morris J.
and Betty
Kempner Fund, Harris and
Eliza
Kimberly-Clark Corp.
Klosk Fund, Louis and Rose
Knox, Sr., and Pearl Wallis
Knox Charitable
Foundation, Robert W.
Koopman Fund
Kresge Foundation
Lasdon Foundation
Laurel Foundation
LBJ Family Foundation
Lea Foundation, Helen Sperry
Lennon Foundation, Fred A.
Levy Foundation, June
Rockwell
Lipton, Thomas J.
Littauer Foundation, Lucius N.
MacArthur Foundation, John
D. and Catherine T.
Mandeville Foundation
Markle Foundation, John and
Mary R.
Marriott Foundation, J. Willard
Mather Charitable Trust, S.
Livingston
Mathis-Pfohl Foundation
Maytag Family Foundation,
Fred
McCune Charitable Trust,
John R.
McFeely-Rogers Foundation
McKenna Foundation, Philip
M.
M.E. Foundation
Mellon Foundation, Andrew W.
Merck & Co.
Merrill Lynch & Co., Inc.
Meyer Fund, Milton and
Sophie
Mitsubishi International Corp.
Mitsubishi Motor Sales of
America, Inc.
Mobil Oil Corp.
Morgan & Company, J.P.
Morrison Knudsen Corporation
Mott Foundation, Charles
Stewart
Mott Fund, Ruth
Mulford Foundation, Vincent
National Westminster Bank
New Jersey
New-Land Foundation
Newman's Own, Inc.
Noble Foundation, Edward
John
Normandie Foundation
North Shore Foundation
Oppenstein Brothers
Foundation
Osborn Charitable Trust,
Edward B.
Overbrook Foundation
Pew Charitable Trusts

Pfizer, Inc.
Phelps Dodge Corporation
PPG Industries, Inc.
Prospect Hill Foundation
Pulitzer Publishing Co.
Putnam Foundation
Quaker Chemical Corp.
Rabb Foundation, Harry W.
Ralston Purina Co.
Reed Foundation
Reynolds Foundation,
Christopher
Rixson Foundation, Oscar C.
RJR Nabisco Inc.
Rockwell International
Corporation
Rohatyn Foundation, Felix and
Elizabeth
Rouse Co.
Rubin Foundation, Samuel
Salomon Foundation, Richard
and Edna
Salvatori Foundation, Henry
Sarkeys Foundation
Schering-Plough Corp.
Seagram & Sons, Inc., Joseph
E.
Sequoia Foundation
Shell Oil Company
Simon Foundation, William E.
and Carol G.
Sloan Foundation, Alfred P.
Speyer Foundation, Alexander
C. and Tillie S.
Starr Foundation
Stein Foundation, Jules and
Doris
Superior Tube Co.
Taconic Foundation
Taubman Foundation, A. Alfred
Taylor Foundation, Ruth and
Vernon
Texaco Inc.
Textron, Inc.
Thomas Foundation, Joan and
Lee
Times Mirror Company, The
Tozer Foundation
Union Bank
Unocal Corp.
Valentine Foundation, Lawson
Vetlesen Foundation, G. Unger
Wean Foundation, Raymond
John
Weil, Gotshal and Manges
Foundation
Westvaco Corporation
Whirlpool Corporation
Whiting Foundation
Williams Companies, The
Wyomissing Foundation
Young Foundation, Irvin L.
Young Foundation, Robert R.
Zachry Co., H.B.

International Relief
Efforts

Alavi Foundation of New York
Allen Brothers Foundation
Aluminum Co. of America
Archer-Daniels-Midland Co.
Arkell Hall Foundation
Babson Foundation, Paul and
Edith
Baldwin Foundation, David
M. and Barbara
Barker Foundation, J.M.R.
Barra Foundation
Bay Foundation
Benenson Foundation, Frances
and Benjamin
Besser Foundation
Blum-Kovler Foundation
Bobst Foundation, Elmer and
Mamdouha
Charina Foundation
Chartwell Foundation
Chatlos Foundation
Chesapeake Corp.
Chevron Corporation
Connelly Foundation
Cowell Foundation, S. H.

Crane Co.
Davis Foundation, Edwin W.
and Catherine M.
Dillon Dunwalke Trust,
Clarence and Anne
Dr. Seuss Foundation
Donner Foundation, William H.
Erpf Fund, Armand G.
Folger Fund
Forbes Inc.
Ford Foundation
Fribourg Foundation
Friedman Family Foundation
Frisch's Restaurants Inc.
Fruehauf Foundation
Fry Foundation, Lloyd A.
Goldsmith Foundation, Horace
W.
Guttman Foundation, Stella
and Charles
Hancock Foundation, Luke B.
Hanson Industries North
America
Hedco Foundation
Heinz Company, H. J.
Hewlett-Packard Co.
Hoffman Foundation,
Maximilian E. and Marion O.
Hunt Foundation
Icahn Foundation, Carl C.
Imperial Bancorp
International Foundation
Jurzykowski Foundation,
Alfred
Kaplan Fund, J. M.
Kempner Fund, Harris and
Eliza
Kreitler Foundation
Lang Foundation, Eugene M.
Lauder Foundation
Loews Corporation
MacLeod Stewardship
Foundation
Mahadh Foundation
Mardigian Foundation
Mattel, Inc.
Mellon Foundation, Richard
King
Merrill Lynch & Co., Inc.
Morgan & Company, J.P.
Muchnic Foundation
Murdock Charitable Trust, M.
J.
Newman's Own, Inc.
Normandie Foundation
North Shore Foundation
OCRI Foundation
O'Quinn Foundation, John M.
and Nancy C.
Overbrook Foundation
PaineWebber
Parvin Foundation, Albert
Pew Charitable Trusts
Price Foundation, Louis and
Harold
Price Foundation, Lucien B.
and Katherine E.
Prouty Foundation, Olive
Higgins
Public Welfare Foundation
Reynolds Foundation,
Christopher
Rixson Foundation, Oscar C.
RJR Nabisco Inc.
Rohatyn Foundation, Felix and
Elizabeth
Rubin Foundation, Samuel
Rubinstein Foundation, Helena
Ryan Foundation, David
Claude
Sandy Hill Foundation
Sawyer Charitable Foundation
Scherman Foundation
Schwob Foundation, Simon
Seaver Charitable Trust,
Richard C.
Seidman Family Foundation
Shaw Foundation, Arch W.
Simon Foundation, William E.
and Carol G.
Skillman Foundation
Smith Foundation, Gordon V.
and Helen C.
Starr Foundation
Texaco Inc.

Titus Foundation, Roy and
Niuta
Trull Foundation
Westerman Foundation,
Samuel L.
Whitecap Foundation
Young Foundation, Irvin L.

Missionary/Religious
Activities

Abell-Hanger Foundation
Ahmanson Foundation
Alavi Foundation of New York
Alexander Foundation, Joseph
Allyn Foundation
Altschul Foundation
Amado Foundation, Maurice
Amoco Corporation
Andreas Foundation
Annenberg Foundation
Atran Foundation
Baldwin Foundation, David
M. and Barbara
Barry Corp., R. G.
Benenson Foundation, Frances
and Benjamin
Bingham Foundation, William
Binswanger Cos.
Blum-Kovler Foundation
Borman's Inc.
Brach Foundation, Helen
Brooks Foundation, Gladys
Burkitt Foundation
Campini Foundation, Frank A.
Carnegie Corporation of New
York
Cassett Foundation, Louis N.
Chartwell Foundation
Chatlos Foundation
Chazen Foundation
Clemens Markets Corp.
Columbia Foundation
Connelly Foundation
Cooperman Foundation, Leon
and Toby
Crown Books
Crown Memorial, Arie and Ida
Dart Group Corp.
Davis Foundations, Arthur
Vining
Duchossois Industries Inc.
Feil Foundation, Louis and
Gertrude
Feild Co-Operative Association
Fikes Foundation, Leland
Fink Foundation
First Hawaiian, Inc.
Fischbach Foundation
Flowers Charitable Trust,
Albert W. and Edith V.
Fohs Foundation
Foster Charitable Trust
Fribourg Foundation
Geifman Family Foundation
Gershman Foundation, Joel
Giant Eagle, Inc.
Glosser Foundation, David A.
Goldberg Family Foundation
Goldie-Anna Charitable Trust
Goldsmith Foundation, Horace
W.
Guttman Foundation, Stella
and Charles
Hafif Family Foundation
Hammer Foundation, Armand
Hanover Foundation
Hassenfeld Foundation
Heinz Endowment, Vira I.
Herzstein Charitable
Foundation, Albert and Ethel
Hillsdale Fund
Hoffman Foundation,
Maximilian E. and Marion O.
Homeland Foundation
Hopkins Foundation,
Josephine Lawrence
Huston Charitable Trust,
Stewart
Huston Foundation
International Foundation
Jaffe Foundation

Kaplun Foundation, Morris J. and Betty
Kardon Foundation, Samuel and Rebecca
Klosk Fund, Louis and Rose
Koret Foundation
Kutz Foundation, Milton and Hattie
LamCo. Communications
Landegger Charitable Foundation
Lasdon Foundation
Lasdon Foundation, William and Mildred
Lichtenstein Foundation, David B.
Littauer Foundation, Lucius N.
MacArthur Foundation, John D. and Catherine T.
Mailman Foundation
Mardigian Foundation
Marshall Trust in Memory of Sanders McDaniel, Harriet McDaniel
Martini Foundation, Nicholas
Matthies Foundation, Katharine
McCann Foundation
McCarty Foundation, John and Margaret
McGee Foundation
McGonagle Foundation, Dextra Baldwin
M.E. Foundation
Meyer Family Foundation, Paul J.
Meyer Fund, Milton and Sophie
Meyerhoff Fund, Joseph
Mnuchin Foundation
Morgan Foundation, Burton D.
Newman's Own, Inc.
Nias Foundation, Henry
North Shore Foundation
OCRI Foundation
Odell Fund, Robert Stewart Odell and Helen Pfeiffer
Park Foundation
Pew Charitable Trusts
Philibosian Foundation, Stephen
Phipps Foundation, Howard
Pitt-Des Moines Inc.
Putnam Foundation
R. F. Foundation
Raymond Corp.
Read Foundation, Charles L.
Reicher Foundation, Anne and Harry J.
Reynolds Foundation, Christopher
Rixson Foundation, Oscar C.
Rohatyn Foundation, Felix and Elizabeth
Rosen Foundation, Joseph
Rosenberg, Jr. Family Foundation, Louise and Claude
Scherman Foundation
Schowalter Foundation
Schwartz Fund for Education and Health Research, Arnold and Marie
Schwob Foundation, Simon
Seagram & Sons, Inc., Joseph E.
Seaver Charitable Trust, Richard C.
Slifka Foundation, Joseph and Sylvia
Smith Foundation, Gordon V. and Helen C.
Smith Trust, May and Stanley
Solow Foundation
Stein Foundation, Jules and Doris
Stevens Foundation, Abbot and Dorothy H.
Stone Charitable Foundation
Sturgis Charitable and Educational Trust, Roy and Christine
Sundet Foundation
Taube Family Foundation
Taubman Foundation, A. Alfred
Timken Foundation of Canton

Travelers Inc.
Trull Foundation
Trust Funds
Turner Charitable Foundation
Weingart Foundation
Weinstein Foundation, J.
Westerman Foundation, Samuel L.
Whitney Fund, David M.
Young Foundation, Irvin L.
Zlinkoff Fund for Medical Research and Education, Sergei S.

Trade

Bank One, Youngstown, NA
Carnegie Corporation of New York
Ford Foundation
Mellon Foundation, Andrew W.
Mott Fund, Ruth
Pew Charitable Trusts
Starr Foundation

Religion

Bible Study/Translation

Berger Foundation, H. N. and Frances C.
Bowen Foundation, Ethel N.
Burchfield Foundation, Charles E.
Chatlos Foundation
Clemens Markets Corp.
Crane Co.
Cuneo Foundation
Flowers Charitable Trust, Albert W. and Edith V.
GSM Industrial
Hallett Charitable Trust, Jessie F.
Huston Foundation
Jewell Memorial Foundation, Daniel Ashley and Irene Houston
Mays Foundation
Murdock Charitable Trust, M. J.
Rixson Foundation, Oscar C.
Ryan Foundation, David Claude
Schowalter Foundation
Schwartz Fund for Education and Health Research, Arnold and Marie
Taubman Foundation, A. Alfred
Trull Foundation
Young Foundation, Irvin L.

Churches

Acushnet Co.
Aetna Life & Casualty Co.
Ahmanson Foundation
AKC Fund
Allegheny Ludlum Corp.
Allianz Life Insurance Co. of North America
AlliedSignal Inc.
Allyn Foundation
American Fidelity Corporation
Amfac/JMB Hawaii Inc.
Andersen Corp.
Andersen Foundation
Anderson Foundation, John W.
Andersons, The
Andreas Foundation
Annenberg Foundation
Ansin Private Foundation, Ronald M.
Ansley Foundation, Dantzler Bond
AON Corporation
Appleby Trust, Scott B. and Annie P.

Arakelian Foundation, Mary Alice
Arcadia Foundation
Archer-Daniels-Midland Co.
Argyros Foundation
Arkelian Foundation, Ben H. and Gladys
Arkell Hall Foundation
Armstrong Foundation
Arnold Fund
Ashtabula Foundation
Asplundh Foundation
Astor Foundation, Vincent
Atherton Family Foundation
Audubon State Bank
Auerbach Foundation, Beatrice Fox
Ayres Foundation, Inc.
Baker Foundation, Dexter F. and Dorothy H.
Baker Trust, George F.
Baldwin Foundation, David M. and Barbara
Baldwin Memorial Foundation, Fred
Barra Foundation
Barry Corp., R. G.
Barth Foundation, Theodore H.
Batts Foundation
Beazley Foundation/Frederick Foundation
Bechtel, Jr. Foundation, S. D.
Beck Foundation, Elsie E. and Joseph W.
Bell Foundation, James F.
Benedum Foundation, Claude Worthington
Berger Foundation, H. N. and Frances C.
Besser Foundation
Betts Industries
Beveridge Foundation, Frank Stanley
Birnschein Foundation, Alvin and Marion
Bishop Foundation, E. K. and Lillian F.
Blake Foundation, S. P.
Blount Educational and Charitable Foundation, Mildred Weedon
Blue Bell, Inc.
Bobst Foundation, Elmer and Mamdouha
Borden, Inc.
Borman's Inc.
Bowen Foundation, Ethel N.
Bowne Foundation, Robert
Brach Foundation, Helen
Brady Foundation
Bremer Foundation, Otto
Breyer Foundation
Bright Family Foundation
Brillion Iron Works
Broadhurst Foundation
Brown Foundation, M. K.
Bryant Foundation
Burchfield Foundation, Charles E.
Burden Foundation, Florence V.
Burkitt Foundation
Cabell Foundation, Robert G. Cabell III and Maude Morgan
Caestecker Foundation, Charles and Marie
Cain Foundation, Effie and Wofford
Cain Foundation, Gordon and Mary
Calder Foundation, Louis
Calhoun Charitable Trust, Kenneth
Callaway Foundation
Campbell Foundation
Campbell Foundation, Ruth and Henry
Carnahan-Jackson Foundation
Carolyn Foundation
Carpenter Foundation, E. Rhodes and Leona B.
Carpenter Technology Corp.
Carter Foundation, Beirne
Cassett Foundation, Louis N.

Cayuga Foundation
CBS, Inc.
Central National Bank
Chadwick Fund, Dorothy Jordan
Champlin Foundations
Chapin Foundation of Myrtle Beach, South Carolina
Chapman Charitable Corporation, Howard and Bess
Chatlos Foundation
Christensen Charitable and Religious Foundation, L. C.
Clarke Trust, John
Clarkson Foundation, Jeniam
Clay Foundation
Clemens Markets Corp.
Clemens Foundation
Close Foundation
Clowes Fund
Coen Family Foundation, Charles S. and Mary
Cogswell Benevolent Trust
Cole Trust, Quincy
Coleman Foundation, George E.
Collins Foundation
Collins Foundation, George and Jennie
Collins, Jr. Foundation, George Fulton
Columbus Dispatch Printing Co.
Commerce Clearing House, Incorporated
Comprecare Foundation
Connelly Foundation
Contran Corporation
Cooke Foundation
Cooperman Foundation, Leon and Toby
Cord Foundation, E. L.
Cornell Trust, Peter C.
Cosmair, Inc.
Coughlin-Saunders Foundation
Crandall Memorial Foundation, J. Ford
Crawford Estate, E. R.
Crestlea Foundation
Crown Books
Culpeper Memorial Foundation, Daphne Seybolt
Culver Foundation, Constans
Cummings Foundation, James H.
Cuneo Foundation
Dalton Foundation, Harry L.
Dana Charitable Trust, Eleanor Naylor
Daniel Foundation of Alabama
Darby Foundation
Daugherty Foundation
Davenport-Hatch Foundation
Davenport Trust Fund
Davis Foundation, Edwin W. and Catherine M.
Davis Foundation, Irene E. and George A.
Davis Foundation, James A. and Juliet L.
Day Foundation, Nancy Sayles
Delavan Foundation, Nelson B.
Dell Foundation, Hazel
Demoulas Supermarkets Inc.
Dentsply International Inc.
DeRoy Foundation, Helen L.
DeRoy Testamentary Foundation
Deuble Foundation, George H.
DeVore Foundation
Dexter Charitable Fund, Eugene A.
Dillon Dunwalke Trust, Clarence and Anne
Dillon Foundation
Dimeo Construction Co.
Dingman Foundation, Michael D.
Dodge Foundation, Cleveland H.
Donaldson Company, Inc.
Donnelley Foundation, Gaylord and Dorothy
Douty Foundation

Dover Foundation
Dow Foundation, Herbert H. and Grace A.
Dreyfus Foundation, Max and Victoria
Duchossois Industries Inc.
Duke Endowment
Dula Educational and Charitable Foundation, Caleb C. and Julia W.
Duncan Foundation, Lillian H. and C. W.
duPont Foundation, Alfred I.
Early Foundation
Eccles Foundation, Ralph M. and Ella M.
Einstein Fund, Albert E. and Birdie W.
Elkins, Jr. Foundation, Margaret and James A.
Emerson Foundation, Inc., Fred L.
Ensign-Bickford Industries
Essick Foundation
Ettinger Foundation
Evans Foundation, T. M.
Evans Foundation, Thomas J.
Everett Charitable Trust
Exchange National Bank
Fair Foundation, R. W.
Fair Play Foundation
Farish Fund, William Stamps
Fenton Foundation
Fikes Foundation, Leland
Finch Foundation, Doak
Finch Foundation, Thomas Austin
First Hawaiian, Inc.
First National Bank
First Union Corp.
Fish Foundation, Ray C.
Flowers Charitable Trust, Albert W. and Edith V.
Folger Fund
Fondren Foundation
Forbes Inc.
Ford Fund, William and Martha
Ford II Fund, Henry
Forest Foundation
Foster Foundation
France Foundation, Jacob and Annita
Frear Eleemosynary Trust, Mary D. and Walter F.
Freeman Charitable Trust, Samuel
Freeport-McMoRan Inc.
French Foundation, D.E.
Frese Foundation, Arnold D.
Friendship Fund
Frohring Foundation, William O. and Gertrude Lewis
Frost National Bank
Fruehauf Foundation
Fry Foundation, Lloyd A.
Fuller Foundation, C. G.
Fuqua Foundation, J. B.
Gallagher Family Foundation, Lewis P.
GAR Foundation
Gebbie Foundation
Gellert Foundation, Carl
Gellert Foundation, Celia Berta
General American Life Insurance Co.
Geneseo Foundation
German Protestant Orphan Asylum Association
Gheens Foundation
Giles Foundation, Edward C.
Gilmore Foundation, William G.
Glanville Family Foundation
Glenn Foundation, Carrie C. and Lena V.
Goddard Foundation, Charles B.
Goldie-Anna Charitable Trust
Goldsmith Foundation, Horace W.
Gordon/Rousmaniere/Roberts Fund
Graham Fund, Philip L.
Green Foundation, Allen P. and Josephine B.

Gregg-Graniteville Foundation
Griswold Foundation, John C.
GSM Industrial
Gulf Coast Medical Foundation
Haas, Jr. Fund, Evelyn and Walter
Habig Foundation, Arnold F.
Hafif Family Foundation
Hagedorn Fund
Hallberg Foundation, E. L. and R. F.
Hallett Charitable Trust, E. W.
Hallett Charitable Trust, Jessie F.
Halsell Foundation, Ewing
Hamilton Bank
Hamman Foundation, George and Mary Josephine
Hammer Foundation, Armand
Hanes Foundation, John W. and Anna H.
Harmon Foundation, Pearl M. and Julia J.
Harrington Foundation, Francis A. and Jacquelyn H.
Harrison Foundation, Fred G.
Hartz Foundation
Harvey Foundation, Felix
Hassenfeld Foundation
Hatch Charitable Trust, Margaret Milliken
Hawn Foundation
Hazen Foundation, Edward W.
Hechinger Co.
Hecht-Levi Foundation
Heckscher Foundation for Children
Heginbotham Trust, Will E.
Heinz Endowment, Vira I.
Helms Foundation
Henderson Foundation, George B.
Herrick Foundation
Herzstein Charitable Foundation, Albert and Ethel
Heydt Fund, Nan and Matilda
High Foundation
Hill Foundation, Sandy
Hillcrest Foundation
Hillsdale Fund
Hoag Family Foundation, George
Hobby Foundation
Hoffmann-La Roche Inc.
Holt Family Foundation
Holzer Memorial Foundation, Richard H.
Homeland Foundation
Hoover Fund-Trust, W. Henry
Hopkins Foundation, Josephine Lawrence
Hopwood Charitable Trust, John M.
Houchens Foundation, Ervin G.
Housatonic Curtain Co.
Houston Endowment
Howe and Mitchell B. Howe Foundation, Lucille Horton
Hoyt Foundation
Hoyt Foundation, Stewart W. and Willma C.
Hugoton Foundation
Huisking Foundation
Hulme Charitable Foundation, Milton G.
Humphrey Fund, George M. and Pamela S.
Hunt Charitable Trust, C. Giles
Hunt Foundation
Hunt Foundation, Samuel P.
Huston Charitable Trust, Stewart
Huston Foundation
Huthsteiner Fine Arts Trust
Hyde and Watson Foundation
Hygeia Dairy Co.
Ittleson Foundation
Jameson Foundation, J. W. and Ida M.
Jaydor Corp.
Jennings Foundation, Mary Hillman
Jewett Foundation, George Frederick
Jockey Hollow Foundation

Johnson Foundation, Burdine
Johnson Foundation, Helen K. and Arthur E.
Johnson Fund, Edward C.
Jones Foundation, Harvey and Bernice
Jones Foundation, Helen
Jordan Charitable Foundation, Mary Ranken Jordan and Ettie A.
Joslin-Needham Family Foundation
Journal-Gazette Co.
Joy Family Foundation
Julia R. and Estelle L. Foundation
Justus Trust, Edith C.
Kaplan Fund, J. M.
Kavanagh Foundation, T. James
Kelly Tractor Co.
Kemper Foundation, William T.
Kent-Lucas Foundation
Kilcawley Fund, William H.
Kinney-Lindstrom Foundation
Kirbo Charitable Trust, Thomas M. and Irene B.
Kirby Foundation, F. M.
Klipstein Foundation, Ernest Christian
Klock and Lucia Klock
Kingston Foundation, Jay E.
Knox, Sr., and Pearl Wallis Knox Charitable Foundation, Robert W.
Knudsen Foundation, Tom and Valley
Komes Foundation
Kreitler Foundation
Kuehn Foundation
Kunkel Foundation, John Crain
Kuyper Foundation, Peter H. and E. Lucille
La-Z-Boy Chair Co.
Ladd Charitable Corporation, Helen and George
Laffey-McHugh Foundation
LamCo. Communications
Landegger Charitable Foundation
Lang Foundation, Eugene M.
Larsen Fund
LBJ Family Foundation
Leavey Foundation, Thomas and Dorothy
Lee Endowment Foundation
LEF Foundation
Leighton-Oare Foundation
Lennon Foundation, Fred A.
Leuthold Foundation
Lichtenstein Foundation, David B.
Link, Jr. Foundation, George
Lockhart Vaughan Foundation
Love Foundation, George H. and Margaret McClintic
Lovett Foundation
Lurie Foundation, Louis R.
Lyon Foundation
MacLeod Stewardship Foundation
Maddox Foundation, J. F.
Magowan Family Foundation
Mahadh Foundation
Mailman Foundation
Mandeville Foundation
Maneely Fund
Mardigian Foundation
Markey Charitable Fund, John C.
Marpat Foundation
Marriott Foundation, J. Willard
Mars Foundation
Marshall Foundation, Mattie H.
Martin Marietta Materials
Martini Foundation, Nicholas
Mathis-Pfohl Foundation
Mattel, Inc.
Mautz Paint Co.
Mays Foundation
McBean Charitable Trust, Alletta Morris
McCann Foundation
McCarty Foundation, John and Margaret

McCasland Foundation
McCormick Trust, Anne
McDermott Foundation, Eugene
McEvoy Foundation, Mildred H.
McFeely-Rogers Foundation
McGee Foundation
McLean Contributionship
McShain Charities, John
M.E. Foundation
Meadows Foundation
Mellon Family Foundation, R. K.
Mellon Foundation, Richard King
Memton Fund
Mengle Foundation, Glenn and Ruth
Mercury Aircraft
Merrick Foundation
Meyer Family Foundation, Paul J.
Mid-Iowa Health Foundation
Middendorf Foundation
Millbrook Tribute Garden
Miller-Mellor Association
Mills Fund, Frances Goll
Monadnock Paper Mills
Monfort Family Foundation
Moore Charitable Foundation, Marjorie
Moore Foundation, Edward S.
Moore & Sons, B.C.
Morgan Charitable Residual Trust, W. and E.
Morgan Foundation, Burton D.
Morgan Foundation, Louie R. and Gertrude
Mosbacher, Jr. Foundation, Emil
Muchnic Foundation
Mulcahy Foundation
Mulford Foundation, Vincent
Mulford Trust, Clarence E.
Muller Foundation
Munger Foundation, Alfred C.
Murphey Foundation, Lluella Morey
Murphy Co. Foundation, G.C.
Murphy Foundation
Musson Charitable Foundation, R. C. and Katharine M.
NewMil Bancorp
Noble Foundation, Samuel Roberts
Norgren Foundation, Carl A.
Norman Foundation, Summers A.
North Shore Foundation
Norton Co.
Oaklawn Foundation
O'Connor Foundation, Kathryn
OCRI Foundation
Odell Fund, Robert Stewart Odell and Helen Pfeiffer
O'Fallon Trust, Martin J. and Mary Anne
Offield Family Foundation
Ohrstrom Foundation
Old Dominion Box Co.
Oliver Memorial Trust Foundation
Olsson Memorial Foundation, Elis
O'Quinn Foundation, John M. and Nancy C.
Osborn Charitable Trust, Edward B.
Osceola Foundation
Osher Foundation, Bernard
Ottley Trust-Watertown, Marion W.
Overbrook Foundation
Overlake Foundation
Owsley Foundation, Alvin and Lucy
PaineWebber
Palisano Foundation, Vincent and Harriet
Palmer Fund, Frank Loomis
Park Foundation
Payne Foundation, Frank E. and Seba B.

Peabody Charitable Fund, Amelia
Pella Corporation
Pennsylvania Dutch Co.
Peppers Foundation, Ann
Peters Foundation, Charles F.
Peters Foundation, R. D. and Linda
Pew Charitable Trusts
Philibosian Foundation, Stephen
Phillips Charitable Trust, Dr. and Mrs. Arthur William
Phillips Foundation, Ellis L.
Phipps Foundation, Howard
Piankova Foundation, Tatiana
Pierce Charitable Trust, Harold Whitworth
Piper Foundation, Minnie Stevens
Plankenhorn Foundation, Harry
Plumsock Fund
Potomac Electric Power Co.
Pott Foundation, Herman T. and Phenie R.
Potts and Sibley Foundation
Prairie Foundation
Price Foundation, Louis and Harold
Price Foundation, Lucien B. and Katherine E.
Priddy Foundation
Prince Trust, Abbie Norman
Proctor Trust, Mortimer R.
Prouty Foundation, Olive Higgins
Providence Journal Company
Prudential Securities, Inc.
Pulitzer Publishing Co.
Putnam Foundation
Quivey-Bay State Foundation
Rabb Foundation, Harry W.
Rachal Foundation, Ed
Ratner Foundation, Milton M.
Read Foundation, Charles L.
Reidler Foundation
Reinberger Foundation
Reynolds Foundation, Christopher
Rice Charitable Foundation, Albert W.
Rich Products Corporation
Richardson Benevolent Foundation, C. E.
Richardson Charitable Trust, Anne S.
Riggs Benevolent Fund
Ritter Charitable Trust, George W. and Mary F.
Robinson-Broadhurst Foundation
Robinson Fund, Maurice R.
Rockefeller Fund, David
Rockwell Fund
Rogers Family Foundation
Rohatyn Foundation, Felix and Elizabeth
Royal Foundation, May Mitchell
Rudin Foundation
Russell Charitable Foundation, Tom
Russell Trust, Josephine G.
Ryan Foundation, David Claude
Sara Lee Hosiery, Inc.
Sargent Foundation, Newell B.
Sasco Foundation
Sawyer Charitable Foundation
Scaife Family Foundation
Schering-Plough Corp.
Schiro Fund
Schlink Foundation, Albert G. and Olive H.
Schmitt Foundation, Kilian J. and Caroline F.
Schoenleber Foundation
Scholl Foundation, Dr.
Schowalter Foundation
Schumann Fund for New Jersey
Schwartz Fund for Education and Health Research, Arnold and Marie
Schwob Foundation, Simon

Scott Foundation, Walter
Scott Foundation, William E.
Scurlock Foundation
Seaver Charitable Trust, Richard C.
Seaver Institute
Seaway Food Town, Inc.
Seidman Family Foundation
Semmes Foundation
Seneca Foods Corp.
Seton Leather Co.
Sheary for Charity, Edna M.
Sheppard Foundation, Lawrence B.
Simon Foundation, William E. and Carol G.
Simpson Investment Company
Smith Charitable Foundation, Clara Blackford Smith and W. Aubrey
Smith Foundation, Gordon V. and Helen C.
Smith Foundation, Ralph L.
Snayberger Memorial Foundation, Harry E. and Florence W.
Snow Foundation, John Ben
Snow Memorial Trust, John Ben
Snyder Foundation, Harold B. and Dorothy A.
Solow Foundation
Specialty Manufacturing Co.
Speer Foundation, Roy M.
Speyer Foundation, Alexander C. and Tillie S.
Sprague Educational and Charitable Foundation, Seth
Springs Foundation
SPX Corp.
Stabler Foundation, Donald B. and Dorothy L.
Stackpole-Hall Foundation
Stanley Charitable Foundation, A.W.
Stanley Works
Starr Foundation
Stauffer Charitable Trust, John
Stauffer Foundation, John and Beverly
Staunton Farm Foundation
Stearns Trust, Artemas W.
Steele Foundation, Harry and Grace
Stein Foundation, Jules and Doris
Steinman Foundation, James Hale
Steinman Foundation, John Frederick
Stemmons Foundation
Sternberger Foundation, Tannenbaum
Stevens Foundation, Abbot and Dorothy H.
Stevens Foundation, John T.
Stokely, Jr. Foundation, William B.
Strauss Foundation, Leon
Strawbridge Foundation of Pennsylvania II, Margaret Dorrance
Strong Foundation, Hattie M.
Sturgis Charitable and Educational Trust, Roy and Christine
Sundet Foundation
Superior Tube Co.
Swalm Foundation
Swanson Family Foundation, Dr. W.C.
Swift Co. Inc., John S.
Symmes Foundation, F. W.
Taconic Foundation
Taylor Foundation, Fred and Harriett
Tecumseh Products Co.
Temple Foundation, T. L. L.
Tennessee Valley Printing Co.
Thornton Foundation
Thornton Foundation, Flora L.
Tiscornia Foundation
Tobin Foundation
Todd Co., A.M.

Towsley Foundation, Harry A. and Margaret D.
Treakle Foundation, J. Edwin
Trexler Trust, Harry C.
Truland Foundation
Trull Foundation
Trust Funds
Turner Charitable Foundation
Unger Foundation, Aber D.
Union Camp Corporation
Upton Foundation, Frederick S.
Utica National Insurance Group
Valentine Foundation, Lawson
van Ameringen Foundation
Van Buren Foundation
Van Every Foundation, Philip L.
Van Houten Memorial Fund
Van Nuys Foundation, I. N. and Susanna H.
Van Wert County Foundation
Vanderbilt Trust, R. T.
Vaughn, Jr. Foundation Fund, James M.
Vetlesen Foundation, G. Unger
Vevay-Switzerland County Foundation
Wahlstrom Foundation
Wallace Foundation, George R.
Walsh Foundation
Warren and Beatrice W. Blanding Foundation, Riley J. and Lillian N.
Warwick Foundation
Washington Forrest Foundation
Washington Mutual Savings Bank
Wean Foundation, Raymond John
Weaver Foundation, Gil and Dody
Webber Oil Co.
Weber Charities Corp., Frederick E.
Weckbaugh Foundation, Eleanore Mullen
Weezie Foundation
Wendt Foundation, Margaret L.
Westerman Foundation, Samuel L.
Weyerhaeuser Memorial Foundation, Charles A.
Wheeler Foundation, Wilmot
White Trust, G. R.
Whiting Foundation
Wickson-Link Memorial Foundation
Widgeon Foundation
Wildermuth Foundation, E. F.
Willard Helping Fund, Cecilia Young
Wilson Fund, Matilda R.
Winthrop Trust, Clara B.
Wise Foundation and Charitable Trust, Watson W.
Witco Corp.
Wood Foundation of Chambersburg, PA
Woodward Fund
Wright Foundation, Lola
Wyman Youth Trust
Y and H Soda Foundation
Yeager Charitable Trust, Lester E.
Young Foundation, Irvin L.
Young Foundation, Robert R.
Zarrow Foundation, Anne and Henry

Dioceses

Ahmanson Foundation
AlliedSignal Inc.
Andreas Foundation
Anheuser-Busch Companies, Inc.
Annenberg Foundation
Argyros Foundation
Bettingen Corporation, Burton G.
Bishop Foundation, E. K. and Lillian F.

Bobst Foundation, Elmer and Mamdouha
Brach Foundation, Helen
Burkitt Foundation
Campbell Foundation, Ruth and Henry
Carvel Foundation, Thomas and Agnes
Chase Manhattan Bank, N.A.
Connelly Foundation
Davis Foundation, Irene E. and George A.
Dunagan Foundation
Firestone, Jr. Foundation, Harvey
France Foundation, Jacob and Annita
Freeport-McMoRan Inc.
Gellert Foundation, Carl
Gilmore Foundation, William G.
Habig Foundation, Arnold F.
Handy and Harman Foundation
Harmon Foundation, Pearl M. and Julia J.
Hearst Foundation, William Randolph
Homeland Foundation
Hugoton Foundation
Huisking Foundation
Humana, Inc.
International Paper Co.
Julia R. and Estelle L. Foundation
Kemper Foundation, William T.
Komes Foundation
Laffey-McHugh Foundation
Leavey Foundation, Thomas and Dorothy
Leuthold Foundation
Levitt Foundation
Mardigian Foundation
Marmot Foundation
Martini Foundation, Nicholas
May Department Stores Company, The
McCann Foundation
Miller-Mellor Association
Mulford Foundation, Vincent
Norman Foundation, Summers A.
North Shore Foundation
PaineWebber
Palisano Foundation, Vincent and Harriet
Payne Foundation, Frank E. and Seba B.
Piper Jaffray Companies Inc.
Price Foundation, Lucien B. and Katherine E.
Rich Products Corporation
Rockwell International Corporation
Sandy Hill Foundation
Seafirst Corporation
Simon Foundation, William E. and Carol G.
Stackpole-Hall Foundation
Trexler Trust, Harry C.
Trust Funds
Union Electric Co.
United Airlines, Inc.
Wiegand Foundation, E. L.
Y and H Soda Foundation

General

Alabama Gas Corp.
CIBC Wood Gundy
CLARCOR Inc.
Cosmair, Inc.
Handy and Harman Foundation
Jaydor Corp.
LamCo. Communications
New York Mercantile Exchange
Old National Bank in Evansville
Pitt-Des Moines Inc.
Thompson Charitable Foundation

Jewish Causes

ACF Industries, Inc.
Acme-McCrary Corp./Sapona Manufacturing Co.
Ahmanson Foundation
Alexander Foundation, Joseph
Allen Brothers Foundation
AlliedSignal Inc.
Altman Foundation
Altschul Foundation
Aluminum Co. of America
Amado Foundation, Maurice
American National Bank & Trust Co. of Chicago
Ames Charitable Trust, Harriett
AMETEK, Inc.
AMR Corp.
Anderson Foundation, M. D.
Andreas Foundation
Annenberg Foundation
Ansin Private Foundation, Ronald M.
AON Corporation
Arcadia Foundation
Archer-Daniels-Midland Co.
Argyros Foundation
Arnhold Foundation
ASDA Foundation
Atran Foundation
Auerbach Foundation, Beatrice Fox
Avery Arts Foundation, Milton and Sally
Barker Foundation, J.M.R.
Barra Foundation
Barry Corp., R. G.
Benedum Foundation, Claude Worthington
Benenson Foundation, Frances and Benjamin
Binswanger Cos.
Blaustein Foundation, Louis and Henrietta
Block, H&R
Blue Bell, Inc.
Blum Foundation, Harry and Maribel G.
Blum-Kovler Foundation
Borkee Hagley Foundation
Borman's Inc.
Bremer Foundation, Otto
Bristol-Myers Squibb Company
Burlington Industries, Inc.
Cain Foundation, Effie and Wofford
Cain Foundation, Gordon and Mary
Campini Foundation, Frank A.
Carpenter Technology Corp.
Cassett Foundation, Louis N.
Charina Foundation
Chartwell Foundation
Chase Manhattan Bank, N.A.
Chazen Foundation
Cheatham Foundation, Owen
Citizens Bank of Rhode Island
City National Bank and Trust Co.
Clemens Markets Corp.
Columbia Foundation
Columbus Dispatch Printing Co.
Connecticut Mutual Life Insurance Company
Continental Corp.
Cooperman Foundation, Leon and Toby
Coors Foundation, Adolph
Coughlin-Saunders Foundation
Cowell Foundation, S. H.
Cranston Print Works Company
Crown Books
Crown Memorial, Arie and Ida
Culver Foundation, Constans
Cummings Foundation, James H.
Daniel Foundation of Alabama
Dart Group Corp.
Davenport-Hatch Foundation
Davis Foundation, Irene E. and George A.
DeRoy Foundation, Helen L.

DeRoy Testamentary Foundation
Duchossois Industries Inc.
Duncan Trust, John G.
Eastman Kodak Company
Einstein Fund, Albert E. and Birdie W.
English Memorial Fund, Florence C. and H. L.
Fair Oaks Foundation, Inc.
Fairchild Foundation, Sherman
Feil Foundation, Louis and Gertrude
Fife Foundation, Elias and Bertha
Fikes Foundation, Leland
Fink Foundation
Firstar Bank Milwaukee, N.A.
Fischbach Foundation
Fleishhacker Foundation
Forbes Inc.
Foster Charitable Trust
Freeman Charitable Trust, Samuel
Freeport-McMoRan Inc.
Fribourg Foundation
Friedman Family Foundation
Geifman Family Foundation
General American Life Insurance Co.
Georgia-Pacific Corporation
German Protestant Orphan Asylum Association
Gershman Foundation, Joel
Gheens Foundation
Giant Eagle, Inc.
Giant Food Inc.
Gifford Charitable Corporation, Rosamond
Glick Foundation, Eugene and Marilyn
Glosser Foundation, David A.
Goldberg Family Foundation
Goldie-Anna Charitable Trust
Goldseker Foundation of Maryland, Morris
Goldsmith Foundation, Horace W.
Goldwyn Foundation, Samuel
Goodstein Family Foundation, David
Graham Fund, Philip L.
Griswold Foundation, John C.
Groome Beatty Trust, Helen D.
Guaranty Bank & Trust Co.
Guggenheim Foundation, Harry Frank
Guttman Foundation, Stella and Charles
Haas, Jr. Fund, Evelyn and Walter
Hammer Foundation, Armand
Hanover Foundation
Harcourt General, Inc.
Hartmarx Corporation
Hassenfeld Foundation
Hauser Foundation
Hebrew Technical Institute
Hechinger Co.
Hecht-Levi Foundation
Heckscher Foundation for Children
Heinz Endowment, Vira I.
Herzstein Charitable Foundation, Albert and Ethel
Higginson Trust, Corina
Hillman Family Foundation, Alex
Hoffman Foundation, Maximilian E. and Marion O.
Holzer Memorial Foundation, Richard H.
Houston Endowment
Hoyt Foundation, Stewart W. and Willma C.
Icahn Foundation, Carl C.
Imperial Bancorp
Ittleson Foundation
Jackson Foundation
Jacobson Foundation, Bernard H. and Blanche E.
Jaffe Foundation
Jarson-Stanley and Mickey Kaplan Foundation, Isaac and Esther

Jaydor Corp.
Jennings Foundation, Mary Hillman
Jewish Healthcare Foundation of Pittsburgh
Kaplun Foundation, Morris J. and Betty
Kardon Foundation, Samuel and Rebecca
Kaufmann Foundation, Henry
Kayser Foundation
Kemper Foundation, William T.
Klipstein Foundation, Ernest Christian
Klosk Fund, Louis and Rose
Kohn-Joseloff Foundation
Koopman Fund
Koret Foundation
Kresge Foundation
Kutz Foundation, Milton and Hattie
Landegger Charitable Foundation
Lang Foundation, Eugene M.
Lasdon Foundation
Lasdon Foundation, William and Mildred
Lauder Foundation
Lazarus Charitable Trust, Helen and Charles
Lebovitz Fund
Lederer Foundation, Francis L.
Lee Enterprises
Leidy Foundation, John J.
Lemberg Foundation
Levitt Foundation
Liberman Foundation, Bertha and Isaac
Lichtenstein Foundation, David B.
Littauer Foundation, Lucius N.
Liz Claiborne, Inc.
Loews Corporation
Lowenstein Foundation, Leon
Lurie Foundation, Louis R.
Maddox Foundation, J. F.
Mailman Family Foundation, A. L.
Mailman Foundation
Management Compensation Group/Dulworth Inc.
Mardigian Foundation
Marpat Foundation
Martin Marietta Corp.
Marx Foundation, Virginia and Leonard
Mattel, Inc.
May Department Stores Company, The
McDonald & Company Securities, Inc.
McGonagle Foundation, Dextra Baldwin
Mellon Foundation, Richard King
Merkley Charitable Trust
Messing Family Charitable Foundation
Meyer Fund, Milton and Sophie
Meyer Memorial Trust
Meyerhoff Fund, Joseph
Miller Fund, Kathryn and Gilbert
Mnuchin Foundation
Monell Foundation, Ambrose
Morris Foundation, Margaret T.
Moses Fund, Henry and Lucy
Musson Charitable Foundation, R. C. and Katharine M.
Nabisco Foods Group
Neuberger Foundation, Roy R. and Marie S.
New-Land Foundation
NewMil Bancorp
Nias Foundation, Henry
Old Dominion Box Co.
Oppenstein Brothers Foundation
Ottenheimer Brothers Foundation
Overbrook Foundation
PaineWebber

Parshelsky Foundation, Moses
L.
Parsons Foundation, Ralph M.
Parvin Foundation, Albert
Pew Charitable Trusts
Phillips Family Foundation,
Jay and Rose
Pick, Jr. Fund, Albert
Piper Jaffray Companies Inc.
Pollock Company Foundation,
William B.
Premier Industrial Corp.
Rabb Charitable Foundation,
Sidney and Esther
Rabb Foundation, Harry W.
Ratner Foundation, Milton M.
Read Foundation, Charles L.
Regenstein Foundation
Reicher Foundation, Anne and
Harry J.
Reisman Charitable Trust,
George C. and Evelyn R.
Rich Products Corporation
Rockwell International
Corporation
Rohatyn Foundation, Felix and
Elizabeth
Rose Foundation, Billy
Rosen Foundation, Joseph
Rosenberg, Jr. Family
Foundation, Louise and
Claude
Rowland Foundation
Rubin Family Fund, Cele H.
and William B.
Rubin Foundation, Samuel
Rubinstein Foundation, Helena
Rudin Foundation
Russell Trust, Josephine G.
Salomon Foundation, Richard
and Edna
Sawyer Charitable Foundation
Scherman Foundation
Schiro Fund
Schwartz Foundation, Arnold
A.
Schwartz Fund for Education
and Health Research, Arnold
and Marie
Schwob Foundation, Simon
Scurlock Foundation
Seafirst Corporation
Seagram & Sons, Inc., Joseph
E.
Seneca Foods Corp.
Seton Leather Co.
Shubert Foundation
Sierra Pacific Resources
Slifka Foundation, Joseph and
Sylvia
Smart Family Foundation
Smeal Foundation, Mary Jean
and Frank P.
Solow Foundation
Speer Foundation, Roy M.
Speyer Foundation, Alexander
C. and Tillie S.
Stans Foundation
Starr Foundation
Staunton Farm Foundation
Stearns Trust, Artemas W.
Stone Charitable Foundation
Strauss Foundation, Leon
Sulzberger Foundation
Taube Family Foundation
Taubman Foundation, A. Alfred
Teleflex Inc.
Texaco Inc.
Texas Commerce
Bank-Houston, N.A.
Thalhimer and Family
Foundation, Charles G.
Thermo Electron Corp.
Thompson Co., J. Walter
Thornton Foundation, Flora L.
Titus Foundation, Roy and
Niuta
TransAmerica Corporation
Travelers Inc.
Truland Foundation
Tuch Foundation, Michael
Tucker Charitable Trust, Rose
E.
Union Electric Co.
Uris Brothers Foundation

Vicksburg Foundation
Weil, Gotshal and Manges
Foundation
Weingart Foundation
Weinstein Foundation, J.
Westerman Foundation,
Samuel L.
Wheat First Butcher Singer,
Inc.
Winnebago Industries, Inc.
Witco Corp.
Wyomissing Foundation
Y and H Soda Foundation
Young Foundation, Robert R.
Zachry Co., H.B.
Zarrow Foundation, Anne and
Henry
Zenkel Foundation
Zlinkoff Fund for Medical
Research and Education,
Sergei S.

Ministries

Abell-Hanger Foundation
Allegheny Ludlum Corp.
AlliedSignal Inc.
American Fidelity Corporation
American National Bank &
Trust Co. of Chicago
AMETEK, Inc.
Andersons, The
Annenberg Foundation
Ansley Foundation, Dantzler
Bond
Bingham Second Betterment
Fund, William
Blue Bell, Inc.
Booth Ferris Foundation
Bothin Foundation
Brach Foundation, Helen
Bridgestone/Firestone, Inc.
Buhl Foundation
Burchfield Foundation,
Charles E.
Burlington Industries, Inc.
Calhoun Charitable Trust,
Kenneth
Carpenter Foundation, E.
Rhodes and Leona B.
Castle Foundation, Harold K.
L.
Cayuga Foundation
Chatlos Foundation
Childs Charitable Foundation,
Roberta M.
Clarke Trust, John
Clowes Fund
Collins Foundation
Columbus Dispatch Printing
Co.
Comprecare Foundation
Connelly Foundation
Coors Foundation, Adolph
Cornell Trust, Peter C.
Crestlea Foundation
Crystal Trust
Davidson Family Charitable
Foundation
Davis Foundation, James A.
and Juliet L.
Deuble Foundation, George H.
Duke Power Co.
Duncan Foundation, Lillian H.
and C. W.
Early Foundation
Einstein Fund, Albert E. and
Birdie W.
English Memorial Fund,
Florence C. and H. L.
Evans Foundation, Thomas J.
Fair Foundation, R. W.
Feild Co-Operative Association
Fish Foundation, Ray C.
Fleming Cos. Food
Distribution Center
Forest Foundation
Freeport-McMoRan Inc.
Fruehauf Foundation
Gallagher Family Foundation,
Lewis P.
Gamble Foundation
Gannett Publishing Co., Guy
Gellert Foundation, Carl

General American Life
Insurance Co.
Gheens Foundation
Good Samaritan
Gulf Coast Medical Foundation
Gulf Power Co.
Hammer Foundation, Armand
Harmon Foundation, Pearl M.
and Julia J.
Hasbro Inc.
Hazen Foundation, Edward W.
Helmerich Foundation
Helms Foundation
Herzstein Charitable
Foundation, Albert and Ethel
Hillsdale Fund
Hook Drugs
Hoover Foundation
Houston Endowment
Howard and Bush Foundation
Hulme Charitable Foundation,
Milton G.
Hunt Foundation
Huston Charitable Trust,
Stewart
Huston Foundation
Janirve Foundation
Jordan Charitable Foundation,
Mary Ranken Jordan and
Ettie A.
Joslin-Needham Family
Foundation
Kantzler Foundation
Kirkpatrick Foundation
Knox, Sr., and Pearl Wallis
Knox Charitable
Foundation, Robert W.
Kreitler Foundation
La-Z-Boy Chair Co.
Ladd Charitable Corporation,
Helen and George
Laffey-McHugh Foundation
Leuthold Foundation
Levy Foundation, June
Rockwell
Lockhart Vaughan Foundation
Longwood Foundation
Markey Charitable Fund, John
C.
Marpat Foundation
Mather Charitable Trust, S.
Livingston
McCarty Foundation, John and
Margaret
McCasland Foundation
McCune Charitable Trust,
John R.
M.E. Foundation
Meadows Foundation
Meyer Family Foundation,
Paul J.
Moore & Sons, B.C.
Morgan Charitable Residual
Trust, W. and E.
Muchnic Foundation
Mulford Foundation, Vincent
Murdock Charitable Trust, M.
J.
Murphy Co. Foundation, G.C.
Musson Charitable
Foundation, R. C. and
Katharine M.
Nias Foundation, Henry
Norgren Foundation, Carl A.
Norton Foundation Inc.
OCRI Foundation
Old National Bank in
Evansville
Olsson Memorial Foundation,
Elis
Oppenstein Brothers
Foundation
PaineWebber
Patterson Charitable Fund, W.
I.
Payne Foundation, Frank E.
and Seba B.
Pella Corporation
Pennsylvania Dutch Co.
Pew Charitable Trusts
Phillips Foundation, Ellis L.
PNC Bank, N.A.
Porter Testamentary Trust,
James Hyde
Priddy Foundation

Prince Trust, Abbie Norman
Prospect Hill Foundation
Ratner Foundation, Milton M.
Rixson Foundation, Oscar C.
Robinson Fund, Maurice R.
Rockwell Fund
Ryan Foundation, David
Claude
Schowalter Foundation
Schuller International
Schwartz Fund for Education
and Health Research, Arnold
and Marie
Scurlock Foundation
Selby and Marie Selby
Foundation, William G.
Sequoia Foundation
Sheary for Charity, Edna M.
Smith Charitable Foundation,
Lou and Lutza
Stans Foundation
Staunton Farm Foundation
Steinhagen Benevolent Trust,
B. A. and Elinor
Stemmons Foundation
Sternberger Foundation,
Tannenbaum
Strauss Foundation, Leon
Strong Foundation, Hattie M.
Sturgis Charitable and
Educational Trust, Roy and
Christine
Sundet Foundation
Symmes Foundation, F. W.
Texas Commerce
Bank-Houston, N.A.
Truland Foundation
Trull Foundation
Union Electric Co.
Upjohn Foundation, Harold
and Grace
Upton Foundation, Frederick S.
Vanderbilt Trust, R. T.
Vogler Foundation, Laura B.
Washington Mutual Savings
Bank
Weaver Foundation, Gil and
Dody
Weckbaugh Foundation,
Eleanore Mullen
Weezie Foundation
Wendt Foundation, Margaret L.
Wheeler Foundation
Williams Charitable Trust,
John C.
Williams Charitable Trust,
Mary Jo
Wilmington Trust Co.
Wyman Youth Trust
Zarrow Foundation, Anne and
Henry

Missionary
Activities (Domestic)

Andreas Foundation
Annenberg Foundation
Ansley Foundation, Dantzler
Bond
Baughman Foundation
Beck Foundation, Elsie E. and
Joseph W.
Brach Foundation, Helen
Bridwell Foundation, J. S.
Burkitt Foundation
Cain Foundation, Effie and
Wofford
Chartwell Foundation
Chatlos Foundation
Collins Foundation, George
and Jennie
Commerce Bancshares, Inc.
Connemara Fund
Cosmair, Inc.
Crandall Memorial
Foundation, J. Ford
Fleishhacker Foundation
Foster Foundation
Fruehauf Foundation
Gallagher Family Foundation,
Lewis P.
Glaser Foundation

Glick Foundation, Eugene and
Marilyn
Hamilton Bank
Hartz Foundation
Hillsdale Fund
Homeland Foundation
Houchens Foundation, Ervin G.
Hunt Charitable Trust, C. Giles
Huston Charitable Trust,
Stewart
Huston Foundation
International Foundation
Kavanagh Foundation, T.
James
Kutz Foundation, Milton and
Hattie
Link, Jr. Foundation, George
Marriott Foundation, J. Willard
Mather Fund, Richard
McGee Foundation
M.E. Foundation
Meyer Family Foundation,
Paul J.
Moore & Sons, B.C.
Munger Foundation, Alfred C.
Norgren Foundation, Carl A.
North Shore Foundation
Owsley Foundation, Alvin and
Lucy
Park Foundation
Philibosian Foundation,
Stephen
Pioneer Trust Bank, NA
Rockefeller Fund, David
Ryan Foundation, David
Claude
Schowalter Foundation
Stauffer Foundation, John and
Beverly
Stokely, Jr. Foundation,
William B.
Sturgis Charitable and
Educational Trust, Roy and
Christine
Trull Foundation
Weckbaugh Foundation,
Eleanore Mullen
Young Foundation, Irvin L.

Religious
Organizations

ACF Industries, Inc.
Achelis Foundation
Acushnet Co.
Air France
Alavi Foundation of New York
Alexander Foundation, Joseph
Allen Brothers Foundation
Allianz Life Insurance Co. of
North America
Altman Foundation
Altschul Foundation
Aluminum Co. of America
Amado Foundation, Maurice
American General Finance
Corp.
Ameritas Life Insurance Corp.
Ames Charitable Trust, Harriett
Amfac/JMB Hawaii Inc.
Andersen Corp.
Andersen Foundation
Andersons, The
Andreas Foundation
Andrews Foundation
Anheuser-Busch Companies,
Inc.
Annenberg Foundation
Ansin Private Foundation,
Ronald M.
Ansley Foundation, Dantzler
Bond
AON Corporation
Arakelian Foundation, Mary
Alice
Archer-Daniels-Midland Co.
Argyros Foundation
Arkelian Foundation, Ben H.
and Gladys
Arkell Hall Foundation
Armstrong Foundation
Asplundh Foundation
Atherton Family Foundation

Meyer Fund, Milton and Sophie
Meyer Memorial Trust
Meyerhoff Fund, Joseph
Middendorf Foundation
Millbrook Tribute Garden
Miller Charitable Foundation, Howard E. and Nell E.
Miller Foundation
Miller-Mellor Association
Mills Fund, Frances Goll
Mnuchin Foundation
Monadnock Paper Mills
Moore & Sons, B.C.
Morgan Charitable Residual Trust, W. and E.
Morgan Foundation, Burton D.
Morgan Foundation, Louie R. and Gertrude
Morris Foundation, Margaret T.
Morrison Charitable Trust, Pauline A. and George E.
Morrison Knudsen Corporation
Moses Fund, Henry and Lucy
Mulford Foundation, Vincent
Mulford Trust, Clarence E.
Mullen Foundation, J. K.
Muller Foundation
Munger Foundation, Alfred C.
Murphey Foundation, Lluella Morey
Musson Charitable Foundation, R. C. and Katharine M.
National Westminster Bank New Jersey
Neuberger Foundation, Roy R. and Marie S.
New York Stock Exchange, Inc.
Nias Foundation, Henry
Noble Foundation, Samuel Roberts
North Shore Foundation
Norton Foundation Inc.
O'Connor Foundation, A. Lindsay and Olive B.
O'Connor Foundation, Kathryn
OCRI Foundation
Odell Fund, Robert Stewart
Odell and Helen Pfeiffer
O'Fallon Trust, Martin J. and Mary Anne
Old National Bank in Evansville
Oliver Memorial Trust Foundation
Olsson Memorial Foundation, Elis
Oppenstein Brothers Foundation
Osher Foundation, Bernard
Overlake Foundation
PaineWebber
Paley Foundation, William S.
Palisano Foundation, Vincent and Harriet
Parshelsky Foundation, Moses L.
Parvin Foundation, Albert
Payne Foundation, Frank E. and Seba B.
Pella Corporation
Peppers Foundation, Ann
Peters Foundation, Charles F.
Peters Foundation, R. D. and Linda
Pettus Crowe Foundation
Pew Charitable Trusts
PHH Corporation
Philibosian Foundation, Stephen
Phillips Family Foundation, Jay and Rose
Pick, Jr. Fund, Albert
Pitt-Des Moines Inc.
Pittsburgh Child Guidance Foundation
Pollock Company Foundation, William B.
Potomac Electric Power Co.
Pott Foundation, Herman T. and Phenie R.
Prairie Foundation
Premier Industrial Corp.

Price Foundation, Lucien B. and Katherine E.
Proctor Trust, Mortimer R.
Prudential Securities, Inc.
Pulitzer Publishing Co.
Putnam Foundation
Quivey-Bay State Foundation
R. F. Foundation
Rabb Foundation, Harry W.
Ralston Purina Co.
R&B Machine Tool Co.
Ratner Foundation, Milton M.
Read Foundation, Charles L.
Reicher Foundation, Anne and Harry J.
Reisman Charitable Trust, George C. and Evelyn R.
Retirement Research Foundation
Reynolds Foundation, Christopher
Rice Foundation
Rich Products Corporation
Richardson Charitable Trust, Anne S.
Ritter Charitable Trust, George W. and Mary F.
Rixson Foundation, Oscar C.
Robinson Fund, Maurice R.
Rockwell Fund
Rose Foundation, Billy
Rosen Foundation, Joseph
Ross Memorial Foundation, Will
Rubin Family Fund, Cele H. and William B.
Rudin Foundation
Ryan Foundation, David Claude
Sandy Hill Foundation
Sargent Foundation, Newell B.
Sarkeys Foundation
Sawyer Charitable Foundation
Scaife Family Foundation
Schiro Fund
Scholl Foundation, Dr.
Schowalter Foundation
Schroeder Foundation, Walter
Schuller International
Schwartz Foundation, Arnold A.
Schwartz Fund for Education and Health Research, Arnold and Marie
Schwob Foundation, Simon
Scurlock Foundation
Seagram & Sons, Inc., Joseph E.
Seaver Charitable Trust, Richard C.
Second Foundation
Sentry Insurance A Mutual Company
Sharon Steel Corp.
Simon Foundation, William E. and Carol G.
Slifka Foundation, Joseph and Sylvia
Smith Foundation, Gordon V. and Helen C.
Smith Memorial Fund, Ethel Sergeant Clark
Smith Trust, May and Stanley
Snow Foundation, John Ben
Snyder Foundation, Harold B. and Dorothy A.
Sonat Inc.
Sordoni Foundation
Speer Foundation, Roy M.
Speyer Foundation, Alexander C. and Tillie S.
SPX Corp.
Stabler Foundation, Donald B. and Dorothy L.
Stackpole-Hall Foundation
Stans Foundation
Stauffer Foundation, John and Beverly
Steele Foundation, Harry and Grace
Steinbach Fund, Ruth and Milton
Steinman Foundation, James Hale

Steinman Foundation, John Frederick
Stevens Foundation, Abbot and Dorothy H.
Stokely, Jr. Foundation, William B.
Stone Charitable Foundation
Strong Foundation, Hattie M.
Sturgis Charitable and Educational Trust, Roy and Christine
Sturgis Charitable and Educational Trust, Roy and Christine
Sulzberger Foundation
Sumners Foundation, Hatton W.
Sundet Foundation
Superior Tube Co.
Swalm Foundation
Swanson Family Foundation, Dr. W.C.
Taube Family Foundation
Taubman Foundation, A. Alfred
Temple Foundation, T. L. L.
Temple-Inland Inc.
Thalhimer and Family Foundation, Charles G.
Thomas Foundation, Joan and Lee
Thompson Co., J. Walter
Thompson Trust, Thomas
Thorne Foundation
Thornton Foundation
Timken Foundation of Canton
Toms Foundation
Tozer Foundation
Travelers Inc.
Truland Foundation
Trull Foundation
Trust Funds
Tuch Foundation, Michael
Tucker Charitable Trust, Rose E.
Tupancy-Harris Foundation of 1986
Turner Charitable Foundation
Unger Foundation, Aber D.
Union Camp Corporation
Union Electric Co.
Union Pacific Corp.
Upjohn Foundation, Harold and Grace
Upton Foundation, Frederick S.
Valmont Industries, Inc.
Van Every Foundation, Philip L.
Vance Charitable Foundation, Robert C.
Vanderbilt Trust, R. T.
Vicksburg Foundation
Wahlstrom Foundation
Wallace Foundation, George R.
Walsh Foundation
Warner Fund, Albert and Bessie
Warren and Beatrice W. Blanding Foundation, Riley J. and Lillian N.
Washington Forrest Foundation
Wean Foundation, Raymond John
Weaver Foundation, Gil and Dody
Weber Charities Corp., Frederick E.
Weckbaugh Foundation, Eleanore Mullen
Weezie Foundation
Wege Foundation
Weil, Gotshal and Manges Foundation
Weinstein Foundation, J.
Wells Foundation, Franklin H. and Ruth L.
Wendt Foundation, Margaret L.
Wheeler Foundation
Wheeler Foundation, Wilmot
White Trust, G. R.
Whitecap Foundation
Whitney Fund, David M.
WICOR, Inc.
Widgeon Foundation
Wiegand Foundation, E. L.
Wiggins Memorial Trust, J. J.

Wildermuth Foundation, E. F.
Willard Helping Fund, Cecilia Young
Williams Charitable Trust, John C.
Wilson Fund, Matilda R.
Witco Corp.
Woolley Foundation, Vasser
Worthington Foods
Wyman Youth Trust
Wyomissing Foundation
Y and H Soda Foundation
Young Foundation, Irvin L.
Young Foundation, Robert R.
Zenkel Foundation

Religious Welfare

Abbott Laboratories
Abell-Hanger Foundation
ACF Industries, Inc.
Achelis Foundation
Acushnet Co.
Ahmanson Foundation
Air Products and Chemicals, Inc.
Akzo Chemicals Inc.
Alabama Gas Corp.
Alcon Laboratories, Inc.
Allegheny Foundation
Allegheny Ludlum Corp.
Allendale Insurance Co.
AlliedSignal Inc.
Allyn Foundation
Altman Foundation
Altschul Foundation
Aluminum Co. of America
American General Finance Corp.
American Natural Resources Company
Ameritas Life Insurance Corp.
Amfac/JMB Hawaii Inc.
AMR Corp.
Andersen Corp.
Andersen Foundation
Anderson Foundation
Anderson Foundation, John W.
Andersons, The
Andreas Foundation
Andrews Foundation
Annenberg Foundation
Ansin Private Foundation, Ronald M.
Ansley Foundation, Dantzler Bond
AON Corporation
Arcadia Foundation
Archer-Daniels-Midland Co.
Argyros Foundation
Aristech Chemical Corp.
Arkansas Power & Light Co.
Arkelian Foundation, Ben H. and Gladys
Arkell Hall Foundation
Armco Inc.
Armstrong Foundation
ASDA Foundation
Ashtabula Foundation
Astor Foundation, Vincent
Atherton Family Foundation
Audubon State Bank
Auerbach Foundation, Beatrice Fox
Avon Products, Inc.
Ayres Foundation, Inc.
Bacon Foundation, E. L. and Oma
Badgeley Residuary Charitable Trust, Rose M.
Baker Foundation, Dexter F. and Dorothy H.
Baker Trust, George F.
Baldwin Foundation, David M. and Barbara
Baldwin Memorial Foundation, Fred
Ball Brothers Foundation
Ball Foundation, George and Frances
Banta Corp.
Barra Foundation
Barry Corp., R. G.
Barth Foundation, Theodore H.

Batts Foundation
Bauervic Foundation, Charles M.
Baughman Foundation
Bay Foundation
Beal Foundation
Bean Foundation, Norwin S. and Elizabeth N.
BE&K Inc.
Beazley Foundation/Frederick Foundation
Beck Foundation, Elsie E. and Joseph W.
Beloit Foundation
Benenson Foundation, Frances and Benjamin
Benwood Foundation
Bettingen Corporation, Burton G.
Betts Industries
Bird Corp.
Birnschein Foundation, Alvin and Marion
Bishop Foundation, E. K. and Lillian F.
Blandin Foundation
Blaustein Foundation, Louis and Henrietta
Bloedorn Foundation, Walter A.
Blount, Inc.
Blum Foundation, Edna F.
Bobst Foundation, Elmer and Mamdouha
Bodman Foundation
Booth Ferris Foundation
Boothroyd Foundation, Charles H. and Bertha L.
Borden, Inc.
Borkee Hagley Foundation
Borman's Inc.
Bothin Foundation
Boutell Memorial Fund
Bowen Foundation, Ethel N.
Bowne Foundation, Robert
Brach Foundation, Helen
Bremer Foundation, Otto
Breyer Foundation
Bridwell Foundation, J. S.
Bright Family Foundation
Brillion Iron Works
Bristol-Myers Squibb Company
Brown Foundation, M. K.
Brunswick Corp.
Bryant Foundation
Buhl Foundation
Burchfield Foundation, Charles E.
Burden Foundation, Florence V.
Burkitt Foundation
Burnett-Tandy Foundation
Bush Foundation
Cabell Foundation, Robert G. Cabell III and Maude Morgan
Caestecker Foundation, Charles and Marie
Cain Foundation, Effie and Wofford
Cain Foundation, Gordon and Mary
Calder Foundation, Louis
Calhoun Charitable Trust, Kenneth
Callaway Foundation
Campbell Foundation
Campbell Foundation, Ruth and Henry
Campini Foundation, Frank A.
Carolyn Foundation
Carpenter Foundation
Carpenter Foundation, E. Rhodes and Leona B.
Carpenter Technology Corp.
Carter Foundation, Beirne
Catlin Charitable Trust, Kathleen K.
CBS, Inc.
Central National Bank
Centralia Foundation
Champlin Foundations
Chartwell Foundation
Chase Manhattan Bank, N.A.

Chastain Charitable Foundation, Robert Lee and Thomas M.
Chatham Manufacturing Co.
Chatlos Foundation
Chazen Foundation
Childs Charitable Foundation, Roberta M.
Christensen Charitable and Religious Foundation, L. C.
CINergy
Citizens Bank of Rhode Island
City National Bank and Trust Co.
Clapp Charitable and Educational Trust, George H.
CLARCOR Inc.
Clark Foundation
Clarke Trust, John
Clarkson Foundation, Jeniam
Clay Foundation
Clemens Markets Corp.
Clorox Co.
Clowes Fund
Coen Family Foundation, Charles S. and Mary
Cogswell Benevolent Trust
Coleman Foundation, George E.
Collins Foundation
Collins Foundation, George and Jennie
Collins, Jr. Foundation, George Fulton
Columbia Foundation
Columbus Dispatch Printing Co.
Comer Foundation
Commerce Bancshares, Inc.
Commerce Clearing House, Incorporated
Connelly Foundation
Consolidated Natural Gas Co.
Consumers Power Co.
Contran Corporation
Cooke Foundation
Cooperman Foundation, Leon and Toby
Coors Foundation, Adolph
Copley Press, Inc.
Cord Foundation, E. L.
Cornell Trust, Peter C.
Coughlin-Saunders Foundation
Cowell Foundation, S. H.
Cowles Charitable Trust
Crandall Memorial Foundation, J. Ford
Crane Co.
Cranston Print Works Company
Crawford Estate, E. R.
Cremer Foundation
Crestlea Foundation
Crocker Trust, Mary A.
Crown Books
Crystal Trust
CS First Boston Corporation
Cullen Foundation
Culpeper Memorial Foundation, Daphne Seybolt
Culver Foundation, Constans
Cummings Foundation, James H.
Cuneo Foundation
Daily News
Daniel Foundation of Alabama
Dater Foundation, Charles H.
Daugherty Foundation
Davenport-Hatch Foundation
Davenport Trust Fund
Davidson Family Charitable Foundation
Davis Foundation, Irene E. and George A.
Davis Foundations, Arthur Vining
Daywood Foundation
Deere & Co.
Dell Foundation, Hazel
Demoulas Supermarkets Inc.
Dentsply International Inc.
Deuble Foundation, George H.
DeVore Foundation
Dexter Charitable Fund, Eugene A.
Dillon Foundation

Dingman Foundation, Michael D.
Dishman Charitable Foundation Trust, H. E. and Kate
Dr. Seuss Foundation
Dodge Foundation, Cleveland H.
Dodge Jones Foundation
Doss Foundation, M. S.
Douty Foundation
Dow Foundation, Herbert H. and Grace A.
Dresser Industries, Inc.
Dreyfus Foundation, Max and Victoria
Duchossois Industries Inc.
Duke Endowment
Duke Power Co.
Dunagan Foundation
Duncan Trust, John G.
duPont Foundation, Alfred I.
Dynamet, Inc.
Eastman Kodak Company
Eaton Corporation
Eccles Foundation, Ralph M. and Ella M.
Eddy Family Memorial Fund, C. K.
Eden Hall Foundation
Einstein Fund, Albert E. and Birdie W.
El Pomar Foundation
Elkins, Jr. Foundation, Margaret and James A.
Emerson Foundation, Inc., Fred L.
English Memorial Fund, Florence C. and H. L.
Essick Foundation
Evans Foundation, Lettie Pate
Evans Foundation, Thomas J.
Exchange National Bank
Fabri-Kal Corp.
Fair Foundation, R. W.
Fair Oaks Foundation, Inc.
Fairchild Foundation, Sherman
Farish Fund, William Stamps
Federal-Mogul Corporation
Feil Foundation, Louis and Gertrude
Feild Co-Operative Association
Fenton Foundation
Fieldcrest Cannon Inc.
Fikes Foundation, Leland
Finch Foundation, Doak
Finch Foundation, Thomas Austin
Fireman's Fund Insurance Co.
First Hawaiian, Inc.
First Interstate Bank of Oregon
First Source Corp.
Firstar Bank Milwaukee, N.A.
Fischbach Foundation
Fish Foundation, Ray C.
Fishback Foundation Trust, Harmes C.
Fleet Financial Group, Inc.
Fleming Cos. Food Distribution Center
Flowers Charitable Trust, Albert W. and Edith V.
Fondren Foundation
Forbes Inc.
Ford Foundation
Ford II Fund, Henry
Forest Foundation
Fort Wayne National Bank
Foster Charitable Trust
Foster Foundation
France Foundation, Jacob and Annita
Frear Eleemosynary Trust, Mary D. and Walter F.
Freed Foundation
Freedom Forge Corp.
French Foundation, D.E.
Frese Foundation, Arnold D.
Friedman Family Foundation
Frohring Foundation, Paul and Maxine
Frohring Foundation, William O. and Gertrude Lewis
Frueauff Foundation, Charles A.

Fruehauf Foundation
Fry Foundation, Lloyd A.
Fuller Foundation, C. G.
Fuqua Foundation, J. B.
Gallagher Family Foundation, Lewis P.
Gannett Publishing Co., Guy
GAR Foundation
Gates Foundation
Gaylord Foundation, Clifford Willard
Gazette Co.
Gebbie Foundation
Geifman Family Foundation
Gellert Foundation, Carl
Gellert Foundation, Celia Berta
General American Life Insurance Co.
General Motors Corp.
Geneseo Foundation
Georgia-Pacific Corporation
German Protestant Orphan Asylum Association
Gheens Foundation
Giant Eagle, Inc.
Giant Food Inc.
Gifford Charitable Corporation, Rosamond
Gilmore Foundation, William G.
Glaser Foundation
Glosser Foundation, David A.
Goddard Foundation, Charles B.
Goldie-Anna Charitable Trust
Goldwyn Foundation, Samuel
Goodstein Family Foundation, David
Gould Electronics Inc.
Graham Fund, Philip L.
Grand Rapids Label Co.
Green Foundation, Allen P. and Josephine B.
Gregg-Graniteville Foundation
Griffis Foundation
Griffith Foundation, W. C.
GSM Industrial
Gulf Power Co.
Guttman Foundation, Stella and Charles
Haas, Jr. Fund, Evelyn and Walter
Habig Foundation, Arnold F.
Hafif Family Foundation
Hagedorn Fund
Haley Foundation, W. B.
Halff Foundation, G. A. C.
Hallberg Foundation, E. L. and R. F.
Hallett Charitable Trust, Jessie F.
Halsell Foundation, Ewing
Hamilton Bank
Hammer Foundation, Armand
Hancock Foundation, Luke B.
Harcourt General, Inc.
Hardin Foundation, Phil
Harland Charitable Foundation, John and Wilhelmina D.
Harmon Foundation, Pearl M. and Julia J.
Harsco Corp.
Hartford Foundation, John A.
Hartmarx Corporation
Harvey Foundation, Felix
Hasbro Inc.
Hatch Charitable Trust, Margaret Milliken
Hawkins Foundation, Robert Z.
Hawn Foundation
Hazen Foundation, Edward W.
HCA Foundation
Hearst Foundation, William Randolph
Hechinger Co.
Heckscher Foundation for Children
Hedco Foundation
Heinz Company, H. J.
Heinz Endowment, Vira I.
Helmerich Foundation
Helms Foundation
Hermann Foundation, Grover
Herrick Foundation

Herzstein Charitable Foundation, Albert and Ethel
Hickory Tech Corp.
High Foundation
Hill Foundation, Sandy
Hillcrest Foundation
Hillman Foundation
Hillsdale Fund
Hoag Family Foundation, George
Hobby Foundation
Hoffman Foundation, Maximilian E. and Marion O.
Homeland Foundation
Hook Drugs
Hoover Fund-Trust, W. Henry
Hopedale Foundation
Hopkins Foundation, Josephine Lawrence
Hopwood Charitable Trust, John M.
Houchens Foundation, Ervin G.
Houston Endowment
Howard and Bush Foundation
Howe and Mitchell B. Howe Foundation, Lucille Horton
Hoyt Foundation, Stewart W. and Willma C.
Hudson-Webber Foundation
Hugoton Foundation
Huisking Foundation
Hulbert Foundation, Nila B.
Hulme Charitable Foundation, Milton G.
Hultquist Foundation
Humana, Inc.
Humphrey Fund, George M. and Pamela S.
Hunt Charitable Trust, C. Giles
Hunt Foundation, Samuel P.
Huston Charitable Trust, Stewart
Huston Foundation
Huthsteiner Fine Arts Trust
Hyde and Watson Foundation
Illinois Consolidated Telephone Co.
Imperial Bancorp
Independence Foundation
International Foundation
Irwin Charity Foundation, William G.
ITT Hartford Insurance Group, Inc.
Jackson Foundation
Jacobs Family Foundation
Jacobson Foundation, Bernard H. and Blanche E.
Jaffe Foundation
Jameson Foundation, J. W. and Ida M.
Janesville Foundation
Janirve Foundation
Jarson-Stanley and Mickey Kaplan Foundation, Isaac and Esther
JELD-WEN, Inc.
Jennings Foundation, Mary Hillman
Jewish Healthcare Foundation of Pittsburgh
JFM Foundation
Johnson Charitable Trust, Keith Wold
Johnson Controls Inc.
Johnson Foundation, Burdine
Johnson Foundation, Helen K. and Arthur E.
Johnson Foundation, M. G. and Lillie A.
Johnson & Son, S.C.
Jones Foundation, Daisy Marquis
Jones Foundation, Fletcher
Jordan Charitable Foundation, Mary Ranken Jordan and Ettie A.
Joslin-Needham Family Foundation
Journal-Gazette Co.
Joy Family Foundation
Julia R. and Estelle L. Foundation
Jurzykowski Foundation, Alfred

Justus Trust, Edith C.
Kaplun Foundation, Morris J. and Betty
Kardon Foundation, Samuel and Rebecca
Kaufmann Foundation, Henry
Kavanagh Foundation, T. James
Kayser Foundation
Kelley and Elza Kelley Foundation, Edward Bangs
Kelly Foundation, T. Lloyd
Kelly Tractor Co.
Kemper Foundation, William T.
Kempner Fund, Harris and Eliza
Kennedy Foundation, Ethel
Kent-Lucas Foundation
Kettering Fund
Kiewit Foundation, Peter
Kilcawley Fund, William H.
Kilroy Foundation, William S. and Lora Jean
Kimball Foundation, Horace A. Kimball and S. Ella
Kingsbury Corp.
Kiplinger Foundation
Kirbo Charitable Trust, Thomas M. and Irene B.
Kirby Foundation, F. M.
Kirkpatrick Foundation
Klock and Lucia Klock Kingston Foundation, Jay E.
Knapp Foundation
Knight Foundation, John S. and James L.
Knox, Sr., and Pearl Wallis Knox Charitable Foundation, Robert W.
Knudsen Foundation, Tom and Valley
Koehler Foundation, Marcia and Otto
Kohn-Joseloff Foundation
Komes Foundation
Koopman Fund
Kreitler Foundation
Kresge Foundation
Kuehn Foundation
Kuyper Foundation, Peter H. and E. Lucille
La-Z-Boy Chair Co.
Ladd Charitable Corporation, Helen and George
Laffey-McHugh Foundation
LamCo. Communications
Lang Foundation, Eugene M.
Lasdon Foundation
Lattner Foundation, Forrest C.
Lauder Foundation
Laurel Foundation
LBJ Family Foundation
Leavey Foundation, Thomas and Dorothy
Lee Enterprises
Lehmann Foundation, Otto W.
Lennon Foundation, Fred A.
Leuthold Foundation
Lichtenstein Foundation, David B.
Life Insurance Co. of Georgia
Link, Jr. Foundation, George
Littauer Foundation, Lucius N.
Liz Claiborne, Inc.
Lockhart Vaughan Foundation
Longwood Foundation
Louisiana-Pacific Corp.
Love Foundation, George H. and Margaret McClintic
Lovett Foundation
Lowenstein Foundation, Leon
Lunda Charitable Trust
Lurie Foundation, Louis R.
Lux Foundation, Miranda
Lyon Foundation
MacArthur Foundation, John D. and Catherine T.
MacLeod Stewardship Foundation
Madison Gas & Electric Co.
Mahadh Foundation
Maneely Fund
Marmot Foundation
Marpat Foundation
Marriott Foundation, J. Willard

Mars Foundation
Marshall Foundation, Mattie H.
Marshall Trust in Memory of Sanders McDaniel, Harriet McDaniel
Martin Marietta Corp.
Martin Marietta Materials
Martini Foundation, Nicholas
Marx Foundation, Virginia and Leonard
Mather Fund, Richard
Mathis-Pfohl Foundation
Mattel, Inc.
Matthies Foundation, Katharine
May Department Stores Company, The
Mayer Foundation, James and Eva
Mayor Foundation, Oliver Dewey
Maytag Family Foundation, Fred
McCann Foundation
McCarty Foundation, John and Margaret
McCasland Foundation
McCune Charitable Foundation, Marshall and Perrine D.
McCune Charitable Trust, John R.
McDonald & Company Securities, Inc.
McDonnell Douglas Corp.-West
McElroy Trust, R. J.
McEvoy Foundation, Mildred H.
McFawn Trust No. 2, Lois Sisler
McFeely-Rogers Foundation
McGee Foundation
McGonagle Foundation, Dextra Baldwin
MCI Communications Corp.
McInerny Foundation
McLean Contributionship
McMahon Foundation
McMillan Foundation, D. W.
McQueen Foundation, Adeline and George
McShain Charities, John
M.E. Foundation
Meadows Foundation
Medtronic, Inc.
Mellon Foundation, Richard King
Mengle Foundation, Glenn and Ruth
Mercury Aircraft
Merkley Charitable Trust
Merrick Foundation
Merrill Lynch & Co., Inc.
Messing Family Charitable Foundation
Meyer Family Foundation, Paul J.
Meyer Memorial Trust
Mid-Iowa Health Foundation
Middendorf Foundation
Millbrook Tribute Garden
Miller Charitable Foundation, Howard E. and Nell E.
Miller-Mellor Association
Mills Fund, Frances Goll
Mine Safety Appliances Co.
Mobil Oil Corp.
Montana Power Co.
Moore Foundation, Edward S.
Moore & Sons, B.C.
Morgan Charitable Residual Trust, W. and E.
Morgan & Company, J.P.
Morgan Construction Co.
Morgan Foundation, Burton D.
Morgan Foundation, Louie R. and Gertrude
Morgan and Samuel Tate
Morgan, Jr. Foundation, Marietta McNeil
Morris Foundation, William T.
Mosbacher, Jr. Foundation, Emil
Moses Fund, Henry and Lucy

Mott Foundation, Charles Stewart
Mulford Foundation, Vincent
Murdock Charitable Trust, M. J.
Murphey Foundation, Lluella Morey
Murphy Co. Foundation, G.C.
Murphy Foundation
Musson Charitable Foundation, R. C. and Katharine M.
Mutual Assurance Co.
Nabisco Foods Group
National Forge Co.
National Steel Corp.
National Westminster Bank New Jersey
Nesholm Family Foundation
New York Stock Exchange, Inc.
Newman's Own, Inc.
NewMil Bancorp
Nias Foundation, Henry
Noble Foundation, Samuel Roberts
Norman Foundation, Summers A.
North Shore Foundation
Northern States Power Co. (Minnesota)
Norton Co.
Norwest Bank Nebraska, N.A.
OCRI Foundation
Odell Fund, Robert Stewart Odell and Helen Pfeiffer
O'Fallon Trust, Martin J. and Mary Anne
Offield Family Foundation
Old National Bank in Evansville
Oppenstein Brothers Foundation
O'Quinn Foundation, John M. and Nancy C.
Osher Foundation, Bernard
Ottenheimer Brothers Foundation
Overbrook Foundation
Overlake Foundation
Owen Industries, Inc.
Owsley Foundation, Alvin and Lucy
Pacific Mutual Life Insurance Co.
PaineWebber
Palisades Educational Foundation
Palisano Foundation, Vincent and Harriet
Palmer Fund, Frank Loomis
Patterson Charitable Fund, W. I.
Payne Foundation, Frank E. and Seba B.
Pella Corporation
Penn Foundation, William
Pennsylvania Dutch Co.
Peppers Foundation, Ann
Peters Foundation, Charles F.
Peters Foundation, R. D. and Linda
Peterson Foundation, Hal and Charlie
Pew Charitable Trusts
Philibosian Foundation, Stephen
Phillips Charitable Trust, Dr. and Mrs. Arthur William
Phillips Family Foundation, Jay and Rose
Pick, Jr. Fund, Albert
Pioneer Trust Bank, NA
Piper Jaffray Companies Inc.
Plankenhorn Foundation, Harry
PNC Bank, N.A.
Polaroid Corp.
Pollock Company Foundation, William B.
Porter Foundation, Mrs. Cheever
Porter Testamentary Trust, James Hyde
Potter Foundation, Justin and Valere
Potts and Sibley Foundation

Prairie Foundation
Premier Industrial Corp.
Price Foundation, Louis and Harold
Price Foundation, Lucien B. and Katherine E.
Prince Trust, Abbie Norman
Providence Journal Company
Prudential Insurance Co. of America, The
Pulitzer Publishing Co.
Puterbaugh Foundation
Putnam Foundation
Quivey-Bay State Foundation
Rabb Foundation, Harry W.
Ralston Purina Co.
R&B Machine Tool Co.
Ratner Foundation, Milton M.
Raymond Corp.
Read Foundation, Charles L.
Regenstein Foundation
Reidler Foundation
Reinberger Foundation
Reisman Charitable Trust, George C. and Evelyn R.
Rennebohm Foundation, Oscar
Retirement Research Foundation
Reynolds Foundation, Edgar
Rice Foundation
Rich Products Corporation
Richardson Benevolent Foundation, C. E.
Richardson Charitable Trust, Anne S.
Riggs Benevolent Fund
Ritter Charitable Trust, George W. and Mary F.
Rixson Foundation, Oscar C.
Robinson-Broadhurst Foundation
Rockefeller Fund, David
Rockwell Fund
Rogers Family Foundation
Rohatyn Foundation, Felix and Elizabeth
Rose Foundation, Billy
Roseburg Forest Products Co.
Ross Memorial Foundation, Will
Rowland Foundation
Ruan Foundation Trust, John
Rubin Foundation, Samuel
Rudin Foundation
Russell Trust, Josephine G.
Ryan Foundation, David Claude
Safety Fund National Bank
Saint Paul Companies, Inc.
Sandy Hill Foundation
Sargent Foundation, Newell B.
Sarkeys Foundation
Sawyer Charitable Foundation
SBC Communications Inc.
Scaife Family Foundation
Schenck Fund, L. P.
Scherer Foundation, Karla
Schering-Plough Corp.
Schiro Fund
Schlink Foundation, Albert G. and Olive H.
Schoenleber Foundation
Scholl Foundation, Dr.
Schowalter Foundation
Schroeder Foundation, Walter
Schumann Fund for New Jersey
Schwartz Foundation, Arnold A.
Schwartz Fund for Education and Health Research, Arnold and Marie
Scurlock Foundation
Seafirst Corporation
Second Foundation
Selby and Marie Selby Foundation, William G.
Sequoia Foundation
Seton Leather Co.
Sharon Steel Corp.
Shaw Foundation, Arch W.
Sheary for Charity, Edna M.
Shell Oil Company
Shott, Jr. Foundation, Hugh I.
Sierra Pacific Resources

Simon Foundation, William E. and Carol G.
Skillman Foundation
Slemp Foundation
Slifka Foundation, Joseph and Sylvia
Smith Foundation, Gordon V. and Helen C.
Smith, Jr. Foundation, M. W.
Smith Trust, May and Stanley
Snayberger Memorial Foundation, Harry E. and Florence W.
Snyder Foundation, Harold B. and Dorothy A.
Sonat Inc.
Spalding Foundation, Eliot
Speer Foundation, Roy M.
Speyer Foundation, Alexander C. and Tillie S.
Sprague Educational and Charitable Foundation, Seth
Springs Foundation
SPX Corp.
Stabler Foundation, Donald B. and Dorothy L.
Stackpole-Hall Foundation
Stanley Charitable Foundation, A.W.
Stanley Works
Stans Foundation
Starr Foundation
Stauffer Charitable Trust, John
Stauffer Foundation, John and Beverly
Staunton Farm Foundation
Steele Foundation, Harry and Grace
Steele-Reese Foundation
Stein Foundation, Jules and Doris
Steinhagen Benevolent Trust, B. A. and Elinor
Steinman Foundation, James Hale
Steinman Foundation, John Frederick
Stemmons Foundation
Sternberger Foundation, Tannenbaum
Stokely, Jr. Foundation, William B.
Stone Charitable Foundation
Strauss Foundation, Leon
Strong Foundation, Hattie M.
Stupp Foundation, Norman J.
Sturgis Charitable and Educational Trust, Roy and Christine
Sturgis Charitable and Educational Trust, Roy and Christine
Sullivan Foundation, Algernon Sydney
Sundet Foundation
Sunnen Foundation
Swanson Family Foundation, Dr. W.C.
Swift Co. Inc., John S.
Symmes Foundation, F. W.
Taube Family Foundation
Taubman Foundation, A. Alfred
Taylor Foundation, Ruth and Vernon
Teichert & Son, A.
Temple Foundation, T. L. L.
Temple-Inland Inc.
Textron, Inc.
Thalhimer and Family Foundation, Charles G.
Thermo Electron Corp.
Thomas Foundation, Joan and Lee
Thomasville Furniture Industries
Thompson Charitable Foundation
Thompson Trust, Thomas
Thorne Foundation
Thornton Foundation
Times Mirror Company, The
Tiscornia Foundation
Tobin Foundation
Todd Co., A.M.

Towsley Foundation, Harry A. and Margaret D.
Tozer Foundation
Travelers Inc.
Trexler Trust, Harry C.
Truland Foundation
Trull Foundation
Trust Funds
Tucker Charitable Trust, Rose E.
Turner Charitable Foundation
Turrell Fund
Unger Foundation, Aber D.
Union Camp Corporation
Union Electric Co.
United Airlines, Inc.
Unocal Corp.
Upjohn Foundation, Harold and Grace
Upton Foundation, Frederick S.
Uris Brothers Foundation
USL Capital Corporation
USX Corporation
Utica National Insurance Group
Valmont Industries, Inc.
van Ameringen Foundation
Van Every Foundation, Philip L.
Van Houten Memorial Fund
Van Nuys Foundation, I. N. and Susanna H.
Vance Charitable Foundation, Robert C.
Vernon Fund, Miles Hodsdon
Vicksburg Foundation
Vogler Foundation, Laura B.
Vollbrecht Foundation, Frederick A.
Wachovia Bank of North Carolina, N.A.
Wahlstrom Foundation
Wal-Mart Stores, Inc.
Walsh Foundation
Warfield Memorial Fund, Anna Emory
Warwick Foundation
Washington Forrest Foundation
Washington Mutual Savings Bank
Waters Charitable Trust, Robert S.
Wean Foundation, Raymond John
Weaver Foundation, Gil and Dody
Weber Charities Corp., Frederick E.
Weckbaugh Foundation, Eleanore Mullen
Wege Foundation
Weingart Foundation
Welfare Foundation
Wendt Foundation, Margaret L.
Wertheim Foundation, Dr. Herbert A.
West Foundation, Harry and Ethel
Westerman Foundation, Samuel L.
Wheeler Foundation
Wheeler Foundation, Wilmot
Whirlpool Corporation
Whitecap Foundation
Whiting Foundation
Whitney Fund, David M.
Wickes Foundation, Harvey Randall
Wickson-Link Memorial Foundation
WICOR, Inc.
Widgeon Foundation
Wiegand Foundation, E. L.
Willard Helping Fund, Cecilia Young
Williams Charitable Trust, Mary Jo
Wilson Foundation, H. W.
Wilson Fund, Matilda R.
Windham Foundation
Winnebago Industries, Inc.
Wiremold Co.
Witco Corp.
Wood Foundation of Chambersburg, PA

Woolley Foundation, Vasser
Wyomissing Foundation
Y and H Soda Foundation
Young Foundation, Irvin L.
Young Foundation, Robert R.
Zachry Co., H.B.
Zarrow Foundation, Anne and Henry

Seminaries

Abell-Hanger Foundation
Alavi Foundation of New York
Altman Foundation
Andersen Foundation
Andrews Foundation
Anheuser-Busch Companies, Inc.
Booth Ferris Foundation
Broadhurst Foundation
Cabell Foundation, Robert G.
Cabell III and Maude Morgan
Campbell Foundation, Ruth and Henry
Carter Foundation, Beirne
Chatlos Foundation
Clemens Markets Corp.
Cornell Trust, Peter C.
Culpeper Foundation, Charles E.
Cuneo Foundation
Davis Foundations, Arthur Vining
English Memorial Fund, Florence C. and H. L.
Fairchild Foundation, Sherman
Fruehauf Foundation
Gellert Foundation, Carl
Gellert Foundation, Celia Berta
Glanville Family Foundation
Hagedorn Fund
Hallett Charitable Trust, Jessie F.
Harriman Foundation, Gladys and Roland
Hearst Foundation, William Randolph
Heinz Endowment, Vira I.
Hillcrest Foundation
Hillman Foundation
Hillsdale Fund
Homeland Foundation
Huisking Foundation
Hyde and Watson Foundation
Johnson Foundation, Helen K. and Arthur E.
Julia R. and Estelle L. Foundation
Knight Foundation, John S. and James L.
Kresge Foundation
Kuehn Foundation
Lasdon Foundation, William and Mildred
Lennon Foundation, Fred A.
Link, Jr. Foundation, George
Lovett Foundation
M/A-COM, Inc.
MacArthur Foundation, John D. and Catherine T.
Marshall Foundation, Mattie H.
McCune Charitable Trust, John R.
McQueen Foundation, Adeline and George
M.E. Foundation
Meyer Memorial Trust
Mulford Foundation, Vincent
Murdock Charitable Trust, M. J.
Norman Foundation, Summers A.
OCRI Foundation
Olsson Memorial Foundation, Elis
Peppers Foundation, Ann
Pew Charitable Trusts
Philibosian Foundation, Stephen
Price Foundation, Lucien B. and Katherine E.
Reisman Charitable Trust, George C. and Evelyn R.

Retirement Research Foundation
Rixson Foundation, Oscar C.
Sandy Hill Foundation
Schowalter Foundation
Smith Foundation, Gordon V. and Helen C.
Sonat Inc.
Sundet Foundation
Travelers Inc.
Trull Foundation
Valentine Foundation, Lawson
Warwick Foundation
Wendt Foundation, Margaret L.
Westerman Foundation, Samuel L.
Wheeler Foundation
Y and H Soda Foundation

Social/Policy Issues

Ahmanson Foundation
Annenberg Foundation
Argyros Foundation
Bauervic Foundation, Charles M.
BE&K Inc.
Benwood Foundation
Binswanger Cos.
Burden Foundation, Florence V.
Chatlos Foundation
Connelly Foundation
Favrot Fund
Feil Foundation, Louis and Gertrude
Fruehauf Foundation
Giant Eagle, Inc.
Giant Food Inc.
Gifford Charitable Corporation, Rosamond
Gulf Power Co.
Hafif Family Foundation
Haynes Foundation, John Randolph and Dora
Herzstein Charitable Foundation, Albert and Ethel
Huber Foundation
Huston Charitable Trust, Stewart
Hygeia Dairy Co.
Jaydor Corp.
Jewish Healthcare Foundation of Pittsburgh
JM Foundation
Johnson Charitable Educational Trust, James Hervey
Kayser Foundation
Leavey Foundation, Thomas and Dorothy
MacArthur Foundation, John D. and Catherine T.
Mailman Family Foundation, A. L.
McKenna Foundation, Philip M.
M.E. Foundation
Meyer Family Foundation, Paul J.
Mutual Assurance Co.
New Jersey Natural Gas Co.
Old Dominion Box Co.
Ottenheimer Brothers Foundation
Pew Charitable Trusts
Phillips Family Foundation, Jay and Rose
Piper Jaffray Companies Inc.
Polaroid Corp.
Public Welfare Foundation
Reicher Foundation, Anne and Harry J.
Scherman Foundation
Schowalter Foundation
Scott Foundation, William E.
Semmes Foundation
Seton Leather Co.
Stone Charitable Foundation
Sunnen Foundation
Thomas Foundation, Joan and Lee
Trust Funds
Turner Charitable Foundation

Weaver Foundation, Gil and Dody

Synagogues/Temples

Ahmanson Foundation
Alexander Foundation, Joseph
Amado Foundation, Maurice
Ames Charitable Trust, Harriett
Amfac/JMB Hawaii Inc.
Annenberg Foundation
Ansin Private Foundation, Ronald M.
Arakelian Foundation, Mary Alice
Astor Foundation, Vincent
Atran Foundation
Auerbach Foundation, Beatrice Fox
Barry Corp., R. G.
Benenson Foundation, Frances and Benjamin
Besser Foundation
Blum Foundation, Harry and Maribel G.
Blum-Kovler Foundation
Borman's Inc.
Callaway Foundation
Chapin Foundation of Myrtle Beach, South Carolina
Charina Foundation
Chazen Foundation
Cheatham Foundation, Owen
Columbia Foundation
Cosmair, Inc.
Crawford Estate, E. R.
DeRoy Foundation, Helen L.
DeRoy Testamentary Foundation
Dimeo Construction Co.
Dow Foundation, Herbert H. and Grace A.
Duncan Trust, John G.
Einstein Fund, Albert E. and Birdie W.
Fife Foundation, Elias and Bertha
Fink Foundation
Foster Charitable Trust
Fribourg Foundation
Frisch's Restaurants Inc.
Geifman Family Foundation
Giant Eagle, Inc.
Gilman Foundation, Howard
Glick Foundation, Eugene and Marilyn
Glosser Foundation, David A.
Goldberg Family Foundation
Goldie-Anna Charitable Trust
Goodstein Family Foundation, David
Hafif Family Foundation
Hagedorn Fund
Hallberg Foundation, E. L. and R. F.
Hassenfeld Foundation
Hechinger Co.
Hecht-Levi Foundation
Herzstein Charitable Foundation, Albert and Ethel
Hill Foundation, Sandy
Hillman Family Foundation, Alex
Holzer Memorial Foundation, Richard H.
Jaffe Foundation
Jaydor Corp.
Jurzykowski Foundation, Alfred
Kardon Foundation, Samuel and Rebecca
Kempner Fund, Harris and Eliza
Kettering Fund
Klosk Fund, Louis and Rose
Koopman Fund
Kutz Foundation, Milton and Hattie
Lasdon Foundation
Lebovitz Fund
Lederer Foundation, Francis L.
Lemberg Foundation
Mailman Foundation

May Department Stores Company, The
McGonagle Foundation, Dextra Baldwin
Mellon Foundation, Richard King
Messing Family Charitable Foundation
Meyer Fund, Milton and Sophie
Meyerhoff Fund, Joseph
Mnuchin Foundation
Neuberger Foundation, Roy R. and Marie S.
Phillips Family Foundation, Jay and Rose
Phillips Family Foundation, L. E.
Price Foundation, Louis and Harold
Prudential Securities, Inc.
Rabb Charitable Foundation, Sidney and Esther
Reicher Foundation, Anne and Harry J.
Reisman Charitable Trust, George C. and Evelyn R.
Ritter Charitable Trust, George W. and Mary F.
Rosen Foundation, Joseph
Rosenberg, Jr. Family Foundation, Louise and Claude
Rudin Foundation
Sawyer Charitable Foundation
Schiro Fund
Schwartz Fund for Education and Health Research, Arnold and Marie
Schwob Foundation, Simon
Seaway Food Town, Inc.
Shawmut National Corp.
Slifka Foundation, Joseph and Sylvia
Speyer Foundation, Alexander C. and Tillie S.
Sternberger Foundation, Tannenbaum
Sulzberger Foundation
Taubman Foundation, A. Alfred
Tecumseh Products Co.
Temple Foundation, T. L. L.
Thalhimer and Family Foundation, Charles G.
Titus Foundation, Roy and Niuta
Union Camp Corporation
Upton Foundation, Frederick S.
Weinstein Foundation, J.
Winston Foundation, Norman and Rosita
Witco Corp.
Zarrow Foundation, Anne and Henry
Zenkel Foundation

Science

General

Alabama Gas Corp.
Aldus Corp.
CIBC Wood Gundy
Cosmair, Inc.
Federated Mutual Insurance Co.
GenRad
Gould Electronics Inc.
Holnam
Kansas City Southern Industries
Kennecott Corporation
Knoll Group
LamCo. Communications
Martin Marietta Materials
Miller Brewing Company/North Carolina
Mitsubishi Motor Sales of America, Inc.
Novell Inc.
Pitt-Des Moines Inc.

Pittsburg Midway Coal Mining Co.
Roseburg Forest Products Co.
Ross Laboratories
Sloan Foundation, Alfred P.
Unitrode Corp.
Zachry Co., H.B.

Observatories & Planetariums

Abbott Laboratories
Armco Inc.
Bedsole Foundation, J. L.
Beech Aircraft Corp.
Blair and Co., William
Brooks Foundation, Gladys
Buhl Foundation
Burdines Inc.
Chevron Corporation
Commerce Clearing House, Incorporated
Donaldson Company, Inc.
Ethyl Corp
Fikes Foundation, Leland
Fireman's Fund Insurance Co.
First Union Corp.
Friedman Family Foundation
GenRad
Illinois Tool Works, Inc.
Kennecott Corporation
Kingsbury Corp.
Komes Foundation
MacArthur Foundation, John D. and Catherine T.
Mine Safety Appliances Co.
New England Business Service
The New Yorker Magazine, Inc.
Norton Co.
Novell Inc.
Peoples Energy Corp.
Pick, Jr. Fund, Albert
PPG Industries, Inc.
Robinson Fund, Maurice R.
Rubin Family Fund, Cele H. and William B.
San Diego Gas & Electric
Sara Lee Corp.
Sedgwick James Inc.
Shenandoah Life Insurance Co.
Teleflex Inc.
Thermo Electron Corp.
TransAmerica Corporation
Trull Foundation
United Airlines, Inc.
Windham Foundation
Zachry Co., H.B.

Science Exhibits & Fairs

Acushnet Co.
Air Products and Chemicals, Inc.
Alabama Power Co.
Aldus Corp.
Alumax Inc.
Aluminum Co. of America
American Natural Resources Company
Bauervic Foundation, Charles M.
Benwood Foundation
Bertha Foundation
Block, H&R
Burdines Inc.
Cabot Corp.
Carpenter Technology Corp.
Carter Foundation, Amon G.
Central Hudson Gas & Electric Corp.
Central Maine Power Co.
Central Vermont Public Service Corp.
Chevron Corporation
Clorox Co.
Cole Foundation, Olive B.
Comer Foundation
Cowles Media Co.
Digital Equipment Corp.
Douglas & Lomason Company
Dow Corning Corp.

du Pont de Nemours & Co., E. I.
Duke Power Co.
Ethyl Corp
Federal-Mogul Corporation
Fikes Foundation, Leland
Fireman's Fund Insurance Co.
First Union Corp.
Freedom Forge Corp.
Freeport-McMoRan Inc.
General Motors Corp.
GenRad
Goodrich Co., The B.F.
HCA Foundation
Hickory Tech Corp.
Illinois Tool Works, Inc.
International Business Machines Corp.
Kansas City Southern Industries
Kennecott Corporation
Kiplinger Foundation
Knoll Group
Komes Foundation
Little, Inc., Arthur D.
Long Island Lighting Co.
Louisiana-Pacific Corp.
McCasland Foundation
McKenna Foundation, Katherine Mabis
Merck & Co.
Merck & Co. Human Health Division
Merkley Charitable Trust
Mitchell Energy & Development Corp.
Mobil Oil Corp.
Norfolk Shipbuilding & Drydock Corp.
Northwest Natural Gas Co.
Norton Co.
NYNEX Corporation
Pennsylvania Dutch Co.
Piper Foundation, Minnie Stevens
Pittsburg Midway Coal Mining Co.
PPG Industries, Inc.
Public Service Electric & Gas Co.
Rockwell Fund
Rockwell International Corporation
Rohm & Haas Co.
San Diego Gas & Electric
Scott Fetzer Co.
Seaway Food Town, Inc.
Shell Oil Company
Shenandoah Life Insurance Co.
Simpson Investment Company
Southern California Edison Co.
Stanley Works
Taubman Foundation, A. Alfred
Tenneco Inc.
Texas Commerce Bank-Houston, N.A.
Textron, Inc.
Thermo Electron Corp.
Transco Energy Co.
Union Camp Corporation
Unitrode Corp.
Unocal Corp.
Valmont Industries, Inc.
Vulcan Materials Co.
Whirlpool Corporation
Williams Companies, The

Science Museums

Abbott Laboratories
Achelis Foundation
AKC Fund
Alcon Laboratories, Inc.
Aldus Corp.
Alexander Foundation, Joseph
Allyn Foundation
Aluminum Co. of America
AMCORE Bank, N.A. Rockford
American Fidelity Corporation
American General Finance Corp.
American National Bank & Trust Co. of Chicago

American President Companies, Ltd.
Andersen Corp.
Andersen Foundation
Anderson Foundation, M. D.
Andrews Foundation
Arcadia Foundation
Argyros Foundation
Asplundh Foundation
Astor Foundation, Vincent
Babson Foundation, Paul and Edith
Bank of Boston Corp.
BankAmerica Corp.
Barker Foundation, J.M.R.
Barth Foundation, Theodore H.
Baughman Foundation
Bay Foundation
BE&K Inc.
Bechtel, Jr. Foundation, S. D.
Bedsole Foundation, J. L.
Bingham Foundation, William
Binswanger Cos.
Bird Corp.
Bishop Foundation, E. K. and Lillian F.
Blum-Kovler Foundation
Bodman Foundation
Boettcher Foundation
Booth Ferris Foundation
Boston Edison Co.
Brach Foundation, Helen
Bryant Foundation
Burnett-Tandy Foundation
Butz Foundation
Cabot Corp.
Cain Foundation, Gordon and Mary
Campbell Foundation, Ruth and Henry
Carpenter Foundation
Carpenter Foundation, E. Rhodes and Leona B.
Carter Foundation, Beirne
Carver Charitable Trust, Roy J.
Champlin Foundation
Chase Manhattan Bank, N.A.
Chastain Charitable Foundation, Robert Lee and Thomas M.
Cheney Foundation, Ben B.
CIGNA Corporation
Claiborne and Art Ortenberg Foundation, Liz
CLARCOR Inc.
Clarke Trust, John
Clay Foundation
Clements Foundation
Collins Foundation
Comer Foundation
Commerce Clearing House, Incorporated
Comprecare Foundation
Connelly Foundation
Cooper Industries, Inc.
Cornell Trust, Peter C.
Crocker Trust, Mary A.
Crown Memorial, Arie and Ida
Cullen Foundation
Culver Foundation, Constans
Cummings Foundation, James H.
Curtice-Burns Foods, Inc.
Daniel Foundation of Alabama
Darling Foundation, Hugh and Hazel
Davenport-Hatch Foundation
Demoulas Supermarkets Inc.
Dewing Foundation, Frances R.
Dodge Foundation, Cleveland H.
Dodge Foundation, Geraldine R.
Dresser Industries, Inc.
Dula Educational and Charitable Foundation, Caleb C. and Julia W.
Dunagan Foundation
Duncan Foundation, Lillian H. and C. W.
Eastman Kodak Company
Eaton Foundation, Cyrus
Einstein Fund, Albert E. and Birdie W.
El Pomar Foundation

Elf Atochem North America, Inc.
English Memorial Fund, Florence C. and H. L.
Erpf Fund, Armand G.
Evans Foundation, Lettie Pate
Exxon Corporation
Fairchild Foundation, Sherman
Farish Fund, William Stamps
Favrot Fund
Federated Mutual Insurance Co.
Fife Foundation, Elias and Bertha
Fikes Foundation, Leland
Fireman's Fund Insurance Co.
Firman Fund
First Interstate Bank of Oregon
First Union Corp.
Fish Foundation, Ray C.
Fishback Foundation Trust, Harmes C.
Fondren Foundation
Forest Oil Corp.
Freeport-McMoRan Inc.
Fribourg Foundation
Frohring Foundation, William O. and Gertrude Lewis
Fuqua Foundation, J. B.
Gates Foundation
GenRad
Georgia-Pacific Corporation
Germeshausen Foundation, Kenneth J.
Gheens Foundation
Gilman Foundation, Howard
Gilmore Foundation, William G.
Glanville Family Foundation
Gleason Foundation
Globe Newspaper Co.
Goldberg Family Foundation
Goldsmith Foundation, Horace W.
Gould Electronics Inc.
Griggs and Mary Griggs Burke Foundation, Mary Livingston
Hamilton Bank
Hanson Industries North America
Harcourt General, Inc.
Harriman Foundation, Gladys and Roland
Harriman Foundation, Mary W.
Harrington Foundation, Francis A. and Jacquelyn H.
Herzstein Charitable Foundation, Albert and Ethel
Hewit Family Foundation
Hewlett-Packard Co.
Hillman Foundation
Hillsdale Fund
Hobby Foundation
Hoffmann-La Roche Inc.
Hopedale Foundation
Houston Endowment
Humana, Inc.
Humphrey Fund, George M. and Pamela S.
Hunt Foundation, Roy A.
Hyde and Watson Foundation
Independence Foundation
Ingalls Foundation, Louise H. and David S.
JELD-WEN, Inc.
Jones Foundation, Daisy Marquis
Jones Foundation, Fletcher
Jonsson Foundation
Jostens, Inc.
Kansas City Southern Industries
Kelley and Elza Kelley Foundation, Edward Bangs
Kemper Foundation, William T.
Kemper National Insurance Cos.
Kettering Fund
Kirby Foundation, F. M.
Knapp Foundation
Knoll Group
Knox, Sr., and Pearl Wallis Knox Charitable Foundation, Robert W.
Komes Foundation

Kreitler Foundation
Kresge Foundation
Kuehn Foundation
LamCo. Communications
Lang Foundation, Eugene M.
Larsen Fund
Lauder Foundation
Leavey Foundation, Thomas and Dorothy
Lebovitz Fund
Lederer Foundation, Francis L.
Lehmann Foundation, Otto W.
Levitt Foundation
Levy Foundation, June Rockwell
Little, Inc., Arthur D.
Longwood Foundation
Louisiana-Pacific Corp.
Lowenstein Foundation, Leon
Lurie Foundation, Louis R.
Lux Foundation, Miranda
M/A-COM, Inc.
Marmot Foundation
Marpat Foundation
Martin Marietta Corp.
Martin Marietta Materials
Mather Charitable Trust, S. Livingston
Mather and William Gwinn Mather Fund, Elizabeth Ring
Mathis-Pfohl Foundation
McCasland Foundation
McDermott Foundation, Eugene
McDonald & Company Securities, Inc.
McEvoy Foundation, Mildred H.
McFawn Trust No. 2, Lois Sisler
McGonagle Foundation, Dextra Baldwin
MCI Communications Corp.
McKenna Foundation, Philip M.
Meadows Foundation
Medtronic, Inc.
Merrick Foundation
Meyer Memorial Trust
Mitsubishi Motor Sales of America, Inc.
Monell Foundation, Ambrose
Morgan & Company, J.P.
Morris Foundation, Margaret T.
Morris Foundation, William T.
Morrison Charitable Trust, Pauline A. and George R.
Muchnic Foundation
Mutual Assurance Co.
New York Times Company
Nias Foundation, Henry
Noble Foundation, Edward John
Norgren Foundation, Carl A.
Novell Inc.
OCRI Foundation
Odell Fund, Robert Stewart
Odell and Helen Pfeiffer
O'Fallon Trust, Martin J. and Mary Anne
Offield Family Foundation
OG&E Electric Services
Osher Foundation, Bernard
Owsley Foundation, Alvin and Lucy
Palisades Educational Foundation
Parker Hannifin Corp.
Pfizer, Inc.
Phillips Family Foundation, Jay and Rose
Phillips Foundation, Ellis L.
Phipps Foundation, Howard
Piankova Foundation, Tatiana
Pick, Jr. Fund, Albert
Pierce Charitable Trust, Harold Whitworth
Piper Jaffray Companies Inc.
Porter Testamentary Trust, James Hyde
Premier Industrial Corp.
Prospect Hill Foundation
Quivey-Bay State Foundation
Rabb Charitable Foundation, Sidney and Esther

Raymond Corp.
Regenstein Foundation
Reicher Foundation, Anne and Harry J.
Reinberger Foundation
Rice Foundation
Rockwell Fund
Roseburg Forest Products Co.
Rosen Foundation, Joseph
Rowland Foundation
Rubin Family Fund, Cele H. and William B.
Saint Paul Companies, Inc.
Saltonstall Charitable Foundation, Richard
Sarkeys Foundation
Sasco Foundation
Sawyer Charitable Foundation
Scherman Foundation
Schlink Foundation, Albert G. and Olive H.
Schlumberger Ltd.
Scholl Foundation, Dr.
Scott Foundation, William E.
Scripps Co., E.W.
Seafirst Corporation
Seaver Institute
Share Trust, Charles Morton
Smith Foundation, Kelvin and Eleanor
Snow Memorial Trust, John Ben
South Waite Foundation
Specialty Manufacturing Co.
Stans Foundation
Stauffer Foundation, John and Beverly
Steele-Reese Foundation
Steinbach Fund, Ruth and Milton
Steinhagen Benevolent Trust, B. A. and Elinor
Stevens Foundation, Abbot and Dorothy H.
Stupp Foundation, Norman J.
Subaru of America Inc.
Sulzberger Foundation
Tait Foundation, Frank M.
Taylor Foundation, Ruth and Vernon
Teleflex Inc.
Texaco Inc.
Thermo Electron Corp.
Thorne Foundation
Thornton Foundation, Flora L.
Times Mirror Company, The
Titus Foundation, Roy and Niuta
Tozer Foundation
Tucker Charitable Trust, Rose E.
Turner Charitable Foundation
Unilever United States, Inc.
United Airlines, Inc.
U.S. Bank of Washington
Unitrode Corp.
USL Capital Corporation
Utica National Insurance Group
Van Nuys Foundation, I. N. and Susanna H.
Vogler Foundation, Laura B.
Walsh Foundation
Warwick Foundation
Weaver Foundation, Gil and Dody
Weckbaugh Foundation, Eleanore Mullen
Weingart Foundation
Wells Foundation, Franklin H. and Ruth L.
Wendt Foundation, Margaret L.
Wheat First Butcher Singer, Inc.
Whitehead Charitable Foundation
Wiegand Foundation, E. L.
Wiley & Sons, Inc., John
Wilson Foundation, H. W.
Winthrop Trust, Clara B.
Wise Foundation and Charitable Trust, Watson W.
Woodward Fund
Zachry Co., H.B.

Scientific Centers & Institutes

Abbott Laboratories
Achelis Foundation
Aetna Life & Casualty Co.
Ahmanson Foundation
AlliedSignal Inc.
Allyn Foundation
American Natural Resources Company
AMETEK, Inc.
AMP Incorporated
Anheuser-Busch Companies, Inc.
Annenberg Foundation
AON Corporation
Arcadia Foundation
Argyros Foundation
Aristech Chemical Corp.
Atherton Family Foundation
Bank of Boston
BankAmerica Corp.
Barker Foundation, J.M.R.
Barra Foundation
Bay Foundation
Bechtel, Jr. Foundation, S. D.
Bedsole Foundation, J. L.
Berwind Corporation
Bethlehem Steel Corp.
Bloedorn Foundation, Walter A.
Blue Bell, Inc.
Borman's Inc.
Brady Foundation
Bridgestone/Firestone, Inc.
Buhl Foundation
Campbell Foundation, Ruth and Henry
Campini Foundation, Frank A.
Carnegie Corporation of New York
Carver Charitable Trust, Roy J.
Castle Foundation, Harold K. L.
CBI Industries, Inc.
Central Maine Power Co.
Chase Manhattan Bank, N.A.
CHC Foundation
Cheney Foundation, Ben B.
Chesapeake Corp.
Chevron Corporation
Clapp Charitable and Educational Trust, George H.
Clowes Fund
Commerce Bancshares, Inc.
Connelly Foundation
Consolidated Papers, Inc.
Consumers Power Co.
Cooper Industries, Inc.
Covington and Burling
Cowell Foundation, S. H.
Cowles Charitable Trust
Crocker Trust, Mary A.
Crystal Trust
Culpeper Memorial Foundation, Daphne Seybolt
Dana Foundation, Charles A.
Daniel Foundation of Alabama
Davenport-Hatch Foundation
DeRoy Foundation, Helen L.
DeRoy Testamentary Foundation
Detroit Edison Co.
Dewing Foundation, Frances R.
Dodge Foundation, Geraldine R.
Donner Foundation, William H.
Dow Corning Corp.
Dow Foundation, Herbert H. and Grace A.
Dresser Industries, Inc.
du Pont de Nemours & Co., E. I.
Duke Power Co.
Dun & Bradstreet Corp.
Dunagan Foundation
Eastman Kodak Company
Eaton Foundation, Cyrus
Eberly Foundation
El Pomar Foundation
Elf Atochem North America, Inc.
Ethyl Corp

Exxon Corporation
Fair Foundation, R. W.
Federal-Mogul Corporation
Feild Co-Operative Association
First Union Corp.
Folger Fund
Ford Foundation
Ford Fund, William and Martha
Ford II Fund, Henry
Forest Foundation
Foster Charitable Trust
Foster Foundation
France Foundation, Jacob and Annita
Frear Eleemosynary Trust, Mary D. and Walter F.
Freed Foundation
Freeport-McMoRan Inc.
Frisch's Restaurants Inc.
Gebbie Foundation
GenCorp Inc.
General American Life Insurance Co.
General Motors Corp.
GenRad
Georgia Power Co.
German Protestant Orphan Asylum Association
Giant Eagle, Inc.
Gifford Charitable Corporation, Rosamond
Gilmore Foundation, William G.
Glaser Foundation
Goddard Foundation, Charles B.
Goldberg Family Foundation
Goldsmith Foundation, Horace W.
Goodrich Co., The B.F.
Green Foundation, Allen P. and Josephine B.
Greenwall Foundation
Groome Beatty Trust, Helen D.
Guaranty Bank & Trust Co.
Gulf Coast Medical Foundation
Hammer Foundation, Armand
Harrington Foundation, Francis A. and Jacquelyn H.
Harvey Foundation, Felix
Hauser Foundation
Hebrew Technical Institute
Hechinger Co.
Hecht-Levi Foundation
Heinz Endowment, Howard
Heinz Endowment, Vira I.
Hershey Foods Corp.
Hillsdale Fund
Hoffman Foundation, Maximilian E. and Marion O.
Hoffmann-La Roche Inc.
Hoover, Jr. Foundation, Margaret W. and Herbert
Hudson-Webber Foundation
Hulme Charitable Foundation, Milton G.
Humphrey Fund, George M. and Pamela S.
Hunt Foundation, Samuel P.
Huston Charitable Trust, Stewart
Huston Foundation
Jacobs Family Foundation
Jacobson Foundation, Bernard H. and Blanche E.
Johnson Controls Inc.
Johnson Foundation, Willard T. C.
Johnson Fund, Edward C.
Jones Foundation, Daisy Marquis
Jones Foundation, Helen
Jonsson Foundation
Journal-Gazette Co.
Jurzykowski Foundation, Alfred
Kansas City Southern Industries
Klock and Lucia Klock Kingston Foundation, Jay E.
Knoll Group
Komes Foundation
Koopman Fund
Kresge Foundation
LamCo. Communications

Larsen Fund
Levitt Foundation
Little, Inc., Arthur D.
Lockhart Vaughan Foundation
Long Island Lighting Co.
Lovett Foundation
MacArthur Foundation, John D. and Catherine T.
Marmot Foundation
Marpat Foundation
Mars Foundation
Martin Marietta Materials
Mather Fund, Richard
Mattel, Inc.
May Department Stores Company, The
MCA Inc.
McCasland Foundation
McDermott Foundation, Eugene
McDonnell Douglas Corp.-West
McEvoy Foundation, Mildred H.
McFawn Trust No. 2, Lois Sisler
McGonagle Foundation, Dextra Baldwin
MCI Communications Corp.
McKenna Foundation, Philip M.
McLean Contributionship
Mead Corporation, The
Meadows Foundation
Mellon Family Foundation, R. K.
Mellon Foundation, Andrew W.
Mellon Foundation, Richard King
Memton Fund
Merck & Co.
Merck & Co. Human Health Division
Merck Family Fund
Mercury Aircraft
Merrick Foundation
Merrill Lynch & Co., Inc.
Meyer Memorial Trust
Middendorf Foundation
Mine Safety Appliances Co.
Mobil Oil Corp.
Monell Foundation, Ambrose
Moore Foundation, Edward S.
Morgan Construction Co.
Morris Foundation, Margaret T.
Murdock Charitable Trust, M. J.
Mutual Assurance Co.
Nabisco Foods Group
The New Yorker Magazine, Inc.
Noble Foundation, Samuel Roberts
Norfolk Shipbuilding & Drydock Corp.
Normandie Foundation
Norton Co.
Novell Inc.
Oaklawn Foundation
Odell Fund, Robert Stewart Odell and Helen Pfeiffer
Olin Corp.
Olin Foundation, Spencer T. and Ann W.
Olsson Memorial Foundation, Elis
Osher Foundation, Bernard
Owsley Foundation, Alvin and Lucy
Packard Foundation, David and Lucile
Palmer Fund, Frank Loomis
Parker Hannifin Corp.
Parsons Foundation, Ralph M.
Pella Corporation
Perkin-Elmer Corp.
Pew Charitable Trusts
Pfizer, Inc.
PHH Corporation
Phillips Foundation, Ellis L.
Pierce Charitable Trust, Harold Whitworth
PNC Bank, N.A.
Pollock Company Foundation, William B.
PPG Industries, Inc.

Public Service Electric & Gas Co.
Puterbaugh Foundation
Ralston Purina Co.
Rice Charitable Foundation, Albert W.
Rockwell International Corporation
Rohm & Haas Co.
Roseburg Forest Products Co.
Ross Memorial Foundation, Will
Rouse Co.
Rowland Foundation
Ruan Foundation Trust, John
Rubin Family Fund, Cele H. and William B.
Rubin Foundation, Samuel
Salomon Inc.
SBC Communications Inc.
Schiff Foundation, Dorothy
Schlumberger Ltd.
Seafirst Corporation
Security Life of Denver Insurance Co.
Seidman Family Foundation
Self Foundation
Semmes Foundation
Shawmut National Corp.
Skillman Foundation
Sloan Foundation, Alfred P.
Smart Family Foundation
Smith Charitable Foundation, Lou and Lutza
SmithKline Beecham Corp.
Sonat Inc.
South Waite Foundation
Southern California Edison Co.
Spang & Co.
Speyer Foundation, Alexander C. and Tillie S.
Sprague Educational and Charitable Foundation, Seth
SPX Corp.
Steele-Reese Foundation
Steinbach Fund, Ruth and Milton
Strawbridge Foundation of Pennsylvania II, Margaret Dorrance
Stupp Foundation, Norman J.
Superior Tube Co.
Swanson Family Foundation, Dr. W.C.
Taubman Foundation, A. Alfred
Teichert & Son, A.
Texaco Inc.
Textron, Inc.
Thalhimer and Family Foundation, Charles G.
Thomasville Furniture Industries
Tobin Foundation
Todd Co., A.M.
Trust Company Bank
Union Electric Co.
Unitrode Corp.
Unocal Corp.
USL Capital Corporation
Vetlesen Foundation, G. Unger
Wachovia Bank of North Carolina, N.A.
Warwick Foundation
Weingart Foundation
Weinstein Foundation, J.
Welfare Foundation
Wendt Foundation, Margaret L.
Wheeler Foundation, Wilmot
Whirlpool Corporation
Whitehead Charitable Foundation
Whitney Fund, David M.
Wilson Fund, Matilda R.
Wise Foundation and Charitable Trust, Watson W.
Witter Foundation, Dean
Wyomissing Foundation
Zachry Co., H.B.

Scientific Labs

Achelis Foundation
Barker Foundation, J.M.R.
Bay Foundation

Bingham Foundation, William
Bodman Foundation
Claiborne and Art Ortenberg Foundation, Liz
Clowes Fund
Cord Foundation, E. L.
Culpeper Foundation, Charles E.
Dana Foundation, Charles A.
Erpf Fund, Armand G.
Exxon Corporation
Ford Fund, William and Martha
Friendship Fund
Gould Foundation, The Florence
Greenwall Foundation
Hanson Industries North America
Hazen Foundation, Edward W.
Hearst Foundation, William Randolph
Hoffmann-La Roche Inc.
Hyde and Watson Foundation
Ingalls Foundation, Louise H. and David S.
Klipstein Foundation, Ernest Christian
Knapp Foundation
Merck & Co.
Merrill Lynch & Co., Inc.
Miller-Mellor Association
Normandie Foundation
Overlake Foundation
Park Foundation
Pfizer, Inc.
Polaroid Corp.
Prairie Foundation
Rockefeller Fund, David
Schering-Plough Corp.
Selby and Marie Selby Foundation, William G.
Seton Leather Co.
SmithKline Beecham Corp.
South Waite Foundation
Sprague Educational and Charitable Foundation, Seth
Strawbridge Foundation of Pennsylvania II, Margaret Dorrance
Texaco Inc.
Vetlesen Foundation, G. Unger
Weezie Foundation
Witter Foundation, Dean

Scientific Organizations

Abell-Hanger Foundation
Air France
Allegheny Foundation
Allendale Insurance Co.
Alumax Inc.
Aluminum Co. of America
American Natural Resources Company
Amoco Corporation
Anheuser-Busch Companies, Inc.
Annenberg Foundation
Arcadia Foundation
Argyros Foundation
Aristech Chemical Corp.
Asplundh Foundation
Atherton Family Foundation
Babcock & Wilcox Co.
Beech Aircraft Corp.
Bell Atlantic Corp.
Benenson Foundation, Frances and Benjamin
Benetton Services Corp.
Bingham Foundation, William
Bird Corp.
Blair and Co., William
Borden, Inc.
Borman's Inc.
Bridgestone/Firestone, Inc.
Brown & Williamson Tobacco Corp.
Cabot Corp.
Cabot Family Charitable Trust
Carnegie Corporation of New York
Chase Manhattan Bank, N.A.

Chevron Corporation
Church & Dwight Co., Inc.
Close Foundation
Clowes Fund
Coltec Industries, Inc.
Cornell Trust, Peter C.
Crocker Trust, Mary A.
Crystal Trust
Detroit Edison Co.
Dewing Foundation, Frances R.
Dodge Jones Foundation
Donner Foundation, William H.
Dresser Industries, Inc.
du Pont de Nemours & Co., E. I.
Duchossois Industries Inc.
Duke Power Co.
Eastman Kodak Company
Edmonds Foundation, Dean S.
Ethyl Corp
Ettinger Foundation
Evans Foundation, T. M.
Fikes Foundation, Leland
First Union Corp.
Ford Foundation
Freeport-McMoRan Inc.
Friendship Fund
Frost National Bank
Gates Foundation
General Motors Corp.
GenRad
Gifford Charitable Corporation, Rosamond
Goddard Foundation, Charles B.
Goodrich Co., The B.F.
Gould Electronics Inc.
Gregg-Graniteville Foundation
Griggs and Mary Griggs Burke Foundation, Mary Livingston
Hafif Family Foundation
Hancock Foundation, Luke B.
Harrington Foundation, Francis A. and Jacquelyn H.
Hearst Foundation, William Randolph
Hebrew Technical Institute
Heinz Company, H. J.
Hershey Foods Corp.
Hewlett-Packard Co.
Hobby Foundation
Hoffman Foundation, Maximilian E. and Marion O.
Hoffmann-La Roche Inc.
Houston Industries Incorporated
Humana, Inc.
ICI Americas Inc.
International Business Machines Corp.
Jones Foundation, Daisy Marquis
Jones Foundation, Helen
Kennecott Corporation
Kerr Foundation
Knudsen Foundation, Tom and Valley
Koopman Fund
Lipton, Thomas J.
Long Island Lighting Co.
Marpat Foundation
Martin Marietta Corp.
Mattel, Inc.
McCasland Foundation
McCormick & Co. Inc.
McLean Contributionship
Mellon Foundation, Andrew W.
Merck & Co.
Merck & Co. Human Health Division
Merck Family Fund
Mercury Aircraft
Mitchell Energy & Development Corp.
Mobil Oil Corp.
Morris Foundation, Margaret T.
Mott Fund, Ruth
National Westminster Bank New Jersey
Nestle USA Inc.
New York Life Insurance Co.
The New Yorker Magazine, Inc.
Noble Foundation, Edward John

Noble Foundation, Samuel Roberts
Norfolk Shipbuilding & Drydock Corp.
Norton Co.
Novell Inc.
Packard Foundation, David and Lucile
Palmer Fund, Frank Loomis
Perkin-Elmer Corp.
Pew Charitable Trusts
Pforzheimer Foundation, Carl and Lily
Pick, Jr. Fund, Albert
Pittsburg Midway Coal Mining Co.
PPG Industries, Inc.
Public Welfare Foundation
Rockwell International Corporation
Rohm & Haas Co.
Rowland Foundation
Russell Charitable Foundation, Tom
San Diego Gas & Electric
Scherman Foundation
Scholl Foundation, Dr.
Schroeder Foundation, Walter
Seaver Institute
Sedgwick James Inc.
Shell Oil Company
Sloan Foundation, Alfred P.
Snow Memorial Trust, John Ben
Southern California Edison Co.
SPX Corp.
Sulzberger Foundation
Texaco Inc.
Unilever United States, Inc.
Union Bank
Union Camp Corporation
Unocal Corp.
USX Corporation
Vetlesen Foundation, G. Unger
Warwick Foundation
Whirlpool Corporation
Whitehead Charitable Foundation
Whitney Fund, David M.
Wiley & Sons, Inc., John
Williams Companies, The
Witco Corp.

Scientific Research

Abbott Laboratories
Achelis Foundation
Aldus Corp.
Anheuser-Busch Companies, Inc.
Baker Trust, George F.
Bay Foundation
Bedsole Foundation, J. L.
Bell Foundation, James F.
Bodman Foundation
Bothin Foundation
Bristol-Myers Squibb Company
Carver Charitable Trust, Roy J.
Cooke Foundation
Dana Charitable Trust, Eleanor Naylor
Dynamet, Inc.
Exxon Corporation
Fairchild Foundation, Sherman
Farish Fund, William Stamps
Firman Fund
First Hawaiian, Inc.
Giant Eagle, Inc.
Greenwall Foundation
Guggenheim Foundation, Harry Frank
Hoover, Jr. Foundation, Margaret W. and Herbert
Humphrey Fund, George M. and Pamela S.
Hygeia Dairy Co.
Ingalls Foundation, Louise H. and David S.
Jacobson Foundation, Bernard H. and Blanche E.
Kansas City Southern Industries
Laurel Foundations

Long Foundation, J.M.
MacArthur Foundation, John D. and Catherine T.
Martin Marietta Corp.
McCune Charitable Trust, John R.
McEvoy Foundation, Mildred H.
Mellon Family Foundation, R. K.
Mellon Foundation, Andrew W.
Monell Foundation, Ambrose
Normandie Foundation
Parsons Foundation, Ralph M.
Pew Charitable Trusts
Potts and Sibley Foundation
Rice Charitable Foundation, Albert W.
Schering-Plough Corp.
Seaver Institute
Sierra Pacific Resources
Simon Foundation, William E. and Carol G.
Sloan Foundation, Alfred P.
Smith Foundation, Kelvin and Eleanor
Texaco Inc.
Thompson Co., J. Walter
Vetlesen Foundation, G. Unger
Wean Foundation, Raymond John
Zachry Co., H.B.

Social Services

Animal Protection

Ahmanson Foundation
Aldus Corp.
Allegheny Foundation
Allendale Insurance Co.
American United Life Insurance Co.
Ames Charitable Trust, Harriett
Andersen Corp.
Andersen Foundation
Andersons, The
Annenberg Foundation
Arcadia Foundation
Arkell Hall Foundation
Arnhold Foundation
Astor Foundation, Vincent
Avon Products, Inc.
Baldwin Memorial Foundation, Fred
Barra Foundation
Bechtel, Jr. Foundation, S. D.
Bedsole Foundation, J. L.
Besser Foundation
Betts Industries
Bingham Foundation, William
Bird Corp.
Blum-Kovler Foundation
Bobst Foundation, Elmer and Mamdouha
Borman's Inc.
Bothin Foundation
Brach Foundation, Helen
Bryant Foundation
Cabell Foundation, Robert G. Cabell III and Maude Morgan
Callaway Foundation
Campbell Foundation
Castle Foundation, Harold K. L.
Champlin Foundations
Chazen Foundation
Cheatham Foundation, Owen
Childs Charitable Foundation, Roberta M.
Church & Dwight Co., Inc.
City National Bank and Trust Co.
Claiborne and Art Ortenberg Foundation, Liz
Colonial Life & Accident Insurance Co.
Columbus Dispatch Printing Co.
Comer Foundation

Commerce Clearing House, Incorporated
Consolidated Papers, Inc.
Cooper Industries, Inc.
Copley Press, Inc.
Cosmair, Inc.
Cowles Charitable Trust
Crary Foundation, Bruce L.
Crestlea Foundation
Curtice-Burns Foods, Inc.
Davis Foundation, Edwin W. and Catherine M.
DEC International, Inc.
Delavan Foundation, Nelson B.
Delaware North Co., Inc.
Dell Foundation, Hazel
Dentsply International Inc.
DeRoy Testamentary Foundation
Dimeo Construction Co.
Dingman Foundation, Michael D.
Dodge Foundation, Geraldine R.
Donnelley Foundation, Gaylord and Dorothy
Douglas & Lomason Company
Dresser Industries, Inc.
Dreyfus Foundation, Max and Victoria
du Pont de Nemours & Co., E. I.
Duke Power Co.
Dula Educational and Charitable Foundation, Caleb C. and Julia W.
Elkins, Jr. Foundation, Margaret and James A.
Emerson Foundation, Inc., Fred L.
Enron Corp.
Everett Charitable Trust
Farish Fund, William Stamps
Federal-Mogul Corporation
Ferebee Endowment, Percy O.
Forest Oil Corp.
Freed Foundation
French Foundation, D.E.
Friedman Family Foundation
Fruehauf Foundation
Gellert Foundation, Carl
Gellert Foundation, Celia Berta
GenRad
Gifford Charitable Corporation, Rosamond
Gilmore Foundation, William G.
Goddard Foundation, Charles B.
Griffith Foundation, W. C.
Guaranty Bank & Trust Co.
Gulf Power Co.
Hachar Charitable Trust, D. D.
Harcourt Foundation, Ellen Knowles
Hatch Charitable Trust, Margaret Milliken
Hawkins Foundation, Robert Z.
Hawn Foundation
Hechinger Co.
Heinz Company, H. J.
Hermann Foundation, Grover
Hill Foundation, Sandy
Hobby Foundation
Hoffmann-La Roche Inc.
Hoover Fund-Trust, W. Henry
Hopkins Foundation, Josephine Lawrence
Houston Endowment
Howe and Mitchell B. Howe Foundation, Lucille Horton
Hoyt Foundation
Hugoton Foundation
Hunt Foundation
Janirve Foundation
Jarson-Stanley and Mickey Kaplan Foundation, Isaac and Esther
Johnson Foundation, Helen K. and Arthur E.
Johnson Fund, Edward C.
Johnson & Son, S.C.
Julia R. and Estelle L. Foundation

Kansas City Southern Industries
Kayser Foundation
Kelley and Elza Kelley Foundation, Edward Bangs
Kelly Tractor Co.
Kennecott Corporation
Kent-Lucas Foundation
Kimball Foundation, Horace A. Kimball and S. Ella
Kingsbury Corp.
Klipstein Foundation, Ernest Christian
Koch Charitable Foundation, Charles G.
Kresge Foundation
Kuehn Foundation
Laffey-McHugh Foundation
Lasdon Foundation
Lemberg Foundation
Lichtenstein Foundation, David B.
Linnell Foundation
Management Compensation Group/Dulworth Inc.
Mandeville Foundation
Mardag Foundation
Markey Charitable Fund, John C.
Mars Foundation
Marshall Foundation, Mattie H.
Mautz Paint Co.
McBean Charitable Trust, Alletta Morris
McCann Foundation
McDonald & Company Securities, Inc.
Meadows Foundation
Memton Fund
Mercury Aircraft
Merkley Charitable Trust
Millbrook Tribute Garden
Miller Brewing Company/North Carolina
Monadnock Paper Mills
Monell Foundation, Ambrose
Monfort Family Foundation
Mosbacher, Jr. Foundation, Emil
Muchnic Foundation
Mulford Trust, Clarence E.
Murphey Foundation, Lluella Morey
Murphy Foundation
Myra Foundation
Norman Foundation, Summers A.
North Shore Foundation
Northwest Natural Gas Co.
Ohrstrom Foundation
Overbrook Foundation
Overlake Foundation
Owsley Foundation, Alvin and Lucy
PaineWebber
Peterson Charitable Foundation, Folke H.
Pettus Crowe Foundation
Phipps Foundation, Howard
Pioneer Trust Bank, NA
Porter Foundation, Mrs. Cheever
Potomac Electric Power Co.
Prairie Foundation
Price Foundation, Louis and Harold
Quivey-Bay State Foundation
Ratner Foundation, Milton M.
Raymond Corp.
Richardson Benevolent Foundation, C. E.
Rieke Corp.
Rockwell Fund
Ross Laboratories
Ruan Foundation Trust, John
Sandusky International Inc.
Sara Lee Hosiery, Inc.
Sargent Foundation, Newell B.
Sarkeys Foundation
Sasco Foundation
Sawyer Charitable Foundation
Scherer Foundation, Karla
Schroeder Foundation, Walter
Schwab & Co., Inc., Charles

Selby and Marie Selby
Foundation, William G.
Sentry Insurance A Mutual
Company
Simon Foundation, William E.
and Carol G.
Slifka Foundation, Joseph and
Sylvia
Smart Family Foundation
Sonat Inc.
South Branch Foundation
Spang & Co.
Sprague Educational and
Charitable Foundation, Seth
Stans Foundation
Stauffer Foundation, John and
Beverly
Stemmons Foundation
Strawbridge Foundation of
Pennsylvania II, Margaret
Dorrance
Swanson Family Foundation,
Dr. W.C.
Taylor Foundation, Fred and
Harriett
Tecumseh Products Co.
Temple Foundation, T. L. L.
Tenneco Inc.
Treakle Foundation, J. Edwin
Upton Foundation, Frederick S.
Van Nuys Foundation, I. N.
and Susanna H.
Van Wert County Foundation
Vanderbilt Trust, R. T.
Vulcan Materials Co.
Wahlstrom Foundation
Wal-Mart Stores, Inc.
Wean Foundation, Raymond
John
Weinstein Foundation, J.
Welch Testamentary Trust,
George T.
Wendt Foundation, Margaret L.
West Foundation, Harry and
Ethel
Westerman Foundation,
Samuel L.
Westvaco Corporation
Whirlpool Corporation
Whiting Foundation
Widgeon Foundation
Wildermuth Foundation, E. F.
Winchester Foundation
Witco Corp.
Witter Foundation, Dean
Woodward Fund
Y and H Soda Foundation
Young Foundation, Robert R.

At-Risk Youth

Abell-Hanger Foundation
ACF Industries, Inc.
Achelis Foundation
Ahmanson Foundation
Alabama Gas Corp.
Aldus Corp.
AlliedSignal Inc.
Aluminum Co. of America
Anderson Foundation, John W.
AON Corporation
Asplundh Foundation
Astor Foundation, Vincent
Atherton Family Foundation
Auerbach Foundation,
Beatrice Fox
Avon Products, Inc.
Baker Trust, George F.
Bank One, Youngstown, NA
Barth Foundation, Theodore H.
Baskin-Robbins USA Co.
Bauervic Foundation, Charles
M.
Bay Foundation
Bean Foundation, Norwin S.
and Elizabeth N.
Beazley Foundation/Frederick
Foundation
Benedum Foundation, Claude
Worthington
Binney & Smith Inc.
Blandin Foundation
Block, H&R
Boettcher Foundation

Borden, Inc.
Bowne Foundation, Robert
Bridwell Foundation, J. S.
Buhl Foundation
Bunbury Company
Burnett-Tandy Foundation
Cabot Corp.
Carnegie Corporation of New
York
Carolyn Foundation
Carpenter Foundation
Carter Foundation, Amon G.
Castle Foundation, Harold K.
L.
Central National Bank
Chase Manhattan Bank, N.A.
Chastain Charitable
Foundation, Robert Lee and
Thomas M.
CHC Foundation
Cheatham Foundation, Owen
CLARCOR Inc.
Clark Foundation
Clay Foundation
Connecticut Mutual Life
Insurance Company
Cooke Foundation
Cooperman Foundation, Leon
and Toby
Cremer Foundation
CS First Boston Corporation
Cullen Foundation
Culver Foundation, Constans
Daniel Foundation of Alabama
Davis Foundation, Irene E. and
George A.
Daywood Foundation
Dentsply International Inc.
DeRoy Foundation, Helen L.
DeVore Foundation
Dewing Foundation, Frances R.
Dexter Charitable Fund,
Eugene A.
Douty Foundation
Dreyfus Foundation, Jean and
Louis
Duchossois Industries Inc.
Duncan Trust, John G.
Favrot Fund
Federated Mutual Insurance
Co.
Fish Foundation, Ray C.
Fletcher Foundation
Fondren Foundation
Ford Foundation
Frueauff Foundation, Charles
A.
GATX Corp.
General American Life
Insurance Co.
General Mills, Inc.
GenRad
German Protestant Orphan
Asylum Association
Gheens Foundation
Giant Eagle, Inc.
Glaser Foundation
Goddard Foundation, Charles
B.
Goldie-Anna Charitable Trust
Goldseker Foundation of
Maryland, Morris
Goldsmith Foundation, Horace
W.
Good Samaritan
Graham Fund, Philip L.
Grand Rapids Label Co.
Greve Foundation, William
and Mary
Griffith Foundation, W. C.
Hancock Foundation, Luke B.
Harcourt General, Inc.
Harland Charitable
Foundation, John and
Wilhelmina D.
Hartford Foundation, John A.
Hartmarx Corporation
Hazen Foundation, Edward W.
Hearst Foundation, William
Randolph
Hechinger Co.
Heinz Endowment, Howard
Heinz Endowment, Vira I.
Heydt Fund, Nan and Matilda
Hillsdale Fund

Hoover Foundation
Hoover Fund-Trust, W. Henry
Houston Endowment
Huisking Foundation
Huston Foundation
Ittleson Foundation
Jackson Foundation
Jacobson Foundation, Bernard
H. and Blanche E.
Jarson-Stanley and Mickey
Kaplan Foundation, Isaac
and Esther
JELD-WEN, Inc.
Joy Family Foundation
Kansas City Southern
Industries
Kayser Foundation
Kennedy Foundation, Ethel
Kirby Foundation, F. M.
Komes Foundation
Laffey-McHugh Foundation
Lehigh Portland Cement Co.
Link, Jr. Foundation, George
Louisiana-Pacific Corp.
Lowenstein Foundation, Leon
Lux Foundation, Miranda
Management Compensation
Group/Dulworth Inc.
Maneely Fund
Margoes Foundation
Marpat Foundation
Marshall Trust in Memory of
Sanders McDaniel, Harriet
McDaniel
Martini Foundation, Nicholas
Massachusetts Mutual Life
Insurance Co.
McDonald & Company
Securities, Inc.
McFeely-Rogers Foundation
M.E. Foundation
Meadows Foundation
Medtronic, Inc.
Merrill Lynch & Co., Inc.
Meyer Memorial Trust
Miller Brewing
Company/North Carolina
Mills Fund, Frances Goll
Mitsubishi Motor Sales of
America, Inc.
Morgan & Company, J.P.
Morgan Stanley & Co., Inc.
Morris Foundation, Margaret T.
Mott Foundation, Charles
Stewart
Munson Foundation Trust, W.
B.
Nesholm Family Foundation
New York Stock Exchange, Inc.
NYNEX Corporation
OCRI Foundation
Odell Fund, Robert Stewart
Odell and Helen Pfeiffer
Old National Bank in
Evansville
Oliver Memorial Trust
Foundation
Overlake Foundation
PaineWebber
Palisades Educational
Foundation
Parsons Foundation, Ralph M.
Peabody Charitable Fund,
Amelia
Peterson Foundation, Hal and
Charlie
Pierce Charitable Trust, Harold
Whitworth
Prairie Foundation
PriMerit Bank
Prudential Insurance Co. of
America, The
R&B Machine Tool Co.
Rockwell Fund
Ross Memorial Foundation,
Will
Saint Paul Companies, Inc.
Sandy Hill Foundation
Schenck Fund, L. P.
Schiff Foundation, Dorothy
Schowalter Foundation
Schuller International
Selby and Marie Selby
Foundation, William G.
Seton Leather Co.

Simon Foundation, William E.
and Carol G.
Skillman Foundation
Smith Charitable Foundation,
Lou and Lutza
Sprague Educational and
Charitable Foundation, Seth
Steinhagen Benevolent Trust,
B. A. and Elinor
Stevens Foundation, Abbot
and Dorothy H.
Strauss Foundation, Leon
Strong Foundation, Hattie M.
Sturgis Charitable and
Educational Trust, Roy and
Christine
Subaru of America Inc.
Sunnen Foundation
Tait Foundation, Frank M.
Thomas Foundation, Joan and
Lee
Thompson Trust, Thomas
Tucker Charitable Trust, Rose
E.
Turner Charitable Foundation
Turrell Fund
U.S. Bank of Washington
Unitrode Corp.
USL Capital Corporation
USX Corporation
van Ameringen Foundation
Vollbrecht Foundation,
Frederick A.
Wallace-Reader's Digest Fund,
DeWitt
Weil, Gotshal and Manges
Foundation
Weingart Foundation
Weinstein Foundation, J.
Welfare Foundation
West Foundation, Harry and
Ethel
Whittenberger Foundation,
Claude R. and Ethel B.
Wickson-Link Memorial
Foundation
Williams Charitable Trust,
Mary Jo
Wilmington Trust Co.
Wilson Fund, Matilda R.
Woodward Fund
Wright Foundation, Lola
Zachry Co., H.B.

Big Brother/Big Sister

Altman Foundation
Aluminum Co. of America
American Fidelity Corporation
Argyros Foundation
Arkell Hall Foundation
Ayres Foundation, Inc.
Beal Foundation
Bean Foundation, Norwin S.
and Elizabeth N.
Bell Foundation, James F.
Besser Foundation
Bishop Foundation, E. K. and
Lillian F.
Bobst Foundation, Elmer and
Mamdouha
Borkee Hagley Foundation
Brady Foundation
Bridwell Foundation, J. S.
Brunswick Corp.
Burnett-Tandy Foundation
Bush Foundation
Carter Foundation, Beirne
Catlin Charitable Trust,
Kathleen K.
Chesebrough-Pond's USA Co.
CLARCOR Inc.
Clowes Fund
Davidson Family Charitable
Foundation
Davis Foundation, Irene E. and
George A.
Davis Foundation, James A.
and Juliet L.
Dekko Foundation
Deuble Foundation, George H.
DeVore Foundation

Fabri-Kal Corp.
Flowers Charitable Trust,
Albert W. and Edith V.
Fort Wayne National Bank
Freeport-McMoRan Inc.
Gellert Foundation, Carl
Giant Eagle, Inc.
Griffith Foundation, W. C.
GSM Industrial
Habig Foundation, Arnold F.
Harcourt General, Inc.
Harriman Foundation, Gladys
and Roland
Harrington Foundation,
Francis A. and Jacquelyn H.
Hartz Foundation
Heckscher Foundation for
Children
Hoag Family Foundation,
George
Hopwood Charitable Trust,
John M.
Jurzykowski Foundation,
Alfred
Kelley and Elza Kelley
Foundation, Edward Bangs
Koehler Foundation, Marcia
and Otto
Ladd Charitable Corporation,
Helen and George
Leidy Foundation, John J.
Lockhart Vaughan Foundation
Lowenstein Foundation, Leon
Mattel, Inc.
Mautz Paint Co.
McCune Charitable
Foundation, Marshall and
Perrine D.
McEvoy Foundation, Mildred
H.
McFawn Trust No. 2, Lois
Sisler
Mid-Iowa Health Foundation
Musson Charitable
Foundation, R. C. and
Katharine M.
Norton Family Foundation,
Peter
Palmer Fund, Frank Loomis
Patterson Charitable Fund, W.
I.
Philibosian Foundation,
Stephen
Pittsburgh Child Guidance
Foundation
Priddy Foundation
Richardson Benevolent
Foundation, C. E.
Rogers Family Foundation
Russell Trust, Josephine G.
Sarkeys Foundation
Slifka Foundation, Joseph and
Sylvia
Smith Charitable Foundation,
Lou and Lutza
Smith Foundation, Gordon V.
and Helen C.
Smith Foundation, Ralph L.
Smith Trust, May and Stanley
Todd Co., A.M.
Unocal Corp.
Walsh Foundation
Weaver Foundation, Gil and
Dody
Whirlpool Corporation
Whiting Foundation
Wickson-Link Memorial
Foundation
Wildermuth Foundation, E. F.

Camps

AKC Fund
Allyn Foundation
Andersen Corp.
Anderson Foundation
Ashtabula Foundation
Auerbach Foundation,
Beatrice Fox
Bauervic Foundation, Charles
M.
Beazley Foundation/Frederick
Foundation
Bedsole Foundation, J. L.

Beloit Foundation
Besser Foundation
Betts Industries
Bingham Foundation, William
Blandin Foundation
Bothin Foundation
Brady Foundation
Brown Foundation, M. K.
Cain Foundation, Effie and
  Wofford
Callaway Foundation
Campbell Foundation
Chazen Foundation
Christensen Charitable and
  Religious Foundation, L. C.
Citizens Bank of Rhode Island
Clarke Trust, John
Clowes Fund
Comer Foundation
Crestlea Foundation
Cummings Foundation, James
  H.
Daniel Foundation of Alabama
Daywood Foundation
Demoulas Supermarkets Inc.
DeRoy Foundation, Helen L.
Deuble Foundation, George H.
Dingman Foundation, Michael
  D.
Dodge Jones Foundation
Doss Foundation, M. S.
Dynamet, Inc.
Eberly Foundation
Eden Hall Foundation
English Memorial Fund,
  Florence C. and H. L.
Federated Mutual Insurance
  Co.
Fikes Foundation, Leland
Fink Foundation
Fohs Foundation
Forest Foundation
French Foundation, D.E.
Frohring Foundation, William
  O. and Gertrude Lewis
Glaser Foundation
Globe Newspaper Co.
Goddard Foundation, Charles
  B.
Grand Rapids Label Co.
Gregg-Graniteville Foundation
Guaranty Bank & Trust Co.
Guttman Foundation, Stella
  and Charles
Halff Foundation, G. A. C.
Hallett Charitable Trust, E. W.
Handy and Harman Foundation
Harland Charitable
  Foundation, John and
  Wilhelmina D.
Heckscher Foundation for
  Children
Hickory Tech Corp.
Hoffman Foundation,
  Maximilian E. and Marion O.
Homeland Foundation
Hook Drugs
Hoyt Foundation
Humphrey Fund, George M.
  and Pamela S.
Hunt Foundation
Hunt Foundation, Roy A.
Ingalls Foundation, Louise H.
  and David S.
Integra Bank of Uniontown
ITT Hartford Insurance Group,
  Inc.
Jennings Foundation, Mary
  Hillman
Journal-Gazette Co.
Kansas City Southern
  Industries
Kaufmann Foundation, Henry
Kavanagh Foundation, T.
  James
Kennedy Foundation, Ethel
Kimball Foundation, Horace
  A. Kimball and S. Ella
Kohn-Joseloff Foundation
Koret Foundation
Kresge Foundation
Kuehn Foundation
LamCo. Communications
Lee Endowment Foundation
LEF Foundation

Leuthold Foundation
Liz Claiborne, Inc.
Long Foundation, J.M.
M/A-COM, Inc.
Management Compensation
  Group/Dulworth Inc.
Mandeville Foundation
Marshall Trust in Memory of
  Sanders McDaniel, Harriet
  McDaniel
Marx Foundation, Virginia and
  Leonard
Mather Charitable Trust, S.
  Livingston
Mather Fund, Richard
McDonald & Company
  Securities, Inc.
McFawn Trust No. 2, Lois
  Sisler
McFeely-Rogers Foundation
McGee Foundation
Meadows Foundation
Miller Brewing
  Company/North Carolina
Moore Foundation, Edward S.
Morgan and Samuel Tate
  Morgan, Jr. Foundation,
  Marietta McNeil
Mosinee Paper Corp.
New York Mercantile Exchange
New York Stock Exchange, Inc.
Norton Co.
OCRI Foundation
Olsson Memorial Foundation,
  Elis
Oppenstein Brothers
  Foundation
Ottley Trust-Watertown,
  Marion W.
Overlake Foundation
Parshelsky Foundation, Moses
  L.
Pella Corporation
Pitt-Des Moines Inc.
Plankenhorn Foundation, Harry
Price Foundation, Lucien B.
  and Katherine E.
PriMerit Bank
Quivey-Bay State Foundation
R&B Machine Tool Co.
Read Foundation, Charles L.
Rixson Foundation, Oscar C.
Robinson-Broadhurst
  Foundation
Rosenberg, Jr. Family
  Foundation, Louise and
  Claude
Ross Laboratories
Ryan Foundation, David
  Claude
Sandusky International Inc.
Sawyer Charitable Foundation
Schiro Fund
Schmitt Foundation, Kilian J.
  and Caroline F.
Schwartz Foundation, Arnold
  A.
Seneca Foods Corp.
Sheary for Charity, Edna M.
Sierra Pacific Resources
Smith Foundation, Kelvin and
  Eleanor
Spang & Co.
Stupp Foundation, Norman J.
Sunnen Foundation
Taubman Foundation, A. Alfred
Temple Foundation, T. L. L.
Temple-Inland Inc.
Thomas Industries
Times Mirror Company, The
Tiscornia Foundation
Todd Co., A.M.
Trees Charitable Trust, Edith L.
Tucker Charitable Trust, Rose
  E.
U.S. Bank of Washington
Unitrode Corp.
Uris Brothers Foundation
Van Houten Memorial Fund
Vernon Fund, Miles Hodsdon
Vollbrecht Foundation,
  Frederick A.
Wahlstrom Foundation
Washington Mutual Savings
  Bank

Weber Charities Corp.,
  Frederick E.
Wege Foundation
Weil, Gotshal and Manges
  Foundation
Weingart Foundation
Weinstein Foundation, J.
Welfare Foundation
Westerman Foundation,
  Samuel L.
Wiegand Foundation, E. L.
Wiremold Co.
Witco Corp.
Wood Foundation of
  Chambersburg, PA
Zachry Co., H.B.

Child Abuse

Abell-Hanger Foundation
Argyros Foundation
BankAmerica Corp.
Buhl Foundation
Connelly Foundation
Crabtree & Evelyn
Crane Co.
Delano Foundation, Mignon
  Sherwood
Doss Foundation, M. S.
Farish Fund, William Stamps
Favrot Fund
Freed Foundation
Friedman Family Foundation
GSM Industrial
Hawn Foundation
Heipz Endowment, Howard
Hoag Family Foundation,
  George
Hook Drugs
Huston Charitable Trust,
  Stewart
Jaydor Corp.
Jostens, Inc.
Kayser Foundation
Klosk Fund, Louis and Rose
Laffey-McHugh Foundation
Lederer Foundation, Francis L.
Leuthold Foundation
Lockhart Vaughan Foundation
Marpat Foundation
Mather Charitable Trust, S.
  Livingston
Meyer Memorial Trust
Parsons Foundation, Ralph M.
Pella Corporation
Pittsburgh Child Guidance
  Foundation
Sarkeys Foundation
Second Foundation
Skillman Foundation
SPX Corp.
Subaru of America Inc.
Travelers Inc.
Washington Forrest Foundation
Weingart Foundation
Whittenberger Foundation,
  Claude R. and Ethel B.
Wickson-Link Memorial
  Foundation

Child Welfare

Abbott Laboratories
Abell-Hanger Foundation
ACF Industries, Inc.
Achelis Foundation
Acushnet Co.
Adams Foundation, Arthur F.
  and Alice E.
Adler Foundation Trust, Philip
  D. and Henrietta B.
Aetna Life & Casualty Co.
Ahmanson Foundation
Air France
Air Products and Chemicals,
  Inc.
Akzo Chemicals Inc.
Alabama Gas Corp.
Alabama Power Co.
Albertson's Inc.
Alcon Laboratories, Inc.
Aldus Corp.
Alexander Foundation, Joseph

Allegheny Foundation
Allegheny Ludlum Corp.
Allendale Insurance Co.
AlliedSignal Inc.
Altman Foundation
Aluminum Co. of America
AMCORE Bank, N.A.
  Rockford
American Brands, Inc.
American National Bank &
  Trust Co. of Chicago
American Natural Resources
  Company
American United Life
  Insurance Co.
Ames Charitable Trust, Harriett
AMETEK, Inc.
Amfac/JMB Hawaii Inc.
Amoco Corporation
AMP Incorporated
AMR Corp.
Andersen Corp.
Andersen Foundation
Anderson Foundation
Anderson Foundation, M. D.
Andersons, The
Andres Charitable Trust, Frank
  G.
Andrews Foundation
Anheuser-Busch Companies,
  Inc.
Annenberg Foundation
Ansley Foundation, Dantzler
  Bond
AON Corporation
Appleby Trust, Scott B. and
  Annie P.
Appleton Papers Inc.
Arcadia Foundation
Archer-Daniels-Midland Co.
Argyros Foundation
Arkansas Power & Light Co.
Arkelian Foundation, Ben H.
  and Gladys
Armco Inc.
Armstrong Foundation
ASDA Foundation
Ashtabula Foundation
Astor Foundation, Vincent
AT&T Corp.
Atherton Family Foundation
Atran Foundation
Auerbach Foundation,
  Beatrice Fox
Avon Products, Inc.
Babson Foundation, Paul and
  Edith
Badgeley Residuary Charitable
  Trust, Rose M.
Baehr Foundation, Louis W.
  and Dolpha
Baker Foundation, Dexter F.
  and Dorothy H.
Baldwin Foundation, David
  M. and Barbara
Baldwin Memorial
  Foundation, Fred
Bank of Boston
Bank of Boston Corp.
Bank of New York Company,
  Inc.
BankAmerica Corp.
Bard Foundation, Robert
Barra Foundation
Barry Corp., R. G.
Barth Foundation, Theodore H.
Baskin-Robbins USA Co.
Battelle Memorial Institute
Bay Foundation
Beal Foundation
Bean Foundation, Norwin S.
  and Elizabeth N.
Beazley Foundation/Frederick
  Foundation
Bedsole Foundation, J. L.
Beech Aircraft Corp.
Bemis Company, Inc.
Benedum Foundation, Claude
  Worthington
Benenson Foundation, Frances
  and Benjamin
Benwood Foundation
Berger Foundation, H. N. and
  Frances C.
Berwind Corporation

Besser Foundation
Bethlehem Steel Corp.
Bettingen Corporation, Burton
  G.
Betts Industries
Beveridge Foundation, Frank
  Stanley
Bigelow Foundation, F. R.
Bingham Foundation, William
Bingham Second Betterment
  Fund, William
Binney & Smith Inc.
Binswanger Cos.
Bird Corp.
Bishop Foundation, E. K. and
  Lillian F.
Blair and Co., William
Blandin Foundation
Blaustein Foundation, Louis
  and Henrietta
Block, H&R
Bloedorn Foundation, Walter
  A.
Blount, Inc.
Blowitz-Ridgeway Foundation
Blue Bell, Inc.
Blum Foundation, Edna F.
Blum Foundation, Harry and
  Maribel G.
Blum-Kovler Foundation
Boatmen's Bancshares, Inc.
Bodman Foundation
Boeing Co., The
Booth Ferris Foundation
Borden, Inc.
Borkee Hagley Foundation
Borman's Inc.
Boswell Foundation, James G.
Bothin Foundation
Boutell Memorial Fund
Bowne Foundation, Robert
Brach Foundation, Helen
Brady Foundation
Bremer Foundation, Otto
Brenner Foundation, Mervyn
Bridgestone/Firestone, Inc.
Bridwell Foundation, J. S.
Bright Family Foundation
Brown Foundation, M. K.
Brown & Williamson Tobacco
  Corp.
Brunswick Corp.
Bryant Foundation
Buhl Foundation
Burchfield Foundation,
  Charles E.
Burden Foundation, Florence
  V.
Burnett-Tandy Foundation
Bush Foundation
Cabell Foundation, Robert G.
  Cabell III and Maude
  Morgan
Cable & Wireless Holdings,
  Inc.
Cabot Corp.
Cafritz Foundation, Morris and
  Gwendolyn
Cain Foundation, Effie and
  Wofford
Cain Foundation, Gordon and
  Mary
Calhoun Charitable Trust,
  Kenneth
Campbell Foundation
Campbell Foundation, Ruth
  and Henry
Campini Foundation, Frank A.
Carnahan-Jackson Foundation
Carnegie Corporation of New
  York
Carolyn Foundation
Carpenter Foundation
Carpenter Foundation, E.
  Rhodes and Leona B.
Carter Foundation, Amon G.
Carter Foundation, Beirne
Catlin Charitable Trust,
  Kathleen K.
Cayuga Foundation
CBI Industries, Inc.
Centerior Energy Corp.
Central Fidelity Banks, Inc.
Central Hudson Gas & Electric
  Corp.

Central Maine Power Co.
Centralia Foundation
Century Companies of America
Chadwick Fund, Dorothy Jordan
Champlin Foundations
Charina Foundation
Chartwell Foundation
Chase Manhattan Bank, N.A.
Chastain Charitable Foundation, Robert Lee and Thomas M.
Chatlos Foundation
Chazen Foundation
CHC Foundation
Cheney Foundation, Ben B.
Chevron Corporation
Chicago Sun-Times, Inc.
Childs Charitable Foundation, Roberta M.
Christensen Charitable and Religious Foundation, L. C.
Chrysler Corp.
CIGNA Corporation
Citibank
Citizens Bank of Rhode Island
City National Bank and Trust Co.
Clapp Charitable and Educational Trust, George H.
CLARCOR Inc.
Clark Foundation
Clarke Trust, John
Clay Foundation
Clements Foundation
Clorox Co.
Clowes Fund
CNA Financial Corporation/CNA Insurance Companies
Coen Family Foundation, Charles S. and Mary
Cogswell Benevolent Trust
Cole Foundation, Olive B.
Collins Foundation
Collins Foundation, George and Jennie
Collins, Jr. Foundation, George Fulton
Collins Medical Trust
Colonial Life & Accident Insurance Co.
Columbus Dispatch Printing Co.
Comer Foundation
Commerce Bancshares, Inc.
Commerce Clearing House, Incorporated
Connecticut Mutual Life Insurance Company
Connelly Foundation
Connemara Fund
Continental Corp.
Contran Corporation
Cooke Foundation
Cooper Industries, Inc.
Cooperman Foundation, Leon and Toby
Coors Foundation, Adolph
Copley Press, Inc.
Cord Foundation, E. L.
Cornell Trust, Peter C.
Cosmair, Inc.
Coughlin-Saunders Foundation
Cowell Foundation, S. H.
Cowles Charitable Trust
Cowles Media Co.
CPC International Inc.
Crabtree & Evelyn
Crandall Memorial Foundation, J. Ford
Crane Co.
Crawford Estate, E. R.
Cremer Foundation
Crestlea Foundation
Crocker Trust, Mary A.
Crown Memorial, Arie and Ida
Crystal Trust
CS First Boston Corporation
CT Corp. System
Culpeper Memorial Foundation, Daphne Seybolt
Culver Foundation, Constans
Cummins Engine Co.
Cuneo Foundation

Curtice-Burns Foods, Inc.
Daily News
Darby Foundation
Dart Group Corp.
Dater Foundation, Charles H.
Daugherty Foundation
Davenport-Hatch Foundation
Davidson Family Charitable Foundation
Davis Foundation, Edwin W. and Catherine M.
Davis Foundation, Irene E. and George A.
Davis Foundation, James A. and Juliet L.
Day Foundation, Nancy Sayles
Daywood Foundation
Dekko Foundation
Delano Foundation, Mignon Sherwood
Dell Foundation, Hazel
Demos Foundation, N.
DeRoy Foundation, Helen L.
DeRoy Testamentary Foundation
Deuble Foundation, George H.
DeVore Foundation
Dewing Foundation, Frances R.
Dexter Charitable Fund, Eugene A.
Digital Equipment Corp.
Dimeo Construction Co.
Dishman Charitable Foundation Trust, H. E. and Kate
Dr. Seuss Foundation
Dodge Foundation, Cleveland H.
Donaldson Company, Inc.
Donnelley Foundation, Gaylord and Dorothy
Doss Foundation, M. S.
Douglas & Lomason Company
Douty Foundation
Dow Jones & Company, Inc.
Dresser Industries, Inc.
Dreyfus Foundation, Jean and Louis
Dreyfus Foundation, Max and Victoria
du Pont de Nemours & Co., E. I.
Duchossois Industries Inc.
Duke Endowment
Duke Power Co.
Dula Educational and Charitable Foundation, Caleb C. and Julia W.
Dun & Bradstreet Corp.
Dunagan Foundation
Duncan Foundation, Lillian H. and C. W.
Duncan Trust, John G.
duPont Foundation, Alfred I.
Early Foundation
Eastman Kodak Company
Eaton Corporation
Eddy Family Memorial Fund, C. K.
Eden Hall Foundation
Einstein Fund, Albert E. and Birdie W.
El Pomar Foundation
Emerson Foundation, Inc., Fred L.
English Memorial Fund, Florence C. and H. L.
Enron Corp.
Ensign-Bickford Industries
Erpf Fund, Armand G.
Essick Foundation
Ettinger Foundation
Everett Charitable Trust
Exxon Corporation
Fabri-Kal Corp.
Fair Play Foundation
Fairchild Foundation, Sherman
Farish Fund, William Stamps
Favrot Fund
Federal-Mogul Corporation
Feild Co-Operative Association
Femino Foundation
Fenton Foundation
Fieldcrest Cannon Inc.

Fife Foundation, Elias and Bertha
Fikes Foundation, Leland
Finch Foundation, Doak
Fireman's Fund Insurance Co.
Firestone, Jr. Foundation, Harvey
Firman Fund
First Fidelity Bank
First Hawaiian, Inc.
First Interstate Bank of Oregon
First Union Corp.
Firstar Bank Milwaukee, N.A.
Fischbach Foundation
Fish Foundation, Ray C.
Fishback Foundation Trust, Harmes C.
Fleet Financial Group, Inc.
Fleishhacker Foundation
Fleming Cos. Food Distribution Center
Flowers Charitable Trust, Albert W. and Edith V.
Fohs Foundation
Folger Fund
Fondren Foundation
Forbes Inc.
Ford Foundation
Ford Fund, William and Martha
Ford II Fund, Henry
Ford Motor Co.
Forest Foundation
Foster Charitable Trust
Foster Foundation
Frear Eleemosynary Trust, Mary D. and Walter F.
Freed Foundation
Freeport-McMoRan Inc.
Fribourg Foundation
Friedman Family Foundation
Frohring Foundation, William O. and Gertrude Lewis
Frost National Bank
Frueauff Foundation, Charles A.
Fry Foundation, Lloyd A.
Fuller Foundation, C. G.
Fund for New Jersey
Fuqua Foundation, J. B.
Gallagher Family Foundation, Lewis P.
Gamble Foundation
Gannett Publishing Co., Guy Gap, Inc., The
Garland Foundation, John Jewett and H. Chandler
Gates Foundation
GATX Corp.
Gaylord Foundation, Clifford Willard
Gebbie Foundation
Gellert Foundation, Carl
Gellert Foundation, Celia Berta
General American Life Insurance Co.
General Mills, Inc.
General Motors Corp.
Geneseo Foundation
GenRad
Georgia-Pacific Corporation
Georgia Power Co.
German Protestant Orphan Asylum Association
Gheens Foundation
Ghidotti Foundation
Giant Eagle, Inc.
Giant Food Inc.
Giant Food Stores
Gifford Charitable Corporation, Rosamond
Glaser Foundation
Gleason Foundation
Glenn Foundation, Carrie C. and Lena V.
Glick Foundation, Eugene and Marilyn
Globe Newspaper Co.
Glosser Foundation, David A.
Goddard Foundation, Charles B.
Goldie-Anna Charitable Trust
Goldseker Foundation of Maryland, Morris
Goldsmith Foundation, Horace W.

Goldwyn Foundation, Samuel
Good Samaritan
Gould Electronics Inc.
Graham Fund, Philip L.
Grand Rapids Label Co.
Green Foundation, Allen P. and Josephine B.
Griffith Foundation, W. C.
Griswold Foundation, John C.
Groome Beatty Trust, Helen D.
Gulf Power Co.
Guttman Foundation, Stella and Charles
Hachar Charitable Trust, D. D.
Hagedorn Fund
Haigh-Scatena Foundation
Halff Foundation, G. A. C.
Hallberg Foundation, E. L. and R. F.
Hallett Charitable Trust, E. W.
Hallett Charitable Trust, Jessie F.
Halsell Foundation, Ewing
Hamilton Bank
Hamman Foundation, George and Mary Josephine
Hancock Foundation, Luke B.
Hanover Foundation
Hanson Industries North America
Harcourt Foundation, Ellen Knowles
Harcourt General, Inc.
Hardin Foundation, Phil
Harland Charitable Foundation, John and Wilhelmina D.
Harriman Foundation, Gladys and Roland
Harrington Foundation, Francis A. and Jacquelyn H.
Hartmarx Corporation
Hasbro Inc.
Hawkins Foundation, Robert Z.
Hazen Foundation, Edward W.
HCA Foundation
Hearst Foundation, William Randolph
Hechinger Co.
Hecht-Levi Foundation
Heckscher Foundation for Children
Heginbotham Trust, Will E.
Heinz Company, H. J.
Heinz Endowment, Howard
Heinz Endowment, Vira I.
Heinz Trust, Drue
Hermann Foundation, Grover
Herrick Foundation
Hershey Foundation, Barry J.
Herzstein Charitable Foundation, Albert and Ethel
Heublein Inc.
Hewit Family Foundation
Hewlett Foundation, William and Flora
Heydt Fund, Nan and Matilda
Hill Foundation, Sandy
Hillcrest Foundation
Hillman Foundation
Hillsdale Fund
Hoag Family Foundation, George
Hobby Foundation
Hoffman Foundation, Maximilian E. and Marion O.
Homeland Foundation
Hoover Foundation
Hopkins Foundation, Josephine Lawrence
Houchens Foundation, Ervin G.
Housatonic Curtain Co.
Houston Endowment
Houston Industries Incorporated
Howe and Mitchell B. Howe Foundation, Lucille Horton
Hoyt Foundation
Hugoton Foundation
Hulme Charitable Foundation, Milton G.
Hultquist Foundation
Humana, Inc.
Humphrey Fund, George M. and Pamela S.

Hunt Charitable Trust, C. Giles
Hunt Foundation
Huston Charitable Trust, Stewart
Huston Foundation
Hyde and Watson Foundation
IBP, Inc.
Icahn Foundation, Carl C.
ICI Americas Inc.
IES Industries, Inc.
Illinois Consolidated Telephone Co.
Imperial Bancorp
Independence Foundation
Ingalls Foundation, Louise H. and David S.
Inland Container Corp.
International Business Machines Corp.
International Paper Co.
Irvine Foundation, James
ITT Hartford Insurance Group, Inc.
Ittleson Foundation
Jackson Foundation
Jacobs Family Foundation
Jacobson Foundation, Bernard H. and Blanche E.
Janirve Foundation
Jarson-Stanley and Mickey Kaplan Foundation, Isaac and Esther
JELD-WEN, Inc.
Jewett Foundation, George Frederick
Jewish Healthcare Foundation of Pittsburgh
JFM Foundation
JM Foundation
Jockey Hollow Foundation
John Hancock Mutual Life Insurance Co.
Johnson Controls Inc.
Johnson Foundation, Helen K. and Arthur E.
Johnson Foundation, M. G. and Lillie A.
Johnson Fund, Edward C.
Johnson & Higgins
Johnson & Son, S.C.
Jones Foundation, Daisy Marquis
Jones Foundation, Fletcher
Jones Foundation, Harvey and Bernice
Jones Foundation, Helen
Jonsson Foundation
Jordan Charitable Foundation, Mary Ranken Jordan and Ettie A.
Journal-Gazette Co.
Julia R. and Estelle L. Foundation
Jurzykowski Foundation, Alfred
Kansas City Southern Industries
Kaplan Fund, J. M.
Kaplun Foundation, Morris J. and Betty
Kaufmann Foundation, Henry
Kayser Foundation
Kelley and Elza Kelley Foundation, Edward Bangs
Kelly Foundation, T. Lloyd
Kemper Foundation, William T.
Kempner Fund, Harris and Eliza
Kennecott Corporation
Kennedy Foundation, Ethel
Kent-Lucas Foundation
Kettering Fund
Kiewit Foundation, Peter
Kilcawley Fund, William H.
Kimball Foundation, Horace A. Kimball and S. Ella
Kimberly-Clark Corp.
Kiplinger Foundation
Kirby Foundation, F. M.
Kirkpatrick Foundation
Kline Foundation, Josiah W. and Bessie H.
Klock and Lucia Klock Kingston Foundation, Jay E.

Knight Foundation, John S. and James L.
Knox, Sr., and Pearl Wallis Knox Charitable Foundation, Robert W.
Knudsen Foundation, Tom and Valley
Koehler Foundation, Marcia and Otto
Komes Foundation
Koopman Fund
Kreitler Foundation
Kresge Foundation
Kuehn Foundation
Kuyper Foundation, Peter H. and E. Lucille
Ladd Charitable Corporation, Helen and George
Laffey-McHugh Foundation
Lang Foundation, Eugene M.
Larsen Fund
Lasdon Foundation
Lattner Foundation, Forrest C.
Laurel Foundation
LBJ Family Foundation
Leavey Foundation, Thomas and Dorothy
Lebovitz Fund
Lee Endowment Foundation
Lehigh Portland Cement Co.
Lehmann Foundation, Otto W.
Leidy Foundation, John J.
Lemberg Foundation
Leuthold Foundation
Levitt Foundation
Levy Foundation, June Rockwell
Lichtenstein Foundation, David B.
Life Insurance Co. of Georgia
Link, Jr. Foundation, George
Little, Inc., Arthur D.
Liz Claiborne, Inc.
Loews Corporation
Longwood Foundation
Louisiana-Pacific Corp.
Love Foundation, George H. and Margaret McClintic
Lowenstein Foundation, Leon
Lurie Foundation, Louis R.
Lux Foundation, Miranda
Lydall, Inc.
Lyon Foundation
M/A-COM, Inc.
MacArthur Foundation, John D. and Catherine T.
MacCurdy Salisbury Educational Foundation
Macy & Co., Inc., R.H.
Maddox Foundation, J. F.
Madison Gas & Electric Co.
Magowan Family Foundation
Mahadh Foundation
Mailman Family Foundation, A. L.
Mailman Foundation
Mandeville Foundation
Maneely Fund
Marbrook Foundation
Mardag Foundation
Maritz Inc.
Marquette Electronics, Inc.
Mars Foundation
Marsh & McLennan Companies, Inc.
Martin Marietta Materials
Martini Foundation, Nicholas
Marx Foundation, Virginia and Leonard
Mascoma Savings Bank
Massengill-DeFriece Foundation
Mather Charitable Trust, S. Livingston
Mather Fund, Richard
Mather and William Gwinn Mather Fund, Elizabeth Ring
Mathis-Pfohl Foundation
Mattel, Inc.
Matthies Foundation, Katharine
May Department Stores Company, The
Mayer Foundation, James and Eva

Maytag Family Foundation, Fred
MCA Inc.
McCasland Foundation
McCune Charitable Foundation, Marshall and Perrine D.
McCune Charitable Trust, John R.
McDonald & Company Securities, Inc.
McDonnell Douglas Corp.-West
McElroy Trust, R. J.
McEvoy Foundation, Mildred H.
McFawn Trust No. 2, Lois Sisler
McGee Foundation
McGonagle Foundation, Dextra Baldwin
MCI Communications Corp.
McInerny Foundation
McMahan Foundation, Catherine L. and Robert O.
McMillan Foundation, D. W.
Mead Corporation, The
Meadows Foundation
Mellon Foundation, Richard King
Mengle Foundation, Glenn and Ruth
Merck & Co.
Merck Family Fund
Merrick Foundation
Merrill Lynch & Co., Inc.
Metropolitan Life Insurance Co.
Meyer Family Foundation, Paul J.
Meyer Memorial Trust
Meyerhoff Fund, Joseph
Mid-Iowa Health Foundation
Middendorf Foundation
Millbrook Tribute Garden
Miller Fund, Kathryn and Gilbert
Miller-Mellor Association
Mine Safety Appliances Co.
Minnesota Mining & Mfg. Co.
Mitsubishi Motor Sales of America, Inc.
Mobil Oil Corp.
Mohasco Corp.
Montana Power Co.
Moore Charitable Foundation, Marjorie
Moore Foundation, Edward S.
Morgan & Company, J.P.
Morgan Foundation, Burton D.
Morris Foundation, Margaret T.
Morrison Knudsen Corporation
Moses Fund, Henry and Lucy
Mott Fund, Ruth
Muller Foundation
Munger Foundation, Alfred C.
Murdock Charitable Trust, M. J.
Murphey Foundation, Lluella Morey
Murphy Co. Foundation, G.C.
Musson Charitable Foundation, R. C. and Katharine M.
Myra Foundation
Nabisco Foods Group
Nalco Chemical Co.
National Westminster Bank New Jersey
Nesholm Family Foundation
Nestle USA Inc.
New Jersey Natural Gas Co.
New-Land Foundation
New York Life Insurance Co.
The New Yorker Magazine, Inc.
Newman's Own, Inc.
NewMil Bancorp
Nias Foundation, Henry
Noble Foundation, Edward John
Noble Foundation, Samuel Roberts
Norfolk Shipbuilding & Drydock Corp.
Norgren Foundation, Carl A.

Normandie Foundation
Northern States Power Co. (Minnesota)
Northwest Natural Gas Co.
Norton Co.
Norton Family Foundation, Peter
Norton Foundation Inc.
Norton Memorial Corporation, Geraldi
Norwest Bank Nebraska, N.A.
OCRI Foundation
Odell Fund, Robert Stewart Odell and Helen Pfeiffer
Offield Family Foundation
Ohrstrom Foundation
Oliver Memorial Trust Foundation
Olsson Memorial Foundation, Elis
Oppenstein Brothers Foundation
O'Quinn Foundation, John M. and Nancy C.
Ottley Trust-Watertown, Marion W.
Overbrook Foundation
Overlake Foundation
Owsley Foundation, Alvin and Lucy
Oxy USA Inc.
Pacific Mutual Life Insurance Co.
Pacific Telesis Group
Packard Foundation, David and Lucile
PaineWebber
Palisades Educational Foundation
Palmer Fund, Frank Loomis
Panhandle Eastern Corporation
Parsons Foundation, Ralph M.
Patterson Charitable Fund, W. I.
Payne Foundation, Frank E. and Seba B.
Peabody Charitable Fund, Amelia
PECO Energy Company
Pella Corporation
Penn Foundation, William
Pennzoil Co.
Peoples Energy Corp.
Peppers Foundation, Ann
Perkin-Elmer Corp.
Pew Charitable Trusts
Pfizer, Inc.
Pforzheimer Foundation, Carl and Lily
PHH Corporation
Philibosian Foundation, Stephen
Phillips Charitable Trust, Dr. and Mrs. Arthur William
Phillips Family Foundation, Jay and Rose
Phillips Foundation, Ellis L.
Piankova Foundation, Tatiana
Pick, Jr. Fund, Albert
Pioneer Trust Bank, NA
Piper Jaffray Companies Inc.
Pittsburg Midway Coal Mining Co.
Pittsburgh Child Guidance Foundation
Plankenhorn Foundation, Harry
PNC Bank, N.A.
Polaroid Corp.
Pollock Company Foundation, William B.
Porter Testamentary Trust, James Hyde
Potomac Electric Power Co.
Pott Foundation, Herman T. and Phenie R.
PPG Industries, Inc.
Premier Industrial Corp.
Price Associates, T. Rowe
Price Foundation, Louis and Harold
Priddy Foundation
Prince Trust, Abbie Norman
Proctor Trust, Mortimer R.
Providence Journal Company
Providian Corporation

Prudential Insurance Co. of America, The
Public Service Electric & Gas Co.
Public Welfare Foundation
Pulitzer Publishing Co.
Puterbaugh Foundation
Quaker Chemical Corp.
Quivey-Bay State Foundation
R. F. Foundation
Rabb Foundation, Harry W.
Ralston Purina Co.
Ratner Foundation, Milton M.
Raymond Corp.
Read Foundation, Charles L.
Regenstein Foundation
Reidler Foundation
Reisman Charitable Trust, George C. and Evelyn R.
Rennebohm Foundation, Oscar
Reynolds Foundation, Donald W.
Reynolds Foundation, Edgar
Rice Foundation
Rich Products Corporation
Richardson Charitable Trust, Anne S.
Rieke Corp.
Riggs Benevolent Fund
Ringier-America
RJR Nabisco Inc.
Robinson-Broadhurst Foundation
Robinson Fund, Maurice R.
Rockwell Fund
Rockwell International Corporation
Rohatyn Foundation, Felix and Elizabeth
Rohm & Haas Co.
Roseburg Forest Products Co.
Rosenberg, Jr. Family Foundation, Louise and Claude
Rose's Stores, Inc.
Ross Laboratories
Rouse Co.
Royal Foundation, May Mitchell
Royal Group, Inc.
Ruan Foundation Trust, John
Rubin Family Fund, Cele H. and William B.
Rubinstein Foundation, Helena
Rudin Foundation
Russell Charitable Foundation, Tom
Russell Trust, Josephine G.
Ryan Foundation, David Claude
Saint Paul Companies, Inc.
San Diego Gas & Electric
Sandusky International Inc.
Sandy Hill Foundation
Santa Fe Pacific Corporation
Sara Lee Corp.
Sara Lee Hosiery, Inc.
Sarkeys Foundation
Sasco Foundation
Sawyer Charitable Foundation
SBC Communications Inc.
Scaife Family Foundation
Schenck Fund, L. P.
Scherer Foundation, Karla
Schering-Plough Corp.
Scherman Foundation
Schiff Foundation, Dorothy
Scholl Foundation, Dr.
Schroeder Foundation, Walter
Schumann Fund for New Jersey
Schwartz Foundation, Arnold A.
Schwartz Fund for Education and Health Research, Arnold and Marie
Scott Foundation, Walter
Scott Foundation, William E.
Scurlock Foundation
Seafirst Corporation
Seaver Charitable Trust, Richard C.
Seaver Institute
Seaway Food Town, Inc.
Second Foundation

Security Life of Denver Insurance Co.
Seneca Foods Corp.
Sequoia Foundation
Seton Leather Co.
Sharon Steel Corp.
Shaw Foundation, Arch W.
Shawmut National Corp.
Sheaffer Inc.
Shell Oil Company
Sheppard Foundation, Lawrence B.
Sierra Pacific Industries
Siltec Corp.
Simon Foundation, William E. and Carol G.
Simpson Investment Company
Skillman Foundation
Slemp Foundation
Slifka Foundation, Joseph and Sylvia
Smart Family Foundation
Smeal Foundation, Mary Jean and Frank P.
Smith Charitable Foundation, Clara Blackford Smith and W. Aubrey
Smith Charitable Foundation, Lou and Lutza
Smith Corp., A.O.
Smith Foundation, Kelvin and Eleanor
Smith, Jr. Foundation, M. W.
Smith Memorial Fund, Ethel Sergeant Clark
Smith Trust, May and Stanley
Snow Foundation, John Ben
Solow Foundation
Sonat Inc.
Sordoni Foundation
Southern California Edison Co.
Southern New England Telephone Company
Spang & Co.
Sprague Educational and Charitable Foundation, Seth
Springs Foundation
Square D Co.
Stabler Foundation, Donald B. and Dorothy L.
Stanley Charitable Foundation, A.W.
Stans Foundation
Starr Foundation
Stauffer Charitable Trust, John
Stauffer Foundation, John and Beverly
Staunton Farm Foundation
Stearns Trust, Artemas W.
Steele Foundation, Harry and Grace
Steele-Reese Foundation
Stein Foundation, Jules and Doris
Steinhagen Benevolent Trust, B. A. and Elinor
Sternberger Foundation, Tannenbaum
Stokely, Jr. Foundation, William B.
Stone Charitable Foundation
Strawbridge Foundation of Pennsylvania II, Margaret Dorrance
Strong Foundation, Hattie M.
Stupp Foundation, Norman J.
Sturgis Charitable and Educational Trust, Roy and Christine
Subaru of America Inc.
Sullivan Foundation, Algernon Sydney
Sumners Foundation, Hatton W.
Sunnen Foundation
Swalm Foundation
Swanson Family Foundation, Dr. W.C.
Taconic Foundation
Tait Foundation, Frank M.
Taper Foundation, Mark
Taubman Foundation, A. Alfred
Taylor Foundation, Fred and Harriett

Taylor Foundation, Ruth and Vernon
Tecumseh Products Co.
Teichert & Son, A.
Teleflex Inc.
Temple-Inland Inc.
Texas Commerce Bank-Houston, N.A.
Textron, Inc.
Thalhimer and Family Foundation, Charles G.
Thermo Electron Corp.
Thomas Foundation, Joan and Lee
Thomas Industries
Thomasville Furniture Industries
Thompson Co., J. Walter
Thorne Foundation
Times Mirror Company, The
Titus Foundation, Roy and Niuta
Todd Co., A.M.
Towsley Foundation, Harry A. and Margaret D.
TransAmerica Corporation
Transco Energy Co.
Travelers Inc.
Trees Charitable Trust, Edith L.
Trexler Trust, Harry C.
Trull Foundation
Trust Company Bank
Tuch Foundation, Michael
Tupancy-Harris Foundation of 1986
Turner Charitable Foundation
Turrell Fund
Union Camp Corporation
Union Electric Co.
Union Pacific Corp.
U.S. Bank of Washington
Unitrode Corp.
Upjohn Foundation, Harold and Grace
Upton Foundation, Frederick S.
Uris Brothers Foundation
US WEST, Inc.
USL Capital Corporation
Vale Foundation, Ruby R.
Valentine Foundation, Lawson
Valmont Industries, Inc.
van Ameringen Foundation
Van Every Foundation, Philip L.
Van Houten Memorial Fund
Van Nuys Foundation, I. N. and Susanna H.
Van Wert County Foundation
Vance Charitable Foundation, Robert C.
Vanderbilt Trust, R. T.
Vernon Fund, Miles Hodsdon
Virginia Power Co.
Vollbrecht Foundation, Frederick A.
Vulcan Materials Co.
Wachovia Bank of North Carolina, N.A.
Wahlstrom Foundation
Wal-Mart Stores, Inc.
Wallace Foundation, George R.
Wallace-Reader's Digest Fund, DeWitt
Walsh Foundation
Warfield Memorial Fund, Anna Emory
Warner Fund, Albert and Bessie
Washington Forrest Foundation
Washington Mutual Savings Bank
Wean Foundation, Raymond John
Weaver Foundation, Gil and Dody
Webber Oil Co.
Weber Charities Corp., Frederick E.
Weckbaugh Foundation, Eleanore Mullen
Wege Foundation
Weingart Foundation
Weinstein Foundation, J.
Welch Testamentary Trust, George T.

Welfare Foundation
Wendt Foundation, Margaret L.
West Foundation, Harry and Ethel
Westerman Foundation, Samuel L.
Western New York Foundation
Weyerhaeuser Co.
Wheat First Butcher Singer, Inc.
Wheeler Foundation
Whirlpool Corporation
White Trust, G. R.
Whiting Foundation
Whitney Fund, David M.
Whittenberger Foundation, Claude R. and Ethel B.
Wickes Foundation, Harvey Randall
Wickson-Link Memorial Foundation
WICOR, Inc.
Wildermuth Foundation, E. F.
Willard Helping Fund, Cecilia Young
Williams Companies, The
Wilson Fund, Matilda R.
Winthrop Trust, Clara B.
Wiremold Co.
Wisconsin Power & Light Co.
Witco Corp.
Woodward Fund
Woolley Foundation, Vasser
Wright Foundation, Lola
Wyman Youth Trust
Yeager Charitable Trust, Lester E.
Young Foundation, Irvin L.
Zachry Co., H.B.

Community Centers

Abbott Laboratories
ACF Industries, Inc.
Achelis Foundation
Acushnet Co.
Alabama Power Co.
Alavi Foundation of New York
Albertson's Inc.
Alcon Laboratories, Inc.
Aldus Corp.
Allegheny Ludlum Corp.
Allendale Insurance Co.
AlliedSignal Inc.
Altman Foundation
Alumax Inc.
Aluminum Co. of America
Amado Foundation, Maurice
Amcast Industrial Corp.
AMCORE Bank, N.A. Rockford
American Brands, Inc.
American National Bank & Trust Co. of Chicago
American President Companies, Ltd.
American United Life Insurance Co.
Amfac/JMB Hawaii Inc.
Andersen Foundation
Anderson Foundation
Andersons, The
AON Corporation
Arkansas Power & Light Co.
Arkell Hall Foundation
Armco Inc.
Ashtabula Foundation
Astor Foundation, Vincent
Atherton Family Foundation
Auerbach Foundation, Beatrice Fox
Avon Products, Inc.
Babcock & Wilcox Co.
Babson Foundation, Paul and Edith
Banc One Wisconsin Corp.
Bank of Boston Corp.
Bank One, Youngstown, NA
Barry Corp., R. G.
Barth Foundation, Theodore H.
Bay Area Foods
Bay Foundation
Beazley Foundation/Frederick Foundation

Bechtel Charitable Remainder Uni-Trust, Marie H.
Benenson Foundation, Frances and Benjamin
Berger Foundation, H. N. and Frances C.
Berwind Corporation
Bethlehem Steel Corp.
Beveridge Foundation, Frank Stanley
Binney & Smith Inc.
Birnschein Foundation, Alvin and Marion
Bishop Foundation, E. K. and Lillian F.
Blair and Co., William
Blandin Foundation
Block, H&R
Blowitz-Ridgeway Foundation
Blue Bell, Inc.
Blue Cross & Blue Shield United of Wisconsin
Blum-Kovler Foundation
Bodman Foundation
Boeing Co., The
Boettcher Foundation
Boise Cascade Corporation
Booth Ferris Foundation
Borman's Inc.
Bothin Foundation
Bowen Foundation, Ethel N.
Bowne Foundation, Robert
BP America Inc.
Brach Foundation, Helen
Bremer Foundation, Otto
Bridgestone/Firestone, Inc.
Brown & Williamson Tobacco Corp.
Brunswick Corp.
Bryant Foundation
Bryn Mawr Trust Co.
Burchfield Foundation, Charles E.
Burlington Industries, Inc.
Bush Foundation
Cable & Wireless Holdings, Inc.
Cabot Corp.
Cafritz Foundation, Morris and Gwendolyn
Cain Foundation, Effie and Wofford
Cain Foundation, Gordon and Mary
Carnahan-Jackson Foundation
Carpenter Foundation
Carvel Foundation, Thomas and Agnes
Catlin Charitable Trust, Kathleen K.
CBI Industries, Inc.
Centerior Energy Corp.
Central Hudson Gas & Electric Corp.
Central Maine Power Co.
Champlin Foundations
Charina Foundation
Chartwell Foundation
Chase Manhattan Bank, N.A.
Chatlos Foundation
Chazen Foundation
Cheney Foundation, Ben B.
Chevron Corporation
Chicago Sun-Times, Inc.
Citibank
Citizens Bank of Rhode Island
Clapp Charitable and Educational Trust, George H.
CLARCOR Inc.
Clark Foundation
Clarke Trust, John
Clorox Co.
Cole Foundation, Olive B.
Colonial Life & Accident Insurance Co.
Coltec Industries, Inc.
Columbia Foundation
Columbus Dispatch Printing Co.
Commerce Bancshares, Inc.
Commerce Clearing House, Incorporated
Consolidated Natural Gas Co.
Continental Corp.
Cooke Foundation

Cooper Industries, Inc.
Coors Foundation, Adolph
Cowles Charitable Trust
Cowles Foundation, Gardner and Florence Call
Cowles Media Co.
CPC International Inc.
Crandall Memorial Foundation, J. Ford
Cremer Foundation
Crestlea Foundation
Crocker Trust, Mary A.
Crystal Trust
CS First Boston Corporation
Cummins Engine Co.
Curtice-Burns Foods, Inc.
Davidson Family Charitable Foundation
DEC International, Inc.
Deere & Co.
Delaware North Co., Inc.
Demoulas Supermarkets Inc.
DeRoy Testamentary Foundation
Detroit Edison Co.
Deuble Foundation, George H.
Dexter Charitable Fund, Eugene A.
Diamond Foundation, Aaron
Diamond Shamrock Inc.
Dimeo Construction Co.
Dodge Foundation, Cleveland H.
Donaldson Company, Inc.
Doss Foundation, M. S.
Douglas & Lomason Company
Dow Corning Corp.
Dow Foundation, Herbert H. and Grace A.
Dresser Industries, Inc.
Dreyfus Foundation, Jean and Louis
du Pont de Nemours & Co., E. I.
Duke Power Co.
Dynamet, Inc.
Eaton Corporation
Eberly Foundation
Eddy Family Memorial Fund, C. K.
Eden Hall Foundation
Einstein Fund, Albert E. and Birdie W.
El Pomar Foundation
Ensign-Bickford Industries
Evans Foundation, Lettie Pate
Evans Foundation, T. M.
Exchange National Bank
Fabri-Kal Corp.
Fair Oaks Foundation, Inc.
Farr Trust, Frank M. and Alice M.
Federal-Mogul Corporation
Federated Mutual Insurance Co.
Feil Foundation, Louis and Gertrude
Feild Co-Operative Association
Fieldcrest Cannon Inc.
Fife Foundation, Elias and Bertha
Fireman's Fund Insurance Co.
Firestone, Jr. Foundation, Harvey
First Fidelity Bank
First Financial Bank FSB
First Hawaiian, Inc.
First Interstate Bank of Oregon
First Union Corp.
Firstar Bank Milwaukee, N.A.
Fischbach Foundation
Fleet Financial Group, Inc.
Fletcher Foundation
Flowers Charitable Trust, Albert W. and Edith V.
Forbes Inc.
Forest Foundation
Forster Charitable Trust, James W. and Ella B.
Foster Charitable Trust
Foster Foundation
Frear Eleemosynary Trust, Mary D. and Walter F.
French Foundation, D.E.
Frese Foundation, Arnold D.

Frost National Bank
Frueauff Foundation, Charles A.
Fry Foundation, Lloyd A.
Gannett Publishing Co., Guy
Gates Foundation
GATX Corp.
Geifman Family Foundation
Gellert Foundation, Carl
General American Life Insurance Co.
General Mills, Inc.
General Motors Corp.
Georgia Power Co.
German Protestant Orphan Asylum Association
Gershman Foundation, Joel
Giant Eagle, Inc.
Giant Food Inc.
Giant Food Stores
Gifford Charitable Corporation, Rosamond
Gillette Co.
Glaser Foundation
Gleason Foundation
Globe Newspaper Co.
Glosser Foundation, David A.
Goldwyn Foundation, Samuel
Goodrich Co., The B.F.
Graham Fund, Philip L.
Grand Rapids Label Co.
Gregg-Graniteville Foundation
Guaranty Bank & Trust Co.
Guttman Foundation, Stella and Charles
Haas, Jr. Fund, Evelyn and Walter
Hafif Family Foundation
Haley Foundation, W. B.
Halff Foundation, G. A. C.
Hamman Foundation, George and Mary Josephine
Handy and Harman Foundation
Harcourt Foundation, Ellen Knowles
Harrington Foundation, Francis A. and Jacquelyn H.
Harsco Corp.
Hartmarx Corporation
Hartz Foundation
Hawn Foundation
HCA Foundation
Hechinger Co.
Heckscher Foundation for Children
Heinz Company, H. J.
Henderson Foundation, George B.
Hillcrest Foundation
Holzer Memorial Foundation, Richard H.
Hoover Foundation
Hopkins Foundation, Josephine Lawrence
Houston Endowment
Houston Industries Incorporated
Howard and Bush Foundation
Hoyt Foundation
Hoyt Foundation, Stewart W. and Willma C.
Huisking Foundation
Hulme Charitable Foundation, Milton G.
Humana, Inc.
Hunt Charitable Trust, C. Giles
Hunt Foundation
Huston Charitable Trust, Stewart
Hyde and Watson Foundation
ICI Americas Inc.
IES Industries, Inc.
Ingalls Foundation, Louise H. and David S.
Inland Container Corp.
International Paper Co.
Jackson Foundation
Janirve Foundation
Jarson-Stanley and Mickey Kaplan Foundation, Isaac and Esther
JELD-WEN, Inc.
Jockey Hollow Foundation
John Hancock Mutual Life Insurance Co.

Bemis Company, Inc.
Benedum Foundation, Claude Worthington
Benenson Foundation, Frances and Benjamin
Benetton Services Corp.
Benwood Foundation
Berger Foundation, H. N. and Frances C.
Besser Foundation
Bethlehem Steel Corp.
Bettingen Corporation, Burton G.
Betts Industries
Beveridge Foundation, Frank Stanley
Bigelow Foundation, F. R.
Bingham Foundation, William
Bingham Second Betterment Fund, William
Binswanger Cos.
Bird Corp.
Birnschein Foundation, Alvin and Marion
Bishop Foundation, E. K. and Lillian F.
Blair and Co., William
Blake Foundation, S. P.
Blaustein Foundation, Louis and Henrietta
Block, H&R
Bloedorn Foundation, Walter A.
Blount Educational and Charitable Foundation, Mildred Weedon
Blount, Inc.
Blowitz-Ridgeway Foundation
Blue Bell, Inc.
Blum Foundation, Edna F.
Blum Foundation, Harry and Maribel G.
Blum-Kovler Foundation
Boatmen's Bancshares, Inc.
Bobst Foundation, Elmer and Mamdouha
Bodman Foundation
Boeing Co., The
Boettcher Foundation
Booth Ferris Foundation
Boothroyd Foundation, Charles H. and Bertha L.
Borden, Inc.
Borkee Hagley Foundation
Borman's Inc.
Boston Edison Co.
Bothin Foundation
Boutell Memorial Fund
Bowne Foundation, Robert
BP America Inc.
Bremer Foundation, Otto
Brenner Foundation, Mervyn
Breyer Foundation
Bridgestone/Firestone, Inc.
Bright Family Foundation
Brillion Iron Works
Bristol-Myers Squibb Company
Broadhurst Foundation
Brown Foundation, M. K.
Brown & Williamson Tobacco Corp.
Brunswick Corp.
Bryant Foundation
Bryn Mawr Trust Co.
Bucyrus-Erie Company
Burchfield Foundation, Charles E.
Burden Foundation, Florence V.
Burkitt Foundation
Burlington Industries, Inc.
Bush Foundation
Cabell Foundation, Robert G. Cabell III and Maude Morgan
Cable & Wireless Holdings, Inc.
Cabot Corp.
Caestecker Foundation, Charles and Marie
Cafritz Foundation, Morris and Gwendolyn
Cain Foundation, Gordon and Mary

Calder Foundation, Louis
Calhoun Charitable Trust, Kenneth
Callaway Foundation
Campbell Foundation
Campbell Foundation, Ruth and Henry
Campini Foundation, Frank A.
Canon U.S.A., Inc.
Cargill Inc.
Carnahan-Jackson Foundation
Carnegie Corporation of New York
Carolyn Foundation
Carpenter Foundation
Carpenter Foundation, E. Rhodes and Leona B.
Carter Foundation, Amon G.
Carter Foundation, Beirne
Carvel Foundation, Thomas and Agnes
Carver Charitable Trust, Roy J.
Cassett Foundation, Louis N.
Catlin Charitable Trust, Kathleen K.
Cayuga Foundation
CBI Industries, Inc.
CBS, Inc.
Centerior Energy Corp.
Central Fidelity Banks, Inc.
Central Hudson Gas & Electric Corp.
Central Maine Power Co.
Central National Bank
Central Vermont Public Service Corp.
Centralia Foundation
Champion International Corporation
Champlin Foundations
Chapin Foundation of Myrtle Beach, South Carolina
Chapman Charitable Corporation, Howard and Bess
Charina Foundation
Chartwell Foundation
Chase Manhattan Bank, N.A.
Chastain Charitable Foundation, Robert Lee and Thomas M.
Chazen Foundation
CHC Foundation
Cheatham Foundation, Owen
Cheney Foundation, Ben B.
Chesapeake Corp.
Chesebrough-Pond's USA Co.
Chevron Corporation
Chicago Sun-Times, Inc.
Childs Charitable Foundation, Roberta M.
Christensen Charitable and Religious Foundation, L. C.
Chrysler Corp.
Church & Dwight Co., Inc.
Citibank
Citizens Bank of Rhode Island
Clapp Charitable and Educational Trust, George H.
CLARCOR Inc.
Clark Foundation
Clarke Trust, John
Clarkson Foundation, Jeniam
Clay Foundation
Clemens Markets Corp.
Clements Foundation
Clorox Co.
Clowes Fund
CNA Financial Corporation/CNA Insurance Companies
Coen Family Foundation, Charles S. and Mary
Cogswell Benevolent Trust
Cole Foundation, Olive B.
Cole Trust, Quincy
Collins Foundation
Collins Foundation, George and Jennie
Collins, Jr. Foundation, George Fulton
Colonial Life & Accident Insurance Co.
Columbia Foundation

Columbus Dispatch Printing Co.
Comer Foundation
Commerce Bancshares, Inc.
Commerce Clearing House, Incorporated
Commonwealth Edison Co.
Comprecare Foundation
Connecticut Mutual Life Insurance Company
Connelly Foundation
Consolidated Natural Gas Co.
Consolidated Papers, Inc.
Consumers Power Co.
Continental Corp.
Cooke Foundation
Cooper Industries, Inc.
Coors Foundation, Adolph
Copley Press, Inc.
Cord Foundation, E. L.
Cornell Trust, Peter C.
Coughlin-Saunders Foundation
Cowell Foundation, S. H.
Cowles Charitable Trust
Cowles Media Co.
CPC International Inc.
CR Industries
Crabtree & Evelyn
Crandall Memorial Foundation, J. Ford
Crane Co.
Cranston Print Works Company
Crary Foundation, Bruce L.
Crawford Estate, E. R.
Cremer Foundation
Crestlea Foundation
Crocker Trust, Mary A.
Crown Books
Crown Memorial, Arie and Ida
Crystal Trust
CS First Boston Corporation
CT Corp. System
Culpeper Memorial Foundation, Daphne Seybolt
Culver Foundation, Constans
Cummings Foundation, James H.
Cummins Engine Co.
Cuneo Foundation
Curtice-Burns Foods, Inc.
Daily News
Dalton Foundation, Harry L.
Daniel Foundation of Alabama
Darby Foundation
Dart Group Corp.
Dater Foundation, Charles H.
Daugherty Foundation
Davidson Family Charitable Foundation
Davis Foundation, Edwin W. and Catherine M.
Davis Foundation, Irene E. and George A.
Davis Foundation, James A. and Juliet L.
Davis Foundations, Arthur Vining
Day Foundation, Nancy Sayles
Daywood Foundation
Deere & Co.
Delavan Foundation, Nelson B.
Dell Foundation, Hazel
Demos Foundation, N.
Demoulas Supermarkets Inc.
Dentsply International Inc.
DeRoy Foundation, Helen L.
DeRoy Testamentary Foundation
Detroit Edison Co.
Deuble Foundation, George H.
DeVore Foundation
Dewing Foundation, Frances R.
Dexter Charitable Fund, Eugene A.
Dexter Corporation
Digital Equipment Corp.
Dillon Foundation
Dimeo Construction Co.
Dishman Charitable Foundation Trust, H. E. and Kate
Dodge Foundation, Cleveland H.
Dodge Jones Foundation
Donaldson Company, Inc.

Donnelley Foundation, Gaylord and Dorothy
Doss Foundation, M. S.
Douglas & Lomason Company
Douty Foundation
Dover Foundation
Dow Corning Corp.
Dow Foundation, Herbert H. and Grace A.
Dresser Industries, Inc.
Dreyfus Foundation, Jean and Louis
Dreyfus Foundation, Max and Victoria
du Pont de Nemours & Co., E. I.
Duchossois Industries Inc.
Duke Power Co.
Dun & Bradstreet Corp.
Dunagan Foundation
Duncan Foundation, Lillian H. and C. W.
Duncan Trust, John G.
duPont Foundation, Alfred I.
Durfee Foundation
Dynamet, Inc.
Early Foundation
Eastman Kodak Company
Eaton Corporation
Eberly Foundation
Eccles Foundation, Ralph M. and Ella M.
Eddy Family Memorial Fund, C. K.
Eden Hall Foundation
Edgewater Steel Corp.
Edmonds Foundation, Dean S.
Einstein Fund, Albert E. and Birdie W.
El Pomar Foundation
Elf Atochem North America, Inc.
Elkins, Jr. Foundation, Margaret and James A.
Emerson Foundation, Inc., Fred L.
English Memorial Fund, Florence C. and H. L.
Enron Corp.
Essick Foundation
Ethyl Corp
Ettinger Foundation
Everett Charitable Trust
Exchange National Bank
Exxon Corporation
Fabri-Kal Corp.
Fair Oaks Foundation, Inc.
Fair Play Foundation
Fairchild Foundation, Sherman
Farish Fund, William Stamps
Farr Trust, Frank M. and Alice M.
Federal-Mogul Corporation
Federated Mutual Insurance Co.
Femino Foundation
Fenton Foundation
Ferebee Endowment, Percy O.
Fieldcrest Cannon Inc.
Fife Foundation, Elias and Bertha
Fikes Foundation, Leland
Finch Foundation, Doak
Finch Foundation, Thomas Austin
Fink Foundation
Fireman's Fund Insurance Co.
Firman Fund
First Fidelity Bank
First Financial Bank FSB
First Interstate Bank of Oregon
First Tennessee Bank
First Union Corp.
First Union National Bank of Florida
Firstar Bank Milwaukee, N.A.
Fischbach Foundation
Fish Foundation, Ray C.
Fishback Foundation Trust, Harmes C.
Fleming Cos. Food Distribution Center
Fletcher Foundation
Flowers Charitable Trust, Albert W. and Edith V.

Folger Fund
Fondren Foundation
Forbes Inc.
Ford Foundation
Ford Fund, William and Martha
Ford II Fund, Henry
Ford Motor Co.
Forest Foundation
Fort Wayne National Bank
Foster Charitable Trust
Foster Foundation
France Foundation, Jacob and Annita
Frear Eleemosynary Trust, Mary D. and Walter F.
Freed Foundation
Freedom Forge Corp.
Freeman Charitable Trust, Samuel
Freeport Brick Co.
Freeport-McMoRan Inc.
French Oil Mill Machinery Co.
Fribourg Foundation
Friedman Family Foundation
Friendship Fund
Frisch's Restaurants Inc.
Frohring Foundation, Paul and Maxine
Frohring Foundation, William O. and Gertrude Lewis
Frost National Bank
Frueauff Foundation, Charles A.
Fruehauf Foundation
Fry Foundation, Lloyd A.
Fujitsu America, Inc.
Fund for New Jersey
Fuqua Foundation, J. B.
Gallagher Family Foundation, Lewis P.
Gamble Foundation
Gannett Publishing Co., Guy
Gap, Inc., The
GAR Foundation
Garland Foundation, John Jewett and H. Chandler
GATX Corp.
Gazette Co.
Gebbie Foundation
Geifman Family Foundation
Gellert Foundation, Carl
Gellert Foundation, Celia Berta
General American Life Insurance Co.
General Mills, Inc.
General Motors Corp.
Geneseo Foundation
GenRad
Georgia-Pacific Corporation
Georgia Power Co.
Gershman Foundation, Joel
Ghidotti Foundation
Giant Eagle, Inc.
Giant Food Inc.
Giant Food Stores
Gifford Charitable Corporation, Rosamond
Giles Foundation, Edward C.
Gilman Foundation, Howard
Gilmore Foundation, William G.
Glanville Family Foundation
Glaser Foundation
Glick Foundation, Eugene and Marilyn
Globe Newspaper Co.
Glosser Foundation, David A.
Goddard Foundation, Charles B.
Goldberg Family Foundation
Goldie-Anna Charitable Trust
Goldseker Foundation of Maryland, Morris
Goldsmith Foundation, Horace W.
Goldwyn Foundation, Samuel
Goodman & Co.
Goodrich Co., The B.F.
Goodstein Family Foundation, David
Gould Electronics Inc.
Graham Fund, Philip L.
Grand Rapids Label Co.
Great-West Life Assurance Co.

Noble Foundation, Samuel Roberts
Norfolk Shipbuilding & Drydock Corp.
Norgren Foundation, Carl A.
Normandie Foundation
North Shore Foundation
Northern States Power Co. (Minnesota)
Norton Co.
Norton Family Foundation, Peter
Norton Foundation Inc.
Norton Memorial Corporation, Geraldi
Novell Inc.
Oaklawn Foundation
O'Connor Foundation, A. Lindsay and Olive B.
O'Connor Foundation, Kathryn
OCRI Foundation
Odell Fund, Robert Stewart Odell and Helen Pfeiffer
O'Fallon Trust, Martin J. and Mary Anne
Offield Family Foundation
OG&E Electric Services
Ohrstrom Foundation
Old Dominion Box Co.
Old National Bank in Evansville
Oliver Memorial Trust Foundation
Olsson Memorial Foundation, Elis
Oppenstein Brothers Foundation
O'Quinn Foundation, John M. and Nancy C.
Osher Foundation, Bernard
Ottley Trust-Watertown, Marion W.
Overbrook Foundation
Overlake Foundation
Owen Industries, Inc.
Owsley Foundation, Alvin and Lucy
Oxy USA Inc.
Pacific Mutual Life Insurance Co.
Packaging Corporation of America
Packard Foundation, David and Lucile
PaineWebber
Palisades Educational Foundation
Palmer Fund, Frank Loomis
Pamida, Inc.
Panhandle Eastern Corporation
Park Foundation
Parshelsky Foundation, Moses L.
Parvin Foundation, Albert
Patterson Charitable Fund, W. I.
Payne Foundation, Frank E. and Seba B.
Peabody Charitable Fund, Amelia
Pella Corporation
Penn Foundation, William
Pennzoil Co.
Peoples Energy Corp.
Perkin-Elmer Corp.
Peters Foundation, Charles F.
Peterson Foundation, Hal and Charlie
Petteys Memorial Foundation, Jack
Pettus Crowe Foundation
Pew Charitable Trusts
Pfizer, Inc.
Pforzheimer Foundation, Carl and Lily
Phelps Dodge Corporation
PHH Corporation
Philibosian Foundation, Stephen
Phillips Charitable Trust, Dr. and Mrs. Arthur William
Phillips Family Foundation, Jay and Rose
Phillips Foundation, Ellis L.
Piankova Foundation, Tatiana

Pick, Jr. Fund, Albert
Pierce Charitable Trust, Harold Whitworth
Pineywoods Foundation
Pioneer Trust Bank, NA
Piper Jaffray Companies Inc.
Pitt-Des Moines Inc.
Pittsburg Midway Coal Mining Co.
Pittsburgh Child Guidance Foundation
Plankenhorn Foundation, Harry
Playboy Enterprises, Inc.
Plumsock Fund
PNC Bank, N.A.
Polaroid Corp.
Pollock Company Foundation, William B.
Porter Foundation, Mrs. Cheever
Porter Testamentary Trust, James Hyde
Potomac Electric Power Co.
Pott Foundation, Herman T. and Phenie R.
PPG Industries, Inc.
Prairie Foundation
Premier Industrial Corp.
Price Associates, T. Rowe
Price Foundation, Lucien B. and Katherine E.
Priddy Foundation
PriMerit Bank
Prince Trust, Abbie Norman
Proctor Trust, Mortimer R.
Providence Gas Co.
Provident Life & Accident Insurance Company of America
Providian Corporation
Prudential Insurance Co. of America, The
Prudential Securities, Inc.
Public Service Co. of New Mexico
Public Service Electric & Gas Co.
Public Welfare Foundation
Pulitzer Publishing Co.
Puterbaugh Foundation
Putnam Foundation
Quaker Chemical Corp.
Quivey-Bay State Foundation
R. F. Foundation
Rabb Foundation, Harry W.
Ralston Purina Co.
Rand McNally & Co.
R&B Machine Tool Co.
Ratner Foundation, Milton M.
Raymond Corp.
Read Foundation, Charles L.
Reed Foundation
Regenstein Foundation
Reicher Foundation, Anne and Harry J.
Reichhold Chemicals, Inc.
Reidler Foundation
Reinberger Foundation
Reisman Charitable Trust, George C. and Evelyn R.
Rennebohm Foundation, Oscar
Republic NY Corp.
Retirement Research Foundation
Reynolds Foundation, Donald W.
Rhone-Poulenc Inc.
Rice Charitable Foundation, Albert W.
Rich Products Corporation
Richardson Benevolent Foundation, C. E.
Rieke Corp.
Riggs Benevolent Fund
Ritter Charitable Trust, George W. and Mary F.
RJR Nabisco Inc.
Robinson Fund, Maurice R.
Rockefeller Fund, David
Rockwell Fund
Rockwell International Corporation
Rogers Family Foundation
Rohatyn Foundation, Felix and Elizabeth

Rohm & Haas Co.
Roseburg Forest Products Co.
Rosenberg Foundation
Rose's Stores, Inc.
Ross Laboratories
Ross Memorial Foundation, Will
Rouse Co.
Royal Foundation, May Mitchell
Royal Group, Inc.
Ruan Foundation Trust, John
Rubin Family Fund, Cele H. and William B.
Rudin Foundation
Russell Charitable Foundation, Tom
Russell Trust, Josephine G.
Ryan Foundation, David Claude
SAFECO Corp.
Safety Fund National Bank
Saint Paul Companies, Inc.
Salomon Foundation, Richard and Edna
San Diego Gas & Electric
Sandusky International Inc.
Sandy Hill Foundation
Santa Fe Pacific Corporation
Sara Lee Corp.
Sara Lee Hosiery, Inc.
Sargent Foundation, Newell B.
Sarkeys Foundation
Sasco Foundation
Sawyer Charitable Foundation
SBC Communications Inc.
Schenck Fund, L. P.
Scherman Foundation
Schiff Foundation, Dorothy
Schiro Fund
Schlink Foundation, Albert G. and Olive H.
Schlumberger Ltd.
Schmitt Foundation, Kilian J. and Caroline F.
Schowalter Foundation
Schroeder Foundation, Walter
Schuller International
Schumann Fund for New Jersey
Schwab & Co., Inc., Charles
Schwartz Foundation, Arnold A.
Schwartz Fund for Education and Health Research, Arnold and Marie
Schwob Foundation, Simon
Scott Fetzer Co.
Scott Foundation, William E.
Scurlock Foundation
Seafirst Corporation
Seaver Charitable Trust, Richard C.
Seaway Food Town, Inc.
Security Life of Denver Insurance Co.
Seidman Family Foundation
Self Foundation
Semmes Foundation
Seneca Foods Corp.
Sentry Insurance A Mutual Company
Seton Leather Co.
Share Trust, Charles Morton
Sharon Steel Corp.
Shaw Foundation, Arch W.
Shawmut National Corp.
Sheaffer Inc.
Sheary for Charity, Edna M.
Shell Oil Company
Shenandoah Life Insurance Co.
Shott, Jr. Foundation, Hugh I.
Sierra Pacific Resources
Simon Foundation, William E. and Carol G.
Simpson Investment Company
Skillman Foundation
Slemp Foundation
Slifka Foundation, Joseph and Sylvia
Smart Family Foundation
Smeal Foundation, Mary Jean and Frank P.
Smith Charitable Foundation, Lou and Lutza

Smith Corp., A.O.
Smith Foundation, Kelvin and Eleanor
Smith Foundation, Ralph L.
Smith, Jr. Foundation, M. W.
Smith Memorial Fund, Ethel Sergeant Clark
Smith Trust, May and Stanley
Snow Foundation, John Ben
Snow Memorial Trust, John Ben
Snyder Foundation, Harold B. and Dorothy A.
Solow Foundation
Sonat Inc.
South Branch Foundation
South Waite Foundation
Southern California Edison Co.
Southern New England Telephone Company
Southwestern Electric Power Co.
Spang & Co.
Speyer Foundation, Alexander C. and Tillie S.
Sprague Educational and Charitable Foundation, Seth
Springs Foundation
SPX Corp.
Square D Co.
Stabler Foundation, Donald B. and Dorothy L.
Stanley Charitable Foundation, A.W.
Stanley Works
Stans Foundation
Starr Foundation
Stauffer Charitable Trust, John
Stauffer Foundation, John and Beverly
Staunton Farm Foundation
Stearns Trust, Artemas W.
Steele Foundation, Harry and Grace
Steele-Reese Foundation
Stein Foundation, Jules and Doris
Steinhagen Benevolent Trust, B. A. and Elinor
Steinman Foundation, James Hale
Steinman Foundation, John Frederick
Stemmons Foundation
Sternberger Foundation, Tannenbaum
Stevens Foundation, Abbot and Dorothy H.
Stevens Foundation, John T.
Stokely, Jr. Foundation, William B.
Stone Charitable Foundation
Stone Trust, H. Chase
Strawbridge Foundation of Pennsylvania II, Margaret Dorrance
Strong Foundation, Hattie M.
Stupp Foundation, Norman J.
Sturgis Charitable and Educational Trust, Roy and Christine
Subaru of America Inc.
Sullivan Foundation, Algernon Sydney
Sulzberger Foundation
Sumitomo Bank of California
Sumners Foundation, Hatton W.
Sundet Foundation
Sunnen Foundation
Superior Tube Co.
Swalm Foundation
Swanson Family Foundation, Dr. W.C.
Swift Co. Inc., John S.
Taconic Foundation
Tait Foundation, Frank M.
Taper Foundation, Mark
Taube Family Foundation
Taubman Foundation, A. Alfred
Taylor Foundation, Fred and Harriett
Teagle Foundation
Teichert & Son, A.
Teleflex Inc.

Temple Foundation, T. L. L.
Tenneco Inc.
Tetley, Inc.
Texaco Inc.
Texas Commerce Bank-Houston, N.A.
Textron, Inc.
Thalhimer and Family Foundation, Charles G.
Thermo Electron Corp.
Thomas Foundation, Joan and Lee
Thomasville Furniture Industries
Thompson Trust, Thomas
Thorne Foundation
Thornton Foundation, Flora L.
Times Mirror Company, The
Timken Foundation of Canton
Tiscornia Foundation
Titus Foundation, Roy and Niuta
Tobin Foundation
Todd Co., A.M.
Toms Foundation
Towsley Foundation, Harry A. and Margaret D.
TransAmerica Corporation
Transco Energy Co.
Travelers Inc.
Treakle Foundation, J. Edwin
Trees Charitable Trust, Edith L.
Trexler Trust, Harry C.
Truland Foundation
Trull Foundation
Trust Company Bank
Trust Funds
Tuch Foundation, Michael
Tucker Charitable Trust, Rose E.
Tupancy-Harris Foundation of 1986
Turner Charitable Foundation
Turrell Fund
Unger Foundation, Aber D.
Unilever United States, Inc.
Union Bank
Union Camp Corporation
Union Electric Co.
Union Pacific Corp.
U.S. Bank of Washington
Unitrode Corp.
Unocal Corp.
Upjohn Foundation, Harold and Grace
Upton Foundation, Frederick S.
Uris Brothers Foundation
USG Corporation
USL Capital Corporation
USX Corporation
Utica National Insurance Group
Vale Foundation, Ruby R.
van Ameringen Foundation
Van Every Foundation, Philip L.
Van Nuys Foundation, I. N. and Susanna H.
Van Wert County Foundation
Vance Charitable Foundation, Robert C.
Vanderbilt Trust, R. T.
Vernon Fund, Miles Hodsdon
Vicksburg Foundation
Vollbrecht Foundation, Frederick A.
Vulcan Materials Co.
Wachovia Bank of North Carolina, N.A.
Wal-Mart Stores, Inc.
Walsh Foundation
Warner Fund, Albert and Bessie
Warren and Beatrice W. Blanding Foundation, Riley J. and Lillian N.
Warwick Foundation
Washington Forrest Foundation
Washington Mutual Savings Bank
Washington Water Power Co.
Weaver Foundation, Gil and Dody
Webber Oil Co.

Weber Charities Corp.,
Frederick E.
Weckbaugh Foundation,
Eleanore Mullen
Weezie Foundation
Wege Foundation
Weil, Gotshal and Manges
Foundation
Weingart Foundation
Weinstein Foundation, J.
Welch Testamentary Trust,
George T.
Welfare Foundation
Wells Foundation, Franklin H.
and Ruth L.
Wendt Foundation, Margaret L.
Wertheim Foundation, Dr.
Herbert A.
West One Bancorp
Westerman Foundation,
Samuel L.
Western New York Foundation
Westvaco Corporation
Weyerhaeuser Co.
Weyerhaeuser Memorial
Foundation, Charles A.
Wheat First Butcher Singer,
Inc.
Wheeler Foundation
Wheeler Foundation, Wilmot
Whirlpool Corporation
Whiting Foundation
Whitney Fund, David M.
Whittenberger Foundation,
Claude R. and Ethel B.
Wickson-Link Memorial
Foundation
Widgeon Foundation
Wiegand Foundation, E. L.
Wilder Foundation
Wildermuth Foundation, E. F.
Willard Helping Fund, Cecilia
Young
Williams Charitable Trust,
John C.
Williams Charitable Trust,
Mary Jo
Williams Companies, The
Wilmington Trust Co.
Wilson Foundation, H. W.
Winchester Foundation
Windham Foundation
Winnebago Industries, Inc.
Winthrop Trust, Clara B.
Wiremold Co.
Wisconsin Power & Light Co.
Wise Foundation and
Charitable Trust, Watson W.
Witco Corp.
Witter Foundation, Dean
Wood Foundation of
Chambersburg, PA
Woodward Fund
Woolley Foundation, Vasser
Wright Foundation, Lola
Wyman Youth Trust
Wyomissing Foundation
Y and H Soda Foundation
Young Foundation, Hugo H.
and Mabel B.
Young Foundation, Irvin L.
Young Foundation, Robert R.
Zachry Co., H.B.
Zarrow Foundation, Anne and
Henry
Zenkel Foundation

Counseling

Abell-Hanger Foundation
Achelis Foundation
Ahmanson Foundation
Air Products and Chemicals,
Inc.
Alcon Laboratories, Inc.
Aldus Corp.
Allegheny Foundation
Allegheny Ludlum Corp.
AlliedSignal Inc.
Aluminum Co. of America
AMCORE Bank, N.A.
Rockford
American United Life
Insurance Co.

Amfac/JMB Hawaii Inc.
Anderson Foundation, John W.
Ansley Foundation, Dantzler
Bond
AON Corporation
Appleton Papers Inc.
Arkell Hall Foundation
Atherton Family Foundation
Badgeley Residuary Charitable
Trust, Rose M.
Banta Corp.
Bard Foundation, Robert
Bean Foundation, Norwin S.
and Elizabeth N.
Bemis Company, Inc.
Bethlehem Steel Corp.
Bingham Second Betterment
Fund, William
Blair and Co., William
Block, H&R
Blowitz-Ridgeway Foundation
Blue Bell, Inc.
Bodman Foundation
Boston Edison Co.
Bothin Foundation
Bowen Foundation, Ethel N.
Brach Foundation, Helen
Bremer Foundation, Otto
Bryn Mawr Trust Co.
Cabot Corp.
Cafritz Foundation, Morris and
Gwendolyn
Campbell Foundation
Carolyn Foundation
Carpenter Foundation
Central Maine Power Co.
Chase Manhattan Bank, N.A.
Chastain Charitable
Foundation, Robert Lee and
Thomas M.
Chazen Foundation
CHC Foundation
Cheney Foundation, Ben B.
Chesebrough-Pond's USA Co.
Chicago Sun-Times, Inc.
Clay Foundation
Clorox Co.
CNA Financial
Corporation/CNA Insurance
Companies
Collins, Jr. Foundation,
George Fulton
Colonial Life & Accident
Insurance Co.
Commerce Bancshares, Inc.
Consolidated Natural Gas Co.
Contran Corporation
Cord Foundation, E. L.
Cowles Charitable Trust
Crandall Memorial
Foundation, J. Ford
Cummins Engine Co.
Delavan Foundation, Nelson B.
Dell Foundation, Hazel
Dewing Foundation, Frances R.
Dimeo Construction Co.
Donaldson Company, Inc.
Dreyfus Foundation, Max and
Victoria
du Pont de Nemours & Co., E.
I.
Duke Power Co.
Dunagan Foundation
Eaton Corporation
Eden Hall Foundation
English Memorial Fund,
Florence C. and H. L.
Ettinger Foundation
Fabri-Kal Corp.
Federated Mutual Insurance
Co.
Fireman's Fund Insurance Co.
First Union Corp.
Fish Foundation, Ray C.
Forest Foundation
Freeport-McMoRan Inc.
Frost National Bank
Frueauff Foundation, Charles
A.
Fry Foundation, Lloyd A.
GATX Corp.
Gazette Co.
Gebbie Foundation
General American Life
Insurance Co.

General Mills, Inc.
GenRad
German Protestant Orphan
Asylum Association
Giant Eagle, Inc.
Glaser Foundation
Globe Newspaper Co.
Goldseker Foundation of
Maryland, Morris
Grand Rapids Label Co.
Griffith Foundation, W. C.
Gulf Power Co.
Habig Foundation, Arnold F.
Hafif Family Foundation
Hagedorn Fund
Haigh-Scatena Foundation
Halff Foundation, G. A. C.
Hancock Foundation, Luke B.
Harcourt General, Inc.
Harland Charitable
Foundation, John and
Wilhelmina D.
Harriman Foundation, Mary W.
Harrison Foundation, Fred G.
Hawkins Foundation, Robert Z.
Hawn Foundation
Hearst Foundation, William
Randolph
Hechinger Co.
Heinz Company, H. J.
Henry Foundation, Patrick
Heydt Fund, Nan and Matilda
Hill Foundation, Sandy
Hillcrest Foundation
Hillsdale Fund
Holzer Memorial Foundation,
Richard H.
Hopkins Foundation,
Josephine Lawrence
Houston Endowment
Hoyt Foundation, Stewart W.
and Willma C.
Hudson-Webber Foundation
Hunt Charitable Trust, C. Giles
Huston Foundation
Icahn Foundation, Carl C.
Ingalls Foundation, Louise H.
and David S.
Ittleson Foundation
Jackson Foundation
Jacobson Foundation, Bernard
H. and Blanche E.
Janirve Foundation
John Hancock Mutual Life
Insurance Co.
Johnson Controls Inc.
Jones Foundation, Harvey and
Bernice
Joy Family Foundation
Kansas City Southern
Industries
Kaufmann Foundation, Henry
Kelly Foundation, T. Lloyd
Kennecott Corporation
Kimberly-Clark Corp.
Kirbo Charitable Trust,
Thomas M. and Irene B.
Ladd Charitable Corporation,
Helen and George
Laffey-McHugh Foundation
Laurel Foundation
Lee Endowment Foundation
Lehigh Portland Cement Co.
Little, Inc., Arthur D.
Longwood Foundation
Lydall, Inc.
Macy & Co., Inc., R.H.
Mardag Foundation
Margoes Foundation
Mars Foundation
Massengill-DeFriece
Foundation
May Department Stores
Company, The
MBIA Inc.
MCA Inc.
McCune Charitable Trust,
John R.
McDonald & Company
Securities, Inc.
McDonnell Douglas
Corp.-West
McFawn Trust No. 2, Lois
Sisler

McQueen Foundation, Adeline
and George
Meadows Foundation
Metropolitan Life Insurance
Co.
Mid-Iowa Health Foundation
Miller Brewing
Company/North Carolina
Miller Foundation
Minnesota Mining & Mfg. Co.
Mnuchin Foundation
Mobil Oil Corp.
Morgan & Company, J.P.
Musson Charitable
Foundation, R. C. and
Katharine M.
Nalco Chemical Co.
New York Life Insurance Co.
New York Mercantile Exchange
Noble Foundation, Edward
John
Norman Foundation, Summers
A.
Northern States Power Co.
(Minnesota)
Northwest Natural Gas Co.
Norton Co.
Norwest Bank Nebraska, N.A.
Ohrstrom Foundation
Oppenstein Brothers
Foundation
Overbrook Foundation
Overlake Foundation
Pacific Mutual Life Insurance
Co.
Packard Foundation, David
and Lucile
PaineWebber
Palmer Fund, Frank Loomis
Penn Foundation, William
Perkin-Elmer Corp.
Pfizer, Inc.
Phillips Family Foundation,
Jay and Rose
Piankova Foundation, Tatiana
Plankenhorn Foundation, Harry
Price Foundation, Louis and
Harold
Priddy Foundation
Prudential Insurance Co. of
America, The
Public Service Electric & Gas
Co.
Public Welfare Foundation
Quaker Chemical Corp.
Retirement Research
Foundation
Reynolds Foundation, Donald
W.
Richardson Charitable Trust,
Anne S.
Rockefeller Fund, David
Rockwell Fund
Rockwell International
Corporation
Roseburg Forest Products Co.
Royal Group, Inc.
Ruan Foundation Trust, John
Rubinstein Foundation, Helena
Saltonstall Charitable
Foundation, Richard
San Diego Gas & Electric
Santa Fe Pacific Corporation
Sara Lee Corp.
Sara Lee Hosiery, Inc.
Scaife Family Foundation
Schoenleber Foundation
Schroeder Foundation, Walter
Schuller International
Schwartz Foundation, Arnold
A.
Seidman Family Foundation
Shawmut National Corp.
Shenandoah Life Insurance Co.
Sheppard Foundation,
Lawrence B.
Skillman Foundation
Southern California Edison Co.
Sprague Educational and
Charitable Foundation, Seth
Starr Foundation
Staunton Farm Foundation
Stearns Trust, Artemas W.
Steele-Reese Foundation
Subaru of America Inc.

Sumners Foundation, Hatton
W.
Taconic Foundation
Tait Foundation, Frank M.
Taper Foundation, Mark
Temple Foundation, T. L. L.
Textron, Inc.
Thermo Electron Corp.
Thompson Trust, Thomas
Tiscornia Foundation
Trull Foundation
Trust Company Bank
Tucker Charitable Trust, Rose
E.
Turrell Fund
Union Camp Corporation
Union Electric Co.
U.S. Bank of Washington
Unitrode Corp.
Upton Foundation, Frederick S.
Uris Brothers Foundation
van Ameringen Foundation
Vulcan Materials Co.
Wal-Mart Stores, Inc.
Walsh Foundation
Weaver Foundation, Gil and
Dody
Webber Oil Co.
Weber Charities Corp.,
Frederick E.
Weezie Foundation
Weingart Foundation
Welfare Foundation
Wendt Foundation, Margaret L.
Westvaco Corporation
Whirlpool Corporation
Wood Foundation of
Chambersburg, PA
Wright Foundation, Lola
Wyman Youth Trust
Wyomissing Foundation
Young Foundation, Robert R.

Crime Prevention

Abell-Hanger Foundation
Ahmanson Foundation
Amado Foundation, Maurice
AMCORE Bank, N.A.
Rockford
Annenberg Foundation
Babson Foundation, Paul and
Edith
Beazley Foundation/Frederick
Foundation
Beech Aircraft Corp.
Blandin Foundation
Bobst Foundation, Elmer and
Mamdouha
Boutell Memorial Fund
Bremer Foundation, Otto
Burden Foundation, Florence
V.
Burnett-Tandy Foundation
Campini Foundation, Frank A.
Carnegie Corporation of New
York
Champlin Foundations
CHC Foundation
Cooke Foundation
Cowles Charitable Trust
Culpeper Foundation, Charles
E.
Darling Foundation, Hugh and
Hazel
Dingman Foundation, Michael
D.
Douty Foundation
Dreyfus Foundation, Jean and
Louis
Dreyfus Foundation, Max and
Victoria
Edgewater Steel Corp.
Einstein Fund, Albert E. and
Birdie W.
Fair Oaks Foundation, Inc.
Feil Foundation, Louis and
Gertrude
Finch Foundation, Doak
Finch Foundation, Thomas
Austin
First Source Corp.
Fletcher Foundation
Freed Foundation

Freeport Brick Co.
Freeport-McMoRan Inc.
Gilman Foundation, Howard
Goddard Foundation, Charles B.
Goldseker Foundation of Maryland, Morris
Goldsmith Foundation, Horace W.
Gould Electronics Inc.
Grundy Foundation
Gulf Coast Medical Foundation
Habig Foundation, Arnold F.
Hafif Family Foundation
Hammer Foundation, Armand
Harrington Foundation, Francis A. and Jacquelyn H.
Hazen Foundation, Edward W.
Heinz Endowment, Vira I.
Helmerich Foundation
Hewlett Foundation, William and Flora
Hillman Family Foundation, Alex
Hook Drugs
Hoover, Jr. Foundation, Margaret W. and Herbert
Hopedale Foundation
Houston Endowment
Hudson-Webber Foundation
Hunt Charitable Trust, C. Giles
Ittleson Foundation
Jacobs Family Foundation
Jewish Healthcare Foundation of Pittsburgh
JM Foundation
Kayser Foundation
Kempner Fund, Harris and Eliza
Kent-Lucas Foundation
Kingsbury Corp.
Koopman Fund
Kreitler Foundation
Kuehn Foundation
Lennon Foundation, Fred A.
MacArthur Foundation, John D. and Catherine T.
MacLeod Stewardship Foundation
Mailman Family Foundation, A. L.
Mailman Foundation
Matthies Foundation, Katharine
Mayor Foundation, Oliver Dewey
McMahon Foundation
Memton Fund
Monfort Family Foundation
Morgan Charitable Residual Trust, W. and E.
Morgan & Company, J.P.
Mott Fund, Ruth
Murphey Foundation, Lluella Morey
Murphy Foundation
Musson Charitable Foundation, R. C. and Katharine M.
Mutual Assurance Co.
Norman Foundation, Summers A.
Osceola Foundation
Overbrook Foundation
Pamida, Inc.
Payne Foundation, Frank E. and Seba B.
Piper Foundation, Minnie Stevens
Pittsburg Midway Coal Mining Co.
Proctor Trust, Mortimer R.
Puterbaugh Foundation
Reynolds Foundation, Edgar
Roseburg Forest Products Co.
Rudin Foundation
Scurlock Foundation
Sequoia Foundation
Skillman Foundation
Smart Family Foundation
Springs Foundation
SPX Corp.
Starr Foundation
Stauffer Foundation, John and Beverly
Staunton Farm Foundation

Stearns Trust, Artemas W.
Stevens Foundation, John T.
Strong Foundation, Hattie M.
Subaru of America Inc.
Sulzberger Foundation
Trexler Trust, Harry C.
Tucker Charitable Trust, Rose E.
Van Buren Foundation
Vicksburg Foundation
Weaver Foundation, Gil and Dody
Weber Charities Corp., Frederick E.
Weingart Foundation
Wheeler Foundation
Wiggins Memorial Trust, J. J.
Wilson Foundation, H. W.
Winnebago Industries, Inc.
Wyomissing Foundation
Young Foundation, Robert R.

Day Care

Abell-Hanger Foundation
Achelis Foundation
Acushnet Co.
Ahmanson Foundation
Air Products and Chemicals, Inc.
Alexander Foundation, Joseph
Allendale Insurance Co.
Allyn Foundation
Altman Foundation
Alumax Inc.
Aluminum Co. of America
AMCORE Bank, N.A. Rockford
American Brands, Inc.
American General Finance Corp.
American United Life Insurance Co.
Archer-Daniels-Midland Co.
Astor Foundation, Vincent
AT&T Corp.
Ayres Foundation, Inc.
Balfour Foundation, L. G.
Ball Foundation, George and Frances
Bank One, Youngstown, NA
Barth Foundation, Theodore H.
Baughman Foundation
Beazley Foundation/Frederick Foundation
Bedsole Foundation, J. L.
Bethlehem Steel Corp.
Betts Industries
Binswanger Cos.
Blair and Co., William
Block, H&R
Blue Bell, Inc.
Boettcher Foundation
Booth Ferris Foundation
Borkee Hagley Foundation
Borman's Inc.
Bothin Foundation
Breyer Foundation
Brown Foundation, M. K.
Bryant Foundation
Bryn Mawr Trust Co.
Bucyrus-Erie Company
Buhl Foundation
Burchfield Foundation, Charles E.
Bush Foundation
Cabot Corp.
Cain Foundation, Gordon and Mary
Carnegie Corporation of New York
Carolyn Foundation
Carpenter Foundation
Carpenter Foundation, E. Rhodes and Leona B.
Carter Foundation, Amon G.
Cassett Foundation, Louis N.
Catlin Charitable Trust, Kathleen K.
CBS, Inc.
Central Maine Power Co.
Centralia Foundation
Charina Foundation
Chase Manhattan Bank, N.A.

Chevron Corporation
Chicago Sun-Times, Inc.
Citibank
Citizens Bank of Rhode Island
CLARCOR Inc.
Clorox Co.
Cole Foundation, Olive B.
Collins Foundation
Colonial Life & Accident Insurance Co.
Connecticut Mutual Life Insurance Company
Connelly Foundation
Cowell Foundation, S. H.
Cowles Media Co.
Crabtree & Evelyn
Crestlea Foundation
Culpeper Memorial Foundation, Daphne Seybolt
Dana Foundation, Charles A.
Davenport-Hatch Foundation
Davidson Family Charitable Foundation
Davis Foundation, Edwin W. and Catherine M.
Davis Foundation, James A. and Juliet L.
Deere & Co.
Dekko Foundation
Dentsply International Inc.
DeRoy Testamentary Foundation
Deuble Foundation, George H.
Dewing Foundation, Frances R.
Dexter Charitable Fund, Eugene A.
Dodge Jones Foundation
Donaldson Company, Inc.
Doss Foundation, M. S.
Dreyfus Foundation, Max and Victoria
du Pont de Nemours & Co., E. I.
Duke Endowment
Dula Educational and Charitable Foundation, Caleb C. and Julia W.
Eden Hall Foundation
El Pomar Foundation
Elkins, Jr. Foundation, Margaret and James A.
Evans Foundation, T. M.
Exxon Corporation
Fabri-Kal Corp.
Fair Play Foundation
Federated Mutual Insurance Co.
Fireman's Fund Insurance Co.
First Hawaiian, Inc.
First Union Corp.
Fishback Foundation Trust, Harmes C.
Frear Eleemosynary Trust, Mary D. and Walter F.
Freed Foundation
GAR Foundation
Gellert Foundation, Celia Berta
General Mills, Inc.
German Protestant Orphan Asylum Association
Gershman Foundation, Joel
Giles Foundation, Edward C.
Glaser Foundation
Globe Newspaper Co.
Goddard Foundation, Charles B.
Goldsmith Foundation, Horace W.
Good Samaritan
GSM Industrial
Gulf Coast Medical Foundation
Hammer Foundation, Armand
Harsco Corp.
Hechinger Co.
Heckscher Foundation for Children
Heinz Endowment, Howard
Heinz Endowment, Vira I.
Hillcrest Foundation
Hillman Foundation
Hook Drugs
Hoover Foundation
Houston Endowment
Hoyt Foundation, Stewart W. and Willma C.

Huisking Foundation
Hunt Charitable Trust, C. Giles
Hunt Foundation
Hyde and Watson Foundation
IBP, Inc.
Icahn Foundation, Carl C.
ICI Americas Inc.
Imperial Bancorp
International Paper Co.
Irvine Foundation, James
ITT Hartford Insurance Group, Inc.
Jackson Foundation
Janirve Foundation
Jewish Healthcare Foundation of Pittsburgh
Johnson Foundation, M. G. and Lillie A.
Jones Foundation, Daisy Marquis
Jones Foundation, Harvey and Bernice
Joy Family Foundation
Kansas City Southern Industries
Kelley and Elza Kelley Foundation, Edward Bangs
Kimball Foundation, Horace A. Kimball and S. Ella
Kingsbury Corp.
Kinney-Lindstrom Foundation
Kirbo Charitable Trust, Thomas M. and Irene B.
Knudsen Foundation, Tom and Valley
Komes Foundation
Kutz Foundation, Milton and Hattie
Kuyper Foundation, Peter H. and E. Lucille
Laffey-McHugh Foundation
Lattner Foundation, Forrest C.
Lee Enterprises
Lehigh Portland Cement Co.
Leuthold Foundation
Levitt Foundation
Liz Claiborne, Inc.
Longwood Foundation
Lunda Charitable Trust
Maddox Foundation, J. F.
Mailman Family Foundation, A. L.
Mardag Foundation
Martini Foundation, Nicholas
Mather Charitable Trust, S. Livingston
Mayer Foundation, James and Eva
MBIA Inc.
McCann Foundation
McConnell Foundation
McElroy Trust, R. J.
McInerny Foundation
McLean Contributionship
Meadows Foundation
Mellon Foundation, Richard King
Merck & Co.
Merck Family Fund
Merrick Foundation
Meyer Memorial Trust
Mid-Iowa Health Foundation
Miller Foundation
Minnesota Mining & Mfg. Co.
Morgan & Company, J.P.
Morris Foundation, Margaret T.
Morrison Knudsen Corporation
Nesholm Family Foundation
New York Life Insurance Co.
New York Mercantile Exchange
New York Stock Exchange, Inc.
NewMil Bancorp
North Shore Foundation
Northern States Power Co. (Minnesota)
Northwest Natural Gas Co.
O'Connor Foundation, A. Lindsay and Olive B.
OCRI Foundation
Odell Fund, Robert Stewart Odell and Helen Pfeiffer
O'Fallon Trust, Martin J. and Mary Anne
Offield Family Foundation

Olin Foundation, Spencer T. and Ann W.
Ore-Ida Foods, Inc.
Pacific Mutual Life Insurance Co.
Pacific Telesis Group
Packard Foundation, David and Lucile
PaineWebber
Parsons Foundation, Ralph M.
Pella Corporation
Penn Foundation, William
Perkin-Elmer Corp.
Peterson Foundation, Hal and Charlie
Pick, Jr. Fund, Albert
Pittsburg Midway Coal Mining Co.
PPG Industries, Inc.
Prudential Insurance Co. of America, The
Public Service Co. of New Mexico
Quivey-Bay State Foundation
Rabb Charitable Foundation, Sidney and Esther
Raymond Corp.
Read Foundation, Charles L.
Robinson-Broadhurst Foundation
Rockefeller Fund, David
Rockwell Fund
Rogers Family Foundation
Roseburg Forest Products Co.
Rubinstein Foundation, Helena
SAFECO
Saint Paul Companies, Inc.
San Diego Gas & Electric
Sara Lee Corp.
Sara Lee Hosiery, Inc.
Schenck Fund, L. P.
Schowalter Foundation
Schumann Fund for New Jersey
Schwartz Foundation, Arnold A.
Scurlock Foundation
Seafirst Corporation
Selby and Marie Selby Foundation, William G.
Semmes Foundation
Shawmut National Corp.
Sheary for Charity, Edna M.
Skillman Foundation
Snayberger Memorial Foundation, Harry E. and Florence W.
Snow Memorial Trust, John Ben
Steinhagen Benevolent Trust, B. A. and Elinor
Steinman Foundation, John Frederick
Sternberger Foundation, Tannenbaum
Subaru of America Inc.
Sundet Foundation
Sunnen Foundation
Temple Foundation, T. L. L.
Thornton Foundation
Timken Foundation of Canton
Travelers Inc.
Trull Foundation
Turrell Fund
Unilever United States, Inc.
Union Camp Corporation
U.S. Bank of Washington
Unitrode Corp.
Uris Brothers Foundation
Vale Foundation, Ruby R.
van Ameringen Foundation
Van Houten Memorial Fund
Van Wert County Foundation
Vernon Fund, Miles Hodsdon
Wachovia Bank of North Carolina, N.A.
Weingart Foundation
Welch Testamentary Trust, George T.
Welfare Foundation
Wendt Foundation, Margaret L.
Western New York Foundation
Whirlpool Corporation
Whittenberger Foundation, Claude R. and Ethel B.

Wilmington Trust Co.
Windham Foundation
Wise Foundation and
  Charitable Trust, Watson W.
Woodward Fund
Y and H Soda Foundation
Zarrow Foundation, Anne and
  Henry

Delinquency & Criminal Rehabilitation

Abbott Laboratories
Abell-Hanger Foundation
Ahmanson Foundation
Air Products and Chemicals,
  Inc.
Alabama Power Co.
Aldus Corp.
AlliedSignal Inc.
Alumax Inc.
Aluminum Co. of America
AMCORE Bank, N.A.
  Rockford
American United Life
  Insurance Co.
Amfac/JMB Hawaii Inc.
Amoco Corporation
Anderson Foundation, John W.
Andrews Foundation
Anheuser-Busch Companies,
  Inc.
Atherton Family Foundation
Avon Products, Inc.
Banc One Wisconsin Corp.
Bean Foundation, Norwin S.
  and Elizabeth N.
BE&K Inc.
Berger Foundation, H. N. and
  Frances C.
Berwind Corporation
Bethlehem Steel Corp.
Betts Industries
Binswanger Cos.
Blair and Co., William
Block, H&R
Boatmen's Bancshares, Inc.
Boeing Co., The
Borman's Inc.
Brunswick Corp.
Buhl Foundation
Burden Foundation, Florence
  V.
Burlington Industries, Inc.
Carpenter Foundation
Carter Foundation, Amon G.
Centerior Energy Corp.
Central Maine Power Co.
Chase Manhattan Bank, N.A.
Chevron Corporation
Chicago Sun-Times, Inc.
Clark Foundation
Clorox Co.
CNA Financial
  Corporation/CNA Insurance
  Companies
Colonial Life & Accident
  Insurance Co.
Commerce Clearing House,
  Incorporated
Connecticut Mutual Life
  Insurance Company
Continental Corp.
Coors Foundation, Adolph
Covington and Burling
Cowles Charitable Trust
Cowles Media Co.
Curtice-Burns Foods, Inc.
Dater Foundation, Charles H.
Day Foundation, Nancy Sayles
DeRoy Foundation, Helen L.
Detroit Edison Co.
Dexter Corporation
Donaldson Company, Inc.
Doss Foundation, M. S.
Douty Foundation
Dreyfus Foundation, Jean and
  Louis
Dreyfus Foundation, Max and
  Victoria
du Pont de Nemours & Co., E.
  I.

Early Foundation
Eaton Corporation
Enron Corp.
Exxon Corporation
Federal-Mogul Corporation
Fieldcrest Cannon Inc.
First Fidelity Bank
First Source Corp.
First Union Corp.
Firstar Bank Milwaukee, N.A.
Ford Foundation
Ford Fund, William and Martha
Ford Motor Co.
Freedom Forge Corp.
Freeport-McMoRan Inc.
Fribourg Foundation
Frost National Bank
Fry Foundation, Lloyd A.
GATX Corp.
General Mills, Inc.
GenRad
Georgia Power Co.
Gershman Foundation, Joel
Giant Eagle, Inc.
Glosser Foundation, David A.
Goldsmith Foundation, Horace
  W.
Good Samaritan
Graham Fund, Philip L.
Habig Foundation, Arnold F.
Hancock Foundation, Luke B.
Harland Charitable
  Foundation, John and
  Wilhelmina D.
Hazen Foundation, Edward W.
HCA Foundation
Hechinger Co.
Heckscher Foundation for
  Children
Heinz Company, H. J.
Heinz Endowment, Vira I.
Hillcrest Foundation
Hillman Foundation
Hoover, Jr. Foundation,
  Margaret W. and Herbert
Houston Industries
  Incorporated
Hoyt Foundation, Stewart W.
  and Willma C.
Hudson-Webber Foundation
Huston Charitable Trust,
  Stewart
International Business
  Machines Corp.
ITT Hartford Insurance Group,
  Inc.
Ittleson Foundation
James River Corp. of Virginia
Jaydor Corp.
John Hancock Mutual Life
  Insurance Co.
Johnson & Son, S.C.
Jones Foundation, Daisy
  Marquis
Jurzykowski Foundation,
  Alfred
Kansas City Southern
  Industries
Kaplun Foundation, Morris J.
  and Betty
Kennecott Corporation
Kimberly-Clark Corp.
KN Energy, Inc.
Kuehn Foundation
Lee Endowment Foundation
Liberman Foundation, Bertha
  and Isaac
Lovett Foundation
Macy & Co., Inc., R.H.
Mailman Family Foundation,
  A. L.
Maneely Fund
Mardag Foundation
Maritz Inc.
Mattel, Inc.
May Foundation, Wilbur
MCA Inc.
McDonald & Company
  Securities, Inc.
Meadows Foundation
Mellon Family Foundation, R.
  K.
Metropolitan Life Insurance
  Co.
Meyer Memorial Trust

Miller Brewing
  Company/North Carolina
Miller-Mellor Association
Minnesota Mining & Mfg. Co.
Mobil Oil Corp.
Monell Foundation, Ambrose
Moore Charitable Foundation,
  Marjorie
Morgan Foundation, Burton D.
Nalco Chemical Co.
National Westminster Bank
  New Jersey
New York Mercantile Exchange
New York Times Company
Newman's Own, Inc.
Northern States Power Co.
  (Minnesota)
Northwest Natural Gas Co.
Norton Co.
OCRI Foundation
Old National Bank in
  Evansville
Osceola Foundation
Oxy USA Inc.
Pacific Mutual Life Insurance
  Co.
Parsons Foundation, Ralph M.
Pennzoil Co.
Perkin-Elmer Corp.
Pfizer, Inc.
Pittsburg Midway Coal Mining
  Co.
Pittsburgh Child Guidance
  Foundation
Playboy Enterprises, Inc.
PNC Bank, N.A.
PriMerit Bank
Prudential Insurance Co. of
  America, The
Public Service Electric & Gas
  Co.
Public Welfare Foundation
Quivey-Bay State Foundation
Ralston Purina Co.
Ratner Foundation, Milton M.
Regenstein Foundation
Reidler Foundation
Rockwell Fund
Rockwell International
  Corporation
Rudin Foundation
SAFECO Corp.
Salomon Inc.
San Diego Gas & Electric
Scaife Family Foundation
Scott Foundation, William E.
Scurlock Foundation
Seneca Foods Corp.
Share Trust, Charles Morton
Shawmut National Corp.
Shell Oil Company
Sierra Pacific Resources
Skillman Foundation
Smeal Foundation, Mary Jean
  and Frank P.
Snow Memorial Trust, John
  Ben
South Waite Foundation
Spang & Co.
Speyer Foundation, Alexander
  C. and Tillie S.
Sprague Educational and
  Charitable Foundation, Seth
Springs Foundation
Stauffer Charitable Trust, John
Staunton Farm Foundation
Stein Foundation, Jules and
  Doris
Stevens Foundation, Abbot
  and Dorothy H.
Strawbridge Foundation of
  Pennsylvania II, Margaret
  Dorrance
Sumners Foundation, Hatton
  W.
Sunnen Foundation
Taubman Foundation, A. Alfred
Tecumseh Products Co.
Teichert & Son, A.
Temple Foundation, T. L. L.
Tenneco Inc.
Texaco Inc.
Texas Commerce
  Bank-Houston, N.A.
Transco Energy Co.

Trull Foundation
Trust Company Bank
Tupancy-Harris Foundation of
  1986
Union Camp Corporation
Union Electric Co.
Unitrode Corp.
USX Corporation
Valentine Foundation, Lawson
Vicksburg Foundation
Vulcan Materials Co.
Wachovia Bank of North
  Carolina, N.A.
Warner Fund, Albert and
  Bessie
Washington Forrest Foundation
Weingart Foundation
Westerman Foundation,
  Samuel L.
Whirlpool Corporation
Wilson Foundation, H. W.
Zachry Co., H.B.

Domestic Violence

Abell-Hanger Foundation
Achelis Foundation
Ahmanson Foundation
Air Products and Chemicals,
  Inc.
Aldus Corp.
AlliedSignal Inc.
Altman Foundation
Aluminum Co. of America
AMCORE Bank, N.A.
  Rockford
American National Bank &
  Trust Co. of Chicago
American President
  Companies, Ltd.
American United Life
  Insurance Co.
Amfac/JMB Hawaii Inc.
Andersen Foundation
Andrews Foundation
Appleton Papers Inc.
Argyros Foundation
Arkansas Power & Light Co.
Arkell Hall Foundation
Atherton Family Foundation
Bacon Foundation, E. L. and
  Oma
Banta Corp.
Baughman Foundation
Beal Foundation
Beazley Foundation/Frederick
  Foundation
Beloit Foundation
Benetton Services Corp.
Berger Foundation, H. N. and
  Frances C.
Besser Foundation
Bethlehem Steel Corp.
Bingham Foundation, William
Binney & Smith Inc.
Birnschein Foundation, Alvin
  and Marion
Blandin Foundation
Blaustein Foundation, Louis
  and Henrietta
Block, H&R
Bodman Foundation
Boeing Co., The
Boettcher Foundation
Borman's Inc.
Bremer Foundation, Otto
Bright Family Foundation
Bucyrus-Erie Company
Bunbury Company
Burden Foundation, Florence
  V.
Bush Foundation
Cafritz Foundation, Morris and
  Gwendolyn
Cain Foundation, Effie and
  Wofford
Calhoun Charitable Trust,
  Kenneth
Campini Foundation, Frank A.
Carolyn Foundation
Carpenter Foundation
Carter Foundation, Beirne
Castle Foundation, Harold K.
  L.

Central Hudson Gas & Electric
  Corp.
Central Maine Power Co.
Chartwell Foundation
Chase Manhattan Bank, N.A.
CHC Foundation
Chevron Corporation
Chicago Sun-Times, Inc.
Clorox Co.
Colonial Life & Accident
  Insurance Co.
Columbia Foundation
Commerce Bancshares, Inc.
Commerce Clearing House,
  Incorporated
Comprecare Foundation
Connelly Foundation
Consolidated Natural Gas Co.
Contran Corporation
Cooke Foundation
Coors Foundation, Adolph
Cord Foundation, E. L.
Cowell Foundation, S. H.
Cowles Media Co.
CPC International Inc.
Crabtree & Evelyn
Crane Co.
Crary Foundation, Bruce L.
Crown Memorial, Arie and Ida
Crystal Trust
Cummins Engine Co.
Curtice-Burns Foods, Inc.
Darby Foundation
Dater Foundation, Charles H.
Daywood Foundation
Dekko Foundation
Delano Foundation, Mignon
  Sherwood
DeRoy Foundation, Helen L.
DeRoy Testamentary
  Foundation
Dexter Corporation
Digital Equipment Corp.
Dodge Foundation, Geraldine
  R.
Donaldson Company, Inc.
Donnelley & Sons Co., R.R.
Douty Foundation
du Pont de Nemours & Co., E.
  I.
Eaton Foundation, Cyrus
Eden Hall Foundation
El Pomar Foundation
Exchange National Bank
Favrot Fund
Federated Mutual Insurance
  Co.
Femino Foundation
Fikes Foundation, Leland
Finch Foundation, Thomas
  Austin
Fireman's Fund Insurance Co.
First Fidelity Bank
First Union Corp.
Forest Foundation
Freed Foundation
Freeport-McMoRan Inc.
Friedman Family Foundation
Frisch's Restaurants Inc.
Frost National Bank
Fry Foundation, Lloyd A.
Fuller Foundation, C. G.
Fund for New Jersey
Gates Foundation
GATX Corp.
Gazette Co.
Gebbie Foundation
General American Life
  Insurance Co.
General Mills, Inc.
GenRad
German Protestant Orphan
  Asylum Association
Giant Eagle, Inc.
Giant Food Stores
Glaser Foundation
Globe Newspaper Co.
Goddard Foundation, Charles
  B.
Goldseker Foundation of
  Maryland, Morris
Gould Electronics Inc.
Graham Fund, Philip L.
Grand Rapids Label Co.
Great-West Life Assurance Co.

Gregg-Graniteville Foundation
Griswold Foundation, John C.
Groome Beatty Trust, Helen D.
Guaranty Bank & Trust Co.
Haas, Jr. Fund, Evelyn and Walter
Haigh-Scatena Foundation
Halsell Foundation, Ewing
Handy and Harman Foundation
Hanson Industries North America
Harcourt General, Inc.
Harland Charitable Foundation, John and Wilhelmina D.
Harmon Foundation, Pearl M. and Julia J.
Harriman Foundation, Gladys and Roland
Hastings Charitable Foundation, Oris B.
HCA Foundation
Hechinger Co.
Heinz Endowment, Howard
Heinz Endowment, Vira I.
Helmerich Foundation
Henry Foundation, Patrick
Hermann Foundation, Grover
Hillcrest Foundation
Hillman Foundation
Hoag Family Foundation, George
Hook Drugs
Hopwood Charitable Trust, John M.
Houston Endowment
Howell Foundation of Florida
Hudson-Webber Foundation
Hunt Charitable Trust, C. Giles
Hunt Foundation, Samuel P.
Icahn Foundation, Carl C.
Irvine Foundation, James
ITT Hartford Insurance Group, Inc.
Jackson Foundation
Janirve Foundation
Jaydor Corp.
Jennings Foundation, Mary Hillman
Jewish Healthcare Foundation of Pittsburgh
Jockey Hollow Foundation
Johnson Foundation, Burdine
Johnson Foundation, M. G. and Lillie A.
Jones Foundation, Daisy Marquis
Kansas City Southern Industries
Kempner Fund, Harris and Eliza
Kennecott Corporation
Kerr Foundation
Kimberly-Clark Corp.
Kirby Foundation, F. M.
Kirkpatrick Foundation
Klosk Fund, Louis and Rose
Kresge Foundation
Ladd Charitable Corporation, Helen and George
Lattner Foundation, Forrest C.
Leavey Foundation, Thomas and Dorothy
Lederer Foundation, Francis L.
Lehigh Portland Cement Corp.
Lehmann Foundation, Otto W.
Leuthold Foundation
Levitt Foundation
Life Insurance Co. of Georgia
Liz Claiborne, Inc.
Lurie Foundation, Louis R.
Lydall, Inc.
Madison Gas & Electric Co.
Mailman Family Foundation, A. L.
Maneely Fund
Mardag Foundation
Maritz Inc.
Markey Charitable Fund, John C.
Mather Charitable Trust, S. Livingston
McDermott Foundation, Eugene

McDonald & Company Securities, Inc.
McElroy Trust, R. J.
McFawn Trust No. 2, Lois Sisler
Mead Corporation, The
Meadows Foundation
Meyer Memorial Trust
Minnesota Mining & Mfg. Co.
Mnuchin Foundation
Mobil Oil Corp.
Monadnock Paper Mills
Montana Power Co.
Morgan & Company, J.P.
Morgan Foundation, Burton D.
Murphey Foundation, Lluella Morey
Musson Charitable Foundation, R. C. and Katharine M.
Nalco Chemical Co.
National Westminster Bank New Jersey
Nesholm Family Foundation
New York Life Insurance Co.
New York Mercantile Exchange
The New Yorker Magazine, Inc.
Newman's Own, Inc.
Northern States Power Co. (Minnesota)
Norton Co.
Overlake Foundation
Oxy USA Inc.
Parsons Foundation, Ralph M.
Payne Foundation, Frank E. and Seba B.
Penn Foundation, William
Peppers Foundation, Ann
Perkin-Elmer Corp.
Pew Charitable Trusts
PHH Corporation
Pick, Jr. Fund, Albert
Pioneer Trust Bank, NA
Piper Jaffray Companies Inc.
Pittsburg Midway Coal Mining Co.
Playboy Enterprises, Inc.
PNC Bank, N.A.
Pott Foundation, Herman T. and Phenie R.
Prairie Foundation
Premier Industrial Corp.
PriMerit Bank
Prouty Foundation, Olive Higgins
Public Welfare Foundation
Richardson Charitable Trust, Anne S.
Rockwell International Corporation
Roseburg Forest Products Co.
Ross Laboratories
Rouse Co.
Royal Foundation, May Mitchell
Sandusky International Inc.
Sandy Hill Foundation
Santa Fe Pacific Corporation
Sara Lee Corp.
Sara Lee Hosiery, Inc.
Scherman Foundation
Schuller International
Scott Foundation, William E.
Seaway Food Town, Inc.
Second Foundation
Security Life of Denver Insurance Co.
Seidman Family Foundation
Selby and Marie Selby Foundation, William G.
Shawmut National Corp.
Siltec Corp.
Skillman Foundation
Smith Charitable Foundation, Lou and Lutza
Smith Foundation, Ralph L.
Smith Memorial Fund, Ethel Sergeant Clark
Smith Trust, May and Stanley
Spang & Co.
Sprague Educational and Charitable Foundation, Seth
Staunton Farm Foundation
Steele Foundation, Harry and Grace

Stevens Foundation, John T.
Stupp Foundation, Norman J.
Sturgis Charitable and Educational Trust, Roy and Christine
Subaru of America Inc.
Sunnen Foundation
Swanson Family Foundation, Dr. W.C.
Taubman Foundation, A. Alfred
Temple Foundation, T. L. L.
Tetley, Inc.
Times Mirror Company, The
Transco Energy Co.
Travelers Inc.
Trull Foundation
Trust Company Bank
Unger Foundation, Aber D.
Union Bank
Union Camp Corporation
Union Pacific Corp.
U.S. Bank of Washington
Unitrode Corp.
Uris Brothers Foundation
USL Capital Corporation
Valentine Foundation, Lawson
van Ameringen Foundation
Van Wert County Foundation
Wahlstrom Foundation
Wal-Mart Stores, Inc.
Wallace Foundation, George R.
Walsh Foundation
Washington Forrest Foundation
Washington Mutual Savings Bank
Weckbaugh Foundation, Eleanore Mullen
Wells Foundation, Franklin H. and Ruth L.
West One Bancorp
Whirlpool Corporation
Wickson-Link Memorial Foundation
WICOR, Inc.
Williams Companies, The
Windham Foundation
Woodward Fund
Wright Foundation, Lola
Y and H Soda Foundation
Zachry Co., H.B.
Zarrow Foundation, Anne and Henry

Emergency Relief

Abbott Laboratories
Adams Foundation, Arthur F. and Alice E.
Ahmanson Foundation
Air Products and Chemicals, Inc.
Albertson's Inc.
Alumax Inc.
Aluminum Co. of America
Amcast Industrial Corp.
AMCORE Bank, N.A. Rockford
American General Finance Corp.
American Natural Resources Company
American United Life Insurance Co.
Amfac/JMB Hawaii Inc.
Andersen Corp.
Andreas Foundation
Appleton Papers Inc.
Archer-Daniels-Midland Co.
AT&T Corp.
Atherton Family Foundation
Audubon State Bank
Baldwin Memorial Foundation, Fred
Beazley Foundation/Frederick Foundation
Beech Aircraft Corp.
Bethlehem Steel Corp.
Beveridge Foundation, Frank Stanley
Block, H&R
Blowitz-Ridgeway Foundation
Borman's Inc.
Bridgestone/Firestone, Inc.
Burnett-Tandy Foundation

Cabot Corp.
Cafritz Foundation, Morris and Gwendolyn
Cain Foundation, Effie and Wofford
Central Maine Power Co.
Chase Manhattan Bank, N.A.
Chazen Foundation
Chesebrough-Pond's USA Co.
Chevron Corporation
Chicago Sun-Times, Inc.
Childs Charitable Foundation, Roberta M.
Chrysler Corp.
Church & Dwight Co., Inc.
Citibank
CLARCOR Inc.
Cole Foundation, Olive B.
Colonial Life & Accident Insurance Co.
Cooke Foundation
Cooper Industries, Inc.
Cosmair, Inc.
Cowles Charitable Trust
Cowles Media Co.
Crocker Trust, Mary A.
Crown Memorial, Arie and Ida
Cummins Engine Co.
Curtice-Burns Foods, Inc.
Davidson Family Charitable Foundation
Davis Foundation, Edwin W. and Catherine M.
Davis Foundation, James A. and Juliet L.
Daywood Foundation
Delaware North Co., Inc.
Digital Equipment Corp.
Dodge Foundation, Cleveland H.
Donaldson Company, Inc.
du Pont de Nemours & Co., E. I.
Duke Power Co.
duPont Foundation, Alfred I.
Eaton Corporation
El Pomar Foundation
Enron Corp.
Federated Mutual Insurance Co.
Fireman's Fund Insurance Co.
First Fidelity Bank
First Union Corp.
Fish Foundation, Ray C.
Foster Foundation
Freeport-McMoRan Inc.
Friedman Family Foundation
Frost National Bank
General American Life Insurance Co.
General Mills, Inc.
Glenn Foundation, Carrie C. and Lena V.
Goldwyn Foundation, Samuel
Goodrich Co., The B.F.
Gordon/Rousmaniere/Roberts Fund
Hafif Family Foundation
Hancock Foundation, Luke B.
Handy and Harman Foundation
Harsco Corp.
Hawn Foundation
Heinz Endowment, Vira I.
Hermann Foundation, Grover
Heublein Inc.
Hillcrest Foundation
Hobby Foundation
Hook Drugs
Huston Charitable Trust, Stewart
Inland Container Corp.
International Business Machines Corp.
ITT Hartford Insurance Group, Inc.
Jarson-Stanley and Mickey Kaplan Foundation, Isaac and Esther
Jennings Foundation, Mary Hillman
Johnson Foundation, Helen K. and Arthur E.
Johnson Foundation, M. G. and Lillie A.
Johnson & Son, S.C.

Kansas City Southern Industries
Kayser Foundation
Kingsbury Corp.
Koopman Fund
Laffey-McHugh Foundation
LamCo. Communications
Lee Enterprises
Lehigh Portland Cement Co.
Lipton, Thomas J.
Little, Inc., Arthur D.
Liz Claiborne, Inc.
Louisiana-Pacific Corp.
Lowenstein Foundation, Leon
Lydall, Inc.
Macy & Co., Inc., R.H.
Mailman Foundation
Mardag Foundation
Maritz Inc.
Mars Foundation
May Foundation, Wilbur
MCA Inc.
McCann Foundation
McCasland Foundation
McCormick Trust, Anne
McDonald & Company Securities, Inc.
McDonnell Douglas Corp.-West
MCI Communications Corp.
Meadows Foundation
Mellon Family Foundation, R. K.
Merrill Lynch & Co., Inc.
Middendorf Foundation
Mine Safety Appliances Co.
Minnesota Mining & Mfg. Co.
Mitsubishi Motor Sales of America, Inc.
Mobil Oil Corp.
Morgan Stanley & Co., Inc.
Murphey Foundation, Lluella Morey
Nesholm Family Foundation
New York Mercantile Exchange
Norfolk Shipbuilding & Drydock Corp.
Normandie Foundation
Northern States Power Co. (Minnesota)
Norton Co.
OG&E Electric Services
Overbrook Foundation
Oxy USA Inc.
Pacific Mutual Life Insurance Co.
Packaging Corporation of America
Palmer Fund, Frank Loomis
Parsons Foundation, Ralph M.
Pennzoil Co.
Perkin-Elmer Corp.
Pfizer, Inc.
PHH Corporation
Phillips Family Foundation, Jay and Rose
Piper Jaffray Companies Inc.
Pitt-Des Moines Inc.
Pittsburg Midway Coal Mining Co.
Plankenhorn Foundation, Harry
Premier Industrial Corp.
Price Foundation, Louis and Harold
Prudential Insurance Co. of America, The
Pulitzer Publishing Co.
Rachal Foundation, Ed
Reisman Charitable Trust, George C. and Evelyn R.
Rockwell Fund
Rockwell International Corporation
Rohm & Haas Co.
Rosenberg Foundation
Rose's Stores, Inc.
Ross Laboratories
SAFECO Corp.
Saint Paul Companies, Inc.
Salomon Inc.
San Diego Gas & Electric
Sandy Hill Foundation
Santa Fe Pacific Corporation
Sara Lee Hosiery, Inc.
Sargent Foundation, Newell B.

Schuller International
Schumann Fund for New Jersey
Schwab & Co., Inc., Charles
Scott Foundation, Walter
Scurlock Foundation
Seagram & Sons, Inc., Joseph E.
Second Foundation
Security Life of Denver Insurance Co.
Shell Oil Company
Shenandoah Life Insurance Co.
Skillman Foundation
Southern California Edison Co.
Southwestern Electric Power Co.
Square D Co.
Starr Foundation
Staunton Farm Foundation
Taylor Foundation, Ruth and Vernon
Tenneco Inc.
Textron, Inc.
Thermo Electron Corp.
Trull Foundation
Trust Company Bank
Union Camp Corporation
Union Electric Co.
United Airlines, Inc.
U.S. Bank of Washington
USG Corporation
Vulcan Materials Co.
Wal-Mart Stores, Inc.
Weber Charities Corp., Frederick E.
Weil, Gotshal and Manges Foundation
Weingart Foundation
Wheeler Foundation, Wilmot
Whitecap Foundation
Wiley & Sons, Inc., John
Williams Charitable Trust, Mary Jo
Williams Companies, The
Winnebago Industries, Inc.
Wisconsin Power & Light Co.
Wright Foundation, Lola
Young Foundation, Robert R.

Family Planning

Abell-Hanger Foundation
Ahmanson Foundation
AKC Fund
Alexander Foundation, Joseph
Allyn Foundation
Aluminum Co. of America
Amcast Industrial Corp.
Andersen Corp.
Anderson Foundation, John W.
Andreas Foundation
Annenberg Foundation
Ansin Private Foundation, Ronald M.
Archer-Daniels-Midland Co.
Audubon State Bank
Auerbach Foundation, Beatrice Fox
Ayres Foundation, Inc.
Babson Foundation, Paul and Edith
Baker Trust, George F.
Baldwin Foundation, David M. and Barbara
Ball Foundation, George and Frances
Bank One, Youngstown, NA
Barker Foundation, J.M.R.
Barra Foundation
Battelle Memorial Institute
Batts Foundation
Beloit Foundation
Bemis Company, Inc.
Berwind Corporation
Bettingen Corporation, Burton G.
Bingham Second Betterment Fund, William
Bishop Foundation, E. K. and Lillian F.
Bissell Foundation, J. Walton
Blaustein Foundation, Louis and Henrietta

Block, H&R
Blowitz-Ridgeway Foundation
Blum Foundation, Edna F.
Boettcher Foundation
Booth Ferris Foundation
Borman's Inc.
Brenner Foundation, Mervyn
Breyer Foundation
Bridgestone/Firestone, Inc.
Brunswick Corp.
Bunbury Company
Burden Foundation, Florence V.
Burkitt Foundation
Burnett-Tandy Foundation
Bush Foundation
Cabell Foundation, Robert G.
Cabell III and Maude Morgan
Cabot Family Charitable Trust
Cafritz Foundation, Morris and Gwendolyn
Cain Foundation, Gordon and Mary
Campbell Foundation
Carnegie Corporation of New York
Carolyn Foundation
Carter Foundation, Amon G.
Carter Foundation, Beirne
Cassett Foundation, Louis N.
Cayuga Foundation
Central Maine Power Co.
Champlin Foundations
Chartwell Foundation
Chase Manhattan Bank, N.A.
Chazen Foundation
CHC Foundation
Chicago Sun-Times, Inc.
Claiborne and Art Ortenberg Foundation, Liz
Clapp Charitable and Educational Trust, George H.
Clark Foundation
Clorox Co.
Clowes Fund
Collins Foundation
Colonial Life & Accident Insurance Co.
Columbus Dispatch Printing Co.
Commerce Bancshares, Inc.
Connelly Foundation
Consolidated Papers, Inc.
Cooke Foundation
Cornell Trust, Peter C.
Corning Incorporated
Cowell Foundation, S. H.
Cowles Charitable Trust
Cowles Foundation, Gardner and Florence Call
Cowles Media Co.
Crary Foundation, Bruce L.
Cremer Foundation
Crestlea Foundation
Crocker Trust, Mary A.
Crystal Trust
Cullen Foundation
Cummins Engine Co.
Curtice-Burns Foods, Inc.
Dana Charitable Trust, Eleanor Naylor
Davenport-Hatch Foundation
Davis Foundation, James A. and Juliet L.
Day Foundation, Nancy Sayles
Delano Foundation, Mignon Sherwood
Delavan Foundation, Nelson B.
DeRoy Testamentary Foundation
Deuble Foundation, George H.
Dexter Charitable Fund, Eugene A.
Dillon Foundation
Dimeo Construction Co.
Dr. Seuss Foundation
Dodge Foundation, Cleveland H.
Dodge Foundation, Geraldine R.
Donaldson Company, Inc.
Douty Foundation
Dover Foundation
Dresser Industries, Inc.

Dreyfus Foundation, Jean and Louis
Dreyfus Foundation, Max and Victoria
Duke Endowment
Duke Power Co.
Dunagan Foundation
Eaton Foundation, Cyrus
Elkins, Jr. Foundation, Margaret and James A.
Ettinger Foundation
Fair Oaks Foundation, Inc.
Farish Fund, William Stamps
Favrot Fund
Federated Mutual Insurance Co.
Fife Foundation, Elias and Bertha
Fikes Foundation, Leland
First Fidelity Bank
First Union Corp.
Fish Foundation, Ray C.
Fishback Foundation Trust, Harmes C.
Fletcher Foundation
Forbes Inc.
Ford Foundation
Ford Fund, William and Martha
Forest Foundation
Foster Foundation
Freed Foundation
Freeman Charitable Trust, Samuel
French Oil Mill Machinery Co.
Friendship Fund
Frohring Foundation, Paul and Maxine
GAR Foundation
Gates Foundation
Gellert Foundation, Carl
General American Life Insurance Co.
General Mills, Inc.
Georgia Power Co.
German Protestant Orphan Asylum Association
Gershman Foundation, Joel
Gheens Foundation
Glanville Family Foundation
Glaser Foundation
Glick Foundation, Eugene and Marilyn
Glosser Foundation, David A.
Goldseker Foundation of Maryland, Morris
Goldsmith Foundation, Horace W.
Goldwyn Foundation, Samuel
Good Samaritan
Grand Rapids Label Co.
Griffith Foundation, W. C.
Griggs and Mary Griggs Burke Foundation, Mary Livingston
Grundy Foundation
GSM Industrial
Guttman Foundation, Stella and Charles
Hagedorn Fund
Haigh-Scatena Foundation
Halff Foundation, G. A. C.
Halsell Foundation, Ewing
Hamman Foundation, George and Mary Josephine
Hanover Foundation
Harriman Foundation, Mary W.
Harrington Foundation, Francis A. and Jacquelyn H.
Harsco Corp.
Hartmarx Corporation
Hasbro Inc.
HCA Foundation
Hechinger Co.
Hecht-Levi Foundation
Heckscher Foundation for Children
Heinz Company, H. J.
Heinz Endowment, Howard
Heinz Endowment, Vira I.
Helms Foundation
Hewlett Foundation, William and Flora
Heydt Fund, Nan and Matilda
Hillman Foundation
Hillsdale Fund
Hobby Foundation

Homeland Foundation
Hoover Foundation
Houston Endowment
Hoyt Foundation, Stewart W. and Willma C.
Huber Foundation
Hulme Charitable Foundation, Milton G.
Humana, Inc.
Humphrey Fund, George M. and Pamela S.
Hunt Charitable Trust, C. Giles
Hunt Foundation
Huston Charitable Trust, Stewart
Huston Foundation
Illinois Tool Works, Inc.
Independence Foundation
Ingalls Foundation, Louise H. and David S.
International Foundation
Irvine Foundation, James
Jackson Foundation
Jacobs Family Foundation
Jaffe Foundation
Janirve Foundation
Jennings Foundation, Mary Hillman
Jewett Foundation, George Frederick
JM Foundation
Jockey Hollow Foundation
Johnson Foundation, Burdine
Johnson Foundation, Helen K. and Arthur E.
Johnson Foundation, Willard T. C.
Jones Foundation, Daisy Marquis
Jonsson Foundation
Journal-Gazette Co.
Jurzykowski Foundation, Alfred
Kansas City Southern Industries
Kaplan Fund, J. M.
Kaufmann Foundation, Henry
Kayser Foundation
Kelly Foundation, T. Lloyd
Kempner Fund, Harris and Eliza
Kennecott Corporation
Kennedy Foundation, Ethel
Kerr Foundation
Kettering Fund
Kiewit Foundation, Peter
Kiplinger Foundation
Kirby Foundation, F. M.
Kirkpatrick Foundation
Kline Foundation, Josiah W. and Bessie H.
Klipstein Foundation, Ernest Christian
KN Energy, Inc.
Koopman Fund
Kresge Foundation
Kunkel Foundation, John Crain
Laffey-McHugh Foundation
Larsen Fund
Lattner Foundation, Forrest C.
Laurel Foundation
Lazarus Charitable Trust, Helen and Charles
Leavey Foundation, Thomas and Dorothy
Leuthold Foundation
Levitt Foundation
Levy Foundation, June Rockwell
Lipton, Thomas J.
Lockhart Vaughan Foundation
Longwood Foundation
Lurcy Charitable and Educational Trust, Georges
MacArthur Foundation, John D. and Catherine T.
Magowan Family Foundation
Mailman Family Foundation, A. L.
Management Compensation Group/Dulworth Inc.
Maneely Fund
Marbrook Foundation
Markey Charitable Fund, John C.

Marmot Foundation
Marpat Foundation
Mars Foundation
Marshall Trust in Memory of Sanders McDaniel, Harriet McDaniel
Martin Marietta Corp.
Marx Foundation, Virginia and Leonard
Mather Charitable Trust, S. Livingston
Mather Fund, Richard
Mather and William Gwinn Mather Fund, Elizabeth Ring
Maytag Family Foundation, Fred
MBIA Inc.
MCA Inc.
McCormick & Co. Inc.
McDonald & Company Securities, Inc.
McElroy Trust, R. J.
McEvoy Foundation, Mildred H.
McFawn Trust No. 2, Lois Sisler
MCI Communications Corp.
McInerny Foundation
McLean Contributionship
McMahan Foundation, Catherine L. and Robert O.
Mellon Foundation, Andrew W.
Mellon Foundation, Richard King
Merck Family Fund
Mercury Aircraft
Meyer Memorial Trust
Mid-Iowa Health Foundation
Middendorf Foundation
Miller-Mellor Association
Morgan & Company, J.P.
Morgan Construction Co.
Morgan Foundation, Burton D.
Morgan Stanley & Co., Inc.
Morris Foundation, Margaret T.
Moses Fund, Henry and Lucy
Mott Foundation, Charles Stewart
Mulford Foundation, Vincent
Munger Foundation, Alfred C.
Murphey Foundation, Lluella Morey
New-Land Foundation
The New Yorker Magazine, Inc.
Nias Foundation, Henry
Noble Foundation, Edward John
Noble Foundation, Samuel Roberts
Norgren Foundation, Carl A.
Normandie Foundation
North Shore Foundation
Norton Co.
Norton Foundation Inc.
Norwest Bank Nebraska, N.A.
O'Fallon Trust, Martin J. and Mary Anne
Offield Family Foundation
OG&E Electric Services
Old National Bank in Evansville
Olin Foundation, Spencer T. and Ann W.
Oppenstein Brothers Foundation
O'Quinn Foundation, John M. and Nancy C.
Osborn Charitable Trust, Edward B.
Osher Foundation, Bernard
Overbrook Foundation
Owsley Foundation, Alvin and Lucy
Pacific Mutual Life Insurance Co.
Packard Foundation, David and Lucile
Palmer Fund, Frank Loomis
Parshelsky Foundation, Moses L.
Parsons Foundation, Ralph M.
Parvin Foundation, Albert
Peabody Charitable Fund, Amelia
Penn Foundation, William

Pew Charitable Trusts
Phelps Dodge Corporation
Phillips Foundation, Ellis L.
Phipps Foundation, Howard
Pick, Jr. Fund, Albert
Pierce Charitable Trust, Harold Whitworth
Pittsburgh Child Guidance Foundation
Playboy Enterprises, Inc.
Plumsock Fund
Pollock Company Foundation, William B.
Pott Foundation, Herman T. and Phenie R.
PriMerit Bank
Prospect Hill Foundation
Providence Journal Company
Prudential Insurance Co. of America, The
Public Welfare Foundation
Pulitzer Publishing Co.
Puterbaugh Foundation
Rabb Charitable Foundation, Sidney and Esther
Ralston Purina Co.
Regenstein Foundation
Reicher Foundation, Anne and Harry J.
Reidler Foundation
Reinberger Foundation
Richardson Charitable Trust, Anne S.
Robinson-Broadhurst Foundation
Rockefeller Fund, David
Rockwell Fund
Rose Foundation, Billy
Rose's Stores, Inc.
Ross Memorial Foundation, Will
Rowland Foundation
Ruan Foundation Trust, John
Rubinstein Foundation, Helena
Salomon Foundation, Richard and Edna
Salomon Inc.
Sara Lee Corp.
Sarkeys Foundation
Sasco Foundation
Scaife Family Foundation
Schenck Fund, L. P.
Scherer Foundation, Karla
Scherman Foundation
Schiff Foundation, Dorothy
Schiro Fund
Schoenleber Foundation
Seidman Family Foundation
Selby and Marie Selby Foundation, William G.
Semmes Foundation
Sequoia Foundation
Seton Leather Co.
Shawmut National Corp.
Sierra Pacific Resources
Simon Foundation, William E. and Carol G.
Skillman Foundation
Slifka Foundation, Joseph and Sylvia
Smith Foundation, Ralph L.
South Waite Foundation
Speyer Foundation, Alexander C. and Tillie S.
SPX Corp.
Sprague Educational and Charitable Foundation, Seth
Stackpole-Hall Foundation
Stanley Charitable Foundation, A.W.
Starr Foundation
Stauffer Charitable Trust, John
Steele Foundation, Harry and Grace
Steele-Reese Foundation
Stein Foundation, Jules and Doris
Steinman Foundation, James Hale
Steinman Foundation, John Frederick
Stone Charitable Foundation
Strawbridge Foundation of Pennsylvania II, Margaret Dorrance

Subaru of America Inc.
Sulzberger Foundation
Sunnen Foundation
Taconic Foundation
Tait Foundation, Frank M.
Taubman Foundation, A. Alfred
Taylor Foundation, Ruth and Vernon
Teichert & Son, A.
Temple Foundation, T. L. L.
Texas Commerce Bank-Houston, N.A.
Textron, Inc.
Tiscornia Foundation
Todd Co., A.M.
Towsley Foundation, Harry A. and Margaret D.
Trull Foundation
Trust Funds
Tucker Charitable Trust, Rose E.
Turner Charitable Foundation
Turrell Fund
Unger Foundation, Aber D.
Union Camp Corporation
Upton Foundation, Frederick S.
Uris Brothers Foundation
Van Houten Memorial Fund
Vance Charitable Foundation, Robert C.
Vanderbilt Trust, R. T.
Wachovia Bank of North Carolina, N.A.
Wallace Foundation, George R.
Washington Forrest Foundation
Wean Foundation, Raymond John
Weaver Foundation, Gil and Dody
Weber Charities Corp., Frederick E.
Weckbaugh Foundation, Eleanore Mullen
Wege Foundation
Weil, Gotshal and Manges Foundation
Welch Testamentary Trust, George T.
Wells Foundation, Franklin H. and Ruth L.
Whirlpool Corporation
Whitney Fund, David M.
Williams Charitable Trust, John C.
Williams Companies, The
Windham Foundation
Winnebago Industries, Inc.
Witco Corp.
Woodward Fund
Wright Foundation, Lola
Wyomissing Foundation
Young Foundation, Robert R.
Zarrow Foundation, Anne and Henry
Zlinkoff Fund for Medical Research and Education, Sergei S.

Family Services

Abbott Laboratories
Abell-Hanger Foundation
Achelis Foundation
Acushnet Co.
Ahmanson Foundation
Air Products and Chemicals, Inc.
Alabama Gas Corp.
Alabama Power Co.
Alcon Laboratories, Inc.
Aldus Corp.
Alexander Foundation, Joseph
Allegheny Ludlum Corp.
Allendale Insurance Co.
AlliedSignal Inc.
Allyn Foundation
Altman Foundation
Aluminum Co. of America
AMCORE Bank, N.A. Rockford
American General Finance Corp.
American National Bank & Trust Co. of Chicago

American United Life Insurance Co.
Ameritas Life Insurance Corp.
Amfac/JMB Hawaii Inc.
AMP Incorporated
AMR Corp.
Andersen Corp.
Andersen Foundation
Anderson Foundation, John W.
Andersons, The
Annenberg Foundation
Ansin Private Foundation, Ronald M.
Ansley Foundation, Dantzler Bond
Aristech Chemical Corp.
Arkelian Foundation, Ben H. and Gladys
Arkell Hall Foundation
AT&T Corp.
Atherton Family Foundation
Auerbach Foundation, Beatrice Fox
Avon Products, Inc.
Ayres Foundation, Inc.
Babson Foundation, Paul and Edith
Baldwin Memorial Foundation, Fred
Ball Brothers Foundation
Ball Foundation, George and Frances
Bank of Boston
Bank of Boston Corp.
Bank of New York Company, Inc.
BankAmerica Corp.
Bard Foundation, Robert
Barker Foundation, J.M.R.
Barra Foundation
Barry Corp., R. G.
Barth Foundation, Theodore H.
Battelle Memorial Institute
Baughman Foundation
Bay Foundation
Beal Foundation
Bean Foundation, Norwin S. and Elizabeth N.
BE&K Inc.
Bedsole Foundation, J. L.
Beloit Foundation
Bemis Company, Inc.
Benedum Foundation, Claude Worthington
Benwood Foundation
Bertha Foundation
Besser Foundation
Bethlehem Steel Corp.
Betts Industries
Beveridge Foundation, Frank Stanley
Bingham Second Betterment Fund, William
Binney & Smith Inc.
Bishop Foundation, E. K. and Lillian F.
Blair and Co., William
Blandin Foundation
Blaustein Foundation, Louis and Henrietta
Block, H&R
Blount, Inc.
Blowitz-Ridgeway Foundation
Blue Cross & Blue Shield United of Wisconsin
Bodman Foundation
Boettcher Foundation
Booth Ferris Foundation
Borden, Inc.
Borman's Inc.
Boston Edison Co.
Bothin Foundation
Bowne Foundation, Robert
Brach Foundation, Helen
Bremer Foundation, Otto
Brenner Foundation, Mervyn
Bridgestone/Firestone, Inc.
Bridwell Foundation, J. S.
Brown & Williamson Tobacco Corp.
Brunswick Corp.
Bucyrus-Erie Company
Bunbury Company
Burden Foundation, Florence V.

Burlington Industries, Inc.
Burnett-Tandy Foundation
Bush Foundation
Cabell Foundation, Robert G. Cabell III and Maude Morgan
Calder Foundation, Louis
Calhoun Charitable Trust, Kenneth
Campini Foundation, Frank A.
Carnegie Corporation of New York
Carolyn Foundation
Carpenter Foundation
Carpenter Foundation, E. Rhodes and Leona B.
Carpenter Technology Corp.
Carter Foundation, Amon G.
Carter Foundation, Beirne
Carver Charitable Trust, Roy J.
Cayuga Foundation
Central Fidelity Banks, Inc.
Central Maine Power Co.
Chartwell Foundation
Chase Manhattan Bank, N.A.
Chazen Foundation
CHC Foundation
Chesapeake Corp.
Chevron Corporation
Chicago Sun-Times, Inc.
Childs Charitable Foundation, Roberta M.
Christensen Charitable and Religious Foundation, L. C.
Citibank
Citizens Bank of Rhode Island
City National Bank and Trust Co.
Clark Foundation
Clarke Trust, John
Clarkson Foundation, Jeniam
Clay Foundation
Clemens Markets Corp.
Clorox Co.
Clowes Fund
CNA Financial Corporation/CNA Insurance Companies
Cogswell Benevolent Trust
Collins Medical Trust
Colonial Life & Accident Insurance Co.
Comer Foundation
Commerce Bancshares, Inc.
Commerce Clearing House, Incorporated
Comprecare Foundation
Connecticut Mutual Life Insurance Company
Consumers Power Co.
Continental Corp.
Contran Corporation
Cooke Foundation
Cooperman Foundation, Leon and Toby
Coors Foundation, Adolph
Cornell Trust, Peter C.
Cowell Foundation, S. H.
Cowles Charitable Trust
Cowles Media Co.
CPC International Inc.
Crandall Memorial Foundation, J. Ford
Cremer Foundation
Crestlea Foundation
Crocker Trust, Mary A.
Crown Books
Crown Memorial, Arie and Ida
Crystal Trust
CT Corp. System
Culpeper Memorial Foundation, Daphne Seybolt
Culver Foundation, Constans
Cummings Foundation, James H.
Cummins Engine Co.
Curtice-Burns Foods, Inc.
Dater Foundation, Charles H.
Davenport-Hatch Foundation
Davis Foundation, Edwin W. and Catherine M.
Daywood Foundation
Deere & Co.
Delano Foundation, Mignon Sherwood

Delavan Foundation, Nelson B.
Demos Foundation, N.
DeRoy Foundation, Helen L.
DeRoy Testamentary Foundation
Detroit Edison Co.
Deuble Foundation, George H.
Dewing Foundation, Frances R.
Diamond Foundation, Aaron
Dishman Charitable Foundation Trust, H. E. and Kate
Dodge Foundation, Cleveland H.
Dodge Foundation, Geraldine R.
Dodge Jones Foundation
Donaldson Foundation, Inc.
Donnelley & Sons Co., R.R.
Doss Foundation, M. S.
Douglas & Lomason Company
Douty Foundation
Dow Foundation, Herbert H. and Grace A.
Dow Jones & Company, Inc.
Dresser Industries, Inc.
Dreyfus Foundation, Max and Victoria
du Pont de Nemours & Co., E. I.
Duchossois Industries Inc.
Duke Endowment
Duke Power Co.
Dula Educational and Charitable Foundation, Caleb C. and Julia W.
Dunagan Foundation
Duncan Trust, John G.
Eastman Kodak Company
Eaton Corporation
El Pomar Foundation
English Memorial Fund, Florence C. and H. L.
Ettinger Foundation
Exxon Corporation
Fair Foundation, R. W.
Fair Play Foundation
Farish Fund, William Stamps
Favrot Fund
Federated Mutual Insurance Co.
Feild Co-Operative Association
Fife Foundation, Elias and Bertha
Fikes Foundation, Leland
Fink Foundation
Fireman's Fund Insurance Co.
Firestone, Jr. Foundation, Harvey
First Fidelity Bank
First Hawaiian, Inc.
First Interstate Bank of Oregon
First Union Corp.
Firstar Bank Milwaukee, N.A.
Fishback Foundation Trust, Harmes C.
Fleishhacker Foundation
Fleming Cos. Food Distribution Center
Folger Fund
Fondren Foundation
Forbes Inc.
Ford Foundation
Forest Foundation
Foster Foundation
France Foundation, Jacob and Annita
Freed Foundation
Freeport-McMoRan Inc.
Frese Foundation, Arnold D.
Fribourg Foundation
Friedman Family Foundation
Frost National Bank
Frueauff Foundation, Charles A.
Fruehauf Foundation
Fuller Foundation
Fund for New Jersey
Fuqua Foundation, J. B.
Gannett Publishing Co., Guy
GAR Foundation
Gates Foundation
GATX Corp.
Gazette Co.
Gebbie Foundation

Selby and Marie Selby Foundation, William G.
Self Foundation
Semmes Foundation
Seneca Foods Corp.
Shaw Foundation, Arch W.
Shawmut National Corp.
Sheaffer Inc.
Sheary for Charity, Edna M.
Shell Oil Company
Simon Foundation, William E. and Carol G.
Skillman Foundation
Slifka Foundation, Joseph and Sylvia
Sloan Foundation, Alfred P.
Smith Charitable Foundation, Lou and Lutza
Smith Corp., A.O.
Smith Foundation, Ralph L.
Smith Trust, May and Stanley
Snyder Foundation, Harold B. and Dorothy A.
Sonat Inc.
Sordoni Foundation
Southern California Edison Co.
Southwestern Electric Power Co.
Sprague Educational and Charitable Foundation, Seth
SPX Corp.
Stanley Charitable Foundation, A.W.
Stanley Works
Starr Foundation
Stauffer Charitable Trust, John
Staunton Farm Foundation
Stearns Trust, Artemas W.
Stein Foundation, Jules and Doris
Stemmons Foundation
Sternberger Foundation, Tannenbaum
Stevens Foundation, Abbot and Dorothy H.
Stokely, Jr. Foundation, William B.
Stone Charitable Foundation
Strong Foundation, Hattie M.
Stupp Foundation, Norman J.
Sturgis Charitable and Educational Trust, Roy and Christine
Subaru of America Inc.
Sumitomo Bank of California
Sumners Foundation, Hatton W.
Sunnen Foundation
Swalm Foundation
Swanson Family Foundation, Dr. W.C.
Tait Foundation, Frank M.
Taube Family Foundation
Taubman Foundation, A. Alfred
Tecumseh Products Co.
Teichert & Son, A.
Temple Foundation, T. L. L.
Thalhimer and Family Foundation, Charles G.
Thomas Foundation, Joan and Lee
Thomas Industries
Thomasville Furniture Industries
Thorne Foundation
Times Mirror Company, The
Timken Foundation of Canton
Towsley Foundation, Harry A. and Margaret D.
Tozer Foundation
TransAmerica Corporation
Travelers Inc.
Trull Foundation
Trust Company Bank
Trust Funds
Tucker Charitable Trust, Rose E.
Turrell Fund
Unger Foundation, Aber D.
Union Bank
Union Camp Corporation
Union Electric Co.
Union Pacific Corp.
U.S. Bank of Washington
Upton Foundation, Frederick S.

Uris Brothers Foundation
US WEST, Inc.
USL Capital Corporation
Utica National Insurance Group
Vale Foundation, Ruby R.
Valentine Foundation, Lawson
van Ameringen Foundation
Vance Charitable Foundation, Robert C.
Vernon Fund, Miles Hodsdon
Vicksburg Foundation
Vollbrecht Foundation, Frederick A.
Wachovia Bank of North Carolina, N.A.
Warfield Memorial Fund, Anna Emory
Washington Forrest Foundation
Washington Mutual Savings Bank
Waters Charitable Trust, Robert S.
Weaver Foundation, Gil and Dody
Weber Charities Corp., Frederick E.
Weezie Foundation
Weil, Gotshal and Manges Foundation
Weingart Foundation
Welfare Foundation
Wells Foundation, Franklin H. and Ruth L.
Wendt Foundation, Margaret L.
Western New York Foundation
Weyerhaeuser Co.
Whirlpool Corporation
Whitecap Foundation
Whiting Foundation
Whittenberger Foundation, Claude R. and Ethel B.
Wickson-Link Memorial Foundation
Williams Charitable Trust, John C.
Williams Companies, The
Windham Foundation
Wiremold Co.
Wisconsin Power & Light Co.
Wood Foundation of Chambersburg, PA
Wright Foundation, Lola
Y and H Soda Foundation
Young Foundation, Robert R.
Zachry Co., H.B.
Zarrow Foundation, Anne and Henry
Zenkel Foundation

Food/Clothing Distribution

Abell-Hanger Foundation
ACF Industries, Inc.
Achelis Foundation
Adler Foundation Trust, Philip D. and Henrietta B.
Ahmanson Foundation
Air Products and Chemicals, Inc.
Alabama Power Co.
Albertson's Inc.
Alcon Laboratories, Inc.
Aldus Corp.
Allegheny Ludlum Corp.
Allendale Insurance Co.
AlliedSignal Inc.
Allyn Foundation
Alumax Inc.
Aluminum Co. of America
AMCORE Bank, N.A. Rockford
American Brands, Inc.
American National Bank & Trust Co. of Chicago
American Natural Resources Company
American United Life Insurance Co.
Ameritas Life Insurance Corp.
Amfac/JMB Hawaii Inc.
AMP Incorporated

Andersen Corp.
Anderson Foundation
Anderson Foundation, John W.
Andersons, The
Anheuser-Busch Companies, Inc.
AON Corporation
Appleton Papers Inc.
Arcadia Foundation
Archer-Daniels-Midland Co.
Argyros Foundation
Aristech Chemical Corp.
Arkansas Power & Light Co.
Arkell Hall Foundation
Arnhold Foundation
Atherton Family Foundation
Auerbach Foundation, Beatrice Fox
Avon Products, Inc.
Ayres Foundation, Inc.
Babcock & Wilcox Co.
Babson Foundation, Paul and Edith
Badgeley Residuary Charitable Trust, Rose M.
Baker Foundation, Dexter F. and Dorothy H.
Baldwin Memorial Foundation, Fred
Banc One Wisconsin Corp.
Bank of Boston Corp.
BankAmerica Corp.
Banta Corp.
Bard Foundation, Robert
Barra Foundation
Barth Foundation, Theodore H.
Batts Foundation
Beal Foundation
Bean Foundation, Norwin S. and Elizabeth N.
Beazley Foundation/Frederick Foundation
Beech Aircraft Corp.
Bemis Company, Inc.
Benedum Foundation, Claude Worthington
Benwood Foundation
Berger Foundation, H. N. and Frances C.
Berwind Corporation
Besser Foundation
Bethlehem Steel Corp.
Bingham Second Betterment Fund, William
Bird Corp.
Birnschein Foundation, Alvin and Marion
Blaustein Foundation, Louis and Henrietta
Block, H&R
Bloedorn Foundation, Walter A.
Blount, Inc.
Blue Bell, Inc.
Blum Foundation, Harry and Maribel G.
Blum-Kovler Foundation
Bobst Foundation, Elmer and Mamdouha
Bodman Foundation
Boeing Co., The
Boettcher Foundation
Booth Ferris Foundation
Borden, Inc.
Borkee Hagley Foundation
Borman's Inc.
Boston Edison Co.
Brach Foundation, Helen
Bremer Foundation, Otto
Breyer Foundation
Bridwell Foundation, J. S.
Bristol-Myers Squibb Company
Brown Foundation, M. K.
Brunswick Corp.
Bryn Mawr Trust Co.
Bucyrus-Erie Company
Buhl Foundation
Bunbury Company
Burdines Inc.
Burnett-Tandy Foundation
Cabell Foundation, Robert G. Cabell III and Maude Morgan
Cabot Corp.

Calhoun Charitable Trust, Kenneth
Campini Foundation, Frank A.
Cargill Inc.
Carpenter Foundation
Carpenter Foundation, E. Rhodes and Leona B.
Carpenter Technology Corp.
Carter Foundation, Amon G.
Castle Foundation, Harold K. L.
Catlin Charitable Trust, Kathleen K.
CBS, Inc.
Central Hudson Gas & Electric Corp.
Central Maine Power Co.
Centralia Foundation
Champlin Foundations
Chapman Charitable Corporation, Howard and Bess
Chartwell Foundation
Chase Manhattan Bank, N.A.
Chatlos Foundation
Cheney Foundation, Ben B.
Chesebrough-Pond's USA Co.
Chevron Corporation
Chicago Sun-Times, Inc.
Chrysler Corp.
Church & Dwight Co., Inc.
CIGNA Corporation
Citibank
Citizens Bank of Rhode Island
Clapp Charitable and Educational Trust, George H.
CLARCOR Inc.
Clay Foundation
Clemens Markets Corp.
Clorox Co.
Clowes Fund
CNA Financial Corporation/CNA Insurance Companies
Cole Foundation, Olive B.
Collins Foundation
Collins, Jr. Foundation, George Fulton
Colonial Life & Accident Insurance Co.
Columbia Foundation
Columbus Dispatch Printing Co.
Commerce Bancshares, Inc.
Connecticut Mutual Life Insurance Company
Connelly Foundation
Consolidated Natural Gas Co.
Cooke Foundation
Cooper Industries, Inc.
Coors Foundation, Adolph
Cord Foundation, E. L.
Cornell Trust, Peter C.
Coughlin-Saunders Foundation
Cowell Foundation, S. H.
Cowles Charitable Trust
Cowles Media Co.
Crane Co.
Crawford Estate, E. R.
Cremer Foundation
Crestlea Foundation
Crown Memorial, Arie and Ida
Crystal Trust
Cullen Foundation
Cummings Foundation, James H.
Cummins Engine Co.
Cuneo Foundation
Curtice-Burns Foods, Inc.
Daily News
Darby Foundation
Dater Foundation, Charles H.
Daugherty Foundation
Davenport Trust Fund
Davidson Family Charitable Foundation
Davis Foundation, Irene E. and George A.
Davis Foundation, James A. and Juliet L.
Daywood Foundation
Dekko Foundation
Demoulas Supermarkets Inc.
Dentsply International Inc.
DeRoy Foundation, Helen L.

Detroit Edison Co.
Deuble Foundation, George H.
Dewing Foundation, Frances R.
Dexter Charitable Fund, Eugene A.
Dexter Corporation
Digital Equipment Corp.
Dishman Charitable Foundation Trust, H. E. and Kate
Dr. Seuss Foundation
Dodge Jones Foundation
Donaldson Company, Inc.
Donner Foundation, William H.
Doss Foundation, M. S.
Dreyfus Foundation, Jean and Louis
Dreyfus Foundation, Max and Victoria
du Pont de Nemours & Co., E. I.
Duke Power Co.
Dun & Bradstreet Corp.
duPont Foundation, Alfred I.
Dynamet, Inc.
Eaton Corporation
Eddy Family Memorial Fund, C. K.
Eden Hall Foundation
Einstein Fund, Albert E. and Birdie W.
El Pomar Foundation
English Memorial Fund, Florence C. and H. L.
Enron Corp.
Ettinger Foundation
Fair Foundation, R. W.
Farish Fund, William Stamps
Federal-Mogul Corporation
Federated Mutual Insurance Co.
Ferebee Endowment, Percy O.
Fikes Foundation, Leland
Finch Foundation, Doak
Finch Foundation, Thomas Austin
Fireman's Fund Insurance Co.
First Fidelity Bank
First Hawaiian, Inc.
First Interstate Bank of Oregon
First Union Corp.
Fischbach Foundation
Fish Foundation, Ray C.
Fishback Foundation Trust, Harmes C.
Ford II Fund, Henry
Forest Foundation
Foster Foundation
Frear Eleemosynary Trust, Mary D. and Walter F.
Freeport Brick Co.
Freeport-McMoRan Inc.
French Oil Mill Machinery Co.
Frese Foundation, Arnold D.
Friedman Family Foundation
Frost National Bank
Frueauff Foundation, Charles A.
Fry Foundation, Lloyd A.
Fuller Foundation
Gallagher Family Foundation, Lewis P.
Gap, Inc., The
GAR Foundation
Gates Foundation
GATX Corp.
Gazette Co.
Gellert Foundation, Carl
Gellert Foundation, Celia Berta
General American Life Insurance Co.
General Mills, Inc.
General Motors Corp.
Georgia-Pacific Corporation
Georgia Power Co.
Germeshausen Foundation, Kenneth J.
Gheens Foundation
Giant Eagle, Inc.
Giant Food Inc.
Gifford Charitable Corporation, Rosamond
Giles Foundation, Edward C.
Gillette Co.
Gilman Foundation, Howard

Gilmore Foundation, William G.
Glaser Foundation
Globe Newspaper Co.
Goldie-Anna Charitable Trust
Goldseker Foundation of Maryland, Morris
Goodstein Family Foundation, David
Graham Fund, Philip L.
Grand Rapids Label Co.
Gregg-Graniteville Foundation
Griffith Foundation, W. C.
Grundy Foundation
Guaranty Bank & Trust Co.
Guardian Life Insurance Company of America
Gulf Power Co.
Haas, Jr. Fund, Evelyn and Walter
Hachar Charitable Trust, D. D.
Hagedorn Fund
Halff Foundation, G. A. C.
Hallberg Foundation, E. L. and R. F.
Hamman Foundation, George and Mary Josephine
Hancock Foundation, Luke B.
Harmon Foundation, Pearl M. and Julia J.
Harsco Corp.
Harvey Foundation, Felix
Hasbro Inc.
Hauser Foundation
Hawkins Foundation, Robert Z.
Hazen Foundation, Edward W.
HCA Foundation
Hechinger Co.
Heinz Endowment, Vira I.
Helmerich Foundation
Hermann Foundation, Grover
Herrick Foundation
Hershey Foods Corp.
Herzstein Charitable Foundation, Albert and Ethel
Heydt Fund, Nan and Matilda
Hickory Tech Corp.
Higginson Trust, Corina
Hillcrest Foundation
Hillman Family Foundation, Alex
Hillsdale Fund
Hoag Family Foundation, George
Hobby Foundation
Hoffman Foundation, Maximilian E. and Marion O.
Homeland Foundation
Hook Drugs
Hoover Foundation
Hopedale Foundation
Hudson-Webber Foundation
Hugoton Foundation
Hulme Charitable Foundation, Milton G.
Humana, Inc.
Hunt Charitable Trust, C. Giles
Huston Foundation
Hyde and Watson Foundation
Hygeia Dairy Co.
IBP, Inc.
IES Industries, Inc.
Imperial Bancorp
International Foundation
International Paper Co.
Irwin Charity Foundation, William G.
ITT Hartford Insurance Group, Inc.
Ittleson Foundation
Jackson Foundation
Jacobson Foundation, Bernard H. and Blanche E.
Jaffe Foundation
Janirve Foundation
Jarson-Stanley and Mickey Kaplan Foundation, Isaac and Esther
Jaydor Corp.
Jewish Healthcare Foundation of Pittsburgh
JFM Foundation
John Hancock Mutual Life Insurance Co.

Johnson Charitable Trust, Keith Wold
Johnson Controls Inc.
Johnson Foundation, Burdine
Johnson Foundation, Helen K. and Arthur E.
Johnson Foundation, M. G. and Lillie A.
Jones Foundation, Daisy Marquis
Jones Foundation, Fletcher
Jonsson Foundation
Jordan Charitable Foundation, Mary Ranken Jordan and Ettie A.
Joslin-Needham Family Foundation
Journal-Gazette Co.
Joy Family Foundation
Julia R. and Estelle L. Foundation
Jurzykowski Foundation, Alfred
Kansas City Southern Industries
Kaplan Fund, J. M.
Kavanagh Foundation, T. James
Kayser Foundation
Kennedy Foundation, Ethel
Kent-Lucas Foundation
Kerr Foundation
Kiewit Foundation, Peter
Kilcawley Fund, William H.
Kimball Foundation, Horace A. Kimball and S. Ella
Kimberly-Clark Corp.
Kingsbury Corp.
Kiplinger Foundation
Kirbo Charitable Trust, Thomas M. and Irene B.
Kirby Foundation, F. M.
Kirkpatrick Foundation
Kline Foundation, Josiah W. and Bessie H.
Kmart Corporation
Knox, Sr., and Pearl Wallis Knox Charitable Foundation, Robert W.
Knudsen Foundation, Tom and Valley
Koopman Fund
Koret Foundation
Kreitler Foundation
Kresge Foundation
Laffey-McHugh Foundation
Lattner Foundation, Forrest C.
Lazarus Charitable Trust, Helen and Charles
LBJ Family Foundation
Leavey Foundation, Thomas and Dorothy
Lebovitz Fund
Lee Enterprises
Lehmann Foundation, Otto W.
Leidy Foundation, John J.
Lennon Foundation, Fred A.
Leuthold Foundation
Levy Foundation, June Rockwell
Lipton, Thomas J.
Liz Claiborne, Inc.
Lockhart Vaughan Foundation
Long Island Lighting Co.
Longwood Foundation
Louisiana-Pacific Corp.
Love Foundation, George H. and Margaret McClintic
Lowenstein Foundation, Leon
Lurie Foundation, Louis R.
Lydall, Inc.
MacLeod Stewardship Foundation
Maddox Foundation, J. F.
Madison Gas & Electric Co.
Mailman Foundation
Mardag Foundation
Mardigian Foundation
Maritz Inc.
Marmot Foundation
Marpat Foundation
Mars Foundation
Martin Marietta Corp.
Mather Charitable Trust, S. Livingston

Mather and William Gwinn Mather Fund, Elizabeth Ring
May Foundation, Wilbur
MBIA Inc.
MCA Inc.
McCormick & Co. Inc.
McCormick Trust, Anne
McCune Charitable Foundation, Marshall and Perrine D.
McDermott Foundation, Eugene
McDonald & Company Securities, Inc.
McDonnell Douglas Corp.-West
McElroy Trust, R. J.
McFawn Trust No. 2, Lois Sisler
McGee Foundation
McInerny Foundation
McKenna Foundation, Philip M.
McMahan Foundation, Catherine L. and Robert O.
McMillan Foundation, D. W.
McQueen Foundation, Adeline and George
Mead Corporation, The
Meadows Foundation
Mellon Foundation, Richard King
Merck Family Fund
Merrick Foundation
Merrill Lynch & Co., Inc.
Metropolitan Life Insurance Co.
Meyer Memorial Trust
Mid-Iowa Health Foundation
Middendorf Foundation
Miller Brewing Company/North Carolina
Miller-Mellor Association
Minnesota Mining & Mfg. Co.
Mitsubishi Motor Sales of America, Inc.
Mnuchin Foundation
Mobil Oil Corp.
Monfort Family Foundation
Morgan & Company, J.P.
Morgan and Samuel Tate Morgan, Jr. Foundation, Marietta McNeil
Morgan Stanley & Co., Inc.
Morris Foundation, Margaret T.
Moses Fund, Henry and Lucy
Mott Fund, Ruth
Mulcahy Foundation
Mullen Foundation, J. K.
Murphy Co. Foundation, G.C.
Musson Charitable Foundation, R. C. and Katharine M.
Nabisco Foods Group
Nalco Chemical Co.
Nestle USA Inc.
New York Life Insurance Co.
New York Mercantile Exchange
New York Stock Exchange, Inc.
New York Times Company
The New Yorker Magazine, Inc.
Newman's Own, Inc.
NewMil Bancorp
Norgren Foundation, Carl A.
Norman Foundation, Summers A.
Normandie Foundation
Northern States Power Co. (Minnesota)
Northwest Natural Gas Co.
Norton Foundation Inc.
Norwest Bank Nebraska, N.A.
Novell Inc.
NYNEX Corporation
OCRI Foundation
O'Fallon Trust, Martin J. and Mary Anne
Offield Family Foundation
Old Dominion Box Co.
Old National Bank in Evansville
Olin Corp.
Olsson Memorial Foundation, Elis

O'Quinn Foundation, John M. and Nancy C.
Ore-Ida Foods, Inc.
Osborn Charitable Trust, Edward B.
Osher Foundation, Bernard
Ottenheimer Brothers Foundation
Overbrook Foundation
Oxy USA Inc.
Pacific Mutual Life Insurance Co.
Packaging Corporation of America
Packard Foundation, David and Lucile
PaineWebber
Palmer Fund, Frank Loomis
Pamida, Inc.
Parshelsky Foundation, Moses L.
Parsons Foundation, Ralph M.
Patterson Charitable Fund, W. I.
Payne Foundation, Frank E. and Seba B.
Pella Corporation
Pennsylvania Dutch Co.
Peppers Foundation, Ann
Perkin-Elmer Corp.
Pfizer, Inc.
PHH Corporation
Phipps Foundation, Howard
Pierce Charitable Trust, Harold Whitworth
Pioneer Trust Bank, NA
Piper Jaffray Companies Inc.
Pittsburgh Child Guidance Foundation
PNC Bank, N.A.
Polaroid Corp.
Porter Testamentary Trust, James Hyde
Potomac Electric Power Co.
Pott Foundation, Herman T. and Phenie R.
PPG Industries, Inc.
Premier Industrial Corp.
Price Associates, T. Rowe
Price Foundation, Louis and Harold
Priddy Foundation
Proctor Trust, Mortimer R.
Providence Gas Co.
Provident Life & Accident Insurance Company of America
Providian Corporation
Prudential Insurance Co. of America, The
Public Service Electric & Gas Co.
Public Welfare Foundation
Pulitzer Publishing Co.
Quaker Chemical Corp.
R. F. Foundation
Ralston Purina Co.
Regenstein Foundation
Reidler Foundation
Reisman Charitable Trust, George C. and Evelyn R.
Rennebohm Foundation, Oscar
Republic NY Corp.
Retirement Research Foundation
Reynolds Foundation, Donald W.
Rich Products Corporation
Richardson Benevolent Foundation, C. E.
Rockwell Fund
Rohm & Haas Co.
Roseburg Forest Products Co.
Rosenberg, Jr. Family Foundation, Louise and Claude
Rose's Stores, Inc.
Ross Laboratories
Ross Memorial Foundation, Will
Rouse Co.
Rubin Family Fund, Cele H. and William B.
Rudin Foundation
Russell Trust, Josephine G.

Ryan Foundation, David Claude
Salomon Inc.
San Diego Gas & Electric
Sandusky International Inc.
Sandy Hill Foundation
Santa Fe Pacific Corporation
Sara Lee Corp.
Sara Lee Hosiery, Inc.
Sargent Foundation, Newell B.
Sarkeys Foundation
Sasco Foundation
Scaife Family Foundation
Schenck Fund, L. P.
Scherman Foundation
Schlink Foundation, Albert G. and Olive H.
Schlumberger Ltd.
Scholl Foundation, Dr.
Schuller International
Schwab & Co., Inc., Charles
Schwartz Foundation, Arnold A.
Scott Fetzer Co.
Seaway Food Town, Inc.
Second Foundation
Security Life of Denver Insurance Co.
Seidman Family Foundation
Selby and Marie Selby Foundation, William G.
Sequoia Foundation
Shaw Foundation, Arch W.
Shawmut National Corp.
Shell Oil Company
Shenandoah Life Insurance Co.
Simon Foundation, William E. and Carol G.
Simpson Investment Company
Skillman Foundation
Slifka Foundation, Joseph and Sylvia
Smith Charitable Foundation, Lou and Lutza
Smith Foundation, Kelvin and Eleanor
Smith Trust, May and Stanley
Sonat Inc.
Spalding Foundation, Eliot
Spang & Co.
Speyer Foundation, Alexander C. and Tillie S.
SPX Corp.
Square D Co.
Stabler Foundation, Donald B. and Dorothy L.
Starr Foundation
Stauffer Charitable Trust, John
Stauffer Foundation, John and Beverly
Stearns Trust, Artemas W.
Steele Foundation, Harry and Grace
Steele-Reese Foundation
Steinhagen Benevolent Trust, B. A. and Elinor
Stevens Foundation, Abbot and Dorothy H.
Stupp Foundation, Norman J.
Sturgis Charitable and Educational Trust, Roy and Christine
Subaru of America Inc.
Sunnen Foundation
Swalm Foundation
Symmes Foundation, F. W.
Taylor Foundation, Fred and Harriett
Tecumseh Products Co.
Temple Foundation, T. L. L.
Tenneco Inc.
Texas Commerce Bank-Houston, N.A.
Textron, Inc.
Thalhimer and Family Foundation, Charles G.
Thermo Electron Corp.
Thornton Foundation, Flora L.
Times Mirror Company, The
Timken Foundation of Canton
Titus Foundation, Roy and Niuta
Toms Foundation
TransAmerica Corporation
Travelers Inc.

Truland Foundation
Trust Company Bank
Trust Funds
Tuch Foundation, Michael
Tucker Charitable Trust, Rose E.
Turner Charitable Foundation
Turrell Fund
Unger Foundation, Aber D.
Unilever United States, Inc.
Union Electric Co.
Union Pacific Corp.
U.S. Bank of Washington
Uris Brothers Foundation
USG Corporation
USL Capital Corporation
Utica National Insurance Group
Valentine Foundation, Lawson
Vernon Fund, Miles Hodsdon
Virginia Power Co.
Vogler Foundation, Laura B.
Vollbrecht Foundation, Frederick A.
Vulcan Materials Co.
Wachovia Bank of North Carolina, N.A.
Wahlstrom Foundation
Wal-Mart Stores, Inc.
Walsh Foundation
Washington Forrest Foundation
Washington Mutual Savings Bank
Wean Foundation, Raymond John
Weaver Foundation, Gil and Dody
Weber Charities Corp., Frederick E.
Weckbaugh Foundation, Eleanore Mullen
Weingart Foundation
Welch Testamentary Trust, George T.
Welfare Foundation
Wells Foundation, Franklin H. and Ruth L.
Wheeler Foundation
Whirlpool Corporation
Whiting Foundation
Whitney Fund, David M.
Wickes Foundation, Harvey Randall
Wilson Fund, Matilda R.
Winnebago Industries, Inc.
Wiremold Co.
Wisconsin Power & Light Co.
Wise Foundation and Charitable Trust, Watson W.
Wood Foundation of Chambersburg, PA
Wright Foundation, Lola
Y and H Soda Foundation
Young Foundation, Irvin L.
Young Foundation, Robert R.
Zarrow Foundation, Anne and Henry
Zenkel Foundation

General

Acme-McCrary Corp./Sapona Manufacturing Co.
Alabama Gas Corp.
Aldus Corp.
Aluminum Co. of America
Amcast Industrial Corp.
AMCORE Bank, N.A. Rockford
Amoco Corporation
Andersen Foundation
Ansley Foundation, Dantzler Bond
Baldwin Foundation, David M. and Barbara
Bank One, Texas-Houston Office
Bank One, Youngstown, NA
Barry Corp., R. G.
Bay Foundation
Benenson Foundation, Frances and Benjamin
Binney & Smith Inc.
Blair and Co., William

Bowen Foundation, Ethel N.
Bryant Foundation
Bryn Mawr Trust Co.
Carter Foundation, Beirne
Central Maine Power Co.
CHC Foundation
Chicago Sun-Times, Inc.
Christian Dior New York, Inc.
CIBC Wood Gundy
CINergy
CNA Financial Corporation/CNA Insurance Companies
Cosmair, Inc.
Cummings Foundation, James H.
Cuneo Foundation
Davis Foundation, Irene E. and George A.
DEC International, Inc.
Diamond Shamrock Inc.
Ebsco Industries, Inc.
Encyclopaedia Britannica, Inc.
Fabri-Kal Corp.
First Union National Bank of Florida
French Oil Mill Machinery Co.
GenRad
Gould Electronics Inc.
Grand Rapids Label Co.
Hagedorn Fund
Handy and Harman Foundation
Harcourt General, Inc.
Hermann Foundation, Grover
Hickory Tech Corp.
Hoag Family Foundation, George
Holnam
Hoyt Foundation, Stewart W. and Willma C.
Integra Bank of Uniontown
International Paper Co.
ITT Hartford Insurance Group, Inc.
Jaydor Corp.
Kansas City Southern Industries
Kardon Foundation, Samuel and Rebecca
Kaye, Scholer, Fierman, Hays & Handler
Kennecott Corporation
Kingsbury Corp.
KN Energy, Inc.
Knoll Group
LamCo. Communications
Lattner Foundation, Forrest C.
Laurel Foundation
Lehigh Portland Cement Co.
Lydall, Inc.
Maddox Foundation, J. F.
Management Compensation Group/Dulworth Inc.
Maritz Inc.
Martin Marietta Materials
Mascoma Savings Bank
Mautz Paint Co.
MBIA Inc.
McDonald & Company Securities, Inc.
Miller Brewing Company/North Carolina
Mitsubishi Motor Sales of America, Inc.
Moore Foundation, Edward S.
Mosinee Paper Corp.
National Forge Co.
New Jersey Natural Gas Co.
New York Mercantile Exchange
New York Times Company
The New Yorker Magazine, Inc.
Nias Foundation, Henry
Norfolk Shipbuilding & Drydock Corp.
Northwest Natural Gas Co.
Norton Co.
Novell Inc.
Old National Bank in Evansville
Packaging Corporation of America
PaineWebber
Pamida, Inc.
PHH Corporation
Pioneer Trust Bank, NA

Piper Jaffray Companies Inc.
Pitt-Des Moines Inc.
Pittsburg Midway Coal Mining Co.
PriMerit Bank
Providence Gas Co.
Providian Corporation
Roseburg Forest Products Co.
Rose's Stores, Inc.
Ross Laboratories
Royal Group, Inc.
Sandusky International Inc.
Sara Lee Hosiery, Inc.
Sarkeys Foundation
Security Life of Denver Insurance Co.
Sedgwick James Inc.
Seneca Foods Corp.
Sheppard Foundation, Lawrence B.
Sierra Pacific Resources
Siltec Corp.
Snow Memorial Trust, John Ben
Solow Foundation
Southwestern Electric Power Co.
SPX Corp.
Stevens Foundation, Abbot and Dorothy H.
Teleflex Inc.
Thompson Co., J. Walter
Thomson Information Publishing Group
Tupancy-Harris Foundation of 1986
Turrell Fund
U.S. Bank of Washington
Unitrode Corp.
Unocal Corp.
Webber Oil Co.
Weber Charities Corp., Frederick E.
West One Bancorp
Westerman Foundation, Samuel L.
Whirlpool Corporation
WICOR, Inc.
Wiremold Co.
Wisconsin Power & Light Co.
Witco Corp.
Zachry Co., H.B.

Homes

Abell-Hanger Foundation
ACF Industries, Inc.
Ahmanson Foundation
Air Products and Chemicals, Inc.
Alexander Foundation, Joseph
Allegheny Ludlum Corp.
Allendale Insurance Co.
AlliedSignal Inc.
Aluminum Co. of America
AMCORE Bank, N.A. Rockford
American National Bank & Trust Co. of Chicago
Ameritas Life Insurance Corp.
AMETEK, Inc.
Amfac/JMB Hawaii Inc.
Amoco Corporation
Andersen Corp.
Andersen Foundation
Ansley Foundation, Dantzler Bond
AON Corporation
Argyros Foundation
Arkansas Power & Light Co.
Arkelian Foundation, Ben H. and Gladys
Atherton Family Foundation
Atran Foundation
Audubon State Bank
Babson Foundation, Paul and Edith
Badgeley Residuary Charitable Trust, Rose M.
Bank One, Youngstown, NA
Barra Foundation
Batts Foundation
Beazley Foundation/Frederick Foundation

Bechtel, Jr. Foundation, S. D.
Beech Aircraft Corp.
Bemis Company, Inc.
Bettingen Corporation, Burton G.
Betts Industries
Bigelow Foundation, F. R.
Bingham Second Betterment Fund, William
Birnschein Foundation, Alvin and Marion
Block, H&R
Bloedorn Foundation, Walter A.
Blount, Inc.
Blowitz-Ridgeway Foundation
Blue Bell, Inc.
Blum-Kovler Foundation
Bodman Foundation
Boeing Co., The
Boise Cascade Corporation
Borden, Inc.
Borkee Hagley Foundation
Bremer Foundation, Otto
Bucyrus-Erie Company
Bunbury Company
Cabot Corp.
Cain Foundation, Gordon and Mary
Campbell Foundation, Ruth and Henry
Carolyn Foundation
Carpenter Technology Corp.
Carter Foundation, Amon G.
Carter Foundation, Beirne
Central Fidelity Banks, Inc.
Central Hudson Gas & Electric Corp.
Centralia Foundation
Champlin Foundations
Chase Manhattan Bank, N.A.
CHC Foundation
Chesapeake Corp.
Chevron Corporation
Chicago Sun-Times, Inc.
Childs Charitable Foundation, Roberta M.
Christensen Charitable and Religious Foundation, L. C.
Citibank
Citizens Bank of Rhode Island
CLARCOR Inc.
Clark Foundation
Clay Foundation
Clemens Markets Corp.
Clowes Fund
Coen Family Foundation, Charles S. and Mary
Cole Trust, Quincy
Collins Foundation
Colonial Life & Accident Insurance Co.
Columbia Foundation
Connecticut Mutual Life Insurance Company
Connelly Foundation
Consolidated Natural Gas Co.
Continental Corp.
Coors Foundation, Adolph
Copley Press, Inc.
Cowell Foundation, S. H.
Crane Co.
Crawford Estate, E. R.
Cremer Foundation
Crestlea Foundation
Crown Memorial, Arie and Ida
Culver Foundation, Constans
Cummings Foundation, James H.
Cuneo Foundation
Curtice-Burns Foods, Inc.
Dater Foundation, Charles H.
Daugherty Foundation
Davenport-Hatch Foundation
Davidson Family Charitable Foundation
Daywood Foundation
Deere & Co.
Demoulas Supermarkets Inc.
DeRoy Testamentary Foundation
Deuble Foundation, George H.
DeVore Foundation
Dewing Foundation, Frances R.

Dishman Charitable Foundation Trust, H. E. and Kate
Donaldson Company, Inc.
Doss Foundation, M. S.
Douty Foundation
Dow Foundation, Herbert H. and Grace A.
du Pont de Nemours & Co., E. I.
Duchossois Industries Inc.
Duke Endowment
Duncan Trust, John G.
duPont Foundation, Alfred I.
Dynamet, Inc.
Early Foundation
Eaton Corporation
Eden Hall Foundation
El Pomar Foundation
Elkins, Jr. Foundation, Margaret and James A.
Emerson Foundation, Inc., Fred L.
Enron Corp.
Evans Foundation, Lettie Pate
Federated Mutual Insurance Co.
Fenton Foundation
Ferebee Endowment, Percy O.
Fikes Foundation, Leland
Finch Foundation, Doak
Fink Foundation
First Fidelity Bank
First Union Corp.
Fish Foundation, Ray C.
Fletcher Foundation
Forbes Inc.
Ford Fund, William and Martha
Forest Foundation
Foster Foundation
Frueauff Foundation, Charles A.
Fruehauf Foundation
Fuller Foundation, C. G.
Fuqua Foundation, J. B.
Gannett Publishing Co., Guy
Gebbie Foundation
Geifman Family Foundation
Gellert Foundation, Carl
Gellert Foundation, Celia Berta
General American Life Insurance Co.
General Mills, Inc.
General Motors Corp.
Georgia Power Co.
German Protestant Orphan Asylum Association
Gershman Foundation, Joel
Gifford Charitable Corporation, Rosamond
Giles Foundation, Edward C.
Glaser Foundation
Globe Newspaper Co.
Goddard Foundation, Charles B.
Gould Electronics Inc.
Groome Beatty Trust, Helen D.
Grundy Foundation
Gulf Power Co.
Guttman Foundation, Stella and Charles
Haas, Jr. Fund, Evelyn and Walter
Habig Foundation, Arnold F.
Hallett Charitable Trust, E. W.
Hallett Charitable Trust, Jessie F.
Hamilton Bank
Hamman Foundation, George and Mary Josephine
Hancock Foundation, Luke B.
Hanes Foundation, John W. and Anna H.
Harland Charitable Foundation, John and Wilhelmina D.
Harsco Corp.
Harvey Foundation, Felix
Hazen Foundation, Edward W.
HCA Foundation
Hechinger Co.
Heginbotham Trust, Will E.
Heinz Company, H. J.
Heinz Endowment, Vira I.
Helmerich Foundation

Blake Foundation, S. P.
Blandin Foundation
Blaustein Foundation, Louis and Henrietta
Block, H&R
Bloedorn Foundation, Walter A.
Blowitz-Ridgeway Foundation
Blum Foundation, Edna F.
Blum-Kovler Foundation
Bodman Foundation
Boeing Co., The
Boettcher Foundation
Booth Ferris Foundation
Borden, Inc.
Borman's Inc.
Boswell Foundation, James G.
Bothin Foundation
Brach Foundation, Helen
Brady Foundation
Bremer Foundation, Otto
Breyer Foundation
Bridgestone/Firestone, Inc.
Bridwell Foundation, J. S.
Brillion Iron Works
Bristol-Myers Squibb Company
Brooks Foundation, Gladys
Brown Foundation, M. K.
Brunswick Corp.
Bucyrus-Erie Company
Buhl Foundation
Bunbury Company
Burnett-Tandy Foundation
Bush Foundation
Butz Foundation
Cabell Foundation, Robert G.
Cabell III and Maude Morgan
Cabot Corp.
Cafritz Foundation, Morris and Gwendolyn
Cain Foundation, Effie and Wofford
Calhoun Charitable Trust, Kenneth
Callaway Foundation
Campbell Foundation
Campbell Foundation, Ruth and Henry
Canon U.S.A., Inc.
Cargill Inc.
Carnahan-Jackson Foundation
Carolyn Foundation
Carpenter Foundation
Carpenter Foundation, E. Rhodes and Leona B.
Carter Foundation, Amon G.
Carter Foundation, Beirne
Carver Charitable Trust, Roy J.
Cassett Foundation, Louis N.
Castle Foundation, Harold K. L.
CBI Industries, Inc.
Centerior Energy Corp.
Central Maine Power Co.
Charina Foundation
Chartwell Foundation
Chase Manhattan Bank, N.A.
Chatlos Foundation
Cheney Foundation, Ben B.
Chevron Corporation
Chicago Sun-Times, Inc.
Childs Charitable Foundation, Roberta M.
Christensen Charitable and Religious Foundation, L. C.
Christian Dior New York, Inc.
CINergy
Citibank
Claiborne and Art Ortenberg Foundation, Liz
CLARCOR Inc.
Clark Foundation
Clay Foundation
Clayton Fund
Clorox Co.
Close Foundation
Clowes Fund
CNA Financial Corporation/CNA Insurance Companies
Coen Family Foundation, Charles S. and Mary
Cogswell Benevolent Trust

Cole Foundation, Olive B.
Collins Foundation
Colonial Life & Accident Insurance Co.
Columbus Dispatch Printing Co.
Comprecare Foundation
Connelly Foundation
Consolidated Natural Gas Co.
Consolidated Papers, Inc.
Continental Corp.
Cooke Foundation
Cooper Industries, Inc.
Coors Foundation, Adolph
Copley Press, Inc.
Cord Foundation, E. L.
Cornell Trust, Peter C.
Cowell Foundation, S. H.
Cowles Charitable Trust
Cowles Media Co.
CPC International Inc.
CR Industries
Crabtree & Evelyn
Crane Co.
Cremer Foundation
Crestlea Foundation
Crocker Trust, Mary A.
Crown Memorial, Arie and Ida
Crystal Trust
CS First Boston Corporation
Culver Foundation, Constans
Cummings Foundation, James H.
Cuneo Foundation
Curtice-Burns Foods, Inc.
Daily News
Dana Foundation, Charles A.
Darling Foundation, Hugh and Hazel
Dart Group Corp.
Dater Foundation, Charles H.
Daugherty Foundation
Davenport-Hatch Foundation
Davenport Trust Fund
Davidson Family Charitable Foundation
Davis Foundation, Irene E. and George A.
Day Foundation, Nancy Sayles
Daywood Foundation
De Queen General Hospital Foundation
Deere & Co.
Dekko Foundation
Delano Foundation, Mignon Sherwood
Delaware North Co., Inc.
Demos Foundation, N.
Demoulas Supermarkets Inc.
Dentsply International Inc.
DeRoy Foundation, Helen L.
DeRoy Testamentary Foundation
Deuble Foundation, George H.
DeVore Foundation
Dewing Foundation, Frances R.
Dexter Corporation
Digital Equipment Corp.
Dillon Foundation
Dr. Seuss Foundation
Dodge Foundation, Cleveland H.
Dodge Jones Foundation
Donaldson Company, Inc.
Donnelley & Sons Co., R.R.
Donner Foundation, William H.
Doss Foundation, M. S.
Douty Foundation
Dow Foundation, Herbert H. and Grace A.
Dow Jones & Company, Inc.
Dresser Industries, Inc.
Dreyfus Foundation, Max and Victoria
du Pont de Nemours & Co., E. I.
Duchossois Industries Inc.
Duke Endowment
Duke Power Co.
Dula Educational and Charitable Foundation, Caleb C. and Julia W.
Dun & Bradstreet Corp.
Duncan Foundation, Lillian H. and C. W.

Duncan Trust, John G.
Dynamet, Inc.
Eastman Kodak Company
Eaton Corporation
Eberly Foundation
Eden Hall Foundation
Edgewater Steel Corp.
Einstein Fund, Albert E. and Birdie W.
El Pomar Foundation
Elf Atochem North America, Inc.
English Memorial Fund, Florence C. and H. L.
Ensign-Bickford Industries
Essick Foundation
Fair Oaks Foundation, Inc.
Farish Fund, William Stamps
Favrot Fund
Federal-Mogul Corporation
Federated Mutual Insurance Co.
Feil Foundation, Louis and Gertrude
Fieldcrest Cannon Inc.
Fife Foundation, Elias and Bertha
Fikes Foundation, Leland
Fink Foundation
Fireman's Fund Insurance Co.
Firestone, Jr. Foundation, Harvey
Firman Fund
First Financial Bank FSB
First Interstate Bank of Oregon
First Source Corp.
First Union Corp.
Firstar Bank Milwaukee, N.A.
Fish Foundation, Ray C.
Fishback Foundation Trust, Harmes C.
Fleet Financial Group, Inc.
Folger Fund
Ford II Fund, Henry
Forest Foundation
Forest Oil Corp.
Fort Wayne National Bank
Foster Charitable Trust
France Foundation, Jacob and Annita
Freed Foundation
Freedom Forge Corp.
Freeman Charitable Trust, Samuel
Freeport-McMoRan Inc.
French Foundation, D.E.
French Oil Mill Machinery Co.
Frese Foundation, Arnold D.
Friedman Family Foundation
Frohring Foundation, Paul and Maxine
Frohring Foundation, William O. and Gertrude Lewis
Frost National Bank
Frueauff Foundation, Charles A.
Fruehauf Foundation
Fry Foundation, Lloyd A.
Fuqua Foundation, J. B.
Gallagher Family Foundation, Lewis P.
Gamble Foundation
Gannett Publishing Co., Guy
GAR Foundation
Gates Foundation
GATX Corp.
Gaylord Foundation, Clifford Willard
Gebbie Foundation
Geifman Family Foundation
Gellert Foundation, Carl
Gellert Foundation, Celia Berta
General American Life Insurance Co.
General Mills, Inc.
General Motors Corp.
GenRad
Georgia-Pacific Corporation
Georgia Power Co.
German Protestant Orphan Asylum Association
Gheens Foundation
Giant Eagle, Inc.
Giant Food Inc.
Giant Food Stores

Gifford Charitable Corporation, Rosamond
Giles Foundation, Edward C.
Gilmore Foundation, William G.
Glaser Foundation
Gleason Foundation
Globe Newspaper Co.
Goddard Foundation, Charles B.
Goldberg Family Foundation
Goldie-Anna Charitable Trust
Goldsmith Foundation, Horace W.
Goldwyn Foundation, Samuel
Goodrich Co., The B.F.
Gould Foundation, The Florence
Graham Fund, Philip L.
Grand Rapids Label Co.
Great-West Life Assurance Co.
Green Foundation, Allen P. and Josephine B.
Gregg-Graniteville Foundation
Greve Foundation, William and Mary
Griffith Foundation, W. C.
Groome Beatty Trust, Helen D.
Grundy Foundation
GSM Industrial
Guaranty Bank & Trust Co.
Guggenheim Foundation, Harry Frank
Gulf Power Co.
Guttman Foundation, Stella and Charles
Haas, Jr. Fund, Evelyn and Walter
Hafif Family Foundation
Hagedorn Fund
Halff Foundation, G. A. C.
Hallberg Foundation, E. L. and R. F.
Hallett Charitable Trust, E. W.
Hallett Charitable Trust, Jessie F.
Halsell Foundation, Ewing
Hamilton Bank
Hammer Foundation, Armand
Hancock Foundation, Luke B.
Hanson Industries North America
Harcourt General, Inc.
Hardin Foundation, Phil
Harland Charitable Foundation, John and Wilhelmina D.
Harriman Foundation, Mary W.
Harsco Corp.
Hartford Foundation, John A.
Hartmarx Corporation
Hawkins Foundation, Robert Z.
Hawn Foundation
HCA Foundation
Hearst Foundation, William Randolph
Hechinger Co.
Heckscher Foundation for Children
Heinz Company, H. J.
Heinz Trust, Drue
Helmerich Foundation
Helms Foundation
Hermann Foundation, Grover
Herrick Foundation
Hershey Foods Corp.
Herzstein Charitable Foundation, Albert and Ethel
Heublein Inc.
Hill Foundation, Sandy
Hillcrest Foundation
Hillman Family Foundation, Alex
Hillman Foundation
Hillsdale Fund
Hoag Family Foundation, George
Hobby Foundation
Hoffman Foundation, Maximilian E. and Marion O.
Hoffmann-La Roche Inc.
Hook Drugs
Hoover Foundation
Hopkins Foundation, Josephine Lawrence

Hopwood Charitable Trust, John M.
Housatonic Curtain Co.
Houston Endowment
Houston Industries Incorporated
Howe and Mitchell B. Howe Foundation, Lucille Horton
Hoyt Foundation, Stewart W. and Willma C.
Hugoton Foundation
Hulme Charitable Foundation, Milton G.
Humana, Inc.
Humphrey Fund, George M. and Pamela S.
Hunt Charitable Trust, C. Giles
Hunt Foundation
Hunt Foundation, Samuel P.
Hyde and Watson Foundation
Hygeia Dairy Co.
Icahn Foundation, Carl C.
ICI Americas Inc.
IES Industries, Inc.
Illinois Tool Works, Inc.
Inland Container Corp.
Integra Bank of Uniontown
International Business Machines Corp.
International Foundation
Iowa-Illinois Gas & Electric Co.
Irwin Charity Foundation, William G.
ITT Hartford Insurance Group, Inc.
Ittleson Foundation
Jackson Foundation
Jaffe Foundation
Janirve Foundation
Jarson-Stanley and Mickey Kaplan Foundation, Isaac and Esther
Jaydor Corp.
JELD-WEN, Inc.
Jennings Foundation, Mary Hillman
Jewett Foundation, George Frederick
Jewish Healthcare Foundation of Pittsburgh
JM Foundation
John Hancock Mutual Life Insurance Co.
Johnson Controls Inc.
Johnson Foundation, Helen K. and Arthur E.
Johnson Foundation, M. G. and Lillie A.
Johnson & Higgins
Jones Foundation, Daisy Marquis
Jones Foundation, Fletcher
Jones Foundation, Helen
Jordan Charitable Foundation, Mary Ranken Jordan and Ettie A.
Journal-Gazette Co.
Joy Family Foundation
Julia R. and Estelle L. Foundation
Jurzykowski Foundation, Alfred
Kansas City Southern Industries
Kantzler Foundation
Kaplun Foundation, Morris J. and Betty
Kardon Foundation, Samuel and Rebecca
Kaufmann Foundation, Henry
Kayser Foundation
Kelly Tractor Co.
Kempner Fund, Harris and Eliza
Kennecott Corporation
Kennedy Foundation, Ethel
Kern Foundation Trust
Kettering Fund
Kiewit Foundation, Peter
Kilcawley Fund, William H.
Kimberly-Clark Corp.
Kiplinger Foundation
Kirbo Charitable Trust, Thomas M. and Irene B.

Thomas Industries
Thorne Foundation
Times Mirror Company, The
Tobin Foundation
Todd Co., A.M.
TransAmerica Corporation
Transco Energy Co.
Trees Charitable Trust, Edith L.
Trexler Trust, Harry C.
Truland Foundation
Trust Company Bank
Tuch Foundation, Michael
Turner Charitable Foundation
Turrell Fund
Unger Foundation, Aber D.
Unilever United States, Inc.
Union Bank
Union Camp Corporation
Union Electric Co.
Union Pacific Corp.
U.S. Bank of Washington
Unitrode Corp.
Unocal Corp.
Upjohn Foundation, Harold
and Grace
Upton Foundation, Frederick S.
USG Corporation
USL Capital Corporation
USX Corporation
Utica National Insurance
Group
Valmont Industries, Inc.
van Ameringen Foundation
Van Nuys Foundation, I. N.
and Susanna H.
Van Wert County Foundation
Vance Charitable Foundation,
Robert C.
Vernon Fund, Miles Hodsdon
Virginia Power Co.
Vogler Foundation, Laura B.
Vollbrecht Foundation,
Frederick A.
Vulcan Materials Co.
Wachovia Bank of North
Carolina, N.A.
Wahlstrom Foundation
Wal-Mart Stores, Inc.
Walsh Foundation
Warren and Beatrice W.
Blanding Foundation, Riley
J. and Lillian N.
Warwick Foundation
Waters Charitable Trust,
Robert S.
Wean Foundation, Raymond
John
Weaver Foundation, Gil and
Dody
Webber Oil Co.
Weber Charities Corp.,
Frederick E.
Weckbaugh Foundation,
Eleanore Mullen
Weezie Foundation
Weingart Foundation
Weinstein Foundation, J.
Welfare Foundation
Wells Foundation, Franklin H.
and Ruth L.
Wendt Foundation, Margaret L.
West One Bancorp
Westerman Foundation,
Samuel L.
Western New York Foundation
Westvaco Corporation
Wheat First Butcher Singer,
Inc.
Wheeler Foundation
Whirlpool Corporation
White Trust, G. R.
Whiting Foundation
Wickes Foundation, Harvey
Randall
Wickson-Link Memorial
Foundation
WICOR, Inc.
Widgeon Foundation
Wilder Foundation
Wildermuth Foundation, E. F.
Willard Helping Fund, Cecilia
Young
Williams Companies, The
Wilson Foundation, H. W.
Wilson Fund, Matilda R.

Wiremold Co.
Wisconsin Power & Light Co.
Wise Foundation and
Charitable Trust, Watson W.
Witco Corp.
Woodward Fund
Woolley Foundation, Vasser
Worthington Foods
Wright Foundation, Lola
Wyomissing Foundation
Yeager Charitable Trust,
Lester E.
Young Foundation, Hugo H.
and Mabel B.
Young Foundation, Robert R.
Zachry Co., H.B.
Zarrow Foundation, Anne and
Henry
Zlinkoff Fund for Medical
Research and Education,
Sergei S.

Recreation & Athletics

Abell-Hanger Foundation
Achelis Foundation
Ahmanson Foundation
Air Products and Chemicals,
Inc.
AKC Fund
Aldus Corp.
Allegheny Foundation
Allegheny Ludlum Corp.
Allen Brothers Foundation
AlliedSignal Inc.
Allyn Foundation
Altman Foundation
Altschul Foundation
Aluminum Co. of America
Amado Foundation, Maurice
American Brands, Inc.
American Fidelity Corporation
American National Bank &
Trust Co. of Chicago
American Natural Resources
Company
American President
Companies, Ltd.
American United Life
Insurance Co.
Ames Charitable Trust, Harriett
Amfac/JMB Hawaii Inc.
Amoco Corporation
AMP Incorporated
Andersen Corp.
Andersons, The
Andreas Foundation
Anheuser-Busch Companies,
Inc.
Annenberg Foundation
Ansley Foundation, Dantzler
Bond
AON Corporation
Appleton Papers Inc.
Archer-Daniels-Midland Co.
Argyros Foundation
Aristech Chemical Corp.
Arkansas Power & Light Co.
Arkelian Foundation, Ben H.
and Gladys
Arkell Hall Foundation
Armco Inc.
Ashtabula Foundation
Asplundh Foundation
Astor Foundation, Vincent
Atherton Family Foundation
Audubon State Bank
Auerbach Foundation,
Beatrice Fox
Avon Products, Inc.
Baehr Foundation, Louis W.
and Dolpha
Baker Foundation, Dexter F.
and Dorothy H.
Baker Trust, George F.
Baldwin Foundation, David
M. and Barbara
Ball Brothers Foundation
Ball Foundation, George and
Frances
Banc One Wisconsin Corp.
Bank of Boston Corp.

Banta Corp.
Battelle Memorial Institute
Baughman Foundation
Beatty Trust, Cordelia
Lunceford
Beazley Foundation/Frederick
Foundation
Bechtel, Jr. Foundation, S. D.
Beloit Foundation
Bemis Company, Inc.
Benenson Foundation, Frances
and Benjamin
Benwood Foundation
Bethlehem Steel Corp.
Betts Industries
Bingham Foundation, William
Bingham Second Betterment
Fund, William
Binswanger Cos.
Bird Corp.
Bishop Foundation, E. K. and
Lillian F.
Block, H&R
Blount, Inc.
Blue Bell, Inc.
Blue Cross & Blue Shield
United of Wisconsin
Blum Foundation, Harry and
Maribel G.
Blum-Kovler Foundation
Boatmen's Bancshares, Inc.
Bobst Foundation, Elmer and
Mamdouha
Bodman Foundation
Boettcher Foundation
Boise Cascade Corporation
Booth Ferris Foundation
Borden, Inc.
Borman's Inc.
Boston Edison Co.
Boswell Foundation, James G.
Bothin Foundation
Boutell Memorial Fund
Bowen Foundation, Ethel N.
Bowne Foundation, Robert
Brady Foundation
Bremer Foundation, Otto
Bridgestone/Firestone, Inc.
Bridwell Foundation, J. S.
Brillion Iron Works
Brown Foundation, M. K.
Brunswick Corp.
Bryant Foundation
Bryn Mawr Trust Co.
Bucyrus-Erie Company
Buhl Foundation
Bunbury Company
Burlington Industries, Inc.
Burnett-Tandy Foundation
Cabell Foundation, Robert G.
Cabell III and Maude
Morgan
Cabot Corp.
Cafritz Foundation, Morris and
Gwendolyn
Cain Foundation, Effie and
Wofford
Cain Foundation, Gordon and
Mary
Calder Foundation, Louis
Callaway Foundation
Campbell Foundation, Ruth
and Henry
Cape Branch Foundation
Carolyn Foundation
Carpenter Foundation
Carter Foundation, Amon G.
Carvel Foundation, Thomas
and Agnes
Carver Charitable Trust, Roy J.
Caspersen Foundation for Aid
to Health and Education, O.
W.
Catlin Charitable Trust,
Kathleen K.
Cayuga Foundation
Central Maine Power Co.
Central National Bank
Century Companies of America
Champlin Foundations
Chartwell Foundation
Chase Manhattan Bank, N.A.
Chazen Foundation
CHC Foundation
Cheatham Foundation, Owen

Cheney Foundation, Ben B.
Chesebrough-Pond's USA Co.
Chicago Sun-Times, Inc.
Christensen Charitable and
Religious Foundation, L. C.
Chrysler Corp.
CINergy
CLARCOR Inc.
Clark Foundation
Clorox Co.
Close Foundation
Clowes Fund
Coen Family Foundation,
Charles S. and Mary
Cole Foundation, Olive B.
Cole Trust, Quincy
Collins Foundation, George
and Jennie
Collins, Jr. Foundation,
George Fulton
Colonial Life & Accident
Insurance Co.
Comer Foundation
Commerce Clearing House,
Incorporated
Connelly Foundation
Consolidated Natural Gas Co.
Consolidated Papers, Inc.
Continental Corp.
Cooke Foundation
Cooper Industries, Inc.
Coors Foundation, Adolph
Copley Press, Inc.
Cord Foundation, E. L.
Corning Incorporated
Crabtree & Evelyn
Crawford Estate, E. R.
Crestlea Foundation
Crystal Trust
CS First Boston Corporation
Culver Foundation, Constans
Cummings Foundation, James
H.
Cuneo Foundation
Curtice-Burns Foods, Inc.
Dalton Foundation, Harry L.
Daniel Foundation of Alabama
Dater Foundation, Charles H.
Daugherty Foundation
Davenport-Hatch Foundation
Davidson Family Charitable
Foundation
Davis Foundation, Edwin W.
and Catherine M.
Davis Foundation, Irene E. and
George A.
Day Foundation, Nancy Sayles
Daywood Foundation
Dekko Foundation
Dell Foundation, Hazel
Demoulas Supermarkets Inc.
Dentsply International Inc.
DeRoy Testamentary
Foundation
Detroit Edison Co.
Deuble Foundation, George H.
Dewing Foundation, Frances R.
Dillon Dunwalke Trust,
Clarence and Anne
Dillon Foundation
Dodge Foundation, Cleveland
H.
Doss Foundation, M. S.
Douglas & Lomason Company
Dow Foundation, Herbert H.
and Grace A.
Dreyfus Foundation, Max and
Victoria
du Pont de Nemours & Co., E.
I.
Duchossois Industries Inc.
Duke Power Co.
Dun & Bradstreet Corp.
Duncan Foundation, Lillian H.
and C. W.
Eaton Corporation
Eccles Foundation, Ralph M.
and Ella M.
Eddy Family Memorial Fund,
C. K.
El Pomar Foundation
Emerson Foundation, Inc.,
Fred L.
English Memorial Fund,
Florence C. and H. L.

Ensign-Bickford Industries
Essick Foundation
Ettinger Foundation
Evans Foundation, Thomas J.
Everett Charitable Trust
Fair Oaks Foundation, Inc.
Fair Play Foundation
Fairchild Foundation, Sherman
Farish Fund, William Stamps
Favrot Fund
Federal-Mogul Corporation
Federated Mutual Insurance
Co.
Fenton Foundation
Fieldcrest Cannon Inc.
Fife Foundation, Elias and
Bertha
Finch Foundation, Doak
Firestone, Jr. Foundation,
Harvey
First Fidelity Bank
First Financial Bank FSB
First Hawaiian, Inc.
First Source Corp.
Firstar Bank Milwaukee, N.A.
Flowers Charitable Trust,
Albert W. and Edith V.
Fohs Foundation
Folger Fund
Forbes Inc.
Ford Fund, William and Martha
Ford II Fund, Henry
Ford Motor Co.
Forest Foundation
Fort Wayne National Bank
Frear Eleemosynary Trust,
Mary D. and Walter F.
Freedom Forge Corp.
Freeport Brick Co.
Freeport-McMoRan Inc.
French Foundation, D.E.
French Oil Mill Machinery Co.
Frese Foundation, Arnold D.
Fribourg Foundation
Frost National Bank
Frueauff Foundation, Charles
A.
Fruehauf Foundation
Gallagher Family Foundation,
Lewis P.
Gamble Foundation
GAR Foundation
Gates Foundation
Gellert Foundation, Carl
Gellert Foundation, Celia Berta
General American Life
Insurance Co.
General Mills, Inc.
Geneseo Foundation
Georgia-Pacific Corporation
Georgia Power Co.
Gershman Foundation, Joel
Giant Eagle, Inc.
Giant Food Inc.
Gifford Charitable
Corporation, Rosamond
Gillette Co.
Glanville Family Foundation
Glaser Foundation
Glick Foundation, Eugene and
Marilyn
Globe Newspaper Co.
Goldsmith Foundation, Horace
W.
Good Samaritan
Goodrich Co., The B.F.
Gordon/Rousmaniere/Roberts
Fund
Graham Fund, Philip L.
Grand Rapids Label Co.
Green Foundation, Allen P.
and Josephine B.
Gregg-Graniteville Foundation
Griffith Foundation, W. C.
Grundy Foundation
GSM Industrial
Gulf Power Co.
Guttman Foundation, Stella
and Charles
Hachar Charitable Trust, D. D.
Hafif Family Foundation
Hagedorn Fund
Hallberg Foundation, E. L. and
R. F.
Hallett Charitable Trust, E. W.

Wahlstrom Foundation
Wal-Mart Stores, Inc.
Walsh Foundation
Warren and Beatrice W.
Blanding Foundation, Riley
J. and Lillian N.
Washington Forrest Foundation
Wean Foundation, Raymond
John
Webber Oil Co.
Weber Charities Corp.,
Frederick E.
Weezie Foundation
Weingart Foundation
Weinstein Foundation, J.
Welch Testamentary Trust,
George T.
Westvaco Corporation
Whirlpool Corporation
Whitney Fund, David M.
Wickes Foundation, Harvey
Randall
Wickson-Link Memorial
Foundation
WICOR, Inc.
Widgeon Foundation
Williams Companies, The
Wilmington Trust Co.
Windham Foundation
Winnebago Industries, Inc.
Winston Foundation, Norman
and Rosita
Wiremold Co.
Witco Corp.
Woodward Fund
Wyman Youth Trust
Yeager Charitable Trust,
Lester E.
Young Foundation, Robert R.
Zenkel Foundation

Refugee Assistance

American President
Companies, Ltd.
Andersen Corp.
Andersons, The
AON Corporation
Barker Foundation, J.M.R.
Benetton Services Corp.
Block, H&R
Blum-Kovler Foundation
Bremer Foundation, Otto
Bush Foundation
Cafritz Foundation, Morris and
Gwendolyn
Chevron Corporation
Colonial Life & Accident
Insurance Co.
Columbia Foundation
Cowles Media Co.
CPC International Inc.
Crown Memorial, Arie and Ida
Davis Foundation, Edwin W.
and Catherine M.
Dewing Foundation, Frances R.
Fohs Foundation
Ford Foundation
Fry Foundation, Lloyd A.
General Mills, Inc.
Haas, Jr. Fund, Evelyn and
Walter
Hasbro Inc.
Hauser Foundation
Hazen Foundation, Edward W.
Higginson Trust, Corina
Houston Industries
Incorporated
Icahn Foundation, Carl C.
International Foundation
Kansas City Southern
Industries
Mardag Foundation
McFawn Trust No. 2, Lois
Sisler
Meadows Foundation
Meyer Memorial Trust
Mobil Oil Corp.
Mott Fund, Ruth
National Westminster Bank
New Jersey
Nesholm Family Foundation
The New Yorker Magazine, Inc.

Northern States Power Co.
(Minnesota)
Parsons Foundation, Ralph M.
Pew Charitable Trusts
Playboy Enterprises, Inc.
Public Welfare Foundation
Royal Group, Inc.
Sara Lee Corp.
Sara Lee Hosiery, Inc.
Schiff Foundation, Dorothy
Shawmut National Corp.
Starr Foundation
Textron, Inc.
Trull Foundation
U.S. Bank of Washington
Unitrode Corp.
Wege Foundation

Scouts

Achelis Foundation
Acushnet Co.
Aetna Life & Casualty Co.
Air Products and Chemicals,
Inc.
Alabama Gas Corp.
Allianz Life Insurance Co. of
North America
Allyn Foundation
AMCORE Bank, N.A.
Rockford
American General Finance
Corp.
Andersen Foundation
Annenberg Foundation
Ansin Private Foundation,
Ronald M.
Ansley Foundation, Dantzler
Bond
Argyros Foundation
Arkell Hall Foundation
Arnold Fund
Audubon State Bank
Auerbach Foundation,
Beatrice Fox
Ayres Foundation, Inc.
Baehr Foundation, Louis W.
and Dolpha
Baker Foundation, Dexter F.
and Dorothy H.
Baldwin Memorial
Foundation, Fred
Ball Foundation, George and
Frances
Barry Corp., R. G.
Baughman Foundation
BE&K Inc.
Beatty Trust, Cordelia
Lunceford
Beck Foundation, Elsie E. and
Joseph W.
Bedsole Foundation, J. L.
Beech Aircraft Corp.
Bell Foundation, James F.
Blount Educational and
Charitable Foundation,
Mildred Weedon
Bodman Foundation
Boettcher Foundation
Borden, Inc.
Boswell Foundation, James G.
Bowen Foundation, Ethel N.
Brady Foundation
Bridwell Foundation, J. S.
Bright Family Foundation
Brillion Iron Works
Brown Foundation, M. K.
Brunswick Corp.
Buhl Foundation
Burnett-Tandy Foundation
Cain Foundation, Effie and
Wofford
Castle Foundation, Harold K.
L.
Cayuga Foundation
Central National Bank
Centralia Foundation
Champlin Foundations
Charina Foundation
CHC Foundation
Chesebrough-Pond's USA Co.
Christy-Houston Foundation
CINergy
CLARCOR Inc.

Clarke Trust, John
Clements Foundation
Clorox Co.
Clowes Fund
Cole Foundation, Olive B.
Comer Foundation
Continental Corp.
Cooke Foundation
Coors Foundation, Adolph
Cord Foundation, E. L.
Corning Incorporated
Cremer Foundation
Cullen Foundation
Curtice-Burns Foods, Inc.
Davenport-Hatch Foundation
Davidson Family Charitable
Foundation
Davis Foundation, James A.
and Juliet L.
Daywood Foundation
DeRoy Foundation, Helen L.
Dishman Charitable
Foundation Trust, H. E. and
Kate
Dr. Seuss Foundation
Dow Corning Corp.
Dreyfus Foundation, Jean and
Louis
Dunagan Foundation
Eberly Foundation
Eden Hall Foundation
English Memorial Fund,
Florence C. and H. L.
Essick Foundation
Everett Charitable Trust
Exchange National Bank
Exxon Corporation
Fair Oaks Foundation, Inc.
Farish Fund, William Stamps
Feil Foundation, Louis and
Gertrude
Fenton Foundation
Fife Foundation, Elias and
Bertha
Flowers Charitable Trust,
Albert W. and Edith V.
Folger Fund
Fondren Foundation
Freedom Forge Corp.
French Foundation, D.E.
Frueauff Foundation, Charles
A.
Fuller Foundation
Gamble Foundation
Gannett Publishing Co., Guy
Gazette Co.
Geneseo Foundation
Gheens Foundation
Giant Eagle, Inc.
Gilmore Foundation, William
G.
Glick Foundation, Eugene and
Marilyn
Glosser Foundation, David A.
Goddard Foundation, Charles
B.
Graham Fund, Philip L.
Grundy Foundation
GSM Industrial
Gulf Power Co.
Habig Foundation, Arnold F.
Hachar Charitable Trust, D. D.
Haley Foundation, W. B.
Hallett Charitable Trust, E. W.
Hallett Charitable Trust, Jessie
F.
Halsell Foundation, Ewing
Hammer Foundation, Armand
Harland Charitable
Foundation, John and
Wilhelmina D.
Hartz Foundation
Heckscher Foundation for
Children
Heinz Trust, Drue
Herzstein Charitable
Foundation, Albert and Ethel
Hickory Tech Corp.
Hill Foundation, Sandy
Hillman Foundation
Hobby Foundation
Hook Drugs
Hoover Fund-Trust, W. Henry
Houston Endowment

Hoyt Foundation, Stewart W.
and Willma C.
Hulme Charitable Foundation,
Milton G.
Hunt Charitable Trust, C. Giles
Hunt Foundation, Samuel P.
Hygeia Dairy Co.
Imperial Bancorp
Jackson Foundation
Janirve Foundation
Jaydor Corp.
JFM Foundation
JM Foundation
Johnson & Son, S.C.
Jones Foundation, Fletcher
Jones Foundation, Helen
Jordan Charitable Foundation,
Mary Ranken Jordan and
Ettie A.
Joslin-Needham Family
Foundation
Jostens, Inc.
Julia R. and Estelle L.
Foundation
Kantzler Foundation
Kardon Foundation, Samuel
and Rebecca
Kayser Foundation
Kelly Tractor Co.
Kemper Foundation, William T.
Kempner Fund, Harris and
Eliza
Kingsbury Corp.
Kinney-Lindstrom Foundation
Kitzmiller/Bales Trust
Klipstein Foundation, Ernest
Christian
Klock and Lucia Klock
Kingston Foundation, Jay E.
Kohn-Joseloff Foundation
Komes Foundation
Kresge Foundation
Kuehn Foundation
Lederer Foundation, Francis L.
Lee Endowment Foundation
Lee Enterprises
Leuthold Foundation
Levy Foundation, June
Rockwell
Long Foundation, J.M.
Madison Gas & Electric Co.
Mahadh Foundation
Marmot Foundation
Marpat Foundation
Marshall Foundation, Mattie H.
Marshall Trust in Memory of
Sanders McDaniel, Harriet
McDaniel
Mascoma Savings Bank
Mautz Paint Co.
Maytag Family Foundation,
Fred
McCasland Foundation
McFeely-Rogers Foundation
McInerny Foundation
Mellon Foundation, Richard
King
Memton Fund
Mengle Foundation, Glenn and
Ruth
Meyer Family Foundation,
Paul J.
Meyerhoff Fund, Joseph
Mid-Iowa Health Foundation
Millbrook Tribute Garden
Monell Foundation, Ambrose
Monfort Family Foundation
Morgan Stanley & Co., Inc.
Morris Foundation, Margaret T.
Mosbacher, Jr. Foundation,
Emil
Mosinee Paper Corp.
Muchnic Foundation
Murphy Foundation
Musson Charitable
Foundation, R. C. and
Katharine M.
New Jersey Natural Gas Co.
Norgren Foundation, Carl A.
Norman Foundation, Summers
A.
Norton Co.
Offield Family Foundation
Old National Bank in
Evansville

Palisades Educational
Foundation
Palmer Fund, Frank Loomis
Parker Hannifin Corp.
Parsons Foundation, Ralph M.
Peppers Foundation, Ann
Peterson Foundation, Hal and
Charlie
Phillips Charitable Trust, Dr.
and Mrs. Arthur William
Phipps Foundation, Howard
Pick, Jr. Fund, Albert
Pioneer Trust Bank, NA
Prairie Foundation
Proctor Trust, Mortimer R.
Putnam Foundation
Quivey-Bay State Foundation
Rand McNally & Co.
Regenstein Foundation
Richardson Benevolent
Foundation, C. E.
Richardson Charitable Trust,
Anne S.
Ritter Charitable Trust, George
W. and Mary F.
Robinson-Broadhurst
Foundation
Rockwell Fund
Roseburg Forest Products Co.
Russell Trust, Josephine G.
Sargent Foundation, Newell B.
Sarkeys Foundation
Sawyer Charitable Foundation
Schuller International
Scott Foundation, William E.
Seneca Foods Corp.
Sentry Insurance A Mutual
Company
Sequoia Foundation
Seton Leather Co.
Share Trust, Charles Morton
Skillman Foundation
Slemp Foundation
Smeal Foundation, Mary Jean
and Frank P.
Snayberger Memorial
Foundation, Harry E. and
Florence W.
Solow Foundation
Sonat Inc.
Springs Foundation
Stackpole-Hall Foundation
Stauffer Charitable Trust, John
Stauffer Foundation, John and
Beverly
Stevens Foundation, John T.
Stokely, Jr. Foundation,
William B.
Swift Co. Inc., John S.
Tait Foundation, Frank M.
Taube Family Foundation
Taubman Foundation, A. Alfred
Thomas Industries
Thompson Co., J. Walter
Times Mirror Company, The
Todd Co., A.M.
Towsley Foundation, Harry A.
and Margaret D.
Travelers Inc.
Treakle Foundation, J. Edwin
Trexler Trust, Harry C.
Truland Foundation
Tucker Charitable Trust, Rose
E.
Turrell Fund
Union Electric Co.
Union Pacific Corp.
Unocal Corp.
USL Capital Corporation
Utica National Insurance
Group
Van Houten Memorial Fund
Vollbrecht Foundation,
Frederick A.
Walsh Foundation
Washington Forrest Foundation
Washington Mutual Savings
Bank
Wean Foundation, Raymond
John
Weaver Foundation, Gil and
Dody
Weckbaugh Foundation,
Eleanore Mullen
Weingart Foundation

Wells Foundation, Franklin H. and Ruth L.
Wheeler Foundation
Whitecap Foundation
Whiting Foundation
Whitney Fund, David M.
Whittenberger Foundation, Claude R. and Ethel B.
Widgeon Foundation
Wiggins Memorial Trust, J. J.
Wilson Fund, Matilda R.
Winnebago Industries, Inc.
Wood Foundation of Chambersburg, PA
Wright Foundation, Lola
Wyomissing Foundation
Young Foundation, Hugo H. and Mabel B.
Young Foundation, Robert R.
Zollner Foundation

Senior Services

Abell-Hanger Foundation
Achelis Foundation
Ahmanson Foundation
Air Products and Chemicals, Inc.
AKC Fund
Alabama Gas Corp.
Alabama Power Co.
Albertson's Inc.
Alexander Foundation, Joseph
Allegheny Foundation
Allegheny Ludlum Corp.
AlliedSignal Inc.
Altman Foundation
Altschul Foundation
Alumax Inc.
Aluminum Co. of America
Amado Foundation, Maurice
Amcast Industrial Corp.
AMCORE Bank, N.A. Rockford
American General Finance Corp.
American United Life Insurance Co.
Ameritas Life Insurance Corp.
Ames Charitable Trust, Harriett
AMETEK, Inc.
Amfac/JMB Hawaii Inc.
Andersen Foundation
Anderson Foundation
Anderson Foundation, M. D.
Andersons, The
Andreas Foundation
AON Corporation
Appleton Papers Inc.
Arcadia Foundation
Archer-Daniels-Midland Co.
Arkansas Power & Light Co.
Arkell Hall Foundation
Armco Inc.
Atherton Family Foundation
Atran Foundation
Audubon State Bank
Auerbach Foundation, Beatrice Fox
Avon Products, Inc.
Ayres Foundation, Inc.
Badgeley Residuary Charitable Trust, Rose M.
Bank One, Youngstown, NA
Barra Foundation
Barry Corp., R. G.
Battelle Memorial Institute
Baughman Foundation
Beech Aircraft Corp.
Bemis Company, Inc.
Benedum Foundation, Claude Worthington
Benwood Foundation
Berwind Foundation
Bethlehem Steel Corp.
Betts Industries
Beveridge Foundation, Frank Stanley
Bigelow Foundation, F. R.
Bird Corp.
Birnschein Foundation, Alvin and Marion
Bissell Foundation, J. Walton
Blair and Co., William

Block, H&R
Bloedorn Foundation, Walter A.
Blount, Inc.
Blowitz-Ridgeway Foundation
Bodman Foundation
Boeing Co., The
Boettcher Foundation
Boise Cascade Corporation
Boothroyd Foundation, Charles H. and Bertha L.
Borman's Inc.
Boston Edison Co.
Bothin Foundation
Brach Foundation, Helen
Bremer Foundation, Otto
Bridwell Foundation, J. S.
Brown Foundation, M. K.
Brown & Williamson Tobacco Corp.
Brunswick Corp.
Bryn Mawr Trust Co.
Bucyrus-Erie Company
Bunbury Company
Burden Foundation, Florence V.
Bush Foundation
Cabell Foundation, Robert G. Cabell III and Maude Morgan
Cabot Corp.
Cafritz Foundation, Morris and Gwendolyn
Calhoun Charitable Trust, Kenneth
Carolyn Foundation
Carpenter Foundation
Carter Foundation, Amon G.
Cassett Foundation, Louis N.
Catlin Charitable Trust, Kathleen K.
Centerior Energy Corp.
Central Fidelity Banks, Inc.
Central Hudson Gas & Electric Corp.
Central Maine Power Co.
Chadwick Fund, Dorothy Jordan
Champlin Foundations
Chapman Charitable Corporation, Howard and Bess
Charina Foundation
Chartwell Foundation
Chase Manhattan Bank, N.A.
CHC Foundation
Cheney Foundation, Ben B.
Chesebrough-Pond's USA Co.
Chevron Corporation
Chicago Sun-Times, Inc.
Childs Charitable Foundation, Roberta M.
Christensen Charitable and Religious Foundation, L. C.
Chrysler Corp.
Citizens Bank of Rhode Island
Clark Foundation
Clorox Co.
Coen Family Foundation, Charles S. and Mary
Cole Foundation, Olive B.
Colonial Life & Accident Insurance Co.
Columbus Dispatch Printing Co.
Comprecare Foundation
Connecticut Mutual Life Insurance Company
Consolidated Natural Gas Co.
Cooke Foundation
Cooper Industries, Inc.
Coors Foundation, Adolph
Copley Press, Inc.
Cornell Trust, Peter C.
Cosmair, Inc.
Covington and Burling
Cowles Charitable Trust
Cowles Foundation, Gardner and Florence Call
CPC International Inc.
Crandall Memorial Foundation, J. Ford
Cremer Foundation
Crestlea Foundation
Crown Memorial, Arie and Ida

Crystal Trust
Culpeper Memorial Foundation, Daphne Seybolt
Cummins Engine Co.
Curtice-Burns Foods, Inc.
Darby Foundation
Davidson Family Charitable Foundation
Daywood Foundation
DEC International, Inc.
Deere & Co.
Dekko Foundation
Delavan Foundation, Nelson B.
Demoulas Supermarkets Inc.
Dentsply International Inc.
DeRoy Testamentary Foundation
Dexter Charitable Fund, Eugene A.
Digital Equipment Corp.
Dillon Foundation
Dimeo Construction Co.
Dr. Seuss Foundation
Dodge Foundation, Cleveland H.
Donnelley Foundation, Gaylord and Dorothy
Douty Foundation
Dover Foundation
Dow Foundation, Herbert H. and Grace A.
Dresser Industries, Inc.
Dreyfus Foundation, Jean and Louis
Dreyfus Foundation, Max and Victoria
du Pont de Nemours & Co., E. I.
Duke Power Co.
Dula Educational and Charitable Foundation, Caleb C. and Julia W.
Duncan Trust, John G.
duPont Foundation, Alfred I.
Dynamet, Inc.
Eaton Corporation
Eden Hall Foundation
Einstein Fund, Albert E. and Birdie W.
El Pomar Foundation
Emerson Foundation, Inc., Fred L.
Enron Corp.
Ensign-Bickford Industries
Fabri-Kal Corp.
Federated Mutual Insurance Co.
Fikes Foundation, Leland
Finch Foundation, Thomas Austin
Fink Foundation
Fireman's Fund Insurance Co.
First Fidelity Bank
First Hawaiian, Inc.
First Interstate Bank of Oregon
First Union Corp.
Firstar Bank Milwaukee, N.A.
Fish Foundation, Ray C.
Fishback Foundation Trust, Harmes C.
Fleming Cos. Food Distribution Center
Fohs Foundation
Forbes Inc.
Foster Foundation
Freeport Brick Co.
Freeport-McMoRan Inc.
French Foundation, D.E.
French Oil Mill Machinery Co.
Friedman Family Foundation
Frohring Foundation, Paul and Maxine
Frohring Foundation, William O. and Gertrude Lewis
Frost National Bank
Frueauff Foundation, Charles A.
Fry Foundation, Lloyd A.
Fuller Foundation, C. G.
Gannett Publishing Co., Guy
GAR Foundation
Gates Foundation
GATX Corp.
Gellert Foundation, Carl
Gellert Foundation, Celia Berta

General American Life Insurance Co.
General Mills, Inc.
General Motors Corp.
Geneseo Foundation
GenRad
Georgia Power Co.
Gershman Foundation, Joel
Gheens Foundation
Giant Eagle, Inc.
Giant Food Inc.
Giant Food Stores
Gifford Charitable Corporation, Rosamond
Glaser Foundation
Gleason Foundation
Glick Foundation, Eugene and Marilyn
Glosser Foundation, David A.
Goldsmith Foundation, Horace W.
Goldwyn Foundation, Samuel
Goodman & Co.
Goodrich Co., The B.F.
Graham Fund, Philip L.
Grand Rapids Label Co.
Green Foundation, Allen P. and Josephine B.
Gregg-Graniteville Foundation
Groome Beatty Trust, Helen D.
Guaranty Bank & Trust Co.
Gulf Power Co.
Guttman Foundation, Stella and Charles
Haas, Jr. Fund, Evelyn and Walter
Habig Foundation, Arnold F.
Hafif Family Foundation
Hancock Foundation, Luke B.
Hartmarx Corporation
Hartz Foundation
Hastings Charitable Foundation, Oris B.
Hatch Charitable Trust, Margaret Milliken
Haynes Foundation, John Randolph and Dora
HCA Foundation
Hearst Foundation, William Randolph
Hechinger Co.
Hedco Foundation
Heinz Company, H. J.
Heinz Endowment, Howard
Heinz Endowment, Vira I.
Hermann Foundation, Grover
Herrick Foundation
Hickory Tech Corp.
Higginson Trust, Corina
Hillcrest Foundation
Hillman Foundation
Hillsdale Fund
Hoag Family Foundation, George
Hook Drugs
Hoover Foundation
Hopedale Foundation
Hopwood Charitable Trust, John M.
Houston Industries Incorporated
Howard and Bush Foundation
Howell Foundation of Florida
Hoyt Foundation, Stewart W. and Willma C.
Hugoton Foundation
Hulme Charitable Foundation, Milton G.
Humana, Inc.
Humphrey Fund, George M. and Pamela S.
Hunt Charitable Trust, C. Giles
Hunt Foundation, Samuel P.
Huston Charitable Trust, Stewart
ICI Americas Inc.
IES Industries, Inc.
Illinois Tool Works, Inc.
Inland Container Corp.
International Business Machines Corp.
International Paper Co.
ITT Hartford Insurance Group, Inc.
Ittleson Foundation

Jackson Foundation
Jameson Foundation, J. W. and Ida M.
Janirve Foundation
Jewett Foundation, George Frederick
Jewish Healthcare Foundation of Pittsburgh
John Hancock Mutual Life Insurance Co.
Johnson Controls Inc.
Johnson Foundation, Burdine
Johnson Foundation, Helen K. and Arthur E.
Johnson Foundation, M. G. and Lillie A.
Johnson Foundation, Willard T. C.
Johnson & Higgins
Jones Foundation, Daisy Marquis
Journal-Gazette Co.
Julia R. and Estelle L. Foundation
Justus Trust, Edith C.
Kansas City Southern Industries
Kantzler Foundation
Kaplan Fund, J. M.
Kaplun Foundation, Morris J. and Betty
Kaufmann Foundation, Henry
Kelley and Elza Kelley Foundation, Edward Bangs
Kennecott Corporation
Kennedy Foundation, Ethel
Kettering Fund
Kiewit Foundation, Peter
Kilcawley Fund, William H.
Kimberly-Clark Corp.
Kingsbury Corp.
Kiplinger Foundation
Kirkpatrick Foundation
Klosk Fund, Louis and Rose
KN Energy, Inc.
Koehler Foundation, Marcia and Otto
Kohn-Joseloff Foundation
Komes Foundation
Kreitler Foundation
Kresge Foundation
La-Z-Boy Chair Co.
Laffey-McHugh Foundation
Lasdon Foundation
Lauder Foundation
Laurel Foundation
Leavey Foundation, Thomas and Dorothy
Lee Endowment Foundation
Lee Enterprises
Life Insurance Co. of Georgia
Link, Jr. Foundation, George
Littauer Foundation, Lucius N.
Liz Claiborne, Inc.
Long Foundation, J.M.
Long Island Lighting Co.
Longwood Foundation
Lurie Foundation, Louis R.
MacArthur Foundation, John D. and Catherine T.
Macy & Co., Inc., R.H.
Madison Gas & Electric Co.
Mardag Foundation
Markle Foundation, John and Mary R.
Marmot Foundation
Marpat Foundation
Marriott Foundation, J. Willard
Mars Foundation
Marshall Trust in Memory of Sanders McDaniel, Harriet McDaniel
Martini Foundation, Nicholas
Mascoma Savings Bank
Mather and William Gwinn Mather Fund, Elizabeth Ring
Mayor Foundation, Oliver Dewey
Maytag Family Foundation, Fred
MBIA Inc.
MCA Inc.
McCann Foundation
McCasland Foundation
McConnell Foundation

Sexual Abuse

Shelters/Homelessness

Ross Laboratories
Ross Memorial Foundation, Will
Rouse Co.
Royal Group, Inc.
Rubin Family Fund, Cele H. and William B.
Rubin Foundation, Samuel
Rubinstein Foundation, Helena
Russell Charitable Foundation, Tom
SAFECO Corp.
Salomon Foundation, Richard and Edna
San Diego Gas & Electric
Sandy Hill Foundation
Santa Fe Pacific Corporation
Sara Lee Corp.
Sara Lee Hosiery, Inc.
Sarkeys Foundation
Sawyer Charitable Foundation
SBC Communications Inc.
Scaife Family Foundation
Scherman Foundation
Schiff Foundation, Dorothy
Schlink Foundation, Albert G. and Olive H.
Schlumberger Ltd.
Scholl Foundation, Dr.
Schuller International
Schumann Fund for New Jersey
Schwab & Co., Inc., Charles
Schwartz Foundation, Arnold A.
Seaway Food Town, Inc.
Security Life of Denver Insurance Co.
Shawmut National Corp.
Shell Oil Company
Shenandoah Life Insurance Co.
Sheppard Foundation, Lawrence B.
Sierra Pacific Industries
Siltec Corp.
Simon Foundation, William E. and Carol G.
Skillman Foundation
Smeal Foundation, Mary Jean and Frank P.
Smith Charitable Foundation, Lou and Lutza
Smith Corp., A.O.
Smith Foundation, Ralph L.
Snyder Foundation, Harold B. and Dorothy A.
Sonat Inc.
Sprague Educational and Charitable Foundation, Seth
Stanley Works
Starr Foundation
Stauffer Foundation, John and Beverly
Staunton Farm Foundation
Stearns Trust, Artemas W.
Steele-Reese Foundation
Stein Foundation, Jules and Doris
Steinhagen Benevolent Trust, B. A. and Elinor
Steinman Foundation, John Frederick
Stokely, Jr. Foundation, William B.
Strong Foundation, Hattie M.
Sulzberger Foundation
Sunnen Foundation
Swalm Foundation
Taconic Foundation
Taylor Foundation, Ruth and Vernon
Temple Foundation, T. L. L.
Tenneco Inc.
Texas Commerce Bank-Houston, N.A.
Textron, Inc.
Thermo Electron Corp.
Thomas Industries
Thompson Trust, Thomas
Thornton Foundation, Flora L.
Tiscornia Foundation
TransAmerica Corporation
Travelers Inc.
Trexler Trust, Harry C.
Truland Foundation

Trull Foundation
Trust Company Bank
Unger Foundation, Aber D.
Unilever United States, Inc.
Union Camp Corporation
Union Electric Co.
Union Pacific Corp.
U.S. Bank of Washington
Unitrode Corp.
Uris Brothers Foundation
USL Capital Corporation
Utica National Insurance Group
van Ameringen Foundation
Van Buren Foundation
Van Every Foundation, Philip L.
Vernon Fund, Miles Hodsdon
Virginia Power Co.
Vogler Foundation, Laura B.
Vulcan Materials Co.
Wahlstrom Foundation
Wal-Mart Stores, Inc.
Warwick Foundation
Washington Forrest Foundation
Waters Charitable Trust, Robert S.
Weaver Foundation, Gil and Dody
Weber Charities Corp., Frederick E.
Weil, Gotshal and Manges Foundation
Weingart Foundation
Welch Testamentary Trust, George T.
West One Bancorp
Weyerhaeuser Co.
Whirlpool Corporation
Whiting Foundation
Whitney Fund, David M.
Wickes Foundation, Harvey Randall
Wickson-Link Memorial Foundation
Wiley & Sons, Inc., John
Williams Companies, The
Wisconsin Power & Light Co.
Wood Foundation of Chambersburg, PA
Woodward Fund
Wright Foundation, Lola
Yeager Charitable Trust, Lester E.
Young Foundation, Irvin L.

Special Olympics

Aluminum Co. of America
Ansley Foundation, Dantzler Bond
Atran Foundation
Ball Brothers Foundation
Ball Foundation, George and Frances
Bauervic Foundation, Charles M.
Borkee Hagley Foundation
Boswell Foundation, James G.
Campbell Foundation
CINergy
Continental Corp.
Crane Co.
Crestlea Foundation
Crystal Trust
CS First Boston Corporation
Daugherty Foundation
DeVore Foundation
Dow Foundation, Herbert H. and Grace A.
English Memorial Fund, Florence C. and H. L.
Essick Foundation
Freedom Forge Corp.
Hanover Foundation
Jostens, Inc.
Kempner Fund, Harris and Eliza
Kingsbury Corp.
Kline Foundation, Josiah W. and Bessie H.
Laffey-McHugh Foundation
Leavey Foundation, Thomas and Dorothy

Marmot Foundation
McCormick Trust, Anne
Mid-Iowa Health Foundation
Moore & Sons, B.C.
Mosinee Paper Corp.
Murphey Foundation, Lluella Morey
Pioneer Trust Bank, NA
Reisman Charitable Trust, George C. and Evelyn R.
Richardson Benevolent Foundation, C. E.
Sarkeys Foundation
Seneca Foods Corp.
Sentry Insurance A Mutual Company
Seton Leather Co.
Sheppard Foundation, Lawrence B.
SPX Corp.
Temple Foundation, T. L. L.
Unocal Corp.
Utica National Insurance Group
Welfare Foundation
Westerman Foundation, Samuel L.
Wickson-Link Memorial Foundation
Wiegand Foundation, E. L.
Winnebago Industries, Inc.

Substance Abuse

Abbott Laboratories
Abell-Hanger Foundation
Achelis Foundation
Acushnet Co.
Ahmanson Foundation
Air Products and Chemicals, Inc.
Alabama Power Co.
Albertson's Inc.
Alexander Foundation, Joseph
AlliedSignal Inc.
Allyn Foundation
Alumax Inc.
Aluminum Co. of America
AMCORE Bank, N.A. Rockford
American Brands, Inc.
American General Finance Corp.
American United Life Insurance Co.
Amfac/JMB Hawaii Inc.
Andersen Corp.
Andersen Foundation
Anderson Foundation
Andrews Foundation
Anheuser-Busch Companies, Inc.
Annenberg Foundation
Ansley Foundation, Dantzler Bond
Appleton Papers Inc.
Archer-Daniels-Midland Co.
Argyros Foundation
Arkansas Power & Light Co.
Arkelian Foundation, Ben H. and Gladys
Astor Foundation, Vincent
AT&T Corp.
Atherton Family Foundation
Auerbach Foundation, Beatrice Fox
Avon Products, Inc.
Bacon Foundation, E. L. and Oma
Badgeley Residuary Charitable Trust, Rose M.
Baker Trust, George F.
Baldwin Foundation, David M. and Barbara
Ball Foundation, George and Frances
Bank of New York Company, Inc.
Bank One, Texas-Houston Office
BankAmerica Corp.
Baskin-Robbins USA Co.
Battelle Memorial Institute
Batts Foundation

Bay Area Foods
Bean Foundation, Norwin S. and Elizabeth N.
Beazley Foundation/Frederick Foundation
Beloit Foundation
Bemis Company, Inc.
Benenson Foundation, Frances and Benjamin
Benetton Services Corp.
Benwood Foundation
Berger Foundation, H. N. and Frances C.
Bertha Foundation
Bethlehem Steel Corp.
Bingham Foundation, William
Bingham Second Betterment Fund, William
Bird Corp.
Bishop Foundation, E. K. and Lillian F.
Blair and Co., William
Blandin Foundation
Block, H&R
Blount Educational and Charitable Foundation, Mildred Weedon
Blue Bell, Inc.
Blue Cross & Blue Shield United of Wisconsin
Blum-Kovler Foundation
Bodman Foundation
Boeing Co., The
Boise Cascade Corporation
Booth Ferris Foundation
Borman's Inc.
Bothin Foundation
Bremer Foundation, Otto
Breyer Foundation
Bridgestone/Firestone, Inc.
Bridwell Foundation, J. S.
Brillion Iron Works
Bristol-Myers Squibb Company
Brown Foundation, M. K.
Brown & Williamson Tobacco Corp.
Brunswick Corp.
Bunbury Company
Burden Foundation, Florence V.
Burlington Industries, Inc.
Burnett-Tandy Foundation
Bush Foundation
Cabot Corp.
Cafritz Foundation, Morris and Gwendolyn
Cain Foundation, Effie and Wofford
Cain Foundation, Gordon and Mary
Callaway Foundation
Carnegie Corporation of New York
Carolyn Foundation
Carpenter Foundation
Carpenter Technology Corp.
Carter Foundation, Amon G.
Castle Foundation, Harold K. L.
Catlin Charitable Trust, Kathleen K.
Central Maine Power Co.
Champion International Corporation
Chartwell Foundation
Chase Manhattan Bank, N.A.
CHC Foundation
Cheatham Foundation, Owen
Chesebrough-Pond's USA Co.
Chevron Corporation
Chicago Sun-Times, Inc.
Childs Charitable Foundation, Roberta M.
Chrysler Corp.
CINergy
Citizens Bank of Rhode Island
Clark Foundation
Clorox Co.
Close Foundation
Clowes Fund
Coen Family Foundation, Charles S. and Mary
Colonial Life & Accident Insurance Co.

Comer Foundation
Commerce Bancshares, Inc.
Commerce Clearing House, Incorporated
Commonwealth Edison Co.
Comprecare Foundation
Connecticut Mutual Life Insurance Company
Connelly Foundation
Consumers Power Co.
Continental Corp.
Contran Corporation
Cooke Foundation
Coors Foundation, Adolph
Copley Press, Inc.
Cord Foundation, E. L.
Cornell Trust, Peter C.
Cosmair, Inc.
Cowell Foundation, S. H.
Cowles Charitable Trust
Cowles Media Co.
CPC International Inc.
CR Industries
Crandall Memorial Foundation, J. Ford
Crane Co.
Cummins Engine Co.
Curtice-Burns Foods, Inc.
Dana Foundation, Charles A.
Daniel Foundation of Alabama
Dart Group Corp.
Davidson Family Charitable Foundation
Deere & Co.
Delano Foundation, Mignon Sherwood
Delaware North Co., Inc.
Demoulas Supermarkets Inc.
Detroit Edison Co.
Deuble Foundation, George H.
DeVore Foundation
Dexter Corporation
Diamond Foundation, Aaron
Digital Equipment Corp.
Dimeo Construction Co.
Dishman Charitable Foundation Trust, H. E. and Kate
Donaldson Company, Inc.
Dow Foundation, Herbert H. and Grace A.
Dresser Industries, Inc.
Dreyfus Foundation, Jean and Louis
Dreyfus Foundation, Max and Victoria
du Pont de Nemours & Co., E. I.
Duchossois Industries Inc.
Duke Power Co.
Duncan Trust, John G.
Dynamet, Inc.
Early Foundation
Eden Hall Foundation
El Pomar Foundation
Elkins, Jr. Foundation, Margaret and James A.
Exxon Corporation
Farish Fund, William Stamps
Federal-Mogul Corporation
Federated Mutual Insurance Co.
Feild Co-Operative Association
Fenton Foundation
Fikes Foundation, Leland
Finch Foundation, Doak
Fireman's Fund Insurance Co.
First Fidelity Bank
First Hawaiian, Inc.
First Interstate Bank of Oregon
First Union Corp.
Firstar Bank Milwaukee, N.A.
Fleet Financial Group, Inc.
Fletcher Foundation
Fondren Foundation
Forbes Inc.
Ford Foundation
Ford Fund, William and Martha
Ford Motor Co.
Forest Oil Corp.
Foster Charitable Trust
Freed Foundation
Freedom Forge Corp.
Freeport-McMoRan Inc.

Friendship Fund
Frohring Foundation, Paul and Maxine
Frost National Bank
Frueauff Foundation, Charles A.
Fruehauf Foundation
Fry Foundation, Lloyd A.
GAR Foundation
Gates Foundation
GATX Corp.
Gazette Co.
Gebbie Foundation
Geifman Family Foundation
Gellert Foundation, Carl
General American Life Insurance Co.
General Mills, Inc.
General Motors Corp.
GenRad
Georgia-Pacific Corporation
Georgia Power Co.
Gheens Foundation
Giant Food Stores
Gifford Charitable Corporation, Rosamond
Glanville Family Foundation
Glaser Foundation
Globe Newspaper Co.
Goddard Foundation, Charles B.
Goldsmith Foundation, Horace W.
Goodrich Co., The B.F.
Graham Fund, Philip L.
Great-West Life Assurance Co.
Griffith Foundation, W. C.
Grundy Foundation
Guaranty Bank & Trust Co.
Guardian Life Insurance Company of America
Gulf Power Co.
Hafif Family Foundation
Halff Foundation, G. A. C.
Halsell Foundation, Ewing
Handy and Harman Foundation
Hanson Industries North America
Harriman Foundation, Gladys and Roland
Harsco Corp.
Hauser Foundation
Hawn Foundation
Haynes Foundation, John Randolph and Dora
HCA Foundation
Hearst Foundation, William Randolph
Hechinger Co.
Heckscher Foundation for Children
Heinz Company, H. J.
Heinz Endowment, Howard
Heinz Endowment, Vira I.
Herrick Foundation
Hershey Foods Corp.
Herzstein Charitable Foundation, Albert and Ethel
Hillcrest Foundation
Hillman Foundation
Hillsdale Fund
Hino Diesel Trucks (U.S.A.)
Hoag Family Foundation, George
Hoffmann-La Roche Inc.
Hook Drugs
Hoover Foundation
Houston Endowment
Houston Industries Incorporated
Hoyt Foundation, Stewart W. and Willma C.
Hudson-Webber Foundation
Humphrey Fund, George M. and Pamela S.
Hunt Charitable Trust, C. Giles
Hunt Foundation
Huston Charitable Trust, Stewart
Hyde and Watson Foundation
Hygeia Dairy Co.
Icahn Foundation, Carl C.
ICI Americas Inc.
Illinois Tool Works, Inc.
Inland Container Corp.

International Business Machines Corp.
International Paper Co.
ITT Hartford Insurance Group, Inc.
Jackson Foundation
Jacobs Family Foundation
James River Corp. of Virginia
Jewett Foundation, George Frederick
Jewish Healthcare Foundation of Pittsburgh
JM Foundation
John Hancock Mutual Life Insurance Co.
Johnson Charitable Educational Trust, James Hervey
Johnson Controls Inc.
Johnson Foundation, Helen K. and Arthur E.
Johnson Foundation, M. G. and Lillie A.
Johnson & Higgins
Jostens, Inc.
Journal-Gazette Co.
Joy Family Foundation
Kansas City Southern Industries
Kayser Foundation
Kelley and Elza Kelley Foundation, Edward Bangs
Kemper National Insurance Cos.
Kempner Fund, Harris and Eliza
Kennecott Corporation
Kimberly-Clark Corp.
Kingsbury Corp.
Kirby Foundation, F. M.
Kline Foundation, Josiah W. and Bessie H.
Klock and Lucia Klock Kingston Foundation, Jay E.
Knox, Sr., and Pearl Wallis Knox Charitable Foundation, Robert W.
Koehler Foundation, Marcia and Otto
Komes Foundation
Kresge Foundation
Kunkel Foundation, John Crain
Laffey-McHugh Foundation
Leavey Foundation, Thomas and Dorothy
Lehigh Portland Cement Co.
Lennon Foundation, Fred A.
Levy Foundation, June Rockwell
Life Insurance Co. of Georgia
Linnell Foundation
Lipton, Thomas J.
Lockhart Vaughan Foundation
Longwood Foundation
Louisiana-Pacific Corp.
Lowenstein Foundation, Leon
Lurie Foundation, Louis R.
Lydall, Inc.
Macy & Co., Inc., R.H.
Maddox Foundation, J. F.
Mahadh Foundation
Mardag Foundation
Maritz Inc.
Mars Foundation
Marsh & McLennan Companies, Inc.
Mather Charitable Trust, S. Livingston
Mattel, Inc.
Matthies Foundation, Katharine
May Department Stores Company, The
Maytag Family Foundation, Fred
MBIA Inc.
McCasland Foundation
McConnell Foundation
McCune Charitable Trust, John R.
McDermott Foundation, Eugene
McDonald & Company Securities, Inc.
McDonnell Douglas Corp.-West

McElroy Trust, R. J.
McEvoy Foundation, Mildred H.
McGraw-Hill, Inc.
M.E. Foundation
Meadows Foundation
Mellon Foundation, Richard King
Merck & Co.
Merrick Foundation
Merrill Lynch & Co., Inc.
Messing Family Charitable Foundation
Metropolitan Life Insurance Co.
Meyer Memorial Trust
Mid-Iowa Health Foundation
Miller Brewing Company/North Carolina
Miller Foundation
Minnesota Mining & Mfg. Co.
Mnuchin Foundation
Mobil Oil Corp.
Monfort Family Foundation
Morgan Construction Co.
Mosbacher, Jr. Foundation, Emil
Muchnic Foundation
Murphey Foundation, Lluella Morey
Musson Charitable Foundation, R. C. and Katharine M.
Nalco Chemical Co.
National Gypsum Co.
National Steel Corp.
National Westminster Bank New Jersey
Nesholm Family Foundation
New Jersey Natural Gas Co.
New York Life Insurance Co.
New York Mercantile Exchange
New York Times Company
The New Yorker Magazine, Inc.
Noble Foundation, Samuel Roberts
Northern States Power Co. (Minnesota)
Northwest Natural Gas Co.
Norton Co.
Offield Family Foundation
Ohrstrom Foundation
Old National Bank in Evansville
Olin Corp.
O'Quinn Foundation, John M. and Nancy C.
Osborn Charitable Trust, Edward B.
Osher Foundation, Bernard
Overbrook Foundation
Overlake Foundation
Oxy USA Inc.
Pacific Mutual Life Insurance Co.
Pacific Telesis Group
PaineWebber
Palmer Fund, Frank Loomis
Pamida, Inc.
Panhandle Eastern Corporation
Parker Hannifin Corp.
Payne Foundation, Frank E. and Seba B.
Pennsylvania Dutch Co.
Pennzoil Co.
Perkin-Elmer Corp.
Pew Charitable Trusts
Pfizer, Inc.
PHH Corporation
Pick, Jr. Fund, Albert
Pineywoods Foundation
Piper Foundation, Minnie Stevens
Pittsburgh Child Guidance Foundation
Pollock Company Foundation, William B.
Potomac Electric Power Co.
Prairie Foundation
PriMerit Bank
Providence Gas Co.
Providence Journal Company
Provident Life & Accident Insurance Company of America

Prudential Insurance Co. of America, The
Public Service Electric & Gas Co.
Puterbaugh Foundation
Rachal Foundation, Ed
Ralston Purina Co.
Republic NY Corp.
Reynolds Foundation, Donald W.
Rhone-Poulenc Inc.
Rice Charitable Foundation, Albert W.
Richardson Charitable Trust, Anne S.
Rieke Corp.
Rockwell Fund
Rockwell International Corporation
Rohm & Haas Co.
Roseburg Forest Products Co.
Rouse Co.
Royal Foundation, May Mitchell
Royal Group, Inc.
Rubinstein Foundation, Helena
Rudin Foundation
SAFECO Corp.
Salomon Inc.
Saltonstall Charitable Foundation, Richard
San Diego Gas & Electric
Santa Fe Pacific Corporation
Sara Lee Corp.
Sara Lee Hosiery, Inc.
Sarkeys Foundation
Sawyer Charitable Foundation
Scaife Family Foundation
Schenck Fund, L. P.
Schering-Plough Corp.
Schuller International
Scott Foundation, William E.
Seagram & Sons, Inc., Joseph E.
Seaver Institute
Seaway Food Town, Inc.
Security Life of Denver Insurance Co.
Seidman Family Foundation
Seneca Foods Corp.
Shawmut National Corp.
Sheaffer Inc.
Shell Oil Company
Siltec Corp.
Simon Foundation, William E. and Carol G.
Skillman Foundation
Sloan Foundation, Alfred P.
Smeal Foundation, Mary Jean and Frank P.
Smith Charitable Foundation, Lou and Lutza
Smith Corp., A.O.
Smith Foundation, Ralph L.
SmithKline Beecham Corp.
Snayberger Memorial Foundation, Harry E. and Florence W.
Solow Foundation
Sonat Inc.
South Waite Foundation
Southern California Edison Co.
Southern New England Telephone Company
Specialty Manufacturing Co.
Sprague Educational and Charitable Foundation, Seth
Springs Foundation
SPX Corp.
Stabler Foundation, Donald B. and Dorothy L.
Stackpole-Hall Foundation
Stanley Works
Starr Foundation
Stauffer Charitable Trust, John
Stauffer Foundation, John and Beverly
Staunton Farm Foundation
Steele-Reese Foundation
Stevens Foundation, Abbot and Dorothy H.
Stone Trust, H. Chase
Strawbridge Foundation of Pennsylvania II, Margaret Dorrance

Stupp Foundation, Norman J.
Sturgis Charitable and Educational Trust, Roy and Christine
Subaru of America Inc.
Sumners Foundation, Hatton W.
Sunnen Foundation
Swalm Foundation
Swift Co. Inc., John S.
Taubman Foundation, A. Alfred
Taylor Foundation, Ruth and Vernon
Teleflex Inc.
Temple Foundation, T. L. L.
Temple-Inland Inc.
Tenneco Inc.
Tetley, Inc.
Texaco Inc.
Texas Commerce Bank-Houston, N.A.
Textron, Inc.
Towsley Foundation, Harry A. and Margaret D.
Transco Energy Co.
Travelers Inc.
Trull Foundation
Trust Company Bank
Tucker Charitable Trust, Rose E.
Turner Charitable Foundation
Turrell Fund
Unilever United States, Inc.
Union Camp Corporation
Union Pacific Corp.
U.S. Bank of Washington
Unitrode Corp.
Unocal Corp.
Upjohn Foundation, Harold and Grace
Uris Brothers Foundation
USX Corporation
van Ameringen Foundation
Van Nuys Foundation, I. N. and Susanna H.
Vanderbilt Trust, R. T.
Virginia Power Co.
Vulcan Materials Co.
Wachovia Bank of North Carolina, N.A.
Wahlstrom Foundation
Wal-Mart Stores, Inc.
Washington Forrest Foundation
Wean Foundation, Raymond John
Weaver Foundation, Gil and Dody
Weber Charities Corp., Frederick E.
Weckbaugh Foundation, Eleanore Mullen
Weezie Foundation
Wege Foundation
Weingart Foundation
Welfare Foundation
Wells Foundation, Franklin H. and Ruth L.
Wendt Foundation, Margaret L.
Western New York Foundation
Westvaco Corporation
Weyerhaeuser Co.
Wheeler Foundation
Whirlpool Corporation
Whiting Foundation
Whittenberger Foundation, Claude R. and Ethel B.
Wickes Foundation, Harvey Randall
WICOR, Inc.
Williams Companies, The
Wilson Foundation, H. W.
Winnebago Industries, Inc.
Wisconsin Public Service Corp.
Young Foundation, Robert R.
Zarrow Foundation, Anne and Henry

United Funds/United Ways

Abbott Laboratories
Abell-Hanger Foundation

Abrams Foundation, Talbert and Leota
ACF Industries, Inc.
Acushnet Co.
AEGON USA Inc.
Aetna Life & Casualty Co.
Air Products and Chemicals, Inc.
AKC Fund
Akzo America
Akzo Chemicals Inc.
Alabama Gas Corp.
Alabama Power Co.
Albertson's Inc.
Aldus Corp.
Alexander Foundation, Joseph
Allegheny Ludlum Corp.
Allendale Insurance Co.
Allianz Life Insurance Co. of North America
AlliedSignal Inc.
Altschul Foundation
Alumax Inc.
Aluminum Co. of America
Amado Foundation, Maurice
Amcast Industrial Corp.
AMCORE Bank, N.A. Rockford
American Brands, Inc.
American Fidelity Corporation
American General Finance Corp.
American National Bank & Trust Co. of Chicago
American Natural Resources Company
American President Companies, Ltd.
American United Life Insurance Co.
Ameritas Life Insurance Corp.
AMETEK, Inc.
Amfac/JMB Hawaii Inc.
Amoco Corporation
AMP Incorporated
AMR Corp.
Andersen Corp.
Andersen Foundation
Anderson Foundation
Anderson Foundation, John W.
Andersons, The
Andrews Foundation
Anheuser-Busch Companies, Inc.
Annenberg Foundation
Ansin Private Foundation, Ronald M.
Ansley Foundation, Dantzler Bond
AON Corporation
Appleton Papers Inc.
Arakelian Foundation, Mary Alice
Archer-Daniels-Midland Co.
Argyros Foundation
Aristech Chemical Corp.
Arkansas Power & Light Co.
Arkelian Foundation, Ben H. and Gladys
Armco Inc.
Armstrong Foundation
Arnold Fund
Ashtabula Foundation
Asplundh Foundation
AT&T Corp.
Atherton Family Foundation
Atran Foundation
Auerbach Foundation, Beatrice Fox
Avon Products, Inc.
Babcock & Wilcox Co.
Babson Foundation, Paul and Edith
Bacon Foundation, E. L. and Oma
Baehr Foundation, Louis W. and Dolpha
Baker Foundation, Dexter F. and Dorothy H.
Baldwin Foundation, David M. and Barbara
Baldwin Memorial Foundation, Fred
Ball Brothers Foundation

Ball Foundation, George and Frances
Banc One Wisconsin Corp.
Bank of Boston
Bank of Boston Corp.
Bank of New York Company, Inc.
Bank One, Texas-Houston Office
Bank One, Youngstown, NA
BankAmerica Corp.
Bankers Trust Company
Banta Corp.
Bard Foundation, Robert
Barker Foundation, J.M.R.
Barra Foundation
Barry Corp., R. G.
Barth Foundation, Theodore H.
Battelle Memorial Institute
Batts Foundation
Bay Area Foods
Beal Foundation
Bean Foundation, Norwin S. and Elizabeth N.
BE&K Inc.
Beatty Trust, Cordelia Lunceford
Beazley Foundation/Frederick Foundation
Bechtel, Jr. Foundation, S. D.
Bedsole Foundation, J. L.
Beech Aircraft Corp.
Beloit Foundation
Bemis Company, Inc.
Benedum Foundation, Claude Worthington
Benenson Foundation, Frances and Benjamin
Benetton Services Corp.
Benwood Foundation
Berwind Corporation
Besser Foundation
Bethlehem Steel Corp.
Betts Industries
Bigelow Foundation, F. R.
Binney & Smith Inc.
Binswanger Cos.
Birnschein Foundation, Alvin and Marion
Bishop Foundation, E. K. and Lillian F.
Blake Foundation, S. P.
Blandin Foundation
Block, H&R
Bloedorn Foundation, Walter A.
Blount Educational and Charitable Foundation, Mildred Weedon
Blount, Inc.
Blue Bell, Inc.
Blue Cross & Blue Shield United of Wisconsin
Blum Foundation, Harry and Maribel G.
Boatmen's Bancshares, Inc.
Boeing Co., The
Boettcher Foundation
Boise Cascade Corporation
Borden, Inc.
Borman's Inc.
Boston Edison Co.
Boswell Foundation, James G.
Boutell Memorial Fund
Bowater Incorporated
Bowen Foundation, Ethel N.
BP America Inc.
Brady Foundation
Bremer Foundation, Otto
Brenner Foundation, Mervyn
Breyer Foundation
Bridgestone/Firestone, Inc.
Bridwell Foundation, J. S.
Bright Family Foundation
Bristol-Myers Squibb Company
Broadhurst Foundation
Brown Foundation, M. K.
Brown & Williamson Tobacco Corp.
Brunswick Corp.
Bryn Mawr Trust Co.
Bucyrus-Erie Company
Burchfield Foundation, Charles E.

Burdines Inc.
Burkitt Foundation
Burlington Industries, Inc.
Burnett-Tandy Foundation
Bush Foundation
Cabell Foundation, Robert G. Cabell III and Maude Morgan
Cable & Wireless Holdings, Inc.
Cabot Corp.
Cafritz Foundation, Morris and Gwendolyn
Cain Foundation, Effie and Wofford
Cain Foundation, Gordon and Mary
Calhoun Charitable Trust, Kenneth
Callaway Foundation
Campbell Foundation
Canon U.S.A., Inc.
Cargill Inc.
Carnahan-Jackson Foundation
Carpenter Foundation
Carpenter Technology Corp.
Carter Foundation, Amon G.
Carvel Foundation, Thomas and Agnes
Cassett, Jr. Foundation, Louis N.
Castle Foundation, Harold K. L.
Cayuga Foundation
CBS, Inc.
Central Fidelity Banks, Inc.
Central Hudson Gas & Electric Corp.
Central Maine Power Co.
Central National Bank
Century Companies of America
Champlin Foundations
Chapman Charitable Corporation, Howard and Bess
Chase Manhattan Bank, N.A.
Chatham Manufacturing Co.
Chazen Foundation
Cheatham Foundation, Owen
Cheney Foundation, Ben B.
Chesapeake Corp.
Chesebrough-Pond's USA Co.
Chevron Corporation
Chicago Sun-Times, Inc.
Childs Charitable Foundation, Roberta M.
Chrysler Corp.
Church & Dwight Co., Inc.
CIBC Wood Gundy
CIGNA Corporation
CINergy
Citibank
Citizens Bank of Rhode Island
City National Bank and Trust Co.
Clapp Charitable and Educational Trust, George H.
CLARCOR Inc.
Clark Foundation
Clay Foundation
Clemens Markets Corp.
Clements Foundation
Clorox Co.
Close Foundation
Clowes Fund
CNA Financial Corporation/CNA Insurance Companies
Coen Family Foundation, Charles S. and Mary
Cogswell Benevolent Trust
Cole Foundation, Olive B.
Cole Trust, Quincy
Collins Foundation, George and Jennie
Colonial Life & Accident Insurance Co.
Coltec Industries, Inc.
Columbus Dispatch Printing Co.
Comer Foundation
Comerica Incorporated
Commerce Bancshares, Inc.
Commerce Clearing House, Incorporated
Commonwealth Edison Co.

Connecticut Mutual Life Insurance Company
Connelly Foundation
Connemara Fund
Consolidated Natural Gas Co.
Consolidated Papers, Inc.
Consumers Power Co.
Continental Corp.
Contran Corporation
Cooke Foundation
Cooper Industries, Inc.
Cooperman Foundation, Leon and Toby
Coors Foundation, Adolph
Copley Press, Inc.
Cord Foundation, E. L.
Cornell Trust, Peter C.
Corning Incorporated
Cosmair, Inc.
Coughlin-Saunders Foundation
Cowell Foundation, S. H.
Cowles Charitable Trust
Cowles Media Co.
CPC International Inc.
CR Industries
Crandall Memorial Foundation, J. Ford
Crane Co.
Cranston Print Works Company
Crawford Estate, E. R.
Cremer Foundation
Crestlea Foundation
Crown Memorial, Arie and Ida
CS First Boston Corporation
CT Corp. System
Cullen Foundation
Culpeper Memorial Foundation, Daphne Seybolt
Culver Foundation, Constans
Cummings Foundation, James H.
Cummins Engine Co.
Cuneo Foundation
Curtice-Burns Foods, Inc.
Daily News
Dalton Foundation, Harry L.
Daniel Foundation of Alabama
Darby Foundation
Dart Group Corp.
Dater Foundation, Charles H.
Daugherty Foundation
Davenport-Hatch Foundation
Davidson Family Charitable Foundation
Davis Foundation, Edwin W. and Catherine M.
Davis Foundation, Irene E. and George A.
Davis Foundation, James A. and Juliet L.
Davis Foundations, Arthur Vining
Daywood Foundation
DEC International, Inc.
Deere & Co.
Delano Foundation, Mignon Sherwood
Dell Foundation, Hazel
Dentsply International Inc.
DeRoy Foundation, Helen L.
DeRoy Testamentary Foundation
Detroit Edison Co.
Deuble Foundation, George H.
DeVore Foundation
Dexter Charitable Fund, Eugene A.
Dexter Corporation
Dillon Dunwalke Trust, Clarence and Anne
Dillon Foundation
Dishman Charitable Foundation Trust, H. E. and Kate
Dodge Jones Foundation
Donaldson Company, Inc.
Donnelley & Sons Co., R.R.
Douglas & Lomason Company
Douty Foundation
Dover Foundation
Dow Corning Corp.
Dow Foundation, Herbert H. and Grace A.
Dow Jones & Company, Inc.
Dresser Industries, Inc.

du Pont de Nemours & Co., E. I.
Duchossois Industries Inc.
Duke Power Co.
Dula Educational and Charitable Foundation, Caleb C. and Julia W.
Dun & Bradstreet Corp.
Dunagan Foundation
Duncan Foundation, Lillian H. and C. W.
duPont Foundation, Alfred I.
Dynamet, Inc.
Early Foundation
Eastman Kodak Company
Eaton Corporation
Eddy Family Memorial Fund, C. K.
Eden Hall Foundation
Edgewater Steel Corp.
Einstein Fund, Albert E. and Birdie W.
El Pomar Foundation
Elf Atochem North America, Inc.
Elkins, Jr. Foundation, Margaret and James A.
Emerson Foundation, Inc., Fred L.
Encyclopaedia Britannica, Inc.
English Memorial Fund, Florence C. and H. L.
Enron Corp.
Ensign-Bickford Industries
Essick Foundation
Ethyl Corp
Everett Charitable Trust
Exxon Corporation
Fabri-Kal Corp.
Fair Foundation, R. W.
Fair Oaks Foundation, Inc.
Favrot Fund
Federal-Mogul Corporation
Federated Mutual Insurance Co.
Femino Foundation
Fenton Foundation
Fieldcrest Cannon Inc.
Fikes Foundation, Leland
Finch Foundation, Doak
Finch Foundation, Thomas Austin
Fireman's Fund Insurance Co.
Firestone, Jr. Foundation, Harvey
Firman Fund
First Fidelity Bank
First Financial Bank FSB
First Hawaiian, Inc.
First Interstate Bank of Oregon
First Source Corp.
First Tennessee Bank
First Union Corp.
Firstar Bank Milwaukee, N.A.
Fischbach Foundation
Fishback Foundation Trust, Harmes C.
Fleet Financial Group, Inc.
Fleming Cos. Food Distribution Center
Fletcher Foundation
Folger Fund
Forbes Inc.
Ford Foundation
Ford Fund, William and Martha
Ford II Fund, Henry
Ford Motor Co.
Forest Oil Corp.
Fort Wayne National Bank
Foster Charitable Trust
Foster Foundation
France Foundation, Jacob and Annita
Frear Eleemosynary Trust, Mary D. and Walter F.
Freedom Forge Corp.
Freeport Brick Co.
Freeport-McMoRan Inc.
French Foundation, D.E.
French Oil Mill Machinery Co.
Frese Foundation, Arnold D.
Fribourg Foundation
Friedman Family Foundation
Frisch's Restaurants Inc.

Frueauff Foundation, Charles A.
Fruehauf Foundation
Fry Foundation, Lloyd A.
Fujitsu America, Inc.
Fund for New Jersey
Fuqua Foundation, J. B.
Gallagher Family Foundation, Lewis P.
Gamble Foundation
Gannett Publishing Co., Guy Gap, Inc., The
GAR Foundation
Garland Foundation, John Jewett and H. Chandler
Gates Foundation
GATX Corp.
Gaylord Foundation, Clifford Willard
Gazette Co.
Gebbie Foundation
Geifman Family Foundation
GenCorp Inc.
General American Life Insurance Co.
General Mills, Inc.
General Motors Corp.
Geneseo Foundation
Georgia-Pacific Corporation
Georgia Power Co.
Gershman Foundation, Joel
Gheens Foundation
Ghidotti Foundation
Giant Eagle, Inc.
Giant Food Inc.
Giant Food Stores
Gifford Charitable Corporation, Rosamond
Giles Foundation, Edward C.
Gillette Co.
Gilmore Foundation, William G.
Glanville Family Foundation
Glaser Foundation
Gleason Foundation
Glenn Foundation, Carrie C. and Lena V.
Glick Foundation, Eugene and Marilyn
Globe Newspaper Co.
Glosser Foundation, David A.
Goddard Foundation, Charles B.
Goldberg Family Foundation
Goldie-Anna Charitable Trust
Goldwyn Foundation, Samuel
Goodrich Co., The B.F.
Goodstein Family Foundation, David
Gould Electronics Inc.
Grand Rapids Label Co.
Great-West Life Assurance Co.
Griffis Foundation
Griffith Foundation, W. C.
Griggs and Mary Griggs Burke Foundation, Mary Livingston
Groome Beatty Trust, Helen D.
Grundy Foundation
GSM Industrial
Guaranty Bank & Trust Co.
Guardian Life Insurance Company of America
Guggenheim Foundation, Harry Frank
Gulf Power Co.
Guttman Foundation, Stella and Charles
Haas, Jr. Fund, Evelyn and Walter
Habig Foundation, Arnold F.
Hachar Charitable Trust, D. D.
Hafif Family Foundation
Hagedorn Fund
Haley Foundation, W. B.
Halff Foundation, G. A. C.
Halsell Foundation, Ewing
Hamilton Bank
Handy and Harman Foundation
Hanes Foundation, John W. and Anna H.
Hanson Industries North America
Harcourt Foundation, Ellen Knowles

Harland Charitable Foundation, John and Wilhelmina D.
Harrington Foundation, Francis A. and Jacquelyn H.
Harrison Foundation, Fred G.
Harsco Corp.
Hartmarx Corporation
Hasbro Inc.
Hatch Charitable Trust, Margaret Milliken
Hawkins Foundation, Robert Z.
Hawn Foundation
Hazen Foundation, Edward W.
HCA Foundation
Hechinger Co.
Hecht-Levi Foundation
Heinz Company, H. J.
Heinz Endowment, Howard
Heinz Endowment, Vira I.
Heinz Trust, Drue
Heller Financial, Inc.
Henkel Corp.
Henry Foundation, Patrick
Herrick Foundation
Hershey Foods Corp.
Herzstein Charitable Foundation, Albert and Ethel
Heublein Inc.
Hewit Family Foundation
Heydt Fund, Nan and Matilda
Hickory Tech Corp.
Higginson Trust, Corina
High Foundation
Hill Foundation, Sandy
Hillman Foundation
Hillsdale Fund
Hobby Foundation
Hoffman Foundation, Maximilian E. and Marion O.
Hook Drugs
Hoover Foundation
Hoover Fund-Trust, W. Henry
Hopedale Foundation
Hopwood Charitable Trust, John M.
Houchens Foundation, Ervin G.
Housatonic Curtain Co.
Houston Endowment
Houston Industries Incorporated
Howe and Mitchell B. Howe Foundation, Lucille Horton
Hoyt Foundation
Hudson-Webber Foundation
Huisking Foundation
Hulbert Foundation, Nila B.
Hulme Charitable Foundation, Milton G.
Hultquist Foundation
Humana, Inc.
Humphrey Fund, George M. and Pamela S.
Hunt Foundation
Hunt Foundation, Roy A.
Hunt Foundation, Samuel P.
Huston Foundation
Hygeia Dairy Co.
Icahn Foundation, Carl C.
ICI Americas Inc.
IES Industries, Inc.
Illinois Tool Works, Inc.
Imperial Bancorp
Independence Foundation
Ingalls Foundation, Louise H. and David S.
Inland Container Corp.
Integra Bank of Uniontown
Interkal, Inc.
International Business Machines Corp.
Iowa-Illinois Gas & Electric Co.
Irvine Foundation, James
Irwin Charity Foundation, William G.
ITT Hartford Insurance Group, Inc.
Ittleson Foundation
Jackson Foundation
Jacobson Foundation, Bernard H. and Blanche E.
Jaffe Foundation
James River Corp. of Virginia
Janesville Foundation

Jarson-Stanley and Mickey Kaplan Foundation, Isaac and Esther
Jaydor Corp.
JELD-WEN, Inc.
Jennings Foundation, Mary Hillman
Jewell Memorial Foundation, Daniel Ashley and Irene Houston
Jewett Foundation, George Frederick
Jewish Healthcare Foundation of Pittsburgh
JFM Foundation
Jockey Hollow Foundation
John Hancock Mutual Life Insurance Co.
Johnson Controls Inc.
Johnson Foundation, Helen K. and Arthur E.
Johnson & Higgins
Johnson & Son, S.C.
Jones Foundation, Harvey and Bernice
Jordan Charitable Foundation, Mary Ranken Jordan and Ettie A.
Joslin-Needham Family Foundation
Jostens, Inc.
Journal-Gazette Co.
Joy Family Foundation
Julia R. and Estelle L. Foundation
Jurzykowski Foundation, Alfred
Justus Trust, Edith C.
Kansas City Southern Industries
Kantzler Foundation
Kaplun Foundation, Morris J. and Betty
Kardon Foundation, Samuel and Rebecca
Kavanagh Foundation, T. James
Kaye, Scholer, Fierman, Hays & Handler
Kayser Foundation
Kelley and Elza Kelley Foundation, Edward Bangs
Kennecott Corporation
Kennedy Foundation, Ethel
Kent-Lucas Foundation
Kiewit Foundation, Peter
Kilcawley Fund, William H.
Kilroy Foundation, William S. and Lora Jean
Kimberly-Clark Corp.
Kingsbury Corp.
Kinney-Lindstrom Foundation
Kiplinger Foundation
Kirby Foundation, F. M.
Kirkpatrick Foundation
Kline Foundation, Josiah W. and Bessie H.
Klipstein Foundation, Ernest Christian
Klock and Lucia Klock Kingston Foundation, Jay E.
Klosk Fund, Louis and Rose
Kmart Corporation
Knapp Foundation
Knight Foundation, John S. and James L.
Knoll Group
Knox, Sr., and Pearl Wallis Knox Charitable Foundation, Robert W.
Kohn-Joseloff Foundation
Komes Foundation
Koopman Fund
Koret Foundation
Kreitler Foundation
Kuehn Foundation
Kunkel Foundation, John Crain
Kuyper Foundation, Peter H. and E. Lucille
La-Z-Boy Chair Co.
Ladd Charitable Corporation, Helen and George
Laffey-McHugh Foundation
LamCo. Communications
Laurel Foundation

LBJ Family Foundation
Lebanon Mutual Insurance Co.
Lebovitz Fund
Lee Endowment Foundation
Lee Enterprises
Lehigh Portland Cement Co.
Lehmann Foundation, Otto W.
Leidy Foundation, John J.
Leighton-Oare Foundation
Lemberg Foundation
Lennon Foundation, Fred A.
Levitt Foundation
Levy Foundation, June Rockwell
Lichtenstein Foundation, David B.
Life Insurance Co. of Georgia
Linnell Foundation
Lipton, Thomas J.
Little, Inc., Arthur D.
Loews Corporation
Long Island Lighting Co.
Longwood Foundation
Louisiana-Pacific Corp.
Love Foundation, George H. and Margaret McClintic
Lovett Foundation
Lowenstein Foundation, Leon
Lurie Foundation, Louis R.
Lydall, Inc.
M/A-COM, Inc.
MacArthur Foundation, John D. and Catherine T.
MacLeod Stewardship Foundation
Macy & Co., Inc., R.H.
Maddox Foundation, J. F.
Madison Gas & Electric Co.
Magowan Family Foundation
Mahadh Foundation
Mailman Family Foundation, A. L.
Mailman Foundation
Management Compensation Group/Dulworth Inc.
Maneely Fund
Marbrook Foundation
Mardag Foundation
Mardigian Foundation
Maritz Inc.
Markey Charitable Fund, John C.
Marmot Foundation
Marquette Electronics, Inc.
Marsh & McLennan Companies, Inc.
Marshall Trust in Memory of Sanders McDaniel, Harriet McDaniel
Martin Marietta Corp.
Martin Marietta Materials
Marx Foundation, Virginia and Leonard
Massengill-DeFriece Foundation
Mather Charitable Trust, S. Livingston
Mather Fund, Richard
Mather and William Gwinn Mather Fund, Elizabeth Ring
Mattel, Inc.
Matthies Foundation, Katharine
Mautz Paint Co.
May Department Stores Company, The
May Foundation, Wilbur
Mayer Foundation, James and Eva
Mayor Foundation, Oliver Dewey
Maytag Family Foundation, Fred
MCA Inc.
McCann Foundation
McCarty Foundation, John and Margaret
McCasland Foundation
McCormick & Co. Inc.
McCormick Trust, Anne
McCune Charitable Foundation, Marshall and Perrine D.
McDermott Foundation, Eugene

McDonald & Company Securities, Inc.
McDonnell Douglas Corp.-West
McEvoy Foundation, Mildred H.
McFawn Trust No. 2, Lois Sisler
McFeely-Rogers Foundation
McGee Foundation
McGonagle Foundation, Dextra Baldwin
McGraw-Hill, Inc.
MCI Communications Corp.
McInerny Foundation
McKenna Foundation, Katherine Mabis
McKenna Foundation, Philip M.
McLean Contributionship
McMahon Foundation
McMillan Foundation, D. W.
Mead Corporation, The
Meadows Foundation
Medtronic, Inc.
Mellon Foundation, Richard King
Memton Fund
Mengle Foundation, Glenn and Ruth
Merck & Co.
Mercury Aircraft
Merrick Foundation
Messing Family Charitable Foundation
Metropolitan Life Insurance Co.
Meyer Family Foundation, Paul J.
Meyerhoff Fund, Joseph
Mid-Iowa Health Foundation
Middendorf Foundation
Miller Brewing Company/North Carolina
Miller Foundation
Miller Fund, Kathryn and Gilbert
Miller-Mellor Association
Mills Fund, Frances Goll
Mine Safety Appliances Co.
Minnesota Mining & Mfg. Co.
Mitchell Energy & Development Corp.
Mitsubishi Motor Sales of America, Inc.
Mobil Oil Corp.
Mohasco Corp.
Monfort Family Foundation
Montana Power Co.
Moore Charitable Foundation, Marjorie
Morgan Construction Co.
Morgan Foundation, Burton D.
Morgan and Samuel Tate Morgan, Jr. Foundation, Marietta McNeil
Morgan Stanley & Co., Inc.
Morris Foundation, William T.
Mosbacher, Jr. Foundation, Emil
Mosinee Paper Corp.
Muchnic Foundation
Mulcahy Foundation
Mulford Foundation, Vincent
Mulford Trust, Clarence E.
Munson Foundation Trust, W. B.
Murdock Charitable Trust, M. J.
Murphey Foundation, Lluella Morey
Murphy Co. Foundation, G.C.
Murphy Foundation
Musson Charitable Foundation, R. C. and Katharine M.
Mutual Assurance Co.
Nabisco Foods Group
National Forge Co.
National Gypsum Co.
National Steel Corp.
National Westminster Bank New Jersey
NBD Indiana, Inc.
Nesholm Family Foundation

Reynolds Foundation,
Christopher
Rubin Foundation, Samuel
Sargent Foundation, Newell B.
Seneca Foods Corp.
Sentry Insurance A Mutual
Company
Simon Foundation, William E.
and Carol G.
Stauffer Foundation, John and
Beverly
van Ameringen Foundation

Volunteer Services

Abbott Laboratories
Aetna Life & Casualty Co.
Air Products and Chemicals,
Inc.
Alabama Gas Corp.
Aldus Corp.
Allendale Insurance Co.
AlliedSignal Inc.
Aluminum Co. of America
AMCORE Bank, N.A.
Rockford
American Brands, Inc.
American General Finance
Corp.
American Natural Resources
Company
American United Life
Insurance Co.
Amfac/JMB Hawaii Inc.
AMR Corp.
Andersen Corp.
Andersen Foundation
Anderson Foundation
Anheuser-Busch Companies,
Inc.
Annenberg Foundation
AON Corporation
Archer-Daniels-Midland Co.
Arkansas Power & Light Co.
Armco Inc.
Atherton Family Foundation
Avon Products, Inc.
Ayres Foundation, Inc.
Baker Foundation, Dexter F.
and Dorothy H.
Bank of New York Company,
Inc.
Bank One, Youngstown, NA
Bard Foundation, Robert
Barker Foundation, J.M.R.
Baskin-Robbins USA Co.
BE&K Inc.
Bechtel, Jr. Foundation, S. D.
Bedsole Foundation, J. L.
Beech Aircraft Corp.
Bethlehem Steel Corp.
Binney & Smith Inc.
Birnschein Foundation, Alvin
and Marion
Bishop Foundation, E. K. and
Lillian F.
Block, H&R
Blue Cross & Blue Shield
United of Wisconsin
Boeing Co., The
Boettcher Foundation
Borden, Inc.
Bothin Foundation
Brach Foundation, Helen
Bridgestone/Firestone, Inc.
Bryn Mawr Trust Co.
Burkitt Foundation
Cabot Corp.
Cafritz Foundation, Morris and
Gwendolyn
Campbell Foundation, Ruth
and Henry
Carnegie Corporation of New
York
Carter Foundation, Amon G.
CBI Industries, Inc.
Centerior Energy Corp.
Central Hudson Gas & Electric
Corp.
Central Maine Power Co.
Chase Manhattan Bank, N.A.
Chazen Foundation
Cheney Foundation, Ben B.
Chesebrough-Pond's USA Co.

Chevron Corporation
Chicago Sun-Times, Inc.
Chrysler Corp.
Citibank
Clark Foundation
Clay Foundation
Clorox Co.
Collins Foundation
Colonial Life & Accident
Insurance Co.
Columbia Foundation
Commerce Clearing House,
Incorporated
Connecticut Mutual Life
Insurance Company
Contran Corporation
Cooke Foundation
Cosmair, Inc.
Cowles Charitable Trust
Cowles Media Co.
Crane Co.
CS First Boston Corporation
Cummins Engine Co.
Curtice-Burns Foods, Inc.
Daily News
Dana Foundation, Charles A.
Davenport-Hatch Foundation
DEC International, Inc.
Dingman Foundation, Michael
D.
Dishman Charitable
Foundation Trust, H. E. and
Kate
Dodge Foundation, Cleveland
H.
Douglas & Lomason Company
Douty Foundation
Dow Jones & Company, Inc.
Dreyfus Foundation, Max and
Victoria
du Pont de Nemours & Co., E.
I.
Duchossois Industries Inc.
Duncan Foundation, Lillian H.
and C. W.
Duncan Trust, John G.
Early Foundation
Eaton Corporation
Eddy Family Memorial Fund,
C. K.
English Memorial Fund,
Florence C. and H. L.
Enron Corp.
Ensign-Bickford Industries
Essick Foundation
Exxon Corporation
Farish Fund, William Stamps
Federal-Mogul Corporation
Federated Mutual Insurance
Co.
Fieldcrest Cannon Inc.
Fikes Foundation, Leland
Firman Fund
First Fidelity Bank
First Tennessee Bank
First Union Corp.
Firstar Bank Milwaukee, N.A.
Fish Foundation, Ray C.
Fondren Foundation
Forbes Inc.
Ford II Fund, Henry
Ford Motor Co.
Freeport-McMoRan Inc.
Frisch's Restaurants Inc.
Frohring Foundation, William
O. and Gertrude Lewis
Frost National Bank
Fry Foundation, Lloyd A.
Gap, Inc., The
GenCorp Inc.
General American Life
Insurance Co.
General Mills, Inc.
General Motors Corp.
GenRad
German Protestant Orphan
Asylum Association
Ghidotti Foundation
Gillette Co.
Gleason Foundation
Goldsmith Foundation, Horace
W.
Graham Fund, Philip L.
Greenwall Foundation

Haas, Jr. Fund, Evelyn and
Walter
Hafif Family Foundation
Hancock Foundation, Luke B.
Hanover Foundation
Harcourt Foundation, Ellen
Knowles
Harcourt General, Inc.
Hardin Foundation, Phil
Harmon Foundation, Pearl M.
and Julia J.
HarperCollins Publishers Inc.
Harriman Foundation, Mary W.
Harsco Corp.
Hartford Foundation, John A.
Hartmarx Corporation
Hasbro Inc.
HCA Foundation
Hearst Foundation, William
Randolph
Hechinger Co.
Heckscher Foundation for
Children
Heinz Company, H. J.
Heinz Endowment, Howard
Heinz Endowment, Vira I.
Hershey Foods Corp.
Hewlett Foundation, William
and Flora
Hickory Tech Corp.
Higginson Trust, Corina
Hill Foundation, Sandy
Hino Diesel Trucks (U.S.A.)
Hoffman Foundation,
Maximilian E. and Marion O.
Hook Drugs
Hoover, Jr. Foundation,
Margaret W. and Herbert
Houston Endowment
Houston Industries
Incorporated
Howe and Mitchell B. Howe
Foundation, Lucille Horton
Humphrey Fund, George M.
and Pamela S.
Hunt Charitable Trust, C. Giles
Huston Charitable Trust,
Stewart
IBP, Inc.
Illinois Tool Works, Inc.
International Business
Machines Corp.
International Paper Co.
Irvine Foundation, James
Ittleson Foundation
Jackson Foundation
Jacobson Foundation, Bernard
H. and Blanche E.
James River Corp. of Virginia
JELD-WEN, Inc.
Jewish Healthcare Foundation
of Pittsburgh
JM Foundation
John Hancock Mutual Life
Insurance Co.
Johnson Foundation, Helen K.
and Arthur E.
Johnson & Higgins
Jones Foundation, Fletcher
Jordan Charitable Foundation,
Mary Ranken Jordan and
Ettie A.
Journal-Gazette Co.
Kansas City Southern
Industries
Kiewit Foundation, Peter
Kimberly-Clark Corp.
Kingsbury Corp.
Kiplinger Foundation
Kline Foundation, Josiah W.
and Bessie H.
Knoll Group
Knox, Sr., and Pearl Wallis
Knox Charitable
Foundation, Robert W.
Laurel Foundation
Leavey Foundation, Thomas
and Dorothy
Levy Foundation, June
Rockwell
Link, Jr. Foundation, George
Lipton, Thomas J.
Little, Inc., Arthur D.
Loews Corporation
Long Island Lighting Co.

Lowenstein Foundation, Leon
Lund Foundation
MacArthur Foundation, John
D. and Catherine T.
Macy & Co., Inc., R.H.
Mahadh Foundation
Mardag Foundation
Marpat Foundation
Mars Foundation
Mautz Paint Co.
Maytag Family Foundation,
Fred
MBIA Inc.
MCA Inc.
McCann Foundation
McCasland Foundation
McConnell Foundation
McCormick & Co. Inc.
McCune Charitable Trust,
John R.
McDonnell Douglas
Corp.-West
McElroy Trust, R. J.
McFawn Trust No. 2, Lois
Sisler
McGraw-Hill, Inc.
McInerny Foundation
McMillan Foundation, D. W.
Meadows Foundation
Medtronic, Inc.
Mellon Foundation, Richard
King
Metropolitan Life Insurance
Co.
Meyerhoff Fund, Joseph
Millbrook Tribute Garden
Minnesota Mining & Mfg. Co.
Mitsubishi Motor Sales of
America, Inc.
Mobil Oil Corp.
Morgan & Company, J.P.
Morgan Stanley & Co., Inc.
Morris Foundation, Margaret T.
Moses Fund, Henry and Lucy
Mosinee Paper Corp.
Mott Foundation, Charles
Stewart
Mulford Foundation, Vincent
B.
Munson Foundation Trust, W.
B.
Musson Charitable
Foundation, R. C. and
Katharine M.
Mutual Assurance Co.
National Westminster Bank
New Jersey
New-Land Foundation
New York Life Insurance Co.
New York Stock Exchange, Inc.
New York Times Company
The New Yorker Magazine, Inc.
Noble Foundation, Edward
John
Northern States Power Co.
(Minnesota)
Northwest Natural Gas Co.
Norton Co.
Norton Foundation Inc.
Novell Inc.
Olin Corp.
Oppenstein Brothers
Foundation
Ore-Ida Foods, Inc.
Overbrook Foundation
Owsley Foundation, Alvin and
Lucy
Pacific Mutual Life Insurance
Co.
Pacific Telesis Group
Palisades Educational
Foundation
Panhandle Eastern Corporation
Parsons Foundation, Ralph M.
Pella Corporation
Penn Foundation, William
Peoples Energy Corp.
Peppers Foundation, Ann
Perkin-Elmer Corp.
Pew Charitable Trusts
Pfizer, Inc.
Phillips Family Foundation,
Jay and Rose
Piper Jaffray Companies Inc.
Pittsburg Midway Coal Mining
Co.

PPG Industries, Inc.
Premier Industrial Corp.
Priddy Foundation
Providian Corporation
Prudential Insurance Co. of
America, The
Quaker Chemical Corp.
Quivey-Bay State Foundation
Ralston Purina Co.
Rand McNally & Co.
Ratner Foundation, Milton M.
Raymond Corp.
Regenstein Foundation
Rennebohm Foundation, Oscar
Retirement Research
Foundation
Rice Foundation
RJR Nabisco Inc.
Rockwell Fund
Rockwell International
Corporation
Rohm & Haas Co.
Roseburg Forest Products Co.
Rosenberg, Jr. Family
Foundation, Louise and
Claude
Rose's Stores, Inc.
Rouse Co.
Royal Group, Inc.
Rudin Foundation
SAFECO Corp.
Saint Paul Companies, Inc.
San Diego Gas & Electric
Sandusky International Inc.
Santa Fe Pacific Corporation
Sara Lee Corp.
Sara Lee Hosiery, Inc.
Sasco Foundation
SBC Communications Inc.
Schenck Fund, L. P.
Scherman Foundation
Scholl Foundation, Dr.
Schroeder Foundation, Walter
Schuller International
Schumann Fund for New
Jersey
Schwab & Co., Inc., Charles
Schwartz Foundation, Arnold
A.
Scott Fetzer Co.
Scott Foundation, William E.
Scurlock Foundation
Seaver Institute
Security Life of Denver
Insurance Co.
Shawmut National Corp.
Shell Oil Company
Siltec Corp.
Sonat Inc.
Southern California Edison Co.
Spang & Co.
Sprague Educational and
Charitable Foundation, Seth
Stabler Foundation, Donald B.
and Dorothy L.
Stackpole-Hall Foundation
Strong Foundation, Hattie M.
Sturgis Charitable and
Educational Trust, Roy and
Christine
Taube Family Foundation
Taubman Foundation, A. Alfred
Teleflex Inc.
Temple Foundation, T. L. L.
Tenneco Inc.
Texaco Inc.
Texas Commerce
Bank-Houston, N.A.
Textron, Inc.
Thermo Electron Corp.
Thomas Industries
Thornton Foundation, Flora L.
Times Mirror Company, The
Tiscornia Foundation
Towsley Foundation, Harry A.
and Margaret D.
Tozer Foundation
Turrell Fund
Union Camp Corporation
Union Electric Co.
U.S. Bank of Washington
Unitrode Corp.
Upton Foundation, Frederick S.
Uris Brothers Foundation
USL Capital Corporation

Valentine Foundation, Lawson
Vetlesen Foundation, G. Unger
Wahlstrom Foundation
Wal-Mart Stores, Inc.
Washington Mutual Savings Bank
Weingart Foundation
Wells Foundation, Franklin H. and Ruth L.
Western New York Foundation
Weyerhaeuser Co.
Whirlpool Corporation
Whiting Foundation
Wickes Foundation, Harvey Randall
Wickson-Link Memorial Foundation
Wilson Fund, Matilda R.
Winter Construction Co.
Wyman Youth Trust
Yeager Charitable Trust, Lester E.

YMCA/YWCA/ YMHA/YWHA

ACF Industries, Inc.
Acushnet Co.
Adler Foundation Trust, Philip D. and Henrietta B.
AKC Fund
Alabama Gas Corp.
Allianz Life Insurance Co. of North America
Allyn Foundation
Aluminum Co. of America
AMCORE Bank, N.A. Rockford
American Fidelity Corporation
American General Finance Corp.
Andersen Foundation
Ansley Foundation, Dantzler Bond
Appleby Trust, Scott B. and Annie P.
Arnold Fund
Ashtabula Foundation
Babson Foundation, Paul and Edith
Baker Foundation, Dexter F. and Dorothy H.
Baldwin Foundation, David M. and Barbara
Ball Brothers Foundation
Ball Foundation, George and Frances
Bank of Boston
BankAmerica Corp.
Banta Corp.
Bard Foundation, Robert
Beal Foundation
Bean Foundation, Norwin S. and Elizabeth N.
Betts Industries
Bishop Foundation, E. K. and Lillian F.
Boettcher Foundation
Borkee Hagley Foundation
Boswell Foundation, James G.
Brackenridge Foundation, George W.
Bridwell Foundation, J. S.
Brunswick Corp.
Bryn Mawr Trust Co.
Burnett-Tandy Foundation
Calder Foundation, Louis
Campbell Foundation
Campbell Foundation, Ruth and Henry
Carpenter Foundation
Carpenter Technology Corp.
Castle Foundation, Harold K. L.
Catlin Charitable Trust, Kathleen K.
Central National Bank
Centralia Foundation
Champlin Foundations
Chapman Charitable Corporation, Howard and Bess
Chase Manhattan Bank, N.A.

Chazen Foundation
Christy-Houston Foundation
CIBC Wood Gundy
City National Bank and Trust Co.
CLARCOR Inc.
Clarke Trust, John
Clay Foundation
Clemens Markets Corp.
Clorox Co.
Collins Foundation, George and Jennie
Collins, Jr. Foundation, George Fulton
Cooper Industries, Inc.
Coors Foundation, Adolph
Cord Foundation, E. L.
Crawford Estate, E. R.
Cremer Foundation
Crestlea Foundation
Crystal Trust
CS First Boston Corporation
Culpeper Memorial Foundation, Daphne Seybolt
Culver Foundation, Constans
Davenport-Hatch Foundation
Davenport Trust Fund
Davidson Family Charitable Foundation
Davis Foundation, Irene E. and George A.
Daywood Foundation
Dekko Foundation
Dentsply International Inc.
DeRoy Foundation, Helen L.
Deuble Foundation, George H.
DeVore Foundation
Dexter Charitable Fund, Eugene A.
Dr. Seuss Foundation
Dodge Foundation, Cleveland H.
Duncan Foundation, Lillian H. and C. W.
Eden Hall Foundation
Einstein Fund, Albert E. and Birdie W.
Everett Charitable Trust
Exchange National Bank
Exxon Corporation
Fabri-Kal Corp.
Fair Foundation, R. W.
Favrot Fund
Fikes Foundation, Leland
Finch Foundation, Doak
Finch Foundation, Thomas Austin
First Source Corp.
Fishback Foundation Trust, Harmes C.
Flowers Charitable Trust, Albert W. and Edith V.
Fort Wayne National Bank
Freeport-McMoRan Inc.
French Foundation, D.E.
Friedman Family Foundation
Frohring Foundation, William O. and Gertrude Lewis
Frueauff Foundation, Charles A.
Gannett Publishing Co., Guy
GAR Foundation
Gates Foundation
Gaylord Foundation, Clifford Willard
Gazette Co.
Gebbie Foundation
German Protestant Orphan Asylum Association
Glosser Foundation, David A.
Good Samaritan
Graham Fund, Philip L.
Griffith Foundation, W. C.
Grundy Foundation
GSM Industrial
Guaranty Bank & Trust Co.
Hafif Family Foundation
Hagedorn Fund
Hammer Foundation, Armand
Hanover Foundation
Harcourt Foundation, Ellen Knowles
Harland Charitable Foundation, John and Wilhelmina D.

Harrington Foundation, Francis A. and Jacquelyn H.
Hartmarx Corporation
Hatch Charitable Trust, Margaret Milliken
Hauser Foundation
Hawn Foundation
Hazen Foundation, Edward W.
Heinz Endowment, Vira I.
Herzstein Charitable Foundation, Albert and Ethel
Hewlett-Packard Co.
Hickory Tech Corp.
Hill Foundation, Sandy
Hillman Foundation
Hillsdale Fund
Hoag Family Foundation, George
Hobby Foundation
Hoover Foundation
Hoover Fund-Trust, W. Henry
Hopedale Foundation
Houston Endowment
Howe and Mitchell B. Howe Foundation, Lucille Horton
Hulbert Foundation, Nila B.
Huston Charitable Trust, Stewart
Hyde and Watson Foundation
Imperial Bancorp
Jackson Foundation
Jacobson Foundation, Bernard H. and Blanche E.
Janirve Foundation
Jewish Healthcare Foundation of Pittsburgh
Johnson Foundation, Helen K. and Arthur E.
Johnson & Son, S.C.
Jones Foundation, Daisy Marquis
Jones Foundation, Helen
Jordan Charitable Foundation, Mary Ranken Jordan and Ettie A.
Julia R. and Estelle L. Foundation
Justus Trust, Edith C.
Kansas City Southern Industries
Kantzler Foundation
Kardon Foundation, Samuel and Rebecca
Kaufmann Foundation, Henry
Kinney-Lindstrom Foundation
Kline Foundation, Josiah W. and Bessie H.
Klock and Lucia Klock Kingston Foundation, Jay E.
Knoll Group
Koehler Foundation, Marcia and Otto
Koopman Fund
Kreitler Foundation
Kresge Foundation
Ladd Charitable Corporation, Helen and George
Lebanon Mutual Insurance Co.
Lee Enterprises
Leighton-Oare Foundation
Lemberg Foundation
Leuthold Foundation
Lockhart Vaughan Foundation
Lowenstein Foundation, Leon
Madison Gas & Electric Co.
Markey Charitable Fund, John C.
Marmot Foundation
Marpat Foundation
Mattel, Inc.
Matthies Foundation, Katharine
Maytag Family Foundation, Fred
McCarty Foundation, John and Margaret
McCasland Foundation
McCormick Trust, Anne
McCune Charitable Trust, John R.
McEvoy Foundation, Mildred H.
McFawn Trust No. 2, Lois Sisler
McFeely-Rogers Foundation
McInerny Foundation

McMahan Foundation, Catherine L. and Robert O.
McQueen Foundation, Adeline and George
Meadows Foundation
Medtronic, Inc.
Mellon Foundation, Richard King
Mengle Foundation, Glenn and Ruth
Merkley Charitable Trust
Merrick Foundation
Meyer Memorial Trust
Meyerhoff Fund, Joseph
Mid-Iowa Health Foundation
Middendorf Foundation
Miller Charitable Foundation, Howard E. and Nell E.
Mingenback Foundation, Julia J.
Monell Foundation, Ambrose
Moore & Sons, B.C.
Morgan & Company, J.P.
Morgan Construction Co.
Morgan and Samuel Tate Morgan, Jr. Foundation, Marietta McNeil
Morgan Stanley & Co., Inc.
Mosbacher, Jr. Foundation, Emil
Moses Fund, Henry and Lucy
Mosinee Paper Corp.
Muchnic Foundation
Mulcahy Foundation
Murphey Foundation, Lluella Morey
Murphy Foundation
Musson Charitable Foundation, R. C. and Katharine M.
Mutual Assurance Co.
New Jersey Natural Gas Co.
New York Times Company
Nias Foundation, Henry
Norton Co.
Old National Bank in Evansville
Olin Foundation, Spencer T. and Ann W.
PaineWebber
Palmer Fund, Frank Loomis
Parshelsky Foundation, Moses L.
Parsons Foundation, Ralph M.
Payne Foundation, Frank E. and Seba B.
Peters Foundation, Charles F.
Peters Foundation, R. D. and Linda
Peterson Foundation, Hal and Charlie
Phillips Charitable Trust, Dr. and Mrs. Arthur William
Pick, Jr. Fund, Albert
Pioneer Trust Bank, NA
Plankenhorn Foundation, Harry
Porter Testamentary Trust, James Hyde
Priddy Foundation
Putnam Foundation
Quivey-Bay State Foundation
Rand McNally & Co.
Read Foundation, Charles L.
Reynolds Foundation, Donald W.
Richardson Benevolent Foundation, C. E.
Ritter Charitable Trust, George W. and Mary F.
Rockefeller Fund, David
Rockwell Fund
Rockwell International Corporation
Russell Trust, Josephine G.
Schumann Fund for New Jersey
Schwartz Foundation, Arnold A.
Scott Foundation, William E.
Seafirst Corporation
Second Foundation
Semmes Foundation
Seneca Foods Corp.
Sheppard Foundation, Lawrence B.

Smith Trust, May and Stanley
Snayberger Memorial Foundation, Harry E. and Florence W.
Snow Memorial Trust, John Ben
South Bend Tribune
South Waite Foundation
SPX Corp.
Stauffer Charitable Trust, John
Staunton Farm Foundation
Stearns Trust, Artemas W.
Stemmons Foundation
Strong Foundation, Hattie M.
Subaru of America Inc.
Sumners Foundation, Hatton W.
Symmes Foundation, F. W.
Tait Foundation, Frank M.
Taubman Foundation, A. Alfred
Temple-Inland Inc.
Thompson Charitable Foundation
Thorne Foundation
Times Mirror Company, The
Timken Foundation of Canton
Tiscornia Foundation
Todd Co., A.M.
Trexler Trust, Harry C.
Tuch Foundation, Michael
Tucker Charitable Trust, Rose E.
Turner Charitable Foundation
Turrell Fund
Union Pacific Corp.
U.S. Bank of Washington
Unocal Corp.
Upjohn Foundation, Harold and Grace
Upton Foundation, Frederick S.
Utica National Insurance Group
Van Wert County Foundation
Vernon Fund, Miles Hodsdon
Vogler Foundation, Laura B.
Wahlstrom Foundation
Wallace Foundation, George R.
Warwick Foundation
Washington Mutual Savings Bank
Weaver Foundation, Gil and Dody
Webber Oil Co.
Weber Charities Corp., Frederick E.
Weingart Foundation
Welfare Foundation
Wendt Foundation, Margaret L.
West Foundation, Harry and Ethel
Whiting Foundation
Widgeon Foundation
Wiegand Foundation, E. L.
Wisconsin Power & Light Co.
Wood Foundation of Chambersburg, PA
Woodward Fund
Woolley Foundation, Vasser
Wyomissing Foundation
Young Foundation, Robert R.
Zarrow Foundation, Anne and Henry
Zollner Foundation

Youth Organizations

Abbott Laboratories
Abell-Hanger Foundation
Abrams Foundation, Talbert and Leota
ACF Industries, Inc.
Achelis Foundation
Acushnet Co.
Adler Foundation Trust, Philip D. and Henrietta B.
Ahmanson Foundation
Air Products and Chemicals, Inc.
AKC Fund
Akzo America
Akzo Chemicals Inc.
Alabama Power Co.
Albertson's Inc.
Alcon Laboratories, Inc.

Eccles Foundation, Ralph M.
and Ella M.
Eddy Family Memorial Fund,
C. K.
Eden Hall Foundation
Edgewater Steel Corp.
Einstein Fund, Albert E. and
Birdie W.
El Pomar Foundation
Elf Atochem North America,
Inc.
Emerson Foundation, Inc.,
Fred L.
Encyclopaedia Britannica, Inc.
English Memorial Fund,
Florence C. and H. L.
Enron Corp.
Ensign-Bickford Industries
Erpf Fund, Armand G.
Essick Foundation
Ethyl Corp
Ettinger Foundation
Evans Foundation, T. M.
Evans Foundation, Thomas J.
Everett Charitable Trust
Exxon Corporation
Fabri-Kal Corp.
Fair Foundation, R. W.
Fair Oaks Foundation, Inc.
Fairchild Foundation, Sherman
Farish Fund, William Stamps
Farr Trust, Frank M. and Alice
M.
Favrot Fund
Federal-Mogul Corporation
Federated Mutual Insurance
Co.
Feild Co-Operative Association
Femino Foundation
Fieldcrest Cannon Inc.
Fikes Foundation, Leland
Finch Foundation, Doak
Finch Foundation, Thomas
Austin
Fireman's Fund Insurance Co.
Firestone, Jr. Foundation,
Harvey
First Fidelity Bank
First Financial Bank FSB
First Hawaiian, Inc.
First Interstate Bank of Oregon
First Source Corp.
First Tennessee Bank
First Union Corp.
First Union National Bank of
Florida
Firstar Bank Milwaukee, N.A.
Fischbach Foundation
Fish Foundation, Ray C.
Fishback Foundation Trust,
Harmes C.
Fleet Financial Group, Inc.
Fleishhacker Foundation
Fletcher Foundation
Flowers Charitable Trust,
Albert W. and Edith V.
Fohs Foundation
Folger Fund
Fondren Foundation
Forbes Inc.
Ford Foundation
Ford Fund, William and Martha
Ford II Fund, Henry
Ford Motor Co.
Forest Foundation
Forster Charitable Trust, James
W. and Ella B.
Foster Charitable Trust
Foster Foundation
France Foundation, Jacob and
Annita
Frear Eleemosynary Trust,
Mary D. and Walter F.
Freedom Forge Corp.
Freeman Charitable Trust,
Samuel
Freeport Brick Co.
Freeport-McMoRan Inc.
French Foundation, D.E.
French Oil Mill Machinery Co.
Frese Foundation, Arnold D.
Fribourg Foundation
Friedman Family Foundation
Frisch's Restaurants Inc.

Frohring Foundation, Paul and
Maxine
Frohring Foundation, William
O. and Gertrude Lewis
Frost National Bank
Frueauff Foundation, Charles
A.
Fruehauf Foundation
Fry Foundation, Lloyd A.
Fuqua Foundation, J. B.
Gallagher Family Foundation,
Lewis P.
Gamble Foundation
Gannett Publishing Co., Guy
Gap, Inc., The
GAR Foundation
Garland Foundation, John
Jewett and H. Chandler
Gates Foundation
GATX Corp.
Gaylord Foundation, Clifford
Willard
Gazette Co.
Gebbie Foundation
Geifman Family Foundation
Gellert Foundation, Carl
Gellert Foundation, Celia Berta
GenCorp Inc.
General American Life
Insurance Co.
General Mills, Inc.
General Motors Corp.
Geneseo Foundation
GenRad
Georgia-Pacific Corporation
Georgia Power Co.
German Protestant Orphan
Asylum Association
Gheens Foundation
Ghidotti Foundation
Giant Eagle, Inc.
Giant Food Inc.
Giant Food Stores
Gifford Charitable
Corporation, Rosamond
Giles Foundation, Edward C.
Gillette Co.
Gilmore Foundation, William
G.
Glanville Family Foundation
Glaser Foundation
Gleason Foundation
Glick Foundation, Eugene and
Marilyn
Globe Newspaper Co.
Glosser Foundation, David A.
Goddard Foundation, Charles
B.
Goldie-Anna Charitable Trust
Goldseker Foundation of
Maryland, Morris
Goldsmith Foundation, Horace
W.
Good Samaritan
Goodrich Co., The B.F.
Gordon/Rousmaniere/Roberts
Fund
Graham Fund, Philip L.
Grand Rapids Label Co.
Great-West Life Assurance Co.
Green Foundation, Allen P.
and Josephine B.
Greenwall Foundation
Gregg-Graniteville Foundation
Griffis Foundation
Griffith Foundation, W. C.
Griswold Foundation, John C.
Groome Beatty Trust, Helen D.
Grundy Foundation
GSM Industrial
Guardian Life Insurance
Company of America
Gulf Power Co.
Guttman Foundation, Stella
and Charles
Haas, Jr. Fund, Evelyn and
Walter
Habig Foundation, Arnold F.
Hachar Charitable Trust, D. D.
Hafif Family Foundation
Hagedorn Fund
Haigh-Scatena Foundation
Haley Foundation, W. B.
Halff Foundation, G. A. C.
Hallett Charitable Trust, E. W.

Hallett Charitable Trust, Jessie
F.
Hamilton Bank
Hamman Foundation, George
and Mary Josephine
Hammer Foundation, Armand
Hancock Foundation, Luke B.
Handy and Harman Foundation
Hanes Foundation, John W.
and Anna H.
Hanover Foundation
Harcourt Foundation, Ellen
Knowles
Harcourt General, Inc.
Hardin Foundation, Phil
Harland Charitable
Foundation, John and
Wilhelmina D.
Harmon Foundation, Pearl M.
and Julia J.
Harriman Foundation, Gladys
and Roland
Harriman Foundation, Mary W.
Harrington Foundation,
Francis A. and Jacquelyn H.
Harrison Foundation, Fred G.
Harsco Corp.
Hartford Foundation, John A.
Hartmarx Corporation
Harvey Foundation, Felix
Hasbro Inc.
Hatch Charitable Trust,
Margaret Milliken
Hawkins Foundation, Robert Z.
Hawn Foundation
Hazen Foundation, Edward W.
HCA Foundation
Hearst Foundation, William
Randolph
Hebrew Technical Institute
Hechinger Co.
Heckscher Foundation for
Children
Hedco Foundation
Heginbotham Trust, Will E.
Heinz Company, H. J.
Heinz Endowment, Howard
Heinz Endowment, Vira I.
Heinz Trust, Drue
Heller Financial, Inc.
Helms Foundation
Henry Foundation, Patrick
Hermann Foundation, Grover
Herrick Foundation
Herzstein Charitable
Foundation, Albert and Ethel
Heublein Inc.
Hewit Family Foundation
Hewlett Foundation, William
and Flora
Hewlett-Packard Co.
Heydt Fund, Nan and Matilda
Hickory Tech Corp.
Higginson Trust, Corina
High Foundation
Hill Foundation, Sandy
Hillcrest Foundation
Hillman Foundation
Hillsdale Fund
Hino Diesel Trucks (U.S.A.)
Hoag Family Foundation,
George
Hobby Foundation
Hoffman Foundation,
Maximilian E. and Marion O.
Homeland Foundation
Hook Drugs
Hoover Foundation
Hoover Fund-Trust, W. Henry
Hopkins Foundation,
Josephine Lawrence
Hopwood Charitable Trust,
John M.
Houchens Foundation, Ervin G.
Housatonic Curtain Co.
Houston Endowment
Houston Industries
Incorporated
Howard and Bush Foundation
Howe and Mitchell B. Howe
Foundation, Lucille Horton
Hoyt Foundation
Hoyt Foundation, Stewart W.
and Willma C.
Hudson-Webber Foundation

Huisking Foundation
Hulbert Foundation, Nila B.
Hulme Charitable Foundation,
Milton G.
Hultquist Foundation
Humana, Inc.
Hunt Charitable Trust, C. Giles
Hunt Foundation
Hunt Foundation, Roy A.
Hunt Foundation, Samuel P.
Huston Charitable Trust,
Stewart
Huston Foundation
Huthsteiner Fine Arts Trust
Hyde and Watson Foundation
Hygeia Dairy Co.
IBP, Inc.
Icahn Foundation, Carl C.
IES Industries, Inc.
Illinois Consolidated
Telephone Co.
Illinois Tool Works, Inc.
Imperial Bancorp
Ingalls Foundation, Louise H.
and David S.
Inland Container Corp.
International Business
Machines Corp.
International Paper Co.
Irvine Foundation, James
Irwin Charity Foundation,
William G.
ITT Hartford Insurance Group,
Inc.
Ittleson Foundation
Jackson Foundation
Jacobson Foundation, Bernard
H. and Blanche E.
Jaffe Foundation
James River Corp. of Virginia
Jameson Foundation, J. W. and
Ida M.
Janesville Foundation
Jarson-Stanley and Mickey
Kaplan Foundation, Isaac
and Esther
Jaydor Corp.
JELD-WEN, Inc.
Jennings Foundation, Mary
Hillman
Jewett Foundation, George
Frederick
Jewish Healthcare Foundation
of Pittsburgh
JFM Foundation
JM Foundation
Jockey Hollow Foundation
John Hancock Mutual Life
Insurance Co.
Johnson Controls Inc.
Johnson Foundation, Helen K.
and Arthur E.
Johnson Foundation, M. G.
and Lillie A.
Johnson Foundation, Willard
T. C.
Johnson & Higgins
Johnson & Son, S.C.
Jones Foundation, Daisy
Marquis
Jones Foundation, Fletcher
Jones Foundation, Harvey and
Bernice
Jones Foundation, Helen
Jonsson Foundation
Jordan Charitable Foundation,
Mary Ranken Jordan and
Ettie A.
Joslin-Needham Family
Foundation
Jostens, Inc.
Journal-Gazette Co.
Joy Family Foundation
Julia R. and Estelle L.
Foundation
Jurzykowski Foundation,
Alfred
Justus Trust, Edith C.
Kansas City Southern
Industries
Kantzler Foundation
Kaplun Foundation, Morris J.
and Betty
Kaufmann Foundation, Henry

Kavanagh Foundation, T.
James
Kayser Foundation
Kelley and Elza Kelley
Foundation, Edward Bangs
Kelly Foundation, T. Lloyd
Kelly Tractor Co.
Kempner Fund, Harris and
Eliza
Kennecott Corporation
Kennedy Foundation, Ethel
Kent-Lucas Foundation
Kerr Foundation
Kettering Fund
Kiewit Foundation, Peter
Kilcawley Fund, William H.
Kilroy Foundation, William S.
and Lora Jean
Kimball Foundation, Horace
A. Kimball and S. Ella
Kimberly-Clark Corp.
Kingsbury Corp.
Kiplinger Foundation
Kirbo Charitable Trust,
Thomas M. and Irene B.
Kirby Foundation, F. M.
Kirkpatrick Foundation
Kline Foundation, Josiah W.
and Bessie H.
Klipstein Foundation, Ernest
Christian
Klock and Lucia Klock
Kingston Foundation, Jay E.
Kmart Corporation
KN Energy, Inc.
Knapp Foundation
Knight Foundation, John S.
and James L.
Knoll Group
Knox, Sr., and Pearl Wallis
Knox Charitable
Foundation, Robert W.
Knudsen Foundation, Tom and
Valley
Koehler Foundation, Marcia
and Otto
Kohn-Joseloff Foundation
Komes Foundation
Koopman Fund
Kreitler Foundation
Kresge Foundation
Kuehn Foundation
Kunkel Foundation, John Crain
Kutz Foundation, Milton and
Hattie
Kuyper Foundation, Peter H.
and E. Lucille
La-Z-Boy Chair Co.
Ladd Charitable Corporation,
Helen and George
Laffey-McHugh Foundation
Lang Foundation, Eugene M.
Larsen Fund
Lasdon Foundation
Lasdon Foundation, William
and Mildred
Lattner Foundation, Forrest C.
Lauder Foundation
Laurel Foundation
Lazarus Charitable Trust,
Helen and Charles
LBJ Family Foundation
Leavey Foundation, Thomas
and Dorothy
Lederer Foundation, Francis L.
Lee Endowment Foundation
Lee Enterprises
LEF Foundation
Lehigh Portland Cement Co.
Lehmann Foundation, Otto W.
Leidy Foundation, John J.
Lenna Foundation, Reginald
A. and Elizabeth S.
Lennon Foundation, Fred A.
Leuthold Foundation
Levy Foundation, June
Rockwell
Liberman Foundation, Bertha
and Isaac
Life Insurance Co. of Georgia
Link, Jr. Foundation, George
Linn-Henley Charitable Trust
Lipton, Thomas J.
Little, Inc., Arthur D.
Liz Claiborne, Inc.

Lockhart Vaughan Foundation
Loews Corporation
Long Foundation, J.M.
Long Island Lighting Co.
Longwood Foundation
Louisiana-Pacific Corp.
Love Foundation, George H.
and Margaret McClintic
Lovett Foundation
Lowenstein Foundation, Leon
Lurie Foundation, Louis R.
Lux Foundation, Miranda
Lydall, Inc.
Lyon Foundation
M/A-COM, Inc.
MacCurdy Salisbury
Educational Foundation
MacLeod Stewardship
Foundation
Macy & Co., Inc., R.H.
Maddox Foundation, J. F.
Madison Gas & Electric Co.
Magowan Family Foundation
Mahadh Foundation
Mailman Family Foundation,
A. L.
Mailman Foundation
Management Compensation
Group/Dulworth Inc.
Mandeville Foundation
Maneely Fund
Marbrook Foundation
Mardag Foundation
Mardigian Foundation
Margoes Foundation
Maritz Inc.
Markey Charitable Fund, John
C.
Marmot Foundation
Marriott Foundation, J. Willard
Mars Foundation
Marshall Foundation, Mattie H.
Marshall Trust in Memory of
Sanders McDaniel, Harriet
McDaniel
Martin Marietta Corp.
Martin Marietta Materials
Martini Foundation, Nicholas
Marx Foundation, Virginia and
Leonard
Mascoma Savings Bank
Massengill-DeFriece
Foundation
Mather Charitable Trust, S.
Livingston
Mather Fund, Richard
Mather and William Gwinn
Mather Fund, Elizabeth Ring
Mathis-Pfohl Foundation
Mattel, Inc.
Matthies Foundation, Katharine
Mautz Paint Co.
May Department Stores
Company, The
May Foundation, Wilbur
Mayer Foundation, James and
Eva
Mayor Foundation, Oliver
Dewey
Maytag Family Foundation,
Fred
MBIA Inc.
MCA Inc.
McCann Foundation
McCasland Foundation
McCormick & Co. Inc.
McCormick Trust, Anne
McCune Charitable
Foundation, Marshall and
Perrine D.
McCune Charitable Trust,
John R.
McDermott Foundation,
Eugene
McDonald & Company
Securities, Inc.
McDonnell Douglas
Corp.-West
McElroy Trust, R. J.
McEvoy Foundation, Mildred
H.
McFawn Trust No. 2, Lois
Sisler
McFeely-Rogers Foundation
McGee Foundation

McGonagle Foundation,
Dextra Baldwin
MCI Communications Corp.
McInerny Foundation
McKenna Foundation,
Katherine Mabis
McKenna Foundation, Philip
M.
McLean Contributionship
McMahon Foundation
McMillan Foundation, D. W.
McQueen Foundation, Adeline
and George
M.E. Foundation
Mead Corporation, The
Meadows Foundation
Mellon Family Foundation, R.
K.
Mellon Foundation, Richard
King
Memton Fund
Mengle Foundation, Glenn and
Ruth
Merck & Co.
Merck & Co. Human Health
Division
Merck Family Fund
Mercury Aircraft
Merkley Charitable Trust
Merrick Foundation
Merrill Lynch & Co., Inc.
Messing Family Charitable
Foundation
Metropolitan Life Insurance
Co.
Meyer Family Foundation,
Paul J.
Meyer Memorial Trust
Mid-Iowa Health Foundation
Middendorf Foundation
Millbrook Tribute Garden
Miller Charitable Foundation,
Howard E. and Nell E.
Miller Foundation
Miller Fund, Kathryn and
Gilbert
Miller-Mellor Association
Mills Fund, Frances Goll
Mine Safety Appliances Co.
Mingenback Foundation, Julia
J.
Minnesota Mining & Mfg. Co.
Mitchell Energy &
Development Corp.
Mitsubishi International Corp.
Mitsubishi Motor Sales of
America, Inc.
Mobil Oil Corp.
Mohasco Corp.
Monadnock Paper Mills
Monell Foundation, Ambrose
Monfort Family Foundation
Montana Power Co.
Moore Charitable Foundation,
Marjorie
Moore Foundation, Edward S.
Morgan & Company, J.P.
Morgan Construction Co.
Morgan Foundation, Burton D.
Morgan and Samuel Tate
Morgan, Jr. Foundation,
Marietta McNeil
Morgan Stanley & Co., Inc.
Morris Foundation, Margaret T.
Morris Foundation, William T.
Morrison Knudsen Corporation
Mosbacher, Jr. Foundation,
Emil
Mosinee Paper Corp.
Mott Foundation, Charles
Stewart
Mott Fund, Ruth
Muchnic Foundation
Mulcahy Foundation
Mulford Foundation, Vincent
Mulford Trust, Clarence E.
Mullen Foundation, J. K.
Muller Foundation
Munger Foundation, Alfred C.
Munson Foundation Trust, W.
B.
Murdock Charitable Trust, M.
J.
Murphey Foundation, Lluella
Morey

Murphy Co. Foundation, G.C.
Murphy Foundation
Musson Charitable
Foundation, R. C. and
Katharine M.
Myra Foundation
Nabisco Foods Group
Nalco Chemical Co.
National Gypsum Co.
National Steel Corp.
National Westminster Bank
New Jersey
NBD Indiana, Inc.
Nesholm Family Foundation
Nestle USA Inc.
Neuberger Foundation, Roy R.
and Marie S.
New-Land Foundation
New York Life Insurance Co.
New York Mercantile Exchange
New York Stock Exchange, Inc.
New York Times Company
The New Yorker Magazine, Inc.
Newman's Own, Inc.
NewMil Bancorp
Nias Foundation, Henry
Noble Foundation, Edward
John
Noble Foundation, Samuel
Roberts
Norgren Foundation, Carl A.
Norman Foundation, Summers
A.
Normandie Foundation
North Shore Foundation
Northern States Power Co.
(Minnesota)
Northwest Natural Gas Co.
Norton Co.
Norton Foundation Inc.
Norton Memorial Corporation,
Geraldi
Norwest Bank Nebraska, N.A.
Oaklawn Foundation
O'Connor Foundation, A.
Lindsay and Olive B.
OCRI Foundation
Odell Fund, Robert Stewart
Odell and Helen Pfeiffer
O'Fallon Trust, Martin J. and
Mary Anne
Offield Family Foundation
OG&E Electric Services
Ohrstrom Foundation
Old Dominion Box Co.
Old National Bank in
Evansville
Olin Corp.
Olin Foundation, Spencer T.
and Ann W.
Oliver Memorial Trust
Foundation
Olsson Memorial Foundation,
Elis
Oppenstein Brothers
Foundation
O'Quinn Foundation, John M.
and Nancy C.
Ore-Ida Foods, Inc.
Osborn Charitable Trust,
Edward B.
Osher Foundation, Bernard
Ottley Trust-Watertown,
Marion W.
Overbrook Foundation
Overlake Foundation
Owen Industries, Inc.
Owsley Foundation, Alvin and
Lucy
Pacific Mutual Life Insurance
Co.
Pacific Telesis Group
Packaging Corporation of
America
Packard Foundation, David
and Lucile
PaineWebber
Paley Foundation, William S.
Palisades Educational
Foundation
Palmer Fund, Frank Loomis
Pamida, Inc.
Parker Hannifin Corp.
Parshelsky Foundation, Moses
L.

Parsons Foundation, Ralph M.
Patterson Charitable Fund, W.
I.
Payne Foundation, Frank E.
and Seba B.
Peabody Charitable Fund,
Amelia
Pella Corporation
Penn Foundation, William
Pennsylvania Dutch Co.
Pennzoil Co.
Peoples Energy Corp.
Peppers Foundation, Ann
Perkin-Elmer Corp.
Peters Foundation, Charles F.
Peterson Foundation, Hal and
Charlie
Pew Charitable Trusts
Pfizer, Inc.
Phelps Dodge Corporation
PHH Corporation
Philibosian Foundation,
Stephen
Phillips Charitable Trust, Dr.
and Mrs. Arthur William
Phillips Family Foundation,
Jay and Rose
Phillips Family Foundation, L.
E.
Phipps Foundation, Howard
Piankova Foundation, Tatiana
Pick, Jr. Fund, Albert
Pickford Foundation, Mary
Pierce Charitable Trust, Harold
Whitworth
Pineywoods Foundation
Pioneer Trust Bank, NA
Piper Foundation, Minnie
Stevens
Piper Jaffray Companies Inc.
Pitt-Des Moines Inc.
Pittsburg Midway Coal Mining
Co.
Pittsburgh Child Guidance
Foundation
Plankenhorn Foundation, Harry
Playboy Enterprises, Inc.
Plumsock Fund
PNC Bank, N.A.
Pollock Company Foundation,
William B.
Porter Foundation, Mrs.
Cheever
Porter Testamentary Trust,
James Hyde
Potomac Electric Power Co.
Pott Foundation, Herman T.
and Phenie R.
Potter Foundation, Justin and
Valere
PPG Industries, Inc.
Prairie Foundation
Premier Industrial Corp.
Price Associates, T. Rowe
Price Foundation, Louis and
Harold
Price Foundation, Lucien B.
and Katherine E.
Priddy Foundation
PriMerit Bank
Prince Trust, Abbie Norman
Proctor Trust, Mortimer R.
Prouty Foundation, Olive
Higgins
Providence Gas Co.
Providence Journal Company
Provident Life & Accident
Insurance Company of
America
Providian Corporation
Prudential Insurance Co. of
America, The
Prudential Securities, Inc.
Public Service Co. of New
Mexico
Public Service Electric & Gas
Co.
Public Welfare Foundation
Pulitzer Publishing Co.
Puterbaugh Foundation
Putnam Foundation
Quaker Chemical Corp.
Quivey-Bay State Foundation
Rabb Foundation, Harry W.
Ralston Purina Co.

Rand McNally & Co.
R&B Machine Tool Co.
Ratner Foundation, Milton M.
Raymond Corp.
Read Foundation, Charles L.
Regenstein Foundation
Reichhold Chemicals, Inc.
Reidler Foundation
Reinberger Foundation
Rennebohm Foundation, Oscar
Republic NY Corp.
Reynolds Foundation, Donald
W.
Reynolds Foundation, Edgar
Rhone-Poulenc Inc.
Rice Charitable Foundation,
Albert W.
Rice Foundation
Rich Products Corporation
Richardson Benevolent
Foundation, C. E.
Richardson Charitable Trust,
Anne S.
Rieke Corp.
Riggs Benevolent Fund
Ringier-America
Ritter Charitable Trust, George
W. and Mary F.
Rixson Foundation, Oscar C.
RJR Nabisco Inc.
Robinson-Broadhurst
Foundation
Rockefeller Fund, David
Rockwell Fund
Rockwell International
Corporation
Rogers Family Foundation
Rohatyn Foundation, Felix and
Elizabeth
Rohm & Haas Co.
Rose Foundation, Billy
Roseburg Forest Products Co.
Rosen Foundation, Joseph
Rose's Stores, Inc.
Ross Laboratories
Ross Memorial Foundation,
Will
Rouse Co.
Royal Foundation, May
Mitchell
Royal Group, Inc.
Ruan Foundation Trust, John
Rubin Family Fund, Cele H.
and William B.
Rubinstein Foundation, Helena
Rudin Foundation
Russell Charitable Foundation,
Tom
Russell Trust, Josephine G.
Ryan Foundation, David
Claude
SAFECO Corp.
Safety Fund National Bank
Saint Paul Companies, Inc.
Salomon Inc.
Saltonstall Charitable
Foundation, Richard
San Diego Gas & Electric
Sandusky International Inc.
Sandy Hill Foundation
Santa Fe Pacific Corporation
Sara Lee Corp.
Sara Lee Hosiery, Inc.
Sargent Foundation, Newell B.
Sarkeys Foundation
Sasco Foundation
Sawyer Charitable Foundation
SBC Communications Inc.
Scaife Family Foundation
Schenck Fund, L. P.
Scherer Foundation, Karla
Schering-Plough Corp.
Scherman Foundation
Schiff Foundation, Dorothy
Schiro Fund
Schlumberger Ltd.
Schoenleber Foundation
Scholl Foundation, Dr.
Schroeder Foundation, Walter
Schuller International
Schumann Fund for New
Jersey
Schwab & Co., Inc., Charles
Schwartz Foundation, Arnold
A.

Schwartz Fund for Education and Health Research, Arnold and Marie
Schwob Foundation, Simon
Scott Fetzer Co.
Scott Foundation, Walter
Scott Foundation, William E.
Scurlock Foundation
Seafirst Corporation
Seagram & Sons, Inc., Joseph E.
Seaver Institute
Seaway Food Town, Inc.
Second Foundation
Security Life of Denver Insurance Co.
Seidman Family Foundation
Selby and Marie Selby Foundation, William G.
Self Foundation
Semmes Foundation
Seneca Foods Corp.
Sentry Insurance A Mutual Company
Sequoia Foundation
Seton Leather Co.
Share Trust, Charles Morton
Sharon Steel Corp.
Shaw Foundation, Arch W.
Shawmut National Corp.
Sheaffer Inc.
Shell Oil Company
Shenandoah Life Insurance Co.
Sheppard Foundation, Lawrence B.
Sierra Pacific Industries
Sierra Pacific Resources
Simon Foundation, William E. and Carol G.
Simpson Investment Company
Skillman Foundation
Slemp Foundation
Slifka Foundation, Joseph and Sylvia
Smeal Foundation, Mary Jean and Frank P.
Smith Charitable Foundation, Clara Blackford Smith and W. Aubrey
Smith Charitable Foundation, Lou and Lutza
Smith Corp., A.O.
Smith Foundation, Gordon V. and Helen C.
Smith Foundation, Ralph L.
Smith, Jr. Foundation, M. W.
Smith Memorial Fund, Ethel Sergeant Clark
Smith Trust, May and Stanley
SmithKline Beecham Corp.
Snayberger Memorial Foundation, Harry E. and Florence W.
Snow Foundation, John Ben
Snow Memorial Trust, John Ben
Snyder Foundation, Harold B. and Dorothy A.

Solow Foundation
Sonat Inc.
Sordoni Foundation
South Bend Tribune
South Waite Foundation
Southern California Edison Co.
Southern New England Telephone Company
Southwestern Electric Power Co.
Spang & Co.
Sprague Educational and Charitable Foundation, Seth
Springs Foundation
SPX Corp.
Square D Co.
Stabler Foundation, Donald B. and Dorothy L.
Stackpole-Hall Foundation
Stanley Charitable Foundation, A.W.
Stanley Works
Stans Foundation
Starr Foundation
Stauffer Charitable Trust, John
Stauffer Foundation, John and Beverly
Staunton Farm Foundation
Stearns Trust, Artemas W.
Steele Foundation, Harry and Grace
Steele-Reese Foundation
Stein Foundation, Jules and Doris
Steinhagen Benevolent Trust, B. A. and Elinor
Steinman Foundation, James Hale
Steinman Foundation, John Frederick
Stemmons Foundation
Sternberger Foundation, Tannenbaum
Stevens Foundation, Abbot and Dorothy H.
Stevens Foundation, John T.
Stokely, Jr. Foundation, William B.
Stone Charitable Foundation
Stone Trust, H. Chase
Strauss Foundation, Leon
Strong Foundation, Hattie M.
Stupp Foundation, Norman J.
Sturgis Charitable and Educational Trust, Roy and Christine
Subaru of America Inc.
Sulzberger Foundation
Sumitomo Bank of California
Sumners Foundation, Hatton W.
Sundet Foundation
Sunnen Foundation
Superior Tube Co.
Swalm Foundation
Swanson Family Foundation, Dr. W.C.
Swift Co. Inc., John S.

Swiss Bank Corp.
Taconic Foundation
Tait Foundation, Frank M.
Taube Family Foundation
Taubman Foundation, A. Alfred
Taylor Foundation, Fred and Harriett
Taylor Foundation, Ruth and Vernon
Teagle Foundation
Tecumseh Products Co.
Teichert & Son, A.
Teleflex Inc.
Temple Foundation, T. L. L.
Temple-Inland Inc.
Tenneco Inc.
Tetley, Inc.
Teubert Charitable Trust, James H. and Alice
Texaco Inc.
Texas Commerce Bank-Houston, N.A.
Textron, Inc.
Thalhimer and Family Foundation, Charles G.
Thomas Foundation, Joan and Lee
Thomas Industries
Thomasville Furniture Industries
Thompson Co., J. Walter
Thompson Trust, Thomas
Thorne Foundation
Thornton Foundation
Times Mirror Company, The
Timken Foundation of Canton
Tiscornia Foundation
Titus Foundation, Roy and Niuta
Tobin Foundation
Todd Co., A.M.
Toms Foundation
Tonya Memorial Foundation
Towsley Foundation, Harry A. and Margaret D.
Tozer Foundation
TransAmerica Corporation
Transco Energy Co.
Travelers Inc.
Treakle Foundation, J. Edwin
Trexler Trust, Harry C.
Truland Foundation
Trull Foundation
Trust Company Bank
Trust Funds
Tuch Foundation, Michael
Tucker Charitable Trust, Rose E.
Tupancy-Harris Foundation of 1986
Turner Charitable Foundation
Turrell Fund
Unilever United States, Inc.
Union Bank
Union Camp Corporation
Union Electric Co.
Union Pacific Corp.
United Airlines, Inc.

U.S. Bank of Washington
Unitrode Corp.
Unocal Corp.
Upjohn Foundation, Harold and Grace
Upton Foundation, Frederick S.
Uris Brothers Foundation
US WEST, Inc.
USG Corporation
USL Capital Corporation
USX Corporation
Utica National Insurance Group
Valmont Industries, Inc.
van Ameringen Foundation
Van Every Foundation, Philip L.
Van Houten Memorial Fund
Van Nuys Foundation, I. N. and Susanna H.
Van Wert County Foundation
Vance Charitable Foundation, Robert C.
Vanderbilt Trust, R. T.
Vernon Fund, Miles Hodsdon
Vicksburg Foundation
Vogler Foundation, Laura B.
Vollbrecht Foundation, Frederick A.
Vulcan Materials Co.
Wachovia Bank of North Carolina, N.A.
Wahlstrom Foundation
Wal-Mart Stores, Inc.
Wallace Foundation, George R.
Wallace-Reader's Digest Fund, DeWitt
Walsh Foundation
Warner Fund, Albert and Bessie
Warwick Foundation
Washington Forrest Foundation
Washington Mutual Savings Bank
Washington Water Power Co.
Wean Foundation, Raymond John
Weaver Foundation, Gil and Dody
Webber Oil Co.
Weber Charities Corp., Frederick E.
Weckbaugh Foundation, Eleanore Mullen
Weezie Foundation
Wege Foundation
Weil, Gotshal and Manges Foundation
Weingart Foundation
Weinstein Foundation, J.
Welfare Foundation
Wells Foundation, Franklin H. and Ruth L.
Wendt Foundation, Margaret L.
Wertheim Foundation, Dr. Herbert A.
West Foundation, Harry and Ethel

West One Bancorp
Westerman Foundation, Samuel L.
Western New York Foundation
Westvaco Corporation
Weyerhaeuser Co.
Wheat First Butcher Singer, Inc.
Wheeler Foundation
Wheeler Foundation, Wilmot
Whirlpool Corporation
White Trust, G. R.
Whitecap Foundation
Whiting Foundation
Whitney Fund, David M.
Whittenberger Foundation, Claude R. and Ethel B.
Wickes Foundation, Harvey Randall
Wickson-Link Memorial Foundation
WICOR, Inc.
Widgeon Foundation
Wiegand Foundation, E. L.
Wiggins Memorial Trust, J. J.
Wildermuth Foundation, E. F.
Willard Helping Fund, Cecilia Young
Williams Charitable Trust, John C.
Williams Charitable Trust, Mary Jo
Williams Companies, The
Wilmington Trust Co.
Wilson Fund, Matilda R.
Windham Foundation
Winnebago Industries, Inc.
Winthrop Trust, Clara B.
Wiremold Co.
Wisconsin Power & Light Co.
Wisconsin Public Service Corp.
Wise Foundation and Charitable Trust, Watson W.
Witco Corp.
Wood Foundation of Chambersburg, PA
Woodward Fund
Woolley Foundation, Vasser
Wright Foundation, Lola
Wyman Youth Trust
Wyomissing Foundation
Y and H Soda Foundation
Yeager Charitable Trust, Lester E.
Young Foundation, Hugo H. and Mabel B.
Young Foundation, Irvin L.
Young Foundation, Robert R.
Zachry Co., H.B.
Zarrow Foundation, Anne and Henry
Zenkel Foundation
Zollner Foundation

Index to Grant Recipients by State

Please refer to the Master Index to Corporations and Foundations for profile page numbers.

Ryan Foundation, David Claude

Chronic Fatigue Immune Disfunction Syndrome Fund ($12,500) see Pettus Crowe Foundation

Church Divinity School ($5,000) see Murphey Foundation, Lluella Morey

Cities-in-Schools ($10,000) see Chartwell Foundation

Citizens for Betterment of Community ($5,000) see West Foundation, Harry and Ethel

City of Anderson, Parks and Recreation Department — instructional and wading pools ($100,000) see McConnell Foundation

City of Daly City — for maintenance and improvement of recreational facilities, equipment, and senior center operating funds ($10,000) see Gellert Foundation, Carl

City of Hope ($25,000) see Chartwell Foundation

City of Hope ($50,000) see Hoag Family Foundation, George

City of Hope ($3,000) see Murphey Foundation, Lluella Morey

City of Hope — over five years for a new doctors' wing, part of a $200-million capital improvement program ($1,000,000) see Parsons Foundation, Ralph M.

City of Hope ($25,000) see Parvin Foundation, Albert

City of Hope ($25,000) see Strauss Foundation, Leon

City of Hope — to support medical services for children without insurance ($510,000) see Weingart Foundation

City of Hope ($100,000) see Stanley Works

City of Hope ($8,000) see USG Corporation

City of Hope ($6,500) see USG Corporation

City of Hope ($2,000) see Altschul Foundation

City of Hope ($10,000) see Reicher Foundation, Anne and Harry J.

City of Hope ($7,500) see Thomasville Furniture Industries

Claremont Graduate School — support the American/Chinese program ($51,316) see Durfee Foundation

Claremont Graduate School — Hispanic gang study ($42,216) see Haynes Foundation, John Randolph and Dora

Claremont Graduate School ($250,000) see Humana, Inc.

Claremont Graduate School and University Center — computer upgrade, final payment ($250,000) see Jones Foundation, Fletcher

Claremont Graduate School and University Center — endowed Hollis P. Allen Chair ($214,000) see Jones Foundation, Fletcher

Claremont Institute — teacher seminars ($175,000) see Salvatori Foundation, Henry

Claremont McKenna College — endowment fund ($2,751,625) see Berger Foundation, H. N. and Frances C.

Claremont McKenna College ($10,000) see Golden West Foundation

Claremont McKenna College ($25,000) see Pickford Foundation, Mary

Claremont McKenna College ($10,000) see Strauss Foundation, Leon

Claremont McKenna College ($100,000) see Olin Foundation, Spencer T. and Ann W.

Claremont McKenna College — Phillip M. McKenna Professorship pledge ($500,000) see McKenna Foundation, Philip M.

Claremont McKenna College — DCM Achievement Awards pledge ($335,000) see McKenna Foundation, Philip M.

Coalition on Homelessness ($10,000) see Friedman Family Foundation

Coleman Advocates for Children and Youth ($10,000) see Friedman Family Foundation

Coleman Chamber Music Association ($7,500) see Scott Foundation, Virginia Steele

College of Notre Dame — for financial aid to students ($10,000) see Gellert Foundation, Carl

College of Notre Dame — for financial aid for deserving students ($12,500) see Gellert Foundation, Celia Berta

College of the Redwoods ($1,750) see Sierra Pacific Industries

College of the Siskiyou — membership ($48,000) see McConnell Foundation

College of the Siskiyous — for computers ($580,936) see Roseburg Forest Products Co.

College of the Siskiyous — for theater improvements ($198,500) see Roseburg Forest Products Co.

Columbia Park Boys Club ($53,300) see Campini Foundation, Frank A.

Commonweal ($15,000) see Bothin Foundation

Commonweal ($25,000) see Hancock Foundation, Luke B.

Community Church of Palm Springs ($15,500) see Philibosian Foundation, Stephen

Community Development Institute ($10,000) see Friedman Family Foundation

Community Foundation of Santa Clara County — for grant to the Silicon Valley Arts Fund ($500,000) see Packard Foundation, David and Lucile

Community Housing Partnership ($125,000) see Cowell Foundation, S. H.

Community of Mindful Living — operating support ($10,000) see Hunt Foundation

Community School of Music and Arts — expand chamber music ensemble opportunities and scholarship assistance for music school students ($26,890) see Heller Charitable Foundation, Clarence E.

Community Television of Southern California — to support LIFE and TIMES ($500,000) see Irvine Foundation, James

Community Trust Fund of VL/SFV ($30,000) see AMR Corp.

Concern America — medical and health training in Honduras ($30,000) see International Foundation

Congregation B'nai Sholom ($5,000) see Geifman Family Foundation

Congregation Emanu-El — a second grant of $250,000 over five years ($100,000) see Columbia Foundation

Congregation Emanu-El ($100,000) see Haas, Jr. Fund, Evelyn and Walter

Constitutional Rights Foundation ($26,500) see Robinson Fund, Maurice R.

Corcoran Scholarship Committee — individual scholarship at Corcoran High School ($169,447) see Boswell Foundation, James G.

Cornerstone Theater ($5,000) see Lea Foundation, Helen Sperry

CORO Foundation ($10,000) see USL Capital Corporation

Costume Council of LACMA — Doris Stein Research and Design Center for Costumes and Textiles ($56,200) see Stein Foundation, Jules and Doris

Coyote Point Museum — for educational program for 1994 ($5,000) see Gellert Foundation, Celia Berta

Crescenta-Canada Family YMCA ($3,000) see Murphey Foundation, Lluella Morey

Criminal Justice Legal Foundation ($5,000) see Boswell Foundation, James G.

Crisis Pregnancy Services — for anti-abortion counseling ($10,000) see Trust Funds

Cuesta College Foundation ($38,500) see Hoag Family Foundation, George

Cultural Heritage Foundation of Southern California ($25,000) see Knudsen Foundation, Tom and Valley

Curtis School ($20,000) see Seaver Charitable Trust, Richard C.

Danish Lutheran Church Relocation Committee ($100,000) see Knudsen Foundation, Tom and Valley

Daughters of Mary and Joseph ($250,000) see Leavey Foundation, Thomas and Dorothy

Davis Science Center — Explorit ($3,000) see Teichert & Son, A.

Deep Springs College — scholarship fund ($5,000) see Darling Foundation, Hugh and Hazel

Descanso Gardens Guild ($10,000) see Golden West Foundation

Descanso Gardens Guild ($2,500) see Scott Foundation, Virginia Steele

Desert Hospital Foundation — health ($60,000) see Nabisco Foods Group

Development Studies Center — to expand the Child Development Study ($500,000) see Hewlett

Foundation, William and Flora

Developmental Studies Center ($85,436) see Rosenberg, Jr. Family Foundation, Louise and Claude

Diffa — Heart Strings ($2,500) see Teichert & Son, A.

Doheny Eye Institute ($112,500) see Argyros Foundation

Doheny Eye Institute ($5,500) see Munger Foundation, Alfred C.

Doheny Eye Institute ($10,000) see Seaver Charitable Trust, Richard C.

Dolores Street Community Center ($15,000) see Bothin Foundation

Dominican College of San Rafael — upgrade three residence halls ($150,000) see Irwin Charity Foundation, William G.

Eagle Forum Education and Legal Defense Fund — essay competition ($100,000) see Salvatori Foundation, Henry

East Bay Center for the Performing Arts ($8,000) see LEF Foundation

East Bay Funders — to help East Oakland neighborhood residents develop their capacity to solve problems in their communities ($50,000) see Clorox Co.

East Los Angeles Community Union Education Foundation ($100,000) see Southern California Edison Co.

East Oakland Youth Development Center/Foundation — for the interim executive director position, general operating support, grant writing, and the Summer Youth Program ($85,000) see Clorox Co.

Elementary Institute of Science — for capacity building ($35,000) see Jacobs Family Foundation

Energy Foundation — in support of general operations over three years ($13,500,000) see MacArthur Foundation, John D. and Catherine T.

English Language Institute of China ($5,000) see MacLeod Stewardship Foundation

English Language Institute of China ($5,000) see Fruehauf Foundation

English Language Institute of China — recruit, train, and send professional Christian teachers to China to teach English ($30,000) see Huston Foundation

English Language Institute of China — general support ($20,000) see Huston Foundation

Enterprise for High School Students — to support their collaborative apprenticeship program ($18,249) see Lux Foundation, Miranda

Entertainment Industry — general ($30,000) see MCA Inc.

Environmental Traveling Companions — for social rehabilitation ($5,000) see Gamble Foundation

Episcopal Community Services of San Francisco ($25,000) see Odell Fund, Robert Stewart Odell and Helen Pfeiffer

Episcopal Sanctuary ($30,000) see Osher Foundation, Bernard

Episcopal School of Theology ($35,000) see Jameson Foundation, J. W. and Ida M.

ETI Institute — support for the Search for Extraterrestrial Intelligence Program ($1,000,000) see Packard Foundation, David and Lucile

Executive Service Corps of Southern California ($37,500) see McDonnell Douglas Corp.-West

Expenses Water District — solar installation project ($43,654) see McConnell Foundation

Exploratorium ($25,000) see Odell Fund, Robert Stewart Odell and Helen Pfeiffer

Falkirk Cultural Center ($10,000) see Fireman's Fund Insurance Co.

Family School ($10,000) see Friedman Family Foundation

Family Service Agency of San Francisco ($125,000) see Cowell Foundation, S. H.

Family Violence Prevention Fund — to fund a national prevention and public awareness advertising campaign entitled, "There's No Excuse for Domestic Violence" ($68,000) see Whirlpool Corporation

Fellows of the Huntington Library ($4,100) see Golden West Foundation

Fellowship Academy — support to acquire property and buildings for school programs serving low-income and minority students and to endow the Future Leaders Scholarship program ($18,000) see Margoes Foundation

Fellowship Academy — support to acquire property and buildings for school programs serving low-income and minority students and to endow the Future Leaders Scholarship program ($14,000) see Margoes Foundation

Film Acquisition Fund ($50,079) see Cabot Family Charitable Trust

Film Arts Foundation, San Francisco — to support new community partnership over two years with the National Asian American Telecommunications Association, Cine Accion, and Frameline ($10,000) see Fleishhacker Foundation

Fine Arts Museums Foundation — third and final year of a $45,000 grant to support the permanent installation of portions of the Teotihuacan murals from Mexico ($20,000) see Fleishhacker Foundation

Fine Arts Museums of San Francisco ($15,000) see Magowan Family Foundation

Fine Arts Museums of San Francisco ($13,000) see USL Capital Corporation

Fisheries Foundation of California ($6,000) see West Foundation, Harry and Ethel

Food Bank for Monterey County ($5,000) see McMahan Foundation, Catherine L. and Robert O.

FoodBank of Southern California ($32,500) see

McDonnell Douglas Corp.-West Foothill Country Day School ($10,000) see Van Nuys Foundation, I. N. and Susanna H.

Foothill Theater Company ($6,000) see Ghidotti Foundation

Ft. Mason Center — to renovate the World Music Showcase; $250,000 over five years ($50,000) see Columbia Foundation

Ft. Mason Center ($25,000) see Hancock Foundation, Luke B.

Foundation for Books to China — for educational purposes ($3,500) see Gamble Foundation

Foundation for the Junior Blind — toward the capital campaign for renovation and new facility construction ($500,000) see Ahmanson Foundation

Foundation for the Retarded Children of the Desert — transportation/vehicle ($25,000) see Dreyfus Foundation, Max and Victoria

Foundation for San Francisco's Architectural Heritage ($15,000) see Davis Foundation, Edwin W. and Catherine M.

Foundation for Technology Access — for general operating support ($79,000) see Mattel, Inc.

Freewheelers Association — for continuance and expansion ($10,000) see Gellert Foundation, Carl

French Foundation ($5,000) see Femino Foundation

French Foundation for Alzheimers Research — general support ($5,000) see Imperial Bancorp

Fresno Unified School District — education center ($25,000) see Long Foundation, J.M.

Friends of Child Advocates ($30,000) see AMR Corp.

Friends of Claremont Public Library ($10,000) see Hafif Family Foundation

Friends of Huntington Library ($2,000) see Howe and Mitchell B. Howe Foundation, Lucille Horton

Friends of Julia Singer Center ($1,000) see Parvin Foundation, Albert

Friends of Le Chambon ($50,000) see Amado Foundation, Maurice

Fromm Institute for Lifelong Learning ($10,000) see Meyer Fund, Milton and Sophie

Fulfillment Fund— for children's programs ($15,000) see Davis Foundation, Edwin W. and Catherine M.

Fulfillment Fund — children's program ($15,000) see Davis Foundation, Edwin W. and Catherine M.

Fuller Graduate School of Psychology ($30,000) see Sequoia Foundation

Fuller Graduate School of Psychology ($30,000) see Sequoia Foundation

Fund for Pediatric Care and Research — general budget ($6,000) see Smith Trust, May and Stanley

Garces Memorial High School ($7,000) see West Foundation, Harry and Ethel

Gay Men's Health Crisis ($25,000) see Gap, Inc., The

Gene Autry Western Heritage Museum ($50,000) see Pickford Foundation, Mary

Glide Memorial Foundation — food program ($50,000) see TransAmerica Corporation

Glide Memorial Foundation — 30th anniversary celebration ($25,000) see TransAmerica Corporation

Global Fund for Women ($25,044) see Cabot Family Charitable Trust

Global Fund for Women — to support specific programs focusing on women's economic autonomy in Brazil ($40,000) see Jurzykowski Foundation, Alfred

Good Samaritan Family Resource Center ($25,000) see Gap, Inc., The

Good Shepard Lutheran Church ($5,000) see Griswold Foundation, John C.

Good Shepard Lutheran School ($10,000) see Griswold Foundation, John C.

Good Shepherd Foundation ($5,000) see Arkelian Foundation, Ben H. and Gladys

Good Shepherd Home ($100,000) see Hedco Foundation

Good Shepherd School ($20,000) see Jameson Foundation, J. W. and Ida M.

Goodwill Industries — partial support of the acquisition of 1500 Mission Street building to expand vocational training and rehabilitation services for people with physical and mental disabilities ($20,000) see Margoes Foundation

Grace Cathedral ($19,650) see Magowan Family Foundation

Grace Cathedral ($50,000) see Skaggs Foundation, L. J. and Mary C.

Grass Valley School District ($12,500) see Ghidotti Foundation

Green Hotel Restoration ($5,000) see Arkelian Foundation, Ben H. and Gladys

Gregorian University Foundation ($25,000) see Landegger Charitable Foundation

Grovemont Theater ($5,000) see McMahan Foundation, Catherine L. and Robert O.

Guide Dogs for the Blind — seeing eye dog training ($2,500) see Sargent Foundation, Newell B.

Happy Valley School ($31,200) see Kern Foundation Trust

Harvard-Westlake School ($720) see Munger Foundation, Alfred C.

Harvard Westlake School ($10,000) see Seaver Charitable Trust, Richard C.

Harvard-Westlake School ($50,000) see Thornton Foundation

Harvard-Westlake School ($20,000) see May Foundation, Wilbur

Harvey Mudd College ($20,000) see Knudsen Foundation, Tom and Valley

Harvey Mudd College — renovation of chemistry lab in Jacobs science center ($50,000) see Stauffer Charitable Trust, John

Harvey Mudd College ($15,000) see Thornton Foundation

Harvey Mudd College — science building construction ($1,051,500) see Olin Foundation, F. W.

Haven — Stanislaus women's refuge center ($8,000) see Bright Family Foundation

Hayfork Volunteer Fire Department ($5,000) see Sierra Pacific Industries

H.C.S.F. Foundation ($8,000) see Brenner Foundation, Mervyn

Healing Kidz — to support various vocational programs ($17,500) see Lux Foundation, Miranda

Hebrew Union College Jewish Institute of Religion — toward furnishing and equipping the Ahmanson Resource Center at the Cultural Center for American Jewish Life ($500,000) see Ahmanson Foundation

Helen Woodward Animal Center ($10,000) see Stauffer Foundation, John and Beverly

Henry E. Huntington Library and Art Gallery ($20,000) see Jameson Foundation, J. W. and Ida M.

Henry E. Huntington Library and Art Gallery — Fletcher Jones Chair, first payment ($500,000) see Jones Foundation, Fletcher

Henry E. Huntington Library and Art Gallery ($2,247,500) see Scott Foundation, Virginia Steele

Henry E. Huntington Library and Art Gallery — toward seventy-fifth anniversary observances ($50,000) see Times Mirror Company, The

Henry E. Huntington Library and Art Gallery ($13,584) see Van Nuys Foundation, I. N. and Susanna H.

Hereditary Disease Foundation ($10,000) see Bay Foundation

Higher Education Policy Institute — core support ($1,200,000) see Irvine Foundation, James

Highland Foundation —for partial funding of the executive director's position ($25,000) see Clorox Co.

Hoag Hospital Foundation ($1,710,000) see Hoag Family Foundation, George

Hollenbeck Police Department ($3,000) see Murphey Foundation, Lluella Morey

Holy Family Day Home — for support of the salary and benefits costs of full-time social worker ($6,500) see Gellert Foundation, Celia Berta

Holy Names College —for the Holy Names Performing Arts Theatre ($25,000) see Clorox Co.

Home Start — for Family Ties program ($30,000) see Jacobs Family Foundation

Homemaker Service of Pasadena ($4,000) see Howe

and Mitchell B. Howe Foundation, Lucille Horton

Honnold Mudd Library — support joint information exchange agreement with UCLA in collaboration with Caltech and Cal Poly ($20,000) see Smith Foundation, Ralph L.

Hoover Institution on War, Revolution, and Peace — Russian archives microfilming ($75,000) see Hoover, Jr. Foundation, Margaret W. and Herbert

Hoover Institution on War, Revolution, and Peace ($104,167) see Donner Foundation, William H.

Hoover Institution on War, Revolution, and Peace ($250,000) see Monell Foundation, Ambrose

Hoover Institution of War, Revolution, and Peace — for educational purposes ($100,000) see Henry Foundation, Patrick

Hospice Program ($200) see Munger Foundation, Alfred C.

Hospital of the Good Samaritan ($50,000) see Essick Foundation

Hospital of the Good Samaritan ($250,075) see Munger Foundation, Alfred C.

Hospital of the Good Samaritan ($339,593) see Van Nuys Foundation, I. N. and Susanna H.

Hospitalier Foundation St. John of God ($5,725) see Stauffer Foundation, John and Beverly

House Ear Institute — development of binaural hearing aid ($51,879) see Hoover, Jr. Foundation, Margaret W. and Herbert

House Ear Institute — general support ($5,000) see Imperial Bancorp

Housing Options for People to Excel — for general operating support ($36,000) see Mattel, Inc.

Humanist Association of Los Angeles — publicize humanism on college campuses ($25,000) see Johnson Charitable Educational Trust, James Hervey

Huntington ($34,377) see Munger Foundation, Alfred C.

Huntington Library — endow the R. Stanton Avery Chair ($100,000) see Durfee Foundation

Huntington Library ($2,000) see Femino Foundation

Huntington Library — cataloging papers of Kenneth Hahn ($28,131) see Haynes Foundation, John Randolph and Dora

Huntington Library — Henry E. Endowment ($250,000) see Munger Foundation, Alfred C.

Huntington Library ($2,000) see Stans Foundation

Huntington Library and Art Gallery ($25,000) see Essick Foundation

Huntington Library and Art Gallery ($15,000) see Knudsen Foundation, Tom and Valley

Huntington Library, Gardens and Art Gallery — for an integrated security and fire

protection system ($1,000,000) see Parsons Foundation, Ralph M.

Huntington Medical Research Institute — research in arteriosclerosis ($41,000) see Hoover, Jr. Foundation, Margaret W. and Herbert

Huntington Medical Research Institute ($50,000) see Jameson Foundation, J. W. and Ida M.

Huntington Medical Research Institutes ($76,000) see Howe and Mitchell B. Howe Foundation, Lucille Horton

Huntington Memorial Hospital ($29,519) see Golden West Foundation

Huntington Memorial Hospital — "Physicians and the Aging Network: A Chronic Care Partnership" ($269,788) see Hartford Foundation, John A.

Immaculate Conception Academy — for endowment fund ($10,000) see Gellert Foundation, Celia Berta

Immaculate Conception Academy ($25,000) see Odell Fund, Robert Stewart Odell and Helen Pfeiffer

Immigrant Legal Resource Center — immigrant children's projects ($106,000) see Rosenberg Foundation

Independence Center — general fund ($20,000) see Lund Foundation

Independent Colleges of Southern California ($23,000) see Pacific Mutual Life Insurance Co.

Independent Colleges of Southern California — for scholarships and fellowships ($40,000) see Unocal Corp.

Inner-City Arts ($100,000) see Taper Foundation, Mark

Institute for Civil Justice ($50,000) see Continental Corp.

Institute for Journalism Education — second payment toward pledge of $125,000, to support core programs in management training and advancement for minorities in journalism ($75,000) see Graham Fund, Philip L.

Institute for Journalism Education ($25,000) see Dow Jones & Company, Inc.

Institute for Sustainable Forestry ($20,000) see Crocker Trust, Mary A.

Interaid ($25,000) see Landegger Charitable Foundation

International Documentary Foundation ($3,000) see Hillman Family Foundation, Alex

International Society for Ecology and Culture ($10,000) see Normandie Foundation

Israel Emergency Fund ($140,000) see Price Foundation, Louis and Harold

Jewish Community Federation — Operation Exodus ($50,000) see Lurie Foundation, Louis R.

Jewish Community Federation ($45,974) see Meyer Fund, Milton and Sophie

Jewish Community Federation ($110,250) see Taube Family Foundation

Paradise Valley Hospital — for Healthy Beginnings Parent Education program ($30,000) see Jacobs Family Foundation

Pasadena City College Foundation — purchase of computer, softwares, and computer-related materials ($118,500) see Berger Foundation, H. N. and Frances C.

Pasadena City College Foundation ($8,000) see Howe and Mitchell B. Howe Foundation, Lucille Horton

Pasadena Enterprise Center — for entrepreneurial technical assistance and one-on-one counseling ($30,000) see Jacobs Family Foundation

Pasadena Historical Society ($7,500) see Stauffer Foundation, John and Beverly

Pasadena Library ($25,000) see Peppers Foundation, Ann

Pasadena Neighborhood Housing Service — for Bilingual Coordinator, NEC program ($35,000) see Jacobs Family Foundation

Pasadena Symphony ($2,000) see Stans Foundation

Pasadena Symphony Association ($9,635) see Golden West Foundation

Pasadena Symphony Association ($3,000) see Howe and Mitchell B. Howe Foundation, Lucille Horton

Pasadena Symphony Association ($10,000) see Scott Foundation, Virginia Steele

Pasadena Unified School District ($15,000) see Knudsen Foundation, Tom and Valley

Pathfinder International ($25,044) see Cabot Family Charitable Trust

Paulist Productions ($165,667) see Leavey Foundation, Thomas and Dorothy

Pediatric AIDS Foundation ($78,000) see Johnson Foundation, Willard T. C.

Pediatric AIDS Foundation see New York Mercantile Exchange

Pediatric AIDS Foundation ($15,000) see PaineWebber

Peninsula Center for Blind and Visually Impaired ($1,500) see Taube Family Foundation

Peninsula Center for Blind and Visually Impaired ($1,025) see Taube Family Foundation

Peninsula Symphony ($5,000) see Y and H Soda Foundation

People Reaching Out ($3,000) see Teichert & Son, A.

Pepperdine University — endowment fund ($250,000) see Darling Foundation, Hugh and Hazel

Pepperdine University — for Ann Peppers Scholarship Fund ($17,500) see Peppers Foundation, Ann

Pepperdine University ($250,000) see Thornton Foundation, Flora L.

Petaluma Wildlife and National Science Museum ($25,000) see Crocker Trust, Mary A.

P.F. Bresee Foundation ($29,300) see Whitecap Foundation

Phoenix House of California — charitable ($250,000) see Bettingen Corporation, Burton G.

Pilgrim Place — to provide additional funding for the Davis Health Endowment ($200,000) see Davis Foundations, Arthur Vining

Pitzer College ($20,000) see Avery Arts Foundation, Milton and Sally

Planned Parenthood of Los Angeles — world population ($75,000) see Munger Foundation, Alfred C.

Planned Parenthood of Los Angeles ($10,000) see Jonsson Foundation

Planned Parenthood of San Francisco ($40,000) see Osher Foundation, Bernard

Planned Parenthood/World Population — Emerson Electric stock; general support ($294,975) see Steele Foundation, Harry and Grace

Point Loma College ($30,000) see Ryan Foundation, David Claude

Points of Light/Volunteer Centers ($30,000) see Hancock Foundation, Luke B.

Police Athletic League ($25,000) see Chase Manhattan Bank, N.A.

Polytechnic School — remodeling of James G Boswell library ($50,000) see Boswell Foundation, James G.

Polytechnic School ($10,500) see Golden West Foundation

Pomona College ($5,000) see Hafif Family Foundation

Popper-Keizer Advanced School ($122,587) see Burchfield Foundation, Charles E.

Prentice Day School ($20,000) see Hoag Family Foundation, George

Project Angel Food — general support ($5,000) see Imperial Bancorp

Project Open Hand ($5,701) see American President Companies, Ltd.

Project Open Hand ($30,000) see Gilmore Foundation, William G.

Project Open Hand ($15,000) see TransAmerica Corporation

Public Counsel — charitable ($200,000) see Bettingen Corporation, Burton G.

Puente Learning Center — for general operating support ($50,000) see Mattel, Inc.

Puente Learning Center — over two years to construct a state-of-the-art learning center in East Los Angeles ($250,000) see Parsons Foundation, Ralph M.

Puente Learning Center ($30,000) see Whitecap Foundation

Puente Project — over four and one-half years to support a program of mentoring, counseling, and writing instruction to improve the high school graduation and college-going rates of Mexican-American and Latino students from 18 high schools in California ($2,050,000) see Wallace-Reader's Digest Fund, DeWitt

Queen of Angels Hospital - Hollywood Presbyterian Foundation — purchase three cardiac monitors for

the emergency department ($50,000) see Stauffer Charitable Trust, John

Queen of the Valley Hospital Foundation ($30,000) see Gilmore Foundation, William G.

R.D. Colburn School of Performing Arts — for expansion of the need based scholarship program for beginning music students ($25,000) see Heller Charitable Foundation, Clarence E.

Reality House West — for social rehabilitation ($5,000) see Gamble Foundation

Reason Foundation ($25,000) see Jameson Foundation, J. W. and Ida M.

Reason Foundation — for educational studies program ($1,000) see Lake Placid Education Foundation

Rebuild Los Angeles ($500,000) see Marriott Foundation, J. Willard

Recreation Center for the Handicapped — for children's afterschool program ($15,000) see Gellert Foundation, Carl

Red Cross ($50,000) see Gap, Inc., The

Redwood City School District ($400,000) see Cowell Foundation, S. H.

Redwood Coast Jazz Festival ($2,000) see Sierra Pacific Industries

Remedial Reading and Learning Center — for software, staff, and volunteer training ($8,000) see Peppers Foundation, Ann

Renaissance Technical Training Institute — for Student Opportunity and Resource program ($17,500) see Lux Foundation, Miranda

Research Libraries Group — for general support of research and development for Research Libraries Information Network ($500,000) see Hewlett Foundation, William and Flora

Resource Renewal Institute — for research and public education on Green Plans ($40,000) see Heller Charitable Foundation, Clarence E.

Richard Nixon Library and Birthplace ($30,000) see Simon Foundation, William E. and Carol G.

Rio Hondo Boys and Girls Club ($10,000) see Strauss Foundation, Leon

Riordan Foundation ($26,000) see Union Camp Corporation

Robert Louis Stevenson School ($25,000) see McMahan Foundation, Catherine L. and Robert O.

Ronald Reagan Presidential Foundation — toward research, educational forums, and publications on domestic issues, final payment of a two-year grant ($50,000) see JM Foundation

Ronald Reagan Presidential Foundation — Presidential Library Education ($30,000) see Barry Corp., R. G.

Ronald Reagan Presidential Library — interactive computer ($250,000) see Salvatori Foundation, Henry

Rudolf Steiner College ($2,500) see Teichert & Son, A.

Rural Community Assistance Corporation — San Diego Farmworker Housing project ($109,250) see Rosenberg Foundation

RX for Reading — Riordan Foundation ($13,000) see Blount, Inc.

RX for Reading ($93,750) see Hasbro Inc.

Sacramento Life Center — for anti-abortion counseling ($15,528) see Trust Funds

Sacramento Neighborhood Housing Services ($2,500) see Teichert & Son, A.

Sacramento Public Library ($10,000) see Teichert & Son, A.

Sacramento Symphony Association ($5,000) see Teichert & Son, A.

St. Anthony Foundation ($100,000) see Odell Fund, Robert Stewart Odell and Helen Pfeiffer

St. Anthony's School — for counselor ($8,000) see Trust Funds

St. Elizabeth Youth Employment ($10,000) see Friedman Family Foundation

St. Francis Hospital ($25,000) see Ensign-Bickford Industries

St. Francis Hospital ($10,000) see New England Business Service

St. Francis Hospital Foundation ($25,000) see Bothin Foundation

St. Ignatius College Preparatory — for the science wing expansion ($10,000) see Gellert Foundation, Celia Berta

St. Ignatius College Preparatory — capital campaign ($300,000) see Irwin Charity Foundation, William G.

St. Ignatius College Preparatory — theatrical equipment ($100,000) see Wiegand Foundation, E. L.

St. John's Hospital — purchase of a computerized patient monitoring system ($50,000) see Stauffer Charitable Trust, John

St. Joseph Hospital — oncology equipment ($106,000) see Wiegand Foundation, E. L.

St. Margaret's Church ($20,500) see Philibosian Foundation, Stephen

St. Marys College — for Carl Gellert Memorial Scholarship Fund ($10,000) see Gellert Foundation, Carl

St. Marys College — to fund scholarships for undergraduate students ($10,000) see Gellert Foundation, Celia Berta

St. Mary's College — toward the cost of a comprehensive program to become a more effective multicultural academic community ($500,000) see Irvine Foundation, James

St. Mary's College ($12,500) see Y and H Soda Foundation

St. Mary's College — science equipment ($97,000) see Wiegand Foundation, E. L.

Salesian Boys and Girls Club ($27,500) see Whitecap Foundation

Salesian Boys and Girls Club ($5,000) see Y and H Soda Foundation

Salk Institute — support AIDS research and gene therapy programs ($250,000) see Berger Foundation, H. N. and Frances C.

Salk Institute ($5,000) see Femino Foundation

Salk Institute — AIDS research ($25,000) see Alexander Foundation, Joseph

Salk Institute ($150,000) see Harriman Foundation, Gladys and Roland

Salk Institute — to establish centers for theoretical neurobiology ($1,387,453) see Sloan Foundation, Alfred P.

Salk Institute for Biological Studies ($25,000) see Schlink Foundation, Albert G. and Olive H.

Salk Institute for Biological Studies — plant cell biology project ($619,148) see Noble Foundation, Samuel Roberts

Salk Institute for Biological Studies — plant cell biology fellowships ($178,333) see Noble Foundation, Samuel Roberts

Salvation Army ($5,000) see Arkelian Foundation, Ben H. and Gladys

Salvation Army — charitable ($150,000) see Bettingen Corporation, Burton G.

Salvation Army ($25,000) see Hancock Foundation, Luke B.

Salvation Army ($25,000) see Hoag Family Foundation, George

Salvation Army — Los Angels earthquake relief ($50,000) see Middendorf Foundation

Salvation Army of the Bay Area ($25,000) see TransAmerica Corporation

Salvation Army Harbor Lights ($12,000) see Campini Foundation, Frank A.

San Diego Community Foundation ($215,000) see Dr. Seuss Foundation

San Diego Council on Literacy ($6,500) see Dr. Seuss Foundation

San Diego Hospice ($7,500) see Dr. Seuss Foundation

San Diego Innovative Preschool Project — to support an early childhood education and social service program for preschool children from low-income families ($416,813) see Weingart Foundation

San Diego Museum of Art ($7,000) see Dr. Seuss Foundation

San Diego National Sports Training Foundation ($300,000) see Copley Press, Inc.

San Diego Rescue Mission ($25,000) see Copley Press, Inc.

San Diego Rescue Mission ($69,667) see Ryan Foundation, David Claude

San Diego State University Project Primer ($9,220) see Dr. Seuss Foundation

San Domenico School Foundation — funding for a modular classroom building ($70,000) see Irwin Charity Foundation, William G.

($12,174) see Goldwyn
Foundation, Samuel

University of California
Regents ($11,000) see
Brenner Foundation, Mervyn

University of California
Regents — for an initiative
to develop sound public
policy options designed to
prevent the damaging public
health effects of pesticide
use an air pollution
($200,000) see Heller
Charitable Foundation,
Clarence E.

University of California
Regents — Dr. Michael
Strober research ($8,000)
see Strauss Foundation, Leon

University of California
Regents — for employee
scholarship ($6,000) see
Quaker Chemical Corp.

University of California
Riverside ($16,667) see
Wilson Foundation, H. W.

University of California San
Francisco — establish the
laboratory for the study of
cancer in women ($150,000)
see Irwin Charity
Foundation, William G.

University of California San
Francisco ($110,000) see
Long Foundation, J.M.

University of California San
Francisco ($30,000) see
Lurie Foundation, Louis R.

University of California San
Francisco — That Man May
See ($20,000) see
TransAmerica Corporation

University of California San
Francisco — degenerative
diseases research ($450,000)
see Fairchild Foundation,
Sherman

University of California San
Francisco — to establish
centers for theoretical
neurobiology ($1,518,530)
see Sloan Foundation, Alfred
P.

University of California San
Francisco Cancer Research
($15,000) see Campini
Foundation, Frank A.

University of California San
Francisco Foundation
($9,500) see Brenner
Foundation, Mervyn

University of California San
Francisco Neurology
Fellowship ($55,000) see
Osher Foundation, Bernard

University of California San
Francisco Pediatric
Oncology Clinical Research
($20,000) see Campini
Foundation, Frank A.

University of California San
Francisco Pediatric
Oncology Research
($20,000) see Campini
Foundation, Frank A.

University of California San
Francisco Pediatric
Oncology Research
($15,000) see Campini
Foundation, Frank A.

University of California Santa
Barbara — religious and
public life in Los Angeles
($92,289) see Haynes
Foundation, John Randolph
and Dora

University of California Santa
Cruz — J.M. Long marine
lab ($200,000) see Long
Foundation, J.M.

University of California
School of Medicine —
pediatric oncology ($5,000)
see Broadhurst Foundation

University of the Pacific —
chair in Entrepreneurship,
final payment ($463,182)
see Jones Foundation,
Fletcher

University of Pacific
($300,000) see Long
Foundation, J.M.

University of Pacific —
conference facility ($53,000)
see Long Foundation, J.M.

University of the Pacific — to
establish the Ralph M.
Parsons Student Revolving
Loan Fund ($225,000) see
Parsons Foundation, Ralph
M.

University of Pacific Friends
of Art Department — for
educational purposes
($5,000) see Gamble
Foundation

University of the Pacific
School of Business and
Public Administration — for
funding to upgrade and
enhance computer resources
($30,000) see Kemper
National Insurance Cos.

University of Redlands —
toward construction of the
University Center
($750,000) see Irvine
Foundation, James

University of Redlands —
chair in American Politics,
final payment ($451,825)
see Jones Foundation,
Fletcher

University of Redlands
($25,000) see Knudsen
Foundation, Tom and Valley

University of Redlands — for
equipment and professor for
Ann Peppers Art Center
($22,600) see Peppers
Foundation, Ann

University of San Diego —
chair in Biology, first
payment ($500,000) see
Jones Foundation, Fletcher

University of San Diego
Center for Public Interest
Law — to support Children's
Advocacy Program and to
enable the employment of a
fund raising director
($470,000) see Weingart
Foundation

University of San Francisco —
for unrestricted use
($15,000) see Gellert
Foundation, Carl

University of San Francisco —
chair in Biology, first
payment ($500,000) see
Jones Foundation, Fletcher

University of San Francisco
($1,000) see Taube Family
Foundation

University of San Francisco —
to purchase IAV, A-V, and
CAI equipment ($64,622)
see Fuld Health Trust,
Helene

University of Southern
California ($200,000) see
BankAmerica Corp.

University of Southern
California — endowment
fund ($125,000) see Darling
Foundation, Hugh and Hazel

University of Southern
California ($27,500) see
Femino Foundation

University of Southern
California ($3,250) see
Hanover Foundation

University of Southern
California — study of
residential overcrowding
($32,173) see Haynes
Foundation, John Randolph
and Dora

University of Southern
California — crime in small
business community in
central Los Angeles
($31,184) see Haynes
Foundation, John Randolph
and Dora

University of Southern
California — library
cataloging of Historical
Society Photography
Collection ($25,459) see
Haynes Foundation, John
Randolph and Dora

University of Southern
California —for electrical
and computer engineering
($817,683) see
Hewlett-Packard Co.

University of Southern
California — for the James
Irvine Foundation Center for
Scholarly Technology
($1,000,000) see Irvine
Foundation, James

University of Southern
California ($55,000) see
Long Foundation, J.M.

University of Southern
California — remainder of
grant made as an
endowment, income of
which underwrites the
international symposia held
by the Loker Hydrocarbon
Research Institute
($500,000) see Stauffer
Charitable Trust, John

University of Southern
California ($15,500) see
Georgia-Pacific Corporation

University of Southern
California ($9,302) see
Helms Foundation

University of Southern
California — "Criminal
Violence and Mental Illness
in a Birth Cohort" ($34,951)
see Guggenheim
Foundation, Harry Frank

University of Southern
California ($4,829,167) see
Annenberg Foundation

University of Southern
California Department of
Nursing ($629,340) see
Leavey Foundation, Thomas
and Dorothy

University of Southern
California Kenneth Norris,
Jr., Cancer Center
($200,000) see Thornton
Foundation, Flora L.

University of Southern
California Library —
scripter ($20,000) see
Femino Foundation

University of Southern
California Norris Cancer
Center — toward the Cancer
Pharmacology Laboratory
Suite in the new Research
Tower of the Kenneth
Norris, Jr. Comprehensive
Cancer Center ($1,000,000)
see Ahmanson Foundation

University of Southern
California School of
Business Administration —
to endow Babcock Chair in
Finance ($50,000) see Times
Mirror Company, The

University of Southern
California School of
Dentists ($10,000) see
Femino Foundation

University of Southern
California School of
Gerontology ($55,000) see
Pickford Foundation, Mary

University of Southern
California School of
Medicine ($5,000) see
Femino Foundation

University of Southern
California School of
Medicine — research in
diabetic induced corneal
changes ($38,200) see
Hoover, Jr. Foundation,
Margaret W. and Herbert

University of Southern
California School of
Medicine ($33,334) see
Ryan Foundation, David
Claude

University of Southern
California School of
Pharmacy — online method
to assess chemotherapeutic
response in real time
($36,490) see Hoover, Jr.
Foundation, Margaret W.
and Herbert

University of Southern
California School of Public
Administration — hospital
trends ($25,195) see Haynes
Foundation, John Randolph
and Dora

US Committee for UNICEF
($25,000) see Chartwell
Foundation

US Ski Team — education
($3,500) see Blum
Foundation, Harry and
Maribel G.

Venice Family Clinic
($15,000) see Goldwyn
Foundation, Samuel

Visionary Inner-City
Partnership ($10,000) see
Van Nuys Foundation, I. N.
and Susanna H.

Volunteer Action Center of
Nevada County ($3,500) see
Ghidotti Foundation

Volunteers of America
($35,000) see McDonnell
Douglas Corp.-West

Walter A. Haas School of
Business ($15,000) see
Argyros Foundation

Walter A. Hass School of
Business ($105,000) see
Witter Foundation, Dean

Walter A. Hass School of
Business ($105,000) see
Witter Foundation, Dean

Wellness Community ($6,000)
see Markey Charitable Fund,
John C.

Western Cardiac Foundation
($50,000) see May
Foundation, Wilbur

Westmont College — Weingart
Foundation Student Loan
Program ($334,407) see
Weingart Foundation

Whittier College — Whittier
science equipment fund
($50,000) see Stauffer
Charitable Trust, John

Wildlife Associates
Conservation Earth — for
educational purposes
($5,000) see Gamble
Foundation

World Research International
— video for classrooms
($1,000) see Pennsylvania
Dutch Co.

World Vision ($31,597) see
Hedco Foundation

World Vision ($3,250) see
MacLeod Stewardship
Foundation

World Vision — medical and
eye surgery and education in
Vietnam ($25,000) see
International Foundation

World Vision — health and
gardening training in
Mauritania ($25,000) see
International Foundation

World Vision International
($10,000) see Ryan
Foundation, David Claude

YMCA ($3,000) see Hanover
Foundation

YMCA ($25,000) see Einstein
Fund, Albert E. and Birdie
W.

YMCA of Kern County
($5,088) see West
Foundation, Harry and Ethel

YMCA of San Diego County
($106,000) see Copley
Press, Inc.

Yosemite Fund ($30,000) see
Long Foundation, J.M.

Yours for Life Ministries
($10,000) see Norgren
Foundation, Carl A.

Youth Development Center
($22,500) see Hancock
Foundation, Luke B.

YWCA ($10,000) see
McMahan Foundation,
Catherine L. and Robert O.

YWCA of San Gabriel Valley
— replacement and
redecorating costs for Wings
Shelter ($124,000) see
Berger Foundation, H. N.
and Frances C.

Zoological Society ($7,500)
see Stauffer Foundation,
John and Beverly

Zoological Society of San
Diego ($19,650) see Dr.
Seuss Foundation

Colorado

Adult Learning Source
($20,000) see JFM
Foundation

Adult Learning Source
($10,000) see Weckbaugh
Foundation, Eleanore Mullen

Allied Jewish Federation
($25,000) see Rabb
Foundation, Harry W.

AMC Cancer Research Center
($5,000) see Duncan Trust,
John G.

American Diabetes
Association ($10,000) see
Fishback Foundation Trust,
Harmes C.

American Indian Science and
Engineering Society —
chemical engineering
scholarship see Nalco
Chemical Co.

American Indian Science and
Engineering Society
($40,125) see Santa Fe
Pacific Corporation

American Lung Association
($5,000) see Schuller
International

American Wildlands ($50,000)
see Carolyn Foundation

Anderson Ranch Arts Center
($6,436) see Adler
Foundation Trust, Philip D.
and Henrietta B.

Anti-Defamation League of
B'nai B'rith ($2,500) see
Rabb Foundation, Harry W.

Arapaho House — advocacy
case management
($130,634) see Johnson
Foundation, Helen K. and
Arthur E.

Arapahoe Library Foundation
($8,000) see Norgren
Foundation, Carl A.

Area Church ($1,550) see
Joslin-Needham Family
Foundation

Arvada Center for the Arts and
Humanities ($5,000) see
Duncan Trust, John G.

Aspen Art Museum ($20,000)
see Kuyper Foundation,
Peter H. and E. Lucille

Aspen Country Dy School
($17,000) see Kuyper

Foundation, Peter H. and E. Lucille

Aspen Foundation ($24,000) see Dingman Foundation, Michael D.

Aspen Foundation ($16,000) see Duncan Foundation, Lillian H. and C. W.

Aspen Institute ($50,000) see Continental Corp.

Aspen/Snowmass Council for the Arts ($10,000) see Kuyper Foundation, Peter H. and E. Lucille

Assistance League of Colorado Springs — Operation School bell program ($7,500) see Stone Trust, H. Chase

Augusta Lutheran Church ($10,000) see Comprecare Foundation

Bayaud Industries ($10,000) see Mullen Foundation, J. K.

Bent County Nursing Service ($10,800) see Comprecare Foundation

Beth Israel at Shalom Park — pledge ($125,000) see Phillips Family Foundation, Jay and Rose

Boy Scouts of America Denver Area Council ($10,000) see Hewit Family Foundation

Boy Scouts of America Denver Area Council ($4,600) see Norgren Foundation, Carl A.

Boys and Girls Club of Metro Denver ($5,000) see Hewit Family Foundation

Boys and Girls Club of Metro Denver — special campaign ($10,000) see O'Fallon Trust, Martin J. and Mary Anne

Boys and Girls Clubs of Metro Denver — remodeling, expansion, and modernization of facilities ($300,000) see Coors Foundation, Adolph

Boys and Girls Clubs of Metro Denver ($200,000) see Gates Foundation

Boys and Girls Clubs of Metro Denver ($200,000) see Gates Foundation

Breckenridge Outdoor Education Center ($32,700) see Scott Foundation, Walter

Brush High School ($2,000) see Joslin-Needham Family Foundation

Brush High School ($2,000) see Joslin-Needham Family Foundation

Business of Art Center — operating expenses ($5,000) see Stone Trust, H. Chase

Busy Hands Preschool — for computer and program ($3,500) see Heginbotham Trust, Will E.

Capuchin Mission Association ($10,000) see Weckbaugh Foundation, Eleanore Mullen

Cenikor Foundation ($100,000) see Johnson Foundation, Helen K. and Arthur E.

Cenikor Foundation ($5,000) see Schuller International

Central City Opera House Association ($15,000) see Weckbaugh Foundation, Eleanore Mullen

Charter Fund ($38,000) see JFM Foundation

Cheetah Preservation Fund ($12,000) see Bay Foundation

Cheyenne Mountain Zoo — for general operating support ($250,000) see El Pomar Foundation

Children's Cancer Center see Piper Jaffray Companies Inc.

Children's Diabetes Foundation —to further programs of care and research on behalf of those afflicted with diabetes ($25,000) see Hanson Industries North America

Children's Diabetes Foundation — to further programs of care and research on behalf of those afflicted with diabetes ($25,000) see Hanson Industries North America

Children's Diabetes Foundation at Denver ($50,000) see Blum-Kovler Foundation

Children's Hospital ($20,000) see Mullen Foundation, J. K.

Children's Hospital Foundation ($6,000) see Norgren Foundation, Carl A.

Children's Hospital Foundation ($10,000) see Banta Corp.

Children's Hospital, Red Wagon Club ($10,000) see Hewit Family Foundation

Choices — therapeutic program ($25,000) see Monfort Family Foundation

Christian Living Campus — expansion project ($250,000) see Johnson Foundation, Helen K. and Arthur E.

Church of the Risen Christ ($10,000) see Weckbaugh Foundation, Eleanore Mullen

City of Brush ($13,564) see Joslin-Needham Family Foundation

City of Brush ($10,000) see Petteys Memorial Foundation, Jack

City of Colorado Springs Drug Abuse Awareness Program — for drug prevention program presented to local fifth and sixth grade students ($12,500) see Stone Trust, H. Chase

City of Grant Junction — economic development ($7,500) see Bacon Foundation, E. L. and Oma

City of Holyoke — for swimming pool roof ($15,000) see Heginbotham Trust, Will E.

City of Wray — volunteer fire department first responder equipment ($6,507) see Kitzmiller/Bales Trust

City of Wray — museum bison antiques project ($4,000) see Kitzmiller/Bales Trust

Coalition of Essential Schools ($100,000) see Gates Foundation

Colorado 4-H Youth Fund ($4,000) see Norgren Foundation, Carl A.

Colorado Action for Healthy People ($53,000) see Comprecare Foundation

Colorado AIDS Project ($3,000) see Rabb Foundation, Harry W.

Colorado College — scholarships ($455,390) see Boettcher Foundation

Colorado College — 1992 scholarships ($260,000) see El Pomar Foundation

Colorado Council on Economic Education ($25,000) see Monfort Family Foundation

Colorado Council on Economic Education

($30,000) see McKenna Foundation, Philip M.

Colorado Historical Society ($10,000) see Fishback Foundation Trust, Harmes C.

Colorado Opera Festival — 1992 production expenses ($5,000) see Stone Trust, H. Chase

Colorado Outdoor Education Center ($5,000) see Norgren Foundation, Carl A.

Colorado School of Mines ($30,000) see Phelps Dodge Corporation

Colorado School of Mines — for Borehole Technologies ($20,000) see Schlumberger Ltd.

Colorado School of Mines Foundation — for computer equipment to be used in the EPICS program ($250,000) see Parsons Foundation, Ralph M.

Colorado School of Mines Foundation — Herman F. Coors Professorial Chair in Ceramics ($141,000) see Coors Foundation, Adolph

Colorado Springs Mounted Patrol — funding for start-up costs ($5,000) see Stone Trust, H. Chase

Colorado State Fair Authority — toward indoor coliseum ($200,000) see Boettcher Foundation

Colorado State Fair Authority — construction of new indoor arena ($700,000) see Coors Foundation, Adolph

Colorado State University — for educational purposes ($500) see First National Bank

Colorado State University Foundation — for the equine teaching and research center ($150,000) see El Pomar Foundation

Colorado State University Foundation ($5,500) see Norgren Foundation, Carl A.

Colorado Symphony Association ($5,250) see Fishback Foundation Trust, Harmes C.

Colorado University Foundation for AIDS Research ($4,500) see Fishback Foundation Trust, Harmes C.

Colorado Uplift — new programs ($150,000) see Johnson Foundation, Helen K. and Arthur E.

Colorado Wildlife Heritage Foundation — Barrier-Free Wildlife Facility ($5,000) see Morrison Charitable Trust, Pauline A. and George R.

Community Hospital Foundation ($5,000) see Bacon Foundation, E. L. and Oma

Community Technical Skill Center ($10,000) see Duncan Trust, John G.

Craig Hospital Foundation — patient and family education program ($50,000) see Frueauff Foundation, Charles A.

Crow Canyon Center for Southwest Archaeology — to partially support scholarship endowment ($100,000) see Scholl Foundation, Dr.

Crystal Ball Foundation ($16,900) see Wertheim Foundation, Dr. Herbert A.

Curtis Park Community Center ($5,000) see Schuller International

Denver Academy ($10,000) see Duncan Trust, John G.

Denver Art Museum ($5,000) see Fishback Foundation Trust, Harmes C.

Denver Art Museum ($50,000) see JFM Foundation

Denver Art Museum ($10,000) see KN Energy, Inc.

Denver Art Museum — Wolf Collection of American Photography ($10,000) see Morrison Charitable Trust, Pauline A. and George R.

Denver Art Museum — for 100th year celebration ($5,000) see O'Fallon Trust, Martin J. and Mary Anne

Denver Art Museum, Center for Central American Art and Archeology ($14,874) see JFM Foundation

Denver Art Museum Foundation — endowment ($200,000) see JFM Foundation

Denver Botanic Gardens ($2,500) see Fishback Foundation Trust, Harmes C.

Denver Botanical Gardens ($800,000) see Gates Foundation

Denver Emergency Housing Coalition ($5,000) see Schuller International

Denver Inner-City Parish ($6,000) see Schuller International

Denver International Film — operating funds ($52,000) see Swanson Family Foundation, Dr. W.C.

Denver Museum of Miniatures, Dolls and Toys — for A. Schoenhut collection ($5,000) see O'Fallon Trust, Martin J. and Mary Anne

Denver Museum of Natural History — toward prehistoric journey exhibits ($350,000) see Boettcher Foundation

Denver Museum of Natural History — for support of the Paleontology exhibit ($150,000) see El Pomar Foundation

Denver Museum of Natural History ($5,000) see Fishback Foundation Trust, Harmes C.

Denver Museum of Natural History ($10,000) see Hewit Family Foundation

Denver Museum of Natural History — operations ($15,000) see Morrison Charitable Trust, Pauline A. and George R.

Denver Museum of Natural History — in support of Prehistoric Journey ($100,000) see O'Fallon Trust, Martin J. and Mary Anne

Denver Museum of Natural History — for general fund ($10,000) see Forest Oil Corp.

Denver Public Library — toward equipment for Western History Department's photo automation project ($342,000) see Boettcher Foundation

Denver Public Library ($5,000) see Hewit Family Foundation

Denver Public Library ($20,090) see Mullen Foundation, J. K.

Denver Public Library ($20,000) see Mullen Foundation, J. K.

Denver Public Library ($15,000) see Weckbaugh Foundation, Eleanore Mullen

Denver Public Library Foundation ($250,000) see Gates Foundation

Denver Rescue Mission ($5,000) see Duncan Trust, John G.

Denver Zoological Foundation — to support the primate conservation center project ($200,000) see El Pomar Foundation

Denver Zoological Foundation ($10,000) see Hewit Family Foundation

Denver Zoological Foundation ($6,500) see Mullen Foundation, J. K.

Denver Zoological Foundation ($4,500) see Norgren Foundation, Carl A.

Denver's Ocean Journey ($30,000) see Taylor Foundation, Ruth and Vernon

Dominican Sisters Home Health Agency of Denver — general support ($5,000) see O'Fallon Trust, Martin J. and Mary Anne

Doo Zoo ($5,000) see Bacon Foundation, E. L. and Oma

East Morgan County Hospital Foundation ($55,000) see Joslin-Needham Family Foundation

East Morgan County Hospital Foundation ($3,000) see Joslin-Needham Family Foundation

East Morgan County Hospital Foundation ($115,000) see Petteys Memorial Foundation, Jack

East Morgan County Library District ($27,000) see Joslin-Needham Family Foundation

East Yuma County School District RJ-2 — capital expenditures ($50,500) see Kitzmiller/Bales Trust

Eastern Colorado Services for the Developmentally Disabled ($3,000) see Petteys Memorial Foundation, Jack

Ebenezer Lutheran Care Center Foundation ($54,757) see Joslin-Needham Family Foundation

Eden Theatrical Workshop ($5,000) see Duncan Trust, John G.

Education and Civic Achievement ($5,000) see Hewit Family Foundation

Education Commission of States ($155,000) see Gates Foundation

Education Commission of States ($150,000) see Gates Foundation

Eleanor Roosevelt Institute — toward library renovation ($210,000) see Boettcher Foundation

Epilepsy Foundation of Colorado ($10,000) see Duncan Trust, John G.

First Steps ($50,000) see Monfort Family Foundation

Florence Crittenton School Human Services ($5,000) see O'Fallon Trust, Martin J. and Mary Anne

Focus on the Family — religious ($10,000) see Fruehauf Foundation

Foothills Foundation ($10,000) see Comprecare Foundation

Foundation Valley School of Colorado — for the renovation of the Froelicher academic building ($500,000) see El Pomar Foundation

Fountain Valley School — to assist replacement of trees on school campus ($5,000) see Stone Trust, H. Chase

Fountain Valley School — for construction of athletic storage facility ($5,000) see Stone Trust, H. Chase

Genesis Jobs ($15,000) see Weckbaugh Foundation, Eleanore Mullen

Girl Scouts of America Mile Hi Council ($10,000) see Hewit Family Foundation

Golden Plains Extension Service — for Baby's First Step program ($2,000) see Heginbotham Trust, Will E.

Gospel Missionary Union ($2,500) see MacLeod Stewardship Foundation

Graland Country Day School — toward campus capital campaign ($400,000) see Boettcher Foundation

Graland Country Day School — rebuild the Graland Campus to enhance delivery of quality education ($250,000) see Coors Foundation, Adolph

Graland Country Day School ($650,000) see Gates Foundation

Grand Valley Senior Daybreak ($10,600) see Comprecare Foundation

Habitat for Humanity ($5,000) see Bacon Foundation, E. L. and Oma

Haxtun RE-2J School District — for balance of new school building grant ($50,000) see Heginbotham Trust, Will E.

High Plains Easter Seal Society ($1,000) see Petteys Memorial Foundation, Jack

Historical Paramount Foundation ($5,000) see Duncan Trust, John G.

Holyoke Housing Authority — for 1993 installment payment per November 1991 grant ($40,000) see Heginbotham Trust, Will E.

Hope Communities — Elm Park townhomes ($75,000) see Johnson Foundation, Helen K. and Arthur E.

Hospice of Metro Denver ($5,000) see Rabb Foundation, Harry W.

Hospice of Peace ($5,500) see Rabb Foundation, Harry W.

Hospice of St. John ($5,000) see Rabb Foundation, Harry W.

Humane Society of Weld County — toward building of animal shelter ($101,884) see Monfort Family Foundation

Iliff School of Theology ($50,000) see Bacon Foundation, E. L. and Oma

International Wilderness Leadership Foundation ($25,000) see Hillsdale Fund

International Wilderness Leadership Society ($16,000) see Erpf Fund, Armand G.

Jefferson County Adult ESL Program ($12,500) see Weckbaugh Foundation, Eleanore Mullen

Jefferson Hall ($3,200) see Rabb Foundation, Harry W.

Jerry Ford Foundation ($3,000) see Wertheim Foundation, Dr. Herbert A.

Jewish Family Service of Colorado — older adults services department ($103,375) see Phillips Family Foundation, Jay and Rose

J.K. Mullen High School ($10,000) see Weckbaugh Foundation, Eleanore Mullen

Junior Achievement — for headquarters expansion and annex building ($800,000) see El Pomar Foundation

Junior Achievement, National — capital improvements to Colorado Springs headquarters; programs provide in-class economic education for young people ($150,000) see Coors Foundation, Adolph

Kids in Need of Dentistry ($12,000) see Comprecare Foundation

KPMA/Channel 6 ($5,000) see Hewit Family Foundation

KRMA-TV — for the learning services center ($250,000) see El Pomar Foundation

KRMA-TV ($4,000) see Petteys Memorial Foundation, Jack

KRMA-TV/Channel 6 — renovation of facility ($200,000) see Coors Foundation, Adolph

Land and Water Fund of the Rockies ($25,000) see New-Land Foundation

Latin American Educational Foundation — 1992-93 scholarship program ($5,000) see O'Fallon Trust, Martin J. and Mary Anne

Les Dames d'Aspen, Limited ($1,000) see Gershman Foundation, Joel

Lions Club see Pittsburg Midway Coal Mining Co.

March of Dimes see Pittsburg Midway Coal Mining Co.

Marillac Clinic — indigent care ($10,000) see Bacon Foundation, E. L. and Oma

Melissa Memorial Hospital — for balance of capital improvement grant ($19,000) see Heginbotham Trust, Will E.

Melissa Memorial Hospital — for partial equipment grant ($6,000) see Heginbotham Trust, Will E.

Melissa Memorial Hospital — for Rose Medical Center consultation program ($3,000) see Heginbotham Trust, Will E.

Mental Health Association of Colorado ($10,000) see Comprecare Foundation

Mesa State College — early childhood education ($5,000) see Bacon Foundation, E. L. and Oma

Mile High United Way ($12,500) see Rabb Foundation, Harry W.

Mile High United Way ($93,200) see United Airlines, Inc.

Mile High United Way ($110,000) see Martin Marietta Corp.

Morgan Community College ($2,500) see Petteys Memorial Foundation, Jack

Mt. St. Vincent Home ($6,000) see Rabb Foundation, Harry W.

Mountain States Legal Foundation ($31,250) see Taylor Foundation, Ruth and Vernon

Music Associates of Aspen — capital campaign for Aspen Meadows Phase I ($500,000) see Boettcher Foundation

Music Associates of Aspen — renovation of Castle Creek Campus; program provides training experience for gifted young musicians from all over the world ($150,000) see Coors Foundation, Adolph

Music Associates of Aspen ($25,000) see Lauder Foundation

National Council on Alcohol and Drug Abuse ($6,000) see Bacon Foundation, E. L. and Oma

National Fragile X Foundation — for research and education ($30,000) see Forest Oil Corp.

National Jewish Center for Immunological and Respiratory Medicine ($3,000) see Blum Foundation, Harry and Maribel G.

National Jewish Center for Immunology and Respiratory Medicine — fellowship program ($11,500) see Broadhurst Foundation

National Jewish Center for Imunology and Respiratory Medicine ($7,000) see Hartmarx Corporation

National Jewish Hospital Research Center ($3,000) see Read Foundation, Charles L.

National Sports Center for the Disabled ($5,000) see Norgren Foundation, Carl A.

Native American Rights Fund ($1,000) see Seidman Family Foundation

Native American Rights Fund — two-year supplement, for program and institutional development on behalf of Native Americans ($1,200,000) see Ford Foundation

Officer McGruff see Pittsburg Midway Coal Mining Co.

Peetz Plateau School District RE-5 ($3,005) see Petteys Memorial Foundation, Jack

Penrose-St. Francis Healthcare Foundation — toward development of Penrose Cancer Center ($40,000) see Stone Trust, H. Chase

Penrose-St. Francis Healthcare System — for new kitchen facilities at Namaste ($335,000) see El Pomar Foundation

Phillips County Commissioners — for 1993 grant for courthouse remodeling project ($30,000) see Heginbotham Trust, Will E.

Pikes Peak Library District for Imagination Celebration — for 1993 functions ($6,000) see Stone Trust, H. Chase

Plan de Salud del Valle ($6,535) see Comprecare Foundation

Planned Parenthood of the Rocky Mountains ($137,500) see Gates Foundation

Porter Hospice ($5,000) see Fishback Foundation Trust, Harmes C.

Presbyterian St. Lukes Institute of Limb Preservation ($2,500) see Fishback Foundation Trust, Harmes C.

Rankin Presyterian Church ($2,700) see Joslin-Needham Family Foundation

RE-1 Valley School District ($10,000) see Petteys Memorial Foundation, Jack

Regis High School ($25,000) see Mullen Foundation, J. K.

Regis/Loretto Heights College ($25,000) see Mullen Foundation, J. K.

Regis University — scholarships ($77,560) see Johnson Foundation, Helen K. and Arthur E.

Regis University ($6,500) see Robinson Fund, Maurice R.

Regis University Weckbaugh — Lascor endowment ($20,000) see Weckbaugh Foundation, Eleanore Mullen

Resource Center — domestic violence ($10,000) see Bacon Foundation, E. L. and Oma

Right to Read ($45,000) see Monfort Family Foundation

Rocky Mountain National Park Associates — for the Colorado River Accessibility Trail project ($25,000) see O'Fallon Trust, Martin J. and Mary Anne

Rocky Mountain National Park Association — Colorado River Handicapped Access Trail ($30,884) see Morrison Charitable Trust, Pauline A. and George R.

Sacred Heart House ($2,500) see Rabb Foundation, Harry W.

Sacred Heart House ($25,000) see Weckbaugh Foundation, Eleanore Mullen

St. Anne's Episcopal School — capital costs of library ($10,000) see O'Fallon Trust, Martin J. and Mary Anne

St. Thomas Seminary ($12,500) see Mullen Foundation, J. K.

St. Thomas Seminary ($12,500) see Mullen Foundation, J. K.

School District No. 1 ($15,000) see JFM Foundation

SET of Colorado Springs ($10,100) see Comprecare Foundation

Sewall Rehabilitation Center Foundation ($5,000) see Norgren Foundation, Carl A.

SHARE ($1,500) see Petteys Memorial Foundation, Jack

Son Scape Ministries — religious ($7,500) see Stemmons Foundation

Southern Ute Community Action Programs ($10,600) see Comprecare Foundation

Spalding Rehabilitation Hospital ($5,000) see Fishback Foundation Trust, Harmes C.

Spalding Rehabilitation Hospital ($50,000) see Reisman Charitable Trust, George C. and Evelyn R.

Stanley British Primary School ($10,000) see Duncan Trust, John G.

Stapleton Redevelopment Foundation ($120,000) see Gates Foundation

Summit Foundation ($10,000) see Scott Foundation, Walter

Temple Center ($10,000) see Duncan Trust, John G.

Town of Haxtun — for final grant for fire truck ($25,000) see Heginbotham Trust, Will E.

United Way ($100,000) see Monfort Family Foundation

United Way of Mesa County ($10,000) see Bacon Foundation, E. L. and Oma

United Way of Morgan County ($1,900) see Joslin-Needham Family Foundation

University of Colorado ($119,658) see Seaver Institute

University of Colorado — scholarships ($390,053) see Boettcher Foundation

University of Colorado — for continuation of the Longitudinal Twin Study, a study of the early development of social, emotional, and cognitive behavior, over five years ($1,361,820) see MacArthur Foundation, John D. and Catherine T.

University of Colorado — to implement model curriculum project ($261,842) see Fuld Health Trust, Helene

University of Colorado at Boulder — Computer Graphics Lap Fund ($100,000) see Bechtel, Jr. Foundation, S. D.

University of Colorado Boulder ($54,900) see Martin Marietta Corp.

University of Colorado at Boulder — to establish endowments to support visiting professionals in their schools of journalism ($200,000) see Hearst Foundation, William Randolph

University of Colorado Boulder Foundation ($200,000) see Martin Marietta Corp.

University of Colorado Foundation — renovation of Dal Ward Center ($500,000) see Coors Foundation, Adolph

University of Colorado Foundation — AIDS research ($125,000) see Johnson Foundation, Helen K. and Arthur E.

University of Colorado Foundation — cancer research ($304,159) see Monfort Family Foundation

University of Colorado Health Sciences Center ($10,000) see Hewit Family Foundation

University of Denver — toward Walter K. Koch Chair in entrepreneurship in the College of Business Administration ($350,000) see Boettcher Foundation

University of Denver — for upgrading the Penrose Library ($235,000) see El Pomar Foundation

University of Denver ($41,113) see JFM Foundation

University of Denver — scholarships ($70,058) see

Delaware

A.C.E.S. see ICI Americas Inc.

Albert Einstein Academy ($18,511) see Kutz Foundation, Milton and Hattie

American Institute for Public Service — support the President's youth service awards ($30,000) see Good Samaritan

Archmere Academy — capital campaign ($50,000) see Laffey-McHugh Foundation

Beebe Hospital — building campaign ($500,000) see Longwood Foundation

Beebe Medical Foundation ($6,000) see Wilmington Trust Co.

Benedictine Home ($3,000) see Kutz Foundation, Milton and Hattie

Benedictine Homes of Delaware — provide scholarship funds ($35,000) see Good Samaritan

Boys Club of Delaware see ICI Americas Inc.

Business/Public Education Council ($2,000,000) see du Pont de Nemours & Co., E. I.

Carlisle Fire Company — for community service ($5,000) see Dentsply International Inc.

Catholic Charities — capital campaign ($50,000) see Laffey-McHugh Foundation

Catholic Diocese of Wilmington — educational trust ($75,000) see Laffey-McHugh Foundation

Delaware Adolescent Program ($5,000) see Wilmington Trust Co.

Delaware Arts Stabilization Fund — capital campaign ($50,000) see Crestlea Foundation

Delaware Arts Stabilization Fund — consortium established to address needs of Delaware's arts organizations ($50,000) see Laffey-McHugh Foundation

Delaware Arts Stabilization Fund — capital campaign ($1,000,000) see Longwood Foundation

Delaware Arts Stabilization Fund ($50,000) see Marmot Foundation

Delaware Arts Stabilization Fund — capital campaign ($100,000) see Welfare Foundation

Delaware Council on Economic Education see ICI Americas Inc.

Delaware Health Plan Consortium — marketing campaign ($75,000) see Welfare Foundation

Delaware Historical Society ($12,000) see Borkee Hagley Foundation

Delaware Hospice see ICI Americas Inc.

Delaware Nature Education Society ($15,000) see Borkee Hagley Foundation

Delaware Nature Society — landowner contact program ($182,645) see Crystal Trust

Delaware Nature Society see ICI Americas Inc.

Delaware Nature Society — purchase of audio-visual equipment ($11,250) see Knapp Foundation

Delaware Special Olympics ($10,000) see Borkee Hagley Foundation

Delaware Special Olympics — capital campaign ($100,000) see Welfare Foundation

Delaware State College see ICI Americas Inc.

Diocese of Wilmington — school upgrade ($10,000) see Huisking Foundation

Diocese of Wilmington Education Trust — scholarships ($400,000) see Longwood Foundation

Easter Seal Society Del-Mar see ICI Americas Inc.

Easter Seal Society of Del-Mar ($25,000) see Vale Foundation, Ruby R.

Eleutherian Mills-Hagley Museum and Library — research library ($250,000) see Crystal Trust

Family and Children's Services of Delaware ($20,000) see Vale Foundation, Ruby R.

Food Bank of Delaware — expansion ($100,000) see Crystal Trust

Food Bank of Delaware ($25,000) see Marmot Foundation

Food Bank of Delaware ($100,000) see Welfare Foundation

Goldey Beacon College ($1,030) see GSM Industrial

Gratz Hebrew High School ($5,790) see Kutz Foundation, Milton and Hattie

Hagley Museum — water mains ($20,000) see Fair Play Foundation

Hagley Museum and Library ($10,000) see Borkee Hagley Foundation

Hagley Museum and Library — endowment campaign ($400,000) see Crestlea Foundation

Hagley Museum and Library ($100,000) see McShain Charities, John

Henry Francis DuPont — exhibition building/Point to Point course ($30,000) see Fair Play Foundation

Henry Francis du Pont Winterhur Museum — challenge grant ($50,000) see Wood Foundation of Chambersburg, PA

Henry Francis du Pont Winterhur Museum — campaign for Winterhur ($50,000) see Wood Foundation of Chambersburg, PA

Henry Francis du Pont Winterhur Museum ($100,000) see Brooks Foundation, Gladys

Historical Society of Delaware — capital campaign ($150,000) see Crystal Trust

Hockessin Library — payment of challenge grant ($100,000) see Crystal Trust

Independence School — capital needs ($250,000) see Crystal Trust

Ingleside Homes — capital campaign ($100,000) see Crystal Trust

Ingleside Homes — improvements to retirement apartments ($425,000) see Longwood Foundation

Interfaith Housing Task Force ($5,000) see Wilmington Trust Co.

Jewish Community Center ($14,915) see Kutz Foundation, Milton and Hattie

Jewish Family Services ($20,009) see Kutz Foundation, Milton and Hattie

Jewish Federation of Delaware ($33,156) see Kutz Foundation, Milton and Hattie

Layton Home for the Aged ($10,000) see Borkee Hagley Foundation

Layton Homes for Aged — building renovations ($100,000) see Welfare Foundation

Literacy Volunteers of America see ICI Americas Inc.

Milford District Free Public Library ($25,000) see Vale Foundation, Ruby R.

Ministry of Caring — capital improvements and work with the homeless ($65,000) see Laffey-McHugh Foundation

Ministry of Caring ($5,000) see Wilmington Trust Co.

Nature Conservancy — land purchase ($25,000) see Crestlea Foundation

New Castle Historical Society — Amstel and Dutch houses ($16,180) see Fair Play Foundation

Newark Senior Center — capital campaign ($500,000) see Longwood Foundation

Newark Senior Center — land acquisition ($80,000) see Welfare Foundation

Oblates of St. Francis de Sales — capital campaign to construct assisted care living facility ($50,000) see Laffey-McHugh Foundation

Pilot School — building repairs ($25,000) see Crestlea Foundation

Planned Parenthood of Delaware — endowment campaign ($500,000) see Longwood Foundation

Police Athletic League of Delaware ($9,000) see Wilmington Trust Co.

Project ASSIST Institute — support the continuation and expansion of services ($30,000) see Good Samaritan

Read Aloud Delaware see ICI Americas Inc.

Riverside Hospital ($5,000) see Wilmington Trust Co.

St. Francis Hospital/St. Clare Outreach — mobile medical office to serve poor and homeless people in Wilmington ($50,000) see Laffey-McHugh Foundation

St. Mark's High School — capital campaign ($75,000) see Crystal Trust

St. Mark's High School — capital campaign ($500,000) see Longwood Foundation

Turnabout Counseling — capital campaign ($500,000) see Longwood Foundation

Union Baptist Day Care Center ($70,055) see Burchfield Foundation, Charles E.

United Way of Delaware — capital campaign ($25,000) see Crestlea Foundation

United Way of Delaware ($50,000) see Marmot Foundation

United Way of Delaware — capital campaign ($80,000) see Welfare Foundation

United Way of Delaware ($24,750) see Westvaco Corporation

University of Delaware — to support Improving School Board Effectiveness program ($48,600) see Good Samaritan

University of Delaware — Hillel Center ($5,000) see Kutz Foundation, Milton and Hattie

University of Delaware — capital campaign ($580,000) see Longwood Foundation

University of Delaware ($8,500) see Wilmington Trust Co.

University of Delaware —for RISE program ($12,500) see Air Products and Chemicals, Inc.

University of Delaware Fluid Mechanics ($20,000) see Schlumberger Ltd.

Widener University School of Law ($15,000) see Vale Foundation, Ruby R.

Wilmington College — capital campaign ($2,500,000) see Crystal Trust

Wilmington Institute Free Library — building fund ($50,000) see Crestlea Foundation

Wilmington Library ($7,000) see Wilmington Trust Co.

Wilmington Music School — capital campaign ($25,000) see Crestlea Foundation

Winterthur Museum and Gardens ($10,000) see Osborn Charitable Trust, Edward B.

YMCA of Delaware — capital campaign ($35,000) see Crestlea Foundation

YMCA of Delaware — capital campaign ($100,000) see Crystal Trust

YMCA Dover — capital campaign ($100,000) see Welfare Foundation

YMCA of New Castle County ($25,000) see Marmot Foundation

YWCA ($50,000) see Good Samaritan

YWCA of New Castle County see ICI Americas Inc.

District of Columbia

Academy for Educational Development ($25,000) see Bowne Foundation, Robert

Academy of Hope — support for new staff position and expanded services of community-based literacy and basic education program for 100 adult students ($5,000) see Strong Foundation, Hattie M.

Accuracy in Media ($2,000) see Stans Foundation

African Wildlife Foundation ($3,150) see Stans Foundation

African Wildlife Foundation ($36,000) see Chadwick Fund, Dorothy Jordan

African Wildlife Foundation — gorilla project in Uganda ($15,000) see Fair Play Foundation

Africare — water project ($26,700) see Besser Foundation

Africare — medical and essential drug distribution in Ghana ($25,000) see International Foundation

Africare — medical ($25,000) see International Foundation

All American Fund ($50,000) see Philibosian Foundation, Stephen

Allen Community Outreach Center — support of expansion of Saturday Academy program for children in grades 1-6 ($5,000) see Strong Foundation, Hattie M.

Alzheimers Disease and Related Disorders Association ($15,000) see Chadwick Fund, Dorothy Jordan

American Alliance for Rights and Responsibilities — grassroots drug enforcement assistance and national registry of alcohol victims ($250,000) see Scaife Family Foundation

American Association of Engineering Societies see Amoco Corporation

American Athletic Association of the Deaf ($3,000) see Dart Group Corp.

American Cancer Society — school program projects ($5,000) see Kinney-Lindstrom Foundation

American Cancer Society ($1,310) see Dart Group Corp.

American Chemical Society — campaign for chemistry, last of five payments on $500,000 pledge ($150,000) see AlliedSignal Inc.

American Council on Education — co-sponsorship of 1995 biannual conference on campus diversity ($50,000) see Aetna Life & Casualty Co.

American Enterprise Institute for Public Policy Research ($25,000) see Blount, Inc.

American Enterprise Institute for Public Policy Research ($30,000) see Fuqua Foundation, J. B.

American Enterprise Institute for Public Policy Research see Amoco Corporation

American Enterprise Institute for Public Policy Research ($39,000) see Coleman Foundation, George E.

American Enterprise Institute for Public Policy Research ($250,000) see Monell Foundation, Ambrose

American Enterprise Institute for Public Policy Research ($50,000) see Rose Foundation, Billy

American Enterprise Institute for Public Policy Research ($100,000) see SmithKline Beecham Corp.

American Farmland Trust ($100,000) see Archer-Daniels-Midland Co.

American Farmland Trust ($27,500) see Donnelley Foundation, Gaylord and Dorothy

American Farmland Trust — support their Florida initiative ($50,000) see Laurel Foundation

American Farmland Trust ($25,000) see Clayton Fund

American Forests Urban Tree Research ($100,000) see Texaco Inc.

International Christian Embassy Jerusalem-USA — to purchase a dual cab Volkswagen truck ($20,000) see Huston Charitable Trust, Stewart

International Council on Monuments and Sites — summer intern program ($25,000) see Marpat Foundation

International Foundation ($1,500) see Rixson Foundation, Oscar C.

International Human Rights Law Group ($6,000) see Covington and Burling

Iona Senior Services — operational ($5,000) see Darby Foundation

Iona Senior Services ($25,000) see Dreyfus Foundation, Max and Victoria

James Madison Foundation — fellowship ($200,000) see Salvatori Foundation, Henry

Jewish Institute for National Security Affairs ($1,000) see Dart Group Corp.

John F. Kennedy Center for the Performing Arts ($50,000) see Chadwick Fund, Dorothy Jordan

John F. Kennedy Center for Performing Arts ($50,000) see Folger Fund

John F. Kennedy Center for the Performing Arts ($10,000) see Kiplinger Foundation

John F. Kennedy Center for the Performing Arts — for education and public service ($6,000) see Butz Foundation

John F. Kennedy Center for the Performing Arts ($20,000) see Hechinger Co.

John F. Kennedy Center for Performing Arts ($2,595) see Truland Foundation

Joint Center for Political Economic Studies — two-year supplement, for research, analysis, and dissemination activities on public policies affecting African Americans, national economic policy, and the military ($1,800,000) see Ford Foundation

Jubilee Enterprise of Greater Washington — for operating and project support ($125,000) see Cafritz Foundation, Morris and Gwendolyn

Julie Gould Fund ($10,000) see Brady Foundation

Kennan Institute for Advanced Russian Studies ($50,000) see Harriman Foundation, Mary W.

Lab School of Washington ($20,000) see Liberman Foundation, Bertha and Isaac

Land Trust Alliance ($3,000) see Friendship Fund

Land Trust Alliance — to provide critical support to land trusts and other land conservation organizations in their efforts to protect rural land resources including funds for startup costs; capacity building; improved land protection and land conservation policy ($100,000) see Kaplan Fund, J. M.

Land Trust Alliance ($7,500) see Sasco Foundation

Latin American Youth Center — in support of multifaceted educational program at the Teen Drop-In Center

($6,000) see Strong Foundation, Hattie M.

Legal Aid Society of the District of Columbia ($25,000) see Covington and Burling

Lend-a-Hand Foundation ($1,000) see Dart Group Corp.

Leukemia Society of America ($10,000) see Dart Group Corp.

Levin School of Music — LINC program ($7,500) see Higginson Trust, Corina

Library of Congress ($50,000) see Pickford Foundation, Mary

Library of Congress — to purchase the Watterston House, to be used as a temporary residence for visiting scholars ($200,000) see Cafritz Foundation, Morris and Gwendolyn

Library of Congress — in support of the Center for American Architecture ($20,000) see Graham Foundation for Advanced Studies in the Fine Arts

Life and Health Insurance Medical Research Fund — Otis Bowen research center ($25,000) see American United Life Insurance Co.

Life and Health Insurance Medical Research Fund — scholarship fund ($15,000) see American United Life Insurance Co.

Life and Health Insurance Medical Research Fund ($5,000) see Ameritas Life Insurance Corp.

Life and Health Insurance Medical Research Fund ($100,000) see New York Life Insurance Co.

Life Skills Center ($5,000) see Bloedorn Foundation, Walter A.

Living Stage Theater ($10,000) see Lea Foundation, Helen Sperry

Local Initiatives Support Corporation — to develop 450 units of affordable housing and for commercial development ($250,000) see Cafritz Foundation, Morris and Gwendolyn

Local Initiatives Support Corporation ($25,000) see Hechinger Co.

Management Institute for Environment and Business — two-year pilot program in Environmental Management Education at the University of Virginia (Darden School) ($40,000) see Virginia Environmental Endowment

Maret School ($5,000) see Bloedorn Foundation, Walter A.

Margaret Thatcher Foundation ($50,000) see Forbes Inc.

Margaret Thatcher Foundation ($10,000) see Osborn Charitable Trust, Edward B.

Marriott Foundation for People with Disabilities ($1,000,000) see Marriott Foundation, J. Willard

Marriott Foundation for People with Disabilities ($500,000) see Marriott Foundation, J. Willard

Marshall Heights Community Development Organization — salary support for new position ($20,000) see Prince Trust, Abbie Norman

Meridian House International — for International classroom project to provide DC school students with an understanding of world cultures through presentations by international college students, resource materials, art exhibits ($20,000) see Marpat Foundation

Mineral Policy Center — education and advocacy to reform environmentally destructive hardrock mining practices and for a media campaign to publicize the facts about US taxpayer subsidies to the mining industry ($40,000) see Merck Family Fund

Mineral Policy Center ($20,000) see New-Land Foundation

Mt. Vernon College ($5,000) see DeRoy Foundation, Helen L.

Mt. Vernon College — educational ($35,000) see Dreyfus Foundation, Max and Victoria

Mt. Vernon College ($15,000) see Osceola Foundation

Museum of American Textile History ($10,000) see Hopedale Foundation

Museum Trustee Association ($1,000) see Holt Family Foundation

N Street Village — for a model low-income permanent rental apartment community ($250,000) see Public Welfare Foundation

NAACP ($45,000) see Huber Foundation

National Abortion Rights Action League Foundation ($5,000) see Pettus Crowe Foundation

National Abortion Rights Action League Foundation ($80,000) see Huber Foundation

National Academy of Engineering ($25,000) see Thermo Electron Corp.

National Academy of Sciences — over two years, toward support of the Board on Children and Families ($650,000) see Carnegie Corporation of New York

National Academy of Sciences — endowment for operation of study center ($66,700) see Jonsson Foundation

National Alliance of Business ($7,500) see Rich Products Corporation

National Business Coalition on Health — "Expanding the Community Health Reform Movement" ($932,260) see Hartford Foundation, John A.

National Coalition Building Institute — for operating expenses ($7,500) see McMahan Foundation, Catherine L. and Robert O.

National Commission Against Drunk Driving see Mitsubishi Motor Sales of America, Inc.

National Committee for Adoption ($7,500) see Morrison Knudsen Corporation

National Community AIDS Partnership ($44,600) see Pacific Mutual Life Insurance Co.

National Community AIDS Partnership ($50,000) see New York Life Insurance Co.

National Community AIDS Partnership ($50,000) see Borden, Inc.

National Community Development Initiative — to increase the scale of community development activities nationwide (over three years; program-related investment) ($6,000,000) see MacArthur Foundation, John D. and Catherine T.

National Consumers League — Fraud Information Center ($100,000) see MCI Communications Corp.

National Crime Prevention Council ($41,000) see Burden Foundation, Florence V.

National Cultural Alliance ($10,000) see PaineWebber

National Environmental Policy Institute ($20,000) see Bethlehem Steel Corp.

National Fish and Wildlife Foundation ($50,000) see Dula Educational and Charitable Foundation, Caleb C. and Julia W.

National Gallery of Art ($34,000) see Chadwick Fund, Dorothy Jordan

National Gallery of Art — special project and general operations ($102,000) see Folger Fund

National Gallery of Art ($1,000) see Haley Foundation, W. B.

National Gallery of Art ($200,000) see Frese Foundation, Arnold D.

National Gallery of Art ($250,000) see Gould Foundation, The Florence

National Gallery of Art ($146,000) see Kress Foundation, Samuel H.

National Gallery of Art — endowment grant in support of three senior positions and associated support activities ($1,500,000) see Mellon Foundation, Andrew W.

National Gallery of Art — Whistler's exhibition ($250,000) see NYNEX Corporation

National Geographic Education Foundation ($50,000) see Westvaco Corporation

National Geographic Society ($100,000) see Seaver Institute

National Geographic Society Education Foundation ($10,000) see Bloedorn Foundation, Walter A.

National Geographic Society Education Foundation ($10,000) see Kerr Foundation

National Health Policy Council ($25,000) see Hasbro Inc.

National Journalism Center — graduate journalism scholarships ($42,000) see Sumners Foundation, Hatton W.

National Kidney Foundation ($1,000) see Crown Books

National Learning Center/Children's Museum — general support ($150,000) see Cafritz Foundation, Morris and Gwendolyn

National Museum of American Art — Thomas Cole ($175,000) see NYNEX Corporation

National Museum of Health and Medicine ($27,250) see Whitehead Charitable Foundation

National Museum of Women in the Arts ($155,000) see Martin Marietta Corp.

National Parks Foundation ($25,000) see TransAmerica Corporation

National Public Radio — establish an Environmental Reporting unit which will produce eight to ten half-hour programs on topical environmental issues ($100,000) see Dodge Foundation, Geraldine R.

National Public Radio — for coverage of technology issues ($595,000) see Sloan Foundation, Alfred P.

National Public Radio — special projects ($50,000) see Bell Atlantic Corp.

National Rehabilitation Hospital ($28,500) see Zarrow Foundation, Anne and Henry

National Science Teachers Association — scholarships ($462,930) see NYNEX Corporation

National Symphony Orchestra ($51,000) see Kiplinger Foundation

National Symphony Orchestra ($25,000) see Hechinger Co.

National Taxpayers Union Foundation — Congressional Budget Tracking System project ($75,000) see McKenna Foundation, Philip M.

National Trust for Historic Preservation — donation ($10,000) see Schwartz Fund for Education and Health Research, Arnold and Marie

National Women's Law Center ($6,000) see Pettus Crowe Foundation

Neediest Kids ($1,333) see Dart Group Corp.

Network of Employers for Traffic Safety see Mitsubishi Motor Sales of America, Inc.

New Israel Fund ($40,000) see Meyerhoff Fund, Joseph

New Israel Fund ($30,000) see Meyerhoff Fund, Joseph

Operation Restoration — Israeli immigrant housing ($50,000) see Fohs Foundation

Peace Action Education Fund ($15,000) see Rubin Foundation, Samuel

Pharmaceutical Manufacturers Association ($75,000) see Abbott Laboratories

Pharmaceutical Manufacturers Association Foundation ($60,000) see Schering-Plough Corp.

Pharmaceutical Manufacturers Association Foundation ($200,000) see Bristol-Myers Squibb Company

Pharmaceutical Manufacturers Association Foundation ($50,000) see SmithKline Beecham Corp.

Phillips Collection — to support corporate donor recognition event ($53,548) see Graham Fund, Philip L.

Physicians for Social Responsibility — for a program in professional and public education of the medical consequences of environmental degradation

($25,000) see Heller Charitable Foundation, Clarence E.

Planned Parenthood ($11,000) see Breyer Foundation

Planned Parenthood of Metropolitan Washington — general support ($400,000) see Cafritz Foundation, Morris and Gwendolyn

Pool Research and Action Center — continued support of the Campaign to End Childhood Hunger ($30,000) see Mott Fund, Ruth

Population Action International ($25,044) see Cabot Family Charitable Trust

Population Action International — public education program and special projects fund ($90,000) see Scherman Foundation

Population Crisis Committee ($30,000) see Clayton Fund

Potomac Institute — support of general program ($36,000) see Taconic Foundation

Prison Fellowship ($21,000) see Sundet Foundation

Prison Fellowship Ministries ($45,000) see M.E. Foundation

Project Nishma ($15,000) see Stone Charitable Foundation

Protestant Episcopal Cathedral Foundation, Mt. St. Albans ($217,500) see Folger Fund

Quality Education for Minorities Network ($700,000) see Carnegie Corporation of New York

Reading is Fundamental ($5,000) see Crown Books

Reading is Fundamental ($208,000) see Chrysler Corp.

Reading Is Fundamental ($208,000) see Chrysler Corp.

Renwick Gallery of the National Museum — general support ($40,000) see MCI Communications Corp.

Resources for the Future — Climate Resources Program ($50,000) see Vetlesen Foundation, G. Unger

Ronald Reagan Presidential Foundation —for general support ($100,000) see Hanson Industries North America

Ronald Reagan Presidential Foundation — for general support ($100,000) see Hanson Industries North America

St. Albans School — capital fund, capital improvements, general operations ($188,850) see Folger Fund

St. Anselm's Abbey ($5,125) see Truland Foundation

Salesianum School — capital campaign ($75,000) see Laffey-McHugh Foundation

Salvation Army — Capital Campaign Office ($5,000) see Bloedorn Foundation, Walter A.

Salvation Army — second payment on pledge of $250,000, to support a capital campaign for expansion and upgrading of facilities throughout the metro area ($80,000) see Graham Fund, Philip L.

Salvation Army see Providian Corporation

Salvation Army — for shelter ($15,000) see Mars Foundation

Salvation Army, Harbor Treatment Facility — toward the construction of the Harbor Light Treatment Facility in Washington ($750,000) see Kresge Foundation

Samaritan Inns — to support the campaign for Tabitha's House, a single-room occupancy residence for women ($60,000) see Graham Fund, Philip L.

Samaritan Inns ($10,000) see Truland Foundation

Scottsdale Center for the Arts ($5,000) see Woodward Fund

Share Our Strength — for hunger relief efforts ($250,000) see Kmart Corporation

Sheridan School ($15,000) see AKC Fund

Sidwell Friends ($29,000) see Lazarus Charitable Trust, Helen and Charles

Sidwell Friends School ($4,000) see Crown Books

Sidwell Friends School ($40,000) see Hechinger Co.

Sidwell Friends School, Chinese Student Exchange ($28,000) see Lea Foundation, Helen Sperry

Smithsonian Institute — James Smithson Society ($2,000) see Goldberg Family Foundation

Smithsonian Institution ($100,000) see Adler Foundation Trust, Philip D. and Henrietta B.

Smithsonian Institution ($10,000) see Lee Enterprises

Smithsonian Institution ($4,500) see Edmonds Foundation, Dean S.

Smithsonian Institution ($50,000) see Arcadia Foundation

Special Olympics ($1,200) see Seneca Foods Corp.

Tax Foundation ($4,000) see Handy and Harman Foundation

Textile Museum ($7,000) see Speyer Foundation, Alexander C. and Tillie S.

Thrift Shop, Washington Antiques Show ($15,000) see Mars Foundation

Trinity College — for general operating support ($25,000) see Mattel, Inc.

Trustees of Amherst College, Folger Shakespeare College — operating support ($30,000) see Prince Trust, Abbie Norman

United Cerebral Palsy of Southwestern Pennsylvania — scientific research ($12,500) see Dynamet, Inc.

United Way — National Capital Area ($145,000) see Hechinger Co.

United Way Campaign ($75,000) see Kiplinger Foundation

United Way of Delaware — annual campaign ($165,000) see Laffey-McHugh Foundation

United Way of National Capital Area ($175,000) see Giant Food Inc.

United Way of the National Capital Area ($82,600) see United Airlines, Inc.

University District of Columbia Foundation

($50,000) see Covington and Burling

University of Maryland Foundation — to create a national resource library on freedom of information issues relating to schools and colleges ($1,112,000) see Knight Foundation, John S. and James L.

Urban Institute — for the endowment ($500,000) see Hewlett Foundation, William and Flora

Urban Institute — over five years, to help meet the institute's endowment goal of $25 million ($7,000,000) see Ford Foundation

US Holocaust Memorial Council ($25,000) see Mailman Foundation

US Holocaust Memorial Museum — cultural and civic ($150,000) see Blum Foundation, Harry and Maribel G.

US Holocaust Memorial Museum ($50,000) see Blaustein Foundation, Louis and Henrietta

US Holocaust Memorial Museum ($200,000) see Chrysler Corp.

US Holocaust Memorial Museum ($50,000) see Lauder Foundation

US Holocaust Memorial Museum ($100,000) see Seagram & Sons, Inc., Joseph E.

US Holocaust Memorial Museum ($77,000) see Hassenfeld Foundation

US Holocaust Memorial Museum Campaign — endowment of the cinema in the museum's cultural and conference center in memory of Helena Rubinstein ($300,000) see Rubinstein Foundation, Helena

US Kids — educational ($5,000) see Darby Foundation

US Telecommunications Training — Telecom Training Program ($35,000) see MCI Communications Corp.

Washington AIDS Partnership — for general support ($25,000) see Freed Foundation

Washington Ballet — community and education outreach program ($7,500) see Higginson Trust, Corina

Washington Ballet ($20,000) see Hechinger Co.

Washington Ballet — performing arts ($40,000) see Dreyfus Foundation, Max and Victoria

Washington Cathedral, Mt. St. Alban — capital improvements and general operations ($32,500) see Folger Fund

Washington Chamber Symphony ($7,500) see Neuberger Foundation, Roy R. and Marie S.

Washington Drama Society ($25,000) see Chadwick Fund, Dorothy Jordan

Washington Drama Society — performing arts ($25,000) see Dreyfus Foundation, Max and Victoria

Washington Educational Telecommunications Associations ($30,000) see Chadwick Fund, Dorothy Jordan

Washington Humane Society ($12,500) see Delavan Foundation, Nelson B.

Washington Journalism Center ($90,000) see Kiplinger Foundation

Washington Lawyer's Committee — public education project ($7,500) see Higginson Trust, Corina

Washington Legal Foundation ($2,500) see Taube Family Foundation

Washington Legal Foundation — fund the Grover Hermann Communications Center in new building ($100,000) see Hermann Foundation, Grover

Washington Legal Foundation — conference center furnishings ($119,000) see Wiegand Foundation, E. L.

Washington Legal Foundation ($11,000) see Goddard Foundation, Charles B.

Washington Opera — two-to-one challenge grant for general support ($300,000) see Cafritz Foundation, Morris and Gwendolyn

Washington Opera ($10,000) see Dart Group Corp.

Washington Regional Association of Grantmakers — for the Community Development Support Collaborative ($150,000) see Cafritz Foundation, Morris and Gwendolyn

Wesley Theological Seminary — President's Discretionary Fund ($28,000) see Smith Foundation, Gordon V. and Helen C.

Wesley Theological Seminary — endowment campaign ($24,000) see Smith Foundation, Gordon V. and Helen C.

Wesley Theological Seminary ($6,600) see Smith Foundation, Gordon V. and Helen C.

WETA — to provide final production funding for "Baseball" ($250,000) see Davis Foundations, Arthur Vining

WETA ($40,000) see Hechinger Co.

WETA National Geographic Specials — to provide capstone funding for 1994-95 ($500,000) see Davis Foundations, Arthur Vining

White House Endowment Fund ($50,000) see Clements Foundation

Wider Opportunities for Women — to promote non-traditional training and employment for women ($45,000) see Merck Family Fund

Wilderness Society ($13,500) see Bothin Foundation

Wilderness Society ($50,000) see Claiborne and Art Ortenberg Foundation, Liz

Wilderness Society — support of the work done in the Everglades in Florida ($25,000) see Dillon Dunwalke Trust, Clarence and Anne

Wilderness Society ($20,000) see OCRI Foundation

Wildlife Conservation Society ($287,500) see Claiborne and Art Ortenberg Foundation, Liz

Women's Legal Defense Fund — Child Support Reform

project ($67,500) see Rosenberg Foundation

Woodrow Wilson International Center for Scholarships ($100,000) see Andreas Foundation

World Wildlife Fund ($10,000) see Magowan Family Foundation

World Wildlife Fund ($152,300) see Claiborne and Art Ortenberg Foundation, Liz

World Wildlife Fund — Windows on the Wild Program ($500,000) see Eastman Kodak Company

World Wildlife Fund ($57,050) see Erpf Fund, Armand G.

World Wildlife Fund ($50,000) see Phipps Foundation, Howard

World Wildlife Fund ($46,000) see Sequoia Foundation

Worldwatch Institute ($150,000) see Noble Foundation, Edward John

YMCA ($5,000) see Appleby Trust, Scott B. and Annie P.

Youth for Understanding — international exchange ($14,070) see Dexter Corporation

Youth for Understanding — Foreign Exchange Scholarships ($18,275) see Inland Container Corp.

Youth for Understanding International Exchange — one Subaru Summer in Japan scholarship for a SOA employee's child ($4,070) see Subaru of America Inc.

YWCA, Harrison Center for Career Education — support of direct training expenses of the practical nursing and home health aid programs ($6,000) see Strong Foundation, Hattie M.

Zero Population Growth ($20,000) see Smith Foundation, Ralph L.

Florida

All Children's Hospital ($75,000) see Dana Charitable Trust, Eleanor Naylor

Allegro Productions — science screen reports ($32,000) see Union Camp Corporation

Alzheimers Association — funds to be used as needed ($440,000) see Lattner Foundation, Forrest C.

American Natural Hygiene Society — produce videotape of convention ($21,900) see Johnson Charitable Educational Trust, James Hervey

American Natural Hygiene Society — publish a book on natural hygiene ($20,000) see Johnson Charitable Educational Trust, James Hervey

American Red Cross — disaster relief fund ($5,000) see Kent-Lucas Foundation

American Red Cross — flood relief disaster fund ($10,000) see Royal Foundation, May Mitchell

American Red Cross ($3,000) see Miller-Mellor Association

American Red Cross of Palm Beach County ($20,000) see Marmot Foundation

Georgia

Idaho

Illinois

American Red Cross
Quad-Cities Chapter
($26,300) see Lee
Enterprises
Americans United for Life —
for anti-abortion initiative
through courts ($15,000) see
Trust Funds
Anshe Emet Synagogue
($4,000) see Geifman
Family Foundation
Anti-Drug Abuse Education
Fund ($1,000) see Swift Co.
Inc., John S.
Archdiocese of Chicago Big
Brothers Shoulders Fund —
pledge payment ($100,000)
see AON Corporation
Arrowhead Ranch ($50,000)
see Geneseo Foundation
Art Institute of Chicago
($7,500) see Blair and Co.,
William
Art Institute of Chicago
($10,000) see Boothroyd
Foundation, Charles H. and
Bertha L.
Art Institute of Chicago —
final payment of a two-year
$100,000 grant for a
curriculum development and
training program for
Chicago high school
teachers ($50,000) see Fry
Foundation, Lloyd A.
Art Institute of Chicago —
endowment challenge in
support of architectural
publications and exhibitions
($100,000 over three years)
($100,000) see Graham
Foundation for Advanced
Studies in the Fine Arts
Art Institute of Chicago —
oral histories of 20 Chicago
architects ($10,000) see
Graham Foundation for
Advanced Studies in the
Fine Arts
Art Institute of Chicago
($15,000) see Illinois Tool
Works, Inc.
Art Institute of Chicago
($10,000) see Lederer
Foundation, Francis L.
Art Institute of Chicago
($110,000) see McCormick
Foundation, Chauncey and
Marion Deering
Art Institute of Chicago —
museum support see Nalco
Chemical Co.
Art Institute of Chicago
($5,000) see Rand McNally
& Co.
Art Institute of Chicago
($271,794) see Regenstein
Foundation
Art Institute of Chicago
($1,750,000) see Rice
Foundation
Art Institute of Chicago
($100,000) see Sara Lee
Corp.
Art Institute of Chicago
($1,500) see Swift Co. Inc.,
John S.
Art Institute of Chicago — for
the arts see Morgan Stanley
& Co., Inc.
Arthritis Foundation, Women's
Board ($20,000) see Rice
Foundation
Arthroscopy Association of
North America ($150,000)
see Bristol-Myers Squibb
Company
Artis Trees/Children Celebrate
Children, Children's
Memorial Hospital ($3,500)
see Rand McNally & Co.
Association House of Chicago
see Amoco Corporation

Augustan College ($35,000)
see Bechtel Testamentary
Charitable Trust, H. R.
Austin Career Education
Center — adult education
see Nalco Chemical Co.
Barbara Olson School of Hope
($4,500) see AMCORE
Bank, N.A. Rockford
Barnesville School — for
handicapped facilities
($7,000) see Butz Foundation
Barnum and Bailey Circus
($15,000) see Chicago
Sun-Times, Inc.
Beat the Champs Bowling
Contest ($14,734) see
Chicago Sun-Times, Inc.
Bensenville Home Society —
foster parents program see
Nalco Chemical Co.
Bethel New Life ($10,000) see
Boothroyd Foundation,
Charles H. and Bertha L.
Bethel New Life — for the
self-sufficiency project
($50,000) see Fry
Foundation, Lloyd A.
Big Shoulders Fund — to help
support long-range planning
process and support for
teaching corps serving 130
inner-city schools
($100,000) see Brach
Foundation, Helen
Big Shoulders Fund — first
payment of five-year
$500,000 grant for teacher
training and staff
development in inner-city
schools of the Archdiocese
of Chicago ($100,000) see
Fry Foundation, Lloyd A.
Blackburn College —
scholarships for women
($10,000) see Monticello
College Foundation
Bonaventure House —
unrestricted ($15,000) see
GATX Corp.
Boy Scouts of America —
pledge payment ($100,000)
see AON Corporation
Boy Scouts of America
Chicago Area ($2,500) see
Rand McNally & Co.
Boy Scouts of America
Chicago Area Council —
in-school scouting program,
Carver Schools ($7,750) see
Pick, Jr. Fund, Albert
Boys and Girls Club — pledge
payment ($200,000) see
AON Corporation
Boys and Girls Club ($20,000)
see Russell Charitable
Foundation, Tom
Boys and Girls Club of
Chicago — capital
improvements, Logan
Square Club ($20,000) see
Blowitz-Ridgeway
Foundation
Boys and Girls Club of
Chicago ($102,500) see
Crown Memorial, Arie and
Ida
Boys and Girls Club of
Chicago ($15,500) see
Cuneo Foundation
Boys and Girls Clubs of
America — legends and
fans; general support
($28,000) see Duchossois
Industries Inc.
Boys and Girls Clubs of
America — scholarships
($5,000) see Lehmann
Foundation, Otto W.
Boys and Girls Clubs of
Chicago — for social service
see Morgan Stanley & Co.,
Inc.
Bradley University ($10,900)
see First Chicago Corp.

Bradley University ($3,000)
see First Financial Bank FSB
Brooks and Hope B.
McCormick Foundation
($50,000) see McCormick
Foundation, Chauncey and
Marion Deering
Buehler Center on Aging —
three-year grant to expand
the summer student program
which provides research,
education, and clinical
experience in geriatrics to
second-year medical
students to four additional
medical colleges in the area
($186,688) see Retirement
Research Foundation
Build ($20,000) see LEF
Foundation
Business and Professional
People for the Public
Interest — exhibition and
symposium about Chicago's
scattered-site housing
program ($16,000) see
Graham Foundation for
Advanced Studies in the
Fine Arts
Business and Professional
People for the Public
Interest — support of
national Gautreaux
implementation ($35,000)
see Taconic Foundation
Cabrini-Green Youth Program
see Heller Financial, Inc.
Cairo Historical Association
($10,000) see Hastings
Charitable Foundation, Oris
B.
Cairo Independent Ambulance
Service ($10,000) see
Hastings Charitable
Foundation, Oris B.
Cairo Public Library ($11,500)
see Hastings Charitable
Foundation, Oris B.
Canal Corridor Association
($25,000) see Donnelley
Foundation, Gaylord and
Dorothy
Carmelite Monastery
($16,000) see Cuneo
Foundation
Catholic Charities ($20,000)
see Cuneo Foundation
Catholic Charities of Chicago
— to continue support for
the Madonna St. Joseph
Center for adolescent/adult
pregnant women ($50,000)
see Brach Foundation, Helen
Catholic Charities of Chicago
— people with special needs
($4,000) see Lehmann
Foundation, Otto W.
Catholic Schools in the Quad
Cities ($100,000) see Deere
& Co.
Center for Economic Policy
Research ($25,000) see
Witter Foundation, Dean
Center for Enriched Living
($5,500) see Hartmarx
Corporation
Centralia Cultural Society
($1,598) see Centralia
Foundation
Centralia Public Library
($2,557) see Centralia
Foundation
CGH Medical Center
($25,000) see Dillon
Foundation
Chicago Anti-Hunger
Federation — for social
service see Morgan Stanley
& Co., Inc.
Chicago Christian Industrial
League ($5,000) see
Hartmarx Corporation
Chicago Cities in Schools see
Heller Financial, Inc.

Chicago Commons
Association — for a literacy
and job training program
serving residents of West
Humboldt Park ($50,000)
see Fry Foundation, Lloyd A.
Chicago Commons
Association — Parents Too
Soon program in Henry
Horner and at Mile Square
Center ($10,000) see Pick,
Jr. Fund, Albert
Chicago Community
Foundation — the
McCormick Family Fund
($65,000) see McCormick
Foundation, Chauncey and
Marion Deering
Chicago Council of Urban
Affairs ($3,600) see USG
Corporation
Chicago Historical Society
($6,000) see Commerce
Clearing House, Incorporated
Chicago Historical Society —
library ($10,000) see
Lederer Foundation, Francis
L.
Chicago Historical Society
($10,000) see Rand McNally
& Co.
Chicago Historical Society
($150,000) see Rice
Foundation
Chicago Horticultural Society
($10,000) see Commerce
Clearing House, Incorporated
Chicago Horticultural Society
($210,000) see Donnelley
Foundation, Gaylord and
Dorothy
Chicago Horticultural Society
— English walled garden
($10,000) see Norton
Memorial Corporation,
Geraldi
Chicago Horticultural Society
— fund exhibit ($250,000)
see Regenstein Foundation
Chicago Horticultural Society
— toward the construction
of the Gateway Center
($500,000) see Kresge
Foundation
Chicago House — general
support ($10,000) see
Duchossois Industries Inc.
Chicago House and Social
Service Agency ($7,500) see
Lederer Foundation, Francis
L.
Chicago Institute for the Study
of Architecture and
Technology — book
documenting technological
advances in Chicago
building, 1950-90 ($10,000)
see Graham Foundation for
Advanced Studies in the
Fine Arts
Chicago International Theater
Festival — 1994 festival
($5,000) see Norton
Memorial Corporation,
Geraldi
Chicago Lighthouse for the
Blind ($10,000) see Rand
McNally & Co.
Chicago Metro History Fair
($15,000) see Russell
Charitable Foundation, Tom
Chicago Opera Theatre
($2,500) see USG
Corporation
Chicago Public Art Group
($7,500) see Butz Foundation
Chicago Public Library
($10,000) see Salomon Inc.
Chicago Public Library
($10,000) see Salomon Inc.
Chicago Public Library
Foundation — education
($200,000) see Blum
Foundation, Harry and
Maribel G.

Chicago Public Library
Foundation ($60,000) see
Donnelley Foundation,
Gaylord and Dorothy
Chicago Sun-Time Sports
Show ($20,640) see Chicago
Sun-Times, Inc.
Chicago Symphony/Lyric
Opera Facilities Fund —
10-year pledge totaling
$2,500,000 ($250,000) see
United Airlines, Inc.
Chicago Symphony Orchestra
($127,500) see Abbott
Laboratories
Chicago Symphony Orchestra
— support symphony
programs ($125,000) see
AON Corporation
Chicago Symphony Orchestra
($110,000) see United
Airlines, Inc.
Chicago United ($3,000) see
USG Corporation
Chicago Urban League
($3,000) see USG
Corporation
Chicago Volunteer Legal
Services Foundation
($10,000) see Boothroyd
Foundation, Charles H. and
Bertha L.
Chicago Zoological Society —
capital campaign ($20,000)
see GATX Corp.
Child Abuse Prevention
Services — children's group
programs ($10,000) see
Lederer Foundation, Francis
L.
Children's Home and Aid
Society ($32,500) see Cuneo
Foundation
Children's Home and Aid
Society of Illinois ($75,000)
see McCormick Foundation,
Chauncey and Marion
Deering
Children's Memorial Hospital
— towards new pediatric
research facility ($25,000)
see Blowitz-Ridgeway
Foundation
Children's Memorial Hospital
($5,000) see R. F. Foundation
Children's Memorial Hospital
($10,000) see Griswold
Foundation, John C.
Children's Memorial Hospital
($8,000) see Love
Foundation, George H. and
Margaret McClintic
Children's Memorial Medical
Center — health facility
($5,000) see Lehmann
Foundation, Otto W.
City of Cairo ($15,000) see
Hastings Charitable
Foundation, Oris B.
City of Centralia ($6,893) see
Centralia Foundation
City of Sterling ($976,458) see
Dillon Foundation
City Year ($1,500) see
American National Bank &
Trust Co. of Chicago
Civic Committee Foundation
($50,000) see Illinois Tool
Works, Inc.
Clarence Darrow Convention
Center ($15,000) see
Boothroyd Foundation,
Charles H. and Bertha L.
Clearbrook Center — funding
for expansion for vocational
rehabilitation center
($125,000) see Scholl
Foundation, Dr.
Columbus-Cabrini Medical
Center — medical ($10,000)
see Blum Foundation, Harry
and Maribel G.
Commercial Club Foundation
($100,000) see Abbott
Laboratories

Roger McCormick Foundation ($50,000) see McCormick Foundation, Chauncey and Marion Deering

Ronald McDonald Children's Charity — general support ($50,000) see MCI Communications Corp.

Rosary College — for the master of arts in educational leadership program for prospective school principals ($75,000) see Fry Foundation, Lloyd A.

Rush Presbyterian — diagnostic center ($700,000) see Regenstein Foundation

Rush-Presbyterian-St. Luke's Medical center — for the Pilsen senior health advocates program ($100,000) see Fry Foundation, Lloyd A.

Rush-Presbyterian-St. Luke's Medical center — Heart Institute, five-year pledge totaling $425,000 ($85,000) see United Airlines, Inc.

Rush Presbyterian-St. Luke's Medical Center ($25,000) see CBI Industries, Inc.

Rush-Presbyterian St. Luke's Medical Center ($10,000) see Kelly Foundation, T. Lloyd

Rush-Presbyterian-St. Lukes Medical Center ($87,000) see R. F. Foundation

Rush-Presbyterian-St. Luke's Medical Center — three-year grant for research to vigorously evaluate whether an integrated, multimodality program of health promotion practices can slow or possibly reverse aging processes in the elderly ($389,663) see Retirement Research Foundation

Sabin Management School ($570) see American National Bank & Trust Co. of Chicago

Sabin School ($2,400) see American National Bank & Trust Co. of Chicago

Sabin School ($1,069) see American National Bank & Trust Co. of Chicago

Sabin School ($787) see American National Bank & Trust Co. of Chicago

Sabin School ($682) see American National Bank & Trust Co. of Chicago

Sabin School ($608) see American National Bank & Trust Co. of Chicago

St. Elizabeth Community Center ($5,000) see AMCORE Bank, N.A. Rockford

St. Ignatius College Prep — scholarship fund ($10,000) see Brunswick Corp.

St. Ignatius College Prep School — to continue re-wiring of 1895 wing of school ($50,000) see Brach Foundation, Helen

St. Joseph Church ($45,000) see Cuneo Foundation

St. Joseph School ($13,000) see Hastings Charitable Foundation, Oris B.

St. Mary's Hospital ($2,557) see Centralia Foundation

St. Mary's Parish ($25,000) see Cuneo Foundation

St. Vincent Home for Children — to replace roof and hire a full-time temporary director of development for this treatment center for emotionally disturbed children ($50,000) see Brach Foundation, Helen

Salvation Army — adults with special needs ($5,000) see Lehmann Foundation, Otto W.

Sara Lee Foundation ($100,000) see Price Foundation, Louis and Harold

Saturday Scholar Program ($617) see American National Bank & Trust Co. of Chicago

Sauk Valley College Foundation ($29,000) see Dillon Foundation

Second Harvest National Food Bank Network ($100,000) see Sara Lee Corp.

Shore Community Services — roof replacement ($96,000) see Regenstein Foundation

Silver Spring Foundation ($50,000) see McCormick Foundation, Chauncey and Marion Deering

Smart Museum of the University of Chicago ($190,270) see Smart Family Foundation

Southern Illinois Hunting and Fishing Days ($2,500) see Harrison Foundation, Fred G.

Species Survival Commission — study declining amphibian population ($60,000) see Fikes Foundation, Leland

Sports Luncheon ($14,569) see Chicago Sun-Times, Inc.

Sterling High School Activity Fund ($38,475) see Dillon Foundation

Sterling Park District ($121,373) see Dillon Foundation

Sterling Park Library ($36,000) see Dillon Foundation

Sterling Schools Foundation ($183,484) see Dillon Foundation

Stritch School of Medicine ($29,000) see Cuneo Foundation

Summit School — Elgin campus ($114,000) see Regenstein Foundation

Swedish American Medical Foundation ($50,000) see CLARCOR Inc.

Teen Living Programs — transitional shelter on City's south side ($15,000) see GATX Corp.

Theosophical Society in America ($533,000) see Kern Foundation Trust

Thresholds — for community rehabilitation program ($7,000) see Butz Foundation

Thresholds Foundation ($15,000) see Babson Foundation, Paul and Edith

Travelers and Immigrants Aid ($75,000) see Blum-Kovler Foundation

Travelers and Immigrants Aid — GATX New Beginning II ($20,000) see GATX Corp.

Travelers and Immigrants Aid — affordable housing initiatives ($10,000) see Lederer Foundation, Francis L.

Travelers and Immigrants Aid of Chicago ($5,000) see Blair and Co., William

Travelers and Immigrants Aid of Chicago — first payment of a three-year $225,000 grant for the Families Building Community project ($75,000) see Fry Foundation, Lloyd A.

Tri City Jewish Center — endowment ($6,000) see Geifman Family Foundation

Tri City Jewish Center ($5,500) see Geifman Family Foundation

Tri City Jewish Center Building Fund ($50,000) see Geifman Family Foundation

Trinity College ($10,000) see Dexter Corporation

Tyndale Theological Seminary — second payment on property purchase commitment ($73,000) see Chatlos Foundation

Tyndale Theological Seminary — capital purchase of present property ($73,000) see Chatlos Foundation

Uniform Law Foundation ($6,000) see Covington and Burling

United Animal Nations — to increase donor base and to continue new-member acquisition program ($100,000) see Brach Foundation, Helen

United Charities of Chicago — life management skills ($33,800) see Pick, Jr. Fund, Albert

United Way ($85,153) see CLARCOR Inc.

United Way ($60,000) see Dillon Foundation

United Way ($18,000) see Illinois Tool Works, Inc.

United Way ($22,445) see Outboard Marine Corp.

United Way ($18,500) see Commerce Bancshares, Inc.

United Way ($1,000) see Goodstein Family Foundation, David

United Way ($6,773) see First Financial Bank FSB

United Way of Chicago ($189,200) see Rockwell International Corporation

United Way Crusade of Mercy ($78,926) see CBI Industries, Inc.

United Way Crusade of Mercy ($42,585) see CBI Industries, Inc.

United Way Crusade of Mercy ($55,000) see Hartmarx Corporation

United Way/Crusade of Mercy ($225,000) see Illinois Tool Works, Inc.

United Way/Crusade of Mercy ($12,500) see Rand McNally & Co.

United Way/Crusade of Mercy ($12,500) see Rand McNally & Co.

United Way Crusade of Mercy ($187,000) see Santa Fe Pacific Corporation

United Way Crusade of Mercy ($381,925) see Sara Lee Corp.

United Way Crusade of Mercy ($286,975) see United Airlines, Inc.

United Way Crusade of Mercy ($25,000) see USG Corporation

United Way Crusade of Mercy — human services ($60,000) see Nabisco Foods Group

United Way Crusade of Mercy ($75,000) see Borden, Inc.

United Way of Elk Grove ($34,716) see Cooper Industries, Inc.

United Way Kankakee County ($24,355) see CBI Industries, Inc.

United Way Lake County ($676,561) see Abbott Laboratories

United Way Services ($55,000) see AMCORE Bank, N.A. Rockford

University of Chicago — for volumes 1 and 2 of "The Reliefs and Inscriptions from Luxor Temple" ($228,000) see Getty Trust, J. Paul

University of Chicago — virtual learning center ($500,000) see Fairchild Foundation, Sherman

University of Chicago — HALP ($221,734) see Smart Family Foundation

University of Chicago — Chicago Brown Book ($15,000) see Boothroyd Foundation, Charles H. and Bertha L.

University of Chicago ($113,578) see Donnelley Foundation, Gaylord and Dorothy

University of Chicago ($32,853) see First Chicago Corp.

University of Chicago — for the 1993 summer seminars for high school teachers ($113,200) see Fry Foundation, Lloyd A.

University of Chicago — scholarship endowment fund ($30,000) see GATX Corp.

University of Chicago — support student/biological science/Pritzker ($20,000) see Lederer Foundation, Francis L.

University of Chicago — Department of Radiation and Cellular Oncology; Gene Therapy, Prostate Cancer ($25,000) see Norton Memorial Corporation, Geraldi

University of Chicago — molecular genetics lab ($20,000) see Norton Memorial Corporation, Geraldi

University of Chicago — Albert Pick, Jr. Lecturer on International Relations ($17,500) see Pick, Jr. Fund, Albert

University of Chicago — library renovation ($1,000,000) see Regenstein Foundation

University of Chicago ($125,000) see Rubin Family Fund, Cele H. and William B.

University of Chicago — scholarship ($4,000) see Scherer Foundation, Karla

University of Chicago ($75,728) see Greenwall Foundation

University of Chicago ($90,000) see Lurcy Charitable and Educational Trust, Georges

University of Chicago, Ben May Institute ($10,000) see Boothroyd Foundation, Charles H. and Bertha L.

University of Chicago Diabetes Research — medical ($100,000) see Blum Foundation, Harry and Maribel G.

University of Chicago Diabetes Research — Kovler Diabetes Center ($100,000) see Blum-Kovler Foundation

University of Chicago Library ($13,200) see Kern Foundation Trust

University of Chicago Medical Center — research on drug-resistant infections ($31,750) see Blowitz-Ridgeway Foundation

University of Illinois — research on chemical reactions in cancer causing agents ($26,000) see Blowitz-Ridgeway Foundation

University of Illinois Foundation — College of Nursing ($10,000) see Boothroyd Foundation, Charles H. and Bertha L.

University of Illinois Foundation ($50,000) see Donnelley Foundation, Gaylord and Dorothy

University of Illinois Foundation ($7,635) see First Chicago Corp.

University of Illinois Foundation ($5,000) see R. F. Foundation

University of Illinois at Urbana-Champaign — for a two-moth research visit by a librarian from Romania ($146,500) see Getty Trust, J. Paul

Uptown Community Learning Center — to support the Math and Science Civil Rights Campaign, a community education initiative designed to gain support for and involvement of parents in the implementation of the Chicago Systemic Initiative in Math and Science ($24,000) see Hazen Foundation, Edward W.

Urban Gateways see Heller Financial, Inc.

Urban Libraries Council ($37,950) see Wilson Foundation, H. W.

Visiting Nurse Association ($5,000) see AMCORE Bank, N.A. Rockford

Visiting Nurses Association ($10,000) see Boothroyd Foundation, Charles H. and Bertha L.

Wheaton Christian Grammer School — capital campaign ($50,000) see Gallagher Family Foundation, Lewis P.

Wheaton College — grant/renovation ($650,000) see Balfour Foundation, L. G.

Woman's Board of Northwestern Memorial Hospital ($10,000) see Norton Memorial Corporation, Geraldi

WTTW/Channel 11 ($50,000) see Payne Foundation, Frank E. and Seba B.

YMCA ($13,600) see Valmont Industries, Inc.

Young Life ($12,500) see Russell Charitable Foundation, Tom

Youth Guidance — Comer Near West Side School community development project ($15,000) see GATX Corp.

Youth Sports Program — Marion County Housing Authority ($5,000) see Centralia Foundation

Zaslow Party ($4,994) see Chicago Sun-Times, Inc.

Zazz Mixer ($19,430) see Chicago Sun-Times, Inc.

Indiana

ABC Stewart School — scholarships ($25,000) see Cummins Engine Co.

AIDS Resource Group of Evansville —for office equipment see Aluminum Co. of America

Allen County Stadium Fund — capital ($28,000) see Journal-Gazette Co.

American Communications Network ($5,500) see Winchester Foundation

American Red Cross ($15,000) see American General Finance Corp.

American Red Cross ($15,000) see American General Finance Corp.

Anthony Wayne Area Council ($1,000) see Rieke Corp.

Anthony Wayne Services — capital ($10,000) see Journal-Gazette Co.

Art Association of Richmond see Aluminum Co. of America

Arts United of Greater Ft. Wayne — for charitable purposes ($41,898) see Fort Wayne National Bank

Associated Colleges of Indiana — operating fund ($4,500) see Ayres Foundation, Inc.

Associated Colleges of Indiana — for educational purposes ($8,000) see Fort Wayne National Bank

Associated Colleges of Indiana ($5,000) see Old National Bank in Evansville

Athenaeum Foundation — roof restoration ($50,000) see Clowes Fund

Auburn Automotive Heritage — Auburn, Cord, Duesenberg ($3,000) see Rieke Corp.

Auburn Board of Public Works — marketing plan of Auburn Chamber of Commerce ($1,500) see Rieke Corp.

Auburn Cord Duesenberg Museum ($75,000) see Cord Foundation, E. L.

Ball Memorial Hospital Foundation — challenge grant ($100,000) see Ball Brothers Foundation

Ball State University Foundation — '93 Wings payment ($600,000) see Ball Brothers Foundation

Ball State University Foundation — academic excellence ($500,000) see Ball Foundation, George and Frances

Ball State University Foundation, Fisher Wellness Institute ($30,000) see Ball Brothers Foundation

Ball State University Foundation, Teachers College — PEP Sesame Street ($100,900) see Ball Brothers Foundation

Baptist Theological College ($10,000) see duPont Foundation, Alfred I.

Bartholomew Consolidated School Corporation — architect fees for expansion of Northside and Schmitt schools ($100,000) see Cummins Engine Co.

Bethel College ($25,000) see Oliver Memorial Trust Foundation

Big Brothers and Big Sisters ($500) see Rieke Corp.

Blaine County School District Education Fund ($10,000) see Whiting Foundation, Macauley and Helen Dow

Bloomington Community Foundation — for endowment building for the community see CINergy

BMH Foundation — facilities ($300,000) see Ball Foundation, George and Frances

Bowling Green Public Library ($5,000) see Houchens Foundation, Ervin G.

Boy Scouts of America ($16,000) see Zollner Foundation

Boy Scouts of America Crossroads of American Council — swimming pool ($75,000) see Clowes Fund

Boys and Girls Club — operating fund ($2,000) see Ayres Foundation, Inc.

Boys and Girls Club of Northwest Indiana ($952,800) see Anderson Foundation, John W.

Boys and Girls Club of Porter County ($476,041) see Anderson Foundation, John W.

Boys and Girls Clubs of Indianapolis ($25,000) see Griffith Foundation, W. C.

Boys and Girls Clubs of Indianapolis ($10,000) see Hook Drugs

Brian Bex Report — scholarship fund ($25,000) see Pennsylvania Dutch Co.

Brian Bex Report — educational material ($2,700) see Pennsylvania Dutch Co.

Brownsburg Community School Corporation — for Challenger Learning Center see CINergy

Butler University — for Partnership for Excellence see CINergy

Butler University ($6,000) see Hook Drugs

Butler University ($5,000) see Hook Drugs

Butler University — Pierre Goodrich Scholarship Fund ($14,000) see Winchester Foundation

Butler University Scholarship ($6,000) see Hook Drugs

Cardinal Greenway — Rails to Trails ($250,000) see Ball Foundation, George and Frances

Carson-Newman College ($66,000) see Stokely, Jr. Foundation, William B.

Carson-Newman College ($22,000) see Stokely, Jr. Foundation, William B.

Catholic Education Endowment Program ($2,500) see Habig Foundation, Arnold F.

Center for Leadership Development ($10,000) see American United Life Insurance Co.

Cerebral Palsy of Northwest Indiana ($125,000) see Anderson Foundation, John W.

Child Protection ($10,000) see Houchens Foundation, Ervin G.

Children's Museum of Indianapolis — for planetarium show see CINergy

Christian Church Foundation — to establish permanent

fund ($6,000) see Hallberg Foundation, E. L. and R. F.

City of Auburn — drug and alcohol resistance education ($2,000) see Rieke Corp.

City of Bluffton Senioride — assist in continued services for senior citizen transportation ($1,000) see Pamida, Inc.

City of Columbus — donation of land to Mill Race Park ($530,000) see Cummins Engine Co.

City of Columbus — support for executive architect ($34,127) see Cummins Engine Co.

City of Columbus — support for Project Self-Sufficiency ($26,000) see Cummins Engine Co.

City of Mish-Immigrants Project ($2,000) see First Source Corp.

Civic Theatre ($5,000) see Old National Bank in Evansville

Clarksville Riverfront Foundation — for Falls of the Ohio Interpretive Center see CINergy

CLASS ($9,000) see American United Life Insurance Co.

Columbus Area Arts Council — general support 1993-94 ($35,000) see Cummins Engine Co.

Community Foundation ($100,000) see First Source Corp.

Community Foundation ($30,000) see First Source Corp.

Community Foundation of Jackson County — for start-up funds see CINergy

Community Foundation of Muncie — economic development ($50,000) see Ball Foundation, George and Frances

Community Foundation of Muncie and Delaware County — Cardinal Greenways ($110,000) see Ball Brothers Foundation

Community Foundation of St. Joseph County ($20,000) see First Source Corp.

Community Foundation of St. Joseph County — endowment fund ($99,600) see Leighton-Oare Foundation

Community Foundation of St. Joseph County ($50,000) see South Bend Tribune

Community Harvest Food Bank ($40,000) see Cole Foundation, Olive B.

Community Harvest Food Bank — capital ($20,100) see Journal-Gazette Co.

Community Hospital Foundation ($10,000) see Griffith Foundation, W. C.

Conner Prairie — capital fund ($20,000) see American United Life Insurance Co.

Corporation of St. Marys College — science hall renovation ($100,000) see Leighton-Oare Foundation

Crossroads Rehabilitation Center ($15,000) see Griffith Foundation, W. C.

Culver Academies — new library ($90,000) see Towsley Foundation, Harry A. and Margaret D.

DeKalb County Council on Aging — William A. Heimach Center ($6,000) see Rieke Corp.

DeKalb County Parent Group for Handicapped Children — preschool for handicapped ($2,000) see Rieke Corp.

DeKalb Humane Society ($2,000) see Rieke Corp.

DePauw University — Pierre Goodrich Scholarship Fund ($15,422) see Winchester Foundation

DePauw University — Pierre Goodrich Scholarship Fund ($15,000) see Winchester Foundation

DePauw University — science building construction ($1,658,000) see Olin Foundation, F. W.

East Enterprise Fire Department ($15,000) see Vevay-Switzerland County Foundation

Eckhart Public Library ($3,000) see Rieke Corp.

Evansville Dance Theater ($20,000) see American General Finance Corp.

Evansville Dance Theater ($20,000) see American General Finance Corp.

Evansville Museum ($8,500) see Old National Bank in Evansville

Evansville Philharmonic ($7,750) see Old National Bank in Evansville

Fairbanks Hospital — capital campaign ($5,000) see Glick Foundation, Eugene and Marilyn

First Presbyterian Church ($50,000) see Dingman Foundation, Michael D.

Ft. Wayne Bicentennial Celebration Council — capital ($25,605) see Journal-Gazette Co.

Ft. Wayne Bicentennial Council — for charitable purposes ($12,500) see Fort Wayne National Bank

Ft. Wayne Children's Zoo — for Indonesian tropical rain forest section ($20,000) see Cole Foundation, Olive B.

Ft. Wayne Community Foundation — for 1993 - 1994 Season ($17,000) see Cole Foundation, Olive B.

Ft. Wayne Community Foundation ($35,000) see Zollner Foundation

Ft. Wayne Zoological Society — for charitable purposes ($10,000) see Fort Wayne National Bank

Ft. Wayne Zoological Society — capital ($10,000) see Journal-Gazette Co.

Four Rivers Resource Conservation and Development ($5,000) see Old National Bank in Evansville

Franklin Retirement Home — operating fund ($2,500) see Ayres Foundation, Inc.

Goodwill Industries of Central Indiana — capital fund ($20,000) see Ayres Foundation, Inc.

Goodwill Industries of Central Indiana — for general operating support see CINergy

Goshen College — scholarships ($10,000) see Schowalter Foundation

Hanover College — Pierre Goodrich Scholarship Fund ($10,000) see Winchester Foundation

Harmony School Corporation — for Statewide School

Transformation Project see CINergy

Headwaters State Park Commission — for charitable purposes ($10,000) see Fort Wayne National Bank

Helen G. Smith Hillel Center — one-half of new sculpture ($5,500) see Glick Foundation, Eugene and Marilyn

Homeless Center ($7,500) see First Source Corp.

Howe Military School — to defray the costs of a new computer system for the cadets attend the school ($100,000) see Herrick Foundation

Howe Military School — to defray the costs of a new computer system for the cadets attending Howe Military School ($100,000) see Tecumseh Products Co.

Hudson Institute — education ($10,000) see Inland Container Corp.

Independent Colleges of Indiana — for general fund ($27,500) see Cole Foundation, Olive B.

Independent Colleges of Indiana Foundation — operating and capital funds ($34,500) see American United Life Insurance Co.

Independent Colleges of Indiana Foundation ($322,500) see Anderson Foundation, John W.

Independent Colleges of Indiana Foundation — annual grant ($50,000) see Ball Brothers Foundation

Independent Colleges of Indiana Foundation ($6,000) see Hook Drugs

Independent Colleges of Indiana Foundation ($10,000) see Inland Container Corp.

Indiana Institute of Technology ($37,000) see Zollner Foundation

Indiana State Museum — operating fund ($6,000) see Ayres Foundation, Inc.

Indiana State University Foundation — insurance program ($25,000) see American United Life Insurance Co.

Indiana University — scholarship ($3,000) see Scherer Foundation, Karla

Indiana University — for expenses for continuing education ($5,000) see Dentsply International Inc.

Indiana University Foundation ($404,000) see Anderson Foundation, John W.

Indiana University Foundation — operating ($61,600) see Journal-Gazette Co.

Indiana University Medical School — capital fund ($25,000) see Ayres Foundation, Inc.

Indiana University Northwest ($106,378) see Anderson Foundation, John W.

Indiana University R.W. Howard Seminar ($32,836) see Scripps Co., E.W.

Indiana Vocational Technical College ($22,000) see Zollner Foundation

Indianapolis Art League ($15,000) see Griffith Foundation, W. C.

Indianapolis Art League Foundation — capital

Kansas

($63,903) see Williams Charitable Trust, Mary Jo

General Conference Mennonite Church — LIFE training video ($5,000) see Schowalter Foundation

General Conference Mennonite Church — CHM-Chinese Essay Contest ($5,000) see Schowalter Foundation

Girl Scouts of America ($1,000) see Central National Bank

Girl Scouts of the Wichita Area ($150,000) see Lattner Foundation, Forrest C.

Goodland Activities Center — for educational purposes ($1,005) see First National Bank

Goodland Public Library — for educational purposes ($150) see First National Bank

Goodwill Industries Easter Seal Society ($5,000) see DeVore Foundation

Greater Goodland Development — for governmental purposes ($1,900) see First National Bank

Haur Hill Prep School ($1,000) see Exchange National Bank

Hesston College — peace studies program ($8,000) see Schowalter Foundation

Highland Community College ($1,000) see Exchange National Bank

Hospice Midland Care ($1,000) see Central National Bank

Hospice of Reno County — new office ($3,000) see Davis Foundation, James A. and Juliet L.

Hutchinson Community College Endowment Association — general scholarships ($6,000) see Davis Foundation, James A. and Juliet L.

Jewish Federation of Greater Kansas City ($40,000) see Oppenstein Brothers Foundation

Jewish Federation of Greater Kansas City ($40,000) see Oppenstein Brothers Foundation

Kansas Action for Children — for health purposes ($1,000) see First National Bank

Kansas Aviation Museum —for culture and the arts ($10,000) see Beech Aircraft Corp.

Kansas Cultural Trust — 1992 program ($85,000) see Koch Charitable Foundation, Charles G.

Kansas Independent College Fund —for universities and schools ($50,000) see Beech Aircraft Corp.

Kansas Independent College Fund ($5,000) see Exchange National Bank

Kansas Independent College Fund — for support of member colleges ($2,000) see Martin Marietta Materials

Kansas Mennonite Disaster Service — disaster relief ($5,000) see Williams Charitable Trust, Mary Jo

Kansas Public Telecommunication Service — Sesame Street ($2,600) see Davis Foundation, James A. and Juliet L.

Kansas State University — over three years to implement Counseling for High Skills: VoTech Career Options ($3,296,464) see Wallace-Reader's Digest Fund, DeWitt

Kansas State University College of Human Ecology ($100,000) see Lattner Foundation, Forrest C.

Kansas State University Foundation ($100,000) see Andreas Foundation

Kansas State University Foundation ($100,000) see Archer-Daniels-Midland Co.

Kansas University Endowment ($200,000) see SBC Communications Inc.

Kansas University Endowment Association ($25,000) see Muchnic Foundation

Kansas University Endowment Association — Engineering Scholarship Fund ($10,000) see Muchnic Foundation

Kansas University Endowment Association — energy research center ($3,000) see Kuehn Foundation

Kansas University Endowment Association ($17,225) see Baehr Foundation, Louis W. and Dolpha

Kids After School ($2,000) see Davis Foundation, James A. and Juliet L.

Lakemary Endowment ($10,000) see Baehr Foundation, Louis W. and Dolpha

LAVTS Foundation — instructional equipment, scholarships ($25,000) see Baughman Foundation

Lee Richardson Zoo ($10,000) see IBP, Inc.

Liberal Good Samaritan Center — part 1992 and all 1993 capital drive ($32,875) see Baughman Foundation

Lindsborg Hospital — new construction ($25,000) see Mingenback Foundation, Julia J.

Living Land Foundation — new library ($30,000) see Davis Foundation, James A. and Juliet L.

Living Land Foundation ($3,000) see Davis Foundation, James A. and Juliet L.

McPherson Memorial Hospital — capital improvements ($60,000) see Mingenback Foundation, Julia J.

McPherson Public Library — programs and operations ($1,500) see Mingenback Foundation, Julia J.

Mexican-American Ministries — aid to needy ($5,000) see Williams Charitable Trust, Mary Jo

Miami County Hospital ($6,278) see Baehr Foundation, Louis W. and Dolpha

Miami County Mental Health Association ($5,000) see Baehr Foundation, Louis W. and Dolpha

Montessori Learning Center — preschool child care ($200,000) see Williams Charitable Trust, Mary Jo

Mt. St. Scholastica Academy ($1,000) see Exchange National Bank

Nature Conservancy — nature conservation ($11,000) see Williams Charitable Trust, Mary Jo

NWK Educational Service Center — for educational purposes ($100) see First National Bank

Oswatomic Library ($5,000) see Baehr Foundation, Louis W. and Dolpha

Our Lady of Perpetual Help Church — for religious purposes ($6,767) see First National Bank

Paola Babe Ruth ($3,000) see Baehr Foundation, Louis W. and Dolpha

Paola Girl Softball ($3,000) see Baehr Foundation, Louis W. and Dolpha

Paola Little League ($3,000) see Baehr Foundation, Louis W. and Dolpha

Presbyterian Church ($16,707) see Central National Bank

Presbyterian Church-Highland Cemetery ($1,257) see Central National Bank

Raymer Society — renovation and maintenance of gallery ($6,667) see Mingenback Foundation, Julia J.

St. Francis Academy — to work with boys with problems ($500) see Collins, Jr. Foundation, George Fulton

St. Josephs Catholic School — capital improvements ($50,000) see Mingenback Foundation, Julia J.

Salvation Army — aid to needy ($5,000) see Williams Charitable Trust, Mary Jo

Santa Fe Depot Enhancement Project ($4,000) see Exchange National Bank

Scholarship Program Beech Aircraft Foundation —for universities and schools ($32,126) see Beech Aircraft Corp.

Sedgwick County Zoological Association —for community service ($25,000) see Beech Aircraft Corp.

Sedgwick County Zoological Society ($5,000) see DeVore Foundation

Seward County Community College Development Foundation — scholarships, public relations, liability insurance ($104,500) see Baughman Foundation

Sherman County — for health purposes ($894) see First National Bank

Skills for the Living — 1993 operation ($20,000) see Baughman Foundation

Southwest Kansas Medical Foundation — capital fund drive ($100,000) see Baughman Foundation

Spirit of the Plains Casa — court appointed special advocate program for children ($7,500) see Williams Charitable Trust, Mary Jo

Sunflower State Games ($2,500) see Central National Bank

Training and Evaluation Center of Hutchinson (TECH) ($3,000) see Davis Foundation, James A. and Juliet L.

Trinity Episcopal Church ($2,000) see Exchange National Bank

Unified School District 368 — Together Project ($70,000) see Baehr Foundation, Louis W. and Dolpha

United Way of Geary County ($6,116) see Central National Bank

United Way of Greater Topeka ($100,000) see Santa Fe Pacific Corporation

United Way of the Plains —for community service ($103,000) see Beech Aircraft Corp.

United Way of the Plains ($5,000) see DeVore Foundation

University of Kansas — to establish endowments to support visiting professionals in their schools of journalism ($200,000) see Hearst Foundation, William Randolph

University of Kansas — McGregor Herbarium ($10,000) see Bridwell Foundation, J. S.

University of Kansas at Spencer ($75,000) see Kress Foundation, Samuel H.

University of Kansas at Spencer ($50,000) see Kress Foundation, Samuel H.

USD 480 — tri-agency ($34,204) see Baughman Foundation

USD 483 — computer instructional equipment ($20,000) see Baughman Foundation

Valley View Care Chapel Fund ($1,257) see Central National Bank

Villages — Children of the Village ($25,000) see Jones Foundation, Helen

Wichita Collegiate School — building fund ($500,000) see Koch Charitable Foundation, Charles G.

Wichita State University Frank E. Hedrick Conference Room —for universities and schools ($25,000) see Beech Aircraft Corp.

Wichita Symphony Society —for culture and the arts ($14,500) see Beech Aircraft Corp.

Wildwood Outdoor Education Center ($5,000) see Kuehn Foundation

YMCA ($2,500) see Central National Bank

YMCA ($50,000) see DeVore Foundation

YMCA — programs and operations ($15,000) see Mingenback Foundation, Julia J.

Kentucky

Actors Theater of Louisville ($100,000) see Shubert Foundation

Actors Theatre of Louisville ($578,500) see Humana, Inc.

Alice Lloyd College ($4,000) see Childs Charitable Foundation, Roberta M.

Alice Lloyd College ($225,000) see Andersen Foundation

Alice Lloyd College ($19,250) see Sullivan Foundation, Algernon Sydney

Alice Lloyd College — capital projects ($150,000) see Eden Hall Foundation

American Indian College Fund — to ensure the survival and growth of their institutions, all of which are located on or near reservations in 12 western and midwestern

states ($5,000) see Brown & Williamson Tobacco Corp.

American Red Cross, Louisville Chapter ($275,000) see Humana, Inc.

Appalshop — for Roadside Theater's regional initiative ($25,000) see Mott Fund, Ruth

Archdiocese of Louisville Catholic Schools — education ($50,000) see Gheens Foundation

Asbury College ($225,000) see Andersen Foundation

Asbury Theological Seminary — renovation of the Estes Chapel pipe organ ($100,000) see Chatlos Foundation

Asbury Theological Seminary — increase endowed World Missions scholarship fund ($100,000) see Chatlos Foundation

Asbury Theological Seminary — scholarship program ($7,500) see Broadhurst Foundation

Audubon Council ($4,000) see Houchens Foundation, Ervin G.

Barren County History Foundation ($5,000) see Houchens Foundation, Ervin G.

Bellarmine College — new library ($250,000) see Gheens Foundation

Bellarmine College — toward the construction of a library ($600,000) see Kresge Foundation

Berea College — construction of physical education auditorium building ($100,000) see Hermann Foundation, Grover

Berea College — capital campaign ($200,000) see Ball Foundation, George and Frances

Berea College ($50,000) see Ball Foundation, George and Frances

Berea College— grant for Hutchins Library Acquisition Fund ($10,000) see Knapp Foundation

Berea College ($4,000) see Childs Charitable Foundation, Roberta M.

Berea College ($10,000) see Westerman Foundation, Samuel L.

Berea College ($10,000) see Westerman Foundation, Samuel L.

Berea College ($45,514) see Hallett Charitable Trust, Jessie F.

Berea College ($29,500) see Sullivan Foundation, Algernon Sydney

Berea College ($54,480) see Second Foundation

Berea College — construction ($200,000) see Eden Hall Foundation

Berea College — nursing professorship ($5,000) see Johnson Foundation, Burdine

Bowling Green State University ($6,000) see Frohring Foundation, William O. and Gertrude Lewis

Boy Scouts of America Old Kentucky Home Council — operating costs ($175,000) see Gheens Foundation

Brescia College ($5,000) see Thomas Industries

Louisiana

Maine

Tulane University ($4,000) see Kuehn Foundation

Tulane University ($500,000) see McCune Charitable Foundation, Marshall and Perrine D.

Tulane University Educational Fund ($300,000) see Shell Oil Company

United Way Greater New Orleans Area ($330,000) see Shell Oil Company

United Way Southwestern Louisiana — charitable contribution ($30,000) see Olin Corp.

YMCA — building program ($44,000) see Coughlin-Saunders Foundation

Youth Service Bureau of St. Tammany — Power of Choice Program ($23,030) see German Protestant Orphan Asylum Association

YWCA — air conditioning and heating repairs ($14,000) see Coughlin-Saunders Foundation

Maine

Atlantic Challenge Foundation ($20,000) see Sprague Educational and Charitable Foundation, Seth

Atlantic Challenge Foundation ($20,000) see Sprague Educational and Charitable Foundation, Seth

Bangor Symphony Orchestra ($4,000) see Webber Oil Co.

Bangor Theological Seminary — to develop a new model for educating lay leaders (Bangor, ME; Hanover, NH; Portland, ME) ($74,625) see Teagle Foundation

Bates College — fund for student research ($100,000) see Hoffman Foundation, Maximilian E. and Marion O.

Bates College ($41,000) see Ladd Charitable Corporation, Helen and George

Bath Area Family YMCA ($8,500) see Davenport Trust Fund

Birth Right Forces ($30,000) see Sprague Educational and Charitable Foundation, Seth

Blue Hill Heritage Trust ($7,500) see Sasco Foundation

Blue Hill Memorial Hospital ($7,500) see Sasco Foundation

Boothbay Railway Village Museum ($37,500) see McEvoy Foundation, Mildred H.

Boothbay Railway Village Museum ($37,500) see McEvoy Foundation, Mildred H.

Boothbay Railway Village Museum ($37,500) see McEvoy Foundation, Mildred H.

Boothbay Railway Village Museum ($37,500) see McEvoy Foundation, Mildred H.

Bowdoin College — for Beckwith Chair ($10,000) see Day Foundation, Nancy Sayles

Bowdoin College — grants ($250,000) see Balfour Foundation, L. G.

Bowdoin College ($3,000) see Morgan Construction Co.

Bowdoin College ($50,000) see Morris Foundation, William T.

Bridgton Public Library ($5,000) see Mulford Trust, Clarence E.

Child Evangelism Fellowship — capital improvement; building construction challenge grant ($44,839) see Gallagher Family Foundation, Lewis P.

Children's Museum of Maine ($2,000) see Webber Oil Co.

Chop Point ($7,000) see Davenport Trust Fund

Church of the New Jerusalem ($7,000) see Mulford Trust, Clarence E.

Colby College ($100,000) see Brooks Foundation, Gladys

Colby College — first installment of a $333,000 two-for-one challenge grant to establish a $1,000,000 nonathletic scholarship endowment fund for students from the city of New York who show high academic promise and whose families have demonstrated an acute financial need ($100,000) see Calder Foundation, Louis

College of Atlantic ($5,000) see Rockefeller Fund, David

Community Health and Counsel ($2,500) see Webber Oil Co.

East Orrington Congregational Church ($3,000) see Webber Oil Co.

Eastern Maine Charities Children's Campaign ($5,000) see Webber Oil Co.

Elmhurst Association for Retarded Citizens ($20,000) see Davenport Trust Fund

Family Planning Association of Maine ($43,000) see Huber Foundation

First Assembly of God Church ($2,000) see Mulford Trust, Clarence E.

Fryeburg Academy ($159,237) see Mulford Trust, Clarence E.

Fryeburg Congregational Church ($7,000) see Mulford Trust, Clarence E.

Fryeburg Library Club ($8,000) see Mulford Trust, Clarence E.

Good Will Hinckley Home for Boys and Girls ($75,000) see Brooks Foundation, Gladys

Gould Academy ($61,800) see Bingham Second Betterment Fund, William

Grand Banks Schooner Museum Trust — restoration of Port Planking ($300,000) see McEvoy Foundation, Mildred H.

Grand Banks Schooner Museum Trust — repayment of promissory note ($79,250) see McEvoy Foundation, Mildred H.

Greater Portland Cares ($35,000) see Gannett Publishing Co., Guy

Haystack Mountain School of Crafts — endowment fund for Maine education program ($30,000) see Bingham Second Betterment Fund, William

Hospital Chaplaincy Services — general operations ($25,000) see Gallagher Family Foundation, Lewis P.

Husson College ($4,000) see Webber Oil Co.

Hyde Foundation ($500,000) see Smart Family Foundation

Islesboro Affordable Property — general support ($25,000) see Dillon Dunwalke Trust, Clarence and Anne

Jackson Laboratory ($50,000) see Barker Foundation, J.M.R.

Jackson Laboratory ($5,000) see Rockefeller Fund, David

Jackson Laboratory — capital ($40,000) see Ingalls Foundation, Louise H. and David S.

Jackson Laboratory — annual fund ($8,000) see South Waite Foundation

Jackson Laboratory ($10,000) see Strawbridge Foundation of Pennsylvania II, Margaret Dorrance

Maine Audubon Society ($10,000) see Borkee Hagley Foundation

Maine Audubon Society — environmental centers project ($5,000) see Woodward Fund

Maine Children's Cancer Program ($34,400) see Bingham Second Betterment Fund, William

Maine Coast Heritage Trust ($15,000) see Rockefeller Fund, David

Maine Coast Heritage Trust ($10,000) see Sasco Foundation

Maine Community Foundation ($82,485) see Bingham Second Betterment Fund, William

Maine-Dartmouth Family Practice Residency ($45,000) see Bingham Second Betterment Fund, William

Maine Development Foundation ($1,000) see Webber Oil Co.

Maine Historical Society ($10,000) see Borkee Hagley Foundation

Maine Medical Center ($25,000) see Davenport Trust Fund

Maine Public Broadcasting ($15,000) see Davenport Trust Fund

Maine Public Broadcasting Network ($15,000) see Ladd Charitable Corporation, Helen and George

Maine State Society for the Protection of Animals ($50,000) see Johnson Fund, Edward C.

Maine Women's Fund ($30,000) see Bingham Second Betterment Fund, William

Mid-Coast Health Services ($7,500) see Davenport Trust Fund

Mission College ($4,000) see Webber Oil Co.

Mt. Desert Island Health Care Foundation/MDI Hospital ($5,000) see Rockefeller Fund, David

Mt. Desert Public Health Nursing Association ($8,000) see Rockefeller Fund, David

Natural Resources Council of Maine ($4,500) see Ladd Charitable Corporation, Helen and George

Nature Conservancy ($10,000) see Whiting Foundation, Macauley and Helen Dow

Nature Conservancy Maine Chapter — toward the cost of securing the protection of

Great Duck Island ($25,000) see Dillon Dunwalke Trust, Clarence and Anne

Piscataquis YMCA ($5,000) see Woodward Fund

Planned Parenthood of Northern New England ($53,000) see Huber Foundation

Portland Performing Arts Center — multicultural program series ($10,000) see Hunt Foundation

Portland Public Library ($1,000) see Gannett Publishing Co., Guy

Portland Symphony Orchestra ($3,500) see Gannett Publishing Co., Guy

Portland YMCA ($8,000) see Gannett Publishing Co., Guy

Preble Street Resource Center ($1,000) see Gannett Publishing Co., Guy

Prop ($1,000) see Gannett Publishing Co., Guy

Riley School ($20,000) see Sprague Educational and Charitable Foundation, Seth

Rockport Apprenticeship — renovation of facilities ($75,000) see Clowes Fund

Rural Community Action Ministry ($5,000) see Ladd Charitable Corporation, Helen and George

St. Elizabeth Ann Seton Church ($2,000) see Mulford Trust, Clarence E.

St. Marys Church of Bath ($7,500) see Davenport Trust Fund

St. Paul's School — annual fund ($10,000) see Hunt Foundation

Salvation Army ($15,000) see Davenport Trust Fund

School Administrative District 72 ($5,000) see Mulford Trust, Clarence E.

Spirit of Springfield ($1,000) see Gannett Publishing Co., Guy

Springfield Technical College ($1,000) see Gannett Publishing Co., Guy

Starlight Foundation ($7,310) see Feil Foundation, Louis and Gertrude

Town of Fryeburg ($55,709) see Mulford Trust, Clarence E.

Town of Wayne ($37,600) see Ladd Charitable Corporation, Helen and George

United Way ($85,360) see Gannett Publishing Co., Guy

United Way of Portland ($60,320) see Bank of Boston Corp.

United Way of Southeastern Maine ($150,000) see Bank of Boston Corp.

University of Maine Farmington ($2,000) see Webber Oil Co.

University of Maine at Farmington ($75,000) see Bingham Second Betterment Fund, William

University of Maine Foundation ($30,000) see Georgia-Pacific Corporation

University of Maine Orono — scholarships ($14,000) see Davenport Trust Fund

University of Maine Pulp and Paper Foundation ($25,000) see Hill Foundation, Sandy

University of Maine Pulp and Paper Foundation ($25,000) see Hill Foundation, Sandy

University of New England ($100,000) see Bingham

Second Betterment Fund, William

University of Southern Maine — scholarships ($10,000) see Davenport Trust Fund

West Street School ($3,464) see American Optical Corp.

WTVL Public Schools ($1,000) see Gannett Publishing Co., Guy

YMCA of Boothbay Region — capital fund ($50,000) see McEvoy Foundation, Mildred H.

Your Choice ($5,000) see Ladd Charitable Corporation, Helen and George

YWCA ($5,100) see Ladd Charitable Corporation, Helen and George

Maryland

Accokeek Foundation — preserve natural, historical, cultural resources of Potomac River basin, foster public education programs to make people aware of its diverse heritage and encourage land stewardship ($25,000) see Marpat Foundation

Advocates for Children and Youth ($119,000) see Goldseker Foundation of Maryland, Morris

Alliance for the Chesapeake Bay see Amoco Corporation

American Association of Colleges of Osteopathic Medicine ($149,696) see SmithKline Beecham Corp.

American Association of Colleges of Pharmacy ($400,000) see SmithKline Beecham Corp.

American Association of Colleges of Pharmacy ($60,000) see SmithKline Beecham Corp.

American College of Cardiology ($210,000) see Merck & Co.

American Council for Drug Education — public education program ($145,000) see Scaife Family Foundation

American Friends of Tel Aviv University ($30,000) see Fribourg Foundation

American Trauma Society see USX Corporation

Annapolis Center for Environmental Quality see USX Corporation

Anxiety Disorders Association of America — for establishment of library ($40,000) see Freed Foundation

AOPA Air Safety Foundation — for operating budget ($50,000) see Baker Trust, George F.

Aspen Institute ($100,000) see Dingman Foundation, Michael D.

Aspen Institute — three-year supplement, for the institute's Nonprofit Sector Research Fund, which promotes the study of philanthropy and the nonprofit sector ($1,650,000) see Ford Foundation

Aspen Institute ($50,000) see Lauder Foundation

Associated Catholic Charities ($500) see Warfield Memorial Fund, Anna Emory

Associated H and LPM Fund ($75,000) see Meyerhoff Fund, Joseph

Associated Jewish Charities ($50,000) see Hecht-Levi Foundation

Associated Jewish Charities ($19,000) see Leidy Foundation, John J.

Associated Jewish Charities ($10,000) see Cooperman Foundation, Leon and Toby

Associated Jewish Charities and Welfare Fund ($625,668) see Blaustein Foundation, Louis and Henrietta

Associated Jewish Community ($119,660) see Goldseker Foundation of Maryland, Morris

Association for Research in Vision and Ophthalmology ($25,000) see Alcon Laboratories, Inc.

Baltimore Chamber Orchestra — to purchase computers and for training ($6,670) see Rouse Co.

Baltimore Commonwealth ($3,000) see Unger Foundation, Aber D.

Baltimore Community Foundation ($119,600) see Goldseker Foundation of Maryland, Morris

Baltimore Community Foundation ($5,000) see Hecht-Levi Foundation

Baltimore Community Foundation — for collaborative children and families initiative ($25,000) see Lockhart Vaughan Foundation

Baltimore Educational Scholarship Trust — for secondary education ($20,000) see Price Associates, T. Rowe

Baltimore Housing Roundtable ($60,500) see Goldseker Foundation of Maryland, Morris

Baltimore International Culinary College — scholarship fund ($5,000) see Rouse Co.

Baltimore Metropolitan Council ($60,000) see Goldseker Foundation of Maryland, Morris

Baltimore Museum of Art ($62,500) see Blaustein Foundation, Louis and Henrietta

Baltimore Museum of Art — for fund drive ($20,000) see Price Associates, T. Rowe

Baltimore Museum of Industry ($10,000) see Blaustein Foundation, Louis and Henrietta

Baltimore Opera Company ($6,500) see Campbell Foundation

Baltimore Symphony Orchestra see AEGON USA Inc.

Baltimore Symphony Orchestra ($50,000) see Blaustein Foundation, Louis and Henrietta

Baltimore Symphony Orchestra — sustaining fund ($100,000) see Hecht-Levi Foundation

Baltimore Symphony Orchestra ($6,000) see Leidy Foundation, John J.

Baltimore Symphony Orchestra ($75,000) see Meyerhoff Fund, Joseph

Baltimore Symphony Orchestra ($25,000) see PHH Corporation

Barnesville School ($16,180) see Truland Foundation

Bethesda United Methodist Church ($6,560) see Smith Foundation, Gordon V. and Helen C.

Big Brothers and Big Sisters of Baltimore ($10,000) see Leidy Foundation, John J.

Big Brothers and Big Sisters of Central Maryland — for general support ($20,000) see Lockhart Vaughan Foundation

Boys and Girls Club of Maryland ($15,000) see Leidy Foundation, John J.

Boys and Girls Club of Maryland ($10,000) see Leidy Foundation, John J.

Boys Latin School of Maryland — acquisition of books and information system ($50,000) see Middendorf Foundation

Brown Memorial Church ($5,000) see Campbell Foundation

Bryn Mawr School ($6,000) see Campbell Foundation

Build ($10,000) see Rouse Co.

Capitol College — equipment for the CD-ROM reference collection ($10,000) see Knapp Foundation

Carroll County General Hospital — for scientific purposes ($2,500) see Lehigh Portland Cement Co.

Center Stage — sustaining fund ($5,000) see Hecht-Levi Foundation

Chase-Brexton Clinic — capital fund ($10,000) see Rouse Co.

Chesapeake Bay Foundation — Nanticoke project ($100,000) see Fair Play Foundation

Chesapeake Bay Foundation — for the water pollution and wetlands initiatives ($126,000) see Cafritz Foundation, Morris and Gwendolyn

Chesapeake Bay Foundation — for its public school program ($5,000) see Higginson Trust, Corina

Chesapeake Bay Foundation — for educational purposes ($20,000) see Lockhart Vaughan Foundation

Chesapeake Bay Foundation — campaign for William B. Mullins and environmental education center at Smith Island ($50,000) see Mellon Family Foundation, R. K.

Chesapeake Bay Foundation ($8,500) see Treakle Foundation, J. Edwin

Chesapeake Bay Foundation — partial support for Phase III of "Managing Growth to Conserve Natural and Cultural Resources in the Lower Rappahannock River Valley" ($50,000) see Virginia Environmental Endowment

Chesapeake Bay Girl Scout Council ($7,000) see Wilmington Trust Co.

Chesapeake Bay Maritime Museum — education program ($15,000) see Fair Play Foundation

Chesapeake Maritime Museum ($3,000) see Widgeon Foundation

Chesapeake Wildlife Heritage — Woodducks/Bluebirds Project ($15,000) see Fair Play Foundation

Citizens Planning and Housing Association ($69,000) see Goldseker Foundation of Maryland, Morris

Citizens Planning and Housing Association — toward the Community Schools Initiative ($25,000) see Hazen Foundation, Edward W.

College Bound Foundation ($40,000) see PHH Corporation

Collegebound Foundation — for secondary education ($15,000) see Price Associates, T. Rowe

Columbus Center see Novell Inc.

Community Foundation of the Eastern Shore ($20,000) see Wood Foundation of Chambersburg, PA

CTY/JMU Talent Search ($77,295) see Seaver Institute

Dorchester County Public Library ($3,000) see Widgeon Foundation

Echo Hill Outdoor School — Billy B. Bay Project ($385,664) see France Foundation, Jacob and Annita

Echo Hill Outdoor School ($119,750) see France Foundation, Jacob and Annita

Enoch Pratt Free Library ($10,000) see Leidy Foundation, John J.

Enterprise Foundation ($20,000) see Gap, Inc., The

Enterprise Foundation — fulfills three-year pledge of $300,000, to support large-scale development of affordable housing in Washington, DC ($100,000) see Graham Fund, Philip L.

Enterprise Foundation — "Greenstreets," the gardening/open space component of the Sandtown-Winchester community revitalization project in Baltimore ($50,000) see Merck Family Fund

Enterprise Foundation — support of the New York City program ($25,000) see Taconic Foundation

Family Life Foundation ($10,000) see Unger Foundation, Aber D.

Foundation for Advanced Education in the Sciences (NEI) ($25,000) see Alcon Laboratories, Inc.

Friends of Jefferson Patterson Park — six-month funding for three staff people to present school programs, manage a visitor center, and conduct special activities for visitors ($28,000) see Marpat Foundation

Friends for Johns Hopkins Medicine ($25,000) see Folger Fund

Fund for Educational Excellence ($50,000) see Meyerhoff Fund, Joseph

Fund for Educational Excellence ($5,000) see Unger Foundation, Aber D.

Fund for Johns Hopkins Medicine ($5,000) see Willard Helping Fund, Cecilia Young

Garrison Forest School ($124,250) see France Foundation, Jacob and Annita

Garrison Forest School ($201,000) see Johnson Fund, Edward C.

GBMC Foundation ($10,000) see PHH Corporation

Gilman School ($144,667) see France Foundation, Jacob and Annita

Gilman School Scholarship Fund — provide funds for financial support ($10,500) see Campbell Foundation

Greater Baltimore Medical Center — redevelopment campaign fund ($20,000) see Rouse Co.

Hammond Harwood House Association — for an endowment ($50,000) see Middendorf Foundation

Health Care for the Homeless — for medical purposes ($25,000) see Lockhart Vaughan Foundation

Hebrew Literacy Publications — education ($2,750) see Kaplun Foundation, Morris J. and Betty

Henry A. Wallace Institute for Alternative Agriculture — for the Alternative Agriculture Policy Studies program ($25,000) see Heller Charitable Foundation, Clarence E.

Howard County General Hospital ($8,333) see Giant Food Inc.

Independent College Fund of Maryland ($5,000) see Campbell Foundation

Independent College Fund of Maryland — for higher education ($12,000) see Price Associates, T. Rowe

Institute for Family Centered Care — training for family-centered care ($37,000) see Mailman Family Foundation, A. L.

International Geographical Congress ($50,000) see Bell Atlantic Corp.

Interns for Peace — Center of Jewish-Arab Economic Development ($10,000) see Unger Foundation, Aber D.

Irvine Natural Science Center — urban environmental education project ($20,000) see Lockhart Vaughan Foundation

Islamic Education Center ($493,100) see Alavi Foundation of New York

Jesuit Hamshedour Mission ($7,000) see Speyer Foundation, Alexander C. and Tillie S.

Jewish National Fund ($1,000) see Dart Group Corp.

Jewish Social Service Agency ($1,250) see Crown Books

Johns Hopkins Cancer Center — building fund ($10,000) see Willard Helping Fund, Cecilia Young

Johns Hopkins Center for Talented Youth — support an Expedition Awards program, which provides educational fieldwork for high school students ($95,380) see Durfee Foundation

Johns Hopkins Children's Center — for medical support ($20,000) see Lockhart Vaughan Foundation

Johns Hopkins Hospital ($10,000) see PHH Corporation

Johns Hopkins Medical Center — for scholarship aid for the School of Medicine ($15,000) see Palisades Educational Foundation

Johns Hopkins Medical Center, School for Advanced Studies for the Najing Center — for general support ($10,000) see Palisades Educational Foundation

Johns Hopkins Medical Fund ($12,000) see Hecht-Levi Foundation

Johns Hopkins Oncology Center — for medical purposes ($20,000) see Lockhart Vaughan Foundation

Johns Hopkins Oncology Center — for medical purposes ($20,000) see Lockhart Vaughan Foundation

Johns Hopkins University ($159,360) see Seaver Institute

Johns Hopkins University — 1993 Medical Science Scholar ($108,000) see Culpeper Foundation, Charles E.

Johns Hopkins University ($80,000) see Blaustein Foundation, Louis and Henrietta

Johns Hopkins University — success for all programs ($243,760) see France Foundation, Jacob and Annita

Johns Hopkins University — Zanvyl Kreiger Mind/Brain Institute ($192,500) see France Foundation, Jacob and Annita

Johns Hopkins University — athletic facility ($137,500) see France Foundation, Jacob and Annita

Johns Hopkins University ($119,660) see Goldseker Foundation of Maryland, Morris

Johns Hopkins University ($5,250) see Hecht-Levi Foundation

Johns Hopkins University ($100,000) see Martin Marietta Corp.

Johns Hopkins University ($25,000) see PHH Corporation

Johns Hopkins University ($50,000) see Benenson Foundation, Frances and Benjamin

Johns Hopkins University — Dana Consortium on the Genetic Basis of Manic-Depressive Illness ($275,000) see Dana Foundation, Charles A.

Johns Hopkins University ($233,694) see Donner Foundation, William H.

Johns Hopkins University — support for a new book, "The Great Surprise: What the Collapse of Communism Means to Us" ($121,194) see Donner Foundation, William H.

Johns Hopkins University — partial support to establish a North American Studies program at the Foreign Policy Institute ($112,500) see Donner Foundation, William H.

Johns Hopkins University ($100,000) see Steinbach Fund, Ruth and Milton

Johns Hopkins University — medical ($10,150) see Lebovitz Fund

Johns Hopkins University ($12,000) see Superior Tube Co.

Johns Hopkins University ($150,000) see Hassenfeld Foundation

Johns Hopkins University Hospital/Brady Institute ($20,000) see Spang & Co.

Johns Hopkins University School of Hygiene and Public Health ($5,000) see Unger Foundation, Aber D.

Johns Hopkins University School of Medicine — for a preschool screening pilot project ($48,987) see Middendorf Foundation

Joseph Richey House ($10,000) see Rouse Co.

Kennedy Kreiger Institute ($20,000) see Blaustein Foundation, Louis and Henrietta

Kennedy Krieger Institute ($10,000) see PHH Corporation

Kent School — for the school's capital and endowment campaign ($100,000) see Bingham Foundation, William

Library Theater — summer books alive ($7,500) see Higginson Trust, Corina

Life Underwriter Training Council — general support ($165,000) see Prudential Insurance Co. of America, The

Loyola College see AEGON USA Inc.

Loyola College ($20,000) see PHH Corporation

Loyola College — for higher education ($10,000) see Price Associates, T. Rowe

Loyola College, Sellinger School of Business Management — special event ($5,000) see Rouse Co.

Maryland Food Bank ($20,000) see Blaustein Foundation, Louis and Henrietta

Maryland Food Bank ($5,000) see Rouse Co.

Maryland Food Committee ($18,000) see Leidy Foundation, John J.

Maryland Institute College of Art ($110,000) see France Foundation, Jacob and Annita

Maryland Institute College of Art ($11,000) see Hecht-Levi Foundation

Maryland School for the Blind — for the complete Wolfe renovation project ($25,000) see Middendorf Foundation

Maryland Science Center ($110,000) see France Foundation, Jacob and Annita

Maryland Society for the Prevention of Blindness ($6,000) see Campbell Foundation

McDonogh School ($50,500) see Kiplinger Foundation

McDonogh School ($12,500) see Campbell Foundation

Mechanics Hall — endowment ($15,000) see Harrington Foundation, Francis A. and Jacquelyn H.

Morgan State University Foundation ($119,660) see

Goldseker Foundation of Maryland, Morris

Muslim Community School ($316,000) see Alavi Foundation of New York

NAACP — annual spring breakfast ($3,000) see Giant Food Inc.

NAACP ($30,000) see Bell Atlantic Corp.

NAACP Special Contribution Fund — operating expenses ($50,000) see Georgia Power Co.

National 4-H ($12,000) see International Paper Co.

National 4-H Council ($50,253) see Bridgestone/Firestone, Inc.

National 4-H Council ($29,000) see Bridgestone/Firestone, Inc.

National 4-H Council ($29,000) see Bridgestone/Firestone, Inc.

National 4-H Council ($29,000) see Bridgestone/Firestone, Inc.

National 4-H Council ($27,750) see Bridgestone/Firestone, Inc.

National 4-H Educational Awards Program ($60,000) see Santa Fe Pacific Corporation

National Aquarium in Baltimore ($5,000) see Giant Food Inc.

National Arts Stabilization Fund ($50,000) see Blaustein Foundation, Louis and Henrietta

National Retinitis Pigmentosa Foundation — partial funding for investigators, technicians and visiting scholars ($75,000) see Scholl Foundation, Dr.

Neighborhood Housing Services ($110,000) see Goldseker Foundation of Maryland, Morris

Pacific Basin Research Institute — support for the development of a market strategy for Vietnam ($137,500) see Donner Foundation, William H.

Park School ($7,000) see Hecht-Levi Foundation

Peabody Institute ($50,000) see Hecht-Levi Foundation

Peabody Institute ($13,000) see Unger Foundation, Aber D.

Prince George's County Memorial Library System ($10,000) see Bell Atlantic Corp.

Retinitis Pigmentosa Foundation Fighting Blindness — final payment on commitment ($196,800) see Chatlos Foundation

Roland Park Country School ($5,000) see Campbell Foundation

Roland Park Country School — for secondary education ($21,225) see Price Associates, T. Rowe

St. Ignatius Loyola Academy ($10,000) see Leidy Foundation, John J.

St. John's College ($27,173) see Kornfeld Foundation, Emily Davie and Joseph S.

St. Paul School — for secondary education ($19,700) see Price Associates, T. Rowe

Salisbury State University ($3,500) see Widgeon Foundation

Salvation Army ($10,000) see PHH Corporation

Sexual Assault Recovery Center — for sexually assaulted and abused children ($20,000) see Lockhart Vaughan Foundation

Shakespeare Globe Centre ($25,000) see Heinz Trust, Drue

Shorebank Advisory Services ($111,500) see Goldseker Foundation of Maryland, Morris

Sisters of Mercy of the Americas ($250,000) see McShain Charities, John

Telecommunications Life Skills — general support ($34,000) see MCI Communications Corp.

Theater Project ($7,500) see Unger Foundation, Aber D.

Trappe Volunteer Fire Department — operational ($5,000) see Darby Foundation

Trinity Church ($10,000) see Campbell Foundation

Union Memorial Hospital ($200) see Warfield Memorial Fund, Anna Emory

Union Memorial Hospital Foundation ($12,500) see Unger Foundation, Aber D.

United Jewish Appeal Federation of Jewish Philanthropies ($159,000) see Hechinger Co.

United Way ($75,000) see Price Associates, T. Rowe

United Way of Central Maryland — 1991-92 pledge ($42,000) see Giant Food Inc.

United Way of Central Maryland see AEGON USA Inc.

United Way Central Maryland ($130,000) see PHH Corporation

United Way of Central Maryland ($100,000) see Rouse Co.

United Way of Central Maryland ($2,500) see Handy and Harman Foundation

United Way Central Maryland ($20,000) see Armco Inc.

United Way of Central Maryland ($215,000) see Bethlehem Steel Corp.

United Way of Central Maryland — for general support ($4,700) see Lehigh Portland Cement Co.

United Way Lower Eastern Shore ($33,000) see Dresser Industries, Inc.

University Baltimore School of Law ($7,500) see Leidy Foundation, John J.

University of Baltimore School of Law Clinical Law Program ($7,500) see Leidy Foundation, John J.

University of Maryland — scholarships ($32,000) see Newcombe Foundation, Charlotte W.

University of Maryland — support George LaNoue's writing at the University of Maryland regarding affirmative action ($35,000) see Laurel Foundation

University of Maryland at Baltimore — Shock Trauma Research Fund ($105,000) see France Foundation, Jacob and Annita

University of Maryland Foundation ($204,000) see Martin Marietta Corp.

University of Maryland Foundation ($10,350) see Widgeon Foundation

University of Maryland Health Systems see AEGON USA Inc.

University of Maryland School of Pharmacy ($5,000) see Giant Food Inc.

US Naval Academy Alumni Association ($2,000) see Price Foundation, Lucien B. and Katherine E.

Villa Julie College ($8,000) see Unger Foundation, Aber D.

Walden School — for heating and cooling equipment ($10,000) see Peppers Foundation, Ann

Walters Art Gallery ($40,000) see Blaustein Foundation, Louis and Henrietta

Walters Art Gallery ($6,000) see Campbell Foundation

Walter's Art Gallery — for culture and the arts ($9,785) see Price Associates, T. Rowe

Washington College — construction and renovation of dormitories ($50,000) see Middendorf Foundation

Waverly Family Center — teen parents ($16,990) see Lockhart Vaughan Foundation

Wesley Home ($200) see Warfield Memorial Fund, Anna Emory

Wildfowl Trust of North America — maintenance of habitat for waterfowl and wildlife for educational purposes ($298,364) see Knapp Foundation

Wilmer Institute ($25,000) see Titus Foundation, Roy and Niuta

Wilmer Institute ($25,000) see Titus Foundation, Roy and Niuta

Massachusetts

5A Sports Program see Massachusetts Mutual Life Insurance Co.

300 Committee — stewardship program ($4,130) see Friendship Fund

ACCION International — to initiate microenterprises near Sao Paulo, Brazil ($15,000) see Cabot Corp.

Action International — expansion of the microlending programs at their Brazilian affiliate, FENAPE ($37,500) see Jurzykowski Foundation, Alfred

Adaptive Environments — universal design project ($50,000) see NYNEX Corporation

Aero Club of New England — scholarship fund ($2,500) see Edmonds Foundation, Dean S.

African American Federation of Greater Boston ($25,000) see Shawmut National Corp.

AIDS Action Committee ($5,000) see Thermo Electron Corp.

Alexis de Tocqueville Society ($11,000) see Breyer Foundation

All Saints Church — operational ($20,000) see

Rice Charitable Foundation, Albert W.

Alumnae Fund of Smith College ($5,000) see Memton Fund

American Academy of Arts and Sciences ($55,000) see Eaton Foundation, Cyrus

American Antiquarian Society ($75,000) see Donnelley Foundation, Gaylord and Dorothy

American Antiquarian Society — to establish endowment to fund the Marcus A. McCorison Librarianship ($30,000) see Harrington Foundation, Francis A. and Jacquelyn H.

American Antiquarian Society — operational ($15,000) see Rice Charitable Foundation, Albert W.

American Health Assistance Foundation — for Alzheimers disease research ($4,000) see Prouty Foundation, Olive Higgins

American Ireland Fund ($200,000) see Heinz Company, H. J.

American Ireland Fund ($150,000) see Heinz Company, H. J.

American Red Cross ($3,000) see Morgan Construction Co.

American Repertory Theater ($10,000) see Day Foundation, Nancy Sayles

American Textile Museum ($25,000) see Demoulas Supermarkets Inc.

Amherst College ($40,000) see Jameson Foundation, J. W. and Ida M.

Amherst College ($5,000) see Fribourg Foundation

Amherst College ($26,000) see Lurcy Charitable and Educational Trust, Georges

Amherst College Alumni Fund ($60,100) see Rosen Foundation, Joseph

Andover Historical Society ($15,000) see Rogers Family Foundation

Anna Jacques Hospital — special care nursery ($25,000) see Arakelian Foundation, Mary Alice

Anna Jacqus Hospital ($2,500) see Gould Electronics Inc.

Anti-Displacement Project ($5,000) see Heydt Fund, Nan and Matilda

Appalachian Mountain Club ($25,040) see Cabot Family Charitable Trust

Appalachian Mountain Club — help pay for data collection and Landsat work involved in the Northern Forest Lands project ($25,000) see Pierce Charitable Trust, Harold Whitworth

Applewild School ($15,359) see Ansin Private Foundation, Ronald M.

Applewild School ($50,000) see Wallace Foundation, George R.

Archdiocese of Boston ($2,500) see Handy and Harman Foundation

Associated Day Care Services ($5,000) see Dewing Foundation, Frances R.

Associated Grantmakers — annual dues ($10,700) see Stevens Foundation, Abbot and Dorothy H.

Associated Grantmakers of Massachusetts ($45,000) see Polaroid Corp.

Jason Foundation ($30,000) see Bell Foundation, James F.

Jewish Family and Children's Services ($40,000) see Stone Charitable Foundation

Jewish Federation for Justice ($10,000) see Stone Charitable Foundation

Jewish Fund for Justice ($10,000) see Stone Charitable Foundation

JFK Library Foundation ($4,500) see Goldberg Family Foundation

Jobs for Youth ($10,000) see New England Business Service

Jobs for Youth of Boston ($10,000) see New England Business Service

John F. Kennedy School of Government — full tuition scholarship for Cambridge city employees to attend Mid-Career Master in Public Education program ($19,650) see Little, Inc., Arthur D.

Joslin Diabetes Center — endowment ($15,000) see Shaw Foundation, Arch W.

Junior Achievement — general support ($6,000) see Acushnet Co.

Junior Achievement ($1,000) see Blake Foundation, S. P.

Junior Achievement see Massachusetts Mutual Life Insurance Co.

Junior Achievement of Western Massachusetts ($68,000) see Davis Foundation, Irene E. and George A.

Just-A-Start — on-going support for job training, education, and counseling services ($9,000) see Little, Inc., Arthur D.

Knights of Don Orione ($10,000) see Sawyer Charitable Foundation

Kodaly Center of America ($75,000) see Rowland Foundation

La Alianza Hispana — for the certified nurses' aide/home health aide training program ($10,000) see Pierce Charitable Trust, Harold Whitworth

Laboure Center ($13,600) see Boston Edison Co.

Lahey Clinic ($25,000) see Scherer Foundation, Karla

Lahey Clinic Foundation ($25,000) see Rogers Family Foundation

Landmark Volunteers ($10,000) see Sasco Foundation

Lawrence Academy ($308,552) see Ansin Private Foundation, Ronald M.

Lawrence Boys and Girls Club ($25,000) see Russell Trust, Josephine G.

Lawrence Boys and Girls Club ($15,000) see Stearns Trust, Artemas W.

Lawrence General Hospital ($70,000) see Russell Trust, Josephine G.

Lawrence General Hospital ($40,000) see Stearns Trust, Artemas W.

Lawrence General Hospital Foundation ($25,000) see Rogers Family Foundation

Lawrence General Hospital Foundation ($25,000) see Stevens Foundation, Abbot and Dorothy H.

Lawrence Memorial ($20,000) see Citizens Bank of Rhode Island

Lawrence Memorial Hospital ($10,000) see Griffis Foundation

Lazarus House ($20,000) see Stearns Trust, Artemas W.

Lesley College — Project Best ($85,000) see NYNEX Corporation

Letters of Intent Higgins Armory ($5,000) see Morgan Construction Co.

Link House — renovations ($15,000) see Arakelian Foundation, Mary Alice

Longy School of Music — assist in making Bakalar Library collection accessible through computerization of its holdings ($10,000) see Phillips Foundation, Ellis L.

MacDuffie School ($125,000) see Davis Foundation, Irene E. and George A.

Marian Manor for Aged and Infirmed ($13,573) see Boston Edison Co.

Marine Biological Laboratory — for the Young Investigators Endowment at Ecosystems Center ($100,000) see Clowes Fund

Marine Biological Laboratory ($250,000) see Vetlesen Foundation, G. Unger

Marthas Vineyard Hospital Foundation ($5,000) see Seton Leather Co.

Mason Square Development Corporation see Massachusetts Mutual Life Insurance Co.

Massachusettes Institute of Technology — general support ($5,000) see Acushnet Co.

Massachusetts 4-H Foundation ($20,000) see Saltonstall Charitable Foundation, Richard

Massachusetts Association for the Blind ($79,583) see Memorial Foundation for the Blind

Massachusetts Audubon Society ($15,000) see Fletcher Foundation

Massachusetts Audubon Society ($100,000) see South Branch Foundation

Massachusetts Coalition for Battered Women Service Corps — Jane Doe Safety Fund ($4,000) see Prouty Foundation, Olive Higgins

Massachusetts Corporation for Educational Telecommunications — support for pilot program, FirstMath ($10,000) see Little, Inc., Arthur D.

Massachusetts General Hospital ($10,000) see Vanderbilt Trust, R. T.

Massachusetts General Hospital ($300,000) see Marriott Foundation, J. Willard

Massachusetts General Hospital — restricted support for Clinic Research project ($25,000) see Cabot Corp.

Massachusetts General Hospital ($50,000) see Davis Foundation, Irene E. and George A.

Massachusetts General Hospital ($50,000) see Levy Foundation, June Rockwell

Massachusetts General Hospital ($120,701) see Rowland Foundation

Massachusetts General Hospital ($20,000) see Saltonstall Charitable Foundation, Richard

Massachusetts General Hospital ($10,000) see Thermo Electron Corp.

Massachusetts General Hospital — Merrill Lynch Cardiology Research Award, first payment of a $1 million pledge ($250,000) see Merrill Lynch & Co., Inc.

Massachusetts General Hospital ($20,000) see Jaffe Foundation

Massachusetts General Hospital Cancer Society ($470,000) see Monell Foundation, Ambrose

Massachusetts General Hospital Neurolinguistics Lab — for Neurolinguistics Lab Fund and precursor program ($25,000) see Cape Branch Foundation

Massachusetts Historical Society ($4,200) see Winthrop Trust, Clara B.

Massachusetts Institute of Technology — Bechtel Lecture Hall ($100,000) see Bechtel, Jr. Foundation, S. D.

Massachusetts Institute of Technology ($1,222,923) see Hewlett-Packard Co.

Massachusetts Institute of Technology —for electrical and computer engineering ($970,533) see Hewlett-Packard Co.

Massachusetts Institute of Technology — silicon retinal implant ($150,000) see Seaver Institute

Massachusetts Institute of Technology ($25,000) see Mulford Foundation, Vincent

Massachusetts Institute of Technology — scholarships ($200,000) see Balfour Foundation, L. G.

Massachusetts Institute of Technology ($50,000) see Bank of Boston Corp.

Massachusetts Institute of Technology — support for the Hoyt Hotel Career Development professorship ($50,000) see Cabot Corp.

Massachusetts Institute of Technology — for general purpose ($100,000) see Germeshausen Foundation, Kenneth J.

Massachusetts Institute of Technology ($1,000,000) see Peabody Charitable Fund, Amelia

Massachusetts Institute of Technology ($50,000) see Thermo Electron Corp.

Massachusetts Institute of Technology —for annual payment on unrestricted operating grant ($500,000) see General Motors Corp.

Massachusetts Institute of Technology ($50,000) see Barker Foundation, J.M.R.

Massachusetts Institute of Technology — capital campaign ($20,000) see Klipstein Foundation, Ernest Christian

Massachusetts Institute of Technology ($30,350) see Lurcy Charitable and Educational Trust, Georges

Massachusetts Institute of Technology ($140,000) see BP America Inc.

Massachusetts Institute of Technology ($101,550) see AMP Incorporated

MCCM Foundation ($17,500) see Fletcher Foundation

MCCM Foundation — to construct Cancer Care Center ($15,000) see Harrington Foundation, Francis A. and Jacquelyn H.

McLean Hospital — Shervert H. Frazier Institute campaign ($13,000) see Rabb Charitable Foundation, Sidney and Esther

Medical Center of Central Massachusetts ($1,500) see Bank of Boston

Medical Center of Central Massachusetts — operational ($33,333) see Rice Charitable Foundation, Albert W.

Medical Foundation ($50,000) see Levy Foundation, June Rockwell

Medical Foundation — funding for one biomedical research fellowship ($28,500) see Pierce Charitable Trust, Harold Whitworth

Memorial Hospital — Kidney Dialysis Unit ($761) see Memorial Foundation for the Blind

Mercy Hospital ($60,000) see Davis Foundation, Irene E. and George A.

Merrimack College ($22,000) see Russell Trust, Josephine G.

Merrimack Repertory Theater ($23,072) see Ansin Private Foundation, Ronald M.

Merrimack Repertory Theater ($11,500) see M/A-COM, Inc.

Merrimack Valley Community Foundation ($48,000) see Stevens Foundation, Abbot and Dorothy H.

Metropolitan Boston Housing Partnership ($50,000) see Shawmut National Corp.

Metropolitan Boston Housing Partnership ($100,000) see Bank of Boston Corp.

Metropolitan Boston Housing Partnership ($40,000) see Globe Newspaper Co.

Metrowest Medical Center ($50,000) see Weezie Foundation

Milford Salvation Army ($5,000) see Hopedale Foundation

Milford-Whitinsville Regional Hospital ($75,000) see Hopedale Foundation

Milton Academy — capital campaign ($5,000) see Memton Fund

Milton Hospital ($141,740) see Pierce Charitable Trust, Harold Whitworth

Minuteman Home Care Corporation ($2,500) see GenRad

Miss Hall's School — capital fund ($30,000) see Firman Fund

Mount Auburn Foundation — Campaign 2000 ($10,000) see Little, Inc., Arthur D.

Mt. Auburn Hospital Foundation ($100,000) see Rowland Foundation

Mt. Holyoke College — for use over three years toward development of the Czech and Slovak Library Information Network ($1,188,000) see Mellon Foundation, Andrew W.

Mt. Holyoke College ($50,000) see Levitt Foundation

Museum of Afro-American History ($10,000) see Tupancy-Harris Foundation of 1986

Museum of American Textile History ($122,557) see Stevens Foundation, Abbot and Dorothy H.

Museum of American Textile History ($100,000) see Stevens Foundation, Abbot and Dorothy H.

Museum of Fine Arts — for Children's Room ($10,000) see Germeshausen Foundation, Kenneth J.

Museum of Fine Arts ($206,000) see Dingman Foundation, Michael D.

Museum of Fine Arts see Unitrode Corp.

Museum of Fine Arts ($4,000) see Wilder Foundation

Museum of Fine Arts of Boston ($43,950) see Johnson Fund, Edward C.

Museum of Science ($30,000) see Babson Foundation, Paul and Edith

Museum of Science — final payment of three-year pledge to build a chemistry laboratory classroom ($50,000) see Cabot Corp.

Museum of Science — for new exhibits plan ($75,000) see Germeshausen Foundation, Kenneth J.

Museum of Science ($2,500) see Hopedale Foundation

Museum of Science — Discovery Center ($100,000) see Pierce Charitable Trust, Harold Whitworth

Museum of Science see Unitrode Corp.

Music Hall ($7,500) see Fuller Foundation

NAACP Special Contribution Fund ($5,250) see Morrison Knudsen Corporation

Nantucket Arts Network ($12,000) see Tupancy-Harris Foundation of 1986

Nantucket Athaeneum ($25,000) see Day Foundation, Nancy Sayles

Nantucket Athenaeum ($25,000) see Jockey Hollow Foundation

Nantucket Atheneum Building ($100,000) see Weezie Foundation

Nantucket Boys and Girls Club ($24,000) see Tupancy-Harris Foundation of 1986

Nantucket Boys and Girls Club ($50,000) see Weezie Foundation

Nantucket Conservation Foundation ($193,000) see Tupancy-Harris Foundation of 1986

Nantucket Conservation Foundation ($5,000) see Osceola Foundation

Nantucket Cottage Hospital ($20,000) see Day Foundation, Nancy Sayles

Nantucket Cottage Hospital — for medical purposes ($26,000) see Larsen Fund

Nantucket Cottage Hospital ($39,000) see Tupancy-Harris Foundation of 1986

Nantucket Cottage Hospital ($26,000) see Osceola Foundation

Nantucket Historical Association ($51,141) see

Tobey Health Systems — medical ($50,000) see Barth Foundation, Theodore H.

Tower Hill Botanical Garden ($3,000) see Bank of Boston

Town of Hopedale Master Plan ($11,782) see Hopedale Foundation

Town of Manchester-by-the-Sea ($5,500) see Winthrop Trust, Clara B.

Town of Winchendon — operations ($25,000) see Robinson-Broadhurst Foundation

Town of Winchendon — equipment ($25,000) see Robinson-Broadhurst Foundation

Travelers Aid of Boston — revolving fund ($7,500) see Weber Charities Corp., Frederick E.

Travelers Aid Society of Boston — operating support ($10,000) see Hunt Foundation, Roy A.

Trustees of Boston University ($6,000) see Edmonds Foundation, Dean S.

Trustees of Phillips Academy of Andover ($50,000) see Phipps Foundation, Howard

Trustees of Reservations — Coolidge Point Reservation and Essex River Estuary ($27,000) see Folger Fund

Trustees of Reservations ($25,040) see Cabot Family Charitable Trust

Trustees of Reservations ($70,000) see Saltonstall Charitable Foundation, Richard

Trustees of Reservations ($4,000) see Winthrop Trust, Clara B.

Trustees of Tufts College — for a Perseus Project of Archaic and Classical Greek sculpture ($200,000) see Getty Trust, J. Paul

Tufts College Trustees ($52,500) see Ames Charitable Trust, Harriett

Tufts College Veterinary School ($100,000) see Rowland Foundation

Tufts University — scholarships ($200,000) see Balfour Foundation, L. G.

Tufts University ($30,000) see Bay Foundation

Tufts University ($55,000) see Porter Foundation, Mrs. Cheever

Tufts University Arts and Sciences ($50,000) see Loews Corporation

Tufts University/Lincoln Filene — New England Institute for nonprofit organization ($13,000) see Rabb Charitable Foundation, Sidney and Esther

Tufts University Lincoln Filene Center — New England Institute for Non-Profit Organizations ($30,000) see Goldberg Family Foundation

Tufts University Medical School ($61,814) see Greenwall Foundation

Tufts University School of Veterinary Medicine — purchase of equipment to modernize the surgical facilities at Wildlife Clinic ($30,000) see Knapp Foundation

Tufts University School of Veterinary Medicine ($5,000) see Childs

Charitable Foundation, Roberta M.

Unh Image Making ($5,000) see Dewing Foundation, Frances R.

United Fund of Merrimack Valley ($34,000) see Rogers Family Foundation

United Fund of North Central ($17,500) see New England Business Service

United Fund of North Central Massachusetts ($17,500) see New England Business Service

United Negro College Fund — general operating and scholarship support for 41 member colleges ($10,000) see Little, Inc., Arthur D.

United Negro College Fund — scholarships for students from Boston ($15,000) see Pierce Charitable Trust, Harold Whitworth

United Way ($23,500) see Babson Foundation, Paul and Edith

United Way ($34,036) see Goldberg Family Foundation

United Way ($70,000) see Morgan Construction Co.

United Way ($2,500) see Reisman Charitable Trust, George C. and Evelyn R.

United Way of Central Massachusetts ($72,000) see Shawmut National Corp.

United Way of Central Massachusetts ($240,000) see Norton Co.

United Way of Central Massachusetts ($25,000) see Rice Charitable Foundation, Albert W.

United Way of Central Massachusetts ($3,875) see Safety Fund National Bank

United Way of Eastern New England ($675,000) see Bank of Boston Corp.

United Way Eastern New England ($358,904) see Polaroid Corp.

United Way of Gardner ($4,000) see Safety Fund National Bank

United Way of Massachusetts ($15,000) see CS First Boston Corporation

United Way Massachusetts Bay ($332,846) see Boston Edison Co.

United Way of Massachusetts Bay ($64,000) see Saltonstall Charitable Foundation, Richard

United Way of Massachusetts Bay ($10,000) see Weber Charities Corp., Frederick E.

United Way of Massachusetts Bay/Child Care Initiative — pledge toward the Child Care Initiative Funding Collaboratives to strengthen nonprofit child care providers by focusing resources on physical facilities and staff retention ($30,000) see Globe Newspaper Co.

United Way of Merrimack Valley ($15,000) see Arakelian Foundation, Mary Alice

United Way of Merrimack Valley ($15,000) see Russell Trust, Josephine G.

United Way of Merrimack Valley ($25,000) see Stearns Trust, Artemas W.

United Way of Merrimack Valley ($15,000) see Stevens Foundation, Abbot and Dorothy H.

United Way of New Bedford — general support ($70,000) see Acushnet Co.

United Way of New England — corporate contribution ($40,000) see Little, Inc., Arthur D.

United Way of North Central Massachusetts ($26,250) see Safety Fund National Bank

United Way of Pioneer Valley ($26,820) see Shawmut National Corp.

United Way of Pioneer Valley ($55,000) see Dow Jones & Company, Inc.

United Way of Pioneer Valley ($31,616) see Westvaco Corporation

United Way Webster/Dudley — operating funds ($12,000) see Cranston Print Works Company

University Christian Movement ($15,000) see Wallace Foundation, George R.

University of Massachusetts ($1,525) see Bird Corp.

University of Massachusetts ($15,000) see Boston Edison Co.

University of Massachusetts — Taylor Scholarship — support the Taylor Scholars Program ($125,000) see Globe Newspaper Co.

University of Massachusetts ($33,333) see GenCorp Inc.

University of Massachusetts Boston — in support of the 1993 Taylor Scholars Program ($50,000) see Globe Newspaper Co.

University of Massachusetts Dartmouth — operating funds ($10,000) see Cranston Print Works Company

University of Massachusetts Foundation ($15,000) see Dexter Charitable Fund, Eugene A.

University of Massachusetts Medical Center ($16,500) see Memorial Foundation for the Blind

Urban League of Springfield ($25,000) see Dexter Charitable Fund, Eugene A.

Urban League of Springfield see Massachusetts Mutual Life Insurance Co.

US Rugby Football Foundation ($4,800) see Dell Foundation, Hazel

Very Special Arts Massachusetts ($9,000) see Robinson Fund, Maurice R.

Visitation Sisters of St. Joseph Convent — construction of new monastery ($75,000) see Laffey-McHugh Foundation

Visiting Nurse Association ($6,000) see Hopedale Foundation

Visiting Nurse Association Home Care ($30,000) see Stevens Foundation, Abbot and Dorothy H.

Wang Center for the Performing Arts ($10,000) see Fuller Foundation

Wediko Children's Services — grant for fund-raising personnel, curriculum development, and engineering and architectural planning in the expansion of this year-round program for emotionally disturbed children ($120,000) see van Ameringen Foundation

Wellesley College — four payments on a five-year commitment in support for the full climate control project of the Mary Cooper Jewett Arts Center ($200,000) see Jewett Foundation, George Frederick

Wellesley College ($67,918) see Van Nuys Foundation, I. N. and Susanna H.

Wellesley College ($125,000) see Caspersen Foundation for Aid to Health and Education, O. W.

Wellesley College — scholarship ($2,000) see American Optical Corp.

Wellesley College ($30,000) see Burden Foundation, Florence V.

Wellesley College ($25,000) see Cowles Charitable Trust

Wellesley College ($100,000) see Pforzheimer Foundation, Carl and Lily

Wellesley Community Center ($50,000) see Babson Foundation, Paul and Edith

Wellesley School-Age Child Care Project — over four years and eight months to establish Wellesley's School-Aged Child Care Project (WSACP) as project manager for the new Community School-Age Child Care Initiative ($7,713,037) see Wallace-Reader's Digest Fund, DeWitt

Wendell P. Clark Memorial — capital improvement and operations ($325,000) see Robinson-Broadhurst Foundation

Wentworth Institute of Technology — support for a new educational technology project to equip laboratory for faculty to develop software to supplement regular classroom instruction ($10,000) see Little, Inc., Arthur D.

Western Massachusetts Food Bank ($20,000) see Heydt Fund, Nan and Matilda

Weston Library — for general purpose ($25,000) see Germeshausen Foundation, Kenneth J.

Westport River Watershed ($4,660) see Dewing Foundation, Frances R.

WGBH — for general purpose ($100,000) see Germeshausen Foundation, Kenneth J.

WGBH — Ralph Lowell Society ($5,000) see Goldberg Family Foundation

WGBH ($50,000) see Saltonstall Charitable Foundation, Richard

WGBH Educational Foundation — endowment for program excellence campaign ($5,000) see Rabb Charitable Foundation, Sidney and Esther

WGBH Educational Foundation ($7,500) see Winthrop Trust, Clara B.

WGBH Educational Foundation ($15,000) see Hunt Foundation, Roy A.

WGBH Public Broadcasting ($100,000) see Rowland Foundation

WGBH Television ($30,000) see Arakelian Foundation, Mary Alice

WGBY/Channel 57 ($2,500) see Blake Foundation, S. P.

Wheaton College — scholarship ($3,000) see American Optical Corp.

Wheaton College — NEH Challenge Program ($100,000) see Mars Foundation

Wheaton College Board of Trustees — athletic facility ($1,000,000) see Haas, Jr. Fund, Evelyn and Walter

WICN — Audio Journal ($35,000) see Memorial Foundation for the Blind

Wilbraham Monson Academy ($167,648) see Blake Foundation, S. P.

Williamstown Regional Art Conservation ($40,000) see Bay Foundation

Winchendon Health Foundation — capital improvements ($50,000) see Robinson-Broadhurst Foundation

Windrush Farm Therapeutic Equitation ($70,000) see Rowland Foundation

Winsor School ($500,000) see Peabody Charitable Fund, Amelia

Winsor School ($7,000) see Winthrop Trust, Clara B.

Woods Hole Oceanographic ($5,500) see Normandie Foundation

Woods Hole Oceanographic Institute ($30,000) see Argyros Foundation

Woods Hole Oceanographic Institute ($121,275) see Seaver Institute

Woods Hole Oceanographic Institute ($400,000) see Vetlesen Foundation, G. Unger

Woods Hole Research Center ($25,000) see Schiff Foundation, Dorothy

Worcester Art Museum ($12,000) see Morgan Construction Co.

Worcester Art Museum — underwrite part of cost of exhibition Women of the Pleasure Quarter ($200,000) see Carpenter Foundation, E. Rhodes and Leona B.

Worcester Chamber of Commerce — convention center ($5,000) see Safety Fund National Bank

Worcester Children's Friend Society ($2,500) see Bank of Boston

Worcester County Horticultural Society ($25,000) see Ansin Private Foundation, Ronald M.

Worcester County Horticultural Society ($5,000) see Morgan Construction Co.

Worcester County Horticultural Society — operational ($10,000) see Rice Charitable Foundation, Albert W.

Worcester Foundation for Experimental Biology ($1,500) see Bank of Boston

Worcester Foundation for Experimental Biology — to assist with the recruitment of new scientists ($50,000) see McEvoy Foundation, Mildred H.

Worcester Foundation for Experimental Biology — research on male contraceptives ($55,000) see Noble Foundation, Edward John

($80,000) see Wilson Fund, Matilda R.

International Aid ($1,067) see Smith Foundation, Gordon V. and Helen C.

Jackson Community Foundation — program support ($30,000) see Consumers Power Co.

Jesse Besser Museum ($153,280) see Besser Foundation

Jewish Ensemble Theater — production costs ($5,675) see DeRoy Foundation, Helen L.

Jewish Family and Children's Services ($15,600) see Merkley Charitable Trust

Jewish Welfare Federation ($11,000) see Ratner Foundation, Milton M.

John Ball Zoological Society ($5,000) see Batts Foundation

John Ball Zoological Society — community development ($39,000) see Wege Foundation

Junior Achievement ($1,000) see Abrams Foundation, Talbert and Leota

Kalamazoo Academic Partnership — operations ($20,000) see Upjohn Foundation, Harold and Grace

Kalamazoo Child Guidance Clinic ($5,000) see Todd Co., A.M.

Kalamazoo Christian Schools ($2,500) see Fabri-Kal Corp.

Kalamazoo College — Dow Science Center ($100,000) see Towsley Foundation, Harry A. and Margaret D.

Kalamazoo College — scholarships ($8,000) see Vicksburg Foundation

Kalamazoo County Co-op ($6,000) see Vicksburg Foundation

Kalamazoo Foundation — YMCA — capital campaign ($5,000) see Todd Co., A.M.

Kalamazoo Foundation — Math and Science Center ($3,000) see Todd Co., A.M.

Kalamazoo Foundation — endowment ($25,000) see Vicksburg Foundation

Kalamazoo Valley Habitat for Humanity — facilities ($50,000) see Upjohn Foundation, Harold and Grace

Kalamazoo Valley Habitat for Humanity — operations ($20,000) see Upjohn Foundation, Harold and Grace

Kellogg Community College — adult scholarships ($10,000) see Miller Foundation

Kirk in the Hills ($11,000) see Westerman Foundation, Samuel L.

Kresge Eye Institute — support research associate for visual lab ($10,000) see Royal Foundation, May Mitchell

Lake Michigan College ($60,725) see Upton Foundation, Frederick S.

Lake Michigan College Education Fund ($5,000) see Tiscornia Foundation

Leader Dogs for the Blind — dog training program ($7,500) see Royal Foundation, May Mitchell

Library ($15,000) see Abrams Foundation, Talbert and Leota

Life Connections Campaign ($800) see Grand Rapids Label Co.

Little Traverse Conservancy ($100,000) see Offield Family Foundation

Loyola Academy ($15,000) see Whitney Fund, David M.

Manistee County Youth Center see Packaging Corporation of America

Marced Productions ($3,000) see Merkley Charitable Trust

Marian Burch Day Care — landscaping ($10,000) see Miller Foundation

Marygrove College ($20,000) see Whitney Fund, David M.

MCHS Infant Mortality Project — jubilee program ($7,500) see DeRoy Foundation, Helen L.

McKenley Foundation — Huron River - North Main Development Project ($165,000) see Towsley Foundation, Harry A. and Margaret D.

McKinley Foundation — to defray, in part, the costs of constructing and equipping its current project, New Center Ann Arbor, Michigan, as an office building for non-profit organizations ($100,000) see Herrick Foundation

McKinley Foundation — to defray, in part, the costs of constructing and equipping its current project, New Center Ann Arbor, MI, as an office building for nonprofit organizations ($100,000) see Tecumseh Products Co.

Mercy Memorial Health Fund ($45,000) see Tiscornia Foundation

Mercy Memorial Hospital Foundation — health ($30,000) see La-Z-Boy Chair Co.

Michigan Botanical Gardens — capital funds ($5,000) see Seidman Family Foundation

Michigan Botanical Gardens — community development ($65,000) see Wege Foundation

Michigan Cancer Foundation ($29,000) see Borman's Inc.

Michigan Colleges Foundation ($254,072) see Chrysler Corp.

Michigan Colleges Foundation — scholarships ($10,000) see Miller Foundation

Michigan Colleges Foundation ($6,000) see Tiscornia Foundation

Michigan Dyslexia Institute ($15,000) see Abrams Foundation, Talbert and Leota

Michigan Humane Society, Cruelty Investigation Division ($33,136) see DeRoy Testamentary Foundation

Michigan Molecular Institute — operating and capital ($400,000) see Dow Foundation, Herbert H. and Grace A.

Michigan Opera Theater see Douglas & Lomason Company

Michigan Opera Theater ($11,000) see Westerman Foundation, Samuel L.

Michigan Opera Theatre — program support ($15,000) see Consumers Power Co.

Michigan Opera Theatre Opera in Residence Petoskey — program support ($15,000) see Consumers Power Co.

Michigan Partnership for New Education —for annual payment on unrestricted operating grant ($300,000) see General Motors Corp.

Michigan State University ($50,000) see Abrams Foundation, Talbert and Leota

Michigan State University — MBA scholarship fund ($25,000) see DeRoy Testamentary Foundation

Michigan State University ($89,000) see Dow Corning Corp.

Michigan State University ($312,500) see Ford Motor Co.

Michigan State University ($312,500) see Ford Motor Co.

Michigan State University —for annual payment on capital campaign 1988-97 ($500,000) see General Motors Corp.

Michigan State University ($25,000) see GenCorp Inc.

Michigan State University — for employee scholarship ($4,000) see Quaker Chemical Corp.

Michigan State University College of Natural Sciences — Center for Science and Mathematics Teachers ($200,000) see Towsley Foundation, Harry A. and Margaret D.

Michigan State University KCMS — building project ($3,500) see Todd Co., A.M.

Michigan Tech Fund ($50,000) see Dow Corning Corp.

Michigan Tech Fund ($2,000) see Van Evera Foundation, Dewitt

Michigan Technological University — scholarship ($7,934) see Caestecker Foundation, Charles and Marie

Michigan Theater Foundation ($2,000) see R&B Machine Tool Co.

Michigan United Conservation — other ($25,000) see La-Z-Boy Chair Co.

Midland Center for the Arts — operating fund ($874,850) see Dow Foundation, Herbert H. and Grace A.

Midland Center for the Arts — renovation of Hall of Ideas ($450,000) see Dow Foundation, Herbert H. and Grace A.

Midland County Project — drug abuse resistance training ($2,500) see Royal Foundation, May Mitchell

Midland Foundation — Riverside Place building fund ($1,500,000) see Dow Foundation, Herbert H. and Grace A.

Mitten Bay Girl Scout Council — new administrative facility ($10,000) see Kantzler Foundation

Mitten Bay Girl Scouts ($10,000) see Dow Corning Corp.

MMU Business College ($7,500) see Fabri-Kal Corp.

Monroe Family YMCA — human services ($25,000) see La-Z-Boy Chair Co.

Mt. Zion Baptist Church ($2,000) see Todd Co., A.M.

Music Hall Center for the Performing Arts — capital ($100,000) see Wilson Fund, Matilda R.

Muskegon Community College — expansion fund ($20,000) see Brunswick Corp.

Muskegon Community College ($30,000) see SPX Corp.

Muskegon Museum of Art ($52,000) see SPX Corp.

National Board for Professional Teaching Standards — to support field testing of an ambitious national, voluntary advanced certification program for school teachers ($750,000) see Knight Foundation, John S. and James L.

National Center for Community Education — to support the continued planning and coordination of a comprehensive national/international community education leadership training program ($500,000) see Mott Foundation, Charles Stewart

Neighborhood Club ($20,000) see Ford II Fund, Henry

Neighborhood House — Christmas baskets ($5,500) see Mills Fund, Frances Goll

Neighborhoods of Battle Creek — housing program ($125,000) see Miller Foundation

New Museum ($5,000) see Lasdon Foundation, William and Mildred

North American Committee for Humanism — publication of Humanism Today magazine and seminar ($33,000) see Johnson Charitable Educational Trust, James Hervey

North American Committee for Humanism — publication of Humanism Today magazine ($10,000) see Johnson Charitable Educational Trust, James Hervey

Northern Michigan Hospital Foundation ($5,000) see Batts Foundation

Northwood University ($20,000) see Whiting Foundation, Macauley and Helen Dow

Northwood University — External Degree program and Master Degree Library additions ($10,000) see Bauervic Foundation, Charles M.

Oakland Community College Foundation ($5,000) see Vollbrecht Foundation, Frederick A.

Oakland Community College Foundation — Project BOLD ($3,600) see Vollbrecht Foundation, Frederick A.

Oakland Family Services — Therapeutic Nursery Program ($26,626) see DeRoy Testamentary Foundation

Oakland University — capital ($95,700) see Wilson Fund, Matilda R.

Office of the Wayne County Executive, Department of

Public Health — youth violence prevention project ($265,000) see Skillman Foundation

Old Regent Theater Company ($15,000) see Delano Foundation, Mignon Sherwood

Olivet College — scholarship fund ($14,000) see Besser Foundation

Olivet College ($5,000) see Tiscornia Foundation

Olivet College ($51,000) see Upton Foundation, Frederick S.

Opportunities Industrialization Center ($80,000) see Boutell Memorial Fund

Opportunities Industrialization Center — building ($50,000) see Eddy Family Memorial Fund, C. K.

Parks Foundation of Kalamazoo County — operations ($15,000) see Upjohn Foundation, Harold and Grace

Pere Marquette Rail Trail ($15,000) see Dow Corning Corp.

Piney Woods Country Life School ($5,000) see Appleby Trust, Scott B. and Annie P.

Planned Parenthood Association ($10,000) see Tiscornia Foundation

Planned Parenthood Centers of West Michigan ($2,500) see Batts Foundation

Planned Parenthood League ($18,000) see Whitney Fund, David M.

Planned Parenthood of Mid-Michigan — peer education program ($60,752) see Towsley Foundation, Harry A. and Margaret D.

Porter Hills Presbyterian ($1,000) see Grand Rapids Label Co.

Prevention of Child Abuse ($20,000) see Delano Foundation, Mignon Sherwood

Pride Place ($2,500) see Todd Co., A.M.

Providence Hospital Foundation — Ambulatory Surgery Center ($100,000) see DeRoy Testamentary Foundation

Providence Hospital Foundtion — Ambulatory Surgery Center ($27,000) see DeRoy Testamentary Foundation

Rainbow Connection ($1,000) see Glanville Family Foundation

Right Place Program ($1,000) see Grand Rapids Label Co.

Ronald McDonald House ($5,000) see R&B Machine Tool Co.

Rotary Club of Lansing Foundation ($2,000) see Abrams Foundation, Talbert and Leota

Ruffed Grouse Society — forest habitat development work ($50,000) see Mellon Family Foundation, R. K.

Saginaw Art Museum — busing students ($5,000) see Mills Fund, Frances Goll

Saginaw Art Museum — operations ($10,000) see Mather and William Gwinn Mather Fund, Elizabeth Ring

Saginaw Business Incubator — building ($50,000) see Eddy Family Memorial Fund, C. K.

The Big Book of Library Grant Money

Upjohn Foundation, Harold and Grace
Walsh College — capital ($100,000) see Wilson Fund, Matilda R.
Walsh College of Accountancy and Business Administration — capital campaign pledge ($30,000) see Vollbrecht Foundation, Frederick A.
Walsh College of Accountancy and Business Administration — scholarship fund ($10,000) see Vollbrecht Foundation, Frederick A.
Washtenaw Community College ($3,000) see R&B Machine Tool Co.
Washtenaw United Way ($151,451) see Johnson Controls Inc.
Wayne County Regional Educational Service Agency ($75,000) see Detroit Edison Co.
Wayne State University — Faculty Research Awards Program ($36,000) see American Natural Resources Company
Wayne State University — Volunteerism Lecture Series ($50,000) see DeRoy Testamentary Foundation
Wayne State University Center for Peace and Conflict Studies — coordination of Community Dispute Resolution Programs ($81,000) see Hudson-Webber Foundation
Wayne State University Center for Urban Studies — Southeastern Michigan Business Assistance Consortium ($75,000) see Hudson-Webber Foundation
West Michigan Children's Museum see Knoll Group
West Shore Symphony ($15,000) see SPX Corp.
Western Michigan University — scholarships ($8,000) see Vicksburg Foundation
Western Michigan University — capital campaign ($40,000) see Eaton Corporation
Western Michigan University Business College ($7,500) see Fabri-Kal Corp.
WKAR-TV/Channel 23 Nature — program support ($15,000) see Consumers Power Co.
Women's Resource Center of Northern Michigan ($100,000) see Offield Family Foundation
Wyoming Community Foundation ($2,500) see KN Energy, Inc.
Yeshiva Beth Yehudah ($27,600) see Borman's Inc.
YWCA ($2,017) see Abrams Foundation, Talbert and Leota
YWCA — facility renovation project ($35,000) see Kantzler Foundation
YWCA ($10,000) see Tiscornia Foundation
YWCA — operations ($6,500) see Upjohn Foundation, Harold and Grace
YWCA Capital Fund ($2,500) see Fabri-Kal Corp.
YWCA Capital Fund ($2,500) see Fabri-Kal Corp.
YWCA of Greater Michigan see Knoll Group
YWCA of Southwestern Michigan ($75,190) see Upton Foundation, Frederick S.

Zuael Memorial Library — computers ($3,100) see Mills Fund, Frances Goll

Minnesota

Abbott-Northwestern Hospital Piper Cancer Center ($10,000) see Marbrook Foundation
Adath Jeshurun Congregation — Phillips endowment ($100,000) see Phillips Family Foundation, Jay and Rose
Adult Abuse Community Service — to sustain services to victims of family violence, sexual assault, and other personal injury crimes while new funding sources are being developed ($60,000) see Bremer Foundation, Otto
Alexandra House — general operating/capital see Northern States Power Co. (Minnesota)
Alexandra House — capital support see Piper Jaffray Companies Inc.
Alliance for the Mentally Ill of Minnesota see Northern States Power Co. (Minnesota)
Alternatives for People with Autism see Northern States Power Co. (Minnesota)
American Indian Opportunities Industrialization Center ($25,000) see Mardag Foundation
American Indian Opportunities Industrialization Center see Northern States Power Co. (Minnesota)
American Indian Opportunities Industrialization Center see Piper Jaffray Companies Inc.
American Library Association ($50,000) see Cargill Inc.
American Red Cross ($148,418) see Minnesota Mining & Mfg. Co.
Anew Dimension Child Enrichment Center — capital see Northern States Power Co. (Minnesota)
Archdiocesan AIDS Ministry Program — emergency needs/relief fund see Northern States Power Co. (Minnesota)
Augsburg College — capital for library see Northern States Power Co. (Minnesota)
Augsburg College ($20,000) see Sundet Foundation
Augsburg College Library Fund see Allianz Life Insurance Co. of North America
Bayport Public Library ($5,000) see Mahadh Foundation
Belwin Foundation — purchase real estate ($50,000) see Bell Foundation, James F.
Benson Public Library — software for public use ($1,000) see Pamida, Inc.
Bethany Lutheran College ($25,000) see Hickory Tech Corp.
Bethel College and Seminary ($225,000) see Andersen Foundation
Bethel College and Seminary ($45,514) see Hallett Charitable Trust, Jessie F.
Big Brothers and Big Sisters of Rice County see Northern

States Power Co. (Minnesota)
Billy Graham Evangelical Association ($20,000) see Fruehauf Foundation
Billy Graham Evangelical Association ($4,000) see Moore & Sons, B.C.
Blake School ($10,000) see Marbrook Foundation
Boy Scouts of America — Indianhead Council ($1,115,000) see Andersen Foundation
Boy Scouts of America Indianhead Council ($97,000) see Andersen Corp.
Boy Scouts of America Indianhead Council — scouting for youth with special needs program see Northern States Power Co. (Minnesota)
Boy Scouts of America Indianhead Council — general ($13,500) see Tozer Foundation
Boys and Girls Club of Minneapolis see Piper Jaffray Companies Inc.
Boys and Girls Club of St. Paul — for health and human services see Jostens, Inc.
Boys and Girls Club of St. Paul ($50,000) see Mardag Foundation
Boys and Girls Clubs of Minneapolis — Phillips endowment ($100,000) see Phillips Family Foundation, Jay and Rose
Boys and Girls club of St. Paul — for capital support for the construction of a new facility on the East Side of St. Paul which will house education and other programs for low-income youth ($150,000) see Saint Paul Companies, Inc.
Breck School — for educational purposes ($22,500) see Larsen Fund
Breck School ($12,000) see Marbrook Foundation
Breck School — for Real Science Partnership ($48,000) see Medtronic, Inc.
Bush Leadership Fellows Programs — 1992 program that provides mid-career study and internship opportunities for selected residents of Minnesota, North Dakota, South Dakota, and western Wisconsin ($496,548) see Bush Foundation
Bush Leadership Fellows Programs — 1993 program that provides mid-career study and internship opportunities for selected residents of Minnesota, North Dakota, South Dakota, and western Wisconsin ($303,785) see Bush Foundation
Business Economic Education Foundation — Stock Market Game see Piper Jaffray Companies Inc.
Business Economics Education Foundation — for education see Jostens, Inc.
Campaign for Harriet Tubman — social, welfare, and health ($50,000) see Bemis Company, Inc.
Carleton College — scholarship ($10,000) see Caestecker Foundation, Charles and Marie

Carleton College — excellence in science program ($150,000) see General Mills, Inc.
Carleton College — construction math and computer science building ($100,000) see Booth Ferris Foundation
Carpenter Nature Center — wildlife rehabilitation program see Northern States Power Co. (Minnesota)
Center School see Piper Jaffray Companies Inc.
Central Minnesota Community Foundation see Piper Jaffray Companies Inc.
Children's Miracle Network ($1,470,433) see Wal-Mart Stores, Inc.
Children's Miracle Network ($106,354) see Wal-Mart Stores, Inc.
Children's Miracle Network ($55,260) see Wal-Mart Stores, Inc.
Children's Museum — capital ($250,000) see General Mills, Inc.
Child's Play Theatre Company — for the arts, civic, and cultural purposes see Jostens, Inc.
Citizens Scholarship Foundation ($75,750) see Mohasco Corp.
Citizens Scholarship Foundation of America — for scholarships and fellowships ($94,000) see Unocal Corp.
Citizens Scholarship Foundation of America ($57,500) see Illinois Tool Works, Inc.
Citizens Scholarship Foundation of America ($21,900) see Hechinger Co.
Citizens Scholarship Foundation of America ($19,000) see Hechinger Co.
Citizen's Scholarship Foundation of America — educational ($63,950) see Bemis Company, Inc.
Citizen's Scholarship Foundation of America ($40,000) see Hickory Tech Corp.
Citizens Scholarship Foundation of America ($83,826) see Norwest Corporation
Citizen's Scholarship Foundation of America see Piper Jaffray Companies Inc.
Citizens Scholarship Foundation of America — postsecondary scholarship support for children of Prudential employees ($111,688) see Prudential Insurance Co. of America, The
Citizens Scholarship Foundation of America —for scholarships for the children of CIGNA employees ($129,660) see CIGNA Corporation
Citizens Scholarship Foundation of America ($125,265) see Weyerhaeuser Co.
Citizens Scholarship Foundation of America/Pathways ($163,958) see Metropolitan Life Insurance Co.
Citizens Scholastic Foundation of America — achievement awards program ($278,500) see BankAmerica Corp.

City of Crosby — community center Steering Committee ($21,000) see Hallett Charitable Trust, E. W.
City of Deerwood — playground equipment ($20,000) see Hallett Charitable Trust, E. W.
City of Grand Rapids — for the capital reserve endowment fund for the Central School Commission ($99,000) see Blandin Foundation
City of Thief River Falls — river walk bridge at Hartz Park ($10,000) see Hartz Foundation
College of St. Benedict — capital challenge grants to Minnesota and Dakota private colleges ($492,000) see Bush Foundation
College of St. Benedict ($17,000) see Van Evera Foundation, Dewitt
College of St. Catherine — capital challenge grants to Minnesota and Dakota private colleges ($353,500) see Bush Foundation
Community Area Recreation Committee — recreational facility for people of all ages ($1,000) see Pamida, Inc.
Community Clinic — annual campaign support ($4,000) see Mahadh Foundation
Community Memorial Hospital — for assistance in the relocation of the emergency services area ($200,000) see Blandin Foundation
Concerts for the Environment ($25,000) see Bell Foundation, James F.
Concordia College ($30,343) see Hallett Charitable Trust, Jessie F.
Courage Center ($100,000) see Mardag Foundation
Courage Center — Phillips endowment ($100,000) see Phillips Family Foundation, Jay and Rose
Courage Center — St. Croix Valley aquatics and therapy facility ($15,000) see Tozer Foundation
Crosby-Ironton Independent School District 182 — electronics laboratory ($57,000) see Hallett Charitable Trust, E. W.
Crosby-Ironton Independent School District 182 — alternative education program ($49,180) see Hallett Charitable Trust, E. W.
Crosby-Ironton Independent School District 182 — scholarship fund ($30,000) see Hallett Charitable Trust, E. W.
Crosby-Ironton Presbyterian Church ($25,341) see Hallett Charitable Trust, E. W.
Cuyana Regional Medical Center — long-term care program ($50,000) see Hallett Charitable Trust, E. W.
Cuyana Regional Medical Center — helicopter landing site ($43,040) see Hallett Charitable Trust, E. W.
Cuyana Regional Medical Center — expanded hospice program ($25,000) see Hallett Charitable Trust, E. W.
Cuyana Regional Medical Center — isokinetic

Mississippi

Missouri

Nelson-Atkins Museum of Art — ten-year pledge to enhance the collection of French impressionistic art ($25,000) see Block, H&R

Nelson Gallery Foundation — annual unrestricted support for museum programs, Horizons ($20,000) see Stein Foundation, Jules and Doris

Nelson Gallery Foundation ($2,700) see Miller-Mellor Association

Nishnabotna Drainage District — interest from funds to be used for pump fuel ($40,000) see Morgan Charitable Residual Trust, W. and E.

NMSU Development Fund Corporation, Northeast Missouri State University — support of research project ($35,000) see Dillon Dunwalke Trust, Clarence and Anne

Older Adult Service and Information System (OASIS) ($216,495) see May Department Stores Company, The

Older Adult Service and Information System (OASIS) ($203,965) see May Department Stores Company, The

Older Adult Service and Information System (OASIS) ($165,745) see May Department Stores Company, The

Operation Food Search — driver's salary for one year ($24,000) see Sunnen Foundation

Ozarks Medical Center — cancer center ($15,000) see Shaw Foundation, Arch W.

Palestine Gardens Senior Citizen Center — to construct the senior citizens center ($30,000) see Block, H&R

Parkview Towers Fund ($5,000) see Messing Family Charitable Foundation

Planned Parenthood ($51,000) see Kelly Foundation, T. Lloyd

Powell Gardens ($20,000) see Kuehn Foundation

Powell Gardens ($6,000) see Kuehn Foundation

PP-St. Louis — library and popular literature ($35,000) see Sunnen Foundation

Presbyterian Children's Services — for installation of a new underground water delivery system on the farm campus and central air conditioning at the Stubble Family and Youth Center in Moberly ($15,500) see Green Foundation, Allen P. and Josephine B.

Provident Counseling — for the support of Union Electric's Dollar More program ($75,000) see Union Electric Co.

Rainbow Village — first year of four-year pledge for endowment program ($25,000) see Sunnen Foundation

Ranken-Jordan Children's Rehabilitation Center ($40,000) see Jordan Charitable Foundation, Mary Ranken Jordan and Ettie A.

Ranken Technical College ($50,000) see Jordan Charitable Foundation, Mary Ranken Jordan and Ettie A.

Ranken Technical Institute — for educational purposes ($3,000) see ACF Industries, Inc.

Rehabilitation Institute ($20,000) see Oppenstein Brothers Foundation

Religious Coalition for Reproduction Choice — clergy counseling program ($30,000) see Sunnen Foundation

Repertory Theater ($5,000) see Van Evera Foundation, Dewitt

Repertory Theater of St. Louis ($20,000) see Jordan Charitable Foundation, Mary Ranken Jordan and Ettie A.

Research Medical Center ($250,000) see Kemper Foundation, William T.

Rockhurst College ($175,000) see Kemper Foundation, William T.

Rockhurst College — support of programs that focus on the Jesuit Mission, and Values ($50,000) see McGee Foundation

Rockhurst College — strengthen undergraduate science, and graduate allied health education ($25,000) see McGee Foundation

Rockhurst High School — debt reduction ($50,000) see McGee Foundation

St. Elizabeth Church ($2,950) see Miller-Mellor Association

St. Louis Art Museum ($50,000) see Pulitzer Publishing Co.

St. Louis Artists Guild ($7,000) see Messing Family Charitable Foundation

St. Louis Association for Retarded Citizens ($1,250) see ACF Industries, Inc.

St. Louis Children's Hospital ($50,000) see Jordan Charitable Foundation, Mary Ranken Jordan and Ettie A.

St. Louis Children's Hospital ($15,000) see Stupp Foundation, Norman J.

St. Louis Children's Hospital ($10,000) see Stupp Foundation, Norman J.

St. Louis Children's Hospital ($1,000) see Swift Co. Inc., John S.

St. Louis College of Pharmacy ($6,000) see Hook Drugs

St. Louis Conservatory — scholarships for women ($10,000) see Monticello College Foundation

St. Louis Jewish Center for the Aged — endowment fund ($10,000) see Lee Enterprises

St. Louis Mercantile Library Association ($40,000) see Pott Foundation, Herman T. and Phenie R.

St. Louis Mercantile Library Association ($30,000) see Pott Foundation, Herman T. and Phenie R.

St. Louis Science Center ($87,500) see Boatmen's Bancshares, Inc.

St. Louis Science Center ($200,000) see May Department Stores Company, The

St. Louis Science Center ($200,000) see Ralston Purina Co.

St. Louis Science Center ($30,000) see Stupp Foundation, Norman J.

St. Louis Science Center ($30,000) see Stupp Foundation, Norman J.

St. Louis Science Center ($5,000) see Salomon Inc.

St. Louis Science Center ($5,000) see Salomon Inc.

St. Louis Science Center ($240,000) see SBC Communications Inc.

St. Louis Symphony Orchestra ($56,000) see Boatmen's Bancshares, Inc.

St. Louis Symphony Orchestra ($30,000) see Ralston Purina Co.

St. Louis Symphony Society ($57,500) see Jordan Charitable Foundation, Mary Ranken Jordan and Ettie A.

St. Louis Symphony Society ($50,000) see Pulitzer Publishing Co.

St. Louis Symphony Society ($50,000) see Pulitzer Publishing Co.

St. Louis Symphony Society ($60,000) see Union Electric Co.

St. Louis University — for educational purposes ($1,100) see ACF Industries, Inc.

St. Louis University ($500,000) see Anheuser-Busch Companies, Inc.

St. Louis University ($300,000) see Anheuser-Busch Companies, Inc.

St. Louis University — to establish scholarship fund ($75,000) see Boatmen's Bancshares, Inc.

St. Louis University ($20,000) see Gaylord Foundation, Clifford Willard

St. Louis University ($209,199) see Lichtenstein Foundation, David B.

St. Louis University ($55,000) see Union Electric Co.

St. Louis University — charitable ($12,000) see Allendale Insurance Co.

St. Louis University, Eye Institute ($50,000) see Stupp Foundation, Norman J.

St. Louis University Hospital, Cardiology Division ($55,720) see Lichtenstein Foundation, David B.

St. Lukes Hospital Foundation ($139,000) see Kemper Foundation, William T.

St. Pauls Episcopal Day School ($150,000) see Kemper Foundation, William T.

St. Vincent DePaul Society St. Louis — for the support of Union Electric's Dollar More program ($60,000) see Union Electric Co.

Salvation Army ($1,000) see Wertheim Foundation, Dr. Herbert A.

Salvation Army — flood relief ($50,000) see Middendorf Foundation

Salvation Army ($80,000) see Boatmen's Bancshares, Inc.

Salvation Army Hope Center ($30,000) see Pott Foundation, Herman T. and Phenie R.

Salvation Army of Kansas City ($167,000) see Kemper Foundation, William T.

Scottish Rite Clinic — speech and language program ($40,000) see Sunnen Foundation

Sheldon Arts Foundation ($25,000) see Jordan Charitable Foundation, Mary Ranken Jordan and Ettie A.

Shriners Children's Hospital ($2,657) see Centralia Foundation

Sisters of St. Joseph of Carondelet — health needs of retired sisters ($6,000) see McGee Foundation

Southside Baptist Church ($105,530) see Lichtenstein Foundation, David B.

State Ballet of Missouri — funding to underwrite "The Miraculous Madarin" ($17,500) see Block, H&R

State Historical Society of Missouri ($7,500) see Gaylord Foundation, Clifford Willard

Students in Free Enterprise ($120,000) see Wal-Mart Stores, Inc.

Students in Free Enterprise ($30,000) see Ralston Purina Co.

Swope Parkway Health Center — to support capital campaign that will create a state-of-the-art medical campus ($25,000) see Block, H&R

Thompson Community Center — for care of and services to elderly ($5,000) see Mielke Family Foundation

Torah Prep of Torah Center ($42,000) see Lichtenstein Foundation, David B.

United States Catholic Conference — for Youville Hospital and Rehabilitation Center ($25,000) see Polaroid Corp.

United Way — third of four payments ($34,713) see Commerce Bancshares, Inc.

United Way — fourth of four payments ($34,713) see Commerce Bancshares, Inc.

United Way — second of four payments ($34,712) see Commerce Bancshares, Inc.

United Way — first of four payments ($34,712) see Commerce Bancshares, Inc.

United Way — third of four payments ($20,000) see Commerce Bancshares, Inc.

United Way — second of four payments ($20,000) see Commerce Bancshares, Inc.

United Way — fourth of four payments ($20,000) see Commerce Bancshares, Inc.

United Way — first of four payments ($20,000) see Commerce Bancshares, Inc.

United Way of Greater ($216,500) see SBC Communications Inc.

United Way of Greater ($216,500) see SBC Communications Inc.

United Way of Greater ($216,500) see SBC Communications Inc.

United Way of Greater Kansas City, MO and Kansas ($22,950) see Santa Fe Pacific Corporation

United Way of Greater St. Joseph ($50,150) see Johnson Controls Inc.

United Way Greater St. Louis ($1,102,250) see Anheuser-Busch Companies, Inc.

United Way of Greater St. Louis ($144,500) see Boatmen's Bancshares, Inc.

United Way of Greater St. Louis ($144,500) see Boatmen's Bancshares, Inc.

United Way of Greater St. Louis ($144,500) see Boatmen's Bancshares, Inc.

United Way of Greater St. Louis ($144,500) see Boatmen's Bancshares, Inc.

United Way of Greater St. Louis ($22,000) see Pott Foundation, Herman T. and Phenie R.

United Way of Greater St. Louis ($90,500) see Pulitzer Publishing Co.

United Way of Greater St. Louis ($221,250) see Ralston Purina Co.

United Way of Greater St. Louis ($221,250) see Ralston Purina Co.

United Way of Greater St. Louis ($221,250) see Ralston Purina Co.

United Way of Greater St. Louis ($640,000) see Union Electric Co.

United Way of Greater St. Louis ($130,000) see Union Pacific Corp.

United Way of the Heart of America ($20,000) see Oppenstein Brothers Foundation

United Way of the Heart of America ($20,000) see Oppenstein Brothers Foundation

United Way Heart of America ($32,000) see Armco Inc.

United Way of St. Louis ($216,500) see SBC Communications Inc.

University of Missouri — charitable contribution ($30,000) see Olin Corp.

University of Missouri ($16,000) see Pulitzer Publishing Co.

University of Missouri Kansas City — to construct the Henry W. Bloch School of Business and Public Administration ($133,200) see Block, H&R

University of Missouri St. Louis ($20,000) see Stupp Foundation, Norman J.

University of Missouri St. Louis ($50,000) see Union Electric Co.

University of Missouri School of Forestry — scholarship ($15,000) see Shaw Foundation, Arch W.

University of Missouri School of Forestry, Fisheries, and Wildlife — scholarship ($15,000) see Shaw Foundation, Arch W.

University of Missouri School of Medicine ($250,000) see Towsley Foundation, Harry A. and Margaret D.

University of Missouri School of Medicine — AIDS research ($10,000) see General American Life Insurance Co.

Vanderschmidt School — continue language lab ($7,600) see Monticello College Foundation

Village of Watson — Community Facility Improvement ($3,000) see Morgan Charitable Residual Trust, W. and E.

Visiting Nurse Association ($3,050) see Miller-Mellor Association

Washington University — Olin Fellowship program

($110,000) see Monticello College Foundation

Washington University — scholarship ($2,200) see American Optical Corp.

Washington University ($200,000) see Boatmen's Bancshares, Inc.

Washington University ($200,000) see Boatmen's Bancshares, Inc.

Washington University ($7,500) see Gaylord Foundation, Clifford Willard

Washington University — AIDS research ($15,000) see General American Life Insurance Co.

Washington University ($100,000) see Jordan Charitable Foundation, Mary Ranken Jordan and Ettie A.

Washington University ($250,000) see May Department Stores Company, The

Washington University — for the Spencer T. and Ann W. Olin Medical Scientist Fellowship Program Endowment ($1,500,000) see Olin Foundation, Spencer T. and Ann W.

Washington University ($30,000) see Pott Foundation, Herman T. and Phenie R.

Washington University ($30,000) see Pott Foundation, Herman T. and Phenie R.

Washington University ($500,000) see Ralston Purina Co.

Washington University — endowed chair ($83,333) see Stupp Foundation, Norman J.

Washington University St. Louis ($110,000) see Union Electric Co.

Washington University School of Law ($100,000) see Gaylord Foundation, Clifford Willard

Watson Fire Department — Watson honor roll students ($5,500) see Morgan Charitable Residual Trust, W. and E.

Watson Fire Department — additional funds for Watson area college students scholarships ($3,000) see Morgan Charitable Residual Trust, W. and E.

Webster University ($25,000) see Jordan Charitable Foundation, Mary Ranken Jordan and Ettie A.

Webster University ($5,000) see Messing Family Charitable Foundation

Webster University — summer sabbatical ($4,500) see Messing Family Charitable Foundation

Webster University ($5,000) see Van Evera Foundation, Dewitt

Westminster College ($200,000) see Hermann Foundation, Grover

Westminster College — scholarships for women ($10,000) see Monticello College Foundation

Whitfield School ($25,000) see Jordan Charitable Foundation, Mary Ranken Jordan and Ettie A.

Whitfield School — scholarships ($25,000) see Pott Foundation, Herman T. and Phenie R.

William Woods University ($100,000) see McCune Charitable Trust, John R.

Winston Churchill Memorial Library see Givenchy Corp.

Woodhaven Learning Center ($7,500) see Gaylord Foundation, Clifford Willard

YMCA see Kansas City Southern Industries

YMCA of the Ozarks ($25,000) see Stupp Foundation, Norman J.

YWCA see Kansas City Southern Industries

Montana

American Wildlands ($28,000) see New-Land Foundation

Butte Central High School — unrestricted contribution ($32,000) see Montana Power Co.

Emerson Cultural Center ($25,000) see Taylor Foundation, Ruth and Vernon

Gallatin Valley Literacy Council ($25,000) see Taylor Foundation, Ruth and Vernon

Greater Yellowstone Coalition ($58,000) see Claiborne and Art Ortenberg Foundation, Liz

Greater Yellowstone Coalition ($25,000) see Ohrstrom Foundation

Intermountain Children's Home — capital contribution ($20,000) see Montana Power Co.

Intermountain Children's Home ($50,000) see Steele-Reese Foundation

Mansfield Foundation — endowment ($50,000) see Lee Enterprises

Maureen and Mike Mansfield Foundation — Mansfield Library ($25,000) see Adler Foundation Trust, Philip D. and Henrietta B.

McLaughlin Research Institute — research project support ($15,000) see Montana Power Co.

Montana Community Foundation — endowment fund ($16,667) see Lee Enterprises

Montana Economic Study — to complement and strengthen a more general study of the US economy ($53,970) see Claiborne and Art Ortenberg Foundation, Liz

Montana Rescue ($4,500) see Sargent Foundation, Newell B.

Montana State University Museum of the Rockies ($75,750) see Taylor Foundation, Ruth and Vernon

Montana Tech Butte — unrestricted contribution ($40,000) see Montana Power Co.

Montana Tech Foundation ($35,000) see Phelps Dodge Corporation

Montana University System — support academic excellence ($960,240) see Montana Power Co.

Museum of the Rockies — capital contribution ($15,000) see Montana Power Co.

Political Economy Research Center — general operations ($50,000) see Cain

Foundation, Gordon and Mary

St. Labre Indian School ($5,000) see Dell Foundation, Hazel

Zoo Montana ($10,000) see Lee Enterprises

Nebraska

Aksarben — charitable ($10,000) see Owen Industries, Inc.

Aksarben — charitable ($10,000) see Owen Industries, Inc.

AkSarBen Agricultural Youth Foundation see Norwest Bank Nebraska, N.A.

Aksarben Agriculture Youth Foundation ($20,000) see Valmont Industries, Inc.

American Red Cross see Norwest Bank Nebraska, N.A.

Applied Information Management Institute — unrestricted ($70,000) see Union Pacific Corp.

Archdiocese of Omaha see Piper Jaffray Companies Inc.

Aurora Housing Development Corporation ($10,000) see Farr Trust, Frank M. and Alice M.

Bellevue College see Norwest Bank Nebraska, N.A.

Boy Scouts of America see Norwest Bank Nebraska, N.A.

Boystown National Institute see Norwest Bank Nebraska, N.A.

Camp Fire Pioneer Council see Norwest Bank Nebraska, N.A.

Campfire-Pioneer Council ($5,000) see Ameritas Life Insurance Corp.

Campus House ($5,000) see Quivey-Bay State Foundation

Central Community College ($25,000) see Reynolds Foundation, Edgar

Central Community College Foundation see Norwest Bank Nebraska, N.A.

Central Nebraska Goodwill — debt retirement and rehab center ($17,250) see Reynolds Foundation, Edgar

Chadron State College ($2,500) see KN Energy, Inc.

Chadron State Foundation ($10,000) see Quivey-Bay State Foundation

Cheyenne County Community Center Foundation ($5,000) see KN Energy, Inc.

Christian Urban Education Service — employability program ($10,000) see Ameritas Life Insurance Corp.

City of Grand Island, Parks and Recreation Department ($15,000) see Reynolds Foundation, Edgar

College Park Fund ($55,300) see Reynolds Foundation, Edgar

College of St. Mary see Norwest Bank Nebraska, N.A.

College of St. Mary ($16,167) see Valmont Industries, Inc.

Community College Foundation see Norwest Bank Nebraska, N.A.

Community Concerts see Norwest Bank Nebraska, N.A.

Creighton University ($25,000) see Valmont Industries, Inc.

Dana College ($10,000) see Valmont Industries, Inc.

Duchesne Academy — fine art endowment fund ($5,000) see Ameritas Life Insurance Corp.

Father Flanagan's Boys Home — charitable ($1,000,000) see Bettingen Corporation, Burton G.

Fremont Family YMCA ($20,000) see Valmont Industries, Inc.

Girls Incorporated of Omaha — to fund acquisition and renovation of Clifton Hills school for use as grantee's main program ($1,600,000) see Kiewit Foundation, Peter

Goodwill Industries — charitable ($12,500) see Owen Industries, Inc.

Goodwill Industries ($12,500) see Owen Industries, Inc.

Grand Island Soccer League Grant ($40,000) see Reynolds Foundation, Edgar

Greater Omaha Women's Fund — charitable ($10,000) see Owen Industries, Inc.

Guiding Star Girl Scout Council ($5,000) see Quivey-Bay State Foundation

Hamilton Community Foundation — Farr Rotary Scholarships ($10,000) see Farr Trust, Frank M. and Alice M.

Hamilton County Agricultural Society ($53,500) see Farr Trust, Frank M. and Alice M.

Hamilton County Historical Society — Edgerton pledge ($60,179) see Farr Trust, Frank M. and Alice M.

Hamilton County Historical Society — Edgerton pledge ($17,500) see Farr Trust, Frank M. and Alice M.

Hamilton County Historical Society — mower ($4,000) see Farr Trust, Frank M. and Alice M.

Hamilton Manor Alzheimers Wing ($50,000) see Farr Trust, Frank M. and Alice M.

Hastings College Foundation ($2,605) see KN Energy, Inc.

Hastings College Foundation — to partially fund the expansion and furnishing of the studio theater ($250,000) see Kiewit Foundation, Peter

Hastings College Foundation ($10,000) see Valmont Industries, Inc.

Hastings Museum — IMAX theater construction ($15,000) see Reynolds Foundation, Edgar

Hastings Museum Foundation ($10,000) see KN Energy, Inc.

Heritage-Joslyn Foundation — to partially fund the cost of collect ion acquisition at Joslyn Art Museum and improvements to the physical plant facilities ($2,000,000) see Kiewit Foundation, Peter

Lincoln Public Schools Foundation — Math, Science, and Technology Institute ($10,000) see Ameritas Life Insurance Corp.

Madonna Centers — capital campaign ($15,000) see Ameritas Life Insurance Corp.

Nebraska Art Collection — to assist the renovation and furnishing of program facility ($250,000) see Kiewit Foundation, Peter

Nebraska Community Law Enforcement ($10,992) see Reynolds Foundation, Edgar

Nebraska Historical Society ($4,000) see KN Energy, Inc.

Nebraska Independent College Foundation ($10,000) see Quivey-Bay State Foundation

Nebraska Independent College Foundation ($10,000) see Reynolds Foundation, Edgar

Nebraska Statewide Arboretum — to fund construction of community landscape assistance program ($260,000) see Kiewit Foundation, Peter

Nebraska Wesleyan University ($25,000) see Ameritas Life Insurance Corp.

Nebraska Western College Scholarship Fund ($10,000) see Quivey-Bay State Foundation

Omaha Zoo Foundation — charitable ($10,500) see Owen Industries, Inc.

Omaha Zoological Society — to partially fund the construction of a restaurant and education facility adjacent to the Lied Jungle ($1,000,000) see Kiewit Foundation, Peter

Pius X School — Embrace the Future campaign ($15,000) see Ameritas Life Insurance Corp.

Regional West Medical Center ($12,000) see Quivey-Bay State Foundation

St. Francis Medical Center ($18,600) see Reynolds Foundation, Edgar

Stuhr Museum ($20,000) see Reynolds Foundation, Edgar

United Arts of Omaha — charitable ($12,000) see Owen Industries, Inc.

United Arts Omaha ($50,000) see Norwest Corporation

United Arts Omaha — support of United Arts Omaha ($439,650) see Kiewit Foundation, Peter

United Arts of Omaha ($25,000) see Valmont Industries, Inc.

United Arts Omaha — unrestricted ($120,000) see Union Pacific Corp.

United Way ($27,000) see Monfort Family Foundation

United Way of Lincoln ($50,500) see Ameritas Life Insurance Corp.

United Way of Mid-Plains ($65,000) see Union Pacific Corp.

United Way of Midlands — for 1990-91 general fund drive campaign ($607,950) see Kiewit Foundation, Peter

United Way of the Midlands ($65,000) see Valmont Industries, Inc.

United Way of Midlands ($230,000) see Union Pacific Corp.

University of Nebraska College of Nursing — nursing education ($90,000) see Teagle Foundation

University of Nebraska Foundation ($2,150) see KN Energy, Inc.

University of Nebraska Foundation — support for Wilson and Peterson chairs

Princeton Day School ($10,000) see Bunbury Company

Princeton Theological Seminary — scholarship ($10,000) see Warwick Foundation

Princeton University — study on superconductivity ($100,000) see Seaver Institute

Princeton University ($10,000) see Whiting Foundation, Macauley and Helen Dow

Princeton University ($50,000) see Hoffmann-La Roche Inc.

Princeton University ($500) see Glanville Family Foundation

Princeton University ($5,000) see Icahn Foundation, Carl C.

Princeton University ($509,000) see Lowenstein Foundation, Leon

Princeton University ($10,000) see Memton Fund

Princeton University — scholarship ($10,000) see Warwick Foundation

Princeton University — scholarship ($10,000) see Warwick Foundation

Princeton University ($205,950) see Mobil Oil Corp.

Princeton University Trustees ($2,000,000) see Bristol-Myers Squibb Company

Recording for the Blind — Anne T. Macdonald Center ($10,000) see Clayton Fund

Renaissance Newark — purchase of office equipment and furnishings ($30,000) see Hyde and Watson Foundation

Rider College — Science Building capital fund ($55,000) see Union Camp Corporation

Riverview Foundation ($100,000) see Brooks Foundation, Gladys

Robert Wood Johnson University Hospital Foundation ($50,000) see Van Houten Memorial Fund

Rumson Country Day School ($25,000) see Smeal Foundation, Mary Jean and Frank P.

Rutgers Preparatory School ($5,500) see Klipstein Foundation, Ernest Christian

Rutgers University ($5,000) see Seton Leather Co.

Rutgers University Center for Advancement ($40,000) see Lipton, Thomas J.

Rutgers University College of Pharmacy ($70,000) see Lipton, Thomas J.

Rutgers University Foundation —for Ceramics/Fiber Optics Program ($25,000) see Corning Incorporated

St. Barnabas Medical Center ($20,000) see Cooperman Foundation, Leon and Toby

St. Benedict's Prep ($16,500) see Beck Foundation, Elsie E. and Joseph W.

St. Benedict's Preparatory School ($6,000) see Seton Leather Co.

St. Columbia Neighborhood Club — operating support for this neighborhood service organization ($30,000) see Schumann Fund for New Jersey

St. Francis Hospital ($100,000) see Link, Jr. Foundation, George

St. Joseph's Hospital and Medical Center Foundation ($75,000) see Van Houten Memorial Fund

St. Joseph's Hospital and Medical Center Foundation ($50,000) see Van Houten Memorial Fund

St. Peters Preparatory ($54,000) see Link, Jr. Foundation, George

St. Vincent's Academy ($30,000) see Beck Foundation, Elsie E. and Joseph W.

Salvation Army New Jersey Divisional Headquarters — program support in Newark ($75,000) see Turrell Fund

Seeing Eye — capital campaign ($200,000) see Kirby Foundation, F. M.

Seton Hall Prep — for capital program ($25,000) see Beck Foundation, Elsie E. and Joseph W.

Seton Hall Prep ($18,500) see Beck Foundation, Elsie E. and Joseph W.

Seton Hall Preparatory School — general fund ($100,000) see Sandy Hill Foundation

Seton Hall University — for restricted Library Room ($40,000) see Beck Foundation, Elsie E. and Joseph W.

Seton Hall University — for restricted scholarship program ($10,000) see Beck Foundation, Elsie E. and Joseph W.

Seton Hall University — library ($399,864) see Sandy Hill Foundation

Social Service Federation, Leonard Johnson Day Nursery ($55,250) see Schenck Fund, L. P.

Somerset Art Association ($25,000) see Brady Foundation

Somerset Art Association — for building fund ($9,000) see Cape Branch Foundation

Spectrum for Living Development ($20,000) see Schenck Fund, L. P.

Stevens Institute of Technology ($27,500) see Greve Foundation, William and Mary

Stevens Institute of Technology —engineering scholarships program ($463,405) see Exxon Corporation

Stevens Institute of Technology ($20,000) see Bell Atlantic Corp.

Stevens Institute of Technology ($50,000) see Johnson Controls Inc.

Stevens Institute of Technology Education Program ($32,000) see Unilever United States, Inc.

Stuart Country Day School ($25,000) see Bunbury Company

Stuart Country Day School ($25,000) see Bunbury Company

Summer Educational Opportunity Award for Principals — 25 grants of $5,000 each were offered to public school principals in 1993; an additional grant of $1,000 each was given to each respective school district to assist with

expenses associated with the grant. ($125,000) see Dodge Foundation, Geraldine R.

Summer Educational Opportunity Awards — since 1985, this foundation initiative has recognized the need for teachers to be supported professionally in pursuing educational dreams during the summer ($125,000) see Dodge Foundation, Geraldine R.

Summit Speech School — essential alterations and improvements and relocation to new facilities to expand program for hearing-impaired children ($50,000) see Hyde and Watson Foundation

Summit Speech School — to name the new Summit speech school building ($1,000,000) see Kirby Foundation, F. M.

Summit Speech School — capital campaign ($50,000) see Turrell Fund

Task ($3,222) see Betts Industries

Tomorrow's Children Fund ($2,750) see Weinstein Foundation, J.

Trust for Public Land — over two years for the Barnegat Bay Initiative ($500,000) see Penn Foundation, William

Turrell Scholarship Program — scholarships ($441,344) see Turrell Fund

Underwood Memorial Hospital Foundation ($150,000) see Mobil Oil Corp.

UNICO National Cedar Grove Chapter ($5,000) see Martini Foundation, Nicholas

Unified Vailsburg Services Organization — child care, meals on wheels, administrative support ($45,000) see Schumann Fund for New Jersey

United Jewish Appeal of Metrowest ($52,000) see Jaydor Corp.

United Jewish Appeal of MetroWest ($10,000) see Cooperman Foundation, Leon and Toby

United Way of Camden County — annual contribution of 18 dollars/employee on behalf of SFS/SDA's 419 employees ($7,542) see Subaru of America Inc.

United Way of Morris County ($175,000) see Kirby Foundation, F. M.

United Way Morris County — human services ($148,000) see Nabisco Foods Group

United Way Princeton Area Communities ($40,000) see Dow Jones & Company, Inc.

United Way of Union County ($360,000) see Merck & Co.

University Heights Science Park — planning ($70,000) see Fund for New Jersey

University of Medicine and Dentistry Foundation ($66,032) see Van Houten Memorial Fund

University of Medicine and Dentistry of New Jersey — Newark women and children grant program ($200,000) see Prudential Insurance Co. of America, The

University of Medicine and Dentistry of New Jersey —

gifted children's program ($58,357) see Turrell Fund

University of Medicine and Dentistry of New Jersey Foundation ($52,100) see Hoffmann-La Roche Inc.

University of Medicine and Dentistry of New Jersey Foundation ($134,910) see Van Houten Memorial Fund

Upper Raritan Watershed Association — for conservation of natural resources ($10,000) see Cape Branch Foundation

US Golf Association — centennial program ($25,000) see Bechtel, Jr. Foundation, S. D.

Van Ost Institute for Family Living ($20,000) see Schenck Fund, L. P.

Walt Whitman Center of Rutgers ($75,000) see Fund for New Jersey

Woodrow Wilson National Fellowship — in support of the programs of Mellon fellowships ($6,280,000) see Mellon Foundation, Andrew W.

YMCA — program support ($60,000) see Turrell Fund

YMCA of Madison Area — to renovate and rename the F. M. Kirby Children's Center ($1,125,000) see Kirby Foundation, F. M.

Youth Consultation Services, Holley House ($50,000) see Schenck Fund, L. P.

New Mexico

Albuquerque Children's Museum — for general support ($15,000) see Public Service Co. of New Mexico

Albuquerque Community Foundation — for general support ($20,000) see Public Service Co. of New Mexico

Albuquerque T-VI — for general support ($10,000) see Public Service Co. of New Mexico

Amigos Bravos ($20,000) see New-Land Foundation

Archaeological Conservancy — matching challenge grant for preservation fund ($25,000) see Laurel Foundation

Assurance Home ($62,500) see Maddox Foundation, J. F.

Ayudantes ($75,000) see McCune Charitable Foundation, Marshall and Perrine D.

Boys and Girls Club of Hobbs ($249,324) see Maddox Foundation, J. F.

Casa Esperanza — for general support ($7,500) see Public Service Co. of New Mexico

Catholic Social Services of Santa Fe ($50,000) see McCune Charitable Foundation, Marshall and Perrine D.

Children's Center of New Mexico ($1,000) see NewMil Bancorp

Community Services Center ($300,000) see Maddox Foundation, J. F.

Eastern New Mexico University — for Distinguished Education award ($15,000) see Public Service Co. of New Mexico

Eunice Public Library ($105,000) see Maddox Foundation, J. F.

Friends of South Broadway Cultural Center — for general support ($7,500) see Public Service Co. of New Mexico

Fund for Folk Culture — to extend the Lila Wallace-Reader's Digest Community Folklife Program, which provides grants and other support services to local and regional organizations involved in representing or documenting folk-arts traditions nationwide ($2,450,000) see Wallace-Reader's Digest Fund, Lila

Habitat for Humanity ($50,000) see McCune Charitable Foundation, Marshall and Perrine D.

Hospice Center ($65,000) see McCune Charitable Foundation, Marshall and Perrine D.

Institute of American Indian Arts — for general support ($15,000) see Public Service Co. of New Mexico

KHME-TV 5 ($50,000) see McCune Charitable Foundation, Marshall and Perrine D.

La Familia Medical Center ($79,218) see McCune Charitable Foundation, Marshall and Perrine D.

La Nueva Vida ($80,000) see McCune Charitable Foundation, Marshall and Perrine D.

Lea County Good Samaritan Village ($1,048,357) see Maddox Foundation, J. F.

Lovington Municipal Schools ($127,000) see Maddox Foundation, J. F.

Maxwell Museum Association — for general support ($6,500) see Public Service Co. of New Mexico

Museum of Indian Arts and Culture ($50,000) see McCune Charitable Foundation, Marshall and Perrine D.

Museum of New Mexico ($25,000) see Herzstein Charitable Foundation, Albert and Ethel

Museum of New Mexico Foundation ($25,000) see Thornton Foundation, Flora L.

New Mexico Boys and Girls Ranch Foundation ($300,000) see Maddox Foundation, J. F.

New Mexico Christian Children's Home ($350,000) see Maddox Foundation, J. F.

New Mexico Highlands University — for support of Kennedy Hall ($8,000) see Public Service Co. of New Mexico

New Mexico Military Institute ($103,900) see Kerr Foundation

New Mexico Symphony Orchestra ($5,000) see Illinois Consolidated Telephone Co.

Partners in Education see Pittsburg Midway Coal Mining Co.

Ridoso Community Concert — for concerts ($2,000) see Huthsteiner Fine Arts Trust

Santa Fe Institute — in support of institute activities over three years ($1,500,000) see MacArthur

New York

Ballet Theatre Foundation ($25,000) see Piankova Foundation, Tatiana

Ballet Theatre Foundation ($5,000) see Salomon Inc.

Ballet Theatre Foundation ($5,000) see Salomon Inc.

Bank Street College of Education — scholarship endowment challenge grant to build a Newcombe Fund ($25,000) see Newcombe Foundation, Charlotte W.

Bank Street College of Education — toward small libraries for the Partners for Success program ($25,000) see Astor Foundation, Vincent

Bank Street College of Education — final renewed support of the Principals Institute ($150,000) see Diamond Foundation, Aaron

Bank Street College of Education — for final payment of $100,000 capital grant and $75,000 for the Principals Institute/Leadership Center ($107,500) see Morgan & Company, J.P.

Bank Street College of Education ($100,000) see Pforzheimer Foundation, Carl and Lily

Bank Street College of Education — over four and one-half years to contract with Bank Street College of Education as the coordinating agency for expansion of the DeWitt Wallace-Reader's Digest Pathways to Teaching Careers Program to colleges and universities ($2,068,502) see Wallace-Reader's Digest Fund, DeWitt

Bank Street College of Education ($79,900) see Levitt Foundation

Bank Street College of Education ($17,000) see Love Foundation, George H. and Margaret McClintic

Bank Street School ($4,000) see Levitt Foundation

Bar Ilan University — for Joseph Alexander library ($50,000) see Alexander Foundation, Joseph

Bar-Ilan University ($5,000) see Kaplun Foundation, Morris J. and Betty

Bard College ($28,000) see Helms Foundation

Bard College ($50,000) see Avery Arts Foundation, Milton and Sally

Bard College ($25,000) see Lang Foundation, Eugene M.

Bargemusic — chamber music concerts ($6,000) see Smith Trust, May and Stanley

Barnard College ($35,000) see Mnuchin Foundation

Barnard College ($270,000) see Overbrook Foundation

Baycrest Centre for Geriatric Care ($35,000) see Cummings Foundation, James H.

Baywith Lepleitot ($12,000) see Rosen Foundation, Joseph

Beaverkill Conservancy — for their Special Projects Fund, which supports efforts to enhance and protect the natural and built environment of New York city and state ($159,000) see Kaplan Fund, J. M.

Bedford Stuyvesant Restoration Corporation see Bank of New York Company, Inc.

Ben-Gurion University of the Negev ($46,500) see Foster Charitable Trust

Bendersville Lutheran Church ($10,000) see Bobst Foundation, Elmer and Mamdouha

Benjamin Banneker Academy in Community Development ($50,000) see Bankers Trust Company

Benjamin N. Cardozo School of Law of Yeshiva University ($10,000) see Fink Foundation

BENS Education Fund ($12,500) see Salomon Foundation, Richard and Edna

Bet Torah ($7,000) see Goldie-Anna Charitable Trust

Beth Israel Foundation ($10,000) see Feil Foundation, Louis and Gertrude

Beth Israel Foundation ($114,500) see McGonagle Foundation, Dextra Baldwin

Beth Israel Hospice ($25,000) see Reicher Foundation, Anne and Harry J.

Beth Israel Medical Center — for the Samuels Planetree Model Hospital Unit ($50,000) see Hearst Foundation, William Randolph

Beth Israel Medical Center — breast diagnostic ($25,000) see Hugoton Foundation

Beth Israel Medical Center ($10,000) see Reicher Foundation, Anne and Harry J.

Bethany Retirement Center — for the activities room ($15,000) see Anderson Foundation

Better Business Bureau of Metropolitan New York see Bank of New York Company, Inc.

Big Apple Circus ($18,000) see Normandie Foundation

Binding Together — job training and employment ($3,500) see Vogler Foundation, Laura B.

Binghamton Area Girls Softball Association — construction of softball complex ($22,207) see Hoyt Foundation, Stewart W. and Willma C.

Binghamton Symphony — moving and marketing expenses ($12,000) see Hoyt Foundation, Stewart W. and Willma C.

Black Leadership Commission on AIDS — for health care see Morgan Stanley & Co., Inc.

Blind Association of Western New York ($10,000) see Joy Family Foundation

Blind Association of Western New York — to upgrade present computer system ($20,000) see Western New York Foundation

Bloomingdale House of Music ($5,000) see Daily News

Blue Ridge Community Health Service ($25,000) see Cummings Foundation, James H.

B'nai B'rith ($135,000) see Seagram & Sons, Inc., Joseph E.

Boquet River Association ($1,000) see Crary Foundation, Bruce L.

Boy Scouts of America — build a cub scout camp ($5,000) see Curtice-Burns Foods, Inc.

Boy Scouts of America Cayuga County Council ($5,000) see Everett Charitable Trust

Boy Scouts of America Five River Council ($22,526) see Taylor Foundation, Fred and Harriett

Boy Scouts of America Greater New York Council ($100,000) see Smeal Foundation, Mary Jean and Frank P.

Boy Scouts of America Greater New York Council ($100,000) see Smeal Foundation, Mary Jean and Frank P.

Boy Scouts of America Greater New York Council ($10,000) see Smeal Foundation, Mary Jean and Frank P.

Boy Scouts of America Greater New York Councils — Cub World/Camp Alpine, second of three payments of a $500,000 pledge ($150,000) see Merrill Lynch & Co., Inc.

Boy Scouts of America Greater New York Councils — for social service see Morgan Stanley & Co., Inc.

Boy Scouts of America Otetiana Council — Camp Cutler campaign ($30,000) see Davenport-Hatch Foundation

Boyce Thompson Institute for Plant Research ($5,000) see Park Foundation

Boys Brotherhood Republic of New York ($20,000) see Achelis Foundation

Boys Club of New York — general ($350,000) see Fairchild Foundation, Sherman

Boys Club of New York ($2,250) see Breyer Foundation

Boys Club of New York — learning center program support ($50,000) see Frueauff Foundation, Charles A.

Boys Club of New York ($35,000) see Harriman Foundation, Mary W.

Boys Club of New York ($15,000) see Johnson Foundation, Willard T. C.

Boys Club of New York ($15,000) see Sprague Educational and Charitable Foundation, Seth

Boys Clubs of America ($50,000) see Ford Fund, William and Martha

Boys and Girls Club of Binghamton — construction of teen center ($20,000) see Hoyt Foundation, Stewart W. and Willma C.

Boys and Girls Clubs of America ($1,100) see Taubman Foundation, A. Alfred

Boys and Girls Clubs of America — to support Outreach Two Million, a three-year plan to serve 2,000,000 disadvantaged youngsters nationwide by 1994, final payment of a two-year grant ($200,000) see JM Foundation

Boys Harbor/The Harbor for Girls and Boys ($20,000) see Achelis Foundation

British Schools and Universities Foundation ($25,000) see Heinz Trust, Drue

Broad Jump Prep for Prep ($40,000) see Greve Foundation, William and Mary

Bronfman Center for Jewish Life ($1,000,000) see Seagram & Sons, Inc., Joseph E.

Bronfman Library ($95,000) see Seagram & Sons, Inc., Joseph E.

Bronfman Youth Fellowships ($460,000) see Seagram & Sons, Inc., Joseph E.

Bronx Council on the Arts ($5,000) see Daily News

Bronx Educational Services — library renovations ($100,000) see Booth Ferris Foundation

Bronx House ($10,000) see Lemberg Foundation

Bronx-Lebanon Hospital ($20,000) see Hagedorn Fund

Bronx-Lebanon Hospital New Directions Fund — for Bronx-Lebanon Hospital Center ($100,000) see Altman Foundation

Bronx Museum of the Arts ($5,000) see Daily News

Brookdale Center on Aging ($38,826) see Burden Foundation, Florence V.

Brookdale Center on Aging ($30,000) see Dreyfus Foundation, Jean and Louis

Brookdale Center on Aging at Hunter College ($50,000) see Weinstein Foundation, J.

Brookdale Hospital and Medical Center ($27,500) see Parshelsky Foundation, Moses L.

Brookdale Hospital and Medical Center — surgery department ($10,000) see Parshelsky Foundation, Moses L.

Brooklyn Academy of Music ($50,000) see Dow Jones & Company, Inc.

Brooklyn Academy of Music ($5,000) see Daily News

Brooklyn Academy of Music ($100,000) see Gilman Foundation, Howard

Brooklyn Academy of Music ($350,000) see Gould Foundation, The Florence

Brooklyn Academy of Music ($107,285) see Hillman Family Foundation, Alex

Brooklyn Academy of Music ($50,000) see Noble Foundation, Edward John

Brooklyn Academy of Music ($12,000) see Tuch Foundation, Michael

Brooklyn Botanic Garden ($5,000) see Culver Foundation, Constans

Brooklyn Bureau of Community Service see Bank of New York Company, Inc.

Brooklyn Bureau of Community Service ($75,000) see Heckscher Foundation for Children

Brooklyn Children's Museum ($100,000) see Altman Foundation

Brooklyn Children's Museum — for the arts see Morgan Stanley & Co., Inc.

Brooklyn Children's Museum — Black Family Forum Series for the exchange of ideas and resources ($3,000) see Vogler Foundation, Laura B.

Brooklyn Historical Society — library modernization ($100,000) see Booth Ferris Foundation

Brooklyn Law School ($3,500) see Hanover Foundation

Brooklyn Mosque ($21,000) see Alavi Foundation of New York

Brooklyn Museum ($50,000) see Moses Fund, Henry and Lucy

Brooklyn Museum ($10,000) see Tuch Foundation, Michael

Brooklyn Music School ($5,000) see Daily News

Brooklyn Philharmonic Orchestra ($10,000) see Tuch Foundation, Michael

Brooklyn Public Library ($17,808) see Tuch Foundation, Michael

Brooklyn in Touch Information Center ($40,500) see Bowne Foundation, Robert

Broome-Chenango Alternative High School ($5,000) see Raymond Corp.

Broome Community College — health science center ($75,000) see O'Connor Foundation, A. Lindsay and Olive B.

Broome Community College Foundation — scholarships to Broome County students ($17,500) see Hoyt Foundation, Stewart W. and Willma C.

Broome County Arts Council — United Cultural Fund ($95,000) see Hoyt Foundation, Stewart W. and Willma C.

Broome County Child Development Council — assistance in development/improvement of day care in Broome County ($30,000) see Hoyt Foundation, Stewart W. and Willma C.

Buffalo and Erie County Public Library ($100,000) see Julia R. and Estelle L. Foundation

Buffalo and Erie County United Way ($90,000) see Fleet Financial Group, Inc.

Buffalo General Hospital ($83,000) see Cummings Foundation, James H.

Buffalo General Hospital ($65,000) see Julia R. and Estelle L. Foundation

Buffalo Museum of Science — establishment of Science Education Center ($100,000) see Wendt Foundation, Margaret L.

Buffalo Philharmonic Endowment — future commitment ($45,000) see Cornell Trust, Peter C.

Buffalo Philharmonic Fund for Music — for extenden grant ($40,000) see Western New York Foundation

Buffalo Philharmonic Orchestra ($17,116) see Joy Family Foundation

Buffalo Philharmonic Orchestra — loan converted to a grant ($250,000) see Wendt Foundation, Margaret L.

Buffalo Philharmonic Orchestra Society ($10,000) see Rich Products Corporation

Buffalo State College Foundation — for purchase of new lighting board ($10,000) see Western New York Foundation

Business Committee for the Arts ($35,873) see Forbes Inc.

Business Council of United Nations ($100,000) see Archer-Daniels-Midland Co.

Business Council for the United Nations — special event ($5,000) see Rouse Co.

Business for Social Responsibility ($25,000) see Mailman Foundation

Cabrini Medical Center ($50,000) see Morris Foundation, William T.

Camelot Family Foundation see New York Mercantile Exchange

Camp Good Days ($2,500) see Seneca Foods Corp.

Camp Good Days — for air exposition ($1,800) see Seneca Foods Corp.

Camp Good Days and Special Times — special international program for sick children ($10,000) see Schmitt Foundation, Kilian J. and Caroline F.

Camp Vacamas ($75,000) see Kaufmann Foundation, Henry

Camp Vacamas Association — children's camp activities ($10,000) see Parshelsky Foundation, Moses L.

Camp Wethersfield — operating expenses ($50,000) see Homeland Foundation

Can/Pal/Root Community Chest — general support ($10,000) see Arkell Hall Foundation

Canajoharie Central School — Barbour scholarships ($50,000) see Arkell Hall Foundation

Canajoharie Community Services — facility repairs and improvements ($27,250) see Arkell Hall Foundation

Canandaigua City School District — grant for new multi-media creation station in library ($10,000) see Knapp Foundation

Cancer Care ($1,000) see Mosbacher, Jr. Foundation, Emil

Cancer Research Institute — to name clinical research program ($150,000) see Kirby Foundation, F. M.

Cancer Research Institute ($6,000) see Hatch Charitable Trust, Margaret Milliken

Cancer Research Institute — medical ($3,525) see Cayuga Foundation

Canisius College ($125,000) see Julia R. and Estelle L. Foundation

Canisius College — for Palisano Religious Vocation program ($55,000) see Palisano Foundation, Vincent and Harriet

Canisius College — for added funding Palisano Religious Vocational program ($20,000) see Palisano Foundation, Vincent and Harriet

Capital District Center for Drug Abuse Research and Treatment — final renewed support for the development and utilization of new drugs for treating drug addiction ($75,000) see Diamond Foundation, Aaron

Caramoor Center for Music and Arts ($5,000) see Icahn Foundation, Carl C.

Caramoor Center for Music and Arts ($25,000) see Phipps Foundation, Howard

Caramoor Garden Guild ($15,000) see Richardson Charitable Trust, Anne S.

Cardinal Hayes Home ($35,000) see Millbrook Tribute Garden

Cardinal's Committee of the Laity ($15,000) see Prudential Securities, Inc.

Caribbean Women's Health Association ($20,000) see Dreyfus Foundation, Jean and Louis

Carmelite Monastery of Rochester ($50,000) see Link, Jr. Foundation, George

Carnegie Art Center ($3,288) see Welch Testamentary Trust, George T.

Carnegie Hall ($10,000) see Holzer Memorial Foundation, Richard H.

Carnegie Hall ($75,000) see Heckscher Foundation for Children

Carnegie Hall — unrestricted ($336,000) see Rohatyn Foundation, Felix and Elizabeth

Carnegie Hall — for general operating support ($300,000) see Travelers Inc.

Carver Statewide Scholarship Program — college and university scholarships ($669,100) see Carver Charitable Trust, Roy J.

Casita Maria Fiesta '92 ($5,000) see Taubman Foundation, A. Alfred

Cast the Sleeping Elephant Trust ($10,000) see Erpf Fund, Armand G.

Cathedral of St. John the Divine — grant for the psychiatric social worker, who treats the mentally ill elderly in the senior outreach program ($55,008) see van Ameringen Foundation

Catholic Charities — archdiocese of New York inner-city scholarship fund ($25,000) see Nias Foundation, Henry

Catholic Charities ($10,000) see Raymond Corp.

Catholic Charities Appeal ($150,000) see Julia R. and Estelle L. Foundation

Catholic Charities, Archdiocese of New York ($100,000) see Altman Foundation

Catholic Charities of the Archdiocese of New York ($25,000) see Badgeley Residuary Charitable Trust, Rose M.

Catholic Charities Diocese of Brooklyn — St. John's community life center and future fund campaign ($50,000) see Frueauff Foundation, Charles A.

Catholic Home Bureau ($100,000) see Altman Foundation

Catholic Near East Welfare Association ($20,000) see

Bobst Foundation, Elmer and Mamdouha

Catskill Area Hospice ($10,000) see Hulbert Foundation, Nila B.

Catskill Center for Conservation and Development — fulltime Main Street manager ($35,000) see O'Connor Foundation, A. Lindsay and Olive B.

Catskill Center for Conservation and Development — marketing project ($30,000) see O'Connor Foundation, A. Lindsay and Olive B.

Catskill Forest Association — general purposes ($28,000) see O'Connor Foundation, A. Lindsay and Olive B.

Cayuga Chamber Orchestra ($2,000) see Delavan Foundation, Nelson B.

Cayuga County Community College ($4,000) see Everett Charitable Trust

Cayuga County Habitat for Humanity — general ($3,525) see Cayuga Foundation

Cazenovia College — unrestricted ($10,000) see Chapman Charitable Corporation, Howard and Bess

Cazenovia College — debt reduction ($100,000) see Emerson Foundation, Inc., Fred L.

Centennial Foundation ($3,250) see Arnhold Foundation

Center on Addiction and Substance Abuse ($25,000) see Chase Manhattan Bank, N.A.

Center on Addiction and Substance Abuse — supplement over 22 months, for a research program that tests comprehensive, community-based services aimed at preventing drug use among at-risk youth ($1,800,000) see Ford Foundation

Center for African Art ($20,000) see Benenson Foundation, Frances and Benjamin

Center for African Art ($50,000) see Mnuchin Foundation

Center for Children and Families ($20,000) see Bowne Foundation, Robert

Center for Collaborative Education ($140,000) see Kornfeld Foundation, Emily Davie and Joseph S.

Center for Constitutional Rights — legal ($50,000) see Rubin Foundation, Samuel

Center for Educational Innovation (Manhattan Institute for Policy Research) — to enable the Center to provide its educational expertise to the East Brooklyn Congregations that, with Rev. Johnny Ray Youngblood's leadership, are establishing two new high schools ($275,000) see Kaplan Fund, J. M.

Center for Family Life in Sunset Park — for social service see Morgan Stanley & Co., Inc.

Center of Governmental Research ($125,000) see Gleason Foundation

Center for Independent Thought — for "Critical Review," their quarterly journal of "classical liberal thought," to enable them to establish a firm financial footing ($100,000) see Kaplan Fund, J. M.

Center for Law and Justice ($23,500) see Howard and Bush Foundation

Center on Learning Assessment and School Structure — to support three programs: a national contest seeking exemplary lessons created by teachers utilizing performance-based methods; the compilation of these lessons into an anthology; and the implementation of these methods ($100,000) see Dodge Foundation, Geraldine R.

Center for Post-Soviet Studies ($40,000) see Greve Foundation, William and Mary

Center for Reproductive Law and Policy ($100,000) see Huber Foundation

Center for the Study of the Presidency ($5,000) see McDonald & Company Securities, Inc.

Center for the Study of Soviet Changes ($75,000) see Greve Foundation, William and Mary

Central Park Conservancy — Shakespeare Garden ($29,000) see Griggs and Mary Griggs Burke Foundation, Mary Livingston

Central Park Conservancy ($5,000) see Daily News

Central Park Conservancy — creation of a "Discovery Center" in Central Park ($750,000) see Dana Foundation, Charles A.

Central Park Conservancy ($27,600) see Lauder Foundation

Central Park Conservancy — capital campaign, final payment of a $500,000 pledge ($200,000) see Merrill Lynch & Co., Inc.

Central Park Conservancy ($50,000) see Moses Fund, Henry and Lucy

Central Park Conservancy ($17,250) see Osborn Charitable Trust, Edward B.

Central Park Conservancy ($10,000) see Sasco Foundation

Central Park Conservancy ($23,350) see Schlumberger Ltd.

Central Park Conservancy ($100,000) see Texaco Inc.

Central Park Conservancy ($10,500) see Thorne Foundation

Central Park Conservancy ($15,000) see Weil, Gotshal and Manges Foundation

Central Park Conservancy — capital campaign ($500,000) see Burnett-Tandy Foundation

Central Park Wildlife Center ($25,000) see Prudential Securities, Inc.

Channel 13/WNET Educational Broadcasting Corporation — first payment of five-year grant totaling $2.5 million to establish the "Cornelius V. Starr Fund for

Arts Programming" ($500,000) see Starr Foundation

Chapin School — for expansion of facilities ($50,000) see Baker Trust, George F.

Chatham Hall ($1,300) see Acme-McCrary Corp./Sapona Manufacturing Co.

Chaut Region Community Foundation — eco dev fund ($3,000) see Lenna Foundation, Reginald A. and Elizabeth S.

Chautauqua Area Girl Scout Council ($50,000) see Hultquist Foundation

Chautauqua Fire Department ($10,000) see Carnahan-Jackson Foundation

Chautauqua Foundation — ESL building ($85,000) see Lenna Foundation, Reginald A. and Elizabeth S.

Chautauqua Institution ($120,000) see Carnahan-Jackson Foundation

Chautauqua Institution ($25,000) see Hultquist Foundation

Chautauqua Institution — restoration of the Massey Memorial Pipe Organ ($100,000) see Wendt Foundation, Margaret L.

Chautauqua Institution Fund — general operations ($15,000) see Lenna Foundation, Reginald A. and Elizabeth S.

Chautauqua Lake Association — for general operating expenses over three years ($100,000) see Gebbie Foundation

Chautauqua Striders ($12,000) see Hultquist Foundation

Chautauqua Striders — general operations ($15,000) see Lenna Foundation, Reginald A. and Elizabeth S.

Chemung Valley Arts Council — for regional cultural plan ($125,000) see Corning Incorporated

Child Development Center ($5,000) see Marx Foundation, Virginia and Leonard

Children Aid Society ($25,000) see Hagedorn Fund

Children of Bellevue see Wiley & Sons, Inc., John

Children of Bellvue ($5,000) see Love Foundation, George H. and Margaret McClintic

Children's Aid Society ($40,000) see Moore Foundation, Edward S.

Children's Aid Society ($23,000) see Blum Foundation, Edna F.

Children's Aid Society ($70,000) see Bodman Foundation

Children's Blood Foundation — for health care see Morgan Stanley & Co., Inc.

Children's Blood Foundation — AIDS research and ongoing support of clinic, training, and research programs for children's blood diseases at the New York Hospital-Cornell Medical Center ($60,000) see Rubinstein Foundation, Helena

Children's Express ($5,000)
see Daily News

Children's Hope Foundation
($17,000) see Witco Corp.

Children's Hospital ($25,600)
see Joy Family Foundation

Children's Hospital of Buffalo
($25,000) see Cummings
Foundation, James H.

Children's Hospital of Buffalo
Foundation — pediatric
intensive care and trauma
center project ($300,000) see
Wendt Foundation, Margaret
L.

Children's Museum —
computer exhibit ($5,000)
see Utica National Insurance
Group

Children's Museum of
Manhattan ($5,000) see
Daily News

Children's Museum of
Manhattan ($50,000) see
Unilever United States, Inc.

Children's Storefront
Foundation ($100,000) see
Altman Foundation

Children's Television
Workshop — to provide
capstone funding for
"Ghostwriters" ($300,000)
see Davis Foundations,
Arthur Vining

Christ Church — unrestricted
($5,000) see Chapman
Charitable Corporation,
Howard and Bess

Christ Church United
Methodist ($5,000) see
Hallberg Foundation, E. L.
and R. F.

Christian Heralds Children
Home ($15,172) see Hallett
Charitable Trust, Jessie F.

Church and Friary of St.
Francis of Assisi ($70,000)
see Link, Jr. Foundation,
George

Church of the Holy Trinity
($5,000) see Memton Fund

Church of St. Michael
($15,000) see Dula
Educational and Charitable
Foundation, Caleb C. and
Julia W.

Cider Mill Playhouse —
capital campaign ($25,000)
see Hoyt Foundation,
Stewart W. and Willma C.

Citizens Budget Commission
($250,000) see Smeal
Foundation, Mary Jean and
Frank P.

Citizens Committee for New
York ($10,000) see Rudin
Foundation

Citizen's Domestic Violence
Program ($3,000) see Crary
Foundation, Bruce L.

Citizens Hose Company
($16,090) see Taylor
Foundation, Fred and
Harriett

City Center 55th Street
Theater Foundation
($15,000) see Rose
Foundation, Billy

City College Fund ($15,000)
see McGonagle Foundation,
Dextra Baldwin

City College Fund ($25,000)
see Moses Fund, Henry and
Lucy

City College Simon H. Rifkind
Center ($100,000) see
Winston Foundation,
Norman and Rosita

City Harvest ($24,000) see
Tuch Foundation, Michael

City Meals on Wheels
($2,500) see Slifka
Foundation, Joseph and
Sylvia

City Opera ($7,500) see
Holzer Memorial
Foundation, Richard H.

City Parks Foundation — for
the citywide Disabled
Playground Project at Asser
Levy Park ($75,000) see
Heckscher Foundation for
Children

Citymeals-on-Wheels ($3,500)
see Crane Co.

Civil Liberties Action League
($41,450) see Borman's Inc.

Clarkson University —for
William C. Decker-Corning
Scholars Program ($25,000)
see Corning Incorporated

Clarkson University ($10,000)
see Snow Foundation, John
Ben

Classroom — for their
professional development
program ($100,000) see
Morgan & Company, J.P.

Clear Pool Camp ($30,000)
see Moore Foundation,
Edward S.

Clear Pool Camp — charitable
($10,000) see New York
Stock Exchange, Inc.

Clearpool — in conjunction
with the Edwin Gould
Foundation for Children;
Clearpool, a residential
summer camp in Carmel,
NY, is collaborating with
Bedford-Stuyvesant School
District 16 to create a model
year-round K-8 grade school
with campuses at both
locations ($25,000) see
Guttman Foundation, Stella
and Charles

Clearpool ($53,000) see Liz
Claiborne, Inc.

Clearpool School ($83,000)
see Bankers Trust Company

Clemens Center — for general
operations ($27,000) see
Anderson Foundation

CNY Community Foundation
— support for Greater
Pulaski Fund ($35,000) see
Snow Memorial Trust, John
Ben

Colbert Foundation see
Givenchy Corp.

Cold Spring Harbor
Laboratory — Allied Signal
Aging Research Award
($100,000) see AlliedSignal
Inc.

Cold Spring Harbor
Laboratory ($50,000) see
Hoffmann-La Roche Inc.

Cold Spring Harbor
Laboratory ($45,000) see
Bodman Foundation

Cold Spring Harbor
Laboratory — Dana
Consortium on the Genetic
Basis of Manic-Depressive
Illness ($670,000) see Dana
Foundation, Charles A.

Cold Spring Harbor
Laboratory ($35,000) see
Westvaco Corporation

Cold Spring Harbor
Laboratory — medical
research seminars
($100,000) see Farish Fund,
William Stamps

Cold Spring Harbor
Laboratory Cancer Research
Institute ($200,000) see
Freeman Charitable Trust,
Samuel

Colgate University — for
general education fund
($12,500) see Palisades
Educational Foundation

College Board — 1992-95,
$440,000 grant for
dissemination of the Equity
2000 program, a $28

million, six-city, multiyear
demonstration program
aimed at enabling all
students to successfully
complete algebra and
geometry ($110,000) see
Aetna Life & Casualty Co.

College Careers see MBIA Inc.

College of Insurance — for
faculty development
($25,000) see Kemper
National Insurance Cos.

College of Physicians and
Surgeons of Columbia
University ($100,000) see
Brooks Foundation, Gladys

Columbia Business School
($5,000) see Chazen
Foundation

Columbia Business School
($10,000) see Hammer
Foundation, Armand

Columbia College of
Physicians and Surgeons
($30,000) see Sulzberger
Foundation

Columbia Law School
($5,000) see Goldie-Anna
Charitable Trust

Columbia Presbyterian
Medical Center — Hatch
Professorship Chair
($1,010,000) see Hatch
Charitable Trust, Margaret
Milliken

Columbia Presbyterian
Medical Center — aid for
research in oral diseases
($10,000) see Vernon Fund,
Miles Hodsdon

Columbia Presbyterian
Medical Center Fund —
capital campaign for
expansion ($200,000) see
Farish Fund, William Stamps

Columbia School of
Journalism ($10,000) see
Robinson Fund, Maurice R.

Columbia University — event
($50,000) see MCA Inc.

Columbia University
($250,000) see Thermo
Electron Corp.

Columbia University —
scholarship ($4,000) see
Scherer Foundation, Karla

Columbia University —
graduate assistance
($56,000) see Griggs and
Mary Griggs Burke
Foundation, Mary Livingston

Columbia University
($50,000) see Pulitzer
Publishing Co.

Columbia University
($20,000) see Dow Jones &
Company, Inc.

Columbia University
($37,500) see Dun &
Bradstreet Corp.

Columbia University
($270,000) see Harriman
Foundation, Gladys and
Roland

Columbia University
($31,000) see Hebrew
Technical Institute

Columbia University
($505,000) see Lang
Foundation, Eugene M.

Columbia University —
Yiddish studies program and
scholarship support for
graduate students ($25,000)
see Littauer Foundation,
Lucius N.

Columbia University
($52,272) see Lurcy
Charitable and Educational
Trust, Georges

Columbia University
($15,000) see Miller Fund,
Kathryn and Gilbert

Columbia University
($419,000) see Seagram &
Sons, Inc., Joseph E.

Columbia University —
Sovern Library ($250,000)
see Shubert Foundation

Columbia University —
presidential scholars
program ($100,000) see
Shubert Foundation

Columbia University — for
support of educational
programs ($5,000) see Fair
Oaks Foundation, Inc.

Columbia University in the
City of New York —
purchase of microfilm
reader/printer ($10,000) see
Knapp Foundation

Columbia University in the
City of New York ($45,000)
see Atran Foundation

Columbia University in the
City of New York Trustees
($25,000) see Ames
Charitable Trust, Harriett

Columbia University College
of Physicians and Surgeons
— Dana Consortium on
Memory Loss and Aging
($270,000) see Dana
Foundation, Charles A.

Columbia University College
of Physicians and Surgeons
— charitable contribution
($12,500) see Klosk Fund,
Louis and Rose

Columbia University College
of Physicians and Surgeons
($250,000) see Lowenstein
Foundation, Leon

Columbia University College
of Physicians and Surgeons
— encephalitis research aid
($30,000) see Vernon Fund,
Miles Hodsdon

Columbia University
Department of Psychiatry
($25,000) see Marmot
Foundation

Columbia University
Externship Program in
Human Rights and Health
Care ($104,905) see
Kornfeld Foundation, Emily
Davie and Joseph S.

Columbia University Graduate
School of Business
($50,000) see Cooperman
Foundation, Leon and Toby

Columbia University Graduate
School of Business
($100,000) see Uris Brothers
Foundation

Columbia University Graduate
School of Journalism —
project to research
establishing a Ph.D. program
($50,000) see New York
Times Company

Columbia University
Knight-Baghot Fellowship
($30,000) see McGraw-Hill,
Inc.

Columbia University Lamont
— DOH Earth Observation
($29,373) see Vetlesen
Foundation, G. Unger

Columbia University Research
Institute of International
Change ($25,000) see
Vetlesen Foundation, G.
Unger

Columbia University, School
of General Studies —
scholarships for women
($60,000) see Rubinstein
Foundation, Helena

Columbia University Teachers
College ($100,000) see
Lowenstein Foundation,
Leon

Columbia University Trustees
— MRI center ($100,000)
see Hugoton Foundation

Columbia University Trustees
— education ($5,000) see
Lebovitz Fund

Comfortcare of Cayuga
County — medical ($4,700)
see Cayuga Foundation

Committee for the Blind of
Poland — for construction
of library at the Institute for
the Blind at Laski, Poland
($141,500) see Jurzykowski
Foundation, Alfred

Committee for Economic
Development ($2,500) see
Goldberg Family Foundation

Committee for Economic
Development ($3,500) see
Rubin Family Fund, Cele H.
and William B.

Committee for Economic
Development — a two-year
grant for the completion of a
policy statement on
inner-city problems and for a
study of the global economy
($150,000) see AT&T Corp.

Committee to Protect
Journalists ($1,000) see
Goodstein Family
Foundation, David

Community Access ($5,000)
see Blum Foundation, Edna
F.

Community Foundation —
other ($20,000) see
La-Z-Boy Chair Co.

Community Health Project
($20,000) see Kornfeld
Foundation, Emily Davie
and Joseph S.

Community Memorial
Hospital — unrestricted
($5,000) see Chapman
Charitable Corporation,
Howard and Bess

Community Partnership
Development Corporation
($150,000) see Uris Brothers
Foundation

Community Research
Initiative on AIDS — to
conduct clinical trials of
promising new AIDS
therapies in New York City's
only community-based
research facility that works
directly with local doctors
and their AIDS patients
($105,000) see Kaplan Fund,
J. M.

Community Theater ($1,500)
see Warner Fund, Albert and
Bessie

Community Youth Center —
operating support ($20,000)
see Arkell Hall Foundation

Comprehensive Community
Revitalization Program
($75,000) see Bankers Trust
Company

Conference Board —
charitable contribution
($30,000) see Olin Corp.

Conference Board ($20,000)
see Dun & Bradstreet Corp.

Congregation Beth Sholom
($5,000) see Fischbach
Foundation

Congregation Emanu-El
($50,000) see Lurie
Foundation, Louis R.

Congregation Emanu-El
($10,000) see Meyer Fund,
Milton and Sophie

Congregation Emanu-El
($3,200) see Lasdon
Foundation

Congregation Emanu El
($5,000) see Lasdon
Foundation, William and
Mildred

Congregation Emanu El
($5,000) see Lasdon
Foundation, William and
Mildred

Gimmel Foundation ($20,000) see Amado Foundation, Maurice

Girl Scout Council of Greater New York ($75,000) see Phipps Foundation, Howard

Girl Scout Council of Greater New York ($25,000) see Prudential Securities, Inc.

Girl Scouts of America —for improvements to program centers ($25,000) see Corning Incorporated

Girls Incorporated ($10,000) see Coltec Industries, Inc.

Glens Falls Home — aid for care of elderly ($6,500) see Vernon Fund, Miles Hodsdon

Glimmerglass Opera ($150,000) see Clark Foundation

Glimmerglass Opera ($100,000) see Clark Foundation

Global Action Plan — support their community-based ecoteam program as a pilot for mass replication; coteams encourage and support people in living an environmentally sustainable lifestyle ($30,000) see Ittleson Foundation

Gloversville Holiday Christmas Lights ($3,000) see City National Bank and Trust Co.

Gloversville Holiday Decoration Fund ($683) see City National Bank and Trust Co.

Gloversville Releaf Fund ($2,500) see City National Bank and Trust Co.

Gloversville YWCA ($5,000) see City National Bank and Trust Co.

Goddard Riverside Community Center — OPTIONS program ($150,000) see Booth Ferris Foundation

Goddard-Riverside Community Center — for final renewed general support and the options program ($75,000) see Diamond Foundation, Aaron

God's Love We Deliver ($10,000) see Tuch Foundation, Michael

Good Samaritan Hospital ($265,000) see Harriman Foundation, Gladys and Roland

Good Shepherd Services — help youngsters with substance and drug abuse problems ($3,500) see Vogler Foundation, Laura B.

Goodwill Industries of Greater New York ($30,000) see Porter Foundation, Mrs. Cheever

Gow School ($11,000) see Joy Family Foundation

Grace Church Building Fund ($5,000) see Culver Foundation, Constans

Grace Episcopal Church ($115,000) see Millbrook Tribute Garden

Graham-Windham Services ($25,375) see Cheatham Foundation, Owen

Grand Street Settlement House — unrestricted ($63,200) see Rohatyn Foundation, Felix and Elizabeth

Grayson-Jockey Club Research Foundation — pledge first installment ($26,000) see Duchossois Industries Inc.

Grayson Jockey Club Research Foundation ($25,000) see Brady Foundation

Greater Buffalo Development Foundation ($25,000) see Rich Products Corporation

Greater New York Hospital Foundation — over five years to support the implementation of Walks of Life, an employment preparation program for youth in two New York City public high schools and some of their "feeder" junior high and elementary schools ($2,685,165) see Wallace-Reader's Digest Fund, DeWitt

Greater Utica United Way ($77,000) see Fleet Financial Group, Inc.

Greater Winfield Medical Building ($5,000) see Utica National Insurance Group

Greene Fire Department ($2,000) see Raymond Corp.

Greene Lions Club ($3,000) see Raymond Corp.

Greene Lions Club Park ($8,000) see Raymond Corp.

Guggenheim Museum — for Spector ($40,000) see Norton Family Foundation, Peter

Guggenheim Museum ($22,000) see Cheatham Foundation, Owen

Guide Dog Foundation ($7,500) see Blum Foundation, Edna F.

Guild Hall Academy of Arts ($5,000) see Icahn Foundation, Carl C.

Guild Hall of East Hampton ($5,000) see Slifka Foundation, Joseph and Sylvia

Gurwin Jewish Geriatric Center ($50,000) see Feil Foundation, Louis and Gertrude

Habitat for Humanity of Fulton County ($1,000) see City National Bank and Trust Co.

Hadassah ($630,010) see Goodstein Family Foundation, Louis and Harold

Hadassah ($12,800) see Price Foundation, Louis and Harold

Hadassah Hospice ($10,000) see Fink Foundation

Hamilton College — scholarship endowment ($100,000) see Emerson Foundation, Inc., Fred L.

Hamilton College ($15,500) see Kennedy Foundation, Ethel

Hamilton Madison House ($17,750) see Blum Foundation, Edna F.

Hammondsport Beautification Committee ($25,774) see Taylor Foundation, Fred and Harriett

Hammondsport Board of Education ($32,180) see Taylor Foundation, Fred and Harriett

Hammondsport Joint Fund Drive ($1,500) see Mercury Aircraft

Hammondsport Methodist Church ($1,500) see Mercury Aircraft

Hammondsport Presbyterian Church ($1,500) see Mercury Aircraft

Hammondsport Volunteer Ambulance ($10,000) see Taylor Foundation, Fred and Harriett

Hand House — for meetings and conferences of community organizations ($8,453) see Crary Foundation, Bruce L.

Hanford Hills Museum — insurance, accounting salaries ($34,027) see O'Connor Foundation, A. Lindsay and Olive B.

Hanford Hills Museum — sending member to a conference in Denver, CO ($24,700) see O'Connor Foundation, A. Lindsay and Olive B.

Harry Frank Guggenheim Foundation Publication Program — To Publish "Understanding Violence," a Review of Research Related to Violence, Aggression, and Dominance" ($103,514) see Guggenheim Foundation, Harry Frank

Hartwick College ($20,000) see Hulbert Foundation, Nila B.

Hartwick College ($50,000) see Morris Foundation, William T.

Hartwick College ($15,000) see Warren and Beatrice W. Blanding Foundation, Riley J. and Lillian N.

Hastings Center ($41,000) see Pettus Crowe Foundation

Health Research — The New York State Community Health Management Information System Program" ($320,433) see Hartford Foundation, John A.

Hebrew Free Loan Society ($250,000) see Kaufmann Foundation, Henry

Hebrew Free Loan Society ($25,000) see Zlinkoff Fund for Medical Research and Education, Sergei S.

Hebrew Home — charitable contribution ($5,000) see Klosk Fund, Louis and Rose

Hebrew Home — charitable contribution ($5,000) see Klosk Fund, Louis and Rose

Helen Hayes Hospital — continuation of doctoral program and general support ($36,000) see Scott Foundation, Walter

Henry Street Settlement — in support of Phase II of the settlement's capital campaign ($25,000) see Guttman Foundation, Stella and Charles

Henry Street Settlement ($25,000) see Kornfeld Foundation, Emily Davie and Joseph S.

Henry Street Settlement ($100,000) see Pforzheimer Foundation, Carl and Lily

Henry Street Settlement ($100,000) see Levitt Foundation

Hetrick-Martin Institute ($40,000) see Burden Foundation, Florence V.

Hetrick-Martin Institute — one-time grant to support the training of child welfare administrators and social workers in mainstream agencies on working with lesbian, gay, and bisexual youth and tolerance training for other youth served by these agencies ($50,000) see Ittleson Foundation

Highland Hospital Foundation — expand, renovate, and family medicine facility

($5,000) see Curtice-Burns Foods, Inc.

Hilbert College — for equipment ($20,000) see Palisano Foundation, Vincent and Harriet

Hillside Children's Center — school building campaign ($25,000) see Davenport-Hatch Foundation

Hispanic AIDS Forum ($46,360) see New York Life Insurance Co.

Historic Hudson Valley ($25,000) see Rockefeller Fund, David

Hobart and William Smith Colleges ($100,000) see Olin Foundation, Spencer T. and Ann W.

Hobart and William Smith Colleges — teaching and learning endowment ($200,000) see Emerson Foundation, Inc., Fred L.

Homespace Corporation — equipment and furnishings ($10,000) see Cornell Trust, Peter C.

HOPE Program ($120,000) see Clark Foundation

Hopevale — toward improvements to the facility ($250,000) see Wendt Foundation, Margaret L.

Horace Mann-Barnard School ($10,000) see Charina Foundation

Hospice — general operations ($10,000) see Lenna Foundation, Reginald A. and Elizabeth S.

Hospice Buffalo — final payment on grant ($25,000) see Cornell Trust, Peter C.

Hospice Buffalo ($100,000) see Julia R. and Estelle L. Foundation

Hospice Buffalo — construction of a centralized hospice health care campus ($200,000) see Wendt Foundation, Margaret L.

Hospice Foundation ($10,000) see Joy Family Foundation

Hospice Foundation — for extended grant ($12,500) see Western New York Foundation

Hospice of Martin ($25,000) see Hagedorn Fund

Hospital Audiences — computer printer in braille ($5,000) see Vogler Foundation, Laura B.

Hospital for Joint Diseases Orthopaedic Institute ($250,000) see Reicher Foundation, Anne and Harry J.

Hospital for Special Surgery — research activities ($37,500) see Morris Foundation, Margaret T.

Hospital for Special Surgery ($37,500) see Morris Foundation, Margaret T.

Hospital for Special Surgery ($3,500) see Mosbacher, Jr. Foundation, Emil

Hospital for Special Surgery ($10,000) see Charina Foundation

Hospital for Special Surgery ($25,000) see Frese Foundation, Arnold D.

Hospital for Special Surgery ($600,000) see Goldsmith Foundation, Horace W.

Hospital for Special Surgery — spine fellowship ($50,000) see Hugoton Foundation

Hospital for Special Surgery — children's summer camp

program for handicapped youngsters ($6,000) see Scott Foundation, Walter

Houghton College — scholarship for missionary children ($20,000) see Gallagher Family Foundation, Lewis P.

Housing Conservation ($21,330) see Hebrew Technical Institute

Housing and Services — expand, enhance and evaluate their pioneering "Continuum of Care" AIDS housing program that offers three models of residential and health care which together provide a range of supportive housing opportunities ($35,000) see Ittleson Foundation

Hudson Riverkeeper Fund — toward their Regulatory Reform Program that works for better enforcement of existing water quality laws and for policy analysis and advocacy to preserve water quality in the New York City reservoir system ($100,000) see Kaplan Fund, J. M.

Hudson Riverkeeper Fund — for public education and media program to bring to public attention the seriousness of the threat to the public health that a polluted New York City water supply would be ($100,000) see Kaplan Fund, J. M.

Hudson Valley Philharmonic — general support ($25,000) see Homeland Foundation

Hudson Valley Philharmonic Society — for 1993 Pops series ($50,000) see McCann Foundation

Human Rights Watch — in support of operations over three years ($1,500,000) see MacArthur Foundation, John D. and Catherine T.

Human Rights Watch ($65,000) see Gilman Foundation, Howard

Human Rights Watch ($11,000) see Hauser Foundation

Human Rights Watch see Wiley & Sons, Inc., John

Hunter College — scholarships ($27,000) see Newcombe Foundation, Charlotte W.

Hunter College ($21,300) see Lang Foundation, Eugene M.

Huntington Memorial Library ($19,000) see Hulbert Foundation, Nila B.

Huntington Memorial Library ($10,000) see Warren and Beatrice W. Blanding Foundation, Riley J. and Lillian N.

Hurlbut Memorial Community Church ($15,000) see Carnahan-Jackson Foundation

Hurricane Allen St. Lucia Rebuilding Fund ($25,000) see Pitt-Des Moines Inc.

Hyde Collection ($24,800) see Hill Foundation, Sandy

Hyde Collection ($24,800) see Hill Foundation, Sandy

I Have A Dream Foundation — scholarship fund ($32,500) see Rohatyn Foundation, Felix and Elizabeth

ICD Ezra K. Zilkha Institute for Communication

Disorders ($25,000) see Nias Foundation, Henry

ICD International Center for the Disabled ($30,000) see Achelis Foundation

ICD-International Center for the Disabled ($50,000) see Bodman Foundation

ICD-International Center for the Disabled — toward the 75th Anniversary fundraising campaign, final payment of a four-year, $1 million challenge grant ($200,000) see JM Foundation

ICD-International Center for the Disabled — for a comprehensive organizational review ($37,500) see JM Foundation

Idyllic Foundation — unrestricted ($5,000) see Chapman Charitable Corporation, Howard and Bess

Immaculate Conception Church ($25,000) see Hagedorn Fund

Independent College Fund ($15,000) see Allyn Foundation

Independent College Fund — matching gift for minority scholarships ($50,000) see Snow Memorial Trust, John Ben

Independent College Fund of New York ($75,000) see Taylor Foundation, Fred and Harriett

Independent Production Fund ($50,000) see Blum-Kovler Foundation

Inner-City Scholarship Fund ($25,000) see Achelis Foundation

Inner-City Scholarship Fund ($60,000) see Bodman Foundation

Inner City Scholarship Fund — general support ($25,000) see Homeland Foundation

Inner-City Scholarship Fund ($10,000) see Smeal Foundation, Mary Jean and Frank P.

Inner-City Schools of Archdiocese of New York ($30,000) see PaineWebber

Institute for Development Anthropology — "The Role of Bolivia's Peasant Union Movement in Reducing Violence Associated with the War on Drugs" ($34,756) see Guggenheim Foundation, Harry Frank

Institute for East-West Studies — two-year supplement, for programs in economics, security, and political culture in Eastern Europe ($1,200,000) see Ford Foundation

Institute for East-West Studies ($40,000) see Salomon Foundation, Richard and Edna

Institute of Ecosystem Studies ($50,000) see Millbrook Tribute Garden

Interfaith Neighbors ($25,000) see Bowne Foundation, Robert

International Association for Jewish Vocational Services ($11,240) see Hebrew Technical Institute

International Association of Psycho-Social Rehabilitation Services/New York Association of Psychiatric Rehabilitation Services — grant for startup costs of an Albany office of NYAPRS, which would protect and expand the clubhouses for the recovering mentally ill in New York ($80,000) see van Ameringen Foundation

International Center for the Disabled ($50,000) see Schering-Plough Corp.

International Center for the Disabled ($25,000) see Freeman Charitable Trust, Samuel

International Center in New York ($10,000) see Richardson Charitable Trust, Anne S.

International Center of Photography ($71,250) see Continental Corp.

International Center of Photography ($11,150) see Hillman Family Foundation, Alex

International Center of Photography ($5,000) see Memton Fund

International Center of Photography ($17,500) see Zenkel Foundation

International Center of Syracuse ($6,500) see Mather Fund, Richard

International Peace Academy ($50,000) see Hauser Foundation

International Rescue Committee — for general operating support ($30,000) see Davis Foundation, Edwin W. and Catherine M.

International Rescue Committee ($30,000) see Davis Foundation, Edwin W. and Catherine M.

International Rescue Committee — social and refugee assistance in Pakistan and Thailand ($25,000) see International Foundation

International Rescue Committee ($25,000) see Allen Brothers Foundation

International Rescue Committee ($5,000) see Icahn Foundation, Carl C.

International Rescue Committee ($15,000) see Normandie Foundation

Iona College — endowment funding ($50,000) see Badgeley Residuary Charitable Trust, Rose M.

Ira Davenport Memorial Hospital ($64,360) see Taylor Foundation, Fred and Harriett

Iroquois Indian Museum ($10,000) see Snow Foundation, John Ben

Isabel Oneil Foundation for the Art of the Painted Finish ($15,000) see Evans Foundation, T. M.

Israel Endowment Fund ($7,000) see Meyer Fund, Milton and Sophie

Israel Endowment Fund ($175,000) see Meyerhoff Fund, Joseph

Israel Heritage ($15,000) see Mailman Foundation

Israel Tennis Centers Association ($900) see Taube Family Foundation

Israel Tennis Centers Association ($1,000) see Altschul Foundation

Ithaca College Endowment ($10,000) see Howell Foundation of Florida

James Prendergast Library — general operations ($4,800) see Lenna Foundation, Reginald A. and Elizabeth S.

James Prendergast Library Association ($12,035) see Carnahan-Jackson Foundation

James Prendergast Library Association ($49,422) see Hultquist Foundation

Jamestown Audubon Society ($45,000) see Carnahan-Jackson Foundation

Jamestown Community College — toward capital construction and renovations ($500,000) see Gebbie Foundation

Jamestown Community College — toward construction and renovations over three years ($250,000) see Gebbie Foundation

Jamestown Community College — matching grant for scholarships over five years ($200,000) see Gebbie Foundation

Jamestown Community College — to continue programs at Jamestown Community Schools over three years ($115,000) see Gebbie Foundation

Jamestown Community College ($300,000) see Hultquist Foundation

Jamestown Community College ($2,210) see Betts Industries

Jamestown Concert Association ($9,000) see Hultquist Foundation

Japan Society — final payment of a $250,000 pledge ($125,000) see Merrill Lynch & Co., Inc.

Jazz Foundation of America ($65,000) see Levitt Foundation

Jericho Project ($5,000) see Goldie-Anna Charitable Trust

Jericho Project ($15,000) see Unilever United States, Inc.

Jerusalem Foundation ($300,000) see Goldsmith Foundation, Horace W.

Jerusalem Foundation — Paley Art Center ($50,000) see Paley Foundation, William S.

Jerusalem Foundation ($118,699) see Hassenfeld Foundation

Jewish Association for Services for the Aged ($25,000) see Nias Foundation, Henry

Jewish Board of Family and Children's Services ($250,000) see Kaufmann Foundation, Henry

Jewish Board of Family and Children's Services ($10,000) see Marx Foundation, Virginia and Leonard

Jewish Braille Institute of America — general purposes ($9,000) see Parshelsky Foundation, Moses L.

Jewish Campus Life Fund ($35,000) see Sulzberger Foundation

Jewish Child Care Association ($50,000) see Kaufmann Foundation, Henry

Jewish Child Care Association ($10,000) see Weil, Gotshal and Manges Foundation

Jewish Child Care Association of New York ($64,000) see Heckscher Foundation for Children

Jewish Community Center ($75,000) see Kaufmann Foundation, Henry

Jewish Community Center of Bensonhurst ($33,000) see Nias Foundation, Henry

Jewish Community Centers Association ($100,000) see Kaufmann Foundation, Henry

Jewish Guild for the Blind ($5,000) see Miller Fund, Kathryn and Gilbert

Jewish Home and Hospital for the Aged ($64,195) see Greenwall Foundation

Jewish Home and Hospital for the Aged ($30,000) see Nias Foundation, Henry

Jewish Labor Committee ($80,000) see Atran Foundation

Jewish Museum ($115,000) see Amado Foundation, Maurice

Jewish Museum ($16,667) see Holzer Memorial Foundation, Richard H.

Jewish Museum ($30,700) see Lemberg Foundation

Jewish Museum ($20,000) see Solow Foundation

Jewish Theological Seminary ($25,000) see Holzer Memorial Foundation, Richard H.

Jewish Theological Seminary ($7,500) see Fink Foundation

Jewish Theological Seminary of America ($5,000) see Lasdon Foundation, William and Mildred

Jewish Theological Seminary of America ($140,000) see Winston Foundation, Norman and Rosita

Joffrey Ballet — general support ($66,200) see Duchossois Industries Inc.

Juilliard School ($75,000) see Seaver Institute

Juilliard School ($50,000) see South Branch Foundation

Juilliard School ($140,000) see Heckscher Foundation for Children

Juilliard School ($12,000) see Arnhold Foundation

Junior Achievement of Central New York ($50,000) see Gifford Charitable Corporation, Rosamond

Junior Achievement of New York ($20,000) see Dun & Bradstreet Corp.

Junior Achievement of New York — educational ($36,000) see New York Stock Exchange, Inc.

Juvenile Diabetes see New York Mercantile Exchange

Juvenile Diabetes Foundation ($30,000) see Norton Memorial Corporation, Geraldi

Juvenile Diabetes Foundation ($10,000) see Fischbach Foundation

Juvenile Diabetes Foundation International ($850,000) see Johnson Foundation, Willard T. C.

Juvenile Diabetes Foundation International — aid for diabetes research ($7,500) see Vernon Fund, Miles Hodsdon

Juvenile Diabetes Foundation International ($50,000) see Ames Charitable Trust, Harriett

J.W. Juckett Park ($16,230) see Hill Foundation, Sandy

J.W. Juckett Park ($16,230) see Hill Foundation, Sandy

Katonah Museum of Art see MBIA Inc.

Kenmore Mercy Foundation — reconstruction and renovation project ($100,000) see Wendt Foundation, Margaret L.

Kenmore Mercy Hospital ($25,000) see Cummings Foundation, James H.

Keren Hayesod (Jewish Agency) ($300,000) see Goldsmith Foundation, Horace W.

Keren Or ($3,000) see Weinstein Foundation, J.

Keuka College — capital campaign ($200,000) see Ball Foundation, George and Frances

Keuka College — capital building campaign ($25,000) see Davenport-Hatch Foundation

Keuka College ($60,000) see Jones Foundation, Daisy Marquis

Keuka College — community associates campaign ($6,000) see Mercury Aircraft

Keuka College — centennial campaign ($5,000) see Mercury Aircraft

Keuka College ($10,000) see Snow Foundation, John Ben

Keuka Swim Team ($1,500) see Seneca Foods Corp.

Kidney Foundation of Upstate New York — transportation for dialysis patients ($2,000) see Schmitt Foundation, Kilian J. and Caroline F.

Kingsbridge Heights Community Center — for capital campaign ($50,000) see Dodge Foundation, Cleveland H.

Kingsbrook Jewish Medical Center — medical equipment ($10,000) see Parshelsky Foundation, Moses L.

Kipps Bay Boys and Girls Club ($10,000) see Evans Foundation, T. M.

Kips Bay Boys and Girls Club — outreach projects ($25,000) see Badgeley Residuary Charitable Trust, Rose M.

Kirby Potter Fund ($40,000) see Dow Jones & Company, Inc.

Kivel Geriatric Center ($1,106,615) see Goldsmith Foundation, Horace W.

Kleinhans Music Hall — renovation and restoration of hall ($100,000) see Wendt Foundation, Margaret L.

Kosciuszko Foundation — in support of Polish scholarship/grants ($120,000) see Jurzykowski Foundation, Alfred

Lacoure School of the Arts ($10,000) see Piankova Foundation, Tatiana

Ladies Christian Union ($3,000) see Hatch Charitable Trust, Margaret Milliken

Lakeside-Beikrich ($38,700) see Jones Foundation, Daisy Marquis

Lambda Legal Defense ($3,000) see Levitt Foundation

Lamont-Doherty Geological Observatory ($500,000) see Vetlesen Foundation, G. Unger

Language Development Program ($15,000) see Joy Family Foundation

Laura Rosenberg Foundation — charitable contribution ($5,000) see Klosk Fund, Louis and Rose

Lawyers Alliance for New York ($15,000) see Weil, Gotshal and Manges Foundation

Lawyers Committee for Human Rights ($25,000) see Valentine Foundation, Lawson

Lawyers Committee on Nuclear Policy ($15,000) see Rubin Foundation, Samuel

LEAD Program in Business ($5,500) see Crane Co.

Lead Program in Business — general support ($35,000) see MCI Communications Corp.

Learning Foundation see MBIA Inc.

Learning Thru Art ($61,500) see Gilman Foundation, Howard

Legal Aid Society ($135,000) see Kaye, Scholer, Fierman, Hays & Handler

Legal Aid Society ($5,000) see Miller Fund, Kathryn and Gilbert

Legal Aid Society ($85,000) see Scherman Foundation

Legal Aid Society ($225,000) see Weil, Gotshal and Manges Foundation

Lehman College Youth Practitioner's Institute ($20,000) see Dreyfus Foundation, Jean and Louis

LeMoyne College — annual fund ($125,000) see Emerson Foundation, Inc., Fred L.

Lenox Hill Hospital ($15,000) see Griffis Foundation

Lenox Hill Hospital ($120,500) see Hillman Family Foundation, Alex

Lenox Hill Hospital — ambulatory surgical center ($200,000) see Hugoton Foundation

Lenox Hill Hospital ($13,300) see Price Foundation, Louis and Harold

Lenox Hill Hospital ($57,500) see Ames Charitable Trust, Harriett

Lenox Hill Neighborhood Association ($30,000) see Landegger Charitable Foundation

Lenox Hill Neighborhood Association — toward "Transitions," a program to identify and assist chronic homeless substance abusers living in the New York City subway system ($30,000) see Astor Foundation, Vincent

Lenox Hill Neighborhood Association — toward the housing placement project ($25,000) see Dillon Dunwalke Trust, Clarence and Anne

Leukemia Society ($15,000) see CS First Boston Corporation

Leukemia Society of America ($25,000) see Allen Brothers Foundation

Leukemia Society of America ($15,000) see Altschul Foundation

Lexington School for the Deaf Foundation — testmobile service for the elderly and hard of hearing free of

charge ($10,000) see Scott Foundation, Walter

LHNA/Lenox Hill Neighborhood Association — unrestricted ($30,000) see Rohatyn Foundation, Felix and Elizabeth

Life Force Women Fighting AIDS — training volunteers to lead prevention education groups at clinics and hospitals, in street outreach, home progress, prisons, and schools ($123,645) see van Ameringen Foundation

Lighthouse for Blind ($100,000) see Steinbach Fund, Ruth and Milton

Lincoln Center Beaumont Theater ($50,000) see New York Times Company

Lincoln Center Consolidated Fund ($100,000) see New York Times Company

Lincoln Center Institute ($60,000) see Pforzheimer Foundation, Carl and Lily

Lincoln Center Institute — support of outreach publications ($25,000) see Snow Memorial Trust, John Ben

Lincoln Center New Building Campaign — screening room for the film society in memory of Nancy Ittleson ($50,000) see Ittleson Foundation

Lincoln Center for Performing Arts ($12,500) see Holzer Memorial Foundation, Richard H.

Lincoln Center for the Performing Arts ($210,000) see Bristol-Myers Squibb Company

Lincoln Center for the Performing Arts — corporate fund program ($100,000) see Citibank

Lincoln Center for the Performing Arts ($15,000) see Coltec Industries, Inc.

Lincoln Center for the Performing Arts ($350,000) see Continental Corp.

Lincoln Center for Performing Arts — Consolidated Corporate Fund ($50,000) see Continental Corp.

Lincoln Center for Performing Arts ($10,000) see Culver Foundation, Constans

Lincoln Center for the Performing Arts ($66,667) see Dana Charitable Trust, Eleanor Naylor

Lincoln Center for the Performing Arts ($50,000) see Gilman Foundation, Howard

Lincoln Center for the Performing Arts ($51,270) see Lemberg Foundation

Lincoln Center for the Performing Arts — new building campaign ($50,000) see McGraw-Hill, Inc.

Lincoln Center for the Performing Arts ($25,000) see McGraw-Hill, Inc.

Lincoln Center for the Performing Arts — for first payment of $200,000 grant for the Consolidated Corporate Fund ($100,000) see Morgan & Company, J.P.

Lincoln Center for the Performing Arts — charitable ($10,000) see New York Stock Exchange, Inc.

Lincoln Center for the Performing Arts — outdoor series ($25,000) see Rose Foundation, Billy

Lincoln Center for the Performing Arts ($10,000) see Thompson Co., J. Walter

Lincoln Center Theater ($14,500) see Cheatham Foundation, Owen

Lincoln Center Theater ($17,000) see Miller Fund, Kathryn and Gilbert

Lincoln Center Theater — the Beaumont ($25,000) see Rose Foundation, Billy

Lincoln Center Theater ($225,000) see Shubert Foundation

Lions Club Sightfirst Campaign ($500) see City National Bank and Trust Co.

Literacy Volunteers ($10,000) see Snow Foundation, John Ben

Literacy Volunteers of America — for general support ($5,000) see Anderson Foundation

Literacy Volunteers of America — for support for literacy program ($5,000) see Lake Placid Education Foundation

Literacy Volunteers of New York City — unrestricted ($10,000) see Rohatyn Foundation, Felix and Elizabeth

Literacy Volunteers of New York City see Wiley & Sons, Inc., John

Local Initiatives Support Corporation — for support of Campaign for Communities, a national effort to expand community development corporation programs ($1,000,000) see Knight Foundation, John S. and James L.

Local Initiatives Support Corporation — Detroit Community Development Funders' Collaborative project ($250,000) see Skillman Foundation

Local Initiatives Support Corporation — for grant to determine the feasibility of developing low-income housing initiatives in London, England ($100,000) see Saint Paul Companies, Inc.

Local Initiatives Support Corporation ($125,000) see Bankers Trust Company

Local Initiatives Support Corporation — for second payment of $200,000 grant for their New York City programs and second payment of $100,000 grant for the Campaign for Communities ($75,000) see Morgan & Company, J.P.

Local Initiatives Support Corporation ($75,000) see Uris Brothers Foundation

Long Island Alzheimers Society — general support ($5,000) see ASDA Foundation

Long Island Alzheimers Society — general support ($5,000) see ASDA Foundation

Long Island University ($150,000) see Clark Foundation

Long Island University School of Pharmacy ($25,000) see Lasdon Foundation

Louis Wise Services ($57,200) see Uris Brothers Foundation

Lucy Moses School for Music and Dance ($25,000) see Moses Fund, Henry and Lucy

Lutheran Film Association ($190,220) see Burchfield Foundation, Charles E.

Lutheran High School Association ($170,800) see Burchfield Foundation, Charles E.

Lutheran Social Services ($5,741) see Geneseo Foundation

Lutheran Social Services ($34,459) see Hultquist Foundation

Lyall Memorial federated Church ($20,000) see Millbrook Tribute Garden

Lynchurst National Trust Preservation — donation ($25,000) see Schwartz Fund for Education and Health Research, Arnold and Marie

MacDowell Colony ($60,000) see Dreyfus Foundation, Jean and Louis

Manhattan Bowery Corporation — Fresh Start ($50,000) see Chase Manhattan Bank, N.A.

Manhattan College ($10,000) see Crane Co.

Manhattan College — environmental science program ($32,000) see du Pont de Nemours & Co., E. I.

Manhattan College — first installment of a $250,000 two-for-one challenge grant to establish a $750,000 nonathletic scholarship endowment fund for students from the city of New York who show high academic promise and whose families have demonstrated an acute financial need ($250,000) see Calder Foundation, Louis

Manhattan Country School ($100,000) see Overbrook Foundation

Manhattan Eye and Ear ($10,000) see Alcon Laboratories, Inc.

Manhattan Eye, Ear, and Throat Hospital ($20,000) see Thorne Foundation

Manhattan Institute for Policy Research ($15,000) see Oaklawn Foundation

Manhattan Theater Club ($150,000) see Shubert Foundation

Manhattanville College — endowment fund ($71,000) see Simon Foundation, William E. and Carol G.

Manna Food Bank ($25,000) see Cummings Foundation, James H.

Mannes College ($19,000) see Osceola Foundation

Manpower Demonstration Research Corporation (MDRC) — two-year supplement, for general support of the MDRC's program development and dissemination activities ($1,400,000) see Ford Foundation

Marine Environmental Science Consortium ($153,000) see Bedsole Foundation, J. L.

Marine Toys for Tots Foundation — community outreach program ($100,000) see MCI Communications Corp.

Marion A. Buckley School of Nursing ($20,000) see Zlinkoff Fund for Medical Research and Education, Sergei S.

Marist College — 1993 scholarships for local students ($50,000) see McCann Foundation

Marist College — for computer programs for nonprofit organizations ($31,808) see McCann Foundation

Markle Foundation-Sponsored Project — election project 1992 ($164,165) see Markle Foundation, John and Mary R.

Markle Foundation-Sponsored Project — Markle commission follow-up ($138,931) see Markle Foundation, John and Mary R.

Markle Foundation-Sponsored Project — political advertising study ($131,966) see Markle Foundation, John and Mary R.

Martha Graham Dance Center ($11,000) see Cheatham Foundation, Owen

Marymount College ($6,000) see Kennedy Foundation, Ethel

Marymount College Tarrytown ($5,000) see Rockefeller Fund, David

Marymount Manhattan College ($88,700) see Brooks Foundation, Gladys

Marymount Manhattan College ($100,000) see Freeman Charitable Trust, Samuel

Masters School ($25,000) see Ingalls Foundation, Louise H. and David S.

Mayfield Parent-Teachers Association ($500) see City National Bank and Trust Co.

Meals on Wheels ($6,000) see R. F. Foundation

Medecins Sans Frontieres US — for health care project in Romania ($50,000) see Medtronic, Inc.

Medical Development for Israel — medical ($6,000) see Kaplun Foundation, Morris J. and Betty

Medical Development for Israel ($20,000) see Price Foundation, Louis and Harold

Memorial Sloan-Kettering Cancer Center ($25,000) see Griffith Foundation, W. C.

Memorial Sloan Kettering Cancer Center — Dream Team ($25,000) see Middendorf Foundation

Memorial Sloan-Kettering Cancer Center — for medical research and care ($25,000) see AMETEK, Inc.

Memorial Sloan-Kettering Cancer Center ($50,000) see Bobst Foundation, Elmer and Mamdouha

Memorial Sloan-Kettering Cancer Center ($45,000) see Bodman Foundation

Memorial Sloan-Kettering Cancer Center ($100,000) see Forbes Inc.

Memorial Sloan-Kettering Cancer Center ($110,000) see Frese Foundation, Arnold D.

Memorial Sloan-Kettering Cancer Center ($100,000) see Gordon/Rousmaniere/Roberts Fund

Memorial Sloan-Kettering Cancer Center — to establish a collaborative outpatient rehabilitation

The Big Book of Library Grant Money

United Cerebral Palsy of New York City ($20,000) see Rudin Foundation

United Hospital Fund ($25,000) see Hagedorn Fund

United Hospital Medical Center ($10,000) see Fischbach Foundation

United Jewish Appeal ($75,000) see Borman's Inc.

United Jewish Appeal — for general welfare ($100,000) see AMETEK, Inc.

United Jewish Appeal ($100,000) see Benenson Foundation, Frances and Benjamin

United Jewish Appeal ($30,000) see Feil Foundation, Louis and Gertrude

United Jewish Appeal ($50,000) see Forbes Inc.

United Jewish Appeal — charitable contribution ($6,000) see Klosk Fund, Louis and Rose

United Jewish Appeal — charitable contribution ($6,000) see Klosk Fund, Louis and Rose

United Jewish Appeal — charitable contribution ($6,000) see Klosk Fund, Louis and Rose

United Jewish Appeal ($100,000) see Lauder Foundation

United Jewish Appeal ($10,000) see Liberman Foundation, Bertha and Isaac

United Jewish Appeal ($800,000) see Seagram & Sons, Inc., Joseph E.

United Jewish Appeal ($5,000,000) see Annenberg Foundation

United Jewish Appeal Federation ($25,000) see Lazarus Charitable Trust, Helen and Charles

United Jewish Appeal Federation ($20,000) see Fife Foundation, Elias and Bertha

United Jewish Appeal Federation ($15,000) see Fife Foundation, Elias and Bertha

United Jewish Appeal Federation ($15,000) see Fife Foundation, Elias and Bertha

United Jewish Appeal Federation ($10,000) see Fischbach Foundation

United Jewish Appeal Federation ($10,000) see Lasdon Foundation

United Jewish Appeal Federation ($75,000) see Lemberg Foundation

United Jewish Appeal Federation ($150,000) see Liz Claiborne, Inc.

United Jewish Appeal Federation ($625,000) see Loews Corporation

United Jewish Appeal Federation ($120,000) see Mailman Foundation

United Jewish Appeal Federation ($100,000) see Marx Foundation, Virginia and Leonard

United Jewish Appeal Federation ($10,000) see Miller Fund, Kathryn and Gilbert

United Jewish Appeal Federation ($50,000) see Mnuchin Foundation

United Jewish Appeal Federation ($25,000) see Mnuchin Foundation

United Jewish Appeal Federation ($10,000) see Rosen Foundation, Joseph

United Jewish Appeal Federation ($100,000) see Slifka Foundation, Joseph and Sylvia

United Jewish Appeal Federation — capital campaign ($100,000) see Solow Foundation

United Jewish Appeal Federation ($40,000) see Zenkel Foundation

United Jewish Appeal Federation ($5,000) see Levitt Foundation

United Jewish Appeal Federation — operating funds ($10,000) see Cranston Print Works Company

United Jewish Appeal Federation ($70,000) see Hassenfeld Foundation

United Jewish Appeal Federation of Greater Washington ($100,000) see Giant Food Inc.

United Jewish Appeal Federation of Greater Washington ($100,000) see Giant Food Inc.

United Jewish Appeal Federation of Jewish Philanthropies ($25,000) see Badgeley Residuary Charitable Trust, Rose M.

United Jewish Appeal Federation of Jewish Philanthropies ($630,010) see Goodstein Family Foundation, David

United Jewish Appeal Federation of Jewish Philanthropies — to support the research and development phase of the NORC supportive services program ($25,000) see Guttman Foundation, Stella and Charles

United Jewish Appeal Federation of Jewish Philanthropies ($500,000) see Moses Fund, Henry and Lucy

United Jewish Appeal Federation of Jewish Philanthropies ($100,000) see Moses Fund, Henry and Lucy

United Jewish Appeal Federation of Jewish Philanthropies ($50,000) see Neuberger Foundation, Roy R. and Marie S.

United Jewish Appeal Federation of Jewish Philanthropies ($15,000) see Neuberger Foundation, Roy R. and Marie S.

United Jewish Appeal Federation of Jewish Philanthropies ($100,000) see Rudin Foundation

United Jewish Appeal Federation of Jewish Philanthropies ($130,000) see Scherman Foundation

United Jewish Appeal Federation of Jewish Philanthropies ($550,000) see Weil, Gotshal and Manges Foundation

United Jewish Appeal Federation of Jewish Philanthropies of New York — in support of Operation Exodus ($100,000) see Guttman Foundation, Stella and Charles

United Jewish Appeal Federation of Jewish Philanthropies of New York ($85,000) see Lowenstein Foundation, Leon

United Jewish Appeal Federation of Jewish Philanthropies of New York ($10,000) see Parshelsky Foundation, Moses L.

United Jewish Appeal Federation of Jewish Philanthropies of New York — general support ($242,000) see Rubinstein Foundation, Helena

United Jewish Appeal Federation of New York ($400,000) see Rudin Foundation

United Jewish Appeal Federation of Rockland County ($45,000) see Chazen Foundation

United Jewish Appeal Foundation ($22,700) see Feil Foundation, Louis and Gertrude

United Jewish Appeal, Israel Emergency Fund ($75,000) see Atran Foundation

United Jewish Welfare Fund ($2,000) see Seneca Foods Corp.

United Methodist Church — capital improvements ($30,722) see Robinson-Broadhurst Foundation

United Ministry — religious ($5,875) see Cayuga Foundation

United Nations International Children Educational Foundation —to support a full range of child survival and developmental programs ($25,000) see Hanson Industries North America

United Nations International Children Educational Foundation — to support a full range of child survival and developmental programs ($25,000) see Hanson Industries North America

United Negro College Fund see Alabama Power Co.

United Negro College Fund — event ($25,000) see MCA Inc.

United Negro College Fund — operating expenses ($100,000) see Georgia Power Co.

United Negro College Fund ($3,000) see R. F. Foundation

United Negro College Fund — general support ($30,000) see Cummins Engine Co.

United Negro College Fund —for annual payment on special project grant ($307,500) see General Motors Corp.

United Negro College Fund — to support Campaign 2000, a campaign to raise $250 million for general endowments for the 41 UNCF member institutions ($2,000,000) see Mott Foundation, Charles Stewart

United Negro College Fund — capital campaign for UNCF member institutions ($250,000) see General Mills, Inc.

United Negro College Fund ($125,000) see Merck & Co.

United Negro College Fund ($75,000) see Avon Products, Inc.

United Negro College Fund ($50,000) see Bodman Foundation

United Negro College Fund — Campaign 2000: An Investment in America's future ($250,000) see Citibank

United Negro College Fund —to help African Americans overcome the cultural and financial obstacles to a higher education ($25,000) see Hanson Industries North America

United Negro College Fund — to help African Americans overcome the cultural and financial obstacles to a higher education ($25,000) see Hanson Industries North America

United Negro College Fund ($50,000) see International Paper Co.

United Negro College Fund — for an undergraduate fellowship program to increase the number of minority students who enroll in Ph.D. programs in the arts and sciences ($2,010,000) see Mellon Foundation, Andrew W.

United Negro College Fund — for a program to increase the number of minority scholars holding doctorates in the arts and sciences ($1,200,000) see Mellon Foundation, Andrew W.

United Negro College Fund — Campaign 2000, first payment of a $250,000 pledge ($100,000) see Merrill Lynch & Co., Inc.

United Negro College Fund ($100,000) see PaineWebber

United Negro College Fund ($150,000) see Pfizer, Inc.

United Negro College Fund ($20,000) see Prudential Securities, Inc.

United Negro College Fund — first payment of five-year grant totaling $5 million in support of Campaign 2000 ($1,000,000) see Starr Foundation

United Negro College Fund ($200,000) see Texaco Inc.

United Negro College Fund ($4,000) see Moore & Sons, B.C.

United Negro College Fund ($202,500) see Borden, Inc.

United Negro College Fund ($5,000,000) see Annenberg Foundation

United Negro College Fund — capital campaign/endowment fund ($75,000) see Union Pacific Corp.

United Negro College Fund —organizational support grant ($1,200,000) see Exxon Corporation

United Negro College Fund - educational ($200,000) see Hobby Foundation

United Negro College Fund Ladders of Hope — general support ($100,000) see Nestle USA Inc.

United Negro College Fund, Morris Brown College — operating expenses ($100,000) see Georgia Power Co.

United Neighborhood Centers ($250,000) see Gleason Foundation

United Neighbors of East Midtown — providing

weekend meals and shopping for frail and homebound elderly ($3,500) see Vogler Foundation, Laura B.

United Way ($3,000) see Mosbacher, Jr. Foundation, Emil

United Way ($12,000) see Taubman Foundation, A. Alfred

United Way — for general support ($12,500) see Anderson Foundation

United Way ($30,000) see Carnahan-Jackson Foundation

United Way — Red Cross campaign ($45,000) see Davenport-Hatch Foundation

United Way ($178,000) see Gleason Foundation

United Way ($14,500) see Hultquist Foundation

United Way ($140,000) see Weil, Gotshal and Manges Foundation

United Way Broome County ($9,500) see Chesapeake Corp.

United Way of Buffalo — operating funds ($33,000) see Cornell Trust, Peter C.

United Way of Buffalo and Erie County ($28,000) see Cummings Foundation, James H.

United Way of Buffalo and Erie County ($105,000) see Julia R. and Estelle L. Foundation

United Way of Buffalo and Erie County ($9,000) see Rich Products Corporation

United Way of Buffalo and Erie County ($26,000) see Bethlehem Steel Corp.

United Way of Cayuga County — annual support ($116,436) see Emerson Foundation, Inc., Fred L.

United Way of Cayuga County ($47,216) see Everett Charitable Trust

United Way of Cayuga County ($5,471) see Everett Charitable Trust

United Way of Central New York — 1993 program ($97,500) see Gifford Charitable Corporation, Rosamond

United Way of Central New York ($6,700) see Mather Fund, Richard

United Way of Central New York ($32,215) see Cooper Industries, Inc.

United Way of Central Steuben County ($3,500) see Mercury Aircraft

United Way of Chemung and Steuben Counties —for general program support ($235,000) see Corning Incorporated

United Way of Fulton County ($13,000) see City National Bank and Trust Co.

United Way, Greater Buffalo Chapter ($14,000) see Hartmarx Corporation

United Way of Greater Rochester ($13,000) see Hartmarx Corporation

United Way of Greater Rochester — housing and homeless programs ($108,000) see Chase Manhattan Bank, N.A.

United Way of Greater Rochester — annual fund drive ($25,000) see Curtice-Burns Foods, Inc.

United Way Greater Rochester — annual fund drive ($24,000) see Curtice-Burns Foods, Inc.

United Way of Greater Rochester ($921,250) see Eastman Kodak Company

United Way of Greater Rochester ($825,000) see Eastman Kodak Company

United Way of Greater Rochester ($825,000) see Eastman Kodak Company

United Way of Greater Rochester ($825,000) see Eastman Kodak Company

United Way of Greater Rochester ($15,000) see Unilever United States, Inc.

United Way Greater Rochester ($58,000) see Fleet Financial Group, Inc.

United Way Greater Rochester ($150,000) see Mobil Oil Corp.

United Way of Greater Utica ($63,000) see Utica National Insurance Group

United Way Long Island ($52,500) see Fleet Financial Group, Inc.

United Way of New York see CIBC Wood Gundy

United Way New York City ($33,000) see Commerce Clearing House, Incorporated

United Way of New York City ($178,750) see Clark Foundation

United Way of New York City ($100,380) see Clark Foundation

United Way of New York City ($50,000) see Thompson Co., J. Walter

United Way of New York City — operating funds ($12,000) see Cranston Print Works Company

United Way of Northeastern New York ($20,000) see Norton Co.

United Way Northeastern New York ($115,000) see Fleet Financial Group, Inc.

United Way Northeastern New York ($115,000) see Fleet Financial Group, Inc.

United Way of Southern Chautauqua County — toward the 1993 annual campaign goal ($300,000) see Gebbie Foundation

United Way of the Tarrytowns ($10,000) see Rockefeller Fund, David

United Way of Tompkins County ($6,500) see Park Foundation

United Way of Tri-State ($355,000) see AlliedSignal Inc.

United Way of Tri-State ($55,000) see Dow Jones & Company, Inc.

United Way Tri-State ($520,000) see Bristol-Myers Squibb Company

United Way of Tri-State ($1,100,000) see Chase Manhattan Bank, N.A.

United Way of Tri-State ($230,000) see Continental Corp.

United Way of Tri-State ($25,000) see CS First Boston Corporation

United Way Tri-State ($317,100) see Dun & Bradstreet Corp.

United Way Tri-State ($57,900) see Dun & Bradstreet Corp.

United Way Tri-State ($25,000) see Dun & Bradstreet Corp.

United Way Tri-State ($27,000) see Handy and Harman Foundation

United Way of Tri-State ($85,000) see McGraw-Hill, Inc.

United Way of Tri-State ($85,000) see McGraw-Hill, Inc.

United Way of Tri-State ($700,000) see Metropolitan Life Insurance Co.

United Way of Tri-State ($400,000) see New York Life Insurance Co.

United Way Tri-State — charitable ($72,850) see New York Stock Exchange, Inc.

United Way of Tri-State ($70,000) see New York Times Company

United Way Tri-State ($275,000) see Prudential Securities, Inc.

United Way of Tri-State ($35,000) see Unilever United States, Inc.

United Way of Tri-State ($70,107) see Westvaco Corporation

United Way of Ulster County ($11,000) see Klock and Lucia Klock Kingston Foundation, Jay E.

United Way of Wayne County ($29,000) see Coltec Industries, Inc.

University of Buffalo — construction of laboratory and equipment for neurosurgical endovascular research ($105,644) see Wendt Foundation, Margaret L.

University at Buffalo Foundation — final payment on grant ($80,000) see Cornell Trust, Peter C.

University at Buffalo Foundation ($150,000) see Cummings Foundation, James H.

University of Buffalo Foundation ($100,000) see Rich Products Corporation

University of Missouri ($35,000) see Greve Foundation, William and Mary

University Neighborhood Housing Program — support of the organizing program ($20,000) see Taconic Foundation

University of Rochester ($6,547) see Essick Foundation

University of Rochester — scholarship fund ($5,000) see Friendship Fund

University of Rochester — University Campaign for the 90s ($40,000) see Davenport-Hatch Foundation

University of Rochester — capital campaign ($40,000) see Davenport-Hatch Foundation

University of Rochester ($300,000) see Eastman Kodak Company

University of Rochester — endowed professorship ($160,000) see Schmitt Foundation, Kilian J. and Caroline F.

University of Rochester — symposium ($10,000) see Schmitt Foundation, Kilian J. and Caroline F.

University Settlement Directors ($5,000) see Levitt Foundation

University Settlement Society of New York ($18,000) see Bowne Foundation, Robert

Urban Foundation ($221,000) see Deere & Co.

Urban League of Albany ($21,000) see Howard and Bush Foundation

Utica Head Start — construction of new center ($7,500) see Utica National Insurance Group

Vassar College ($5,050) see American President Companies, Ltd.

Vassar College — scholarship ($25,000) see Koopman Fund

Vassar College Annual Fund — general use ($11,000) see Firestone, Jr. Foundation, Harvey

Villa Maria College — for computer-room equipment ($5,000) see Palisano Foundation, Vincent and Harriet

Village of Cayuga — general ($5,875) see Cayuga Foundation

Village of Hobart — rebuilding sewer system ($600,000) see O'Connor Foundation, A. Lindsay and Olive B.

Village of Hobart — water and sewer project ($150,000) see O'Connor Foundation, A. Lindsay and Olive B.

Village of Stamford — capital improvement ($116,058) see Robinson-Broadhurst Foundation

Visions ($25,000) see Blum Foundation, Edna F.

VISIONS/Services for the Blind and Visually Impaired — year-end ($17,500) see Parshelsky Foundation, Moses L.

Visiting Nurse Association of Brooklyn ($3,500) see Vogler Foundation, Laura B.

Visiting Nurse Service — capital building campaign ($25,000) see Davenport-Hatch Foundation

Visiting Nurse Service of Rochester ($70,000) see Jones Foundation, Daisy Marquis

Vitrous Research Fund ($5,000) see Fischbach Foundation

Volunteer Counseling Service of Rockland County ($25,000) see Chazen Foundation

Volunteer Lawyers for the Arts ($2,500) see Miller Fund, Kathryn and Gilbert

Volunteer Services for the Elderly ($3,000) see Hatch Charitable Trust, Margaret Milliken

VVS Dollars for Scholars — unrestricted ($2,000) see Chapman Charitable Corporation, Howard and Bess

Weizmann Institute of Science American Committee — Helena Rubinstein Postdoctoral fellowship in biomedical sciences and cancer research in perpetuity, for a women scientist ($83,334) see Rubinstein Foundation, Helena

Wells College — for Pauline M. Dodge '16 Endowment Scholarship Fund ($25,000)

see Dodge Foundation, Cleveland H.

Wells College ($90,000) see Hagedorn Fund

Wells College — educational ($5,875) see Cayuga Foundation

Westchester Association for Retarded Citizens ($40,000) see Frese Foundation, Arnold D.

Westchester Association for Retarded Citizens ($25,000) see Witco Foundation

Westchester Clubman see MBIA Inc.

Westchester Community College ($250,000) see Marx Foundation, Virginia and Leonard

Westchester Conservatory of Music ($7,300) see Goldie-Anna Charitable Trust

Westchester Education Coalition — principals program ($59,007) see NYNEX Corporation

Westchester Exceptional Children's School see MBIA Inc.

Westchester Library System ($26,600) see Marx Foundation, Virginia and Leonard

Western New York Public Broadcasting Association — construction of a new state-of-the-art public broadcasting center in downtown Buffalo ($200,000) see Wendt Foundation, Margaret L.

Western Wall Heritage Foundation — Herodian street excavations ($25,000) see Alexander Foundation, Joseph

Westminster Presbyterian Church ($10,943) see Everett Charitable Trust

White Plains Hospital Medical Center ($250,000) see Lowenstein Foundation, Leon

White Plains Medical Center ($50,200) see McGonagle Foundation, Dextra Baldwin

Whitney Museum of American Art ($1,000) see Jaydor Corp.

Whitney Museum of American Art ($5,000) see Lasdon Foundation, William and Mildred

Whitney Museum of American Art — annual fund ($50,000) see Lauder Foundation

Whitney Museum of American Art ($22,000) see Lauder Foundation

Whitney Museum of American Art ($90,500) see Mnuchin Foundation

Whitney Museum of American Art — fellowship endowment and annual fellowships for the Independent Study Program providing curatorial training for college and graduate students ($100,000) see Rubinstein Foundation, Helena

Whitney Museum of American Art ($9,000) see Thompson Co., J. Walter

Whitney Point Daycare/Preschool — construction of new building for preschool and daycare center ($15,000) see Hoyt Foundation, Stewart W. and Willma C.

Wilmington Cooper Memorial — for reading program ($2,500) see Lake Placid Education Foundation

Wilmington Cooper Memorial — for computers ($2,500) see Lake Placid Education Foundation

Wilmington Cooper Memorial — for general support ($1,000) see Lake Placid Education Foundation

Windward School ($15,000) see Connemara Fund

Winston Preparatory School ($15,000) see Neuberger Foundation, Roy R. and Marie S.

WNET/Channel 13 ($1,000) see Alavi Foundation of New York

WNET/Channel 13 ($5,000) see Marx Foundation, Virginia and Leonard

WNET/Channel 13 — educational ($15,000) see New York Stock Exchange, Inc.

WNET/Channel 13 — unrestricted ($365,000) see Rohatyn Foundation, Felix and Elizabeth

WNET/Channel 13 ($50,000) see Salomon Foundation, Richard and Edna

WNET/Channel 13 ($10,000) see Thorne Foundation

WNET/Channel Thirteen — sponsorship of children's television program ($200,000) see Rubinstein Foundation, Helena

Wolfeboro Area Children's Center — aid for child care programs ($30,000) see Vernon Fund, Miles Hodsdon

Women's League for Israel ($5,000) see Fischbach Foundation

Women's League for Israel ($15,300) see Weinstein Foundation, J.

Woodstock School of Art ($3,000) see Avery Arts Foundation, Milton and Sally

World Jewish Congress ($1,004,600) see Seagram & Sons, Inc., Joseph E.

World Monuments Fund ($210,000) see Gould Foundation, The Florence

World Monuments Fund ($200,000) see Kress Foundation, Samuel H.

World Monuments Fund ($125,000) see Kress Foundation, Samuel H.

World Monuments Fund ($75,000) see Kress Foundation, Samuel H.

World Monuments Fund ($50,000) see Kress Foundation, Samuel H.

World Rehabilitation Fund ($1,000) see Glanville Family Foundation

World Union for Progressive Judaism ($15,000) see Reicher Foundation, Anne and Harry J.

World University Games 1993 — to assist in administering and marketing ($25,000) see Western New York Foundation

Writers Voice see HarperCollins Publishers Inc.

WSKG Public Television and Radio — for general support ($5,000) see Anderson Foundation

WXII Public Broadcasting ($2,500) see Schmitt Foundation, Kilian J. and Caroline F.

WXXI Public Broadcasting —
capital building campaign
($30,000) see
Davenport-Hatch Foundation
WXXI Public Broadcasting
($35,000) see Jones
Foundation, Daisy Marquis
Yeshiva Beth Yehudah
($2,000) see Taubman
Foundation, A. Alfred
Yeshiva University — Joseph
Alexander science education
enhancement program at
Stern/Yeshiva college
($50,000) see Alexander
Foundation, Joseph
Yivo Institute for Jewish
Research ($75,000) see
Atran Foundation
Yivo Institute for Jewish
Research ($8,500) see Icahn
Foundation, Carl C.
YMCA ($25,000) see
Carnahan-Jackson
Foundation
YMCA Capital Fund
($25,000) see Hill
Foundation, Sandy
YMCA Capital Fund, Glens
Falls Family YMCA
($25,000) see Hill
Foundation, Sandy
YMCA of Greater New York
— capital campaign
($50,000) see Chase
Manhattan Bank, N.A.
YMCA of Greater New York
— for second installment of
a $1,000,000 grant for
Endowment for Youth
($400,000) see Dodge
Foundation, Cleveland H.
YMCA of Greater New York
— balance of a $325,000
grant for national expansion
of the Writers Community
project, a program offering
residencies for writers in
mid-career who during their
residencies give readings
and conduct workshops for
other writers ($275,000) see
Bingham Foundation,
William
YMCA of New York see CIBC
Wood Gundy
YMCA-WEIU ($5,472) see
Everett Charitable Trust
Yonkers Public Schools —
playgrounds ($150,000) see
Carvel Foundation, Thomas
and Agnes
Young Adult Institute ($6,000)
see Commerce Clearing
House, Incorporated
Young Audiences ($28,000)
see Fribourg Foundation
Youth Advocacy Center — to
support the foster Care
Youth Training and
Advocacy Project, designed
to help foster care teens
advocate for themselves, as
well as for changes in the
child welfare system
($25,000) see Hazen
Foundation, Edward W.
Youth Counseling League
($10,000) see Piankova
Foundation, Tatiana
Youth Counseling League
($35,000) see Weezie
Foundation
Youth for Understanding
($8,360) see American
Optical Corp.
YWCA —
three-and-a-half-year grant
for SB6 Grant and expansion
of "TLC" program ($73,156)
see Gebbie Foundation
YWCA — toward operating
expenses for family violence
and sexual assault network

program for 1994 ($66,000)
see Gebbie Foundation
YWCA ($150,000) see
Gordon/Rousmaniere/Roberts
Fund
YWCA — paging system used
in rape crisis ($5,900) see
Utica National Insurance
Group
YWCA of Cortland —
coalition for children
($25,000) see Allyn
Foundation
YWCA of the USA
($100,000) see Digital
Equipment Corp.

North Carolina

African American Atlier
Gallery see Miller Brewing
Company/North Carolina
AIDS Community Residence
Association ($4,000) see
Akzo America
AIDS Council ($15,000) see
Glenn Foundation, Carrie C.
and Lena V.
Alamance Health Services —
to construct a single new
hospital to replace both
Alamance County and
Alamance Memorial
hospitals ($250,000) see
Duke Endowment
Alleghany Fairgrounds
($25,000) see Chatham
Manufacturing Co.
American Association for
Gifted Children — provide
$1,000 awards for 141
presidential scholars, all of
whom are graduating high
school seniors, representing
50 states, the District of
Columbia, and the territories
($145,000) see Dodge
Foundation, Geraldine R.
American Friends of Paris
Ballet and Opera ($100,000)
see Gould Foundation, The
Florence
American Social Health
Association ($10,000) see
Overlake Foundation
Arts Council ($1,000) see
Toms Foundation
Arts Council for Davidson
County ($10,000) see
Thomasville Furniture
Industries
Arts and Science Council
($106,753) see First Union
Corp.
Arts and Science Council —
annual fund drive ($5,000)
see National Gypsum Co.
Arts and Science Council —
for third quarter payment on
annual pledge ($11,875) see
Royal Group, Inc.
Arts and Science Council —
for second quarter payment
on capital commitment
($11,875) see Royal Group,
Inc.
Arts and Science Council —
for payment four of
corporate pledge ($11,875)
see Royal Group, Inc.
Arts and Science Council
Charlotte Mecklenburg
($107,890) see Duke Power
Co.
Asheville Community Theater
($50,000) see Janirve
Foundation
Asheville School ($75,000)
see Steele-Reese Foundation
Associated New Jersey
Environmental Commission
— state plan ($110,000) see
Fund for New Jersey

Bowman Gray School of
Medicine — capital
campaign ($900,000) see
RJR Nabisco Inc.
Bowman Gray School of
Medicine — for J. Paul
Sticht Center on Aging
($5,000) see Chatham
Manufacturing Co.
Boy Scouts of America Old
North State Council
($1,000) see Acme-McCrary
Corp./Sapona Manufacturing
Co.
Brevard Music Center
($100,000) see Janirve
Foundation
Building Together ($29,000)
see Hillsdale Fund
Burlington City Schools —
teacher technology lab
($13,200) see Burlington
Industries, Inc.
Canterbury School ($25,000)
see Hillsdale Fund
Center for Research on
Population and Security
($25,000) see Zlinkoff Fund
for Medical Research and
Education, Sergei S.
Central Piedmont Community
College — educational
institution general support
($2,000) see National
Gypsum Co.
Charlotte City Ballet —
general support ($500) see
National Gypsum Co.
Charlotte Country Day School
($43,100) see Dalton
Foundation, Harry L.
Charlotte-Mecklenburg
Hospital ($125,000) see Van
Every Foundation, Philip L.
Charlotte-Mecklenburg
Hospital ($125,000) see Van
Every Foundation, Philip L.
Children's Home Society
($5,000) see Finch
Foundation, Doak
Children's Home Society of
North Carolina ($15,000)
see Sternberger Foundation,
Tannenbaum
City of Lenoir — aquatic and
fitness center ($7,925) see
Thomasville Furniture
Industries
City of Winston-Salem
($20,000) see Hanes
Foundation, John W. and
Anna H.
Clay County Historical and
Arts Council — grant for
matting, framing, and
preparing pictures ($1,250)
see Ferebee Endowment,
Percy O.
Cleveland Community College
School of Nursing ($10,000)
see Dover Foundation
Cleveland Memorial Library
($12,500) see Dover
Foundation
Community Arts Council of
Western North Carolina
(Arts Alliance) ($45,000)
see Janirve Foundation
Community General Hospital
($25,000) see Thomasville
Furniture Industries
Community General Hospital
of Thomasville ($20,000)
see Finch Foundation,
Thomas Austin
Court Watch of North Carolina
($26,821) see Sternberger
Foundation, Tannenbaum
Crisis Assistance Ministry
($264,912) see Duke Power
Co.
Crisis Assistance Ministry
($18,000) see Glenn
Foundation, Carrie C. and
Lena V.

Crisis Control Ministry
($154,503) see Duke Power
Co.
Crossnore School ($24,184)
see Willard Helping Fund,
Cecilia Young
Davidson College ($100,000)
see Steele-Reese Foundation
Davidson College ($775,013)
see First Union Corp.
Davidson College —
charitable ($7,000) see
Allendale Insurance Co.
Davidson County Arts Council
($5,000) see Finch
Foundation, Doak
Davidson County Community
College ($5,000) see Finch
Foundation, Doak
Davidson County Library
Foundation ($20,000) see
Thomasville Furniture
Industries
Department of Social Services
Emergency Energy
Committee ($78,151) see
Duke Power Co.
Discovery Place ($10,871) see
Glenn Foundation, Carrie C.
and Lena V.
Dover Baptist Church
($17,000) see Dover
Foundation
Downtown Goldsboro
Association, Paramount
Center for the Performing
Arts ($25,000) see Hillsdale
Fund
Duke Comprehensive Cancer
Center ($20,000) see Russell
Charitable Foundation, Tom
Duke Fuqua School ($15,000)
see Harvey Foundation, Felix
Duke University ($25,000) see
Muchnic Foundation
Duke University ($2,000) see
Kelly Tractor Co.
Duke University ($2,000,000)
see Whitehead Charitable
Foundation
Duke University ($9,925) see
First Chicago Corp.
Duke University ($25,000) see
Benenson Foundation,
Frances and Benjamin
Duke University — final
installment of a $250,000
two-for-one challenge grant
to establish a $1,000,000
nonathletic scholarship
endowment fund for
students from the city of
New York who show high
academic promise and
whose families have
demonstrated an acute
financial need ($250,000)
see Calder Foundation, Louis
Duke University — to be
applied to their financial aid
program and used to assist
students from the city of
New York who show high
academic promise and
whose families have
demonstrated an acute
financial need ($100,000)
see Calder Foundation, Louis
Duke University ($25,000) see
Dula Educational and
Charitable Foundation,
Caleb C. and Julia W.
Duke University ($250,000)
see Lowenstein Foundation,
Leon
Duke University ($45,600) see
Sulzberger Foundation
Duke University ($5,025) see
Dalton Foundation, Harry L.
Duke University — Dover
scholarships ($10,000) see
Dover Foundation
Duke University —
scholarships ($106,000) see

Sternberger Foundation,
Tannenbaum
Duke University Department
of Cultural Anthropology —
"Cultural Redefinition of
Peace and Violence: The
Invention and Diffusion of
Gandhian Nonviolent
Revolution" ($44,977) see
Guggenheim Foundation,
Harry Frank
Duke University Libraries
($25,000) see Thompson
Co., J. Walter
Duke University Libraries —
renovation of conference
room in Perkins Library
($150,000) see Carpenter
Foundation, E. Rhodes and
Leona B.
Duke University Medical
Center ($11,000) see Akzo
America
Duke University Medical
Center — to construct the
Medical Sciences Research
Building, a 90,000
square-foot biomedical
science research facility
($1,000,000) see Duke
Endowment
Duke University Medical
Center — to support the
Levine Science Research
Center, a 170,000
square-foot facility for
interdisciplinary research for
the School of the
Environment, the
Department of Computer
Science, and components of
biomedical engineering
($750,000) see Duke
Endowment
Duke University Medical
Center — to develop a
statewide case management
service for HIV-positive
children and their families
($170,000) see Duke
Endowment
Duke University Medical
Center, Duke
Comprehensive Cancer
Center ($25,000) see
Hillsdale Fund
Duke University Parents Fund
($25,000) see Mathis-Pfohl
Foundation
East Carolina University
($7,000) see Harvey
Foundation, Felix
East Carolina University
Foundation ($133,400) see
Wachovia Bank of North
Carolina, N.A.
Eastern Carolina
Exchange/Exchangette Child
Abuse Prevention Center
($54,000) see Hanes
Foundation, John W. and
Anna H.
Eden United Way see Miller
Brewing Company/North
Carolina
Eden YMCA see Miller
Brewing Company/North
Carolina
Elizabeth Baptist ($5,000) see
Morgan Foundation, Louie
R. and Gertrude
Empty Stocking Fund ($200)
see Toms Foundation
Family and Children's
Services ($22,503) see
Sternberger Foundation,
Tannenbaum
Fellowship of Christian
Athletes ($2,000) see
Harvey Foundation, Felix
Fieldcrest — scholarships
1990 ($36,000) see
Fieldcrest Cannon Inc.

Columbus Foundation — for culture and the environment ($26,000) see Columbus Dispatch Printing Co.

Columbus Foundation — Greenlawn Cemetery Roads — for culture and the environment ($23,800) see Columbus Dispatch Printing Co.

Columbus Foundation Trilogy — for culture and the environment ($200,000) see Columbus Dispatch Printing Co.

Columbus Jewish Federation — Jewish Community programs ($166,666) see Barry Corp., R. G.

Columbus Municipal School District ($100,000) see Weyerhaeuser Co.

Columbus Symphony Orchestra — for challenge grant ($45,425) see Columbus Dispatch Printing Co.

Columbus Urban League ($37,500) see Borden, Inc.

Committee for Economic Development ($1,000) see French Oil Mill Machinery Co.

Community Christian Church ($25,000) see Hoover Fund-Trust, W. Henry

Community Christian Church ($10,000) see Hoover Fund-Trust, W. Henry

Community Preparatory School ($25,000) see Providence Journal Company

Copeland Oaks Crandall Medical Center — for capital improvement program ($60,000) see Crandall Memorial Foundation, J. Ford

Corinne Dolan Alzheimers Center ($100,000) see Frohring Foundation, William O. and Gertrude Lewis

Cultural Center for the Arts — handicapped accessibility project and annual campaign for fund for the arts ($77,700) see Hoover Foundation

Cultural Center for the Arts ($10,000) see Hoover Fund-Trust, W. Henry

Cultural Center for the Arts ($3,900) see Hoover Fund-Trust, W. Henry

Cuyahoga Community College — general scholarship fund ($25,000) see Andrews Foundation

Cuyahoga Valley Christian Academy — capital improvements ($15,000) see Gallagher Family Foundation, Lewis P.

Dayton Area Chamber of Commerce ($5,000) see Amcast Industrial Corp.

Dayton Art Institute ($750) see Amcast Industrial Corp.

Dayton Art Institute — equipment support for new exhibit ($6,000) see Tait Foundation, Frank M.

Dayton Contemporary Dance Company — arts advancement program ($10,090) see Tait Foundation, Frank M.

Dayton Foundation — Human Services Education Fund ($7,500) see Tait Foundation, Frank M.

Dayton Museum of Natural History ($67,772) see Kettering Fund

Dayton Society of Natural History — Bieser Discovery Center ($30,009) see Tait Foundation, Frank M.

Defiance College ($10,000) see Markey Charitable Fund, John C.

Denison University ($20,000) see Carnahan-Jackson Foundation

Denison University — math and physical science building construction ($970,000) see Olin Foundation, F. W.

Dublin School ($16,600) see Putnam Foundation

Dublin School ($8,400) see Putnam Foundation

East Sparta Ohio Baseball Association ($3,000) see Flowers Charitable Trust, Albert W. and Edith V.

Easter Seals see Seaway Food Town, Inc.

Education Enhancement Partnership — to finance education initiatives ($50,000) see Deuble Foundation, George H.

Education Enhancement Partnership — funds for continuation of programs ($150,000) see Hoover Foundation

Education Enhancement Partnership ($3,000) see Hoover Fund-Trust, W. Henry

Eleanor B. Rainey Memorial Institute ($6,000) see Frohring Foundation, William O. and Gertrude Lewis

Epilepsy Foundation see Seaway Food Town, Inc.

Family Planning Association ($2,500) see Williams Charitable Trust, John C.

Family Service Association of Steubenville ($20,000) see Williams Charitable Trust, John C.

Fine Arts Continuing Education Trust ($600) see French Oil Mill Machinery Co.

Firelands Habitat for Humanity ($2,000) see Sandusky International Inc.

First Call for Help ($5,000) see Schuller International

First United Church of Christ — renovations ($25,000) see Ashtabula Foundation

First United Methodist Church — renovations ($13,444) see Ashtabula Foundation

Flower Hospital ($9,035) see Ritter Charitable Trust, George W. and Mary F.

Flower Memorial Hospital Foundation — to defray, in part, the cost of the construction of its barrier free inpatient rehabilitation center ($100,000) see Herrick Foundation

Flower Memorial Hospital Foundation — to be used to defray, in part, the cost of the construction of its barrier free inpatient rehabilitation center ($100,000) see Tecumseh Products Co.

Foundation Center ($6,500) see Second Foundation

Frank and Edna Memorial Fund ($17,500) see Hoover Fund-Trust, W. Henry

Fred Hutchinson Cancer Research Center — capital needs ($100,000) see Forest Foundation

Fred Hutchinson Cancer Research Center ($20,000) see Foster Foundation

Free Medical Clinic of Greater Cleveland ($17,000) see Eaton Foundation, Cyrus

Friends of the Cleveland School of the Arts ($5,000) see Eaton Foundation, Cyrus

Furnace Street Mission Victim Assistance ($12,500) see Calhoun Charitable Trust, Kenneth

Garden Center — general support ($5,000) see Frohring Foundation, Paul and Maxine

Gilmour Academy — endowment fund Matthew A. Baxter Middle School ($40,000) see Andrews Foundation

Gilmour Academy ($100,400) see Lennon Foundation, Fred A.

Gish Film Theatre ($20,000) see Pickford Foundation, Mary

Good Samaritan Hunger Center — truck ($10,000) see Musson Charitable Foundation, R. C. and Katharine M.

Goodrich-Gannett Neighborhood Center — intergenerational art program ($12,000) see Mather Charitable Trust, S. Livingston

Goodwill Industries — literacy program expansion ($7,500) see Tait Foundation, Frank M.

Great Lakes Museum of Science, Environment, and Technology — general fund ($17,000) see McDonald & Company Securities, Inc.

Great Lakes Theater Festival — production of play ($150,000) see Smith Foundation, Kelvin and Eleanor

Greater Akron Musical Association ($6,000) see Calhoun Charitable Trust, Kenneth

Greater Cincinnati Foundation ($15,000) see Griswold Foundation, John C.

Greater Cleveland Roundtable — operating support ($38,000) see Eaton Corporation

Greater Erie County Marketing Group ($5,000) see Sandusky International Inc.

Habitat for Humanity — construction of home for indigent families ($7,500) see Van Wert County Foundation

Habitat for Humanity of Greater Canton — construction and renovation of homes ($180,000) see Timken Foundation of Canton

Halom House ($35,000) see Reicher Foundation, Anne and Harry J.

Halvern, Ohio Baseball Association ($3,000) see Flowers Charitable Trust, Albert W. and Edith V.

Hanna Perkins School ($10,000) see Calhoun Charitable Trust, Kenneth

Harding Evans Foundation — building fund for care of children and adolescents ($3,500) see Worthington Foods

Hathaway Brown School ($12,500) see Eaton Foundation, Cyrus

Hathaway Brown School — general support ($10,000) see Frohring Foundation, Paul and Maxine

Hathaway Brown School — capital campaign ($25,000) see Humphrey Fund, George M. and Pamela S.

Hathaway Brown School ($100,000) see Kettering Fund

Hathaway Brown School — capital campaign ($150,000) see Smith Foundation, Kelvin and Eleanor

Hathaway Children's Service ($10,000) see Van Nuys Foundation, I. N. and Susanna H.

Haven of Rest Ministries — general ($10,000) see Musson Charitable Foundation, R. C. and Katharine M.

Hawken School — for renovation of facilities to establish a preschool program ($50,000) see Bingham Foundation, William

Hawken School — gymnasium ($20,000) see Humphrey Fund, George M. and Pamela S.

Heart and Hand Foundation — general fund ($83,050) see McDonald & Company Securities, Inc.

Heath Athletic Boosters — ticket booth and concession stand ($10,000) see Evans Foundation, Thomas J.

Heidelberg College ($6,000) see Osceola Foundation

Heimlich Institute Foundation ($10,000) see Griswold Foundation, John C.

Henry H. Stambauh Auditorium ($10,000) see Kilcawley Fund, William H.

Hipple Cancer Research Center ($1,625) see French Oil Mill Machinery Co.

Hiram College ($10,000) see Frohring Foundation, William O. and Gertrude Lewis

Hiram College — for library equipment and materials ($500,000) see GAR Foundation

Hiram College — for Presidential Discretionary Fund ($25,000) see Morgan Foundation, Burton D.

Hiram House — summer camperships ($12,500) see Mather Charitable Trust, S. Livingston

Hiram House — second-year payment of endowment pledge ($7,500) see Mather Charitable Trust, S. Livingston

Hitchcock House ($5,000) see Eaton Foundation, Cyrus

Hoban Trust Fund — to establish an endowment fund which will support the "work study" program and for endowment ($110,000) see GAR Foundation

Holden Arboretum — Science Center ($50,000) see Mather and William Gwinn Mather Fund, Elizabeth Ring

Holden Arboretum — operations ($10,000) see Mather and William Gwinn Mather Fund, Elizabeth Ring

Holden Arboretum — first payment of $500,000

commitment toward greenhouse/nursery research facility construction ($100,000) see Reinberger Foundation

Holden Arboretum — horticulture science center ($33,500) see Smith Foundation, Kelvin and Eleanor

Holden Arboretum — operations ($5,000) see South Waite Foundation

Holly Hills ($7,000) see Flowers Charitable Trust, Albert W. and Edith V.

HOME Communication Channel ($20,000) see Russell Charitable Foundation, Tom

Hospice ($12,500) see Scott Fetzer Co.

Hudson School District — Barlow Scholarship Endowment Fund ($25,000) see Gallagher Family Foundation, Lewis P.

Human Life Center, University of Steubenville — for salary of research assistant ($18,000) see Trust Funds

Interfaith Home Maintenance Service ($2,500) see Pollock Company Foundation, William B.

Jewish Community Federation ($500,100) see Premier Industrial Corp.

Jewish Federation ($82,000) see Jarson-Stanley and Mickey Kaplan Foundation, Isaac and Esther

John Carroll University — educational physics ($50,000) see Hugoton Foundation

John Carroll University ($28,390) see Centerior Energy Corp.

John Carroll University — capital campaign ($50,000) see Eaton Corporation

John Carroll University ($23,000) see Ingalls Foundation, Louise H. and David S.

John Carroll University — for capital fund ($28,572) see Parker Hannifin Corp.

Johnny Appleseed Council Boy Scouts ($4,000) see Young Foundation, Hugo H. and Mabel B.

Joy of Life Ministries — property improvements ($15,000) see Evans Foundation, Thomas J.

Judean Hills Foundation ($50,000) see Hassenfeld Foundation

Julie Billiart School ($8,000) see Second Foundation

Junior Achievement ($2,000) see Amcast Industrial Corp.

Junior Achievement ($2,000) see Freedom Forge Corp.

Junior Achievement ($2,000) see Gould Electronics Inc.

Kawken School — capital ($100,000) see Ingalls Foundation, Louise H. and David S.

Kent State University ($10,000) see Wilson Foundation, H. W.

Kent State University Foundation — for the Margaret C. Morgan Endowed Scholarship Fund at the School of Fashion Design and Merchandising ($18,000) see Morgan Foundation, Burton D.

Kent-Sussex Industries ($4,000) see Wilmington Trust Co.

Kenyon College ($5,500) see Koopman Fund

Kenyon College ($15,350) see First Chicago Corp.

Kenyon College — operations ($12,000) see Mather and William Gwinn Mather Fund, Elizabeth Ring

Kettering Medical Center ($2,000,000) see Kettering Fund

Kettering Medical Center Fund — education scholarship ($2,000) see Worthington Foods

Kettering Mohican Area Medical Center ($155,000) see Young Foundation, Hugo H. and Mabel B.

Lakewood Christian Service Center ($5,000) see Second Foundation

Laurel School — in memory of MHS ($5,000) see South Waite Foundation

Licking County Foundation — COIC/University of Southern Ohio, bell tower ($50,000) see Evans Foundation, Thomas J.

LifeCare Alliance — programs for the elderly ($6,000) see Barry Corp., R. G.

Little Sisters of the Poor ($10,000) see Sawyer Charitable Foundation

Local Initiatives Support Corporation ($8,334) see Andersons, The

Loudonville Agricultural Society ($3,500) see Young Foundation, Hugo H. and Mabel B.

Loudonville-Perrysville Scholarship ($8,000) see Young Foundation, Hugo H. and Mabel B.

Loudonville-Perrysville School ($96,230) see Young Foundation, Hugo H. and Mabel B.

Loudonville Public Library ($31,000) see Young Foundation, Hugo H. and Mabel B.

Magnificat High School — Convent construction and renovation ($40,000) see Andrews Foundation

Malone College — for construction of the college's Centennial Center ($100,000) see Bingham Foundation, William

Malone College — capital drive for construction of the Centennial Center ($50,000) see Deuble Foundation, George H.

March of Dimes see Seaway Food Town, Inc.

Marietta College ($28,000) see Fenton Foundation

Marietta College ($10,000) see Fenton Foundation

Marietta Memorial Hospital ($10,000) see Fenton Foundation

Marietta Memorial Hospital ($10,000) see Fenton Foundation

Marietta United Way ($3,300) see Fenton Foundation

Marion Polk Food Share ($1,000) see Pioneer Trust Bank, NA

Martin Luther Lutheran Church ($15,000) see Flowers Charitable Trust, Albert W. and Edith V.

Martins Ferry City Schools — renewed support of Project

Ohio River Education in Martins Ferry City Schools to increase knowledge and awareness of the Ohio River environment ($34,000) see Virginia Environmental Endowment

Mary Scott Nursing Center ($82,223) see Kettering Fund

Masonic Toledo Trust ($10,000) see Andersons, The

Massillon Museum — renovate Giltz Building ($125,000) see Timken Foundation of Canton

Mather Museum — operations ($40,000) see Mather and William Gwinn Mather Fund, Elizabeth Ring

Merry-Go-Round Museum ($5,000) see Sandusky International Inc.

Miami Valley Cultural Alliance — annual campaign ($19,000) see Tait Foundation, Frank M.

Miami Valley Health Foundation ($5,000) see Amcast Industrial Corp.

Middletown Area United Way ($12,000) see Mosinee Paper Corp.

Mill Creek Park Foundation — for public improvement program ($75,000) see Crandall Memorial Foundation, J. Ford

Mill Creek Park Foundation — for capital improvement program ($75,000) see Crandall Memorial Foundation, J. Ford

Millcreek Child Development Center — for capital improvement program ($50,000) see Crandall Memorial Foundation, J. Ford

Millcreek Child Development Center — for capital improvement program ($25,000) see Crandall Memorial Foundation, J. Ford

Millcreek Child Development Center ($20,000) see Kilcawley Fund, William H.

Mobile Meals ($14,856) see McFawn Trust No. 2, Lois Sisler

Mohican Area Community Fund ($2,500) see Young Foundation, Hugo H. and Mabel B.

Mohican Area Growth Foundation ($30,000) see Young Foundation, Hugo H. and Mabel B.

Morgan Memorial Goodwill Industries ($2,500) see Pollock Company Foundation, William B.

Multiple Sclerosis Society Friendly Visitor Program — general ($15,000) see Musson Charitable Foundation, R. C. and Katharine M.

Museum Center Foundation — renovation of Union Terminal ($15,000) see Dater Foundation, Charles H.

Museum Guild ($4,000) see Hoover Fund-Trust, W. Henry

Musical Arts Association — support of Cleveland Orchestra 75th Anniversary Campaign ($335,000) see BP America Inc.

Musical Arts Association ($11,000) see Calhoun Charitable Trust, Kenneth

Musical Arts Association — challenge grant ($66,667) see Mather and William Gwinn Mather Fund, Elizabeth Ring

Musical Arts Association — operations ($12,000) see Mather and William Gwinn Mather Fund, Elizabeth Ring

Musical Arts Association — support of symphony orchestra ($5,000) see Mather Charitable Trust, S. Livingston

Musical Arts Association ($20,000) see McFawn Trust No. 2, Lois Sisler

Musical Arts Association ($30,000) see Premier Industrial Corp.

Musical Arts Association — artistic initiative ($150,000) see Smith Foundation, Kelvin and Eleanor

Musical Arts Association ($100,000) see Smith Foundation, Kelvin and Eleanor

National Alliance of Business ($5,000) see Crane Co.

National Family Service see Seaway Food Town, Inc.

National Foundation for Ileitis and Colitis ($5,000) see Gould Electronics Inc.

National Invention Center ($25,000) see GenCorp Inc.

National Invention Center ($20,000) see McFawn Trust No. 2, Lois Sisler

National Merit Scholarship Program — for colleges and universities ($32,900) see Parker Hannifin Corp.

National Pro Football Museum — expansion project ($200,000) see Timken Foundation of Canton

Neighborhood House ($30,000) see Williams Charitable Trust, John C.

Neighborhood Progress ($500,000) see BP America Inc.

Neighborhood Progress ($125,000) see Premier Industrial Corp.

New Cleveland Campaign ($100,000) see Lennon Foundation, Fred A.

New Life Community — general support ($28,500) see Nestle USA Inc.

Newark City Schools — blacktop basketball courts ($29,506) see Evans Foundation, Thomas J.

Newbury Local Schools Library Program ($5,000) see Frohring Foundation, William O. and Gertrude Lewis

North Canton Medical Foundation — major expansion project ($500,000) see Hoover Foundation

North Canton Memorial Fund — improvements to Hoover Memorial Stadium complex ($25,000) see Deuble Foundation, George H.

North Coast Youth Services ($3,150) see Sandusky International Inc.

Northcoast Fund — minority entrepreneurship ($62,500) see Eaton Corporation

Northeastern Ohio Roundtable ($75,000) see Lennon Foundation, Fred A.

Northwest Jackson Soccer Association ($4,000) see Flowers Charitable Trust, Albert W. and Edith V.

Notre Dame Cathedral Latin School ($100,000) see Lennon Foundation, Fred A.

Oberlin College ($128,000) see BP America Inc.

Oberlin College — to match the grant of the National Science Foundation to renovate the ground floor for the Wright Physics Laboratory ($125,000) see GAR Foundation

Oberlin College — annual fund ($15,000) see Hunt Foundation, Roy A.

Ohio Foundation of Independent Colleges ($1,000) see Amcast Industrial Corp.

Ohio Foundation of Independent Colleges ($28,000) see Centerior Energy Corp.

Ohio Foundation of Independent Colleges — to benefit the operation of the Ohio Foundation of Independent Colleges' 36 member institutions located throughout the state of Ohio ($125,000) see GAR Foundation

Ohio Foundation of Independent Colleges ($30,000) see Goodrich Co., The B.F.

Ohio Foundation of Independent Colleges — support for scholarship programs ($43,000) see Hoover Foundation

Ohio Foundation of Independent Colleges — general fund ($10,000) see McDonald & Company Securities, Inc.

Ohio Foundation of Independent Colleges — for colleges and universities ($36,000) see Parker Hannifin Corp.

Ohio Foundation of Independent Colleges ($6,000) see Pollock Company Foundation, William B.

Ohio Foundation of Independent Colleges ($5,000) see Sandusky International Inc.

Ohio State Bar Foundation ($9,034) see Ritter Charitable Trust, George W. and Mary F.

Ohio State University ($305,000) see Ford Motor Co.

Ohio State University ($279,659) see Gleason Foundation

Ohio State University ($38,307) see Borden, Inc.

Ohio State University ($20,000) see Armco Inc.

Ohio State University College of Optometry ($48,334) see Wildermuth Foundation, E. F.

Ohio State University Kiplinger Fellows ($30,000) see Kiplinger Foundation

Ohio University College of Engineering and Technology ($100,000) see Cooper Industries, Inc.

Ohio University E.W. Scripps School of Journalism ($100,000) see Scripps Co., E.W.

Ohio University Foundation — to establish endowments for visiting professionals in the Department of Journalism ($200,000) see Hearst

Foundation, William Randolph

Ohio University Foundation ($10,000) see Scott Fetzer Co.

Ohio University Midwest Newspapers Workshop for Minorities ($10,000) see Scripps Co., E.W.

Ohio Wesleyan University ($20,000) see Smith Foundation, Gordon V. and Helen C.

Ohio Wesleyan University — David Warren Jay Walk ($1,000) see Smith Foundation, Gordon V. and Helen C.

Ohio Wesleyan University ($10,000) see Hoover Fund-Trust, W. Henry

Old Ft. Steuben Project ($25,000) see Williams Charitable Trust, John C.

Otterbein College — nursing education ($90,000) see Teagle Foundation

Par-Excellence Learning School — operating capital ($20,000) see Evans Foundation, Thomas J.

Park College ($2,897) see Gould Electronics Inc.

Park Vista Life Care Fund ($7,000) see Pollock Company Foundation, William B.

Perry Local School District — adult booster club ($3,000) see Flowers Charitable Trust, Albert W. and Edith V.

Phillips Osborne School — capital campaign ($25,000) see Humphrey Fund, George M. and Pamela S.

Pilot Dogs ($9,000) see Wildermuth Foundation, E. F.

Piqua Chamber of Commerce Veterans Memorial Fund ($1,000) see French Oil Mill Machinery Co.

Planned Parenthood Association ($700) see French Oil Mill Machinery Co.

Planned Parenthood Association — general support ($2,500) see Frohring Foundation, Paul and Maxine

Planned Parenthood Association ($10,000) see Pollock Company Foundation, William B.

Planned Parenthood Association of Miami Valley ($40,000) see Kettering Fund

Playhouse Square Foundation ($5,000) see Eaton Foundation, Cyrus

Premier Industrial Philanthropic Fund ($550,000) see Premier Industrial Corp.

Pro Football Hall of Fame — expansion program ($45,000) see Hoover Foundation

Project Learn — general support ($1,500) see Frohring Foundation, Paul and Maxine

Public Broadcasting Foundation of Northwest Ohio ($5,290) see Andersons, The

Public Library of Cincinnati and Hamilton County — for the Westwood Branch Library children's programs and services ($20,000) see Dater Foundation, Charles H.

Public Library of Youngstown and Mahoning County

($10,000) see Kilcawley
Fund, William H.
PVA for Retarded Children
and Adults — unrestricted
($25,000) see Andrews
Foundation
Rainbow Babies and
Children's Hospital —
unrestricted ($20,000) see
Humphrey Fund, George M.
and Pamela S.
Ritter Library ($22,585) see
Ritter Charitable Trust,
George W. and Mary F.
Riverside Foundation for
Riverside Hospital ($9,034)
see Ritter Charitable Trust,
George W. and Mary F.
Robert Casadesus International
Piano Competition ($5,000)
see Frohring Foundation,
William O. and Gertrude
Lewis
Rock and Roll Hall of Fame
($50,000) see Consolidated
Natural Gas Co.
St. Bernadette Church —
Jewel Tomer Scholarship
Fund ($50,000) see Andrews
Foundation
St. Francis DeSales —
building addition ($25,000)
see Evans Foundation,
Thomas J.
St. Francis Rehabilitation
Hospital ($26,500) see
Schlink Foundation, Albert
G. and Olive H.
St. Joseph Home — purchase
therapeutic equipment
($10,000) see Dater
Foundation, Charles H.
St. Luke Lutheran Home
($25,000) see Flowers
Charitable Trust, Albert W.
and Edith V.
St. Michael's Church —
chimes ($15,000) see Blount
Educational and Charitable
Foundation, Mildred Weedon
St. Pauls Episcopal Church —
for construction of a
memorial garden ($23,000)
see Morgan Foundation,
Burton D.
St. Vincent Hospital ($9,035)
see Ritter Charitable Trust,
George W. and Mary F.
Salvation Army — building
renovation ($33,333) see
Evans Foundation, Thomas J.
Salvation Army — general
support ($2,500) see
Frohring Foundation, Paul
and Maxine
Salvation Army — pledge
payment/community center
($25,000) see JELD-WEN,
Inc.
Salvation Army Camp
Swonkey — purchase cots
and mattresses ($8,000) see
Dater Foundation, Charles H.
Sandusky High School
Scholarship Fund ($4,000)
see Sandusky International
Inc.
Sandusky Schools — Mills
Aquatic program ($1,500)
see Sandusky International
Inc.
Sandusky State Theater
($18,600) see Sandusky
International Inc.
Santa Maria Community
Services — activities and
programs for disadvantaged
children ($10,000) see Dater
Foundation, Charles H.
Shrine Hospital for Crippled
Children and Burn Institute
($17,857) see Ritter
Charitable Trust, George W.
and Mary F.

Shriners Hospital for Crippled
Children ($2,000) see
Flowers Charitable Trust,
Albert W. and Edith V.
Sight Center — unrestricted
($15,000) see Humphrey
Fund, George M. and
Pamela S.
Sight Center ($38,500) see
Schlink Foundation, Albert
G. and Olive H.
Sisters of Charity of St.
Augustine ($25,000) see
Kilcawley Fund, William H.
Sisters of St. Augustine
($10,000) see Kilcawley
Fund, William H.
Society for Rehabilitation —
special MHS endowment
($10,000) see South Waite
Foundation
Southern Christian Leadership
Conference ($3,000) see
Giant Food Inc.
Springer School — challenge
campaign ($10,000) see
Dater Foundation, Charles H.
Stark County — courthouse
renovation ($124,251) see
Timken Foundation of
Canton
Stark County Christian
Academy ($5,000) see
Flowers Charitable Trust,
Albert W. and Edith V.
Stark County Foundation — to
meet outstanding challenge
grants ($240,000) see GAR
Foundation
Stark County Historical
Society ($5,000) see Flowers
Charitable Trust, Albert W.
and Edith V.
Stark County Treasurer —
funds for courthouse
renovation ($372,356) see
Hoover Foundation
Stark County Treasurer for
Courthouse Restoration —
restoration of courthouse
($58,678) see Deuble
Foundation, George H.
Stark County Treasurer for
Courthouse Restoration —
courthouse restoration
($58,594) see Deuble
Foundation, George H.
Stein Hospice ($7,500) see
Sandusky International Inc.
Stein Hospice ($8,157) see
Schlink Foundation, Albert
G. and Olive H.
Stepping Stone Center —
abused and battered
children's fund ($8,000) see
Dater Foundation, Charles H.
Steubenville Concerts
($10,000) see Williams
Charitable Trust, John C.
Summer Home for the Aged
($6,000) see Calhoun
Charitable Trust, Kenneth
Summit County Historical
Society of Akron ($15,000)
see Calhoun Charitable
Trust, Kenneth
Summit Educational
Partnership Foundation
($25,000) see Morgan
Foundation, Burton D.
Sumner Home for the Aged —
general ($10,000) see
Musson Charitable
Foundation, R. C. and
Katharine M.
Sunshine Youth Services
($8,000) see Williams
Charitable Trust, John C.
Toledo Hospital ($33,878) see
Ritter Charitable Trust,
George W. and Mary F.
Toledo Museum of Art
($22,586) see Ritter
Charitable Trust, George W.
and Mary F.

Toledo Museum of Art see
Seaway Food Town, Inc.
Toledo Opera see Seaway
Food Town, Inc.
Toledo Repertoire Theatre see
Seaway Food Town, Inc.
Toledo Rotary Club ($9,034)
see Ritter Charitable Trust,
George W. and Mary F.
Toys for Tots see Seaway Food
Town, Inc.
Trilogy Fund of the Columbus
Foundation — fourth
installment of grant to fund
proposal ($100,000) see
Reinberger Foundation
Trinity United Church of
Christ — purchase of
carillon ($32,180) see
Deuble Foundation, George
H.
Trumbull Memorial Hospital
— building fund ($50,000)
see Wean Foundation,
Raymond John
United Community Fund
Knox County ($28,400) see
JELD-WEN, Inc.
United Community Services
— operational ($62,000) see
Vance Charitable
Foundation, Robert C.
United Fund — general
($33,000) see Musson
Charitable Foundation, R. C.
and Katharine M.
United Way ($8,000) see
Amcast Industrial Corp.
United Way — corporate
pledge ($1,435,085) see BP
America Inc.
United Way ($11,250) see
Scott Fetzer Co.
United Way Ashtabula County
($33,000) see Centerior
Energy Corp.
United Way of Central Stark
County — campaign
contribution ($27,000) see
Deuble Foundation, George
H.
United Way, Central Stark
County — operating funds
and community initiative
program ($130,000) see
Hoover Foundation
United Way of Cincinnati
($11,000) see Jarson-Stanley
and Mickey Kaplan
Foundation, Isaac and Esther
United Way Corporate — for
community fund ($148,450)
see Parker Hannifin Corp.
United Way Dayton Area
($215,000) see Mead
Corporation, The
United Way of Erie County
($12,000) see Sandusky
International Inc.
United Way Franklin County
($242,442) see Abbott
Laboratories
United Way of Franklin
County ($57,519) see
Continental Corp.
United Way Franklin County
($18,614) see Andersons,
The
United Way of Franklin
County — local community
fund ($18,535) see Barry
Corp., R. G.
United Way of Franklin
County ($184,800) see
Borden, Inc.
United Way of Franklin
County — for 1993
campaign ($336,000) see
Columbus Dispatch Printing
Co.
United Way Greater Cleveland
($483,000) see Centerior
Energy Corp.
United Way of the Greater
Dayton Area — Venture

grant program ($21,000) see
Tait Foundation, Frank M.
United Way Greater Toledo
($170,000) see Centerior
Energy Corp.
United Way of Lake County
($12,627) see Gould
Electronics Inc.
United Way of Portage County
($103,500) see Sentry
Insurance A Mutual
Company
United Way Richland County
($25,000) see Armco Inc.
United Way Ross County
($76,000) see Mead
Corporation, The
United Way Services
($26,000) see Firman Fund
United Way Services ($3,328)
see Gould Electronics Inc.
United Way Services —
operations ($15,000) see
Mather and William Gwinn
Mather Fund, Elizabeth Ring
United Way Services —
annual support ($32,000) see
Mather Charitable Trust, S.
Livingston
United Way Services
($11,250) see Scott Fetzer
Co.
United Way Services
($11,250) see Scott Fetzer
Co.
United Way Services
($11,250) see Scott Fetzer
Co.
United Way Services —
operations ($12,000) see
South Waite Foundation
United Way Services
($75,000) see Consolidated
Natural Gas Co.
United Way Services
($75,000) see Consolidated
Natural Gas Co.
United Way Services
($75,000) see Consolidated
Natural Gas Co.
United Way Services
($75,000) see Consolidated
Natural Gas Co.
United Way Services
($20,000) see Wheat First
Butcher Singer, Inc.
United Way Services of
Cleveland — unrestricted
($31,000) see Humphrey
Fund, George M. and
Pamela S.
United Way of Summit County
— to provide 1994 funding
for program/services of 53
affiliated agencies and for a
study to answer the question
"Are there more effective
ways for the United Ways of
Summit County and
Barberton to work together
to meet the community
needs?" ($230,000) see
GAR Foundation
United Way Summit County
($60,375) see GenCorp Inc.
United Way of Summit County
($22,000) see McFawn Trust
No. 2, Lois Sisler
United Way Toledo ($165,200)
see Andersons, The
United Way of Trumbull
County ($12,500) see
Freedom Forge Corp.
Univeristy of Akron Musson
Chair — education
($85,000) see Musson
Charitable Foundation, R. C.
and Katharine M.
University of Akron —
educational ($50,000) see
Bemis Company, Inc.
University of Akron ($25,000)
see GenCorp Inc.

University of Akron ($50,000)
see McFawn Trust No. 2,
Lois Sisler
University of Akron
Foundation ($10,500) see
Calhoun Charitable Trust,
Kenneth
University of Akron
Foundation — $1 million to
create the Lisle M.
Buckingham Memorial
Endowment Fund by the
GAR Foundation, the
income from which will be
used for full scholarships for
honors students for tuition
and books based on merit
and financial aid
($1,250,000) see GAR
Foundation
University of Cincinnati
College of Medicine Library
($150,000) see
Jarson-Stanley and Mickey
Kaplan Foundation, Isaac
and Esther
University Circle — capital
campaign ($20,000) see
Firman Fund
University Circle —
endowment fund ($25,000)
see Humphrey Fund, George
M. and Pamela S.
University Circle —
operations ($626,189) see
Mather and William Gwinn
Mather Fund, Elizabeth Ring
University Circle ($500,000)
see Second Foundation
University of Dayton
($475,000) see Kettering
Fund
University Hospitals —
Pediatric Hospital ($30,000)
see Firman Fund
University Hospitals of
Cleveland ($60,000) see
GenCorp Inc.
University Hospitals of
Cleveland — unrestricted
($25,000) see Humphrey
Fund, George M. and
Pamela S.
University Hospitals of
Cleveland — research and
education fund ($25,000)
see Humphrey Fund, George
M. and Pamela S.
University School Library
($33,300) see Kilroy
Foundation, William S. and
Lora Jean
University of Toledo ($61,050)
see Andersons, The
Ursuline College ($100,000)
see Lennon Foundation, Fred
A.
Ursuline Nuns — St. Angela
Health Care Center
construction ($40,000) see
Andrews Foundation
Ursuline Sisters of
Motherhouse ($25,000) see
Kilcawley Fund, William H.
Ursuline Sisters of
Youngstown — for capital
improvement program
($8,333) see Crandall
Memorial Foundation, J.
Ford
Ursuline Sisters of
Youngstown Beatitude
House ($25,000) see
Kilcawley Fund, William H.
Ursuline Sisters of
Youngstown Preschool
Project ($25,000) see
Kilcawley Fund, William H.
Van Wert City Schools —
indigent children ($16,674)
see Van Wert County
Foundation
Van Wert City Schools —
music department ($8,460)

Hospice ($25,000) see Puterbaugh Foundation

Jasmine Moran Children's Museum ($10,000) see Blue Bell, Inc.

Kirk of the Hills Presbyterian ($5,000) see Harmon Foundation, Pearl M. and Julia J.

Lawton Philharmonic Society — support music competition ($25,000) see McMahon Foundation

Lawton Public Schools — support special programs ($30,858) see McMahon Foundation

McAlester Economic Development Council — economic development ($15,750) see Puterbaugh Foundation

McAlester Public Schools Foundation ($33,750) see Puterbaugh Foundation

McAlester United Way ($35,000) see Puterbaugh Foundation

McMahon Memorial Auditorium Authority ($28,593) see McMahon Foundation

Memorial Hospital of Southern Oklahoma ($50,000) see Goddard Foundation, Charles B.

Mental Health Services of S. Oklahoma ($10,000) see Merrick Foundation

Mercy Health Center ($300,000) see McCune Charitable Trust, John R.

Mutual Girls Club — new van ($10,000) see Lyon Foundation

National Cowboy Hall of Fame ($50,000) see OG&E Electric Services

National Cowboy Hall of Fame and Western Heritage Center — Wilson Hurley Triptych western landscape ($500,000) see Noble Foundation, Samuel Roberts

National Cowboy Hall of Fame and Western Heritage Center — support for office of development ($100,000) see Noble Foundation, Samuel Roberts

Neighbor for Neighbor ($15,000) see Zarrow Foundation, Anne and Henry

North Care Mental Health Center ($110,000) see McCune Charitable Trust, John R.

North Tulsa Heritage Foundation — cultural center furnishings ($50,000) see Helmerich Foundation

Northern Oklahoma Youth Services ($3,500) see Beatty Trust, Cordelia Lunceford

Northwestern Oklahoma State University Foundation ($19,000) see Share Trust, Charles Morton

Nowata Historical Society ($5,000) see Harmon Foundation, Pearl M. and Julia J.

Oak Hall Alphabetic Phonics Program ($80,000) see Goddard Foundation, Charles B.

Oak Hall Alphabetic Phonics Program ($25,000) see Goddard Foundation, Charles B.

Oak Hall Episcopal School — building campaign ($100,000) see Goddard Foundation, Charles B.

Oakdale School Foundation ($100,000) see McCune Charitable Trust, John R.

OK Mozart — computer system/laser printer ($7,349) see Lyon Foundation

Oklahoma Arts Institute — McCasland Foundation Scholars Fund ($50,000) see McCasland Foundation

Oklahoma Arts Institute ($5,000) see Share Trust, Charles Morton

Oklahoma Christian University of Science and Arts ($50,000) see OG&E Electric Services

Oklahoma City Community Foundation ($631,500) see Kirkpatrick Foundation

Oklahoma City Economic Development Foundation ($30,000) see OG&E Electric Services

Oklahoma City Metro Alliance for Safer Cities ($25,000) see Kerr Foundation

Oklahoma City Philharmonic Orchestra ($10,584) see American Fidelity Corporation

Oklahoma City Public School Foundation ($12,155) see American Fidelity Corporation

Oklahoma City Public Schools Foundation ($20,500) see Kirkpatrick Foundation

Oklahoma City Public Schools Foundation ($15,000) see OG&E Electric Services

Oklahoma City University ($115,000) see Kerr Foundation

Oklahoma City University ($35,000) see OG&E Electric Services

Oklahoma City University School of Law — building fund ($100,000) see Sumners Foundation, Hatton W.

Oklahoma Department of Public Safety — replace roof on local highway patrol building ($35,630) see McMahon Foundation

Oklahoma Health Center Foundation ($10,000) see Kerr Foundation

Oklahoma Independent Living Resource Center — handicapped citizens self-support program ($30,000) see Puterbaugh Foundation

Oklahoma Lions Club Eye Bank ($15,000) see Share Trust, Charles Morton

Oklahoma Medical Research Foundation ($12,500) see Merrick Foundation

Oklahoma Medical Research Foundation — biomedical research support ($1,414,051) see Noble Foundation, Samuel Roberts

Oklahoma Medical Research Foundation ($25,000) see Puterbaugh Foundation

Oklahoma Special Olympics — building project ($150,000) see Noble Foundation, Samuel Roberts

Oklahoma State Chamber of Commerce and Industry ($10,000) see Merrick Foundation

Oklahoma State University ($10,000) see Reynolds Foundation, Donald W.

Oklahoma State University Foundation — baseball stadium ($150,000) see Helmerich Foundation

Oklahoma State University Foundation ($13,913) see Kerr Foundation

Oklahoma State University Foundation ($12,980) see Kerr Foundation

Oklahoma State University Foundation — Laserscope KTP/532 Fiberoptic System ($75,000) see McCasland Foundation

Oklahoma State University Foundation ($50,000) see OG&E Electric Services

Oklahoma State University Foundation — library program ($37,500) see Puterbaugh Foundation

Oklahoma State University Foundation ($33,334) see Williams Companies, The

Oklahoma University Foundation — Oklahoma Museum of Natural History ($100,000) see McCasland Foundation

Oklahoma University Foundation — Museum of Natural History Building Fund ($100,000) see McCasland Foundation

Oklahoma University Foundation — Catlett Music Building Fund ($100,000) see McCasland Foundation

Oklahoma University Foundation — summer scholars program ($15,000) see Puterbaugh Foundation

Oklahoma Zoological Society ($20,000) see Kirkpatrick Foundation

Omniplex — Investing In Curiosity campaign ($33,333) see McCasland Foundation

Omniplex Science and Arts Museum ($20,000) see American Fidelity Corporation

Operation Aware ($2,000) see Collins Foundation, George and Jennie

Operation Aware ($2,000) see Collins, Jr. Foundation, George Fulton

Panhandle State University — scholarships ($20,000) see Baughman Foundation

Park Friends — police camcorders ($100,000) see Helmerich Foundation

Parkside for New Beginning ($5,000) see Harmon Foundation, Pearl M. and Julia J.

Philbrook Museum of Art ($4,950) see Broadhurst Foundation

Philbrook Museum of Art — building expansion ($25,000) see Collins Foundation, George and Jennie

Philbrook Museum of Art — building expansion ($25,000) see Collins, Jr. Foundation, George Fulton

Philbrook Museum of Art — endowment funds ($1,000,000) see Helmerich Foundation

Phillips Graduate Seminary — scholarship program ($5,000) see Broadhurst Foundation

Pittsburg County Health Department — guidance center program ($25,000) see Puterbaugh Foundation

Planned Parenthood ($20,000) see Kirkpatrick Foundation

Rogers State College — contribution ($7,500) see Oxy USA Inc.

Ronald McDonald House ($25,000) see Kirkpatrick Foundation

St. John Medical Center Foundation — building fund ($10,000) see Oxy USA Inc.

St. John Medical Center Foundation ($30,000) see Williams Companies, The

St. Simeon's Episcopal Home — building expansion for patients with Alzheimers and dementia related illnesses ($25,000) see Collins Foundation, George and Jennie

St. Simeon's Episcopal Home — building addition for patients with Alzheimers and dementia ($25,000) see Collins, Jr. Foundation, George Fulton

Salvation Army — camp fund ($1,000) see Collins Foundation, George and Jennie

Salvation Army ($1,000) see Collins, Jr. Foundation, George Fulton

Salvation Army — capital funds drive ($250,000) see Helmerich Foundation

Salvation Army — addition-challenge grant ($50,000) see Lyon Foundation

Salvation Army — building fund ($15,000) see Oxy USA Inc.

Salvation Army ($10,000) see Zarrow Foundation, Anne and Henry

Salvation Army, Arkansas-Oklahoma Division ($15,000) see Kirkpatrick Foundation

Second Presbyterian Church ($5,000) see Harmon Foundation, Pearl M. and Julia J.

Senior Citizens of Pryor — senior citizen center ($60,000) see Mayor Foundation, Oliver Dewey

Senior Citizens of Pryor — soil test and low-income housing project ($23,500) see Mayor Foundation, Oliver Dewey

Sertoma Handicapped Opportunity Program ($10,000) see Zarrow Foundation, Anne and Henry

Skyline Urban Ministry ($22,000) see Kirkpatrick Foundation

Southeast Area Health Center ($50,000) see Kirkpatrick Foundation

Southern Nazarene University — scholarship program ($7,500) see Broadhurst Foundation

State of Oklahoma Department of Corrections ($200,000) see Share Trust, Charles Morton

Support Center ($25,000) see Avon Products, Inc.

Thomas Gilcrease Museum Association — renovations ($100,000) see Helmerich Foundation

Thomas Gilcrease Museum Association ($51,000) see Williams Companies, The

Town and Country School ($10,000) see Broadhurst Foundation

Town and Country School ($10,000) see Zarrow Foundation, Anne and Henry

Trinity Episcopal Church ($10,000) see Mulford Foundation, Vincent

Tulsa Area United Way — contribution ($100,000) see Oxy USA Inc.

Tulsa Area United Way ($510,463) see Williams Companies, The

Tulsa Ballet Theatre — education program and school program ($10,000) see Oxy USA Inc.

Tulsa Ballet Theatre ($70,000) see Williams Companies, The

Tulsa Center for Physically Limited ($40,000) see Zarrow Foundation, Anne and Henry

Tulsa Education Fund — elementary school capital improvements ($62,500) see Helmerich Foundation

Tulsa Metro Ministry — building fund ($10,000) see Oxy USA Inc.

Tulsa Opera ($5,000) see Harmon Foundation, Pearl M. and Julia J.

Tulsa Performing Arts Center Trust ($30,000) see Williams Companies, The

Tulsa Philharmonic — education program and annual fund ($7,000) see Oxy USA Inc.

Tulsa Philharmonic Society ($8,000) see Mulford Foundation, Vincent

Tulsa Zoo Development ($41,666) see Williams Companies, The

United Way ($37,522) see American Fidelity Corporation

United Way ($35,823) see American Fidelity Corporation

United Way ($108,000) see AMR Corp.

United Way of Ada County ($27,433) see Morrison Knudsen Corporation

United Way of Lawton ($50,000) see McMahon Foundation

United Way Oklahoma City — annual fund ($10,000) see Oxy USA Inc.

United Way of South Central Oklahoma ($15,000) see Merrick Foundation

University of Oklahoma — for Geology and/or Petroleum and Geological Engineering ($50,000) see Unocal Corp.

University of Oklahoma ($7,500) see Reynolds Foundation, Donald W.

University of Oklahoma Foundation ($50,000) see McCormick Foundation, Chauncey and Marion Deering

University of Oklahoma Foundation ($115,000) see Kerr Foundation

University of Oklahoma Foundation — scholarships for Journalism department ($25,000) see McMahon Foundation

University of Oklahoma Foundation ($33,334) see Williams Companies, The

University of Oklahoma Returning Gift Foundation ($25,000) see Bay Foundation

Western Kay Literacy Council ($1,500) see Beatty Trust, Cordelia Lunceford

Westminster Church ($18,000) see American Fidelity Corporation

Westside Community Center — new building on existing

land ($50,000) see Lyon Foundation
Westside YMCA — ropes course and building repairs ($21,050) see Collins Foundation, George and Jennie
Westside YMCA — ropes course and building repairs ($21,050) see Collins, Jr. Foundation, George Fulton
Women and Children in Crisis — child advocacy center ($10,000) see Lyon Foundation
World Neighbors ($25,000) see Valentine Foundation, Lawson
World Neighbors — farmer training, dryland methods in India ($25,000) see International Foundation
World Neighbors ($5,000) see Johnson Foundation, Burdine
World Neighbors — reproductive health activities ($20,000) see Trull Foundation
YMCA ($27,500) see Williams Companies, The
YMCA Metro Tulsa — capital campaign contribution ($15,000) see Oxy USA Inc.
YMCA Second Century Campaign ($50,000) see OG&E Electric Services

Oregon

1,000 Friends of Oregon — capital building project ($20,000) see Tucker Charitable Trust, Rose E.
Albina Ministerial Alliance ($10,000) see Jackson Foundation
American Jewish Community see Piper Jaffray Companies Inc.
American National Red Cross ($10,000) see Jackson Foundation
Assistance League of Salem — Operation School Bell ($1,000) see Pioneer Trust Bank, NA
Beaverton Education Foundation — for education see Washington Mutual Savings Bank
Beaverton United School District ($6,000) see Brenner Foundation, Mervyn
Boy Scouts of America ($7,500) see Jackson Foundation
Boy Scouts of America ($16,000) see Wheeler Foundation
Boy Scouts of America Oregon Trails ($15,000) see Hunt Charitable Trust, C. Giles
Boys and Girls Club ($30,000) see Boise Cascade Corporation
Britt Festivals — in support of Britt Classical Festival ($15,000) see Carpenter Foundation
Campaign for Equal Justice ($15,000) see Tucker Charitable Trust, Rose E.
Center for National Independence in Politics ($5,000) see Memton Fund
CERVS — toward a permanent facility ($15,000) see Carpenter Foundation
Children's Oncology Services — Ronald McDonald house ($12,500) see Wheeler Foundation
Children's Oncology Services of Oregon — for expansion

of Ronald McDonald house ($150,000) see Roseburg Forest Products Co.
City of Roseburg Stewart Park ($12,500) see Hunt Charitable Trust, C. Giles
City of Sutherlin ($8,000) see Hunt Charitable Trust, C. Giles
Concordia College — new science education facilities ($500,000) see Murdock Charitable Trust, M. J.
Crater High School ($2,204) see Sierra Pacific Industries
Craterian Performances Company — toward a regional community and cultural events facility ($25,000) see Carpenter Foundation
Crisis Intervention — toward parenting education for families at high risk of child abuse or neglect ($14,750) see Carpenter Foundation
D.A.R.E. — drug awareness program see Siltec Corp.
Deschutes County Children's Foundation — pledge payment ($25,000) see JELD-WEN, Inc.
Deschutes United Way ($25,000) see JELD-WEN, Inc.
Douglas County Library Foundation ($15,000) see Hunt Charitable Trust, C. Giles
Douglas Education Service District — for mental health therapists for Douglas County Schools ($264,200) see Roseburg Forest Products Co.
Ecotrust — program support ($25,000) see Forest Foundation
Ecumenical Ministries of Oregon — Hopewell House ($100,000) see Collins Foundation
Episcopal Laymen's Mission Society ($7,000) see Jackson Foundation
Fohs Hall — toward outstanding liabilities ($25,000) see Fohs Foundation
Friendly House ($12,500) see Adler Foundation Trust, Philip D. and Henrietta B.
Friendly Kitchen ($100,900) see Hunt Charitable Trust, C. Giles
George Fox College — to support the construction of a new science building ($500,000) see Meyer Memorial Trust
George Fox College ($33,000) see Wheeler Foundation
Gilbert House Children's Museum ($1,000) see Pioneer Trust Bank, NA
Gilbert House Children's Museum see Siltec Corp.
Heart Institute at St. Vincent Hospital ($100,000) see Louisiana-Pacific Corp.
High Desert Museum ($12,000) see OCRI Foundation
Humane Society of the Willamette Valley — building fund ($2,000) see Pioneer Trust Bank, NA
Jesuit High School ($10,000) see Wheeler Foundation
Lebanon Community Hospital ($10,000) see Wheeler Foundation
Lewis and Clark College — signature program

($300,000) see Collins Foundation
Lewis and Clark College — to renovate and expand the Aubrey Watzek Library ($550,000) see Meyer Memorial Trust
Lewis and Clark College — scholarships ($30,000) see Tucker Charitable Trust, Rose E.
Lewis and Clark College ($13,000) see Wheeler Foundation
Linfield College — for debt retirement ($150,000) see Roseburg Forest Products Co.
Linfield College School of Nursing — for JFP Scholarship Fund ($25,000) see Collins Medical Trust
Little League — Basketball/Baseball/Soccer see Siltec Corp.
Lutheran Family Service — building refurbishing ($20,000) see JELD-WEN, Inc.
March of Dimes Birth Defects — general support ($38,650) see MCI Communications Corp.
Marylhurst College ($25,000) see Bay Foundation
Marylhurst College ($20,280) see First Interstate Bank of Oregon
Marylhurst College — for improvements to the library building ($373,000) see Meyer Memorial Trust
Marylhurst College ($12,500) see Wheeler Foundation
Medical Research Foundation of Oregon ($51,567) see Collins Medical Trust
Meridian Park Medical Foundation ($10,000) see Collins Medical Trust
Mid-Columbia Health Foundation — for library grant ($20,000) see Collins Medical Trust
Mid-Columbia Medical Center — video endoscopy system ($92,000) see Wiegand Foundation, E. L.
Mid-Valley Children's Guild — building fund ($1,500) see Pioneer Trust Bank, NA
Middle Oregon Indian Historical Society — permanent exhibit in museum ($150,000) see Collins Foundation
Natural Resources Defense Council ($15,000) see Tucker Charitable Trust, Rose E.
Nature Conservancy — first of two payments toward acquisition of parcel at Lower Table Rock ($15,000) see Carpenter Foundation
Nature Conservancy ($5,000) see Jackson Foundation
OnTrack — toward afterschool program for primary grade students in White City ($25,076) see Carpenter Foundation
Oregon Coast Aquarium — for two years ($10,000) see Jackson Foundation
Oregon Coast Aquarium — expansion ($12,500) see Tucker Charitable Trust, Rose E.
Oregon Community Foundation — for the Dension Family Foundation ($58,500) see Smith Foundation, Ralph L.

Oregon Community Foundation — for Women's Foundation of Oregon Fund ($25,000) see Smith Foundation, Ralph L.
Oregon Conservancy ($50,000) see Georgia-Pacific Corporation
Oregon Food Bank ($6,000) see OCRI Foundation
Oregon Graduate Institute ($30,000) see Gilmore Foundation, William G.
Oregon Graduate Institute — for building renovation and construction of the Center for Lifelong Learning, which will include dining facilities, classrooms, a campus center, office space, and meeting rooms ($500,000) see Meyer Memorial Trust
Oregon Graduate Institute of Science and Technology ($22,000) see First Interstate Bank of Oregon
Oregon Graduate Institute of Science and Technology — new chemical and biological sciences/environmental science and engineering building ($2,000,000) see Murdock Charitable Trust, M. J.
Oregon Health Decisions ($7,000) see Collins Medical Trust
Oregon Health Sciences University Foundation ($20,000) see Collins Medical Trust
Oregon Historical Society — "Trails to Oregon" project ($150,000) see Collins Foundation
Oregon Historical Society ($30,000) see First Interstate Bank of Oregon
Oregon Historical Society — permanent exhibit of Portland history ($12,500) see Tucker Charitable Trust, Rose E.
Oregon Historical Society ($40,000) see Wheeler Foundation
Oregon Independent College Foundation ($90,287) see First Interstate Bank of Oregon
Oregon Independent College Foundation — for general support ($350,000) see Roseburg Forest Products Co.
Oregon Museum of Science and Industry ($22,500) see First Interstate Bank of Oregon
Oregon Museum of Science and Industry — to launch a capital campaign to finance construction of a new state-of-the-art facility on the east bank of the Willamette River ($500,000) see Meyer Memorial Trust
Oregon Museum of Science and Industry Capital Campaign ($100,000) see Louisiana-Pacific Corp.
Oregon Public Broadcasting ($7,000) see OCRI Foundation
Oregon Public Broadcasting ($1,000) see Pioneer Trust Bank, NA
Oregon Public Broadcasting/NOVA ($25,500) see Gilmore Foundation, William G.
Oregon School for the Deaf see Siltec Corp.

Oregon Shakespeare Festival ($25,000) see Skaggs Foundation, L. J. and Mary C.
Oregon Shakespeare Festival ($5,000) see Dalton Foundation, Harry L.
Oregon Shakespeare Festival — underwrite student and senior half-price matinees for Rouge Valley residents ($22,500) see Carpenter Foundation
Oregon Shakespearean Festival — seating pavilion ($100,000) see Collins Foundation
Oregon State University — to support the construction of the Environmental Computing Center to house an advanced computer system and research team for the NASA Earth Observing System project ($575,000) see Meyer Memorial Trust
Oregon State University Foundation — accounting development fund ($5,000) see Brenner Foundation, Mervyn
Oregon State University Foundation ($56,000) see Long Foundation, J.M.
Oregon Symphony — for two years ($7,500) see Jackson Foundation
Oregon Symphony Association — support of assistant resident conductor ($12,500) see Tucker Charitable Trust, Rose E.
OSU Foundation ($40,000) see Vaughn, Jr. Foundation Fund, James M.
Pacific Crest Outward Bound School ($22,500) see Hancock Foundation, Luke B.
Pacific Institute of Natural Sciences — creation of natural history museum ($15,000) see Carpenter Foundation
Pacific Northwest Museum of Natural History — for the development of this new natural history museum ($1,000,000) see Meyer Memorial Trust
Pacific University — science education center ($100,000) see Collins Foundation
Pacific University — new science center ($1,000,000) see Murdock Charitable Trust, M. J.
Portland Christian Schools ($12,000) see OCRI Foundation
Portland Opera Association ($7,500) see Jackson Foundation
Portland State University — honors, scholarships, and development ($19,000) see Tucker Charitable Trust, Rose E.
Portland Youth for Christ ($6,000) see OCRI Foundation
Reed College ($5,000) see AKC Fund
Reed College — for construction of a state-of-the-art chemistry building which will provide laboratories, classrooms, and research space ($500,000) see Meyer Memorial Trust
Rice Hill Rural Fire District ($6,525) see Hunt Charitable Trust, C. Giles

River Network ($500,000) see Anheuser-Busch Companies, Inc.

Roseburg Rescue Mission ($10,000) see Hunt Charitable Trust, C. Giles

Sacred Heart School — building renovation ($34,015) see JELD-WEN, Inc.

St. Mary's Academy of Portland — for building restoration ($400,000) see Meyer Memorial Trust

St. Vincent Medical Foundation — support Center of Excellence in Laser Medicine and Surgery ($150,000) see Collins Foundation

St. Vincent Medical Foundation ($6,500) see Jackson Foundation

St. Vincent Medical Foundation ($15,000) see Wheeler Foundation

Salem Boys and Girls Club see Siltec Corp.

Salem Foundation Friends of Pioneer Cemetery ($1,000) see Pioneer Trust Bank, NA

Salem Public Library Foundation — endow two chairs ($1,500) see Pioneer Trust Bank, NA

Salem Public School see Siltec Corp.

Salem Symphony see Siltec Corp.

Salem Theater-Auditorium Group Enterprise — to purchase and renovate the Elsinore Theater for use as a performing arts center for Salem ($400,000) see Meyer Memorial Trust

Salmon and Trout Enhancement Program ($25,000) see Boise Cascade Corporation

Salvation Army ($7,500) see Jackson Foundation

Shangri La — workshop for the mentally and physically handicapped see Siltec Corp.

SOSC — Faculty Development Scholarship Grant ($20,000) see Carpenter Foundation

Teen Challenge of Oregon Women's Center — construction of new facility ($25,000) see JELD-WEN, Inc.

Tucker-Maxon Oral School — continuing support ($18,000) see Tucker Charitable Trust, Rose E.

Umpqua Community Action Network ($10,000) see Hunt Charitable Trust, C. Giles

Umpqua Community Action Network, Food Shares ($9,000) see Hunt Charitable Trust, C. Giles

Umpqua Community College — for child care facility ($573,890) see Roseburg Forest Products Co.

United Way see Siltec Corp.

United Way Columbia-Willamette ($339,000) see First Interstate Bank of Oregon

United Way of Columbia-Willemette Area ($22,490) see Georgia-Pacific Corporation

United Way of Klamath Basin ($53,000) see JELD-WEN, Inc.

United Way Lane County ($25,085) see First Interstate Bank of Oregon

University of Portland — endowed chair in science ($200,000) see Collins Foundation

University of Portland ($124,570) see Louisiana-Pacific Corp.

University of Portland ($100,000) see Louisiana-Pacific Corp.

Western Biomedical Research — research in multiple sclerosis ($112,542) see Hoover, Jr. Foundation, Margaret W. and Herbert

Willamette University — Collins Legal Center ($500,000) see Collins Foundation

Willamette University — G. Herbert Smith scholarships ($250,000) see Collins Foundation

Willamette University — sesquicentennial campaign ($35,000) see Tucker Charitable Trust, Rose E.

Williamette University — general purposes ($100,000) see Olin Foundation, F. W.

Winston-Dillard Fire District 5 ($5,000) see Hunt Charitable Trust, C. Giles

Women's Crisis Center see Siltec Corp.

Women's Foundation of Oregon ($35,000) see Smith Foundation, Ralph L.

World Forestry Center ($20,000) see Georgia-Pacific Corporation

World Forestry Center ($100,000) see Louisiana-Pacific Corp.

World Forestry Center ($18,000) see Wheeler Foundation

YMCA — support the initiation and construction of day-care services in the Rogue Valley ($15,000) see Carpenter Foundation

Pennsylvania

Abington Memorial Health Care Corporation ($2,500) see Asplundh Foundation

AC Chemical People ($250) see Lebanon Mutual Insurance Co.

Academy Annual Fund ($3,000) see Asplundh Foundation

Academy of Music — anniversary concert and ball and the restoration and preservation fund ($2,410) see Maneely Fund

Academy of Music ($2,225) see Gershman Foundation, Joel

Academy of Music Restoration Fund ($5,000) see Cassett Foundation, Louis N.

Academy of Natural Sciences ($50,000) see Arcadia Foundation

Academy of Natural Sciences ($3,000) see Groome Beatty Trust, Helen D.

Academy of Natural Sciences of Philadelphia — toward building and equipping new Estuarine Research center ($20,000) see Marpat Foundation

Academy of the New Church ($6,000) see Asplundh Foundation

Academy of Vocal Arts see Bryn Mawr Trust Co.

Academy of Vocal Arts ($3,000) see Levitt Foundation

Academy of Vocal Arts ($45,000) see Superior Tube Co.

Aces ($10,000) see Kunkel Foundation, John Crain

Action Housing — development fund ($100,000) see Eden Hall Foundation

ACTION Housing — development fund ($140,000) see Scaife Family Foundation

Adams Memorial Library — for endowment fund ($20,000) see McFeely-Rogers Foundation

Adelphoi —for Human Services Center construction see Aluminum Co. of America

Adelphoi, Inc. ($50,000) see McKenna Foundation, Katherine Mabis

Agricultural and Industrial Museum — for community service ($5,000) see Dentsply International Inc.

Akiba Hebrew Academy — to provide funding for Science and Technology Initiative to apply computers and high technology in a variety of disciplines for its students, administration, and faculty ($15,000) see Huston Charitable Trust, Stewart

Alanon Association — building fund ($10,000) see Kunkel Foundation, John Crain

Alanon Association — renovations to fellowship house ($10,000) see Wells Foundation, Franklin H. and Ruth L.

Alcohol/Drug Help Others — prevention/education ($500) see Snayberger Memorial Foundation, Harry E. and Florence W.

All Souls Church ($5,000) see Cassett Foundation, Louis N.

All Souls Episcopal Church ($1,000) see Peters Foundation, Charles F.

Allegheny College — campuswide communication network ($100,000) see Buhl Foundation

Allegheny College — construction costs for Hall of Biology ($100,000) see Wells Foundation, Franklin H. and Ruth L.

Allegheny Conference on Community Development ($15,000) see Aristech Chemical Corp.

Allegheny Conference on Community Development ($15,000) see Clapp Charitable and Educational Trust, George H.

Allegheny Conference on Community Development ($500) see Edgewater Steel Corp.

Allegheny Conference on Community Development ($25,000) see Giant Eagle, Inc.

Allegheny Conference on Community Development — support for emerging international city ($25,000) see Laurel Foundation

Allegheny Conference of Community Development ($20,000) see Mine Safety Appliances Co.

Allegheny Conference on Community Development — general contribution ($33,333) see PNC Bank, N.A.

Allegheny Council to Improve Our Neighborhoods-Housing — recapitalize development fund ($1,000,000) see Mellon Foundation, Richard King

Allegheny County Community College — for capital campaign ($50,000) see PPG Industries, Inc.

Allegheny County League of Women Voters see Aluminum Co. of America

Allegheny Highlands Regional Theater ($8,000) see Kavanagh Foundation, T. James

Allegheny Lutheran Home ($4,000) see Waters Charitable Trust, Robert S.

Allegheny Singer Research Institute — research grant to evaluate the Family Growth Center Pilot Project which supports young mothers with first-born babies ($10,318) see Pittsburgh Child Guidance Foundation

Allegheny Trails Council ($5,000) see Pitt-Des Moines Inc.

Allegheny Valley Hospital Sponsoring Committee ($30,000) see Allegheny Ludlum Corp.

Allegheny Valley School — sprinkler system for group homes ($135,000) see Eden Hall Foundation

Allegheny Valley School ($60,000) see Jennings Foundation, Mary Hillman

Allegheny Valley School — capital campaign ($75,000) see Trees Charitable Trust, Edith L.

Allegheny Valley Trails Association ($15,000) see Justus Trust, Edith C.

Allegheny Valley Trails Association ($5,000) see Justus Trust, Edith C.

Allentown Area Food Bank ($5,000) see Baker Foundation, Dexter F. and Dorothy H.

Allentown Art Museum ($50,000) see Payne Foundation, Frank E. and Seba B.

Allentown Art Museum ($40,000) see Holt Family Foundation

Allentown College of St. Francis de Sales — toward scholarships ($55,000) see Trexler Trust, Harry C.

Allentown Public Library ($1,000) see Holt Family Foundation

Allentown Public Library — cost of addition ($66,000) see Trexler Trust, Harry C.

Allied Arts Fund ($20,000) see AMP Incorporated

Allied Jewish Appeal ($10,000) see Kardon Foundation, Samuel and Rebecca

ALS and Neuromuscular Research Center ($50,000) see Hedco Foundation

ALS and Neuromuscular Research Center ($30,000) see Hedco Foundation

Alzheimers Disease and Related Disorders Association — support startup of an adult day care program in the Allegheny River corridor in partnership with NAMSC, Department of Aging, and the Alzheimer Association ($75,000) see Jewish Healthcare Foundation of Pittsburgh

American Cancer Society —for "Bridging the Gap, Cancer and the Poor" project see Aluminum Co. of America

American Cancer Society ($15,000) see Clapp Charitable and Educational Trust, George H.

American Cancer Society ($525) see GSM Industrial

American Cancer Society — for medical purposes ($6,000) see McCormick Trust, Anne

American Cancer Society — cancer research ($2,000) see Patterson Charitable Fund, W. I.

American Cancer Society — support of service and rehabilitation programs ($10,000) see Phillips Charitable Trust, Dr. and Mrs. Arthur William

American Cancer Society — Hanover Branch ($2,000) see Sheppard Foundation, Lawrence B.

American Friends of Hebrew University ($20,000) see Stone Charitable Foundation

American Friends Service Committee ($27,000) see Valentine Foundation, Lawson

American Friends Service Committee — rice integrated farming systems in Laso ($40,918) see Reynolds Foundation, Christopher

American Heart Association see Integra Bank of Uniontown

American Heart Association — cardivascular research and educational programs ($10,000) see Phillips Charitable Trust, Dr. and Mrs. Arthur William

American Interfaith Institute ($2,500) see Chazen Foundation

American Red Cross see Bryn Mawr Trust Co.

American Red Cross ($25,000) see Elf Atochem North America, Inc.

American Red Cross ($7,500) see Hulme Charitable Foundation, Milton G.

American Red Cross ($2,000) see Plankenhorn Foundation, Harry

American Red Cross Disaster Relief Fund — flood disaster relief ($100,000) see Eden Hall Foundation

American Red Cross Hanover Chapter ($2,000) see Sheppard Foundation, Lawrence B.

American Red Cross Lawrence County ($10,000) see Hoyt Foundation

American Rescue Workers ($1,500) see LamCo. Communications

American Rescue Workers — offset deficit in general operating fund ($10,000) see Plankenhorn Foundation, Harry

American Society of Ancient Instruments ($15,000) see North Shore Foundation

American Waterways Wind Orchestra —for joint

performance with Harmonie Drunen see Aluminum Co. of America

American Wind Symphony ($4,100) see Freedom Forge Corp.

American Zionist Fund, Pittsburgh Zionist District and Tri-State Zionist Region ($8,000) see Giant Eagle, Inc.

Andrew Kaul Memorial Hospital ($14,955) see Stackpole-Hall Foundation

Annenberg Research Institute ($2,000,000) see Annenberg Foundation

Annville Free Library ($500) see Lebanon Mutual Insurance Co.

ARC Allegheny County — camping sessions and respite services ($240,000) see Trees Charitable Trust, Edith L.

ARC-Allegheny Foundation see USX Corporation

ARC Westmoreland Chapter — parent support services department ($65,000) see Trees Charitable Trust, Edith L.

Arnold Volunteer Fire Department see Aluminum Co. of America

Arsenal Family and Children's Center — conduct two programs for children ages zero to three ($27,345) see Pittsburgh Child Guidance Foundation

Ashland Trusts — Helping Hand ($21,000) see Reidler Foundation

ASPIRA ($5,000) see Douty Foundation

Assumption Church ($10,000) see Murphy Co. Foundation, G.C.

Athenaeum ($3,000) see Groome Beatty Trust, Helen D.

Athenaeum of Philadelphia ($80,000) see Barra Foundation

Atwater Kent Museum — education program ($40,000) see Kent-Lucas Foundation

Auberle Home ($12,500) see Murphy Co. Foundation, G.C.

Auberle Home ($1,000) see Peters Foundation, Charles F.

Bach Choir of Bethlehem ($5,000) see South Branch Foundation

Baum School of Art — challenge grant to eliminate all mortgage debt ($55,000) see Trexler Trust, Harry C.

Bedford County Regional Campus see Integra Bank of Uniontown

Beginning with Books — for gift book program ($7,500) see Miller Charitable Foundation, Howard E. and Nell E.

Beginnings Child Early Intervention ($2,000) see Glosser Foundation, David A.

Belleville Mennonite School ($2,000) see Freedom Forge Corp.

Benedictine Sisters — purchase industrial dryer and dining room tables and chairs ($4,000) see Kavanagh Foundation, T. James

Benzinger Township — defray expenses incurred by city transition committee

($22,275) see Stackpole-Hall Foundation

Berks Education Coalition — education improvement initiative ($25,000) see Wyomissing Foundation

Berks Festivals — sponsor of 1993 Sparks River Days ($70,000) see Wyomissing Foundation

Beth Sholom Congregation ($1,000) see Glosser Foundation, David A.

Beth Sholom Congregation Religious School ($400) see Glosser Foundation, David A.

Bethesda Mission ($11,000) see Harsco Corp.

Betsy Ross House Foundation ($7,000) see Kent-Lucas Foundation

Better Homes, Inc. of Bucks County — purchase and rehabilitate low-income housing (Towpath Apartments) in Morrisville ($50,000) see Grundy Foundation

Better Housing for Chester ($20,000) see Smith Memorial Fund, Ethel Sergeant Clark

Biblical Theological Seminary ($1,000) see Rixson Foundation, Oscar C.

Biblical Theological Seminary — build library ($26,000) see Huston Foundation

Big Brothers and Big Sisters — over four years to develop training programs for executive staff and board members to increase participation of minority volunteers and staff ($1,782,988) see Wallace-Reader's Digest Fund, DeWitt

Big Brothers and Big Sisters of Beaver County — on campus mentoring relationships between college students in Beaver County and children from single-parent households ($6,733) see Pittsburgh Child Guidance Foundation

Big Sisters of Philadelphia ($3,000) see Groome Beatty Trust, Helen D.

Borough of Bristol — improvements to Riverfront Park Wharf ($26,000) see Grundy Foundation

Borough of Bristol, CZM — rehabilitate Mill Street Wharf structure ($36,000) see Grundy Foundation

Borough of Rimersburg — sewage system lagoons ($3,874) see Eccles Foundation, Ralph M. and Ella M.

Boy Scouts of America ($5,000) see Binswanger Cos.

Boy Scouts of America ($13,934) see Dynamet, Inc.

Boy Scouts of America ($500) see GSM Industrial

Boy Scouts of America — for 1993 grant ($56,101) see Mengle Foundation, Glenn and Ruth

Boy Scouts of America Allegheny Trails Council ($15,000) see Aristech Chemical Corp.

Boy Scouts of America Hawk Mountain Council ($1,500) see Snayberger Memorial Foundation, Harry E. and Florence W.

Boy Scouts of America Lancaster-Lebanon Council ($9,000) see Hamilton Bank

Boy Scouts of America Minsi Trails Council — for capital improvements to camp Trexler ($70,000) see Trexler Trust, Harry C.

Boy Scouts of America Westmoreland Fayette Council — for new Exploring executive position ($15,000) see McFeely-Rogers Foundation

Boys Club of Harrisburg ($9,250) see Harsco Corp.

Boys Club of Harrisburg — expansion and renovations ($20,000) see Kline Foundation, Josiah W. and Bessie H.

Boys and Girls Club ($15,000) see Schoenleber Foundation

Boys and Girls Club of Lancaster — camping facility ($10,000) see High Foundation

Boys and Girls Club of Western Pennsylvania ($15,000) see Clapp Charitable and Educational Trust, George H.

Boys and Girls Clubs Western Pennsylvania ($30,000) see PPG Industries, Inc.

Bradford Hospital ($30,000) see Dresser Industries, Inc.

Bradford Regional Medical Center — for building fund ($20,000) see Forest Oil Corp.

Brandywine Conservancy — conservation easement program ($200,000) see Welfare Foundation

Brandywine Museum ($11,550) see Philibosian Foundation, Stephen

Breachmenders ($15,000) see Miller Charitable Foundation, Howard E. and Nell E.

Bristol Riverside Theater — to support the 1992-93 season's operating budget and expand marketing activity ($80,000) see Grundy Foundation

BRSI Beaumont ($25,000) see Lovett Foundation

Bryn Athyn Church Building fund ($4,500) see Asplundh Foundation

Bryn Athyn Church of the New Jerusalem ($152,000) see Asplundh Foundation

Bryn Mawr Beautification Plan see Bryn Mawr Trust Co.

Bryn Mawr College — professorship in science and public policy ($280,000) see Clowes Fund

Bryn Mawr College ($250,000) see Neuberger Foundation, Roy R. and Marie S.

Bryn Mawr College — scholarship fund ($25,000) see Fohs Foundation

Bryn Mawr College ($10,000) see Warwick Foundation

Bryn Mawr College campaign for Bryn Mawr ($7,500) see Memton Fund

Bryn Mawr Hospital ($90,000) see Superior Tube Co.

Bryn Mawr Hospital Foundation ($10,000) see Lovett Foundation

Bryn Mawr Rehabilitation — for purchase of Eye Gaze computer equipment for on-site diagnostic evaluation of patients ($15,000) see

Huston Charitable Trust, Stewart

Bucknell University — summer program ($10,000) see Wells Foundation, Franklin H. and Ruth L.

Bucks County Association of Retired and Senior Citizens — repairs to kitchen and dining room of Lower Bucks Activity Center ($50,000) see Grundy Foundation

Bucks County Audubon Society — to acquire 88 acres of land from PECO for conservation ($25,000) see Grundy Foundation

Bucks County Community College School of Nursing — fellowship program ($200,000) see Independence Foundation

Bucks County Historical Society — capital campaign ($80,000) see Warwick Foundation

Bucks County Historical Society ($10,000) see Warwick Foundation

Buffalo Valley Lutheran Village ($25,000) see Sheary for Charity, Edna M.

Bunker Challenge ($6,000) see Edgewater Steel Corp.

Butler Public Library ($2,000) see Spang & Co.

Buxmont Jewish Appeal — for Operation Exodus ($3,000) see Clemens Markets Corp.

California Senior Care ($5,000) see Coen Family Foundation, Charles S. and Mary

Calvary Episcopal Church ($60,000) see Love Foundation, George H. and Margaret McClintic

Cambodian Association of Greater Philadelphia ($5,000) see Douty Foundation

Cambria Free Library — educational ($4,000) see Waters Charitable Trust, Robert S.

Camp Hill Public Library ($10,000) see Kunkel Foundation, John Crain

Camp Mt. Luther Corporation — building ($100,000) see Sheary for Charity, Edna M.

Camp Spears-Eljabar YMCA — cabin renovations and aid for youth programs ($49,000) see Vernon Fund, Miles Hodson

Camphill Foundation ($56,160) see Smart Family Foundation

Camphill Special Schools ($10,000) see Lazarus Charitable Trust, Helen and Charles

Camphill Village ($12,000) see Bard Foundation, Robert

Canonsburg General Hospital Foundation ($5,000) see Coen Family Foundation, Charles S. and Mary

Capital Cultural Campaign ($30,000) see AMP Incorporated

Capital Cultural Campaign — for charitable purposes, second pledge payment ($5,000) see McCormick Trust, Anne

CARE Center — new program focused on parenting skills for adults recovering from drug and alcohol addiction ($5,000) see Pittsburgh Child Guidance Foundation

Carlow College ($10,000) see Aristech Chemical Corp.

The Carnegie ($52,500) see Allegheny Ludlum Corp.

Carnegie ($20,000) see Aristech Chemical Corp.

Carnegie ($1,000) see Edgewater Steel Corp.

Carnegie — for support of programs ($5,000) see Fair Oaks Foundation, Inc.

Carnegie — Hall of African Wildlife ($35,000) see Hunt Foundation, Roy A.

Carnegie — capital campaign ($25,000) see Hunt Foundation, Roy A.

The Carnegie — support Powdermill Nature Reserve ($45,000) see Laurel Foundation

The Carnegie ($50,000) see Mine Safety Appliances Co.

The Carnegie — general contribution ($93,750) see PNC Bank, N.A.

The Carnegie — for capital ($100,000) see PPG Industries, Inc.

Carnegie — Second Century fund ($1,000,000) see Scaife Family Foundation

Carnegie Free Library ($40,000) see Crawford Estate, E. R.

Carnegie Free Library of McKeesport ($1,000) see Peters Foundation, Charles F.

Carnegie Institute — expansion of Pittsburgh Wayfinding Project ($381,250) see Buhl Foundation

Carnegie Institute ($15,000) see Clapp Charitable and Educational Trust, George H.

Carnegie Institute — scientific research organization ($5,000) see Dynamet, Inc.

Carnegie Institute — scientific research organization ($5,000) see Dynamet, Inc.

Carnegie Institute ($200,000) see Heinz Company, H. J.

Carnegie Institute — towards the capital campaign Second Century Fund ($1,000,000) see Heinz Endowment, Howard

Carnegie Institute, Museum of Art — in support of the Andy Warhol Museum ($850,000) see Heinz Endowment, Vira I.

Carnegie Institute, Museum of Art — in support of the Andy Warhol Museum ($800,000) see Heinz Endowment, Vira I.

Carnegie Institute Second Century Fund ($4,000) see Pitt-Des Moines Inc.

Carnegie Library ($15,000) see Clapp Charitable and Educational Trust, George H.

Carnegie Library ($8,000) see Murphy Co. Foundation, G.C.

Carnegie Library of Homestead ($77,000) see Allegheny Foundation

Carnegie Library of Pittsburgh ($10,000) see Hunt Foundation

Carnegie Library of Pittsburgh see Neville Chemical Co.

Carnegie Library of Pittsburgh ($23,335) see Patterson Charitable Fund, W. I.

Carnegie Mellon University ($8,000) see M/A-COM, Inc.

Carnegie Mellon University ($100,000) see Merck & Co.

Carnegie Mellon University ($20,000) see CS First Boston Corporation

Carnegie Mellon University ($50,000) see Evans Foundation, T. M.

Carnegie Mellon University ($15,000) see Witco Corp.

Carnegie Mellon University ($12,500) see Aristech Chemical Corp.

Carnegie Mellon University ($20,000) see Armco Inc.

Carnegie Mellon University — Journey to the Center of the Cell Project ($150,000) see Buhl Foundation

Carnegie Mellon University ($15,000) see Foster Charitable Trust

Carnegie Mellon University ($165,000) see Heinz Company, H. J.

Carnegie Mellon University — endowment for Botanical Institute ($958,958) see Hunt Foundation

Carnegie Mellon University — support for Center for the Neural Basis of Cognition ($1,500,000) see Mellon Foundation, Richard King

Carnegie Mellon University — toward cost of an addition to the Graduate School of Industrial Administration Building ($1,000,000) see Mellon Foundation, Richard King

Carnegie Mellon University — for chemistry ($50,000) see PPG Industries, Inc.

Carnegie Mellon University — for employee scholarship ($4,000) see Quaker Chemical Corp.

Carnegie Mellon University ($20,000) see Speyer Foundation, Alexander C. and Tillie S.

Carnegie Mellon University Graduate School of Industrial Administration —for education ($7,500) see Air Products and Chemicals, Inc.

Carnegie-Mellon University Hunt Institute — operation support for Botanical Institute ($50,000) see Hunt Foundation, Roy A.

Carnegie-Mellon University Hunt Institute — operation support for Botanical Institute ($50,000) see Hunt Foundation, Roy A.

Carnegie-Mellon University Hunt Institute — operation support for Botanical Institute ($50,000) see Hunt Foundation, Roy A.

Carnegie-Mellon University Hunt Institute — operation support for Botanical Institute ($50,000) see Hunt Foundation, Roy A.

Carnegie Mellon University, School of Computer Science — to continue research on computer-based models of cognition and interactive media ($152,767) see Markle Foundation, John and Mary R.

Carnegie Museum of Art ($1,500,000) see Heinz Trust, Drue

Carnegie Museum of Art ($1,500,000) see Heinz Trust, Drue

Carnegie Museum of Art ($1,204,000) see Heinz Trust, Drue

Carnegie Museum of Natural History — three-year pledge, toward purchase of mineral specimens and developing new and

refurbishing existing mineral exhibits in Hillman Hall of Minerals and Gems ($110,600) see Hillman Foundation

Carnegie Second Century Fund ($25,000) see Foster Charitable Trust

Carnegie Second Century Fund ($100,000) see Jennings Foundation, Mary Hillman

Carnegie Second Century Fund ($5,000) see Love Foundation, George H. and Margaret McClintic

Cathedral Church of the Nativity — capital improvements ($100,000) see Payne Foundation, Frank E. and Seba B.

Catholic Diocese of Allentown — scholarship fund ($45,000) see Stabler Foundation, Donald B. and Dorothy L.

Catholic Diocese of Harrisburg — scholarship fund ($45,000) see Stabler Foundation, Donald B. and Dorothy L.

Catholic Life 2000 — general support ($4,000) see Maneely Fund

Cedar Crest College ($50,000) see Arcadia Foundation

Cedar Crest College — scholarships ($75,000) see Trexler Trust, Harry C.

Cedar Crest Rodale Aquatic Center — social welfare ($5,000) see Lebovitz Fund

Center for Alternative Learning — support activities ($50,000) see McLean Contributionship

Center for Autistic Children ($3,000) see Binswanger Cos.

Central Pennsylvania Youth Ballet — support of the arts ($1,000) see Pennsylvania Dutch Co.

Central Philadelphia Development ($2,500) see Mutual Assurance Co.

Central Philadelphia Development Corporation — Avenue of the Arts corridor project ($41,000) see Barra Foundation

Chambersburg Area United Way ($13,000) see Wood Foundation of Chambersburg, PA

Chambersburg Hospital Health Services ($20,000) see Wood Foundation of Chambersburg, PA

Channel 39 —for Scholastic Scrimmage Awards ($6,000) see Air Products and Chemicals, Inc.

Chatham College ($15,000) see Clapp Charitable and Educational Trust, George H.

Chemical Dependency Grant — support second year of chemical dependency program at Taylor Allderdice and Mt. Lebanon high schools ($205,000) see Jewish Healthcare Foundation of Pittsburgh

Chester County 4-H — YEPCC ($15,000) see Fair Play Foundation

Chester County Historical Society — history/resource ($50,000) see Barra Foundation

Chester Education Foundation ($10,000) see Smith Memorial Fund, Ethel Sergeant Clark

Chestnut Hill Academy ($5,000) see Levitt Foundation

Chestnut Hill Hospital HealthCare ($250,000) see Barra Foundation

Children's Advocacy Center ($7,000) see Hoyt Foundation

Children's Crisis Treatment Center ($3,000) see Teleflex Inc.

Children's Hospital ($500) see Edgewater Steel Corp.

Children's Hospital ($1,494) see Spang & Co.

Children's Hospital Department of Adolescent Medicine ($5,000) see Douty Foundation

Children's Hospital Foundation — to furnish and equip a new pediatric research building at Children's Hospital of Philadelphia ($1,000,000) see Pew Charitable Trusts

Children's Hospital of Philadelphia — The Campaign for CHOP ($25,000) see Kent-Lucas Foundation

Children's Hospital of Pittsburgh — to design and implement Preventing Childhood injuries, a health education curriculum for children ($210,000) see Benedum Foundation, Claude Worthington

Children's Hospital of Pittsburgh ($20,000) see Clapp Charitable and Educational Trust, George H.

Children's Hospital of Pittsburgh — scientific charity - handicapped children research ($5,000) see Dynamet, Inc.

Children's Hospital of Pittsburgh ($20,000) see Mine Safety Appliances Co.

Children's Hospital of Pittsburgh — over three years, family advocate program ($97,500) see Staunton Farm Foundation

Children's House — teachers enrichment and childrens cultural enrichment programs ($3,000) see Maneely Fund

Children's Literacy Institute — for follow-up training sessions at Sumner and Forest Hills Schools ($7,000) see Subaru of America Inc.

Choices Pregnancy Options Center — salary for two part-time people ($20,000) see Huston Foundation

Christ Church Hospital — to provide independent living for senior citizens ($500,000) see Penn Foundation, William

Christ Soul Saving Station ($1,000) see Peters Foundation, Charles F.

Christian Concern ($25,000) see Arcadia Foundation

Christian Home ($4,000) see Waters Charitable Trust, Robert S.

Christy Park United Methodist Church ($1,000) see Peters Foundation, Charles F.

Church of the Assumption, B.V.M. — construction ($100,000) see Payne Foundation, Frank E. and Seba B.

Church of the Covenant ($7,000) see Coen Family

Foundation, Charles S. and Mary

Church Farm School ($3,000) see Breyer Foundation

Church of the Mediator ($3,500) see Holt Family Foundation

Circle C Group Homes ($5,000) see Miller Charitable Foundation, Howard E. and Nell E.

Cities in Schools in Fayette County see Integra Bank of Uniontown

Citizens Crime Commission see Berwind Corporation

Citizens Library ($12,500) see Coen Family Foundation, Charles S. and Mary

Citizens Library ($40,000) see Hopwood Charitable Trust, John M.

City of Allentown — for the improvement, extension, and maintenance of all city parks ($594,709) see Trexler Trust, Harry C.

City of Harrisburg — memorial park ($368,920) see Kunkel Foundation, John Crain

City of Oil City Heritage Society ($15,000) see Justus Trust, Edith C.

City Theater ($10,000) see Miller Charitable Foundation, Howard E. and Nell E.

City of Uniontown Redevelopment Authority ($64,700) see Eberly Foundation

City of Warren ($4,319) see Betts Industries

Civic Light Opera Association —general support ($3,000) see Patterson Charitable Fund, W. I.

Clarion University of Pennsylvania ($20,000) see Wilson Foundation, H. W.

Clearview Terrace II ($2,500) see Sheppard Foundation, Lawrence B.

Clelian Heights Schools — remove and replace boilers and pumps, refurbish playground ($118,478) see Trees Charitable Trust, Edith L.

Cognitive Therapy — endowment ($250,000) see Independence Foundation

Collaboration for West Philadelphia Schools ($5,000) see Douty Foundation

Collegiate Museum of Art ($43,000) see Sordoni Foundation

Colonial Pennsylvania Plantation ($10,000) see Smith Memorial Fund, Ethel Sergeant Clark

Committee for Economic Growth ($5,000) see Sordoni Foundation

Commonwealth Foundation of Public Policy Alternatives ($85,000) see McKenna Foundation, Philip M.

Commonwealth Service Corps — intern coordinator ($15,000) see Wells Foundation, Franklin H. and Ruth L.

Community Care — health care services ($5,000) see National Forge Co.

Community College of Allegheny County ($15,000) see Crawford Estate, E. R.

Community College of Allegheny County — general contribution

($50,000) see PNC Bank, N.A.

Community College of Philadelphia School of Nursing — endowed nursing chair ($400,000) see Independence Foundation

Community College of Philadelphia School of Nursing — fellowship grant ($200,000) see Independence Foundation

Community Education Center ($5,000) see Douty Foundation

Community Foundation of Greater Johnstown ($1,000) see Glosser Foundation, David A.

Community Human Services Corporation — replicate the program, Families Facing the Future in Bedford Dwellings, Pittsburgh ($66,980) see Pittsburgh Child Guidance Foundation

Community Services of Venango County ($20,000) see Justus Trust, Edith C.

Conamough Valley Hospital ($4,500) see Waters Charitable Trust, Robert S.

Conestoga House Foundation ($483,056) see Steinman Foundation, James Hale

Congregation Adath Jeshurun ($10,000) see Superior Tube Co.

Congregation Rodelph Shalom ($5,000) see Cassett Foundation, Louis N.

Conservation Center for Art and Historic Artifacts — over three years to help museums develop disaster and response plans and provide related information and services ($435,909) see Penn Foundation, William

Conservation Company ($24,000) see Dun & Bradstreet Corp.

Corporate Alliance for Drug Education — general operating for substance abuse prevention programs ($2,500) see Subaru of America Inc.

County of Lehigh — for campaign to construct the Sports Field of Lehigh County ($77,000) see Trexler Trust, Harry C.

Cross Trainers ($15,000) see Miller Charitable Foundation, Howard E. and Nell E.

Cumberland Valley Mental Health — deck installation ($76,356) see Wood Foundation of Chambersburg, PA

Curtis Institute of Music ($800) see Gershman Foundation, Joel

Curtis Institute of Music ($14,000) see Kardon Foundation, Samuel and Rebecca

David A. Glosser Memorial Library ($10,000) see Glosser Foundation, David A.

Delaware County Community College School of Nursing — fellowship grant ($200,000) see Independence Foundation

Delaware Valley College ($4,000) see Kavanagh Foundation, T. James

Delco Blind/Sight Center ($25,000) see Smith Memorial Fund, Ethel Sergeant Clark

Dickinson College — land development ($50,000) see Kline Foundation, Josiah W. and Bessie H.

Dickinson School of Law ($35,000) see Vale Foundation, Ruby R.

Domestic Abuse Project of Delaware County ($25,000) see Smith Memorial Fund, Ethel Sergeant Clark

Drexel University ($48,000) see Muchnic Foundation

Drexel University — undergraduate engineering ($105,000) see du Pont de Nemours & Co., E. I.

Drug and Alcohol Abuse Services — elementary school pilot program ($26,090) see Stackpole-Hall Foundation

DuBois Area United Way — for 1993 grant ($20,000) see Mengle Foundation, Glenn and Ruth

DuBois Area YMCA — for 1993 grant ($38,000) see Mengle Foundation, Glenn and Ruth

DuBois Area YMCA Endowment Fund — for 1993 grant ($20,000) see Mengle Foundation, Glenn and Ruth

DuBois Regional Medical Center — for 1993 grant ($61,000) see Mengle Foundation, Glenn and Ruth

Duquesne University ($110,000) see Heinz Company, H. J.

Easter Seal Society ($5,000) see Spang & Co.

Easter Seal Society ($16,667) see Wood Foundation of Chambersburg, PA

Eccles-Lesher Memorial Library ($66,515) see Eccles Foundation, Ralph M. and Ella M.

Eisenhower Exchange Fellowships — for scholarships and fellowships ($30,000) see Johnson & Son, S.C.

Elizabethtown College — library ($150,000) see High Foundation

Elizabethtown College — construction of new library ($50,000) see Kline Foundation, Josiah W. and Bessie H.

Elizabethtown College — library fund ($10,000) see Stabler Foundation, Donald B. and Dorothy L.

Elizabethtown College ($75,000) see Steinman Foundation, John Frederick

Elk County Christian High School — computer lab ($15,000) see Stackpole-Hall Foundation

Elk County Development Foundation — provide low interest loans for job creation ($150,000) see Stackpole-Hall Foundation

Ellis School ($4,000) see Waters Charitable Trust, Robert S.

Emlenton United Methodist Church — assist in establishing a parking lot ($12,700) see Phillips Charitable Trust, Dr. and Mrs. Arthur William

Ephrata Public Library ($1,500) see GSM Industrial

Episcopal Academy ($20,000) see Mandeville Foundation

Episcopal Academy, Merion Campus — equip a library/resource center and implement a program in environmental studies ($50,000) see McLean Contributionship

Episcopal Diocese of Northwest Pennsylvania ($37,388) see Stackpole-Hall Foundation

Esperanza Health Center — helping the Hispanic community with all phases of health care ($30,000) see Huston Foundation

Evangelical Community Hospital — building ($102,655) see Sheary for Charity, Edna M.

Evangelical Congregational Church ($1,000) see Peters Foundation, Charles F.

Executive Service Corps of Delaware Valley ($10,000) see Superior Tube Co.

Exodus — meet the health care needs of Soviet immigrants ($200,000) see Jewish Healthcare Foundation of Pittsburgh

Extra Mile Education Foundation — library facilities ($70,000) see Allegheny Foundation

Extra Mile Education Foundation — Crossroads scholarship fund ($50,000) see Allegheny Foundation

Extra Mile Education Foundation — endowment fund ($375,000) see Eden Hall Foundation

Extra Mile Education Foundation ($10,000) see Miller Charitable Foundation, Howard E. and Nell E.

Extra Mile Education Foundation — scholarship fund for inter-city elementary schools ($200,000) see Scaife Family Foundation

Eye and Ear Institute of Pittsburgh ($50,000) see Jennings Foundation, Mary Hillman

Fairmont Park Commission ($3,215) see Binswanger Cos.

Faith Presbyterian Church — building fund ($10,000) see Stabler Foundation, Donald B. and Dorothy L.

Family and Children's Services ($10,000) see McCormick Trust, Anne

Family Communication — for special projects fund ($33,000) see McFeely-Rogers Foundation

Family Hospice ($3,750) see Miller Charitable Foundation, Howard E. and Nell E.

Family House — charitable organizations for terminally ill patients ($17,500) see Dynamet, Inc.

Family Life Institute of North Central — operational ($42,000) see Sheary for Charity, Edna M.

Family Life Institute of Northeast Pennsylvania — family wellness project ($10,000) see Plankenhorn Foundation, Harry

Family Resources — replicate an existing successful program, From Birth to Five, in two new communities by training volunteers to conduct the program ($10,000) see Pittsburgh Child Guidance Foundation

Family Service Association of Wyoming Valley ($2,000) see Sordoni Foundation

Family Services of Montgomery County — Meals on Wheels ($20,000) see Bard Foundation, Robert

Family Social Services ($5,000) see Waters Charitable Trust, Robert S.

Family Support Services — over two years for a child abuse and violence prevention program in communities and child care centers ($333,270) see Penn Foundation, William

Fay-Penn Economic Development Corporation ($100,000) see Eberly Foundation

Fay-Penn Economic Development Corporation ($100,000) see Eberly Foundation

Federation of Allied Jewish Appeal ($15,000) see Cassett Foundation, Louis N.

First Baptist Church Lansdale — for building fund ($5,000) see Clemens Markets Corp.

First Presbyterian Church — final organ ($10,000) see Hoyt Foundation

First Presbyterian Church of Allentown — support local church ($56,000) see Baker Foundation, Dexter F. and Dorothy H.

Forbes Fund — towards the establishment of the Forbes Fund on a permanent basis ($1,250,000) see Heinz Endowment, Howard

Forbes Fund — to establish the Forbes Fund on a permanent basis ($750,000) see Heinz Endowment, Vira I.

Ft. Hunter Mansion ($10,000) see Kunkel Foundation, John Crain

Ft. Ligonier Association — purchase of a portrait of General Sir John St. Clair ($45,000) see Mellon Family Foundation, R. K.

Foundation for Independent Colleges ($1,600) see Betts Industries

Foundation for Independent Colleges ($1,500) see LamCo. Communications

Foundation for Independent Colleges — better communication and understanding between business community and independent higher education ($2,000) see National Forge Co.

Foundation for Independent Colleges — area college support ($3,000) see Patterson Charitable Fund, W. I.

Foundation of Independent Colleges of Pennsylvania ($2,500) see Pitt-Des Moines Inc.

Foundation for Reading Area Community College — support of Library Learning Resource Center ($25,000) see Wyomissing Foundation

Foundation for the Reading Public Museum — endowment fund, second installment ($25,000) see Wyomissing Foundation

Fox Chase Cancer Center — for medical research and care ($22,000) see AMETEK, Inc.

Fox Chase Cancer Center ($5,000) see Binswanger Cos.

Franklin Institute ($50,000) see Arcadia Foundation

Franklin Institute see Berwind Corporation

Franklin and Marshall College ($100,000) see Kunkel Foundation, John Crain

Franklin YMCA ($17,500) see Justus Trust, Edith C.

Free Enterprise Partnership — operating support ($50,000) see Allegheny Foundation

Freeport Area Library Association ($1,000) see Freeport Brick Co.

Freeport Community Park Corporation — community recreation ($25,000) see Freeport Brick Co.

Freeport Volunteer Fire department ($1,000) see Freeport Brick Co.

Friends Council on Education ($125,000) see Clark Foundation

Friends of George C. Marshall see Integra Bank of Uniontown

Friends Hospital ($3,000) see Groome Beatty Trust, Helen D.

Friends of Philadelphia Heart Institute ($2,500) see Gershman Foundation, Joel

Friends of Rittenhouse ($10,000) see Binswanger Cos.

Friends of Rittenhouse Square ($1,000) see Gershman Foundation, Joel

Friends of Ronald McDonald House ($5,150) see Cassett Foundation, Louis N.

Friends of the State Museum ($15,000) see Kunkel Foundation, John Crain

Fulton Opera House ($14,500) see Hamilton Bank

Fulton Opera House Foundation ($26,000) see Steinman Foundation, James Hale

Fund for Historic Rittenhouse Town ($2,500) see Groome Beatty Trust, Helen D.

Gannon University — for faculty and curriculum development in business ($25,000) see Kemper National Insurance Cos.

Gateway Rehabilitation Center ($1,000) see Edgewater Steel Corp.

Gateway Rehabilitation Center — adolescent treatment program ($150,000) see Scaife Family Foundation

Gateway Rehabilitation Centers ($30,000) see Jennings Foundation, Mary Hillman

Gaudenzia ($17,500) see AMP Incorporated

Geisinger Foundation ($10,500) see Reidler Foundation

Geisinger Foundation ($15,000) see Sordoni Foundation

General Church of the New Jerusalem ($13,000) see Asplundh Foundation

General Church of the New Jerusalem ($3,000) see Asplundh Foundation

Genesis of Tamaqua ($500) see Snayberger Memorial Foundation, Harry E. and Florence W.

Gettysburg College — renovations of athletic complex ($50,000) see Kline Foundation, Josiah W. and Bessie H.

Girl Scouts of America Council Beaver-Castle ($30,000) see Hoyt Foundation

Girl Scouts of Southwestern Pennsylvania — upgrade camps and program center ($200,000) see Eden Hall Foundation

Girls Club of Lancaster ($45,000) see Steinman Foundation, John Frederick

Good Samaritan Hospital Street Fair ($150) see Lebanon Mutual Insurance Co.

Good Samaritan Medical Center ($5,000) see Cassett Foundation, Louis N.

Good Shepherd Home Long-Term Care Facility — kitchen and dining area renovations designed to make the raker Center more supportive of independent living on the part of its physically challenged residents ($55,000) see Trexler Trust, Harry C.

Goodwill Industries ($115,630) see Eberly Foundation

Goodwill Industries — recycling plant ($100,000) see Eberly Foundation

Goodwill Industries — relocation and renovation ($82,000) see Trees Charitable Trust, Edith L.

Goodwill Industries of Central Pennsylvania ($13,500) see AMP Incorporated

Goodwill Industries of Fayette County see Integra Bank of Uniontown

Goodwill Industries of Pittsburgh ($100,000) see McCune Charitable Trust, John R.

Grace Episcopal Church ($48,604) see Stackpole-Hall Foundation

Grand View Hospital — for hospitals ($20,000) see AMETEK, Inc.

Graystone Society — restoration of the chimney and the repair and replacement of the eaves in portion of the rehabilitation of Terracins ($60,000) see Huston Charitable Trust, Stewart

Graystone Society — director's salary ($15,000) see Huston Charitable Trust, Stewart

Graystone Society — coverage of basic operating expenses and completion of second floor rooms ($20,000) see Huston Charitable Trust

Greater Erie YMCA — for 1993 grant ($22,000) see Mengle Foundation, Glenn and Ruth

Greater Philadelphia Federation of Settlements — over three years to provide coordination, training, and technical assistance to member human-services organizations ($315,371) see Penn Foundation, William

Greater Philadelphia Urban Affairs Coalition ($2,700) see Mutual Assurance Co.

Greater Pittsburgh Community Food Bank ($10,000) see Murphy Co. Foundation, G.C.

Greater Pittsburgh Guild for the Blind — blind training

1993-94 school year bio-search project, documenting memory ($2,000) see Mascoma Savings Bank

Lebanon Valley College — construction sports center ($80,000) see Kline Foundation, Josiah W. and Bessie H.

Lebanon Valley College ($1,000) see Lebanon Mutual Insurance Co.

Lebanon Valley College ($10,750) see Reidler Foundation

Lehigh County Conference of Churches — toward purchase of leasehold interest in Alliance Hall ($61,118) see Trexler Trust, Harry C.

Lehigh County Velodrome —for developmental cycling program ($31,400) see Air Products and Chemicals, Inc.

Lehigh University ($814,000) see Payne Foundation, Frank E. and Seba B.

Lehigh University — general fund ($210,000) see Sandy Hill Foundation

Lehigh University ($5,000) see Baldwin Foundation, David M. and Barbara

Lehigh University — general operations ($1,000) see Lenna Foundation, Reginald A. and Elizabeth S.

Lehigh University — support Baker auditorium ($30,000) see Baker Foundation, Dexter F. and Dorothy H.

Lehigh University — Baker scholarship program ($5,000) see Baker Foundation, Dexter F. and Dorothy H.

Lehigh University ($9,000) see Holt Family Foundation

Lehigh University — Stabler scholarship fund ($50,000) see Stabler Foundation, Donald B. and Dorothy L.

Lehigh Valley Chamber Orchestra —for culture and art ($7,000) see Air Products and Chemicals, Inc.

Lehigh Valley Chamber Orchestra ($10,000) see Baker Foundation, Dexter F. and Dorothy H.

Lehigh Valley Child Care —for community investment ($7,500) see Air Products and Chemicals, Inc.

Library Company of Philadelphia — endowment of two cataloguing positions ($50,000) see McLean Contributionship

Life Service Systems — general ($85,000) see Trees Charitable Trust, Edith L.

Light of Life Ministries — toward the Resident Counseling Component ($204,800) see Staunton Farm Foundation

Light of Life Ministries — over three years, counseling component at Serenity Village ($100,000) see Staunton Farm Foundation

Light of Life Rescue Mission ($50,000) see Allegheny Foundation

Lincoln Fire Company Number One ($500) see GSM Industrial

Linden Hall ($26,000) see Steinman Foundation, James Hale

Linden Hall ($25,000) see Steinman Foundation, John Frederick

Local Initiatives Support Corporation ($10,000) see Douty Foundation

Longwood Gardens — project expenses ($6,350,000) see Longwood Foundation

Louise Child Care Center for Advancement of Child Care Professionals — a new project that aims to improve the quality of child care in Allegheny County by becoming the focal point for child care quality, offering assessment, guidance, and training for child care providers ($100,000) see Buhl Foundation

Lower Bucks Hospital — capital campaign; hospital expansion ($50,000) see Grundy Foundation

Lower Merion Preservation Trust — Phase I of project to establish a Lower Mill Creek Preserve ($40,000) see McLean Contributionship

Ludington Library ($10,000) see Lovett Foundation, Constans

Lutheran Home at Topton —capital campaign ($15,000) see Carpenter Technology Corp.

Lycoming County District Attorney — special video equipment ($7,940) see Plankenhorn Foundation, Harry

Magee Women's Health Foundation ($100,000) see McCune Charitable Trust, John R.

Main Line Art Center see Bryn Mawr Trust Co.

Make-A-Wish Foundation of Western Pennsylvania — programs for children with life threatening illnesses ($3,000) see Patterson Charitable Fund, W. I.

Mann Music Center — donation to 1992 concert ($3,360) see Maneely Fund

Marble Public Library ($10,000) see Smith Memorial Fund, Ethel Sergeant Clark

March of Dimes Birth Defects Foundation ($2,000) see Freedom Forge Corp.

March of Dimes Birth Defects Foundation ($2,000) see Freedom Forge Corp.

Marian Manor ($20,000) see Clapp Charitable and Educational Trust, George H.

Marriage Council of Philadelphia ($1,000) see Gershman Foundation, Joel

Martin Luther King, Jr. Memorial Scholarship ($625) see GSM Industrial

Mayfair — support art festival ($7,000) see Baker Foundation, Dexter F. and Dorothy H.

Mayor's Private Sector Task Force ($2,500) see Binswanger Cos.

McKeesport Boys and Girls Club ($15,000) see Murphy Co. Foundation, G.C.

McKeesport Heritage Center ($45,000) see Crawford Estate, E. R.

McKeesport Hospital ($10,000) see Crawford Estate, E. R.

McKeesport Hospital Foundation ($15,000) see Crawford Estate, E. R.

McKeesport Meals on Wheels ($25,000) see Crawford Estate, E. R.

McKeesport Preschool for Exceptional Children — preschool program ($60,000) see Trees Charitable Trust, Edith L.

McKeesport Symphony Society ($17,000) see Crawford Estate, E. R.

McKeesport Symphony Society ($2,000) see Peters Foundation, Charles F.

McKeesport YMCA ($5,000) see Miller Charitable Foundation, Howard E. and Nell E.

McNell Chemical Senses Center ($600,000) see Monell Foundation, Ambrose

Meadowbrook Christian School — equipment ($22,526) see Sheary for Charity, Edna M.

Media-Providence Friends School ($25,000) see Smith Memorial Fund, Ethel Sergeant Clark

Melmark Home ($5,000) see Culver Foundation, Constans

Melmark Home ($3,000) see Groome Beatty Trust, Helen D.

Mendelssohn Choir of Pittsburgh ($13,500) see Mine Safety Appliances Co.

Mengle Memorial Library — for 1993 grant ($25,000) see Mengle Foundation, Glenn and Ruth

Mengle Memorial Library — for 1993 grant ($20,000) see Mengle Foundation, Glenn and Ruth

Mengle Scholarship Fund — for 1993 grant National Merit and DuBois Educational Foundation ($25,000) see Mengle Foundation, Glenn and Ruth

Mennonite Central Committee — Prey Veng Public Health Cambodia ($38,975) see Reynolds Foundation, Christopher

Mental Health Association of Beaver County — support the position of an advocate for children with severe emotional problems ($10,000) see Pittsburgh Child Guidance Foundation

Mental Health Association in Westmoreland County — over two years, advocacy services at Torrance State Hospital ($80,000) see Staunton Farm Foundation

Mercersberg Academy ($100,000) see Regenstein Foundation

Mercersburg Academy ($50,000) see Wood Foundation of Chambersburg, PA

Mercersburg Academy ($24,500) see Close Foundation

Mercy Hospital ($4,500) see Waters Charitable Trust, Robert S.

Mercy Vocational High School — faculty endowment to bring salary and benefits to parity with diocesan package ($536,500) see Connelly Foundation

Messiag College — construction of fitness center ($20,000) see Kline Foundation, Josiah W. and Bessie H.

Messiah College — operating expenses ($20,000) see High Foundation

Messiah College — construction of academic center ($50,000) see Kline Foundation, Josiah W. and Bessie H.

Messiah College — for educational purposes, first pledge payment ($5,000) see McCormick Trust, Anne

Messiah College — annual appeal ($1,000) see Pennsylvania Dutch Co.

Messiah College — Donald B. and Dorothy L. Stabler scholarship fund ($40,000) see Stabler Foundation, Donald B. and Dorothy L.

Messiah College ($25,000) see Steinman Foundation, John Frederick

Messiah College — nursing scholarships ($12,000) see Wells Foundation, Franklin H. and Ruth L.

Metro Arts ($40,000) see Kunkel Foundation, John Crain

Meyersdale Area Historical Society see Integra Bank of Uniontown

Milton S. Hershey Medical Center ($50,000) see Schering-Plough Corp.

Milton S. Hershey Medical Center — for medical purposes, third pledge payment ($5,000) see McCormick Trust, Anne

Minersville Midget Football Association ($500) see Snayberger Memorial Foundation, Harry E. and Florence W.

Minsi Trails Council — support inner-city scouting program ($10,100) see Baker Foundation, Dexter F. and Dorothy H.

Misericordia Hospital — toward pledge to implement maternity program ($1,000,000) see Connelly Foundation

Mon Valley Education Consortium — to support the operations of the Mon Valley Education Consortium ($330,000) see Heinz Endowment, Vira I.

Moravian Academy ($2,000) see Holt Family Foundation

Moravian College ($12,000) see International Paper Co.

Morvian College — endowment fund ($100,000) see Payne Foundation, Frank E. and Seba B.

Moss Rehabilitation Hospital ($50,000) see Kardon Foundation, Samuel and Rebecca

Mt. Aloysius College — library automation ($150,000) see Buhl Foundation

Mt. Olivet Cemetery Association ($2,000) see Sheppard Foundation, Lawrence B.

MPC Corporation — for Common Knowledge: Pittsburgh; the Pittsburgh Public School District and the Pittsburgh Supercomputing Center have joined together toward a five-year project, partially funded by the National Science Foundation ($110,000) see Buhl Foundation

M.S. Hershey Medical Center Biomedical Research Building ($50,000) see Hershey Foods Corp.

Muhlenberg College — support the college's theatre, music, and drama departments ($50,000) see Baker Foundation, Dexter F. and Dorothy H.

Museum of Scientific Discovery — Starlab System ($13,500) see Wells Foundation, Franklin H. and Ruth L.

National Flag Foundation — educational organization ($5,500) see Dynamet, Inc.

National Flag Foundation ($5,000) see Love Foundation, George H. and Margaret McClintic

The Nature Conservancy ($2,000) see Holt Family Foundation

Nature Conservancy — establish a Stewardship endowment fund ($50,000) see McLean Contributionship

Neffsville Mennonite Church — operating expenses ($5,000) see High Foundation

Neshaminy Warwick Presbyterian Church ($100,000) see Warwick Foundation

New Castle Public Library ($22,000) see Hoyt Foundation

New Covenant Under Church of Christ — special bequest ($2,500) see Plankenhorn Foundation, Harry

New Covenant United Church of Christ — emergency fund ($45,000) see Plankenhorn Foundation, Harry

North Central Sight Services — building fund ($80,000) see Plankenhorn Foundation, Harry

North Penn United Way ($215,900) see Merck & Co.

North Penn United Way ($6,800) see Clemens Markets Corp.

North Penn YMCA — for building fund ($6,000) see Clemens Markets Corp.

North Pennsylvania Valley Boys and Girls Club ($5,000) see Teleflex Inc.

Northeast Pennsylvania Philharmonic ($2,500) see Sordoni Foundation

NorthStep Neighborhood Watch and Rent Fund ($5,000) see Plankenhorn Foundation, Harry

Notre Dame Church — funds to help young people participate in retreats, conferences and conventions, duplicating equipment and educational materials ($5,000) see Kavanagh Foundation, T. James

Ohio Valley General Hospital ($20,000) see Hopwood Charitable Trust, John M.

Oil City Community Development Corporation ($50,000) see Justus Trust, Edith C.

Oil City Library ($20,000) see Justus Trust, Edith C.

Olivet Boys Club — improvements to existing facilities and erect a new building ($50,000) see Wyomissing Foundation

Olivet Boys and Girls Club —capital campaign

Please Touch Museum ($3,000) see Groome Beatty Trust, Helen D.

Please Touch Museum — over three years to create, document, and disseminate models of effective and culturally sensitive informal learning for preschool children ($400,000) see Penn Foundation, William

Point Park College — automation and networking for the Library Center ($183,000) see Buhl Foundation

Polyclinic Medical Center — expansion and renovations ($150,000) see Kline Foundation, Josiah W. and Bessie H.

Presbyterian Association on Aging ($100,000) see Coen Family Foundation, Charles S. and Mary

Presbyterian Hospital ($600,000) see Love Foundation, George H. and Margaret McClintic

Presbyterian University Hospital ($25,000) see Allegheny Ludlum Corp.

Presbyterian University Hospital ($10,000) see Spang & Co.

Project Home — for help for disadvantaged ($9,000) see Mautz Paint Co.

Project Outreach ($7,500) see Bard Foundation, Robert

Project STAR, Rehabilitation Institute — counseling for adopted boys with developmental difficulties who have experienced sexual abuse prior to adoption, and for their families in Beaver County ($8,000) see Pittsburgh Child Guidance Foundation

Public/Private Ventures — over 30 months, toward evaluations of voluntary youth-serving organizations ($625,000) see Carnegie Corporation of New York

Public/Private Ventures — over five years to launch WORK-PLUS ($3,000,000) see Wallace-Reader's Digest Fund, DeWitt

QED Communications ($500,000) see Avon Products, Inc.

QED Communications — five-year pledge, toward endowment in support of program development ($300,000) see Hillman Foundation

QED Communications — for capital ($50,000) see PPG Industries, Inc.

Quaker Valley School District — for the creation of a mathematics and science learning network involving area school systems and Allegheny College ($288,100) see Heinz Endowment, Vira I.

Reach ($2,500) see Clemens Markets Corp.

Reading Area Community College — capital campaign ($10,000) see Carpenter Technology Corp.

Reading Musical Foundation —operating support ($6,500) see Carpenter Technology Corp.

Reading Public Museum Foundation —operating support ($15,000) see Carpenter Technology Corp.

Reading Public Museum Foundation ($15,000) see Hamilton Bank

Reading Symphony Orchestra ($10,000) see Hamilton Bank

Rehabilitation Institute of Pittsburgh — five-year pledge, toward renovation and expansion of program facilities and construction of underground parking garage ($75,000) see Hillman Foundation

Rehabilitation Institute of Pittsburgh ($30,000) see Jennings Foundation, Mary Hillman

Reilly-Branch Townships ($500) see Snayberger Memorial Foundation, Harry E. and Florence W.

Retired Senior Volunteer Program ($8,000) see Bard Foundation, Robert

Rimersburg Medical Center ($16,947) see Eccles Foundation, Ralph M. and Ella M.

Ringtown Borough — construction of recreation complex ($25,000) see JELD-WEN, Inc.

Riverview Children's Center — over three years, for expansion of mental health services ($150,000) see Staunton Farm Foundation

Rodale Institute — support to develop an internship program for African nationals to attend Rodale Institute Research Center ($10,760) see Margoes Foundation

Rodef Shalom ($10,000) see Speyer Foundation, Alexander C. and Tillie S.

Rodef Shalom Temple Restoration Fund ($15,000) see Foster Charitable Trust

Rodin Museum, Philadelphia Museum of Art — restoration of the sculpture The Thinker ($5,000) see Maneely Fund

Roman Catholic Diocese of Allentown — benefit of Holy Family Manor toward cost of a new wing ($60,000) see Trexler Trust, Harry C.

Roman Catholic High School — scholarship fund ($3,000) see Maneely Fund

Roman Catholic High School — for renovations and expansion of facilities to serve the over 800 students ($500,000) see Connelly Foundation

Roman Catholic High School ($85,000) see McShain Charities, John

Rosemont College ($200,000) see McShain Charities, John

Rosemont College ($100,000) see McShain Charities, John

Rosemont College ($85,600) see McShain Charities, John

Rotary of South Lebanon County ($100) see Lebanon Mutual Insurance Co.

Royersford Community Chest ($10,087) see Bard Foundation, Robert

Safe Harbor — capital fund campaign for homeless ($4,000) see Pennsylvania Dutch Co.

St. Albans Episcopal Church — building fund ($5,000) see Kavanagh Foundation, T. James

St. Andrews United Methodist Church ($20,000) see Sheary for Charity, Edna M.

St. Anthony's Center ($500) see LamCo. Communications

St. Christophers Hospital for Children ($7,000) see Douty Foundation

St. Clair Hospital Foundation ($30,000) see Hopwood Charitable Trust, John M.

St. Edmond's Home — Love Bond appeal ($3,000) see Maneely Fund

St. Edmund's Academy — annual fund ($8,000) see Hunt Foundation

St. Francis College — funds put into the Dorothy day center which assists the poor and needy families in the area ($5,000) see Kavanagh Foundation, T. James

St. Francis Xavier Church — improve church property and aid needy students in parish school ($10,000) see Kavanagh Foundation, T. James

St. James Church ($2,500) see Steinman Foundation, James Hale

St. Joseph Hospital — operating expenses ($5,000) see High Foundation

St. Joseph Hospital Foundation ($1,500) see GSM Industrial

St. Joseph's Hospital — capital campaign, third and final installment ($25,000) see Wyomissing Foundation

St. Joseph's Hospital ($25,000) see Citizens Bank of Rhode Island

St. Josephs-in-the-Hills ($100,000) see McShain Charities, John

St. Josephs Preparatory School ($250,000) see McShain Charities, John

St. Joseph's Preparatory School ($150,000) see Superior Tube Co.

St. Josephs School — learning assistance program ($15,000) see Kavanagh Foundation, T. James

St. Luke United Methodist Church ($10,000) see Lovett Foundation

St. Lukes Hospital — construction ($1,300,000) see Payne Foundation, Frank E. and Seba B.

St. Luke's Hospital — in-kind gift of structural steel for new Education Pavilion ($39,505) see Bethlehem Steel Corp.

St. Margaret Memorial Hospital ($25,000) see Mine Safety Appliances Co.

St. Margaret's Memorial Hospital Foundation ($1,000) see Edgewater Steel Corp.

St. Matthias Church ($10,000) see Lovett Foundation

St. Oddment's Academy — three-year pledge, toward purchase of property for and construction of athletic field ($81,000) see Hillman Foundation

St. Peters Child Development Centers — salary and pension plan expense ($150,000) see Trees Charitable Trust, Edith L.

St. Vincent Archabbey — for Archabbot's discretionary fund ($20,000) see McFeely-Rogers Foundation

St. Vincent College ($20,000) see Armco Inc.

St. Vincent College ($50,000) see McKenna Foundation, Katherine Mabis

Salvation Army — flood relief ($5,000) see Kent-Lucas Foundation

Salvation Army ($48,333) see Allegheny Ludlum Corp.

Salvation Army —for first installment of a five-year pledge ($10,000) see Giant Eagle, Inc.

Salvation Army ($1,000) see Glosser Foundation, David A.

Salvation Army — five-year pledge — toward purchase, renovation, and expansion of facility for emergency disaster services and purchase of disaster-related equipment ($100,000) see Hillman Foundation

Salvation Army ($15,000) see Hulme Charitable Foundation, Milton G.

Salvation Army ($1,500) see LamCo. Communications

Salvation Army — campaign to improve countywide facilities ($1,500,000) see Mellon Foundation, Richard King

Salvation Army ($9,000) see Murphy Co. Foundation, G.C.

Salvation Army — international charity ($3,000) see Patterson Charitable Fund, W. I.

Salvation Army ($2,000) see Peters Foundation, Charles F.

Salvation Army ($10,000) see Plankenhorn Foundation, Harry

Salvation Army — general contribution ($50,000) see PNC Bank, N.A.

Salvation Army ($6,000) see Warwick Foundation

Saunders House — to complete the Watchmate Security System ($50,000) see McLean Contributionship

Scheie Eye Institute — to establish and name the F. M. Kirby Center for Molecular Ophthalmology ($5,000,000) see Kirby Foundation, F. M.

School for Blind Children ($1,000) see Spang & Co.

School District of Philadelphia — Hunter Elementary School ($8,000) see Douty Foundation

Schuylkill Center for Environmental Education — capital ($11,250) see Simpson Investment Company

Science in the Summer ($84,000) see SmithKline Beecham Corp.

Seton Hill College — for scholarship fund ($20,000) see McFeely-Rogers Foundation

Settlement Music School ($34,125) see Kardon Foundation, Samuel and Rebecca

Sexual Assault and Prevention ($10,500) see Steinman Foundation, John Frederick

Shady Side Academy — to assist the academy in meeting the major capital needs ($500,000) see Benedum Foundation, Claude Worthington

Shadyside Academy ($13,500) see Hulme Charitable Foundation, Milton G.

Shadyside Hospital Foundation — five-year pledge, toward relocation of Mary Hillman Jennings Radiation Oncology Center and purchase of equipment ($200,000) see Hillman Foundation

Shadyside Hospital Foundation ($50,000) see Hopwood Charitable Trust, John M.

Shadyside Hospital Foundation ($15,000) see Hulme Charitable Foundation, Milton G.

Shadyside Presbyterian Church ($10,000) see Hulme Charitable Foundation, Milton G.

Sharon Fire Department ($1,000) see NewMil Bancorp

Sharon Regional Health System ($5,000) see Kavanagh Foundation, T. James

Shepherd of the Streets ($750) see LamCo. Communications

Shipley School ($5,000) see Caspersen Foundation for Aid to Health and Education, O. W.

Sisters of Mercy — renovation of three floors on the east wing of the Motherhouse ($500,000) see Connelly Foundation

Sisters of St. Francis of Millvale — support a "learn-earn motivational" after-school program for 30 elementary school children in a public housing community ($6,738) see Pittsburgh Child Guidance Foundation

Sligo Little League — playing field ($2,500) see Eccles Foundation, Ralph M. and Ella M.

Society of Automotive Engineers ($5,000) see Teleflex Inc.

Society of Automotive Engineers/Warrendale ($100,000) see Rockwell International Corporation

Society for Contemporary Crafts ($2,500) see Miller Charitable Foundation, Howard E. and Nell E.

Society for the Preservation of Duquesne Heights Incline — endowment and expenses ($2,341) see Patterson Charitable Fund, W. I.

Somerset House Art History Foundation — fellowships for American graduates to attend the Courtauld Institute and support the Witt and Conway libraries ($50,000) see Mellon Family Foundation, R. K.

South Buffalo Township Volunteer Fire Department ($500) see Freeport Brick Co.

South Central Pennsylvania Food Bank ($10,000) see Harsco Corp.

South Central Pennsylvania Food Bank — construction of warehouse and office facility ($25,000) see Wells Foundation, Franklin H. and Ruth L.

South Central Pennsylvania Housing Development Foundation — operating expenses ($15,000) see

($40,000) see Close
Foundation
Youth Alternatives — repairs
and maintenance of their
building ($13,000) see
Phillips Charitable Trust, Dr.
and Mrs. Arthur William
Youth Baseball/Softball
Association ($2,900) see
Betts Industries
Youth Enhancement Services
— operating expenses
($25,000) see Wells
Foundation, Franklin H. and
Ruth L.
Youth Opportunities Unlimited
— Fairywood projects
($120,900) see Allegheny
Foundation
YWCA ($30,000) see
Crawford Estate, E. R.
YWCA — building repairs
and replacement of old
equipment ($11,554) see
Phillips Charitable Trust, Dr.
and Mrs. Arthur William
Zembo Shrine Circus Fund
($50) see Lebanon Mutual
Insurance Co.
Zoological Society ($2,500)
see Mutual Assurance Co.
Zoological Society of
Philadelphia see Berwind
Corporation
Zoological Society of
Philadelphia — for a
collaborative,
community-based effort to
encourage families to
participate in
science-education programs
at regional museums
($997,000) see Pew
Charitable Trusts
Zoological Society of
Pittsburgh — for a new
education complex and a
children's zoo ($400,000)
see Heinz Endowment, Vira
I.

Puerto Rico

Puerto Rico Community
Foundation ($100,000) see
Hoffmann-La Roche Inc.
Puerto Rico Community
Foundation ($100,000) see
Schering-Plough Corp.

Rhode Island

Boys and Girls Club ($30,000)
see Young Foundation,
Robert R.
Bradley Hospital ($200,000)
see Champlin Foundations
Brick Market Foundation
($175,000) see McBean
Charitable Trust, Alletta
Morris
Brown University ($3,500) see
Wheeler Foundation, Wilmot
Brown University ($200,000)
see Crown Memorial, Arie
and Ida
Brown University ($100,000)
see Reisman Charitable
Trust, George C. and Evelyn
R.
Brown University ($10,000)
see Fruehauf Foundation
Brown University ($15,000)
see Cooperman Foundation,
Leon and Toby
Brown University ($500,000)
see Forbes Inc.
Brown University — for the
Coalition of Essential
Schools' national expansion
program ($50,000) see
Hearst Foundation, William
Randolph

Brown University — expand
the environmental studies
program ($400,000) see
Ittleson Foundation
Brown University ($40,000)
see Salomon Foundation,
Richard and Edna
Brown University ($550,000)
see Champlin Foundations
Brown University ($100,000)
see Fleet Financial Group,
Inc.
Brown University ($65,000)
see Jaffe Foundation
Brown University Center for
Foreign Policy Development
($25,000) see Valentine
Foundation, Lawson
Brown University School of
Medicine ($26,500) see
Zlinkoff Fund for Medical
Research and Education,
Sergei S.
Bryant College ($25,000) see
Levy Foundation, June
Rockwell
Bryant College ($26,500) see
Providence Journal Company
Burrilville School Department
($20,000) see Levy
Foundation, June Rockwell
Canonicus Camp and
Conference Center
($10,000) see Clarke Trust,
John
Choices ($5,000) see Clarke
Trust, John
Community Preparatory
School ($8,800) see Clarke
Trust, John
Dana Farber Cancer Institute
($15,000) see Levy
Foundation, June Rockwell
Elmwood Neighborhood
Housing Services ($30,000)
see Citizens Bank of Rhode
Island
Glocester-Manton Free Public
Library ($15,000) see Levy
Foundation, June Rockwell
Hamilton School at Wheeler
($3,500) see Clarke Trust,
John
Institute for International
Sport ($25,000) see Hasbro
Inc.
Interfaith Health Care
Ministries — "Aging 2000:
Systemic Change in Care for
the Elderly in Rhode Island"
($387,275) see Hartford
Foundation, John A.
International Institute of
Rhode Island ($15,000) see
Citizens Bank of Rhode
Island
International Institute of
Rhode Island ($30,000) see
Providence Journal Company
Jewish Federation of Rhode
Island ($420,000) see
Hassenfeld Foundation
John Carter Brown Library
($80,000) see Adams
Foundation, Arthur F. and
Alice E.
Johnson and Wales University
($17,000) see Citizens Bank
of Rhode Island
Lincoln School ($28,000) see
Levy Foundation, June
Rockwell
Marathon House — for
construction of an arts and
recreation center ($50,000)
see Bingham Foundation,
William
Memorial Hospital of Rhode
Island ($200,000) see
Champlin Foundations
Miriam Hospital ($18,000) see
Levy Foundation, June
Rockwell
Miriam Hospital ($200,000)
see Champlin Foundations

Miriam Hospital ($40,000) see
Citizens Bank of Rhode
Island
Miriam Hospital ($42,817) see
Jaffe Foundation
Miriam Hospital ($40,000) see
Providence Journal Company
Miriam Hospital Foundation
($50,000) see Hasbro Inc.
Nature Conservancy
($1,300,000) see Champlin
Foundations
Nature Conservancy Rhode
Island Field Office
($10,000) see Kimball
Foundation, Horace A.
Kimball and S. Ella
New Visions for Newport City
($10,000) see Clarke Trust,
John
Newport Art Museum
($50,000) see McBean
Charitable Trust, Alletta
Morris
Newport Art Museum
($15,000) see Young
Foundation, Robert R.
Newport Cultural Commission
($15,000) see McBean
Charitable Trust, Alletta
Morris
Northwest Community
Nursing and Health Services
($28,000) see Levy
Foundation, June Rockwell
Preservation Society of
Newport ($172,400) see
McBean Charitable Trust,
Alletta Morris
Providence College ($60,000)
see Fleet Financial Group,
Inc.
Providence College ($41,500)
see Providence Journal
Company
Providence College
($1,100,000) see Textron,
Inc.
Providence Education
Foundation ($25,000) see
Providence Journal Company
Providence Performing Arts
Center ($25,000) see
Citizens Bank of Rhode
Island
Providence Public Library
($200,000) see Champlin
Foundations
Providence Public Library
($5,000) see Clarke Trust,
John
Redwood Library Athenaeum
($17,500) see McBean
Charitable Trust, Alletta
Morris
Rhode Island Hospital
($50,000) see Bank of
Boston Corp.
Rhode Island Hospital
($200,000) see Champlin
Foundations
Rhode Island Hospital
($519,000) see Hasbro Inc.
Rhode Island Hospital
($80,000) see Providence
Journal Company
Rhode Island Public
Expenditure Council —
charitable ($9,672) see
Allendale Insurance Co.
Rhode Island School of
Design — scholarships
($200,000) see Balfour
Foundation, L. G.
Rhode Island School of
Design ($29,000) see
Providence Journal Company
Rhode Island State Council of
Churches ($35,000) see
Hassenfeld Foundation
Roger Williams Medical
Center ($200,000) see
Champlin Foundations
Rose Island Lighthouse
Foundation ($20,000) see

McBean Charitable Trust,
Alletta Morris
Rose Island Zoological
Society ($25,000) see Greve
Foundation, William and
Mary
St. George's School
($100,000) see McBean
Charitable Trust, Alletta
Morris
St. Georges School ($50,000)
see Dingman Foundation,
Michael D.
St. Georges School —
educational ($4,000) see
Darby Foundation
St. John the Evangelist
($27,500) see McBean
Charitable Trust, Alletta
Morris
Salve Regina University
($30,000) see Young
Foundation, Robert R.
Salve Regina University
($4,000) see Clarke Trust,
John
Save the Bay — first payment
of $90,000 grant for
activities to protect
Narragansett Bay ($40,000)
see Prospect Hill Foundation
Town of Charlestown ($5,000)
see Kimball Foundation,
Horace A. Kimball and S.
Ella
Trinity Church ($50,000) see
McBean Charitable Trust,
Alletta Morris
United Baptist Church
($4,000) see Clarke Trust,
John
United Way of New England
($165,000) see May
Department Stores
Company, The
United Way of Southeastern
New England ($40,000) see
Levy Foundation, June
Rockwell
United Way of Southeastern
New England — charitable
($182,474) see Allendale
Insurance Co.
United Way of Southeastern
New England — charitable
($7,600) see Allendale
Insurance Co.
United Way Southeastern New
England ($193,000) see
Citizens Bank of Rhode
Island
United Way Southeastern New
England — operating funds
($12,000) see Cranston Print
Works Company
United Way of Southeastern
New England ($150,000) see
Hasbro Inc.
United Way of Southeastern
New England ($208,000) see
Providence Journal Company
University of Rhode Island —
River Rescue Project
($31,000) see Citizens Bank
of Rhode Island
University of Rhode Island —
scholarship to dependent
child of donor employee
($14,598) see Cranston Print
Works Company
University of Rhode Island
Foundation ($318,787) see
Champlin Foundations
US International Sailing
Association ($25,000) see
Strawbridge Foundation of
Pennsylvania II, Margaret
Dorrance
YMCA of Greater Providence
($371,870) see Champlin
Foundations
YWCA of Greater Rhode
Island ($5,000) see Clarke
Trust, John

South Carolina

Anderson College — building
fund ($25,000) see Dreyfus
Foundation, Max and
Victoria
Archibald Rutledge Academy
($10,000) see Griswold
Foundation, John C.
Bailey Manor — cost of
heating and air conditioning
west wing of renovation
project (challenge grant)
($25,000) see Self
Foundation
Barnwell County Library
($6,500) see Fuller
Foundation, C. G.
Barnwell County Office of
Aging ($2,500) see Fuller
Foundation, C. G.
Belle Baruch Institute for
Marine Biology ($30,000)
see Moore Foundation,
Edward S.
Bennettsville Historical
Society ($2,000) see Fuller
Foundation, C. G.
Bethlehem Baptist Church
($4,100) see Fuller
Foundation, C. G.
Bruce Hospital System — to
design and establish an early
intervention program in the
Pee Dee school for children
three to five years of age
($150,000) see Duke
Endowment
Cambridge Academy — assist
with capital campaign to
build classrooms and arts
center (challenge grant)
($100,000) see Self
Foundation
Campaign to Save Hitchcock
Woods — capital campaign
pledge; second installment
($20,000) see Duchossois
Industries Inc.
Center for Cancer Treatment
($7,500) see Fuller
Foundation, C. G.
Chester County Department of
Education — school
assistance programs
($20,472) see Springs
Foundation
Chester County Hospital —
physicians' office building
($25,000) see Springs
Foundation
Christ Church Episcopal
School ($30,000) see
Symmes Foundation, F. W.
Christ School ($100,000) see
Steele-Reese Foundation
Citadel ($100,000) see Daniel
Foundation of Alabama
Clemson University — capital
($55,000) see Georgia
Power Co.
Clemson University ($30,000)
see Close Foundation
Clemson University
Foundation — general
operation fund ($10,000) see
Jewell Memorial
Foundation, Daniel Ashley
and Irene Houston
Clemson University
Foundation — for student
center ($20,000) see
Burlington Industries, Inc.
Clemson University
Foundation ($50,000) see
Gregg-Graniteville
Foundation
Coastal Carolina College —
scholarship ($9,915) see
Caestecker Foundation,
Charles and Marie
Columbia College ($25,000)
see Close Foundation

Florence Crittenton Agency ($1,500) see Toms Foundation

Girls, Inc. ($5,000) see Massengill-DeFriece Foundation

Girls Preparatory School — general operation fund ($3,000) see Jewell Memorial Foundation, Daniel Ashley and Irene Houston

Girls Preparatory School ($330,000) see Benwood Foundation

Girls Preparatory School — endowment ($417,000) see Tonya Memorial Foundation

Hunter Museum of Art ($30,000) see Sulzberger Foundation

Ijams Nature Center ($2,000) see Toms Foundation

Interfaith Health Clinic — various medical equipment ($100,000) see Thompson Charitable Foundation

Johnson Bible College ($100,000) see Thompson Charitable Foundation

Knoxville College — renovation of dormitories ($125,000) see Thompson Charitable Foundation

Knoxville Museum of Art ($22,500) see Stokely, Jr. Foundation, William B.

Knoxville Zoological Gardens ($750) see Toms Foundation

Lifelong Learning Center — seventh payment ($35,000) see Cornell Trust, Peter C.

Literacy Academy of Bristol Lab ($2,860) see Massengill-DeFriece Foundation

Little Theatre ($200,000) see Benwood Foundation

Madonna Day School — summer camp scholarship ($5,000) see Gallagher Family Foundation, Lewis P.

Martha O'Bryan Center ($7,000) see Ansley Foundation, Dantzler Bond

Martha O'Bryan Center — support for a $2 million capital and endowment campaign ($50,000) see HCA Foundation

Martin Luther King Avenue Redevelopment Corporation ($75,000) see Bedsole Foundation, J. L.

McCallie School — general operation fund ($10,000) see Jewell Memorial Foundation, Daniel Ashley and Irene Houston

McCallie School ($620,000) see Benwood Foundation

McCallie School — capital campaign ($600,000) see Tonya Memorial Foundation

McNeilly Center for Children — support for a $500,000 capital campaign to rebuild the building serving school-age children ($50,000) see HCA Foundation

Meharry Medical Center ($30,000) see Potter Foundation, Justin and Valere

Meharry Medical College ($30,000) see Moore Foundation, Edward S.

Meharry Medical College — funding to strengthen the surgical education program ($33,000) see HCA Foundation

Memphis Arts Council ($20,000) see International Paper Co.

Memphis Arts Council ($20,000) see International Paper Co.

Memphis Arts Council — challenge board members to give gifts over and above their regular gifts ($62,500) see Clarkson Foundation, Jeniam

Memphis Business Group on Health — "Implementation of the MidSouth Health Care Alliance — A Community Health Management Information System" ($352,738) see Hartford Foundation, John A.

Memphis Concert Ballet ($2,500) see Clarkson Foundation, Jeniam

Middle Tennessee State University — for nursing department classroom building ($1,295,276) see Christy-Houston Foundation

Middle Tennessee State University — for student scholarship fund ($30,000) see Christy-Houston Foundation

Montgomery Bell Academy ($22,500) see Ansley Foundation, Dantzler Bond

Nashville Ballet — general support for the 1994-95 season ($60,000) see HCA Foundation

Nashville Opera Association — general support for the 1994-95 season ($40,000) see HCA Foundation

Nashville Symphony ($1,000) see Christy-Houston Foundation

Oneida Special School District — completion of high school, gym, middle school, and cafeteria ($536,875) see Thompson Charitable Foundation

Opera Memphis ($75,000) see Adams Foundation, Arthur F. and Alice E.

Orange Grove Center ($250,000) see Benwood Foundation

PENCIL Foundation — 1994 HCA Teacher Awards program ($40,000) see HCA Foundation

Playhouse on the Square — renovate and computerize the ticket office and subscription/mailing lists ($11,500) see Clarkson Foundation, Jeniam

Porter Leath Children's Center ($25,000) see Adams Foundation, Arthur F. and Alice E.

READ of Chattanooga — general operation fund ($3,000) see Jewell Memorial Foundation, Daniel Ashley and Irene Houston

Rhea Family YMCA — human services ($20,000) see La-Z-Boy Chair Co.

Rhodes College — toward the renovation of recreational facilities as part of the construction and renovation of buildings for a Campus Life Center ($750,000) see Kresge Foundation

Rhodes College — Seidman Awards program ($25,000) see Seidman Family Foundation

RiverCity Company — for expenses relating to design and construction of Vistors Center ($2,782,206) see Tonya Memorial Foundation

RiverCity Company — for Miller Plaza Fund ($28,140) see Tonya Memorial Foundation

RiverCity Company — for payment of work on Riverwalk ($6,313) see Tonya Memorial Foundation

RiverCity Company — for expenses relating to Tennessee Riverpark ($5,883) see Tonya Memorial Foundation

Rotary Club of Bristol ($3,000) see Massengill-DeFriece Foundation

St. Jude Children's Research Hospital ($10,000) see Cooperman Foundation, Leon and Toby

Salvation Army ($7,000) see Ansley Foundation, Dantzler Bond

Salvation Army — general support ($100,000) see Thompson Charitable Foundation

Sarah Cannon Cancer Foundation ($10,000) see Ansley Foundation, Dantzler Bond

Stokely Memorial Library ($25,000) see Stokely, Jr. Foundation, William B.

Tennessee Committee for the National Museum of Women in Arts ($500) see Toms Foundation

Tennessee Outdoor Drama Association — operating fund ($65,000) see Tonya Memorial Foundation

Tennessee Performing Arts Center — support for the 1994-95 Humanities Outreach in Tennessee program ($40,000) see HCA Foundation

Tennessee State University Foundation — funding to retain a director for the alumni scholarship fund campaign ($50,000) see HCA Foundation

Tennessee Technological University — for employee scholarship ($4,834) see Quaker Chemical Corp.

Traveller's Rest Historic House Museum ($40,000) see Potter Foundation, Justin and Valere

United Way — general operation fund ($5,500) see Jewell Memorial Foundation, Daniel Ashley and Irene Houston

United Way ($6,600) see Park Foundation

United Way ($50,000) see Ansley Foundation, Dantzler Bond

University of the South Sewanee ($20,250) see Sullivan Foundation, Algernon Sydney

University of Tennessee Academy for Teachers of Math/Science ($235,000) see Martin Marietta Corp.

University of Tennessee Law School ($4,000) see Toms Foundation

Vanderbilt TV Archives ($35,000) see Potter Foundation, Justin and Valere

Vanderbilt University — operating grant ($10,000) see Marshall Trust in Memory of Sanders McDaniel, Harriet McDaniel

Vanderbilt University — operating grant ($10,000) see Marshall Trust in

Memory of Sanders McDaniel, Harriet McDaniel

Vanderbilt University — three-year grant for research to assess the benefits elderly individuals with hearing loss receive from personal amplification ($265,066) see Retirement Research Foundation

Vanderbilt University ($15,000) see Bay Foundation

Vanderbilt University ($20,000) see Cheatham Foundation, Owen

Vanderbilt University — for field trials at several colleges and universities of a simulated engineering laboratory for on- and off-campus students ($399,910) see Sloan Foundation, Alfred P.

Vanderbilt University School of Medicine — for Justin Potter Merit Scholarship ($245,000) see Potter Foundation, Justin and Valere

Volunteer Federal Bank ($10,000) see Schuller International

Webb School ($50,000) see Stokely, Jr. Foundation, William B.

Webb School ($20,000) see Stokely, Jr. Foundation, William B.

YCAP (YMCA) ($35,000) see Potter Foundation, Justin and Valere

YMCA ($10,000) see Ansley Foundation, Dantzler Bond

YMCA — for new building ($1,000,000) see Christy-Houston Foundation

YMCA Community Action Project ($8,000) see Ansley Foundation, Dantzler Bond

YMCA of Nashville and Middle Tennessee — additional support for the Outdoor Family Center at the East Nashville YMCA ($50,000) see HCA Foundation

YWCA ($100,000) see Avon Products, Inc.

Texas

Abilene Chamber of Commerce Foundation — to support the Abilene Educational Council on Educational Projects ($100,000) see Dodge Jones Foundation

Abilene Christian University — to help fund renovation of educational facilities ($200,000) see Dodge Jones Foundation

Abused Children's Shelter — building renovations ($30,000) see Doss Foundation, M. S.

Admiral Nimitz Foundation — construction of George Bush Gallery of the Pacific War in Nimitz Museum ($25,000) see Peterson Foundation, Hal and Charlotte

Alamo Community College District — operation ($12,500) see Koehler Foundation, Marcia and Otto

Alamo Public Telecommunications — for phase II capital campaign for new headquarters ($50,000) see Halsell Foundation, Ewing

Alamo Public Telecommunications Council — purchase of equipment need at new site ($10,000) see Piper Foundation, Minnie Stevens

Alamo Public Telecommunications Council ($2,500) see Piper Foundation, Minnie Stevens

All Saints Episcopal Hospital ($10,000) see McQueen Foundation, Adeline and George

All Saints Health Foundation ($10,000) see Weaver Foundation, Gil and Dody

All Saints School — educational ($10,000) see Wise Foundation and Charitable Trust, Watson W.

All Saints School — educational ($10,000) see Wise Foundation and Charitable Trust, Watson W.

Alley Theatre see USX Corporation

Alley Theatre ($5,000) see Knox, Sr., and Pearl Wallis Knox Charitable Foundation, Robert W.

Alpha Home — operation ($10,000) see Koehler Foundation, Marcia and Otto

Alpine Montessori School ($5,000) see Potts and Sibley Foundation

Alvin Community College see Amoco Corporation

Amarillo College — to implement an on-line testing center project ($54,533) see Fuld Health Trust, Helene

Amarillo College ($3,080) see Mays Foundation

Amarillo Community Center ($4,000) see Mays Foundation

Amarillo Education Foundation ($3,000) see Mays Foundation

Amarillo Multiservice Center for the Aging dba Jan Werner Adult Day Care Center — toward facility expansion for the Jan Werner Adult Day Care Center ($250,000) see Meadows Foundation

Amarillo Wesley Community Center ($132,000) see Burchfield Foundation, Charles E.

American Airpower Heritage Foundation — challenge grant for debt retirement resulting from construction of the Confederate Air Force Headquarters ($250,000) see Abell-Hanger Foundation

American Cancer Society — Camp Discovery see Freeport-McMoRan Inc.

American Cancer Society — medical treatment ($13,500) see Hamman Foundation, George and Mary Josephine

American Cancer Society ($500) see Walsh Foundation

American Cancer Society Hale County Unit — assist in the underwriting of the Hale County Cotton Baron's Ball ($5,000) see Mayer Foundation, James and Eva

American Enterprise Forum for Economic Understanding — teacher training and student programs in economics and American Heritage ($30,134) see Armstrong Foundation

American Heart Association — medical treatment ($17,000) see Hamman

Foundation, George and Mary Josephine

American Lung Association ($5,000) see Clayton Fund

American National Red Cross — disaster relief services ($50,000) see Rockwell Fund

American Red Cross see Freeport-McMoRan Inc.

American Red Cross — operating budget ($5,000) see Bridwell Foundation, J. S.

American Red Cross — help provide relief to victims of disaster ($2,000) see Kayser Foundation

American Red Cross see Management Compensation Group/Dulworth Inc.

Amon Carter Museum — general support ($4,624,975) see Carter Foundation, Amon G.

Angel House ($25,567) see Meyer Family Foundation, Paul J.

Anglina County Illegal Dumping — for general operations ($10,000) see Pineywoods Foundation

Any Baby Can ($5,000) see Willard Helping Fund, Cecilia Young

ARC of the United States — development of equipment for the handicapped ($54,000) see Cain Foundation, Effie and Wofford

Archdiocese of San Antonio Pilot Program for Deaf Children — pilot project mainstreaming deaf students into high schools ($2,500) see Piper Foundation, Minnie Stevens

Armand Bayou Nature Center — community funds ($10,000) see Hamman Foundation, George and Mary Josephine

Arts Council of Ft. Worth — for cultural purposes ($40,000) see Scott Foundation, William E.

Assistance Fund ($10,000) see Duncan Foundation, Lillian H. and C. W.

Association for the Advancement of Mexican Americans see Amoco Corporation

Association for Community Television see USX Corporation

Austin Adopt-a-School see Freeport-McMoRan Inc.

Austin Business Committee for the Arts see Freeport-McMoRan Inc.

Austin College — endowed scholarships ($50,000) see Cain Foundation, Effie and Wofford

Austin College — recruitment program for Hispanic students ($25,000) see Fish Foundation, Ray C.

Austin College ($5,000) see Knox, Sr., and Pearl Wallis Knox Charitable Foundation, Robert W.

Austin College — scholarships ($17,300) see Mayor Foundation, Oliver Dewey

Austin College — for NEH challenge grant ($10,000) see Munson Foundation Trust, W. B.

Austin College ($25,000) see Smith Charitable Foundation, Clara Blackford Smith and W. Aubrey

Austin College — Clinica Promesa project/Mexico ($50,000) see Trull Foundation

Austin Museum of Art — toward acquisition of land for a downtown multicultural art museum ($250,000) see Meadows Foundation

Austin Parks Foundation (Texas) and Trust for Public Land (San Francisco) — over four years to develop parks in east and southeast Austin, TX, and encourage community involvement in the development ($800,000) see Wallace-Reader's Digest Fund, Lila

Austin Presbyterian Theological Seminary — construction of a community center ($100,000) see Abell-Hanger Foundation

Austin Special — capital needs, sheltered workshop for mentally disabled ($28,090) see Blowitz-Ridgeway Foundation

Austin Symphony ($5,000) see Potts and Sibley Foundation

Ballet of Americas — for general support ($2,500) see Huthsteiner Fine Arts Trust

Ballet El Paso — for general support ($4,000) see Huthsteiner Fine Arts Trust

Bank One/Denison Credit Account — for Denison Community Foundation Sister Cities Division ($15,000) see Munson Foundation Trust, W. B.

Bank One/Denison Credit Account — for balance of contribution for delegates from Cognac, France ($14,620) see Munson Foundation Trust, W. B.

Bank One/Sherman Credit Account — for St. Mary's Catholic School computer fund ($17,500) see Munson Foundation Trust, W. B.

Baptist General Convention of Texas — for work with young men and retirees ($10,000) see White Trust, G. R.

Baptist Hospital ($40,000) see Temple-Inland Inc.

Baptist Seminary — for monetary contribution ($10,000) see Norman Foundation, Summers A.

Baptist Spanish Publishing House — for equipment ($2,000) see Huthsteiner Fine Arts Trust

Bastian School — salary for person to work in the Quiet Room ($37,000) see Favrot Fund

Battle of Flowers Association ($2,000) see Tobin Foundation

Bay City Day Care — for home renovation ($50,000) see Gulf Coast Medical Foundation

Bay City Library Association — for library relocation ($25,000) see Gulf Coast Medical Foundation

Bay City Library Association — expansion and modernization ($15,000) see Trull Foundation

Baylor College of Medicine — endowed research chair in cardiology ($250,000) see Cain Foundation, Effie and Wofford

Baylor College of Medicine — endowment for molecular genetics ($580,000) see Cullen Foundation

Baylor College Medicine — research ($100,000) see Herzstein Charitable Foundation, Albert and Ethel

Baylor College of Medicine ($400,000) see Shell Oil Company

Baylor College of Medicine — Alzheimers research ($500,000) see Temple Foundation, T. L. L.

Baylor College of Medicine Department of Opthamology — establish an eye research lab center ($100,000) see Farish Fund, William Stamps

Baylor College of Medicine Vascular Biology Laboratory ($340,000) see Fondren Foundation

Baylor University ($10,000) see Reynolds Foundation, Donald W.

Baylor University ($117,600) see Fair Foundation, R. W.

Baylor University — toward construction of the Jesse H. Jones library ($3,000,000) see Houston Endowment

Baylor University ($25,800) see Mays Foundation

Baylor University — education ($10,000) see Wise Foundation and Charitable Trust, Watson W.

Baylor University Department of Environmental Studies — further education of students in environmental studies ($5,000) see Hallberg Foundation, E. L. and R. F.

Baylor University Medical Center — for Baylor Pediatric Center for Restorative Care ($100,000) see Hillcrest Foundation

Baylor University School of Law ($50,000) see Anderson Foundation, M. D.

Baylor University Waco — contribution to scholarship fund ($5,000) see Kayser Foundation

Bayou Bend Capital Campaign ($50,000) see Kilroy Foundation, William S. and Lora Jean

Be An Angel Fund — for general support ($25,000) see O'Quinn Foundation, John M. and Nancy C.

Beaumont Public Schools Foundation — contribution to Start Up Foundation ($10,000) see Dishman Charitable Foundation Trust, H. E. and Kate

Because We Care — drug counseling in the public schools ($35,000) see Sumners Foundation, Hatton W.

Believe in Me Project — training and operating funds ($31,200) see Wright Foundation, Lola

Ben Richey Boys Ranch — to forgive the loan given to construct new cottages ($420,022) see Dodge Jones Foundation

Bexar County Community Corrections Department — equipment purchase ($5,000) see Semmes Foundation

Big Brothers and Big Sisters ($10,000) see Halff Foundation, G. A. C.

Big Brothers and Big Sisters — operation ($10,000) see

Koehler Foundation, Marcia and Otto

Big Brothers and Big Sisters ($500) see Walsh Foundation

Blaffer Gallery see Management Compensation Group/Dulworth Inc.

Bluebonnet Youth Ranch — to construct a recreation center and meeting place ($60,000) see Johnson Foundation, M. G. and Lillie A.

Boy Scouts of America ($5,000) see Norton Co.

Boy Scouts of America ($24,000) see Hachar Charitable Trust, D. D.

Boy Scouts of America ($24,000) see Hachar Charitable Trust, D. D.

Boy Scouts of America — help to aid in the development of tomorrows leaders ($2,000) see Kayser Foundation

Boy Scouts of America ($5,000) see Prairie Foundation

Boy Scouts of America — urban scouting program ($35,000) see Rockwell Fund

Boy Scouts of America ($500) see Walsh Foundation

Boy Scouts of America Buffalo Trail Council ($5,000) see Dunagan Foundation

Boy Scouts of America Rio Grande Council ($2,500) see Hygeia Dairy Co.

Boys Club — computers and operating support ($54,943) see Mayor Foundation, Oliver Dewey

Boys and Girls Club of Galveston ($20,000) see Kempner Fund, Harris and Eliza

Boys and Girls Club of Waco ($101,561) see Meyer Family Foundation, Paul J.

Boys and Girls Clubs of Abilene — to provide operational support and the hiring of a well-qualified executive director ($90,000) see Dodge Jones Foundation

Boys and Girls Clubs of Greater Ft. Worth — capital campaign/East Side facility ($300,000) see Burnett-Tandy Foundation

Boys and Girls Clubs of Laredo ($90,000) see Hachar Charitable Trust, D. D.

Boys and Girls Clubs of San Angelo — to fund the building and expansion project of the club ($100,000) see Dodge Jones Foundation

Boys Harbor ($30,000) see Steinhagen Benevolent Trust, B. A. and Elinor

Brazosport Health Foundation — cancer therapy center see Nalco Chemical Co.

Briarwood School ($10,000) see Elkins, Jr. Foundation, Margaret and James A.

Broadway Baptist Church ($10,000) see Walsh Foundation

Brooks County Area Volunteer Emergency Response Team ($25,000) see Rachal Foundation, Ed

Brooks County Independent School District ($200,000) see Rachal Foundation, Ed

Brookwood Community ($50,000) see Anderson Foundation, M. D.

Brookwood Community — expansion of home for dysfunctional adults

($100,000) see Farish Fund, William Stamps

Brookwood Community Volunteers — streets of Sante Fe Underwriter Pledge and new men's hom ($25,000) see Early Foundation

Brownsville Public Library Foundation ($5,000) see Norton Co.

Buckner Baptist Benevolence — dorm renovations ($73,313) see Doss Foundation, M. S.

Buckner Baptist Benevolence — toward construction of a new Activity Center for elderly residents of Buckner Retirement Home and youth from Buckner Children's Home ($300,000) see Meadows Foundation

Buckner Baptist Benevolences — help build Ledbetter Community Center at Buckner Retirement Village ($60,000) see Hillcrest Foundation

Bullard Independent School District — for tennis courts ($20,000) see Norman Foundation, Summers A.

Bush Presidential Library Foundation — educational ($50,000) see Darby Foundation

Bush Presidential Library Foundation — to help establish the George Bush Presidential Library Foundation at Texas A&M University ($500,000) see Starr Foundation

Bynum School Development Disabilities Center — for general operating support ($50,000) see Davidson Family Charitable Foundation

Cabbages and Kings ($7,500) see Geifman Family Foundation

Cal Farley's Boys Ranch see Management Compensation Group/Dulworth Inc.

Camp Fire Council of North Texas ($10,000) see Priddy Foundation

Camp Fire Girls ($10,000) see Quivey-Bay State Foundation

Cancer Therapy and Research ($30,000) see Halff Foundation, G. A. C.

Cancer Therapy and Research Center — capital campaign ($100,000) see Semmes Foundation

Cancer Therapy and Research Foundation of South Texas — toward constructing and equipping of a patient treatment/clinical research building ($500,000) see Meadows Foundation

Cancer Therapy and Research Foundation of South Texas — general funding ($40,000) see Zachry Co., H.B.

Capital Area Food Bank of Texas ($6,300) see Priddy Foundation

CARE — small business enterprise development projects in Peru, Guatemala, and Costa Rica ($25,000) see Contran Corporation

Caring for Children of Ward County ($4,520) see Dunagan Foundation

Carver Cultural Center ($2,500) see Tobin Foundation

Casa de Amigos ($10,000) see Beal Foundation

Casa de Amigos — for diabetic screening program for "working poor" ($25,000) see Davidson Family Charitable Foundation

Casa Manana ($5,000) see Hallberg Foundation, E. L. and R. F.

Cathedral High School — building renovations and expansion ($5,000) see Burkitt Foundation

Cathedral of St. John the Divine ($25,000) see Tobin Foundation

Catholic Family and Children — operation ($12,000) see Koehler Foundation, Marcia and Otto

Ceden Family Resource Center — Volunteer Program ($37,880) see Wright Foundation, Lola

Center for Battered Women — Shelter Fund ($10,000) see Clayton Fund

Center for Battered Women — van and stove ($28,375) see Wright Foundation, Lola

Centers for Children and Families ($10,000) see Beal Foundation

CEO Foundation — education ($30,000) see Zachry Co., H.B.

Cherokee County Crisis Center — for monetary contribution ($25,000) see Norman Foundation, Summers A.

Chi Omega Community Charities ($2,000) see Walsh Foundation

Child Advocates — for general support ($10,500) see O'Quinn Foundation, John M. and Nancy C.

Child Advocates — public civic ($10,000) see Owsley Foundation, Alvin and Lucy

Child Advocates — for expenses to recruit, train, and supervise court-appointed special advocacy volunteers to serve 40 children for a 12-month period ($52,000) see Swalm Foundation

Child Advocates Endowment — for the first installment of a two-year pledge to support an endowment campaign to secure future funding for programs that supply volunteer advocates for abused and neglected children ($50,000) see Swalm Foundation

Child and Family Service — computer system ($25,000) see Wright Foundation, Lola

Child Study Center — for educational purposes ($50,000) see Scott Foundation, William E.

Child Study Center ($11,000) see Weaver Foundation, Gil and Dody

Children's Assessment Center — expenses for the center to hire an additional therapist to serve sexually abused children and their families ($36,611) see Swalm Foundation

Children's Assessment Center — operating expenses and salaries ($20,000) see Turner Charitable Foundation

Children's Home — building renovation ($135,000) see Doss Foundation, M. S.

Children's Medical Center — expansion and renovation ($100,000) see Fikes Foundation, Leland

Children's Medical Foundation ($40,000) see Sturgis Charitable and Educational Trust, Roy and Christine

Children's Museum of Houston ($50,000) see Anderson Foundation, M. D.

Children's Museum of Houston — toward construction of the Mary Gibbs Jones building ($1,000,000) see Houston Endowment

Children's Museum of Houston ($5,000) see Knox, Sr., and Pearl Wallis Knox Charitable Foundation, Robert W.

Children's Museum of Houston — for capital campaign ($25,000) see O'Quinn Foundation, John M. and Nancy C.

Children's Village — endowed scholarship fund ($100,000) see Sumners Foundation, Hatton W.

Chinquapin School ($5,000) see Clayton Fund

Chinquapin School — general support ($5,000) see Semmes Foundation

Christ Church Cathedral — churches and affiliated organizations ($15,000) see Hamman Foundation, George and Mary Josephine

Christian Mission Concerns ($26,000) see Meyer Family Foundation, Paul J.

Christmas in Spring of Wichita County ($5,000) see Priddy Foundation

Church of the Heavenly Rest — capital campaign ($200,000) see Burnett-Tandy Foundation

City of Abilene — to fund Redbud Park development costs ($118,722) see Dodge Jones Foundation

City of Alto — for baseball program ($20,000) see Norman Foundation, Summers A.

City of Angelo, Texas — toward construction and landscaping of the Plaza to serve as a site for a farmers' market and community festivals as part of a comprehensive effort to revitalize the Historic City Center ($500,000) see Meadows Foundation

City of Dallas ($250,000) see Mobil Oil Corp.

City of Diboll ($62,053) see Temple-Inland Inc.

City of El Campo — for a new ambulance ($35,000) see Gulf Coast Medical Foundation

City of Galveston ($6,000) see Kempner Fund, Harris and Eliza

City of Galveston Police Department ($20,000) see Kempner Fund, Harris and Eliza

City of Galveston Police Department ($15,000) see Kempner Fund, Harris and Eliza

City of Graham — trees for the park ($2,450) see Bertha Foundation

City of Houston Parks and Recreation Department — development of Cullen Park

($3,108,407) see Cullen Foundation

City of Jacksonville — for K-9 vehicle ($10,000) see Norman Foundation, Summers A.

City of Kerrville — fund purchase of four ambulances for fire department's newly established Emergency Medical Services Unit ($311,760) see Peterson Foundation, Hal and Charlie

City of Kerrville — recycling program ($39,000) see Peterson Foundation, Hal and Charlie

City of Kyle Community Library ($15,000) see Johnson Foundation, Burdine

City of Lufkin — for general operations ($6,400) see Pineywoods Foundation

City of Pampa ($7,500) see Brown Foundation, M. K.

City of Pineland — day care center project ($303,217) see Temple Foundation, T. L. L.

Clarendon College — to help fund construction for the ranch operations program at the college ($100,000) see Dodge Jones Foundation

College of St. Thomas More ($2,500) see Piper Foundation, Minnie Stevens

Common Ground Community Economic Development Corporation — salary support for two new staff persons ($15,000) see Contran Corporation

Common Ground University — renovate abandoned and condemned houses in East Dallas-Fair Park South Dallas-Oak Cliff for poor and homeless people ($50,000) see Hillcrest Foundation

Communities Foundation of Texas ($182,500) see Priddy Foundation

Communities in School Houston — to support "at-risk" children in schools ($7,500) see Early Foundation

Communities in Schools ($20,000) see Duncan Foundation, Lillian H. and C. W.

Communities in Schools Houston — community funds ($10,000) see Hamman Foundation, George and Mary Josephine

Community Enrichment Center ($25,000) see McQueen Foundation, Adeline and George

Community Food Bank — to construct new building ($153,000) see Johnson Foundation, M. G. and Lillie A.

Community Guidance Center ($10,000) see Halff Foundation, G. A. C.

Concerned Citizens of Central Texas ($30,546) see Meyer Family Foundation, Paul J.

Concordia Lutheran College — additional funds for the reconstruction of the Science Building, Beto Hall ($150,000) see Johnson Foundation, M. G. and Lillie A.

Concordia Lutheran College — provide additional funds for the renovation and expansion of the Science Building, Beto Hall ($100,000) see Johnson

Foundation, M. G. and Lillie A.

Country Day School of Arlington — for charitable purposes ($40,000) see Scott Foundation, William E.

County of Refugio ($10,000) see O'Connor Foundation, Kathryn

Court Appointed Special Advocates — to provide a bilingual supervisor of volunteers ($30,000) see Favrot Fund

Court Appointed Special Advocates ($8,143) see Steinhagen Benevolent Trust, B. A. and Elinor

Cowboy Artists of America Museum Foundation — general operating funds ($21,000) see Fish Foundation, Ray C.

Crystal Charity Ball ($50,000) see Contran Corporation

Crystal Charity Ball ($13,700) see Hammer Foundation, Armand

Dallas Child Guidance Clinic — repair erosion of creek bank behind their building ($75,000) see Fikes Foundation, Leland

Dallas Museum of Art ($50,000) see JFM Foundation

Dallas Museum of Art — community cultural assistance ($55,000) see Hawn Foundation

Dallas Museum of Art — expansion campaign of Hamon Building for advancement of eduction ($50,000) see Hillcrest Foundation

Dallas Museum of Art — for Mexican Vice Regal Cabinet ($300,000) see McDermott Foundation, Eugene

Dallas Museum of Art — for the Eugene McDermott Director's Chair ($200,000) see McDermott Foundation, Eugene

Dallas Museum of Art — for big chest of drawers circa 1700-1725 ($50,000) see McDermott Foundation, Eugene

Dallas Museum of Art — public civic ($29,989) see Owsley Foundation, Alvin and Lucy

Dallas Museum of Art ($80,000) see Sturgis Charitable and Educational Trust, Roy and Christine

Dallas Museum of Natural History ($10,000) see Jonsson Foundation

Dallas Museum of Natural History Association ($50,000) see Clements Foundation

Dallas Opera — general support ($2,500) see National Gypsum Co.

Dallas Opera — community cultural assistance ($50,000) see Hawn Foundation

Dallas Opera — cultural ($10,000) see Stemmons Foundation

Dallas Symphony Association —special grant $1,500,000 over five years ($300,000) see Exxon Corporation

Dallas Symphony Association — cultural ($10,000) see Stemmons Foundation

Dallas Symphony Orchestra — for the Eugene McDermott Orchestra Endowment Fund

($200,000) see McDermott Foundation, Eugene

Dallas Symphony Orchestra — for concert hall ($150,000) see McDermott Foundation, Eugene

Dallas Symphony Orchestra — for orchestra travel fund ($80,000) see McDermott Foundation, Eugene

Dallas Theological Seminary — part of cost for new computer for main campus computer for student registration ($51,000) see Hillcrest Foundation

Day Nursery of Abilene — building construction ($54,000) see Doss Foundation, M. S.

Deaf Action Center — toward renovation of agency offices and apartments for elderly, deaf persons ($285,000) see Meadows Foundation

Deep East Texas Development — for general operations ($2,000) see Pineywoods Foundation

Deep East Texas Regional MH-HR Services — residential facilities for mentally ill ($651,900) see Temple Foundation, T. L. L.

Deep East Texas Regional MH-MR Services — residential facilities for mentally retarded ($421,946) see Temple Foundation, T. L. L.

Denison Community Foundation — for Eisenhower birthplace capital improvement ($60,000) see Munson Foundation Trust, W. B.

Denison Community Foundation — renovation ($50,000) see Smith Charitable Foundation, Clara Blackford Smith and W. Aubrey

Denison Public Library — for heating and air conditioning project ($45,626) see Munson Foundation Trust, W. B.

DePelchin Children's Center — to aid children and families in need ($15,000) see Duncan Foundation, Lillian H. and C. W.

DePelchin Children's Center — to aid children/families in need ($30,000) see Early Foundation

Depelchin Children's Center ($15,000) see Texas Commerce Bank-Houston, N.A.

Desert Research Institute ($10,000) see Sierra Pacific Resources

Diboll Independent School District — computer technology implementation ($1,250,000) see Temple Foundation, T. L. L.

Diocese of Amarillo — University Catholic Student Center ($5,000) see Burkitt Foundation

Diocese of Victoria ($100,000) see O'Connor Foundation, Kathryn

Earth Promise — public civic ($6,500) see Owsley Foundation, Alvin and Lucy

East Texas Baptist College ($41,000) see Fair Foundation, R. W.

East Texas Baptist University ($30,000) see Meyer Family Foundation, Paul J.

Ebenezer Child Development Center — furnish classrooms ($25,000) see Wright Foundation, Lola

El Pasiano Girl Scouts ($12,000) see Hachar Charitable Trust, D. D.

El Paso Art Association — for art award show ($2,500) see Huthsteiner Fine Arts Trust

El Paso Community Foundation ($5,000) see R. F. Foundation

El Paso Philharmonic Strings — for computers for music department ($12,500) see Huthsteiner Fine Arts Trust

El Paso Pro-Musica — for general support ($2,500) see Huthsteiner Fine Arts Trust

El Paso Symphony Orchestra — for concerts and general support ($29,000) see Huthsteiner Fine Arts Trust

Elflouise ($10,000) see Overlake Foundation

Endow a Child - Houston School for Deaf Children — to support on-going programs and 1991 gala ($10,000) see Early Foundation

Epilepsy Association of Houston — help children with epilepsy enjoy a camping experience and help with research ($2,800) see Kayser Foundation

Episcopal Church of the Good Shepherd ($1,000) see Acme-McCrary Corp./Sapona Manufacturing Co.

Episcopal High School ($120,000) see Anderson Foundation, M. D.

Episcopal High School — capital fund campaign ($330,000) see Cullen Foundation

Episcopal High School ($50,000) see Elkins, Jr. Foundation, Margaret and James A.

Episcopal High School — land purchase, retirement, and language enrichment program ($236,000) see Farish Fund, William Stamps

Episcopal High School — capital campaign ($25,000) see Fish Foundation, Ray C.

Episcopal High School — debt retirement ($250,000) see Fondren Foundation

Episcopal High School — toward the school's property acquisition program ($1,000,000) see Houston Endowment

Episcopal High School ($35,000) see Scurlock Foundation

Episcopal School of Dallas — education ($50,000) see Stemmons Foundation

ESCAPE (Exchange Club Center for the Prevention of Child Abuse) ($25,000) see Favrot Fund

Escape Family Resource Center — to support a Parent Education Program that teaches parents how to prevent child abuse; a Children's Enhancement Program that builds self-esteem, develops cognitive, psychological, social, and motor skills among children of parents attending ($50,000) see Swalm Foundation

Faith in Sharing House — purchase building for office space and storage ($20,000) see Mayer Foundation, James and Eva

Family Life Ministry ($10,607) see Steinhagen Benevolent Trust, B. A. and Elinor

Family Service Association — to establish volunteer database program ($50,000) see Halsell Foundation, Ewing

Fellowship of Christian Athletes ($10,000) see Kilroy Foundation, William S. and Lora Jean

Fellowship of Christian Athletes, Greater Dallas Chapter — Tom Landry FCA Open Golf Tournament ($25,000) see Contran Corporation

Fire Department ($50,000) see Temple-Inland Inc.

First Baptist Church ($55,000) see Fair Foundation, R. W.

First Baptist Church ($10,000) see Hallberg Foundation, E. L. and R. F.

First Baptist Church ($6,300) see Mays Foundation

First Baptist Church ($427,000) see Meyer Family Foundation, Paul J.

First Baptist Church — religious ($10,000) see Wise Foundation and Charitable Trust, Watson W.

First Baptist Church — religious ($10,000) see Wise Foundation and Charitable Trust, Watson W.

First Baptist Church — religious ($10,000) see Wise Foundation and Charitable Trust, Watson W.

First English Lutheran Church Cancer Aid Fund ($10,000) see Overlake Foundation

First Presbyterian Church ($5,000) see Knox, Sr., and Pearl Wallis Knox Charitable Foundation, Robert W.

First Presbyterian Church — for monetary contribution ($75,000) see Norman Foundation, Summers A.

First Presbyterian Church — pipe organ competition ($2,500) see Piper Foundation, Minnie Stevens

First United Methodist Church ($7,500) see Hallberg Foundation, E. L. and R. F.

First United Methodist Church ($450,783) see Herzstein Charitable Foundation, Albert and Ethel

First United Methodist Church ($3,000) see Potts and Sibley Foundation

First United Methodist Church ($33,000) see Rachal Foundation, Ed

F.M. Buck Richards Memorial Library — purchase of equipment and improvements ($165) see White Trust, G. R.

Food Bank of Greater Tarrant County ($1,000) see Walsh Foundation

Food Bank of Greater Tarrant County — memorial donation ($15,000) see Weaver Foundation, Gil and Dody

Ft. Worth Ballet ($50,000) see McQueen Foundation, Adeline and George

Ft. Worth Ballet — for cultural purposes ($25,000) see Scott Foundation, William E.

Ft. Worth Educational Council — for general support ($10,000) see O'Quinn Foundation, John M. and Nancy C.

Ft. Worth Museum of Science and History — for cultural purposes ($25,000) see Scott Foundation, William E.

Ft. Worth Opera Association ($5,000) see Walsh Foundation

Ft. Worth Symphony ($12,500) see Alcon Laboratories, Inc.

Ft. Worth Symphony Orchestra ($6,000) see Hallberg Foundation, E. L. and R. F.

Ft. Worth Symphony Orchestra ($5,000) see Hallberg Foundation, E. L. and R. F.

Ft. Worth Theater Greater Community ($1,300) see Walsh Foundation

Ft. Worth Zoological Association — capital and renovation campaign ($400,000) see Burnett-Tandy Foundation

Ft. Worth Zoological Association — for charitable purposes ($150,000) see Scott Foundation, William E.

Ft. Worth Zoological Society ($30,000) see McQueen Foundation, Adeline and George

Foster Home for Children — building construction ($33,310) see Doss Foundation, M. S.

Foto Fest Innovative Design Center ($25,000) see Vale Foundation, Ruby R.

Foundation for the Retarded — building campaign ($50,000) see Fish Foundation, Ray C.

Foundation of Temple Public Library — purchase of building ($1,500,000) see Carpenter Foundation, E. Rhodes and Leona B.

Friends of Children — for charitable purposes ($25,000) see Scott Foundation, William E.

Friends of Dr. Martin Luther King — contribution of 1993 birthday celebration ($3,000) see Dishman Charitable Foundation Trust, H. E. and Kate

Friends of Elder Citizens — nutrition program ($15,000) see Trull Foundation

Friends of the Midland Public Library — for Children and Youth Department fixtures ($25,000) see Davidson Family Charitable Foundation

Friends of Milam Park — operation ($25,000) see Koehler Foundation, Marcia and Otto

Friends of Reading is Fundamental of Austin ($5,000) see Johnson Foundation, Burdine

Friends of Ronald McDonald House ($20,000) see Clayton Fund

Friends of Unger Memorial Library — purchase hardware, software and furniture to be used in library ($14,344) see Mayer Foundation, James and Eva

Fund for Excellence in Education in the Dallas Independent School District — school performance improvement award fund

($100,000) see Fikes Foundation, Leland

Funding Information Center — library support ($3,000) see Semmes Foundation

Gaines County — building construction, equipment ($46,601) see Doss Foundation, M. S.

Galveston Historical Foundation — to implement project to build or renovate home in historical district for qualified low-income buyer with special training in home ownership ($25,000) see Favrot Fund

Galveston Historical Foundation ($6,000) see Knox, Sr., and Pearl Wallis Knox Charitable Foundation, Robert W.

George Bush Presidential Library — capital campaign ($50,000) see Fish Foundation, Ray C.

German Heritage Park — operation ($10,000) see Koehler Foundation, Marcia and Otto

Gideons ($3,000) see Mays Foundation

Girl Scouts of America ($5,000) see Prairie Foundation

Gladney Center — equipment ($50,000) see Doss Foundation, M. S.

Gladney Fund ($40,000) see Hillsdale Fund

Glassell School of Art Benefit — 1992 Glassell School of Art Benefit ($6,000) see Early Foundation

Goals for Dallas ($10,000) see Jonsson Foundation

Good Samaritan Center ($10,000) see Halff Foundation, G. A. C.

Good Samaritan Center — annual grant ($100,000) see Cain Foundation, Gordon and Mary

Good Samaritan Foundation — nursing scholarships ($28,000) see Turner Charitable Foundation

Goodfellows Association — help needy children at Christmas time ($2,500) see Kayser Foundation

Goodwill Industries ($11,547) see Knox, Sr., and Pearl Wallis Knox Charitable Foundation, Robert W.

Goodwill Industries of Abilene — to provide operating support and loan forgiveness of $30,000 ($60,000) see Dodge Jones Foundation

Goodwill Industries of Central Texas — fire sprinkler system ($30,000) see Wright Foundation, Lola

Graham Area Literacy Council ($1,000) see Bertha Foundation

Graham Art Guild ($300) see Bertha Foundation

Graham Concert Association — membership ($1,000) see Bertha Foundation

Graham General Hospital — health fair ($1,850) see Bertha Foundation

Graham Independent School District — computers and conferences ($6,685) see Bertha Foundation

Graham Public Library — building construction ($1,193,487) see Bertha Foundation

Gray County Association for the Retarded ($10,000) see Brown Foundation, M. K.

Grayson Adult Literacy Team — for children's one-on-one reading program ($24,948) see Munson Foundation Trust, W. B.

Grayson Adult Literacy Team ($24,948) see Munson Foundation Trust, W. B.

Grayson Adult Literacy Team Advisory Council — for read to win project ($30,890) see Munson Foundation Trust, W. B.

Grayson County College — lab learning center ($62,265) see Smith Charitable Foundation, Clara Blackford Smith and W. Aubrey

Grayson County College — nursing program ($25,270) see Smith Charitable Foundation, Clara Blackford Smith and W. Aubrey

Grayson County Crisis Center — capital expenses ($25,000) see Smith Charitable Foundation, Clara Blackford Smith and W. Aubrey

Grayson County Rehabilitation Center — computer network ($53,500) see Smith Charitable Foundation, Clara Blackford Smith and W. Aubrey

Greater Houston Hemophilia Society ($6,000) see Murphy Co. Foundation, G.C.

Greenhill School — faculty support ($33,000) see Contran Corporation

Gulf Coast Regional Blood Center — toward building expansion ($2,000,000) see Houston Endowment

Habitat for Humanity ($60,000) see Temple-Inland Inc.

Harlingen Area Educational Foundation — for educational purposes ($3,000) see Hygeia Dairy Co.

Harmony Family Services — boys residential treatment center ($100,000) see Bridwell Foundation, J. S.

Harper Independent School District — track portion of athletic facility plan ($40,000) see Peterson Foundation, Hal and Charlie

Harris County Juvenile Probation Department — for salary and travel expenses to hire an Assistant Volunteer Coordinator to attract volunteers to help serve the needs of the youth of Harris County involved with the Juvenile Probation Department ($36,009) see Swalm Foundation

Hays Consolidated Independent School District — Kodaly music program, playgrounds, and landscaping ($288,500) see Johnson Foundation, Burdine

Hays Youth Athletic Association — septic system ($15,000) see Johnson Foundation, Burdine

Health Care Foundation ($25,000) see McQueen Foundation, Adeline and George

Heirborn Ministries of Gulf Coast — for the Boiling Youth program ($25,000) see Gulf Coast Medical Foundation

Henderson Civic Center see Southwestern Electric Power Co.

Hermann Eye Fund — distinguished professorship endowment ($35,000) see Rockwell Fund

High Sky Children's Ranch ($7,500) see Prairie Foundation

Highland Park Presbyterian Church ($100,000) see Hawn Foundation

Hill Country Crisis Council — funds to the children's program, construction of counseling house, and shelter repair ($51,500) see Peterson Foundation, Hal and Charlie

Hilltop Baptist Temple ($250,000) see Speer Foundation, Roy M.

History in Action — produce video, student guide, leader's guide, quiz, and Aware of Excellence program on life of Mark Twain ($50,000) see Hillcrest Foundation

Hockaday School ($10,000) see Clements Foundation

Holy Name Catholic School — student tuition assistance ($5,000) see Burkitt Foundation

Hope of South Texas ($10,400) see Overlake Foundation

Hospice in the Pines ($48,398) see Temple-Inland Inc.

Hospice of South Texas ($50,000) see O'Connor Foundation, Kathryn

Hospice at the Texas Medical Center — patient care center ($166,800) see Fondren Foundation

Hospice of Wichita Falls — operating budget ($2,500) see Bridwell Foundation, J. S.

HOT Council Boy Scouts ($125,010) see Meyer Family Foundation, Paul J.

Houston Arboretum and Nature Center — capital campaign ($30,000) see Fish Foundation, Ray C.

Houston Ballet see Management Compensation Group/Dulworth Inc.

Houston Ballet ($30,000) see Texas Commerce Bank-Houston, N.A.

Houston Ballet Foundation ($5,000) see Kilroy Foundation, William S. and Lora Jean

Houston Ballet Foundation ($5,000) see Kilroy Foundation, William S. and Lora Jean

Houston Baptist University — seminar room in McNair Center ($25,000) see Turner Charitable Foundation

Houston Food Bank ($2,500) see Hygeia Dairy Co.

Houston Foto Fest — fund the Fotofest Literacy through Photography program ($20,000) see Favrot Fund

Houston Foundation ($10,000) see Knox, Sr., and Pearl Wallis Knox Charitable Foundation, Robert W.

Houston-Galveston Area Food Bank ($50,000) see Rockwell Fund

Houston Grand Opera ($13,900) see Texas Commerce Bank-Houston, N.A.

Houston Grand Opera ($1,000) see Wilder Foundation

Houston Host Committee Fund — for construction cost inside the Astrodome for GOP national convention ($250,000) see Tenneco Inc.

Houston Housing Partnership ($15,000) see Texas Commerce Bank-Houston, N.A.

Houston Humane Society ($500) see Elkins, Jr. Foundation, Margaret and James A.

Houston Jewish Geriatric Foundation see Management Compensation Group/Dulworth Inc.

Houston Leadership Circle — to support on-going programs ($20,000) see Early Foundation

Houston Museum of Natural Science — for the arts ($50,000) see Schlumberger Ltd.

Houston Museum of Natural Science — general operations ($50,000) see Cain Foundation, Gordon and Mary

Houston Museum of Natural Science — capital campaign, Phase II Face of the Future ($300,000) see Cullen Foundation

Houston Museum Natural Science ($20,000) see Dresser Industries, Inc.

Houston Museum of Natural Science — to support Face of the Future: 2001 Phase II Campaign ($12,500) see Duncan Foundation, Lillian H. and C. W.

Houston Museum of Natural Science — community funds ($100,000) see Hamman Foundation, George and Mary Josephine

Houston Museum of Natural Science ($15,000) see Texas Commerce Bank-Houston, N.A.

Houston Museum of Natural Sciences — capital campaign ($180,000) see Fondren Foundation

Houston Parks Board — Memorial Golf Course restoration ($50,000) see Turner Charitable Foundation

Houston School for Deaf Children ($10,000) see Clayton Fund

Houston Symphony ($100,000) see Anderson Foundation, M. D.

Houston Symphony see Management Compensation Group/Dulworth Inc.

Houston Symphony Orchestra — community funds ($20,000) see Hamman Foundation, George and Mary Josephine

Houston Symphony Society ($200,000) see Shell Oil Company

Houston Texas Exes — public educational ($3,000) see Owsley Foundation, Alvin and Lucy

HOW Center — contribution for center repairs ($15,833) see Dishman Charitable Foundation Trust, H. E. and Kate

HOW Center ($7,667) see Dishman Charitable Foundation Trust, H. E. and Kate

HOW Center — kitchen and dining facility ($5,000) see

Steinhagen Benevolent Trust, B. A. and Elinor

Hull Country Youth Ranch — Performing Arts Theater challenge ($40,000) see Turner Charitable Foundation

Human Enrichment of Life Program ($10,000) see Elkins, Jr. Foundation, Margaret and James A.

Hurricane Allen St. Lucia Foundation ($20,000) see Scurlock Foundation

I Have A Dream Foundation ($500) see Walsh Foundation

I Have A Dream Houston — general operations ($30,000) see Cain Foundation, Gordon and Mary

Incarnate Word College — for books ($25,000) see Brackenridge Foundation, George W.

Incarnate Word College — Chapel Preservation campaign ($2,500) see Piper Foundation, Minnie Stevens

Institute of Nautical Archaeology ($25,000) see JFM Foundation

Institute of Religion ($25,000) see Turner Charitable Foundation

InterCultura — for cultural purposes ($31,000) see Scott Foundation, William E.

Inwood Baptist — educational ($25,000) see Herzstein Charitable Foundation, Albert and Ethel

Irving Humane Society — community ($5,000) see Stemmons Foundation

Jacksonville Rodeo Association — for monetary contribution ($62,750) see Norman Foundation, Summers A.

James Dick Center for the Performing Arts ($2,500) see Piper Foundation, Minnie Stevens

James Dick Foundation for Performing Arts — building fund ($200,000) see Johnson Foundation, Burdine

James Dick Foundation for Performing Arts — toward sound booth ($25,000) see Wright Foundation, Lola

James L. West Presbyterian Special Care Center — for charitable purposes ($75,000) see Scott Foundation, William E.

Jarvis Christian College ($15,000) see McQueen Foundation, Adeline and George

Jasper Memorial Hospital ($70,000) see Temple-Inland Inc.

Jewel Charity Ball ($25,000) see McQueen Foundation, Adeline and George

Jewish Federation ($15,000) see Weil, Gotshal and Manges Foundation

Jordan School — memorial endowment fund ($200,000) see Fondren Foundation

Judson Montessori — purchase of land ($100,000) see Brackenridge Foundation, George W.

Judson Montessori School — acquisition of land for new campus ($80,000) see Halsell Foundation, Ewing

Julia C. Hester House — for support to complete a capital campaign to build a new building to house Juila C. hester House in the Fifth Ward Area; and provide

expenses to teach entreprenurial skills to cildren to prevent juvenile delinquency ($72,993) see Swalm Foundation

Junior Achievement of East Texas see Southwestern Electric Power Co.

Junior Achievement of Tarrant County ($27,000) see Alcon Laboratories, Inc.

Junior Helping Hand for Children — furnishings ($23,368) see Wright Foundation, Lola

Junior League of Dallas ($2,500) see Clements Foundation

Justin Paul Foundation — developmental disabilities and other programs ($80,000) see Cain Foundation, Effie and Wofford

Juvenile Diabetes Foundation — medical research ($76,000) see Hawn Foundation

Karitas ($12,500) see Texas Commerce Bank-Houston, N.A.

KERA/Channel 13 ($5,000) see Stemmons Foundation

Kerrville Independent School District — funding of various programs for each of the district's schools ($166,177) see Peterson Foundation, Hal and Charlie

Kerrville Independent School District — fund purchase of Chamber Building for the district's mentoring program ($34,000) see Peterson Foundation, Hal and Charlie

Kinkaid School — educational ($125,000) see Hobby Foundation

Kinkaid School — computer purchase ($50,000) see Kilroy Foundation, William S. and Lora Jean

Kinkaid School — computer purchase ($25,000) see Kilroy Foundation, William S. and Lora Jean

Kinkaid School ($63,000) see Wilder Foundation

KLRN ($6,000) see Tobin Foundation

KPAC — operation ($17,000) see Koehler Foundation, Marcia and Otto

KSCE Television — for Joy of Music program ($1,500) see Huthsteiner Fine Arts Trust

KUHT — for general support ($50,000) see O'Quinn Foundation, John M. and Nancy C.

Lady Lex Museum/Bay Association ($2,500) see Hygeia Dairy Co.

Lake County Christian Foundation — building program ($150,000) see Carter Foundation, Amon G.

Laredo Independent School District ($250,000) see Hachar Charitable Trust, D. D.

Laredo Junior College Nursing Program ($27,123) see Hachar Charitable Trust, D. D.

Laredo Philharmonic Orchestra ($12,751) see Hachar Charitable Trust, D. D.

LaRue Learning Center ($37,000) see Meyer Family Foundation, Paul J.

Law Focused Education — teacher training institutes

($308,396) see Sumners Foundation, Hatton W.

LBJ Museum and Library ($5,000) see LBJ Family Foundation

Leadership for the Future ($66,000) see Union Pacific Corp.

Lone Star Girl Scouts Council — matching grant ($25,000) see Wright Foundation, Lola

Lubbock Area Foundation ($18,000) see Hallberg Foundation, E. L. and R. F.

Lubbock International Cultural Center — building fund ($25,000) see Jones Foundation, Helen

Lufkin Independent School District — for general operations ($3,029) see Pineywoods Foundation

Lutheran Social Services of the South — grant for the Texas Money Management Project ($4,500) see Dishman Charitable Foundation Trust, H. E. and Kate

Lyndon B. Johnson School ($6,000) see LBJ Family Foundation

Make-A-Wish Foundation ($10,000) see Overlake Foundation

Manos De Cristo — pastoral care director position ($10,000) see Trull Foundation

Marine Military Academy — for building purposes ($4,000) see Hygeia Dairy Co.

Marshall Regional Arts Council see Southwestern Electric Power Co.

Marvin United Methodist ($54,000) see Fair Foundation, R. W.

McNay Art Institute ($50,000) see Tobin Foundation

Mcnay Art Museum ($10,000) see Halff Foundation, G. A. C.

McNay Art Museum — security equipment, general support ($55,600) see Semmes Foundation

M.D. Anderson Cancer Center ($11,000) see Glanville Family Foundation

M.D. Anderson Cancer Center ($100,000) see Elkins, Jr. Foundation, Margaret and James A.

M.D. Anderson Cancer Center ($50,050) see Hobby Foundation

M.D. Anderson Cancer Center — capital improvement campaign ($150,000) see McDermott Foundation, Eugene

M.D. Anderson Cancer Center ($21,666) see Scurlock Foundation

M.D. Anderson Cancer Center ($58,000) see Smith Charitable Foundation, Clara Blackford Smith and W. Aubrey

M.D. Anderson Cancer Center ($5,000) see Wilder Foundation

M.D. Anderson Hospital — help with more technologically sophisticated facilities ($20,000) see Kayser Foundation

M.D. Anderson Hospital and Tumor Institute ($220,000) see Shell Oil Company

Meals on Wheels ($15,000) see Weaver Foundation, Gil and Dody

Rio Grande Radiation Treatment/Cancer Foundation — for building purposes ($5,000) see Hygeia Dairy Co.

Ronald McDonald House ($44,883) see Temple-Inland Inc.

Rotary Club Activities of Houston and Harris County — toward a housing facility for patients at the M.D. Anderson Cancer Center ($1,000,000) see Houston Endowment

Rotary Club of Graham — scholarship fund ($5,000) see Bertha Foundation

Rotary Scholarship — for monetary contribution ($10,000) see Norman Foundation, Summers A.

Rummell Creek Elementary School — awards ($250,000) see RJR Nabisco Inc.

Rusk Independent School District — for computers ($38,784) see Norman Foundation, Summers A.

SA Council on Alcohol and Drug Abuse ($10,000) see Halff Foundation, G. A. C.

Sacred Heart Church ($25,000) see Rachal Foundation, Ed

St. Andrew's Episcopal School — school expansion ($75,000) see Cain Foundation, Effie and Wofford

St. Andrews Episcopal School ($125,000) see Hobby Foundation

St. Dennis Church ($45,870) see O'Connor Foundation, Kathryn

St. Edward's University ($50,000) see Hobby Foundation

St. John the Divine Episcopal Church — capital campaign ($208,500) see Fondren Foundation

St. John's Episcopal Church ($11,000) see Weaver Foundation, Gil and Dody

St. John's School ($126,000) see Hobby Foundation

St. John's School — public educational ($22,000) see Owsley Foundation, Alvin and Lucy

St. Joseph Academy — building renovation and expansion ($7,500) see Burkitt Foundation

St. Joseph High School ($50,000) see O'Connor Foundation, Kathryn

St. Joseph Hospital — capital program ($150,000) see Carter Foundation, Amon G.

St. Luke's Episcopal Hospital ($25,000) see Ford Fund, William and Martha

St. Lukes Methodist Church Foundation — capital campaign ($50,000) see Rockwell Fund

St. Luke's United Methodist Church — building fund ($20,000) see Turner Charitable Foundation

St. Mark's School of Texas — phase III of a building campaign ($250,000) see Fikes Foundation, Leland

St. Mary's Hall ($39,000) see Taylor Foundation, Ruth and Vernon

St. Mary's University — scholarship ($34,500) see Brackenridge Foundation, George W.

St. Michael and All Angels Church ($250,000) see Fikes Foundation, Leland

St. Michael's Church ($15,000) see Clements Foundation

St. Paul Medical Center — medical assistance ($50,000) see Hawn Foundation

St. Peter Episcopal Church — building expansion fund ($75,000) see Turner Charitable Foundation

St. Philips School ($1,800) see Clements Foundation

St. Stephen's Episcopal School ($15,000) see JFM Foundation

St. Stephen's Episcopal School — building and operating funds ($438,200) see Johnson Foundation, Burdine

St. Thomas High School — payment of construction debt ($10,000) see Burkitt Foundation

Salvation Army — capital campaign for renovation of construction ($4,000) see Barry Corp., R. G.

Salvation Army — operating budget ($2,500) see Bridwell Foundation, J. S.

Salvation Army — building construction ($50,000) see Steinhagen Benevolent Trust, B. A. and Elinor

Salvation Army Beaumont Corps ($50,000) see Dishman Charitable Foundation Trust, H. E. and Kate

Salvation Army of Dallas — five-year pledge to support the Salvation Army School for Officers' Training Southern Territory ($25,000) see Contran Corporation

Samaritan Counseling Center ($5,000) see Dunagan Foundation

San Antonio Academy ($32,000) see Taylor Foundation, Ruth and Vernon

San Antonio Art Institute ($10,000) see Halff Foundation, G. A. C.

San Antonio Little Theater — operation ($11,250) see Koehler Foundation, Marcia and Otto

San Antonio Museum — furniture and equipment ($65,000) see Brackenridge Foundation, George W.

San Antonio Museum of Art — operation ($18,000) see Koehler Foundation, Marcia and Otto

San Antonio Museum Association — donation ($12,000) see Schwartz Fund for Education and Health Research, Arnold and Marie

San Antonio Museum Association ($10,000) see Halff Foundation, G. A. C.

San Antonio Museum Association — contribution toward Latin American Wing, Museum of Art ($400,000) see Halsell Foundation, Ewing

San Antonio Museum Association — acquisition of contemporary Mexican art ($50,000) see Halsell Foundation, Ewing

San Antonio Public Library Foundation — acquisition of major art piece for permanent exhibition at new library ($250,000) see Halsell Foundation, Ewing

San Antonio Public Library Foundation — towards construction library ($20,000) see Semmes Foundation

San Antonio Public Library Foundation — general funding ($50,000) see Zachry Co., H.B.

San Antonio Public Library Foundation — education ($50,000) see Zachry Co., H.B.

San Antonio Symphony ($10,000) see Tobin Foundation

San Antonio Symphony — general funding ($80,000) see Zachry Co., H.B.

Save Our Schools — for general support ($25,000) see O'Quinn Foundation, John M. and Nancy C.

Scenic Houston — help in new forestery for parks in Houston ($3,500) see Kayser Foundation

School of the Woods — capital improvement drive ($196,000) see Fondren Foundation

Schreiner College — Weir building renovation/library ($55,000) see Fish Foundation, Ray C.

Schreiner College — funding of nursing program and Senior Vice President's position ($135,000) see Peterson Foundation, Hal and Charlie

Schreiner College — startup expenses for senior vice president ($10,000) see Trull Foundation

Science Spectrum — grant ($25,000) see Jones Foundation, Helen

Scott and White Hospital — equipment purchase ($500,000) see Carter Foundation, Amon G.

Scott and White Memorial Hospital — Fastrac CT Scanner ($500,000) see Noble Foundation, Samuel Roberts

Search ($500,000) see Herzstein Charitable Foundation, Albert and Ethel

Sears Methodist Centers — alzheimer care program ($5,000) see Bridwell Foundation, J. S.

Senior Citizens Service of North Texas ($10,000) see Priddy Foundation

Service of Emergency Aid Resource Center ($12,500) see Weil, Gotshal and Manges Foundation

Seton Fund — parent counseling room ($25,000) see Wright Foundation, Lola

SFA Minority Scholarships — for general operations ($1,500) see Pineywoods Foundation

Shelby Foundation — for general operations ($5,000) see Pineywoods Foundation

Shepherd's Adult Day Care Center —to purchase wheel chair lift equipped van ($25,000) see Davidson Family Charitable Foundation

Sibley Environmental Learning Center ($4,000) see Potts and Sibley Foundation

Society for the Prevention of Cruelty to Animals of Texas — community ($10,000) see Stemmons Foundation

Some Other Place — grant for the Back to School Clothing Program ($10,000) see Dishman Charitable Foundation Trust, H. E. and Kate

Some Other Place ($11,000) see Steinhagen Benevolent Trust, B. A. and Elinor

South Plains Council 694 Boys Scouts of America — renovation of camp ($25,000) see Jones Foundation, Helen

South Plains Food Bank — equipment ($75,000) see Doss Foundation, M. S.

South Plains Food Bank — final funding for innovative surplus food drying and distribution operation ($1,250,000) see Meadows Foundation

South Texas College of Law — capital fund drive ($50,000) see Rockwell Fund

South Texas Drug and Alcohol Rehabilitation ($25,000) see Rachal Foundation, Ed

Southeast Texas Arts Council — contribution to continue Sub Grant Program ($7,500) see Dishman Charitable Foundation Trust, H. E. and Kate

Southeast Texas Arts Council ($15,000) see Steinhagen Benevolent Trust, B. A. and Elinor

Southern Methodist University ($16,000) see Oaklawn Foundation

Southern Methodist University — Free Enterprise Institute ($15,000) see Armstrong Foundation

Southern Methodist University ($61,000) see Clements Foundation

Southern Methodist University — library renovation ($380,000) see Fondren Foundation

Southern Methodist University — arts library fund ($100,000) see Hawn Foundation

Southern Methodist University — for Underwood Law Library renovation ($125,000) see Hillcrest Foundation

Southern Methodist University — endowment ($25,000) see Jonsson Foundation

Southern Methodist University — political science partial tuition grants endowment ($100,000) see Sumners Foundation, Hatton W.

Southern Methodist University School of Archaeology ($3,000) see Potts and Sibley Foundation

Southwest Foundation — operation ($15,000) see Koehler Foundation, Marcia and Otto

Southwest Medical Foundation — medical assistance ($50,000) see Hawn Foundation

Southwestern Exposition and Livestock Show — capital campaign ($500,000) see Burnett-Tandy Foundation

Southwestern Medical Foundation ($40,000) see Goddard Foundation, Charles B.

Southwestern Theological Seminary ($20,000) see McQueen Foundation, Adeline and George

Southwestern University — endowed scholarships ($75,000) see Cain Foundation, Effie and Wofford

Southwestern University ($300,000) see Cullen Foundation

Southwestern University ($10,000) see Duncan Foundation, Lillian H. and C. W.

Southwestern University — to support on-going programs ($10,000) see Early Foundation

Southwestern University ($15,000) see Scurlock Foundation

Square House Museum ($39,300) see Brown Foundation, M. K.

State Preservation Board — for capital fund for restoration of Legislative Library ($150,000) see McDermott Foundation, Eugene

State of Texas Department of Health — three-year, $500,000 grant for the funding of statewide community-based immunization grants program ($200,000) see Aetna Life & Casualty Co.

Stehlin Foundation — medical treatment ($15,000) see Hamman Foundation, George and Mary Josephine

Stehlin Foundation for Cancer Research — cancer research ($50,000) see Fish Foundation, Ray C.

Stephen F. Austin State University ($51,266) see Temple-Inland Inc.

Su Casa de Esperanza — parenting and pregnant teen programs ($10,000) see Trull Foundation

Sul Ross State University ($3,000) see Potts and Sibley Foundation

Susan G. Komen Foundation — regional breast cancer summits ($230,000) see General Mills, Inc.

TAMU Development Foundation — rice research program ($10,000) see Trull Foundation

Tarrant County Hospital District — community health centers in the Stop Six and Diamond Hill neighborhoods ($400,000) see Burnett-Tandy Foundation

Tarrant County Housing Partnership — special program ($350,000) see Carter Foundation, Amon G.

Tarrant County Junior College — to purchase IAV and CAI equipment and to fund a workshop ($77,870) see Fuld Health Trust, Helene

Teen Challenge of Grayson County — transportation ($23,876) see Smith Charitable Foundation, Clara Blackford Smith and W. Aubrey

Temple B'nai Israel ($50,000) see Kempner Fund, Harris and Eliza

Texas A&I University Foundation ($900,000) see Rachal Foundation, Ed

Texas A&M Development Foundation — improvements to G. Rollie White Center of Animal

The Big Book of Library Grant Money

Women's Crisis Center ($10,000) see Overlake Foundation

Women's Haven of Tarrant County ($11,000) see Weaver Foundation, Gil and Dody

YMCA ($25,000) see Duncan Foundation, Lillian H. and C. W.

YMCA — to support Second Century Development Programs ($25,000) see Early Foundation

YMCA ($50,000) see Herzstein Charitable Foundation, Albert and Ethel

YMCA of Metropolitan Dallas — community ($10,000) see Stemmons Foundation

YMCA of Metropolitan Dallas ($200,000) see Sturgis Charitable and Educational Trust, Roy and Christine

Young Audiences of Greater Dallas — cultural ($10,000) see Stemmons Foundation

Young Life ($15,000) see McQueen Foundation, Adeline and George

Youth Alternatives — renovate emergency shelter and acquire new security system ($52,500) see Halsell Foundation, Ewing

YWCA — special needs daycare program ($15,000) see Weaver Foundation, Gil and Dody

Utah

Avatar, Inc. — operating funds ($39,500) see Swanson Family Foundation, Dr. W.C.

Boy Scouts of America — operating funds ($30,000) see Swanson Family Foundation, Dr. W.C.

Brigham Young University — technology, education, and construction management ($5,000) see Bright Family Foundation

Brigham Young University — for Kemper Scholar Grants ($29,200) see Kemper National Insurance Cos.

Brigham Young University ($7,500) see Reynolds Foundation, Donald W.

Brigham Young University School of Management ($100,000) see Marriott Foundation, J. Willard

Diocese of Salt Lake City ($10,000) see Price Foundation, Lucien B. and Katherine E.

Family Support Center — operating funds ($30,000) see Swanson Family Foundation, Dr. W.C.

Holy Cross Hospital see Packaging Corporation of America

Judge Memorial High School ($12,500) see Price Foundation, Lucien B. and Katherine E.

Junior Achievement see Novell Inc.

Notre Dame School ($10,000) see Price Foundation, Lucien B. and Katherine E.

Ogden City Downtown Civic Center — building funds ($100,000) see Swanson Family Foundation, Dr. W.C.

Ogden City School — building funds ($195,000) see Swanson Family Foundation, Dr. W.C.

Ogden River Parkway — building funds ($32,000) see Swanson Family Foundation, Dr. W.C.

Orem High School — awards ($250,000) see RJR Nabisco Inc.

Primary Children's Medical Center — to help build a new hospital serving the Intermountain West ($25,000) see Boise Cascade Corporation

Primary Children's Medical Center ($5,000) see Sargent Foundation, Newell B.

Timpanogos Storytelling Festival see Novell Inc.

Treehouse Children's Museum — operating funds ($38,900) see Swanson Family Foundation, Dr. W.C.

University of Utah —for computer science ($576,352) see Hewlett-Packard Co.

University of Utah Library ($200,000) see Marriott Foundation, J. Willard

University of Utah Library ($200,000) see Marriott Foundation, J. Willard

Utah Opera see Novell Inc.

Waterford Institute — development of a computer-based reading program to help solve reading problems of disadvantaged students ($35,000) see Hyde and Watson Foundation

Weber County School Foundation — to purchase equipment ($35,000) see Swanson Family Foundation, Dr. W.C.

Weber State University — operating funds ($30,000) see Swanson Family Foundation, Dr. W.C.

Vermont

Appalachian Mountain Club — an outreach and communications coordinator for the Northern Forest Alliance ($50,000) see Merck Family Fund

Bennington College ($30,000) see Harriman Foundation, Mary W.

Bennington College ($10,000) see Lemberg Foundation

Bennington College Corporation ($62,000) see Valentine Foundation, Lawson

Brattleboro Mutual Aid Association ($30,500) see Thompson Trust, Thomas

Champlain Islands Parent-Child Center — program support ($50,000) see Turrell Fund

CIRMA ($59,500) see Plumsock Fund

Critical Languages and Area Studies Consortium — toward Japanese language and culture studies for high school students ($127,400) see Culpeper Foundation, Charles E.

East School — community publishing center ($3,000) see Windham Foundation

Experiment in International Living ($25,000) see Thompson Trust, Thomas

Experiment in International Living ($25,000) see Bunbury Company

Gailer School at Middlebury ($25,000) see Barker Foundation, J.M.R.

Grace Cottage Hospital ($17,500) see Thompson Trust, Thomas

Grafton Church — building renovations ($20,000) see Windham Foundation

Jimmie Heuga Center — scholarship assistance ($3,000) see Windham Foundation

King Street Area Youth Program — capital campaign ($145,000) see Turrell Fund

Lake Champlain Maritime Museum — partially underwrite the printing of an illustrated museum education publication ($5,000) see Phillips Foundation, Ellis L.

Landmark College — support the college's outreach program and provide student scholarships for summer skills development session ($30,000) see Good Samaritan

Marlboro Press — support to establish, staff, and maintain office in Brattleboro, VT ($40,000) see Laurel Foundation

Middlebury College ($102,800) see Overbrook Foundation

Planned Parenthood of New England — medical training of nurses and midwives in Uganda ($29,000) see International Foundation

Preservation Trust of Vermont ($2,500) see Windham Foundation

Proctor Free Library — book budget ($3,000) see Proctor Trust, Mortimer R.

Proctor School District ($27,950) see Proctor Trust, Mortimer R.

Putney School — renovation of physical plant ($150,000) see Clowes Fund

Putney School ($18,500) see Goldberg Family Foundation

Rescue ($30,000) see Thompson Trust, Thomas

Rutland Central Supervisor Union — repair and paint the clock tower at Proctor Elementary School ($4,575) see Proctor Trust, Mortimer R.

St. Dominics Catholic Church — repairs of dormer windows, parish windows, and stained glass windows ($9,735) see Proctor Trust, Mortimer R.

St. Dominics Catholic Church — insulation, installation of vinyl siding, and repairs to the rectory ($7,500) see Proctor Trust, Mortimer R.

Salzburg Seminar ($5,000) see Hauser Foundation

Shelburne Farms — charitable ($150,000) see Bettingen Corporation, Burton G.

Smokey House Project — support of general program ($300,000) see Taconic Foundation

Stratton Mountain School — scholarship fund ($10,000) see Windham Foundation

Town of Grafton — Village Bridge repair ($25,000) see Windham Foundation

Town of Proctor — fire department, purchase of new

pumper ($30,000) see Proctor Trust, Mortimer R.

Town of Proctor — maintenance of Taranovich field, youth league, pool operations, and skating rink ($28,639) see Proctor Trust, Mortimer R.

Union Church of Proctor — restoration of pipe organ ($18,000) see Proctor Trust, Mortimer R.

University of Vermont ($26,300) see Holzer Memorial Foundation, Richard H.

University of Vermont — general fund ($210,000) see Sandy Hill Foundation

University of Vermont — scholarship fund ($150,000) see Simon Foundation, William E. and Carol G.

University of Vermont — to purchase CAI and IAV equipment ($70,000) see Fuld Health Trust, Helene

University of Vermont Capital Campaign ($3,000) see Windham Foundation

US Olympic Committee, Vermont State Committee — olympic program funding ($5,000) see Windham Foundation

Vermont Community Foundation ($10,000) see Bunbury Company

Vermont Land Trust ($5,000) see Pettus Crowe Foundation

Vermont Studio Center ($10,000) see Avery Arts Foundation, Milton and Sally

Vermont Studio School ($10,000) see South Branch Foundation

Vermont Symphony Orchestra ($10,000) see Windham Foundation

Wheatstone Brook Pathway Project ($15,000) see Thompson Trust, Thomas

Wilmington Middle-High School — soccer field lights ($3,000) see Windham Foundation

Winston L. Prouty Center ($16,500) see Thompson Trust, Thomas

World Learning ($5,000) see AKC Fund

Youth Services — roof repair ($22,925) see Thompson Trust, Thomas

Virginia

Abingdon Volunteer Fire Company ($11,400) see Treakle Foundation, J. Edwin

Abingdon Volunteer Rescue Squad ($11,400) see Treakle Foundation, J. Edwin

Academy of Model Aeronautics — hire development staff ($50,000) see Ball Brothers Foundation

Alexandria Library — community welfare ($30,000) see Bryant Foundation

American Diabetes Association — first of five payments ($100,000) see AlliedSignal Inc.

American Frontier Culture Foundation ($25,000) see Fleming Cos. Food Distribution Center

American National Red Cross ($1,000) see Altschul Foundation

American Press Institute/Ted Scripps Fellows ($20,000) see Scripps Co., E.W.

American Red Cross see Shenandoah Life Insurance Co.

American Spectator Educational Foundation see USX Corporation

American Truck Stop Foundation ($100,000) see Bridgestone/Firestone, Inc.

Amherst County Public Library ($5,000) see Old Dominion Box Co.

Animal Care Society ($10,200) see Treakle Foundation, J. Edwin

Antietam Elementary School — restricted purpose in support of the Accelerated Reader program ($10,000) see Washington Forrest Foundation

Appalachia Fire Department ($15,000) see Slemp Foundation

Appalachia Rescue Squad — funds to purchase equipment and an ambulance ($19,685) see Slemp Foundation

Arlington Community Foundation — restricted purpose in support of a neighborhood tutoring program ($15,000) see Washington Forrest Foundation

Arlington Free Clinic — general operating support ($7,500) see Washington Forrest Foundation

Arlington Public Schools Transitional First Grade Program — restricted purpose for paying the salary of a part-time teacher for the At-Risk first-grade language arts class ($20,284) see Washington Forrest Foundation

Arlington United Methodist Church — restricted purpose in support of asbestos removal ($16,000) see Washington Forrest Foundation

Ashoka — in support of 10 Brazilian fellows identified as innovators in the areas of working with street children and the environment ($88,125) see Jurzykowski Foundation, Alfred

Ashoka ($30,000) see Zlinkoff Fund for Medical Research and Education, Sergei S.

Ashoka ($10,000) see Kempner Fund, Harris and Eliza

Big Gig — Richmond's international music festival ($10,000) see Cole Trust, Quincy

Blue Ridge School ($25,000) see Fleming Cos. Food Distribution Center

Bluefield State College — renovation of enrollment management suite ($10,000) see Richardson Benevolent Foundation, C. E.

Boissevain Coal Miner's Museum and Park ($50,000) see Shott, Jr. Foundation, Hugh I.

Boys and Girls Clubs of Richmond ($10,100) see Thalhimer Family Foundation, Charles G.

Business Consortium for Arts ($16,550) see Norfolk Shipbuilding & Drydock Corp.

Camp Virginia Jaycees ($20,000) see Morgan and Samuel Tate Morgan, Jr. Foundation, Marietta McNeil

Candii House ($3,672) see Goodman & Co.

Center for Biomedical Ethics of University of Virginia ($300,000) see Kornfeld Foundation, Emily Davie and Joseph S.

Center for Economic and Policy Education — library automation pledge ($50,000) see McKenna Foundation, Philip M.

Center for Economic and Policy Education — AGM Economic Education Series and economic directions ($32,810) see McKenna Foundation, Philip M.

Center for Excellence in Education ($10,000) see Bell Atlantic Corp.

Center for Foreign Journalists — for the Knight International Press Fellowship Program ($3,000,000) see Knight Foundation, John S. and James L.

Center for Foreign Journalists ($20,000) see Dow Jones & Company, Inc.

Center for the Study of Market Process — new faculty and student assistance ($160,000) see Koch Charitable Foundation, Charles G.

Center for the Study of Market Process — summer faculty and student fund ($96,000) see Koch Charitable Foundation, Charles G.

Central Fidelity Bank Special Education Initiatives ($322,342) see Central Fidelity Banks, Inc.

Charities Fund ($301,356) see Sonat Inc.

Charities Funds Transfers ($500,000) see SmithKline Beecham Corp.

Chelonia Institute ($30,000) see Truland Foundation

Chesapeake Volunteers in Youth Services — operation of restaurant ($32,000) see Beazley Foundation/Frederick Foundation

Children ($145,000) see Philibosian Foundation, Stephen

Children's Hospital of the King's Daughters — operating expense ($33,600) see Beazley Foundation/Frederick Foundation

Christ Church, St. Annes Parish ($15,000) see Carter Foundation, Beirne

Christchurch School ($20,000) see Olsson Memorial Foundation, Elis

Christchurch School — restricted support for the construction of a field house in honor of Edward M. Smith ($15,000) see Washington Forrest Foundation

Church of the Good Shepherd ($29,000) see North Shore Foundation

Citizen's Clearinghouse for Hazardous Wastes — to provide technical assistance to communities and grassroots organizations i protecting Virginia's water resources ($15,000) see

Virginia Environmental Endowment

City of Department of Public Health — city dental clinic ($186,791) see Beazley Foundation/Frederick Foundation

City of Portsmouth Parks and Recreation — youth against drugs program ($40,000) see Beazley Foundation/Frederick Foundation

Clinic of Central Virginia ($15,000) see Morgan and Samuel Tate Morgan, Jr. Foundation, Marietta McNeil

College of William and Mary ($8,000) see Chesapeake Corp.

College of William and Mary ($20,000) see Wheat First Butcher Singer, Inc.

Collegiate Schools ($65,000) see Thalhimer and Family Foundation, Charles G.

Colonial Williamsburg — program to teach American values ($50,000) see Salvatori Foundation, Henry

Colonial Williamsburg Foundation ($30,000) see Skaggs Foundation, L. J. and Mary C.

Colonial Williamsburg Foundation ($10,000) see Van Nuys Foundation, I. N. and Susanna H.

Colonial Williamsburg Foundation — education ($10,000) see American Fidelity Corporation

Colonial Williamsburg Foundation ($10,000) see American Fidelity Corporation

Colonial Williamsburg Foundation ($1,000) see Old Dominion Box Co.

Conservation Fund — support a focused effort to establish a national network of linked open spaces ($25,000) see Good Samaritan

Conservation Fund — to establish a land acquisition fund as part of the implementation of a plan for the environmentally sustainable economic development of Canaan Valley and surrounding communities ($1,000,000) see Benedum Foundation, Claude Worthington

Conservation Fund ($100,000) see Mellon Family Foundation, R. K.

Corporation for Jefferson's Poplar Forest — for Thomas Jefferson's Poplar Forest ($160,000) see Getty Trust, J. Paul

Corporation for Jefferson's Poplar Forest — architectural restoration of poplar forest ($50,000) see Cabell Foundation, Robert G. Cabell III and Maude Morgan

Corporation for Jefferson's Poplar Forest ($25,000) see Fleming Cos. Food Distribution Center

Council for America's First Freedom — monument to the Virginia Statute for Religious Freedom ($25,000) see Cole Trust, Quincy

County of Pulaski — fund heritage exhibitions in the old and new courthouses ($5,000) see Richardson Benevolent Foundation, C. E.

CS Lewis Institute — operating funds, challenge grant ($10,000) see Gallagher Family Foundation, Lewis P.

Cystic Fibrosis Foundation ($1,500) see Thalhimer and Family Foundation, Charles G.

Diabetes Institution Foundation — renovation of foundation building ($100,000) see Cabell Foundation, Robert G. Cabell III and Maude Morgan

Diocese of Southern Virginia-Episcopal ($30,000) see North Shore Foundation

Easter Seal Society of Virginia — dormitory annex, Camp Easter Seal East ($50,000) see Cabell Foundation, Robert G. Cabell III and Maude Morgan

Empowerment Network Foundation (TEN) — to launch the Empowerment Network: a national clearinghouse, resource bank, and grassroots coalition ($35,000) see JM Foundation

Enough is Enough Campaign ($10,000) see Morrison Knudsen Corporation

Episcopal High School ($100,000) see Olsson Memorial Foundation, Elis

Episcopal Theological Seminary ($50,000) see Olsson Memorial Foundation, Elis

Episcopal Theological Seminary ($50,000) see Olsson Memorial Foundation, Elis

Fairfax Symphony ($2,000) see Smith Foundation, Gordon V. and Helen C.

Falls Church Episcopal Church ($3,865) see Smith Foundation, Gordon V. and Helen C.

Ferrum College — partial financing of two-story addition to Garber Hall science building ($20,000) see Richardson Benevolent Foundation, C. E.

Fieldale Virginia Community Center ($24,000) see Fieldcrest Cannon Inc.

Fine Arts Center for New River Valley — partial financing of general operating expenses ($5,000) see Richardson Benevolent Foundation, C. E.

First Nations Development Institute ($25,000) see Bay Foundation

Flight Safety Foundation — internship ($10,000) see Friendship Fund

Forward Hampton Roads ($30,000) see Central Fidelity Banks, Inc.

Foundation Endowment ($8,000) see Stauffer Foundation, John and Beverly

Foundation Endowment ($10,000) see Vaughn, Jr. Foundation Fund, James M.

Foundation for International Community Assistance ($10,000) see Friedman Family Foundation

Foundation for Roanoke Valley see Shenandoah Life Insurance Co.

Foxcroft School — one-for-one grant/annual

fund ($25,000) see Prince Trust, Abbie Norman

Foxcroft School ($20,000) see AKC Fund

Foxcroft School — general use ($10,000) see Firestone, Jr. Foundation, Harvey

Freedom House ($5,000) see Schuller International

Friends of Charlotte County Library ($8,500) see Priddy Foundation

Friends of Richmond Public Library ($50,000) see Morgan and Samuel Tate Morgan, Jr. Foundation, Marietta McNeil

General Douglas MacArthur Foundation ($5,000) see Norfolk Shipbuilding & Drydock Corp.

George Mason University — curriculum development of the Community Youth Leadership component for Project LEAD ($6,000) see Strong Foundation, Hattie M.

Gesundheit Institute ($60,000) see Plumsock Fund

Gloucester Library Endowment ($13,600) see Treakle Foundation, J. Edwin

Gloucester-Mathews Humane Society ($10,200) see Treakle Foundation, J. Edwin

Gloucester Volunteer Fire Company and Rescue Squad ($22,800) see Treakle Foundation, J. Edwin

Hampden-Sydney College ($12,500) see Fuqua Foundation, J. B.

Hampden-Sydney College ($20,250) see Sullivan Foundation, Algernon Sydney

Hampden-Sydney College — part of the cost of construction of the third Carpenter House ($750,000) see Carpenter Foundation, E. Rhodes and Leona B.

Hampden-Sydney College — student scholarship assistance ($2,500) see Richardson Benevolent Foundation, C. E.

Hampden-Sydney College ($20,000) see Wheat First Butcher Singer, Inc.

Hampden-Sydney College Endowment — education fund ($50,000) see Bryant Foundation

Hampton University — nursing education ($90,000) see Teagle Foundation

Hampton University — Bemis laboratory restoration ($50,000) see Cabell Foundation, Robert G. Cabell III and Maude Morgan

Hanover Tavern Foundation ($25,000) see Carter Foundation, Beirne

Henricus Foundation ($25,000) see Cole Trust, Quincy

Hensel Eckman YMCA — pool therapy and disability swim programs and for membership scholarships ($5,000) see Richardson Benevolent Foundation, C. E.

Highland Medical Center ($5,000) see Memton Fund

Hill School Corporation ($25,000) see Hillsdale Fund

Hollins College ($50,000) see Hillsdale Fund

Horatio Alger Association ($80,000) see Louisiana-Pacific Corp.

Horatio Alger Association ($45,000) see Louisiana-Pacific Corp.

Horatio Alger Association ($25,000) see Louisiana-Pacific Corp.

Hospice — to support the renovation of the in-patient facility ($10,000) see Washington Forrest Foundation

Humane Studies Foundation — 1992-93 Charles G. Koch Fellowship ($50,000) see Koch Charitable Foundation, Charles G.

Image ($15,000) see M.E. Foundation

Inova Health System Foundation ($3,000) see Truland Foundation

Ivy Hill Cemetery — community welfare ($20,000) see Bryant Foundation

James Madison University ($11,552) see Helms Foundation

James Madison University ($20,000) see Wheat First Butcher Singer, Inc.

Jamestown-Yorktown Educational Trust — 18th century artifacts ($50,000) see Cabell Foundation, Robert G. Cabell III and Maude Morgan

Jefferson Center Foundation see Shenandoah Life Insurance Co.

Jewish Center of Richmond ($1,000) see Fife Foundation, Elias and Bertha

Jewish Community Federation ($15,300) see Thalhimer and Family Foundation, Charles G.

Julian Stanley Wise Foundation see Shenandoah Life Insurance Co.

Junior League of Richmond ($15,000) see Fleming Cos. Food Distribution Center

Lee County High School — final installment of pledge for auditorium ($50,000) see Slemp Foundation

Lee County Public Schools — demonstration teaching project pledged ($10,000) see Slemp Foundation

Lee County Public Schools ($10,000) see Slemp Foundation

Leukemia Society of America ($3,000) see Truland Foundation

Little River Foundation ($206,000) see Ohrstrom Foundation

Little River Foundation ($124,000) see Ohrstrom Foundation

Lower James River Association — match a grant from the Virginia Environmental Endowment Fund ($4,000) see Friendship Fund

Lynchburg College — renovation of science facilities ($50,000) see Cabell Foundation, Robert G. Cabell III and Maude Morgan

Lynchburg College ($20,000) see Old Dominion Box Co.

Lynchburg Fine Arts Center ($1,000) see Old Dominion Box Co.

Madeira School — capital campaign ($100,000) see Prince Trust, Abbie Norman

Madiera School — new facility ($250,000) see

Payne Foundation, Frank E. and Seba B.

Marrow Foundation — three-year pledge to promote expansion of national registry of bone marrow donors ($100,000) see Contran Corporation

Mary Baldwin College — support program in healthcare and ministry ($174,600) see Carpenter Foundation, E. Rhodes and Leona B.

Mary Washington College ($15,000) see Morgan and Samuel Tate Morgan, Jr. Foundation, Marietta McNeil

Marymount University ($26,370) see Truland Foundation

Maryview Hospital - Bon Secours — Elm Avenue Center for Health ($30,000) see Beazley Foundation/Frederick Foundation

Mathews Memorial Library ($13,600) see Treakle Foundation, J. Edwin

Mathews Volunteer Fire Department ($11,400) see Treakle Foundation, J. Edwin

Maymont Foundation ($100,000) see Carter Foundation, Beirne

Maymont Foundation — environmental education programs for teachers ($17,130) see Virginia Environmental Endowment

Maymount Foundation — aviary and small animal habitat ($11,848) see Thalhimer and Family Foundation, Charles G.

Maymount Foundation ($1,500) see Thalhimer and Family Foundation, Charles G.

Media Research Center — Publication 50,000: Free Enterprise and Media Institute ($100,000) see Hermann Foundation, Grover

Media Research Center — free enterprise and Media Institute ($25,000) see Armstrong Foundation

Medical College of Hampton Roads — geriatric evaluation clinic in Portsmouth ($85,000) see Beazley Foundation/Frederick Foundation

Medical College of Hampton Roads Foundation ($8,000) see Norfolk Shipbuilding & Drydock Corp.

Medical College of Virginia ($38,200) see Carter Foundation, Beirne

Medical College of Virginia Foundation ($20,000) see Olsson Memorial Foundation, Elis

Mini Bible College ($42,500) see M.E. Foundation

Mountain Empire Community College — scholarship fund ($10,000) see Slemp Foundation

Mountain Mission School ($100,000) see Shott, Jr. Foundation, Hugh I.

National Association of Secondary School Principals — scholarships ($200,000) see Balfour Foundation, L. G.

National Association of Secondary School Principals ($350,000) see Shell Oil Company

National Community Education Association — to strengthen the financial stability of the association by helping establish a $1.5 million endowment fund ($500,000) see Mott Foundation, Charles Stewart

National Maritime Center Foundation ($20,000) see Norfolk Shipbuilding & Drydock Corp.

National Right to Work Legal Defense and Education Foundation ($6,000) see Stauffer Foundation, John and Beverly

National Right to Work Legal Defense and Education Foundation ($2,000) see French Oil Mill Machinery Co.

National Right to Work Legal Defense and Education Fundation ($2,000) see Pitt-Des Moines Inc.

National Right to Work Legal Defense Foundation ($100,000) see Andersen Corp.

Nature Conservancy ($10,000) see Richardson Charitable Trust, Anne S.

Nature Conservancy ($30,000) see Kerr Foundation

Nature Conservancy — to design, develop, and operate four model conservation lodges in the United States and Caribbean ($4,450,000) see Pew Charitable Trusts

Nature Conservancy ($12,000) see Mars Foundation

New America Schools Development Corporation ($165,000) see Eastman Kodak Company

New American Schools Development Corporation ($600,000) see Martin Marietta Corp.

New American Schools Development Corporation ($200,000) see Bristol-Myers Squibb Company

New American Schools Development Corporation ($10,000,000) see Annenberg Foundation

New American Schools Development Corporation ($250,000) see Rockwell International Corporation

New American Schools Development Corporation —in general support of its efforts to create a new generation of American schools ($833,333) see Exxon Corporation

New Community School — multipurpose activity center ($25,000) see Cole Trust, Quincy

New River Community College Educational Foundation — partial financing of equipment for mathematics and computer information system departments ($5,000) see Richardson Benevolent Foundation, C. E.

Norfolk Community Playground ($6,000) see AKC Fund

North Cross School ($16,000) see Carter Foundation, Beirne

Operation Smile see MBIA Inc.

Operation Smile ($20,000) see North Shore Foundation

Ozone Society ($25,000) see Magowan Family Foundation

Parent Child Development Center ($12,000) see Chesapeake Corp.

Planned Parenthood of the Blue Ridge ($36,114) see Carter Foundation, Beirne

Planned Parenthood of Southeastern Virginia ($27,500) see North Shore Foundation

Portsmouth Community Development Group — salary for executive director ($32,500) see Beazley Foundation/Frederick Foundation

Portsmouth Public Schools — planetarium ($79,167) see Beazley Foundation/Frederick Foundation

Portsmouth Public Schools — scholarship ($78,000) see Beazley Foundation/Frederick Foundation

Prestwould Foundation ($30,000) see Carter Foundation, Beirne

Prince Edward Academy ($77,848) see Fuqua Foundation, J. B.

Prince Edward Academy ($6,142) see Fuqua Foundation, J. B.

Prince Edward Academy Foundation ($27,000) see Fuqua Foundation, J. B.

Pro-Art — Campbell Edmonds Concert ($15,000) see Slemp Foundation

Project Hope ($50,000) see Hoffmann-La Roche Inc.

Project Horizon — conference with high school guidance counselors and high school students ($713) see Crary Foundation, Bruce L.

Public Broadcasting System —for support of "A Woman's Health" ($206,979) see CIGNA Corporation

Radford University Foundation — student scholarship assistance ($6,000) see Richardson Benevolent Foundation, C. E.

Randolph-Macon College ($21,750) see Sullivan Foundation, Algernon Sydney

Randolph-Macon College — faculty development ($100,000) see Cabell Foundation, Robert G. Cabell III and Maude Morgan

Randolph-Macon Woman's College ($17,500) see North Shore Foundation

Randolph-Macon Woman's College Indoor Riding Arena Fund ($10,000) see Old Dominion Box Co.

Randolph-Macon Women's College — renovation of Martin science building ($100,000) see Cabell Foundation, Robert G. Cabell III and Maude Morgan

Regent University ($18,400) see McCarty Foundation, John and Margaret

Regent University ($11,231) see Helms Foundation

Richard Wright Foundation, George Mason University ($1,000) see Crown Books

Richmond Ballet — scenery for performance ($30,000) see Cole Trust, Quincy

Richmond Better Housing Coalition ($25,000) see

Morgan and Samuel Tate Morgan, Jr. Foundation, Marietta McNeil

Richmond Hill — historic restoration ($15,000) see Morgan and Samuel Tate Morgan, Jr. Foundation, Marietta McNeil

Richmond Recreation and Parks Foundation Fund — Billy Austin sidewalk project ($15,000) see Cole Trust, Quincy

Richmond Renaissance — 7th Street fountain ($125,000) see Cabell Foundation, Robert G. Cabell III and Maude Morgan

Richmond Renaissance ($25,000) see Central Fidelity Banks, Inc.

Richmond Symphony ($15,000) see Central Fidelity Banks, Inc.

Richmond Symphony Foundation ($3,000) see Thalhimer and Family Foundation, Charles G.

River Foundation ($250,000) see Carter Foundation, Beirne

River Foundation see Shenandoah Life Insurance Co.

Roanoke College Library see Shenandoah Life Insurance Co.

Robert E. Lee Memorial ($50,000) see Dula Educational and Charitable Foundation, Caleb C. and Julia W.

St. Catherine's School ($8,000) see Campbell Foundation, Ruth and Henry

St. Catherines School ($25,000) see Carter Foundation, Beirne

St. Christopher's School ($25,000) see Fleming Cos. Food Distribution Center

St. John's Episcopal Church ($15,000) see Olsson Memorial Foundation, Elis

St. John's Episcopal Church — restricted purpose of repair, renovation and upgrading of the sanctuary and nave of the church, reworking the heating system, replacing a roof, and correcting a drainage problem ($10,000) see Washington Forrest Foundation

St. Pauls College ($7,500) see Treakle Foundation, J. Edwin

St. Paul's University ($50,000) see Morgan and Samuel Tate Morgan, Jr. Foundation, Marietta McNeil

Salvation Army ($25,000) see Morgan and Samuel Tate Morgan, Jr. Foundation, Marietta McNeil

Seton Home Study School — Macintosh computer and laser printer ($6,000) see Bauervic Foundation, Charles M.

Shenandoah University — capital improvement Smith Library ($50,000) see Gallagher Family Foundation, Lewis P.

Shenandoah University — education fund ($50,000) see Bryant Foundation

Snohomish County Youth Foundation — social services teen philanthropy ($10,000) see Glaser Foundation

Society for the Preservation of the Greek Heritage

($13,500) see Lea Foundation, Helen Sperry

Southampton County ($37,100) see Campbell Foundation, Ruth and Henry

Southampton Memorial Hospital ($8,000) see Campbell Foundation, Ruth and Henry

Southeast 4-H Educational Center ($43,500) see Campbell Foundation, Ruth and Henry

Southern Environmental Law Center — the Southern Forest Protection Project ($50,000) see Merck Family Fund

Southern Virginia College for Women — partial financing of construction of student center and laundry facility ($5,000) see Richardson Benevolent Foundation, C. E.

Southwest Virginia Community College — new building construction ($200,000) see Thompson Charitable Foundation

Steward School ($6,900) see Widgeon Foundation

Stratford Hall — capital ($105,000) see Ingalls Foundation, Louise H. and David S.

Sugar Plum ($15,000) see Fleming Cos. Food Distribution Center

Sweet Briar College — faculty development ($100,000) see Cabell Foundation, Robert G. Cabell III and Maude Morgan

Tidewater Community College ($3,000) see Norfolk Shipbuilding & Drydock Corp.

Trail of Lonesome Pine — 1994 school touring program ($10,000) see Slemp Foundation

Union Mission ($5,000) see Bowen Foundation, Ethel N.

United Way Central Virginia ($40,000) see Central Fidelity Banks, Inc.

United Way of Central Virginia ($2,115) see Old Dominion Box Co.

United Way of Greater Franklin ($31,852) see Union Camp Corporation

United Way of Greater Richmond ($32,400) see Westvaco Corporation

United Way Greater Richmond ($76,875) see Central Fidelity Banks, Inc.

United Way National Capital Area ($275,000) see Mobil Oil Corp.

United Way of Roanoke Valley ($1,908) see Park Foundation

United Way Services ($5,000) see Park Foundation

United Way Services ($20,591) see Central Fidelity Banks, Inc.

United Way Services ($13,500) see Thalhimer and Family Foundation, Charles G.

United Way South Hampton Roads ($35,300) see Central Fidelity Banks, Inc.

University of Richmond ($15,000) see Central Fidelity Banks, Inc.

University of Richmond — construction of the arts center complex ($25,000) see Cole Trust, Quincy

University of Richmond ($15,000) see Wheat First Butcher Singer, Inc.

Washington

West Virginia

Wisconsin

United Way Neenah-Menasha
($21,500) see Chesapeake
Corp.
United Way of Northern Rock
County ($100,000) see
Janesville Foundation
United Way of Northern Rock
County ($100,000) see
Janesville Foundation
United Way Portage County —
for general welfare
($21,800) see AMETEK, Inc.
United Way, Portage County
($6,025) see Banc One
Wisconsin Corp.
United Way Portage County
($30,379) see Consolidated
Papers, Inc.
United Way of South Wood
County ($48,297) see
Georgia-Pacific Corporation
United Way South Wood
County ($131,580) see
Consolidated Papers, Inc.
United Way of Washington
County ($8,100) see Banc
One Wisconsin Corp.
United Way Waukesha
($57,250) see Dresser
Industries, Inc.
University of Wisconsin —
capital funds ($40,000) see
Wisconsin Public Service
Corp.
University of Wisconsin Eau
Claire Foundation —
visiting professorship
($32,500) see Phillips
Family Foundation, L. E.
University of Wisconsin Eau
Claire Foundation —
internship program
($17,500) see Phillips
Family Foundation, L. E.
University of Wisconsin
Foundation — scholarships
($7,500) see Blue Cross &
Blue Shield United of
Wisconsin
University of Wisconsin
Foundation — for funding
for epidemiologist at
University of Wisconsin
Medical School ($15,000)
see Cremer Foundation
University of Wisconsin
Foundation ($75,755) see
Madison Gas & Electric Co.
University of Wisconsin
Foundation — for youth
welfare ($4,400) see Mautz
Paint Co.
University of Wisconsin
Foundation — education
($855,630) see Rennebohm
Foundation, Oscar
University of Wisconsin
Foundation ($50,000) see
Schoenleber Foundation
University of Wisconsin
Foundation at Madison —
capital campaign ($43,000)
see Firstar Bank Milwaukee,
N.A.
University of Wisconsin Green
Bay Foundation — for
scholarship program
($8,000) see Sentry
Insurance A Mutual
Company
University of Wisconsin
Oshkosh Foundation — for
scholarship program
($8,000) see Sentry
Insurance A Mutual
Company
University of Wisconsin
Stevens Point — for
matching gift ($12,370) see
Sentry Insurance A Mutual
Company
University of Wisconsin
Stevens Point Foundation —
for scholarship program
($55,000) see Sentry

Insurance A Mutual
Company
University of Wisconsin at
Stevens Point Pulp and
Paper Foundation —
scholarships ($31,000) see
Consolidated Papers, Inc.
UPAF ($25,901) see Marquette
Electronics, Inc.
UPAF ($65,000) see Ross
Memorial Foundation, Will
Waukesha Memorial Hospital
($5,000) see First Financial
Bank FSB
Wausau Area Community
Foundation ($10,200) see
Mosinee Paper Corp.
Wausau YMCA Foundation
($10,000) see Mosinee Paper
Corp.
Wisconsin Foundation of
Independent Colleges
($7,500) see Banta Corp.
Wisconsin Foundation of
Independent Colleges —
scholarships ($52,000) see
Consolidated Papers, Inc.
Wisconsin Foundation for
Independent Colleges
($25,000) see Sentry
Insurance A Mutual
Company
Wisconsin Foundation of
Independent Colleges
($20,000) see Wisconsin
Power & Light Co.
Wisconsin Public Radio — for
support of arts and education
($4,600) see Mielke Family
Foundation
Wisconsin Public Television
($4,850) see Brillion Iron
Works
Wisconsin Public Television
— for support of arts and
education ($8,000) see
Mielke Family Foundation
Wisconsin Vietnam Veterans
Memorial Project —
Vietnam memorial
construction ($10,000) see
Phillips Family Foundation,
L. E.
Wiscraft — for restricted use
($10,000) see Birnschein
Foundation, Alvin and
Marion
YMCA ($5,000) see Madison
Gas & Electric Co.
YMCA — for grounds
improvements ($25,000) see
Peters Foundation, R. D. and
Linda
YMCA of Green Bay —
capital funds ($20,000) see
Wisconsin Public Service
Corp.
YMCA of Neenah-Menasha
($15,000) see Banta Corp.
YMCA of Neenah-Menasha
($6,000) see Banta Corp.
YMCA of South Wood County
($37,000) see Consolidated
Papers, Inc.
YWCA — Waukesha Home
for Disabled ($3,500) see
First Financial Bank FSB
Zoological Society of
Milwaukee County
($29,250) see Marquette
Electronics, Inc.
Zoological Society of
Milwaukee County — to
maintain membership with
the Platypus Society
($32,500) see Smith Corp.,
A.O.

Wyoming

Boys and Girls Club of Central
Wyoming — building fund
($2,500) see Sargent
Foundation, Newell B.

Buffalo Bill Historical Center
see USX Corporation
Casper Civic Symphony
($2,000) see KN Energy, Inc.
Central Wyoming Rescue
Mission — building fund
and Christmas dinner
($2,500) see Sargent
Foundation, Newell B.
Ducks Unlimited ($95,200)
see Whitecap Foundation
Ducks Unlimited see Pittsburg
Midway Coal Mining Co.
Friends of Washakie County
Museum ($12,000) see
Sargent Foundation, Newell
B.
New Horizons Care Center —
Alzheimers wing ($3,000)
see Sargent Foundation,
Newell B.
Southwest Wyoming
Rehabilitation Center see
Pittsburg Midway Coal
Mining Co.
Sublette County ($30,000) see
Taylor Foundation, Ruth and
Vernon
Sublette County Retirement
Center ($30,000) see Taylor
Foundation, Ruth and Vernon
Wyoming Centennial
Community Foundation —
future museum ($115,000)
see Sargent Foundation,
Newell B.

International

Australia

Big Brothers and Big Sisters
($16,000) see Newman's
Own, Inc.
Camp Quality ($16,000) see
Newman's Own, Inc.
Child Abuse Prevention
Service ($40,000) see
Newman's Own, Inc.
Comite Newman's Own
($9,000) see Newman's
Own, Inc.
Hear and Say Centre for Deaf
Children ($14,400) see
Newman's Own, Inc.
Malcolm Sargent Cancer Fund
for Children ($16,000) see
Newman's Own, Inc.
National Aunties and Uncles
($21,800) see Newman's
Own, Inc.
New South Wales Scholarship
Program — undergraduate
scholarship ($105,140) see
Boswell Foundation, James
G.
Royal Blind Society ($20,000)
see Newman's Own, Inc.
Shepherd Centre for Deaf
Children ($16,800) see
Newman's Own, Inc.
Women's and Children's
Hospital ($74,000) see
Newman's Own, Inc.

Bahamas

Lyford Cay Foundation —
educational ($3,000) see
Darby Foundation

Botswana

Okavango Wilderness School
($5,000) see Allen Brothers
Foundation

Canada

1995 Canada Winter Games
Host Society ($99,125) see
Weyerhaeuser Co.
Canadian Centre for
Architecture ($500,000) see
Seagram & Sons, Inc.,
Joseph E.
Columbia Christian
Counseling Group Society
— subsidizing fees for
low-income clients ($6,000)
see Smith Trust, May and
Stanley
Community Justice Initiatives
Association —
victim/offender
reconciliation program
($6,000) see Smith Trust,
May and Stanley
Lake of the Woods Hospital
($150,000) see Boise
Cascade Corporation
Ridley College ($49,385) see
Mandeville Foundation
Samuel and Daidye Bronfman
Family Foundation —
general support ($160,700)
see ASDA Foundation
Samuel and Saidye Bronfman
Family Foundation —
general support ($160,700)
see ASDA Foundation
United Way Ontario ($16,180)
see Inland Container Corp.
United Ways ($106,920) see
Metropolitan Life Insurance
Co.
World Leisure and Recreation
— growth and development
of recreation and leisure
movement ($15,000) see
National Forge Co.

People's Republic of China

State Bureau of Cultural
Relics — fund to purchase
Tong Ting Panels and
reinstallation in the Summer
Palace in Beijing as a
cultural relic of the Chinese
people ($515,000) see Starr
Foundation

England

American Trust for Oxford
University ($20,000) see
Reed Foundation
Bath Abbey Trust ($50,000)
see Skaggs Foundation, L. J.
and Mary C.
Cambridge Foundation —
partially fund assessment
room in clinical suite
($100,000) see Scholl
Foundation, Dr.
National Trust ($25,000) see
Skaggs Foundation, L. J. and
Mary C.
Royal Caledonian Schools —
operating grant ($38,776)
see Glencoe Foundation
Royal Caledonian Schools —
facilities grant ($29,338) see
Glencoe Foundation
Thoroughbred Breeders
Association — provide staff
salary support for the equine
fertility unit ($40,000) see
Mellon Family Foundation,
R. K.
University of Cambridge —
support research on quantum
theory of gravity and other
topics ($20,000) see Smith
Foundation, Ralph L.

Westminster Abbey Trust
($150,000) see Skaggs
Foundation, L. J. and Mary
C.

France

Association Claude Bernard
($150,000) see
Bristol-Myers Squibb
Company
Fondation de France — for
indigent patient services at
Ho Chi Minh Ville Heart
Hospital ($100,000) see
Medtronic, Inc.
Friends of Vieilles Maisons
Francaises ($220,000) see
Gould Foundation, The
Florence
Institute of American
Universities — to support
Marchuz School Minibus
fund for school
transportation ($4,000) see
Maneely Fund

Greece

Anatolia College ($25,000)
see Demos Foundation, N.
Friends of the Deaf of
Thessaloniki ($10,000) see
Demos Foundation, N.
Society for Thalassemic
Children ($20,000) see
Demos Foundation, N.
Spastics Society ($50,000) see
Demos Foundation, N.

Guatemala

Center for Regional
Mesoamerican
Investigations ($148,500)
see Plumsock Fund

Indonesia

Institute of Teaching,
Bandbung ($90,000) see
Gleason Foundation

Ireland

Mercy International Centre —
restoration of original House
of Mercy in Dublin and
development of endowment
fund to maintain mission
and preserve heritage
($500,000) see Connelly
Foundation
Mercy International Centre —
restoration of original House
of Mercy in Dublin and
development of endowment
fund to preserve mission and
heritage ($250,000) see
Connelly Foundation

Israel

Hadassah — charitable
contribution ($6,000) see
Klosk Fund, Louis and Rose
Hebrew University of
Jerusalem — for the survey,
documentation, and research
of Jewish art in Poland
($268,000) see Getty Trust,
J. Paul
Omer — assistance programs
($25,000) see Fohs
Foundation
Technion-Israel Institute —
research ($50,000) see

Herzstein Charitable
Foundation, Albert and Ethel

Italy

Bologna Center of the John
Hopkins University —
tuition fellowship for two
Brazilian students ($32,960)
see Good Samaritan
John Cabot International
College — general support
($500,000) see Frohring
Foundation, Paul and Maxine

Lebanon

Syrian Orthodox Church —
land for high school

($86,000) see Hoffman
Foundation, Maximilian E.
and Marion O.

Mexico

American British Cowdray
Hospital Foundation — to
furnish a suite in hospital for
families of terminal care and
intensive care patients
($25,000) see Favrot Fund

Rwanda

Free Methodist World
Missions Kibogora Hospital
— housing for doctor

($21,500) see Young
Foundation, Irvin L.

Scotland

Clan Donald Lands Trust —
operating grant ($154,836)
see Glencoe Foundation
Clan Donald Lands Trust —
small project grants
($63,040) see Glencoe
Foundation
Clan Donald Lands Trust —
cottage area laundry
($15,330) see Glencoe
Foundation
Crieff Trust ($14,721) see
M.E. Foundation
Glasgow University
Department of Archaeology

— provide support for
student research and field
work done in the north of
Scotland ($20,300) see
Durfee Foundation
Lomond School — scholarship
funds ($15,521) see Glencoe
Foundation
National Museum of Scotland
— project funds ($8,877)
see Glencoe Foundation
National Trust for Scotland —
project funds ($16,576) see
Glencoe Foundation

Vatican City

Vatican Museums — tapestry
project ($80,000) see
Homeland Foundation

Wales

Centre for Advanced Welsh
and Celtic Studies ($20,000)
see Skaggs Foundation, L. J.
and Mary C.

Zaire

Christian Missions in Many
Lands — building funds
($31,675) see Young
Foundation, Irvin L.

Index to Library Recipients by State

Please refer to the Master Index to Corporations and Foundations for profile page numbers.

Alabama

B.B. Comer Memorial Library
— library ($19,500) see
Comer Foundation
Escambia County Co-operative
Library System ($1,000) see
McMillan Foundation, D. W.
Escambia County Co-operative
Library System ($1,000) see
McMillan Foundation, D. W.
Escambia County Co-operative
Library System ($1,000) see
McMillan Foundation, D. W.
Gulf County Public Library
($6,900) see duPont
Foundation, Alfred I.
Henley Research Library
($50,000) see Linn-Henley
Charitable Trust
Henley Research Library
($50,000) see Linn-Henley
Charitable Trust
Regional Library Board —
purchase of children's books
($5,000) see JELD-WEN,
Inc.
Reynolds Historical Library
($5,000) see Linn-Henley
Charitable Trust
Spring Hill College — library
upgrade ($24,000) see
Huisking Foundation
Tuscaloosa Public Library see
Alabama Power Co.
Wheeler Basin Regional
Library — for educational
purposes ($2,909) see
Tennessee Valley Printing
Co.
White Smith Memorial
Library ($10,000) see
Bedsole Foundation, J. L.

Arizona

Arizona State University
Foundation — to partially
fund the construction of a
new library ($5,000) see
Kiewit Foundation, Peter
Art Libraries Society of North
America — for
representatives from Central
and Eastern Europe to attend
the 1993 Art Libraries
Society of North American
conference ($30,000) see
Getty Trust, J. Paul
Libraries Limited ($2,000) see
Spalding Foundation, Eliot
Navajo Nation Museum and
Library Fund — for general
support ($10,000) see Public
Service Co. of New Mexico
Sedona Public Library
($50,000) see Offield Family
Foundation

Arkansas

Barton Library — endowment
fund in the form of stocks
($20,531) see Murphy
Foundation
Booneville Library ($2,000)
see Spang & Co.
Central Arkansas Library
System ($15,000) see
Sturgis Charitable and
Educational Trust, Roy and
Christine

Clark County Public Library
($10,000) see Bedsole
Foundation, J. L.
County of Sevier, Arkansas —
library building fund
($50,000) see De Queen
General Hospital Foundation
Friends of the Library Newton
Company ($5,000) see Mays
Foundation
Hendrix College Library Fund
($12,500) see Riggs
Benevolent Fund
Hot Spring County Library
($5,000) see Sturgis
Charitable and Educational
Trust, Roy and Christine
Hot Spring County Library
($1,500) see Sturgis
Charitable and Educational
Trust, Roy and Christine
Searcy County Library
($3,600) see Mays
Foundation
University of Arkansas Little
Rock — special endowment
fund and materials for
library of college of science
and engineering technology
($12,500) see Jonsson
Foundation
University of Arkansas Little
Rock Foundation —
establish a Hershel H. Friday
Library Endowment Fund
and name a courtroom in the
new Little Rock Center in
Mr. Friday's honor
($31,250) see Union Pacific
Corp.
University of Arkansas Little
Rock Law Library ($5,000)
see Ottenheimer Brothers
Foundation
University of Arkansas Little
Rock Ottenheimer Library
Expansion ($150,000) see
Ottenheimer Brothers
Foundation

California

Academy Foundation —
Herrick Library ($10,000)
see Goldwyn Foundation,
Samuel
Bala Cynwyd Library ($7,000)
see Amado Foundation,
Maurice
Bancroft Library, Friends
University of California
($7,000) see Auerbach
Foundation, Beatrice Fox
California Historical Society
— develop visual imaging
system for library
automation program
($12,000) see Durfee
Foundation
California Institute of
Technology — toward
restoration of the Gates and
Morgan Libraries
($323,500) see Ahmanson
Foundation
California State Bakersfield
Foundation — W. Stern
Library ($10,000) see Long
Foundation, J.M.
Carmel Public Library
Foundation — for first
installment of pledge
($12,500) see McMahan
Foundation, Catherine L.
and Robert O.

Claremont University Center
— toward acquisition of
endowment for the Honnold
Library ($250,000) see
Ahmanson Foundation
College of Notre Dame — to
computerize the library
catalog system ($120,000)
see Irvine Foundation, James
Community Library ($500) see
Parvin Foundation, Albert
Fellows of the Huntington
Library ($4,100) see Golden
West Foundation
Ft. Jones Library ($5,000) see
Smith Foundation, Ralph L.
Foundation Center — for
general support ($1,000) see
Heller Charitable
Foundation, Clarence E.
Foundation Center — for
support of library research
publication for foundations
($1,000) see Trust Funds
Foundation for Monterey
County Free Libraries —
help fund the Hopework
Center program ($3,000) see
McMahan Foundation,
Catherine L. and Robert O.
Friends of Bancroft Library —
for support of the arts
($2,500) see Gamble
Foundation
Friends of Bancroft Library —
for support of the arts
($2,500) see Gamble
Foundation
Friends of Claremont Public
Library ($10,000) see Hafif
Family Foundation
Friends of Huntington Library
($2,000) see Howe and
Mitchell B. Howe
Foundation, Lucille Horton
Friends of San Francisco
Public Library ($7,715) see
Bothin Foundation
Friends of the San Francisco
Public Library — in support
of the City Guides project, a
program of historical and
architectural walks in San
Francisco's neighborhoods
($10,000) see Jewett
Foundation, George
Frederick
Friends of Turlock Public
Library ($2,000) see Bright
Family Foundation
Friends of Vacaville Library
($10,000) see Long
Foundation, J.M.
Graduate Theological Union
— for its library automation
project ($25,000) see Teagle
Foundation
Henry E. Huntington Library
and Art Gallery — general
support ($50,000) see
Ahmanson Foundation
Henry E. Huntington Library
and Art Gallery — general
support ($50,000) see
Ahmanson Foundation
Henry E. Huntington Library
and Art Gallery — for
restoration of the Tempietto
and complete relandscaping
of the Rose Garden
($100,000) see Berger
Foundation, H. N. and
Frances C.
Henry E. Huntington Library
and Art Gallery ($20,000)
see Jameson Foundation, J.
W. and Ida M.

Henry E. Huntington Library
and Art Gallery — Fletcher
Jones Chair, first payment
($500,000) see Jones
Foundation, Fletcher
Henry E. Huntington Library
and Art Gallery — operating
($25,000) see Jones
Foundation, Fletcher
Henry E. Huntington Library
and Art Gallery ($2,247,500)
see Scott Foundation,
Virginia Steele
Henry E. Huntington Library
and Art Gallery — toward
seventy-fifth anniversary
observances ($50,000) see
Times Mirror Company, The
Henry E. Huntington Library
and Art Gallery — for
unrestricted annual support
($12,500) see Times Mirror
Company, The
Henry E. Huntington Library
and Art Gallery ($13,584)
see Van Nuys Foundation, I.
N. and Susanna H.
Honnold Mudd Library —
support joint information
exchange agreement with
UCLA in collaboration with
Caltech and Cal Poly
($20,000) see Smith
Foundation, Ralph L.
Huntington Library — endow
the R. Stanton Avery Chair
($100,000) see Durfee
Foundation
Huntington Library — support
the American/Chinese
program ($5,000) see Durfee
Foundation
Huntington Library ($2,000)
see Femino Foundation
Huntington Library —
cataloging papers of
Kenneth Hahn ($28,131) see
Haynes Foundation, John
Randolph and Dora
Huntington Library — history
fellowships ($21,600) see
Haynes Foundation, John
Randolph and Dora
Huntington Library —
photography, missions, and
Native Americans ($12,800)
see Haynes Foundation,
John Randolph and Dora
Huntington Library — Henry
E. Endowment ($250,000)
see Munger Foundation,
Alfred C.
Huntington Library ($5,000)
see Seaver Institute
Huntington Library ($2,000)
see Stans Foundation
Huntington Library ($2,300)
see Thornton Foundation
Huntington Library —
education and arts ($2,000)
see Booth Ferris Foundation
Huntington Library and Art
Gallery ($25,000) see Essick
Foundation
Huntington Library and Art
Gallery ($15,000) see
Knudsen Foundation, Tom
and Valley
Huntington Library and Art
Gallery ($4,000) see Seaver
Charitable Trust, Richard C.
Huntington Library, Gardens
and Art Gallery — for an
integrated security and fire
protection system
($1,000,000) see Parsons
Foundation, Ralph M.

Kern County Library
Foundation ($13,000) see
West Foundation, Harry and
Ethel
Kern County Library Fund
($35,840) see Arkelian
Foundation, Ben H. and
Gladys
La Jolla Country Day School
— Lower School Library
($500) see Klipstein
Foundation, Ernest Christian
Library Foundation of Los
Angeles — toward the
Public Library Collection's
Endowment Fund
($250,000) see Ahmanson
Foundation
Library Foundation of Los
Angeles — $100,000 grant
payable over four years for
repair and renovation of the
historic library building and
collection, restoration, and
catalogue ($25,000) see
BankAmerica Corp.
Library Foundation of Los
Angeles ($2,000) see
Hanover Foundation
Library Foundation of Los
Angeles — for general
operating budget ($5,000)
see Mattel, Inc.
Library Foundation of Los
Angeles — for Sunday
public service hours at the
Central Library of Los
Angeles ($100,000) see
Parsons Foundation, Ralph
M.
Library Foundation of Los
Angeles ($2,500) see Seaver
Charitable Trust, Richard C.
Library Foundation of Los
Angeles — for two-year,
$150,000 grant toward the
capital campaign of the
Central Library to establish
the Los Angeles Times
Literacy Center ($75,000)
see Times Mirror Company,
The
Library Foundation of Los
Angeles ($25,000) see Van
Nuys Foundation, I. N. and
Susanna H.
Library Foundation of Los
Angeles ($25,000) see
Whitecap Foundation
Library Foundation of Los
Angeles ($50,000) see
Crown Books
Library Foundation of San
Francisco — capital support
$250,000 over five years
($50,000) see BankAmerica
Corp.
Library Foundation of San
Francisco ($5,000) see
Campini Foundation, Frank
A.
Library Foundation of San
Francisco ($50,000) see
Chevron Corporation
Library Foundation of San
Francisco — for the capital
campaign for a new public
library for San Francisco;
$250,000 over five years
($150,000) see Columbia
Foundation
Library Foundation of San
Francisco ($200,000) see
Cowell Foundation, S. H.
Library Foundation of San
Francisco ($25,000) see

Colorado

Connecticut

Sarasota County Public Library System ($5,000) see Beattie Foundation Trust, Cordelia Lee
Sarasota County Public Library System — materials/equipment ($5,000) see Beattie Foundation Trust, Cordelia Lee
Washington County Public Library — capital funds ($1,000) see Gulf Power Co.

Georgia

Agnes Scott College — to help fund the library computerization project ($100,000) see Davis Foundations, Arthur Vining
APPLE Corps — to support efforts to obtain a Readers Digest/DeWitt-Wallace Library Power Grant for the Atlanta public schools ($3,000) see Woolley Foundation, Vasser
Atlanta-Fulton Public Library Foundation ($5,000) see English Memorial Fund, Florence C. and H. L.
Atlanta-Fulton Public Library Foundation — operating grant ($5,000) see Marshall Trust in Memory of Sanders McDaniel, Harriet McDaniel
Augusta Public Library ($5,000) see Appleby Trust, Scott B. and Annie P.
Carter Presidential Library ($50,000) see Kirbo Charitable Trust, Thomas M. and Irene B.
Chattoga County Georgia Library ($500) see Fieldcrest Cannon Inc.
Chickamauga Public Library — general operation fund ($15,000) see Jewell Memorial Foundation, Daniel Ashley and Irene Houston
Effingham County Library Board — for construction of a new county public library ($25,000) see Evans Foundation, Lettie Pate
James Hyde Porter Memorial Library — purchase of books, microfilm, periodicals, and genealogical aids ($7,000) see Porter Testamentary Trust, James Hyde
LaGrange Memorial Library — for expansion project ($658,622) see Callaway Foundation
LaGrange Memorial Library — for operating support ($138,048) see Callaway Foundation
Lake Blackshear Regional Library ($5,000) see Marshall Foundation, Mattie H.
Medical Center — library fund ($2,500) see Schwob Foundation, Simon
Ogelthorpe University — expansion of library holdings ($35,000) see Frueauff Foundation, Charles A.
Oglethorpe University — to fund the library acquisitions project ($100,000) see Davis Foundations, Arthur Vining
Paine College — for an endowment to support the Collins-Callaway Library ($20,000) see Heller

Charitable Foundation, Clarence E.
Porter Library ($20,000) see Arnold Fund
Southern Education Foundation — for use over four years in support of a program to strengthen the libraries of leading private Black colleges ($1,200,000) see Mellon Foundation, Andrew W.
Southern Education Foundation — to strengthen libraries of leading private black colleges ($1,150,000) see Mellon Foundation, Andrew W.

Hawaii

Haleakala School Library ($10,000) see Baldwin Memorial Foundation, Fred
Hawaii Preparatory Academy — for upgrade and renovation of Dyer library ($15,000) see Atherton Family Foundation
Imua Rehab ($3,000) see Baldwin Memorial Foundation, Fred
Koloa Early School — replace books and equipment in the library corner following Hurricane Iniki ($1,500) see Frear Eleemosynary Trust, Mary D. and Walter F.
Seabury Hall — capital fund drive for new gymnasium and library ($100,000) see Castle Foundation, Harold K. L.

Idaho

Caldwell Public Library — foundation center ($2,500) see Whittenberger Foundation, Claude R. and Ethel B.
Community Library Association ($8,000) see Whiting Foundation, Macauley and Helen Dow
Hackay Free Library District ($3,500) see CHC Foundation
Halley Library Friends ($1,000) see Hanover Foundation
Idaho Falls Public Library — eastern Idaho science and technology MTRL ($9,000) see Daugherty Foundation
Jefferson Free Library District — Henan-Annis ($4,135) see CHC Foundation
Ririe City Library ($1,625) see CHC Foundation

Illinois

American Library Association — link health clinics and libraries to reach at-risk parents and their babies through Born to Read demonstration project ($275,000) see Prudential Insurance Co. of America, The
American Library Association — over four years to serve as the central coordinator of the National Library Power Program ($2,838,000) see Wallace-Reader's Digest Fund, DeWitt

American Library Association ($9,600) see Wilson Foundation, H. W.
American Library Association ($10,000) see Scott Fetzer Co.
American Library Association ($96,341) see Bell Atlantic Corp.
Anshe Emet Library Fund ($2,000) see Lederer Foundation, Francis L.
Cairo Public Library ($11,500) see Hastings Charitable Foundation, Oris B.
Centralia Public Library ($2,557) see Centralia Foundation
Chicago Athenaeum — exhibition: "20th Century Industrial Design in Chicago" ($5,000) see Graham Foundation for Advanced Studies in the Fine Arts
Chicago Historical Society — library ($10,000) see Lederer Foundation, Francis L.
Chicago Public Library ($10,000) see Salomon Inc.
Chicago Public Library ($10,000) see Salomon Inc.
Chicago Public Library Foundation see Amoco Corporation
Chicago Public Library Foundation — education ($200,000) see Blum Foundation, Harry and Maribel G.
Chicago Public Library Foundation ($50,000) see Crown Memorial, Arie and Ida
Chicago Public Library Foundation ($60,000) see Donnelley Foundation, Gaylord and Dorothy
Chicago Public Library Foundation ($10,000) see Sara Lee Corp.
Chicago Public Library Foundation — four-year pledge totaling $100,000 ($25,000) see United Airlines, Inc.
College of St. Francis — for faculty and curriculum development and library enhancement ($15,000) see Kemper National Insurance Cos.
De Paul University — toward construction costs of new library on Lincoln Park Campus ($50,000) see Brach Foundation, Helen
Friends of Libraries USA see HarperCollins Publishers Inc.
Greenville College — for programs to improve retention of high-risk students; to enhance library holdings for academic computing hardware and software; and to help increase alumni giving ($50,000) see Teagle Foundation
Herrin City Library ($5,000) see Harrison Foundation, Fred G.
Library of International Relations ($7,000) see Cuneo Foundation
Library of International Relations ($10,000) see Rice Foundation
Newberry Library ($25,000) see Smart Family Foundation
Newberry Library — pledge payment ($20,000) see AON Corporation

Newberry Library ($1,000) see Boothroyd Foundation, Charles H. and Bertha L.
Newberry Library ($75,000) see Donnelley Foundation, Gaylord and Dorothy
Newberry Library ($10,000) see Illinois Tool Works, Inc.
Newberry Library ($3,500) see Illinois Tool Works, Inc.
Newberry Library ($1,000) see Norton Memorial Corporation, Geraldi
Newberry Library ($35,090) see Rand McNally & Co.
Newberry Library — endowment reading room ($250,000) see Regenstein Foundation
Newberry Library ($2,000) see Regenstein Foundation
Newbury Library — post-doctoral scholarship for women ($12,500) see Monticello College Foundation
Northwestern University — Deering Library fund ($25,000) see McCormick Foundation, Chauncey and Marion Deering
Northwestern University Library ($2,500) see Rand McNally & Co.
Rock Island Library Foundation — endowment fund ($20,000) see Geifman Family Foundation
Sterling Park Library ($36,000) see Dillon Foundation
University of Chicago — library renovation ($1,000,000) see Regenstein Foundation
University of Chicago Library ($13,200) see Kern Foundation Trust
University of Chicago Library Society ($200) see Kelly Foundation, T. Lloyd
University of Illinois at Urbana-Champaign — for a two-moth research visit by a librarian from Romania ($146,500) see Getty Trust, J. Paul
Urban Libraries Council ($37,950) see Wilson Foundation, H. W.

Indiana

Allen County Public Library Foundation — for charitable purposes ($4,000) see Fort Wayne National Bank
Athenaeum Foundation — roof restoration ($50,000) see Clowes Fund
Bowling Green Public Library ($5,000) see Houchens Foundation, Ervin G.
Culver Academies — new library ($90,000) see Towsley Foundation, Harry A. and Margaret D.
Eckhart Public Library ($3,000) see Rieke Corp.
Evansville Association for the Blind — for parent-infant program and toy lending library see Aluminum Co. of America
Indiana Libraries — for Summer Family Reading Program see CINergy
Indiana University Lilly Library — Ball/Fisher fellowships for visiting scholars ($15,000) see Ball Brothers Foundation
Indianapolis Library Foundation — operating

fund ($1,500) see Ayres Foundation, Inc.
Indianapolis Marion County Public Library Foundation — support of summer reading program ($1,000) see Glick Foundation, Eugene and Marilyn
Jasper Public Library ($90) see Habig Foundation, Arnold F.
Joyce Public Library — for upgrading and expansion ($5,000) see Cole Foundation, Olive B.
LaGrange County Library ($22,483) see Dekko Foundation
Noble County Community Fair — to establish library flag fund ($10,000) see Dekko Foundation
Notre Dame Library ($1,000) see American Optical Corp.
Notre Dame Library ($1,000) see Morgan Construction Co.
Willard Library ($500) see American General Finance Corp.
Willard Library ($500) see Kuehn Foundation
Winchester Community Library ($5,000) see Winchester Foundation

Iowa

Audubon Library ($250) see Audubon State Bank
Audubon Library ($25) see Audubon State Bank
Bettendorf Public Library — endowment fund ($3,000) see Lee Enterprises
Birmingham Public Library — Ralph Schott Memorial ($640) see Van Buren Foundation
City of Newton Library ($50,000) see Maytag Family Foundation, Fred
Coe College — capital growth annual fund, expansion of library, general operations, endowment for faculty salaries, endowment for student financial aid, faculty and program development, instructional equipment, and sponsor cultural events ($12,375) see IES Industries, Inc.
Cresco Public Library ($2,500) see Donaldson Company, Inc.
Eddyville Public Library — for new library building ($5,000) see Pella Corporation
Fairfield Public Library — construction project ($3,500) see IES Industries, Inc.
Fertile Public Library ($500) see Winnebago Industries, Inc.
Forest City Public Library ($500) see Winnebago Industries, Inc.
Friends of Public Library ($500) see Gazette Co.
Herbert Hoover Presidential Library ($35,000) see Bechtel Testamentary Charitable Trust, H. R.
Hoover Presidential Library Association — to provide educational programming ($25,000) see McElroy Trust, R. J.
Hoover Presidential Library Association — for five year commitment ($5,000) see Pella Corporation

Kentucky

Bellarmine College — new library ($250,000) see Gheens Foundation
Bellarmine College — toward the construction of a library ($600,000) see Kresge Foundation
Berea College— grant for Hutchins Library Acquisition Fund ($10,000) see Knapp Foundation
Henderson County Public Library ($4,000) see Thomas Industries
Henderson County Public Library ($5,000) see Yeager Charitable Trust, Lester E.
Kentucky Historical Society — toward construction and equipment of a museum and library to house and exhibit Kentucky's history for all Kentuckians ($15,000) see Marpat Foundation
Louisville Library see Providian Corporation
Louisville Presbyterian Theological Seminary — to fund a joint library automation project with Southern Baptist Theological Seminary ($62,500) see Davis Foundations, Arthur Vining
Manchester Christian Academy — library books and playground equipment ($1,800) see Thompson Charitable Foundation
Olive Hill Public Library ($500) see Commercial Bank
Southern Baptist Theological Seminary — to fund a joint library automation project with Louisville Presbyterian Theological ($62,500) see Davis Foundations, Arthur Vining

Louisiana

Friends of New Orleans Public Library see Freeport-McMoRan Inc.
Rapides Parish Library — books and equipment ($10,000) see Coughlin-Saunders Foundation

Maine

Albert F Totman Library ($1,500) see Read Foundation, Charles L.
Bridgton Public Library ($5,000) see Mulford Trust, Clarence E.
Brownfield Public Library ($500) see Mulford Trust, Clarence E.
Denmark Public Library ($250) see Mulford Trust, Clarence E.
Friends of Alice L. Pendleton Library — toward the cost of a new library addition ($5,000) see Dillon Dunwalke Trust, Clarence and Anne
Friends of Guilford Memorial Library ($524) see Woodward Fund
Fryeburg Library Club ($8,000) see Mulford Trust, Clarence E.
Northeast Harbor Library ($1,000) see Kent-Lucas Foundation

Keosauqua Public Library (continued)
Keosauqua Public Library — copier ($732) see Van Buren Foundation
Manchester Public Library — construction project ($5,000) see IES Industries, Inc.
Marion Public Library ($25) see Guaranty Bank & Trust Co.
Mason City Public Library ($13,000) see Lee Endowment Foundation
Mechanicsville Public Library — to purchase reference materials for students ($5,000) see McElroy Trust, R. J.
Mt. Mercy College — construction of new library and support academic programs ($31,100) see IES Industries, Inc.
Rock Rapids Public Library — purchase of art prints ($5,000) see Forster Charitable Trust, James W. and Ella B.
Rockwell Public Library ($1,000) see Winnebago Industries, Inc.
St. Ambrose University — toward the construction of a new library ($750,000) see Kresge Foundation
University of Iowa Library — library linking research ($40,000) see Carver Charitable Trust, Roy J.
West Branch Public Library — construction project ($4,000) see IES Industries, Inc.

Kansas

Ashland City Library — computer equipment ($2,500) see Baughman Foundation
Atchison Library ($8,000) see Muchnic Foundation
Atchison Library — funds for special big print books ($2,000) see Muchnic Foundation
Atchison Public Library Multi-Media ($250) see Exchange National Bank
Bradford Memorial Library ($25,000) see Texaco Inc.
City of Kismet — library software ($2,700) see Baughman Foundation
City of Oxford — computer for city library ($4,350) see Broadhurst Foundation
Dwight D. Eisenhower Library —for culture and the arts ($5,000) see Beech Aircraft Corp.
Frank Carlson Library ($1,164) see Central National Bank
Goodland Public Library — for educational purposes ($150) see First National Bank
Liberal Memorial Library — book purchases ($2,000) see Baughman Foundation
Living Land Foundation — new library ($30,000) see Davis Foundation, James A. and Juliet L.
McPherson Public Library — programs and operations ($1,500) see Mingenback Foundation, Julia J.
Oswatomic Library ($5,000) see Baehr Foundation, Louis W. and Dolpha
Wichita Public Library Foundation ($1,000) see DeVore Foundation

Northeast Harbor Library ($2,000) see Strawbridge Foundation of Pennsylvania II, Margaret Dorrance
Patten Free Library ($3,400) see Davenport Trust Fund
Portland Public Library ($1,000) see Gannett Publishing Co., Guy
Southwest Harbor Public Library ($35,000) see Peabody Charitable Fund, Amelia
William Farnsworth Library and Museum ($500) see Webber Oil Co.
Woman's Library Club of Lovell ($1,000) see Mulford Trust, Clarence E.

Maryland

Anxiety Disorders Association of America — for establishment of library ($40,000) see Freed Foundation
Board of Library Trustees ($3,500) see Leidy Foundation, John J.
Dorchester County Public Library ($3,000) see Widgeon Foundation
Enoch Pratt Free Library ($50,000) see Goldseker Foundation of Maryland, Morris
Enoch Pratt Free Library ($10,000) see Leidy Foundation, John J.
Enoch Pratt Free Library — for educational purposes ($10,000) see Lockhart Vaughan Foundation
Goucher College — purchase of new copiers for Julia Rogers Library ($10,000) see Knapp Foundation
Johns Hopkins University — library acquisitions ($50,000) see Booth Ferris Foundation
Kennedy Kreiger Institute — establishment of a lending library for assistive technology equipment ($25,000) see Chatlos Foundation
Library Theater — summer books alive ($7,500) see Higginson Trust, Corina
Museum and Library of Maryland History ($1,000) see Campbell Foundation
Prince George's County Memorial Library System ($10,000) see Bell Atlantic Corp.
St. Johns College — library retrospective conversion project ($4,400) see Knapp Foundation
Villa Julie College — support for library acquisitions ($10,000) see Knapp Foundation
Washington College — purchase of equipment for card catalogue ($10,000) see Knapp Foundation

Massachusetts

American Antiquarian Society — to establish endowment to fund the Marcus A. McCorison Librarianship ($30,000) see Harrington Foundation, Francis A. and Jacquelyn H.
Boston Athenaeum ($25,000) see Rowland Foundation

Boston Medical Library ($50,000) see Dana Charitable Trust, Eleanor Naylor
Boston Public Library — a 1991 donation to the "Endowment for Literacy" campaign, partial payment on a multiyear $1,000,000 pledge ($100,000) see Globe Newspaper Co.
Boston Public Library — casting a copy of MacMonnies' Bacchante ($30,000) see Henderson Foundation, George B.
Boston Public Library — capital campaign ($4,000) see Rabb Charitable Foundation, Sidney and Esther
Boston Public Library ($10,000) see Weber Charities Corp., Frederick E.
Boston Public Library ($5,000) see Fuller Foundation
Boston Public Library Foundation ($50,000) see Shawmut National Corp.
Boston Public Library Foundation ($50,000) see Bank of Boston Corp.
Boston Public Library Foundation — capital campaign to restore historic library ($25,000) see Cabot Corp.
Boston Public Library Foundation ($25,044) see Cabot Family Charitable Trust
Boston Public Library Foundation ($50,000) see Harcourt General, Inc.
Boston Public Library Foundation ($10,000) see M/A-COM, Inc.
Boston Public Library Foundation ($1,000,000) see Peabody Charitable Fund, Amelia
Boston University Friends of Libraries ($1,000) see Linnell Foundation
Bradford Library Building Fund ($10,000) see Witco Corp.
Brookline Public Library ($2,500) see Fife Foundation, Elias and Bertha
Center for Coastal Studies — purchase of a computerized reference filing system and inter-library communications system for the library ($3,800) see Pierce Charitable Trust, Harold Whitworth
Clark University — library cataloging project ($5,000) see McEvoy Foundation, Mildred H.
Concord Free Public Library — in support of the Concord Collections project, to survey and document historic book and document collections ($10,000) see Phillips Foundation, Ellis L.
Crandall Public Library ($5,000) see Dewing Foundation, Frances R.
East Longmeadow Public Library ($5,000) see Davis Foundation, Irene E. and George A.
Emmanuel College Library — purchase of equipment for library automation system ($10,000) see Knapp Foundation
French Library in Boston ($100,000) see Beaucourt Foundation

Friends of Harvard-Radcliffe Hillel — for the Judah J. Shapiro Library in Rosovsky Hall, second installment ($75,000) see Littauer Foundation, Lucius N.
Friends of Hopedale Library ($1,500) see Hopedale Foundation
Friends of Libraries, Boston University ($1,000) see Linnell Foundation
Friends of the Libraries of Boston University ($1,000) see Edmonds Foundation, Dean S.
Friends of Manchester Library ($8,000) see Plumsock Fund
Friends of the Newburyport Public Library ($15,000) see Arakelian Foundation, Mary Alice
Friends of West Springfield Public Library ($3,500) see Heydt Fund, Nan and Matilda
Hampshire College — to be used toward the Library Foreign Periodical Fund ($15,000) see Globe Newspaper Co.
Harvard College Library — addition to endowment, sixth payment ($175,000) see Littauer Foundation, Lucius N.
Harvard Medical School Countway Library ($50,000) see Uris Brothers Foundation
Harvard University — for use over two years by its Center for Italian Renaissance Studies toward development of a consortium of libraries in Florence, Italy ($327,000) see Mellon Foundation, Andrew W.
Harvard University Center for Italian Renaissance — Villa I Tatti-Library Catalog ($10,000) see Jones Foundation, Fletcher
Harvard University Italiam Library Consortium — for use over two years by its Center for Italiam Renaissance Studies toward development of a consortium of libraries in Florence, Italy ($327,000) see Mellon Foundation, Andrew W.
Harvard University Library ($25,000) see Phipps Foundation, Howard
Harvard University Library ($5,000) see Hunt Foundation, Roy A.
Haverhill Public Library ($1,500) see Rogers Family Foundation
Insurance Library of Boston ($2,000) see Royal Group, Inc.
JFK Library Foundation ($4,500) see Goldberg Family Foundation
John F. Kennedy Library Foundation ($2,000) see Ansin Private Foundation, Ronald M.
John F. Kennedy Library Foundation ($5,000) see Forbes Inc.
John F. Kennedy Library Foundation Dinner ($10,000) see Boston Edison Co.
Lawrence Public Library ($2,000) see Rogers Family Foundation
Lawrence Public Library ($12,000) see Russell Trust, Josephine G.

Michigan

Minnesota

Mississippi

Missouri

J.W. Barriger III National RR Library — Library Endowment Campaign ($10,000) see Duchossois Industries Inc.

Kansas City Public Library ($10,000) see Oppenstein Brothers Foundation

Mary Institute — Library Foundation ($1,000) see Messing Family Charitable Foundation

Mercantile Library Association ($10,000) see Gaylord Foundation, Clifford Willard

Missouri Botanical Gardens — library automation and capital campaign ($50,000) see Sunnen Foundation

Missouri Botanical Gardens — for use over three years toward the costs of integrating the library and herbarium collections ($350,000) see Mellon Foundation, Andrew W.

National Railroad Library Endowment ($5,000) see Freedom Forge Corp.

PP-St. Louis — library and popular literature ($35,000) see Sunnen Foundation

Rockhurt College Library Guild ($250) see Miller-Mellor Association

St. Louis Mercantile Library ($3,500) see Jordan Charitable Foundation, Mary Ranken Jordan and Ettie A.

St. Louis Mercantile Library ($3,000) see Stupp Foundation, Norman J.

St. Louis Mercantile Library Association ($40,000) see Pott Foundation, Herman T. and Phenie R.

St. Louis Mercantile Library Association ($30,000) see Pott Foundation, Herman T. and Phenie R.

St. Louis Mercantile Library/Barriger National Railroad Library ($10,000) see Santa Fe Pacific Corporation

St. Louis Public Library ($25,000) see Anheuser-Busch Companies, Inc.

St. Louis Public Library ($10,000) see Dula Educational and Charitable Foundation, Caleb C. and Julia W.

St. Louis University — library associates ($1,200) see Messing Family Charitable Foundation

Thomas Jefferson Library-UMSL ($1,500) see Pulitzer Publishing Co.

Westminster College — to help fund a joint library automation project with William Woods College ($66,000) see Davis Foundations, Arthur Vining

William Woods College — to help fund a joint library automation project with Westminster College ($66,000) see Davis Foundations, Arthur Vining

Winston Churchill Memorial Library see Givenchy Corp.

Winston Churchill Memorial and Library —for restoration of memorial and library building ($5,000) see Hanson Industries North America

Winston Churchill Memorial and Library in the US Westminister College in Fulton, Missouri — for restoration of memorial and library building ($5,000) see Hanson Industries North America

Montana

Chouteau County Free Library Foundation ($5,000) see Steele-Reese Foundation

Kohrs Memorial Library ($2,500) see Lee Enterprises

Maureen and Mike Mansfield Foundation — Mansfield Library ($25,000) see Adler Foundation Trust, Philip D. and Henrietta B.

Northern Montana College — library automation project ($67,500) see Murdock Charitable Trust, M. J.

William K. Kohrs Memorial Library ($5,000) see Louisiana-Pacific Corp.

Nebraska

Beatrice Public Library Foundation — to partially fund the construction of grantee's program facility ($50,000) see Kiewit Foundation, Peter

Central City Library Foundation — to partially fund the construction of a new library facility ($25,000) see Kiewit Foundation, Peter

City of Kearney Library and Information Center Bookmobile ($2,000) see KN Energy, Inc.

Dakota City Library ($1,500) see IBP, Inc.

Hastings Library Foundation see Norwest Bank Nebraska, N.A.

Kearney Public Library ($1,500) see CLARCOR Inc.

Lincoln Public Schools Foundation — over three years to implement Library Power in 36 elementary and middle schools that service 23,200 students ($1,222,000) see Wallace-Reader's Digest Fund, DeWitt

O'Neill Friends of the Library ($2,000) see KN Energy, Inc.

Sidney Public Library ($2,000) see Reynolds Foundation, Edgar

Nevada

Friends of Washoe County Library — assistance grant ($5,000) see Hawkins Foundation, Robert Z.

University of Nevada Reno Savitt Medical Library ($30,000) see Cord Foundation, E. L.

New Hampshire

Amherst Town Library — to purchase and install on-line phone access catalogs to replace the card catalog system ($4,380) see Bean Foundation, Norwin S. and Elizabeth N.

Dartmouth University — for renovation and improvement of the Baker Library and for support for programs of the Baker and Berry library facilities ($3,000,000) see Baker Trust, George F.

Jackson Memorial Library ($2,000) see Dingman Foundation, Michael D.

Keene Public Library — final pledge payment/Library campaign ($4,000) see Kingsbury Corp.

Library Campaign — Keene Public Library ($10,000) see Putnam Foundation

Manchester Historic Association — salary support for librarian ($12,500) see Hunt Foundation, Samuel P.

Manchester Historic Association — salary support for librarian ($12,500) see Hunt Foundation, Samuel P.

New Hampshire State Library — video equipment ($5,000) see Cogswell Benevolent Trust

Richards Free Library — challenge grant to provide continued support to the Mill Tapestry Project ($2,500) see Phillips Foundation, Ellis L.

Richards Free Library — continued support for the Mill Tapestry Project ($25,000) see Mott Fund, Ruth

New Jersey

A.A. Schwartz Memorial — update computer Children's Library ($9,800) see Schwartz Foundation, Arnold A.

Barnegat Branch of Ocean County Library ($6,000) see Bell Atlantic Corp.

Belleville Public Library ($7,500) see Martini Foundation, Nicholas

Bernardsville Public Library ($26,000) see Jockey Hollow Foundation

Blair Academy — library and faculty study ($50,000) see Wean Foundation, Raymond John

Bloomfield Public Library ($2,500) see Martini Foundation, Nicholas

City of Long Branch — computerize elementary school libraries ($59,000) see Freed Foundation

Clarence Dillon Public Library — annual operating needs ($500,000) see Dillon Dunwalke Trust, Clarence and Anne

Clarence Dillon Public Library Project 91 — for new building fund ($5,000) see Cape Branch Foundation

Demarest Public Library ($300) see Holzer Memorial Foundation, Richard H.

Englewood Public Library ($11,276) see Schenck Fund, L. P.

Foundation at New Jersey Institute of Technology — purchase of technical journal abstracts in electronic format and software to increase efficiency and capacity of library services and educational programs ($25,000) see Hyde and Watson Foundation

Friends of the Clifton Public Library ($13,000) see Link, Jr. Foundation, George

Glen Ridge Public Library ($2,000) see Martini Foundation, Nicholas

Joint Free Public Library of Chester Borough and Chester Township ($250) see Klipstein Foundation, Ernest Christian

Kean College of New Jersey Foundation — alteration and modernization of library facility ($15,000) see Hyde and Watson Foundation

Library of Chathams ($2,000) see Read Foundation, Charles L.

Manville Public Library ($6,000) see Schuller International

Matheny School — operating funds for library ($10,000) see Schwartz Foundation, Arnold A.

Monmouth College Library Association ($650) see New Jersey Natural Gas Co.

Montclair Public Library — trustee grant ($2,500) see Schumann Fund for New Jersey

Morristown and Morris Township Library Foundation — to replenish reserve fund ($150,000) see Kirby Foundation, F. M.

New Jersey Historical Society — renovation of historic building for museum and library ($15,000) see Snow Memorial Trust, John Ben

New Jersey Institute of Technology — acquisition of EI database for library ($10,000) see Knapp Foundation

Oceanic Free Library ($10,000) see Brooks Foundation, Gladys

Princeton Public Library ($6,000) see Dow Jones & Company, Inc.

Recording for the Blind — purchase of materials for special services library ($2,000) see Knapp Foundation

Recording for the Blind — to provide recorded and computerized textbooks and library services to the blind ($5,000) see Hanson Industries North America

Recording for the Blind —to provide recorded and computerized textbooks and library services to the blind ($5,000) see Hanson Industries North America

Recording for the Blind — first payment of two-year grant totaling $350,000 for expansion project with master tape library ($175,000) see Starr Foundation

Seton Hall University — for restricted Library Room ($40,000) see Beck Foundation, Elsie E. and Joseph W.

Seton Hall University — library ($399,864) see Sandy Hill Foundation

New Mexico

Eunice Public Library ($105,000) see Maddox Foundation, J. F.

Mora County Community Library ($20,000) see McCune Charitable Foundation, Marshall and Perrine D.

St. John's College — to help endow a teaching chair and to help fund library renovation ($125,000) see Davis Foundations, Arthur Vining

Sierra Vista Elementary School — books for school library ($5,000) see Seidman Family Foundation

Tatum Public Library ($218,651) see Maddox Foundation, J. F.

New York

Alice and Hamilton Fish Library — to maintain high-quality video collection ($5,000) see Favrot Fund

American Foundation for the Blind — educational materials for special library services ($2,000) see Knapp Foundation

American Friends of Hebrew University — Jewish National and University Library project to microfilm the Jewish Press Collection in the Russian State Library, second and final payment ($50,000) see Littauer Foundation, Lucius N.

American Friends of Tel Aviv Museum of Art — renovation of the Helena Rubinstein Art Library ($60,000) see Rubinstein Foundation, Helena

American Friends of Tel Aviv Museum of Art — book, periodical, microfilm, and equipment purchases for the Helena Rubinstein Art Library ($50,000) see Rubinstein Foundation, Helena

Ardsley Public Library — for the Thomas and Agnes Carvel Foundation Children's Library ($150,000) see Carvel Foundation, Thomas and Agnes

Aurora Free Library Association — general ($4,700) see Cayuga Foundation

Aurora Library — Morgan Opera House Renovation Project ($9,650) see Emerson Foundation, Inc., Fred L.

Bank Street College of Education — toward small libraries for the Partners for Success program ($25,000) see Astor Foundation, Vincent

Bar Ilan University — for Joseph Alexander library ($50,000) see Alexander Foundation, Joseph

Bard College — fourth and final payment of four-year grant totaling $1 million in support of new Library project ($250,000) see Starr Foundation

Blue Mountain Center National Library Support Project — to develop a campaign to raise public awareness of the importance of public libraries on local, state, and national levels; to organize multiple constituencies in support of public libraries ($60,000) see Kaplan Fund, J. M.

Bronfman Library ($95,000) see Seagram & Sons, Inc., Joseph E.

New York Public Library ($25,000) see Rowland Foundation

New York Public Library ($2,000) see Lazarus Charitable Trust, Helen and Charles

New York Public Library ($6,000) see Lipton, Thomas J.

New York Public Library ($500) see Alavi Foundation of New York

New York Public Library ($100,000) see Altman Foundation

New York Public Library ($250) see Altschul Foundation

New York Public Library ($1,250) see Arnhold Foundation

New York Public Library — general support ($500) see ASDA Foundation

New York Public Library ($3,000) see Atran Foundation

New York Public Library ($2,700) see Avery Arts Foundation, Milton and Sally

New York Public Library see Bank of New York Company, Inc.

New York Public Library — charitable ($25,000) see Barth Foundation, Theodore H.

New York Public Library ($4,000) see Bay Foundation

New York Public Library ($50,000) see Benenson Foundation, Frances and Benjamin

New York Public Library ($15,000) see Blum Foundation, Edna F.

New York Public Library — restorations of the reference collections ($100,000) see Booth Ferris Foundation

New York Public Library ($25,000) see Bristol-Myers Squibb Company

New York Public Library — final payment of a $500,000 grant to "adopt" the Sedgwick Branch Libary at 176th Street and University Avenue in the Bronx and support its renovation and reconstruction ($150,000) see Calder Foundation, Louis

New York Public Library ($2,500) see Charina Foundation

New York Public Library see CIBC Wood Gundy

New York Public Library ($7,000) see Coltec Industries, Inc.

New York Public Library ($100,000) see Continental Corp.

New York Public Library ($10,000) see Cowles Charitable Trust

New York Public Library ($20,000) see CS First Boston Corporation

New York Public Library ($2,500) see Culver Foundation, Constans

New York Public Library ($5,000) see Daily News

New York Public Library — to convert records into machine-readable form ($50,000) see Dana Foundation, Charles A.

New York Public Library — for Lifelong Learning Collection of the Branch Libraries ($10,000) see

Dodge Foundation, Cleveland H.

New York Public Library ($5,000) see Dodge Foundation, Cleveland H.

New York Public Library ($5,000) see Dun & Bradstreet Corp.

New York Public Library — Schomberg Center for Research in Black Culture ($50,000) see Eastman Kodak Company

New York Public Library ($10,000) see Erpf Fund, Armand G.

New York Public Library ($500) see Feil Foundation, Louis and Gertrude

New York Public Library ($500) see Feil Foundation, Louis and Gertrude

New York Public Library ($300) see Fife Foundation, Elias and Bertha

New York Public Library ($1,200) see Fribourg Foundation

New York Public Library ($1,750) see Goldie-Anna Charitable Trust

New York Public Library ($125,000) see Goldsmith Foundation, Horace W.

New York Public Library ($75,000) see Gould Foundation, The Florence

New York Public Library ($15,000) see Greve Foundation, William and Mary

New York Public Library — toward general support ($6,000) see Guttman Foundation, Stella and Charles

New York Public Library ($25,000) see Hagedorn Fund

New York Public Library — to support various programs ($3,000) see Hanson Industries North America

New York Public Library —to support various programs ($3,000) see Hanson Industries North America

New York Public Library see HarperCollins Publishers Inc.

New York Public Library ($35,000) see Harriman Foundation, Gladys and Roland

New York Public Library ($20,000) see Hebrew Technical Institute

New York Public Library — conservation project ($10,000) see Homeland Foundation

New York Public Library — research ($5,000) see Hugoton Foundation

New York Public Library — in support of research libraries ($10,000) see Jurzykowski Foundation, Alfred

New York Public Library — charitable contribution ($1,500) see Klosk Fund, Louis and Rose

New York Public Library ($1,000) see Lang Foundation, Eugene M.

New York Public Library ($1,250) see Lasdon Foundation, William and Mildred

New York Public Library ($700) see Lasdon Foundation, William and Mildred

New York Public Library ($2,000) see Lauder Foundation

New York Public Library ($2,500) see Lemberg Foundation

New York Public Library ($25,000) see Liberman Foundation, Bertha and Isaac

New York Public Library — renewed support for Microcomputer Page Project at branch libraries ($10,000) see Littauer Foundation, Lucius N.

New York Public Library ($13,000) see Liz Claiborne, Inc.

New York Public Library ($100,000) see Loews Corporation

New York Public Library ($6,000) see Lowenstein Foundation, Leon

New York Public Library ($5,000) see Marx Foundation, Virginia and Leonard

New York Public Library ($25,000) see McGraw-Hill, Inc.

New York Public Library ($5,000) see Memton Fund

New York Public Library — research libraries ($25,000) see Merrill Lynch & Co., Inc.

New York Public Library ($20,000) see Metropolitan Life Insurance Co.

New York Public Library ($100,000) see Monell Foundation, Ambrose

New York Public Library ($50,000) see Morris Foundation, William T.

New York Public Library ($10,000) see Moses Fund, Henry and Lucy

New York Public Library ($1,250) see Neuberger Foundation, Roy R. and Marie S.

New York Public Library ($15,000) see New-Land Foundation

New York Public Library — educational ($2,500) see New York Stock Exchange, Inc.

New York Public Library — $25,000 is for U.S. Newspaper Project ($55,000) see New York Times Company

New York Public Library ($9,000) see Nias Foundation, Henry

New York Public Library — Music Division's work-study project for Juilliard graduate students ($42,570) see Noble Foundation, Edward John

New York Public Library ($1,000) see Normandie Foundation

New York Public Library ($10,000) see Osborn Charitable Trust, Edward B.

New York Public Library ($25,000) see PaineWebber

New York Public Library — general program ($30,000) see Paley Foundation, William S.

New York Public Library — in support of Jewish Division ($2,000) see Parshelsky Foundation, Moses L.

New York Public Library ($98,465) see Pforzheimer Foundation, Carl and Lily

New York Public Library ($2,000) see Porter Foundation, Mrs. Cheever

New York Public Library — toward conservation

laboratory ($25,000) see Prospect Hill Foundation

New York Public Library ($35,000) see Prudential Securities, Inc.

New York Public Library ($10,000) see Richardson Charitable Trust, Anne S.

New York Public Library — unrestricted ($50,000) see Rohatyn Foundation, Felix and Elizabeth

New York Public Library ($3,000) see Rosen Foundation, Joseph

New York Public Library ($55,000) see Rudin Foundation

New York Public Library ($25,000) see Salomon Foundation, Richard and Edna

New York Public Library ($100,000) see Scherman Foundation

New York Public Library ($25,000) see Schiff Foundation, Dorothy

New York Public Library ($1,000) see Slifka Foundation, Joseph and Sylvia

New York Public Library ($25,000) see Solow Foundation

New York Public Library — second payment of three-year grant totaling $1.5 million in support of the new Science, Industry, and Business Library ($500,000) see Starr Foundation

New York Public Library — challenge grant met for Center for Japan-US Business and Economic Studies at New York University ($1,000,000) see Starr Foundation

New York Public Library ($25,000) see Steinbach Fund, Ruth and Milton

New York Public Library ($1,000) see Thompson Co., J. Walter

New York Public Library ($2,000) see Thorne Foundation

New York Public Library ($5,000) see Titus Foundation, Roy and Niuta

New York Public Library ($5,000) see Titus Foundation, Roy and Niuta

New York Public Library ($10,000) see Unilever United States, Inc.

New York Public Library ($60,000) see Uris Brothers Foundation

New York Public Library see Wiley & Sons, Inc., John

New York Public Library ($10,000) see Wilson Foundation, H. W.

New York Public Library ($25,000) see Winston Foundation, Norman and Rosita

New York Public Library ($1,250) see Zenkel Foundation

New York Public Library ($15,000) see Zlinkoff Fund for Medical Research and Education, Sergei S.

New York Public Library ($20,000) see Fohs Foundation

New York Public Library Astor and Lenox Tilden ($5,000) see Ames Charitable Trust, Harriett

New York Public Library, Astor, Lenox and Tilden Foundation — toward opening the research library on Mondays ($25,000) see Astor Foundation, Vincent

New York Public Library, Astor, Lenox and Tilden Foundation — general support ($5,000) see Astor Foundation, Vincent

New York Public Library, Astor, Lenox and Tilden Foundation ($20,000) see Hartford Foundation, John A.

New York Public Library, Astor, Lenox, and the Tilden Foundations — general book fund ($33,000) see van Ameringen Foundation

New York Public Library of Contemporary Art ($25,000) see Norton Family Foundation, Peter

New York Public Library Department of Rare Books ($25,000) see Schiff Foundation, Dorothy

New York Public Library Schomburg Center ($5,000) see Continental Corp.

New York Public Library Schomburg Center — library projects ($500,000) see RJR Nabisco Inc.

New York Society Library ($15,000) see Achelis Foundation

New York Society Library ($2,000) see Porter Foundation, Mrs. Cheever

NYSERNET for Project GAIN (Global Access Information Network) — a pilot community information system to enable rural libraries in New York State to broaden their services through innovative telecommunications technologies ($65,000) see Kaplan Fund, J. M.

Oneida Library Building Fund — unrestricted ($20,000) see Chapman Charitable Corporation, Howard and Bess

Pace University — for first payment of $50,000 grant for the Center for Academic Excellence and $185,000 start-up grant for the College Library Usage Project ($210,000) see Morgan & Company, J.P.

Palisades Free Library ($500) see Normandie Foundation

Patterson Library of Westfield — toward new handicap accessible entrance project ($25,000) see Gebbie Foundation

Pavilion Public Library — for renovation of library ($10,000) see Western New York Foundation

Peirpont Morgan Library ($13,750) see Erpf Fund, Armand G.

Petersburgh Public Library ($1,000) see Ottley Trust-Watertown, Marion W.

Pierpont Morgan Library — capital campaign ($50,000) see Morris Foundation, Margaret T.

Pierpont Morgan Library ($2,500) see Crane Co.

Pierpont Morgan Library — endowment ($1,000,000) see Fairchild Foundation, Sherman

Pierpont Morgan Library ($1,250) see Mulford Foundation, Vincent

Bartlesville Library Trust Authority — book endowment fund ($100,000) see Lyon Foundation

Blackwell Public Library — children's books ($1,000) see Beatty Trust, Cordelia Lunceford

Comanche County Clerk — purchase video tapes and films for county school film library ($3,948) see McMahon Foundation

Endowment Trust of Metro Library System ($5,000) see American Fidelity Corporation

Endowment Trust of Metro Library System — urban/civic ($5,000) see American Fidelity Corporation

McAlester Public Library ($500) see Puterbaugh Foundation

Metropolitan Library System Endowment Trust ($3,333) see OG&E Electric Services

Oklahoma City University School of Law — library fund ($25,000) see Sumners Foundation, Hatton W.

Oklahoma State University Foundation — library program ($37,500) see Puterbaugh Foundation

Oklahoma University Foundation — Bizzell Library ($10,000) see McCasland Foundation

Western Plains Library System — children's library area ($10,000) see McCasland Foundation

Oregon

C. Giles Hunt Memorial Library ($3,000) see Hunt Charitable Trust, C. Giles

Canyonville Branch Library ($1,200) see Hunt Charitable Trust, C. Giles

Cottin Gabel School — new library, middle school ($30,000) see Collins Foundation

Douglas County Library Foundation ($15,000) see Hunt Charitable Trust, C. Giles

Glendale Branch Library ($2,150) see Hunt Charitable Trust, C. Giles

Klamath County Library — update book collection ($10,000) see JELD-WEN, Inc.

Lewis and Clark College — to renovate and expand the Aubrey Watzek Library ($550,000) see Meyer Memorial Trust

Lorraine Williams-Oregon Children's Library Center ($1,000) see Dr. Seuss Foundation

Marylhurst College — for improvements to the library building ($373,000) see Meyer Memorial Trust

Marylhurst College — Schoe Library collection ($10,000) see Tucker Charitable Trust, Rose E.

Marylhurst Education Center — Shoen Library Automation ($394,500) see Murdock Charitable Trust, M. J.

Mid-Columbia Health Foundation — for library grant ($20,000) see Collins Medical Trust

Mid-Columbia Health Foundation ($4,000) see Wheeler Foundation

Mt. Angel Abbey and Seminary — library enhancement program ($25,000) see Collins Foundation

Oakland Branch Library ($4,000) see Hunt Charitable Trust, C. Giles

Reedsport Branch Library ($900) see Hunt Charitable Trust, C. Giles

Riddle Branch Library ($600) see Hunt Charitable Trust, C. Giles

St. Mary of the Valley School — library automation; equipment ($36,400) see Wiegand Foundation, E. L.

Salem Public Library Foundation — endow two chairs ($1,500) see Pioneer Trust Bank, NA

Salem Public Library Foundation ($25) see Pioneer Trust Bank, NA

University of Oregon — to expand public access to the Knight Library by renovating and upgrading the Technical Service Center and creating a union catalog by merging the bibliographic databases of the University of Oregon and several other state-supported colleges ($256,500) see Meyer Memorial Trust

Winston Branch Library ($2,500) see Hunt Charitable Trust, C. Giles

Yoncalla Branch Library ($3,000) see Hunt Charitable Trust, C. Giles

Pennsylvania

Adams Memorial Library — for endowment fund ($20,000) see McFeely-Rogers Foundation

Adams Memorial Library — for Children's Library ($7,500) see McFeely-Rogers Foundation

Adams Memorial Library — for collections additions ($1,000) see McFeely-Rogers Foundation

Adams Memorial Library ($4,000) see McKenna Foundation, Katherine Mabis

Adams Memorial Library — collection development pledge ($10,000) see McKenna Foundation, Philip M.

Agnes Irwin School ($6,000) see Strawbridge Foundation of Pennsylvania II, Margaret Dorrance

Allentown Public Library ($1,000) see Holt Family Foundation

Allentown Public Library — cost of addition ($66,000) see Trexler Trust, Harry C.

Allentown Public Library — budgetary support ($33,000) see Trexler Trust, Harry C.

American Philosophical Society — for use over three years by its library to support the archiving of documents in 20th century science and a program of training in the history of recent science and technology ($285,000) see Mellon Foundation, Andrew W.

Annville Free Library ($500) see Lebanon Mutual Insurance Co.

Athenaeum ($5,000) see Copley Press, Inc.

Athenaeum ($3,000) see Groome Beatty Trust, Helen D.

Athenaeum ($3,000) see Superior Tube Co.

Athenaeum — community welfare ($5,000) see Bryant Foundation

Athenaeum of Philadelphia — exhibition, catalog and symposium about American perspective drawings prior to Latrobe ($5,000) see Graham Foundation for Advanced Studies in the Fine Arts

Athenaeum of Philadelphia ($80,000) see Barra Foundation

Athenaeum of Philadelphia — building project ($20,000) see McLean Contributionship

Athenaeum of Philadelphia ($1,000) see Warwick Foundation

Atheneum ($1,100) see Erpf Fund, Armand G.

Bayard Taylor Memorial Library — computerize card file ($60,000) see Longwood Foundation

Beaverdale Public Library ($200) see Glosser Foundation, David A.

Bethlehem Public Library ($26,000) see Payne Foundation, Frank E. and Seba B.

Biblical Theological Seminary — build library ($26,000) see Huston Foundation

Blairsville Library Association ($20,000) see Allegheny Foundation

Braddock's Field Historical Society — restoration of Braddock Carnegie library ($24,000) see Allegheny Foundation

Braddocks Field Historical Society — step and walkway replacement at Braddock Carnegie Library and Community Center ($10,000) see Buhl Foundation

Braddock's Field Historical Society — for continued support of the Community Center at the Braddock Carnegie Library ($30,000) see Heinz Endowment, Vira I.

Bucks County Free Library ($1,000) see Asplundh Foundation

Butler Public Library ($10,000) see Armco Inc.

Butler Public Library ($2,000) see Spang & Co.

California University of Pennsylvania, Foundation for California University of Pennsylvania — video/CD library; computer equipment ($25,500) see Trees Charitable Trust, Edith L.

Cambria Free Library — educational ($4,000) see Waters Charitable Trust, Robert S.

Camp Hill Public Library ($10,000) see Kunkel Foundation, John Crain

Carnegie — Second Century fund ($1,000,000) see Scaife Family Foundation

Carnegie Free Library ($40,000) see Crawford Estate, E. R.

Carnegie Free Library — for general support ($500) see Fair Oaks Foundation, Inc.

Carnegie Free Library of McKeesport ($1,000) see Peters Foundation, Charles F.

Carnegie Institute — county-wide public library planning study ($25,000) see Buhl Foundation

Carnegie Institute — fellows fund ($1,000) see Foster Charitable Trust

Carnegie Institute ($200,000) see Heinz Company, H. J.

Carnegie Institute ($91,667) see Heinz Company, H. J.

Carnegie Institute ($30,000) see Heinz Company, H. J.

Carnegie Institute — towards the capital campaign Second Century Fund ($1,000,000) see Heinz Endowment, Howard

Carnegie Institute ($500) see Spang & Co.

Carnegie Library ($15,000) see Clapp Charitable and Educational Trust, George H.

Carnegie Library ($8,000) see Murphy Co. Foundation, G.C.

Carnegie Library for the Blind and Physically Handicapped ($5,000) see Hulme Charitable Foundation, Milton G.

Carnegie Library of Homestead ($77,000) see Allegheny Foundation

Carnegie Library of Homestead — renovations ($25,000) see Eden Hall Foundation

Carnegie Library of Homestead — support for purchase of computer equipment ($15,000) see Laurel Foundation

Carnegie Library of Pittsburgh — science and technology department ($1,000) see Aristech Chemical Corp.

Carnegie Library of Pittsburgh ($10,000) see Hunt Foundation

Carnegie Library of Pittsburgh — to fund Family Literacy Program ($100,000) see Mellon Foundation, Richard King

Carnegie Library of Pittsburgh — three-year operational support for Children's Programming Initiative ($70,000) see Mellon Foundation, Richard King

Carnegie Library of Pittsburgh ($1,000) see Mine Safety Appliances Co.

Carnegie Library of Pittsburgh see Neville Chemical Co.

Carnegie Library of Pittsburgh ($23,335) see Patterson Charitable Fund, W. I.

Carnegie Library of Pittsburgh, Homewood Branch — to expand Project Beacon, an early intervention literacy program targeted to children 0-5 ($145,200) see Heinz Endowment, Howard

Carnegie Mellon University — for the development of prototype to demonstrate new technology that will enhance learning through interactive video libraries ($150,000) see Heinz Endowment, Vira I.

Carnegie Second Century Fund ($100,000) see Jennings Foundation, Mary Hillman

Carnegie Second Century Fund ($5,000) see Love Foundation, George H. and Margaret McClintic

Catholic Library Association ($5,000) see Wilson Foundation, H. W.

Catholic Library Association ($1,500) see Scott Fetzer Co.

Citizens Library ($12,500) see Coen Family Foundation, Charles S. and Mary

Citizens Library ($40,000) see Hopwood Charitable Trust, John M.

Citizen's Library Association of Washington Pennsylvania — educational program ($5,000) see Dynamet, Inc.

Civil War Library and Museum — for an exhibition on women and the Civil War ($17,000) see Penn Foundation, William

Community Library of Allegheny Valley ($10,000) see Allegheny Ludlum Corp.

Coyle Free Library ($2,500) see Wood Foundation of Chambersburg, PA

Dauphin County Library System — building expansion ($10,000) see Kline Foundation, Josiah W. and Bessie H.

Dauphin County Library System — general ($1,000) see Stabler Foundation, Donald B. and Dorothy L.

David A. Glosser Memorial Library ($10,000) see Glosser Foundation, David A.

David Library of the America Revolution ($2,000) see Groome Beatty Trust, Helen D.

DuBois Public Library — for 1993 grant ($2,500) see Mengle Foundation, Glenn and Ruth

Eastern College — to increase the library's holdings for students preparing for careers in Christian service ($5,000) see Huston Charitable Trust, Stewart

Eccles-Lesher Memorial Library ($66,515) see Eccles Foundation, Ralph M. and Ella M.

Elizabethtown College — library ($150,000) see High Foundation

Elizabethtown College — construction of new library ($50,000) see Kline Foundation, Josiah W. and Bessie H.

Elizabethtown College — library fund ($10,000) see Stabler Foundation, Donald B. and Dorothy L.

Ephrata Public Library ($1,500) see GSM Industrial

Episcopal Academy, Merion Campus — equip a library/resource center and implement a program in environmental studies ($50,000) see McLean Contributionship

Extra Mile Education Foundation — library facilities ($70,000) see Allegheny Foundation

Foundation for Reading Area Community College — support of Library Learning Resource Center ($25,000) see Wyomissing Foundation

Franklin and Marshall College — construction of science library ($10,000) see Kline

Puerto Rico

Rhode Island

South Carolina

South Dakota

Tennessee

The Big Book of Library Grant Money

City of Lavergne — for public library building ($50,000) see Christy-Houston Foundation

Harriman Public Library ($2,500) see Blue Bell, Inc.

Meharry Medical College — purchase of books for medical library ($5,000) see Knapp Foundation

Metropolitan Nashville Public Education Foundation — to develop a plan to implement Library Power in Nashville schools ($18,000) see Wallace-Reader's Digest Fund, DeWitt

Sequatchie County — for the costs of new bookshelves, furniture and equipment to complete the Sequatchie County Library Renovation Project ($20,000) see Tecumseh Products Co.

Sequatchie County, Tennessee — to pay and defray, in part, the costs of new bookshelves, furniture, and equipment to complete the Sequatchie County Library Renovation project ($20,000) see Herrick Foundation

Stokely Memorial Library ($25,000) see Stokely, Jr. Foundation, William B.

Tellico Plains Library ($5,000) see Stokely, Jr. Foundation, William B.

Vanderbilt University — funding of the Divinity School's Roman Catholic Studies Program for scholarships, faculty support, and library additions ($90,000) see Connelly Foundation

Vanderbilt University — for Jean and Alexander Heard Library ($1,000) see Ansley Foundation, Dantzler Bond

Texas

Anson Public Library — to promote the Cowboy Christmas Ball, which showcases cowboy heritage ($7,500) see Dodge Jones Foundation

Austin College — political science library acquisition ($5,500) see Sumners Foundation, Hatton W.

Bay City Library Association — for library relocation ($25,000) see Gulf Coast Medical Foundation

Bay City Library Association — to furnish and equip a new library ($95,000) see Meadows Foundation

Bay City Library Association — expansion and modernization ($15,000) see Trull Foundation

Baylor University — toward construction of the Jesse H. Jones library ($3,000,000) see Houston Endowment

Beautify Hallettsville — to purchase furniture and fixtures for public library ($29,500) see Johnson Foundation, M. G. and Lillie A.

Brackett Independent School District — school library furniture and equipment, one PLATO Site license, computer education literacy, and GED for students and adults ($35,000) see Hillcrest Foundation

Brownsville Public Library Foundation ($5,000) see Norton Co.

Bush Presidential Library Foundation — educational ($50,000) see Darby Foundation

Bush Presidential Library Foundation — to help establish the George Bush Presidential Library Foundation at Texas A&M University ($500,000) see Starr Foundation

Cameron Jarvis Library — educational ($5,000) see Wise Foundation and Charitable Trust, Watson W.

Christian Education for the Blind — library ministry to blind persons ($2,000) see Patterson Charitable Fund, W. I.

Christian Education for the Blind — library services for visually impaired ($1,000) see Hawn Foundation

City of Bullard — for library ($2,000) see Norman Foundation, Summers A.

City of Frankston — for library ($5,000) see Norman Foundation, Summers A.

City of Kyle Community Library ($15,000) see Johnson Foundation, Burdine

Degolyer Library ($1,000) see Overlake Foundation

Denison Public Library — for heating and air conditioning project ($45,626) see Munson Foundation Trust, W. B.

Denison Public Library Endowment Fund ($1,500) see Munson Foundation Trust, W. B.

F.M. Buck Richards Memorial Library — purchase of equipment and improvements ($165) see White Trust, G. R.

Ft. Worth Library ($10,000) see McQueen Foundation, Adeline and George

Foundation of Temple Public Library — purchase of building ($1,500,000) see Carpenter Foundation, E. Rhodes and Leona B.

Friench Simpson Library — cultural ($1,000) see Herzstein Charitable Foundation, Albert and Ethel

Friends of Dallas Public Library — education ($2,500) see Stemmons Foundation

Friends of the Library — for operating expenses ($250) see Wiggins Memorial Trust, J. J.

Friends of the Library ($5,000) see Wilson Foundation, H. W.

Friends of Mansfield Public Library — towards purchase of additional books for library ($3,875) see Hallberg Foundation, E. L. and R. F.

Friends of Mansfield Public Library — purchase of children's books ($500) see Weaver Foundation, Gil and Dody

Friends of the Midland Public Library — for Children and Youth Department fixtures ($25,000) see Davidson Family Charitable Foundation

Friends of Midland Public Library — furnishings for new addition ($5,000) see Early Foundation

Friends of Public Library of Buda ($1,000) see Johnson Foundation, Burdine

Friends of the Sherman Public Library ($1,000) see Reynolds Foundation, Donald W.

Friends of the Sherman Public Library ($7,900) see Munson Foundation Trust, W. B.

Friends of Unger Memorial Library — purchase hardware, software and furniture to be used in library ($14,344) see Mayer Foundation, James and Eva

Funding Information Center — library support ($3,000) see Semmes Foundation

George Bush Presidential Library — capital campaign ($50,000) see Fish Foundation, Ray C.

George Bush Presidential Library Foundation — toward Library Center at Texas A&M University ($250,000) see Weingart Foundation

Graham Public Library — building construction ($1,193,487) see Bertha Foundation

Happy Hill Farm Academy — library acquisitions ($10,000) see Sumners Foundation, Hatton W.

Harlingen Public Library — for building purposes ($1,000) see Hygeia Dairy Co.

Houston Public Library ($20,000) see Anderson Foundation, M. D.

Houston Public Library ($1,800) see Clayton Fund

Houston Public Library — support Library Enhancement Campaign ($5,000) see Duncan Foundation, Lillian H. and C. W.

Houston Public Library — support Library Enhancement Campaign ($5,000) see Early Foundation

Houston Public Library — community funds ($5,000) see Hamman Foundation, George and Mary Josephine

Houston Public Library ($7,500) see Hobby Foundation

Houston Public Library — help to add up-to-date quality material ($1,500) see Kayser Foundation

J.R. Huffman Public Library ($10,000) see Temple-Inland Inc.

Kerrville Independent School District — replacement of water-damaged books at Starkey Elementary School Library ($5,000) see Peterson Foundation, Hal and Charlie

Kurth Memorial Library ($10,100) see Temple-Inland Inc.

LBJ Museum and Library ($5,000) see LBJ Family Foundation

Midland County Public Library ($7,000) see Beal Foundation

Newton County Library — for general operations ($3,500) see Pineywoods Foundation

Newton County Library Board — purchase of books and other materials ($25,000)

see Porter Testamentary Trust, James Hyde

Nita Stewart Haley Memorial Library ($25,000) see Abell-Hanger Foundation

Nita Stewart Haley Memorial Library/aka Haley Library — for general operating support ($5,000) see Davidson Family Charitable Foundation

Oil Information Library of Ft. Worth ($2,500) see Piper Foundation, Minnie Stevens

Our Lady of the Lake University — automation of library and capital campaign ($421,000) see Halsell Foundation, Ewing

Permian Basin Petroleum Museum, Library, and Hall of Fame — challenge grant for the permanent endowment ($250,000) see Abell-Hanger Foundation

Permian Basin Petroleum Museum, Library, and Hall of Fame ($175,000) see Abell-Hanger Foundation

Real County — assist library in establishing a branch in Camp Wood ($7,656) see Peterson Foundation, Hal and Charlie

Recording Library for the Blind ($2,000) see Potts and Sibley Foundation

Redeemer Episcopal School — library automation equipment and books ($18,500) see Halsell Foundation, Ewing

River Oaks Baptist School — new library and media center ($166,667) see Cullen Foundation

River Oaks Baptist School — books for new library ($30,000) see Farish Fund, William Stamps

Rosenberg Library ($5,000) see Knox, Sr., and Pearl Wallis Knox Charitable Foundation, Robert W.

San Antonio Public Library ($8,000) see Halff Foundation, G. A. C.

San Antonio Public Library Foundation — acquisition of major art piece for permanent exhibition at new library ($250,000) see Halsell Foundation, Ewing

San Antonio Public Library Foundation ($2,500) see Piper Foundation, Minnie Stevens

San Antonio Public Library Foundation — towards construction library ($20,000) see Semmes Foundation

San Antonio Public Library Foundation — education ($50,000) see Zachry Co., H.B.

San Antonio Public Library Foundation — general funding ($50,000) see Zachry Co., H.B.

Schreiner College — Weir building renovation/library ($55,000) see Fish Foundation, Ray C.

Schreiner College — library acquisitions ($25,000) see Sumners Foundation, Hatton W.

Schreiner College — library challenge ($15,000) see Turner Charitable Foundation

Slocum Independent School District — construct school library ($68,700) see Temple Foundation, T. L. L.

Southern Methodist University — library renovation ($380,000) see Fondren Foundation

Southern Methodist University — arts library fund ($100,000) see Hawn Foundation

Southern Methodist University — for Underwood Law Library renovation ($125,000) see Hillcrest Foundation

Southern Methodist University School of Law Library Fund — educational institution library fund ($500) see National Gypsum Co.

Southwest Adventist College — library program ($75,000) see Carter Foundation, Amon G.

State Preservation Board — for capital fund for restoration of Legislative Library ($150,000) see McDermott Foundation, Eugene

Stella Link Redevelopment Association — toward acquisition of a site for construction of a new public library in the educational/recreational service corridor being developed in the Stella Link area of Houston ($750,000) see Houston Endowment

Texas State Library — support for Blind Programs ($2,000) see Semmes Foundation

Texas University General Libraries ($6,500) see Scurlock Foundation

Thorndale Independent School District —for library, computer equipment, and software see Aluminum Co. of America

T.L.L. Temple Memorial Library — support archives budget ($242,600) see Temple Foundation, T. L. L.

T.L.L. Temple Memorial Library ($24,430) see Temple-Inland Inc.

University of Houston — M.D. Anderson Foundation ($100,000) see Anderson Foundation, M. D.

University of Houston University Park — library collections ($25,000) see Rockwell Fund

Waco McLennan County Library Foundation ($250) see Meyer Family Foundation, Paul J.

Weise Memorial Academy — upgrade library materials, learning materials for disabled, purchase computers, science lab equipment, and physical education equipment ($30,000) see Hillcrest Foundation

Westbank Community Library — endowment see Freeport-McMoRan Inc.

Utah

Park City Municipal Court — children's library ($10,000) see McCarty Foundation, John and Margaret

Salt Lake Community College — establish a learning resource center at the new library ($25,000) see Union Pacific Corp.

Vermont

Cavendish Fletcher Community Library — program funding ($1,000) see Windham Foundation

Greensboro Free Library — children's room and staffing ($25,000) see Turrell Fund

Proctor Free Library — book budget ($3,000) see Proctor Trust, Mortimer R.

St. Johnsbury Athenaeum ($1,000) see Windham Foundation

Visiting Nurse Association, Maternal Child Health Division — parent education library project ($1,500) see Windham Foundation

Virginia

Alexandria Library — community welfare ($30,000) see Bryant Foundation

Amherst County Main Library ($6,000) see Central Fidelity Banks, Inc.

Amherst County Public Library ($5,000) see Old Dominion Box Co.

Arlington Public Schools Patrick Henry Elementary — Parent Resource Library ($400) see Washington Forrest Foundation

Blue Ridge School — for library ($5,000) see Butz Foundation

Center for Economic and Policy Education — library automation pledge ($50,000) see McKenna Foundation, Philip M.

Center for the Study of Public Choice — Buchanan Library project ($10,000) see Koch Charitable Foundation, Charles G.

City of Franklin Library Fund ($25,000) see Union Camp Corporation

Ells Olsson Memorial Library Fund ($7,000) see Chesapeake Corp.

Friends of Charlotte County Library ($8,500) see Priddy Foundation

Friends of Richmond Public Library ($50,000) see Morgan and Samuel Tate Morgan, Jr. Foundation, Marietta McNeil

Friends of the West Point Library — renovation of museum ($20,000) see Cabell Foundation, Robert G. Cabell III and Maude Morgan

Gloucester Library Endowment ($13,600) see Treakle Foundation, J. Edwin

Hampden-Sydney College — to help meet the cost of completion of reclassification from Dewey Decimal System to Library of Congress and conversion of bibliographic records to machine readable format ($15,000) see Huston Foundation

Hollins College — purchase of equipment for library automation system ($10,000) see Knapp Foundation

Lancaster County Public Library ($5,000) see Carter Foundation, Beirne

Lancaster County Public Library ($3,500) see Olsson Memorial Foundation, Elis

Langley School — for learning center/library ($10,000) see Mars Foundation

Lonesome Pine Library Literacy Project — purchase of books for Literacy Project ($4,000) see Slemp Foundation

Lonesome Pine Regional Library — toward the purchase of new cargo van ($5,000) see Slemp Foundation

Marymount University — purchase of automated equipment for Emerson G. Reinsch Library ($5,500) see Knapp Foundation

Mathews Memorial Library ($13,600) see Treakle Foundation, J. Edwin

Middlesex County Public Library ($12,500) see Olsson Memorial Foundation, Elis

National Sporting Library ($5,000) see Ohrstrom Foundation

Norfolk Academy — new library project ($25,000) see Beazley Foundation/Frederick Foundation

Portsmouth Public Library — forum ($800) see Beazley Foundation/Frederick Foundation

Roanoke College Library see Shenandoah Life Insurance Co.

Ruth Camp Campbell Memorial Library ($5,000) see North Shore Foundation

Shenandoah University — capital improvement Smith Library ($50,000) see Gallagher Family Foundation, Lewis P.

University of Virginia Darden School of Business — Camp Library ($50,000) see Union Camp Corporation

Virginia Foundation for Independent Colleges — strengthening library services on fifteen member colleges' campuses ($5,000) see Richardson Benevolent Foundation, C. E.

Virginia State Library and Archives — fund processing and housing of Charles Gilette's correspondence ($36,000) see Cole Trust, Quincy

West Point Public Library ($15,000) see Chesapeake Corp.

Washington

Gonzaga University — instructional media services center in new library ($500,000) see Murdock Charitable Trust, M. J.

Heritage College — construction of library and learning center ($100,000) see Booth Ferris Foundation

Heritage College — build library and learning center ($25,000) see Cheney Foundation, Ben B.

Heritage College — library and learning center ($500,000) see Murdock Charitable Trust, M. J.

Seattle Public Library ($15,000) see Foster Foundation

Seattle Public Library Foundation ($10,000) see Bishop Foundation, E. K. and Lillian F.

Seattle Public Library Foundation — social services teen health education ($5,000) see Glaser Foundation

Seattle Public Library Foundation ($15,000) see Nesholm Family Foundation

Washington Library for the Blind and Physically Handicapped — social services radio reader ($10,000) see Glaser Foundation

West Virginia

Craft Memorial Library ($5,000) see Bowen Foundation, Ethel N.

Davis and Elkins College ($17,250) see Sullivan Foundation, Algernon Sydney

Greenbrier County Library ($5,000) see Daywood Foundation

Kanawha County Public Library ($4,550) see Jacobson Foundation, Bernard H. and Blanche E.

McDowell County Public Library ($10,000) see Shott, Jr. Foundation, Hugh I.

Ohio-West Virginia YMCA — Camp Horseshoe library ($10,000) see Daywood Foundation

Parkersburg and Wood County Public Library — to construct a new library at the Waverly School ($27,000) see Cabot Corp.

Wisconsin

Appleton Public Library Foundation — for educational purposes ($20,000) see Mielke Family Foundation

Beloit College — library ($100,000) see Beloit Foundation

Black River Public Library ($2,000) see Lunda Charitable Trust

Brillion Public Library Trust — for general support ($3,000) see Peters Foundation, R. D. and Linda

Caestecker Public Library Foundation — library building ($1,268,604) see Caestecker Foundation, Charles and Marie

City of Abbotsford Library — Clements Encyclopedia of World Governments ($945) see Christensen Charitable and Religious Foundation, L. C.

City Libraries ($10,369) see Outboard Marine Corp.

Deer Park Public Library — to construct a new library ($25,000) see Bremer Foundation, Otto

Deerfield Public Library — for funding for a handicap accessible entrance ($2,200) see Cremer Foundation

International Crane Foundation — Ron Sauey Memorial Library ($10,000) see Griggs and Mary Griggs Burke Foundation, Mary Livingston

L. E. Phillips Memorial Public Library — building remodeling ($24,260) see Phillips Family Foundation, L. E.

Library of Congress Madison ($10,000) see Liz Claiborne, Inc.

Library for Wisconsin Artists — equipment ($25,000) see Rennebohm Foundation, Oscar

Lodi City Library ($2,500) see Madison Gas & Electric Co.

Marathon County Public Library ($5,000) see Mosinee Paper Corp.

Marathon County Public Library Foundation — capital funds ($5,000) see Wisconsin Public Service Corp.

Mazomanie Depot Library ($1,000) see Madison Gas & Electric Co.

Milwaukee Public Library — computer equipment ($7,000) see Firstar Bank Milwaukee, N.A.

Milwaukee Public Library ($1,000) see Marquette Electronics, Inc.

Milwaukee Public Library ($1,000) see Ross Memorial Foundation, Will

Milwaukee Public Library ($15,000) see Schoenleber Foundation

Milwaukee Public Library — education ($6,000) see Schroeder Foundation, Walter

Milwaukee Public Library — to aid in the purchase of books and materials for the new Center Street Library ($5,000) see Smith Corp., A.O.

Milwaukee Public Library Foundation — for restricted use ($10,000) see Birnschein Foundation, Alvin and Marion

Osceola Public Library — capital drive ($5,000) see Tozer Foundation

Pittsville Community Library — capital ($5,000) see Consolidated Papers, Inc.

Portage County Library Fund ($1,500) see Blue Cross & Blue Shield United of Wisconsin

Portage County Public Library Foundation — capital funds ($3,000) see Wisconsin Public Service Corp.

Portage Library Building Fund — for government programs ($100) see Mautz Paint Co.

Somerset Library — capital drive ($5,000) see Tozer Foundation

Stevens Point Library — capital ($20,000) see Consolidated Papers, Inc.

Stevens Point Public Library ($5,000) see First Financial Bank FSB

Tomah Public Library — on-line computer catalog ($7,890) see Andres Charitable Trust, Frank G.

Twin Lakes Library ($500) see First Financial Bank FSB

Waupaca Public Library Foundation ($5,000) see Wisconsin Public Service Corp.

Whitewater Public Library — building fund ($2,500) see First Financial Bank FSB

Whitewater Public Library ($1,000) see Fleming Cos. Food Distribution Center

International

Canada

Canadian Library Association ($2,500) see Scott Fetzer Co.

Czech Republic

National Library of Prague — for equipment ($20,000) see Getty Trust, J. Paul

El Salvador

Universidad Centroamericana Jose — for use over three years toward the development of its library ($335,000) see Mellon Foundation, Andrew W.

England

Winston Churchill Memorial and Library ($250) see Kuehn Foundation

France

American Library in Paris ($50,000) see Gould Foundation, The Florence

Hungary

National Szechenyi Library — for use over two years toward costs of developing the Hungarian-Slovak Library Network ($425,000) see Mellon Foundation, Andrew W.

Poland

Marie Curie Sklodowska University — for use over three years toward costs of automating the libraries of the Lublin Consortium ($951,000) see Mellon Foundation, Andrew W.

University of Poznan — for library acquisitions ($40,000) see Getty Trust, J. Paul

University of Wroclaw — for use over two years in automating its library system ($465,000) see Mellon Foundation, Andrew W.

Slovakia

Slovak National Gallery — for library acquisitions ($50,000) see Getty Trust, J. Paul

Republic of South Africa

Read Education Trust — Read Library advisor ($86,805) see Timken Foundation of Canton

Master Index to Corporations and Foundations

O

P